FICTION CORE COLLECTION

NINETEENTH EDITION

CORE COLLECTION SERIES

FORMERLY
STANDARD CATALOG SERIES

KENDAL SPIRES, MLIS, GENERAL EDITOR

CHILDREN'S CORE COLLECTION
MIDDLE AND JUNIOR HIGH CORE COLLECTION
SENIOR HIGH CORE COLLECTION
FICTION CORE COLLECTION
PUBLIC LIBRARY: NONFICTION CORE COLLECTION
GRAPHIC NOVELS CORE COLLECTION
YOUNG ADULT FICTION CORE COLLECTION

FICTION
CORE COLLECTION

NINETEENTH EDITION

EDITED BY

KENDAL SPIRES

H. W. Wilson
A Division of EBSCO Information Service, Inc.
Ipswich, Massachusetts
2018

GREY HOUSE PUBLISHING

ISBN 978-1-68217-083-0

Fiction Core Collection, published by Grey House Publishing, Inc., Amenia, NY, under exclusive license from EBSCO Information Services, Inc.

A catalog record for this title is available from the Library of Congress.

PRINTED IN CANADA

TABLE OF CONTENTS

Preface. vii

Purpose and Organization ix

Acknowledgments xi

Part 1. List of Fictional Works 1

Part 2. Indexes

Name Index. 851

Title and Subject Index 865

PREFACE

FICTION CORE COLLECTION is a selective list of classic and contemporary works of adult fiction either written or translated into English. This Core Collection is a print version of the database available via EBSCO*host* from EBSCO Information Services, which has an additional two recommendation levels, Lexile® measures, book reviews, and expanded metadata, and is updated weekly. Contact your EBSCO sales rep for a free trial. EBSCO invites feedback from Core Collections customers at corecollections@ebsco.com.

What's New in this Edition?

This edition includes more than 7,600 titles at the Most Highly Recommended and Core Collection recommendation levels. For supplemental titles, please consult the online database. A star (★) at the start of an entry indicates that a book is a "most highly recommended" title. These titles constitute a shortlist of the essential books in a given category or on a given subject. There are often a number of recommended titles on a single subject, and the star designation helps a user who wants only one or two.

Scope

The items in the FICTION CORE COLLECTION are considered appropriate for libraries serving adult readers and have been selected with guidance from review sources and the advice of librarian advisors with expertise in fiction. Titles selected for inclusion include popular works deemed to have lasting value to readers as well as new literary and genre titles that have been recognized as significant achievements in their respected areas of literature. The Core Collection excludes non-English-language materials, with the exception of bilingual materials.

Books listed are both hardcover and paperback editions published in the United States, or published in Canada or the United Kingdom and distributed in the United States. Out-of-print titles have been retained in the belief that good fiction is not obsolete simply because it happens to go out of print.

FICTION CORE COLLECTION is a guide to works of fiction only. Users who seek literary criticism, literary history, biographies of authors, and books on the writing of fiction are referred to FICTION CORE COLLECTION's companion publication, PUBLIC LIBRARY: NONFICTION CORE COLLECTION

Database

Additional metadata for the titles in this volume, plus full-text book reviews, full-color cover art, Lexile® measures, and all of the Supplementary and Archival book recommendations appear only in the FICTION CORE COLLECTION database available from EBSCO. For more information or for a free trial, contact your EBSCO sales rep or visit https://www.ebsco.com/products/research-databases/core-collections.

Preparation

Books included in this edition were selected by experienced librarians representing public library systems, school libraries, and academic libraries across the United States who also act as a committee of advisors on library policy and trends. The names of participating librarians and their affiliations are listed in the Acknowledgments.

Additional Products

For additional recommendations of children's books, librarians are encouraged to investigate these other databases and their print versions:

CHILDREN'S CORE COLLECTION

GRAPHIC NOVELS CORE COLLECTION

SENIOR HIGH CORE COLLECTION

PURPOSE AND ORGANIZATION

PURPOSE

FICTION CORE COLLECTION is designed to serve a number of purposes:

As an aid in purchasing. The Core Collection is designed to assist in the selection and ordering of titles. Annotations are provided for each title along with information concerning the publisher, ISBN, price, and availability. In evaluating the suitability of a work each library will want to consider the special character of the patron base it serves.

As an aid to the readers' advisor. Every title in this Core Collection is a recommended work and can be given with confidence to a user who expresses a need based on topic, genre, etc. Readers' advisory and user service are further aided by information about sequels, series, and companion volumes; by the descriptive and critical annotations; and by the subject headings in the Title and Subject Index.

As an aid in verification of information. For this purpose full bibliographical data are provided in the List of Works. Notes describe editions available, awards, publication history, and other titles in the series. For the most up-to-date metadata please consult the EBSCO*host* FICTION CORE COLLECTION database.

As an aid in curriculum support. The classified approach, subject indexing, and annotations are helpful in identifying materials appropriate for classroom use.

As an aid in collection maintenance. Information about titles available on a subject facilitates decisions to rebind, replace, or discard items. If a book has been demoted to Supplementary or Archival recommendation level (usually because it is no longer in print but sometimes for other reasons), and therefore no longer appears in the print abridgement of the database, that demotion is not intended as a sign that the book is no longer valuable or that it should necessarily be weeded from library collections.

As an instructional aid. The Core Collection is useful in courses that deal with literature and book selection for young people.

ORGANIZATION

The Core Collection is organized into two parts: the List of Fictional Works and the Indexes.

Part 1. List of Fictional Works

Part 1 lists works of fiction in alphabetical order by the last name of the author or by title, if the title is the main entry. References are made from variant forms of authors' names, from names of joint authors, and from names of editors or compilers of short story collections.

Each listing consists of a full bibliographical description. Prices, which are always subject to change, have been obtained from the publisher, when available, and are as current as possible. Entries include notes regarding sequels and publication history, and, whenever possible, an evaluation from a quoted source. The following is an example of a typical entry and a description of its components:

Machado, Carmen Maria

★**Her** body and other parties; stories. Carmen Maria Machado. Graywolf Press 2017 245p. (alk. paper) $16 ISBN 9781555977887; 155597788X

LC 2017930115

Kirkus Prize Finalist: Fiction (2017)

National Book Award Finalist: Fiction (2017)

In this collection of stories, author Carmen Maria Machado "blithely demolishes the arbitrary borders between psychological realism and science fiction, comedy and horror, fantasy and fabulism. . . . A wife refuses her husband's entreaties to remove the green ribbon from around her neck. A woman recounts her sexual encounters as a plague slowly consumes humanity. A salesclerk in a mall makes a horrifying discovery

within the seams of the store's prom dresses." (Publisher's note)

"Machado creates eerie, inventive worlds shimmering with supernatural swerves in this engrossing debut collection. Her stories make strikingly feminist moves by combining elements of horror and speculative fiction with women's everyday crises." Pub Wkly

The name of the author, Carmen Maria Machado, is given in conformity with *Anglo-American Cataloguing Rules,* 2nd edition, 2002 revision. The star at the start of the title indicates this is a "most highly recommended" title. The title of the book is *Her body and other parties.* The book was published by Graywolf Press in 2017

The book has 245 pages. If it were part of a series, then the series name would follow the page count. It sells for $16.

The ISBN (International Standard Book Number) is included to facilitate ordering. The Library of Congress control number is provided when available.

Following are two notes supplying additional information about the book. The first is a listing of awards it was shortlisted for or won. The second is a description of the book. The third is a critical note from *Publishers Weekly*. Such annotations are useful in evaluating books for selection and in determining which of several books on the same subject is best suited for the individual reader. Notes are also made to describe special features, sequels and companion volumes, editions available, and publication history.

Part 2. Indexes

The Title and Subject Index is a single alphabetical list of all the books entered in the Core Collection. Each book is entered under title, which is followed by the name of the author under which the entry for the book will be found in Part 1. Books are also listed under their main subjects or themes, as well as under headings for genre, form, or literary technique, if appropriate. Subject headings and subject cross references are printed in capital letters.

"See" references are made from forms of names or subjects that are not used as headings. "See also" references are made to related or more specific headings.

The following are examples of Index entries for the book cited above:

Title **Her** body and other parties. Machado, C. M.

Subject **WOMEN -- IDENTITY**

Machado, C. M. Her body and other parties

The Name Index is a list of names and pseudonyms used by authors included in Part 1. This list is included as a separate index for ease of reference, readers' advisory, and display creation.

ACKNOWLEDGMENTS

H. W. Wilson and EBSCO Information Services express special gratitude to the following librarians who both advised the company in editorial matters and assisted in the selection and weeding of titles for this Core Collection:

Advisory Board

Jennifer Baker
Librarian, Ret.
Seattle, WA

Brian Flota
Humanities Librarian
James Madison University
Harrisonburg, VA

Francisca Goldsmith
Consulting Librarian
Worcester, MA

Mary Griffin
Library Administrator, Ret.
Omaha, NE

Steven Jablonski
Collection Development Librarian
Skokie Public Library
Skokie, IL

Liza Oldham
Research and Instructional Design Librarian
Phillips Academy
Andover, MA

James Stubbs
Digital Services Librarian
Florence County Library System
Florence, SC

The editors would like to thank librarians Kim Burton, Hannah Callahan, Elizabeth Coleman, Halle Eisenman, Claire Fielder, Shauna Griffin, Maria Hugger, Lisa Schimmer, and Emily Young, and the EBSCO Proprietary Publishing team, whose help was instrumental in the creation of this collection.

FICTION CORE COLLECTION

NINETEENTH EDITION

A

Aaronovitch, Ben

Midnight riot; by Ben Aaronovitch. Del Rey/Ballantine 2011 310 p. (Rivers of London) (pbk.) $7.99

ISBN 034552425X; 9780345524256

LC 2013658945

Originally published in the U.K. as Rivers of London

In this book, by Ben Aaronovitch, "Probationary Constable Peter Grant dreams of being a detective in London's Metropolitan Police. Too bad his superior plans to assign him to the Case Progression Unit, where the biggest threat he'll face is a paper cut. But Peter's prospects change in the aftermath of a puzzling murder, when he gains exclusive information from an eyewitness who happens to be a ghost. Peter's ability to speak with the lingering dead brings him to the attention of Detective Chief Inspector Thomas Nightingale, who investigates crimes involving magic and other manifestations of the uncanny." (Publisher's note)

Other titles in this series are:

Moon over Soho (2011)

Whispers under ground (2012)

Broken homes (2014)

Foxglove summer (2015)

The hanging tree (2017)

Abani, Christopher

GraceLand. Farrar, Straus, and Giroux 2004 321p $24

ISBN 0-374-16589-0

LC 2003-12705

"This book works brilliantly in two ways. As a convincing and unpatronizing record of life in a poor Nigerian slum, and as a frighteningly honest insight into a world skewed by casual violence, it's wonderful." N Y Times Book Rev

Abani, Christopher, 1966-

The **secret** history of Las Vegas; a novel. Chris Abani. Penguin Books 2014 336 p. pbk $16

ISBN 0143124951; 9780143124955

LC 2013033496

Edgar Award: Best Paperback Original (2015)

In this book, by Chris Abani, "Las Vegas detective Salazar is determined to solve a recent spate of murders. When he encounters a pair of conjoined twins with a container of blood near their car, he's sure he has apprehended the killers, and enlists the help of Dr. Sunil Singh, a South African transplant who specializes in the study of psychopaths. As Sunil tries to crack the twins, the implications of his research grow darker." (Publisher's note)

"[A]n intricate braid of story strands, enriched by vivid descriptions, intriguingly dysfunctional characters, and abundant metaphors." Booklist

Abbott, Jeff

Blame; Jeff Abbott. Grand Central Publishing 2017 377 p. (hardcover) $26

ISBN 1455558435; 9781455558438; 9781455595662

LC 2017008122

In this book, by Jeff Abbott, "two years ago, Jane Norton crashed her car on a lonely road, killing her friend David and leaving her with amnesia. At first, everyone was sympathetic. Then they found Jane's note: I wish we were dead together. . . . From that day the town turned against her. But even now Jane is filled with questions: Why were they on that road? Why was she with David? Did she really want to die?" (Publisher's note)

"The unconventional plot, the constant surprises, and above all the psychological depth of the characters all make this a first-rate crime novel." Kirkus

Abbott, Megan E.

Bury me deep. Simon & Schuster Paperbacks 2009 240p il pa $15

ISBN 978-1-4165-9909-8; 978-1-4165-9909-6

LC 2008-30676

Working "from a true crime, the infamous Brighton Trunk Murders of 1934, Edgar-winner Abbott brings the era to life, inhabiting the 'bright-eyed and twitchy-tailed' party girls in all their enthusiasm and desperation. Her nearly stream-of-consciousness narration is direct and powerful, straight from Marion's addled and passionate brain. . . . But for all the classic-noir simplicity, such as the use of repetition rather than elaboration for emphasis, her prose carries an urgency that brings hard-boiled crime fiction kicking and screaming into the modern age." Kirkus

Abbott, Megan E., 1971-

Dare me; a novel. Megan Abbott. Reagan Arthur Books 2012 290 p. $24.99

ISBN 0316097772; 9780316097772

LC 2011051323

This novel tells the story of cheerleaders and best friends Addy Hanlon and Beth Cassidy. Addy has always followed Beth's leadership, but the young and cool new coach "Colette French draws Addy and the other cheerleaders into her life," leaving Beth unsettled and jealous. A suicide "focuses a police investigation on Coach and her squad." When "Addy tries to uncover the truth behind the death," she "learns that the boundary between loyalty and love can be dangerous terrain." (Publisher's note)

"Abbott has a keen sense for the beauty, danger, and vulnerability of teenage girls; her spare, elegant prose cuts straight to the heart of the high school pecking order and brings the girls' world to life." LJ

Abbott, Megan E., 1971-

The **fever**; Megan Abbott. Little, Brown & Co. 2014 320 p. (hardcover) $26

ISBN 0316231053; 9780316231053

LC 2014933201

In this book, by Megan Abbott, "the Nash family is close-knit. Tom is a popular teacher, father of two teens: Eli, a hockey star and girl magnet, and his sister Deenie, a diligent student. Their seeming stability, however, is thrown into chaos when Deenie's best friend is struck by a terrifying, unexplained seizure in class. Rumors of a hazardous outbreak spread through the family, school and community. As hysteria and contagion swell, a series of tightly held secrets emerges." (Publisher's note)

"Once again, Abbott makes an unforgettable inquiry into the emotional lives of young people, this time balanced with parents' own fears and failings. It's also a powerful portrait of community, with interesting echoes of The Crucible." Booklist

Abbott, Megan E., 1971-

★ **You** will know me; a novel. Megan Abbott. Little, Brown and Co. 2016 352 p. (hardcover) $26; (ebook) $78

ISBN 9780316231077; 9780316365918

LC 2015026542

This novel, by Megan Abbott, is "about family and ambition. . . . How far will you go to achieve a dream? That's the question a celebrated coach poses to Katie and Eric Knox after he sees their daughter Devon, a gymnastics prodigy and Olympic hopeful, compete. For the Knoxes there are no limits--until a violent death rocks their close-knit gymnastics community and everything they have worked so hard for is suddenly at risk." (Publisher's note)

"It's vivid, troubling, and powerful—and Abbott totally sticks the landing." Booklist

Abdul-Jabbar, Kareem, 1947-

★ **Mycroft** Holmes; by Kareem Abdul-Jabbar, Anna Waterhouse. Random House Inc. 2015 336 p. $25.99

ISBN 1783291532; 9781783291533

In this novel, by Kareem Abdul-Jabbar and Anna Waterhouse, Sherlock Holmes' brother "Mycroft's comfortable existence is overturned when [his friend] Douglas receives troubling reports from home. . . . Upon hearing the news, Georgiana abruptly departs for Trinidad. Near panic, Mycroft convinces Douglas that they should follow her, drawing the two men into a web of dark secrets that grows more treacherous with each step they take." (Publisher's note)

"The authors hit all the right notes here, combining fascinating historical detail (on Trinidadian culture and folklore, on tobacco importation in London, even on the development of the Gatling gun) with rousing adventure, including some cleverly choreographed fight scenes and a pair of protagonists whose rich biracial friendship, while presented realistically, given the era (Douglas must sometimes pose as a butler), is the highlight of the book." Booklist

Abe, Kobo

The **woman** in the dunes; translated from the Japanese by E. Dale Saunders; with drawings by Machi Abé. Knopf 1964 239p il

Original Japanese edition, 1962

The protagonist of this novel "is Niki Jumpei, an amateur entomologist who, on a weekend trip from the city, discovers a bizarre village in the dunes where residents live in deep sand pits. Imprisoned with a widow in one of the pits, he must shovel the omnipresent sand that threatens to bury the community. The novel relates Niki's attempts to escape the pit, his relationship with the woman, and his gradual acceptance of a new identity." Merriam-Webster's Ency of Lit

Abercrombie, Joe

Before they are hanged. Pyr Books 2008 543p pa $15.98

ISBN 978-159102-641-9; 1-59102-641-5

LC 2007-51694

Sequel to: The blade itself

"As savage Northmen invade Angland, the northernmost province of the unwieldy Union, honorable, hardworking Union soldier Colonel West watches his notions of civilized warfare erode in one horrible battle after another. In Dagoska, a southern city threatened by Gurkish soldiers and left undefended as Union troops head to Angland, dreadfully maimed Inquisitor Glokta employs tortures and deceptions to ferret out conspiracies against the king. Ignoring these worldly concerns, disreputable magus Bayaz of Calcis drives a squabbling little band through a wasteland in search of a relic that can open a gate to the realm of demons. Abercrombie leavens the bloody action with moments of dark humor, developing a story suffused with a rich understanding of human darkness and light." Publ Wkly

Followed by: Last argument of kings

Abercrombie, Joe

The **blade** itself. Pyr 2007 531p pa $15

ISBN 978-1-59102-594-8; 1-59102-594-X

LC 2007-28499

This is a "fantasy novel full of enough ironic and slightly self-deprecating humor and Scorcese-esque violence to make the average hipper than thou non-fantasy reader want to learn more about the genre . . . , yet filled with enough touchstones to make your average Tolkien weaned fantasy reader quite happy indeed." Blade & Thruster

Followed by: Before they are hanged

Abercrombie, Joe

Half a King; Joe Abercrombie. Random House Inc 2014 352 p. map (Shattered Sea) (hardcover) $26

ISBN 0804178321; 9780804178327

LC 2014017107

In this fantasy novel, by Joe Abercrombie, "among the royalty of Gettland, only strong, fearless, cold-eyed warriors have value. So Prince Yarvi, born with a withered hand, had only one option: to train as a minister (counselor). After years studying . . . Yarvi is ready to take the ministry's test when news arrives that his father and elder brother have been treacherously murdered by [a] neighboring rival King." (Publisher's note)

"The world building here is complete and convincing, and the characters are arresting in their all-too-human nature." Booklist

Followed by: Half the World (2015)

Abercrombie, Joe

Half a war; Joe Abercrombie. Del Rey 2015 384 p. (Shattered sea) $26

ISBN 0804178453; 9780804178457

LC 2015018064

In this fantasy novel, by Joe Abercrombie, the concluding volume of the "Shattered sea" series, "Princess Skara of Throvenland watches helplessly as Bright Yilling, the High King's war leader, callously kills her grandfather King Fynn, burns his halls, and lays waste to her homeland after what the king thought was an agreement turned out to be a betrayal. . . . The allies will need elf-weapons, hidden and deadly dangerous, designed to kill a god." (Kirkus Reviews)

"The narrative, well-sprinkled with gory action and impelled by characters at this stage not just familiar, but gratifying, moves along at a brisk clip. Best of all, the relentless intrigues, plots, and schemes bubble just below the surface." Kirkus

Abercrombie, Joe

Half the world; Joe Abercrombie. Del Rey 2015 366 p. map (hardcover : acid-free paper) $26

ISBN 0804178429; 9780804178426

LC 2014038766

Alex Award (2016)

"This stand-alone sequel to the author's popular Half a King (2014) features a new protagonist: 16-year-old Thorn, who finds herself pressed into service to Father Yarvi, the cunning minister to King Uthil of Gettland and his queen, Laithlin. Thorn will accompany Yarvi on a voyage designed to turn enemies into friends and allies as Gettland faces the possibility of war with the High King. Along the way, she will be trained in fighting by a woman named Skifr, whom some call a witch, and find her feelings for a boy named Brand changing." (Booklist)

"Abercrombie has a knack for building characters with pathos and wit. Both plot and setting are believable, and readers will easily immerse themselves in Thorn and Yarvi's world." Pub Wkly

Followed by: Half a War (2015)

Abercrombie, Joe

The **heroes**; Joe Abercrombie. 1st ed. Orbit 2011 xi, 541p.p ill.

ISBN 9780316044981; 0316193569; 9780316193566

This fantasy novel tells the story of a "three-day battle . . . set in the same world as [author Joe] Abercrombie's First Law Trilogy. . . . Union commander Lord Marshal Kroy coordinates the fight with the aid of a motley group of incompetent, self-important officers. . . . Col. Bremer dan Gorst is officially a royal observer who nurses a burning desire to kill or be killed. Leading a much smaller army against the Union is Black Dow, whose grip on the throne of the Northmen is tenuous and based on fear and brutality. Calder, a slippery and cunning egotist, advocates peace while plotting to take Black Dow's place." (Publishers Weekly)

Abercrombie, Joe

Red country; Joe Abercrombie. Orbit 2012 464 p.

ISBN 0316187216; 9780316187213

In this novel by Joe Abercrombie "Shy South . . . [will] have to sharpen up some bad old ways to get her family back. . . . She sets off in pursuit with only a pair of oxen and her cowardly old step father Lamb for company. But it turns out Lamb's buried a bloody past of his own. . . . Their journey will take them across the barren plains to a frontier town gripped by gold fever, through feud, duel and massacre, high into the unmapped mountains to a reckoning with the Ghosts." (Publisher's note)

Abrahams, Peter

Dog on it; a Chet and Bernie mystery. [by] Spencer Quinn. Atria Books 2008 305p $25

ISBN 978-1-4165-8583-1; 1-4165-8583-4

"Chet the Jet is a dog who failed K-9 school (cats in the open country played a role in his demisc), but now he is a dedicated PI and works with Bernie, owner of the Little Detective Agency. The story is told entirely from Chet's point of view, which will delight dog-loving mystery readers, but the book is also an excellent PI tale, dogs aside, as Chet and Bernie investigate the disappearance of a teenage girl whose developer dad may be up to no good. . . . Excellent and fully fleshed primary and secondary characters, a consistently doggy view of the world, and a sprightly pace make this a not-to-be-missed debut." Booklist

Abrams, David

Fobbit. Black Cat 2012 372 p. $15

ISBN 0802120326; 9780802120328

This book is a "satire of the Iraq War. . . . The Fobbits of the title are U.S. Army support personnel, stationed at Baghdad's enclave of desk jobs: Forward Operating Base Triumph. . . . The soul of the book is Staff Sgt. Chance Gooding Jr., a public relations NCO who spends his days crafting excruciating press releases and fending off a growing sense of moral bankruptcy." (Publishers Weekly)

Abu-Jaber, Diana, 1960-

Birds of paradise; a novel. W. W. Norton & Co. 2011 362p $25.95

ISBN 978-0-393-06461-2; 0-393-06461-1

LC 2011-14575

"After 13-year-old Felice Muir runs away from her Miami hom. . . , her mother, Avis, retreats to her kitchen, where she creates elaborate pastries as part therapy, part offering to her absent daughter. Felice's father, Brian, buries himself in his lawyering and fantasizes about the young Cuban woman in the office next door, and her brother, Stanley, throws himself into the organic market he's opened in lieu of going to college. They all vacillate between willing themselves to forget Felice and constant wondering—why she left, where she is, if she's alive—until the approach of her eighteenth birthday and a storm named Katrina upsets their fragile holding patterns. Abu-Jaber . . . employs her descriptive talents in bringing Miami to steamy, pulsing life, but it is Birds of Paradise's neither predictable nor merely haphazard momentum and its rich cast of characters that make us feel we're in deliciously capable hands." Elle

Abu-Jaber, Diana

Crescent. Norton 2003 349p hardcover o.p. pa $13.95

ISBN 0-393-05747-X; 0-393-32554-7 pa

LC 2002-152907

"Sirine's now-deceased missionary parents were Iraqi and American; she's been raised since she was nine by her beloved Iraqi uncle. Her world is his house, the cafe where she is chef, and the air of Los Angeles. She's nearly 40, and inside her pale skin and green eyes she feels the rhythms of her uncle's Arabic stories and the scent of Eastern spices. Hanif ('Han'), a professor of Arabic literature at the local university comes to the cafe for the tastes of home, and he and Sirine fall into an affair of wild, sweet tenderness. . . . Abu-Jaber's language is miraculous, whether describing the texture of Han's skin or Sirine's way with an onion. It is not possible to stop reading." Booklist

Abu-Jaber, Diana

Origin; a novel. W.W. Norton & Co. 2007 384p $24.95

ISBN 978-0-393-06455-1; 0-393-06455-7

LC 2007-4963

"For all its internal chill, the drama that unfolds around fingerprint expert Lena Dawson is a struggle toward spring and the light. Haunting and compelling, Origin combines the traditions of the crime novel with an examination of Lena's unusual upbringing. It's a little film noir, a bit independent-woman-detective thriller, and winningly fresh in its approach." PopMatters

Acampora, Lauren

★ The **Wonder** Garden; Lauren Acampora. Grove Press 2015 368 p. (hardcover) $24

ISBN 0802123554; 9780802123558; 9780802124814

This short story collection, by Lauren Acampora, "bring[s] to the page the myriad lives of a suburban town, and reveal at each turn the unseen battles we play out behind drawn blinds, the creeping truths from which we distract ourselves, and the massive dreams we haul quietly with us and hold close." (Publisher's note)

"Acampora not only meticulously conveys the allure of an outwardly paradisiacal suburban community, with its perfectly restored Victorian homes and well-tended lawns; she also clearly captures the inner turmoil of its residents, homing in on their darkest impulses and beliefs. Some of the stories' starring characters make cameos in others, adding considerable complexity to the whole." Booklist

Acevedo, Chantel

The **Distant** Marvels; Chantel Acevedo. Penguin Group USA 2015 304 p. $17

ISBN 1609452526; 9781609452520

LC 2015410975

In this book, by Chantel Acevedo, "the elderly Maria Sirena has lived through and, as a young girl, participated in the Cuban war for independence; now, in 1963, at the dawn of Castro's new Cuba, with Hurricane Flora on the way, she is evacuated with other women to a historic mansion for shelter, where she entertains her fellow refugees with personal and richly imagined stories." (Booklist)

"This extraordinary narrative tells, from these women's perspectives, how war brings lovers together and tears families apart. This is a major, uniquely powerful, and startlingly beautiful novel that should bring Acevedo's name to the top echelon of this generation's writers." Booklist

Achebe, Chinua

★ **Things** fall apart. Astor-Honor 1959 215p $15.95

ISBN 0-8392-1113-9

First published 1958 in the United Kingdom; first United States edition published by McDowell, Obolensky

"The novel chronicles the life of Okonkwo, the leader of an Igbo (Ibo) community, from the events leading up to his banishment from the community for accidentally killing a clansman, through the seven years of his exile, to his return. The novel addresses the problem of the intrusion in the 1890s of white missionaries and colonial government into tribal Igbo society. It describes the simultaneous disintegration of its protagonist Okonkwo and of his village. The novel was praised for its intelligent and realistic treatment of tribal beliefs and of psychological disintegration coincident with social unraveling." Merriam-Webster's Ency of Lit

Aciman, Andre A.

Call me by your name; [by] André Aciman. Farrar, Straus and Giroux 2007 248p $23

ISBN 0-374-29921-8

LC 2006-11720

Lambda Literary Award: Gay General Fiction (2008)

"Aciman's novel describes a passionate affair between two young men." (N Y Times Book Rev)

"When Oliver, a handsome young American philosopher, arrives in a seaside town in Italy to work on a book about Heraclitus, as the guest of an Italian professor, the son of the house, Elio—seventeen, studious, moody, and ravenous—falls for him. Elio's edgy rapture as he forms himself in relation to another plays out against the background of a scorching Mediterranean summer, and Aciman introduces a small universe of characters who are themselves altered by the charged air that surrounds the lovers: Elio's mother, who calls Oliver il cauboi (the cowboy); his generous, hazy father; and the households cantankerous cook, who every morning carefully cracks open the American's soft-boiled eggs." New Yorker

Aciman, André

Enigma variations; André Aciman. Farrar, Straus and Giroux 2017 266 p. (hardcover) $26

ISBN 9780374148430; 9780374714772

LC 2016020262

This novel, by André Aciman, "charts the life of a man named Paul, whose loves remain as consuming and as covetous throughout his adulthood as they were in his adolescence. . . . Ahead of every step Paul takes, his hopes, denials, fears, and regrets are always ready to lay their traps. Yet the dream of love lingers." (Publisher's note)

"Aciman's sensuous, subtle language supports not only his marvelous descriptive power but also how deeply and resonantly he constructs his fondly and fully conceived characters." Booklist

Aciman, André

Harvard Square; a novel. André Aciman. 1st ed. W.W. Norton & Co Inc. 2013 304 p. (hardcover) $25.95

ISBN 039308860X; 9780393088601

LC 2012050738

This book's narrator, "a young Jewish man originally from Egypt, is a graduate student at Harvard in the mid 1970s. After failing exams he questions his goal of a career in academia. When he's not studying, he frequents Cambridge bars and restaurants that cater to a Middle Eastern clientele, and there he meets Kalaj, a man of Tunisian descent with a magnetic personality. With much in common, the two bond and spend the fall carousing in Cambridge and reminiscing about their pasts." (Library Journal)

Ackerman, Elliot

Dark at the Crossing; by Elliot Ackerman. Alfred A. Knopf 2017 237 p. hardcover $25.95

ISBN 9781101947371; 1101947373

LC 2016954679

National Book Award Finalist: Fiction (2017)

In this book, by Elliot Ackerman, "Haris Abadi is a man in search of a cause. An Arab American with a conflicted past, he is now in Turkey, attempting to cross into Syria and join the fight against Bashar al-Assad's regime. But he is robbed before he can make it, and is taken in by Amir, a charismatic Syrian refugee and former revolutionary, and Amir's wife, Daphne, a sophisticated beauty haunted by grief." (Publisher's note)

"Here is a thriller, psychological fiction, political intrigue, and even a love story all wrapped into a stunningly realistic and sometimes horrifying package." LJ

Ackroyd, Peter

The **trial** of Elizabeth Cree; a novel of the Limehouse murders. Talese 1995 261p

ISBN 0-385-47707-4

LC 94-37348

First published 1994 in the United Kingdom with title: Dan Leno and the Limehouse Golem

"Well-known but incidental Victorian 'characters'—Karl Marx and the novelist George Gissing—converge in this mystery/anti-suspense fiction about a former music-hall actress, Elizabeth Cree, and her husband, an apparent serial killer. Chapters of Mr. Cree's diary alternate with transcripts of Mrs. Cree's trial for his murder and sections of third-person narrative." New Yorker

Adams, Alice

After the war; a novel. Knopf 2000 305p $25

ISBN 0-375-40683-2

LC 99-47104

Adams' final novel, set in 1940s North Carolina, "picks up where her previous book, 'A Southern Exposure,' left off. Cynthia Baird, a transplanted Yankee, is floating from one affair to another while her husband, Harry, is off fighting in Europe; her housekeeper, Odessa, the moral center of this particular universe, keeps turning out her ham biscuits; the local girls, including Melanctha Byrd, who is heading North to Radcliffe . . . are growing sly and eager to leave town. There are so many subplots—

about race relations, sex, politics, and adolescence—that it's as if Adams wanted both to capture an era entirely and to make things, this once, come out right. The result is lovely, tender, and a little hokey, like that moment just before the birthday candles are blown out." New Yorker

Adams, Alice

A **southern** exposure; a novel. Knopf 1996 305p
ISBN 0-679-44452-1

LC 95-16109

"Though this plot teeters on the edge of soap opera, it never slips into the slush, thanks in part to the sobering imminence of war, which casts an air of gravity over all these amorous proceedings. Ms. Adams's breezy, wistful lyricism perfectly captures this lovely place and golden time, just before things got so damn serious forever." NY Times Book Rev

Adams, Alice

★ The **stories** of Alice Adams. Knopf 2002 622p $30
ISBN 0-375-41285-9

LC 2002-70940

"Taken together, these stories betray the changing mores of the past half-century; taken in sequence, they trace the changes in the American short story over the past 40 years, some of those changes wrought by Adams herself." Publ Wkly

Adams, Douglas

The **hitchhiker's** guide to the galaxy; 25th anniversary illustrated collector's ed.; Harmony Books 2004 271p il $35
ISBN 1-4000-5293-9

LC 2004-558987

First published 1980

"Based on a BBC radio series, . . . this is the episodic story of Arthur Dent, a contemporary Englishman who discovers first that his unpretentious house is about to be demolished to make way for a bypass, and second that a good friend is actually an alien galactic hitchhiker who announces that Earth itself will soon be demolished to make way for an intergalactic speedway. A suitably bewildered Dent soon finds himself hitching . . . rides throughout space, aided by a . . . reference book, The Hitchhiker's Guide to the Galaxy, a compendium of 'facts,' philosophies, and wild advice." Libr J

Other titles in this series are:
Life, the universe, and everything
The restaurant at the end of the universe
So long, and thanks for all the fish
Mostly harmless

Adams, Douglas

Life, the universe, and everything. Harmony Bks. 1982 227p hardcover o.p. pa $12.95
ISBN 0-517-54874-7; 0-345-41890-6 pa

LC 82-15470

Third volume in The hitchhiker's series

"Arthur Dent and his motley crew do tie up most of the loose ends and manage to prevent the destruction of the universe, but the first two novels . . . 'must' be read to understand the situation, and even then it's confusing." Libr J

Followed by So long, and thanks for all the fish

Adams, Douglas

Mostly harmless. Harmony Bks. 1992 277p hardcover o.p. pa $12.95
ISBN 0-517-57740-2; 0-345-37933-0 pa

LC 92-25457

"A Grebulon reconnaissance ship with faulty programming, a news reporter suffering from a bad case of missed opportunities, a fugitive from the new 'improved' offices of the Hitchhiker's Guide to the Galaxy, and a hitchhiker lost in a parallel universe come together in grand style in the fifth installment of Adams's best-selling 'trilogy.'" Libr J

Adams, Douglas

The **restaurant** at the end of the universe. Harmony Bks. 1981 250p hardcover o.p. pa $12.95
ISBN 0-517-54535-7; 0-345-41892-1 pa

LC 81-6563

Second volume in The hitchhiker's series

First published 1980 in the United Kingdom

"Poor uprooted Arthur Dent finds himself swept along in the wake of Zaphod Beeblebrox, former President of the Galaxy, as Zaphod searches for the man who rules the Universe. They and their companions tumble from one scrape into another, with the erratic aid of Zaphod's dead great-grandfather and Marvin, their perpetually depressed robot. Adams's lively sense of the ridiculous has concocted many hilarious episodes, though the inspired lunacy of the first book has become rather uneven here. Still, this is one of the best pieces of sf humor available." Libr J

Followed by Life, the universe, and everything

Adams, Douglas

So long, and thanks for all the fish. Harmony Bks. 1985 204p hardcover o.p. pa $7.99
ISBN 0-517-55439-9; 0-345-39183-4 pa

LC 84-19350

Fourth volume in The hitchhiker's series

Arthur Dent "returns to a supposedly destroyed Earth to build a hyperspace bypass. The night of his return, Arthur falls in love with a sedated girl (her brother says she's 'barking mad'), only to lose her, then accidentally find her twice more. She is Fenchurch, the girl who in . . . 'Guide' . . . discovered the secret of Earth's potential happiness moments before it was demolished. Her 'madness' stems from the time when Earth should have been destroyed, and wasn't, but when all the dolphins disappeared. . . . The humor is still off-the-wall, but less forced and more gentle than the other books. . . . The series seems to be winding down, but it is still an addictive commodity to its fans." SLJ

Followed by Mostly harmless

Adams, Henry

★ **Democracy**; an American novel. introduction by Arthur Schlesinger, Jr. Modern Library 2003 xx, 209p pa $12.95
ISBN 0-375-76058-X

LC 2002-19645

First published anonymously 1880

"A social and political satire based on the corruption of the second Grant administration, the book includes characters modeled on President Hayes and James G. Blaine. A charming and intelligent young widow, Madeleine Lee, moves to Washington 'to touch with her own hands the massive machinery of society.' She finally rejects an offer of marriage from a senator who has compromised his moral integrity for political advantage." Reader's Ency. 3d edition

Adams, Richard

Watership Down; Scribner classics ed.; Scribner 1996 429p $30; pa $15
ISBN 0-684-83605-X; 0-7432-7770-8 pa

"Faced with the annihilation of its warren, a small group of male rabbits sets out across the English downs in search of a new home. Internal struggles for power surface in this intricately woven, realistically told adult adventure when the protagonists must coordinate tactics in order to defeat an enemy rabbit fortress. It is clear that the author has done research on rabbit behavior, for this tale is truly authentic." Shapiro Fic for Youth. 3d edition

Adamson, Gil

The **outlander**; a novel. Ecco 2008 389p $25.95

ISBN 978-0-06-149125-2; 0-06-149125-X

LC 2007-41062

First published in 2007 in Canada

"Of course, the Girl Being Chased is one of the most enduring figures of chivalric and chauvinistic literature, a staple of television dramas and horror films. . . . But Gil is short for Gillian, and her strange and complicated heroine has nothing in common with Hollywood's wornout damsels in distress. . . there are pages here you can't read slowly enough to catch every word." Washington Post Book World

Addison, Corban

A **harvest** of thorns; Corban Addison. Thomas Nelson 2017 359 p. (hardcover : alk. paper) $24.99

ISBN 9780718042387; 9780718042400

LC 2016027881

In this novel, by Corban Addison, "in Dhaka, Bangladesh, a garment factory burns to the ground, claiming the lives of hundreds of workers, mostly young women. . . . A year later in Washington DC, Joshua Griswold, a disgraced former journalist from the 'Washington Post,' receives an anonymous summons from a corporate whistleblower who offers him confidential information about Presto and the fire." (Publisher's note)

"Through his broad, intelligent research and insightful writing, Addison prods the conscience, trumpeting justice while acknowledging that the cost of a globalized society is incalculably higher than the price of a T-shirt." Pub Wkly

Addison, Katherine

The **Goblin** Emperor; Katherine Addison. Tor Books 2014 448 p. (hardcover) $25.99

ISBN 076532699X; 9780765326997

LC 2013025454

Locus Award: Fantasy Novel (2015)

"The youngest, half-goblin son of the Emperor has lived his entire life in exile, distant from the Imperial Court and the deadly intrigue. . . . But when his father and three sons in line for the throne are killed in an 'accident,' he has no choice but to take his place as the only surviving rightful heir." (Publisher's note)

"There are powerful character studies and a plot full of small but deadly traps among which the sweet-natured, perplexed Maia must navigate. The result is a spellbinding and genuinely affecting drama." Kirkus

Adebayo, Ayobami

★ **Stay** with me; a novel. Ayobami Adebayo. Alfred A. Knopf 2017 257 p. (hardcover) $25.95

ISBN 9780451494610; 9780451494603; 0451494601

LC 2016031296

Baileys Women's Prize for Fiction: Shortlist (2017)

In this book, by Ayobami Adebayo, "Yejide and Akin have been married since they met and fell in love at university. Though many expected Akin to take several wives, he and Yejide have always agreed: polygamy is not for them. But four years into their marriage[,] . . . Yejide is still not pregnant. She assumes she still has time--until her family arrives on her doorstep with a young woman they introduce as Akin's second wife." (Publisher's note)

". . . Adebayo's novel captures how the turmoil of Nigerian life in the 1980s and '90s seeps into the most personal of decisions—to fight for, and protect, one's family. Adebayo's debut marks the emergence of a fine young writer." Kirkus

Adichie, Chimamanda Ngozi, 1977-

★ **Americanah**; a novel. Chimamanda Ngozi Adichie. 1st ed. Alfred A. Knopf 2013 496 p. (hardcover) $26.95

ISBN 0307271080; 9780307271082

LC 2012043875

Carnegie Medal: Shortlist (2014)

In this book, "Ifemelu, beautiful and naturally aristocratic, has the good fortune to escape Nigeria during a time of military dictatorship. . . . Ifemelu's high school sweetheart, Obinze . . . he has been denied a visa to enter post-9/11 America . . ., and now he is living illegally in London, delivering refrigerators and looking for a way to find his beloved. . . . The years pass, and Ifemelu is involved in the usual entanglements." Can they reunite? (Kirkus Reviews)

"Witty, wry, and observant, Adichie is a marvelous storyteller who writes passionately about the difficulty of assimilation and the love that binds a man, a woman, and their homeland." LJ

Adichie, Chimamanda Ngozi

Half of a yellow sun. Alfred A. Knopf 2006 435p $24.95

ISBN 978-1-4000-4416-0; 1-4000-4416-2

LC 2005-57784

The author has a "gift for capturing the rhythms of African middle-class life: not just its political awareness but the aspirations and cultural imperatives that lend it its varied character. . . . For its portrayal of Nigeria's political and cultural past, [this book] is a welcome addition to the corpus of African letters." Times Lit Suppl

Adichie, Chimamanda Ngozi

The **thing** around your neck. Alfred A. Knopf 2009 240p $24.95

ISBN 978-0-307-27107-5; 0-307-27107-2

LC 2008-41271

"The stories are set both in the United States and in Nigeria, where things continue to fall apart. . . . Adichie, a brilliant writer whose characters stay with you for a long time, deserves to be more widely known." Libr J

Adiga, Aravind

★ **Last** man in tower; a novel. Alfred A. Knopf 2011 381p $26.96

ISBN 978-0-307-59409-9; 0-307-59409-2

LC 2011-03406

"In the rapidly expanding city of Mumbai, where new buildings sprout like weeds, the construction business isn't just a front for illegal activity, it's a raison d'être. When a less-than-ethical developer tries to lure, and later coerce, a community of longstanding tenants out of their apartment complex, it is only the widowed schoolteacher of 3A who continues to rebuff him. . . . [Adiga] maps out, in luminous prose, India's ambivalence toward its accelerated growth, while creating an engaging protagonist in the stubborn resident: a man whose ambition and independence have been tempered with an understanding of the important, if almost imperceptible, difference between development and progress." Entertainment Wkly

Adiga, Aravind

Selection day; a novel. Aravind Adiga. Scribner 2017 289 p. (hardcover) $26

ISBN 9781501150838; 9781501150852; 1501150839

LC 2017288219

This novel, by Aravind Adiga, is about "two brothers in a Mumbai slum who are raised by their obsessive father to become cricket stars, and whose coming of age threatens their relationship, future, and sense of themselves. . . . Filled with unforgettable characters from across India's social strata—the old scout everyone calls Tommy Sir; Anand Mehta, the big-dreaming investor; Sofia, a wealthy, beautiful girl and the boys' biggest fan." (Publisher's note)

"A master class in integrating character and landscape, Adiga's novel also portrays Mumbai as alternatively stifling and liberating." Booklist

Adiga, Aravind

The **white** tiger; a novel. Free Press 2008 336p $24

ISBN 978-1-416-56259-7; 1-416-56259-1

LC 2007-45527

"In this darkly comic début novel set in India, Balram, a chauffeur, murders his employer, justifying his crime as the act of a 'social entrepreneur.' In a series of letters to the Premier of China, in anticipation of the leader's upcoming visit to Balram's homeland, the chauffeur recounts his transformation from an honest, hardworking boy growing up in 'the Darkness'—those areas of rural India where education and electricity are equally scarce, and where villagers banter about local elections 'like eunuchs discussing the Kama Sutra'—to a determined killer. He places the blame for his rage squarely on the avarice of the Indian élite, among whom bribes are commonplace, and who perpetuate a system in which many are sacrificed to the whims of a few. Adiga's message isn't subtle or novel, but Balram's appealingly sardonic voice and acute observations of the social order are both winning and unsettling." New Yorker

Adler, H. G., 1910-1988

Panorama; a novel. [by] H.G. Adler; translated from the German by Peter Filkins. Random House 2010 xxii, 450p $26

ISBN 978-1-4000-6851-7; 1-4000-6851-7

LC 2010-15079

Original German edition, 1968

"Adler chronicles various moments in the life of protagonist Josef: unhappy childhood in Prague, brutish boarding school, teenage adventures in the bucolic Czech forest, political and bureaucratic frustrations as a young academic, and, finally, hardship and bleakness in a concentration camp. It is written in a captivating stream-of-consciousness style that wanders yet comes to circle certain salient observations, and readers may note stylistic and philosophical continuities between this and the work of W. G. Sebald, who claimed Adler as a major influence. But, in part, the beauty of this work is that it can't be easily categorized: it's not quite a bildungsroman; it's delightfully if erratically satirical; it's hauntingly bleak yet possesses echoes of the transcendent." Booklist

Adler, H. G., 1910-1988

The **wall**; a novel. H. G. Adler; translated by Peter Filkins. Random House Inc 2014 672 p. (hardback) $30

ISBN 0812993063; 9780812993066

LC 2014003513

Written by H. G. Adler and translated by Peter Filkins, "Drawing upon Adler's own experiences in the Holocaust and his postwar life, 'The Wall,' like the other works in the trilogy, nonetheless avoids detailed historical specifics. The novel tells the story of Arthur Landau, survivor of a wartime atrocity, a man struggling with his nightmares and his memories of the past as he strives to forge a new life for himself." (Publisher's note)

"Adler's novel has a Kafkaesque dimension as well, save that Landau has at least the saving grace of an understanding wife who does what she can to make him feel safe, or at least safer, in the world: 'She was happy to see,' Landau tells us, 'that I had achieved a partial and tolerable sense of resignation.' An eloquent record of suffering—and perhaps of redemption as well." Kirkus

Includes bibliographical references and index

Adler-Olsen, Jussi

The **absent** one; by Jussi Adler-Olsen ; translated by K.E. Semmel. Dutton 2012 406 p. (hardcover) $26.95

ISBN 9780525952893

LC 2012021473

This novel, by Jussi Adler-Olsen, is the second book in the "Department Q" series. It follows "detective Carl Mørck, a deeply flawed, brilliant detective newly assigned to . . . Copenhagen's coldest cases. . . . A brother and sister were brutally murdered two decades earlier. . . . But once Mørck reopens the files, it becomes clear that all is not what it seems. Looking into the supposedly solved case leads him to Kimmie, a woman living on the streets, stealing to survive." (Publisher's note)

Adler-Olsen, Jussi

A **Conspiracy** of Faith; Jussi Adler-Olsen. Penguin Group USA 2013 512 p. (hardcover) $26.95

ISBN 0525954007; 9780525954002

This novel, by Jussi Adler-Olsen, is part of the "Department Q" series. "Detective Carl Mørck holds . . . [an] old and decayed message, written in blood. It is a cry for help from two young brothers, tied and bound in a boathouse by the sea. Could it be real? . . . Carl's investigation will force him to cross paths with a woman stuck in a desperate marriage. . . . But enough is enough. She will find out the truth, no matter the cost to her husband--or to herself." (Publisher's note)

Adler-Olsen, Jussi

The **keeper** of lost causes; Jussi Adler-Olsen; translated by Lisa Hartford. Dutton 2011 396 p. (hardcover) $25.95

ISBN 0525952489; 9780525952480

LC 2011014873

This novel, by Jussi Adler-Olsen, first entry in the "Department Q" series, "features the deeply flawed chief detective Carl MØrck, who used to be . . . one of Copenhagen's best. . . . [Now] Carl's been selected to run Department Q, a new special investigations division that turns out to be a department of one. With a stack of Copenhagen's coldest cases to keep him company, . . . Carl may have the last laugh, and redeem himself in the process." (Publisher's note)

Other titles in this series are:

The absent one (2012)

A conspiracy of faith (2013)

The purity of vengeance (2013)

The Marco effect (2014)

The hanging girl (2015)

The scarred woman (2017)

Adrian, Chris

The **children's** hospital. McSweeney's Books 2006 615p $24

ISBN 1-932416-60-9

"Adrian's vast floating world of a novel is a marvel. The Children's Hospital is intelligent, seductive and beautifully realized." Hartford Courant

Adrian, Chris

The **great** night. Farrar, Straus and Giroux 2011 292p $26

ISBN 978-0-374-16641-0; 0-374-16641-2

LC 2010-47603

"Inventive and scarily beautiful, this could wipe out casual readers, but it is an extraordinary novel." Libr J

Afrika, Tatamkulu, 1920-2002

Bitter Eden; a novel. Tatamkhulu Afrika. First U.S. edition Picador 2014 240 p. (hardcover) $25

ISBN 1250043662; 9781250043665

LC 2013038598

Stonewall Honor Book - Literature (2015)

This book "is based on [author] Tatamkhulu Afrika's own capture in North Africa and his experiences as a prisoner of war during World War II in Italy and Germany. [It] deals with three men who must negotiate the emotions that are brought to the surface by the physical closeness of survival in the male-only camps. The complex rituals of camp life and the strange loyalties and deep bonds among the men are . . . depicted." (Publisher's note)

"First published in Britain in 2002 (and written years earlier), this sole novel from Egyptian-born, South African-raised Afrika is based on his experiences in Italian and German prisoner-of-war camps in World War II...Afrika focuses on aspects of prison camp life that have been little explored. While the novel's theme of repressed desire might have had more power and perhaps a bit of shock value had it been published at the time it was written, it's still notable for its compelling depiction of an individual's struggle to maintain some measure of humanity and tenderness under the most inhuman of conditions." LJ

Agawa, Yoko

The **housekeeper** and the professor; translated by Stephen Snyder. Picador 2009 180p pa $14

ISBN 0-312-42780-8 pa; 978-0-312-42780-1 pa

LC 2006-41568

In this novel, "a strange relationship blossoms between a brilliant math professor suffering from short-term memory problems following a traumatic head injury and the young housekeeper, the mother of a ten-year-old son, hired to care for him." (Publisher's note)

"A mysterious, suspenseful, and radiant fable. . . . The smart and resourceful housekeeper, the single mother of a baseball-crazy 10-year-old boy the Professor adores, falls under the spell of the beautiful mathematical phenomena the Professor elucidates, as will the reader, and the three create an indivisible formula for love." Booklist

Agee, Jonis

The **bones** of paradise; Jonis Agee. William Morrow, an imprint of HarperCollinsPublishers 2016 432 p. (ebook) $24.99; (hardback) $25.99

ISBN 9780062413499; 9780062413475; 9780062413482

LC 2015037302

This novel, by Jonis Agee, is "a multigenerational family saga set in the unforgiving Nebraska Sand Hills in the years following the massacre at Wounded Knee. . . . Ten years after the Seventh Cavalry massacred more than two hundred Lakota men, women, and children at Wounded Knee, J.B. Bennett, a white rancher, and Star, a young Native American woman, are murdered in a remote meadow on J.B.'s land. The deaths bring together the scattered members of the Bennett family." (Publisher's note)

"The story's several parts—gritty Western, family saga, mystery—work together for a memorable tale of heartbreak and redemption." Pub Wkly

Agee, James

★ A **death** in the family. McDowell, Obolensky 1957 339p

"Six-year-old Rufus Follet, his younger sister Catherine, his mother, and various relatives all react differently to the unexpected announcement that Rufus's father has been fatally injured in an automobile accident. The poignancy of sorrow, the strength of personal beliefs, and the comforting love and support of a family are all elements of this compassionate novel." Shapiro. Fic for Youth. 3d edition

Agee, James, 1909-1955

Let us now praise famous men; A death in the family, and shorter fiction; . Library of America 2005 818p il $35

ISBN 1-931082-81-2

LC 2005-45098

This volume presents Agee's "Let Us Now Praise Famous Men (1941), a collaboration with photographer Walker Evans that began as an assignment from Fortune magazine to report on the lives of Alabama sharecroppers. . . . A Death in the Family, the Pulitzer Prize-winning novel that he worked on for over a decade and that was published posthumously in 1957, recreates . . . Agee's childhood in Knoxville, Tennessee, and the upheaval his family experienced after his father's death in a car accident when Agee was six years old. . . . This volume also includes The Morning Watch (1951), an autobiographical novella, . . . and three short stories." (Publisher's note)

Agnon, Shmuel Yosef

★ **Only** yesterday; [by] S.Y. Agnon; translated by Barbara Harshav. Princeton Univ. Press 2000 652p

ISBN 0-691-00972-4

LC 00-21147

"Though Agnon would go on to write much of compelling interest during his remaining 25 years, this would be his masterpiece—a novel that deserves comparison with Kafka's The Trial, Mann's The Magic Mountain and Hermann Broch's The Sleepwalkers as a deployment of the resources of fiction for plumbing those abysses of cultural and personal crisis that haunted so many imaginations in the modernist period." Los Angeles Times Book Rev

Ahmad, A. X.

The **Caretaker**. St. Martin's Press 2013 304 p. (hardcover) $24.99

ISBN 1250016843; 9781250016843

LC 2013006966

This novel "introduces Ranjit Singh, a former captain in the Indian army currently trying to make ends meet as a landscaper on Martha's Vineyard." Singh gets the caretaker position at the home of Sen. Clayton Neals. "Singh's family moves into the Neals's home, but they must flee when a break-in occurs. As they leave, Singh's daughter, Shanti, grabs a doll that contains a hidden microfilm chip that proves to be the key to the family's survival." (Library Journal)

Ahmad, Jamil, 1933-2014

The **wandering** falcon. Penguin Books 2011 243p $25.95

ISBN 978-0-241-114515-9; 0-241-14515-5

LC 20110323153

A novel "set in the forbidding remote tribal areas of Pakistan and Afghanistan. . . . [The author] has written [a] . . . portrait of a world of custom and compassion, of love and cruelty, of hardship and survival, a place fragile, unknown, and unforgiving." (Publisher's note)

"A gripping book, as important for illuminating the current state of this region as it is timeless in its beautiful imagery and rhythmic prose." Publ Wkly

Aiken, Joan

The **monkey's** wedding, and other stories. Small Beer Press 2011 203p $24

ISBN 978-1-931520-74-4; 1-931520-74-7

LC 2011-04625

"Brisk, matter-of-fact accounts of annoying mermaids, hospitable devils, unionizing mice and robot prototypes that make flipping light switches an act of menace. And the women range from self-willed wives to beautiful stunt motorcyclists to knitting spinsters. Sometimes they conform to the stereotypes of the times they were created in, but Aiken is full of surprises: Her plots and characters continually wander off the beaten track, leaving far behind what fantasist Lord Dunsany called 'the fields we know.'" Seattle Times

Aira, Cesar

Ghosts; translated by Chris Andrews. New Directions 2008 139p pa $12.95

ISBN 978-0-8112-1742-2 pa; 0-8112-1742-6 pa

LC 2008-47193

Original Spanish edition, 1990

A "novel about a migrant Chilean family living in an apartment house under construction in Buenos Aires. New Year's Eve finds the hard-drinking Chilean night watchman, Raúl Vinas, hosting a party with his wife, Elisa, their four small children and Elisa's pensive 15-year-old daughter, Patri. Moreover, ghosts reside in the house: naked, dust-covered floating men, mostly unseen except by Elisa and Patri. The novel engineers a clever layering of metaphorical details about the building, but gradually focuses on Elisa's preparations for the party and her conversations with her daughter about finding a 'real man' to marry. Prodded perhaps by her isolation within the family, Patri accepts the ghosts' invitation to a midnight feast, at her life's peril." Publ Wkly

Aira, Cesar

The **literary** conference; translated by Katherine Silver. New Directions 2010 90p pa $9.95

ISBN 978-0-8112-1878-8 pa; 0-8112-1878-3 pa

LC 2009-45914

Original Spanish edition, 2006

"At a literary conference, César, the protagonist—author and translator by day, mad scientist by night—hatches a plan to rule the world by creating an army cloned from the Mexican author Carlos Fuentes. But César accidentally clones a cell that's not from Fuentes but from Fuentes's silk tie, thus loosing lumbering, thousand-foot-long electric-blue silkworms upon the city of Mérida. Aira writes, 'It seems like the insertion of a different plot line, from an old B-rated science fiction movie.' It sure does. But Aira's writerly self-reference, while hardly subtle, is disarming, and the result is amusing, self-conscious camp." New Yorker

Aira, Cesar

The **seamstress** and the wind; translated by Rosalie Knecht. New Directions 2011 132p pa $12.95

ISBN 978-0-8112-1912-9; 0-8112-1912-7

LC 2011-06006

Original Spanish edition, 1994

The novel "is simultaneously minimalist and epic. Aira's voice is clear, his characters are palpable, and his ideas—elucidations on literary theory, existential ruminations, and thought experiments—are evocative and infectious. The story, which concerns a seamstress and her husband who travel the Patagonia desert in pursuit of their accidentally kidnapped son, careens with each chapter at dizzying speed. Seamstress might be thought confusing and possibly incomplete, because the story's inciting incident—the kidnapped child—goes completely unresolved, even forgotten by the seamstress and her husband. But that is the point: It's part of Aira's style; he is mysterious without obfuscating." Zyzzyva

Akhtar, Ayad, 1970-

American dervish; by Ayad Akhtar. Little, Brown and Co. 2012 357p

ISBN 9780297865445 Weidenfeld and Nicolson; 0316183318 Little, Brown and Co.; 9780316183314 Little, Brown and Co.

LC 2011019737

This book tells the story of "Hayat Shah [who] is a young American in love for the first time. His normal life of school, baseball, and video games had previously been distinguished only by his Pakistani heritage and by the frequent chill between his parents, who fight over things he is too young to understand. Then Mina arrives, and everything changes. . . . Her deep spirituality brings the family's Muslim faith to life in a way that resonates with Hayat as nothing has before." (Publisher's note)

al-Shaykh, Hanan

★ **One** thousand and one nights; a sparkling retelling of the beloved classic. Hanan al-Shaykh ; with an introduction by Mary Gaitskill. Pantheon Books 2013 320 p.

ISBN 9780307958860

LC 2012039272

In this book, Lebanese novelist Hanan al-Shaykh "takes the hundreds of stories that make up the traditional 'One Thousand and One Nights' and . . . pares them down to 19. Focusing on tales that expose misogyny—of men who kill their wives and lovers, who injure them, or who leave them for dead—al-Shaykh is interested in how women grapple with a society that is stacked against them." (Library Journal)

Alameddine, Rabih

★ An **Unnecessary** Woman; Rabih Alameddine. First edition Grove Press 2014 320 p. hc $25

ISBN 9780802122148; 0802122140

National Book Award Shortlist: Fiction (2014)

This book, by Rabih Alameddine, follows "seventy-two-year-old Beirut native Aaliya Sobhi. . . . Divorced at 20 after a negligible marriage, she lived alone and began her life's work of translating the novels she most loved into Arabic from other translations, then simply storing them, unread, in her apartment. Sustained by her 'blind lust for the written word' and surrounded by piles of books, she anticipates beginning a new translation project each year until disaster appears to upend her life." (Booklist)

"Alameddine's storytelling is rich with a bookish humor that's accessible without being condescending. A gemlike and surprisingly lively study of an interior life." Kirkus

Alarcón, Daniel, 1977-

At Night We Walk in Circles; a novel. by Daniel Alarcón. Penguin Group USA 2013 374 p. $27.95

ISBN 1594631719; 9781594631719

LC 2013019446

PEN/Faulkner Award for Fiction: Shortlist (2014)

In this book, by Daniel Alarcón, "Nelson's life is not turning out the way he hoped. . . . until he lands a starring role in a touring revival of The Idiot President, a legendary play by Nelson's hero, Henry Nunez, leader of the storied guerrilla theater troupe Diciembre. . . . With each performance, Nelson grows closer to his fellow actors, becoming hopelessly entangled in their complicated lives, until . . . a long-buried betrayal surfaces to force the troupe into chaos." (Publisher's note)

"[A] fast-unraveling mystery of role-playing and retribution, told in compelling prose that is smart, subtle, and totally engrossing." Booklist

Alarcon, Daniel

Lost City Radio; a novel. HarperCollins 2007 257p $24.95

ISBN 0-06-059479-9

LC 2006-046498

This "is a fable for an entire continent, and is no less pertinent in other parts of the world where different languages are spoken in different climates but where the same ruinous dance is played out." Washington Post Book World

Albert, Elisa

After Birth; Elisa Albert. Houghton Mifflin Harcourt 2015 208 p. (hardback) $23

ISBN 0544273737; 9780544273733

LC 2014006756

In this novel by Elisa Albert "a year has passed since Ari gave birth to Walker, though it went so badly awry she has trouble calling it 'birth' and still she can't locate herself in her altered universe. When Mina, a one-time cult musician--older, self-contained, alone, and nine-months pregnant--moves to town, Ari sees the possibility of a new friend, despite her unfortunate habit of generally mistrusting women." (Publisher's note)

"Irreverent, hilarious, and honest, Albert's newest novel loudly decries the isolation of new mothers in today's world. Her opinionated protagonist is sympathetic, if not entirely likable, and will pull readers along on her journey toward a new normal with great humor and wit." Booklist

Albert, Elisa

The **book** of Dahlia; a novel. Free Press 2008 276p $23

ISBN 978-0-7432-9129-3; 0-7432-9129-8

LC 2007-33839

"Dahlia Finger, the heroine of this début novel, is a sarcastic, self-absorbed Jewish American Princess, twenty-nine years old and living in a desirable bungalow in Venice, California, bought for her by her lawyer father. She's also, thanks to Albert's control of tone and timing, one of the most likable characters in recent fiction, as self-aware about her bad habits (smoking pot, wallowing in hopelessness, refusing to engage with her broken family) as she is incapable of changing them, even when diagnosed with a 'level four' tumor in the left temporal lobe of her brain. Basing her chapters on a self-help book that Dahlia buys ('It's Up to You: The Cancer To-Do List'), Albert writes with the black humor of Lorrie Moore and a pathos that is uniquely her own, all the more blistering for being slyly invoked." New Yorker

Albert, Susan Wittig

The **Darling** Dahlias and the cucumber tree; Susan Wittig Albert. Berkley Prime Crime 2010 xii, 290p (Darling Dahlias mysteries) (hc) $24.95; $7.99

ISBN 9780425234457; 0425234452; 9780425242162; 0425242161

LC 2010010033

"The Dahlias comprise the 12 members of a gardening club dedicated to beautifying their town while struggling to survive the Depression. Even small towns can have their share of mysteries, and Darling is no exception--fortunately, the Dahlias are sleuths as well as gardeners. Before long, they are searching for an escaped prisoner and a stolen car and investigating troubles at the local bank. And then there is the mysterious death of a young woman." (Booklist)

Albert "brings a small Southern town to life and vividly captures an era and culture-the Depression, segregation, class differences, the role of women in the South--with authentic period details." LJ

Other titles in this series are:

The Darling Dahlias and the naked ladies (2011)
The Darling Dahlias and the Confederate rose (2012)
The Darling Dahlias and the Texas star (2013)
The Darling Dahlias and the silver dollar bush (2014)
The Darling Dahlias and the Eleven O'clock Lady (2015)
The Darling Dahlias and the unlucky clover (2018)

Alcott, Kate

A **touch** of stardust; Kate Alcott. Doubleday 2015 304 p. (hardcover) $25

ISBN 0385539045; 9780385539043

LC 2014020972

This novel, by Kate Alcott, "takes you behind the scenes of the filming of 'Gone with the Wind,' while turning the spotlight on the passionate romance between its dashing leading man, Clark Gable, and the blithe, free-spirited actress Carole Lombard. . . . Julie is given a front-row seat to not one but two of the greatest love affairs of all time: the undeniable on-screen chemistry between Scarlett and Rhett, and offscreen, the deepening love between Carole and Clark." (Publisher's note)

"The briskly paced narrative captivates as it lets readers view the creation of silver-screen magic, and it's also a terrific tribute to the industry pioneers, like screenwriter Frances Marion, who helped others jump-start their dreams." Booklist

Alcott, Louisa May

★ **Little** women; Little men; Jo's boys; [Elaine Showalter, editor] Library of America, Distributed to the trade in the U.S. by Penguin Putnam 2005 1092p il (The library of America) $40

ISBN 1-931082-73-1

LC 2004-48828

"Little Women (1868-69), set in New England during the Civil War, introduces the charming, unforgettable March sisters Meg, Jo, Amy, and Beth as they begin to make their way into the world. Little Men (1871) follows the intellectual tomboy Jo, now married, into adulthood, as she finds herself the caretaker of a houseful of rambunctious children at Plumfield school. Jo's Boys (1886) returns to Plumfield a decade later. Now grown, Jo's children recount adventures of their own." Publisher's note

Alderman, Naomi

★ The **power**; Naomi Alderman. First North American edition Little, Brown & Co. 2017 386 p. (hardcover) $26

ISBN 0316547611; 9780316547611; 9780316558372

LC 2017936787

Baileys Women's Prize for Fiction (2017)

In this novel, by Naomi Alderman, " the world is a recognizable place: there's a rich Nigerian boy who lounges around the family pool; a foster kid whose religious parents hide their true nature. . . . But then a vital new force takes root and flourishes, causing their lives to converge with devastating effect. Teenage girls now have immense physical power--they can cause agonizing pain and even death. And, with this small twist of nature, the world drastically resets." (Publisher's note)

"Both the main story and the frame narrative ask interesting questions about gender, but this isn't a dry philosophical exercise. It's fast-paced, thrilling, and even funny." Kirkus

Aldiss, Brian Wilson

★ **Helliconia** spring; [by] Brian W. Aldiss. Atheneum Pubs. 1982 361p

ISBN 0-689-11196-9

LC 81-66036

"Aldiss has not only written a science fiction novel about another world, he has created another universe complete with it's own language and flavor, peopled with colorful characters (both human and otherwise) who engage sympathy and interest." Best Sellers

Followed by Helliconia summer

Aldiss, Brian Wilson

★ **Helliconia** summer; [by] Brian W. Aldiss. Atheneum Pubs. 1983 398p

ISBN 0-689-11388-9

LC 83-45062

"In this second novel in Aldiss's trilogy, the planet Helliconia . . . is presented as an epic miniature of humanity's loftiest aspirations and basest shortcomings. The action takes place on two levels, represented by the geometrical symbol of the planet's supreme god Akhanaba. Some events proceed along the inner rim, driven by incessant racial wars between the cohabitant Helliconian humans and the 'ahuman' Phagors. Along the outermost rim are the concerns of the king of Borlien . . . and the nefarious intrigues of court hangers-on ranging from chancellors to child prostitutes." Publ Wkly

Followed by Helliconia winter

Aldiss, Brian Wilson

★ **Helliconia** winter. Atheneum Pubs. 1985 281p

ISBN 0-689-11541-5

LC 84-45607

"This conclusion to the Helliconia trilogy ranks as a landmark of fictional world-building." Libr J

Alenyikov, Michael

Ivan and Misha; stories. Michael Alenyikov. TriQuarterly Books 2010 199 p.

ISBN 0810127180; 9780810127180

LC 2010024016

This collection of short stories, the 2011 winner of the Northern California Book Award for Fiction, "revolves around a pair of fraternal twins, Ivan and Misha, brought to America as children, along with their father, Louie. Ivan inherited his father's dark good looks and his mother's bipolar disease . . . Misha has his mother's blond coloring and the burden of responsibility for his brother. Both brothers become involved in gay relationships, which strain their own bonds. . . . [The author captures] the world the father and brothers have made for themselves in contemporary New York City, . . . the jitteriness of Ivan's manic episodes, the tensions of urban gay life, and the coping with family acceptance and AIDS." (Libr J)

Alexander, Tamera, 1961-

A **beauty** so rare; Tamera Alexander. Bethany House 2014 480 p. (A Belmont Mansion novel) (pbk.) $14.99

ISBN 0764206230; 9780764206238

LC 2013047195

In this book, by Tamera Alexander, "Eleanor Braddock . . . knows she will never marry. But with a dying soldier's last whisper, she believes her life can still have meaning and determines to find his widow. Impoverished and struggling to care for her ailing father, Eleanor arrives at Belmont Mansion, home of her aunt, Adelicia Acklen, the richest woman in America. . . . Adelicia insists on finding her niece a husband, but a simple act of kindness leads Eleanor down a far different path." (Publisher's note)

"Alexander's . . . exquisitely written historical tale is filled with unforgettable characters, a romance that seems hopeless, and a close-up look at the aftermath of a war that nearly destroyed the country." Booklist

Alexander, V. S.

The **Magdalen** girls; V.S. Alexander. Kensington Books 2016 294 p. (paperback) $15

ISBN 1496706129; 9781496706133; 9781496706126

LC 2017289010

In this novel, by V. S. Alexander, "within the gated grounds of the convent of The Sisters of the Holy Redemption lies one of the city's Magdalen Laundries. . . . Some inmates are 'fallen' women . . . [but] most are ordinary girls whose only sin lies in being too pretty, too independent, or tempting the wrong man. Among them is sixteen-year-old Teagan Tiernan, sent by her family when her beauty provokes a lustful revelation from a young priest." (Publisher's note)

Alexander, Victoria

The **lady** travelers guide to scoundrels & other gentlemen; Victoria Alexander. Harlequin Books 2017 538 p. $7.99

ISBN 0373803982; 9780373803989

In this book in the Lady Travelers Society series, by Victoria Alexander, "when Derek Saunders's . . . elderly aunt and her . . . Lady Travelers Society loses one of their members, what's a man to do but step up to the challenge? Now he's escorting [his aunt] . . . to find her missing relative. While India Prendergast only suspects his organization defrauds . . . travelers, she's certain a man with as scandalous a reputation as Derek. Saunders cannot be trusted any farther." (Publisher's note)

"Alexander celebrates the spirit of adventure, elevates dubious scheming with good intentions, and advocates for the yielding of judgment and practicality to hedonism and happiness. Readers will savor every page." Pub Wkly

Alexander, Victoria

The **Scandalous** Adventures of the Sister of the Bride; Victoria Alexander. Kensington Pub Corp 2014 400 p. $7.99

ISBN 1420132245; 9781420132243

"When Lady Delilah Hargate throws her customary propriety to the wind during a trip to New York and indulges in a scandalous interlude with a man she's just met, she thinks it is just an unforgettable adventure. Yet her "adventure" turns out to be her future brother-in-law's good friend and sometimes business partner Sam Russell and he's now in England for the wedding." (Library Journal)

"With dialogue reminiscent of those classic screwball comedies of the 1930s and 1940s, Alexander's latest wickedly funny historical romance is the perfect synthesis of love and laughter." Booklist

Alexie, Sherman, 1966-

★ **Blasphemy**; new and selected stories. by Sherman Alexie. Grover Pr 2012 viii, 465 p.p (hardcover) $27.00; (ebook) $24.99

ISBN 0802120393; 9780802120397; 9781921942969

Author Sherman Alexie presents a short story collection. "A son envisions his dead father's 'impossibly small corpse' peering out of his morning omelet in the page-long 'Breakfast.' In 'Gentrification,' a white narrator's do-gooder intentions go predictably awry in his all-black neighborhood. 'Night People' finds a sex-starved insomniac and a connection-hungry manicurist at a 24-hour New York City salon finding common ground in their loneliness and lack of sleep." (Publishers Weekly)

Alexie, Sherman

Flight; a novel. Black Cat 2007 181p pa $13

ISBN 978-0-8021-7037-8; 0-8021-7037-4

LC 2006-52656

"Many of [the] allegorical, action-packed vignettes tread familiar thematic territory—the continuing fight for survival, the anger of racial divides, the absence of fathers—of Mr. Alexie's earlier works. . . . But with 'Flight,' he takes these themes a step further: he skillfully explores both sides of the proverbial war. Zits witnesses brutal violence through the eyes of whites and Indians, fathers and sons, and he begins to understand what it means to be the hero, the villain and the victim." N Y Times (Late N Y Ed)

Alexie, Sherman

Indian killer. Atlantic Monthly Press 1996 420p
ISBN 0-871-13652-X

LC 96-27996

"Sherman Alexie is too good a writer, too devoted to the complexities of a story, to settle for a diatribe. His vigorous prose, his haunted , surprising characters and his meditative exploration of the sources of human identity transform into a resonant tragedy what might have been a melodrama in less assured hands." N Y Times Book Rev

Alexie, Sherman

Reservation blues. Atlantic Monthly Press 1995 306p
ISBN 0-871-13594-9

LC 94-46132

"Hilarious but poignant, filled with enchantments yet dead-on accurate with regard to modern Indian life, this tour de force will leave readers wondering if Alexie himself hasn't made a deal with the Gentleman in order to do everything so well." Publ Wkly

Algren, Nelson

★ The **man** with the golden arm; a novel. Doubleday 1949 343p

"Set in the slums of Chicago, the novel, which won a National Book Award in 1950, tells the story of Frankie Machine (Francis Majcinek) who is said to have a 'golden arm' because of his sure touch with pool cues, dice, his drumsticks, his heroin needle, and his deck of cards. Unable to free himself from his slum environment, Frankie is finally driven to suicide." Reader's Ency. 4th edition

Algren, Nelson

A **walk** on the wild side. Farrar, Straus & Cudahy 1956 346p

A novel about the residents of a slum street in New Orleans during the early years of the Depression

"Algren's vivid writing gives this degenerate cast the power to shock or appall, and if a glimmer of compassion leaks through occasionally it is slapped down before it gets out of hand." Libr J

Ali, Monica

★ **Brick** lane; a novel. Scribner 2003 369p $25
ISBN 0-7432-4330-7

LC 2003-42795

"Nazeen, a young Bangladeshi woman, moves to London's Bangla Town (around the street of the title) in the mid-nineteen eighties after an arranged marriage with an older man. Seen through Nazeen's eyes, England is at first utterly baffling, but over the seventeen years of the narrative (which takes us into the post-September 11th era), she gradually finds her way, bringing up two daughters and eventually starting an all-female tailoring business. . . . In Ali's subtle narration, Nazeen's mixture of traditionalism, and adaptability, of acceptence and restlessness, emerges as a quiet strength." New Yorker

Ali, Monica

In the kitchen; a novel. Scribner 2009 436p $25.99
ISBN 978-1-4165-7168-1; 1-4165-7168-X

LC 2009-01551

"Gabriel plans to serve 'Classic French, a modern twist, cooked with precision' in his restaurant. Translated into literary terms, it's a fair description of what Ali herself dishes up in this rich, classically structured novel that tackles big social issues." San Francisco Chron

Ali, Monica

Untold story; a novel. Scribner 2011 259p $25
ISBN 1-4516-3548-6; 978-1-4516-3548-5

In this novel, Ali "imagines what the fate of Princess Diana might have been had she not died in Paris in 1997. . . . If Diana had lived, would she ever have found peace and happiness, or would the curse of fame always have been too great? Fast forward a decade after the (averted) Paris tragedy, and an Englishwoman named Lydia is living in a small, nondescript town somewhere in the American Midwest. She has a circle of friends: one owns a dress shop; one is a Realtor; another is a frenzied stay-at-home mom. Lydia volunteers at an animal shelter, and swims a lot. Her lover, who adores her, feels she won't let him know her. Who is she?" (Publisher's note)

"After a series of moves from one American town to another, Lydia finally settles in a generic hamlet called Kensington, where she becomes friends with three middle-aged women: a bubbly blonde named Amber; a stressed out, brunette mom named Suzie; and a red-haired, New-Agey realtor named Tevis. These three pals are kinder, gentler versions of John Updike's witches of Eastwick — or maybe older, hipper versions of the gals in Rona Jaffe's 'Best of Everything.' . . . Like Curtis Sittenfeld, who tried to channel Laura Bush in 'American Wife,' Ms. Ali does an engaging job of creating sympathy for her heroine." N Y Times (Late N Y Ed)

Aliu, Xhenet

★ **Brass**; a novel. Xhenet Aliu. Random House 2018 295 p.
ISBN 9780399590245; 9780399590252

LC 2017002763

In this novel, by Xhenet Aliu, "Elsie . . . meets Bashkim, . . . a married man . . . [from] Albania. . . . Elsie . . . falls in love quickly, . . . [and becomes] pregnant. . . . Seventeen years later, . . . Luljeta receives a rejection letter from NYU and her first-ever suspension from school. . . . She's stuck in Connecticut with her mother, Elsie. . . . Lulu decides to find out what . . . her mother has been hiding about the father she never knew." (Publisher's note)

"Aliu's riveting, sensitive work shines with warmth, clarity, and a generosity of spirit. Her characters are nuanced and real, capable of taking risks, making mistakes, and growing in unexpected ways." Kirkus

Allen, Jeffery Renard, 1962-

Song of the shank; Jeffery Renard Allen. Graywolf Press 2014 608 p. illustrations, map pbk $18
ISBN 1555976808; 9781555976804

LC 2013958011

PEN/Faulkner Award for Fiction: Finalist (2015)

A historical novel by Jeffery Renard Allen, "'Song of the Shank' opens in 1866 as Tom and his guardian, Eliza Bethune, struggle to adjust to their fashionable apartment in the city in the aftermath of riots that had driven them away a few years before. But soon a stranger arrives from the mysterious island of Edgemere--inhabited solely by African settlers and black refugees from the war and riots--who intends to reunite Tom with his now-liberated mother." (Publisher's note)

"One of America's most gifted novelists projects dark and daring speculations upon the incredible-but-true 19th-century story of a child piano prodigy who was blind, autistic and a slave. . . . Allen's psychological insight and evocative language vividly bring to life all the black and white people in Tom's life who, in seeking to understand or exploit Tom's unholy gifts, are both transformed and transfixed by his inscrutable, resolutely self-contained personality." Kirkus

Allen, Sarah Addison

First Frost; Sarah Addison Allen. St. Martin's Press 2015 304 p. $25.99

ISBN 1250019834; 9781250019837

LC 2014032166

"A tale set 10 years after the events in Garden Spells finds Claire's happy contentment shattered by her father's revelations, which challenge everything she ever believed about herself." - Publisher's note.

"Fans of Allen (The Peach Keeper; The Sugar Queen) will recognize familiar characters from her 2007 Garden Spells. This novel features charming characters, exploration of the family ties that bind and captivate us, and a touch of the supernatural, which will especially please longtime Allen readers." LJ

Allen, Sarah Addison

Garden Spells; by Sarah Addison Allen. Bantam Discovery 2008 290 p. $16

ISBN 055338483X; 9780553384833

LC 2007000195

In this novel, by Sarah Addison Allen, "The Waverleys have always been a curious family, endowed with peculiar gifts that make them outsiders even in their hometown of Bascom, North Carolina. Even their garden has a reputation, famous for its feisty apple tree that bears prophetic fruit, and its edible flowers, imbued with special powers. Generations of Waverleys tended this garden. Their history was in the soil. But so were their futures." (Publisher's note)

"Spellbindingly charming, Allen's impressively accomplished debut novel will bewitch fans of Alice Hoffman and Laura Esquivel, as her entrancing brand of magic realism nimbly blends the evanescent desires of hopeless romantics with the inherent wariness of those who have been hurt once too often." Booklist

Allen, Sarah Addison

The **girl** who chased the moon; a novel. Bantam Books 2010 269p $25; pa $15

ISBN 978-0-553-80721-9; 0-553-80721-8; 978-0-553-38559-5 pa; 0-553-38559-3 pa

LC 2009-42254

Emily Benedict came to Mullaby, North Carolina, hoping to solve at least some of the riddles surrounding her mother's life. But the moment Emily enters the house where her mother grew up and meets the grandfather she never knew—a reclusive, real-life gentle giant—she realizes that mysteries aren't solved in Mullaby, they're a way of life.

"That it is never too late to change the future and that high school sins can be forgiven—these are wonderful messages, but Allen's warm characters and quirky setting are what will completely open readers' hearts to this story. Nothing in it disappoints." Libr J

Allen, Sarah Addison

The **sugar** queen. Bantam Books 2008 276p $22

ISBN 978-0-553-80549-9; 0-553-80549-5

LC 2007-48178

"Allen's characters are darling, and even the bad guys are charming and charismatic in this novel written as a modern-day fairy tale. In Allen's town of Bald Slope, magic lets books choose their owners and passion fry eggs in their carton. Best of all, it lets friends discover one another in the most mysterious ways." St. Petersburg Times

Allende, Isabel

Daughter of fortune; a novel. translated from the Spanish by Margaret Sayers Peden. HarperCollins Pubs. 1999 399p hardcover o.p. pa $16.95

ISBN 0-06-019491-X; 0-06-156533-4 pa

LC 99-26021

Original Spanish edition, 1999

"This novel has pretensions, but they are overridden by Allende's riproaring girl's adventure story. . . . Throughout it all, Allende projects a woman's point of view with confidence, control and an expansive definition of romance as a fact of life." Time

Allende, Isabel

★ **Eva** Luna; translated by Margaret Sayers Peden. Knopf 1988 271p hardcover o.p. pa $14

ISBN 0-394-57273-4; 0-553-38382-5 pa

LC 88-45272

Original Spanish edition, 1987

This "wonderful novel, crammed with the strange and fantastical, the sensuous and the erotic, also speaks powerfully in the cause of freedom." Publ Wkly

Allende, Isabel

★ The **house** of the spirits; translated from the Spanish by Magda Bogin. Knopf 1985 368p $29.95; pa $16

ISBN 0-394-53907-9; 0-553-38380-9 pa

LC 84-48516

Original Spanish edition, 1982

"The style is superbly controlled (and/or the translation is marvelously sensitive), balancing detail rich in associations with a deadpan humor that completely demystifies things that would be otherwise inexplicable. In other words, sentimentality never intrudes on the emotions you develop for these hopelessly well-meaning people and their equally errant children." Best Sellers

Allende, Isabel, 1942-

In the midst of winter; a novel. Isabel Allende ; translated from the Spanish by Nick Castor and Amanda Hopkinson. Atria Books 2017 342 p. (hardcover) $28

ISBN 150117813X; 9781501178139; 9781501178153

LC 2017027807

In this novel, by Isabel Allende, translated by Nick Castor and Amanda Hopkinson, "Richard Bowmaster--a 60-year-old human rights scholar--hits the car of Evelyn Ortega--a young, undocumented immigrant from Guatemala--in the middle of a snowstorm in Brooklyn. What at first seems just a small inconvenience takes an unforeseen and far more serious turn when Evelyn turns up at the professor's house seeking help." (Publisher's note)

"Filled with Allende's signature lyricism and ingenious plotting, the book delves wonderfully into what it means to respect, protect, and love." Pub Wkly

Allende, Isabel

Island beneath the sea; a novel. translated from the Spanish by Margaret Sayers Peden. Harper 2010 457p $26.99; pa $14.99

ISBN 978-0-06-198824-0; 0-06-198824-3; 978-0-06-198825-7 pa; 0-06-198825-1 pa

LC 2009-46251

Original Spanish edition, 2009

"In a many-faceted plot, Allende animates irresistible characters authentic in their emotional turmoil and pragmatic adaptability. She also captures the racial, sexual, and entrepreneurial dynamics of each society in sensuous detail while masterfully dramatizing the psychic wounds of slavery. Sexually explicit, Allende is grace incarnate in her evocations of the spiritual energy that still sustains the beleaguered people of Haiti and New Orleans." Booklist

Allende, Isabel, 1942-

The **Japanese** Lover; A Novel. by Isabel Allende. Pocket Books 2015 352 p. $28

ISBN 1501116975; 9781501116971

This novel, by Isabel Allende, is a "love story and multigenerational epic. . . . In 1939, as Poland falls under the shadow of the Nazis, young Alma Belasco's parents send her away to live in safety with an aunt and uncle in their opulent mansion in San Francisco. There, as the rest of the world goes to war, she encounters Ichimei Fukuda, the quiet and gentle son of the family's Japanese gardener. Unnoticed by those around them, a tender love affair begins to blossom." (Publisher's note)

"Allende's latest (Maya's Notebook), a glorious family saga, with its rich cast of decent, complex characters caught up in America's struggles with war, prejudice, AIDS, and society's old taboos that are fast disappearing, is a beautiful tribute to devotion." LJ

Allende, Isabel, 1942-

★ **Maya's** Notebook. HarperCollins 2013 400 p. (hardcover) $27.99

ISBN 0062105620; 9780062105622

In this book, set in 2009, "Berkley-born and -bred Maya arrives in Chiloé, an isolated island community in southern Chile, to escape the drug dealers and law enforcement officials on her trail. Her eponymous notebook combines a record of Maya's not-so-gradual immersion into the Chiloé community with her memories of an idyllic childhood and horrifically wayward adolescence." (Kirkus Reviews)

Allende, Isabel

Portrait in sepia; translated from the Spanish by Margaret Sayers Peden. HarperCollins Pubs. 2001 304p

ISBN 0-06-621161-1

LC 00-54127

Sequel to Daughter of fortune

Original Spanish edition, 2000

"Through Aurora, Allende exercises her supreme storytelling abilities, of which strong, passionate characters are paramount." Publ Wkly

Allingham, Margery

Crime and Mr. Campion. Doubleday 1959 575p

An omnibus volume containing the complete texts of three mystery novels all starring the British detective Albert Campion. Death of a ghost (1934) is based on art forgery, Flowers for the judge (1936) is about the murder of a publisher and Dancers in mourning (1937) concerns a group of theatrical characters

Allingham, Margery

Three cases for Mr. Campion. Doubleday 1961 604p

"The Gyrth chalice mystery" unravels Mr. Campion's solution to the secret in the locked room of Gyrth Tower; "The fashion in shrouds" involves the theft of dress designs, sixty cages of canaries, and blackmail, as Albert Campion investigates a three-year-old murder; "Traitor's purse" finds Albert Campion, an amnesia victim haunted by an urgency to do something of immense consequence before time runs out

Allison, Dorothy

★ **Bastard** out of Carolina. Dutton 1992 309p hardcover o.p. pa $16

ISBN 0-525-93425-1; 0-452-28705-7 pa

LC 91-34607

"Set in the rural South, this tale centers around the Boatwright family, a proud and closeknit clan known for their drinking, fighting, and womanizing. Nicknamed Bone by her Uncle Earle, Ruth Anne is the bastard child of Anney Boatwright, who has fought tirelessly to legitimize her child. When she marries Glen, a man from a good family, it appears that her prayers have been answered. However, Anney suffers a miscarriage and Glen begins drifting. He develops a contentious relationship with Bone and then begins taking sexual liberties with her. . . . Unaware of her husband's abusive behavior, Anney stands by her man. Eventually, a violent encounter wrests Bone away from her stepfather." Libr J

Alvar, Mia

★ **In** the country; stories. Mia Alvar. Alfred A. Knopf 2015 368 p. (hardback) $26.95

ISBN 9780385352819; 9780804171496; 0385352816

LC 2014036940

This book, by Mia Alvar, presents nine short stories that "give voice to the women and men of the Filipino diaspora. Here are exiles, emigrants, and wanderers uprooting their families from the Philippines to begin new lives in the Middle East, the United States, and elsewhere--and, sometimes, turning back again." (Publisher's note)

"Both intrepid readers and armchair tourists eager to explore debut narratives that straddle multiple countries and cultures—à la Violet Kupersmith's The Frangipani Hotel or Rajesh Parameswaran's I Am an Executioner—will be opulently rewarded here." LJ

Alvarez, Julia

★ **How** the Garcia girls lost their accents. Algonquin Bks. 1991 290p hardcover o.p. pa $13.95

ISBN 0-945575-57-2; 1-56512-975-X pa

LC 90-48575

"This is an account of parallel odysseys, as each of the four daughters adapts in her own way, and a large part of Alvarez's accomplishment is the complexity with which these vivid characters are rendered." Publ Wkly

Alvarez, Julia

Yo! Algonquin Bks. 1997 309p $18.95

ISBN 1-56512-157-0

LC 96-24611

Sequel to How the Garcia girls lost their accents

"Yolanda Garcia's mother and sisters are furious at her for having plagiarized their lives in her all-too-celebrated novel. The balance of this novel is a rebuttal of sorts, narrated by her defenders. For everyone else who has come into contact with Yo and her storytelling prowess—from her repressed professor to her downtrodden landlady—life has changed for the better. These high-spirited accounts indulge the pleasing fantasy that we are the heroes not only of our own lives but of everyone else's as well." New Yorker

Alyan, Hala

Salt houses; Hala Alyan. Houghton Mifflin Harcourt 2017 312 p. (hardback) $26

ISBN 9780544912588; 9780544912380

LC 2016046956

In this novel, by Hala Alyan, "Salma is forced to leave her home in Nablus; Alia's brother gets pulled into a politically militarized world he can't escape; and Alia and her gentle-spirited husband move to Kuwait City, where they reluctantly build a life with their three children. When Saddam Hussein invades Kuwait in 1990, Alia and her family once again lose their home, their land, and their story as they know it, scattering to Beirut, Paris, Boston, and beyond." (Publisher's note)

"A deeply moving look inside the Palestinian diaspora." Kirkus

Amado, Jorge

★ **Dona** Flor and her two husbands; a moral and amorous tale. translated from the Portuguese by Harriet de Onís. Knopf 1969 553p

Original Portuguese edition published 1966 in Brazil

"Dona Flor has such a harridan of a mother (Dona Rozilda) that you would like her to have her cake and eat it, too, and she very nearly does. Dona Flor's first husband, Vadinho, is a scamp, a prevaricator, and a 'shameless lover.' On Carnival Sunday, at the height of the gaiety, filled with rum, he drops dead. Dona Flor is desolate but cuts a handsome figure as a widow. She lives through the wake (a gem of a scene) and her mourning quite well, with memories and her cooking school to sustain her. Then suitors appear. None appeal but Dr. Teodoro Madureira, pharmacist and bassoonist, a pillar of propriety. Dona Rozilda is ecstatic, but the well-rounded Dona Flor has her troubles, for alas, Dr. Teodoro is no lover. Dreams haunt her and strange things begin to happen. Thanks to a Yoruba charm, Vadinho returns to ravish our bewildered heroine, and then the fun begins. Bahia in Brazil is the setting for this delectable rum cake of a novel." Publ Wkly

Amado, Jorge

Gabriela, clove and cinnamon; translated from the Portuguese by James L. Taylor and William L. Grossman. Knopf 1962 425p

Original Portuguese edition published 1958 in Brazil

"Ilhéus, a Brazilian town near Bahia, is fortunate in the wealth it is realizing from its cacao crop. Money flows freely and is spent in cabarets, in bordellos, and on gambling during the period 1925-1926. . . . The removal of a sand bar blocking the harbor is the basis of this fascinating portrait of politics in a provincial Brazilian town. Amado also tells the love story of Nacib, the Arab owner of the most popular café in town, and Gabriela, a child of nature. Amoral rather than immoral, with skin the color of cinnamon and smelling of cloves, Gabriela gives her love readily and freely. Her skillful cooking makes her more valuable to Nacib as a mistress than as a wife. The atmosphere of this entertaining novel is lusty, sensual, and humorous." Shapiro. Fic for Youth. 3d edition

Amend, Allison

A **nearly** perfect copy; a novel. Allison Amend. Nan A. Talese/Doubleday 2013 304 p. (alk. paper) $25.95

ISBN 0385536690; 9780385536691

LC 2012020699

In this novel, by Allison Amend, "Elm Howells has a loving family and a distinguished career at an elite Manhattan auction house. But after a tragic loss . . . , she pursues a reckless course of action that jeopardizes her personal and professional success. Meanwhile, talented artist Gabriel Connois wearies of remaining at the margins of the capricious Parisian art scene, and, desperate for recognition, he embarks on a scheme that threatens his burgeoning reputation." (Publisher's note)

American fantastic tales: terror and the uncanny from Poe to the pulps; Peter Straub, editor. Library of America 2009 746p $35

ISBN 978-1-59853-047-6

LC 2009-927073

"A valuable collection of excellent, often deeply disturbing stories." Kirkus

American fantastic tales: terror and the uncanny from the 1940s to now; Peter Straub, editor. Library of America 2009 713p $35

ISBN 978-1-59853-048-3

LC 2009-927074

This volume's "contents reflect confused and perturbed reactions to radical changes in people's daily lives and the larger world around them during periods of instability beginning around the time of World War II and extending into the dizzying technological changes of the past quarter-century. . . . A terrific, must-have collection." Kirkus

American odysseys; writings by new Americans. The Vilcek Foundation. 1st Dalkey ed. Dalkey Archive Press 2013 600 p. (paperback) $16

ISBN 1564788067; 9781564788061

LC 2012049513

This "anthology is composed of selections from 22 writers recognized by the 2011 Vilcek Prize for Creative Promise, an award given annually to a young American immigrant (Dinaw Mengestu won in 2011). The anthology, with a foreword by Charles Simic, is composed of poetry, short stories, and excerpts of novels. . . . Across the works, identity and memory emerge as common themes of the immigrant experience." (Publishers Weekly)

Amirrezvani, Anita

★ **Equal** of the sun; a novel. Anita Amirrezvani. 1st Scribner hardcover ed. Scribner 2012 431 p. (hardcover) $26

ISBN 1451660464; 9781451660463

LC 2011277836

Author Anita Amirrezvani tells the story of "Javaher, a eunuch . . . [and] the loyal servant of Princess Pari, a wise if occasionally headstrong daughter of the shah. . . . He is determined to learn who among the nation's elite is responsible for his father's murde. . . . [The] shah dies and is replaced with his son Isma'il, who begins a reign . . . that threatens to break down the fragile truces with neighboring lands. . . . [Pari] begins a scheme to end his reign, with Javaher serving as assistant, sounding board and spy . . . [which] allows him to navigate the highest and lowest castes of Iranian society." (Kirkus Reviews)

Includes bibliographical references (p. [429]-431).

Amis, Kingsley

★ **Lucky** Jim; a novel. Doubleday 1954 256p

First published 1953 in the United Kingdom

"The title is ironic, since the story is about the comic misfortunes of Jim Dixon, a young lower-middle-class instructor at an English university. The book satirizes the academic 'racket' and cultural pretensions." Reader's Ency. 4th edition

Amis, Kingsley

The **Russian** girl. Viking 1994 296p

ISBN 0-670-85329-1

First published 1992 in the United Kingdom

"What makes 'The Russian Girl' such a jolly good read is precisely {its} scathing level of insight, to say nothing of Amis's dazzling virtuosity with the old bons mots. They litter the floor. He also manages to be very, very funny, even when he's being very, very serious." NY Times Book Rev

Amis, Martin

House of meetings. Alfred A. Knopf 2007 256p $23

ISBN 1-400-04455-3

LC 2006-47397

First published 2006 in the United Kingdom

"In previous novels Amis has been something of a meta-fictioneer, but the outstanding virtue of House of Meetings is its traditional psychological realism. Its themes of the camps, the misery, the overwhelming sense of sin, and the presentation of Russia as an emblem of human fate all recall Dostoyevsky, and, like Dostoyevsky, Amis fails to offer any answer to the question of human evil that the book raises." New Yorker

Amis, Martin, 1949-

Lionel Asbo; state of England. by Martin Amis. 1st American ed. Alfred A. Knopf 2012 255 p. (paperback) $15.00; (hardcover) $25.95

ISBN 9780307948083; 0307958086; 9780307958082

LC 2012006340

This novel is "two stories, a satirical take on the rise and fall of Lionel Abso, small-time criminal, and the coming-of-age story of Desmond 'Des' Pepperdine." Lionel has been a thug since age three, in and out of prison his whole life. "Des is Lionel's nephew. He is gifted" and "booksmart. . . . When Lionel's not in jail the two live in a . . . housing estate in . . . Diston." Then "Lionel wins the lottery, becomes a multimillionaire and starts living the celebrity life." (Library Journal)

Amis, Martin

★ **London** fields. Harmony Bks. 1989 470p

ISBN 0-517-57718-6

LC 89-49558

"Amis's technical virtuosity is extraordinary. . . . {This is} the most intellectually interesting fiction of the year, and a work beyond the reach of any British contemporary. Amis's figures, like those of Dickens, are caricatures that have their own gigantic reality." London Rev Books

Amis, Martin

★ The **pregnant** widow; inside history. Alfred A. Knopf 2010 370p $26.95

ISBN 978-1-4000-4452-8; 1-4000-4452-9

LC 2009-41689

"When Amis shows us the sexual revolution in action and reaction, when he tells us how people dressed and what it meant, when he depicts the effects of women's sexual aggression on men's egos, how women talked about men and vice versa when he is pretending to be a well-behaved comic-naturalist novelist, the book works. But when he philosophises he can sound just like tedious-clever journalism. . . . And the narrative is slowed and blurred by Amis' unwillingness ever to say anything in a simple or straightforward way." Age

Amis, Martin

Time's arrow; or, The nature of the offense. Harmony Bks. 1991 168p

ISBN 0-517-58515-4

LC 91-4144

This novel "shoots us into the past as it reveals the true identity of a man called Tod Friendly. As Tod lies in a hospital bed, his consciousness distances itself from the present and assesses his life in reverse, like a film run backwards. Every action is reversed and every conversation inverted. This voice, this estranged soul, watches Tod create food and beverages at meals, get paid for bringing items into stores, and grow younger. As his American identity is stripped away, his hideous past as a German doctor and executioner at a Nazi extermination camp is revealed." Booklist

Amis, Martin, 1949-

★ The **zone** of interest; a novel. Martin Amis. 1st U.S. ed. Vintage 2014 320 p. photographs (hardback) $26.95

ISBN 9780385353496; 0385353499

LC 2014011667

"Taking place in the most notorious concentration camp, the book introduces a cast of characters that includes the officious Commandant, Paul Doll, an alcoholic tyrant thriving on petty vindictiveness; Golo Thomsen, the well-placed nephew of Martin Bormann, tasked with building a rubber production plant inside the camp; and the Jewish Szmul, a former teacher, victimized into collaborating with his tormentors." (Library Journal)

"An audaciously satiric and brilliantly realized tale about personal angst and mass psychosis, and the immolation of self and soul." Booklist

Ampuero, Roberto

The **Neruda** case; Roberto Ampuero ; translated by Carolina De Robertis. Riverhead Books 2012 340 p.

ISBN 159448743X; 9781594487439

LC 2012001890

This book by Roberto Ampuero presents a "fictional interpretation of Nobel laureate Pablo Neruda's final days in 1973 . . . Neruda, who's ill with cancer as Chile teeters toward upheaval because of his friend President Allende's reform platform, seeks out unemployed Cuban Cayetano Brûlé in Valparaíso and hires him to investigate the whereabouts of a former acquaintance, Dr. Ángel Bracamonte. Never mind that Brûlé is no detective. The aging poet-cum-political activist persuades the young Brûlé . . . travel to Mexico City, the last place Neruda saw Bracamonte. The mission seems cut and dried, except Neruda has not only withheld critical information, he has sworn Brûlé to secrecy. Nobody must know the identity of who Brûlé is looking for or why he is looking for him." (Publishers Weekly)

Includes bibliographical references and index.

Amsterdam, Steven

Things we didn't see coming; [by] Steven Amsterdam. Pantheon Books 2010 199p $24

ISBN 0307378500; 9780307378507

LC 2009-17843

This debut collection of linked short stories "follows a single man over three decades as he tries to survive in an increasingly savage apocalyptic world that is at once utterly fantastic and disturbingly familiar. Here, coming-of-age is complicated not only by family troubles and mercurial love affairs, but treacherous weather, unstable governments, pandemic, and technology run amuck." (Publisher's note)

Amsterdam's unsettling debut story collection . . . envisions a not-too-distant future plagued by pollution, disease, corruption, turbulent climate conditions and a society whose members readily sacrifice morality for survival. Despite their bleakness, each of the nine entries is wildly original and engaging, yet not for the faint of heart or those seeking an optimistic escape from the everyday. . . . Amsterdam's writing is consistently bold and daring, dense yet somehow accessible. Edge

Anam, Tahmima, 1975-

The **Bones** of Grace; A Novel. by Tahmima Anam. HarperCollins 2016 416 p. (ebook) $24.99; $25.99

ISBN 9780062199317; 0061478946; 9780061478949

LC 2016013384

This book, by Tahmima Anam, is a "love story about belonging, migration, tragedy, survival, and the mysteries of origins. On the eve of her departure to find the bones of the walking whale—the fossil that provides a missing link in our evolution—Zubaida Haque falls in love with Elijah Strong, a man she meets in a darkened concert hall in Boston. Their connection is immediate and intense, despite their differences." (Publisher's note)

"In having Zubaida come to terms with her origins and her own contentment, Anam captures two very different cultures in an introspective character study that will mesmerize readers from the very first page." Pub Wkly

Anatoli, A.

Babi Yar; a document in the form of a novel. {by} A. Anatoli (Kuznetsov). Translated by David Floyd. Farrar, Straus & Giroux 1970 477p

ISBN 0-374-10761-0

Original Russian edition published 1966 in censored form under author's former name A. Kuznetsov; English translation by Jacob Guralsky of this version published 1967 by Dial Press

A documentary novel about the period from 1941 to 1943 in which the Germans systematically murdered some 2,000,000 people, including 50,000 Jews, at the ravine on the outskirts of Kiev known as Babi Yar. The author, who was twelve years old at the time, based his work on interviews, newspaper clippings, diaries and other documents

Anaya, Rudolfo A.

The **man** who could fly and other stories. University of Oklahoma Press 2006 197p (Chicana & Chicano visions of the Américas) $19.95

ISBN 0-8061-3738-X

LC 2005-51426

"The stories showcase 30 years of Anaya's Chicano literary voice, simultaneously innocent and omniscient and always rooted in the landscape, especially the windswept llanos of New Mexico. . . . The characters' passionate force radiates from Anaya's simple prose as they confront ethical dilemmas in varied regional settings." Libr J

Anders, Adriana

Under Her Skin; by Adriana Anders. Sourcebooks Casablanca 2017 376 p. (Blank Canvas) (paperback) $7.99

ISBN 1492633844; 9781492633853; 9781492633846

In this book, by Adriana Anders, "Ivan thought the world was through giving him second chances. . . . But the moment Uma walked into his life, Ivan knew he had to put all that crap aside and do everything he could to help. She was like nothing he'd ever known. Beautiful, lost, alone, she had the kind of sad eyes that were just begging for someone to save her..." (Publisher's note)

"An incredibly sexy, heartbreaking, and intense romantic debut." Kirkus

Other titles in this series are:

By her touch (2017)

In his hands (2017)

Anders, Charlie Jane

★ **All** the birds in the sky; Charlie Jane Anders. TOR Books 2016 320 p. (hardback) $25.99

ISBN 9780765379948; 0765379945

LC 2015031481

Hugo Nominee: Best Novel (2017)

Nebula Award: Best Novel (2016)

In this novel, by Charlie Jane Anders, "the planet is falling apart. . . . Laurence is an engineering genius who's working with a group that aims to avert catastrophic breakdown through technological intervention. Patricia . . . works with a small band of other magicians to secretly repair the world's every-growing ailments. Little do they realize that something bigger than either of them, something begun years ago in their youth, is determined to bring them together." (Publisher's note)

"Anders clearly has an intimate understanding of how hard it is to find friends when you're perceived as 'different' as well as a sweeping sense of how nice it would be to solve large problems with a single solution (and how infrequently that succeeds)." Kirkus

Andersen, Laura

The **Boleyn** King; a novel. Laura Andersen. Ballantine Books Trade Paperbacks 2013 368 p. (pbk.) $15

ISBN 0345534093; 9780345534095

LC 2013004505

This novel by Laura Andersen is "the first book in an enthralling trilogy that [imagines]: What if Anne Boleyn had actually given Henry VIII a son who grew up to be king? Henry IX, known as William, is a king bound by the restraints of the regency yet anxious to prove himself. [He] trusts only three people: his older sister Elizabeth; his best friend . . . Dominic; and Minuette, a young orphan. When he and Dominic both fall in love with Minuette, romantic obsession looms over a new generation of Tudors." (Publisher's note)

Other titles in this series are:

The Boleyn deceit (2013)

The Boleyn reckoning (2014)

Anderson, Poul

Genesis. TOR Bks. 2000 253p

ISBN 0-312-86707-7

LC 99-58829

"Christian Brannock agrees to have his personality uploaded into a computer so that his mind can explore the stars long after the death of his body. When his billion-year journey brings him back to an Earth that has undergone many cosmic changes, Brannock encounters another uploaded personality who restores to him the wonder of being 'human.' The lyrical approach of this sf master to the meaning of human existence gives his latest effort a surreal, allegorical feel." Libr J

Anderson, Poul

War of the Gods. TOR Bks. 1997 304p

ISBN 0-312-86315-2

LC 97-19383

"Anderson writes with a spare style, often relying on the alliterative, rhythmic prose of Scandinavian folklore, giving this epic tale an original spirit and tone. Readers bored with Tolkien-clone fantasies will be enthralled by the intricately detailed world and characters Anderson brings to life here." Publ Wkly

Anderson, Sherwood, 1876-1941

★ **Winesburg,** Ohio. Modern Lib. 1995 231p

ISBN 0-679-60146-5

LC 94-23229

A reissue of the title first published 1919 by B.W. Huebsch

"A series of twenty-three vignettes, Winesburg, Ohio is a character study of a small town. It highlights individual residents and scrutinizes who they are and why this reality often conflicts with their dreams. The short stories are linked through George Willard, a young newspaper reporter who is disenchanted with the narrow-mindedness of small towns." Shapiro. Fic for Youth. 3d edition

Anderton, Jo

Debris. Angry Robot 2011 432p (Veiled worlds trilogy)
ISBN 085766154X pa; 9780857661548 pa

This book tells the story of a woman who "is among the highest in her far-future society -- a skilled pioneer, able to use a mixture of ritual and innate talent to manipulate the particles that hold all matter together. But an accident brings her life crashing down around her ears." (Publisher's note) "Stripped of her powers, bound inside a bizarre powersuit, . . . Tanyana must adjust to a new life collecting 'debris,' the stuff left behind by pions. But as she tries to find who has done all of this to her, she also starts to realize that debris is more important than anyone could guess." (angryrobotbooks.com)

Andrew, Sally ✓

Recipes for Love and Murder; Sally Andrew. HarperCollins 2015 432 p. (Tannie Maria Mystery) $26.99
ISBN 0062397664; 9780062397669
LC 2015041162

In this book, by Sally Andrew, "Tannie Maria is a middle-aged widow who likes to cook—and eat. She shares her culinary love as a recipe columnist for the local paper—until The Gazette decides its readers are hungrier for advice on matters of the heart rather than ideas for lunch and dinner. Tannie Maria . . . helps . . . a woman desperate to escape her abusive husband. When the woman is murdered, Tannie Maria . . . is involved in something much more sinister than perfecting her chocolate cake." (Publisher's note)

"The mystery takes on the worldwide problem of abused women while revealing both the beauties and problems of South Africa. And the recipes will make you want to drop everything and start cooking." Kirkus

Andrews, Ilona

White Hot; Ilona Andrews. HarperCollins 2017 410 p. $7.99
ISBN 006228925X; 9780062289254
LC bl2017021596

In this novel in the Hidden Legacy series, by Ilona Andrews, "Nevada Baylor has a unique and secret skill--she knows when people are lying--and she's used that magic (along with plain, hard work) to keep her colorful and close-knit family's detective agency afloat. But her new case pits her against the shadowy forces that almost destroyed the city of Houston once before, bringing Nevada back into contact with Connor 'Mad' Rogan." (Publisher's note)

"Add breathtaking romance and sexual tension plus a complex, layered plot, and you have a book that's hard to put down." Kirkus

Andrews, Mary Kay

Every crooked nanny. HarperCollins Pubs. 1992 286p
ISBN 0-06-017923-6
LC 91-58359

"This quick-paced thriller provides an intriguing introduction to a delightfully down-to-earth sleuth." Booklist

Andrews, Mary Kay

Irish eyes; a Callahan Garrity mystery. HarperCollins Pubs. 2000 296p $24
ISBN 0-06-019421-9
LC 99-55680

"Former Atlanta cop Garrity returns to crime solving when her ex-partner, Bucky Deavers, is shot on the way home from a party he finagled her into attending at the Shamrock Society. With the help of the eccentric staff of her housecleaning business, Garrity vows to get to the bottom of the shooting. This is an entertaining, suspenseful romp." Booklist

Andrews, Mary Kay

Summer rental; Mary Kay Andrews. 1st ed.; St. Martin's Press 2011 viii, 402p
ISBN 9780312642693; 0312642695
LC 2011004404

This book tells the story of "three lifelong friends who grew up together in Savannah--unemployed banker Ellis, model Julia, teacher Dorie--and reunite in Nags Head, N.C., for a month-long holiday at a rundown rental elegantly named the Ebbtide. But when the 30-somethings BFFs, each of whom is struggling with life-changing crises, take in Maryn, a stranger and runaway-wife, the beachy holiday takes on a dangerous edge. To the rescue comes handsome landlord Ty, who's renting out his ramshackle family home in hopes of staving off foreclosure." (Publishers Weekly)

Anolik, Lili

Dark Rooms; a novel. Lili Anolik. HarperCollins 2015 336 p. $25.99
ISBN 0062345869; 9780062345868
LC 2014504331

This novel, by Lili Anolik, is "about murder and glamour set in the ambiguous and claustrophobic world of an exclusive New England prep school. Death sets the plot in motion: the murder of Nica Baker, beautiful, wild, enigmatic, and only sixteen. The crime is solved, and quickly--a lonely classmate, unrequited love, a suicide note confession--but memory and instinct won't allow Nica's older sister, Grace, to accept the case as closed." (Publisher's note)

"As much as this is a crime drama, it's also a coming-of-age novel. The plot is high-suspense, but it's the strength of the characters—and the strength of Anolik's hypnotic, unfussy prose—that gives the book its lasting force. Wholly absorbing and emotionally rich, this novel dodges Law & Order: Special Victims Unit clichés to deliver something deeply satisfying." Kirkus

Ansay, A. Manette

River angel. Morrow 1998 243p
ISBN 0-688-15243-0
LC 97-31006

"With 'River Angel,' A. Manette Ansay has moved beyond her prior mastery of the family scene to a lucid, eloquent representation of the commingled and conflicting lives of a town." N Y Times Book Rev

Anshaw, Carol

Carry the one; Carol Anshaw. Simon & Schuster 2012 253 p.
ISBN 9781451636888; 9781451636895; 9781451656930
LC 2011013428

This book "begins in the hours following Carmen's wedding reception, when a car filled with stoned, drunk, and sleepy guests accidentally hits and kills a girl on a dark country road. For the next twenty-five years, those involved, including Carmen and her brother and sister, craft their lives in response to this single tragic moment. As one character says, 'When you add us up, you always have to carry the one.' Through friendships and love affairs; marriage and divorce; parenthood, holidays, and the modest calamities and triumphs of ordinary days, 'Carry the One' shows how one life affects another and how those who thrive and those who self-destruct are closer to each other than we'd expect." (Publisher's note)

Anton, Maggie

Rav Hisda's daughter, book I, apprentice; a novel of love, the Talmud, and sorcery. Maggie Anton. Plume 2012 xxvi, 452 p. p ill., map (paperback) $16.00

ISBN 0452298091; 9780452298095

LC 2012014785

In this novel by Maggie Anton "Hisdadukh, blessed to be beautiful and learned, is the youngest child of Talmudic sage Rav Hisda. . . . Rome, fast becoming Christian, battles Zoroastrian Persia for dominance while Rav Hisda and his colleagues struggle to establish new Jewish traditions after the destruction of Jerusalem's Holy Temple. Against this backdrop Hisdadukh embarks on the tortuous path to become an enchantress in the very land where the word 'magic' originated." (Publisher's note)

Antopol, Molly

The **Unamericans**; stories. by Molly Antopol. W W Norton & Co Inc 2014 256 p. (hardcover) $24.95

ISBN 0393241130; 9780393241136

LC 2013044212

National Jewish Book Award Finalist: Fiction (2014)

This book, by Molly Antopol, is an "exploration of characters shaped by the forces of history. . . . A former dissident from communist-era Prague needles his adult daughter for details about her newly commissioned play. . . . An Israeli soldier, forced to defend a settlement filled with American religious families, still pines for a chance to discover the United States for himself. [And] a young Israeli journalist . . . questions her life path." (Publisher's note)

"Antopol depicts with bold strokes and uncanny intelligence the intimate links between family, history, and politics, never failing to capture the grit and hurt of intergenerational confrontation." Booklist

Antunes, Antonio Lobo

The **inquisitors'** manual; translated by Richard Zenith. Grove Press 2003 435p $25

ISBN 0-8021-1732-5

LC 2002-33858

Original Portuguese edition, 1997

"Lobo Antunes, one of the most skillfull psychological portraitists writing anywhere, renders the turpitude of an entire society through an impasto of intensely individual voices." New Yorker

Appelfeld, Aharon

★ **Badenheim** 1939; [by] Aharon Appelfeld; translated by Dalya Bilu. Godine 1980 148p

ISBN 0-879-23342-7

LC 80-66192

Originally published in Hebrew

"The most shocking thing about this novel is not its satirical humor, but its charm. Appelfeld manages to treat his appalling theme with grace." N Y Rev Books

Appelfeld, Aharon

Blooms of darkness; translated from the Hebrew by Jeffrey M. Green. Schocken Books 2010 279p $25.95

ISBN 978-0-8052-4280-5; 0-8052-4280-5

LC 2009-33532

Original Hebrew edition, 2006

Appelfeld "narrates Blooms of Darkness in a taut, terse present-tense voice that refuses the consolations of retrospect. His decision to use the present tense is particularly shrewd since it eliminates—for the reader, as for Hugo—any possibility of a future. . . Like Anne Frank's diary—a work to which it will draw justified comparison—Blooms of Darkness, beautifully translated from the Hebrew by Jeffrey M. Green, records a brutal process of education." N Y Times Book Rev

Appelfeld, Aharon

The **man** who never stopped sleeping; Aharon Appelfeld ; Translated from the Hebrew by Jeffrey M. Green. Schocken Books 2017 272 p. (hardback) $26; (ebook) $65

ISBN 9780805243192; 9780805243208

LC 2016028875

In this book, by Aharon Appelfeld, "Erwin doesn't remember much about his journey across Europe when the war finally ended because he spent most of it asleep, carried by other survivors as they emerged from their hiding places or were liberated from the camps and made their way to the shores of Naples, where they filled refugee camps and wondered what was to become of them. As he struggles to stay awake, Erwin becomes part of a group of boys being rigorously trained both physically and mentally by an emissary from Palestine for life in their new home." (Publisher's note)

"Appelfeld's style is never flashy, but the plainness of his writing gives post-Holocaust events both starkness and power." Kirkus

Appelfeld, Aharon

Until the dawn's light. Schocken Books 2011 231p $26

ISBN 978-0-8052-4179-2; 0-8052-4179-5

LC 2011-07286

Original Hebrew edition, 1995

"A beautiful and affecting novel, Tolstoyan in its compassion for humanity." Kirkus

Apple, Max

The **Jew** of Home Depot and other stories. Johns Hopkins University Press 2007 170p $19.95

ISBN 978-0-8018-8738-3; 0-8018-8738-0

LC 2007-18864

"Comic movies don't often get Oscar nods. In fiction, too, tragedy wears the capital L for Literature, whereas comedy—good luck, happy endings, pleasure itself—is deemed to be the fluffy stuff of chick lit and beach books. With The Jew of Home Depot, his first collection of stories in two decades, Max Apple challenges the canard that misery reveals more about our identity than joy does. . . . The 13 delightful, utterly cynicism-free stories collected here are mostly tales of courtship, and as the title not so shyly suggests, they often star Jews." Washington Post Book World

Arango, Sascha

The **truth** and other lies; a novel. Sascha Arango. Atria Books 2015 256 p. (hardback) $24.99

ISBN 147679555X; 9781476795553

LC 2014046309

In this novel, by Sascha Arango, "follows a famous author whose wife--the brains behind his success--meets an untimely death, leaving him to deal with the consequences. . . . Now not only are the police after Henry, but his past--which he has painstakingly kept hidden--threatens to catch up with him as well." (Publisher's note)

"Arango uses dark humor to probe the depths of human depravity in Henry's borderline psychotic profile. Fans of psychological thrillers will be eager to see whether Henry's increasingly detailed spin job will protect him or if the chaos he has created will blow his own cover." Booklist

Archer, Jeffrey

And thereby hangs a tale. St. Martin's Press 2010 301p $25.99

ISBN 978-0-312-53953-5; 0-312-53953-3

LC 2010-21666

"Archer assembles 15 more of the clever stories for which he is known. They are split between tales of trickery, as with 'Stuck on You,' where an eager young man is played by a diamond thief, and decidedly sentimental stories, such as 'Members Only,' about a man who wants nothing more than to join a private country club. . . . His trademark twists—sometimes a surprise to the reader, sometimes not—and genial tone will endear these mostly cozy stories to his many fans." Publ Wkly

Archer, Jeffrey, 1940-

Best kept secret; Jeffrey Archer. 1st ed. St. Martin's Press 2013 384 p. (hardcover) $27.99

ISBN 125000098X; 9781250000989

LC 2013000638

This historical family saga, by Jeffrey Archer, is book three of "The Clifton Chronicles." It is set in "1945, London. The vote in the House of Lords as to who should inherit the Barrington family fortune has ended in a tie. The Lord Chancellor's deciding vote will cast a long shadow on the lives of Harry Clifton and Giles Barrington. . . . In 1957, Sebastian wins a scholarship to Cambridge, and a new generation of the Clifton family marches onto the page." (Publisher's note)

Archer, Jeffrey

Only time will tell. St. Martin's Press 2011 386p $27.99

ISBN 978-0-312-53955-9; 0-312-53955-X

LC 2011-25823

"This first title from the Clifton Chronicles introduces readers to Harry Clifton, a boy growing up in Bristol whose father mysteriously died a full year before his birth, supposedly killed in WWI. Though Harry dreams of becoming a stevedore like his Uncle Stan, crazy Old Jack Tar shows Harry the truths of the stevedore life and becomes his surrogate father. After hearing an angelic treble voice, Harry decides to join the choir and learns to read. The choir in turn gains him a scholarship to boys' boarding school St. Bede'sa gateway to the life his mother wants for him, far from the harbor and shipping industry. He meets scholarly Deakins and wealthy Giles Barrington, who become his best friends, and the three strive to gain acceptance to Bristol Grammar School. Though Giles' father has a particular aversion to Harry, the boys' friendship proves stronger than any paternal dictates." Publ Wkly

Other titles in this series are:

The sins of the father (2012)

Best kept secret (2013)

Be careful what you wish for (2014)

Mightier than the sword (2015)

Cometh the hour (2016)

This was a man (2016)

Arden, Katherine

★ The **bear** and the nightingale; a novel. Katherine Arden. Del Rey 2017 336 p. (hardback) $27; (ebook) $65

ISBN 9781101885932; 9781101885949

LC 2016011345

In this novel, part of the Winternight Trilogy, by Katherine Arden, "winter lasts most of the year at the edge of the Russian wilderness, and in the long nights, Vasilisa and her siblings love to gather by the fire to listen to their nurse's fairy tales. Above all, Vasya loves the story of Frost, the blue-eyed winter demon. . . . Fiercely devout, Vasya's [new] stepmother forbids her family from honoring their household spirits, but Vasya fears what this may bring." (Publisher's note)

"Arden has shaped a world that neatly straddles the seen and the unseen, where readers will hear echoes of stories from childhood while recognizing the imagination that has transformed old material into something fresh." Kirkus

Another title in this series is:

The girl in the tower (2017)

Arden, Katherine

The **girl** in the tower; a novel. Katherine Arden. Del Rey 2018 362 p. (Winternight trilogy) (hardcover : acid-free paper) $27

ISBN 9781101885970; 1101885963; 9781101885963

LC 2017039509

In this book, by Katherine Arden, "Vasilisa has grown up at the edge of a Russian wilderness, where snowdrifts reach the eaves of her family's wooden house and there is truth in the fairy tales told around the fire. Vasilisa's gift for seeing what others do not won her the attention of Morozko—Frost, the winter demon from the stories—and together they saved her people from destruction. But Frost's aid comes at a cost, and her people have condemned her as a witch." (Publisher's note)

"A masterfully told story of folklore, history, and magic with a spellbinding heroine at the heart of it all." Booklist

Aridjis, Chloe

Asunder; Chloe Aridjis. Mariner Books 2013 208 p. $13.95

ISBN 0544003462; 9780544003460

LC 2013026088

In this book from Prix du Premier Roman Etranger prize-winner Chloe Aridjis, "narrator Marie, a museum guard at London's National Gallery, has an intimate knowledge of the paintings around her. She watches the behavior of visitors and absorbs art history lessons from the experts passing through. . . . Marie's passive and unassuming demeanor matches her seemingly aimless personal life": a friendly but distant roommate and a noncommittal relationship with poet Daniel. (Library Journal)

Arimah, Lesley Nneka

★ **What** it means when a man falls from the sky; Lesley Nneka Arimah. Riverhead Books 2017 230 p. (hardback) $26

ISBN 9780735211025

LC 2016036303

Kirkus Prize: Fiction (2017)

Author Lesley Nneka Arimah's "debut collection explores the ties that bind parents and children, husbands and wives, lovers and friends to one another and to the places they call home. . . . In 'Wild,' a disastrous night out shifts a teenager and her Nigerian cousin onto uneasy common ground. In 'The Future Looks Good,' three generations of women are haunted by the ghosts of war, while in "Light," a father struggles to protect and empower the daughter he loves." (Publisher's note)

"This speculative turn joins everything from fabulism to folk tale as Arimah confidently tests out all the tools in her kit while also managing to create a wholly cohesive and original collection." Kirkus

Arnott, Jake

The **house** of rumour; Jake Arnott. Houghton Mifflin Harcourt 2013 448 p. (hardcover) $26

ISBN 0544077792; 9780544077799

LC 2012042359

This novel, by Jake Arnott, "explores WWII spy intrigue (featuring Ian Fleming), occultism (Aleister Crowley), the West Coast science-fiction set (Heinlein, L. Ron Hubbard, and Philip K. Dick all appear), and the new wave music scene of the '80s. The decades-spanning, labyrinthine plot . . . [is] told through multiple narrators, what at first appears to be a constellation of random events begins to cohere as the work of a shadow organization--or is it just coincidence?" (Publisher's note)

Arnow, Harriette Louisa Simpson

The **dollmaker**; [by] Harriette Simpson Arnow. Macmillan 1954 549p

"It is hard to believe that anyone who opens its pages will soon forget {Gertie} and her sufferings as traced in Harriette Arnow's long, heavily packed masterwork." NY Times Book Rev

Arsenault, Emily

The **broken** teaglass; a novel. Delacorte Press 2009 370p $25; pa $15

ISBN 978-0-553-80733-2; 0-553-80733-1; 978-0-553-38653-0 pa

LC 2008-39167

"College graduate Billy Webb takes a job at the Samuelson Company, a venerable dictionary publisher in out-of-the-way Claxton, Massachusetts. While he learns the ropes of research reading, defining, and answering the phone, wondering whether his hushed workplace is really the 'real world,' he finds an unusual citation (for the word editrix) from The Broken Teaglass, by Dolores Beekmim. Though it's not the only such excerpt in the files, no such novel has even been published. Stranger still, the story seems to be set at Samuelson. Working with his arch, cryptic colleague Mona Minot, Billy tries to find the rest of the citations, which seem to make reference to murder. . . . [This] novel has a delightful premise, crisply drawn characters, and a subtle sense of humor. Word nerds, too, will enjoy the peeks at the procedure of making a dictionary." Booklist

Arsenault, Emily

In search of the Rose notes. William Morrow 2011 369p pa $14.99

ISBN 978-0-06-201232-6

Drawn back to her old neighborhood and to her former best friend Charlotte when the bones of their babysitter Rose are found, Nora must revisit the events surrounding Rose's disappearance and her own troubled adolescence.

"Instead of dwelling on fear and pain, Arsenault guides the reader through grief, compassion, and understanding in this emotionally complex and deeply satisfying read." Publ Wkly

Arudpragasam, Anuk

The **story** of a brief marriage; Anuk Arudpragasam. Flatiron Books 2016 193 p. (hardcover) $24.99

ISBN 9781250072405; 9781250074751

LC 2016020830

"Anuk Arudpragasam's 'The Story of a Brief Marriage' is a feat of extraordinary sensitivity and imagination, a meditation on the fundamental elements of human existence---eating, sleeping, washing, touching, speaking--that give us direction and purpose, even as the world around us collapses. Set over the course of a single day and night, this unflinching debut confronts marriage and war, life and death, bestowing on its subjects the highest dignity, however briefly." (Publisher's note)

"Dinesh finds beauty in the worst of situations, which contributes to making this debut deeply moving and hopeful." Pub Wkly

Arvin, Reed

Blood of angels; a novel. Reed Arvin. HarperCollins Publishers 2005 viii, 354p (pbk.) $7.99

ISBN 9780060596354; 0060596341; 9780060596347

LC 2004060931

This book tells the story of "Thomas Dennehy, assistant DA of Davidson County, Tenn., [who will] be certified as the first lawyer in the country to have sent the wrong man to the death chamber. As if that isn't enough, he must also prosecute a charismatic member of the local Sudanese community, Moses Bol, accused of killing a prostitute, in a trial that threatens to engulf Nashville in a full-scale race riot. Dennehy is tough, in court and out, and has plenty of . . . personal problems—primarily an ex-wife for whom he has conflicting feelings and an 11-year-old daughter he adores. . . . While trying to sort through his problems, Dennehy falls for an unlikely lady, Fiona Towns, a local minister and Moses Bol's alibi." (Publishers Weekly)

Asaro, Catherine

Primary inversion. Tor 1995 317p

ISBN 0-312-85764-0

LC 94-47207

"In a distant future where three empires battle for control of the galaxy, Sauscony Valdoria, the heir apparent of the Skolian Empire, finds herself inexplicably attracted to Jaibriol Qox, the son of the Emperor of Tarnth and the symbol of everything Sauscony has been taught to despise. Asaro's sf debut features strong male and female protagonists and a well-realized far-future world. Blending hard science with a familiar tale of star-crossed lovers." Libr J

Asch, Sholem

The **Apostle**; translated by Maurice Samuel. Putnam 1943 804p

In "'The Apostle,' Sholem Asch has written a book which should stand beside 'The Nazarene.' Its erudition, its essential reverence for the two faiths concerned, its scholarly and dramatic portrayal of the Jew who spread the gospel to the gentiles will call forth the respect of every civilized and intelligent reader." N Y Her Trib Books

Asch, Sholem

The **Nazarene**; translated by Maurice Samuel. Putnam 1939 698p

A novel based on the life of Christ told from three different points of view. First there is the narrative as a modern Polish Jewish scholar hears it from lips of one who claims to be the reincarnation of the Roman military governor of Jerusalem. Then there is the 'fifth gospel' written by Judas Iscariot, and finally there is the story as the young Jew remembers it when he realizes that he himself is the reincarnation of a disciple of the Pharisee, Rabbi Nicodemon

"Judged purely as a novel, The Nazarene is a superb achievement. Even on the factual side, a work such as Papini's Life is thin beside it. This is because Mr. Asch has taken an infinite amount of trouble to build up an historical background against which the figure of Jesus may move authentically, with that sense of reality which we should expect of fiction as of life." Atlantic

Ashford, Jane

What the duke doesn't know; Jane Ashford. Sourcebooks Inc 2016 384 p. (The Duke's sons) (ebook) $7.99; (ebook) $7.99; $7.99

ISBN 9781492621614; 9781492621607; 1492621595; 9781492621591

LC 2016036596

In this book in the Duke's Sons series, by Jane Ashford, "Captain James Gresham is the fifth son of the Duke of Langford and has made his fortune in the Royal Navy. The time has come to find a proper wife and establish his home, but the adventurous possibilities of the sea entice him. Enter Kawena Benson-half-English, half-Polynesian, and all spunk. She has one mission: avenge her father and reclaim the jewels stolen from him. And she has her target: Lord James Gresham." (Publisher's note)

"Throw in Ashford's gift for creating intriguingly different characters and her dry sense of humor, and you have a romance worth cherishing." Booklist

Asimov, Isaac

The **complete** stories. Doubleday 1990 2v v1 pa $19.95

ISBN 0-385-41627-X

LC 90-3136

This set contains all of Asimov's science fiction stories including the "collections 'Earth Is Room Enough' and 'Nine Tomorrows' from the 1950s as well as . . . 'Nightfall and Other Stories.'" SLJ

Asimov, Isaac

★ **Forward** the Foundation. Doubleday 1993 415p (Foundation)

ISBN 0-385-24793-1

LC 92-46655

This volume and Prelude to Foundation predate the other Foundation novels in terms of internal chronology

Although "Asimov leans rather heavily on dialogue to carry the story, we are privileged to learn something more of Seldon, whom Asimov regards as his alter ego—intellectually vigorous, witty, vulnerable, and deeply concerned about the fate of his fallible species." Christ Sci Monit

Asimov, Isaac

★ **Foundation**. Gnome Press 1951 255p (Foundation)

"A story of a Galactic Empire of the future, and its successor in the government of the Milky Way." Publ Wkly

Followed by Foundation and empire

Asimov, Isaac

★ **Foundation** and earth. Doubleday 1986 356p (Foundation)

ISBN 0-385-23312-4

LC 86-2130

In the fifth novel of the Foundation series "Golan Trevize rejects the vaunted Selden Plan of Foundation and Empire in favor of a bold experiment in galactic unity. To ferret out the reason for his instinctive decision, Trevize embarks on a journey through uncharted space in search of a legendary planet known as Earth. Asimov's latest entry in his epic series features his usual cast of intelligent, likeable characters and just enough action to give substance to this novel of lucid speculations." Libr J

Asimov, Isaac

★ **Foundation** and empire. Gnome Press 1952 247p (Foundation)

In this second volume of the Foundation series "two groups struggle for control of the world's destiny in a future time when mankind has settled in the Milky Way. Then a mutant appears bringing with him a new threat for everyone." Chicago Public Libr

Followed by Second Foundation

Asimov, Isaac

★ **Foundation's** edge. Doubleday 1982 366p (Foundation)

ISBN 0-385-17725-9

The fourth novel in the Foundation series "shows us the Seldon Plan at midpoint and still surprisingly on target in spite of the passage of time and unforeseen events. The focus has narrowed to power struggles between the Foundations, both wishing to be the controlling element in the planned Second Galactic Empire, quite unlike Seldon's idealistic vision. And new players have been introduced into the game." Libr J

Followed by Foundation and earth

Asimov, Isaac

The **gods** themselves. Doubleday 1972 288p

"Imagination is the fount of Isaac Asimov's mastery. The suspense he generates . . . is low-key and subtle, and he has a gifted knack for making wild and indescribable superbeings (for he never quite describes them) seem lifelike, though scarcely human." Best Sellers

Asimov, Isaac

★ **I,** robot; Bantam hardcover ed.; Bantam Books 2004 224p (Robot series) $24; pa $7.99

ISBN 0-553-80370-0; 0-553-29438-5 pa

LC 2003-69139

First published 1950 by Gnome Press

"These loosely connected stories cover the career of Dr. Susan Calvin and United States Robots, the industry that she heads, from the time of the public's early distrust of these robots to its later dependency on them. This collection is an important introduction to a theme often found in science fiction: the encroachment of technology on our lives." Shapiro. Fic for Youth. 3d edition

Asimov, Isaac

★ **Prelude** to Foundation. Doubleday 1988 403p (Foundation)

ISBN 0-385-23313-2

LC 87-33086

This novel and Forward the Foundation are set chronologically prior to other volumes in the Foundation series

This "is vintage Asimov, a novel that places ideas ahead of all its other elements but doesn't stint on characterization or entertaining plot lines. It also contains a fair number of mysteries, and . . . all of this is handled in a simple, direct style that never gets between the reader and the story." West Coast Rev Books

Asimov, Isaac

★ **Second** Foundation. Gnome Press 1953 210p (Foundation)

Third book of the Foundation series about the efforts of a group of scientists who are trying to subdue the chaos and conflict of the galactic world. The story centers on fourteen-year-old Arkady Darrell's search for this secret group

Followed by Foundation's edge

Aslam, Nadeem

★ The **Blind** Man's Garden; Nadeem Aslam. Alfred A. Knopf 2013 384 p. (First Edition) $26.95

ISBN 0307961710; 9780307961716

LC 2012041083

This book by Nadeem Aslam is a "novel set in Pakistan and Afghanistan in the months following 9/11: a story of war, of one family's losses. Jeo and Mikal are foster brothers from a small town in Pakistan. Jeo is a . . . medical student. Mikal has been a vagabond . . . in love with a woman he can't have. When Jeo decides to sneak across the border into Afghanistan . . . to help care for wounded civilians . . . Mikal determines to go with him." (Publisher's note)

Includes bibliographical references

Aslam, Nadeem

★ The **golden** legend; a novel. Nadeem Aslam. First American edition Alfred A. Knopf 2017 319 p. (hardcover) $27.95

ISBN 9780451493781; 9780451493798

LC 2016034887

In this novel by Nadeem Aslam, "for weeks someone has been broadcasting people's secrets from the minaret of the local mosque, and, in a country where even the accusation of blasphemy is a currency to be bartered, the mysterious broadcasts have struck fear in Christians and Muslims alike. When the loudspeakers reveal a forbidden romance between a Muslim cleric's daughter and Nargis's Christian neighbor, Nargis finds herself trapped in the center of the chaos." (Publisher's note)

"Brooding and beautiful: a mature, assured story of the fragility of the world and of ourselves." Kirkus

Aslam, Nadeem

Maps for lost lovers; Nadeem Aslam. 1st American ed. Knopf 2005 xii, 379 p o.p.; (pbk.) $14.95

ISBN 1400042429; 9781400076970

LC 2004059428

Kiriyama Prize: Fiction (2005)

In this book, author Nadeem "Aslam . . . explores the interwoven lives of Pakistani immigrants in an English town they have rechristened Dasht-e-Tanhaii, 'the Wilderness of Solitude' or 'the Desert of Loneliness.' The disappearance of Jugnu and Chanda, lovers who broke Islamic law to live in sin, throws the small community into upheaval. The police arrest Chanda's brothers, whom they believe murdered the couple to avenge their family's shame. . . . Aslam depicts an insular ex-pat Pakistani community fighting to preserve its cultural heritage and losing the battle to its Western-born children. . . . At the heart of the turmoil is sexual freedom, and Aslam illustrates the many ways women's lives are restricted and romantic love is denied in the name of religion." (Publishers Weekly)

Aslam, Nadeem

The **wasted** vigil. Alfred A. Knopf 2008 319p $25

ISBN 978-0-307-26842-6; 0-307-26842-X

LC 2008-17772

"The prose in The Wasted Vigil is usually so generous with startling perceptions that the reader rarely feels overwhelmed by the social and historical facts that Aslam, writing about a country largely unknown to his readers, has to constantly smuggle into his narrative. . . . Aslam's determination to gaze resolutely at the darkest side of our many cold and hot wars is what gives The Wasted Vigil its depth and power." N Y Rev Books

Atkins, Ace

✓**Devil's** garden. G.P. Putnam's Sons 2009 354p $24.95

ISBN 978-0-399-15536-9; 0-399-15536-8

LC 2008-46361

"The 1921 rape/manslaughter trial of silent film star Roscoe 'Fatty' Arbuckle provides the gritty backdrop for Atkins's outstanding crime novel, in which Dashiell Hammett, then a Pinkerton operative living in San Francisco, plays a significant role. A wild party Arbuckle throws at San Francisco's posh St. Francis Hotel results in tragedy after an actress, Virginia Rappe, is mysteriously injured and later dies. . . . With enviable ease, Atkins . . . brings to life Hammett, Arbuckle, William Randolph Hearst and other real figures of the period. Those familiar with the historical case will be impressed by how well the book meshes fact and fiction. Genre fans who enjoy the grim realism of James Ellroy's post-WWII Los Angeles will find a lot to like in Atkins's Prohibition-era San Francisco." Publ Wkly

Atkins, Ace

✓The **forsaken**; Ace Atkins. G.P. Putnam's Sons 2014 384 p. illustrations, map (Quinn Colson) (hardback) $26.95

ISBN 0399161791; 9780399161797

LC 2014015440

"Thirty-six years ago, a nameless black man wandered into Jericho, Mississippi. . . . Less than two days later, he was accused of rape and murder, hunted down by a self-appointed posse, and lynched. Now evidence has surfaced of his innocence, and county sheriff Quinn Colson sets out not only to identify the stranger's remains, but to charge those responsible for the lynching." (Publisher's note)

"The dive into Jericho's dark past makes for great reading as Atkins rolls through a handful of perspectives, propelling the story's threads toward an adrenaline-laced, Wild West-style conclusion." Booklist

Atkins, Ace

✓The **ranger**. G.P. Putnam's Sons 2011 334p $25.95

ISBN 978-0-399-15748-6; 0-399-15748-4

LC 2011-02785

"Fresh from his tour of duty in Afghanistan, Quinn returns to his hometown of Jericho, Miss., for the funeral of his uncle, Sheriff Hampton Beckett. The sheriff's death was ruled a suicide but Deputy Lillie Virgil believes he was murdered and appeals to Quinn to help find his murderer. But as he tries to find the truth behind his uncle's death, Quinn plunges into a morass of violence and corruption that has overpowered his rural hometown and the environs of remote Tibbehah County. An 'invisible confederacy of crooks' includes a compound of meth dealers, shady land deals and a general disregard for the law. While Quinn acts as the archetypical character who has come to clean up the town, 'The Ranger' avoids stereotypes and clichés. Quinn isn't molded as a superhero but a man struggling with his role and duties as a soldier and what he owes his family and hometown." South Florida Sun-Sentinel

Other titles about Quinn Colson are:

✓The lost ones (2012)
✓The broken places (2013)
✓The forsaken (2014)
The redeemers (2015)
✓The innocents (2016)
✓The fallen (2017)

Atkins, Ace

✓**White** shadow. Putnam 2006 370p $24.95

ISBN 0-399-15355-1

LC 2005-56683

This novel "slowly unfurls itself, strolling along with the readers, as it evokes the heat and humidity of a setting where the languorousness stands in sharp contrast to the life and death stakes at hand. Murder, corruption, and organized crime are all present, but the heat seems to suck the speed out of them, so even death is dispatched in slow motion. Ultimately, the atmosphere of this novel is the star. Atkins nails all the period details and describes the city perfectly." PopMatters

Atkins, Ace

✓**Wicked** city. G. P. Putnam's Sons 2008 336p $24.95

ISBN 978-0-399-15457-7

LC 2007-32774

"It's 1954, and the attorney-general-elect of Alabama has been assassinated near a downtown street. Among the gathering crowd stands a young teen still wearing 3-D glasses from the John Wayne movie he's just seen. So begins Ace Atkins' novel, Wicked City, a vivid depiction of the real-life Phenix City, a den of gambling, prostitution and corruption that rivaled any Hollywood creation. Atkins provides a 3-D view through two narrators, an omniscient teller and Lamar Murphy, an ex-boxer enlisted to help solve Albert Patterson's murder. . . . A character warns that the sweetness of Phenix City moonshine masks the embalming fluid that provides its kick. Atkins has likewise crafted a smart tale of a decadent place; Southern sweetness laced with poison." Paste

Atkinson, Kate, 1951-

★ **Case** histories; a novel. Little, Brown 2004 312p $23.95

ISBN 0-316-74040-3 Little, Brown; 0-385-60799-7 Doubleday

LC 2004-2379

This novel is set in Cambridge, England. "Olivia Land, youngest and most beloved of the Land girls, goes missing in the night and is never seen again. Thirty years later, two of her surviving sisters unearth a shocking clue to Olivia's disappearance. . . . Theo delights in his daughter Laura's wit, effortless beauty, and selfless love. But her first day as an associate in his law firm is also the day when Theo's world turns upside down. . . . Michelle looks around one day and finds herself trapped. . . . A very needy baby and a very demanding husband make her every waking moment a reminder that . . . she'd made a grave mistake and would spend the rest of her life paying for it—until a fit of rage creates a grisly, bloody escape. As Private Detective Jackson Brodie investigates all three cases, startling connections and discoveries emerge. Inextricably caught up in his clients' grief, joy, and desire, Jackson finds their unshakable need for resolution very much like his own." (Publisher's note)

"The novel is packed with women whose appetites are large, and Atkinson's prose is correspondingly loose and louche: no single point of view predominates, and everyone's thoughts effortlessly rollick along." N Y Times Book Rev

Atkinson, Kate, 1951-

★ A **God** in Ruins; Kate Atkinson. Little, Brown & Co. 2015 400 p. $28

ISBN 0316176532; 9780316176538

LC 2015933947

Sequel to: Life After Life (2013)

This novel by Kate Atkinson "tells the dramatic story of the 20th Century through Ursula's beloved younger brother Teddy--would-be poet, heroic pilot, husband, father, and grandfather-as he navigates the perils and progress of a rapidly changing world. After all that Teddy endures in battle, his greatest challenge is living in a future he never expected to have. " (Publisher's note)

"As in Life After Life, Atkinson isn't just telling a story: she's deconstructing, taking apart the notion of how we believe stories are told. Using narrative tricks that range from the subtlest sleight of hand to direct address, she makes us feel the power of storytelling not as an intellectual conceit, but as a punch in the gut." Pub Wkly

Includes bibliographical references

Atkinson, Kate, 1951-

★ **Life** After Life; Kate Atkinson. Little Brown & Co 2013 544 p. $27.99

ISBN 0316176486; 9780316176484

This book is the story of Ursula Todd, who has an apparently infinite number of lives. "As she grows, she also dies, repeatedly, in a variety of ways, while the young century marches on towards its second cataclysmic world war. Does Ursula's apparently infinite number of lives give her the power to save the world from its inevitable destiny? And if she can—will she?" (Publisher's note)

Atkinson, Kate

Started early, took my dog; a novel. Little, Brown and Company 2011 371p $24.99

ISBN 978-0-316-06673-0; 0-316-06673-7

LC 2010-32217

First published 2010 in the United Kingdom

"A delight: an intricate construction that assembles itself before the reader's eyes, populated by idiosyncratic, multidimensional characters and written with shrewd, mordant grace. . . . Atkinson's Jackson Brodie books are like high-wire acts in which she is forever defying gravity (in the form of crime fiction's improbable conventions) by making the work fresh, unpredictable and alive." Salon.com

Atkinson, Kate

★ **When** will there be good news? Little, Brown & Co. 2008 388p $24.99

ISBN 978-0-316-15485-7; 0-316-15485-7

LC 2008-14738

"As always, Atkinson inhabits her characters with fluency, clarity and a good eye and ear for quirks and habits of mind." Times Lit Suppl

Atlee, Alison

★ The **typewriter** girl; Alison Atlee. 1st Gallery Books trade pbk ed Gallery Books 2013 367 p. (paperback) $15

ISBN 1451673256; 1451673272; 9781451673258; 9781451673272

LC 2012007883

In this book, Betsey Dobson travels to the Idensea seaside resort and is hired by manager John Jones. "John, who has spent four years supervising construction of the resort's pleasure railway and indoor amusement park, clashes with Sir Alton Dunning, who wants to maintain his hotel's elegant exclusivity. In addition to completing the park, John's plans also include finding a rich wife. Yet Betsy intrigues him, even after he learns how she was seduced and abandoned" while working as a housemaid. (Library Journal)

Attenberg, Jami

★ The **Middlesteins**; Jami Attenberg. Grand Central Pub. 2012 288 p. $24.99

ISBN 1455507210; 9781455507214

LC 2011025990

In "[Jami] Attenberg's multigenerational novel about a Midwestern Jewish family, shifting points of view tell the story of the breakup and aftermath of Edie and Richard Middlestein's nearly 40-year marriage as Edie slowly eats herself to death. . . . When complications surrounding Edie's diabetes precipitate Richard's filing for divorce, the already tightly wound [daughter-in-law] Rachelle becomes obsessed with the family's physical and moral health." (Publishers Weekly)

Atwood, Margaret, 1939-

Alias Grace. Talese 1996 468p il
ISBN 0-385-47571-3

LC 96-21689

"Always a powerful writer, Atwood outdoes herself with compelling prose, expert control of the material, and fine attention to historical detail." Libr J

Atwood, Margaret, 1939-

The **blind** assassin. Talese 2000 521p $26
ISBN 0-385-47572-1

LC 99-462109

"Within the novel, stories produce anguish and arousal, charges and vindications, guilt and vengeance. For readers of the novel, all this may foster something like delight, although the fictional universe is hardly a pleasant one." Women's Rev Books

Atwood, Margaret, 1939-

★ **Cat's** eye. Doubleday 1989 446p
ISBN 0-385-26007-5

LC 88-24345

First published 1988 in Canada

"Atwood's achievement is the decoding of childhood's secrets, and the creation of a flawed and haunting work of art." Time

Atwood, Margaret, 1939-

★ The **Handmaid's** tale; with an introduction by Valerie Martin. Everyman's Library 2006 xxxiii, 350p
ISBN 9780099511663

LC 2006042618

First published 1986 by Houghton Mifflin

This is a new edition of Atwood's 1986 novel with an introduction by Valerie Martin. The book is "set in the near future, in a fundamentalist Christian totalitarian state called the Republic of Gilead. . . . Because of environmental pollution, the number of fertile women is low and those who can still bear children are effectively prisoners of the government. When the Christian fundamentalists took power they removed fertile women from their husbands and children and sent them to live with government leaders—or 'Commanders'—and their infertile wives—so that they could conceive and bear children who would then be raised by the Commanders and their wives as their own. The novel is narrated by one of these fertile women, called Handmaids." (N Y Rev Books)

"A gripping suspense tale, The Handmaid's Tale is an allegory of what results from a politics based on misogyny, racism, and anti-Semitism." Ms

Atwood, Margaret, 1939-

The **Heart** Goes Last; A Novel. by Margaret Atwood. Random House Inc 2015 320 p. $26.95
ISBN 0385540353; 9780385540353

LC 2015016476

In this book, by Margaret Atwood, "there are 'not enough jobs, and too many people,' which drives married couple Stan and Charmaine to become interested in the Positron Project, a community that purports to have achieved harmony. There is a catch . . . citizens are required to share their home with other couples, alternating each month between time in prison and time at home." (Publishers Weekly)

"Atwood is fond of intricate plot work, and the novel takes a long time to set up the action, but once it hits the last third, it gains an unstoppable momentum. The novel is full of sly moments of peripeteia and lots of sex, which play alongside larger ideas about the hidden monsters lurking in facile totalitarianism, and, as implied by the title, the ability of the heart to keep fighting despite long odds." Pub Wkly

Atwood, Margaret, 1939-

Life before man. Simon & Schuster 1980 317p
ISBN 0-671-25115-5

LC 79-20281

This "is a powerful, introspective view of contemporary marriage and the changing roles of the sexes. . . . {This novel} returns to the survival and identity theme of Atwood's early thematic guide to Canadian literature, but at a level that transcends the national. With men and mores rooted in the prehistoric past, Atwood forces us to confront a harrowing present that anticipates an ecologically and culturally doomed future." Choice

Atwood, Margaret, 1939-

★ **Maddaddam**; a novel. by Margaret Atwood. Nan A. Talese 2013 416 p. (hardback) $27.95
ISBN 0385528787; 9780385528788

LC 2013018715

In this book by Margaret Atwood, "after the Waterless Flood pandemic has wiped out most of humanity, Toby and Ren have rescued their friend Amanda from the vicious Painballers. They return to the MaddAddamite cob house, newly fortified against man and giant pigoon alike. Accompanying them are the Crakers, the gentle, quasi-human species engineered by the brilliant but deceased Crake." (Publisher's note)

Atwood, Margaret, 1939-

★ **Stone** mattress; Nine Tales. Margaret Atwood. Random House Inc 2014 256 p. $25.95
ISBN 0385539126; 9780385539128

LC 2014013010

In this short story collection author Margaret Atwood presents "nine tales of acute psychological insight and turbulent relationships. A recently widowed fantasy writer is guided through a stormy winter evening by the voice of her late husband. A man who bids on an auctioned storage space has a surprise.A woman born with a genetic abnormality is mistaken for a vampire." (Publisher's note)

"Most of the nine stories feature women who have been wronged as girls but recover triumphantly as adults. Atwood brings her biting wit to bear on the battle of the sexes." Pub Wkly

Atwood, Margaret, 1939-

The **year** of the flood; a novel. Nan A. Talese/Doubleday 2009 448p $26.95
ISBN 978-0-385-52877-1; 0-385-52877-9

LC 2009-05901

"Structurally, the book can be overwhelming. The story begins with the end and is told from the disparate points of view of Ren, a young sex-club trapeze dancer; Toby, who becomes one of God's Gardeners; and Adam One, the leader of the Gardeners. Narratives jump back and forth in time to show how and why the destruction came about. Keeping the story line straight can be challenging because of the multiple narrators, but it's easy enough to tell the good guys from the bad guys. The good guys are green. (Not literally, although in a book like this, that is a possibility.) Atwood gives each main character an imaginative life history." Dallas Morning News

Atxaga, Bernardo

Seven houses in France; Bernardo Atxaga ; translated from the Spanish by Margaret Jull Costa. Farrar Straus & Giroux

2012 250 p. (paperback : alk. paper) $15.00; (hardcover) $29.40

ISBN 1555976239; 1846554470; 9781555976231; 9781846554476

LC 2011507407

This historical novel "is set in the Belgian Congo in the early part of the last century, [where] the arrival of a devout and taciturn young officer into a contingent of colorful colonial soldiers on a remote jungle outpost on the River Congo sets off a . . . chain of events." The marksman, Chrysostome Liège, is abused by his commander, Captain Biran, who is "engage[d] in a risky contraband scheme with his covetous subordinate, the psychotic Lieutenant Van Thiegel." (Publishers Weekly)

Auel, Jean M.

★ The **Clan** of the Cave Bear; a novel. Crown 1980 468p (Earth's children)

ISBN 0-517-18918-6

LC 80-14581

"It's subject matter, its vast research . . . make this fictional excursion into prehistory a thing of wonder. But it's an enjoyable story, too, though leisurely and not notable for the quality of its prose. . . . The depiction of how the cave-dwelling Neanderthals lived—how they performed their totemistic rituals, gathered medicinal plants, slew mammoths and other animals—is solid, convincing and sometimes exciting." Publ Wkly

Other titles in this series are:

The valley of horses (1982)

The mammoth hunters (1985)

The plains of passage (1990)

The shelters of stone (2002)

The land of painted caves (2011)

Auel, Jean M.

The **land** of painted caves. Broadway Books 2011 757p (Earth's children) $30

ISBN 978-0-517-58051-6; 0-517-58051-9

LC 2010-21873

The sixth and final book in the author's Earth's Children series which began with The Clan of the Cave Bear (1980)

"Ayla is the mate of Jondalar, the mother of Jonayla, their infant daughter, and an acolyte of the First of the Zelandonii, the spiritual leaders of the caves of her husband's people. But all is not well with Ayla. She is separated from her husband and daughter while training for her new position, which takes a terrible physical toll on her health, and her innovative ideas and unusual history create conflict among the people. . . . Though one must occasionally suspend disbelief that one young woman, no matter how intelligent, can really be responsible for introducing concepts such as animal husbandry, sign language, and the role of men in sexuality and conception, the book is compelling." Libr J

Auslander, Shalom

Hope; a tragedy. Shalom Auslander. Riverhead Books 2011 292 p.

ISBN 9781594488382

LC 2011046843

The novel tells the story of "a young Jewish business writer and his family, who buy a house in rural New York. They find that their purchase has included a whole lot more than they bargained for. The protagonist, Solomon Kugel, discovers there's a secret tenant in the attic - none other than Holocaust writer-victim Anne Frank. The iconic Anne Frank, now very old, miraculously survived the Nazi death camps and took up residence in this bucolic enclave, camping in Kugel's attic and writing a book about her life. Kugel targets . . . all sorts of social worries, such as anti-Semitism; and oddities from gluten allergies to the tanning fad to the real estate business." (NPR)

Austen, Jane

★ **Emma**; with an introduction by Marilyn Butler. Knopf 1991 xlvii, 498p $19

ISBN 0-679-40581-X

LC 91-52988

First published 1815

"Emma is a pretty girl of sterling character and more will than she can properly manage. She thinks she knows what is best for everybody, and is a prey to many deceptions. She is imposed upon, and imposes upon herself; it is a long while before she sees things as they are, and recognizes where her own happiness lies. Her hero is one of Jane's sober, clear-eyed, and perfect men. The Fairfax and Churchill subplot furnishes a comedy of dissimulation contrasting didactically with Emma's honesty. A formidable snob and vulgarian, Mrs. Elton, and a good-natured bore, Miss Bates, who would be insufferable outside these pages, are among the more laughable characters." Baker. Guide to the Best Fic

Austen, Jane

★ **Mansfield** Park; with an introduction by Peter Conrad. Alfred A. Knopf 1992 xxxvii, 488p $21

ISBN 0-679-41269-7

LC 91-58689

First published 1814

"Her most considerable piece of work, not in mere dimensions, but in the mastery of a difficult problem. . . . In truth, nowhere is the difference between true comedy and satire better exemplified." Baker. Guide to the Best Fic

Austen, Jane

Northanger Abbey. Vintage Classics 2007 241p pa $6.95

ISBN 978-0-307-38683-0; 0-307-38683-X

LC 2007-281091

First published 1818

"Though not published until 1818, this was written 1798-9 and entitled 'Susan', revised in 1803 and sold for publication; it may perhaps have been rewritten or touched up later, before it appeared posthumously. Begun as a parody of sentimentalism and the romantics, it developed into the genre which was to be peculiarly Jane Austen's—the portrayal in sober and faithful tints of the quiet middle-class life she knew; the satire restrained, the comedy all-pervasive." Baker. Guide to the Best Fic

Austen, Jane

Persuasion. Alfred A. Knopf 1992 xxxvii, 260p $18

ISBN 0-679-40986-6

LC 91-53181

First published 1818

"The heroine, Anne Elliott, and her lover, Captain Wentworth, had been engaged eight years before the story opens but Anne had broken the engagement in deference to family and friends. Upon his return he finds her 'wretchedly altered,' but after numerous obstacles have been overcome, the lovers are happily united." Gerwig. Handb for Readers and Writers

Austen, Jane

★ **Pride** and prejudice; introduction by Anna Quindlen. Modern Library 1995 281p $14.95

ISBN 0-679-60168-6

LC 95-6310

First published 1813

"The characters are drawn with humor, delicacy, and the intimate knowledge of men and women that Miss Austen always shows." Keller. Reader's Dig of Books

Austen, Jane

★ **Sense** and sensibility; with an introduction by Peter Conrad. Knopf 1992 xxxix, 367p $16

ISBN 0-679-40987-4

LC 91-53182

First published 1811

"A study of character and manners in a very delicate, precise, miniature style; the characters just everyday people, drawn as they are without exaggeration; the minute differences of human nature delicately penciled; the satire directed against mere commonplace foolishness, conceit, and vulgarity, rather than vice or eccentricity. In truth, the social failings and personal foibles are self-revealed rather than satirized and make spontaneous comedy." Baker. Guide to the Best Fic

Auster, Paul, 1947-

★ **4** 3 2 1; a novel. Paul Auster. Henry Holt & Co. 2017 880 p. (hardcover) $32.50; (ebook) $60

ISBN 9781627794466; 9781627794473

LC 2016020041

Man Booker Prize Shortlist (2017)

In this novel, by Paul Auster, "on March 3, 1947, in the maternity ward of Beth Israel Hospital in Newark, New Jersey, Archibald Isaac Ferguson, the one and only child of Rose and Stanley Ferguson, is born. From that single beginning, Ferguson's life will take four simultaneous and independent fictional paths. Four identical Fergusons made of the same DNA, four boys who are the same boy, go on to lead four parallel and entirely different lives." (Publisher's note)

"With this novel, Auster reminds us that not just life, but also narrative is always conditional, that it only appears inevitable after the fact." Kirkus

Auster, Paul

The **Brooklyn** follies. Holt 2006 306p $24

ISBN 0-8050-7714-6

LC 2005-40201

This "is a departure for Auster. Instead of tight plotting and theoretical figure work, there is domestic realism. The result is a novel far more passionately American than Auster's previous ones." Times Lit Suppl

Auster, Paul

In the country of last things. Viking 1987 188p

ISBN 0-670-81445-8

LC 86-40257

This novel "is distinguished by an uncanny grasp of the day-to-day realities of homelessness. This is a scary but highly relevant book." Libr J

Auster, Paul

★ **Invisible**. Henry Holt and Co. 2009 308p $25

ISBN 978-0-8050-9080-2; 0-8050-9080-0

LC 2009-02237

This novel "novel opens in New York City in the spring of 1967, when twenty-year-old Adam Walker, an aspiring poet and student at Columbia University, meets the enigmatic Frenchman Rudolf Born and his silent and seductive girfriend, Margot. Before long, Walker finds himself caught in a perverse triangle that leads to a sudden, shocking act of violence that will alter the course of his life. Three different narrators tell the story of Invisible, a novel that travels in time from 1967 to 2007 and moves from Morningside Heights, to the Left Bank of Paris, to a remote island in the Caribbean." Publisher's note

Auster, Paul

Oracle night. Holt 2003 243p $23

ISBN 0-8050-7320-5

"A novelist writing about a novelist writing about an editor reading a novel: these Russian dolls might come across as merely cute, were it not for the fact that the lucid Mr Auster is a natural storyteller, with a seemingly inexhaustible trove of yarns at his disposal. All of the stories within stories are compelling in their own right." Economist

Auster, Paul

Sunset Park. Henry Holt and Co. 2010 309p $25

ISBN 978-0-8050-9286-8; 0-8050-9286-2

LC 2009-45726

"The novel is graphically sexual and, more surprisingly, insistently phallic. This is a little bewildering until, as the novel progresses, one comes to accept that, for Auster's characters, the body – in its fragility and strength – is one of the only certainties in a time of increasing darkness. In a way, Sunset Park is Auster's most Whitmanesque novel and it's very entertaining." Globe and Mail

Austin, Lynn

All she ever wanted; Lynn Austin. Bethany House 2005 400p (pbk.) $14.99

ISBN 0764228897; 9780764228896

LC 2005018574

In this book, "Kathleen Seymour's carefully constructed world starts to collapse when her teenage daughter, Joelle, is caught shoplifting and a row with her boss leaves Kathleen unemployed. After a few sessions with a therapist, Kathleen tries reconnecting with her daughter by taking her to a party hosted by the estranged family members Kathleen left years ago. Through multiple points of view and . . . [several] flashbacks to previous generations, [author Lynn N.] Austin . . . illustrates how shame and bad choices can affect families for years." (Publishers Weekly)

Ausubel, Ramona

No one is here except all of us; Ramona Ausubel. Riverhead Books 2012 336p.

ISBN 9781594487941

LC 2011046846

'This novel takes place "[i]n 1939, [when] the families in a remote Jewish village in Romania feel the war close in on them. Their tribe has moved and escaped for thousands of years-across oceans, deserts, and mountains-but now, it seems, there is nowhere else to go. . . . At the suggestion of an eleven-year-old girl and a mysterious stranger who has washed up on the riverbank, the villagers decide to reinvent the world: deny any relationship with the known and start over from scratch. . . . Time and history are forgotten. Jobs, husbands, a child, are reassigned. And for years, there is boundless hope. But the real world continues to unfold alongside the imagined one, eventually overtaking it, and soon our narrator-the girl, grown into a young mother-must flee her village, move from one world to the next, to find her husband and save her children, and propel them toward a real and hopeful future." (Publisher's note)

Avery, Ellis

The **last** nude; Ellis Avery. Riverhead Books 2012 310 p. $25.95

ISBN 1594488134; 9781594488139

LC 2011027708

This book relies on historical events that occurred "[i]n 1927 . . . [when] Polish artist Tamara de Lempicka encountered 17-year-old Rafaela while in Paris's Bois de Boulogne and took her home, using her as a model for six significant paintings (including Beautiful Rafaela) and briefly becoming her lover. . . . Inspired by these bare facts, [author Ellis] Avery . . . has crafted a . . . work that imagines the relationship between artist and model." (Library Journal)

Includes bibliographical references.

Awad, Mona

★ **13** ways of looking at a fat girl; fiction. Mona Awad. Penguin Books 2015 224 p. (softcover) $16

ISBN 9780143128489; 0143128485

LC 2015011712

Scotiabank Giller Prize Shortlist (2016).

In this novel, by Mona Awad, "Lizzie has never liked the way she looks--even though her best friend Mel says she's the pretty one. With punishing drive, she counts almonds consumed, miles logged, pounds dropped. She fights her way into coveted dresses. She grows up and gets thin, navigating double-edged validation from her mother, her friends, [and] her husband. . . . But no matter how much she loses, will she ever see herself as anything other than a fat girl?" (Publisher's note)

"Lizzie's particular sadness is unsettlingly sharp: she gets under your skin, and she stays there. Beautifully constructed; a devastating novel but also a deeply empathetic one." Kirkus

B

Babel, I. (Isaak), 1894-1940

★ The **complete** works of Isaac Babel; edited by Nathalie Babel; translated with notes by Peter Constantine; introduction by Cynthia Ozick. Norton 2001 1072p il maps $39.95

ISBN 0-393-04846-2

LC 2001-44036

In addition to the stories this volume contains sketches, journalistic pieces, a diary, plays, and screenplays

"Few writers possess Babel's level of genius and temerity, and this first complete collection should acquaint more readers with his unjustly neglected work." Publ Wkly

Includes bibliographical references

Bachelder, Chris, 1971-

The **throwback** special; a novel. Chris Bachelder. W W Norton & Co Inc 2016 224 p. (hardcover) $25.95

ISBN 0393249468; 9780393249460

LC 2015028394

National Book Award Finalist: Fiction (2016)

This novel, by Chris Bachelder, "is the absorbing story of twenty-two men who gather every fall to painstakingly reenact what ESPN called 'the most shocking play in NFL history' and the Washington Redskins dubbed the 'Throwback Special': the November 1985 play in which the Redskins' Joe Theismann had his leg horribly broken by Lawrence Taylor of the New York Giants live on Monday Night Football." (Publisher's note)

Bacigalupi, Paolo

★ The **water** knife; A Novel. Paolo Bacigalupi. Alfred A. Knopf 2015 371 p. (hardcover) $25.95

ISBN 9780385352871; 9780804171533; 0385352875

LC 2015001576

This novel, by Paolo Bacigalupi, is "a near-future thriller that casts new light on how we live today--and what may be in store for us tomorrow. The American Southwest has been decimated by drought. . . . Into the fray steps Las Vegas water knife Angel Velasquez. Detective, assassin, and spy, Angel 'cuts' water for the Southern Nevada Water Authority and its boss, Catherine Case. . . . When rumors of a game-changing water source surface in Phoenix, Angel is sent to investigate." (Publisher's note)

"The way the novel's environmental nightmare affects society, as individuals and larger entities--both official and criminal--vie for a limited and essential resource, feels solid, plausible, and disturbingly believable." Kirkus

Bacigalupi, Paolo

★ The **windup** girl. Night Shade Books 2009 361p $24.95; pa $14.95

ISBN 978-1-59780-157-7; 978-1-59780-158-4 pa

In this novel Bacigalupi follows the interconnected stories of several people caught "in the genome industry's web: We have a covert 'calorie man' called Anderson who tries to sniff out uncontaminated genomes for a Monsanto-esque multinational called AgriGen; a 'yellow card' Chinese refugee named Hock Seng who is trying to climb to the top of the energy-generator black market in Thailand; Environment Ministry shock troops Jaidee and Kanya, whose job is to protect Thailand from contaminated genomes, foreign imports, and dirty energy; and the mysterious whore Emiko, a genetically-engineered 'windup' person abandoned by her former owner in Thailand, where GMO people are illegal. We follow these characters through every eschelon of Thai society, from backroom meetings between government officials to backroom performances at the strip club where Emiko is fetishistically degraded every night. . . . One of the strengths of The Windup Girl, other than its intriguing characters, is Bacigalupi's world building. You can practically taste this future Thailand he's built." io9

Backman, Fredrik, 1981-

A **man** called Ove; a novel. by Fredrik Backman. Atria Books 2014 352 p. (hardcover) $25

ISBN 1476738017; 9781476738017; 9781476738024

LC 2014015618

In this novel by Fredrik Backman, readers will "meet Ove. He's a curmudgeon--the kind of man who points at people he dislikes as if they were burglars caught outside his bedroom window. He has staunch principles, strict routines, and a short fuse. People call him 'the bitter neighbor from hell.' But must Ove be bitter just because he doesn't walk around with a smile plastered to his face all the time?" (Publisher's note)

Backman, Fredrik, 1981-

My grandmother asked me to tell you she's sorry; a novel. by Fredrik Backman ; translated from the Swedish by Henning Koch. Atria Books 2015 352 p. (hardcover) $25

ISBN 1501115065; 9781501115066

LC 2015000829

This novel, by Fredrik Backman, translated from the Swedish by Henning Koch, is "about a young girl whose grandmother dies and leaves behind a series of letters, sending her on a journey that brings to life the world of her grandmother's fairy tales. . . . Her grandmother's letters lead her to an apartment building full of drunks, monsters, attack dogs, and totally ordinary old crones, but also to the truth about fairy-tales and kingdoms and a grandmother like no other." (Publisher's note)

"A delectable homage to the power of stories to comfort and heal, Backman's tender tale of the touching relationship between a grandmother and granddaughter is a tribute to the everlasting bonds of deep family ties." Booklist

Baggott, Julianna

Pure; Julianna Baggott. Grand Central Publishing 2012 431p.

ISBN 9781455503063; 9781455503032; 9781611733563; 9781455503056

LC 2011010209

Alex Award (2013)

This book is set "sometime in the unspecified future, [where] a series of detonations as all but destroyed the world. A handpicked few were given refuge in the Dome, a high-tech bubble designed to withstand environmental disaster. Those left outside were not so fortunate. The intensity of the explosions not only devastated the landscape but changed forever those who survived it, fusing people with animals, with objects, with the earth." It follows Pressia, a "survivor . . . In a few days' time, on her 16th birthday, Pressia will be claimed by the OSR . . a paramilitary force that terrorizes the ravaged city. She will be 'untaught to read' and either trained as a killer or, if her deformations are too debilitating, used for target practice. . . . Meanwhile, life in the Dome has its own privations. The younger inhabitants, known as Pures because of their unblemished bodies, are being subjected to a series of 'codings,' devised to enhance their physical capabilities and suppress potentially rebellious behavior." (N Y Times)

Bahr, Howard

The **Judas** Field; a novel of the Civil War. H. Holt 2006 292p $25

ISBN 978-0-8050-6739-2

LC 2005-055011

The author "recreates this seminal moment in American history with prose that is vivid, unflinching and often incantatory. The book's pace and detail are wrenching, and it is starkly devoid of romanticism. Within the battlefield scenes, Bahr's accomplishment is magnificent: a fully realized depiction of controlled mass butchery on a field of blood, body parts and utterly obliterated human beings. The reader puts down the book with a sense of shock to find he is not actually inside a level of hell." Washington Post Book World

Bailey, Martine

An **appetite** for violets; a novel. Martine Bailey. Thomas Dunne Books/St. Martin's Press 2015 391 p. illustrations, map (hardback) $26.99

ISBN 1250056918; 9781250056917

LC 2014032365

In this novel, by Martine Bailey, "Irrepressible Biddy Leigh, undercook at forbidding Mawton Hall, only wants to marry her childhood sweetheart and set up her own tavern. But when her elderly master marries young Lady Carinna, Biddy is unwittingly swept up in a world of scheming, secrets, and lies. Forced to accompany her new mistress to Italy, she documents her adventures and culinary discoveries in an old household book of recipes." (Publisher's note)

"Though the novel seems to have too many ingredients, everything is kneaded together at the end. This is a delectable dish that will appeal to readers with a taste for historical mysteries as well as fiction about food." Booklist

Bainbridge, Beryl, 1932-2010

Every man for himself; Beryl Bainbridge. Carroll & Graf Publishers 1996 224 p.

ISBN 0786703490

LC 96032518

This novel "takes place on the ill-fated Titanic. The story is narrated by Morgan, a young American, and follows the events between boarding and rescue by the Carpathia." (Libr J)

"Bainbridge hits a tremendous pace as her story reaches its climax. In a remarkably concise book, shot through with laconic wit, she establishes complex characters who engage first the reader's curiosity, then affection. The elegiac theme extends far beyond the historical event." New Statesman (1913)

Baker, Dorothy

★ **Young** man with a horn. Houghton Mifflin 1938 243p

"Rick Martin is not interested in school but is intrigued by music. Learning how to play the jazz trumpet from black musicians, Rick becomes a genius in the art of 'swing' and quickly rises to fame in the Phil Morrison orchestra. The inability to cope with success, as well as a bad marriage and gin, lead to his fatal end." Shapiro. Fic for Youth. 3d edition

Baker, Jo

★ **Longbourn**; By Jo Baker. Alfred A. Knopf 2013 352 p. (alk. paper) $25.95

ISBN 0385351232; 9780385351232

LC 2013016430

This historical novel by Jo Baker is intertwined with Jane Austen's classic novel "Pride and Prejudice." "In this irresistibly imagined belowstairs answer to 'Pride and Prejudice,' the servants take center stage. Sarah, the orphaned housemaid, spends her days scrubbing the laundry, polishing the floors, and emptying the chamber pots for the Bennet household. But there is just as much romance, heartbreak, and intrigue downstairs at Longbourn as there is upstairs." (Publisher's note)

Baker, Jo

The **undertow**; Jo Baker. Alfred A. Knopf 2012 335 p.

ISBN 0307957098; 9780307957092

LC 2012002079

This historical novel by Jo Baker traces "a family, constructed over decades, through relationships, wars and secrets . . . Starting in London in 1914, it introduces young sweethearts William and Amelia Hastings. . . . Amelia, pregnant with Billy, will always stay faithful to William's memory . . . and when shipmate George Sully . . . threatens, Amelia and Billy see him off together. Billy has a talent for cycling, but his prospects . . . are clouded by issues of money and class, and then World War II intervenes. Billy survives to marry Ruby . . . The couple's first child is Will, partly disabled by Perthes disease. . . . Clever Will achieves academic success at Oxford, but marries unhappily. It's with his artistic daughter Billie that the book reaches its . . . conclusion." (Kirkus)

Baker, Kage

★ The **bird** of the river. Tor 2010 268p $25.99

ISBN 978-0-7653-2296-8; 0-7653-2296-X

LC 2010-30146

"A vivid setting . . . with minimal fantasy elements, agreeably complemented by solid plotting, mysteries, surprises and characters that grow in the telling. A sparkling farewell from a writer whose illustrious career proved all too brief." Kirkus

Baker, Kage

The **house** of the stag. Tor 2008 350p $25.95

ISBN 978-0-7653-1745-2; 0-7653-1745-1

LC 2008-30212

"Baker's fantasy is completely different from her science fiction, but it's just as good. Gently humorous and ironic, Gard is a character readers will pull for as he moves from foundling to outcast to slave to ruler. Baker's worldbuilding is consistently topnotch, and the various supporting characters are just as well drawn as her antihero." Romantic Times

Baker, Kage

★ **In** the garden of Iden; a novel of the company. Harcourt Brace & Co. 1998 329p

ISBN 0-15-100299-1

LC 97-23284

"The initial assignment for 18-year-old Mendoza, transformed into an immortal cyborg by the 24th-century Company, is to retrieve from Renaissance England an endangered plant that cures cancer. Posing as a Spanish lady accompanying her doctor father, she falls in love with the mortal Nicholas Harpole, secretary to the owner of Iden Hall and its exotic gardens. Amidst the raging Catholic/Protestant powerplays revolving around the English throne and the fervent religious bloodlust of common folk, Mendoza is torn between her task and her love. Baker's story comments powerfully on religious hypocrisy and xenophobia." Libr J

Baker, Kage

The **sons** of heaven. Tor 2007 430p $25.95

ISBN 978-0-7653-1746-9; 0-7653-1746-X

LC 2007-9541

This is the concluding volume of the "saga of The Company and its immortal, time-traveling minions. As this volume opens, it is very nearly July 9, 2355, the end of recorded time, after which there is only silence regarding the fate of humankind. Various factions of cyborgs, mortals and other mysterious entities have differing opinions about what should occur after that date, and some of their plans involve armed insurrection and genocide. From the first volume, 'In the Garden of Iden,' Botanist Mendoza has always been at the center of the narrative, and for a certain subset of Baker's readers, Mendoza's star-crossed love affairs with three eerily similar men across literally countless centuries inspire the most devotion to the series. Others may find Mendoza something of an annoying pill and prefer the adventures of the supporting cast, especially Preservationist Lewis and Facilitator Joseph, two secret agents never sure of who their true enemies might be. No matter. 'The Sons of Heaven' gives equal time to both Mendoza and her subordinates, and Baker resolves the apocalyptic conflict with flair and enviable skill." San Francisco Chronicle

Baker, Kevin

Strivers Row. HarperCollins 2006 550p $26.95

ISBN 0-06-019583-5

LC 2005-52679

In this "novel—the final volume of a New York trilogy called 'City of Fire' [previous titles: Dreamland and Paradise Alley]—Kevin Baker plunges into the world of Harlem in the early 1940's to imagine the lives of two African-American men. . . . One of his main characters was known in the 'real' world of 1943 as Malcolm Little, a rootless 18-year-old who would later become famous as Malcolm X. The other is the invention of Baker: a young, bourgeois, light-skinned Harlem clergyman named Jonah Dove. Malcolm is poor. Jonah is comfortably middie-class. In different ways, each is tormented by the world. . . . In the end, Baker has written a brave, honorable work, taking us into a vanished world that should be better known. More important, he imagines his human subjects with a sense of pity and compassion and embrace, thus making them visible in ways that are fresh and new." N Y Times Book Rev

Baker, Lori

★ The **Glass** Ocean; Lori Baker. Penguin Group USA 2013 352 p. $25.95

ISBN 1594205361; 9781594205361

LC 2013007696

This novel "is narrated by red-haired, six-foot-plus Carlotta Dell'oro, who relates the story of her parents' lives. On an 1841 expedition aboard the Narcissus, during which he's expected to sketch sea creatures, Leonardo Dell'oro falls for remote, lovely Clotilde Girard, whose father funded the voyage. Leonardo brings Clotilde to remote Whitby, England, when her father goes missing, but they aren't the perfect couple." (Library Journal)

Baker, Nicholson

The **anthologist**. Simon & Schuster 2009 243p $25

ISBN 1-4165-7244-9; 978-1-4165-7244-2

LC 2009-01205

Baker's novel "is narrated by Paul Chowder—a once-in-a-while-published kind of poet who is writing the introduction to a new anthology of poetry. He's having a hard time getting started because his career is floundering, his girlfriend Roz has recently left him, and he is thinking about the great poets throughout history who have suffered far worse and deserve to feel sorry for themselves. He has also promised to reveal many wonderful secrets and tips and tricks about poetry, and it looks like the introduction will be a little longer than he'd thought." (Publisher's note)

"The narrator, Paul Chowder, is a poet who is struggling to write the introduction to an anthology of rhyming poems he's collected. He's also trying to win back Roz, the woman who has just left him. These dilemmas make for some enlightening, absorbing reflections on poetry, the creative process, and life itself. While Chowder admits that he despises teaching, the narrative offers a wonderful explanation of what poetry is and the relationship between form and meaning. In the process, Chowder comes to understand himself better and pulls out of a slump. The novel's subtle sense of humor comes through as Chowder deals with injured fingers, a misbehaving dog, and the perils of reading his poetry in public." Libr J

Baker, Nicholson, 1957-

House of holes; a book of raunch. Simon & Schuster 2011 262p $25

ISBN 978-1-4391-8951-1; 1-4391-8951-X

LC 2010-47433

In this book, author Nicholson Baker "uses an alternative reality, the house of holes, as a playground of latent desires in which characters experience their most erotic fantasies. The characters travel to this place, drawn with a touch of the magical, through portals such as washing machines and wooden sculptures. A world seemingly constructed from sexual energy, the house of holes encourages individuals to indulge rather than repress their sexual desire." (Library Journal)

This novel is comprised of "a series of fantasies that a very imaginative 14-year-old boy might have: They all involve metamorphoses that enable more sexual possibilities than are human. Genitals can be swapped, people can shrink to miniature size (you can guess where they go). These transformations occur, to a long list of characters, in a parallel universe, an uninhibited plane of existence (perhaps something like the unconscious) that resembles nothing more than a high-end holiday resort. It has a sprawling landscape of beaches, hotel rooms and parodic attractions (Upskirt Street, the masturboats, pussyboarding). Magical objects – the Belt of Jingly Bells, the Cable of Induhash, drops from King Bohuslav's beard – can heal and arouse. You get to this House of Holes through actual holes in the real world – the end of a straw, the back of a clothes dryer. The land of enchantment is run by a matter-of-fact headmistress, the plump, fiftyish Lila, who assigns and withholds its pleasures. . . . You might think this is too adolescent to be arousing, but you'd be surprised by the effect prolonged exposure to all this mad splashing might have. It's a bit repetitive, for sure, and the characters are hard to tell apart, which doesn't really matter, as there is no unifying plot. They are interchangeable bodies, reflecting the theme of mutability in their own stories." Globe and Mail

Baker, Tiffany

The **little** giant of Aberdeen County; a novel. Grand Central Pub. 2009 341p $24.99

ISBN 978-0-446-19420-4; 0-446-19420-4

LC 2008-774

"Baker enters Alice Hoffman territory in this parable about beauty and ugliness, meanness and mercy and magic, and does it with considerable dark humor." Hartford Courant

Bakker, Gerbrand

The **twin**; translated from the Dutch by David Colmer. Archipelago Books 2009 343p $25

ISBN 978-0-9800330-2-1; 0-9800330-2-0

LC 2008-45725

Original Dutch edition, 2006; this translation first published 2008 in the United Kingdom

"Helmer Van Wonderen ditches university to return home to the family farm in north Holland when his twin brother, Henk, is killed in a car accident. Nearly forty years later, Helmer, now 57, ponders the path his life has taken while waiting for his invalid father to die. The catalyst arrives in the form of Riet, Henk's teenage sweetheart, who now has an adolescent son. Helmer has inherited the life of his dead twin, and Bakker's great skill is to characterise the mixture of grief, guilt, rage and regret that shadows Helmer, without resorting to caricature or clunky exposition." TNT Magazine

Balaskovits, A. A.

Magic for unlucky girls; A.A. Balaskovits. SFWP 2017 226 p. (trade paper : alk. paper) $14.95

ISBN 9781939650665; 9781939650689

LC 2016033041

This book in the SFWP Literary Awards series, by A.A. Balaskovits, presents fourteen stories that "take the familiar tropes of fairytales and twist them into new and surprising shapes. These unlucky girls, struggling against a society that all too often oppresses them, are forced to navigate strange worlds as they try to survive." (Publisher's note)

"In this reimagining and reinventing of traditional, patriarchal fairy tales, Balaskovits creates a safe—and often startling—space for girls and women in her book of short stories." Booklist

Includes bibliographical references and index

Baldwin, James

★ **Another** country. Dial Press (NY) 1962 436p

This novel is set in "New York City and focuses mainly on Harlem society. The death—perhaps suicide—of the main character, Rufus Scott, is representative of the treatment individuals receive in an environment which is essentially hostile and which erects barriers to their desire for love." Camb Guide to Lit in Engl

Baldwin, James

Early novels and stories. Library of Am. 1998 970p $35

ISBN 1-88301-151-5

LC 97-23028

Gathered in this collection are three early Baldwin novels, namely, Go Tell It On the Mountain, Giovanni's Room, and Another Country. Also included are the contents of his short story collection Going to Meet the Man.

Baldwin, James

★ **Giovanni's** room; a novel. Dial Press (NY) 1956 248p

"Mr. Baldwin has taken a very special theme and treated it with great artistry and restraint." Saturday Rev

Baldwin, James

★ **Go** tell it on the mountain. Knopf 1953 303p $15.95; pa $6.99

ISBN 0-679-60154-6; 0-440-33007-6 pa

This novel is an "autobiographical story of a Harlem child's relationship with his father against the background of his being saved in the pentecostal church." Benet's Reader's Ency of Am Lit

Baldwin, James

Going to meet the man. Dial Press (NY) 1965 249p

Contents: The rockpile; The outing; The man child; Previous condition; Sonny's blues; This morning, this evening, so soon; Come out the wilderness; Going to meet the man

Baldwin, James

If Beale Street could talk. Dial Press (NY) 1974 197p hardcover o.p. pa $12.95

ISBN 0-803-74169-3; 0-307-27593-0 pa

"Tish, aged 19, and Fonny, 22 years old, are in love and pledged to marry, a decision hastened by Tish's unexpected pregnancy. Fonny is falsely accused of raping a Puerto Rican woman and is sent to prison. The families of the desperate couple search frantically for evidence that will prove his innocence in order to reunite the lovers and provide a safe haven for the expected child. There is some explicit sex but it is not treated in a sensational manner, nor is the use of street language gratuitous." Shapiro. Fic for Youth. 3d edition

Baldwin, James

Tell me how long the train's been gone; a novel. Dial Press (NY) 1968 484p

Leo Proudhammer, a successful black "actor has a serious heart attack on stage. Barbara King, his leading lady . . . and in a strange way his inamorata, stays by his side. In a series of flashbacks . . . Leo relives his past from his Harlem boyhood on. Although he learned early to hate 'the man,' Leo's own betrayal as a man and as a human being is not limited to the white man's corruption. It encompasses his painful relationship with his brother, who lures him into homosexuality. Paralleling this story is the tale of Leo's career. The third thread is his bisexual private life in which the two main figures are white Barbara, his true but unattainable love, and black Christopher, worshipful and available." Publ Wkly

Ball, Jesse, 1978-

A **cure** for suicide; a novel. Jesse Ball. Pantheon Books 2015 256 p. (hardcover : acid-free paper) $24

ISBN 1101870125; 9781101870129

LC 2014026919

In this novel, by Jesse Ball, a "man and a woman have moved into a small house in a small village. The woman is an 'examiner,' the man, her 'claimant.' The examiner is both doctor and guide, charged with teaching the claimant a series of simple functions: this is a chair, this is a fork, this is how you meet people. She makes notes in her journal about his progress: he is showing improvement yet his dreams are troubling." (Publisher's note)

"Ball is playing with a lot of conceptual territory here, contemplating memory, identity, and isolation, among other themes. The novel eventually pulls back the curtain on "the Process of Villages," this strange therapeutic transformation invented to allow men to start over completely with different identities. There are times it feels rushed between the spare, meticulous play going on between the claimant and the examiner and other breathless sections with unbroken waves of narrative exposition—the shift in tones can be jarring. This may be Ball's most self-contained work, but it's also one of his most fragile and one that may not hold up under focused scrutiny by a wider audience." Kirkus

Ball, Jesse, 1978-

How to set a fire and why; A novel. Jesse Ball. Pantheon Books 2016 304 p. hbk $24.95

ISBN 9781101870570; 1101870575

LC 2015017989

In this novel by Jesse Ball, "Lucia's father is dead, her mother is in a mental hospital, and she's living in a garage-turned-bedroom with her aunt. And now she's been kicked out of school—again. . . . But when she discovers that her new school has a secret Arson Club, she's willing to do anything to be a part of it, and her life is suddenly lit up. As Lucia's fascination with the Arson Club grows, her story becomes one of misguided friendship and, ultimately, destruction." (Publisher's note)

Ball, John Dudley

In the heat of the night; by John Ball. Harper & Row 1965 184p

"Virgil Tibbs is found with a full wallet in the waiting room of a railroad station in Wells, a small town in the Carolinas. Because he is black he becomes the prime suspect for the murder of the town's musical director. The local police chief learns that Tibbs is a homicide expert from the Pasadena police department and enlists his assistance. Tibbs solves the crime, despite the bigotry to which he is exposed." Shapiro. Fic for Youth. 2d edition

Ballantyne, Lisa, 1973-

The **guilty** one; Lisa Ballantyne. William Morrow 2013 480 p. $14.99

ISBN 0062195514; 9780062195517

LC 2012013279

This novel, by Lisa Ballantyne, "is a psychological thriller about the darkness in each of us. . . . Solicitor Daniel Hunter is called to defend 11-year-old Sebastian who has been charged with the murder of a young boy on a London playground. While examining Sebastian's life in order to save it, Daniel can't help but be transported to his own difficult youth spent in foster care--a time when the one he trusted the most was the one who betrayed him." (Publisher's note)

Ballard, J. G., 1930-2009

★ The **complete** stories of J.G. Ballard. W.W. Norton & Company 2009 1199p $35; pa $24.95

ISBN 978-0-393-07262-4; 0-393-07262-2; 978-0-393-33929-1 pa; 0-393-33929-7 pa

LC 2009-18456

"An astonishing record of a vibrant and vital mind at work. This volume includes 92 stories, most of which are set in some kind of nightmarish future world or alternate 'visionary present,' to use Ballard's phrase from his introduction to the book. The variety of stories here is impressive, even dizzying." Libr J

Includes bibliographical references and index

Ballard, J. G., 1930-2009

★ The **day** of creation. Farrar, Straus & Giroux 1988 254p

ISBN 0-374-13527-4

LC 87-37525

First published 1987 in the United Kingdom

The narrator of this novel, Dr. Mallory, "is a physician with the World Health Organization, working in a mythical central African country, who launches what appears to be a vain search for water to forestall the desertification of the region. He accidentally releases the flow—and in fact thinks he is the creator—of a new river. . . . {He later} embarks on a dangerous journey to find its source and destroy it." (Books Can)

The narrator of this novel, Dr. Mallory, "is a physician with the World Health Organization, working in a mythical central African country, who launches what appears to be a vain search for water to forestall the desertification of the region. He accidentally releases the flow—and in fact thinks he is the creator—of a new river. . . . {He later} embarks on a dangerous journey to find its source and destroy it." Books Can

Ballard, J. G., 1930-2009

Empire of the Sun; a novel. Simon & Schuster 1984 279p hardcover o.p. pa $13

ISBN 0-671-53051-8; 0-7432-6523-8 pa

LC 84-10630

"This novel is much more than the gritty story of a child's miraculous survival in the grimly familiar setting of World War II's concentration camps. There is no nostalgia for a good war here, no sentimentality for the human spirit at extremes. Mr. Ballard is more ambitious than romance usually allows. He aims to render a vision of the apocalypse, and succeeds so well that it can hurt to dwell upon his images." N Y Times Book Rev

Followed by The kindness of women (1991)

Ballard, J. G., 1930-2009

Kingdom come; J.G. Ballard. Liveright 2012 304 p. $24.95

ISBN 0393081788; 9780393081787; 9780871404039

LC 2011041724

In this book, set in a fascist suburban future, mental patient Duncan Christie is held for the murder of a man shot and killed at the mall. "This seems to be a cut-and-dried case, even to Richard Pearson, narrator and son of the victim, but a few anomalies crop up." Plus, "Pearson has other problems, for he has recently lost his job . . . . Pearson watches with some amazement the rise of quasi-fascist elements in this quasi-suburban setting that's starting to create its own reality." (Kirkus)

Ballard, J. G., 1930-2009

Millennium people. W.W. Norton & Company 2011 288p $26.95

ISBN 978-0-393-08177-0; 0-393-08177-X

LC 2010-52504

First published 2003 in the United Kingdom

"Ballard is a natural surrealist; his is a world where the unthinkable is commonplace and rationality chucked in the towel long ago. . . . Ballard's phrasing is as sure as ever. He writes wonderfully well about London. His characterization is as vivid as it is strange. An extremely unsettling novel. Reading it is like having all the planks that underpin your life removed one by one and being forced to confront the brutality and emptiness that lies below." Scotsman

Balogh, Mary

The **escape**; Mary Balogh. Random House Inc 2014 394 p. (Survivors' Club) $7.99

ISBN 0345536061; 9780345536068

In this historical romance novel, by Mary Balogh, "a hopeful widow and a resilient war hero discover the promise of love. . . . After surviving the Napoleonic Wars, Sir Benedict Harper is struggling to move on, his body and spirit in need of a healing touch. . . . After the lingering death of her husband, Samantha McKay is at the mercy of her oppressive in-laws--until she plots an escape to distant Wales to claim a house she has inherited." (Publisher's note)

"As always, Balogh's scarred protagonists find deep wells of strength and generosity within as well as experiencing great sexual tension and forging tender relationships." Booklist

Balogh, Mary

More than a mistress. Delacorte Press 2000 343p

ISBN 0-385-33531-8

LC 99-462117

"When Jane Ingleby tries to stop a duel, Jocelyn Dudley, Duke of Tresham, is wounded. So it's surprising that she ends up employed as his nurse—and ultimately his mistress as well. But as their relationship blossoms, Jocelyn commits the unpardonable sin of falling in love. In this refreshingly unconventional romance, which boasts an outspoken, memorable heroine, the author again pushes the edges of the genre." Libr J

Balogh, Mary

Only a Promise; A Survivors' Club Novel. Mary Balogh. Penguin Group USA 2015 400 p. (Other titles in this series are: Only Beloved; Only a Kiss; Only a Promise; Only Enchanting; The Escape; The Arrangement; The Proposal) (paperback) $7.99

ISBN 9780451469670; 0451469674

In this historical romance novel, by Mary Balogh, part of the "Survivor's Club" series, follows "six men and one woman, all wounded in the Napoleonic Wars, their friendship forged during their recovery at Penderris Hall in Cornwall. . . . Ralph Stockwood . . . must move on . . . and find a wife so as to secure an heir to his family's title and fortune. Since her Seasons in London ended in disaster, Chloe Muirhead is resigned to spinsterhood . . . , [until] she meets Ralph" (Publisher's Note)

"As in the other books in Balogh's Survivor's Club series, including Only Enchanting (2014), two wounded and independent people find strength, love, and community. This entrancing tale will delight those who have read the stories of Ralph's close friends, as well as readers new to the series." Booklist

Balogh, Mary

The **secret** mistress. Delacorte Press 2011 309p $24

ISBN 978-0-385-34331-2; 0-385-34331-0

LC 2010-52864

Balogh "pairs a staid young nobleman with a vivacious debutante in this topnotch tale. When the headstrong Lady Angeline Dudley, sister of the wealthy duke of Tresham, is accosted by the rakish Lord Windrow, she immediately falls for the ordinary-looking gentleman who intervenes. Her rescuer, Edward Ailsbury, is the earl of Heyward, whose family-unaware of his affection for his bluestocking confidante, Eunice Goddard-plans to match him with the very eligible Angeline. An unusually accurate portrayal of Regency society, laden with colorful period detail, makes a sparkling backdrop, and the supporting characters are delightful." Publ Wkly

Balogh, Mary

Seducing an angel. Delacorte Press 2009 325p $23

ISBN 978-0-385-34105-9

LC 2009-01662

"Cassandra Belmont, the widowed Lady Paget, is in London on a desperate mission. Rumored to have killed her husband and banished penniless from his estate by the heir, Cassie has no option but to find a protector for herself and her small household—and wealthy, young, angelically handsome Stephen Huxtable, Earl of Merton, seems the perfect choice. Marriage is definitely not her goal, nor is it his, until an impulsive public kiss changes everything. The gradually developing relationship between these fully realized, three-dimensional characters is complex, believable, and exquisitely rendered." Libr J

Balogh, Mary

Someone to Love; Mary Balogh. Penguin Group USA 2016 400 p. ill., genealogical tables (A Westcott novel) (ebook) $23.97; $7.99

ISBN 9780698411340; 0451477790; 9780451477798

LC 2016028439

In this first Westcott novel, by Mary Balogh, "Anna Snow grew up in an orphanage in Bath knowing nothing of the family she came from. Now she discovers that the late Earl of Riverdale was her father and that she has inherited his fortune. She is also overjoyed to learn she has siblings. However, they want nothing to do with her or her attempts to share her new wealth. But the new earl's guardian is interested in Anna." (Publisher's note)

"Fans will be delighted to meet the Westcotts here and anticipate future installments of their series." Pub Wkly

Balzac, Honore de

The **country** doctor; Translated by Ellen Marriage; introd. by Marcel Girard. Dutton 1961 xxv, 290p

Original French edition, 1833. Part of the series: Scenes of provincial life

The device with which this character study is held together concerns the visit of Pierre Joseph Genastas, an ex-soldier, who is searching for the saintly doctor Benassis. "A minute description of country life in the hilly region about Grenoble; the agricultural doings, the wretchedness of the peasantry, and M. Benassis' persevering attempts to ameliorate their condition, furnish a good example of Balzac's indefatigable realism. In this practical philanthropist, the reformed sinner who becomes a public benefactor, an ideal figure is created, a great soul, unselfish, full of love for man, unconquerably patient." Baker. Guide to the Best Fic

Balzac, Honore de

Cousin Bette; translated from the French by James Waring. Knopf 1991 xliii, 484p

ISBN 0-679-40671-9

LC 91-52964

Original French edition, 1846. Part of the series: Scenes of Parisian life

"This powerful story is a vivid picture of the tastes and vices of Parisian life in the middle of last century. Lisbeth Fischer, commonly called Cousin Bette, is an eccentric poor relation, a worker in gold and silver lace. The keynote of her character is jealousy, the special object of it her beautiful and nobel-minded cousin Adeline, wife of Baron Hector Hulot. The chief interest of the story lies in the development of her character, of that of the unscrupulous beauty Madame Marneffe, and the base and empty voluptuary Hulot. . . . Gloomy and despairing . . . {it is} yet terribly powerful." Keller. Reader's Dig of Books

Balzac, Honore de

★ **Pere** Goriot (Old Goriot) a new translation: responses, contemporaries and other novelists, twentieth-century criticism. translated by Burton Raffel; edited by Peter Brooks. W.W. Norton & Co. 1998 370p map pa $11.25

ISBN 0-393-97166-X

LC 97-19938

Original French edition, 1835. Part of the series: Scenes of Parisian life

"Goriot, a retired manufacturer of vermicelli, is a good man and a weak father. He has given away his money in order to ensure the marriage of his two daughters, Anastasie and Delphine. Because of his love for them, he has to accept all kinds of humiliations from his sons-in-law, one a 'gentilhomme,' M. de Restaud, and the other a financier, M. de Nucingen. Both young women are ungrateful. They gradually abandon him. He dies without seeing them at his bedside, cared for only by young Rastignac, a law student who lives at the same boarding house, the pension Vauquer." Haydn. Thesaurus of Book Dig

Bambara, Toni Cade

Gorilla, my love. Random House 1972 177p

ISBN 0-394-48201-8

"Toni Cade Bambara gives us compelling portraits of a wide range of unforgettable characters, from sassy children to cunning old men, in scenes shifting between uptown New York and rural North Carolina." (Publisher's note)

Bambara, Toni Cade

The **salt** eaters. Random House 1980 295p

ISBN 0-394-50712-6

LC 79-4806

This novel "with its beautiful, difficult prose, is a work at once intensely personal and political that will assure Bambara's place in black American fiction." Libr J

Banasky, Carmiel

The **suicide** of Claire Bishop; A Novel. Carmiel Banasky. Dzanc Books 2015 280 p. $24.95

ISBN 9781938103087

LC 2015000623

In this novel, by Carmiel Banasky, in 1959 "Claire Bishop sits for a portrait—a gift from her husband—only to discover that what the artist has actually depicted is Claire's suicide. Haunted by the painting, Claire is forced to redefine herself within a failing marriage and a family history of madness. Shifting ahead to 2004, we meet West, a young man with schizophrenia obsessed with a painting he encounters in a gallery: a mysterious image of a woman's suicide." (Publisher's note)

"Although the novel's structure suggests a chronological approach, its nonlinear sections make story elements more challenging to follow. But a careful reader is rewarded by Banasky's skillful character development, innovative points-of-view technique, and fresh language. The book is full of quotable sentences, including one descriptive of the book itself, 'Here's the truth: we're all connected, but not in a straight line. More like constellations, or islands.'" Booklist

Bandi

The **accusation**; forbidden stories from inside North Korea. Bandi. Grove Press 2017 vii, 247 p.p (hardcover : alk. paper) $25

ISBN 0802126200; 9780802126207

LC 2016058764

This book, by Bandi, translated by Deborah Smith, "is a deeply moving and eye-opening work of fiction that paints a powerful portrait of life under the North Korean regime. Set during the period of Kim Il-sung and Kim Jong-il's leadership, the seven stories that make up . . . [this book] give voice to people living under this most bizarre and horrifying of dictatorships." (Publisher's note)

"With these uncompromising stories, the pseudonymous Bandi gives a rare glimpse of life in the "truly fathomless darkness" of North Korea." Pub Wkly

Bank, Melissa

The **wonder** spot; Melissa Bank. Viking 2005 324p (pbk.) $14.00; o.p.

ISBN 9780143037217; 0670034118 (acid-free paper)

LC 2004061189

This book follows "Sophie Applebaum, a sarcastic, self-deprecating middle child from a suburban Jewish family who moves from a fish-out-of-water adolescence to a how-did-I-get-here adulthood. . . . Sophie's (mis)adventures in life and love include an attempt to use lyrics from Bob Dylan's 'It Ain't Me, Babe' to argue against the necessity of attending Hebrew school and a penchant for imagining her future life with men she barely knows." Also described in the story are "a grandmother's slip into senility, Sophie's mother's dip into infidelity, a brother's turn toward Orthodox Judaism. Through it all, Sophie never quite escapes the sense of being a 'solid trying to do a liquid's job'" (Publishers Weekly)

Banks, Iain, 1954-2013

The **hydrogen** sonata; Iain M. Banks. Orbit 2012 517 p. (hardcover) $25.99

ISBN 0316212377; 9780316212366; 9780316212373; 9780316212380; 9781619695481

LC 2012944666

This novel, by Iain M. Banks, is a science fiction story set in space. "[T]he Gzilt . . . [have] made the collective decision to . . . Sublime, elevating themselves to a new and . . . complex existence. Amid preparations though, the Regimental High Command is destroyed. . . . Vyr Cossont appears to have been involved. . . . Aided only by an . . . android and a suspicious Culture avatar, Cossont must complete her last mission given to her by the High Command." (Publisher's note)

Banks, Iain

Matter; a Culture novel. [by] Iain M. Banks. Orbit 2008 593p $25.99

ISBN 9780316005364; 0316005363

LC 2007-941828

This novel in the author's series about "the Culture, an interstellar posthuman civilization of incredible wealth and technological sophistication, centers on three siblings: Ferbin and Oramen, the misfit heirs of conquering King Hausk of the Sarl, who rules a backward and patriarchal realm deep beneath the surface of the artificial 'Shellworld' Sursamen, and their exiled sister, Djan, now a powerful agent of the Culture's Special Circumstances division. When King Hausk is murdered, Ferbin narrowly avoids the conspirators and sets out across the galaxy to ask Djan's help with revenge against the killer, now serving as Oramen's regent. Soon they learn of the horrific forces a hidden enemy is about to unleash on Sursamen, and must race to save the home that has rejected them both. Beautifully written and filled with memorable characters and startling technology" Publ Wkly

Banks, Iain, 1954-2013

Stonemouth; a novel. by Iain Banks. Pegasus Crime 2012 357 p. $25.95

ISBN 1605983829; 9781605983820

LC 2012462689

In this book, "Stewart Gilmour . . . has returned . . . to Stonemouth, the Scottish town of his upbringing. . . . [H]e had to flee Stonemouth after falling foul of a local crime family. . . . Donald Murston, the current head of the family, has given him grudging permission . . . to attend the funeral of Donald's father Joe. . . . [W]e find that the funeral is merely a pretext for him to determine what happened to the first and only love of his life, Donald's daughter Ellie." (TLS)

Banks, Russell

★ **Affliction**. Harper & Row 1989 355p

ISBN 0-06-016142-6

LC 89-45075

This novel is "psychological portraiture of a high order, and like all profound portraits it finds in its subject astonishing contradictions." N Y Times Book Rev

Banks, Russell, 1940-

Lost memory of skin. Ecco 2011 416p $25.99

ISBN 978-0-06-185763-8; 0-06-185763-7

LC 2011276214

This novel by Russell Banks follows "'The Kid,' a young sex offender . . . After a police raid, the Kid meets 'the Professor,' a pompous, rotund man claiming to be researching homelessness. He wants to study--and cure--the Kid in order to prove his theories about society. But just as the study commences, the Professor, claiming that his life is in danger because of past work as a government spy, turns the tables, paying the Kid to interview him instead." (Publishers Weekly)

"Set in a fictional part of Florida in a time of paranoia (possibly the near future), Lost Memory of Skin is the story of a twentyish sex offender (known simply as the Kid) on parole and the affable but troubled sociology instructor (called the Professor) on a misguided mission to help him become better adjusted. The Kid is a wastrel addicted to Internet porn, with only his pet iguana for company, until an unfortunate series of events—beginning with an Internet chat with a underage girl and ending To Catch a Predator–style—lands him in prison. Upon his release, he is forced to live with other sex offenders under a causeway because of a law that keeps them 2,500 feet from anywhere children are playing. The Professor, a behemoth in a suit, begins interviewing the Kid for academic research purposes; as he learns more about the Kid's crime, he begins to reveal his own troubled history, which only undermines his efforts to help. Banks inhabits unsympathetic voices well, and it is a pleasure to see his gift turned to big, semisurreal characters. The grand, rambling examination of guilt and blame takes place against a ravishingly bleak backdrop, lyrically described, while each revelation of character is like a quiet explosion." Time Out N Y

Banks, Russell

★ The **sweet** hereafter. HarperCollins Pubs. 1991 257p

ISBN 0-06-016703-3

LC 90-56404

"Banks handles his dark theme with judicious restraint, empathy and compassion." Publ Wkly

Bannalec, Jean-Luc

Death in Brittany; a mystery. Jean-Luc Bannalec. Minotaur Books 2015 320 p. map (hardcover) $24.99

ISBN 1250061741; 9781250061744

LC 2015011388

In this mystery novel, by Jean-Luc Bannalec, translated by Sorcha McDonagh, "Commissaire Georges Dupin, a Parisian-born caffeine junkie recently relocated from the glamour of Paris to the remote (if picturesque) Breton coast, is not happy when he is dragged from his morning croissant and coffee to the scene of a curious murder. . . . The legendary ninety-one-year-old hotelier Pierre-Louis Pennec, owner of the Central Hotel, has been found dead." (Publisher's note)

"Bannalec feeds the reader with intriguing bits of history (for example, Bretons are descended from the Celts, who fled Britain during the Anglo-Saxon invasions) and culture, along with bracing glimpses of centuries-old stone buildings, river banks, and the sea." Booklist

Another title in this series is:

Murder on Brittany Shores (2016)

Banner, Catherine

The **house** at the edge of night; Catherine Banner. Random House 2016 432 p. (ebook) $65; $27

ISBN 9780812998801; 9780812998795

LC 2015023813

This book, by Catherine Banner, is a "saga about four generations of a family who live and love on an enchanting island off the coast of Italy. . . . Castellamare is an island far enough away from the mainland to be forgotten, but not far enough to escape from the world's troubles. At the center of the island's life is a café draped with bougainvillea called the House at the Edge of Night, where the community gathers to gossip and talk." (Publisher's note)

"Banner deftly touches on weightier themes while weaving an enchanting narrative, the events of which extend to the present." Pub Wkly

Bannon, James

I2; James Bannon. Banco Picante Press 2011 260 p. $9.99

ISBN 9780983912439; 0983912432

This science-fiction and psychological thriller revolves around a terminally ill bio-software scientist's attempt to upload his mind into the consciousness of an unborn baby to once again be with the woman he loves. Neuroscientist Edward Frame's plan results in the creation of Adam, a child born with the mind and awareness of a grown man. The plot follows Adam as he grows into a young man and faces the unintended consequences Edward's actions. "[James] Bannon's debut novel is a science-fiction thriller . . . but . . . ultimately a . . . romance and . . . [an] exploration into the frailty and preciousness of human existence." (Kirkus)

Banville, John, 1945-

Ancient light; John Banville. Alfred A. Knopf 2012 287 p. $25.95

ISBN 0307957055; 9780307957054

LC 2012019891

This novel by John Banville is "about an actor in the twilight of his life and his career. . . . Is there any difference between memory and invention? . . . [This] is the question that haunts Alexander Cleave . . . as he plumbs the memories of his first--and perhaps only--love . . . and of his daughter, lost to a kind of madness of mind and heart that Cleave can only fail to understand." (Publisher's note)

Banville, John, 1945-

The **blue** guitar; John Banville. Alfred A. Knopf 2015 255 p. (hardcover) $25.95

ISBN 0385354266; 9780385354264

LC 2015006555

"Oliver Otway Orme . . . is a painter of some renown and a petty thief who has never before been caught and steals only for pleasure. And his last act of thievery . . . has been discovered. The fact that the purloined possession was the wife of the man who was, perhaps, his best friend has compelled him to run away." (Publisher's note)

"Banville delights in descriptions of people and nature, and here he has the added excuse of writing through a painter's gifted eye. The artist Orme is not a pleasant creation to spend several hours with, but in the hands of this gifted Irish writer, even a potbellied, melancholic petty thief and Lothario offers countless delights." Kirkus

Banville, John

★ The **book** of evidence. HarperCollins Pubs. 1990 219p

ISBN 0-684-19180-6

LC 89-10985

First published 1989 in the United Kingdom

"This novel, the inventive testimony of a murderer more interested in making an impression than escaping conviction, is . . . hauntingly beautiful and original. . . . Mr. Banville shows his uncanny ability to make everything he describes seem new and rare, yet instantly recognisable." Economist

Banville, John

★ **Christine** Falls; a novel. [by] Benjamin Black. H. Holt 2006 340p $25

ISBN 978-0-8050-8152-7; 0-8050-8152-6

LC 2006-43581

"As the story moves from Ireland to Boston, the push and pull of the novel's dual existence as 'literary thriller' becomes almost as absorbing as the plot; the tension between the two halves of that troublesome equation regularly rippling the book's surface. . . . At its best, the prose here is every bit as acute as one would expect from John Banville, even Banville in disguise—the baroque flourishes are held in check . . . , but the stern elegance remains, and its marriage to a thriller's momentum can have startling results." Times Lit Suppl

Other titles in this series are:
The silver swan (2008)
Elegy for April (2010)
A death in summer (2011)
Vengeance (2012)
Holy orders (2013)
Even the dead (2016)

Banville, John, 1945-

The **infinities**. Alfred A. Knopf 2010 273p $25.95

ISBN 978-0-307-27279-9; 0-307-27279-6

LC 2009-48331

First published 2009 in the United Kingdom

"Sure, 'The Infinities' will have you looking up 'invigilate' in the dictionary (I'll save you the time: 'to keep watch') and Googling 'Amphitryon' (a Greek myth dramatized by the 19th century German writer Heinrich von Kleist). But none of this legwork feels like a chore; because 'The Infinities' is constructed as a tantalizing puzzle you're eager to piece together. And Hermes is a delightfully cheeky and amiable narrator, constantly mocking randy old Zeus and guiding us through the multiple worlds of the novel. Moreover, Banville is a glorious stylist whose prose holds sustaining pleasures, both large and small." Newsday

Banville, John

The **sea**. Knopf 2005 195p $23

ISBN 0-307-26311-8

LC 2005-50418

"What's strangest about 'The Sea' is that the novel somehow becomes simpler and clearer as it gets more selfconscious: a consequence, I suppose, of its author dropping the pretense of being one kind of writer and giving in to his authentic and much more complicated creative nature. This misshapen but affecting novel turns out to be about something even more familiar than the loss of innocence: it's about grief, the misery and confusion the narrator feels on losing his wife." N Y Times Book Rev

Bao Ninh

The **sorrow** of war; a novel of North Vietnam. translated from the Vietnamese by Phan Thanh Hao; edited by Frank Palmos. Scribner 1995 233p

ISBN 0-679-43961-7

LC 94-22390

Original Vietnamese edition, 1991

"The word classic is bandied about with ridiculous laxity, but in this case it is hard not to fall back on it. Nothing else really fits the elemental simplicity of theme and treatment: love, war, death, disillusionment, betrayal." New Statesman (1913)

Barber, Ros, 1964-

The **Marlowe** papers; a novel. Ros Barber. St. Martin's Press 2013 464 p. (hardback) $24.99

ISBN 1250017173; 9781250017178

LC 2012037986

In this novel by Ros Barber "Christopher Marlowe reveals . . . that his 'death' was an elaborate ruse to avoid a conviction of heresy; . . . that he continued to write plays and poetry, hiding behind the name of a colorless man from Stratford--one William Shakespeare. This novel . . . in verse gives voice to . . . a cobbler's son who counted nobles among his friends, a spy in the Queen's service, a fickle lover and a declared religious skeptic." (Publisher's note)

Barbery, Muriel

The **elegance** of the hedgehog; translated from the French by Alison Anderson. Europa Editions 2008 325p pa $15

ISBN 1933372605; 9781933372600

Original French edition, 2006

"The novel's two narrators alternate chapters, but the book is dominated by Renée, a widowed concierge in her 50s. . . . [Her] counterpart is Paloma, a precocious 12-year-old whose family lives in the fashionable building Renée cares for." (N Y Times Book Rev)

In this novel, "the unschooled middle-aged concierge of an upper-class Paris apartment building acts like a stereotypical concierge, leaving the television on all day and sharing her quarters with an old, fat cat, but she secretly consumes vast quantities of literature. A few floors above her, the brilliant and prematurely disillusioned twelve-year-old daughter of a 'holier-than-thou-left-wing-intellectual' family is planning arson and suicide, unless she can find something worth living for beyond the 'vacuousness of bourgeois existence.' Unbeknown to each other, the two autodidacts share an allergy to grammatical errors (the concierge considers a misplaced comma an 'underhanded attack') and a love of tea and moments of ineffable beauty. Barbery's sly wit, which bestows lightness on the most ponderous cogitations, keeps her tale aloft." New Yorker

Barclay, Linwood

★ **Trust** your eyes; a thriller. Linwood Barclay. New American Library 2012 498 p. (hardcover) $25.95; (paperback) $9.99

ISBN 0451237900; 9780451237903; 9780451414175

LC 2011053176

This book by Linwood Barclay follows "Thomas Kilbride . . . a map-obsessed schizophrenic. . . . With a computer program . . . he travels the world while never so much as stepping out the door. . . . Then he sees something . . . in a street view of downtown New York City . . . that looks like a woman being murdered. . . . Thomas's brother, Ray . . . humors him with a half-hearted investigation. But Ray soon realizes he and his brother have stumbled onto a deadly conspiracy." (Publisher's note)

Barkan, Josh

Mexico; stories. Josh Barkan. Hogarth 2017 242 p. (hardcover) $25

ISBN 9781101906309; 9781101906293; 1101906294

LC 2016036402

This book, by Josh Barkan, presents "stories about transformation and danger, passion and heartbreak, terror and triumph. They . . . tap into the most universal and enduring human experiences: love even in the face of danger and loss, the struggle to grow and keep faith amidst hardship and conflict, and the pursuit of authenticity and courage over apathy and oppression." (Publisher's note)

"Masterful stories that peel away at the thin border between everyday life and profane violence in modern-day Mexico." Kirkus

Barker, Clive

Coldheart Canyon. HarperCollins Pubs. 2001 676p

ISBN 0-06-018297-0

LC 2001-279145

Years ago, many film stars and "their colleagues were drawn by the beautiful, rapacious film star Katya Lupi to her magnificent home in Los Angeles's Coldheart Canyon. What kept them at the house, even after death, is the incredible room in its lowest story. Assembled from thousands of painted tiles, that room—brought to California in the 1920s from an ancient monastery in Romania—is literally alive with evil. . . . The room's powers bestow timeless youth on some, including Katya, but give rise to monstrous entities as well. In the present day, into this horrific place enter several modern sorts, most notably A-list film hero Todd Pickett and a dowdy woman, head of Todd's fan club, whose courage and good sense mark her as the novel's hero." Publ Wkly

Barker, Clive

★ **Imajica**. HarperCollins Pubs. 1991 824p

ISBN 0-06-017922-8

LC 90-56405

"Barker's prodigious imagination delivers magicians, doppelgängers, Boschean creatures of staggeringly various descriptions and a pantheon of gods and goddesses seduced by power and redeemed by love in a story of violence, occasional unconventional eroticism and mesmerizing invention." Publ Wkly

Barker, Clive

★ **Weaveworld**. Poseidon Press 1987 584p

ISBN 0-671-61268-9

LC 87-18602

Barker "creates a fantastic romance of magic and promise that is at once popular fiction and utopian conjuring. . . . There is great wit in the struggle that ensues, and keen attention to the facts of poverty and exile." NY Times Book Rev

Barker, Nicola

Darkmans. Harper Perennial 2008 838p pa $16.95

ISBN 978-0-06-157521-1; 0-06-157521-6

LC 2007-40012

First published 2007 in the United Kingdom

"Darkmans is set in Ashford, the Kent town now best known as the home of the Channel Tunnel's International Passenger Station. But in becoming a 'geographical hub', the town in Barker's imagination is robbed of its history, sterilised in the present, and abandoned to an uncertain future. . . . [The central character, Daniel] Beede, is a diligent local worthy turned Puritan avenger by, and against, the brash homogenisation of his hometown. The novel introduces the reader to a remarkable cast of characters: one circle encompasses Beede's drug-dealing son Kane, his ex-girlfriend Kelly Broad (of the infamous Broad clan) and Gaffar, a Kurdish refugee mildly besotted with Kelly and 'employed' by Kane, who has a morbid fear of salads. Another circle links Beede's chiropodist Elen and her husband, the paranoid, narcoleptic Isidore, and their eerie child-prodigy son Fleet. . . . [The plot] is twisted and braided with an intricacy so delicate you barely notice the links until the whole web engulfs you." Scotland on Sunday

Barker, Pat

★ The **eye** in the door. Dutton 1994 280p

ISBN 0-525-93808-7

LC 93-43833

First published 1993 in the United Kingdom

This work "succeeds as both historical fiction and as sequel. Its research and speculation combine to produce a kind of educated imagination that is persuasive and illuminating about this particular place and time. . . . The novel's greatest success, however, has to do with the insight it provides into its central doctor-patient relationships." N Y Times Book Rev

Followed by The ghost road

Barker, Pat

★ The **ghost** road. Dutton 1996 278p

ISBN 0-525-94191-6

LC 95-46863

First published 1995 in the United Kingdom

"The Ghost Road is a startlingly good novel in its own right. With the other two volumes of the trilogy, it forms one of the richest and most rewarding works of fiction of recent times. Intricately plotted, beautifully written, skillfully assembled, tender, horrifying and funny, it lives on in the imagination, like the war it so imaginatively and so intelligently explores." Times Lit Suppl

Barker, Pat

★ **Regeneration**. Dutton 1992 251p

ISBN 0-525-93427-8

LC 91-41264

First published 1991 in the United Kingdom

"'Regeneration' is an antiwar war novel, in a tradition that is by now an established one, though it tells a part of the whole story of war that is not often told—how war may batter and break men's minds—and so makes the madness of war more than a metaphor, and more awful." N Y Times Book Rev

Followed by The eye in the door

Barker, Susan

★ The **incarnations**; Susan Barker. Simon & Schuster 2015 384 p. (hardback) $26

ISBN 1501106783; 9781501106781; 9781501106798

LC 2014043145

This novel by Susan Barker is "about a Beijing taxi driver whose past incarnations . . . haunt him through searing letters . . . , filled with the stories of Wang's previous lives--from escaping a marriage to a spirit bride, to being a slave on the run from Genghis Khan, to living as a fisherman during the Opium Wars, and being a teenager on the Red Guard during the cultural revolution--bound to his mysterious 'soulmate,' spanning one thousand years of betrayal and intrigue." (Publisher's note)

"Barker's historical tour de force is simultaneously sweeping and precise. It would be easy for the novel to teeter into overwrought melodrama; instead, Barker's psychologically nuanced characters and sharp wit turn the bleakness and the gore into something seriously moving." Kirkus

Barlow, Toby

Babayaga; by Toby Barlow. 1st ed. Farrar Straus & Giroux 2013 383 p. ill. (hardcover) $27.00

ISBN 0374107874; 9780374107871

LC 2013008712

In this book, the "reader is introduced to Zoya, a babayaga, or witch, living in Paris some years after WWII, as she gets rid of a lover who has noticed her failure to visibly age. The messy results lead her to drag in

Elga, her mentor; Elga in turn gets heat from a detective and turns him into a flea. Zoya then meets, charms, and falls for a CIA agent named Will who has problems of his own." (Publishers Weekly)

Barnard, Robert

Death of a literary widow. Scribner 1980 192p
ISBN 0-684-16648-8

LC 80-13128

First published 1979 in the United Kingdom with title: Posthumous papers

"Two elderly women, Viola and Hilda, live in the same house, avoiding each other like the plague. Both have been married to the same man, the late writer Walter Mackin, who is the object of a sudden, intense renewal of interest—articles are written about him, his books are reissued. The great concern of the two wives is who will profit from Mackin's posthumous reputation. One of the old ladies dies in a fire, leaving everyone wondering whether she went out in an accidental blaze or as the result of someone's murderous rage." Booklist

Barnard, Robert

A **fall** from grace. Scribner 2007 261p $24
ISBN 978-0-7432-7220-9; 0-7432-7220-X

LC 2006-51427

Leeds cop Charlie Peace is a "newly made inspector, relocating with his wife to the village of Slepton Edge, a move somewhat darkened by the parallel move of Peace's detested father-inlaw to a house nearby. . . . Peace and his wife, Felicity, learn that her father had to leave his former village hurriedly, after he struck a young woman. And now the old man is hitting on a teenage girl. Before the Peaces have a chance to figure out how to protect her, the old man is found dead at the bottom of a quarry. Suspects abound, including a clutch of murderous children and Felicity herself. Peace moves into full detective mode with a murder on his doorstep and his wife a prime suspect. This very satisfying riff on the traditional village mystery finds Barnard at the top of his game." Booklist

Barnes, Djuna

★ **Nightwood**. Modern Lib. 2000 xxxii, 169p
ISBN 0-679-64024-X

LC 99-56308

First published 1936 in the United Kingdom; first United States edition 1937 by Harcourt, Brace

"An account of the tangled sexual and psychological relationships between various expatriates in Paris and Berlin. Narrated in part through an alcoholic haze of stream of consciousness, it owes its reputation as an avant-garde work partially to its frank treatment of lesbianism." Benet's Reader's Ency of Am Lit

Barnes, John

The **armies** of memory. Tor 2006 429p $25.95
ISBN 0-7653-0330-2

LC 2005-18807

"Set in the same far-future universe as A Million Open Doors and A Sky So Big and Black, Barnes's novel concludes the adventures of one of the genre's most distinctive 'special agents,' the cultured, talented, and deadly Giraut Leones. At the same time, the author depicts a future in which the coexistence of divergent human cultures remains a major force in the development of human society. A superb blending of adventure and scientific speculation." Libr J

Barnes, John

The **sky** so big and black. TOR Bks. 2002 315p $24.95
ISBN 0-7653-0303-5

LC 2002-22307

"As always, Barnes's character are beautifully natural. His sense of how the conditions of a place can create a culture and individual sensibilities is outstanding, and here he even allows his slang to evolve." Publ Wkly

Barnes, Jonathan

The **somnambulist**. William Morrow & Co. 2008 353p $23.95
ISBN 978-0-06-137538-5; 0-06-137538-1

First published 2007 in the United Kingdom

"There is much that is strange, magical and darkly hilarious in this book, at least if one savors the sardonic and the bizarre. At various points it recalls Dickens, Alice in Wonderland and Frankenstein, but it remains an original and monumentally inventive piece of work." Washington Post Book World

Barnes, Julian

★ A **history** of the world in 10 1/2 chapters. Knopf 1989 307p
ISBN 0-394-58061-3

LC 89-45266

This book "shapes up not only as Barnes's funniest novel but also his most richly cargoed and imaginatively designed. . . . As satirist and story-teller he has few equals at present." New Statesman Soc

Barnes, Julian, 1946-

The **noise** of time; A Novel. Julian Barnes. Alfred A. Knopf 2016 224 p. (hardcover) $25.95
ISBN 9781101947241; 9781101971185

LC 2015043444

In this novel, by Julian Barnes, "in 1936, Shostakovich, just thirty, fears for his livelihood and his life. Stalin, hitherto a distant figure, has taken a sudden interest in his work and denounced his latest opera. Now, certain he will be exiled to Siberia . . . , Shostakovich reflects on his predicament, his personal history, his parents, various women and wives, his children--and all who are still alive themselves hang in the balance of his fate." (Publisher's note)

"A moody, muted composition about art under the thumb of tyranny." Kirkus

Barnes, Julian

Pulse; stories. Julian Barnes. Alfred A. Knopf 2011 227p il (hbk.) $25
ISBN 9780307595263; 0307595269

LC 2011002736

In this book author Julian Barnes, "returns with [14] stories about longing and loss, friendship and love, whose mysterious natures he examines with his trademark wit and observant eye. . . . Whether domestic or extraordinary, each story pulses with the resonance, spark, and poignant humor for which Barnes is justly heralded." (Publisher's note)

In this collection "Barnes' main focus is on love and intimacy — how it starts, and what accounts for its endurance or failure to thrive. Many of his characters suffer the loss of one of their five senses, or of a close relationship. . . . Interspersed through the first half of Pulse is a quartet of witty, clever dinner party conversations, 'At Phil & Joanna's,' presented with little exposition. The tight-knit group of aging boomers who gather every few months manage to preserve their high spirits even as they banter about serious subjects, including American politics, global warming, health care, 'the marmalade theory of Britishness,' and gender distinctions in talking about love and sex. These snappy running dialogues evoke Barnes' conversational novels . . . . They also demonstrate, along with the other stories in this graceful collection, that Barnes has his finger firmly planted on the pulse of topics that continue to matter to us." NPR

Barnes, Julian, 1946-

★ The **sense** of an ending. Alfred A. Knopf 2011 163p.

ISBN 0-307-95712-8; 978-0-307-95712-2

LC 2011025433

Man Booker Prize (2011)

The novel, a recipient of the Man Booker Prize, takes place in "the North London suburbia. . . . The narrator, Tony Webster, now well into middle age, looks back to his school days when he was one of a group of clever, articulate, and opinionated youths. A few years later one of them, Adrian Finn, commits suicide, and the novel follows Tony's attempts to understand this tragic event. Eventually he discovers that the reasons for it are not at all what he (and the readers) had assumed." (Commonweal)

"Tony Webster, a contented man settling comfortably into middle age, fondly carries his youth with him until a long-ago first love and an old childhood friend begin to haunt his present, forcing him to question the core of his character. Barnes' latest—a meditation on memory and aging—occasionally feels more like a series of wise, underline-worthy insights than a novel. But the many truths he highlights make it worthy of a careful read." Entertainment Wkly

Barnes, Linda

The **Perfect** Ghost; Linda Barnes. St Martins Pr 2013 304 p. (hardcover) $24.99

ISBN 1250023637; 9781250023636

LC 2013002519

This novel from Anthony Award-winner Linda Barnes focuses on "Em Moore, an agoraphobe who ghostwrites celebrity biographies under the joint pseudonym T.E. Blakemore, [who] worries whether she can complete her current project--an 'autobiography' of famed actor-director Garrett Malcolm--without her writing partner, Teddy Blake, after his death in a car crash." (Publishers Weekly)

Barnes, Steven

Domino Falls; a novel. Steven Barnes and Tananarive Due. Pocket Books 2013 384 p. $15

ISBN 145161702X; 9781451617023

LC 2012048451

In this fantasy sequel, "a ragtag 'family' of survivors makes it to Domino Falls, the California town that is home to New Age guru Joseph Wales and his Threadrunner Ranch. After the survivors' ordeal on the road, the town's comfortable accommodations seem almost too good to be true—and indeed they are, because the 'Threadies' are a dangerous cult that has abducted and murdered people to cover up Wales's role in the apocalypse." (Publishers Weekly)

Barnett, LaShonda Katrice

Jam on the Vine; A Novel. by LaShonda Barnett. Grove Press 2015 336 p. $24

ISBN 0802123341; 9780802123343

Stonewall Honor Book in Literature (2016)

In this novel, by LaShonda Barnett, "Ivoe Williams, the precocious daughter of a Muslim cook and a metalsmith from central-east Texas, first ignites her lifelong obsession with journalism when she steals a newspaper from her mother's white employer. . . . Ivoe eventually flees the Jim Crow South with her family and settles in Kansas City, where she and her former teacher and lover, Ona, found the first female-run African American newspaper, 'Jam! On the Vine.'" (Publisher's note)

Barr, Nevada

✓**Destroyer** angel; an Anna Pigeon novel. Nevada Barr. Minotaur Books 2014 352 p. (Anna Pigeon mysteries) (hardcover) $26.99

ISBN 0312614586; 9780312614584

LC 2013032879

In this book, by Nevada Barr, "Anna Pigeon, a ranger for the U.S. Park Services, sets off on . . . an autumn canoe trip [with friends] in the to the Iron Range in upstate Minnesota. . . . On their second night out, Anna goes off on her own for a solo evening float on the Fox River. When she comes back, she finds that four thugs . . . have taken the two women and their teenaged daughters captive. With limited resources . . . Anna has only two days to rescue them." (Publisher's note)

"Barr's gift for depicting breathtaking scenery elevates the story, as does Anna's complex, ever-evolving personality." Pub Wkly

Barr, Nevada

✓The **rope**; by Nevada Barr. Minotaur Books 2011 357 p.

ISBN 1410444864; 9781410444868 978-0-312-61457-7

LC 2011035837

This book tells the story of fictional character Anna Pigeon, who, "[i]n 1995 and 35 years old, fresh off the bus from New York City, . . . takes a . . . job as a seasonal employee of the Glen Canyon National Recreational Area. On her day off, Anna goes hiking into the park never to return. . . . Anna . . . wakes up, trapped at the bottom of a dry natural well, naked, without supplies and no clear memory of how she found herself in this situation. . . . [I]t soon becomes clear that someone has trapped her there, in an inescapable prison, and no one knows that she is even missing. . . . Anna Pigeon must muster the courage, determination and will to live that she didn't even know she still possessed to survive, outwit and triumph." (Publisher's note)

Barrett, A. Igoni, 1979-

Love is power, or something like that; A. Igoni Barrett. Farrar Straus & Giroux 2013 176 p. (paperback) $15

ISBN 1555976409; 9781555976408

LC 2012956123

This collection of short stories, by A. Igoni Barrett, centers on Nigeria. "In these wide-ranging stories, A. Igoni Barrett roams the streets with people from all stations of life. A man with acute halitosis navigates the chaos of the Lagos bus system. A minor policeman, full of the authority and corruption of his uniform, beats his wife. A family's fortunes fall from love and wealth to infidelity and poverty as poor choices unfurl over three generations." (Publisher's note)

Barrett, Andrea

Archangel; Fiction. by Andrea Barrett. 1st ed. W W Norton & Co Inc 2013 238 p. (hardcover) $24.95; (pbk.) $14.95

ISBN 0393240002; 9780393240009; 0393348776; 9780393348774

LC 2013016958

This is a collection of science-focused stories from National Book Award winner Andrea Barrett. "In 'The Ether of Space,' set in 1920, astronomer Phoebe Wells struggles with the implications of Einstein's theories; in 'The Island,' set in 1873, young biologist Henrietta Atkins, initially worshipful of a creationist professor, succumbs to Darwinism. (Publishers Weekly)

Barrett, Andrea

Ship fever and other stories. Norton 1996 254p $21

ISBN 0-393-03853-X

LC 95-14562

Barrett "tells her stories through alternating voices, diaries, letters—whatever seems to hint at the most promising results. Seen against a larger fictional landscape overpopulated with the sensational and affectless, her work stands out for its sheer intelligence, its painstaking attempt to discern and describe the world's configuration." N Y Times Book Rev

Barrett, Colin

Young skins; Colin Barrett. The Stinging Fly 2013 179 p. $15

ISBN 0802123325; 1906539278; 9780802123329; 9781906539276

LC 2013433890

This collection of short stories by Colin Barrett is "set for the most part in the fictional County Mayo town of Glanbeigh [and] explore the wayward lives and loves of young men and women in contemporary post-boom Ireland. A recovering addict drifts closer to the oblivion he'd hoped to avoid by returning to his home town; two estranged friends hide themselves away in a darkened pub, reluctant to attend the funeral of the woman they both loved." (Publisher's note)

"This is a powerful dark shadow of a tale, the heart of this collection of six stories and one longer novella. . . . Barrett has given us moments that resonate true to a culture, a population and a geography that are fertile with the stuff of good fiction." Kirkus

Barrett, William E.

★ The **lilies** of the field; drawings by Burt Silverman. Doubleday 1962 92p

"Homer Smith is an amiable Southern black man. Driving through the Southwest after getting out of the Army, he stops to help four German refugee nuns build a church. After teaching them English and survival skills, he disappears, leaving behind the legend of his faithful help." Shapiro. Fic for Youth. 3d edition

Barrows, Annie

The **Guernsey** Literary and Potato Peel Pie Society; [by] Mary Ann Shaffer & Annie Barrows. The Dial Press 2008 277p $22

ISBN 0-385-34099-0; 978-0-385-34099-1

LC 2008-15477

This novel opens in London in 1946. "Writer Juliet Ashton is looking for her next book subject . . . in a letter from a man she's never met, a native of the island of Guernsey, who has come across her name written inside a book by Charles Lamb. . . . As Juliet and her new correspondent exchange letters, Juliet is drawn into the world of this man and his friends . . . [in the] Guernsey Literary and Potato Peel Pie Society—born as a spur-of-the-moment alibi when its members were discovered breaking curfew by the Germans occupying their island." (Publisher's note)

"Juliet's ready wit is enchanting, as are the discussion of authors from Catullus to Shakespeare. . . . There is the occasional false note. . . . However, 'The Guernsey Literary and Potato Peel Pie Society' is a labor of love, and it shows on almost every page." Christ Sci Monit

Barry, Brunonia

The **lace** reader. William Morrow 2008 390p $24.95

ISBN 978-0-06-162476-6; 0-06-162476-4

Self-published 2006

"Set in Salem, Mass., the story is that of a 32-year-old woman who fled when she was 17 to California but returns when her 85-year-old great-aunt, Eva, is reported missing. Like Eva, Towner Whitney is a 'reader,' though she suppresses the talent. Eva could see a picture in a piece of Ipswich lace that would foretell what was to come. . . . Towner ran off after an extended stay in a high-end looney bin, where she ended up following the suicide of her twin sister, Lyndley. It was that, more than anything, that caused her to reject the family heritage of reading minds as well as lace, though such gifts certainly hold a respected place in Salem. Or did until her Uncle Cal, a wife batterer who sexually abused Lyndley, form a fundamentalist cult to torment and harass the modern-day wiccans? That includes Great-Aunt Eva, a wise and knowing woman, who is found dead and may have been murdered. Cal is a suspect, and it seems he also may have killed a young woman carrying his child. This time it's not so easy for Towner to run, but in staying she confronts pervasive menace." N Y Daily News

Barry, Brunonia

The **map** of true places. William Morrow & Co. 2010 406p $25.99

ISBN 978-0-06-162478-0

"Although marred by unnecessary 'come-to-realize' moments, this woman-in-jeopardy thriller retooled with gothic elements—shifting identities, secrets and portents, a deserted cottage and a missing suicide note—manages to transcend its component cliches." Kirkus

Barry, Kevin

Beatlebone; Kevin Barry. Random House Inc 2015 256 p. $24.95

ISBN 0385540299; 9780385540292

LC 2015035098

In this novel, by Kevin Barry, "it is 1978, and John Lennon has escaped New York City to try to find the island off the west coast of Ireland he bought eleven years prior. Leaving behind domesticity, his approaching forties, his inability to create, and his memories of his parents, he sets off to calm his unquiet soul in . . . isolation. But when he puts himself in the hands of a shape-shifting driver full of Irish charm and dark whimsy, what ensues can only be termed a magical mystery tour." (Publisher's note)

"Nothing at all like Barry's award-winning debut novel, this may be a risky follow-up, but it's intriguing at every turn, and Barry's prose can be as mesmerizing as some of his hero's songs." Kirkus

Barry, Kevin

City of Bohane; Kevin Barry. Cape 2011 277 pp.

ISBN 9780224090575; 0224090577

LC 2011431407

The book explores the "imagined, decivilized Irish city" of Bohane, which "has taken 40 years to fall into utter decay. The setting is a rich stew of ethnicities, loyalties, gangster cred, vices and technologically barren conflicts. . . . Pulling the strings on this criminality is Logan Hartnett, a gaunt, pale rake called 'The Albino.' Hartnett is beleaguered by harpy wife Immaculata and protected by a trio of young warriors: ambitious Wolfie Stanners, irrepressible F##ker Burke and razor-cool Jenni Ching, who works all sides with equal aplomb. A 'welt of vengeance' threatens to jump off, after a Cusack of the Rises gets 'Reefed' in Smoketown. . . . Stirring the pot is the fact that Hartnett's mortal enemy, 'The Gant Broderick,' has sashayed back into town." (Kirkus)

Barry, Kevin

Dark lies the island; Stories. Kevin Barry. Graywolf Press 2013 185 p. $24

ISBN 9781555976514 (alk. paper); 0224090585; 1555976514; 9780224090582

LC 2013937003

This is Kevin Barry's second short story collection. Here, a "postmodern lens reflects youthful ineptness in 'Across the Rooftops.' In 'Wifey Redux,' . . . Saoirse, 'blonde and wispily slight with a delicate, bone-china complexion,' marries, births Ellie and turns to Pinot Grigio, while her dutiful husband becomes consumed by their daughter's beauty and her sex-obsessed suitors. A blocked poet turned innkeeper herds horny Belarus staff and droning, alcoholic locals in 'Fjord of Killary.'" (Kirkus Reviews)

Barry, Max

★ **Lexicon**; a novel. Max Barry. The Penguin Press 2013 400 p. (hardcover) $26.95

ISBN 1594205388; 9781101604908; 9781594205385

LC 2012046980

Alex Award (2014)

In this novel, there is "a secret society of 'poets' who collect and wield special words to control others. Emily Ruff, a teenager living on the street, has been recruited by the organization but leaves in seeming disgrace. Years later, Wil Parke is caught in a firefight between the factions—over him. He is the only survivor of a horrifying event unleashed by an ultimate word of power. But there is a deeper connection between Wil and Emily and the organization that comes between them." (Library Journal)

Barry, Quan

She weeps each time you're born; Quan Barry. Pantheon Books 2014 288 p. (hard cover : alk. paper) $24.95

ISBN 0307911772; 9780307911773

LC 2014006309

This novel, by Quan Barry, "brings us the tumultuous history of modern Vietnam as experienced by a young girl born under mysterious circumstances a few years before the country's reunification, a child gifted with the otherworldly ability to hear the voices of the dead. . . . The novel reconstructs a turbulent historical period through a painterly human lens." (Publisher's note)

"Barry's rich narrative entwines one personal tale with an evocative and haunting exploration of Vietnam's painful past." Booklist

Includes bibliographical references

Barry, Sebastian, 1955-

Days Without End; Sebastian Barry. Viking 2017 259 p. (hardcover) $26

ISBN 0525427368; 9780698168633; 9780525427360

LC 2017288108

In this book, by Sebastian Barry, "Thomas McNulty, aged barely seventeen and having fled the Great Famine in Ireland, signs up for the U.S. Army in the 1850s. With his brother in arms, John Cole, Thomas goes on to fight in the Indian Wars—against the Sioux and the Yurok—and, ultimately, the Civil War. Orphans of terrible hardships themselves, the men find these days to be vivid and alive, despite the horrors they see and are complicit in." (Publisher's note)

"A lively, richly detailed story of one slice of the Irish immigrant experience in America." Kirkus

Barry, Sebastian, 1955-

On Canaan's side. Viking 2011 256p $25.95

ISBN 978-0-670-022922; 0-670-02292-6

LC 2011-13207

"A masterful novel filled with the bittersweet ruminations of an 89-year-old woman as she reflects on her rich life while contemplating death. . . . A novel to be savored." Kirkus

Barth, John

★ **Giles** goat-boy; or, The revised new syllabus. Doubleday 1966 xxxi, 710p

"The novel's protagonist, Billy Bockfuss (also called George Giles, the goat-boy), was raised with herds of goats on a university farm after being found as a baby in the bowels of the giant West Campus Automatic Computer (WESCAC). The WESCAC plans to create a being called GILES (Grand-Tutorial Ideal, Laboratory Eugenical Specimen) that would possess superhuman abilities. Billy's foster father, who tends the herd, suspects Billy of being GILES but tries to groom him to be humanity's savior and to stop WESCAC's domination over humans." Merriam-Webster's Ency of Lit

Barth, John

The **sot**-weed factor. Doubleday 1967 806p

Picaresque novel "originally published in 1960 and revised in 1967. A parody of the historical novel, it is based on and takes its title from a satirical poem published in 1708 by Ebenezer Cooke, who is the protagonist of Barth's work. The novel's black humor is derived from its purposeful misuse of conventional litarary devices." Merriam-Webster's Ency of Lit

Barthelme, Donald

★ **Sixty** stories. Putnam 1981 457p

ISBN 0-399-12659-7

LC 81-8646

Contents: Margins; A shower of gold; Me and Miss Mandible; For I'm the boy; Will you tell me; The balloon; The President; Game; Alice; Robert Kennedy saved from drowning; Report; The dolt; See the moon; The Indian uprising; Views of my father weeping; Paraguay; On angels; The Phantom of the Opera's friend; City life; Kierkegaard unfair to Schlegel; The falling dog; The Policemen's Ball; The glass mountain; Critique de la vie quotidienne; The sandman; Träumerei; The rise of capitalism; A city of churches; Daumier; The party; Eugénie Grandet; Nothing: a preliminary account; A manual for sons; At the end of the mechanical age; Rebecca; The captured woman; I bought a little city; The sergeant; The school; The great hug; Our work and why we do it; The crisis; Cortés and Montezuma; The new music; The zombies; The king of jazz; Morning; The death of Edward Lear; The abduction from the Seraglio; On the steps of the conservatory; The leap; Aria; The emerald; How I write my songs; The farewell; The emperor; Thailand; Heroes; Bishop; Grandmother's house

Barton, Emily

Brookland. Farrar, Straus & Giroux 2006 478p $25

ISBN 0-374-11690-3

LC 2005-16269

"So much modern fiction thinks small, feels small. Emily Barton will never be accused of either. The large and complex storytelling in 'Brookland' is divided between a traditional third-person narrative and the much older Prudence's letters to her daughter. Both feature a large and complex cast." N Y Times Book Rev

Barton, Fiona

The **child**; by Fiona Barton, read by Mandy Williams, Rosalyn Landor, Jean Gilpin, Katharine McEwan, and Steve West. First edition. Berkley 2017 364 p. (hardback) $26

ISBN 1101990481; 9781101990483

LC 2016055096

In this audiobook, by Fiona Barton, read by Mandy Williams, Rosalyn Landor, Jean Gilpin, Katharine McEwan and Steve West, "as an old house is demolished in a gentrifying section of London, a workman discovers a tiny skeleton, buried for years. For journalist Kate Waters, it's a story that deserves attention. She cobbles together a piece for her newspaper, but at a loss for answers, she can only pose a question: Who is the Building Site Baby?" (Publisher's note)

"Barton's second missing-child story is a gut-wrenching tale of narcissism, cunning predators, and bare-knuckle survival." Booklist

Bass, Rick, 1958-

All the Land to Hold Us; Rick Bass. Houghton Mifflin Harcourt 2013 336 p. $25

ISBN 0547687125; 9780547687124

LC 2013019224

This book by Rick Bass presents the "interwoven tale of the generations of residents living in and around the harsh landscape of Midland, TX. . . . Geologist Richard . . . works for the oil industry and is in love with Clarissa, a young beauty dreaming big dreams. Then there's Herbert Mix, an obsessed desert treasure hunter; the widowed Marie, a woman seeking peace after years of harsh living out on salt flats; and Ruth, a gifted, isolated Mormon schoolteacher." (Library Journal)

Bass, Rick

★ **Nashville** chrome. Houghton Mifflin Harcourt 2010 253p $24

ISBN 978-0-54731-726-7; 0-54731-726-3

LC 2010-05732

"Bass gives us Maxine, Bonnie and Jim Ed Brown, three of the five children of Floyd and Birdie Brown; their childhood in the backwoods of post-Depression south-central Arkansas; and their rise to fame as singers and songwriters, members of the fledgling Grand Ole Opry and contemporaries of Elvis Presley. The trio's biggest hit was 'The Three Bells,' and they broke up in 1965. Maxine, who had the strongest pull to fame, went on to release a solo album and write her autobiography. . . . Bass does what he does — sluicing their lives, traveling up Maxine's bloodstream to create a parallel story, a work of fiction full of real names, dates and facts. And when he is done with the Browns, those facts sit, like so many fish bones, on history's clean plate." Los Angeles Times

Bates, H. E.

★ **Fair** stood the wind for France. Little, Brown 1944 270p

A British bomber, returning from a mission over Italy, crashed in occupied France. The members of the crew managed to escape via the underground route, all but the pilot who was too ill. He was cared for by a family of French peasants, whose innate goodness made such an impression on him that when he finally left France he took with him the daughter of the family, as his wife

"An almost unbearable suspense, the romance of the two young people and a true portrait of the little people of France, defenseless but possessed of an enduring power, all these go to make an unforgettable story, beautifully told." Bookmark

Bates, Judy Fong

Midnight at the Dragon Café; Judy Fong Bates. McClelland & Stewart 2004 317 p. Library binding $22.95

ISBN 9781417697786; 0771010982

LC 2004381288

This book, "[s]et in the 1960s, [tells] . . . the story of a young girl, the daughter of a small Ontario town's solitary Chinese family, whose life is changed over the course of one summer when she learns the burden of secrets. Through Su-Jen's eyes, the hard life behind the scenes at the Dragon Café unfolds. . . . Su-Jen's . . . mother, a beautiful but embittered woman, settles uneasily into their new life. Su-Jen feels the weight of her mother's unhappiness as Su-Jen's life takes her outside the restaurant and far from the customs of the traditional past. When Su-Jen's half-brother arrives, smouldering under the responsibilities he must bear as the dutiful Chinese son, he forms an alliance with Su-Jen's mother, one that will have devastating consequences." (Publisher's note)

Batuman, Elif

★ The **idiot**; Elif Batuman. Penguin Press 2017 423 p. (hardback) $27

ISBN 9780143111061 ; 9781101622513; 9781594205613

LC 2016029596

Women's Prize for Fiction Longlist (2018)

In this novel, by Elif Batuman, "the year is 1995, and email is new. Selin, the daughter of Turkish immigrants, arrives for her freshman year at Harvard. She signs up for classes in subjects she has never heard of, befriends her charismatic and worldly Serbian classmate, Svetlana, and, almost by accident, begins corresponding with Ivan, an older mathematics student from Hungary." (Publisher's note)

"A sweetly caustic first novel...Self-aware, cerebral, and delightful." Kirkus

Bauer, Belinda

Blacklands. Simon & Schuster 2010 221p $23

ISBN 978-1-4391-4944-7; 1-4391-4944-5

LC 2009-08548

"Bauer displays remarkable talent in pacing, plotting and, most important of all, getting beneath the skin of even her most repellent characters." Kirkus

Bauer, Belinda

Darkside; a novel. Simon & Schuster Paperbacks 2011 287p $15

ISBN 978-1-4516-1275-2; 1-4516-1275-3

LC 2010-28109

"Given the shallow pool of prospective victims and suspects, it takes real skill to write a plausible whodunit about an undetected serial killer running amok in an English village. . . . Arriving in the bleak midwinter to investigate the murder of an elderly woman as she lay paralyzed in her bed, the citybred Detective Chief Inspector John Marvel is so appalled to find himself in the boondocks, obliged to waste his talents 'on the low and the stupid,' that out of sheer spite, he repeatedly subjects the local constable, Jonas Holly, to public humiliation. Jonas, a sweet, conscientious policeman who sacrificed his career ambitions to care for his dying wife, knows he doesn't deserve this ridicule. But the taunting notes the killer leaves behind as he continues his rampage touches some core of guilt Jonas can't bring himself to face. Set against a landscape that would tax anyone's sanity, Bauer's grim tale deploys a morbid wit that's positively wicked." N Y Times Book Rev

Bauer, Carlene

★ **Frances** and Bernard; Carlene Bauer. Houghton Mifflin Harcourt 2013 195 p. (hardcover) $23

ISBN 0547858248; 9780547858241

LC 2012014028

In this book, set in the late 1950s, "over the course of one long lunch at a writer's workshop, Frances and Bernard begin a journey of love and loss. They banter about writing and the workshop's limitations, and, while falling in love, they struggle with the meaning of religion and the nature of friendship. In the end, their relationship is tested to the limits when Bernard suffers a manic episode." (Library Journal)

Bauermeister, Erica

Joy for beginners. Putnam 2011 272p $24.95

ISBN 978-0-399-15712-7; 0-399-15712-3

LC 2010-26587

This novel "centers around seven women. Kate is a cancer survivor, and the friends that supported her through it all come together to celebrate her recovery. In honor of that, Kate makes a bargain with them. She's going to do something she has always been terrified of: white-water rafting. In return, they each have to do something they've always said they wouldn't. But they don't get to choose. Kate does. The novel tells the story of each of the characters separately. The reader gets to know these women intimately; their pasts, their lives, their hopes, their dreams. Most importantly, their secret fears. The challenges Kate sets for all of them speak to their innermost—and unrealized—longings and sets them on the paths to true happiness and fulfillment." Fort Worth Examiner

Bausch, Richard

Peace; a novel. Knopf 2008 171p $19.95

ISBN 978-0-307-26833-4; 0-307-26833-0

LC 2007-37096

"A story cleanly told — void of trickery or plot shifting, without the faux drama of point-of-view shifts or uninvited monologue on the state of the cultural landscape — well, that's a thing to behold. . . . Bausch, among the most prolific and accomplished story writers of the last two decades, provides a gift to those who like to swallow their stories whole, in one sitting, without digression or narrative handstands." Esquire

Bausch, Richard

Something is out there; stories. Alfred A. Knopf 2010 268p $25.95

ISBN 978-0-307-26627-9; 0-307-26627-3

LC 2009-27437

"In this fine new collection, Bausch presents us with young people and old people; married, single and divorced people; straight and gay people; professional and blue-collar people; and people who are simply layabouts. They make bad choices, occasionally even deadly choices, because they can't help themselves—and because the universe is full of peril and temptation. . . . Again and again, [Bausch] excavates the darkest corners of his characters' lives without giving in to despair." N Y Times Book Rev

Bausch, Richard

★ The **stories** of Richard Bausch. HarperCollins 2003 651p $29.95

ISBN 0-06-019649-1

LC 2003-42318

"Failure and its exactions this is Bausch's big subject. These 42 stories test the play of hope and disappointment in the lives of spouses and lovers, of parents and children and siblings. And while Bausch does in several instances write with insight and authority from a woman's perspective, it is the sons, fathers and husbands in their daily trials that he registers most memorably. Indeed, so alive are these characters, with their credible flaws, their complaints and loud excitements, that closing the book feels like pushing the door shut on some clamorous party." N Y Times Book Rev

Baxter, Charles

The **feast** of love. Pantheon Bks. 2000 308p

ISBN 0-375-41019-8

LC 99-53088

National Book Award Finalist: Fiction (2000)

"An insomniac Mid-western novelist named Charlie Baxter becomes the unwitting audience of a neighbor's midnight confession, and is drawn into a tale of love in its manifold guises—confused, ecstatic, unrequited. We hear the story of Kathryn, who left her husband for the female shortstop of a local softball team; of Diana, a capricious lawyer who doesn't want anyone to want her too much; and of Chloé, a pierced teenager with a strong sense of justice and a doomed passion for a former drug addict. Baxter's novel is a modern Symposium, unexpectedly hilarious in its attempt to get at the evasive truths of love; unlike Plato's treatise, though, its strength lies in its recognition that such truths aren't universal." New Yorker

Baxter, Charles

Gryphon; new and selected stories. Pantheon Books 2011 400p $27.95

ISBN 978-0-307-37921-4; 0-307-37921-3

LC 2010-13785

"The strength of Charles Baxter's 'Gryphon' stories collection is characters who struggle with shame in an age when the burden of knowledge is compounded by the inability to act properly. Most of the stories are set in snowy Midwestern cities whose economic and social misfortunes weigh on his characters like an alp. . . . Baxter's writing is spare but, like a flash of cat eyes in the night, well-crafted images and wit flit onto the pages to keep the narrative moving." Providence J

Baxter, Charles

Saul and Patsy. Pantheon Bks. 2003 317p $24

ISBN 0-375-41029-5

LC 2003-42027

"Baxter's prose is succulent, his characters magnetic, his humor incisive, his decipherment of the human psyche felicitous, and his command of the storyteller's magic absolute." Booklist

Baxter, Charles

★ **There's** something I want you to do; stories. Charles Baxter. Pantheon Books 2015 240 p. (hardcover) $24

ISBN 9781101870013; 110187001X

LC 2014003352

In author Charles Baxter's short story collection, stories "are held together by a surreally intricate web of cause and effect--one that slowly ensnares both fictional bystanders and enraptured readers. The result is a portrait of human nature as seen from the tightrope that spans the distance between dreams and waking life--a portrait that could have arisen only from Baxter's singular vision." (Publisher's note)

"Rooted in Minneapolis, its industrial ruins so poetically rendered, these ravishing, funny, and compassionate stories redefine our perceptions of vice and virtue, delusion and reason, love and loss." Booklist

Baxter, Stephen

Manifold; space. Stephen Baxter. Ballantine Pub. Group 2001 452p (pbk.) $7.99; o.p.

ISBN 9780345430786; 9780345430779

LC 00050804

This book takes place in "2020. Fueled by an insatiable curiosity, Reid Malenfant ventures to the far edge of the solar system, where he discovers a strange artifact left behind by an alien civilization: A gateway that functions as a kind of quantum transporter, allowing virtually instantaneous travel over the vast distances of interstellar space. . . . [H] e will soon be faced with an impossible choice that will push him beyond terror, beyond sanity, beyond humanity itself. Meanwhile on Earth the Japanese scientist Nemoto fears her worst nightmares are coming true. Startling discoveries reveal that the Moon, Venus, even Mars once thrived with life . . . that was snuffed out not just once but many times, in cycles of birth and destruction." (Publisher's note)

Bayard, Louis

The **black** tower. William Morrow 2008 352p $24.95

ISBN 978-0-06-117350-9; 0-06-117350-9

LC 2008-5059

The author sets his "historical adventure in the streets of Paris as the blood lust of the revolution subsides. It is 1818 when Vidocq, a former convict and the (real-life) founder of the newly created plainclothes investigative force known as the Sûreté, tracks down obscure medical student Hector Carpentier, whose name was found in the pocket of a dead man. As they work through the clues together, they move from the slums of Paris out to the royal gardens of Saint-Cloud. The duo soon realizes that the murders they are investigating may be connected to the whereabouts of Marie Antoinette's lost son, said to have died in the Black Tower." Libr J

Bayard, Louis

The **pale** blue eye; a novel. Louis Bayard. HarperCollins Publishers 2006 432 p. $24.95

ISBN 978-0-06-073397-1; 0-06-073397-7

LC 2005044741

"Bayard scatters seeds of Poe's short stories and poems throughout the novel, culminating in a grisly set piece that out-Goths 'The Fall of the House of Usher.' But just when a reader's eyes start rolling, Bayard's ending brilliantly upends the entire novel." Christ Sci Monit

Bayard, Louis

The **school** of night; a novel. Henry Holt and Company 2011 338p $25

ISBN 978-0-8050-9069-7; 0-8050-9069-X

LC 2010-24961

A "fabricated account of a secret society of brilliant Elizabethan thinkers who challenge conventional 16th-century wisdom by exercising 'the freedom to speak their minds.' Henry Cavendish, the 21st-century scholar who narrates the story, tumbles to this academic crew when an unscrupulous collector (who would 'lay down his life for a Shakespeare quarto') hires him to search the archives of a fellow bibliophile who committed suicide. Leaving Henry to puzzle out the clues in the library, Bayard shifts the story to Tudor England, where members of the elite circle that meets at Sir Walter Ralegh's Dorset estate are immersed in their esoteric arts. From either perspective, the story is fascinating. And yes, there's a good reason that Shakespeare is not welcome in this company." N Y Times Book Rev

Beach, Edward Latimer

Run silent, run deep; {by} Edward L. Beach. Holt & Co. 1955 364p

"If ever a book has the ring of reality, this is it. From the moment the reader steps aboard a training boat in New London, Conn., to the time when the submarine Walrus dives deeply to avoid the depth charges of the enemy's destroyers, there is awe and respect for the author who created them." N Y Times Book Rev

Beach-Ferrara, Jasmine

Damn love; Jasmine Beach-Ferrara. Ig Publishing 2013 200 p. (pbk.) $15.95

ISBN 1935439782; 9781935439783

LC 2013012280

Lambda Literary Awards Finalist: Gay General Fiction (2014)

This book, by Jasmine Beach-Ferrara, "set in San Francisco and North Carolina, . . . introduce[s] us to characters struggling with love in all its complicated forms, including a young doctor getting over a breakup with the help of a patient, a newly married gay man who reconnects with his estranged mother, a trio of physicists caught in a surprising love triangle, and a soldier who takes secrets with her to the Iraqi desert." (Publisher's note)

"Expressive and sincere, Beach-Ferrara's stories give voice to common, yet often uncomfortable, themes in society: same-sex love and issues of marriage, identity, religious beliefs, military service and intolerance." Kirkus

Beagle, Peter S.

★ The **last** unicorn. Viking 1968 218p hardcover o.p. pa $14.95

ISBN 0-670-41908-7; 0-451-45052-3 pa

"Beagle is a true magician with words, a master of prose and a deft practitioner in verse. He has been compared, not unreasonably, with Lewis Carroll and J. R. R. Tolkien, but he stands squarely and triumphantly on his own feet." Saturday Rev

Beagle, Peter S.

Summerlong; by Peter S. Beagle. Tachyon Publications 2016 236 p. (paperback) $15.95

ISBN 9781616962449; 1616962445

In this book, by Peter S. Beagle, "it was a typically unpleasant Puget Sound winter before the arrival of Lioness Lazos. An enigmatic young waitress with strange abilities, when the lovely Lioness comes to Gardner Island even the weather takes notice. And as an impossibly beautiful spring leads into a perfect summer, Lioness is drawn to a complicated family. She is taken in by two disenchanted lovers—dynamic Joanna Delvecchio and scholarly Abe Aronson." (Publisher's note)

"In his first new novel in more than a decade, Beagle creates an intimate drama between the members of a family who are slowly blindsided by myth and magic spilling into their ordinary world." Kirkus

Beah, Ishmael, 1980-

Radiance of tomorrow; a novel. Ishmael Beah. Sarah Crichton Books, Farrar, Straus and Giroux 2014 256 p. (hardback) $25

ISBN 0374246025; 9780374246020

LC 2013036856

This novel, by Ishmael Beah, is "about postwar life in Sierra Leone. . . . Benjamin and Bockarie . . . return to their hometown, Imperi, after the civil war. . . . [They] try to forge a new community by taking up their former posts as teachers, but they're beset by obstacles . . . and the depredations of a foreign mining company. . . . As Benjamin and Bockarie search for a way to restore order, they're forced to reckon with the uncertainty of their past and future alike." (Publisher's note)

"The power of the story is in the close-up, heartbreaking detail of the struggle for survival, the cruelty, and also the kindness." Booklist

Bear, Elizabeth

All the windwracked stars. Tor 2008 368p (The edda of burdens) $24.95

ISBN 978-0-7653-1882-4; 0-7653-1882-2

LC 2008-34076

The author's "ability to create breathtaking variations on ancient themes and make them new and brilliant is, perhaps, unparalleled in the genre." Libr J

Bear, Elizabeth

Blood and iron. ROC 2006 432p pa $7.99

ISBN 978-0-451-46092-9; 0-451-46092-8

LC 2005-33954

"Ancient grudges and ruthless schemes are simply business as usual to the Faerie court in Bear's complex and involving contemporary fantasy. Seeker, formerly Elaine Andraste, is a changeling bound to the Mebd, the queen of the Daoine Sidhe, to find other changelings and bring them to the Faerie court. There, like legendary Tam Lin, and Seeker's own son, Ian, they entertain the queen until she tires of them. Now the queen needs Seeker to find—and win the heart of—the new Merlin, latest incarnation of a being who, in the hands of the Prometheans, could be used to destroy the Fae. Pragmatic college professor Carel Bierce, the first female Merlin, is not easily swayed by Fae—or Promethean—advances. Long-forgotten rivalries and unsuspected blood ties arise to tug at Seeker's loyalties, even as the queen promises to free Ian when she succeeds." Publ Wkly

Bear, Elizabeth

Ink and steel; a novel of the Promethean Age. Roc 2008 427p pa $14

ISBN 978-0-451-46209-1

LC 2008-746

"Bear reveals the secret war between fae and the Elizabethan court in this dramatic prequel to Blood and Iron and Whiskey and Water. Framed with the intrigues of queens and courtiers, the story focuses on the mutual respect and growing love of Kit Marley (aka Christopher Marlowe) and Will Shakespeare. As Morgan le Fey rescues Kit from assassins, various factions recruit Will to bolster their political machinations with the magic of poetry. Kit pulls Will into Faerie and both are forced to face their own deepest desires and fears, which cannot be resolved until they deal with a power even higher than mortal Queen Elizabeth or fae Queen Mab. Copious quotes and intelligent speculation about their lives and works mark this sensitive and sensual look at the two supreme playwrights of the English Renaissance." Publ Wkly

Bear, Elizabeth

Range of ghosts; Elizabeth Bear. Tor 2012 334p.

ISBN 9780765327543

LC 2011025171

In this fantasy book, "Temur, grandson of the Great Khan, is walking away from a battlefield where he was left for dead. All around lie the fallen armies of his cousin and his brother, who made war to rule the Khaganate. Temur is now the legitimate heir by blood to his grandfather's throne. . . . Once-Princess Samarkar is climbing the thousand steps of the Citadel of the Wizards of Tsarepheth. She was heir to the Rasan Empire until her father got a son on a new wife. . . . These two will come together to stand against the hidden cult that has so carefully brought all the empires of the Celadon Highway to strife and civil war through guile and deceit and sorcerous power." (Publisher's note)

Bear, Elizabeth

Shattered pillars; Elizabeth Bear. Tor Books 2013 336 p. (Eternal sky) (hardcover) $26.99

ISBN 0765327554; 9780765327550; 9781429947770

LC 2012038826

This is Elizabeth Bear's second installment in her Mongolia-inspired fantasy epic series. "The necromancer priest al-Sepehr is bringing war to the world, placing his allies and minions throughout the nations to see them crumble. But beyond his control are Edene, who has stolen the green ring that makes her ruler of the ancient and treacherous realm of Erem; bold imperial scion Temur;" and his companions Samarkar, Hrahima, and Hsiung. (Publishers Weekly)

Bear, Elizabeth

Steles of the sky; Elizabeth Bear. Tor Books 2014 432 p. map (hardback) $26.99

ISBN 0765327562; 9780765327567

LC 2013029676

Sequel to: Shattered pillars (2013)

"Elizabeth Bear concludes her award-winning epic fantasy trilogy, The Eternal Sky, with 'Steles of the Sky.' Re Temur, exiled heir to his grandfather's Khaganate, has finally raised his banner and declared himself at war with his usurping uncle. With his companions--the Wizard Samarkar, the Cho-tse Hrahima, and the silent monk Brother Hsiung--he must make his way to Dragon Lake to gather in his army of followers." (Publisher's note)

"Battles are fought on both a personal level and a grand scale, with artifacts of obscure ancient civilizations, spirit animals, magical creatures, and poetry and politics. The conclusion is both untelegraphed and completely appropriate." Pub Wkly

Bear, Greg

★ **Anvil** of stars. Warner Bks. 1992 434p

ISBN 0-446-51601-5

LC 91-50411

Sequel to The forge of God

"Bear is superlatively competent in the English language and a master of both technical wizardry and powerful scenes. Throughout the book, he addresses the question of an ethical basis for genocide, leaving the matter sufficiently open to make one wonder whether the story is yet completed." Booklist

Bear, Greg

The **collected** stories of Greg Bear. TOR Bks. 2002 653p hardcover o.p. pa $17.95

ISBN 0-7653-0160-1; 0-7653-0161-X pa

LC 2002-20466

In addition to Blood music (1985), a novelette where a genetic engineer injects himself with experimental intelligent microorganisms with disasterous results, this "volume subsumes Bear's earlier collections, The wind from a burning woman (1983) and Tangents (1989), while also including more recent work." Anatomy of Wonder 5

Bear, Greg

★ The **forge** of God. TOR Bks. 1987 474p

ISBN 0-312-93021-6

LC 87-50482

"Three geologists discover an alien artifact in Death Valley and set off a chain of events leading to the discovery that Earth is about to be invaded by two alien races. One race sends out planet-wrecking machines; . . . the other is trying to enlist the survivors of humanity in tracking down and destroying the planet wreckers. The battle over Earth is seen through the eyes of a large cast of well-drawn characters, crowned by a climax of enormous power." Booklist

Followed by Anvil of stars

Beard, Jo Ann

In Zanesville. Little, Brown and Co. 2011 289 p. $23.99

ISBN 978-0-316-08447-5; 0-316-08447-6

LC 2010041808

Alex Award (2012)

The events of the novel take place in the 1970s. In Zanesville is "titled after the Illinois township where the story is set. . . . [The book opens] inside the house of the six children whom the narrator and her best friend, Felicia, babysit all summer." (Bookforum)

This novel is "set in an Illinois factory town in the 1970s. The coming-of-age material is familiar: the panic that accompanies the first sight of a tampon; the drowsy-making thrill of a boy's hand creeping up your back; the impotent worry over a broken parent. And yet somehow Beard makes the daily rituals and discoveries of her nameless 14-year-old narrator and her best friend Felicia ('Flea') epic and profound. These thoughtful, funny, awestruck, slightly peculiar girls are so endearing, so painfully true, that they almost make a reader wish she were back in high school so she could be friends with them." Entertainment Wkly

Beaton, M. C.

✓**Death** of a macho man. Mysterious Press 1996 216p

ISBN 0-89296-531-2

LC 96-7268

"Befuddled, earnest and utterly endearing, Hamish makes his triumphs sweetly satisfying." Publ Wkly

Beaton, M. C.

✓**Pushing** up daisies; M. C. Beaton. Minotaur Books 2016 280 p. (Agatha Raisin mysteries) (hardcover) $25.99

ISBN 9781466861190; 9781250057440

LC 2016010568

In this book, by M. C. Beaton, "Lord Bellington, a wealthy land developer, wants to turn the community garden into a housing estate. And when Agatha and her friend Sir Charles Fraith attempt to convince Lord Bellington to abandon his plans, he scoffs, 'Do you think I give a damn about what a lot of pesky villagers want?' So it's no surprise that some in the town are feeling celebratory when Agatha finds his obituary in the newspaper two weeks later." (Publisher's note)

"A twisty plot, a familiar cast of eccentric characters, and a charming English country setting mean that lovers of cozy mysteries will be satisfied indeed." Pub Wkly

Beattie, Ann

★ **Chilly** scenes of winter. Doubleday 1976 280p

ISBN 0-385-11658-6

"Beattie has an instinct for the grotesque that verges on the edge of real wit and pain. She is obviously a first-rate craftswoman with an eye for idiosyncratic detail." Saturday Rev

Beattie, Ann

Follies; new stories. Scribner 2005 305p $25

ISBN 0-743-26961-6

LC 2004-65087

"The tales in this volume showcase a newly flexible voice that accommodates both the author's patented gift for social observation and her more recent interest in her characters' inner lives, a voice that allows her to move fluently back and forth in time, back and forth from memory to rumination." N Y Times (Late N Y Ed)

Beattie, Ann, 1947-

The **New** Yorker stories. Scribner 2010 514p $30

ISBN 978-1-4391-6874-5; 1-4391-6874-1

LC 2010-32933

The book presents a compilation of short stories by author Ann Beattie which she has published in the "New Yorker" magazine since the 1970s. "In 'The Burning House,' . . . [a] man destroys the delicate ecosystem that exists among himself, his exwife, their young daughter and his lover (his gay lover—this is all the way back in 1979) by taking a job in San Francisco. . . . By the early 1980s—the pieces later included, for the most part, in her fourth collection, 'Where You'll Find Me'—Beattie's work has changed again. Now the stories are almost all quite brief, six pages or less. . . . 'The New Yorker Stories''s final pieces, which represent Beattie's work since the early '90s, reflect . . . a mellowing. . . . The characters have aging parents, or are ones." (Nation)

"Beattie made her mark as an audaciously understated yet resoundingly on-the-mark writer in the 1970s in the New Yorker, and it is testimony both to her unceasing artistic growth and the magazine's unshakable commitment to exceptional short stories that the final works in this grand retrospective collection are as provocative as the first. Forty-eight Beattie stories appeared in the New Yorker between 1974 and 2006, and until now nearly half remained uncollected. This scintillating volume showcases Beattie's stunning insights into the eternal isolation of individuals and each decade's signature longings and conflicts." Booklist

Beattie, Ann, 1947-

★ **Picturing** Will. Random House 1989 230p

ISBN 0-394-56987-3

LC 89-42781

"Aspiring photographer Jody, abandoned by husband Wayne—now on his third wife—is deeply devoted to her young son Will but hesitant to commit to lover Mel. Still, she visits Mel in faraway New York City, where Mel's friend, gallery owner Haverford (whose name she can recall only as Haveabud), takes a shine to her work—or to her. When Mel takes Will to visit his father in Florida, Haveabud goes along for the ride, bringing Spencer, a former protegé's son. . . . Meanwhile, Wayne demonstrates his continued instability by cheating flagrantly on his new wife, Corky." (Libr J)

Beattie "has almost as many narrative voices as characters in this book, yet the result is never confusing. . . . 'Picturing Will' would be admirable for its technique alone; what makes it Beattie's best novel is her new and fearless way with emotional complexity." Newsweek

Beattie, Ann, 1947-

★ The **state** we're in; Maine Stories. by Ann Beattie. Simon & Schuster 2015 224 p. (hardcover) $25

ISBN 9781501107818; 150110781X

LC 2015374895

This short story collection, by Ann Beattie, "is about how we live in the places we have chosen--or have been chosen by. . . . The collection is woven around Jocelyn, a wry, disaffected teenager living with her aunt and uncle for the summer, forging new friendships, avoiding her mother's calls, taking writing classes, and encountering mortality for the first time." (Publisher's note)

"Some pieces read like sketches with promising characters but little movement: a 77-year-old writer discusses poetry with an IRS agent, a doctor reminisces about her life in New York before moving north, an author interviews a local for a book about "people who have negative effects on other people's lives." A full novel on Jocelyn might be more fulfilling, but Beattie clearly enjoys wandering around the neighborhood. An engaging collection of varied characters, if varying degrees of substance." Kirkus

Beatty, Paul, 1962-

★ The **sellout**; a novel. Paul Beatty. 1st edition Farrar, Straus & Giroux 2015 304 p. (hardcover) $26

ISBN 0374260508; 9780374260507

LC 2014027451

National Book Critics Circle Award Finalist: Fiction (2015)
Man Booker Prize (2016)

This book by Paul Beatty, winner of the 2016 Man Booker Prize for Fiction, is a satire "about a young man's isolated upbringing and the race trial that sends him to the Supreme Court. . . . It challenges the sacred tenets of the United States Constitution, urban life, the civil rights movement, the father-son relationship, and the holy grail of racial equality--the black Chinese restaurant." (Publisher's note)

"Beatty . . . creates a wicked satire that pokes fun at all that is sacred to life in the United States, from father-son dynamics right up to the Supreme Court. His story is full of the unexpected, resulting in absurd and hilarious drama." LJ

Beatty, Paul

Slumberland; a novel. Bloomsbury 2008 256p

ISBN 978-1-59691-240-3; 1-59691-240-5

LC 2007-45049

"The protagonist of the novel, DJ Darky, is a Los Angeles DJ who comes to Berlin to be a jukebox sommelier. He is in search of a virtuoso saxophonist, Charles Stone nicknamed the Shuwa who is in many ways his doppelgänger. DJ Darky has created a sonic masterpiece, layering nearly every sound he can find into a flawless testament, a musical ars poetica. Now, despite offers from the gangsta rap community, he wants the Shuwa to play some avant-garde mystical voodoo music over the beat. DJ Darky arrives in Germany, having already declared the end of blackness, to find himself once more the subject of racism amid constant reminders of his obsolete ethnicity. His real quest, we soon learn, is for meaning and a place in the increasingly chaotic post-Cold War world. 'Slumberland' is laugh-out-loud funny in many places, and its wit and satire can be burning, regardless of where they are pointed: blackness or whiteness." Los Angeles Times Book Rev

Beauvoir, Simone de

★ The **mandarins**; a novel. World Pub. 1956 610p

Original French edition, 1954

This "semiautobiographical novel addressed the attempts of post-World War II leftist intellectuals to abandon their elite, 'mandarin' status and to engage in political activism. The characters of psychologist Anne Dubreuilh and her husband Robert were roughly based on de Beauvoir and her lifelong associate Jean-Paul Sartre; de Beauvoir's account of Anne's affair with the American Lewis Brogan was a thinly veiled account of her own relationship with novelist Nelson Algren." Merriam-Webster's Ency of Lit

Beckett, Samuel

★ **Molloy,** Malone dies, The unnamable; with an introduction by Gabriel Josipovici. Knopf 1997 xliii, 476p $22

ISBN 0-375-40070-2

LC 98-119494

A reissue of the title first published 1959 by Grove Press; Original French editions of Molloy and Malone dies published 1951; The unnamable, 1953. These translations published separately 1955, 1956 and 1958, respectively

The trilogy "is concerned with the search for identity, for the true self which can rest from self-caricature; and as a parallel it is concerned with the true silence which is the end of speech. Molloy, Malone and their final unnamable incarnation are paradigms of humanity in general and of the artist in particular. . . . The trilogy seen as a whole composes one of the most remarkable, most original and most haunting prose-works of the century." Times Lit Suppl

Beckett, Samuel

★ **Murphy**. Grove Press 1957 282p

First published 1938 in the United Kingdom

"The story concerns an Irishman in London who yearns to do nothing more than sit in his rocking chair and daydream. Murphy attempts to avoid all action; he escapes from a girl he is about to marry, takes up with a kind prostitute, and finds a job as a nurse in a mental institution, where he plays nonconfrontational chess. His disengagement from the world is shattered when his fiancée, with a detective and two new lovers in tow, discovers him. He is killed when someone accidentally turns on the gas in his apartment." Merriam-Webster's Ency of Lit

Begley, Louis

About Schmidt; Louis Begley. 1st ed. Alfred Knopf; Distributed by Random House 1996 273p $23

ISBN 0679450335; 9780679450337

LC 96008244

This book tells the story of Schmidt, a "retired lawyer whose lucrative practice was notable for its meticulousness but is now all but anarchistic, . . . [who] misses his late wife and is uneasy alone in their stately Long Island mansion. His sense of isolation is compounded by his estrangement from his only child, Charlotte, whom he uncharitably thinks of as a 'smug, overworked yuppie,' and by his displeasure over her impending marriage to a lawyer he claims not to like because he's a dull-witted workaholic, when, in fact, it's his Jewishness Schmidt can't abide." (Booklist)

Belcher, R. S.

The **six** -gun tarot; R. S. Belcher. Tor Books 2013 364 p. (hardcover) $25.99

ISBN 0765329328; 9780765329325; 9781429946988

LC 2012026479

In this debut novel from R.S. Belcher, when "young Jim Negrey and his long-suffering horse find sanctuary in the cattle town of Galgotha, NV, Jim notices that the sheriff bears the marks of a noose round his neck; his deputy calls the coyotes his kin, and a nameless evil inhabits the nearby silver mine." (Library Journal)

"Against the backdrop of Chinese and Mormon mythology and the Civil War, with a bit of Frankenstein for color, the mix of theology, frontier justice, and zombies is merely cover for an intense and irreverent exploration of good, evil, and free will." Pub Wkly

Belfer, Lauren

And after the fire; a novel. Lauren Belfer. Harper 2016 464 p. (hardcover : acid-free paper) $26.99

ISBN 0062428519; 9780062428516; 9780062428523

LC 2015038472

In this novel, by Lauren Belfer, "at the end of World War II, American soldier Henry Sachs takes . . . an old music manuscript, from a seemingly deserted mansion. In America in 2010, Henry's niece, Susanna . . . becomes determined to discover what it is and to return it to its rightful owner. In Berlin, Germany, in 1783 . . . Sara Itzig Levy, a renowned musician, conceals the manuscript of an anti-Jewish cantata by Johann Sebastian Bach. Interweaving the stories of Susanna and Sara, and their families, 'And After the Fire' traverses over two hundred years of history." (Publisher's note)

"Based on impressive research, this remarkable novel spans centuries and continents, touching finally on the Holocaust and serving as a paean to Bach's music while acknowledging the composer's expressed hatred of Jews." Booklist

Belfer, Lauren

A **fierce** radiance; a novel. Harper 2010 400p $25.99

ISBN 978-0-06-125251-8; 0-06-125251-4

LC 2009-40116

"Belfer fuses fiction and history cleverly and seamlessly. . . . A Fierce Radiance resonates precisely because the characters Belfer creates, and the ones she borrows from history, feel real—as organic and natural as the molds from which these miracle drugs come." USA Today

Belfoure, Charles

The **Paris** Architect; A Novel. Charles Belfoure. Sourcebooks Landmark 2013 384 p. $25.99

ISBN 1402284314; 9781402284311

LC 2013017034

In this book, set in 1942 Paris, "architect Lucien Bernard hates the occupying Germans but feels no love for the Jews, who have been asked to surrender to authorities. Times are tough, though, and Lucien takes on a dangerous job designing hiding spots for Jews, While he's initially motivated by the challenge and the satisfaction of outsmarting the Germans, the job becomes unexpectedly personal when tragedy strikes an occupant in one of his designs." Lucien has a change of heart. (Library Journal)

Includes bibliographical references and index

Bell, Alden

The **reapers** are the angels; a novel. Alden Bell. Henry Holt and Company 2010 225 p. pa $15

ISBN 9780805092431; 0805092439

LC 2009048158

Alex Award (2011)

This book follows "15-year-old Temple," who was "[b]orn into a crumbling society plagued by zombies. . . . When she is assaulted at a safe house, she murders her human attacker, Abraham Todd, and runs from his vengeful brother, Moses. Temple soon acquires a traveling partner, a slow mute by the name of Maury, and begrudgingly takes responsibility for his care, remembering a young boy she swore to protect but couldn't save. Fleeing Moses, the 'meatskins,' and her own battered conscience, Temple still finds moments of simple joy in the brutal world." (Publishers Weekly)

Bell, Lenora

★ **How** the Duke Was Won; Lenora Bell. HarperCollins 2016 384 p. (The Disgraceful Dukes) $7.99

ISBN 0062397729; 9780062397720

"James, the scandalously uncivilized Duke of Harland, requires a bride with a spotless reputation for a strictly business arrangement. . . . Charlene Beckett, the unacknowledged daughter of an earl and a courtesan, has just been offered a life-altering fortune to pose as her half-sister, Lady Dorothea, and win the duke's proposal. . . . Charlene must decide if the promise of a new life is worth risking everything." (Publisher's note)

"Charlene is smart and tough and easily steals the show with her gutsy nonconformity." LJ

Other titles in this series include:

If I Only Had a Duke (2016)

Blame It on the Duke (2017)

Bell, Madison Smartt

All souls' rising. Pantheon Bks. 1995 530p

ISBN 0-679-43989-7

LC 95-12339

"Set during the struggle for Haiti's independence in the late 1700s, this intensely imagined epic novel of racial hatred and bloody upheaval illuminates the enmities among the astonishingly complex ethnic populations of the Caribbean island. Bell evokes a society caught in the crucible of violence with superb characterizations, ranging from the arrogant grand blanc plantation owners to the black slaves—including Toussaint L'Ouverture, the leader of the black revolt." Publ Wkly

Belle, Kimberly

The **marriage** lie; Kimberly Belle. Mira Books 2016 334 p. (paperback) $15.99

ISBN 0778319768; 9780778319764; 9781460396353

In this novel, by Kimberly Belle, "Iris and Will have been married for seven years, and life is as close to perfect as it can be. But on the morning Will flies out for a business trip to Florida, Iris's happy world comes to an abrupt halt: another plane headed for Seattle has crashed into a field, killing everyone on board and, according to the airline, Will was one of the passengers. . . . Why did Will lie about where he was going? And what else has he lied about?" (Publisher's note)

"With plot twists around every corner, Belle isn't afraid to keep her readers guessing until the very last page of this heart-pounding story of one woman's desperate search for answers." Booklist

Bellow, Saul

★ The **adventures** of Augie March; with an introduction by Martin Amis. Knopf 1995 xxxvii, 616p

ISBN 0-679-44460-2

A reissue of the title first published 1953 by Viking

"It is a picaresque story of a poor Jewish youth from Chicago, his progress, sometimes highly comic, through the world of the 20th century, and his attempts to make sense of it." Merriam-Webster's Ency of Lit

Bellow, Saul

★ **Henderson** the rain king; a novel. Viking 1959 341p

This novel, "designed on a grand and mythic scale, records American millionaire Gene Henderson's quest for revelation and spiritual power in Africa, where he becomes rainmaker and heir to a kingdom." Oxford Companion to Engl Lit

Bellow, Saul

★ **Humboldt's** gift. Viking 1975 487p

ISBN 0-670-38655-3

"The story of Charlie Citrine, a successful writer and academic plagued by women, lawsuits, and mafiosi, whose present career is interwoven with memories of the early success, failing powers, and squalid death of his friend Von Humboldt Fleischer, whose poetic destiny he fears he may inherit, together with his manuscripts." Oxford Companion to Engl Lit

Bellow, Saul

Mr. Sammler's planet. Viking 1970 313p

ISBN 0-670-33319-0

"Artur Sammler, in his seventies and an escapee from the horrors of Nazi atrocities and the memory of having had to dig himself out of his own grave, theorizes about the possibility of finding a similar escape from the assaults of life in New York City, its muggings, crime, dirt, noise. Living with his bizarre daughter, Shula, also saved from death in Europe but somewhat deranged, perhaps the result of traumas suffered, is not possible, and living with his niece Margotte also has its drawbacks. The most important person to Sammler is his nephew Elya, by whose generosity Sammler and Shula are able to exist. But Elya's escape from the horrors of his own life—his son Wallace's irresponsible behavior and his daughter Angela's sexually promiscuous behavior—is by way of death. For our desire to find relief from the outrages of life in this decade, Bellow has made a metaphor of man's desire to go to the moon." Shapiro. Fic for Youth. 3d edition

Bellow, Saul

Novels, 1944-1953. Library of America 2003 1029p $35

ISBN 1-931082-38-3

LC 2003-40144

Dangling man and The adventures of Augie March are entered separately. The victim (1947) tells the story of Asa Leventhal, who once held a position on a New York trade journal, and had won a certain security, but a few sultry weeks while his wife was away almost wrecked him. The remembrance of his insane mother, and the constant harrying of a Gentile friend, who insisted that Asa had ruined his career, brings him to the verge of insanity.

Bellow, Saul

Novels, 1970-1982. Library of America 2010 1064p $40

ISBN 978-1-59853-079-7; 1-59853-0798

LC 2010-924272

"In Mr. Sammler's Planet, the anarchic forces of late-1960s America are set loose on Artur Sammler. . . . A Holocaust survivor living out his latter days in Manhattan, Sammler endures the city's everyday barbarism, as shocking as it is casual, and must contend with absurd complications when a manuscript goes missing. . . . Humboldt's Gift depicts the deep and troubled friendship between the tormented poet Von Humboldt Fleisher and the renowned writer Charlie Citrine. . . . In The dean's December, Albert Corde experiences totalitarianism firsthand when he travels to Bucharest to visit his dying mother-in-law. As a college dean in Chicago he has attracted controversy through his journalism and his role in a racially charged murder trial. Alternating between Romanian and American settings, the novel is . . . [an] indictment of official hypocrisy and corruption on both sides of the Iron Curtain." Publisher's note

Bellow, Saul

Seize the day; with three short stories and a one-act play. Viking 1956 211p

"Seize the Day gives contemporary literature a story which will be explained, expounded, and argued, but about which a final reckoning can be made only after it ripples out in the imagination of the generations of readers to come. I suspect that it is one of the central stories of our day." Nation

Benaron, Naomi

★ **Running** the rift; Naomi Benaron. Algonquin Books of Chapel Hill 2012 365p.

ISBN 9781616200428; 1616200421

LC 2011026349

Bellwether Prize for Fiction (2010)

This book, the winner of the 2010 Bellwether Prize, tells the story of "Jean Patrick Nkuba, a gifted Rwandan boy. . . . Born a Tutsi, he is thrust into a world where it's impossible to stay apolitical—where the man who used to sell you gifts for your family now spews hatred . . . where your Hutu coach is secretly training the very soldiers who will hunt down your family. Yet in an environment increasingly restrictive for the Tutsi, he holds fast to his dream of becoming Rwanda's first Olympic medal contender in track, a feat he believes might deliver him and his people from this violence. When the killing begins, Jean Patrick is forced to flee, leaving behind the woman, the family, and the country he loves. Finding them again is the race of his life." (Publisher's note)

Includes bibliographical references (p. 364-365).

Benchley, Peter

Jaws. Random House 2005 311p $15.95

ISBN 1-4000-6456-2

LC 2005-46451

First published 1974

This is a "story about what happens when a great white shark terrorizes a small Long Island town. . . . A woman swimmer is devoured by the shark, and Police Chief Martin Brody insists on closing the beaches. But he's overruled by the town fathers who remind him that the community is dependent on summer visitors for economic survival. Two deaths later, the news can no longer be suppressed and Brody, an oceanographer and a fisherman go after the monster in an exciting chase." Publ Wkly

Bender, Aimee

The **particular** sadness of lemon cake; a novel Aimee Bender. 1st ed. Doubleday 2010 292 p. $25.95

ISBN 0385501129; 9780385501125

LC 2009032541

Alex Award (2011)

This book follows "young, needy Rose Edelstein, who can literally taste the emotions of whoever prepares her food, giving her unwanted insight into other people's secret emotional lives--including her mother's, whose lemon cake betrays a deep dissatisfaction." (Publishers Weekly) "When her mother begins an affair, Rose can taste that, too. Her brilliant older brother, Joseph, seems to have some type of autism spectrum disorder, though it is never named. Rose grows up and manages what she now considers her food skill, discerning not only the city of production but also the personality and temperament of the growers and pickers. She also draws closer to her father, finally understanding his prepossessions." (Library Journal)

"Nine-year-old Rose Edelstein bids adieu to normality after taking a bite of her mother's lemon cake. Immediately, she is overwhelmed by the emptiness of her mother's life. All food has this effect on her. She can taste emotions, particularly those that are hidden or repressed. . . . While the time period is never specified—the book appears to open in the 1970s—the setting is forever-sunny Los Angeles. Until the emergence of her super sense, Rose had been the unexceptional child of a supposedly unexceptional nuclear family. As we follow her into maturity, however, she discovers she has more in common with her father and her brother Joseph than previously thought. Each of them possesses a special ability as well." Miami Herald

Bender, Karen E.

Refund; stories. Karen Bender. Counterpoint Press 2015 256 p. (hardcover) $25

ISBN 1619024551; 9781619024557

LC 2014034079

National Book Award Finalist: Fiction (2015)

In this short story collection, author Karen E. Bender "creates an award-winning collection of stories that deeply explore the ways in which money and the estimation of value affect the lives of her characters. The stories in 'Refund' reflect our contemporary world--swindlers, reality show creators, desperate artists, siblings, parents--who try to answer the question: What is the real definition of worth?" (Publisher's note)

"Although her tone can veer toward bitterness, Bender excels at characters on the edge of despair, particularly mothers who resent the children they love." Kirkus

Benet, Stephen Vincent, 1898-1943

The **Devil** and Daniel Webster; illustrated by Harold Denison. Farrar & Rinehart 1937 61 p. ill.

ISBN 9780848807894; 9780895987020

"Jabez Stone, a New Hampshire farmer, receives a decade of material wealth in return for selling his soul to the Devil—Mr. Scratch. When the Devil comes to claim Stone's soul, the farmer has the statesman and orator Daniel Webster argue his case at midnight before a jury of historic American villains." Merriam-Webster's Ency of Lit

Benford, Gregory

Foundation's fear. HarperPrism 1997 425p (Second Foundation trilogy)

ISBN 0-06-105243-4

LC 96-45296

"Mr. Benford picks up the story as Seldon is about to become First Minister to Emperor Cleon I, who rules the 25 million inhabited planets of the galaxy from the imperial capital of Trantor. I have no idea whether anyone unfamiliar with the original Foundation series—which spells out what happened to Seldon and his predictions—will be able to make sense of 'Foundation's Fear.' But for the legions of readers who have long been tantalized by Asimov's cryptic references to psychohistory, Mr. Benford provides some fascinating insights into its development." N Y Times Book Rev

Followed by Foundation and chaos, by Greg Bear

Benford, Gregory

★ **Timescape**. Simon & Schuster 1980 412p

ISBN 0-671-25327-1

"As the world lurches toward disaster, scientists in 1998 try to transmit a warning message to 1962 by means of tachyons. Their story is told in parallel with that of the scientists trying to decode the transmission, and the two plots converge on the possibility of paradox. Unusual for the realism of its depiction of scientists at work; admirably serious in handling the implications of its theme." Anatomy of Wonder 4

Benioff, David

City of thieves; a novel. Viking 2008 258p $24.95

ISBN 978-0-670-01870-3; 0-670-01870-8

LC 2007-42784

In this novel, a writer depicts his grandfather's experiences during the siege of Leningrad. "Having elected to stay in Leningrad during the siege, 17-year-old Lev Beniov is caught looting a German paratrooper's corpse. The penalty for this infraction (and many others) is execution. But when Colonel Grechko confronts Lev and Kolya, a Russian army deserter also facing execution, he spares them on the condition that they acquire a dozen eggs for the colonel's daughter's wedding cake. Their mission exposes them to the most ghoulish acts of the starved populace and takes them behind enemy lines to the Russian countryside. There, Lev and Kolya take on an even more daring objective: to kill the commander of the local occupying German forces." Publ Wkly

Benjamin, Chloe

The **immortalists;** a novel. Chloe Benjamin. G. P. Putnam's Sons 2018 346 p. (hardcover) $26

ISBN 0735213186; 9780735213180; 9780735213197

LC 2016053641

In this novel, by Chloe Benjamin, "it's 1969 . . . and word has spread of the arrival of a . . . traveling psychic who claims to be able to tell anyone the day they will die. The Gold children . . . sneak out to hear their fortunes. The prophecies inform their next five decades. Goldenboy Simon escapes to the West Coast, searching for love . . . and bookish Varya throws herself into longevity research, where she tests the boundary between science and immortality." (Publisher's note)

"Benjamin has created mesmerizing characters and richly suspenseful predicaments in this profound and glimmering novel of death's ever-shocking inevitability and life's wondrously persistent whirl of chance and destiny." Booklist

Benjamin, Melanie

Alice I have been. Delacorte Press 2010 351p il $25

ISBN 978-0-385-34413-5; 0-385-34413-9

LC 2009-35353

A "fictionalized autobiography of Alice Liddell Hargreaves, the real-life inspiration for one of the most beloved characters in children's literature. . . . When we first meet 7-year-old Alice Liddell circa 1859, in the novel's first and best section, she is just a charmingly ordinary little girl: the sprightly, strong-willed fourth child of an Oxford dean who befriends a stuttering math tutor named Charles Dodgson (the Carroll pen name came later). Through their unlikely companionship, Alice finds relief from the often stultifying confines of Victorian girlhood, quickly becoming a favorite subject for both his amateur photography and the tall tales he concocts to entertain her and her sisters. . . . By the time Alice I Have Been leaps forward to Alice's early 20s and her star-crossed affair with a sickly young prince, however, the consequences of a lurid, long-ago incident between the author and his young muse have cast an enduring pall over both their lives." Entertainment Wkly

Benjamin, Melanie

★ The **aviator's** wife; a novel. Melanie Benjamin. 1st ed. Delacorte Press 2013 416 p. (hardcover) $26.00; (ebook) $26

ISBN 0345528670; 9780345528674; 9780345534699

LC 2012017014

This biographical novel, by Melanie Benjamin, follows Anne Morrow, wife of aviator Charles Lindbergh. "Anne Morrow, the shy daughter of [a] U.S. ambassador, . . . meets Colonel Charles Lindbergh, fresh off his celebrated 1927 solo flight across the Atlantic. . . . The two marry in a headline-making wedding. Hounded by adoring crowds and . . . an insatiable press, Charles shields himself and his new bride from prying eyes, leaving Anne to feel her life falling back into the shadows." (Publisher's note)

Benn, James R.

Billy Boyle; a World War II mystery. Soho Press 2006 284p $23

ISBN 1-569474-33-8

LC 2006-42300

"Benn provides historically accurate background and appealing characters, spices the narrative with romance and emotion, and ruminates about the consequences of actions, all in a suitably straightforward prose style. A solid addition to mystery collections." Libr J

Other titles in this series are:
The first wave (2007)
Blood alone (2008)
Evil for evil (2009)
Rag and bone (2010)
A mortal terror (2011)
Death's door (2012)
A blind goddess (2013)
The rest is silence (2014)
The white ghost (2015)
Blue Madonna (2016)
The devouring (2017)

Bennett, Alan, 1934-

Smut; stories. Alan Bennett. 1st U.S. ed. Picador 2012 152 p. (paperback) $14.00; (downloadable audio) $29.95

ISBN 1250003164; 9781250003164; 9780792785217 unabridged

LC 2011035090

Author Alan Bennett's "book consists of two stories, 'The Greening of Mrs. Donaldson' and 'The Shielding of Mrs. Forbes.' In the first, widowed, cash-strapped 55-year-old Mrs. Donaldson rents out a bedroom in her home to a young couple . . . [and takes] a job at the hospital. . . . In Bennett's next tale, Betty is smitten with [her gay] fiancé Graham Forbes. . . . But Graham, who'd married for money, in time startles himself by actually liking Betty. . . . Eventually, Graham's secret comes out--as do others, [and] the Betty/Graham union continues." (Kirkus Reviews)

Bennett, Brit

The **mothers**; a novel. Brit Bennett. Riverhead Books 2016 288 p. (hardback) $26; (ebook) $76

ISBN 0399184511; 9780399184512; 9780735288287

LC 2016010837

In this novel, by Brit Bennett, "it is the last season of high school life for Nadia Turner, a rebellious, grief-stricken, seventeen-year-old beauty. Mourning her own mother's recent suicide, she takes up with the local pastor's son. Luke Sheppard is twenty-one, a former football star whose injury has reduced him to waiting tables at a diner. They are young; it's not serious. But the pregnancy that results from this teen romance . . . will have an impact that goes far beyond their youth." (Publisher's note)

"Chapel provides further context and an extra layer to an already exquisitely developed story." Pub Wkly

Bennett, Jenn

Bitter Spirits; by Jenn Bennett. Berkley Pub Group 2014 336 p. (Roaring Twenties) (pbk) $7.99

ISBN 0425269574; 9780425269572

LC 2014656623

"Aida Palmer performs a spirit medium show onstage at Chinatown's illustrious Gris-Gris speakeasy. Winter Magnusson is a notorious bootlegger [and] the recent target of a malevolent hex that renders him a magnet for hauntings. After Aida's supernatural assistance is enlisted to banish the ghosts [they] hunt for the curseworker responsible for the hex . . . and the closer they become." (Publisher's note)

"The details of the Prohibition era are well researched but not intrusive, providing a solid and tangible backdrop for the developing romance and supernatural mystery." Pub Wkly

Bennett, Robert Jackson

American elsewhere; Robert Jackson Bennett. Orbit 2012 688 p. $13.99

ISBN 0316200204; 9780316200202

LC 2012016166

In this book by Robert Jackson Bennett, "Mona Bright, a former cop with a tragic past, inherits her long-dead mother's house in Wink, N. Mex., a picture-perfect hamlet built as a support community for a government lab conducting experiments in quantum physics. As Mona pieces together a history that bears no resemblance to the childhood she remembers, Bennett's . . . narrative unveils a chronicle of dysfunction masked by Wink's mechanical obsession with normalcy." (Publishers Weekly)

Bennett, Robert Jackson

City of blades; Robert Jackson Bennett. Broadway Books 2016 496 p. (The Divine Cities) $15

ISBN 0553419714; 9780553419719

LC 2015020205

Sequel to: City of stairs

In this book, by Robert Jackson Bennett, "the city of Voortyashtan was the stronghold of the god of war and death. . . . Now, the city's god is dead. The city itself lies in ruins. And to its new military occupiers, the once-powerful capital is a wasteland of sectarian violence and bloody uprisings. So it makes perfect sense that General Turyin Mulaghesh . . . has been exiled there to count down the days until she can draw her pension and be forgotten." (Publisher's note)

"Bennett continues his theme of the influence of imperialism on what appears to be a very similar world to ours (albeit one in which gods helped shape the geopolitics), seamlessly melding spycraft and mythology. Turyin, a physically and emotionally wounded warrior who both loathes battle and excels at it, serves as a fascinating character to shoulder the book's heavy burden of tragedy." Pub Wkly

Bennett, Robert Jackson

City of stairs; a novel. Robert Jackson Bennett. 1st ed Broadway Books 2014 448 p. $15

ISBN 080413717X; 9780804137171

LC 2013040422

In this novel by Robert Jackson Bennett "the city of Bulikov . . . has become just another colonial outpost of the world's new geopolitical power. Into this broken city steps Shara Thivani. Unofficially, she is one of her country's most accomplished spies, dispatched to catch a murderer. As Shara pursues the killer, she starts to suspect that the beings who ruled this terrible place may not be as dead as they seem. (Publisher's note)

"The world Bennett . . . has constructed is a complex political landscape of a subjugated people holding onto the memories of their glory days and protective gods and the conquerors reaping revenge for their own previous subjugation. An excellent spy story wrapped in a vivid imaginary world." LJ

Other titles in this series are:
City of blades (2016)
City of miracles (2017)

Bennett, Robert Jackson

The **company** man; Robert Jackson Bennett. 1st ed.; Orbit 2010 466p.

ISBN 9780316054706 pa; 0316054704

LC 2010011247

This book, "an alternate history novel," is set in a reality where "by 1919 . . . 50 years of mind-boggling technological innovations flowing from quiet Lawrence Kulahee have changed the face of the world. After a chance meeting with Kulahee, ruthless entrepreneur William McNaughton realizes the economic potential of the unassuming genius. In short order, the skies are full of airships, the roads with automobiles, and the U.S. becomes the most powerful nation on Earth. . . . Disparities in wealth have produced a society that seems headed towards social collapse. Unrest has spurred the formation of a labor-union movement, many of whose members and organizers are dropping like flies, killed in inexplicable circumstances. . . . Enter quasi-policeman Hayes to sort things out. He's a highly troubled man but also seems to have psychic gifts rivaling in scale the intellectual gifts of Kulahee." (Booklist)

Bennett, Robert Jackson

The **troupe**; Robert Jackson Bennett. Orbit 2012 505 p.

ISBN 9780316187527

LC 2011018068

The author "melds an energetic reimagining of medieval myth with [a] . . . backdrop of impresarios, puppeteers, and amazing feats of strength in this tale of turn-of-the-century vaudevillians. The performances of Hieronomo 'Harry' Silenus's quartet leave audiences dazzled yet unable to remember what they have seen. Teen piano prodigy George Carole, believing that Harry is his father, joins the quartet and learns their actual mission: to sing the song of creation that keeps the world alive and safe. As darkness closes in, the exhausted and increasingly fractious performers gamble everything for one more bit of the song." (Publishers Wkly)

Bennett, Vanora

The **queen's** lover. William Morrow 2010 578p $25.99

ISBN 978-0-06-168986-4; 0-06-168986-6

The "tale of young Catherine de Valois, the fifteenth-century French princess sacrificed on the altar of national honor and political expediency. Hastily married off to King Henry V of England as a battle prize, she must learn to navigate the intricacies and intrigues of the English royal court after Henry's untimely death. Luckily, she has Owain Tudor, the Welsh-born controller of her household, to assist her in doing so. Especially unique and compelling is the story of Catherine's friendship with feminist poet Christine de Pizan. Historical fiction with enough heft to satisfy discriminating fans." Booklist

Berg, Elizabeth

Once upon a time, there was you; a novel. Random House 2011 280p $26

ISBN 978-1-4000-6865-4; 1-4000-6865-7

LC 2010-49690

"In St. Paul, Minn. John — a phlegmatic architect — is just beginning to date again. One day he gets a call from his ex-wife, Irene, in San Francisco, worried that their 18-year-old daughter Sadie has not come back from a weekend away with friends and does not answer her cell phone. Sadie, feeling smothered by her high-strung, controlling mother, had actually been on her way to a tryst with her new boyfriend but, frustrated by his tardiness, had accepted a ride from a stranger who turns out to be the archetypal villain of a horror story. As often happens in a Berg novel, the plot seems momentarily derailed into stereotype at this point. But, once again, Berg manages to restrain the melodrama through a lucky coincidence. . . . Berg's psychological wisdom about love, family, and aging always make her well-paced novels a good read." Providence J

Berg, Elizabeth, 1948-

★ **Tapestry** of fortunes; a novel. Elizabeth Berg. Random House 2013 240 p. (hardback) $26

ISBN 0812993144; 9780679644699; 9780812993141

LC 2012033033

In this novel, by Elizabeth Berg, "four women venture into their pasts in order to shape their futures. . . . Cecilia Ross . . . moves into a[n] . . old house in Saint Paul, . . . with . . . three housemates: Lise, the home's owner . . . ; Joni, a top-notch sous chef . . . ; and Renie, the . . . most mercurial of the group, who is trying to rectify a teenage mistake. These women embark on a journey together in an attempt to connect with parts of themselves long denied." (Publisher's note)

Berg, Elizabeth

We are all welcome here; a novel. Random 2006 187p hardcover o.p. pa $15

ISBN 1-4000-6161-X; 0-8129-7100-0 pa

LC 2005-48956

"Full of humor, devoid of self-pity, with lively characters that rise above their circumstances, this is the story of an adolescent accepting adult responsibilities, encountering the temptations of boys and booze, and experiencing the tensions between race and class in the 1960s." SLJ

Berg, Elizabeth

★ **What** we keep; a novel. Random House 1998 272p

ISBN 0-375-50099-5

LC 97-42070

As the novel "opens, Ginny is flying to California to join her sister in a meeting with their mother, whom neither daughter has seen for 35 years. Ginny uses her travel time to reflect upon her memories of the summer when her mother withdrew from the family and became an outsider in her daughters' lives. Berg's precise, evocative descriptions create vivid images of Ginny's physical world, while Berg's understanding and perception are an eloquent testimony to Ginny's emotional turmoil." Libr J

Berger, Thomas

Arthur Rex. Delacorte Press/Seymour Lawrence 1978 499p

ISBN 0-440-00362-8

LC 78-7241

This is a "splendid, satiric retelling of the legend of Camelot. . . . The curious truth is that Mr. Berger's revisions are most authentic, most profound, when the admixture of parody is strongest. At those times—a good three-fourths of the book—he is never merely a parodist after all, but also a compelling yarnspinner in his own right." N Y Times Book Rev

Berger, Thomas

★ **Being** invisible; a novel. Little, Brown 1987 262p

ISBN 0-316-09158-8

LC 86-20897

"There is much in 'Being Invisible' to celebrate—the pleasures of invention, humor, surprise, of Mr. Berger's enraged, unforgiving view. That so much of his vision seems neither freakish nor admonitory but rather, oddly tonic, says something about the era in which we live. . . . It is a sign of the times that we feel such affection for Thomas Berger's dogged, cranky courage, and for the denizens of his unwelcoming and chaotic corner of the fictional world." N Y Times Book Rev

Berger, Thomas

★ **Little** Big Man. Dial Press (NY) 1979 xxii, 440p

"The author purports to write the story of Jack Crabb, adopted Cheyenne, gunfighter, buffalo hunter, and survivor of Custer's last stand, whom he has located at the Marville Center for Senior Citizens. In the few months before his death at the self-professed age of 111, Crabb recounts his version of life in the Old West." Shapiro. Fic for Youth. 3d edition

Followed by The return of Little Big Man (1999)

Berger, Thomas

★ **Neighbors**. Delacorte Press/Seymour Lawrence 1980 275p

ISBN 0-440-06556-9

LC 79-20307

Berger "quickly conditions the reader to expect the unexpected but manages to be consistently surprising nevertheless, introducing new twists and outrages that not even the most warped spectator could have foreseen. The novel adopts a formal, almost fussy style to convey lunacy, as if Berger were describing low deeds to a maiden aunt. . . . {The book} is not at all interested in being socially redeeming, and those who read books to gain warm feelings or philosophic nuggets will come away from this one empty-handed and probably angry. . . .What Berger has produced is a tour de force." Time

Bergman, Megan Mayhew

Almost Famous Women; Stories. Megan Mayhew Bergman. Simon & Schuster 2015 256 p. illustrations $25

ISBN 1476786569; 9781476786568

LC 2015295882

This short story collection, by Megan Mayhew Bergman, profiles "heroines, born in proximity to the spotlight, struggle to distinguish themselves: Lord Byron's illegitimate daughter, Allegra; Oscar Wilde's wild niece, Dolly; Edna St. Vincent Millay's talented sister, Norma; James Joyce's daughter, Lucia." (Publisher's note)

"The author has infused her characters with passion and yearning; they are so lifelike we feel we know them... Writing with brilliant cadence and economy, Bergman is an impressionist who uses her brilliant palette to illuminate facets of the lives of these brave and creative lesser-known strivers." LJ

Bergman, Megan Mayhew

Birds of a lesser paradise; stories. Megan Mayhew Bergman. Scribner 2012 224 p.

ISBN 9781451643350; 9781451643367; 9781451643374

LC 2011019400

This book features a "collection of [short] stories, most of them revolving around motherhood, animals and conflicting loyalties. . . . [In] "Housewifely Arts," a single mom drives her 7-year-old son nine hours south to a roadside zoo near Myrtle Beach in hopes of hearing one last time her mother's voice . . . or rather the perfect mimicry of that voice by the 36-year-old African gray parrot. . . . In "The Cow That Milked Herself," a young mother-to-be gets an ultrasound in the office of her husband, a loving but distracted and harried veterinarian. . . . In "Every Vein a Tooth," a woman who shelters refugee animals . . . watches helplessly as her boyfriend . . . drifts away. . . . The woman's response is . . . to carry on as she always has, no matter the human consequences." (Kirkus)

Berlin, Lucia, 1936-2004

★ A **manual** for cleaning women; selected stories. Lucia Berlin ; edited by Stephen Emerson. Farrar, Straus & Giroux 2015 432 p. (hardcover) $26

ISBN 0374202397; 9780374202392; 9780374712860

LC 2014047119

Kirkus Prize Finalist: Fiction (2015)

This book, by Lucia Berlin, is a "posthumous collection of stories, almost uniformly narrated by hard-living women. . . . The title story, for instance, balances wry commentary about housecleaning work. . . . 'Tiger Bites' [is] narrated by an El Paso woman who heads to Juarez for an illegal abortion. . . . And 'Mijito' . . . exposes how an immigrant woman's best intentions to care for her ailing son are easily derailed by circumstance and obligation." (Kirkus Reviews)

"As characters recur and settings and predicaments vary, Berlin unflinchingly strips bare casual and catastrophic cruelty and injustice. . . . An essential collection of jazzy, jolting, incisive, wryly funny, and keenly compassionate, virtuoso tales." Booklist

Berney, Lou

The **Long** and Faraway Gone; A Novel. by Lou Berney. HarperCollins 2015 464 p. $14.99

ISBN 0062292439; 9780062292438

LC 2015296629

This novel, by Lou Berney, is a "crime story that explores the mysteries of memory and the impact of violence on survivors. . . . In the summer of 1986, two tragedies rocked Oklahoma City. Six movie-theater employees were killed in an armed robbery, while one inexplicably survived. Then, a teenage girl vanished from the annual State Fair. Neither crime was ever solved. Twenty-five years later, the reverberations of those unsolved cases quietly echo through survivors' lives." (Publisher's note)

"Berney's first two novels (Gutshot Straight, 2011; Whiplash River, 2012) were delightful, Elmore Leonard-style crime novels. This time he's focused, very insightfully, on love, loss, and memory, and he astutely portrays the immediate and long-term psychological impact of the loss of the most important people in his characters' young lives. Wyatt, Juli, Genevieve, and Wyatt's dead coworkers are all fully realized creations that readers won't soon forget. A genuinely memorable novel of ideas." Booklist

Bernhard, Thomas

★ The **loser**; translated from the German by Jack Dawson; afterword by Mark M. Anderson. Knopf 1991 189p

ISBN 0-394-57239-4

LC 90-45942

Original German edition, 1983

"Dawson's translation is superb. . . . The Loser is undoubtedly one of the most fascinating works of contemporary Austrian literature, and given its extraordinary meditations on art, the artist, and the reception of the creative process, it is a work that should find international readership." American Book Rev

Bernhard, Thomas

★ **Woodcutters**; translated from the German by David McLintock. Knopf 1987 181p

ISBN 0-394-55152-4

LC 87-45123

Original German edition, 1984

"Mr. Bernhard's portrait of a society in dissolution has a Scandinavian darkness reminiscent of Ibsen and Strindberg, but it is filtered through a minimalist prose of obsessive repetition and ever so slight modulations." N Y Times Book Rev

Berry, Steve

The **Charlemagne** pursuit; a novel. Ballantine Books 2008 509p il $26

ISBN 978-0-345-48579-3; 0-345-48579-3

LC 2008-28357

"Using his connections in the federal government, Cotton [Malone] asks to see a classified file that details the mission that resulted in his father's death. He knew his father died on a submarine but none of the shocking details about where or why he died. But Cotton is not the only person who wants this file, and they kill to get it. Nazi missions to the Antarctic, ancient societies, and a valuable artifact from Charlemagne's tomb all play key roles as Malone uncovers the truth. So much is going on that there is enough material for two good books, let alone one great one." Libr J

Berry, Steve

The **lost** order; Steve Berry. Minotaur Books 2017 x, 493 p.p illustrations (hardback) $28.99

ISBN 9781250056252; 9781466862623

LC 2016050194

In this novel, by Steve Berry, "the Knights of the Golden Circle was the largest and most dangerous clandestine organization in American history. It amassed billions in stolen gold and silver, all buried in hidden caches across the United States. . . . Now, one hundred and sixty years later, two factions of what remains of the Knights of the Golden Circle want that lost treasure--one to spend it for their own ends, the other to preserve it." (Publisher's note)

"The fusion of contemporary and historical adventure makes this a page-turner of the highest order." Pub Wkly

Berry, Wendell

Jayber Crow; a novel. Counterpoint 2000 363p

ISBN 1-58243-029-2

LC 00-35889

"Orphaned at 4 by the flu epidemic of 1918, and again at 10, when age claims the elderly relatives who took him in, Jonah 'Jayber' Crow finds a valued place as a humble barber in a Kentucky river township. He finds love, too, though he never speaks of it." Booklist

Berry, Wendell

★ **That** distant land; the collected stories of Wendell Berry. Shoemaker & Hoard 2004 440p $26

ISBN 1-593-76027-2

LC 2003-25213

"Set in a small Kentucky farming village, this collection of Berry's Port William stories illuminates the evolution of rural American life over the course of the 20th century. In 23 stories, Berry chronicles Port William from the 1880s to the 1980s, evoking the connectedness of the small town's denizens to each other and to the land." Publ Wkly

The Best American mystery stories of the century; Tony Hillerman, editor; Otto Penzler, series editor; with an introduction by Tony Hillerman. Houghton Mifflin 2000 813p hardcover o.p. pa $17.95

ISBN 0-618-01267-2; 0-618-01271-0 pa

"This anthology is a cornerstone volume for any mystery library." Publ Wkly

Best American mystery stories [date] Otto Penzler, series editor. Houghton Mifflin

Annual. First published 1997. Editors vary

An annual volume of mystery stories culled from a variety of magazines, collections, and anthologies. Loren D. Estleman, Lawrence Block, Michael Connelly, Joyce Carol Oates, Bill Pronzini, Hannah Tinti, James Lee Burke, and Holly Goddard Jones are among the authors represented

★ **The best American noir of the century**; edited by James Ellroy & Otto Penzler; with an introduction by James Ellroy. Houghton Mifflin Harcourt 2010 731p $30

ISBN 978-0-547-33077-8

LC 2010-17204

This anthology "features noir of the literary kind. For those of you for whom the shot glass is always half empty and the forecast is always grim, you can't do much better this sterling collection of 39 tales from the darkness at the edge of town, full of characters doomed to bad choices and worse luck. You can gripe about the editors' definition of noir or some of their omissions, but they've done a great job here, offering lesser known tales by such expected perpetrators as Cornell Woolrich, Jim Thompson, James M. Cain, Mickey Spillane, Evan Hunter and Patricia Highsmith as well as a few outliers, such as Dorothy B. Hughes, David 'Rambo' Morrell and Lorenzo 'Sleepers' Carcaterra and a few authors even the most devoted noir devotee may not be familiar with. Tod Robbins, anyone?" Mystery Scene

The Best American short stories; selected from U.S. and Canadian magazines. Houghton Mifflin

This annual series began in 1915 under the editorship of Edward J. O'Brien with title: Best short stories. Editors vary

An annual anthology of stories by American and Canadian writers culled from a variety of magazines. Authors represented include: Raymond Carver, Alice Munro, Tobias Wolff, John Updike, Rick Bass, and Jamaica Kincaid

The Best from Fantasy & Science Fiction; 1st-20th, 22nd-24th series. Doubleday 1952 23v

24th series published by Scribner. No volume bearing 21st series designation published; Special 25th anniversary volume published instead

Collection culled from a journal, founded in 1949, that "continues to publish an unusual number of first stories and award winners, to discover new, literary writers, to maintain a circulation of about half to two-thirds that of the most popular magazines, and to remain the most consistently reliable magazine in the field." New Ency of Sci Fic

The Best from fantasy & science fiction: the fiftieth anniversary anthology; edited by Edward L. Ferman and Gordon Van Gelder. Doherty Assocs. 1999 381p $24.95

ISBN 0-312-86973-8

LC 99-40560

"This anthology includes 22 stories published . . . between 1993 and 1998. . . . Their authors include such luminaries as Ursula Le Guin, Gene Wolfe, and Ray Bradbury, and the distinguished if less conspicuous likes of Paul Di Filippo, Terry Bisson, and Esther Friesner." Booklist

Betts, Doris

★ **Souls** raised from the dead; a novel. Knopf 1994 339p

ISBN 0-679-42621-3

LC 93-30900

"Mary's life and death are superbly and unsentimentally accomplished. . . . Yet none of this should sound grim, only appropriately sad, because Ms. Betts seems to be possessed of high spirits and a generous wisdom. And that is what buoys up her characters and makes a lot of the proceedings very funny even as her people struggle with their anger and bewilderment." N Y Times Book Rev

Beukes, Lauren

★ **Broken** monsters; A Novel. Lauren Beukes. Mulholland Books / Little, Brown and Co. 2014 448 p. (hardcover) $26

ISBN 0316216828; 9780316216821

LC 2014937377

"Detective Gabriella Versado has seen a lot of bodies. But this one is unique even by Detroit's standards: half boy, half deer, somehow fused together. As stranger and more disturbing bodies are discovered, how can the city hold on to a reality that is already tearing at its seams?" (Publisher's note)

"Beukes avoids predictability by leading readers to doubt their interpretations of motives and events, blending detection and atmospheric horror to court both hard-boiled mystery and literary-horror fans." Booklist

Beukes, Lauren

Zoo city; Lauren Beukes. Angry Robot 2011 317 p. (pbk.) $15

ISBN 9780857662163

LC 2010475248

Arthur C. Clarke Award (2011)

This book, the winner of the 2011 Arthur C. Clarke Award, offers a "parallel world . . . [where] those who cause someone's death are both blessed and cursed with companion animals who mark them as killers while giving them special powers. In a run-down slum in Johannesburg, journalist and former addict Zinzi December uses the power provided by her Sloth to find lost objects, supplementing her meager income by running 419 scams. When a rich client is murdered, Zinzi is drawn into an investigation that involves teen pop stars, sleazy record producers, and ethics-challenged newspapermen." (Publishers Weekly)

Beverly, Bill

Dodgers; a novel. Bill Beverly. Crown Publishers 2016 304 p. $26

ISBN 1101903732; 9781101903735

LC 2015027588

This novel, by Bill Beverly, "is the story of a young LA gang member named East, who is sent by his uncle along with some other teenage boys--including East's hothead younger brother--to kill a key witness hiding out in Wisconsin. The journey takes East out of a city he's never left and into an America that is entirely alien to him, ultimately forcing him to grapple with his place in the world and decide what kind of man he wants to become." (Publisher's note)

"Highly recommended for fans of Richard Price, this is a searing novel about crime, race, and coming-of-age, with characters who live, breathe, and bleed." Booklist

Bezmozgis, David

★ The **Betrayers**; a novel. David Bezmozgis. 1st ed Little, Brown & Co. 2014 225 p. (hardcover) $26

ISBN 0316284335; 9780316284332; 9780316284356

LC 2014937342

National Jewish Book Award: Fiction (2014)

Scotiabank Giller Prize Shortlist (2014)

This book, by David Bezmozgis, focuses on "Baruch Kotler, a Soviet Jewish dissident who now finds himself a disgraced Israeli politician. When he refuses to back down from a contrary but principled stand regarding the settlements in the West Bank, his political opponents expose his affair with a mistress decades his junior, and the besieged couple escapes to Yalta, the faded Crimean resort of Kotler's youth." (Publisher's note)

"Though the action is fixed largely in one location, Bezmozgis's novel feels vast, its pages heavy with the complicated debts we owe one another, which are impossible to leave behind." Pub Wkly

Bezmozgis, David

The **free** world. Farrar, Straus & Giroux 2011 356p

ISBN 0-374-28140-8; 978-0-374-28140-3

LC 2010-33122

In this novel, after "refusing the Kremlin's order to relocate to Israel, the Jewish Krasnansky family of 1978 Russia makes their way across Italy at the sides of thousands of other immigrants." (Publisher's note)

The novel "opens on the platform of Vienna's Western Terminal, where 'the representatives of Soviet Jewry — from Tallinn to Tashkent — roiled, snarled, and elbowed to deposit their belongings onto the waiting train.' Among them are two brothers, Alec and Karl Krasnansky, their wives, children and elderly parents, all jostling west from Riga, Latvia toward Rome. The novel takes place in 1978 during the five-month interlude the family spends in Italy awaiting word on where they will go: America, Canada, Australia or Israel. The gifted Bezmozgis is interested in what must be left behind, what is and is not in the suitcases. His characters must navigate the pull of places and relationships, language and ideologies. One must weigh whether to keep or end a pregnancy. Out of the stream of the everyday, Bezmozgis brings his considerable talent for observation and humor." Cleveland Plain Dealer

Bhattacharya, Rahul

The **sly** company of people who care; Rahul Bhattacharya. 1st American ed. Farrar, Straus and Giroux 2011 278p.

ISBN 0374265852; 9780374265854; 978-0-374-26585-4; 0-374-26585-2

LC 2010047596

"The narrator of this novel journeys into Guyana's interior to seek answers about the country's past." (N Y Times Book Rev)

Bialosky, Jill

The **prize**; a novel. Jill Bialosky. Counterpoint Press 2015 349 p. (hardcover) $25

ISBN 1619025701; 9781619025707

LC 2015023052

In this book, by Jill Bialosky, "Edward Darby has . . . a rising career as a partner at an esteemed gallery. . . . Influenced by his father, a brilliant Romantics scholar, Edward has always been more of a purist. . . . But when a celebrated artist controlled by her insecurities betrays him, and another very different artist awakens his heart and stirs up secrets from his past, Edward will find himself unmoored from his marriage, his work, and the memory of his beloved father." (Publisher's note)

"This fluently sophisticated and exquisitely pleasurable novel is radiant with precise and sensuous descriptions and intricately laced with discerning and affecting insights into the passion and business of art and the meaning and struggles of marriage." Booklist

Bierce, Ambrose

★ The **complete** short stories of Ambrose Bierce; compiled with commentary by Ernest Jerome Hopkins. Doubleday 1970 496p

ISBN 9780803260719

LC 79103758

The Big book of adventure stories; edited and with a introduction by Otto Penzler; foreword by Douglas Preston. Vintage Crime/Black Lizard 2011 874p pa $25

ISBN 978-0-307-47450-6; 0-307-47450-X

LC 2011-02226

"Otto Penzler has ranged far and wide to make this anthology. (What fun he must have had!) It is divided into 11 sections: Sword & Sorcery; Megalomania Rules; Man vs. Nature; Island Paradise; Sand and Sun; Something Feels Funny; Go West, Young Man; Future Shock; I Spy; Yellow Peril; In Darkest Africa. Much of it is, as Mr. Penzler happily warns readers, politically most incorrect. Almost all the authors are more than comfortable with the idea of Anglo-Saxon superiority, and lesser breeds are treated with disdain and contempt—even when there is reason to fear their vile schemes and vindictive nature. . . . The range of stories Mr. Penzler has collected is wide, the range of talent too." Wall Street J

The big book of science fiction; edited by Ann VanderMeer and Jeff VanderMeer. Vintage Crime/Black Lizard, Vintage Books 2016 1216 p. (pbk.) $25; (ebook) $65

ISBN 9781101910092; 9781101910108

LC 2015042397

This anthology of science fiction, edited by Ann VanderMeer and Jeff VanderMeer, "showcases classic contributions from H. G. Wells, Arthur C. Clarke, Octavia E. Butler, and Kurt Vonnegut, alongside a century of the eccentrics, rebels, and visionaries who have inspired generations of readers. Within its pages, you'll find beloved worlds of space opera, hard SF, cyberpunk, the New Wave, and more." (Publisher's note)

"A necessity for those wishing to broaden their understanding of science fiction as a genre...or just those looking for some darn good stories." Kirkus

★ **The big book of Sherlock Holmes stories**; edited and with an introduction by Otto Penzler. Pantheon Books 2015 xxii, 789 p.p (hardcover) $40

ISBN 1101870893; 9781101870891

LC 2015373175

This book, edited by Otto Penzler, is "the largest collection of Sherlockian tales ever assembled. . . . Penzler collects eighty-three wonderful stories about Sherlock Holmes and Dr. John Watson, published over a span of more than a hundred years. . . . [Besides Arthur Conan Doyle's originals, stories include those] by Laurie R. King, Colin Dexter, Anthony Burgess, Anne Perry, Stephen King, P.G. Wodehouse, Kingsley Amis, and many, many more." (Publisher's note)

Penzler "has composed a short history of Holmes and also provides a brief introduction to each tale, which covers the author, the work itself, how it came to be published and why it is included. The pieces are separated into categories, which makes choosing a story more fun for the reader. For example, one can decide to read a famous O. Henry or Stephen King story, or elect to read a parody of Holmes by R.C. Leyman or by Doyle himself." LJ

Bijan, Donia

The **last** days of Café Leila; a novel. Donia Bijan. Algonquin Books of Chapel Hill 2017 292 p. (hardcover) $25.95

ISBN 9781616207120; 9781616205850

LC 2016043555

This novel, by Donia Bijan, "is a powerful story of food, family, and a bittersweet homecoming. When we first meet Noor, she is living in San Francisco, missing her beloved father, Zod, in Iran. Now, dragging her stubborn teenage daughter, Lily, with her, she returns to Tehran and to Café Leila, the restaurant her family has been running for three generations. Iran may have changed, but Café Leila, still run by Zod, has stayed blessedly the same." (Publisher's note)

"Bijan has crafted a richly layered story of the deep connections within a family, resilient links that survive tragedy and distance." Booklist

Bilenchi, Romano

★ The **chill**; translated from the Italian by Ann Goldstein. Europa 2009 99p pa $15

ISBN 978-1-933372-90-7

Original Italian edition, 1982

"Following an unnamed teenager's initiation into adulthood in Tuscany in the Fascist years, [this novelette consists of] a series of episodes of alienation, narrated in a frank, flat voice. In a sickeningly swift eighty pages, the protagonist becomes aware of the petty and vicious nature of his fellow-townspeople, of his increasing estrangement from friends and family, and of his first grotesque (if fascinating) stirrings of sexuality. Manipulated and dominated by the adults around him, he concludes that 'it wasn't possible to live among other people if all of a sudden they could attack one another with such ferocity.' Most coming-of-age novels illuminate the tumultuous inner world of adolescence; Bilenchi's reveals the brutality of the adulthood that surrounds it." New Yorker

Binchy, Maeve

★ **Circle** of friends. Delacorte Press 1991 565p

ISBN 0-385-30149-9

LC 90-3944

First published 1990 in the United Kingdom

"There is nothing fancy about 'Circle of Friends.' There is no torrid sex, no profound philosophy. There are no stunning metaphors. There is just a wonderfully absorbing story about people worth caring about. And that is a rare pleasure." N Y Times Book Rev

Binchy, Maeve

The **glass** lake. Delacorte Press 1995 584p

ISBN 0-385-31354-3

LC 94-36104

First published 1994 in the United Kingdom

This novel "focuses on the inhabitants of a small town in Ireland. Helen, wife and mother of the McMahon household, is presumed to have drowned in a nearby lake. Actually, she shook off her dull, staid life and fled to London with her lover. Successful at business, she yearns for some communication with her now teenaged daughter, Kit. She begins a casual correspondence with Kit under the guise of being an old friend of her mother." Libr J

Binchy, Maeve

★ **Silver** wedding. Delacorte Press 1989 306p

ISBN 0-385-29826-9

LC 89-1276

"An elegant literary construction, a comedy of manners as well as a soap opera. Each chapter has its own story, yet each story connects with all the others to produce a satisfying whole. Add to this a sly, understated tone and you have a book that's an effortless pleasure to read." NY Times Book Rev

Binchy, Maeve, 1940-2012

A **week** in winter; by Maeve Binchy. 1st U.S. ed. Alfred A. Knopf 2013 336 p. (hardcover) $26.95

ISBN 0307273571; 9780307273574

LC 2012039948

In this book, Stone House is a rundown house in western Ireland. "When Chicky Starr decides to buy the property and turn it into a hotel, the town thinks she's gone crazy. The project brings unexpected peace and understanding to Chicky and her staff," but the "first out-of-towners arrive with disappointment, disgrace, and doubt." Yet "all experience a catharsis on the cliffs and trails and in the gardens that can be found in the surrounding countryside." (Library Journal)

Binchy, Maeve

Whitethorn Woods. A.A. Knopf 2007 339p $25.95

ISBN 978-0-307-26578-4; 0-307-26578-1

LC 2006-48803

First published 2006 in the United Kingdom

"Story by story, voice by voice, Binchy builds the fictional community of Rossmore so that, by the end of the novel, we know Rossmore's inhabitants better than our own neighbours . . . . Few contemporary novelists match Binchy's gift for giving us the world through her characters' eyes." Toronto Globe and Mail

Binet, Laurent, 1972-

★ **HHhH**; Laurent Binet ; translated from the French by Sam Taylor. Farrar, Straus and Giroux 2012 327 p.

ISBN 0374169918; 9780374169916

LC 2011046063

In this book, which "tak[es] its title from the German for 'Himmler's brain is called Heydrich,' [author Laurent] Binet . . . tells two stories: primarily that of the daring mission to assassinate Reinhard Heydrich, the prominent Nazi Protector of Bohemia and Moravia known as . . . 'The Man with the Iron Heart.' . . . It is also, however, the metafictional tale of Binet's struggles with shaping the story." (Publishers Weekly)

Bingham, Harry

★ **Talking** to the dead; a novel. Harry Bingham. Delacorte Press 2012 337 p. $26

ISBN 0345533739; 9780345533739; 9780345533746

LC 2011041365

In this novel, by Harry Bingham, "a young woman undone by drugs and prostitution, her six-year-old daughter dead alongside her. But then detectives find . . . the platinum credit card of a very wealthy . . . steel tycoon. What is a heroin-addicted hooker doing with the credit card of a well-known . . . man who died months ago? This is the question that the most junior member of the investigative team, Detective Constable Fiona Griffiths, is assigned to answer." (Publisher's note)

Another title in this series is:

Love story, with murders (2014)

Bingham, Sallie

Mending; new and selected stories. Sarabande Books 2011 260p $23; pa $16.95

ISBN 9781936747009; 1936747006; 9781936747016 pa; 1936747014 pa

LC 2011-06208

"Spanning 50 years, this omnibus of Bingham's tight, sparkling short fiction includes stories from her earliest collection, The Touching Hand (1967), to her latest, Red Car (2008). . . . [Her work] remains sharp and deliciously unsettling, ripe for discovery by a new generation of readers." Publ Wkly

Birch, Carol

★ **Jamrach's** menagerie. Doubleday 2011 295p il $25.95
ISBN 978-0-385-53440-6; 0-385-53440-X
LC 2010-38082

"Jaffy's experience could well move the reader as profoundly as it changed the narrator." Kirkus

Bishop, Anne

Written in red; a novel of the Others. Anne Bishop. Roc 2013 448 p. (hardcover) $26.95
ISBN 0451464966; 9780451464965
LC 2012036432

In this novel, Meg Corbyn is a Cassandra sangue, a blood prophet who sees the future when her skin is cut. Along with others like her, she has lived under the tight reins of her Controllers, with no actual experiences of the real world. Knowing that eventually blood prophets lose their usefulness and, usually, their lives, Meg seeks refuge at the Lakeside Courtyard, a part of the city owned and operated by the Others—shapeshifters and other supernatural creatures." (Library Journal)

Other titles in this series are:
Murder of crows (2014)
Vision in silver (2015)
Marked in flesh (2016)
Etched in bone (2017)
Lake Silence (2018)

Bisson, Terry

Numbers don't lie; Terry Bisson. Tachyon Publications 2005 176p
ISBN 1892391325; 9781892391322

This collection of science fiction short stories is centered around "Wilson Wu. . . . No piker, Wu manages to walk, in 'one long step for mankind,' from an auto repair garage in a nondescript part of Brooklyn directly to the moon in 'The Hole in the Hole.' He even brings back half of a dune buggy left behind by astronauts and casually explains the situation as 'a periodic incongruent neotopological metaeuclidean adjacency.' In the second tale, 'The Edge of the Universe,' Wu saves the expanding universe from shrinking. Finally, he patches 'a hole in the fabric of space-time' in 'Get Me to the Church on Time.'" (Publishers Weekly)

The Black Lizard big book of Black Mask stories; edited and with a foreword by Otto Penzler; introduction by Keith Alan Deutsch. Vintage Crime/Black Lizard 2010 1116p pa $25
ISBN 978-0-307-45543-7
LC 2010-24508

"Launched by H.L. Mencken and George Jean Nathan in the 1920s, Black Mask would springboard the careers of a handful of writers, raising the level of penny dreadful pulp mysteries to that of literature, while also publishing plenty of quickly hacked-out swill. This gathers the cream produced by legends like Dashiell Hammett (the godfather of hardboiled detective fiction), Erle Stanley Gardner, Raymond Chandler, Carroll John Daly, Cornell Woolrich, and other aces. There are more than 50 stories in all, including 'The Maltese Falcon' (the original serialized version, which differs from the published novel, is reproduced here for the first time since its initial 1929 publication), Chandler's 'Try the Girl' (which, ultimately, became Farewell, My Lovely), and Horace McCoy's 'Dirty Work.' Each author receives a brief bio and the stories sport original artwork—it's a complete education on vintage crime mysteries between two covers. . . . A hefty hunk of hardboiled heaven and a noir lover's dream." Libr J

Black, Cara

Murder below Montparnasse; Cara Black. Soho Press 2013 319 p. (hardcover) $25.95
ISBN 1616952156; 9781616952150
LC 2012032374

This novel, by Cara Black, is an episode in the "Aimée Leduc Investigation" mystery series. "A long-lost Modigliani portrait, a grieving brother's blood vendetta, a Soviet secret that's been buried for 80 years--Parisian private investigator Aimée Leduc's current case is her most exciting one yet. . . . Aimée has to find the painting, stop her attackers, and figure out what her long-missing mother . . . has to do with all this." (Publisher's note)

Black, Cara, 1951-

Murder in Passy. Soho Press 2011 273p $25
ISBN 978-1-56947-882-0; 1-56947-882-1
LC 2010-34816

"Leduc is always a reliable and charming guide to the city's lesser-known corners." Seattle Times

Black, Cara

Murder in the Bastille; Cara Black. Soho Press 2003 276 p. (hardcover) $24
ISBN 1569473242; 9781569473245
LC 2002042625

In this book by Cara Black, part of the Aimée Leduc series, "after a mysterious attack leaves her blinded. . . Aimee and her partner, computer expert Ren Friant, face dual dilemmas. . . . The diminutive Ren must become the eyes of the team while Aimee makes do as best she can with her other senses. Meanwhile, with her attacker still on the loose and the police off on a wrong scent chasing a serial killer, Aimee remains a vulnerable target." (Publishers Weekly)

Black, Cara

Murder in the Marais; Cara Black. Soho Press 1999 354 p. (hardcover) $22
ISBN 1569471592; 9781569471593
LC 98052070

In this book by Cara Black, part of the Aimée Leduc series, "[p]rivate investigator Aimée Leduc . . . discovers the body of an elderly Jewish woman whose forehead has been inscribed with a swastika. With the arrival of a German trade delegation, meanwhile, the existence of a powerful covert group comprising former SS officers becomes clear. Aimée's subsequent investigation exposes the connection between a war-time romance gone wrong and the modern-day murder." (Library Journal)

Black, Cara

Murder in the rue de Paradis; Cara Black. Soho Crime 2008 305 p. map (hardcover) $24.00
ISBN 9781569474747; 1569474745
LC 2007009194

This novel, by Cara Black, is an episode in the "Aimée Leduc Investigation" mystery series. "As Aimée is about to find happiness at last, Yves, her fiancé of a single night, is killed. . . . Finding out who cut her lover's throat involves Aimée in Kurdish and Turkish politics as she tries to track down his contacts above and beneath the streets of Paris." (Publisher's note)

Black, Cara

Murder in the Sentier; Cara Black. Soho Press 2002 322 p. (hardcover) $24.00

ISBN 1569472785; 9781569472781

LC 2002017566

This book is the third in author Cara Black's Aimée Leduc series. It follows "the daughter of an American, Sydney Leduc, who disappeared when Aimee was eight years old, and a Parisian cop, Jean-Claude Leduc, . . . from whom she inherited a detective agency. . . . Aimée has always wanted to know the truth about her missing mother, so when she gets a phone call from a woman . . . claiming to have known her mother in prison she agrees to meet the mysterious caller." (Publishers Weekly)

In this mystery, sleuth Aimee Leduc scours Paris' Second Arrondissement "in pursuit of a tip to the whereabouts of her American mother, a political fugitive since the early 1970's for her anarchist activities with a group very much like the Baader-Meinhof gang. The plot that has Aimee pounding the cobblestones of this quaint quarter is a circular affair that entails much chasing after aging urban guerrillas who tend to be incoherent, hostile or dead when found. . . . But if it lacks design, the story provides a street map to this idiosyncratic area." N Y Times Book Rev

Black, Cara

Murder on the Champ de Mars; Cara Black. Soho Crime 2015 320 p. map (An Aimée Leduc investigation) (hardcover) $27.95

ISBN 1616952865; 9781616952860

LC 2014044512

In this book, by Cara Black, "Aimée Leduc has her work cut out for her—running her detective agency and fighting off sleep deprivation as she tries to be a good single mother to her new bébé. The last thing she has time for now is to take on a personal investigation for a poor manouche (Gypsy) boy. But he insists his dying mother has an important secret she needs to tell Aimée, something to do with Aimée's father's unsolved murder a decade ago. How can she say no?" (Publisher's note)

"Black once again delivers what her readers crave: high-speed Parisian peregrinations, chic suspense, a touch of humor, and the indomitable Aimée, as unstoppable with a baby strapped to her hip as she was with one growing in her belly... The popularity of Black's series, especially in libraries, has grown steadily over the years, with Aimée and company finally assuming a perch they are not likely to surrender on most bestseller lists." Booklist

Black, Elizabeth

The **drowning** house; a novel. Elizabeth Black. Nan A. Talese/Doubleday 2013 288 p. (alk. paper) $25.95

ISBN 0385535864; 9780385535861

LC 2011046222

In this novel by Elizabeth Black "photographer Clare Porterfield's once-happy marriage is coming apart, unraveling under the strain of a family tragedy. When she receives an invitation to direct an exhibition in her hometown of Galveston, Texas, she jumps at the chance to escape her grief and reconnect with the island she hasn't seen for ten years. There Clare will . . . search for answers about her troubled past and her family's complicated relationship with the wealthy and influential Carraday family." (Publisher's note)

Black, Lisa

Blunt Impact; Lisa Black. Severn House Pub Ltd 2013 224 p. (hardcover) $28.95

ISBN 072788252X; 9780727882523

This novel, by Lisa Black, is an entry in the author's "Theresa Maclean" mystery series. "Forensic scientist Theresa MacLean is puzzled by the questionable death of a female construction worker at a Cleveland building site. A witness to the death--a young girl nicknamed Ghost--may be able to help. . . . Soon Theresa finds herself in a race against time to protect Ghost from an unknown killer before he is able to find the little girl and silence her for good." (Publisher's note)

Black, Lisa

Takeover. William Morrow 2008 341p $24.95

ISBN 978-0-06-154445-3; 0-06-154445-0

LC 2007-45606

As this thriller "opens, thirty-eight year old forensic scientist Theresa MacLean is working a murder scene along with her cousin, homicide detective Frank Patrick, and his partner, Theresa's fiancé, Paul Cleary. The deceased is a middle-aged man whose head had been bashed in. His name is Mark Ludlow, and he had worked as an examiner for the Federal Reserve Bank of Cleveland. Coincidentally, two armed men later enter that same bank in an apparent robbery attempt. Since the Federal Reserve is no ordinary savings and loan, the perpetrators fail to get their hands on any ready cash. Knowing that they cannot escape without being gunned down by snipers, the two criminals, Lucas Parrish and Bobby Moyers, take hostages while they consider their options. Much to Theresa's horror, her future husband, Paul, is among the people being held captive. . . . Black skillfully creates a claustrophobic and tension-laden atmosphere." Mostly Fiction

Black, Saul

★ The **killing** lessons; A Novel. Saul Black. St. Martin's Press 2015 400 p. (hardback) $25.99

ISBN 9781250057341

LC 2015017805

In this book, by Saul Black, "two strangers turn up at Rowena Cooper's isolated Colorado farmhouse. . . . For the two haunted and driven men . . . it's just another stop on a long and bloody journey. And they still have many . . . victims to sacrifice, before their work is done. For San Francisco homicide detective Valerie Hart, their trail of victims . . . has brought her from obsession to the edge of physical and psychological destruction." (Publisher's note)

"Aficionados may fault Black for allowing the police at least one major oversight, but most readers will likely be too engrossed or happily grossed out to do anything but whip through the pages." Kirkus

Blackmore, R. D.

Lorna Doone; a romance of Exmoor. edited with an introduction and notes by Sally Shuttleworth. Oxford University Press 2009 xxix, 680p (Oxford world's classics) pa $13.95

ISBN 978-0-19-953759-4; 0-19-953759-3

First published 1869

A romantic love-story of Exmoor and the North Devon Coast of England, telling of the outlaw Doones, the maid brought up in the midst of them, and plain John Ridd's herculean power and his service to James II during Monmouth's Rebellion

"The scenic descriptions of the lovely region befits the tale, and many local worthies have their lineaments preserved here. Though 'Lorna Doone' made little stir at the time of its appearance, it has had innumerable imitations since, and it initiated a return to . . . romanticism in historical fiction." Baker. Guide to the Best Fic

Blackstock, Terri

Shadow in Serenity; Terri Blackstock. Zondervan 2011 352p.

ISBN 9780310332312; 9780310332329

This book tells the story of Carny Sullivan, who "grew up in the zany world of a traveling carnival. Quaint and peaceful Serenity, Texas, has given her a home, a life, and a child. Logan Brisco is the smoothest, slickest, handsomest man Serenity, Texas has ever seen. But Carny Sullivan knows a con artist when she sees one . . . [F]rom his Italian shoes to his movie-actor smile, Logan has the rest of the town snowed. Carny is determined to reveal Brisco's selfish intentions before his promise to the townspeople for a cut in a giant amusement park sucks Serenity dry. Yet, as much as she hates his winning ways, there is a man behind that suave smile, a man who may win her heart against her will." (Publisher's note)

Blackwood, Caroline

Never breathe a word; the collected stories of Caroline Blackwood. Counterpoint 2010 366p $26

ISBN 978-1-58243-569-5; 1-58243-569-3

LC 2009-38105

"It is clear that we read for pleasure; what is less obvious are the varieties of pleasures we experience. Pleasing isn't always pleasant. Take Caroline Blackwood's stories they are rare in their brutal exposure and are deeply troubling to read. Yet 'Never Breathe a Word' is nothing less than a marvelous slide into an emotional abyss. In Blackwood's stories, women—almost always women—have quietly slipped outside their conventional roles. . . . They inhabit danger zones of keen intelligence, amused manipulation and something else — self-indulgence, or maybe self-importance. They are sometimes funny, unwittingly revealing and rarely nice. At the core, they're out of sync with underlying societal assumptions, women who are unselfconsciously and dominantly at the center of their worlds." Los Angeles Times Book Rev

Blake, James Carlos, 1947-

The **house** of Wolfe; a border noir. James Carlos Blake. Mysterious Press 2015 288 p. (hardcover) $24

ISBN 0802122469; 9780802124746; 9780802122469

In this suspense novel, by James Carlos Blake, "on a rainy winter night in Mexico City, a ten-member wedding party is kidnapped in front of the groom's family mansion. The perpetrator is a small-time gangster . . . who wants nothing more than to make his crew part of a major cartel and hopes that this crime will be his big break." (Publisher's note)

"Blake excels at ensemble pieces and plays to his strengths here. Like a director with a small army of camera teams at his disposal, he wheels from one location to another, racking the focus with such intensity that, at any moment, the story you're in feels like the only story there is until he cuts away again. A hard-edged, fast-moving thriller that will hold your attention hostage—good luck getting away." Booklist

Blake, Robin

A **dark** anatomy; Robin Blake. Macmillan 2011 359 p. map $11.04

ISBN 023074835X; 9780230748354

LC 2011431238

In this mystery novel, "[t]he Lancashire estate of Garlick Hall is the scene of a gruesome murder and Titus Cragg, lawyer and coroner, is called upon to investigate and arrange a coroner's jury. When Dolores Brockletower, the wife of the squire, is found with her throat cut in the woods near her home, Titus calls upon his friend doctor Luke Fidelis to help investigate. . . . [W]hen the corpse is stolen . . . it is obvious someone is willing to go to great lengths to prevent an investigation." (Kirkus)

Other titles in this series are:
Dark waters (2013)
The hidden man (2015)
Skin and bone (2016)

Blake, Sarah

The **postmistress**. Amy Einhorn Books 2010 326p $25.95

ISBN 978-0-399-15619-9; 0-399-15619-9

LC 2009-24532

"Frankie Bard is an American radio gal reporting from the Blitz in London, desperate for her dawdling countrymen back home to understand the need to enter World War II. Frankie's tough and fun. She can quip and quaff as quick as any of her male colleagues. She's one of three terrifically moving women—each of whom responds in her own way to the horrors of the war—in Sarah Blake's novel. Frankie's reports of an escalating conflict, and the terrifying waves of Jews flung from their homes, hold a young bride named Emma Fitch spellbound in tiny Franklin, Mass. Emma longs for a letter from her doctor husband, who has left her behind so that he can care for London's wounded and fallen. Yet it isn't Emma who first learns of the doctor's fate—it is Iris James, the town's postmistress, who delivers, daily, the letters that change people's lives. Iris, an ungainly 40-year-old with unflattering red lipstick and a crush on the town mechanic, ultimately proves to be the heart of Blake's novel." Entertainment Wkly

Blatty, William Peter

Dimiter. Forge 2010 302p $24.99

ISBN 978-0-7653-2512-9; 0-7653-2512-8

LC 2010-13285

"In 1973 Albania, a nameless prisoner is arrested by authorities and put through horrific torture, but he refuses to reveal his name or purpose. A year later in Jerusalem, a doctor contemplates a series of seemingly mystical occurrences at his hospital, while his police-detective friend still mourns the deaths of his wife and son. All three are brought together by a mystery involving murder, international intrigue, and Christian belief. Blatty's greatest strength has also always been his most mockable weakness: his complete, unabashed sincerity. Dimiter is so unhampered by the agonies of irony and self-awareness that it's occasionally impossible to read with a straight face. . . . And yet that same unwinking intensity gives the story its power." A.V. Club

Blatty, William Peter

★ The **exorcist**. Harper & Row 1971 340p

ISBN 0-06-010365-5

"Blatty has done his homework. He discourses, a bit bookishly, on the history of possession and the relation of autosuggestion to masked guilt. . . . Blatty maintains headlong thrust, slowly increasing Regan's agony until the reader winces; no more, a part of us says, but of course we want more because Blatty handles the horror so well." Newsweek

Bledsoe, Alex

The **hum** and the shiver. Tor Books 2011 349p $15.99

ISBN 978-0-7653-2744-4

LC 2011021573

"Bledsoe turns standard urban fantasy tropes on their head by reimagining modern elves as a tiny, isolated ethnic group unsure of their own origins, like the Lemkos of Poland or the Melungeons of the southern Appalachians. The plot is a bit thin, but the slowly unfolding mystery of the Tufa is a fascinating and absorbing masterpiece of world-building." Publ Wkly

Other titles in this series are:
Wisp of a thing (2013)
Long black curl (2015)
Chapel of ease (2016)
Gather her round (2017)
The fairies of Sadieville (2018)

Bledsoe, Alex

Wisp of a thing; Alex Bledsoe. 1st ed. Tor 2013 352 p. (hardcover) $25.99

ISBN 0765334135; 9780765334138

LC 2013003720

In this novel, by Alex Bledsoe, named in "Kirkus Reviews'" Best Fiction Books of 2011, "touched by a very public tragedy, musician Rob Quillen comes to Cloud County, Tennessee, in search of a song that might ease his aching heart. All he knows of the mysterious and reclusive Tufa is what he has read on the internet: they are an enigmatic clan of swarthy, black-haired mountain people whose historical roots are lost in myth and controversy." (Publisher's note)

Block, Lawrence

All the flowers are dying. Morrow 2005 288p $24.95

ISBN 0-06-019831-1

LC 2004-53643

"Although Scudder's hunt for the killer turns into a companionable tour of colorful neighborhoods, his thoughts on the city run deep and reflect real feelings about its humanity." N Y Times Book Rev

Block, Lawrence

★ The **burglar** in the library; a Bernie Rhodenbarr mystery. Dutton 1997 342p

ISBN 0-525-94301-3

LC 96-37537

"Panting after a copy of 'The Big Sleep' inscribed by Raymond Chandler for Dashiell Hammett ('the ultimate association copy in American crime fiction'), Bernie drags Carolyn to an inn, 'a genuine English country house' in the Berkshires, so he can relieve the unsuspecting owners of this treasure. But before he can pull the heist, the inn is snowbound, the phone lines are cut, the bridge is down and Bernie's ex-girlfriend shows up with her new husband. What next? A body in the library? Yes, and, even better, the drollest sendup of a murder-in-a-teacup mystery that you will ever hope to beg, borrow—or steal." N Y Times Book Rev

Block, Lawrence

A **drop** of the hard stuff; a Matthew Scudder novel. Mulholland Books/Little, Brown and Co. 2011 319p $25.99

ISBN 978-0-316-12733-2

LC 2010-41792

"More than any of the previous entries, the mystery in A Drop of the Hard Stuff is interwoven with the 12-Step program that's such an intimate part of Scudder's life. Told in flashback, the story begins when Scudder bumps into a childhood neighbor at an AA meeting. Matt and Jack Avery were casual friends for a brief period during their youths, but as adults they drifted to opposite sides of the law – Scudder joining the police while Avery opted for a life of crime. Apart from a brief glimpse a rookie cop Scudder got of Avery in a police lineup years back, the two haven't seen each other in decades. . . . While Matt still harbors reservations about the A.A. program, Jack's on the 9th step, which requires him to make amends to the people he's harmed. It's during this process that Jack is brutally murdered. Since the cops won't spend much time searching for the murderer of a 'known criminal,' Jack's sponsor asks Matt to investigate. . . . Another solid entry in one of mystery's most reliable series." Spinetingler

Block, Lawrence

Eight million ways to die. Arbor House 1982 319p

ISBN 0-87795-405-4

LC 81-71698

This "novel is both a rousing private-eye story and an extended meditation on the whimsical ways of death—through freak accident, premeditated murder, and self-destruction. Private eye Matthew Scudder solves murders while he battles his own alcoholism. . . . In {this} tale, a 23-year old prostitute, Kim Dakkinen, wants out of 'the life' and asks Scudder to speak to her pimp, Chance. Scudder does, and a few days later Kim is found stabbed to death. Chance does the unexpected by hiring Scudder to find Kim's murderer, and while Scudder investigates, another one of Chance's prostitutes commits suicide; then another slashing occurs. A magnificently plotted, sensitive portrayal of two kinds of death—the kind that comes as an intruder and the kind that comes as an invited guest." Booklist

Block, Lawrence, 1938-

★ **Hit** me; a Keller novel. Lawrence Block. Mulholland Books 2013 352 p. $26.99

ISBN 0316127353; 9780316127356; 9780316224147

LC 2012019988

This book by Lawrence block opens with "philatelist and killer for hire John Keller . . . living in New Orleans under a new name with his wife, Julia, and their baby daughter. Despite having a legitimate job in real estate, Keller can't resist resuming his old life. . . . In inventive ways, Keller deals with a cheating wife in Dallas, a 'felonious monk' in New York City, a cruise ship in Florida with a protected witness aboard, and a wandering husband in Denver." (Publishers Weekly)

Block, Lawrence

Killing Castro. Hard Case Crime 2009 204p pa $6.99

ISBN 978-0-8439-6113-3; 0-8439-6113-9

First published 1961 by Monarch under the pseudonym Lee Duncan with title: Fidel Castro assassinated

An "absorbing yarn about five men vying for a $100,000 prize put on Fidel Castro's head by a mysterious guy named Hiraldo. Bounty hunter Ray Garrison only works on his own; hardened murderer Michael Turner is paired with 19-year-old Jim Hines, avenging his brother's execution; and Earl Fenton, longing to do some good before he dies of cancer, teams up with jack-of-all-trades Matt Garth, who just wants the money. As they make their way to the Cuban coast, sympathetic locals support the five would-be killers in their titular goal despite their penchant for rape and mayhem. Passages discussing Castro's life and times add depth to this intense, taut thriller, just as good now as it was in 1961." Publ Wkly

Block, Lawrence

The **sins** of the fathers; a Matthew Scudder novel. introduction by Stephen King. Dark Harvest 1992 179p

ISBN 0-913165-66-2

First published 1976 in paperback

This novel introduced the then-hard-drinking ex-cop Matt Scudder. "The father of murdered Wendy Hanniford comes to Scudder to try to find out more about his errant daughter—not to find her killer, who was apparently her living partner, a brittle young man who was found in the street raving and covered with her blood and who killed himself shortly after he was arrested. In his dour, methodical, oddly empathetic way, Scudder finds out a great deal, altering several lives in the process. . . . This is a fine opportunity to get in on the start of what has become one of the most rewarding PI series currently in progress." Publ Wkly

Block, Lawrence

A **ticket** to the boneyard; a Matthew Scudder novel. Morrow 1990 302p

ISBN 0-688-09070-2

LC 90-5710

The author "has a fine nose for the pungencies of New York's after-dark street life, and he gives his hero wonderful opportunities to swap syllables with the city's most articulate riffraff. This is primo stuff, and Scudder doesn't get any sharper than when he's interviewing transvestite hookers, desk clerks in fleabag hotels and bouncers in gay leather bars." N Y Times Book Rev

Block, Lawrence

★ **When** the sacred ginmill closes. Arbor House 1986 239p

ISBN 0-87795-774-6

LC 85-18682

"The writing is realistic in the best sense of the word. There are no artificial heroics, forced lines of dialogue or false moves. Mr. Block knows his New York and the way people speak." N Y Times Book Rev

Bloom, Amy, 1953-

★ **Lucky** us; a novel. Amy Bloom. Random House Inc 2014 256 p. (alk. paper) $26

ISBN 1400067243; 9781400067244

LC 2013017648

In this novel, by Amy Bloom, "Iris, the hopeful star and Eva the sidekick, journey through 1940s America in search of fame and fortune. Iris's ambitions take the pair across the America of Reinvention in a stolen station wagon, from small-town Ohio to . . . Hollywood, and to the jazz clubs and golden mansions of Long Island. With their friends in high and low places, Iris and Eva stumble and shine though a landscape of big dreams, scandals, betrayals, and war." (Publisher's note)

"At its core, this is a novel of resilience. . . . Full of intriguing characters and lots of surprises." LJ

Blume, Judy, 1938-

In the unlikely event; Judy Blume. Alfred A. Knopf 2015 432 p. (hardcover) $27.95

ISBN 1101875046; 9781101875049

LC 2015007629

In this novel by Judy Blume, set "in 1987, Miri Ammerman returns to her hometown of Elizabeth, New Jersey, to attend a commemoration of the worst year of her life. Thirty-five years earlier, when Miri was fifteen, and in love for the first time, a succession of airplanes fell from the sky, leaving a community reeling. Against this backdrop of actual events that Blume experienced in the early 1950s . . . she paints a vivid portrait of a particular time and place." (Publisher's note)

"Maintaining her knack for personal detail, Blume mixes Miri's familiar coming-of-age melodrama with an exploration of how disasters test character, alter relationships, and reveal undercurrents of a seemingly simple world. She evokes '50s music, ethnic neighborhoods, and Las Vegas in the early days." Pub Wkly

Blume, Judy

Summer sisters; a novel. Delacorte Press 1998 400p $21.95

ISBN 0-385-32405-7

LC 98-9911

This is a "coming-of-age story set during a series of summers on Martha's Vineyard in the late 1970s and early '80s. At 12, Vix Weaver, the eldest daughter of a blue collar Santa Fe couple, can't believe her luck when Caitlin Somers, the most popular girl in the sixth grade, invites her to vacation with the eclectically aristocratic Somers clan on the Vineyard. The girls declare themselves 'summer sisters' and vow to 'never be ordinary' as they forge a friendship marked by sexual awakening, angst and adventure." Publ Wkly

"The strength of this novel is its vivid portrait of teens in the 1980s. Interspersed viewpoints of various characters add interest and depth to what is a relentlessly readable book." Libr J

Bock, Charles

★ **Alice** & Oliver; a novel. Charles Bock. Random House Inc 2016 416 p. (hardcover) $28; (ebook) $95

ISBN 9781400068388; 9780399569555

LC 2015022303

In this novel by Charles Bock, "Alice Culvert is a caring wife, a doting new mother, a loyal friend, and a soulful artist—a fashion designer who wears a baby carrier and haute couture with equal aplomb. In their loft in Manhattan's gritty Meatpacking District, Alice and her husband, Oliver, are raising their infant daughter, Doe. . . . Their life together feels so vital and full of promise, which makes Alice's sudden cancer diagnosis especially staggering." (Publisher's note)

"The illness doesn't interrupt humanity; humanity grows from the illness, which is a narrative strategy that makes the book one of the most moving in recent memory. A stunning book about Alice and Oliver, yes, but also about the way illness shatters us all." Kirkus

Alice and Oliver

Bock, Charles

Beautiful children; a novel. Random House 2008 417p $25

ISBN 978-1-4000-6650-6; 1-4000-6650-6

LC 2007-4166

"In the no-man'sland of Bock's Vegas there remain only the survival strategies of the hopelessly inept young. I cannot think of another novelist who has dared to attack this most pressing and complex issue so ferociously." Washington Post Book World

Bock, Dennis

The **ash** garden; a novel. Knopf 2001 281p $23

ISBN 0-375-41302-2

LC 2001-29872

"Bock's writing is both dense and immensely readable, as engaging when it focuses on life's minutiae as when it explores life's catastrophes. The Ash Garden is difficult to forget and it rewards repeated readings in a way that few novels can." Quill Quire

Bognanni, Peter

The **house** of tomorrow; Peter Bognanni. Amy Einhorn Books/G.P. Putnam's Sons 2010 354p o.p.; (pbk.) $15

ISBN 0399156097; 9780425238882

LC 2009023542

Alex Award (2011)

This book follows teenager Sebastian Prendergast, who "lives in Iowa's first geodesic dome with his grandmother, a devout follower of futurist philosopher Buckminster R. Fuller. But when Nana has a stroke, Sebastian is thrown together with Janice and teenage Jared Whitcomb, who were touring the home when Nana was stricken. Soon, Sebastian and Jared form an unlikely bond via the great teenage tradition of punk rock, starting their own band despite the objections of everyone around them and Sebastian's lack of musical ability . . . And while Jared succeeds to some degree in socializing Sebastian—teaching him about music, smoking, and curse words—Sebastian ends up getting more than he bargained for when the two get caught up in Whitcomb family drama." (Publishers Weekly)

"Sebastian's first stumble out of the woods into the sweet and vicious real world may not break any new ground, but it's worthwhile, distracting and delightful. Bognanni . . . captures that breath we take before we jump out into our life" Minneapolis Star Tribune

Bohjalian, Chris

The **night** strangers; a novel. [by] Chris Bohjalian. Crown 2011 378p $25

ISBN 978-0-307-39499-6; 0-307-39499-9

LC 2010-45401

"Chip Linton is at the controls of a jet that flies into a flock of birds and goes down in Lake Champlain. Although Linton does everything correctly, an errant wave tips the plane over. Thirty-nine of the 48 people aboard die, and the captain's life, obviously, is changed forever. His lawyer wife, Emily, and their 10-year-old twins decide they need to start over. So they leave Pennsylvania for the small town of Bethel, N.H. But things do not get better. The ghost of several drowned passengers haunts him, particularly Ashley, a young girl, and her dad. They are stuck in purgatory and alone. Linton believes he's responsible, and that Ashley deserves company, and he's prepared to kill his own daughters to provide it. He's crazy, of course or is he? The denouement is not only unexpected but is also perfect and true to the story. Bohjalian is a terrific writer and parsimonious in the way he issues information, slowly building an increasing sense of dread and excitement." Minneapolis Star Tribune

Bohjalian, Chris

The **sandcastle** girls; a novel. Chris Bohjalian. Doubleday 2012 299 p. $25.95

ISBN 0385534795; 9780385534796

LC 2011050285

In this book, "Elizabeth Endicott, a recent Mount Holyoke graduate, accompanies her Bostonian banker father on his philanthropic mission to Aleppo, Syria, to aid Armenian refugees fleeing atrocities committed by the Ottoman government. Her friendship with Armenian engineer Armen . . . flourishes . . . in letters. Years later, Laura Petrosian, seeking out a photograph of a woman rumored to be her Armenian grandmother, uncovers these letters." (Library Journal)

"Bohjalian powerfully narrates an intricately nuanced romance with a complicated historical event at the forefront." LJ

Bohjalian, Christopher A.

Secrets of Eden; a novel. [by] Chris Bohjalian. Shaye Areheart Books 2010 370p $25

ISBN 978-0-307-39497-2

LC 2009-23946

"Alice Hayward, the town of Haverill knows, is a battered wife, struggling to find meaning in her life with her brutal husband. The same day that she is baptized by the town's minister, Stephen Drew, she is murdered by her husband, who then turned a gun on himself. These facts emerge in the book's first dozen pages, and the rest of the novel rotates around the events of that night. Four narrative voices, with varying degrees of directness, tell their versions of the story: the Reverend Drew, who has a not entirely spiritual connection with Alice; state's attorney Catherine Benincasa, concerned that the full story may not yet have been told; self-help author Heather Laurent, a specialist in angels who's haunted by her own parents' murder/suicide; and the Haywards' daughter Katie, a newly orphaned highschooler sorting out the messiness left behind." Seattle Times

Bohjalian, Christopher A.

Skeletons at the feast; a novel. by Chris Bohjalian. Shaye Areheart Books 2008 372p map $25

ISBN 978-0-307-39495-8; 0-307-39495-6

LC 2007-40800

"Inspired by the World War II diary of an East Prussian woman, Skeletons describes the horrific final months of the war as a motley crew of characters struggle to make their way across the Polish countryside to reach British and American lines. With Russian troops on their flanks and remnants of the Third Reich dotted dauntingly here and there, their journey is a daring and terrifying exodus. Key to the group are Uri Singer, a German Jew who dove to freedom from a train headed to Auschwitz and thereafter assumes the identity of various dead German soldiers; Anna Emmerich, a daughter of Prussian aristocrats who is fleeing with her family; and Callum Finnella, a Scottish prisoner of war who hides in the Emmerich family wagon and has become Anna's lover." Rocky Mountain News

Bolano, Roberto

2666; translated from the Spanish by Natasha Wimmer. Farrar, Straus and Giroux 2008 898p $30

ISBN 978-0-374-10014-8; 0-374-10014-4

LC 2008-18295

Original Spanish edition, 2004

"More vast and more lurid than his previous novels that have been translated into English, '2666' is not Roberto Bolaño's masterpiece but almost a compendium, in individual scenes, of the qualities that made him a great writer. His themes are violence, dislocation, and the sexiness of literature, and here these strands are recombined endlessly, in Europe, Detroit, and Mexico, through multiple narrators and prose styles. The action converges on the Sonoran desert, where Bolaño anatomizes, in brutal and eerie detail, the true-life murders of hundreds of women, most of which remain unsolved. By the end, after close to nine hundred pages, the reader will be impressed by the range and power on display but might wish that the novel cohered, rather than merely concluding." New Yorker

Bolano, Roberto

★ **By** night in Chile; translated from the Spanish by Chris Andrews. New Directions 2004 130p pa $13.95

ISBN 0-81121-547-4 pa

Original Spanish edition, 2000

"Postwar Chilean politics and literature infuse this densely learned, richly evocative novel. In Chris Andrews's lucid translation, Bolano's febrile narrative tack and occasional surreal touches bring to mind the classics of Latin American magic realism; his cerebral protagonist and nonfiction borrowings are reminiscent of Thomas Bernhard and W. G. Sebald." N Y Times Book Rev

Bolano, Roberto

Last evenings on Earth; translated from the Spanish by Chris Andrews. New Directions 2006 219p $23.95

ISBN 978-0-8112-1634-0; 0-8112-1634-9

LC 2006-3819

"These 14 bleakly luminous stories are all told in the first person by men (usually young) who yearn for something just out of their grasp (fame, talent, love) and who harbor few hopes of attaining what they desire. . . . The stories are similar, in theme and voice (though not in locale), and they are perfectly calibrated: Bolaño limns the capacity of a voice to carry despair without shading into bitterness." Publ Wkly

Bolano, Roberto

Monsieur Pain; translated by Chris Andrews. New Directions 2010 134p $22.95

ISBN 978-0-8112-1714-9; 0-8112-1714-0

LC 2009-37431

Original Spanish edition, 1999

"Paris, 1938: Two shadowy Spaniards seem to be stalking Monsieur Pain, a middle-aged mesmerist hopelessly in love with a young widow, who appears with a desperate plea: She needs his help to heal Monsieur Vallejo, a Peruvian dying of inexplicable hiccups. Monsieur Pain tries to visit the ailing man in the clinic, which turns out to be a Kafkaesque maze of circular halls and hostile nurses. Meanwhile, the mysterious Spaniards issue Pain a cash bribe and a demand: Under no circumstances must he use his occult abilities to heal the Peruvian. The Peruvian in question is none other than the poet César Vallejo, widely considered one of the most innovative surrealists of the 20th century. Bolaño draws on actual facts the real Vallejo was hospitalized in Paris in 1938, and his wife called in practitioners of occult sciences when doctors failed to cure him to weave his brilliant, noir-steeped fictional world. As Pain wanders the rainy streets of Paris, convinced of a plot to assassinate Vallejo, haunted by his own complicity and helpless rebellion, we enter a hallucinatory dreamscape flooded with resonant symbols." San Francisco Chron

Bolano, Roberto

★ **Nazi** literature in the Americas; translated from the Spanish by Chris Andrews. New Directions 2008 227p $23.95

ISBN 978-0-8112-1705-7; 0-8112-1705-1

LC 2007-37800

Original Spanish edition, 1996

This novel, "a wicked, invented encyclopedia of imaginary fascist writers and literary tastemakers, is Bolaño playing with sharp, twisting knives. As if he were Borges's wisecracking, sardonic son, Bolaño has meticulously created a tightly woven network of far-right litterateurs and purveyors of belles lettres for whom Hitler was beauty, truth and great lost hope. Cross-referenced, complete with bibliography and a biographical list of secondary figures, Nazi Literature is composed of a series of sketches, the compressed life stories of writers in North and South America who never existed, but all too easily could have. Goose-stepping caricatures a la 'The Producers' they are not; instead, they are frighteningly subtle, poignant and plausible." N Y Times Book Rev

Includes bibliographical references

Bolano, Roberto

★ The **savage** detectives; translated from the Spanish by Natasha Wimmer. Farrar, Straus & Giroux 2007 577p il $27

ISBN 978-0-374-19148-1; 0-374-19148-4

LC 2006-22176

Original Spanish edition, 1998

"'Though the fragmented narrative can be frustrating at times, the late-20th-century panorama emerging from the cacophony is simultaneously frightening and spectacular. At every turn, Bolaño examines the individual lives history discards. The result is a large, sprawling and—most of all—sublime novel." Paste

Bolaño, Roberto, 1953-2003

★ The **Third** Reich; a novel. translated from the Spanish by Natasha Wimmer. 1st American ed. Farrar, Straus and Giroux 2011 277p. $25

ISBN 9780374275624; 978-0-374-27562-4; 9781250013934

LC 2011025798

Original Spanish edition, 2010

This book tells the story of "Udo Berger and his girlfriend Ingeborg, Germans in their 20s, [who] arrive on Spain's Costa Brava for their vacation. . . . War games are Udo's passion, and he's the German champion . . . [and] he's brought with him a World War II game, the eponymous Third Reich. . . . [T]he core of the novel [is] the game and . . . [Udo's] obsession with a mysterious, badly scarred guy known as El Quemado (the Burn Victim). . . . No one is sure of his background; South America? There's even a suggestion he's the re-incarnation of an Incan warrior. At first Udo idealizes him as a Noble Savage, but he's plenty smart, a poetry lover. Udo teaches him the game; El Quemado catches on fast. Power shifts from the cocksure Udo to his humble opponent as the German crumbles, on the board and off." (Kirkus)

"Not long after his death, [Bolaño's] heirs discovered an unpublished manuscript, The Third Reich, written more than 20 years ago, and now translated into English by Natasha Wimmer. While it might not feature the narrative fireworks of his award-winning The Savage Detectives (1998) or the epic sprawl of 2666, it's no less brilliant. . . . The novel chronicles a month in the life of Udo Berger, a young German on vacation in northeast Spain with his girlfriend, Ingeborg. Udo is a prodigy, a widely respected master of 'war games' — a type of strategy-based board game popular among hobbyists in the 1970s and 1980s. He plans to use his time off to research an article he's writing about The Third Reich, a challenging World War II simulation . . . . His plans are derailed, though, once he and Ingeborg meet Charly, a charming, impulsive fellow German tourist, and El Quemado ('The Burned One'), a mysterious beach dweller who shows an unexpected interest in the game. After Charly disappears while windsurfing, it doesn't take long for Udo to realize that no amount of skill or strategy can keep his life from falling apart." NPR

Boll, Heinrich

The **clown**; translated from the German by Leila Vennewitz. McGraw-Hill 1965 247p

Original German edition, 1963

This novel revolves around the loss of meaning in the life of Hans Schnier, a twenty-seven-year-old clown and mime who returns home to Bonn after a disastrous performance tour. Flashbacks reconstruct Schnier's life in Hitler's Germany and his bitter experiences of the postwar period

"What Schnier (and the author) seem to be asking is: How can an honest man profess Christianity when Christian culture in the West failed to stop the rise of Nazism . . . and when the Church thrives in a society that worships nothing but the values of the marketplace? Hard questions but embodied in a bitter and brilliant book." NY Times Book Rev

Boll, Heinrich

The **silent** angel; translated by Breon Mitchell. St. Martin's Press 1994 182p

ISBN 0-312-11064-2

LC 94-2052

Written in 1950; first German edition, 1992

"While the bleakness Böll portrays might have made German publishers wary in 1950, the artistry of his portrayal makes 'The Silent Angel' a rich novel, one still pertinent to our own hunger for the bread of meaning amid the rubble of history. Heinrich Böll's gift to us is the skill with which he captures its first pangs." NY Times Book Rev

Bollen, Christopher

Orient: a novel. by Christopher Bollen. HarperCollins 2015 624 p. map (hardcover) $26.99

ISBN 9780062329950; 9781471136153; 0062329952

In this novel, by Christopher Bollen, "one late summer morning, the body of a local caretaker is found in the open water; the same day, a monstrous animal corpse is found on the beach, presumed a casualty from a nearby research lab. With rumors flying, eyes turn to Mills Chevern. . . . As the deaths continue and fear in town escalates, Mills is enlisted by Beth, an Orient native in retreat from Manhattan, to help her uncover the truth." (Publisher's note)

Bolton, S. J.

Now you see me. Minotaur Books 2011 395p il $25.99

ISBN 978-0-312-60052-5; 0-312-60052-6

LC 2011-08751

"On the anniversary of the original Ripper's first killing, Det. Constable Lacey Flint is horrified to find a dying woman, 'her abdomen . . . a mass of scarlet,' leaning against the detective's car in a London car park. The guilt-ridden Flint wonders whether different actions on her part might have saved the victim's life or caught the killer. The connection with the 1888 autumn of terror becomes clear after a journalist receives a letter obviously derived from some of the correspondence Scotland Yard received back then, ostensibly from the Ripper himself. By coincidence, Flint is something of a Ripper expert, and her knowledge proves useful in what develops into a multiple murder investigation. Avoiding gratuitous violence, Bolton . . . skillfully plays with the reader's expectations." Publ Wkly

Borges, Jorge Luis

★ **Collected** fictions; translated by Andrew Hurley. Viking 1998 565p

ISBN 0-670-84970-7

LC 98-21217

This is a collection of all the stories written by Borges over a 50-year period

"A Borges invention . . . always takes the reader on a roller-coaster ride into some previously unsuspected dimension. This collection of the great magician's work is a new translation and includes one piece never before put into English." Atl Mon

Borland, Hal

When the legends die. Lippincott 1963 288p hardcover o.p. pa $6.50

ISBN 0-553-25738-2

"Thomas Black Bull, a Ute Indian, is being reared in the traditional Native American way when his parents are forced to flee from the world of the white man. After the death of his parents Tom is returned to the white world, where he suffers the disintegration of his native heritage and traditions as he experiences school, sheep herding, and rodeo life. Following a serious accident at a rodeo he returns to the mountains and is drawn back into his past." Shapiro. Fic for Youth 3rd edition

Boswell, Robert

Century's son. Knopf 2002 307p $24

ISBN 0-375-41237-9

LC 2001-38101

"Morgan, whose first name has fallen away 'from disuse,' was once a fearless labor organizer for his fellow sanitation workers; it was his uncompromising idealism that led Zhenya, his college-professor wife, to fall in love with him. But, ten years later, Morgan has abandoned his activism; he spends his days collecting garbage and contemplating his decline, which began when his son hanged himself, at the age of twelve. As if the Morgan marriage didn't have enough to deal with, Zhenya's father, the famous Russian writer Peter Ivanovich Kamenev, is coming to visit. . . . A moving portrait of a family both torn apart and united by grief." New Yorker

Boswell, Robert

Tumbledown; Robert Boswell. Graywolf Press 2013 448 p. (alk. paper) $26

ISBN 1555976492; 9781555976491

LC 2013931489

"Set at a California counseling center and sheltered workshop, this story [by author Robert Boswell] focuses on the emotionally disrupted lives of its large set of characters. Candler is a counselor in line for the center's directorship but isn't sure he wants the responsibility. . . . Lise is a former patient of Candler's . . . who believes she is in love with him. . . . Maura is in love with teenage Mick, a schizophrenic struggling to get back to the life he knew before his illness." (Library Journal)

Boucher, Christopher

How to keep your Volkswagen alive. Melville House 2011 239p pa $15

ISBN 978-1-935554-63-9; 1-935554-63-8

This book "is set in a zany, modern-day western Massachusetts, where time is literally money, inanimate objects walk and talk, words take on new meaning, and, like the narrator's ever-shifting metaphors, the landscape alters its form at will. Based on a veritable hippie bible, a 1969 Volkswagen maintenance manual, Boucher's loosely structured, surreal interpretation portrays a man struggling to raise his sickly, illegitimate son, a 1971 VW Beetle (he often vomits oil) who was born shortly after the narrator's father was abducted and killed by a Heart Attack Tree. When the narrator sets out to investigate his father's death, his attempts to save time to heal his ailing son result in one long how-to on fatherhood. . . . With wicked, postmodern playfulness and a heart of tenderness, Boucher introduces a supercharged novel that reaffirms the vast and rousing possibilities of fiction." Booklist

Includes bibliographical references

Bouchet, Amanda

★ **Breath** of fire; Amanda Bouchet. Sourcebooks Casablanca 2017 440 p. (The Kingmaker chronicles) (pbk.) $7.99

ISBN 9781492626053; 9781492626046; 149262604X

Sequel to: A promise of fire (2016)

In this romance novel in The Kingmaker Chronicles series, by Amanda Bouchet, "Griffin knows Cat is destined to change the world--for the better. As the realms are descending into all-out war, Cat and Griffin risk sacrificing everything they've fought for. Gods willing, they will emerge side-by-side in the heart of their future kingdom...or die trying." (Publisher's note)

"With breathtaking storytelling, high-octane action and adventure, intense romance, and threads to ancient Greek mythology . . . Bouchet sets the bar for high-concept fantasy romance." Kirkus

Boulle, Pierre

★ The **bridge** over the River Kwai; translated by Xan Fielding. Vanguard Press 1954 224p

Original French edition, 1952

"In 1942 the Japanese military under the command of Col. Saito orders its British prisoners of war to construct a bridge over the 400-foot-wide River Kwai in the Siamese jungle. Complications arise when prisoner Col. Nicholson insists that officers not be treated like regular lower-class soldiers. Medical officer Clipton is much more humane, and this difference brings the two fellow prisoners into frequent conflict. When the bridge is finally completed, a British demolition team prepares to destroy it." Shapiro. Fic for Youth. 3d edition

Boulle, Pierre

★ **Planet** of the apes; translated by Xan Feilding. Ballantine 2001 268p pa $6.99

ISBN 0-345-44798-0

First published 1963 by Vanguard Press; published in the United Kingdom with title: Monkey planet

"In this Swiftian fable Boulle gives full play to his not inconsiderable gift for irony and satire." Libr J

Bouman, Tom

★ **Dry** bones in the valley; a novel. Tom Bouman. W.W. Norton & Co Inc. 2014 288 p. (hardcover) $24.95

ISBN 0393243028; 9780393243024

LC 2014002224

Edgar Award: Best First Novel (2015)

This crime novel by Tom Bouman describes how as "The lone policeman in a small township . . . , Henry Farrell expected to spend his mornings hunting and fishing. . . . Instead, he has watched the steady encroachment of gas drilling bring new wealth and erode neighborly trust. The drug trade is pushing heroin into the territory. . . . When a stranger turns up dead, Henry's search for the killer will open old wounds, dredge up ancient crimes, and exact a deadly price." (Publisher's note)

"Henry's growth from a grief-stricken widower to a lawman with an inner resolve fuels the brisk plot, as does an evocative look at a changing landscape." Pub Wkly

Bournc, Joanna

★ The **black** hawk; Joanna Bourne. Berkley Sensation 2011 336p.

ISBN 9780425244531 pa; 9781410447456

LC 2012659025

This espionage thriller tells the story of two spies. "Adrian Hawker spied on France for England while Justine DeCabrillac gathered intelligence for the Police Sècrete. They were teens when they met in Paris in 1794, and as they grew up, their paths crossed often in a changing world. Sometimes they were on the same side, and sometimes they were opposed, but it was inevitable that they fall bittersweetly in love, knowing that any minute duty could take precedence over passion. Their tempestuous love affair unfolds in flashbacks, alternating with scenes from 1818 London, where somebody tries to kill Justine and frame Hawker, now head of the British Intelligence Service with as many enemies in England as in France." (Publishers Weekly)

Bourne, Joanna

My lord and spymaster. Berkley Sensation 2008 324p pa $7.99

ISBN 978-0-425-22246-1; 0-425-22246-2

"Jess Whitby, daughter of suspected spy Josiah Whitby, is doing everything in her power to exonerate her imprisoned father. In order to free him, she must prove that someone other than her father is the Cinq, a notorious mole. But Jess has met her match in Capt. Sebastian Kennett, wealthy bastard son of an English nobleman, equally as clever at keeping tabs on Jess as she is at tracking him. Sebastian is responsible for Josiah's arrest; Jess believes that Sebastian may be the Cinq; their mutual attraction proves a lovely foil for their suspicious minds. Glimpses of the leads' sordid pasts add depth, and Bourne's consummate way with a story line and an explosive denouement do the rest." Publ Wkly

Bourne, Joanna

★ **Rogue** Spy; Joanna Bourne. Berkley Pub Group 2014 336 p. (Spymasters) (pbk) $7.99

ISBN 0425260828; 9780425260821

In this novel by Joanna Bourne, "former French spy Camille Leyland is dragged from her safe rural obscurity by threats and blackmail. Dusting off her spy skills, she sets out to track down a ruthless French fanatic and rescue the innocent victim he's holding--only to find an old colleague already on the case. Pax. Old friendship turns to new love, and as Pax and Camille's dark secrets loom up from the past." (Publisher's note)

Bourne "continues to demonstrate a remarkable flair for deftly mixing danger and desire in an impeccably crafted Regency setting." Booklist

Bourne, Joanna

The **spymaster's** lady. Berkley Publishing Group 2008 373p pa $7.99

ISBN 978-0-425-21960-7

"Annique Villiers, the elusive spy known as the Fox Cub, has outwitted, outmaneuvered and outfoxed every man she's ever met, until British spymaster Robert Grey steps into a French prison. Grey's mission is to capture the Cub and uncover exactly what she knows and who she works for. As enemies, they hate one another; as fellow prisoners they must band together to escape. Their truce is filled with suspicion, but there's also a spark of something more a forbidden passion that threatens their missions." Romantic Times

Bova, Ben

★ **Mars**. Bantam Bks. 1992 502p

ISBN 0-553-07892-5

LC 91-29466

"A Native American geologist finds himself the center of political controversy as he becomes one of the first humans to set foot on the red planet. Bova's imaginary chronicle of the first human mission to Mars offers a field day for science buffs as his characters experience the challenges of exploring Earth's nearest neighbor." Libr J

Followed by Return to Mars

Bowen, Elizabeth

The **heat** of the day. Knopf 1949 372p

Essentially this novel presents character studies of Stella Rodney, and the two men who loved her. The background is London after Dunkirk, a London of blitzes and buzz bombs; and peaceful Ireland. The two men are Robert Kelway, Stella's lover, and the mysterious Harrison, who betrays Kelway's secret in order to gain Stella for himself

"Miss Bowen's novel expertly flicks the rawness of several unsolved queries concerning loyalty and love and ponders the degree to which human beings are strangers to each other. More densely written than her earlier work, this study of behavior is a soberly shocking, compassionate baring of the confused and vulnerable human heart." N Y Her Trib Books

Bowen, Kelly

You're the Earl That I Want; Kelly Bowen. Forever 2015 365 p. (pbk.) $7.99

ISBN 145558388X; 9781455583881

LC 2015656958

"Once a shy slip of a girl, Joss is now brilliant, beautiful chaos in a ball gown. In her heart, Joss has always loved Heath, the one person she's always been able to count on. . . . Joss can do as she pleases-and now it pleases her to solve the mystery of an encoded file given to Heath by a dying man. . . . And to remind him that what she lacks in convention, she makes up for in passion." (Publisher's note)

"Bowen's thrilling plot, spot-on pacing, and savvy characterization will delight her current fans and seduce new ones." Pub Wkly

Bowen, Lila

Wake of vultures; Lila Bowen. Orbit 2015 320 p. map (hardback) $25

ISBN 9780316264310

LC 2015010160

In this book, by Lila Bowen, "Nettie Lonesome dreams of a better life than toiling as a slave in the sandy desert. But late one night, a stranger attacks her -- and Nettie wins more than the fight. Now she's got everything she ever wanted: friends, a good horse, and a better gun. But if she can't kill the thing haunting her nightmares and stealing children across the prairie, she'll lose it all -- and never find out what happened to her real family." (Publisher's note)

"Incorporating Native American and Western myths, plus Nettie's multicultural heritage and characters from a wide range of backgrounds, this is a must-have for all modern fantasy collections and a great choice for adults and teens. Suggest to readers who enjoyed Western-themed fantasies such as Emma Bull's Territory." LJ

Bowen, Peter

Badlands. St. Martin's Minotaur 2003 250p $23.95
ISBN 0-312-26252-3

LC 2002-37196

Montana sheriff Gabriel Du Pré's "suspicions are aroused when the Host of Yahweh immediately destroys the ranch buildings, sells the livestock and erects a makeshift metal chapel for secret rites. Soon, reportsof mass murders and suicides bring in cautious FBI agents ever mindful of the Waco debacle. Du Pré's blunt speech and sometimes opaque thought patterns can be hard to follow, but his pursuits of wrongdoers over cliffs, canyons and arid river beds are truly riveting." Publ Wkly

Bowles, Paul

Collected stories & later writings. Library of America 2002 1062p $40
ISBN 1-931082-20-0

LC 2002-19452

Fifty-two of the short stories in this volume have appeared in the five books: The delicate prey (1950); A hundred camels in the courtyard (1962); The time of friendship (1967); Things gone and things still here (1977); and Midnight mass (1981). Six selected later stories are also included. Up above the world (1966) is a novella where an American couple visiting Central America have a frightening experience with an apparently wealthy local couple. Their heads are green and their hands are blue (1963) is a collection of travel essays.

Includes bibliographical references

Bowles, Paul

★ The **sheltering** sky. New Directions 1949 318p

"Port and Kit Moresby, an American couple of independent means, have been traveling aimlessly for 12 years. By the time they reach Morocco they have become disaffected and alienated. They take up with a series of unreliable, rootless wanderers. On a trip to the interior Port contracts typhoid fever—out of apathy he has neglected to be vaccinated—and dies. Kit has an affair with an Arab and joins his household, but their relationship soon falls apart. Kit is found and returned to Oran. She is teetering on the brink of insanity and finds an opportunity to disappear into the crowded bazaar." Merriam-Webster's Ency of Lit

Bowles, Paul

The **sheltering** sky; Let it come down; The spider's house. Library of America 2002 938p $35
ISBN 1-931082-19-7

LC 2002-19453

The sheltering sky is entered separately. "In Let It Come Down (1952), Bowles plots the doomed trajectory of Nelson Dyar, a New York bank teller who comes to Tangier in search of a different life and ends up giving in to his darkest impulses. . . . The Spider's House (1955) . . . is set against the end of French rule in Morocco. Its characters—ranging from a Moroccan boy gifted with spiritual healing power to an American writer who regrets the passing of traditional ways—are caught up in the clash between colonial and nationalist factions, and are forced to confront cultural gulfs widened by political violence." Publisher's note

Bowles, Paul

The **stories** of Paul Bowles; introduction by Robert Stone. Ecco Press 2001 657p $39.95
ISBN 0-06-621273-1

LC 2001-51231

"Earthy, violent and comfortable with corruption, these deeply affecting stories are distinguished by their lyrical rhythms and meticulous regard for language." Publ Wkly

Bowman, Valerie

The **Accidental** Countess; Valerie Bowman. St. Martin's Press 2014 320 p. $7.99
ISBN 1250042089; 9781250042088

In this novel by Valerie Bowman, set after the Napoleonic Wars, " Lady Cassandra Monroe has waited for the man of her dreams to return from the war. Unfortunately, he happens to be engaged to her flighty cousin. What Cass wouldn't give to take her cousin's place! When he mistakes Cass for Patience Bunbury, a fictitious friend her cousin has invented to escape social obligations--even with her future husband, Cass thinks this is her chance." (Publisher's note)

"The second in Bowman's thoroughly entertaining, Regency-set Playful Brides series (The Unexpected Duchess, 2014) will delight readers with its madcap plot and buoyant sense of humor." Booklist

Bowman, Valerie

The **Unexpected** Duchess; Valerie Bowman. St. Martin's Press 2014 368 p. $7.99
ISBN 1250042070; 9781250042071

In this book, by Valerie Bowman, "Lady Lucy Upton's tongue may be too sharp to attract suitors but her heart is good, and when her painfully shy friend Cassandra needs help she devises a brilliant scheme to help her discourage an unwanted suitor, the Duke of Claringdon. Lucy will hide behind the hedgerow and tell Cass just what to say to discourage the Duke of Claringdon… but it turns out that he's made of sterner stuff than either of them anticipated." (Publisher's note)

"Lucy is the Regency shrew to Hunt's gentle-warrior hero who falls for her quick wit, then recognizes the wounded girl behind the virago mask. A fun, smart comedy of errors and a sexy, satisfying romance." Kirkus

Box, C. J.

✓**Back** of beyond. Minotaur Books 2011 372p $25.99
ISBN 978-0-312-36574-5

LC 2011-10134

"A disgraced cop with a history of alcoholism, Cody Hoyt is also a bulldog investigator. When his AA sponsor turns up dead, Cody determines that the killer is one of 14 dudes on a weeklong expedition in Yellowstone National Park; Cody's son is also on the trip. While struggling to figure out who and why, and where they are in the wilderness, Cody also searches for redemption on behalf of his friend." Libr J

Box, C. J.

✓★ **Badlands**; a novel. C. J. Box. Minotaur Books 2015 278 p. (hardcover) $26.99
ISBN 0312583214; 9780312583217

LC 2015017001

"Twenty miles across the North Dakota border, where the scenery goes from rolling grass prairie to pipeline fields, detective Cassie Dewell has been assigned as the new deputy sheriff of Grimstad-a place people used to be from, but were never headed to. Grimstad is now the oil capital of North Dakota. With oil comes money, with money comes drugs, and with drugs come the dirtiest criminals hustling to corner the market." (Publisher's note)

"Cassie arrives just as a series of brutal murders signals a war between drug gangs--although the missing duffle bag the criminals are searching for has accidentally wound up in the hands of a special-needs paperboy, 12-year-old Kyle Westergaard. . . . The story's brisk action is broken into alternating sections as Cassie and Kyle try to figure out what's going on and what they must do. The vulnerable boy's plight gives emotional heft to the criminal investigation, balancing cynicism with warm empathy." Pub Wkly

Box, C. J.

Breaking point; C. J. Box. G. P. Putnam's Sons 2013 384 p. (hardcover) $26.95

ISBN 0399160752; 9780399160752

This thriller, by C. J. Box, is an entry in the author's "Joe Pickett" novels. "It was always good to see Butch Roberson, Joe thought. . . . Little did he know that . . . the man was about to disappear. He was heading into the mountains to scout elk, he said, but instead he was running. Two EPA employees had just been murdered, and all signs pointed to him as the killer. . . . But was it the whole story? The more Joe looks into it, the more he begins to wonder." (Publisher's note)

Box, C. J.

Force of nature; C.J. Box. G. P. Putnam's Sons 2012 385 p. (Joe Pickett novel)

ISBN 039915826X; 9780399158261

LC 2011047681

In this book, "set just weeks after fugitive Nate Romanowski's double loss of his lover and a trusted ally, . . . Nate realizes that his former Air Force mentor is hunting him down and systematically eliminating all his known associates. A bloody confrontation along the Twelve Sleep River injures Nate and sets the tone for a series of violent attacks stretching from Colorado into Wyoming and Idaho. Getting ever closer to Nate's best friends, game warden Joe Pickett and his wife Marybeth, the killer taunts his intended victims. Nate, up against a skilled falconer, expects only the worst outcome, but still he perseveres. And Joe, always honorable, plans to save Nate's life, no matter what it takes." (Libr J)

Box, C. J.

Free fire; by C.J. Box. G.P. Putnam's Sons 2007 352p map o.p.; (pbk.) $7.99; o.p.

ISBN 9780399154270; 9780425221242; 0399154272

LC 2007000539

In this book, "Joe Pickett, having recently been fired from his job as a Wyoming game warden, is working on his father-in-law's ranch when he receives a call from the governor's office . . . [regarding] Clay McCann, a lawyer who slaughtered four campers in cold blood in a far-off corner of Yellowstone National Park. After the murders, McCann immediately turned himself in at the nearest park ranger station. . . . [But] the crimes were committed in a thin sliver of land with zero residents and overlapping jurisdiction, the so-called free-fire zone. McCann had taken advantage of a loophole in the law: neither the state of Wyoming nor the federal government can try him for his crime, so he walks out of prison a free man. Governor Rulon . . . wants his own investigation into the murders. The governor will reinstate Joe as a game warden if he'll go to Yellowstone to investigate." (Publisher's note)

Box, C. J.

The **highway**; C. J. Box. Minotaur Books 2013 400 p. (hardcover) $25.99

ISBN 0312583206; 9780312583200

LC 2013009869

In this novel by C.J. Box "two sisters set out across . . . Montana [and] the girls . . . simply vanish. Former police investigator Cody Hoyt, . . . convinced by his son and his former rookie partner, Cassie Dewell, . . . begins the drive . . . to the girls' last known location. This . . . landscape is the hunting ground for a killer whose viciousness is outmatched only by his intelligence. Can Cody Hoyt battle his own demons and find this killer before another victim vanishes on the highway?" (Publisher's note)

Box, C. J.

Nowhere to run. G.P. Putnam's Sons 2010 356p $25.95

ISBN 978-0-399-15645-8; 0-399-15645-3

LC 2009-46027

"Joe Pickett, exiled to the 'warden's graveyard' in a remote district of southern Wyoming, has one week left before regaining his old job in Twelve Sleep County, where his family still lives. On a final horseback patrol, however, a routine citation for unlicensed fishing turns into a deadly confrontation with twin brothers Caleb and Camish Grim, whose anger at the government is downright murderous. The first hundred pages are as good as anything Box has written, highlighting both the dangerous beauty of the West and the risks of a job where a lone civil servant interacts with a well-armed populace. As events escalate and a complex conspiracy comes to light, momentum is maintained by the dogged determination of Pickett, who could have walked away, and probably should have, but didn't." Booklist

Box, C. J.

Open season; C.J. Box. G.P. Putnam 2001 293p. (pbk.) $7.99; (acid-free paper) o.p.

ISBN 9780425185469; 0399147489

LC 00050992

Anthony Award: Best First Novel (2002)

Macavity Award: Best First Mystery Novel (2002)

"Joe Pickett is the new game warden in Twelve Sleep, Wyoming, a town where nearly everyone hunts and the game warden--especially one like Joe who won't take bribes or look the other way--is far from popular. When he finds a local hunting outfitter dead, splayed out on the woodpile behind his state-owned home, he takes it personally. There had to be a reason that the outfitter, with whom he's had run-ins before, chose his backyard, his woodpile to die in. Even after the 'outfitter murders,' as they have been dubbed by the local press after the discovery of the two more bodies, are solved, Joe continues to investigate, uneasy with the easy explanation offered by the local police." (Publisher's note)

Other titles about Joe Pickett are:

Savage run (2002)
Winterkill (2003)
Trophy hunt (2004)
Out of range (2005)
In plain sight (2006)
Free fire (2007)
Blood trail (2008)
Below zero (2009)
Nowhere to run (2010)
Cold wind (2011)
Force of nature (2012)
Breaking point (2013)
Stone cold (2014)
Endangered (2015)
Off the grid (2016)
Vicious circle (2017)
The disappeared (2018)

Box, C. J.

Vicious circle; a Joe Pickett novel. C. J. Box. G.P. Putnam's Sons 2017 367 p. (A Joe Pickett novel) $27

ISBN 0399176616; 9780399176616

LC 2016046699

In this book in the Joe Pickett series, by C. J. Box, "the Cates family had always been a bad lot. Game warden Joe Pickett had been able to strike a fierce blow against them when the life of his daughter April had been endangered. . . . Joe knows they're coming after him and his family now. He has his friend Nate by his side, but will that be enough this time? All he can do is prepare . . . and wait for them to make the first move." (Publisher's note)

"Box masterfully tightens the suspense until we're caught in a vicious circle of our own and unable to stop reading." Booklist

Boyce, Trudy Nan

Old bones; Trudy Nan Boyce. G.P. Putnam's Sons 2017 337 p. (Detective Sarah Alt) (hardback) $27

ISBN 9780399167270; 9780698140714

LC 2016036562

In this book, in the Detective Sarah Alt Novel series, by Trudy Nan Boyce, "in a city burdened by history and a community erupting in pain and anger, [Detective Sarah 'Salt'] . . . must delve into the past for answers. [This novel is] a gripping and astute story about what it means to serve and protect." (Publisher's note)

"An exceptional police procedural, with a compelling protagonist and strong moral underpinning." Booklist

Boyd, William

Any human heart; a novel. by William Boyd. Knopf 2003 498p $26

ISBN 0-375-41493-2; 9780375414930

LC 2002027451

Boyd's novel "purports to be the intimate journals of one Logan Gonzago Mountstuart. 'LMS', as the notional 'editor' calls him, made his first appearance in 1998 as a source for Boyd's . . . hoax biography Nat Tate: An American Artist 1928-60. The book even included a small black and white photograph, captioned 'Logan Mountstuart, 1959', that showed a round-faced, faintly-smiling man with abbreviated eyebrows and incipient jowls. . . . Now we have the diaries—nine in all, running to nearly five hundred pages and complete with 12-page index. The earliest dates from 1923, when Mountstuart is a precocious public schoolboy; . . . the last ends with his death in 1991." (London Rev Books)

"This flawed yet immensely appealing protagonist is one of Boyd's most distinctive creations, and his voice—articulate, introspective, urbane, stoically philosophical in the face of countless disappointments—engages the readers empathy." Publ Wkly

Boyd, William

Sweet Caress; The Many Lives of Amory Clay. by William Boyd. Bloomsbury USA 2015 352 p. illustrations, portraits $28; $28

ISBN 1632863324; 9781632863324

In this novel, by William Boyd, "[w]hen Amory Clay was born, in the decade before the Great War, her disappointed father gave her an androgynous name and announced the birth of a son. But this daughter was not one to let others define her; Amory became a woman who accepted no limits to what that could mean, and, from the time she picked up her first camera, one who would record her own version of events." (Publisher's note)

"In avidly precise scenes of stylish romance, candid eroticism, thorny irony, crushing defeat, and reclaimed independence, Boyd portrays a mesmerizingly determined and clever protagonist created in homage to such pioneering real-life photographers as Lee Miller and Margaret Bourke-White. He also dramatizes with empathy and sharp intent the insidious psychic damage caused by war. The result is a seductively glossy yet gritty portrait of a strong, adventurous woman and an epoch-spanning novel veined with unsettling psychological and social insights." Booklist

Boyd, William

Waiting for sunrise; a novel. William Boyd. Harper 2012 353 p.

ISBN 9780061876769

LC 2011036857

This book follows, "former espionage agent . . . Lysander Rief . . . [who,] having gone to consult a Freudian psychoanalyst . . . encounters Hettie Bull, a highly strung expat Englishwoman. . . . [T]hey begin an affair. But she accuses him of raping her and he's arrested, only to be rescued by British diplomatic officials, kicking off a web of intrigue that enmeshes Rief in ever more mysterious circumstances." (Publishers Weekly)

Boyden, Joseph

Three-day road; a novel. Joseph Boyden. Viking 2005 354 p. o.p.; (pbk.) $15

ISBN 0670034312; 9780143037071

LC 2004066149

CBA Libris Awards (Canadian Booksellers Association): Fiction Book of the Year (2006), Roger Writers' Trust Fiction Prize (2005)

This book follows "Cree Indians Xavier Bird and Elijah Whiskyjack [who] join the Canadian Army in 1915 . . . expect[ing] to go to France, become warriors and kill Germans. What they don't expect is that the war will drive one of them mad and make the other a morphine-addicted cripple. . . . Elijah is outgoing and boastful, while Xavier is quiet and reserved, but both are deadly efficient soldiers. A parallel story line tells of Niska, Xavier's aunt, a Cree Indian prophet and healer, as she tells of the sad decline of Cree culture and waits for her nephew to come home. . . . [O]ne of the men's addiction to drugs and killing causes him to take extreme risks; when he finally commits murder to hide the ugly truth, his friend sees only one solution to save his own soul." (Publishers Weekly)

Boylan, Jennifer Finney, 1958-

Long Black Veil; A Novel. by Jennifer Finney Boylan. First edition. Random House Inc 2017 290 p. $25

ISBN 0451496329; 9780451496324

In this novel, by Jennifer Finney Boylan, "on a warm August night in 1980, six college students sneak into the dilapidated ruins of Philadelphia's Eastern State Penitentiary, looking for a thrill. . . . But it's not long before they realize they are locked in—and not alone. When the friends get lost and separated, the terrifying night ends in tragedy, and the unexpected, far-reaching consequences reverberate through the survivors' lives." (Publisher's note)

Boyle, Elizabeth

Along Came a Duke; Rhymes with Love. Elizabeth Boyle. Avon 2012 384 p.

ISBN 0062089064; 9780062089069

In this historical romance novel, author Elizabeth Boyle launches the Rhymes with Love Regency series with this . . . Cinderella story. The duke of Preston is the worst sort of rake, ruining young men with reckless wagers and seducing innocent misses during parties. Tabitha Timmons is an orphan who lives with her aunt and uncle and works her fingers to the bone as a scullery maid. A sensible girl who speaks her mind, she immediately pegs Preston as a ne'er-do-well. It takes a late-night dinner and an impromptu dancing lesson for her to sense hints of Prince Charming. Tabitha may be naive about many things, but she is resourceful and practical when it comes to saving herself from greedy relatives interested in her inheritance." (Publishers Weekly)

Boyle, T. Coraghessan, 1948-

The **Harder** They Come; A Novel. by T.C. Boyle. HarperCollins 2015 400 p. $27.99

ISBN 0062349376; 9780062349378

LC 2015296230

This book by T. C. Boyle follows "an ex-Marine and retired school principal 'Sten' Stensen and his schizophrenic son, Adam, who arms himself against shadowy 'hostiles' and identifies with heroic 19th-century wilderness guide John Colter. On vacation in Costa Rica, Sten kills a gunman attempting to rob his tour group. . . . Meanwhile, Adam forms a tenuous, lust-fueled bond with anti-government activist Sara Jenning." (Publishers Weekly)

"Boyle remains a master at sustaining narrative momentum as the sense of foreboding darkens and deepens." Kirkus

Boyle, T. Coraghessan, 1948-

The **relive** box and other stories; T. C. Boyle. Ecco, an imprint of HarperCollins Publishers 2017 252 p. (hardcover) $25.99

ISBN 9780062673398; 0062673394; 9780062673404

In this book, author T. C. Boyle's "sharp wit and rich imagination combine with a penetrating social consciousness to produce . . . expansive short stories defined by an inimitable voice. . . . In stories that span a variety of styles and genres, Boyle addresses the enduring concerns of the human mind and heart while taking on timely social concerns." (Publisher's note)

"Boyle's substantial collection is funny, disarming, and crushing, haunting and beautiful . . . ." Booklist

Boyle, T. Coraghessan

Road to Wellville; a novel. Viking 1993 476p il

ISBN 0-670-83766-0

LC 92-50731

The author "evokes the world of the senses with remarkable skill. As always, his prose is a marvel, enjoyable from beginning to end, alive with astute observations, sharp intelligence and subtle musicality. Possibly as an effect of his highly developed style, Mr. Boyle's vision has been one of the most distinctive and original of his generation." N Y Times Book Rev

Boyle, T. Coraghessan, 1948-

The **Terranauts**; a novel. T. C. Boyle. HarperCollins 2016 528 p. (hardcover) $25.99; (ebook) $25.99

ISBN 9780062349408; 9780062349460; 0062349406

LC 2016035720

In this novel, by T. C. Boyle, "it is 1994 . . . in the desert near Tillman, Arizona. . . . As climate change threatens the earth, eight scientists, four men and four women dubbed the 'Terranauts,' have been selected to live under glass in E2, a prototype of a possible off-earth colony. Their sealed, three-acre compound comprises five biomes—rainforest, savanna, desert, ocean, and marsh—and enough wildlife, water, and vegetation to sustain them." (Publisher's note)

"Beneath the high-tech sheen is a rather old-fashioned theme: how idealistic enterprises can crumble owing to the foibles and fragility of human nature. This is one of Boyle's best—and quite possibly one of the best of the year." LJ

Boyle, T. Coraghessan

★ The **tortilla** curtain. Viking 1995 355p

ISBN 0-670-85604-5

LC 95-1970

"What Boyle does, and does well, is lay on the line our national cult of hypocrisy. Comically and painfully he details the snug wastefulness of the haves and the vile misery of the have-nots. . . . Americans of every stripe will find themselves rooting for Cándido and América, right up to the riproaring deus ex machina ending that screams out that we are all in this together." Nation

Boyle, T. Coraghessan

When the killing's done. Viking 2011 369p $26.95

ISBN 978-0-670-02232-8; 0-670-02232-2

LC 2010-46488

"The novel never reduces its narrative to polemics—there are no heroes here—while underscoring the difficult decisions that those who consider themselves on the side of the angels must face. Narrative propulsion is laced with delicious irony in this winning novel." Kirkus

Boyle, T. Coraghessan

Wild child; stories. Viking 2010 304p $25.95

ISBN 978-0-670-02142-0; 0-670-02142-3

LC 2009-26518

In this "collection of short stories, Boyle captures characters facing a range of critical turning points. Some of these moments are quiet: An unexpected emotional connection is made in a rundown recording studio ('Three Quarters of the Way to Hell'); a college graduate wonders whether she should accept a menial dog-sitting job ('Admiral'). Others are more obviously dramatic: A woman encounters an escaped tiger in her suburban garden ('Question 62'); a Venezuelan baseball player discovers his mother has been kidnapped ('The Unlucky Mother of Aquiles Maldonado'). In Boyle's world, they all have the potential to become peak experiences. While the scenarios may be surreal, the characters experiencing them are decidedly down-to-earth." Boston Globe

Boyle, T. Coraghessan

The **women**; a novel. Viking 2009 451p $27.95

ISBN 978-0-670-02041-6; 0-670-02041-9

LC 2008-42462

"Boyle's latest novel takes on the architect Frank Lloyd Wright by examining his notoriously tumultuous relationships with four women, each unique in her own histrionic way. Narrated in reverse chronological order by a fictional Japanese apprentice, the book is extremely readable and deftly builds a portrait of the artist as pure egoist. Unfortunately, the novel avoids any sustained consideration of Wright's relationship to his art—a passion arguably more important in forming his genius than any of the women in his life were. Still, it proves an effective showcase for Boyle's own strengths as a craftsman. His prose is full of vivid descriptions and turns of phrase that pop with a preternatural precision." New Yorker

Boyle, T. Coraghessan

World's end; a novel. Viking 1987 456p

ISBN 0-670-81489-X

LC 87-40023

"The themes Mr. Boyle develops as his story shuttles between epochs make us grasp in new terms their connection with the American social and political experiment. His mastery of history is the secret of the accomplishment here. Mr. Boyle has lost none of the qualities that marked him a wit writer before, but now he has challenged his own disengagement; passion, need and belief breathe with striking force and freedom through this smashing good novel." N Y Times Book Rev

Boyne, John

The **absolutist**; John Boyne. Other Press 2011 309 p. (trade paperback) $16.95; (ebook) $14.99; (audiobook) $40.95

ISBN 1590515528; 9781590515525; 9781590515532; 9781452629360

LC 2012000433

This book by John Boyne "documents the lives of two inseparable men navigating the trenches of WWI and the ramifications of a taboo involvement. . . .Tristan Sadler [is] a soldier en route to visit his dead comrade Will Bancroft's older sister Marian in Norwich, England. . . . The story oscillates between Sadler's trip in 1919 to return Will's letters to Marian, and recollections of wartime, including a forbidden and fleeting homosexual affair with Bancroft." (Publishers Weekly)

Boyne, John

Crippen; a novel of murder. Thomas Dunne Books 2006 337p $24.95

ISBN 978-0-312-34358-3; 0-312-34358-2

LC 2005-56011

First published 2004 in the United Kingdom

"Boyne starts with the basic facts. . . but he has altered the story to suit his dramatic needs and authorial whims. The result of his reinvention is a dark comedy that is supremely readable, always suspenseful, sometimes laugh-out-loud funny and, finally, a monumental piece of misogyny. In Boyne's sardonic telling, Cora Crippen was a monster who richly deserved to die, and her long-suffering husband was a man more sinned against than sinning." Washington Post Book World

Boyne, John

The **house** of special purpose; by John Boyne. Other Press 2012 480 p. (paperback) $16.95

ISBN 1590515986; 9781590515983; 9781590515990

LC 2012030175

In this historical novel, by John Boyne, "eighty-year-old Georgy Jachmenev is haunted by his past--a past of death, suffering, and scandal. . . . Living in England with his beloved wife, Zoya, Georgy prepares to make one final journey back to the Russia he once knew and loved. . . . As Georgy remembers days gone by, we are transported to St. Petersburg, to the Winter Palace of the czar, in the early twentieth century--a time of change, threat, and bloody revolution." (Publisher's note)

Bracewell, Patricia

Shadow on the crown; Patricia Bracewell. Viking 2013 xi, 416 p.p map (hardcover) $27.95

ISBN 0670026395; 9780670026395

LC 2012028932

This book by Patricia Bracewell "begins with Emma of Normandy crossing the 'Narrow Sea' in 1002 C.E. to marry the much older King Aethelred. Emma is ill-prepared for the trials that come with her new position. . . .The king, regretting the hasty decision of 'taking a Norman slut to wife,' quickly tires of his demanding new bride; jealous rivals vie for Emma's crown; and the threat of a Viking invasion constantly looms." (Publishers Weekly)

Bradbury, Ray

★ **Bradbury** stories; 100 of his most celebrated tales. Morrow 2003 893p hardcover o.p. pa $17.95

ISBN 0-06-054242-X; 0-06-054488-0 pa

LC 2003-42189

"This massive retrospective of self-selected Bradbury stories offers a compendium of his eccentrics, misfits, losers, and small-town dreamers, who typically inhabit an uncanny setting or confront a strange, unsettling situation." Libr J

Bradbury, Ray

★ **Dandelion** wine; a novel. Avon Books 1999 267p $15.95

ISBN 0-380-97726-5

LC 98-93914

First published 1957 by Doubleday

A novel about one summer in the life of a twelve-year-old boy, Douglas Spaulding: the summer of 1928. The place is Green Town, Illinois, and Doug and his brother Tom wander in and out among their elders, living and dreaming, sometimes aware of things, again just having a wonderful time. Doug's big discovery that summer was that he was alive.

"The writing is beautiful and the characters are wonderful living people. A rare reading experience—highly recommended to all libraries." Libr J

Followed by Farewell summer (2006)

Bradbury, Ray, 1920-2012

★ **Fahrenheit** 451. Simon & Schuster 2003 190p $23

ISBN 0-7432-4722-1

LC 2003-66160

First published 1953 in paperback by Ballantine Bks.

Dystopian novel about a bookburner official in a future fascist state.

Bradbury, Ray

The **illustrated** man. Doubleday 1951 251p

In this work "the stories are given a linking framework; they are all seen as magical tattoos becoming living stories, springing from the body of the protagonist." Sci Fic Ency

Bradbury, Ray

★ The **Martian** chronicles. Avon Books 1997 268p $15.95

ISBN 0-380-97383-9

LC 96-95071

First published 1950 by Doubleday

This book's "closely interwoven short stories, linked by recurrent images and themes, tell of the repeated attempts by humans to colonize Mars, of the way they bring their old prejudices with them, and of the repeated, ambiguous meetings with the shape-changing Martians." Sci Fic Ency

Bradbury, Ray

★ **Something** wicked this way comes. Avon Bks. 1999 293p $15.95; pa $7.99

ISBN 0-380-97727-3; 0-380-72940-7 pa

A reissue of the title first published 1962 by Simon and Schuster

"We read here of the loss of innocence, the recognition of evil, the bond between generations, and the purely fantastic. These forces enter Green Town, Illinois, on the wheels of Cooger and Dark's Pandemonium Shadow Show. Will Halloway and Jim Nightshade, two 13-year-olds, explore the sinister carnival for excitement, which becomes desperation as the forces of the dark threaten to engulf-them. Bradbury's gentle humanism and lyric style serve this fantasy well." Shapiro. Fic for Youth. 3d edition

Braden, Kara

The **Longest** Night; by Kara Braden. Sourcebooks Inc 2014 320 p. $7.99

ISBN 140229185X; 9781402291852

In this book, by Kara Braden, "Ian Fairchild, a brilliant and sophisticated criminal defense lawyer from Manhattan, is left with major back pain and an addiction to narcotic painkillers after an accident. His brother, Preston, calls in a debt and sends Ian to recover at the cabin home of former marine captain Cecily Knight. . . . Cecily has been fighting her own demons for seven years since being captured and tortured while deployed." (Booklist)

"The two of them grow to respect, like, and then lust for one another, their relationship hindered by Ian's overly logical approach to life and Cecily's self-doubt and fear. Their blossoming is slow, steady, inevitable, and entrancing." Pub Wkly

Bradford, Barbara Taylor

★ A **woman** of substance. Doubleday 1979 755p

ISBN 0-385-12050-8

LC 77-9231

"It's a life worth the telling, and Ms. Bradford has told it well, sparing no detail. She writes competently, if not extraordinarily, against an accurate and well drawn historical background." West Coast Rev Books

Followed by Hold the dream

Bradley, Alan

As chimney sweepers come to dust; a Flavia de Luce novel. Alan Bradley. Delacorte Press 2015 416 p. (Flavia de Luce) (hardcover : acid-free paper) $25

ISBN 0345539931; 9780345539939

LC 2014029962

In this novel by Alan Bradley, "Twelve-year-old Flavia de Luce laments her predicament, when her father and Aunt Felicity ship her off to Miss Bodycote's Female Academy, the boarding school that her mother, Harriet, once attended . . . in Canada. The sun has not yet risen . . . when a gift lands at her feet. . . . Now, while attending classes . . . , Flavia is on the hunt for the victim's identity and time of death, as well as suspects, motives, and means." (Publisher's note)

"Flavia's resourcefulness away from her English village with a whole new set of well-drawn characters is reason to rejoice. Fans of Dorothy Sayers, Gladys Mitchell, and Agatha Christie will delight in this engaging series." LJ

Bradley, Alan ✓

I am half-sick of shadows; Alan Bradley. Delacorte Press 2011 297 p.

ISBN 9780385344012 (hardback); 9780345532152 (ebook); 0385344015

LC 2011022373

This book tells the story of "the precocious Flavia de Luce -- an eleven-year-old-sleuth with a passion for chemistry and a penchant for crime solving. . . . [W]hen a film crew arrives at Buckshaw, the de Luces' decaying English estate, to shoot a movie starring the famed Phyllis Wyvern . . . nobody is prepared for the evening's shocking conclusion: a body found, past midnight, strangled to death with a length of film." (Publisher's note) "Despite the murder and subsequent investigation, 'Shadows' is more about the de Luce family than anything else. . . . [T] he real plot revolves around Flavia's simultaneous desire to understand more about he de Luces and nervousness about what she might learn." (arts.nationalpost.com)

Bradley, Alan ✓

A **red** herring without mustard; a Flavia de Luce novel. Delacorte Press 2011 399p $23

ISBN 978-0-385-34232-2

LC 2010-49325

"Think preteen Nancy Drew, only savvier and a lot richer, and you have Flavia de Luce, an 11-year-old sleuth of the English gentry who's morbidly interested in both corpses and poison (she's got a chemistry lab in the attic). When a body turns up on the lawn of the family estate — skewered by an heirloom sterling lobster fork — she gets to work. Don't be fooled by Flavia's age or the 1950s setting: A Red Herring isn't a dainty tea-and-crumpets sort of mystery. It's shot through with real grit." Entertainment Wkly

Bradley, Alan ✓

Speaking from among the bones; a Flavia de Luce novel. Alan Bradley. Delacorte Press 2012 400 p. (ebook) $24

ISBN 0385344031; 9780345538680; 9780385344036

LC 2012028396

In this mystery novel by Alan Bradley, part of the Flavia de Luce series, "Eleven-year-old amateur detective and ardent chemist Flavia de Luce . . . finds . . . the body of Mr. Collicutt, the church organist, . . . [in a] patron's saint's tomb. . . . Who held a vendetta against Mr. Collicutt, and why would they hide him in such a sacred resting place? The irrepressible Flavia decides to find out." (Publisher's note)

Bradley, Alan ✓

★ The **sweetness** at the bottom of the pie; Alan Bradley. Delacorte Press 2009 373p (Flavia de Luce) (pbk.) $15

ISBN 9780385343497; 9780385342308

LC 2008041787

Macavity Award: Best First Mystery Novel (2010)

Agatha Award: Best First Novel (2009)

Arthur Ellis Award: Best First Novel (2010)

Dilys Award (2010)

This book follows "11-year-old sleuth Flavia de Luce. . . . In an early 1950s English village, Flavia is preoccupied with retaliating against her lofty older sisters when a rude, redheaded stranger arrives to confront her eccentric father, a philatelic devotee. Equally adept at quoting 18th-century works, listening at keyholes and picking locks, Flavia learns that her father, Colonel de Luce, may be involved in the suicide of his long-ago schoolmaster and the theft of a priceless stamp. The sudden expiration of the stranger in a cucumber bed, wacky village characters with ties to the schoolmaster, and a sharp inspector with doubts about the colonel and his enterprising young detective daughter mean complications for Flavia." (Publishers Weekly)

"Mystery fans, Anglophiles, and science buffs will delight in this book and may come away with a slightly altered view of what is possible for a headstrong girl to achieve." SLJ

Other titles about Flavia de Luce are:

The weed that strings the hangman's bag (2010)

A red herring without mustard (2011)

I am half-sick of shadows (2011)

Speaking from among the bones (2013)

The dead in their vaulted arches (2014)

As chimney sweepers come to dust (2015)

Thrice the brinded cat hath mew'd (2016)

The grave's a fine and private place (2018)

Bradley, Alan

The **weed** that strings the hangman's bag; a Flavia de Luce mystery. Alan Bradley. Delacorte Press 2010 364p map $24

ISBN 9780385342315

LC 2009043002

This is the second mystery novel featuring girl detective Flavia de Luce, introduced in The Sweetness at the Bottom of the Pie (2009). When master puppeteer Robert Porson's "van breaks down in the village of Bishop's Lacey, Flavia . . . helps Rupert and his charming assistant, Nialla, put together a performance in the local church. . . . But even as the newcomers . . . set the stage for Jack and the Beanstalk, there are signs that something just isn't right: Nialla's strange bruises and solitary cries in the churchyard, Rupert's unexplained disappearances and a violent argument with his BBC producer, the disturbing atmosphere at Culverhouse Farm, and the peculiar goings-on in nearby Gibbet Wood—where young Robin Ingleby was found hanging . . . While the local police do their best to keep up with Flavia in solving Rupert's murder, his killer may pull Flavia in way over her head." (Publisher's note)

Bradley, Celeste

I Thee Wed; Celeste Bradley. Penguin Group USA 2016 352 p. (The wicked Worthingtons series) (paperback) $7.99

ISBN 9780451475978; 0451475976

In this novel by Celeste Bradley in the Wicked Worthington Series, "Orion Worthington aspired to be like his mentor, the acclaimed scientist Sir Geoffrey Blayne. Logically, Sir Geoffrey's daughter would be Orion's perfect match. So why can't he keep his mind off the unruly girl who works in Sir Geoffrey's lab? Orphaned fire-cracker Francesca Penrose hopes that London is modern enough to accept her brilliant mind despite her womanhood." (Publisher's note)

"This hugely fun novel is charming and delightful the whole way through." Pub Wkly

Bradley, Marion Zimmer

The **mists** of Avalon. Ballantine Pub. Group 2000 876p $30; pa $16.95

ISBN 0-345-44118-4; 0-345-35049-9 pa

LC 00-712415

A reissue of the title first published 1982 by Knopf

This retelling of the Arthurian legend is dominated by the character of Morgan le Fay (here called Morgaine), the powerful sorceress who symbolizes the historical clash betweeen Christianity and the early pagan religions of the British Isles." Publ Wkly

Other novels in the Avalon series written with Diana L. Paxson are: The forest house (1993); Lady of Avalon (1997); Priestess of Avalon (2000). Following Bradley's death Paxson continued the series with: Ancestors of Avalon (2004); Ravens of Avalon (2007); Sword of Avalon (2009)

Braffet, Kelly

Save yourself; a novel. Kelly Braffet. Crown Publishers 2013 352 p. (alk. paper) $25

ISBN 0385347340; 9780385347341

LC 2012048148

In this book, set in Ratchetsburg, Pa., "Patrick Cusimano blames his brother, Mike, for the fact that, their father, John, was sent to prison for the hit-and-run death of a child while in an alcoholic haze. Mike believes that if Patrick hadn't called the police, their father would never have been arrested, despite the damaged, bloody car. The residents of Ratchetsburg also fault the brothers for waiting 19 hours before calling the police." (Publishers Weekly)

Bragg, Melvyn

The **soldier's** return. Arcade Pub. 2002 384p $25.95

ISBN 1-55970-639-2

LC 2002-21558

First published 1999 in the United Kingdom

"Bragg weaves a powerful, deeply moving story of a family and a society torn apart by war. His straightforward prose and the measured pace of his writing allow readers to savor every nuance of life in a small town in postwar England, and the depth and reality of his characters and his ability to bring the horrors of war alive are nothing short of brilliant." Booklist

Bragg, Melvyn

A **son** of war; a novel. Arcade Pub. 2003 426p $25.95

ISBN 1-559-70686-4

LC 2002-44058

"A hauntingly evocative slice of postwar life." Booklist

Brand, Max

Beyond the outposts. Five Star 1997 254p

ISBN 0-7862-0745-0

LC 97-9308

Earlier version of this story was serialized in 1925 in Western Story magazine

This western adventure follows the "journeys of young Lew Dorset as he searches for his father, an escaped convict. His skill with firearms gets him a job as a hunter with a trader's freight train heading onto the prairies to barter with the Indians. There he meets young Chuck Morris, and together they take on a Cheyenne attack party. Finding shelter in a Sioux village, they absorb the native culture. . . . Lew goes on to play a decisive role in a battle between the Sioux and Pawnee, but returns to find that Chuck has deserted his wife and son. His attempts to reconcile them culminate in great danger and, ultimately, a threat to his life." Publisher's note

Brand, Max

Chinook; a north-western story. Five Star 1998 271p

ISBN 0-7862-1155-5

LC 98-22718

"Joe Harney heads to Alaska during the great gold rush of 1898 and finds himself impressed by a great wolf dog owned by Andrew Steen, a crusty, bad-tempered loner. When Harney saves Steen's life, Steen grudgingly agrees that they can travel overland together. On that harsh journey, they meet Kate Winslow and learn that she's headed for Circle City to meet up with a man who wants her dead. This is a tale of the tough and often ruthless folks who risked their lives to get to the frozen north and, with any luck, to find their fortune." Publisher's note

Brand, Max

★ The **collected** stories of Max Brand; edited, with story prefaces, by Robert and Jane Easton; introduction by William Bloodworth. centennial ed; University of Neb. Press 1994 xx, 342p $40

ISBN 0-8032-1244-5

LC 93-43938

Brand, Max

Max Brand's best western stories; edited with a biographical introduction by William F. Nolan. Dodd, Mead 1981 3v

LC 81-3204

Contents v1 Wine on the desert; Virginia creeper; Macdonald's dream; Partners; Dust across the range {novelette}; The bells of San

Carlos; v3 Reata's peril trek; Crazy rhythm; Dust storm; A lucky dog; The third bullet; Half a partner; The sun stood still; v2 Outcasts {novelette}; The fear of Morgon the Fearless; Dark Rosaleen {novelette}; Cayenne Charlie; The golden day

Brand, Max

★ The **Stingaree**. Dodd, Mead 1968 216p

"Jimmy Green is a wild, half-Indian, half-civilized, thirteen-year-old who is undisputed king of the small village of Fort Anxious. One day, a tramp wanders into the village, and ultimately into the life of Jimmy, changing it from the complacent existence of a boy into the desperate flight of a fugitive. The stranger, also known as the Stingaree, has come from Alabama to revenge the death of his partner by the leading citizen of Fort Anxious. Although he succeeds in forcing the man to confess, he is thwarted by the police in his attempt to kill Stanley Parker. The Stingaree, along with Jimmy Green, an Indian companion, and a wild dog is forced to flee into the wilderness, beginning one of the best chase episodes." Libr J

Brandt, Harry

The **Whites**; a novel. Richard Price writing as Harry Brandt. Henry Holt & Co. 2015 352 p. (hardback) $28

ISBN 0805093990; 9780805093995

LC 2014028457

In this novel by Richard Price, "Night Watch is summoned to the four a.m. fatal slashing of a man in Penn Station, and this time Billy's investigation moves beyond the usual handoff to the day tour. And when he discovers that the victim was once a suspect in . . . a savage case with connections to the former members of the Wild Geese--the bad old days are back in Billy's life with a vengeance." (Publisher's note)

"In the wake of rage and sorrow, ordinary people respond by going crazy and screwing up. In this far-from-ordinary novel, Price/Brandt explores the hows and whys. Fasten your seat belt." Kirkus

Braun, Lilian Jackson

The **cat** who ate Danish modern. Dutton 1967 192p

"The mystery is mild, the satire on interior decorating fads and fancies amusing, and the Siamese cat who helps play detective delightful." Publ Wkly

Braun, Lilian Jackson

★ The **cat** who went underground. Putnam 1989 223p

ISBN 0-399-13431-X

LC 88-32185

"Qwill's saving grace is that he is properly humble before the superior intelligence of his pets, while the author is shrewd enough to balance the cats' amazing antics with many amusing character studies of the Mooseville natives." N Y Times Book Rev

Brave new worlds; edited by John Joseph Adams. Night Shade Books 2011 481p pa $15.99

ISBN 978-1-59780-221-5

"Familiar classics by such luminaries as Shirley Jackson, Ursula K. Le Guin, and J.G. Ballard rub shoulders with new standouts in this dark anthology of 33 dystopian futures and alternate worlds. In Joseph Paul Haines's 'Ten with a Flag,' a government uses confusion to manipulate the governed. Sarah Langan's 'Independence Day' shows a tyrannical future U.S. through a teenager's eyes. Matt Williamson's 'Sacrament' offers the torturer's perspective on his 'art.' Adam-Troy Castro's 'Of a Sweet Slow Dance in the Wake of Temporary Dogs' asks how much of our souls we would surrender for nine days of guaranteed happiness plus one of horror. Grinding inevitability runs through Vylar Kaftan's interactive 'Civilization.' Most of the stories are bleak, many are hopeless, and all serve as powerful warnings of what we may let ourselves become." Publ Wkly

Brekke, Jorgen

The **fifth** element; Jorgen Brekke. First U.S. edition Minotaur Books 2017 314 p. (hardcover) $26.99

ISBN 9781250073914; 9781466885417

LC 2016043769

In this book, by Jorgen Brekke, "Police Inspector Odd Singsaker has been captured, imprisoned on an island off the Northern coast of Norway. He wakes to find himself holding a shotgun. Next to him is a corpse. But what events led him to this point? And how did he get here? A few weeks earlier, Felicia, his wife, disappeared. Though he didn't know it, she was trying to find her way back to Odd to reconcile, but then she vanished into a snowstorm." (Publisher's note)

"It's Brekke's prodigious powers of invention, his ability to keep coming up with unforgettable characters and indelible episodes, that lift this above his own earlier work and most of the heavy Nordic competition." Kirkus

Brennan, Marie

A **natural** history of dragons; a memoir by Lady Trent. Marie Brennan. Tor 2013 336 p. (hardcover) $16.99

ISBN 0765331969; 9780765331960

LC 2012038819

In this book, "Isabella, Lady Trent, is a naturalist and adventurer in a country that . . . resembles 19th-century England, yet fantastical creatures roam. . . . Isabella has been obsessed with studying dragons since childhood, but a formal scientific career is off limits to a woman. Instead she . . . joins her husband's expedition to see the wild dragons of Vystrana. Along the way, Isabella solves a mystery and proves her worth as a naturalist." (Publishers Weekly)

Brett, Simon

Mrs Pargeter's Principle; Simon Brett. Severn House Pub Ltd 2015 192 p. (Mrs Pargeter Mysteries) (hardcover) $28.95

ISBN 9781780290744; 1780290748

This cozy mystery novel, by Simon Brett, features the return of the character Mrs. Pargeter. "It is a matter of principle that she should complete any of her late husband's unfinished business. Amongst the many bequests he made to her, perhaps the most valuable is his little black book. . . . This means that whenever Mrs P has a crime to solve she can readily contact someone with the relevant expertise to help in her enquiries." (Publisher's note)

"Brett's customary wit and good humor abound." Pub Wkly

Brett, Simon

★ **Murder** unprompted; a Charles Paris novel. Scribner 1982 160p

ISBN 0-684-17659-9

LC 82-5578

"Here Paris is less drunk than usual, which enables us to believe that he can think as shrewdly as he does. And the situation is delightful: he gets at last a chance to act in a play that may move to a big West End theater if all goes well in the tryouts. The interplay among the cast is splendid, funny, and also touching. Murder in full view, on the first night, might bring good publicity, but other troubles develop—the whole mess handled in masterly fashion." Barzun. Cat of Crime. Rev and enl edition

Brett, Simon

The **torso** in the town; a Fethering mystery. Berkley Prime Crime 2002 340p

ISBN 0-425-18502-8

LC 2002-18482

"A dinner party in a richly restored country house in a Sussex village that is 'riddled with class consciousness' is interrupted by a scream. A body, arms and legs neatly removed, has been discovered in the cellar. There to witness the discovery is an outsider, a middle-aged woman from the seaside village of Fethering. The woman, Jude brings news of the grisly find back to her pal Carole Seddon another middle-aged woman from Fethering, in hopes that a little mystery will pull her out of a depression brought on by a lapsed love affair. . . . The ladies from Fethering once again proceed totally outside the bumbling police investigation in a somehow utterly credible way, gaining access and insight where the police can't." Booklist

Brill, Amy

The **movement** of stars; Amy Brill. Riverhead Books 2013 400 p. (hardcover) $27.95

ISBN 1594487448; 9781101602058; 9781594487446

LC 2012027241

In this book, introverted Quaker "Hannah Gardner Price spends her days working at the local Nantucket Atheneum and her nights scanning the stars in search of a comet that she hopes will earn her a prestigious King of Denmark Prize. . . . Hannah soon finds herself at a crossroad when her father announces he's remarrying and moving to Philadelphia, meaning Hannah must either marry . . . or abandon her night-sky vigils." She embarks on a controversial interracial relationship. (Bust Magazine)

Brin, David

Existence; David Brin. Tor 2012 556 p. (hardcover) $27.99

ISBN 9780765303615; 9781429946964

LC 2012017272

This science fiction book tells the story of "Gerald Livingston [who] is an orbital garbage collector. For a hundred years, people have been abandoning things in space, and someone has to clean it up. But there's something spinning a little bit higher than he expects, something that isn't on the decades' old orbital maps. An hour after he grabs it and brings it in, rumors fill Earth's infomesh about an 'alien artifact.' Thrown into the maelstrom of worldwide shared experience, the Artifact is a game-changer. A message in a bottle; an alien capsule that wants to communicate. The world reacts as humans always do: with fear and hope and selfishness and love and violence. And insatiable curiosity." (Publisher's note)

Includes bibliographical references [p. [556] [558])

Brink, Andre Philippus

★ The **other** side of silence; [by] André Brink. Harcourt 2003 311p

ISBN 0-15-100770-5

LC 2002-32748

First published 2002 in the United Kingdom

This novel "takes as its point of departure a German program at the turn of the twentieth century whereby women were shipped out to Germany's colonies in South-West Africa (now Namibia) to be wives—or, failing that, sexual fodder—for the colonizers. Brink's protagonist, Hannah X., an abused orphan from Bremen, is eager for the imagined romance of the desert, but life in the colonies turns out to be even worse than what she has known before. . . .Brink's powerful and brutal story is an effective response to those who suspected that the end of apartheid would leave him without a subject, and a shrewd meditation on the dehumanizing power of hatred." New Yorker

Brink, André P. (André Philippus), 1935-2015

★ **Philida**; a novel. by Andre Brink. Vintage Books 2012 310 p. (paperback) $15

ISBN 0345805038; 9780345805034

LC 2012031043

This book, "set on South Africa's Cape ('Caab') in the 1830s as slavery is being abolished, and four characters and one outsider narrate the action. Philida is the most sympathetic, seeking justice when a promise of freedom from her 'baas' with whom she bore four children is reneged on, and she is put to auction." (Library Journal)

"With alternating present-tense viewpoints, the aching personal drama is set against the history of lechery, power, and violent abuse... [a] stirring novel." Booklist

Brkic, Courtney Angela

The **First** Rule of Swimming; by Courtney Angela Brkic. Little, Brown and Co. 2013 384 p. $26

ISBN 0316217387; 9780316217385

In this novel by Courtney Angela Brkic "Magdalena does not panic when she learns that her younger sister has disappeared. A free-spirit, Jadranka has always been prone to mysterious absences. But when weeks pass with no word, Magdalena leaves the isolated Croatian island where their family has always lived and sets off to New York to find her sister. Her search begins to unspool the dark history of their family, reaching back three generations to a country torn by war." (Publisher's note)

Brockmeier, Kevin

The **brief** history of the dead; Kevin Brockmeier. Pantheon Books 2006 252p $22.95

ISBN 0375423699

LC 2005-48882

"The City is inhabited by the recently departed, who reside there only as long as they remain in the memories of the living. Among the current residents of this afterlife are Luka Sims, who prints the only newspaper in the City, with news from the other side; Coleman Kinzler, a vagrant who speaks the cautionary words of God; and Marion and Phillip Byrd, who find themselves falling in love again after decades of marriage. On Earth, Laura Byrd is trapped by extreme weather in an Antarctic research station." (Publisher's note)

"Although it never quite lives up to its promising premise, the novel's Borges-like spirit will appeal to select readers." Booklist

Brockmeier, Kevin

The **Illumination**. Pantheon Books 2011 257p $24.95

ISBN 0375425314; 9780375425318

LC 2010-20732

In the aftermath of a fatal car accident, a private journal of love notes written by a husband to his wife passes into the keeping of a hospital patient, and from there through the hands of five other suffering people.

"For a novel so relentlessly fixed on elucidating human suffering in all its permutations, 'The Illumination' is surprisingly uplifting. This is a testament to Brockmeier's considerable stylistic gifts — the man writes exquisite sentences — and to the palpable compassion with which he frames each of his characters." Cleveland Plain Dealer

Brockmeier, Kevin

The **view** from the seventh layer. Pantheon Books 2008 267p $21.95

ISBN 978-0-375-42530-1; 0-375-42530-6

LC 2007-23404

"This work compiles 13 wondrous tales—four fables, eight stories, and one choose-your-own-adventure. . . . [Brockmeier's] stories have a bit less of the troubling, possibly ironic distancing that can be a pitfall in the fiction of peers like David Foster Wallace. Instead, we're invited to empathize with the characters via his clean lines and attentive crafting. The comparisons to Italo Calvino are certainly valid (Calvino's novel The Baron in the Trees is even referenced), and yet Brockmeier's tales feel distinctly contemporary." Libr J

Brockway, Connie

The **golden** season; Connie Brockway. Onyx 2010 388p. (pbk.) $7.99

ISBN 9780451412836; 0451412834

LC 2010479420

This book follows "Lydia Eastlake, . . . the toast of the town . . . [who] never thought her considerable fortune would ever run out. Now she is left with one option if she doesn't want to learn how to economize: find a wealthy man to marry before word of her financial reversal gets out. After meeting kind and sexy Captain Ned Lockton, Lydia thinks she may have found her perfect match, but what she doesn't know is that Ned, whose own family is rapidly draining the ancestral coffers, is hunting for a spouse too, and only heiresses need apply." (Booklist)

Brockway, Connie

No Place for a Dame; by Connie Brockway. Amazon Pub 2013 292 p. $12.95

ISBN 1477808582; 9781477808580

LC 2013906195

In this book, by Connie Brockway, "Avery dreams of becoming a member of the Royal Astronomical Society--and the only way she can join the all-male society is to disguise herself as a boy. After helping Giles, Lord Strand, escape a disastrous engagement, she is certain he will assist in her daring masquerade. No lady would ever come up with such a preposterous scheme, and no gentleman would accept...but fortunately for Avery, Giles is no gentleman." (Publisher's note)

Brockway "delivers a unique, engaging historical storyline with fun, intriguing elements and with a delicious arc of two star-crossed misfits who share a deep love and deserve an exceptional future." Kirkus

Bronsky, Alina

The **Hottest** Dishes of the Tartar Cuisine; translated from German by Tim Mohr. Europa Editions 2011 304p.

ISBN 9781609450069 pa

This book tells the story of "Rosa Achmetowna . . . [who] lives in a cramped Soviet apartment with her husband, teenage daughter Sulfia, and a nosy, disagreeable roommate. . . . [W]hen the 'rather stupid' Sulfia winds up pregnant, Rosa immediately tries a variety of crude home remedies for aborting Sulfia's baby—but nine months later, Aminat is born." (Publishers Weekly)

"When Aminat, now a wild and willful teenager, catches the eye of a sleazy German cookbook writer researching Tartar cuisine, Rosa is quick to broker a deal that will guarantee all three women a passage out of the Soviet Union. But as soon as they are settled in the West, the . . . dysfunctional ties that bind mother, daughter and grandmother begin to fray." (Publisher's note)

Bronte, Anne

The **tenant** of Wildfell Hall. Modern Lib. 1997 510p

ISBN 0-679-60279-8

LC 97-14200

First published 1848

"This epistolary novel presents a portrait of debauchery that is remarkable in light of the author's sheltered life. It is the story of young Helen Graham's disastrous marriage to the dashing drunkard Arthur Huntingdon—said to be modeled on the author's wayward brother Branwell—and her flight from him to the seclusion of Wildfell Hall. Pursued by Gilbert Markham, who is in love with her, Graham refuses him and, by way of explanation, gives him her journal. There he reads of her wretched married life. Eventually, after Huntingdon's death, they marry." Merriam-Webster's Ency of Lit

Bronte, Charlotte

★ **Emma**; by Charlotte Brontë and Another Lady J.M. Dent 1980 201p

Fragments of a story left unfinished at Brontë's death form the opening two chapters of this novel completed by Constance Savery

"In the full-blown literary manner and circuitous story-telling characteristic of Charlotte Brontë, . . . an intriguing melodrama unrolls in this tale of wrongs finally righted. Most wronged is adolescent Martina, deprived of her natural mother by the machinations of her stepbrothers, led on by their sister, the cruel, enigmatic beauty Emma. The events that lead to familial reconciliation include Martina's sentence to ladies' boarding school, abduction to a French convent and graveyard visitations before some fancy detective work by an old friend unravels the ingenious but dastardly plot. The author of this Gothic romp is obviously steeped in the period and felicitous style of the brilliant English novelist, providing entertainment on the same grand scale." Publ Wkly

Bronte, Charlotte

★ **Jane** Eyre; [by] Charlotte Brontë with an introduction by Lucy Hughes-Hallet. Knopf 1991 xxxviii, 284p $20

ISBN 0-679-40582-8

LC 91-52968

First published 1847

"In both heroine and hero the author introduced types new to English fiction. Jane Eyre is a shy, intense little orphan, never for a moment, neither in her unhappy school days nor her subsequent career as a governess, displaying those qualities of superficial beauty and charm that had marked the conventional heroine. Jane's lover, Edward Rochester, to whose ward she is governess, is a strange, violent man, bereft of conventional courtesy, a law unto himself. Rochester's moodiness derives from the fact that he is married to an insane wife, whose existence, long kept secret, is revealed on the very day of his projected marriage to Jane. Years afterward the lovers are reunited." Reader's Ency. 4th edition

Bronte, Emily

★ **Wuthering** Heights; with an introduction by Katherine Frank. Knopf 1991 xxxiii, 385p $22

ISBN 0-679-40543-7

LC 91-52969

First published 1847

Forced by a storm to spend the night at the home of the somber and unsociable Heathcliff, Mr. Lockwood has an encounter with the spirit of Catherine Linton. He gradually learns that Catherine's father, Mr. Earnshaw, had taken in Heathcliff as a young orphan. Heathcliff and Catherine began to fall in love, but after Mr. Earnshaw's death Catherine's brother treated Heathcliff in a degrading manner and Catherine married rich Edgar Linton. Heathcliff gradually worked his revenge against those who injured him.

Includes bibliographical references

Brookmyre, Christopher, 1968-
✓ **When** the Devil Drives; a Liberty Lane mystery. by Christopher Brookmyre. Pgw 2013 288 p. (hardcover) $24
ISBN 080212089X; 9780802120892

In this book, "young women are being scooped off the streets of 1839 London under the cover of darkness, and folks think the devil himself is driving the coach. When the bodies of two victims are later positioned near prominent London monuments, the fear factor rises. Even Liberty Lane, a female private investigator, is shaken by this development. She has been probing the disappearance of a young man's fiancée—who has been murdered—and her client is AWOL." (Library Journal)

Brookmyre, Christopher, 1968-
✓ **Where** the bodies are buried; Christopher Brookmyre. Atlantic Monthly Press 2012 293 p. $25
ISBN 0802120253; 9780802120250

Originally published: London : Little, Brown, 2011.

In this book, Christopher "Brookmyre . . . introduces Det. Insp. Catherine McLeod and PI Jasmine Sharp in . . . [this] Glasgow crime series. . . . [P]erceptive Catherine looks into the murder of a drug dealer, ... while inexperienced Jasmine searches for her PI uncle/boss, who went missing while working a case involving a family that disappeared decades before. Jasmine's only lead is Glen Fallan, a professional assassin who's rumored to have been dead for 20 years." (Publishers Weekly)

"Red herrings and plot convolutions abound, but it's Brookmyre's sense of the city and its no-nuance criminals that makes this one a winner." Booklist

Brookner, Anita
★ **Brief** lives. Random House 1991 260p
ISBN 0-394-58548-8

LC 90-38904

First published 1990 in the United Kingdom

"This short, subtle, beautifully organised and orchestrated novel positively gains from the deliberate restraint and detachment of the writing." London Rev Books

Brookner, Anita
Family and friends. Pantheon Bks. 1985 187p
ISBN 0-394-54616-4

LC 85-6373

"Anita Brookner's prose is impeccably elegant and she is unsentimental with it. . . . There is a closeness of atmosphere, almost claustrophobic, in Family and Friends, as if we were alternating between a discreetly perfumed lady's boudoir and the smoking room of a superior gentleman's club. There is no mistaking the originality as well as the skill and consistency with which the novel so beautifully conforms to its genre and its intentions." N Y Rev Books

Brookner, Anita
★ **Hotel** du Lac. Pantheon Bks. 1985 184p
ISBN 0-394-54215-0

LC 84-20641

First published 1984 in the United Kingdom

The tone of this novel is "oddly detached, very small-scale, faintly humorous. . . . It is by means of this very remoteness that Edith manages to hold our interest throughout this achingly uneventful holiday, with its empty chasms of time, its murmuring respectability, its dining room scattered sparsely with people who mean nothing to her. . . . There are

some uncomfortable patches. . . . But generally, the writing is graceful and attractive." N Y Times Book Rev

Brookner, Anita
Undue influence; a novel. Random House 2000 231p $24
ISBN 0-375-50334-X

LC 99-36282

"The novel contains a fine brace of supporting characters whose behavior implicitly reflects on Claire's fall into limbo, and Brookner's narrative skill works like a scalpel exposing the complexity of each of their lives." Publ Wkly

Brooks, Bill
Frontier justice; a John Henry Cole story. Bill Brooks. Five Star 2012 322 p. (hardcover) $25.95
ISBN 1432826077; 9781432826079

LC 2012016329

This is Bill Brooks' second John Henry Cole story. Here, Cole "hits the trail of revenge after his partner, Ike Kelly, is found dead, apparently the victim of a gigantic, vengeful black man named Leviticus Book. Cole is joined on the trail by bounty hunter Will Harper in an arduous pursuit through bad winter weather and worse luck, taunted all the while by Book, who, with his big Sharps rifle, makes both Cole and Harper seem like fools." (Booklist)

Brooks, Bill
Winter kill; a John Henry Cole story. by Bill Brooks. Five Star, A part of Gale, Cengage Learning 2013 262 p. (A John Henry Cole story) (hardcover) $25.95
ISBN 1432826344; 9781432826345

LC 2013005469

In this Western novel, by Bill Brooks, "John Henry Cole was three miles out of town on his small ranch waiting out the storm that was quickly killing his cattle and horses and starting to feel a little crazy himself. . . . [Then] Teddy Green a Texas Ranger arrives in Cheyenne and seeks Cole's help in locating Ella Mims, a woman who once lived in Cheyenne and with whom Cole had once been intimate. Green wants to question her concerning her involvement in a murder in Denver City." (Publisher's note)

Brooks, Geraldine
Caleb's crossing. Viking 2011 306p $26.95
ISBN 978-0-670-02104-8; 0-670-02104-0

LC 2010-51207

In this book, the narrator, "Bethia Mayfield, grow[s] up in the tiny settlement of Great Harbor amid a small band of pioneers and Puritans. . . . As often as she can, she slips away to . . . observe . . . [the] native Wampanoag inhabitants. At twelve, she encounters Caleb, the young son of a chieftain, and the two forge a tentative secret. . . . Bethia's minister father tries to convert the Wampanoag, awakening the wrath of the tribe's shaman, against whose magic he must test his own beliefs. One of his projects becomes the education of Caleb, and a year later, Caleb is in Cambridge, studying Latin and Greek among the colonial elite. There, Bethia finds herself reluctantly indentured as a housekeeper and can closely observe Caleb's crossing of cultures." (Publisher's note)

A historical novel "inspired by Caleb Cheeshahteaumauck, the first Native American to graduate from Harvard. Brooks brings the 1660s to life with evocative period detail, intriguing characters, and a compelling story narrated by Bethia Mayfield, the outspoken daughter of a Calvinist preacher. While exploring the island now known as Martha's Vineyard, Bethia meets Caleb, a Wampanoag native to the island, and they become close, clandestine friends. After Caleb loses most of his family to smallpox, he begins to study under the tutelage of Bethia's father. Since Bethia isn't allowed to pursue education herself, she eavesdrops on Caleb's and her own brother's lessons. Caleb is a gifted scholar who eventually travels, along with Bethia's brother, to Cambridge to continue his education. Bethia tags along and her descriptions of 17th-century Cambridge and Harvard are as entertaining as they are enlightening." Publ Wkly

Brooks, Geraldine

People of the book. Viking 2008 372p

ISBN 9780670018215

LC 2007-18082

"In 1996, Hanna Heath, an Australian rare-book expert, is offered the job of a lifetime: analysis and conservation of the famed Sarajevo Haggadah, which has been rescued from Serb shelling during the Bosnian war. Priceless and beautiful, the book is one of the earliest Jewish volumes ever to be illuminated with images. . . . In Bosnia during World War II, a Muslim risks his life to protect it from the Nazis. In the hedonistic salons of fin-de-siècle Vienna, the book becomes a pawn in the struggle against the city's rising anti-Semitism. In Venice during the time of the inquisition, a Catholic priest saves it from burning. In Barcelona in 1492, the scribe who wrote the text sees his family destroyed by the agonies of enforced exile. And in Seville in 1480, the reason for the Haggadah's extraordinary illuminations is finally disclosed. Hanna's investigation unexpectedly plunges her into the intrigues of fine art forgers and ultranationalist fanatics." (Publisher's note)

"When an Australian rare-book conservator named Hanna Heath finds a butterfly wing, a salt crystal, a white hair, and bloodstains in the recently rediscovered Sarajevo Haggadah, a late-medieval illuminated codex of uncertain provenance, she sets out to solve the mystery of the book's origins. To her disappointment, analysis of the specimens reveals little. . . . Brooks, beginning where science leaves off, uses Hanna's finds as entry points to richly imagined historical landscapes peopled by the Haggadah's creators, protectors, and would-be destroyers—a female Muslim slave in Convivencia Spain, a Jewish doctor in fin-de-siècle Vienna, an alcoholic priest in seventeenth-century Venice. Their narratives alternate with Hanna's own, and the final, multilayered effect is complex and moving." New Yorker

Brooks, Geraldine

The **Secret** Chord; A Novel. by Geraldine Brooks. Penguin Group USA 2015 320 p. maps $27.95

ISBN 0670025771; 9780670025770

LC 2015373206

This novel, by Geraldine Brooks, "takes on one of literature's richest and most enigmatic figures: a man who shimmers between history and legend. Peeling away the myth to bring David to life in Second Iron Age Israel, Brooks traces the arc of his journey from obscurity to fame, from shepherd to soldier, from hero to traitor, from beloved king to murderous despot and into his remorseful and diminished dotage." (Publisher's note)

"A skillful reimagining of stories already well-known to any well-versed reader of the Bible, gracefully and intelligently told." Kirkus

Brooks, Geraldine

Year of wonders; a novel of the plague. Viking 2001 308p

ISBN 0-670-91021-X

LC 00-52757

"In 1665, the intense young pastor of a plague-stricken Derbyshire village persuades his parish to quarantine itself from the outside world. This selfless decision leads to the deaths of two-thirds of the inhabitants but saves the surrounding towns, as it did in the case of the historical village that inspired the tale. The novel glitters with careful research into such arcana as seventeenth-century lead-mining, sheep-farming, and of course, medicine, but its true strength is a deep imaginative engagement with how people are changed by catastrophe. . . . A rare few—including the narrator, a young widow who is a servant of the pastor—discover new strengths and abilities." New Yorker

Brooks, Max

★ **World** War Z; an oral history of the zombie war. Crown 2006 342p $24.95

ISBN 0-307-34660-9

LC 2006-9517

"Brooks tells the story of the world's desperate battle against the zombie threat with a series of first-person accounts 'as told to the author' by various characters around the world. A Chinese doctor encounters one of the earliest zombie cases at a time when the Chinese government is ruthlessly suppressing any information about the outbreak that will soon spread across the globe. The tale then follows the outbreak via testimony of smugglers, intelligence officials, military personnel and many others who struggle to defeat the zombie menace. Despite its implausible premise and choppy delivery, the novel is surprisingly hard to put down." Publ Wkly

Brooks, Terry

The **druid** of Shannara. Ballantine Bks. 1991 423p (Heritage of Shannara)

ISBN 0-345-36298-5

LC 90-42424

"Broadening the landscape of his magic world, Brooks has produced a deep and thoughtful fantasy." Publ Wkly

Followed by The elfqueen of Shannara

Brooks, Terry

First king of Shannara. Ballantine Bks. 1996 489p

ISBN 0-345-39652-9

LC 95-52321

"To defend his followers and escape subjugation from the evil Warlock Lord, Druid Bremen must possess the magical Black Elfstone. This . . . answers fans' questions about the early history of the Shannara family." Libr J

Brooks, Terry

The **measure** of the magic; legends of Shannara. Del Rey/ Ballantine Books 2011 383p $27

ISBN 978-0-345-48420-8; 0-345-48420-7

LC 2011-14440

Sequel to: The bearer of the Black Staff (2010)

Sider Ament, the "wielder of the power of the Black Staff, is dead. With his dying breath, he has given possession of the Black Staff over to Panterra Qu, a young Tracker. Panterra, though, doesn't know how to unlock the power of the Staff. Time is not on his side, however. The Elf king of Arborlon has been assassinated, and Trolls are massing for an invasion. Elsewhere, Panterra's companion, Prue Liss, is desperately trying to find her way back to safety. Trolls hunt her, but if that were all, it would be bad enough. Coming in their wake is a darker and more sinister foe: The Ragpicker, a Demon bent on locating magic. In particular he seeks the Black Staff, and whomever happens to possess it will fall under his assault. The main storyline Brooks weaves with Panterra is extraordinarily fun. The tension is ramped up as Panterra struggles to understand the Staff and how to control it. Throw in the mystery and the conspiracy surrounding the death of the King of the Elves, and you have more than enough excitement and intrigue." Bookreporter

Brooks, Terry

The **sword** of Shannara; illustrated by the Brothers Hildebrandt. Random House 1977 726p il

ISBN 0-394-41333-4

LC 77-151532

"Reminiscent of Tolkien's fantasies though lacking the originality of his vision and the beauty of his language, this is still an engrossing saga of hardship and adventure with well-maintained action that will keep readers captive right up to a nicely-wrought finish." SLJ

Followed by The Elfstones of Shannara

Brooks, Terry, 1944-

Wards of Faerie; Terry Brooks. Del Rey 2012 371 p. (Dark legacy of Shannara) (hardcover) $28

ISBN 0345523474; 9780345523471

LC 2012020292

This epic fantasy novel, by Terry Brooks, is part of the "Dark Legacy of Shannara" series. "When the world was young, . . . the Elfstones warded the race of Elves and their lands, keeping evil at bay. . . . Thousands of years later, tumultuous times are upon the world. . . . The young Druid Aphenglow Elessedil has stumbled upon the secret account of an Elven girl's heartbreak and the shocking truth about the vanished Elfstones." (Publisher's note)

Broun, Bill

★ **Night** of the Animals; A Novel. by Bill Broun. HarperCollins 2016 560 p. (ebook) $25.99; $26.99

ISBN 9780062400819; 0062400797; 9780062400796

LC 2016020957

In this novel by Bill Broun, "the tale of Noah's Ark is . . . recast as a story of fate and family, set in a near-future London. . . . In 2052, . . . Cuthbert Handley sets out on a . . . quest: to release the animals of the London Zoo. . . . But his grand plan is not the only thing that threatens to disturb the . . . city. Around him is greater turmoil, as the world. . . anticipates the rise of a suicide cult set on destroying the world's animals along with themselves." (Publisher's note)

"Broun's novel is strange, witty, and engrossing, skipping through madness and into the realm of myth." Pub Wkly

Brown, Dan, 1964-

Angels & demons; Dan Brown. Atria Books 2000 713 p. maps hbk $27.99

ISBN 0743486226; 9780743486224; 1416524797; 9781416524793

LC 2006275719

"When world-renowned Harvard symbologist Robert Langdon is summoned to his first assignment to a Swiss research facility to analyze a mysterious symbol -- seared into the chest of a murdered physicist -- he discovers evidence of the unimaginable: the resurgence of an ancient secret brotherhood known as the Illuminati...the most powerful underground organization ever to walk the earth. The Illuminati has now surfaced to carry out the final phase of its legendary vendetta against its most hated enemy -- the Catholic Church." (Publisher's note)

Brown, Dan

The **Da** Vinci code; a novel. Doubleday 2003 454p $24.95

ISBN 0-385-50420-9

LC 2002-40918

"In a two-day span, American symbologist Robert Langdon finds himself accused of murdering the curator of the Louvre, on the run through the streets of Paris and London, and teamed up with French-cryptologist Sophie Neveu to uncover nothing less than the secret location of the Holy Grail. It appears that a conservative Catholic bishop might be on the verge of destroying the Grail, which includes an alternate history of Christ that could bring down the church. . . .The story is full of brain-teasing puzzles and fascinating insights into religious history and art." Booklist

Brown, Dan, 1964-

Inferno; a novel. Dan Brown. Doubleday 2013 x, 461 p.p (hardback) $29.95

ISBN 0385537859; 9780385537858

LC 2012533166

In this book, Dan Brown's Robert Langdon "wakes up in a Florence hospital unable to remember the last several days. A bullet has grazed his head, and some bad people are after him, but with the help of the lovely Dr. Sienna Brooks, he's able to escape--and escape and escape, as he slowly comprehends that a plague is quite deliberately about to be released, and it's his job to figure out the puzzles and symbols that lead to its location." (Booklist)

Brown, Dee Alexander

★ **Creek** Mary's blood; a novel. [by] Dee Brown. Holt, Rinehart & Winston 1980 401p il

ISBN 0-03-044281-8

LC 79-9060

"Through the words and memories of Dane, grandson of Creek Mary (or Akusa Amayi), we follow the history of the men, children, and grandchildren in the life of that indomitable exemplar of the American Indian. The action—and there is plenty of it—takes place in the period after the Revolutionary War and continues through the nineteenth century. The customs, rituals, courting, fighting, and celebrating are all described in detail. One of the most painful sections of the book depicts the forced removal west of the Mississippi of Indian tribes. . . . The relationships among the various tribes—Creek, Cheyenne, Cherokee, and others—is of great interest. Many famous names are recalled, among them Tecumseh, Andrew Jackson, Teddy Roosevelt, and the great chiefs Crazy Horse and Sitting Bull." Shapiro. Fic for Youth. 3d edition

Brown, E. R.

Almost criminal; by E. R. Brown. Dundurn Press 2013 285 p. ill. (paperback) $17.99

ISBN 1459705831; 9781459705838

LC 2013376771

This novel, written by E.R. Brown, focuses on Randle Kennedy, "British Columbia's most prolific producer of boutique marijuana," who meets Tate MacLane who is "brilliant, miserable, and broke. Randle wants a fresh face to front his transactions. Tate desperately needs a mentor and yearns for respect. Soon Tate finds out that it's harder to get out of the business than to get in." (Publisher's note)

Brown, Eleanor

The **weird** sisters; Eleanor Brown. Amy Einhorn Books/ G.P. Putnam's Sons 2011 320p.

ISBN 0399157220; 9780399157226; 978-0-399-15722-6

LC 2010029599

"There is no problem that a library card can't solve. The Andreas family is one of readers. Their father, a . . . Shakespeare professor who speaks almost entirely in verse, has named his three daughters after famous Shakespearean women. When the sisters return to their childhood home, ostensibly to care for their ailing mother, but really to lick their wounds and bury their secrets, they are horrified to find the others there. . . . But the sisters soon discover that everything they've been running from—one another, their small hometown, and themselves—might offer more than they ever expected." (Publisher's note)

Brown, Joe David

Addie Pray; a novel. Simon & Schuster 1971 313p

ISBN 0-671-20962-0

"Brown has a special feeling for the Depression-era South. . . . {Addie's speech} is vulgar, pungent country talk, which adds greatly to the book's easygoing charm. Looking at Long Boy with his floozy, she observes that 'he got that silly, dazed grin like a tom cat being choked to death with cream.' Like that extravagant expression, the book is a long tall, oldtime tale. But as Addie might put it, in the right hands that kind of yarn has a lot of prance left." Time

Brown, Karen

The **longings** of wayward girls; a novel. Karen Brown. Washington Square Press 2013 336 p. $15

ISBN 1476724911; 9781476724911

LC 2012044427

In this novel, "back in the '70s, a quiet middle-class neighborhood is rocked by the disappearance of two young girls who vanish five years apart. Sadie Watkins bears a close resemblance to the first, 9-year-old Laura Loomis, and is grudgingly forced to play with the second, Francie Bingham. Francie, with her awkward appearance, unhappy home life and a desire to be liked, makes an easy target for Sadie and her best friend, Betty." Now an adult, Sadie must confront her past. (Kirkus Reviews)

Brown, Larry

★ **Joe**; a novel. Algonquin Bks. 1991 345p

ISBN 0-945575-61-0

LC 91-12026

A novel about "poor 'white trash' in rural Mississippi. Joe Ranson is a middle-aged redneck with a soul. He fights and spits, drinks beer by the gallon from a cooler embedded in his truck, and endures bad relationships with women. But within the society he inhabits, he is a moral man, more or less following the rituals and established 'codes' of fair play. Unfortunately, he is involved in a classic feud, the roots of which are never revealed, that threatens to destroy him. Also destined to cross paths with Joe is the nomadic Jones family. Gary Jones is a hardworking and painfully naive teenager. His father is pure evil, his mother nearly insane, and his siblings barely human. Joe offers Gary work, fueling hope that these two very different men will learn enough from each other to save themselves." Booklist

Brown, Pierce

Golden Son; Pierce Brown. First edition Del Rey 2015 xii, 446 p.p $25

ISBN 0345539818; 9780345539816

LC 2014031015

This dystopian science fiction novel, by Pierce Brown, book 2 of "The Red Rising Trilogy" series, "continues the . . . saga of Darrow, a rebel forged by tragedy, battling to lead his oppressed people to freedom. . . . Darrow sacrifices himself in the name of the greater good for which Eo, his true love and inspiration, laid down her own life. He becomes a Gold, infiltrating their privileged realm so that he can destroy it from within." (Publisher's note)

"The stakes are even higher than they were in Red Rising, and the twists and turns of the story are every bit as exciting. The jaw-dropper of an ending will leave readers hungry for the conclusion to Brown's wholly original, completely thrilling saga." Booklist

Brown, Pierce

Morning Star; Pierce Brown. Del Rey 2016 544 p. ill (Red Rising trilogy) $27

ISBN 0345539842; 9780345539847

LC 2015048261

"Darrow would have lived in peace, but his enemies brought him war. The Gold overlords demanded his obedience, hanged his wife, and enslaved his people. But Darrow is determined to fight back. Risking everything to transform himself and breach Gold society, Darrow has battled to survive the cutthroat rivalries that breed Society's mightiest warriors, climbed the ranks, and waited patiently to unleash the revolution that will tear the hierarchy apart from within." (Publisher's note)

"Brown's vivid, first-person prose puts the reader right at the forefront of impassioned speeches, broken families, and engaging battle scenes that don't shy away from the gore as this intrastellar civil war comes to a most satisfying conclusion." Pub Wkly

Brown, Pierce

Red Rising; Pierce Brown. Del Rey 2014 400 p. $25

ISBN 0345539788; 9780345539786

LC 2013020634

In this science fiction novel, by Pierce Brown, "Darrow is a Red, a member of the lowest caste in the . . . society of the future. . . . He works all day, believing that he and his people are making the surface of Mars livable for future generations. . . . Darrow sacrifices everything to infiltrate the legendary Institute, . . . where the next generation of humanity's overlords struggle for power. He will be forced to compete for his life and the very future of civilization." (Publisher's note)

"This is a very ambitious novel, with a fully realized society . . . and a cast of well-drawn characters." Booklist

Other titles in this series are:

Golden Son (2015)

Morning Star (2016)

Iron Gold (2018)

Brown, Rita Mae, 1944-

✓The **litter** of the law; a Mrs. Murphy mystery. Rita Mae Brown & Sneaky Pie Brown; Illustrated by Michael Gellatly. Bantam Books 2013 256 p. (alk. paper) $26

ISBN 0345530489; 9780345530486

LC 2013007940

In this entry in Rita Mae Brown's Mrs. Murphy series, "Mary 'Harry' Haristeen . . . and her loyal brood of animals stumble upon a scarecrow whose straw form has been replaced with a corpse. Harry didn't know the late Joshua Hill and can't seem to find a reason anyone would want him dead. . . . With Halloween fast approaching, Harry would love to get to the truth before the spooky mood settles over her little Virginia town." (Kirkus Reviews)

Brown, Rita Mae

✓**Murder** at Monticello; or, Old sins; [by] Rita Mae Brown & Sneaky Pie Brown; illustrations by Wendy Wray. Bantam Bks. 1994 298p il

ISBN 0-553-08140-3

LC 94-16711

"Tiger cat Mrs. Murphy and corgi Tee Tucker . . . help Mary Minor 'Harry' Haristeen, postmistress of Crozet, Virginia, solve a nearly 200-year-old mystery. It begins with a skeleton discovered in a slave cabin during restorations at Monticello—and continues with the present-day murder of Kimball Haynes, head of archaeology there, who has discovered secrets of miscegenation recorded in a doctor's long-hidden journals. . . . An entertaining treat for animal-loving mystery/history fans." Booklist

Brown, Rita Mae, 1944-

✓★ **Rubyfruit** jungle; Rita Mae Brown. Bantam Books 1988 xii, 193 p.p (paperback) $16; (ebook) $48

ISBN 9781101965122; 1101965126; 9780804152761

LC 88019239

This coming-of-age novel by Rita Mae Brown, winner of the Lambda Literary Pioneer Award and the Lee Lynch Classic Book Award, "tells the story of Molly Bolt, the adoptive daughter of a dirt-poor Southern couple who boldly forges her own path in America. With her startling beauty and crackling wit, Molly finds that women are drawn to her wherever she goes—and she refuses to apologize for loving them back." (Publisher's note)

Brown, Rita Mae

✓ **Wish** you were here; [by] Rita Mae Brown & Sneaky Pie Brown; illustrations by Wendy Wray. Bantam Bks. 1990 242p il

ISBN 0-553-05881-9

LC 90-1071

"Ms. Brown writes with wise, disarming wit about her country-bred characters and their not-always-neighborly ways." N Y Times Book Rev

Brown, Rosellen

★ **Before** and after. Farrar, Straus & Giroux 1992 354p

ISBN 0-374-10999-0

LC 92-81571

This novel begins "on the day that Carolyn Reiser, a New Hampshire pediatrician with two teenage kids, gets called to the emergency room. A girl has been bludgeoned to death. The chief suspect is Carolyn's son, and he has disappeared. . . . Carolyn and her husband, Ben, can't believe their son, Jacob, is guilty, even as the evidence builds up; but . . . they are forced to grapple with unthinkable possibilities. . . . Neither can spare much thought for their daughter, Judith, who is wrestling with her own memories of a secretive, sometimes puzzling brother." (Newsweek)

Brown is "tenacious in her examination of each major character. Deftly, artfully, she strips away the delicate shelter of conventional relationships." N Y Times Book Rev

Brown, Rosellen

Half a heart. Farrar, Straus & Giroux 2000 402p

ISBN 0-374-44013-1

LC 00-22926

"The situation is an intriguing one rendered all the more so by Brown's skillful and sympathetic handling of her two central characters." Time

Brown, Rosellen

Tender mercies. Knopf 1978 259p

ISBN 0-394-42741-6

LC 78-1315

"What impresses one most about Tender Mercies is its dignity and restraint. While we learn a great deal about the physical details of paralysis, catheters and such, Brown makes no case for any horror of the body, nor does Laura's suffering prompt a garish loathing of the universe. . . . The language is spare and clean, with flashes of quiet poetry, perfectly suited to the plain but by no means simple New Englanders it portrays." Saturday Rev

Brown, Sandra

The **witness**. Warner Bks. 1995 422p

ISBN 0-446-51631-7

LC 94-42733

"This story pivots on the relationship between Kendall Deaton Burnwood, an idealistic public defender, and U.S. Marshal John McGrath, who is returning her to Prosper, S.C., as a material witness when their car crashes into a ravine in Georgia. With her three-month-old in tow, Kendall tries repeatedly to abandon John, who's hobbled by temporary amnesia and a leg injury. Kendall fears the town of Prosper for good reason: it's where she witnessed her husband and father-in-law, ringleaders of a white-supremacist vigilante group, ritualistically execute one of her clients. . . . The push-pull generated by John's memory loss and Kendall's terror sparks a sexual tension that is deftly and vividly consummated, and secrets keep popping out until the last page." Publ Wkly

Brown, Taylor

★ **Fallen** land; a novel. Taylor Brown. St. Martin's Press 2016 276 p. (hardback) $25.99

ISBN 1250077974; 9781250077974

LC 2015037367

This novel, by Taylor Brown, is "set in the final year of the Civil War. . . . Callum [is] a seasoned horse thief at fifteen years old. . . . Ava . . . hides in her crumbling home until Callum determines to rescue her from the bands of hungry soldiers pillaging the land, leaving destruction in their wake. Ava and Callum have only each other in the world and their remarkable horse, Reiver, who carries them through the destruction that is the South." (Publisher's note)

"Picaresque in style--tracing the couple's wanderings from danger to devastation--with photographic precision and a stunning descriptive style reminiscent of a mournful ballad, this historical novel bleeds sorrow and regret. And the reader cannot look away or forget. Brown uses lovely language to describe the horrific, and dramatizes humanity's best and worst in wartime." Booklist

Brown, William Wells

Clotel, or, The president's daughter; William Wells Brown; edited with an introduction and notes by M. Giulia Fabi. Penguin Books 2004 xxxii, 285 p.p (paperback) $14; (ebook) $39

ISBN 0142437727; 9780142437728; 9780307419279

LC 2003053661

This novel by William Wells Brown, with an introduction by M. Giulia Fabi, was originally published in 1853 amid rumors that Thomas Jefferson had fathered children with one of his slaves. "The story begins with the auction of his mistress, here called Currer, and their two daughters, Clotel and Althesa. The Virginian who buys Clotel falls in love with her, gets her pregnant, seems to promise marriage—then sells her." (Publisher's note)

Includes bibliographical references (p. [249]-285)

Browne, S. G.

Lucky bastard; S.G. Browne. Gallery Books 2012 358 p.

ISBN 1451657196; 9781451657197; 9781451657203

LC 2011050997

This "supernaturally themed comedy" novel from "[S.G.] Browne introduces P.I. Nick Monday . . . [who] is . . . one of the few hundred people in America who are able to poach luck, and then sell it on the black market. . . . Nick's trouble begins when a knockout named Tuesday Knight breezes in with an offer of $100,000 to recover her father's stolen luck. Not long after, a Chinese crime boss named Tommy Wong tries to strong-arm Nick into poaching a particularly rare form of luck. Meanwhile, a couple of government agents are on Nick's tail, and who knows what motivates the mysterious Scooter Girl orbiting around the whole scene." (Kirkus)

Bruen, Ken

Cross. St. Martin's Minotaur 2008 288p $23.95

ISBN 978-0-312-34142-8; 0-312-34142-3

LC 2007-42421

First published 2007 in the United Kingdom

"Bruen riffs on different meanings and implications of the word cross throughout, and his insights into pain, loss and Irishness are unforgettable." Publ Wkly

Bruen, Ken

The **guards**. St. Martin's Minotaur 2003 291p $23.95

ISBN 0-312-30355-6

LC 2002-35855

"Bruen's astringent prose and death's-head humor keep this quest for redemption from getting maudlin, just as his 'tapestry of talk' makes somber poetry of the bar-stool laments that serve as dialogue." N Y Times Book Rev

Other titles about Jack Taylor are:
The killing of the tinkers (2002)
The magdalen martyrs (2003)
The dramatist (2006)
Priest (2006)
Cross (2007)
Sanctuary (2008)
The devil (2010)
Headstone (2011)
Purgatory (2013)
Green hell (2015)
The emerald lie (2016)
The ghosts of Galway (2017)

Brundage, Elizabeth

★ **All** things cease to appear; A novel. Elizabeth Brundage. Alfred A. Knopf 2016 416 p. (hardcover) $26.95

ISBN 9781101875599; 9781101911488; 9781101875605

LC 2015024682

In this novel, by Elizabeth Brundage, "[art teacher] George Clare comes home to find his wife killed and their three-year-old daughter alone . . . in her room across the hall. . . . George is of course the immediate suspect. . . . While his parents rescue him from suspicion, a persistent cop is stymied at every turn in proving Clare a heartless murderer. And three teenage brothers (orphaned by tragic circumstances) find themselves entangled in this mystery." (Publisher's note)

"Succeeding as murder mystery, ghost tale, family drama, and love story, her novel is both tragic and transcendent." Pub Wkly

Brunner, John

★ **Stand** on Zanzibar. Grove Press 1968 505p

"Extrapolating from current politics, social and sexual mores, the communications revolution, the use of computers, brainwashing, drug use, psychology, philosophy, and sociology, Brunner has fashioned a mammoth work that is an intricate tapestry depicting a possible future. The dozens of characters interspersed in a complex fashion make the novel difficult to read but well worth the effort. Brunner's brand of cynicism and radical social commentary may not appeal to the taste of all readers, but in the time that has elapsed since the publication of the book, we have seen changes that bear startling similarities to several of Brunner's predictions." Shapiro. Fic for Youth. 3d edition

Brunt, Carol Rifka

★ **Tell** the wolves I'm home; a novel. Carol Rifka Brunt. Dial Press 2012 360 p. (hbk. : acid-free paper) : $25

ISBN 0679644199; 081299292X; 9780679644194; 9780812992922

LC 2011027932

Alex Award (2013)

Carol Rifka Brunt's novel "is an exploration of an unlikely friendship that blossoms in the wake of a terrible loss. It's 1987, and 14-year-old June Elbus is reeling from the death of her beloved uncle Finn, a famous painter who has succumbed to AIDS. . . . Finn's death leaves a gaping hole in June's life, and she's shocked when Toby, her uncle's lover and the man her mother holds responsible for his death, makes a bid to fill that emptiness by contacting June secretly." (Booklist)

Buchan, John

★ The **thirty**-nine steps. Doran, G.H. 1915 231p

"A bored, well-to-do Englishman, Richard Hannay, returns home to England after growing up in South Africa. Drifting between his club and the sights of London, he is drawn into the confidences of a secret agent in the thick of espionage. The agent is murdered in Hannay's apartment and Richard finds himself on the run from Scotland Yard and the cult of the 'Black Stone.'" Shapiro. Fic for Youth. 3d edition

Buchanan, Cathy Marie

★ The **painted** girls; Cathy Marie Buchanan. Riverhead Books 2013 368 p. $27.95

ISBN 1594486247; 9781594486241

LC 2012038433

In this novel by Cathy Marie Buchanan, "following their father's sudden death, the van Goethem sisters find their lives upended. . . . Marie throws herself into dance and is soon modeling in the studio of Edgar Degas. . . . There she meets a wealthy male patron of the ballet. . . . Meanwhile Antoinette, derailed by her love for the dangerous Émile Abadie, must choose between honest labor and the more profitable avenues open to a young woman of the Parisian demimonde." (Publisher's note)

"Buchanan brings the unglamorous reality of the late-19th-century Parisian demimonde into stark relief while imagining the life of Marie Van Goethem, the actual model for the iconic Degas statue Little Dancer Aged Fourteen... the moving yet unsentimental portrait of family love, of two sisters struggling to survive with dignity, makes this a must-read." Kirkus

Buchanan, Edna

Love kills; a Brit Montero novel. Simon and Schuster 2007 308p $25

ISBN 978-0-7432-9476-8; 0-7432-9476-9

LC 2006-39050

"Miami crime reporter Britt Montero, on the mend emotionally after losing her fiance in a shootout . . . , decides work is the best medicine. Her first case is actually an old one. The body of Nathan York is excavated by construction workers. Years earlier York was the subject of Britt's first big story. He was a militant advocate for men's rights in custody cases and would snatch children from their mothers and deliver them to their estranged fathers. Britt is also trying to track down Marsh Holt, the Honeymoon Killer. A hunky thirtysomething lothario operating with aliases in various states, Holt married a string of women across the country who all suffered fatal 'accidents' while on their honeymoons." Booklist

Buchanan, Edna

You only die twice; a Britt Montero mystery. Morrow 2001 292p $24

ISBN 0-380-97655-2

LC 00-49543

"A fascinating amalgam of red herrings, misdirection, and guilt by personality. . . . An intelligent, thoroughly entertaining crime novel." Booklist

Buck, Pearl S.

★ The **good** earth. Washington Square Press 2004 357p (Contemporary classics) pa $14

ISBN 0-7432-7293-5

First published 1931 by Day

This novel set in prerevolutionary China "describes the rise of Wang Lung, a Chinese peasant, from poverty to the position of a rich landowner, helped by his patient wife, O-lan. Their vigor, fortitude, persistence, and enduring love of the soil are emphasized throughout. Generally regarded as Pearl Buck's masterpiece, the book won universal acclaim for its sympathetically authentic picture of Chinese life." Reader's Ency. 4th edition

Buckley, Fiona

The **doublet** affair; a mystery at Queen Elizabeth I's court : featuring Ursula Blanchard. Fiona Buckley. Scribner 1998 294 p. (hbk.) o.p.; (pbk.) $22.99

ISBN 0684838427; 9780743489089

LC 98043016

This book follows "Ursula Blanchard, . . . lady-in-waiting to Queen Elizabeth I, [who] is the only female spy employed by the queen's right-hand man, William Cecil. . . . Ursula is requested by the queen and Cecil to retire temporarily from court and to stay . . . at the home of Leonard and Ann Mason, who are suspected of harboring sympathies for the Catholic Mary, Queen of Scots. Working undercover as a governess, Ursula seeks to gather information on a conspiracy that may involve a London clockmaker and the Masons' tutor. She is helped significantly by her married servants, Fern Dale and Roger Brockley. . . . Ursula finds her life threatened but forges on, unraveling the conspiracy and, ultimately, making a fateful decision regarding her future." (Publishers Weekly)

Buckley, Fiona

The **siren** queen; an Ursula Blanchard mystery at Queen Elizabeth I's court. Fiona Buckley. Scribner 2004 277p $25

ISBN 0743237528; 9780743237529

LC 2004045284

This book follows "Ursula Blanchard, half sister to Queen Elizabeth I and occasional spy for the realm. . . . While paying a reluctant visit to the seemingly foolish duke of Norfolk to discuss the possibility of an early betrothal for her young daughter, Ursula learns that her host has been conducting an ill-considered correspondence with the incarcerated Mary, queen of Scots. Determined to leave the duke's estate before the impressionable Meg becomes even more besotted with the icy Edmund Dean, she is prevented from returning home by the brutal murders of a courier and a servant. As Ursula attempts to untangle a treasonous web of deceit and double-cross, she places her own life in danger in order to protect the queen and the sister she has pledged to love and serve in secrecy." (Booklist)

Buckley, William F.

★ **Mongoose,** R.I.P; a Blackford Oakes novel. [by] William F. Buckley, Jr. Random House 1988 322p

ISBN 0-394-55931-2

LC 87-28344

"The best of the Blacky books, this is an entertainment of the Graham Greene order that truly entertains, excites, and edifies. . . . The story builds with considerable suspense up to Blackford's horrendous dilemma on the day of JFK's assassination." Natl Rev

Buehlman, Christopher

The **Necromancer's** house; by Christopher Buehlman. Ace Books 2013 416 p. (hardcover) $25.95

ISBN 0425256650; 9780425256657

LC 2013011502

In this book, by Christopher Buehlman, "Andrew Ranulf Blankenship is a . . . recovering alcoholic and a practicing warlock, able to speak with the dead through film. His house is a maze of sorcerous booby traps and escape tunnels, as yours might be if you were sitting on a treasury of Russian magic stolen from the Soviet Union thirty years ago. Now a monster straight from the pages of Russian folklore is coming for him, and frost and death are coming with her." (Publisher's note)

Buehlman, Christopher

The **suicide** motor club; Christopher Buehlman. Berkley Books 2016 368 p. (ebook) $65; (hardback) $26

ISBN 9781101988749; 9781101988732

LC 2015050513

In this book, by Christopher Buehlman, "remember that car that passed you near midnight on Route 66, doing 105 with its lights off? You wondered where it was going so quickly on that dark, dusty stretch of road, motor roaring, the driver glancing out the window as he blew by. . . . You just saw the founder of the Suicide Motor Club. Be grateful his brake lights never flashed. Be grateful his car was already full." (Publisher's note)

"Buehlman's latest is gripping the whole way through, with a perfectly poignant ending." Pub Wkly

Buffett, Jimmy

A **salty** piece of land. Little, Brown and Co 2004 462p $27.95

ISBN 0-316-90845-2

LC 2004-16508

"Perhaps it is because Buffett has long been a writer of lyrics that his prose style now seems to flow in a fresh, fanciful, finely imagined fashion. . . . What makes the incredible so credible to the reader, what makes the old lighthouse shine again, is the spiritual savvy Buffett has gleaned from the beach of life as he's wandered in the raw poetry of time." N Y Times Book Rev

Bujold, Lois McMaster

The **paladin** of souls. Eos 2003 456p hardcover o.p. pa $7.99

ISBN 0-380-97902-0; 0-380-81861-2 pa

LC 2003-40884

Sequel to The curse of Chalion

"Three years free of the madness that kept her imprisoned in her family's castle, Ista is finally released from her last remaining duties by the death of her mother. She undertakes a pilgrimage, but doesn't get far before she is overtaken by trouble, sorrow, need, and a host of other adversities. Chalion is in trouble again, thanks to the plots, counterplots, machinations, and follies of men and of gods. . . . What really keeps one turning the pages is the fascinating cast of characters—not that the plot is anything to sneeze at." Booklist

Bulawayo, NoViolet, 1981-

We need new names; a novel. by NoViolet Bulawayo. Back Bay Books 2014 304 p. (hbk.) $25; (pbk.) $15

ISBN 0316230812; 0316230847; 9780316230810; 9780316230841

LC 2012038068

Man Booker Prize Shortlist (2013)

In this novel, by NoViolet Bulawayo, "Darling is only ten years old, and yet she must navigate a fragile and violent world . . . in Zimbabwe. But Darling has a chance to escape: she has an aunt in America. She travels to this new land in search of America's famous abundance only to find that her options as an immigrant are perilously few." (Publisher's note)

Bulgakov, Mikhail Afanas'evich

★ The **master** and Margarita; translated from the Russian by Michael Glenny. Knopf 1992 xxvii, 446p $19

ISBN 0-679-41046-5

LC 91-53220

Written in the 1930s. Original Russian edition published 1966-67 in censored form. This translation, first published 1967 by Harper, is based on the unexpurgated version that was subsequently published 1973 in the Soviet Union

This novel "juxtaposes two planes of action—one set in Moscow in the 1930s and the other in Jerusalem at the time of Christ. The three central characters of the contemporary plot are the Devil, disguised as one Professor Woland; the 'Master,' a repressed novelist; and Margarita, who, though married to a bureaucrat, loves the Master. The Master has burned his manuscript and gone willingly into a psychiatric ward when critics attacked his work—a portrayal of the story of Jesus. Margarita sells her soul to the Devil in order to obtain the Master's release from the psychiatric ward. A parallel plot presents the action of the Master's destroyed novel, the condemnation of Yeshua (Jesus) in Jerusalem." Merriam-Webster's Ency of Lit

Buntin, Julie

★ **Marlena**; a novel. Julie Buntin. Henry Holt & Co. 2017 288 p. (hardback) $26

ISBN 9781627797641

LC 2016021949

This book, by Julie Buntin, presents "the story of two girls and the feral year that will cost one her life, and define the other's for decades. Everything about fifteen-year-old Cat's new town in rural Michigan is lonely and off-kilter, until she meets her neighbor, the manic, beautiful, pill-popping Marlena. Cat, inexperienced and desperate for connection, is quickly lured into Marlena's orbit by little more than an arched eyebrow and a shake of white-blond hair." (Publisher's note)

"Jumping between their teenage friendship in Michigan and Cat's adult life in New York City, Buntin creates a world so subtle and nuanced and alive that it imprints like a memory. Devastating; as unforgettable as it is gorgeous." Kirkus

Bunyan, John

The **pilgrim's** progress; edited with an introduction and notes by W.R. Owens. Oxford University Press 2003 lvi, 333p il (Oxford world classics) pa $8.95

ISBN 0-19-280361-1

LC 2003-283122

First published 1678

"The 'immortal allegory,' next to the Bible the most widely known book in religious literature. It was written in Bedford jail, where Bunyan was for twelve years a prisoner for his convictions. It describes the troubled journey of Christian and his companions through this life to a triumphal entrance into the Celestial city. Bunyan 'wrote with virgin purity utterly free from mannerisms and affectations; and without knowing himself for a writer of fine English, produced it.'" Pratt Alcove

Includes bibliographical references

Burdett, John

Bangkok 8. Knopf 2003 317p $24

ISBN 1-400-04044-2

LC 2002-40658

"The narrator, a Buddhist cop named Sonchai Jitplecheep, finds himself plunged into a dangerous investigation of the deaths of his partner Pichai Apiradee and U. S. Embassy Sgt. William Bradley. Sonchai is an unusual character on several levels, from the mysteries of his violent past to his conversations with the ghost of Pichai. His ambiguous feelings toward Kimberley Jones, an American FBI agent brought in to work the case, reflect his upbringing as the child of a Thai mother and an unknown American father. . . .The mix of detective work, Bangkok street life, the Thai sex trade and drug smuggling forms a powerful mélange of images and insight." Publ Wkly

Other titles in this series are:
Bangkok Tattoo (2005)
Bangkok Haunts (2007)
The Godfather of Kathmandu (2009)
Vulture Peak (2011)
The Bangkok Asset (2015)

Burdick, Eugene

Fail-safe; by Eugene Burdick & Harvey Wheeler. McGraw-Hill 1962 286p

"With mounting tension this gripping thriller tells of a possible nuclear holocaust. An American attack squadron is accidentally and irretrievably launched to obliterate Moscow. The frantic U.S. president and the Russian premier begin a dramatic hotline race against time to halt the bombers' flight and prevent disaster. The crisis is seen through the eyes of several characters, and their differing perceptions provide an effective story-telling technique." Shapiro. Fic for Youth. 3d edition

Burgess, Anthony, 1917-1993

★ A **clockwork** orange; the restored edition. Anthony Burgess ; edited with an Introduction and notes by Andrew Biswell. W.W. Norton & Co. 2012 246 p. (hardcover) $24.95

ISBN 0393089134; 9780393089134

LC 2012029687

This book is the 50th anniversary edition of Anthony Burgess's novel, which offered a "nightmare vision of the future told in its own fantastically inventive lexicon." Editor "Andrew Biswell, PhD, director of the International Burgess Foundation, has taken a close look at the three varying published editions alongside the original typescript to recreate the novel as Anthony Burgess envisioned it." (Publisher's note)

"Paradox is at the heart of this book, as this newly restored, fiftieth-anniversary edition makes more clear than ever...a fitting publication of a book that remains...shocking and thought provoking." Booklist

Includes bibliographical references

Burgess, Matt

Dogfight, a love story; a novel. Doubleday 2010 290p $24.95

ISBN 978-0-385-53298-3; 0-385-53298-9

LC 2009-41885

"With an acute ear for dialogue and the poetry of the street, Burgess . . . gives us the pizzerias and bodegas, playgrounds and schoolyards, barbershops and bowling alleys of his home turf. His is a cliché-free depiction of gritty urban reality, reminiscent of Richard Price. But Burgess's city novel is less Clockers than Portrait of the Artist as an Ambivalent Drug Dealer, less an inner city whodunit than an outer borough how-will-he-do-it." N Y Times Book Rev

Burgess, Matt

Uncle Janice; a novel. Matt Burgess. Doubleday 2014 288 p. $25.95

ISBN 0385536801; 9780385536806

LC 2014003337

In this novel, by Matt Burgess, "Janice Itwaru is an 'uncle'-- NYPD lingo for an undercover narcotics officer. . . . With an ailing mother at home, her cover nearly blown, quota pressures from her superiors, and rumors circulating that Internal Affairs has her unit under surveillance, Janice is running terribly short on luck. . . . Now she has to decide which evil to confront: the absurd bureaucrats at One Police Plaza, or the violent drug dealers who may already be on to her identity." (Publisher's note)

"As in his well-received debut, Dogfight, a Love Story (2010), Burgess puts a humorous slant on deadly serious drug matters in this vivid portrayal of life on the streets, which swings from funny to gut-tighteningly suspenseful. Not likely to gain recruits for narcotics squads, but a tour-de-force of its type." Booklist

Burke, James Lee

Black cherry blues. Little, Brown 1989 290p

ISBN 0-316-11699-8

LC 89-7977

"A stunning novel that takes detective fiction into new imaginative realms. . . . All the main characters in this darkly beautiful, lyric saga carry heavy emotional baggage, and Robicheaux's sleuthing is a simultaneous exorcism of demons of grief, loss, fear, rage, vengeance." Publ Wkly

Burke, James Lee

Heaven's prisoners. Holt & Co. 1988 292p

ISBN 0-8050-0665-6

LC 87-26878

"There is a pronounced streak of poetry in Mr. Burke's prose. He has the knack of combining action with reflection; he has pity for the human condition, and even his villains can have some sympathetic and redeeming qualities. Mr. Burke writes in an unhurried manner, but the book never loses tension because he is so wrapped up in his characters and their locale." N Y Times Book Rev

Burke, James Lee, 1936-

House of the rising sun; James Lee Burke. Simon & Schuster 2015 435 p. (cloth) $27.99

ISBN 1501107100; 9781501107108; 9781501107139

LC 2015012518

This novel, by James Lee Burke, offers "the story of a father and son separated by war and circumstance—and whose encounter with the legendary Holy Grail will change their lives forever. . . . After a violent encounter that leaves four Mexican soldiers dead, Hackberry escapes the country in possession of a stolen artifact, earning the ire of a bloodthirsty Austrian arms dealer who then places Hack's son Ishmael squarely in the cross hairs of a plot to recapture his prize." (Publisher's note)

"Crisp dialogue highlights this tale of redemption and the bonds of family, and the breathtaking conclusion is one that readers won't soon forget." Pub Wkly

Burke, James Lee, 1936-

Wayfaring Stranger; a novel. James Lee Burke. Simon & Schuster 2014 448 p. (hardback) $27.99

ISBN 1476710791; 9781476710792; 9781476710808

LC 2014000147

"In 1934, sixteen-year-old Weldon Avery Holland happens upon infamous criminals Bonnie Parker and Clyde Barrow after one of their notorious armed robberies. . . . Ten years later, Second Lieutenant Weldon Holland barely survives the Battle of the Bulge. . . . In just a few years' time Weldon will spar with the jackals of the [oil] industry, rub shoulders with dangerous men, and win and lose fortunes twice over." (Publisher's note)

"Burke takes a break from his Dave Robicheaux series to offer an ambitious, deeply satisfying historical thriller that fills in backstory on the author's other fictional family, the Hollands. With two series already in place starring contemporary members of the Holland clan, Burke now steps back in time to tell the story of oilman Weldon Avery Holland and his struggle to carve a life for himself on his own terms." Booklist

Burke, Shannon

Into the Savage Country; Shannon Burke. Pantheon Books 2014 272 p. (hard cover : alk. paper) $24.95

ISBN 0307908925; 9780307908926

LC 2014006429

Written by Shannon Burke, "This . . . adventure set in the American West of the 1820s is at once a tale of complex friendships, a love story, and a panoramic retelling of a crucial moment in American history. When the young William Wyeth leaves St. Louis for a fur-trapping expedition, he nearly loses his life and quickly discovers the depth of loyalty among the men who must depend on one another to survive." (Publisher's note)

"Burke includes fine episodes of derring-do, two involving bears, and there is a thrilling climax, but character is his overriding interest, the way it's shaped by tests of endurance in magnificent, alien landscapes. A grand immersion in the past." Kirkus

Burnet, Graeme MaCrae

His Bloody Project; Documents Relating to the Case of Roderick Macrae. by Graeme MaCrae Burnet. Skyhorse Publishing 2016 288 p. map $24.99

ISBN 1510719210; 9781510719217

Man Booker Prize Shortlist (2016)

This book, by Graeme MaCrae Burnet, focuses on "a brutal triple murder in a remote Scottish farming community in 1869 [that] leads to the arrest of seventeen-year-old Roderick . . . . Presented as a collection of documents discovered by the author, [it] opens with a series of police statements. . . . Chief among the papers is Roderick Macrae's own memoirs. . . . There follow medical reports, psychological evaluations, [and] a courtroom transcript from the trial." (Publisher's note)

"Although Burnet paints a disturbing picture of the hopelessness and hardships of tenant farmers, as well as providing an eye-opening introduction to the fallibility of so-called expert witnesses, this is not a bleak book. Rather, it is sly, poignant, gritty, thought-provoking, and sprinkled with wit." Pub Wkly

Burns, Charles, 1955-

★ **Black** hole; Charles Burns. Pantheon Books 2005 1 v. ill. $29.95

ISBN 9780375714726; 9780375423802; 037542380X

LC 2005046431

Eisner Awards: Best Graphic Album - Reprint (2006); Harvey Awards: Best Graphic Album - Previously Published (2006); Ignatz Awards: Outstanding Anthology or Collection (2006)

This book takes place in "[s]uburban Seattle, [in] the mid-1970s. We learn from the out-set that a strange plague has descended upon the area's teenagers, transmitted by sexual contact. The disease is manifested in any number of ways—from the hideously grotesque to the subtle (and concealable)—but once you've got it, that's it. There's no turning back. As we inhabit the heads of several key characters—some kids who have it, some who don't, some who are about to get it—what unfolds isn't the expected battle to fight the plague, or bring heightened awareness to it , or even to treat it. What we become witness to instead is a fascinating and eerie portrait of the nature of high school alienation itself—the savagery, the cruelty, the relentless anxiety and ennui, the longing for escape. And then the murders start." (Publisher's note)

Burroughs, William S.

★ **Naked** lunch; the restored text edited by James Grauerholz and Barry Miles. Grove Press 2003 289p pa $14

ISBN 978-0-8021-4018-0; 0-8021-4018-1

LC 2001-23190

First published 1959 in France; first published 1962 in the United States

"An autobiographical novel that discards . . . conventional narrative prose . . . to present a surrealistic vision of a liberated, hallucinatory counterculture set in opposition to a mass-produced, technological society bent on mass destruction. In this and the books of the next few years, Burroughs relied on such techniques as random cutting and pasting to create an extreme montage effect. Surviving obscenity trials in the U. S., Naked Lunch became an icon of the emancipated sixties." Benet's Reader's Ency Am Lit

Burrowes, Grace

The **heir**; Grace Burrowes. Sourcebooks Casablanca 2010 471 p.

ISBN 1402244347; 9781402244346

"The earl of Westhaven is determined to avoid his father's marital machinations by remaining in sweltering London while Society departs for the country. Westhaven takes great pleasure in his well-run household until his new housekeeper, Anna Seaton, mistakes his intentions toward a chambermaid and knocks him flat with a fireplace poker. Anna is too educated and polished to have been born to service, but she makes a tender nurse. As their affections grow, Westhaven believes he's found a candidate for marriage who would please him and satisfy his father, but Anna refuses Westhaven's proposal. Her hidden background contains ugly obligations, and she's determined to keep outrunning them even as he tries to change her mind." (Publishers Weekly)

Burrowes, Grace

Lady Maggie's secret scandal; Grace Burrowes. Sourcebooks Casablanca 2012 416p $7.99

ISBN 9781402263774

In this romance novel, "thirty, independent, and firmly on the shelf, Lady Magdalene Windham, the adopted illegitimate daughter of the Duke of Moreland, lives a quiet, sedate life. But Maggie is being plagued by her past, and when her reticule goes missing--and with it some letters she is desperate to have back--she goes to her family's discreet, incredibly observant private investigator, Benjamin Hazlit, the one man who can help her. Although he hides it, Ben quickly realizes that Maggie is not revealing the whole truth; getting her to trust him with her secrets--or her heart--is not going to be easy." (Libr J)

Burrowes, Grace

Tremaine's True Love; Grace Burrowes. Sourcebooks Inc 2015 416 p. $7.99

ISBN 1492621021; 9781492621027

In this novel by Grace Burrowes, "Tremaine St. Michael is half French, half Scottish, and all business. He prowls the world in search of more profits, rarely settling in one place for long. When he meets practical, reserved Lady Nita Haddonfield, he sees an opportunity to mix business with pleasure by making the lady his own." (Publisher's note)

"The second installment of Burrowes' (The Duke's Disaster, 2015, etc.) new True Gentlemen series is a tightly woven story that deals with many of the world's timeless moral issues—poverty, domestic violence, professional recognition for women, and animal rights. The characters are complicated and compelling and experience enough personal growth during the course of the novel to keep the reader enthralled. Burrowes is at the top of her game, and this latest offering is not to be missed." Kirkus

Busch, Frederick

Rescue missions; stories. W.W. Norton & Co. 2006 316p $24.95

ISBN 978-0-393-06252-6; 0-393-06252-X

LC 2006-13011

"'Need trumps love,' in the words of one of Busch's indelible characters, and need in all its permutations infuses the final collection of stories from this master of the genre. Whether it's the obligation of a son to his dying father, the unfulfilled duty of a soldier fresh from the war in Iraq, or the demand for revenge of a former lover, the drive for recognition, connection, and affirmation is revealed as an essential life force. In Busch's hands, it thrums with an elegiac cadence, so subtle at times as to be barely perceptible, so strong at others as to take one's breath away." Booklist

Butcher, Jim

★ The **aeronaut's** windlass; by Jim Butcher. ROC 2015 640 p. maps $27.95

ISBN 9780451466808

LC 2015009056

In this book, by Jim Butcher, "Spires have sheltered humanity, towering for miles over the mist-shrouded surface of the world. Within their halls, aristocratic houses have ruled for generations, developing scientific marvels, fostering trade alliances, and building fleets of airships to keep the peace. Captain Grimm commands the merchant ship, Predator. Fiercely loyal to Spire Albion, he has taken their side in the cold war with Spire Aurora." (Publisher's note)

"The author blends familiar steampunk and fantasy elements (airships, wizardry, and heroes from a monarch's guard) in a fresh and wonderful way that results in a fantastic ride. This should well satisfy fans of fantasy, sf, or their stepchild steampunk." LJ

Butcher, Jim

Proven guilty; a novel of the Dresden files. Jim Butcher. ROC 2006 404p o.p.; (paperback) $9.99

ISBN 0451460855 (hardcover); 9780451461032

LC 2005030130

In this novel, "Harry Dresden, Chicago's only consulting wizard, takes on phobophages, creatures that feed on fear who attack a horror film convention, in the . . . eighth installment of [author Jim] Butcher's increasingly complicated Dresden Files series. . . . Harry finds that fighting monsters is only the prelude to maneuvers amid the warring wizards of the White Council and the vampire Red Court. Less and less V.I. Warshawski with witchcraft, Harry aims his deductive powers at political intrigues rather than crime solving. . . . Harry, taking on an apprentice, has to face up to the consequences of his all-too-human failings." (Publishers Weekly)

Butler, Nickolas

★ The **Hearts** of Men; a novel. Nickolas Butler. HarperCollins 2017 400 p. (ebook) $25.99; $26.99

ISBN 9780062469700; 0062469681; 9780062469687

LC 2017002946

In this novel, by Nickolas Butler, "Nelson, irrevocably scarred from the Vietnam War, becomes Scoutmaster of Camp Chippewa, while [his friend] Jonathan marries, divorces, and turns his father's business into a highly profitable company. And when something unthinkable happens at a camp get-together with Nelson as Scoutmaster and Jonathan's teenage grandson and daughter-in-law as campers, the aftermath demonstrates the depths—and the limits—of Nelson's selflessness and bravery." (Publisher's note)

"Butler demonstrates enormous command over the material and sympathy for his flawed characters. This beautiful novel might be his best yet." Pub Wkly

Butler, Octavia E.

Adulthood rites. 1988 277p (Xenogenesis)

ISBN 0-446-51422-5

LC 87-34620

In the second novel in the Xenogenesis trilogy "the alien Oankali have rescued the dying remnants of humanity after Earth's nuclear war. Now, though, the children of the two races, called constructs, are resented and feared by the original survivors. This is the story of one such construct, Akin, who possesses an adult mind and voice before he is two years old. Stolen by a barren human community, he grows up knowing both races." Publ Wkly

Followed by Imago

Butler, Octavia E.

★ **Dawn**; [by] Octavia Butler. Warner Bks. 1987 264p (Xenogenesis)

ISBN 0-446-51363-6

LC 87-6195

In this first volume in the Xenogenesis trilogy "a band of nuclear holocaust survivors is in the hands of an alien race that offers to save them. The price is high though: the survivors must participate in the evolution of the aliens by bearing children that incorporate some of the aliens' characteristics. Butler is one of the few sf writers who can handle effectively a slow-moving plot that emphasizes characters' emotions. Her command of the language is superior, and her aliens are quite convincing creations." Booklist

Followed by Adulthood rites

Butler, Octavia E.

Fledgling; a novel. Seven Stories 2005 317p $24.95

ISBN 1-58322-690-7

LC 2005-5664

"In the feisty Shori, Butler has created a new vampire paradigm–one that's more prone to sci-fi social commentary than gothic romance–and given a tired genre a much-needed shot in the arm." Publ Wkly

Butler, Octavia E.

Imago. Warner Bks. 1989 264p (Xenogenesis)

ISBN 0-446-51472-1

LC 88-27975

First published 1985 in the United Kingdom

The concluding volume of the Xenogenesis trilogy "considers a post-holocaust humanity whose only chance for survival is to be absorbed by the alien Oankali. Totally uninterested in domination, this race thrives on a symbiosis that Earthlings find difficult to credit. That distrust hampers the narrator, an ooloi (neuter) named Jodahs, as it tries to find life partners in the same ratio as its five parents: a human couple, an Oankali couple and itself, the essential ooloi who joins all five and melds their genetic legacy. Butler's achievement here is less the abstract reassignment of sexual roles than a warmth and urgency that dramatizes and personalizes these conflicts and transformations." Publ Wkly

Butler, Octavia E.

★ **Kindred**; 25th anniverary ed; Beacon Press 2003 287p (Black women writers series) pa $14

ISBN 0-8070-8369-0

LC 2003-62862

First published 1979 by Doubleday

"Dana, a well-educated contemporary African American woman, suddenly finds herself pulled into the past to save the life of a distant ancestor, an early-19th-century southern white boy named Rufus Weylin. Although she returns to the present moments later, she soon finds herself saving Rufus again and again. Although only a short time passes for her between each bout of time travel, years pass for Rufus, who gradually grows into adulthood and becomes a slave owner. This sometimes painful novel features superb character development." Anatomy of Wonder 5

Includes bibliographical references

Butler, Robert Olen

A **good** scent from a strange mountain; stories. Robert Olen Butler. Holt & Co. 1992 249p $19.95

ISBN 9780805019865; 0-8050-1986-3

LC 91-31359

This book by Robert Olen Butler is a collection of stories "about the aftermath of the Vietnam War and its enduring impact on the Vietnamese . . . [and blends] Vietnamese folklore and contemporary American realities. . . . This new edition includes two previously uncollected stories—'Missing' and 'Salem'—that brilliantly complete the collection's narrative journey, returning to the jungles of Vietnam to explore the experiences of a former Vietcong soldier and an American MIA." (Publisher's note)

"Recommended for all literary fiction collections and essential for libraries seeking to expand Asian American literature collections." LJ

Butler, Robert Olen

Hell; a novel. Grove Press 2009 232p $24

ISBN 978-0-8021-1901-8; 0-8021-1901-8

"Butler's lust for the tabloid romp and his stream of the never-ending punch line both irritates and illuminates. The reader's taste will have to be the final arbiters of worth." Publ Wkly

Butler, Robert Olen

Perfume River; A Novel. Robert Olen Butler. Atlantic Monthly Press 2016 272 p. (ebook) $25; (hardcover) $25

ISBN 9780802190109; 9780802125750; 0802125751

In this novel by Robert Olen Butler, "Robert Quinlan is a seventy-year-old historian, teaching at Florida State University, where his wife Darla is also tenured. Their marriage, forged in the fervor of anti-Vietnam-war protests, now bears the fractures of time, both personal and historical. . . . The divisions in Robert's own family are more apparent: he has almost no relationship with his brother Jimmy, . . . [who] refuses to appear at his [sick] father's bedside." (Publisher's note)

"This is thoughtful, introspective fiction of the highest caliber, but it carries a definite edge, thanks to an insistent backbeat that generates suspense with the subtlest of brushstrokes." Booklist

Butler, Sarah

Ten things I've learnt about love; a novel. by Sarah Butler. The Penguin Press 2013 320 p. (hardcover) $26.95

ISBN 1594205337; 9781594205330

LC 2012046987

Author Sarah Butler presents "a story about finding love in unexpected places, about rootlessness and homecoming, and the power of the ties that bind. Alice is the youngest of three daughters, and the black sheep of her family. Drawn to traveling in far-flung and often dangerous countries, she has never enjoyed the closeness with her father that her two older sisters have. [She] is late to hear the news that her father is dying. She returns to the family home only just in time to say good-bye." (Publisher's note)

Buwalda, Peter

★ **Bonita** Avenue; a novel. by Peter Buwalda, translated by Jonathan Reeder. First American edition Hogarth 2015 560 p. hbk $26

ISBN 0553417851; 9780553417852

In this novel, by Peter Buwalda, translated by Jonathan Reeder, "Siem Sigerius is a beloved, brilliant professor of mathematics with a promising future in politics. . . . But there are elements of Siem's past that threaten to upend the peace and stability that he has achieved, and when he stumbles upon a deception that's painfully close to home, things begin to fall apart." (Publisher's note)

"The rich layer of detail would be impressive when applied to one topic, but Buwalda creates multiple complex worlds around vastly different subjects: the porn industry, mathematics, music, and judo, among others. An outstanding literary suspense story." LJ

Byatt, A. S. (Antonia Susan), 1936-

The **children's** book; a novel. Alfred A. Knopf 2009 675p $26.95

ISBN 0-307-27209-5; 978-0-307-27209-6

LC 2009-16334

Byatt's novel ranges from the Victorian era through World War I. "When Olive Wellwood's oldest son discovers a runaway named Philip sketching in the basement of the new Victoria and Albert Museum—a talented working-class boy who could be a character out of one of Olive's magical tales—she takes him into the storybook world of her family and friends—a world that conceals more treachery and darkness than Philip has ever imagined and that will soon be eclipsed by far greater forces." (Publisher's note)

"This is a moving book. Its words are beautifully chosen. . . . Everything connects. A S Byatt is Gaudi and Christopher Wren rolled into one." Scotsman

Byatt, A. S.

Possession; a romance. Modern Lib. 2000 605p

ISBN 0-679-64030-4

LC 99-56297

A reissue of the edition first published 1990 by Random House

"Intelligent, ingenious and humane, {this} bids fair to be looked back upon as one of the most memorable novels of the 1990s." Times Lit Suppl

Byatt, A. S. (Antonia Susan), 1936-

★ **Ragnarok**; A.S. Byatt. Grove Press 2011 177p. ill.

ISBN 1-84767-064-4; 978-1-84767-064-9; 9780802129925; 9780753188842

LC 2011508517

"Recently evacuated to the British countryside and with World War Two raging around her, one young girl is struggling to make sense of her life. Then she is given a book of ancient Norse legends." (Publisher's note)

Includes bibliographical references.

Byers, Michael

Percival's planet; a novel. Henry Holt and Co. 2010 414p $27

ISBN 978-0-8050-9218-9; 0-8050-9218-8

LC 2009-40107

This "novel, set mainly in the 1930s, tells the true story of the search for Pluto and those looking for it as their lives swing slowly and surely into alignment. Michael Byers occasionally gets bogged down in his prodigious research, but his characters remain strong enough to pull you in. They may be attempting to better understand the vast expanse of the universe, but what Byers has created is really just an endearing story of underdogs, both the ragtag crew of astronomers and the tiny celestial body they're hoping to find." Entertainment Wkly

Bynum, Sarah Shun-Lien

Ms. Hempel chronicles. Harcourt 2008 193p $23

ISBN 978-0-15-101496-5; 0-15-101496-5

LC 2008-08924

"Ms. Hempel's consciousness is a joy to inhabit. Kind, scrupulous, curious, wistful, and odd, she has the vitality of a bright, nervous child, overlaid by the premature world-weariness of someone in their late twenties. . . . This is not a saccharine novel, and heartache, sexual confusion, and resignation rear their heads." Bookforum

Byrne, Kerrigan

The **Duke**; by Kerrigan Byrne. St. Martin's Press 2017 377 p. (Victorian Rebels) (paperback) $7.99

ISBN 1250118247; 9781250118240; 9781250118257

In this book, by Kerrigan Byrne, "Collin 'Cole' Talmage, Duke of Trewyth, is the stuff that legends are made of. He's the English Empire's golden son--until fate has its way with him. . . . Imogen Pritchard is a beautiful lass who works in a hospital by day and as a serving maid at night. Years ago, . . . she ended up spending a scandalous night with Cole. . . . Imogen entered a marriage of convenience—one that left her a wealthy widow—but she never forgot Cole." (Publisher's note)

"Byrne's complex characterizations make her characters believable and real in this page-turning novel full of historical details and sensuous romance." Pub Wkly

Börjlind, Rolf

Spring Tide; by Cilla Börjlind and Rolf Börjlind. Trafalgar Square 2014 480 p. $16.95

ISBN 1843915154; 9781843915157

In this book, by Cilla Börjlind and Rolf Börjlind, "[a] gang has been killing homeless people in parks, filming their attacks, and broadcasting them on the internet. The police have their work cut out trying to keep abreast of the crime wave. Olivia Rönning hopes to follow in her father's footsteps and join their ranks in the next few months as she completes her training; she has only one last hurdle to overcome, . . . a challenge from her professor to pick a cold case and solve it." (Publisher's note)

"Two Swedish scriptwriters (TV series Wallander and Beck) deliver an intense, action-packed first novel. They smoothly transition among the many well-developed characters and set a chilling mood with an excellent evocation of the Swedish landscape. In addition, the authors effortlessly blend two mysteries to create a plot with many twists and turns that will be sure to appeal to fans of Henning Mankell, Maj Sjöwall and

Per Wahlöö, and Camilla Läckberg. While the English translation is excellent, the British slang might be off-putting to some U.S. readers." LJ

C

Cadwalladr, Carole

The **family** tree. Dutton 2005 384p il $23.95

ISBN 0-525-94842-2

LC 2004-52756

"Set in late-20th-century Britain, the novel is narrated by Rebecca Monroe, a pop culture researcher who tells of her marriage to Alistair, a behavioral geneticist; her childhood leading up to her mother's suicide; and her grandmother's doomed biracial romance with Cecil, a Jamaican immigrant. In an effort to better understand herself, the child she can't decide whether or not to have, and the people she still can't believe make up her family, Rebecca considers both sides of the nature/nurture debate, with any romantic notions she might be on the brink of reaching debunked by her husband's passionless scientific postulations. Cadwalladr explicates her tale with a slew of definitions, scientific charts and graphs, detailed family anatomies, examples of deductive fallacies and footnotes expounding on such essential '70s pop culture references as Dallas and The Sale of the Century. Her mastery of time and place, wry humor and sporadic bouts of self-doubt will endear her to readers, while her fascination with the choices people make combined with a morbid curiosity about her own fate add depth and texture to this utterly winning tale of one lovable, dysfunctional family." Publ Wkly

Cain, Chelsea

Heartsick. St. Martin's Minotaur 2007 326p $23.95

ISBN 978-0-312-36846-3; 0-312-36846-1

LC 2007-18005

"In addition to spiky characters, Cain has a crisp voice, a wicked sense of humor, and an imagination for all the horrors that can unfold in a locked basement." Entertainment Wkly

Other titles in this series are:

Sweetheart (2008)
Evil at Heart (2009)
The Night Season (2011)
Kill You Twice (2012)
Let Me Go (2013)

Cain, Chelsea

Kill you twice; Chelsea Cain. Minotaur Books 2012 336 p. (hardcover) $25.99

ISBN 9780312619787; 9781250014887

LC 2012013604

In this mystery novel, part of a series following "the 'Beauty Killer,' Gretchen Lowell . . . Portland, Oregon, police detective Archie Sheridan . . . is healing, slowly, from all the wounds, physical and psychological, that Gretchen has inflicted upon him, and Gretchen is safely ensconced in the Oregon State Mental Hospital. . . . Archie gets a call from Gretchen's psychiatrist with a message that the killer Archie is hunting is after Gretchen's child." (Booklist)

Cain, Chelsea

Let me go; Chelsea Cain. Minotaur Books 2013 336 p. (hardcover) $25.99

ISBN 0312619812; 9780312619817

LC 2013009825

This novel by Chelsea Cain focuses on Detective Archie Sheridan and "with escaped serial killer Gretchen Lowell on the loose . . . Archie finds himself crashing a masked ball on a private island owned by Jack Reynolds, a . . . drug kingpin. Archie's nemesis and sometimes lover has something special in mind for [him]. On Halloween Eve, with time running out, and the life of someone close to Archie on the line, Archie knows his only chance is to give Gretchen exactly what she wants." (Publisher's note)

Cain, Chelsea

★ **One** Kick; a novel. Chelsea Cain. Simon & Schuster 2014 384 p. (hardback) $25.99

ISBN 9781476749785; 9781476749822

LC 2013044441

This book, by Chelsea Cain, focuses on "Kick Lannigan, a young woman whose complicated past has given her a very special skill set. Famously kidnapped at age six, Kick captured America's hearts when she was rescued five years later. Now, twenty-one, she finds herself unexpectedly entangled in a missing child case that will put her talents to the test." (Publisher's note)

"The subject matter is uncomfortable, even stomach-churning at times, but Cain manages to deal sensitively with her material while still allowing Kick's character to emerge with multifaceted humanity--and even snatches of humor." Booklist

Cain, James M. (James Mallahan), 1892-1977

The **postman** always rings twice, double indemnity, Mildred Pierce and selected stories. Alfred A. Knopf 2003 xxxix, 594p (Everyman's library) $25

ISBN 0-375-41438-X; 978-0-375-41438-1

LC 2003-277292

The postman always rings twice, (1934) is the tale of a drifter who stumbles into a job, into an erotic obsession, and into a murder. Double indemnity (1934) is a story of blind passion, duplicity, and murder. Mildred Pierce (1943) is the tale of a woman with a taste for shiftless men and an unreasoned devotion to her monstrous daughter. Also included here are five stories:Pastorale; The baby in the icebox; Dead man; Brush fire; The girl in the storm

Caldwell, Erskine

Tobacco road. Scribner 1932 241p

"Jeeter Lester is an impoverished Georgia sharecropper who lives on Tobacco Road with his starving old mother, his sickly wife, Ada, and his two children, sixteen-year-old Dude and Ellie May, who has a harelip. A third child, Pearl, has been married at the age of twelve to Lov Bensey, a railroad worker. When Jeeter's widowed preacher sister, Bessie Rice, induces Dude to marry her by buying him a new automobile, Dude accidentally wrecks the car and kills his grandmother. Pearl runs away from Lov Bensey; Ellie May happily goes to live with him; and Jeeter and Ada, left alone one night, perish when their shack burns down." Reader's Ency. 4th edition

Caldwell, Ian, 1976-

The **Fifth** Gospel; A Novel. by Ian Caldwell. Simon & Schuster 2015 448 p. $25.99

ISBN 1451694148; 9781451694147

LC 2014041909

In this novel, by Ian Caldwell, "a mysterious exhibit is under construction at the Vatican Museums. A week before it is scheduled to open, its curator is murdered. . . . That same night, a violent break-in rocks the home of the curator's research partner, Father Alex Andreou, a Greek Catholic priest who lives inside the Vatican with his five-year-old son. When the papal police fail to identify a suspect in either crime, Father Alex . . . undertakes his own investigation." (Publisher's note)

"An intelligent and deeply contemplative writing style, along with more than a few bombshell plot twists, set this one above the pack, but it's the insightful character development that makes this redemptive story so moving." Pub Wkly

Caldwell, Ian

The **rule** of four; [by] Ian Caldwell & Dustin Thomason. Dial Press 2004 372p $24

ISBN 0-385-33711-6

LC 2003-70124

"A Princeton student has only twenty-four hours to complete his senior thesis—hardly the nail-biting stuff of thrillers, except that the thesis in question purports to solve the mystery of an erotic fifteenth-century allegory littered with ciphers and algorithms. . . . As the student races to meet his deadline, mayhem engulfs the campus: a chase through steam tunnels beneath the grassy quads, an inferno at the school's toniest eating club, and nude frolics in the snow (this last not fiction but a real Princeton tradition). The authors . . . keep up a frantic, somewhat exhausting pace, but the most riveting action sequences take place inside the mind, as the hero wrestles with the manuscript." New Yorker

Calisher, Hortense

The **collected** stories of Hortense Calisher; Hortense Calisher. Open Road Media 2013 502 p. ebook $29.99

ISBN 1480437387; 9781480437388

Originally published 1975 by Arbor House

National Book Award Finalist: Fiction (1976)

This book "gathers short pieces that chart the author's best-loved themes of mindful consciousness and social worlds. This collection includes one of her well-known New Yorker stories, 'In Greenwich There Are Many Gravelled Walks,' in which a young man drops his mother off at a sanitarium and acquires a new friend who finally awakens him to the world. Also included are 'The Sound of Waiting,' one of the chapters in the Elkin family saga; the chilling, Jamesian 'The Scream on Fifty-seventh Street,' in which a New York widow hears a scream late one night but cannot decide how to investigate without appearing to her neighbors to have gone mad; and the nearly novella-length 'The Summer Rebellion.'" (Publisher's note)

Callihan, Kristen

Firelight. Forever 2012 400 p. (pbk) $5.99

ISBN 9781455508594

This book tells the story of "Miranda Ellis, [who] has an unearthly talent for creating fire from thin air. Lord Benjamin Archer has lived for decades under the influence of a dark curse and wears a black mask over his disfigured face. After Miranda's family is ruined, she weds Benjamin for his money and is surprised when passion and romance follow. Shortly after the wedding, Benjamin stands accused of a gruesome series of homicides. As he and Miranda hunt the true killer, Miranda soon sees the innocent, passionate man behind the mask, while wary Benjamin begins to trust in his wife's love even though it endangers them both." (Publishers Weekly)

Calling the wind; twentieth century African-American short stories. edited and with an introduction by Clarence Major. HarperCollins Pubs. 1993 xxv, 622p hardcover o.p.

ISBN 0-06-018337-3

LC 92-52620

This "could become the anthology of black American short fiction for wide use in the high school and college classroom as well as by the general reading public." Booklist

Calvino, Italo

Baron in the trees; translated by Archibald Colquhoun. Harcourt 1977 217p pa $12

ISBN 0-15-610680-9

LC 76-039704

Original Italian edition, 1957; this translation first published 1959 by Random House

Calvino's "status as one of Italy's greatest writer's was confirmed by the acclaim which met the fantasy, The baron in the trees (1957), in which a nineteenth-century nobleman opts to pursue life without ever setting foot on the ground. The story examines the meeting-points of reality and imagination." Good Fiction Guide

Calvino, Italo

★ **If** on a winter's night a traveler. Knopf 1993 254p $18

ISBN 0-679-42025-8

LC 92-54302

Original Italian edition, 1979; this is a reissue of the edition published 1981 by Harcourt Brace Jovanovich

The novel "begins with a man discovering that the copy of a novel he has recently purchased is defective, a Polish novel having been bound within its pages. He returns to the bookshop the following day and meets a young woman who is on an identical mission. They both profess a preference for the Polish novel. Interposed between the chapters in which the two strangers attempt to authenticate their texts are 10 excerpts that parody genres of contemporary world fiction, such as the Latin-American novel and the political novel of eastern Europe." Merriam-Webster's Ency of Lit

Calvino, Italo

Invisible cities; translated from the Italian by William Weaver. Harcourt Brace Jovanovich 1974 165p

ISBN 0-15-145290-3

Original Italian edition, 1972

"Italo Calvino is recognized as one of the consummate stylists among writers today, a novelist whose superbly imaginative mind conjures up metaphorical fables of exquisite beauty to transcribe his personal visions of man and the universe." Choice

Cambias, James L.

★ A **Darkling** Sea; James L. Cambias. Tor 2014 352 p. (hardcover) $25.99

ISBN 0765336278; 9780765336279

LC 2013025215

"On the planet Ilmatar, under a roof of ice a kilometer thick, a team of deep-sea diving scientists investigates the blind alien race that lives below. The Terran explorers have made an uneasy truce with the Sholen, their first extraterrestrial contact: so long as they don't disturb the Ilmataran habitat, they're free to conduct their missions in peace. But when Henri Kerlerec, media personality and reckless adventurer, ends up sliced open by curious Ilmatarans, tensions between Terran and Sholen erupt, leading to a diplomatic disaster that threatens to escalate to war." (Publisher's note)

"Cambias makes the Sholen and Ilmataran people and cultures as real as the more familiar human component. Beautifully written, with a story that captures the imagination." Booklist

Cameron, Claire

The **last** Neanderthal; a novel. Claire Cameron. Little, Brown & Co. 2017 x, 277 p.p illustration (hardcover) $26

ISBN 9780316314480; 9780316314473

LC 2016955674

In this novel, by Claire Cameron, "forty thousand years in the past, the last family of Neanderthals roams the earth. . . . Girl, the oldest daughter, is just coming of age and her family is determined to . . . find her a mate. But . . . Girl is left alone to care for Runt, a foundling of unknown origin. . . . In the modern day, archaeologist Rosamund Gale works well into her pregnancy, racing to excavate newly found Neanderthal artifacts before her baby comes." (Publisher's note)

"The contrasting and similar reactions to motherhood are emblematic of the book's greatest strength—its ability to collapse time and space to draw together seemingly dissimilar species: ancestors and successors, writer and reader." Pub Wkly

Cameron, Peter, 1959-

The **city** of your final destination. Farrar, Straus & Giroux 2002 312p $24

ISBN 0-374-28197-1

LC 2001-51127

In this "novel, Omar Razaghi, a graduate student in Kansas by way of Iran and Canada, travels to Uruguay to research a biography of Jules Gund, a critically ignored expatriate writer who published only a single novel before his death. In an attempt to obtain permission to proceed with his work, Omar finds himself entangled in, and even falling a bit in love with, the family Jules left behind: his homosexual brother, Adam; Jules's wife, Caroline; and his mistress Arden. . . . The characters discover themselves not through the books they have read (as Omar first believes) or the places they have been (as the title would suggest) but through Cameron's precisely rendered conversations." New Yorker

Cameron, Peter

Coral Glynn; Peter Cameron. Farrar, Straus and Giroux 2012 210 p.

ISBN 0374299013; 9780374299019

LC 2011034926

This book tells the story of "Coral, a nurse, sent to Hart House in 1950 to tend the dying Mrs. Hart." (Libr J) Her son Major Hart "has an aversion to spending the rest of his life alone. He had been badly wounded in the war and has few social contacts beyond his childhood friend Robin, who's in love with the major. . . . Hart somewhat ambivalently returns some of Robin's affection, but . . . he and Coral get engaged. . . . On their wedding night their marriage is immediately thwarted by Inspector Hoke, who's investigating a mysterious murder that occurred in the woods near Hart House. . . . Uncertain whether Coral has any culpability in the crime, Hart urges her to disappear to London, where she lives for two years. . . . Their on-again/off-again relationship teeters on the brink until Coral finally makes up her mind." (Kirkus)

Campbell, Bebe Moore

Brothers and sisters. Putnam 1994 476p

ISBN 0-399-13929-X

LC 94-14196

"What makes 'Brothers and Sisters' different from the traditional potboiler is Ms. Campbell's genuine attempt to address the complexities of race in the modern age." N Y Times Book Rev

Campbell, Bonnie Jo

American salvage; stories. Wayne State University Press 2009 170p pa $18.95

ISBN 978-0-8143-3412-6; 0-8143-3412-1

LC 2008-51203

National Book Award Finalist: Fiction (2009)

"Campbell's knockout short stories about postindustrial rural Michigan portray damaged, discarded, and busted-broke people rich in yearning, forgiveness, and love." Booklist

Campbell, Bonnie Jo, 1962-

Mothers, tell your daughters; stories. Bonnie Jo Campbell. W W Norton & Co Inc 2015 264 p. (hardcover) $25.95

ISBN 0393248453; 9780393248456

LC 2015022459

In this short story collection, by Bonnie Jo Campbell, "strong but flawed women . . . must negotiate a sexually charged atmosphere as they love, honour, and betray one another against the backdrop of all the men in their world. Such richly fraught mother-daughter relationships can be lifelines, anchors, or they can sink a woman like a stone." (Publisher's note)

"From a bittersweet variation on the Lolita predicament to a cheating dead ex-fiancé possibly reincarnated as a dog to the title story, a tour de force performed by a tough old gal whose life has been shaped by grueling chores, a 'fearsome' husband, six children, and sexual crimes, Campbell delivers 16 commanding, piquant, and reverberating stories about womanhood besieged and triumphant." Booklist

Campbell, Bonnie Jo, 1962-

★ **Once** upon a river; Bonnie Jo Campbell. W. W. Norton & Co. 2011 348p. map $25.95

ISBN 978-0-393-07989-0; 0-393-07989-9; 9780393341775

LC 201101499

'This novel, a National Book Award and National Book Critics Circle Award finalist, tells the story of "Margo Crane, a beauty whose unflinching gaze and uncanny ability with a rifle have not made her life any easier. After the violent death of her father, in which she is complicit, Margo takes to the Stark River in her boat, with only a few supplies and a biography of Annie Oakley, in search of her vanished mother. But the river . . . is a dangerous place for a young woman traveling alone, and she must be strong to survive, using her knowledge of the natural world and her ability to look unsparingly into the hearts of those around her. Her river odyssey through rural Michigan becomes a defining journey, one that leads her beyond self-preservation and to the decision of what price she is willing to pay for her choices." (Publisher's note)

"What happens to Margo unfolds as a gripping story, old-fashioned in its fullness of event and character development. And all the while, an assured Campbell narrates in a graceful, gliding, confident voice that steers the action smoothly from one bend in the plot to the next — a demonstration of outstanding skills on the river of American literature." Entertainment Wkly

Camus, Albert

★ The **fall**; translated from the French by Justin O'Brien. Knopf 1957 147p

Original French edition, 1956

"A former Parisian lawyer explains to a stranger in an Amsterdam bar his current profession of judge-penitent. His bitter honesty prevented him first from winning his own self-esteem through good deeds, then from exhausting his own self-condemnation through debauchery. Knowing that no man is ever innocent, he is still trying to forestall personal judgment by confession, by judging others, and by avoiding any situation demanding action." Reader's Ency. 4th edition

Camus, Albert

The **plague**; translated from the French by Stuart Gilbert. Knopf 1948 278p hardcover o.p. pa $12.95

ISBN 0-394-44061-7; 0-679-72021-9 pa

Original French edition, 1947

"Using an epidemic of bubonic plague in an Algerian city as a symbol for the absurdity of man's condition, Albert Camus has in this novel articulated his firm belief in mankind's heroism in struggling against the ultimate futility of life. The plague makes everyone in the city intensely aware both of mortality and of the fact that cooperation is the only logical consolation anyone will find in the face of certain death. Though each character, from doctor to priest, represents some aspect of mankind's attempts to deal with the absurd, none is a cardboard figure. The reader cares what happens to the men depicted here. One takes pleasure in the moments of deep human connection that leave us with the conviction that men are, on the whole, admirable." Shapiro. Fic for Youth. 3d edition

Camus, Albert

★ The **stranger**; translated from the French by Matthew Ward. Knopf 1988 123p $25

ISBN 0-394-53305-4

LC 83-48885

Original French edition, 1942; published in the United Kingdom with title: The outsider

This novel "reveals the 'Absurd' as the condition of man, who feels himself a stranger in his world. Meursault refuses to 'play the game,' by telling the conventional social white lies demanded of him or by believing in human love or religious faith. The unemotional style of his narrative lays naked his motives—or his absence of motive—for his lack of grief over his mother's death, his affair with Marie, his killing an Arab in the hot Algerian sun. Having rejected by honest self-analysis all interpretations which could explain or justify his existence, he nevertheless discovers, while in prison awaiting execution, a passion for the simple fact of life itself." Reader's Ency. 4th edition

Canin, Ethan

America America; a novel. Random House 2008 458p $27

ISBN 978-0-679-45680-3; 0-679-45680-5

LC 2008-2341

"Sifter is, at times, too perfect a lead, and his Saline coming-of-age is an idealized yesteryear, a mythic America encased in amber. But it is so passionately imagined that it is hard to resist Mr. Canin's retreat to simpler times and his vision of those who would forfeit comfort for the possibility of unknown highs (or lows)." N Y Sun

Canin, Ethan

★ A **Doubter's** Almanac; a novel. Ethan Canin. Random House 2015 576 p. (hardback) $28

ISBN 1400068266; 9781400068265

LC 2014022315

"Milo Andret is born with an unusual mind. A lonely child growing up in the woods of northern Michigan in the 1950s, he gives little thought to his own talent. But with his acceptance at U.C. Berkeley he realizes the extent, and the risks, of his singular gifts. California in the seventies is a seduction, opening Milo's eyes to the allure of both ambition and indulgence." (Publisher's note)

"A moving, spiritual journey, this poetic novel clocks in at well over 500 pages but begs to be read in one sitting. It will delight literary fiction readers of all stripes with its diverse themes, from coming of age to love, grief, and addiction. But a warning; it's tough to keep a dry eye through this one." LJ

Canty, Kevin

The **underworld**; a novel. Kevin Canty. W W Norton & Co Inc 2017 253 p. (hardcover) $24.95

ISBN 9780393293067; 9780393293050

LC 2016035694

In this novel, author "Kevin Canty tells a story inspired by the facts of a disastrous fire that took place in an isolated silver mining town in Idaho in the 1970s. . . . [it] imagines the fates of a handful of fictional survivors and their loved ones--Jordan, a young widow with twin children; David, a college student trying to make a life for himself, . . . [and] Lionel, a lifelong hard-rock miner--as they struggle to come to terms with the loss." (Publisher's note)

"His sculpted, lapidarian cadence deftly navigates the terrain separating numbness and pain, second guesses and second chances, to illuminate the fragility and preciousness of life." Booklist

Cao, Lan

The **lotus** and the storm; a novel. Lan Cao. Viking 2014 400 p. (hardback) $27.95

ISBN 0670016926; 9780670016921

LC 2013047861

This novel, by Lan Cao, is describes events in the Vietnam War. "Minh is a former South Vietnamese commander . . . who left his homeland with his daughter, Mai. . . . Forty years later, . . . as Mai discovers a series of devastating truths about . . . her family during those years, Minh reflects upon his life and the story of love and betrayal that has remained locked in his heart since the fall of Saigon." (Publisher's note)

"Written with acute psychological insight and poetic flair, this deeply moving novel illuminates the ravages of war as experienced by a South Vietnamese family. In a rewarding follow-up to her well-received debut, Monkey Bridge (1997), the author returns to the conflict that shaped her own destiny before she was airlifted from her native Saigon to live in Virginia... A novel that humanizes the war in a way that body counts and political analyses never will." Kirkus

Capote, Truman

★ **Breakfast** at Tiffany's: a short novel and three stories. Random House 1958 179p

ISBN 0-394-41770-4

"'Breakfast at Tiffany's' tells the story of haunting and neurotic Holiday Golightly, Texan child-bride, girl-about-New York and friend of gangster czar, Sally Tomato, in a remarkable novelette that bears the Capote trademark of neat prose, multiple dimensions and unusual atmosphere." Ont Libr Rev

Capote, Truman, 1924-1984

★ The **complete** stories of Truman Capote; By Truman Capote, introduction by Reynolds Price. Random House 2004 300p $24.95

ISBN 0-679-64310-9; 9780812994377

LC 2004-46876

"Ranging from the gothic South to the chic East Coast, from rural children to aging urban sophisticates, all the unforgettable places and people of [Truman] Capote's oeuvre are here, in stories as elegant as they are heartfelt, as haunting as they are compassionate. Reading them reminds us of the miraculous gifts of a beloved American original." (Publisher's note)

"Now, for the first time, all of Capote's short stories are being published together, an event that signifies a renewed appreciation of his overall contribution to literature, for evidence is presented in this one volume that he should be ranked as a major American short story writer." Booklist

Capote, Truman

The **grass** harp. Random House 1951 181p

"After the death of his parents, Collin goes to live with his two aunts, Verna and Dolly. The former is wealthy and practical, the latter, whimsical and romantic. Dolly produces a cure for dropsy that she bottles and sells through the mail. Verna is ready to take over the operation and realize a large profit. To avoid this scheme, Collin, Dolly, and Catherine, a servant, go off to live in a treehouse, where they are joined by other eccentric characters. When Dolly dies, Collin is ready for his independence, having learned a valuable lesson about love and nonconformity." Shapiro. Fic for Youth. 3d edition

Caputo, Philip

Acts of faith. Knopf 2005 669p $26.95

ISBN 0-375-41166-6

LC 2004-48982

"Mr. Caputo writes with such authority that he's able to invest events that might seem improbable in another novelist's hands with an uncommon degree of verisimilitude, delineating not only the viewpoints of his Western visitors, but also those of the Sudanese rebels and their Islamic opponents with equally sure-handed drama and psychological ballast" N Y Times (Late N Y Ed)

Caputo, Philip

Crossers. Alfred A. Knopf 2009 447p $26.95

ISBN 978-0-375-41167-0; 0-375-41167-4

LC 2009-19096

This "is at once a color-filled action tale; a generational saga with a moral; a touching love story; and a bold lesson in history and its inevitabilities." Dallas Morning News

Capó Crucet, Jennine

Make Your Home Among Strangers; a novel. Jennine Capo Crucet. St. Martin's Press 2015 400 p. $26.99

ISBN 1250059666; 9781250059666

LC 2015017167

In this novel, by Jennine Capó Crucet, longlisted for the 2015 Center for Fiction First Novel Prize, "when Lizet-the daughter of Cuban immigrants and the first in her family to graduate from high school-secretly applies and is accepted to an ultra-elite college, her parents are furious at her decision to leave Miami. . . . Amidst this turmoil, Lizet begins her first semester at Rawlings College, distracted by both the exciting and difficult moments of freshman year." (Publisher's note)

"An emblematic story of both immigrant America and the coming-of-age struggle, told by an a PEN/O. Henry and Iowa Short Fiction award winner." LJ

Card, Orson Scott

Ender's game. TOR Bks. 1991 xxi, 226p $24.95; pa $6.99

ISBN 0-312-93208-1; 0-8125-5070-6 pa

A reissue of the title first published 1985

ALA YALSA Margaret A. Edwards Award (2008)

"The key, of course, is Ender Wiggin himself. Mr. Card never makes the mistake of patronizing or sentimentalizing his hero. Alternately likable and insufferable, he is a convincing little Napoleon in short pants." N Y Times Book Rev

Other titles in the author's distant future series about Ender Wiggin include:

Children of the mind (1996)
Ender in exile (2008)
Ender's shadow (1999)
Shadow of the giant (2005)
Shadow of the Hegemon (2001)
Shadow of the giant (2005)
Shadow puppets (2002)
Speaker for the dead (1986)
A war of gifts (2007)
Xenocide (1991)

Card, Orson Scott

Keeper of dreams. TOR 2008 656p $27.95

ISBN 978-0-7653-0497-1; 0-7653-0497-X

LC 2007-46720

"These short science fiction, fantasy and 'literary' stories, along with a handful of Hatrack River tales (related to the Alvin Maker series) and four stories 'written by a Mormon, about Mormon culture, for Mormon readers,' illustrate Card's fascination with complex child protagonists. . . . Card intended several of the included stories, like the powerful 'In the Dragon's House,' to open novels not yet written, but even on their own they provide significant examples of his perennial themes: morality, salvation and redemption." Publ Wkly

Card, Orson Scott

Maps in a mirror; the short fiction of Orson Scott Card. TOR Bks. 1990 675p $19.95

ISBN 0-312-85047-6

LC 90-38896

This collection features "46 pieces by an exceptional writer. Card's talents are represented by fantasy, science fiction, horror, poetry, and the stories that launched his sagas of Alvin Maker and Ender Wiggins. A substantial amount of autobiographical discussion of each story's origin enhances the volume's high value." Booklist

Card, Orson Scott

Seventh son. Doherty Assocs. 1987 241p (Tales of Alvin Maker) hardcover o.p. pa $6.99

ISBN 0-312-93019-4; 0-812-53305-4 pa

LC 86-51490

"This beguiling book recalls Robert Penn Warren in its robust but reflective blend of folktale, history, parable and personal testimony, pioneer narrative." Publ Wkly

Other titles in this series about Alvin Maker are:

Alvin Journeyman (1995)
The crystal city (2003)
Heartfire (1998)
Prentice Alvin (1989)
Red prophet (1988)

Carey, Jacqueline

Autumn bones; agent of hel. Jacqueline Carey. ROC, Published by the Penguin Group, Penguin Group (USA) Inc. 2013 432 p. (alk. paper) $26.95

ISBN 0451465180; 9780451465184

LC 2013017119

This is the second in Jacqueline Carey's suburban fantasy series. Here, "though still attracted to werewolf cop Cody and psychic vampire leader Stefan, Daisy Johanssen--half-demon advisor to the police of Pemkowet, Mich., and liaison to the goddess of the tiny underworld that lies beneath it--is enjoying the human normality of her new boyfriend, tour bus driver Sinclair Palmer. Then his mother releases his grandfather's duppy on the town to convince Sinclair to return to Jamaica." (Publishers Weekly)

Carey, Jacqueline

Banewreaker; Jacqueline Carey. Tor 2004 431p map (pbk.) $7.99

ISBN 9780765344298; 9780765305213; 0765305216

LC 2004048093

The background for this fantasy novel takes place at a time when "the Seven Shapers dwelled in accord and Shaped the world to their will. But Satoris, the youngest among them, was deemed too generous in his gifts to the race of Men, and so began the Shapers' War, which Sundered the world. Now six of the Shapers lay to one end of a vast ocean, and Satoris to the other, reviled by even the race of Men. Satoris sits in his Darkhaven, surrounded by his allies. Chief among them is Tanaros Blacksword, immortal Commander General of his army. . . . Now there is a new prophecy that tells of Satoris's destruction and the redemption of the world. To thwart it, Satoris sends Tanaros to capture the Lady of the Ellylon, the beautiful Cerelinde, to prevent her alliance with the last High King of Men." (Publisher's note)

Another title in this series is:
Godslayer (2005)

Carey, Jacqueline

Dark currents; agents of Hel. Jacqueline Carey. Roc 2012 368 p. $26.95

ISBN 0451464788; 9780451464781

LC 2012007049

This urban fantasy novel tells the story of "Daisy Johanssen," who lives in a Michigan town that is a tourist destination and "home to a thriving 'eldritch community' of supernatural entities, thanks to the presence of the local underworld controlled by the Norse goddess Hel." Daisy is Hel's assistant as well as a clerk at the human police station. She "is called in to help investigate the drowning of a local college boy when signs of both foul play and magical residue are found on the body." (Publishers Weekly)

Other titles in this series are:
Autumn Bones (2013)
Poison Fruit (2014)

Carey, Jacqueline

Kushiel's dart. Tor 2001 701p

ISBN 0-312-87238-0

LC 2001-21945

"Making a marvelous debut, Carey spins a breathtaking epic starring an unflinching yet poignantly vulnerable heroine. The tale blends Christianity and paganism with fascinating results." Booklist

Followed by Kushiel's chosen (2002) and Kushiel's avatar (2003)

Carey, Jacqueline

★ **Kushiel's** Scion; Jacqueline Carey. Warner Books 2006 xii, 753p map (pbk.) $7.99; o.p.; o.p.

ISBN 9780446610025; 044650002X; 9780446500029

LC 2005023648

This volume of the "Legacy series marks the start of a new trilogy set in Terre d'Ange, the author's reimagined Renaissance world. The story picks up where volume three, 'Kushiel's Avator' (2003), left off, though Imriel nó Montrève de la Courcel, a prince of the blood, now narrates in place of the . . . heroine of the previous books, Phèdre nó Delauney. As a boy, Imriel is abandoned by his treasonous parents and subjected to terrible indignities by pirates. Later rescued and adopted by Phèdre, he grows into a position of authority and learns many skills, including sexual prowess. He has a torrid affair with a married woman, and finally survives a terrible siege at a walled city he courageously defends." (Publishers Weekly)

Other titles in this series are:
Kushiel's Justice (2007)
Kushiel's Mercy (2008)

Carey, Jacqueline

Poison fruit; Agent of Hel novel. Jacqueline Carey. Roc 2014 448 p. (hardback) $26.95

ISBN 0451465318; 9780451465313

LC 2014015080

In this novel by Jacquelin Carey "as a result of a recent ghost uprising, an unknown adversary--represented by a hell-spawn lawyer has instigated a lawsuit against the town. If Pemkowet loses, Hel's sovereignty will be jeopardized, and the fate of the eldritch community will be at stake. The only one who can prevent it is Daisy--but she's going to have to confront her own worst nightmare to do it." (Publisher's note)

"This third urban fantasy series outing (after 2013's Autumn Bones) is the opposite of Carey's epic fantasies (Kushiel's Dart), but it is light and fun. With Daisy's romantic triangles, she will appeal to readers who miss Charlaine Harris's Sookie Stackhouse. The small-town setting and variety of inhuman creatures keep things lively." LJ

Carey, Lisa

The **stolen** child; Lisa Carey. Harper Perennial 2017 373, 15 p.p (paperback) $15.99

ISBN 9780062492180; 9780062492203

LC 2016032315

In this book, by Lisa Carey, is a "novel set on an enchanted island off the west coast of Ireland where magic, faith, and superstition pervade the inhabitants' lives and tangled relationships. . . . Steeped in Irish history and lore, . . . [it] is a mesmerizing descent into old world beliefs, and a captivating exploration of desire, myth, motherhood, and love in all its forms." (Publisher's note)

"Magical realism of the best kind, utterly devoid of whimsy." Kirkus

Carey, Peter, 1943-

The **chemistry** of tears; by Peter Carey. Alfred A. Knopf 2012 229 p.

ISBN 0307592715; 9780307592712

LC 2012005880

"The principal narrator of Peter Carey's . . . novel is [museum horologist] Catherine Gehrig." Her "boss . . . gives her a new project to work on, a set of tea chests containing the parts of a nineteenth-century mechanical bird, along with a stack of notebooks written by a man named Henry Brandling. . . . Two parallel quests begin: in 1854, Henry, . . . find[s] someone who will make a bird for his young son . . . ; in 2010, Catherine . . . tries to unravel his story and rebuild his bird." (Times Literary Supplement)

Carey, Peter

His illegal self. Alfred A. Knopf 2008 272p $24.95

ISBN 978-0-307-26372-8; 0-307-26372-X

LC 2007-42862

"Hippie communal disintegration has been done before, and better by T.C. Boyle in 'Drop City,' but Carey keeps us reading with his vivid lyricism, his finely tuned sense of the ridiculous and his focus on two very specific characters: a boy aching for mother love and a woman who is trying to make sense of having maternal love thrust upon her. In the end, this is a love story, an unconventional but emotionally compelling one." St. Louis Post-Dispatch

Carey, Peter

★ **My** life as a fake. Knopf 2003 266p $24

ISBN 0-375-41498-3

LC 2003-52746

A novel told through the "eyes of Lady Sarah Wode-Douglass, editor of a struggling but prestigious London poetry journal, who one day in the early 1970s finds herself accompanying an old family friend, poet and novelist John Slater, out to Malaysia. There they encounter an eccentric Australian expatriate, Christopher Chubb, who concocted, Slater says, a huge literary hoax in Australia just after the war, creating an imaginary genius poet, Bob McCorkle, whose publication by a litle magazine led to the suicide of the magazine's editor. Now Chubb offers

Lady Sarah a page of poetry that shows undoubted genius and claims it is from a book in his possession. Lady Sarah's every acquisitive instinct is inflamed, but to get her hands on the book she has to listen, as Chubb inflicts on her, Ancient Mariner-like, the amazing story of his own epic struggle with McCorkle." Publ Wkly

This work "is so confidently brilliant, so economical yet lively in its writing, so tightly fitted and continuously startling in its plot that something, we feel, must be wrong with it. It ends in a bit of a rush, and left several questions dangling in this reader's mind. Unfortunately, to spell out those questions would be to betray too much of an intricate fictional construct where little is as it first seems and fantastic developments unfold like scenes on a fragile paper fan." New Yorker

Carey, Peter

★ **Parrot** and Olivier in America. Knopf 2010 379p $26.95

ISBN 978-0-307-59262-0; 0-307-59262-6

LC 2009-47435

National Book Award Finalist: Fiction (2010)

Olivier-Jean-Baptiste de Clarel de Garmont "has been bundled off to America at the behest of his mother, who suffered brutally under the French Terror of 1793 and thinks only of how to save her son from a similar fate. Accompanying him is Parrot, an English orphan with artistic aspirations, trained as a printer, who is yoked to Olivier de Bahbah Garmont as servant, gadfly and spy. Both men wrestle with demon love: Olivier for his democratic American girl who can never be taken to home to Paris and maman; Parrot for his mistress, a beautiful and lusty painter, all that smeary wine and meat and fat glistening on her lips, and whose talent outstrips his own. In short, it's a buddy novel. But what a novel! . . . . Funny, bawdy, brainy and moving, Parrot & Olivier in America is an utter delight." Globe and Mail

Cargill, C. Robert

Dreams and Shadows. HarperCollins 2013 448 p. $24.99

ISBN 0062190423; 9780062190420

In this book, "[C. Robert] Cargill chronicles the friendship and adventures of Ewan, stolen as a baby by the fairy-goblin crossbreeds called Bendith Y Mamau, and Colby, an eight-year-old who encounters a djinn. . . . The two boys travel from the faerie lands known as the Limestone Kingdom, a realm filled with creatures of myth—Coyote, changelings, the Wild Hunt, and more—to Austin, Tex., where they must learn to navigate the often treacherous path to adulthood." (Publishers Weekly)

Another title in this series is:

Queen of the Dark Things (2014)

Carlson, Ron

Five skies. Viking 2007 244p $23.95

ISBN 0-670-03850-4; 978-0-670-03850-3

LC 2006-51760

"High in the desert plains of southern Idaho, three men gather for a summer of hard work: an aging rancher, whose wife was killed in a freak accident; a nineteen-year-old fleeing both family and law; and an engineer whose career is built on precision but whose brother died in a poorly planned stunt. Time and talk, so often friends to Carlson's characters, slowly heal the wounds, but the men's commission, a ramp for a Knievel-style canyon jump, makes hazardous any hope for moral uplift and serves, in the end, as the stage for tragedy." New Yorker

Carlyle, Liz, 1958-

The **bride** wore scarlet; Liz Carlyle. Avon 2011 375 p. (paperback) $7.99

ISBN 0061965766; 9780061965760

LC 2012658231

This book is part of Liz Carlyle's Fraternitas paranormal Victorian trilogy. Here, "Anaïs de Rohan has spent much of her life training, hoping to join the male-only Fraternitas. The earl of Bessett reluctantly allows her to accompany him on a mission to Brussels where they must pose as husband and wife in order to rescue a young child who has the ability to see into the future. The pretense leads to real attraction that Bessett and Anaïs find impossible to ignore." (Publishers Weekly)

Carnoy, David

The **big** exit; David Carnoy. Overlook Press 2012 319 p. $25.95

ISBN 1590205154; 9781590205150

In this crime novel by David Carnoy "Richie Forman is freshly out of prison. By night, he makes a living impersonating Frank Sinatra in San Francisco's lounges and corporate parties. But then his ex-best friend--the man who stole his fiancée while he was in prison--is found hacked to death in his garage, and Richie is the prime suspect." (Publisher's note)

Carr, Caleb

★ The **alienist**. Random House 1994 496p

ISBN 0-679-41779-6

LC 93-32766

"A society-born reporter and an enigmatic abnormal psychologist—the 'alienist' of the title—are recruited in 1896 by New York's reform police commissioner Teddy Roosevelt to track down a serial killer who is slaughtering boy prostitutes. The investigators are opposed at every step by crime bosses and the city's hidden rulers (including J. Pierpont Morgan); they distrust the alienist's novel methods and would rather conceal evidence of the murders than court publicity." (Libr J)

Followed by The angel of darkness

Carr, Robyn

The **Wanderer**; A thunder point novel. Robyn Carr. Harlequin Books 2013 377 p. (paperback) $7.99

ISBN 0778314472; 9780778314479

This novel, by Robyn Carr, is set in a small town "on the Oregon coast. . . . Locals love the land's unspoiled beauty. Developers see it as a potential gold mine. When newcomer Hank Cooper learns he's been left an old friend's entire beachfront property, he finds himself with a community's destiny in his hands. Cooper has never been a man to settle in one place, and Thunder Point was supposed to be just another quick stop. But Cooper finds himself getting involved with the town." (Publisher's note)

Other titles in this series are:

The Newcomer (2013)
The Hero (2013)
The Chance (2014)
The Promise (2014)
The Homecoming (2014)
One Wish (2015)
A New Hope (2015)
Wildest Dreams (2015)

Carroll, Jonathan, 1949-

Bathing the Lion; Jonathan Carroll. St. Martin's Press 2014 288 p. $25.99

ISBN 1250048265; 9781250048264

LC 2014021408

"In Jonathan Carroll's surreal masterpiece, 'Bathing the Lion,' five people who live in the same New England town go to sleep one night and all share the same hyper-realistic dream. Some of these people know each other; some don't. When they wake the next day all of them know what has happened. All five were at one time 'mechanics,' a kind of cosmic repairman whose job is to keep order in the universe." (Publisher's note)

"Cosmic conspiracies, paranoia, and awe are grounded in the everyday, the impossible made probable by Carroll's authoritative wordplay." Pub Wkly

Carroll, Jonathan

The **ghost** in love. Sarah Crichton Books/Farrar, Straus and Giroux 2008 308p $25

ISBN 978-0-374-16186-6; 0-374-16186-0

LC 2008-7877

"Ben Gould hits his head on the sidewalk in an accident that should have killed him. Somehow he survives, but he's changed in ways that he cannot understand. So starts a magical tale in which Ben talks to his dog, Pilot; the ghost sent to monitor Ben falls in love with his girlfriend; and a mysterious knife-wielding man threatens them all. . . . Love, memory, and balancing the needs of our many selves are themes in this occasionally scary, often luminous work of unconventional fantasy." Libr J

Carter, Angela

★ **Burning** your boats; the collected short stories. with an introduction by Salman Rushdie. Holt & Co. 1996 462p

ISBN 0-8050-4462-0

LC 95-26312

"Gathered from 30 years of Carter's writing life, this collection is arranged chronologically to reveal her evolution as a writer as well as her consistent preoccupation with the Gothic. . . . As her friend Salman Rushdie writes in his moving introduction, Carter is not an easy read, but there are many rewards for the persistent." Libr J

Carter, Angela, 1940-1992

★ **Nights** at the circus. Viking 1985 294p

ISBN 0-670-80375-8

LC 84-40459

The protagonist of this novel is "a six-foot-two-inch woman aerialist with wings. The setting is turn of the century London, St. Petersburg, and Siberia. An American journalist, Jack Walser, has been sent to interview Sophia, known as Fevvers to her friends, and is so intrigued by her account of her childhood that he joins the circus as a clown. Then begin the . . . 'nights at the circus,' with a train derailment in Siberia, where Walser starts his apprenticeship as a shaman." (Libr J)

"Carter describes a locale as exotic to the traditional reader as her women are to Walser and, by implication, all men; and she undercuts accepted Western history as she goes." New Republic

Carter, M. J.

The **Strangler** Vine; by M.J. Carter. Fig Tree 2014 352 p. maps (Avery and Blake novels) $27.95

ISBN 0241146224; 0399171673; 9780241146224; 9780399171673

LC 2014017351

This book, by M.J. Carter, is "set in the untamed wilds of nineteenth-century colonial India. . . . William Avery is a young soldier; . . . Jeremiah Blake is a secret political agent gone native, a genius at languages and disguises, disenchanted with the whole ethos of British rule, but who cannot resist the challenge of an unresolved mystery. What starts as a wild goose chase for this unlikely pair . . . becomes very much more sinister." (Publisher's note)

"Making pleasing use of the developing bromance/adventure formula and a wealth of research, Carter delivers an engaging, skeptical, modern take on empire." Kirkus

Other titles in this series are:

The Infidel Stain (2016)

The Devil's Feast (2017)

Carter, Stephen L.

The **emperor** of Ocean Park. Knopf 2002 657p $26.95

ISBN 0-375-41363-4

LC 2001-38227

This "tale of ambition, revenge and the power of familial obligations is set in the privileged environs of an Ivy League law school, Martha's Vineyard, and Washington, D.C. Oliver Garland is the demanding but emotionally distant patriarch of an elite, affluent African American family used to special privileges and close relationships with the powerful in government, business, and the criminal underworld. Oliver's death sparks renewed interest in his political career—as a vitriolic conservative, embittered by a failed bid for the U.S. Supreme Court—and concern in many quarters about 'arrangements' he has made in the event of his demise. Garland's son Talcott, a law professor, is very reluctantly drawn into the intrigue. . . . An elegantly nuanced novel, with finely drawn characters, a challenging plot, and perfect pacing." Booklist

Carter, Stephen L.

New England white. Alfred A. Knopf 2007 555p $24.95

ISBN 978-0-375-41362-9; 0-375-41362-6

LC 2006-19721

Carter "creates an invigorating and often scathing portrait of the Carlyles' community. He refutes political correctness, preferring to explore the contradictions warring within Julia. . . . [He] is equally intense in his portrayal of the Carlyles' outwardly perfect, inwardly turbulent marriage, a delicate balance of duty and endurance, even love of a sort." PopMatters

Carter, Stephen L.

Palace council. Alfred A. Knopf 2008 513p $26.95

ISBN 978-0-307-26658-3; 0-307-26658-3

LC 2007-52134

"Set primarily in the years between 1954 and 1974—what Carter calls the 'two decades' of the sixties—this political thriller leaves virtually no important person or event unturned. Richard Nixon, Langston Hughes, and dissident groups all play roles as the action shifts from Harlem to Washington and Saigon. After Eddie Wesley stumbles upon the body of a prominent lawyer who died clutching the talisman of a secret society in his fist, he finds himself caught up in the machinations of spies and assassins. Untangling the so-called Palace Council's purpose gains new urgency when Eddie's sister suddenly vanishes. At the same time, Aurelia, the ex-girlfriend for whom he still carries a torch, is on her own path to discovering the enigmatic group's secrets. . . . Carter offers a finely drawn picture of the complicated black social world." New Yorker

Carver, Raymond

★ **Collected** stories; [William L. Stull & Maureen P. Carroll, editors] Library of America 2009 1019p $40

ISBN 978-1-59853-046-9; 1-59853-046-1

LC 2009-23633

"The Library of America Collected Stories is a fascinating event . . . if you haven't read it you cannot claim, in the fullest sense, to have read Raymond Carver." Tmes Lit Suppl

Carver, Raymond

★ **What** we talk about when we talk about love; stories. Vintage Books 1989 159p pbk $15

ISBN 0679723056; 9780679723059

LC 80-21752

Originally published 1981

"In spare, deft, precise prose, whole lives are portrayed in a single second as Carver briefly exposes his doom-ridden characters to one startling flash of agonizing self-recognition. These disturbing images remain long in the memory even after their immediate impression has disappeared." Booklist

Carver, Tania

The **surrogate**; a novel. Pegasus Crime 2011 438p $25.95

ISBN 978-1-60598-256-4

"A serial killer is on the loose in Colchester, England, where pregnant women are being brutally slain, their babies ripped from their wombs. Veteran officer Phil Brennan is desperate to solve the mystery. After the third such murder occurs, this time with the baby almost certainly taken alive, Phil and his team call upon their colleague, psychologist Marina Esposito, to assist in profiling and capturing the killer. Pregnant, Marina is drawn deeper and deeper into the hunt for a monster. . . . This well-written . . . novel grips the reader from the start, with plenty of violence, gore, and psychological suspense." Libr J

Another title in this series is:

The Creeper (2012)

Cash, Wiley

★ A **land** more kind than home; a novel. Wiley Cash. William Morrow 2012 309 p. (hardcover) $24.99

ISBN 0062088149; 9780062088147; 9780062088239; 9780062088246

LC 2011022819

In this book, set "up beyond Asheville, near where Gunter Mountain falls into Tennessee . . . Jess Hall is the 9-year-old son of Ben and Julie and beloved younger brother of gentle Stump, his mute, autistic sibling. Clem Barefield is county sheriff, a man with a moral code as tough, weathered and flexible as his gun belt. Adelaide Lyle, once a midwife, is now community matriarch of simple faith and solid conscience. Carson Chambliss is pastor of River Road Church of Christ. He has caught Stump spying, peering into the bedroom of his mother Julie, while she happened to be entertaining the amoral pastor. . . .Chambliss convinces Julie to bring Stump to the church to be cured by the laying on of hands. There, Stump suffers a terrible fate." (Kirkus Reviews)

Cash, Wiley

This dark road to mercy; a novel. Wiley Cash. William Morrow 2014 240 p. (hardback) $25.99

ISBN 0062088254; 9780062088253; 9780062088260

LC 2013022221

In this novel, by Wiley Cash, "when their mother dies unexpectedly, twelve-year-old Easter Quillby and her six-year-old sister, Ruby, are shuffled into the foster care system in Gastonia, North Carolina, a little town not far from the Appalachian Mountains. But just as they settle into their new life, their errant father, Wade, an ex-minor league baseball player whom they haven't seen in years, suddenly reappears and steals them away in the middle of the night." (Publisher's note)

"A story of family, blood loyalty and making choices that can seem right but end up wrong." Kirkus

Castellani, Christopher

All this talk of love; a novel. by Christopher Castellani. Algonquin Books of Chapel Hill 2013 320 p. $13.95

ISBN 9781616201708

LC 2012030841

In this book by Christopher Castellani, "it's been fifty years since Antonio Grasso married Maddalena and brought her to America. That was the last time she would see . . . everything she knew and loved in the village of Santa Cecilia, Italy. . . . But . . . ['their] American-born daughter . . . hatches the idea to take the entire family back to Italy. . . . It is an idea that threatens to tear the Grasso family apart." (Publisher's note).

Castellanos Moya, Horacio, 1957-

Tyrant memory; translated from the Spanish by Katherine Silver. New Directions 2011 270p pa $15.95

ISBN 978-0-8112-1917-4; 0-8112-1917-8

LC 2011-02587

"Haydee is surrounded by a host of vibrant and resilient family and friends, whose lives of relative comfort evoke the grande bourgeoisie 'decent people' society that she inhabits. . . It's an extremely appealing world, both exotic and restrained. The literary style is no less interesting, with sharp divisions between the dignified voice of Haydee recording events in her diary and the bawdy Clemente's attempts to leave El Salvador, narrated playwright style. It's truly innovative writing which the accomplished Moya carries off with ease, while simultaneously managing to let the serious, yet politically recalcitrant, Pericles dominate the work, despite his near total absence from any of the events recorded." Metro Eireann

Castillo, Linda

Breaking silence; 1st ed.; Minotaur Books 2011 320p (Kate Burkholder thrillers)

ISBN 9780312374990

LC 2011005103

When the fatal accidents of three Amish farmers are proven to be murders, former Amish woman Kate investigates a possible link between the killings and recent hate crimes, a case that is complicated by a dark secret and her precarious relationship with agent John Tomasetti. (Publisher's note)

"In addition to creating exceptionally well drawn characters and crafting a gripping plot that takes some shocking turns on the way to a heart-pounding conclusion, Castillo probes with keen sensitivity the emotional toll taken by police work." Booklist

Castillo, Linda

The **dead** will tell; Linda Castillo. Minotaur Books 2014 320 p. (Kate Burkholder) (hardback) $25.99

ISBN 1250029570; 9781250029577

LC 2014008870

In this book, by Linda Castillo, "[e]veryone . . . knows the abandoned Hochstetler farm is haunted. But only a handful of the residents remember the terrible secrets lost in the muted/hushed whispers of time—and now death is stalking them, seemingly from the grave. On a late-night shift, Chief of Police Kate Burkholder is called to the scene of an apparent suicide—an old man found hanging from the rafters in his dilapidated barn. But evidence quickly points to murder." (Publisher's note)

"As always, the introspective but determined Kate straddles both worlds with remarkable dexterity. Castillo shows again why the phrase 'gritty Amish mystery' is no oxymoron." Booklist

Castillo, Linda

Her last breath; Linda Castillo. Minotaur Books 2013 320 p. (hardcover) $25.99

ISBN 0312658575; 9780312658571

LC 2013006979

In this book by Linda Castillo "an . . . Amish woman . . .is the central figure in a story that reveals a dark side of Painters Mill and its . . . Amish world. What . . . seems like a tragic . . . car accident suddenly takes on a more sinister cast as evidence emerges that nothing about the crash is accidental. Desperate to find out who killed her best friend's husband and why, Kate begins to suspect she is . . . on the trail of a cold blooded killer." (Publisher's note)

Castillo, Linda

Sworn to silence. Minotaur Books 2009 336 p. (Kate Burkholder thrillers)

ISBN 978-0-312-37497-6; 0-312-37497-6

LC 2008-45671

Kate Burkholder, a former Amish resident of Painters Mill, is returning as police chief sixteen years after a series of brutal murders took place there, but when a new victim is found under her watch, she struggles with a secret that could hurt both her and her family. (Publisher's note)

"Deeply flawed characters in a distinctive setting make this a crackling good series opener." Booklist

Other titles about Kate Burkholder are:
Pray for silence (2010)
Breaking silence (2011)
Gone missing (2012)
Her last breath (2013)
The dead will tell (2014)
After the storm (2015)
Among the wicked (2016)
Down a dark road (2017)

Castro, Joy

Hell or high water; a novel. Joy Castro. Thomas Dunne Books 2012 352 p. (hardcover) $25.99

ISBN 1250004578; 9781250004574; 9781250015112

LC 2012009377

In "this suspense novel . . . the central crime is the kidnapping of a college girl from a packed restaurant. The nerve center for the book is the features section of the New Orleans Times-Picayune, where heroine Nola Céspedes churns out entertainment pieces and yearns for an actual news story. Her editor assigns her to an in-depth feature on the rehabilitation of sex offenders. As Nola (her Cuban single mother thought the name would give her daughter roots) interviews victims and offenders, she realizes that her story is evolving into an investigation of the college girl's disappearance and probable fate. Most of the book follows Nola on her interviews." (Booklist)

Cather, Willa

★ **Death** comes for the archbishop. Knopf 1992 xxvii, 297p $17; pa $11.95

ISBN 0-679-41319-7; 0-679-72889-9 pa

First published 1927

"Bishop Jean Latour and his vicar Father Joseph Vaillant together create pioneer missions and organize the new diocese of New Mexico. . . . The two combine to triumph over the apathy of the Hopi and Navajo Indians, the opposition of corrupt Spanish priests, and adverse climatic and topographic conditions. They are assisted by Kit Carson and by such devoted Indians as the guide Jacinto. When Vaillant goes as a missionary bishop to Colorado, they are finally separated, but Latour dies soon after his friend, universally revered and respected, to lie in state in the great Santa Fe cathedral that he himself created." Oxford Companion to Am Lit. 6th edition

Cather, Willa

★ **My** Antonia; with an introduction by Lucy Hughes-Hallett. Knopf 1996 xxxiii, 272p $20

ISBN 0-679-44727-X

LC 96-223945

First published 1918 by Houghton Mifflin

"Told by Jim Burden, a New York lawyer recalling his boyhood in Nebraska, the story concerns Antonia Shimerda, who came with her family from Bohemia to settle on the prairies of Nebraska. The difficulties related to pioneering and the integration of immigrants into a new culture are clearly portrayed." Shapiro. Fic for Youth. 3d edition

Cather, Willa

★ **O** pioneers! edited with an introduction and notes by Marilee Lindemann. Oxford University Press 2008 xxxi, 179p (Oxford world's classics) pa $9.95

ISBN 978-0-19-955232-0

LC 2009-291007

First published 1913 by Houghton Mifflin

"The heroic battle for survival of simple pioneer folk in the Nebraska country of the 1880's. John Bergson, a Swedish farmer, struggles desperately with the soil but dies unsatisfied. His daughter Alexandra resolves to vindicate his faith, and her strong character carries her weak older brothers and her mother along to a new zest for life. Years of privation, are rewarded on the farm. But when Alexandra falls in love with Carl Linstrum, and her family objects because he is poor, he leaves to seek a different career. After Alexandra's younger brother Emil is killed by the jealous husband of the French girl Marie Shabata, however, Carl gives up his plans to go to the Klondike, returns to marry Alexandra and take up the life of the farm." Haydn. Thesaurus of Book Dig

Includes bibliographical references

Cather, Willa

The **song** of the lark. Houghton Mifflin 1915 580p

This novel "tells the story of Thea Kronborg, a Colorado girl, the daughter of a Swedish clergyman, who has a talent for music. She goes to Chicago to study, has an unhappy love affair with Fred Ottenburg, a wealthy young man who cannot obtain a divorce to marry her, and eventually becomes a soprano at the Metropolitan Opera House in New York City, famous for her Wagnerian roles." Reader's Ency. 3d edition

Catling, B.

The **Erstwhile**; a novel. B. Catling. Vintage Books, a division of Penguin Random House, LLC 2017 462 p. (paperback) $16.95

ISBN 9781101972724; 9781101972731

LC 2016030228

Sequel to: The Vorrh (2015)

In this book, by Brian Catling, "in London and Germany, strange beings are reanimating themselves. They are the Erstwhile, the angels that failed to protect the Tree of Knowledge, and their reawakening will have major consequences. In Africa, the colonial town of Essenwald has fallen into disarray because the timber workforce has disappeared into the Vorrh. Now a team of specialists are dispatched to find them." (Publisher's note)

"Catling combines fantasy, history, mythology, and the supernatural to create a menacing and dreamlike novel that is disturbing, immersive, and, ultimately, entertaining." Booklist

Catton, Eleanor, 1985-

★ The **luminaries**; by Eleanor Catton. Little, Brown and Co. 2013 848 p. $27

ISBN 0316074314; 9780316074315

LC 2013941814

Man Booker Prize (2013)

In this book by Eleanor Catton, winner of the 2013 Man Booker Prize, "it is 1866, and Walter Moody has come to make his fortune upon the New Zealand goldfields. He stumbles across a tense gathering of twelve local men, who have met in secret to discuss a series of unsolved crimes. A wealthy man has vanished, a prostitute has tried to end her life, and an enormous fortune has been discovered in the home of a luckless drunk. Moody is soon drawn into the mystery." (Publisher's note)

Celine, Louis-Ferdinand

Journey to the end of the night; translated from the French by John H. P. Marks. Little, Brown 1934 509p

Original French edition, 1932

"Ferdinand Bardamu, the cynical, disillusioned hero, wanders aimlessly through war-torn Europe, surrounded by destruction and putrefaction. Man, as Céline portrays him, attempts to flee from the solitude of his existence and the impossibility of helping his fellow humans but succeeds only in embracing evil and death. The novel caused a scandal when it was published because of the coarsness of its language and the unrelieved blackness of its pessimism. Yet the language is a highly original attempt to reproduce the proletarian argot that reflects the horror and intimacy of war, and the pessimism shows Céline's desire to arouse the reader and make him aware of his condition." Reader's Ency. 4th edition

A **Century** of great Western stories; edited by John Jakes. Forge 2000 525p hardcover o.p. pa $18.95

ISBN 0-312-86986-X; 0-312-86985-1 pa

LC 99-462096

This anthology of 30 short stories includes pieces by such writers as Owen Wister, Zane Grey, Max Brand, Bill Pronzini, Elmer Kelton and Marcia Muller.

"Romance, murder, action, mystery and suspense are mixed with hefty doses of moral dilemma, guilt and redemption in these carefully plotted tales. . . . Many of the stories are appearing here for the first time since they were published in the pulps of the '30s, '40s and '50s, but their appeal is as fresh as ever." Publ Wkly

Includes bibliographical references

Cervantes Saavedra, Miguel de

★ **Don** Quixote de la Mancha; [by] Miguel de Cervantes; translated, with a critical text based on the first editions of 1605 and 1615, and with variant readings, variorum notes, and an introduction by Samuel Putnam. Modern Library 1998 xl, 1239p $25.95

ISBN 0-679-60286-0

LC 97-47415

Original Spanish edition, published in two parts, 1605 and 1615

"Originally conceived as a comic satire against the chivalric romances then in literary vogue, the novel describes realistically what befalls an elderly knight who, his head bemused by reading romances, sets out on his old horse Rosinante, with his pragmatic squire Sancho Panza, to seek adventure. In the process, he also finds love in the person of the pleasant Dulcinea. Contemporaries evidently did not take the book as seriously as later generations have done, but by the end of the 17th century it was deemed highly significant, especially abroad. It came to be seen as a mock epic in prose, and the 'grave and serious air' of the author's irony was much admired. In the history of the modern novel the role of Don Quixote is recognized as seminal." Merriam-Webster's Ency of Lit

Chabon, Michael, 1963-

The **amazing** adventures of Kavalier and Clay; a novel. Random House 2000 639p $26.95

ISBN 0679450041

LC 00-29063

Joe Kavalier, a Czech war refugee, and his American-born cousin Sammy Clay are {this} novel's protagonists. They create a comic-book crusader known as the Escapist. . . . A young artist with Harry Houdini's ability to pick locks while holding his breath, Kavalier has escaped Nazi-occupied Czechoslovakia by hiding in a coffin containing the mythic Golem of Prague." (Time)

"Themes are masterfully explored, leaving the book's sense of humor intact and characters so highly developed they could walk off the page." Newsweek

Chabon, Michael, 1963-

Moonglow; A Novel. Michael Chabon. HarperCollins 2016 448 p. $28.99

ISBN 0062225553; 9780062225559

Carnegie Medal Finalist: Fiction (2017)

This novel, by Michael Chabon, "unfolds as the deathbed confession of a man the narrator refers to only as 'my grandfather.' It is a tale of madness, of war and adventure, of sex and marriage and desire, of existential doubt and model rocketry, of the shining aspirations and demonic underpinnings of American technological accomplishment at midcentury, and, above all, of the destructive impact--and the creative power--of keeping secrets and telling lies." (Publisher's note)

"As towering a figure as the grandfather is, all of Chabon's characters are complex and commanding." Booklist

Chabon, Michael, 1963-

Telegraph Avenue; a novel. Michael Chabon ; photographs by Malik Johnson. 1st ed. Harper 2012 480 p. (hardcover) $27.99; (trade paperback) $15.99; (ebook) $21.99; (paperback) $27.99

ISBN 0061493341; 9780061493348; 9780061493355; 9780062124609; 9780062201454 (large print)

LC 2012001355

This book by Michael Chabon is "anchored by Brokeland Records, a funky used-vinyl paradise. . . . The proprietors are . . . Archy Stallings and high-strung Nat Jaffe, whose wives, too, work together, in a midwifery partnership. . . . A difficult birth puts Gwen and Aviva's business in jeopardy, just as Archy and Nat face potentially insurmountable competition in the form of a planned megastore." (Booklist)

Chabon, Michael

Wonder boys. Villard Bks. 1995 368p

ISBN 9781857024050

LC 94-28921

"Bright promise gone awry is the theme of this exuberantly comic novel, whose convoluted plot sparkles with inventiveness and wit." Publ Wkly

Chabon, Michael

The **Yiddish** policemen's union; a novel. HarperCollins Publishers 2007 414p $26.95

ISBN 978-0-00-714982-7; 0-00-714982-4

LC 2006-49751

"Though the ultimate secret behind the murder that kick-starts the story involves a religious-political scheme that tips over clumsily into surreal satire, the remainder of the book is so authoritatively and minutely imagined that the reader, absorbed in the plight of [the author's] shambling hero, really doesn't mind. . . . Mr. Chabon has so thoroughly conjured the fictional world of Sitka—its history, culture, geography, its incestuous and byzantine political and sectarian divisions—that the reader comes to take its existence for granted." N Y Times (Late N Y Ed)

Chakraborty, S. K.

The **city** of brass; S. A. Chakraborty. Harper Voyager 2017 532 p. map (hardcover) $25.99

ISBN 9780062678126; 9780062678102

LC 2017020068

In this book, by S. A. Chakraborty, "Nahri has never believed in magic. Certainly, she has power; on the streets of eighteenth-century Cairo, she's a con woman. . . . But she knows better than anyone that the trades she uses to get by—palm readings, zars, and a mysterious gift for healing—are all tricks. . . . But when Nahri accidentally summons Dara, an equally sly, darkly mysterious djinn warrior, to her side during one of her cons, she's forced to reconsider her beliefs." (Publisher's note)

"There is enough material here—a feisty, independent lead searching for answers, reminiscent of Star Wars's Rey, and a richly imagined alternate world—to support a potential series." Pub Wkly

Chancellor, Bryn

Sycamore; a novel. Bryn Chancellor. First edition Harper 2017 323 p. (hardback) $26.99

ISBN 9780062661098

LC 2016042150

In this novel, by Bryn Chancellor, "out for a hike one scorching afternoon in Sycamore, Arizona, a newcomer to town stumbles across what appear to be human remains embedded in the wall of a dry desert ravine. . . . Sycamore's longtime residents fear the bones may belong to Jess Winters, the teenage girl who disappeared suddenly some eighteen years earlier, an unsolved mystery that has soaked into the porous rock of the town and haunted it ever since." (Publisher's note)

"This is a movingly written, multivoiced novel examining how one tragic circumstance can sow doubt about fundamental things." Pub Wkly

Chandler, Raymond

★ The **big** sleep. Knopf 1939 277p

"A tale of degeneracy in southern California, in which two Hollywood heiresses become mixed up in blackmail and murder; and Philip Marlowe is the private detective, who tells the story." Washington, D.C. Public Libr

Chandler, Raymond

The **long** goodbye. Houghton Mifflin 1953 316p

Detective Philip Marlowe provides moral support for Terry Lennox who is running away to Mexico because he thinks he committed a murder

This novel is one of Chandler's "most meticulously plotted and by some stretches his most corrosive. What he gives us here is painful if exciting pleasure." N Y Her Trib Books

Chang, Lan Samantha

All is forgotten, nothing is lost. W. W. Norton & Company 2010 208p $23.95

ISBN 978-0-393-06306-6; 0-393-06306-2

LC 2010-17503

"Among the many threads Chang elegantly pursues—the fraught relationships between mentors and students, the value of poetry, the price of ambition—it is her indelible portrait of the loneliness of artistic endeavor that will haunt readers the most in this exquisitely written novel about the poet's lot." Booklist

Chanter, Catherine

★ The **well**; a novel. by Catherine Chanter. Atria Books 2015 390 p. (hardcover) $26

ISBN 1476772762; 9781476772769

LC 2015010422

"When Ruth Ardingly and her family make that first long drive up from the city in their grime-encrusted car and view The Well, they are enchanted by a jewel of a farm that appears to offer everything they need: an opportunity for Ruth, an escape for her husband, and a home for their grandson. But when the drought begins, everything changes. Surrounded by thirty acres of lush greenery, the farm mysteriously thrives while the world outside crumbles under the longest dry spell in recorded history." (Publisher's note)

"Combining gripping mystery, nuanced psychological drama, and striking prose, this debut is a mesmerizing read." Pub Wkly

Chaon, Dan

Await your reply; a novel. Ballantine Books 2009 324p $25

ISBN 978-0-345-47602-9; 0-345-47602-6

LC 2009-21245

"Lucy is a recent high school graduate who leaves a small town in Ohio with her high-school teacher after her parents are killed. Only just above-average in intelligence, she's led to believe she's a stellar thinker by her witty, Maserati-driving, Yale-educated history teacher, George Orson. Miles is searching for his long-gone twin brother, Hayden, a probable schizophrenic. Flashbacks to the twins' childhoods reveal that Miles feels inferior to Hayden, who antagonized him throughout childhood. . . . College student Ryan, who was adopted, leaves a structured life in small-town Iowa to live with his biological father. . . . These stories, at first, present a lot of detail but not a lot of direction, but all the ink spent on backstory and character development prove to be worth it when the characters' lives intersect, and the novel turns from stories about people trying to find themselves to a page-turning mystery." Pittsburgh Post-Gazette

Chaon, Dan

★ **Ill** will; Dan Chaon. Ballantine Books 2017 480 p. (hardback) $28

ISBN 9780345476043; 0345476042

LC 2016034066

In this novel, by Dan Chaon, "Dustin is drifting through his forties when he hears the news: His adopted brother, Rusty, is being released from prison. Thirty years ago, Rusty received a life sentence for the massacre of Dustin's parents, aunt, and uncle. The trial came to epitomize the 1980s hysteria over Satanic cults; despite the lack of physical evidence, the jury believed the outlandish accusations. . . . Now, . . . DNA analysis has overturned the conviction." (Publisher's note)

"Chaon has mastered multiple psychologically complex and often fearsome characters. A shadowy narrative that's carried well by the author's command and insight." Kirkus

Charlton, Blake

Spellbound. Tor 2011 409p $24.99

ISBN 978-0-7653-1728-5; 0-7653-1728-1

LC 2011-13451

"Ten years after the events of Spellwright (2010), the physician Francesca DeVega discovers that her city of Avel is now secretly controlled by the demon Typhon, in preparation for the Disjunction, a prophesied demonic invasion. She is apparently key to Typhon's plot to recruit Nicodemus Weal, the outlaw spellwright destined to play a (as yet undefined) role in the Disjunction and whose cacography causes him to misspell most magical texts and prevents him from touching other living beings. Tensions rise as the city becomes overrun by various political, religious and magical factions who have their own beliefs about the looming Disjunction. To make matters worse, the Savanna Walker, Typhon's half-draconic creation, roams the streets, causing blindness and aphasia; a second threatened dragon remains hidden. As Francesca (at first reluctantly) joins Nicodemus in his quest to thwart Typhon, find the second dragon and recover the emerald that will cure his cacography, she learns one more devastating truth—about herself. Middle volumes are always tricky, but Charlton succeeds brilliantly here." Kirkus

Charlton, Blake

Spellbreaker; by Blake Charlton. St. Martin's Press 2016 480 p. map (Spellwright Trilogy) $26.99

ISBN 076531729X; 9780765317292

In this book, by Blake Charlton, "Leandra Weal has a bad habit of getting herself in dangerous situations. While hunting neodemons in her role as Warden of Ixos, Leandra obtains a prophetic spell that provides a glimpse one day into her future. She discovers that she is doomed to murder someone she loves, soon, but not who. . . . Leandra's quest to unravel the mystery . . . becomes more urgent when her chronic disease flares up." (Publisher's note)

"Vivid, intelligent, and painful in an authentically laudable way." Kirkus

Charlton, Blake

★ **Spellwright**. Tor 2010 350p $24.99

ISBN 978-0-7653-1727-8; 0-7653-1727-3

A "a fantastic first novel, set in an intriguing world of magic based on the written word. Charlton uses his own experiences with dyslexia to create a protagonist, Nicodemus, whose learning disability could unmake the world. Reading Spellwright as a bibliophile is a real treat, and the focus on language, reading, writing and understanding as a wizardly trait is something that seems somewhat new, and honestly, something long overdue in the fantasy realm." Io9

Charyn, Jerome

Johnny One-Eye; a tale of the American Revolution. W.W. Norton & Co. 2008 479p $25.95

ISBN 978-0-393-06497-1; 0-393-06497-2

LC 2007-34343

"What 'Johnny One-Eye' lacks in narrative momentum it handily supplies in antics and atmosphere. Here are the founding fathers out on a lark; here is the Revolution waged at the gaming table and in the bedroom. . . . Charyn hasn't woven a taut narrative from a lurching plot. What he has done is to create a rollicking tale in which — true to the dictates of the genre — our hapless rogue makes good. That he should do so in Washington's 'runt of a republic' isn't such a stretch. When you think about it, the American Revolution was something of a picaresque too." International Herald Tribune

Chase, Loretta

★ **Dukes** Prefer Blondes; Loretta Chase. HarperCollins 2015 384 p. (Avon romance) (paperback) $7.99; (ebook) $7.99

ISBN 9780062100344; 9780062098276; 0062100343

In this novel in the "Dressmakers" series by Loretta Chase, "marriage proposals from men who can't see beyond her . . . looks are starting to get on Lady Clara Fairfax's nerves. Desperate . . . , she escapes to her favorite charity. When a child is in trouble, she turns to tall, dark, and annoying barrister Oliver Radford. Though he's . . . in line to inherit a dukedom, Radford's never been part of fashionable society, and the blonde beauty . . . isn't part of his plans." (Publisher's note)

"Chase's tongue-in-cheek tone captures tender and humorous nuances in character descriptions and actions, creating fully realized characters and a rich plot." Pub Wkly

Chase, Loretta

The **last** hellion; [by] Loretta Chase. Five Star 1999 393p (Five Star standard print romance series)

ISBN 0-7862-1989-0

LC 99-26433

"When Vere Mallory, the seventh Duke of Ainswood and the last of the infamous 'Mallory Hellions,' ends up in the mud after being properly slugged by an outspoken, crusading journalist of Amazonian proportions, he decides to teach her a lesson—and ends up learning a few things himself. Well-matched, appealing protagonists, a lively, witty writing style, and excellent dialog complement this compelling story that addresses some of the more relevant social issues of the Regency era." Libr J

Chase, Loretta

Scandal wears satin; Loretta Chase. Avon 2012 371 p.

ISBN 0062100319; 9780062100313

In this novel by Loretta Chase a "family scandal has made" dressmaker Sophy Noirot "an enemy of one of society's fashion leaders, . . . leaving her little patience for a big, reckless rakes like the Earl of Longmore. . . . But when Longmore's sister, Noirot's wealthiest, favorite customer, runs away, Sophy can't let him bumble after her on his own. In hot pursuit with the one man who tempts her beyond reason, she finds desire has never slipped on so smoothly." (Publisher's note)

Chase, Loretta

Silk is for seduction. Avon 2011 371p (Avon historical romance) pa $7.99

ISBN 978-0-06-163268-6

"With a sharp eye for both upper-class society and the cutthroat world of high-class London mantua makers, Chase mixes snappy dialogue, erotic tension, and the fanciful styles of the era into a sparkling love story as Marcelline's strategy ensnares not only Clevedon's patronage but his heart." Publ Wkly

Chase, Loretta

Vixen in Velvet; Loretta Chase. HarperCollins 2014 384 p. (Dressmakers) $7.99

ISBN 0062100327; 9780062100320

"Lethally charming Simon Blair, Marquess of Lisburne, has reluctantly returned to London for one reason only: a family obligation. Still, he might make time for the seduction of a certain redheaded dressmaker--but Leonie Noirot hasn't time for him. She's obsessed with transforming his cousin, the dowdy Lady Gladys, into a swan." (Publisher's note)

"With her gorgeously rendered prose, flawless sense of characterization, and rare gift for effortlessly matching sparkling wit and seductive passion, Chase will once again charm readers into swooning with delight." Booklist

Chase, Loretta

Your scandalous ways; Loretta Chase. Avon 2008 374p pa $6.99; $6.99

ISBN 006123124X; 9780061231247

LC 2008-577455

"A world-weary British spy and master of disguises living in Regency Venice, James Cordier has been dispatched by the government to retrieve highly sensitive letters in courtesan Francesca Bonnard's possession. A few mishaps later, it's clear that Cordier isn't the only one wanting something from the notorious Francesca, who fled England following an affair that left her humiliated, divorced and friendless. Lord Elphick, her ex-husband, is a man with multiple mistresses and great political ambitions. Cordier's mission and Francesca's inability to ever trust a man again lead the two into a marvelously and intricately danced tango of a romance." Publ Wkly

Chatterjee, Upamanyu

English, August; an Indian story. introduction by Akhil Sharma. New York Review Books 2006 326p (New York Review Books classics) pa $14.95

ISBN 1-59017-179-9

LC 2005-22842

First published 1988 in India

"This satiric novel chronicles the reluctant coming of age of a privileged young man who has just entered the prestigious Indian Administrative Service. Posted to a small town deep in the interior, he finds himself a foreigner in his own country, wary of cholera, defenseless against mosquitoes, and shocked by the sight of a tribal woman: 'They exist, he shrieked silently, outside arty films about tribal exploitation and agrarian reform.' In revolt, he sneaks out of meetings, pretends to be the son of Antarctic explorers, and smokes copious amounts of pot. He's an avatar of the Western slacker: overeducated, bored, plagued with doubts, and incapable of action. Still, Chatterjee's story is uniquely Indian, as he plumbs his hero's fear of being 'just one more urban Indian bewitched by America's hard sell in the Third World.'" New Yorker

Chatwin, Bruce

Utz. Viking 1989 154p

ISBN 0-670-82497-6

LC 88-40310

"The hero of Mr. Chatwin's provocative short novel is a successful survivor. He is part Jewish but has managed to survive Hitler. . . . {Utz is} required to bequeath the collection to the state, and what he does about that insult to his elegant eighteenth-century companions becomes his own peculiar final solution. Mr. Chatwin has created an intriguing proposition—that obedient passivity can amount to successful rebellion." Atlantic

Chaudhuri, Amit, 1962-

★ **Odysseus** Abroad; A Novel. by Amit Chaudhuri. Random House Inc. 2015 224 p. $24

ISBN 1101874511; 9781101874516

LC 2014042574

"It is 1985. Twenty-two-year-old Ananda has been in London for two years, practicing at being a poet. He's homesick, thinks of himself as an inveterate outsider, and yet he can't help feeling that there's something romantic, even poetic, in his isolation. His uncle, Radhesh, a magnificent failure who lives in genteel impoverishment and celibacy, has been in London for nearly three decades. [The book] follows them on one of their weekly, familiar forays about town." (Publisher's note)

"The . . . strangeness may frustrate some readers, as may Chaudhuri's ambling sense of story arc, but they add another kind of music to a work that captivates almost in spite of itself. Like Joyce, Chaudhuri recognizes that the seemingly artless rhythms and repetitions of daily life can have, in thoughtful hands, the depth and breadth of true art." Kirkus

Chee, Alexander

The **queen** of the night; Alexander Chee. Houghton Mifflin Harcourt 2015 576 p. (hardcover) $28

ISBN 0618663029; 9780618663026

LC 2014014409

This novel, by Alexander Chee, "follows one woman's rise from circus rider to courtesan to world-renowned diva. . . . Lilliet Berne is a sensation of the Paris Opera, a legendary soprano with every accolade except an original role. . . . When one is finally offered to her, she realizes with alarm that the libretto is based on a hidden piece of her past. Only four could have betrayed her: one is dead, one loves her, one wants to own her. And one, she hopes, never thinks of her at all." (Publisher's note)

"Richly researched, ornately plotted, this story demands, and repays, close attention." Kirkus

Cheever, John

Bullet Park; a novel. Knopf 1969 245p

LC 69-14730

The author "mixes compassion and high comedy brilliantly, holding up to view an America that is fatally schizoid in many of its manifestations. The confrontation that finally comes between Hammer and Nailles is a horrifying dark allegory of our times." Publ Wkly

Cheever, John

Falconer. Knopf 1977 211p

ISBN 0-394-41071-8

"John Cheever uses prison as an emblem for the world in this stunning novel about love, mysticism, and man's relationship with God. . . . The surface events include a prison riot, a massacre of prison cats by an enraged guard who had his steak stolen by one of them, a homosexual love affair, and a couple of breathtaking escapes, one by Farragut's lover, who dons a cassock to escape in a helicopter with a visiting bishop. Woven in and out are threads of Farragut's past life, his relationship to his wife and the other women in his life, the secret behind his hatred for his brother." Choice

Cheever, John

★ The **Wapshot** chronicle. Harper & Row 1957 307p

National Book Award: Fiction (1958)

"Based in part on Cheever's adolescence in New England, the novel takes place in a small Massachusetts fishing village and relates the breakdown of both the Wapshot family and the town. Part One focuses on Leander, a gentle ferryboat operator harried by his tyrannical wife and his eccentric sister; he eventually swims out to sea and never returns. Part Two chronicles the disastrous lives of Leander's sons, Coverly and Moses. Told in a comic rather than a tragic vein, the novel uses experimental prose techniques to convey a nostalgic vision of a lost world." Merriam-Webster's Ency of Lit

Followed by The Wapshot scandal

Cheever, John

The **Wapshot** scandal. Harper & Row 1964 309p

This sequel to The Wapshot chronicle "continues the tale of the decline of the fortunes of the Wapshot family and of the mythical New England town of St. Botolphs. The 'scandal' is the discovery that Aunt Honora has never paid her income taxes, and the principal disaster stems from the long-standing oversight. The novel also traces the misfortunes of two Wapshot nephews, Coverly, a public relations man at a missile site, and Moses, an alcoholic. Despite the somberness of the main line of events, the book is not depressing; it is lighted by the high gloss of Mr. Cheever's style, by glints of humor, and especially by the warm glow of human fortitude under stress." Libr J

Chekhov, Anton Pavlovich

Early short stories, 1883-1888; edited by Shelby Foote; translated by Constance Garnett. Modern Lib. 1999 642p

ISBN 0-679-60317-4

LC 98-20049

Following his introduction Foote presents seventy of Chekhov's early stories

Chekhov, Anton Pavlovich

Later short stories, 1888-1903; edited by Shelby Foote; translated by Constance Garnett. Modern Lib. 1999 628p

ISBN 0-679-60316-6

LC 98-20048

This volume contains forty-two short stories

Chekhov, Anton Pavlovich

Longer stories from the last decade; {by} Anton Chekhov; translated by Constance Garnett. Modern Lib. 1993 611p

ISBN 0-679-60063-9

LC 93-14536

"Some six hundred tales bear Chekhov's name, not a few of which are the famous 'long short stories' written during roughly the last decade of his brief life. This volume gives us eleven of these, in eminent translations by Constance Garnett and chosen by Shelby Foote." (Publisher's note)

Chen, Da

Brothers; a novel. Shaye Areheart Books 2006 421p $25

ISBN 1-4000-9728-2

LC 2005-36267

"Da Chen has achieved something that sounds simple but is, in fact, close to impossible: he brings the Western reader into the guts of the conflict, the agonies and the revelations of events that shook the world's largest population in the 35 years after 1960, when Shento and his brother were born. Make no mistake, this is not contemporary history retold. This is magnificent fiction. It transcends the events it chronicles and does what fiction at its best should do: it changes our internal landscape." Washington Post Book World

Cheng, Bill

★ **Southern** Cross the Dog; Bill Cheng. HarperCollins 2013 336 p. (hardcover) $25.99

ISBN 0062225006; 9780062225009

This book, by Bill Cheng, follows how "the bonds between three childhood friends are upended by the Great Mississippi Flood of 1927. In its aftermath, one young man must choose between the lure of the future and the claims of the past. Having lost virtually everything in the fearsome storm--home, family, first love--Robert Chatham embarks on an odyssey that takes him through the deep South, from the desperation of a refugee camp . . . into the Mississippi hinterland." (Publisher's note)

Cherryh, C. J.

Foreigner; a novel of first contact. DAW Bks. 1994 378p

ISBN 0-88677-590-6

LC 94-179662

"Cherryh plays her strongest suit in this exploration of human/alien contact, producing an incisive study-in-contrast of what it means to be human in a world where trust is nonexistent." Libr J

Followed by Invader

Chesnutt, Charles Waddell

★ **Stories,** novels, & essay; Stories, novels, & essays. [by] Charles W. Chesnutt. Library of Am. 2002 939p $35

ISBN 1-931082-06-5

LC 2001-38120

The house behind the cedars (1900) is " concerned with a light-complexioned black woman who is undecided whether to enjoy comfort as a white man's mistress or the sincere love of a black man."

The house behind the cedars (1900) is "concerned with a light-complexioned black woman who is undecided whether to enjoy comfort as a white man's mistress or the sincere love of a black man." Oxford Companion to Am Lit. 6th edition

Includes bibliographical references (p. 929-939)

Chevalier, Tracy

★ **Girl** with a pearl earring. Dutton 2000 240p hardcover o.p. pa $16

ISBN 0-525-94527-X; 0-452-28702-2 pa

LC 99-32493

Chevalier examines the world of artist Johannes Vermeer and the city of Delft in the 17th century through the eyes of Griet, an illiterate 17-year-old. In this novel the fictional character of Griet, a servant in the Vermeer household, acts as the model for the artist's portrait Girl With a Pearl Earring.

The author "has done very well in creating the feel of a society with sharp divisions of status and creed. . . . Griet is a memorable character—reserved, wary, observant, and, although she does not know it, afflicted with a serious and ultimately dangerous crush on her employer. The situation makes a fine story, which is exceptionally well told." Atl Mon

Chevalier, Tracy, 1962-

The **last** runaway; Tracy Chevalier. Dutton 2013 320 p. $26.95

ISBN 0525952993; 9780525952992

LC 2012034693

This is New York Times bestselling author Tracy Chevalier's seventh novel. Here, "leaving home after suffering a disappointment, English Quaker Honor Bright ends up in 1850 Ohio, where she finds folks—even Quakers—pragmatically unprincipled and becomes involved in the Underground Railroad." (Library Journal)

"Chevalier offers a cast of strong characters wrestling with thorny personalities, the harsh realities of the frontier, and the legal and moral complexities of American slavery." Booklist

Chiang, Ted

The **life** cycle of software objects. Subterannean Press 2010 150p $25

ISBN 978-1-59606-317-4; 1-59606-317-3

"Ana Alvarado is a former zookeeper turned software tester. When Blue Gamma offers her a job as animal trainer for their digients—digital entities, spawned by genetic algorithms to provide pets for players in the future virtual reality of Data Earth—she discovers an unexpected affinity for her charges. So does Derek Brooks, an animator who designs digient body parts. The market for digients develops and expands, cools and declines after the pattern of the software industry. Meanwhile Ana, Derek, and their friends become increasingly attached to their cute and talkative charges, who are neither pets nor children but something wholly new. But as Blue Gamma goes bust and Data Earth itself fades into obsolescence, Ana and the remaining digient keepers face a series of increasingly unpleasant dilemmas, their worries sharpened by their charges' growing awareness of the world beyond their pocket universe, and the steady unwinding of their own lives and relationships into middle-aged regrets for lost opportunities." Publ Wkly

Chiang, Ted

Stories of your life and others; Ted Chiang. First Vintage Books edition Vintage 2016 281 p. (paperback) $16

ISBN 1101972122; 9781101972120

LC 2016001193

Originally published 2002

This book, by Ted Chiang, "delivers dual delights of the very, very strange and the heartbreakingly familiar, often presenting characters who must confront sudden change—the inevitable rise of automatons or the appearance of aliens—with some sense of normalcy. With sharp intelligence and humor, Chiang examines what it means to be alive in a world marked by uncertainty, but also by beauty and wonder." (Publisher's note)

"Chiang writes seldom, but his almost unfathomably wonderful stories tick away with the precision of a Swiss watch--and explode in your awareness with shocking, devastating force." Kirkus

Chiaverini, Jennifer

Mrs. Lincoln's dressmaker; a novel. Jennifer Chiaverini. Dutton 2013 352 p. (hardcover) $26.95

ISBN 0525953612; 9780525953616

LC 2012036366

In this novel, freed slave Elizabeth "Lizzy" Keckley "gains fame as a dressmaker for Northerners and Southerners alike . . . . She becomes the modiste for Mary Todd Lincoln and is privy to the innermost workings of the Lincoln White House, Mary Todd's reckless spending, President Lincoln's death, and his widow's subsequent penury. When Lizzy writes a memoir about her experiences, she's denigrated by the public." (Publishers Weekly)

Child, Lee

Killing floor; Lee Child. Putnam 1997 p. cm (Jack Reacher) hbk o.p.; pbk $16

ISBN 0-399-14253-3; 9780425264355; 0425264351

LC 96-34452

"Former military policeman Jack Reacher is drifting through Margrave, Georgia, looking for the grave site of an old blues pioneer when he's arrested for the execution-style murders of two men. He's cleared and ready to leave town when he learns that one of the dead men is his brother, Joe, an undercover agent for the Treasury Department. Now it's personal. Reacher follows the trail to the world of international counterfeiting, but he still needs to figure out how the jerk-water town of Margrave fits into the picture." (Booklist)

"Child serves up a big, rangy plot, menace as palpable as a ticking bomb, and enough battered corpses to make an undertaker grin." Kirkus

Other books about Jack Reacher are:
Die trying (1998)
Tripwire (1999)
Running blind (2000)
Echo burning (2001)
Without fail (2002)
Persuader (2003)
The enemy (2004)
One shot (2005)
The hard way (2006)
Bad luck and trouble (2007)
Nothing to lose (2008)
Gone tomorrow (2009)
61 hours (2010)
Worth dying for (2010)
The affair (2011)
A wanted man (2012)
Never go back (2013)
Personal (2014)
Make me (2015)
Night school (2016)
The midnight line (2017)
Past Tense (2018)

Child, Lee

One shot; a Jack Reacher novel. Delacorte Press 2005 376p $25

ISBN 0-385-33668-3

LC 2004-58246

"Mr. Child's idea of heroism has nihilism around the edges but a fierce, fighting spirit at its core. In marked contrast to the brooding figures who otherwise dominate contemporary detective stories, Reacher is not one for self-doubt. His is a two-fisted decency. But Mr. Child also gives him amazing powers of deduction, a serious conscience and the occasional touch of tenderness. It's a wildly improbable mixture, one that can't be beat." N Y Times (Late N Y Ed)

Childress, Mark

Crazy in Alabama. Putnam 1993 383p

ISBN 0-399-13855-2

LC 92-38334

This novel comprises two "stories that alternate. The first concerns Peejoe's coming of age during the summer of 1965, as the town swimming pool in Industry, Ala., is painfully integrated. The second details {his} Aunt Lucille's cross-country crime spree, her sexual awakening and her overnight television stardom." (N Y Times Book Rev)

"It is a measure of Mr. Childress's skill as a novelist—not to mention a triumphant example of style over content—that he soon had me eating out of his hand. I don't know how he did it but he managed to confront every cliché, every convention of the genre head on and pound it into submission, so that his novel seems not only fresh and original but also positively inspired." NY Times Book Rev

Cho, Zen, 1986-

★ **Sorcerer** to the crown; Zen Cho. Ace 2015 384 p. (Sorcerer Royal) (hardback) $26.95

ISBN 0425283372; 9780425283370

LC 2015007899

"Zacharias Wythe, Sorcerer Royal of the Unnatural Philosophers and eminently proficient magician, ventures to the border of Fairyland to discover why England's magical stocks are drying up. But when his adventure brings him in contact with a most unusual comrade, a woman with immense power and an unfathomable gift, he sets on a path which will alter the nature of sorcery in all of Britain." (Publisher's note)

"Cho's entertaining, fantastical debut brings past and current issues of diversity and social class to light with charm, wit, and magic." Booklist

Choi, Susan

My education; Susan Choi. Viking 2013 296 p. (pbk.) $16; (hardcover) $26.95

ISBN 0143125575; 9780143125570; 9780670024902; 9781101622681

LC 2013001605

Lambda Literary Award: Bisexual Fiction (2014)

This book, by Susan Choi, is a "novel of desire and disaster. . . . Regina Gottlieb had been warned about Professor Nicholas Brodeur long before arriving as a graduate student at his prestigious university high on a pastoral hill. He's said to lie in the dark in his office while undergraduate women read couplets to him. . . . But no one has warned Regina about his exceptional physical beauty, or his charismatic, volatile wife." (Publisher's note)

"Choi's talent resides in her densely layered prose and her slowing down the pace to draw readers into the inner worlds of her characters. The result is a deeply human tale of intentional mistakes, love and lust, and the search for a clearer vision of one's self." LJ

Chopin, Kate

Complete novels and stories. Library of America 2002 1071p $40

ISBN 1-931082-21-9

LC 2002-19450

At fault (1890) is a melodrama set in Louisiana centered on a love triangle between a young widow, a St. Louis businessman who purchases timber rights to her plantation, and his alcoholic wife. The awakening (1899) depicts a Southern woman's revolt against her husband and her quest for sexual and emotional fulfillment

Christie, Agatha

✓ ★ The **A.B.C.** murders; a Hercule Poirot mystery. Black Dog & Leventhal Publishers 2006 252p $12

ISBN 1-57912-624-3; 978-1-57912-624-7

LC 2006-45734

First published 1936 by Dodd, Mead & Company

This novel is "about a serial killer who announces his apparently unmotivated killings in advance to Poirot; the only clue is a railway guide left at the scene of each crime. In the opinion of many critics, this is one of Dame Agatha's greatest detective novels." Ency of Mystery & Detection

Christie, Agatha

✓ ★ **And** then there were none. St. Martin's Griffin 2004 264p pa $12.95

ISBN 0-312-33087-1

LC 2004-41165

First published 1939 in the United Kingdom with title: Ten little niggers; first United States edition, 1940, by Dodd, Mead. Variant title: Ten little Indians

"A tour de force on the following trapeze: invitations go out to a group of people, all of whom have been responsible for the death of someone by negligence of intent. The island on which the party is gathered is owned by the would-be avenger of all those deaths. The events and the tension produced by the gradual polishing off of the undetected culprits are beautifully done. One improbability, well hidden, makes the whole thing plausible." Barzun. Cat of Crime. Rev and enl edition

Christie, Agatha

✓ The **body** in the library. Dodd, Mead 1942 245p

"The body that turns up in the married colonel's library is that of a dancing hostess from a neighboring seaside hotel. The setting is St. Mary Mead, whence Miss Marple has drawn her knowledge of human evil and duplicity and applies it to the case at hand, predicting a second murder and averting a third." Barzun. Cat of Crime. Rev and enl edition

Christie, Agatha

✓ ★ **Curtain**. Dodd, Mead 1975 238p

ISBN 0-396-07191-0

"In this her last book, which contrives Poirot's death proprio motu, the old grand master shows that her powers of invention and execution remained strong and fresh till the end. Her villain acts villainous in an entirely new way and from an original yet convincing motive. As for Poirot's performance, it is charged with a new purposefulness, ending in a fine display of moral conscience. The story may have one or two moments of weak writing and even an unparsable sentence, but it is an astonishing piece of work nevertheless." Barzun. Cat of Crime. Rev and enl edition

Christie, Agatha

✓ **Endless** night. Dodd, Mead 1968

First published 1967 in the United Kingdom

"A sharp break with all her previous work: none of her usual detectives. No résumé would be fair since the impact of the book depends upon a skillfully worked-out volte-face involving two characters. The creator of Roger Ackroyd has done it again, in a different way, but without any pretense at detection." Barzun. Cat of Crime. Rev and enl edition

Christie, Agatha

✓ The **Hollow**. Putnam 1992 296p

ISBN 0-399-13727-0

LC 91-31855

First published 1946; copyright renewed 1974

"A triumph of Christie's art, not so much of characterization—for the detective story does not really permit true character study—but of motive-building. That is where A.C. is unrivaled. She knows how to make plausible the divergence between action and motive that maintains uncertainty until the physical clues, the times, and other objective facts mesh with motive to disclose the culprit. The great art is to multiply the ambiguities of feeling, action, and gesture without falling into obvious patterns about greed, revenge, and the like. Here the familiar figure of the able, virile, brilliant man whom women go for is admirably sketched and provided with three possible women murderers and their possibly jealous men. In addition, an elderly femme folle very well done—and Poirot." Barzun. Cat of Crime. Rev and enl edition

Christie, Agatha

Mrs. McGinty's dead. Dodd, Mead 1952 243p

First published 1951 in the United Kingdom with title: Blood will tell

"A Poirot story with Mrs. Oliver thrown in for humor, otherwise, an ingenious plot involving the discovery of one of the offspring of some scandals of 20 years earlier, so as to account for the murder of a charwoman who presumably found an incriminating photograph. Complex and well handled, as well as amusing." Barzun. Cat of Crime. Rev and enl edition

Christie, Agatha

✓ The **murder** at the vicarage; a detective story. Dodd, Mead 1930 319p

Colonel Protheroe, the heartily disliked squire of St Mary Mead, is the victim. The fact that his wife is desperately in love with another man seems to have supplied motive for murder on the part of two people at least. But shrewd Miss Marple points out several other possibilities

"The plot of this tale is intricate. . . . But it is well constructed and holds the reader's attention on the problem of who wanted Col. Protheroe out of the way. The byplay between the vicar and his flirtatious wife is also an amusing innovation." Barzun. Cat of Crime. Rev and enl edition

Christie, Agatha

✓ A **murder** is announced. Dodd, Mead 1950 248p

"A well-told story—her 50th—of blackmail and murder in an English village. Miss Marple does the detecting, and the author plays very fair with the reader in the laying down of a trail leading to the unmasking of a most satisfactory least likely person." Barzun. Cat of Crime. Rev and enl edition

Christie, Agatha

✓ ★ The **murder** of Roger Ackroyd. Dodd, Mead 1926 306p

"Roger Ackroyd, a retired business man, is found dead in his study shortly after the suicide of the woman he was to have married. Suspicion and the police point to Ackroyd's adopted son as the murderer, but the outcome of the story is a complete surprise. As in others of Miss Christie's tales, the mystery is solved by . . . M. Poirot." Booklist

Christie, Agatha

★ **Murder** on the Orient Express. Dodd, Mead 1934 302p

A man is murdered on a train going from Istanbul to Calais. The famous detective Hercule Poirot happens to be on board and unravels the mystery

"This is the tour de force in which Agatha makes conspiracy believable and enlivens it by a really satisfying description of the Taurus Express (part of the Orient system)." Barzun. Cat of Crime. Rev and enl edition

Christie, Agatha

★ The **pale** horse. Dodd, Mead 1962 242p

First published 1961 in the United Kingdom

"This story relies on Mrs. Oliver without Poirot: detection is carried out by an oldish-young scholar called Mark Easterbrook, and what he investigates is superbly organized murder compounded with black magic. A classic treatment of the paralytic suspect-cum-wheelchair is thrown in for good measure." Barzun. Cat of Crime. Rev and enl edition

Christie, Agatha

Three blind mice and other stories. Dodd, Mead 1950 250p

A collection of eight stories and one novelette most of the puzzles solved either by Miss Marple or Hercule Poirot. The title story is a novelette, first published 1948, which was also published with the title: The mousetrap, and appeared as a play with that title. It involves a murder at a boarding-house where several people have taken shelter during a snowstorm. After a policeman arrives on skis, another murder takes place

Christie, Agatha

Towards zero. Blakiston 1944

"Agatha has always liked the combination of the big house on the cliff, the large party composed of relatives and in-laws at odds with one another, plus a couple of mysterious and possibly good-for-nothing male visitors. All these give sufficient reason for fastening the murder(s) upon almost any one of the group. The present brew is one of her best servings, enhanced by almost too many cleverly arranged clues, some of them laid by the murderer to bring off a double bluff. Poirot functions only to the extent of being wished for by Insp. Battle, who is solid and acceptable." Barzun. Cat of Crime. Rev and enl edition

Christie, Alix

Gutenberg's apprentice; a novel. Alix Christie. Harper 2014 416 p. (hardcover) $27.99

ISBN 0062336010; 9780062336019; 9780062336026

LC 2014012878

"Youthful, ambitious Peter Schoeffer is on the verge of professional success as a scribe in Paris when his foster father, wealthy merchant and bookseller Johann Fust, summons him home to corrupt, feud-plagued Mainz to meet 'a most amazing man.' Johann Gutenberg, a driven and caustic inventor, has devised a revolutionary--and to some, blasphemous--method of bookmaking: a machine he calls a printing press." (Publisher's note)

"An inspiring tale of ambition, camaraderie, betrayal, and cultural transformation based on actual events and people." Booklist

Chu, Wesley

The **Lives** of Tao; Wesley Chu. Angry Robot 2013 464 p. $7.99

ISBN 0857663291; 9780857663290

Alex Award (2014)

"When out-of-shape IT technician Roen woke up and started hearing voices in his head, he naturally assumed he was losing it. He wasn't. He now has a passenger in his brain - an ancient alien life-form called Tao, whose race crash-landed on Earth before the first fish crawled out of the oceans. Now split into two opposing factions - the peace-loving, but under-represented Prophus, and the savage, powerful Genjix - the aliens have been in a state of civil war for centuries. Both sides are searching for a way off-planet, and the Genjix will sacrifice the entire human race, if that's what it takes." (Publisher's note)

"Imagine humans are not Earth's dominant species, and aliens live among us in plain sight. This is the conceit of Chu's hip, wise-cracking military SF debut." Pub Wkly

Other titles in this series are:
The Deaths of Tao (2014)
The Rebirths of Tao (2015)
The days of Tao (2016)

Chung, Catherine

Forgotten country; Catherine Chung. Riverhead Books 2012 304 p.

ISBN 9781594488085

LC 2011047577

In this book, "[o]n the night Janie waits for her sister, Hannah, to be born, her grandmother tells her a story: Since the Japanese occupation of Korea, their family has lost a daughter in every generation, so Janie is charged with keeping Hannah safe. . . . Years later, when Hannah inexplicably cuts all ties and disappears, Janie embarks on a mission to find her sister and finally uncover the truth beneath her family's silence." (Publisher's note)

Church, James

Bamboo and blood; James Church. Thomas Dunne Books / St. Martin's Minotaur 2008 294p $13.99

ISBN 9780312372910; 0312372914

LC 2008030116

This book takes place "[i]n the winter of 1997, [when,] trying to stay alive during a famine that has devastated much of North Korea, Inspector O is ordered to play host to an Israeli agent who appears in Pyongyang. When the wife of a North Korean diplomat in Pakistan dies under suspicious circumstances, O is told to investigate, with a curious proviso: Don't look too closely at the details, and stay away from the question of missiles. O knows he can't avoid finding out what he is supposed to ignore on a trail that leads him from the dark, chilly rooms of Pyongyang to an abandoned secret facility deep in the countryside, guarded by a lonely general; and from the streets of New York to a bench beneath a horse chestnut tree on the shores of Lake Geneva, where the Inspector discovers he is up to his ears in missiles---and worse." (Publisher's note)

Church, James

★ A **corpse** in the Koryo; James Church. 1st ed. Thomas Dunne Books/St. Martin's Minotaur 2006 280p $23.95

ISBN 9780312352080; 0312352085

LC 2006045471

This book, written by "the pseudonymous [James] Church, a former intelligence officer, provides a rare look into one of the world's most closed societies, North Korea. When Inspector O, a state security officer, is called on the carpet for botching a sensitive surveillance assignment, O soon realizes that competing forces in the military and intelligence hierarchies set him up to fail and that his personal and professional well-being depend on his walking a tightrope. The detective's pragmatic if unwavering commitment to the ideals of pursuing justice in the face of serious obstacles makes him a heroic figure." (Publishers Weekly)

Other titles in this series are:
Hidden moon (2007)
Bamboo and blood (2008)
The man with the Baltic stare (2010)
A drop of Chinese blood (2012)
The gentleman from Japan (2016)

Church, James

A **drop** of Chinese blood; James Church. Thomas Dunne Books 2012 304 p. map (hardcover) $24.99

ISBN 0312550634; 9780312550639; 9781250017925
LC 2012033780

In this novel by James Church "Major Bing . . . [is] the long-suffering chief of the Chinese Ministry of State Security operations on the border with North Korea. . . . As suddenly as she shows up. . . a woman Headquarters wants closely watched . . . mysteriously disappears across the river into North Korea, leaving in her wake both consternation and a highly sensitive assignment for Bing to bring back from the North a long missing Chinese security official." (Publisher's note)

Ciotta, Beth

Her Sky Cowboy; Beth Ciotta. Signet Eclipse 2012 342 p. $7.99

ISBN 0451238478; 9780451238474

This steampunk romance novel is set in "an alternate Victorian England. Spunky airship mechanic Amelia Darcy is smitten with an obsession for flight and a longtime yen for Tucker Gentry, the Sky Cowboy, an American . . . antihero." After her father's death, she competes for a scientific prize, encounters Tucker, and the "two pursue an airborne quest for Leonardo da Vinci's fabled ornithopter while fending off sky pirates employed by dastardly and lascivious Lord Bingham." (Publishers Weekly)

Cisneros, Sandra, 1954-

★ The **house** on Mango Street. Knopf 1994 134p $24

ISBN 0-679-43335-X
LC 93-43564

Originally published by Arte Público Press in 1984

In this book by Sandra Cisneros, "Esperanza Cordero, a girl coming of age in the Hispanic quarter of Chicago, uses poems and stories to express thoughts and emotions about her . . . environment." (Publishers Weekly) It is "told in a series of vignettes--sometimes heartbreaking, sometimes deeply joyous". (Publisher's note)

This is "a composite of evocative snapshots that manages to passionately recreate the milieu of the poor quarters of Chicago." Commonweal

Clancy, Tom, 1947-2013

Clear and present danger. Putnam 1989 656p

ISBN 0-399-13440-9
LC 89-10287

This novel begins with National Security Adviser, Vice Admiral James "Cutter's winning presidential approval for a covert operation against the Colombian drug cartel. The ill-conceived plan: insert four platoons of élite U.S. Army light infantrymen into the Colombian jungle to identify drug-running planes and disrupt cocaine production. . . . Clancy recounts the training of Sergeant 'Ding' Chavez and the other 'light-fighters' (fast-moving small units unencumbered by heavy equipment) for their quasi-legal mission. Almost as soon as Chavez and his fellow grunts hit the ground, things begin to go awry. . . . {The book's protagonist}, CIA man Jack Ryan, mounts a . . . maneuver to rescue the light-fighters." (Time)

"A president decides that drug smuggling has become a 'clear and present danger' to national security. The response is a complex and covert military campaign against the 'Colombian Cartel.' Clancy presents the technology of special operations and the details of light infantry warfare with his usual facility. Superior even to his descriptions of tools and techniques, however, is Clancy's analysis of the legal and moral problems of operating in a twilight zone, where the rules are ambiguous and an open society makes secrecy impossible." Publ Wkly

Clancy, Tom, 1947-2013

★ The **hunt** for Red October. Naval Inst. Press 1984 387p $27.95

ISBN 0-87021-285-0
LC 84-16569

"Based on a true incident—the attempted defection of a Soviet destroyer in 1975—the plot concerns the defection of the 'Red October', a Soviet submarine carrying 26 Seahawk missiles able to destroy 200 cities. Russia's fleet is ordered to find and destroy the sub; the U.S. Navy wants to find it and get it to an American port. An 18-day, 4,000-mile hunt across the Atlantic ensues." Booklist

Clancy, Tom, 1947-2013

Patriot games. Putnam 1987 540p $27.95

ISBN 0-399-13241-4
LC 87-6910

In this novel by the author of Red Storm Rising (BRD 1986), Jack Ryan, the protagonist of Mr. Clancy's first work of fiction, The Hunt for Red October (1984), foils an attack on members of the British royal family by the Ulster Liberation Army (U.L.A.), a Maoist splinter group of the provisional wing of the Irish Republican Army. When Ryan returns to the United States where he teaches history at Annapolis, U.L.A. terrorists attempt to take their revenge.

"On a visit with his wife and daughter in London, Ryan stumbles onto an attempt by a new Irish revolutionary group to kidnap the Prince and Princess of Wales and their eldest son. Using his Marine Corps training, Ryan saves the royals (which leads to several visits between the Ryans and the residents of Buckingham Palace), but Ryan becomes the target of the surviving terrorists." Publ Wkly

Clark, Georgia

The **regulars**; a novel. Georgia Clark. Emily Bestler Books/Atria 2016 394 p. (hardcover) $26

ISBN 1501119591; 9781501119590; 9781501119613
LC 2016011398

In this novel, by Georgia Clark, "best friends Evie, Krista, and Willow are just trying to make it through their mid-twenties in New York. With average looks and typical quarter-life crises, they're trying to make it up the corporate ladder, make sense of online dating, and make rent. Until they come across Pretty, a magic tincture that makes them, . . . supermodel gorgeous. . . . But there's a dark side to Pretty, too." (Publisher's note)

"Clark, the author of two YA novels, crosses over to women's fiction with this raunchy and very funny tale, which has a distinctly hip, modern feel." Booklist

Clark, Marcia

Guilt by association. Little, Brown & Company 2011 368 p.

ISBN 9780316129510; 0316129518
LC 2010031573

In this book, "[s]omeone has been watching D.A. Rachel Knight--someone who's Rachel's equal in brains, but with more malicious intentions. It began when a near-impossible case fell into Rachel's lap, the suspectless homicide of a homeless man. In the face of courthouse backbiting and a gauzy web of clues, Rachel is determined to deliver justice. She's got back-up: tough-as-nails Detective Bailey Keller. As Rachel and Bailey stir things up, they're shocked to uncover a connection with the vicious murder of an LAPD cop a year earlier. Something tells Rachel someone knows the truth, someone who'd kill to keep it secret." (Publisher's note)

Clark, Martin

The **legal** limit. Knopf 2008 356p $24.95

ISBN 978-0-307-26835-8; 0-307-26835-7

LC 2007-042861

This is a "model for how to write a literary thriller with a wry sense of humor. . . . Compelling characters, surprising twists, rich details, all told in a knowing voice that will affect the way you view destiny, God, the human condition and the heady concept of justice." Oregonian

Clark, Mary Higgins, 1927-

The **sleeping** beauty killer; an Under Suspicion novel. Mary Higgins Clark and Alafair Burke. Simon & Schuster 2016 301 p. (Under suspicion novel) (hardcover) $26.99

ISBN 9781501108587; 9781501108600

LC 2016040599

In this Under Suspicion novel, by Mary Higgins Clark and Alafair Burke, "Casey Carter was convicted of murdering her fiancé . . . fifteen years ago. And Casey . . . has always claimed she's innocent. Although she was charged and served out her sentence in prison, she is still living 'under suspicion.' . . . Her story attracts the attention of Laurie Moran and the 'Under Suspicion' news team--it's Casey's last chance to finally clear her name." (Publisher's note)

"This third series entry (following All Dressed in White, 2015) is a quick suspense read from two very popular writers and will satisfy plenty of eager readers." Booklist

Clark, Walter Van Tilburg

The **Ox**-bow incident. Random House 1940 309p

"Rustlers are systematically stealing cattle near Bridger's Gulch, Nevada, in the late 1880s. After a cattleman is killed, an illegal posse is formed to apprehend the criminals. In a remote valley they surprise three men, hold a makeshift trial, and hang the three. Soon afterward it is discovered that the wrong men have been punished. This is a western with psychological insight." Shapiro. Fic for Youth. 3d edition

Clarke, Arthur C.

★ **2001**: a space odyssey. New Am. Lib. 1968 221p hardcover o.p. pa $7.99

ISBN 0-451-45799-4 pa

Astronauts of the spaceship Discovery, aided by their computer, HAL, blast off in search of proof that extraterrestrial beings had a part in the development of intelligent life forms on Earth millions of years ago.

"By standing the universe on its head, the author makes us see the ordinary universe in a different light. . . . [This novel becomes] a complex allegory about the history of the world." New Yorker

Clarke, Arthur C.

Childhood's end. Ballantine Bks. 1953 214p hardcover o.p. pa $13.95

ISBN 0-345-44405-1 pa

This novel is "paradigmatic of Clarke's more speculative, transcendental novels. Structured as a succession of apocalytic revelations, it depicts the sudden metamorphosis of humanity, under the protective midwifery of the alien Overlords, into the next evolutionary stage, a group mind that ultimately merges with the cosmic Overmind, destroying the Earth in the process. . . . The alien other that transcends humanity yet paradoxically represents humanity's destiny is a recurring theme in the author's speculative novels." New Ency of Sci Fic

Clarke, Arthur C.

★ The **collected** stories of Arthur C. Clarke. TOR Bks. 2001 966p hardcover o.p. pa $19.95

ISBN 0-312-87821-4; 0-312-87860-5 pa

First published 2000 in the United Kingdom

"Although most of these stories date from between 1946 and 1970, seven earlier tales, rescued from what would now be called fanzines, extend coverage back to 1937, and a few snippets stretch it toward the present. At least two dozen stories bear titles that are household words among sf readers. . . . The stories demonstrate Clarke's dazzling and unique combination of command of the language, scientific and other kinds of erudition, and inimitable wit." Booklist

Clarke, Arthur C.

★ The **Garden** of Rama; by Arthur C. Clarke and Gentry Lee. Bantam Bks. 1991 441p (Rama)

ISBN 0-553-07261-7

LC 91-2888

This is the third title in the Rama saga. "Trapped aboard the massive Raman spacecraft as it leaves Earth's solor system, three cosmonauts begin a 13-year voyage toward an unknown destination. Combining the best of space adventure (as the spacefarers encounter other life forms within the multi-habitat vessel) with human drama (as children are born and raised in an unearthly environment), this third novel in the Rama cycle asks as many questions as it answers." Libr J

Followed by Rama revealed

Clarke, Arthur C.

Rendezvous with Rama. Harcourt Brace Jovanovich 1973 303p (Rama)

ISBN 0-15-176835-8

This work contains "flights of prose where the language fairly purrs. And here too one finds the questioning and probing of man and his place in the cosmos that marks good fiction and good science fiction." Libr J

Other titles in this series are:

Rama II (1989)

The Garden of Rama (1991)

Rama Revealed (1993)

Clarke, Brock

An **arsonist's** guide to writers' homes in New England; a novel. Algonquin Books Of Chapel Hill 2007 303p $23.95

ISBN 978-1-56512-551-3; 1-56512-551-7

LC 2006-100732

"This straight-faced, postmodern comedy scorches all things literary, from those moldy author museums to the excruciating question-and-answer sessions that follow public readings. There are no survivors here: women's book clubs, literary critics, Harry Potter fans, bookstores, English professors, memoir writers, librarians, Jane Smiley, even the author himself—they're all singed under Clarke's crisp wit." Washington Post Book World

Clarke, Brock

Exley; a novel. Algonquin Books of Chapel Hill 2010 303p $24.95

ISBN 978-1-56512-608-4

LC 2010-15518

"Frederick Exley's classic 1968 account of his epic alcoholism, A Fan's Notes, bears the oxymoronic subtitle 'A Fictional Memoir.' It is the space between those words, between real and fabricated memory, that Clarke examines in his flawed but forceful new novel, Exley. Miller is a precocious 9-year-old who lives in a cloud of self-delusion, especially when it comes to his dad, an acolyte of A Fan's Notes who may or may not be in a coma at the VA hospital. The boy goes on a search for the inconveniently dead Exley, a mission that is ultimately less about finding the truth than avoiding it. With humor as black as Exley's liver, Clarke picks apart the fictions we tell one another — and those we tell ourselves." Entertainment Wkly

Clarke, Maxine Beneba

★ **Foreign** soil and other stories; Maxine Beneba Clarke. 37 Ink 2017 256 p. (hardcover) $22

ISBN 9781501136368; 9781501136375; 1501136364

LC 2017299703

This short story collection, by Maxine Beneba Clarke, "gives voice to the disenfranchised, the lost, and the mistreated. . . . Within these pages, a desperate asylum seeker is pacing the hallways of Sydney's notorious Villawood detention centre; a seven-year-old Sudanese boy has found solace in a patchwork bike; an enraged black militant is on the war-path through the rebel squats of 1960s Brixton . . . and a Sydney schoolgirl loses her way." (Publisher's note)

"Australian writer and poet Clarke's powerful debut collection of award-winning short stories addresses oppressed, downtrodden, and mistreated outsiders of society." Booklist

Clarke, Susanna, 1959-

★ **Jonathan** Strange & Mr. Norrell; illustrations by Portia Rosenberg. Bloomsbury 2004 782p il $27.95

ISBN 1-582-34416-7

LC 2004-2402

This fantasy novel is set in England during the Napoleonic Wars. Mr. Norrell has "regained some of the powers of England's [ancient] magicians. He goes to London and raises a beautiful young woman from the dead. Soon he is lending his help to the government in the war against Napoleon. . . . . A rival magician appears. Jonathan Strange is handsome, charming, and talkative—the very opposite of Mr. Norrell. . . . Mr. Norrell accepts Strange as a pupil. But it soon becomes clear that their ideas of what English magic ought to be are very different. For Mr. Norrell, their power is something to be cautiously controlled, while Jonathan Strange will always be attracted to the . . . most perilous forms of magic. He becomes fascinated by the ancient, shadowy figure of the Raven King, a child taken by fairies who became king of both England and Faerie. . . . Eventually Strange's heedless pursuit of long-forgotten magic threatens to destroy not only his partnership with Norrell, but everything that he holds dear." (Publisher's note)

"This fantasy novel is set in early-nineteenth-century England, where two men, Gilbert Norrell and his pupil Jonathan Strange, revive the once-thriving practice of the dark arts. After aiding the British against Napoleon, the magicians fall out over interpretations of wizardly philosophy. Meanwhile, a malevolent fairy accidentally set loose by Norrell enchants, among others, Strange's wife. Clarke's ability to construct a fully imagined world-much of it explained in long, witty footnotes-is impressive." New Yorker

Clarkson, John

Among thieves; John Clarkson. Minotaur Books 2015 418 p. hardcover $25.99

ISBN 1250047242; 9781250047243

LC 2014033881

In this book, by John Clarkson, "Olivia Sanchez--smart, driven, and beautiful--started at the bottom and worked her way up the ranks of a brokerage firm only to be unjustly, brutally fired, then blackballed. With no place else to go, she turns to her cousin, Manny Guzman, ex-con and ex-gang leader, for help. Manny's first instinct is to hit back. Hard. But his partner, James Beck knows that out in the real world, things aren't done that way." (Publisher's note)

"With crisp prose, masterful plotting, and building suspense, this is a real treat for fans of gritty crime fiction, who will want more from Clarkson." Booklist

Claudel, Philippe

The **investigation**; a novel. Philippe Claudel ; translated from the French by John Cullen. Random House 2012 221 p.

ISBN 0385535341; 9780385535342

LC 2011034662

In this satire-mystery by Philippe Claudel, translated by John Cullen, "[t]he Investigator . . . has been assigned to conduct an Investigation of a series of suicides (twenty-two in the past eighteen months) that have taken place at the Enterprise, a huge, sprawling complex located in an unnamed Town. . . . Time and time again, regulations hamstring him, street layouts befuddle him, and all the while he senses someone watching him, recording his every movement." (Publisher's note)

Clavell, James

Shogun; a novel of Japan. Atheneum Pubs. 1975

ISBN 0-689-10565-7

First novel in the author's Asian saga

This book by James Clavell "fictionalizes the life of Will Adams, the English sailor who became a retainer to the brilliant Tokugawa Iyeyasu at the time he was moving toward power. That power endured for more than 250 years." (Library Journal) "Sixteenth-century English pilot John Blackthorne becomes entangled in politics and civil war when he is shipwrecked off the coast of Japan." (Booklist)

"Clavell creates a world: people, customs, settings, needs and desires all become so enveloping that you forget who and where you are. 'Shōgun' is history infused with fantasy. It strives for epic dimension and occasionally it approaches that elevated state. It's irresistible, maybe unforgettable." N Y Times Book Rev

Cleage, Pearl

What looks like crazy on an ordinary day-- a novel. Avon Bks. 1997 244p

ISBN 0-380-97584-X

LC 97-17708

"Despite the early bad news, Cleage's funny, irreverent, and hopeful novel is stunningly real and evocative of the conditions behind the high unemployment, aimlessness, and drug culture that permeate the urban landscape and have invaded smaller towns as well." Booklist

Cleave, Chris

★ **Gold**; a novel. Chris Cleave. Simon & Schuster 2012 336 p.

ISBN 1451672721; 9781451672725; 9781451672732; 9781451672749

LC 2011043699

This "novel [is] about the world of professional cycling. Zoe Castle and Kate Meadows met at age 19 trying out for the British Cycling Team and have been friends and rivals for 13 years now. Kate might have more natural ability, but Zoe is the more driven of the two. Kate is married to a fellow racer, Jack Argall, and they have an eight-year-old daughter, Sophie, who suffers from leukemia. Zoe is pursued by her own demons and has a tabloid reputation for sleeping around, which doesn't sit well with her agent. Things begin to heat up when the International Olympic Committee changes its rules so that only one cyclist, either Zoe or Kate, will be eligible to compete in the 2012 London Games." (Publishers Weekly)

Cleave, Chris

Little Bee. Simon & Schuster 2009 271p $24

ISBN 978-1-4165-8963-1; 1-4165-8963-5

LC 2008-30689

First published 2008 in the United Kingdom with title: The other hand

"The novel begins in the middle of the story when Little Bee is illegally released from a prison outside of London after two years of incarceration for attempting to sneak into the country. . . . Without any papers, legal documentation or identification, Little Bee is forced to visit the only person she knows in England—Sarah Summers. . . .Sarah Summers and her husband, Andrew O'Rourke, met Little Bee on a beach in Nigeria. Having grown apart in their marriage, Andrew and Sarah traveled to Nigeria to get away from city life. Inadvertently, the couple stumbles across Little Bee and her sister while taking a romantic walk on the beach, only to be surrounded by a group of mercenaries intent on killing the girls. . . . In a gruesome twist, the soldiers agree to let the girls live if Andrew will cut off his middle finger. As Andrew is unable to comply with their terms, Sarah picks up a machete and slices off her own finger—effectively dooming their marriage. The soldiers initially take both girls away, but in the end spare Little Bee. When she appears at Sarah and Andrew's household outside of London, a series of tragic, beautiful and emotionally turbulent events unfold which will change all of their lives forever." PopMatters

Cleave, Paul

Cemetery Lake; a thriller. by Paul Cleave. 1st Atria paperback ed. Atria Books 2013 416 p. (paperback) $16

ISBN 1451677839; 9781451677836

LC 2012047800

This is Paul Cleave's third Christchurch mystery, introducing PI Theodore Tate. "Two years earlier, the grown daughter of bank manager Henry Martins asked Tate, then a policeman, to investigate what she believed to have been her father's murder. Tate found nothing, but now the second husband of Martins's widow has died, possibly of poisoning. Martins's body is exhumed . . . and three bodies surface in a lake adjacent to the cemetery, one belonging to a missing 19-year-old girl." (Publishers Weekly)

Cleave, Paul

★ **Five** minutes alone; a thriller. by Paul Cleave. Atria Paperback 2014 464 p. pbk $16

ISBN 1476779155; 9781476779157

LC 2014011039

In this mystery, by Paul Cleave, "someone is helping rape victims exact revenge on their attackers. . . . Carl Schroder and Theodore Tate, labeled 'The Coma Cops' by the media, are finally getting their lives back into shape. . . . When the body of a convicted rapist is found, obliterated by an oncoming train, Tate works the case, trying to determine if this is murder or suicide." (Publisher's note)

"Cleave's masterful plotting skills are matched with superior pacing and characterization." Pub Wkly

Cleeves, Ann, 1954- ✓

The **crow** trap; Ann Cleeves. First U.S. edition Minotaur Books 2017 535 p. (Vera Stanhope) (hardcover) $27.99

ISBN 1250122732; 1250122740; 9781250122742; 9781250122735; 9781250122759

In this mystery novel in the Vera Stanhope series, by Ann Cleeves, "three very different women come together. . . . Three women who . . . know the meaning of betrayal....For team leader Rachael Lambert the project is the perfect opportunity to rebuild her confidence. . . . Botanist Anne Preece . . . sees it as a chance to indulge in a little deception of her own. And . . . Grace Fulwell, a strange, uncommunicative young woman with plenty of her own secrets to hide..." (Publisher's note)

Cleeves, Ann, 1954- ✓

Thin air; a Shetland mystery. Ann Cleeves. Minotaur Books 2015 400 p. (hardcover) $25.99

ISBN 9781250069948

LC 2015002537

In this mystery, by Ann Cleeves, a "group of old university friends leave . . . London and travel to Shetland to celebrate the marriage of one of their friends. But, one of them, Eleanor, disappears. . . . And then Eleanor's body is discovered lying in a small loch close to the cliff edge. Detectives Jimmy Perez and Willow Reeves are dispatched to investigate. Before she went missing, Eleanor claimed to have seen the ghost of a local child who drowned in the 1920s." (Publisher's note)

"This nicely detailed procedural and rich character study pairs beautifully with Peter May's Lewis trilogy." Booklist

Clegg, Bill

★ **Did** you ever have a family; Bill Clegg. Gallery Books 2015 304 p. (hardcover) $26

ISBN 1476798176; 9781476798172

LC 2014037087

This novel, by Bill Clegg, is "about a circle of people who find solace in the least likely of places as they cope with a horrific tragedy. . . . June Reid's life is completely devastated when a shocking disaster takes the lives of . . . her entire family. . . . Alone and directionless, June drives across the country, away from her small Connecticut town. In her wake, a community emerges, weaving a beautiful and surprising web of connections through shared heartbreak." (Publisher's note)

"Clegg is both delicately lyrical and emotionally direct in this masterful novel, which strives to show how people make bearable what is unbearable, offering consolation in small but meaningful gestures." Booklist

Clement, Jennifer

Prayers for the stolen; a novel. Jennifer Clement. Hogarth 2014 224 p. hc $23

ISBN 9780804138789; 0804138788

LC 2013025756

PEN/Faulkner Award for Fiction: Finalist (2015)

In this novel, by Jennifer Clement, "Ladydi Garcia Martínez is fierce, funny and smart. She was born into a world where being a girl is a dangerous thing. . . . Here in the shadow of the drug war, bodies turn up on the outskirts of the village to be taken back to the earth by scorpions and snakes. . . . Despite the odds against her, this spirited heroine's resilience and resolve bring hope to otherwise heartbreaking conditions." (Publisher's note)

"Clement's deft first-person narrative style imbues authenticity to her depiction of a world turned upside down by drug cartels, police corruption, and American exploitation." Booklist

Clements, Rory

Revenger; Rory Clements. Bantam Books 2011 429p.

ISBN 9780385342841; 0385342845

LC 2010053015

Dagger Awards: CWA Ellis Peters Historical Award (2010)

This book tells the story of "John Shakespeare, the playwright's older brother, [who] has left the intelligence world behind to teach at a small school, but he's drawn back into the treacherous world of spying by two powerful and competing rivals -- the earl of Essex and Queen Elizabeth's new spymaster, Sir Robert Cecil. Essex asks Shakespeare to find the truth behind the mysterious disappearance of the colonists of Roanoke, Va. One of them has reportedly been seen walking the streets of London, and Essex wants the intelligencer to confirm or dispel those rumors. Meanwhile, Cecil, who fears that Essex's scheming threatens the monarch, seeks to have Shakespeare work as a double agent." (Publishers Weekly)

Clemmons, Zinzi

What we lose; Zinzi Clemmons. Viking 2017 213 p. (hardcover) $22

ISBN 0735221715; 9780735221710; 9780735221727

LC 2017019757

In this novel, by Zinzi Clemmons, "raised in Pennsylvania, Thandi views the world of her mother's childhood in Johannesburg as both impossibly distant and ever present. She is an outsider wherever she goes, caught between being black and white, American and not. She tries to connect these dislocated pieces of her life, and as her mother succumbs to cancer, Thandi searches for an anchor—someone, or something, to love." (Publisher's note)

"A compelling exploration of race, migration, and womanhood in contemporary America." Kirkus

Clinch, Jon

Finn; a novel. Random House 2007 287p $23.95

ISBN 978-1-4000-6591-2; 1-4000-6591-7

LC 2006-45802

"Shocking and charming. Clinch creates a folk-art masterpiece that will delight, beguile and entertain as it does justice to its predecessor. . . . In Finn, Clinch expands the bloodlines and scope of the original story and casts new light on the troubled legacy of our country's infamous past." N Y Post

Cline, Emma, 1989-

The **girls**; A Novel. Emma Cline. Random House 2016 368 p. (hardcover) $27

ISBN 081299860X; 9780812998603

LC 2015012714

This book, by Emma Cline, "a lonely and thoughtful teenager, Evie Boyd, sees a group of girls in the park, and is immediately caught by their freedom, their careless dress, their dangerous aura of abandon. Soon, Evie is in thrall to Suzanne, a mesmerizing older girl, and is drawn into the circle of a soon-to-be infamous cult and the man who is its charismatic leader." (Publisher's note)

"Cline pushes past the myths, vividly imagining how the darkness crept in and turned a group of idealistic young adults into cold-blooded killers. In her impressive debut, Cline illuminates the darkest truths of a girl's coming-of-age, telling a story that is familiar on multiple levels in a unique and compelling way." Booklist

Cline, Ernest

Ready player one; [by] Ernest Cline. Crown Publishers 2011 374p. $24

ISBN 978-0-307-88743-6; 0-307-88743-X; 9780307887450; 9780307887443; 9780307887436

LC 2011015247

Alex Award (2012)

The events in this novel take place in 2044. Many of the students of 1980s trivia are interested in that particular time period "because a billionaire inventor, James Halliday, died and left behind a mischievous legacy. Whoever first cracks Halliday's series of '80s-related riddles, clues and puzzles that are included in a film called 'Anorak's Invitation' will inherit his fortune." (N Y Times (Late N Y Ed))

"Cultural items from VH1's I Love the 80's series and early G4 programming like Icons or Portal cover a basic swath of the material, but Monty Python, John Hughes, Dungeons & Dragons, WarGames, Blade Runner, Pac-Man, Rush, and infinitely more highly regarded geek cultural touchstones appear both as delightful inclusions and ingenious plot devices. Ready Player One lends itself easily to mash-up comparisons, since in its more complicated passages, it amounts to long strings of cultural references pumped through well-worn story arcs. The adventure comedy of Mike Judge's Idiocracy meets South Park's Imaginationland with a dash of Willy Wonka, except all of the cynicism has been replaced by sheer geeky love." A.V. Club

Coady, Lynn

The **antagonist**; Lynn Coady. Alfred A Knopf 2013 304 p. $25.95

ISBN 0307961354; 0887842968; 9780307961358; 9780887842962

In this book, 40-year-old "Gordon 'Rank' Rankin discovers that a close friend from university days has used him as a primary character in a novel. Infuriated with Adam's portrayal of him as a teenager, Rank begins to blister Adam with angry e-mails to set the record straight and, ultimately, to come to terms with Rank's own deeply conflicted feelings about himself and his life." (Booklist)

Coben, Harlan

✓ **Caught**. Dutton 2010 388p $27.95

ISBN 978-0-525-95158-2; 0-525-95158-X

LC 2010-02056

"As usual with Coben, there are dark secrets from the past, plenty of quips and pithy insults, and some colorful specimens along the trail. Despite the touchy subject matter, 'Caught' earns a PG-13 rating. We're not talking soaring prose here, but Coben is an engaging companion." Portland Oregonian

Coben, Harlan, 1962-

✓ **Fool** Me Once; Harlan Coben. Penguin Group USA 2016 390 p. (hardcover) $28

ISBN 9780525955092; 0525955097

LC 2015050593

In this thriller by Harlan Coben, the main character seeks to uncover a profound family deception. "Horrified when she spots the husband who was reported dead weeks earlier playing with their toddler on her nanny cam, former special ops pilot Maya confronts deep secrets and deceit in her own past in order to discern the truth." (Publisher's note)

"Once again, Coben marries his two greatest strengths—masterfully paced plotting that leads to a climactic string of fireworks and the ability to root all the revelations in deeply felt emotions—in a tale guaranteed to fool even the craftiest readers a lot more than once." Kirkus

Coben, Harlan

✓ **Hold** tight. Dutton 2008 416p $26.95

ISBN 978-0-525-95060-8; 0-525-95060-5

LC 2007-51582

"The story is about Tia and Mike Baye, whose son, Adam, has been somewhat isolated since his best friend killed himself. The parents, not knowing where he is going and what he is doing, consider putting some sophisticated spyware on their son's computer. Even though troubled by their invasion of his privacy they do so, anyway, using their worries about his welfare as an excuse. Once they find out where Adam is going and what he is doing, Mike all but abandons his medical practice to search for him and interact with some very dangerous people. Coben's style is laid back initially, but it builds into a strong, smart, suspenseful novel including at least five different storylines. " Deseret News

Coben, Harlan, 1962-

Stay close; Harlan Coben. Dutton 2012 400p.
ISBN 9780525952275

LC 2012001871

In this book, "three people are haunted by the disappearance of Stewart Green 17 years earlier in Atlantic City: photographer Ray Levine; housewife Megan Pierce; and Detective Broome, who investigated the disappearance and befriended Green's wife and kids. The disappearance of Carlton Flynn on February 18, the same date Green went missing, helps reignite the smoldering case, pointing the way to other victims and a strange pattern. Flynn's case also results in a pair of preppie, very scary sadists calling themselves Ken and Barbie entering the scene." (Publishers Weekly)

Coben, Harlan

The **woods**. Dutton 2007 404p $26.95
ISBN 978-0-525-95012-7; 0-525-95012-5

LC 2007-8329

The author "has created another surprising and emotional story that will remain with the reader long after the last page is finished. One of Coben's best." Libr J

Coco, Giovanni

Shadows on the lake; Giovanni Cocco and Amneris Magella; translated by Stephen Sartarelli. Penguin Books 2017 310 p. (Stefania Valenti mystery) (paperback) $16
ISBN 9780143127253; 9780698185722

LC 2016012231

In this book in the Stefania Valenti Mystery, by Giovanni Cocco and Amneris Magella "during the construction of a new road to the Swiss border in the mountains above Lake Como, the remains of a young man are unearthed on the . . . Cappelletti family's property. On the case is Stefania Valenti, forty-five, divorced with a young daughter, and a brilliant, determined police inspector. Her investigation takes her back to World War II and deep into the history of the region." (Publisher's note)

"A well-crafted piece of crime fiction cleverly enhanced by an inviting travel narrative from a husband-and-wife writing team who live in the region." Booklist

Coe, Jonathan

The **Rotters'** Club. Knopf 2002 419p
ISBN 0-375-41383-9

LC 2001-42523

First published 2001 in the United Kingdom

"The Rotter's Club, for all its occassional overegging and its self-conscious deployment of issues, is a superior entertainment. The pages seem to turn themselves, and Coe's oblique humor allows the romantic and satirical to combine without undercutting each other." New Statesman (1913)

Coel, Margaret

Blood memory. Berkley Prime Crime 2008 305p $24.95
ISBN 978-0-425-22345-1; 0-425-22345-0

LC 2008-22197

"The story sails along like an eagle riding the wind, and Coel provides plenty of plausible misdirection before revealing the surprising hand behind the plot to take her life. . . . Coel does a nice job of making Denver and the nearby environs into a charming 'character'—not the easiest task." Daily Camera (Boulder, Co.)

Coelho, Paulo, 1947-

★ The **alchemist**; Paulo Coelho; translated by Alan R. Clarke. HarperOne 2014 x, 182 p.p (pbk.) $16.99
ISBN 0062315005; 9780062315007

LC 2013041007

This novel by Paulo Coelho "tells the mystical story of Santiago, an Andalusian shepherd boy who yearns to travel in search of a worldly treasure. His quest will lead him to riches far different--and far more satisfying--than he ever imagined. Santiago's journey teaches us about the essential wisdom of listening to our hearts, of recognizing opportunity and learning to read the omens strewn along life's path, and, most importantly, to follow our dreams." (Publisher's note)

"The story has the comic charm, dramatic tension and psychological intensity of a fairy tale, but it's full of specific wisdom as well, about becoming self-empowered, overcoming depression, and believing in dreams. The cumulative effect is like hearing a wonderful bedtime story from an inspirational psychiatrist. Comparisons to The Little Prince are appropriate; this is a sweetly exotic tale for young and old alike." Pub Wkly.

Coetzee, J. M., 1940-

The **Childhood** of Jesus; by J. M. Coetzee. Viking Adult 2013 288 p. $26.95
ISBN 0670014656; 9780670014651

LC 2013016960

In this book, by J.M. Coetzee, David is "separated from his mother as a passenger on a boat bound for a new land. The piece of paper explaining his situation is lost, but a fellow passenger, Simón, vows to look after the boy. When the boat docks, David and Simón are issued . . . virtually a whole new life. Strangers in a strange land, knowing nothing of their surroundings, nor the language or customs, they are determined to find David's mother." (Publisher's note)

Coetzee, J. M.

★ **Disgrace**. Viking 1999 220p
ISBN 0-670-88731-5

"A novel that not only works its spell but makes it impossible for us to lay it aside once we've finished reading it. . . . Coetzee's sentences are coiled springs, and the energy they release would take other writers pages to summon." New Yorker

Coetzee, J. M.

Foe. Viking 1987 157p
ISBN 0-670-81398-2

LC 86-40267

First published 1986 in the United Kingdom

"In adding to Defoe's repertory company, Coetzee has introduced urgencies that are neither fresh nor illumined, only brilliantly disguised. Flashing back and forward, scattering allusions, adopting a series of poses and styles, the author is less reminiscent of a prior novelist than of contemporary street mimes who build hints until the audience shouts in recognition." Time

Coetzee, J. M.

★ **Life** & times of Michael K. Viking 1984 184p
ISBN 0-670-42789-6

LC 83-47860

First published 1983 in the United Kingdom

"Born with a harelip and brought up in an uncaring orphanage, Michael K. struggles through a desperate life in South Africa. When his sick mother persuades him to bring her back to her homeland, he must endure not only the terrible journey, pulling her in a cart he has made, but also risk the dangers of military checkpoints since he does not have the necessary permits. His undying attachment is to the land, but he is not allowed to remain the gardener he wishes to be. The details of Michael's suffering in camps, hospitals, and labor gangs are harrowing and underscore a courage that never forsakes him." Shapiro. Fic for Youth. 3d edition

Coetzee, J. M., 1940-

The **schooldays** of Jesus; J. M. Coetzee. Viking 2017 260 p. (hardcover) $27

ISBN 0735222665; 9780735222663; 9780735222687

LC 2016478250

Sequel to: The Childhood of Jesus (2013)

Author J.M. Coetzee won the Nobel Prize in Literature in 2003.

In this novel, by J. M. Coetzee, "Davíd is enrolled in the Academy of Dance. It's here, in his new golden dancing slippers, that he learns how to call down the numbers from the sky. But it's here, too, that he will make troubling discoveries about what grown-ups are capable of. In this mesmerizing allegorical tale, [J. M.] Coetzee deftly grapples with the big questions of growing up . . . and how we choose to live our lives." (Publisher's note)

"As compelling, and confounding, as its predecessor, Coetzee's newest also invites questions about what his protagonist's next years may bring." Booklist

Coetzee, J. M.

★ **Summertime**. Viking 2009 256p $25.95

ISBN 978-0-670-02138-3; 0-670-02138-5

LC 2009-37527

"In the early seventies, a young unpublished writer returns to his native South Africa after a disgrace abroad. His name is John Coetzee, and he both is and isn't the Nobel-winning author of this unorthodox book. Where the real Coetzee had a wife and children at the time, his doppelgänger shares a crumbling house with his widowed father and engages in fitful affairs with married women, one of whom judges him 'autistic' in bed. These 'facts' emerge from interviews conducted by a biographer nearly four decades later, after Coetzee's (imagined) death. At stake is what it means to commit oneself: to a person, a place, a moral imperative. . . . Not since 'Disgrace' has he written with such urgency and feeling." New Yorker

Coffey, Michael

The **Business** of Naming Things; Michael Coffey. Bellevue Literary Press 2015 224 p. $15.95

ISBN 1934137863; 9781934137864

LC 2014025375

In this collection of short stories, by Michael Coffey, "a fan of writer (and fellow adoptee) Harold Brodkey gains an audience with him at his life's end, two pals take a Joycean sojourn, a man whose business is naming things meets a woman who may not be what she seems, and a father discovers his son is a suspect in an assassination attempt on the president." (Publisher's note)

"In his first book of short fiction, poet Coffey, former coeditorial director of Publishers Weekly, delivers startlingly original and at times darkly funny stories that interrogate the very act of reading as well as human ambitions and the self-deception sometimes needed to realize them. His characters are as flawed and complicated as they are recognizable and sympathetic; all fiction readers can enjoy." LJ

Cogman, Genevieve

The **invisible** library; Genevieve Cogman. ROC 2016 352 p. (The invisible library novel) (softcover) $15

ISBN 9781101988640

LC 2016000476

In this novel, by Genevieve Cogman, "Irene is a professional spy for the mysterious Library, a shadowy organization that collects important works of fiction from all of the different realities. Most recently, she and her enigmatic assistant Kai have been sent to an alternative London. Their mission: Retrieve a particularly dangerous book. The problem: By the time they arrive, it's already been stolen." (Publisher's note)

"Intriguing characters and fast-paced action are wrapped up in a spellbinding, well-built world." LJ

Cohen, Joshua

★ **Book** of numbers; a novel. Joshua Cohen. Random House Inc 2015 592 p. (hardcover) $28

ISBN 0812996917; 9780812996913

LC 2014040735

"The enigmatic billionaire founder of Tetration, the world's most powerful tech company, hires a failed novelist, Josh Cohen, to ghostwrite his memoirs. The mogul, known as Principal, brings Josh behind the digital veil, tracing the rise of Tetration, which started in the earliest days of the Internet by revolutionizing the search engine before venturing into smartphones, computers, and the surveillance of American citizens." (Publisher's note)

"A dense, thrilling, and occasionally perplexing work, Cohen's encyclopedic epic is about many things--language, art, divinity, narrative, desire, global politics, surveillance, consumerism, genealogy--but it is above all a standout novel about the Internet, humanity's 'first mutual culture,' in which our identities are increasingly defined by a series of ones and zeroes." Pub Wkly

Cohen, Joshua

Four new messages; Joshua Cohen. Farrar Straus & Giroux 2012 193 p. (alk. paper) $14.00

ISBN 1555976182; 9781555976187

LC 2012936219

This collection of short stories, by Joshua Cohen, "capture[s] the pathos and absurdity of life in the age of the internet." Story characters include "a hapless drug dealer in Princeton . . . , a frustrated pharmaceutical copywriter . . . , a father visiting NYU with his daughter [who] remembers a former writing teacher, . . . [and] an aspiring journalist. . . . Highbrow and low-down, these four . . . stories explain what happens when the virtual begins to colonize the real." (Publisher's note)

Cohen, Leah Hager

The **grief** of others. Riverhead Books 2011 371p $26.95

ISBN 978-1-59448-805-4; 1-59448-805-3

LC 2011-09414

"Occasionally, the action of Cohen's novel seems forced when it moves outside the family circle, particularly when John goes to his job managing the theatrical scene shop at a community college. Sometimes, too, in shifting the perspective from one character to another, Cohen lets her own voice intrude, breaking the spell she's cast. But those are quibbles about a novel that's otherwise graceful, satisfying, and closely observed." Boston Globe

Coldsmith, Don

The **long** journey home. Forge 2001 400p $24.95

ISBN 0-312-87617-3

LC 00-48459

Coldsmith portrays a "Native American athlete who bears an intentional resemblance to the great Jim Thorpe. . . . This well-researched piece of historical fiction interweaves a compelling life story with many of the pivotal events of the early twentieth century." Booklist

Coldsmith, Don

Tallgrass; a novel of the Great Plains. Bantam Bks. 1997 454p

ISBN 0-553-10632-5

LC 96-19672

Coldsmith's saga concerns "the opening of the Santa Fe Trail. Starting with the coming of the Spanish conquistadors in 1541, his work spans 300 years to a time when the fur trade has died, Eastern Native Americans have been relocated onto lands west of the Mississippi, and conflict is building between the Plains Indians and Eastern interlopers, both Indian and white. Coldsmith focuses on a tribe of Pawnee and the devastation that contact with whites brings. This powerful novel demonstrates the diversity of the Native American culture while treating the tribes and their history with dignity and understanding." Libr J

Cole, Alyssa

★ An **Extraordinary** Union; by Alyssa Cole. Kensington Pub Corp 2017 258 p. (The Loyal League) $15.00

ISBN 1496707443; 9781496707444

In this book, by Alyssa Cole, "Elle Burns is a former slave with a passion for justice and an eidetic memory. Trading in her life of freedom in Massachusetts, she returns to the indignity of slavery in the South—to spy for the Union Army. Malcolm McCall is a detective for Pinkerton's Secret Service. Subterfuge is his calling, but he's facing his deadliest mission yet—risking his life to infiltrate a Rebel enclave in Virginia." (Publisher's note)

"Any reader who thinks romance novels are pure fluff will be schooled by Cole's richly drawn characters, who must overcome generations of trauma in order to let themselves love each other. A masterful tale that bodes well for future work from Cole." Kirkus

Cole, Alyssa

★ A **hope** divided; Alyssa Cole. First Kensington trade pbk Kensington Pub Corp 2017 320 p. (The Loyal League) paperback $15

ISBN 9781496707468; 149670746X

LC 2017048672

In this novel in The Loyal League series, by Alyssa Cole, "for all of the War Between the States, Marlie Lynch has helped the cause in peace: with coded letters about anti-Rebel uprisings in her Carolina woods, tisanes and poultices for Union prisoners, and silent aid to fleeing slave and Freeman alike. . . . [U]ntil the vicious Confederate Home Guard claims Marlie's home for their new base of operations in the guerilla war against Southern resistors of the Rebel cause." (Publisher's note)

"Thoughtfully portrayed characters with deep minds and passionate hearts make this second novel in Cole's Loyal League series, following An Extraordinary Union (2017), sparkle." Booklist.

Other titles in this series are:

An Extraordinary Union (2017)

Cole, Daniel

Ragdoll; Daniel Cole. Ecco, an imprint of HarperCollinsPublishers 2017 374 p. (hardcover) $27.99

ISBN 0062653954; 9780062653970; 9780062653956

LC 2016288714

In this novel, by Daniel Cole, "William Fawkes, a controversial detective known as The Wolf, has just been reinstated to his post after he was suspended for assaulting a vindicated suspect. . . . When his former partner and friend, Detective Emily Baxter, calls him to a crime scene, he's sure this is it: the body is made of the dismembered parts of six victims, sewn together like a puppet--a corpse that becomes known as 'The Ragdoll.'" (Publisher's note)

"With a third-person omniscient narrator, the briskly paced story line allows readers into the mind-sets of the various characters—from the multiple detectives to potential victims." LJ

Cole, Teju

Every day is for the thief; a novel. Teju Cole. Random House Inc 2014 162 p. illustrations hbk $23

ISBN 0812995783; 9780812995787

LC 2014004326

In this book, by Teju Cole, "a young Nigerian living in New York City goes home to Lagos for a short visit, finding a city both familiar and strange. In a city dense with story, the unnamed narrator moves through a mosaic of life, hoping to find inspiration for his own. He witnesses . . . email frauds from an Internet café, longs after a mysterious woman reading on a public bus, . . . and recalls the tragic fate of an eleven-year-old boy accused of stealing at a local market." (Publisher's note)

"The structure is loose, a collection of observances of daily life in Lagos in which Cole presents the complexities of culture and poverty. In addition, Cole sprinkles dramatic black-and-white photos throughout the book, but it's his willingness to explore so many uncomfortable paradoxes that sears this narrative into our brains." Pub Wkly

Cole, Teju

★ **Open** city; a novel. Random House 2011 259p $25

ISBN 978-1-4000-6809-8; 1-4000-6809-6

LC 2010-08927

"Cole's writing is assured, his ideas are well developed, and his imagery is delicious. . . . His readers will be those who understand that all stories are interconnected, that literature is not mere entertainment, and that art is nothing if not an extended conversation spanning eras, nations and languages. The novel's importance lies in its honesty." N Y Times Book Rev

Coleman, Reed Farrel

★ **Where** it hurts; a Gus Murphy novel. Reed Farrel Coleman. G. P. Putnam's Sons 2016 368 p. $27

ISBN 9780399173035; 039917303X

LC 2015017115

In this novel, by Reed Farrel Coleman, "four months earlier, Tommy's son T.J.'s battered body was discovered in a wooded lot, yet the Suffolk County PD doesn't seem interested in pursuing the killers. In desperation, Tommy seeks out the only cop he ever trusted--Gus Murphy. Gus reluctantly agrees to see what he can uncover. As he begins to sweep away the layers of dust that have collected over the case during the intervening months, Gus finds that Tommy was telling the truth." (Publisher's note)

"Coleman's moving portrayal of a man in deep, deep pain, a tightly constructed plot, and a gift for making Long Island seem like James Ellroy's L.A. add up to a winner." Pub Wkly

Colette

The **collected** stories of Colette; edited, and with an introduction, by Robert Phelps; translated by Matthew Ward, et al. Farrar, Straus & Giroux 1983 605p

ISBN 0-374-12629-1

LC 83-16449

"Includes two novellas that rank as classics, not only in Colette's canon, but in all of 20th century French literature. The Tender Shoot is the story of a singularly nasty middle-aged roué's pursuit of a 15-year-old peasant girl. Upon this squalid tale, Colette lavished her most lyrical language and poetic fancies, heightening the sense of evil. . . . As Colette remarked of her writing, her 'great landscape was always the human face.' No work demonstrates this better than The Kepi, the portrait of a doomed 46-year-old French lieutenant." Time

Colette

The **complete** Claudine; Claudine at school, Claudine in Paris, Claudine married, Claudine and Annie. translated by Antonia White. Farrar, Straus & Giroux 1976 632p

Omnibus edition of four semi-autobiographical novels written by Colette in 1900-1903. The first three appeared under the pen name of her husband and the fourth novel was published under both their names. These translations have copyright dates 1956, 1958, 1960 and 1962 respectively. Variant title for English translation of third volume: Indulgent husband; of final volume: Innocent wife

In the first novel we meet Claudine as a precocious school girl peeping and spying on both her contemporaries and her boarding school teachers. The second novel depicts a girl approaching womanhood discovering the exciting world of Paris and meeting a varied assortment of escorts. Claudine married is not so much the story of the heroine's marriage as the story of Claudine's love affair with Rézi, another married woman. The final volume has Claudine as one of its principal characters, but it is largely the story of an innocent young wife, who during the absence of her domineering husband begins to see more of her sister-in-law and her sophisticated friends and her eyes open to the true ways of life and love

Colette

Six novels. Modern Lib. 697p

Contents: Claudine at school; Music-hall sidelights; Mitsou; Chéri; The last of Chéri; Gigi

Colfer, Eoin, 1965-

Plugged; a novel. Overlook Press 2011 254p $24.95

ISBN 978-1-59020-463-4

LC 2011025335

"Daniel McEvoy has a problem. Well, really, he has several, but for this Irish ex-pat bouncer at a seedy, small-time casino the fact that his girlfriend was just murdered in the parking lot is uppermost in his mind. That is until lots of people around him start dying, and not of natural causes. Suddenly Daniel's got half the New Jersey mob, dirty cops and his man-crazy upstairs neighbor after him and he still doesn't know what's going on." (Publisher's note)

"Outrageous characters, . . . uproariously funny plot twists, and brutal, nonstop action make this a sure-fire winner." Publ Wkly

Another title in this series is:
Screwed (2013)

Collins, Ciarán

The **gamal**; Ciarán Collins. Bloomsbury USA 2013 480 p. (alk. paper) $17

ISBN 1608198758; 9781608198757

LC 2012046539

In this novel by Ciarán Collins "Charlie has a story to tell, about his best friends Sinead and James and the bad things that happened. Charlie has promised Dr Quinn he'll write 1,000 words a day, but it's hard to know which words to write. And which secrets to tell. This is the story of the dark heart of an Irish village, of how daring to be different can be dangerous, and how there is nothing a person will not do for love." (Publisher's note)

Collins, Max Allan, 1948-

Ask not; Nathan Heller Mystery. Max Allan Collins. Forge Books 2013 320 p. (Nathan Heller mysteries) (hardback) $25.99

ISBN 076533626X; 9780765336262

LC 2013018440

This is the 17th Nate Heller book by Max Allan Collins. Here, in "September 1964, a Cuban that the PI knows was involved in an attempt on J.F.K.'s life in Chicago three weeks before Dallas tries to run down Heller and his 16-year-old son on a Chicago street after a Beatles concert. With the permission of senatorial candidate Robert Kennedy, an old friend, Heller joins forces with journalist Flo Kilgore . . . to investigate an apparent conspiracy." (Publishers Weekly)

Collins, Wilkie, 1824-1889

★ The **moonstone**. Knopf 1992 473p $19

ISBN 0-679-41722-2

LC 92-52918

First published 1868

This book by Wilkie Collins is "a classic Victorian romance/adventure novel with detective insertions. When a valuable Indian diamond with a horrid history disappears from an English country home, Inspector Cuff of Scotland Yard is called in to investigate. The details of the story are revealed in a series of separate . . . witness accounts written by individuals of varying classes and viewpoints, ending with the now customary, but then new, deductive summing up." (Library Journal)

This novel "concerns the disappearance of the Moonstone, an enormous diamond that once adorned a Hindu idol and came into the possession of an English officer. The heroine, Miss Verinder, believes her lover, Franklin Blake, to be the thief; other suspects are Blake's rival and three mysterious Brahmins. The mystery is solved by Sergeant Cuff, possibly the first detective in English fiction." Reader's Ency. 4th edition

Collins, Wilkie

★ The **woman** in white. Knopf 1991 xxxvii, 569p $20

ISBN 0-679-40563-1

LC 91-52971

First published 1860; first Everyman's library edition 1910

"Practically the first English novel to deal with the detection of crime. The plot is based on the resemblance between the heroine and a mysterious woman in white, and involves an infamous attempt to obtain the heroine's money." Lenrow. Reader's Guide to Prose Fic

Colwin, Laurie

A **big** storm knocked it over; a novel. HarperCollins Pubs. 1993 259p

ISBN 0-06-017019-0

LC 92-56219

"The novel makes the idea of happy endings for decent people seem entirely plausible, almost inevitable—no small feat for a writer these days and no small pleasure for a reader." N Y Times Book Rev

Colwin, Laurie

Family happiness; a novel. Knopf 1982 271p

ISBN 0-394-52511-6

LC 82-23

"What is so striking about this wrenching novel is not the plot itself . . . but, rather, the absolutely convincing way that Colwin portrays Polly's slow awakening to selfhood." Booklist

Colwin, Laurie

Goodbye without leaving. Poseidon Press 1990 253p

ISBN 0-671-70706-X

LC 90-6797

"The tone here is disarmingly light, the humor intimate, and the plot inventive. A cheerfully irreverent look at an identity crisis and its unexpected resolution." Booklist

Colwin, Laurie

Happy all the time; a novel. Knopf 1978 213p

ISBN 0-394-50190-X

LC 78-2425

Set in New York City, this love story involves four quite normal people, "two men, two women. The men are cousins and close friends, the women are very different from each other, but full of spunk and individuality. Guido and Holly come together first, Vincent and Misty meet later. The men, long-time associates, are terribly nervous about their women liking each other. The women, in turn, eye each other warily. What we, as readers are treated to, however, is one of the most engaging and funniest dual courtships in a long time. The dialogue is sparkling and crisp, the encounter situations perfectly believable and perfectly ridiculous, as these four people, who really are 'happy all the time,' go through the 'angst' of realizing it." Publ Wkly

Conde, Maryse

I, Tituba, black witch of Salem; translated by Richard Philcox; foreword by Angela Y. Davis; afterword by Ann Armstrong Scarboro. University Press of Va. 1992 227p

ISBN 0-8139-1398-5

LC 92-8134

Original French edition, 1986

"Part historical novel, part literary fable, part exploration of the clash of irreconcilable cultures, {this} is most of all an affirmation of a courageous and resourceful woman's capacity for survival." N Y Times Book Rev

Conklin, Tara

The **house** girl; a novel. Tara Conklin. 1st ed. William Morrow Paperbacks 2013 384 p. (hardcover) $20.99; (paperback) $14.99; (ebook) $20.99

ISBN 0062207393; 9780062207395; 9780062207517; 9780062207524

LC 2012027370

This book follows "Lina Sparrow . . . a first-year associate at a prestigious New York law firm; in 1852, Josephine Bell is the titular 'house girl,' a slave on a Virginia farm. Assigned to work on a class-action suit involving slavery reparations, Lina searches out a suitable plaintiff for the case. . . . Lina's father, an artist, suggests that Lina research the story of Josephine, speculated to be the real artist behind paintings attributed to . . . her white master." (Publishers Weekly)

Conley, Robert J.

Mountain windsong; a novel of the Trail of Tears. University of Okla. Press 1992 218p

ISBN 0-8061-2452-0

LC 92-54150

"Its historical accuracy and its political correctness aside, the novel is a timeless love story about young people buffeted by a changing world over which they have no control." Booklist

Conlon, Edward

★ **Red** on red; Edward Conlon. 1st ed.; Spiegel & Grau 2011 442p.

ISBN 9780385519175; 9780385519182

LC 2010017534

This book "tells the . . . story of two NYPD detectives, Meehan and Esposito: one damaged and introspective, the other ambitious and unscrupulous. Meehan is compelled by haunting and elusive stories that defy easy resolution, while Esposito is drawn to cases of rough and ordinary combat. A fierce and unlikely friendship develops between them and plays out against a tangle of mysteries: a lonely immigrant who hangs herself in Inwood Hill Park, a serial rapist preying on upper Manhattan, a troubled Catholic schoolgirl who appears in the wrong place with uncanny regularity, and a savage gang war that erupts over a case of mistaken identity." (Publisher's note)

Conn, Brian

The **fixed** stars; thirty-seven emblems for the perilous season. FC2 2010 311p pa $19.95

ISBN 978-1-57366-153-9; 1-57366-153-8

LC 2009-38689

"An intricate, innovative, and beautifully realized book about a far-future society contending with mysterious plagues and its own violent customs, The Fixed Stars is speculative fiction at once challenging and deeply rewarding, alive with a kind of mythic strangeness." Rain Taxi

Connell, Evan S.

Deus lo volt! chronicle of the Crusades. Counterpoint 2000 462p OP

ISBN 1-58243-065-9; 9781619026933; 9781582431406

LC 99-54831

A chronicle "of the crusades from the point of view of a French knight. Jean Joinville, a participant in the disastrous second crusade under Louis IX, begins his chronicle with the first crusade, in 1095, and ends with the taking of Acre in 1290 by the forces of Ashraf Khalil, which effectively ended the mad attempt to make Palestine a Christian protectorate." Publ Wkly

What enlivens Connell's historial fiction "is first, his boyish fascination with how much has been buried alongside the victims: lost books and alphabets, artworks, cities, enigmatic treasures of all kinds. Second, there is the glittering anger of his style." Yale Rev

Connell, Evan S.

Lost in Uttar Pradesh; new and selected stories. Counterpoint 2008 359p $27

ISBN 978-1-59376-175-2; 1-59376-175-9

LC 2007-43829

"The stories in 'Lost in Uttar Pradesh'—seven of which are published here for the first time—vary in setting and length, but it is not hard to identify the common thread running through them: Connell's characters, whether recurring or simply enjoying a walk-on, find themselves suddenly shellacked by the realization that the world is not as it appears—moral, ordered, progressing toward some comprehensible end but is, in fact, the opposite. . . . If these narratives sometimes feel less like fully realized stories and more like fragments of an ongoing conversation Connell is having with the world, so be it—what he's working to do here is express both rage and its futility, and it's fascinating to watch this theme morph and play out in various scenarios." Star Tribune (Minneapolis, Minn.)

"Connell combines the master fiction writer's skills (brisk characterization, supple stylistic precision) with those of a compulsive traveler, ruminative antiquarian and borderline-eccentric obsessive." (Kirkus)

Connell, Evan S.

Mrs. Bridge; [by] Evan S. Connell, Jr. Viking 1959 254p

"India Bridge is a country club matron in Kansas City. Her husband, a successful lawyer, is seldom home so Mrs. Bridge copes—not too well—with her children, who are very different from one another. Ruth, the eldest, keeps aloft; Douglas, the youngest, is mostly off on his own projects and not interested in the fine rules of behavior that Mrs. Bridge finds essential. She seems able to communicate most easily with Carolyn, the middle child. We follow the family as the children grow. Mrs. Bridge, eager to be a proper upper-middle-class wife and mother, finds no happiness despite her affluence and good intentions." Shapiro. Fic for Youth. 3d edition

Connelly, Michael, 1956-

The **burning** room; Michael Connelly. Little Brown & Co. 2014 400 p. (hardcover) $28

ISBN 0316225932; 9780316225939

LC 2014940681

In this mystery novel by Michael Connelly, "when a man succumbs to complications from being shot by a stray bullet ten years earlier, [detective Harry] Bosch catches a case in which the body is still fresh, but any other clues are virtually nonexistent. Even a veteran cop would find this one tough going, but Bosch's new partner, Detective Lucia Soto, has no homicide experience." (Publisher's note)

"Bosch is very much of the old school in this high-tech world, but his hands-on tenacity serves him and the case well—just as Connelly serves his readers well with his encyclopedic knowledge and gifts as a storyteller." Pub Wkly

Connelly, Michael, 1956-

The **crossing**; a novel. by Michael Connelly. Little, Brown & Co. 2016 400 p. (hardback) $28

ISBN 9780316225885

LC 2015027456

In this book, by Michael Connelly, "Detective Harry Bosch has retired from the LAPD, but his half-brother, defense attorney Mickey Haller, needs his help. The murder rap against his client seems ironclad, but Mickey is sure it's a setup. . . . Bosch takes the case. With the secret help of his former LAPD partner Lucia Soto, he turns the investigation inside the police department. But as Bosch gets closer to discovering the truth, he makes himself a target." (Publisher's note)

"As always, Connelly's blackboard work is as precise as his finale is exciting." Booklist

Connelly, Michael, 1956-

The **Gods** of Guilt; by Michael Connelly. Little Brown & Co 2013 416 p. (Lincoln Lawyer) $28

ISBN 0316069515; 9780316069519

LC 2013032952

This book is Michael Connelly's "fifth novel featuring Mickey Haller . . . the L.A. defense attorney who uses a Lincoln town car as a mobile office. . . . Andre La Cosse, a high-tech pimp, is charged with murdering one of his clients, Giselle Dallinger. . . . Haller's strategy is not to uncover the truth but to develop a credible alternative theory of the crime, and the investigation that follows is like a police procedural seen from the other side of the criminal justice world." (Publishers Weekly)

Connelly, Michael

★ The **Lincoln** lawyer; a novel. Little, Brown 2005 404p $26.95

ISBN 0-316-73493-4

LC 2005-12863

"The book is haunted by Mickey's worst nightmare: the thought of having to defend an innocent man. He starts out without the foggiest idea of what to do with someone like that. But by the end of the story an Honest Abe conscience has begun to kick in. That's when Mickey becomes a Connelly character through and through." N Y Times (Late N Y Ed)

Connelly, Michael

The **scarecrow**; a novel. Little, Brown and Co. 2009 419p $27.99

ISBN 978-0-316-16630-0

LC 2009-00855

This novel "begins with Jack McEvoy—the crime reporter who was the hero of Connelly's 1996 The Poet—being given two weeks' notice at the Los Angeles Times. He's expected to spend his last days training his replacement: a young reporter whose real advantage, for the bosses, is that her salary is much lower than Jack's. . . . Jack decides that the ultimate 'fuck you' to the paper will be a final story so good that the suits will look like fools to fire him. He decides on the case of a teen gang-banger charged with a stripper's rape and murder. It doesn't take long for Jack to suss out that the police have the wrong man, and to link the murder with another that makes it clear both are the work of a serial killer. The Scarecrow is swift and engrossing, and it marks a development that has needed to happen in Connelly's novels for a while." Boston Phoenix

Connolly, John

The **book** of lost things. Atria Books 2006 339p $23

ISBN 978-0-7432-9885-8; 0-7432-9885-3

LC 2006-049340

A "novel about a 12-year-old English boy, David, who is thrust into a realm where eternal stories and fairy tales assume an often gruesome reality. Books are the magic that speak to David, whose mother has died at the start of WWII after a long debilitating illness. His father remarries, and soon his stepmother is pregnant with yet another interloper who will threaten David's place in his father's life. When a portal to another world opens in time-honored fashion, David enters a land of beasts and monsters where he must undertake a quest if he is to earn his way back out. Connolly echoes many great fairy tales and legends (Little Red Riding Hood, Roland, Hansel and Gretel), but cleverly twists them to his own purposes." Libr J

Connolly, John

The **burning** soul; a thriller. Atria Books 2011 406p $26

ISBN 978-1-4391-6527-0

LC 2011-21367

"An intelligent, plausible thriller, both harrowing and memorable." Kirkus

Connolly, Tina

Ironskin; Tina Connolly. Tor 2012 304 p. (hardcover) $24.99

ISBN 0765330598; 9780765330598; 9781429993043

LC 2012019874

This fantasy novel by Tina Connolly is "set in a gothic, alternate version of the Victorian era, in the aftermath of a war with powerful, forest-dwelling beings called the fey. . . . Jane Eliot, a young teacher and former governess dedicates herself to teaching the peculiar, stubborn [Dorie] but wonders whether Dorie's disquieting powers can be curtailed. Jane soon comes to realize that the war with the fey may not, in fact, be over after all." (Kirkus Reviews)

Other titles in this series are:

Copperhead (2013)

Silverblind (2014)

Conrad, Hy

Toured to Death; by Hy Conrad. Kensington Pub Corp 2015 320 p. $25

ISBN 1617736783; 9781617736780

LC 2014953078

In this book, by Hy Conrad, "[w]hile Fanny takes care of the business end of Amy's Travel in New York City, Amy is traipsing around Monte Carlo, managing their first mystery-themed excursion. . . . Amy still has reservations about partnering up with her mother. But both women . . . need a fresh beginning. The trip starts off without a hitch. . . . [But] just when the suspense is peaking, the writer they hired to script their made-up mystery is found murdered." (Publisher's note)

"Fast paced with an appealing international flair, this story will likely cross gender and genre lines, appealing to both men and women as well as to readers of more than just cozies. Characters with plenty of flaws offer enough red herrings to keep the ending a surprise, even for seasoned mystery fans." Booklist

Another title in this series is:

Dearly Departed (2016)

Death on the Patagonian Express (2016)

Conrad, Joseph

The **complete** short fiction of Joseph Conrad; edited with an introduction by Samuel Hynes. Ecco Press 1991 2v

ISBN 0-88001-307-9 v1; 0-88001-308-7 v2

LC 91-27115

Contents: v1 The idiots; The lagoon; An outpost of progress; Karain: a memory; The return; Youth: a narrative; Amy Foster; To-morrow; Gaspar Ruiz: a romantic tale; v2 An anarchist: a desperate tale; The informer: an ironic tale; The brute: an indignant tale; The black mate; Il conde: a pathetic tale; The secret sharer: an episode from the coast; Prince Roman; The partner; The Inn of the Two Witches: a find; Because of the dollars; The warrior's soul; The tale

Conrad, Joseph

★ **Heart** of darkness; with an introduction by Verlyn Klinkenborg. Knopf 1993 110p $15

ISBN 0-679-42801-1

LC 93-1855

Originally published 1902 in the United Kingdom in the collection Youth, and two other stories

"Marlow tells his friends of an experience in the (then) Belgian Congo, where he once ran a river steamer for a trading company. Fascinated by reports about the powerful white trader Kurtz, Marlow went into the jungle in search of him, expecting to find in his character a clue to the evil around him. He found Kurtz living a depraved and abominable life, based on his exploitation of the natives. Without the pressures of society, and with the opportunity to wield absolute power, Kurtz succumbs to atavism." Reader's Ency. 4th edition

Conrad, Joseph

Lord Jim; a tale. Knopf 1992 xxxiii, 437p $19

ISBN 0-679-40544-5

LC 91-53223

First published 1899; first Everyman's library edition 1935

"The title character is a man haunted by guilt over an act of cowardice. He becomes an agent at an isolated East Indian trading post. There his feelings of inadequacy and responsibility are played out to their logical and inevitable end." Merriam-Webster's Ency of Lit

Conrad, Joseph

Nostromo; a tale of the seaboard. Knopf 1992 532p $20

ISBN 0-679-40990-4

LC 91-53185

First published 1904; first Everyman's library edition 1957

"Set in the South American republic of 'Costaguana,' it is an exciting, complicated story about capitalist exploitation and revolution on the national scene and about personal morality and corruption in individuals. Charles Gould's silver mine helps to maintain the country's stability and its reactionary government. Gould's idealistic preoccupation with the mine warps his character and makes him neglect his gentle wife, Dona Emilia. When the revolution comes, Gould puts a consignment of silver in the charge of Nostromo, the magnificent, 'incorruptible' capataz de cargadores ('foreman of the dock workers'). A chance happening makes Nostromo decide to bury the silver and pretend that it was lost at sea. He is eventually killed on the island where his riches are buried, when he is mistaken by his fiancée's father for a prowler. . . . Conrad's characterization is strong, his narration is complex and oblique. The story starts halfway through the events of the revolution and proceeds by way of flashbacks and glimpses into the future." Reader's Ency. 4th edition

Conrad, Joseph

Victory; an island tale. with an introduction by Tony Tanner. Knopf 1998 lxi, 385p $20

ISBN 0-375-40047-8

LC 98-27677

First published 1915

The novel's "central character, Axel Heyst, a Swedish aristocrat, lives on an island in the Malay Archipelego. Influenced by the sceptical philosophy of his father, and trying to avoid forming any attachments, his way of life is challenged when he rescues Lena, who has been touring the islands as part of a Ladies' Orchestra, from the sexual harassment of the hotelkeeper, Schomberg. The novel explores their relationship and the difficulties precipitated by the arrival of the devilish 'Mr Jones' and his two companions." Oxford Companion to 20th-century Lit in Engl

Includes bibliographical references (p. xliv-xlv)

Conroy, Pat

The **prince** of tides. Houghton Mifflin 1986 567p $35

ISBN 0-395-35300-9

LC 86-10689

"Savannah Wingo, a successful feminist poet who has suffered from hallucinations and suicidal tendencies since childhood, has never been able to reconcile her life in New York with her early South Carolina tidewater heritage. Her suicide attempt brings her twin brother, Tom, to New York, where he spends the next few months, at the request of Savannah's psychiatrist . . . helping to reconstruct and analyze her early life." Libr J

Conroy, Pat

South of Broad; a novel. Doubleday 2009 514p $29.95

ISBN 978-0-385-41305-3; 0-385-41305-X; 9780385344074; 9780385532143

LC 2008-45681

In this novel "Charleston, S.C., gossip columnist Leopold Bloom King narrates a paean to his hometown and friends. . . . In the late '60s and after his brother commits suicide, then 18-year-old Leo befriends a cross-section of the city's inhabitants: scions of Charleston aristocracy; Appalachian orphans; a black football coach's son; and an astonishingly beautiful pair of twins, Sheba and Trevor Poe, who are evading their psychotic father. The story alternates between 1969, the glorious year Leo's coterie stormed Charleston's social, sexual and racial barricades, and 1989, when Sheba, now a movie star, enlists them to find her missing gay brother in AIDS-ravaged San Francisco." Publ Wkly

"In the great Southern tradition of storytelling, the city of Charleston, S.C., is the principal 'character' in Pat Conroy's new novel. . . . Like the Southern Gothic masters, William Faulkner and Flannery O'Connor, Conroy understands that a compelling sense of place will lend grace to his narrative, inhabiting the minds of his readers like the mournful strains of an old folk song." Boston Globe

Constantine, Liv

★ The **Last** Mrs. Parrish; Liv Constantine. HarperCollins 2017 393 p. (hardcover) $25.99

ISBN 9780062667595; 0062667572; 9780062667571

In this novel, by Liv Constantine, "Amber Patterson is fed up. She's tired of being a nobody: . . . She deserves more—a life of money and power like the one blond-haired, blue-eyed goddess Daphne Parrish takes for granted. To everyone in the exclusive town of Bishops Harbor, Connecticut, Daphne—a socialite and philanthropist—and her real-estate mogul husband, Jackson, are a couple straight out of a fairy tale. Amber's envy could eat her alive . . . if she didn't have a plan." (Publisher's note)

"A Gone Girl-esque confection with villainy and melodrama galore." Kirkus

Cook, Claire, 1955-

Best staged plans; Claire Cook. 1st ed.; Voice-Hyperion 2011 viii, 238p

ISBN 9781401341176; 9781401341855

LC 2010041839

This book tells the story of Sandra, "a professional home stage based out of the Boston area. Knowledgeable about home design and full of ideas, she somehow can't manage to get her own house ready for the market, thanks to her slacking-off husband and son. When she gets an offer to stage a boutique hotel in Atlanta, she leaps at the chance to run away and get some distance and perspective." (Libr J)

Cook, Elizabeth

Achilles. Picador 2002 115p

ISBN 0-312-28884-0

LC 2001-52398

First published 2001 in the United Kingdom

"This forceful re-creation of the life of Achilles sacrifices nothing to modernity: gods mate violently with mortals, ghosts feast on sheep's blood, and Achilles rages and slays, unburdened by psychology. At the same time, this brief, intense novel is unmistakably modern in intent, turning a war epic into a meditation on the limits of human perfectibility." New Yorker

"This forceful re-creation of the life of Achilles sacrifices nothing to modernity: gods mate violently with mortals, ghosts feast on sheep's blood, and Achilles rages and slays, unburdened by psychology. At the same time, this brief, intense novel is unmistakably modern in intent, turning a war epic into a meditation on the limits of human perfectibility." New Yorker

Cook, Robin

Coma; a novel. Little, Brown 1977 306p

ISBN 0-316-15510-1

LC 76-52951

"A female medical student uses her charms and femininity to obtain forbidden charts and computer read-outs on certain patients who have gone into coma on the operating table and never come out of it, remaining like vegetables due to extensive brain damage. Susan feels there is something wrong and sets out to find what it is. As a second-year med student, she knows practically nothing of medical terms or practices, so spends all of her class time in the library trying to learn the terminology before she can try to solve a mystery that has puzzled the finest surgeons in the hospital. She does manage to uncover a ring of doctors who are selling various organs for transplant from the coma victims as soon as they can declare them dead, and is almost a victim herself for her pains." West Coast Rev Books

Cook, Robin

Marker; Robin Cook. Putnam 2005 533p $25.95

ISBN 0-399-15293-8

LC 2005-45812

"True love runs a rocky course, and the plot thickens before the denouement crackles to an electric edge-of-the-seat finale." Publ Wkly

Cook, Robin

Vector. Putnam 1999 404p

ISBN 0-399-14471-4

LC 98-49058

In this "novel, the People's Aryan Army (PAA) is planning a major terrorist attack against a big government building in New York, hoping that will spark nationwide revolution. PAA founder Curt recruits immigrant Russian technician Yuri to prepare bioweapons for the attack. Yuri sets up a basement lab to produce anthrax, and a package 'bomb' becomes the vector for the anthrax when Yuri tries it out on a Greek rug dealer. Desiring proof of the merchant's death. Yuri meets Jack Stapleton from the medical examiner's office, and Jack's sidekick, Laurie, gets involved. . . . Vector is Cook at his best, providing both thrills and an urgent message." Booklist

Cook, Thomas H.

The **Chatham** School affair. Bantam Bks. 1996 292p

ISBN 0-553-09652-4

LC 96-4021

"Cook is a marvelous stylist, gracing his prose with splendid observations about people and the lush, potentially lethal landscape surrounding them. Events accelerate with increasing force, but few readers will be prepared for the surprise that awaits at novel's end." Publ Wkly

Cook, Thomas H.

The **cloud** of unknowing. Harcourt 2007 320p $24

ISBN 978-0-15-101260-2; 0-15-101260-1; 9780547538150

LC 2006-13951

"David and Diana Sears, the children of a paranoid schizophrenic father, were left deeply scarred by the abuse that resulted from his illness. David, too, is anxious about the genetic legacy of his father's condition, a legacy that seems to play itself out when Diana's son, Jason, is born with schizophrenia. Her ambitious scientist husband, Mark, is never able to reconcile himself to Jason's condition, and after Jason drowns, Diana can't accept the authorities' conclusion that his death was accidental. She becomes obsessed to the point of madness with the notion of Mark's involvement an obsession that will ultimately have disastrous consequences." Libr J

"Although Cook is maddeningly coy about who actually killed whom, he writes eloquently about the fears that lead people to equate intelligence with madness, suppressing the imagination and taking refuge in mediocrity." N Y Times Book Rev

Cook, Thomas H.

The **fate** of Katherine Carr. Houghton Mifflin Harcourt 2009 276p $25

ISBN 978-0-15-101401-9; 0-15-101401-9

LC 2008-49203

"Adept at merging past and present plot lines, Cook eloquently examines the often cathartic act of storytelling." Publ Wkly

Cook, Thomas H.

Instruments of night. Bantam Bks. 1998 293p

ISBN 0-553-10554-X

LC 97-52760

"Although it's easy to miss the very real clues that Cook drops so artfully into the story, there's no ignoring his savage imagery, or escaping the airless chambers of his disturbing imagination." N Y Times Book Rev

Cook, Thomas H.

Master of the delta. Harcourt 2008 367p $24

ISBN 978-0-15-101254-1; 0-15-101254-7

LC 2007-26506

"Cook writes in a multiplicity of voices and time frames, and with a profusion of literary references that in another context might seem showy. But from the perspective of a learned narrator who has lived long enough to rue the day he tried to play God, the convolutions of both plot and thought—so tortured and twisted and ultimately so futile—are entirely in character." N Y Times Book Rev

Cook, Thomas H.

Sandrine's Case. Pgw 2013 352 p. $24

ISBN 0802126081; 9780802126085

In this novel, "Sam Madison and his wife, Sandrine, both professors at Georgia's Coburn College (he of literature, she of history) and parents of a grown daughter, appear to have a solid marriage. But below the surface there are problems, which culminate in Sandrine's death from a cocktail of Demerol and vodka. While the coroner rules the death a suicide, the police suspect foul play and soon zero in on Sam as his wife's killer." (Publishers Weekly)

Cooke, Carolyn

Daughters of the revolution; a novel. Alfred A. Knopf 2011 173p $24.95

ISBN 978-0-307-59473-0; 0-307-59473-4

LC 2011-02743

In this novel "the '60s are encroaching upon the prestigious Goode School, where headmaster Goddard Byrd — 'God' for short — stands staunchly opposed to coeducation until Carole Faust, a gifted African-American girl, is admitted via clerical error. The shock waves from this period permeate the decades that follow in unexpected ways, throughout the school and beyond. Cooke's slim but muscular novel asks a lot of the reader, switching perspectives and taking narrative detours. But her exquisitely hewn sentences and fiercely original characters brilliantly capture a moment of social change without ever resorting to simplistic, black-and-white depictions of feminism." Entertainment Wkly

Cooley, Martha

✓The **archivist**; a novel. Little, Brown 1998 328p

ISBN 0-316-15872-0

LC 97-38385

The novel "treats serious questions in a humane and passionate manner, and leaves one thinking about these questions long after one has read the last page. Cooley is an accomplished stylist—there's scarcely a graceless or unintelligent sentence in the book—and a subtle chronicler of the inner life." N Y Times Book Rev

Cooper, Isabel

No proper lady; Isabel Cooper. Sourcebooks Casablanca 2011 368p.

ISBN 9781402259524 pa; 9781402259531

This book tells the story of "a woman from a dystopian future . . . where humanity is losing the war against demonic forces unleashed by a 200-year-old evil wizard, Alex Reynell. To destroy Reynell, Joan goes back to England in 1888, where magician Simon Grenville becomes her guide to a completely different way of life. When she practices proper Victorian flirtation on Simon, their heady attraction flairs." (Publishers Weekly)

Cooper, J. California

The **future** has a past; stories. Doubleday 2000 265p $23.95

ISBN 0-385-49680-X

LC 00-34602

Stories about "African-American women struggling to make something of their smalltown lives. . . . Navigating poverty, unwanted pregnancy, single motherhood and inexperience, all Cooper's heroines triumph, to lesser and greater degrees, finding 'real love' despite being surrounded by 'no good men'." Publ Wkly

Cooper, J. California

Wild stars seeking midnight suns. Doubleday 2006 209p

ISBN 0-385-51133-7

LC 2005-56004

"Cooper's talent for capturing the lives of ordinary people penetrates this collection of short stories. These are simple stories about personal struggles in settings from small towns to urban centers. An awkward young woman, pushed into a loveless marriage by her mother, eventually finds her own way professionally and emotionally. Two successful urban professionals cross paths in a nightclub, and neither is satisfied when the evening ends as so many have–in disappointment. A 14-year-old in love with her best friend's much older brother observes the sexual tensions he stirs in others. Many of the stories are told from the perspective of a narrator, close but far away enough for sharp discernment. Cooper fans will enjoy this collection, and those who are new to her work will appreciate her character development and artful storytelling." Booklist

Cooper, James Fenimore

The **last** of the Mohicans; introduction by Leslie A. Fiedler. Modern Library 2001 xxxii, 350p (The Modern Library classics) pa $9.95

ISBN 0-375-75764-3

LC 00-68105

First published 1826

This Leatherstocking tale "presents Chingachgook and his son Uncas as the last of the Iroquois aristocracy. Natty Bumppo, the scout Hawkeye, is in the prime of his career in the campaign of Fort William Henry on Lake George under attack by the French and Indians. The commander's daughters, Cora and Alice Munro, with the latter's fiancé Major Duncan Heyward, are captured by a traitorous Indian but rescued and conveyed to the fort by Hawkeye. Later Munro surrenders to Montcalm, and the girls are seized again by Indians. Uncas and Cora are killed, and the others return to civilization." Haydn. Thesaurus of Book Dig

Cooper, Tom

The **marauders**; a novel. by Tom Cooper. Crown Publishers 2015 304 p. $26

ISBN 0804140561; 9780804140560

LC 2013049483

In this book by Tom Cooper, set "in post-BP-oil-spill Louisiana, several men--two of whom may have been cursed--set out to try to make their fortune by selling drugs, stealing drugs, hunting for pirate treasure, and swindling people out of their right to sue BP." (Esquire) "At the center of it all is Gus Lindquist, a pill-addicted, one armed treasure hunter obsessed with finding the lost treasure of pirate Jean Lafitte." (Publisher's note)

"With withering contempt for BP, Cooper offers a believable portrait of a bayou town and a cast of deeply engaging characters wrestling inchoately with the likely extinction of the only life they know. There is real substance and humanity in this fine debut novel." Booklist

Coover, Robert

Noir. Overlook 2010 192p $24.95

ISBN 978-1-59020-294-4; 1-59020-294-5

LC 2009-40215

"With its flashbacks and glittering allusions, Noir is an exuberant, edgy laugh in the dark. . . . If you're looking for a Sam Spade, Mr. Noir is not your sleuth. He's an empty trench coat, which makes the ending so delicious. If you're a Coover groover, you'll love how the writer gooses this classic subgenre. Noir is an obsidian gem." Dallas Morning News

Coplin, Amanda

★ The **orchardist**; a novel. Amanda Coplin. Harper, an imprint of HarperCollinsPublishers 2012 426 p. $26.99

ISBN 006218850X; 9780062188502

LC 2012005466

This book is set "in the Pacific Northwest during the early years of the 20th century, [where] middle-aged Talmadge tends his orchards, . . . Two barely pubescent sisters, Jane and Delia, both pregnant by an opium-addicted, violent brothel owner from whom they have escaped, touch Talmadge's otherwise stoic heart, and he shelters and protects them until the arrival of the girls' pursuers precipitates tragic consequences." (Publishers Weekly)

Corby, Gary

The **Marathon** conspiracy; Gary Corby. Soho Crime 2014 352 p. illustrations (Athenian Mysteries) (hardback) $26.95

ISBN 161695387X; 9781616953874

LC 2013033925

In this historical mystery novel by Gary Corby, "Nicolaos, Classical Athens's favorite sleuth, and his partner in investigation, the clever ex-priestess Diotima, have taken time out of their assignments to come home to get married. But if Nico was hoping they'd be able to get hitched without a hitch, he was overly optimistic. When they arrive in Athens, there's a problem waiting for them." (Publisher's note)

"Corby serves up a bubbly cocktail of clear history, contemporary wit, and heart-stopping action." Booklist

Corby, Gary

The **Pericles** Commission; Gary Corby. 1st ed.; Minotaur Books 2010 xiii, 335 p.p $34.99

ISBN 0312599021; 9780312599027

LC 2010030462

In this mystery, by Gary Corby, "Nicolaos walks the mean streets of Classical Athens as an agent for the promising young politician Pericles. His mission is to find the assassin of the statesman Ephialtes. . . . But murder and mayhem don't bother Nico; what's really on his mind is how to get closer (much closer) to Diotima, the intelligent and annoyingly virgin priestess of Artemis, and how to shake off his irritating twelve-year-old brother Socrates." (Publisher's note)

Other titles in this series are:
The Ionia sanction (2011)
Sacred games (2013)
The marathon conspiracy (2014)
Death ex machina (2015)
The singer from Memphis (2016)

Corey, James S. A.

Abaddon's Gate; by James S. A. Corey. 1st ed. Orbit 2013 576 p. (paperback) $17

ISBN 0316129070; 9780316129077

LC 2012041860

This novel, written by James S.A. Corey, is the third in the Expanse series. An "alien artifact . . . has appeared in Uranus' orbit, where it has built a massive gate that leads to a starless dark. Jim Holden and the crew of the Rocinante are part of a vast flotilla of scientific and military ships going out to examine the artifact. The emissaries of the human race try to find whether the gate is an opportunity or a threat. But behind the scenes, a complex plot is unfolding, with the destruction of Holden at its core." (Publisher's note)

Corey, James S. A.

Caliban's war; by James S. A. Corey. Orbit 2012 624 p. $15.99

ISBN 9780316129060

LC 2011031646

This book by James S. A. Corey "returns to the politically charged future solar system setting of 'Leviathan Wakes.' . . . Eighteen months have passed since the now defunct corporation Protogen tried--with horrifying results--to harness an alien molecule with the power to rearrange living and inanimate matter. . . . The shaky détente among Mars, Earth, and the Outer Planets Alliance shatters after aliens attack Earth and Mars forces on Ganymede, making it look like Earth was the aggressor." (Publishers Weekly)

Corey, James S. A.

Cibola burn; James S. A. Corey. Orbit 2014 592 p. (The Expanse) (hardback) $27

ISBN 031621762X; 9780316217620

LC 2013045273

In this book, by James S. A. Corey, "[t]he gates have opened the way to a thousand new worlds. . . . Ilus, the first human colony on this vast new frontier, is being born in blood and fire. Independent settlers stand against the overwhelming power of a corporate colony ship. . . . The struggle on Ilus threatens to spread all the way back to Earth. James Holden and the crew of his one small ship are sent to make peace in the midst of war and sense in the midst of chaos." (Publisher's note)

"Combining an exploration of real human frailties with big sf ideas and exciting thriller action, Corey (pen name for authors Ty Franck and Daniel Abraham) cements the series as must-read space opera." LJ

Corey, James S. A.

★ **Leviathan** Wakes; James S.A. Corey. 1st ed. Orbit 2011 582p. (The Expanse)

ISBN 9780316129084 pa; 0316129089

LC 2010046442

This book tells the story of "Jim Holden, [who] is XO of an ice-hauler swinging between the rings of Saturn and the mining stations of the Belt. . . . His ship's captain . . . orders Holden and a shuttle crew to investigate what proves to be a derelict. Holden realizes it's some sort of trap, but an immensely powerful, stealthed warship destroys the ice-hauler, leaving Holden and the shuttle crew the sole survivors. This unthinkable act swiftly brings Earth . . . Mars . . . and the . . . Belt to the brink of war. Meanwhile, . . . cynical, hard-drinking detective Miller . . . receives orders to track down . . . a girl. . . . [T]he trail leads towards Holden, the derelict, and what might prove to be a horrifying biological experiment." (Kirkus)

Other titles in this series are:
Caliban's war (2012)
Abaddon's gate (2013)

Cibola burn (2014)
Nemesis games (2015)
Babylon's ashes (2016)
Persepolis rising (2017)

Corleone, Douglas

Good as gone; Douglas Corleone. Minotaur Books 2013 304 p. (hardcover) $24.99

ISBN 1250017203; 9781250017208

LC 2013009828

In this book, "a child's kidnapping leads a specialist in child recovery on a torrid chase across two continents. Simon Fisk's stint as a U.S. Marshal ended when his daughter Hailey was kidnapped. . . . Now, Simon makes his living recovering children abducted by estranged parents. . . . Vince and Lori Sorkin'[s] . . . daughter Lindsay has been grabbed by somebody who's not her parent. . . . Lindsay's trail takes him to Germany, Poland, Ukraine and Belarus." (Kirkus Reviews)

Other titles in this series are:
Payoff (2014)
Gone cold (2015)

Cornwell, Bernard, 1944-

1356; Bernard Cornwell. HarperCollins 2013 432 p. $28.99

ISBN 0061969672; 9780061969676

This book is the fourth book in Bernard Cornwell's Grail Quest series. English archer Sir Thomas of Hookton's lord orders him to find the mystical sword of Saint Peter before the French do, so he 'begins, with his men, a perilous journey of raiding and plundering across southern France. . . . Thomas and his men reach the decisive Battle of Poitiers, a vicious melee that killed thousands, unseated a king, and forced a devastating and short peace on a land ravaged by warfare." (Publishers Weekly)

Cornwell, Bernard

The **archer's** tale. HarperCollins Pubs. 2001 374p

ISBN 0-06-621084-4

LC 2001-24333

First published 2000 in the United Kingdom with title Harlequin

"Authentically detailed and appropriately gruesome, the medieval battle scenes fairly crackle with tension; however, what sets Cornwell's work apart from most run-of-the-mill military adventures are his meticulously developed story lines and his razor-sharp characterizations." Booklist

Cornwell, Bernard, 1944-

Death of kings. HarperCollins 2011 xii, 320 p.p $27.99

ISBN 9780061969652

LC 2012371564

This book follows Uhtred, an "irreverent but deadly ninth-century Saxon-born, Viking raised warrior" who has sworn loyalty to English leader Alfred the Great. Alfred is dying and "wishes to cement the line of succession, thus guaranteeing his son, Edward, the throne." (Libr J)

Cornwell, Bernard

Enemy of God; a novel of Arthur. St. Martin's Press 1997 396p (Warlord chronicles)

ISBN 0-312-15523-9

LC 96-51740

"This complex and superbly wrought narrative easily eclipses the more sanitized and tepid versions of Arthur's exploits." Booklist

Followed by Excalibur

Cornwell, Bernard, 1944-

The **Empty** Throne; Bernard Cornwell. HarperCollins 2015 336 p. illustration $27.99

ISBN 006225071X; 9780062250711

In this novel by Bernard Cornwell "Æthelred, the ruler of Mercia, is dying, leaving no legitimate heir. The West Saxons want their king, but Uhtred has long supported Æthelflaed. Widely loved and respected, Æthelflaed has all the makings of a leader-- but could Saxon warriors ever accept a woman as their ruler? The stage is set for rivals to fight for the empty throne. Uhtred is still suffering from the wounds he received in battle. To recover his strength he needs to find the sword that caused the injury." (Publisher's note)

"Despite Cornwell's use of ancient names and places, the lusty, rollicking narrative (accompanied by a map) is totally accessible and great good fun. Cornwell's done it again. New readers: Draw a flagon of ale, and be prepared to find the first seven in the series." Kirkus

Cornwell, Bernard

Excalibur; a novel of Arthur. St. Martin's Press 1998 340p (Warlord chronicles)

ISBN 0-312-18575-8

LC 98-10247

"The action is gripping and skillfully paced, cadenced by passages in which the characters reveal themselves in conversation and thought, convincingly evoking the spirit of the time. Ways of ancient ritual, battle and daily life are laid out in surprising detail." Publ Wkly

Cornwell, Bernard, 1944-

The **last** kingdom; a novel. Bernard Cornwell. HarperCollins Publishers 2005 333p map o.p.; o.p.; (pbk.) $14.99

ISBN 0060530510 (acid-free paper); 9780060530518; 9780060887186

LC 2004054236

This book is "set in medieval England prior to the unification of the four Anglo-Saxon kingdoms. . . . Northumbria is invaded by the fearless Danes, and Uhtred, the rightful heir to the earldom of Bebbanburg, is captured by the enemy. Raised as a Viking warrior by Ragnar the Terrible, his beloved surrogate father, Uhtred is still torn by an innate desire to reclaim his birthright. Fighting as a Dane but realizing that his ultimate destiny lies along another path, he seizes the opportunity to serve Alfred, king of Wessex, after Ragnar is horribly betrayed and murdered by Kjartan, a fellow Dane. . . . Uhtred awaits his chance to settle the blood feud with Kjartan and to seize Bebbanburg from his treacherous uncle." (Booklist)

Cornwell, Bernard

★ The **winter** king; a novel of Arthur. St. Martin's Press 1996 431p (Warlord chronicles)

ISBN 0-312-14447-4

LC 96-1421

First published 1995 in the United Kingdom

"Cornwell's Arthur is fierce, dedicated and complex, a man with many problems, most of his own making. His impulsive decisions sometimes have tragic ramifications, as when he lustfully takes Guinevere instead of the intented Ceinwyn, alienating his friends and allies and inspiring a bloody battle. The secondary characters are equally unexpected, and are ribboned with the magic and superstition of the times." Publ Wkly

Followed by Enemy of God

Cortazar, Julio

Hopscotch; translated from the Spanish by Gregory Rabassa. Pantheon Bks. 1966 564p

Original Spanish edition published 1963 in Argentina

"Considered to be Cortázar's masterwork, it is an open-ended novel; after reading the first 56 chapters, the reader is asked to reread the chapters in a different order. . . . The novel's antihero is Horacio Oliveira, an Argentine existentialist who lives among cultured expatriates in Paris while searching for his telepathic mistress. Returning to Buenos Aires, Oliveira meets Traveler and Talita, who are the doubles of his mistress and himself. None of the characters understands or cares more than superficially about the others, and impulse motivates their choices and actions. Narrative progress in the story is insignificant and its end is inconclusive." Merriam-Webster's Ency of Lit

Cosse, Laurence

A **novel** bookstore; translated from the French by Alison Anderson. Europa Editions 2010 416p pa $15

ISBN 978-1-933372-82-2; 1-933372-82-6

Original French edition, 2009

"The book begins with descriptions of the committee members' menacings, provoking a reader's quick interest and sympathy. Then follows the booksellers' lengthy interview with a sympathetic police inspector, in which the history of their individual lives and mutual enterprise is told. After that, the rest of the plot unfolds. Several mysteries are plumbed, if not necessarily solved, in this most engaging and winning novel." San Francisco Chron

Costello, Mark

Big if. Norton 2002 315p $24.95

ISBN 0-393-05116-1

LC 2002-512

National Book Award Finalist: Fiction (2002)

"The novel ends not with a bang but a shiver—in a masterfully orchestrated scene that is vividly cinematic. But true to his materials and vision—and to life—Costello slyly defuses the emotional catharsis in a manner that would be anathema to the feel-good demands of a major Hollywood production." N Y Times Book Rev

Coster, Naima

Halsey Street; Naima Coster. Little A 2018 320 p. (hardcover) $24.95

ISBN 1503941175; 9781503941175

In this novel, by Naima Coster, "Penelope Grand has . . . moved back to Brooklyn to keep an eye on her ailing father. . . . When Penelope moves into the attic apartment of the affluent Harpers, she thinks she's found a semblance of family--and maybe even love. But her world is upended again when she receives a postcard from Mirella asking for reconciliation. As old wounds are reopened, and secrets revealed, a journey across an ocean of sacrifice and self-discovery begins." (Publisher's note)

"Coster is a masterful observer of family dynamics: her characters, to a one, are wonderfully complex and consistently surprising. Absorbing and alive, the kind of novel that swallows you whole." Kirkus

Cotterill, Colin

The **coroner's** lunch; Colin Cotterill. Soho Press 2004 257 p. $24

ISBN 1569473765; 9781569473764

LC 2004048191

"Confronted by the poisoning of an important official's wife and the sudden appearance of three bodies that may create an international incident between Laos and Vietnam, 72-year-old state coroner Dr. Siri Paiboun keeps his cool in Cotterill's engaging whodunit, set in Laos a year after the 1975 Communist takeover." Pub Wkly

Other titles in this series are:

Thirty-Three Teeth (2005)
Disco for the Departed (2006)
Anarchy and Old Dogs (2007)
Curse of the Pogo Stick (2008)
The Merry Misogynist (2009)
Love Songs from a Shallow Grave (2010)
Slash and Burn (2011)
The Woman Who Wouldn't Die (2013)
Six and a Half Deadly Sins (2015)
I Shot the Buddha (2016)
The Catcher's Olympics (2017)
Don't Eat Me (2018)

Cotterill, Colin

Killed at the whim of a hat. Minotaur Books 2011 374p map $24.99

ISBN 978-0-312-56453-7; 0-312-56453-8

LC 2011-08722

"Cotterill combines plenty of humor with fascinating and unusual characters, a solid mystery, and the relatively unfamiliar setting of southern Thailand to launch what may be the best new international mystery series since the No. 1 Ladies' Detective Agency." Booklist

Cotterill, Colin

Slash and burn; Colin Cotterill. Soho Crime 2011 290p. (paperback) $15.00; (hardcover) $25.00

ISBN 9781616951788; 9781616951160

LC 2011030330

This novel tells the story of "Dr. Siri, . . . Laos's national coroner, . . . [who is] dragged into one last job for the Lao government: supervising an excavation for the remains of U.S. fighter pilot who went down in the remote northern Lao jungle ten years earlier. The presence of American soldiers in Laos is a hot-button issue for both the Americans and the Lao involved, and the search party includes high-level politicians and scientists. But one member of the party is found dead, setting off a chain of accidents Dr. Siri suspects aren't completely accidental. Everyone is trapped in a cabin in the jungle, and the bodies are starting to pile up." (Publisher's note)

Coulter, Catherine

The **end** game; Catherine Coulter and J. T. Ellison. G.P. Putnam's Sons 2015 464 p. illustrations (hardcover) $26.95

ISBN 9780399173806

LC 2015024632

In this book, by Catherine Coulter and J. T. Ellison, "FBI agent Nicholas Drummond and his partner, Mike Caine, are deep into an investigation of COE—Celebrants of the Earth. . . . While investigating a tip from a civilian . . . the Bayway Refinery in New Jersey explodes. Nicholas and Mike race to the scene and barely escape being killed by a secondary device. Returning to the civilian's home to continue their interrogation, they discover the tipster—and the FBI team left to guard him—dead." (Publisher's note)

Coulter, Catherine

The **Final** Cut; by Catherine Coulter and J. T. Ellison. Putnam Adult 2013 400 p. $26.95

ISBN 0399164731; 9780399164736

LC 2013024511

In this book, by Catherine Coulter and J.T. Ellison, "Det. Chief Insp. Nicholas Drummond . . . travels from London to Manhattan, where a thief known only as the Fox has stolen the Koh-i-Noor diamond, the centerpiece of the Queen Mother's crown on display at the Metropolitan Museum of Art. The Fox's relationship with the man who hired her to steal the diamond, Saleem Singh Lanighan, and the man who trained her, William Mulvaney, complicate matters. Drummond connects . . . with Coulter's main series heroes, FBI agents Dillon Savich and Lacey Sherlock." (Publishers Weekly)

Other titles in this series are:
The lost key (2014)
The end game (2015)
The Devil's Triangle (2017)
The sixth day (2018)

Coulter, Catherine

Split second. G. P. Putnam's Sons 2011 419p $26.95

ISBN 978-0-399-15743-1

LC 2011-08016

In this "15th FBI thriller featuring husband-wife agents Dillon Savich and Lacey Sherlock (after Whiplash), Dillon arrives one night at a Georgetown convenience store in Washington, D.C., just in time to thwart an armed robbery. While the robbery, which left one gunman wounded and a female accomplice dead, is never far from his thoughts, Dillon soon has an important case to pursue with Lacey—investigating a serial killer who may be related to the notorious Ted Bundy and has a chameleonlike ability to change appearances. . . . A tight plot full of unexpected twists will keep readers turning the pages." Publ Wkly

Couto, Mia

Sleepwalking land; translated by David Brookshaw. Serpent's Tail 2006 213p pa $14.95

ISBN 1-85242-897-X

Original Portuguese edition, 1992

"Many great novels have shown a world torn to shreds by the brutality of war. To do so, their authors ground their texts in the details of destruction and decay. But Couto's novel stands apart: it shows the world that war creates, a dreamscape of uncertainty where characters and readers alike marvel not at the abnormal becoming normal but at the way we come to accept the impossible as reality." N Y Times Book Rev

Cox, Michael

The **glass** of time; the secret life of Miss Esperanza Gorst. narrated by herself. W. W. Norton 2008 586p $24.95

ISBN 978-0-393-06773-6; 0-393-06773-4

LC 2008-23909

An "entirely wonderful mock Victorian novel. . . . It's a melodrama, of course, chock-full of revenge, romance, duplicity, concealed identities and murder most frequent—but melodrama on a grand scale." Washington Post Book World

Cox, Michael

The **meaning** of night; a confession. W. W. Norton 2006 703p $25.95

ISBN 978-0-393-06203-8; 0-393-06203-1

LC 2006-18941

"Cox has delivered almost everything Victorian readers might have expected (mystery, wit, romance, an evil double) and some (explanatory footnotes) they might not. Throughout [the book], he winks slyly at the era's literary conventions while twisting story lines back on one another. The result is a narrative as beguiling as it is intelligent, full of great country houses, epic loves, fierce anger and vicious habits of every sort." N Y Times Book Rev

Includes bibliographical references

Crace, Jim

Being dead. Farrar, Straus & Giroux 2000 193p

ISBN 0-374-11013-1

LC 99-45082

First published 1999 in the United Kingdom

"The style is agile, precise, and vigorous. Words hit their target directly and unerringly. Images are colorful, evocative, forceful." Commonweal

Crace, Jim, 1946-

★ **Harvest**; Jim Crace. 1st American ed. Nan A. Talese/ Doubleday 2013 224 p. (hardcover) $24.95

ISBN 0385520778; 9780385520775

LC 2012026208

Man Booker Prize Shortlist (2013)

This book is set in a premodern English village. "One morning, Master Kent's stable is found burning, and strangers who have peaceably signaled their presence by sending up the customary smoke plume are blamed; their heads are shaved, and the two men are put in stocks. The only one to show them sympathy is odd Mr. Quill, hired to map the village lands." (Library Journal)

Crace, Jim

The **pesthouse**; a novel. Nan A. Talese 2007 255p $24.95

ISBN 978-0-385-52075-1; 0-385-52075-1

LC 2006-26555

"The story is a gripping, harrowing adventure tale and Crace's language is extraordinary: he has immersed himself in his own kind of variant American idiom . . . which is simple, often beautiful, as tough and workable as leather." New Statesman

Crace, Jim

Quarantine. Farrar, Straus & Giroux 1998 242p

ISBN 0-374-23962-2

LC 97-61489

First published 1997 in the United Kingdom

Crace's "prose is startingly specific about ancient life and Judea's harsh, terrible beauty. Unlike many authors of biblical fiction, he blends his research smoothly into his narrative and adds a leavening pinch of humor." Time

Crafts, Hannah

The **bondswomans** narrative; edited by Henry Louis Gates Jr. Warner Bks. 2002 lxxiv, 338p il $24.95

ISBN 0-446-53008-5

LC 2001-98325

"Published from a manuscript bought at auction by Henry Louis Gates Jr., {this} is quite probably the first novel written by a black woman, as well as the only novel written by a female fugitive slave. It is also one of the few purely firsthand accounts of the slave experience available." N Y Times Book Rev

Includes bibliographical references (p. 333-336)

Craig, Charmaine

Miss Burma; Charmaine Craig. Grove Press 2017 x, 355 p.p (hardcover) $26

ISBN 9780802189523; 9780802126450

LC 2016047415

This novel, by Charmaine Craig, "tells the story of modern-day Burma through the eyes of Benny and Khin, husband and wife, and their daughter Louisa. . . . Based on the story of the author's mother and grandparents, . . . [it] is a captivating portrait of how modern Burma came to be and of the ordinary people swept up in the struggle for self-determination and freedom." (Publisher's note)

"In her epic new novel, Craig (The Good Men) takes readers on a journey through the political history of Burma (today's Myanmar) from 1920s British colonialism to 1960s military rule." LJ

Craig, Philip R.

A **shoot** on Martha's Vineyard; a Martha's Vineyard mystery. Scribner 1998 285p map $22

ISBN 0-684-83454-5

LC 97-51141

When "J.W. Jackson's long-time nemesis arrives in town and is murdered, J.W. can avoid suspicion only by finding the murderer. A handsome Hollywood movie scout, meanwhile, takes a shine to Jackson's new wife. A lively and entertaining addition to the series." Libr J

Craig, Philip R.

Third strike; a Brady Coyne/J.W. Jackson mystery. [by] Philip R. Craig and William G. Tapply. Scribner 2007 323p $24

ISBN 978-1-4165-3256-9; 1-4165-3256-0

LC 2007-9103

"Tapply's Boston lawyer, Brady Coyne, responds to an anguished call for help from an old client living on Martha's Vineyard, where the late Philip Craig's ex-cop, J.W. Jackson, is being urged by his wife to investigate the death of a striking ferry boat worker. . . . The two friends pursue their cases separately and together as tensions caused by the ferry strike mount and a murder raises the stakes. This marks the highly enjoyable and poignant end to a short, sweet series." Publ Wkly

Craig, Philip R.

A **vineyard** killing; a Martha's Vineyard mystery. Scribner 2003 229p $24

ISBN 0-7432-0524-3

LC 2002-42878

This installment "begins with a bang: an unknown assailant shoots someone outside the delicatessen where series private investigator J. W. Jackson is eating with his wife. Jackson is soon embroiled in a murder case involving grabby real estate developers and recalcitrant islanders. Off-season atmosphere and the usual high-caliber sleuthing." Libr J

Crain, Caleb, 1967-

Necessary errors; a novel. Caleb Crain. Perseus Books Group 2013 480 p. pbk $16

ISBN 9780143122418

LC 2013006551

Lambda Literary Awards Finalist: Gay General Fiction (2014)

This book, by Caleb Crain, presents the "coming-of-age story of Jacob Putnam. He is a gay man, a recent graduate of Harvard . . . who is teaching English as a second language on contract in Prague just after the triumph of the Velvet Revolution. . . . Jacob is part of a group of young expatriates . . . similarly employed, transitionally bohemian. He is in the foreground of a group portrait of new friends that develops . . . over the course of a year." (New York Review of Books)

"The plot is compelling, but Crain's talent for nuance and dialog, particularly in the gay bar scenes, is an observational wonder. Through a historic lens, Crain details the beautiful East European capital city's transition from Communist to democratic rule." LJ

Crais, Robert

Chasing darkness; an Elvis Cole novel. Simon & Schuster 2008 273p $25.95

ISBN 978-0-7432-8164-5; 0-7432-8164-0

LC 2008-10709

"While clearing houses in the path of a forest fire in Laurel Canyon, police officers find the body of Lionel Byrd, an apparent suicide. Three years earlier, Cole, working for Byrd's attorney, uncovered evidence that cleared Byrd of a murder charge. Now new evidence suggests that he was guilty of that murder and six others, two of them committed after Cole helped exonerate him. Torn by guilt, Cole plunges into his own investigation, which leads in startling directions." Publ Wkly

Crais, Robert

Demolition angel; a novel. Doubleday 2000 386p

ISBN 0-385-49584-6

LC 00-29054

"The book features one of the most complex heroines to grace a thriller since Clarice Starling locked eyes with Hannibal Lecter, a deliciously spooky villain in the person of a mad bomber known as Mr. Red, and an aggressively involving plot." Publ Wkly

Crais, Robert

First rule. G.P. Putnam's Sons 2010 308p $26.95

ISBN 978-0-399-15613-7; 0-399-15613-5

LC 2009-36928

"Righteous vengeance, a reckless pace, a stratospheric body count and just enough surprises to keep you turning the pages. The pleasures may be primitive, but they're genuine." Kirkus

Cramer, W. Dale

★ **Bad** ground; W. Dale Cramer. Bethany House 2004 382p $12.99

ISBN 076422784X (pbk.); 9780764227844

LC 2004002023

In this book, "[t]he day before his mother's funeral, newly orphaned 17-year-old Jeremy Prine is given a letter in which she tells him, 'When the time is right I want you to go find your Uncle Aiden. . . . You have something I couldn't give him, and he has something I couldn't give you.' He hitchhikes to where Aiden, aka Snake, works a hard-rock tunnel south of Atlanta, and Jeremy manages to wangle a job. [Author W. Dale] Cramer invites the reader into the life of the rock tunnel workers—hard-bitten, simple men with simple desires—as Jeremy wrestles with change, loss and becoming a man." (Publishers Weekly)

Cramer, W. Dale

Levi's will; a novel. W. Dale Cramer. Bethany House 2005 394p (pbk.) $14.99

ISBN 9780739456378; 0739456377; 0764207121; 9780764207129

LC 2005004602

Christy Award: Contemporary Stand Alone (2006)

This book begins "[i]n 1943, [when] 19-year-old Will Mullet flees his pacifist Amish community of Apple Creek, Ohio, leaving behind a pregnant girl and a rigid, God-fearing home to find a new life. He enlists in the military, marries a southern belle and tries to erase every trace of his past. But he can't completely disengage from his roots, and nor, he belatedly discovers, does he want to. Levi, Will's father, is slow to accept the prodigal son. Decades pass, and . . . Will's life and relationship with his own children unfolds. . . . [Author W. Dale] Cramer shifts eras and narrative styles from chapter to chapter, sometimes following Will's life in the 1940s as a young single man, sometimes chronicling other decades leading up to and including the 1980s." (Publishers Weekly)

Crane, Elizabeth

You must be this happy to enter; stories. Punk Planet Books 2008 183p pa $14.95

ISBN 978-1-933354-43-9

LC 2007-926133

"Zombies, time travelers, reality TV contestants and even a few normalish folks populate the pages of Elizabeth Crane's quirky, charming new collection. . . . Crane writes like she's running out of air: fast and a little babbly, but she's endlessly entertaining." PopMatters

Crane, Stephen, 1871-1900

The **complete** novels of Stephen Crane; edited with an introduction by Thomas A. Gullason. Doubleday 1967 xvi, 821 p.p

ISBN 9780385041829

LC 67010369

Includes: Maggie: a girl of the streets (1893); The red badge of courage (1895); George's mother (1896); The third violet (1897); Active service (1899); The O'Ruddy (1903)

Crane, Stephen, 1871-1900

The **complete** short stories & sketches of Stephen Crane; edited with an introduction by Thomas A. Gullason. Doubleday 1963 790p

Crane, Stephen, 1871-1900

★ **Maggie**: a girl of the streets (a story of New York) an authoritative text, backgrounds and sources, the author and the novel, reviews and criticism, edited by Thomas A. Gullason. Norton 1979 258p

ISBN 0-393-01222-0

LC 78-24596

First published privately in 1893 under the pseudonym Johnston Smith

"Maggie Johnson is the daughter of a brutal father and a drunken mother. She goes to work in a collar factory, falls in love with Pete, a bartender who is a friend of her brother Jimmie, and is seduced by him. Her mother disowns her, she becomes a prostitute; and in despair she finally kills herself. Her final degeneration becomes almost an allegory." Reader's Ency. 4th edition

Crane, Stephen, 1871-1900

The **portable** Stephen Crane; edited, with an introduction and notes, by Joseph Katz. Viking 1969 xxvi, 550p

ISBN 0-670-01068-5

Contains sixteen short stories, plus sketches, letters, pieces of journalism, some poetry and three novels: Maggie: a girl of the streets (1893); George's mother (1896); and The red badge of courage (1895)

Crane, Stephen, 1871-1900

Prose and poetry. Library of Am. 1984 1379p $40; pa $15.95

ISBN 0-940450-17-8; 1-883011-39-6 pa

LC 83-19908

Maggie: a girl of the streets and The red badge of courage are entered separately. George's mother (1896) focuses on a woman who sacrifices everything for her own son, whom she mistakenly believes to be destined for greatness. The third violet (1896-97) deals with an artist and his bohemian life. In The monster (1898) "Henry Johnson, a black servant in the home of Dr. Trescott, rescues the physician's son from a fire. He is terribly disfigured and loses his sanity, so that no home can be found for him in the town. Horrified by the 'monster,' the townspeople ostracize the doctor and his family because they harbor the man." Oxford Companion to Am Lit. 6th edition

Crane, Stephen, 1871-1900

★ The **red** badge of courage; an episode of the American Civil War. introduced by Wendell Minor. Complete and unabridged ed.; Puffin 2009 215p (Puffin classics) pa $4.99

ISBN 978-0-14-132752-5

First published 1895 by D. Appleton and Co.

"A young Union soldier, Henry Fleming, tells of his feelings when he is under fire for the first time during the battle of Chancellorsville. He is overcome by fear and runs from the field. Later he returns to lead a charge that reestablishes his own reputation as well as that of his company. One of the great novels of the Civil War." Cincinnati Public Libr

Crews, Harry

A **feast** of snakes. Atheneum 1976 177p

ISBN 0-689-107293

LC 76-8206

The novel is set in the backwoods hamlet of Mystic, Georgia, where the annual festival "begins with the crowning of the high-school Rattlesnake Queen , continues with a pit-bull championship fight, and ends with a Rattlesnake Roundup. The festival this year is a total nightmare: a black girl with a razor emasculates Sheriff Buddy Matlow, Big Joe Mackey kicks his losing dog to death, and Joe Lon Mackey–aged twenty-two, practically illiterate, miserably married, with two screaming babies, his years of glory as an all-around athlete . . . behind him–goes out of control with a twelve-gauge shotgun." New Yorker

Crichton, Michael

★ The **Andromeda** strain. Avon Books 2003 331p pa $7.99

ISBN 0-06-054181-4

First published 1969 by Knopf

"In these days of interplanetary exploration, this tale of the world's first space-age biological emergency may seem uncomfortably believable. When a contaminated space capsule drops to earth in a small Nevada town and all the town's residents suddenly die, four American scientists gather at an underground laboratory of Project Wildfire to search frantically for an antidote to the threat of a worldwide epidemic." Shapiro. Fic for Youth. 3d edition

Crichton, Michael, 1942-2008

★ **Jurassic** Park; a novel. Knopf 1990 399p pa $7.99; $28.95

ISBN 0-345-37077-5 pa; 0-394-58816-9

LC 90-52960

This novel "tells of a modern-day scientist bringing to life a horde of prehistoric animals." (N Y Times Book Rev)

"Crichton is a master at blending technology with fiction. . . . Suspense, excitement, and good adventure pervade this book." SLJ

Followed by The lost world (1995)

Crichton, Michael

Pirate latitudes; a novel. Harper 2009 312p map $27.99

ISBN 978-0-06-192937-3; 0-06-192937-9

LC 2009-49965

The Caribbean, 1665. Pirate captain Charles Hunter, with backing from a powerful ally, assembles a crew of ruffians to take the Spanish galleon, "El Trinidad," guarded by the bloodthirsty Cazalla, a favorite commander of the Spanish king himself.

"Capt. Charles Hunter is the protagonist, a swashbuckling rake from the Massachusetts Bay Colony (with a degree from a new college called Harvard) who is bumming around Jamaica looking for trouble when he hears about a boatload of Spanish booty waiting to be stolen. This being a Crichton novel, Hunter promptly assembles a crackerjack team of 'privateers' — an eagle-eyed helmsman named Enders, the master assassin Sanson, an explosives expert nicknamed simply 'The Jew' — and sails off to raid King Philip's coffers. Along the way he rescues a comely kidnapped Englishwoman from island cannibals, crosses swords with a sadistic villain called Cazalla, and outflanks Spanish gunships with bold tactical maneuvers that would leave Jack Sparrow gasping." Entertainment Wkly

Crichton, Michael

Prey; novel. HarperCollins Pubs. 2002 376p $26.95

ISBN 0-06-621412-2

LC 2002-32338

"Despite its absurd moments, 'Prey' is irresistibly suspenseful. You're entertained on one level and you learn something on another, even if the two levels do ultimately diverge." N Y Times Book Rev

Crichton, Michael

Sphere; a novel. Knopf 1987 385p

ISBN 0-394-56110-4

LC 86-46321

The author "sends a team of civilian experts to the floor of the Pacific to investigate an enormous spaceship that appears to have rested there for some 300 years. In it, they discover a huge sphere, made of a mysterious metal, which they cannot force open despite its having a door. Then, when one of the group inspects the ship on his own, it opens, he enters, and the real fun begins. . . . Crichton's prose, pedestrian but not clumsy, lets the story spin itself out, and few readers who grab its thread will let go until the web is broken in a 'Wizard of Oz'-style ending." Booklist

Crichton, Michael

Timeline. Knopf 1999 449p

ISBN 0-679-44481-5

LC 99-461985

In this novel, a billionaire planning a theme park uses time travel to send historians working on an excavation in the Dordogne back to the France of 1357, where they become involved in a war

"Crichton is a master of an odd hybrid: entertaining novels that educate. 'Timeline' is a page turner and a very lucid look at life in the late Middle Ages. He teaches you how to think like a knight during a joust by putting you in the saddle." Newsweek

✓ **Crime** novels: American noir of the 1930s and 40s; [edited by Robert Polito] Library of Am. 1997 990p il $35

ISBN 1-88301-146-9

LC 97-2485

The postman always rings twice and The big clock are entered in main catalog. They shoot horses, don't they? (1935) explores the turbulent world of a Hollywood dance marathon. Thieves like us (1937) follows a fugitive band of Oklahoma bank robbers. Nightmare alley (1946) presents a psychological portrait of a doomed carnival hustler. I married a dead man (published 1948 under pseudonym William Irish) is a title of switched identities set in suburbia

Crime novels: American noir of the 1950s; [edited by Robert Polito] Library of Am. 1997 892p $35

ISBN 1-883011-49-3

LC 97-2487

The killer inside me (1952) portrays a small town Texas deputy sheriff who is a psychopathic killer. The talented Mr. Ripley (1955) is about an opportunistic social parasite. Pick-up (1955) explores the seedy world of an alcoholic African American painter. Down there (1956; variant title: Shoot the piano player) is a psychological portrait of a barroom pianist. The real cool killers (1959) features Harlem police officers Coffin Ed Johnson and Grave Digger Jones

Cristofano, David

The **girl** she used to be. Grand Central Pub. 2009 241p $22.99

ISBN 978-0-446-58222-3; 0-446-58222-0

LC 2008-03280

"The novel is told from Melody's point of view, and Cristofano is largely able to pull off the female perspective. . . . Snappy dialogue and scenes with unpredictable outcomes keep the novel going at a steady pace." PopMatters

Criswell, Millie

What to do about Annie? Millie Criswell. Ivy Books 2001 316p

ISBN 0804119511

LC 2001116593

In this book, "[h]aving grown up in Baltimore's Little Italy with a Jewish father and an Italian mother, Annie Goldman feels caught between two worlds and is determined to flaunt her individuality. She . . . drives Father 'what-a-hunk' Joe Russo crazy with her curve-hugging clothes. Annie once dreamed that she would have a future with Joe, but her hopes were dashed when he left her to join the priesthood. Now, 15 years later, Joe has decided to hang up his rosary beads and give love another try. . . . While the two attempt to rekindle their romance, Annie becomes a part owner of her father's outdated clothing store. . . . Joe has his own problems to contend with as well—namely, his domineering mother and her matchmaking machinations." (Publishers Weekly)

Crombie, Deborah

✓ **Water** like a stone. William Morrow 2007 407p $24.95

ISBN 978-0-06-052527-9; 0-06-052527-4

LC 2006-46841

"As in books by Elizabeth George and P. D. James, the intriguing personal relationships and family dynamics drive this well-crafted, impressive mystery-drama." Booklist

Crompton, Richard

Hell's gate; a novel. Richard Crompton. Sarah Crichton Books/Farrar, Straus & Giroux 2015 256 p. (Detective Mollel) (hardback) $26

ISBN 0374280584; 9780374280581

LC 2014030528

In this book, by Richard Crompton, "Mollel . . . the former Masai warrior turned Nairobi detective sergeant, has been demoted and sent to a small town near Hell's Gate National Park. It's an undercover assignment to investigate the frequent disappearances of local bad guys there. But the local cops Mollel joins are suspicious of him, and Mollel knows they might kill him at any moment. Even worse, an investigator from the International Criminal Court is poking the same hornet's nest." (Booklist)

"In this second Mollel novel (after Hour of the Red God), Crompton writes about Kenya's social problems—including wildlife poaching, violence against women, and corruption—in a way both searing and compassionate. Mollel's love for and commitment to his country, despite its many problems, is evident throughout. A classic lone-wolf detective story with enough plot twists to keep readers guessing until the end, this novel will appeal to those looking for both a psychological and an action thriller." LJ

Crompton, Richard

Hour of the Red God; Richard Crompton. Sarah Crichton Books/Farrar, Straus and Giroux 2013 304 p. (Detective Mollel mysteries) (hardcover : alk. paper) $26

ISBN 0374171998; 9780374171995

LC 2012034612

In this mystery novel, Nairobi police detective Mollel, a single parent who lost his wife to the 1998 al-Qaeda bombing of the U.S. embassy, looks into the murder of a fellow Maasai tribe member, a woman whose genitals were freshly mutilated. Mollel's less-than-honest boss, who quickly labels the victim a prostitute, directs him to wrap things up quickly. But the dogged Mollel follows the evidence wherever it leads him, even if it means stepping on the toes of the rich and powerful." (Publishers Weekly)

"[Crompton's] debut novel combines a sinuous plot, a wonderfully complex and tragic protagonist, and a remarkable portrait of a city that is simultaneously exotic yet familiar." Booklist

Cronin, A. J.

★ The **citadel**. Little, Brown 1937 401p

"In 1921 Andrew Manson, newly graduated at the top of his medical-school class, accepts his first position as assistant to a dying physician in an impoverished Welsh mining town. Hard-working and conscientious at first, Andrew is promoted to a more socially desirable post in London, where he abandons his principles. A faulty operating-room procedure magnifies his increasing incompetence and jolts him back to a career of integrity." Shapiro. Fic for Youth. 3d edition

Cronin, A. J.

★ The **keys** of the kingdom. Little, Brown 1941 344p

ISBN 0-316-16189-6

"A child of Scottish fisher folk, Father Francis Chisholm, even as a young lad, yearned to enter the Catholic priesthood. After graduation from the seminary and a few years of parish work at home, he was sent to China as a missionary. With the years of toil he acquired saintliness and tolerance. Pestilence and famine, bandits and flood, and unappreciative superiors only served to strengthen his character and fortitude. Excellent character delineation." Libr J

Cronin, Justin

The **city** of mirrors; a novel. Justin Cronin. Ballantine Books 2016 624 p. (Passage trilogy) (hardcover) $28

ISBN 9780345505002; 034550500X

LC 2015050523

In this post-apocalyptic novel by Justin Cronin, "the story picks up several years after the destruction of the Homeland and the evacuation of many of its citizens to Texas. With 11 of the 12 virals destroyed, a period of relative peace has settled on the landscape. Yet the remaining viral, Zero, still haunts the ruins of New York City, preparing for his final standoff with humankind." (Library Journal)

"Not only does this title bring the series to a thrilling and satisfying conclusion, but it also exhibits Cronin's moving exploration of love as both a destructive force and an elemental need, elevating this work among its dystopian peers." LJ

Cronin, Justin

★ The **passage**; a novel. Ballantine Books 2010 766p $27

ISBN 978-0-345-50496-8

LC 2010-07455

This first novel in a proposed trilogy, "set in the near American future (Texas is now overseen by Gov. Jenna Bush), expertly draws together the parallel story lines of an unusually watchful, stoic little girl named Amy and a covert Army experiment to turn the human body into a bioweapon, using death-row inmates as test subjects. Cronin painstakingly weaves the threads of a narrative so involving and immediate that when he jumps ahead almost a century, it's hard at first to release those characters and invest in the dozens of new ones that emerge in the Stand–meets–The Road journey that follows. The Passage owes a substantial debt to both King's 1978 epic and Cormac McCarthy's 2007 Pulitzer winner, and he is not immune to some of the hoarier tropes of Armageddon fiction (mystical children, cryptic-wisdom-spouting old folks, impossibly arduous vision quests). But his bogeymen, the vampiric, blood-hungry beasts known as 'virals,' are magnificently unnerving, and his power to compel readers to the next page seldom flags." Entertainment Wkly

Cronin, Justin

The **twelve**; a novel. Justin Cronin. Ballantine Books 2012 xvii, 568 p.p maps (Passage trilogy) (hardcover : acid-free paper) $28

ISBN 9780345504982; 9780345534897; 0345504984

LC 2012028427

"In this second book of his epic vampire trilogy (after The Passage), Cronin once again deposits readers on the front lines of a human-made apocalypse. On the North American continent, a failed government experiment has turned most of humanity into lethal, vampirelike creatures called virals and destroyed the world as we know it. Cronin's story follows the human survivors, moving smoothly between "Year Zero," when the outbreak began, and a period 97 years later, when the remaining pockets of humanity seek not only to survive but also to eradicate the viral plague and defeat a despotic regime that has risen to power." (Library Journal)

Cross, Amanda

The **collected** stories of Amanda Cross. Ballantine Bks. 1997 184p

ISBN 0-345-40817-9

LC 96-42006

"Kate Fansler, a university professor normally involved with things academic, also dabbles in solving mysteries. In these short stories, she deals with cases ranging from missing persons to murder. Cross presents a complex jumble of seemingly enigmatic clues that Kate proceeds to study and resolve into a simple answer based on logic and deduction. The author camouflages the clues, facts, and answers by placing them in total view during the entire story." SLJ

Cross, Janine

Touched by venom; Janine Cross. ROC 2005 353p o.p.

ISBN 0451460480

LC 2005014310

This book, "set in Malacar, a land with a repressive patriarchal society that both worships and enslaves dragons, . . . introduces headstrong nine-year-old Zarq Darquel, who lives a harsh but not completely unpleasant life as a member of the pottery clan on a dragon estate. When destitution forces her father to sell Waisi, Zarq's beautiful older sister, into sexual slavery, her mother, Kavarria, who belongs to the disdained Djimbi race, tries to save Waisi at all costs, but more tragedy follows.

Zarq, her life governed by her mother's madness and obsession, eventually winds up as a sexually mutilated nun caring for retired bull dragons." (Publishers Weekly)

Followed by: Shadowed by Wings (2006)

Cross, Neil

Luther; the calling. Simon & Schuster 2012 326 p.

ISBN 1451673094; 9781451673098

LC 2012462320

This novel by Neil Cross is "the first in a series . . . featuring DCI John Luther . . . [and] takes us into Luther's past and into his mind. It is the story of the case that tore his personal and professional relationships apart and propelled him over the precipice. Beyond fury, beyond vengeance. All the way to murder." (Publisher's note)

Crouch, Blake

Dark matter; A Novel. by Blake Crouch. Crown Publishers 2016 352 p. (hardcover) $26.99

ISBN 1101904224; 9781101904220

LC 2015040107

In this thriller novel, by Blake Crouch, "in this world he's woken up to, Jason's life is not the one he knows. His wife is not his wife. His son was never born. And Jason is not an ordinary college physics professor, but a celebrated genius who has achieved something remarkable. Something impossible. Is it this world or the other that's the dream? . . . The answers lie in a journey more wondrous and horrifying than anything he could've imagined." (Publisher's note)

"Suspenseful, frightening, and sometimes poignant--provided the reader has a generously willing suspension of disbelief." Kirkus

Crowley, John

Four freedoms. William Morrow 2009 389p $25.99

ISBN 978-0-06-123150-6; 0-06-123150-9

LC 2008-46338

"Although nominally about life at an American aircraft factory during World War II, Crowley's complex and subtle novel is much grander. He explores the minds and hearts of people compelled by history to radically change their lives. Unaccountably optimistic Prosper Olander, orphaned as a child and crippled by a failed surgery, discovers that even he can find important work at a distant aircraft company in rural Oklahoma. Connie Wrobleski, frightened of nearly everything except her infant son, also travels to Oklahoma to reunite with her domineering husband, only to see him desert his family by enlisting. Prosper, Connie, and half a dozen other characters are developed in intricate detail and used as lenses on the massive relocation, dislocation, and societal change caused by the war." Booklist

Crowley, John

★ **Lord** Byron's novel; the evening land. William Morrow 2005 465p $25.95

ISBN 0-06-055658-7

LC 2004-63575

"Crowley's real achievement in Lord Byron's Novel is not a convincing imitation of Byron—not even Byron, who was pudgy and pale and walked with a limp, could always pull that off. More persuasive by far is the suffocating world of encryption and code, coincidence and conspiracy, paranoia and parapsychology that Crowley summons from his 19th-century documents and 21st-century decoders." N Y Times Book Rev

Crumley, James

Bordersnakes. Mysterious Press 1996 320p

ISBN 0-89296-573-8

LC 96-34405

"The plot, such as it is, takes the pair from one violent encounter to the next, each with its separate cast of sublimely weird characters. . . . Mr. Crumley saves his fiercest prose for El Paso, where the villains of the piece have their day; but the sheer originality of his style tears up every pit stop on this hellishly funny adventure." NY Times Book Rev

Crumley, James

The **final** country. Mysterious Press 2001 310p

ISBN 0-89296-666-1

LC 2001-30640

"Plot twists and details seem loose and easy, yet every thread is sewn tight as a hardball. This is a brilliant achievement, with Crumley returned to his full powers, seeming to say with each assured sentence, Yeah, I'm an old dog, but I still wag the baddest bone." Publ Wkly

Crumley, James

The **last** good kiss; a novel. Random House 1978 259p

ISBN 0-394-41946-4

LC 77-90286

"C. W. Sughrue is hired to trace the missing and drunken writer Abraham Trahearne by the man's divorced first wife, Catherine. Catherine Trahearne is sexy, elegant, and ice-cold. She lives with Trahearne's ancient mother, Edna, across the creek from the house where Trahearne lives with Melinda, his second wife. The plot is episodic and keeps one bleary eye loosely focused on Trahearne's dysfunctional extended family." Murphy. Ency of Murder and Mystery

Crumley, James

★ The **wrong** case; a novel. Random House 1975 272p

ISBN 0-394-49198-3

LC 74-29598

Milton "Milo" Milodragovitch is a private detective in Meriwether, Montana. This case involves the suicide of a homosexual heroin pusher

This is "an exceptionally good example of the genre. Properly deferring to hallowed conventions, Crumley writes about damaged people seen through a haze of jaded romanticism, but he asserts his own tone of voice . . . . Crumley is a vivid writer. He makes Milo much more vulnerable, more involved in this sordid case than Hammett or Chandler would have done." Newsweek

Crummey, Michael

Galore; a novel. Other Press 2011 338p pa $15.95

ISBN 978-1-59051-434-4; 1-59051-434-3

LC 2010-40763

First published 2009 in Canada

Crummey "has created an unforgettable place of the imagination. Paradise Deep belongs on the same literary map as Faulkner's Yoknapatawpha and Garcia Marquez's Macondo." Boston Globe

Crummey, Michael

Sweetland; a novel. Michael Crummey. W W Norton & Co Inc 2015 336 p. $24.95

ISBN 0871407906; 9780871407900

LC 2014031404

This novel, by Michael Crummey, follows "an endangered Newfoundland community and the struggles of one man determined to resist its extinction. . . . Moses Sweetland, whose ancestors founded the village, is the only one to refuse [a government resettlement offer]. As he watches his neighbors abandon the island, he recalls the town's rugged history and its eccentric cast of characters." (Publisher's note)

The "small cast of accompanying characters is well and wittily delineated, and Crummey's characteristic switching between past and present is done craftily." Booklist

Cruse, Howard

The **complete** Wendel; by Howard Cruse. Universe Pub. 2011 288 p. ill.

ISBN 0789322161; 9780789322166

LC 2010934608

This book is a compilation of Howard Cruse's comic strip "Wendel," which was published in the newspaper "The Advocate" in the 1980s. "Cruse's feature was an episodic chronicle of life as experienced by young Wendel Trupstock, his lover Ollie and their friends, who collectively represented a particular slice of the American LGBT demographic during a particularly stressful period in recent history, when the afterglow of gay liberation collided with the AIDS epidemic and the ascendancy of Moral Majority-fueled homophobia. Simultaneously a mirror of the days' new events and a comedic portrayal of everyday queer life, drawing Wendel required . . . what the cartoonist calls an "elasticity of tone," balancing lightheartedness with pain, erotic mischief with mundane follies." (Kirkus)

Cumming, Charles, 1971-

A **divided** spy; Charles Cumming. St. Martin's Press 2017 358 p. (Thomas Kell novels) (hardback) $26.99

ISBN 9781250021045; 9781250021038

LC 2016037568

In this book, by Charles Cumming, "Thomas Kell thought he was done with spying. A former MI6 officer, he devoted his life to the Service, but it has left him with nothing but grief and a simmering anger against the Kremlin. Then Kell is offered an unexpected chance at revenge. Taking the law into his own hands, he embarks on a mission to recruit a top Russian spy who is in possession of a terrifying secret." (Publisher's note)

"Cumming not only tells a moving human story here, he also constructs an airtight espionage plot full of unanticipated twists and leading up to a perfectly orchestrated finale." Booklist

Cumming, Charles, 1971-

★ The **Trinity** Six. St. Martin's Press 2011 356p

ISBN 0-312-67529-1; 978-0-312-67529-5

LC 2010-40197

This novel imagines a sixth man, Sam Gaddis, among the Cambridge spies "Kim Philby, John Cairncross, Guy Burgess, Donald Maclean and Anthony Blunt." (N Y Times Book Rev)

"Over a wine-soaked dinner with his friend Charlotte, Sam Gaddis, university professor and author of several widely unread books on Soviet history, learns a tantalizing piece of information: that the Cambridge Five, a real-life KGB cell that operated in 1930s England, was actually six spies strong, and Charlotte has access to someone who claims to be privy to the sixth spy's memoirs. Gaddis, who is in desperate need of quick cash, happily accepts his friend's offer to collaborate on a book, but when she dies of a heart attack that night, it is up to Gaddis to find her contact—an elderly man named Thomas Neame—and complete the book on his own. Gaddis doesn't realize that Charlotte was actually murdered by an agent of the FSB (the post-Soviet successor to the KBG) because of her interest in the truth about the Cambridge Five. . . . Taut, atmospheric and immersive—an instant classic." Kirkus

Cunningham, Michael

By nightfall. Farrar, Straus and Giroux 2010 238p $25

ISBN 978-0-374-29908-8; 0-374-29908-0

LC 2010-12614

"Cunningham is a cool observer of the New York art scene, and he has fun with the contrasts between the makers of art, toiling away in obscurity, and the buyers cocooned in expensive suburbs. His descriptions of the objects themselves are also worth the price of the book. . . . [This] is a good book, even a challenging one. But for a story about the power of passion to upend lives, it lacks juiciness and messiness. Cunningham's prose is so exact and so careful that it actually takes away from the story, putting an arid, intellectual distance between Peter and the reader. The result: Instead of a novel overflowing with flesh and sweat, rage and craziness, Cunningham has given us a well-considered treatise." Cleveland Plain Dealer

Cunningham, Michael

Flesh and blood. Farrar, Straus & Giroux 1995 465p

ISBN 0-374-18113-6

LC 94-24628

"Fairly brief episodes, often occuring years apart, recount key moments in the establishment, disintegration, and reconfiguration of the family. Thoroughly realized action, vivid character delineation, and the splendid control of language guarantee both the unity and powerful impact of this successful novel." Libr J

Cunningham, Michael

★ The **hours**. Farrar, Straus & Giroux 1998 229p $23

ISBN 0-374-17289-7

LC 98-34188

"After a brief prologue, the stories alternate in an intricate sequence, rather like a rhyme scheme. . . . The whole book does sound a little fussy in description, an exercise in echoes, but it doesn't read that way." N Y Times Book Rev

Cunningham, Michael, 1952-

The **snow** queen; Michael Cunningham. 1st ed Farrar, Straus & Giroux 2014 272 p. hc $26

ISBN 9780374266325; 0374266328

LC 2013038712

This book follows "Barrett Meeks, a poetically minded man in his late thirties who . . . shares a Brooklyn apartment with Tyler, his older musician-bartender brother, and Beth, Tyler's great love. . . . Beth is undergoing full-throttle treatment for cancer. Tyler is struggling to write the perfect love song for their wedding, and breaking [his] promise not to do drugs. Barrett . . . remains in an altered state after seeing a . . . 'celestial light' over dark and snowy Central Park." (Booklist)

"In concise yet descriptive language, Cunningham weaves the secret of transcendence through the mundane occurrences of everyday life." LJ

Cunningham, Michael

Specimen days. Farrar, Straus and Giroux 2005 308p $25

ISBN 0-374-29962-5

LC 2005-40518

"As much as Cunningham's novel is haunted by the ghost of Whitman's prophecies, it is profoundly informed by the events of September 11, 2001. . . . Cunningham's brilliantly imagined dystopian future represents the final betrayal of Walt Whitman's joyously democratic America." New Leader

Currie, Ron

Everything matters! [by] Ron Currie, Jr. Viking 2009 305p $25.95

ISBN 978-0-670-02092-8; 0-670-02092-3

LC 2008-46686

"Junior Thibodeau of Waterville, ME—the fourth-smartest person in human history—is born with the certain knowledge that an asteroid will destroy Earth in 36 years. In that case, what is the point of living? In this radical reimagining of Frank Capra's It's a Wonderful Life, Junior tells his own story, while in alternating chapters his wildly dysfunctional family and friends provide commentary." Libr J

Currie, Ron

Flimsy little plastic miracles; a true story. Ron Currie, Jr. Viking 2013 352 p. $26.95

ISBN 0670025348; 9780670025343

LC 2012028931

In this book by Ron Currie Jr., his "protagonist, a blend of fact and fiction from his own life, is so distraught by his father's death, a book lost to fire, and an unreciprocated love that he hides out on a Caribbean island to write a new book about the mess. Then he fakes his own death, which brings him fame, fortune, and big trouble." (Library Journal)

Cusk, Rachel

★ The **Bradshaw** variations. Farrar, Straus and Giroux 2010 234p $25

ISBN 978-0-374-10081-0

LC 2009-31888

First published 2009 in the United Kingdom

"By dropping a man into what Philip Larkin once called 'the hollows of afternoons', and chaining the father to the sink instead, Cusk flips the notion of the unfulfilled, bored mother on its head, and delivers a thought-provoking, rich and powerful study of family life." Scotland on Sunday

Cusk, Rachel

In the fold; a novel. Little, Brown and Co. 2005 262p $23.95

ISBN 0-571-22813-5

LC 2005-02589

This novel is the "cleverest portrait of narcissism since Charles Allen Gilbert's 1892 painting 'All Is Vanity.' Like that image, an optical illusion that can be seen either as a young woman at her mirror or as a human skull, 'In the Fold' is at once a shimmering vision of privilege and a wise meditation on disillusionment." N Y Times Book Rev

Cusk, Rachel

★ **Outline**; a novel. Rachel Cusk. Farrar Straus & Giroux 2015 256 p. (hardback) $26

ISBN 0374228345; 9780374228347

LC 2014016969

Scotiabank Giller Prize Shortlist (2015).

"Rachel Cusk's 'Outline' is a novel in ten conversations. . . . It follows a novelist teaching a course in creative writing during one oppressively hot summer in Athens. She leads her students in storytelling exercises. She meets other visiting writers for dinner and discourse. She goes swimming in the Ionian Sea with her neighbor from the plane. The people she encounters speak volubly about themselves: their fantasies, anxieties, pet theories, regrets, and longings." (Publisher's note)

"And as the profile of her main character grows more defined in relief, so does Cusk's underlying message about love, loss, and feminine identity in the modern world, evident not only in her story but also in its delivery." Booklist

Cusk, Rachel

Transit; Rachel Cusk. Farrar, Straus & Giroux 2017 272 p. (ebook) $60; (hardback) $26

ISBN 9780374714574; 0374278628; 9780374278625

LC 2016025619

Sequel to: Outline

In this novel, by Rachel Cusk, "in the wake of her family's collapse, a writer and her two young sons move to London. The process of this upheaval is the catalyst for a number of transitions—personal, moral, artistic, and practical—as she endeavors to construct a new reality for herself and her children. In the city, she is made to confront aspects of living that she has, until now, avoided, and to consider questions of vulnerability and power, death and renewal." (Publisher's note)

"Brilliantly written and structured, which is nothing new from this superlatively gifted writer, but with a chastened empathy for human weakness that was absent from her last two novels. Its return is most welcome." Kirkus

Cussler, Clive

Fire ice; a novel from the NUMA(r) files. {by} Clive Cussler, with Paul Kemprecos. Putnam 2002 434p

ISBN 0-399-14872-8

LC 2002-19050

Previous titles in the Kurt Austin series: Serpent (1999) and Blue Gold (2000), published in paperback

In this thriller Kurt Austin and "the men from NUMA (Native Underwater & Marine Agency) team up with former KGB spies to face down a Russian mobster with czarist aspirations and a zealot's hatred for the 'corruption and materialism' of the Western lifestyle. . . . Cussler is in top form here, working in a role for Old Ironsides and Czar Nicholas II's crown while throwing in enough derringdo and eco-lore to leave his fans breathless." Publ Wkly

Cussler, Clive

The **kingdom**; [by] Clive Cussler with Grant Blackwood. G. P. Putnam's Sons 2011 392p $27.95

ISBN 978-0-399-15742-4; 0-399-15742-5

LC 2011-09207

In this "adventure featuring treasure hunters extraordinaire Sam and Remi Fargo . . . , the couple get on the trail of a sacred object, the Theurang, 'said to have been a life-sized statue of a manlike creature or . . . the skeleton of the creature itself.' Or maybe it's a chest holding the creature's bones. Reclusive wealthy entrepreneur Charles King (aka 'King Charlie') is also searching for this artifact. King's girlfriend, Zhilan Hsu, and their grown children, Russell and Marjorie, will stop at nothing to fulfill King's deadly demands. . . . Fresh prose, a smart and amusing husband-and-wife team, interesting history and science, and a wildly imaginative plot all add up to a good time for Cussler's many fans as well as series newcomers." Publ Wkly

Cussler, Clive

Lost city; a novel from the NUMA files. [by] Clive Cussler with Paul Kemprecos. Putnam 2004 420p $26.95

ISBN 0-399-15177-X

LC 2004-50556

"Kidnappings, hair's breadth escapes, fierce battles, strange science, beautiful women and plenty of action add up to vintage Cussler." Publ Wkly

Cussler, Clive, 1931-

The **Mayan** secrets; Clive Cussler and Thomas Perry. G. P. Putnam's Sons 2013 384 p. (A Fargo adventure) $28.95

ISBN 0399162496; 9780399162497

LC 2013015387

This is Clive Cussler's fifth Fargo novel. Here, while bringing medical supplies to an isolated Mexican village, Sam and Remi Fargo "stumble across a hidden Mayan tomb that contains a tremendous find: an extremely rare 486-year-old codex." They take it "home to La Jolla, Calif., where Mayan expert David Caine fills them in on the value of their find." However, wealthy amateur archeologist Sarah Allersby wants it and "first tries to buy it, then later tries to steal it." (Publishers Weekly)

Cussler, Clive

White death; a novel from the NUMA files. {by} Clive Cussler with Paul Kemprecos. Putnam 2003 419p $26.95

ISBN 0-399-15041-2

LC 2003-46501

This thriller "chronicles the exploits of Kurt Austin, leader and hero of NUMA's Special Assignment Team. The plot involves Austin and his partner Zavala, who are investigating a feud between a radical environmentalist group and a Danish cruiser. Austin and Zavala must come to the rescue of men trapped on the ship. They find that a giant multinational corporation is seeking to kill anyone who attempts to stop its efforts to control the seas." Booklist

Cutter, Kimberly

The **maid**. Houghton Mifflin Harcourt 2011 287p

ISBN 9780547427522; 978-0-547-42752-2

LC 2011-09146

This book tells "the story of Joan of Arc. . . . After an unremarkable childhood as the youngest of five children in rural France, we see the . . . moment in her adolescence when she first hears heavenly voices. Three saints impart to Joan the sacred mission of both raising an army against England and crowning the dauphin king of France in Reims. [Author Kimberly] Cutter builds a . . . case for how a 15th-century peasant girl from Domrémy could embolden an army to reclaim their land from the English in the name of God. She . . . describes Jehanne's transformation from an innocent, curious child into a confident, driven young woman who conquers souls, brings thousands to her support, and convinces a wary would-be king that she can make him realize his destiny." (Publishers Weekly)

"Was Joan of Arc a messenger from God, a lunatic, or just a petulant kid? She's a little of each in this beautifully written novel, which follows Jehanne from her girlhood to the Hundred Years' War — during which, as a teenager, she insisted that God had commanded her to lead the French army — to her death at 19, burned at the stake in the Rouen marketplace. Cutter presents Jehanne as part mystic, but also part mascot used by France to rally support from the peasants. In The Maid's best scenes, she couldn't be more human." Entertainment Wkly

Czepiel, Kathy Leonard

A **violet** season; A novel. Kathy Leonard Czepiel. 1st Simon & Schuster pbk. ed. Simon & Schuster Paperbacks 2012 254, [10] p.p (trade paperback) $15.00

ISBN 1451655061; 9781451655063; 9781451655087

LC 2011031733

This book "traces a struggling rural family at the turn of the 20th century." Frank Fletcher, in order to pay his debts and regain his share in the Fletcher family's profitable violet farm, brings his daughter Alice to work as housekeeper at a brothel in New York City, though he "tells his wife that Alice is working in a factory. . . . By the time Ida finally learns where Alice is, she has been raped and fallen into a serious depression." (Publishers Weekly)

Czerneda, Julie E.

A **Turn** of Light; Julie E. Czerneda. Penguin Group USA 2013 896 p. $20

ISBN 0756407079; 9780756407070

In this fantasy novel, Julie E. Czerneda introduces the world of Marrowdell "and a beautiful but restless heroine who holds the key to Marrowdell's security. Although she longs to travel beyond the well-trod byways of her village, Jenn Nalynn, the miller's daughter, is moored to Marrowdell by the curse of her birth. Turn-born, she unwittingly provides the balance between Marrodell and the darkly feral Verge." These two worlds "can only coexist if Jenn . . . remains firmly rooted in place." (Booklist)

D

D'Abo, Christine

30 Days; by Christine d'Abo. Kensington Pub Corp 2015 320 p. $9.95

ISBN 1617739545; 9781617739545

LC 2015297366

In this book, by Christine d'Abo, "[s]ome people wait their whole lives to find their soul mate, but not Alyssa Barrow. She met Rob at nineteen, and they were set to live happily ever after—until he became ill. In his final days, Rob urged his beautiful, young wife not to abandon happiness—or pleasure. He even left her a special gift, a sexy game plan to help her move on: Thirty cards with instructions for thirty days of passion." (Publisher's note)

"The premise could have become awkward or maudlin in less skilled hands, but D'Abo makes it feel charming and plausible. Well-developed and engaging characters, major and minor, lead to conflicts that feel both realistic and fresh, and difficult subjects are handled with empathy and gentle humor. Romance fans will delight in this sweet and spicy expedition." Pub Wkly

D'Ambrosio, Charles

The **dead** fish museum. Knopf 2006 236p $22

ISBN 1-4000-4286-0

LC 2005-44672

"A gemlike set of eight stories in which wayward, self-deceiving characters set out to make order of their customary chaos–and realize they are more likely to find unhappy company than catharsis." Publ Wkly

D'Erasmo, Stacey

The **Sky** Below. Houghton Mifflin 2009 320p $24

ISBN 0-618-43925-0; 978-0-618-43925-6

LC 2008-25673

"At thirty-seven, Gabriel Collins works halfheartedly as an obituary writer at a fading newspaper in lower Manhattan. . . . [He is] an adult who trades in petty crimes. His wealthy, older boyfriend is indulgent of him—to a point. But after a brush with his own mortality, Gabriel must flee to Mexico in order to put himself back together." (Publisher's note)

This "novel tells the story of a misanthropic obituary writer for a dying New York newspaper, who views his life through a series of memory boxes modelled on the assemblage art of Joseph Cornell. 'I assiduously collected interesting junk, filling my pockets with pebbles and wire and old nails: the stuff of transformation,' he says. He narrates the drudgery of the daily grind and scrutinizes his dysfunctional, fatherless childhood, during which he rebelled against his mother by dealing drugs and engaging in sex with men for money. Now nearing forty and spiritually broken, he is given a diagnosis of cancer and travels to a commune in Mexico, where he reluctantly receives the help of a clairvoyant eight-year-old girl. Although the book strays into portentous magic realism, its lyrical prose and telling detail create a powerful atmosphere." New Yorker

D'Souza, Tony

The **Konkans**. Harcourt 2008 320p $25

ISBN 978-0-15-101519-1; 0-15-101519-8

LC 2007-15303

This is "more than an ethnographic study—D'Souza stays character-focused throughout the novel, gently mixing irony and fatalism with a warm affection for humans and the stupid things they do." Washington City Paper

D'Souza, Tony

Mule; a novel of moving weight. Mariner Books 2011 292p pa $14.95

ISBN 978-0-547-57671-8; 0-547-576714

LC 2011-16050

"After the recession and an unexpected baby, James, an out-of-work journalist, agrees to transport a stash of prime-grade weed from California to Florida as a temporary money fix. But when he gets a taste of the fast cash, he becomes addicted to the thrill of the operation, continuing long after money ceases to be a necessity. In Mule, an acutely detailed page-turner, D'Souza depicts the moral free fall of a decent — albeit weak-willed — man so believably, readers may start buying James' brand of hazy moral justification." Entertainment Wkly

D'Souza, Tony

Whiteman. Harcourt 2006 279p $22

ISBN 0-15-101145-1

LC 2005-25459

"One significant virtue of D'Souza's storytelling rests in his ability to present Jack's experiences of African life with a vividness that reveals the continent's allure without sentimentalizing its exoticism. . . . Much of the drama that unfolds in the 12 loosely chronological parts of 'Whiteman' (each a story that could stand on its own) rests in the gentle progression that ferries Jack away from a form of blindness to a new kind of sight." N Y Times Book Rev

Dabbagh, Selma

Out of It. St Martins Pr 2013 $15.00

ISBN 1608198766; 9781608198764; 9789992178744; 9992178744

This novel by Selma Dabbagh "follows the lives of Rashid and Iman as they try to forge paths for themselves in the midst of occupation, religious fundamentalism and the divisions between Palestinian factions. It tells of family secrets, unlikely love stories and unburied tragedies . . . of the modern Arab world." (Author's note)

Dahl, Arne

Bad Blood; by Arne Dahl ; translated by Rachel Willson-Broyles. Pantheon Books 2013 341 p. (hardcover) $25.95

ISBN 0375425365; 9780375425363

LC 2012046772

In this novel by Arne Dahl "the Intercrime team is assigned the task of tracking down an American serial killer on the loose in Sweden. Detectives Paul Hjelm and Kerstin Holm of Intercrime's A-Unit take over the investigation. They learn that the method of torture used . . . a highly specialized means of extracting information secretly developed during the Vietnam War. Hjelm and Holm fly to New York, hoping to discover both the killer's identity and the source of his interest in Sweden." (Publisher's note)

Dahl, Arne

Misterioso; translated from the Swedish by Tiina Nunally. Pantheon Books 2011 339p $25.95

ISBN 978-0-375-42535-6

LC 2010-32837

Original Swedish edition, 1999

"It's 1997, and a serial killer is methodically killing Sweden's wealthiest businessmen while listening to a tape of Thelonious Monk's haunting classic Misterioso. The National Police, still traumatized by the unsolved assassination of Prime Minister Olaf Palme a decade before, decide to create a special unit to hunt down the killer. Paul Hjelm, a detective in Stockholm's southern suburbs, is selected as one of the unit's six seemingly mismatched members. . . . [The author] sets a full plate for himself in the first of a series about Hjelm and his colleagues. He describes a once comfortable country fragmented by racial malaise; East European Mafias; a financial collapse brought on by greedy, reckless bankers and government deregulation; postindustrial capitalism; and a gnawing fear that Sweden has lost its way." Booklist

Dahl, Julia

Conviction; Julia Dahl. Minotaur Books 2017 312 p. (Rebekah Roberts) (hardcover) $25.99

ISBN 1250083699; 9781250083692; 9781250083715

LC 2016047069

In this novel, by Julia Dahl, "a year after riots exploded between black and Jewish neighbors in Crown Heights, a black family is brutally murdered in their Brooklyn home. A teenager is quickly convicted. . . . Twenty-two years later, journalist Rebekah Roberts gets a letter: I didn't do it. . . . Rebekah starts to dig . . . and as she gets closer to the truth of that night, Rebekah finds herself in the path of a killer with two decades of secrets to protect." (Publisher's note)

"Dahl excels at revealing the inner workings of enigmatic subcultures while maintaining peak suspense." Pub Wkly

Dahl, Roald

Collected stories; edited and introduced by Jeremy Treglown. Everyman's Library/Alfred A. Knopf 2006 xxxvii, 850p $30

ISBN 978-0-307-26490-9; 0-307-26490-4

First published 1991 in the United Kingdom with title: The collected stories of Raold Dahl. The introduction is new to this volume

"With the inventive power of a Thomas Edison and the imagination of a Lewis Carroll . . . Roald Dahl is a wizard of comedy and the grotesque, an artist with a marvelously topsy-turvy sense of the ridiculous in life." Cleveland Plain Dealer

Dai Sijie

Once on a moonless night; translated from the French by Adriana Hunter. Alfred A. Knopf 2008 277p $24.95

ISBN 978-0-307-27158-7

LC 2008-41089

Original French edition, 2007

"This strange and beautiful novel ponders the nature of language, the history of China, filial and romantic love, and intellectual passion. . . . Though it plays with ideas, the novel is most impressive as a stream of striking images and vignettes." N Y Times Book Rev

Daisley, Stephen

Coming rain; Stephen Daisley. Text Publishing 2016 268 p. (pbk.) $15.95

ISBN 1922182028; 9781922182029; 9781925095029

LC 2014472767

In this book, by Stephen Daisley, "Lew McLeod has been travelling and working with Painter Hayes since he was a boy. Shearing, charcoal burning—whatever comes. Painter made him his first pair of shoes. It's a hard and uncertain life, but it's the only one he knows. But Lew's a grown man now. And with this latest job, shearing for John Drysdale and his daughter Clara, everything will change." (Publisher's note)

Dallas, Sandra

The **Persian** Pickle Club. St. Martin's Press 1995 196p

ISBN 0-312-13586-6

LC 95-31032

This is a "simple but endearing story that depicts small-town eccentricities with affection and adds dazzle with some latebreaking surprises. Dallas hits all the right notes, combining an authentic look at the social fabric of Depression-era life with a homespun suspense story." Publ Wkly

Dallas, Sandra

Tallgrass. St. Martin's Press 2007 305p $23.95

ISBN 978-0-312-36019-1; 0-312-36019-3

LC 2006-51271

"Rennie Stroud looks back to 1942, when she was 13, to tell a powerful coming-of-age story. That year, the U.S. government opened a Japanese internment camp outside Ellis, CO, less than a mile from where Rennie and her family farmed sugar beets. Rennie observes the prejudice of some of the townspeople as well as her parents' strong moral code and their entanglement in the emotions of the time. Her father, Loyal, not only shows open support for the Japanese, whom he views as Americans, but offers to hire them to work on the farm. When a young girl is murdered, suspicion naturally turns to the camp, and the town is divided by fear. Dallas's strong, provocative novel is a moving examination of prejudice and fear that addresses issues of community discord, abuse, and rape." Libr J

Dalton, John

The **inverted** forest; a novel. Scribner 2011 323p

ISBN 1-4165-9602-X; 978-1-4165-9602-8

LC 2011-05574

"A story set at a summer camp can go a number of different ways. The Inverted Forest — a gripping, tender, and at times disturbing tale — takes the road less traveled. It's the summer of 1996, and a small group of inexperienced counselors find themselves unprepared to care for more than 100 severely developmentally disabled adult campers from a state facility. A shocking act of violence will affect the young staff for years to come, and Dalton nimbly delves into his characters' perspectives, uncovering past secrets and future dreams (and eventual disappointments). While some of what's described is anything but pleasant, reading it certainly is." Entertainment Wkly

Daly, Paula

Just What Kind of Mother Are You? Grove Press 2013 256 p. $24

ISBN 0802121624; 9780802121622

This book "revolves around two mothers of teenage girls. Perpetually stretched by obligations to family and work, Lisa Kallisto knows she's partly to blame when Lucinda, the daughter of her friend Kate Riverty, is abducted. . . . As Det. Constable Joanne Aspinall compares the disappearance to a series of similar unsolved crimes, Lisa battles her self-doubt and tries to save the enviably perfect Kate from crumbling." (Publishers Weekly)

★ **Dangerous** women; George R.R. Martin and Gardner Dozois, ed. Tor Books 2013 784 p. (hardback) $32.50

ISBN 076533206X; 9780765332066

LC 2013018473

This book, edited by George R. R. Martin and Gardner Dozois, presents "21 stories . . . including a new "Outlander" story by Diana Gabaldon, a tale of Harry Dresden's world by Jim Butcher, a story from Lev Grossman set in the world of The Magicians, and a 35,000-word novella by George R. R. Martin about the Dance of the Dragons, the vast civil war that tore Westeros apart nearly two centuries before the events of A Game of Thrones." (Publisher's note)

Daniel, Susanna

Stiltsville; a novel. HarperCollins 2010 310p $24.99

ISBN 978-0-06-196307-0

This is a "love story but not one that should be mistaken for a romance. This lyrically written work, which follows the ebb and flow of a long marriage, is just intimate enough to draw the reader close. It isn't until well into the novel that you realize just how much you've come to care about author Susana Daniel's narrator and her story." Denver Post

Danielewski, Mark Z.

The **familiar**; one rainy day in May. Mark Z. Danielewski. Pantheon Books 2015 880 p. illustrations (some color) (softcover : acid-free paper) $25

ISBN 0375714944; 9780375714948

LC 2014028320

This book, by Mark Z. Danielewski, "ranges from Mexico to Southeast Asia, from Venice, Italy, to Venice, California, with nine lives hanging in the balance, each called upon to make a terrifying choice. . . . At the very heart, though, is a twelve-year-old girl named Xanther who one rainy day in May sets out with her father to get a dog, only to end up trying to save a creature as fragile as it is dangerous." (Publisher's note)

"Strangely, it works, though not without studied effort on the reader's part. And as for all the loose ends? No worries--there are 26 volumes to come in which to tie them up." Kirkus

The familiar. Volume 2, Into the forest

The familiar. Volume 3, Honeysuckle & pain

The familiar. Volume 4, Hades

The familiar. Volume 5, Redwood

Danielewski, Mark Z.

★ **House** of leaves. Pantheon Bks. 2000 720p ill. pa $21; $50

ISBN 9780375703768; 9780375420528

LC 99-36024

In this horror novel by Mark Z. Danielewski, "a young family that moves into a small home on Ash Tree Lane where they discover something is terribly wrong: their house is bigger on the inside than it is on the outside. Of course, neither Pulitzer Prize-winning photojournalist Will Navidson nor his companion Karen Green was prepared to face the consequences of that . . . until the day their two little children wandered off and their voices eerily began to return another story." (Publisher's note)

"This work is a kaleidoscopically layered and deconstructed H. P. Lovecraft-style horror story. It hums and resonates with wonder, dread, and insight." Booklist

Includes bibliographical references and index.

Danielewski, Mark Z.

Only revolutions. Random House 2006 384p $26

ISBN 0-375-42176-9; 0-385-61138-2

LC 2006-40996

National Book Award Finalist: Fiction (2006)

This novel "consists of the dual free-verse narratives of 16-year-old Hailey and Sam, which are meant to be read in tandem; eight pages of Hailey's story are to be read first, then the volume needs to be flipped upside down and read in reverse for Sam's story, until the two narratives meet in the middle. With a Jack Kerouac-like reverence for the open road and a Dr. Seuss-like feel for wordplay, Danielewski tells an epic love story as the two teens travel across time, from the Civil War to the year 2063, in vehicles ranging from a Model T to a Mustang. Though outside forces threaten to undermine them, the two remain forever 16 and madly in love. . . . This creative paean to the velocity of young lovers and the vibrancy of American culture is sure to wow the experimental-fiction camp." Booklist

Danler, Stephanie

Sweetbitter; A Novel. Stephanie Danler. Alfred A. Knopf 2016 368 p. (hardback) $25

ISBN 1101875941; 9781101875940

LC 2015037137

"Tess comes to New York . . . alone, knowing no one, living in a rented room in Williamsburg. She manages to land a job as a 'backwaiter' at a celebrated downtown Manhattan restaurant. This begins the year we spend with Tess as she starts to navigate the chaotic, enchanting, punishing, and privileged life she has chosen, as well as the remorseless and luminous city around her." (Publisher's note)

"Throughout, Danler evokes Tess's voice--intimate, confiding, wonderstruck, depressed--with deft skill." Pub Wkly

Danticat, Edwidge, 1969-

Claire of the sea light; Edwidge Danticat. Alfred A. Knopf 2013 256 p. (hardback) $25.95

ISBN 030727179X; 9780307271792

LC 2012043876

Carnegie Medal: Shortlist (2014)

In this novel, "Claire Limyè Lanmè ('Claire of the Sea Light'), whose mother died in childbirth and whose fisherman father has made the wrenching decision to give her a better life by relinquishing her, goes missing just before her seventh birthday. As the entire community searches for her, secrets emerge that clarify our relationships with one another and with the natural world, even as we see the beauty and heartbreak of Haiti." (Library Journal)

"In interlocking stories moving back and forth in time, Danticat weaves a beautifully rendered portrait of longing in the small fishing town of Ville Rose in Haiti." Booklist

Danticat, Edwidge

The **dew** breaker. Knopf 2004 244p $22

ISBN 1-400-04114-7

"Beautifully written fiction about the real-life horror that is Haiti. Seamlessly blending the personal and political, it deals with what happens to a country and its people when mothers and fathers disappear for their political transgressions." USA Today

Danticat, Edwidge

The **farming** of bones; a novel. Soho Press 1998 312p $23

ISBN 1-56947-126-6

LC 98-3655

"It's a testament to Danticat's skill that Amabelle's musical, sorrowing voice never falters, even during her stark descriptions of the bloodbath." New Yorker

Danticat, Edwidge

Krik? Krak! Soho Press 1995 224p

ISBN 1-56947-025-1

LC 94-41999

The author "touches upon life both in Haiti and in New York's Haitian community, though we spend most of our time in Port-au-Prince and the country town of Ville Rose. The best of these stories humanize, particularize, give poignancy to the lives of people we may have come to think of as faceless emblems of misery, poverty and brutality." N Y Times Book Rev

Daoud, Kamel

The **Meursault** investigation; Kamel Daoud; translated by John Cullen. Other Press 2015 160 p. (paperback) $14.95

ISBN 1590517512; 9781590517512

LC 2015010736

This novel, by Kamel Daoud, translated by John Cullen, follows "the brother of 'the Arab' killed by the infamous Meursault, the antihero of [Albert] Camus's classic novel ['The Stranger']. Seventy years after that event, Harun, who has lived since childhood in the shadow of his sibling's memory, refuses to let him remain anonymous: he gives his brother a story and a name--Musa--and describes the events that led to Musa's casual murder on a dazzlingly sunny beach." (Publisher's note)

"An eye-opening, humbling read, splendid whether or not you know and love the original." LJ

Dare, Tessa

Any Duchess Will Do; Tessa Bare. HarperCollins Publishers 2013 384 p. (paperback) $5.99

ISBN 0062240129; 9780062240125

This is Tessa Dare's fourth Spindle Cove romance novel. Here, "Griffin York, the marriage-shy eighth Duke of Halford, is dragged to the town by his mother, who orders him to pick a bride. He brashly selects Pauline Simms, a proud tavern serving girl. Griff's mother declares she can turn Pauline into duchess material; Griff retorts that if she fails, he'll be off the hook. He offers Pauline £1,000 to go to London and fail the training," but things become complicated when attraction arises. (Publishers Weekly)

Dare, Tessa

Do you want to start a scandal; Tessa Dare. HarperCollins 2016 384 p. (Avon romance) (ebook) $7.99; $7.99

ISBN 9780062349057; 006234904X; 9780062349040

LC 2016035310

In this book in the Castles Ever After series, by Tessa Dare, "on the night of the Parkhurst ball, someone had a scandalous tryst in the library. . . . All Charlotte Highwood knows is this: it wasn't her. But rumors to the contrary are buzzing. Unless she can discover the lovers' true identity, she'll be forced to marry Piers Brandon, Lord Granville--the coldest, most arrogantly handsome gentleman she's ever had the misfortune to embrace." (Publisher's Note)

"The irresistibly provocative, classy love scenes set the bar high for other historical romance novels." Pub Wkly

Dare, Tessa

A **night** to surrender. Avon 2011 400 p.

ISBN 9780062049834

In this book, "[Tessa] Dare . . . pairs up an educated spinster and a wounded hero in this . . . the first in the 'Spindle Cove series.' Lt. Col. Victor "Bram" Bramwell is traveling with fellow soldiers when a flock of sheep stalls them. They set explosives to scatter the sheep, but Susanna Finch, a woman living nearby, gets too close. Fortunately, Bram knocks her out of harm's way just in time. The instant attraction between Susanna and Bram is complicated by Bram's having just inherited a title, a crumbling castle, and the right to summon a militia. The last will be nearly impossible in the peaceful woman-dominated community of Spindle Cove, where few are thrilled by the military newcomers." (Publishers Wkly)

Dare, Tessa

★ **Romancing** the duke; by Tessa Dare. HarperCollins 2014 384 p. (Castles ever after) $7.99

ISBN 0062240196; 9780062240194

In this book, by Tessa Dare, "Isolde Ophelia Goodnight grew up on tales of brave knights and fair maidens. She never doubted romance would be in her future, too. The storybooks offered endless possibilities. And as she grew older, Izzy crossed them off. One by one by one. . . . Now Izzy's given up yearning for romance. She'll settle for a roof over her head. What fairy tales are left over for an impoverished twenty-six year-old woman who's never even been kissed? This one." (Publisher's note)

"Humor, whimsy, and joy overflow as a most unlikely pair find their happy ending in this fairy tale-come-to-life." LJ

Dare, Tessa

Say Yes to the Marquess; Tessa Dare. HarperCollins 2014 384 p. $7.99

ISBN 006224020X; 9780062240200

In this romance novel, by Tessa Dare, part of the "Castles Ever After" series, "Clio Whitmore is thrilled when her surprise inheritance of Twill Castle means she no longer needs to marry for security and can call off her upcoming wedding. Now all she needs is for her fiancé's reprobate, prizefighting brother to sign the papers to dissolve the betrothal in the Marquess's continuing absence. . . . Naturally, it doesn't work out that way." (Library Journal)

"With the latest sterling addition to her Castles Ever After series, RITA award-winning Dare (Romancing the Duke, 2014) continues to charm and captivate readers with her droll sense of humor, clever plotting, and engaging characters. This flawlessly written Regency historical is guaranteed to hit the sweet spot for most romance readers." Booklist

Dare, Tessa

A **week** to be wicked. Avon 2012 375 p.

ISBN 0062049879; 9780062049872

The plot of this romance novel "unites an unlikely pair as a wastrel viscount comes to the aid of a serious scientist. Minerva Highwood asks Colin Sandhurst, Lord Payne, to accompany her on a journey from spinster haven Spindle Cove to Edinburgh, where she plans on winning a prize for her presentation to the geological society. The journey will appear as an aborted elopement, but Minerva is willing to risk social stigma to achieve fame. She promises Colin her cash winnings, as the confirmed bachelor can't access his trust fund until he marries. Minerva and Colin's mishap-filled trip results in passion that neither expected." (Publishers Weekly)

Dare, Tessa

★ **When** a Scot Ties the Knot; by Tessa Dare. HarperCollins 2015 384 p. $7.99

ISBN 0062349023; 9780062349026

In this book, by Tessa Dare, "Miss Madeline Gracechurch . . . was certain to be a dismal failure on the London marriage mart. So Maddie . . . invented a . . . Scottish sweetheart. . . . Maddie poured her heart into writing the imaginary Captain MacKenzie . . . and by pretending to be devastated when he was (not really) killed in battle, she managed to avoid the pressures of London society entirely. Until years later, when this kilted Highland lover of her imaginings shows up." (Publisher's note)

"Dare's latest begins with a fairy-tale twist of fate, then leads readers on a mesmerizing and intense emotional journey that explores love in many forms and the powerful pull of dreams. A brilliant, enchanting, and soul-satisfying romance." Kirkus

The **dark**; new ghost stories. edited by Ellen Datlow. TOR Bks. 2003 378p $25.95

ISBN 0-7653-0444-9

LC 2003-54336

"Datlow has cast her net beyond the horror genre's usual names and pulled in contributors whose stories are the equal of their best work, as well as mystery, fantasy and SF writers whose tales seem to be the ghost story they've always wanted to tell." Publ Wkly

Dark matter; a century of speculative fiction from the African diaspora. edited by Sheree R. Thomas. Warner Bks. 2000 427p

ISBN 0-446-52583-9

LC 00-22288

"Ranging in variety from the lilting cadence of Nalo Hopkinson ('Greedy Choke Puppy') to the understated bleakness of Derek Bell ('The space traders'), this collection of 28 tales by African American sf and fantasy authors showcases a wealth of talent that spans over 100 years." Libr J

Darnielle, John, 1967-

Universal harvester; John Darnielle. Farrar, Straus & Giroux 2017 224 p. (ebook) $60; (hardback) $25

ISBN 9780374714024; 9780374282103

LC 2016025809

In this novel, by John Darnielle, "Jeremy works at the Video Hut in Nevada, Iowa. . . . This is the late 1990s. . . . A local schoolteacher comes in to return her copy of Targets, . . . she has an odd complaint: 'There's something on it,' she says, but doesn't elaborate. Two days later, a different customer returns a different tape, a new release, and says it's not defective, exactly, but altered. . . . Jeremy doesn't want to be curious, but he brings the movies home to take a look." (Publisher's note)

"Darnielle's contemporary ghost story may confound with its elusiveness (who is the mysterious "I" narrator?), but its impact will stick with readers." LJ

Darnielle, John, 1967-

Wolf in white van; a novel. John Darnielle. First edition Farrar, Straus & Giroux 2014 224 p. (hardback) $24

ISBN 0374292086; 9780374292089

LC 2014015427

Alex Award (2015)

In this novel, by John Darnielle, "[i]solated by a disfiguring injury since the age of seventeen, Sean Phillips crafts imaginary worlds for strangers to play in. From his small apartment in southern California, he orchestrates fantastic adventures where possibilities, both dark and bright, open in the boundaries between the real and the imagined." (Publisher's note)

"Sean Phillips was an unremarkable, moody teenager until tragedy left him with a horrific injury, changing his life forever. Who or what drove him to his fate? Can anyone be blamed? Is there a lesson to be learned? These questions are explored but never fully answered in Darnielle's first full-length novel...As senseless as a car accident, and as hard to look away from, the inconclusiveness of this journey will either captivate or madden readers." Booklist

Dau, Stephen

The **book** of Jonas; Stephen Dau. Blue Rider Press 2012 256p

ISBN 9780399158452

LC 2011047494

This book tells the story of "Younis, a perceptive . . . boy in a nameless Central Asian land, [who] is caught up in the war on terror. His village has been destroyed, his family killed, and now he must remake himself as Jonas Iskander, refugee. A charity sends Jonas to live with the Martins, an evangelical family in Pennsylvania. There he attends high school, an outcast . . he is also bullied, until he finally responds to an ugly attack by beating the bully senseless. The school mandates counseling . . . the young refugee's fractured recollections lead the counselor to connect Jonas's story with that of Rose Henderson, whose son, Christopher, went missing while in combat in Jonas' home country. To Rose, trapped in a limbo of loss, Jonas reluctantly tells his story—of the attack on his village and of his mountain cave sanctuary where he was found by the soldier." (Kirkus)

Davidar, David

The **house** of blue mangoes. HarperCollins Pubs. 2002 421p

ISBN 0-06-621254-5

A multigenerational family saga set on the "Dorai estate in a tiny village in southern India. Tamil Christians, the Dorais are fortunate to have the contemplative patriarch Solomon at the helm in 1899, a time of violent unrest. Solomon has high hopes for his good-looking and athletic son, Aaron, but the heir apparent gets drawn into a radical terrorist group, so it's shy and studious Daniel, who makes a fortune in cosmetics, who takes his father's place. An avid student of the history and cultures of India, Davidar tracks the fortunes of the Dorai clan over the course of five turbulent decades as the independence movement coalesces, British rule ends, and India is drawn into two world wars." Booklist

Davidson, Andrew

The **gargoyle**. Doubleday 2008 468p $25.95

ISBN 978-0-385-52494-0; 0-385-52494-3

"Likely to ignite the passion of anyone who loves a mix of romance and the macabre. . . . Nothing [the narrator]—or you—can assume about this spectacularly imaginative journey will help navigate its twists and turns. Before it's all over, like Dante before him, our narrator must visit Hades, and like every chapter of The Gargoyle, that's a hell of a story, too." Washington Post Book World

Davies, J. D.

Gentleman captain; J.D. Davies. 1st U.S. ed.; Houghton Mifflin Harcourt 2010 336 p. $25

ISBN 0547382618; 9780547382616

LC 2010005737

In this novel by, J. D. Davies, "Captain Matthew Quinton is determined to complete his second mission without loss of life or honor. Rebellion is stirring in the Scottish Isles, and King Charles II needs loyal officers to sail north and face the threat. But aboard His Majesty's Ship the Jupiter, the young 'gentleman captain' leads a resentful crew and has but few on whom he can rely. . . . [He has] a growing conviction that betrayal lies closer to home than he had thought." (Publisher's note)

Includes bibliographical references

Davies, J. D.

The **mountain** of gold; J.D. Davies. Houghton Mifflin Harcourt 2012 359 p. (hardback) $25

ISBN 0547580991; 9780547580999

LC 2011028559

Sequel to: Gentleman Captain

This book "begins when a captured Barbary pirate speaks of . . . a mountain of gold. Rather than hang this enemy of England, King Charles II hands him back over to the man who apprehended him, Capt. Matthew Quinton. Quinton and the pirate devise an expedition to Africa and the treasure, which the king desires for his campaign against the Dutch. . . . Once out to sea, the captain's mission takes on new complications that test his crew and England's reputation as a maritime power." (Library Journal)

"A naval adventure that goes well beyond the usual outlines of the genre to paint a lively portrait of England in the 1600s." Kirkus

Davies, Peter Ho

The **Fortunes**; Peter Ho Davies. Houghton Mifflin Harcourt 2016 288 p. illustration (ebook) $27; (hardback) $27

ISBN 9780544263789; 9780544263703

LC 2016005161

This book, by Peter Ho Davies, "recasts American history through the lives of Chinese Americans. . . . Inhabiting four lives—a railroad baron's valet who unwittingly ignites an explosion in Chinese labor, Hollywood's first Chinese movie star, a hate-crime victim whose death mobilizes Asian Americans, and a biracial writer visiting China for an adoption—[it] captures and capsizes over a century of our history." (Publisher's note)

"Davies' nuanced contemplation of how America has affected the Chinese (and vice versa) forces the reader to confront what is both singular and similar about all cross-cultural transactions." Kirkus

Davies, Peter Ho

The **Welsh** girl; a novel. Houghton Mifflin 2007 338p $24

ISBN 978-0-618-00700-4; 0-618-00700-8

LC 2006-15358

This novel is "set during World War II in northern Wales, where German POWs are held in a low-security prison. The intertwining stories involve a farm girl named Esther, who becomes pregnant after being raped by an English soldier; German POW Karsten, who is ashamed of surrendering in battle; and Jewish interrogator Rotheram, who is trying to refute captured Hitler deputy Rudolf Hess's claims of amnesia. From behind the prison fence, Karsten becomes friendly with Esther. He later escapes and hides at Esther's farm. Karsten and Esther share their fears, humiliation, and shame, which eventually leads to an affectionate sexual episode before Karsten gives himself up and returns to prison. . . . The characters are heartfelt and real and events vividly and memorably described." Libr J

Davies, Robertson

The **cunning** man; a novel. Viking 1995 469p

ISBN 0-670-85911-7

LC 94-31874

Robertson Davies "entertains with an old-fashioned fictional mixture that he seems to have invented anew: keen social observations delivered with wit, intelligence and free-floating philosophical curiosity." Time

Davies, Robertson

Fifth business. Viking 1970 308p

The first volume in the Deptford trilogy, followed by The manticore and World of wonders

This novel "achieves a richness and depth that are exceptional in a modern novel and rare at any time. On its simplest and most obvious level it is a remarkably colorful tale of ambition, love and weird vengeance. At its deepest, it is a work of theological fiction that approaches Graham Greene at the top of his form." Book World

Davies, Robertson

Murther & walking spirits; a novel. Viking 1991 357p

ISBN 0-670-84189-7

LC 91-29844

"The films convey more than sight and sound, making our hero eerily privy to his relatives' thoughts and feelings. Davies has great fun with this device, giving full rein to his sense of drama, love of gritty, historical detail, and delight in satire." Booklist

Davies, Robertson

★ The **rebel** angels. Viking 1982 326p

ISBN 0-670-59063-0

LC 81-51907

First volume in the Cornish trilogy, followed by What's bred in the bone and The lyre of Orpheus

First published 1981 in Canada

"The names of Rabelais and Paracelsus are not gratuitously invoked by the plot. There is a Rabelaisian quality . . . in Mr. Davies's own writing; while the hermetic and heterodox ideas associated with the name of Paracelsus are exploited in a fashion that is at once playful and serious." New Repub

Davies, Valentine

Miracle on 34th Street. Harcourt Brace & Co. 1947 120p

ISBN 0-15-160239-5

"Nice blend of fantasy, fun and humor with the universal and wholesome appeal of the Christmas spirit." Libr J

Davis, Amanda

Wonder when you'll miss me. William Morrow 2003 259p $24.95; pa $12.95

ISBN 0-688-16781-0; 0-06-053426-5 pa

LC 2002-24118

Alex Award (2004)

"Davis's writing is at its finest when the protagonist is struggling through the constant trials with her distant mother, her ineffectual teachers, and her one true friend's suicide. . . . The author succeeds in making this character unique, with flaws that teens will relate to. Readers will root for Faith, and the heartwarming conclusion will leave them satisfied." SLJ

Includes bibliographical references

Davis, Kathryn

Duplex; Kathryn Davis. Graywolf Press 2013 208 p. (alk. paper) $24

ISBN 1555976530; 9781555976538

LC 2013936988

In this book, by Kathryn Davis, "Mary and Eddie are meant for each other--but love is no guarantee, not in these suburbs. Like all children, they exist in an eternal present; time is imminent, and the adults of the street live in their assorted houses like numbers on a clock. . . . Soon a sorcerer's car will speed down Mary's street, and as past and future fold into each other, the resonant parenthesis of her girlhood will close forever." (Publisher's note)

Davis, Kathryn

The **thin** place. Little Brown 2006 277p $23.95

ISBN 0-316-73504-3

LC 2005-07981

"In the opening pages of this . . . book, three small-town girls discover a man's corpse at the edge of a lake, and one of them, Mees Kipp, mysteriously brings him back to life. Davis writes hallucinatory, literate prose, and adopts a cosmic perspective: she is concerned with nothing less than describing the town's every waking moment. The experiences of Mees's dog, trotting through a clearing that smells of porcupine, stand alongside those of a minister's wife reading her morning paper and 'confronting whatever form the devil had chosen to assume overnight.' In any other book, a magical resurrection would be a central event; for Davis, it's just another moment in a particular place." New Yorker

Davis, Kathryn

Versailles. Houghton Mifflin 2002 206p $21

ISBN 0-618-22136-0

LC 2002-510048

This "idiosyncratic novel begins when Marie Antoinette, née Maria Antonia Josephina Johanna, Archduchess of Austria, aged fourteen, is riding in a blue-satin-lined carriage on her way to be married to the Dauphin of France. It ends with her death. Except for the brief, witty playlets studded throughout the narrative (in which various minor actors try to figure out what's going on), the Queen tells her own story, and the voice Davis has given her is by turns sage, mercurial, and ravishing. It is also edged with doom, each word bordered in black by the reader's own premonitions." New Yorker

Davis, Lindsey, 1949-

✓The **Ides** of April; a Flavia Albia mystery. Lindsey Davis. 1st U.S. ed. Minotaur Books 2013 352 p. (Flavia Albia mysteries) (hardcover) $25.99

ISBN 1250023696; 9781250023698

LC 2013011921

In this historical mystery novel, by Lindsey Davis, is part of the "Flavia Albia Mysteries" series. "Flavia Albia is the adopted daughter of Marcus Didius Falco and Helena Justina. . . . Now, working as a private informer in Rome during the reign of Domitian, Flavia has taken over her father's . . . Fountain Court in the Surbura district, where she plies her trade with energy, determination, and the usual Falco luck." (Publisher's note)

Other titles in this series are:
Enemies at home (2014)
Deadly election (2015)
The graveyard of the Hesperides (2016)
The third Nero (2017)
Pandora's boy (2018)

Davis, Lindsey, 1949-

Master and God; Lindsey Davis. 1st US ed. St. Martin's Press 2012 452 p. (hardcover) $25.99; (hardcover) $25.99; (downloadable audio) $69.95; (paperback) $16.99

ISBN 0312606648; 146680243X; 9780312606640; 9781466802438; 9780792787815; 9781250021557

LC 2012024195

This book is a "novel about the reign of Emperor Domitian (51-96 C.E.). . . . The novel's action revolves around Gaius Vinius, a soldier promoted to the emperor's Praetorian Guard, and Flavia Lucilla, the daughter of a freed slave who takes up her mother's profession as a hairdresser to high-ranking members of society. The two characters navigate wars, fires, business, real estate, scandals, and multiple marriages as Domitian's once-successful reign deteriorates." (Kirkus Reviews)

Davis, Lydia

Can't and Won't; Lydia Davis. Farrar, Straus and Giroux 2014 304 p. (hardcover) $26

ISBN 0374118582; 9780374118587

LC 2013033909

In this book, author Lydia Davis presents a collection of short stories that "may be literal one-liners . . . [or] they may be lengthier investigations of the havoc wreaked by the most mundane disruptions to routine. The stories may appear in the form of letters of complaint; they may be extracted from Flaubert's correspondence; or they may be inspired by the author's own dreams, or the dreams of friends." (Publisher's note)

Includes bibliographical references

Davis, Lydia

★ The **collected** stories of Lydia Davis. Farrar, Straus and Giroux 2010 733p $30

ISBN 978-0-374-27060-5; 0-374-27060-0

LC 2009-25451

This volume presents a "body of work probably unique in American writing, in its combination of lucidity, aphoristic brevity, formal originality, sly comedy, metaphysical bleakness, philosophical pressure, and human wisdom. I suspect that The Collected Stories of Lydia Davis will in time be seen as one of the great, strange American literary contributions, distinct and crookedly personal, like the work of Flannery O'Connor, or Donald Barthelme, or J. F. Powers." New Yorker

Day, Cathy

The **circus** in winter; Cathy Day. 1st ed; Harcourt 2004 274p il $23

ISBN 0-15-101048-X

LC 2003-25033

In this "collection of interrelated short stories, [Day] succeeds in appropriating much of the garish pungency of the world of freaks, geeks and sideshow Houdinis without succumbing to its ready banalities. Although once or twice she treads close to cliche must the revelations of two-bit fortunetellers in fiction always turn out to be true? most of the time she steers clear of tired expectations. This is one circus act that doesn't rely on dependable gimmicks to keep the audience amused." N Y Times Book Rev

Dazieri, Sandrone

Kill the father; Sandrone Dazieri ; translated by Antony Shugaar. Scribner 2017 498 p. (Caselli and Torre series) (hardcover : alk. paper) $28

ISBN 9781501130731; 9781501130755

LC 2016015605

In this novel, in the Caselli and Torre Series, by Sandrone Dazieri, translated by Antony Shugaar, "two people, each shattered by their past, team up to solve a series of killings and abductions--a ruthlessly planned escalation that turns out to be merely the surface of something far more sinister." (Publisher's note)

"Dazieri's dazzling U.S. debut, the first in a series, introduces Deputy Capt. Colomba Caselli, a Rome police detective recuperating from major work-related PTSD, and Dante Torre, a near-incapacitated claustrophobic private consultant on missing-person cases." Pub Wkly

Includes bibliographical references and index

De Bernieres, Louis

Birds without wings; Louis de Bernieres. 1st American ed; Knopf 2004 553p $25.95

ISBN 1-400-04341-7

LC 2004-14529

"This epic about the tragedy of borders is likely to cross all borders, moving readers everywhere as it describes the harrowing cost of remaking faraway places in the image of our dreams." Christ Sci Monit

De Bernieres, Louis

The **dust** that falls from dreams; a novel. by Louis de Bernieres. Pantheon Books 2015 528 p. (hard cover : alk. paper) $27.95

ISBN 9781101946480

LC 2015011829

This novel, by Louis de Bernieres, is "about a British family whose lives and loves are indelibly shaped by the horrors of World War I. . . . In the brief golden years of the Edwardian era the McCosh sisters—Christabel, Ottilie, Rosie and Sophie—grow up in an idyllic household in the countryside south of London. . . . In childhood this band is inseparable, but the days of careless camaraderie are brought to an abrupt halt by the outbreak of The Great War." (Publisher's note)

"This heartrending saga of love, loss, and endurance paints a vivid portrait of the steep price paid by an entire generation of young men and women who participated in and endured the Great War... Patrons will remember this author's blockbuster novel, made into a popular movie, so expect demand for this latest." Booklist

De Bernieres, Louis

A **partisan's** daughter. Alfred A. Knopf 2008 193p $23.95

ISBN 978-0-307-26887-7; 0-307-26887-X

LC 2008-17773

This novel's main "characters are Chris and Roza. He's a 40-year-old English pharmaceuticals salesman, locked in a loveless suburban marriage; she's an undocumented Yugoslav girl, scraping out an existence amid the economic hardship of pre-Thatcher 1970s London. They meet when, on an impulse—and for the first time in his life—Chris approaches a girl he believes to be a streetwalker. Roza protests she is not a 'working girl,' but she accepts a ride from him because she judges him, rightly, to be safe and kind. Before they part, she admits that she was once a prostitute, and charged 500 pounds for her services. Obsessed with the idea of sleeping with her, Chris begins to squirrel away money, but in the meantime he regularly visits Roza as friend rather than client, enjoying her company and listening to her stories. . . . Roza shocks Chris with the revelation that she once seduced her father, who was a comrade of Tito, and details her rape at the hands of a British thug. But Chris, like readers of the novel, is never quite sure when Roza is telling the truth or when she is weaving a tale to make herself more fascinating—to this humdrum man who so obviously adores her, and to herself." BookPage

De Bodard, Aliette

The **house** of shattered wings; Aliette de Bodard. Roc 2015 416 p. (hardcover) $26.95

ISBN 9780451477385

LC 2015013751

In this book, by Aliette de Bodard, "the streets of Paris are lined with haunted ruins, the aftermath of a Great War. . . . The Great Houses still vie for dominion over France's once grand capital. Once the most powerful and formidable, House Silverspires now lies in disarray. . . . Within the House, three . . . people must come together: a naive but powerful Fallen angel; an alchemist with a self-destructive addiction; and a resentful young man wielding spells of unknown origin." (Publisher's note)

"De Bodard (author of award-winning short fiction as well as the "Obsidian and Blood" novels) has spun a fascinating Paris of decay and cruelty. Phillippe is a marvel of a character, unreliable as a narrator but compelling in his flaws and his deep well of homesickness." LJ

Another title in this series is:

The house of binding thorns (2017)

De Giovanni, Maurizio, 1958-

The **Crocodile**; Maurizio de Giovanni ; translated from the Italian by Antony Sgugaar. Penguin Group USA 2013 336 p. $17

ISBN 1609451198; 9781609451196

In this detective novel, disgraced Sicilian Insp. Giuseppe Lojacono is exiled to Naples and "spends his working days playing computer poker. He gets a chance to exercise his dormant gray cells when a gunman kills a 16-year-old boy, and the detective, one of the first on the scene, notices that the killer left behind some used tissues." He's ignored until "his theory that this death isn't related to organized crime attracts the interest of the investigating prosecutor." (Publishers Weekly)

De Kretser, Michelle

The **Hamilton** case. Little, Brown and Co 2004 307p $24.95

ISBN 0-316-73548-5

LC 2003-60759

Having come of age on the island nation of Ceylon, Sam Obeysekere is a lawyer whose life is guided by the British culture that dominates his homeland. . . . Sam's undoing arrives in the form of the Hamilton case, a scandalous murder that shakes the upper echelons of island society. Guided by grandiose visions of Sherlock Holmes, he becomes convinced he can solve the mysterious case-and that his good standing with the English will insulate him from the unrest the case has exposed." Publisher's note

De la Cruz, Melissa

Witches of East End. Hyperion 2011 273p

ISBN 1-4013-2390-1; 978-1-4013-2390-5

LC 2010-52857

This first title in the author's series about witchcraft is "the tale of the Beauchamp women—Joanna and her daughters Freya and Ingrid, who had their powers stripped back in the 17th century. But as they say, magic will out, and the women begin to dabble again just as a bunch of mysterious happenings start plaguing their small Long Island town. De la Cruz balances the supernatural high-jinksery with unpredictable twists and a conclusion that nicely sets up book 2." Entertainment Wkly

De la Pava, Sergio

A **naked** singularity; a novel. Sergio de la Pava. The University of Chicago Press 2012 678 p. (paperback : alkaline paper) $18

ISBN 0226141799; 9780226141794

LC 2011032343

The author, Sergio de la Pava, "tells the story of Casi, a child of Colombian immigrants who lives in Brooklyn and works in Manhattan as a public defender--one who, tellingly has never lost a trial. . . . [Readers see Casi's] sense of justice and even his sense of self begin to crack--and how his world then slowly devolves. . . . [Pava] takes readers through crime and courts, immigrant families and urban blight, savagery and media satire, scatology and boxing, and even a breathless heist worthy of any crime novel." (Publisher's note)

De la Pava, Sergio

Personae; a novel. by Sergio De La Pava. University of Chicago Press 2013 216 p. (paperback : alkaline paper) $17

ISBN 022607899X; 9780226078991

LC 2013016557

In this book, by Sergio de la Pava, readers "meet Detective Helen Tame as she investigates a crime scene, before diving into the writings Tame discovers at the victim's house. Notebook scribblings include pronouncements against filling with allusive arcana for dimwit professors. The conclusions for Helen and the victim, and especially the novella, which wraps up the book, are darker, and more touching." (Publisher's note)

De la Roche, Mazo

Jalna. Little, Brown 1927 347p

Jalna is the family home of the Whiteoaks. Gathered under its roof are representatives of each generation from the time the grandparents drifted to Canada, via England from India and there built their homestead on a lavish scale. Renny, 37, is the present head of the household which includes Gran—a formidable old lady of 99—two uncles, an aunt, an elderly sister, and four half-brothers. An affectionate, warring group of strong personalities from the old lady down to Wakefield, the youngest, aged nine. Two of the boys marry and bring their wives home

De Lint, Charles

Widdershins. Tor Books 2006 560p $27.95

ISBN 0-765312-85-9

LC 2005-34475

"On her way home from a gig in the small Canadian town of Sweetwater, Celtic fiddler Lizzie Mahone disrupts the feasting of a band of faerie thugs and becomes a target for their hostility, also winning the respect of a pair of Native American spirits. These new complications bring her into the orbit of Jilly Coppercorn, a brilliant painter and a favorite of the many faerie folk who dwell unseen in the nearby town of Newford, and Jilly's friend, master fiddler Geordie Riddell. As familiarly as though he were chronicling the lives of old friends, de Lint . . . spins yet another magical story of the intersections between reality and the faerie and spirit world in this latest addition to the Newford opus." Libr J

De los Santos, Marisa

The **Precious** One; A Novel. by Marisa de los Santos. HarperCollins 2015 352 p. $25.99

ISBN 0061670898; 9780061670893

LC 2015295746

In this novel, by Marisa de los Santos, "Eustacia 'Taisy' Cleary has given her heart to only three men: her first love, Ben Ransom; her twin brother, Marcus; and Wilson Cleary--professor, inventor, philanderer, self-made millionaire, brilliant man, breathtaking jerk: her father. Seventeen years ago, Wilson ditched his first family for Caroline, a beautiful young sculptor. . . . Why then, is Wilson calling Taisy now, inviting her for an extended visit?" (Publisher's note)

De Robertis, Carolina

The **gods** of tango; Carolina De Robertis. Alfred A. Knopf 2015 384 p. (hardcover) $26.95

ISBN 9781101872857; 9781101874493

LC 2014023450

Stonewall Book Award: Barbara Gittings Literature Award (2016)

In this book, by Carolina De Robertis, "seventeen-year-old Leda, clutching a suitcase and her father's cherished violin, leaves her small Italian village for a new home (and husband) halfway across the world in Argentina. Upon her arrival in Buenos Aires, Leda is shocked to find that her bridegroom has been killed. Unable to fathom the idea of returning home, she remains in this unfamiliar city, living in a commune, without friends or family, on the brink of destitution." (Publisher's note)

"The novel is a plea to embrace 'the bright jagged thing you really are,' and in its hero's more contemplative, interior moments, De Robertis captures the enormity of that struggle." Kirkus

De Robertis, Carolina

★ **Perla**; by Carolina De Robertis. Alfred A. Knopf 2012 256p.

ISBN 9780307947840; 9780307599599

LC 2011041833

This book tells the story of "Perla, the narrator, . . . [who] is a young university student . . . [with] a dark secret: Her father was a naval officer who during the late 1970s and early '80s helped round up the 'disappeared,' dissidents who were arrested and executed by the military regime, often dropped into the Atlantic Ocean from airplanes. . . . But that legacy becomes unavoidable to her when a man appears in Perla's home, soaked and dank-smelling and constantly thirsty. He's a ghost of one of the disappeared, but also quite real: The water that he can't shake off soaks the apartment. His surreal presence unlocks a host of memories for Perla, and the novel alternates between her perspective, as she recalls her difficult relationship with her father, and the stranger's perspective, as he recalls the horrific rapes and other abuses he suffered while in military custody." (Kirkus)

De Rosnay, Tatiana

Sarah's key; Tatiana de Rosnay. St. Martin's Press 2007 294p $25.95

ISBN 9780312370831; 0312370830

LC 2007010080

This novel begins in "Paris, July 1942 . . . [when] Sarah, a ten-year-old girl, is taken with her parents by the French police as they go door to door arresting Jewish families in the middle of the night. Desperate to protect her younger brother, Sarah locks him in a bedroom cupboard—their secret hiding place—and promises to come back for him as soon as they are released. Sixty Years Later: Sarah's story intertwines with that of Julia Jarmond, an American journalist investigating the roundup. In her research, Julia stumbles onto a trail of secrets that link her to Sarah, and to questions about her own future." (Publisher's note)

Dean, Anna

Bellfield Hall, or, The observations of Miss Dido Kent; Anna Dean. 1st U.S. ed.; Minotaur Books 2010 300 p.

ISBN 0312562942; 9780312562946

LC 2009041130

Originally published: A moment of silence. London : Allison & Busby, 2008

The book tells the tale of "[s]pinster aunt Miss Dido Kent [who] is summoned to Bellfield Hall, the Montague country estate, by her niece Catherine, who wants her to discover why Richard Montague, her fiancé, ran off after declaring he was a ruined man. Before Dido can solve this puzzle, an unknown woman is found murdered in the Hall's shrubbery, and Richard's strange departure makes him a prime suspect. Can Dido discover the truth hidden behind a wealth of secrets, or will this house party have a decidedly unhappy ending? (Libr J)

Dean, Anna

A **gentleman** of fortune, or, The suspicions of Miss Dido Kent; Anna Dean. Minotaur Books 2011 335 p.

ISBN 0312596960; 9780312596965

LC 2010042003

Sequel to: Bellfield Hall

In this detective novel, a "murder among the English gentility . . . challenges the inquisitive prowess of Miss Dido Kent. . . . Dido is residing in the fashionable town of Richmond with her cousin, Mrs. Flora Beaumont, when the ladies learn that the charming, eligible bachelor Mr. Lansdale has finally come into his fortune on the death of his invalid aunt. This happy occasion is disrupted by the vicious gossip of Mrs. Midgely, a neighbor who insinuates that Mrs. Lansdale was murdered. . . . When Mrs. Midgely prevails upon the local apothecary to bring the case to the magistrates, Dido gives in to her natural curiosity. By paying visits, eavesdropping in shops and attending to the subtleties of parlor games, Dido aspires to defend Mr. Lansdale's innocence." (Kirkus)

Dean, Anna

★ A **place** of confinement; the investigations of Miss Dido Kent. Anna Dean. A Thomas Dunne Book For Minotaur Books, An imprint of St. Martin's Pub. Group 2013 416 p. (The Dido Kent series) (hardcover) $25.99

ISBN 1250029678; 9781250029676

LC 2013011842

In this book by Anna Dean, "30-ish spinster Dido Kent . . . bristles at serving as companion to her Aunt Manners during the latter's visit to Charcombe Manor. . . . One reason for the underlying tension is the disappearance two days earlier of 19-year-old Letitia Verney, who was under the care of Dido's host, Lancelot Fenstanton. Letitia was last seen with a young man of dubious reputation, Tom Lomax, who just happens to be the son of the man Dido is in love with." (Publishers Weekly)

Dean, Anna

A **woman** of consequence; the investigations of Miss Dido Kent. Anna Dean. Minotaur Books / A Thomas Dunne Book 2012 383 p. (Dido Kent mystery)

ISBN 0312626843; 9780312626846; 9781429942560

LC 2012003258

This book, "[s]et in 1806," is "[Anna] Dean's . . . third mystery featuring Miss Dido Kent. . . . Dido writes to her sister, Eliza, of Penelope Lambe's falling and hitting her head at ruined Madderstone Abbey, where the "sweet-tempered, good-natured girl" had gone in the hope of getting a glimpse of the abbey ghost known as the Grey Nun. Penelope's claim to have seen the Grey Nun shortly before losing consciousness leads Dido to investigate Madderstone for herself. The discovery in a drained pool on the abbey grounds of a human skeleton raises the stakes. Dean . . . integrates a wealth of historical detail, especially regarding the rights of women and the inheritance laws in effect in the early 19th century." (Publishers Wkly)

Dean, Debra

The **madonnas** of Leningrad; a novel. William Morrow 2006 231p hardcover o.p. pa $13.99

ISBN 0-06-082530-8; 0-06-082531-6 pa

LC 2005-50233

"Like her adoring museum audiences 60 years earlier, readers will absorb Marina's glorious, lush accounts of classical beauties as she traces them in her mind. Dean eloquently depicts the ravages of Alzheimer's disease and convincingly describes the inner world of the afflicted." Libr J

Dean, Margaret Lazarus

The **time** it takes to fall. Simon & Schuster 2007 305p $24

ISBN 978-0-7432-9722-6; 0-7432-9722-9

LC 2006-52213

"This first novel looks at the tragedy of the Challenger space shuttle from the unique perspective of a teenage girl named Dolores, whose father works for NASA. Dolores is obsessed with becoming an astronaut and keeps a scrapbook of stories associated with the space program that includes a journal of her attendance at the successful launches. After Dolores befriends a schoolmate named Eric, she comes to suspect that his father, the director of launch safety, is having an affair with her mother. Dolores is forced to consider the wobbly direction her young life is beginning to take when her mother leaves the family and when her father is involved in the investigation of the space program's cover-ups after the Challenger disaster. . . . A gripping judgment of American culture with a harrowing depiction in the epilog of the last few minutes in the lives of the Challenger's seven astronauts." Libr J

Dean, Michael

★ **I,** Hogarth. Penguin Group USA 2013 272 p. $26.95

ISBN 1468303422; 9781468303421

This book is a fictional biography of artist William Hogarth. "Born in 1697 . . . , Hogarth was apprenticed to an engraver, only to maneuver his way into tutelage from and assistantship to the court painter Sir James Thornhill. Hogarth's family fractures when father Richard lands in debtors' prison." In a moneylender's mansion, "Hogarth glimpses Kate, a strumpet, the vision unleashing the artist's lifelong appreciation for fleshly sensuality." (Kirkus Reviews)

Deane, Seamus

★ **Reading** in the dark. Knopf 1997 245p

ISBN 0-394-57440-0

LC 96-49635

First published 1996 in the United Kingdom

"A Catholic boy growing up hard by the border between Donegal and Derry is fascinated by the local ghost stories and neighborhood lore, and this fascination leads him to secrets at the heart of a family feud. His search for the truth runs through a labyrinth of Irish detours and delights: elaborate catechisms, mad poets, mute idiots, drunken hyperbole, deathbed revelations, and a clever reprisal involving an unwitting bishop." New Yorker

Deaver, Jeff

Edge; a novel. Jeffery Deaver. Simon & Schuster 2010 397p $26.99; pbk $15

ISBN 978-1-4391-5635-3; 1-4391-5635-2; 9781476726427

LC 2010-26347

"Henry Loving is a lifter, hired to get information by any means--including torture. His expertise is in getting an 'edge' by kidnapping or threatening someone close to his principal, exerting pressure until they cave. When Washington, D.C., police detective Ryan Kessler inexplicably becomes Loving's target, the job of keeping Kessler's family alive falls to a senior federal protection officer named Corte, who lost a friend to Loving's ruthless machinations six years earlier. As Corte and his team race to counter Loving, the lifter moves in on his prey--and Corte must choose between protecting his charges and exposing them to a killer in the name of long-awaited revenge." (Publisher's note)

Deaver, Jeff

Garden of beasts; a novel of Berlin 1936. {by} Jeffery Deaver. Simon & Schuster 2004 404p $24.95

ISBN 0-7432-2201-6

LC 2004-45206

"Top Nazis, including Hitler, Himmler and Göring, make colorful cameos, but it's the smart, shaded-gray characterizations of the principals that anchor the exciting plot." Publ Wkly

Deaver, Jeffery

The **October** list; Jeffery Deaver. Grand Central Pub. 2013 320 p. (hardback) $26

ISBN 1455576646; 9781455576647

LC 2013018524

This book by Thriller Award-winner Jeffery Deaver "moves backward in time over the span of a three-day weekend, from Sunday evening to early Friday morning." Office manager Gabriela McKenzie's six-year-old daughter, Sarah, has been kidnapped. "Gabriela must not only pay a $500,000 ransom but also fork over the mysterious 'October List,' which belongs to her former boss Charles Prescott, the head of Prescott Investments, who has fled from a police investigation." (Publishers Weekly)

Deb, Siddhartha

The **point** of return. Ecco Press 2003 304p $24.95

ISBN 0-06-050151-0

LC 2002-35300

"To allow Dr. Dam to evolve through most of the book in a self-generated fog of benevolence and to shatter it in the last pages is a brillant stroke. . . . Storytelling of the kind Deb lavishes, for most of his book, on Dr. Dam is rare and precious and uplifting." N Y Times Book Rev

Deborde, Rob

Portlandtown; a tale of the Oregon Wyldes. Rob DeBorde. St. Martin's Griffin 2012 384 p.

ISBN 1250006643; 9781250006646

LC 2012037424

This novel by Rob DeBorde is "a supernatural western. . . . When [Joseph Wylde's] father-in-law's grave-digging awakens more than just ghosts, Joseph invites him into their home. . . . Unfortunately, the old man's past soon follows, unleashing a terrible storm on a city already knee deep in floodwaters. As the dead mysteriously begin to rise, the Wyldes must find the truth before an unspeakable evil can spread across the West and beyond." (Publisher's note)

Decarlo, Melissa

The **Art** of Crash Landing; a novel. Melissa DeCarlo. HarperCollins 2015 432 p. (paperback) $15.99

ISBN 0062390546; 9780062390547

LC 2015010374

In this novel, by Melissa DeCarlo, "Mattie Wallace has really screwed up this time. Broke and knocked up, she's got all her worldly possessions crammed into six giant trash bags, and nowhere to go. . . . Mattie can no longer deny that she really is turning into her mother, a broken alcoholic who never met a bad choice she didn't make. When Mattie gets news of a possible inheritance left by a grandmother she's never met, she jumps at this one last chance to turn things around." (Publisher's note)

"DeCarlo bursts on the scene with a fascinating, mysterious novel. The pacing is excellent and the prose fluid as the story unfolds in a combination of flashbacks and present-day scenes. This debut is thick with secrets; it will cause readers to question everyone and everything. The author does an outstanding job combining suspense with heartache, adding a dash of romance and, at the end, hope." LJ

Dee, Jonathan

The **privileges**; a novel. Random House 2010 258p $25

ISBN 1-4000-6867-3; 978-1-4000-6867-8

LC 2009-12900

"Smart, socially gifted, and chronically impatient, Adam and Cynthia Morey . . . marry young and have two children before Cynthia reaches the age of twenty-five. Adam is a rising star in the world of private equity and becomes his boss's protégé. With a beautiful home in . . . Manhattan, gorgeous children, and plenty of money, they are, by any reasonable standard, successful. But the Moreys' standards are not the same as other people's. The future in which they have always believed for themselves and their children—a life of almost boundless privilege— . . . is not arriving fast enough to suit them." (Publisher's note)

The "tale of a family scaling the heights of finance in New York City, a family born, nursed and prep-schooled on the fiscally rich milk of the hedge fund. The novel begins with the wedding of Cynthia and Adam—two glossy, self-absorbed 22-year-olds. . . . [They] go on to live the life of insider-trading zillionaires, obtaining the Manhattan penthouse, the villa in Anguilla, the halfhearted charitable trust. But where a lesser novelist might rely on sarcasm and satire, Dee opts for old-fashioned complexity. The wedding scene, a 32-page masterpiece, begins with a panoramic perspective that dips into the brains of all involved, from the wedding planner to her stoned son to Cynthia's jealous mother. His characters are stories in and of themselves, particularly Cynthia, a sexy savant who calls people skanks and pays off her estranged father's girlfriend to leave his deathbed. Yet Dee approaches her—and all his characters—with understanding." Time Out N Y

Dee, Jonathan

A **thousand** pardons; a novel. Jonathan Dee. Random House 2012 224 p. (ebook) $26; (hardcover) $26

ISBN 0812993217; 9780679645009; 9780812993219

LC 2012018513

In this novel, by Jonathan Dee, "once a privileged and loving couple, the Armsteads have now reached a breaking point. . . . Thrust back into the working world, Helen finds a job in public relations and relocates . . . to an apartment in Manhattan. There, Helen discovers . . . she can convince arrogant men to admit their mistakes, spinning crises into second chances. Yet redemption is more easily granted in her professional life than in her personal one." (Publisher's note)

Defoe, Daniel

★ **Moll** Flanders; with an introduction by John Mullan. Knopf 1991 xxxiii, 338p $19

ISBN 0-679-40548-8

LC 91-52994

First published 1722. Variant title: The fortunes and misfortunes of the famous Moll Flanders

"This purports to be the autobiography of the daughter of a woman who had been transported to Virginia for theft soon after her child's birth. The child, abandoned in England, is brought up in the house of the compassionate mayor of Colchester. The story relates her seduction, her subsequent marriages and liaisons, and her visit to Virginia, where she finds her mother and discovers that she has unwittingly married her own brother. After leaving him and returning to England, she is presently reduced to destitution. She becomes an extremely successful pickpocket and thief, but is presently detected and transported to Virginia in company with one of her former husbands, a highwayman. With the funds that each has amassed they set up as planters, and Moll moreover finds that she has inherited a plantation from her mother. She and her husband spend their declining years in a atmosphere of prosperity and ostensible penitence." Oxford Companion to Engl Lit. 6th edition

Defoe, Daniel

★ **Robinson** Crusoe; edited with an introduction by Thomas Keymer and notes by Thomas Keymer and James Kelly. Oxford University Press 2007 368p (Oxford world's classics) pa $7.95

ISBN 0-19-283342-1; 978-0-19-283342-6

LC 2006-26022

First published 1719

"A minutely circumstantial account of the hero's shipwreck and escape to an uninhabited island, and the methodical industry whereby he makes himself a comfortable home. The story is founded on the actual experiences of Alexander Selkirk, who spent four years on the island of Juan Fernandez in the early 18th century." Lenrow. Reader's Guide to Prose Fic

Deford, Frank

Bliss, remembered; Frank Deford. Overlook Press 2010 352p $25.95; pbk $15

ISBN 9781590203590; 9781590206423; 1590203593

LC 2010023590

"When American swimmer Sydney Stringfellow arrives at the 1936 Berlin Olympics, she never expects to fall in love with a handsome young German, but she does. When politics separate them, she goes home to nurse her broken heart and meets Jimmy, a kind young American who restores her faith in love and marries her before being shipped off to the Pacific theater of WWII. When Horst shows up on her doorstep, though, Sydney is torn and must decide what she is willing to do for love." (Publishers Weekly)

Deighton, Len

Berlin game. Knopf 1984 345p

ISBN 0-394-53407-7

LC 83-48104

The first volume of an espionage trilogy; other volumes are Mexico set and London match

This novel "is a decent entertainment that rattles swiftly along to its payoff. Two things especially recommend it—a devious contrivance of plot that has probably never been used before in an espionage novel; and the city of Berlin, mecca to spies and spy novelists. The second is the greater asset. Although the book is elaborately plotted, its best moments derive from the setting and from the force of this particular setting upon behavior and psychology." N Y Times Book Rev

Deighton, Len

★ The **Ipcress** file. Simon & Schuster 1963 287p

First published 1962 in the United Kingdom

"A British secret-service agent is assigned to help recover a kidnapped biochemist. The international intrigue, involving brainwashing, spies, and counter-spies of uncertain loyalties, takes the agent from London to the Far East, to an atomic test site in the Pacific, and behind the Iron Curtain." Shapiro. Fic for Youth. 3d edition

Deighton, Len

London match. Knopf 1985 407p

ISBN 0-394-54937-6

LC 85-40454

"The strength of (this novel) is not in its plot but its characterization. . . . Mr. Deighton portrays each character of his large cast fully and sympathetically. However, the best character is the city of Berlin. It is a living presence, and in some of the descriptions one can almost hear the stones breathing." N Y Times Book Rev

Dekker, Ted

A.D. 30; a novel. Ted Dekker. Center Street 2014 432 p. maps (hardback) $25

ISBN 1599954184; 9781599954189

LC 2014017802

In this novel, by Ted Dekker, "the outcast daughter of one of the most powerful Bedouin sheikhs in Arabia, Maviah is called on to protect the very people who rejected her. . . . But Maviah's path leads her unexpectedly to another man. An enigmatic teacher who speaks of a way in this life which offers greater power than any kingdom. His name is Yeshua, and his words turn everything known on its head." (Publisher's note)

"This first entry in a new series about the life of Yeshua (Jesus Christ) showcases the New York Times best-selling author's gift ("Circle" series) for immersing readers in ancient settings, believable characters, and high-octane story lines. An accessible and suspenseful tale reminiscent of novels by Tosca Lee and Anita Diamant, this is biblical fiction of the highest caliber." LJ

Dekker, Ted

Mortal; Ted Dekker and Tosca Lee. Faithwords 2012 432 p. (downloadable audio) $59.99; (paperback) $7.99; (hardcover) $24.99; (hardcover) $24.99

ISBN 9781619690943; 9781599953571; 1599953587; 9781599953588

This book, the second in the "Books of Mortals" series, is set "five hundred years into the post-apocalyptic future . . . [where most people] have been emptied of all emotion but fear. . . . Hope rests in Jonathan's ability to reawaken humanity. The megalomaniac Saric, who commands a race of lowly, foul-smelling Dark Bloods, will have something to say about that. So will Saric's sister Feyn, newly revived from a suspended state." (Kirkus Reviews)

Delaney, Edward J.

★ **Broken** Irish. Turtle Point Press 2011 379p pa $18.50

ISBN 978-1-933527-50-5; 1-933527-50-1

LC 2010-938747

"After alcoholic copywriter Jimmy Gilbride loses his job, a rich entrepreneur offers him a lucrative ghostwriting opportunity; crestfallen widow Colleen mourns her military husband and struggles to raise her secretive 13-year-old son, Christopher, while offering clandestine help to Jeanmarie, a reckless teenage runaway with a sketchy boyfriend. Meanwhile, Father John is retiring from the priesthood with an overwhelming sense of uselessness and a guilty conscience. Christopher starts spending time with Jeanmarie, which doesn't sit well with her boyfriend. As the boy braces for violence and Colleen appeals to the church, blackouts, memory lapses, and liver problems get in the way of Jimmy's new job." Publ Wkly

Delaney, Frank, 1942-2017

The **matchmaker** of Kenmare; Frank Delaney. 1st ed.; Random House 2011 x, 397 p.p

ISBN 9781400067848; 0679604332; 1400067847; 9780679604334

LC 2010035301

Sequel to: Venetia Kelly's traveling show.

In this book, "[a]s World War II rages on, Ben remains haunted by the mysterious disappearance of his wife, the actress Venetia Kelly. Searching for purpose by collecting stories for the Irish Folklore Commission, he travels to a remote seaside cottage to profile the . . . Matchmaker of Kenmare. Ben is immediately captivated by the forthright Miss Begley, who is remarkably self-assured in her instincts but provincial in her experience. . . . But when Charles Miller, a striking American military intelligence officer, arrives on the scene, Miss Begley develops an intense infatuation and looks to make a match for herself. Miller needs a favor, but it will be dangerous. Under the cover of their neutrality as Irish citizens, Miss Begley and Ben travel to London and effectively operate as spies. As they are drawn more deeply and painfully into the conflict, both discover the perils of neutrality--in both love and war." (Publisher's note)

Delaney, J. P.

The **girl** before; a novel. JP Delaney. Ballantine Books 2017 352 p. (hardback) $27

ISBN 0425285049; 9780425285046

LC 2016029751

In this book, by JP Delaney, "[after] a traumatic break-in, Emma wants a new place to live. But none of the apartments she sees are affordable or feel safe. Until One Folgate Street. The house is an architectural masterpiece. . . . After a personal tragedy, Jane needs a fresh start. When she finds One Folgate Street she is instantly drawn to the space–and to its aloof but seductive creator. Moving in, Jane soon learns about the untimely death of the home's previous tenant." (Publisher's note)

"This haunting Big Brother-esque novel will consume psychological thriller enthusiasts and keep them thinking long after the final page." LJ

Delany, Samuel R., 1942-

★ **Babel**-17; Empire star; Samuel R. Delany. Vintage Books 2001 219, 92 p.p ill. pbk $15.95

ISBN 0375706690; 9780375706691

LC 2001025844

Nebula Award: Best Novel (1966)

"Babel-17 . . . is a fascinating tale of a famous poet bent on deciphering a secret language that is the key to the enemy's deadly force, a task that requires she travel with a splendidly improbable crew to the site of the next attack. For the first time, Babel-17 is published as the author intended with the short novel Empire Star, the tale of Comet Jo, a simple-minded teen thrust into a complex galaxy when he's entrusted to carry a vital message to a distant world." (Publisher's note)

Delany, Samuel R.

Stars in my pocket like grains of sand. Bantam Bks. 1984 384p

ISBN 0-553-05053-2

LC 84-45180

"Reading this novel is like learning another language, only to realize how much it teaches you about your own, and how relative it makes your cultural assumptions." Publ Wkly

DeLillo, Don

Falling man; a novel. Scribner 2007 246p $26

ISBN 978-1-416-54602-3; 1-416-54602-2

LC 2006-52306

"Scenes are laid out like cards face up in some mysterious game of solitaire, except that each card, each sequence, seems to carry some larger import. It's not clear even at the novel's end what its finishing up might mean. On one narrative level, the game is already over — the characters are living in an unknown afterworld. But on another level — DeLillo inserts several time-jumps into the pre-Sept. 11 past — we see his terrorist preparing himself. . . . Though the setup feels stylized, it is also riveting." Los Angeles Times Book Rev

DeLillo, Don, 1936-

Point Omega; a novel. Scribner 2010 117p $24

ISBN 1-4391-6996-9; 978-1-4391-6995-7

LC 2009-42232

"Jim Finley, a young filmmaker, attempts to convince Richard Elster, a former secret war advisor, to tell his story on film, an endeavor complicated by the arrival of Richard's daughter from New York and a devastating event that throws everything into question." (Publisher's note)

"An academic, hired by the Defense Department to 'conceptualize' the Iraq War. A struggling postmodern filmmaker who visits the academic in his desert retreat to enlist him as the subject of a documentary. Hitchcock's 'Psycho' slowed down to run at two frames a second, or some 24 hours in all, in an installation at New York's Museum of Modern Art. All three figure in Don DeLillo's spectral, difficult, and sometimes brilliant novel, 'Point Omega.' They are linked, but that is to overstate the clarity; it would be truer to say that they haunt each other." Boston Globe

DeLillo, Don

Underworld. Scribner 1997 827p

ISBN 0-684-84269-6

LC 97-13825

"The dialogue is a rockingly comic attack on our mental excreta: the distortions and sound bites of the television age. DeLillo was absent from his fiction before, an unbodied intelligence, but here is an undertow of personal pain he has never touched. This is his most demanding novel and yet his most transparent, giving the reader the privileged intimacy that comes from seeing a writer whole." N Y Times Book Rev

DeLillo, Don, 1936-

★ **Zero** K; a novel. Don DeLillo. Scribner 2016 288 p. hbk $27

ISBN 9781501135392; 9781501138058

LC 2015040210

In this novel by Don DeLillo, "Jeffrey Lockhart's father, Ross, is a billionaire . . . with a younger wife, Artis Martineau, whose health is failing. Ross is the primary investor in a remote and secret compound where death is exquisitely controlled and bodies are preserved until a future time when . . . new technologies can return them to a life of transcendent promise. Jeff joins Ross and Artis at the compound to say 'an uncertain farewell' to her as she surrenders her body." (Publisher's note)

"DeLillo's rich language and rhythmic prose draw readers deep into a rumination on both the inescapability and alluring possibilities of the eternal return." LJ

Delinsky, Barbara

The **secret** between us; Barbara Delinsky. Doubleday 2007 343 p. pbk $14

ISBN 9780385518680; 9780767925198; 076792519X

LC 2007031294

"Deborah Monroe and her daughter, Grace, are driving home from a party when their car hits a man running in the dark. Grace was at the wheel, but Deborah sends her home before the police arrive, determined to shoulder the blame for the accident. Her decision then turns into a deception that takes on a life of its own and threatens the special bond between mother and daughter." (Publisher's note)

Delinsky "deftly and realistically addresses family issues like parental expectations and disapproval, divorce and secrets, as well as small-town issues like preferential treatment and gossip." LJ

Delinsky, Barbara

Sweet salt air; Barbara Delinsky. 1st ed. St. Martin's Press 2013 416 p. (hardcover) $25.99

ISBN 1250007038; 9781250007032

LC 2013004041

In this novel, by Barbara Delinsky, "Charlotte and Nicole were once the best of friends. . . . But many years, and many secrets, have kept the women apart. . . . When Nicole is commissioned to write a book about island food, she invites her old friend Charlotte back to Quinnipeague, for a final summer, to help. . . . But what both women don't know is that they are each holding something back that may change their lives forever." (Publisher's note)

Delius, Friedrich Christian, 1943-

Portrait of the mother as a young woman; Friedrich Christian Delius ; translated from the German by Jamie Bulloch. Farrar, Straus and Giroux 2012 119p.

ISBN 0374533296; 9780374533298; 9780956284006

LC 2011046065

This book follows "the heavily pregnant young narrator" as she "takes a long walk though the streets of Rome. . . . But while that is all that actually happens, her thoughts wander freely, touching often on her absent husband, Gert, a soldier stationed in North Africa. . . . The specific horrors of the war figure little in her thoughts, other than a vague recognition that the Führer who 'places himself above God' should not be obeyed blindly." (Kirkus Reviews)

DeMille, Nelson

Plum Island. Warner Bks. 1997 511p

ISBN 0-446-51506-X

LC 97-7221

"Key to the novel's sway is its boisterous plot, as DeMille expertly melds medical mystery, police procedural and nautical adventure, adding assorted love interests and capping matters with a ferocious storm at sea." Publ Wkly

Other titles in this series are:
The lion's game (2000)
Night fall (2004)
Wild fire (2006)
The lion (2010)
The panther (2012)
Radiant angel (2015)

DeMille, Nelson

Wild fire; a novel. Warner Books 2006 519p $26.99

ISBN 978-0-446-57967-4; 0-446-57967-X

LC 2006-20982

This thriller features "John Corey, the ex-NYPD detective who now works on a government anti-terrorism task force. . . . Bain Madox, a brilliant and probably insane villain, has hatched a fiendishly clever plot to force the U.S. to launch an all-out nuclear attack against the entire Islamic world. It's up to Corey, with the help of his FBI agent wife, to stop Madox before he can detonate nuclear weapons on American soil. Set in 2002, barely a year after 9/11, the novel presents a what-if scenario that's so plausible we have to remind ourselves that DeMille is making the whole thing up. Or is he? As usual, DeMille appears to have done a ton of research; what sets his thrillers apart from those of some of his competitors is the way he seamlessly incorporates real technology and real government organizations into his stories." Booklist

Dennis-Benn, Nicole Y.

Here Comes the Sun; A Novel. by Nicole Dennis-Benn. W. W. Norton & Co. 2016 352 p. $26.95

ISBN 1631491768; 9781631491764

LC 2016011646

In this novel by Nicole Dennis-Benn, "women battle for independence while a maelstrom of change threatens their Jamaican village. . . . At an opulent resort in Montego Bay, Margot hustles to send her younger sister, Thandi, to school. Taught as a girl to trade her sexuality for survival, Margot is ruthlessly determined to shield Thandi from the same fate. . . . As they face the impending destruction of their community, each woman . . . must confront long-hidden scars." (Publisher's note)

"Haunting and superbly crafted, this is a magical book from a writer of immense talent and intelligence." Kirkus

Deón, Natashia

★ **Grace**; A Novel. by Natashia Deon. Counterpoint 2016 404 p. $26

ISBN 1619027208; 9781619027206

In this novel, by Natashia Deon, "for a runaway slave in the 1840s south, life on the run can be just as dangerous as life under a sadistic Massa. That's what fifteen-year-old Naomi learns after she escapes the brutal confines of life on an Alabama plantation. Striking out on her own, she must leave behind her beloved Momma and sister Hazel and takes refuge in a Georgia brothel run by a freewheeling, gun-toting Jewish madam named Cynthia." (Publisher's note)

"Deón stays in control of her complex material, from its clever parallel structure to the women's psychological reactions to relentless tension." Booklist

Dépestre, René, 1926-

Hadriana in all my dreams; René Depestre ; translated by Kaiama L. Glover ; with a foreword by Edwidge Danticat. Akashic Books 2017 256 p. map (trade pbk. original) $15.95

ISBN 9781617755330; 9781617755552

LC 2016953896

This book, by René Depestre, translated by Kaiama L. Glover, "takes place . . . during Carnival in 1938 in the Haitian village of Jacmel. A beautiful young French woman, Hadriana, is about to marry a Haitian boy. . . . But on the morning of the wedding, Hadriana drinks a mysterious potion and collapses at the altar. Transformed into a zombie, her wedding becomes her funeral. She is . . . revived by an evil sorcerer, and then disappears into popular legend." (Publisher's note)

"Depestre presents a rich and nuanced exploration of large and significant themes expertly couched in one fantastical, expertly translated tale." Booklist

Desai, Anita

★ **Clear** light of day. Houghton Mifflin 2000 182p pa $13

ISBN 0-618-07451-1

LC 00-61326

First published 1980 by Harper & Row

This work "does what only the best novels can do: it totally submerges us. It takes us so deeply into another world that we almost fear we won't be able to climb out again." N Y Times Book Rev

Desai, Kiran

The **inheritance** of loss. Atlantic Monthly 2006 324p $24

ISBN 0-87113-929-4

LC 2005-52416

"In a crumbling, isolated house at the foot of Mount Kanchenjunga lives an embittered old judge who wants to retire in peace when his orphaned granddaughter Sai arrives on his doorstep. The judge's chatty cook watches over her, but his thoughts are mostly with his son, Biju, hopscotching from one New York restaurant job to another, trying to stay a step ahead of the INS, forced to consider his country's place in the world. When a Nepalese insurgency in the mountains threatens Sai's new-sprung romance with her handsome Nepali tutor and causes their lives to descend into chaos, they, too, are forced to confront their colliding interests." (Publisher's note)

This "novel is set in the nineteen-eighties in the northeast corner of India, where the borders of several Himalayan states—Bhutan and Sikkim, Nepal and Tibet—meet. At the head of the novel's teeming cast is Jemubhai Patel, a Cambridge-educated judge who has retired from serving a country he finds 'too messy for justice.' He lives in an isolated house with his cook, his orphaned seventeen-year-old granddaughter, and a red setter, whose company Jemubhai prefers to that of human beings. The tranquillity of his existence is contrasted with the life of the cook's son, working in grimy Manhattan restaurants, and with his granddaughter's affair with a Nepali tutor involved in an insurgency that irrevocably alters Jemubhai's life. Briskly paced and sumptuously written, the novel ponders questions of nationhood, modernity, and class, in ways both moving and revelatory." New Yorker

DeSilva, Bruce

Providence Rag; a Liam Mulligan novel. Bruce DeSilva. Forge Books 2014 352 p. (A Liam Mulligan novel) (hardback) $25.99

ISBN 0765374293; 9780765374295

LC 2013025786

This book, by Bruce DeSilva, "melds moral dilemmas with a suspenseful plot in [the] third novel featuring Providence, R.I.-based reporter Liam Mulligan. . . . In 1992, . . . an editor assigns him to help cover a gory double murder. . . . Mulligan ends up cracking the case, but the main action concerns the fate of the convicted killer, who is due to be released after six years thanks to a legal fluke." (Publisher's Weekly)

"[T]here is real suspense here. And Mulligan's character, played off the vicissitudes of his job, is skillfully layered and engaging." Booklist

DeSilva, Bruce

Rogue island; Bruce DeSilva. Forge 2010 304 p. ill.

ISBN 0765327260; 9780765327260

LC 2011389934

Macavity Award: Best First Mystery Novel (2011)

Edgar Allan Poe Award: Best First Novel by an American Author (2011)

This crime mystery novel by Bruce DeSilva follows the journalist Liam Mulligan. "His beat is Providence, Rhode Island, and he knows every street and alley. He knows the priests and prostitutes, the cops and street thugs. He knows the mobsters and politicians--who are pretty much one and the same. Someone is systematically burning down the neighborhood Mulligan grew up in, people he knows and loves are perishing in the flames, and the public is on the verge of panic. With the police looking for answers in all the wrong places, and with the whole city of Providence on his back, Mulligan must find the hand that strikes the match." (Publisher's note)

DeSilva, Bruce

A **Scourge** of Vipers; Bruce DeSilva. St. Martin's Press 2015 320 p. $25.99

ISBN 0765374315; 9780765374318

LC 2015936660

In this novel by Bruce DeSilva, "to solve Rhode Island's budget crisis, the state's colorful governor, Attila the Nun, wants to legalize sports gambling; but her plan has unexpected consequences. Organized crime, professional sports leagues, and others who have a lot to lose--or gain--if gambling is made legal flood the state with money to buy the votes of state legislators." (Publisher's note)

"DeSilva is spot-on, as only a journalist with a 40-year newspaper career behind him can be, when it comes to corruption. His dialogue, however, has everyone, including the former nun, sounding as if they've just completed a 'Talk like a Martin Scorsese thug' course." Booklist

Deutermann, P. T.

★ The **ghosts** of Bungo Suido; a novel. by P. T. Deutermann. 1st ed. St. Martin's Press 2013 343 p. (hardcover) $25.99

ISBN 1250018021; 9781250018021

LC 2013009264

In this novel by P.T. Deutermann, set during World War II, "America's naval forces face what seems an insurmountable threat from Japan: immense Yamato-class battleships, which dwarf every other ship at sea. Built in secrecy, these ships seem invincible, and lay waste to any challengers. Lieutenant Commander Gar Hammond . . . is now captain of a new submarine. Hammond may be the navy's only hope to locate and stop the Japanese super-ship before it launches." (Publisher's note)

Deutermann, Peter T., 1941-

Pacific glory; P.T. Deutermann. St. Martin's Press 2011 vii, 389p.p

ISBN 9780312599447; 0312599447

LC 2010041944

This book tells "the story of Annapolis friends Marsh Vincent, who barely survives the Savo [Island] debacle [during World War II,] and Mick McCarty, whose dive bombing at Midway sinks a Japanese aircraft carrier that helped devastate Pearl Harbor, and Glory Hawthorne, a woman both love who has become a navy nurse. Having seen the savagery of naval war, Marsh fears he may not have the courage to face it again. Mick, an Annapolis football hero, has problems with alcohol and authority. He fears that he may be grounded. Ultimately, both are off Samar when a small group of tiny escort carriers and destroyers finds itself facing an overwhelming force of cruisers—and the Yamato, the largest battleship ever built." (Booklist)

Dev, Sonali

A **Bollywood** affair; Sonali Dev. Kensington Pub Corp 2014 304 p. $15

ISBN 1617730130; 9781617730139

In this book, by Sonali Dev, "Bollywood . . . director, Samir Rathod, has come to Michigan to secure a divorce for his older brother. Persuading a naïve village girl to sign the papers should be easy. . . . But Mili is neither a fool nor a gold-digger. Open-hearted yet complex, she's trying to reconcile her independence with cherished traditions. And before he can stop himself, Samir is immersed in Mili's life." (Publisher's note)

"Dev's heartfelt debut novel is rich in scenes and images illuminating Indian culture, leaving readers with a greater understanding and appreciation of Indian traditions while beautifully capturing the struggle between familial duty and self-discovery." Booklist

Dewitt, Helen

Lightning rods. New Directions 2011 273p $24.95

ISBN 978-0-8112-1943-3; 0-8112-1943-7

This is an "exercise in novel as extrapolation. Ms. Dewitt's method is to introduce a device into the world as we know it and systematically explore how the world reacts to that device. Joe's original moment of epiphany is almost superfluous; the real fun results once the idea exists and must be dealt with. Ms. Dewitt creates the problems, identifies the problems, and then figures out how to solve them. It's an appealingly practical way to think about writing fiction, and one that ignores any distinction between realism and fantasy." N Y Observer

DeWitt, Patrick

The **Sisters** brothers. Ecco Press 2011 328p il $24.99

ISBN 978-0-06-204126-5; 0-0-6204126-6

LC 2011282605

Governor General's Literary Awards: English-Language Fiction (2011)

Rogers Writers' Trust Fiction Prize (2011)

A novel about the "life and times of two gunslingers, Eli and Charlie Sisters. Contracted by their boss, the mysterious Commodore, the brothers are ordered to hightail it out of 1851 Oregon City and head to California's gold-rush camps. There, they'll meet a dandy named Henry Morris (a man who 'is not above biting') who will lead them to their intended target: prospector Hermann Kermit Warm. The brothers don't really know why the Commodore wants Warm dead, or even whether he's innocent (it wouldn't surprise them if he was), but taking lives is their job, and they set out on the trail with two ramshackle horses. It seems like a plot straight out of a spaghetti western, but from the start, deWitt has more than a few tricks in his saddlebag. Narrated in delicious deadpan by Eli, the kinder of the two brothers, ('Our blood is the same, we just use it differently,' Eli explains) the two men embark on a series of picaresque misadventures. . . . When the brothers finally get to California and find their victim, all expectations are gleefully reversed. The brothers discover that nothing is really what it seems to be, that a career change could be in the works, and the plot peels away like onion skin, revealing startling secrets that lead to a transformative ending as unexpectedly moving as it is satisfying." Boston Globe

DeWitt, Patrick

Undermajordomo Minor; Patrick deWitt. Ecco 2015 320 p. $26.99

ISBN 0062281208; 9780062281203

LC 2015373926

"Lucien (Lucy) Minor is the resident odd duck in the bucolic hamlet of Bury. Friendless and loveless, young and aimless, Lucy is a compulsive liar, a sickly weakling in a town famous for producing brutish giants. Then Lucy accepts employment assisting the Majordomo of the remote, foreboding Castle Von Aux. While tending to his new post as Undermajordomo, Lucy soon discovers the place harbors many dark secrets, not least of which is the whereabouts of the castle's master, Baron Von Aux." (Publisher's note)

"DeWitt has delivered another intriguing, compelling, and thought-provoking winner that will appeal to anyone who wants to be captivated by a smart, entertaining read." Booklist

DeWoskin, Rachel

Big girl small; Rachel DeWoskin. Farrar, Straus and Giroux 2011 294p. $25

ISBN 978-0-374-11257-8; 9781250002532; 9780374112578; 9781611731132

LC 201033106

Alex Award (2012)

"Bright and sardonic Judy Lohden, a 16-year-old dwarf freshly enrolled in Ann Arbor's Darcy Arts Academy, falls victim to 'the worst Steven King Carrie prank in the history of dating' at the hands of popular boy Jeff Legassic, who becomes an object of desire as soon as he and Judy meet cute the first week of school. The book opens with Judy hiding out in a seedy motel; throughout the novel, she slowly unveils her secret and reveals her two visions of herself—that of a pretty teenage girl with an hourglass figure who happens to be three feet nine inches tall, and that of a sideshow attraction. It's a rare author who is willing to subject her protagonist to the extreme ranges of degradation and redemption to which DeWoskin subjects Judy; thankfully, she manages it beautifully." Publ Wkly

Dexter, Colin

The **daughters** of Cain. Crown 1995 295p

ISBN 0-517-70067-0

First published 1994 in the United Kingdom

In this Inspector Morse case "the crime is the murder of a retired Oxford don, and the stratagem is to make the homicide seem easy to solve. . . . Mr. Dexter is a superb technician who torments the reader with logistical details that contradict every previously established point in his puzzle. Red herrings are a specialty. But the canny author also strews the path with literary quotations to think on, polysyllabic words to look up and characters whose lives are so complicated they turn into richly distracting mini-dramas." N Y Times Book Rev

Dexter, Colin

The **remorseful** day. Crown 2000 363p

ISBN 0-609-60622-0

LC 99-59840

First published 1999 in the United Kingdom

"A two-year-old murder has baffled the police in Burford, a rural English village. Inspector Morse, who excels at this sort of puzzle, refuses to touch it, despite anonymous phone calls offering new evidence. Then his sidekick, Sergeant Lewis, discovers that the inspector knew the murdered woman." Libr J

Dexter, Colin

The **way** through the woods. Crown 1993 296p

ISBN 0-517-59444-7

LC 92-40762

First published 1992 in the United Kingdom

"To say that the investigation is tricky is only to hint at the technical density of the plot, which, once all the tantalizing enigmas have been packed up, hinges on the most basic human frailties. Dazzling." N Y Times Book Rev

Dexter, Pete

★ **Deadwood**. Random House 1986 365p

ISBN 0-394-53669-X

LC 85-19635

This novel "is unpredictable, hyperbolic and, page after page, uproarious; a joshing book written in high spirits and a raw appreciation for the past." N Y Times Book Rev

Dexter, Pete

Paris Trout. Random House 1988 306p

ISBN 0-394-56370-0

LC 87-43314

"Paris Trout, the small-town Georgia store owner . . . sleeps with a sheet of lead under his mattress. He's afraid someone is going to hide under his bed and shoot him in the middle of the night—and for no good reason, as Trout sees it. He was only taking care of business, trying to collect on Henry Ray Boxer's debt. That little black girl, Rosie Sayers, who got shot and killed in the scuffle, shouldn't have got in his way, or the woman with Rosie, who still walks around with Trout's bullet in her chest. . . . Mr. Dexter has created a character whose racism is a blunt, unregenerate fact, as primitive and willful as an earthquake or a rainstorm—and just as sealed off from argument, examination or questions of mercy. What the town's polite society takes care to disguise in Sunday-go-to-meeting euphemisms, Paris sets in defiant, ugly relief; he makes it easy for them to believe they are innocent of racism." N Y Times Book Rev

Dexter, Pete

Spooner. Grand Central Pub. 2009 469p $26.99

ISBN 978-0-446-54072-8; 0-446-54072-2

LC 2009-06087

"The title character is one Warren Spooner, a kid dogged by the fact that his mother's favorite child, Spooner's twin brother, died at birth. Spooner's dad dies soon afterward. Into the family's life arrives Ottosson, [a] disgraced young naval officer turned schoolteacher. He is a man of great virtues: smart, tough, capable and wreathed in infinite patience. He will need the latter quality in spades to deal with his troubled stepson. . . . Despite the autobiographical elements in 'Spooner,' the book lacks a narrative arc that permits a complete picture of the protagonist's life. This is not cited as a fault. It is a function of how this picaresque novel serves as a work of memory, real or imagined." Denver Post

Diamant, Anita

The **Boston** girl; a novel. Anita Diamant. Scribner 2015 336 p. (hardcover) $26

ISBN 1439199353; 9781439199350; 9781439199367

LC 2014019284

This novel, by Anita Diamant, is "about a young Jewish woman growing up in Boston in the early twentieth century. . . . Addie is . . . the spirited daughter of an immigrant Jewish family. . . . Growing up in the North End of Boston, then a teeming multicultural neighborhood, Addie's intelligence and curiosity take her to a world her parents can't imagine--a world of short skirts, movies, celebrity culture, and new opportunities for women." (Publisher's note)

Diamant, Anita

Last days of Dogtown; a novel. Scribner 2005 263p il $25

ISBN 0-7432-2573-2

LC 2005-45191

This novel "weaves together seemingly disparate stories of a dying Massachusetts town. . . . In the early 1800s, Dogtown is a village on Cape Ann populated by spinsters, free slaves, and prostitutes, all of whom are reviled by the surrounding communities. Beginning with the death of a town patriarch and ending when the last resident expires, Dogtown's final days are filled with all the secrets a town can keep. Several characters stand out, including Tammy Younger, the town pariah, and Judy Rhines, whose affair with a free African is kept secret to heartbreaking effect. Diamant has a gift for storytelling and breathes life into this dying town and its eccentric inhabitants." Libr J

Diamant, Anita

★ The **red** tent. St. Martin's Press 1997 321p $24.95; pa $16.95

ISBN 0-312-16978-7; 0-312-35376-6 pa

LC 97-16825

"Diamant's fiction debut links the passions of the early Israelites to the ongoing traditions of modern Jews, while the red tent of her title (where women retreat for menstruation, childbirth and illness) becomes a resonant symbol of womanly strength, love and wisdom. Despite a few unprofitable digressions, Diamant succeeds admirably in depicting the lives of women in the age that engendered our civilization and our most enduring values." Publ Wkly

Diamond, De'nesha

A **gangster** and a gentleman; Kiki Swinson, De'nesha Diamond. Dafina 2012 320 p. $15

ISBN 0758251823; 9780758251824

This book contains two novellas, one by Kiki Swinson and one by De'Nesha Diamond. In Swinson's "I Need a Gangsta," "Melody Goldman isn't about to let her rich, cheating, ungrateful husband walk out and leave her with nothing" so she hires ex-con Scott Harris to help her." In Diamond's "Gentlemen Prefer Bullets," "publicist Blake Scott" has kept "far, far away from her gangsta kingpin father. But now the only person who can protect her is his enforcer, Eli Hardwick." (Publisher's note)

Diaz, Junot

The **brief** wondrous life of Oscar Wao; Junot Díaz. Riverhead Books 2007 339 p.

ISBN 1-59448-958-0; 978-1-59448-958-7

LC 2007017251

In this novel "Díaz presents a slice of the vast history of Santo Domingo and the intricate past and present of a doomed family. . . . Oscar de León [is] Díaz's sci-fi obsessed, overweight, romantic hero who hopes to someday be the 'Dominican Stephen King.' Oscar is the ultimate outcast both at home and at school. This 'ghetto nerd' lacks the philandering, macho finesse expected of a Dominican male. His bookish manner and unappealing looks relegate his high school experience to the level of 'a medieval spectacle,' an experience 'like being put in the stocks and forced to endure the pelting and outrages of a mob of deranged half-wits.' But this is more than a tale of mere adolescent anguish. Oscar and his family appear to be the hapless victims of a so-called Dominican curse, or the 'fukú,' that has followed them for generations from the shores of their homeland to New Jersey. Díaz weaves the stories of Lola, his troubled but supportive sister, and Belicia, his hardened mother, along with various other family members, to portray a colorful and complex portrait of mad love, old-world superstition, and the continual strivings of a diaspora." Christ Sci Monit

Díaz, Junot, 1968-

★ **This** is how you lose her; Junot Díaz. Riverhead Books 2012 213 p. $26.95

ISBN 1594487367; 9781594487361

LC 2012024051

National Book Award Finalist: Fiction (2012)

This short story collection, by Pulitzer Prize-winning author Junot Díaz, "turns . . . to the haunting, impossible power of love--obsessive love, illicit love, fading love, maternal love. . . . At the heart of these stories is the irrepressible, irresistible Yunior, a young hardhead whose longing for love is equaled only by his recklessness--and by the extraordinary women he loves and loses." (Publisher's note)

Dibdin, Michael

Blood rain; an Aurelio Zen mystery. Pantheon Bks. 2000 273p

ISBN 0-375-40915-7

LC 99-46938

First published 1999 in the United Kingdom

Didbin "uses the somber tones, circuitous locutions and dense plot structure appropriate to a region where every gesture—from a chess game to a political assassination—sends a subtle and dangerous message." N Y Times Book Rev

Dibdin, Michael

Ratking; Michael Dibdin. Bantam Books 1989 266p. (pbk.) $13.95; o.p.

ISBN 9780679768548; 055305337X

LC 88-47832

In this book, the winner of the 1988 Gold Dagger award, "Italian Police Commissioner Aurelio Zen is dispatched to investigate the kidnapping of Ruggiero Miletti, a powerful Perugian industrialist. But nobody much wants Zen to succeed: not the local authorities, who view him as an interloper, and certainly not Miletti's children, who seem content to let the head of the family languish in the hands of his abductors -- if he's still alive. Was Miletti truly the victim of professionals? Or might his kidnapper be someone closer to home: his preening son Daniele, with his million-lire wardrobe and his profitable drug business? His daughter, Cinzia, whose vapid beauty conceals a devastating secret?" (Publisher's note)

Followed by: Vendetta (1998)

Dick, Philip K.

★ The **collected** stories of Philip K. Dick. Underwood/Miller 1987 5v

ISBN 0-88733-053-3

Dick, Philip K.

★ **Do** androids dream of electric sheep? Ballantine Books 1996 244p pa $13.95

ISBN 0-345-40447-5

LC 96-96117

First published 1968

"In a future where technological sophistication has made the ersatz virtually indistinguishable from the real, the hero is a bounty hunter who must track down and eliminate androids passing for human. . . . A key novel in Dick's canon." Anatomy of Wonder 5

Dick, Philip K.

Five novels of the 1960s & 70s; Martian time-slip; Dr. Bloodmoney; Now wait for last year; Flow my tears, the policeman said; A scanner darkly. Library of America 2008 1128p $40

ISBN 978-1-59853-025-4

"Martian Time-Slip (1964) unfolds on a parched and thinly colonized Red Planet where the unscrupulous seek to profit from a troubled child's time-fracturing visions. Dr. Bloodmoney, or How We Got Along After the Bomb (1965) chronicles the interwoven stories of a multiracial community of survivors, including the scientist who may have been responsible for World War III. . . . Now Wait for Last Year (1966) explores the effects of JJ-180, a hallucinogen that alters not only perception, but reality. In Flow My Tears, the Policeman Said (1974), a television star seeks to unravel a mystery that has left him stripped of his identity. A Scanner Darkly (1977), the basis for the 2006 film, envisions a drug-addled world in which a narcotics officer's tenuous hold on sanity is strained by his new surveillance assignment: himself." Publisher's note

Dick, Philip K.

★ **Four** novels of the 1960s; The man in the high castle; The three stigmata of Palmer Eldritch; Do androids dream of electric sheep?; Ubik. Library of America 2007 830p $35

ISBN 978-1-59853-009-4; 1-598-53009-7

LC 2006-48776

"These novels grapple with spirituality, rather than science. In The Man in the High Castle [1962], set in a United States that has been defeated by the Axis powers in World War II, the characters use the ancient Chinese text I Ching to determine their actions. In The Three Stigmata [1965], hallucinogenic drugs provide virtual reality experiences that lead to discussions of the existence and nature of God. Do Androids Dream [1968] features a religion, Mercerism, in which adherents experience real suffering through a machine that registers their empathy for a sacrificial victim. Ubik [1969] utilizes the Tibetan Book of the Dead to examine the existence and consciousness of an afterlife. I don't want this to sound as if Dick is some dry-as-bones, proselytizing prophet. These novels are also funny, thrilling and stimulating. There are shootouts with renegade androids and undercover spies. There are parodies of consumer culture. There are debates about historicity and drug use. Each novel offers a reading experience that is cathartic while reading, yet offers fruit for continued thought afterward." Philadelphia Inquirer

Dick, Philip K.

★ The **man** in the high castle. Vintage Books 1992 259p pa $12

ISBN 0-679-74067-8

LC 91-50895

First published 1962 by Putnam

"An alternate history in which Germany and Japan won World War II and partitioned the U.S., except for the Rocky Mountain States, which were left in a kind of political limbo. Faction-ridden Nazism oppressively rules the eastern U.S. In the west, the Japanese overlords are reconciling Oriental and American cultural values. . . . This is Dick's most important early book." Anatomy of Wonder 5

Dick, Philip K.

The **minority** report. Pantheon Bks. 2002 103p $12.95

ISBN 0-375-42187-4

LC 2002-72313

Originally published posthumously as a short story

"Police Commissioner John Anderton finds himself at the mercy of his own crime-prevention system when the prescient precogs he's hired to stop crime before it starts peg him as a soon-to-be murderer." Publ Wkly

Dick, Philip K.

VALIS and later novels; edited by Jonathan Lethem. Library of America 2009 849p $35

ISBN 9781598530445

"The collection opens with A Maze of Death (1970). . . . Mysteriously summoned to the planet Delmak-O, a motley group of colonists attempts to survive together in a hostile new world. . . . . [VALIS (1981) is a] self-portrait of a man confronting a 'Vast Active Living Intelligence System,' torn between conflicting interpretations of what might be gnostic illumination or mental collapse. In The Divine Invasion (1981), the life of a solitary off-world colonist is hijacked by a local alien, who turns out to be the Yahweh of Judeo-Christian tradition. Returning to Earth with his pregnant wife in tow, Dick's hapless Herb Asher finds himself thrust into the middle of an apocalyptic war between Good and Evil. . . . The Transmigration of Timothy Archer (1982), Dick's last novel, is by turns a theological mystery story, a roman à clef, and a starkly disillusioned portrait of contemporary California life. Based loosely on the career of Bishop James Pike, Dick's close friend and a kindred spirit, the novel's title character gives up his comfortable place in the church hierarchy in a tragic quest for enlightenment." Publisher's note

Dickens, Charles

★ **Bleak** House; with the original illustrations by Phiz; introduced by Barbara Hardy. Knopf 1991 xlix, 891p il $23

ISBN 0-679-40568-2

LC 91-52974

First published 1853

"In this novel, Dickens attacks the delays and archaic absurdities of the courts, which he knew about firsthand." Reader's Ency. 4th edition

Dickens, Charles

★ A **Christmas** carol; with illustrations by Arthur Rackham. Knopf 1994 155p il $13.95

ISBN 0-679-43639-1

LC 95-163031

Written in 1843

"This Christmas story of nineteenth century England has delighted young and old for generations. In it, a miser, Scrooge, through a series of dreams, finds the true Christmas spirit. . . . The story ends with the much-quoted cry of Tiny Tim, the crippled son of Bob Cratchit, whom Scrooge now aids: 'God bless us, everyone!'" Haydn. Thesaurus of Book Dig

Dickens, Charles

★ **David** Copperfield; with the original illustrations by Phiz; introduced by Michael Slater. Knopf 1991 xlii, 891p il $25

ISBN 0-679-40571-2

LC 91-52995

First published 1850

This novel "incorporates material from the autobiography Dickens had recently begun but soon abandoned and is written in the first person, a new technique for him. Although Copperfield differs from his creator in many ways, Dickens uses many early personal experiences that had meant much to him—his own period of work in a factory while his father was jailed, his schooling and reading, his passion for Maria Beadnell (a woman much like Dora Spenlow), and (more cursorily) his emergence from parliamentary reporting into successful novel writing." Merriam-Webster's Ency of Lit

Dickens, Charles

Dombey and Son; with forty illustrations by `Phiz; introduced by Lucy Hughes-Hallett. Knopf 1994 xlvii, 889p il $23

ISBN 0-679-43591-3

LC 94-4778

First published 1848

"The proud, unfeeling Mr. Dombey has but one ambition: to have a son so that his firm might be called Dombey and Son. When his son Paul is born, he promises to fulfill this ambition, which overrides even grief at the death of Mrs. Dombey. Young Paul, a delicate, sensitive boy, is quite unequal to the great things expected of him; he is sent to Mr. Blimber's school and gives way under the strain of the discipline. . . . Mr. Dombey is embittered by Paul's death. Florence, his daughter, lives on with him, trying desperately to win his love, but she has succeeded only in incurring his hatred because she lives while her brother died. Dombey marries again, but his second wife, Edith Granger, runs off with Mr. Carker, his business manager. Florence marries the kind young Walter Gay. Dombey's firm fails, and alone and miserable, he finds himself longing for the sweet and kind daughter whom he treated so coldly. The two are reconciled, and Dombey tries to expiate his past through his grandchildren." Reader's Ency. 4th edition

Dickens, Charles

★ **Great** expectations; illustrated by F.W. Pailthrope with an introduction by Michael Slater. Knopf 1992 xxxiv, 469p il $21

ISBN 0-679-40579-8

LC 91-53219

First published 1861

"The first-person narrative relates the coming-of-age of Pip (Philip Pirrip). Reared in the marshes of Kent by his disagreeable sister and her sweet-natured husband, the blacksmith Joe Gargery, the young Pip one day helps a convict to escape. Later he is sent to live with Miss Havisham, a woman driven half-mad years earlier by her lover's departure on their wedding day. . . . When an anonymous benefactor makes it possible for Pip to go to London for an education, he credits Miss Havisham. . . . Pips benefactor turns out to have been Abel Magwitch, the convict he once aided, who dies awaiting trial after Pip is unable to help him a second time. Joe rescues Pip from despair and nurses him back to health." Merriam-Webster's Ency of Lit

Dickens, Charles

Little Dorrit. Knopf 1992 xxxvii, 836p il $22

ISBN 0-679-41725-7

LC 92-52919

First published 1857

"Satirizes the Civil Service under the style of the Circumlocution Office. Also pictures prison life. Little Dorrit's father being Father of the Marshalsea. The melodramatic element appears in the history of the House of Clennam: with the usual complement of originals: Mr. F.'s Aunt, the Meagles, Pancks, Mr. Nanby, Mr. Casby, Flora Finching, Miss Wade, Tallycoram." Baker. Guide to the Best Fic

Dickens, Charles

Martin Chuzzlewit; with forty illustrations by Phiz; introduced by William Boyd. Knopf 1994 xlvii, 851p il $20

ISBN 0-679-43884-X

LC 95-136833

"The story's protagonist, Martin Chuzzlewit, is an apprentice architect who is fired by Seth Pecksniff and is also disinherited by his own eccentric, wealthy grandfather. Martin and a servant, Mark Tapley, travel to the United States, where they are swindled by land speculators and have other unpleasant but sometimes comic experiences. Thoroughly disillusioned with the New World, the pair returns to England, where a chastened Martin is reconciled with his grandfather, who gives his approval to Martin's forthcoming marriage to his true love, Mary Graham." Merriam-Webster's Ency of Lit

Dickens, Charles

The **mystery** of Edwin Drood; with 12 illustrations by Luke Fildes and 2 by Charles Collins, and an introduction by S. C. Roberts. Oxford Univ. Press 1956 278p il

ISBN 0-19-254516-7

First published 1870

"This novel Dickens left unfinished at his death. The striking opening scene shows John Jasper, precentor of Cloisterham cathedral, in an opium den. He is the uncle of Edwin Drood, and persecutes with his evil passion Rosa Bud, to whom Drood is betrothed by an arrangement made by the late respective fathers of the two orphans. Actually Edwin is cool to Rosa, and it is another orphan, Neville Landless, who is attracted to her. The sinister Jasper foments a quarrel between Edwin and Neville, not knowing that the engagement has already been broken off. The same night Edwin disappears, and there is circumstantial evidence pointing to Neville as his murderer. The latter is arrested, but as no body has been found, is released. There turns up in the neighborhood a white-haired stranger who calls himself Datchery and acts like a detective on the trail of Jasper. Here the story breaks off with no indication as to how it would have ended." Haydn. Thesaurus of Book Dig

Dickens, Charles

★ **Nicholas** Nickleby; with an introduction by John Carey. Knopf 1993 lvii, 843p il $24

ISBN 0-679-42307-9

LC 93-1856

First published 1839

After Nicholas Nickleby's father dies bankrupt, Nicholas, his sister and their mother go to London to seek aid from Nicholas' uncle, a moneylender. At the scheming miser's insistence, Nicholas "first serves as usher to Mr. Wackford Squeers, schoolmaster at Dotheboys Hall; the brutality of Squeers and his wife, especially toward a poor, half-witted boy named Smike, causes Nicholas to leave in disgust. Smike runs away from school to follow Nicholas, remaining his follower until he dies. Next Nicholas joins the theatrical company of Mr. Crummles, and finally he secures a good post in a counting house owned by the benevolent Cheeryble brothers, Ned and Charles, self-made merchants ready to help those struggling against ill fortune." Reader's Ency. 4th edition

Dickens, Charles

The **old** curiosity shop; with seventy-five illustrations by Cattermole and `Phiz'; introduced by Peter Washington. Knopf 1995 569p il $24

ISBN 0-679-44373-8

LC 95-75208

First published 1841; first Everyman's library edition 1907

This is the "story of Little Nell Trent and the evil dwarf Quilp. When Little Nell's grandfather gambles away his curiosity shop to his creditor Quilp, the girl and the old man flee London. Nell's friend Kit Nubbles and a mysterious Single Gentleman (who turns out to be the wealthy brother of Nell's grandfather) attempt to find them but are thwarted by Quilp, who drowns while fleeing the law. Little Nell dies before Kit and the Single Gentleman arrive, and her brokenhearted grandfather dies days later." Merriam-Webster's Ency of Lit

Dickens, Charles

Oliver Twist; with twenty-four illustrations by George Cruikshank; introduced by Michael Slater. Knopf 1992 xlvi, 427p il $20

ISBN 0-679-41724-9

LC 92-52899

First published 1837-1838

"A boy from an English workhouse falls into the hands of rogues who train him to be a pickpocket. The story of his struggles to escape from an environment of crime is one of hardship, danger and the severe obstacles overcome." Natl Counc of Teachers of Engl

Dickens, Charles

Our mutual friend; with an introduction by Andrew Sanders. Knopf 1994 xliii, 832p $22

ISBN 0-679-42028-2

LC 93-81033

First published 1865

"John Harmon, 'our mutual friend,' will inherit a fortune if he marries Bella Wilfer. He assumes the names of Julius Handford and later John Rokesmith, and his supposed death helps him conceal his identity. John's father's foreman, Nicodemus Boffin, and his wife, Henrietta, help him with the ruse. He enters the employ of Boffin, who has adopted Bella. Bella has had her head turned by wealth, but reforms when her eyes are opened to its evils; she marries Harmon. Other characters are: Jesse Hexam; his son Charley, and daughter, Lizzie; Bradley Headstone, schoolmaster, who is jealous of Eugene Wrayburn's love for Lizzie Hexam; Fanny Cleaver (Jenny Wren), a doll's dressmaker; one-legged Silas Wegg, the villain in the main plot, as Headstone is in the secondary one. Here again Dickens protests against the poor laws through the character Betty Hidger, who fears the workhouse." Haydn. Thesaurus of Book Dig

Dickens, Charles

The **posthumous** papers of the Pickwick Club; with forty-three illustrations by Seymour and `Phiz and an introduction by Bernard Darwin. Oxford Univ. Press 1959 xxiii, 801p il

ISBN 0-19-254501-9

First published 1837

"Episodes of the doings and foibles of the Pickwick Club. . . . The book is made up of letters and manuscripts about the club's actions. Among the incidents are: the army parade; trip to Manor Farm; the saving of Rachel Wardle from the villain, Alfred Jingle; trip to Eatonsville; Mrs. Leo Hunter's party of authors, including Count Smorltork and

Charles FitzMarshall; ice skating. Pickwick's landlady, Mrs. Bardell, faints in his arms and compromises the unsophisticated gentleman. She sues him for breach of promise and an amusing court trial follows. Pickwick refuses to pay damages and is put in Fleet prison. Sam Weller, his faithful servant, accompanies him. Mrs. Bardell is also incarcerated for not paying the costs of the trial. When Pickwick is released he retires to a house outside London, with Weller, and the latter's new bride, Mary, as housekeeper. He dissolves the club and spends his time arranging its memoranda." Haydn. Thesaurus of Book Dig

Dickens, Charles

★ A **tale** of two cities; with an introduction by Simon Schama and sixteen illustrations by Phiz. Knopf 1993 xxviii, 413p il $20

ISBN 0-679-42073-8

LC 92-73542

First published 1859

"Although Dickens borrowed from Thomas Carlyle's history, The French Revolution, for his sprawling tale of London and revolutionary Paris, the novel offers more drama than accuracy. The scenes of large-scale mob violence are especially vivid, if superficial in historical understanding. The complex plot involves Sydney Carton's sacrifice of his own life on behalf of his friends Charles Darnay and Lucie Manette. While political events drive the story, Dickens takes a decidedly anti-political tone, lambasting both aristocratic tyranny and revolutionary excess." Merriam-Webster's Ency of Lit

Dickey, Eric Jerome

One night; by Eric Jerome Dickey. Dutton 2015 368 p. (hardcover) $26.95

ISBN 0525954856; 9780525954859

LC 2014030840

"A couple checks in to an upscale hotel. The pair seem unlikely companions, from opposing strata of society, but their attraction is palpable to all who observe them—or overhear their cries of passion. In the course of twelve hours, con games, erotic interludes, jealousy, violence, and murder swirl around them. Will they part ways in bliss, in sorrow, or in death?" (Publisher's note)

Dickey, James

★ **Deliverance**. Houghton Mifflin 1970 278p

ISBN 9780385313872

LC 82462524

"The plot revolves around a canoe trip undertaken by four city men as a break in routine and to see a wilderness river before it is dammed. Early in the journey two of the men are attacked by brutal mountaineers and another member of the quartet is killed. Dickey probes the diverse personalities of each man, showing clearly that leadership devolves on the one most able to solve a problem rationally rather than the one most given to theorizing about how to cope with the issue of basic survival." Booklist

Dickinson, Peter

★ The **yellow** room conspiracy. Mysterious Press 1994 261p

ISBN 0-89296-556-8

LC 94-1980

"Like the labyrinthine route one must take to the Yellow Room, the resolution of the mystery is lengthy and winding and delightfully disorienting." N Y Times Book Rev

Dickinson, Seth

The **traitor** Baru Cormorant; Seth Dickinson. TOR 2015 400 p. map (hardback) $25.99

ISBN 9780765380722; 0765380722

LC 2015019187

In this book, by Seth Dickinson, "Baru Cormorant believes any price is worth paying to liberate her people--even her soul. When the Empire of Masks conquers her island home, overwrites her culture, criminalizes her customs, and murders one of her fathers, Baru vows to swallow her hate, join the Empire's civil service, and claw her way high enough to set her people free. . . . But the cost of winning the long game of saving her people may be far greater than Baru imagines." (Publisher's note)

"Dickinson's worldbuilding is ambitious and his language deviously subtle; both are seductive in their complexity. He combines social engineering, economic trickery, and coldhearted pseudoscientific theories to weave a compelling, utterly surprising narrative that keeps readers guessing until the end." Pub Wkly

Dicks, Matthew

Memoirs of an imaginary friend; Matthew Dicks. 1st ed. St. Martin's Press 2012 314 p. (hardcover) $24.99

ISBN 125000621X; 9781250006219; 9781250024008

LC 2012028234

In this novel by Matthew Dicks "imaginary friend Budo . . . thinks constantly of the day when eight-year-old Max Delaney will stop believing in him. When that happens, Budo will disappear. . . . Some people say that [Max] has Asperger's Syndrome, but most just say he's 'on the spectrum.' . . . [When] Mrs. Patterson, the woman who works with Max in the Learning Center . . . kidnaps Max, it is up to Budo and a team of imaginary friends to save him." (Publisher's note)

Didion, Joan

A **book** of common prayer. Simon & Schuster 1977 272p

ISBN 0-671-22491-3

LC 76-50067

Didion's "exposition of situations and details adroitly conceals their significance—until much later their meaning flares before our eyes. This is a remarkably good novel." Newsweek

Didion, Joan

★ **Play** it as it lays; a novel. Farrar, Straus & Giroux 1970 214p

"Using a phrenetic millieu of drugs, pills, sexual aberrancy, Didion elliptically etches the self-destructive life of Maria Wyeth. Didion with authorial legerdemain skillfully controls the suspense as Maria dangerously exists: she cannot relate and adjust. Her father has told her life was a crap game and to play it as it lays, not the hard way. But Maria plays it the hardest way, trying to anesthetize herself against pain (almost everyone, anything) and pleasure (Kate, her neurally damaged child), and trying to lose herself in the dead-end life around her." Choice

Diffenbaugh, Vanessa

The **language** of flowers; Vanessa Diffenbaugh. Ballantine Books 2011 322 p. $25

ISBN 978-0-345-52554-3; 0-345-52554-X; 9780345525567

LC 201051026

The book tells the story of orphan "Victoria [who] was placed with a woman named Elizabeth, on a picturesque Napa vineyard. . . . Unable to trust her turn of luck, the furious little girl tried to sabotage her new situation. . . . But Elizabeth refused to be baited, offering consequences but not ultimatums, making it clear that no matter what, Victoria was there to stay. . . . But something went terribly wrong. We meet the girl as she walks away from her last group home, only to unfurl her sleeping bag at a park on Potrero Hill, scrounge leftovers off cafe tables and begin a job search, with no diploma or work experience. . . . In chapters taking us back to the past, we learn that although Victoria failed at school, Elizabeth recognized that she was bright and curious, and taught her everything about the grapes and the flowers on her vineyard. . . . As an adult, Victoria . . . serendipitously find[s] work at an upscale flower shop." (SFGate)

"After more than 32 homes, 18-year-old Victoria Jones, abandoned as a baby, has given up on the idea of love or family. Scarred, suspicious and defiant, she has nothing: no friends, no money, just an attitude, an instinct for flowers and an education in their meaning from Elizabeth, the one kind foster parent who persevered with her. Now graduating out of state care, Victoria must make her own way and starts out by sleeping rough in a local San Francisco park. But a florist gives her casual work and then, at a flower market, she meets Grant, Elizabeth's nephew, another awkward soul who speaks the language of flowers. Diffenbaugh narrates Victoria and Grant's present-day involvement, over which the cloud of the past hangs heavy, in parallel with the history of Elizabeth's foster care, which we know ended badly. . . . An unusual, overextended romance, fairy tale in parts but with a sprinkling of grit." Kirkus

Dillard, Annie

The **Maytrees**; a novel. HarperCollinsPublishers 2007 216p $24.95

ISBN 978-0-06-123953-3; 0-06-123953-4

LC 2006-52599

"The good news is that in The Maytrees, despite the big words and the name-dropping . . . there is also good old straight narrative and prose that is often, yes, breathtakingly illuminative." N Y Times Book Rev

Dinesen, Isak

★ **Seven** Gothic tales; with an introduction by Dorothy Canfield. Modern Lib. 1994 422p

ISBN 0-679-60086-8

LC 91-50030

First published 1934 by H. Smith and analyzed in Short story index

"Distinguished by a romantic style and an aura of mystery, these tales of nineteenth-century aristocratic life in northern Europe remain favorites of a wide audience. A major plot device in some stories is the revealing of illegitimacy (sometimes of legitimacy), while a strong element of the supernatural is to be found in others." Shapiro. Fic for Youth. 3d edition

Dinesen, Isak

Winter's tales. Random House 1942 313p

Contents: The sailor-boy's tale; The young man with the carnation; The pearls; The invincible slaveowners; The heroine; The dreaming child; Alkmene; The fish; Peter and Rosa; Sorrow-acre; A consolatory tale

Divakaruni, Chitra Banerjee, 1956-

★ **Oleander** girl; a novel. by Chitra Banerjee Divakaruni. Free Press 2013 304 p. (hardcover) $24

ISBN 1451695659; 9781451695656

LC 2012025671

In this novel, by Chitra Banerjee Divakaruni, "the wild and headstrong Korobi Roy has enjoyed a privileged childhood with her adoring grandparents. . . . However, a sudden heart attack kills Korobi's grandfather, revealing serious financial problems and a devastating secret about Korobi's past. Shattered by this discovery and by her grandparents' betrayal, Korobi decides to undertake a courageous search across post-9/11 America to find her true identity." (Publisher's note)

"Divakaruni... introduces a cast of characters who defy their stereotypes... [and] has crafted a beautiful, complex story in which caste, class, religion, and race are significant factors informing people's world views." LJ

Dixon, Stephen, 1936-

★ **Interstate**; a novel. Holt & Co. 1995 374p

ISBN 0-8050-2654-1

LC 94-40174

In this novel, "eight narratives are alternative replays of a . . . moment that transpires in the book's opening pages: an act of random violence in which a man [Nathan Frey]and his two daughters are shot at by punks in a passing van, and one of the girls is killed." Libr J

Dixon, Stephen, 1936-

Old friends; a novel. Melville House Pub 2004 220p $22.95

ISBN 0-9749609-2-6

LC 2004-16101

"Dixon follows the lives of two writers from the time they meet as young men until late middle age. Neither Irv nor Leonard has achieved any great fame, and though there's a good deal of writerly chatter, it's really background music to the story of the daily struggles of two aging men and their families. Their lives are tragic, but not dramatically so—Leonard slowly fades into Lyme disease-induced dementia while Irv is busy caring for his crippled wife. What makes this book so good is Dixon's ability to invent characters just average enough that readers can identify with the banality of their pain." Publ Wkly

Dobyns, Stephen, 1941-

Is fat Bob dead yet? a novel. Stephen Dobyns. Blue Rider Press 2015 368 p. (hardcover) $26.95

ISBN 0399171452; 9780399171451

LC 2015017213

This novel, by Stephen Dobyns, is "a comic suspense novel about a small-time con operation, a pair of combative detectives, and the pride, revenge, and deception. . . . In the seaport city of New London, Connecticut, and newcomer Connor Raposo has just witnessed a gruesome motorcycle accident on Bank Street. At least he thinks it was an accident. But then he sees a familiar man--who else would wear an Elvis pompadour in this day and age?--lurking around the crime scene." (Publisher's note)

"The latest offering from veteran novelist and poet Dobyns . . . delights with quirky characters, absurd situations, language play, and keen insights. Recommended for those who enjoy dark humor and complicated plots in their mysteries." LJ

Doctorow, Cory

Down and out in the Magic Kindgom. TOR Bks. 2003 208p $22.95

ISBN 0-7653-0436-8

LC 2002-73277

"Jules, a relative youngster at more than a century old, is a contented citizen of the Bitchun Society that has filled Earth and near-space since shortage and death were overcome. . . . What Jules wants to do is move to Disney World, join the ad-hoc crew that runs the park and fine-tune the Haunted Mansion ride to make it even more wonderful. When his prudently stored consciousness abruptly awakens in a cloned body, he learns that he was murdered; evidently he's in the way of somebody else's dreams. . . . Doctorow has served up a nicely understated dish: meringue laced with caffeine." Publ Wkly

Doctorow, Cory

Overclocked; stories of the future present. Thunder's Mouth Press 2007 285p pa $15.95

ISBN 978-1-56025-981-7; 1-56025-981-7

"As these stories illustrate, [Doctorow] has a knack for identifying those seminal trends of our current landscape that will in all likelihood determine the shape of our future(s). Add in a recursive affection for past landmarks of SF . . . , and a gentle empathy for the underdogs in such scenarios, and you get a winning narrative and ideational combination." Sci Fi Wkly

Doctorow, Cory

Rapture of the nerds; Cory Doctorow and Charles Stross. Tor 2012 349 p.

ISBN 0765329107; 9780765329103; 9781429944915

LC 2012019450

This novel, by Cory Doctorow and Charles Stross, takes places "at the dusk of the twenty-first century. . . . [T]here's Tech Jury Service: random humans . . . charged with assessing dozens of new inventions and ruling on whether to let them loose. Young Huw, a technophobic, misanthropic Welshman, has been selected, . . . a task he does his best to perform despite an itchy technovirus, the apathy of the proletariat, and a couple of truly awful moments on bathroom floors." (Publisher's note)

Doctorow, Cory

Walkaway; a novel. Cory Doctorow. First edition St. Martin's Press 2017 379 p. $26.99

ISBN 0765392763; 9780765392763

LC 2017288508

In this novel, by Cory Doctorow, "Hubert, Etc-was too old to be at that Communist party. . . . After falling in with Natalie, an ultra-rich heiress, . . . the two decide to give up fully on formal society--and walk away. . . . When the initial pioneer walkaways flourish, more people join them. Then the walkaways discover the one thing the ultra-rich have never been able to buy: how to beat death. Now it's war–a war that will turn the world upside down." (Publisher's note)

"Doctorow sticks the landing with a multigenerational saga that extends this tale of the 'first days of a better nation' to a thrilling and unexpected finale. A truly visionary techno-thriller that not only depicts how we might live tomorrow, but asks why we don't already." Kirkus

Doctorow, E. L.

All the time in the world; new and selected stories. Random House 2011 277p $26

ISBN 978-1-4000-6963-7

LC 2010-42500

"In the preface to his new book, [Doctorow] reiterates a position he has advocated many times: 'You write to find out what you're writing.' . . . . The surprises in this book come at you as slaps on the back of the head. Even while the plots make the surprises seem inevitable the moment you see them, you have to imagine Doctorow's own shock and relief that the story has come so far from its premise. You can only imagine it, though, because the writer and his agenda are nowhere to be found. At the emotional heights of this book, you communicate less with Doctorow than with the presiding god of the world of the story. Doctorow is only the medium. The effect is egoless, frank, spontaneous and altogether wonderful." San Francisco Chron

Doctorow, E. L., 1931-2015

Andrew's Brain; a novel. by E.L. Doctorow. Random House Inc 2014 224 p. $26

ISBN 1400068819; 9781400068814

This book, by E. L. Doctorow, "is structured as an extended series of conversations between Andrew, a cognitive neuroscientist by training, and an unnamed man who initially appears to be his psychotherapist. The book opens with Andrew's description of leaving his infant daughter with an ex-wife. When the baby's mother dies, Andrew claims to be too incapacitated by grief and self-doubt to care for the child." (Publishers Weekly)

Doctorow, E. L.

★ **Billy** Bathgate; a novel. Random House 1989 323p

ISBN 0-394-52529-9

LC 88-42820

This is the "story of Billy's education, conducted on an extravagant scale. Doctorow brings a nice sense of moral ambiguity and creates characters who develop or deteriorate at an appropriate pace. His fecund run-on sentences are a pleasure to read. It all adds up to that rarity: a formal literary work that's also hugely entertaining." Newsweek

Doctorow, E. L., 1931-2015

Doctorow; collected stories. E.L. Doctorow. Random House 2016 321 p. (hardcover : acid-free paper) $30

ISBN 9780399588358

LC 2016006619

This book, by E.L. Doctorow, contains fifteen stories. "In 'A House on the Plains,' a mother has a plan for financial independence, which may include murder. In 'Walter John Harmon,' a man starts a cult using subterfuge and seduction. 'Jolene: A Life' follows a teenager who escapes her home for Hollywood on a perilous quest for success. [And] 'Heist,' the account of an Episcopal priest coping with a crisis of faith, was expanded into the bestseller 'City of God.'" (Publisher's note)

"This new volume was compiled by the author just before his death, and it includes revised and updated versions of all of his best stories, which makes it an essential acquisition for many libraries." LJ

Doctorow, E. L.

Homer & Langley; a novel. Random House 2009 208p $26

ISBN 978-1-4000-6494-6; 1-4000-6494-5

LC 2009-06959

"Cunningly panoramic. . . . Doctorow has packed this tale with episodes of existential wonder that capture the brothers in all their fascinating wackiness." Elle

Doctorow, E. L.

The **march**. Random House 2005 363p $25.95

ISBN 0-375-50671-3

LC 2005-46452

National Book Award Finalist: Fiction (2005)

"The march in question is that of General William Tecumseh Sherman and his Union soldiers as they slash and burn their way through Georgia and the Carolinas, and the 'march to freedom' as liberated slaves fall in step with the liberating army. But it is also, given the poetic depth of Doctorow's vision, the great march of time and of humanity in all its cruelty and glory. As Doctorow dramatizes the fury, conviction, and chaos of the Civil War, he portrays historical figures, as he is wont to do, most electrifyingly Sherman himself. But he focuses most on brilliantly imagined characters who embody the epic conflicts of that cataclysmic era, including Pearl, the smart and courageous daughter of a slave and slave owner; an excessively clinical military surgeon; the valiant daughter of a Southern judge; a freed slave who becomes a war photographer; and Arly, a scheming Rebel soldier who provides shrewdly comic relief. Doctorow writes with blazing clarity about the 'brutal romance' of war and its gruesome realities, with lyrical splendor about nature, and with wry wisdom and nimble satire about human folly." Booklist

Doctorow, E. L.

★ **Ragtime**. Modern Library 1997 320p $18.95

ISBN 0-679-60297-6

LC 97-42251

This is a reissue of the title first published 1975 by Random House

"The lives of an upper-middle-class family in New Rochelle; a black ragtime musician who loses his love, his child, and his life because of bigotry; and a poor immigrant Jewish family are interwoven in this early-twentieth-century story. There are cameo appearances by wellknown figures of that period: Houdini, anarchist Emma Goldman, actress Evelyn Nesbit, Henry Ford, and J.P. Morgan, whose magnificent library plays an important part in the story. The book mingles fact and fiction in portraying the era of ragtime." Shapiro. Fic for Youth. 3d edition

Doctorow, E. L.

Sweet land stories. Random House 2004 147p $22.95

ISBN 1-400-06204-7

LC 2003-58780

"As one might expect of Doctorow, the title is ironic. In settings that range across the U.S., most of the alienated characters in the five stories here find life anything but sweet as they struggle to surmount the stigmas of poverty, lack of education and their instincts to gamble against the odds. . . . In this knowing treatment of the cynical abuse of power, Doctorow uses the spare, laconic style endemic to thrillers and builds suspense with sure strokes. Boring like a laser into the failures of the American dream, he captures the resilience of those who won't accept defeat." Publ Wkly

Doctorow, E. L.

The **waterworks**. Random House 1994 253p

ISBN 0-394-58754-5

LC 93-44735

"Martin Pemberton, renegade son of rich, unscrupulous Augustus Pemberton and favorite freelance of the persevering editor of the New York Telegram, . . . narrates this tale. First, Martin claims to have seen his dead father on a horse-drawn omnibus, and then he disappears. The worried editor contacts Inspector Edmund Donne—the only honest cop in 1870s New York, where the Tweed Ring holds sway—and eventually they discover that the ailing Augustus is part of an experiment by the brilliant Dr. Sartorius to prolong the lives of several old men rich enough to foot the bill." Libr J

Doctorow, E. L., 1931-2015

★ **World's** fair; E. L. Doctorow. Random House 2007 288p pbk $16

ISBN 081297820X; 9780812978209

Originally published 1985

National Book Award: Fiction (1986)

This is a "fictional memoir of life in New York City in the 1930s as observed by a child who recounts his first nine years. Interspersed in Edgar's narrative are chapters by his mother and his older brother, Donald. . . . The family faces hard times as the father's business fails, Donald leaves home, Edgar's senile grandmother dies, and Edgar is hospitalized with a burst appendix. But the World's Fair (Edgar wins free admission in an 'American Boyhood' essay contest) holds promise for the future; and his experience there offers Edgar the recognition that he's growing up, finding his place in the world." (Libr J)

Dodd, Christina

The **woman** who couldn't scream; Christina Dodd. St. Martin's Press 2017 viii, 342 p.p (Virtue Falls series) (hardcover) $27.99

ISBN 9781250028495; 9781250028488; 1250028485

LC 2017022278

In this novel in the Virtue Falls series, by Christina Dodd, "Merida Falcon is a world-class beauty, a trophy wife who seems to have it all... except she has no voice. For nine bitter years, Merida served her wealthy elderly husband, never leaving his side, always doing his bidding... On his death, Merida vanishes...and reappears in Virtue Falls with a new name, a new look, and a plot to take revenge on the man who loved her, betrayed her and walked away." (Publisher's note)

"Dodd's (Because I'm Watching, 2017, etc.) new title delivers complex storytelling, a rollicking pace, and surprising twists and turns, plus sly humor, a touch of the supernatural, and a full cast of interesting and diverse characters." Kirkus

Doerr, Anthony

★ **All** the light we cannot see; a novel. Anthony Doerr. First edition Scribner 2014 448 p. (hardback) $27

ISBN 1476746583; 9781476746586; 9781476746593

LC 2013034107

Pulitzer Prize: Fiction (2015)

Alex Award (2015)

National Book Award Shortlist: Fiction (2014)

Carnegie Medal: Fiction (2015)

This book, by Anthony Doerr, is told from "multiple viewpoints but focus[es] mostly on blind French teenager Marie-Laure and Werner, a brilliant German soldier just a few years older than she. . . . They are on opposite sides of the horrors of World War II, and their fates ultimately collide in connection with the radio--a means of resistance for the Allies and just one more avenue of annihilation for the Nazis." (Library Journal)

"Doerr captures the sights and sounds of wartime and focuses, refreshingly, on the innate goodness of his major characters." Kirkus

Doerr, Anthony

Memory wall; stories. Scribner 2010 243p $24

ISBN 1-4391-8280-9; 978-1-4391-8280-2

LC 2009-52245

This is a collection of six stories by the author of The Shell Collector (2002), About Grace (2004), and Four Seasons in Rome (2007).

"The characters in these six stories struggle to recall loved ones who are gone, or choose to bury their memories, or are displaced from their homes, left with nothing but memories. Such is Doerr's skill and sensitivity that he seems to be his characters' caretaker rather than their creator. It's as if he possesses a photographic memory of all of their lives, but as a discriminating photographer he knows exactly which pictures to include in the exhibition, and which to leave out, the whole more powerful through their absence." San Francisco Chron

Doerr, Harriet

★ **Stones** for Ibarra. Viking 1984 214p

ISBN 0-670-19203-1

LC 83-47861

"When Sara and Richard Everton pack up their belongings and mortgage themselves to leave California for a small village in Mexico, their friends think they are crazy. Many of the Mexican natives in the village of Ibarra also consider the two gringos incredible. While Sara restores the house that had belonged to Richard's grandparents, Richard restores a copper mine that had been his family's, and thereby gives employment to many of the villagers. We learn that Richard has leukemia and has been given just a few years to live, but it is the lives of the villagers that are more full of tragedy, religious commitment, and reliance on talismans and prayers. There is a strength among these people and an acceptance of all that life brings which make them memorable. Learning from them, perhaps, Sara finally accepts the inevitability of her husband's death." Shapiro. Fic for Youth. 3d edition

Doetsch, Richard

Half-past dawn. Atria Books 2011 356 p.

ISBN 9781439183977; 143918397X ; 1439183996; 9781439183991

LC 2011034027

In this story, "Jack Keeler, a district attorney for the city of New York, . . . wakes up one morning to an empty house. He has a stitched-up bullet wound on his chest and a bizarre tattoo covering his arm. Jack has no memory of what happened." After seeing a newspaper article describing a car crash in which he and his wife supposedly died, "Jack begins a desperate mission to restore his life and find answers to what has happened." (Miami Herald) Other elements of the story include "an Asian people out of legend, an assassin who will stop at nothing to avenge his death sentence, and a diary whose contents tell the future." (Publisher's note)

Doig, Ivan, 1939-2015

★ The **bartender's** tale; Ivan Doig. Riverhead Books 2012 400 p. $27.95

ISBN 1594487359; 9781594487354

LC 2012017498

In this book, "[a]fter living half his life in Phoenix, Ariz., with his aunt, 12-year-old Russell 'Rusty' Harry comes back to the tiny town of Gros Ventre to live with his father, Tom, the owner of a popular saloon. . . . Rusty entertains himself in the cavernous back room, which Tom operates like a pawnshop." Soon, "12-year-old Zoe Constantine shows up and soon becomes Rusty's partner in crime in the backroom, listening to the bar through a concealed air vent." (Publishers Weekly)

Doig, Ivan

Bucking the sun; a novel. Simon & Schuster 1996 412p

ISBN 0-684-81171-5

LC 96-3814

The author "begins this saga with adultery and death, then moves backward to examine the causes. Just as the building of the mammoth Fort Peck Dam transforms the Montana countryside, it radically alters the lives of its Depression-era inhabitants. In particular, members of the Duff clan abandon subsistence farming and move to the construction boomtowns. There a father, three brothers, and their wives confront the task of building the largest earthen dam in the world, brave the dangers of such labor, and battle among themselves. . . . This richly detailed narrative offers comedy, passion, and adventure." Libr J

Doig, Ivan

★ **Dancing** at the Rascal Fair. Atheneum Pubs. 1987 405p

ISBN 0-689-11764-7

LC 87-18672

Chronologically the first in the author's Montana trilogy

"If the thorny individualism of Rob and Angus results in lives that are never easy, they are rich in incident and growth, beautifully described in Doig's strong, savory prose. America's frontier history comes vividly to life in this absorbing saga filled with memorable characters." Publ Wkly

Doig, Ivan

The **eleventh** man. Harcourt 2008 406p $26

ISBN 978-0-15-101243-5; 0-15-101243-1

LC 2008-10046

In this novel, "11 starters of a close-knit Montana college championship football team enlist as the U.S. hits the thick of WWII and are capriciously flung around the globe in various branches of the service. Ben Reinking, initially slated for pilot training, is jerked from his plane and more or less forced to become a war correspondent for the semisecret Threshold Press War Project, a propaganda arm of the combined armed forces. His orders: to travel the world, visiting and writing profiles on each of his heroic teammates. The fetching Women's Airforce Service Pilot who flies him around, Cass Standish, is married to a soldier fighting in the South Pacific, which leads to anguish for them both . . . . Meanwhile, Ben's former teammates are being killed one by one, often, it seems, being deliberately put into harm's way. Doig adroitly keeps Ben on track, offering an old-fashioned greatest generation story, well told." Publ Wkly

Doig, Ivan

English Creek. Atheneum Pubs. 1984 339p

ISBN 0-689-11478-8

LC 84-45051

This volume in the Montana trilogy chronologically follows Dancing at the Rascal Fair

This "is a sensitive coming-of-age story as well as a portrait of a society still looking to its frontier past, but about to be engulfed by the future. The result is both highly personal and deeply engaging." Best Sellers

Doig, Ivan, 1939-2015

★ **Last** bus to wisdom; a novel. Ivan Doig. Riverhead Books 2015 464 p. (hardcover) $18.99

ISBN 9781594632020

LC 2015014721

In this novel, by Ivan Doig, awarded Best Book of the Year by the Seattle Times and Kirkus Reviews, "Aunt Kate-bossy, opinionated, argumentative, and tyrannical. . . . After one contretemps too many, Kate packs [Donal] back to the authorities in Montana on the next Greyhound. But as it turns out, Donal isn't traveling solo: [her husband] Herman the German has decided to fly the coop with him." (Publisher's note)

"Doig's superb storytelling does not disappoint. The dialog is snappy, funny, and true to the charming characters. With the author's passing in April, this is the last journey into familiar Doig territory we've come to admire." LJ

Doig, Ivan, 1939-2015

Sweet thunder; a novel. Ivan Doig. Riverhead Books 2013 320 p. $27.95

ISBN 1594487340; 9781594487347

LC 2013015397

This is Ivan Doig's second book with Morrie Morgan. Here, "back in Butte after a yearlong honeymoon with Grace . . . , Morrie needs to find a job fast. Not only has he nearly run through his winnings from a savvy bet on the fixed 1919 World Series, but he has an expensive mansion to maintain. . . . So Morrie goes to work as the editorial writer for a new newspaper funded by the miners' union to counter Anaconda's propaganda for unfettered capitalism." (Kirkus Reviews)

Doig, Ivan

The **whistling** season. Harcourt 2006 345p hardcover o.p. pa $14.95

ISBN 978-0-15-101237-4; 0-15-101237-7; 978-0-15-603164-6 pa; 0-15-603164-7 pa

LC 2005-25457

"Set in the early 1900s, this novel is a nostalgic, bittersweet story about a widower, his three sons, and the year these boys spend in a one-room country schoolhouse. The novel begins with the father, Oliver, hiring a widowed housekeeper named Rose from Minneapolis (her advertisement reads 'Can't Cook but Doesn't Bite'). She arrives with her unconventional brother, Morrie, in tow. Morrie is something of a scholar, and he soon finds himself pressed into service as a replacement teacher. During the course of the novel, these intriguing and unpredictable characters come together in surprising and uplifting ways. This is an affectionate, heartwarming tale that also celebrates a vanished way of life and laments its passing." Libr J

Doig, Ivan, 1939-2015

Work song. Riverhead Books 2010 275p $25.95

ISBN 1594487626; 9781594487620; 978-1-59448-762-0; 1-59448-762-6

LC 2009-42647

This novel featuring Morrie Morgan, the hero of The Whistling Season (2006), depicts post-World War I Butte, Montana, in thrall to the Anaconda mining company.

This "sequel to The Whistling Season (2006) begins ten years later in 1919, when Morrie Morgan gets off the train in Butte, MT, "the richest hill on earth," run by Anaconda Copper. He settles into a boardinghouse run by the widow Grace and is befriended by her other boarders, Griff and Hoop, two retired miners who tell Morrie what's going on in town. Scholarly Morrie finds his niche at the public library, the domain of a crusty retired rancher named Sandison, who comes with the territory because the entire library is his own magnificent book collection. Before long, Morrie discovers he's being shadowed by Anaconda's thugs for being a strike agitator." Libr J

Doiron, Paul

Bad Little Falls; a novel. Paul Doiron. 1st ed. Minotaur Books 2012 310 p. ill. (hardcover) $24.99; (paperback) $14.99

ISBN 0312558481; 9780312558482; 9781250010919; 9781250031471

LC 2012007787

This is the "third novel from Edgar-finalist [Paul] Dorion featuring game warden Mike Bowditch." Bowditch has been transferred to Washington County, Maine "after he became an embarrassment to the powers-that-be by shooting a murderer in self-defense." His strict rule-following earns him enemies. One night during a blizzard, veterinarian Doc Larrabee "needs his help with a person suffering from a severe case of frostbite." Further, Bowditch must find the victim's lost partner. (Publishers Weekly)

Doiron, Paul

The **poacher's** son. Minotaur Books 2010 336p $24.99

ISBN 978-0-312-55846-8; 0-312-55846-5

LC 2009-41136

"Along with nostalgic laments about the old-growth woods and modest settlements that have already fallen to civilization, Doiron provides wonderful scenes of present-day bear-tracking and man-hunting through the kind of terrain that attracts hikers, hunters and the odd 'paranoid militia freak' like the one causing so much trouble in this story." N Y Times Book Rev

Other titles in this series are:
Trespasser (2011)
Bad Little Falls (2012)
Massacre pond (2013)
The bone orchard (2014)
The precipice (2015)
Widowmaker (2016)
Knife Creek (2017)

Doiron, Paul

The **Precipice**; A Novel. by Paul Doiron. St. Martin's Press 2015 320 p. (Mike Bowditch Mysteries) $25.99

ISBN 1250063698; 9781250063694

LC 2015013520

"When the chewed-up bodies of two young female hikers who disappeared along a remote stretch of the Appalachian Trail are found, biologist Stacey Stevens, Mike's new girlfriend, insists coyotes were not the culprits. When she disappears along the trail where the girls had vanished, Mike must uncover the truth." (Library Journal)

"Bowditch is an uncomplicated good guy who might even be considered boring except for the lively conversations on topics as diverse as atheism, sexuality, and animal rights. This unexpected thoughtfulness makes his character appealing enough for readers to cheer him on." LJ

Dolan, Harry

Bad things happen. Amy Einhorn Books/G. P. Putman's Sons 2009 338p $24.95

ISBN 978-0-399-15563-5

LC 2008-54628

Prequel: The last dead girl (2014)

"Although the plot is fairly outlandish, the narrative comes with startling developments and nicely tricky reversals. There's also something appealingly offbeat about the wry, dry tone of its academic humor, which has much to do with the self-important authors who figure in the hectic plot." N Y Times Book Rev

Dolan, Harry

Very bad men. Amy Einhorn Books 2011 412p $25.95

ISBN 978-0-399-15749-3; 0-399-15749-2

LC 2011-06877

Sequel to: Bad things happen (2009)

"Anthony Lark's mission is simple: to kill three of the men involved in a fatally botched bank robbery 17 years ago. He's already dispatched two of his targets—an impressive feat, considering that one of them, Terry Dawtrey, is serving 30 years in Kinross Prison—when he identifies them both and announces his third, nurse practitioner Sutton Bell, in an anonymous letter to Loogan . . . , who promptly shares it with his ladylove, police detective Elizabeth Waishkey. The timely intervention of aspiring tabloid reporter Lucy Navarro saves Bell from Lark's initial attempt and gives Dolan a chance to fill in some back story. . . . Dolan mixes his pitches with an ace's judgment, steadily complicating Lark's quest while keeping the psychology of his characters considerably more plausible than in Loogan's equally baroque debut. The rare crime novel with something for everyone who reads crime fiction." Kirkus

The **Doll** Collection; Seventeen Brand-New Tales of Dolls. edited by Ellen Datlow. St. Martin's Press 2015 352 p. illustrations $27.99

ISBN 0765376806; 9780765376800

This book, edited by Ellen Datlow, is a collection of "dark stories about dolls of all types. . . . Datlow has assembled a list of beautiful and terrifying stories from bestselling and critically acclaimed authors such as Joyce Carol Oates, Seanan McGuire, Carrie Vaughn, Pat Cadigan,

Tim Lebbon, Richard Kadrey, Genevieve Valentine, and Jeffrey Ford." (Publisher's note)

"Dolls, like clowns, are one of the totems of childhood that somehow seem sinister in adulthood. Award-winning editor Datlow has arranged a strong, themed anthology without ever resorting to the "evil doll" cliché of horror movies. There isn't a bad story in the bunch, making this a great addition to horror collections." LJ

Donaldson, Stephen R.

The **Illearth** war. Holt, Rinehart & Winston 1977 407p il (Chronicles of Thomas Covenant, the Unbeliever)

ISBN 0-03-022776-3

LC 77-8621

In this second volume, Lord Foul the Despiser continues his attack against the Land with the Illearth Stone. Covenant and the daughter of the High Lord, Elena, undertake a mission into a mountain region, where they hope they will find the ancient gnostic power that will combat the Stone

Donaldson, Stephen R.

Lord Foul's bane. Holt, Rinehart & Winston 1977 369p il (Chronicles of Thomas Covenant, the Unbeliever)

LC 77-73868

Thomas Covenant, a man burdened with a stigma that has isolated him, is suddenly sent to a mysterious magic world known as the Land. The Land has an immortal enemy—Lord Foul the Despiser—who wishes to destroy it. In Thomas, who does not believe in the Land's life-restoring powers, Lord Foul thinks he has found the perfect tool for his purpose

Donaldson, Stephen R.

The **power** that preserves. Holt, Rinehart & Winston 1977 379p il (Chronicles of Thomas Covenant, the Unbeliever)

ISBN 0-03-022781-X

LC 77-10814

In this final volume of the first trilogy Covenant makes his way to the stronghold of Lord Foul the Despiser. He is accompanied by his friend Saltheart Foamfollower, a Giant. But it is Covenant who must meet Foul in final combat, to ensure survival for the Land and to achieve salvation for himself

"Below the stirring adventure tale is a poignant and profoundly religious chronicle of a quest for self-esteem and peace." Booklist

Donaldson, Stephen R.

The **runes** of the earth. G.P. Putnam's Sons 2004 xx, 532p (Last chronicles of Thomas Covenant) $26.95

ISBN 0-399-15232-6

LC 2004-50526

"It is 10 years since Thomas Covenant's death, and Linden Avery runs the small mental hospital in which Covenant's widow, Joan, is confined. Roger Covenant, newly turned 21, visits Avery and tries to get his mother released. Failing at that, he kidnaps Joan as well as Avery's adopted son, then commits several murders and flees to the Land, the other world of Covenant sagas. Roger is clearly doing Lord Foul's bidding, and Avery has no choice but to follow him. She discovers that in the Land three and a half millennia have passed. The Haruchai are now called the Masters and distrust Earthpower, and an old man, Anele, who is full of Earthpower, is key to finding the lost and essential Staff of Law. . . . Expect readers to swarm." Booklist

Other titles in this series are:

Fatal revenant (2007)

Against all things ending (2010)

The last dark (2013)

Donaldson, Stephen R.

The **wounded** Land. Ballantine Bks. 1980 497p il (Chronicles of Thomas Covenant, the Unbeliever)

ISBN 0-345-28647-2

LC 79-20644

This is the first volume of the second trilogy about the Land

"In the first of the second trilogy of his adventures, leper Thomas Covenant returns to the mysterious Land after nearly 4000 years have passed there (ten years in earth time). Dr. Linden Avery unexpectedly joins him and goes through the same denial and disbelief he had suffered before. Now the Land is suffering from unending plagues called the Sunbane, inflicted by the evil Lord Foul whom Covenant had defeated but not destroyed on his last visit. Although it is not necessary to have read the previous three to appreciate the breadth and scope of this grim fantasy, for those who have 'The Wounded Land' is absolutely compelling." SLJ

Donoghue, Emma

★ **Frog** music; a novel. Emma Donoghue. Little, Brown and Co. 2014 405 p. (hardback) $27

ISBN 9780316404587; 9780316371452; 9780316324687

LC 2014000840

Stonewall Honor Book - Literature (2015)

This novel, by Emma Donoghue, is set in "Summer of 1876: San Francisco is in the fierce grip of a record-breaking heat wave and a smallpox epidemic. Through the window of a railroad saloon, a young woman named Jenny Bonnet is shot dead.The survivor, her friend Blanche Beunon, is a French burlesque dancer. Over the next three days, she will risk everything to bring Jenny's murderer to justice--if he doesn't track her down first." (Publisher's note)

"[A]n engrossing and suspenseful tale about moral growth, unlikely friendship, and breaking free from the past." Booklist

Donoghue, Emma

★ **Room**; a novel. Emma Donoghue. Little, Brown and Co. 2010 321p

ISBN 0316098337; 9780316098335

LC 2010006983

Alex Award (2011), CBA Libris Awards (Canadian Booksellers Association): Fiction Book of the Year (2011), Rogers Writers' Trust Fiction Prize (2010), Indies' Choice Book Awards: Adult Fiction (2011)

"The narrator of Emma Donoghue's 'Room' is a 5-year-old boy. . . . He and his mother have been trapped in the 11-by-11-foot room of the title since the day he was born." (N Y Times (Late N Y Ed))

"Though the story's chilling circumstances reflect the horrors endured by tabloid-famous abductees, Donoghue avoids all sensationalism. Instead, she gracefully distills what it means to be a mother — and what it's like for a child whose entire world measures just 11 x 11." Entertainment Wkly

Donoghue, Emma

The **sealed** letter. Harcourt 2008 396p $26

ISBN 978-0-15-101549-8; 0-15-101549-X

LC 2008-14677

Donoghue "has sifted through court records, newspapers, correspondence, and even Faithfull's later novels. She makes 150-year-old events immediate. . . . What could have been mere Victorian melodrama resonates here with emotional truth." Quill Quire

Donoghue, Emma

Slammerkin. Harcourt 2001 336p $30

ISBN 0-15-100672-5

LC 00-49867

First published 2000 in the United Kingdom

"In her storytelling, the author shrewdly alternates the point of view, a technique that, rather than feeling gratuitous and shticky as it so often does these days, works to put Mary in a delicious pickle, since the satisfaction of her deepest desires, and the revelation of her secret career, could crush those for whom she—and we—come to feel real affection." N Y Times Book Rev

Donoghue, Emma

Touchy subjects; stories. Harcourt 2006 280p $24

ISBN 978-0-15-101386-9; 0-15-101386-1

LC 2005-26170

Donoghue "exhibits adeptness in the short story form in this collection of 19 tales that, without a hint of pretension but with wisdom extending far beyond the placidness of her prose style, isolates aspects of a character or a moment of revelation for a character. . . . Her stories find secure footing where poignancy and humor intersect, and their geniality will prove an asset to librarians encouraging readers exclusively devoted to the novel to–come on–try some short stories." Booklist

Donoghue, Emma

★ The **wonder**; Emma Donoghue. Little, Brown & Co. 2016 304 p. (hardcover) $27; (ebook) $81

ISBN 0316393878; 9780316393874; 9780316395632

LC 2016930971

Scotiabank Giller Prize Shortlist (2016).

In this novel by Emma Donoghue, "an English nurse brought to a small Irish village to observe what appears to be a miracle-a girl said to have survived without food for months-soon finds herself fighting to save the child's life. Tourists flock to the cabin of eleven-year-old Anna O'Donnell, who believes herself to be living off manna from heaven, and a journalist is sent to cover the sensation." (Publisher's note)

"Donoghue's most recent offering is as startlingly rewarding as her celebrated novel Room. Heart-hammering suspense builds as Lib monitors Anna's quickening pulse, making this book's bracing conclusion one of the most satisfying in recent fiction." LJ

Donohue, Keith

Centuries of June; a novel. Crown 2011 342p $24

ISBN 978-0-307-45028-9; 0-307-45028-7

LC 2010-23574

This is "an episodic novel that's part ghost story, part psychological mystery and part vaudeville show. Think Scheherazade by way of 'Tristram Shandy' by way of 'The Sixth Sense.' . . . For all of its complexity and ambition, 'Centuries of June' captivates mostly in the small things, the little bits of textual and theatrical sleight-of-hand that Donohue pulls off without much apparent effort." Washington Post Book World

Donohue, Keith

The **stolen** child; a novel. Nan A. Talese 2006 319p hardcover o.p. pa $15

ISBN 0-385-51616-9; 1-4000-9653-7 pa

LC 2005-53828

"On the surface, Donohue may seem to have written a clever debut novel about fairies. But the real triumph of the book is that, while our backs were turned, he has performed a switch and delivered a luminous and thrilling novel about our humanity." Washington Post Book World

Dorris, Michael

Cloud chamber; a novel. Scribner 1997 316p

ISBN 0-684-81567-2

LC 96-42544

"Though not unflawed—a few voices sound confusingly similar and a few characters are more types than people—this is a compellingly readable and emotionally satisfying novel, full of secrets and surprises." Booklist

Dorris, Michael

★ A **yellow** raft in blue water. Holt & Co. 1987 343p hardcover o.p. pa $14

ISBN 0-8050-0045-3; 0-312-42185-0 pa

LC 86-26947

"The bitter rifts and inevitable bonds between generations are highlighted as a teenaged daughter, mother, and grand matriarch of an American Indian family tell their life stories. Humorous and poignant, with unique characters." SLJ

Dos Passos, John

Manhattan transfer. Harper 1925 404p

"Dos Passos creates a portrait of New York City in the first quarter of this century by telling the stories of many people. They include the daughter of an accountant, who loses hope for any future happiness when her first love commits suicide; a milkman who rises in status to become a union boss; and an immigrant sailor who starts as a bartender and becomes a wealthy bootlegger during Prohibition. There are happy and unhappy endings to these stories, but always the city plays an important role." Shapiro. Fic for Youth. 3d edition

Dos Passos, John

★ **Novels,** 1920-1925. Library of America 2003 873p (The library of America) $35

ISBN 1-931082-39-1

LC 2003-47529

One man's initiation, 1917 (1920) focuses on a young American's experiences in France during a time of war. Three soldiers (1921) describes the lives of three men with three different backgrounds—an Indiana farmboy, an Italian-American store clerk, and a musician hoping to become a composer—and how they cope with life both on and off the battlefield. Manhattan transfer is entered separately.

Dos Passos, John

★ **U.S.A.** Library of Am. 1996 1288p $40

ISBN 1-883011-14-0

LC 95-49282

An omnibus volume containing the trilogy titles: The 42nd parallel, first published 1930; 1919, first published 1932 and The big money, first published 1936

"U.S.A. tries to capture, through a diversity of fictional techniques, the variety and multiplicity of American life in the first decades of the 20th cent.; it presents various interlocking and parallel narratives, against a panoramic collage of real-life events, snatches of newsreel and popular song, advertisements, etc., with a commentary by the author as 'The Camera Eye.'" Oxford Companion to Engl Lit

Dos Passos, John, 1896-1970

1919. Harcourt Brace & Co. 1932 473p

In this second volume of the trilogy, the author continues his chronicle of life in America through the war years, giving glimpses of the lives and characters of five young Americans—a low caste sailor, the daughter of a Chicago minister, a young girl from Texas, a radical Jew, a young poet

"'1919' is literally what so many books are erroneously called, 'a slice of life.' With infinite skill that slicing is done by the author, and the raw surface which meets the reader's eye is the actual living, breathing record of a period in its most intense manifestation." Chicago Daily Trib

Followed by The big money (1936)

Dostoyevsky, Fyodor

The **best** short stories of Dostoevsky; translated with an introduction by David Magarshack. Modern Lib. 1992 xxvii, 348p

ISBN 0-679-60020-5

LC 92-50214

First Modern Library edition 1955

Dostoyevsky, Fyodor

★ The **brothers** Karamazov; translated by Constance Garnett. Modern Library 1996 xxi, 880p $21

ISBN 0-679-60181-3

Written 1880

"The main plot involves Fyodor Pavlovich 'Karamazov' and his four sons: Dmitry, Ivan, Alyosha, and the bastard Smerdyakov. Fyodor Pavlovich, a depraved buffoon, is Dmitry's rival for the affections of the local siren, Grushenka, despite her checkered past and blemished reputation. Fyodor Pavlovich is a model of animation and irrationalism, who enjoys his depravity and is only encouraged by the shock and disapproval of others. After violent quarrels over Grushenka and over Dmitry's disputed inheritance, Fyodor Pavlovich is murdered. Dmitry is arrested and brought to trial for the crime. This basic line of action is complicated throughout the novel by a host of other factors masterfully linked to the main plot. . . . The literal, religious, social, and ethical levels of the novel are buttressed by the psychological probings for which Dostoyevsky is well known." Reader's Ency. 4th edition

Dostoyevsky, Fyodor

★ **Crime** and punishment; translated from the Russian by Constance Garnett; with an introduction by Ernest J. Simmons. Modern Library 1994 xxiv, 629p $19.95

ISBN 0-679-60100-7

Written 1866

"The novel is a psychological analysis of the poor student Raskolnikov, whose theory that humanitarian ends justify evil means leads him to murder a St. Petersburg pawnbroker. The act produces nightmarish guilt in Raskolnikov. The narrative's feverish, compelling tone follows the twists and turns of Raskolnikov's emotions and elaborates his struggle with his conscience and his mounting sense of horror as he wanders the city's hot, crowded streets. In prison, Raskolnikov comes to the realization that happiness cannot be achieved by a reasoned plan of existence but must be earned by suffering." Merriam-Webster's Ency of Lit

Dostoyevsky, Fyodor

Notes from underground; translated from the Russian by Richard Pevear and Larissa Volkhonsky [sic]; with an introduction by Richard Pevear. Knopf 2004 xxxi, 126p $18

ISBN 1-4000-4191-0

LC 2003-59216

Written 1864. Variant titles: Letters from the underworld and Memoirs from underground

"The work, which includes extremely misanthropic passages, contains the seeds of nearly all of the moral, religious, political, and social concerns that appear in Dostoyevsky's great novels. Written as a reaction against Nikolay Chernyshevsky's ideological novel What Is to Be Done? (1863), which offered a planned utopia based on 'natural' laws of self-interest, Notes from the Underground attacks the scientism and rationalism at the heart of Chernyshevsky's novel. The views and actions of Dostoyevsky's underground man demostrate that in asserting free will humans often act against self-interest." Merriam-Webster's Ency of Lit

Dostoyevsky, Fyodor

The **possessed**; a novel in three parts. from the Russian by Constance Garnett. Macmillan Pub. Co. 1913 637p

Original Russian edition, 1892. Variant titles: Demons; The devils

"Loosely based on sensational press reports of a Moscow student's murder by fellow revolutionists, The possessed depicts the destructive chaos caused by outside agitators who move into a moribund provincial town. The enigmatic Stavrogin dominates the novel. His magnetic personality influences his tutor, the liberal intellectual poseur Stepan Verkhovensky, and the teacher's revolutionary son Pyotr, as well as other radicals. Stavrogin is portrayed as a man of strength without direction, capable of goodness and nobility. When Stravrogin loses his faith in God, however, he is seized by brutal desires he does not fully understand. In the end, Stavrogin hangs himself in what he believes is an act of generosity, and Stepan Verkhovensky is received into the church on his deathbed." Merriam-Webster's Ency of Lit

Doughty, Louise

Whatever you love; a novel. Louise Doughty. Harper Perennial 2012 369 p.

ISBN 0062094661; 9780062094667

LC 2011028521

This book, a finalist for the Orange Prize and the Costa Novel Award, looks at "the loss of life, love, and rationality. Laura Needham is a single mother raising two children." Her 9-year-old daughter dies in a hit-and-run accident on page one. "As Laura grapples with her daughter's death, her already complicated relationship with her ex-husband grows more so." Laura slowly loses her mind and "moves to the brink of a breakdown that might end in violence." (Publishers Weekly)

Dovey, Ceridwen

Blood kin. Viking 2008 183p $23.95

ISBN 978-0-670-01856-7; 0-670-01856-2

LC 2007-019876

In this "novel, the deposed president of an unnamed country is imprisoned in his residence with, among others, his chef, his barber, and his portraitist. These three servants, awaiting their fate, reveal, in alternating chapters, their ties to the president and their reasons for serving his corrupt regime. Dovey connects her main characters to the president first through their work—their tasks of feeding, grooming, and painting give them an uneasy intimacy with the president—and then through various women in their lives. The narratives of these women, halfway through the book, expose the full extent of the president's depravity. In lively, straightforward prose, Dovey gets to the heart of the complicit nature of the master-servant relationship." New Yorker

Dovey, Ceridwen

Only the animals; stories. Ceridwen Dovey. Farrar, Straus and Giroux 2015 256 p. (hardcover) $25

ISBN 9780374226633

LC 2014049062

In this short story collection by Ceridwen Dovey, "the souls of ten animals caught up in human conflicts over the last century and connected to both famous and little-known writers in surprising ways tell their astonishing stories of life and death. In a trench on the Western Front, a cat recalls her owner Colette's theatrical antics in Paris. In Nazi Germany, a dog seeks enlightenment." (Publisher's note)

"The inner monologues of animals, all of them doomed by human tragedy, is high-risk terrain: too earnest and it's sentimental, too moralistic and it's preachy, too clownish and it's a cartoon. But Dovey's stories, at once charming and haunting, are something else altogether. "Absorbing" is not quite the right word for them—their poetic oddness keeps them at arm's length—but they are intoxicating nonetheless. As unsettling as they are beautiful, these quietly wise stories wedge themselves into your mind—and stay there." Kirkus

Dowlatabadi, Mahmoud

The **colonel**; Mahmoud Dowlatabadi; translated by Tom Patterdale. Melville House 2012 v, 247 p.p (paperback) $17.95

ISBN 1612191320; 9781612191324

LC 2012934610

This Iranian novel, by Mahmoud Dowlatabadi, "begins on a . . . rainy night, when there's a knock on the Colonel's door. Two policemen have come to summon him to collect the tortured body of his youngest daughter. . . . As we watch him struggle with the death of his innocent child, we find him wracked with guilt and anger over the condition of his country, particularly as represented by his own children." (Publisher's note)

Down, David

Masaryk Station; David Downing. Soho Crime 2013 330 p. (hardcover) $26.95

ISBN 1616952237; 9781616952235

LC 2012042044

This book by David Downing, "the sixth novel in the John Russell series . . . opens in 1948 with postwar Berlin and Eastern Europe in disarray. . . . John Russell's situation is just as complex: The Brits and the Americans think he's their double agent, working against the Soviets. . . . Posing as a journalist, he carries out missions in Trieste, Belgrade, and Prague. . . . Meanwhile, Russell's wife, Effi, an actress, faces her own challenges." (Library Journal)

Downie, Ruth

Caveat emptor; a novel of the Roman Empire. Bloomsbury USA 2011 338p $25

ISBN 978-1-59691-608-1; 1-59691-608-7

LC 2010-34525

"Serial physician (medicus) and de facto detective Gaius Petreius Ruso is assigned to investigate the suspicious disappearance of both tax collector Julius Asper and money owed to the coffers of Emperor Hadrian. Ruso traces a path between the Roman command center in Londinium and the northern metropolis (Verulamium) whence Asper and his brother (also 'missing') have presumably fled. When it appears both fugitives were murdered, Asper's pregnant common-law wife begins hurling accusations. Ruso's former servant and present wife Tilla does what she usually does, helping out, investigating on her own and attracting the threatening attentions of assorted suspects. . . . As always, Downie displays a virtuoso's command of pertinent period detail." Kirkus

Downie, Ruth

Medicus; a novel of the Roman Empire. Bloomsbury Pub. 2006 386p (Medicus investigation) $23.95

ISBN 978-1-59691-231-1; 1-59691-231-6

LC 2006-13179

"The plot is suspenseful and fluidly told, but the evolving bond between master and servant is at the heart of this excellent first work, as Downie carefully details the pained conscience of the former and the latter's sorrow that both her family and her country have been ravaged." Libr J

Other titles in this series are:
Terra incognita (2008)
Persona non grata (2008)
Caveat emptor (2010)
Semper fidelis (2013)
Tabula rasa (2014)
Vita brevis (2016)
Memento mori (2018)

Downie, Ruth

Semper Fidelis; A Novel of the Roman Empire. Ruth Downie. St. Martin's Press 2013 352 p. (hardcover) $26.00

ISBN 1608197093; 9781608197095

This historical novel, by Ruth Downie, is part of the "Novels of the Roman Empire" series. "As mysterious injuries, and even deaths, begin to appear in the medical ledgers, it's clear that all is not well amongst the native recruits to Britannia's imperial army. . . . Bound by his sense of duty and ill-advised curiosity, Ruso begins to ask questions nobody wants to hear. Meanwhile his barbarian wife, Tilla, is finding out some of the answers." (Publisher's note)

Downie, Ruth

Tabula Rasa; A Crime Novel of the Roman Empire. Ruth Downie. St. Martin's Press 2014 352 p. map (Gaius Ruso) $26

ISBN 1608197085; 9781608197088

"As Ruso and Tilla try to solve the mystery of . . . two disappearances--while at the same time struggling to keep the peace between the Britons and the Romans--an intricate scheme involving slavery, changed identities, and fur trappers emerges, and it becomes imperative that Ruso find Branan before it's too late." (Publisher's note)

"Downie writes with quiet authority and surprising depth, offering an engaging depiction of an obscure slice of history." Kirkus

Downie, Ruth

Terra incognita; a novel of the Roman Empire. Bloomsbury 2008 384p $23.95

ISBN 978-1-59691-232-8; 1-59691-232-4

LC 2007-44474

"Having just solved the mysterious deaths of several prostitutes . . . , Ruso accepts a posting to the northern border of Roman Britain in the hopes of getting a much-deserved rest and a return to actual medical practice. Instead, he finds himself at the center of an investigation into the death of a Roman soldier. The murder victim's missing head, an overzealous military aide who doesn't hesitate to use torture to force confessions from the local natives, a drug-addled fellow medic who has confessed to the murder, a stag-headed rabble-rouser, and Ruso's housekeeper all play a part in the drama. Saving this novel from a certain gritty grimness often found in mysteries is Downie's wry and witty humor." Libr J

Downing, David

Potsdam station. Soho Press 2011 340p $25

ISBN 978-1-56947-917-9

LC 2010-39801

This episode finds "well-traveled Anglo-American journalist [John Ressell] in Moscow in the spring of 1945, angling for a way to get back into Berlin, where his German girlfriend is still trapped, before the Reich falls and the Red Army starts exacting its revenge on the surviving populace — starting with the women. Russell gets his pass; but it's not free. He must guide an expedition to Berlin on a secret hunt for documents from the German atomic research program. Downing provides no platform for debate in this unsentimental novel, leaving his hero to ponder the ethics of his pragmatic choices while surveying the ground-level horrors to be seen in Berlin. The assaults on the ear are no less shocking, from the screams of women in the night to the appalling silence at the end of it all." N Y Times Book Rev

Doyle, Arthur Conan, Sir, 1859-1930

The **adventures** and the memoirs of Sherlock Holmes; by Arthur Conan Doyle ; illustrated by Scott McKowen. Sterling Pub. Co. 2004 vi, 569 p.p ill. (hardcover) $9.95

ISBN 140271453X; 9781402714535

LC 2004016067

This book is a collection of Sir Arthur Conan Doyle's mystery stories featuring detective "Sherlock Holmes, with his unequalled powers of deduction." This edition has illustrations created by Scott McKowen "in scratchboard, an engraving medium which evokes the look of popular art from the period of these stories." (Publisher's note)

Doyle, Arthur Conan

★ The **complete** Sherlock Holmes; with a preface by Christopher Morley. Doubleday 1960 1122p $27.95

ISBN 0-385-00689-6

First published 1930

This book contains the following four Sherlock Holmes novels: A study in scarlet (1887); The sign of the four (1890); The hound of the Baskervilles (1902); The valley of fear (1915). It also contains fifty-eight Sherlock Holmes stories which were originally published in the following separate volumes: Adventures of Sherlock Holmes (1892); Memoirs of Sherlock Holmes (1894); The return of Sherlock Holmes (1905); His last bow (1917); The case book of Sherlock Holmes (1927).

Doyle, Roddy

Bullfighting and other stories. Viking 2011 214p $25.95

ISBN 978-0-670-02287-8; 0-670-02287-X

LC 2010-53424

"A kind of composite central character emerges in the course of these 13 stories (many of which have appeared in the New Yorker). He is a middle-aged Dubliner who can't "really imagine life before the children" or marriage. Though he might take an occasional holiday from responsibility (such as the boys' week in Spain detailed in the title story), he is typically conscientious to a comical fault." Minneapolis Star Tribune

Doyle, Roddy

The **dead** republic. Viking 2010 329p $26.95

ISBN 978-0-670-02177-2; 0-670-02177-6

LC 2009-44778

The novel "reads almost like a hallucinatory dream of the making and unmaking of the idea of modern Ireland. While it is not quite the successor to the trilogy's first two novels that fans might have envisioned, it remains a fine if imperfect farewell to one of the more memorable protagonists in recent literature." Denver Post

Doyle, Roddy, 1958-

The **Guts**; Roddy Doyle. Viking Adult 2014 336 p. $27.95; pbk $16

ISBN 0670016438; 9780670016433; 0143126091; 9780143126096

LC 2013036812

Sequel to: The Commitments (1989)

In this book by Roddy Doyle, "Jimmy Rabbitte--last seen as the brash, young manager of the Commitments--is now middle-aged. He's still kicking around Dublin, married, with four kids, and working as a reasonably successful promoter of nostalgia bands--one-hit wonders that have been generally forgotten. When Jimmy is diagnosed with bowel cancer, however, he finds himself suddenly reevaluating his life, his decisions, and his legacy." (Publishers Weekly)

Doyle, Roddy

★ **Paddy** Clarke, ha ha ha. Viking 1993 282p pbk $16; hbk o.p.

ISBN 0670853453; 0140233903; 9780140233902; 9780670853458

Doyle's "triumph in this novel is to replenish our sense of how children think and speak and explain the adult world to themselves." London Rev Books

Doyle, Roddy, 1958-

★ **Smile**; a novel. Roddy Doyle. Viking 2017 214 p. (hardcover) $25

ISBN 9780735224452; 0735224447; 9780735224445

LC 2017031415

In this novel, by Roddy Doyle, "alone for the first time in years, Victor Forde goes every evening to Donnelly's for a pint, a slow one. One evening his drink is interrupted. A man in shorts and a pink shirt comes over and sits down. He seems to know Victor's name and to remember him from secondary school. His name is Fitzpatrick. Victor dislikes him on sight, dislikes, too, the memories that Fitzpatrick stirs up of five years being taught by the Christian Brothers." (Publisher's note)

"Doyle's ability to convey so much meaning through rapid-fire dialog in the Irish vernacular is unsurpassed. His commentary about the Catholic Church, sexuality, and repression is searing." LJ

Doyle, Roddy

A **star** called Henry. Viking 1999 343p

ISBN 0-670-88757-9

LC 99-25310

"In Doyle's hands, the grand patriotic narrative is tempered with a sharp sense of humanity and human frailty." Times Lit Suppl

Doyle, Roddy

★ The **woman** who walked into doors. Viking 1996 226p

LC 95-41850

Doyle "is a very, very good writer. 'The Woman Who Walked Into Doors' honors not the female experience in the abstract, but the experience of this one woman, Paula Spencer; it examines it with tenderness, but with fearless clearsightedness. And it's funny in places too. Paula Spencer is neither a victim nor a flawless Madonna; she inhabits the complexity of her mind and history; she acts to buy a better future for her children." N Y Times Book Rev

Drabble, Margaret, 1939-

★ The **dark** flood rises; a novel. Margaret Drabble. Farrar, Straus & Giroux 2017 336 p. (ebook) $60; (hardcover) $26

ISBN 9780374715762; 9780374134952

LC 2016025620

This novel, by Margaret Drabble, is a "tale about the many ways in which we confront aging and living in a time of geopolitical rupture. . . . [It] moves between . . . [Francesca Stubbs'] interconnected group of family and friends in England and a seemingly idyllic expat community in the Canary Islands. In both places, disaster looms. In Britain, the flood tides are rising, and in the Canaries, there is always the potential for a seismic event." (Publisher's note)

"For women of a certain age, it is a pure pleasure to grow older alongside Drabble... For all others, there's plenty of joy to be had in this thoughtful meditation on aging and mortality." LJ

Drabble, Margaret, 1939-

A **day** in the life of a smiling woman; complete short stories. Margaret Drabble ; edited by José Francisco Fernández. Houghton Mifflin Harcourt 2011 xxii, 227p (hbk.) $24; (pbk.) $13.95

ISBN 9780547550404; 0547550405; 0547737351; 9780547737355

LC 2010049798

This short story collection "chronicle[s] relationships . . . from first meetings through marriages, love affairs, betrayals, abuses, and estrangements," focusing on "the experiences of women in their eras. 'Hassan's Tower' . . . deals with a disastrous honeymoon where magnified misunderstandings and unexpressed resentments underline how very little love exists in this new marriage. 'Crossing the Alps' is the tale of a long-planned illicit getaway for a pair of lovers that goes terribly wrong when an illness makes one of them incapable of romance. In the . . . title story, a popular television personality who appears to balance work and life cheerfully and capably, actually lives with an abusive husband and is suffering from a serious malignancy." (Libr J)

"The discursive spaciousness of Margaret Drabble's voice and vision lends itself to the long form, as her 17 splendid novels demonstrate. This may help to explain why her 'complete short stories' make up so slender a volume. Drabble, it seems, just didn't have enough time to write short stories (with apologies to Mark Twain). Of those collected here, 14 in all, the earliest dates from the 1950s, the most recent from the 1990s. Some are reed slim, but many glimmer with the irony, lyricism, moral vision and (despite their page counts) amplitude we associate with Drabble's novels. They reflect back to us the last half of the 20th century, albeit in Drabble's often 19th-century voice." N Y Times Book Rev

Drabble, Margaret, 1939-

The **pure** gold baby; Margaret Drabble. Houghton Mifflin Harcourt 2013 304 p. pbk $14.95

ISBN 9780544158900; 0544158903 ; 9780544228030

LC 2013021736

"Jessica Speight, a young anthropology student in 1960s London, is at the beginning of a promising academic career when an affair with her married professor turns her into a single mother. Anna is a pure gold baby with a delightful sunny nature. But as it becomes clear that Anna will not be a normal child, the book circles questions of responsibility, potential, even age." (Publisher's note)

Drabble, Margaret, 1939-

The **radiant** way. Knopf 1987 407p

ISBN 0-394-56143-0

LC 87-45126

This novel covers five years (from New Year's Eve, 1979 to July 1985) in the lives of three women who have been friends since their student days at Cambridge in the 1950s. Liz Headleand is a "psychotherapist, Alix {Bowen} a teacher of literature in a women's prison, and Esther {Breuer} an art historian specializing in the Italian Renaissance." (Libr J)

Drabble "charts every hill and dale in the increasingly brighter landscape of middle-class women's roles (a progression that takes place, ironically, as Britain's economic power erodes). Drabble is a master of delicate phrasing set amid a big, robust narrative." Booklist

Followed by A natural curiosity (1989) and The gates of ivory (1992)

Drabble, Margaret, 1939-

The **sea** lady; a late romance. Harcourt, Inc. 2007 345p $24

ISBN 978-0-15-101263-3; 0-15-101263-6

LC 2006-23778

First published 2006 in the United Kingdom

The author "has a keen sense of the past and the ways in which intellectual fashions evolve. She is pitiless—and very funny—about the flimsiness of Ailsa's various posturings. Where Humphrey craves knowledge, Ailsa craves exposure. Their love affair mirrors the age they are living through. . . . Drabble writes beautifully about the passing of time and the sad, incomplete experience of human love." New Staesman

Drabble, Margaret, 1939-

The **witch** of Exmoor. Harcourt Brace & Co. 1997 281p

ISBN 0-15-100363-7

LC 97-10952

First published 1996 in the United Kingdom

"Can politics ever amount to more than the conspiracies we hatch against our parents and the spells we cast on our children? The humbling surprise of Drabble's novel is not that it refuses to resolve this question but that we gradually lose our lofty perspective and begin to have an emotional stake in the answer." New Yorker

Drayson, Nicholas

Guide to the birds of East Africa. Houghton Mifflin 2008 201p $22

ISBN 978-0-547-15258-5; 0-547-15258-2

LC 2008-17183

"With captivating character sketches and glimpses into Kenyan life and politics, Drayson meets the inevitable comparisons to Alexander McCall Smith without breaking a sweat." Publ Wkly

Dreiser, Theodore

★ An **American** tragedy. Boni & Liveright 1925 2v

"Clyde Griffiths, product of a poor and pious home, is driven by ambition to acquire money and social status. He is loved by Roberta, a factory coworker, but is dazzled by Sondra, who would be a passport to the country-club set. When Roberta, pregnant and no longer desirable, becomes an obstacle to Clyde's fulfilling his dream, he plans her death, for which he is caught and convicted." Shapiro. Fic for Youth. 3d edition

Dreiser, Theodore

★ **Sister** Carrie; historical editors, John C. Berkey, Alice M. Winters; textual editor, James L.W. West III; general editor Neda M. Westlake; introduction by Alfred Kazin. Penguin Books 1994 499p pa $12.95

ISBN 0-14-018828-2

First published 1900

"A powerful account of a young working girl's rise to the 'tinsel and shine' of worldly success, and of the slow decline of her lover and protector Hurstwood." Oxford Companion to Engl Lit

Dreiser, Theodore

Sister Carrie; Jennie Gerhardt; Twelve men. Library of America 1987 1168p il $40

ISBN 0-940450-41-0

Sister Carrie and Jennie Gerhardt are entered separately. Twelve men (1919) presents brief biographical sketches of twelve men that have influenced the author's life

Dreyer, Eileen

Barely a lady. Forever 2010 418p pa $6.99

ISBN 978-0-446-54208-1

"Five years ago Olivia's husband, Jack, nearly destroyed her life, and now he is about to do it again. Accepting scurrilous rumors as fact, Jack divorced Olivia early in their marriage, leaving her destitute. She has finally rebuilt her life, and now all her hard work is threatened when Jack's old valet suddenly turns up and insists that Olivia accompany him to Waterloo, where Olivia discovers that Jack is badly wounded and attired in a French officer's uniform. Helping her ex could very well destroy Olivia, but she knows Jack is no traitor. . . . [The novel is] addictively readable thanks to exquisitely nuanced characters, a brilliantly realized historical setting, and a captivating plot encompassing both the triumph and tragedy of war." Booklist

Dreyer, Eileen

Once a Rake; by Eileen Dreyer. Grand Central Pub 2013 416 p. (Drake's Rakes) $8

ISBN 1455519324; 9781455519323

LC 2014657982

In this book, by Eileen Dreyer, "Colonel Ian Ferguson may be a rake, but he's no traitor. Accused of trying to kill the Duke of Wellington, the disgraced Scotsman is now a fugitive-from the law, the army, and the cunning assassin who hunts him. Wounded and miles from his allies, Ian finds himself at the mercy of an impoverished country wife. The spirited woman is . . . hiding some dangerous secrets of her own." (Publisher's note)

"Exquisite writing, historical accuracy, a clever plot, and complex, enthralling, walk-off-the-page characters make this another fascinating gem." LJ

Dreyer, Eileen

Twice tempted; by Eileen Dreyer. Grand Central Pub 2014 379 p. $8

ISBN 1455519340; 9781455519347

In this book, by Eileen Dreyer, "it feels like a lifetime ago that Alex Knight saved Fiona from certain doom . . . and stole a soul-shattering kiss for good measure. Wanting nothing more than to keep her safe, he left her in the care of her grandfather, the Marquess of Dourne. But Fiona was hardly safe. As soon as he could, the marquess cast her and her sister out on the streets with only her wits to keep them alive." (Publisher's note)

"In the latest thrilling addition to her Drake's Rakes series, following Once a Rake (2013), Dreyer's brilliantly complex characters, addictively tart sense of humor, and flair for crafting sizzling sexual chemistry once again prove to be irresistible, and her skillful incorporation of the contributions of Regency women to science provides the perfect historical counterpoint to the story's danger-rich plot." Booklist

Drndić, Daša, 1946-

★ **Trieste**; Daša Drndić ; translated by Ellen Elias-Bursać. Houghton Mifflin Harcourt 2014 368 p. (hardback) $27

ISBN 0547725140; 9780547725147

LC 2013044258

This "novel of WWII and its aftermath is acclaimed Croatian author [Daša] Drndić's American debut. In 2006, elderly Haya Tedeschi is awaiting a reunion with her son, who disappeared as an infant during WWII.. . . Interspersed with [protagonist] Haya's account are photographs, interviews, and personal testimonies, and, in one case, pages listing the names of all 9,000 Jews deported from or murdered in northern Italy during the war." (Publishers Weekly)

"Trieste's originality lies not just in its structure and forceful, unflinching imagery . . . but also in how it brings the lingering effects of the Nazis' merciless racial policies forward into the present." Booklist

Druon, Maurice

The **Iron** King; a novel. Translated from the French by Humphrey Hare. HarperCollins 2013 368 p. (paperback) $14.99

ISBN 0007491263; 9780007491261

LC 56010197

This book is the first in "a seven-part historical series that chronicles the beginnings of the Hundred Years' War and the fall of the Capetian kings" from author Maurice Druon. At the heart of this entry "is the French monarch, Philip the Fair (1268-1314), grandson of Saint Louis, who rules with an iron fist; it's his persecution of the Knights Templar, including burning its Grand Master at the stake, that sets the stage for his downfall." (Library Journal)

Drury, Tom

The **driftless** area. Atlantic Monthly Press 2006 215p $22

ISBN 0-87113-943-X

LC 2006-40787

"Deadpan wit, cosmic melancholy, characters both ethereal and down and dirty, predicaments a Beckett character would accept as inevitable, and a porous divide between the living and the dead add up to a delectably unnerving outlaw fairy tale." Booklist

Du Maurier, Daphne

Frenchman's Creek. Doubleday, Doran 1942 310p

"The lovely Lady St. Columb fled by coach from the boredom of London society, and an unloved husband to their wild and unused Cornish coast estate. There she discovered an aristocratic French pirate who secreted his ship and crew in the hidden creek and as a game preyed gaily upon the dull Cornish gentry. {The book describes} the love between the two and the thrilling adventure they shared." Booklist

Du Maurier, Daphne

Jamaica Inn. Doubleday, Doran 1936 332p

"A stirring tale of an old inn on the desolate moors of Cornwall, where Mary Yellan, left alone in the world at her mother's death, took refuge with her aunt. Her uncle, the landlord, directed smugglers who wrecked ships on the nearby coast, and the inn was a place of horror and mystery. Mary's hope of rescuing her aunt, and escaping, was soon complicated by her unwilling interest in the landlord's brother, who stole horses but drew the line at murder." Booklist

Du Maurier, Daphne

★ **Rebecca**. Doubleday 1938 457p $29.95

ISBN 0-385-04380-5

"Rebecca, lovely and charming wife of English aristocrat Maxim de Winter, dies unexpectedly, and the mystery surrounding her death haunts all who remain at the Manderley country estate. Eight months after the sailing accident in which Rebecca lost her life Maxim remarries. Through his new wife's writing, the reader learns the truth about Rebecca's death and character." Shapiro. Fic for Youth. 3d edition

Dubus, Andre, 1959-

Dirty Love; by Andre Dubus III. 1st ed. W W Norton & Co Inc 2013 320 p. (hardcover) $25.95

ISBN 0393064654; 9780393064650

LC 2013017214

This book contains four loosely connected short works. In 'Listen Carefully as Our Options Have Changed,' Mark Welch is a middle-aged project manager who suspects that his wife is having an affair. . . . One shorter work deals with Maria, an overweight bank teller, and the surprising things she discovers about herself after she falls in love for the first time; another follows Robert Doucette, a bartender-cum-poet who cheats on his pregnant wife." (Publishers Weekly)

Dubus, Andre, 1959-

The **garden** of last days; a novel. [by] Andre Dubus III. W.W. Norton 2008 537p $24.95

ISBN 0393041654; 9780393041651; 978-0-393-04165-1; 0-393-04165-4

LC 2008-1294

This is a novel by the author of House of Sand and Fog (1999) and Bluesman (2001). "One early September night in Florida, a stripper brings her daughter to work. . . . April works at the Puma Club for Men. And tonight she has an unusual client, a foreigner both remote and too personal, and free with his money. . . . His name is Bassam. Meanwhile, another man, AJ, has been thrown out of the club for holding hands with his favorite stripper, and he's drunk and angry." (Publisher's note)

The "narrative mostly unfolds at a Florida strip club, and the evening is spent with a terrorist who drives a leased Neon, a stripper who brings her toddler to work, a patron who gets bounced for innocently touching a dancer, and a landlord who, had she not taken ill, might have saved everyone. . . . When the critics weigh in, there will be plenty of chatter about how Dubus so deeply inhabits even the most disturbing characters. And rightly so. But the book's most profound achievement is a far more difficult one: the omnipresence of hope in a hopeless place. [The novel] is riveting and disturbing, as beautiful as it is bleak, and if there are cowards among the cast of broken characters, I couldn't find them." Esquire

Due, Tananarive

Blood colony; a novel. Atria Books 2008 422p $25

ISBN 978-0-7432-8735-7; 0-7432-8735-5

LC 2008-12403

Due "expertly mixes genres and intertwines sociopolitical issues into the framework of a story about a group of ancient African immortals who are battling to end the AIDS/HIV epidemic. Like the late, great Octavia Butler, Due fearlessly tackles contemporary issues." Baltimore Sun

Due, Tananarive

Ghost summer; Stories. Tananarive Due. Prime Books 2015 256 p. (paperback) $15.95

ISBN 160701453X; 9781607014539

LC 2015036171

NAACP Image Award Nominee: Outstanding Literary Work - Fiction (2016)

This supernatural short story collection, by Tananarive Due "uses a clear-eyed view of history to explain (but never excuse) the present. Sexual predators are recast as lake creatures ('The Lake'), and werewolves choose cosmetic treatment to disguise their monthly changes ('Aftermoon'); Due craftily employs these shape-shifters to explore how humans embrace transformations in ourselves and one another, even when the result is monstrous." (Publishers Weekly)

Duenas, Maria, 1964-

The **time** in between; Maria Duenas; translated by Daniel Hahn. 1st Atria Books hardcover ed. Atria Books 2011 615 p.

ISBN 9781451616880; 1451616880

LC 2011019250

This book "opens during the mid-1930s as Spain is on the brink of civil war and young Sira Quiroga is preparing a simple wedding in Madrid, where she lives. Sira's plans are thrown off track when she meets Ramiro Arribas, the cunning older manager of a typewriter shop who convinces her to embark on an exotic life in Morocco. The future that he envisions for her differs from what he imagines for himself, however, and he abandons Sira after pilfering her inheritance and leaving her saddled with debt. Newly adrift, Sira travels to northern Morocco, where she is reluctantly taken in by Candeleria, a disreputable woman known for housing dispossessed souls. In Candeleria's care, Sira returns to her roots as a dressmaker's apprentice. Realizing her talent with a needle and thread, Candeleria takes advantage, quietly financing Sira's efforts and taking half the profits." (Publishers Weekly)

Includes bibliographical references.

Duffy, Brendan

House of echoes; a novel. Brendan Duffy. Ballantine Books 2015 400 p. genealogical table (hardback) $26

ISBN 0804178119; 9780804178112

LC 2014024343

In this novel by Brendan Duffy "Ben and Caroline Tierney and their two young boys are hoping to start over. When Ben inherits land in the village of Swannhaven, in a remote corner of upstate New York, the Tierneys believe it's just the break they need, and they leave behind all they know to restore a sprawling estate. But as Ben uncovers Swannhaven's chilling secrets and Charlie ventures deeper into the surrounding forest, strange things begin to happen." (Publisher's note)

"Debut author Duffy has delivered a fluid, suspenseful yet subtle thriller, with touches of humor, evocative writing, and characters that are both familiar and uniquely fascinating. A wonderfully tense and heart-wrenching debut." Kirkus

Duffy, Stella

Theodora; actress, empress, whore. Stella Duffy. Penguin Books 2011 352 p. $15

ISBN 0143119877; 9780143119876

LC 2011007869

This book by Stella Duffy presents the fictional "retelling of the true story of a woman (500-548) who rose from lowly beginnings to become Empress of the Byzantine Empire. . . . Theodora was trained as a dancer, singer, and actress who performed on the stage and in the bedrooms of anyone who could afford her, from the time she was a child. . . . When Theodora finds herself cast off in a few short years, she must make her way back to her beloved Constantinople." (Library Journal)

Includes bibliographical references

Dufresne, John

Deep in the shade of paradise. Norton 2002 364p $25.95

ISBN 0-393-02020-7

LC 2001-44487

"The people in this small town are surprisingly endearing, despite their quirks. Numerous asides sprinkled throughout the novel make for a clever and memorable narrative style." Booklist

Dufresne, John

Requiem, Mass. a novel. W. W. Norton & Co. 2008 316p $24.95

ISBN 978-0-393-05790-4; 0-393-05790-9

LC 2008-1343

"The book unfolds like a series of nesting dolls: John meanders around his coastal Florida home, writing his novel, visiting with friends and going on appointments for teaching jobs, while Johnny lives with his mother's worsening condition, his father's absences, his mother's hospitalization and a momentous trip South. Then there are stories within the memoir within the story, including the one a woman tells about her friend, Ginger Rae, who talks of writing a neighbor's suicide note, then claims it's part of a story she herself is writing. John is a very amusing unreliable narrator, and Dufresne's witty, sardonic take on life's fictions leaps off the page." Publ Wkly

Dugoni, Robert

Murder one; a novel. Simon & Schuster 2011 374p $24.99

ISBN 978-1-4516-0669-0; 1-4516-0669-9

LC 2011-05010

In this legal thriller Seattle attorney David Sloane "attends his first public event since his wife's murder a year earlier, a benefit to promote legal aid services, where he literally runs into attorney Barclay Reid, an adversary from a previous case. Reid is also in mourning-for her college age daughter, Carly, who died of a heroin overdose. Reid mounts a charm offensive to persuade Sloane to represent her in a wrongful death suit against the Russian gangster, Filyp Vasiliev, who was behind the heroin sale that killed Carly and who has just beaten federal criminal charges after a judge tossed out crucial evidence at a pretrial hearing. The shooting death of Vasiliev in his Seattle home derails the developing romance between Sloane and Reid as well as the civil case. While many will anticipate the ending twist, Dugoni conveys the legalese in digestible form." Publ Wkly

Dugoni, Robert

My sister's grave; Robert Dugoni. Thomas & Mercer 2014 416 p. (Tracey Crosswhite) (trade pbk : alk. paper) $15.95

ISBN 1477825576; 9781477825570

LC 2014939862

In this novel by Robert Dugoni, "Tracy Crosswhite has spent twenty years questioning . . . her sister Sarah's disappearance and the murder trial. Motivated by the opportunity to obtain real justice, Tracy became a homicide detective. When Sarah's remains are finally discovered near their hometown in the northern Cascade mountains of Washington State, Tracy is determined to get the answers she's been seeking." (Publisher's note)

Other titles in this series are:
Her final breath (2015)
In the clearing (2016)
The trapped girl (2017)
Close to home (2017)
A steep price (2018)

Dumas, Alexandre

★ **Camille**; the lady of the camellias. by Alexandre Dumas fils; translated by Edmund Gosse; with a new introduction by Toril Moi. Signet Classic 2004 255p il pa $6.95

ISBN 978-0-451-52920-6; 0-451-52920-0

Original French edition, 1848; first United States edition published 1857 by E.J. Hincken with title: The camelia-lady. Variant title: Lady with the camellias

Camille "is a beautiful courtesan who has become part of the fashionable world of Paris. Scorning the wealthy Count de Varville, who has offered to relieve her debts should she once more become his mistress, she escapes to the country with her penniless lover Armand Duval. Here Camille makes her great sacrifice. Giving Armand, whom she truly loves, the impression that she has tired of their life together, but actually at the request of his family, she returns to Paris and her life of frivolity. The tale concludes with the ultimate tragic reunion of Armand and the dying Camille." Reader's Ency. 4th edition

Dumas, Alexandre

★ The **Count** of Monte Cristo. Modern Library 1996 1462p $25.95

ISBN 0-679-60199-6

LC 96-3397

Original French edition, 1844

"Edmond Dantes, a young sailor unjustly accused of helping the exiled Napoleon in 1815, has been arrested and imprisoned in the Chateau d'If, near Marseille. After fifteen years, he finally escapes by taking the place of his dead companion, the Abbe Faria; enclosed in a sack, he is thrown into the sea. He cuts the sack with his knife, swims to safety, is taken to Italy on a fisherman's boat. From Genoa, he goes to the caverns of Monte Cristo and digs up the fabulous treasures of which the dying Faria had told. He then uses the money to punish his enemies and reward his friends." Haydn. Thesaurus of Book Dig

Dumas, Alexandre

★ The **man** in the iron mask; translated by Joachim Neugroschel ; introduction by Francine du Plessix Gray. Penguin Books 2003 xxv, 470p (Penguin classics) pa $16

ISBN 978-0-14-043924-3; 0-14-043924-2

LC 2002-193017

Original French edition published 1850 as part of Le Vicomte de Bragelonne

The identity of the man in the iron mask—is an unsolved mystery. Dumas' "iron mask episode is found toward the end . . . of the third volume of 'Vicomte De Bragelonne'. . . . The present volume remains essentially the story of the . . . closing years of those four men who had performed such prodigies—attacking armies, assaulting castles, terrifying death itself—Athos, Porthos, Aramis, and their captain, D'Artagnan." Preface for the reader

Dumas, Alexandre

★ The **three** musketeers; translated with an introduction by Richard Pevear. Viking 2006 704p $35

ISBN 0-670-03779-6

LC 2005-58468

Original French edition, 1844

"Richard Pevear's brisk, agile new translation succeeds, I think, because it does justice to the pure nuttiness of Dumas's writing: the nonindustrial, nonformulaic, downright peculiar qualities that make a work of popular fiction memorable." N Y Times Book Rev

Dumas, Alexandre

Twenty years after; edited with an introduction and notes by David Coward. Oxford University Press 1998 xxv, 845p il pa $15.95

ISBN 0-19-283843-1

LC 99-188043

Sequel to The three musketeers

Original French edition, 1845; first United States edition published 1846 by Taylor, Wilde and Company

"Anne of Austria's regency, the insurrection of the Fronde, and the execution of Charles I of England mark out the period (1648-9)." Baker. Guide to the Best Fic

Followed by The Vicomte de Bragelonne (1848-1850)

Dunant, Sarah

The **birth** of Venus; a novel. Random House 2004 394p $21.95

ISBN 1-400-06073-7

LC 2003-46932

In this novel, "the fictional narrator is Alessandra Cecchi, 14, the daughter of a wealthy cloth merchant in the Florence of Michelangelo and Botticelli. Alessandra yearns to live with a brush in her hand. For that matter, she would be happy just to get out of the house. But it's the 1490s, so her best hope is an agreeable arranged marriage." (Time)

"Part feverish thriller, part historical romance, the story of the outspoken heroine's sentimental education—a comprehensive curriculum including every conceivable transgression—sometimes comes off as a heady blend of Browning's My Last Duchess and Anaïs Nin. But Dunant's skill lies in combining these elements with a finely textured and pertinent depiction of a cultured citizenry in the grip of rampant fundamentalism." New Yorker

Dunant, Sarah

★ **Blood** and beauty; the Borgias : a novel. Sarah Dunant. 1st U.S. ed. Random House Inc. 2013 506 p. map (hardcover) $27

ISBN 1400069297; 9781400069293

LC 2012042215

In this work of "biofiction" by Sarah Dunant presents an "account of Rodrigo Borgia's ascent to the papacy as Alexander VI in 1492 and his subsequent tireless efforts to build a power base through the strategic use of his four children. Cesare is the sly, shrewd son . . . who moves ruthlessly from cardinal to soldier as politics and advancement dictate. Beloved daughter Lucrezia makes one strategic marriage after another while nursing a powerful attachment to Cesare." (Kirkus Reviews)

"An impressively confident, capable sweep through the corrupt politics and serpentine relationships of a legendary family." Kirkus

Dunant, Sarah

In the company of the courtesan; a novel. Random House 2006 371p $23.95

ISBN 1-4000-6381-7

LC 2005-51649

This historical novel "follows the fortunes of a beautiful, flame-haired courtesan, Fiammetta Bianchini, who, after escaping from the 1527 pillage of Rome, sets up shop in Venice. The novel, narrated by Fiammetta's servant, a dwarf, chronicles the pair's horrific scrapes and their dizzying triumphs, which include Fiammetta's becoming Titian's model for his 'Venus of Urbino.' Along the way, Dunant presents a lively and detailed acccount of the glimmering palaces and murky alleys of Renaissance Venice, and examines the way the city's clerics and prostitutes alike are bound by its peculiar dynamic of opulence and restraint." New Yorker

Dunant, Sarah

Sacred hearts; Sarah Dunant. Random House 2009 415p $25; pbk $15

ISBN 978-1-4000-6382-6; 1400063825; 9780812974058

LC 2009002246

"Sixteen-year-old Serafina, a talented songstress with a broken heart, literally enters the cloister kicking and screaming, the victim of her nobleman father's callous intent to quash an unsuitable romance. Despite the fact that Serafina strikes up a strong friendship with Suora Zuanna, the gifted mistress of the dispensary, Serafina has one goal in mind: to escape the confines of a life imposed on her by her time, her circumstances, and her station. As Serafina's determination to take control of her own life takes root, her discontent has a domino effect on the other nuns." (Booklist)

Duncan, Dave

When the saints; Dave Duncan. Tor 2011 332 p. (Brothers Magnus)

ISBN 0765323486; 9780765323484

LC 2011021617

This book is "set in Jorgary, a fictional country in late 15th-century Central Europe. Certain individuals possess a form of magic called Speaking, which involves invoking saints . . . to work miracles. The Magnus clan has loyally served the kings of Jorgary for centuries. However, Cardinal Zdenek, the real ruler of Jorgary . . . knows that Duke Wartislaw of Pomerania has invaded Jorgary with an army of Wends. . . . The four surviving Magnus brothers, Wulf, Otto, Anton and Vlad, have . . . been dispatched to Gallant to organize the defenses. Young Wulf is a Speaker, powerful but untrained and ignorant of magic's rules, wracked with doubts as to whether his talents truly emanate from saints or demons. Zdenek arranges for another Speaker, from a mysterious organization known as the Saints, to assist with Wulf's education." (Kirkus)

Duncan, Glen

By blood we live; Glen Duncan. Alfred A. Knopf 2014 368 p. (hardback) $25.95

ISBN 0307595102; 9780307595102

LC 2013044988

This novel by Glen Duncan presents "a stunningly erotic love story that gives us the final battle for survival between werewolves and vampires, and one last searing--and brilliantly ironic--look at what it means to be, or not to be, human. . . . as the novel unfolds, Talulla and Remshi are inexorably drawn to each other--and toward the moment when an ancient prophecy may finally come to pass." (Publisher's note)

"[T]here are plenty of battles, blood, and sexy escapades; but the real treats continues to be Duncan's beautifully twisted way with language and the profound thesis he poses about humanity." Booklist

Duncan, Glen

Death of an ordinary man; Glen Duncan. Grove Press 2005 304p pa $13

ISBN 0-8021-7004-8

LC 2004-56727

"As this novel opens, Nathan finds himself falling into darkness and emerges to float above his own funeral. . . . Along with the reader, Nathan pieces together his life and death mosaiclike as he hovers around his family after the funeral, able to sense their feelings and falling into the memories thus invoked. We see his passion for his edgy, intense wife, who ultimately betrayed him with his best friend; we register his concern for his floundering son and budding, tough-as-nails older daughter. We learn that a younger daughter has died and are eventually rubbed raw by the details of her horrific death. Duncan layers on brilliant prose—sometimes a little heavily, as the narrative seems to slow halfway through. In the end, however, he has produced an arresting story, and he writes convincingly and affectingly of the consequences of a child's death, which is pretty rare indeed." Libr J

Duncan, Glen

The **last** werewolf. Knopf 2011 293p

ISBN 0-307-59508-0; 978-0-307-59508-9

LC 2011-11667

A "yarn about a Kant-quoting lycanthrope on the run from monster hunters bent on rendering his species extinct. Jake Marlowe, whose name recalls the hero of Joseph Conrad's Heart of Darkness and the author of Doctor Faustus, was infected nearly 200 years ago and has grown weary of the chase and his monthly feedings. Unlike Jeff Lindsay's Dexter Morgan, the serial killer who targets only fellow killers, Jake is generally less discriminating in his selection of victims. But even he gives in to charitable impulses, of a sort: 'Two nights ago I'd eaten a forty-three-year-old hedge fund specialist. I've been in a phase of taking the ones no one wants.' Jake is not only quite the raconteur, he's also a major horndog — the book's many sex scenes are just as graphic as the kills. 'The werewolf gets dyslexia and a permanent erection,' Duncan notes, while the vampires whose presence makes Jake physically ill are immortal and sexless. Take that, True Blood fans! Duncan creates a world that is completely imagined, if occasionally implausible." Entertainment Wkly

Duncan, Glen

Talulla rising; by Glen Duncan. Alfred A. Knopf 2012 351 p. (hardcover : alk. paper) $25.95; (paperback) $15.00; (ebook) $25.95

ISBN 0307595099; 9780307595096; 9780307742186; 9780307958433

LC 2012005881

Sequel to: The Last Werewolf.

This book by Glen Duncan "finds newly turned werewolf Talulla Demetriou hiding out in a remote hunting lodge . . . mourning her dead werewolf lover, Jake Marlowe, by whom she's pregnant. After Talulla delivers boy-girl befurred twins, vampires kidnap her newborn son as a sacrifice to bring back their mythic progenitor. With baby daughter Zoë in tow, Talulla sets out after the vampires in a quest to regain her son that will bring her in contact with more of her kind." (Publishers Weekly)

Dunmore, Helen

The **betrayal**. Black Cat 2011 331p pa 14.95

ISBN 978-0-8021-7088-0; 0-8021-7088-9

First published 2010 in the United Kingdom

"In her sequel to The Siege (2002), Dunmore returns to Leningrad in 1952, compressing the anxiety and terror of the postwar Stalinist years into the intimate details of one family's crisis. A sense of doom takes over from the first page when pediatrician Andrei is approached by a nervously sweating colleague who twists his arm to consult on a case they both know will bring trouble. Volkov, the head of State Security, has brought in his 10-year-old son Gorya with a badly swollen leg. X-rays show a cancerous tumor; Gorya's leg must be amputated. Andrei, whose specialty is arthritis, has no expertise in oncology, but Volkov demands he take charge of the case because Gorya likes him. Anti-Semitic Volkov even agrees to Andrei's recommendation of a Jewish surgeon. Although the amputation is successful and Gorya appears on the road to recovery, the surgeon immediately transfers out of Leningrad and recommends Andrei do the same to lower his visibility. Instead, he and his wife Anna, who fell in love during the Nazi's siege on the city, take a fatalistic approach, barely altering their routine. . . . Historical fiction of the highest order." Kirkus

Dunmore, Helen, 1952-2017

★ **Exposure**; by Helen Dunmore. Atlantic Monthly Press 2016 391 p. $25

ISBN 0802124933; 9780802124937

This book, by Helen Dunmore, is a "Cold War espionage tale. . . . It's London, 1960. . . . Two colleagues, Giles Holloway and Simon Callington, face a terrible dilemma over a missing top-secret file. At the end of a suburban garden, in the pouring rain, Simon's wife, Lily, buries a briefcase containing the file. . . . She believes that in doing so she is protecting her family. What she will learn is that no one is immune from betrayal or the devastating consequences of exposure." (Publisher's note)

"Dunmore deftly creates a noir atmosphere, revealing layers of complexity in personal relationships darkened by non-battlefield conflict and blending psychological observations reminiscent of Henry James with le Carré-esque betrayals." Pub Wkly

Dunmore, Helen, 1952-2017

The **lie**; by Helen Dunmore. Pgw 2014 304 p. $24

ISBN 080212254X; 9780802122544

LC 2015295381

In this book, by Helen Dunmore, "Daniel Branwell has survived the First World War and returned to the small fishing town where he was born. Behind him lie the trenches and the most intense relationship of his life. As he works on the land, struggling to make a living in the aftermath of war, he is drawn deeper and deeper into the traumas of the past and memories of his dearest friend and his first love. . . . Daniel is haunted by the terrible, unforeseen consequences of a lie." (Publisher's note)

"From the first page, Dunmore shares Daniel's inner life, building an increasing sense of dread while exposing the tragedy of great promise thwarted by forces beyond Daniel's control. Dunmore's crystalline prose is almost too good; the pain she describes is often unbearable to read, yet the emotional power resonates, and Daniel is impossible to forget." Kirkus

Dunn, Katherine, 1945-2016

★ **Geek** love. Knopf 1989 347p

ISBN 0-394-56902-4

LC 88-45776

In this book by Katherine Dunn, "Olympia's parents are circus performers seeking a cost-effective solution to the financial throes of a moribund industry. Her mother, Crystal Lil, agrees to ingest heaps of toxic chemicals and drugs during a gaggle of pregnancies in order to deliberately induce deformities in her offspring. Many don't make it" but "a blessed--or is that accursed?--few achieve a measure of success on the stage." (Bookforum)

"The narrator is a bald female albino hunchback dwarf, raised in her family's carnival show, Binewski's Fabulon. (By using drugs and other methods, her parents succeeded in producing children with physical 'attributes' perfect for performance in a freak show.) This picaresque tale follows the life of the narrator during her family's carnival existence, through times both strange and awful." Booklist

Dunn, Mark

Ella Minnow Pea; a progressively lipogrammatic epistolary fable. by Mark Dunn. MacAdam/Cage Pubs. 2001 205p (alk. paper) $22.00

ISBN 9780967370163; 0967370167

LC 2001042585

This novel "takes place in the present day on the fictional island of Nollop off the coast of South Carolina, where over a century earlier, the great Nevin Nollop invented a 35-letter panagram (a phrase, sentence or verse containing every letter in the alphabet). . . . Nollop was deified for his achievement. . . . Life seems almost utopian in its simplicity until letters of the alphabet start falling from the inscription on the statue erected in Nollop's honor, and the island's governing council decrees that as each letter falls, it must be extirpated from both spoken and written language. Forced to choose from a gradually shrinking pool of words, the novel's protagonists—a family of islanders—seek ways to communicate without employing the forbidden letters." (Publishers Weekly)

Dunne, Dominick

Too much money; a novel. Crown Publishers 2009 275p $26

ISBN 978-0-609-60387-1; 0-609-60387-6

LC 2009-39443

Sequel to: People like us

"The novel opens with an Easter luncheon in a vast Park Avenue apartment that ironically marks the decline of its owner, a well-bred old guard woman named Lil Altemus. Gus Bailey, Dunne's alter ego, is in attendance. He's a journalist who works for a high-society magazine and is about to write a novel about widowed Perla Zacharias, one of the wealthiest women in the world, who, because of dubious origins, has been held down from New York society's highest ranks. Zacharias is not happy with the news about the novel and takes appropriate measures to block it. . . . Dunne shows a little more affection for his subjects than Capote, but not that much. Too little sympathy and you have acid satire. Too much and you have a sentimental portrait. Dunne does it just about right. After you finish his portrayal of the very rich, you may somehow be satisfied with the knowledge of just how poorly they live." San Francisco Chron

Dunnett, Dorothy

★ **Niccolo** rising. Knopf 1986 470p (House of Niccolò)

ISBN 0-394-53107-8

LC 86-45306

This novel "displays all the author's strengths: strong characterization, subtle wit (with a dash of slapstick), lively action, and labyrinthine plot." Wilson Libr Bull

Followed by The spring of the ram

Dunnett, Dorothy

Pawn in frankincense. Putnam 1969 486p

Previous titles in this series of interlocking novels about Scottish adventurer Francis Crawford are: The game of kings (1961); Queen's play (1964) and The disorderly knights (1966)

This installment of Crawford's adventures finds him in "the eastern Mediterranean region searching for his bastard son, who is being held hostage. Plots and counterplots, blood and gore lead to an excruciating climax in the form of a chess contest (a game this is not), in which Crawford and his old adversary Graham Mallett play with living pieces, themselves included. Penalty for capture is death, and Crawford's son, whom he can't recognize, is involved." Libr J

Followed by The ringed castle (1971)

Dunnett, Dorothy

Race of scorpions. Knopf 1990 534p (House of Niccolò)

ISBN 0-394-57107-X

LC 89-45292

"Through precisely rendered scenes, whether depicting a battle on the high seas, the operations of a dye works, a cleverly plotted ambush (using insects) or the gruesome tactics employed to destroy a proud city under siege, Dunnett furnishes fascinating images while spinning her admirable narrative web." Publ Wkly

Followed by Scales of gold

Dunnett, Dorothy

To lie with lions. Knopf 1996 xxiv, 626p (House of Niccolò)

ISBN 0-394-58629-8

LC 95-50422

First published 1995 in the United Kingdom

This sixth book in the House of Niccolo series focuses on 15th century adventurer Nicholas de Fleury's "marriage to quick-witted, self-sufficient Gelis van Borselen. It's a war of wills, egos and attrition that erupts in 1471 as de Fleury (aka Nicholas vander Poele) snatches his infant son, Jordan, from Gelis's arms and kidnaps the boy, a pawn in a bitter power struggle that will take the lives of friends and rivals. . . . With her usual dramatic flair, Dunnett mixes historical and fictive characters in a tale that sweeps from Venice to Antwerp, Edinburgh, Iceland, France and Cyprus." Publ Wkly

Followed by Caprice and Rondo

Dunning, John

★ **Booked** to die; a mystery introducing Cliff Janeway. Scribner 1992 321p $24

ISBN 0-684-19383-3

LC 91-26889

Homicide detective and rare book collector Cliff "Janeway turns in his badge, opens a shop called Twice Told Books on Denver's Book Row and for a time becomes preoccupied with the enchanting lore of his trade. But Janeway discovers that not all book folk are gentlefolk. Two inoffensive book scouts are murdered after making a rare find, and the young clerk in Twice Told Books is dispatched with equal brutality. Thinking like a cop again, Janeway starts suspecting all his new friends on Book Row, including the woman with whom he has fallen in love. . . . This is a soundly plotted, evenly executed whodunit in the classic mode." N Y Times Book Rev

Dunning, John ✓

The **bookman's** wake; a mystery with Cliff Janeway. Scribner 1995 351p

ISBN 0-684-80003-9

LC 94-34328

The author "can't resist writing lengthy, luxurious passages about the craftsmanship of the great print men. Strictly speaking, these eloquent lectures on the art of the printer and the beauty of the book get in the way of the action; but that shouldn't bother anyone who loves books—and their covers." N Y Times Book Rev

DuPree, Kia

Silenced; a novel. Kia DuPree. Grand Central Pub. 2011 336 p. $13.99

ISBN 9780446547741 pa

LC 2011000858

In this book, "30-year-old Nicola "Cola" Hampton struggles to keep her family together. Told from the perspectives of both Cola and her young daughter, Teyona ("Tinka"), the novel opens with Cola losing her job and moving Tinka and her older sons--14-year-old Marquan and 12-year-old Taevon--into Sursum Corda, a notorious D.C. housing project. Cola desperately wants to prevent her children from making the same mistakes that she and their fathers have made: Marquan's father is serving a life sentence for murder; Taevon's is a womanizer; and Tinka's has simply disappeared. Despite Cola's best efforts, Marquan steals a car, is associated with a double homicide, and a few years later is charged with capital murder; Taevon deals drugs; and Tinka's boyfriend robs liquor stores and gas stations." (Publishers Wkly)

Duran, Meredith

A **lady's** code of misconduct; Meredith Duran. Pocket Books 2017 385 p. (Rules for the reckless) (paperback) $7.99

ISBN 1501139029; 9781501139031; 9781501139024

In this novel in the Rules for the Reckless series, by Meredith Duran, "trapped in the countryside, facing an unwanted marriage and the theft of her fortune, Jane Mason is done behaving nicely. To win her freedom, she'll strike a deal with . . . [Crispin Burke.] The bitter past has taught . . . Burke to trust no one. He'll gladly help a lovely young heiress, provided she pays a price. Yet when a single mistake shatters his life, it is Jane who holds the key to his salvation." (Publisher's note)

"A masterful tale of suspense, forgiveness, and love." Kirkus

Duran, Meredith

Luck Be a Lady; Meredith Duran. Pocket Books 2015 368 p. (Rules for the Reckless) pbk $7.99

ISBN 1476741360; 9781476741369

LC 2015028905

"They call her the 'Ice Queen.' Catherine Everleigh is London's loveliest heiress, but a bitter lesson in heartbreak has taught her to keep to herself. All she wants is her birthright--the auction house that was stolen from her. To win this war, she'll need a powerful ally. Who better than infamous and merciless crime lord Nicholas O'Shea? A marriage of convenience will no doubt serve them both." (Publisher's note)

"These intelligent, multilayered characters embody the best aspects of this wonderfully indulgent series." Pub Wkly

Durham, David Anthony

Acacia; book one: The war with the Mein. Doubleday 2007 576p $26.95

ISBN 978-0-385-50606-9; 0-385-50606-6

LC 2006-29726

"Leodan Akaran wants only to be a devoted father and political reformer, but his Acacian empire is based on forced labor, drugged pacification, and a dark deal that trades children into slavery. His chance for reform ends abruptly when the Meins, a fierce people subjugated by the Acacians, revolt through assassination, warfare, and biological terror. The four Akaran children scatter to their respective hiding places—and destinies—around the empire. . . . A series opener that combines the moral ambiguity and brutality of George R.R. Martin's Song of Ice and Fire with Guy Gavriel Kay's emotional sweep and Ursula K. Le Guin's ethnic diversity." Libr J

Durham, David Anthony

★ **Gabriel's** story. Doubleday 2001 291p hardcover o.p. pa $13.95

ISBN 0-385-49814-4; 0-385-72033-5 pa

LC 00-25291

Alex Award (2002)

In this "novel, set in the eighteen-seventies, Gabriel, a fifteen-year-old black boy from Baltimore, resents his new life on the Kansas plains when his widowed mother marries a homesteader. But then he falls in with a charismatic cowpunch and horse thief, and as they travel west to New Mexico a series of violent episodes brings Gabriel to swift maturity. The moral gravity of Durham's narrative is offset by his attentiveness to the primacy of nature in the Western landscape." New Yorker

Durrell, Lawrence

The **Alexandria** quartet: Justine; Balthazar; Mountolive {and} Clea. Dutton 1962 884p

Omnibus edition of four titles entered separately

Durrell, Lawrence

★ **Balthazar**; a novel. Dutton 1958 250p

The second volume of the Alexandria quartet

"Once again {Durrell} writes of Justine, Melissa, Clea, Nessim, Pursewarden, Scobie, Pombal—but from a fresh point of view. The new insights are provided by the psychiatrist, Balthazar, who convinces the narrator that the first volume of the story was almost wholly inaccurate. . . . So this second volume is a correction and an expansion of the first." N Y Times Book Rev

Followed by Mountolive

Durrell, Lawrence

★ **Clea**; a novel. Dutton 1960 287p

Final volume of the Alexandria quartet

"'The Alexandria Quartet' is one of the major achievements of fiction in our time, distinguished not only by its power of language, by its evocation of a place, by its creation of character, by the drama of many of its incidents, but also by its boldly original design. 'Clea' perfects the work, as a spire crowns a cathedral, but the spire is not to be judged in isolation." Saturday Rev

Durrell, Lawrence

★ **Justine**. Dutton 1957 253p

First volume of the Alexandria quartet

"Set in Alexandria the story concerns the amorous adventures of a penniless young man, a prostitute who lives with him, the rich and beautiful Justine with whom he has an affair, and Justine's husband." Publ Wkly

Followed by Balthazar

Durrell, Lawrence

★ **Mountolive**; a novel. Dutton 1959 318p

Third volume of the Alexandria quartet

First published 1958 in the United Kingdom

The perspective is "that of David Mountolive, the British ambassador: and what appeared to be 'the intrigues of desire' are shown to be intrigues motivated by politics. We learn that the beautiful Jewess, Justine, and her Coptic (Christian) husband, Nessim, are passionately united by a common cause: he believes that the formation of a Jewish state will save other minorities in the Arab world from Muslim domination and he is the leader of a group which is smuggling arms to the Jews in Palestine. The discovery of this conspiracy by Nessim's loyal English friends, Pursewarden and the ambassador, and their reactions to it form the plot line of Mountolive." Atlantic

Followed by Clea

Durrow, Heidi W.

★ The **girl** who fell from the sky; a novel. Algonquin Books of Chapel Hill 2010 264p $22.95

ISBN 978-1-56512-680-0; 1-56512-680-7

LC 2009-27572

"Set in the 1980s and focusing luminously on one unusually sympathetic girl overcoming apocalyptic tragedy and navigating her way through nascent sexuality and racial tensions, Durrow's novel transcends topicality." Christ Sci Monit

Durst, Sarah Beth

The **queen** of blood; Sarah Beth Durst. Harper Voyager, an imprint of HarperCollins Publishers 2016 368 p. map (The queens of Renthia) (ebook) $18.99; (hardcover) $19.99

ISBN 9780062413369; 9780062413345

LC 2015044319

Alex Award (2017)

This book in the Queens of Renthia series, by Sarah Beth Durst, is "set in the magical world of Renthia . . . [where] everything has a spirit. . . . But the spirits that reside within this land want to rid it of all humans. . . . The queen . . . alone has the magical power to prevent the spirits from destroying every man, woman, and child. But queens are still just human, and no matter how strong or good, the threat of danger always looms." (Publisher's note)

"In addition to a solid cast of characters and great political intrigue, Durst delivers some fascinating worldbuilding, and the spirits are malevolent, cunning, wild, and mysterious antagonists." Pub Wkly

Dyachenko, Marina

The **scar**; Sergey Dyachenko and Marina Dyachenko. Tor 2012 336p.

ISBN 9780765329936

LC 2011025177

This book "is the story of a man driven by his own feverish demons to find redemption and the woman who just might save him. . . . Egert is a brash, confident member of the elite guards and an egotistical philanderer. But after he kills an innocent student in a duel, a mysterious man known as 'The Wanderer' challenges Egert and slashes his face with his sword, leaving Egert with a scar that comes to symbolize his cowardice. Unable to end his suffering by his own hand, Egert embarks on an odyssey to undo the curse and the horrible damage he has caused, which can only be repaired by a painful journey down a long and harrowing path." (Publisher's note)

Dybek, Stuart

I sailed with Magellan. Farrar, Straus and Giroux 2003 307p $24

ISBN 0-374-17407-5

LC 2003-49052

The "episodes that intersect and surround young Perry Katzek's upbringing in the Polish-Mexican ghetto of Chicago's South Side are simultaneously daring and compassionate, intimate in detail and mythic in scale. Dybek has the rare ability to dart back and forth in time and slide around recklessly in space while carrying the reader effortlessly with him." Washington Post Book World

Dyer, Geoff

Jeff in Venice, death in Varanasi. Pantheon Books 2009 296p $24

ISBN 978-0-307-37737-1; 0-307-37737-7

LC 2008-23759

This novel is "zany and deceptively light, even as Atman explores the meaning of life and enlightenment. Does it matter whether the unnamed hero of the second part is Jeff or Geoff? Or whether the stories in Venice and Varanasi are the same story? You can read this novel as if you're munching a burger or savoring a ribeye." St. Louis Post-Dispatch

E

Earle, Steve

I'll never get out of this world alive. Houghton Mifflin Harcourt 2011 243p $26

ISBN 978-0-618-82096-2; 0-618-82096-5

LC 2010-49825

"With its Charles Portis vibe and the author's immense cred as a musician and actor, this should have no problem finding the wide audience it deserves." Publ Wkly

Earley, Tony

The **blue** star; a novel. Little, Brown 2008 286p $23.99

ISBN 978-0-316-19907-0; 0-316-19907-9

LC 2007-9921

Sequel to: Jim the boy

"It's late summer 1941, and Jim Glass, now a high school senior, has an earnest, unshakable passion for classmate Chrissie Steppe. But as straightforward as his feelings are, the circumstances of his nascent romance are complex: Chrissie's family is indebted to their landlord, whose sailor son Bucky claimed Chrissie as his girl before shipping out to serve on the USS California at Pearl Harbor. Throughout Jim's fraught final year at school, he relies on the advice of his uncles, but after Pearl Harbor is bombed, they can't protect him from the war's toll. Questions of patriotism, sexuality and poverty weave their way into a narrative that's deceptive in its simplicity: the growing pains that Jim and his friends experience pack a startling emotional punch." Publ Wkly

Earley, Tony

Jim the boy; a novel. Little, Brown 2000 227p $23.95

ISBN 0-316-19964-8

LC 99-42901

"The genius of a novel like this is Earley's trust in the purity of his style and the plainness of his story. Perhaps all things done very well look simple." Christ Sci Monit

Earley, Tony

Mr. Tall; a novella and stories. Tony Earley. Little, Brown & Co. 2014 256 p. (hardcover) $25

ISBN 0316246123; 9780316246125

LC 2014937379

This book, by Tony Earley, presents short stories that "introduce us not only to ordinary people seeking to live extraordinary lives, but also to the skunk ape (a southern variant of Bigfoot), the ghost of Jesse James, and a bone-tired Jack the Giant Killer. Whether it's Appalachia, Nashville, the Carolina Coast, or a make-believe land of talking dogs, each world Earley creates is indelible." (Publisher's note)

Eastland, Sam

The **Beast** in the Red Forest; An Inspector Pekkala Novel of Surprise. Sam Eastland. Hal Leonard Corp 2014 340 p. $22.95

ISBN 1623160499; 9781623160494

In this book, by Sam Eastland, "the world of Soviet espionage is shaken with the shocking disappearance of Stalin's invincible Inspector Pekkala whose charred remains are reported from the frontlines. But Stalin refuses to accept the demise of his indomitable lieutenant and dispatches Pekkala's assistant deep into the wild forests of Western Russia, to follow a wilderness trail of clues, each one leading to a more tortured turn of fate." (Publisher's note)

"Fans of this gripping series of literary thrillers will be glued to their chairs until the final pages. A real corker." Booklist

Eastland, Sam

Eye of the Red Tsar; a novel of suspense. Sam Eastland. Bantam Books 2010 278p $25

ISBN 978-0-553-80781-3; 0-553-80781-1

LC 2009-52898

"The tale is a bit tooreliant on flashbacks, but hair-raising action sequences and spellbinding settings make up for that minor flaw." Kirkus

Includes bibliographical references

Other titles in this series are:

Shadow pass (2011)
Archive 17 (2012)
Red moth (2012)
The beast in the red forest (2014)
Red icon (2015)
Berlin red (2017)

Eastland, Sam

Shadow pass; a novel of suspense. Sam Eastland. Bantam Books 2011 289 p.

ISBN 055380782X; 9780553807820; 9780553908091

LC 2010027234

In this book, "[d]eep in the Russian countryside, a thirty-ton killing machine known officially as T-34 is being developed in total secrecy. Its inventor is a rogue genius whose macabre death is considered an accident only by the innocent. Suspecting assassins everywhere, Stalin brings in his best—if least obedient—detective to solve a murder that's tantamount to treason. Answerable to no one, Inspector Pekkala has the dictator's permission to go anywhere and interrogate anyone. But the closer Pekkala gets to answers, the more questions he uncovers—first and foremost, why is the state's most dreaded female operative, Commissar Major Lysenkova, investigating the case when she's only assigned to internal affairs?" (Publisher's note)

Ebershoff, David

The **19th** wife; a novel. Random House 2008 514p $26

ISBN 978-1-4000-6397-0; 1-4000-6397-3

LC 2008-00074

This "novel tells two parallel stories of polygamy. The first recounts Brigham Young's expulsion of one of his wives, Ann Eliza, from the Mormon Church; the second is a modern-day murder mystery set in a polygamous compound in Utah. Unfolding through an impressive variety of narrative forms—Wikipedia entries, academic research papers, newspaper opinion pieces—the stories include fascinating historical details. . . . Ebershoff demonstrates abundant virtuosity, as he convincingly inhabits the voices of both a nineteenth-century Mormon wife and a contemporary gay youth excommunicated from the church, while also managing to say something about the mysterious power of faith." New Yorker

Ebershoff, David

The **Danish** Girl; a novel. by David Ebershoff. Penguin Books 2001 270 p. pbk $16

ISBN 9780140298482; 0140298487

LC 9934890

This book, by David Ebershoff, "starts with a question, a simple favor asked by a wife of her husband while both are painting in their studio, setting off a transformation neither can anticipate. . . . [It] portrays the unique intimacy that defines every marriage and the . . . story of Lili Elbe, a pioneer in transgender history, and the woman torn between loyalty to her marriage and her own ambitions and desires." (Publisher's note)

Ebershoff's "poignant and visionary conclusion is a fitting one for what is, above all, and despite its sensationalist trimmings, a profound and beautifully realized love story." Pub Wkly

Echenoz, Jean

Lightning; translated from the French by Linda Coverdale. New Press 2011 142p $19.95

ISBN 978-1-59558-649-0

This is a "fictional portrait of Nikola Tesla (here depicted as Gregor), a talented immigrant who begins life in the U.S. as an underpaid troubleshooter for Thomas Edison but whose exceptional gifts eventually make him Edison's formidable rival. But readers see much more than the extensively chronicled Edison-Tesla rivalry. Probing deep into Tesla's tangled psyche, Echenoz illuminates unexpected tensions. . . . Coverdale's nuanced translation of Echenoz's highly successful French original permits English-speaking readers to contemplate the human mystery that persists long after the scientific puzzles have been solved." Booklist

Echlin, Kim

The **disappeared**. Black Cat 2009 235p pa $14

ISBN 978-0-8021-7066-8

"There is something of Marguerite Duras in these pages, something of the lust between the young Western girl and the Asian man that drove novels like The Lover and The North China Lover. But while Duras focuses mostly on desire, Echlin focuses on absolute love—physical desire coupled with the need to know everything about the beloved, to follow him even to the grave and beyond. . . . [An] exquisite novel." N Y Times Book Rev

Eco, Umberto

Baudolino; translated from the Italian by William Weaver. Harcourt 2002 522p $27

ISBN 0-15-100690-3

LC 2002-2345

Original Italian edition, 2000

"In this whimsical yet deadly earnest tale, Eco puts forth the question that perpetually beguiles him and with which he beguiles the rest of us: If a teller of tales tells us he's telling the truth, how can we know for sure what really happened?." New Yorker

Eco, Umberto

Foucault's pendulum; translated from the Italian by William Weaver. Harcourt Brace Jovanovich 1989 641p $33

ISBN 0-15-132765-3

LC 89-32212

Original Italian edition, 1988

This book "is not meant to be easy. . . . {But} great are the rewards for those who actually manage to read it. For while it is not a novel in the strict sense of the word, it is a truly formidable gathering of information delivered playfully by a master manipulating his own invention—in effect, a long, erudite joke." N Y Times Book Rev

Eco, Umberto

The **island** of the day before; translated from the Italian by William Weaver. Harcourt Brace & Co. 1995 515p

ISBN 0-15-100151-0

LC 95-7594

Original Italian edition, 1994

In this novel, set in 1643, "Roberto della Griva is shipwrecked on a ship. His own ship has been rent apart by a storm, and, tied to a plank, he has drifted to the Daphne, anchored in the bay of a South Pacific island. The deserted Daphne has no boat, and Roberto can't swim, so he is effectively a prisoner. As he explores the Daphne, he recalls his life as a young man at the siege of Casale, his years spent in hot philosophical debate in Paris, and his devotion to an adored but unapproachable woman. But there is an intruder on board, which brings to mind Ferrante, the evil twin Roberto imagines he has. The intruder turns out to be a monk obsessed with issues of time and the meridians." Libr J

Eco, Umberto

The **mysterious** flame of Queen Loana; translated from the Italian by Geoffrey Brock. Harcourt, Inc. 2005 469p il $27

ISBN 0-15-101140-0

LC 2004-29105

Original Italian edition, 2004

"Those who don't enjoy the occasional ramble through 'Bartlett's Quotations' may quickly lose patience with 'Queen Loana,' but bookworms will get an added kick out of puzzling out the dozens of literary allusions." Christ Sci Monit

Eco, Umberto, 1932-2016

★ The **name** of the rose; translated from the Italian by William Weaver. Harcourt Brace Jovanovich 1983 502p $35

ISBN 0-15-144647-4

LC 82-21286

Original Italian edition, 1982

The story in this "novel takes place in seven days, in a Benedictine monastery in Northern Italy, in late November 1327. The characters are almost all monks and other churchmen who become involved in a series of bizarre deaths at the monastery. The form of the novel is a detective story; the principal sleuth, Brother William of Baskerville, a Franciscan, solves the mystery of the deaths only after he solves the mystery of the classification of the great library in the monastery. . . . The story is told, many years after it takes place, by Adso of Melk, a Benedictine." (America)

This novel "is an antidetective-story detective story; as a semiotic murder mystery it is superbly entertaining; it is also an extraordinary work of novelistic art." Harpers

Eco, Umberto, 1932-2016

Numero Zero; A novel. Umberto Eco ; translated from the Italian by Richard Dixon. Houghton Mifflin Harcourt 2015 208 p. $24

ISBN 0544635086; 9780544635081

LC 2015028187

This novel, by Umberto Eco, translated by Richard Dixon, "is about a newspaper that aims mainly to dig up dirt (good for blackmail), an editor overly absorbed with reconstructing the story of Mussolini's double, the murder of Pope John Paul I, links between red terrorists and the secret services, and the love affair between a failed ghost-writer and a sweet-souled young woman who purveys celebrity gossip. . . . And then someone turns up dead in Milan. (Library Journal)

"Eco combines his delight in suspense with astute political satire in this brainy, funny, neatly lacerating thriller." Booklist

Edgarian, Carol

Three stages of amazement; a novel. Scribner 2011 298p $25

ISBN 978-1-4391-9830-8; 1-4391-9830-6

LC 2010-44448

"Edgarian's characters fully inhabit this all-too-familiar world of marital squabbles, wounded pride and unpaid bills. Her depiction of the frustrations and joys of motherhood is hilariously on target, when it's not tragic. Her characters are caught in the rhythms of trying, failing and trying again—patterns that superbly mimic those of everyday life." BookPage

Edgerton, Clyde

The **Bible** salesman; a novel. Little, Brown and Co. 2008 241p $23.99

ISBN 978-0-316-11751-7; 0-316-11751-X

LC 2007-45410

"Edgerton is a master of comic timing, and 'The Bible Salesman' is a font of wildly creative comedy. . . . But it's the novel's quiet, introspective moments that are most memorable." Richmond Times-Dispatch

Edgerton, Clyde

The **night** train; a novel. Little, Brown and Company 2011 215p $23.99

ISBN 978-0-316-11759-3; 0-316-11759-5

LC 2010-41546

In this book set "in 1963, at the age of 17, Dwayne Hallston discovers James Brown and wants to perform just like him. His band, the Amazing Rumblers, studies and rehearses Brown's Live at the Apollo album in the storage room of his father's shop in their small North Carolina town. Meanwhile, Dwayne's forbidden black friend Larry--aspiring to play piano like Thelonius Monk--apprentices to a jazz musician called the Bleeder. His mother hopes music will allow him to escape the South." (Publisher's note)

Edgerton's "affinity for simple sentences and clean chapter breaks give this slim novel an almost fable-like power. [His] knowledge about music is on full display, as is his understanding of the subtleties of race relations as the Civil Rights Movement picked up steam." Kirkus

Edgerton, Clyde

★ **Walking** across Egypt; a novel. Algonquin Bks. 1987 216p $17.95

ISBN 0-912697-51-2

LC 86-20645

This novel is "warm, innocent, and has a charming central character." Booklist

Followed by Killer diller

Edghill, India

Queenmaker; a novel of King David's Queen. St. Martin's Press 2002 376p

ISBN 0-312-28918-9

LC 2001-48603

"With its excellent writing, dynamic characters, and galloping pace, Edghill's work is highly recommended for all historical fiction collections." Libr J

Edmonds, Walter D.

Drums along the Mohawk. Little, Brown 1936 592p

A "regional novel about early settlers in the Mohawk river valley in New York state during the Revolutionary war. The little community is made up of . . . individuals to whom Indian raids, British invasions, and militia gatherings are evidences of a distraught world outside. Their own understanding of the difficulties is rather vague. Gil Martin and his wife, clearing their home in the forest, and their not-very-near neighbors, are the main characters." Booklist

Edugyan, Esi

Half-blood blues; Esi Edugyan. Picador 2012 343p.

ISBN 9781250012708

LC 2011044816

Scotiabank Giller Prize (2011)

This novel, shortlisted for the 2011 Man Booker Prize, tells the story of "Hieronymous Falk, a rising star on the cabaret scene [in 1940s Paris, France], [who] was arrested in a cafe and never heard from again. He was twenty years old. He was a German citizen. And he was black. Fifty years later, Sid, Hiero's bandmate and the only witness that day, is going back to Berlin. Persuaded by his old friend Chip, Sid discovers there's more to the journey than he thought when Chip shares a mysterious letter, bringing to the surface secrets buried since Hiero's fate was settled." (themanbookerprize.com)

Edwards, Kim

The **memory** keeper's daughter; Kim Edwards. Viking 2005 x, 401p (pbk.) $15; $24.95

ISBN 9780670034161; 9780143037149; 0670034169

LC 2005042257

British Book Awards (the Nibbies): Popular Fiction Award (2005)

This book "hinges on the birth of fraternal twins, a healthy boy and a girl with Down syndrome. . . . [W]hen young Norah Henry goes into labor, her husband, orthopedic surgeon Dr. David Henry, must deliver their babies himself, aided only by a nurse. Seeing his daughter's handicap, he instructs the nurse, Caroline Gill, to take her to a home and later tells Norah . . . that their son Paul's twin died at birth. Instead of institutionalizing Phoebe, Caroline absconds with her to Pittsburgh.

David's deception becomes the defining moment of the main characters' lives. . . . David's undetected lie warps his marriage; he grapples with guilt; Norah mourns her lost child; and Paul not only deals with his parents' icy relationship but with his own yearnings for his sister as well." (Publishers Weekly)

Edwards, Yvvette

A **Cupboard** full of coats. Oneworld Publications 2011 260 p.

ISBN 9781851687978; 1851687971

In this book, which was long-listed for the Man Booker Prise, "fourteen years after the tragic death of her mother, Jinx cannot reconcile her overwhelming sense of guilt and move on with her life. Her marriage has dissolved, her relationship with her young son is in shambles, and she hasn't learned to love since her mother's violent exit from this world at the hands of her lover. But when an unexpected visitor from the past returns, Jinx is forced to face the twisted tale of her mother's last months and uncover secrets." (Booklist)

Edwardson, Åke

Sail of stone; Åke Edwardson; translated by Rachel Willson-Broyles. Simon & Schuster 2012 402 p.

ISBN 1451608500; 9781451608502

LC 2011028497

This book presents "a pair of fresh cases for Erik Winter and Aneta Djanali, of the Gothenburg Police. Though she hasn't made any complaints herself, her neighbors have repeatedly indicated that Anette Lindsten has been attacked. . . . Imagine her surprise when, on a return visit, she finds Anette's father and brother packing up her things--and then her even greater surprise when she learns that Anette has no brother and that the solicitous men were a pair of thieves. . . . Winter, meanwhile, is chasing his own will-o'-the-wisp at the urging of his old girlfriend Johanna Osvald, who's worried because her fisherman father Axel has vanished during a trip to Scotland. It soon becomes clear that Axel was investigating the disappearance of his own father, John Osvald, from a fishing trawler during the war." (Kirkus)

Egan, Elisabeth

A **window** opens; a novel. Elisabeth Egan. Simon & Schuster 2015 416 p. (hardback) $26

ISBN 1501105434; 9781501105432; 9781501105456

LC 2014047742

In this novel, author "Elisabeth Egan brings us Alice Pearse, a compulsively honest, longing-to-have-it-all, sandwich generation heroine for our social-media-obsessed, lean in (or opt out) age. . . . She is a mostly-happily married mother of three, an attentive daughter, an ambivalent dog-owner, a part-time editor, a loyal neighbor and a Zen commuter. . . . But when her husband makes a radical career change, Alice is ready to lean in." (Publisher's note)

"Egan, herself the books editor at Glamour, packs an incredible amount of humor, observation, and insight into her buoyant debut novel, a sort-of The Way We Live Now for 21st-century moms who grew up loving the bookish heroines of Anne of G reen Gables and Betsy-Tacy. Women may not be able to have it all, but this novel can." Kirkus

Includes bibliographical references and index

Egan, Greg

Schild's ladder. Eos 2002 342p $25.95

ISBN 0-06-105093-8

LC 2001-55583

First published 2001 in the United Kingdom

"Egan writes rather forbidding novels, always grounded in real science and imbued with serious scientific speculations. This is his most uncompromising book to date." Booklist

Includes bibliographical references (p. 341-342)

Egan, Greg

Zendegi. Night Shade 2010 279p $24.95; pa $14.99

ISBN 978-1-59780-174-4; 1-59780-174-7; 978-1-59780175-1 pa; 1-59780-175-5 pa

"Zendegi is two stories told in parallel. The first is the story of Martin Seymour, an Australian journalist sent to Iran to cover another disputed election (this one in 2012), and fifteen years afterward, of the new life that he and his family have built in Iran. The second is Nasim Golestani, an Iranian expatriate who, using a new method of electronically mapping human consciousness, has inadvertently created the framework for the future world's most popular MMORPG, 'Zendegi.' Martin and Nasim discover each other by unfortunate happenstance, and while Zendegi is slowly being destroyed, Nasim and the now-dying Martin try to use the game to preserve a copy of his consciousness, to ensure that Martin's son will always have his father." io9

Egan, Jennifer, 1962-

The **keep**. Alfred A. Knopf 2006 239p $23.95

ISBN 1-4000-4392-1

LC 2006-11573

This novel "makes us think hard about one of the murkiest mysteries of all: the mystery of perception, that uncertain border where reality and imagination meet. . . . In a novel full of unexpected shifts and interruptions, it's amazing how deftly Egan builds a logic for her characters." Los Angeles Times

Egan, Jennifer, 1962-

★ **Manhattan** Beach; a novel. Jennifer Egan. Scribner 2017 438 p. (hardcover) $28

ISBN 9781476716756; 9781476716732; 1476716730

LC 2017029043

Carnegie Medal: Fiction (2018)

Women's Prize for Fiction Longlist (2018)

In this book, by Jennifer Egan, "Anna Kerrigan, nearly twelve years old, accompanies her father to visit Dexter Styles, a man who, she gleans, is crucial to the survival of her father and her family. She is mesmerized by the sea beyond the house and by some charged mystery between the two men. Years later, her father has disappeared and the country is at war." (Publisher's note)

"Realistically detailed, poetically charged, and utterly satisfying: apparently there's nothing Egan can't do." Kirkus

Egan, Jennifer, 1962-

★ A **visit** from the Goon Squad. Knopf 2010 273p il $25.95

ISBN 0-307-59283-9; 978-0-307-59283-5

LC 2009-46496

"Interlocking narratives circle the lives of Bennie Salazar, an aging former punk rocker and record executive, and Sasha, the passionate, troubled young woman he employs. Although Bennie and Sasha never discover each other's pasts, the reader does, . . . along with the secret lives of . . . other characters whose paths intersect with theirs, over many years, in locales as varied as New York, San Francisco, Naples, and Africa. We first meet Sasha in her mid-thirties, on her therapist's couch in New York City, confronting her longstanding compulsion to steal. Later, we . . . see her as the child of a violent marriage, then as a runaway living in Naples, then as a college student. . . . We meet Bennie Salazar at the melancholy nadir of his adult life—divorced, struggling to connect with his nine-year-old son . . . —and then revisit him in 1979." (Publisher's note)

This novel is "centered, nominally, on the aging owner of an independent record label and his comely, kleptomania-prone assistant. But it is in fact a frequently dazzling piece of layer-cake meta-fiction, told via a sprawling constellation of characters and linked vignettes that spill from the late'70s Bay Area punk scene to the African plains, the dissolute slums of Naples, and the flush New York suburbs of the '90s boom. Egan's expert flaying of human foibles has the compulsive allure of poking at a sore tooth: excruciating but exhilarating, too." Entertainment Wkly

Eggers, Dave, 1970-

The **Circle**; a novel. by Dave Eggers. Knopf 2013 504 p. (hardback) $27.95

ISBN 0385351399; 9780385351393

LC 2013032894

"Mae Holland is hired to work for the Circle, the world's most powerful internet company. . . . The Circle, run out of a sprawling California campus, links users' personal emails, social media, banking, and purchasing with their universal operating system, resulting in one online identity. . . . Mae can't believe her luck, . . . even as a strange encounter with a colleague leaves her shaken." (Publisher's note)

Eggers, Dave, 1970-

Heroes of the frontier; Dave Eggers. Alfred A. Knopf 2016 400 p. (hardcover) $28.95

ISBN 9780451493811; 9780451493804

LC 2016938204

In this novel by Dave Eggers, "Josie and her children's father have split up, she's been sued by a former patient and lost her dental practice, and she's grieving the death of a young man senselessly killed. When her ex asks to take the children to meet his new fiancée's family, Josie makes a run for it, figuring Alaska is about as far as she can get without a passport." (Publisher's note)

"This uproarious quest, this breathless journey from lost to found, this delirious American road-trip saga, is fueled by uncanny insight, revolutionary humor, and profound pleasure in the absurd and the sublime." Booklist

Eggers, Dave, 1970-

★ A **hologram** for the king; a novel. by Dave Eggers. McSweeney's Books 2012 312 p. $25

ISBN 193636574X; 9781936365746

National Book Award Finalist (2012)

Author David Eggers "takes us around the world to show how one man fights to hold himself and his splintering family together in the face of the global economy's gale-force winds. . . . In a rising Saudi Arabian city, far from weary, recession-scarred America, a struggling businessman pursues a last-ditch attempt to stave off foreclosure, pay his daughter's college tuition, and finally do something great." (Publisher's note)

Eggers, Dave, 1970-

How we are hungry; stories. by Dave Eggers. Vintage Books 2005 218p (pbk.) $15.00

ISBN 1400095565; 9781400095568

LC 2005042321

This book offers a collection of short stories. "The collection starts with 'Another,' a story of a middle-aged divorcee galloping through the Egyptian deserts and subjecting himself to the pain of the relentless jolting of the horse's gait until he finally learns to absorb its rhythm. His search for more sights and further experiences is endless, and on he goes, disappointed but insatiable, streaming into the wilderness. . . . 'The Only Meaning of the Oil-Wet Water' is a . . . long short story in which Pilar, a dermatologist, flies to Costa Rica to meet her friend Hand . . . in the knowledge that they'll end up having sex, but uncertain what emotions will bind them beyond lust and friendship." (The Guardian)

Eggers, Dave, 1970-

What is the what; the autobiography of Valentino Achak Deng : a novel. Dave Eggers. McSweeney's 2006 475 p. map (pbk.) $16; $26

ISBN 9780307385901; 1932416641; 9781932416640

LC 2007276445

This "novel's subtitle, 'The Autobiography of Valentino Achak Deng,' refers to a real-life Sudanese refugee who informs us in a brief preface that 'over the course of many years, I told my story orally to the author. He then concocted this novel, approximating my voice and using the basic events of my life as the foundation.'" The book presents the fictionalized story of Deng's "odyssey from his village in southern Sudan to temporary shelter in Ethiopia to a vast refugee camp in Kenya and finally to Atlanta." (New York Times)

Eggers "has made the outlines of the tragedy in East Africa—so vague to so many Americans—not only sharp and clear but indelible. An eloquent testimony to the power of storytelling, What Is the What is an extraordinary work of witness, and of art." N Y Times Book Rev

Eisenberg, Deborah

The **collected** stories of Deborah Eisenberg. Picador/Farrar, Straus And Giroux 2010 992p $22

ISBN 978-0-312-42989-8; 0-312-42989-4

LC 2010-02081

This volume gathers all the stories from four previously published collections: Transactions in a foreign currency (1986); Under the 82nd Airborne (1992); All around Atlantis (1997); Twilight of the superheroes (2006)

"Eisenberg's tales, their milieus vividly defined, their dialogue unsettlingly real, are long and leisurely; her characters, hyper-observant but helpless. They often have just enough drive and sense of purpose to thrust themselves into the stream of life, but then they are just carried along, baffled or passive. . . . Wry humor surfaces just often enough to keep desolation at bay. After all, while Eisenberg recognizes that there is no escaping selfishness, weakness, and confusion (both intimate and geopolitical)—let alone illness, age, and misfortune—humanity must keep drifting on somehow." Atlantic

Eisenberg, Deborah

Twilight of the superheroes. Farrar, Straus & Giroux 2006 225p $23

ISBN 978-0-374-29941-5; 0-374-29941-2

LC 2005-42659

"Using her playwright's ear for dialogue and a journalistic eye for the askew detail, Ms. Eisenberg gives us—in just a handful of pages—a visceral sense of these characters' daily routines, the worlds they inhabit and the families they rebel against or allow to define them. . . . Instead of forcing her characters' stories into neat, arbitrary, preordained shapes, she allows them to grow asymmetrical narratives—narratives that possess all the surprising twists and dismaying turns of real life." N Y Times (Late N Y Ed)

Eisler, Barry, 1964-

The **God's** Eye View; by Barry Eisler. Amazon Pub 2016 400 p. $24.95

ISBN 1503951510; 9781503951518

In this book, by Barry Eisler, "NSA director Theodore Anders . . . knows unlimited surveillance is the only way to keep America safe.

Evelyn Gallagher . . . just wants to keep her head down and manage the NSA's camera network and facial recognition program so she can afford private school for her deaf son, Dash. But when Evelyn discovers the existence of an NSA program code-named God's Eye . . .her doubts put her and Dash in the crosshairs of a pair of government assassins." (Publisher's note)

"The agent sent to monitor her is not quite what the boss thinks, and the personal and cyberfink stories are blended beautifully." Booklist

Includes bibliographical references in unnumbered pages at end of work.

El Akkad, Omar

★ **American** war; a novel. Omar El Akkad. Alfred A. Knopf 2017 333 p. illustrations, maps (hardback) $26.95

ISBN 9780451493583

LC 2016042308

This novel, by Omar El Akkad, focuses on "a second American Civil War, a devastating plague, and one family caught deep in the middle. . . . Sarat Chestnut, born in Louisiana, is only six when the Second American Civil War breaks out in 2074. But even she knows that oil is outlawed, that Louisiana is half underwater, and that unmanned drones fill the sky. When her father is killed and her family is forced into Camp Patience for displaced persons, she begins to grow up." (Publisher's note)

"El Akkad has created a brilliantly well-crafted, profoundly shattering saga of one family's suffering in a world of brutal power struggles, terrorism, ignorance, and vengeance." Booklist.

Elias, Gerald

Danse macabre; Gerald Elias. Minotaur Books 2010 278 p. $24.99

ISBN 0312541899; 9780312541897

LC 2010021994

In author Gerald Elias' book, "blind and cranky Daniel Jacobus, a former concert violinist, reluctantly agrees to investigate the murder of maestro René Allard after . . . musician BTower, who had a tumultuous relationship with Allard, is seen standing over the body literally with blood on his hands. As BTower sits on death row . . . , Jacobus . . . uncovers shady activities on Allard's part. Puzzling transactions involving violins, an attempt on Jacobus's life, and the suicide of an elevator operator indicate that Jacobus may be closing in on uncomfortable truths." (Publishers Weekly)

Elias, Gerald

★ **Death** and transfiguration; a Daniel Jacobus novel. Gerald Elias. Minotaur Books 2012 322 p.

ISBN 9780312678357; 9781250014801

LC 2012005488

This book tells the story of "Vaclav Herza . . . [who] has been music director of Harmonium for forty years. . . . It is the eve of the opening of a dramatic new concert hall designed by Herza himself. It is also the eleventh hour of intense contract negotiations with the musicians that have strained relations within the organization. When the acting concertmaster, Schehcrazade O'Brien, is summarily dismissed by the despotic Herza for the permanent concertmaster position, an audition she was poised to win, O'Brien slits her wrists and the orchestra becomes convulsed. Now, blind, cantankerous violin teacher Daniel Jacobus . . . investigates Herza's dark past." (Publisher's note)

Eliot, George

★ **Middlemarch**; a study of provincial life. with an introduction by E.S. Shaffer. Knopf 1991 xxxix, 888p $22

ISBN 0-679-40567-4

LC 91-52976

First published 1872

A novel "with a double plot interest. The heroine, Dorothea Brooke, longs to devote herself to some great cause and, for a time, expects to find it in her marriage to Rev. Mr. Casaubon, an aging scholar. Mr. Casaubon lives only eighteen months after their marriage, a sufficient period to disillusion her completely. He leaves her his estate, with the ill-intentioned proviso that she will forfeit if she marries his young cousin Will Ladislaw, whom she had seen frequently in Rome. Endeavoring to find happiness without Ladislaw, whom she has come to care for deeply, Dorothea throws herself into the struggle for medical reforms advocated by the young Dr. Lydgate. Finally, however, she decides to give up her property and marry Ladislaw. The second plot deals with the efforts and failure of Dr. Lydgate to live up to his early ideals." Reader's Ency. 4th edition

Eliot, George

★ The **mill** on the Floss. Knopf 1992 xxxi, 597p $22

ISBN 0-679-41726-5

LC 92-52920

First published 1860

"Deeply significant tragedy of the inner life, enacted amidst the quaint folk and old-fashioned surroundings of a country town (St. Ogg's is Gainsborough). The conflict of affection and antipathy between a brother and sister, and again in the family relations of their father, is a dominant motive; but the emotional tension rises to a climax in Maggie's unpremeditated yielding to an unworthy lover and betrayal of her finer nature. Brother and sister . . . are purified and reconciled only in death." Baker. Guide to the Best Fic

Eliot, George

★ **Silas** Marner; the weaver of Raveloe. Knopf 1993 xxx, 206p $18

ISBN 0-679-42030-4

LC 92-54293

First published 1861

"Silas Marner is a handloom weaver, a good man, whose life has been wrecked by a false accusation of theft, which cannot be disproved. For years he lives a lonely life, with the sole companionship of his loom: and he is saved from his own despair by the chance finding of a little child. On this baby girl he lavishes the whole passion of his thwarted nature, and her filial affection makes him a kindly man again. After sixteen years the real thief is dicovered, and Silas's good name is restored. On this slight framework are hung the richest pictures of middle and low class life that George Eliot has painted." Keller. Reader's Dig of Books

Elison, Meg

The **book** of Etta; Meg Elison. 47North 2017 305 p. (The road to Nowhere) (paperback) $14.95

ISBN 9781503941823; 1503941825

Sequel to: The Book of the Unnamed Midwife (2016)

In this book in the Road to Nowhere series, by Meg Elison, "Etta comes from Nowhere, a village of survivors of the great plague that wiped away the world that was. In the world that is, . . . childbearing is dangerous…yet desperately necessary for humankind's future. . . . As a scavenger. Loyal to the village but living on her own terms, Etta roams the desolate territory beyond: salvaging useful relics of the ruined past and braving the threat of brutal slave traders." (Publisher's note)

"Elison continues to startle her readers with unexpected gender permutations and fascinating relationships worked out in front of a convincingly detailed landscape." Pub Wkly

Elison, Meg

★ The **Book** of the Unnamed Midwife; Meg Elison. 47North 2016 291 p. (The road to Nowhere) (paperback) $14.95

ISBN 9781503939110; 1503939111

Philip K. Dick Award Winner (2015)

In this book, by Meg Elison, "in the wake of a fever that decimated the earth's population—killing women and children and making childbirth deadly for the mother and infant—the midwife must pick her way through the bones of the world she once knew to find her place in this dangerous new one. Gone are the pillars of civilization. All that remains is power—and the strong who possess it." (Publisher's note)

"Elison takes readers on an exciting and often excruciating journey, navigating issues of gender and sex in a scorched, disease-ridden world." Booklist

Elkins, Aaron J.

Dying on the vine; Aaron Elkins. Berkley Prime Crime 2012 294 p. $25.95

ISBN 0425247880; 9780425247884

LC 2012035917

Author Aaron J. Elkins' book "takes the man 'known throughout the world of forensic science as the Skeleton Detective' to Tuscany, where he looks into the apparent murder-suicide of Pietro Cubbiddu, the strong-willed patriarch of the famous Cubbiddu wine-making family, and Pietro's wife, Nola. After examining the remains, Gideon concludes that it's an unusual double homicide instead. The family and its confidantes had motive and opportunity for killing the couple--but why push the bodies off a cliff, then shoot them after they're already dead?" (Publishers Weekly)

Elkins, Aaron J.

Good blood; [by] Aaron Elkins. Berkley Prime Crime 2004 293p $23.95

ISBN 0-425-19411-6

LC 2003-62799

In this mystery, forensic anthropologist Gideon Oliver and his park ranger wife, Julie, "are on holiday in Italy, helping a friend host a tour featuring canoeing and bicycle riding. Since neither activity is Gideon's idea of fun, he lounges around the picturesque town of Stresa and is pulled, consequently, into the investigation of recently uncovered bones, which turn out to be connected to a 40-year-old secret baby swap. In turn, the swap is tied to a recent kidnapping involving the wealthy, influential family to which Gideon's tour guide friend is related. . . . This is vintage Elkins: well-drawn supporting characters, lovely scenery, and a bit of interesting science." Libr J

Elkins, Aaron J.

Unnatural selection. Berkley Prime Crime 2006 281p $23.95

ISBN 0-425-21005-7

LC 2006-2173

"Elkins keeps things moving with plenty of local atmosphere, compelling characterization, and a refreshingly low level of violence." Natural Hist

Ellis, Bret Easton

Imperial bedrooms. Alfred A. Knopf 2010 169p $24.95

ISBN 978-0-307-26610-1; 0-307-26610-9

LC 2009-41690

Sequel to: Less than zero (1985)

Clay, a successful screenwriter, has returned from New York to Los Angeles to help cast his new movie, and he's soon drifting through a long-familiar circle that will leave him no choice but to plumb the darkest recesses of his character and come to terms with his proclivity for betrayal.

"As with Chandler's work, the details of the twists and turns are beside the point — particularly since Ellis puckishly reveals at the start which character is going to wind up as a corpse in a Tom Ford suit. But the author uses the thriller framework to infuse nerve-rending unease into this look at Tinseltown mores, a dissection that also comes nicely weighted with both bleak hilarity and firsthand authorial experience." Entertaiment Wkly

Ellis, Bret Easton

Lunar Park. Alfred A. Knopf 2005 308p $24.95

ISBN 0-375-41291-3

LC 2005-40923

"The whole book swirls, surreally, pushing the limits of tolerable confusion while sending up laughably familiar horror story shticks. For a while, it looks as if nothing will be resolved. It works precisely because it is a ghost story, replete with eviscerated livestock, freshly dug graves, and messages written in ash—and because everything, ultimately, is resolved." New Criterion

Ellis, David

In the company of liars; David Ellis. G.P. Putnam's Sons 2005 378p (pbk.) $1.99; o.p.

ISBN 9780425204290; 0399152474

LC 2004057342

This "novel is centered on a woman who is on trial for murder-Allison Pagone, a mother caught between competing forces, each represented by someone who may not care if the pressure kills her in the end. A prosecutor wants Allison convicted and put on death row. An FBI agent believes she can squeeze her into ratting on her family. A daughter and an ex-husband need to save their own skins. And circling them all: a group who would prefer to eliminate her quietly and anonymously, but who also are not what they seem. Our first picture of Allison is in the moments following her death. The story then moves backward in time." (vjbooks.com)

Ellis, David

The **last** alibi; David Ellis. G.P. Putnam's Sons 2013 480 p. $26.95

ISBN 0399158804; 9780399158803

LC 2013015329

This is David Ellis's fourth legal thriller featuring Midwestern attorney Jason Kolarich. "Jason, who's on trial for murder, is sure of only one thing: if he testifies, he won't tell the truth. The clock turns back six months to when Jason meets beautiful court reporter Alexa Himmel, whom he's soon dating. He also has an odd-looking new client, James Drinker, who tells Jason that he's afraid that he'll be accused of murder." (Publishers Weekly)

Ellis, Helen

American housewife; stories. Helen Ellis. Doubleday 2016 208 p. (hbk.) $24.00; (pbk.) $15.00

ISBN 1101970995; 9780385541039; 0385541031; 9781101970997

LC 2015021779

This book, by Helen Ellis, offers a "delightfully unhinged collection of stories set in the dark world of domesticity. . . . These twelve irresistible stories take us from a haunted prewar Manhattan apartment building to the set of a rigged reality television show, from the unique initiation ritual of a book club to the getaway car of a pageant princess on the lam, from the gallery opening of a tinfoil artist to the fitting room of a legendary lingerie shop." (Publisher's note)

"With monstrous children and cats, hopeless husbands, and covertly dangerous women, Ellis takes down the entire housewife concept with a sniper's precision. These are delectably revved up, marauding, sometimes macabre tales of ruined marriages, illness, infertility, crass commercialism (literary product placement), desperation, ghosts, even murder, featuring women of shrewd calculation, secret sorrows, and deep sympathy." Booklist

Ellison, Ralph

★ **Invisible** man; preface by Charles Johnson. Modern Lib. 1994 xxxiv, 572p $19.95; pa $12

ISBN 0-679-60139-2; 0-679-73276-4 pa

LC 94-176953

A reissue of the title first published 1952 by Random House

"Acclaimed as a powerful representation of the lives of blacks during the Depression, this novel describes the experiences of one young black man during that period. Dismissed from a Negro college in the South for showing one of the founders how Negroes live there, he is used later as a symbol of repression by a Communist group in New York City. After a Harlem race riot, he is aware that he must contend with both whites and blacks, and that loss of social identity makes him invisible among his fellow beings." Shapiro. Fic for Youth. 3d edition

Ellison, Ralph, 1914-1994

Three days before the shooting-- edited by John F. Callahan and Adam Bradley. Modern Library 2010 1101p $50

ISBN 0375759530; 9780375759536

LC 2010-277049

"At his death in 1994, Ralph Ellison left behind roughly two thousand pages of his second unfinished novel. . . . Five years later, Random House published Juneteenth, drawn from the central narrative of Ellison's unfinished epic. Three Days Before the Shooting . . . gathers together in one volume, for the first time, all the parts of that planned opus, including . . . sequences never before published." (Publisher's note)

"Culled from Ellison's drafts, his notes, and those of his wife, Fanny, this book brings together four decades of work, a portion of which was published posthumously as Juneteenth in 1999. The allegorical, lyrical novel is presented in three books in various stages of completion. It centers on the complex relationship between A. Z. Hickman, a blues musician turned preacher, and Bliss, an orphan of undetermined race, whom Hickman raises as a boy preacher. As a teen, Bliss runs off and develops his skills as a flimflammer, ultimately emerging in the U.S. Senate as Senator Sunraider. Hickman searches in vain for Bliss, but when he learns of a threat to Sunraider, the two are reunited in an orgy of reexamination of their lives and circuitous paths. Book 1 is a first-person narrative by McIntyre, a white reporter who witnesses the shooting of Sunraider on the floor of the Senate and the attempt by Hickman to save a man known as a charismatic race-baiter. Book 2, the basis for Juneteenth, traces the relationship between Hickman and Bliss/Sunraider through a dialogue between them, an inner reflection of their coming together and their falling apart. Book 3 includes several fragments of earlier portions of the novel, deeper character portrayals, and alternative paths of action as Ellison struggled to bring all the pieces together. He is masterful at evoking the language of common black folks, preachers, press and politicians, and charlatans and flimflammers." Booklist

Ellory, Roger Jon

The **Anniversary** Man. Overlook 2010 400p $24.95

ISBN 978-1-59020-327-9; 1-59020-327-5

First published 2009 in the United Kingdom

"Ellory is a patient storyteller, willing to stretch beyond the necessities of his plot and illuminate people who occupy the peripheries of his captivating tale. He also doesn't stint in fleshing out his central players, even if in doing so he swings far from the demands of a police procedural." January

Ellory, Roger Jon

A **simple** act of violence; R.J. Ellory. Overlook Press 2011 464p.

ISBN 9781590203187

LC 2011016139

This book presents the story of "a serial murder investigation in Washington DC, told in parallel with a history of the most squalid period in the annals of the CIA -- its shocking activities in Nicaragua, financed by the smuggling of tons of cocaine into America." (guardian.co.uk)

Ellroy, James

American tabloid; a novel. Knopf 1995 571p

ISBN 0-679-40391-4

LC 94-42898

"The dizzying number of covert alliances and compromised loyalties that link the Mob, the C.I.A., Howard Hughes, J. Edgar Hoover, and the Kennedys comes across less like a cancer of epic proportions that like a kind of institutional dyspepsia. Ellroy's tabloidization of this chapter of American history makes it all the more queasy and real." New Yorker

Ellroy, James

★ The **black** dahlia. Mysterious Press 1987 325p

LC 87-7952

"The author manages a gripping re-creation of LA street life in the 1940s, and his characters are powerfully written and terrifyingly real. The bare-bones plot, the slew of false conclusions, and the hazy evocation of the murder victim give the narrative a dreamlike atmosphere, ideal for a tale of immoral heroes and wasted lives." Booklist

Ellroy, James

Blood's a rover; a novel. Alfred A. Knopf 2009 633p $28.95

ISBN 978-0-679-40393-7; 0-679-40393-0

LC 2009-24460

"The final novel of Ellroy's 'Underworld U.S.A.' trilogy, following 'American Tabloid' and 'The Cold Six Thousand,' is a fittingly crazed and violent account of the years 1968 to 1972. Alternating chapters follow three henchmen with ties to a labyrinth of interconnected schemes—one cooks dope for Howard Hughes while facilitating his Vegas hotel takeover; another subverts black militant groups for J. Edgar Hoover; and the third kills revolutionaries in Cuba. Ellroy employs a huge cast and hyper-pulp prose to create a convincingly horrific universe run by the F.B.I., the Mob, and a host of other sinister organizations." New Yorker

Ellroy, James

The **cold** six thousand. Knopf 2001 672p $25.95

ISBN 0-679-40392-2

Sequel to American tabloid

"Ellroy's prose is easy to absorb sentence by sentence, thanks to his simple subject-verb-object constructions, but monstrous as it acquires cumulative force over hundreds of pages. . . . The novel is an exhausting, masochistic, often revelatory rereading of the allegedly idealistic sixties—an assassination, finally, of the decade rather than of its leaders." New Yorker

Ellroy, James

★ **L.A.** confidential. Mysterious Press 1990 496p $32

ISBN 0-89296-293-3

LC 89-40523

The author "merges raw-edged period detail with sleazy celluloid lore, producing a dark and dazzling descent into the criminal underworld of the 1950s." Booklist

Ellroy, James, 1948-

Perfidia; A Novel. James Ellroy. Random House Inc 2014 608 p. $28.95

ISBN 0307956997; 9780307956996

LC 2014009939

In this novel, by James Ellroy, "it is December 6, 1941. America stands at the brink of World War II. Last hopes for peace are shattered when Japanese squadrons bomb Pearl Harbor. Los Angeles has been a haven for loyal Japanese-Americans--but now, war fever and race hate grip the city and the Japanese internment begins. The hellish murder of a Japanese family summons three men and one woman. . . . The investigation throws them together and rips them apart." (Publisher's note)

"Regardless of what Ellroy intends or means, what he's achieved is a disturbing, unforgettable, and inflammatory vision of how the men in charge respond to the threat of war." Booklist

Emshwiller, Carol

★ The **secret** city. Tachyon 2007 209p pa $14.95

ISBN 978-1-892391-44-5; 1-892391-44-9

"First and foremost, Emshwiller is a poet—with a poet's sensibility, precision, and magic. She revels in the sheer taste and sound of words, she infuses them with an extraordinary vitality and sense of life." Newsday

Endo, Shusaku

★ **Deep** river; translated by Van C. Gessel. New Directions 1995 216p

ISBN 0-8112-1289-0

LC 94-38913

This is a "beautifully wrought, lyrically suggestive story. . . . If Christianity holds up to us the lonely individual challenged by a God who entered history, Buddhism gives us people who are ready to surrender, finally, a measure of their human and spiritual particularity and who, with acceptance, join their fellow creatures as part of the great tide of humanity. Mr. Endo manages to merge both of these streams of faith, bringing them together in a flow that is, indeed, deep. His work is a soulful gift to a world he keeps rendering as unrelievedly parched." N Y Times Book Rev

Endo, Shusaku

The **final** martyrs; translated by Van C. Gessel. New Directions 1994 199p $21.95

ISBN 0-8112-1272-6

LC 94-746

"This deftly translated collection, comprised of stories written as early as 1959 and as late as 1985, also includes semi-autobiographical tales in which Endo deals with the traumatic impact that his parent's divorce had on his boyhood. He also writes with grace, compassion and gentle humor about old age, love betrayed, Japanese tourists and the marks we leave on the lives of others." Publ Wkly

Endo, Shusaku

★ **Silence**; translated by William Johnston. Taplinger 1979 294p

LC 78-27168

Original Japanese edition, 1966; this translation first published 1969 in Japan

"The story is based on events in early 17th-century Japan, when Japanese Christians and Christian missionaries were brutally persecuted. In the novel, Sebastian Rodrigues, a Portuguese seminarian, journeys to Japan to investigate why his former teacher, a missionary to Japan, has chosen apostasy over martyrdom. Pervading the novel is the belief that Christianity is incomparible with Japanese culture. In the end, seeing the selfishness of martyrdom, Rodrigues also chooses apostasy." Merriam-Webster's Ency of Lit

Eng, Tan Twan

The **gift** of rain. Weinstein Books 2008 435p $23.95

ISBN 978-1-60286-024-7; 1-60286-024-6

First published 2007 in the United Kingdom

"Eng's characters are as deep and troubled as the time in which the story takes place, and he draws on a rich palette to create a sprawling portrait of a lesser explored corner of the war. Hutton's first-person narration is measured, believable and enthralling." Publ Wkly

Engelmann, Karen

★ The **Stockholm** Octavo; Karen Engelmann. HarperCollins 2012 432 p. $26.99

ISBN 0061995347; 9780061995347

In this book, "political and social intrigue are merged through the medium of the mystical card layout called the Octavo. . . . In the reign of the alternately enlightened and autocratic King Gustav III, his brother Karl and the society doyenne known as the Uzanne scheme to return control of Sweden to the nobility, opposed secretly by the mysterious gambling club owner Sofia Sparrow, whose prophetic visions link Gustav with the doomed king and queen of France." (Publishers Weekly)

Enger, Lin

The **high** divide; a novel. by Lin Enger. Algonquin Books of Chapel Hill 2014 352 p. map $24.95

ISBN 1616203757; 9781616203757

LC 2014014702

"In 1886, Gretta Pope wakes one morning to discover that her husband is gone. Ulysses Pope has left his family behind on the far edge of Minnesota's western prairie. It doesn't take long for Gretta's young sons, Eli and Danny, to set off after him . . . where they need to go, and ending up in the rugged badlands of Montana. Gretta has no choice but to search for her sons and her husband, leading her to the doorstep of a woman who seems intent on making Ulysses her own." (Publisher's note)

Enger, Lin

Undiscovered country. Little, Brown and Co. 2008 308p $23.99

ISBN 978-0-316-00694-1; 0-316-00694-7

LC 2007-30138

"A modern-day Hamlet story set in rural northern Minnesota. Teenage Jesse's father, the mayor of Battlepoint, apparently committed suicide with his own hunting rifle. But Jesse suspects his Uncle Clay, who had more than one motive for murder. Is Jesse's suspicion simply his inability to accept his father's senseless act? Or is Clay really guilty—and how complicit is Jesse's mother? If Clay is guilty, what should he do about it? The obvious parallels with Shakespeare's play are even acknowledged by some of the characters, but Enger doesn't let this conceit overwhelm the story. He skillfully draws a portrait of small-town life and all its barely concealed secrets and effectively narrates Jesse's torment." Libr J

Englander, Nathan

The **Ministry** of Special Cases. Alfred A. Knopf 2007 339p $25

ISBN 978-0-375-40493-1; 0-375-40493-7

LC 2006-48731

The author "bravely wrangles the themes of political liberty and personal loss with the swift style and knowing humor of folklore. In the spirit of the simple ambiguity of its title, The Ministry of Special Cases is carefully contradictory, wise and off-kilter, funny and sad." N Y Observer

Englander, Nathan

★ **What** we talk about when we talk about Anne Frank; stories. Nathan Englander. Alfred A. Knopf 2012 224p

ISBN 9780307949608; 9780307958709

LC 2011033756

2013 Sophie Brody Medal Honor Book

This book offers a collection of short stories. "The title story . . . is a . . . portrait of two marriages in which the Holocaust is played out as a devastating parlor game. In the . . . [short story] 'Camp Sundown' vigilante justice is undertaken by a group of geriatric campers in a bucolic summer enclave. 'Free Fruit for Young Widows' is a small, sharp study in evil, . . . told by a father to a son. 'Sister Hills' chronicles the history of Israel's settlements from the eve of the Yom Kippur War through the present, a political fable constructed around the tale of two mothers who strike a terrible bargain to save a child." (Publisher's note)

In this book of "eight stories [about Jewish identity and victimhood], three center on a preoccupation with the Holocaust, one on the related subject of anti-Semitism, and another on the also related subject of the loss of dear ones in the Israeli-Arab conflict. . . . In 'Camp Sundown,' a camp for Jewish elders . . . the aged campers decide for reasons that remain unclear that one of their number was actually a concentration-camp guard, and they gather together and murder him." (New Republic)

Enright, Anne

★ The **forgotten** waltz. W. W. Norton & Co. 2011 263p $25.95

ISBN 978-0-393-07255-6; 0-393-07255-X

LC 2011-21006

"As Gina accepts that she has been forced into a place where she no longer has the power to walk away, The Forgotten Waltz meditates on the way personal responsibility can twist the most well-meaning, loving relationship into a holding tank for accusations and tears. . . . Enright allows her main character the thrill of remembered joys, without letting her slip away from blame." A V Club

Enright, Anne

The **gathering**. Black Cat 2007 261p pa $14

ISBN 978-0-8021-7039-2; 0-8021-7039-0

"You will love this book or loathe it. It doesn't take prisoners, it doesn't simper or seek to be liked. Abrasively honest and toweringly moving, it grabs and shakes you, rabbiting on in a manic monologue, comical, tragic, lost and profound." Scotsman

Enright, Anne, 1962-

★ The **Green** Road; A Novel. by Anne Enright. W.W. Norton & Co. Inc. 2015 304 p. $26.95

ISBN 0393248216; 9780393248210

LC 2015004414

Man Booker Prize: Longlist (2015)

This book, by Anne Enright, "tells the story of Rosaleen, matriarch of the Madigans, a family on the cusp of either coming together or falling irreparably apart. As they grow up, Rosaleen's four children leave the west of Ireland for lives they could have never imagined in Dublin, New York, and Mali, West Africa." (Publisher's note)

"Long introductions to the principal characters precede the theatrical format of the reunion, allowing Enright plenty of space to convey her brilliant ear for dialogue, her soft wit, and piercing, poetic sense of life's larger abstractions." Kirkus

Enright, Anne

Yesterday's weather. Grove Press 2008 308p $24

ISBN 978-0-8021-1874-5; 0-8021-1874-7

"Enright's subjects are family, children, love, domestic horror. The stories are strong and hard bitten. Something in them is always snagging and catching on grief, large or small. She is a confident writer, letting stories unfold at their own speed. Her best pieces have a fluid shape that feels close to the way we actually think, choose, muse." Washington Post Book World

Ephron, Hallie

Night Night, Sleep Tight; A Novel of Suspense. by Hallie Ephron. HarperCollins 2015 288 p. $26.99

ISBN 0062117637; 9780062117632

LC 2014504706

This book, by Hallie Ephron, is a "tale of domestic noir. . . . When Deirdre Unger arrived in Beverly Hills to help her bitter, disappointed father sell his dilapidated house, she discovers his lifeless body floating face down in the swimming pool. At first, Deirdre assumes her father's death was a tragic accident. But the longer she stays in town, the more she suspects that it is merely the third act in a story that has long been in the making." (Publisher's note)

"As the daughter of screenwriters, Ephron (There Was an Old Woman, 2013) knows the old Hollywood scene and re-creates it vividly in her fourth novel, inspired in part by the 1958 stabbing of Lana Turner's lover. A fast-moving tale, with building suspense and the price of fame at its center." Booklist

Epperson, Tom

Sailor; Tom Epperson. Forge 2012 352 p.

ISBN 0765328925; 9780765328922; 9781429998604

LC 2011047593

This book is a thriller novel by Tom Epperson. "After years of suffering the terror of being married to a criminal, [Gina] took the one thing he ever gave her that she wanted—her son, Luke. . . . With her husband behind bars, her father-in-law will stop at nothing for revenge. . . . With a vast network that stretches across the country, every favor is called in to kill Gina and return Luke to his grandfather. Gina can trust no one. . . . So with a gun and stolen diamonds in her purse, and derelicts, the law, and hit men on her tail, Gina takes Luke and runs. . . . then they meet Gray. He says he's a sailor, but he seems to be hiding a lot. And when the time comes, he's the only thing standing between her and the grave." (Publisher's note)

Epstein, Joseph

★ The **love** song of A. Jerome Minkoff and other stories. Houghton Mifflin Harcourt 2010 260p $24

ISBN 978-0-618-72195-5; 0-618-72195-9

LC 2009-34898

"It's a rare and welcome thing to find a collection of short stories that define a place. . . . Epstein delivers one about a neighborhood on the far north of Chicago called West Rogers Park. It is a polyglot area, but Epstein has chosen to write about the Jews who dominate it. . . . If his voice is wry, it is also sympathetic. Life is hard, and he knows it. He invests his collection with a peerless take on a particular slice of Jewish life today. Each story stands strong as a discrete work, but together they become profound." Boston Globe

Erdrich, Louise

★ The **Beet** Queen; a novel. Holt & Co. 1986 338p

ISBN 0-8050-0058-5

LC 86-4788

Second installment in the author's North Dakota Quartet

This novel "concerns a brother and sister, Karl and Mary Adare, who are abandoned by their mother, who runs away with a barnstorming pilot. Flight is a recurring theme in this . . . tale of loneliness set against a stark North Dakota landscape. Karl spends his life as an itinerant salesman, running from his troubled family and his own sexual ambivalence; Mary, who grows up with her aunt and uncle, uses self-reliance as a way of hiding from the pain of human relationships; and Sita, Mary's cousin, retreats into insanity to avoid facing the realization that her idealized dreams of a glamorous life have evaporated. Only Celestine, Mary's friend and the mother of Karl's child, accepts reality on its own terms as she struggles to protect her daughter from the suffering that has engulfed those around her." Booklist

Erdrich, Louise

Four souls. HarperCollins Publishers 2004 210p $23.95

ISBN 0-06-620975-7

LC 2003-65243

Fleur Pillager takes her mother's name, Four Souls, for strength and walks away from her Ojibwe reservation to the cities of Minneapolis and Saint Paul. She is seeking restitution from and revenge on the lumber baron who has stripped her reservation." Publisher's note

Erdrich, Louise, 1954-

Future home of the living god; a novel. Louise Erdrich. HarperCollins 2017 269 p. (hardcover) $28.99

ISBN 0062694057; 9780062694058; 9780062694072

This novel, by Louise Erdrich, "paints a startling portrait of a young woman fighting for her life and her unborn child against oppressive forces that manifest in the wake of a cataclysmic event. The world as we know it is ending. . . . Cedar Hawk Songmaker . . . is as disturbed and uncertain as the rest of America around her. But for Cedar, this change is profound and deeply personal. She is four months pregnant." (Publisher's note)

"A tornadic, suspenseful, profoundly provoking novel of life's vulnerability and insistence." Booklist

Erdrich, Louise, 1954-

★ **LaRose**; Louise Erdrich. Harper 2016 x, 373 p.p (hardcover) $27.99

ISBN 0062277022; 9780062277022

LC 2016299026

National Book Critics Circle Award: Fiction (2017)

"North Dakota, late summer, 1999. Landreaux Iron stalks a deer along the edge of the property bordering his own. He shoots with easy confidence—but when the buck springs away, Landreaux realizes he's hit something else, a blur he saw as he squeezed the trigger. When he staggers closer, he realizes he has killed his neighbor's five-year-old son, Dusty Ravich." (Publisher's note)

"After accidentally shooting his friend and neighbor's young son, a man on a Native American reservation subscribes to 'an old form of justice' by giving his own son, LaRose, to the parents of his victim. . . . Electric, nimble, and perceptive, this novel is about 'the phosphorous of grief' but also, more essentially, about the emotions men need, but rarely get, from one another." Kirkus

Erdrich, Louise

The **last** report on the miracles at Little No Horse; a novel. HarperCollins Pubs. 2001 361p hardcover o.p. pa $14.95

ISBN 0-06-018727-1; 0-06-157762-6 pa

LC 00-47198

National Book Award Finalist: Fiction (2001)

"Even the small incidents in this novel are moments of tremendous power, stripped of sentimentality or pretension. Erdrich has developed a style that can sound as serious as death or ring with the haunting simplicity of ancient legend." Christ Sci Monit

Erdrich, Louise

★ **Love** medicine; new and expanded version. Holt & Co. 1993 367p

ISBN 0-8050-2798-X

LC 93-15166

Original version published 1984

"The story opens in 1981 when June Kashpaw, an attractive, leggy Chippewa prostitute who has idled away her days on the main streets of oil boomtowns in North Dakota, decides to return to the reservation on which she was raised. Before leaving Williston, N.D., however, June takes on one more client and, afterward, decides to walk back to her home. En route she dies in the freezing Dakota countryside. But her memory and the legacy she passes on to her family prompt various relatives and acquaintances to recall their relationships with her and to reminisce about their own lives." N Y Times Book Rev

Erdrich, Louise

The **Master** Butchers Singing Club. HarperCollins Pubs. 2002 289p $25.95

ISBN 0-06-620977-3

LC 2002-68501

"Erdrich is demonstrably capable of pursuing a potent image or theme throughout a narrative. And although this novel's leitmotif of violent, gruesome death is a bit too obvious, its smaller symbols succeed better, perhaps because they're accompanied by less fanfare." N Y Times Book Rev

Erdrich, Louise

The **painted** drum. HarperCollins 2005 277p $25.95

ISBN 0-06-051510-4

LC 2005-40227

"There is searing pain and loss aplenty in this book, but one of Erdrich's strengths as a writer is the way in which she controls emotion. . . . Readers familiar with her works will recognize characters from the North Dakota native families who populate other of her works. But again, it doesn't really matter. Her themes transcend that terrain." Christ Sci Monit

Erdrich, Louise, 1954-

The **plague** of doves. HarperCollins 2008 313p $25.95

ISBN 0-06-0515512-0; 978-0-06-051512-6

LC 2007-33626

"The unsolved murder of a farm family haunts the small, white, off-reservation town of Pluto, North Dakota. . . . Evelina Harp is a witty, ambitious young girl, part Ojibwe, part white, who is prone to falling hopelessly in love. Mooshum, Evelina's grandfather, is a seductive storyteller, a repository of family and tribal history with an all-too-intimate knowledge of the violent past. Nobody understands the weight of historical injustice better than Judge Antone Bazil Coutts, a thoughtful mixed blood who witnesses the lives of those who appear before him, and whose own love life reflects the entire history of the territory." (Publisher's note)

This novel is about the unsolved murder of a farm family, "but it is also an allegory about blood (and bloody) connections that develop as the descendants of killers and victims continue to live alongside one another near the Ojibwe reservation in North Dakota. As always with Erdrich, the bloodlines are both white and Native American, churned by the passions of characters with wonderful names like Mooshum Milk and Holy Track, whose lives and stories make the question of whodunit seem like an afterthought. Mooshum, one of three Indians falsely accused of the 1911 crime and the only one who survives the lynch mob tells of finding the murdered farm family and the infant who lived. Evelina, his granddaughter, becomes the central narrator of Mooshum's story amidst the intertwining tales of 'deathless romantic encounters' that follow. Evelina and others detail the dramas of her family, including her own budding romantic encounters with the descendant of the murdered family and a nun whose lineage goes back to the lynch mob." N Y Daily News

Erdrich, Louise

The **red** convertible; selected and new stories, 1978-2008. HarperCollins 2009 496p $27.99

ISBN 978-0-06-153607-6; 0-06-153607-5

"Louise Erdrich is an immensely satisfying storyteller who molds her novels from the clay of her short fiction. . . . This anthology returns 30 of those stories, which eventually became parts of 11 novels, to their original, unentangled forms. The book also includes six other stories, some of which are being published for the first time. Like Faulkner, Erdrich has created a fictional community an Ojibwe reservation in North Dakota from which her work can unfold. Her stories stretch back 100 years or more and venture as far away as New Hampshire, looping elliptically, intersecting through a priest, a place, a hidden parentage. But where her novels develop these relationships, 'The Red Convertible,' in dislodging the stories, creates a new arc between them." Los Angeles Times Book Rev

Erdrich, Louise, 1954-

★ The **round** house; Louise Erdrich. 1st ed. Harper 2012 321 p. (ebook) $21.99; (paperback) $14.99; (hardcover) $27.99

ISBN 9780062065261; 9780062065254; 9780062065247; 0062065246

LC 2012005381

National Book Award: Fiction (2012)

Alex Award (2013)

This book by Louise Erdrich, "[s]et on an Ojibwe reservation in North Dakota . . . focuses on 13-year-old Joseph. After his mother is brutally raped yet refuses to speak about the experience, Joe must not only cope with her slow physical and mental recovery but also confront his own feelings of anger and helplessness. Questions of jurisdiction and treaty law complicate matters. Doubting that justice will be served, Joe enlists his friends to help investigate the crime." (Library Journal)

Erdrich, Louise

★ **Shadow** tag; a novel. Harper 2010 255p $25.99

ISBN 978-0-06-153609-0; 0-06-153609-1

LC 2009-33699

"Irene America, the protagonist of . . . [this] novel, is a woman whose identity has never been entirely her own. For while she is both a mother and a serious academic, she is best known as the subject of her husband Gil's esteemed art—large, assertive and overtly sexual portraits that exemplify his love, but also his constant need to subjugate and own her. This power dynamic has always troubled Irene, but at the novel's start, she discovers that Gil has reached a new level in his quest for possession; he is reading her diary in an attempt to both quell and verify fears that the marriage is deteriorating. Unable to confront Gil directly, but unwilling to let him know everything, Irene reacts by creating another hidden diary in which she records the actual truth. She continues to write in the original diary, however, leaving it where she knows her husband will find it and crafting her words in order to manipulate him. . . . Erdrich is a muscular and fearless writer, and she explores her characters with both compassion and criticism and through lyrical and visceral prose." BookPage

Erdrich, Louise

Tracks; a novel. Holt & Co. 1988 226p

ISBN 0-8050-0895-0

LC 88-9321

"Ms. Erdrich is, as always, the generous kind of storyteller, passing along not only everything her characters know, but the story of the stories as well. Giving life and shape and sense to what's happened, she lets the designs spring clear." N Y Times Book Rev

Erickson, Steve

Zeroville. Europa Editions 2007 329p pa $14.95

ISBN 978-1-933372-39-6; 1-933372-39-7

"Over his entire career Erickson has challenged readers with a fiercely intelligent and surprisingly sensual brand of American surrealism that can, at times, seem impenetrable. For this reason, it surprised me that almost everything in Erickson's new novel Zeroville entertains so readily without seeming watered down or slight. Zeroville is funny, sad and darkly beautiful, built around short chapters that allow the author to capture the essential moment and move effortlessly through time." Washington Post Book World

Eriksson, Kjell

The **princess** of Burundi; translated from the Swedish by Ebba Segerberg. St. Martin's Press 2006 300p hardcover o.p. pa $13.95

ISBN 0-312-32767-6; 0-312-32768-4 pa

LC 2005-50965

Original Swedish edition, 2002

"When a jogger finds a dead body in the snow, the members of Sweden's Uppsala police force uncover a victim with an unsettling history. John Jonsson, known to everyone as Little John, was a respectable family man and a local expert on tropical fish. But he had been quite a troublemaker, and his delinquent past seems to have caught up with him. Despite being on maternity leave, Inspector Ann Lindell is determined to find John's murderer. The cruel cat-and-mouse game that follows leads Ann to a deadly confrontation with a treacherous killer." (Publisher's note)

"When the badly mutilated body of John Harald Jonsson—a working-class family man and an expert on the tropical fish known as cichlids—is found in the snow in the provincial Swedish town of Libro, homicide detective Ola Haver and his colleague, Ann Lindell, quickly identify a suspect, an embittered sociopath. The brilliance of Eriksson's richly detailed crime novel, . . . lies in its psychological and even sociological insights. Eriksson not only reveals a deep, sympathetic understanding for his large cast of characters but also evokes a pervasive sense of despair, reminiscent of Henning Mankell's, in the face of the violent, amoral nature of contemporary society and the challenges it places on the police." Publ Wkly

Other titles about Ann Lindell are:
The cruel stars of the night
The demon of Dakar
The hand that trembles
Black lies, red blood
Open grave
Stone coffin

Erpenbeck, Jenny

The **book** of words; translated, with an afterword, by Susan Bernofsky. New Directions 2007 96p pa $14.95

ISBN 9780811217064; 0-8112-1706-X

LC 2007-23569

"Erpenbeck's narrator speaks in the language and consciousness of a little girl, attending school, going on day trips with her wet nurse though she's long past the age of breastfeeding, and living in a beautiful country 'where the sun almost always shines'. Darker hints begin to appear. Playmate Alice casually refers to the gunshots heard outside the schoolyard. The wet nurse's young daughter doesn't return home one day, and other people start to disappear, too. There is a nightmare coming, revealed finally when the narrator's father, a high-ranking government official, takes her on a trip into the countryside and calmly tells her of horror upon horror. Erpenbeck . . . eschews specific geographical detail, letting the eeriness rise to the universal. Susan Bernofsky's remarkably fluid translation does a seamless job of capturing Erpenbeck's swirl of language as the voice of her narrator trips along like uninterrupted thought.. . . . This is writing so intense you don't even notice the brevity." Guardian

Erpenbeck, Jenny

Visitation; translated from the German by Susan Bernofsky. New Directions Pub. 2010 151p

ISBN 0-8112-1835-X; 978-0-8112-1835-1

LC 2010-11144

Original German edition, 2008

This novel's "central character is a place. In a grand house and its grounds, by a lake in Brandenburg, a succession of occupants dislodge each other, borne along by the political calamities of 20th century Europe. The Jewish family who own the property in the 1930s are forced to sell while they wait for visas out of the Third Reich. An architect renovates the house; at the end of the second world war, it's requisitioned by the Russian army; then, under the GDR, the architect has to flee for having done illegal business with the west. The place is reclaimed by returning exiles from Siberia, then resold by estate agents. . . . The one person known to all the owners and occupants—and thus the thread that binds the narrative together—is the gardener. Periodic updates are given of his activities, describing his routines in detail. . . . No word is ever heard from him, and Erpenbeck allows no access to his mind, but we end up feeling great relief whenever he reappears, and deep sadness as this increasingly frail figure does what he can to forestall his Eden's incremental slide into ruin. Indeed, the amount of emotional engagement Erpenbeck manages to win from us, in a mere 150 pages, is just one proof of her mastery." Guardian (UK)

Eschbach, Andreas

The **carpet** makers; Andreas Eschbach; translated by Doryl Jensen; [with a foreword by Orson Scott Card]. Tom Doherty Associates Books 2005 300p $24.95; (pbk.) $15.99

ISBN 0765305933 (alk. paper); 9780765314901

LC 2004058866

This book, "[s]et on a low-tech world where the main industry is the manufacture of carpets of human hair," this book presents a "mosaic of stories of myriad people and cultures trapped in stagnation by one powerful man's petty anger. Intended for the emperor on a distant planet, the carpets are so finely made that each carpet maker can only finish one in his lifetime, working with hairs from the bodies of his wives, who are chosen for the quality and color of their tresses. And so life goes, generation after generation, even after rumors and, finally, ships from the new government arrive with word of the emperor's removal. The new interstellar government learns the emperor secretly maintained thousands of carpet-making planets." (Publishers Weekly)

Eskens, Allen

The **heavens** may fall; by Allen Eskens. Seventh Street Books, an imprint of Prometheus Books 2016 301 p. (paperback) $15.95

ISBN 9781633882065; 9781633882058

LC 2016018139

Minnesota Book Award (Genre Fiction 2017); Barry Award Nominee (Best Paperback Original 2017)

In this novel, by Allen Eskens, "Detective Max Rupert and attorney Boady Sanden's friendship is being pushed to the breaking point. Max is convinced that Jennavieve Pruitt was killed by her husband, Ben. Boady is equally convinced that Ben, his client, is innocent. As the case unfolds, the two are forced to confront their own personal demons." (Publisher's note)

"Eskens keeps the reader guessing as the tale takes several unexpected twists before reaching the satisfying denouement." Pub Wkly

Esquivel, Laura

★ **Like** water for chocolate; translated by Carol Christensen and Thomas Christensen. Doubleday 1992 245p $26; pa $13.95

ISBN 0-385-42016-1; 0-385-42017-X pa

LC 91-47188

Original Spanish edition published 1989 in Mexico

"A poignant, funny story of love, life, and food which proves that all three are entwined and interdependent." Libr J

Essbaum, Jill Alexander

Hausfrau; a novel. Jill Alexander Essbaum. Random House 2015 336 p. (hardcover : acid-free paper) $26

ISBN 0812997530; 9780812997538

LC 2014026118

In this novel by Jill Alexander Essbaum "Anna Benz, an American in her late thirties, lives with her Swiss husband, Bruno--a banker--and their three young children in a postcard-perfect suburb of Zürich. Though she leads a comfortable, well-appointed life, Anna is falling apart inside. Anna tries to rouse herself with new experiences: German language classes, Jungian analysis, and a series of sexual affairs she enters with an ease that surprises even her." (Publisher's note)

"Isolated and tormented, Anna shares more than her name with that classic adulteress, Anna Karenina, but Essbaum has given a deft, modern facelift to the timeless story of a troubled marriage and tragic love." Booklist

Essex, Karen

Leonardo's swans; a novel. Doubleday 2006 344p $21.95

ISBN 0-385-51706-8

LC 2005-048468

"Readers of Tracy Chevalier's Girl with a Pearl Earring or Sarah Dunant's The Birth of Venus will welcome this novel, which brings Renaissance Italy vividly to life." Libr J

Estleman, Loren D.

The **adventures** of Johnny Vermillion. Forge 2006 269p $24.95

ISBN 978-0-765-30914-3

LC 2006-42532

"Johnny Vermillion, operator and featured performer of the Prairie Rose Repertory Company, travels the Wild West putting on plays in towns like Lockjaw, Diablo, and Purgatory. But that's just his cover: in fact, he and his small troop are bank robbers. And when a determined Pinkerton agent tips to what Johnny has been up to, an all-out pursuit results, culminating in a wickedly clever trap. Once again, Estleman proves why he is among the best of our contemporary western novelists . . . . Johnny and his merry band of thieves are thoroughly delightful characters, a bunch of good-natured rogues, colorful without being cartoony." Booklist

Estleman, Loren D.

★ **Amos** Walker; the complete story collection. Tyrus Books 2010 637p il $32.95

ISBN 978-1-935562-24-5; 1-935562-24-X

"All the elements that have made Estleman one of the best hard-boiled writers of all time—just a notch below Chandler and Hammett—are present in these 32 short stories. Remarkably, he has kept his Detroit-based Amos Walker series (Motor City Blue) fresh after three decades and 20 novels, and any fan of the genre who has yet to encounter the ex-cop turned PI will get a great introduction through this collection. What's most impressive is Estleman's ability to blend sharp-edged language, cynical characters, betrayals, twists, and a memorable narrative voice within the short story format. He also manages to inject dark humor into his work that keeps the violence, corruption, and double-crosses from becoming too grim. . . . Longtime fans will welcome the author's informative introduction." Publ Wkly

Estleman, Loren D.

★ The **book** of Murdock. Forge 2010 271p $24.99

ISBN 978-0-7653-1600-4

"This is one of Estleman's best, a smart, tightly wrapped story about an honest lawman who drinks Old Forester and knows the difference between a Presbyterian and a Unitarian." Publ Wkly

Estleman, Loren D.

Frames. Forge 2008 269p (Valentino mysteries) $23.95

ISBN 978-0-7653-1575-5; 0-7653-1575-0

LC 2008-4505

"Estleman first introduced Valentino in a series of short stories for Ellery Queen Mystery Magazine and promises that 'Frames' is the first in a series of novels featuring the 'film detective.' As with every Estleman novel, 'Frames' is written in crisp, vivid prose, the characters well-drawn. And the author's meticulous research of movie history adds another layer of richness." San Francisco Chron

Other titles in this series are:

Alone (2009)

Alive! (2013)

Shoot (2016)

Brazen (2016)

Estleman, Loren D.

★ **Gas** City. Forge 2008 299p $24.95

ISBN 978-0-7653-1956-2; 0-7653-1956-X

LC 2007-34927

"The shades of Frank Norris and Upton Sinclair must have been looking over Loren D. Estleman's shoulder when he wrote Gas City. Set in a Midwestern metropolis that grew up around a refinery, his muscular novel initially takes a long view of the cynical bargain struck between civic leaders and organized crime—and only moves in for the kill when a key figure in this devil's dance decides to reform. Like earlier muckraking writers, Estleman is always looking for the tipping point where our frontier values of independent entrepreneurship and community justice tumble into criminality. And his characters never stop asking whether it's possible to go back and get it right." N Y Times Book Rev

Estleman, Loren D.

Infernal angels. Forge 2011 270p $24.99

ISBN 978-0-7653-1955-5; 0-7653-1955-1

LC 2011-13480

A "novel featuring Detroit PI Amos Walker. . . . Reuben Crossgrain, proprietor of Past Presence ('Everything you require for the Modern Regressive Lifestyle'), hires Walker to recover 25 TV converter boxes that allow the owner to watch HDTV on an analog set, although the total value of the loss isn't much more than Walker's standard retainer. The detective hits the pavement to identify the likely recipients of the hot items, and his digging soon attracts the attention of ex-Detroit police detective Mary Ann Thaler, who now works in D.C. on homeland security. As the bodies start to drop, Estleman presents a powerful view of the battered inner city, where federally funded housing ends up derelict. Three decades on, Estleman and Walker show no signs of slowing down." Publ Wkly

Estleman, Loren D.

★ The **master** executioner. Forge 2001 270p $23.95

ISBN 0-312-86970-3

LC 2001-23181

"Estleman has created an unforgettable character in Stone. . . . A dark, compelling journey into a previously unexplored facet of the old West." Booklist

Estleman, Loren D.

A **smile** on the face of the tiger. Mysterious Press 2000 295p $24.95

ISBN 0-89296-706-4

LC 00-22284

Detroit gumshoe Amos Walker, "a serious drinker-thinker who lives by a tough-guy code that went out of fashion with the Edsel, is sick of hearing that he looks as if he just slouched out of a 1950's paperback novel. But when a publisher hires him to find Eugene Booth, a has-been pulp legend who skipped out on a lucrative contract to reissue his best book, Walker finds himself staring at a streaky mirror image of himself—if he lives so long. . . . Estleman pays handsome homage to Goodis and Woolrich and all the other 'paper tigers' to whom he dedicates this wonderful book." N Y Times Book Rev

Estleman, Loren D.

★ **Something** borrowed, something black; a Peter Macklin novel. Forge 2002 236p $24.95

ISBN 0-312-87863-X

LC 2001-54752

Peter Macklin "has retired from the hit-man business and married Laurie, a young woman who knows nothing of his former career. They're on their honeymoon in Los Angeles when Macklin is forced back into his old calling by a Midwestern crime lord who's interested in expanding his territory. . . . Back in L.A., Laurie is being held hostage. At first she thinks the lanky cowboy named Abilene is just keeping her company while her husband is away 'on business,' but a fist in the face changes her take on things. . . . The story vibrates with letter-perfect details, and the plot, with changing locations and changing points of view, is deftly handled." Publ Wkly

Eugenides, Jeffrey

Fresh complaint; stories. Jeffrey Eugenides. Farrar, Straus & Giroux 2017 285 p. (hardcover) $27

ISBN 9780374203061; 9780374717384

LC 2017007576

This short story collection, by Jeffrey Eugenides, "presents characters in the midst of personal and national emergencies. We meet a failed poet who, envious of other people's wealth during the real-estate bubble, becomes an embezzler; . . . and, in 'Fresh Complaint,' a high school student whose wish to escape the strictures of her immigrant family lead her to a drastic decision that upends the life of a middle-aged British physicist." (Publisher's note)

"Pulitzer Prize-winning Eugenides' first story collection . . . is gifted with the strong voices and luminous prose his novels are known for." Booklist

Eugenides, Jeffrey

★ The **marriage** plot. Farrar, Straus and Giroux 2011 406p $28

ISBN 0-374-20305-9; 978-0-374-20305-4

LC 2011-22099

College English major "Madeleine Hanna is writing her senior thesis on Jane Austen and George Eliot." (Publisher's note)

The novel's "plot, as it were, centers on the lopsided love triangle of three bright young things at Brown University, class of '82: WASPy beauty Madeleine Hanna; charismatic manic-depressive Leonard Bankhead; and Mitchell Grammaticus, who is, Madeleine tells herself, exactly 'the kind of smart, sane, parent-pleasing boy she should fall in love with and marry.' But it's the brilliant, volatile Leonard whom she falls for when the pair meet in a Semiotics 211 seminar. . . . If chronicling the Derrida debates and romantic travails of perpetually self-regarding undergrads, even ones as sharply drawn as the trio here, sounds beneath Eugenides' considerable gifts, well, it can feel that way at times. Plot's story line wobbles and ultimately loses its way. Still, there are serious pleasures here for people who love to read: diamond-sharp observations and dazzling sentences." Entertainment Wkly

Eugenides, Jeffrey

Middlesex. Farrar, Straus & Giroux 2002 529p $26

ISBN 0-374-19969-8

LC 2002-19921

A coming of age story about Cal, a hermaphrodite, born in 1960 Detroit as a baby girl and reborn in 1974 as a teenage boy

"Eugenides pitches a big tent, but one of the delights of 'Middlesex' is how soundly it's constructed, with motifs and characters weaving through the novel's various episodes, pulling it tight." N Y Times Book Rev

Eugenides, Jeffrey

★ The **virgin** suicides. Farrar, Straus & Giroux 1993 249p

ISBN 0-374-28438-5

LC 92-33466

"The Lisbon girls, all five of whom committed suicide in the early 1970s, haunt the memories of boys next door in a wealthy Detroit suburb. A nameless narrator, one of the boys, 20 years later collects and weaves together the impressions that friends, neighbors, and parents had of the dead girls. Except for school and group outings to two ill-fated parties, the girls' lives played out confined to their dwelling, a cloistered existence protected by a mother vigilant for their virtue and by a meek father." (Booklist)

The author's "engrossing writing style keeps one reading despite a creepy feeling that one shouldn't be enjoying it so much. A black, glittering novel that won't be to everyone's taste but must be tried by readers looking for something different." Libr J

Evanovich, Janet

One for the money. Scribner 1994 290p $25

ISBN 0-684-19639-5

LC 93-50733

"A wonderful sense of humor, an eye for detail, and a self-deprecating narrative endow Stephanie Plum with the easy-to-swallow believability that accounts for her appeal as heroine. . . . A witty, well-written, and gutsy debut." Libr J

Other titles about Stephanie Plum are:
Two for the dough (1996)
Three to get deadly (1997)
Four to score (1998)
High five (1999)
Hot six (2000)
Seven up (2001)
Hard eight (2002)
To the nines (2003)
Ten big ones (2004)
Eleven on top (2005)
Twelve sharp (2006)
Lean mean thirteen (2007)
Fearless fourteen (2008)
Finger lickin' fifteen (2009)
Sizzling sixteen (2010)
Smokin' seventeen (2011)
Explosive eighteen (2011)
Notorious nineteen (2012)
Takedown twenty (2013)
Top secret twenty-one (2014)
Tricky twenty-two (2015)
Turbo twenty-three (2016)
Hardcore twenty-four (2017)

Evans, Danielle

Before you suffocate your own fool self. Riverhead Books 2010 232p $25.95

ISBN 978-1-59448-769-9; 1-59448-769-3

LC 2010-07179

"This debut collection is contemporary, powerful, and very real. While race is a factor throughout, with biracial characters, mixed-race romantic relationships, and plenty of interaction among people of different ethnicities, it remains subsidiary to themes like family relationships, romantic attachments, coming-of-age, belonging, and searching or yearning for direction in life. . . . A smartly written and enjoyable collection from an up-and-coming author." Libr J

Evans, Justin

The **white** devil. Harper 2011 366p

ISBN 9780061728273; 0061728276; 9780061728280 pa; 0061728284 pa

LC 2010051662

"When Andrew Taylor is sent to the Harrow School, a British institution for privileged adolescents, he is spurned by nearly all of his peers, and becomes immersed in a two-hundred-year-old literary mystery when he finds a friend in the school's poet-in-residence." (Publisher's note)

Evans, Nicholas

★ The **horse** whisperer. Delacorte Press 1995 404p $24.95

ISBN 0-385-31523-6

LC 95-17742

"Evans can give equally clipped but clear descriptions of a prosthetic device or a Montana vista, and the lead characters emerge through carefully constructed, seemingly effortless scenes and dialog, not in histrionics." Libr J

Evaristo, Bernardine

Blonde roots. Riverhead Books 2009 269p $24.95

ISBN 978-1-59448-863-4; 1-59448-863-0

LC 2008-46308

First published 2008 in the United Kingdom

"The whole story is a riotous, bitter course in the arbitrary nature of our cultural values. Don't be fooled; slavery might have ended 150 years ago, but you've still got time to be enlightened by this bracing novel." Washington Post Book World

Evaristo, Bernardine, 1959-

Mr. Loverman; a novel. Bernardine Evaristo. Akashic Books 2014 284 p. pbk $15.95

ISBN 9781617752728; 1617752894; 161775272X; 9781617752896

LC 2013956051

In this novel by Barnardine Evaristo, "Barrington Jedidiah Walker is seventy-four and leads a double life. Born and bred in Antigua, he's lived in Hackney, London, for years. A flamboyant, wise-cracking character with a dapper taste in retro suits and a fondness for Shakespeare, Barrington is a husband, father, grandfather--and also secretly gay, lovers with his childhood friend, Morris." (Publisher's note)

"In this vibrant novel, Evaristo draws wonderful character portraits of complex individuals as well as the West Indian immigrant culture in Britain." Booklist

Everett, Percival, 1956-

★ **Erasure**; A Novel. Percival Everett. Graywolf Press 2011 272 p. (ebook) $20; (paperback) $16

ISBN 9781555970390; 1555975992; 9781555975999

In this satire by Percival Everett about race and writing, "Thelonious 'Monk' Ellison's writing career has bottomed out: his latest manuscript has been rejected by seventeen publishers. . . . In his rage and despair, Monk dashes off a novel meant to be an indictment of Juanita Mae Jenkins's bestseller. He doesn't intend for My Pafology to be published, let alone taken seriously, but it is—under the pseudonym Stagg R. Leigh—and soon it becomes the Next Big Thing." (Publisher's note)

Everett, Percival, 1956-

God's country; a novel. by Percival Everett (Author), Madison Smartt Bell (Introduction) Beacon Press 2003 ix, 219 p.p (paperback) $18

ISBN 0807083631; 9780807083635

LC 2002036119

This novel by Percival Everett, with an introduction by Madison Smartt Bell, is set in the American West of the 1870s. The story begins with "Curt Marder, Union Army deserter and indolent homesteader, [watching] from a safe distance as white renegades pillage his farm, carry off his wife, and, worst of all, kill his dog. After hiring a tracker, an ex-slave named Bubba, he sets off to recover a wife for whom he cares little." (Library Journal)

Everett, Percival L.

I am Not Sidney Poitier; a novel. [by] Percival Everett. Graywolf Press 2009 234p pa $16

ISBN 978-1-55597-527-2; 1-55597-527-5

"Everett's latest tells the story of a young man named Not Sidney Poitier who bears an uncanny resemblance to the famed actor and is adept at deploying a hypnotic technique called Fesmerism. When Not Sidney is young, his mother dies, but not before becoming an early investor in Ted Turner's enterprises. The boy then moves to Atlanta, into the home of Ted Turner. Despite his vast wealth and celebrity looks, when Not Sidney ventures out into the world as a young adult, he faces bizarre, stinging and potentially deadly forms of racism. . . . Not only is the novel smart and without a trace of pretentiousness, it shows Everett as a novelist at the height of his narrative and satirical powers." Publ Wkly

Everett, Percival, 1956-

Percival Everett by Virgil Russell; Percival Everett. Graywolf Press 2013 256 p. (alk. paper) $15

ISBN 1555976344; 9781555976347

LC 2012952759

PEN/Faulkner Award for Fiction: Shortlist (2014)

This metaphysical novel, by Percival Everett, is "a story inside a story inside a story. A man visits his aging father in a nursing home, where his father writes the novel he imagines his son would write. Or is it the novel that the son imagines his father would imagine, if he were to imagine the kind of novel the son would write?" (Publisher's note)

Everett, Percival, 1956-

Suder; A Novel. Percival L. Everett. Louisiana State University Press 1999 171 p. (paperback) $19.95

ISBN 9780807123874; 0807123870

LC 98051110

In this novel in the Voices of the South series by Percival L. Everett, "Craig Suder has problems. A black ballplayer for Seattle, he's in a bad slump that embarrasses his son, and he's having problems with his wife. When he's told to take some time off, an obsession with Charlie Parker's 'Ornithology' and the idea of flight/escape brings him to Portland and involvement with a group of gay Chinese, an Indian, a nine-year-old runaway girl, and an elephant." (Library Journal)

Evison, Jonathan

All about Lulu; a novel. Soft Skull Press 2008 340p pa $14.95

ISBN 978-1-59376-196-7; 1-59376-196-1

LC 2007-46761

"William Miller Jr. is a scrawny loner whose mother dies of cancer when he is seven years old, leaving him an awkward vegetarian with an ominously macho father and idiot twin brothers in mid-1970s Santa Monica. William's father, Big Bill, remarries a grief counselor named Willow, and Will spends the following decades in love with Louisa (Lulu, as she prefers to be called), his new stepsister. They are close throughout adolescence, but after a summer at cheerleading camp, Lulu returns home distant and hostile, leaving Will to pine for her in solitary desperation. Will finally appears to be on the path to normalcy in the early 1990s when he lucks into a radio talk-show hosting gig, but the stroke of good fortune is short-lived, as he discovers things about Lulu he'd rather not know. Evison provides readers a viciously funny and deeply felt portrayal of a blended family and one man's thwarted longing." Publ Wkly

Evison, Jonathan

The **revised** fundamentals of caregiving; a novel. by Jonathan Evison. 1st ed. Algonquin Books of Chapel Hill 2012 288 p. (hardcover) $23.95; (audiobook) $52.43; (paperback) $14.95; (ebook) $23.95

ISBN 1616200391; 9781616200398; 9781611749007; 9781616203153; 9781616201852

LC 2012002956

In this novel by Jonathan Evison, "when Ben is assigned to tyrannical nineteen-year-old Trevor, who is in the advanced stages of Duchenne muscular dystrophy, he soon discovers . . . the reality of caring for a fiercely stubborn . . . adolescent. . . . The relationship between Trev and Ben evolves into a close camaraderie, and the traditional boundaries between patient and caregiver begin to blur as they embark on a road trip to visit Trev's ailing father." (Publisher's note)

Evison, Jonathan

This is your life, Harriet Chance! a novel. by Jonathan Evison. Algonquin Books of Chapel Hill 2015 304 p. (hardcover) $25.95

ISBN 9781616202613

LC 2015004221

In this book, by Jonathan Evison, "seventy-eight-year-old Harriet Chance impulsively sets sail on an ill-conceived Alaskan cruise that her late husband had planned. . . . There, amid the overwhelming buffets and the incessant lounge singers, between the imagined appearances of her late husband and the very real arrival of her estranged daughter midway through the cruise, Harriet is forced to take a long look back." (Publisher's note)

"Evison writes humanely and with good humor of his characters, who, like the rest of us, muddle through, too often without giving ourselves much of a break. A lovely, forgiving character study that ' s a pleasure to read." Kirkus

Evison, Jonathan

★ **West** of here; a novel. Jonathan Evison. Algonquin Books of Chapel Hill 2011 486p maps

ISBN 1565129520; 9781565129528; 978-1-56512-952-8; 1-56512-952-0

LC 201020224

"The book charts the trajectory, over 127 years, of Port Bonita, a fictional outpost on the Olympic Peninsula, west of Seattle." (N Y Times Book Rev)

Extence, Gavin, 1982-

The **Universe** Versus Alex Woods; Gavin Extence. Little Brown & Co. 2014 320 p. $15

ISBN 031624659X; 9780316246590

Alex Award (2014)

In this book, by Gavin Extence, "a rare meteorite struck Alex Woods when he was ten years old, leaving scars and marking him for an extraordinary future. The son of a fortune teller, bookish, and an easy target for bullies, Alex hasn't had the easiest childhood. But when he meets curmudgeonly widower Mr. Peterson, he finds an unlikely friend. Someone who teaches him that that you only get one shot at life. That you have to make it count." (Publisher's note)

"Most teens think the universe is against them at some point. Seventeen-year-old Alex Woods has plenty of evidence for his case: a tarot-reading witch for a mother, his father a one-night Solstice stand long since forgotten, a chunk of meteorite crashing through the roof and smashing into him, the onset of epileptic seizures, and school bullies eager to target him...A bittersweet, cross-audience charmer, this debut novel will appeal to guys, YA readers, and Vonnegut and coming-of-age fiction fans." (Library Journal)

F

Faber, Michel

The **Book** of Strange New Things; a novel. Michel Faber. Random House Inc 2014 480 p. $28

ISBN 055341884X; 9780553418842

LC 2014013938

This novel by Michel Faber "begins with Peter, a devoted man of faith, as he is called to the mission . . . that takes him galaxies away from his wife, Bea. Peter becomes immersed in the mysteries of an astonishing new environment, overseen by an enigmatic corporation. But Peter is rattled when Bea's letters from home become increasingly desperate: typhoons and earthquakes are devastating whole countries, and governments are crumbling." (Publisher's note)

Faber, Michel

The **courage** consort; three novellas. Harcourt 2004 232p $23.00

ISBN 0-15-101061-7

LC 2004-5912

"In 'The Courage Consort,' the soprano of a vocal quintet her husband directs progresses from suicidal anxiety to relative equanimity as the group rehearses a difficult new piece that sudden death prevents them from premiering. In 'The Hundred Ninety-Nine Steps,' a woman resolves her trauma over losing a leg and her lover because of a senseless accident; by means romantic and eerie, a handsome young doctor, his late father's dog, and a manuscript in a bottle are the catalysts of her transformation. In the entrancing 'The Fahrenheit Twins'—perhaps a coming-of-age parable—brother and sister Marko'cain and Tainto'lilith, born and reared in arctic isolation, quest far from home for a signal from the universe telling them what to do with their mother's corpse. Faber's literary artistry in all three pieces is consummate." Booklist

Faber, Michel

The **crimson** petal and the white. Harcourt 2002 838p $26

ISBN 0-15-100692-X

LC 2002-24138

"The large themes that interwine the characters with one another—religion, health, sexuality, death, and, reluctantly, love—are juxtaposed against the most minute and intimate details of Victorian life. . . . This massive work is startling and absorbing." Booklist

Fagan, Jenni

The **panopticon**; a novel. by Jenni Fagan. Hogarth 2013 304 p. $22

ISBN 0385347863; 9780385347860

LC 2013006072

In this novel, by Jenni Fagan, "Anais Hendricks, fifteen, is headed for the Panopticon, a home for chronic young offenders. She can't remember what's happened, but across town a policewoman lies in a coma and Anais's school uniform is covered in blood. Anais finds a sense of belonging among the residents of the Panopticon--they form intense bonds, and she soon becomes part of an ad hoc family. Together, they struggle against the adults that keep them confined." (Publisher's note)

Fairstein, Linda

Entombed; [by] Linda A. Fairstein. Scribner 2005 400p $26

ISBN 0-7432-5488-0

LC 2004-52189

"Alexandra Cooper returns in another case featuring two seemingly unrelated crimes that the talented sex-crimes prosecutor is hell-bent on connecting. A serial rapist is terrorizing Manhattan's tony Upper East Side. Dubbed the Silk Stocking rapist, his usual M.O. is to terrorize the victim but not kill her. When one girl winds up dead, Alex and her trusted detective partners, Mercer Wallace and Mike Chapman, believe that perhaps a copycat perpetrator is out there who takes his crimes one step further. At the same time, Alex becomes obsessed with the stories of Edgar Allan Poe, especially after a young person's skeleton is found in an old home Poe once inhabited." Booklist

Fairstein, Linda

Night watch; Linda Fairstein. Dutton Adult 2012 402 p. (hardback) $26.95

ISBN 0525952632; 9780525952633

LC 2012009632

In this mystery novel by Linda Fairstein, "[w]hile visiting her boyfriend, Luc, an acclaimed chef, in the charming French town of Mougins, NYC prosecutor Alexandra Cooper trips over . . . a serial murder case that just might be her undoing. The local authorities appear clueless about forensics; the only thing they seem capable of doing is pointing a finger at Luc. . . . At the same time, Alex learns that a prominent West African leader living in France is accused of rape by a housekeeper while he was staying in New York, and her colleagues, investigators Mercer and Chapman, get the case. When the couple returns to New York, Alex dives into the rape case as Luc prepares to reopen one of the city's most famous French restaurants, Lutece." (Booklist)

Faletti, Giorgio, 1950-

A **pimp's** notes; Giorgio Faletti ; translated from the Italian by Antony Shugaar. Farrar, Straus and Giroux 2012 325 p.

ISBN 0374231400; 9780374231408

LC 2011046064

Author Giorgio Faletti tells the story of Bravo, the narrator, who "discovers that he's been framed as part of a complicated scheme that's left some of Italy's prominent movers and shakers dead . . . not long after taking a new prostitute under his wing . . . Bravo is a black-humored, streetwise narrator with an appealingly flinty demeanor even when he's in over his head, and he has an excellent femme fatale in Carla, an initially pliable woman who turns out to be much more manipulative than he expected." (Kirkus)

Fallon, Siobhan

★ **You** know when the men are gone. G.P. Putnam's Sons 2011 226 p. $23.95

ISBN 978-0-399-15720-2

LC 2010029597

This book offers a collection of short stories about "[t]he crucial role of military wives, . . . where the women are linked by absence and a pervading fear that they'll become war widows. In the title story, a war bride from Serbia finds she can't cope with the loneliness and her outsider status, and chooses her own way out. The wife in 'Inside the Break' realizes that she can't confront her husband's probable infidelity with a female soldier in Iraq; as in other stories, there's a gap between what she can imagine and what she can bear to know. In 'Remission,' a cancer patient waiting on the results of a crucial test is devastated by the behavior of her teenage daughter, and while the trials of adolescence are universal, this story is particularized by the unique tensions between military parents and children." (Publishers Weekly)

"In this book of eight stories, connected by young families stationed at Fort Hood, Texas, Siobhan Fallon sees military life as an alternate universe. It can be many times better and so much worse than its civilian counterparts. . . . Fallon is a superb writer with a delicate perception of this raw material. Her characters may be invented or based on people she herself knew as an army wife. In either case, the stories are powerful." Providence J

Farah, Nuruddin, 1945-

Crossbones. Riverhead Books 2011 389p $27.95

ISBN 1-59448-816-9; 978-1-59448-816-0

LC 2011-18748

"Gripping but utterly humane thriller set in one of the least-understood regions on earth." Kirkus

Includes bibliographical references

Farah, Nuruddin

Knots. Riverhead Books 2006 422p $25.95

ISBN 978-1-59448-924-2; 1-59448-924-6

LC 2006-23107

"Despite its weaknesses, there is beauty in this story of reclamation and resurrection. When Farah's heroine sheds her veil of conformity, it is as if Somalia itself is emerging from a cocoon of despair." Time Out New York

Farah, Nuruddin

Links. Riverhead Books 2004 336p $24.95

ISBN 1-573-22265-8

LC 2003-65969

First published 2003 in South Africa

This novel is "both alien and familiar, a haunting exploration of the desire to help and the attendant costs of doing so." Christ Sci Monit

Farmer, Philip Jose

The **classic** Philip Jose Farmer, 1952-1964--1964-1973; edited and introduction by Martin H. Greenberg; foreword by Isaac Asimov. Crown 1984 2v

Farmer, Philip Jose

The **dark** design. Berkley Pub. Group 1977 412p (Riverworld)

ISBN 0-399-12031-9

LC 77-5138

The third volume of the Riverworld series

"Some threads in the design are loose or overknotted, but the dash and grand scope of the project and this installment of it are compellingly fascinating." Publ Wkly

Followed by The magic labyrinth

Farmer, Philip Jose

The **fabulous** riverboat; a science fiction novel. Putnam 1971 253p

ISBN 9780345419682; 9780399102738 out of print

LC 98096315

This second novel in the Riverworld series "is set in an 'after-Earth-life' of resurrected people over the age of five from time immemorial. The main character is . . . Sam Langhorne Clemens, alias Mark Twain, who attempts to build a metal riverboat. His goal, not obtained in this novel, is to sail upriver to reach the Misty Tower and discover the secret of its guardians, the Ethicals." Libr J

Followed by The dark design

Farmer, Philip Jose

Gods of Riverworld. Putnam 1983 331p (Riverworld)

ISBN 0-399-12843-3

LC 83-9552

The fifth volume of the Riverworld series

"The members of the intrepid band that achieved its quest for the end of the River in the previous books now find themselves in command of the Ethicals' polar control center. When they're not trying to track down an unknown enemy, they're building private worlds and resurrecting a few friends. . . . It's the two varieties of god-playing, culminating in a disastrous tea party in Alice Pleasance Liddell's Wonderland, that give the book its interest." Publ Wkly

Farmer, Philip Jose

The **magic** labyrinth. Berkley Pub. Group 1980 339p (Riverworld)

ISBN 0-399-12381-4

LC 80-144

In this fourth volume in the Riverworld series "Farmer brings his large and bizarre cast of characters (including King John Lackland of England, Samuel Clemens, Sir Richard Burton, Hermann Göring, and Alice Liddell, who inspired 'Alice in Wonderland') to the end of their quest and reveals the secret of the Riverworld. For readers prepared to accept it on its own terms, this book will be rewarding, even exciting. Farmer's imagination does not flag from beginning to end." Booklist

Followed by Gods of Riverworld

Farmer, Philip Jose

To your scattered bodies go; a science fiction novel. Putnam 1971 221p (Riverworld)

The first volume of the Riverworld series

"The fabulous Riverworld, site of the resurrection of every human being who has died, is one of the great fictional creations. Sir Richard Burton, Victorian explorer and rogue, finds himself reborn and sets off on an epic journey to learn the truth of its existence." Shapiro. Fic For Youth. 3d edition

Followed by The fabulous riverboat

Farnsworth, Christopher

Blood oath. G. P. Putnam's Sons 2010 390p $24.95

ISBN 978-0-399-15635-9; 0-399-15635-6

LC 2009-36951

"Here we have a tale of contemporary guardianship — the fact that unbeknownst to most, a vampire has been part of the American political system for over a hundred years, serving democracy and defending America against opposition from things not usually noticed by your typical American citizen. To this tale arrives Zach Barrows, up and coming political figure. In circumstances that are a little embarrassing (caught en flagrante with Candace, the President's daughter) the result is a promotion of sorts, to being the political liaison officer to Nathaniel Cade. Cade is the vampire: blood-oathed for over 130 years to the President. Much of the book then is spent assisting Cade in dealing with those supernatural issues that appear from time to time. . . . Generally this book is well-written, has a definite film/TV style (perhaps not too farfetched considering that Farnsworth is also a screenwriter) and if you can live with the impracticalities, a solid, fun read." SFFWorld.com

Farrell, Henry, 1920-2006

★ **What** ever happened to Baby Jane? by Henry Farrell. 1st edition. Grand Central Pub 2013 304 p. (trade pbk.) $15

ISBN 1455546755; 9781455546756

LC 2013939629

Author Henry Farrell presents a novel "about a former vaudevillian child star, Baby Jane Hudson, who torments her wheelchair-bound sister, Blanche, who was once a glamorous movie star. Farrell delves into Baby Jane's psyche, showing a woman mourning her childhood success and stymied by her inability to act on her emotional needs." (Publishers Weekly)

Farrell, James T.

Studs Lonigan; a trilogy. Library of America 2004 988p (The library of America) $35

ISBN 1-931082-55-3

LC 2003-44207

First published as a trilogy 1935 by Vanguard Press

A trilogy "about life among lower-middle-class Irish Roman Catholics in Chicago during the first third of the 20th century. . . . As a boy, William Lonigan (always referred to as 'Studs') makes a slight effort to rise above his squalid urban environment. However, the combination of his own personality, unwholesome neighborhood friends, a small-minded family, and his schooling and religious training all condemn him to the life of futility and dissipation that are his inheritance." Merriam-Webster's Ency of Lit

Includes bibliographical references

Farrow, John

★ The **Storm** Murders; A Thriller. by John Farrow. St. Martin's Press 2015 320 p. (Emile Cinq-Mars) $25.99

ISBN 125005768X; 9781250057686

LC 2015011403

In this mystery, by John Farrow, "the day after a massive blizzard, two policemen are called to an isolated farm house sitting all by itself in the middle of a pristine snow-blanketed field. Inside the lonely abode are two dead people. But there are no tracks in the snow leading either to the house or away. What happened here? Is this a murder/suicide case? Or will it turn into something much more sinister?" (Publisher's note)

"Farrow (a pseudonym for Canadian author Trevor Ferguson) brings a literary fiction writer's sensitivity to nuance and feel for landscape to this fine, character-rich thriller with a bang-up finish." Booklist

Faulkner, William

★ **Absalom,** Absalom! corrected text. Random House 1986 313p

ISBN 0-394-55634-8

LC 86-6488

First published 1936

"During the summer of 1910, prior to Quentin Compson's leaving the South for his first year at Harvard, old Rosa Coldfield insists upon a private conference with the youth to divulge her recollections of Thomas Sutpen. Driven by a great plan to become a Southern aristocrat, Sutpen builds a mansion, only to see his life ruined. The title of the book reveals the story's basic tragedy: Sutpen's disappointment in his children. One is a spinster and thus has no offspring to continue the family lineage; the other is a son who has disappeared. Sutpen himself falls victim to a murder for retribution. Faulkner depicts the South before and after the Civil War in this powerfully written novel." Shapiro. Fic for Youth. 3d edition

Faulkner, William

★ **As** I lay dying. Modern Lib. 2000 $16.95

ISBN 0-375-50452-4

This is a reissue of the title first published 1930 by H. Smith

This book focuses on "the Bundrens, a down-at-the-heels family of dirt farmers in Yoknapatawpha County. Who lays dying is Addie Bundren, the mother. . . . . And when Addie Bundren dies, having just once raised herself to the window to look at her coffin, her presumed desires direct the action of the rest of the book, for she has chosen to be buried among her 'own people' in the town of Jefferson, forty miles away." (New York Review of Books)

"Experimental in both subject and narrative structure, this novel treats the events surrounding the illness, death and burial of Addie Bundren, wife of Anse and mother of Cash, Darl, Jewel, Dewey Dell, and Vardaman. It is divided into 59 short interior monologues, predominantly in the present tense, spoken both by the seven members of the family and by various other characters, including the Reverend Whitfield, Dr. Peabody, and the Bundrens' neighbours, Vernon and Cora Tull." Camb Guide to Lit in Engl

Faulkner, William

Collected stories of William Faulkner. Random House 1950 900p hardcover o.p. pa $19.95

ISBN 0-679-76403-8 pa

"Forty-two short stories, including all from These Thirteen (1931), all but two from Doctor Martino and other stories (1934) and seventeen published in magazines, 1932-1948. . . . Many of the stories deal with characters and incidents related to those in his novels set in the mythical Yoknapatawpha County, Mississippi." Libr J

Faulkner, William

A **fable**. Random House 1954 437p

ISBN 0-394-42400-X

"Set in France a few months before the end of World War I, 'A Fable' is both an allegory of the passion of Christ and a study of a world that has chosen submission to authority and the secular values of power and chauvinism instead of the individuality and the exercise of free will. The novel centers on the fate of a young corporal . . . {who} with the aid of twelve companions, incites a mutiny in the trenches which results in a temporary armistice. Betrayed by a member of his own regiment, the corporal is executed for cowardice along with two other military criminals, becoming a martyr to his principles and his belief in humanity." Benet's Reader's Ency of Am Lit

Faulkner, William

The **Faulkner** reader; selections from the works of William Faulkner. Random House 1954 682p

Contains the following: The sound and the fury {complete} (1929); The bear, excerpt from Go down, Moses; Old man, excerpt from The wild palms; Spotted horses, excerpt from The hamlet; A rose for Emily; Barn burning; Dry September; That evening sun; Turnabout; Shingles for the Lord; A justice; Wash; An odor of verbena, excerpt from The Unvanquished; Percy Grimm, excerpt from Light in August; The courthouse, excerpt from Requiem for a nun

Faulkner, William

★ **Go** down, Moses; introduction by Stanley Crouch. Modern Lib. 1995 xxii, 367p

ISBN 0-679-60174-0

LC 95-4715

A reissue of the Random House edition published 1942 with title: Go down Moses, and other stories which was analyzed in Short story index

"The voices of Faulkner's South—black and white, comic and tragic—ring through this sprawling tale of the McCaslin clan. The tone ranges from the farcical to the profound. As the title suggests, the stories are rife with biblical themes. Although the seven stories were originally published separately, Go Down, Moses is best read as a novel of interconnecting generations, races, and dreams." Merriam-Webster's Ency of Lit

Faulkner, William

The **hamlet**; 3rd ed; Random House 1964 366p

ISBN 0-394-42759-9

First published 1940

First volume in the trilogy about the "Snopes family who descended upon Yoknapatawpha County, Mississippi in the latter years of the nineteenth century. It "tells how Ab Snopes, ex-bushwhacker, horse trader and sharecropper won immunity in Frenchman's Bend because of his reputation as a barn burner and how his son Flem became a clerk in Will Varner's store. Before long other members of the family descend like swarming locusts on the village. . . . Led by Flem, who has set himself up in the world by marrying Eula Varner when she was pregnant with another man's child, they then move on to Jefferson, the county seat." Magill. Masterpieces of World Lit in Dig Form

Followed by The town

Faulkner, William

Intruder in the dust. Random House 1948 247p

ISBN 0-394-43074-3

"When Lucas, an elderly Negro, is accused of murdering a white man, Charles, a 16-year-old white boy, works to save him from being lynched. Charles gets the help he needs in his sleuthing from an old aristocratic lady and a young black boy. The trio visits the church graveyard at night to dig up the corpse of the supposed victim. The book can be read as a mystery and, on a deeper level, as a social commentary on the South." Shapiro. Fic for Youth. 3d edition

Faulkner, William, 1897-1962

Light in August; the corrected text. Modern Library 2002 512p $21.95

ISBN 0-679-64248-X

LC 2001-57933

First published 1932 by Harrison Smith & Robert Haas, Inc.

This novel by William Faulkner chronicles "Lena Grove's resolute search for the father of her unborn child," presenting a "story of perseverence in the face of mortality". Characters include "Reverend Gail Hightower, plagued by visions of Confederate horsemen, and Joe Christmas, a ragged, itinerant soul obsessed with his mixed-race ancestry." (Publisher's note)

The novel "reiterates the author's concern with a society that classifies men according to race, creed, and origin. Joe Christmas, the central character and victim, appears to be white but is really part black; he has an affair with Joanna Burden, a spinster whom the townsfold of Jefferson regard with suspicion because of her New England background. Joe eventually kills her and sets fire to her house; he is captured, castrated, and killed by the outraged townspeople, to whom his victim has become a symbol of the innocent white woman attacked and killed by a black man. Other important characters are Lena Grove, who comes to Jefferson far advanced in pregnancy, expecting to find the lover who has deserted her, and Gail Hightower, the minister who ignores his wife and loses his church because of his fanatic devotion to the past." Reader's Ency. 4th edition

Faulkner, William

Novels, 1926-1929. Library of Am. 2006 1182p $40

ISBN 1-931082-89-8

LC 2005-49444

Soldiers' pay (1926) explores the disillusionment provoked by World War I. Mosquitoes (1927) is a satire of artistic poseurs. In Flags in the dust (published in truncated form in 1929 as Sartoris) Faulkner began his exploration of Yoknapatapha County, Mississippi. The sound and the fury (1929) tells of the decline of the Compson clan

Faulkner, William

Novels, 1930-1935. Library of Am. 1985 1034p $35

ISBN 0-940450-26-7

LC 84-23424

Faulkner, William

Novels, 1936-1940. Library of Am. 1990 1117p map $37.50

ISBN 0-940450-55-0

LC 89-62931

Absalom, Absalom!, The unvanquished, and The hamlet are entered seperately. If I forget thee, Jerusalem (published 1939 with title The wild palms) depicts, in alternating narratives, the "effects of a Mississippi flood on the lives of a hillbilly convict and a New Orleans doctor and his mistress." Oxford Companion to Am Lit. 6th edition

Faulkner, William

Novels, 1942-1954. Library of Am. 1994 1115p $35

ISBN 0-940450-85-2

LC 94-2942

Contents: Go down, Moses; Intruder in the dust; Requiem for a nun; A fable

Faulkner, William

Novels, 1957-1962. Library of Am. 1999 1008p $35

ISBN 1-88301-169-8

LC 99-18348

Contents: The town; The mansion; The reivers

Faulkner, William

Pylon. H. Smith and R. Haas, Inc. 1935 315p

The scene is a Southern city where a Mardi Gras celebration is in progress. The action covers four days in the lives of a strange set of people, all of them connected in some way with the airplane contests which are being held in celebration of the opening of a new airport. The main characters are: Shumann, an airplane pilot; Jiggs, his mechanic; Jackson, a parachute jumper; Laverne, Shumann's wife; and a nameless reporter who adopts the group for the time being

Faulkner, William

The **reivers**; a reminiscence. Vintage Books 1992 305p pa $12.95

ISBN 0-679-74192-5

LC 92-50095

First published 1932 by Harrison Smith & Robert Haas, Inc.

"Told to his grandson as 'A Reminiscence,' Lucius Priest's monologue recalls his adventures in 1905 as an 11-year-old, when he, the gigantic but childish part-Indian Boon Hogganbeck, and a black family servant, Ned William McCaslin, become reivers (stealthy plunderers) of the automobile of his grandfather, the senior banker of Jefferson, Miss." Oxford Companion to Am Lit. 5th edition

Faulkner, William

Requiem for a nun. Random House 1951 286p

"Written in three prose sections, which provide the background, and three acts which present the drama in the courthouse and the jail, the novel centers on Temple Drake, one of the main characters of Sanctuary. In the interval of the eight years separating the events of the two books, Temple has married Gowan Stevens and borne two children; she is being blackmailed by Pete, brother of her lover in Sanctuary, and is planning to run away with him when Nancy Manningoe, her black servant, kills Temple's youngest child. Her attempts to gain a pardon from the governor for Nancy finally bring out Temple's own involvement in and responsibility for the crime." Reader's Ency. 4th edition

Faulkner, William

★ **Sanctuary**. J. Cape & H. Smith 1931 380p

"Horace Benbow, an ineffectual intellectual, becomes involved in the violent events centering on Temple Drake, a provocative, irresponsible young coed. Temple is raped by Popeye, who murders a man trying to protect her. Popeye is a figure of evil, but is also a victim of his environment. Carried off to a Memphis brothel by Popeye, Temple later protects him and testifies against Lee Goodwin, who is accused of the murder. Benbow defends Goodwin at the trial and unsuccessfully tries to give shelter to Goodwin's common-law wife. Temple's perjured testimony ends all hope for Goodwin, who is lynched by the townspeople." Reader's Ency. 4th edition

Faulkner, William

Snopes; The hamlet, The town, The mansion. introduction by George Garrett. Modern Lib. 1994 1065p $27.95

ISBN 0-679-60092-2

An omnibus volume of three novels entered separately

Faulkner, William

★ The **sound** and the fury; New, corrected ed.; Random House 1984 326p

ISBN 0-394-53241-4

LC 84-42626

First published 1929

"The story is told in four parts, through the stream of consciousness of three characters (the sons of the Compson family, Benjy, Quentin, and Jason), and finally in an objective account. The Compson family, formerly genteel Southern patricians, now lead a degenerate, perverted life on their shrunken plantation near Jefferson, Miss. The disintegration of the family, which clings to outworn aristocratic conventions, is counterpointed by the strength of the black servants, who include old Dilsey and her son Luster." Oxford Companion to Am Lit. 6th edition

Faulkner, William

Uncollected stories of William Faulkner; edited by Joseph Blotner. Random House 1979 716p

ISBN 0-394-40044-5

LC 78-21803

Contents: Ambuscade; Retreat; Raid; Skirmish at Sartoris; The unvanquished; Vendée; Fool about a horse; Lizards in Jamshyd's courtyard; The hound; Spotted horses; Lion; The old people; A point of law; Gold is not always; Pantaloon in black; Go down, Moses; Delta autumn; The bear; Race at morning; Hog pawn; Nympholepsy; Frankie and Johnny; The priest; Once aboard the Lugger (I); Once aboard the Lugger (II); Miss Zilphia Gant; Thrift; Idyll in the desert; Two dollar wife; Afternoon of a cow; Mr. Acarius; Sepulture South; Gaslight; Adolescence; Al Jackson; Don Giovanni; Peter; Moonlight; The big shot; Dull tale; A return; A dangerous man; Evangeline; A portrait of Elmer; With caution and dispatch; Snow

Faulks, Sebastian

★ **Birdsong**. Random House 1996 402p

LC 95-23721

First published 1993 in the United Kingdom

"In 1910, England's Stephen Wraysford, a junior executive in a textile firm, is sent by his company to northern France. There he falls for Isabelle Azaire, a young and beautiful matron who abandons her abusive husband and sticks by Stephen long enough to conceive a child. Six years later, Stephen is back in France, as a British officer fighting in the trenches. Facing death, embittered by isolation, he steels himself against thoughts of love. But despite rampant disease, harrowing tunnel explosions and desperate attacks on highly fortified German positions, he manages to survive, and to meet with Isabelle again. . . . {The author} proves himself a grand storyteller here." Publ Wkly

Faulks, Sebastian

Charlotte Gray; a novel. Random House 1999 399p

ISBN 0-375-50169-X

LC 98-33658

First published 1998 in the United Kingdom

Faulks "has written one of those rare books that is adventurous enough to attract a popular audience while thoughtful enough to sustain the more serious reader." Libr J

Faulks, Sebastian

Devil may care; [by] Sebastian Faulks, writing as Ian Fleming. Doubleday 2008 278p $24.95

ISBN 978-0-385-52428-5; 0-385-52428-5

LC 2007-43052

"Mr. Faulks-writing-as-Fleming does not fall short of the rest of Fleming's posthumous output. Nor does he tinker with the series's surefire recipe for success. What he delivers is a serviceable madeleine for Bond nostalgists and a decent replica of past Bond escapades." N Y Times (Late N Y Ed)

Faulks, Sebastian

Engleby; a novel. Doubleday 2007 319p $24.95

ISBN 978-0-385-52405-6

LC 2007-16044

Readers are "plunged without introduction into the journals of Mike Engleby, a fiercely intelligent, acerbic and curiously disturbing young man who's studying natural sciences at Cambridge University in the early 1970's. . . . Engleby drinks and smokes a lot, and skulks, and does drugs—but not in a way that could be described as recreational. He pops little blue pills (also unnamed) but never seems to lose his capacity for lucid, almost clinical analysis of his surroundings. . . . Then there's his creepy infatuation with a pretty fellow student, Jennifer Arkland, who disappears in their final year—missing and presumed dead. Has Engleby killed her? The novel generates an unusual kind of suspense, a nagging puzzlement. Jennifer's fate is a worry, of course, but the persistent question is, What's his problem? . . . . The best way to enjoy Engleby is to concentrate, as the bizarre suspense percolates, on Mr. Faulks' exceptionally precise writing." N Y Observer

Faulks, Sebastian

On Green Dolphin Street; a novel. Random House 2002 351p

ISBN 0-375-50225-4

LC 2001-41753

"The outline of this archetypal love story may sound familiar, but everything about Faulks' telling of it is fresh. . . . It is a love story above all, but it is also a New York story, the sights, sounds, and smells of the city perfectly evoked to capture one of those moments when the forces of change collide with the proprieties of the past." Booklist

Faulks, Sebastian

★ **Jeeves** and the Wedding Bells; Sebastian Faulks. St. Martin's Press 2013 336 p. $25.99

ISBN 1250047595; 9781250047595

LC 2013027676

In this book by Sebastian Faulks, "P.G. Wodehouse's debonair Bertie Wooster and redoubtable butler Jeeves are back, with Bertie downcast because Georgina Meadowes is marrying someone else. His promise to help friend Peregrine 'Woody' Beeching with his own star-crossed romance leads to Jeeves's impersonating a lord and Bertie acting as manservant, all in the vicinity of the doubtless puzzled Georgina." (Library Journal)

Faulks, Sebastian

A **week** in December. Doubleday 2010 392p $27.95

ISBN 978-0-385-53291-4; 0-385-53291-1

LC 2009-30109

First published 2009 in the United Kingdom

"The events of the novel span seven days close to Christmas, 2007. It's a time when fears of terrorism are, as now, real and the financial markets are on the brink of disaster. Faulks employs a sizable cast, and a fast bicyclist who rides without a light, to reveal a social DNA that reverberates through the present. The characters are introduced on Sunday, Dec. 16, as Sophie Topping begins final preparations for an important dinner party the following Saturday. Her husband, Lance, has recently been elected to Parliament, and this gathering is meant to show party leadership that Lance moves in powerful circles. The guest list is a combination of financial, social, business, journalism and sports figures, culled from Sophie's broad network. From this assemblage, which Faulks will allow the reader to follow over the coming week, several leading characters emerge. . . . This, at its heart, is fiction about folks, and it's darned compelling." Denver Post

Faust, Christa

Choke hold. Hard Case Crime 2011 250p pa $9.95

ISBN 978-0-8576-8285-7

"The second in a series featuring Angel Dare, a hard-bitten former porn star on the run from Croatian mobsters. When Hold opens, our heroine is working as a waitress down in Yuma, Arizona, after her Wit-Sec cover has been violently blown. A chance encounter with a former industry flame, Thick Vic Ventura, forces her out of hiding after Vic is gunned down at the diner where she's been working. The catalyst for this sudden burst of gunplay turns out to be Vic's son Cody Noon, a dumb-ass would-be fighter beholden to an Arizona businessman with ties to south of the border extreme fighting and drug trafficking. Teaming up with Cody's trainer, a somewhat addled former pugilist named Hank 'The Hammer' Hammond, Angel comes up against Mexican thugs and also winds up drawing the attention of the aforementioned Croatian mobsters. It all comes together in a high body count set of showdowns that ends in Las Vegas." Seattle Post-Intelligencer

Faust, Christa

Money shot. Hard Case Crime 2008 250p pa $6.99

ISBN 978-0-8439-5958-1

"Former porn star Angel Dare (nee Gina Moretti), who stopped acting to establish Daring Angels, a firm that manages women in the business, is lured to perform once more by a hot young male star. Instead, she's beaten, raped, shot, and left for dead in the trunk of a car, and that's just the start—all because of money from the international sex trade. With the help of her company's ex-cop security escort, Lalo Malloy, Angel untangles the plot and players, depending finally on nothing but her own resources for the vengeance she craves. A rip-roaring story with nonstop action and an inside look at X-rated movie making, this is clearly not for all readers or collections; but the title (which originated in the porn industry) and cover art are indicators of its contents." Libr J

Faverón Patriau, Gustavo, 1966-

★ The **Antiquarian**; by Gustavo Faverón Patriau ; translated by Joseph Mulligan. Pgw 2014 240 p. $16

ISBN 0802121608; 9780802121608

In this book, by Gustavo Faverón Patriau, "[t]hree years have passed since Gustavo, a renowned psycholinguist, last spoke to his closest friend, Daniel, who has been interned in a psychiatric ward for murdering his fiancée. When Daniel unexpectedly calls to confess the truth behind the crime, Gustavo's long buried fraternal loyalty resurfaces and draws him into the center of a quixotic investigation." (Publisher's note)

Fay, Juliette

Deep down true; Juliette Fay. Penguin Books 2011 xi, 399, 13 p.p

ISBN 014311851X; 9780143118510

LC 2010038552

This book tells the story of recent divorcée Dana Stellgarten. "Her 7-year-old, Grady, is struggling with the absence of his father and becoming moody and morose. She discovers that her 12-year-old, Morgan, is bulimic and succumbing to pressure from her popular friends. Her 16-year-old niece, Alder, literally crashes into their lives and begs Dana to take her in for several months. . . . To top it all off, Dana's well-to-do ex-husband is suddenly struggling with his child-care payments." (Booklist)

Fay, Juliette

The **shortest** way home; Juliette Fay. Penguin Books 2013 386 p. $15

ISBN 014312191X; 9780143121916

LC 2012025149

In this novel, by Juliette Fay, winner of the 2012 Library Journal Award for Best Women's Fiction, "Sean has spent twenty years in . . . disaster areas, . . . but when burnout sets in, Sean is reluctantly drawn home to Belham, Massachusetts. . . . There, he discovers that his . . . [family is] having a little natural disaster of their own. When he reconnects with a woman from his past, Sean has to wonder if the bonds of love and loyalty might just rewrite his destiny." (Publisher's note)

Fay, Kim

★ The **map** of lost memories; a novel. Kim Fay. Ballantine Books 2012 viii, 326 p.p (hardcover : acid-free paper) $26.00

ISBN 9780345531346; 9780345531353; 0345531345

LC 2012004142

This adventure novel, by Kim Fay, follows an "expedition to a remote land, where the search for an elusive treasure becomes a journey into the darkest recesses of the mind and heart. In 1925, . . . Irene Blum, . . . [s]killed at acquiring priceless, often illicitly trafficked artifacts, . . . is given a rare map believed to lead to a set of copper scrolls that chronicle the lost history of Cambodia's ancient Khmer civilization." (Publisher's note)

Faye, Lyndsay

The **gods** of Gotham; Lyndsay Faye. Amy Einhorn Books 2012 414 p. $25.95

ISBN 9780399158377

LC 2011047675

This book is "[s]et in 1845 New York City. . . . Timothy Wilde, a 27-year-old former bartender, adjusts to life as a policeman in New York's newly formed police force. . . . In short order on his lower Manhattan beat, he runs across an infanticide and the body of a 12-year-old Irish boy whose spleen has been removed. The investigation the novice detective launches into the boy's murder brings him deep into the heart of human darkness." (Publishers Weekly)

Other titles in this series are:
Seven for a secret (2013)
The fatal flame (2015)

Faye, Lyndsay

Jane Steele; by Lyndsay Faye. Penguin Group USA 2016 432 p. $27

ISBN 0399169490; 9780399169496

LC 2016006511

"At age nine, Jane fights off the advances of her creepy 13-year-old cousin, Edwin Barbary, who winds up at the bottom of a ravine with a broken spine. She succeeds in selling Edwin's subsequent death as an accident, but her aunt ships her off to a Dickensian boarding school, run by a sadistic headmaster who puts his charges through a daily reckoning that ends with most of them going without food." (Publishers Weekly)

"Faye's skill at historical mystery was evident in her nineteenth-century New York trilogy, but this slyly satiric stand-alone takes her prowess to new levels. A must for Brontë devotees; wickedly entertaining for all." Booklist

Faye, Lyndsay

Seven for a secret; by Lyndsay Faye. Amy Einhorn Books 2013 464 p. $26.95

ISBN 0399158383; 9780399158384

LC 2013008127

In this book, by Lyndsay Faye, "six months after the formation of the NYPD . . . Timothy Wilde, thinks himself well versed in his city's dark practices--until he learns of . . . 'blackbirders,' who snatch free Northerners of color . . . and sell them South . . . as plantation property. Lucy Adams staggers into Timothy's office to report a robbery and is asked what was stolen, her reply is, 'My family.'" (Publisher's note)

Faye, Lyndsay ✓

The **whole** art of detection; lost mysteries of Sherlock Holmes. Lyndsay Faye. Mysterious Press 2017 viii, 352 p.p (hardcover) $25

ISBN 9780802125927; 9780802189363

LC 2016037116

This collection of stories about Sherlock Holmes, by Lyndsay Faye, "spans Holmes's career, from self-taught young upstart to publicly lauded detective, both before and after his faked death . . . in 1894. In 'The Lowther Park Mystery,'. . . [Holmes] improvises a bit of theater to foil a conspiracy against the government. 'The Adventure of the Thames Tunnel' brings Holmes's attention to the baffling murder of a jewel thief in . . . an underground railway passage." (Publisher's note)

"Fans and neophytes alike should cheer Faye's reinvigoration of Conan Doyle's hero and his panoramic world." Kirkus

Includes bibliographic references (page [351]-352).

Feldman, Ellen

Next to love; a novel. Spiegel & Grau 2011 291p $25

ISBN 978-0-8129-92717

LC 2010-52486

Follows the stories of three young couples whose lives are irrevocably changed in the years following World War II, a period during which they struggle with difficult losses and witness profound transformations in American culture.

"At turns brave, frustrating, and fragile, Feldman's characters live and love with breathtaking intensity, and her deft juggling of several zigzagging plots makes the pages flow past with the force of a slow but mighty river. Equally impressive is her understanding of the period and of the assumptions not only about race and sex but also about keeping private pain private, which made the Greatest Generation not only flawed but often deeply, quietly miserable." Booklist

Ferber, Edna

So Big. Doubleday, Page 1924 360p

Selina DeJong would look up from her work and say, 'How big is my man?' Then little Dirk DeJong would answer in the time-worn way, 'So-o-o big!' And he was so nicknamed. Though So Big gives the book its title his mother is the outstanding figure. Until Selina was nineteen she traveled with her gambler-father. At his sudden death she secured a teacher's post in the Dutch settlement of High Prairie, a community of hardworking farmers and their thrifty, slaving wives—narrow-minded people indifferent to natural beauty. Soon Selina married Pervus DeJong, a plodding, goodnatured boy. With her marriage the never-ending drudgery of a farmer's wife began. Through all the years of hardship she never lost her gay indomitable spirit. Unfortunately, she was unable to transmit these qualities to her son

Fergus, Jim

The **wild** girl: the notebooks of Ned Giles, 1932; a novel. Hyperion 2005 355p $23.95

ISBN 1-401-30054-5

LC 2004-54161

"After the death of his parents, 17-year-old Giles leaves behind his job at a Chicago country club to join the Great Apache Expedition, a journey organized by citizens of the U.S and Mexico to recover the kidnapped son of a Mexican rancher. Exploring Mexico's Sierra Madres is an opportunity too rich to resist for Giles, who lucks into a job as one of the expedition's photographers. But when he captures the chilling image of a wild Apache girl in a Mexican jail, the young man cannot, in good conscience, turn his back and walk away. . . . Fans of both Larry McMurtry and Louis L'Amour will relish this deftly rendered tale of survival, self-discovery, and the precarious boundaries between man and beast. " Booklist

Ferrante, Elena

★ The **lost** daughter; translated from the Italian by Ann Goldstein. Europa 2008 125p pa $14.95

ISBN 978-1-933372-42-6; 1-933372-42-7

Original Italian edition, 2006

"In this brutally frank novel of maternal ambivalence, the narrator, a forty-seven-year-old divorcée summering alone on the Ionian coast, becomes obsessed with a beautiful young mother who seems ill at ease with her husband's rowdy, slightly menacing Neapolitan clan. When this woman's daughter loses her doll, the older woman commits a small crime that she can't explain even to herself. Although much of the drama takes place in her head, Ferrante's gift for psychological horror renders it immediate and visceral." New Yorker

Ferrante, Elena, 1943-

My brilliant friend. Europa Editions 2012 331 p.

ISBN 1609450787; 9781609450786

This novel by Elena Ferrante is a "story about two friends, Elena and Lila . . . in a poor but vibrant neighborhood on the outskirts of Naples. . . . [A]s their paths repeatedly diverge and converge, Elena and Lila remain best friends whose respective destinies are reflected and refracted in the other. They are likewise the embodiments of a nation undergoing momentous change." (Publisher's note)

Ferrante, Elena, 1943-

★ The **Story** of the Lost Child; Elena Ferrante; translated from the Italian by Ann Goldstein. Penguin Group USA 2015 464 p. (Neapolitan Novels) $18

ISBN 1609452860; 9781609452865

This book by Elena Ferrante is the "saga of two women, the brilliant, bookish Elena and the fiery, uncontainable Lila. In this book, both are adults; life's great discoveries have been made, its vagaries and losses have been suffered. Through it all, the women's friendship, examined in its every detail over the course of four books, remains the gravitational center of their lives." (Publisher's note)

"Although the eponymous child is of profound importance here, it's the disappearance revealed at the series' onset and to which Ferrante returns, after navigating the 40-plus-year span covered in the story, that will compel readers forward, puzzling over it and anticipating resolution. As Elena ages, struggling to understand her relationship to her books' success, she writes--and we read, a level removed--a story about story and its authorship. A friendship so reflective and yet so repellent, so truthfully plumbed, is a rare thing written." Booklist

Ferrante, Elena, 1943-

★ The **Story** of a New Name; Elena Ferrante ; translated from the Italian by Ann Goldstein. Penguin Group USA 2013 480 p. $18

ISBN 1609451341; 9781609451349

This book, by Elena Ferrante, is "the second in a trilogy. . . . [It] rejoins narrator Elena Greco and her 'brilliant friend' Lina Cerullo as they leave behind their claustrophobic Italian girlhood and enter the tumultuous world of young womanhood. . . . Against the backdrop of 1960s/70s Naples, the previously inseparable girls embark on diverse paths. At 16, Lila has married the prosperous local grocer. . . . Conversely Elena has chosen education." (Publishers Weekly)

"Ferrante's writing is captivating and insightful. She delves deeply into the character of the girls' friendship, ushering them into womanhood with an honesty that is acutely personal." Booklist

Ferrante, Elena, 1943-

★ **Those** Who Leave and Those Who Stay; by Elena Ferrante; translated from the Italian by Ann Goldstein. Penguin Group USA 2014 400 p. (Neapolitan novels) $18

ISBN 160945233X; 9781609452339

In this third Neapolitan Novel, by Elena Ferrante, "Elena and Lila, . . . have become women. Lila married at sixteen and has a young son; she has left her husband and the comforts her marriage brought and now works as a common laborer. Elena has left the neighborhood, earned her college degree, and published a successful novel, all of which has opened the doors to a world of learned interlocutors and richly furnished salons." (Publisher's note)

"Ferrante continues to imbue this growing saga with great magic, treating the girls' years of marriage and motherhood with breathtaking honesty while envisaging the turbulence of political and social unrest in 1970s Italy." Booklist

Ferraris, Zoe

Finding Nouf. Houghton Mifflin 2008 305p $24

ISBN 978-0-618-87388-3; 0-618-87388-0

LC 2007-38411

Alex Awards (2009)

"Sixteen-year-old Nouf ash-Shrawi, daughter of a wealthy Saudi Arabian family, mysteriously disappears and is eventually found drowned in the desert. . . . Nouf's brother, Othman, asks his friend Nayir Sharqi, a local desert guide, to find out what happened to his sister. Nayir's investigation leads him into unknown territory—notably, the secret realm of women in a segregated Middle Eastern society. In an unusual partnership that challenges his traditional ideas, Nayir works on the case with Othman's fiancée, a laboratory technician in the medical examiner's office. Ferraris's debut novel gives a fascinating peek into the lives and minds of devout Muslim men and women while serving up an engrossing mystery." Libr J

Ferraris, Zoe

Kingdom of strangers; a novel. Zoë Ferraris. Little, Brown and Company 2012 363 p.

ISBN 0316074241; 9780316074247

LC 2011046158

In this novel, a "secret grave is unearthed in the desert revealing the bodies of 19 women and the shocking truth that a serial killer has been operating undetected in Jeddah for more than a decade. However, lead inspector Ibrahim Zahrani is distracted by a mystery closer to home. His mistress has suddenly disappeared, but he cannot report her missing since adultery is punishable by death. . . . [This is] a tale of psychological suspense around . . . the sinister forces trafficking in human lives in Saudi Arabia." (Publisher's note)

Ferris, Joshua

To Rise Again at a Decent Hour; a novel. Joshua Ferris. Little, Brown and Co. 2014 352 p. $26

ISBN 0316033979; 9780316033978

LC 2014931908

National Jewish Book Award Finalist: Fiction (2014)

Man Booker Prize Shortlist (2014)

In this novel by Joshua Ferris, "Paul O'Rourke is a man made of contradictions: he loves the world, but doesn't know how to live in it. He's . . . an atheist not quite willing to let go of God. Then someone begins to impersonate Paul online. . . . As Paul's quest to learn why his identity has been stolen deepens, he is forced to confront his troubled past and his uncertain future in a life disturbingly split between the real and the virtual." (Publisher's note)

"The protagonist's sharp inner dialogues are laugh-out-loud hilarious, combining Woody Allen's New York nihilism with an Ivy League vocabulary." Booklist

Ferris, Joshua

★ The **unnamed**. Little, Brown and Co. 2010 320p $24.99

ISBN 978-0-316-03401-2; 0-316-03401-0

LC 2009-10264

"Audacious, risky and powerfully bleak, with the author's unflinching artistry its saving grace." Kirkus

Festing, I. A.

The **birdkeeper**; I.A. Festing. Book Guild 2010 228 p.

ISBN 1846244943; 9781846244940

LC 2010674521

In this novel, "[w]hen two Siberian cranes return to breed at Naagpur, a bird sanctuary in Rajasthan, their presence stirs bittersweet memories in Satchin Rai. The son of a wealthy businessman, Satchin has turned his back on his family obligations and lineage to work as an ornithologist at Naagpur. . . . When he meets Peter, a charming and handsome Englishman, and agrees to be his guide, he becomes strangely drawn to the confident and charismatic tourist. Their ensuing affair and plans to elope together are at once tantalising and terrifying to Satchin, who is torn between family loyalty and this all-consuming passion that dare not speak its name. . . . When Indira Gandhi is assassinated, the country is plunged into violent unrest, and Satchin is further torn between his country, his father and his secret love." (Publisher's note)

Fforde, Jasper

The **Eyre** affair; a novel. Viking 2002 374p hardcover o.p. pa $14

ISBN 0-670-03064-3; 0-14-200180-5 pa

LC 2001-43775

First published 2001 in the United Kingdom

Alex Award (2003)

"It's 1985 in England, at least on the calendar; the Crimean War is in its hundred-and-thirty-first year; time travel is nothing new; Japanese tourists slip in and out of Victorian novels; and the literary branch of the special police, led gamely by the beguiling Thursday Next, are pursuing Acheron Hades, who has stolen the manuscript of 'Martin Chuzzlewit' and set his sights on kidnapping the character Jane Eyre, a theft that could have disastrous consequences for Brontë lovers who like their story straight. This rambunctious caper could be taken as a warning about what might happen if society considered literature really important—like, say, energy futures or accounting." New Yorker

Other titles featuring Thursday Next are:

Thursday Next in Lost in a good book (2003)

Thursday Next in Something rotten (2004)

Thursday Next in The well of lost plots (2004)

Fforde, Jasper

Lost in a good book; a Thursday Next novel. Viking 2003 399p il hardcover o.p. pa $15

ISBN 0-670-03190-9; 0-14-200403-0 pa

LC 2002-71304

Companion volume to: The Eyre affair

First published 2002 in the United Kingdom with title: Lost in a good book

"Time flies—and leaps and zigzags—while reading this wickedly funny and clever fantasy. Would-be wordsmiths and mystery fans will find the surreal genre-buster irresistible." Publ Wkly

Fforde, Jasper

Shades of grey; the road to High Saffron. Viking 2009 390p $25.95

ISBN 978-0-670-01963-2; 0-670-01963-1

LC 2009-30813

"The world is wildly but closely imagined, so the result is as internally coherent as it is unlikely. Distinctive wordplay abounds. All the fooling around is built on a good mystery, and Fforde telegraphs no punches. In short, 'Shades of Grey' is everything that Fforde fans love, and distinctly different from what has come before." Denver Post

Fielding, Helen

Bridget Jones's diary; a novel. Viking 1998 271p $22.95

ISBN 0-670-88072-8

LC 98-18687

First published 1996 in the United Kingdom

"Brimming with a deliciously irreverent sense of humor and a keen sense of women's deepest insecurities, Bridget Jones's Diary is a must-read." Booklist

Fielding, Helen, 1958-

Bridget Jones; Mad About the Boy. Helen Fielding. Random House Inc 2013 400 p. $26.95

ISBN 0385350864; 9780385350860

LC 2013362253

In this book, by Helen Fielding, "Bridget is once again looking for romance. . . . She is now 51 and the mother of two young children. . . . The opening pages find Bridget fretting about her new man, Roxby McDuff. . . . Roxster, as he's called, is 20 years Bridget's junior. She met him on Twitter. This 'toyboy' is fun and flirty, but is he someone who can commit long term? The book considers the role of social media and mobile devices in modern dating." (Kirkus Reviews)

Fielding, Henry

★ The **history** of Tom Jones, a foundling. Knopf 1991 xxxvi, 408, 427p $20

ISBN 0-679-40569-0

LC 91-52996

First published 1749. Variant title: Tom Jones

"Squire Allworthy suspects that the infant whom he adopts and names Tom Jones is the illegitimate child of his servant Jenny Jones. When Tom is a young man, he falls in love with Sophia Western, his beautiful and virtuous neighbor. In the end his true identity is revealed and he wins Sophia's hand, but numerous obstacles have to be overcome, and in the course of the action the various sets of characters pursue each other from one part of the country to another, giving Fielding an opportunity to paint an incomparably vivid picture of England in the mid-18th century." Merriam-Webster's Ency of Lit

Fielding, Henry

Joseph Andrews and Shamela; edited by Douglas Brooks-Davies. Oxford University Press 2008 xliv, 410p (Oxford world's classics) pa $9.95

ISBN 978-0-19-953698-6; 0-19-953698-8

LC 2009-290678

"Henry Fielding wrote both Joseph Andrews (1742) and Shamela (1741) in response to Samuel Richardson's book Pamela (1740), of which Shamela is a splendidly bawdy travesty. Joseph Andrews begins as a parody, too, but soon outgrows its origins, and its deepest roots lie in Cervantes and Marivaux. In both stories, Fielding demonstrates his concern for the corruption of contemporary society, politics, religion, morality, and taste. This revised and expanded edition follows the text of Joseph Andrews established by Martin C. Battestin for the definitive Wesleyan Edition of Fielding's works. The text of Shamela is based on the first edition, and two substantial appendices reprint the preliminary matter from the second edition of Richardson's Pamela and Conyers Middleton's Life of Cicero, which is also closely parodied in Shamela." Publisher's note

Fielding, Joy

Heartstopper; a novel. Atria Books 2007 387p $24.95

ISBN 978-0-7432-9598-7; 0-7432-9598-6

LC 2006-50801

In this "suspense novel set in tiny Torrance, Florida, a serial killer's journal entries are interspersed with the stunned reactions of various of the town's citizens when two teenage girls go missing. Sandy Crosbie, a highschool English teacher and the mother of two teenagers, has relocated to remote Torrance from Rochester, New York, at the urging of her handsome doctor husband. But his reasons for the move soon become apparent when he leaves her for Kerri Franklin, a 'Barbie clone and Internet paramour extraordinaire.' Sandy, along with the rest of the town's citizens, is jolted out of her self-absorption when the body of the most popular girl in school is found buried in a shallow grave. Now it's up to exhausted, overweight Sheriff John Weber, unhappily married to the TV-addicted Pauline, to calm residents' fears and find out what happened to the pretty blonde teen. But even as he fends off the town's obnoxious mayor, intent on calling in the FBI, Sandy's daughter goes missing. Fielding crafts a suspenseful plot, with a stunner of a twist, while giving her characters a depth of humanity not frequently found in formula fiction." Booklist

Fielding, Joy

Someone Is Watching; A Novel. by Joy Fielding. Random House Inc 2015 384 p. $27

ISBN 0553390635; 9780553390636

LC 2014037390

In this novel, by Joy Fielding, "as a special investigator for a hotshot Miami law firm, Bailey Carpenter is smart, savvy, and fearless. When she's assigned to spy on a deadbeat dad in the middle of the night, Bailey thinks nothing of the potential dangers, only that she needs to gather evidence. Then she is blindsided—attacked and nearly killed." (Publisher's note)

"Still, the mystery is not the point in Fielding's work: A page-turning ride wit h a likable protagonist is, and here, she succeeds admirably." Kirkus

Fields, Jennie

The **age** of desire; a novel. Jennie Fields. Pamela Dorman Books/Viking 2012 x, 352 p.p $27.95

ISBN 067002368X; 9780670023684

LC 2011042393

This novel, by Jennie Fields, offers a "glimpse into the life of Edith Wharton and the scandalous love affair that threatened her closest friendship. . . . When . . . Edith falls . . . in love with a dashing younger journalist, . . . it threatens . . . her abiding friendship with Anna . . . Bahlmann--her . . . nurturing friend. . . . As Edith's marriage crumbles and Anna's disapproval threatens to shatter their lifelong bond, the women must face the fragility at the heart of all friendships." (Publisher's note)

Finch, Charles

✓A **beautiful** blue death; Charles Finch. St. Martin's Minotaur 2007 309 p. $24.95

ISBN 0312359772; 9780312359775

LC 2007011273

In this mystery novel by Charles Finch "Charles Lenox, Victorian gentleman and armchair explorer, . . . cannot resist the chance to unravel a mystery . . . when his lifelong friend Lady Jane asks for his help. . . . Prudence Smith, one of Jane's former servants, is dead of an apparent suicide. But Lenox suspects something far more sinister: murder, by a rare and deadly poison. . . . Was it jealousy that killed Prudence Smith? Or was it something else entirely?" (Publisher's note)

Other titles in this series are:

The September Society (2008)

The Fleet Street murders (2009)

A stranger in Mayfair (2010)

A burial at sea (2011)

A death in the small hours (2012)

An old betrayal (2013)

The laws of murder (2014)

Home by nightfall (2015)

The inheritance (2016)

The woman in the water (2018)

Finch, Charles

The **last** enchantments; Charles Finch. St. Martin's Press 2014 336 p. (hardback) $24.99

ISBN 1250018714; 9781250018717

LC 2013031731

In this novel, by Charles Finch, "a young American embarks on a year at Oxford and has an impassioned affair that will change his life forever. . . . Will expects nothing more than a year off before resuming the comfortable life he's always known, but he's soon caught up in a whirlwind of unexpected friendships and romantic entanglements that threaten his safe plans." (Publisher's note)

Finch, Charles (Charles B.)

The **September** Society. St. Martin's Minotaur 2008 310p $26.95

ISBN 978-0-312-35978-2; 0-312-35978-0

LC 2008-3452

"When Oxford student George Payson goes missing, his mother asks Charles Lennox to find him. All avenues of investigation point to foul play, and then Payson's garroted body is found in the Christ Church Meadow. Wealthy, intelligent, Oxford-educated, and a detective of some repute, Charles seeks to determine what role the little-known student club, the September Society, might have played in Payson's death and what lies behind the threats against Payson's friends and now Lennox's beloved Lady Jane Grey. . . . Finch, a superb hand at plotting, gives nothing away, and even the most astute reader will be guessing to the end." Libr J

Finder, Joseph

Buried secrets. St. Martin's Press 2011 390p $25.99

ISBN 978-0-312-37914-8

LC 2011-04443

"Finder's compulsively readable sequel to Vanished opens fast and never slows down. When 17-year-old Alexa Marcus, the spoiled daughter of Marshall Marcus, a wildly successful money manager, is kidnapped from a Boston club and buried alive in a coffin equipped with an air hose and a video camera (for Internet streaming, of course!), Marshall asks his old intelligence expert friend, Nick Heller, to find her. The search leads into an expanding world of 'buried secrets,' from Marshall's gold-digging trophy wife, Belinda, and his crumbling investment empire to allegations of government funding for covert operations and the Russian mafia. . . . Self-effacing, wry, and ridiculously competent, Heller makes a reasonably engaging protagonist, but this thriller's real star is the suspenseful, expertly paced plot." Publ Wkly

Finder, Joseph

Vanished. St. Martin's Press 2009 388p $25.99

ISBN 978-0-312-37908-7; 0-312-37908-0

LC 2009-13029

The first title in a "new series featuring Nick Heller, a high-powered international investigator and corporate security consultant. Through a brilliant piece of detection, Heller has just tracked down 12 cargo containers packed with $1 billion in cash when he gets a call from his nephew Gabe in Washington, DC. Heller's brother Roger, the kid's stepfather, has vanished, and the boy's mother, Lauren, is in the hospital, the victim of a late-night attack. Both Roger and Lauren work for Gifford Industries, a multibillion-dollar corporation where Roger mostly handled mergers and acquisitions. . . . Using his Special Forces skills and the latest high-tech wizardry, Heller counters lethal adversaries as he peels back layers of secrets that hide not only high-level corporate crimes but the troubled affairs of his own family." Libr J

Other titles in this series are:

Buried Secrets (2011)

Guilty Minds (2016)

Findley, Timothy

The **piano** man's daughter. Crown 1996 461p il

ISBN 978-0002243797

LC 96-171372

First published 1995 in Canada

"Set in turn-of-the-century Canada, the story tells, in a series of evocative flashbacks, the engaging tale of Lily Kilworth, and her son, Charlie. Conceived when her mother, Ede, falls in love with a musician, Lily is born in a field of flowers and grows into an odd, lonely child whose world is exotically tip-tilted. As she matures, she becomes more and more alienated from real life, but this doesn't keep her from having a brief, mysterious affair while she's a student in wartime England. The result is her son, Charlie, who has perfect musical pitch and a high tolerance for his mother's eccentric ways. . . . Brilliantly told, powerfully affecting." Booklist

Finn, A. J.

The **woman** in the window; A.J. Finn. William Morrow, an imprint of HarperCollins Publishers 2018 427 p. (hardcover) $26.99

ISBN 0062678418; 9780062678416; 9780062678447

LC 2017002312

In this novel, by A.J. Finn, "Anna Fox lives alone--a recluse in her New York City home. . . . She spends her day drinking wine . . . , watching old movies, recalling happier times . . . and spying on her neighbors. Then the Russells move into the house across the way: a father, a mother, their teenage son. The perfect family. But when Anna, gazing out her window one night, sees something she shouldn't, her world begins to crumble--and its shocking secrets are laid bare." (Publisher's note)

"An astounding debut from a truly talented writer, perfect for fans in search of more like Gone Girl and The Girl on the Train." Booklist

Finney, Jack

From time to time; a novel. Simon & Schuster 1995 303p il

LC 94-24497

"This mind-stretching escapist adventure is studded with period photos and news clippings that function as an integral part of the story." Publ Wkly

Finney, Jack

★ **Time** and again. Simon & Schuster 1970 399p

The author "re-creates the world of nineteenth-century New York City and at the same time critically appraises modernity. His hero, Simon Morley, agrees to live in the Dakota apartments and, assisted by hypnosis, to share a series of experiences in the year 1882. Eager to cooperate with the U.S. governmental agencies conducting the test Simon observes the manners and mores of the past and falls in love with Julia, a girl of the period. Simon's enthusiasm palls, however, when he is asked to alter historical events in the interest of the agency's evidently nefarious designs." Booklist

Followed by From time to time

Fisher, Suzanne Woods

Anna's crossing; an Amish beginnings novel. Suzanne Woods Fisher. Revell 2015 336 p. (softcover) $15.99

ISBN 0800723198; 9780800723194

LC 2014038587

In this novel, by Suzanne Woods Fisher, "on a hot day in 1737 in Rotterdam, Anna König reluctantly sets foot on . . . a merchant ship that will carry her and her fellow Amish believers across the Atlantic to start a new life. As the only one in her community who can speak English, she feels compelled to go. But Anna is determined to complete this journey and return home." (Publisher's note)

"Readers beware: the rolling ocean waves, grime, and festering lower-deck quarters are not for the faint of stomach. Those who summon the courage to read about the raw immigrant experience on this treacherous crossing will find a deeply satisfying story of conviction and hope." Booklist

Fishman, Boris

A **replacement** life; a novel. Boris Fishman. Harper 2014 336 p. (hardback) $25.99

ISBN 0062287877; 9780062287878; 9780062287885

LC 2013048444

National Jewish Book Award Finalist: Fiction (2014)

"Slava Gelman has distanced himself from his immigrant family of Russian Jews so that he can become truly American. When his grandmother dies, his grandfather convinces Slava to submit a claim to the German government program for restitution to Holocaust survivors. The catch is that his dead grandmother qualified but his living grandfather does not. Slava amends the story, making the application in his grandfather's name. He suddenly finds that his grandfather has spread the word to the entire Russian community and that everyone wants Slava to write (read: invent) their narratives." (Library Journal)

"Fishman thoughtfully raises questions of what Holocaust-era suffering is deserving of recompense.A smart first novel that's unafraid to find humor in atrocity." Kirkus

Fitch, Janet

Paint it black; a novel. Little, Brown & Co. 2006 387p $24.99

ISBN 978-0-316-18274-4; 0-316-18274-5

LC 2006-10211

"Fitch has given us a courageous and interesting young woman who handles the bad cards she has been dealt with grace and resolve. No one, not even Cinderella, knows better than Josie Tyrell that life isn't fair—and no one, despite some very long odds, seems more likely to transcend the role of victim and succeed with or without her fairy-tale prince." Washington Post Book World

Fitch, Janet

White oleander; a novel. Little, Brown 1999 390p $24.95

ISBN 0-316-28526-9

LC 98-50371

"This sensitive exploration of the mother daughter terrain . . . offers a convincing look at what Adrienne Rich has called 'this womanly splitting of self,' in a poignant, virtuosic, utterly captivating narrative." Publ Wkly

Fitzgerald, F. Scott

★ The **beautiful** and damned. Scribner 449p

ISBN 0-684-15153-7

First published 1922; copyright renewed 1950

"Anthony Patch pursues and wins the beautiful and sought-after Gloria Gilbert. He decides that they can survive on his limited income until he comes into a large fortune he stands to inherit from his grandfather. Through the ensuing years, their lives deteriorate into mindless alcoholic ennui. Anthony's grandfather makes a surprise appearance at one of their wild parties and, in disgust, disinherits him. After his grandfather's death, Anthony institutes a lawsuit that takes years to settle. Although the Patches eventually win, by then Anthony's spirit is broken, he and Gloria have grown apart, and they care about nothing." Merriam-Webster's Ency of Lit

Fitzgerald, F. Scott

★ The **great** Gatsby; preface by Matthew J. Bruccoli. Scribner Classics 1996 170p

ISBN 0684830426

LC 96016596

First published 1925

"The mysterious Jay Gatsby lives in a luxurious mansion on the Long Island shore. . . . Nick Carraway, the narrator, lives next door to Gatsby, and Nick's cousin Daisy and her crude but wealthy husband Tom Buchanan live directly across the harbor. Gatsby reveals to Nick that he and Daisy had a brief affair before the war and her marriage to Tom. . . . He persuades Nick to bring him and Daisy together again but ultimately he is unable to win her away from Tom. Daisy, driving Gatsby's car, runs over and kills Tom's mistress Myrtle, unaware of her identity. Myrtle's husband traces the car and shoots Gatsby, who has remained silent in order to protect Daisy. Gatsby's friends and business associates have all deserted him, and only Gatsby's father, and one former guest attend the funeral." Reader's Ency. 4th edition

Fitzgerald, F. Scott

★ The **last** tycoon; an unfinished novel. Scribner 163p

ISBN 0-684-15311-4

First published 1941 with The Great Gatsby, and selected stories; copyright renewed 1969

"The work is an indictment of the Hollywood film industry, where Fitzgerald had had a disappointing career as a screenwriter. Monroe Stahr is a studio executive who has worked obsessively to produce high-quality films without regard to their financial prospects. He takes a personal interest in every aspect of the studio. At age 35 he is almost burned out, and the novel is the story of how he loses control of the studio and his life." Merriam-Webster's Ency of Lit

Fitzgerald, F. Scott

Novels and stories, 1920-1922. Library of Am. 2000 1082p $35

ISBN 1-88301-184-1

LC 00-24287

Includes bibliographical references

Contents: This side of paradise (1920); Flappers and philosophers (1920); The beautiful and the damned (1922); Tales of The jazz age (1922)

Fitzgerald, F. Scott

★ The **short** stories of F. Scott Fitzgerald; edited and with a preface by Matthew J. Bruccoli. Scribner Classics 1998 797p $37.50

ISBN 0-684-84250-5

LC 98-121806

Reissue of the 1989 edition analyzed in Short story index

Fitzgerald, F. Scott

Six tales of the jazz age, and other stories. Scribner 1960 192p

Contents: The jelly-bean; The camel's back; The curious case of Benjamin Button; Tarquin of Cheapside; "O Russet witch"; The lees of happiness; The adjuster; Hot and cold blood; Gretchen's forty winks

Fitzgerald, F. Scott

★ **This** side of paradise. Scribner 282p

ISBN 0-684-15601-6

First published 1920; copyright renewed 1948

"Immature though it seems today, the work when it was published was considered a revelation of the new morality of the young in the early Jazz Age; and it made Fitzgerald famous. The novel's hero, Amory Blaine, is a handsome, spoiled young man who attends Princeton, becomes involved in literary activities, and has several ill-fated romances. A portrait of the Lost Generation, the novel addresses Fitzgerald's later theme of love distorted by social climbing and greed." Merriam-Webster's Ency of Lit

Fitzgerald, Penelope

The **blue** flower. Houghton Mifflin 1997 225p pa $13

ISBN 0-395-85997-2 pa

LC 96-52911

First published 1996 in the United Kingdom

This "is a historical novel based on the life of the poet, aphorist, novelist, Friedrich von Hardenberg, a Saxon nobleman who wrote under the name of Novalis. . . . Novalis had a vision of a unique blue flower as the goal of a quest. . . . In the waking life of Fritz von Hardenberg the part of the flower was played by Sophie von Kühn. She is 12 years old when he meets her and at once designates her his future bride and his incarnation of Wisdom. Reluctant parental permission is obtained for their betrothal, but Sophie (as well as not being noble) is tubercular. . . . Their relationship, and Fritz's dealings with his own family and Sophie's, are the main business of the novel." (London Rev Books)

This novel "ranges far beyond itself. It is an interrogation of life, love, purpose, experience and horizons, which has found its perfect vehicle in a few years from the pitifully short life of a German youth about to become a great poet." N Y Times Book Rev

Fitzgerald, Penelope

The **means** of escape. Houghton Mifflin 2000 117p $18

ISBN 0-618-07994-7

LC 00-38914

"Strange, whimsical, sometimes gothic or bizarre, these tales demonstrate Fitzgerald's cool and civilized wit and the merciless eye she casts on worldly pretensions." Publ Wkly

Flagg, Fannie

★ **Fried** green tomatoes at the Whistle-Stop Cafe. Random House 1987 403p

ISBN 0-394-56152-X

LC 87-12813

This novel is "set in a rural hamlet outside of Birmingham, Alabama. Bulletins from a gossipy town newsletter produced in the 1940s by Dot Weems are interspersed with the recollections of Mrs. Cleo (Vinnie) Throughgoode uttered (40 years later) in a nursing home to a depressed, menopausal visitor, Evelyn Couch (whose life is rejuvenated by these Sunday afternoon chats). Flagg also supplies basic narrative passages illuminating the news shared by Dot and Vinnie. The pace of the novel is as swift as the life of the small town is slow—at least it seems slow until Vinnie drops hints of a murder and of riotous pranks played upon the local minister. The story is carefully plotted, with the moods and people of pre- and post-World War II Alabama splendidly evoked." Booklist

Flagg, Fannie

Standing in the rainbow; a novel. Random House 2002 493p

ISBN 0-679-42615-9

LC 2002-21977

"Beneath the sentlmentality, there's a real celebration of life here, an affirmation that success and happiness are the results of simple kindness gratituder and courage." Sci Monit

Flanagan, Richard

Gould's book of fish; a novel in twelve fish. Grove Press 2002 404p il

ISBN 0-8021-1711-2

LC 2001-55747

"This remarkable novel is a meditation on colonialism—indeed, on history itself—couched in the story of an English guttersnipe." New Yorker

Flanagan, Richard

★ The **narrow** road to the deep north; Richard Flanagan. Vintage Books 2013 467 p. (hardcover) $26.95

ISBN 0385352859; 9780385352857

LC 2014010405

Man Booker Prize (2014)

This novel by Richard Flanagan is set in "August, 1943. In the despair of a Japanese POW camp on the Thai-Burma Death Railway, Australian surgeon Dorrigo Evans is haunted by his affair with his uncle's young wife two years earlier. His life is a daily struggle to save the men under his command from starvation, from cholera, from pitiless beatings. Until he receives a letter that will change him forever." (Publisher's note)

A "supple meditation on memory, trauma, and empathy that is also a sublime war novel." Pub Wkly

Flanagan, Richard

The **unknown** terrorist. Grove Press 2007 320p $24

ISBN 978-0-8021-1851-6; 0-8021-1851-8

First published 2006 in Australia

A "page-turning thriller worthy of John le Carré, with a plot so credible a reader might feel it's nonfiction, except for a few too many coincidences. But even those can't dampen the chilling effect of the story, written in a fresh, exhilarating prose style in which the author makes each sentence a small work of art." Seattle Times

Flanagan, Richard

Wanting. Atlantic Monthly Press 2009 256p $24

ISBN 978-0-8021-1900-1; 0-8021-1900-X

First published 2008 in Australia

This novel is a "meditation on the nature and character of the Tasmanian landscape and its bloody history; and it is an exploration of the ways human beings imprison themselves emotionally, and label their prisons reason, science, religion; and it is a musing on illusions and lies, on the awful and wonderful implications of desire." Portland Oregonian

Flanagan, Thomas, 1923-2002

★ The **tenants** of time. Dutton 1988 824p

ISBN 0525246061; 9780525246060

LC 87-13632

This novel is about the "time in Irish history between the Fenian Rising of 1867 through the death of Charles Stewart Parnell in 1891 and on into the summer of 1908. . . . The primary setting is the town of Kilpeder in Munster, and the action is centered on the efforts of a young historian, Patrick Prentiss, to make something out of his belief 'that what happened in Kilpeder between the rising of 1867 and the fall of Parnell had a shape, a design, a theme which worked itself out in the variations of a dozen lives.' He is helped and guided in this research by the retired schoolmaster Hugh MacMahon, {who} . . . was close friends with fellow Fenians Robert Delaney, Vincent Tully and the American Capt.

Edward (Ned) Nolan. All were involved—and variously punished for their involvement—in the failed attempt to capture the police barracks in 1867." (N Y Times Book Rev)

This "novel is enormously long and unfalteringly rich in its delineation of the sometimes thorny connection between the public associations and private needs and loyalties of people who live energetically, and even recklessly, through times of political turbulence." Commonweal

Flanagan, Thomas

★ The **year** of the French; a novel. Holt, Rinehart & Winston 1979 516p

LC 78-23539

The author "writes well, taking care to approximate . . . the spoken and written language of the time. The result is, I'm convinced, not only a serious book, free of the irony and satire that informs so many of the more literary historical fictions written today, but a distinguished one as well." Newsweek

Flanery, Patrick, 1975-

Absolution; Patrick Flanery. Riverhead Books 2012 388 p.

ISBN 9781594488177

LC 2011049338

In this novel, "Sam Leroux has a publisher's assignment to write the biography of a famous South African author, Clare Wald, imperious, reticent, evasive about her writing and disinclined to discuss her catastrophic personal life. . . . Told from alternating points of view, the novel shifts from . . . present to bloody past, from today's fractured economic and social environment to the historic struggle to end apartheid." (Kirkus Reviews)

Flanery, Patrick, 1975-

★ **Fallen** land; Patrick Flanery. Riverhead Books 2013 416 p. $27.95

ISBN 1594631808; 9781594631801

LC 2013015004

In this book, the widowed Louise must sell her land to Paul Krovik, who "erects his new housing development, beginning with his own home. But Paul's vision is ill-founded, and when he loses everything, he sinks into madness and goes into hiding in a bunker beneath his house." Julia and Nathaniel buy the house, unwitting of Paul. "As they become increasingly mindful of an unexplainable presence in their home, Nathaniel's reservations about the move grow to the point of insanity." (Booklist)

Flash fiction international; very short stories from around the world. edited by James Thomas, Robert Shapard, Christopher Merrill. W. W. Norton & Company 2015 288 p. (pbk.) $15.95

ISBN 0393346072; 9780393346077

LC 2014043259

This book, edited by James Thomas, Robert Shapard, and Christopher Merrill, is a "new anthology of the very best very short fiction from around the world. . . . These short shorts, usually no more than 750 words, range from linear narratives to the more unusual: stories based on mathematical forms, a paragraph-length novel, [or] a scientific report on volcanic fireflies that proliferate in nightclubs." (Publisher's note)

"Flash fiction—short, short stories only several hundred words in length—is celebrated as an international phenomenon in this exceptional anthology whose 83 selections span six continents... Natasza Goerke, in 'Stories,' may as well be describing this entire collection when she writes, 'The stories are short, but concise.... The final sentence is contained in the first.'" Pub Wkly

Includes bibliographical references

Flaubert, Gustave

★ **Madame** Bovary; patterns of provincial life. translated from the French by Francis Steegmuller; with an introduction by Victor Brombert. Alfred A. Knopf 1993 xxxviii, 330p $17

ISBN 0-679-42031-2

LC 92-54294

Original French edition, 1857

A novel about the "life and fate of the Norman bourgeoise Emma Bovary. Unhappy in her marriage to a good-hearted but stupid village doctor, Emma finds her pathetic dreams of romantic love unfulfilled. A sentimental, discontented, and hopelessly limited person, she commits adultery, piles up enormous debts, and finally takes her own life in desperation. The novel's subject, the life of a very ordinary woman, and its technique, the amassing of precise detail, make Madame Bovary one of the crowning works in the development of the novel." Reader's Ency. 4th edition

Flaubert, Gustave

★ **Sentimental** education; or, The history of a young man. Magee 2v

Original French edition, 1869

"The background of this novel is the decline and fall of the Monarchy of Louis Philippe and the Revolution of 1848. . . . The hero, Frederic Moreau, has many of the traits of young Flaubert. Madame Arnous, with whom he falls in love, is very like Madame Schlesinger whom Flaubert had admired at Trouville as early as 1836. The subject of the novel is really the futility of existence." Haydn. Thesaurus of Book Dig

Fleming, Ian, 1908-1964

★ **Casino** Royale. Macmillan 1954 176p

ISBN 9781567310566; 9781612185439

"Against the background of a French resort the book describes Bond's destruction of the French branch of SMERSH, the Soviet espionage ring. The climax of the story is a tense game of baccarat in which Bond ruins the leader of the ring, Le Chiffre. The girl in the case is a compliant Soviet agent named Vesper Lynd, and there is much closely described violence." Wakeman. World Authors, 1950-1970

Fleming, Ian, 1908-1964

Doctor No. Macmillan 1958 256 p.

ISBN 9780425086797; 9781567310542

LC 58011083

The setting is the Caribbean, where James Bond is trying to trace the disappearance of two agents who had trespassed on the isolated island kingdom of the Eurasian Dr. No. The maniacal doctor, equipped with two pairs of steel pincers for hands, dreams of world conquest and is stockpiling a deadly arsenal for that time. Bond, with female companion in tow, survives a manhunt through the island's mangrove swamps to foil the doctor's plans

Fleming, Ian, 1908-1964

From Russia, with love. Macmillan 1957 253p

ISBN 9781567310535; 9780685112106

LC 57010292

James Bond, the British secret agent here meets the Soviet murder organization SMERSH once more. His execution has been ordered but Bond's counter activities seem successful—until the last page

Fleming, Ian, 1908-1964

★ **Goldfinger**. Macmillan 1959 318p

ISBN 9781612185507; 9781567310511

In this novel by Ian Fleming "Auric Goldfinger is the richest man in England—though his wealth can't be found in banks. He's . . . attracted the suspicion of 007's superiors at MI6. Sent to investigate, Bond uncovers an ingenious gold-smuggling scheme, as well as Goldfinger's most daring caper yet: Operation Grand Slam, a gold heist so audacious it could bring down the world economy and put the fate of the West in the hands of SMERSH." (Publisher's note)

"James Bond, British Secret Service Agent 007, must retrieve British gold from a Mr. Auric Goldfinger whose ruthless obsession is suggesting in his goal—personal possession of half the supply of mined gold in the world." Publ Wkly

Fleming, Ian, 1908-1964

The **man** with the golden gun. New Am. Lib. 1965 183p

ISBN 9780859974400 out of print; 9781840236903

This adventure "begins with a brainwashed Bond ready to do the bidding of the K.G.B. in headquarters of the Secret Service, and thrashes through to a climax in Jamaica where the adversary is Scaramonga, the most ruthless death-dealing instrument forged in the 20th century." Libr J

Fleming, Ian, 1908-1964

On Her Majesty's Secret Service. New Am. Lib. 1963 299 p.

ISBN 9781567310795; 9781840236743

LC 63018007

James Bond, British secret agent 007, forsakes his bachelorhood for Countess Teresa di Vicenzo, who involves him in another adventure with Ernst Stavro Blofeld, head of an international crime syndicate and architect of an atomic blackmail scheme. The story is set against an Alpine background

Fleming, Ian, 1908-1964

You only live twice. New Am. Lib. 1964 240p

ISBN 9780685116319; 9781567310801

LC 64021144

"Bond, near-prostrate from his bride's death, is given a Japanese assignment to snap him out of his torpor. . . . {The story} involves Bond's making up as a Japanese and venturing into the den of a foreign 'death collector,' a madman who has set up a poisonous garden complete with noxious plants, volcanic geysers, snakes, and, in a lake, piranha fish. Very grisly and chilling. The ending is an epitome of horror." Publ Wkly

Flint, Emma

★ **Little** deaths; Emma Flint. Hachette Books 2017 320 p. (ebook) $78; (hardback) $26

ISBN 9780316272513; 0316272477; 9780316272476

LC 2016037331

In this book, by Emma Flint, "it's 1965 in a tight-knit working-class neighborhood in Queens, New York, and Ruth Malone--a single mother who works long hours as a cocktail waitress--wakes to discover her two small children, Frankie Jr. and Cindy, have gone missing. Later that day, Cindy's body is found in a derelict lot a half mile from her home, strangled. Ten days later, Frankie Jr.'s decomposing body is found. Immediately, all fingers point to Ruth." (Publisher's note)

"This accomplished debut novel will intrigue fans of both true crime and noir fiction. Flint, a technical writer in London, is a welcome addition to the world of literary crime fiction." LJ

Flournoy, Angela, ca. 1985-

The **Turner** house; Angela Flournoy. Houghton Mifflin Harcourt 2015 320 p. (hardback) $23

ISBN 0544303164; 9780544303164

LC 2014034423

National Book Award Finalist: Fiction (2015)

NAACP Image Award Nominee: Outstanding Literary Work- Debut Author (2016)

In this novel by Angela Flournoy, "the Turners have lived on Yarrow Street for over fifty years. Their house has seen thirteen children grown and gone--and some returned; it has seen the arrival of grandchildren, the fall of Detroit's East Side, and the loss of a father. But now, as ailing matriarch Viola finds herself forced to leave her home and move in with her eldest son, the family discovers that the house is worth just a tenth of its mortgage. The Turner children are called home to decide its fate." (Publisher's note)

"Flounoy's debut is a lively, thoroughly engaging family saga with a cast of fully realized characters. . . . [She] evokes the intricacies of domestic situations and sibling relationships, depicting how each of the Turners' lives has been shaped by the social history of their generation." Pub Wkly

Flynn, Gillian

Dark places. Shaye Areheart Books 2009 349p $24

ISBN 978-0-307-34156-3; 0-307-34156-9

LC 2008-40244

"Libby Day, the protagonist of Flynn's disturbing second novel, was, as a seven-year-old, the only survivor of her family's brutal murder by her older brother, an event dubbed by the media the 'Satan Sacrifice of Kinnakee, Kansas.' Twenty-five years later, she has become a hardened, selfish young woman with no friends or family. Since the tragedy, her life has been paid for by donations of well-wishers, but, with that fund now empty, Libby must find a way to make money. Her search leads her to The Kill Club, a secret society of people obsessed with the details of notorious murders. As Libby tries to gather artifacts to sell to The Kill Club (whose members, it turns out, doubt the guilt of her brother), she is forced to reëxamine the events of the night of the murder. Flynn's well-paced story deftly shows the fallibility of memory and the lies a child tells herself to get through a trauma." New Yorker

Flynn, Gillian, 1971-

★ **Gone** girl; a novel. Gillian Flynn. Crown 2012 419 p.

ISBN 030758836X; 9780307588364; 9780307588388

LC 2011041525

In this book, "[w]hen Nick Dunne's beautiful and clever wife, Amy, goes missing on their fifth wedding anniversary, the media descend. . . . And Nick stumbles badly, for, as it turns out, he has plenty to hide, and under the pressure of police questioning and media scrutiny, he tells one lie after another. Juxtaposed with Nick's first-person narration of events are excerpts from Amy's diary, which completely contradict Nick's story and depict a woman who is afraid of her husband." (Booklist)

Flynn, Gillian, 1971-

Sharp objects; a novel. Shaye Areheart Books 2006 245p $24

ISBN 0-307-34154-2

LC 2005-35046

The author "offers up a literary thriller that's a doozy. . . and she does it with wit and grit, a sort of Hitchcock visits Stephen King, with plenty of the former's offstage and often only implied violence, and the latter's sense of pacing and facility with dialogue. . . . This is not a comfortable novel of touchy-feely family fun. Rather, it is a tough tale told with remarkable clarity and dexterity." Denver Post

Flynn, Michael

Eifelheim. Tor Book 2006 320p $25.95

ISBN 0-7653-0096-6

LC 2006-5468

"Tom, a young historian, obsesses about Eifelheim, a German village that mysteriously disappeared from all maps in 1349. His lover Sharon, a theoretical physicist, occupies herself with testing the limits of conventional theories of time and space. Their interests merge when they discover the remarkable story of Father Dietrich, Eifelheim's parish priest during the Black Death and a believer in travelers from the stars. With a sure grasp of both speculative science and medieval history, Flynn . . . compellingly weaves past and present together in a dialog of faith and science." Libr J

Flynn, Michael

In the Lion's Mouth; Michael Flynn. Tor 2012 303 p. ill

ISBN 0765322854; 9780765322852

LC 2011025168

This book tells the story of a future universe "wherein two human empires, the Confederation of Central Worlds and the United League of the Periphery, struggle for dominance. . . . Bridget ban, a Hound or agent of the League, seeks news of Donovan buigh, a scarred former Shadow, or operative of the Confederation, her former lover. . . . The great powers of the Confederacy, Those of Name, tortured Donovan to fragment his mind into seven distinct personalities. . . . A civil war . . . smolders in the Lion's Mouth the control arm of the Shadows. . . . Donovan miraculously escaped the horrors inflicted by the Names, and now the rebels . . . [intend] to recruit or at least capture him. Unknown to everybody . . . Donovan's separated personalities have begun to communicate and access their common memories, making him even more formidable than before." (Kirkus)

Flynn, Michael

The **January** dancer. Tor 2008 350p il $24.95

ISBN 978-0-7653-1817-6; 0-7653-1817-2

LC 2008-29772

"The characters zip through so many worlds that it's hard to keep track of them, but Flynn includes enough clever references to the long-abandoned Earth to keep the journey amusing. . . . The balladic framework can be heavy-handed at times, but it adds a mythical quality to what could have been run-of-the-mill space fantasy." Washington Post Book World

Flynn, Michael

On the razor's edge; Michael Flynn. Tor 2013 352 p. (hardback) $25.99

ISBN 0765334801; 9780765334800

LC 2013006328

In this book by Michael Flynn "the secret war among the Shadows of the Name is escalating, and there are hints that it is not so secret as the Shadows had thought. The scarred man, Donovan buigh, half honored guest and half prisoner, is carried deeper into the Confederation, all the way to Holy Terra herself, to help plan the rebel assault on the Secret City. Meanwhile, Bridget ban has organized a posse . . . to go in pursuit of her kidnapped daughter." (Publisher's note)

Flyte, Magnus

City of dark magic; a novel. Magnus Flyte. Penguin Books 2012 464 p. $16

ISBN 0143122681; 9780143122685

LC 2012028676

In this romantic mystery novel, "musicologist Sarah Weston has been summoned to Prague to catalog Beethoven manuscripts at the Lobkowicz Palace." Weird stuff happens as she prepares to go, including the apparent suicide of her mentor Sherbatsky. "As Sarah dutifully sifts through the manuscripts, she discovers clues not only about the 'Immortal Beloved,' but also Sherbatsky's strange behavior leading up to his death," which may have had to do with time-travel drugs.. (Kirkus)

Flyte, Magnus

City of lost dreams; a novel. Magnus Flyte. Penguin Books 2013 368 p. $16

ISBN 0143123270; 9780143123279

LC 2013031311

In this novel, by Magnus Flyte, "we find musicologist Sarah Weston in Vienna in search of a cure for her friend Pollina, who is now gravely ill and who may not have much time left. . . . Nicolas Pertusato, in London [is] in search of an ancient alchemical cure for the girl . . . In Prague, Prince Max tries to unravel the strange reappearance of a long dead saint while being pursued by a seductive red-headed historian with dark motives of her own." (Publisher's note)

"Sensual, witty and sometimes laugh-out-loud funny, set forth in sparkling prose and inhabited by characters well-worth getting to know." Kirkus

Foer, Jonathan Safran

Everything is illuminated; a novel. Houghton Mifflin 2002 276p il $24

ISBN 0-618-17387-0

LC 2001-51610

"Foer deftly handles the intricate story-within-a-story plot, and the layers of suspense build as the shtetl hurtles toward the devastation of the 20th century while Alex and Jonathan and Grandfather close in on the object of their search. An impressive, original debut." Publ Wkly

Foer, Jonathan Safran

Extremely loud & incredibly close. Houghton Mifflin 2005 326p il $24.95; pa $13.95

ISBN 0-618-32970-6; 0-618-71165-1 pa

LC 2004-65131

The author's "depiction of Oskar's reaction to phone messages left by his father as he awaited rescue in the burning World Trade Center, his description of Oskar's grandfather's love affair . . . and his experiences during the bombing of Dresden—these passages underscore Mr. Foer's ability to evoke, with enormous compassion and psychological acuity, his characters' emotional experiences, and to show how these private moments intersect with the great public events of history." N Y Times (Late N Y Ed)

Foer, Jonathan Safran, 1977-

Here I am; a novel. Jonathan Safran Foer. Farrar, Straus & Giroux 2016 571 p. (hardcover) $28

ISBN 0374280029; 9780374280024; 9780374712501

LC 2016007096

This novel by Jonathan Safran Foer "is the story of a fracturing family in a moment of crisis. As Jacob and Julia Bloch and their three sons are forced to confront the distances between the lives they think they want and the lives they are living, a catastrophic earthquake sets in motion a quickly escalating conflict in the Middle East. At stake is the meaning of home—and the fundamental question of how much aliveness one can bear." (Publisher's note)

"That he can provide such a redemptive denouement, at once poignant, inspirational, and compassionate, is the mark of a thrillingly gifted writer." Pub Wkly

Follett, Ken, 1949-

A **column** of fire; Ken Follett. Viking 2017 916 p. map (Kingsbridge) (hardcover) $36

ISBN 052595497X; 9780525954972; 9780735224476

LC 2017025384

In this book in the Kingsbridge series, by Ken Follett, "in 1558, . . . [a]s power in England shifts . . . between Catholics and Protestants, royalty and commoners clash, testing friendship, loyalty, and love. Ned Willard wants . . . to marry Margery Fitzgerald. But [they] . . . find themselves on opposing sides of the religious conflict dividing the country. . . [T]he love between Ned and Margery seems doomed as extremism sparks violence from Edinburgh to Geneva." (Publisher's note)

"Follett's sprawling novel is a fine mix of heart-pounding drama and erudite historicism." Pub Wkly

Follett, Ken, 1949-

Edge of Eternity; by Ken Follett. Dutton 2014 1120 p. hc $36

ISBN 0525953094; 9780525953098

LC 2014005306

The Century Trilogy

This final book in the Century Trilogy "follows the fortunes of five intertwined families--American, German, Russian, English, and Welsh--as they make their way through the twentieth century. . . . [It] covers one of the most tumultuous eras of all: the 1960s through the 1980s, encompassing civil rights, assassinations, Vietnam, the Berlin Wall, the Cuban Missile Crisis, presidential impeachment, revolution--and rock and roll." (Publisher's note)

"This mesmerizing final installment is an exhaustive but rewarding reading experience dense in thematic heft, yet flowing with spicy, expertly paced melodrama, character-rich exploits, familial histrionics, and international intrigue." Pub Wkly

Follett, Ken

★ **Eye** of the needle; a novel. Arbor House 1978 313p

LC 77-90670

"An absolutely terrific thriller, so pulse-pounding, so ingenious in its plotting, and so frighteningly realistic that you simply cannot stop reading, this World War II espionage tale is right up there with the best of them." Publ Wkly

Follett, Ken, 1949-

Fall of giants; book one of the Century trilogy. Dutton 2010 985p $36

ISBN 0-525-95165-2; 978-0-525-95165-0

LC 2010-09279

This is the first installment of Follet's fictional trilogy spanning the entire twentieth century. It "follows the fates of five interrelated families—American, German, Russian, English and Welsh—as they move through the world-shaking dramas of World War I, the Russian Revolution and the struggle for women's suffrage." (Publisher's note)

"Follett entwines fiction and factual events well. Creating characters of numerous, actual historical figures is a big risk. How do you write about Trotsky without being facile? Follett successfully assails the dilemma from a couple of angles, most importantly by knowing a lot about the period but not making the reader aware of how arduously he is working." Chicago Sun-Times

Follett, Ken

Hornet flight. Dutton 2002 420p $26.95

ISBN 0-525-94689-6

LC 2002-37903

"Tale of amateur spies pursued by Nazi collaborators in occupied Denmark in 1941. Harald Olufsen is an 18-year-old physics student who stumbles into espionage when he accidentally discovers a secret German radar installation on the island where he lives. . . . Follett starts out fast and keeps up the pace, revealing how ordinary people who want to do the right thing are undone by their own enthusiasm and inexperience. He also paints a vivid and convincing picture of life in occupied Denmark, of easy collaboration with the Nazis and of the insidious, creeping persecution of the Jews. Publ Wkly

Follett, Ken

Jackdaws. Dutton 2001 451p

ISBN 0-525-94628-4

LC 2001-37087

This thriller is about a mission "to take out a German telephone exchange near Reims in the last few hours before D-Day. A full-frontal assault led by British SOE (Special Operations Executives) Felicity 'Flick' Clariet and her husband, a French Resistance leader, has failed, leaving the Allies with only a last-minute desperation plan: a team of six women, posing as a cleaning detail, will infiltrate the exchange and dismantle it. . . . The assembled team includes two lesbians, a German transvestite, and a gypsy. All of this may sound like cliched melodrama, but when Follett starts the clock and slips the narrative gearshift into synchromesh, one's literary misgivings are abandoned in the wake of the plot's forward thrust." Booklist

Follett, Ken, 1949-

The **pillars** of the earth; Ken Follett. Morrow 1989 973p ill. (hbk.) $34.99

ISBN 0688046592 ; 9780688046590

LC 89009405

This book takes place in "the twelfth century; the place—feudal England; and the subject—the building of a glorious cathedral. [Author Ken] Follett has re-created the . . . England of the Middle Ages. . . . The vast forests, the walled towns, the castles, and the monasteries become a familiar landscape. Against this . . . backdrop, filled with the ravages of war and the rhythms of daily life, the . . . storyteller draws the reader . . . into the intertwined lives of his characters—into their dreams, their labors, and their loves: Tom, the master builder; Aliena, the ravishingly beautiful noblewoman; Philip, the prior of Kingsbridge; Jack, the artist in stone; and Ellen, the woman of the forest who casts a terrifying curse." (Publisher's note)

"Follett has skillfully crafted an extraordinary epic buttressed by a succession of suspenseful subplots. A towering triumph of romance, rivalry, and spectacle from a major talent." Booklist

Follett, Ken, 1949-

Winter of the world; Ken Follett. Dutton 2012 940 p.

ISBN 0525952926; 9780525952923

LC 2012004653

This historical novel, by Ken Follett, is the second book in "The Century Trilogy." "[Picking] up right where the first book left off, . . . its five interrelated families . . . enter a time of enormous . . . turmoil, beginning with the rise of the Third Reich, . . . up to the explosions of the American and Soviet atomic bombs. . . . These characters . . . find their lives inextricably entangled as their experiences illuminate the cataclysms that marked the century." (Publisher's note)

Follett, Ken

World without end. Dutton 2007 1014p $35

ISBN 978-0-525-95007-3; 0-525-95007-9

LC 2007-26639

"Some 200 years after Pillars, the town of Kingsbridge is still dominated by its magnificent cathedral. But times have changed. War and plague have dramatically affected the infrastructure of the Middle Ages, shifting the base of power from the noble and religious to the rising merchant and artisan classes. Populated with an immense cast of truly remarkable characters-the rich and powerful, the weak and downtrodden, clergy, guildsmen and nobility-this novel explores the lives and fortunes of the ancestors of the original inhabitants of Kingsbridge." Libr J

Ford, Ford Madox

★ The **good** soldier; a tale of passion. Knopf 1991 (Everyman's library) $24

ISBN 0-679-40665-4

LC 91-52977

First published 1915 in the United Kingdom

This novel "consists of the first-person narration of American John Dowell (an archetypally unreliable narrator), who relates the history of relationships that begin in 1904, when his wife Florence meet Edward and Leonora Ashburnham in a hotel in Nauheim. The two couples form a foursome, and meet regularly. In August 1913 the Ashburnhams take their young ward Nancy Rufford to Nauheim with them, and Florence commits suicide. Later that year the Ashburnhams send Nancy to India (where she goes mad) and Edward also commits suicide. Dowell becomes Nancy's 'male sick nurse'; Leonora remarries. The substance of the novel lies in Dowell's growing understanding of the intrigues that lay behind the orderly Edwardian fąсade both couples had presented to the world." Oxford Companion to Engl Lit. 6th edition

Ford, Ford Madox

★ **Parade's** end. Knopf 1992 906p $22

ISBN 0-679-41728-1

LC 92-52922

A reissue of the title first published 1950; A one volume edition of the author's tetralogy that includes: Some do not (1924); No more parades (1925); A man could stand up (1926); and The last post (1928)

This series of novels "describes the adventures in love and war of Christopher Tietjens, an old-fashioned gentleman of the English governing class. Ford draws a brilliant picture of the social changes brought about by the First World War. Before the war, Tietjens is nobly faithful to his impossible wife. But trench warfare seems to him a symbol of the disintegration of his whole society. He has a mental breakdown, goes to live with a woman he loves, and gives up his position, wealth, and historic family ties." Reader's Ency. 4th edition

Ford, Jamie

Songs of Willow Frost; a novel. by Jamie Ford. Ballantine Books 2013 352 p. (hardcover : alk. paper) $26

ISBN 0345522028; 9780345522023

LC 2013011007

This book is a follow-up to Jamie Ford's book "Hotel on the Corner of Bitter and Sweet." Here, "on a birthday outing, William Eng, a Chinese American boy living at Seattle's Sacred Heart Orphanage during the Depression, sees actress Willow Frost onscreen and is convinced that she is his mother." (Library Journal)

Ford, Jeffrey

The **drowned** life. Harper Perennial 2008 290, 16p pa $14.95

ISBN 978-0-06-143506-5; 0-06-143506-6

LC 2008-13181

"This collection of short stories from the author of The Shadow Year contains some of the most unusual and provocative settings and plots this reviewer has ever encountered, which will make it perfect for book talking to patrons. . . . Sometimes shocking, sometimes mesmerizing, sometimes humorous, this collection will please fans of Raymond Carver and Flannery O'Connor." Libr J

Ford, Jeffrey

The **empire** of ice cream; with an introduction by Jonathan Carroll. Golden Gryphon Press 2006 319p $24.95

ISBN 1-930846-39-8

LC 2005-24035

"Giants and unidentifiable alien creatures, fairy tales, the intertwining of wonder and terror, and fantastic views of both the strange and the ordinary all appear in this marvelous collection, with Ford's comments on his inspiration and motivations appended to each story. Ford is nothing if not versatile, as this collection confirms to great effect." Booklist

Ford, Jeffrey

The **shadow** year. William Morrow 2008 289p $25.95

ISBN 978-0-06-123152-0; 0-06-123152-5

LC 2007-37319

"A masterly literary adventure that is at once a hypnotically compelling mystery and a stunningly evocative portrait of small-town adolescence." Pittsburgh Press

Ford, Richard, 1944-

Canada; a novel. Richard Ford. Ecco 2012 420 p. $27.99

ISBN 0061692042; 9780061692048

LC 2011279175

This novel tells the story of "15-year-old Dell Parsons, whose world collapses when his parents are jailed for a bank robbery, his twin sister flees, and he is transported across the border by a family friend to an obscure town in Canada. . . . Segmented into three parts, the narrative slowly builds into a . . . commentary on life's biggest question: Why are we here?" (Library Journal)

Ford, Richard

★ **Independence** Day. Knopf 1995 451p

ISBN 0-679-49265-8

LC 95-3126

One is "constantly struck by the rich, dense mixture of Ford's narrative. No one writes better—and with more inventive brio—about the bland wasteland of US suburbia; that shopping-malled, subdivisioned terrain that has rapidly become the true defining landscape of late 20th-century America." New Statesman (1913)

Ford, Richard

The **lay** of the land. Alfred A. Knopf 2006 496p $26.95

ISBN 0-679-45468-3; 978-0-679-45468-7

LC 2006-25570

This third novel featuring sports journalist Frank Bascombe, who appeared previously in The Sportswriter (1986) and Independence Day (1995), finds the protagonist facing health problems (prostate cancer), the end of the Clinton era, and family issues.

This is as "as vibrant a book as any that Richard Ford has written. It bristles with energy, with a natural assurance on the part of its writer. . . . And what a slice of life at the turn of the century and millennium this novel is. There is so much trenchant criticism of what is wrong with American society: the economic royalism, the greed, the lack of common decency and civility in so many walks of life, and above all perspective. . . . As people today read Theodore Dreiser for his acute portraits of industrialized America in its gilded age and Sinclair Lewis for his insights into his nation's struggles to come to terms with 20th-century changes in its social structures, one day readers will turn to Richard Ford to discover just what the United States was like on the homefront during his particular fin de siecle." Christ Sci Monit

Ford, Richard, 1944-

Let Me Be Frank With You; Richard Ford. HarperCollins 2014 272 p. (Frank Bascombe) $27.99

ISBN 0061692069; 9780061692062

In this novel, author Richard Ford "reinvents [character Frank] Bascombe in the aftermath of Hurricane Sandy. In four richly luminous narratives, Bascombe (and Ford) attempts to reconcile, interpret and console a world undone by calamity. It is a moving and wondrous and extremely funny odyssey through the America we live in at this moment." (Publisher's note)

"In each neatly linked tale, Frank ruminates misanthropically, wittily, and wisely about love, family, friendship, race, politics, and the mystery of the self." Booklist

Ford, Richard

A **multitude** of sins; stories. Knopf 2002 286p

ISBN 0-375-41212-3

LC 2001-38402

"Tracing the blueprint of human interaction in this latest collection . . . Ford signals the master text of lust standing behind the multitude of small sins he so tersely and poignantly chronicles. To err is human, and, in Ford's worldview, little is so human as the act of cheating on a wife or husband." Publ Wkly

Forester, C. S.

Admiral Hornblower in the West Indies. Little, Brown 1958 329p

"Recounted with taste, with psychological insight, and with a sure sense of story. This is top grade adventure fiction." N Y Her Trib Books

Forester, C. S.

★ The **African** Queen. Little, Brown 1935 275p

ISBN 0-89244-065-1

"At her brother's death Rose Sayer is left alone in an isolated African mission. She is determined to fight against the Germans, who have taken her brother's black converts into custody. She joins forces with a Cockney, Alnutt, and they take a long and dangerous trip down-river in Alnutt's dilapidated launch in order to reach the German boat they intend to blow up. The journey points up the differences between this ill-matched pair, and their bravery as well." Shapiro. Fic for Youth. 3d edition

Forester, C. S.

★ **Beat** to quarters. Little, Brown 1937 324p

A sea story of the British navy in the early nineteenth century. Essentially it is a portrait of a man, captain of an English frigate. Hornblower, son of a country doctor, is a man uncertain of his own powers, of his technical skill and of the admiration of his men, yet when he is sent under sealed orders to the Pacific coast of Central America, he accomplishes his mission brilliantly, and fights two successful battles with the same Spanish warship

"There is plenty of action. But there is also an unusual character study." N Y Times Book Rev

Followed by Ship of the line

Forester, C. S.

Commodore Hornblower. Little, Brown 1945 384p

"It is a spirited piece of work, and full of interesting detail where matters naval, military, and diplomatic in that year of decision are concerned." Times Lit Suppl

Followed by Lord Hornblower

Forester, C. S.

Flying colours. Little, Brown 1939 294p

Third book in a series which began with Beat to quarters and Ship of the line. Captain Hornblower, his crippled first mate, Bush, and his servant, Brown, escape from their escort on the way to Paris to be tried for piracy. The story is of their recapture of an English vessel and return to England, where they are covered with honors

Followed by Commodore Hornblower

Forester, C. S.

Hornblower and the Atropos. Little, Brown 1953 325p

This is a series of episodes in the early life of the Captain; a journey across England from Gloucester to London by canal; his part in the funeral of Nelson; and his battles on the coast of Turkey, where he recovers a huge treasure from a sunken English ship

Forester, C. S.

Hornblower and the Hotspur. Little, Brown 1962 344p

ISBN 0-316-28899-3

"The story opens just before Horatio sails on a cruise in his first command. His rank is Commander; his ship something less than a frigate but something more than a sloop; his task to act as the eyes of the Channel Fleet which is to be in position to blockade Brest upon the imminent declaration of hostilities with France. In the course of action Hornblower is detained at sea for almost two years as, in his own inimitable and logically necessary style, he helps cripple the Napoleonic effort to invade England, the last block to conquest of Europe." Best Sellers

Forester, C. S.

Hornblower during the crisis, and two stories: Hornblower's temptation and The last encounter. Little, Brown 1967 174p

ISBN 0-316-28915-9

"Because Forester died before completing this novel, the reader is left with a summary sketch and his own imagination for final details of the plot. For Forester devotees, this will not detract from the essential verve and dash of Hornblower's last chase." Christ Sci Monit

Forester, C. S.

Lieutenant Hornblower. Little, Brown 1952 306p

ISBN 0-316-28907-8

The author "interprets the navy, certainly in its Napoleonic period, with the help of a character that represents the navy at its best and action that is grandly exciting without being melodramatic; helped, too, by a sense of order and a mastery of technique that puts his work on a high plane of artistry." Christ Sci Monit

Forester, C. S.

Lord Hornblower. Little, Brown 1946 322p

ISBN 0-316-28908-6

In this "Hornblower novel Horatio continues his adventures and helps defeat Napoleon by aiding the heir to the Bourbon throne to enter France. Barbara goes to the Congress of Vienna to act as hostess for her brother while Horatio returns to France to visit old friends and renew an old love. When Napoleon escapes from Elba danger threatens Hornblower as he forms a guerrilla band in the south of France. But, saved by the defeat of the French at Waterloo, he returns to the arms of Barbara and new honors as Lord Hornblower." Booklist

Forester, C. S.

Mr. Midshipman Hornblower. Little, Brown 1950 310p

ISBN 0-316-28909-4

Chronologically this is the first book of the Hornblower series. "The book details, in a series of incidents, the genesis of the Hornblower career from the day he first stepped aboard ship as a kings-letter man to the day when he received his commission as Lieutenant in a Spanish prison. Actually the story is told as a series of incidents . . . with only a thin thread of continuity connecting them." Best Sellers

Forester, C. S.

Ship of the line. Little, Brown 1938 298p

In this sequel to Beat to quarters, Captain Hornblower is given command of the ship Sutherland and sent to join the forces blockading the Spanish coast in the war with Napoleon

Followed by Flying colours

Forman, Gayle

Leave Me; A Novel. Gayle Forman. Workman Pub Co. 2016 352 p. (hardcover) $26.95

ISBN 9781616206178; 1616206179

LC 2016006430

In this novel by Gayle Forman, Maribeth Klein is "a harried working mother who's so busy taking care of her husband and twins, she doesn't even realize she's had a heart attack. Surprised to discover that her recuperation seems to be an imposition on those who rely on her, Maribeth does the unthinkable: she packs a bag and leaves. But, as is often the case, once we get where we're going we see our lives from a different perspective." (Publisher's note)

"With humor and pathos, Forman depicts Maribeth's complicated situation and her thoroughly satisfying arc, leaving readers feeling as though they've really accompanied Maribeth on her journey." Pub wkly

Forna, Aminatta

Ancestor stones. Atlantic Monthly Press 2006 317p $24

ISBN 0-87113-944-8

LC 2006-47708

This is an "optimistic, truthful novel and if we accept Ben Okri's notion of writers as 'the barometer of the vitality of the spirit of the nation', then we should be optimistic about an indisputably talented young novelist and for the future of Africa too." Times Lit Suppl

Forna, Aminatta

The **Hired** Man; by Aminatta Forna. Atlantic Monthly Press 2013 304 p. $24

ISBN 0802121918; 9780802121912

LC 2013375768

In this book, by Aminatta Forna, "an English woman, Laura, and her two children arrive in the small Croatian town of Gost. They've come to renovate a . . . blue house. . . . Their neighbour, Duro, offers to help the family with repairs, and . . . he uncovers a mosaic concealed beneath the plaster. As they restore it, hidden resentments among the townfolk begin to surface. What the family doesn't know is that Duro has a long association with the blue house." (Times Literary Supplement)

"A low-key but sophisticated portrait of history--and evil--at a local level." Kirkus

Forna, Aminatta

The **memory** of love; Aminatta Forna. Bloomsbury 2010 445p.

ISBN 978-1-4088-0813-9 Bloomsbury; 1-4088-0813-7 Bloomsbury; 978-0-8021-1965-0 Atlantic Monthly Press; 0-8021-1965-4 Atlantic Monthly Press

LC 2010413660

Commonwealth Writers' Prize: Best Book (2011)

Commonwealth Writers' Prize: Regional Award: Africa: Best Book (2011)

This book tells the story of "British psychiatrist Adrian Lockheart, [who] has fled his failing marriage in England in the hopes of doing some good in Sierra Leone. Adrian becomes fascinated by two of his patients, elderly Elias Cole, a former university professor, and Agnes, a woman lost in a fugue state. The dying Cole reveals to Adrian . . . how he fell in love with a radical colleague's wife in the late 1960s, while Adrian must piece together the details of Agnes' life. Adrian finds a friend in a haunted young surgeon, Kai, who is contemplating leaving the country. Kai questions some of Adrian's risky decisions, such as his intention to track Agnes down once she leaves the hospital, but it is Adrian's involvement with a local woman from Kai's past that shocks the young doctor." (Booklist)

Foroutan, Parnaz

★ The **girl** from the garden; a novel. Parnaz Foroutan. HarperCollins 2015 288 p. $26.99

ISBN 006238838X; 9780062388384

In this novel by Parnaz Foroutan, "Asher Malacouti--the head of a prosperous Jewish family living in the Iranian town of Kermanshah--cannot have the one thing he desires above all: a male son. His young wife Rakhel . . . is made desperate by her failure to conceive, and grows jealous and vindictive. Frustrated by his wife's inability to bear him an heir, Asher makes a fateful choice that will shatter the household and drive Rakhel to dark extremes to save herself." (Publisher's note)

"Foroutan draws on her own family history to integrate the lore and traditions of old Iran. Suspenseful and haunting, this riveting story of jealousy, sacrifice, and betrayal and the intimately drawn characters within will not be easily forgotten." Booklist

Forster, E. M.

The **collected** tales of E. M. Forster. Knopf 1947 308p

The celestial omnibus: The story of a panic; The other side of the hedge; The celestial omnibus; Other kingdom; The curate's friend; The road from Colonus; The eternal moment: The machine stops; The point of it: Mr. Andrews; Co-ordination; The story of the siren; The eternal moment

Forster, E. M.

★ **Howards** End. Knopf 1991 xxxiii, 359p $19

ISBN 0-679-40668-9

LC 91-52997

First published 1910

This novel "deals with an English country house called Howards End and its influence on the lives of the materialistic Wilcoxes, the cultural and idealistic Schlegel sisters, and the poor bank clerk Leonard Bast. The Schlegels try to befriend Bast. Mr. Wilcox, whom Margaret Schlegel later marries, gives him financial advice which ruins him. Helen Schlegel becomes his mistress for a short time and bears his son; thereupon Charles Wilcox thrashes and accidentally kills him. The house passes from intuitive, half-mystical Mrs. Wilcox to her husband's second wife Margaret Schlegel, to Margaret's nephew, Leonard Bast's son. Illustrating Forster's motto 'Only connect,' the house brings together three important elements in English society: money and successful business in the Wilcoxes, culture in the Schlegels, and the lower classes in Leonard Bast." Reader's Ency. 4th edition

Forster, E. M.

Maurice. Norton 1971 256p

"This posthumous novel with a homosexual theme would have been sensational had it been published when written in 1913. Appearing in the 1970's, it is not sensational, but it is an interesting novel—well written as all of E. M. Forster's works are. . . . It is filled with keen insight and sympathetic character analysis, valuable for an understanding of the author and his works." Choice

Forster, E. M.

★ A **passage** to India; with an introduction by P.N. Furbank. Knopf 1991 xxxix, 293p $18

ISBN 0-679-40549-6

First published 1924

"Politics and mysticism are potent forces in India just after World War I. Ronald Heaslop, magistrate of Chandrapore, has asked his mother, Mrs. Moore, to visit him along with his fiancee, Adela Quested. To add to their knowledge of the real India, Dr. Aziz, a young Moslem doctor, offers to take them to the Marabar Caves outside the city. The visit is a shattering experience. Mrs. Moore is struck by the thought that all her ideas about life are no more than the hollow echo she hears in the cave. Adela, entering another cave alone, emerges in a panic and accuses Dr. Aziz of having attacked her in the gloom of the cave. The trial that results from her accusation divides the groups in the city so acutely that a reconciliation appears impossible." Shapiro. Fic for Youth. 3d edition

Forster, E. M.

A **room** with a view; introduction and notes by Malcolm Bradbury. Penguin Books 2000 xxviii, iv, 206p (Penguin twentieth-century classics) pa $9.95

ISBN 0-14-118329-2

LC 99-462172

First published 1908 in the United Kingdom; first United States edition 1911

The novel "is set mostly in Italy, a country which represents for the author the forces of true passion. The heroine, upper-class Lucy Honeychurch, is visiting Italy with a friend. When she regrets that her hotel room has no view, lower-class Mr. Emerson offers the friends his own room and that of his son. Lucy becomes caught between the world of the Emersons and that of Cecil Vyse, the shallow, conventional young man of her own class to whom she becomes engaged on her return to England. Finally, she overcomes her own prejudice and her family's opposition and marries George Emerson." Reader's Ency. 4th edition

Forsyth, Frederick

Avenger. Thomas Dunne Bks. 2003 370p $24.95

ISBN 0-312-31951-7

LC 2003-53163

"World War II, Vietnam, Bosnia, and Cambodia take turns commanding center stage, held together by two protagonists: a middle-age lawyer and an aging business tycoon, who have both suffered devastating losses. The tycoon's loss, that of his grandson on a relief mission in Bosnia, becomes subsumed in the mission of attorney Calvin Dexter, grieving father and former 'Nam tunnel rat, whose mission in life is to bring justice to those who have gotten away with murder. . . . Forsyth's extraordinary care with detail, his solid voice, and his exquisite pacing make this a totally engrossing thriller." Booklist

Forsyth, Frederick

★ The **day** of the jackal. Viking 1971 380p

"Dissident OAS officers hire a mercenary, known by the code name 'Jackal', to assassinate General Charles deGaulle. The officers hope to cash in on the political chaos that would follow. The methodical, ingenious preparations of 'Jackal' are paralleled by the attempts of the combined French law-enforcement agencies to uncover and stop the plot. The suspense is acute." Shapiro. Fic for Youth. 3d edition

Forsyth, Frederick

★ The **Odessa** file. Viking 1972 337p

"Forsyth skillfully blends fact and fiction into a suspenseful and detailed story which is often downright chilling in its credibility." Libr J

Fortier, Anne

Juliet; a novel. Ballantine Books 2010 447p $25

ISBN 978-0-345-51610-7; 0-345-51610-9

LC 2010-02093

"American Julie Jacobs travels to Siena in search of her Italian heritage—and possibly an inheritance—only to discover she is descended from 14th-century Giulietta Tomei, whose love for Romeo defied their feuding families and inspired Shakespeare's Romeo and Juliet. Julie's hunt leads her to the families' descendants, still living in Siena, still feuding, and still struggling under the curse of the friar who wished a plague on both their houses. Julie's unraveling of the past is assisted by a Felliniesque contessa and the contessa's handsome nephew, and complicated by mobsters, police, and a mysterious motorcyclist. . . . Fortier navigates around false clues and twists, resulting in a dense, heavily plotted love story that reads like a Da Vinci Code for the smart modern woman." Publ Wkly

Fortier, Anne

The **lost** sisterhood; a novel. Anne Fortier. Ballantine Books 2014 608 p. illustrations (hardback) $27

ISBN 0345536223; 9780345536228

LC 2014002152

Written by Anne Fortier, this is a "novel about a young scholar who risks her reputation--and her life--on a thrilling journey to prove that the legendary warrior women known as the Amazons actually existed. Oxford lecturer Diana Morgan is an expert on Greek mythology. Her obsession with the Amazons started in childhood when her eccentric grandmother claimed to be one herself--before vanishing without a trace." (Publisher's note)

Fossum, Karin

Bad intentions; translated from the Norwegian by Charlotte Barslund. Houghton Mifflin Harcourt 2011 213p $24

ISBN 978-0-547-48334-4; 0-547-48334-1

LC 2010-49773

Original Norwegian edition, 2008; this translation first published 2010 in the United Kingdom

This Konrad Sejer mystery "focuses on three young men—the disturbingly intuitive Axel Frimann, the bumbling drug addict Philip Reilly, and the painfully sensitive Jon Moreno. They've been friends forever, but something happens that alters the dynamic among them and causes the unbalanced Moreno to abruptly throw himself out of a small boat into a lake outside Oslo called, appropriately, Dead Water. Sejer and his partner, Jacob Skarre, find no evidence of murder, but something is off, as suggested by Frimann and Reilly altering the details of the suicide. When the body of a 17-year-old Vietnamese immigrant, Kim Van Chau, surfaces in another lake, Sejer discovers that the trio were at the same party as Chau the night he went missing." Publ Wkly

Fossum, Karin

Broken; translated from the Norwegian by Charlotte Barslund. Houghton Mifflin Harcourt 2010 265p $25

ISBN 978-0-15-101366-1; 0-15-101366-7

LC 2010-05730

Original Norwegian edition, 2006; English translation first published 2008 in the United Kingdom

"A woman wakes up in the middle of the night. A strange man is in her bedroom. She lies there in silence, paralyzed with fear. The woman is an author and the man one of her characters, one in a long line that waits in her driveway for the time when she'll tell their stories. He is so desperate that he has resorted to breaking into her house and demanding that she begin. He, the author decides, is named Alvar Eide, forty-two years old, single, works in a gallery. He lives a quiet, orderly life and likes it that way—no demands, no unpleasantness. Until the icy winter morning when a young drug addict, skinny and fragile, walks into the gallery." Publisher's note

Fossum, Karin

Eva's eye; Karin Fossum; translated from the Norwegian by James Anderson. Houghton Mifflin Harcourt 2013 304 p. $25

ISBN 9780547738758

LC 2012039063

Author Karin Fossum's book is the first in the Inspector Sejer Mystery book series. "Eva and her young daughter Emma are walking by the river when Emma spots something floating in the water. It's the body of a man, and what's more, a man Eva recognizes. Sejer and Skarre piece together the stories behind two unsolved murders . . . does it all lead back to Eva?" (Publisher's note)

Foster, Lori

Under Pressure; by Lori Foster. Harlequin Books 2017 475 p. (Body Armor) (paperback) $7.99

ISBN 9781460396124; 9780373789931; 0373789939

In this book, by Lori Foster, "Leese Phelps's road hasn't been an easy one, but it's brought him to the perfect job—working for the elite Body Armor security agency. And what his newest assignment lacks in size, she makes up for in fire and backbone. But being drawn to Catalina Nicholson is a dangerous complication, especially since it could be the very man who hired Leese who's threatening her." (Publisher's note)

"Romantic thriller veteran Foster has been honing her skill for a long time, and it's clear she's at the top of her game here." Kirkus

Foulds, Adam

In the wolf's mouth; a novel. Adam Foulds. Farrar Straus & Giroux 2014 336 p. (hardback) $26

ISBN 0374175829; 9780374175825

LC 2013034421

"Set in North Africa and Sicily at the end of World War II, 'In the Wolf's Mouth' follows the Allies' botched 'liberation' attempts as they chased the Nazis north toward the Italian mainland. . . . The book also explores the continuity of organized crime in Sicily through the eyes of two men." (Publisher's note)

"Foulds writes like no one else; while individual scenes are rendered with poetic simplicity, they fit together into an elliptical, complex plot readers will puzzle over long after finishing this novel." Kirkus

Foulds, Adam

The **quickening** maze. Penguin Books 2010 258p pa $15

ISBN 978-0-14-311779-7; 0-14-311779-3

LC 2009-40218

First published 2009 in the United Kingdom

"To be sure, there are inherent drawbacks to historical fiction. To guess at the words and thoughts of long gone people risks inaccuracy at best and disservice at worst. Foulds's Clare is a less sophisticated version of the real poet. But the essence of the man, his sweet, courageous, fine spirit, is real enough in this deeply rewarding fiction." Boston Globe

Founds, Kathleen

When mystical creatures attack! Kathleen Founds. University of Iowa Press 2014 206 p. (John simmons short fiction award) (pbk : alk. paper) $16

ISBN 1609382838; 9781609382834; 9781609382902

LC 2014935648

In this book, by Kathleen Founds, "Ms. Freedman's high school English class writes essays in which mystical creatures resolve the greatest sociopolitical problems of our time. Students include Janice Gibbs . . . and Cody Splunk. Following a nervous breakdown, Ms. Freedman corresponds with Janice and Cody from an insane asylum run on the capitalist model of cognitive-behavioral therapy." (Publisher's note)

"Each story adds a layer of feeling, understanding and history to the characters as they slide back and forth through time and relationships. They handle, gracefully, the whiplash switch between depression and hilarity, between the ghost of a suicidal mother and a love-struck boy promising to invent a time machine. A surreal, dark and very funny collection that has the emotional punch of a novel." Kirkus

Fountain, Ben

★ **Billy** Lynn's long halftime walk; Ben Fountain. Ecco 2012 307 p.

ISBN 0060885599; 9780060885595

LC 2011275813

National Book Award Finalist: Fiction (2012)

This "novel takes place over a single Thanksgiving Day, when the eight soldiers [of the Iraq War] . . . find themselves at the promotional center of an all-American extravaganza, a nationally televised Dallas Cowboys football game. Providing the novel with its moral compass is protagonist Billy Lynn, a 19-year-old virgin from small-town Texas who has been . . . documented by an embedded Fox News camera." (Kirkus Reviews)

Fowler, Christopher, 1953-

Bryant & May; strange tide. Christopher Fowler. Bantam Books 2016 436 p. (Bryant & May : Peculiar Crimes Unit mystery) (hardback) $27

ISBN 9781101887042; 9781101887035; 1101887036

LC 2016029725

In this book in the Peculiar Crimes Unit series, by Christopher Fowler, "near the Tower of London, along the River Thames, the body of a woman has been discovered chained to a stone post and left to drown. Curiously, only one set of footprints leads to the tragic spot. 'The Bride in the Tide,' as the London press gleefully dubs her, has the PCU stumped. Why wouldn't the killer simply dump her body in the river--as so many do?" (Publisher's note)

"Fowler once again perfectly balances farce and deduction." Pub Wkly

Fowler, Karen Joy

The **Jane** Austen book club. Putnam 2004 288p $23.95

ISBN 0-399-15161-3

LC 2003-47244

This novel is essentially a "character study of six people who meet regularly over several months to discuss six of Austen's works. Jocelyn, in her 50s and never married, is the originator of the club, a control freak who handpicked all the members; Sylvia, her good friend, is in a funk because her husband of 32 years has just left her for another woman; Sylvia's daughter, Allegra, is an attractive 30-year-old lesbian who recently broke up with her lover; Prudie is a twentysomething high school French teacher; the much-married Bernadette, 67, is now single; and Grigg, in his 40s, would love to get married." Libr J

Fowler, Karen Joy

★ **Sarah** Canary. Holt & Co. 1991 290p

ISBN 0-8050-1753-4

LC 91-9746

"This novel is similar in scope to E. L. Doctorow's 'Ragtime,' and yet Ms. Fowler's book is as much a dreamscape as a panorama. Each of her 19 chapters has a contemporaneous and often cryptic epigraph from Emily Dickinson's poetry that, amazingly, seems to dictate the narrative that follows." N Y Times Book Rev

Fowler, Karen Joy

★ **We** Are All Completely Beside Ourselves; Karen Joy Fowler. GP Putnam And Sons 2013 320 p. (hardcover) $26.95

ISBN 0399162097; 9780399162091

LC 2013000988

Man Booker Prize Shortlist (2014)

PEN/Faulkner Award for Fiction (2014)

This novel, by Karen Joy Fowler, follows "the Cooke family: Mother and Dad, brother Lowell, sister Fern, and our narrator, Rosemary, who begins her story in the middle. . . . 'I spent the first eighteen years of my life . . . raised with a chimpanzee,' she tells us. . . . 'She was my twin, my funhouse mirror, my whirlwind other half, and I loved her as a sister.'" (Publisher's note)

"A fantastic novel: technically and intellectually complex, while emotionally gripping." Kirkus

Fowler, Karen Joy

What I didn't see and other stories. Small Beer Press 2010 197p $24

ISBN 978-1-932520-68-3; 1-931520-68-2

LC 2010-25911

An "engrossing and thought-provoking set of short stories that mix history, sci-fi, and fantasy elements with a strong literary voice. Whether examining the machinations of a Northern California cult, in 'Always,' or a vague but obviously horrific violent act in the eerie title story, the PEN/Faulkner finalist displays a gift for thrusting familiar characters into bizarre, off-kilter scenarios. Fowler never strays from the anchor of human emotion that makes her characters so believable, even when chronicling the history of epidemics, ancient archeological digs, single family submersibles, or fallen angels." Publ Wkly

Fowler, Therese Anne

★ **Z**; A Novel of Zelda Fitzgerald. Therese Anne Fowler. 1st ed. St. Martin's Press 2013 375 p. (hardcover) $25.99

ISBN 1250028655; 9781250028655

LC 2013003452

This novel by Therese Anne Fowler follows "Jazz Age legends F. Scott and Zelda Fitzgerald. . . . The famous couple have a whirlwind courtship in Montgomery, Ala., where Scott was briefly stationed at the end of WWI, and Zelda was the talk of the town. Then Fowler unfolds the next 20 years: the couple's New York celebrity after 'This Side of Paradise'; the years in Paris with the other 'Lost Generation' expats; and their return to the U.S. to treat Zelda's schizophrenia." (Publishers Weekly)

Fowles, John

★ The **French** lieutenant's woman. Little, Brown 1969 467p

"The setting is Victorian England. The hero is Charles, respectable, well-to-do, thoughtful, progressive. He is engaged to Ernestina, a rich, attractive, but highly conventional girl, but he falls in love with the beautiful, tragic, mysterious Sarah who is known to Lyme Regis (where the action begins) as 'the French lieutenant's woman' because of some disreputable but romantic episode in her past life. The situation, that of the amorous triangle, is familiar in fiction. What makes this book highly original is that it has three possible endings, all different. . . . We have here a highly readable and informative book, compelling, thrilling, erotic, but we are not permitted to relax as if we were reading Dickens or Thackeray. A very modern mind is manipulating us as well as the characters." Burgess. 99 Novels

Fowles, John

The **magus**; a revised version. with a foreword by the author. Little, Brown 1978 656p

ISBN 0-440-35162-6

LC 77-17343

Originally published 1966; this version first published 1977 in the United Kingdom

"With the narrative skill and literary sleight of hand . . . Fowles again provides hours of engrossing entertainment for an audience susceptible to a massive blend of sensuous realism, suspenseful romanticism, hypertheatrical mystification, psychic intervention, and a gallery of unusual or exotic characters in the vivid setting of the golden, craggy, threatening beauty of an isolated Greek island." Booklist

Fox, Lauren

Days of awe; a novel. by Lauren Fox. Alfred A. Knopf 2015 272 p. $24.95

ISBN 0307268128; 9780307268129

LC 2015013533

This novel, by Lauren Fox, "is the story of a woman who, in the wake of her best friend's sudden death, must face the crisis in her marriage, the fury of her almost-teenage daughter, and the possibility of opening her cantankerous heart to someone new. . . . As the relationships that long defined Isabel--wife, mother, daughter, best friend--change before her eyes, Isabel must try to understand who she really is." (Publisher's note)

Frame, Janet, 1924-2004

★ **Between** my father and the king; new and uncollected stories. by Janet Frame. Pgw 2013 256 p. (hardcover) $26.00

ISBN 1619021692; 9781619021693

This book is a collection of stories from award-winning late author Janet Frame. "Thirteen of the 28 stories in this collection were unpublished in her lifetime." Included are "The Gravy Boat," "I Got a Shoes," "A Night at the Opera" and "Gorse is Not People." The last three "concern themselves with the insane and the institutions where they waste away, patronized and abused." (Kirkus Reviews)

Frame, Janet, 1924-2004

In the memorial room; a novel. Janet Frame. Counterpoint 2013 208 p. (hardback) $24

ISBN 1619021757; 9781619021754

LC 2013018057

In this book, author Janet Frame "portray[s] historical fiction writer Harry Gill's travails after being awarded the annual Watercress-Armstrong Fellowship. The award, given in honor of the (fictional) poet Margaret Rose Hurndell, requires him to travel to Menton, [France] where

Hurndell once lived. Harry finds himself struggling to turn his good fortune into productivity." (Publishers Weekly)

Frame, Janet

Prizes; selected short stories. Counterpoint 2009 294p $26

ISBN 978-1-58243-515-2

Frame "is as famous for her epic personal history as for her career. Her first collection, The Lagoon and Other Stories, published in 1954, was written while Frame stayed in a mental hospital. This new anthology spans her lifetime and includes the best of four published collections—The Lagoon and Other Stories, Snowman Snowman: Fables and Fantasies, The Reservoir: Stories and Sketches, and You Are Now Entering the Human Heart—plus five previously unpublished stories. Often melancholy but containing wonderful detail, imagery, and emotion, her works cover a wide range of topics like childhood, madness, relationships, identity, and more." Libr J

Frame, Janet

Towards another summer. Counterpoint 2009 216p $24

ISBN 978-1-58243-476-6; 1-58243-476-X

LC 2008-50515

Written in 1963; first published 2007 in New Zealand

"Like every writer worth remembering, Frame exploits—or creates on the page, to be absolutely puristic about it—her peculiar sensibility, her private window into the universal.. . . Frame's sad, slyly comic fish-out-of-water story . . . looks back to Virginia Woolf in its focus on the tortuous internal positionings beneath the surface of apparently casual conversation." N Y Times Book Rev

Frame, Ronald

★ **Havisham**; By Ronald Frame. Faber & Faber 2013 357 p. $26

ISBN 0571288286; 1250037271; 9780571288281; 9781250037275

Written by Ronald Frame, this novel describes how "Before she became the immortal and haunting Miss Havisham of [Charles Dickens's novel] 'Great Expectations,' she was Catherine, a young woman with all of her dreams ahead of her." This book "unfurls the psychological trauma that made young Catherine into Miss Havisham and cursed her to a life alone, roaming the halls of the mansion in the tatters of the dress she wore for the wedding she was never to have." (Publisher's note)

Frame, Ronald

The **lantern** bearers; a novel. Counterpoint 2001 224p $24

ISBN 1-58243-155-8

LC 2001-28897

First published 1999 in the United Kingdom

"Neil Pritchard, told that he will die of cancer within two years, presses forward with his book on the Scottish composer Euan Bone. He also tells in this book the story of his encounter with Bone shortly before the composer's death. Neil, 14 then and a superb boy soprano, was summering with his aunt in a southern Scottish coastal town when Bone enlisted him to help prepare a vocal score based on a Robert Louis Stevenson essay. All went beautifully, and Neil was falling in love with Bone; then his voice changed, ending the collaboration. . . . In a resentful funk, he told the lie that Bone had molested him, which led, Neil came to think, to Bone's demise." Booklist

Frampton, Megan

The **Duke's** Guide to Correct Behavior. HarperCollins 2014 384 p. $5.99

ISBN 0062352202; 9780062352200

In this novel by Megan Frampton "when Miss Lily Russell crosses the threshold of the Duke of Rutherford's stylish townhouse, she knows she has come face to face with sensual danger. As for the duke himself, it was bad enough when his unknown child landed on his doorstep. Now Lily, with her unassuming beauty, has aroused his most wicked fantasies--and, shockingly, his desire to change his wanton ways." (Publisher's note)

"Frampton's romance has charm to spare, and readers will find it impossible to resist her flawless characterization, fanciful plotting, and deliciously fizzy wit." Booklist

Frampton, Megan

Put Up Your Duke; Megan Frampton. HarperCollins 2015 384 p. (paperback) $7.99

ISBN 9780062352224; 0062352229

In this romance novel, by Megan Frampton, part of the "Dukes Behaving Badly" series, "to keep his estate afloat, the new Duke of Gage must honor an agreement to marry Lady Isabella Sawford. Stunningly beautiful, utterly tempting, she's also a bag of wedding night nerves, so Nicholas decides to wait to do his duty. . . .To his utter shock, Nicholas discovers that no previous exploits were half as pleasurable as wooing his own wife." (Publisher's note)

"Rich in subtle characterization, deftly seasoned with plenty of piquant wit, and spiced with just the right amount of sexy passion, the second tale in the Dukes Behaving Badly series (following The Duke's Guide to Correct Behavior, 2014) is a romantic tour de force. With this splendidly satisfying love story, Frampton proves that she is one of the rising new stars in the historical romance genre." Booklist

Francis, David

Wedding Bush Road; a novel. David Francis. Counterpoint Press 2016 263 p. (hardcover) $25

ISBN 9781619028746; 9781619027879

LC 2016020224

In this book, by David Francis, "when he learns of his mother's ailing health, Daniel Rawson must leave Los Angeles and travel half a world away to the family's horse farm on Wedding Bush Road, one hundred miles outside of Melbourne. Estranged from his parents, Daniel is hesitant to revisit their history: long divorced, his mother still maintains the farm having put out her cheating, rakish husband, and even in these later years her anger burns brightly." (Publisher's note)

"Domestic drama with an offbeat, rural flavor." Kirkus

Francis, Dick

★ **Bolt**. Putnam 1987 318p

LC 86-25167

"As adept on a race-course as he is in an Eaton Square drawing room, Fielding is a match for any menace. . . . In mystery circles, Francis again demonstrates that he is both a win and a nice read." Time

Francis, Dick

✓**Even** money; [by] Dick Francis and Felix Francis. G.P. Putnam's Sons 2009 350p $26.95

ISBN 978-0-399-15591-8; 0-399-15591-0

LC 2009-24109

"Ever since he started writing with his son Felix, Dick Francis seems to have found fresh inspiration at the racetrack." N Y Times Book Rev

Francis, Dick

Longshot. Harper & Row 1990 320p

LC 90-41145

"Francis remains one of the most incandescent talents in the mystery game. His plot positively shimmers, and his sleuth easily hurdles that always difficult jump from credible character to believable amateur detective. Perhaps best of all, Francis extracts a wealth of weird and wonderful shadings from his suspects." Booklist

Francis, Dick

Nerve. Harper & Row 1964 273p

"Rob Finn, a young steeplechase jockey, had been near Art Mathews when Mathews shot himself at the Dunstable races. When asked why the man had killed himself, Finn replied, 'Mr Kellar might know.' Then other jockeys began having trouble and finally Finn was involved." Publisher's note

Francis, Dick

Proof. Harper & Row 1985 334p

LC 84-15940

"Wine merchant Tony Beach is engaged to supply a horse trainer's garden party. During the party a horse van careens into the marquee, bringing disaster. One of the casualties is a restaurant owner suspected of serving cheap liquor under false labels, and Beach, as an expert taster, is enlisted to track the bootleggers. Francis gives the same fascinating and authoritative detail about the liquor trade as he does about the racing world (which figures intermittently in this book as background)." Libr J

Francis, Dick

Smokescreen. Harper & Row 1973 213p

First published 1972 in the United Kingdom

"Even given Francis's high standards {this novel is} an elegant construction, in which we see the parts and their potentialities, and are as much excited to discover how he put them together as what happens when he does. . . . A symphony tumultuous with thrills." Times Lit Suppl

Francis, Dick

★ **Whip** hand. Harper & Row 1980 293p

First published 1979 in the United Kingdom

"The book contains moments of breathless suspense, much information about the sport of kings, and perceptive insights into Halley's character that explain some of the reasons for the breakdown of his marriage." Shapiro. Fic for Youth. 3d edition

Francis, Felix

Dick Francis's Damage; a novel of suspense. Felix Francis. Putnam Adult 2014 400 p. (hardcover : acid-free paper) $26.95

ISBN 0399168222; 9780399168222

LC 2014026856

In this suspense novel, by Felix Francis, "undercover investigator Jeff Hinkley is assigned by the British Horseracing Authority to look into the activities of a suspicious racehorse trainer, but as he's tailing his quarry through the Cheltenham Racing Festival, the last thing he expects to witness is a gruesome murder. Could it have something to do with the reason the trainer was banned in the first place--the administration of illegal drugs to his horses?" (Publisher's note)

Another title in this series is:

Front Runner (2015)

Franck, Julia

Back to Back; by Julia Franck and translated by Anthea Bell. Grove Press 2013 320 p. $24

ISBN 0802121675; 9780802121677

This book by Julia Franck "begins in 1954, and centers around a single family living in Berlin in the socialist East. The mother, Käthe, is a sculptor of Jewish heritage, who has been leveraging her party connections in order to get more important and significant commissions. Devoted entirely to becoming a success in the socialist state, she is a cruel and completely unaffectionate mother, putting the party above her children. Käthe's hard-nosed brutality . . . means Thomas and Ella are unable to live the lives they want." (Publisher's note)

Franck, Julia

The **blindness** of the heart; translated from the German by Anthea Bell. Grove Press 2010 424p $24.95

ISBN 978-0-8021-1967-4; 0-8021-1967-0

Original German edition, 2007; this translation first published 2009 in the United Kingdom

The novel's "central character, Helene Würsich, is the daughter of a printer who returns maimed and ruined from the battlefields of World War I, leaving Helene and her older sister Martha in the power of their mentally unstable mother Selma, 'the foreign woman'—meaning Jewish, in the disapproving view of the local community. Martha, a nurse, develops a taste for drugs while clever but introverted Helen, unsympathetically treated by Selma, never fulfills her potential. A legacy saves the family's fortunes, the girls move to Berlin to live with a racy aunt and Helene falls in love with a student, only to lose him. As the political mood darkens and Selma is incarcerated for possible hereditary disorders, Helene's future is shaped by another man, Wilhelm, a keen supporter of the new regime who nevertheless agrees to risk 'racial disgrace' and arrange false papers certifying her Aryan descent. But their marriage brings no happiness and a prologue and epilogue expose the emotional damage arising from a long sequence of disasters." Kirkus

Frank, Dorothea Benton

Folly Beach. Harper 2011 358p $25.99

ISBN 978-0-06-196127-4; 0-06-196127-2

"The recently widowed protagonist's journey to rediscovering joy and love will thrill readers, especially with the addition of a suavely integrated story-within-a-story involving a one-woman play about the lovers who wrote Porgy and Bess. There's a certain authenticity to the lives Frank tells that will resonate with many women. Frank's telling of this tale will help readers celebrate love and sexuality after 60." Publ Wkly

Frank, Pat

Alas, Babylon; a novel. Lippincott 1959 253p

"This is an extraordinarily real picture of human beings numbed by catastrophe but still driven by the unconquerable determination of living creatures to keep on being alive. The writing is simple and straightforward and practical." New Yorker

Frankel, Laurie

Goodbye for now; a novel. Laurie Frankel. 1st ed. Doubleday 2012 289 p. (paperback) $15.00; (hardcover) $25.95

ISBN 9780307951274; 0385536186; 9780385536189

LC 2011051266

This novel, by Laurie Frankel, follows "Sam Elling[, who] works for an internet dating company . . . [and] meets the love of his life, . . . Meredith. . . . When Meredith's grandmother . . . dies suddenly, Sam . . . create[s] a computer program that will allow Meredith to have one last conversation with her grandmother . . . from all her correspondence. . . . Meredith loves it, and the couple begins to wonder if this is something that could help more people through their grief." (Publisher's note)

Frankel, Laurie

This is how it always is; a novel. Laurie Frankel. Flatiron Books 2017 336 p. (ebook) $60; (hardback) $25.99

ISBN 9781250118523; 9781250088550

LC 2016037633

This novel, by Laurie Frankel, is "about revelations, transformations, fairy tales, and family. And it's about the ways this is how it always is: Change is always hard and miraculous and hard again, parenting is always a leap into the unknown with crossed fingers and full hearts, children grow but not always according to plan. And families with secrets don't get to keep them forever." (Publisher's note)

"This is a wonderfully contradictory story—heartwarming and generous, yet written with a wry sensibility." Pub Wkly

Franklin, Ariana

Mistress of the art of death. Putnam 2007 384p $25.95

ISBN 978-0-399-15414-0; 0-399-154140

LC 2006-24710

"It is 1171 in Cambridge, England, and Henry II is beside himself. Four children have been found murdered and mutilated, and the townsfolk of Cambridge are blaming the Jews, who have taken shelter in the castle. King Henry is less concerned about the murderer than the tax revenue he is losing while the Jewish community languishes in the fortress. He appeals to the king of Sicily to send him a master of the art of death—one who can look at the deceased and determine how he or she died. Adelia, a mistress of this art, arrives with a group of returning pilgrims. Along with a eunuch escort named Mansur and Simon of Naples, a Jew with an affinity for detection, she must piece together the mystery of these hideous crimes before the monster kills again. I. . . This novel will surely please mystery fans as well as lovers of historical fiction." Libr J

Franklin, Ariana

The **serpent's** tale. G. P. Putnam's Sons 2008 371p $25.95

ISBN 978-0-399-15464-5

LC 2007-38585

"This excellent adventure delivers high drama and lively scholarship from its heroine's feminist perspective." N Y Times Book Rev

Franklin, Ariana

The **Siege** Winter; Ariana Franklin; Samantha Norman. HarperCollins 2015 352 p. $25.99

ISBN 0062282565; 9780062282569

This novel by Ariana Franklin and Samantha Norman is a "tour de force mystery and murder, adventure and intrigue, a battle for a crown, told by two courageous young women whose fates are intertwined in twelfth century England's devastating civil war." (Publisher's note)

"The cheeky wit and precise descriptions that were Franklin's hallmarks are as sharp as ever, and the major characters are delightfully human. The book also has a genuine feel for medieval life and times. This unique collaboration is a worthy conclusion to one remarkable career and a promising beginning to another." Booklist

Franklin, Miles

★ **My** brilliant career. Putnam 1980 232p

First published 1901 in Scotland

"The novel's heroine, Sybylla Melvyn, a girl of sixteen, rebels against the stagnant life on her parents' dairy farm at Possum Gully and against the inevitable fate of teaching or marriage that awaits her; both forms of 'slavery' are distasteful to her but she sees marriage as particularly degrading. Rescued temporarily by a period with her affluent grandmother at the congenial station homestead, Caddagat, she faces interwoven problems—her sexual ambivalence which is characterized by strong physical attraction to eligible young squatter, Harold Beecham, and an equally strong physical revulsion." Oxford Companion to Australian Lit

Followed by The end of my career

Franklin, Tom

Crooked letter, crooked letter. William Morrow 2010 274p

ISBN 0-06-059466-7; 978-0-06-059466-4

LC 2010005423

"Franklin writes with quiet economy. There are no great flights of dialogue or rambling description; everything is sharply focused to achieve its purpose. The resulting novel winds through its path as crookedly as the letters of its title, and arrives at a nicely achieved ending. It's an ending that isn't without complication but, given what precedes it, a conclusion that is fitting and right." Denver Post

Franklin, Tom

Hell at the breech; a novel. Morrow 2003 520p $23.95

ISBN 0-688-16741-1

LC 2002-40982

"When a storekeeper campaigning for the state legislature is assassinated, Mitcham Beat is swept by a wave of violence that includes lynchings and shootings, barn burnings, and robberies. A gang of hooded men known as the Hell-at-the-Breech gang is terrorizing the community, and the only man to stop them is an aging sheriff ready to retire with his whiskey bottle. It sounds like the wild, wild West, but Franklin. . . has taken a little-known event in Alabama history, the Mitcham Beat War, and transformed it into a Faulknerian tale of bloody revenge and vigilante justice." Libr J

Franzen, Jonathan

★ The **corrections**. Farrar, Straus & Giroux 2001 568p $25

ISBN 0-374-12998-3

LC 2001-33478

National Book Award: Fiction (2001)

The novel "has the absorbing treacheries of married life, the comic squalors of cruise-shop travel and the shenanigans of global capitalism. It also has language that builds in powerful, rolling strides. And it has characters, the separately unraveling Lamberts, who get very deeply under your skin." Time

Franzen, Jonathan, 1959-

★ **Freedom**. Farrar, Straus and Giroux 2010 562p $28

ISBN 0374158460; 9780374158460

LC 2010-10273

This multigenerational novel follows the fortunes of the Berglund family of St. Paul.

"Patty and Walter Berglund meet at the University of Minnesota, settle in an initially rundown section of St. Paul, and raise two precocious kids. She's a former student athlete rebelling against her politician mom back East; he's a lawyer–turned–environmental advocate bristling at the legacy of his distant, alcoholic dad. Each has a charged relationship with Walter's ex-roommate, alt-rock musician Richard Katz, but the pair's biggest obstacle to happiness is each other — and themselves. Franzen performs a kind of literary MRI on the marriage, micro-slicing its many nuances. He innately grasps how desires can shift in an instant, and how getting what we want can lead to disappointment or self-doubt. And he remains a keen observer of modern culture. . . . Freedom isn't flawless: Patty's journal reads more like Franzen than his character, and he gets sidetracked by quirky tangents. But this is a deep dive into a fascinating family that feels very real, and fully grounded in our time." Entertainment Wkly

Franzen, Jonathan, 1959-

★ **Purity**; a novel. Jonathan Franzen. Farrar, Straus & Giroux 2015 563 p. (hardcover) $28

ISBN 9780374239213

LC 2015010131

In this novel, by Jonathan Franzen, "Young Pip Tyler . . . doesn't have a clue who her father is, why her mother chose to live as a recluse with an invented name, or how she'll ever have a normal life. . . . A glancing encounter with a German peace activist leads Pip to an internship in South America with The Sunlight Project, an organization that traffics in all the secrets of the world--including, Pip hopes, the secret of her origins." (Publisher's note)

"... here, Franzen is burrowing deep into each person's questionable sense of his or her own goodness and suggests that the moral rot can metastasize to the levels of corporations and government. And yet the novel's prose never bogs down into lectures, and its various back stories are as forceful as the main tale of Purity's fate. Franzen is much-mocked for his primacy in the literary landscape (something he himself mocks when Charles grouses about "a plague of literary Jonathans"). But here, he's admirably determined to think big and writ e well about our darkest emotional corners. An expansive, brainy, yet inviting novel that leaves few foibles unexplored." Kirkus

Frayn, Michael

Headlong; a novel. Metropolitan Bks. 1999 342p

ISBN 0-8050-6285-8

LC 99-20717

Martin Clay "seems to have all he might reasonably wish for: a new career as an art historian, a loving wife, an adorable baby daughter, and a summer cottage in the English countryside, where he is supposed to be completing his book on fifteenth-century Netherlandish art. Instead, he stumbles upon an unsigned Brueghel (at least, he's almost positive it's a Brueghel) stashed in a fireplace of his neighbor's crumbling estate. Overwhelmed by high-minded professional curiosity and base greed, Martin resolves to acquire it by whatever means necessary. What follows is part detective story, part art-history lesson, part cautionary tale, and entirely funny." New Yorker

Frayn, Michael

Spies; a novel. Metropolitan Bks. 2002 261p

ISBN 0-8050-7058-3

LC 2001-39840

"A compelling story about secrecy and betrayal. . . . What is truly remarkable about this novel, though, is the way Frayn perfectly captures the dynamics of childhood friendships." Booklist

Frazier, Charles, 1950-

★ **Cold** Mountain. Atlantic Monthly Press 1997 356p $19.95

ISBN 0-87113-679-1

LC 97-275

"After Inman, a Confederate soldier, is gravely wounded outside Petersburg, he decides to flee the war. With his fearsome LeMat's pistol for protection, he sets out for Cold Mountain, where he was raised and where he left Ada, the woman he loves, on uncertain terms four years earlier. In the meantime, Ada, a preacher's daughter transplanted to the country from Charleston, has begun to learn the hard reality of a farmer's life. This novel's landscape is finely drawn, full of dark beauty and presentiment, and so are its characters. They give voice to a classical, peculiarly American feeling of nostalgia—the pain of returning home" New Yorker

Frazier, Charles, 1950-

Nightwoods; a novel. Random House 2011 259p $26

ISBN 978-1-4000-6709-1; 1-4000-6709-X

LC 2011-14629

"At the center of Frazier's tale — set in Appalachia in the early 1960s — is Luce, a scarred woman with a dark past who's taken a job as the caretaker of an abandoned old lodge. The solitude suits her. . . . But the outside inevitably intrudes on Luce's isolated retreat, first in the form of her recently murdered sister's mute twin children, then with the unexpected appearance of the murderer, Bud, who's chasing the two terrified young witnesses to his crime. Not surprisingly, things get messy, but Nightwoods is no typical thriller. It hits hard because you come to care so much about the characters, all of them drawn with that precise enchanted prose. By the book's climactic scenes in the shadowy mountain forest that gives Nightwoods its title, the unhurried, poetic suspense is both difficult to bear and impossible to shake." Entertainment Wkly

Frazier, Charles, 1950-

Thirteen moons; a novel. Random House 2006 422p $26.95

ISBN 0-375-50932-1

LC 2007-270081

The author "uses his sense of time and place and his lyrical, pointillist prose to give the reader an aching appreciation of the Indians' plight. . . . [He] recounts Will's melancholy adventures with plenty of narrative brio, giving the reader a succession of suspenseful—and in some cases touching—set pieces." N Y Times (Late N Y Ed)

Freedman, Benedict

Mrs. Mike; the story of Katherine Mary Flannigan. by Benedict and Nancy Freedman; drawings by Ruth D. McCrea. Coward-McCann 1947 312p

"At 16, Boston-reared Katherine Mary O'Fallon is sent north to Alberta, Canada, to find relief for the pleurisy from which she has been suffering. While residing with her Uncle John, she falls in love with Mike, a handsome Canadian Mounted Policeman. Life in the wilderness in the early 1900s is harsh, but the newly married couple finds joy and challenge in their adventures." Shapiro. Fic for Youth. 3d edition

Freeman, Anna

The **fair** fight; a novel. Anna Freeman. Riverhead Books 2015 480 p. (hardback) $27.95

ISBN 1594633290; 9781594633294

LC 2014019046

This novel, by Anna Freeman, is "set in . . . late eighteenth-century England. . . . Born in a brothel, Ruth doesn't expect much for herself beyond abuse. . . . That is until she meets pugilist patron George Dryer and discovers her true calling--fighting bare knuckles in the prize rings of Bristol. Manor-born Charlotte has a different cross to bear. . . . After a disastrous, life-changing fight sidelines Ruth, the two women meet." (Publisher's note)

"Freeman doesn't shy away from the grim realities of sexism, homophobia, and illness that afflict the lives of her characters, and readers will appreciate her blunt look at the English caste system. Freeman is at her best in moments when the characters transcend their societal roles and break free of expectations." Booklist

Freeman, Brian

Goodbye to the dead; Brian Freeman. Quercus 2016 416 p. (A Jonathan Stride novel) $26.99

ISBN 9781623659110; 1623659116

LC 2015956914

In this novel, by Brian Freeman, "Detective Jonathan Stride's first wife, Cindy, died of cancer eight years ago, but her ghost hangs over Stride's relationship with current lover, and fellow detective, Serena Dial. When Serena witnesses a brutal murder outside a Duluth bar, she stumbles onto a case with roots that go all the way back to the last year of Cindy Stride's life." (Publisher's note)

"Freeman skillfully weaves together diverse story lines, from the old murder to a sex-slavery operation, with twists that build suspense, in this fine, character-driven addition to a strong series." Booklist

Freeman, Brian

Spilled blood; a novel. Brian Freeman. Silver Oak 2012 347 p. (hardcover) $24.95; (downloadable audio) $59.95

ISBN 1402798121; 9781402798122; 9781402798382; 9781455135028; 9781623651275

LC 2011279593

This book by Brian Freeman "pits the residents of two southwestern Minnesota towns against each other. One town is home to a thriving chemical research plant; the other, downstream, is the center of a cancer cluster (five girls have died from leukemia in a couple of years). This town's residents blame the company for dumping toxic chemicals in the river. Tensions finally result in a murder." (Booklist)

Freeman, Castle

All that I have; a novel. [by] Castle Freeman Jr. Steerforth Press 2009 164p pa $13.95

ISBN 978-1-58642-151-9; 1-58642-151-4

LC 2008-43223

"Sheriff Lucian Wing, the narrator of Freeman's wonderfully wry fourth novel, is a laconic, old-fashioned lawman who discovers an outpost of nefarious Russians in his sleepy Vermont county. Wing's Fargo-esque delivery is hysterical, but what makes this spare tale a standout is Freeman's keen ear for dialogue and his affection for the quietly complex characters of small-town life." People

Freeman, Castle

★ **Go** with me; [by] Castle Freeman, Jr. Steerforth Press 2008 160p $21.95

ISBN 978-1-58642-139-7; 1-58642-137-9

LC 2007-42572

"This nimble thriller is the literary equivalent of a fierce bantamweight fighter: Short but muscular and lightning quick, it packs a surprising punch . . . . Freeman has a flawless ear for dialogue and a sharp eye for quirky detail." People

Frei, Max

The **stranger's** magic; Max Frei ; translated by Polly Gannon and Astamur Moore. Overlook Press 2012 320 p. $27.95

ISBN 1590204794; 9781590204795

This is the third book in the "Labyrinth of Echo" series. Max Frei has "come into some good luck by having been placed in a position of power in the Unified Kingdom, chasing around the ever-weird city of Echo 'to investigate cases of illegal magic and battle trespassing monsters from other worlds.'" Frei "investigates some . . . capers, including the possibility of a palace coup, an attempted murder and a bungled burglary." (Kirkus)

French, Albert

★ **Billy**. Viking 1993 214p

ISBN 0-670-85013-6

LC 93-14676

"The story, once in motion, gathers momentum like a landslide. . . . 'Billy' is tragedy in the classical mode, mythic in the sense that instead of the surprise, the twists of plot we might discover in a more typical contemporary novel, here we are confirmed in our worst dreads as destiny immutably and shockingly unfolds." NY Times Book Rev

French, Marilyn

★ The **women's** room. Summit Bks. 1977 471p

LC 77-24918

"Dealing with the interlocking lives of dozens of American women, who know each other at some point of time between the 1950s and the 70s, and concentrating in particular on the evolution of Mira from petted baby girl wife to independent womanhood, it speaks from the heart to women everywhere. . . . {The author's} dialogue, her characterizations, her knowledge of the changing relationships, sexual and otherwise, between men and women in a complex world of shifting values, are all extraordinary. Mira, the suburban housewife and mother, the unexpected divorcee groping her way out of a marriage that she never understood, going back to Harvard at 38 as a graduate student, meeting other women, some tougher, some weaker, coming to terms with herself against all odds, even if it means a bleak and lonely parting from a man she loves, is memorable." Publ Wkly

French, Nicci

★ **Blue** Monday; Nicci French. Pamela Dorman Books/ Viking 2012 322 p. map (Frieda Klein novels)

ISBN 0670023361; 9780670023363

LC 2011039747

Other titles in this series are: Tuesday's gone (2013); Waiting for Wednesday (2014); Thursday's children (2016); Friday on my mind (2016); Dark Saturday (2017); Sunday Silence (2018)

"The abduction of five-year-old Matthew Farraday provokes national outcry and a desperate police hunt. And when his face is splashed over the newspapers, psychotherapist Frieda Klein is left troubled: one of her patients has been relating dreams in which he has a hunger for a child. A child he can describe in perfect detail, a child the spitting image of Matthew. Detective Chief Inspector Karlsson doesn't take Frieda's concerns seriously until a link emerges with an unsolved abduction twenty years ago and he summons Frieda to interview the victim's sister." (Publisher's note)

"With its smart plot, crisp prose, and a stunning final twist, this is psychological suspense at its best. Absolutely riveting." Booklist

French, Nicci

★ **Thursday's** children; Nicci French. Penguin Books 2015 368 p. illustrations (Frieda Klein mysteries) (softcover) $16

ISBN 9780143127215; 0143127217

LC 2014038883

"Frieda Klein is uninterested in catching up on old times when her former classmate, Maddie Capel, shows up at her door—until she hears about Maddie's troubled daughter, Becky. The teenager claims she was raped in her own bed one night while her mother was downstairs. Her assailant left her with a warning: 'Don't think of telling anyone, sweetheart. Nobody will believe you.' And no one does—except Frieda." (Publisher's note)

"A skillfully woven plot and deftly drawn characters complement the central mystery, which engages and satisfies while developing the series arc." Pub Wkly

French, Nicci

Tuesday's gone; Nicci French. Pamela Dorman Books/ Viking 2013 384 p. (hardcover) $27.95

ISBN 0670025674; 9780670025671

LC 2012040052

This novel, by Nicci Gerard and Sean French, writing as Nicci French, follows their character Frieda Klein. "A London social worker makes a routine home visit only to discover her client, Michelle Doyce, serving afternoon tea to a naked, decomposing corpse. . . . Chief Inspector Karlsson again calls upon Frieda for help. She discovers that the body belongs to Robert Poole, con man extraordinaire. But Frieda can't shake the feeling that the past isn't done with her yet." (Publisher's note)

French, Nicci

Waiting for Wednesday; Nicci French. Pamela Dorman Books/Viking 2014 384 p. map (Freida Klein) hbk $27.95

ISBN 0670015776; 9780670015771

LC 2013016793

"In [Nicci] French's third novel . . . featuring London psychotherapist Frieda Klein, seemingly average mother Ruth Lennox is found murdered without apparent reason. As details of her secret life emerge, the cast of characters expose a web of tangled lives. Frieda gets involved when her teenage niece befriends the dead woman's son. The pace picks up after one of Frieda's patients, during therapy, makes an offhand remark that leads Frieda to believe a serial killer is at work." (Library Journal)

"French's darkly ambitious tale piles on the complications until you beg for mercy. Hard-core fans of detective work as a vehicle for revealing the depths of the human soul will find it irresistible." Kirkus

French, Tana, 1973-

★ **Broken** Harbor; Tana French. Viking 2012 464 p. (alk. paper) $27.95

ISBN 9780670023653

LC 2011042397

This crime novel by Tana French follows "Mick 'Scorcher' Kennedy, the Dublin Garda's top homicide detective. . . . When he and his brand-new partner are assigned a savage triple homicide in a distant housing development, abandoned before completion when the Irish housing bubble burst, Scorcher is shaken; the development is located in a place that gave him the best -- and worst -- moments of his life." (Booklist)

French, Tana, 1973-

Faithful Place; a novel. Viking 2010 400p $25.95

ISBN 978-0-670-02187-1; 0-670-02187-3

LC 2010-03212

In this book, the "third novel about the Dublin Murder squad, [Tana] French takes readers into the mind of Frank Mackey, the hotheaded mastermind of 'The Likeness,' as he wrestles with his own past and the family, the lover, and the neighborhood he thought he'd left behind for good." (Publisher's note)

"The first thing that Ms. French does so well in 'Faithful Place' is to inhabit fully a scrappy, shrewd, privately heartbroken middle-aged man. The second is to capture the Mackey family's long-brewing resentments in a way that's utterly realistic on many levels. Sibling rivalries, class conflicts, old grudges, adolescent flirtations and memories of childhood violence are all deftly embedded in this novel, as is the richly idiomatic Dublinese." N Y Times (Late N Y Ed)

French, Tana

In the woods. Viking 2007 429p $24.95

ISBN 978-0-670-03860-2; 0-670-03860-1

LC 2006-33498

French sets a vivid scene for her complex characters, who seem entirely capable of doing the unexpected. Drawn by the grim nature of her plot and the lyrical ferocity of her writing, even smart people who should know better will be able to lose themselves in these dark woods. N Y Times Book Rev

French, Tana

The **likeness**. Viking 2008 448p $25.95

ISBN 978-0-670-01886-4; 0-670-01886-4

LC 2008-003940

"Cassie Maddox, the partner of the self-destructing detective who narrated 'In the Woods,' is drawn into a ménage à cinq of college students living a seeming charmed existence in an Irish country house. One of the five, a girl who is Cassie's doppelgänger and has been living under an alias Cassie once used as an undercover narcotics agent, turns up murdered in a ruined cottage. Cassie is given the unlikely task of pretending to be a woman who was pretending to be a woman whom Cassie once pretended to be. As you might expect, 'The Likeness' wrestles with matters of identity and intimacy as its heroine comes to prefer this triply false life to her real one. The hypnotic prose and eerie atmosphere conspire to make this ostensible mystery novel much, much more than it appears to be." Salon.com

French, Tana, 1973-

★ The **secret** place; Tana French. Viking 2014 464 p. $27.95

ISBN 0670026328; 9780670026326

LC 2014004500

In this novel by Tana French "Detective Stephen Moran has been waiting for his chance to [join] Dublin's Murder Squad. A board where the girls at St. Kilda's School can pin up their secrets anonymously, is normally a mishmash of gossip and covert cruelty, but today someone has used it to reignite the stalled investigation into [a] murder. Stephen joins forces with the abrasive Detective Antoinette Conway to find out who and why." (Publisher's note)

"Beyond the murder mystery, which leaves the reader in suspense throughout, the novel explores the mysteries of friendship, loyalty and betrayal, not only among adolescents, but within the police force as well. Everyone is this meticulously crafted novel might be playing--or being played by--everyone else." Kirkus

Freudenberger, Nell

The **dissident**. Ecco 2006 427p $25.95

ISBN 978-0-06-075871-4; 0-06-075871-6

LC 2006-42617

This "novel centers on a Chinese performance artist and former political prisoner, who travels to Los Angeles to accept a teaching fellowship at a prestigious girls' school. His hosts are a well-off family whose matriarch, Cece Travers, is trapped in a loveless marriage with Gordon, a psychiatrist obsessed with tracing his genealogy back to 'the crossing ancestor.' A large cast of secondary characters includes Gordon's sister Joan, an accomplished but discontented novelist who stays skinny 'by worrying,' and his charming but irresponsible brother Phil, who is single-mindedly in love with Cece. Freudenberger demonstrates great talent for capturing the subtleties of cross-cultural and intergenerational relationships, as the dissident's struggles with his past and with his art intersect with Cece's unravelling." New Yorker

Freudenberger, Nell

★ The **newlyweds**; a novel. Nell Freudenberger. Knopf 2012 337 p.

ISBN 0307268845; 9780307268846

LC 2011044116

This book by Nell Freudenberger "examines a marriage arranged via the Internet. . . . Amina wanted to escape from her family's straitened circumstances in Bangladesh; George wanted someone who "did not play games". . . . So here she is, in the fall of 2005 in . . . Rochester, N.Y., recently married, working in retail while she studies for a teaching certificate. . . . [S]he's uncertain how to bridge the gulf between [her] two selves. She makes a much-needed friend in George's cousin Kim . . . so when it turns out that she and George have been hiding something important from Amina, it's . . . shattering. However, it does prompt George to agree to bring Amina's parents to America, and she goes to collect them in Bangladesh, where several old family conflicts flare anew." (Kirkus Reviews)

Fridlund, Emily

★ **History** of wolves; a novel. Emily Fridlund. Atlantic Monthly Press 2017 288 p. (hardback) $25; paperback $16; ebook $25

ISBN 9780802125873; 9780802127389; 9780802189776

LC 2016027800

Man Booker Prize Shortlist (2017)

In this novel, by Emily Fridlund, "fourteen-year-old Linda. . . . is drawn to the enigmatic, attractive Lily and new history teacher Mr. Grierson. When Mr. Grierson is charged with possessing child pornography, the implications of his arrest deeply affect Linda. . . . The young Gardner family moves in across the lake and Linda finds herself welcomed . . . as a babysitter. . . . Over the course of a few days, Linda makes a set of choices that reverberate throughout her life." (Publisher's note)

"The novel has a tinge of fairy tale, wavering on the blur between good and evil, thought and action. But the sharp consequences for its characters make it singe and sing—a literary tour de force." Kirkus

Includes bibliographical references and index

Friedman, Daniel

★ **Don't** ever get old; Daniel Friedman. Minotaur Books 2012 viii, 294 p.p

ISBN 0312606931; 9780312606930

LC 2012005485

This book "introduces a highly unusual hero, 87-year-old, politically incorrect Buck Schatz, a former member of the Memphis PD. . . . [H] e agrees to a request to visit Jim Wallace, a soldier he served with in WWII who's on his deathbed. Wallace reveals that Heinrich Ziegler, the SS officer who ran the POW camp where both Schatz and Wallace were imprisoned, survived the war. On top of that shocker, Wallace reveals that he facilitated the Nazi's escape in exchange for a gold bar." (Publishers Weekly)

Friedman, Daniel

Riot most uncouth; a Lord Byron mystery. Daniel Friedman. Minotaur Books 2015 304 p. (hardcover) $24.99

ISBN 9781250027597

LC 2015033767

In this novel, by Daniel Friedman, set in "1807, Cambridge, England, a young woman is murdered . . . nobody knows what to do about it. . . . In a situation such as this, it's very easy for a gentleman with a romantic disposition to mistake himself for one. . . . 19 year-old Lord Byron, the outlaw poet, is a student at Trinity College. . . . Catching a killer seems like a fine diversion, . . . and Byron decides that solving the crime must take precedence over other . . . matters" (Publisher's note)

"Friedman manages to make one of the most obnoxious leads in recent memory oddly endearing and even sympathetic." Pub Wkly

Fuentes, Carlos

The **crystal** frontier; a novel in nine stories. translated from the Spanish by Alfred Mac Adam. Farrar, Straus & Giroux 1997 266p

ISBN 0-374-13277-1

LC 97-11230

Original Spanish edition published 1995 in Mexico

"Leonardo Barroso is an unscrupulous Mexican oligarch whose fortress of a villa is only a short drive from the 'crystal frontier' of the title, and each one of the nine stories comprising this work explores the life of someone touched by him." Libr J

Fuentes, Carlos

★ The **death** of Artemio Cruz; translated from the Spanish by Alfred MacAdam. Farrar, Straus & Giroux 1991 307p

LC 90-43280

Original Spanish edition published 1962 in Mexico; first English translation by Sam Hileman published 1964

"As the novel opens, Artemio Cruz, former revolutionary turned capitalist, lies on his deathbed. He drifts in and out of consciousness, and when he is conscious his mind wanders between past and present. The story reveals that Cruz became rich through treachery, bribery, corruption, and ruthlessness. As a young man he had been full of revolutionary ideals. Acts committed as a means of self-preservation soon developed into a way of life based on opportunism. A fully realized character, Cruz can also be seen as a symbol of Mexico's quest for wealth at the expense of moral values." Merriam-Webster's Ency of Lit

Fuentes, Carlos

Destiny and desire; a novel. translated by Edith Grossman. Random House 2011 415p $27

ISBN 978-1-4000-6880-7; 1-4000-6880-0

LC 2010-15078

Original Spanish edition, 2008

"A towering work. No character enters its pages lightly, and escape for each carries a price. Fuentes's language is rich, evoking character, place and, perhaps most memorably, the human decisions that propel society. It is a novel of wheels turning within wheels and of convoluted but ultimately meaningful connections." Denver Post

Fuentes, Carlos

The **eagle's** throne; translated by Kristina Cordero. Random House 2006 336p $26.95

ISBN 1-4000-6247-0

LC 2006-40806

Original Spanish edition, 2003

While Fuentes is "concerned, as always, about the destiny of his native country, his story focuses more on down-and-dirty political means than serious political ends, leaving us to draw our own conclusions about what sort of good can possibly come of his characters' byzantine strategies and counterstrategies–their opportunistic alliances, their calculated secret-keeping and secret-leaking, their posturing, their watchful waiting, their sly brutalities. What results is the most wickedly entertaining novel of Fuentes's career." N Y Times Book Rev

Fuentes, Carlos

★ The **old** gringo; translated by Margaret Sayers Peden. Farrar, Straus & Giroux 1985 199p

ISBN 0-374-22578-8

LC 85-16266

Original Spanish edition published in Mexico

"We have in this novel a fastidious American governess stranded in Pancho Villa's revolution, where she attracts the erotic interest of an intellectual fellow countryman and a nature-boy Mexican general. On this inanely trite foundation Mr. Fuentes has erected a narrative of brilliant complexity and sophistication, describing brisk military action and philosophically contrasting national character, or social tradition, or styles of revolt, or regional strengths, weaknesses, and prejudices." Atlantic

Fuentes, Carlos

The **years** with Laura Diaz; translated by Alfred MacAdam. Farrar, Straus & Giroux 2000 516p

ISBN 0-374-29341-4

LC 00-37648

"The novel begins in 1999 when photographer Santiago Lopez-Alfare arrives in Detroit to film a documentary about Mexican muralists in the U.S. There he comes across the image of an unnamed woman immortalized on the mural of the famous Diego Rivera. He soon realizes that @those almost golden eyes, mestizo, between European and Mexican' belonged to his great-grandmother, Laura Diaz. Thereafter, the novel recounts the life of Diaz, from the settlement of her German grandparents in Mexico in the late 1800s . . . to her experience of the Mexican Revolution and its aftermath." Booklist

Fuentes, Norberto

The **autobiography** of Fidel Castro; translated by Anna Kushner. W.W. Norton & Co. 2009 572p il $27.95

ISBN 978-0-393-06899-3; 0-393-06899-4

LC 2009-31601

An abridged version of a two-volume edition originally published in Spanish, 2004

"Most Cubaphiles will find Fuentes' effort to be a masterful act of ventriloquism, offering a Castro who is prideful, intuitively Machiavellian and relentlessly cynical. . . . Fuentes is the beneficiary of the superb editing and translation of Anna Kushner, whose deftness reminds one of Natasha Wimmer." San Francisco Chron

Includes bibliographical references.

Furnivall, Kate

The **red** scarf; a novel. Berkley Books 2008 470p pa $15

ISBN 978-0-425-22164-8; 0-425-22164-4

LC 2007-40037

"Sophia Morozova's relationship with fragile Anna Fedorina begins through a small act of kindness at a 1930s Siberian labor camp. As the two inmates struggle daily to survive, they increasingly rely on each other for hope and comfort; when Anna falls ill, Sophia escapes, intending to find Anna's lifelong love, Vasily, and rescue Anna. Beautiful and charismatic, Sophia quickly becomes a force to reckon with in the town of Tivil, where she hopes to find Vasily, and her connections with powerful gypsy Rafik, the handsome factory director Mikhail Pashin and the stern but unreadable Aleksei Fomenko become satisfying sources of danger and desire. Furnivall . . . paints a stark picture of rampant scarcity, grim regimentation and blaring propaganda in pre-WWII Soviet Russia." Publ Wkly

Furst, Alan

Blood of victory; a novel. Random House 2002 237p

ISBN 0-375-50574-1

LC 2002-21312

This thriller "revolves around a plan to disrupt the flow of Romanian oil to the Third Reich. As usual, Furst adheres strictly to the rules of the genre: the protagonist, a Russian expatriate writer, is seduced into service both by the prospect of heroism and by a mysterious Frenchwoman, and embarks on a globetrotting, spy-versus-spy adventure. But his debts to convention work in his favor. Densely atmospheric and genuinely romatic, the novel is most reminiscent of the Hollywood films of the forties, when moral choices were rendered not in black-and-white but in smoky shades of gray." New Yorker

Furst, Alan

Dark voyage; a novel. Random House 2004 256p $24.95

ISBN 1-400-06018-4

LC 2004-46674

The protagonist of this novel is "E. M. DeHaan, the captain of the Dutch tramp freighter Noordenham, a ship without a home since the Nazis invaded Holland. It's 1941 when DeHaan accepts . . . his new assignment: disguised as a Spanish freighter, the Noordendam will be deployed on secret assignments for the British." Booklist

Furst, Alan

The **foreign** correspondent; a novel. Random House 2006 273p $24.95

ISBN 1-4000-6019-2

LC 2006-40417

"In an interview in 2002, Furst said that he had difficulty understanding why none of his bestselling novels had yet been filmed. With no apparent preciousness about what might be lost in a transfer to the screen, he added, 'These really are movies.' In a sense, this is true. He has the ability to invent plots that work all on their own, which is, as Somerset Maugham once pointed out, a very rare gift indeed." Atlantic Monthly

Furst, Alan

★ A **Hero** of France; A Novel. Alan Furst. Random House Inc 2016 256 p. maps $27

ISBN 0812996496; 9780812996494

This book is set in France in 1941 when "small groups of ordinary men and women are determined to take down the occupying forces of Adolf Hitler. Mathieu, a leader of the French Resistance, leads one such cell, helping downed British airmen escape back to England. . . . As the German military police heighten surveillance, Mathieu and his team face a new threat, dispatched by the Reich to destroy them all." (Publisher's note)

Furst, Alan

★ **Mission** to Paris; a novel. Alan Furst. Random House 2012 272 p. map (hbk.) $27.00; (hbk.) $27.00

ISBN 1400069483; 9781400069484

LC 2012450028

This book is set in 1938, when "film star Fredric Stahl is on his way to Paris to make a movie for Paramount France. The Nazis know he's coming--a secret bureau within the Reich Foreign Ministry has for years been waging political warfare against France . . . . For their purposes, Fredric Stahl is a perfect agent of influence, and they attack him. What they don't know is that Stahl . . . has become part of an informal spy service being run out of the American embassy in Paris." (Publisher's note)

Furst, Alan

★ **Spies** of the Balkans; a novel. Random House 2010 268p $26

ISBN 978-1-4000-6603-2; 1-4000-6603-4

LC 2010-07755

Furst "is not in the least imitative—he has own style, and intricate sense of detail—but in his hands the mastery of the traditional spy novel has firmly passed to the other side of the Atlantic, and all I can say is that Eric Ambler and Graham Greene would have read his books with pleasure, and that somebody like Orson Welles (think of him playing Harry Lime in The Third Man) or Otto Preminger could have made a marvelous movie out of Spies of the Balkans. A pity that it probably won't happen—somehow, Furst seems to write in black and white, not Technicolor, just as Greene did—but in the meantime, this is a book, written for adults, to sit down and read in one gulp if you can." Daily Beast

Furst, Alan

The **spies** of Warsaw; a novel. Random House 2008 266p $25

ISBN 978-1-4000-6602-5; 1-4000-6602-6

"Rather than Eric Ambler thrillers or Graham Greene entertainments, the comparisons Mr. Furst's novels most often draw, they might more accurately be seen as extended series of Talk of the Town pieces. There's the same soupÐon of irony, the expert deployment of detail and, above all, a thick helping of knowingness—only with military secrets, machine pistols and Gestapo agents instead of celebrity quirks or outer-borough oddities." N Y Observer

The **Future** Is Japanese. Haikasoru 2012 365 p. (paperback) $14.99

ISBN 9781421542232

This anthology of Japanese-themed fiction, edited by Nick Mamatas, Masumi Washington, and Haikasoru, contains "thirteen stories from and about the Land of the Rising Sun [which] run the gamut from fantasy to cyberpunk." Topics include "[a] web browser that threatens to conquer the world, . . . [t]he longest, loneliest railroad on Earth, . . . [a]nd yes, giant robots." (Publisher's note)

G

Gabaldon, Diana

A **breath** of snow and ashes. Delacorte Press 2005 979p $28

ISBN 0-385-32416-2

LC 2005-51948

Previous titles in the Oulander series: Outlander (1991); Dragonfly in amber (1992); Voyager (1994); Drums of autumn (1997); The fiery cross (2001)

In this sixth title in the Outlander series, the author "unfolds the continuing story of the Frasers, heartbreakingly heroic highlander Jamie and his time-traveling wife Clare. Set during the three years leading up to the American Revolution, this . . . [novel] maps both violent loss and strong family ties. On the eve of war much is changing on Fraser's Ridge and Jamie and Claire encounter much harm. This vivid and haunting novel, therefore, brings an aching sadness, but it is balanced with sheer joy, revelation, and solace. The large scope of the novel allows Gabaldon to do what she does best, paint in exquisite detail the lives of her characters." Booklist

Followed by: An echo in the bone

Gabaldon, Diana

An **echo** in the bone. Delacorte Press 2009 820p $30

ISBN 978-0-385-34245-2; 0-385-34245-4

This seventh Outlander title "covers approximately two years during the heart of the Revolutionary War, beginning in July 1776. Brianna and Roger Mackenzie have traveled back through the stones to 1980 to get the health care for their infant daughter that was unavailable in the 18th century. Jamie Fraser and his beloved time-traveling wife Claire, having survived the fire that burned down their home in the hills of North Carolina, are making plans to sail back to Scotland to retrieve Jamie's printing press so he can fight on the American side with the pen instead of the sword. Meanwhile rich, powerful but tormented homosexual Lord John Grey finds himself in coastal North Carolina catching up with his adoptive son William Ransom, who is anxiously waiting to prove his worth in the British army. . . . There's no lack of action in the novel, and the Revolutionary War setting provides an opportunity for the characters to cross paths with such notable luminaries as Benjamin Franklin, Nathan Hale and Benedict Arnold." Romance Reader

Gabaldon, Diana, 1952-

The **fiery** cross; Diana Gabaldon. Delacorte Press 2001 ix, 979p $30

ISBN 0385315279 (alk. paper)

LC 2001047063

Romantic Times Reviewers' Choice Award: Historical (2001)

This book follows "time traveler Claire Randall, now firmly ensconced in the past with her daughter, Brianna, and Brianna's husband, Roger, [who] finds herself and her . . . husband, Jamie, at a critical juncture. It is 1771, and the first stirrings of the American Revolution are being felt in the mountains of North Carolina where Jamie, despite being a Catholic, has been given an enormous tract of land by the governor and is ordered to raise a militia. Having learned about the Revolution from his 20th-century wife and daughter, Jamie uneasily complies with the governor's orders and is immensely relieved when the crisis passes and the militia is disbanded." (Publishers Weekly)

Gabaldon, Diana, 1952-

Outlander; Diana Gabaldon. Delacorte Press 1991 627p. (hc) $30.00

ISBN 9780385302302; 0385302304

LC 90019122

RITA Awards: Romance of the Year (1991)

In this novel, "English nurse Claire Beauchamp Randall and husband Frank take a second honeymoon in the Scottish Highlands in 1945. When Claire walks through a cleft stone in an ancient henge, she's somehow transported to 1743. She encounters Frank's evil ancestor, British captain Jonathan 'Black Jack' Randall, and is adopted by another clan. Claire nurses young soldier James Fraser, a gallant, merry redhead, and the two begin a romance. . . . Scenes of the Highlanders' daily life blend . . . with Scottish wit and humor. Eventually Sassenach (outlander) Claire finds a chance to return to 1945, and must choose between distant memories of Frnak [sic] and her happy, uncomplicated existence with Jamie." (Publishers Weekly)

Gabaldon, Diana, 1952-

Written in my own heart's blood; a novel. Diana Gabaldon. 1st ed. Delacorte Press 2014 825 p. genealogical table (Outlander) (hardback) $35

ISBN 9780385344432; 0385344430

LC 2013043591

In this novel, by Diana Gabaldon, "France declares war on Great Britain, the British army leaves Philadelphia, and George Washington's troops leave Valley Forge in pursuit. At this moment, Jamie Fraser returns from a presumed watery grave to discover that his best friend has married his wife, his illegitimate son has discovered (to his horror) who his father really is, and his beloved nephew, Ian, wants to marry a Quaker." (Publisher's note)

Gaddis, William

Agape agape; afterword by Joseph Tabbi. Viking 2002 113p

ISBN 0-670-03131-3

LC 2002-20676

"Gaddis has compressed 50 years of research on the social history of the player piano into a novel narrated by a dying elderly man who is as concerned with his own physical collapse as he is with his piano-based literary project. . . . As usual, Gaddis's avant-garde style requires patience and staying power from readers, who must parse long, elliptical sentences that wander from idea to idea while barely advancing the narrative. But his thoughts and ruminations remain fascinating and challenging." Publ Wkly

Includes bibliographical references

Gaddis, William

A **frolic** of his own; a novel. Poseidon Press 1994 586p

ISBN 0-671-66984-2

LC 93-26098

"The medium is exceptionally dense. The mere effort of sorting out the voices, of tracking them, can be exhausting. . . . In any case, I hope the reader will persevere. 'A Frolic of His Own' is an exceptionally rich, even important novel." N Y Times Book Rev

Gaddis, William, 1922-1998

★ The **recognitions**; William Gaddis ; introduction by William H. Gass. Dalkey Archive Press 2012 956p.

ISBN 9781564786913

LC 2011031304

This book "is a . . . work about art and forgery, and the increasingly thin line between the counterfeit and the fake. [Author William] Gaddis anticipates by almost half a century the crisis of reality that we currently face, where the real and the virtual are combining in alarming ways, and the sources of legitimacy and power are often obscure to us." (Publisher's note)

Gaige, Amity

Schroder; Amity Gaige. Twelve 2013 288 p. $21.99

ISBN 1455512133; 9781455512133

LC 2012013882

In this novel by Amity Gaige "young Eric Schroder--a first-generation East German immigrant--adopts the last name Kennedy to more easily fit in, a fateful white lie that will set him on an improbable and ultimately tragic course. 'Shroder' relates the story of Eric's urgent escape years later to Lake Champlain, Vermont, with his six-year-old daughter, Meadow, in an attempt to outrun the authorities amid a heated custody battle with his wife." (Publisher's note)

Gailey, Sarah

River of Teeth; Sarah Gailey. Tor.com 2017 176 p. illustration paperback $14.99

ISBN 9780765395238; 0765395231

Nebula Finalist: Best Novella (2017)

Hugo Finalist: Best Novella (2018)

"In the early 20th Century, the United States government concocted a plan to import hippopotamuses into the marshlands of Louisiana to be bred and slaughtered as an alternative meat source. This is true. Other true things about hippos: they are savage, they are fast, and their jaws can snap a man in two. This was a terrible plan." (Publisher's note)

"The tight pace, complex relationships, and twisting motivations of the characters keep the reader engaged, and the alternate history of American hippo farming is clearly illustrated without clumsy exposition." Pub Wkly

Gaiman, Neil, 1960-

★ **American** gods; a novel. Morrow 2001 465p $26

ISBN 0-380-97365-0

LC 2001-30407

This is a "sci-fi road trip novel. . . . Early in 'American Gods' we are introduced to Shadow, a man who has been released from prison only to learn that his wife has died in a car crash. With nothing to return home to, Shadow accepts a job protecting Mr. Wednesday, an omniscient one-eyed grifter. . . . Soon the ex-convict finds himself in an alternate universe, where he is haunted by prophetic nightmares and visited by his dead wife." (N Y Times Book Rev)

"A noirish sci-fi road trip novel in which the melting pot of the United States extends not merely to mortals but to a motley assortment of disgruntled gods and deities. Early in 'American Gods' we are introduced to Shadow, a man who has been released from prison only to learn that his wife has died in a car crash. With nothing to return home to, Shadow accepts a job protecting Mr. Wednesday, an omniscient one-eyed grifter. . . . Soon the ex-convict finds himself in an alternate universe, where he is haunted by prophetic nightmares and visited by his dead wife." N Y Times Book Rev

Gaiman, Neil

★ **Anansi** boys. William Morrow 2005 336p il $26.95; pa $7.99

ISBN 978-0-06-051518-8; 0-06-051518-X; 978-0-06-051519-5 pa; 0-06-051519-8 pa

LC 2005-47176

"Fat Charlie's life is about to be spiced up–his estranged father dies in a karaoke bar, and the handsome brother he never knew he had shows up on his doorstep with a gleam in his eye. Next thing he knows, Fat Charlie is being investigated by the police, his fiancée's falling in love with the wrong brother, and he finds out that his father was the god Anansi, Trickster and Spider, and that the beast gods of folklore are plotting their own revenge upon his family bloodline. A fun book with a little of everything–horror, mystery, magic, comedy, song, romance, ghosts, scary birds, ancient grudges, and trademark British wit." Libr J

Gaiman, Neil

Fragile things; short fictions and wonders. William Morrow 2006 xxxi, 360p $26.95

ISBN 978-0-06-051522-5; 0-06-051522-8

LC 2006-48135

"Gaiman follows no overarching theme, but that is what makes these stories charming, at times creepy, and good fun. They read like dreams and meditations, with a stream-of-consciousness quality to their presentation. Gaiman also explains some of the inspiration behind the stories to help put them in perspective." Libr J

Gaiman, Neil, 1960-

Good omens; the nice and accurate prophecies of Agnes Nutter, witch: a novel. [by] Neil Gaiman and Terry Pratchett. Workman 1990 354p

ISBN 0-89480-853-2

LC 90-50362

"The end of the world is nigh! At least according to the prophecies of Agnes Nutter, a witch whose predictions are usually accurate but seldom heeded. Eleven years before the deadly Last Saturday Night, the ancient rivals of good and evil personified by the angelic Aziraphale (otherwise living as a London book dealer) and the demonic devil and former serpent Crowley clash in substituting the Antichrist during the birth of a baby." (SLJ)

Gaiman, Neil, 1960-

★ **Norse** mythology; Neil Gaiman. W W Norton & Co Inc 2017 304 p. illustrations (ebook) $50; (hardcover) $25.95

ISBN 9780393609103; 039360909X; 9780393609097

LC 2016046917

This book, by Neil Gaiman, "stays true to the myths in envisioning the major Norse pantheon: Odin, the highest of the high, wise, daring, and cunning; Thor, Odin's son, incredibly strong yet not the wisest of gods; and Loki—son of a giant—blood brother to Odin and a trickster and unsurpassable manipulator." (Publisher's note)

"Just the thing for the literate fantasy lover and the student of comparative religion and mythology alike." Kirkus

Gaiman, Neil, 1960-

★ The **Ocean** at the End of the Lane; Neil Gaiman. HarperCollins 2013 192 p. (hardcover) $25.99

ISBN 0062255657; 9780062255655

In this speculative fiction novel, by Neil Gaiman, a 7-year old boy seeks to banish an evil spirit with the help of the odd Hempstock family. "Despite his determination and well-developed sense of right and wrong, he's also a scared little boy drawn into adventures beyond his understanding, forced into terrible mistakes through innocence." (Kirkus Reviews)

Gaiman, Neil

Stardust. Avon Bks. 1999 238p hardcover o.p. pa $13.95; $30.00

ISBN 0-380-97728-1; 0-06-114202-6 pa; 9780062200396

LC 98-8773

"Young Tristran Thorn has grown up in the isolated village of Wall, on the edge of the realm of Faerie. When Tristran and the lovely Victoria see a falling star during the special market fair, Victoria impulsively offers him his heart's desire if he will retrieve the star for her. Tristran crosses the border into Faerie and encounters witches, unicorns, and other strange creatures." Libr J

Gaiman, Neil, 1960-

Trigger warning; short fictions and disturbances. Neil Gaiman. William Morrow, an imprint of HarperCollins Publishers 2015 xxxvii, 310 p.p (hardcover) $26.99

ISBN 0062330268; 9780062330260

LC 2015300197

This short story collection, by Neil Gaiman, "explores the masks we all wear and the people we are beneath them to reveal our vulnerabilities and our truest selves. Here is a rich cornucopia of horror and ghosts stories, science fiction and fairy tales, fabulism and poetry that explore the realm of experience and emotion." (Publisher's note)

"Full of all manner of witches and monsters and things that creep in the night, this collection will thoroughly satisfy faithful fans and win new ones—if there's anyone out there left unconverted." Kirkus

Gaines, Ernest J.

★ The **autobiography** of Miss Jane Pittman. Dial Press (NY) 1971 245p hardcover o.p. pa $6.99

ISBN 0-553-26357-9 pa

LC 77-144380

"In the epic of Miss Jane Pittman, a 110-year-old ex-slave, the action begins at the time she is a small child watching both Union and Confederate troops come into the plantation on which she lives. It closes with the demonstrations of the sixties and the freedom walk she decides to make. This is a log of trials, heartaches, joys, love—but mostly of endurance." Shapiro. Fic for Youth. 3d edition

Gaines, Ernest J.

★ A **gathering** of old men. Knopf 1983 213p hardcover o.p. pa $11.95

ISBN 0-394-51468-8; 0-679-73890-8 pa

LC 82-49000

"The story opens with the murder of Beau Boutan, a Cajun farmer, on the Louisiana plantation of Candy Marshall, a headstrong white owner. She claims to have done the shooting because she wished to protect one of her black workers, Mathu, who has been like a guardian to her following the death of her parents. In the plan to stand between Mapes, the local sheriff, and Mathu, Candy has set into motion an idea that has brought together a group of old black men with shotguns (unloaded), all claiming to have done the shooting. The threat of the South's way of punishing blacks by lynching hangs over the story like a pall. It meets opposition from Beau's young brother who has been friends with a black fellow-student and team-mate at his university." Shapiro. Fic for Youth. 3d edition

Gaines, Ernest J.

★ A **lesson** before dying. Knopf 1997 256p $26; pa $12.95

ISBN 0-679-45561-2; 0-375-70270-9 pa

LC 92-20335

First published 1993

"YAs who seek thought-provoking reading will enjoy this glimpse of life in the rural South just before the civil rights movement." SLJ

Gaitskill, Mary

Don't cry; stories. Pantheon Books 2009 226p $23.95

ISBN 978-0-375-42419-9; 0-375-42419-9

LC 2008-25231

"There is always a moment in a Mary Gaitskill story when you wince. And then you shrug. The wince means, 'Wow, that's a pretty creepy aspect of human nature to point out,' while the shrug is a way of acknowledging, 'But it's true. Life's really like that, isn't it?' The Gaitskill two-step—that wince-and-shrug maneuver her work inspires—is what elevates her above other fiction writers who, though talented, are content to give us surfaces. Gaitskill never stops at surfaces. She's too adventurous for that, too reckless. " Newsday

Gaitskill, Mary

The **mare**; a novel. by Mary Gaitskill. Pantheon Books 2015 464 p. (hard cover : alk. paper) $26.95

ISBN 9780307379740

LC 2015007973

In this novel, by Mary Gaitskill, "Velveteen Vargas is eleven years old, a Fresh Air Fund kid from Brooklyn. Her host family is a couple in upstate New York: Ginger, a failed artist and shakily recovered alcoholic, and her academic husband, Paul, who wonder what it will mean to "make a difference" in such a contrived situation. Gaitskill illuminates their shifting relationship with Velvet over several years, as well as Velvet's encounter with the horses at the stable down the road." (Publisher's note)

"Gaitskill explores the complexities of love (mares, meres...) to bring us a novel that gallops along like a bracing bareback ride on a powerful thoroughbred." Kirkus

Gaitskill, Mary

Veronica. Pantheon 2005 227p $23

ISBN 0-375-42145-9

LC 2005-43143

National Book Award Finalist: Fiction (2005)

The author's "fierce, night-blooming new novel is about a close friendship between two women. But it should not be confused with anything cozy. Imagine a buddy story from the mind of William S. Burroughs, illustrated with images by Robert Mapplethorpe or David Cronenberg, and you get some idea of the tenderness to be found here. . . . Ms. Gaitskill writes so radiantly about violent self-loathing that the very incongruousness of her language has shocking power." N Y Times (N Y Late Ed)

Galbraith, Robert

Career of evil; Robert Galbraith. Mulholland Books 2015 497 p. $28

ISBN 0316349933; 9780316349932

LC 2015948930

"When a mysterious package is delivered to Robin Ellacott, she is horrified to discover that it contains a woman's severed leg. Her boss, private detective Cormoran Strike, is less surprised but no less alarmed. There are four people from his past who he thinks could be responsible. With the police focusing on the one suspect Strike is increasingly sure is not the perpetrator, he and Robin take matters into their own hands." (Publisher's note)

"The real appeal here . . . is Robin and Strike's relationship. A contemporary thriller with characters whose emotional journey is just as page-turningly gratifying as the most high-stakes manhunt." Booklist

Galbraith, Robert

The **silkworm**; Robert Galbraith. 1st American ed. Mulholland Books / Little, Brown and Co. 2014 464 p. (Cormoran Strike) (hardcover) $28

ISBN 9780316206877; 9780316206891; 9780316206914

LC 2014938182

In this mystery by Robert Galbraith, "novelist Owen Quine goes missing [and] his wife calls in private detective Cormoran Strike. . . . [A]s Strike investigates, it becomes clear that there is more to Quine's disappearance than his wife realizes. The novelist has just completed a manuscript featuring poisonous pen-portraits of almost everyone he knows. If the novel were to be published, it would ruin lives-meaning that there are a lot of people who might want him silenced." (Publisher's note)

"In her Galbraith persona, author J.K. Rowling has created memorable characters who develop and grow throughout the course of the novel. The mystery itself is clever, and the frequent darts aimed at the publishing world are entertaining." LJ

Galchen, Rivka

★ **American** innovations; Rivka Galchen. Farrar, Straus & Giroux 2014 192 p. (hardcover) $24

ISBN 9780374280475; 0374280479

LC 2013039912

This book is a collection of short stories by Rivka Galchen. "In one of the . . . stories, . . . a young woman's furniture walks out on her. In another, the narrator feels compelled to promise to deliver a takeout order that has incorrectly been phoned in to her. In a third, the petty details of a property transaction illuminate the complicated pains and loves of a family." (Publisher's note)

"Galchen's stories feel remarkably believable, despite their suggestion of alternate worlds and lives." Kirkus

Galchen, Rivka

Atmospheric disturbances. Farrar, Straus and Giroux 2008 240p il $24

ISBN 978-0-374-20011-4; 0-374-20011-4

LC 2007-47327

It is on the "level of psychological realism rather than postmodern invention, that 'Atmospheric Disturbances' succeeds, and where Ms. Galchen displays her real gifts as a writer. As we come to learn, in a series of dropped hints, the real story of Leo and Rema and their marriage, it becomes clear that the particular form of Leo's delusion is anything but accidental." N Y Sun

Gallagher, Matt

Youngblood; a novel. Matt Gallagher. Atria Books 2016 336 p. (ebook) $16.99; (hardcover) $26

ISBN 9781501105760; 9781501105746

LC 2015014772

In this book, by Matt Gallagher, "the US military is preparing to withdraw from Iraq, and newly-minted lieutenant Jack Porter struggles to accept how it's happening--through alliances with warlords who have Arab and American blood on their hands. Day after day, Jack tries to assert his leadership in the sweltering, dreary atmosphere of Ashuriyah." (Publisher's note)

"Gallagher's riveting combination of gritty military jargon, sharply drawn characters, and suspenseful story line adds up to one of the best modern war novels since Tim O'Brien's Vietnam classic, The Things They Carried (1990). Highly recommended." Booklist

Gallagher, Stephen

The **bedlam** detective; a novel. Stephen Gallagher. Crown Publishers 2012 305 p.

ISBN 9780307406644; 9780307952783

LC 2011018605

In this book, "Sebastian Becker . . . his fast-track career abruptly derailed, contemplates an uncertain future. . . . [H]e faces 1912 back in his native England, employed as the special investigator to the Masters of Lunacy. Englishmen of property deemed too loopy to look after anyone's property face Bedlams of one sort or another, their property removed from their care. It's up to Sir James Crichton-Browne, acting for His Majesty's Government, to render judgments informed by evidence his special investigator Sebastian provides. The job . . . is nuanced enough to be interesting. And it gets even more so when Sebastian meets Sir Owain Lancaster, a scientist who's been widely respected until he blames the failure of his lavish Amazonian expedition on a series of attacks by horrific monsters only he can see." (Kirkus)

Gallagher, Stephen

The **kingdom** of bones; a novel. Shaye Areheart Books 2007 366p $24.95

ISBN 978-0-307-38280-1; 0-307-38280-X

LC 2007-13288

"Vividly set in England and America during the booming industrial era of the late 19th and early 20th centuries, this stylish thriller conjures a perfect demon to symbolize the age and its appetites, an entity that inhabits characters eager to barter their souls for fame and fortune." N Y Times Book Rev

Galloway, Gregory

As simple as snow; Gregory Galloway. Putnam 2005 308p $23.95

ISBN 9780399152313; 9780425207802; 0399152318 (alk. paper)

LC 2004044500

Alex Award (2006)

In this book which takes place "[i]n a small town near a river not far from a city, the narrator, an unnamed high school sophomore, encounters new Goth arrival, Anna Cayne. . . . The narrator is unsure why anyone would pursue him, . . . but pursue him Anna does, charming him with intriguing postcards, reading recommendations and long walks by the river. He's soon completely, hopelessly in love. But halfway through the story Anna disappears, leaving the narrator and the reader feeling lost and betrayed. The book becomes a search for Anna, complete with ciphers, codes, sightings and buried maps. Does affable art teacher Mr. Devon have something to do with her disappearance? Who was really driving the night fellow student Bryce Druitt slammed his car into the side of the bridge?" (Publishers Weekly)

Galsworthy, John

★ The **Forsyte** saga; with a preface by Ada Galsworthy. Scribner 1922 xx, 921p

In chancery relates the further fortunes of the Forsyte family. Irene Forsyte's first effort toward emancipation from her husband Soames ended with the accidental death of the architect who loved her. Meeting Irene again, after a separation of fifteen years, awakens in Soames the old desire to possess her, and failing of her consent, files for divorce. This action forces his cousin Jolyon into the role of correspondent. Soames eventually marries Annette Lamotte, who presents him with a daughter, Fleur, instead of a longed-for male heir. Jolyon and Irene marry and have a son, Jon

Followed by A modern comedy

Gao Xingjian

Buying a fishing rod for my grandfather; stories. translated from the Chinese by Mabel Lee. HarperCollins Pubs. 2004 127p $17.95

ISBN 0-06-057555-7

LC 2003-51138

Original Chinese edition, 1989

"Though few in number, the stories in this collection are richly diverse. One is a bittersweet reflection of a newlywed on his honeymoon; another a Pinteresque dialogue in a park; a third a traffic accident recounted in realtime with all its voyeuristic detail and authentic philosophical questioning, and still another, a strong memory-driven, first-person tale that follows the mental trail of a man who passes a fishing equipment shop and begins to remember his grandfather. For variety of content, stylistic experimentation, graceful language, and poignant insight, Xingjian is a writer who does it all beautifully." Booklist

Gao Xingjian

Soul mountain; translated from the Chinese by Mabel Lee. HarperCollins Pubs. 2000 510p

ISBN 0-06-621082-8

LC 2001-269378

"It is not easy to say what the novel is about—and yet the marvel is that somehow it is still both engaging and elegant." N Y Times Book Rev

List of author's works: p. 507-510

Garcia Marquez, Gabriel

★ The **autumn** of the patriarch; translated from the Spanish by Gregory Rabassa. Harper & Row 1976 269p

Original Spanish edition, 1975

"A highly sophisticated novel about an unnamed dictator (the patriarch), who, at the time of his death, is somewhere between 107 and 232 years of age. The patriarch embodies the archtypal evils of despotism, but even more significant is his extreme, and often pathetic, solitude, which becomes increasingly evident with his advancing age and which emerges as the principal theme. Despite its political and psychological overtones, the autumn of the patriarch can best be described as a lyrical novel, whose plot and character development are subordinate to formal design and symbolic imagery." Ency of World Lit in the 20th century

Garcia Marquez, Gabriel

Chronicle of a death foretold; translated from the Spanish by Gregory Rabassa. Knopf 1983 120p $25

ISBN 0-394-53074-8

LC 82-48884

Original Spanish edition published 1981 in Colombia; this translation first published 1982 in the United Kingdom

This "investigation of an ancient murder takes on the quality of a hallucinatory exploration, a deep groping search into the gathering darkness of human intentions for a truth that continually slithers away." N Y Rev Books

Garcia Marquez, Gabriel

Collected novellas. HarperCollins Pubs. 1990 249p

LC 89-46106

English translations of the three novellas included in this volume were first published 1972, 1968 and 1982 respectively

Garcia Marquez, Gabriel

Collected stories. Harper & Row 1984 311p

LC 84-47826

This volume includes stories from the author's three previous collections: No one writes to the colonel, and other stories; Leaf storm, and other stories, and Innocent Eréndira, and other stories

Garcia Marquez, Gabriel

The **general** and his labyrinth; translated from the Spanish by Edith Grossman. Knopf 1990 285p

ISBN 0-394-58258-6

LC 90-52957

Original Spanish edition, 1989

"Seldom has there been a more fitting match between author and subject. Mr. Garcia Márquez wades into his flamboyant, often improbable and ultimately tragic material with enormous gusto, heaping detail upon sensuous detail, alternating grace with horror." N Y Times Book Rev

Garcia Marquez, Gabriel

In evil hour; translated from the Spanish by Gregory Rabassa. Harper & Row 1979 183p

Original Spanish edition, 1968

"The reader is carried along effortlessly in the current of this gifted storyteller's prose. Both heroes and villains elicit sympathy because their basic human foibles, while true to local circumstances, can be recognized by people of any culture." Libr J

Garcia Marquez, Gabriel

Leaf storm, and other stories; translated from the Spanish by Gregory Rabassa. Harper & Row 1972 146p

The title novella (originally published 1955) covers three generations of boom and decline in the mythical Colombian town Macondo. "The small river town changes with the leaf storm of people—strangers who come there as a result of civil war and the establishment of a banana company. Marquez begins with the end, the death of one mysterious wanderer, a doctor who . . . withdraws from the world. As the narrators, a man, his daughter, her young son, reveal the doctor's story, so too do the tellers' own melancholy lives emerge, symbolic yet specific, representing the everlasting variety of man's inhumanity to man." Publ Wkly

Garcia Marquez, Gabriel

Love in the time of cholera; translated from the Spanish by Edith Grossman; with an introduction by Nicholas Shakespeare. Knopf 1997 xxxiii, 422p $22

ISBN 0-375-40069-9

Original Spanish edition published 1985 in Colombia, this is a reissue of the 1988 edition

"The story, which concerns the themes of love, aging, and death, takes place between the late 1870s and the early 1930s in a South American community troubled by wars and outbreaks of cholera. It is a tale of two lovers, artistic Florentino Ariza and wealthy Fermina Daza, who reunite after a lifetime apart. Their spirit of enduring love contrasts ironically with the surrounding corporeal decay." Merriam-Webster's Ency of Lit

García Márquez, Gabriel, 1927-2014

Memories of my melancholy whores; translated from the Spanish by Edith Grossman. Knopf 2005 115p $20

ISBN 1-4000-4460-X

LC 2005-43591

Original Spanish edition, 2004

"Measured by the highest standards, Memories is not a major achievement, but its goal is brave: to speak on behalf of the desire of older men for underage girls, or, in other words, pedophilia. The conceptual strategy that Garcia Marquez uses toward this end is to break down the barrier between erotic passion and the passion of veneration." N Y Rev Books

García Márquez, Gabriel, 1927-2014

★ **One** hundred years of solitude; translated from the Spanish by Gregory Rabassa. Harper & Row 1970 422p

ISBN 0-06-011418-5

Original Spanish edition published 1967 in Argentina

This novel "relates the founding of Macondo by Jose Arcadio Buendia, the adventures of six generations of his descendants, and, ultimately, the town's destruction. It also presents a vast synthesis of social, economic, and political evils plaguing much of Latin America. Even more important from a literary point of view is its aesthetic representation of a world in microcosm, that is, a complete history, from Eden to Apocalypse, of a world in which miracles such as people riding on flying carpets and a dead man returning to life tend to erase the thin line between objective and subjective realities." Ency of World Lit in the 20th Century

Garcia Marquez, Gabriel

Strange pilgrims; twelve stories. translated from the Spanish by Edith Grossman. Knopf 1993 188p

ISBN 0-679-42566-7

LC 93-12257

"Exile and loss are the principal subjects of these 12 stories . . . which capture with lyrical precision the emotions of disorientation and fear, coupled with a sense of new possibility, experienced by Latin Americans in Europe." Publ Wkly

Garcia, Cristina

The **Aguero** sisters. Knopf 1997 299p

ISBN 0-679-45090-4

LC 96-52204

"The story of the middle-aged Agüero sisters—independent Reina, an electrician living in Havana, and thoroughly urbanized Constancia, a successful cosmetics salesperson living in New York—is also the story of how personal tragedy and the legacy of Castro's revolution impact one family's history and collective memory. The narrative is filtered through many voices, both past and present, including the women's parents, famous naturalists, and Reina's daughter, a sometime prostitute who is sick to death of poverty-stricken Havana." Booklist

Garcia, Cristina

★ **Dreaming** in Cuban; a novel. Knopf 1992 244p

LC 91-20755

"While taking very seriously those ideas that have truly riven so many families in recent years, leaving many obsessed with the politics of Cuba, Ms. Garcia also portrays the costliness of such an obsession and the fading of the light between mothers and daughters, between lovers, as communication fails." N Y Times Book Rev

Garcia, Cristina

A **handbook** to luck. Knopf 2007 259p $24

ISBN 978-0-307-26436-7; 030726436X

LC 2006-48736

"García's characters have a lot to teach us about playing life's odds, and about resilience . . . . With an ear for language and its cadence, García writes with humor, tenderness and an intuitive sense of how ordinary people weather fortune's turns. If you long for a 'handbook' that reveals how ordinary people become extraordinary, you are in luck." N Y Daily News

García, Cristina, 1958-

King of Cuba; a novel. Cristina García. Scribner 2013 256 p. (hardcover : alk. paper) $26

ISBN 1476710244; 9781476710242; 9781476714530; 9781476725666

LC 2012037553

This book "explores the hatred Goyo Herrera, an expatriate geriatric Cuban, harbors toward his arch enemy El Comandante, a contemporary who still wields formidable power in their homeland. El Comandante reminisces about the bygone days of revolutionary glory while expressing disgust for the current state of Cuba. In contrast, the widower Goyo lives in Miami with his daughter . . . concocting revenge schemes against his nemesis." (Publishers Weekly)

Garcia, Cristina

The **lady** matador's hotel; a novel. Scribner 2010 209p $24

ISBN 978-1-4391-8174-4; 1-4391-8174-8

LC 2009-49749

"García has created a half-magical world in which blood runs close to the surface and flesh is transitory, opening the door to the big questions of existence: Who am I, and what is my purpose in life? The answers she offers — such as they are — come with a sly wit and strong visual style that explodes with color and life." Miami Herald

Garcia, Cristina

Monkey hunting. Knopf 2003 251p $23

ISBN 0-375-41056-2

LC 2002-35916

"For all the ground Garcia covers, the most beautiful and moving parts of her novel are the chapters on Chen Pan's youthful sufferings. Here, horror and wonder alternate unblinkingly, as if they are random occurrences in a dark once-upon-a-time." N Y Times Book Rev

Garcia-Roza, Luiz Alfredo

Alone in the crowd; an Inspector Espinosa mystery. translated by Benjamin Moser. Henry Holt and Co. 2009 225p $23

ISBN 978-0-8050-7959-3; 0-8050-7959-9

LC 2008-50135

Original Portuguese edition published 2007 in Brazil

"At a bank in Rio de Janeiro, pensioner Dona Laureta withdraws her money from the same teller Hugo Breno every month like clockwork. She leaves the bank, goes to the grocery and pharmacy, and then she travels to the police of the Twelfth Precinct in Copacabana. She asks to speak with the chief, but Espinoza is tied up in a meeting. She decides to leave and come back later, but instead is run over by a bus; bystanders believe she was deliberately pushed. The police interrogate Breno who remains a person of interest. Espinoza has him under surveillance. . . . Espinoza is unaware that Breno has been watching him for decades and even came to the same park when they were children. A memory of a child's death makes the cop wonder if the teller was involved. They meet at a restaurant and Hugo tells his story to Espinoza. A day later Laureta's friend is killed. Espinoza is sure that Breno killed both women, but has no evidence. Both adversaries risk their lives with similar yet differing purposes." Mystery Gazette

Garcia-Roza, Luiz Alfredo

December heat; translated by Benjamin Moser. Holt & Co. 2003 273p $23

ISBN 0-8050-6890-2

LC 2002-38825

Original Portuguese edition published 1998 in Brazil

"An exciting procedural, infused with exotic ambience, sympathetic detectives, and a little romance." Libr J

Gardam, Jane

The **flight** of the maidens. Carroll & Graf Pubs. 2001 278p $25

ISBN 0-7867-0879-4

LC 00-343383

First published 2000 in the United Kingdom

Gardam "has thrown out the usual too-sensitive-for-you boilerplate of the coming-of-age novel, for which we can be thankful. Luckily, the generational conflict that remains is usually all the better for her wry indirection." N Y Times Book Rev

Gardam, Jane

God on the rocks. Europa Editions 2010 195p $15

ISBN 9781933372761 pa; 1933372761 pa

First published 1978 in the United Kingdom; first American edition published 1979 by Morrow

This novel "dexterously exposes the misapprehensions wrought by class, sex, love, and religion among the members of two families in a seaside town in the north of England during the interwar years. Gardam has been compared to Anita Brookner, but her view, though equally dark, is far less dreary. Few can present tragedy with such humor." Atlantic

Gardam, Jane

Last Friends. Penguin Group USA 2013 304 p. (Old Filth trilogy) $16

ISBN 1609450930; 9781609450939

With this book, author Jane Gardam finishes her Old Filth trilogy. Here, "when Sir Terence and Sir Edward die within months of each other, only a few people at their memorial services can personally recall the details of the venerable yet tumultuous lives they led. But old Dulcie, widow of judge William Willy, and Sir Frederick Fiscal-Smith, perennial houseguest of the upper class, share fleeting recollections of earlier lives through reminisces that are clouded with the haze of old age." (Kirkus Reviews)

Gardam, Jane

The **man** in the wooden hat. Europa Editions 2009 233p pa $15

ISBN 1-933372-89-3; 978-1-933372-89-1

This novel tells the story of the fifty-year marriage of the barrister Edward Feathers, "Old Filth", and his wife Betty.

"In this understated novel, Gardam returns to the successful barrister and judge Sir Edward Feathers, the protagonist of her deliciously acerbic 'Old Filth.' The complementary tale, told largely from the point of view of Feathers's wife, Betty, a fellow 'Raj orphan,' begins as the two make 'a prudent marriage not for love,' in Hong Kong after the Second World War. The story briskly follows their fifty-year union from adulterous beginnings and unhappy childlessness to a companionable old age in England, after the handover of Hong Kong." New Yorker

Gardam, Jane

Old Filth. Europa 2006 289p pa $14.95

ISBN 1-933372-13-3

LC 2005-36039

First published 2004 in the United Kingdom

This "novel examines the life of Sir Edward Feathers, a desiccated barrister known to colleagues and friends as Old Filth (the nickname stands for 'Failed in London Try Hong Kong'). After a lucrative career in Asia, Filth settles into retirement in Dorset. With anatomical precision, Gardam reveals that, contrary to appearances, Sir Edward's life is seething with incident: a 'raj orphan,' whose mother died when he was born and whose father took no notice of him, he was shipped from Malaysia to Wales (cheaper than England) and entrusted to a foster mother who was cruel to him. What happened in the years before he settled into school, and was casually adopted by his best friend's kindly English country family, haunts, corrodes, and quickens Filth's heart; Gardam's prose is so economical that no moment she describes is either gratuitous or wasted." New Yorker

Gardam, Jane

★ The **people** on Privilege Hill and other stories. Europa Editions 2008 196p $15.95

ISBN 978-1-933372-56-3

"The 14 stories in Gardam's marvelously titled new collection, The People on Privilege Hill, focus to a large extent on members of her generation (she was born July 11, 1928, soon to turn 80) or that of her parents. These generally feisty individuals recall sometimes troubling events from their prime while they cope with the affronts of aging in a changing world. Not all the stories are winners, but even the slightest offer the pleasures of Gardam's brisk, sharp sensibility. The title story brings back the splendid character Filth from her last novel. He's approaching 90, a widower who's retired to Dorset and misses the warm tropical rains of the Orient, where he practiced law for many years." Christ Sci Monit

Gardiner, Meg

The **Dirty** Secrets Club. Dutton 2008 355p $24.95

ISBN 978-0-525-95066-0; 0-525-95066-4

LC 2007-46757

"As Beckett gets in touch with her inner Rambo, Ericksen's acid-tinged delivery suddenly works just fine." Publ Wkly

Gardner, Lisa

Alone. Bantam Books 2005 324p $24
ISBN 0-553-80253-4

LC 2004-57577

The protagonist of this thriller is "Massachusetts police sniper Bobby Dodge. He meets his match in Catherine Gagnon, who as a girl was snatched, raped and nearly murdered. Now she's the wife of erratic, rich Jimmy Gagnon and mother of perpetually ill four-year-old Nathan. When Bobby kills Jimmy during a hostage situation at the Gagnons, he does it to save Catherine and Nathan. But was it a righteous shoot, or did Catherine engineer the killing? Judge James Gagnon and his wife, Maryanne, think Bobby murdered their son out of lust for Catherine. As other people start dying, very messily, and the DA and cops come down hard on Bobby, Gardner keeps the tension high and the pace fast." Publ Wkly

Gardner, Lisa

Catch me. Dutton 2012 400 p.
ISBN 9781455870561; 9780525952763

LC 2011043577

This book follows the adventures of "Boston Sgt. Det. D.D. Warren." In this case, "Charlene Rosalind Carter Grant, a 28-year-old police dispatch officer with a horrific childhood, expects to be murdered on January 21. One of her two best friends was strangled at home on January 21 two years earlier; exactly a year later, her other best friend suffered the same fate. On January 17, Grant seeks out Warren at a crime scene and asks the homicide detective to investigate her expected murder. Meanwhile, Warren is looking into the execution-style slayings of two pedophiles. Rookie sex crime detective Ellen O brings her expertise to this second case." (Publishers Weekly)

Gardner, Lisa

Find Her; by Lisa Gardner. Penguin Group USA 2016 416 p. (Detective D.D. Warren) $27
ISBN 0525954570; 9780525954576

LC 2015038503

In this psychological thriller by Lisa Gardner, "college student Flora was kidnapped while on spring break. . . . Alive after her ordeal, Flora has spent the past five years reacquainting herself with the rhythms of normal life. . . . When Boston detective D. D. Warren is called to the scene of a crime—a dead man and the bound, naked woman who killed him—she learns that Flora has tangled with three other suspects since her return to society. Is Flora a victim or a vigilante?" (Publisher's note)

"A gritty, complicated heroine like Flora Dane deserves a better plot than this needlessly complicated story." Kirkus

Gardner, Lisa

Live to tell; a detective D.D. Warren novel. Lisa Gardner. Bantam Books 2010 388 p. (acid-free paper) o.p.; (pbk.) $7.99
ISBN 9780553807240; 9780553591910

LC 2010003473

This detective novel follows "D.D. [Warren who investigates] . . . the mass murder of a family. . . . While D.D. labors to crack the case with the help of sidekick Alex Wilson, a . . . professor training as a criminologist by taking a police rotation, single mother Victoria is just trying to make it through another day. Her life revolves around her emotionally disturbed son Evan, whose constant death threats and physical abuse rule her every move even though he's only eight. The third vein in the story is Danielle's tale of survival. When she was still a child, Danielle's family was killed by her father, but her life was spared. Adult Danielle, who wonders why, spends her time giving back by working late hours as a pediatric nurse with disturbed children." (Kirkus)

Gardner, Lisa

Love you more; a novel. Bantam Books 2011 356p $26
ISBN 978-0-553-80725-7; 0-553-80725-0

LC 2010-42093

In this novel featuring Boston PD Sgt. Det. D.D. Warren, "D.D.'s former partner and one-time lover, Det. Bobby Dodge, of the Massachusetts State Police, asks her to look into what appears to be a clear-cut homicide case. The evidence suggests that Tessa Leoni, a state trooper colleague of Bobby's, shot and killed her abusive husband, Brian Darby, who may have kidnapped her six-year-old daughter, Sophie. But Tessa won't talk about her bruises, her husband, or what might have happened to her child. D.D. examines every detail about the family, while Tessa uses her skills to manipulate the investigation. . . . Gardner sprinkles plenty of clues and inventive twists to keep readers off-kilter as the suspense builds to a realistic, jaw-dropping finale." Publ wkly

Gardner, Lisa

The **neighbor**; Lisa Gardner. Bantam Books 2009 373 p. o.p.; o.p.; $7.99
ISBN 9780553807233; 0553807234; 9780553591903

LC 2009009861

Thriller Awards (International Thriller Writers): Best Novel (2010)

This book follows "Boston police detective D. D. Warren," who is investigating the case of a "schoolteacher [who] vanishes from her home, leaving behind a young daughter and a husband. . . [I]t becomes apparent that her departure was not voluntary and the suspects begin to mount up: the not-so-grieving husband, who seems to be hiding some pretty big secrets; a neighbor who happens to be a registered sex offender; one of the victim's students, a boy who might have some misguided feelings for the victim; even the woman's estranged father . . . the woman herself is deeply troubled and is perhaps not quite the innocent victim she appears to be." (Booklist)

Garey, Juliann

Too bright to hear too loud to see; Juliann Garey. Soho Press 2012 289 p. (hbk. : alk. paper) $25
ISBN 161695129X; 9781616951290; 9781616951306

LC 2012026028

This book is the "story of one man's descent into madness and his painful struggle to recover" from manic depression through electric shock treatments. Formerly a movie studio executive, "the tools of [Greyson Todd's] trade—lying, manipulation, negotiation—were skills that came naturally . . . . Greyson snaps under this constant pressure to pretend, leaves his family, and travels around the world, visiting sex clubs in Thailand and disease-ridden villages in Africa." (Library Journal)

Garner, Helen

The **spare** room; a novel. Henry Holt 2009 175p $22
ISBN 978-0-8050-8888-5; 0-8050-8888-1

LC 2008-10107

First published 2008 in Australia

"Humour is not just an occasional relief in The Spare Room, it's actually the lifeblood of the book. The old cliché that 'you've got to laugh' in the face of tragedy is given new meaning by Garner. For all the sickness and suffering and thankless service involved in the story, it's only an acute sense of the absurdity of the situation that keeps the heroine . . . sane. Garner's dealings with terminal illness are truly refreshing. Instead of focusing on the sufferer, Nicola, she delves inwards, exploring the impact on the carer. And she dares to express the unspeakable thoughts we often think when confronted by another's illness." PopMatters

Gash, Jonathan

Prey dancing; a Dr. Clare Burtonall mystery. Viking 1998 272p

ISBN 0-670-87764-6

LC 98-2830

"Brilliantly written, mysterious, menacing, and filled with unforgettable characters." Booklist

Gash, Jonathan

The **rich** and the profane; a Lovejoy novel. Viking 1999 344p

ISBN 0-670-88346-8

LC 98-38951

First published 1998 in the United Kingdom

"With this dervish of comic activity and a romp that ends in a circus-like venue, Gash is in top form." Publ Wkly

Gaskell, Elizabeth Cleghorn

★ **Cranford**; [by] Elizabeth Gaskell. Oxford University Press 1998 xxxii, 194p (Oxford world classics) pa $9.95

ISBN 0-19-283209-3

LC 98-204713

First published 1853

This novel "centres on the formidable Miss Deborah Jenkyns and her gentle sister Miss Matty, daughters of the former rector. Moments of drama are provided by the death of the genial Captain Brown, run over by a train when saving the life of a child; by the panic caused in the village by rumours of burglars; by the surprising marriage of the widowed Lady Glenmire with the vulgar Mr. Hoggins, the village surgeon; by the failure of a bank which ruins Miss Matty, and her rescue by the fortunate return from India of her long-lost brother Peter. But the greatest charm of 'Cranford,' which has kept it unfailingly popular, is its amused but loving portrayal of the old-fashioned customs and 'elegant economy' of a delicately observed group of middle-aged figures in a landscape." Oxford Companion to Engl Lit. 5th edition

Gaspar de Alba, Alicia, 1958-

Desert blood; the Juárez murders. by Alicia Gaspar de Alba. Arte Publico Press 2005 vi, 346p (pbk.) $16.95; o.p.; o.p.

ISBN 9781558855182; 1558854460 (alk. paper); 9781558854468 (alk. paper)

LC 2004055417

Lambda Literary Awards: Lesbian Mystery (2005)

This novel tells the story of a "visiting professor at an L.A. college, Ivon [Villa, who] is smart, beautiful, and gay. She and her partner, Brigit, decide to adopt a baby from Mexico, and Ivon travels to her native El Paso to see the child. On the plane, she reads an article about the murdered bodies of more than 100 women found in the desert outside Juarez. The crime wave hits home when the mother of the baby she was to adopt becomes one of the victims. Then Ivon's little sister, Irene, goes missing after an evening in Juarez. With the help of her cousin and a nervous priest, Ivon desperately searches for Irene while dealing with their accusatory mother and corrupt border patrol officers." (Booklist)

Gass, William H., 1924-2017

★ **Middle** C; a novel. by William H. Gass. Alfred A. Knopf 2013 416 p. $28.95

ISBN 0307701638; 9780307701633

LC 2012017087

This novel, by William H. Gass, "begins in Graz, Austria, 1938. Joseph Skizzen's father . . . leaves his country for England. . . . In London . . . , he disappears under mysterious circumstances. The family is relocated to a small town in Ohio, where Joseph Skizzen grows up, becomes a decent amateur piano player, in part to cope with the abandonment of his father, and creates as well a fantasy self--a professor with a fantasy goal: to establish the Inhumanity Museum." (Publisher's note)

Gavin, Jim

★ **Middle** men; stories. Jim Gavin. Simon & Schuster 2012 224 p.

ISBN 9781451649314

LC 2011045956

This collection of short stories by Jim Gavin presents a "panoramic vision of California, portraying a group of men, from young dreamers to old vets, as they make valiant forays into middle-class respectability. . . . The men in Gavin's stories all find themselves stuck somewhere in the middle, caught half way between their dreams and the often crushing reality of their lives." (Publisher's note)

Gay, Roxane

Difficult women; Roxane Gay. Grove Press 2017 272 p. (hardcover) $25; (ebook) $25

ISBN 0802125395; 9780802125392; 9780802189646

LC 2016030262

This book, by Roxane Gay, is a "collection of stories of rare force and beauty, of hardscrabble lives, passionate loves, and quirky and vexed human connection. The women in these stories live lives of privilege and of poverty, are in marriages both loving and haunted by past crimes or emotional blackmail. . . . From a girls' fight club to a wealthy subdivision in Florida where neighbors conform, compete, and spy on each other, Gay delivers a . . . vision of modern America." (Publisher's note)

"Whether focusing on assault survivors, single mothers, or women who drown their guilt in wine and bad boyfriends, Gay's fantastic collection is challenging, quirky, and memorable." Pub Wkly

Gay, Roxane

★ An **Untamed** State; Roxane Gay. Pgw 2014 368 p. $16

ISBN 0802122515; 9780802122513

In this novel by Roxane Gay, "Mireille Duval Jameson is living a fairy tale. The strong-willed youngest daughter of one of Haiti's richest sons, she has an adoring husband, a precocious infant son, by all appearances a perfect life. The fairy tale ends one day when Mireille is kidnapped in broad daylight by a gang of heavily armed men, in front of her father's Port au Prince estate." (Publisher's note)

"Among the strongest achievements of this novel is that Mireille's story feels complete and whole while emphasizing its essential brokenness. A cutting and resonant debut." Kirkus

Gay, William

I hate to see that evening sun go down; collected stories. Free Press 2002 303p $24

ISBN 0-7432-4088-X

LC 2002-73945

"Gay is richly gifted: a seemingly effortless storyteller, a writer of prose that's fiercely wrought, pungent in detail, yet poetic in the most welcome sense." N Y Times Book Rev

Gay, William

Twilight; a novel. MacAdam/Cage 2006 224p $25

ISBN 978-1-59692-058-3; 1-59692-058-0

LC 2006-19865

The "absence of a soothing depth—of motive, reasons, understanding—is one of the great achievements of the novel. It sets up a central tension for the reader, who deaires to know more, while the writer resolutely adheres to the truth of his universe—that such comforts aren't available and that the quiverings of the individual consciousness aren't substantial enough in the face of life's darkly malevolent forces." Paste

Geagley, Brad

Year of the hyenas; Brad Geagley. Simon & Schuster 2005 291p $23; (pbk.) $20

ISBN 074325080X; 9781439124697

LC 2004058979

This book, set in Thebes, Egypt in 1153 B.C., follows "an embittered, self-loathing, near-alcoholic named Semerket, . . . the Clerk of Investigations and Secrets, . . . a cop charged with nailing the killer of [a] beloved local priestess. . . . Semerket learns soon enough that responsibility has fallen on his shoulders precisely because the powers-that-be expect him to collapse under its weight." (Kirkus) "[H]e ultimately uncovers a conspiracy aimed at overthrowing the current pharaoh, Ramses III." (Library Journal)

Gear, Kathleen O'Neal

People of the masks; [by] Kathleen O'Neal Gear & W. Michael Gear. Forge 1998 416p

ISBN 0-312-85857-4

LC 98-8695

"Great trouble begins for two tribes in what is now northeastern North America when Jumping Badger, a sadistic war leader, raids and destroys Paint Rock village and kidnaps the dwarf child Rumbler, whose power in the spirit world is legendary. Blue Raven, Jumping Badger's cousin, believes that the tribes need to work together to survive attacks from fiercer enemies. But as warriors begin to die, Rumbler is accused of casting evil spells, and Blue Raven can no longer protect him." Libr J

Gear, Kathleen O'Neal

People of the mist; [by] Kathleen O'Neal Gear and W. Michael Gear. Forge 1997 432p maps

ISBN 0-312-85854-X

LC 97-14682

"Simple prose brightened by atmospheric detail sweeps this fluid, suspenseful mix of anthropological research and character-driven mystery to a solid, satisfying resolution." Publ Wkly

Gear, W. Michael

People of the thunder; [by] W. Michael Gear and Kathleen O'Neal Gear. Forge 2009 383p $25.95

ISBN 978-0-7653-1439-0; 0-7653-1439-8

LC 2008-38017

"Set in the 1300s largely in what is now Alabama and Mississippi, this complex novel tracks three wanderers' quest to create peace in violent times. The Sky Hand people control their territory from Split Sky City (Moundville, Ala.), ruled by scheming chief Flying Hawk and his ruthless nephew, war chief Smoke Shield. While they plot to suppress the enslaved Albaamaha people and to conquer their neighbors, three people pursue a mission to restore peace. Old White is a prophet and 'the most dangerous man alive'; Trader is a man with blood on his hands and a stunning secret; Two Petals is a shaman woman who says and does everything backwards. Together this curious trio must bring down Flying Hawk and Smoke Shield. The story is loaded with early Native American lore, spirituality, economics, government and daily life; however, it is not for the squeamish, as it also contains plenty of blood and gore, hideous torture, rape and chilling cruelty. . . . A terrific tale." Publ Wkly

Geni, Abby

The **last** animal; stories. Abby Geni. Counterpoint 2013 304 p.

ISBN 9781619021822

LC 2013014415

This book, by Abby Geni, is a "series of stories unified around one theme: people who use the interface between the human and the natural world to contend with their modern challenges in love, loss, and family life. . . . Through a menagerie of settings and landscapes . . . it underscores the connection among all living things." (Publisher's note)

"The characters and events here are unusual and far-reaching, but Geni's careful craftsmanship renders them immediate and real." Kirkus

Geni, Abby

★ The **lightkeepers**; a novel. Abby Geni. Counterpoint 2016 340 p. (hardcover) $25

ISBN 9781619026001; 1619026007

LC 2015037125

In this novel, by Abby Geni, "we follow Miranda, a nature photographer who travels to the Farallon Islands, an exotic and dangerous archipelago off the coast of California, for a one-year residency capturing the landscape. Her only companions are the scientists studying there. . . . Shortly after her arrival, Miranda is assaulted by one of the inhabitants of the islands. A few days later, her assailant is found dead, perhaps the result of an accident." (Publisher's note)

"As the plot turns violent and suspenseful, and the mesmerizingly vivid descriptions reach shivery crescendos of shocking revelations, Geni dramatically meshes the grand, menacing power of the ruthless wild with the mysteries and aberrations of the equally untamed human psyche." Booklist

Genova, Lisa

Inside the O'Briens; a novel. Lisa Genova. Gallery Books 2015 352 p. (hardcover : acid-free paper) $26

ISBN 147671777X; 9781476717777; 9781476717791

LC 2014034832

In this novel, by Lisa Genova, "Joe O'Brien is a 44-year-old Boston cop who still lives in the Charlestown neighborhood where he grew up. He begins experiencing involuntary, jerky movements, and his fellow cops suspect he might be a drunk, but a doctor's visit and extensive testing reveal that he suffers from Huntington's disease, which is hereditary and incurable." (Booklist)

George, Elizabeth, 1949-

A **Banquet** of Consequences; A Lynley Novel. by Elizabeth George. Penguin Group USA 2015 592 p. $28.95

ISBN 0525954333; 9780525954330

In this mystery, by Elizabeth George, "[a]s Inspector Thomas Lynley investigates the London angle of an ever more darkly disturbing case, his partner, Barbara Havers, is looking behind the peaceful façade of country life to discover a twisted world of desire and deceit. The suicide of William Goldacre is devastating to those left behind . . . could there be a link between the young man's leap from a Dorset cliff and a horrific poisoning in Cambridge?" (Publisher's note)

"This nineteenth Lynley novel is a sterling addition to George's acclaimed character-centered series: even the most minor characters are full-bodied, and the personal lives of Lynley and Havers are advanced nicely." Booklist

George, Elizabeth, 1949-

Believing the lie; Elizabeth George. Dutton 2012 610p. maps

ISBN 1410445151; 9781410445155; 0525952586 ; 9780525952589

LC 2011043105

This book tells the story of "Inspector Thomas Lynley, [who] is mystified when he's sent undercover to investigate the death of Ian Cresswell at the request of the man's uncle, the wealthy and influential Bernard Fairclough. The death has been ruled an accidental drowning, and nothing on the surface indicates otherwise. But when Lynley enlists the help of his friends Simon and Deborah St. James, the trio's digging soon reveals that the Fairclough clan is awash in secrets, lies, and motives. . . . As the investigation escalates, the Fairclough family's veneer cracks, with deception and self-delusion threatening to destroy everyone." (Publisher's note)

George, Elizabeth

Careless in red; a novel. Harper 2008 626p $27.95

ISBN 978-0-06-116087-5; 0-06-116087-3

LC 2007-44629

"As with George's other books, the reader is soon plunged into a vast back story of relationships and psychologically complex characters. It's a level of literary sophistication readers have come to expect from George." Seattle Times

George, Elizabeth, 1949-

★ **Just** one evil act; by Elizabeth George. Dutton, Penguin Group (USA) Inc. 2013 736 p. (Inspector Lynley) $29.95

ISBN 0525952969; 9780525952961

LC 2012049712

In this book by Elizabeth George Detective Sergeant Barbara Havers "is at a loss: The daughter of her friend Taymullah Azhar has been taken by her mother, and Barbara can't really help. Azhar is just beginning to accept his soul-crushing loss when Angelina reappears with shocking news: Hadiyyah is missing, kidnapped from an Italian marketplace. Barbara and her partner, Inspector Thomas Lynley, soon discover, the case is far more complex than a typical kidnapping." (Publisher's note)

George, Elizabeth

This body of death; a novel. Harper 2010 692p $28.99

ISBN 978-0-06-116088-2; 0-06-116088-1

LC 2009-35547

"As always, [George's] story is credible and commanding, and her characters—particularly Lynley and Havers—continue to evolve while remaining the reader's old and dear friends. George's perceptive characterizations find a worthy complement in her descriptive powers, which evoke a strong sense of place. . . . A book for neither the faint of heart nor the short of patience, "This Body of Death" is a rich, unsettling work, one whose darkness is lightened by Lynley's steady emergence from grief." Richmond Times-Dispatch

George, Elizabeth

What came before he shot her. HarperCollins 2006 548p $26.95

ISBN 0-06-054562-3

LC 2006-43520

"This is crime writing at its finest, with an almost painfully sharp view of the world and evil." Rocky Mountain News

George, Margaret

The **confessions** of young Nero; Margaret George. Berkley Books 2017 514 p. (hardcover) $28

ISBN 9780698184763; 9780451473387

LC 2016024945

This book, by Margaret George, focuses on "Emperor Nero, one of the most notorious and misunderstood figures in history. . . . [It relates Nero's] ruthless ascension to the throne. Detailing his journey from innocent youth to infamous ruler, it is an epic tale of the lengths to which man will go in the ultimate quest for power and survival." (Publisher's note)

"Highly acclaimed for the detail and personality she gives to epic subjects, George's heavily researched novel flows dynamically among multiple points of view." LJ

George, Margaret

Elizabeth I; a novel. Viking 2011 671p $30

ISBN 978-0-670-02253-3; 0-670-02253-5

LC 2010-35382

"Set in the final 20 years of Elizabeth's reign, George's novel is the portrait of an aging powerful woman, one who struggles at times with her waning sexual allure even as she refuses to let its loss diminish her power. . . . This historical novel has considerable strengths, from impressive detail and a wonderfully evocative setting to dialogue that feels appropriately 'old' without ever veering into hokeyness. George brings the queen's two major foreign-policy challenges—conflict with Spain and with Ireland—to life in a way that feels both immediate and relevant. But these achievements are at times outweighed both by the inclusion of (seemingly) everything that happened in England during the time period covered, and by the jarring choice to divide the story between two first-person narrators: Elizabeth herself, and her cousin, Lettice Knollys, who was wife to one of Elizabeth's favorite courtiers and mother to another. The two narrators slow the pace down—a problem in such a lengthy tome — and the stories don't intersect enough for a reader to gain traction. . . . Nevertheless, the contrast between the two narrative voices successfully illustrates two very different modes of female power: the Virgin Queen vs. the seductive noblewoman." Boston Globe

Includes bibliographical references

George, Margaret

Helen of Troy. Viking 2006 611p $27.95

ISBN 0-670-03778-8

LC 2005-58473

George's "characters are precisely crafted, and the lovely Helen, clear-eyed and intelligent, is a sympathetic narrator. Despite the novel's length, the pages practically turn themselves. An absorbing retelling of the classic Trojan War myth, and a sobering look at the utter futility of trying to change one's fate." Booklist

George, Nina, 1973-

The **little** Paris bookshop; a novel. Nina George ; translated by Simon Pare. Crown 2015 400 p. map (hardback) $25

ISBN 9780553418774; 0553418777

LC 2014040459

"Monsieur Perdu calls himself a literary apothecary. From his floating bookstore in a barge on the Seine, he prescribes novels for the hardships of life. Using his intuitive feel for the exact book a reader needs, Perdu mends broken hearts and souls. The only person he can't seem to heal through literature is himself; he's still haunted by heartbreak after his great love disappeared." (Publisher's note)

"Through its well-drawn characters, this novel carefully explores these relationships between lovers, friends, and family, and the painful sacrifices made selflessly for them." Booklist

Gerritsen, Tess

Body double. Ballantine Bks. 2004 339p $24.95

ISBN 0-375-43374-0

LC 2004-49807

"An electric series of startling twists, the revelation of ghoulishly practical motives and a nail-biting finale make this Gerritsen's best to date." Publ Wkly

Gerritsen, Tess, 1953-

Playing with fire; a novel. Tess Gerritsen. Ballantine Books 2015 250 p. (hardcover : alk. paper) $28

ISBN 1101884347; 9781101884348

LC 2015026566

In this novel, by Tess Gerritsen, "violinist Julia Ansdell happens upon a curious piece of music—the Incendio waltz. . . . From the moment Julia's bow moves across the strings, . . . something strange is stirred. . . . The music has a terrifying and inexplicable effect on her young daughter, who seems violently transformed. Convinced that the hypnotic strains of Incendio are weaving a malevolent spell, Julia sets out to discover the man and the meaning behind the score." (Publisher's note)

"Gerritsen's narrative weaves back and forth between Julia's time and that of musical prodigy Lorenzo Todesco, who faces the growing anti-Semitism in WWII Italy. These story lines arch, intertwine, and combust in a riveting finale." Booklist

Includes historical notes and bibliographical references

Gessen, Keith

All the sad young literary men. Viking 2008 242p il $24.95

ISBN 978-0-670-01855-0; 0-670-01855-4

LC 2007-21009

"Gessen's humor is persistently Seinfeldian, avoiding the excesses of savage comedy or satire, or anything like raging spiritual despair, for All the Sad Young Literary Men is a post-postmodernist work of fiction in which spiritual impotence is the great subtextual theme, even as sexual promiscuity is the norm." N Y Rev Books

Gholson, Christien

A **fish** trapped inside the wind. Parthian Books 2011 268p pa $14.95

ISBN 978-1-906998-90-5

This book tells the story of "a small town in Belgium near the French border, [where] on the morning of Saint Woelfred's festival, dead fish lie on the ground, scattered everywhere, as if blown in by the wind. The quarries that were once active now stand empty and will soon be used as toxic waste dumps. Are the fish a sign from the saint? Or simply a cruel trick played by Contexture, the dance group who once stripped naked at the Vatican? . . . Journeys of self-discovery are experienced through the eyes of a magician, a writer, the town Casanova, a clairvoyant married to a drunk, a priest and a Rimbaud scholar: each seeking answers to their individual tribulations." (Publisher's note)

"Like the most finely cadenced, beautifully fanciful works of surrealism, this novel beckons with its subtle nuances before it leaps into a dazzling mastery that will ensnare even the casual reader. The town of Villon, Belgium, is experiencing an extremely odd phenomenon. Dead fish are strewn everywhere. Flung over yards and stoops and fields, the fish puzzle the residents no end as they speculate on the significance of such a bizarre happening. Other intersecting events include a rally meant to protest a decision to use local quarries as toxic dumps and the festival of St. Woelfred, who fled into the wilderness in the seventh century to live out her days reflecting in prayer." Booklist

Ghosh, Amitav, 1956-

Flood of fire; a novel. by Amitav Ghosh. Farrar, Straus and Giroux 2015 624 p. maps (hardcover) $28

ISBN 9780374174248

LC 2015010118

In this novel, by Amitav Ghosh, it "is 1839 and China has embargoed the trade of opium, yet too much is at stake in the lucrative business and the British Foreign Secretary has ordered the colonial government in India to assemble an expeditionary force for an attack to reinstate the trade. Among those consigned is Kesri Singh, a soldier in the army of the East India Company. He makes his way eastward on the Hind, a transport ship that will carry him from Bengal to Hong Kong." (Publisher's note)

"Forbidden and betrayed love are the primary forces here, enacted with bawdy comedy and outright melodrama amid family concerns, secret deals, brutality, military battles, and the horrors of the drug trade. This feverishly detailed, vividly panoramic, tumultuous, funny, and heartbreaking tale offers a vigorous conclusion to Ghosh's astutely complex and profoundly resonant geopolitical saga." Booklist

Ghosh, Amitav

The **glass** palace; a novel. Random House 2001 474p $25.95

ISBN 0-375-50148-7

LC 00-41477

This narrative "stretches from the British invasion of Burma, in 1885, through the country's independence, to the uneasy military rule of the present day. The novel is presided over by the Indian-born Rajkumar, a poor orphan, who falls for Dolly, a servant of the exiled queen. Ghosh renders the polite imprisonment of the Burmese royal family in India and the lush, dangerous atmosphere of teak camps in the Burmese forest with fine detail—a perfect balance for the broad stroke of romance and serendipity that drive the story forward." New Yorker

Includes bibliographical references (p. {475})

Ghosh, Amitav, 1956-

The **hungry** tide; Amitav Ghosh. Houghton Mifflin 2005 333p map (pbk.) $14.95

ISBN 0618329978; 9780618711666

LC 2004060942

This book is "set in the Sundarbans, a[n] . . . archipelago . . . that's also a fragile ecosystem. . . . A young marine biologist, born in India but raised in Seattle, is investigating the few remaining freshwater dolphins in this alluring landscape, a vast string of islands and mangrove forests in the Bay of Bengal. She is accompanied by a local fisherman, stubbornly devoted to the old ways of life, who acts as her guide, and by a Delhi-based translator revisiting the region to help an aunt sort through some long-lost family papers. To each, the Sundarbans represent something different, but for all they become ' . . . a meeting not just of many rivers, but a roundabout people can use to pass in many directions—from country to country and even between faiths.'" (New York Times)

Ghosh, Amitav, 1956-

River of smoke. Farrar, Straus and Giroux 2011 522p $28

ISBN 978-0-374-17423-1

LC 2011-24409

Sequel to Sea of poppies (2008)

"Ghosh's fascination with the multicultural ferment of Canton inspires thrilling descriptions of everything from local cuisine to the geopolitics of the opium wars. And his delight in language, especially the inventiveness of pidgin, further vitalizes his canny and dazzling tale, which, for all its historical exactitude, subtly reflects the hypocrisy and horrors of today's drug trafficking." Booklist

Ghosh, Amitav

Sea of poppies. Farrar, Straus and Giroux 2008 515p map $26

ISBN 978-0-374-17422-4; 0-374-17422-9

LC 2008-30854

"An adventure story set in nineteenth-century Calcutta against the backdrop of the Opium Wars. On the Ibis, a ship engaged in transporting opium across the Bay of Bengal, varied life stories converge. A fallen raja, a half-Chinese convict, a plucky American sailor, a widowed opium farmer, a transgendered religious visionary are all united by the 'smoky paradise' of the opium seed. Ghosh writes with impeccable control, and with a vivid and sometimes surprising imagination." New Yorker

Gibb, Camilla

Sweetness in the belly. Penguin Press 2006 338p $23.95

ISBN 1-59420-084-X

LC 2005-53451

First published 2005 in Canada

"Utterly convincing and authentic . . . a novel that will take you to a place so far from yourself that you may wonder, from time to time, whether you are ever coming back." San Francisco Chronicle

Gibbons, Kaye

Divining women. G. P. Putnam's Sons 2004 205p $23.95

ISBN 0-399-15160-5

LC 2003-60661

In this "tale of marital strife and female resilience, Gibbons considers conflicts between blacks and whites and men and women within the context of the First World War and the Spanish influenza epidemic. Martha has sent her intelligent daughter, Mary, to North Carolina to help Martha's half-brother, Troop, and his expectant wife, Maureen, and Mary is amazed to find herself in a household as miserable as it is opulent. Troop is a coldhearted, possibly insane despot; lovely and muddled Maureen is his prisoner; and Zollie and Mamie, their kind African American employees, are treated with appalling indifference. The hate, lies, and machinations at work in this psychotic hothouse rival that of the most gothic of southern melodramas, a tradition Gibbons shrewdly subverts as she divines the true nature of feminine power and points the way toward justice in this gorgeously moody and piquant fairy tale." Booklist

Gibbons, Kaye

★ **Ellen** Foster; a novel. Algonquin Bks. 1987 146p $16.95

ISBN 1-56512-205-4

LC 86-22136

"What might have been grim, melodramatic material in the hands of a less talented author is instead filled with lively humor, . . . compassion and intimacy. This short novel focuses on Ellen's strengths rather than her victimization, presenting a memorable heroine who rescues herself." N Y Times Book Rev

Followed by The life all around me by Ellen Foster (2006)

Gibbons, Kaye

The **life** all around me by Ellen Foster. Harcourt 2006 218p $23

ISBN 0-15-101204-0

LC 2005-14552

Sequel to Ellen Foster (1987)

In this sequel, "Ellen is now 15 and driven to succeed. She and her foster mother, Laura, scrape together enough money to send her to an academic enrichment weekend program at Johns Hopkins University, and she composes an ambitious letter to a professor at Harvard asking him to consider her for admission despite her youth. Yet as she writes poetry to finance her trip to Baltimore, Ellen still clings to her hometown and friends." Libr J

Gibbons, Kaye

On the occasion of my last afternoon. Putnam 1998 273p

ISBN 0-399-14299-1

LC 98-12947

"Gibbons is unsparing in her depiction of the gruesome reality of the carnage, and unflinching in her effort to convey the madness of that time and the havoc it wreaked on people's souls." Booklist

Gibbons, Kaye

Sights unseen. Putnam 1995 209p $19.95

ISBN 0-399-13986-9

LC 95-9781

"Gibbons has her quietly heroic narrator relate one wild and poignant incident after another, holding us rapt with wonder and empathy for Maggie and her loving, self-sacrificing family. This is a novel that deserves unwavering attention from start to finish." Booklist

Gibson, William

★ **Neuromancer**; with a new introduction by the author; with an afterword by Jack Womack. 20th anniversary ed; Ace Books 2004 371p $25

ISBN 0-441-01203-5

LC 2004048718

First published 1984

"In a highly urbanized future dominated by cybernetics and bioengineering, anti-hero Case is rescued from wretchedness and given back the ability to send his persona into the cyberspace of the world's computer networks, where he must carry out a hazardous mission for an enigmatic employer. An adventure story much enlivened by elaborate technical jargon and sleazy, streetwise characters—the pioneering 'cyberpunk' novel and arguably the most influential SF novel of the 1980s." Anatomy of Wonder 5

Gibson, William

★ **Pattern** recognition. Putnam 2003 356p $25.95

ISBN 0-399-14986-4

LC 2002-67955

This novel "tells the story of Cayce Pollard, a 'coolhunter' who gets paid to spot hot new trends for marketers. In her private life, Cayce is obsessed with a series of short films that have appeared anonymously on the Internet. . . . Trouble arises when the two sides of Cayce's life short-circuit: a billionaire marketer gets wind of the films and hires her to find their creator, so he can use them as a marketing tool." (Time)

"Cayce Pollard is a brand consultant whose father disappeared on September 11th. She becomes fascinated by mysterious scraps of film footage—seemingly random scenes, luminously shot—that are disseminated on the Web and have spawned cults of viewers. Gibson wisely avoids addressing the import of 9/11 head on, but he somehow establishes a powerful correlative for it in Cayce's strange quest—through the Tokyo red-light district and the Moscow underworld—to find the anonymous filmmaker. In Gibson's eerie vision of our time, the future has come crashing upon us, fragmentary and undecipherable." New Yorker

Gibson, William, 1948-

The **peripheral**; William Gibson. Putnam's Sons 2014 496 p. (hardback) $28.95

ISBN 0399158448; 9780399158445

LC 2014028558

In this science fiction novel by William Gibson, "where Flynne and her brother, Burton, live, jobs outside the drug business are rare. . . .

Then one night Burton has to go out, but there's a job he's supposed to do--a job Flynne didn't know he had. Beta-testing part of a new game, he tells her. . . . What she sees, though, isn't what Burton told her to expect. It might be a game, but it might also be murder." (Publisher's note)

"All of Gibson's characters are intensely real, and Flynne is a clever, compelling, stereotype-defying, unhesitating protagonist who makes this novel a standout." Pub Wkly

Gibson, William

Spook country. G.P. Putnam's Sons 2007 371p $25.95

ISBN 978-0-399-15430-0; 0-399-15430-2

LC 2007-3138

This novel portrays a "post-9/11 America, which, in thrall to ubiquitous media and vague threats of annihilation, has 'developed Stockholm syndrome toward its own government.' The convoluted and politically insistent plot involves a missing shipping container, a former rock star, a Cuban-Chinese crime-facilitating family, and an Ativan addict coerced into domestic espionage. Fanciful touches include the creation of virtual art in public spaces using satellite mapping and Wi-Fi; texting in Volapuk, a Cyrillic-Latin amalgam; encrypting data within songs on an iPod; and the C.I.A.'s recruitment of sea pirates in the war on terrorism. (All but the last are verifiably real.) If Gibson's vision has got bleaker, his eye for the eerie in the everyday still lends events an otherworldly sheen." New Yorker

Gibson, William

Zero history. G.P. Putnam's Sons 2010 404p $26.95

ISBN 0-399-15682-8; 978-0-399-15682-3

LC 2010-16974

Third book in Gibson's Bigend Trilogy, which includes Pattern recognition and Spook country

"In 'Spook Country' (2007), [Hubertus] Bigend employed Hollis Henry, former lead singer of the fictional '90s band the Curfew, to investigate 'locative' technologies. Now, in 'Zero History,' Henry reluctantly accepts a second commission from Bigend, to track down the designer behind the super-fashionable but anti-fashion 'secret brand' Gabriel Hounds." (N Y Times Book Rev)

"Hollis Henry finds herself once again under Bigend's employ. This time she is hired to discover the identity of the designer of a secret brand of clothing called Gabriel Hounds, whom Bigend hopes to enlist in his bid to get into the design, contracting, and manufacture of U.S. military clothing (and its inevitable spinoff into the mainstream consumer market). Military contracting, according to Bigend, is essentially recession proof. Meanwhile, the translator and cryptologist Milgrim . . . , a former Ativan addict (now in recovery on Bigend's dime) with 'zero history' (being off the grid, he has no credit or address history), is asked to assist Hollis in her investigation. What begins as a seemingly innocent apparel-related project takes on more sinister overtones when the two are followed from London to Paris by a competitor with shady dealings in the arms trade and a personal ax to grind with Milgrim." Booklist

Gide, Andre

★ The **counterfeiters** (Les faux-monnayeurs) translated from the French of André Gide by Dorothy Bussy. Knopf 1927 365p

Original French edition, 1925

"The novelist Edouard keeps a journal of events in order to write a novel about the nature of reality. The intrigues of a gang of counterfeiters symbolize the 'counterfeit' personalities with which people disguise themselves to conform hypocritically to convention or to deceive themselves. The adolescent boys Bernard Profitendieu and Olivier Molinier, having left home in order to be free to find and develop their true selves, encounter many varieties of hyprocrisy and self-deception in human relationships and barely escape falling into such poses themselves. Both begin by seeking a close emotional tie with Edouard. Each, however, comes to recognize that Edouard is inadequate as an ideal for emulation, particularly when the novelist cannot recognize the psychological reality of the schoolboy Boris' useless suicide, which is an indirect result of the counterfeiters' machinations." Reader's Ency. 4th edition

Gide, Andre

★ The **immoralist**; translated by Richard Howard. Modern Lib. 1984 171p

ISBN 0-394-60500-4

LC 83-42856

Original French edition, 1902. First United States edition, translated by Dorothy Bussy, published 1930 by Knopf; this translation first published 1970 by Knopf

"Michel takes his bride, Marceline, to North Africa, where he develops tuberculosis and becomes hyperconscious of physical sensations, particularly of his attraction to young Arab boys. Back on his French estate after being cured, he is encouraged by his friend Ménalque to rise above conventional good and evil and give free rein to all his passions. When Marceline falls ill with the tuberculosis she caught while nursing him, he takes her south. He neglects her demands on him more and more, however, in order to keep himself free, since his new doctrine demands that the weak be suppressed if necessary for the preservation of the strong. She dies, and he, guilt-ridden and debilitated by his excesses, tries to justify his conduct to a group of friends." Reader's Ency. 4th edition

Gideon, Melanie

Wife 22; a novel. Melanie Gideon. Ballantine Books 2012 380 p.

ISBN 034552795X; 9780345527950; 9780345527974

LC 2012004405

This novel by Melanie Gideon is about "a woman losing herself . . . and finding herself again . . . in the middle of her life. . . . [A]fter almost twenty years of marriage my husband and I seemed to be running out of things to say to each other. But when the anonymous online study . . . showed up in my inbox, I had no idea how profoundly it would change my life. . . . I was assigned both a pseudonym (Wife 22) and a caseworker (Researcher 101). . . . My anonymous correspondence with Researcher 101 has taken an unexpectedly personal turn." (Publisher's note)

Giffin, Emily

Heart of the matter. St. Martin's Press 2010 386p $26.99

ISBN 978-0-312-55416-3; 0-312-55416-8

LC 2009-45700

"Giffin's chronicle of fluid, almost casual marital disconnect is a powerful cautionary tale. The slow erosion of marriage leaves Tessa with a litany of unanswered questions. . . . While the ending provides no pat answers, as one would hope, there is the very deliberate turning of a page as, despite transgressions, each of the main characters finds a pathway for looking forward and moving ahead." Boston Globe

Gifford, Barry

The **stars** above Veracruz. Thunder's Mouth Press 2006 262p $24

ISBN 1-56025-807-1

LC 2006-282377

"While the stories take place in cities from berlin to Havana to San Francisco and involve characters as disparate as a prizefighter, a schoolboy, and a one-legged ex-Legionnaire, each concerns the naked bravery of characters stepping into maturity. Gifford's great talent is capturing defining moments with the casual grace of anecdote.

Each of these 16 stunning tales makes the anecdotal monumental." San Francisco Magazine

Gilb, Dagoberto

The **flowers**. Grove Press 2008 250p $24

ISBN 978-0-8021-1859-2; 0-8021-1859-3

"A tightly woven narrative about a boy coming of age in a community bubbling with racial tension. It's beautifully rendered in part because Mr. Gilb nails the voice of 15-year-old narrator Sonny Bravo with pinpoint accuracy." Dallas Morning News

Gilbert, David

& sons; a novel. David Gilbert. Random House Inc 2013 448 p. (acid-free paper) $27

ISBN 0812993969; 9780812993967; 9780812993974

LC 2012031308

This book focuses on "the funeral of Charles Henry Topping on Manhattan's Upper East Side. . . . As [reclusive novelist] Andrew Newbold Dyer delivers the eulogy for his oldest friend, he suffers a breakdown over the life he's led and the people he's hurt and the novel that will forever endure as his legacy. He must gather his three sons for the first time in many years--before it's too late." (Publisher's note)

Gilbert, Elizabeth, 1969-

★ The **Signature** of All Things; a novel. Elizabeth Gilbert. Penguin Group USA 2013 512 p. $28.95

ISBN 0670024856; 9780670024858

LC 2013017045

This book follows Alma Whittaker. "Born in 1800, Alma learns Latin and Greek, understands the natural world, and reads everything in sight. Despite her wealth and education, Alma is a woman, and a plain one at that, two facts that circumscribe her opportunities. Resigned to spinsterhood, ashamed and tormented by her erotic desires, Alma finds a late-in-life soul mate in Ambrose Pike, a talented botanical illustrator and spiritualist." (Publishers Weekly)

Gilchrist, Ellen

The **age** of miracles; stories. Little, Brown 1995 260p

LC 94-37441

In several of the stories in this collection, the author recounts the adventures of her recurring heroine Rhoda Manning. "Elegant, independent, and successful, Rhoda is approaching 60 with unwavering nerve, delighted with the freedom age brings." Booklist

Gilchrist, Ellen

★ **Ellen** Gilchrist: collected stories. Little, Brown 2000 563p $38

ISBN 0-316-29948-0

"Gilchrist is an important voice in contemporary Southern fiction, and this book belongs in every library." Libr J

Gilchrist, Ellen

Flights of angels; stories. Little, Brown 1998 327p $34

ISBN 0-316-31486-2

LC 98-21420

This collection "features some of Gilchrist's familiar, endearingly eccentric narrators. . . . There are also some new, young and engaging characters and, throughout the book, a convincing evocation of the changing South." Publ Wkly

Gill, John Freeman

★ The **gargoyle** hunters; a novel. by John Freeman Gill. Alfred A. Knopf 2017 339 p. (hardcover) $27.95

ISBN 9781101946886; 9781101946893

LC 2016012828

In this novel, by John Freeman Gill, "thirteen-year-old Griffin Watts is recruited into his estranged father's illicit and dangerous architectural salvage business. . . . Griffin is charged with stealing . . . gargoyles . . . right off the faces of unsung tenements and iconic skyscrapers all over town. . . . [He] is slow to recognize that his father's deepening obsession with preserving the architectural treasures of Beaux Arts New York is also a destructive force." (Publisher's note)

"A bildungsroman rich with symbolism, wistful memory, and unabashed longing, this is a remarkably tender love letter to a city and imaginative fiction par excellence." Booklist

Gillham, David R.

City of women; David R. Gillham. Amy Einhorn Books 2012 392 p. (hardcover) $25.95; (paperback) $16.00

ISBN 039915776X; 9780399157769; 9780425252963

LC 2012011002

This book is the story of Sigrid Schröder, "an unassuming stenographer stuck in a loveless marriage and living in Berlin [during World War II] with her sour, difficult mother-in-law. But . . . she has . . . a Jewish lover, and if that were not risky enough, Sigrid becomes entangled with a neighbor who is helping to shelter Jews. As the war progresses, and Sigrid's husband is sent to the Russian front, she's drawn deeper into a world where trust is a hard-won commodity." (Publishers Weekly)

Gilman, Carolyn Ives

Dark orbit; by Carolyn Ives Gilman. Tor Books 2015 304 p. (hardback) $25.99

ISBN 0765336294; 9780765336293

LC 2015015036

In this book, by Carolyn Ives Gilman, "Saraswati Callicot is a Waster--a scientist who spends her life traveling light-years from home to explore new worlds, leaping across decades in an instant, stepping in and out of the flow of ordinary human time. Her latest mission is her farthest, and strangest, trip yet: she's traveled 58 light-years to explore a new planet surrounded by dark matter and secretly observe her crewmate Thora Lassiter, a member of the interplanetary elite." (Kirkus Reviews)

"Blending mystery, philosophy, and science gracefully in a twisty plot, Gilman (Ison of the Isles) has written a challenging but ultimately satisfying space adventure that explores how the most basic preconceptions can distort our outlook. It's a winner for any sf fan, of special appeal to those with interests in epistemology, ethics, or physics." LJ

Gilman, Charlotte Perkins

The **Charlotte** Perkins Gilman reader; The yellow wallpaper and other fiction. edited and introduced by Ann J. Lane. Pantheon Bks. 1980 208p

LC 80-7711

The editor "has selected representative pieces by the early-twentieth-century American feminist socialist, including her best known (and best) quasi-autobiographical story, 'The Yellow Wallpaper,' plus excerpts from four novels and three writings about utopias." Booklist

Gilman, Charlotte Perkins

Charlotte Perkins Gilman's Utopian novels; edited and with an introduction by Minna Doskow. Fairleigh Dickinson Univ. Press 1999 389p

ISBN 0-8386-3761-2

LC 98-23510

In Moving the mountain, an explorer, lost in Tibet for thirty years, returns to the United States in 1940 and finds a society totally transformed by women

Includes bibliographical references (p. 388-389)

Gilman, Charlotte Perkins

Herland; with an introduction by Ann J. Lane. Pantheon Bks. 1979 xxiv, 147p

"Written in 1915, Herland was serialized in Gilman's monthly magazine, 'The Forerunner.'" Introduction

"On the eve of World War I, three American male explorers stumble onto an all-female society somewhere in the distant reaches of the earth. Unable to believe their eyes, they promptly set out to find the men of the society, convinced that, since 'this is a "civilized" country . . . there must be men.' . . . {The novel examines} what is masculine and what is feminine, what is culturally learned and what is biologically determined in our society." Publisher's note

Gilman, Charlotte Perkins

With her in Ourland; sequel to Herland. edited by Mary Jo Deegan and Michael R. Hill; with an introduction by Mary Jo Deegan. Greenwood Press 1997 200p $100.95

ISBN 0-313-27614-5

LC 96-51135

Written in 1916, With her in Ourland was serialized in Gilman's magazine, The Forerunner

"He's a brash American adventurer; she's an independent, albeit sheltered, sociologist from Herland, a 2000-year-old, all-female society. Not surprisingly, when Vandyck (Van) and Ellador marry, most everything becomes a point of negotiation, if not contention: sexual relations, family obligations and attitudes about race, class and the welfare state." Publ Wkly

Gilman, Dorothy

The **amazing** Mrs. Pollifax. Doubleday 1970 234p

Mrs. Emily Pollifax, widow and grandmother, combats international espionage at the request of the C.I.A. in this spy adventure. The scene is Istanbul where Mrs. Pollifax must help a double agent escape. That she does, outwitting the enemy with her own special brand of logic

Gilman, Dorothy

The **elusive** Mrs. Pollifax. Doubleday 1971 240p

Mrs. Pollifax "the genteel grandmother-heroine swings into action for the CIA by transporting in her hat some forged passports to the Bulgarian underground which turns out to be a group of five amateurs. In her travels Mrs. Pollifax meets some young Americans, one of whom is ostensibly imprisoned for espionage but actually held for ransom, and Mrs. Pollifax involves the underground and a paid informer in a daring rescue plan. Amusing spy adventure with more appeal for readers of light fiction than for espionage buffs." Booklist

Gilman, Dorothy

Kaleidoscope; a Countess Karitska novel. Ballantine Bks. 2002 244p $21

ISBN 0-345-44820-0

LC 2002-277874

"Madame Karitska's trade as a fortune teller attracts a strange array of clients, including an artistic woman whose husband abandons her to join a religious cult and an Italian immigrant with a 'cursed' child. Karitska also helps her good friend, Detective-Lieutenant Pruden, solve the hit-and-run death of a young violinist and the murder of a local philanthropist. Her most troubling case, however, occurs when a subway incident leaves her with an attaché case full of diamonds. This {is a} well-written episodic adventure." Libr J

Gilman, Dorothy

Mrs. Pollifax and the whirling dervish. Doubleday 1990 196p

LC 89-25796

"The countryside is depicted in great detail, and so are the native people. Gilman's eye for background matches her marvelous sense of adventure." Booklist

Gilman, Dorothy

Mrs. Pollifax pursued. Fawcett Columbine 1995 198p

LC 94-27625

Mrs. Pollifax "discovers a young woman in her hall closet hiding from some men in a white van. Eager as always, she elicits the girl's story, eludes the villains, and enables the CIA to resolve the situation, which involves kidnapping, shady investments, attempted murder, and the grandson of Ubangiba's last king. Agents actually consult reference books for essential background information, and a few literary allusions build character or relate to earlier Pollifax appearances. This fast-moving tale sports a lively, energetic style." Libr J

Gilman, Dorothy

Mrs. Pollifax, innocent tourist. Fawcett Columbine 1997 203p

LC 96-47715

Mrs. Pollifax is on "a trip to the Middle East with her CIA friend Farrell to retrieve a manuscript written by a murdered dissident. The manuscript, thinly disguised as fiction, provides provocative details of Saddam Hussein's reign of terror. The pickup, arranged through an intermediary, proves much more difficult than Farrell or Mrs. Pollifax anticipated, what with smugglers disguised as businessmen, attacks by knife-wielding sheikhs, car chases, and rides on berserk camels. . . . Fun and entertaining, this one is sure to be a hit with the legion of Mrs. Pollifax fans." Booklist

Gilman, Dorothy

Thale's Folly. Ballantine Pub. Group 1999 199p

ISBN 0-449-00364-7

LC 98-27657

"At first, it seems Gilman is rounding up the usual literary suspects, but her genial and well-paced writing, vivid landscapes, and quirky characters are greater than the sum of the clichés." Booklist

Gilman, Dorothy

The **unexpected** Mrs. Pollifax. Doubleday 1966 216p

A "tale of espionage with the chase in Mexico and through the mountains of Albania. Emily Pollifax, a widow of 63, was startled by her doctor's suggestion that the cure for her depression was a job. The only career that inspired Emily was spying, and despite her lack of qualifications, off she went to CIA headquarters in Langly, Virginia, to apply. How she became a routine courier, and why unexpected developments brought into play every scrap of skill and knowledge she had acquired in her former secure life, is an exciting discovery for the reader." Libr J

Gilman, Felix

★ The **half**-made world. Tor 2010 479p $25.99

ISBN 978-0-7653-2552-5; 0-7653-2552-7

LC 2010-32564

"Sick of predictable books that fill your subgenre bingo card with the same subgenre elements over and over? . . . . Felix Gilman has blended elements from alternate history, Steampunk, Westerns, and epic fantasy to create something truly original." io9

Gilman, Laura Ann

Flesh and fire; Laura Anne Gilman. Pocket Books 2009 374p (hbk.) o.p.; (pbk.) $9.99

ISBN 9781439101414; 9781439126875; 9781439191545

LC 2009012786

In this fantasy novel, "[o]nce, all power in the Vin Lands was held by the prince-mages, who alone could craft spellwines, and selfishly used them to increase their own wealth and influence. But their abuse of power caused a demigod to break the Vine, shattering the power of the mages. Now, fourteen centuries later, it is the humble Vinearts who hold the secret of crafting spells from wines, the source of magic, and they are prohibited from holding power. But now . . . [s]trange, terrifying creatures, sudden plagues, and mysterious disappearances threaten the land. Only one Vineart senses the danger, and he has only one weapon to use against it: a young slave. His name is Jerzy, and his origins are unknown. . . . Yet his uncanny sense of the Vinearts' craft offers a hint of greater magics within -- magics that his Master, the Vineart Malech, must cultivate and grow." (Publisher's note)

Followed by: Weight of Stone (2012)

Gilman, Laura Anne

★ The **cold** eye; Laura Anne Gilman. First edition Saga Press 2017 334 p. illustrations (Gilman, Laura Anne. Devil's West) (hardcover : acid-free paper) $27.99; (softcover : acid-free paper) $16.99; (hardcover : acid-free paper) $27.99; (softcover : acid-free paper) $16.99

ISBN 9781481429719; 9781481429726; 148142971X; 1481429728

LC 2016029456

In this book in The Devil's West series, by Laura Anne Gilman, "Isobel is riding circuit through the Territory as the Devil's Left Hand. But when she responds to a natural disaster, she learns the limits of her power and the growing danger of something mysterious that is threatening not just her life, but the whole Territory." (Publisher's note)

While serving as the Left Hand of the Devil, Isobel has her power tested as she tries to figure out the cause of a growing and mysterious danger throughout the Territory, in a sequel to Silver on the Road.

Gilman, Laura Anne

Hard magic. Luna 2010 329p pa $14.95

ISBN 978-0-373-80313-2; 0-373-80313-3

"Spinning off a minor character from the Retrievers books (Staying Dead, etc.), Gilman launches an entertaining new series set in her Cosa Nostradamus world of magic-using Talented humans. Following up on a mysterious job lead, college grad Bonita Torres joins the Private Unaffiliated Paranormal Investigations (PUPI), a freelance CSI-style unit for Talent-related crimes. The puppies refine and practice spells until they get their first big case: an apparent double suicide. As they follow the evidence, trail and interrogate suspects, and defend themselves against attacks, the investigators develop comfortable and engaging team dynamics and create the field of forensic magic. Gilman's deft plotting and first-class characters complement her agile blend of science and spell craft." Publ Wkly

Gilman, Laura Anne

Silver on the Road; Laura Anne Gilman. Simon & Schuster 2015 400 p. map (Gilman, Laura Anne. Devil's West) hardcover $26.99

ISBN 9781481429689; 148142968X

LC 2016287058

In this novel in the Devil's West series by Laura Anne Gilman, "Isobel, upon her sixteenth birthday, makes the choice to work for the devil in his territory west of the Mississippi. But this is not the devil you know. This is a being who deals fairly with immense—but not unlimited—power, who offers opportunities to people who want to make a deal, and they always get what they deserve. But his land is a wild west that needs a human touch, and that's where Izzy comes in." (Publisher's note)

"Refreshingly, her vision of the American West includes respectful portrayals of Native Americans. Isobel's coming-of-age story is very accessible to teens, and there's plenty for adventure-minded adults to enjoy as well." Pub Wkly

Other titles in this series are:

The cold eye

Red waters rising

Gilman, Susan Jane

The **Ice** Cream Queen of Orchard Street; a novel. by Susan Jane Gilman. Grand Central Publishing 2014 512 p. (hardcover) $26

ISBN 0446578932; 9780446578936

LC 2013030543

National Jewish Book Awards Finalist: Debut Fiction (2014)

In this book, by Susan Jane Gilman, "Malka Treynovsky flees Russia with her family. . . . [N]o sooner do they land on the squalid Lower East Side of Manhattan, than Malka is crippled and abandoned in the street. Taken in by a tough-loving Italian ices peddler, she manages to survive through cunning and inventiveness. . . . She falls in love with a gorgeous, illiterate radical named Albert, and they set off across America in an ice cream truck." (Publisher's note)

"At the heart of memoirist Gilman's (Hypocrite in a Pouffy White Dress; Kiss My Tiara) first novel is ice cream entrepreneur Lillian Dunkle, a fascinating character who, like American businesswoman Leona Helmsley, believes that "only the little people pay taxes." At 75, Lillian is bravely facing federal tax evasion charges...With its vivid depictions of old New York City tenement life and its tale of the American ice cream business set against the backdrop of the major events of the 20th century, this rags-to-riches saga will appeal greatly to readers of American historical novels." LJ

Gilmore, Jennifer

Golden country; a novel. Scribner 2006 315p $25

ISBN 978-0-7432-8863-7; 0-7432-8863-7

LC 2005-57586

"An ingeniously plotted family yarn. Gilmore's careful planning results in a satisfying blend of story lines, and her refusal to settle on one simple perspective enlivens the myth of the American Dream." N Y Times Book Rev

Gilmore, Jennifer

The **Mothers**; 1st Scribner hardcover ed. Simon & Schuster 2013 288 p. (hardcover) $26

ISBN 1451697252; 9781451697254

LC 2012533117

This third novel from Jennifer Gilmore is the "cry of a woman who desperately wants a baby. Jesse Weintraub, a history professor in Manhattan, is postcancer and almost 40. After years of trying to get pregnant, she and husband Ramon Aragon pursue open adoption. The chronicle of their 10-year marriage, forged when Jewish Jesse met Spanish-Italian Ramon in Italy, is a paradoxical tale of marital love surmounting cultural and religious differences and then veering into obsessive desperation." (Publishers Weekly)

Gilmore, Jennifer

Something red; a novel. Scribner 2010 307p $25

ISBN 9781416571704; 1416571701

LC 2009-40482

"When their oldest child, Ben, leaves for college, Dennis and Sharon Goldstein—one-time young idealists who became a bureaucrat and a society caterer, respectively—begin to discover their family's secrets. Not only is Sharon having an affair but daughter Vanessa is anorexic. Indeed, it's soon evident that the family secrets transcend generations. The story is told in chapters from the point of view of each family member, detailing Dennis's travel for the U.S. Department of Agriculture and recollections of when his children were young, Sharon's extramarital affair and her relationship with Vanessa, Ben's college experimentation and activism, and Vanessa's high school relationships and eating disorder." Libr J

Gingrich, Newt

Gettysburg; a novel of the Civil War. {by} Newt Gingrich and William Forstchen; and Albert S. Hanser, contributing editor. St. Martin's Press 2003 463p il $24.95

ISBN 0-312-30935-X

LC 2003-41381

"On July 1, 1863, the Army of Virginia, under the command of Gen. Robert E. Lee, and the Army of the Potomac, under Gen. George G. Meade, clashed in deadly combat near Gettysburg, PA. Of course, Union forces won, but Gingrich and Forstchen imagine a different outcome in which Confederate forces do a surprise march around Union lines to flank and cut off the Union troops from their supply and information routes. In the course of their narrative, the authors depict the gallantry and heroism of Lee, Longstreet, Chamberlain, Hancock, Hunt, and many other officers and enlisted men on both sides of the conflict." Libr J

Gingrich, Newt

Grant comes east; a novel of the Civil War. [by] Newt Gingrich, William R. Forstchen and Albert S. Hanser, contributing editor. 1st ed; Thomas Dunne Books\St. Martin's Press 2004 404p il map $24.95

ISBN 0-312-30937-6

LC 2004-43894

This alternate-history sequel to the author's Gettysburg "centers on the Union government's bringing General Grant eastward from his recent victory in Vicksburg; of course, the immediate ramification of Lee's win at Gettysburg . . . is the threatened safety of Washington, D.C.–and further down the line, the possibility of actual and official recognition of the Confederacy by the European powers. Gingrich and Forstchen's readjustments to history are notably original." Booklist

Giolito, Malin Persson

Quicksand; Malin Persson Giolito ; translated from the Swedish by Rachel Willson-Broyles. Other Press 2016 501 p. (hardcover) $25.95

ISBN 1590518578; 9781590518571; 9781590518588

LC 2016032468

In this book, by Malin Persson Giolito, translated by Rachel Willson-Broyles, "a mass shooting has taken place at a prep school in Stockholm's wealthiest suburb. Eighteen-year-old Maja Norberg is charged for her involvement in the massacre that left her boyfriend and her best friend dead. She has spent nine months in jail awaiting trial. . . . How did Maja--popular, privileged, and a top student--become a cold-blooded killer in the eyes of the public?" (Publisher's note)

"Giolito's astonishing English-language debut . . . is a dark exploration of the crumbling European social order and the psyches of rich Swedish teens." Booklist

Giordano, Paolo

The **human** body; Paolo Giordano ; English translation by Anne Milano Appel. Pamela Dorman Books/Viking 2014 318 p. (hardback) $27.95

ISBN 0670015644; 9780670015641

LC 2014006927

In this novel, by Paolo Giordano, "a platoon of young men and one woman soldier leaves Italy for . . . Forward Operating Base (FOB) in the Gulistan district of Afghanistan. Each member in the platoon manages the toxic mix of boredom and fear that is life at the FOB in his own way. . . . But when a much-debated mission goes devastatingly awry, the soldiers find their lives changed in an instant." (Publisher's note)

"The Human Body is a memorable entry in the literature of the Afghan war, the characters crisply drawn and the writing full of telling details." Booklist

Giordano, Paolo

Like Family; Paolo Giordano. Penguin Group USA 2015 160 p. $22

ISBN 0525428763; 9780525428763

LC 2015040695

In this novel, by Paolo Giordano, "when Mrs. A. first enters the narrator's home, his wife, Nora, is experiencing a difficult pregnancy. First as their maid and nanny, then their confidante, this older woman begins to help her employers negotiate married life, quickly becoming the glue in their small household. But the family's delicate fabric comes undone when Mrs. A. is diagnosed with cancer." (Publisher's note)

"And at his best, Giordano muses gorgeously on our inability to blend our life essences; even love leaves us lonely. A lovely remembrance played in a minor key." Kirkus

Giordano, Paolo

The **solitude** of prime numbers. Pamela Dorman Books/ Viking 2010 271p $25.95

ISBN 978-0-670-02148-2

LC 2009-41165

Original Italian edition, 2008; This translation first published 2009 in the United Kingdom

"Alice has been crippled in a childhood skiing accident, Mattia is consumed by guilt after playing an unintended but key role in his twin sister's disappearance. Upon meeting in their early teens, they develop a frequently uncomfortable yet enveloping friendship. . . . This is a book about communication: in lacking a facility for self-expression, our stunted protagonists exist almost solely, and safely, in their own minds. Despite its heavy subject matter, it reads easily, due in part to the almost seamless translation. A quietly explosive ending completes the novel in just the fashion it was started, as an intimate psychological portrait of two 'prime numbers'—together alone and alone together." Booklist

Glass, Julia

I see you everywhere. Pantheon Books 2008 287p $24.95

ISBN 978-0-375-42275-1; 0-375-42275-7

LC 2008-00212

"Mourning, a dish that never grows cold, is the subtext of I See You Everywhere, but it is only part of the feast. Rich, intricate and alive with emotion, the book reconstructs the complicated bonds between Louisa and Clem, making neither sister a villain, neither a hero." N Y Times Book Rev

Glass, Julia

★ **Three** Junes. Pantheon Bks. 2002 353p
ISBN 0-375-42144-0

LC 2001-55448

National Book Award: Fiction (2002)

"Free of gimmickry, @Three Junes' brilliantly rescues, then refurbishes, the traditional plot-driven novel." N Y Times Book Rev

Glass, Julia

The **whole** world over. Pantheon Books 2006 506p $25.95
ISBN 0-375-42274-9

LC 2005-54043

"Glass is too capable to need recipes and four-legged friends to make her fiction a pleasure. It's a tribute to this unassuming but conspicuously talented novelist that even with far too many of them, The Whole World Over so often manages to sing." N Y Times Book Rev

Glass, Julia

The **widower's** tale. Pantheon Books 2010 402p $25.95
ISBN 978-0-307-37792-0; 0-307-37792-X

LC 2010-02854

"Percy Darling, 70, is the titular widower, a rigid man still sorely missing his long-deceased wife. He holds the center of Glass' [novel], . . . set in a bucolic town outside of Boston. Orbiting around Percy are two grown daughters: one a divorced flibbertigibbet and the other a renowned oncologist who is as stern with her family as she is open and available to her patients. Add to the mix a wayward Harvard grandson, a Guatemalan gardener, a gay preschool teacher, and a salt-of-the-earth artist who reminds Percy that he is still very much alive. It's a large, endearing cast, bursting with emotional and social issues, and Glass slips effortlessly between their individual and enmeshed dramas." Entertainment Wkly

Gloss, Molly

The **hearts** of horses. Houghton Mifflin Co. 2007 289p $24
ISBN 978-0-618-79990-9; 0-618-79990-7

LC 2007-8521

Gloss bases her novel on "historical accounts of cowgirls in the American West. With obvious appeal for horse lovers, it has a homespun quality, and varies in action between a gentle canter and energetic gallop." Libr J

Glynn, Alan

Bloodland; Alan Glynn. Faber and Faber 2011 417 p.
ISBN 0571275427; 0571275435; 9780571275427; 9780571275434

LC 2011514786

This book follows "a hungry young journalist named Jimmy Gilroy" who is investigating the case of "Susie Monaghan . . . on the cusp of stardom when her life was cut short by a tragic helicopter crash. . . . Before dying, Susie's path had crossed with an unlikely gallery of powerful men: an ex-Prime minister with a carefully guarded secret; the businessman brother of a U.S. Senator angling for the Oval Office; and a billionaire investor with his eye on an extremely rare commodity. Might there also be a link between Susie's death and a deranged security contractor operating in Congo? Piece by piece, Jimmy uncovers a bizarre nexus of coincidence among these disparate people and events." (Publisher's note)

Goddard, Robert

Beyond recall; a novel. Holt & Co. 1998 310p
ISBN 0-8050-5110-4

LC 97-28895

First published 1997 in the United Kingdom

"There's an elegant arc to Goddard's fluid style, which gracefully orchestrates the story over its broad time span and through the ambiguous testimony of its complex characters." N Y Times Book Rev

Goddard, Robert

★ **Into** the blue. Poseidon Press 1990 415p
ISBN 0-671-70482-6

LC 90-42481

"During this quest, Harry's courage is tested as well as his judgment of people—all of whom turn out to be totally and depressingly human. An everyman's hero, against all mental and emotional odds, Harry finds Heather and renewed self-respect. A very satisfying novel in every way." Booklist

Goddard, Robert

★ **Long** time coming; a novel. Bantam Books Trade Paperbacks 2010 420p pa $15
ISBN 978-0-385-34361-9; 0-385-34361-2

LC 2009-44547

In this thriller the author "shifts effortlessly between 1976, when 68-year-old Eldritch Swan, thought killed in the Blitz, resurfaces from 36 years in an Irish prison, and 1940, when Eldritch, a cocksure secretary for an unscrupulous Antwerp diamond merchant, Isaac Meridor, prepares to leave for America. The older Eldritch, who appears as weird as his given name implies, assures his nephew, Stephen, he'd been framed in Dublin for unspecified offenses against the state, though he admits to helping steal Meridor's Picasso collection. Eldritch needs Stephen's help to prove the collection rightfully belongs to Meridor's wife, daughter, and granddaughter, Rachel Banner. Bit by tantalizing bit the convoluted tale of Eldritch's unknowing involvement in high wartime crimes and misdemeanors during Britain's finest hour emerges, deftly counterpointed by Stephen's growing attachment to Rachel." Publ Wkly

Goddard, Robert

Never go back. Delta Trade Paperbacks 2007 336p pa $12
ISBN 978-0-385-34063-2; 038534063X

LC 2007-6336

First published 2006 in the United Kingdom

"In 1955, Harry Barnett and a group of fellow Royal Air Force servicemen participated in a teaching experiment in a castle on the outskirts of Aberdeen, Scotland. (Each agreed to be a guinea pig in lieu of punishment for bad behavior.) Now, 50 years later, surviving RAF alumni are invited to a reunion at the same royal locale. Though Barnett, now 70, is reluctant to be away from his wife and young daughter in Vancouver, British Columbia, he decides to go. Tragedy strikes when one of the retired servicemen jumps from the train en route from London (or was he pushed?). In the midst of the reunion, a suspicious automobile accident kills another, and suddenly this get-together doesn't seem like such a good plan. Police soon name Harry and former business partner Barry, whose shady financial dealings once landed him in prison, as prime suspects. Certain the violence is linked to the experiments carried out half a century ago, the two men launch an investigation of their own. Goddard's latest offering marks the return of unlikely hero Harry Barnett, star of Into the Blue (1990) and Out of the Sun (1997). It's a crackling good read, with clipped prose, complex characters, and a smart, sinuous plot." Booklist

Godden, Rumer

The **battle** of the Villa Fiorita. Viking 1963 312p

Godden's "characters live and linger in the mind, and the very feel of golden Italy counterpoints the sharp battle in which both sides so tragically lose." Libr J

Godden, Rumer

★ **Black** Narcissus. Little, Brown 1939 294p

A "story of a small group of Anglican nuns newly settled in a convent, formerly a general's pleasure palace, on a high ledge facing Himalayan winds and snows. How the strange pagan environment and unusual experiences affect each of the Sisters, and how a year's effort to teach and heal the natives come to naught is related in a portrayal impressive for its beauty, poignancy and insight." Bookmark

Godden, Rumer

★ The **greengage** summer; a novel. Viking 1958 218p

"There is real evil in Miss Godden's novel as well as real good: sex and theft and even murder intrude upon her dewy world as baldly as on the daily papers. But even violence she handles with consummate delicacy. If she allows a moral to creep in, it is that we lose something valuable in gaining maturity." N Y Her Trib Books

Godden, Rumer

Pippa passes. Morrow 1994 171p

ISBN 0-688-13397-5

LC 94-18336

"In less able hands, these highly romantic goings-on would seem contrived, but Godden's graceful storytelling keeps readers enthralled, with gorgeous Venice and the nitty-gritty of the dance troupe's routine providing a convincing backdrop for her winsome ingenue." Publ Wkly

Godwin, Gail

Evensong. Ballantine Bks. 1999 405p

ISBN 0-345-37244-1

LC 98-15861

Sequel to Father Melancholy's daughter

Godwin "has created a character who has enough flaws to satisfy contemporary skeptics but who also struggles convincingly with the old-fashioned task of being a good person. For all its leisurely pace, Evensong turns out, near the end, to have wasted few words." Time

Godwin, Gail

★ The **finishing** school. Viking 1985 322p

ISBN 0-670-31494-3

LC 84-40069

"'The Finishing School' is a strikingly accurate examination of the affinity between adolescence and middle age." N Y Times Book Rev

Godwin, Gail, 1937-

★ **Flora**; a novel. Gail Godwin. Bloomsbury 2013 288 p. $26

ISBN 1620401207; 9781620401200

LC 2012036741

In this book, "Helen, a writer, looks back to the fateful summer of 1945, when she was a precocious, motherless 10-year-old trying to make sense of a complicated and unjust world. Young Helen lives on a hill in North Carolina in an old . . . house that was once a sanatorium for folks she calls the Recoverers. Raised by her . . . grandmother, whom she worships, Helen is bereft after Nonie's sudden death" and she must live with her guileless cousin Flora. (Booklist)

Godwin, Gail

The **good** husband. Ballantine Bks. 1994 468p

LC 94-5651

"Godwin's intensely drawn characters are vividly portrayed during the most intimate times of love, marriage, and death." Libr J

Godwin, Gail

A **mother** and two daughters. Viking 1982 564p

ISBN 0-670-49021-0

LC 81-65286

"Suddenly widowed Nell Strickland and her two daughters, reunited in grief, are all on the verge of change as the story begins. Bohemian Cate is twice divorced, almost 40, out of a teaching job and threatened by losses, while younger Lydia, who just left her husband, is winning: a college degree, a new lover, and fame as a TV personality. Ambivalent about accommodation and possibility but 'hospitable . . . to whatever came next,' each has created herself anew by the end. The North Carolina setting is as precisely evoked as {are} the many unusual, amusing characters." Libr J

Godwin, Gail

Queen of the underworld; a novel. Random House 2006 336p $24.95

ISBN 0-345-48318-9

LC 2005-48592

"A master stylist with a dozen novels to her credit, Godwin has never written more voluptuously, nor had as much fun with a character or setting." Booklist

Godwin, Gail

★ **Unfinished** desires; a novel. Random House 2010 393p $26

ISBN 978-0-345-48320-1; 0-345-48320-0

LC 2008-49320

"Told from multiple points of view, 'Unfinished Desires' puts the author's twin talents storytelling and characterization on dazzling display. Godwin brings each of the girls and women fully alive and tells her well-conceived and well-executed story in a leisurely but suspenseful fashion." Richmond Times-Dispatch

Goethe, Johann Wolfgang von

★ The **sorrows** of young Werther, and Novella; translated by Elizabeth Mayer and Louise Brogan; poems translated by W. H. Auden; foreword by W. H. Auden. Modern Lib. 1993 xx, 201p

ISBN 0-679-60064-7

LC 93-5007

A translation of two of Goethe's works, originally published 1774 and 1828 respectively; this is a reissue of the 1971 edition published by Random House

Novella, is an example of a specific literary genre, the idyll. A tame tiger which escapes during a fire pursues a princess and is killed. The animal trainer and his family, lamenting its death, persuade the prince, who has been out hunting a lion, to let them tame that animal rather than kill it. According to W. H. Auden it is "a parable about the relation between wild nature and human craft"

"Werther is a sensitive artist, ill at ease in society and hopelessly in love with Charlotte, who is engaged to someone else. This novel, with the eventual suicide of the hero, caused a sensation throughout Europe." Oxford Companion to Engl Lit

Gogol', Nikolai Vasil'evich

The **collected** tales of Nikolai Gogol; translated and annotated by Richard Pevear and Larissa Volokhonsky. Pantheon Bks. 1998 xxii, 435p

ISBN 0-679-43023-7

LC 97-37228

Contents: St. John's Eve; The night before Christmas; The terrible vengeance; Ivan Fyodorovich Shponka and his aunt; Old world landowners; Viy; The story of how Ivan Ivanovich quarreled with Ivan Nikiforovich; Nevsky Prospect; The diary of a madman; The nose; The carriage; The portrait; The overcoat

Gogol', Nikolai Vasil'evich

★ **Dead** souls; [by] Nikolai Gogol; translated and annotated by Richard Pevear and Larissa Volokhonsky. Pantheon Bks. 1996 xxiv, 402p

ISBN 0-679-43022-9

LC 95-24357

Original Russian edition, 1842

"Considered one of the world's finest satires, this picaresque work traces the adventures of the social-climbing Pavel Ivanovich Chichikov, a dismissed civil servant out to seek his fortune. It is admired not only for its enduring comic portraits but also for its sense of moral purpose." Merriam-Webster's Ency of Lit

Gogol', Nikolai Vasil'evich

The **overcoat,** and other tales of good and evil; {by} Nikolai V. Gogol; translated with an introduction by David Magarshack. Norton 1965 271p

This collection was first published 1957 in paperback by Doubleday with title: Tales of good and evil

Gohlke, Cathy

I have seen him in the watchfires; Cathy Gohlke. Moody Publishers 2008 331P (pbk.) $13.99

ISBN 9780802487742; 0802487742

LC 2008013224

Christy Award: Young Adult (2009)

In this book, a "Civil War . . . [novel], Robert Glover is . . . 17 years old. Although he promised his father not to join the Union Army until he became of age, circumstances force Robert to head for the war. He must also cope with his mother's growing mental illness and rely on his own faith to carry him through his trials." (Library Journal) "When he unwittingly gets entangled in a Confederate escape plot, Robert must forge his anger and shame into a new determination to save his family. And, perhaps, he must also realize that the saving might not be entirely up to him. Honor and duty to God and country aren't as clear-cut as he hoped them to be." (Publisher's note)

Gohlke, Cathy

Promise me this; Cathy Gohlke. Tyndale House Publishers 2012 407p (softcover) 13.99

ISBN 9781414353074

LC 2011034977

In this book, "[t]aking a break from work to watch the 'Titanic' set sail on its maiden voyage, Michael Dunnagan meets passenger Owen Allen and decides to stow away in hopes of convincing Owen to let him join his uncle's business in America. But the . . . ship strikes an iceberg, and a dying Owen extracts a promise from Michael that he will care for Owen's relatives in America and his sister Annie, still in England. Annie can't bear the thought that Michael lived when her brother was lost, but the two develop a friendship through the letters they exchange. When World War I breaks out and Annie's letters stop, Michael drops everything to find the woman he has come to love." (Libr J)

Gold, Glen David

Sunnyside. Alfred A. Knopf 2009 559p $26.95

ISBN 978-0-307-27068-9; 0-307-27068-8

LC 2009-03804

This novel "novel tells the story of early Chaplin, the beginning of Hollywood as we know it and a young America getting ready to flex its muscles. Sunnyside starts shortly before America's involvement in World War I, on a day when Chaplin is simultaneously spied in hundreds of places around the country. It is told by a young Chaplin, already a star but not yet a legend; an Adonis-like lighthouse keeper; and an over-educated ne'erdowell. While the latter two do cross paths with Chaplin, their story is the story of a war fought by dregs and managed by idiots. . . . Chaplin does not go to war. Instead he tours with archrival Mary Pickford and friend Douglas Fairbanks, raising money for the cause. We travel with Chaplin, underneath that hat with his thoughts as he blunders his way past self-doubt and contempt and into greatness." BookPage

Goldberg, Myla

Bee season; a novel. Doubleday 2000 275p hardcover o.p. pa $13.95

ISBN 0-385-49879-9; 0-385-49880-2 pa

LC 99-47933

"Some of the events that unfold . . . seem a little contrived. But Goldberg engenders considerable suspense around both Eliza's string of spelling successes and the fates of the other Naumanns." Time

Goldberg, Myla

Wickett's remedy. Doubleday 2005 326p $24.95

ISBN 0-385-51324-0

LC 2005-48103

"In the margins of each page are voices from the dead commenting on or clarifying plot points. . . . There's a lot going on here, some of which is underdeveloped. Other parts are just plain distracting, particularly the notes from beyond, which are more often hokey than profound. But Goldberg is a skillful, smooth writer who has clearly done her research, and readers who can tune out the noise will be rewarded." Time

Goldberg, Paul

The **Yid**; a novel. Paul Goldberg. Picador 2016 320 p. (hardcover) $26

ISBN 1250079039; 9781250079039

LC 2015029503

"Moscow, February 1953. A week before Stalin's death, . . . three government goons arrive . . . to arrest Solomon Shimonovich Levinson, an actor from the defunct State Jewish Theater. But Levinson . . . is a veteran of past wars, and his shocking response to the intruders sets in motion a series of events both zany and deadly as he proceeds to assemble a ragtag group to help him enact a mad-brilliant plot: the assassination of a tyrant." (Publisher's note)

"Goldberg ingeniously captures the brutality and lunacy of Stalin's rule as well as Russia's stoicism in this spectacularly incisive, humanizing, and comedically cathartic theater of the absurd." Booklist

Goldberg, Tod

★ **Gangsterland**; a novel. Tod Goldberg. Counterpoint Press 2014 464 p. (hardback) $26

ISBN 161902344X; 9781619023444

LC 2014014920

In this book, by Tod Goldberg, "Sal Cupertine is a legendary hit man for the Chicago Mafia. . . . His first-ever mistake forces Sal to botch an assassination, killing three undercover FBI agents in the process. . . . [H]e knows this botched job will be his death sentence to the Mafia. So he agrees to their radical idea to save his own skin. A few surgeries and some intensive training later, and Sal Cupertine is gone, disappeared into the identity of Rabbi David Cohen." (Publisher's note)

"Clever plotting, a colorful cast of characters and priceless situations make this comedic crime novel an instant classic." Kirkus

Golden, Arthur

★ **Memoirs** of a geisha; a novel. Knopf 1997 434p il $26.95; pa $7.99

ISBN 0-375-40011-7; 1-4000-9689-8 pa

LC 97-74747

"Rarely has a world so closed and foreign been evoked with such natural assurance, from the aesthetics of the Kyoto geisha's 'art'—to the fetishized sexuality of Gion in the thirties and forties, at once delicate and crude, repressed and flagrant." New Yorker

Golding, William

★ **Close** quarters. Farrar, Straus & Giroux 1987 281p

LC 87-5351

This second volume of the trilogy begun with Rites of passage is a "tale of the tragic misadventures befalling an 18th century fighting ship now converted to transporting cargo and passengers on the treacherous voyage from England to Australia. The novel is cast as a journal written by Edmund FitzHenry Talbot, a well-meaning, somewhat uncertain, slightly pompous officer and gentleman enroute to Sydney and a career in His Majesty's service. As a result of a green sailor's blunder, the ship's masts shatter, and it founders. Golding's principal achievement is the vivid, detailed depiction of a disintegrating vessel in the tropical seas, its progressive decay, and the wretchedness and despair of its passengers." Publ Wkly

Followed by Fire down below

Golding, William

★ **Darkness** visible. Farrar, Straus & Giroux 1979 265p

LC 79-19206

"A child hideously maimed in the bombing of London during World War II grows up to inspire the messianic fantasies of the people with whom he comes in contact. In Golding's dark world the horrors of the physically deformed are mirrored in—but are no match for—the spiritual monsters who inhabit the novel's strange vision of contemporary life. A powerful contemplation of the evil at the root of human behavior." Booklist

Golding, William

★ **Fire** down below. Farrar, Straus & Giroux 1989 313p

LC 88-18079

Golding is "translucent and economical. In his writing, allegorical motifs are revealed fleetingly in the everyday and in the ordinary. He is at once a complex and highly readable novelist." Economist

Golding, William

The **inheritors**. Harcourt 1962 233p

First published 1955 in the United Kingdom

A narrative "inhabiting the near-animal consciousness of Lok, a Neanderthal man, and describing in his clumsy terms and with great pathos the casual destruction of his species by Homo sapiens. The reader is shown his ancestors, already armed, arrogant, murderous, and corrupt—not superior to the Neanderthalers, only more clever and more evil." Wakeman. World Authors, 1950-1970

Golding, William

★ **Lord** of the flies; introduction by E. M. Forster; with a biographical and critical note by E. L. Epstein; illustrated by Ben Gibson. 50th anniversary ed; Berkley 2003 315p $23.95; pa $13

ISBN 0-399-52920-9; 0-399-50148-7 pa

LC 2003-54825

First published 1954 in the United Kingdom; first United States edition, 1955, by Coward-McCann

"Stranded on an island, a group of English schoolboys leave innocence behind in a struggle for survival. A political structure modeled after English government is set up and a hierarchy develops, but forces of anarchy and aggression surface. The boys' existence begins to degenerate into a savage one. They are rescued from their microcosmic society to return to an adult, stylized milieu filled with the same psychological tensions and moral voids. Adventure and allegory are brilliantly combined in this novel." Shapiro. Fic for Youth. 3d edition

Golding, William

★ **Rites** of passage. Farrar, Straus & Giroux 1980 278p

LC 80-16809

"In a sense the novel seems highly artificial, not only in its careful, detailed recreation of the period, but also in the elaborate system of correspondences and parallels—some clear, some obscure—which underpins the narration. Yet at the same time it is an extremely lively, enjoyable piece of work. Readers who know only the early Golding will be surprised by its humor." Times Lit Suppl

Followed by Close quarters

Goldman, Francisco

Say her name. Grove Press 2011 350p

ISBN 0802119816; 9780802119810; 0-8021-1981-6; 978-0-8021-1981-0

LC 2011283024

Francisco Goldman has written a novel based on a true story: the life and death of his "young wife, Aura Estrada, who died as a result of a bodysurfing accident in Mexico in 2007." (N Y Times (Late N Y Ed))

The author's "wife, Aura Estrada, died unexpectedly in 2007. She was 30 years old, a fiction writer and academic who loved Jorge Luis Borges and Belle & Sebastian and looked, Goldman writes, 'like a Mexican Björk.' This quietly devastating novel finds him grappling with Aura's life and death: the four years they spent as a couple, her childhood and budding literary career, and his own terrible struggle with her loss, which sits in him like 'a hard hollow rectangle filled with tepid blank air.' His story unfolds gently, like a muted conversation in an empty bar, the tone numb and hushed. Goldman doesn't keep his wife's passing a secret—he reveals it in the very first sentence of Say Her Name. But for most of the book he explores the before and after while dancing around the details of what actually happened. The effect is powerful. As the story builds—inevitably, unbearably—toward Aura's last day, Goldman has so convincingly brought her to life that her death still somehow comes as a shock." Entertainment Wkly

Goldman, William

★ **Marathon** man. Delacorte Press 1974 309p

"Babe" Levy, a graduate student, spends his free time running, and dreams of being a great marathon runner. The death of his brother in Babe's apartment starts a chain of mysterious and terrifying events. Pursued by government agents and ex-Nazis, Babe struggles to escape being assassinated. The torture scenes may make this suspenseful story an ordeal for some readers." Shapiro. Fic for Youth. 3d edition

Goldman, William, 1931-

The **princess** bride; S. Morgenstern's classic tale of true love and high adventure. the "good parts" version, abridged by William Goldman. Ballantine Books 2003 xli, 429 p.p ill. o.p.; (hbk.) $25

ISBN 0345418263; 9780151015443

LC 2003272241

This book offers the 30th anniversary edition of William Goldman's book "The Princess Bride." "As a boy, William Goldman claims, he loved to hear his father read the S. Morgenstern classic, 'The Princess Bride.' But as a grown-up he discovered that the boring parts were left out of good old Dad's recitation, and only the 'good parts' reached his ears. . . . [With this book, h]e's reconstructed the 'Good Parts Version.' . . . What's it about? Fencing. Fighting. True Love. Strong Hate. Harsh Revenge. A Few Giants. Lots of Bad Men. Lots of Good Men. Five or Six Beautiful Women. Beasties Monstrous and Gentle. Some Swell Escapes and Captures. Death, Lies, Truth, Miracles, and a Little Sex. In short, it's about everything." (Publisher's note)

Goldstein, Rebecca

36 arguments for the existence of God; a work of fiction. [by] Rebecca Newberger Goldstein. Pantheon Books 2010 402p $27.95

ISBN 978-0-307-37818-7; 0-307-37818-7

LC 2009-17022

This "is without a doubt the funniest work of existential philosophy you'll read all year. Thoughtful, witty, and – I cannot stress enough – really entertaining, '36 Arguments' is part campus comedy, part romantic farce, part philosophical treatise." Christ Sci Monit

Gonzales, Laurence

★ **Lucy**. Alfred A Knopf 2010 307p $24.95

ISBN 978-0-307-27260-7; 0-307-27260-5

LC 2010-03898

"Lucy is a genetic experiment: part person, part chimpanzee. She looks and sounds just like any normal 15-year-old girl—in fact, she can recite Shakespeare's sonnets by heart—it's just that she sometimes eats bananas without peeling them and swings from treetop to treetop. . . . Splicing DNA has been a science-fiction plot device as far back as the 19th century, when H.G. Wells was mixing the test tubes. But the results were always horrific crimes against nature. Here, the mutant hybrid couldn't be lovelier or more charming—it's the people who behave like monsters. . . . [The author has] Crichton's gift for page-turning storytelling, but also a vivid, literary-grade prose style, and a knack for getting inside his characters' heads." Entertainment Wkly

Goodis, David

Nightfall; a novel. with a new introduction by Bill Pronzini. Millipede Press 2007 213p $40; pa $14

ISBN 978-1-933618-18-0; 1-933618-18-3; 9781933618173 pa; 1933618175 pa

First published 1947 by Messner

"Jim Vanning, a commercial artist living in Manhattan, is being hunted by a group of bank robbers who believe he ran off with $300,000 of their ill-gotten money. He's also being watched by a detective who's trying to suss out what Vanning did with the satchel of cash. Vanning denies stealing the money, but the money hardly matters—the satchel is just a MacGuffin. Nightfall's real story is about Vanning's despair about how to behave rationally when he knows he's being watched and the detective's self-questioning about whether a man can ever act with integrity without falling under suspicion. It's a relatively big theme for a noir, but Goodis keeps the story earthbound, rooting it in cynical observations designed to keep the mood of paranoia going." Washington City Paper

Goodman, Allegra

★ The **cookbook** collector; a novel. Dial Press 2010 394p $26

ISBN 978-0-385-34085-4; 0-385-34085-0

LC 2009-47594

"As the story opens in 1999, twentysomething sisters Emily and Jessamine Bach are a study in contrasts: One's a driven tech executive in Silicon Valley; the other, an impoverished Berkeley grad student/bookstore employee with a penchant for sprout sandwiches and seductive tree huggers. A revolving constellation of characters — Emily's golden-boy fiancé and instant-millionaire colleagues, Jess' brusque, ponytailed boss, George — are made fully flesh and blood by Goodman; sometimes more so, even, than her protagonists. She especially excels at capturing the precipitous rush of the then-nascent tech boom, with its breakneck innovations and backroom intrigues, while simultaneously recounting Jess' increasing absorption into the ornate and distinctly analog world of high-end bibliophilia. Even as Cookbook strikes a rare bum note with a late, left-field revelation, Goodman delivers a novel of impressive élan and real emotional resonance." Entertainment Wkly

Goodman, Allegra

Intuition; a novel. Dial Press 2006 344p $25; pa $13

ISBN 0-385-33612-8; 0-385-33610-1 pa

LC 2005-51940

"The prestigious Philpott Institute in Cambridge, MA, is a virtually closed community dominated by a charismatic leader, oncologist Sandy Glass. Dr. Glass's enthusiasm galvanizes his ambitious scientists to work round the clock when experimental results yield a possible cancer cure, until one young researcher publicizes her suspicions of fraud." Libr J

Goodman, Allegra

Kaaterskill Falls; a novel. by Allegra Goodman. Delta Trade Paperbacks 1999 324 p. $13

ISBN 0385323905; 9780385323901

LC 9753051

National Book Award Finalist

In this book, by by Allegra Goodman, "Kaaterskill Falls is a small town in upstate New York, summer home to Orthodox Jews who come from their tightly knit community in New York City. . . . The women of the community are bound by traditions that dictate their dress, manners, and preoccupations. Elizabeth Shulman, driven by ambitions beyond raising five daughters, opens a store . . . and later runs afoul . . . when she violates a tradition." (Booklist)

"...the author relies on quiet moments of tentative reconciliation to wrap up her story. You don't read Goodman for thrills, but for rich characterizations and faultless evocation of a cloistered culture--pleasures in ample supply here." Kirkus

Goodman, Allegra

Paradise park; a novel. Dial Press (NY) 2001 360p

ISBN 0-385-33416-8

LC 00-49376

"Like Saul Bellow and Philip Roth before her, Goodman has achieved a breakthrough book by discovering and recording a thoroughly uninhibited narrative voice." Time

Goodman, Carol

Arcadia Falls; a novel. Ballantine Books 2010 355p $25

ISBN 978-0-345-49753-6; 0-345-49753-8

LC 2009-44550

"The tone of 'Arcadia Falls,' suffused as it is with foreboding, is a far cry from gloomy. Goodman's touch is sure-handed, even light, dropping hints and shockers with calibrated ease. She knows just what information the reader needs to turn the pages but has enough trust that the same reader won't rush and gobble up paragraphs to reach the finish line, instead pacing the story for a more languid experience where each sentence, layered on top of another, really counts." Los Angeles Times

Goodman, Carol

The **night** villa; a novel. Ballantine Books 2008 413p pa $14

ISBN 978-0-345-47960-0; 0-345-47960-2

LC 2008-8519

"The pleasure of a Carol Goodman novel is in her enviable command of the classical canon–and the deft way she [writes] a book that's light enough for a weekend on the beach but literary enough for a weekend in the Hamptons." Chicago Tribune

Goodman, Carol

River Road; A Novel. Carol Goodman. Touchstone 2016 276 p. (cloth) $25

ISBN 1501109901; 9781501109904; 9781501109911

LC 2015012488

In this novel, by Carol Goodman, "Nan Lewis—a creative writing professor . . . in upstate New York—is driving home from a faculty holiday party. . . . On her way, she hits a deer, but when she gets out of her car, . . . the deer is nowhere to be found. . . . The next morning, Nan is woken up by a police officer. . . . One of her students, Leia Dawson, was killed in a hit-and-run on River Road the night before. And because of the damage to her car, Nan is a suspect." (Publisher's note)

"Goodman provides an insightful look at revenge, grief, and rebuilding one's life after a horrific loss." Pub Wkly

Goodman, Jo

A **place** called home. Kensington Pub. Corp. 2011 432p.

ISBN 9780821774182

This book tells the story of a man and a woman who "learn they've been named joint guardians for their late friends' three children. . . . Something about Mitch's forthright intensity has always left ad exec Thea feeling off-balance, while Mitch makes no secret of his disdain when Thea offers him financial assistance if he'll take sole guardianship." (Publisher's note) "Neither is prepared to become a parent -- and certainly not alone . . . as they work to solve their separate dilemmas, Thea and Mitch discover that they need each other, as well." (Libr J)

Goodwin, Daisy

The **American** heiress; a novel. St. Martin's Press 2011 46880p $25.99

ISBN 978-0-312-65865-6

LC 2010-48539

First published 2010 in the United kingdom with title: My last dutchess

"A shrewd, spirited historical romance with flavors of Edith Wharton, Daphne du Maurier, Jane Austen, Upstairs, Downstairs and a dash of People magazine that charts a bumpy marriage of New World money and Old World tradition." Kirkus

Goolrick, Robert

A **reliable** wife; a novel. Algonquin Books of Chapel Hill 2009 291p $23.95

ISBN 978-1-56512-596-4; 1-56512-596-7

LC 2008-49700

Goolrick is a ticky, mannered writer with an unusual love of clauses that can sometimes give you comma whiplash. This, combined with the graphic problems they are having throughout the novel may be enough to turn some readers off. And that would be a shame, because in the middle of this book a secret is revealed that pushes the plot forward. Freed into clearer storytelling, A Reliable Wife relaxes into an entertaining novel full of all kinds of juicy thingsdeception, betrayal, murder, sex, and even love. PopMatters

Goonan, Kathleen Ann

In war times. Tor 2007 348p $25.95

ISBN 978-0-7653-1355-3; 0-7653-1355-3

LC 2007-5165

This is "the story of Sam Dance, who, while studying mathematics and electronics for the Army just before WW II, is seduced by a mysterious female physicist teaching one of his classes. Dr. Hadntz has plans for a device that might end war forever, by changing humanity's seeming need for conflict. From this premise, Goonan weaves a remarkable tale of quantum physics, human nature and jazz." SF Signal

Goonan, Kathleen Ann

Light music. HarperCollins Pubs. 2002 406p $25.95

ISBN 0-380-97712-5

LC 2001-55602

Sequel to Crescent city rhapsody

In this concluding volume of the Nanotech Quartet "the microscopic machines of the 22nd century have gone beyond creating sentient cities and controlling all communications on Earth—they are themselves evolving. When mysterious lights point to an alien presence and disappearing people arouse stark fear, three human survivors, including Argentine refugee Angelina, set out to solve the mystery and measure the threat to humanity. A lot of picaresque adventures ensue. . . . This classic novel of ideas, with state-of-the-art technology as its subject, remains the work of a powerful imagination with a superior command of language." Publ Wkly

Gordimer, Nadine

Beethoven was one-sixteenth black; and other stories. Farrar, Straus and Giroux 2007 177p $21

ISBN 978-0-374-10982-0; 0-374-10982-6

LC 2007-33474

"A story narrated by a tapeworm. A vignette about a parrot unhappy at losing his usual cafe perch. A tale about a cockroach trapped inside a Kafka fan's typewriter . . . South African Nobel laureate Nadine Gordimer has come up with some true curiosities in her new short-story collection. . . . At its best, the book offers compelling psychosexual journeys, probing at marital tensions and the hazardous play of memory in the bereaved (Gordimer's husband, Reinhold Cassirer, to whom the book is dedicated, died in 2001). Some tales also afford glancing, revealing takes on life in post-apartheid South Africa." Seattle Times

Gordimer, Nadine

The **conservationist**. Viking 1975 252p

First published 1974 in the United Kingdom

The author probes "the way of life that exists in South Africa today, and some aspects of the tensions that exist among English and Afrikaaners, Blacks, coloreds, Indian shopkeepers. . . . Mehring is rich, white, bored. His farm is a weekend pleasure place to which he once brought the mistress whose flirtations with left wing causes have now exiled her forever. His teenage son won't even come home for the holidays and wants out of all that South Africa stands for. Mehring is kind enough to his blacks, keeps them in their place, avoids his Boer neighbors with whom he has nothing in common. A loner, living for himself, deliberately isolated from any unpleasantness that might intrude, only gradually does he begin to perceive that there are forces at work in nature, in the closeness between the blacks and the land by which some day his way of life will be forever changed." Publ Wkly

Gordimer, Nadine

Get a life. Farrar, Straus & Giroux 2005 187p $21

ISBN 0-14303-792-7

LC 2005-07199

"Gordimer confronts the reader with questions of conservation, social welfare, and emotional ecosystems. The austere Gordimer's mastery of her craft means she never needs to point at herself, thus highlighting the difference between art and performance." Harper's

Gordimer, Nadine

A **guest** of honor. Viking 1970 504p

The hero of this novel, James "Bray is a 54-year-old former administrator for one of Her Majesty's former African colonies. . . . He was cashiered for showing too much sympathy for the local independence movement. After independence, Bray accepts an invitation to return as an educational consultant to Miss Gordimer's nameless, composite, new African nation. His professional commitment to the excruciating process of Third World nation building is complicated because the country's opposing political factions—one moderate, the other revolutionary—are led by two of his former protégés." Time

Gordimer, Nadine

★ **July's** people. Viking 1981 160p

ISBN 0-670-41048-9

LC 80-24877

"When revolution breaks out against the whites in South Africa, Bamford and Maureen Smales are forced to flee. Their black servant July, loyal to them for fifteen years, takes them away to his people in a bush village. His role changes slowly to one not only of savior but also overseer. The change in their manner of living from the good, clean, well-regulated life of 'the ruling class' to that of the customs of July's people raises havoc within both the white and black families and in the delicate tissue of understanding between the Smales and their servant. There is much to be learned from this powerful story written by an author who lives in South Africa and who writes with authority on a subject that has import for any society where race relations or colonial conditions are fragile and explosive." Shapiro. Fic for Youth. 3d edition

Gordimer, Nadine

Life times; stories, 1952-2007. Farrar, Straus and Giroux 2010 549p $30

ISBN 978-0-374-27053-7; 0-374-27053-8

LC 2010-23403

Gordimer "has been writing for more than 60 years now, but her concerns have been constant: race, justice, the South African land. In a typical story, the landscape is austere, tough and unforgiving, just the sort of thing to bring out the best in a few hardy people, but calculated to wear down the spirits of most others. . . . Some of the stories clearly date to the early days of resistance to apartheid, politically charged and with passing references to the first stirrings of the African National Congress; others take place in the thick of the battle for justice, amid 'beer-serious conversations about the possibility of the end of the world.' Four of the stories are new, an added pleasure for admirers of Gordimer's work. A welcome collection by a master of English prose—lucid and precisely written, if often bringing news only of disappointment, fear and loss." Kirkus

Gordimer, Nadine

Loot, and other stories. Farrar, Straus & Giroux 2003 240p $23

ISBN 0-374-19090-9

LC 2002-42601

In Karma a deceased insurance executive's spirit makes successive returns to earth in various guises. Mission statement is about a middle-aged Englishwomanwho has a sexual relationship with a native while working for an international aid agency in an impoverished African country

"This compelling collection presents a bleak view of human existence in general and of Africa's colonial past in particular. Written with a sharp sense of irony, it should be a part of every fiction collection." Libr J

Gordimer, Nadine

★ **My** son's story. Penguin Books 1991 277p pa $9.95

ISBN 0-14-015975-4

LC 91-17273

First published 1990 by Farrar, Straus & Giroux

"Sonny is a teacher of mixed race. He and his wife are . . . sympathetic to the plight of the 'real blacks,' yet ambitious that they may someday be accepted by the whites. Sonny's political education begins when he's fired for helping black children demonstrate in their township. Jailed for promoting boycotts and participating in illegal gatherings, Sonny meets and falls in love with a blond, blue-eyed woman who works for a human-rights organization. Sonny's adolescent son, Will, tells the story of his father's political and erotic development, the resentments and betrayals that ensue." Newsweek

Gordimer, Nadine, 1923-2014

No time like the present; Nadine Gordimer. Farrar, Straus and Giroux 2012 421 p.

ISBN 9780374222642; 0374222649

LC 2012930442

The plot of "Nobel laureate [Nadine] Gordimer's . . . novel, . . . set in contemporary South Africa, revolves around Steve, who's Jewish, and Jabulile (Jabu), who's black. Both were 'comrades' in the fight for racial equality. . . . Married and starting a family in a middle-class suburb, they've 'bought ourselves a house while others including comrades . . . are still under tin and cardboard.' . . . [A]s their children grow up, civil and political unrest keeps pace, forcing them to re-evaluate their position in this new South Africa." (Publishers Weekly)

Gordimer, Nadine

None to accompany me. Farrar, Straus & Giroux 1994 324p

ISBN 0-374-22297-5

LC 94-7553

"A novel that raises more questions than it answers, 'None to Accompany Me' is an unflinching and perceptive exploration of people living on the brink of changes—political and personal—with little but their own sense of self-reliance to guide them." Christ Sci Monitor

Gordimer, Nadine

The **pickup**. Farrar, Straus & Giroux 2001 270p $23

ISBN 0-374-23210-5

LC 2001-23041

"Gordimer writes so tenderly and so searchingly about Julie's gradual transcendence of her western self that she manages to hold sceptism at bay." Women's Review of Books

Includes bibliographical references (p. {269}-270)

Gordon, Jaimy

★ **Lord** of Misrule; a novel. McPherson & Co. 2010 294p $25

ISBN 9780929701837; 0-929701-83-6

LC 2010-35030

National Book Award: Fiction (2010)

Gordon "clearly loves the subculture of grifters and ne'er-do-wells whose lives center on a venue that obviously has never and will never bring them success. Her lowlifes have names like Two-Tie, Medicine Ed, Kidstuff and Deucey, and they're capable of speaking a kind of race-track patois occasionally reminiscent of Damon Runyon characters. . . . Exceptional writing and idiosyncratic characters make this an engaging read." Kirkus

Gordon, Mary

★ The **company** of women. Knopf 1981 291p

LC 80-5284

"Given its scope, depth, and the perfection of its lyrical passages (which are the more impressive because of Gordon's natural inclination toward the austere), it is fair to call this a brilliant novel." Saturday Rev

Gordon, Mary

★ **Final** payments. Random House 1978 297p

LC 77-90259

"Isabel Moore spends 11 years almost totally absorbed in caring for her invalid father, who suffered a paralyzing stroke after discovering his daughter in a compromising situation with one of his students. When she is thirty, her father dies; she is freed from responsibility for his welfare but not yet able to accept responsibility for her own life. Her involvement with two men adds complications as, guilt-ridden and filled with religious skepticism, Isabel searches for answers and begins to heal. Two childhood friends, Eleanor, an independent woman, and Liz, a tough married mother of two children, are instrumental in helping Isabel grow toward self-realization." Shapiro. Fic for Youth. 3d edition

Gordon, Mary, 1949-

The **liar's** wife; four novellas. Mary Gordon. Pantheon Books 2014 304 p. (hardback) $25.95

ISBN 0307377431; 9780307377432

LC 2013043926

In this collection of four novellas, by Mary Gordon, "we meet the ferocious Simone Weil during her final days as a transplant to New York City; a vulnerable American grad student who escapes to Italy after her first, compromising love affair; the charming Irish liar of the title story, who gets more out of life than most of us; and Thomas Mann, opening the heart of a high-school kid in the Midwest." (Publisher's note)

Gordon, Mary, 1949-

The **love** of my youth. Pantheon 2011 302p $25.95

ISBN 978-0-307-37742-5; 0-307-37742-3

LC 2011-08966

"Miranda and Adam were each other's first love, but they've had no contact for 30 years. Their heady reunion takes place in Rome, a city of myths and ghosts Adam knows well, allowing him to show Miranda, there for an environmental health conference, the sights and allowing Gordon to make the most of gorgeous settings redolent with ancient secrets and sorrows. The ensuing intense conversations between Miranda and Adam are so psychologically intricate and complexly metaphysical and aesthetic that they seem impossibly theatrical. And yet, as the novel deepens in extended flashbacks, their intoxicating exchanges become exquisitely involving. We learn that their blissful love bloomed when they were 16 in the mid-1960s and slowly withered during their twenties as Adam devoted himself to becoming a great pianist and Miranda searched for a way to help make the world a better place. The more they talk on their Roman rambles, the more the reader burns to know what finally drove them apart." Booklist

Gorman, Edward

Bad moon rising; [by] Ed Gorman. Pegasus Crime 2011 196p $25

ISBN 978-1-60598-260-1

"In 1968, a hippie commune near Black River Falls, Iowa, both horrifies and entices the townsfolk with its uninhibited lifestyle. Sardonic lawyer and investigator McCain becomes involved after the discovery of the body of Vanessa Mainwaring, the teenage daughter of a well-to-do local, at the commune, and a Vietnam vet who's one of its members flees. Interference by a bigoted sheriff, an opportunistic preacher, and a hysterical father makes matters even worse as Sam tries not just to solve the murder but to help the people around him caught in an intensely stressful situation." Publ Wkly

Gorman, Edward

Fools rush in; a Sam McCain mystery. [by] Ed Gorman. Pegasus Books 2007 229p $25

ISBN 978-1-933548-32-3

"Black River Falls, Iowa, 1963: the violence of the civil-rights era lurks behind the double murder of a Peeping Tom photographer and a handsome black lothario, David Leeds, who was dating the daughter of a white Republican senator. Young Sam McCain, a lawyer and sometime private detective, is on the case. Motives are widespread. The senator was having an affair. Local bikers hated Leeds' success with a white woman to whom they could never aspire. The photographer was a blackmailer, and the white ex-boyfriend of the senator's daughter was a violent bully. . . . Readers unfamiliar with this fine series should hop onboard now and watch as an Iowa Mr. Marple starts to behave like a cornbelt Spenser." Booklist

Gorman, Edward

Riders on the Storm; by Ed Gorman. W W Norton & Co Inc 2014 252 p. $25.95

ISBN 1605986259; 9781605986258

LC 2015295402

Sam McCain mystery

In this novel by Ed Gorman, "a brutal murder in the midst of an anti-Vietnam War group sparks an investigation by Sam McCain. . . . Sam returns to his hometown . . . where he works as a lawyer (and part-time investigator). . . . Two of Sam's oldest friends are caught up in this same battle . . . Steve Donovan . . . [and] Will Cullen. . . . When Cullen is found murdered, the obvious suspect is Steve Donovan, but Sam has serious doubts about the man's guilt.." (Publisher's note)

"This is an extended, nuanced fictional biography with an occasional mystery thrown in. Great reading." Booklist

Gorman, Edward

★ **Save** the last dance for me; [by] Ed Gorman. Carroll & Graf Pubs. 2002 230p $24

ISBN 0-7867-0968-5

A "dead-on perfect journey to the underside of the late '50s and early '60s, exposing the anti-intellectualism and anti-Semitism that lurked beneath the era's placid surface." Booklist

Gorman, Edward

Sleeping dogs; [by] Ed Gorman. Thomas Dunne Books/St. Martin's Minotaur 2008 238p $23.95

ISBN 978-0-312-36784-8; 0-312-36784-8

LC 2007-51733

"Unleashing a new series, Gorman gives us political speechwriter and sleuth-by-necessity Dev Conrad. He's just signed onto the unexpectedly troubled reelection campaign of a U.S. senator, and must deal with dirty tricks, campaign sabotage, a suicide and his increasing suspicions about the very man he's supposed to be helping stay in Congress." January

Other titles about Dev Conrad are:
Stranglehold (2010)
Blindside (2012)
Flashpoint (2013)
Elimination (2015)

Gorman, Edward

Ticket to ride; [by] Ed Gorman. Pegasus Books 2009 225p $25

ISBN 978-1-605980-70-6

An entry in the Sam McCain series set in Black River Falls, Iowa. "It's 1965, different stances on the Vietnam War have divided the town, and the anti-war Sam McCain seems to have found himself on the unpopular side. Things start to heat up when Lou Bennett, whose son was killed in the war, crashes McCain's anti-war rally and starts a fight with the charismatic young protester Harrison Doran. From there, things only get worse: Bennett is found dead the next day, and Doran is arrested under suspicion of murder. With the whole town convinced of Doran's guilt, McCain begrudgingly agrees to defend Doran as a favor to a friend. Complicating things even further are McCain's crush on Bennett's daughter-inl-aw Wendy, and a skeleton in the family closet revels a web of secrets that Black River Falls would have preferred to keep buried and forgotten. The reasons for Gorman's reputation as a first-rate novelist are on full display." Pulp Serenade

Gottlieb, Eli

★ **Best** boy; a novel. by Eli Gottlieb. Liveright Publishing Corporation, a division of W.W. Norton & Co. 2015 256 p. illustration, map (hardcover) $24.95

ISBN 9781631490477

LC 2014048573

This novel, by Eli Gottlieb, is "about autism, memory, and, ultimately, redemption. Sent to a 'therapeutic community' for autism at the age of eleven, Todd Aaron, now in his fifties, is the 'Old Fox' of Payton LivingCenter. A joyous man who rereads the encyclopedia compulsively, he is unnerved by the sudden arrivals of a menacing new staffer and a disruptive, brain-injured roommate. His equilibrium is further worsened by Martine, a one-eyed new resident who has romantic intentions." (Publisher's note)

"Gottlieb merits praise for both the endearing eloquence of Todd's voice and a deeply sympathetic parable that speaks to a time when rising autism rates and long-lived elders force many to weigh tough options." Kirkus

Gottlieb, Eli

Now you see him. William Morrow 2008 261p $22.95

ISBN 978-0-06-128464-9; 0-06-128464-5

This is a "haunting and affecting potrait not only of an unthinkable act of violence but also a deeply personal grief and the self-questioning that follows a psychologically scarring event." Vancouver Sun

Goudge, Eileen

Garden of lies. Viking 1989 528p

ISBN 0-670-82458-5

LC 88-40395

"The characters intrigue, the situations hold attention, and the sex scenes simmer near the boiling point." Booklist

Followed by Thorns of truth

Goudge, Eileen

Thorns of truth. Viking 1998 398p

ISBN 0-670-87942-8

LC 97-53231

"Forty-six years after Sylvie Rosenthal abandoned Rose as a dark-haired newborn and stole blonde, blue-eyed baby Rachel to take her place, their lives are still intertwined, and Rachel still doesn't know the truth. Now Rose has problems of her own: her husband's death a year ago has left her with a law firm to manage; her stepdaughter is a drunk; and her eldest son, Drew, is planning to marry Rachel's mentally unstable daughter, Iris, against his mother's wishes. Rachel's life is starting to fray at the edges, too. Her job running a women's health clinic has caused a rift in her marriage to Brian, and, even medicated, Iris remains a constant worry." Publ Wkly

Goudge, Elizabeth

Green Dolphin Street; a novel. Coward-McCann 1944 502p

Published in the United Kingdom with title: Green Dolphin country

This novel is set on one of the English Channel Islands and in frontier New Zealand. "The principal characters are two sisters and the boy who had been their neighbor and companion in Green Dolphin Street on the island. The sisters are Marianne, stern and intellectual, and Marguerite, radiant and beautiful. It is Marguerite whom William loves, but when he writes the letter from New Zealand asking her father for her hand he unaccountably confuses the names and it is Marianne, who comes to be his wife." Wis Libr Bull

Gould, Emily

Friendship; Emily Gould. Fararr, Straus & Giroux 2014 272 p. (hardback) $26

ISBN 0374158614; 9780374158613

LC 2013034422

This novel, by Emily Gould, is "about two friends learning the difference between getting older and growing up. Bev Tunney and Amy Schein have been best friends for years; now, at thirty, they're at a crossroads. Bev is a Midwestern striver. . . . Amy is an East Coast princess. . . . As Bev and Amy are dragged, kicking and screaming, into real adulthood, they have to face the possibility that growing up might mean growing apart." (Publisher's note)

"Gould nails the complex blend of love, loyalty, and resentment that binds female friends." Pub Wkly

Gowdy, Barbara

Helpless; a novel. Metropolitan Books 2007 307p $24

ISBN 978-0-8050-8288-3

LC 2006-47348

"There is a clean urgency to Gowdy's tale. We are helpless before her sure and beguiling hand because ultimately—and breathlessly—we are drawn in." Vancouver Sun

Gowdy, Barbara

The **romantic**; a novel. Metropolitan Bks. 2003 305p $24
ISBN 0-8050-7190-3

LC 2002-29904

"Each of the characters, even minor ones, has a unique voice and a vivid, quirky personality. Louise's need to have Abel create the world for her resonates with unfulfilled passion." Publ Wkly

Gracie, Anne

The **Autumn** Bride; Anne Gracie. Berkley Pub Group 2013 320 p. $7.99
ISBN 0425259250; 9780425259252

This historical romance novel, by Anne Gracie, is part of the "Chance Sisters Romance" series. When "Abigail Chantry . . . finds . . . Lady Beatrice Davenham, bedridden and neglected. . . . Abby rousts Lady Beatrice's predatory servants and [she, with her sister and two friends] . . . become her 'nieces.' . . . It's the perfect situation, until Lady Beatrice's dashing and arrogant nephew, Max, Lord Davenham, returns from the Orient." (Publisher's note)

Gracie, Anne

To catch a bride; Anne Gracie. Berkley Sensation 2009 308 p. (pbk.) $7.99; (pbk.) $7.99
ISBN 0425230228; 9780425230220

LC 2010414788

This book follows "a cynical, restless nobleman [who] flees an unwanted betrothal and heads to Egypt to track down the long-lost granddaughter of a family friend, . . . [and] the last thing he expects is to find love in the form of an elusive, cross-dressing Arab street urchin. Yet once he snares the fiercely loyal, independent Ayisha, Rafe Ramsey knows she is exactly what he wants--if only he can convince her." (Libr J)

Gracie, Anne

The **Winter** Bride; Anne Gracie. Berkley Pub Group 2014 336 p. (Chance Sisters) pbk $7.99
ISBN 0425259269; 9780425259269

LC 2014657916

"Damaris Chance's unhappy past has turned her off the idea of marriage forever. But her guardian, Lady Beatrice Davenham, convinces her to make her coming out anyway--and have a season of carefree, uncomplicated fun. When Damaris finds herself trapped in a compromising situation with the handsome rake Freddy Monkton-Coombes, she has no choice but to agree to wed him." (Publisher's note)

"A pretend engagement devolves into a forced marriage when plans go awry in this exquisitely written, perfectly plotted story that features deeply wounded but resilient protagonists." LJ

Grady, James

Six days of the condor. Norton 1974 192p

"When a branch of the CIA is mass murdered, Malcolm, the only survivor, becomes the object of an intense chase involving the Washington police, the CIA, the FBI, the NSC, and a host of other intelligence agencies. Trying to stay one jump ahead of his pursuers, Malcolm struggles to find out who within the agency has sold out his comrades." Libr J

Graedon, Alena

★ The **word** exchange; a novel. Alena Graedon. Doubleday 2014 384 p. (hardback) $26.95
ISBN 0385537654; 9780385537650

LC 2013033165

This book "explores a near-future America that's shifted almost exclusively to smart technologies, where print is only a nostalgia. . . . Anana Johnson works closely with her . . . father Doug, a famous lexicographer, at the North American Dictionary of the English Language. But when Doug goes missing, what once seemed like a luddite's quaint conspiracy theory takes on new plausibility . . . as the city quickly falls victim to a fast-spreading 'word flu' virus." (Publishers Weekly)

"A wildly ambitious, darkly intellectual and inventive thriller about the intersection of language, technology and meaning." Kirkus

Graeme-Evans, Posie

The **island** house; a novel. by Posie Graeme-Evans. Atria Books 2012 451 p. (paperback) $16
ISBN 0743294432; 9780743294430; 9781451672022

LC 2012010046

This novel, by Posie Graeme-Evans, is about "a young archaeologist who unearths ancient secrets. . . . [In the present,] Freya Dane . . . arrives on the ancient Scottish island of Findnar. . . . [In] AD 800, . . . Signy, a Pictish girl, loses her entire family. Taken in by survivors of the island's Christian community. . . . Signy will call out to Freya across the centuries. Ancient wrongs must be laid to rest in the present and the mystery at the heart of Findnar's violent past exposed." (Publisher's note)

Grafton, Sue

★ **A is for alibi**; a Kinsey Millhone mystery. Holt & Co. 1990 274p $27
ISBN 0-8050-1334-2

A reissue of the title first published 1982 by Holt, Rinehart & Winston

"Kinsey Millhone is a cut above the usual woman private eye who flounces through fiction. Millhone is neither a sex bomb nor a detached cerebrum, but a believable, straightforward character." Booklist

Grafton, Sue

B is for burglar. Holt & Co. 1985 229p $27
ISBN 0-8050-1632-5

LC 84-22378

"Grafton's plot is solid p.i. procedural, but it is her sense of style that will truly delight readers. Her characters, from a punk dope pusher to a brave and resourceful eighty-eight-year-old woman, are completely convincing, and Grafton's ear for natural dialogue is among the best in the business." Wilson Libr Bull

Grafton, Sue

C is for corpse; a Kinsey Millhone mystery. Holt & Co. 1986 243p $27
ISBN 0-8050-2818-8

LC 85-24797

Kinsey Millhone "meets a young man, Buddy Callahan, at the gym where she works out and agrees to take his case. He wants her to investigate an auto accident in which he was badly injured because he claims that it was a murder attempt. When a second attempt results in his death, Kinsey, although she no longer has him as a client, pursues the matter and, in a hair-raising finale that takes place in a morgue, she unmasks the murderer." Shapiro. Fic for Youth. 3d edition

Grafton, Sue

D is for deadbeat; a Kinsey Millhone mystery. Holt & Co. 1987 229p $27
ISBN 0-8050-0248-0

LC 86-25843

"Social awareness and human weakness play a great part in the Millhone books, which always manage to finish with a heart-stopping climax." Libr J

Grafton, Sue

E is for evidence; a Kinsey Millhone mystery. Holt & Co. 1988 227p $27

ISBN 0-8050-0459-9

LC 87-28100

"The plot is just fine and does what a plot ought to in a good detective novel: it keeps us turning pages and serves as a vehicle for the really interesting stuff, an unveiling of the characters' foibles by the worldly-wise but uncorrupt private eye." NY Times Book Rev

Grafton, Sue

F is for fugitive; a Kinsey Millhone mystery. Holt & Co. 1989 261p $27

ISBN 0-8050-0460-2

LC 88-27284

Kinsey Millhone "becomes involved in ugly doings in a California coastal town, where she attempts to prove a man's innocence on a 17-year-old murder rap. Floral Beach appears to be a cozy little place, but it's a hotbed of dirty secrets, most of them involving the long-dead Jean Timberlake, a confused yet apparently sexually quite precocious teenager. Kinsey's investigation opens closet doors, and some tawdry skeletons jump out." Booklist

Grafton, Sue

G is for gumshoe; a Kinsey Millhone mystery. Holt & Co. 1990 261p

LC 89-24652

"Millhone, whose background has made her believe that all families are dysfunctional, has unwittingly taken on another case of domestic violence. Grafton excels in this milieu. Never morally oblique, here she is slyly didactic about (among other things) attitudes toward the mentally ill." Newsweek

Grafton, Sue

H is for homicide. Holt & Co. 1991 256p $27

ISBN 0-8050-1084-X

LC 90-25016

Detective Kinsey Millhone is "hired by California Fidelity to investigate a string of fraudulent automobile insurance claims filed by someone named Bibianna Diaz. To track down the elusive Bibianna, Kinsey adopts an undercover identity as Hannah Moore, a wisecracking, reckless vamp. As Hannah, she befriends Bibianna, a sexy young woman on the run. Both are quickly swept up in an evening of kidnapping and gunplay that ends with the two of them in jail. Through her relationship with Bibianna, Kinsey also stumbles onto a much bigger network of crime." N Y Times Book Rev

Grafton, Sue

I is for innocent. Holt & Co. 1992 286p $27

ISBN 0-8050-1085-8

LC 91-45165

Kinsey Millhone "lands the job of hunting up evidence for a wrongful-death suit against a high-living architect who couldn't be nailed in court for his wife's murder. It's a sobering case, weighted with the survivors' anger and suspicions and darkened by their sordid domestic affairs." N Y Times Book Rev

Grafton, Sue

J is for judgment. Holt & Co. 1993 288p $27

ISBN 0-8050-1935-9

LC 92-35769

"Ms. Grafton writes a smart story and wraps it up with a wry twist; but she takes care to sweeten her tart characterizations with amused understanding and, in the case of Jaffe, even affection." N Y Times Book Rev

Grafton, Sue

K is for killer. Holt & Co. 1994 284p $27

ISBN 0-8050-1936-7

LC 94-1242

"Despite an abrupt ending that has the reader frantically paging back for missed clues, the sturdily engineered plot drags Kinsey into the kind of joints that never seem to close: bars, nightclubs, diners, hospital emergency rooms. All this night crawling serves as an eye-opening experience for Kinsey, who is physically exhausted but mentally energized by her encounters with sad young prostitutes and other fascinating creatures of the night." N Y Times Book Rev

Grafton, Sue

N is for noose. Holt & Co. 1998 289p $25

ISBN 0-8050-3650-4

LC 97-49320

"Even when people are not nice to Kinsey, Grafton always deals fairly with them in this clean, well-constructed story about small-town insecurities." N Y Times Book Rev

Grafton, Sue

O is for outlaw. Holt & Co. 1999 318p $26

ISBN 0-8050-5955-5

LC 99-14967

"Everything that has always worked for this first class series works better here: the sturdy plotting, the animated characters, the breezy style and a heroine with foibles you can laugh at and faults you can forgive." N Y Times Book Rev

Grafton, Sue

P is for peril. Putnam 2001 352p $26.95

ISBN 0-399-14719-5

LC 00-46024

"Private investigator Kinsey Milhone is hired by Dr. Fiona Purcell to find her ex-husband, Dowan, a prominent physician who vanished with his passport and $30,000 in cash nine weeks earlier. Wondering what she can do that the Santa Rosa police haven't done already, Kinsey takes the case and quickly discovers that the nursing home Purcell administered is being investigated for Medicare fraud." Libr J

Grafton, Sue

Q is for quarry. Putnam 2002 385p $26.95

ISBN 0-399-14915-5

LC 2002-68368

"In the summer of 1969, the decomposed corpse of a young white female was discovered near a quarry off California's Highway 1. Her hands had been bound and her throat slashed. Despite months of investigation, 'Jane Doe' remained unidentified and the case unsolved. Now years later, Con Donlan and Stacey Oliphant, the police officers who had found her body, want Kinsey to help them to identify the girl and find her killer before they retire. At the same time, having learned that the body was found on a ranch owned by her estranged grandmother, Kinsey journeys into the past to retrace her own family history. Once again, an intriguing plot, fully drawn characters, and wry humor prove why Grafton's series is one of the best." Libr J

Grafton, Sue

S is for Silence. Putnam 2005 374p $26.95

ISBN 0-399-15297-0

LC 2005-48923

"Grafton uses the mystery of Violet's disappearance as a window into Serena Station, a sad little hamlet of boarded-up houses, abandoned oil rigs and rusting railroad tracks. Something vital went out of the place when Violet disappeared, and Kinsey's investigation forces the onetime neighbors of this lusty Jezebel to recall her unbridled sexual energy and reflect on their own joyless lives. By alternating Kinsey's brisk first-person narrative with dramatic flashbacks that catch the spirit of the town during its volatile postwar period, Grafton allows Violet to emerge as a dynamic but dangerous life force—irresistible to men, threatening to women and too reckless for her own good." N Y Times Book Rev

Grafton, Sue

T is for trespass. G. P. Putnam's Sons 2007 387p

ISBN 9780399154485; 0-399-15448-5

LC 2007-29368

"Gus Vronsky, Kinsey's elderly next-door neighbor, suffers a fall and needs in-home care. A health-care nurse named Solana Rojas is hired, and Kinsey even does the background check, finding nothing out of order. As Gus's condition deteriorates and Solana limits access to her patient, Kinsey and her landlord, Henry, suspect that something is a little off with Solana-and 'little off' doesn't fully describe this identity thief and true sociopath. Digging around more carefully, Kinsey unearths horrifying details of Solana's past and must act quickly to save Gus. This is vintage Grafton, set in the 1980s but scarily current, carefully plotted, and fast paced." Libr J

Grafton, Sue, 1940-

★ **X**; by Sue Grafton. Marian Wood Books/Putnam 2015 416 p. (hardcover : acid-free paper) $28.95

ISBN 9780399163845

LC 2015025108

This book, by Sue Grafton, "features a remorseless serial killer who leaves no trace of his crimes. Once again breaking the rules and establishing new paths, Grafton wastes little time identifying this sociopath. The test is whether Kinsey can prove her case against him before she becomes his next victim." (Publisher's note)

"Grafton's endless resourcefulness in varying her pitches in this landmark series (W Is for Wasted, 2013, etc.), graced by her trademark self-deprecating humor, is one of the seven wonders of the genre." Kirkus

Graham, Jo

Black ships; a novel. Orbit 2008 431p map pa $14.99

ISBN 978-0-316-06800-0; 0-316-06800-4

LC 2007-46166

"Born to a slave taken at the fall of Troy, the child named Gull is chosen by the oracle Pythia to succeed her in service to the Lady of Death because of her prophetic visions. When survivors of a later assault on Troy, called Wilusa by its inhabitants, free their enslaved people, Gull accompanies the captain of the seven black ships, the Trojan Prince Aeneas, as they search for a place to call home. Drawing her inspiration from Virgil's The Aeneid, debut author Graham recreates a vivid picture of the ancient world, a mysterious place in which gods and goddesses speak to their chosen." Libr J

Graley, Lisa

The **current** that carries; stories. by Lisa Graley. University of Georgia Press 2016 xii, 160 p.p (Flannery O'Connor Award for Short Fiction) (hardcover : acid-free paper) $24.95

ISBN 9780820349886; 0820349879; 9780820349879

LC 2015047529

Flannery O'Connor Award for Short Fiction (2016)

This book, by Lisa Graley, is a short story collection as pat of the Flannery O'Connor Award for Short Fiction Series that "bristles and hums with the rugged resilience one encounters in southern and Appalachian fiction, where ghosts of loved ones and livestock alike haunt an underworld of lonely trails." (Publisher's note)

"Eight stories that give voice to incommunicable aspects of love and loss." Kirkus

Gran, Sara

Claire DeWitt and the city of the dead. Houghton Mifflin Harcourt 2011 273p $24

ISBN 978-0-547-42849-9

LC 2010-21449

The novel is "is difficult to categorize, offering a strangely appealing mix of the mystical and the hardboiled. The book is beautifully written in a tight, quirky style that distinguishes Gran as one of the more original writers working today." Miami Herald

Grant, Donna

The **Protector**; by Donna Grant. St. Martin's Press 2017 294 p. (Sons of Texas) (paperback) $7.99

ISBN 9781250083432; 9781250083401; 1250083400

In this book, by Donna Grant, "when Marine Force Recon captain Cullen Loughman learns that his father's been kidnapped, he will do whatever it takes to find him. . . . Cullen will need to team up with the best of the best--someone who just happens to be the most stunning woman he's ever laid eyes on... This isn't the first rodeo for ex-Air Force pilot Mia Carter. Still, Cullen's bad-boy good looks and charm are distracting her from duty... and it appears that the feeling is mutual." (Publisher's note)

"The second in Grant's Sons of Texas trilogy (after The Hero) combines danger and desire in an intoxicating mix." Pub Wkly

Grant, Helen

The **glass** demon; Helen Grant. Bantam Books Trade Paperbacks 2010 305p. ill. pa $15

ISBN 978-0-385-34420-3; 0-385-34420-1; 9780345527585

LC 2011000738

First published 2010 in the United Kingdom.

This book tells the story of "Lin Fox, [who] finds herself in a falling-down castle deep in the woods of Germany while her father attempts to resuscitate his academic career. For generations, the village has lived with the legend of the Allerheiligen Glass-medieval stained glass windows that are said to have been cursed by a demon, bringing death to those who gaze upon them. . . . On Lin's first day, she meets Michel, a mysterious boy who eventually becomes her only ally. . . .What's unclear is if the escalating threats to her family and mounting village deaths are the result of Michel's mad father, or the Glass Demon himself. Combined with the mystery is the story of Lin's everyday teenage concerns: fitting in at school, pining over a crush, and worrying about family dynamics." (School Libr J)

"With its fascinating information on medieval folklore, unique setting, and increasingly claustrophobic sense of terror, this is an exhilarating page-turner that offers a cerebral blend of horror and mystery." Booklist

Grant, Helen

The **vanishing** of Katharina Linden; a novel. Helen Grant. Delacorte Press 2010 287 p. (hbk.) $24; (pbk.) $15

ISBN 9780385344173; 9780440339618; 9780385344180

LC 201003415

First published 2009 in the United Kingdom

Alex Award (2011)

This book follows "ten-year-old Pia Kolvenbach, [who] becomes known in her German hometown of Bad Münstereifel as 'The Girl Whose Grandmother Exploded.' Pia, whose mother is one of only three British citizens in the area, is already familiar with the peculiarities of this insular town, but the ostracism she now faces leaves her with only two confidantes: StinkStefan, a classmate and fellow outcast, and grouchy, secretive Herr Schiller, a source of town lore. Attention soon shifts from Pia when a local girl, Katharina Linden, becomes neither the first nor the last girl to go missing. Pia and Stefan, inspired . . . by Herr Schiller's gruesome stories, become determined to investigate the disappearances." (Library Journal)

"Set in the small German town of Bad Münstereifel during a cold, dreary winter when little girls seem to be disappearing left and right, this dark story gains immeasurably from Grant's choice of narrator: Pia Kolvenbach, who is socially ostracized (shunned as 'the Potentially Explosive Schoolgirl') after her grandmother dies in a bizarre accident. Feeling even more isolated when her English mother and German father begin quarreling, Pia finds companionship with 'StinkStefan,' 'the most unpopular boy in the class,' and Herr Schiller, a kindly old gent who spins terrifying but oddly comforting horror stories. Although thin on plot, the novel has nice atmosphere and takes a tender view of lonely children trying to make sense of a grown-up world." N Y Times Book Rev

Grant, Linda

We had it so good; a novel. Scribner 2011 325p $25

ISBN 978-1-4516-1740-5

LC 2011-04179

"Linda Grant traces the force of time on a group of friends from their hippie days in the Oxford of the late 1960s all the way to the present, through the conventional and unconventional choices they make, the professionals they become, the children they have, the choices those children make. At the center of the novel is the marriage of Stephen and Andrea Newman. He's an American with a Jewish father and a Cuban mother who arrives in England as a Rhodes scholar, making the crossing by boat with one Bill Clinton. She's British, the smart, sensitive daughter of small-time hotel owners in Cornwall. . . . In due course, they fall into bed, into something like love, into a marriage to keep him out of the American draft and then, unexpectedly, into a real marriage of obligations, children, a shared history, a life in London. Time passes. Arranged around this marriage are Grace, Andrea's dear friend, a raving blond beauty with significant psychic scars; Ivan, an advertising man, formerly a freewheeling daredevil given to spouting Reichian theories of the orgone box; Andrea and Stephen' children and parents; their trysts and crushes; their discarded selves." N Y Times Book Rev

Grant, Mira, 1978-

Deadline. Orbit 2011 560 p.

ISBN 9780316081061; 031608106X

This book is set in "2041, a year after Shaun Mason's sister and co-blogger, Georgia, became infected with the zombie virus. . . . After nearly three decades of rampant zombiism, procedures and protocols have evolved to keep humans safe, constrained, and scared. As Shaun struggles to cope with Georgia's death, a doctor from the Centers for Disease Control sets the After the End Times blogging crew to investigating a conspiracy around people with a reservoir condition--a state in which the virus goes live in just one area of the body--and the high death rate among reputable scientists trying to study them." (Publishers Weekly)

Grant, Mira, 1978-

★ **Down** Among the Sticks and Bones; Seanan McGuire. First edition. St. Martin's Press 2017 187 p. (Wayward Children) $17.99

ISBN 0765392038; 9780765392039

LC bl2017021577

Alex Award (2018)

Hugo Finalist: Best Novella (2018)

In this novel by Seanan McGuire, part of the Wayward Children series, "twin sisters Jack and Jill were seventeen when they found their way home and were packed off to Eleanor West's Home for Wayward Children. This is the story of what happened first. They were twelve when they walked down the impossible staircase and discovered that the pretense of love can never be enough to prepare you a life filled with magic in a land filled with mad scientists and death and choices." (Publisher's note)

"Beautifully crafted and smartly written, this fairy-tale novella is everything that speculative fiction readers look for: fantastical worlds, diverse characters, and prose that hits home with its emotional truths." LJ

Grant, Mira, 1978-

Every Heart a Doorway; by Seanan McGuire. St. Martin's Press 2016 176 p. $17.99

ISBN 0765385503; 9780765385505

LC 2015298654

Nebula Award: Best Novella (2016)

Alex Award (2017)

Hugo Award: Best Novella (2017)

This book, by Seanan McGuire, takes place at "Eleanor West's Home for Wayward Children. . . . Children have always disappeared under the right conditions; slipping through the shadows under a bed or at the back of a wardrobe . . . and emerging somewhere... else. . . . Nancy tumbled once, but now she's back. The things she's experienced... they change a person. The children under Miss West's care understand all too well. And each of them is seeking a way back to their own fantasy world." (Publisher's note)

Other titles in this series are:

Down Among the Sticks and Bones (2017)

Beneath the Sugar Sky (2018)

Grant, Mira

Feed. Orbit 2010 599p pa $9.99

ISBN 978-0-316-08105-4; 0-316-08105-1

This fantasy is set in a "postapocalyptic 2039. Twin bloggers Georgia and Shaun Mason and their colleague Buffy are thrilled when Sen. Peter Ryman, the first presidential candidate to come of age since social media saved the world from a virus that reanimates the dead, invites them to cover his campaign. Then an event is attacked by zombies, and Ryman's daughter is killed. As the bloggers wield the newfound power of new media, they tangle with the CDC, a scheming vice presidential candidate, and mysterious conspirators who want more than the Oval Office. Shunning misogynistic horror tropes in favor of genuine drama and pure creepiness, McGuire has crafted a masterpiece of suspense with engaging, appealing characters who conduct a soul-shredding examination of what's true and what's reported." Publ Wkly

Grant, Mira, 1978-

Feedback; Mira Grant. Orbit 2016 489 p. (Newsflesh) (hardcover) $25

ISBN 9780316379342; 9780316379335

LC 2016013017

In this book in the Newsflesh series, by Mira Grant, "a team of scrappy underdog reporters relentlessly pursue the facts while competing against the brother-and-sister blog superstars, the Masons. Surrounded by the infected, and facing more insidious forces working in the shadows, they must hit the presidential campaign trail and uncover dangerous truths. Or die trying." (Publisher's note)

"This mashup of medical and media ethics, politics and the living undead, is a whip-smart thriller overflowing with sharp ideas and social commentary." Kirkus

Grant, Mira, 1978-

Parasite; by Mira Grant. Orbit 2013 512 p. (Parasitology) (hardcover) $20

ISBN 0316218952; 9780316218955

LC 2013005713

In this book by Mira Grant, set "a decade in the future, humanity thrives in the absence of sickness and disease. We owe our good health to a humble parasite - a genetically engineered tapeworm developed by the pioneering SymboGen Corporation. When implanted, the Intestinal Bodyguard worm protects us from illness, boosts our immune system. But these parasites are getting restless. They want their own lives . . . and will do anything to get them." (Publisher's note)

Followed by Symbiont (2014) and Chimera (2015)

Grant, Mira, 1978-

Rosemary and Rue; by Seanan McGuire. DAW 2009 358 p. (DAW Book Collectors ; no. 1487) paperback $7.99

ISBN 9780756405717; 0756405718

LC 2010668298

In this book by Seanan McGuire in the October Daye series, "the world of Faerie never disappeared . . . [and] when the fae and mortal worlds collide, changelings are born. . . . These half-human, half-fae children spend their lives fighting for the respect of their immortal relations. Or, in the case of October 'Toby' Daye, rejecting it completely. . . . Toby has denied the fae world, retreating into a 'normal' life. Unfortunately for her, Faerie has other ideas." (Publisher's note)

"Like Dreams and Shadows, this dark, gritty, and richly detailed urban fantasy introduces characters who awkwardly straddle the boundary between the mortal and supernatural worlds, presenting an inventive contemporary take on classic fairy tale lore." LJ

Grant, Stephanie

Map of Ireland; a novel. Scribner 2008 197p $22

ISBN 978-1-416-55622-0; 1-416-55622-2

LC 2007-45912

"Ann's descriptions of life in Southie are so compelling that some readers may miss those passages, with their very specific, idiosyncratic details, when she steps out of this world she knows best into the wider world. But Grant emerges on the other side with her firm grip on originality, and ultimately, in spite of the wonderful epigraph by Heraclitus — 'Geography is fate' — Ann represents not so much her community, but herself. . . . Early on, she muses that 'the problem with the movies was that they made you think you had more experience than you actually did.' That, too, is the gift of a well-worded novel. 'Map of Ireland' is admirably ambitious, bold, and smart." Boston Globe

Grass, Gunter

The **box**; tales from the darkroom. translated from the German by Krishna Winston. Houghton Mifflin Harcourt 2010 194p $23

ISBN 978-0-547-24503-4; 0-547-24503-3

LC 2010-08479

Original German edition, 2008

"The premise is that for his 80th birthday, Grass has asked his children eight in all, with four different mothers to gather together to record their memories of life with their father. The slender book comprises nine sections. Each consists of the children's uninterrupted (and generally unidentified) voices, bracketed by the author's short preface and concluding reflection. . . . While Grass is the subject of their memories, another figure emerges as equally important: Marie, the author's longtime friend and eventual assistant (and perhaps lover), who constantly takes photographs with her old Agfa box camera as a memory aid for his novels. . . . [This novel] should serve as no one's introduction to Grass; its charm and poignancy hinge on prior knowledge of the author's books." San Francisco Chron

Grass, Gunter

The **call** of the toad; translated by Ralph Manheim. Harcourt Brace Jovanovich 1992 248p il

LC 92-20233

This book is a "skillful balancing act that juggles some very timely questions about the conflict between calls for ethnic self-determination and calls for international unity and cooperation." Christ Sci Monit

Grass, Gunter

Cat and mouse; translated by Ralph Manheim. Harcourt, Brace & World 1963 189p

Original German edition, 1961

A novel about Mahlke, a teenager growing up in a Baltic port city during World War II who is set apart from his fellows by his huge Adam's apple. When a classmate attracts a cat to this 'mouse' he launches Mahlke on his career. Mahlke becomes an excellent swimmer and athlete, and later a hero to his nation. But the symbolic cat watching him is a society of petty men and Mahlke is eventually doomed

Grass, Gunter

Crabwalk; translated from the German by Krishna Winston. Harcourt 2002 234p $25

ISBN 0-15-100764-0

LC 2002-13205

"A writer who refuses to avert his eyes from unpleasant truths, Grassremains an eloquent explorer of his country's troubled 20th-century history." Publ Wkly

Grass, Gunter

The **Danzig** trilogy; translated by Ralph Manheim. Harcourt Brace Jovanovich 1987 1030p

ISBN 0-15-123816-2

LC 87-8725

Contents: The tin drum; Cat and mouse; Dog years

Grass, Gunter

★ **Dog** years; translated by Ralph Manheim. Harcourt, Brace & World 1965 570p

Original German edition, 1963

"A monumental parable on 'mass man,' materialism, and transcendence, written in the richly encrusted, playful, brutal, ironic, subtle, sensitive, surrealist, erudite, unique modern baroque. . . . {This novel tells} of Eduard Amsel, rumored to be half Jew, designer of fantastic scarecrows, endlessly ingenious and talented; of Walter Matern, athlete and compulsive tooth grinder, Amsel's blood brother, his defender, and helper until association with a Nazi S. A. group leads him to beat Amsel unmercifully; of Hitler's favorite dog Prinz of notable lineage and the howling dog days echoing down the centuries through World War II and aftermath. The cast is large; the canvas is chiefly Danzig and villages along the Vistula; and the scarecrow prevails as dominant symbol." Booklist

Grass, Gunter

The **flounder**; translated by Ralph Manheim. Harcourt Brace Jovanovich 1978 547p

LC 78-53891

Original German edition, 1977

"Grass's first-person narrator is the legendary fisherman who caught the magic fish and might have fared well had it not been for the foolishness of his wife Ilsebill. Grass uses the well-known fairy tale as a frame for his chronicler to relate his various lives' experiences (between the late Neolithic and {1970}) . . . to his pregnant wife Ilsebill in the course of nine months. While his story unfolds, the fish is on trial in a feminist courtroom after he has been caught again, this time by three women in West Berlin." Libr J

Grass, Gunter

My century; translated by Michael Henry Heim. Harcourt Brace & Co. 1999 280p $31

ISBN 0-15-100496-X

LC 99-38690

Original German edition, 1999

"The best thing {this book} offers non-Germans, even if inadvertently, is the opportunity to hear, or to overhear, how Germans speak to one another about their history when the rest of us are not supposed to be listening." Natl Rev

Grass, Gunter

★ The **tin** drum; translated from the German by Ralph Manheim; with an introduction by John Reddick. Knopf 1993 xxxvii, 551p

ISBN 0-679-42033-9

LC 92-54295

Original German edition, 1959; this translation first published 1962 in the United Kingdom, 1963 in the United States by Pantheon Books

"Oskar Matzerath, born with an unusually sharp mind, describes the amoral conditions through which he has lived in twentieth-century Germany, both during and after the Hitler regime. This strange narrator stops growing when he is three years old and remains three feet tall until some time late, when he decides to grow a few inches more. After the war he escapes to West Germany, where he works in such capacities as an artist's model, a night-club performer, and a black marketeer. Depicted as a freak (Oskar becomes a hunchback later in his life), this character symbolizes the deformed society of this century. It is through his tin drum, which he uses to stimulate recollections of his life, that Oskar describes his past while he is an inmate in a mental hospital." Shapiro. Fic for Youth. 3d edition

Grass, Gunter

Too far afield; translated from the German by Krishna Winston. Harcourt 2000 658p $30

ISBN 0-15-100230-4

LC 00-29586

Original German edition published 1995

The narrative's "focus is German reunification, in particular, the fate of the German Democratic Republic after the Wall came down in 1989. At the center of the novel are two characters, locked in a sort of political marriage: Theo Wuttke, a former East German cultural figure and long-winded raconteur, and Ludwig Hoffstaller, a professional spy who served for years as Wuttke's shadow. They are both about to turn 70 in this new Germany and are now both employees of the agency responsible for privatizing state-held companies." Booklist

Grau, Shirley Ann

The **keepers** of the house. Knopf 1964 309p

"This multigenerational novel deals with the twentieth-century heirs of a Southern dynasty, their relations to the past, and their involvement in the racial and political complexities of the present. The narrator is Abigail Mason Tolliver, granddaughter of William Howland, whose second wife had been a Freejack Negro. The townspeople have always assumed that she had been no more than William's mistress, but the truth of the legality of their marriage surfaces when Abigail's husband, John Tolliver, enters the race for governor. In addition to leading to Tolliver's defeat, the story of the marriage also incites a mob to burn down the old Howland house. Abigail saves the house but withdraws the economic support that the Howland family has always supplied the town, and lets it 'shrivel and shrink to its real size.'" Shapiro. Fic for Youth. 3d edition

Graves, Robert

Claudius, the god and his wife Messalina. H. Smith & R. Haas 1935 583p

"A vivid picture of profligate Rome during the years in which Claudius conquered Britain and instituted many reforms at home. A story complete in itself, though a continuation of 'I, Claudius.'" Booklist

Graves, Robert

Complete short stories; edited by Lucia Graves. St. Martin's Press 1996 331p

ISBN 0-312-16055-0

LC 96-5343

"Graves is a master storyteller, and the stories collected here are both masterly and charming. Especially noteworthy are the sweetly humorous tales about school days in Edwardian England and the breezy, gently witty stories about everyday life in Majorca, Graves's adopted home." Libr J

Graves, Robert

★ **I,** Claudius; from the autobiography of Tiberius Claudius, born B.C. 10, murdered and deified A.D. 54. H. Smith and R. Haas 1934 494p

"Claudius is lame and a stammerer who seems unlikely to carry on the family tradition of power in ancient Rome. Immersing himself in scholarly pursuits, Claudius observes and lives through the plots hatched by his grandmother, Livia, political conspiracies, murders, and corruption, and he survives a number of emperors. He becomes emperor at last and is a just and well-liked ruler, in contrast to those who preceded him." Shapiro. Fic for Youth. 3d edition

Followed by Claudius, the god and his wife Messalina

Gray, Alasdair

★ **Poor** things; episodes from the early life of Archibald McCandless M.D., Scottish public health officer. edited by Alasdair Gray. Harcourt Brace Jovanovich 1993 317p il

ISBN 0-15-173076-8

LC 92-40018

First published 1992 in the United Kingdom

"Mr. Gray contrasts the political and moral bleakness of contemporary Britain with the civic energy that characterized the best of Victorian values, now lost. He underlines the harm done to Scotland. 'Poor Things' is a political book. It is also witty and delightfully written, if at times two-dimensional. Attention to Victorian Glasgow with its civic fountains, domestic interiors and medical schools gives the book texture. It is the characters, and strangely enough its phantasmagoria, that give it life." N Y Times Book Rev

Gray, Amelia

Gutshot; stories. Amelia Gray. FSG Originals 2015 224 p. (softcover) $14

ISBN 0374175446; 9780374175443

LC 2014031210

This book is a short story collection by Amelia Gray. "In 'Year of the Snake,' a large reptile divides a small town into North Snake and South Snake, and a local scientist turns an unusual discovery into a booming business. In 'House Heart,' two lovers rent the services of a young woman and then enclose her inside the home's air ducts. 'Western Passages' follows a narrator who befriends a young woman on a bus, determined to protect her from a leering passenger." (Booklist)

"Gray's bountiful five-part collection incorporates tales and vignettes both absorbing and unconventional: gods hold a yearly contest in which the winner (whoever can feel the most grief) is reunited with a lost loved one; a deceased mother's voice begins to emanate from her daughter's pimple; young twins place a curse on their mother; "Fifty Ways to Eat Your Lover" is a how-to list. While eccentricities are on display, Gray's stories also deftly capture the startling moments when her characters pull off their armor and reveal their genuine selves." Booklist

Gray, Juliana

A **Duke** Never Yields; Juliana Gray. Berkley Pub Group 2013 320 p. (Affairs by moonlight) $7.99

ISBN 0425251187; 9780425251188

In this historical romance novel, by Juliana Gray, "impatient with the strictures of polite British society, Miss Abigail Harewood has decided to live life on her own terms--and the first thing she requires is a lover. When the commanding Duke of Wallingford arrives on the doorstep of her leased holiday castle, she thinks she's found the perfect candidate: handsome, dashing, and experienced in the art of love." (Publisher's note)

Gray, Juliana

How to School Your Scoundrel; Juliana Gray. Berkley Pub Group 2014 320 p. $7.99

ISBN 0425265684; 9780425265680

In this romance novel by Juliana Gray, part of the Princess in Hiding series, "Princess Luisa has devoted her life to duty, quietly preparing to succeed her father as ruler. . . . The earl is just the man to help her reclaim her throne, but Luisa is drawn to her powerful employer in ways she never imagined. . . . Philip, Earl of Somerton, has spent six years married to a woman in love with another man--he refuses to become a fool due to imprudent emotions ever again."

"Witty banter, sharp humor, and delectable sexual chemistry spice up this exquisitely written, nonstop adventure that takes the cross-dressing theme to the max, adds a dollop of farce, and beautifully wraps up this offbeat late Victorian trilogy." LJ

Gray, Juliana

How to Tame Your Duke; by Juliana Gray. Berkley Pub Group 2013 320 p. $7.99

ISBN 0425265668; 9780425265666

This book, by Juliana Gray, is set in England in 1888. "Princess Emilie . . . disguise[s] herself as a tutor in the household of the imposing Duke of Ashland, a former soldier disfigured in battle. Emilie can't resist the opportunity to learn what lies behind his forbidding mask. The duke never imagines that his son's tutor and his mysterious . . . beauty are one and the same. When the true identity of his lover is laid bare, Ashland must . . . safeguard both his lady--and his heart." (Publisher's note)

Other titles in this series are:

How to master your marquis (2014)

How to school your scoundrel (2014)

Gray, Juliana

A **lady** never lies; by Juliana Gray. Berkley Sensation 2012 311 p.

ISBN 042525092X; 9780425250921

Author Juliana Gray tells the story of "Lady Alexandra Morley, an alluring widow, [who] is desperate to devise a plan to reverse her fortunes. When fate lands her in the arms of Phineas 'Finn' Burke, an attractive inventor, she despairs of ever getting what she needs...until they kiss . . . Despite the brewing scandal, Finn longs to make Alexandra his wife, but he must first convince the maddening lady that their love is the only thing that matters." (Amazon)

Greaney, Mark

Gunmetal gray; Mark Greaney. Berkley 2017 xiv, 494 p.p (Gray man) (hardcover) $27

ISBN 9780698406858; 9780425282854

LC 2016037708

Sequel to: Back blast (2016)

In this book in the Gray Man series, by Mark Greaney, "after five years on the run Court Gentry is back on the inside at the CIA. But his first mission makes him wish he had stayed on the outs when a pair of Chinese agents try to take him down in Hong Kong. . . . Court's high stakes hunt for answers takes him across Southeast Asia and leads to his old friend, Donald Fitzroy, who is being held hostage by the Chinese." (Publisher's note)

"Nonstop thrills and terrific set pieces make this a strong addition to the series and a definite must for fans of Brad Taylor or Tom Clancy." Booklist

Greatest hits; original stories of assassins, hitmen, and hired guns. edited by Robert J. Randisi. Carroll & Graf 2005 318p $26

ISBN 978-0-7867-1581-7; 0-78671-581-2

LC 2006-297413

Randisi "has gathered 15 memorable tales of contract killers, antiheroes paid to carry out murders for a variety of clients and motives. . . . While the moral code that guides the actions of some of the murderers requires a measure of suspension of disbelief, the taut language and suspenseful plot twists that mark virtually all the stories should draw in even non-hardboiled devotees." Publ Wkly

Greaves, C. Joseph

Hard twisted; a novel. C. Joseph Greaves. St. Martin's Press 2012 304 p.

ISBN 1608198553; 9781608198559

LC 2011051902

Author C. Joseph Greaves' book received the 2010 Best Historical Novel award in the SouthWest Writers Annual Writing Contest. "In May of 1934, outside of Hugo, Oklahoma, a homeless man and his 13 year-old daughter are befriended by a Texas drifter . . . [who] lures father and daughter to Texas . . . [There,] the father, Dillard Garrett, mysteriously disappears, and . . . his daughter Lucile begins a one-year ordeal that culminates in four Utah killings and Palmer's notorious Greenville, Texas 'skeleton murder' trial of 1935." (chuckgreaves.com)

Greaves, Chuck

★ **Hush** money; a mystery. Chuck Greaves. Minotaur Books 2012 326 p.

ISBN 125000523X; 9781250005236; 9781466802483

LC 2012004489

In this book, "[w]hen Sydney Everett's Olympic-caliber jumping horse, Hush Puppy, dies suddenly, her law firm jumps into action, sending out young Pasadena, CA, attorney Jack MacTaggart. Sydney is worth watching because another horse she owned died under suspicious circumstances just a few years earlier. Jack . . . learns that Sydney was guilty of insurance fraud that first time, and someone within the club has been blackmailing her ever since. Jack knows he's hot on the trail when the next death turns out to be that of his mentor at the law firm. Stable manager Tara Flynn clues in Jack to the riding club's dirt and also provides romantic interest and an investigative assistant he can trust. Meanwhile, Jack's other case, about medical insurance, gives him the break he needs." (Libr J)

Grebe, Camilla

The **ice** beneath her; a novel. Camilla Grebe; translated by Elizabeth Clark Wessel. Ballantine Books 2016 368 p. (ebook) $65; (hardcover : alk. paper) $27

ISBN 9780425284339; 9780425284322

LC 2016013298

In this novel, by Camilla Grebe, translated by Elizabeth Clark Wessel, "winter's chill has descended on Stockholm as police arrive at the scene of a shocking murder. An unidentified woman lies beheaded in a posh suburban home—a brutal crime made all the more disturbing by its uncanny resemblance to an unsolved killing ten years earlier. But this time there's a suspect: the charismatic and controversial chain-store CEO Jesper Orre, who owns the home but is nowhere to be found." (Publisher's note)

"A tour de force that lifts its author to the front rank among the increasingly crowded field of Nordic noir." Kirkus

Green, George Dawes

Ravens. Grand Central Pub. 2009 325p $24.99

ISBN 978-0-446-53896-1; 0-446-53896-5

LC 2008-48331

"When Shaw and Romeo pull up at a convenience store off I-95 in Georgia, their only thought is to fix a leaky tire and be on their way again to Florida—away from their dull Ohio tech-support jobs. But this happens to be the store from which a $318,000,000-million jackpot ticket has been sold. When a pretty clerk accidentally reveals to Shaw the identity of the winning family, he hatches a ferociously audacious scheme: he and Romeo will squeeze the family for half their prize." Publisher's note

Green, Jane

Another piece of my heart; Jane Green. St. Martin's Press 2012 400p (hardcover) $25.99

ISBN 9780312591823; 9781429962735

LC 2011041347

This book tells the story of "Andi [who] has spent much of her adult life looking for the perfect man, and at thirty-seven, she's finally found him. Ethan--divorced with two daughters, Emily and Sophia--is a devoted father and even better husband. Always hoping one day she would be a mother, Andi embraces the girls like they were her own. But in Emily's eyes, Andi is an obstacle to her father's love, and Emily will do whatever it takes to break her down. When the dynamics between the two escalate, they threaten everything Andi believes about love, family, and motherhood--leaving both women standing at a crossroad in their lives . . . and in their hearts." (Publisher's note)

Green, Jane

Tempting fate; Jane Green. First edition St. Martin's Press 2014 352 p. (hardback) $25.99

ISBN 0312591845; 9780312591847

LC 2013031011

"Gabby and Elliott have been happily married for eighteen years. . . . Forty-three year old Gabby is the last person to have an affair. She can't relate to the way her friends desperately try to cling to the beauty and allure of their younger years. . . . And yet, she too knows her youth is quickly slipping away. She could never imagine how good it would feel to have a handsome younger man show interest in her--until the night it happens." (Publisher's note)

Green, Norman

The **angel** of Montague Street. HarperCollins Pubs. 2003 293p $24.95

ISBN 0-06-018819-7

LC 2002-32885

Silvano Iurata "should never be in Brooklyn in the first place. It's 1973, the city is broke and mean, and he's ben bumming around since he got out of Vietnam, avoiding his Mafia-employed family and keeping clear of his loco cousin, Domenic, who wants to settle and old family quarrel by killing him with his bare hands. But Iurata is on some private redemptive mission, and he figures that if he can find out what happened to his sweet, mildly retarded brother, last seen in Brooklyn Heights, he might be able to give up the dead and rejoin the living. . . . Green writes about mobster families with a knowledge that is unnerving in its intimacy." N Y Times Book Rev

Greenberg, Joanne

★ **I** never promised you a rose garden; a novel. [by] Hannah Green. Holt & Co. 1964 300p

ISBN 0-8050-0872-1

"The hospital world and Deborah's fantasy world are strikingly portrayed, as is the girl's violent struggle between sickness and health, a struggle given added poignancy by youth, wit, and courage." Libr J

Greenberg, Joanne

In this sign. Holt, Rinehart & Winston 1970 275p

"The life of deaf-mutes Abel and Janice Ryder is followed from their marriage to their old age. After they leave the cloistered world of the institution for those with their handicap, they are plunged, unprepared, into the terrifying world of the hearing. They are never fully assimilated into that society. When they have a daughter who can hear, they gain new perspectives, but poverty and personal tragedy—the death of a son—further separate them from others, even from other deaf people. Greenberg's insights into the lives of the deaf are sensitive and painful." Shapiro. Fic for Youth. 2d edition

Greene, Amy

Bloodroot; a novel. Alfred A. Knopf 2010 291p $24.95

ISBN 978-0-307-26986-7; 0-307-26986-8

LC 2009-19483

"As a first novel, Bloodroot has its awkward moments, and some segments that work less well than others. . . . When Bloodroot works, however, its power is awesome, peeling away layers of the human experience like an onion until it reaches a message of redemption. Greene proves herself a newcomer to watch." Wilmington Star News

Greene, Amy

★ **Long** Man; A novel. Amy Greene. Alfred A. Knopf 2014 271 p. (hardcover) $25.95

ISBN 0307593436; 9780307593436

LC 2013018846

Written by Amy Greene, this book is a "novel of a family in turmoil, set against the backdrop of real-life historical event--the story of three days in the summer of 1936, as a government-built dam is about to flood an Appalachian town, and a little girl goes missing. . . . The Tennessee Valley Authority's plans to dam the river and flood the town of Yuneetah for the sake of progress--to bring electricity and jobs to the region--are about to take effect." (Publisher's note)

"A smart and moody historical novel that evokes the best widescreen Southern literature." Kirkus

Greene, Graham, 1904-1991

3: This gun for hire, The confidential agent, The ministry of fear. Viking 1952 3v in 1

A one-volume edition of three suspense stories. The titles were first published 1936, 1939 and 1943, respectively

Greene, Graham, 1904-1991

★ **Brighton** rock; an entertainment. Viking 1938 358p

"This novel presents the story of Pinkie Brown, a chilling, utterly evil 17-year-old gang leader who marries the plodding Rose in order to insure her silence about his crimes. Both Pinkie and Rose were reared as Roman Catholics, and that background continues to inform their thoughts, if not their actions. In the end Pinkie dies while attempting to kill Rose; later, a priest tells Rose that her love for Pinkie may have saved her, as the mercy of God may have saved Pinkie." Merriam-Webster's Ency of Lit

Greene, Graham, 1904-1991

The **captain** and the enemy. Viking 1988 188p

LC 87-40664

The author "wastes not a word in distilling the fictional preoccupations of a lifetime, omitting descriptive padding and elaborate transitions. But stripped down, the narrative runs fast and true across that bleak and poignant emotional landscape that is uniquely, immortally his." Time

Greene, Graham, 1904-1991

Collected stories; including May we borrow your husband? A sense of reality {and} Twenty-one stories. Viking 1973 561p

Greene, Graham, 1904-1991

★ The **end** of the affair. Viking 1951 240p

"The novel is set in wartime London. The narrator Maurice Bendrix, a bitter, sardonic novelist, has a five-year affair with a married woman, Sarah Miles. When a V-1 bomb explodes in front of Bendrix's apartment and Sarah finds Bendrix pinned beneath the front door, she believes him dead. She promises a God in whom she does not believe that she will give Bendrix up if he is allowed to live. Just then, Bendrix walks into the room and Sarah begins her religious journey; she breaks off with Bendrix, railing against God even as she begins to take religious instruction. Gradually she comes to a profound religious faith." Merriam-Webster's Ency of Lit

Greene, Graham, 1904-1991

★ The **heart** of the matter; introduction by James Wood. Deluxe ed; Penguin Books 2004 255p (Penguin classics) pa $15

ISBN 0-14-243799-9

LC 2004-275122

First published 1948

"Set in West Africa, it is a suspense story ingeniously made to hinge on religious faith. . . . The hero is Scobie, an English Roman Catholic who has vowed to make his devout wife happy though he no longer loves her. He borrows money from a local criminal to send her out of harm's way to South Africa; then he falls in love with a young woman from a group of castaways whose ship has been torpedoed. The return of his wife, the development of an adulterous affair, and blackmail drive Scobie deeper into deception and lies. Forced to betray someone, he betrays his god and himself, and finally commits suicide." Reader's Ency. 4th edition

Greene, Graham, 1904-1991

The **honorary** consul. Simon & Schuster 1973 315p

This "novel relates the story of the politically motivated kidnapping of a minor British functionary near Argentina's Paraguayan border. The novel's major characters exemplify the kinds of personal sacrifices one must make in order to live in good conscience in a world where there is too much tyranny and injustice. A minor machismo novelist endures privation; a priest joins the radical underground movement; a physician gives up a lucrative Buenos Aires practice." Libr J

Greene, Graham, 1904-1991

★ The **human** factor. Knopf 1992 xxviii, 338p $18

ISBN 0-679-40992-0

LC 91-53189

A reissue of the title first published 1978 by Simon & Schuster

"In the British Foreign Service 'the human factor' becomes a liability for employees and a conduit for suspense, intrigue, and tragedy. Maurice Castle, head of a division in which information seems to have been leaked, presents a very positive image that appears to assure his innocence, but Davis, directly responsible to him, is an object of speculation. For a secret agent, the normal relationships of love and family are fraught with danger. As is true of many of Greene's novels, there are questions in this book about the loyalty owed to a government whose activities are suspect." Shapiro. Fic For Youth. 3d edition

Greene, Graham, 1904-1991

The **last** word and other stories. Reinhardt Bks. 1990 149p

LC 90-81665

"This modest volume gathers uncollected stories from the entire range of Greene's career. The earliest dates from 1923 (!) and the latest from 1989." Libr J

Greene, Graham, 1904-1991

Our man in Havana; an entertainment. Viking 1958 247p

"Set in Cuba before the communist revolution, the book is a comical spy story about a British vacuum-cleaner salesman's misadventures in the British Secret Intelligence Service. Although many critics found fault with the book's overly farcical style, it was also admired for its skillful rendering of the Cuban locale." Merriam-Webster's Ency of Lit

Greene, Graham, 1904-1991

The **power** and the glory; introduction by John Updike. Viking 1990 295p hardcover o.p. pa $14

ISBN 0-670-83536-6; 0-14-243730-1 pa

LC 90-50052

First published 1940 with title: The labyrinthine ways

Set in Mexico, this novel "describes the desperate last wanderings of a whisky priest as outlaw in his own state, who, despite a sense of his own worthlessness (he drinks, and has fathered a bastard daughter), is determined to continue to function as priest until captured. . . . Like many of Greene's works, it combines a conspicuous Christian theme and symbolism with the elements of a thriller." Oxford Companion to Engl Lit

Greene, Graham, 1904-1991

★ The **quiet** American. Modern Lib. 1992 247p

ISBN 0-679-60014-0

LC 92-50219

First published 1955 in the United Kingdom; first United States edition published 1956 by Viking

"Mr. Greene has always been a master of suspense, and the particular excellence of 'The Quiet American' lies in the way in which he builds up the situation finally to explode the moral problem which for him lies at the heart of the matter." Times Lit Suppl

Greene, Graham, 1904-1991

The **tenth** man. Simon & Schuster 1985 157p

LC 84-29830

"A fatal series of events follows, entwining narrative excitement with broader questions of identity, fate, and morality. As always with Greene, the basic plot is heightened by the novelist's compelling view of the human condition." Libr J

Greene, Graham, 1904-1991

Travels with my aunt; a novel. Viking 1969 244p

"The book unmistakably turns its back on the Orphic preoccupations with the hereafter that characterized Greene's Catholic novels, and wholeheartedly embraces a Bacchic emphasis on the here and now." N Y Times Book Rev

Greenfeld, Karl Taro, 1964-

Triburbia; a novel. Karl Taro Greenfeld. Harper 2012 253 p. map

ISBN 0062132393; 9780062132390

LC 2012462007

"In this . . . novel, [Karl Taro] Greenfeld . . . brings to life the capacious lofts, self-involved chefs, and occasional rent control holdouts of Manhattan's affluent TriBeCa neighborhood. . . . Each chapter . . . is told from the perspective of a different local character. . . . Their lives intersect and overlap because their children attend the same school, they're sleeping with one another's spouses, or, in Sadie's case, because she's the babysitter or, in Cooper's case, because she's queen of the fourth grade." (Publishers Weekly)

Greenidge, Kaitlyn

We love you, Charlie Freeman; a novel. by Kaitlyn Greenidge. Algonquin Books of Chapel Hill 2016 336 p. (ebook) $25.95; $25.95

ISBN 9781616206079; 9781616204679

LC 2015031336

In this novel, by Kaitlyn Greenidge, "the Freeman family . . . have been invited to . . . participate in a research experiment. They will live . . . with Charlie, a young chimp. . . . The Freemans were selected . . . because they know sign language; they are supposed to teach it to Charlie and welcome him as a member of their family. Isolated in their new, nearly all-white community not just by their race but by their strange living situation, the Freemans come undone." (Publisher's note)

"A vivid and poignant coming-of-age story that is also an important exploration of family, race, and history." Kirkus

Greenleaf, Stephen

False conception; a John Marshall Tanner novel. Penzler Bks. 1994 273p

ISBN 1-883402-87-5

LC 94-17371

"Stuart and Millicent Colbert can't conceive a child, but they have the resources to hire a surrogate mother. San Francisco private eye, Marsh Tanner is employed to investigate the surrogate, Greta Hammond. The catch: Hammond must never know the identity of the Colberts nor that she's being investigated. . . . Tanner novels are never just mysteries; Greenleaf always weaves in a larger human dilemma, and here he does it more successfully than ever before." Booklist

Greenleaf, Stephen

Strawberry Sunday; a John Marshall Tanner novel. Scribner 1999 287p

ISBN 0-684-84954-2

LC 98-40955

"The Tanner books often have been built around a specific social or political issue, and this one is no exception. Greenleaf takes a long, hard look at the miserable conditions in which many farmworkers live and toil, and builds a complex, absorbing plot around the topic." Publ Wkly

Greenwell, Garth, 1978-

What belongs to you; a novel. Garth Greenwell. Farrar, Straus & Giroux 2016 208 p. (hardcover) $23

ISBN 0374288224; 9780374288228

LC 2015003932

In this novel, by Garth Greenwell, "on an unseasonably warm autumn day, an American teacher enters a public bathroom beneath Sofia's National Palace of Culture. There he meets Mitko, a charismatic young hustler, and pays him for sex. He returns to Mitko again and again over the next few months, drawn by hunger and loneliness and risk." (Publisher's note)

"The book breaks up the adult protagonist's story with a long middle section devoted to exploring the professor's difficult childhood, as well as his first love, and it is here that the man's struggles--sexual and emotional--come alive." Pub Wkly

Greenwood, Kerry

★ **Medea**; by Kerry Greenwood. Poisoned Pen Press 2013 250 p. map $24.95

ISBN 1464201439; 1863304916; 9781464201431

LC 97169609

Originally published 1997 in Australia

In this novel by Kerry Greenwood "Medea, Princess of Colchis, is a priestess of Hecate. She is the custodian of the wood in which the Golden Fleece is hung. She alone can tame the giant serpent which guards the grove. And then Jason and his Argonauts come along, and she falls . . . in love. She helps him steal the Golden Fleece ans sails with him to claim his throne. And that's when things go wrong... and she must attempt to reclaim her humanity through . . . murder, grief and heavy seas." (Publisher's note)

Includes bibliographical references

Other titles in this series are:

Cassandra
Electra

Greenwood, Kerry

Out of the black land; Kerry Greenwood. Poisoned Pen Press 2013 250 p. (hardcover : alk. paper) $24.95

ISBN 1464200386; 9781464200380; 9781464200403
LC 2012953055

In this novel by Kerry Greenwood "Eighteenth Dynasty Egypt is peaceful and prosperous under the dual rule of the Pharaohs Amenhotep III and IV, until the younger Pharaoh begins to dream new and terrifying dreams. . . . Ptah-hotep . . . wants to live a simple life . . . but Amenhotep IV appoints him as Great Royal Scribe. . . . Not content with his own devotion to one god alone, the newly-renamed Akhnaten plans to suppress the worship of all other gods in the Black Land." (Publisher's note)

Greenwood, Kerry ✓

Unnatural Habits; Kerry Greenwood. Poisoned Pen Press 2013 250 p. (Phryne Fisher Mysteries) $24.95

ISBN 1464201234; 9781464201233

"1929: Girls are going missing in Melbourne. . . . Polly Kettle, a pushy, self-important Girl Reporter with ambition and no sense of self preservation, decides to investigate--and promptly goes missing herself. It's time for Phryne and Dot to put a stop to this and find Polly Kettle before something quite irreparable happens to all of them." (Publisher's note)

Greer, Andrew Sean

The **Impossible** Lives of Greta Wells; Andrew Sean Greer. HarperCollins 2013 304 p. illustrations, map $26.99

ISBN 0062213784; 9780062213785
LC 2013474292

This novel, by Andrew Sean Greer, is the "story of a woman who finds herself transported to the "other lives" she might have lived. After the death of her beloved twin brother and the abandonment of her long-time lover, Greta Wells undergoes electroshock therapy. Over the course of the treatment, Greta finds herself repeatedly sent to 1918, 1941, and back to the present." (Publisher's note)

"Philosophically intriguing as well as gorgeously imagined and executed, this novel will catch fire with the same audience that propelled Audrey Niffenegger's The Time Traveler's Wife (2003) to the top of the best-seller list." Booklist

Greer, Andrew Sean

The **story** of a marriage. Farrar, Straus & Giroux 2008 195p $22

ISBN 978-0-374-10866-3; 0-374-10866-8
LC 2007-46835

"Greer's short novel feels admirably worked over like a long-simmered sauce. He near-brilliantly juxtaposes the nuances of love, sexual awakening and the sometimes suffocating sacrifices marriage demands against broader cultural observations about political turmoil, the physical and emotional effects of war, sexual repression and racism. His book is a perfect mix of what we seek from literature — captivating storytelling; a complex, finely tuned structure; stunning language; and astute observations about both the mundane intricacies of everyday relationships and society as a whole." Los Angeles Times Book Rev

Greer, Robert O.

★ **First** of state. North Atlantic Books 2010 380p $24.95

ISBN 978-1-55643-915-5; 1-55643-915-6
LC 2010-20235

"CJ Floyd is 22 years old, but he seems much older somehow and certainly more disillusioned than his peers in early-1970s Denver. He finds an emotional anchor and kindred soul in Wiley Ames, a World War II amputee and antique dealer. When Wiley is murdered and his case unsolved, CJ vows to find the killer; in the meantime, he throws himself into his uncle Ike's bail-bond business, if only to push his painful memories into the shadows. Five years later one of Ames' most treasured antiques surfaces at a Denver flea market. It's the thread Floyd needs to unravel the murder. This prequel to Greer's always thoughtful and multilayered Floyd series reveals the pain behind the protagonist's curmudgeonly, emotionally guarded personality and his reluctance to employ violence. CJ Floyd is one of crime fiction's hidden gems, and this is a satisfying entry in a rewarding, underappreciated series." Booklist

Gregory, Daryl

Afterparty; Daryl Gregory. Tor Books 2014 302 p. (hardback) $26.99

ISBN 0765336928; 9780765336927
LC 2013025194

This book, by Daryl Gregory, "begins in Toronto, in the years after the smart drug revolution. . . . A seventeen-year-old street girl finds God through a new brain-altering drug called Numinous, used as a sacrament by a new Church that preys on the underclass. But she is arrested and put into detention, and without the drug, commits suicide. Lyda Rose, another patient in that detention facility, has a dark secret: she was one of the original scientists who developed the drug." (Publisher's note)

"This taut, brisk, gripping narrative, dazzlingly intercut with flashbacks and sidebars, oozes warmth and wit. A hugely entertaining, surprising and perhaps prophetic package." Kirkus

Gregory, Daryl

The **devil's** alphabet. Ballantine Books 2009 388p pa $15

ISBN 0-345-50117-9; 978-0-345-50117-2
LC 2009-36180

"The larger question, of what eventually might become of these evolutionary exiles as they move into second and third generations, seems to move us back into Theodore Sturgeon territory, and it's fortunately a territory that Gregory has mastered well. The novel's quiet ending, in a snowbound South Dakota winter, is haunting." Locus

Gregory, Daryl

Pandemonium. Del Rey 2008 288p pa $13

ISBN 978-0-345-50116-5; 0-345-50116-0
LC 2008-300445

"Gregory has produced a debut novel that combines suspense, philosophical conundrums, Jungian psychological theory, aspects of American pop culture, and a touch of neuroscience with skillful and ambitious storytelling." Strange Horizons

Gregory, Daryl

Raising Stony Mayhall. Ballantine Books 2011 422p pa $15

ISBN 978-0-345-52237-5
LC 2011-10016

"Driving home in a winter snowstorm, Wanda Mayhall and her three daughters come upon the corpses of a young woman and her infant, frozen by the side of the road. When the infant opens its eyes, Wanda realizes the child is one of the living dead. In spite of everything they know about the zombie outbreak and the ruthless measures taken to prevent its spread, the Mayhalls keep the child, naming him Stony. In doing so, they cross a line that has repercussions encompassing a new vision of what it means to be alive. . . . Part superhero fiction, part zombie horror story, and part supernatural thriller, this luminous and compelling tale deserves a wide readership beyond genre fans. Highly recommended." Libr J

Gregory, Daryl

We Are All Completely Fine; by Daryl Gregory. Pgw 2014 192 p. $14.95; (ebook) $9.99

ISBN 1616961716; 9781616961718; 9781616961749

In this book, by Daryl Gregory, "Harrison was the Monster Detective. . . . Now he's in his mid-thirties and spends most of his time popping pills and not sleeping. Stan became a minor celebrity after being partially eaten by cannibals. Barbara is haunted by unreadable messages carved upon her bones. Greta may or may not be a mass-murdering arsonist. . . . No one believes the extent of their horrific tales, not until they are sought out by psychotherapist Dr. Jan Sayer." (Publisher's note)

"Blending the stark realism of pain and isolation with the liberating force of the fantastic, Gregory (Afterparty) makes it easy to believe that the world is an illusion, behind which lurks an alternative truth—dark, degenerate, and sublime." Pub Wkly

Gregory, Philippa

The **Boleyn** Inheritance. Touchstone 2006 518p $25.95

ISBN 0-7432-7250-1; 978-0-7432-7250-6

An historical novel focusing on the family of Henry VIII. "Among the cast, who alternately narrate: Henry's fourth wife, Bavarian-born Anne of Cleves; his fifth wife, English teenager Katherine Howard; and Lady Rochford (Jane Boleyn), the jealous spouse whose testimony helped send her husband, Thomas, and sister-in-law Anne Boleyn to their execution. Attended by Lady Rochford, 24-year-old Anne of Cleves endures a disastrous first encounter with the twice-her-age king—an occasion where Henry takes notice of Katherine Howard. . . . Rich in intrigue and irony, this is a tale where readers will already know who was divorced, beheaded or survived, but will savor Gregory's sharp staging of how and why." Publ Wkly

Gregory, Philippa, 1954-

The **constant** princess; Philippa Gregory. Simon & Schuster 2005 393p $24.95

ISBN 074327248X; 9780743272483

LC 2005052303

This work of historical fiction follows "Katherine of Aragon, the 16-year-old daughter of King Ferdinand and Queen Isabella of Spain. Katherine knows from a very young age that she is promised to marry Prince Arthur, heir to the English throne, and she never wavers in her conviction that she will one day become queen. That determination is sorely tested, however, upon Arthur's premature death after two years of marriage. Although she loves her husband (a passion that is kept hidden from the court), Katherine agrees to his dying wish that he be declared impotent so that she can marry his younger brother, Henry, and eventually reign as queen." (Library Journal)

Includes bibliographical references (p. 392-393).

Gregory, Philippa, 1954-

The **kingmaker's** daughter; Philippa Gregory. 1st Touchstone hardcover ed Simon & Schuster 2012 417 p. map, geneal. table (hardcover) $26.99; (paperback) $16.00

ISBN 145162607X; 9781451626070; 9781451626087; 9781451626148

LC 2012011787

This work of historical fiction by Philippa Gregory follows "Anne Neville . . . the daughter of the Earl of Warwick, who put Edward of York on the throne after battling the Lancasters. . . . The earl uses his daughters as pawns in the fluid political situation. Anne eventually marries Richard, the youngest of the three York brothers after an ill-fated first marriage." (Library Journal)

Includes bibliographical references (p. 413-417).

Gregory, Philippa, 1954-

The **lady** of the rivers; the cousins war. Philippa Gregory. Touchstone 2011 448 p. $27.99

ISBN 1416563709; 9781416563709

LC 2011015093

This historical novel by Philippa Gregory tells "the story of Jacquetta, mother of . . . Elizabeth Woodville. Given first to a husband who desires only the magical powers she might possess, Jacquetta marries second for love, much below her station. Still, she manages to keep her family in the good graces of the ineffectual King Henry VI, placing them ultimately on the losing side of the Wars of the Roses." (Library Journal)

Includes bibliographical references (p. [441]-443)

Gregory, Philippa, 1954-

The **other** Boleyn girl; a novel. Scribner Paperback Fiction 2002 664p

ISBN 0-7432-2744-1

LC 2001057646

This is "as much a tale of love and lust as it is a saga about an ambitious family who used their kin as negotiable assets. . . . Absorbing tale of a Renaissance family determined to climb as high as they can, whatever the cost." Kirkus

Gregory, Philippa, 1954-

The **red** queen; Philippa Gregory. Simon & Schuster 2010 382 p. map tab (Cousins' war) $25.99

ISBN 1416563725; 9781416563723; 9781416563938 (ebk.)

LC 2010514092

This novel, by Philippa Gregory, is book 2 in "The Cousins' War" series. "The opposite of her alluring Yorkist rival, plain Lancastrian heiress Margaret Beaufort grows up knowing women are useful only for bearing sons. . . . While England seethes with discord during the turbulent Wars of the Roses, Margaret's transformation from powerless innocent to political mastermind progresses . . . as rival heirs to England's throne are killed in battle, executed, or deliberately eliminated." (Booklist)

Includes bibliographical references (p. 380-382)

Gregory, Philippa, 1954-

The **taming** of the queen; Philippa Gregory. Touchstone 2015 448 p. ill. (some col.), maps, tables pbk $16.99; hbk $27.99

ISBN 9781476758817; 1476758794; 9781476758794; 1476758816

LC 2015018375

This book, by Philippa Gregory, is a "Tudor tale featuring King Henry VIII's sixth wife Kateryn Parr, the first English queen to publish under her own name. . . . Kateryn has no doubt about the danger she faces: the previous queen lasted sixteen months, the one before barely half a year. But Henry adores his new bride and Kateryn's trust in him grows as she unites the royal family, creates a radical study circle at the heart of the court, and rules the kingdom as Regent." (Publisher's note)

"Tracing Kateryn's path to intellectual independence requires more religious discussion than some readers will prefer, but Gregory's portrait of the complex, aging king and his sensual, scholarly bride will satisfy Tudor enthusiasts." Pub Wkly

Includes bibliographical references

Gregory, Philippa, 1954-

The **white** princess; Philippa Gregory. Touchstone 2013 544 p. (hardcover) $27.99; (paperback) $16.00

ISBN 1451626096; 9781451626094; 9781451626100

LC 2013931637

In this book, part of the "Cousins' War series, marriage unites the upstart House of Tudor with its long-time enemies, the declining House of York, to rule over volatile 1485 England. . . . Narrator Elizabeth of York . . . still loves the vanquished Richard III when she dutifully marries his triumphant challenger, Henry VII. The royal pair produces an heir and two spares but mistrust continues to abound, particularly between the two mothers-in-law." Publishers Weekly)

Gremillon, Helene

The **confidant**; [a novel : secrets can be keep forever] Hélène Grémillon ; translated by Alison Anderson. Penguin Books 2012 245 p. (pbk.) $15

ISBN 0143121561; 9780143121565

LC 2012028555

In this book by Helene Gremillon, "Camille Werner receives a[n] unsigned, handwritten letter among the condolence notes after her mother's death. . . . Camille becomes fascinated with the correspondent's tale of a budding romance between two teenage friends, Annie and Louis, in a small town on the cusp of WWII. . . . When he reveals that Annie has a daughter born around the time of Camille's own birth, Camille becomes obsessed with locating Louis and getting the whole story behind his letters." (Publishers Weekly)

Grenville, Kate

The **idea** of perfection. Viking 2002 401p $24.95

ISBN 0-670-03080-5

LC 2001-58133

First published 2000 in the United Kingdom

"Grenville does her characters the honor of taking their pain seriously and is gracious enough to allow them their hard-earned pleasure. Her ability to move between these elements gives her novel a beautiful balance." N Y Times Book Rev

Grenville, Kate

The **lieutenant**. Atlantic Monthly Presss 2009 307p $24

ISBN 978-0-8021-1916-2; 0-8021-1916-6

First published 2008 in Australia

"Grenville's novel, based on the true story of William Dawes, who was among the soldiers accompanying the first prisoners sent to Australia, concerns Daniel Rooke, a lonely, introverted sort whose skill as an astronomer earns him a privileged position in the first colonial mission sent to New South Wales, in 1787. Living apart from his regiment for the purpose of studying stars, Rooke befriends a young Aboriginal girl and begins to compile a vocabulary and grammar of her language. But as tensions between the two groups escalate he must choose between what he feels is right and what he considers his duty. Grenville's thematic relentlessness can be stultifying, but the honest beauty of her story wins out." New Yorker

Grenville, Kate, 1950-

Sarah Thornhill; Kate Grenville. Grove Press 2011 307 p. (paperback) $15.00; (hardcover) $25.00

ISBN 9780802121219; 0802120245; 9780802120243; 9781921758621

LC 2011459910

Sequel to: The secret river

Australian Book Industry Awards: General Fiction Book of the Year (2012)

In this final book of the Thornhill trilogy, "Sarah Thornhill, the youngest daughter of a wealthy yet provincial British ex-convict, grows up in 19th-century Australia learning not to ask questions about her family's past." She has a love affair with a half-Aboriginal man, but "her chance at happiness is shattered by the racial and class prejudice churning within her family and Australia's burgeoning white society." (Library Journal)

Grenville, Kate, 1950-

The **secret** river. Canongate 2006 334p $24

ISBN 1-84195-682-4

LC 20060365651

First published 2005 in Australia

"On his first night in New South Wales, in 1806, William Thornhill—Thames boatman, thief, banished convict—gazes despairingly into the forest outside his flimsy hut. A spear-wielding Aborigine appears before him, and his dejection turns to rage. All he has is his family—'those soft parcels of flesh,' sleeping behind him—and 'the dirt under his bare feet, his small grip on this unknown place,' and he is not about to give them up to a naked black stranger. The Aborigine responds with equal vehemence: 'Be off, be off!' The episode shows, in miniature, the project of Grenville's magnificent novel—an unflinching exploration of modern Australia's origins. Like the settlers, we instinctively turn away from the ugly truths behind every cleared riverbank and every posted fence. But Grenville's psychological acuity, and the sheer gorgeousness of her descriptions of the territory being fought over, pulls us ever deeper into a time when one community's opportunity spelled another's doom." New Yorker

Grey, Zane

★ **Riders** of the purple sage; edited with an introduction and notes by Lee Clark Mitchell. Oxford University Press 2008 xxxviii, 265p (Oxford world's classics) pa $9.95

ISBN 978-0-19-955387-7

LC 2008-482024

First published 1912 by Harper

"Well handled melodramatic story of hairbreadth escapes from Mormon vengeance in southwestern Utah in 1871." Booklist

Includes bibliographical references

Grey, Zane

West of the Pecos. Harper 1937 314p

"Romantic western which tells of Colonel Terrill, broken by the Civil War, and his tomboy daughter, their efforts to get a start in the new world of the west, the Colonel's brutal murder and Pecos Smith's ride to rescue the girl, left alone in a land of desperados." Wis Libr Bull

Grey, Zane

Woman of the frontier; a western story. Five Star 1998 320p $19.95

ISBN 0-7862-1156-3

LC 98-22717

"This tale, written in 1934, was rejected by magazines because of its vivid portrayal of the hardships of pioneer life, including the rape of Grey's heroine by a renegade Apache. A heavily edited version called 30,000 on the Hoof was finally published in 1940, a year after the author's death. This version, completely restored by Grey's son, Loren, recounts the trials and tribulations of Arizona rancher Logan Huett, his heroic wife, Lucinda, their three sons, and a girl named Barbara, who is abandoned by wagon-train travelers and raised by the Huetts." Booklist

Griesemer, John

Signal & noise. Picador 2003 593p $26

ISBN 0-312-30082-4

LC 2003-42938

Griesemer "has created some fine set pieces of disaster: the failed launch of the Great Eastern, two spectacular fires, a train crash that wrecks Ludlow's invention of a great Civil War cannon and, best of all, a breathtaking storm at sea. At the other end of the scale, the detail that fleshes out the novel's world is equally convincing." N Y Times Book Rev

Griffin, Kate

Glass God; Kate Griffin. Orbit 2013 464 p. (trade pbk.) $15

ISBN 0316187275; 9780316187275; 9780316235525

LC 2013932405

This novel by Kate Griffin features "Sharon Li: apprentice shaman and community support officer for the magically inclined. It wasn't the career Sharon had in mind, but she's getting used to running Magicals Anonymous. When the Midnight Mayor goes missing, leaving only a suspiciously innocent-looking umbrella behind him, Sharon finds herself promoted. Her first task: find the Midnight Mayor. The only clues she has are a city dryad's cryptic message of doom and several pairs of abandoned shoes." (Publisher's note)

Griffin, Kate

Stray souls; Kate Griffin. Orbit 2012 464 p. (trade pbk.) $14.99

ISBN 0316187267; 9780316187268; 9780316231749

LC 2012944764

In this book by Kate Griffin, "when . . . Sharon Li discovers that she is a shaman, her first act is to start Magicals Anonymous, a support group that draws a mix of some of London's more unusual inhabitants. . . . She soon learns that someone is stealing the souls of London's buildings and leeching life from the city. Somehow, she and her tribe of misfits must find out the identity of their enemy and save London from spiritual destruction." (Library Journal)

Griffin, W. E. B.

By order of the President; W.E.B. Griffin. Putnam 2004 528p $26.95

ISBN 0-399-15207-5

LC 2004-53417

"Proving himself solidly in control of cutting-edge military material, Griffin bases his new series not on wars past but on today's murky exigencies of terrorism and international political intrigue. . . . In the end, there are a few bodies to account for, but it's the meticulous investigation that leaves readers standing on the tarmac waiting for Charley Castillo and his newly minted band of can-do compatriots to touch down and carry them away again on a new adventure." Publ Wkly

Griffin, W. E. B.

Special ops. Putnam 2001 665p (Brotherhood of war) $25.95

ISBN 0-399-14646-6

LC 00-62779

"In 1964, Cuba's Fidel Castro tried to export communism to Africa under the leadership of the legendary Che Guevera, and Special Ops details the efforts of the U.S. military and the CIA to stop him. With the world's attention focused on Vietnam and Europe, the deadly fighting in some of the world's most remote and primitive places went unnoticed. . . . This is an exciting, intriguing, and fast-paced novel about an often-ignored period in our recent history." Libr J

Griffin, W. E. B.

Under fire. Putnam 2002 576p

ISBN 0-399-14788-8

LC 2001-48245

In this novel "Captain Ken @Killer' McCoy, a protégé of ex-OSS officer Fleming Pickering, who knows a senator, who knows President Truman, has reported to General MacArthur that North Korea will be invaded. The report disappears, McCoy gets busted to the ranks . . . and the Communists start pouring across the thirty-eighth parallel. Truman, suspicious of MacArthur, gets wind of the report, and appoints Pickering and McCoy to the CIA. Boats, bullets, and carrier-launched avengers and corsairs make up the balance of this expansively told story." Booklist

Griffith, Michael

Trophy. TriQuarterly Books/Northwestern University Press 2011 277 p.

ISBN 9780810152182

LC 2010050767

In this novel, "Vada Prickett is a 29-year-old Hose Associate at a car wash in South Carolina, and Darla, the woman he loves, is about to marry his friend, rival, and life-long neighbor, Wyatt Yancey. . . . Vada, as this . . . novel opens, is being crushed to death by Wyatt's latest animal trophy, a stuffed grizzly bear Vada has been helping him to smuggle--against Darla's wishes--into Wyatt's house. It turns out that the cliché is true--at the moment of death, your life does flash before your eyes. Trophy, the account of a man's final, fleeting instant on earth, joins Vada as he attempts to make that flash last as long as possible. As he lies dying, too soon and too absurdly, Vada tries to unravel the mysteries of his life." (Publisher's note)

Griffith, Nicola

Hild; a novel. Nicola Griffith. Farrar Straus & Giroux 2013 560 p. $27

ISBN 0374280878; 9780374280871

LC 2013022510

Lambda Literary Awards Finalist (2014)

This book by Nicola Griffith presents a "fictional coming-of-age story about real-life Saint Hilda of Whitby, who grew up pagan in seventh-century Britain. Daughter of a poisoned prince and a crafty noblewoman, quiet, bright-minded Hild arrives at the court of King Edwin of Northumbria, where the six-year-old takes on the role of seer/consiglieri for a monarch troubled by shifting allegiances and Roman emissaries attempting to spread their new religion." (Publishers Weekly)

Griffiths, Elly

✓The **crossing** places; Elly Griffiths. 1st U.S. ed. Houghton Mifflin Harcourt 2010 303 p. map (Ruth Galloway mysteries) (hardcover) $25

ISBN 0547229895; 9780547229898

LC 2009007006

This book "introduces archeologist Ruth Galloway. . . .When Det. Chief Insp. Harry Nelson asks for her expertise in identifying human remains . . . he's disappointed when Ruth determines they date to the Iron Age. Harry, who's been haunted . . . by the kidnapping of five-year-old Lucy Downey, hoped the bones could bring closure to the girl's family. Drawn into the investigation, Ruth . . . studies the letters Harry has received over the years, presumably from the kidnapper." (Publishers Weekly)

Other titles about Ruth Galloway are:

The Janus stone (2011)

The house at sea's end (2011)
A room full of bones (2012)
A dying fall (2013)
The outcast dead (2014)
The ghost fields (2015)
The woman in blue (2016)
The chalk pit (2017)
The dark angel (2018)

Griffiths, Elly

✓A **Dying** Fall; A Ruth Galloway Mystery. 1st U.S. ed. Houghton Mifflin Harcourt 2013 400 p. (hardcover) $26.00

ISBN 0547798164; 9780547798165

LC 2013001330

In this book, part of the Ruth Galloway mystery series, "Ruth, a forensic archeologist and teacher, learns of the death by fire of a college friend and colleague, Dan Golding, the day before receiving a letter from Dan requesting her professional opinion. Dan has excavated the bones of a 'Raven King,' who may be Arthur Pendragon. Single mother Ruth and various others . . . take summer holiday trips to the vicinity of the site of the murder and dig." (Publishers Weekly)

Griffiths, Elly

✓★ The **house** at sea's end; Elly Griffiths. Houghton Mifflin Harcourt 2012 353 p. (Ruth Galloway mystery) (hbk.) $25

ISBN 0547506147; 9780547506142

LC 2011029652

This book is part of a series following forensic archaeologist Ruth Galloway. After the discovery of "skeletons of six men with their arms bound . . . Home Guard veteran Archie Whitcliffe reveals the existence of a secret the old soldiers have vowed to protect with their lives. But then Archie is killed and a German journalist arrives, asking questions about Operation Lucifer, a plan to stop a German invasion, and a possible British war crime." (Publisher's note)

Solid characterization, believable forensic science, great atmosphere, and a mystery that stretches back decades all make this another winner from the talented Griffiths." Booklist

Griffiths, Emily ✓

The **Janus** stone; Elly Griffiths. 1st U.S. ed. Houghton Mifflin Harcourt 2011 327p. (paperback) $14.95; (hardcover) $26.00

ISBN 9780547577401; 9780547237442; 0547237448

LC 2010005740

This mystery novel tells the story of a murder investigation conducted with the help of "archaeologist Ruth Galloway. . . . [W]hen construction workers demolishing a large old house in Norwich uncover the bones of a child beneath a doorway--minus its skull--Ruth is . . . called upon to investigate. . . . When carbon dating proves that the child's bones . . . relate to a time when the house was privately owned, Ruth is drawn ever more deeply into the case." (Publisher's note)

Grimes, Linda

In a fix; Linda Grimes. 1st ed. Tor 2012 334 p.

ISBN 0765331802; 9780765331809; 9781429947534

LC 2012019453

This novel by Linda Grimes focuses on "Ciel Halligan, . . . [a] kind of human chameleon . . . able to take on her clients' appearances and slip seamlessly into their lives, solving any sticky problems they don't want to deal with themselves. . . . Snagging a marriage proposal for her client while on an all-expenses-paid vacation should be a simple job . . . until Ciel's island resort bungalow is blown to smithereens and her client's about-to-be-fiance is snatched by modern-day Vikings." (Publisher's note)

Other titles in this series are:
Quick fix (2013)
The big fix (2015)
All fixed up (2016)

Grimes, Linda

Quick fix; Linda Grimes. Tor Books 2013 352 p. (pbk.) $15.99

ISBN 0765331810; 9780765331816

LC 2013017712

This is the second book in Linda Grimes's urban fantasy series "starring Ciel Halligan, 'aura adaptor,' meaning that she can take on the physical characteristics of another person. . . . This time out, Ciel visits the National Zoo with hot-hot-hot adoptive cousin (and adaptor) Billy and his 10-year-old sister, Molly. Precocious Molly may be an adaptor herself. But when she touches a baby orangutan, she turns into an ape—and can't change back!" (Kirkus Reviews)

Grimes, Martha

★ The **Anodyne** Necklace. Little, Brown 1983 250p

LC 83-880

"Sixteen-year-old Katie O'Brien, playing her violin in an underground London station to make some money, is mysteriously attacked. From that incident begins a mystery involving the theft of an emeral necklace, the murder of a young man whose fingers have been chopped off, and still another murder. The characters in this absorbing tale include not only the residents of Littlebourne, Katie's village, but some East End Londoners like the Cripps family, whose squalid home and bizarre behavior will not soon be forgotten by the reader. Satirical humor enlivens the careful and patient unraveling done by the special detective featured in Grimes' mysteries—the attractive Scotland Yard Superintendent Richard Jury." Shapiro. Fic for Youth. 3d edition

Grimes, Martha

✓The **case** has altered. Holt & Co. 1997 370p

ISBN 0-8050-5620-3

LC 97-20791

"Psychologically complex and muted in tone, with the characters' elliptical relationships reflecting the setting of England's dreamlike fen country, the novel also boasts Grimes's delicious wit." Publ Wkly

Grimes, Martha

✓**Dakota**; a novel. Viking 2008 414p $25.95

ISBN 978-0-670-01869-7

LC 2007-41715

This novel, featuring the young woman who calls herself Andi Oliver [introduced in the author's Biting the moon], "begins with Andi, who's still unaware of her real name or her past, adrift in the Dakota badlands. After rescuing an abandoned donkey, Andi makes a temporary home for herself in the small town of Kingdom, where she soon creates a stir by standing up to some local bullies. She really begins to shake things up in the placid community, however, when she takes a job at a pig farm to try to save the cruelly treated animals bred there. . . . While one late plot development stretches credibility, Grimes succeeds in sustaining suspense while graphically portraying the ugliness of animal abuse." Publ Wkly

Grimes, Martha

The **five** bells and bladebone. Little, Brown 1987 299p

LC 87-3148

"Visiting his friend Melrose Plant in Plant's ancestral village, Jury is at the local antique shop when Simon Lean's body is found in a flaptop desk. The dealer has just bought the piece from Lady Summerston, mistress of the lush estate of Watermeadows where Simon had lived with his wife Hannah, the lady's granddaughter. Questioning the women, Jury sees the strong resemblance between the widow and Sadie Diver, who was murdered in London's notorious Limehouse district. . . . The splendid mystery has a tragic core, but the gloom is offset by the author's quiet humor." Publ Wkly

Grimes, Martha

Help the poor struggler. Little, Brown 1985 225p

LC 85-109

"This fine novel features a plot that startles, characters that convince, and an atmosphere that sparkles." Booklist

Grimes, Martha

The **Horse** You Came In On. Knopf 1993 331p

LC 92-55069

"Notable for its themes of authorship and authenticity and for the cast of delightfully eccentric characters—who gather each day at a blue-collar bar called The Horse You Came In On—this mystery, with its feathery plot and fey, lighthearted tone, moves in quite a different direction than earlier Jury tales. Not bad, just different." Publ Wkly

Grimes, Martha

Hotel Paradise. Knopf 1996 347p

ISBN 0-679-44187-5

LC 95-49356

"Emma's take on the colorful characters in her small-town world . . . makes this both a provocative study of lonely people and a delightful read." Publ Wkly

Grimes, Martha

I am the only running footman. Little, Brown 1986 206p

LC 86-15305

"Scotland Yard's wise, kind Superintendent Richard Jury must determine if the case of Ivy Childess, strangled in London, is related to a similar crime in Devon. Ivy had left her sometime lover, David Marr, after a tiff in the Footman, so he heads the list of suspects. Jury's interrogation ends with Marr offering a strong alibi, backed by his prestigious family. Calling on the man's sister and other kin, the superintendent senses private fears behind a gracious facade. Jury is right, but his suspicions produce no evidence of collusion until a shocking truth sends him racing to save the killer's third intended victim. An artist at plotting, Grimes concludes this urbanely humorous, knife-edge thriller with a double twist." Publ Wkly

Grimes, Martha

The **Old** Contemptibles. Little, Brown 1991 333p

LC 90-48647

Inspector "Jury is considering marriage to recently met widow Jane Holdsworth at the moment her teenaged son Alex finds her dead, apparently a suicide. Alex runs away, and Jury, required, as a suspect, to remain in London, sends old friend Melrose Plant up to the Lakes to learn what he can about the wealthy Holdsworth family, among whom Jane's death is the fourth suspicious one." Publ Wkly

Grimes, Martha

The **old** fox deceiv'd. Little, Brown 1982 299p

LC 82-7719

"The central mystery that confronts Inspector Richard Jury of Scotland Yard is not whounit, but to whom was it 'dun.' Was the young woman found mutilated with an ice-pick-like instrument Dillys March, the ward of Colonel Titus Crael who left home 15 years previously and recently returned to reclaim her inheritance? Or was the victim Gemma Temple, Dillys' look-alike, who tried to pass herself off as Dillys to gain the inheritance? The tiny English fishing village of Rackmoor is divided and tormented by this mystery, which threatens to rock its social structure." Booklist

Grimes, Martha

★ The **Old** Silent. Little, Brown 1989 425p

LC 89-31650

"The calm moments in this moody mystery about parental ties and family schisms and relationships thicker than blood are as fine as anything Ms. Grimes has written." N Y Times Book Rev

Grimes, Martha

The **Old** Wine Shades; a Richard Jury mystery. Viking 2006 352p $25.95

ISBN 0-670-03479-7

LC 2005-58460

In this Richard Jury "mystery, the Scotland Yard detective is on suspension because he decided to save lives rather than wait for a warrant in his previous outing . . . . With time on his hands, Jury is ensnared by the intriguing tale spun by Harry Johnson, a man who, apparently, just happens upon him in a London pub, the Old Wine Shades. Despite himself, Jury is drawn in by Johnson's account of the baffling disappearance of a mother, her autistic son and their dog–and the more baffling reappearance of the pet nine months later. The detective diligently follows every lead to determine the fate of the missing people, even as Johnson's digressions into the paradoxes of quantum physics lead Jury to question the truth of the man's narrative. The scheme Jury ultimately detects is ingeniously clever and sufficiently consistent with the personalities Grimes has created to overcome disbelief." Publ Wkly

Grimes, Martha

Rainbow's end; a Richard Jury novel. Knopf 1995 383p

ISBN 0-679-44188-3

LC 94-48876

In this Richard Jury mystery, three women "die suddenly in public places: an aged textile restorer in Exeter Cathedral, a society matron in the Tate Gallery and an American tourist in the ruins of Old Sarum, near Salisbury. The deaths appear to be natural and unrelated, but the clever Brits come up with a connection: both Englishwomen had recently visited Santa Fe, N.M., where the American had a silver shop. Once in the Southwest, Jury follows his wispy lead to eye-catching locations like a movie set in Santa Fe. . . . Meanwhile, back home, Jury's sidekick, Melrose Plant, pays nostalgic visits to people and places from previous novels, while mourning the passing of the grand old pubs." N Y Times Book Rev

Grimes, Martha

The **Stargazey**; a Richard Jury mystery. Holt & Co. 1998 354p

ISBN 0-8050-5622-X

LC 98-21214

"Jury is on the Fulham Road bus when he spots a beautiful blonde in a fur coat and feels compelled to follow her to the Fulham Palace grounds. Later she is found murdered on the palace grounds. But is it really she? Jury doubts it and follows a winding path to the truth." Libr J

Grimes, Martha

The **winds** of change; a Richard Jury mystery. Viking 2004 407p $25.95

ISBN 0-670-03327-8

LC 2004-52636

This Richard Jury mystery involves "the murder of an anonymous five-year-old girl, shot in the back. . . . When he learns that the child was found near a house frequented by pedophiles, he's convinced there's a link. His suspicions grow stronger when the man supposedly behind the operation turns out to be the father of a child who mysteriously disappeared three years before from a country estate." Booklist

Grimsley, Jim

The **ordinary**. Tor Bks. 2004 368p map $24.95

ISBN 0-7653-0528-3

LC 2003-71148

"Set in the same future world as Kirith Kirin (2000) . . . , Grimsley's latest SF novel intimately explores the conflicts between magic and science, subconscious and conscious action, the past and the future. The planet of the tech-using Hormling of Senal is connected to the land of Irion, home of the magic-believing Erejhen, via the mysterious Twil Gate, a portal of unknown origins in the ocean. Although traders on both sides enjoy brisk commerce through the gate, Hormling leaders look more and more to Irion as a means to provide land and resources for their expanding civilization. Translator Jedda Martele, member of a Senal diplomatic mission to Irion, is caught in the middle when the delegation's true purpose is revealed. . . . Grimsley's finely textured societies have a clockwork intricacy that fascinates even as it dispels surprise." Publ Wkly

Grindle, Lucretia

Villa triste; Lucretia Grindle. Grand Central Pub. 2013 640 p. (trade pbk.) $14.99

ISBN 1455505374; 9781455505371

LC 2012951450

In this book, "[Lucretia] Grindle . . . combines a contemporary mystery with historical fiction in her . . . narrative about Italian partisans in World War II and a modern-day police inspector determined to uncover certain truths." The story follows an Italian young woman, Caterina, during the Nazi occupation of Italy. Caterina keeps a journal of her work as a Resistance nurse, which is later found by police Inspector Alessandro Pallioti, eager to solve some related murders. (Kirkus)

Grippando, James

Born to run; a novel of suspense. HarperCollins 2008 328p $25.99

ISBN 978-0-06-155611-1; 0-06-155611-4

LC 2008-23282

Miami attorney Jack Swyteck comes to the aid of his former governor father as he investigates the suspicious hunting death of the vice president.

"Grippando ratchets up the action to a breakneck pace in the last half of the novel, stopping to liberally sprinkle the proceedings with snarky dialogue, pointed satire, and some touching father-son moments." Booklist

Grippando, James

Lying with strangers. HarperCollins 2007 389p $24.95

ISBN 978-0-06-113838-6; 0-06-113838-X

LC 2006-50956

First published in slightly different form 2006 by Madison Park Press for Doubleday Entertainment's book clubs

"Grippando excels at the ordinary-person-in-extraordinary-circumstances story, and this one uses the premise expertly, building enough suspense to keep readers looking in dark corners and over their shoulders." Booklist

Grippando, James

Money to burn; a novel of suspense. Harper 2010 360p $25.99

ISBN 978-0-06-155630-2; 0-06-155630-0

LC 2009-24828

"Michael Cantella is one of the rock stars of his Wall Street investment firm. Despite his fancy job and his fancy second wife, Michael has never gotten over his first wife, Ivy, who died on their honeymoon four years before. Michael gets another shock when, on the eve of his 35th birthday, his accounts are cleaned out, which also affects the firm for which he works. The wipeout is made to look as if Michael was behind it. The FBI accuses him of money laundering and insider trading, his second marriage is over and Michael is the target of a cruel, seemingly invisible hit man. Grippando keeps the energy level high in "Money To Burn" while also showing the behind-the-scenes machinations of money schemes. A surprise twist is not only believable but also seamlessly woven into the plot." South Florida Sun-Sentinel

Grisham, John

The **brethren**. Doubleday 2000 366p $30

ISBN 0-385-49746-6

LC 00-23841

This suspense novel revolves around two subplots. In the first three ex-judges, serving time in a federal prison in Florida, concoct a blackmail scheme that targets closeted gay men. The second storyline relates the CIA-backed presidential bid of a corrupt congressman

"Every personage in this novel lies, cheats, steals and/or kills, and while Grisham's fans may miss the stalwart lawyer-heroes and David vs. Goliath slant of his earlier work, all will be captivated by this clever thriller that presents as crisp a cast as he's yet devised, and as grippingly sardonic yet bitingly moral a scenario as he's ever imagined." Publ Wkly

Grisham, John, 1955-

The **client**. Doubleday 1993 422p $29.95; pa $7.99

ISBN 0-385-42471-X; 0-440-21352-5 pa

LC 92-39079

This novel's "hero is 11-year-old Mark Sway, who, with his 8-year-old brother, witnesses a Mafia-defending {lawyer's} . . . suicide, unfortunately not before he's learned . . . a secret that one Barry the Blade in particular is not going to let the lawyer live with. Now that Mark knows it, he's in danger, too, and not only from the bad guys. A politically ambitious U.S. attorney . . . is hot on Barry's case, and he'll pull any string, ruin any life, to get ahead. So the cops and the FBI start coming down hard on Mark. But Mark . . . finds an attorney, Reggie Love, a . . . specialist in defending children." (Booklist)

"While sneaking into the woods to smoke forbidden cigarettes, preteen brothers Mark and Ricky find a lawyer committing suicide in his car. Mark tries to save the man but is instead grabbed by him and told the location of the body of a murdered U.S. senator—a murder for which the lawyer's Mafia-connected client is accused. Witnessing the successful suicide sends Ricky into shock and Mark into a web of lies, half-truths, and finally into refusal to tell the confided secret to the police. Mark accidentally but fortuitously hires a lawyer, Reggie Love, who steers him through a maze of FBI agents, legal proceedings, judges, ambitious lawyers, and hit men. . . . This thriller is unique in its theme and in its suspense mixed with humor. A sure 'all-night' read." SLJ

LP Fiction

some that had previ-
›reaks under control,
ıg, positivity rates are
ds are being set – and
People in Texas, Flor-
Jersey are bracing for
ks in the fall, even as
lly recede. The root of
scientists and health
e to fully incorporate
lerstanding of what it
; society. Until we do
effectively respond to
one prevent them.
› and her advisers have
or-coded warning sys-
v how dire the threat
tious they need to be.
was clear and concise,
vith all the orders was
ng them to tune out,"
colors and numbers
ne and some people
ıst want this to stick."
at the highest threat
nat the outbreak there
nd that people should
ential needs. As with
d, it will take a while
ssage and heed it.
tical and cultural bat-
he coronavirus crisis

Answers to puzzles of 7.12.20

CHORES GALORE

I	G	L	E	S	I	A	S	■	J	E	M	I	M	A	■	O	R	A	T	E
D	U	A	L	R	O	L	E	■	O	S	I	R	I	S	■	N	O	T	A	X
T	A	K	E	O	U	T	T	H	E	T	R	A	S	H	■	P	A	T	T	I
A	V	E	C	■	■	A	R	I	■	D	O	T	H	E	D	I	S	H	E	S
G	A	R	T	H	■	■	A	D	S	■	S	E	A	■	A	T	T	E	S	T
■	■	■	E	I	N	S	T	E	I	N	■	■	P	O	N	C	H	O	■	■
S	W	E	E	P	T	H	E	F	L	O	O	R	■	V	S	H	A	P	E	D
O	I	L	■	S	H	A	■	■	V	E	N	I	C	E	■	■	M	E	T	A
W	I	I	G	■	■	M	E	S	A	■	P	O	O	R	A	T	■	R	O	N
N	U	M	E	R	O	U	N	O	■	G	O	T	O	T	H	E	B	A	N	K
■	■	■	S	I	A	■	A	D	M	I	T	I	T	■	A	L	E	■	■	■
S	O	R	T	T	H	E	M	A	I	L	■	N	I	B	B	L	E	S	O	N
U	D	O	■	E	U	R	O	P	A	■	A	G	E	E	■	■	N	I	K	E
M	I	D	I	■	■	A	R	O	M	A	S	■	■	S	A	Y	■	L	A	W
O	N	E	N	E	S	S	■	P	I	C	K	U	P	T	H	E	T	O	Y	S
■	■	W	E	A	K	E	R	■	■	H	E	R	E	S	H	O	W	■	■	■
S	C	A	R	R	Y	■	A	I	G	■	D	I	E	■	■	H	O	S	E	R
P	A	Y	T	H	E	B	I	L	L	S	■	C	P	A	■	■	S	U	R	I
I	N	I	G	O	■	C	L	E	A	N	T	H	E	G	U	T	T	E	R	S
T	O	N	A	L	■	C	A	N	D	I	D	■	R	U	N	S	A	M	O	K
S	E	N	S	E	■	S	T	E	E	P	S	■	S	E	C	U	R	E	L	Y

KENKEN

1	5	4	3	2
4	1	3	2	5
3	2	5	4	1
2	3	1	5	4
5	4	2	1	3

1	7	2	6	5	3	4
7	6	4	2	3	1	5
5	2	7	3	6	4	1
4	3	5	1	2	7	6
3	1	6	7	4	5	2
6	4	3	5	1	2	7
2	5	1	4	7	6	3

DIAGRAMLESS

Grisham, John, 1955-

The **confession**. Doubleday 2010 418p $28.95

ISBN 978-0-385-52804-7; 0-385-52804-3; 0385528043; 9780385528047

LC 20100513753

"Death penalty proponents might not rush to buy this book. It's a no-apologies, flagrantly one-sided story that would only annoy the heck out of them. But Grisham is the master of the legal thriller. Readers who share his views as well as those sitting on the fence will find much to love and lament in the tragic story of Donté Drumm." USA Today

Grisham, John

★ The **firm**. Doubleday 1991 421p hardcover o.p. pa $9.99

ISBN 0-385-41634-2; 0-440-24592-6 pa

LC 90-3945

"The aphorism 'between a rock and a hard place' aptly describes the dilemma of a young attorney pressed by the FBI to reveal crime-related secrets of his firm, while also hounded by his employers to simply take his huge salary and zip his lip. No aphorism, though, can convey the suspense, wit, and polished writing of this laser-sharp candidate for the best recent updating of the David and Goliath story." Libr J

Grisham, John

Ford County; stories. Doubleday 2009 308p $24

ISBN 978-0-385-53245-7; 0-385-53245-8

LC 2009-32845

"In Ford County, John Grisham's first collection of stories, we meet a weird and endearing group of misfits with one thing in common: each has lived in Clanton, the seat of fictional Ford County, Mississippi. . . . Grisham's prose is smooth and controlled as he deftly moves between narrators and storylines, and his skilled storytelling makes even the wackier scenes believable. One of Ford County's greatest assets is its abundant but understated humor." BookPage

Grisham, John

The **last** juror. Doubleday 2004 355p $27.95

ISBN 0-385-51043-8

"The novel will satisfy those with an appetite for legal thrillers and those who believe Grisham possesses more talent than those breathless page-turners sometimes reveal. It ranks among his best-written and most atmospheric novels." USA Today

Grisham, John

The **partner**. Doubleday 1997 366p $30

ISBN 0-385-47295-1

LC 96-54702

"Money is essentially the principal character in {this novel}. It is a very large sum of it—$90 million, to be exact—that has motivated Gulf Coast lawyer Patrick Lanigan to concoct a scheme to disappear. . . . It is money that drove a crooked defense contractor to try to pry loose a huge sum from Washington, and got Patrick's greedy law firm involved in the first place. And it is varying sums of money that enable Patrick to bribe his way out of a collection of indictments against him a yard long—including one for first-degree murder—when he is eventually found in his Brazilian hide-away and brought back to the U.S. to face the music. . . . To call the plot of The Partner mechanical is at least partly a compliment: it is well-oiled, intricate and works smoothly." Publ Wkly

Grisham, John, 1955-

★ The **pelican** brief. Doubleday 1992 371p $30

ISBN 0-385-42198-2

LC 91-33235

In this novel "two liberal Supreme Court justices have been assassinated. No one can come up with a motive. Darby Shaw, a young law student at Tulane University in New Orleans, has a theory: someone coming before the Court might want to give the conservative President an opportunity to replace the two liberals. Checking appeals pending in the Federal courts, she finds what she is looking for and produces a four-page memorandum. This is the pelican brief. . . . Soon people who have seen the brief, or even know about it, start to die." (N Y Times Book Rev)

"Mr. Grisham has written a genuine page-turner. He has an ear for dialogue and is a skillful craftsman. Like a composer, he brings all his themes together at the crucial moment for a gripping, and logical, finale." NY Times Book Rev

Grisham, John

Playing for pizza. Doubleday 2007 262p $21.95

ISBN 978-0-385-52500-8; 0-385-52500-1

LC 2007-27656

"Third-string Cleveland Browns quarterback Rick Dockery becomes the greatest goat ever by throwing three interceptions in the closing minutes of the AFC championship game. Fleeing vengeful fans, he finds refuge in the grungiest corner of professional football, the Italian National Football League as quarterback of the inept but full-of-heart Parma Panthers. What ensues is a winsome football fable, replete with team bonding and character-building as the underdog Panthers challenge the powerhouse Bergamo Lions for a shot at the Italian Superbowl. The book is also the author's love letter to Italy." Publ Wkly

Grisham, John, 1955-

Sycamore Row; John Grisham. First edition Doubleday 2013 464 p. $28.95

ISBN 0385537131; 9780385537131

LC 2013362251

Sequel to Time to Kill

"Jake Brigance once again finds himself embroiled in a fiercely controversial trial . . . that will expose old racial tensions and force Ford County, [Mississippi] to confront its tortured history. Seth Hubbard is a wealthy man dying of lung cancer. . . . Before he hangs himself from a sycamore tree, Hubbard leaves a new, handwritten, will. It is an act that drags his adult children, his black maid, and Jake into . . . conflict." (Publisher's note)

Grisham, John

A **time** to kill. Doubleday 1993 487p $30

ISBN 0-385-47081-9

LC 93-32545

A reissue of the title first published 1989 by Wynwood Press

In this novel, set in rural Mississippi, local criminal lawyer Jake Brigance defends a black man on trial for murdering the men who raped his daughter

Grodstein, Lauren

★ A **friend** of the family; a novel. Algonquin Books of Chapel Hill 2009 302p $23.95

ISBN 978-1-56512-916-0; 1-56512-916-4

LC 2009-24476

"The novel is spot-on in its depiction of affection and jealousy among longtime friends, boozy suburban bashes; unrequited love; and adjusting to middle age. . . . [It] beautifully captures the ever-striving angst of parents who will take any step to ensure their children's lives are easier or better." USA Today

Grodstein, Lauren

Our short history; Lauren Grodstein. Algonquin Books of Chapel Hill 2017 342 p. $26.95

ISBN 9781616206222

LC 2016038075

In this novel, by Lauren Grodstein, "Karen Neulander, a successful New York political consultant and single mother, has always been fiercely protective of her son, Jacob. . . . When Jacob's father, Dave, found out Karen was pregnant and made it clear that fatherhood wasn't in his plans, Karen walked out of the relationship, never telling Dave her intention was to raise their child alone. But now Jake is asking to meet his dad, and with good reason: Karen is dying." (Publisher's note)

"Grodstein's...heartbreaking, character-driven story is told in the remarkable, believable voice of a courageous, sympathetic character." LJ

Groff, Lauren, 1978-

★ **Arcadia**; Lauren Groff. Hyperion 2012 291 p.

ISBN 9781401340872

LC 2011009956

This book offers an "examination of life on a commune [that] follows Bit, . . . born in the late '60s in a spot that will become Arcadia, a utopian community his parents help to form. Despite their idealistic goals, the family's attempts at sustainability bring hunger, cold, illness, and injury. . . . The . . . child whose purposeful lack of speech is sometimes mistaken for slowness finds comfort in Grimms' fairy tales and is lost in the outside world once Arcadia's increasingly entitled spiritual leader falls from grace and the community crumbles. . . . [T]he book's second half tracks the ways in which Bit, now an adult, . . . has been shaped by Arcadia; a career in photography was the perfect choice for a man who 'watches life from a good distance.'" (Publishers Weekly)

Groff, Lauren

Delicate edible birds and other stories. Hyperion 2009 306p $23.95

ISBN 978-1-4013-4086-5

LC 2008-44002

An "innovative and beautifully written collection that covers a wide swath of humanity, from east coast resort towns, to the early 20th century flu epidemic, to WWII Europe. . . . Even in the less successful stories, Groff's prose is lovely, and when she nails a story—like the title story about journalists fleeing Nazi-occupied Paris—the results are sublime." Publ Wkly

Groff, Lauren, 1978-

★ **Fates** and furies; Lauren Groff. Riverhead Books 2015 400 p. (hardback) $27.95

ISBN 1594634475; 9781594634475

LC 2015013565

National Book Award Finalist: Fiction (2015)

National Book Critics Circle Award Finalist: Fiction (2015)

"At age twenty-two, Lotto and Mathilde are tall, glamorous, madly in love, and destined for greatness. A decade later, their marriage is still the envy of their friends, but . . . we understand that things are even more complicated and remarkable than they have seemed." (Publisher's note)

"The first half of the novel, entitled 'Fates,' gives lanky lothario Lotto's perspective on the marriage. He sees nothing but Mathilde's goodness ('the best person I know') and her unerring belief in his talent, and, after some years of struggling as an actor, Lotto finds great success as a playwright, which brings the couple both fame and wealth. The second half of the novel, 'Furies,' turns the lens on Mathilde and will upend readers' expectations, for she is possessed of a cold calculation that will surprise and even dismay." Booklist

Groff, Lauren

The **monsters** of Templeton; a novel. Voice/Hyperion 2008 364p il map $24.95

ISBN 978-1-4013-2225-0; 1-4013-2225-5

LC 2007-41360

"Forget the ghouls and cheap scares. What Groff is really digging at here is the enigma of the human spirit and how redemption and resilience shape our lives. The Monsters of Templeton is part mystery and part history, generating much of its appeal through the delightfully cranky, persistent Willie and a host of voices—maybe a few too many—from her tangled family tree." PopMatters

Groom, Winston

El Paso; Winston Groom. Liveright Pub. Corp., A Division of W. W. Norton & Co. 2016 xii, 477 p.p (hardcover) $27.95

ISBN 9781631492242; 9781631492259

LC 2016021007

"Long fascinated with the Mexican Revolution and the vicious border wars of the early twentieth century, . . . author Winston Groom brings to life a much-forgotten period of history in this episodic saga set in six parts.. . . . Replete with shootouts, daring escapes, and an unforgettable bullfight, 'El Paso' brings to life a crucial moment in history and, in the process, becomes an indelible portrait of the American Southwest in the final days of the wild frontier." (Publisher's note)

"An engaging epic that could be headed for the best-seller lists and then the big screen." Booklist

Groot, Tracy

Flame of resistance; Tracy Groot. Tyndale House Publishers, Inc. 2012 403 p. (sc) $13.99

ISBN 1414359470; 9781414359472

LC 2011052924

In this book, "years of Nazi occupation have stolen hope from French prostitute Brigitte Durand. But when downed American pilot Tom Jaeger is picked up by the Resistance, she finds herself in the middle of a plot to infiltrate a Germans-only brothel and smuggle out critical intelligence to Tom." (Christianbook.com)

"This is a superior, page-turning entry." Pub Wkly

Groot, Tracy

The **sentinels** of Andersonville; Tracy Groot. Tyndale House Publishers, Inc. 2014 368 p. map (hc) $24.99

ISBN 1414359489; 9781414359489

LC 2013031516

Christy Award: Historical (2015)

In this book, Tracy Groot "uses the Civil War atrocity at Andersonville Prison, where 13,000 Union prisoners died in a single year, as the background for a . . . retelling of the story of the Good Samaritan. Three young Southerners--two Confederate soldiers and a young woman who lives in the town nearest Andersonville--come to understand the true conditions in the prisoner-of-war camp, and must decide what they can do." (Publishers Weekly)

Groot "unflinchingly examines the consequences of becoming a good Samaritan in this richly detailed, engrossing historical fiction." Kirkus

Gross, Andrew

Eyes wide open. William Morrow 2011 338p $25.99

ISBN 978-0-06-165596-8; 0-06-165596-1

LC 2010-48025

"Estranged from his brother, Jay Erlich is surprised when he gets a call from Charlie. Unfortunately, the news isn't pleasant. Charlie's son is dead. Jay decides to visit his brother to offer comfort and help. As he learns more about his nephew's death, Jay begins to suspect that it's not as straightforward as it may appear. The police don't seem interested in investigating. Since his nephew was mentally ill, the authorities assume he wasn't taking his medication. Jay cannot stop until he knows the truth, but that will open up secrets hidden for almost two decades. The issues of what family truly means, the struggles of mental illness that affect both the victims and those surrounding them, and the bad decisions of the past that come back with a vengeance are all displayed like an open wound. . . . Gross has written his best book to date." Denver Post

Gross, Andrew

★ The **one** man; Andrew Gross. Minotaur Books 2016 432 p. (hardcover) $26.99; (ebook) $60

ISBN 9781250079503; 9781466892187

LC 2016007570

In this book, by Andrew Gross, it is "1944. Alfred Mendl and his family are brought on a crowded train to a Nazi concentration camp after being caught trying to flee Paris with forged papers. His family is torn away from him on arrival, his life's work burned before his eyes. To the guards, he is just another prisoner, but in fact Mendl—a renowned physicist—holds knowledge that only two people in the world possess. And the other is already at work for the Nazi war machine." (Publisher's note)

"Alternating between scenes of American hope-against-hope optimism and Nazi brutality, Blum's deadly odyssey into and out of this 20th-century hell drives toward a compelling celebration of the human will to survive, remember, and overcome." Pub Wkly

Includes bibliographical references (pages 415-416).

Gross, Andrew

Reckless. William Morrow 2010 404p $25.99

ISBN 978-0-06-165595-1; 0-06-165595-3

LC 2009-44799

"A pulsating thriller that turns on international conspiracies and financial sleight of hand. While thrillers wrapped around the economic crisis and stock-market meltdowns are becoming more common, Gross makes 'Reckless' a fresh and original take on the genre." South Florida Sun-Sentinel

Gross, Gwendolen

When she was gone; Gwendolen Gross. 1st Gallery Books trade pbk ed Gallery Books 2013 304 p. (paperback) $16

ISBN 1451684746; 9781451684742; 9781451684766

LC 2012022605

This novel, by Gwendolen Gross, asks "what happened to Linsey Hart? When the Cornell-bound teenager disappears into the steamy blue of a late-summer morning, her quiet neighborhood is left to pick apart the threads of their own lives and assumptions. Linsey's neighbors are just ordinary people--but even ordinary people can keep terrible secrets hidden close. . . . As the days of Linsey's absence tick by, dread and hope threaten to tear a community apart." (Publisher's note)

Grossman, Austin

Soon I will be invincible. Pantheon Books 2007 287p $22.95

ISBN 978-0-375-42486-1; 0-375-42486-5

LC 2006-33296

"A heartbreaking genius of staggering evil, Doctor Impossible avenges lost love, a lonely adolescence, and a plethora of foiled doomsday devices. . . . Every comic-book cliché in this witty, stunning debut is lovingly embraced, then turned inside out." Wired

Grossman, David

Be my knife; translated by Vered Almog and Maya Gurantz. Farrar, Straus & Giroux 2002 307p

ISBN 0-374-29977-3

LC 2001-33645

Original Hebrew edition, 1998

"When a thirty-three-year-old man named Yair catches a glimpse of Miriam at a class reunion, he senses a bond with her that goes beyond sexual attraction; because he is a practiced philanderer who is in search of something extraordinary, he implores her to enter a ruthlessly honest correspondence with him, on the understanding that they will never meet. . . . Most of the book is devoted to Yair's letters, and so we don't get to hear Miriam's responses until near the end. But it is Grossman's achievement that we understand from the start that Yair's vision of Miriam (and thus ours) is almost painfully incomplete." New Yorker

Grossman, David

Falling out of time; by David Grossman ; translated by Jessica Cohen. Alfred A. Knopf 2014 208 p. (hardcover) $24.95

ISBN 0385350139; 9780345805850; 9780385350136; 9780385350143

LC 2013017532

In this book by Daniel Grossman, "a bereaved father, who, after five years, still cannot come to terms with his son's death, leaves his wife and home to try to find the 'there,' where the boy's soul resides. As he relentlessly walks through and around his village, the Walking Man is joined by others who have lost their children." (Publishers Weekly)

"Grossman's lyrical approach to the silent suffering of mourning is both a literary study in processing grief and a reminder that healing often comes through the action of putting into words the pain we thought was unspeakable." LJ

Grossman, David

★ **Someone** to run with; translated by Vered Almog and Maya Gurantz. Farrar, Straus and Giroux 2004 343p $24

ISBN 0-374-26657-3

LC 2002-29778

Original Hebrew edition, 2000

In Jerusalem, teenage Assaf "a shy misfit, embarks upon a quixotic journey with a lost dog to find its mistress. Tamar, a caustic fifteen-year-old who can sing Mozart and Leonard Cohen on demand, runs away from home to find the criminals who have ensnared her older brother. A young street musician, in the grip of a heroin habit as formidable as his talent, stumbles through his routines with death close behind. The resulting picaresque is a cross between 'Run Lola Run' and 'Oliver Twist,' and as the reader waits for these solitary odysseys to intersect, the urgency becomes almost unbearable. Grossman evokes teenage nobility and self-hatred in all its pimply particularity, while slyly suggesting that the arduous quest for connections should never be outgrown." New Yorker

Grossman, David

★ **To** the end of the land; translated from the Hebrew by Jessica Cohen. Alfred A. Knopf 2010 575p $26.95

ISBN 978-0-307-59297-2; 0-307-59297-9

LC 2010-03915

Original Hebrew edition, 2008

Grossman "weaves the essences of private life into the tapestry of history with deliberate and delicate skill; he has created a panorama of breathtaking emotional force, a masterpiece of pacing, of dedicated storytelling, with characters whose lives are etched with extraordinary, vivid detail. While his novel has the vast sweep of pure tragedy, it is also at times playful, and utterly engrossing." N Y Times Book Rev

Grossman, Lev

The **magicians**; a novel. Viking 2009 402p $26.95; pa $16

ISBN 978-0-670-02055-3; 0-670-02055-9; 978-0-452-29629-9 pa; 0-452-29629-3 pa

LC 2008-55900

Alex Award (2010)

"Quentin Coldwater is a geeky high-school senior in Brooklyn who is convinced that happiness and 'the life he should be living' are elsewhere—for example, in the series of nineteen-thirties British adventure novels that he was obsessed with as a child. When Quentin stumbles on a portal that takes him to a college for magicians in upstate New York, he learns that the world depicted in these novels, known as Fillory, is real, and he is forced to square his youthful ideas with the realities that exist there, too—boredom, regret, shame, and despair. Quentin's journey becomes an unexpectedly moving coming-of-age story in which he learns that magical worlds are much like the real one." New Yorker

Grossman, Lev, 1969-

The **magician** king; Lev Grossman. Viking 2011 400p. $26.95

ISBN 978-0-670-02231-1; 0-670-02231-4

LC 2011019733

Sequel to: The magicians (2009)

"After Quentin and his old friend Julia leave Fillory on a magical sailing ship, they end up back in Quentin's home in Chesterton, Massachusetts, and only Julia's dark magic can get them back to the realm they have grown to love." (Publisher's note)

"Quentin Coldwater, the wizard who traveled to a mythical land to be its king in the first book, has gotten past most of his misery and settled into bored complacency, wondering whether hanging out in a castle and getting drunk is really all there is to rulership. Isn't he meant for great things? Shouldn't he be carrying out some giant quest? In the book's opening chapter, the quest he's already on unravels disappointingly, so he decides to embark to the farthest edge of the land he rules, a speck of an island in the middle of the sea, and he winds up on an even stranger journey. The Magicians was terrific, but loose, with a plot that moved from incident to incident with only the barest connecting material. The Magician King, which is better in almost every way, feels as if it might be even looser in the early going, with plenty of opportunities to worry whether Grossman can pull his narrative together. But once he reaches his devastating climax, neatly knitting together story threads readers won't have even realized were major plot points, the novel reaches a level of poignancy the first could only hope to attain." A V Club

Grossman, Lev, 1969-

The **magician's** land; a novel. Lev Grossman. Viking 2014 416 p. (Magicians trilogy) (hardback) $27.95

ISBN 0670015679; 9780670015672

LC 2014010097

"Quentin Coldwater has been cast out of Fillory, the secret magical land of his childhood dreams. With nothing left to lose he returns to where his story began, the Brakebills Preparatory College of Magic. . . . Along with Plum, a brilliant young undergraduate with a dark secret of her own, Quentin sets out on a crooked path through a magical demimonde of gray magic and desperate characters." (Publisher's note)

Tthis novel serves as an elegantly written third act to Quentin's bildungsroman, in which he at last learns responsibility and to not simply put childish things aside but understand them--and himself--anew." Pub Wkly

Grossman, Paul

Children of wrath; Paul Grossman. St. Martin's Press 2012 324 p. (audiobook) $34.95

ISBN 9781611748451; 9780312601911; 9781429988940

LC 2011041101

This thriller novel is "set in early 1930s Berlin. . . . Berlin headlines scream about people being sickened by tainted sausages. Bags of bones show up in the city's sewer system. Detective Willi Kraus quickly learns the bones are the remains of children--and young boys are disappearing from the city. His superiors take the spectacular murder case away from him because he is Jewish and hand him the case of the bad sausages instead. . . . A father himself, he cannot--will not--ignore the boys and the bones." (Kirkus Reviews)

Gruber, Michael

The **book** of air and shadows. William Morrow 2007 466p $24.95

ISBN 978-0-06-087446-9; 0-06-087446-5

LC 2006-46767

"Few thrillers will surpass [this book] when it comes to energetic writing, compellingly flawed characters, literary scholarship and mathematical conundrums." USA Today

Gruber, Michael

The **forgery** of Venus; a novel. William Morrow 2008 318p $24.95

ISBN 978-0-06-087448-3; 0-06-087448-1

LC 2008-2363

"Gruber writes passionately and knowledgeably about art and its history—and he writes brilliantly about the shadowy lines that blur reality and unreality. Fans of intelligent, literate thrillers will be well rewarded." Publ Wkly

Gruber, Michael

The **good** son; a novel. Henry Holt and Co. 2010 383p $26

ISBN 0-8050-9128-9; 978-0-8050-9128-1

"This novel slides in and out of conventional identities with a facility that would be disturbing if it weren't so damn smooth. Adeptly plotted yet philosophical, worldly yet preoccupied with moral truth, it's a book to provoke comparisons with John le Carré and Graham Greene, while at the same time eluding the ideological constraints that weigh so heavy on those masters." Salon

Gruber, Michael

The **return**; a novel. Michael Gruber. Henry Holt and Co. 2013 384 p. (hardback) $28

ISBN 0805091297; 9780805091298

LC 2012045307

In this novel by Michael Gruber "a shattering piece of news awakens [Richard] Marder's buried desire for vengeance, and with nothing left to lose, he sets off to punish the people whose actions, years earlier, changed his life. Uninvited, [an army buddy from Vietnam Patrick] Skelly shows up and together the two of them raise the stakes far beyond anything Marder could have envisioned. Marder learns that good motives and sense of justice can't always protect the people a man loves." (Publisher's note)

Gruber, Michael

Valley of bones. William Morrow 2005 436p $24.95

ISBN 0-06-057766-5

"When a Sudanese oil baron is thrown to his death from his hotel balcony, Miami detective Jimmy Paz finds a mysterious woman named Emmylou Dideroff vehemently praying at the scene of the crime; she quickly becomes the main suspect. The plot immediately thickens as Emmylou begins to write a lengthy confession about her disturbing childhood, how she reformed from a criminal to a woman of God, and what led her to the Miami hotel room that day. Is she crazy or does God really speak to her? Jimmy and criminal psychologist Lorna Wise investigate and are thrown into a whirlwind journey involving prostitution, white supremacists, the Sudanese civil war, and massive government cover-ups." Libr J

Gruen, Sara

Ape house; a novel. Spiegel & Grau 2010 320p $26

ISBN 0-385-52321-1; 978-0-385-52321-9

LC 2010-08928

When a family of bonobo apes who know American Sign Language are kidnapped from a language laboratory, their mysterious appearance on a reality TV show propels scientist Isabel Duncan, together with reporter John Thigpen, on a personal mission to rescue them.

This novel portrays "group of six bonobo apes housed in the fictional Great Ape Language Lab in Kansas City and the humans who either come to love them or seek to profit from their surprisingly advanced communication skills. Led by Bonzi, the matriarch and undisputed leader, the bonobo group includes Sam, the charismatic oldest male, Jelani, an adolescent showoff, and Makena, 'Jelani's biggest fan,' who is pregnant and due any day. Isabel Duncan is a research scientist overseeing the bonobos and their unique ability to communicate via lexigrams on their computers, supplemented by American Sign Language. . . . Gruen enlivens this charming story of their emotional bonding with multiple villains—including Isabel's fiancé, the head of the Great Ape Language Lab, who she discovers has a history of animal cruelty and a desire to profit from the bonobos under his control. There's also a purveyor of porn who sees the bonobos as the perfect stars for his new reality TV show, enticing viewers with their healthy sex lives 24 hours a day. Ape House turns into a romp, but Gruen never loses the thread of the enviable bond Isabel has nurtured with her ape friends." BookPage

Gruen, Sara

Water for elephants; a novel. Algonquin Books 2006 335p il $23.95

ISBN 1-565-12499-5

LC 2005-52700

"Life is good for Jacob Jankowski. He's about to graduate from veterinary school and about to bed the girl of his dreams. Then his parents are killed in a car crash, leaving him in the middle of the Great Depression with no home, no family, and no career. Almost by accident, Jacob joins the circus. There he falls in love with the beautiful performer Marlena, who is married to the circus' psychotic animal trainer. He also meets the other love of his life, Rosie the elephant. This lushly romantic novel travels back and forth in time between Jacob's present day in a nursing home and his adventures in the surprisingly harsh world of 1930s circuses. The ending of both stories is a little too cheerful to be believed, but just like a circus, the magic of the story and the writing convince you to suspend your disbelief. The book is partially based on real circus stories and illustrated with historical circus photographs." Booklist

Grumbach, Doris

The **book** of knowledge; a novel. Norton 1995 248p

ISBN 0-393-03770-3

LC 94-37901

"Grumbach's latest novel is grimly compelling in its portrayal of four lives filled with stifled desires, major depression, incest, self-sacrifice, and thwarted love. . . . Grumbach paints a glowing picture of warmth, security, and safety that is shattered by the Great Depression." Booklist

Grunberg, Arnon

Tirza; by Arnon Grunberg ; translated from the Dutch by Sam Garrett. Open Letter 2013 452 p. (paperback) $16.95

ISBN 1934824690; 9781934824696

LC 2012044299

In this book, former book editor Jörgen's life has suffered considerably after the 9/11 terror attacks. The "plot centers on a graduation party for Jörgen's eldest daughter, Tirza, who is planning a trip to Namibia with her boyfriend, who reminds Jörgen of Mohammed Atta, the lead 9/11 hijacker. Jörgen is suffering from the hectoring of his shallow, judgmental wife, and his daughters haven't always shown shrewd judgment. . . . But it's also clear that something is broken within Jörgen himself." (Kirkus)

Grunwald, Lisa

The **irresistible** Henry House; a novel. Random House 2010 412p $25

ISBN 978-1-4000-6300-0

LC 2009-19720

Henry's "story will no doubt garner comparisons to fellow Zelig-like figures Benjamin Button and Forrest Gump. But Grunwald's writing, while sometimes painted in the brushstrokes of allegory, rarely indulges in that kind of soft-focus sentimentality." Entertainment Wkly

Grushin, Olga

The **dream** life of Sukhanov. G.P. Putnam's Sons 2005 354p $24.95

ISBN 0-399-15298-9

LC 2005-43175

"On one level, Grushin recounts the comfortable life of fiftysomething art critic and former artist Anatoly Sukhanov, who enjoys all the perks of a pre-Gorbachev existence, until the arrival of a mysterious cousin at his family's capacious Moscow apartment. As his secure life begins to fray and then unravel, Sukhanov, who had the potential of brilliance as a young artist but eventually joined the Soviet establishment, is forced to confront the loss of his beloved wife, his two children, his editorship at the country's leading art magazine, in a word, his identity. Though an absorbing chronicle of life at the end of the Soviet era, this is really much more–a meditation on society, art, truth, and life." Libr J

Grushin, Olga

★ The **line**. G.P. Putnam's Sons 2010 322p $25.95

ISBN 978-0-399-15616-8; 0-399-15616-X

LC 2009-42733

"In the world of The Line, no desire, no matter how trifling, is met without a herculean struggle, and Anna's stymied attempts to present her family with something as simple as a date cake sometimes devolve into farce. But for the most part, Grushin expertly maintains a dreamlike tone to sell the novel's more preposterous (albeit historically grounded) elements, and characters who initially appear one-dimensional become intensely empathetic by the novel's end, as they bristle or cave under a society that grinds down the exceptional to make way for the pedestrian." A. V. Club

Guene, Faiza

Kiffe kiffe tomorrow; [translated from the French by Sarah Adams] Harcourt 2006 179p pa $13

ISBN 0-15-603048-9; 978-0-15-603048-9

LC 2005-30456

Original French edition, 2004

"Doria, 15, a child of Muslim immigrants, describes her daily struggle in Paris' rough housing projects in a contemporary narrative that's touching, furious, and very funny." Booklist

Guest, Judith

★ **Ordinary** people. Viking 1976 263p hardcover o.p. pa $13

ISBN 0-670-52831-5; 0-14-006517-2 pa

"When his older brother drowns in a boating accident, seventeen-year-old Conrad Jarrett feels responsible and makes an unsuccessful attempt at suicide. After eight months in a mental institution, Conrad returns home to parents whose marriage is crumbling, friends who are wary of him, and a psychiatrist who works with him to help put the pieces together. The pain of adolescent anxiety and fragile family relationships are authentically depicted." Shapiro. Fic for Youth. 3d edition

Guhrke, Laura Lee

How to lose a duke in ten days; by Laura Lee Guhrke. Avon Books 2014 371 p. (An American Heiress in London) pbk $7.99

ISBN 0062118196; 9780062118196

This book, by Laura Lee Guhrke, is "the story of a bargain, a marriage of convenience . . . and the chance for love to last a lifetime. From the moment she met the . . . Duke of Margrave, Edie knew he could change her life. And when he agreed to her outrageous proposal of a marriage . . . she was transformed from ruined American heiress to English duchess. Five years later, she's delighted with their arrangement, especially since her husband is living on another continent." (Publisher's note)

"A spirited yet emotionally fragile heroine and a resourceful hero find love in this flawlessly written, lushly sensual tale that balances sexual abuse issues with flashes of humor and treats readers to a beautifully depicted and tender courtship." LJ

Guhrke, Laura Lee

When the Marquess Met His Match; An American Heiress in London. by Laura Lee Guhrke. HarperCollins 2013 384 p. (An American heiress in London) $7.99

ISBN 006211817X; 9780062118172

In this book, by Laura Lee Guhrke, "Lady Belinda Featherstone, a former American heiress and now the quite happy widow of the Earl of Featherstone, has become the matchmaker of choice for aspiring American debutantes in London—and keeping them safe from philandering fortune hunters is one of her goals. So when the infamous . . . Marquess of Trubridge asks for her help, naturally she refuses." (Library Journal)

"Graced with an abundance of memorable characters and rich in lush sensuality." Booklist

Guillory, Jasmine

The **wedding** date; Jasmine Guillory. Jove 2018 viii, 310 p.p (softcover) $15

ISBN 0399587667; 9780399587665; 9780399587672

LC 2017034041

In this novel, by Jasmine Guillory, "on the eve of his ex's wedding festivities, Drew is minus a plus one. Until a power outage strands him with the perfect candidate for a fake girlfriend... After Alexa and Drew have more fun than they ever thought possible, Drew has to fly back to Los Angeles and his job as a pediatric surgeon, and Alexa heads home to Berkeley, where she's the mayor's chief of staff. Too bad they can't stop thinking about the other." (Publisher's note)

"This incredibly delicious meet-cute brings two people together who would not have met otherwise, and though it could have become predictable, Guillory keeps this contemporary romance fresh with well-drawn multicultural characters navigating the perils of long-distance relationships." Booklist

Guinn, Matthew

The **resurrectionist**; a novel. Matthew Guinn. W W Norton & Co Inc 2013 304 p. (hardcover) $25.95

ISBN 0393239314; 9780393239317

LC 2013003760

This novel by Matthew Guinn takes place at "South Carolina Medical College, where . . . bones of African American slaves, over a century old, are unearthed. Out of the college's dark past, these bones threaten to . . . condemn the present. In the . . . nineteenth century, Dr. Frederick Augustus Johnston . . . purchased a slave. Nemo ("no man") would become . . . responsible for procuring bodies for medical study. Insouciant, tormented, and brilliant, and . . . almost supernatural, Nemo [seizes] his self-respect." (Publisher's note)

Guinn, Matthew

The **scribe**; a novel. Matthew Guinn. W W Norton & Co Inc 2015 304 p. (hardcover) $25.95

ISBN 0393239292; 9780393239294

LC 2015013780

In this novel, by Matthew Guinn, "Thomas Canby is called back to the city on the eve of Atlanta's 1881 International Cotton Exposition to partner with Atlanta's first African American police officer, Cyrus Underwood. The case they're assigned is chilling: a serial murderer who seems to be violently targeting Atlanta's wealthiest black entrepreneurs. . . . The oligarchy of Atlanta's most prominent white businessmen . . . is anxious to solve the murders before they lose . . . money." (Publisher's note)

"This is an absorbing historical mystery filled with evocative period detail, a brooding atmosphere of corruption and pervasive evil, and compelling characters who could be developed further." Booklist

Gulik, Robert Hans van

The **Chinese** bell murders; three cases solved by Judge Dee. a Chinese detective story suggested by three original Chinese plots; with 15 plates drawn by the author in Chinese style. Harper 1959 262p il

First published 1958 in the United Kingdom

Judge Dee, a legendary magistrate and detective, who is based on a real 7th century Chinese person and was the subject of Chinese detective tales during the 17th and 18th centuries, made his American debut in this murder-rape case. The judge solves three interwoven crimes in the provincial city of Pooyang. A postscript provides information on ancient Chinese detection and court procedure and on the Chinese sources of the story

Gulik, Robert Hans van

The **haunted** monastery; a Chinese detective story. {by} Robert van Gulik; with eight illustrations drawn by the author in Chinese style. Scribner 1969 159p il

First published 1961 in Malaysia; first United States edition published 1963 in paperback

This mystery "finds Judge Dee and his family and retainers stranded because of a broken axle and a howling storm. He has to spend the night solving three murders and a problem of impersonation before he can proceed on his journey the following day." Ency of Mystery & Detection

Gulik, Robert Hans van

The **lacquer** screen; a Chinese detective story. {by} Robert van Gulik; with ten illustrations drawn by the author in Chinese style. Scribner 1970 180p il

First published 1962 in Malaysia; first United States edition published 1963 in paperback

This tale is set in 7th century China. Magistrate detective Judge Dee and his lieutenant join the underworld in a district under the Judge's jurisdiction in order to solve three crimes. They share the life of the gangster-boss and his entourage while the underworld people unwittingly help them in their inquiries. The Judge eventually reveals the ugly secret hidden by the panels of a beautiful lacquer screen

Gulik, Robert Hans van

The **Red** Pavilion; a Chinese detective story. {by} Robert van Gulik; with six illustrations drawn by the author in Chinese style. Scribner 1968 173p il

First published 1961 in Malaysia

Judge Dee, "solves more than one knotty criminal problem, all of them stemming out of the fact that he elects to stay in the infamous Red Pavilion on Paradise Island, not knowing it has been the scene of several mysterious deaths in the past. The Chinese atmosphere is suitably exotic and there is a lovely, mistreated courtesan for the judge to protect." Publ Wkly

Gulik, Robert Hans van

The **willow** pattern; a Chinese detective story. by Robert van Gulik; with fifteen illustrations drawn by the author in Chinese style. Scribner 1965 183p il

"This adventure of the legendary Judge Dee, of Seventh Century China, is a strange, brooding tale of crime, cholera, and corruption. . . . The emperor and his court have fled the plague-ridden city and left the judge and his Colonels, Ma Joong and Chiao Tai, in charge of affairs. They quickly become involved in three murders: 'The Case of the Willow Pattern', 'The Case of the Steep Stairs', and 'The Case of the Murdered Bond-Maid.'" Libr J

Gundar-Goshen, Ayelet

★ **Waking** lions; Ayelet Gundar-Goshen ; translated from the Hebrew by Sondra Silverston. Little, Brown & Co. 2017 341 p. (hc) $26

ISBN 0316395439; 9780316395434

LC 2016957622

In his book, by Ayelet Gundar-Goshen, "neurosurgeon Eitan Green has the perfect life--married to a beautiful police officer and father of two young boys. Then, speeding along a deserted moonlit road after an exhausting hospital shift, he hits someone. Seeing that the man, an African migrant, is beyond help, he flees the scene." (Publisher's note)

"As characters reveal previously hidden facets, Gundar-Goshen's mesmerizing novel, her first to be published in English, moves continually into unexpected territory." Booklist

Gunesekera, Romesh

The **match**; a novel. New Press 2008 308p $24.95

ISBN 978-1-59558-198-3; 1-59558-198-7

LC 2007-21883

First published 2006 in the United Kingdom

"Many a novelist, drizzling throwaway contemporary references over the text, looks clumsy and laboured in the attempt. Here the forty-year narrative arc is traced across a sequence of precisely judged topical allusions, embracing everything from Skants underwear to Cherie Blair's late baby. Each emerges quite naturally from narrative and dialogue. Time never hangs too heavily on the story, but we are encouraged to value the experience of its passing. Few novelists have so skilfully underlined the beauty of patience as a redeeming virtue." Times Lit Suppl

Gunn, James E., 1923-

Transcendental; by James Gunn. Tor Books 2013 304 p. (hardcover) $25.99

ISBN 0765335018; 9780765335012

LC 2013023856

In this book, by James Gunn, "Riley, a veteran of interstellar war, is one of many beings from many different worlds aboard a ship on a pilgrimage that spans the galaxy. However, he is not journeying to achieve transcendence, a vague mystical concept that has drawn everyone else on the ship to this journey into the unknown at the far edge of the galaxy. His mission is to find and kill the prophet who is reputed to help others transcend." (Publisher's note)

Another title in this series is:
Transgalactic (2016)

Gunning, Sally

The **rebellion** of Jane Clarke. William Morrow 2010 273p $24.99

ISBN 978-0-06-178214-5; 0-06-178214-9

LC 2010-20340

"Gripping, romantic, historically sound, and completely satisfying." Historical Novels Rev

Guo, Xiaolu, 1973-

A **concise** Chinese-English dictionary for lovers. Nan A. Talese/Doubleday 2007 283p $23.95

ISBN 978-0-385-52029-4; 0-385-52029-8

LC 2007-3118

The novel "cleverly courts our assumptions about the chasm between Chinese and Western cultures, only to upend them. It is an utterly captivating, and disorientating, journey both through language and through love." Independent (London)

Guo, Xiaolu, 1973-

I am China; Xiaolu Guo. Nan A. Talese/Doubleday 2014 384 p. $16.95

ISBN 0804170479; 9780385538718; 9780804170475

LC 2013049786

In this book, by Xiaolu Guo, "London translator Iona Kirkpatrick is at work on a new project: a collection of letters and diaries by a Chinese punk guitarist named Kublai Jian. As she translates the handwritten pages, a story of romance and revolution emerges between Jian, who believes there is no art without political commitment, and Mu, a poet whom he loves as fiercely as his ideals." (Publisher's note)

Guo, Xiaolu, 1973-

Twenty fragments of a ravenous youth. Nan A. Talese/Douleday 2008 204p il $21.95

ISBN 978-0-385-52592-3

LC 2008-1671

"Guo's début novel, first published eleven years ago in China and now reworked in English, distills the rush to modernization through the experience of Fenfang, a young peasant who leaves her village for Beijing. Part of the post-Cultural Revolution generation, Fenfang is untethered from history and profoundly alone, and Guo imbues her flailing efforts to establish herself with a raw, adolescent pain. Pirated books and DVDs provide an education, as Fenfang takes cues from 'Betty Blue,' 'Chungking Express,' Marguerite Duras, and Tennessee Williams, progressing from work as an extra in state film productions to a screenwriting career. Guo is a filmmaker herself, and, if her recurrent homages occasionally cloy, Fenfang's rage to express herself carries an unmistakable autobiographical intensity." New Yorker

Gurganus, Allan, 1947-

★ **Local** souls; novellas. Allan Gurganus. Liveright Publishing Corporation 2013 352 p. (hardcover) $25.95

ISBN 087140379X; 9780871403797

LC 2013016662

Lambda Literary Awards Finalist (2013)

This book by Allan Gurganus presents "three novellas set in Falls, NC, the mythic town in his . . . first novel, 'Oldest Living Confederate Widow Tells All'. In 'Fear Not,' a banker's daughter hunts for the child she was forced to give up at birth. In 'Saints Have Mothers,' a cult grows up around a vanished high school valedictorian. In 'Decoy,' the eroticized bond between two married men is tested by an epic flood." (Library Journal)

Gurganus, Allan

★ The **oldest** living Confederate widow tells all. Knopf 1989 718p

ISBN 0-394-54537-0

LC 88-45870

"In a way, 'Oldest Living Confederate Widow Tells All' is as much about language and myth-making as it is about love and war. Whether one feels that it succeeds depends on how much leeway one is willing to give to this indomitable 'veteran of the veteran,' as Lucy describes herself." N Y Times Book Rev

Gurganus, Allan

The **practical** heart; four novellas. Knopf 2001 322p $25

ISBN 0-679-43763-0

LC 2001-32665

"In 'The Practical Heart,' the narrator recalls the proclivities of his great-aunt, daughter of a Scottish immigrant to Chicago. . . . 'Preservation News' is a fey portrait of a man who has just lost his battle with AIDS but who spent his last breath in the pursuit of the preservation of historic properties. . . . 'He's One, Too' offers an ironically sympathetic portrayal of a married man arrested for lewd acts with a younger man. And in the longest and most moving piece, 'Saint Monster,' a son remembers how the relationship between his ugly but kind father and his beautiful but faithless mother forced him into prematurely dealing with the rawer aspects of adulthood." Booklist

Gurganus, Allan

White people. Knopf 1991 252p

ISBN 0-394-58841-X

LC 90-52943

The novella A hog loves its life concerns a grandfather and his boyish grandson, the other novella Blessed assurance: a moral tale "is a funny, sad, confessional tale told by a man reflecting on his traumatic youth, when he collected funeral insurance premiums from poor blacks. Gurganus is a champion storyteller with particularly American roots, in the tradition of Mark Twain. This is a collection to be savored and reread." Publ Wkly

Gustine, Amy

You should pity us instead; stories. Amy Gustine. Sarabande Books 2016 256 p. (paperback : acid-free paper) $15.95

ISBN 9781941411193

LC 2015017017

This collection of short stories, by Amy Gustine, "explores some of our toughest dilemmas: the cost of Middle East strife at its most intimate level, the likelihood of God considered in day-to-day terms, the moral stakes of family obligations, and the inescapable fact of mortality. Amy Gustine exhibits an extraordinary generosity toward her characters, instilling them with a thriving, vivid presence." (Publisher's note)

"Gustine's language is uniformly remarkable for its clarity and forthrightness." Pub Wkly

Guterson, David

Ed King; a novel. Alfred A. Knopf 2011 301p $26.95

ISBN 978-0-307-27106-8; 0-307-27106-4

LC 2011-10255

"Guterson's narrative voice — by turns savage and sad, amused and outraged — becomes a kind of Greek chorus of one. From the self-reverential blather of Seattle liberals to the gaming industry's nihilistic love of violence to the winner-take-all world of software and search engines, Guterson skewers it all. . . . He interweaves the story with enough mythological references to keep even the most ardent classicist entertained." Seattle Times

Guterson, David

The **other**. Alfred A. Knopf 2008 255p $24.95

ISBN 978-0-307-26315-5; 0-307-26315-0

LC 2007-41098

"With prose that's as careful and quiet as a mountain lion, The Other asks, and helps answer, two of life's most perplexing questions: How do we live in an imperfect world, and what are our obligations to those we love?" Outside

Guterson, David

Our Lady of the Forest. Knopf 2003 323p $25.95

ISBN 0-375-41211-5

LC 2002-43322

"When Ann Holmes starts having visions of the Virgin Mary, the bedraggled teen runaway becomes the last hope for the inhabitants of a dank, economically depressed logging town and the hordes of miracle-seekers who descend on it. In this panoramic, psychologically dense novel, she also becomes a symbol of the intimate intertwining of the sacred and the profane in American life." Publ Wkly

Guterson, David

★ **Snow** falling on cedars. Harcourt Brace & Co. 1994 345p $25

ISBN 0-15-100100-6

LC 94-7535

"Japanese American Kabuo Miyomoto is arrested in 1954 for the murder of a fellow fisherman, Carl Heine. Miyomoto's trial, which provides a focal point to the novel, stirs memories of past relationships and events in the minds and hearts of the San Piedro Islanders. Through these memories, Guterson illuminates the grief of loss, the sting of prejudice triggered by World War II, and the imperatives of conscience. With mesmerizing clarity he conveys the voices of Kabuo's wife, Hatsue, and Ishmael Chambers, Hatsue's first love who, having suffered the loss of her love and the ravages of war, ages into a cynical journalist now covering Kabuo's trial." Libr J

Guthrie, A. B.

★ The **big** sky; [by] A. B. Guthrie, Jr. Sloane 1947 386p

"After a quarrel and fight with his father, 17-year old Boone Caudill leaves his home in Kentucky headed for St. Louis and the west, where he hopes to hunt buffalo and shoot Indians. The story follows his adventurous course, by foot and horseback, to the Mississippi, then by keel boat to the land of the big sky at the headwaters of the Missouri, where for 13 years he leads the typical life of a mountain man for his period and in that short times sees the Indian degraded, the game killed off and the life he loved destroyed." Wis Libr Bull

Guthrie, A. B.

The **way** West. Sloane 1949 340p

A story of an emigrant trek from Independence, Missouri, to Oregon in the 1840s. Dick Summers, one of the principal characters of the author's earlier novel, 'The Big Sky' reappears in this novel

"Where most writers of Western fiction concentrate on what their characters do, Mr. Guthrie concentrates on how they think and feel. It is this emphasis which gives his book depth and sense of reality." Christ Sci Monit

Guttridge, Peter

The **thing** itself; Peter Guttridge. Severn House 2012 213 p. $28.95

ISBN 0727880810; 9780727880819

This novel, by Peter Guttridge, is book three in the "Brighton Mystery" series. "Thriller writer Victor Tempest is dead and his son, the disgraced ex-Chief Constable Bob Watts, is discovering what really happened in the unsolved Brighton Trunk Murder of 1934. At the same time, DS Sarah Gilchrist has a lead that may establish the truth about the Milldean Massacre. If she can stay alive long enough to follow it." (Publisher's note)

Gyasi, Yaa, 1989-

★ **Homegoing**; a novel. Yaa Gyasi. Alfred A. Knopf 2016 320 p. (hardback) $26.95

ISBN 9781101947135; 1101947136; 9780451493835

LC 2015039411

In this novel, by Yaa Gyasi, "two half-sisters, Effia and Esi, are born into different villages in eighteenth-century Ghana. Effia is married off to an Englishman and lives in comfort. Esi is . . . sold with thousands of others into the Gold Coast's booming slave trade, and shipped off to America. One thread of Homegoing follows Effia's descendants through centuries of warfare in Ghana, The other thread follows Esi and her children into America." (Publisher's note)

"Gyasi's characters are vividly drawn, sympathetic yet not simplistically heroic. It's wrenching to leave them behind, but readers will be quickly enthralled by the next generation's story." LJ

H

Haasse, Hella S.

In a dark wood wandering; revised and edited by Anita Miller from an English translation from the Dutch by Lewis C. Kaplan. Academy Chicago 1989 574p

ISBN 0-89733-336-5

LC 89-17814

Original Dutch edition, 1949

"This novel exemplifies historical fiction at its best; the author's meticulous research and polished style bring the medieval world into vibrant focus." Libr J

Habila, Helon

Measuring time; a novel. W. W. Norton & Co. 2007 383p pa $13.95

ISBN 978-0-393-05251-0; 0-393-05251-6

LC 2006-30790

"Habila's beautifully (and deceptively) simple style is matched by a story that is strong, clear and richly evocative." New Statesman (London, England: 1996)

Hacker, Christopher

The **Morels**; Christopher Hacker. Soho Press 2013 368 p. (hardcover) $25.95

ISBN 1616952431; 9781616952433

LC 2012036639

This novel focuses on "Arthur Morel, who as a child was a talented violinist with a flair for self-sabotage, [and who] has just finished his second novel (also called The Morels), a barely fictionalized account of his relationship with his wife Penelope and their son, Will. His book's last scene, however, depicts Arthur and an eight-year-old Will engaging in a sexual act that shocks the public and quickly scuttles his relationship with his family, who are unmoved by his claims of poetic license." (Publishers Weekly)

Haddad, Saleem

Guapa; by Saleem Haddad. Other Press 2016 368 p. (softcover) $16.95

ISBN 9781590517697; 9781590517703

LC 2015039123

Stonewall Honor Book in Literature (2017)

This novel, by Saleem Haddad, follows Rasa, a gay man living in an Arab country. "Rasa finds hope and comfort in the arms of his lover, Taymour. . . . One morning, Rasa's grandmother . . . [discovers them] in bed together. . . . The tumultuous day takes Rasa from his grandmother's apartment, to slums to interview Islamist rebels; to a police station to bail out his best friend . . . ; to the underground gay bar Guapa; and eventually to Taymour's lavish wedding to a woman." (Publishers Weekly)

"The titular Guapa is a dive bar in an unnamed city in the Middle East that has the feel of present-day Cairo. Guapa offers its habitués an escape from the watchful eye of a hard-line regime. Protagonist Rasa, a young, educated (in America) gay man, is a visitor to the underground club, where he meets friends and his lover, Taymour. At the start of this affecting novel, Rasa's indomitable grandmother Teta, with whom he's lived since the death of his father and the disappearance of his mother, discovers him and Taymour in flagrante delicto in Rasa's room. . . Warmly recommended to all readers who are interested in issues of diversity and the Middle East." LJ

Haddam, Jane

Cheating at solitaire; a Gregor Demarkian novel. St. Martin's Minotaur 2008 391p $24.95

ISBN 978-0-312-34308-8; 0-312-34308-6

LC 2007-49770

"When the outrageous behavior of a movie crew filming on Margaret's Harbor (a fictionalized Martha's Vineyard) results in the death of a crew member, the island's one-person police department requests the assistance of former FBI agent Gregor Demarkian. Moving slowly through the landscape of her story, Haddam turns the island and its ambiance into a vividly visual experience for readers. Brilliantly introspective, intellectual ruminations and multiple narrators—who fully convey the craziness of the paparazzi and the cutthroat attitudes of those with power—intersperse with Haddam's own unique and frequently unexpected conclusions." Libr J

Haddam, Jane

Hardscrabble road. St. Martin's Minotaur 2006 309p $24.95

ISBN 0-312-35373-1

LC 2005-54793

"Those new to Haddam will snap up her earlier work based on this captivating literate mystery, which shows how well a classic fair play whodunit can work in a contemporary setting." Publ Wkly

Haddam, Jane

True believers. St. Martin's Press 2001 328p

ISBN 0-312-20929-0

LC 00-51794

"Haddam's large cast pulses with petty jealousies, vanities and fears as they confront the mysteries of life and religion. This is an engrossingly complex mystery that should win further acclaim for its prolific and talented author." Publ Wkly

Haddon, Mark

The **curious** incident of the dog in the night-time; Today Show Book Club ed; Doubleday 2003 226p il $24.95

ISBN 0-385-51210-4

Alex Award (2004)

Despite his overwhelming fear of interacting with people, Christopher, a mathematically-gifted, autistic fifteen-year-old boy, decides to investigate the murder of a neighbor's dog and uncovers secret information about his mother

"Unable to feel emotions himself, his story evokes emotions in readers—heartache and frustration for his well-meaning but clueless parents and deep empathy for the wonderfully honest, funny, and lovable protagonist. Readers will never view the behavior of an autistic person again without more compassion and understanding." SLJ

Haddon, Mark, 1962-

The **red** house; a novel. Mark Haddon. Doubleday 2012 264 p.

ISBN 0385535775; 9780385535779

LC 2011029883

In this book, "Richard and Angela, estranged siblings, try to mend their past by spending a week together with their families at a house on the Welsh border. But the ingredients are not promising. Richard arrives with his glossy new wife and stuck-up stepdaughter. Angela brings her loveless marriage and duly troubled children. . . . The proximity and forced intimacy of the holiday exposes the many cracks in their relationships." (Economist)

"Refreshingly, Haddon takes the risk of making the ordinary extraordinary and succeeds; each character is poignantly real and each small trauma a revelation." LJ

Haddon, Mark

A **spot** of bother. Doubleday 2006 354p $24.95

ISBN 978-0-385-52051-5; 0-385-5205-1-4

LC 2006-16578

This novel "pulls off the smart trick of delivering fully human characters whose flaws make them almost impossible to live with, then depicts their love for one another as completely convincing." Cleveland Plain Dealer

Hadley, Tessa

Bad dreams and other stories; Tessa Hadley. HarperCollins 2017 viii, 224 p.p (hardcover) $26.99

ISBN 0062476661; 9780062476685; 9780062476661

In this collection of short stories, by Tessa Hadley, "two sisters quarrel over an inheritance and a new baby; a child awake in the night explores the familiar rooms of her home, made strange by the darkness; a housekeeper caring for a helpless old man uncovers secrets from his past. The first steps into a turning point and a new life are made so easily and carelessly: each of these stories illuminates crucial moments of transition, often imperceptible to the protagonists." (Publisher's note)

"Achingly lovely, though never sentimental, Hadley's collection renders common lives with exquisite grace." Kirkus

Hadley, Tessa

Clever Girl; A Novel. by Tessa Hadley. Harper 2013 256 p. $25.99

ISBN 0062270397; 0224096524; 9780062270399; 9780224096522

In this book, by Tessa Hadley, "one relatively ordinary life, chronicled from the 1950s to the 1990s in England, mirrors enormous shifts in style, attitude and choice, especially for women. . . . Growing up in the postwar decade without a father . . . [Stella] experiences a childhood bound by convention and a shortage of cash. . . . Stella falls pregnant and becomes a single mother herself, a choice which derails her hopes for college." (Kirkus Reviews)

Hadley, Tessa

The **London** train. Harper Perennial 2011 324p pa $14.99

ISBN 978-0-06-201183-1; 0-06-201183-9

"Cora has abandoned the bright lights of London for Cardiff, where she's found a job at a local library. Meanwhile, Paul has been enticed away from Wales. Their lives, distinct yet connected, form the basis of this enchanting novel, which considers the significance of coincidence and its potential impact upon ordinary lives." Culture Critic

Hadley, Tessa

Married love and other stories; Tessa Hadley. Jonathan Cape 2012 232 p. $14.99

ISBN 0062135643; 9780062135643; 9780224096423

LC 2012358423

In this collection, Tessa Hadley "considers private fears, bad decisions, tipping points and unexpected assertions of free will, via 12 short fictions. . . . 'The Trojan Prince' introduces a young merchant seaman in the 1920s, flirting with the daughter of a wealthy family but ultimately choosing not to respond to her signals of attraction. In 'A Mouthful of Cut Glass,' . . . two college students take their partners home to meet the family and come face to face with the class divide." (Kirkus)

Hadley, Tessa

The **past**; a novel. Tessa Hadley. HarperCollins 2016 320 p. (hardcover) $25.99

ISBN 0062270419; 9780062270412

LC 2015054014

This novel, by Tessa Hadley, follows "a dramatic family reunion . . . over three long, hot summer weeks. . . . Three sisters, a brother, and their children assemble at their country house. . . . [It] may be their last time there; the upkeep is prohibitive, and they may be forced to sell this beloved house. . . . Yet beneath the idyllic pastoral surface, hidden passions, devastating secrets, and dangerous hostilities threaten to consume them." (Publisher's note)

"Hadley is the patron saint of ordinary lives; her trademark empathy and sharp insight are out in force here." Kirkus

Hadley, Tessa

Sunstroke and other stories. Picador 2007 177p pa $13

ISBN 978-0-312-42599-9; 0-312-42599-6

LC 2007-13103

"Deft and resonant, [these stories] encapsulate moments of hope and humiliation in a kind of shorthand of different lives lived. Hadley never fails to surprise, but her surprises are understated—not the 'aha' fakery of some gimmicky short fiction but the small shift in expectations or results that's deeply felt but doesn't show, like the twitch of a rudder that sets a boat gliding on a new course." N Y Times Book Rev

Hagberg, David

Abyss. Forge 2011 496p $24.99

ISBN 978-0-7653-2410-8; 0-7653-2410-5

LC 2011-07891

When an NOAA scientist has a breakthrough that could enable a sustainable energy source and prevent dangerous weather systems, former CIA director Kirk McGarvey begins a cat-and-mouse chase with a contract killer seeking to trigger a nuclear disaster.

"This is a timely and frightening novel. Readers will be left thinking, This could really happen." Kirkus

Hage, Rawi

De Niro's game. Steerforth Press 2007 277p $23.95

ISBN 978-1-58195-223-0; 1-58195-223-6

LC 2007-23905

First published 2006 in Canada

"This is a grim, flat book. Hage's flatness gives it the right tone of bruised emotion, disconnectedness, and violence; it's what makes this such an effective debut." Quill & Quire

Hagedorn, Jessica Tarahata

Toxicology; [by] Jessica Hagedorn. Viking 2011 225p $25.95

ISBN 978-0-670-02257-1; 0-670-02257-8

LC 2010-35379

"In this engaging novel, Hagedorn employs a number of stylistic tricks. She drops in footnotes to explain dream sequences, creates a section in the form of a literary journal (modeled on the Paris Review), and pauses the narrative to announce digressions and 'a bit of exposition.' These experimental touches don't justify themselves in every instance, but they sustain the story in a lively way. One of the best reasons to read this novel is its beautifully precise descriptions of New York City." Boston Globe

Haggard, H. Rider

★ **King** Solomon's mines; introduction by Alexandra Fuller; illustrations by Walter Paget; notes by James Danly. Modern Library 2002 xxv, 264p il pa $9.95

ISBN 0-8129-6629-5

LC 2002-29519

First published 1885

"Highly coloured romance of adventure in the wilds of Central Africa in quest of King Solomon's Ophir; full of sensational fights, bloodcurdling perils and extraordinary escapes." Baker. Guide to the Best Fic

Haggard, H. Rider

★ **She**; edited with an introduction and notes by Daniel Karlin. Oxford University Press 1998 xxxviii, 332p pa $9.95

ISBN 0-19-283550-5

First published 1885

"'She,' or Ayesha, is an African sorceress whom death apparently cannot touch. The young English hero, Leo Vincey, sets out to avenge the murder of his ancestor, an ancient priest of Isis. The setting of this weird romance is an extinct volcano." Univ Handbk for Readers and Writers

Hagy, Alyson

Boleto; a novel. Alyson Hagy. Graywolf Press 2012 251 p.

ISBN 1555976123; 9781555976125

LC 2012931912

This book "opens with Will [Testerman] buying a beautiful 2-year-old filly for a bargain price. She will be a 'development project' for the patient Will. He talks to her a lot, building trust. He won't ride her yet . . . but they'll be going to California together to meet Don Enrique. . . . It turns out Don Enrique is an Argentine businessman who hosts polo games. His manager is a swine. Five frightened, underfed Argentine teenagers do the barn work. Will's fantasy of learning the polo business, unwisely based on a single conversation with the Don, begins to crumble. Will his innate decency hobble him with this tough, mercenary crowd? And can he protect his beloved filly from these rapacious rich folks?" (Kirkus Reviews)

Haig, Francesca

★ The **fire** sermon; a novel. by Francesca Haig. Gallery Books 2015 384 p. (hardback) $26

ISBN 1476767181; 9781476767185

LC 2014031292

In this book, by Francesca Haig, "four hundred years in the future, the Earth has turned primitive following a nuclear fire that has laid waste to civilization and nature. Though the radiation fallout has ended, for some unknowable reason every person is born with a twin. Of each pair, one is an Alpha--physically perfect in every way; and the other an Omega--burdened with deformity, small or large." (Publisher's note)

"Haig's experience as a poet shows in her writing, which is clear, forceful and laced with bright threads of beauty. [A] well-built world [with] vivid characters and [a] suspenseful plot." Kirkus

Other titles in this series are:

The map of bones (2016)

The forever ship (2017)

Haig, Francesca

The **map** of bones; Francesca Haig. Gallery Books 2016 416 p. (Fire sermon) (hardcover) $24.99

ISBN 9781476767192; 9781476767222

LC 2015046667

This book, by Francesca Haig, is part of the Fire Sermon trilogy. "Four hundred years in the future, the Earth has turned primitive following a nuclear fire that has laid waste to civilization and nature. Though the radiation fallout has ended, for some unknowable reason every person is born with a twin. Of each pair, one is an Alpha—physically perfect in every way; and the other an Omega—burdened with deformity, small or large." (Publisher's note)

"A powerful post-apocalyptic story with unusual emotional depth and clear, often beautiful language, this is one genre fans won't want to miss." Kirkus

Haig, Matt

The **dead** fathers club. Viking 2007 328p $23.95

ISBN 0-670-03833-4

LC 2006-50108

First published 2006 in the United Kingdom

This novel is "clearly inspired by Shakespeare's Hamlet, and part of the fun for the reader is discovering the many droll and unforced parallels. But the real draw is the extraordinary voice that Haig has created for his first-person narrator. Given to panic attacks, Philip is a breathless storyteller who seldom stops for punctuation but whose honesty and innocence, which shine from every sentence, are utterly captivating and heartbreakingly poignant. The result is an absolutely irresistible read." Booklist

Haig, Matt

The **humans**; a novel. Matt Haig. Simon & Schuster 2013 304 p. (hardcover : alk. paper) $25

ISBN 1476727910; 9781476727912; 9781476730592

LC 2013003203

In this novel by Matt Haig "an extraterrestrial visitor arrives on Earth. Taking the form of Professor Andrew Martin . . . the visitor is eager to complete the gruesome task assigned him and [return] to the utopian world of his own planet. Unexpectedly, he forges bonds with Martin's family, and in picking up the pieces of the professor's shattered personal life, he begins to see hope and beauty in the humans' imperfections and begins to question the mission that brought him there." (Publisher's note)

Includes bibliographical references and index

Haig, Matt

The **Radleys**. Free Press 2010 371p $25

ISBN 978-1-4391-9401-0; 1-4391-9401-7

LC 2010-04459

Alex Award (2011)

Struggling with overwork and parenting angst, English village doctor Peter Radley endeavors to hide his family's vampire nature until their daughter's oddly satisfying act of violence reveals the truth, an event that is complicated by the arrival of a practicing vampire family member.

"Dr. Peter Radley, his wife, Helen, and their two teenage children, Rowan and Clara, appear to be an ordinary English family living a quiet suburban life — except that they're a family of nonpracticing vampires (or, in the book's AA-like speak, they're following the rules of The Abstainer's Handbook). Rowan and Clara aren't even aware of what they are — or why they must always wear heavy sunblock — until the night Clara has a run-in with a local thug and nature overcomes nurture. With a body to dispose of, Peter must reach out to his estranged practicing-vampire brother, Will, who holds all manner of dark and dirty family secrets. The Radleys is effortlessly sleek and witty." Entertainment Wkly

Haigh, Jennifer

Baker towers; a novel. William Morrow 2005 334p $24.95

ISBN 0-06-050941-4

LC 2004-49073

This novel is "set in Bakerton, a mining town in post-World World II Pennsylvania. Haigh's focus is the Novak family, particularly the five children being raised by their Italian mother after their Polish father drops dead. All five make attempts to escape Bakerton at one point or another; some are successful, others are not. George, a veteran of WW II, neglects his Bakerton fiancee and marries a cold socialite. Dorothy goes to the nation's capital to work, but a nervous breakdown brings her home. Brilliant, cold Joyce thinks her future lies with the military, but she is sorely disappointed. Sandy is the golden son who escapes to dubious success. And Lucy is the youngest, who finds herself in college despite the nagging feeling that she never wanted to leave home in the first place. Haigh creates a real sense of a community and brings her mining town to life through a large cast of minor characters who pass in and out of the Novaks' lives." Booklist

Haigh, Jennifer

The **condition**; a novel. HarperCollins 2008 390p $25.95

ISBN 978-0-06-075578-2; 0-06-075578-4

"The point of view in 'The Condition' shifts repeatedly, as each character replays the relevant scenes of his or her life. This structure adds dimension, but it slows momentum because time doesn't move forward in a linear fashion. Still, the inner lives of these people are so richly developed that they keep us engaged." Chicago Tribune

Haigh, Jennifer

Faith; a novel. Harper 2011 318p $25.99

ISBN 978-0-06-075580-5; 0-06-075580-6

LC 2010-43160

The tale "goes down with deceptive ease. Haigh's smooth prose belies its hard truths. It is relatively easy to tell a story in black and white. The art lies in writing nuanced shades of gray. 'Faith' is painted with a palette of many tones, its outlines of its character sharp and sharply human." Denver Post

Haigh, Jennifer

Mrs. Kimble. Morrow 2003 394p $24.95

ISBN 0-06-050939-2

LC 2002-70304

The title "refers to three women, each of whom marries an opportunist named Ken Kimble. The first wife, Birdie, is Ken's student at a small Christian college. With her, he has two children. Then he seduces another student and deserts his family, leaving Birdie to bring up the children alone. The second Mrs. Kimble is a successful career woman, reassessing her priorities in the wake of her mastectomy. Ken capitalizes on Joan's neediness and sweeps her off her feet. He also ingratiates himself with her uncle, a real estate tycoon. When Joan and Uncle Floyd die, Ken inherits from both. The third Mrs. Kimble had been the first Mrs. Kimble's babysitter. . . . Original and compelling. Libr J

Haimoff, Michelle

These days are ours; Michelle Haimoff. Grand Central Pub. 2012 290 p.

ISBN 9781455500291

LC 2011012929

This novel, "which unfolds in Manhattan soon after 9/11, chronicles rich kid Hailey's attempts to make a life and come to an understanding with her parents. . . . As the daughter of publishing heavyweights, Hailey knows she'll never trump their accomplishments. Though she's highly connected, she's determined to find a job on her own--and land golden boy Michael Brenner, whose close family and cozy apartment fill a void. Hailey tries to stay on Michael's radar despite his propensity for bed hopping. Unlike Michael, the Pennsylvania-born Adrian, an interloper in Hailey's social circle, works for his rent, and Hailey isn't sure how she feels about him, even though they share a similar thoughtfulness and sense of humor." (Publishers Weekly)

Hair, David

★ **Mage's** blood; David Hair. Quercus 2013 704 p. (hardcover) $26.95

ISBN 1623650143; 9781623650148; 9781623650155

LC 2013937925

This book is the first in David Hair's "Moontide Quartet" series. "After the mage Antonin Meiros created the 300-mile-long Leviathan Bridge, which appears every 13 years at the Moontide, the formerly isolated continents of wealthy Yuros (modeled on Europe) and impoverished Antipoia (modeled on India and the Middle East) have interacted through both trade and two bloody crusades. . . . As the next Moontide and crusade approach, turmoil abounds." (Publishers Weekly)

Hair, David

Scarlet tides; David Hair. Quercus 2014 704 p. illustrations $26.99

ISBN 1623658292; 9781623658298

LC 2014945600

In this novel by David Hair "with the Leviathan Bridge now uncovered from the sea, it re-opens the East to the Rondian legions and the Third Crusade ensues in the name of Emperor Constant. Rondians are determined to succeed in their latest Crusade and have recruited the strongest and most lethal magi of the Church's Inquisition to lead the way." (Publisher's note)

"The second volume in Hair's Moontide Quartet (after Mage's Blood) is mostly dizzying movement, plunging headfirst into a convoluted series of plots, unraveling alliances, and tightening nooses... Some parts of the plot that feel slower or less tense are only the eye of the storm, and will keep Hair's fans satisfied while the storm builds." Pub Wkly

Haldane, Seán ✓

★ The **devil's** making; a mystery. Seán Haldane. Minotaur Books 2015 368 p. (hardcover) $25.99

ISBN 1250069408; 9781250069405

LC 2015002683

In this mystery, by Sean Haldane, "a few thousand settlers aspire to the values of the Victorian age while coexisting beside a population of native Indians. . . . Their cautious peace is challenged when a body is discovered: Dr. McCrory, an American alienist whose methods included phrenology, Mesmerism, and sexual-mystical magnetation. Chad Hobbes, recently arrived from England, is the policeman who must solve the crime." (Publisher's note)

A "good match for readers who relish suspense drawn out at a leisurely pace, lavish details of Pacific Northwest Coast Indian life, and the particular edginess of unreliable narrators." Booklist

Haldeman, Joe W.

The **accidental** time machine; [by] Joe Haldeman. Ace Books 2007 278p $23.95

ISBN 978-0-441-01499-6

LC 2007-6935

"Lowly MIT research assistant Matt Fuller toils away in a physics lab until one day he makes an odd discovery. A sensitive quantum calibrator keeps disappearing and reappearing moments later when he hits the reset button. With a little tinkering, Matt realizes that the device functions as a crude, forward-traveling time machine. With visions of Nobel Prizes dancing in his head, he latches it to a car and leaps into the future. The interesting wrinkle here is that each jump ahead is 12 times longer than the last. Matt's successive futures involve jail time, unwelcome celebrity, and assorted holocausts in the earth's climate. He begins to long for his native era. As usual, Haldeman's ingenuity delivers cutting-edge technological speculation and irresistibly compelling reading." Booklist

Haldeman, Joe W.

The **coming**; {by} Joe Haldeman. Ace Bks. 2000 216p

ISBN 0-441-00769-4

LC 00-29306

"On 1 October 2054, astronomy professor Rory Bell receives a message, 'We're coming,' from an Earthbound object way out in space that will arrive on New Year's Day. Soon Rory, her composer husband, her chief faculty protege, the university president, a mob shakedown artist, a Gainesville cop, the mayor, the governor of Florida, and, finally, the president and her cabinet are all conniving away in response to the momentous announcement. . . . Haldeman's fast-paced, cannily constructed yarn is ultimately most like that granddaddy of first-contact flicks, The Day the Earth Stood Still. Maybe better." Booklist

Haldeman, Joe W.

Forever free; [by] Joe Haldeman. Ace Bks. 1999 277p

ISBN 0-441-00697-3

LC 99-33231

This novel "reintroduces readers to William Mandella {featured in Forever War} who has been living peacefully on the planet called Middle Finger, a refuge for humans who refuse to become part of the group mind known as Man. But after decades of this peace, Mandella and others are tired of living like zoo animals. They're ready for a challenge, and they'd like to see Earth again. So they steal a starship—and embark upon a voyage that will forever change their understanding of the universe . . . and themselves." Publisher's note

Haldeman, Joe W.

Forever peace; {by} Joe Haldeman. Ace Bks. 1997 326p

ISBN 0-441-00406-7

LC 96-52650

The author "writes with uncommon intelligence and acuity about the terror of war and the horror of the human heritage in the middle of the next century." Publ Wkly

Haldeman, Joe W.

★ The **forever** war; [by] Joe Haldeman. St. Martin's Press 1975 236p

"A naturalistic description of a war that lasts more than a thousand years, although the main characters age only a few years because of the relativistic effects of faster-than-light space travel. The situation of the soldiers fighting in this kind of war is complicated, however, by their alienation from their own societies by the time-dilation effect, and their growing disillusionment with the war." New Ency of Sci Fic

Haldeman, Joe W.

Marsbound; [by] Joe Haldeman. Ace Books 2008 296p $24.95

ISBN 978-0-441-01595-5; 0-441-01595-6

LC 2008-19356

"Recalling Robert A. Heinlein's Red Planet and Podkayne of Mars, Haldeman updates the Martian setting while keeping faith in his characters' ability to respond to unexpected challenges." Publ Wkly

Haldeman, Joe W.

Starbound; [by] Joe Haldeman. Ace Books 2010 292p $24.95

ISBN 978-0-441-01817-8; 0-441-01817-3

LC 2009-40932

"Haldeman's crisp storytelling and juicy plot twists keep us captivated throughout." Booklist

Hale, Benjamin

The **evolution** of Bruno Littlemore. Twelve 2011 578p $25.99

ISBN 978-0-446-57157-9; 0-446-57157-1

LC 2010-12098

Bruno, the novel's "singular protagonist, is a 25-year-old chimp born at a zoo and raised by researchers who taught him to read, write, and speak. The trappings of humanity, unfortunately, have come with unexpected wants and desires, and Bruno ends up falling in love with one of his handlers. Deeply. Making your main character a talking ape — and one who engages in a romantic liaison with a human being, no less — is ambitious, to say the least. But from the first page, it is clear that Bruno is more than mere literary gimmickry; he is fascinating and fully formed. You learn as much by what he withholds as by what he provides, and he withholds a lot . . . . Where the novel should be offensive, it is often tender, and where it should be risible, it is genuinely funny." Entertainment Wkly

Hale, Shannon

Austenland; a novel. Bloomsbury 2007 197p $19.95
ISBN 1-59691-285-5; 978-1-59691-285-4

LC 2006-34165

The author's "charming first book for adults is chick lit with soul. Though there's a laugh on nearly every page—Hale, like Austen, is adept at subtly skewering the ridiculous—there's also the more serious story of a woman learning the difference between fantasy and reality, and discovering that real life can be better than your dreams." Bookpage

Hall, Adam

Quiller Balalaika. Carroll & Graf/Otto Penzler 2003 242p $24
ISBN 0-7867-1265-1
First published 1996 in the United Kingdom

"The detritus of the cold war in the former Soviet Union comprises self-serving bureaucracies, opportunistic ex-KGBers, and organized criminals who make their U.S. mafioso counterparts seem like mischievous delinquents. Into the mix drops pseudonymous Brit agent Quiller, with the intent of taking out a British national-Basil Seckes, aka Vasyl Sakkas-who is secretly heading up the burgeoning Russian criminal empire. To bring down Sakkas' empire, Quiller needs the help of one Marius Antonov, currently residing in a Gulag prison. Freeing Antonov entails Quiller making his way into the prison and then escaping with his target, no small feat because the prison is virtually escape proof. . . . The book is a typically atmospheric, exciting Quiller adventure." Booklist

Hall, Adam

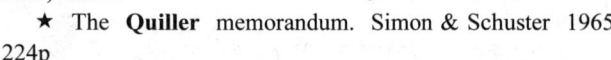

★ The **Quiller** memorandum. Simon & Schuster 1965 224p
Published in the United Kingdom with title: The Berlin memorandum

"Quiller is a British 'Shadow executive', employed by 'the Bureau', a government agency assigned to carry out delicate tasks, and it is so secret it does not exist. As we follow Quiller's 'brain-think' sequences we learn that during the Second World War he was an infiltrator who arranged escapes from Nazi concentration camps. Quiller and others like him with specialised skills, do the jobs that M15 and M16 cannot do. Quiller is used only at the authorisation of the Prime Minister. In The Quiller Memorandum he exposes a large, well-organised neo-Nazi conspiracy in Berlin." McCormick and Fletcher. Spy Fic

Hall, Adam

Quiller Salamander. Penzler Bks. 1994 247p
ISBN 1-883402-40-9

LC 94-17372

"Mr. Hall, a master of intense prose and tense situations, has again come up with a story that wil not disappoint his admirers." N Y Times Book Rev

Hall, Adam

Quiller solitaire. Morrow 1992 286p
ISBN 0-688-10730-3

LC 91-31060

"When a fellow agent who has called upon him for protection is murdered before his eyes, an enraged and embarrassed Quiller pressures his superiors into giving him the dead man's assignment to investigate the murder of a British cultural attache in Berlin. The murder is apparently tied to former East German national Dieter Klaus, a madman who wants to gain attention for his terrorist splinter group." Publ Wkly

Hall, Barbara

The **music** teacher; a novel. Algonquin Books of Chapel Hill 2009 292p
ISBN 978-1-56512-463-9

LC 2008-41336

"It feels like an ancient story—the tired, disappointed teacher who has long since given up on her own talent meets the young student who truly has a shot at greatness. . . . Pearl Swain is a violin teacher. Her 14-year-old student, Hallie Bolaris, is brimming with promise, but Pearl's vicarious desires become a problem. She crosses too many boundaries and punishes her student for pushing her away. 'The Music Teacher' is a study of the many ways to crush the creative human spirit. 'Did you get anything from me?' Pearl asks her estranged student. The question echoes long after the novel ends." Los Angeles Times Book Rev

Hall, James W.

Buzz cut; by James W. Hall. Delacorte Press 1996 374p

LC 95-50425

In this mystery, "Thorn and Sugar take security detail on a luxury Caribbean cruiseship only to find that a brilliant madman named Butler Jack has hijacked the ship for reasons clear only to himself. Butler creates general havoc on board, altering the ship's course, causing near collisions, and randomly killing crew and passengers in spectacularly bloody fashion. Thorn and Sugar slowly unravel the twisted tale of greed and madness that drives the mind of the hijacker, finally reaching a very surprising truth." Libr J

Hall, James W.

Going Dark; James W. Hall. Minotaur Books 2013 304 p. (Thorn P.I.) (hardcover) $25.99
ISBN 1250005000; 9781250005007

LC 2013024718

In this book, by James W. Hall, "Earth Liberation Front, known as ELF, is a loosely knit organization comprised of environmental activists . . . Flynn Moss, Thorn's newly discovered son, has naively fallen in with an ELF cell in Miami which has its sights on Turkey Point, the largest nuclear power plant in the state. . . . With a growing sense of dread about the group's true intentions, Flynn summons Thorn to help him escape from Prince Key . . . where the ELF group is camped." (Publisher's note)

Hall, James W.

Off the chart; a novel. St. Martin's Minotaur 2003 337p $24.95
ISBN 0-312-27178-6

LC 2002-191965

"Yes, we like to imagine ourselves wearing Thorn's deck shoes, in a full-frontal assault on all those who endanger our world, but Hall, unlike most thriller writers, portrays the collateral damage wreaked when rugged individualists go into overdrive. This remains one of the best series in the genre." Booklist

Hall, James W.

Red sky at night; by James W. Hall. Delacorte Press 1997 326p
ISBN 0-385-31638-0

LC 96-45621

"Ensconced in his Key Largo beach house, Thorn seems to have carved a lasting separate peace with the modern world until a senseless crime drives the other side of his personality to the fore, the side that says, 'There's something broken, and I have to fix it.' What's broken this time, though, is Thorn himself, mysteriously paralyzed from the waist down after attempting to confront an apparent prowler. The story begins with the slaughter of several dolphins—killed for their endorphins, the key ingredient in a miracle, pain-killing drug—and extends to Thorn's distant past and his relationship with his best childhood friend, who has been nursing a grudge against Thorn for decades. . . . Popular fiction at its absolute best." Booklist

Hall, Louisa

Speak; Louisa Hall. Ecco 2015 336 p. $27.99

ISBN 0062391194; 9780062391193

Author Louisa Hall presents a "novel that explores the creation of Artificial Intelligence--illuminating the very human need for communication, connection, and understanding.Characters [attempt] to communicate across gaps—to estranged spouses, lost friends, future readers, or a computer program that may or may not understand them." (Publisher's note)

"Much like Daniel H. Wilson's Robopocalypse (2011), Speak relies on primary-source documents to tell its story. An even better comparison is to David Mitchell's Cloud Atlas (2004) for the way Hall subtly weaves a thread through a temporally diverse cast of narrators. Like all good robot novels, Speak raises questions about what it means to be human as well as the meaning of giving voice to memory." Booklist

Hall, Radclyffe

The **well** of loneliness; with a commentary by Havelock Ellis. Covici 1928 506p

This autobiographical novel traces "the life of the wealthy young woman Stephen Gordon from birth to her full realization that she is a 'congenital invert' (as she terms it), a lesbian by nature. . . . It is the first full, rich portrait of a lesbian in literature. At the time the publication was an act of outstanding bravery." British Women Writers

Hall, Steven

The **raw** shark texts. Canongate 2007 428p il $24

ISBN 1-84195-902-2

"The novel's great virtue is its structure. Narrative tricks keep the reader surprised. Information is released in pieces, like time-release drugs in a capsule, their order derived from the progressive revelation of truths rather than the forward march of events. Only at the end do we accelerate towards a more conventional action-packed climax, though even that takes place in a sort of collective unconscious. In many ways, this is cyberfiction, a battle between archetypes in a virtual reality." Times Lit Suppl

Hall, Tarquin

The **case** of the deadly butter chicken; from the files of Vish Puri, India's most private investigator. Tarquin Hall. Simon & Schuster 2012 341 p.

ISBN 9781451613155

LC 2011052702

This book is the third in the Vish Puri detective series. Here, Puri tries to solve the case of the mysterious death of Faheem Khan, "a Pakistani cricket-ace's father. . . . Unfortunately, Faheem's son Kamran, bowler for the Kolkata Colts, has gone back to Rawalpindi to mourn. So Puri, who had never met a Pakistani in person before the Khans, must travel across a most-feared border in pursuit of justice." (Kirkus)

Hall, Tarquin

The **case** of the love commandos; from the files of Vish Puri, India's most private investigator. by Tarquin Hall. Simon & Schuster 2013 320 p. (hardcover) $24.99

ISBN 1451613261; 9781451613261; 9781451613285

LC 2013009100

In this book by Tarquin Hall, "when Ram and Tulsi fall in love, [her] parents are dead set against the union. She's from a high-caste family; he's an Untouchable. Tulsi's father locks her up and promises to hunt down [Ram]. Volunteers dedicated to helping mixed-caste couples, come to the rescue. After they liberate Tulsi, Ram is mysteriously snatched from . . . hiding. It falls to Vish Puri to track down Ram and reunite the star-crossed lovers." (Publisher's note)

Hallberg, Garth Risk

★ **City** on fire; A Novel. by Garth Risk Hallberg. Alfred A. Knopf 2015 944 p. illustrations (hardcover) $30

ISBN 9780385353779; 9780804172950; 0385353774

LC 2014041963

This novel, by Garth Risk Hallberg, takes place in "New York City, 1976. Meet Regan and William Hamilton-Sweeney, estranged heirs to one of the city's great fortunes; Keith and Mercer, the men who, for better or worse, love them; Charlie and Samantha, two suburban teenagers seduced by downtown's punk scene; an obsessive magazine reporter and his idealistic neighbor—and the detective trying to figure out what any of them have to do with a shooting in Central Park on New Year's Eve." (Publisher's note)

"Graceful in execution, hugely entertaining, and most concerned with the longing for connection, a theme that reaches full realization during the blackout of 1977, this epic tale is both a compelling mystery and a literary tour de force." Booklist

Hallgrimur Helgason

101 Reykjavik; a novel. translated by Brian FitzGibbon. Scribner 2003 339p $23

ISBN 0-7432-2514-7

LC 2002-29434

"This novel uses caustic and irreverent humor to paint a vivid picture of Icelandic youth ideas and culture. . . . While the protagonist is confused, depressed, and futureless, the humor saves the book from being depressing." Libr J

Hallinan, Timothy

Crashed; a Junior Bender novel. Timothy Hallinan. Soho Crime 2012 356 p. (hbk. : alk. paper) $25

ISBN 1616952741; 9781616952747; 9781616952754

LC 2012033577

In this book, by Timothy Hallinan, "Junior Bender, a burglar with a magic touch, is being blackmailed into taking on a new freelance job. One of LA's biggest crime bosses is producing a porn movie that someone keeps sabotaging; Junior's job is to figure out who's responsible and keep the movie on track. The trouble is, he's not sure he can go through with the job, blackmail or no blackmail." (Publisher's note)

Other books about Junior Bender are:

Little Elvises (2013)

The Fame Thief (2013)

Herbie's Game (2014)

King Maybe (2016)

Fields Where They Lay (2016)

Hallinan, Timothy

★ **Fields** where they lay; a Junior Bender holiday mystery. Timothy Hallinan. Soho Press 2016 376 p. (Junior Bender Series) (hardcover) $25.95

ISBN 9781616957476; 9781616957469

LC 2016017076

In this book in the Junior Bender Mysteries series, by Timothy Hallinan, "Junior Bender . . . finds himself stuck inside the Edgerton Mall. . . . The mall is a fossil of an industry in decline; . . . [it has] a rampant shoplifting problem. The murderous Russian mobster who owns the place has decided it takes a thief to catch a thief and hires Junior . . . to solve the shoplifting problem for him. But Junior's surveillance operation doesn't go well." (Publisher's note)

"A plum pudding stuffed with cynical disillusionment, organized and disorganized crime, two Santas, a seasonal miracle, and an ending that earns every bit of its uplift." Kirkus

Halter, Marek

Sarah; a novel. Crown Publishers 2004 294 p. map $22

ISBN 1-400-05272-6

LC 2003-19648

Original French edition, 2003

"Sarah is the favorite daughter of a lord of Ur, a city-state of Sumeria. Raised in luxury and privilege, she defies her father on the day of her marriage and escapes into the lower city, where she meets Abraham of the nomadic mar.Tu people. Although soldiers take her home, she can't forget the young man who captured her heart and imagination. Owing to an injudicious use of infertility herbs in an effort to stave off marriage, Sarah renders herself sterile and is dedicated to the temple of Ishtar, where she serves as a revered Sacred Handmaid of the Blood for several years until she meets Abraham again. This time, she successfully escapes, and the two dedicate themselves to the one, true, invisible God and create a nation." Libr J

Hambly, Barbara

★ **Days** of the dead. Bantam Bks. 2003 314p il maps $23.95

ISBN 0-553-10954-5

LC 2002-38571

"An extreme case of culture shock awaits Benjamin January. . .when he leaves cosmopolitan New Orleans, a city that loves life, for bellicose Mexico, a country that lives for its dead. Traveling with his bride, Rose, by overland coach in 1835, this Paris-trained surgeon (and former slave) encounters bloodthirsty bandits, fierce soldiers from Santa Anna's army, rebellious Yankees from uncivilized Texas and a hacienda teeming with feuding relatives on the country estate of the Spanish grandee Don Prospero's only son." N Y Times Book Rev

Hambly, Barbara

Dead water; Barbara Hambly. Bantam Books 2004 297p $25

ISBN 0-553-10964-2

LC 2004-40766

This Benjamin January adventure "finds the amateur sleuth investigating a couple of mysteries. The bank that holds all his money has suddenly and suspiciously collapsed, and someone has apparently put a curse on a former student in the small school operated by January's wife, Rose. Just goes to show: New Orleans, circa 1836, is a wild and dangerous place. . . . Where many writers of historical mysteries get bogged down in exposition, or in cataloging details that most readers are not interested in, Hambly keeps things moving, always focused on her characters and her story, and not on showing off the quantity of research she's done." Booklist

Hambly, Barbara

Die upon a kiss. Bantam Bks. 2001 333p

ISBN 0-553-10924-3

LC 00-69666

In antebellum New Orleans "cultural war is declared between rival American and Creole opera houses when an Italian company attempts to open the season for the upstart Americans with an original and provocative version of 'Othello.' The composer is knifed in the alley, the lead soprano is poisoned, a prominent opera patron is murdered, and—oh, yes, the theater is torched. Benjamin January, a former slave and accomplished musician who plays in the orchestra, is well positioned for this backstage investigation." N Y Times Book Rev

Hambly, Barbara

A **free** man of color. Bantam Bks. 1997 311p hardcover o.p. pa $5.99

ISBN 0-553-10258-3; 0-553-57526-0 pa

LC 96-44942

"A few suspenseful moments not-withstanding, this isn't an action-packed or suspenseful whodunit. Rather, it's a richly detailed, telling portrait of an intricately structured racial hierarchy." Booklist

Hambly, Barbara

Good man Friday; by Barbara Hambly. Severn House 2013 250 p. (hardcover) $29.95

ISBN 0727882554; 9780727882554

This is the 12th installment in Barbara Hambly's Benjamin January mystery series. Here, "when money becomes tight, January takes on an unusual assignment that requires him to leave New Orleans for Washington. Needless to say, 1838 wasn't the safest of times for a free man of color." (Library Journal)

Hambly, Barbara

Graveyard dust. Bantam Bks. 1999 315p

ISBN 0-553-10259-1

LC 98-43456

"Hambly's plot, which revolves around evils confined to no race or class, is complex and often hard to track, but its emotional authenticity, varied cast and rich historical trappings give the novel power and depth." Publ Wkly

Includes bibliographical references

Hambly, Barbara

Patriot hearts; a novel of the founding mothers. Bantam Dell 2007 430p $25

ISBN 978-0-553-80428-7; 0-553-80428-6

LC 2006-24174

This historical novel "opens with First Lady Dolley Madison waiting anxiously for husband 'Jemmy' and deciding what to save if they must flee the White House during the War of 1812. She is thus reminded of her predecessors Martha Washington and Abigail Adams, as well as Sally Hemings, and each of these women has her turn at personal narratives, which take place at critical points in the nation's early years and in their personal lives. The perspective offered is distinctly feminine and gives readers a sense of peeking backstage at a play they know well." Libr J

Hambly, Barbara

Ran away; Barbara Hambly. Severn House 2011 244p.

ISBN 9780727880826

This novel follows the story of fictional character Ben January, who "fled New Orleans to escape its racism, . . . [and] settled in Paris, where he eked out a living as a musician while studying medicine. He met, fell in love with and married Ayasha, who asked him to help out Shamira, a sick, pregnant concubine in the household of Hüseyin Pasha, a wealthy Turk. . . . When Ayasha was abducted and Shamira's fate necessitated exchanging her infant son for her freedom, Ben came to believe Pasha honorable and trustworthy. That's why five years on, back home in New Orleans after Ayasha's death from cholera, Ben disputes the findings that declare that Pasha . . . tossed two of his concubines, Noura and Karida, from a window in his house. With an assist from his current wife Rose and his friend, ex-opium addict Hannibal, Ben steps in to prove Pasha innocent of murder." (Kirkus)

Hambly, Barbara

★ **Sold** down the river. Bantam Bks. 2000 317p $23.95

ISBN 0-553-10257-5

LC 99-54845

A historical mystery "featuring Benjamin January, a freed slave whose Paris education earns him a living in New Orleans and whose refined sense of justice puts him in peril wherever he goes. . . . Ben bends his back to the pain and humiliation of being a slave again when he goes undercover at a sugar cane plantation 20 miles up the river, were a rebellion may be brewing." N Y Times Book Rev

Hambly, Barbara

Wet grave. Bantam Bks. 2002 288p

ISBN 0-553-10935-9

LC 2001-43401

"As with any good historical mystery, we are at least as captivated by the characters, dialogue, and environment as we are with the mystery itself." Booklist

Hamer, Kate

The **girl** in the red coat; Kate Hamer. Melville House 2016 384 p. (hardback) $25.95

ISBN 9781612195001; 1612195008

LC 2015019006

"Beth has one constant, gnawing worry: that her dreamy eight-year-old daughter, Carmel, who has a tendency to wander off, will one day go missing. And then one day, it happens: . . . they get separated in the crowd, and Carmel is gone. Beth sets herself on the grim and lonely mission to find her daughter. Carmel, meanwhile, is on a strange and harrowing journey of her own--to a totally unexpected place that requires her to live by her wits." (Publisher's note)

"Telling the story in two remarkable voices, with Beth's chapters unfurling in past tense and Carmel's in present tense, the author weaves a page-turning narrative. The trajectories of the novel's two leads--through despair, hope, and redemption--are believable and nuanced, resulting in a morally complex, haunting read." Pub Wkly

Hamid, Mohsin, 1971-

★ **Exit** West; Mohsin Hamid. Penguin Group USA 2017 240 p. (hardcover) $26

ISBN 0735212171; 9780735212176

LC 2016036296

Kirkus Prize Finalist: Fiction (2017)

Man Booker Prize Shortlist (2017)

National Book Critics Circle Award Finalist: Fiction (2017)

In this novel, by Mohsin Hamid, "in a country teetering on the brink of civil war, two young people meet . . . [and] embark on a furtive love affair. . . . They begin to hear whispers about doors--doors that can whisk people far away, if perilously and for a price. As the violence escalates, Nadia and Saeed decide that they no longer have a choice. Leaving their homeland and their old lives behind, they find a door and step through." (Publisher's note)

"Hamid's storytelling is stripped down, and the book's sweeping allegory is timely and resonant." Pub Wkly

Hamid, Mohsin, 1971-

★ **How** to Get Filthy Rich in Rising Asia; Mohsin Hamid. Riverhead Books Inc. 2013 240 p. $26.95

ISBN 1594487294; 9781594487293

LC 2012039847

This book, by Mohsin Hamid, presents the "tale of a man's journey from impoverished rural boy to corporate tycoon [and] steals its shape from the business self-help books devoured by ambitious youths all over 'rising Asia.' It follows its nameless hero to the sprawling metropolis where he begins to amass an empire built on that most fluid, and increasingly scarce, of goods: water. Yet his heart remains set on something else, on the pretty girl whose star rises along with his." (Publisher's note)

Hamid, Mohsin, 1971-

The **reluctant** fundamentalist. Harcourt 2007 184p $22

ISBN 0-15-101304-7; 9780151013043

LC 2006-21732

The narrator is "a young Pakistani man named Changez. . . . The novel begins a few years after 9/11. Changez happens upon [an] American in Lahore, invites him to tea and tells him the story of his life in the months just before and after the attacks." (N Y Times Book Rev)

"This is a deeply provocative, excellent addition to the burgeoning sub-genre of September 11 novels. But it would be an understatement to call it merely that. Here is a novel rich in irony and intelligence. Hamid shows us the post-September 11 world from another angle. In doing so he offers up a mirror to the complex business of East-West encounters in these troubled times." Sydney Morning Herald

Hamill, Pete

Forever; a novel. Little, Brown 2002 613p $25.95

ISBN 0-316-34111-8

LC 2002-114241

"In 1740, an Irish Jew named Cormac O'Connor heads to New York in pursuit of the man who killed his father and gets tangled up in a rebellion against the English. Through a series of events involving an African slave with shamanistic powers, he is granted eternal life, provided that he never leaves Manhattan. There follows a tour of the city's history through Cormac's eyes: the political corruption and the poverty, but also the majestic growth of the metropolis through its culture, its buildings, and its people." New Yorker

Hamill, Pete

Tabloid city; a novel. Little, Brown and Co. 2011 278p $26.99

ISBN 978-0-316-02075-6; 0-316-02075-3

LC 2010-26166

"Just as the last ever edition of the New York World is getting put to bed, veteran editor Sam Briscoe stops the presses for a sensational murder: socialite Cynthia Harding and her personal secretary are found stabbed to death in Harding's Manhattan town house. The story unfolds in time-stamped, you-are-there bursts that follow a large cast, including several journalists; Cynthia's adopted daughter; a disgraced Madoff-like financier; a media blogger; the murdered secretary's husband, a police officer assigned to a counterterrorism task force, as well as their son, a convert to radical Islam; and best of all by the weary and worldly Briscoe himself. Hamill is at his best in the Briscoe portions, rich in print anecdotes and mournful for a passing age." Publ Wkly

Hamilton, Jane

Disobedience; a novel. Doubleday 2000 272p $24.95

ISBN 0-385-50117-X

LC 00-29504

"Hamilton has written a novel so disturbing that no one will enjoy reading it. But 'Disobedience' is so provocative that you must." Christ Sci Monit

Hamilton, Jane

★ A **map** of the world. Doubleday 1994 389p

ISBN 0-385-47310-9

LC 93-45723

This is "not an easy or light read; indeed, it takes on some of the toughest issues of modern life. But the writer's skill in describing a community and a way of life, as well as her insight into the hearts of her characters, render this story difficult to forget." Christ Sci Monit

Hamilton, Jane

The **short** history of a prince; a novel. Random House 1998 349p

ISBN 0-679-45755-0

LC 97-31627

"Hamilton has an amazing way with the varieties of human pain. Her characters live with ordinary and sometimes extraordinary torment, yet her writing remains bouyant and her sensibility full of light." Newsweek

Hamilton, Jane

When Madeline was young; a novel. Doubleday 2006 273p $22.95

ISBN 0-385-51671-1

LC 2006-40238

"Hamilton has never written more finely nuanced or beguiling prose, imagined more fascinating characters, or posed more provocative moral dilemmas. In each surprising permutation, Hamilton offers fresh perspectives on the puzzles of time, memory, and consciousness, and keenly gauges the many shades of guilt and audacity, grief and sacrifice, tenacity and goodness." Booklist

Hamilton, Masha

The **camel** bookmobile. Harper Collins 2007 308p $24.95

ISBN 978-0-06-117348-6; 0-06-117348-7

LC 2006-41316

"Hamilton's portrayal of nomadic culture is lovingly and colorfully told. It's a painterly glimpse into a world that few Westerners will ever see." USA Today

Hamilton, Peter F.

The **dreaming** void. Del Rey/Ballantine Books 2007 630p $26.95

ISBN 978-0-345-49653-9; 0-345-49653-1

LC 2007-29244

"There is a generous cast of characters and a handful of storylines involved here and it takes the overall story a while to get going. But once it does, it feels like putting on a comfortable jacket; space opera is what Hamilton does and he does it well." SF Signal

Hamilton, Peter F.

★ **Great** north road; Peter F. Hamilton. Del Rey/Ballantine Books 2012 976 p. (hardcover : alk. paper) $30

ISBN 034552666X; 9780345526663; 9780345526687

LC 2012033593

In author Peter F. Hamilton's book, "Sid is a solid investigator" who "must navigate through a Byzantine minefield of competing interests within the police department and the world's political and economic elite . . . all the while hunting down a brutal killer poised to strike again. And on St. Libra, Angela," a "convicted slayer . . . newly released from prison, joins a mission to hunt down the elusive alien, only to learn that the line between hunter and hunted is a thin one." (Publisher's note)

Hamilton, Peter F.

Pandora's star. Del Rey\Ballantine Books 2004 758p $26.95

ISBN 0-345-46162-2

LC 2003-68753

"By the 24th century, the vast human Commonwealth has spread from Earth via artificial wormholes. Various benign or seemingly indifferent alien races have been encountered during exploration of new planets, but an astronomer sparks curiosity by announcing that a pair of stars is enclosed by a mysterious energy barrier. Unfortunately, a space expedition discovers that the shield was created to imprison an insatiably greedy mass mind that sees any other race as a mortal threat. When the barrier somehow is lowered, the alien immediately attacks the largely unprepared Commonwealth, while humans begin wondering if yet another inhuman power has manipulated events that unleashed this threat. The author deftly juggles many characters in multiple plot lines." Publ Wkly

Hamilton, Steve

★ The **lock** artist; Steve Hamilton. Minotaur Books 2010 304 p. $24.99

ISBN 0312380429; 9780312380427

LC 2009034523

Dagger Awards: CWA Ian Fleming Steel Dagger (2011), Edgar Allan Poe Awards: Best Novel (2011), Alex Award (2011)

In this book, "traumatized at the age of eight, Michael, now eighteen, is no ordinary young man. Besides not uttering a single word in ten years, he discovers the one thing he can somehow do better than anyone else. Whether it's a locked door without a key, a padlock with no combination, or even an eight-hundred pound safe, . . . he can open them all. . . . [His] talent . . . will make young Michael a hot commodity with the wrong people and, whether he likes it or not, push him ever close to a life of crime. Until he finally sees his chance to escape, and with one desperate gamble risks everything to come back home to the only person he ever loved, and to unlock the secret that has kept him silent for so long." (Publisher's note)

Hamilton, Steve

★ The **second** life of Nick Mason; Steve Hamilton. G. P. Putnam's Sons 2016 288 p. hbk $26

ISBN 0399574328; 9780399574320

LC 2016007258

In this novel, by Steve Hamilton, "Nick Mason has already spent five years inside a maximum security prison when an offer comes that will grant his release twenty years early. . . . Now, . . . whenever his cell phone rings, day or night, Nick must answer it and follow whatever order he is given. It's the deal he made with Darius Cole, a criminal mastermind serving a double-life term who runs an empire from his prison cell." (Publisher's note)

Hammett, Dashiell

★ **Complete** novels. Library of Am. 1999 967p $35

ISBN 1-88301-167-1

LC 98-53911

In Red harvest the nameless operative for the Continental Detective Agency in San Francisco known as the Continental Op fights political corruption in the town of Personville, referred to by its citizens as "Poisonville." In The Dain curse Continental Op solves a jewel burglary, multiple murders, and deals with drug addiction and a family curse

Hammett, Dashiell

The **glass** key. Knopf 1931 282p

Appointed special investigator in the district attorney's office to track down the murderer of a Senator's son, Ned Beaumont becomes involved with political bosses, bootlegging gangsters and romance

"One of the two best novels by the man who is generally regarded as the creator and still the acknowledged master of the 'hard-boiled' school of detective fiction. Brutal in its subject matter but excellently written." Howard Haycraft

Hammett, Dashiell

★ The **Maltese** falcon. Knopf 1930 276p

This novel "called the best American detective novel by some critics, opens with Space accepting a case from Brigid O'Shaughnessy, a statuesque redhead masquerading as a Miss Wonderly. Almost immediately, his partner, Miles Archer is killed. Spade hated him and has been having an affair with his wife, but feels duty-bound to find his killer. He becomes involved with an odd assortment of characters, each searching for a statue of a black bird, about a foot high, said to be worth a fortune." Ency of Mystery & Detection

Hammett, Dashiell

★ The **thin** man. Knopf 1934 259p

"One of the first works to bring humor, and of a distinctly native brand, to the detective story in this country." Howard Haycraft

Han, Kang, 1970-

★ **Human** Acts; A Novel. Han Kang. Portobello Books Ltd 2016 224 p. (ebook) $65; (pbk.) $22

ISBN 9781101906729; 9781101906736; 1846275962; 9781846275968

LC 2016002979

This historical novel, written by Han Kang and translated by Deborah Smith, tells how "in the midst of a violent student uprising in South Korea, a young boy named Dong-ho is shockingly killed. The story of this tragic episode unfolds in a sequence of interconnected chapters as the victims and the bereaved encounter suppression, denial, and the echoing agony of the massacre." (Publisher's note)

"A fiercely written, deeply upsetting, and beautifully human novel." Kirkus

Han, Kang, 1970-

★ The **vegetarian**; Han Kang ; translated from the Korean by Deborah Smith. Hogarth 2015 188 p. (hardcover) $21

ISBN 0553448188; 9780553448184; 9781101906118

LC 2015002206

Man Booker International Prize (2016)

In this novel, by Han Kang, translated by Deborah Smith, winner of the 2016 Man Booker International Prize, "before the nightmares began, Yeong-hye and her husband lived an ordinary, controlled life. But the dreams—invasive images of blood and brutality—torture her, driving Yeong-hye to purge her mind and renounce eating meat altogether. It's a small act of independence, but it interrupts her marriage and sets into motion an increasingly grotesque chain of events at home." (Publisher's note)

"Divided into three novellas, The Vegetarian shows how one woman's step toward independence destroys a family that thrives on oppression and what they consider to be normal." Booklist

Han, Suyin

The **enchantress**. Bantam Bks. 1985 345p

LC 84-45185

"This is an extremely well-told tale of life and love in the 18th Century. History comes alive, and there is a masterful blending of magic and science at a time when the division between the two were not so great." SLJ

Hand, Elizabeth, 1957-

Available dark; a thriller. Elizabeth Hand. Minotaur Books 2012 246 p.

ISBN 9780312585945

LC 2011032833

In this mystery novel, a "moody loner heads to Helsinki and beyond, while murder and general creepiness follow. Photographer Cass Neary likes to live under the radar. . . . When Anton Bredahl, a collector of obscure art, contacts Cass to have her verify the authenticity of some prints, the job takes her all the way to Helsinki, where she meets with . . . photographer Ilkka Kaltunnen. . . . These aren't your standard point-and-shoots; they're morbid and macabre scenes of death, almost like stills from a snuff film. Cass . . . starts to grow suspicious of why Anton might want to spend so much on these pictures. . . . Cass hightails it to Reykjavik to locate her old love Quinn. Somehow, finding him enfolds her further in the creepy world she thought she left behind in Helsinki." (Kirkus)

Hand, Elizabeth

★ **Generation** loss; a novel. Small Beer Press 2007 265p $24

ISBN 978-1-931520-21-8; 1-931520-21-6

LC 2006-102024

This is a "crossover novel, difficult to classify, uncomfortable, spiky. Hand is one of those writers who has challenged the restrictions of genre writing. Here, she both fights with and against the conventions of the thriller genre to get at an evil deeper than its mere perpetrator. . . . So although Generation Loss moves like a thriller, it detonates with greater resound. It's a dark and beautiful novel that should not be read by anyone under the age of 30." Washington Post Book World

Other titles about Cass Neary are:
Available dark (2012)
Hard light (2016)

Handke, Peter

★ **Don** Juan; his own version. translated from the German by Krishna Winston. Farrar, Straus and Giroux 2010 101p $22

ISBN 978-0-374-14231-5; 0-374-14231-9

LC 2009-29526

Original German edition, 2004

"In this quick and airy fantasia, the quintessential womanizer becomes instead a sad and mostly passive man, possessing a certain magnetism but emphatically not a seducer, who feels pursued by time itself. Handke's multilayered structure has a sympathetic narrator relaying Don Juan's account of travel through contemporary Europe, the Middle East, and North Africa. Women everywhere are drawn to him, and in his brief affairs he drops into 'womantime,' a dreamlike state free of the usual self-consciousness and sorrow. The novel's action is obscured behind screens of philosophically tinted analysis touching on the nature of relationships, storytelling, and time. And yet the story itself is suffused with the freshness of the French countryside in which it largely takes place." New Yorker

Handler, Daniel

Adverbs. Ecco 2006 272p $23.95

ISBN 0-06-072441-2

LC 2005-52101

This novel is composed of "intertwining vignettes about love in all of its adverbial misery. Each piece, with an adverb for a title, focuses on young men and women negotiating the minefields of intimate relationships. People disappear, only to reappear in later stories skewering assumptions that were first developed in the earlier tales. . . . The stories feature two recurring images: that of the magpie picking up glittering pieces of material and depositing them in other stories, reflecting reality at different angles, and that of a catastrophic explosion–possibly natural, possibly human-made–that destroys everything and everyone in its wake." Libr J

Handler, Daniel, 1970-

We are pirates; a novel. Daniel Handler. Bloomsbury USA 2015 288 p. (hardcover : acid-free paper) $26

ISBN 1608196887; 9781608196883

LC 2014021908

In this book by Daniel Handler, "Phil Needle, a semi-successful radio producer (also semi-successful as a father, spouse, and son), hires a new (young, attractive, outspoken) assistant and sets out to further his career. His daughter, Gwen (14, in trouble again), yearns for something more, makes a few new friends, and proceeds to literally steal a boat and attempt old-fashioned piracy in the modern San Francisco Bay, consequences be damned." (Booklist)

"The reader will delight in Gwen and old Errol's escapades, which involve plenty of jawboning but some good old-fashioned larcenous action, too, all of which affords her the street cred to say piratical things like, 'You take one more step away and I'll split your gullet' and 'Totally verily.' Affecting, lively and expertly told. Just the sort of thing to make grown-ups and teenagers alike want to unfurl the black flag." Kirkus

Hannah, Kristin, 1960-

Fly Away; Kristin Hannah. 1st ed. St Martins Pr 2013 416 p. (hardcover) $27.99

ISBN 0312577214; 9780312577216

LC 2013009097

In this novel, by Kristin Hannah, "Tully Hart has always been larger than life, a woman fueled by big dreams and driven by memories of a painful past. She thinks she can overcome anything until her best friend, Kate Ryan, dies. Tully tries to fulfill her deathbed promise to Kate---to be there for Kate's children--but Tully knows nothing about family or motherhood or taking care of people." (Publisher's note)

Hannah, Kristin, 1960-

★ The **great** alone; Kristin Hannah. First U.S. edition St. Martin's Press 2018 448 p. (hardcover) $28.99; (paperback) $16.99

ISBN 9780312577230; 9781250193773

LC 2017036271

In this novel, Kristin Hannah, "reveals the indomitable character of the modern American pioneer and the spirit of a vanishing Alaska--a place of incomparable beauty and danger. The . . . [book] is a daring, beautiful, stay-up-all-night story about love and loss, the fight for survival, and the wildness that lives in both man and nature." (Publisher's note)

When her volatile, former POW father impulsively moves the family to mid-1970s Alaska to live off the land, young Leni and her mother are forced to confront the dangers of their lack of preparedness in the wake of a dangerous winter season.

Hannah, Kristin, 1960-

Home again; Kristin Hannah. Fawcett Crest 1996 436 p. (pbk.) $6.99

ISBN 0449226352; 9780449226353

LC 97810570

In this book, "[w]hen movie star Angel DeMarco suffers his first heart attack on location near Seattle, his survival depends on a heart transplant. He's medevac-ed to a local hospital famed for its cardiology unit and placed under the care of Dr. Madelaine Hillyard--the pregnant girlfriend he'd abandoned 17 years earlier. Facing death, he's forced to come to terms with his misspent life and attempt to make things right with Madelaine; his saintly priest brother, Francis; and his rebellious teenaged daughter." (Publishers Weekly)

Hannah, Kristin, 1960-

Home front; Kristin Hannah. St. Martin's Press 2012 390p.

ISBN 9780312577209

LC 2011033805

This novel tells the story of "Michael and Jolene Zarkades [who] have to face the pressures of everyday life---children, careers, bills, chores---even as their twelve-year marriage is falling apart. Then an unexpected deployment sends Jolene deep into harm's way and leaves defense attorney Michael at home, unaccustomed to being a single parent to their two girls. . . . In her letters home, she paints a rose-colored version of her life on the front lines, shielding her family from the truth. But war will change Jolene in ways that none of them could have foreseen. When tragedy strikes, Michael must face his darkest fear and fight a battle of his own---for everything that matters to his family." (Publisher's note)

Hannah, Kristin, 1960-

The **nightingale**; Kristin Hannah. St. Martin's Press 2015 440 p. (hardcover) $27.99

ISBN 0312577222; 9780312577223

LC 2014033303

In this book, by Kristin Hannah, "Vianne Mauriac says goodbye to her husband, Antoine, as he heads for the Front. She doesn't believe that the Nazis will invade France … but invade they do. . . . When a German captain requisitions Vianne's home, she and her daughter must live with the enemy or lose everything. . . . Vianne's sister, Isabelle, . . . joins the Resistance and never looks back, risking her life time and again to save others." (Publisher's note)

Hannah, Kristin

On Mystic lake. Crown 1999 323p $19.95

ISBN 0-609-60249-7

LC 98-26448

"Never one to gush, {Hannah} is more than ever disciplined in her writing, and the result is a clean, deep thrust into the reader's heart." Publ Wkly

Hannah, Kristin

★ **Winter** garden. St. Martin's Press 2010 394p $26.99

ISBN 978-0-312-36412-0; 0-312-36412-1

LC 2009-39230

"This tearjerker weaves a convincing historical novel and contemporary family drama with elements of romance. It is sure to please fans of Danielle Steel, Luanne Rice, and Nicholas Sparks." Libr J

Hannah, Sophie

The **cradle** in the grave. Penguin Books 2011 456p pa $15

ISBN 978-0-14-311994-4; 0-14-311994-X

LC 2011-14075

First published 2010 in the United Kingdom with title: Room swept white

The novel "concludes in a fashion that manages to be both surprising and, in retrospect, somewhat inevitable, which is further testament to Hannah's storytelling prowess. The author has certainly chosen to work with a lot of ingredients here, and yet the subtlety with which she does so makes for a hearty literary meal-one in which each part feels as if it's essential. If good books are those that entertain while simultaneously provoking thought, then this one certainly qualifies." Hartford Examiner

Hannah, Sophie

The **wrong** mother. Penguin Books 2009 415p pa $15

ISBN 978-0-14-311630-1; 0-14-311630-4

LC 2009-27521

First published 2008 in the United Kingdom with title: The point of rescue

"Shockingly (and refreshingly) blunt riffs about the violent emotions of motherhood and the familial yearnings of men, along with chilling and darkly funny revelations about lust and loyalty, make this novel one of the season's most absorbing reads." O magazine

Hannaham, James

★ **Delicious** Foods; a novel. James Hannaham. Little, Brown & Co. 2015 384 p. $26

ISBN 0316284947; 9780316284943

LC 2014955137

PEN/Faulkner Award for Fiction (2016)

In this novel by James Hannaham, "Darlene, once an exemplary wife and a loving mother to her young son, Eddie, finds herself devastated by the unforeseen death of her husband. . . . Unbeknownst to eleven-year-old Eddie, now left behind in a panic-stricken search for her, Darlene has been lured away with false promises of a good job and a rosy life. A shady company named Delicious Foods shuttles her to a remote farm, where she is held captive." (Publisher's note)

"If the plot sounds like tough going, Hannaham's masterpiece is anything but. The writing makes it 'great,' and the themes of pain, forgiveness, exploitation, and self-creation make it American." Booklist

Hansen, Ron

★ The **assassination** of Jesse James by the coward Robert Ford. Knopf 1983 304p

ISBN 0-394-51647-8

LC 83-47851

"Hansen's Jesse is in no way romanticized; his interest derives from the complexity of his psychopathology. The Jesse that emerges here is prematurely decrepit; he'll murder when he doesn't need to, but he reads his Bible and talks about God's peace. Canny, intuitive, he seems to welcome the disciple who will betray him, even gives him the pistol for the job. . . . The novel works not despite our knowledge of what will happen, but because of it a sense of fatality hangs over every scene." Newsweek

Hansen, Ron

Exiles. Farrar, Straus and Giroux 2008 227p $23

ISBN 978-0-374-15097-6; 0-374-15097-4

LC 2007-46836

An historical novel "about 19th-century poet Gerard Manley Hopkins. . . . [It] zeroes in on one short period of Hopkins' life — circa 1875, when, as a Jesuit seminarian in Wales, he read about the death of five nuns in the sinking of a steamship and wrote what became a famous poem, 'The Wreck of the Deutschland.' Hansen conveys a man conflicted by his callings as both a spiritual vessel and a full-blooded artist." Entertainment Wkly

Hansen, Ron

★ **Mariette** in ecstasy. Burlingame Bks. 1991 179p

ISBN 0-06-018214-8

LC 90-56362

"The novel pulls its taut plot-thread smartly along from start to finish, weaving flash-forward patches of dialogue from the investigation of Mariette's 'case' into the unfolding action of her entry into the life of the convent. The finale is a stunner." N Y Times Book Rev

Hansen, Ron

A **wild** surge of guilty passion; a novel. Scribner 2011 256p $25

ISBN 978-1-4516-1755-9

LC 2011-05571

This "is a gripping, entertaining novel. You can feel Hansen's fascination with this story—and his delight at the wealth of material; the memoirs written by both murderers, the news and court reports, the testimony of lesser characters, the secondary material that flowed for years following the trial and execution of Ruth and Gray. The restraint is evident in his measured tone—this is fiction but the author still relies on the factual material—the times, dates, places." Los Angeles Times

Harbach, Chad

The **art** of fielding; Chad Harbach. Little, Brown and Co. 2011 512 p. $25.99

ISBN 0316126691; 9780316126694

LC 2011-14912

In this novel, college shortstop phenom Henry Skrimshander accidentally beans teammate Owen Dunne with a misplaced throw . . . start[ing] a chain reaction on the campus of Westish College. . . . Owen is solicitously visited in the hospital by school president Guert Affenlight, a widower, who falls in love with the seductive gay student. . . . Affenlight's daughter, Pella, after a failed marriage in San Francisco, returns to become part of a love triangle with Henry and Mike Schwartz, the team captain and Henry's unofficial mentor. And just when Henry's hopes of playing for the St. Louis Cardinals come within reach, he suffers a crisis of confidence, even as his team makes a rousing run at the championship. (Publishers Weekly)

"Henry Skrimshander—the gawky, blank-faced star of Westish College's overachieving baseball squad—is a flawless shortstop, the definition of defensive perfection. He's headed for greatness, or at least a major-league contract; big-time scouts and agents are starting to hover. But then . . . something happens. Henry's brain betrays him. He loses confidence, botching even the most routine throws. He has no idea why, and nothing seems to help. . . . Harbach spins this simple premise into a wide-ranging book about desire and loss, friendship and loneliness. It's about baseball, of course, but also campus life, dishwashing, and Moby-Dick (you'll find yourself reaching for a copy to brush up on the famous 'Lee Shore' chapter). Most of Harbach's characters are desperately chasing something. Henry's mentor, Mike Schwartz, covets a national championship and a law career. Westish president Guert Affenlight is infatuated with Henry's brilliant roommate, Owen Dunne. Affenlight's daughter, Pella, longs for a fresh start after a bad marriage. Their struggles get tangled up in and amplified by Henry's collapse and make for a rich, engrossing story." Entertainment Wkly

Harding, Georgina

Painter of silence; Georgina Harding. Bloomsbury 2012 312 p. (hardcover : alk. paper) $26.00

ISBN 1608197700; 9781608197705

LC 2011042284

This book, which was "shortlisted for the Orange Prize for Fiction . . . [is] set in Romania and span[s] several decades up the early 1950s". It follows "Safta . . . a daughter of an aristocratic family . . . [whose] past returns in the form of Augustin, a deaf mute from her childhood . . . [who] is found outside a hospital in a provincial town, where she works as a nurse." (Times Literary Supplement)

Harding, Paul

★ **Enon**; Paul Harding. Random House Inc 2013 256 p. $26

ISBN 1400069432; 9781400069439

LC 2013007985

This book by Paul Harding "covers a year in the life of Charlie Crosby . . . as he mourns the death of his 13-year-old daughter in an accident. After smashing his hand against a wall in a rage, he loses his wife and develops a slow-growing addiction to painkillers and alcohol that leads him to break-ins and other foolhardy decisions. But Harding is less concerned with plot as with what's swimming in Charlie's head, and themes of nature and time abound." (Kirkus Reviews)

Harding, Paul

Tinkers. Bellevue Literary Press 2008 191p $14.95

ISBN 9781934137123 pa; 1-934137-12-X pa

LC 2008-39887

"This compact, adamantine début dips in and out of the consciousness of a New England patriarch named George Washington Crosby as he lies dying on a hospital bed in his living room. . . . The story traces Crosby's life back to his hardscrabble Maine childhood, where his father was a tinker and travelling salesman who suffered from epileptic seizures. Crosby's emotional life is dominated by his father's abandonment of the family on learning that his wife was planning to have him institutionalized, but the most memorable parts of Harding's novel may be his depiction of a nineteenth-century landscape complete with mule-drawn carts and 'frozen wood so brittle that it rang when you split it.' In Harding's skillful evocation, Crosby's life, seen from its final moments, becomes a mosaic of memories." New Yorker

Hardy, Thomas

★ **Far** from the madding crowd; with an etching by H. Macbeth-Raeburn and a map of Wessex. Knopf 1991 xxxiii, 243p $22

ISBN 0-679-40576-3

LC 91-52978

First published 1874

"Bathsheba Everdene is loved by Gabriel Oak, a young farmer who becomes bailiff of the farm she inherits; by William Boldwood, who owns a neighboring farm; and by Sergeant Troy, a handsome inconsiderate young adventurer. She marries Troy, who mistreats her and squanders her money. When he leaves her and is presumed drowned at sea, Bathsheba becomes engaged to Boldwood. Troy, however, reappears, and is murdered by Boldwood, who goes mad as a result of his action and is sent to a mental institution. Bathsheba then marries Gabriel, the steadiest and most faithful of her three suitors." Reader's Ency. 4th edition

Hardy, Thomas

★ **Jude** the obscure. Knopf 1992 518p $20

ISBN 0-679-40993-9

LC 92-52925

First published 1895

"Jude Fawley, a poor villager, wants to enter the divinity school at Christminster (Oxford University). Sidetracked by Arabella Donn, an earthy country girl who pretends to be pregnant by him, Jude marries her and is then deserted. He earns a living as a stonemason at Christminster; there he falls in love with his independent-minded cousin, Sue Bridehead. Out of a sense of obligation, Sue marries the schoolmaster Phillotson, who has helped her. Unable to bear living with Phillotson, she returns to live with Jude and eventually bears his children out of wedlock. Their poverty and the weight of society's disapproval begin to take a toll on Sue and Jude. . . . The novel's sexual frankness shocked the public, as did Hardy's criticisms of marriage, the university system, and the church." Merriam-Webster's Ency of Lit

Hardy, Thomas

★ The **return** of the native. Knopf 1992 xxxix, 497p map $22

ISBN 0-679-41730-3

LC 92-52901

First published 1878

"The novel is set on Egdon Heath, a barren moor in the fictional Wessex in southwestern England. The native of the title is Clym Yeobright, who has returned to the area to become a schoolmaster after a successful but, in his opinion, a shallow career as a jeweler in Paris. He and his cousin Thomasin exemplify the traditional way of life, while Thomasin's husband, Damon Wildeve, and Clym's wife, Eustacia Vye, long for the excitement of city life. Disappointed that Clym is content to remain on the heath, Eustacia, willful and passionate, rekindles her affair with the reckless Damon. After a series of coincidences Eustacia comes to believe that she is responsible for the death of Clym's mother. Convinced that fate has doomed her to cause others pain, Eustacia flees and is drowned (by accident or intent). Damon drowns trying to save her." Merriam-Webster's Ency of Lit

Hardy, Thomas

★ **Tess** of the D'Urbervilles; with an introduction by Patricia Ingham. Knopf 1991 xlviii, 472p map $22

ISBN 0-679-40586-0

LC 91-52998

First published in complete form 1891

"The tragic history of a woman betrayed. . . . Tess the author contends, is sinned against, but not a sinner; her tragedy is the work of tyrannical circumstances and of the evil deeds of others in the past and the present, and more particularly of two men's baseness, the seducer, and the well-meaning intellectual who married her. . . . The pastoral surroundings, the varying aspects of field, river, sky, serve to deepen the pathos of each stage in the heroine's calamities, or to add beauty and dignity to her tragic personality." Baker. Guide to the Best Fic

Harkaway, Nick, 1972-

Angelmaker; by Nick Harkaway. Alfred A. Knopf 2012 496 p. $26.95

ISBN 9780307743626; 9780307595959

LC 2011028261

This book tells the story of Joe Spork, an antique clock repairman who "has turned his back on his family's mobster history and aims to live a quiet life. That orderly existence is suddenly upended when Joe activates a particularly unusual clockwork mechanism. . . . It's a 1950s doomsday machine. Having triggered it, Joe now faces the wrath of both the British government and a diabolical South Asian dictator who is also [his client] Edie's old arch-nemesis. . . . With Joe's once-quiet world suddenly overrun by mad monks, psychopathic serial killers, scientific geniuses and threats to the future of conscious life in the universe, he realizes that the only way to survive is to muster the courage to fight, help Edie complete a mission she abandoned years ago and pick up his father's old gun." (Publisher's note)

Harkaway, Nick

The **gone**-away world. Alfred A. Knopf 2008 497p $24.95

ISBN 978-0-307-26886-0; 0-307-26886-1

LC 2008-8701

This novel "is set in a dystopian future where humanity huddles in the shadow of the Jorgmund Pipe. The ragtag bunch of heroes are sent to put out a fire on the Pipe, a mission both dangerous and imperative, since the Pipe, like a vast futuristic Glade room-freshener, releases the only substance that keeps the psychic stinks and foul odours of this post-apocalyptic world at bay. On the way there, the unnamed narrator reminisces about his upbringing, college days, military service, the Go Away Bombs that created their surreal present, and above all his friend Gonzo, to whom he's always felt closer than a brother. Somehow their story brings in ninjas, first loves, pirate-kings, mime-artists, human monsters and, well, monster monsters. . . . The revelation of Gonzo's relationship to his nameless best friend (and the ways in which Harkaway keeps on teasing around us not knowing his name is one of the novel's joys) is both unexpected and obvious. The Gone-Away World is brakes-off fiction." Scotsman

Harkaway, Nick, 1972-

★ **Tigerman**; a novel. Nick Harkaway. Alfred A. Knopf 2014 352 p. (hardback) $26.95

ISBN 0385352417; 9780385352413

LC 2014002571

In this novel by Nick Harkaway, "Sergeant Lester Ferris is a good man in need of a rest. After a long career of being shot at, he's about to be retired. The mildly larcenous, backwater island of Mancreu is the ideal place to serve out his time, a former British colony in legal limbo, belching toxic clouds of waste and facing imminent destruction by an international community concerned for their own safety. [Mancreu] is also the perfect location for . . . shady businesses." (Publisher's note)

Harkaway "has created an immensely likable hero who rises to the occasion in amusing and spectacularly improbable fashion." Pub Wkly

Harkness, Deborah E., 1965-

The **Book** of Life; A Novel. Deborah Harkness. Penguin Group USA/Viking 2014 592 p. (All souls trilogy) $28.95

ISBN 0670025593; 9780670025596

LC 2014004495

In this book, by Deborah Harkness, "historian and witch Diana Bishop and vampire scientist Matthew Clairmont return to the present to face new crises and old enemies. . . . But the real threat to their future has yet to be revealed, and when it is, the search for Ashmole 782 and its missing pages takes on even more urgency. In the trilogy's final volume, Harkness deepens her themes of power and passion, family and caring, past deeds and their present consequences." (Publisher's note)

"There is no shortage of action in this sprawling sequel, and nearly every chapter brings a wrinkle to the tale. The storytelling is lively and energetic, and Diana remains an appealing heroine even as her life becomes ever more extraordinary." Pub Wkly

Harkness, Deborah E., 1965-

A **discovery** of witches; a novel. Viking 2011 579p $28.95

ISBN 0-670-02241-1; 978-0-670-02241-0

LC 2010-30425

"A riveting tale full of romance and danger that will have you on the edge of your seat, yet its chief strength lies in the wonderfully rich and ingenious mythology underlying the story. Entwining strands of science and history, Harkness creates a fresh explanation for how such creatures could arise that is so credible, you'll have to keep reminding yourself this is fiction." BookPage

Harkness, Deborah E., 1965-

Shadow of night; Deborah Harkness. Viking 2012 584 p. (hardcover) $28.95; (paperback) $17.00

ISBN 9780670023486; 0670023485; 9780143123620

LC 2012005843

In this sequel, newlywed "vampire/scientist Matthew de Clermont" and "historian/untrained witch Diana Bishop" time-travel "to Elizabethan England so Diana can study witchcraft. . . . There, they hope to retrieve magical manuscript Ashmole 782, last seen in Oxford's 21st-century Bodleian library. Diana gets in touch with her inner firedrake, Matthew with his father, but they can't find a tutor for ages, and they can't rescue the manuscript without a trip to Prague." (Publishers Weekly)

Harlem Renaissance: five novels of the 1920s; Rafia Zafar, editor. Library of America 2011 867p $35

ISBN 978-1-59853-099-5; 1-59853-099-2

This collection "leads off with Jean Toomer's Cane (1923), a unique fusion of fiction, poetry, and drama rooted in Toomer's experiences as a teacher in Georgia. . . . Claude McKay's Home to Harlem (1928), whose freewheeling, impressionistic, bawdy kaleidoscope of Jazz Age nightlife made it a best seller, traces the picaresque adventures of Jake, a World War I veteran, within and beyond Harlem. Nella Larsen's Quicksand (1928), the poignant, nuanced psychological portrait of a woman caught between the two worlds of her mixed Scandinavian and African American heritage; Jessie Redmon Fauset's Plum Bun (1928), the richly detailed account of a young art student's struggles to advance her career in a society full of obstacles both overt and insidiously concealed; and Wallace Thurman's The Blacker the Berry (1929), with its anguished, provocative look at prejudice and exclusion as it tells of a new arrival in Harlem searching for love, each in its distinct way testifies to the enduring power of the Harlem ferment." Publisher's note

Harlem Renaissance: four novels of the 1930s; Rafia Zafar, editor. Library of America 848p $35

ISBN 978-1-59853-101-5; 1-59853-101-8

"Langston Hughes's Not Without Laughter (1931)—the poet's only novel, an elegiac, elegantly realized coming-of-age tale suffused with childhood memories of Missouri and Kansas—follows a young man from his rural origins to the big city. George S. Schuyler's Black No More (1931), a satire founded on the science-fiction premise of a wonder drug permitting blacks to change their race, savagely caricatures public figures white and black alike in its raucous, carnivalesque send-up of American racial attitudes. Considered the first detective story by an African American writer, Rudolph Fisher's The Conjure-Man Dies (1932) is a mystery that comically mixes and reverses stereotypes, placing a Harvard-educated African 'conjureman' at the center of a phantasmagoric charade of deaths and disappearances. Black Thunder (1936), Arna Bontemps's stirring fictional recreation of Gabriel Prosser's 1800 slave revolt, which, though unsuccessful, shook Jefferson's Virginia to its core, marks a turn from aestheticism toward political militance in its exploration of African American history." Publisher's note

Harman, Patricia

The **midwife** of Hope River; a novel. by Patricia Harman. HarperCollins 2012 382 p.

ISBN 0062198890; 9780062198891

LC 2012010944

This historical novel, by Patricia Harman, follows "[m]idwife Patience Murphy. . . . Working in the hardscrabble conditions of Appalachia during the Depression, Patience takes the jobs that no one else wants, helping those most in need--and least likely to pay. She knows a successful midwifery practice must be built on a foundation of openness and trust--but the secrets Patience is keeping are far too intimate and fragile for her to ever let anyone in." (Publisher's note)

Harper, Jane ✓

★ The **dry**; a novel. Jane Harper. Flatiron Books 2017 320 p. (hardback) $25.99

ISBN 9781250105608

LC 2016016416

In this novel, by Jane Harper, "after getting a note demanding his presence, Federal Agent Aaron Falk arrives in his hometown for the first time in decades to attend the funeral of his best friend, Luke. . . . As Falk reluctantly investigates to see if there's more to Luke's death than there seems to be, long-buried mysteries resurface, as do the lies that have haunted them. And Falk will find that small towns have always hidden big secrets." (Publisher's note)

"From the ominous opening paragraphs, all the more chilling for their matter-of-factness, Harper, a journalist who writes for Melbourne's Herald Sun, spins a suspenseful tale of sound and fury as riveting as it is horrific." Pub Wkly

Another title in this series is:

Force of nature (2018)

Harper, Karen

Fall from pride. Mira Books 2011 342p pa $14.95

ISBN 978-0-7783-1249-9

"Sarah Kauffman is an artist who paints murals on barns in her Amish community. When one of the barns mysteriously burns down, the local papers are quick to print the story. State arson inspector Nate MacKenzie drives down to Columbus to work on the case. He and Sarah make an unusual duo—Nate, the outsider with little knowledge of Amish culture, and Sarah, the Amish woman who often feels like an outsider in her own village. As they discover clues about the crime, they also come to know more and more about one another. . . . Readers will likely enjoy a trip into the heart of Ohio's famed religious community and may be tempted to find out what lies ahead for this unlikely crime-solving couple." Publ Wkly

Harper, Karen

The **Poyson** garden. Delacorte Press 1999 310p

ISBN 0-385-33283-1

LC 98-36420

"Elizabeth's active role may strain credulity a bit, but this one is great fun all the same." Booklist

Harrigan, Stephen

A **friend** of Mr. Lincoln; a novel. Stephen Harrigan. Knopf 2016 432 p. (hardback) $27.95

ISBN 9780307700674; 9781101946862

LC 2015015853

In this historical novel, by Stephen Harrigan, "cage both admires and clashes with Lincoln, sometimes questioning his legal ethics and his cautious stance on slavery. But he is by Lincoln's side as Lincoln slips back and forth between high spirits and soul-hollowing sadness and depression, and as he recovers from a disastrous courtship of one woman to marry the beautiful, capricious, politically savvy Mary Todd." (Publisher's note)

"In a first-rate rendering, Harrigan shows a young Lincoln in all his moods and temperaments, providing context with vividly detailed historical events." LJ

Harrington, Matthew Joseph

The **goliath** stone; Larry Niven and Matthew Joseph Harrington. Tor 2013 320 p. (hardcover) $24.99

ISBN 0765333236; 9780765333230

LC 2012049701

In this novel, by Larry Niven and Matthew Joseph Harrington, "Doctor Toby Glyer has effected miracle cures with the use of nanotechnology. But Glyer's controversial nanites are more than just the latest technological advance, they are a new form of life. . . . Twenty-five years ago, . . . [a] mission took nanomachinery out to divert an Earth-crossing asteroid. . . . Now, a much, much larger asteroid is on a collision course with Earth--and the Briareus nanites may be responsible." (Publisher's note)

Harris, Charlaine

✓ **Dead** reckoning. Ace Books 2011 325p $27.95

ISBN 978-0-441-02031-7; 0-441-02031-3

LC 2010-54261

"God knows it's not easy being Sookie Stackhouse. The telepathic barmaid at the center of so many supernatural occurrences in the sleepy burg of Bon Temps, La., seems to spend most of her time fending off murderous attackers or the romantic advances of vampires, werewolves, shape-shifters and the like. . . . Her relationship with handsome Viking vampire Eric Northman is still acutely complicated — and old flame Bill Compton and werewolf Alcide Herveaux haven't stopped proclaiming their love for Sookie either. And that just might be part of the problem. Certainly, some things have changed in Bon Temps. Right out of the gate, Ms. Stackhouse loses some of her blond locks when her boss Sam Merlotte's bar is fire-bombed, adding insult to the already critical injury of losing business to Vic's Redneck Roadhouse, the new joint in town. Eric is forcing Pam, the vampire he made, to keep a troubling bit of knowledge from Sookie, even as she learns some personal, painful secrets about her beloved late grandmother Adele and comes into possession of a rare magical object called a 'cluviel dor.' " Los Angeles times Book Rev

Harris, Charlaine

A **secret** rage. Severn House 2011 198p $27.95

ISBN 978-0-7278-8026-0

First published 1984 by Houghton Mifflin

"Former model Nickie returns to her hometown to finish college and moves in with her best friend from boarding school. But coming home means more than going back to school, as she must deal with her estranged parents and confront her long-suppressed feelings for her best friend's older brother. Matters are complicated by the presence of a rapist on campus who attacks both Nickie and her advisor. Convinced that the assailant is someone she knows, Nickie sets out to track him down. Mixing a touch of romance with a suspenseful thriller plot, Harris turns out a top-notch read with wide appeal to genre fans." Booklist

Harris, E. Lynn

And this too shall pass; a novel. Doubleday 1996 347p

ISBN 0-385-48030-X

LC 95-38844

Among the African American characters featured in this novel are "Zurich Robinson, a gay pro-football quarterback; MamaCee, aka Miss

Cora, his grandmother; Caliph Taylor, a Chicago cop who is devoted to his daughter; successful attorney Tamela Coleman; sports anchor Mia Miller; and gay sports reporter Sean Elliott. The major plot concerns Zurich's acceptance of his gayness and his developing relationship with Sean. Subplots involve Mia and Tamela, who both struggle with their careers, their relationships with men, and one another. . . . Ultimately both fun and moving, the book has something to impress nearly any reader." Booklist

Harris, E. Lynn

If this world were mine; a novel. Doubleday 1997 318p

ISBN 0-385-48655-3

LC 97-18795

"Members of a monthly journal-writing group, four African American friends from college days who all live in the Chicago area, help each other through the dramas of their respective lives. They're all approaching 40 and looking for answers: Riley Woodson, a self-proclaimed Black Princess immured in a stultifying marriage; Yolanda Williams, a media consultant; gay psychiatrist Leland Thompson; and Dwight Scott, a computer engineer simmering with hatred for white people. . . . A supple raconteur, Harris explores the intimacies of friendship with a sensitive eye." Publ Wkly

Harris, Eve

The **Marrying** of Chani Kaufman; Eve Harris. Grove Press, Black Cat 2014 384 p. $16

ISBN 0802122736; 9780802122735

National Jewish Book Awards Finalist: Debut Fiction (2014)

This book is set in 2008 in London's Orthodox Jewish community, where "Chani Kaufman and Baruch Levy are getting married after a mere three dates. Opening with their wedding ceremony, the story loops back to the couple's first encounter, the matchmaker's involvement, the courtship, the parents' reactions (his mother doesn't approve) and the proposal." (Kirkus Reviews)

"Intelligent, revealing characters who command conviction and connection; the tug between the old ways and modern life; and the universal themes of desire, guilt, manipulation and submission will resonate with readers from all backgrounds." Pub Wkly

Harris, Joanne

Chocolat; a novel. Viking 1999 242p

ISBN 0-670-88179-1

LC 98-21771

"When Vianne Rocher and her daughter arrive in the small French town of Lansquenet-sous-Tannes, they open a shop specializing in exquisite, voluptuous chocolates. This is the first breath of giddiness the town has ever felt. So isolated is the place, it still rigorously maintains Lenten abstinences, and the town priest takes umbrage at the effrontery of this arriviste scheduling a festival of chocolate for Easter Sunday. . . . Harris' writing conveys a multitude of images and captures the self-absorption of small town life in France." Booklist

Harris, Joanne

Five quarters of the orange. Morrow 2001 307p $25

ISBN 0-06-019813-3

LC 00-48952

"Harris has constructed a multilayered plot, punctuated with scrumptious descriptons of French delicacies and telling depictions of the war's jolting effects on one fragile family. This intense work brims with sensuality and sensitivity." Publ Wkly

Harris, Joanne

Peaches for Father Francis; a novel. Joanne Harris. Viking 2012 453 p. $26.95

ISBN 0670026360; 9780670026364

LC 2012015089

In this novel, by Joanne Harris, "when Vianne Rocher receives a letter from beyond the grave, she has no choice but to follow the wind that blows her back to Lansquenet, the beautiful French village in which eight years ago she opened a chocolate shop and first learned the meaning of home. Vianne, with her daughters, Anouk and Rosette, finds Lansquenet changed in unexpected ways. . . . Most surprising of all, her old nemesis, Father Francis Reynaud, desperately needs her help." (Publisher's note)

Harris, Mark

Bang the drum slowly; by Henry W. Wiggen; certain of his enthusiasms restrained by Mark Harris. Knopf 1956 243p

A baseball novel which centers on Bruce, a black catcher, who is slowly dying of Hodgkin's disease. The narrator tries to keep the matter a secret, but eventually it comes out. The rest of the book concerns the loyalty of Bruce's teammates to their doomed member

"Narrated by 'Author' in the raucous speech of the ball park, yet with an elegiac dignity." Booklist

Harris, Robert

Archangel; a novel. Random House 1999 373p

ISBN 0-679-42888-7

LC 98-33655

"The sinewy plot never slackens, but what makes the book memorable are the vividly observed backgrounds. . . . No less authentic are the fragmented but undead relics of the old Soviet system." Natl Rev

Harris, Robert

Conclave; A novel. Robert Harris. Alfred A. Knopf 2016 304 p. map (ebook) $65; (hbk.) $26.95

ISBN 9780451493453; 9780091959166; 0451493443; 9780451493446

LC 2016954899

In this novel, by Robert Harris, "the pope is dead. Behind the locked doors of the Sistine Chapel, one hundred and eighteen cardinals from all over the globe will cast their votes in the world's most secretive election. They are holy men. But they have ambition. And they have rivals. Over the next seventy-two hours one of them will become the most powerful spiritual figure on Earth." (Publisher's note)

"This is another impressive outing from an extremely versatile author." Pub Wkly

Harris, Robert

★ **Enigma**. Random House 1995 320p

LC 95-11335

"As one expects from a thriller-writer, Harris ensures the tension builds inexorably as the plot unfolds. Unlike some, however, he creates characters that linger in the mind, and he never bores his readers with gratuitous technical detail." New Sci

Harris, Robert

★ **Fatherland**. Random House 1992 338p

LC 91-51026

"'Fatherland' is a bleak book. But what concerns the author is the indestructibility of the human spirit, as exemplified by Xavier March. If Hitler's Germany is hell, at least a few angels are floating around." N Y Times Book Rev

Harris, Robert

The **fear** index; Robert Harris. Alfred A. Knopf 2012 285p.

ISBN 0307957934; 9780307957931

LC 2011043472

In this book, the "story takes place over a . . . twenty-four hour period in the life of Dr. Alexander Hoffmann, computer scientist, mathematical genius, and, of late, hedge fund billionaire. It begins . . . when Hoffmann is awoken by an intruder inside his sixty million dollar villa on the shores of Lake Geneva. A confrontation occurs, Hoffmann is injured, and in his attempt to solve just how someone was able to gain entry into his well-guarded palace, Hoffmann comes face to face with the greatest danger he can imagine: himself. . . . Hoffmann . . . began his career as a computer scientist at CERN (European Organization for Nuclear Research) where his work in artificial intelligence involved modeling sophisticated algorithms that programmed computers to teach themselves. It is this mastery of algorithms, and how they train computers to mimic human behavior, that he has turned to such profitable use at Hoffmann Investment Technologies. And it is this mastery that will come to haunt him." (Amazon.com)

Harris, Robert

The **ghost**. Simon & Schuster 2007 335p $26

ISBN 978-1-4165-5181-2; 1-4165-5181-6

LC 2007-29670

"Adam Lang was Britain's longest serving-and most controversial-prime minister of the last half century, whose career ended . . . after he sided with America in an unpopular war on terror. Now, after stepping down in disgrace, Lang is hiding out in . . . Martha's Vineyard to finish his much sought-after, potentially explosive memoir, for which he accepted one of history's largest cash advances. But the project runs aground when his ghostwriter suddenly and mysteriously disappears and later washes up, dead, on the island's deserted shore." Publ Wkly

Harris, Robert

Pompeii; a novel. Random House 2003 278p map hardcover o.p. pa $13.95

ISBN 0-679-42889-5; 0-8129-7461-1 pa

LC 2003-58446

"An upstanding Roman engineer rushes to repair an aqueduct in the shadow of Mount Vesuvius, which, in A.D. 79, is getting ready to blow its top. . . . Lively writing, convincing but economical period details and plenty of intrigue keep the pace quick." Publ Wkly

Harris, Thomas

Hannibal. Delacorte Press 1999 486p $27.95

ISBN 0-385-29929-X

LC 99-29774

"Where Silence haunted and tantalized, Hannibal grosses out and gratifies. Yet there's still a basso ostinato of serious questions, and the answers are darker than in Silence." Nation

Harris, Thomas

Hannibal rising; a novel. Delacorte Press 2006 323p $27.95

ISBN 978-0-385-33941-4; 0-385-33941-0

"There are images of morbid beauty here. . . . Harris' handling of the wartime violence is also impressive, as swift and vicious as the blitzkrieg itself." Los Angeles Times

Harris, Thomas

Red Dragon. Dutton 2000 348p $26.95

ISBN 0-525-94556-3

LC 00-22500

A reissue of the title first published 1981 by Putnam

"This is a chilling, tautly written, and well-realized psychological thriller. . . . The suspense is sustained by deft characterizations, fascinating crime-lab details, a twisting plot, and understated prose." Saturday Rev

Harris, Thomas

★ The **silence** of the lambs. St. Martin's Press 1988 338p $24.95

ISBN 0-312-02282-4

LC 88-18203

"Harris places his clues with precision, and his characterizations . . . are superbly developed and richly complex." Booklist

Followed by Hannibal

Harrison, Colin

The **finder**; a novel. Farrar, Straus and Giroux 2008 322p $25

ISBN 978-0-374-29949-1; 0-374-29949-8

LC 2007-36574

"A few pages into the story, a young Chinese woman, Jin Li, witnesses the grisly murder of two Mexican girls. The killers are really after Jin Li, who heads a cleaning company that handles document-shredding and other services for Manhattan firms. That role allows for all manner of discreet snooping – and fuels the illegal stock speculating ring led by her brother back in Shanghai. A forlorn firefighter who survived a nightmarish assignment inside the collapsed World Trade Center towers on 9/11 serves as the novel's hero. He's capable, brooding – and often lost in the maze of subplots. When he's on the stage, though, he grabs the reader's attention, as does Bill Martz, a conniving and captivating billionaire who's been burned by a mysterious plunging stock price engineered by You Know Who. Harrison mostly moves his pieces around the board in expert fashion and, Wolfean tics (exclamation points run amok!) aside, writes with a crisp authority. He's done his homework, too, as the detailed aside on sewage services will attest." Christ Sci Monit

Harrison, Harry

The **Stainless** Steel Rat joins the circus. TOR Bks. 1999 269p

ISBN 0-312-86934-7

LC 99-34005

Following The Stainless Steel Rat goes to Hell (1996), the master criminal takes on a new assignment. "After taking a job infiltrating a suspicious circus on a four million credit a day retainer, DiGriz finds himself and his family bound up, literally at times, in a planet-wide swindle. Someone is robbing banks and other sources of wealth using The Rat's good name while he dutifully performs his magic act under the big top. Soon DiGriz is hunted by endless factions of the police, his son Bolivar is jailed, his wife Angelina kidnapped, his formerly benevolent employer is getting more sinister by the hour and worst of all, The Stainless Steel Rat is actually losing money!" Publ Wkly

Harrison, Harry

The **Stainless** Steel Rat sings the blues. Bantam Bks. 1994 229p

LC 93-31809

"Caught in the act of robbing the new mint on the planet Paskonjak, master thief Jim DiGriz, a.k.a. the Stainless Steel Rat, is offered a deal by the Galactic League: discover a stolen artifact thought to be somewhere on the prison planet Liokukae within 30 days and go free—or die. In the same vein as previous adventures featuring Harrison's irrepressible antihero . . . this latest outing boasts fast-paced action, a hint of melodrama, and a sizable dose of satirical tweaks at modern culture." Libr J

Harrison, Jim, 1937-2016

The **Ancient** Minstrel; Novellas. by Jim Harrison. Grove Press 2017 272 p. (pbk.) $16.00; (hbk.) $25; (ebook) $24.99

ISBN 9780802126344; 0802126340; 0802124569; 9780802124562; 9780802190215

In this book, author Jim Harrison "delivers three novellas that highlight . . . the human condition. . . . In 'Eggs,' a Montana woman reminisces about staying in London with her grandparents, and collecting eggs at their country house. . . . And in 'The Case of the Howling Buddhas,' retired Detective Sunderson . . . is hired as a private investigator to look into a bizarre cult that achieves satori by howling along with howler monkeys at the zoo." (Publisher's note)

"The unnamed and restless narrator, like Harrison himself, refuses to allow death's imminence to keep him from living fully, embodying this witty and inspired collection." Booklist

Harrison, Jim, 1937-2016

Brown Dog; Novellas. Jim Harrison. Pgw 2013 448 p. $27

ISBN 0802120113; 9780802120113

This book collects Jim Harrison's "five previously published Brown Dog stories and adds a new one. Brown Dog exists primarily off the grid of contemporary society and subsists on odd jobs (some legal, some not) and the occasional generosity of his (maybe) Uncle Delmore and the kind but troubled social worker Gretchen, who is the object of Brown Dog's unrequited passion. Motivated primarily by alcohol and sex . . . , Brown Dog can't seem to stay out of trouble." (Library Journal)

Harrison, Jim

The **English** major. Grove Press 2008 255p $24

ISBN 978-0-8021-1863-9; 0-8021-1863-1

"The protagonist of this wistfully comic novel is a sixty-year-old English teacher turned farmer, whose wife has left him for another man, and who takes to the road in the quixotic pursuit of renaming all the birds and all the states. Along the way, he picks up a neurotic, sex-hungry former student; despairs of road food; wanders into the desert without enough water; and muses on the ways life can suddenly turn upside down. . . . The premise is well-worn, but Harrison has created a character of such appeal and self-deprecating wisdom that even the more fantastical episodes—a nubile young woman cavorting in the nude for his pleasure—acquire a charmingly philosophical air." New Yorker

Harrison, Jim, 1937-2016

★ The **great** leader; a faux mystery. Grove Press 2011 329p $24

ISBN 978-0-8021-1970-4; 0-8021-1970-0

"Some of the funniest and profoundest bits in 'The Great Leader' are the detective's alcohol-soaked musings just before he passes out. The novel serves up Sunderson's old-school field notes, which range from serious case observations to stream-of-consciousness ramblings. This is all the better, for it is fun to hear police quote Marx to each other in the field, where the outlaw and his pursuer find they have things in common, and where religion and sex intersect under the canopy of trees in the Upper Peninsula." Cleveland Plain Dealer

Harrison, Jim

Returning to earth. Grove 2007 280p $24.95

ISBN 978-0-8021-1838-7; 0-8021-1838-0

LC 2006-50802

"This could almost be Hemingway, in some of the Michigan stories, but it's even more stripped than Hemingway. . . . [The novel] is both familiar and strange, rooted and rootless, endlessly dark and occasionally hilarious." San Diego Union-Tribune

Harrison, Jim

★ The **road** home. Atlantic Monthly Press 1998 446p $25

ISBN 0-87113-724-0

LC 98-8391

Sequel to Dalva (1988)

"This saga is as homespun as an old quilt. A woman and her grown son, whom she'd put up for adoption, are reunited. An old man makes his peace as he approaches death. Each family member stitches in a piece of the family history. They are such good company you forget they exist nowhere but in Harrison's imagination." Newsweek

Harrison, Kathryn, 1961-

Enchantments; by Kathryn Harrison. 1st ed. Random House 2012 314 p.

ISBN 9781400063475

LC 2010053369

This book tells the story of Masha, the daughter of the Russian mystic Rasputin, who after his death "is sent to live at the imperial palace with Tsar Nikolay and his family. . . . Desperately hoping that Masha has inherited Rasputin's miraculous healing powers, Tsarina Alexandra asks her to tend to [Prince] Aloysha, who suffers from hemophilia, a blood disease that keeps the boy confined to his sickbed. . . . Two months after Masha arrives at the palace, the tsar is forced to abdicate, and Bolsheviks place the royal family under house arrest. . . . To escape the confinement of the palace, they tell stories—some embellished and some entirely imagined—about Nikolay and Alexandra's courtship, Rasputin's many exploits, and the wild and wonderful country on the brink of an irrevocable transformation." (Publisher's note)

Harrison, Kathryn

The **seal** wife; a novel. Random House 2002 224p

ISBN 0-375-50629-2

LC 2001-48979

"Painterly in its pearlescent evocation of the Alaskan landscape, steeped in myth and the magic of science, this is a delectably moody, erotic, and provocative cross-cultural love story." Booklist

Harrison, M. John

Nova swing. Bantam Books 2007 252p pa $16

ISBN 978-0-553-38501-4; 0-553-38501-1

LC 2007-8288

First published 2006 in the United Kingdom

"The world Harrison has painted for us isn't pretty, and is often incomprehensible. But look around. It's that way already. Nova Swing is witty, mind-expanding, and entertaining. It's a book not to miss." scifidimensions.com

Harrison, Mette Ivie

The **Bishop's** Wife; Mette Ivie Harrison. Soho Crime 2014 352 p. $26.95

ISBN 1616954760; 9781616954765

LC 2014019275

In this novel by Mette Ivie Harrison, part of the Linda Wallheim Novel series, "Linda Wallheim is a devout Mormon, the mother of five boys and the wife of a bishop. But Linda is increasingly troubled by her church's structure and secrecy, especially as a disturbing situation takes shape in her ward. . . . As Linda snoops in the Helm family's circumstances, she becomes convinced that Jared has murdered his wife and painted himself as a wronged husband." (Publisher's note)

"This decidedly adult tale adds twists aplenty to an insider's look at a religion replete with its own mysteries." Kirkus

Another book about Linda Wallheim is:
His Right Hand (2015)

Harrod-Eagles, Cynthia

Blood lines; an Inspector Bill Slider mystery. Scribner 1996 281p

ISBN 0-684-80047-0

LC 96-8555

Inspector Slider investigates the "death of a prominent music critic who comes to a violent end in the men's room of a BBC recording studio. Each plot twist, including one devious turn that throws suspicion on a former member of Slider's murder squad, hangs on the testimony of the complicated characters, who are among the author's finest stock." N Y Times Book Rev

Harrod-Eagles, Cynthia

Death to go. Scribner 1994 281p

ISBN 0-684-19650-6

LC 93-10374

First published 1993 in the United Kingdom with title: Necrochip

"Murder provides the foundation for this extraordinary novel, but, it's finally an examination of love, love lost, and ways in which people cope with both." Booklist

Harrod-Eagles, Cynthia

Death watch. Scribner 1993 280p

LC 92-30924

First published 1992 in the United Kingdom

"This is a fine example of the British procedural—a simmering rather than boiling narrative, plenty of quick wit, and a splash of romantic intrigue, all skillfully written and solidly plotted." Booklist

Harrod-Eagles, Cynthia

Game over; a Bill Slider mystery. Severn House 2008 234p $28.95

ISBN 978-0-7278-6615-8

In this "11th Bill Slider mystery . . . the detective inspector investigates the murder of civil servant Ed Stonax, a former high-profile BBC correspondent, found dead with his skull smashed on the floor of his West London flat. . . . The various plot lines neatly intersect at the highest levels of government by the end of this appealing English whodunit." Publ Wkly

Harrod-Eagles, Cynthia

Grave music; an Inspector Bill Slider mystery. Scribner 1995 234p

ISBN 0-684-80046-2

LC 94-39222

First published 1994 in the United Kingdom with title: Dead end

"Though readers may guess the murderer early on in this . . . {novel, Slider's} police cohorts, and his violinist love, Joanna, are among the most appealing cast in recent memory. Their relationships, the music world setting, and the clever dialog . . . recommend this to all collections." Libr J

Harrod-Eagles, Cynthia

Killing time; an Inspector Bill Slider mystery. Scribner 1998 313p

ISBN 0-684-83776-5

LC 97-26290

First published 1996 in the United Kingdom

In this mystery London's Inspector Bill Slider's "attention is divided between solving the murder of a male striptease dancer—a case that extends from seedy Soho cabarets to the posh country homes of cabinet ministers—and sorting out the needs and demands of his estranged wife and new lover. . . . Many readers may guess the killer early on, but that shouldn't interfere with their appreciation for the rumpled, empathetic Slider, whose ability to see the complexity in the people around him is both his strength and his weakness." Booklist

Harrod-Eagles, Cynthia

★ **Old** bones; Cynthia Harrod-Eagles. Severn House Pub Ltd 2017 249 p. (Bill Slider mysteries) (hardcover) $29.99

ISBN 0727886657; 9781780108353; 9780727886651

In this novel in the Bill Slider Mystery series, by Cynthia Harrod-Eagles, "a young couple discover human remains buried in the garden of their new house: could this be the resting place of 14-year-old Amanda Knight, who disappeared from the same garden two decades before, and was never seen again?" (Publisher's note)

"Another sterling entry in a truly outstanding series." Booklist

Harrod-Eagles, Cynthia

Orchestrated death; a mystery introducing Inspector Bill Slider. Scribner 1992 266p

ISBN 0-684-19388-4

LC 91-29042

First published 1991 in the United Kingdom

A novel "remarkable for its rich, romantic tone, assured technique and perfect literary pitch." N Y Times Book Rev

Other titles in this series are:
Death watch (1993)
Death to go (1993)
Grave music (1994)
Blood lines (1996)
Killing time (1996)
Shallow grave (1998)
Blood sinister (1999)
Gone tomorrow (2001)
Dear departed (2004)
Game over (2008)
Fell purpose (2010)
Body line (2010)
Kill my darling (2012)
Blood never dies (2012)
Hard going (2014)
Star fall (2015)
One under (2016)
Old bones (2017)
Shadow play (2018)

Harrod-Eagles, Cynthia

Shallow grave; a Bill Slider mystery. Scribner 1999 312p $22

ISBN 0-684-83777-3

LC 99-21351

First published 1998 in the United Kingdom

"It isn't Inspector Bill Slider's passion for architectural oddities that brings him to the Mimpriss Estate, but the body on the terrace of the

Old Rectory. . . . The way the neighbors tell it, the victim was 'an unprincipled slut,' the unfaithful wife of a local builder, a 'jealous beast' with means and motive to throttle his spouse. But Slider, whose own convulsive extramartial affairs in this refreshingly grown-up series have made him sensitive to the complexities of modern relationships, believes in looking beneath surfaces." N Y Times Book Rev

Hart, Brian

The **bully** of order; a novel. Brian Hart. Harper 2014 400 p. (hardback) $25.99

ISBN 0062297740; 9780062297747; 9780062297754

LC 2013048447

This novel, by Brian Hart, is "[s]et in a logging town on the lawless Pacific coast of Washington State at the turn of the twentieth century. . . . Keen to make his fortune, Jacob Ellstrom, armed with his medical kit and new wife, Nell, lands in The Harbor. . . . But Jacob is not a doctor, and a botched delivery exposes his ruse, driving him onto the streets in a plunge towards alcoholism. Alone, Nell scrambles to keep herself and their young son, Duncan, safe in this dangerous world." (Publisher's note)

"Not a writer of half-measures, Hart brilliantly re-creates the rugged life in the Pacific Northwest logging camps of the 1890s. A riveting, powerful tale." LJ

Hart, Brian

Then came the evening; a novel. Bloomsbury USA 2009 272p $25

ISBN 978-1-60819-014-0; 1-60819-014-5

LC 2009-16969

This novel "begins with a calamitous misunderstanding. Bandy Dorner, hungover and in trouble with two police officers, is told that his cabin burned down the night before. Bandy assumes his wife, Iona, was inside, and in a confused fury he shoots one of the cops, killing him. But Iona, we soon learn, did not die in the fire. She took off with her new man earlier that night—just after she burned down the cabin. The rest is fallout. From the early '70s we fast-forward to 1990. Bandy's son, Tracy, conceived not long before the fire, comes to visit his father in an Idaho prison. The young man has left home and plans to refurbish an old house that belonged to Bandy's parents. Bandy gets out of prison not long after the visit and joins his son in fixing up the home. Iona is there, too. Over the next several months, they live together uncomfortably, broken, a family that never was. Then Came the Evening may seem ostentatiously bleak—full of prison beatings, drunken fights, sex with truckers for drugs; and all this in the rugged American West—but Hart avoids macho sentimentalism." Bookforum

Hart, Carolyn G.

Death walked in; a death on demand mystery. [by] Carolyn Hart. William Morrow 2008 293p $23.95

ISBN 978-0-06-072405-4; 0-06-072405-6

LC 2007-43589

A fortune in gold coins stolen from a house filled with visiting family members lies at the root of this Max and Annie Darling mystery.

"This tight, Agatha Christie-style puzzler will keep readers guessing to the end." Publ Wkly

Hart, Carolyn

Ghost gone wild; Carolyn Hart. Berkley Hardcover 2013 320 p. (A Bailey Ruth ghost novel) (hardback) $25.95

ISBN 0425260755; 9780425260753

LC 2013025898

This is Agatha Award-winner Carolyn Hart's fourth novel featuring departed spirit Bailey Ruth Raeburn. Here, "Bailey Ruth of heaven's Department of Good Intentions arrives at the Adelaide, Okla., home of video-game millionaire Nick Magruder just in time to prevent a gunman from shooting him. Since the shade of Nick's doting Aunt Dee engineered this mission on the sly, Bailey Ruth must operate on earth without her otherworldly powers" to clear Nick when he's accused of murder. (Publishers Weekly)

Hart, Carolyn G.

Letter from home; {by} Carolyn Hart. Berkley Prime Crime 2003 262p $22.95

ISBN 0-425-19179-6

LC 2003-51953

"Set in a small-town America that lives only in memory, this artfully narrated whodunit observes the residents of an unnamed Oklahoma hamlet over the hot and dusty summer of 1944 as they ration their food, count their war dead and turn on their neighbors." N Y Times Book Rev

Hart, Carolyn G.

Murder walks the plank; a death on demand mystery. [by] Carolyn Hart. HarperCollins Publishers 2004 298p $23.95

ISBN 0-06-000474-6

LC 2003-51095

This novel "can only reinforce Hart's high standing among the cozy mystery cognoscenti." Publ Wkly

Hart, Carolyn G.

Resort to murder; a Henrie O mystery. {by} Carolyn Hart. Morrow 2001 294p $24

ISBN 0-380-97773-7

LC 00-59446

"Recovering from pneumonia, Henrie O isn't sure she feels up to the task of dealing with the emotional maelstrom stewing around the Bermuda wedding of her son-in-law, Lloyd Drake, and beautiful Connor Bailey, a wealthy widow. . . . The hotel where the party has gathered witnessed tragedy the year before, when Roddy Worrell, the manager's husband, plunged to his death from a tower. According to rumor, Roddy had been infatuated with Connor, who spurned his advances. When a ghost is sighted at the tower, word spreads that Roddy has come back to haunt Connor. The subsequent death of a hotel employee who knew more than he should about the apparition puts Henrie O on the murder scent once again." Publ Wkly

Hart, Carolyn G.

White elephant dead; {by} Carolyn Hart. Avon Twilight 1999 277p $23

ISBN 0-380-97530-0

LC 99-20833

This "Death on Demand mystery, delivers charming characters, . . . a tantalizing mystery, and plenty of appealing descriptions of coastal landscapes." Booklist

Hart, Carolyn G.

Yankee Doodle dead; a death on demand mystery. {by} Carolyn Hart. Avon Bks. 1998 273p

ISBN 0-380-97529-7

LC 98-13565

Sleuth Annie Darling, "owner of an island resort mystery bookstore, witnesses the murder of a much-hated man during a Fourth of July fundraiser for the local library." Libr J

Hart, Erin

The **book** of Killowen; Erin Hart. Scribner 2013 352 p. (hardcover) $26

ISBN 1451634846; 9781451634846; 9781451634853; 9781451634860

LC 2012028465

In this book, by Erin Hart, "an ancient volume of philosophical heresy provides a motive for murder. . . . After a year away from working in the field, archaeologist Cormac Maguire and pathologist Nora Gavin are back in the bogs, investigating a ninth-century body. . . . They discover that the ancient corpse is not alone--pinned beneath it is the body of Benedict Kavanagh, missing for mere months. . . . Both men were viciously murdered, but centuries apart." (Publisher's note)

Hart, Erin

Haunted ground; Erin Hart. Scribner 2003 328 p. maps (hardcover) $24

ISBN 0743235053; 9780743235051

LC 2002030679

In this crime novel, by Erin Hart, "when farmers cutting turf in a peat bog make a grisly discovery--the perfectly preserved severed head of a young woman with long red hair--Irish archaeologist Cormac Maguire and American pathologist Nora Gavin team up in a case that will open old wounds." (Publisher's note)

Hart, Erin

Lake of sorrows; Erin Hart. Scribner 2004 328 p. maps (hardcover) $24

ISBN 0743247965; 9780743247962

LC 2004052234

In this novel, by Erin Hart, "American forensic pathologist Nora Gavin has been called to an archaeological site in the bleak midlands west of Dublin to assist at an excavation where a well-preserved Iron Age body has been found buried in a peat bog. . . . Nora and archaeologist Cormac Maguire, embroiled in a tumultuous love affair, must team up again professionally, and are soon enmeshed in the web of tangled desires and terrible secrets that surround this untimely death." (Publisher's note)

Hart, John

Down river. Thomas Dunne Books/St. Martin's 2007 325p $24.95

ISBN 978-0-312-35931-7; 0-312-35931-4

LC 2007-21540

"A small North Carolina town is torn apart when a power company wants to buy up all the farmland on the river; some residents cling to their bucolic way of life, while others see only dollar signs. Adam Chase's family has owned the largest parcel in the area for centuries, and his father has no desire to sell. But tempers flare, and soon a young woman is severely beaten, a body is found on the Chase farm, and Adam is the chief suspect. Newly arrived after five years away, Adam is the town pariah. His stepmother had accused him of murdering a family friend, and while the court acquitted him, his family and friends did not. While time has softened some, others seem ready to unleash their stored-up anger. This work is reminiscent of Raymond Chandler's novels, hardboiled and rich with evocative metaphors." Libr J

Hart, John

Iron house. Thomas Dunne Books/St. Martin's Press 2011 421p $25.99

ISBN 9780312380342

LC 2011-06909

This book "focuses on two brothers, Michael and Julian, both raised and abused at the Iron House of the title, an orphanage in the mountains of North Carolina. As a boy, Michael flees the place and ends up on the streets of New York City, where Otto Kaitlin, 'the most powerful crime boss in recent memory,' rescues him and fashions him into an accomplished killing machine and a surrogate son. When Kaitlin dies, his real son, Stevan, fueled by a mixture of jealousy and greed, sets out to destroy everything the now grownup Michael has. Stevan kidnaps Michael's girlfriend, Elena, and threatens emotionally fragile Julian, a creative, tortured genius who is now living at the North Carolina mansion of his adoptive parents. Hart deftly interweaves a complex family history story with Stevan's intense, bloody quest for vengeance." Publ Wkly

Hart, John

The **king** of lies. St. Martin's Minotaur 2006 310p $22.95

ISBN 0-312-34161-X

LC 2005-49774

"More than anything else—more than a terrific whodunit, an unsentimental, clear-eyed story of love and forgiveness, and a gripping family saga—The King of Lies is a masterful piece of writing." Raleigh News & Observer

Hart, John

The **last** child. Minotaur Books 2009 373p $24.95

ISBN 978-0-312-35932-4; 0-312-35932-2

LC 2008-45678

After his twin sister Alyssa disappears, thirteen year-old Johnny Merrimon is determined to find her. When a second girl disappears from his rural North Carolina town, Johnny makes a discovery that sends shock waves through the community.

The author has produced "a novel that is elegant, haunting, and memorable. His characters are given an emotional depth that genre characters seldom have, and the graceful, evocative prose lifts his stories right out of their genre and into the realm of capital-L literature. A must-read for every variety of fiction reader." Booklist

Hart, John, 1965-

Redemption road; A Novel. John Hart. Thomas Dunne Books 2016 432 p. (hardcover) $27.99

ISBN 0312380364; 9780312380366

LC 2015048657

In this novel, by John Hart, a "boy with a gun waits for the man who killed his mother. A troubled detective confronts her past in the aftermath of a brutal shooting. After thirteen years in prison, a good cop walks free as deep in the forest, on the altar of an abandoned church, a body cools in pale linen. . . . This is a town on the brink. This is Redemption Road." (Publisher's note)

"Hart plays brilliantly on the tradition of the southern gothic, but his grasp of character gives this novel--and all his works--the extra dimension that extends his audience well beyond adrenaline junkies." Booklist

Hart, Josephine

★ **Damage**; a novel. Knopf 1991 195p

ISBN 0-679-40135-0

LC 90-53393

"Erotic obsession is a risky subject for fiction. No matter how besotted the victims of this malady may be, their behavior is likely to strike mere witnesses, i.e., readers, as distasteful, hilarious or both. This first novel . . . sidesteps such unintended responses, thanks to old-fashioned British reserve. . . . The understatement works wonders." Time

Hart, Josephine

The **reconstructionist**. Overlook Press 2001 218p $26.95
ISBN 1-58567-170-3

LC 2001-33963

"Jack Harrington, a well-to-do London psychiatrist, immerses himself in the familial problems of his patients' pasts, while admirably repressing his own childhood trauma. His sister, Kate, a seductive writer of 'fluffy things,' is less able to cope with that trauma, and readers learn early on that Jack's good-natured protectiveness toward his sister belies a far more disturbing sort of sibling bond. . . . Hart has packed this little gem of a novel with sparkling aphoristic insights befitting Jack's profession, and her sketches of fragile, childlike characters masquerading as capable adults are deftly drawn." Publ Wkly

Hart, Josephine

The **truth** about love; a novel. Alfred A. Knopf 2009 205p $24
ISBN 978-0-307-27261-4

LC 2009-21375

This "novel explores the grief of the O'Hara family in an unnamed Irish town after the violent death of a teenage son. It is 1962, and the boy, who is also unnamed, is blown up in his own backyard while building a bomb. He was at the age when 'warriors' held a special fascination, his father explains, and the Christian Brothers at school had filled his head with stories of Irish heroes who had fought for independence against the British. . . . It is the second death in the O'Hara family. Shortly before the book opens, a young daughter has died after a long illness, and the loss of a second child is too great for Mrs. O'Hara, who collapses into a deep depression. . . . [This] is a serious, at times compelling, look at family and memory, despair and redemption." Wall Street J

Harte, Bret, 1836-1902

★ The **best** short stories of Bret Harte; edited, and with an introduction, by Robert N. Linscott. Modern Lib. 1947 x, 517 p.p
ISBN 9780394602509 out of print

LC 47030278

Harte, Bret, 1836-1902

The **Luck** of Roaring Camp, and other tales; with pictures of the author and his environment and illustrations of the setting of the book together with an introduction by Louis B. Salomon. Dodd, Mead 1961 309p il

Hartnett, Annie

Rabbit cake; by Annie Hartnett. Tin House Books 2017 331 p. (alk. paper) $15.95
ISBN 9781941040560

LC 2016036583

In this book, by Annie Hartnett, "twelve-year-old Elvis Babbitt has a head for the facts. . . . She knows she should plan to grieve her mother, who has recently drowned while sleepwalking. . . . But there are things Elvis doesn't yet know--like how to keep her sister Lizzie from poisoning herself while sleep-eating. . . . Elvis investigates the strange circumstances of her mother's death and finds comfort, if not answers, in the people (and animals) of Freedom, Alabama." (Publisher's note)

"In Hartnett's winning debut, a memorable young narrator's desire for rationality wrestles with her grief." Pub Wkly

Includes bibliographical references and index

Haruf, Kent, 1943-2014

★ **Benediction**; Kent Haruf. Alfred A. Knopf 2013 272 p. $25.95
ISBN 0307959880; 9780307959881

LC 2012028744

This book looks at the "last, dying days of old Dad Lewis." He "owns a store in a small Colorado town, and his terminal illness draws out the compassion his adult daughter, whom Dad wants to take over the business upon his imminent passing, and sparks an arousal in his long-devoted wife to seek some degree of resolution to an unhealed family wound." (Booklist)

Haruf, Kent

★ **Eventide**. Knopf 2004 300p $24.95
ISBN 0-375-41158-5

LC 2003-60480

This novel takes up where the author's Plainsong left off, "in the windy high-plains country in and around the tiny town of Holt, Colorado. Distress is general: out on their ranch, two stolid elderly brothers discover loneliness after the wayward girl they took in leaves for college; various troubles—illness, death, basic inability to cope—afflict the adults in town; and some young children are set adrift from disintegrating homes, with dangerous consequences. Every action in Holt casts a long shadow, and the gist of Haruf's story is what happens when those shadows touch. (The results are equal parts grace and calamity.) It's rare that such slow, deliberate prose is this highly charged, but Haruf's writing draws power from his sense of character—its limitations and its possibilities—and how it propels action." New Yorker

Haruf, Kent, 1943-2014

★ **Our** souls at night; Kent Haruf. Alfred A. Knopf 2015 192 p. (hardback) $24
ISBN 1101875895; 9781101875896; 9781101911921

LC 2014045500

In this novel by Kent Haruf, "Addie Moore and Louis Waters have been neighbors in the eastern Colorado farming town of Holt for over 40 years. Now . . . Addie has asked Louis to come over every evening and to stay with her in bed, just to get through the lonely nights. Louis is not a risk taker, but he's lonely, too, and so begins their companionable routine, as they talk not only about trivial matters but also about important things in the past." (Library Journal)

"Haruf, who died in 2014, returns to the landscape and daily life of Holt County, Colo., where his previous novels (Plainsong, Eventide, The Tie That Binds) have also been set, this time with a stunning sense of all that's passed and the precious importance of the days that remain." Pub Wkly

Haruf, Kent

★ **Plainsong**. Knopf 1999 301p $27.50
ISBN 0-375-40618-2

LC 99-15606

"From simple strands of language and cuttings of talk, from the look of the high Colorado plains east of Denver almost to the place where Nebraska and Kansas meet, Haruf has made a novel so foursquare, so delicate and lovely, that it has the power to exalt the reader." N Y Times Book Rev

Another available title about the residents of Holt, Colorado is: Eventide (2004)

Harvey, John

Cold in hand. Harcourt 2008 376p $26
ISBN 978-0-15-101462-0; 0-15-101462-0

LC 2008-5630

"Resnick is now living with a much younger DI, Lynn Kellog, and their relationship is one of the best aspects of this fine crime novel, subtly described and convincing. . . . Cold in Hand reveals modern England in all its most depressing messiness while engaging the reader with characters whose warmth and humanity give real pleasure. There is no melodrama here; all the actions and motives that are eventually revealed are rooted in reality; and yet at the heart of the novel is an event so shocking in the context that it could rival anything in the most lurid thriller." Times Lit Suppl

Harvey, John

✓**Cold** light. Holt & Co. 1994 370p
ISBN 0-8050-2046-2

LC 93-6263

"Nice men, murderers, child batterers, discarded lovers, grieving parents, weary probation officers, cynical cops—they all hurt, they all count and they all speak a kind of poetry in this writer's book." N Y Times Book Rev

Harvey, John

✓A **darker** shade of blue; stories. Pegasus Crime 2012 366 p.
ISBN 1605982849; 9781605982847

This book is "[a] collection of 18 previously published short stories. . . . In "Billie's Blues" and "The Sun, the Moon and the Stars," Charlie [Resnick] tries to help out Eileen, a stripper turned whore turned witness to murder, with dour results. . . . Resnick makes a cameo appearance in "Trouble in Mind," which features [author John] Harvey's leading short-story protagonist, Jack Kiley, who . . . notes that Charlie looks like aging lawman Mario Balzic. Kiley, the former footballer and Met copper now eking out a living as a private eye, faces the usual Harvey suspects . . . with the gals usually in for a bad day. Frank Elder, who stars in three Harvey novels, loses his wife and begins his retirement in "Due North," while Tom Whitemore, a minor character in one of the Elder books, faces his own marriage troubles in "Sack O' Woe."" (Kirkus)

Harvey, John

✓**Darkness** and light. Harcourt 2006 350p
ISBN 978-0-15-101133-9; 0-15-101133-8

LC 2005-37771

"A satisfying look at the twists and turns of police work, through a man who can't quite leave his former life behind." Arizona Republic

Harvey, John

✓**Darkness,** Darkness; John Harvey. W W Norton & Co Inc 2014 352 p. $25.95
ISBN 160598616X; 9781605986166

LC 2014434571

In this novel by John Harvey "the discovery of the body of a young woman who disappeared during the [British Miners'] Strike brings Resnick back to the front line to assist in the investigation into the woman's murder--forcing him to confront his past--in what will assuredly be his last case." (Publisher's note)

"Harvey's first Resnick novel, 1989's Lonely Hearts, is one of the London Times List of 100 Best Crime Novels of the last century and there has been no diminishment in quality in the 11 books since. This is Resnick's final case, and every reader of contemporary mystery fiction should be acquainted with this outstanding series and its jazz-loving protagonist whose stories limn the changing world around him. Increasingly, Charlie is an observer more than an actor, but he remains an unforgettable creation." LJ

Harvey, John

✓**Easy** meat. Holt & Co. 1996 388p

LC 96-7307

"As Resnick's eyes are opened, Mr. Harvey writes with painful urgency about the kind of sexual and psychological abuse that no child can completely outgrow. If this is one of Mr. Harvey's darkest books, it is also one of his most enlightened." N Y Times Book Rev

Harvey, John

★ **Far** cry. Houghton Mifflin Harcourt 2010 500p $26
ISBN 978-0-547-31594-2; 0-547-31594-5

LC 2009-29048

First published 2009 in the United Kingdom

"The architecture of Harvey's storytelling begs to be admired, with its multiple narratives, shifting time lines and elaborate plot details. But it's his handling of difficult characters and provocative themes that gives the book weight. All the adults in this story love children, some selflessly and others in ways that make your skin crawl, and they all react differently when the children they love are taken away from them. Harvey's touch is so subtle, his style so seductive, that he distracts us from the fact that Ruth isn't the only person whose choices are determined, or tragically derailed, by love for a child—even if it's someone else's child." N Y Times Book Rev

Harvey, John

Flesh and blood. Carroll & Graff Pubs. 2004 370p $25
ISBN 0-7867-1359-3

"If anyone could make you feel sorry for a serial killer, it's John Harvey, who always writes with tender feeling about commonplace people killers among them damaged by criminal violence." N Y Times Book Rev

Harvey, John

✓**Gone** to ground. Harcourt 2008 387p $25
ISBN 978-0-15-101363-0; 0-15-101363-2

LC 2006-37390

First published 2007 in the United Kingdom

The author, "best known for his now-complete Charlie Resnick series, follows Cambridge police detectives Will Grayson and Helen Walker as they investigate the disfiguring murder of gay film professor Stephen Bryan. Initially focused on Bryan's love life, they soon sense secrets around a book he was writing on '50s movie queen Stella Leonard. Flashbacks from the star's last film add a noir chill to the tale. Bryan's sister, a journalist, uses her position to look into things on her own, with potentially dangerous results as Leonard's family grows fiercely protective. Harvey keeps the devastating secret at the center of the tale well hidden until the end." Rocky Mountain News

Harvey, John

★ **Last** rites. Holt & Co. 1999 312p
ISBN 0-8050-4150-8

LC 98-33766

First published 1998 in the United Kingdom

This final Charlie Resnick mystery "finds Resnick and colleagues attempting to end a local drug war and track down an escaped killer. As always, Resnick slouches his way to understanding, recognizing eventually that the catalyst for much of the mayhem is a love story, as perverted as it is wrenchingly tender. Meanwhile, strands of stories left incomplete in earlier novels come together, some offering more snapshots of wasted lives, others providing glimmers of hope. Harvey ends his story, yes, but he avoids wrapping it all into too neat a package. The great strength of the Resnick series has always been Harvey's grasp of the mess and muddle of human life and his ability to find poetry in the midst of that mess." Booklist

Harvey, John

★ **Still** waters. Holt & Co. 1997 311p

ISBN 0-8050-4149-4

LC 97-12324

"Charlie Resnick, the laconic British police investigator . . . is faced with the death of an abused woman, a friend of his lover, Hannah. At the same time, he tracks down the circumstances of an idiosyncratic art theft. This standard police procedural formula is given a bit of depth by passages detailing relationships, both business and personal, between the members of the Serious Crime Squad." Libr J

Harvey, John

Wasted years. Holt & Co. 1993 339p

LC 93-247

"By now Harvey's economy of prose is a given, as is his ability to pull together the many composite parts—the interlocking crimes, the boozing, infidelity and Resnick's very human bunch of underlings—that make a Charlie Resnick mystery such satisfying reading." Publ Wkly

Harvey, Michael

Brighton; A Novel. by Michael Harvey. HarperCollins 2016 357 p. $27.99

ISBN 006244297X; 9780062442970

In this book, by Michael Harvey, "Kevin Pearce . . . was fifteen when he left town in the back of his uncle's cab. He and his buddy Bobby Scales had just committed heinous violence for what they thought were the best of reasons. . . . Twenty-six years later, Kevin is a Pulitzer Prize-winning journalist for the Boston Globe. He's never been back to his old block. . . . Then he learns his old friend is the prime suspect in a string of local murders." (Publisher's note)

"Sharp as the blades used to gut the guilty and innocent alike, Harvey's fierce stand-alone is a blood-soaked tribute to finding your past and living with the consequences." Kirkus

Harvey, Michael

The **governor's** wife; by Michael Harvey. Alfred A. Knopf 2015 256 p. (hardcover) $24.95

ISBN 0307958647; 9780307958648

LC 2014014535

In this novel by Michael Harvey "it's been two years since disgraced Illinois governor Ray Perry disappeared from a federal courthouse in Chicago moments after being sentenced to thirty-seven years in prison on corruption charges. P.I. Michael Kelly is sitting in his office when he gets an anonymous e-mail offering to pay him nearly a quarter of a million dollars if he will find Perry, no questions asked." (Publisher's note)

"Harvey makes political corruption personal: this isn't a story of anonymous millions being shuffled between various offshore accounts. The consequence of every decision in Kelly's gritty world bleeds." Kirkus

Harvey, Michael T.

The **Chicago** way; [by] Michael Harvey. Knopf 2007 303p $23.95

ISBN 978-0-307-26686-6; 0-307-26686-9

LC 2007-7796

"Harvey's tightly plotted evocation of the Chicago underworld is set in the present but brings to mind the voices of Chandler and Hammett." New York

Harvey, Michael T.

The **Fifth** Floor; [by] Michael Harvey. Alfred A. Knopf 2008 277p $23.95

ISBN 978-0-307-26687-3; 0-307-26687-7

LC 2008-1484

This Michael Kelly thriller "has the ex-Chicago cop taking on what he thinks is a simple domestic violence case. But when he tails Johnny Woods, a fixer for the city's powerful mayor, to what turns out to be a grisly murder scene, Kelly realizes he's stumbled onto a scandal that began with the great Chicago Fire of 1871. Digging deeper, Kelly unearths what was once considered an urban legend: two of Chicago's most eminent families conspiring to eradicate Irish immigrants by burning down the city's slums. As more bodies pile up and he becomes romantically involved with a judge with secrets of her own, Kelly vows to expose the conspiracy, even if that means putting himself on the wrong side of the city's most powerful men. Harvey's plot twists in all the right places, and his noir-inspired dialogue crackles without sounding showy. Marlowe and Spade would readily welcome Michael Kelly into their fold." Publ Wkly

Harvey, Michael T.

We all fall down; [by] Michael Harvey. Alfred A. Knopf 2011 297p $24.95

ISBN 978-0-307-27251-5

LC 2011-04681

Chicago cop turned private investigator Michael Kelly is on a hunt for the people who poisoned his city by unleashing a pathogen in a subway tunnel.

"A gripping crime novel with a frightening message about very plausible biological warfare." Booklist

Harwood, John

The **ghost** writer. Harcourt 2004 369p $25

ISBN 0-15-101074-9

LC 2003-24918

"Gerard Freeman grows up on the windswept southern coast of Australia in the late 20th century with a controlling mother strangely silent about the details of her childhood in England. His only solace is steadfast English pen friend, Alice, to whom he confides everything. What was Gerard's mother, Phyllis, hoping to escape when she left England? The protagonist slowly pieces together his mother's past with the aid of short stories written by his great-grandmother, Viola. These cunning tales, filled with supernatural occurrences and séances, are seamlessly embedded in the main narrative, offering Gerard—and readers—enticing clues into his troubled family's history. After Phyllis's death, her newly liberated son travels to England, hoping to learn more and to pursue elusive Alice. As he searches through the country house his mother inhabited long ago, Gerard finds past and present fusing in horrifying fashion." Publ Wkly

Haslett, Adam

★ **Imagine** me gone; a novel. Adam Haslett. Little, Brown & Co. 2016 368 p. (hardcover) $26

ISBN 0316261351; 9780316261357

LC 2015028890

Pulitzer Prize Finalist: Fiction (2017)

In this book, by Adam Haslett, "when Margaret's fiancé, John, is hospitalized for depression in 1960s London, she faces a choice: carry on with their plans despite what she now knows of his condition, or back away from the suffering it may bring her. She decides to marry him." (Publisher's note)

"This touching chronicle of love and pain traces half a century in a family of five from the parents' engagement in 1963 through a father's and son's psychological torments and a final crisis." Kirkus

Haslett, Adam

Union Atlantic; a novel. Nan A. Talese/Doubleday 2009 304p $26

ISBN 978-0-385-52447-6; 0-385-52447-1

LC 2009-11875

A novel about "Doug Fanning, a handsome, renegade Boston securities trader whose imprudent bets on the Japanese markets threaten to cause systemic bank failure. . . . Unfolding in the fictional town of Finden, Massachusetts, the novel's central narrative pits Doug in an oblique battle of wills with his neighbor Charlotte Graves, a former history teacher and dismayed old-school liberal who resents the size and style of his massive new house. While the two ostensibly wrangle over property rights, the real stakes of their disagreement is not taste but ideology—or perhaps better, pathology. . . . Set during the run-up to the invasion of Iraq, Union Atlantic is like a pressure-compacted version of a Tom Wolfe zeitgeist doorstop, complete with a diffuse cast of characters (bankers, pot-smoking teenagers, a conflicted corporate whistleblower, the president of the Federal Reserve Bank of New York) and myriad cultural obsessions: about the corporatization of war, the joyless hedonism of American society and the soullessness of suburban life." Time Out N Y

Hassman, Tupelo

Girlchild; Tupelo Hassman. Farrar, Straus and Giroux 2012 275 p.

ISBN 9780374162573

LC 2011041209

Alex Award (2013)

In this novel, a "bright young girl must endure family dysfunction and sexual abuse while coming of age in a Reno trailer park during the late 1980s. Life in the Calle de Las Flores trailer park, as Rory Dawn Hendrix tells it, comes with its own unique rituals and social mores. . . . Her hard-drinking mother Johanna . . . entrusts Rory to a sullen teenage neighbor, Carol. It turns out that Carol's father . . . has been molesting Carol, and preys upon Rory as well. And when he in turn moves away, taking that secret with him, it is left to Rory to rebuild her shattered self-esteem. Taking inspiration from a battered library copy of The Girl Scout Handbook, Rory does a remarkable job raising herself, while trying to let go of the people (and hurts) that no longer serve her." (Kirkus)

Hatcher, Robin Lee

Catching Katie; Robin Lee Hatcher. Tyndale House Publishers 2003 353p o.p.; o.p.

ISBN 0842360999; 9780842360999

LC 2003013281

This book takes place "[i]n 1916 Idaho, [when] Katie Jones has dedicated her life to the campaign for women's suffrage. Until now she has successfully avoided the ties of marriage, fearing it would obscure her message. Will her growing love for childhood chum Ben Rafferty compromise her calling?" (Publisher's note)

Hatcher, Robin Lee

A **promise** kept; Robin Lee Hatcher. Thomas Nelson 2014 304 p. (pbk.) $15.99

ISBN 1401687652; 9781401687656

LC 2013029521

In this book by Robin Lee Hatcher, "the day Allison issued her husband an ultimatum, . . . she never expected he would actually leave. She was certain God had promised to heal; it was clear that she'd misunderstood. But when she finds a wedding dress and a collection of journals in Emma's attic, a portrait of her aunt emerges that takes Allison completely by surprise: a portrait of a heartbroken woman. She is forced to ask a difficult question: Does she really surrender every piece of her life to the Lord?" (Publisher's note)

"[N]arrated alternately by Emma and Allison, Hatcher's latest is an uplifting and heartwarming story about the power of faith to set people free from the pain of their pasts." LJ

Hatoum, Milton

The **brothers**; translated from the Portuguese by John Gledson. Farrar, Straus & Giroux 2002 240p $23

ISBN 0-374-14118-5

LC 2002-17054

Original Portuguese edition, 2000

"Set in a Lebanese immigrant community in the Brazilian port town of Manaus, this is the story of identical twins, Yaqub and Omar, whose lives take radically different paths: one toward professional success in Brazil's metropolis São Paulo, the other to drunken dissipation in the lowly port of his birth. Set against the backdrop of a city whose very character is undergoing radical change, it is also the story of a family on the verge of conflagration from incestuous passion and riddled with secrets and guilt. . . . Hatoum suggests much while fully revealing little; he's content to unfold his lush narrative—replete with the dances, exotic sights, smells and fragrances of his luscious Brazil—one vivid bolt of cloth at a time." Publ Wkly

Hauck, Rachel

How to catch a prince; Rachel Hauck. Zondervan 2015 368 p. (Royal wedding series) (softcover) $15.99

ISBN 0310315549; 9780310315544

LC 2014033423

In this book, by Rachel Hauck, "American heiress Corina Del Rey caught her prince once. But the tragedy of war kept her too long in a fog of grief. . . . Prince Stephen of Brighton is one of the world's most eligible bachelors and a star rugby player, trying to make sense of his life. His days in Afghanistan with the Royal Air Command will mark him forever. . . . With a little heavenly help, Prince Stephen and Corina embark on a journey of truth." (Publisher's note)

"Hauck has written a sensitive, emotion-filled story about the effects of war on a relationship. Her characters are flawed and realistic. This engaging, faith-based book is part of the Royal Wedding Series" Booklist

Hauser, Emily

For the most beautiful; a novel of the women of Troy. Emily Hauser. Pegasus Books 2017 391 p. maps (hardcover) $25.95

ISBN 1681773015; 9781681773018; 9781681773681

This book, by Emily Hauser, "is a breathtaking tale of love and revenge, destiny and the determination, as these two brave women, . . . [Krisayis, the ambitious, determined daughter of the High Priest of Troy, and Briseis, loyal and passionate princess of Pedasus,] . . . the heroes of the Trojan War, and the gods themselves come face to face in an epic battle that will decide the fate of Troy." (Publisher's note)

"Hauser turns the reader's attention to the women driving the story behind the scenes in this consuming debut novel, the first installment of the Golden Apple Trilogy." Pub Wkly

Includes bibliographical references.

Havley, Noah

The **good** father; by Noah Hawley. Doubleday 2012 320p.

ISBN 9780385535533

LC 2011017657

This book tells the story of "[t]he father of a man who assassinates a presidential candidate [and] tries to make sense of his son's crime. . . . Dr. Paul Allen is a successful rheumatologist happily living with his second wife and their twin sons in a chic Connecticut enclave. Contact with Daniel, his aloof son from a previous marriage, is sporadic, and when Daniel drops out of Vassar in his first year to 'see the country,' Dr. Allen shrugs it off as a youthful foible, . . . so the Secret Service agents who appear at his door are a great surprise. Daniel, aka Carter Allen Cash, has shot and killed the Democratic presidential front-runner. . . . Despite the overwhelming evidence against Daniel, Dr. Allen won't believe that his son is guilty . . . and becomes convinced of a conspiracy involving a second man." (Publishers Weekly)

Hawke, Ethan

Ash Wednesday; a novel. Knopf 2002 221p

ISBN 0-375-41326-X

LC 2002-20811

"Hawke's text at times reads raw, but the novel's conversational tone, dual first-person narration and, above all, direct exploration of the simple truths of life and love make this a worthwhile tale and an honest one." Publ Wkly

Hawkes, John

★ The **blood** oranges. New Directions 1971 271p

"This highly rhapsodic, sensual novel suggests both in title and substance the decline of vitality and enlightenment in the characters' lives as in each new day. Reminiscent of Lawrence in the concern with atmosphere and lushness of description, the book is powerfully evocative of a sometimes comic, sometimes hallucinatory sense of timelessness, obsession, and escape from reality." Choice

Hawkins, Paula

★ The **girl** on the train; a novel. Paula Hawkins. Riverhead Books, a member of Penguin Group (USA) 2015 323 p. $26.95

ISBN 1594633665; 9781594633669; 9781594634123

LC 2014027001

In this book, by Paula Hawkins, "Rachel takes the same commuter train every morning. Every day she rattles down the track . . . and stops at the signal that allows her to daily watch the same couple breakfasting on their deck. . . . And then she sees something shocking. It's only a minute until the train moves on, but it's enough. Now everything's changed. Unable to keep it to herself, Rachel offers what she knows to the police, and becomes inextricably entwined in what happens next." (Publisher's note)

"The novel is alternately narrated by three equally unlikable women, and Hawkins very deliberately doles out tantalizing information, but what really gives this novel its compulsive readability is the way she so expertly mines female archetypes: the jealous ex-wife, the smug mistress, the emotionally damaged femme fatale." Booklist

Hawkins, Scott

★ The **Library** at Mount Char; Scott Hawkins. Random House Inc. 2015 400 p. (hardcover) $26

ISBN 0553418602; 9780553418606

LC 2014045600

In this fantasy novel, by Scott Hawkins, "Carolyn's . . . ordinary suburban subdivision was destroyed and the man she now calls Father took her and 11 other children to study in his very unusual Library. Carolyn studied languages--and not only human ones. The other children studied the ways of beasts, learned healing and resurrection, and wandered in the lands of the dead or in possible futures. Now they're all in their 30s, and Father is missing." (Kirkus Reviews)

"Hawkins's cunning plotting is backed up by crisp dialogue, a sensation of constant dread, and a solid, subtly weird setting." Pub Wkly

Hawley, Noah

Before the Fall; Noah Hawley. Grand Central Publishing 2016 400 p. $26

ISBN 1455561789; 9781455561780

In this novel, by Noah Hawley, "eleven people--ten privileged, one down-on-his-luck painter--depart Martha's Vineyard on a private jet headed for New York. Sixteen minutes later . . . the plane plunges into the ocean. The only survivors are Scott Burroughs--the painter--and a four-year-old boy, who is now the last remaining member of [a] . . . powerful media mogul's family. With chapters weaving between the aftermath of the crash and the backstories of the passengers and crew members . . . the mystery surrounding the tragedy heightens." (Publisher's note)

"This is a gritty tale of a man overwhelmed by unwelcome notoriety, with a stunning, thoroughly satisfying conclusion." Pub Wkly

Hawthorne, Nathaniel

★ **Collected** novels. Literary Classics of the United States 1983 1272p $39.50

ISBN 0-940450-08-9

LC 82-18031

In Fanshawe (1828), two students at Harley College— one normal and outgoing, the other isolated and scholarly—both fall in love with a third student, Ellen Langdon. When Ellen is kidnapped, the isolated Fanshawe rescues her, only to turn down her marriage proposal afterward. The scarlet letter, The House of the Seven Gables, The Blithedale romance, and The marble faun are entered separately.

Hawthorne, Nathaniel

Complete short stories of Nathaniel Hawthorne. Hanover House 1959 615p

Hawthorne, Nathaniel

★ The **House** of the Seven Gables; introduction by Mary Oliver. Modern Library 2001 312p pa $8.75

ISBN 0-375-75687-6

LC 00-64585

First published 1851

"Follows the fortunes of a decayed New England family, consisting of four members—Hephzibah Pyncheon, her brother Clifford, their cousin Judge Pyncheon, and other cousin Phoebe, a country girl. At the time the story opens Hephzibah is living in great poverty at the old homestead, the House of the Seven Gables. With her is [her brother] Clifford, just released from prison, where he had served a term of thirty years for the supposed murder of a rich uncle. Judge Pyncheon, who was influential in obtaining the innocent Clifford's arrest, that he might hide his own wrongdoing, now seeks to confine him in an asylum on the charge of insanity. Hephzibah's pitiful efforts to shield this brother, to support him and herself by keeping a scentshop, to circumvent the machinations of the judge, are described through the greater portion of the novel. The sudden death of the malevolent cousin frees them and makes them possessors of his wealth." Keller. Reader's Dig of Books

Hawthorne, Nathaniel

★ The **scarlet** letter; with an introduction by Alfred Kazin. Knopf 1992 xxvii, 273p $18

ISBN 0-679-41731-1

LC 92-52902

"Set in 17th-century Salem, the novel is built around three scaffold scenes, which occur at the beginning, the middle, and the end. The story opens with the public condemnation of Hester Prynne, and the exhortation that she confess the name of the father of Pearl, her illegitimate child. Hester's husband, an old and scholarly physician, just arrived from England, assumes the name of Roger Chillingworth in order to seek out Hester's lover and revenge himself upon him. He attaches himself as physician to a respected and seemingly holy minister, Arthur Dimmesdale, suspecting that he is the father of the child. The Scarlet Letter traces the effect of the actual and symbolic sin on all the characters." Benet's Reader's Ency of Am Lit

Hay, Elizabeth

Late nights on air; a novel. Counterpoint 2008 363p $24

ISBN 978-1-58243-408-7; 1-582-43408-5

LC 2007-43785

First published 2007 in Canada

"The plot of this novel is a faint signal, a series of short moments, sometimes funny, sometimes poignant, often flecked with intimations of tragedy. Hay's writing is so alluring and her lost souls so endearing that you'll lean in to catch the story's delicate developments as these characters shuffle along through quiet desperation and yearning." Washington Post Book World

Hay, Elizabeth

A **student** of weather. Counterpoint 2001 368p

ISBN 1-58243-123-X

LC 00-64445

This novel "begins circa 1930 on the drought-ravished prairies of Saskatchewan, the home of two motherless sisters. The elder, Lucinda, is fair and diligent, Norma Joyce dark and willful, and both fall for a handsome, rambling botanist from fabled Ottawa, Maurice Dove. . . . As the sisters embark on a tragic rivalry that will determine the course of their lives, their story becomes a fairy tale in which solitude, work, art, and desire acquire mystical significance as Hay adroitly weaves their passions into luminous descriptions of extreme weather and the grand cycle of the seasons." Booklist

Hayder, Mo

Birdman; Mo Hayder. 1st ed. Doubleday 1999 327 p. (hardcover) $23.95

ISBN 038549694X; 9780385496940

LC 99015941

In this mystery novel, as the newest member of the Area Major Investigation Pool, Detective Inspector Jack Caffrey "is called to examine the deaths of five women, each found with a bird in her chest cavity. When other investigators take the case in a wrong direction, Caffery risks his new position to find the truth." (Library Journal)

Hayder, Mo

Gone. Atlantic Monthly Press 2011 415p $24

ISBN 978-0-8021-1964-3; 0-8021-1964-6

A crime novel featuring "Detective Inspector Jack Caffery of Bristol's Major Crime Investigation Unit and Sgt. Flea Marley, who heads up the Underwater Search Unit. This artfully constructed procedural opens with a car-jacking that becomes a kidnapping after the thief drives off with a little girl in the back seat. The narrative takes its first chilling turn when Caffery's team detects a pattern of other 'accidental' kidnappings, indicating that the carjacker was stalking little girls all along. More shocks are in store, but for once the visceral thrills don't come at the expense of character. By giving her villain the intelligence to inflict as much emotional as physical pain, Hayder makes him less of a monster and more of a terror." N Y Times Book Rev

Hayder, Mo

Hanging hill; Mo Hayder. Atlantic Monthly Press 2012 432 p.

ISBN 0802120067; 9780802120069

The story in this book "centers around a pair of estranged sisters--one policewoman--and the gruesome homicide of a teenage beauty, which leads them deeper than they ever anticipated into an underground world of sex and violence. One morning in picture-perfect Bath, England, a teenage girl's body is found on the towpath of a canal: Lorne Woods--beautiful, popular, and apparently the victim of a disturbingly brutal murder. . . . Zoe Benedict . . . is convinced the department head needs to look beyond the usual domestic motives to solve the case. . . . When Zoe's investigation turns up evidence that Lorne's attempts to break into modeling had delivered her into the world of webcam girls and amateur porn, a crippling secret from Zoe's past seems determined to emerge." (Publisher's note)

Hayder, Mo

Poppet; Mo Hayder. Pgw 2013 400 p. (hardcover) $25

ISBN 0802121071; 9780802121073

This horror-thriller novel, by Mo Hayder, is part of the "Jack Caffery" series. "Everything goes according to procedure when a patient, Isaac is released into the community from a high security mental health ward. But when the staff realize that he was connected to a series of unexplained episodes of self-harm amongst the ward's patients, and . . . was released in error, they call on Detective Jack Caffery to investigate, and to track Isaac down before he can kill again." (Publisher's note)

Hayder, Mo

Ritual. Atlantic Monthly Press 2008 410p $24

ISBN 978-0-87113-992-4

At the start of this crime novel featuring Det. Insp. Jack Caffery, "Sgt. Phoebe Flea Marley, a police diver, retrieves a severed hand from Bristol harbor. Without a corpse, the investigation stalls, until fingerprints identify the hand as belonging to Ian Mossy Mallows, a known heroin junkie. While Caffery pursues the drug angle, Flea uncovers a possible connection to muti, a brand of African witchcraft and traditional medicine that incorporates body parts into its rituals. Digging deeper, Caffery and Flea discover that Mallows may still be alive and the men responsible may be using muti as a cover for even darker purposes. . . . Hayder vividly evokes torture and drug abuse, but the violence is never gratuitous. Readers looking for visceral thrills need look no further than this gritty English series." Publ Wkly

Hayder, Mo

Skin; Mo Hayder. Bantam Press 2009 384 p. (ebook) $13.00; (paperback) $13.00; (hardcover) $22.00

ISBN 9780802198013; 9780802145178; 9780802119308 out of print

LC 2009437589

In this novel, by Mo Hayder, "when the decomposed body of a young woman is found near some railway tracks just outside Bristol one hot May morning, all indications are that she committed suicide. . . . But DI Jack Caffery is not so sure. . . . Police diver Flea Marley is working alongside Caffery. . . . And then she makes a discovery that changes everything." (Publisher's note)

Hayder, Mo

The **treatment**; Mo Hayder. 1st ed. Doubleday 2002 357 p. (hardcover) $23.95

ISBN 0385496958; 9780385496957

LC 2002280302

This is Mo Hayder's second Jack Caffery novel. Here, a "man and his wife lie tied up and imprisoned in their own home. When they are discovered, badly dehydrated and bearing the marks of a brutal beating, they reveal one final horror: Their young son has disappeared. Called in to investigate, Jack Caffery uses all the tricks of the forensic investigator's trade to piece together the scanty clues at the crime scene." (Publisher's note)

Haydon, Elizabeth

Destiny: child of the sky. TOR Bks. 2001 556p $27.95

ISBN 0-312-86750-6

LC 2001-27473

Sequel to: Prophecy: child of earth

"Though obviously inspired by music theory, Norse and Celtic folklore, and seemingly such authors as Tolkien, C.S. Lewis, Patricia A. McKillip, Anne McCaffrey and Palmer Brown (Cheerful), the author uses a fluid writing style to build a world uniquely and compellingly her own." Publ Wkly

Haydon, Elizabeth

The **Merchant** Emperor; Elizabeth Haydon. Tor Books 2014 432 p. (The symphony of ages) (hardback) $25.99

ISBN 0765305666; 9780765305664; 9781429943970

LC 2014014085

This novel, by Elizabeth Haydon, book 7 in her fantasy "The symphony of ages" series, "The war that they had feared is now upon them. Ashe and Rhapsody, leaders of the Cymrian Alliance, are gathering their allies to combat the machinations of Talquist, who will soon be crowned emperor of Sorbold. . . . [In this episode] beloved characters are forced to make soul shattering sacrifices." (Publisher's note)

"For those familiar with the history of Rhapsody and Ashe, two of the main characters from previous books, this volume will provide additional depth to their personalities as they are forced to make difficult decisions to save not only themselves and those they love but also perhaps the world they live in... followers of the series will be delighted with it." Booklist

Haydon, Elizabeth

Prophecy; child of earth. TOR Bks. 2000 480p $27.95

ISBN 0-312-86751-4

LC 00-26836

Sequel to Rhapsody (1999)

"The skysinger Rhapsody and her two FirBolg companions seek to carve out a place for themselves in a new world even as their lives move inexorably toward the fulfillment of an ancient prophecy. As momentous events take shape around the three heroes, other forces work hard to undermine their hope and bring the powers of evil closer to victory. . . . Haydon's epic saga of the endless battle between light and darkness resounds with the richness of ancient myths reworked into new forms." Libr J

Hayes, Terry

★ **I** Am Pilgrim; A Thriller. by Terry Hayes. Pocket Books 2014 624 p. $26.99

ISBN 1439177724; 9781439177723

This book, by Terry Hayes, "depicts the collision course between two geniuses, one a tortured hero and one a determined terrorist. . . . PILGRIM is the code name for a world class and legendary secret agent. His adversary is a man known only to the reader as the Saracen. . . . In offering the NYPD some casual assistance with [a] case, Pilgrim gets pulled back into the intelligence underground. . . . The inevitable encounter between Pilgrim and the Saracen will come in Turkey." (Publisher's note)

"[T]he race against time to save the world has been done before but seldom this well. . . . [A] taut and muscular thriller." LJ

Haynes, Dana

Crashers. Minotaur Books 2010 343p $24.99

ISBN 978-0-312-59988-1; 0-312-59988-9

LC 2009-46155

"The premise is simple: a crack team of National Transportation Safety Board experts investigate airplane crashes. Normally they take months to sift through wreckage and evidence, but this time they have mere days: if they can't figure out what and who brought down CascadeAir Flight 818, more planes will fall from the sky. The lead characters, the Crashers, are cut from familiar molds: the hotshot engineer, the voice-recorder specialist, the veteran pathologist, and so on. . . . The plot itself relies on familar assembly-cast TV crime dramas, but it is well paced and generates plenty of tension. A solid debut that, with some fine-tuning, could become an engaging series." Booklist

Haynes, Elizabeth

Dark tide; a novel. Elizabeth Haynes. HarperCollins 2012 400 p. (hardcover) $25.99; (paperback) $14.99

ISBN 0062197339; 9780062197320; 9780062197337

LC 2012024422

This novel, by Elizabeth Haynes, is a "thriller about a woman caught in an underworld of corruption and murder. . . . Genevieve has finally . . . [left] the stress of London behind and start a new life aboard a houseboat in Kent. . . . But the night of her boat-warming party, a body washes up, and to Genevieve's horror, she recognizes the victim. . . . The death can't have anything to do with her. Or so she thinks." (Publisher's note)

Hayter, Sparkle

Bandit queen boogie. Three Rivers Press 2004 290p pa $13

ISBN 1-4000-4744-7 pa

LC 2003-25853

"Two childhood friends travel across Europe the summer after their college graduation. The trip was meant for Chloe and her boyfriend, but after he dumps her, Blackie agrees to go instead. Unfortunately, brokenhearted Chloe is not much fun to be around—until the two decide to start robbing the sleazy married men who proposition them. Chloe soon perks up, getting addicted to the thrill and the possibility of being caught. Although the story centers on Chloe and Blackie, numerous characters and story lines come together when they steal a statue of the Hindu god Ganesh that contains a valuable treasure belonging to an Indian crime boss. . . . The characters are vividly rendered, and Hayter deftly weaves together the varying story lines and settings." Libr J

Haywood, Gar Anthony

Cemetery Road. Severn House 2010 216p $28.95

ISBN 978-0-7278-6851-0; 0-7278-6851-9

First published 2009 in the United Kingdom

"Errol 'Handy' White is working as a handyman in the Twin Cities when he gets word that his old friend, R. J. Burrows, has been murdered in Los Angeles. Handy knows he must return to L.A. to attend the funeral, but he also knows that when he sets foot in L.A., where he, R. J., and another friend, O'Neal Holden, now a rising politician, came up together, a terrible secret is in danger of coming to light. As young men, the three friends dabbled in crime in South Central L.A. until a revenge heist at a drug dealer's home went tragically awry. Handy has been running ever since, from the crime and from himself, but now realizes that if he is to help R. J.'s daughter find her father's killer, his running days are over. Haywood melds an intricately plotted but highly suspenseful thriller to a moving story of belated coming-of-age, as the introspective, deeply troubled Handy forces himself to confront what has gone wrong with his life." Booklist

Hazzard, Shirley

★ The **great** fire. Farrar, Straus & Giroux 2003 278p $24

ISBN 0-374-16644-7

LC 2003-49189

National Book Award: Fiction (2003)

"The time is 1947-48, and the place is, primarily, East Asia. . . . Our hero, and indeed he fills the requirements to be called one, is Aldred Leith, who is English and part of the occupation forces in Japan; his particular military task is damage survey. He has an interesting past, including, most recently, a two-year walk across civil-war-torn China to write a book. In the present. . .he meets the teenage daughter and younger son of a local Australian commander. And, as Helen is growing headlong into womanhood, this novel of war's aftermath becomes a story of love—or more to the point, of the restoration of the capacity for love once global and personal trauma have been shed." Booklist

Hazzard, Shirley

★ The **transit** of Venus. Viking 1980 337p

LC 79-21754

This "is an exceedingly ambitious novel; a stunning and at times bewildering galaxy of ideas. From a literary and intellectual standpoint it is a challenge. . . . Miss Hazzard's greatest achievement in this novel is the suspense she creates from unfinished relationships. Instead of spinning off in different directions through space, these characters collide once again, drawn together by an ineluctable magnetism." Christ Sci Monit

Heacox, Kim

Jimmy Bluefeather; a novel. Kim Heacox. Alaska Northwest Books 2015 264 p. (hardcover) $26.99

ISBN 9781941821688

LC 2015007906

In this novel, by Kim Heacox, "Old Keb Wisting is . . . the last living canoe carver in the village of Jinkaat, in Southeast Alaska. . . . When his grandson, James, a promising basketball player, ruins his leg in a logging accident and tells his grandpa that he has nothing left to live for, Old Keb comes alive and finishes his last canoe, with help from his grandson. Together . . . they embark on a great canoe journey." (Publisher's note)

"Heacox does a superb job of transcending his characters' unique geography to create a heartwarming, all-American story. Jinkaat, Alaska, can stand beside Twain's Missouri and Anderson's Winesburg, Ohio." Booklist

Healey, Emma

Elizabeth is missing; Emma Healey. Harper 2014 320 p. (hardcover : alk. paper) $25.99

ISBN 0062309668; 9780062309662; 9780062309686

LC 2013036932

"Maud, an aging grandmother, is slowly losing her memory--and her grip on everyday life. Yet she refuses to forget her best friend Elizabeth, whom she is convinced is missing and in terrible danger. But no one will listen to Maud--not her frustrated daughter, Helen, not her caretakers, not the police, and especially not Elizabeth's mercurial son, Peter. Armed with handwritten notes she leaves for herself and an overwhelming feeling that Elizabeth needs her help, Maud resolves to discover the truth and save her beloved friend." (Publisher's note)

"Part mystery, part meditation on memory, part Dickensian revelation of how apparent charity may hurt its recipients, this is altogether brilliant." Booklist

Heathcock, Alan

Volt; stories. Graywolf Press 2011 207p pa $15

ISBN 978-1-55597-577-7; 1-55597-577-1

This is a collection of eight linked stories set in an imaginary rural town.

"In these eight stories, four previously published in literary journals, the settings are small towns in the mountains and valleys of the northern plains states. No peaceful rural areas exist in Heathcock's imagination. There's a violent death, whether accidental or planned, in every story. The last six stories constitute a terrific cycle, set in the same town, with the repeating characters of sheriff, mayor, and minister and plots that provide climaxes and resolutions that suit the cycle. . . . Heathcock displays a real talent for describing a character in a telling phrase and shows a deep appreciation of the petty and serious violence of daily life. Recommend Volt to fans of Cormac McCarthy, Larry Brown, and Tom Franklin." Booklist

Hedges, Peter

The **Heights**. Dutton 2010 295p $25.95

ISBN 978-0-525-95113-1; 0-525-95113-X

LC 2009-20781

"Hedges brings a touch of farce into the many twists before the climax. Warmhearted yet unsentimental, a smooth weave of marital and neighborhood dynamics." Kirkus

Hedges, Peter

What's eating Gilbert Grape. Washington Square Press 1999 319p pa $14

ISBN 978-0-671-03854-0; 0-671-03854-0

"Just about everything in Endora, Iowa (pop. 1,091 and dwindling) is eating Gilbert Grape, a twenty-four-year-old grocery clerk who dreams only of leaving. His enormous mother, once the town sweetheart, has been eating nonstop ever since her husband's suicide, and the floor beneath her TV chair is threatening to cave in. Gilbert's long-suffering older sister, Amy, still mourns the death of Elvis, and his knockout younger sister has become hooked on makeup, boys, and Jesus -- in that order. But the biggest event on the horizon for all the Grapes is the eighteenth birthday of Gilbert's younger brother, Arnie, who is a living miracle just for having survived so long." (Publisher's note)

Heffernan, William

The **Dinosaur** Club; a novel. Morrow 1997 303p

ISBN 0-688-14988-X

LC 96-46637

"At age 49, Jack Fallon discovers that his life is plummeting out of control. In one fell swoop, his wife leaves him and corporate downsizing threatens his livelihood. Always the warrior, Jack organizes other fifty-ish management employees to fight their ruthless corporate leaders, and the 'Dinosaur Club' is born. Working against formidable odds, the Dinosaurs engage in hilarious hijinks and serious espionage to foil their chief executives. What Jack does not count on is falling in love with Samantha Moore, legal counsel for the corporation. . . . Heffernan is masterly in examining the scruples of corporate downsizing with a discerning eye and blends levity in his cauldron of good and evil." Libr J

Heggen, Thomas

Mister Roberts; with an introduction by David P. Smith. Naval Inst. Press 1992 xxii, 200p $34.95

ISBN 1-55750-723-6

LC 92-9422

A reissue of the title first published 1946 by Houghton Mifflin

"The leisurely narrative is told in a very few incidents, all centering about an admirable young lieutenant miserably defeated in his desire to get into fighting. A quiet, credible story of the corroding effects of apathy and boredom on men who, in battle, might have been heroes." New Yorker

Hegi, Ursula

Children and fire; a novel. Scribner 2011 272p $25

ISBN 978-1-4516-0829-8; 1-4516-0829-2

LC 2011-08398

"A thoughtful, sidelong approach to the worst moment in Germany's history that invites us to understand how decent people come to collaborate with evil." Kirkus

Hegi, Ursula

Stones from the river. Poseidon Press 1994 507p

ISBN 0-671-78075-1

LC 93-33533

"This moving, elegiac novel commands our compassion and respect for the wisdom and courage to be found in unlikely places, in unlikely times." N Y Times Book Rev

Hegi, Ursula

The **vision** of Emma Blau. Simon & Schuster 2000 432p $25

ISBN 0-684-82997-5

LC 99-56392

"Hegi has created a milieu full of sexual energy—the book is often erotic—and has captured both the tension and love endemic to all tight-knit families. Compelling and absorbing, this old-fashioned saga is rife with passion, tragedy, and redemption." Libr J

Heinlein, Robert A.

★ The **moon** is a harsh mistress. Putnam 1966 383p

"Colonists of the Moon declare independence from Earth, and contrive to win the ensuing battle with the aid of a sentient computer. Action-adventure with some exploration of new possibilities in social organization and fierce assertion of the motto 'There Ain't No Such Thing as a Free Lunch.'" Anatomy of Wonder 4

Heinlein, Robert A.

Starship troopers; Ace trade pbk. ed.; Ace Books 2006 279p pa $15

ISBN 0-441-01410-0; 978-0-441-01410-1

LC 2006-40451

First published 1959 by Putnam

"Originally intended as a juvenile, although not published as such, this violent novel of interstellar 'war' won a 1960 Hugo but also gained RAH the reputation of being a militarist, even a 'fascist.'" Sci Fic Ency

Heinlein, Robert A.

★ **Stranger** in a strange land. Putnam 1961 408p hardcover o.p. pa $16.95

ISBN 0-441-78838-6 pa

"The hero is a human born of space travelers from earth and raised by Martians. He is brought to the totalitarian post-World War III world that is in many ways depicted as a satire of the U.S. in the 1960s, marked by repressiveness in sexual morality and religion. The plot, which tells how the heroic stranger creates a Utopian society in which people preserve their individuality but share a brotherhood of community, made Heinlein and his novel cult objects for young people dedicated to a counterculture." Oxford Companion to Am Lit. 5th edition

Heinlein, Robert A.

Variable star; Robert A. Heinlein and Spider Robinson. Tor 2006 318p (pbk.) $7.99; (hbk.) $24.95

ISBN 9780765351685; 076531312X

LC 2006006865

This science fiction book, based on "a fifties-era outline" by author Robert A. Heinlein, tells the story of "a young space explorer colonizing a new world. After discovering his fiancee and supposed fellow orphan is really a wealthy mogul's granddaughter, struggling musician Joel Johnston gets cold feet and grabs the next outbound starship. With his formative agricultural training on Ganymede, Joel has skills that come in handy tending goats and crops in preparation for landfall on Brasil Novo. Yet his vow to abandon love in favor of farming meets some surprising--and romantically intriguing--challenges." (Booklist)

Heiny, Katherine

Single, carefree, mellow; stories. by Katherine Heiny. Alfred A. Knopf 2015 240 p. (hardcover) $23.95

ISBN 0385353634; 9780385353632; 9780804173155

LC 2014003558

In this short story collection by Katherine Heiny, women "are grappling with unwelcome houseguests, disastrous birthday parties, needy but loyal friends, and all manner of love, secrets, and betrayal. Heiny chronicles the ways in which we are unfaithful to each other, both willfully and unwittingly." (Publisher's note)

"Heiny's 11 stories are heightened by her depictions of her characters' internal struggles as they candidly confront their infidelities and other desires." Booklist

Hellenga, Robert

The **Italian** lover; a novel. Little, Brown 2007 343p $23.99

ISBN 978-0-316-11763-0; 0-316-11763-3

LC 2007-8716

"Hellenga smoothly merges past and present while injecting Margot's story with fresh talent. . . . This being Italy, there are affairs, fiery outbursts and lots of rich food. This being Hellenga, the story is just as rich." N Y Times Book Rev

Heller, Joseph

★ **Catch**-22; a novel. Simon & Schuster 1999 415p $26

ISBN 0-684-86513-0

LC 00-265132

"A comic, satirical, surreal, and apocalyptic novel . . . which describes the ordeals and exploits of a group of American airmen based on a small Mediterranean island during the Italian campaign of the Second World War, and in particular the reactions of Captain Yossarian, the protagonist." Oxford Companion to Engl Lit. 6th edition

Followed by Closing time

Heller, Joseph

Good as Gold. Simon & Schuster 1979 447p

ISBN 0-671-22923-0

LC 78-23894

"Dr. Bruce Gold, forty-eight-year-old professor (Jewish) of literature (English) and author of many seminal articles in small journals (unread), finds himself facing the prospect of becoming a high Washington official. The offer comes from Ralph Newsome (Protestant), a presidential aide. . . . {Gold accepts} and soon meets Andrea Conover, the tall, beautiful, gifted daughter (also Protestant) of a wealthy, retired career diplomat (anti-Semite), clearly the suitable mate for a man with a potential of becoming the country's (very first Jewish) Secretary of State." Publisher's note

Heller, Peter

Celine; a novel. Peter Heller. Alfred A. Knopf 2017 333 p. (hardcover) $25.95

ISBN 0451493893; 9780451493897

LC 2016026943

This novel, by Peter Heller, presents "the story of Celine, an elegant, aristocratic private eye who specializes in reuniting families, trying to make amends for a loss in her own past. Working out of her jewel box of an apartment at the base of the Brooklyn Bridge, Celine has made a career of tracking down missing persons, and she has a better record at it than the FBI. But when a young woman, Gabriela, asks for her help, a world of mystery and sorrow opens up." (Publisher's note)

"Heller (The Painter) blends suspense with beautiful descriptive writing of both nature and civilization to create a winner." LJ.

Heller, Peter

★ The **dog** stars; a novel. Peter Heller. 1st ed. Alfred A. Knopf 2012 272 p. (hardcover) $24.95; (ebook) $24.95; (paperback) $15.00

ISBN 0307959945; 9780307959942; 9780307960931; 9780307950475

LC 2011050429

This book by Peter Heller "takes place nine years after a superflu has killed off much of mankind. Hig, an amateur pilot living in Colorado, has retreated to an abandoned airport. . . . Hig's one real comfort . . . is his dog, Jasper. But when that comfort is withdrawn, Hig flies west in search of the radio voice that called out to him three years before. Instead, he ends up being shot down and restrained by a doctor named Cima and her shotgun-toting father, a former Navy SEAL." (Publishers Weekly)

Heller, Peter

★ The **painter**; a novel. Peter Heller. Alfred A. Knopf 2014 384 p. (hardback) $24.95

ISBN 0385352093; 9780385352093

LC 2013045522

In this novel by Peter Heller, "One afternoon, on a dirt road, Jim comes across a man beating a small horse, and a brutal encounter rips his quiet life wide open. Fleeing Colorado, chased by men set on retribution, Jim returns to New Mexico, tormented by his own relentless conscience. . . . 'The Painter' is the story of a man who longs to transcend the shadows in his heart, a man intent on using the losses he has suffered to create a meaningful life." (Publisher's note)

"[E]mbraces themes of personal loss and growth, drama and suspense, while also including plenty for those who enjoy art or nature fiction." LJ

Heller, Zoe

What was she thinking? notes on a scandal. Holt & Co. 2003 258p $23

ISBN 0-8050-7333-7

LC 2002-38809

"Barbara Covett, a sixtyish history teacher, is the kind of unmarried-woman-with-cat whose female friends sooner or later decide she is 'too intense.' Thus when a beautiful new pottery teacher, Sheba Hart. . .chooses Barbara as a confidante, she is deeply, even rather sinisterly, gratified. Sheba's secret is explosive: married with two kids, she is having an affair with a fifteen-year-old student. . . .Equally adroit at satire and at psychological suspense, Heller charts the course of a predatory friendship and demonstrates the lengths to which some people go for human company." New Yorker

Hellström, Börge, 1957-2017

Cell 8; by Anders Roslund and Borge Hellstrom. SilverOak 2012 384p $24.95

ISBN 9781410445117; 1410445119; 9781402787157

LC 2011041325

This book tells the story of "dour sociopathic copper Ewert Grens" who investigates the seemingly routine case of "John Schwartz, a crooner on a cruise ship between Stockholm and Finland," arrested for assaulting "a drunken passenger harassing females on the dance floor. . . . But the uncooperative prisoner is in fact a man called John Meyer Frey. And Frey, it seems, died several years ago while awaiting execution on death row in an Ohio prison. Grens becomes obsessed with the case -- as does another man, whose life has been ruined buy the unfulfilled retribution he has thirsted for after many years." (independent.co.uk)

Helprin, Mark

★ **In** sunlight and in shadow; Mark Helprin. Houghton Mifflin Harcourt 2012 xiv, 705 p.p

ISBN 0547819234; 9780547819235

LC 2012016242

This novel by Mark Helprin focuses on a "love story . . . in post-war America. Harry Copeland, . . . a former paratrooper, . . . [p]ursues [Catherine Thomas Hale], and in time he wins her over, only to find that Catherine harbors many secrets--and that her family harbors more than a few hidden prejudices and is not at all happy when Harry comes a-courting in the place of Catherine's longtime beau." (Kirkus Reviews)

Helprin, Mark

★ **Winter's** tale. Harcourt Brace Jovanovich 1983 673p $35

ISBN 0-15-197203-6

LC 83-273

The author "describes the impossible with microscopic precision, and he summons the moods and myriad landscapes of the city with breathtaking poetry. . . . Again and again Helprin celebrates selfless love, a devotion to beauty, the desire to explore, and an acceptance of responsibility. . . . Helprin's freewheeling use of fantasy at times eclipses his essential seriousness, diminishing the novel as a whole. Yet there is unquestionable genius in the book's marvelous individual pieces." Saturday Rev

Hemingway, Ernest

★ A **farewell** to arms. Scribner Classics 1997 297p $27.50

ISBN 0-684-83788-9

LC 96-53356

A reissue of the title first published 1929

This novel "deals with a love-affair conducted against the background of the war in Italy. Its excellence lies in the delicacy with which it conveys a sense of the impermanence of the best human feelings; the unobstrusive force of its symbolism of mountain and plain; above all the vast scope of its vision of war—the retreat from Caporetto is one of the great war-sequences of literature." Penguin Companion to Am Lit

Hemingway, Ernest

For whom the bell tolls. Scribner 1996 495p $27.50; pa $14

ISBN 0-684-83048-5; 0-684-80335-6 pa

LC 96-7706

"In 1937 Ernest Hemingway traveled to Spain to cover the civil war there for the North American Newspaper Alliance. Three years later he completed the greatest novel to emerge from 'the good fight,' For

Whom the Bell Tolls. The story of Robert Jordan, a young American in the International Brigades attached to an antifascist guerilla unit in the mountains of Spain, it tells of loyalty and courage, love and defeat, and the tragic death of an ideal." (Publisher's note)

Hemingway, Ernest

The **Nick** Adams stories. Scribner 268p pa $12

ISBN 0-684-16940-1

First published 1972

Arranged chronologically, this collection of 24 tales contains all the semi-autobiographical Nick Adams stories

"The volume presents Nick as a child in the northern woods, as adolescent, as soldier, veteran, writer, husband and parent. The last Nick Adams story appeared in 1933, and what surprises here, in these . . . {stories} of varying length, quality and intent, is their freshness and immediacy." Publ Wkly

Hemingway, Ernest

★ The **old** man and the sea; illustrations by C.F. Tunnicliffe and Raymond Sheppard. Scribner Classics 1996 93p il $20

ISBN 0-684-83049-3

LC 96-11419

A reissue of the title first published 1952

"The old fisherman Santiago had only one friend in the village, the boy Manolin. Everyone else thought he was unlucky because he had caught no fish in a long time. At noon on the 85th day of fishing, he hooked a large fish. He fought with the huge swordfish for three days and nights before he could harpoon it, but the battle came to nought when sharks destroyed the fish before Santiago could get back to the village." Shapiro. Fic for Youth. 3d edition

Hemingway, Ernest

★ The **short** stories. Scribner Classics 1997 457p $30

ISBN 0-684-83786-2

LC 96-53349

Originally published 1938 in collection with the play The fifth column

Hemingway, Ernest

The **snows** of Kilimanjaro and other stories. Scribner Classics 1995 143p $25

ISBN 0-684-86221-2

LC 95-4764

A reissue of the title first published 1961

Contents: The snows of Kilimanjaro; A clean, well-lighted place; A day's wait; The gambler, the nun, and the radio; Fathers and sons; In another country; The killers; A way you'll never be; Fifty grand; The short happy life of Francis Macomber

Hemingway, Ernest

★ The **sun** also rises. Scribner Classics 1996 222p $25

ISBN 0-684-83051-5

LC 96-11420

A reissue of the title first published 1926

"Set in the 1920s, the novel deals with a group of aimless expatriates in France and Spain. They are members of the cynical and disillusioned post-World War I Lost Generation, many of whom suffer psychological and physical wounds as a result of the war. Two of the novel's main characters, Lady Brett Ashley and Jake Barnes, typify this generation. Lady Brett drifts through a series of affairs despite her love for Jake, who has been rendered impotent by a war wound. Friendship, stoicism, and natural grace under pressure are offered as the values that matter in an otherwise amoral and often senseless world." Merriam-Webster's Ency of Lit

Hemingway, Ernest

To have and have not. Scribner Classics 1999 174p $25

ISBN 0-684-85923-8

LC 00-266244

A reissue of the title first published 1937

This novel "deals with the effort of Harry Morgan, a native of Key West, to earn a living for himself and his family. He has operated a boat for rental to fishing parties, but, during the Depression of the 1930s, he is forced to turn to the smuggling of Chinese immigrants and illegal liquor. While assisting a gang of bank robbers to escape, he is shot and mortally wounded. He dies gasping, 'One man alone ain't got . . . no chance.'" Reader's Ency. 4th edition

Hemmings, Kaui Hart

★ The **possibilities**; a novel. Kaui Hart Hemmings. Simon & Schuster 2014 288 p. (hardback) $25

ISBN 1476725799; 9781476725796; 9781476725802

LC 2013027385

"Three months ago, her twenty-two-year-old son, Cully, died in an avalanche. Though single, Sarah is hardly alone in her grief. Her father, a retiree, tries to distract her with gadgets from the QVC home shopping channel. Sarah's best friend offers life advice by venting details of her own messy divorce. . . . Kaui Hart Hemmings highlights the subtle poignancies of grief and relationships in this stunning look at people faced with impossible choices in the wake of a tragedy." (Publisher's note)

"Hemmings writes a piercing, empathetic story about parenthood and unfathomable heartbreak and manages to bring humor and hope to her characters. Emotionally complex and relatable to all." Kirkus

Hemon, Aleksandar

Nowhere man; the Pronek fantasies. Doubleday 2002 242p $23.95

ISBN 0-385-49924-8

LC 2002-66208

"Pronek's constantly reconfiguring life makes the novel a wild, twisty read, and Hemon's inimitable voice and the wry urgency of his storytelling should cement his reputation as a talented young writer." Publ Wkly

Hempel, Amy

The **collected** stories of Amy Hempel; with an introduction by Rick Moody. Scribner 2006 409p $27.50

ISBN 0-7432-8946-3

LC 2005-57608

"You could call Hempel part of a movement in the trajectory of the American short story, and Rick Moody, in his intelligent introduction, places her alongside Alice Munro, Grace Paley, Ann Beattie and others—women writers who rise above what he sees as the 'rage' and posturing of their male counterparts. But in the end such comparisons don't matter. Amy Hempel is herself. You read her stories and wonder, Why are they so wonderful? The answer comes to you at the very end of this volume, in a line toward the close of 'Offertory.' 'Because a human being made this.' That's all you need to know." N Y Times Book Rev

Henderson, Eleanor

Ten thousand saints; Eleanor Henderson. Ecco 2011 388p.

ISBN 0062021028; 9780062021021

LC 2011283405

This book is "a coming-of-age story set in the 1980s that departs from the genre's familiar tropes to find a panoramic view of how the imperfect escape from our parents' mistakes makes (equally imperfect) adults of us. Jude Keffy-Horn and Teddy McNicholas are drug-addled adolescents stuck in suburban Vermont and dreaming of an escape to

New York City. But after Teddy dies of an overdose, Jude makes good on their dream and forms a de facto family with Teddy's straight-edge brother, Johnny; Jude's estranged pot-farmer father, Lester; and the troubled Eliza Urbanski, who may be carrying Teddy's child. What results is an odyssey encompassing the age of CBGB, Hare Krishnas, zincs, and the emergence of AIDS." (Publishers Weekly)

"Henderson is a versatile ventriloquist, taking us briskly and believably into the minds and hearts of most of her major characters (though Eliza, while briefly vivid, turns into exactly what the boys treat her as, which is a passive plot device). Though it loses some steam as it hurtles toward a happy ending, 'Ten Thousand Saints' is at its best when depicting the punk scene in New York in the 1980s and its amalgam of homeless junkies, vegan Hinduists, early AIDS victims, and antigentrification activists. It's an auspicious debut, and gives us reason to hope that Eleanor Henderson will mature as satisfyingly as her subjects do." Boston Globe

Henkin, Joshua

The **world** without you; Joshua Henkin. Pantheon Books 2012 321 p.

ISBN 0375424369; 9780375424366

LC 2011046780

In this novel, Joshua "Henkin . . . explores family dynamics. . . . One year after the death of their kidnapped journalist son, Leo, in Iraq, David and Marilyn Frankel, non-practicing Jews, call their entire mishpocha to their summer home . . . to attend his memorial service: Clarissa and her husband . . . are having a difficult time getting pregnant; . . . Noëlle, an Orthodox Jew who arrives from Jerusalem with her husband, Amram, and their four children." (Publishers Weekly)

Henry, O.

The **best** short stories of O. Henry; selected and with an introduction by Bennett A. Cerf, and Van H. Cartmell. Modern Lib. 1994 340p $22.95

ISBN 0-679-60122-8

First Modern Library edition published 1945

O. Henry "is best known for his observations on the diverse lives of everyday New Yorkers, 'the four million' neglected by other writers. He had a fine gift of humor and was adept at the ingenious depiction of ironic circumstances, in plots frequently dependent upon coincidence." Oxford Companion to Am Lit. 6th edition

Henry, O.

★ The **complete** works of O. Henry; foreword by Harry Hansen. Doubleday 1953 1692p $15.95

ISBN 0-385-00961-5

An omnibus volume of 13 short story collections: The four million (1906); Heart of the West (1907); The gentle grafter (1908); Roads of destiny (1909); Cabbages and kings (1904); Whirligigs (1910); Options (1909); Sixes and sevens (1911); Rolling stones (1912); The voice of the city (1908); The trimmed lamp (1907); Strictly business (1910); Waifs and strays (1917)

Henry, Patti Callahan

And then I found you; Patti Callahan Henry. 1st ed. St. Martin's Press 2013 272 p. (hardcover) $24.99

ISBN 0312610769; 9780312610760

LC 2013004029

Here, Katie Vaughn panics when she thinks her boring boyfriend might propose. She "casts her memory back to the first day of spring when she was 13. She had experienced her first kiss and first brush with love with classmate Jack Adams. She promised to love him always, but now, at age 35, Katie no longer has Jack in her life. A secret she shared with him so long ago has resurfaced, and this has caused Katie to revisit the past and reevaluate her life." (Library Journal)

Henry, Patti Callahan

Coming up for air. St. Martin's Press 2011 261p $24.99

ISBN 978-0-312-61039-5; 0-312-61039-4

LC 2011019507

"An affecting Southern tale about second chances and banishing the ghosts of regret. . . . Romantic storytelling at its simple best." Kirkus

Hensher, Philip, 1965-

King of the badgers. Faber & Faber 2011 436p $26

ISBN 978-0-865-47863-3; 0-865-47863-5

"A rich and ambitious novel, which manages both to offer a convincing picture of different levels of English society today and to explore the shifting certainties of individual lives. It is certainly easier to read than to summarise, and this is as it should be." Scotsman

Hensher, Philip, 1965-

Scenes from early life; Philip Hensher. Faber and Faber 2013 320 p. (hardcover : alk. paper) $27

ISBN 0865477612; 9780865477612

LC 2012022169

Philip Hensher's "novel takes the form of a memoir of Bangladesh in the 1970s, a time when both nation and narrator were on their first feet. . . . The novel has 13 chapters in all and they . . . carr[y] . . . detail[s] about Bengali life in the uncertain years before independence and in the period after, when the horrors of the liberation war were still fresh in everyone's minds." (New Statesman)

Henson, Jim, 1936-1990

Jim Henson's tale of sand; written by Jim Henson and Jerry Juhl ; as realized by Ramón K. Pérez ; colors by Ian Herring with Ramón K. Pérez ; lettering and font design by Deron Bennett based on the handwriting of Jim Henson ; edited by Stephen Christy. Archaia Entertainment 2012 152 p.

ISBN 1936393093; 9781936393091

This graphic novel "follows its hapless protagonist as he is cast out into the desert by the cheerful Sheriff Tate. . . . The scruffy hero is a pawn in a game whose rules are concealed from him, pursued across a surrealistic southwest U.S. by an implacable hunter and hindered by the eccentric, bizarre inhabitants of the great desolation. The prize waiting for him at the end of the chase, should he survive to reach the end, is one he will never guess at." (Publishers Weekly)

Hepworth, Sally

The **Secrets** of Midwives; Sally Hepworth. St. Martin's Press 2015 320 p. $25.99

ISBN 1250051894; 9781250051899

LC 2014033628

In this novel by Sally Hepworth "Neva Bradley, a third-generation midwife, is determined to keep the details surrounding her own pregnancy . . . hidden from her family and co-workers for as long as possible. Her mother, Grace, finds it impossible to let this secret rest. The more Grace prods, the tighter Neva holds to her story, and the more the lifelong differences between private, quiet Neva and open, gregarious Grace strain their relationship." (Publisher's note)

"Hepworth makes some interesting, though not always successful, choices in her narratives (chapters alternate among Neva, Grace and Floss), painting an irksome portrait of Grace and a rather opaque picture of Neva, whose secret is kept from the reader until the finale. Fans of

Call the Midwife will enjoy the vignettes of childbirth and the multigenerational female saga." Kirkus

Herbert, Brian

Dune: House Atreides; [by] Brian Herbert and Kevin J. Anderson. Bantam Bks. 1999 604p

ISBN 0-553-11061-6

LC 99-17726

"Though the plot here is intricate, even readers new to the saga will be able to follow it easily." Publ Wkly

Herbert, Brian

Dune: House Corrino; [by] Brian Herbert and Kevin J. Anderson. Bantam Bks. 2001 496p

ISBN 0-553-11084-5

LC 2001-25777

"As Emperor Shaddam IV seeks to consolidate his power as Emperor of a Million Worlds through the monopoly of the spice trade, other forces array themselves in opposition to his increasingly tyrannical rule. . . . Though dependent on the previous books, this complex and compelling tale of dynastic intrigue and high drama adds a significant chapter to the classic Dune saga." Libr J

Herbert, Brian

Dune: The Butlerian jihad; {by} Brian Herbert and Kevin J. Anderson. TOR Bks. 2002 621p $27.95

ISBN 0-7653-0157-1

LC 2002-28581

The authors "continue their prehistory of Frank Herbert's 'Dune' series with a new trilogy opener set in the distant past of Herbert's galactic saga. The authors reveal the origins of the Spacing Guild and the Bene Gesserit, as well as the root of the ancient feud between Houses Atreides and Harkonnen. This compelling saga of men and women struggling for their freedom is required reading for Dune fans." Libr J

Herbert, Brian

Paul of Dune; [by] Brian Herbert and Kevin J. Anderson. Tor 2008 512p $27.95

ISBN 978-0-7653-1294-5; 0-7653-1294-8

LC 2008-30213

"Paul Muad'Dib and his army of Fremen desert warriors have succeeded in their overthrow of the Emperor Shaddam IV, but holding onto a universe of fractious planets proves a challenge even for a man revered by his followers as a god. Set in the years following the late Frank Herbert's classic Dune and its sequel, Dune Messiah, . . . [this book] fills in the missing years of empire building and looks into the formative years of Paul's childhood as well as the histories of those closest to him. . . . A priority purchase for libraries of all sizes." Libr J

Herbert, Frank

★ **Dune**. Ace Bks. 1999 517p il $27.95

ISBN 0-441-00590-X

First published 1965 by Chilton

"Herbert combines several classic elements: a Machiavellian world of political intrigue worthy of fourteenth-century Italy, a huge cast of characters, and a detailed picture of a culture. Duke Leto Atreides and his family are coerced into exchanging their rich lands for a barren planet, Dune, which produces a unique drug. Duke's son, Paul, becomes the leader of a group that leads the Fremen of Dune against the enemy. This is a science fiction story with sociological and ecological import." Shapiro. Fic for Youth. 3d edition

Other titles about Dune are:

Chapterhouse: Dune (1985)
Children of Dune (1976)
Dune messiah (1969)
God Emperor of Dune (1981)
Heretics of Dune (1984)

Herbert, Frank

Dune messiah. Putnam 1969 220p (Dune)

In this second volume of the Dune series "the Bene Gesserit, a mystic sisterhood, plot to overthrow the god/emperor Paul Atreides, whom they created by special breeding but whom they cannot now control. Presented here via the narrative and quotes from journals and legends of the people of Dune, the imperial intrigue is engineered by such diverse characters as Bene Gesserit Mother Superior, a Tleilaxu face dancer, a 'ghola' re-creation of Paul's dead friend, and the Princess Consort. Paul's eventual victory because of his future-vision makes fascinating reading." SLJ

Followed by Children of Dune

Herlihy, James Leo

★ **Midnight** cowboy; [by] James L. Herlihy. Simon & Schuster 1965 253p

"An appalling story, told with great skill and important because Joe Buck is a characteristic product of the way we live and yet he cannot be adequately discussed outside of a novel." Saturday Rev

Hern, Candice

The **bride** sale; Candice Hern. Avon Books 2002 375p.

ISBN 038080901X

LC 2002580398

This romance novel takes place "[i]n 1818 Gunnisloe, [where] Baron James Harkness . . . hears a nearby auction whose bidding and commentary seem strange to him. He . . . is stunned to see a woman on the block instead of cattle. . . . Gilbert Russell sells his wife Verity to 'Lord Heartless' as the locals call James in order to pay off his debts. Though she starts with doubts about her savior due to the rumors that he killed his wife and child, Verity quickly notices his compassion towards people even those not deserving of it. She begins to fall in love with her benefactor and he feels the same attraction, but the secrets he keeps from everyone including her leaves no hope for a real relationship." (thebestreviews.com)

Hern, Candice

Once a gentleman; Candice Hern. Avon Books 2004 373p. (pbk.) $5.99

ISBN 0060565144

LC 2004573984

In this book, "Nicholas Parrish wakes one morning to pounding at the front door of his London townhouse. Standing before him is the irate father of Prudence Armitage and several of her scowling brothers. They accuse him of compromising Prudence, and to his astonishment the woman in question walks out of his study, looking as if she's just been roused from her bed! Prudence had . . . [fallen] asleep at her desk, and when she walks out of the office and sees her family ready to murder the man she had secretly had a crush on, Prudence is appalled. And when a marriage is forced between them, she is devastated. The damage is done, though, and now she's determined to make things right between herself and her new husband." (Publisher's note)

Hernandez, Felisberto

★ **Lands** of memory; translated by Ester Allen. New Directions 2002 190p $24.95

ISBN 0-8112-1483-4

LC 2001-42589

The Lands of memory is an uncoventinal fictional autobiography and Around the time of Clements Colling is a bildungsroman about a one-eyed blind piano teacher and his pupil

"Hernandez revels in images that are simple and repetitive: arms, light and shadow, the houses of the wealthy and their odd contents. The stories acquire a luxurious sheen from the ease with which they navigate memories, taking pleasure in recounting them with no intention other than tracking the mind's twists and turns." Publ Wkly

Herrin, Lamar

★ **Fractures**; A Novel. Lamar Herrin. Thomas Dunne Books/St. Martin's Press 2013 320 p. (hardcover : alk. paper) $25.99

ISBN 1250032768; 9781250032768

LC 2013023588

This book, by Lamar Herrin, focuses on the "hydrofracking controversy as a beleaguered patriarch must decide the fate of his land and children . . . The Joyner family sits atop prime Marcellus Shale. When landmen for the natural gas companies begin to lease property all around the family's hundred acres, the Joyners start to take notice. Undecided on whether or not to lease the family land, Frank Joyner must weigh his heirs' competing motivations." (Publisher's note)

Herron, Mick

Spook street; Mick Herron. Soho Crime 2017 310 p. (Slough house) (hardcover) $26.95

ISBN 9781616956479; 9781616956486

LC 2016025804

In this book in the Slough House series, by Mick Herron, "a shakeup at MI5 and a terrorist attack on British soil set in motion clandestine machinery known to few modern spies. David Cartwright isn't a modern spy, . . . he's . . . a . . . Cold War hero. . . . His stories of 'stotes' hiding in the bushes, . . . have been dismissed by friends and family. . . . [But] Cartwright . . . [is] certain about one thing: Old spooks don't go quietly and neither do the secrets they keep." (Publisher's note)

"All espionage aficionados are—or soon will be—reading Herron. But it's high time, too, that readers of literary fiction embrace him in the way they have John le Carré." Booklist

Hersey, John

★ A **bell** for Adano. Knopf 1944 269p

"The town bell of Adano is transformed into material for a cannon, and its loss symbolizes a moral loss to the very life of the people. When the town falls into the hands of the Americans and the Fascist forces are in retreat, Major Joppolo, a Brooklyn-born Italian, becomes a favorite of the townspeople because of the concern he has for them. Not only does he help Tina find her missing sweetheart, but he finds a replacement for the bell, retrieving it from a U.S. ship named after an Italian-American hero of World War I. To the town's dismay, Major Joppolo is relieved of his command by an American general whose unreasonable orders he ignores." Shapiro. Fic for Youth. 3d edition

Hershon, Joanna

The **German** bride; a novel. Ballantine Books 2008 304p $25

ISBN 978-0-345-46845-1; 0-345-46845-7

LC 2007-32842

"Though sometimes stilted, the novel, with its colorful cast, setting and redemptive conclusion, eventually wins the reader over." Publ Wkly

Hess, Joan

Busy bodies. Dutton 1995 246p

LC 94-46120

In this Claire Malloy mystery, "painter Zeno Gorgias, who has recently moved to the small Arkansas town's historic neighborhood, is staging performance pieces, starring a nearly naked young woman with a rubber snake, on his front lawn. Not only are Claire's hyperbolic teenage daughter and her friend involved, but Claire's policeman lover has his hands full with crowd control. Zeno's estranged wife arrives and threatens to have him institutionalized for incompetence; she is found murdered, her body recovered from charred ashes of Zeno's house after it—and half a million dollars' worth of his paintings—are burned." Publ Wkly

Hess, Joan

★ **Death** by the light of the moon. St. Martin's Press 1992 227p

LC 91-37884

"Ms. Hess handles the complicated plot logistics with a deft touch, and although her overblown caricatures lack the affection she lavishes on the characters in her 'Maggody' series, she has a warm spot for teenagers, whose insufferable ways elicit her funniest and kindest satirical swipes." N Y Times Book Rev

Hess, Joan

Madness in Maggody. St. Martin's Press 1991 231p

LC 90-49306

"Chief of police Arly Hanks, lately of New York City, takes an offhand attitude toward crime or the lack of it in Maggody, Arkansas, until the tamales hit the fan during the grand opening of a supermarket that none of the other merchants in town wants to see succeed. Now Arly's got one death, and reams of rumors to unravel. Although the situation is loaded with humor and small-town high jinks, the solution to the murder shocks Arly so much she promises herself that in the future she will take her job more seriously." Booklist

Hess, Joan

Maggody and the moonbeams; an Arly Hanks mystery. Simon & Schuster 2001 254p

ISBN 0-7432-0229-5

LC 2001-20208

Police chief Arly Hanks, "to her extreme horror, gets railroaded by Mrs. Jim Bob Buchanon into acting as chaperone for a church youth group at Camp Pearly Gates in nearby Dunkicker. Unbeknownst to all, the camp is also the home of a weird commune, the Daughters of the Moon, which is made up of a group of women (known locally as 'Beamers') who sport shaved heads, magenta lipstick, and white robes. The typical Maggody madness and mayhem begins when one of the campers stumbles over the body of a Beamer whose head has been pulverized." Booklist

Hess, Joan

Mischief in Maggody; an Ozarks murder mystery. St. Martin's Press 1988 202p

LC 88-1867

"Maggody, a little Ozark town where nothing ever happens, has problems. Its first female police chief, Arly Hanks, . . . comes back from vacation to find the community in an uproar . . . local prostitute and moonshiner Robin Buchanon has disappeared, leaving behind five hungry children. . . . Arly manages to foist them onto Mrs. Jim Bob while she goes hunting for the mother, whom she finds with her head blown off in the middle of a marijuana patch. . . . Another death and the public humiliation of two of the town's most righteous citizens take place before peace comes to Maggody once again. Hess writes an engaging tale, although the raunchy characters impart a certain vulgarity to the text." Publ Wkly

Hess, Joan

Misery loves Maggody; an Arly Hanks mystery. Simon & Schuster 1999 285p $22

ISBN 0-684-84562-8

LC 98-28728

Maggody, Arkansas police chief Arly Hanks "investigates after out-of-town police arrest the mayor of Maggody in connection with the death of a riverboat showgirl." Libr J

Hess, Joan

Murder@maggody.com. Simon & Schuster 2000 253p

ISBN 0-684-84563-6

LC 99-46821

"Maggody's eccentric inhabitants and Hess's comic touch infuse this cozy with a refreshing dose of spunk, resulting in another triumph for both small-town America and Hess." Publ Wkly

Hesse, Hermann

The **fairy** tales of Hermann Hesse; translated and with an introduction by Jack Zipes; woodcut illustrations by David Frampton. Bantam Bks. 1995 xxxi, 266p il hardcover o.p. pa $14.95

ISBN 0-553-37776-0 pa

LC 94-49166

"Quirky and evocative, Hesse's fairy tales stand alone, but also amplify the ideas and utopian longings of such counterculture avatars as Siddhartha and Steppenwolf." Publ Wkly

Hesse, Hermann

★ **Siddhartha**; translated by Hilda Rosner. New Directions 1951 153p $16.95; pa $6.95

ISBN 0-8112-0292-5; 0-8112-0068-X pa

Original German edition, 1923

"The young Indian Siddhartha endures many experiences in his search for the ultimate answer to the question, what is humankind's role on earth? He is also looking for the solution to loneliness and discontent, and he seeks that solution in the way of a wanderer, the company of a courtesan, and the high position of a successful businessman. His final relationship is with a humble but wise ferryman. This is an allegory that examines love, wealth, and freedom while the protagonist struggles toward self-knowledge." Shapiro. Fic for Youth. 3d edition

Hesse, Hermann

★ **Steppenwolf**; translated from the German by Basil Creighton. Holt & Co. 1929 309p hardcover o.p. pa $14

ISBN 0-312-27867-5

Original German edition, 1927

"The hero, Harry Haller . . . is torn between his own frustrated artistic idealism and the inhuman nature of modern reality, which, in his eyes, is characterized entirely by philistinism and technology. It is his inability to be a part of the world and the resulting loneliness and desolation of his existence that cause him to think of himself as a 'Steppenwolf' (wolf of the Steppes). The novel, which is rich in surrealistic imagery throughout, ends in what is called the magic theater, a kind of allegorical sideshow. Here, Haller learns that in order to relate successfully to humanity and reality without sacrificing his ideals, he must overcome his own social and sexual inhibitions." Reader's Ency. 4th edition

Hewson, David

The **garden** of evil. Delacorte Press 2008 470p $24

ISBN 978-0-385-33957-5; 0-385-33957-7

LC 2007-45762

"A thought-provoking blend of art history and mystery, The Garden of Evil is . . . a treat for readers who like their entertainment literate." Richmond Times-Dispatch

Hewson, David

A **season** for the dead. Delacorte Press 2004 386p $21.95

ISBN 0-385-33722-1

LC 2003-62522

"Outsized, eccentric characters, a complex story and an abundance of historical detail make this engrossing book more than just another cookie-cutter, religious-nut serial killer thriller." Publ Wkly

Heyer, Georgette

★ **Black** sheep. Sourcebooks 2008 279p pa $13.95

ISBN 978-1-4022-1078-5; 1-4022-1078-7

LC 2007-50205

First published 1966 in the United Kingdom

"A lovely young spinster is both charmed and infuriated by the wealthy, unconventional black sheep uncle of the fortune hunter on whom her young niece has her heart set. This character-driven novel . . . is considered one of Heyer's best." Libr J

Heyer, Georgette

The **grand** Sophy; Georgette Heyer. Sourcebooks Casablanca 2009 372 p. (pbk.) $13.99

ISBN 140221894X; 9781402218941

LC 2009012751

Originally published 1950

"When Lady Ombersley agrees to take in her young niece, no one expects Sophy, who sweeps in and immediately takes the ton by storm. Sophy discovers that her aunt's family is in desperate need of her talent for setting everything right: Ceclia is in love with a poet, Charles has tyrannical tendencies that are being aggravated by his grim fiancee, her uncle is of no use at all, and the younger children are in desperate need of some fun and freedom. By the time she's done, Sophy has commandeered Charles's horses, his household, and finally, his heart." (Publisher's note)

Heyer, Georgette

These old shades; Georgette Heyer. Sourcebooks Casablanca 2009 378 p. (ebook) $13.99; (pbk.) $13.99

ISBN 9781402228049; 1402219474; 9781402219474

LC 2009029781

This Regency novel, by Georgette Heyer, "features . . . Justin Alastair, the Duke of Avon, and Leonie, whom he rescues from a life of ignomy and comes to love and marry. . . . Late one evening, [the Duke] is accosted by a young person dressed in ragged boy's clothing running away from a brutal rustic guardian. The Duke buys 'Leon' and makes the child his page. 'Leon' is in fact Leonie, and she serves the Duke with deep devotion." (Publisher's note)

Heyns, Michiel

The **typewriter's** tale; Michiel Heyns. St. Martin's Press 2017 270 p. (hardcover) $25.99

ISBN 9781250119001; 9781250119018

LC 2016038740

In this novel, by Michiel Heyns, "'live all you can; it's a mistake not to.' This is the maxim of celebrated author Henry James and one which his typist Frieda Wroth tries to live up to. Admiring of the great author, she nevertheless feels marginalized and undervalued in her role. But when the dashing Morton Fullerton comes to visit, Frieda finds herself at the center of an intrigue every bit as engrossing as the novels she types." (Publisher's note)

"Literary history blends masterfully with a plot of intrigue in this slim and delightful novel." Kirkus

Includes bibliographical references.

Hiassen, Carl, 1953-

Bad monkey; Carl Hiaasen. 1st ed. Alfred A. Knopf 2013 336 p. (hardcover) $26.95

ISBN 0307272591; 9780307272591

LC 2013005863

In this book, disgraced cop Andrew Yancy has a chance to redeem himself. New sheriff Sonny Summers "tells Yancy to take a severed, shark-bitten arm snagged by a fisherman to Miami, where DNA identifies the limb as belonging to Nick Stripling, a retiree in his 40s whose boat was wrecked at sea. Stripling's grown daughter, Caitlin Cox, claims . . . that her hated stepmother murdered her father, and Yancy sees proving the stepmother's guilt as a way to return to the force." (Publishers Weekly)

Hiaasen, Carl

Basket case. Knopf 2002 317p

ISBN 0-375-41107-0

LC 2001-38317

"In laying out the tale of Jack Tagger, a maladjusted, middle-aged Florida obituary writer who stumbles across a hot news story in the supposed scuba-diving death of Jimmy Stoma, former lead singer for a band called Jimmy and the Slut Puppies, Hiaasen skewers both corporate media operations and the world of pop stardom." N Y Times Book Rev

Hiaasen, Carl

Lucky you; a novel. Knopf 1997 353p

ISBN 0-679-45444-6

LC 97-36885

"Hiaasen writes witty dialogue that crackles, and his characters are eccentrically colorful." N Y Times Book Rev

Hiaasen, Carl

Nature girl. Alfred A. Knopf 2006 305p $25.95

ISBN 978-0-307-26299-8; 0-307-26299-5

LC 2006-49360

"As usual, Hiaasen throws his colorful characters into an increasingly frenetic mix, and the fun lies in watching how, or if, they'll manage to extricate themselves. One reason Nature Girl works so well is the fact that much of the action is confined to a single island, allowing the characters to intermingle and weave in and out of view." San Francisco Chronicle

Hiaasen, Carl

Skin tight. Putnam 1989 319p

ISBN 0-399-13489-1

LC 89-31580

"When Mick Stranahan, a retired investigator, is the attempted victim of murder, he becomes a little curious to find out who wants him dead. He trails the killer to a quack plastic surgeon who was a suspect in a murder case Stranahan investigated four years before. Someone is about to blab that the surgeon had a more than passing interest in the old case and Stranahan gets back in the harness to investigate." West Coast Rev Books

Hiaasen, Carl

Skinny dip; a novel. Alfred A. Knopf 2004 355p $24.95

ISBN 0-375-41108-9

LC 2004-44106

"Joey Perrone and her husband, Chaz, are taking a cruise to celebrate their wedding anniversary. One night, as the rain pours down, Chaz throws Joey overboard. He then proceeds to convince the authorities that he has no idea what happened to her. Unfortunately for him, Joey is rescued and begins to plot her ultimate revenge against her soon-to-be-patsy of a husband. The squirm-inducing mayhem that follows in this sometimes sidesplitting novel almost makes you feel sorry for Chaz. It has rarely been this much fun to read about the act of revenge. All of the trademark characters and Florida locales are used to maximum effect." Libr J

Hiaasen, Carl

Star Island. Alfred A. Knopf 2010 337p $26.95

ISBN 978-0-307-27258-4; 0-307-27258-3

LC 2010-22584

"Trying to follow the plot, which involves a supporting cast of crooked politicians and predatory developers, is a little like walking a puppy. But the outlandish events soar on the exuberance of Hiaasen's manic style, a canny blend of lunatic farce and savage satire." N Y Times Book Rev

Hiaasen, Carl

★ **Strip** tease; a novel. Knopf 1993 353p

ISBN 0-679-41981-0

LC 93-12358

The novel "starts in a Fort Lauderdale strip joint, the Eager Beaver, when a seriously inebriated {congressman} Dilbeck attacks a fellow customer who has draped himself around the legs of the congressman's favorite stripper. Blackmail is the inevitable byproduct of this episode." (Booklist)

In among Hiaasen's "freaks and obsessives, his corrupters and corrupted, his brain-dead and his frenetically active, the author has dropped a real honest-to-God human being, an appealing young woman named Erin Grant. Her presence, her history and goals, make the cartoon nastiness around her less cartoony and more nasty than in previous Hiaasen novels." N Y Times Book Rev

Hickam, Homer H.

The **keeper's** son; a novel. [by] Homer Hickam. 1st ed; Thomas Dunne Books 2003 353p $24.95

ISBN 0-312-30189-8

LC 2003-54964

"This is the first novel of a planned series about rough and tumble Coast Guard Lt. Josh Thurlow and his unusual patrol boat crew during WWII. Josh, 31, is a career officer assigned to Killakeet Island, along North Carolina's treacherous Outer Banks. Both he and his father-the keeper of the Killakeet Lighthouse-are haunted by the loss at sea and presumed death of Josh's two-year-old baby brother 17 years earlier. Shaken from his brooding by the appearance of German U-boats, Josh must try to protect the merchant ships torpedoed every night offshore. . .

. Well-crafted characters, gripping naval warfare and colorful island life come together in this dynamic and exciting tale." Publ Wkly

Hicks, Robert

The **widow** of the south; Robert Hicks. Warner Books 2005 426p ill., map o.p.; $43; (pbk.) $14.99

ISBN 0446500127; 0446578827 (lg. print); 9780446697439

LC 2005010568

This book, "based on true events in [the author's] hometown, follows the saga of Carrie McGavock, a lonely Confederate wife who finds purpose transforming her Tennessee plantation into a hospital and cemetery during the Civil War. . . . Before the 1864 battle of Franklin, Confederate Gen. Nathan Bedford Forrest commandeers her house as a field hospital. In alternating points of view, the battle is recounted by different witnesses, including . . . Confederate Sgt. Zachariah Cashwell, who loses a leg. By the end of the battle, 9,000 soldiers have perished, and thousands of Confederates are buried in a field near the McGavock plantation. Zachariah ends up in Carrie's care at the makeshift hospital . . . while Carrie fights to relocate the buried soldiers when her wealthy neighbor threatens to plow up the field after the war." (Publishers Weekly)

Includes bibliographical references (p. [419]-421).

Higashino, Keigo

★ The **devotion** of suspect X; Keigo Higashino ; translated by Alexander O. Smith with Elye J. Alexander. 1st U.S. ed.; Minotaur Books 2011 298p. (Detective Galileo mysteries) $24.99

ISBN 9780312375065; 0312375069

LC 2010039022

Naoki Prize (Japan) (2005)

This book is "about a desperate woman, Yasuko, who, craving a peacefull life with her daughter, Misato, kills her abusive lout of an ex-husband. The next-door neighbor, Ishigami, helps hide the body and improvises a cover-up. When the body is eventually found, however, determined investigator Kusanagi, with the help of Dr. Yukawa, a physicist who knew Ishigami in college, senses that something is amiss with Yasuko's story. A cat-and-mouse, Dostoevsky-like investigation ensues." (Booklist)

Other titles in this series are:
Salvation of a saint (2012)
A midsummer's equation (2016)

Higashino, Keigo

Malice; A Mystery. Keigo Higashino ; translated by Alexander O. Smith with Elye Alexander. Minotaur Books 2014 276 p. (hardcover) $24.99

ISBN 1250035600; 9781250035608

LC 2014019885

In this book, by Keigo Higashino, "novelist Kunihiko Hidaka is found brutally murdered in his home . . . by his wife and his best friend. . . . At the crime scene, Police Detective Kyochiro Kaga recognizes Hidaka's best friend, Osamu Nonoguchi, . . . a full-time writer, though with not nearly the success of his friend Hidaka. As Kaga investigates, he eventually uncovers evidence that indicates that the two writers' relationship was very different that they claimed." (Publisher's note)

"Each time you're convinced Higashino's wrung every possible twist out of his golden-age setup, he comes up with a new one. If you still miss the days of The Murder of Roger Ackroyd, you can't do better than this fleet, inventive retro puzzler." Kirkus

Higgins, C. A.

Lightless; C.A. Higgins. Del Rey 2015 304 p. (hardcover) $25

ISBN 9780553394429

LC 2014037514

In this science fiction novel, by C. A. Higgins, "serving aboard . . . an experimental military spacecraft . . . , computer scientist Althea has established an intense emotional bond . . . with the ship's electronic systems, which speak more deeply to her analytical mind than human feelings do. But when a pair of fugitive terrorists gain access to the Ananke, Althea must draw upon her heart and soul for the strength to defend her beloved ship." (Publisher's note)

"A suspenseful, emotional story that asks plenty of big questions about identity and freedom." Kirkus

Another title in this series is:
Supernova (2016)

Higgins, George V.

The **Digger's** game; George V. Higgins. Penguin Books 1988 169 p.

ISBN 0140102523; 9780140102529

LC 87019761

In this book, "Jerry 'Digger' Doherty is an ex-con and proprietor of a workingman's Boston bar, who supplements his income with the occasional 'odd job,' like stealing live checks and picking up hot goods. His brother's a priest, his wife's a nag, and he's got a deadly appetite for martinis and gambling. But when the Digger loses eighteen grand in borrowed money on a trip to Vegas, he quickly finds himself in the sights of mob loanshark 'the Greek,' who will have to make the Digger pay up one way or another. Luckily—if you call it luck—the Digger has been let in on a little job that can turn his gambling debt into a profit, as long as he can pull it off without getting killed." (Publisher's note)

Higgins, George V.

★ The **friends** of Eddie Coyle. Knopf 1972 183p

ISBN 0-394-47327-2

"Written entirely in riveting dialogue, this novel is a compelling study of motive." Oxford Companion to Am Lit. 6th edition

Higgins, Jack

Bad company. Putnam 2003 287p $25.95

ISBN 0-399-14970-8

LC 2003-41365

"As the war is drawing to a close in 1945, Hitler gives his diary to an aide for safekeeping. The diary contains an account of a meeting between representatives of Hitler and President Roosevelt at which they discussed ways to negotiate a peace treaty and then to attack Russia. The aide, Max von Berger, is now (in 2003) a billionaire industrialist and a silent partner with an international crime family. Seeking revenge for a killing, Berger vows to reveal the diary's secret that would destroy the current U.S. president. It's up to an American and a British agent to get the diary before it falls into the hands of the president's enemies." Booklist

Higgins, Jack

Confessional. Stein & Day 1985 278p

ISBN 0-8128-3025-3

LC 884-40777

"The hero of this spy-thriller is three people—a KGB agent, an ordained Catholic priest and an IRA terrorist, which means that he goes through a lot of cloak-and-dagger changes as he slips from role to role. In 1958 the Russians set up a mock Irish village in the Ukraine to train future KGB agents so that they could more easily blend into the Irish landscape and go about their nefarious activities of destabilizing English-Irish relations by working through the IRA. Mikhail Kelly was a first-rate candidate because his Irish father had been hung by the British as an IRA activist and he had been raised by his Russian mother in Ireland." Best Sellers

Higgins, Jack

Day of reckoning. Putnam 2000 295p $25.95

ISBN 0-399-14585-0

LC 99-34847

The journalist wife of Sean Dillon's "old comrade Blake Johnson is killed in Brooklyn on orders of her latest object of investigation, Jack Fox, heir apparent to the powerful Solazzo crime family. The law can't touch Fox, but Blake and Dillon can and will. Aided by Dillon's black-ops boss Brigadier Charles Ferguson, and his crew, plus a father/son team of British gangsters, Blake and Dillon strike again and again at Fox's wallet: shutting down his London gambling den; sinking a boat laden with his gold; destroying a cache of his weapons in Ireland; foiling his plans for a major robbery in London. . . . The action is sleek and intensely absorbing." Publ Wkly

Higgins, Jack

The **eagle** has flown; a novel. Simon & Schuster 1991 335p

LC 91-4368

"Mr. Higgins is an expert storyteller, and he goes about 'The Eagle Has Flown' with typical gusto. Everything is carefully arranged, little pieces fitting into other little pieces to form an action-packed mosaic." NY Times Book Rev

Higgins, Jack

★ The **eagle** has landed. Simon & Schuster 1991 399p

LC 90-44042

A revised edition containing the full text of the title first published 1975 by Holt, Rinehart & Winston

"There are elements of heroism, duplicity, and heavy irony, plus considerable bloodshed, in this action-oriented yarn." Christ Sci Monit

Followed by The eagle has flown

Higgins, Jack

Edge of danger. Putnam 2001 273p $25.95

ISBN 0-399-14701-2

LC 00-40268

"Pitting returning antihero Sean Dillon, once of the IRA, now with British intelligence, against an aristocratic English-Arab family bent on vengeance that threatens world order, the story whips along. From London to the Middle East, from Ireland to the White House, it swirls with intrigue and snaps with violence." Publ Wkly

Higgins, Jack

Eye of the storm. Putnam 1992 320p

LC 91-46736

"Early in 1991, while the Gulf war is in full bloom, operatives of Saddam Hussein hire legendary terrorist Sean Dillon to take the war to the enemy. A master of disguise and subterfuge, Dillon began his career with the IRA, earning the enmity of Liam Devlin—the unforgettable antihero of The Eagle Has Landed, who makes a featured appearance here—and of Martin Brosnan, an American Special Forces hero and IRA member turned college professor. After Dillon's attempt to assassinate former Prime Minster Margaret Thatcher during a visit to France fails, he decides to go after her successor John Major. . . . Although readers can be sure that Dillon's scheme will be foiled, fun remains in the how and why." Publ Wkly

Followed by Thunder point (1993)

Higgins, Jack

Flight of eagles. Putnam 1998 328p

ISBN 0-399-14376-9

LC 97-37582

The author traces the exploits of twins Max and Harry Kelso "from 1917, when their wealthy American father marries a German baroness, through 1944. . . . Upon her husband's death in 1930, the baroness returns to Germany with Max in tow, leaving Harry in the care of his American grandfather. By the early 1940s Max is Germany's premier flying ace–he eventually downs more than 300 Allied planes–and is famed as the Black Baron. Harry, meanwhile, has enlisted with the RAF and distinguished himself equally in the Battle of Britain and beyond. The narrative cuts briskly from one twin's adventures to the other's as the dashing, daring young men intersect with historical greats including Hitler, Himmler, Goring, FDR and Eisenhower." Publ Wkly

Higgins, Jack

Luciano's luck. Stein & Day 1981 238p

LC 881-40330

"It is 1943 and the Allied invasion of Sicily is imminent. General Eisenhower plans to enlist Sicilian Mafia support for the invasion by sending two emissaries into Sicily to sway Luca, the Sicilian 'capo di tutti capi.' Logically, perhaps, one emissary is the chief U.S. capo, Lucky Luciano (who is in prison); the second is Luca's alienated granddaughter. The commando expedition to effect a meeting between these three in German-occupied Sicily forms the basis for a fast-paced, action-crammed plot, suspenseful to the last page. The fictionalized Luciano is sympathetically portrayed, and although the romanticizing of the Mafia figures jars a little, the historical premises are acceptably plausible." Libr J

Higgins, Jack

Midnight runner. Putnam 2002 289p

ISBN 0-399-14833-7

LC 2001-48124

This suspense novel finds "former IRA enforcer Sean Dillon and his present boss, Gen. Charles Ferguson, . . . responding to various revenge gambits by the beautiful and fabulously wealthy half-bedu, half-English Lady Kate Rashid, countess of Loch Dhu and head of the Rashid Bedu tribe of Hazar, whose three brothers were killed by Dillon and his comrades . . . after, among other acts of infamy, a Rashid assassination attempt on U.S. President Jack Cazalet." Publ Wkly

Higgins, Jack

Night of the fox. Simon & Schuster 1986 316p

LC 86-29662

"Higgins combines powerful narrative with documentary detail in an exceptional tale that relies upon the interweaving histories of the various characters." Libr J

Higgins, Jack

Rough justice. G.P. Putnam's Sons 2008 326p $25.95

ISBN 978-0-399-15513-0; 0-399-15513-9

LC 2008-8905

This entry in the Sean Dillon thriller series "finds aging, arthritic ex-gangster Harry Salter retired from active operations, leaving Dillon, once the IRA's most feared enforcer, as the real leader of the loose gang of stalwart lads who covertly battle the foes of Western civilization. A newcomer to the team, Maj. Harry Miller, on the surface a mild-mannered MP who's in reality the British prime minister's secret hit man, hooks up with series regular Blake Johnson in Kosovo, where the

Russians, intent on reclaiming old glory, are stirring up trouble. Meanwhile, Islamic fundamentalists are intent on bringing Britain to its knees. The action moves swiftly amid a variety of foreign locales, including Moscow, London and Beirut, to a climax that will leave readers asking themselves, evidence to the contrary, whether the great game is really over." Publ Wkly

Higgins, Jack

Touch the devil. Stein & Day 1982 251p

LC 82-40080

"Charles Ferguson of British intelligence persuades Devlin {featured in the Eagle novels} to join forces with Martin Brosnan, former comrade in the fight for Irish independence, to find and stop (by killing if necessary) another onetime rebel, Frank Barry, now in the pay of the Soviets. Barry, a cold assassin and thief of NATO secret weapons, is a match in cunning for Devlin and Brosnan, and he learns about the plot against him from a mole in Ferguson's office. He knows that Devlin and Brosnan's lover, Anne-Marie Audin, get help from the British to spirit Brosnan from a French prison, as grim as Devil's Island, where his revolutionary activities have landed him. Anne-Marie takes the two men to her secluded farm house in southern France, where Barry and his hirelings lurk in ambush." Publ Wkly

Higgins, Jack

The **White** House connection. Putnam 1999 323p $25.95

ISBN 0-399-14489-7

LC 98-42577

"When it comes to thrillers, Jack Higgins wrote the book. In fact, he wrote lots of them, and this is one of the best." Booklist

Higgins, Kristan

Anything for You; by Kristan Higgins. Harlequin Books 2015 384 p. (Blue Heron) $26.99

ISBN 0373789750; 9780373789757

In this book, by Kristan Higgins, "Connor O'Rourke has been waiting for Jessica Dunn to take their on-again, off-again relationship public, and he thinks the time has come. His restaurant is thriving, she's got her dream job at Blue Heron Vineyard—it's the perfect time to get married. When he pops the question, however, her answer is a fond but firm no. If it ain't broke, why fix it?" (Publisher's note)

"A heroine who believes she can only count on herself, a persistent, protective hero who won't give up, and a wonderful cavalcade of Blue Heron folk lead to an irresistible, often touching story that is tender, sexy, and hilarious." LJ

Higgins, Kristan

★ The **Best** Man; Kristan Higgins. Harlequin Books 2013 432 p. $7.99

ISBN 0373777922; 9780373777921

In this contemporary romance novel, by Kristan Higgins, "Faith Holland left her hometown after being jilted at the altar. Now a little older and wiser, she's ready to return to the Blue Heron Winery, her family's vineyard, to confront the ghosts of her past, and maybe enjoy a glass of red. After all, there's some great scenery there. . . . Like Levi Cooper, the local police chief." (Publisher's note)

Higgins, Kristan

In Your Dreams; Kristan Higgins. Harlequin Books 2014 480 p. $7.99

ISBN 0373779313; 9780373779314

In this love story, by Kristan Higgins, Emmaline Neal's "ex-fiancé is getting married in Malibu . . . can't go to the wedding alone. . . . Tall, blond and gorgeous Jack Holland is practically a cottage industry when it comes to rescuing desperate women. . . . Em figures . . . he won't get the wrong idea. . . . But Jack's pushing for more, and if she lets down her guard, either she'll get her heart crushed again, or discover that Jack's worth more than just dreaming about." (Publisher's note)

"A reluctant hero haunted by the reckless teen he couldn't save and a smart, plucky heroine with issues of her own are blindsided by love in a spirited, truly funny, and emotionally satisfying romance you won't want to put down. Humor and heart in one stunning package!" LJ

Higgins, Kristan

My one and only; Kristan Higgins. HQN Books 2011 382p.

ISBN 9781611730708; 9780373775576

This book follows "divorce attorney Harper James . . . [who] is horrified when her stepsister, Willa, announces that she's marrying the brother of Harper's ex-husband, Nick Lowery. Harper and Nick married young, and while their relationship quickly flamed out, the spark between them never really died. Due to a travel snafu after Willa's wedding, Harper and Nick are forced to journey across the country together. Soon, Harper is examining the reasons their marriage failed, her unresolved feelings for Nick, and her abandonment issues." (Publishers Weekly)

Higgins, Kristan

The **Perfect** Match; Kristan Higgins. Harlequin Books 2013 448 p. $7.99

ISBN 0373778198; 9780373778195

In this book by Kristan Higgins, "Honor Holland has just been . . . rejected by her lifelong crush. And now [he] is engaged to her best friend. British professor Tom Barlow just wants to do right by his unofficial stepson, Charlie, but his visa is about to expire. Honor agrees to help Tom with a marriage of convenience--and make her ex jealous. As sparks start to fly between Honor and Tom, they might discover that [the] relationship is far too perfect to be anything but true love." (Publisher's note)

"Higgins once again blends sweet romance, quirky humor, and realistic emotion in a story that will keep readers entranced." Booklist

Higgins, Kristan

Waiting on You; Kristan Higgins. Harlequin Books 2014 464 p. (Blue Heron) pbk $7.99

ISBN 0373778589; 9780373778584

LC 2014658530

In this romance novel by Kristan Higgins, "Colleen O'Rourke is in love with love . . . just not when it comes to herself. . . . Ten years ago, Lucas Campbell broke her heart . . . an experience Colleen doesn't want to have again. . . . But a family emergency has brought Lucas back to town, handsome as ever and still the only man who's ever been able to crack her defenses." (Publisher's note)

"At times [the characters'] imperfections can almost make them unlikable, but their ability to forgive each other's worst aspects makes their ultimate reconciliation especially gratifying." Kirkus

Highsmith, Patricia

The **boy** who followed Ripley. Lippincott & Crowell 1980 291p

LC 79-29678

In this novel "two people meet casually, but their fates become inextricably, and dangerously, joined. Tom Ripley is an American expatriate living on the outskirts of Paris; he meets a 16-year-old American runaway, who turns out to be the son of a recently deceased food products tycoon. The boy is haunted by guilt over his father's death and pursued through Europe by kidnappers. Engrossing and shiver packed." Booklist

Highsmith, Patricia

Patricia Highsmith: selected novels and short stories; edited with an introduction by Joan Schenkar. W. W. Norton & Co. 2011 644p $35

ISBN 978-0-393-08013-1; 0-393-08013-7

LC 2010-34589

"Highsmith's first book, 'Strangers on a Train' (1950), is the disturbing tale of a forced folie à deux between an alcoholic young psychopath and the architect he ensnares in a nightmarish, homicidal scheme. Her second novel, 'The Price of Salt' (1952), done under the pseudonym Claire Morgan, is the semi-lyrical chronicle of a love affair between two women. Each a commercial success, these works are quite different in tone and content, but both are done with a skill and an artistry that utterly convince." Los Angeles Times Book Rev

Highsmith, Patricia

✓ ★ The **talented** Mr. Ripley; Ripley under ground; Ripley's game. Knopf 1999 877p $26

ISBN 0-375-40792-8

LC 99-38147

In Ripley under ground Tom impersonates a dead artist and is drawn into murder when his deception is about to be discovered

In the talented Mr. Ripley "Tom Ripley is hired by the wealthy Herbert Greenleaf to help him find his son, Dickie. Ripley travels to Europe and catches up to Dickie in Italy, meanwhile corresponding with Greenleaf through the mail. Later, after he has assumed Dickie's identity himself, he keeps up the imposture by writing to Dickie's friends and avoiding personal contact. He continues, however, to be 'Tom Ripley' when the occasion demands. Highsmith takes us into the mind of a repellent character but, through the sheer force of her communication of his personality, compels a sympathetic fascination on the part of the reader." Murphy. Ency of Murder and Mystery

Higley, T. L.

Pompeii; L.T. Higley. B & H Books 2011 xxiii, 338p

ISBN 9781433668579; 1433668572

LC 2011282808

This book tells the story of "Ariella, a young Jewish woman fleeing Jerusalem, and Cato, a Roman merchant famous for his wines. During the fall of Jerusalem, the Roman emperor forces Ariella into slavery; she sneaks away one night, disguises herself as a young man, and joins a gladiator troupe. The gladiators soon journey to Pompeii, where her secret is almost exposed. In Pompeii, she meets Cato, who discovers right away that she's a woman and seeks to watch over her. Through a series of adventures, the two begin secretly to attend meetings led by a Jewish slave named Jeremiah, who expounds the Jewish scriptures and talks about the newly emerging Christian sect." (Publishers Weekly)

Hijuelos, Oscar, 1951-2013

Beautiful Maria of my soul; or, the true story of Maria Garcia y Cifuentes, the lady behind a famous song: a novel. Hyperion 2010 340p $25.99

ISBN 978-1-4013-2334-9; 1-4013-2334-0

LC 2009-35386

"The rare sequel that can be enjoyed independently of the original work or as a complement to it. . . . There's a simmering backdrop of revolution in the middle of the book that provides the story with historical heft. And, in the novel's bold ending, Hijuelos seamlessly welds fact and fiction, with the author himself making an appearance to discuss his books with the characters that inhabit them." Cleveland Plain Dealer

Hijuelos, Oscar

★ The **Mambo** Kings play songs of love; a novel. Farrar, Straus & Giroux 1989 407p

LC 89-1248

"The novel alternates crisp narrative with opulent musings—the language of everyday and the language of longing. When Mr. Hijuelos falters, as from time to time he does, it's through an excess of self-consciousness: he strives too hard for all-encompassing description or grows distant and dutiful in an effort to get period details just right." N Y Times Book Rev

Hijuelos, Oscar, 1951-2013

★ **Twain** and Stanley Enter Paradise; by Oscar Hijuelos. Grand Central Publishing 2015 496 p. $28

ISBN 1455561495; 9781455561490

This book, by Oscar Hijuelos, is a "work of fiction inspired by the real-life, 37-year friendship between two towering figures of the late nineteenth century, famed writer and humorist Mark Twain and legendary explorer Sir Henry Morton Stanley. . . . It is also a study of Twain's complex bond with Mrs. Stanley, the bohemian portrait artist Dorothy Tennant, who introduces Twain and his wife to the world of séances and mediums after the tragic death of their daughter." (Publisher's note)

"The novel, which contains letters, speeches, fragments of Stanley's autobiography, diary entries, and dialog, all of which Hijuelos evidently created, succeeds in conjuring a bygone era from rural 19th-century Cuba to upper-class London society. Well written and engaging, this novel may lack some of the fire of the author's best-known work, but it is a intriguing entry in his output and will appeal to his fans and those who enjoy historical fiction." LJ

Hilderbrand, Elin

The **island**; a novel. Little, Brown 2010 407p $25.99

ISBN 978-0-316-04387-8; 0-316-04387-7

LC 2010-06268

This tale "zips along with the kind of well-limned romantic drama that keeps poolside readers out of the water for hours." Entertainment Wkly

Hilderbrand, Elin

Silver girl; a novel. Little, Brown and Co. 2011 408p $26.99

ISBN 978-0-316-09966-0; 0-316-09966-X

LC 2011-02750

"Connie is profoundly lonely following her husband's death and the estrangement from her daughter. Meanwhile, Meredith's husband's investment firm has been revealed as a Ponzi scheme, and the ensuing investigation has, in a very Ruth Madoff–like way, separated her from the life she's known. The women retreat to Connie's Nantucket home, where they repair their relationships and their own broken hearts while a series of threatening events keeps Meredith in hiding. Though Meredith's guilty feelings about missing clues to her husband's dishonesty are overwhelming, the kindness shown by people who support her-including Connie's tentative new flame-encourages her to make good where she can. Much of the novel is told in flashback as Connie and Meredith work through their crises, but Hilderbrand's talents keep those memories as resonant as the present day." Publ Wkly

Hilderbrand, Elin

Summerland; a novel. Elin Hilderbrand. 1st ed. Reagan Arthur Books/Little, Brown and Co. 2012 392 p. (hardcover) $26.99; (paperback) $14.99; (audiobook) $59.99

ISBN 031609983X; 9780316099837; 9780316099899; 9781619690769 unabridged

LC 2012004929

In this book by Elin Hilderbrand, "what begins as a graduation night celebration ends in tragedy after a horrible car crash leaves the driver of the car, Penny Alistair, dead, and her twin brother in a coma. The other passengers, Penny's boyfriend Jake and her friend Demeter, are physically unhurt - but the emotional damage is overwhelming, and questions linger about what happened before Penny took the wheel." (Publisher's note)

Hill, Antonio

The **good** suicides; a thriller. Antonio Hill ; translation by Laura McGloughlin. First American edition Crown Publishers 2014 352 p. hc $26

ISBN 0770435904; 9780770435905

LC 2013019691

"After a company retreat in a remote country house, senior employees of Alemany Cosmetics return with a dark secret. . . . When they begin killing themselves, one by one, the connection . . . baffles Barcelona law enforcement and corporate think tanks alike, threatening a terrifying end for everyone involved. Breaking through the insular power structures of these enigmatic executives isn't easy, but Inspector Salgado has his own ways." (Publisher's note)

"The characters are intriguingly complex and the author skillfully pulls the rug out with a flourish at the end." LJ

Hill, Antonio

The **summer** of dead toys; a novel. Antonio Hill. 1st ed. Crown 2013 368 p. (hardcover) $26

ISBN 0770435874; 9780770435875

LC 2012034335

This novel, by Antonio Hill, is part of the author's "Inspector Salgado" series. "His boss . . . assigns Salgado to a routine accidental death: a college student fell from a balcony in one of Barcelona's ritzier neighborhoods. As Salgado begins to piece together the life and world of the victim, he realizes that his death was not all that simple. . . . Hector begins to follow a trail that will lead him deep into the underbelly of Barcelona's high society." (Publisher's note)

Hill, Joe

The **fireman**; a novel. Joe Hill. William Morrow 2016 768 p. (hardcover) $28.99

ISBN 9780062200631; 0062200631

LC 2015042212

This novel, by Joe Hill, is "about a worldwide pandemic of spontaneous combustion that threatens to reduce civilization to ashes and a band of improbable heroes who battle to save it, led by one powerful and enigmatic man known as the Fireman. . . . He strolls the ruins of New Hampshire, a madman afflicted with Dragonscale who has learned to control the fire within himself, using it as a shield to protect the hunted . . . and as a weapon to avenge the wronged." (Publisher's note)

"This is a long book, but with a curiously ominous tone set from the very first line, a brisk pace throughout, and dozens of detailed action scenes, readers will be hard-pressed to stop turning the pages." Booklist

Hill, Joe

Heart-shaped box. William Morrow 2007 376p $24.95

ISBN 978-0-06-114793-7; 0-06-114793-1

LC 2006-46548

The author has created a "wild, mesmerizing, perversely witty tale of horror. In a book much too smart to sound like the work of a neophyte, he builds character invitingly and plants an otherworldly surprise around every corner." N Y Times (Late N Y Ed)

Hill, Joe

★ **Horns**. William Morrow 2010 370p $25.99

ISBN 978-0-06-114795-1; 0-06-114795-8

"The strange thing about Horns is that its opening scenes aren't all that strange. Its author, Joe Hill, is able to make Ig's problem seem like the most natural thing in the world. Mr. Hill writes with such palpable enthusiasm that he has no trouble hooking readers. . . . [He] is able to combine intrigue, editorializing, impassioned romance and even fiery theological debate in one well-told story." N Y Times (Late N Y Ed)

Hill, Joe

★ **Nos4a2**; a novel. Joe Hill. HarperCollins 2013 704 p. $28.99

ISBN 0062200577; 9780062200570

LC 2013008897

This book "follows Vic, from 8-year-old girl to troubled teen to embattled mother, as she struggles to survive as a 'strong creative'--one who has access . . . to an alternate universe constructed from imagination. Problem is, a chief attraction of this other America is Christmasland, a snowy Neverland carnival controlled by cheery, ageless child-abductor Charlie Manx. . . . Manx tries to take Vic to Christmasland as a kid, and years later . . . he tries to take her son." (Booklist)

Hill, Joe

Strange Weather; Four Short Novels. Joe Hill. William Morrow 2017 432 p. illustrations (hardcover) $27.99

ISBN 0062663119; 9780062663115; 9780062663139

This book, by Joe Hill, is "a collection of four chilling novels. . . . 'Snapshot' is the disturbing story of a Silicon Valley adolescent. . . . A young man takes to the skies to experience his first parachute jump. . . . On a seemingly ordinary day in Boulder, Colorado, the clouds open up in a downpour of nails. . . . In 'Loaded,' a mall security guard in a coastal Florida town courageously stops a mass shooting." (Publisher's note)

"Hill is back with a collection of four short novels that each showcases his talent for mining modern lives for fear." Booklist

Hill, Lawrence

Someone knows my name; a novel. W.W. Norton & Co. 2007 486p $24.95

ISBN 978-0-393-06578-7; 0-393-06578-2

LC 2007-8035

What makes this novel "extraordinary is Hill's ability to transcend the facts—to make something magical out of them. Despite the unpalatable subject matter, he compels our attention and manages to delight. His Aminata is a heroic figure, a little larger than life, residing within and outside of history. You can never forget this character. She embeds herself in your heart." Toronto Star

Hill, Nathan

★ The **Nix**; A Novel. Nathan Hill. Alfred A. Knopf 2016 640 p. (hardback) $27.95

ISBN 9781101946619; 110194661X

LC 2015046704

In this book, by Nathan Hill, "a Nix can take many forms. In Norwegian folklore, it is a spirit who sometimes appears as a white horse that steals children away. . . . It's 2011, and Samuel Andresen-Anderson—college professor, stalled writer—has a Nix of his own: his mother, Faye. He hasn't seen her in decades, not since she abandoned the family when he was a boy. Now she's re-appeared, having committed an absurd crime." (Publisher's note)

"As more subplots build, including the mesmerizing tale of young Samuel's relationships with twins fearless Bishop and violin prodigy Bethany, Hill takes aim at hypocrisy, greed, misogyny, addiction, and vengeance with edgy humor and deep empathy." Booklist

Hill, Reginald

Arms and the women; an elliad. Delacorte Press 1999 408p $23.95

ISBN 0-385-33279-3

LC 99-35873

"Andy Dalziel and Peter Pascoe, the ranking Yorkshire police officers in this series, marshal the troops when Pascoe's wife, Ellie and their little girl narrowly escape being abducted in broad daylight from their home. Suspicion naturally falls on any number of criminals with deep grudges against Pascoe; but once these obvious bad guys are eliminated, it begins to look as if Ellie has acquired an enemy of her own, perhaps within the circle of strong-minded political activists in her women's rights group." N Y Times Book Rev

Hill, Reginald

Bones and silence. Delacorte Press 1990 332p

LC 89-48836

"A complex, challenging and diverting novel, from one of the most cogent of detective writers." Times Lit Suppl

Hill, Reginald

Death comes for the Fat Man. HarperCollins 2007 404p $24.95

ISBN 978-0-06-082082-4; 0-06-082082-9

LC 2006-48655

"Hill delivers his usual bundle of literary treats, from a single fragrant reference to Voltaire to the voluptuous visions of earthly delights Dalziel clings to as he hovers near death. Characters major and minor march boldly through the dense plot, confident of being remembered for their singular personalities and inexhaustible verbal resources, while Pascoe, who catches himself trying to keep his boss alive by assuming his 'blunt and brutish' ways, fears he's losing his own identity." N Y Times Book Rev

Hill, Reginald

Singing the sadness; a private eye Joe Sixsmith mystery. Thomas Dunne Bks. 1999 251p

ISBN 0-312-24238-7

LC 99-16864

Black private eye Joe Sixsmith "a member of the local choir, is traveling with his fellow singers to the Llanffugiol Choral Festival when the bus passes a burning cottage; without thinking, Joe rushes into the inferno and rescues a woman from the flames. He is pronouced a hero, but there's a mystery brewing: the cottage was supposed to be empty, so who is the woman Joe rescued?" Booklist

Hill, Reginald

The **Stranger** House. HarperCollins 2005 480p $24.95

ISBN 0-06-082081-0

LC 2005-40274

"Twentysomething Aussie math whiz Samantha Flood has fiery red hair and a fierce determination to learn the truth about her paternal grandmother, an orphan shipped from her native England to Australia under suspicious circumstances. Sober Spaniard Miguel Madero, who experiences ghostly visions and painful sensations in his feet and hands, has abandoned pursuit of the priesthood to engage in research about English Catholics during the Reformation. The paths of Samantha and Miguel (known to all as 'Mig') cross in the tiny English village of Illthwaite, home to the Stranger House, an inn that has hosted weary travelers for more than 500 years. Samantha and Mig, an unlikely duo, are drawn to one another as each discovers secrets simmering beneath the surface of Illthwaite's deceptively serene facade." Booklist

Hill, Reginald

The **woodcutter**; a novel. Harper 2011 519p $25.99

ISBN 978-0-06-206074-7; 0-06-206074-0

LC 2010-53608

"Near the end, a character refers to the fate of 'the dreadful, drab English.' There's nothing drab about this dark and compelling novel, although some of its characters are dreadful human beings." Kirkus

Hill, Robert

When all is said and done. Graywolf Press 2006 220p $20

ISBN 1-55597-442-2

LC 2005-926374

This is a "portrait of an unusual early 1960s American marriage. Myrmy is a stylish and successful Madison Avenue advertising copywriter, wife, and mother. Her hunky and loving husband, Dan, is a war veteran turned tie salesman. Overriding anti-Semitic obstacles, Myrmy has moved her family out of the city into a suburb, where she remains a dynamo while Dan is plagued by strange maladies. Could his troubles be the result of a little radiation experiment conducted by the military? It's hard to find time for a diagnosis with three young boys to care for. Every aspect of this agile, intoxicating, hilarious, and poignant novel is compelling, but what elevates it is the exuberant language. Hill writes with velocity, rhythm, and wit, conveying a world of subtle emotions and social nuance in brilliantly syncopated inner monologues and staccato dialogue, creating a bravura and resounding performance." Booklist

Hill, Ruth Beebe

Hanta yo. Doubleday 1979 834p

LC 77-74792

"The practice of using the multi-generational family story to reflect changing times and/or historical events is almost a genre unto itself. This is such a novel. . . . The historical accuracy, linguistic acrobatics, and ethnological acuity do not limit the book's appeal. A superb style transcends the few minor flaws, and despite the scholarly impression given by the introduction, chronology notes, and glossaries, this book is first and foremost a well-written story." Libr J

Hill, Susan

The **pure** in heart; a Simon Serrailler crime novel. Overlook Press 2007 370p $24.95

ISBN 978-1-58567-928-7; 1-58567-928-3

First published 2005 in the United Kingdom

"A nine-year-old boy is kidnapped in broad daylight while waiting for his school ride outside his home in the British cathedral town of Lafferton, and the case falls squarely in the lap of Detective Chief Inspector Serrailler. It's a copper's worst nightmare—broken and grieving parents, intense media interest, and extreme pressure from the top police brass to solve the case "yesterday." But there are few leads and no apparent motive, and as the days go by and the child isn't found, hope drains away. Although the case hits Simon and his team exceptionally hard, he has other problems to deal with. . . . This is realistic, gritty, and gut-wrenching crime fiction, but it's also a poignant and thoughtful character study." Booklist

Hill, Susan

The **risk** of darkness; a Simon Serrailler mystery. by Susan Hill. Overlook Press 2010 374 p. $15.95

ISBN 9780701176822; 1590202902; 9781590202906

LC 2006491232

In this novel by Susan Hill, part of the Simon Serrailler Mystery series, "the . . . opening chapters introduce the two main plot lines: a spate of child abductions that have been unnerving the residents of the British town of Lafferton is pinned on an emotionally disturbed young woman, and a man unhinged by grief over his wife's death goes on a psychotic rampage in pursuit of women who look like her." (Publishers Weekly)

Hill, Susan

Shadows in the street; a Simon Serrailler mystery. Susan Hill. Overlook Press 2010 372 p. $24.95

ISBN 9780701179977; 1590204085; 9781590204085

LC 2010444442

In this novel by Susan Hill, part of the Simon Serrailler series, "Two local prostitutes have been found strangled. When the wife of the St. Michael's Cathedral Dean goes missing and then another respectable woman is taken on her way to work, the townspeople grow angry and afraid. Serrailler is in the greatest danger of his life." (Publisher's note)

Hill, Susan

The **various** haunts of men; a Simon Serrailler crime novel. Overlook Press 2007 437p $24.95

ISBN 978-1-58567-876-1; 1-58567-876-7

LC 2006-51546

"Lafferton, an idyllic village just far enough from the madness of London, is a paragon of tranquility and peace, with a lovely cathedral and a stand of ancient stones on 'the Hill.' But then a woman goes missing from there, and then another, and another. Young policewoman Freya Graffham is assigned to investigate the suspected serial killings. Recently transferred from London, she is young, bright, inquisitive, dedicated, and smitten with Detective Chief Inspector Simon Serrailler. . . . As their relationship and the investigation unfold, the killer is revealed in a series of eerie first-person passages. . . . Readers will be instantly drawn to her likable characters and beautiful landscape and will be carried along by the plot, right up to the shocking final twist." Libr J

Hill, Tobias

The **love** of stones. Picador 2002 396p

ISBN 0-312-28773-9

LC 2001-50038

"Obsessed with finding a legendary stone set called 'The Three Brethren,' [jewel dealer Katharine] Sterne starts her search in Turkey, where she must first locate a rich, eccentric British woman who teases her with a lead about the whereabouts of the gems. As Sterne's quest continues, Hill introduces a parallel historical subplot dealing with the provenance of the stones." Publ Wkly

Hilleman, Andrew

World, chase me down; a novel. Andrew Hilleman. Penguin Books 2017 332 p. (paperback) $16

ISBN 9780143111474; 9781101992784

LC 2016023546

This novel, by Andrew Hilleman, retells the story of "how in 1900 the out-of-work former butcher [Pat Crowe] kidnapped the teenage son of Omaha's wealthiest meatpacking tycoon for a ransom of $25,000 in gold, and then burgled, safe-cracked, and bond-jumped his way across the country and beyond, inciting a manhunt . . . and a showdown in the court of public opinion between the haves and have-nots--all the while plotting a return to the woman he never stopped loving." (Publisher's note)

"Pat makes for an enthusiastic narrator, and he ends his story on a surprising note that affirms man's infinite capacity for resilience in the face of life's harsh vicissitudes." Pub Wkly

Hillerman, Tony

The **blessing** way. Harper & Row 1970 201p

ISBN 9780060548131; 9780914001126; 9780061808357; 9781442079977

LC 73096009

"When Bergen McKee, a disillusioned anthropologist, goes to the reservation to continue his research on Navajo witchcraft, he finds himself involved in murder, intrigue, adventure, and, worst of all, what appears to be genuine witchcraft. . . . Investigating the crime is Lt. Joe Leaphorn of the Navajo Law and Order Division." Libr J

Hillerman, Tony

Hunting badger. HarperCollins Pubs. 1999 275p hardcover o.p. pa $9.99

ISBN 0-06-019289-5; 0-06-196782-3 pa

LC 99-47906

This offers "several new insights into the mysteries of Navajo culture and a story with enough twists and surprises to make readers glad they checked in." Publ Wkly

Hillerman, Tony

The **Jim** Chee mysteries. HarperCollins Pubs. 1990 566p $26.95

ISBN 0-06-016478-6

Contents: People of darkness; The dark wind; The ghostway

Hillerman, Tony

Listening woman. Harper & Row 1978 200p

ISBN 9780060547639; 9780061967764; 9781442079984

LC 77011788

In this novel detective "Joe Leaphorn of the Navajo Tribal Police . . . {is} tracking down the murderer of a harmless old man and searching for a missing helicopter used for the getaway in a Brinks-style robbery pulled off by a militant Indian-rights group called the Buffalo Society. The desecration of some ritual sand paintings and the rumor of a sacred cave lead Leaphorn into a violent confrontation with the fanatical Buffalo Society. The terrorists are plotting to avenge the victims of a long-forgotten atrocity by recreating it—with white children as the pawns—in a vicious kidnapping/mass-murder scheme." N Y Times Book Rev

Hillerman, Tony

Sacred clowns. HarperCollins Pubs. 1993 305p

ISBN 9780061808364; 9780060547516; 9781442079960

LC 91050470

This is the twelfth mystery novel featuring Navajo "tribal policemen Joe Leaphorn and Jim Chee. Unorthodox maverick Chee hates detail . . . and works best solo. . . . {Leaphorn} plays strictly by the book. But with a heavy caseload (including two murder cases, a hit-and-run accident, a possible bribery and corruption scandal within the tribe, and a counterfeit racket involving sacred tribal artifacts) and some tricky personal problems (a love match with a lady lawyer for Chee, a trip to China with a female professor for Leaphorn), the two quickly learn the importance of understanding and teamwork." (Booklist)

"Lt. Joe Leaphorn and Officer Jim Chee of the Navajo police resolve personal issues as they investigate the murders of a tribal dancer and a white schoolteacher." Publ Wkly

Hillerman, Tony ✓

The **shape** shifter. HarperCollins 2006 276p $26.95

ISBN 0-06-056345-1

LC 2005-52602

"Only Hillerman could so masterfully connect such disparate elements as an ancient cursed weaving, two stolen buckets of piñon sap and the Vietnam War. The conclusion is sure to startle longtime fans of this acclaimed mystery series." Publ Wkly

Hillerman, Tony ✓

The **sinister** pig. HarperCollins Pubs. 2003 228p hardcover o.p. pa $7.99

ISBN 0-06-019443-X; 0-06-109878-7 pa

LC 2003-42316

"With his usual up-front approach to issues concerning Native Americans such as endlessly overlapping jurisdictions, Hillerman delivers a masterful tale that both entertains and educates." Publ Wkly

Hillerman, Tony ✓

Skinwalkers. Harper & Row 1987 216p hardcover o.p. pa $7.99

ISBN 0-06-015695-3; 0-06-100017-5 pa

In this mystery "Leaphorn has three unsolved murders to contend with, and then an attempt is made on Chee's life. Much to Leaphorn's dismay bone head figures are the sole clues found, indicating the work of a skinwalker or witch. Hillerman's Leaphorn and Chee novels convey the Navaho culture with all its intricacies set forth in a meaningful way." Libr J

Hillerman, Tony

Talking God. Harper & Row 1989 239p

ISBN 9780061967832; 9780060547318

LC 88045914

This "complex tale hinges on the mysterious murder of a man in shiny old shoes who was apparently killed on his way to an ancient tribal ceremony. Leaphorn and Chee's investigation reveals a conflict over ceremonial masks, which in turn takes them from their familiar New Mexico haunts to Washington, D.C., where they must foil an assassination attempt. As in his previous works, Hillerman combines P. D. James' taut, precise narrative style with a consistently sensitive portrayal of the native American experience. The rural landscapes shimmer with realism, while the plot is crafted with skill and passion, like the masks that figure so strongly in the action." Booklist

Hillerman, Tony

A **thief** of time; a novel. Harper & Row 1988 209p

ISBN 0060159383; 9780060159382

LC 87046147

"When a noted anthropologist arrives at an ancient Anasazi Indian ruin to dig for clay pots, she is at first angry to discover that the pre-Navajo burial site has already been despoiled, then terrified by what looms out of the darkness. Weeks later, Lieutenant Joe Leaphorn, investigating a report to the Navajo Tribal Police that the anthropologist has been stealing precious artifacts, discovers she has also been reported as missing. . . . {Then} Officer Jim Chee, on a routine search for missing excavating equipment, finds more than he expected near a similar dig. Leaphorn joins forces with Chee to . . . {solve a} series of murders that seem to have only one thing in common the beautiful and very valuable Anasazi pots." (Publisher's note)

In this novel "Lieut. Joe Leaphorn and Officer Jim Chee of the Navajo Tribal Police . . . combine forces . . . in the search for a missing archeologist, Prof. Eleanor Friedman-Bernal. A specialist in Anasazi pots, she's on the verge of a major breakthrough—the identification of a specific artist, dead a thousand years—when, beneath a full desert moon, she seems simply to vanish." N Y Times Book Rev

Hillerman, Tony

★ The **wailing** wind. HarperCollins Pubs. 2002 232p

ISBN 0-06-019444-8

LC 2001-51734

"Hillerman is never better than when he is circling a puzzle from various angles, playing with the perceptions of his detectives as well as the reader's." N Y Times Book Rev

Hilton, Erica

Dirty money Honey; Erica Hilton, Nisa Santiago and introducing Kim K. Melodrama Pub. 2011 223 p.

ISBN 1934157449; 9781934157442

LC 2011927243

In this novel, "[a]t only twenty-five, Honey has a long list of exes in her life—an ex-con father, an ex-husband, and an ex-career as an ATF agent. . . . [S]he's now working as a blackjack dealer in one of the most profitable casinos in alluring Las Vegas. Soon, her life's training is put to good use as Honey develops a master plan to get that dirty money! The city is taken by surprise when an armored truck is high-jacked in broad daylight. . . . [T]he Las Vegas police are baffled by this blatant crime, and pressure from the public and casino owners drive them to desperation. Honey and her crew of loyal followers pull off one of the most rewarding and masterful heists in Las Vegas history, but not everyone will get to enjoy the loot. Someone has to take the fall." (Publisher's note)

Hilton, James

★ **Good**-bye Mr. Chips; illustrated by H.M. Brock. Little, Brown 1962 132p il $22

ISBN 0-316-36420-7

First published 1934

"In 1870 Mr. Chipping begins a career teaching the classics at Brookfield Boys' Boarding School in England. After teaching three generations of Brookfield boys, Mr. Chips, as he is fondly called, retires to the boarding house directly across the street from the school. He continues to keep a close watch over the new group of boys and host afternoon teas as a way of sharing his reminiscences. This is a warm testimonial to a caring teacher." Shapiro. Fic for Youth. 3d edition

Hilton, James

★ **Lost** horizon; a novel. Morrow 1995 262p hardcover o.p. pa $12.95

ISBN 0-688-14656-2; 0-06-059452-7 pa

LC 96-160022

A reissue of the title first published 1933

"Hugh Conway is a British consul at Baskul when trouble erupts in 1931 and all civilians are evacuated. He and three others board a plane lent by a Maharajah. After they are airborne for several hours, they realize that they are headed in the wrong direction. When the pilot finally lands, the passengers find themselves in Shangri-La, a utopian lamasery whose inhabitants know the secret of attaining long life. Believing that war is going to destroy all civilization, the High Lama summons the newcomers to form the nucleus of a new civilization." Shapiro. Fic for youth. 3d edition

Hilton, James

Random harvest. Little, Brown 1941 326p

"Charles Rainier, wealthy business man and M.P., for nearly twenty years unable to recall that period of his life between his World War injury and 1919 suddenly has his memory restored. The dramatic suspense is great as Rainier faces his two pasts, passionately resolved to find the Paula of his lost years, at whatever cost to his present marriage and position. . . . Part of the story is related in the first person by Rainier's secretary and confidante who is interested in psychology." Libr J

Hilton, L. S.

Maestra; by L.S. Hilton. Penguin Group USA 2016 320 p. $27

ISBN 0399184260; 9780399184260

LC 2016006514

In this book, by L.S. Hilton, "Judith Rashleigh has worked hard to make something of herself. A put-upon assistant at a prestigious London art house, she's well-educated, well-groomed, and impeccably behaved--the darker desires she indulges on nights off are her own little secret. But when Judith uncovers a dangerous heist, her carefully created life is shattered and soon she's on the run." (Publisher's note)

"With the book already optioned for a movie, interest will be high for this scandalous, thrilling tour through Europe and the art world." LJ

Himes, Chester

The **collected** stories of Chester Himes; foreword by Calvin Hernton. Thunder's Mouth Press 1991 429p

LC 90-25682

Contents: Headwaiter; Lunching at the Ritzmore; All God's chillun got pride; A nigger; Let me at the enemy-an' George Brown; With malice toward none; A penny for your thoughts; Two soldiers; So softly smiling; Heaven has changed; Looking down the street; The song says 'Keep on smiling'; Her whole existence; He seen it in the stars; Make with the shape; Dirty deceivers; A modern marriage; Black laughter; A night of new roses; The night's for cryin'; Face in the moonlight; Strictly business; Prison mass; Money don't spend in the stir; I don't want to die; The meanest cop in the world; On dreams and reality; The way of flesh; The visiting hour; The things you do; There ain't no justice; Every opportunity; I'm not trying to hurt you; Pork chop paradise; Friends; To what red hell; His last day; In the rain; The ghost of Rufus Jones; Whose little baby are you?; Mama's missionary money; My but the rats are terrible; The snake; In the night; All he needs is feet; Christmas gift; The revelation; Daydream; Da-da-dee; Marihuana and a pistol; One more way to die; Naturally, the Negro; Winter coming on; Spanish gin; The something in a colored man; Tang; One night in New Jersey; A modern fable; Prediction; Life everlasting

Himes, Chester

★ **Cotton** comes to Harlem. Vintage Books 1988 159p pa $11.95

ISBN 0-394-75999-0

LC 88-40045

First published 1965 by Putnam

In this mystery featuring "Coffin" Ed Johnson and "Grave Digger" Jones " which, revolves around a cotton bale filled with $87,000, [the author] parodies Marcus Garvey's back to Africa movement. Himes treats the black community with humor and respect, but does not hesitate to show blacks victimizing each other." Murphy. Ency of Murder and mystery

Himes, Chester B., 1909-1984

Lonely crusade; a novel. Chester Himes, foreword by Graham Hodges. Thunder's Mouth Press Distributed by Publishers Group West 1986 x, 398 p.p $17.50

ISBN 1560251425; 9781560251422

LC 98162554

This novel by Chester Himes with foreword by Graham Hodges, "a classic of African-American fiction, . . . Himes's tale of a young black man who becomes a union organizer during WWII examines major problems in American life: racism, anti-Semitism, labor strife, and corruption." (Publisher's note)

Hoag, Tami

Dark horse. Bantam Bks. 2002 435p

ISBN 0-553-80192-9

LC 2002-74583

"A tangled web of deceit and double-dealing makes for a fascinating look into the wealthy world of horses juxtaposed with the realistic introspection of one very troubled ex-cop." Booklist

Hoag, Tami

Dust to dust. Bantam Bks. 2000 354p

ISBN 0-553-10634-1

LC 00-39786

"Minneapolis detective Sam Kovac and his young female partner, Nikki Liska, find themselves hot on the trail of some bad cops. It all starts when they are called to the scene of a homicide, where they find the nude, hanging body of a young Internal Affairs officer, the son of a department hero. Department brass want to declare the case a suicide and close it quickly. But after nosing around a bit, Kovac and Liska begin to suspect something much more sinister. . . . A classic whodunit with many twists and turns and a surprise ending." Booklist

Hoag, Tami

Guilty as sin. Bantam Bks. 1996 470p

ISBN 0-553-09959-0

LC 95-38214

Sequel to Night sins

This suspense novel opens "with an accused kidnapper and child molester sitting in jail awaiting trial. But is the suspect—a respected and beloved college professor—really the author of a devilishly sick scheme to terrorize the families of idyllic Deer Lake, Minn.? Ellen North is the tough county prosecutor, armed with evidence and anger; Tony Costello is the flashy big-town lawyer intent on winning fame and fortune with a headline case; and Jay Butler Brooks is the reporter, a self-centered firebrand who appears to derive pleasure from the suffering of others. . . . As the criminal's clever plot unravels and North and her team come closer to the truth, the tangled relationships that lie just beneath the surface of Deer Lake are tantalizingly revealed." N Y Times Book Rev

Hoag, Tami

Kill the messenger. Bantam Bks. 2004 419p $26

ISBN 0-553-80195-3

LC 2004-47612

"A link to Hollywood provides a burst of fresh energy in the later chapters of this character-driven, solidly constructed thriller." Publ Wkly

Hoag, Tami

Night sins. Bantam Bks. 1995 483p

ISBN 0-553-09961-2

LC 94-23910

The "community of Deer Lake, Minn., takes a turn toward Stephen King territory when the local lady doctor's son is snatched by a fiend who leaves enigmatic notes. Attempting to crack the case, feisty feminist Megan O'Malley—who hopes to become the first female field agent for the male-dominated Minnesota Bureau of Criminal Apprehension—finds herself paired with Mitch Holt, the town's love-scarred sheriff (and recovering alcoholic) who is facing assorted personal demons." Publ Wkly

Hoagland, Edward, 1932-

Children are diamonds; an African apocalypse. by Edward Hoagland. 1st ed. Arcade Publishing 2013 240 p. (hardcover) $23.95

ISBN 161145834X; 9781611458343

LC 2013013603

This novel, by Edward Hoagland, focuses on Hickey, "an American school teacher who . . . goes to Africa as an aid worker. Working for an agency in Nairobi, one of his jobs is to drive food and medical supplies to Southern Sudan to an aid station run by Ruth, a middle-aged woman, who acts as nurse, doctor, [and] feeder of starving children. When the violence . . . in the region increase . . . and aid workers are being slaughtered or evacuated, Hickey is asked to save Ruth." (Publisher's note)

Hoban, Russell

Her name was Lola. Arcade Pub. 2003 207p $24

ISBN 1-559-70726-7

LC 2003-20375

"Hoban apparently wants to see how much outrageous artifice and wilful exposure of literary technique he can get away with while still working his magic on the reader. The answer is plenty. Far from being an arid exercise, the novel has great charm and grace." New Statesman

Hoban, Russell

★ **Riddley** Walker; afterword, notes, and glossary by Russell Hoban. Expanded ed; Indiana Univ. Press 1998 235p il

ISBN 0-253-33448-9

LC 98-14996

A reissue of the title first published 1980 by Summit Bks.

"No review can do more than suggest the range and effect of this extraordinary book. It is 'sui generis,' its inspirations both particular and diverse, its references legion, its craft remarkable—contributing to a whole that is vivid, compelling and certainly unforgettable." Encounter

Hobb, Robin

Assassin's apprentice. Bantam Books 1995 356p map

ISBN 0-553-37445-1

LC 94-28942

"As a royal bastard in the household of King Shrewd, a boy called 'Fitz' spends his early years in the king's stables. When the magic in his blood marks him for destiny, he begins receiving secret instruction, by order of the king, in the art of assassination, a calling that places him in the midst of a nest of intrigue and arcane maneuverings. Firmly grounded in the trappings of high fantasy, Hobb's first novel features a protagonist whose coming of age revolves around the discovery of the meaning of loyalty and trust. [A] gracefully written fantasy." Libr J

Followed by: Royal assassin (1996) and Assassin's quest (1997)

Hobson, Laura Keane Zametkin

Gentleman's agreement; a novel. by Laura Z. Hobson. Simon & Schuster 1947 275p

"Phil Green, a member of the editorial staff of 'Smith's Weekly,' is assigned to write a series of ariticles about anti-Semitism in America. He decides to pose as a Jew for six months, and he has some extraordinary experiences." Benet's Reader's Ency of Am Lit

Hockensmith, Steve

Holmes on the range. St. Martin's Minotaur 2006 294p $22.95

ISBN 978-0-312-34780-2; 0-312-34780-4

LC 2005-50406

"This is a great reworking of the Holmes conceit, and one suspects Hockensmith will have a steady readership as long as the Amlingmeyers are on the case." Booklist

Hockensmith, Steve

On the wrong track. St. Martin's Minotaur 2007 292p $23.95

ISBN 978-0-312-34781-9; 0-312-34781-2

LC 2007-5176

"As a lively Holmes takeoff, as an inventive melding of mystery and western genres, and as a new source of damn good reading, this series demands attention." Booklist

Hodder, Mark

Expedition to the Mountains of the Moon; by Mark Hodder. Pyr 2012 399p

ISBN 9781616145354

LC 2011037544

This book explores "an alternate steampunk universe" in which "famed explorer and polyglot Sir Richard Burton" travels through time in order to prevent both the assassination of Queen Victoria and a previous attempt to avert the murder which led to the twisting of reality. "Meanwhile . . . in 1863, British Prime Minister Lord Palmerston . . . instructs Burton, ostensibly to seek the source of the Nile, actually to recover a third set of psychoactive diamonds left by a now-extinct non-human race, by which means Palmerston hopes to defeat Germany before the world is engulfed in war. In 1914, Burton arrives in East Africa, where an appalling conflict already rages . . . but this time with few memories and little idea of who he is or what he's supposed to do." (Kirkus)

Hodder, Mark

The **strange** affair of Spring Heeled Jack; by Mark Hodder. Pyr 2010 378 p. (pbk.) $17.00

ISBN 9781616142407

LC 2010020632

Philip K. Dick Award (2010)

In this book, "London in the middle of the 19th century suffers from a plague of dog-faced men, thought by some to be werewolves; in addition, a strange apparition bearing a resemblance to the . . . mythical creature known as Spring-Heeled Jack rampages through the city, savagely attacking young women. Lord Palmerston commissions the famous adventurer Sir Richard Burton as a special agent to investigate these occurrences, and Burton acquires the assistance of the notoriously decadent poet and libertine Algernon Charles Swinburne. Together, the mismatched pair traverses the streets of a city filled with mechanical splendors, genetically engineered animals, and unspeakable squalor. Their investigations lead them to the suspicion that they are living in a nonexistent time." (Library Journal)

Other titles in this series are:

The curious case of the clockwork man (2011)

Expedition to the Mountains of the Moon (2012)

The secret of Abdu el Yezdi (2013)

The return of the discontinued man (2014)

The rise of the automated aristocrats (2015)

Hodgen, Christie

Elegies for the brokenhearted; a novel. W. W. Norton & Co. 2010 271p $23.95

ISBN 039306140X; 9780393061406; 978-0-393-06140-6; 0-393-06140-X

LC 2010-11149

This "novel pulls readers into the life of Mary Murphy, who has, along with her older sister, Malinda, endured her mother's five marriages with a silent stoicism. Mary's uncle Mike is the idol of her youth and a semipermanent male presence, despite being 'the chump, the slouch, the drunk, the bum' of the family, until he takes off for New York City and dies of an overdose. A schoolmate's refusal to give Mary and her family a ride results in her mother meeting her fourth husband, an African American who draws Mary out of her shell and becomes a real father. A college roommate then shows her the impossibility of ever leaving family behind. After she graduates, Mary mounts a search for her runaway sister and ends up living a routine existence in a small town in Maine, her only friends a gay pianist and an older German woman, each paralyzed by their past promise."

"Despite its gritty realities, 'Elegies for the Brokenhearted' ultimately has an almost mythic grandeur, in part because the story is propelled by associative rather than linear logic, in part because the action, played out largely in places that are entirely familiar but hardly ever named, acquires a strange universality, and in part because Hodgen's interest lies in questions of blood and parentage — of the ties that bind us together or drive us apart." N Y Times Book Rev

Hodgkinson, Amanda

22 Britannia Road. Pamela Dorman Books/Viking 2011 323p $25.95

ISBN 0-670-02263-2; 978-0-670-02263-2

LC 2010-45353

Silvana is a survivor of the Polish Holocaust. During the war she and her son Aurek hid out in the forest. "They are rescued from a refugee camp by Janusz, the husband and father from whom they were separated at the beginning of the fighting. Janusz brings them to Ipswich, to the small house and garden that give the novel its title." (N Y Times Book Rev)

This "novel moves between wartime Poland and postwar England as it follows the shifting fortunes of Janusz Nowak and his wife, Silvana. Their young marriage is tested by the German invasion as Janusz enlists and Silvana finds herself left behind in Warsaw with their young son, Aurek. Janusz loses his regiment and ends up in England after spending time on a farm in France, where he has a passionate love affair. Silvana and Aurek escape into the forest and endure years of privation and abuse at the hands of their protectors. Their unexpected postwar family reunion is marred by the guilty secrets they each harbor." Libr J

Hodgson, Antonia

★ The **last** confession of Thomas Hawkins; Antonia Hodgson. Houghton Mifflin Harcourt 2016 400 p. (ebook) $27; (hardcover) $27

ISBN 9780544715943; 9780544639683

LC 2015028196

In this book, by Antonia Hodgson, it is "London, 1728. Tom Hawkins is headed to the gallows, accused of murder. Gentlemen don't hang and Tom's damned if he'll be the first. He may not be much of a gentleman, but he is innocent. He just always finds his way into a spot of bad luck." (Publisher's note)

"Hodgson maintains pitch-perfect suspense, craftily constructs a fairly clued whodunit, and convincingly evokes the period." Pub Wkly

Hoeg, Peter

Borderliners; translated by Barbara Haveland. Farrar, Straus & Giroux 1994 277p

ISBN 0-374-11554-0

LC 94-18892

Original Danish edition, 1993

"The author avoids simple storytelling, preferring instead to explore the nature of time. 'What is time?' are the book's opening words, and later Mr. Hoeg actually provides brief historical passages on the development of theories of time. In a related device, the novel employs a dreamy, associative narrative, moving back and forth through the years, including flash-forwards to the adult Peter's family life. . . . 'Borderliners' is written from the heart, and its portrait of the embittered survivor Peter is moving." N Y Times Book Rev

Høeg, Peter

The **elephant** keepers' children; Peter Høeg ; translated from the Danish by Martin Aitken. Other Press 2012 499 p. (hardcover : acid-free paper) $27.95

ISBN 1590514904; 9781590514900; 9781590514917

LC 2012015734

This book by Peter Hoeg "concerns two children, 14-year-old Peter and his older . . . sister, Tilte, who go on the run from the authorities . . . following their parents' mysterious disappearance. The parents work in their hometown church . . . where miracles may have occurred during the father's sermons; lately, they have become involved with shady business dealings as well. . . . The children learn . . . that a theft of priceless religious artifacts may be in the works." (Library Journal)

Hoeg, Peter

The **history** of Danish dreams; translated by Barbara Haveland. Farrar, Straus & Giroux 1995 356p

ISBN 0-374-17138-6

LC 95-18355

Original Danish edition, 1988

"If Dreams is regarded not as a novel, but as a marvelous trunkful of loosely related funny bits, . . . it is a great success." Time

Hoeg, Peter

★ **Smilla's** sense of snow; translated by Tiina Nunnally. Farrar Straus Giroux 1993 453p

ISBN 0-374-26644-1

LC 93-17742

Original Danish edition, 1992; published in the United Kingdom with title: Miss Smilla's feeling for snow

"Selfishness, menace and systematic corruption form the fabric of this mysterious novel. Relationships are all based on suspicion, and love has to be 'like a military operation.'. . . Peter Høeg has a remarkable feeling for sinister surprises." Times Lit Suppl

Hoff, B. J.

River of mercy; BJ Hoff. Harvest House Publishers 2012 304 p. (pbk.) $13.99

ISBN 0736924205; 9780736924207

LC 2012012455

This novel, by B. J. Hoff, is the "conclusion to her . . . Riverhaven Years trilogy. . . . In this third book, young Gideon Kanagy faces a life-changing challenge--and an unexpected romance with his young Amish friend, Emma Knepp. Gideon's sister, Rachel, and the 'outsider' Jeremiah Gant add to the drama with their own dilemma and its repercussions for the entire community of Riverhaven." (Publisher's note)

Hoffman, Alice

Blackbird house. Doubleday 2004 225p

ISBN 0-385-50761-5

LC 2004-07958

"The relationship of the characters to their surroundings is seen as a kind of magical bond, expressed in language that is both eerie and beautiful. The house of the title is one in which, from story to story, we glimpse various families over the course of two centuries. . . . Hoffman lets Blackbird House stand as an emblem for the transforming power of any long-established home, while reveling in the haunting quality of her own distinctive literary style." N Y Times Book Rev

Hoffman, Alice

The **dovekeepers**; a novel. Scribner 2011 504p $27.99

ISBN 978-1-4516-1747-4; 1-4516-1747-X

LC 2011-18099

"Hoffman put years of research into The Dovekeepers, and at times the story slows from a scholar's desire to dwell on details of custom or ritual. But for those like me who'll follow the novelist anywhere, that pacing becomes its own powerful incantation." Entertainment Wkly

Hoffman, Alice

The **ice** queen; a novel. Little, Brown 2005 224p $23.95

ISBN 0-316-05859-9

LC 2004-26610

"Ever since she was eight years old, Hoffman's narrator, a devoted reference librarian, has believed that her temper tantrum caused her mother's death. Her guilt turned her solitary, stoic, and somewhat misanthropic, and she envisions herself as an ice queen. Even after she is struck by lightning. As her damaged narrator reluctantly joins a lightning-strike-survivor support group, Hoffman dramatizes the bizarre effects experienced by real-life lightning strike survivors, and orchestrates a highly erotic and risky romance between the ice queen and a fellow survivor known as Lazarus, whose breath ignites paper. As Hoffman's spellbinding and wonderfully insightful tale unfurls, she pays charming tribute to librarians, revels in metaphors of hot and cold, and poetically explores the meaning of trust, the chemistry of healing, and the reach of love." Booklist

Hoffman, Alice

Illumination night. Putnam 1987 224p

LC 86-30472

"A young couple's marriage has survived struggles and poverty in a countercultural transplant to the off-season isolation of Martha's Vineyard only to face a more unlikely and dangerous threat. A teen-age girl, who has moved next door to care for her sick grandmother, develops an erotic fixation on the husband. Hoffman probes the mythic connotations of the situation as she supplies convincing portraits of the man and woman and of the young girl who is determined to come between them. . . . All of this is delineated with both depth and clarity in a novel that encapsulates and transforms the characters' experiences into broader symbols of yearning and passion." Booklist

Hoffman, Alice

Local girls. Putnam 1999 197p $22.95

ISBN 0-399-14507-9

LC 98-50632

A collection of "interlinked stories about a Jewish Long Island family locked in a downward spiral after the parents' divorce. Most of the stories are told from the viewpoint of Gretel Samuelson as she moves from high-school years to young adulthood. . . . Hoffman doesn't sentimentalize her characters' lives: the tragedies they suffer are ordinary, after all. She has a light touch and a poet's knack for making diffuse elements fall into place with seeming effortlessness." Publ Wkly

Hoffman, Alice

Practical magic. Putnam 1995 244p

ISBN 0-399-14055-7

LC 94-47013

"The tale of the Owenses' struggle is charmingly told, and a good deal of fun. Dark comedy and a light touch carry the story along to a truly Gothic climax." N Y Times Book Rev

Hoffman, Alice

The **probable** future. Doubleday 2003 322p hardcover o.p. pa $13.95

ISBN 0-385-50760-7; 0-345-45591-6 pa

LC 2003-40960

"Filled with vivid (if sometimes sketchy) characters and cinematic descriptions of New England landscapes, this book will be a hit wherever Hoffman is in demand." Libr J

Hoffman, Alice

The **red** garden. Crown Pubs. 2010 270p $25

ISBN 978-0-307-39387-6; 0-307-39387-9

LC 2010-06246

This "a collection of 14 stories set in Blackwell, Mass., a fictional village deep in the woods of the Berkshires. Beginning with Blackwell's founding in 1786 by a handful of inept, unprepared settlers, these stories span more than 200 years. Each one, complete in itself, offers a time-stamped snapshot of the lives of Blackwell's inhabitants — the temporal equivalent of a holograph. If this book has a plot, it is not the usual kind. Instead, against a background of far-off historical events Hoffman sets the ongoing life of one small town and its episodic interaction with the natural world that surrounds it." Boston Globe

Hoffman, Alice

The **river** king. Putnam 2000 324p

ISBN 0-399-14599-0

LC 00-23870

"It can be hard to find an example of good old-fashioned storytelling these days, but storytelling, refreshingly, is Alice Hoffman's strength." N Y Times Book Rev

Hoffman, Alice

The **rules** of magic; Alice Hoffman. Simon & Schuster 2017 367 p. (hardcover) $27.99

ISBN 9781501137471; 9781501137488; 9781501137495

LC 2016054138

In this novel in the Practical Magic series, by Alice Hoffman, "for the Owens family, love is a curse that began in 1620, when Maria Owens was charged with witchery for loving the wrong man. Hundreds of years later, in New York City at the cusp of the sixties, . . . Susanna Owens knows that her three children are dangerously unique. . . . But when her children visit their Aunt Isabelle, . . . they uncover family secrets and begin to understand the truth of who they are." (Publisher's note)

"The spellbinding story, focusing on the strength of family bonds through joy and sorrow, will appeal to a broad range of readers." Pub Wkly

Hoffman, Alice

Skylight confessions. Little, Brown and Co. 2007 262p $24.99

ISBN 978-0-316-05878-0; 0-316-05878-5

LC 2006-01391

This novel, "about the magic of love and the perils of fate, may be the saddest book [Hoffman's] ever written, but it is also one of her very best. . . . [Arlie's] ephemeral self is what fuels the tale—she is a fairy-tale creature, to be sure, and yet she is also obviously a flesh-and-blood woman with deep and compelling desires." Baltimore Sun

Hoffman, Alice

The **story** sisters; a novel. Shaye Areheart Books 2009 325p $25

ISBN 978-0-307-39386-9; 0-307-39386-0

LC 2008-51054

"The Story sisters, Elv, Meg, and Claire, are dark-haired beauties clustered in the attic of their old Long Island house, while their lonely mother broods below. Their all-female household, a sly variation on Little Women, is under a grim fairy-tale spell, and not even sojourns with their fairy-godmother-like grandmother in Paris can protect them. . . . Meg is practical, while Elv and Claire share a tragic secret, and Elv channels her anguish into elaborate, demon-haunted tales of an imaginary parallel world until she discovers more effective means of self-punishment." Booklist

Hoffman, Alice

The **third** angel; a novel. Shaye Areheart Books 2008 278p $25

ISBN 978-0-307-39385-2; 0-307-39385-2

LC 2007-28071

This is the "tale of three women, all terribly in love with the wrong men. The novel is . . . constructed in three sections, narrated in three different time periods. The women in each section stay on the seventh floor of the haunted Lion Park Hotel in London. The first woman, Maddy Heller, stays at the Lion Park in 1999 for her sister's wedding. Her story is compelling in that she is secretly and tragically in love with her sister's fiance. In 1966, the second woman, Frieda Lewis, falls in love with a guest at the hotel: an American rock star and drug addict who happens to be engaged to someone else. And in 1952, the third woman, Bryn Evans, betrays her fiance at the Lion Park, to disastrous results. At the very end of the novel, Hoffman reveals the tragedy of the Lion Park ghost, the suspenseful event that connects all the women in powerful and mystical ways." Rocky Mountain News

Hoffman, Alice

Turtle Moon. Putnam 1992 255p

ISBN 0-399-13720-3

LC 91-37222

"Hoffman handles romance, suspense, and the healing properties of love and understanding with aplomb and a dash of magic." Booklist

Hoffman, Cara

Be safe I love you; Cara Hoffman. Simon & Schuster 2014 304 p. (hardcover) $26; (trade pbk.) $16

ISBN 1451641311; 9781451641318; 9781451641325

LC 2013011118

In this book, by Cara Hoffman, "Lauren Clay has returned from a tour of duty in Iraq just in time to spend the holidays with her family. Before she enlisted, Lauren, a classically trained singer, and her brother Danny, a bright young boy obsessed with Arctic exploration, made the most of their modest circumstances, escaping into their imaginations and forming an indestructible bond. Joining the army allowed Lauren to continue to provide for her family, but it came at a great cost." (Publisher's note)

"Though Hoffman manages to incorporate comic elements, this is a searing, unforgettable, and beautifully written tale about the corrosive effects of war on the psyche." LJ

Hoffman, Nina Kiriki

Catalyst. Tachyon Publications 2006 171p pa $14.95

ISBN 1-892391-38-4

"Kaslin—and Histly, for that matter—are vibrant creations, their psychology utterly credible for smart adolescents. That the book ends with everything but Kaslin and Histly's relationship up in the air may indicate merely that Hoffman knew when she had achieved perfection." Booklist

Hogan, Chuck

Devils in exile; a novel. Scribner 2010 312p $26

ISBN 978-1-4165-5886-6; 1-4165-5886-1

LC 2009-43459

"This is a compelling portrait of a good man who makes bad choices and in the end must battle his way out of a destructive and deadly life." Publ Wkly

Holland, Cecelia

Jerusalem. Forge 1996 318p

LC 95-38814

"The narrative structure may be simple, but Holland's masterful layering of subplots, historical detail and multiple perspectives makes for a great read." Publ Wkly

Holland, Cecelia

An **ordinary** woman; a dramatized biography of Nancy Kelsey. Forge 1999 223p

ISBN 0-312-86528-7

LC 98-48929

A "fictionalized biography of Nancy Kelsey, the first American woman to reach California. Traveling by horse and on foot, 17-year-old Nancy leaves Missouri with a baby on her hip in search of California's holy grail. Part of the 1841 Bidwell-Bartleson party, Nancy and her husband, Ben, decide against the meandering Santa Fe Trail in order to take a more—direct and uncharted—course directly across the continent: traversing the Great Plains, the Rockies, the desert and the Sierra Nevadas. . . . The thorough research lends authority to a vivid and engaging narrative that suffers only a little from Holland's evident fervent admiration for her heroine." Publ Wkly

Includes bibliographical references (p. {221}-223)

Holland, Cecelia

Valley of the Kings; a novel of Tutankhamun. Forge 1997 231p

LC 97-5499

First published 1977 by Dutton under the pseudonym Elizabeth Eliot Carter

The first half of the "novel is narrated by a fictionalized Howard Carter, the Englishman who discovered Tut's tomb in 1922. Holland does an excellent job of rendering Carter's strained relationship with his upper-crust patron, Lord Carnarvon, while surrounded by obtuse British bureaucrats, archeologists more interested in treasure than history and a culture that Carter loves despite its otherness. . . . The second half of the book flashes back to the ancient Egypt of Tut and concerns three common Egyptians—a mason, a beggar and a maid—who are variously damaged and nurtured by the royals, who have their own problems." Publ Wkly

Holland, Travis

The **archivist's** story. Dial Press 2007 239p $23

ISBN 978-0-385-33995-7; 0-385-33995-X

LC 2006-31932

"There is a quiet authenticity about Holland's writing that draws you in, and soon you will find yourself sitting on the edge of your seat, silently cheering for his characters." Libr J

Hollinghurst, Alan, 1954-

The **stranger's** child. Alfred A. Knopf 2011 435p $27.95

ISBN 978-0-307-27276-8; 0-307-27276-1

LC 2011-10256

A tale about "poet-aristocrat Cecil Valance who in the first section of the novel is an omnisexual wildcard, filled with 'airy aggressions' that alarm and/or seduce just about everyone around him. Forty-four years later Cecil is seen, by a young aspiring gay writer contemplating writing his biography, as 'a very minor poet' of World War I 'who just happened to have written lines here and there that had stuck.' He's on school syllabuses. His life was 'dramatic as well as short.' And the people who remember him, loved him and were apparently 'loved back' are still around to be interviewed. The contrast between living Cecil, as extravagant and carnal a creature as they come, and dead Cecil, who posthumously draws all his surviving circle into 'false piety and dutiful suppression,' couldn't be more striking. . . . Hollinghurst divides the novel into five novella-length sections set in 1913, 1926, 1967, 1980 and 2008. In each of them, he demonstrates his knack for conjuring the moments between events, the seeming down time in which the ramifications of turning points in life sort themselves out. His immersion in each period is fluid and free of false notes, collectively fusing into a single symphonic epic." Seattle Times

Hollingshead, Greg

Bedlam. Thomas Dunne Books 2006 312p $24.95

ISBN 978-0-312-35474-9; 0-312-35474-6

LC 2006-44416

First published 2004 in Canada

This novel "begins in 1797 with a jolt: in the bedroom of a real (if minor) historical woman surprised by the unexpected arrival of her naked husband, James Tilly Matthews, an escapee from a London madhouse who is soon back within its walls. After this wrenching, lunatic scene, the novel details, in three different narrative voices, a prolonged struggle both to release him and to discover the possibly political reason for his incarceration. Interspersed are the emotional letters husband and wife write to each other and one touching note from their son. . . . 'Bedlam' has no end of gorgeous writing. Ostentatious language is always a danger when using narrators from the distant past, but Hollingshead's descriptions stand tastefully back from such overexuberance." N Y Times Book Rev

Holmes, Lauren

Barbara the slut and other people; Lauren Holmes. Riverhead Books 2015 272 p. (hardback) $27.95

ISBN 1594633789; 9781594633782

LC 2015004287

This book, by Lauren Holmes, is a "collection about family, friends, and lovers, and the flaws that make us most human. . . . In 'Desert Hearts,' a woman takes a job selling sex toys in San Francisco. . . . In 'Pearl and the Swiss Guy Fall in Love,' a woman realizes she much prefers the company of her pit bull. . . . And in 'Barbara the Slut,' a young woman with an autistic brother, a Princeton acceptance letter, and a love of sex navigates her high school's toxic, slut-shaming culture." (Publisher's note)

"Holmes' 10 tales smartly explore her characters' varied internalizations and vulnerabilities in light of the heavy influence of appearances and unwise attachments." Booklist

Holt, Tom

Doughnut; Tom Holt. Orbit 2013 400 p. (paperback) $13.99

ISBN 0316226106; 9780316226097; 9780316226103

LC 2012951499

In this book by Tom Holt, "physicist Theo Bernstein loses his job when he accidentally blows up Switzerland's Very Very Large Hadron Collider. As his life plummets into chaos, he receives an unexpected inheritance from an old friend, Professor Pieter van Goyen, and careens into a world of impossible possibilities that not only defy the laws of physics but also demand a rewrite. In between, Theo travels to many worlds; meets a cast of friends, relatives, and enemies." (Library Journal)

Holt, Victoria

The **black** opal. Doubleday 1993 275p

LC 92-33830

In this "romantic mystery, Dr. Marline and his ailing wife adopt young Carmel March after she is found wandering among the azaleas on their estate, Commonwood House. Soon she is on her way to a new life in Australia. When Carmel finally returns as a young woman, she realizes that she was hustled away to shield her from a mysterious murder at Commonwood House, and she is convinced that the wrong man has been convicted for the crime." Libr J

Holt, Victoria

Bride of Pendorric. Doubleday 1963 288p

Favel Farrington is a young bride, married to handsome Roc Pendorric. She is fearful that he has chosen her for her money and that she will become another of the legendary brides of Pendorric Castle to die young and tragically

Holt, Victoria

The **Judas** kiss. Doubleday 1981 400p

LC 81-43138

"Pippa Ewing discovers that her beloved older sister Francine has been murdered as she lay in bed with her husband Baron Rudolph. As evidence accumulates to show that Francine had not married him after all, Pippa is launched on a quest to solve her sister's murder and vindicate her name, a journey that takes her to the duchy of Bruxenstein; a job as a governess; and another encounter with Nordic, handsome Conrad, who had caused Pippa to 'fall down the slippery slope' one romantic evening. Mysteries pile up as two similar midnight fires take the lives of a pious and cruel grandfather and a young countess. . . . Plenty of romance, an agreeable amount of sex, lots of danger and suspense in Gothic and exotic settings ensure that this will please Holt fans." Publ Wkly

Holt, Victoria

Secret for a nightingale. Doubleday 1986 371p

LC 86-2206

"In this Victorian romance, Susanna Pleydell loses her husband to drugs and her dearly loved child to her husband's neglect. She develops an obsessive hatred for Damien Adair, the physician she holds responsible for both tragedies. She tries to forget by taking up a nursing career, eventually going to the Crimea. There, working beside Dr. Adair, she finds herself attracted to him despite her hatred. . . . This is one of the better Holt novels, with a well-drawn historical background." Libr J

Holthe, Tess Uriza

When the elephants dance; a novel. Crown 2002 368p il
ISBN 0-609-60952-1

A novel set "in the final days of the battle for the Philippines. During MacArthur's assault on Manila, a group of neighbors seek shelter in the cellar of an abandoned house. Cramped, starving and terrified, they begin to tell each other stories in order @to stay alive when you have died inside'. . . . Full of weird, fantastic twists and folkloric wisdom, the stories become both a touchstone to and a respite from the horrific events unfolding outside." N Y Times Book Rev

Homes, A. M.

This book will save your life. Viking 2006 372p $24.95
ISBN 0-670-03493-2

LC 2005-54697

"Richard Novak's day-trading fortune has given him the good life in the hills above 21st-century Los Angeles, but a heart-attack scare exposes his isolation, and a rapidly expanding sinkhole in his front yard forces him to move to a Malibu rental. These crises throw Richard into the paths of such diverse characters as a donut shop owner, a runaway housewife, and a reclusive, iconic author. His eventual return to humanity culminates in a confrontational and emotional visit with teenage son Ben. . . . Overall, this is an engaging and timely tale told with a balanced mix of dark humor and sympathy for individuals enduring the foibles of everyday living." Libr J

Hood, Ann

An **Italian** Wife; Ann Hood. W W Norton & Co Inc 2014 272 p. genealogical table $25.95
ISBN 0393241661; 9780393241662

LC 2014013801

This novel by Ann Hood "begins in turn-of-the-century Italy, when fourteen-year-old Josephine . . . is forced into an arranged marriage to a man . . . about to depart for America, where she later joins him. Bound by tradition, Josephine gives birth to seven children. The last . . . is conceived in passion, born in secret, and given up for adoption. Josephine spends the rest of her life searching for her lost child." (Publisher's note)

"With each chapter a coming-of-age tale of an individual family member, Hood offers a poignant view of the turbulent 20th century. She successfully displays the connected, ordinary lives of her characters, whom readers will come to love, appreciate, and enjoy. This intricately woven, engrossing narrative will delight Hood's readers and attract fans of literary family sagas." LJ

Hood, Ann

The **knitting** circle. W. W. Norton 2007 346p
ISBN 978-0-393-05901-4; 0-393-05901-4

LC 2006-32223

This novel was "written after Hood's own tragic loss, the death of her young daughter, and it is not hard to imagine the ways in which writing this novel must have been both painful and therapeutic. It is a wondrously simple book about something complicated: the nearly unendurable process of enduring after a great loss. The novel, like knitting, seems to make itself up as it goes along, the threads bound and gathered into a whole. In the end, there is something where there once was nothing." Washington Post Book World

Hood, Ann

The **Obituary** Writer; Ann Hood. 1st ed. W W Norton & Co Inc 2013 320 p. (hardcover) $26.95
ISBN 0393081427; 9780393081428

LC 2012040074

This book is set in 1919, where "Vivien Lowe still hunts for a lover lost in the Great San Francisco Earthquake of 1906 even as she writes obituaries to help herself and others become reconciled to loss. Readers eventually uncover her connection to Claire, a young wife and mother who on the day of JFK's inauguration considers whether she should leave her safe, airless marriage for the man she loves." (Library Journal)

Hood, Ann

The **red** thread; a novel. W.W. Norton & Co. 2010 304p $23.95
ISBN 978-0-393-07020-0; 0-393-07020-4

LC 2009-42605

"Maya started The Red Thread Adoption Agency, referring to a Chinese saying that a red thread connects people destined to be together. . . . Interspersed throughout are italicized vignettes about Chinese mothers forcedby the quota on children and prejudice against girls to make wrenching decisions. The raw and riveting Chinese stories siphon narrative juice from the more conventional American angst that dominates the novel. Still, the tale ends with a pleasing sense that the red thread is more than a myth, especially in Maya's case." Kirkus

Hooker, Richard

★ **MASH**. Morrow 1968 219p hardcover o.p. pa $13
ISBN 0-688-14955-3 pa

LC 68-29610

"Captains Hawkeye Pierce, Duke Forrest, and 'Trapper' John McIntyre, all M.D.'s, are stationed in Korea with the 4077th MASH (Mobile Army Surgical Hospital). The reader is soon involved in many operations and medical jargon. It is, however, the off-duty activities of these three that engages one's attention and laughter. Full of martinis, or bored, or tired, or all three, the men soon start raising hell. . . . Hilarious, occasionally very serious, full of warm, appealing eccentric characters, one could enjoy a very pleasant evening with this sMASHing novel." Libr J

Hooper, Emma

Etta and Otto and Russell and James; a novel. Emma Hooper. Simon & Schuster 2015 320 p. (hardcover) $26
ISBN 1476755671; 9781476755670; 9781476755687

LC 2013045400

In this book, "eighty-three-year-old Etta embarks on a 3,200-kilometer journey walking from Saskatchewan to Halifax in order to see the ocean for the first time. . . . Her husband, Otto, passes the time until her return by writing Etta letters he never mails, learning to bake from her ancient recipe cards, and creating papier-mâché animal sculptures. Russell, who lives on the neighboring farm, goes after Etta, and, in the process, decides that it's time to begin his own journey." (Library Journal)

"Hooper has written an irresistibly enchanting debut novel that explores mysteries of love old and new, the loyalty of animals and dependency of humans, the horrors of war and perils of loneliness, and the tenacity of time and fragility of memory." Booklist

Hooper, Kay

Blood sins. Bantam Books 2009 296p $25
ISBN 978-0-553-80485-0; 0-553-80485-5

LC 2008-34883

In this "paranormal thriller, the second in a trilogy (after Blood Dreams) . . . , Noah Bishop, of the FBI's Special Crimes Unit, and Haven, a civilian investigative organization, take on the fanatical Rev. Adam Deacon Samuel. At age 10, Samuel murdered his abusive prostitute mother by using psychic powers, which a few years later increased after lightning struck him during a tent revival. Noah and his colleagues suspect Samuel, the leader of the Church of the Everlasting Sin, of killing at least eight people via supernatural means and of abusing young girls to enhance his powers. Tessa Gray, a Haven operative posing as a recent widow, reluctantly infiltrates Samuel's compound in the small town of Grace, N.C., near where the body of a fellow Haven operative surfaced in a river. Hooper pulls out all the stops in depicting the unholy preacher's apocalyptic breakdown as Noah's elite team tackles one of their nastiest assignments yet." Publ Wkly

Hooper, Kay

Blood ties; a Bishop/Special Crimes Unit novel. Bantam Books 2010 311p $26

ISBN 978-0-553-80486-7; 0-553-80486-3

LC 2009-37219

The conclusion to Hooper's "paranormal thriller trilogy that began with Blood Dreams and Blood Sins. When a serial killer tortures, dismembers, and dumps eight women in eight weeks in Tennessee and adjacent states, Noah Bishop, head of the FBI's Special Crimes Unit, gets on the case, along with Noah's touch-telepath and seer wife, Miranda, and special agent Hollis Templeton, a profiler-in-training and medium who can selfheal and see auras. Hollis and special investigator Diana Brisco, also a medium and healer, travel to the 'gray time,' a corridor between life and death where a young spirit, Brooke, helps them connect the killings to a past threat. Series fans and newcomers alike will appreciate the appendixes, which include bios of Special Crime Unit agents and definitions of their various paranormal abilities." Publ Wkly

Hooper, Kay

Finding Laura. Bantam Bks. 1997 322p il

LC 97-10116

At the Kilbourne estate auction in Atlanta "striking redhead Laura Sutherland is delighted to acquire a beautiful 200-year-old mirror for her collection. But she's no longer convinced her purchase is a bargain when magnetic Peter Kilbourne turns up dead only hours after attempting to buy back the mirror, and the police immediately consider her a suspect. . . . Hooper keeps the intrigue pleasurably complicated, with gothic touches of suspense and a statisfying resolution." Publ Wkly

Hooper, Tobe

Midnight movie; a novel. [by] Tobe Hooper, with Alan Goldsher. Three Rivers Press 2011 315p pa $14

ISBN 978-0-307-71701-6; 0-307-71701-1

LC 2010-40358

"Hooper leaps from one viewpoint character to the next, never lingering on one scene long enough for the reader to become bored or for the characters to become developed. Though constrained by the conventions of the genre, Hooper demonstrates an undeniable talent, using established horror tropes with considerable skill and ingenuity." Publ Wkly

Hoover, Colleen

November 9; a novel. Colleen Hoover. Atria Books 2015 320 p. (ebook) $11.99; (paperback) $16

ISBN 9781501110351; 9781501110344

LC 2015029360

In this novel, by Colleen Hoover, "Fallon meets Ben, an aspiring novelist, . . . their untimely attraction leads them to spend Fallon's last day in L.A. together, and her eventful life becomes the creative inspiration Ben has always sought for his novel. Over time, . . . they continue to meet on the same date every year. Until one day Fallon becomes unsure if Ben has been telling her the truth or fabricating a perfect reality for the sake of the ultimate plot twist." (Publisher's note)

"Hoover continues her spot-on streak of NA winners, with a relatable, appealing cast and vivid scenarios." Booklist

Hoover, Michelle

The **quickening**; a novel. Other Press 2010 216p pa $14.95

ISBN 978-1-59051-346-0; 1-59051-346-0

LC 2010-05199

"In Hoover's début, the quiet struggle between two Midwestern farm women has the stark simplicity of a Biblical parable. After the First World War, stoic, industrious Enidina Current and her husband draw life from the hard earth of their fields, but at home Enidina suffers violent miscarriages. Their only neighbors for miles—Mary Morrow, bred to 'walk in heels and carry cups of tea,' and her tempestuous husband—have two boys. Mary, seeing refinement in the town's anemic preacher, bears him an illegitimate son, whose actions eventually set the two families against one another. If Hoover's symbolism, like the characters' heavy-handed surnames, is at times too overt, the book's lament for a lost way of life . . . has a mournful beauty." New Yorker

Hope, Anthony

The **prisoner** of Zenda; being the history of three months in the life of an English gentleman. Holt & Co. 1894 226p

"Rudolf Rassendyll, an Englishman, makes a three month's visit to the kingdom of Ruritania. He arrives on the eve of the coronation of King Rudolf. The king has an enemy in his brother, Duke Michael, who aspires to the throne himself. During the festivities at Zenda Castle, the Duke drugs King Rudolf so that he is unable to attend his own coronation. Later, Rassendyll, . . . succeeds in impersonating the King and is crowned in his stead. In the meantime, Princess Flavia, the king's betrothed, falls in love with Rassendyll, who in turn loves her. After many dramatic and dangerous escapades, duels, and intrigues King Rudolf is rescued from Zenda Castle where he is held prisoner by Duke Michael. Rassendyll and Princess Flavia renounce each other when the King is restored, and Rassendyll returns to England." Haydn. Thesaurus of Book Dig

Horan, Nancy

Loving Frank. Ballantine Books 2007 362p

ISBN 0345494997; 9780345494993

LC 2007-14810

In this historical novel, the author draws upon research into the life of Frank Lloyd Wright to explore his relationship with Mamah Borthwick Cheney.

"In 1904, Frank Lloyd Wright started work on a house for an Oak Park couple, Edwin and Mamah Cheney, and, before long, he and Mamah had begun a scandalous affair. In her first novel, Horan, viewing the relationship from Mamah's perspective, does well to avoid serving up a bodice-ripper for the smart set. If anything, she cleaves too faithfully to the sources, occasionally giving her story the feel of a dissertation masquerading as a novel. But she succeeds in conveying the emotional center of her protagonist, whom she paints as a proto-feminist, an educated woman fettered by the role of bourgeois matriarch. Horan best evokes Mamah's troubled personality by means of delicately rendered reflections on the power of the natural world, from which her lover drew inspiration." New Yorker

Horlock, Mary

The **book** of lies; a novel. Harper Perennial 2011 347p pa $14.99

ISBN 978-0-06-206509-4

LC 2010-46608

In this book set in the 1980s, "fifteen-year-old Cat, a smart, overweight outsider, has pushed her bullying classmate Nicolette off the cliffs without remorse. 'For the most part, I am glad she's gone.' After her confession, Cat tracks back through the previous months, presenting a chronicle of Nic's chillingly shrewd, mean-girl torture. At home, Cat takes refuge in her father's study, relatively untouched since his recent death. A passionate historian, he collected wartime accounts of the German occupation of Guernsey, and excerpts of those testimonies, interspersed with Cat's passages, bring heartrending family revelations. The narrative shifts may initially disorient readers, but their subtle, skillfully built connections underscore Horlock's themes of the powerful, shadowy reach of history and the slippery nature of truth . . . while Cat's indelible, darkly funny voice offers unsparing insights into the adolescent jungle." Booklist

Horn, Dara

All other nights; a novel. W.W. Norton & Co. 2009 363p $24.95

ISBN 978-0-393-06492-6

LC 2008-53412

The author "both unearths a fascinating, relatively unexplored aspect of American history—the role of Jewish Americans in the Civil War—and delivers a novel rich in human emotion and ambiguity. A triumph." Booklist

Includes bibliographical references

Horn, Dara

Eternal life; a novel. Dara Horn. W W Norton & Co Inc 2018 236 p. (hardcover) $25.95

ISBN 9780393608533; 9780393608540

LC 2017044684

In this novel, by Dara Horn, "Rachel is a woman with a problem: she can't die. . . . In the 2,000 years since she made a spiritual bargain to save the life of her first son back in Roman-occupied Jerusalem, she's tried everything to free herself, and only one other person in the world understands: a man she once loved passionately, who has been stalking her through the centuries, convinced they belong together forever." (Publisher's note)

"Horn constructs a deeply satisfying novel, rich not only in history and the great philosophical conundrums of living and dying but also in humor and passion." Booklist

Horn, Dara

The **world** to come; a novel. W.W. Norton & Co. 2006 314p $24.95

ISBN 0-393-05107-2

LC 2005-14586

There is "much to be said for this novel. Dara Horn is skillful with words. She is serious about writing 'Jewish literature,' and she knows her Jewish sources and treats them sensitively. Good at describing people and places, she is also good at dialogue. And she has the ability to construct a complex story from a large number of components and to build an utterly coherent whole out of them. The World to Come is architecturally complicated, but as architecture it 'works' beautifully." Commentary

Hornby, Nick

About a boy. Riverhead Bks. 1998 307p

ISBN 1-57322-087-6

LC 97-46499

The protagonist of this satire set in London is 36-year-old underachieving bachelor Will Lightman. "Targeting single mothers, he joins a single parents' group under false pretenses and is soon drawn into the lives of depressed Fiona and her bright 12-year-old son, Marcus. Suddenly, his life is messy and complicated. . . . {Hornby} has an uncanny ability for homing in on wholly contemporary, often serious topics and serving them up in truly hilarious fashion." Booklist

Hornby, Nick

Funny girl; a novel. Nick Hornby. Riverhead Books 2015 256 p. illustrations $27.95

ISBN 1594205418; 9781594205415

LC 2014038381

In this novel, by Nick Hornby, "Barbara Parker idolizes Lucille Ball and dreams of emulating her. . . . She realizes she has to go to London, a city where she has no connections or realistic prospects. . . . Through a series of chance encounters that seem like destiny, she does achieve her dreams, getting cast on a popular BBC comedy and even meeting Lucy." (Kirkus Reviews)

"In his seventh novel (and the first in five years), Hornby pens a homage to light entertainment, sending up the stodgier side of the BBC via snobby critic Vernon Whitfield. He also delivers a winning example of the form, crafting fast-paced, witty dialogue and lovable characters set against a time of creative breakthroughs, both in the culture and in the media. And the final chapters, in which the team must deal with the infirmities of age and illness, highlight Hornby's great gift for effortlessly moving from humor to heartbreak." Booklist

Hornby, Nick

★ **High** fidelity. Riverhead Bks. 1995 323p

ISBN 1-57322-016-7

LC 95-8469

"Owner of a small London record shop and musical snob of a high degree, [thirty-five-year-old protagonist Rob Fleming] . . . finds his life thrown into turmoil when live-in girlfriend Laura suddenly leaves. He embarks on a journey through the past, tracking down old lovers while finding solace with Marie, an American folk/country singer living in London, even as he yearns for Laura's return." Libr J

"Happily, Hornby does not rely on pop-cultural allusion to limn his characters' inner lives, but uses it instead to create a rich, wry backdrop for them." Time

Hornby, Nick

How to be good. Riverhead Bks. 2001 305p

ISBN 1-57322-193-7

LC 2001-19395

"@I'm not a bad person. I'm a doctor,' says Katie Carr, liberal 1990s North London mother of two. This is her hollow mantra, the only comfort that she can feign while her 20-year marriage to surly David falls to pieces. Just when she is about to be kicked out of the house after confessing to an affair, David returns from a visit with an ecstasy-dropping club kid-turned-faith healer named DJ GoodNews a changed—a good—man." Libr J

Hornby, Nick

Juliet, naked. Riverhead Books 2009 406p $25.95

ISBN 978-1-59448-887-0; 1-59448-887-8

LC 2009-23773

"Duncan is a middle-aged Brit living in the dreary seaside town of Gooleness. He's unhealthily obsessed with Tucker Crowe, a mostly obscure American singer-songwriter who hasn't put out an album since the 1980s. Annie is Duncan's girlfriend of 15 years. . . . Annie tolerates Duncan's musical obsession, but when she disagrees with his fawning review of a new Crowe outtakes album, she realizes her boyfriend is a bit of a wanker. She leaves him. Soon, she serendipitously strikes up an email correspondence with Crowe himself, who's been living out of the public eye on a farm in Pennsylvania. Like Annie, he feels like he's wasted the last 15 years of his life. . . . [Hornby] shows how obsessing over music isn't the road to love and self-actualization. It's the road to heartbreak." N Y Post

Hornby, Nick

A **long** way down. Riverhead Books 2005 333p $24.95

ISBN 1-57322-302-6

LC 2004-58837

"Whatever limited consolations the book's survivors find in each other, Hornby resists melodramatic resolutions or glorious moments of redemption, and he doesn't smuggle away or refute all the reasons his characters took with them to the rooftop where they met, the ones that urged them toward the edge rather than down to the ground the slow way, back into the world." N Y Times Book Rev

Horowitz, Anthony

The **House** of Silk; a Sherlock Holmes novel. Mulholland Books 2011 294p $27.99

ISBN 978-0-316-19699-4; 0-316-196991

LC 2011030839

"A year after Sherlock Holmes's death (from natural causes), Watson takes up his pen one last time to recount a case they shared in 1890 that was 'too monstrous, too shocking' to appear in print. The opening is prosaic enough. London art dealer Edmund Carstairs asks for the detective's help after a shadowy figure in a flat cap, apparently an Irish-American thug bent on revenge, surfaces near Carstairs's Wimbledon home. When a murder follows Holmes getting involved, the trail leads him and the good doctor to a powerful secret society known as the House of Silk." Publ Wkly

Horowitz, Anthony

★ **Magpie** murders; Anthony Horowitz. First U.S. edition Harper 2017 446 p. (hardback) $27.99

ISBN 9780062645227; 9780062645234

LC 2016045021

In this book, by Anthony Horowitz, "when editor Susan Ryeland is given the manuscript of Alan Conway's latest novel, she has no reason to think it will be much different from any of his others. After working with the bestselling crime writer for years, she's intimately familiar with his detective, Atticus Pünd. . . . Conway's latest tale has Atticus Pünd investigating a murder at Pye Hall. . . . But the more Susan reads, the more she's convinced that there is another story." (Publisher's note)

"Fans who still mourn the passing of Agatha Christie, the model who's evoked here in dozens of telltale details, will welcome this wildly inventive homage /update/commentary as the most fiendishly clever puzzle--make that two puzzles--of the year." Kirkus

Horowitz, Anthony

Moriarty. HarperCollins 2014 304 p. $26.99

ISBN 0062377183; 9780062377180

"Author Anthony Horowitz's . . . novel plunges us back into the dark and complex world of detective Sherlock Holmes and Moriarty--dubbed the Napoleon of crime by Holmes--in the aftermath of their fateful struggle at the Reichenbach Falls. . . . Moriarty's death has left an immediate, poisonous vacuum in the criminal underworld, and there is no shortage of candidates to take his place--including one particularly fiendish criminal mastermind." (Publisher's note)

"Horowitz's mystery bona fides are impeccable: not only did his previous Sherlock Holmes novel, The House of Silk, sell over 450,000 copies worldwide in more than 35 countries, but he created both Midsomer Murders and the BAFTA-winning Foyle's War. Here he reimagines what happened after the presumably lethal scuffle between Holmes and Moriarty at the Reichenbach Falls." LJ

Hosking, Jay

Three years with the rat; Jay Hosking. Thomas Dunne Books 2017 273 p. (hardcover) $25.99

ISBN 9781250116314; 9781250116307; 1250116309

LC 2016036615

This book, by Jay Hosking, offers a "time-looping tale [that] deftly teases the reader with well-deployed reveals and intrigues...Hosking's prose is limpid and tonally sophisticated; he's a graceful wordsmith as well as a cerebral idea man...A potent, sophisticated combination of science-fiction novel and psychological thriller." (Kirkus Reviews)

"A potent, sophisticated combination of science-fiction novel and psychological thriller." Kirkus

Hospital, Janette Turner

Due preparations for the plague. Norton 2003 401p $24.95

ISBN 0-393-05764-X

LC 2002-156598

"Using the form of a politico-literary thriller, Janette Turner Hospital has attempted a meta-physical novel of evil. . . .'Due preparations for the Plague'—the title and the frequent quotes from Camus indicate the author's larger intentions—is a descent through Dantean circles of governmental conspiracy and betrayal." N Y Times Book Rev

Hosseini, Khaled, 1965-

★ **And** the Mountains Echoed; by Khaled Hosseini. Penguin Group USA 2013 404 p. (hardcover) $28.95

ISBN 159463176X; 9781594631764

LC 2013004004

This novel by Khaled Hosseini is "about how we love, how we take care of one another, and how the choices we make resonate through generations. In this tale revolving around not just parents and children but brothers and sisters, cousins and caretakers, Hosseini explores the many ways in which families nurture, wound, betray, honor, and sacrifice for one another; and how often we are surprised by the actions of those closest to us, at the times that matter most." (Publisher's note)

Hosseini, Khaled, 1965-

★ The **kite** runner. Riverhead Bks. 2003 324p $24.95; pa $14

ISBN 1-57322-245-3; 1-59448-000-1 pa

LC 2003043106

The narrator, "a thirty-eight-year-old writer named Amir, recounts the odyssey of his life from Kabul to San Francisco via Peshwar, Pakistan. The protagonist was born into a wealthy family in Kabul. Raised by his father, . . . Amir lives a relatively happy life until the Soviet tanks roll into Afghanistan. Then he and his father flee to Pakistan and end up in America. In the United States, his father becomes a gas-station manager. . . . Amir meets Soraya, the daughter of a former Afghan general, and soon [marries]. . . . For fifteen years the young couple tries in vain to have children. Then Amir receives a call from Rahim Khan, a friend and former business partner of his now-deceased father. Amir flies to Peshwar to meet with him. Rahim Khan reveals that Hassan, Amir's childhood friend, the presumed son of the family servant Ali, was in reality Amir's half-brother, his father's illegitimate son with Ali's wife. Hassan and his wife were killed by the Taliban. Rahim Khan wants Amir to go to Kabul and bring Hassan's son to Peshwar." (World Lit Today)

"Khaled Hosseini gives us a vivid and engaging story that reminds us how long his people have been struggling to triumph over the forces of violence." N Y Times Book Rev

Hosseini, Khaled, 1965-

A **thousand** splendid suns. Riverhead Books 2007 372p $25.95

ISBN 978-1-59448-950-1; 1-59448-950-5

LC 2007-8679

"The texture of these characters' journey around the craters of their country is no doubt well known to readers of international news. Rendered as fiction . . . , however, it devastates in a new way." Minneapolis Star Tribune

Houellebecq, Michel, 1958-

The **map** and the territory; Michel Houellebecq ; translated from the French by Gavin Bowd. First American edition. Alfred A. Knopf 2012 269p.

ISBN 9782081246331; 9780307946539; 9780307701558

LC 2010540592

Prix Goncourt (France) (2010)

This book, which won the French literary prize the Prix Goncourt, tells "the story of an artist, Jed Martin, and his family and lovers and friends. . . . Global fame and fortune arrive when he turns to painting. . . . Then, while his aging father . . . flirts with oblivion, a police inspector seeks Martin's help in solving an unspeakably gruesome crime. . . . Jed Martin somehow discovers serenity and manages to add another startling chapter to his artistic legacy." (Publisher's note)

Houellebecq, Michel, 1958-

The **possibility** of an island; translated from the French by Gavin Bowd. Alfred A. Knopf 2006 337p $24.95

ISBN 0-307-26349-0

LC 2005-54527

Original French edition, 2005

The power of the novel is "limited by its utter nihilism, and its refusal to countenance the possibility of any enduring good in human life. . . . Houellebecq's novel wants to be both a contemporary satire of empty satisfactions and a dystopic fantasy about their unchecked proliferations, provocative in its moral alarums and blasé about the whole business. It's a book fit for an age done in by wanting too musch for itself." Walrus

Houellebecq, Michel, 1958-

Submission; Michel Houellebecq; translated by Lorin Stein; edited by Mitzi Angel. Farrar, Straus & Giroux 2015 246 p. (hardcover) $25

ISBN 0374271577; 9780374271572; 9780374714482

LC 2015949676

In this novel by Michel Houellebecq "it's 2022. François is bored. He's a middle-aged lecturer at the New Sorbonne University. Meanwhile, it's election season. In an alliance with the Socialists, France's new Islamic party sweeps to power. Islamic law comes into force. Women are veiled, polygamy is encouraged, and François is offered an irresistible academic advancement--on the condition that he convert to Islam." (Publisher's note)

"Submission is well crafted, but the pornographic sex scenes are as tired as their rationale. Houellebecq's faltering is François' failure writ large: the inability to believe there might be any meaning in or meaningful differences between diverse points of view or ways of life." Booklist

House, Silas

A **parchment** of leaves; a novel. Algonquin Bks. 2002 278p $23.95

ISBN 1-565-12367-0

LC 2002-66570

"This is a moving love story set against a stunningly beautiful background, and House seems to capture it all—the deep emotion, the love of land, the customs of mountain people—in quietly eloquent prose." Booklist

Houston, Pam

Cowboys are my weakness; stories. Norton 1992 171p

LC 91-12920

"Short stories, mostly first-person, told with verve and perfect pitch by women entangled with wild men in a cruel world." N Y Times Book Rev

Howard, Linda

Cry no more. Ballantine Books 2003 368p

ISBN 0-345-45341-7

LC 2003-45140

"Milla is a woman with a mission: 10 years after her baby son, Justin, was snatched from her arms, she still hunts for him every day. Her dedicated passion led her to start Finders, an agency set up to help others like her find taken loved ones. Although she has learned some sketchy details about Justin's abductors, they never led anywhere; all she has to go on is a name, Diaz. An anonymous tip about Diaz's location leads to a sighting of the one-eyed man who snatched Justin. When one of Finders' generous grantors offers a tip on finding Diaz, alleged to be a dangerous assassin, Milla takes it upon herself to seek Diaz out, only to learn that he is not tied to the abduction but can help find out who is. . . . At once heart-wrenching and thrilling." Booklist

Howard, Maureen

The **rags** of time; a novel. Viking 2009 238p il $26.95

ISBN 978-0-670-02132-1; 0-670-02132-6

LC 2009-15167

"Like all of Howard's work, 'The Rags of Time' is extremely ambitious, not only in scale but also in points of reference. . . . As such, Howard invites the reader to try to make sense of it all, to stare at the structure whole, as if at one of Joseph Cornell's boxes full of minutely arranged objects, and give it a name and a theme. But looking at her writing from this perspective misses the most interesting part: her sentences. No one writing in English today produces anything quite like them." N Y Times Book Rev

Howard, Ravi

Driving the king; a novel. Ravi Howard. Harper 2015 336 p. (hardback) $25.99

ISBN 006052961X; 9780060529611; 9780060529628

LC 2014015054

NAACP Image Award Nominee: Outstanding Literary Work - Fiction (2016)

In this historical novel by Ravi Howard, "the war is over, the soldiers are returning, and Nat King Cole is back in his hometown of Montgomery, Alabama, for a rare performance. His childhood friend, Nat Weary, plans to propose to his sweetheart, and the singer will honor their moment with a special song. . . . When a white man attacks Cole with a pipe, Weary leaps from the audience to defend him--an act that will lead to a ten-year prison sentence." (Publisher's note)

"Alternating between the cities and Weary's past and present, Howard explores race relations in the pre-civil rights era and the strong ties forged between two extraordinary men." Booklist

Howatch, Susan

Cashelmara. Simon & Schuster 1974 702p

"With a copiousness of detail studded with adventure, rape, depravity, intrigue, and murder, the story plays out with clarity and brilliance." Best Sellers

Howatch, Susan

Glamorous powers. Knopf 1988 403p

LC 88-45347

This "novel, the second in the Church of England series that began with 'Glittering Images,' weaves an intriguing and wholly involving story out of the otherwise sober subject of Christian mysticism in the 20th-century Church of England. Howatch's chief characters are a clerical odd couple, rivals since their Cambridge days: Jonathan Darrow, a 60-year-old Anglo-Catholic monk with 'glamorous' psychic powers, and his Abbot-General, Francis Ingram, a practical, eloquent, urbane man with sophisticated insight into modern psychology. . . . The wisdom of 'Glamorous Powers' lies in the deft way it aligns psychological and spiritual truths to bring about healing in the broadest sense." N Y Times Book Rev

Followed by Ultimate prizes

Howatch, Susan

The **heartbreaker**. Knopf 2004 483p $25

ISBN 1-4000-4147-3

LC 2003-62493

"Plot improbabilities and long sections of spiritual musing are redeemed by Howatch's strongly drawn characters: if Carta can come across as brittle and prudish, Gavin's self-absorbed cant is continually entertaining." Publ Wkly

Howatch, Susan

Scandalous risks. Knopf 1990 385p

LC 90-53076

"With sculptor's hands fashioning rich, lustrous three-dimensional characters, Howatch brilliantly shows how and why the situation between Venetia and her 'Mr. Dean' arose, flourished, then died away." Booklist

Followed by Mystical paths

Howatch, Susan

Ultimate prizes. Knopf 1989 387p

LC 89-45303

This, third novel in the Church of England series, "is narrated by Neville Aysgarth, an ambitious archdeacon in the fictional English diocese of Starbridge. A brilliant administrator with a firm, practical faith in God and the Church of England, Neville has steadily moved up in life by 'chasing the prizes,' overcoming his humble birth and troubled youth to win for himself a perfect wife, a flock of delightful children and a powerful position, all before age 40. During his climb to success he has kept his mind as tidy as his diocese by relentlessly 'ringing down the curtain'—a mental curtain, that is—on disturbing memories and desires. But alas for Neville, his curtain is shortly to be twitched off its rod, first by an infatuation with a young society girl, then by a death in his family." N Y Times Book Rev

Followed by Scandalous risks

Howe, Katherine

The **physick** book of Deliverance Dane; a novel. Hyperion 2009 371p $25.99

ISBN 978-1-4013-4090-2; 1-4013-4090-3

LC 2008-51627

"A Harvard doctoral candidate, Connie learns that 'Physick' is the 17th-century word for an herbal remedy, and that Deliverance Dane was a Massachusetts woman who knew this medicinal craft and kept her recipes—which she called receipts—in an almanac. Connie must discover the hidden location of this old volume of spells (there's no better word for what they are), but she discovers so much more along the way: great personal danger, unanticipated self-knowledge and love, in both its natural and preternatural aspects. The Salem witch trials of 1692 epitomize a moment when a society felt threatened by the notion of women's uncanny power. At strategic points in the novel, Howe recreates, with harrowing vividness, intimate scenes from that historical crisis." BookPage

Howrey, Meg

Blind sight; Meg Howrey. Pantheon Books 2011 289p. $24.95

ISBN 978-0-307-37916-0; 0-307-37916-7; 9780307739292

LC 201012935

The book tells the story of a teenaged boy, "Luke Prescott, who has been brought up in a bohemian matriarchy by his divorced New Age mother, a religious grandmother, and two precocious half-sisters. . . . Luke is writing his college applications when his father -- a famous television star whom he never knew -- calls and invites him to Los Angeles for the summer. Luke accepts and is plunged into a world of location shooting, celebrity interviews, glamorous parties, and premieres. As he begins to know the difference between his father's public persona and his private one, Luke finds himself sorting through his own personal mythology." (Publisher's note)

"The novel resonates with authenticity, both with its description of the world of women from which Luke emerges and the world of easy celebrity in which he is tempered. Even many of Howrey's minor characters—Luke's sisters, for example—shine . . . . A wonderfully intriguing examination of what makes, and might break, a family." Kirkus

Howrey, Meg

The **wanderers**; Meg Howrey. G.P. Putnam's Sons 2017 384 p. (ebook) $54; (hardback) $27

ISBN 9780399574658; 0399574638; 9780399574634

LC 2016036564

In this book, by Meg Howrey, "aerospace giant Prime Space will put the first humans on Mars. Helen Kane, Yoshihiro Tanaka, and Sergei Kuznetsov must prove they're the crew for the historic voyage by spending seventeen months in the most realistic simulation ever created. . . . Helen, Yoshi, and Sergei must appear ever in control. But as their surreal pantomime progresses, each soon realizes that the complications of inner space are no less fraught than those of outer space." (Publisher's note)

"Although the contours of a space drama may seem familiar to a 21st-century readership, Howrey, through the poetry of her writing and the richness of her characters, makes it all seem new. A lyrical and subtle space opera." Kirkus

Hoyt, Elizabeth

Duke of Midnight. Grand Central Pub. 2013 400 p. (Maiden Lane series) $8

ISBN 1455508349; 9781455508341

This is the sixth installment of Elizabeth Hoyt's "1740s Maiden Lane series. The rather silly Lady Penelope Greaves has been making eyes at Maximus Batten, the Duke of Wakefield; Maximus is more interested in Artemis, Penelope's sensible cousin, but he feels obligated to marry a titled lady. When Artemis discovers that Maximus is the masked vigilante called the Ghost of St. Giles, she blackmails him into helping get her brother, Apollo, out of Bedlam." (Publishers Weekly)

Hoyt, Elizabeth

Thief of Shadows; Elizabeth Hoyt. Grand Central Pub. 2012 367 p. (pbk.) $7.99; (pbk.) $7.99

ISBN 1455508322; 9781455508327

This book is the fourth in the Maiden Lane romance series. Here, "[t] he masked Ghost of St. Giles rescues orphaned children from" London's street. "Widowed baroness Isabel Beckinhall rescues the unconscious 'ghost' after finding him injured in the street; before she can ascertain his identity, he awakens and begs her to leave his mask in place. Little does she know he is Winter Makepeace, manager of a local orphanage, whom Isabel finds 'dour.'" (Publishers Weekly)

Hrabal, Bohumil

★ **I** served the King of England; [translated by Paul Wilson] Harcourt Brace Jovanovich 1989 243p

ISBN 0-15-145745-X

LC 88-16482

This novel "is a flood of meandering garrulous narration, with dreamlike, filmlike sequences, hyperbolic, grotesque and farcical analogues of familiar historical fact. No sober account, this, of how it might actually have been, yet still it projects through its debunking prism the shallowness, absurdity and cruelty of how it indeed was." Times Lit Suppl

Hubbard, Ladee

The **talented** Ribkins; a novel. Ladee Hubbard. Melville House 2017 295 p. (hardcover) $25.99

ISBN 9781612196367; 9781612196374

LC 2017018187

In this novel, by Ladee Hubbard, "at seventy-two, Johnny Ribkins . . . [has] got one week to come up with the money he stole from his mobster boss or it's curtains. What may or may not be useful to Johnny as he flees is that he comes from an African-American family that has been gifted with super powers that are a bit, well, odd. . . . [The book is] about race, class, politics, and the unique gifts that, while they may cause some problems from time to time, bind a family." (Publisher's note)

"Hubbard's voice mixes wry humor and superhero pop culture while addressing issues that continue to challenge our country's African American community." LJ

Hudgins, Andrew

The **joker**; a memoir. Andrew Hudgins. Simon & Schuster 2013 352 p.

ISBN 9781476712710; 9781476712727

LC 2013009292

In this memoir, by Andrew Hudgins, "Hudgins tells and analyzes the jokes that explore the contradictions in the Baptist religion he was brought up in, the jokes that told him what his parents would not tell him about sex, and the racist jokes that his uncle loved, his father hated, and his mother, caught in the middle, was ambivalent about. This book is both a memoir and a meditation on jokes and how they educated, delighted, and occasionally horrified him as he grew." (Publisher's note)

Includes bibliographical references and index.

Hughes, Anita

Market Street; Anita Hughes. St. Martin's Press 2013 304 p. (paperback) $14.99

ISBN 0312643330; 9780312643331

LC 2013002660

In this book by Anita Hughes, "raised to take the reins [of the department store owned by her family], Cassie [Fenton] instead chose marriage, to Aidan, a UC Berkeley professor. . . . Around the time Aidan has an affair with one of his students, Cassie's mother presents her with a project that promises even more turmoil. . . . The work, and a new friendship with James, the architect for the project, gives Cassie the space to decide whether or not to forgive her husband." (Publishers Weekly)

Hughes, Langston

Not without laughter. Knopf 1930 324p

This novel portrays the lives of a poor black family in a small Kansas town

"A sympathetic portrayal, unmarred by bitterness or sentimentality, of a people to whom life, no matter how hard, was not without laughter." Booklist

Hughes, Langston

★ **Short** stories of Langston Hughes; edited by Akiba Sullivan Harper; with an introduction by Arnold Rampersad. Hill & Wang 1996 299p hardcover o.p. pa $16

ISBN 0-8090-1603-6

LC 95-19554

"Dating from 1919 to 1963, these pieces vary in theme, covering life at sea, the trials and tribulations of a young pianist and her elderly white patron, a visiting writer's experience in Cuba, a young girl's winning an art scholarship but losing it when it's learned she is black, and an ambitious black preacher trying to gain fame by being nailed to a cross. If you crave good reading don't pass up this gem." Libr J

Hughes, Langston

★ **Simple** speaks his mind. Simon & Schuster 1950 231p

The central figure, is a Harlem black who expresses his views on many subjects, but always from the point of view of his own race. He dislikes whites, and makes no bones of it. Some of his favorite topics are women, landladies especially, parties, and beer

"Simple is completely frank in his opinions about white people; he dislikes them intensely. The race problem is never absent, but the flow of the book is light-hearted and easy." N Y Times Book Rev

Hughes, Langston

Simple's Uncle Sam. Hill & Wang 1965 180p

Contents: Census; Swinging high; Contest; Empty houses; The blues; God's other side; Color problems; The moon; Domesticated; Bomb shelters; Gospel singers; Nothing but a dog; Roots and trees; For President; Atomic dream; Lost wife; Self-protection; Haircuts and Paris; Adventure; Minnie's hype; Yachts; Ladyhood; Coffee break; Lynn Clarisse; Interview; Simply Simple; Golden Gate; Junkies; Dog days; Pose-outs; Soul food; Flay or pray; Not colored; Cracker prayer; Rude awakening; Miss Boss; Dr. Sidesaddle; Wigs for freedom; Concernment; Statutes and statues; American dilemma; Promulgations; How old is old; Weight in god; Sympathy; Uncle Sam

Hughes, Mary-Beth

Double happiness; stories. Black Cat 2010 201p $14

ISBN 978-0-8021-7074-3; 0-8021-7074-9

"The stories in this excellent collection meander with the sureness of streams discovering their paths. Hughes keeps her prose close to her characters' thoughts, and doles out the most crucial information on the sly. Many stories deal with women or girls coming to terms with the failings, or deaths, of the men in their lives. . . . If some of Hughes's stories can initially seem scattered or arbitrary, further reading nearly always discloses careful but unobtrusive organization, giving even the saddest revelations—and most revelations here are sad—an air of the miraculous." New Yorker

Hughes, Matthew

Hespira; a tale of Henghis Hapthorn. Night Shade Books 2009 233p $24.95

ISBN 978-1-59780-101-0; 1-59780-101-1

This novel features a "planet-hopping, gourmandizing, insufferably self-important private eye named Henghis Hapthorn. His task is to help a young lady who's lost her memories recollect her life. Though Hapthorn has suffered his own loss — his intuition has decamped to a private estate halfway around the world — his investigative skills remain impressive. And Hughes' account of this far future detective at work is grand, elaborate fun. Still, the most engaging thing about 'Hespira' is the Alice-in-Wonderland complexity of this curiouser and curiouser story." Cleveland Plain Dealer

Hughes, Richard Arthur Warren

★ A **high** wind in Jamaica; [by] Richard Hughes; introduction by Francine Prose. New York Review Books 1999 279p hardcover o.p. pa $12.95

ISBN 0-940322-15-3

LC 99-14565

First published 1929 by Harper with title: The innocent voyage

"A family of children living in Jamaica in the 19th century are sent to England after a hurricane has partly destroyed their home. Amiable pirates capture them by mistake, and the children bring about the pirates' ruin: one girl becomes a murderess. The irrationality and impenetrability of the child's amoral world and the horror of the whole situation are brilliantly conveyed." Reader's Ency. 3d edition

The **Hugo** winners; edited by Isaac Asimov. Doubleday 1962 5v

The stories and novelettes included in these volumes won the Hugo Awards from 1939-1982

Hugo, Victor

★ The **hunchback** of Notre Dame; revised translation and notes by Catherine Liu; introduction by Elizabeth McCracken. Modern Library 2002 xxviii, 483p pa $11.95

ISBN 0-679-64257-9

LC 2002-18917

Original French edition, 1831. Variant title: Notre Dame de Paris

The hidden force of fate is symbolized by the superhuman grandeur and multitudinous imageries of the cathedral. "The first part . . . is a panorama of medieval life—religious, civic, popular, and criminal—drawn with immense learning and an amazing command of spectacular effect. These elements are then set in motion in a fantastic and grandiose drama, of which the personages are romantic sublimations of human virtues and passions—Quasimodo the hunchback, faithful unto death; Esmeralda, incarnation of innocence and steadfastness; Claude Frolla, Faust-like type of the antagonism between religion and appetite. Splendors and absurdities, the sublime and the grotesque are inextricably mingled in this strange romance. The date is fixed at the year 1482." Baker. Guide to the Best Fic

Hugo, Victor

★ **Les** miserables; translated from the French by Charles E. Wilbour; with an introduction by Peter Washington. Knopf 1997 xxxvii, 1432p $27

ISBN 0-375-40317-5

LC 98-156450

Original French edition, 1862

"A panorama of French life in the first half of the [nineteenth] century, aiming to exhibit the fabric of civilization in all its details, and to reveal the cruelty of its pressure on the poor, the outcast, and the criminal. Jean Valjean, a man intrinsically noble, thru the tyranny of society becomes a criminal. His conscience is reawakened by the ministrations of the saintly Bishop Myriel . . . and Valjean, reformed and prosperous, follows in the good bishop's footsteps as an apostle of benevolence, only to be doomed again by the law to slavery and shame. The 'demimondaine' Fantine, another victim of society; her daughter Cosette one of those whom suffering makes sublime; Marius, an ideal of youth and love; Myriel, the incarnation of Christian charity, are the leading characters of this huge morality, which is thronged with representatives of the good in man and the cruelty of society. Magnificent description . . . scenes invested with terror, awe, repulsion, alternate with tedious rhapsodies. Realism mingles with the incredible." Baker. Guide to the Best Fic

Hulme, Kathryn

★ The **nun's** story. Little, Brown 1956 339p

"Convent life, with its rigors and its compensations, has seldom been as fairly depicted as in this biographical account. An unhappy love affair was one of the reasons why 'Gabrielle Van der Mal' {fictitious name} entered a convent in Belgium, but her love of God and desire to serve her fellow men were also important influences. For 17 years she tried diligently to discipline her analytical and independent mind through prayer and hard work as a nurse, first in a hospital for the insane, then in a Congo mission, and finally in a TB sanatorium in occupied Holland. Ultimately, she faced the bitter truth that the religious life, with its inflexible authority, was not for her, and she was released from her vows." Libr J

Hulme, Keri

★ The **bone** people; a novel. Louisiana State Univ. Press 1985 450p

ISBN 0-8071-1284-4

LC 85-12937

First published 1984 in New Zealand

"This novel is unforgettably rich and pungent. . . . Set on the harsh South Island beaches of New Zealand, bound in Maori myth and entwined with Christian symbols, Miss Hulme's provocative novel summons power with words, as in a conjurer's spell." N Y Times Book Rev

Hulse, S. M.

★ **Black** River; S. M. Hulse. Houghton Mifflin Harcourt 2015 240 p. (hardback) $24

ISBN 0544309871; 9780544309876

LC 2014027025

This novel, by S. M. Hulse, "tells the story of a man marked by a prison riot as he returns to the town, and the convict, who shaped him. . . . How can a man who once embodied evil ever come to good? How can he pay for such crimes with anything but his life? As Wes considers his own choices and grieves for all he's lost, he must decide what he believes and whether he can let Williams walk away." (Publisher's note)

"Hulse clearly loves Montana, and her own experience playing the fiddle and knowledge of horses shine through the novel. She maintains suspense and manages to avoid the clichés of redemption stories." Booklist

Humphreys, Helen

Afterimage; a novel. Metropolitan Bks. 2001 240p $23

ISBN 0-8050-6666-7

LC 00-46907

First published 2000 in Canada

"It's 1865, in England, and both Isabelle Dashell and her husband, Eldon, are making pictures. She's intent on mastering a new medium, photography, and he's seeking renown as a cartographer. When Annie Phelan, a sober beauty orphaned by the Irish famine, answers their ad for a housemaid, she becomes Isabelle's muse and Eldon's confidante, and finds herself pressed into the service of art. Inspired by the work of Julia

Margaret Cameron, this urgent, well-made novel charts the boundaries where light becomes shadow, and the known can suddenly appear awful and astonishing." New Yorker

Humphreys, Josephine

Nowhere else on earth. Viking 2000 341p

ISBN 0-670-89176-2

LC 00-36666

"In 1864, Rhoda Strong is a teenager of mixed ancestry in Scuffletown, an Indian settlement on the Lumbee River, in North Carolina. As the town's inhabitants find themselves caught between marauding Union soldiers and Confederates attempting to conscript their children for labor, Rhoda falls in love with a local outlaw who is fighting to protect the community. Humphreys has always been a master of telling a larger story through a deceptively intimate narrative, and Rhoda's tale, with its clear, distinct voice, is no exception." New Yorker

Huneven, Michelle

Blame. Sarah Crichton Books 2009 291p $25

ISBN 0-374-11430-7; 978-0-374-11430-5

LC 2008-54299

"Huneven makes Patsy's story unfold like a thriller, creating a sense of urgency and mystery even about everyday matters. . . . Huneven's prose moves like a hummingbird, in small bursts that are improbably fast and graceful." N Y Times Book Rev

Hunt, Andrew

City of saints; Andrew Hunt. Minotaur Books 2012 336 p. (Art Oveson) (hardcover) $24.99

ISBN 1250015790; 9781250015792; 9781250015808

LC 2012030078

"When a beautiful socialite turns up dead, Art Oveson, a twenty-something husband, father, and devout Mormon just getting his start as a sheriff's deputy, finds himself thrust into the role of detective. With his partner, a foul-mouthed former strikebreaker, he begins to pursue the murderer--or murderers. His search takes him into the underbelly of Salt Lake City, a place rife with blackmail, corruption, and death." (Publisher's note)

Another title in this series is:

A killing in Zion (2015)

Hunt, Laird

The **evening** road; Laird Hunt. Little, Brown & Co. 2017 288 p. $26

ISBN 9780316391283

LC 2016057649

In this book, by Laird Hunt, "meet Ottie Lee Henshaw, a startling, challenging beauty in small-town Indiana. . . . One day in the summer of 1930 [she goes on] an odyssey across the countryside to witness a dark and fearful celebration. Meet Calla Destry, a determined young woman desperate to escape the violence of her town and to find the lover who has promised her a new life. On this day, the countryside of Jim Crow-era Indiana is no place for either." (Publisher's note)

"Though the novel's meandering odysseys sometimes feel frustrating, Hunt's striking prose and visionary imagery capture America's community bonds, violent prejudices, falling darkness, and searing light." Pub Wkly.

Hunt, Laird

Neverhome; a novel. Laird Hunt. Little, Brown & Co. 2014 256 p. (hardcover) $26

ISBN 0316370134; 9780316370134

LC 2014938585

This novel by Laird Hunt "tells the harrowing story of Ash Thompson during the battle for the South. Through bloodshed and hysteria and heartbreak, she becomes a hero, a folk legend, a madwoman and a traitor to the American cause. She calls herself Ash, but that's not her real name. She is a farmer's faithful wife, but she has left her husband to don the uniform of a Union soldier in the Civil War." (Publisher's note)

"Historical fiction fans will not be disappointed by this wonderful story of Ash's struggles with her identity and of her personal ties to the war. An amazing book." LJ

Hunt, Rebecca

Mr. Chartwell; a novel. Dial Press 2010 242p $24

ISBN 978-1-4000-6940-8

LC 2010-15012

"It is July 1964, and in London, young library clerk Esther Hammerhans, widowed for two years, decides to rent her late husband's study to a lodger. But when Mr. Chartwell, the prospective tenant, arrives to inspect the premises, Esther is stunned to discover that he is a dog — an enormous, hideous, and loquacious black Labrador. Known more informally as Black Pat, the animal is in town to serve his client, Sir Winston Churchill. About to retire from Parliament and live out his remaining days in his country estate — Chartwell — the 89-year-old Churchill is coping with the return of his lifelong nemesis, what he calls the 'black dog' of depression. A drooling, stinky, but coy combination of The Joker, Hannibal Lecter, and children's book character Clifford, Black Pat is that dog. And visible only to Churchill and to Esther — still raw and reeling from her husband's suicide — he is all but irresistible. . . . [This debut novel] is as delicious as it is audacious." Boston Globe

Hunt, Samantha

The **dark** dark; stories. Samantha Hunt. Farrar, Straus & Giroux 2017 241 p. (paperback) $15

ISBN 9780374282134; 9780374716523

LC 2016050909

In this book "acclaimed novelist Samantha Hunt, debuts her first collection of short stories and conjures entire universes in just a few pages. . . . Each of these ten haunting, inventive tales brings us to the brink--of creation, mortality and immortality, infidelity and transformation, technological innovation and historical revision, loneliness and communion, and every kind of love." (Publisher's note)

"This excellent, inventive collection . . . is rife with observant asides, sly humor, and surprises." Pub Wkly

Hunt, Samantha

The **invention** of everything else. Houghton Mifflin Co. 2007 257p $24

ISBN 978-0-618-80112-1; 0-618-80112-X

LC 2007-9416

"Set in New York City in 1943, the book focuses on Nikola Tesla, the underappreciated Serbian inventor. . . . Hunt's story unfolds over the last week of Tesla's life: He is 86 years old, destitute, and maybe a little crazy. He is also, of course, a genius. Tesla is an ideal person to bring back to life through fiction; technically, he's famous, but he's also largely unfamiliar. Because his actual story is so incredible (he was pals with Mark Twain, he fell in love with a bird, he tried to invent a 'death ray'), it's tricky to separate the pieces of Hunt's account that are drawn from fact from those that she's invented. Tesla is well balanced by the entirely fictional character of Louisa, a sensible, inquisitive young chambermaid who works at the hotel and befriends the inventor after he catches her snooping through his things. A classic sort of heroine, she treats the fading man like an oracle as she juggles her own daily dramas." Village Voice

Hunt, Samantha

★ **Mr.** Splitfoot; Samantha Hunt. Houghton Mifflin Harcourt 2016 336 p. (hardcover) $24

ISBN 0544526708; 9780544526709

LC 2015016712

In this novel, by Samantha Hunt, "Ruth and Nat are orphans, packed into a house full of abandoned children run by a religious fanatic. To entertain their siblings, they channel the dead. Decades later, Ruth's niece, Cora, finds herself accidentally pregnant. After years of absence, Aunt Ruth appears, mute and full of intention. She is on a mysterious mission, leading Cora on an odyssey across the entire state of New York on foot." (Publisher's note)

"Hunt's use of a split narrative to measuredly disclose snippets of Ruth's past and Cora's present in alternating, interconnected chapters builds suspense while keeping readers guessing about what crazy turn might happen next. Hints of what's in store for readers include a cult of Etherists, a noseless man, a pile of lost money, and a scar-like pattern of meteorite landings." Pub Wkly

Hunter, Evan

★ The **blackboard** jungle. Simon & Schuster 1954 309p

"The author has not used his shocking material merely to appall. With a superb ear for conversation, with competence as a storyteller, and with a tolerant and tough-minded sympathy for his subject, he has built an extremely good novel." N Y Her Trib Books

Hunter, Evan

Candyland; a novel in two parts. [by] Evan Hunter and Ed McBain. Simon & Schuster 2001 301p $25

ISBN 0-7432-1316-5

LC 00-49684

This novel "is written in two parts. The first half, attributed to Hunter, probes the psyche of Benjamin Thorpe, a sexually obsessed Los Angeles architect on the prowl in New York. The second half, attributed to McBain, is a police procedural in which a detective, Emma Boyle, investigates the murder of a prostitute and identifies the architect as a prime suspect. The novel is a gimmick, and it is a surprise that it works at all. That it works so superbly is a tribute to the skills of this great storyteller." N Y Times Book Rev

Hunter, Evan

The **moment** she was gone; a novel. Simon & Schuster 2002 208p $25

ISBN 0-7432-0269-4

LC 2002-70532

"Carella and Meyer must team up on a murder investigation with Fat Ollie Weeks of the 88th because the lion habitat at the Isola Zoo straddles the boundary between the two precincts and one of the lions dragged part of a victim's body onto the 88th's turf. The body in the lion's den leads the detectives to several things: to a burglary, or at least the burglar; to some strange doings by the Secret Service; to some pretty big local drug dealers; and, finally, to some big-time dealers who don't mind leaving bodies strewn about." Libr J

Hunter, Evan

Privileged conversation. Warner Bks. 1996 326p

LC 95-11148

"Mr. Hunter is smart enough to poke fun at the book's echoes of 'Fatal Attraction.' Even better, he has a good feel for Dr. Chapman's midlife crisis and for the petty annoyances of New York social life." N Y Times Book Rev

Hunter, Madeline

The **conquest** of Lady Cassandra. Jove Books 2013 336 p. (paperback) $7.99

ISBN 0515151114; 9780515151114

In this Regency-era historical romance from RITA Award-winner Madeline Hunter, Cassandra Vernham "desperately needs the money she counted on from auctioning her jewels to keep [her aunt] Sophie safe," but the buyer of a pair of her earrings, Yates Elliston, Viscount Ambury, won't pay her. "Not only does Ambury believe the earrings are hot property, he is almost certain they were stolen from his family." (Booklist)

Hunter, Stephen, 1946-

The **47th** samurai; a Bob Lee Swagger novel. Simon & Schuster 2007 372p $26

ISBN 978-0-7432-3809-0; 0-7432-3809-5

LC 2007-6627

This Bob Lee Swagger adventure "begins in the closing days of World War II, when Bob Lee's father, Earl (Havana), earns the Medal of Honor on Iwo Jima and takes a Japanese officer's samurai sword as a souvenir. Decades later, Bob returns the sword to the dead officer's son and family. But the sword turns out to be historically and politically important, and the Japanese family is slaughtered to get it. This horror causes Bob Lee to obsess about both avenging the family and retrieving the sword. In effect, he becomes a samurai, and his confrontations with the murderers are extremely bloody. Although heavy on both the explanations of Japanese customs and the sordid world of incredibly savage Japanese criminals, this work is compelling, exciting, and satisfying, a dark adventure that will appeal to thriller fans." Libr J

Hunter, Stephen, 1946-

Black light. Doubleday 1996 463p

LC 95-43079

"Mr. Hunter, who is a powerful and disturbing writer, tells this unholy story in a heroic style that gives mythic sweep to the generational waves of violence that seem to have had no beginning and threaten to have no end." N Y Times Book Rev

Hunter, Stephen, 1946-

Dead zero; a Bob Lee Swagger novel. Stephen Hunter. Simon & Schuster 2010 406p. (hardcover) $26.00

ISBN 9781439138656; 9781439149935; 9781439138663; 1439138656; 1439138664

LC 2010046773

Sequel to: I, sniper (2009).

In this book, "[s]everal months after the betrayal of a covert operation in Afghanistan leaves a Marine sniper team dead, the target of that mission, top Taliban commander Ibrahim Zarzi (aka 'the Beheader'), changes sides. . . . Zarzi travels to the U.S., where he meets the president and key congressional leaders and offers the State Department its best chance at achieving a stable, reliable Afghan government. Meanwhile, a Marine radio operator receives a message from Gunnery Sgt. Ray Cruz (aka 'the Cruise Missile'), one of the snipers believed to have been killed. Cruz has returned stateside to continue the mission. The FBI calls in retired Marine sniper ace Bob Lee Swagger to help find Cruz before he blows off the Beheader's head, but someone is following 'Bob the Nailer' to get to Cruz first." (Publishers Weekly)

Hunter, Stephen, 1946-

★ **Dirty** white boys; a novel. Random House 1994 436p

LC 94-15359

"The blood-soaked packaging of Mr. Hunter's big, mythic theme is thrilling, in the manner of the ancient storytellers, with battles fierce enough for a war and characters crazy enough to fight them to the death.

There is no place to run for cover from this author's prose—no glades of pretty writing to cool his vision of a land of lost children, forgotten values and total desolation." NY Times Book Rev

Hunter, Stephen, 1946-

Havana; an Earl Swagger novel. Simon & Schuster 2003 403p $24.95

ISBN 0-7432-3808-7

LC 2003-54461

"Havana's story line bobs and weaves like a prizefighter, taking the reader in many directions, from barely exciting scenes to intense ones." USA Today

Hunter, Stephen, 1946-

Hot Springs; a novel. Simon & Schuster 2000 478p $25

ISBN 0-684-86360-X

LC 99-88530

"Once upon a time, hard-boiled implied more than a style; Hunter shows us what the real thing was all about." Booklist

Hunter, Stephen, 1946-

I, sniper; a Bob Lee Swagger novel. Simon & Schuster 2009 418p $26

ISBN 978-1-4165-6515-4; 1-4165-6515-9

LC 2009-19792

"Someone is killing the aging antiwar radicals of the 1970s and using incredible sniping skills to do it. With bodies piling up, the FBI calls on the skills and knowledge of Bob Lee Swagger . . . , who quickly determines that an American war hero has been framed and then murdered. The chase is on to find out who's responsible and why. As with all of Hunter's Swagger novels, there is much more than meets the eye, with cover-ups and nasty villains galore. Swagger is a loner, a paladin, and a violent and politically incorrect corrector of injustice, a cousin to Lee Child's Jack Reacher." Libr J

Hunter, Stephen, 1946-

Pale horse coming; a novel. Simon & Schuster 2001 491p

ISBN 0-684-86361-8

LC 2001-47386

In this sequel to Hot Springs, "Hunter continues the story of Arkansas state cop Earl Swagger. It's 1951, and Swagger is once again called on to clean up an evil empire. Deep in the swamps of Thebes, Mississippi, a prison for black criminals run by a gang of redneck thugs harbors a sinister conspiracy. After rescuing his friend Sam Vincent from Thebes and narrowly escaping from the prison himself, Earl gathers a team of legendary gunfighters . . . and sets out to liberate Thebes the only way he knows how—violently. . . . The character of Earl Swagger, equal parts gristle and determination, remains compelling, both as archetype and as complex human being." Booklist

Hunter, Stephen, 1946-

Soft target; Stephen Hunter. Simon & Schuster 2011 256 p.

ISBN 9781439138700; 9781439138717; 9781439149942

LC 2011030150

The book, a novel, tells the story of "Ray Cruz . . . a marine sniper . . . Ray is doing a little shopping on Black Friday with his fiancée at 'America the Mall' in rural Minnesota when a gunman kills Santa Claus, and thousands of shoppers are taken hostage in the middle of the ultimate symbol of American consumerism. Terrorists, right? Well, not exactly. The leader of 'Brigade Mumbai' is just a kid who has 'always liked to wreck things.' It's up to Cruz, a human killing machine who finds himself in the wrong place at the right time (but without a gun), to neutralize the assailants before they begin to empty their automatic weapons—and before the headline hunting bureaucrats from the state police can bungle matters completely." (Booklist)

Hunter, Stephen, 1946-

Time to hunt; a novel. Doubleday 1998 467p

ISBN 0-385-48043-1

LC 97-46985

"Swagger is a near-mythic character without peer in mystery fiction. He was born to soldier but longs to stop. As we revel in his adventures and triumphs, we also experience his pain." Booklist

Hurley, Kameron

The **Mirror** Empire; Kameron Hurley. Angry Robot 2014 544 p. map (Worldbreaker saga) $14.99

ISBN 0857665561; 9780857665560

"In the frozen kingdom of Saiduan, invaders from another realm are decimating whole cities, leaving behind nothing but ash and ruin. At the heart of this war lie the pacifistic Dhai people, once enslaved by the Saiduan and now courted by their former masters to provide aid against the encroaching enemy." (Publisher's note)

"This is a hugely ambitious work, bloody and violent, with interestingly gender-flipped politics and a host of factions to keep straight, as points of view switch often." LJ

Hurston, Zora Neale

The **complete** stories; introduction by Henry Louis Gates, Jr. and Sieglinde Lemke. HarperCollins Pubs. 1995 xxiii, 305p hardcover o.p. pa $14.99

ISBN 0-06-016732-7; 0-06-135018-4 pa

LC 91-50438

This collection of Hurston's short fiction contains nineteen stories originally published between 1921 and 1951, arranged in the order in which they were published, and seven previously unpublished stories.

Includes bibliographical references

Hurston, Zora Neale

★ **Novels** and stories. Library of Am. 1995 1041p $35

ISBN 0-940450-83-6

LC 94-25757

Companion volume to Folklore, memoirs, and other writings

This collection contains Hurston's four novels: Jonah's gourd vine, Their eyes were watching God, Moses, man of the mountain, and Seraph on the Suwanee. Also included are nine short stories

"Libraries without a complete set of Hurston's fiction will find this volume a necessary and easy purchase to fill that unfortunate gap." Booklist

Hurston, Zora Neale

★ **Their** eyes were watching God; with a foreword by Edwidge Danticat. HarperCollins Pubs. 2000 xxii, 231p $22; pa $15.95

ISBN 0-06-019949-0; 0-06-112006-0 pa

LC 00-58186

First published 1937 by Lippincott

This novel "treats social problems from a racial and feminist perspective. Janie Crawford, raised by her grandmother in rural poverty, flees her old and dictatorial husband with Joe Starks, an ambitious man who becomes the mayor of Florida's first town run by African Americans. When Joe dies, Janie falls in love with the younger Teacake and follows him to the truck farming area of the Florida swamps. In the floods following a hurricane, he is bitten by a rabid dog and, crazed, attacks Janie. She shoots him, is charged with murder, and finally exonerated. When she returns to the town she and Joe built, she tells her story to a friend." HarperCollins Reader's Ency of Am Lit

Hurwitz, Gregg

The **crime** writer. Viking 2007 301p $24.95

ISBN 978-0-670-06321-5; 0-670-06321-5

LC 2006-52822

"Successful crime-novelist Drew Danner has gained true tabloid fame-as the murderer of his ex-fiance. Found by the police in the midst of a brain-tumor-induced grand mal seizure, with her blood covering his hands and his fingerprints on the murder weapon, Danner seems to be the only person in L.A. who isn't sure he is a killer. Emergency surgery after his arrest removes the tumor, and a temporary insanity defense frees him, but his comfortable life is shattered. He can't live without knowing if he killed a woman he once loved. His only choice is to become a character in a story he hasn't written. Danner's anguish is compellingly described, and the plot has more twists and turns than Mulholland Drive." Booklist

Hurwitz, Gregg, 1973-

The **Nowhere** Man; Gregg Hurwitz. St. Martin's Press 2017 368 p. (ebook) $60; $25.99

ISBN 9781466876521; 1250067855; 9781250067852

LC 2016037565

In this novel in the Evan Smoak series, by Gregg Hurwitz, "Evan was raised and trained as part of the Orphan Program, an off-the-books operation designed to create deniable intelligence assets—i.e. assassins. Evan was Orphan X. He broke with the Program, using everything he learned to disappear and reinvent himself as the Nowhere Man. But his new life is interrupted when a surprise attack comes from an unlikely angle and Evan is caught unaware." (Publisher's note)

"Thriller fans craving action and violence will enjoy this one." Kirkus

Hurwitz, Gregg, 1973-

Orphan X; Gregg Hurwitz. St. Martin's Press 2016 368 p. (hardcover) $25.99

ISBN 9781250067845; 1250067847

LC 2015038311

In this suspense novel, by Gregg Hurwitz, first book in the "Nowhere Man" series, "it's said that when he's reached by the truly desperate and deserving, the Nowhere Man can and will do anything to protect and save them. But he's no legend. . . . Chosen as a child, he was raised and trained as part of the off-the-books black box Orphan program, designed to create the perfect deniable intelligence assets---i.e. assassins." (Publisher's note)

"Hurwitz, known for this kind of adrenaline-producing fiction . . . adds enough humanity to the action to make this a standout, and readers should get in at the start." Booklist

Another title in this series is:

Nowhere Man (2017)

Hurwitz, Gregg

They're watching. St. Martin's 2010 357p $24.99

ISBN 978-0-312-53490-5; 0-312-53490-6

LC 2009-47039

"This is a very well constructed thriller, full of twists and turns and unexpected revelations. Hurwitz frequently sets us up to expect one thing but delivers something entirely different. He keeps us constantly on our toes, and—this is especially good—he keeps us guessing right until the very last pages about exactly who has targeted Patrick and why. Highly recommended, especially for fans of Dean Koontz, Linwood Barclay, and Harlan Coben." Booklist

Hurwitz, Gregg

You're next. St. Martin's Press 2011 407p $24.99

ISBN 978-0-312-53491-2

LC 2011-06869

The Boss Man has an unexpected motive in destroying Mike Wingate, who's worked his way up from the bottom to become a successful home contractor in Lost Hills, California. To protect his family and himself, Mike, who was raised in a foster home, summons his only friend from those days, the formidable Shep, who has grown up to be a career criminal of considerable skill.

"A thriller that grabs readers by the seat of the pants and gives them a Wow, what next! action thrill ride." Kirkus

Hurwitz, Gregg, 1973-

The **survivor**; Gregg Hurwitz. 1st ed. St. Martin's Press 2012 374 p. (paperback) $9.99; (hardcover) $25.99

ISBN 9781250029430; 0312625510; 9780312625511; 9781250009722

LC 2012013914

This novel by Gregg Hurwitz follows "36-year-old Nate Overbay. Diagnosed with Lou Gehrig's disease . . . Nate is about to leap off an 11th-floor ledge of a bank building . . . when he notices a robbery in progress. . . . In revenge, the thwarted theft's mastermind, a notorious Ukrainian mobster, vows to brutally kill Nate and his teenage daughter unless Nate can retrieve the robbery's objective: an envelope stored in one of the bank's safe deposit boxes." (Publishers Weekly)

Huston, Charlie

Already dead. Ballantine Books 2005 268p map pa $14

ISBN 0-345-47824-X

LC 2004-62323

"Huston's intricate, fast-paced, Chandleresque vampire-crime story has plenty of action, violence, and raw language. An excellent story but not for the squeamish in public libraries." Libr J

Huston, Charlie

Caught stealing. Ballantine Books 2004 240p

ISBN 0-345-46477-X

LC 2004-299530

"Having fled California for New York City after an injury cut short his promising baseball career, Hank Thompson settles into an aimless life as an alcoholic bartender. Still, Hank prides himself on making Manhattan a bit more hospitable by helping his friends, so how can he refuse when a neighbor asks him to cat-sit? One lost kidney later, Hank realizes that an Elmore Leonardesque collection of Russian mobsters, short-fused cons, and renegade cops will snuff out all 10 lives he and the cat share between them if that's what it takes to find the not-so-good neighbor. . . . [This book] definitely belongs on every Elmore Leonard fan's to-read list. One note of caution: Lovers of mystery-solving felines should place paws over eyes during the hair-raising cat torture scene." Booklist

Huston, Charlie

Every last drop; a novel. Del Rey 2008 252p il pa $14

ISBN 978-0-345-49588-4; 0-345-49588-8

LC 2008-26441

New York vampire PI Joe Pitt "has been exiled to the South Bronx. He's doing his best to keep a low profile and eke out enough of a living to keep him in blood, bullets and smokes. It's not easy. He's there on sufferance — despite the tolerance and interest of local boss Esperanza — and he's down to his last three bullets. Staying out of trouble doesn't come naturally to him either. So when Dexter Predo of the Coalition offers him a chance to go back to Manhattan, Joe takes it. Sure, Predo wants him dead but it's not like he's the only one. Joe is sent to spy on Manhattan's new vampire clan: the Cure. They were set up by Amanda Horde a broken, brilliant, teenage millionaire with a soft spot for Pitt — and are dedicated to finding a cure for Vyrus, the cause and carrier of vampirism. Some vampires consider the Cure to be heretics, others, like the Coalition, consider them a threat to the status quo. Dexter Predo wants to know what they are doing and what they have planned for the future. . . . [Huston] has crafted a riveting and enjoyable story." SF Site

Huston, Charlie

Half the blood of Brooklyn; a novel. Del Rey/Ballantine Books 2008 223p map pa $13.95

ISBN 978-0-345-49587-7

LC 2007-28330

"Huston's third Joe Pitt vampire novel . . . takes his Manhattan-based hardboiled hero on a dangerous trip into the undead communities across the bridge in Brooklyn. The various vampire clans in New York are on the brink of conflict. Leadership has fallen apart, and to make things worse, a 'Van Helsing' is running amok and has recently murdered a longtime supplier of contraband blood. Worst of all, Pitt's AIDS-stricken girlfriend, Evie, is in the hospital failing fast. . . . Huston's formidable writing chops are on full display: his action scenes are unparalleled in crime fiction and his dialogue is so hip and dead-on that Elmore Leonard should be getting nervous." Publ Wkly

Huston, Charlie

The **mystic** arts of erasing all signs of death. Ballantine Books 2009 319p $25

ISBN 978-0-345-50111-0; 0-345-50111-X

LC 2008-35293

"Oddly, given the willfully grisly subject matter and the rocket-like propulsive quality of Huston's short sentences (a paragraph with more than five lines in it comes to seem almost Proustian), this is a book with something tender and almost mushy at its core. The real subjects here are grief and the quest for friendship and family. . . . The dialogue is terrific . . . and Huston is excellent too on Los Angeles. He doesn't so much evoke the city as allow a sense of it to sink into his prose like blood into a carpet." Los Angeles Times Book Rev

Huston, Charlie

The **shotgun** rule; a novel. Ballantine Books 2007 248p $21.95

ISBN 978-0-345-48135-1; 0-345-48135-6

LC 2007-20511

"In the summer of 1983, four teenage boys (a brainiac, a punk rocker, an army wannabe, and an ex-drug-runner) reclaim their stolen bicycle. They also find a crystal-meth lab and rip-off a half a kilo to sell and perhaps buy their dream car with. The dope-pimp Arroyo brothers—led by obese stoner-hippie, Geezer—kick off a vengeful search. Mayhem, much of it over-the-top and delivered in gruesome detail—rocks the California suburb, and dysfunctional parents deal with their own demons while the boys prove surprisingly clever in a tough spot. From a sharp pitch, staccato dialogue and volatile action, durable characters and an intricate plot emerge, demonstrating Huston can still deliver the expected thriller goods." Paste

Huston, Charlie

Skinner; Charlie Huston. Mulholland Books/Little, Brown and Company 2013 400 p. (hardback) $26

ISBN 0316133728; 9780316133722

LC 2013001055

This novel by Charlie Huston focuses on Skinner, who "founded his career in 'asset protection' on fear. An . . . effective methodology, until Skinner's CIA handlers began to fear him as much as his enemies did and banished him. Now, [a] . . . cyber-terrorist attack is about to end that long exile. His asset is Jae, a roboticist with a gift for seeing the underlying systems violently shaping a new era of global guerrilla warfare." (Publisher's note)

Hustvedt, Siri

The **blazing** world; Siri Hustvedt. Simon & Schuster 2014 368 p. (hardback) $26

ISBN 1476747237; 9781476747231; 9781476747248

LC 2013027172

This novel by Siri Hustvedt presents a "purported collection of writings by and about an enigmatic artist, Harriet Burden, the tall, strong, erudite widow of a famous and secretive art dealer. Long enraged over the dismissive response to her work, Harriet launches a high-stakes gambit to expose the art world's persistent sexism. She convinces three male artists to pose as the creators of a sequence of her elaborate, allusive, and wildly provocative installations." (Booklist)

"Hustvedt subtly explores the intricate workings of the brain and the mysteries of the mind as she shrewdly investigates gender differences, parodies art criticism, and contrasts diabolical ambition and the soul-scouring inquiries of expressive art." Booklist

Hustvedt, Siri

The **sorrows** of an American; a novel. Henry Holt and Co. 2008 306p $25

ISBN 978-0-8050-7908-1; 0-8050-7908-4

LC 2007-31046

"The novel opens with narrator Erik Davidsen, a psychiatrist, and his sister Inga, an academic, flying from New York City home to Minnesota, where the pair begins the painful process of sorting through the study of their deceased father, Lars. . . [This] is a novel of secrets and ghosts: Lars' ghosts, which follow him back to Minnesota after his service in World War II; Erik, divorced, lonely, plagued by a patient's suicide; the widowed Inga, who learns her husband, famous writer Max Blaustein, led a secret life during their tumultuous marriage. Even Sonia, Inga's 18-year-old daughter, carries painful burdens, including what she saw from her schoolroom window on September 11, 2001. . . . In a lesser writer's hands, this glut of thematic material could wind a novel into a hopeless knot. Hustvedt's facility is such that instead, we are lead through the inseparable interactions of mind and body as her characters move through the story. The effect is exhilarating rather than jarring, as events urge us forward, each secret offering up a truth that in turn unlocks another door." PopMatters

Huxley, Aldous, 1894-1963

★ **Brave** new world; a novel. Doubleday, Doran & Co. 1932 311p

"The ironic title, which Huxley has taken from Shakespeare's The Tempest, describes a world in which science has taken control over morality and humaneness. In this utopia humans emerge from test tubes, families are obsolete, and even pleasure is regulated. When a so-called savage who believes in spirituality is found and is imported to the community, he cannot accommodate himself to this world and ends his life." Shapiro. Fic for Youth. 3d edition

Huyler, Frank

The **laws** of invisible things. H. Holt 2004 320p $25

ISBN 0-8050-7330-2

LC 2003-51116

This novel "focuses on Michael Grant, a newly divorced doctor who has just moved to North Carolina and joined the practice of widower Ronald Gass, a much older physician. Grant's lonely personal life is soon in turmoil as it intersects with the black Williams family. Soon after his arrival, Grant treats the granddaughter of Rev. Thomas Williams; the little girl dies, probably due to an oversight by Grant. As a favor to the minister, Grant agrees to see his son Jonas, the girl's father, who has bizarre symptoms that Grant thinks may indicate a previously unknown disease; Gass is skeptical, almost scornful of this idea. Within days, Gass dies of natural causes, Jonas is dead from the disease, and Grant himself is hospitalized with the same symptoms." Libr J

Hyatt, Martin

Beautiful gravity; a novel. Martin Hyatt. Antibookclub 2016 224 p. $16

ISBN 9780997592306

LC 2016941641

Stonewall Honor Book in Literature (2017)

In this book, by Martin Hyatt, "Loner Boz Matthews spends his days working at his grandfather's Louisiana highway diner. His only friends are the Pentecostal preacher's anorexic daughter, Meg, and the ghosts of dead movie stars. But when country music outlaws Catty Mills and Kyle Thomas come to town, Boz's world is turned upside-down, leading to an emotionally turbulent and sexually liberating four-way relationship that challenges small-town beliefs and changes lives forever." (Publisher's note)

Hynes, James

Kings of infinite space. St. Martin's Press 2004 341p $24.95

ISBN 0-312-45645-X

LC 2003-58563

This "is social satire that slides smoothly and surreally into horror, and if it loses a little of its emotional heft in the process, you don't really miss it. The glee with which Hynes choreographs an in-office zombie-vs.-stapler fight scene is compensation enough." Time

Hynes, James

★ **Next**; a novel. Little, Brown and Co. 2010 308p $23.99

ISBN 978-0-316-05192-7; 0-316-05192-6

LC 2009-08490

"This is a book that begins innocently and is careful not to tip its hand, even though there's something very unusual at work. The title signals nothing. The cover art depicts an empty sky. Blurbs on the back allow four very different writers to skip the hosannas and cut to the chase. They find roundabout ways to say that Next took nerve to write, is much more potent than it may initially appear and has an ending that beggars description." N Y Times (Late N Y Ed)

I

Ignatius, David

Bloodmoney; David Ignatius. W.W. Norton & Co. 2011 372p.

ISBN 9780393078114; 0393078116; 9780393341799

LC 2011003003

This book by David Ignatius tells the story of "Sophie Marx, a CIA officer working for the Hit Parade, a new agency offshoot for covert action. Operating well beyond the reach of headquarters, the Hit Parade's minions roam the globe under deep cover with bags of cash and unorthodox marching orders: Buy peace in the borderlands, warlord by warlord. But the Hit Parade has sprung a leak in Pakistan, and its operatives have begun to disappear." (washingtonpost.com)

Ignatius, David

Body of lies; a novel. W.W. Norton & Co. 2007 349p $24.95

ISBN 978-0-393-06503-9; 0-393-06503-0

LC 2006-102362

"Unlike most of the folks writing fiction about the CIA these days, [Ignatius] understands the gestalt of the place and the internal and external pressure under which the agency's denizens operate." Washington Times

Ignatius, David

A **firing** offense. Random House 1997 333p

ISBN 0679448608; 9780679448600

LC 96-29518

In this "thriller, an up-and-coming journalist finds he has made a Faustian bargain when he takes information from the CIA. New York Mirror foreign correspondent Eric Truell's exposé of French governmental corruption leads him to probe the dynamics of power behind a pending French-Chinese communications contract—a deal that could mean the loss of billions for American businesses. Truell's CIA sources use their information to lure the ambitious but naive reporter into playing their own dangerous game in the murky new world order, where real power resides not with governments but with private enterprise." (Libr J)

"Thanks to great writing and an all-too-human protagonist, the preaching is kept to a minimum, but the sermon—about good journalism and bad, truth and lies—is there in bold letters." Publ Wkly

Ignatius, David

The **increment**; a novel. W.W. Norton & Co. 2009 390p $26.95

ISBN 978-0-393-06504-6

LC 2008-53857

The author "immerses readers in a totally believable universe. Jargon, geography and detail all ring true as his meticulously crafted, tightly woven tale moves from Washington to London and Iran. The plot grabs everything in its path like a snowball rolling down a hill." Kirkus

Ignatius, David

The **Sun** King; a novel. Random House 1999 305p

ISBN 0-679-44861-6

LC 99-13490

"A thoroughly involving narrative with a sharp, satiric edge, Ignatius's contemporary take on the tragic confluence of love, power and ambition is a sophisticated look at the media mystique and the movers and shakers in our nation's capitol. His stylish, fluent prose, anchored with fine atmospheric detail, gives the story texture and momentum." Publ Wkly

Iles, Greg

Black cross. Dutton 1995 516p

LC 94-34642

This novel "tells the story of a physician from Georgia and a German Jew who manage to forestall Hitler's use of poison nerve gas during World War II by destroying a secret laboratory hidden in a Nazi death camp. The rash plan for infiltrating the camp and destroying the laboratory has been developed by the Allies and led by Winston Churchill and will require nerves of steel, physical and emotional stamina, unparalleled bravery, and incredible luck. If it works, millions of lives will be saved. But there is a horrible price to pay for the larger victory—hundreds of Jewish prisoners interred in the camp may also die. From the very first page, Iles takes his readers on an emotional roller-coaster ride, juxtaposing tension-filled action scenes, horrifying depictions of savage cruelty, and heart-stopping descriptions of sacrifice and bravery." Booklist

Iles, Greg

★ The **bone** tree; Greg Iles. William Morrow, an imprint of HarperCollinsPublishers 2015 804 p. (hbk.) $27.99

ISBN 0062311115; 9780062311115

LC 2014042113

Sequel to Natchez Burning (2014)

This book, by Greg Iles, is the "second installment of an epic trilogy. . . . Former prosecutor Penn Cage and his fiancée, reporter and publisher Caitlin Masters, have barely escaped with their lives after being attacked by wealthy businessman Brody Royal and his Double Eagles, a KKK sect with ties to some of Mississippi's most powerful men. But the real danger has only begun as FBI Special Agent John Kaiser warns Penn that Brody wasn't the true leader of the Double Eagles." (Publisher's note)

"In a scenario swarming with FBI agents . . . villains, reporters, and a red herring or two, Iles allows Cage and Masters plenty of room to operate--and so they do, with all the missteps of ordinary people, unlike the supercops and superagents of so many other procedurals." Kirkus

Iles, Greg

The **devil's** punchbowl. Scribner 2009 580p $26.99

ISBN 978-0-7432-9251-1; 0-7432-9251-0

LC 2008-49551

Penn Cage, "a former prosecuting attorney-turned-novelist, is now mayor of Natchez, MS, his hometown. But all is not well, for the promises he made as a candidate seem all but impossible to achieve as a working mayor. When one of his childhood friends is murdered a day after contacting him with information concerning dog fighting, prostitution, drugs, and money laundering presided over by the manager of a Natchez gambling casino, Cage takes on an investigation that makes him the target of organized crime, endangers the lives of his family and closest friends, and draws the wrath of the Justice Department and Homeland Security. . . . Provides a thrill a minute." Libr J

Iles, Greg

The **footprints** of God. Scribner 2003 459p $25.95

ISBN 0-7432-3469-3

LC 2003-45733

"Readers interested in the exploration of religious themes without the usual New Age blather or window-dressed dogma will snap up this novel of cutting-edge science." Publ Wkly

Iles, Greg

★ **Mississippi** blood; a novel. Greg Iles. William Morrow, an imprint of HarperCollins Publishers 2017 694 p. (Natchez Burning) (hardback) $28.99

ISBN 0062311158; 9780062311153

LC 2016043631

In this third novel in the Natchez Burning series, by Greg Iles, "shattered by grief and dreaming of vengeance, Penn Cage sees his family and his world collapsing around him. The woman he loves is gone, his principles have been irrevocably compromised, and his father, once a paragon of the community that Penn leads as mayor, is about to be tried for the murder of a former lover. Most terrifying of all, Dr. Cage seems bent on self-destruction." (Publisher's note)

"Iles wraps up his massively ambitious Natchez Burning trilogy with a book that is (in keeping with its predecessors) compelling, dark, surprising, and morally ambiguous." Booklist

Iles, Greg

Mortal fear. Dutton 1997 564p

LC 97-194514

"Despite the artifice of the characters operating it, the technology involved in their ingenious computer chase— which gives new meaning to the term 'network'—is fascinating." N Y Times Book Rev

Iles, Greg

★ **Natchez** burning; a novel. Greg Iles. HarperCollins 2014 800 p. (Penn Cage series ; 4) (hardcover) $27.99

ISBN 0062311077; 9780062311078; 9780062311085

LC 2013031971

"Growing up in the rural Southern hamlet of Natchez, Mississippi, Penn Cage learned everything he knows about honor and duty from his father, Tom Cage. But now the beloved family doctor and pillar of the community is accused of murdering Violet Turner, the beautiful nurse with whom he worked in the dark days of the early 1960s. A fighter who has always stood for justice, Penn is determined to save his father, even though Tom . . . refuses to speak up in his own defense." (Publisher's note)

"Much more than a thriller. . . . This superlative novel's main strength comes from the lead's struggle to balance family and honor." Pub Wkly

Iles, Greg

Third degree. Scribner 2007 385p $25.95

ISBN 978-0-7432-9250-4; 0-7432-9250-2

LC 2007-48097

"When Laurel Shields, a 35-year-old mother of two, discovers she's pregnant, she can't be sure her physician husband, Warren, is the father. Meanwhile, Warren is in trouble with the IRS. Laurel believes his obsessive search for a document in their Athens Point, Miss., home is related to a federal Medicaid fraud investigation focusing on his medical partner, Kyle Auster. As the Feds prepare to swoop down on Warren and Kyle's office to collect the evidence of false billings and bribes to patients without any actual illnesses, Warren takes Laurel and their two children hostage. Iles squeezes every drop of suspense out of the prolonged standoff between the doctor and the police." Publ Wkly

Iles, Greg

Turning angel. Scribner 2005 501p $25.95

ISBN 0-7432-3471-5

LC 2005-54469

"All this is lurid in the extreme and, in Iles's hands, entirely gripping, but there is more to Turning Angel than sex and scandal. Iles offers an insider's heartfelt picture of a Southern town that is dying because of lousy schools, a failing economy and racial tensions–and, again, there is no reason to think Natchez is unique. Iles populates this town with characters who are all too real and makes clear that its privileged young people no longer live isolated lives. . . . This is a powerful piece of popular fiction." Washington Post Book World

In sunlight or in shadow; stories inspired by the paintings of Edward Hopper. edited by Lawrence Block. Pegasus Books 2016 ix, 278 p.p color illustrations (hardcover) $25.95

ISBN 9781681772455; 9781681772882; 1681772450

This short story collection, edited by Lawrence Block, is a "commissioned anthology of seventeen superbly-crafted stories inspired by the paintings of Edward Hopper, including [works by authors] Jeffery Deaver, Joyce Carol Oates, Stephen King, Lee Child, and Robert Olen Butler, among many others." (Publisher's note)

"This strong collection begins in a spirit of homage but winds up showing how powerful inspiration can be." Kirkus

Indridason, Arnaldur ✓

Outrage; an Inspector Erlendur novel. Arnaldur Indridason ; translated from the Icelandic by Anna Yates. Minotaur Books 2012 281 p.

ISBN 0312659113; 9780312659110; 9781250012760

LC 2012035781

In this novel by Arnaldur Indridason "Detective Erlunder decides to take a short leave of absence, putting a female detective, Elínborg, in charge while he is gone. . . . [S]he's quickly thrust into a violent and volatile situation with extremely high stakes. Soon, her investigation uncovers a twisted tale of double lives that may be connected to the unsolved disappearance of a young girl. The clock is ticking to solve the case before a serial rapist strikes again." (Publisher's note)

Indridason, Arnaldur ✓

The **shadow** district; Arnaldur Indriðason ; translated from the Icelandic by Victoria Cribb. Minotaur Books 2017 344 p. (hardcover) $25.99

ISBN 9781250124036; 9781250124029

LC 2017025692

In this novel, by Arnaldur Indriðason, translated by Victoria Cribb, "in wartime Reykjavik, Iceland, a young woman is found strangled in 'the shadow district', a rough and dangerous area of the city. . . . A 90-year-old man is discovered dead on his bed, smothered with his own pillow. Konrad, a former detective . . . , finds newspaper cuttings reporting the WWII shadow district murder in the dead man's home. . . Why, after all this time, would an old crime resurface?" (Publisher's note)

"With minimalist prose, Indridason skillfully weaves the present-day murder with the past in this classic whodunit that ends with a satisfying and logical resolution." Kirkus

Invisible planets; contemporary Chinese science fiction in translation. edited and translated by Ken Liu. SDC Publications 2016 384 p. (hardcover) $24.99; (ebook) $60

ISBN 9781784978815; 9780765384195; 9780765384188; 0765384191

LC 2016047153

In this book "award-winning translator and author Ken Liu presents a collection of short speculative fiction from China. Some stories have won awards (including Hao Jingfang's Hugo-winning novella, 'Folding Beijing'); some have been included in various 'Year's Best' anthologies; some have been well reviewed by critics and readers; and some are simply Ken's personal favorites. . . . In addition, three essays at the end of the book explore Chinese science fiction." (Publisher's note)

"A phenomenal anthology of short speculative fiction." Kirkus

Irving, John, 1942-

Avenue of mysteries; by John Irving. Simon & Schuster 2015 480 p. (hardcover : alk. paper) $28

ISBN 9781451664164; 9781451664171

LC 2015005193

In this book, by John Irving, "Juan Diego—a fourteen-year-old boy, who was born and grew up in Mexico—has a thirteen-year-old sister. Her name is Lupe, and she . . . is a mind reader. . . . Regarding what has happened, as opposed to what will, Lupe is usually right about the past; without your telling her. . . . As an older man, Juan Diego will take a trip to the Philippines, but what travels with him are his dreams and memories As we grow older . . . we live in the past." (Publisher's note)

"Irving works his familiar themes—Catholicism, sex, death—with a light and assured touch, and though the dream-narrative construct is a little shelf-worn, it serves the story well. Though not as irresistible as early works such as The World According to Garp and The Hotel New Hampshire, a welcome return to form." Kirkus

Irving, John

The **cider** house rules; a novel. Modern Library 1999 571p $24.95

ISBN 978-0-679-60335-1; 0-679-60335-2

LC 99-30034

First published 1985 by Morrow

"The Cider House Rules is filled with people to love and to feel for. . . . The characters in John Irving's novel break all the rules, and yet they remain noble and free-spirited. Victims of tragedy, violence, and injustice, their lives seem more interesting and full of thought-provoking dilemmas than the lives of many real people." Houston Post

Irving, John

The **fourth** hand; a novel. Random House 2001 316p

ISBN 0-375-50627-6

LC 2001-18155

"Irving's set pieces are on that high level of American gothic comedy he has made uniquely his own." Publ Wkly

Irving, John, 1942-

★ **In** one person; a novel. John Irving. Simon & Schuster 2012 425 p.

ISBN 9781451664126; 9781451664133; 9781451664157

LC 2011039707

The novel tells a story of Billy, a boy growing up in the town of First Sister, Vermont in the 1960s, who comes to realize that he is bisexual. John Irving reintroduces "his signature motifs (New England life, wrestling, praising great writers, forbidden sex) while animating a . . . cast of misfit characters within a complicated plot. . . . Billy navigates fraught relationships with men and women and witnesses the horrors of the AIDS epidemic." (Booklist)

Irving, John

★ A **prayer** for Owen Meany; a novel. Modern Library 2002 xxiv, 641p $24.95

ISBN 0-679-64259-5

LC 2002-26479

First published 1989 by Morrow

This novel is set in New Hampshire in the 1950s and 1960s. Owen Meany is a short boy with a squeaky voice, who foresees his own death and sees himself as an instrument of God. He hits a baseball that kills the mother of John Wheelwright, the novel's narrator. Because of Owen, John becomes a Christian

"Despite its theological proppings, A Prayer for Owen Meany is a fable of political predestination. As usual, Irving delivers a boisterous cast, a spirited story line and a quality of prose that is frequently underestimated even by his admirers. On the other hand, the novel invites trespass by symbol hunters. . . . To get lost in critical rummage would be to miss the point. Irving's litany of error and folly may strike some as too righteous; but it is effective." Time

Irving, John

A **widow** for one year; a novel. Random House 1998 537p

ISBN 0-375-50137-1

LC 97-49166

"It is clearly not the outline of the plot that makes the book obstinately memorable. Rather, it is Irving's special gift for farcical incident . . . his piercing sense of the wonderful and terrible vulnerability of children, his poetic evocation of the ravages of time." Publ Wkly

Irving, John

★ The **world** according to Garp. Dutton 1978 437p

LC 77-15564

This "is a long family novel, spanning four generations and two continents, crammed with incidents, characters, feelings and craft. The components of black comedy and melodrama, pathos and tragedy, mesh effortlessly in a tale that can also be read as a commentary on art and the imagination." Time

Irving, Washington

★ The **complete** tales of Washington Irving. Doubleday 1975 xxxvii, 798p

Irwin, Stephen M.

The **broken** ones; a novel. Stephen M. Irwin. 1st American ed. Doubleday 2012 356 p. (hardcover) $26.00; (ebook) $78.00; (paperback) $15.95

ISBN 0385534655; 9780385534659; 9780385534666; 9780307744449

LC 2011039733

In this book by Stephen M. Irwin, "the world is reeling from a natural disaster that occurred a few years earlier. In just one day, Earth's poles shifted to affect climate, agriculture, and governmental infrastructure and setting off a global economic crisis. This event is known as Gray Wednesday, the day when the spectral and living worlds became one. . . . Each person is haunted by a ghost, someone from his or her past." (Library Journal)

Irwin, Stephen M.

The **dead** path; a novel. Doubleday 2010 374p $25.95

ISBN 978-0-385-53343-0; 0-385-53343-8

LC 2009-53661

First published 2009 in Australia

"Irwin writes in a lyrical style that expresses both the poignancy of Nicholas's distressing supernatural experiences and the mood of horror those experiences conjure." Publ Wkly

Isaacs, Susan

After all these years. HarperCollins Pubs. 1993 343p

ISBN 0060170603; 9780060170608

LC 92-56200

"Rose Meyers was just an ordinary Jew from Queens who married her sweetheart, became a teacher, moved to the suburbs, and had two kids. Then her husband's business made him a millionaire. Suddenly, Rose and Richie have a Long Island mansion, a fleet of BMWs, and invitations to all the right soirees. Rose is in for a shock, though, when Richie announces he's leaving her for a younger woman. The divorce papers aren't even signed when Rose, stricken with insomnia, goes downstairs one night for a glass of milk and trips over Richie's corpse. The cops immediately peg Rose as the prime suspect, but she knows she didn't kill her husband, and she's determined to find out who did." (Booklist)

Isaacs "has a field day lampooning upper-class mores . . . but also weaves into this thoroughly diverting caper unexpected moments of genuine tenderness and sly social commentary." Publ Wkly

Isaacs, Susan

Almost paradise. Harper & Row 1984 483p

LC 83-48357

"Nicholas is the scion of a wealthy family, although Jane's bloodline is anything but aristocratic. They marry after Jane convinces Nick that his true talent lies with acting rather than law. In no time Nick is the rage of Broadway and Hollywood. The marriage remains idyllic until Jane develops a fear of crowds so great she is unable to walk to her own mailbox. But she continues to make their Connecticut farmhouse the ideal place for her husband to entertain his many guests. The arrangement works for twenty years, as Nick resists the attempts of countless women to seduce him. Nick finally succumbs to a timid film student and Jane takes up with her shrink." West Coast Rev Books

Isaacs, Susan

As husbands go; a novel. Scribner 2010 342p $25

ISBN 978-1-4165-7301-2; 1-4165-7301-1

LC 2009-52241

"The mystery is barely there, but Isaacs' fans will enjoy another sharp-tongued romp through the New York privileged classes and their foibles." Kirkus

Isaacs, Susan

Close relations. Lippincott 1980 270p

LC 80-7858

"Besides being simultaneously romantic, feminist, and political, the novel is also a satire: of Jewish mothers and success-orientation, late-marrying Irishmen, American political campaigns, WASP mores, and human relations." Best Sellers

Isaacs, Susan

★ **Compromising** positions. Times Bks. 1978 248p

LC 77-13896

"Judith Singer is a nice, average Jewish housewife—on the surface—but beneath that placid exterior lurks a secret longing for high adventure. . . . When a local dentist-Lothario is murdered in his office and a neighbor who was his last patient is a suspect, Judith cannot resist getting into the act. Meddling, gossiping, she turns detective, and when she learns that the elegant late Dr. Fleckstein was not only bedding virtually every woman in town but getting them to pose for exceedingly porno photos, there's no stopping her. Enter detective Nelson Sharpe, much more attractive than Judith's stodgy husband. The two make a wild pair of sleuths as Sharpe tracks down the murderer and an accomplice and exposes smug suburban hypocrisy." Publ Wkly

Isaacs, Susan

Lily White; a novel. HarperCollins Pubs. 1996 459p

LC 96-17399

"Susan Isaac's real subject here isn't murder or legal thrills, of course, but the drama and suspense of middle-class women's lives. In her rendition, it's white-knuckle stuff." N Y Times Book Rev

Isaacs, Susan

Red, white and blue; a novel. HarperCollins Pubs. 1998 402p

ISBN 0-06-017608-3

LC 98-34568

"It is no easy task to hold a reader's attention when a novel's outcome is obvious from the very first page. But Susan Isaacs has such a knack for entertaining her reader with the details of American pop culture . . . that it's easy to be distracted from the predictability of her plot." N Y Times Book Rev

Isherwood, Christopher, 1904-1986

★ The **Berlin** stories; Christopher Isherwood; introduction by Armistead Maupin ; preface by Christopher Isherwood. New Directions Pub 2008 207 p. pbk $17.95

ISBN 9780811218047; 081121804X

LC 2008023325

Goodbye to Berlin contains six short stories or sketches of life in Berlin in the last years before Hitler came to power. Though written in first person by one calling himself Christopher Isherwood, according to the author's statement, the material is not to be regarded as autobiographical. The sketches are entitled: A Berlin diary (Autumn 1930); Sally Bowles; On Ruegan Island (Summer 1931); The Nowaks; The Landauers; A Berlin diary (Winter 1932-3)

The last of Mr. Norris, set in Berlin during Hitler's rise to power, "is the story of the narrator's innocent friendship with odd, corrupt Mr. Norris. While pretending to be a sincere Communist, Mr. Norris is actually selling information to fascists and foreigners. Mr. Norris's masochistic sexual aberrations add to the impression that he is a symbol of the whole corrupt, disintegrating society." Reader's Ency. 4th edition

Ishiguro, Kazuo

An **artist** of the floating world. Putnam 1986 206p
ISBN 0-399-13119-1

LC 85-25759

Author Kazuo Ishiguro won the Nobel Prize in Literature in 2017.

"The tensions stay tight. And this is what makes Mr. Ishiguro not only a good writer but also a wonderful novelist." N Y Times Book Rev

Ishiguro, Kazuo

The **buried** giant; a novel. Kazuo Ishiguro. Alfred A. Knopf 2015 320 p. (hardcover) $26.95
ISBN 030727103X; 9780307271037

LC 2014028378

Author Kazuo Ishiguro won the Nobel Prize in Literature in 2017.

In this fantasy novel by Kazuo Ishiguro, "the Romans have long since departed and Britain is steadily declining into ruin. But, at least, the wars that once ravaged the country have ceased. Axl and Beatrice, a couple of elderly Britons, decide that now is the time, finally, for them to set off across this troubled land of mist and rain to find the son they have not seen for years, the son they can scarcely remember." (Publisher's note)

"Ishiguro's story is a deceptively simple one, for enfolded within its elemental structure are many profound truths, including its beautiful and memorable portrait of a long-term marriage and its subtle commentary on the eternity of war, all conveyed in the author's mesmerizing prose." Booklist

Ishiguro, Kazuo

Never let me go. Knopf 2005 288p
ISBN 1400043395

LC 2004048966

Author Kazuo Ishiguro won the Nobel Prize in Literature in 2017.

This is a novel by the author of The Remains of the Day (1989). "Kathy, Ruth and Tommy were pupils at Hailsham—an idyllic establishment situated deep in the English countryside. The children there were tenderly sheltered from the outside world, brought up to believe they were special, and that their personal welfare was crucial. But for what reason were they really there? It is only years later that Kathy, now aged 31, finally allows herself to yield to the pull of memory. What unfolds is the . . . story of how Kathy, Ruth and Tommy slowly come to face the truth about their seemingly happy childhoods—and about their futures." (Publisher's note)

This novel is "set in late 1990s England, in a parallel universe in which humans are cloned and raised expressly to 'donate' their healthy organs and thus eradicate disease from the normal population." Publ Wkly

Ishiguro, Kazuo

★ The **remains** of the day. Knopf 1989 245p

LC 89-80445

Author Kazuo Ishiguro won the Nobel Prize in Literature in 2017.

"Mr. Stevens is a butler of high quality now employed by the American owner of Darlington Hall. His position as butler was quite different when Lord Darlington was his employer. Then there was a large staff, including Miss Kenton, whose friendly overtures to Stevens were met only by his inability to unbend or find some humor as an outlet offsetting his customary snobbish personality. As Stevens reflects on the past the reader gains insight into Lord Darlington's political connections after World War I with important government officials including Ribbentrop, representive of Germany's movement toward a dictatorship. Questions regarding an employee's unquestioning loyalty toward his employer and awareness of the political situation in the period just before Hitler's rise to power make this a thought-provoking novel." Shapiro. Fic for Youth. 3d edition

Ishiguro, Kazuo

The **unconsoled**. Knopf 1995 544p
ISBN 0-679-40425-2

LC 95-15829

Author Kazuo Ishiguro won the Nobel Prize in Literature in 2017.

In this novel, "prominent concert pianist Ryder is at odds with his surroundings. Ryder arrives in an unidentified European city at a bit of a loss. Everyone he meets seems to assume that he knows more than he knows, that he is well acquainted with the city and its obscure cultural crisis. A young woman he kindly consents to advise seems to have been an old lover and her son quite possibly his own; he vaguely recalls past conversations. The world he has entered is a surreal, Alice-in-Wonderland place where a door in a cafe can lead back to a hotel miles away. The result is at once dreamy, disorienting, and absolutely compelling; Ishiguro's paragraphs, though Proust-like, are completely lucid and quite addictive to read." Libr J

Ishiguro, Kazuo

When we were orphans. Knopf 2000 335p $25
ISBN 0-375-41054-6

LC 00-26120

Author Kazuo Ishiguro won the Nobel Prize in Literature in 2017.

"For all its ellipses and evasions, When We Were Orphans, will linger in the mind as an often fascinating, imaginative work of surpassing intelligence and taste." Times Lit Suppl

Itani, Frances

Deafening. Atlantic Monthly Press 2003 378p $24
ISBN 0-87113-902-2

LC 2003-45108

"This novel is not only a beautifully crafted love story but also an exploration of the possibilities of language and the eloquence of silence." Libr J

Itani, Frances

Remembering the bones. Atlantic Monthly Press 2007 282p $24
ISBN 978-0-87113-977-1; 0-87113-977-4

"On the way to a party for Queen Elizabeth II, Georgie Witley, an Anglophile Canadian born the same day, crashes and is thrown from the driver's seat of her car. Lying on her back, like a beetle, at the bottom of a ravine, Georgie dutifully recites a passage from her grandfather's volume of 'Gray's Anatomy': 'Femur, tibia, fibula. Radius, ulna.' The litany of bones anchors Georgie in her broken body, and also helps her to coax eight decades of memories from their hiding places. She reflects on a life given shape by marriage, motherhood, and world war, milestones that she and the Queen have in common. In unpretentious, quietly penetrating prose, Itani exposes the richness and depth beneath the surface of one ordinary life." New Yorker

Itani, Frances

Requiem; Frances Itani. Atlantic Monthly Press 2012 317 p. $24

ISBN 0802120229; 9780802120229

This book by Frances Itani "examines the internment of Japanese Canadian citizens during WWII and its impact on one family. In 1997, artist Binosuke Okuma drives from Montreal to the site of the camp on the Fraser River where his family has been interned when Bin was very young, and where his father made a decision that would cut him off from his family--and permit him to fulfill his potential as an artist. But at first memories of Bin's wife, Lena, who died of a stroke, chase him." (Publishers Weekly)

Itani, Frances

Tell; Frances Itani. Grove Press 2015 272 p. $15

ISBN 0802123368; 9780802123367

Scotiabank Giller Prize Shortlist (2014)

This novel by Frances Itani, sequel to the novel "Deafening," "picks up from the return of the sisters' husbands from the war, and follows Tress's partner Kenan, a young shell-shocked soldier who confines himself indoors, venturing outside only at night to visit the frozen bay where he skated as a boy." (Publisher's note)

"The slow-moving novel circulates among Kenan and Tress, Maggie and Am; an exceptionally awkward ending is summarized in a letter. Though attentive to period detail, Itani seems more constricted than liberated by the past in her sixth novel." Kirkus

Ivey, Eowyn, 1973-

The **snow** child; Eowyn Ivey. Little, Brown and Co. 2012 389p.

ISBN 9780316175661; 9780316175678

LC 2011024937

This book takes place in Alaska in "1920, and frontier living means building your own log cabin with logs you felled yourself. Mabel, born in Pennsylvania, is facing her second winter up north, and she is wilting in the cold and isolation. . . . Jack, is still tainted by grief. He, exhausted by trying to scratch a living from the wilderness, barely talks and never smiles. One evening, though, their mood lifts, and the couple play in the newly fallen snow. They build a little snowman, complete with scarf and mittens. . . . In the morning, nothing remains but a broken heap of snow and a trail of small footprints leading away. . . . Suffice to say that a pale little girl in that same scarf and mittens eventually emerges from the forest and comes to play a crucial role in Jack and Mabel's life. But they have very different ideas about who or what she is, and what she means to them." (The Guardian)

Ivey, Eowyn, 1973-

★ **To** the bright edge of the world; a novel. Eowyn Ivey. Little, Brown & Co. 2016 432 p. ill. (some color), map (ebook) $78; (hardback) $26

ISBN 0316242853; 9780316365598; 9780316242851

LC 2015953904

In this book, by Eowyn Ivey, "in the winter of 1885, decorated war hero Colonel Allen Forrester leads a small band of men on an expedition that has been deemed impossible: to venture up the Wolverine River and pierce the vast, untamed Alaska Territory. Leaving behind Sophie, his newly pregnant wife, Colonel Forrester records his extraordinary experiences in hopes that his journal will reach her if he doesn't return." (Publisher's note)

"In this splendid adventure novel, Ivey captures Alaska's beauty and brutality, not just preserving history, but keeping it alive." Pub Wkly

J

Jacka, Benedict

Fated; Benedict Jacka. Ace Books 2012 295 p. (Alex Verus)

ISBN 1937007294; 9781937007294

This "urban fantasy [novel] . . . introduces cheeky British diviner Alex Verus, who's caught in the middle of a conflict between Light and Dark mages over an ancient magical weapon. Alex can not only see all possible futures but can often choose which ones to make real, so both sides want to use him as a tool. Alex, alienated from other mages because he has developed empathy for the beings around him, refuses to take sides. To save himself and his dependents--Luna, a lonely, cursed young woman, and Starbreeze, an ancient air elemental who's 'dumb as a sack of rocks'--he's forced to think and move nimbly through London and its associated magical realms." (Publishers Weekly)

Other titles in this series are:
Cursed (2012)
Taken (2012)
Chosen (2013)
Hidden (2014)
Veiled (2015)
Burned (2016)
Bound (2017)
Marked (2018)

Jackson, Brenda

Forged in desire; Brenda Jackson. Harlequin Books 2017 407 p. (The protectors) (paperback) $7.99

ISBN 9780373790005; 9781460397794; 0373790007

In this book, by Brenda Jackson, "when good girl Margo Connelly becomes Lamar 'Striker' Jennings's latest assignment, she knows she's in trouble. And not just because he's been hired to protect her from an underworld criminal. The reformed bad boy's appeal is breaching all her defenses, and as the threats against her increase, Margo isn't sure which is more dangerous: the gangster targeting her, or the far too alluring protector tempting her to let loose." (Publisher's note)

"Jackson's deft plotting and effective red herrings keep the suspense high as her multidimensional characters command the reader's attention." Pub Wkly

Jackson, Charles

★ The **lost** weekend. Rinehart 1944 244p

Psychological study of a drunkard. The actual time covered is five days, but in those five days the story of a man's life is told. Don Biram, a sensitive, charming and well-read man, left alone for a few days by his brother, struggles with his overwhelming desire for alcohol, succumbs to it, and in the resulting prolonged agony, goes over much of his life up to and including the long weekend

"It's written with complete lack of literary pretensions; yet Jackson's sheer ability to lick the problems of flashback, stream of consciousness, mind wandering, twisted recollection and alcoholic delirium is spectacular. . . . Its frankness is sometimes shocking but never aimed to shock. The aim, and it is unerring, is always for accuracy and the complete truth" Book Week

Jackson, Joshilyn

The **almost** sisters; Joshilyn Jackson. William Morrow and Co. 2017 342 p. (hardcover) $26.99

ISBN 9780062105738; 9780062105714

LC 2016056529

This book, by Joshilyn Jackson, confronts the truth about privilege, family, and the distinctions between perception and reality. . . . Leia returns to Alabama to put her grandmother's affairs in order, . . . and tell her family that she's pregnant. . . . She learns that illness is not the only thing Birchie's been hiding. Tucked in the attic is a dangerous secret with roots that reach all the way back to the Civil War. Its exposure threatens the family's freedom and future." (Publisher's note)

"Jackson (The Opposite of Everyone, 2016, etc.) has written another spirited page-turner set in a new South still haunted by the ghosts of the old." Kirkus

Jackson, Joshilyn

Between, Georgia. Warner 2006 294p $22.99

ISBN 0-446-52442-5

LC 2005-23748

"Underneath all the pyrotechnics, Joshilyn Jackson is cleverly exploring the nature of family and belonging. . . . Jackson loads her novel with eccentrics straight from Southern Gothic central casting, but her writing brims with enough humor to make it compulsively readable." Christ Sci Monit

Jackson, Joshilyn

A **grown** up kind of pretty; Joshilyn Jackson. Grand Central Pub. 2012 336p.

ISBN 9780446582353

LC 2011004744

This book is about the "Slocumb women [who] suffer from a . . . curse: every 15 years something bad happens. Ginny gave birth to Liza when she was 15. And Liza had Mosey when she was 15. Now it's Mosey who's 15, and she's nervous. But the curse strikes in a different form, bringing a stroke to Liza that renders her mute and crippled, leaving her husband 'Big' to care for her. Wanting to put a pool in the yard for Liza's water therapy, Ginny has a willow uprooted, unearthing the bones of a baby—Liza's baby. This macabre discovery sends Mosey, Ginny, and Big in search of answers about the baby and Mosey's identity." (Publishers Weekly)

Jackson, Joshilyn

The **opposite** of everyone; A Novel. Joshilyn Jackson. William Morrow 2016 352 p. $26.99

ISBN 9780062105684; 006210568X; 0062105698

LC 2015008623

In this novel, by Joshilyn Jackson, "Paula Vauss spent the first decade of her life on the road with her free-spirited young mother, Kai, an itinerant storyteller who blended Hindu mythology with southern oral tradition to re-invent their history as they roved. But everything, including Paula's birth name Kali Jai, changed when she told a story of her own—one that landed Kai in prison and Paula in foster care." (Publisher's note)

"A bit too heavy on the Hindu mythology, this novel, nonetheless, makes some affecting points about the importance of the stories we tell to each other and to ourselves." Booklist

Jackson, Naomi

The **Star** Side of Bird Hill; Naomi Jackson. Penguin Group USA 2015 304 p. $25.95

ISBN 1594205957; 9781594205958

LC 2014504545

NAACP Image Award Nominee: Outstanding Literary Work- Debut Author (2016)

In this novel, by Naomi Jackson, "two sisters are suddenly sent from their home in Brooklyn to Barbados to live with their grandmother. . . . Dionne spends the summer in search of love, testing her grandmother's limits, and wanting to go home. Phaedra explores Bird Hill, where her family has lived for generations, accompanies her grandmother in her role as a midwife, and investigates their mother's mysterious life." (Publisher's note)

A "charming, laid-back bildungsroman and an uplifting story about the importance of a stable, loving home and the embrace of one's culture." Booklist

Jackson, Neta

Who do I talk to? Neta Jackson. Thomas Nelson 2009 ix, 406p (pbk.) $15.99

ISBN 1595545247; 9781595545244

LC 2009024971

Christy Award: Contemporary Series, Sequels, and Novellas (2010)

In this book, "Gabby Fairbanks's husband locks her out and disappears with her sons. . . . With her frail mother and a mutt named Dandy, Gabby must take refuge at the women's shelter where she works. . . . There, her new friends-including Lucy the bag lady and sisters from the Yada Yada Prayer Group-prop her up. But a midnight intruder brings unwanted media attention to the shelter and threatens to undermine Gabby's chances of getting her sons back. Still hoping to put her family together again, Gabby puzzles over what to do with the warm attentions of a sympathetic lawyer who rebuilds her confidence and soothes her wounded spirit." (Publisher's note)

Jackson, Shirley

★ The **haunting** of Hill House. Viking 1959 246p hardcover o.p. pa $14

ISBN 0-14-303998-9 pa

"Dr. John Montague, an anthropologist, is interested in the analysis of supernatural manifestations. He rents Hill House, which is reported to be haunted, and plans to spend the summer there with research assistants. Eleanor Vance, one of the researchers, is at first repelled by the house but soon adjusts. Other people come and signs of psychic activity are rampant, many of them centered on Eleanor. When Dr. Montague insists that she leave to insure her safety, the house does not release her." Shapiro. Fic for Youth. 3d edition

Jackson, Shirley

★ The **lottery** and other stories; introduction by Patrick McGrath. Modern Lib. 2000 292p

ISBN 0-679-64039-8

LC 00-36064

A reissue of The lottery; or, The adventures of James Harris, published 1949 by Farrar, Straus

Jackson, Shirley

Novels and stories; [edited by Joyce Carol Oates] Library of America 2010 827p $35

ISBN 978-1-59853-072-8; 1-59853-072-0

LC 2009-943938

Includes the "short novels The Haunting of Hill House (1959), the tale of an achingly empathetic young woman chosen by a haunted house to be its new tenant, and We Have Always Lived in the Castle (1962), the unrepentant confessions of Miss Merricat Blackwood, a cunning adolescent who has gone to quite unusual lengths to preserve her ideal of family happiness." Publisher's note

Jackson, Shirley

We have always lived in the castle. Viking 1962 214p hardcover o.p. pa $14

ISBN 0-14-303997-0 pa

"Since the time that Constance Blackwood was tried and acquitted of the murder of four members of her family, she has lived with her sister Mary Catherine and her Uncle Julian in the family mansion. Mary Catherine takes care of family chores and Uncle Julian is busy with the writing of a detailed account of the six-year-old murders. Cousin Charles's arrival on the scene disrupts the quiet peace of the family, and Mary Catherine's efforts to get rid of him unloose a chain of events that bring everything down in ruins." Shapiro. Fic for Youth. 3d edition

Jacob, Mira

The **sleepwalker's** guide to dancing; by Mira Jacob. Random House Inc 2014 512 p. $26

ISBN 0812994787; 9780812994780

LC 2013020098

In this book, "novelist Mira Jacob takes us on a . . . journey that ranges from 1970s India to suburban 1980s New Mexico to Seattle during the dot.com boom. . . . [B]rain surgeon Thomas Eapen has been sitting on his porch, talking to dead relatives. At least that is the story his wife, Kamala . . . tells their daughter, Amina. . . . Reluctantly Amina returns home and finds a situation that is far more complicated than her mother let on." (Publisher's note)

"Jacob has written a closely observed, scrupulously detailed story of an extended family dealing with the difficulties of living in America and with each other. That the past is always present in their lives provides a dramatic tension that at once brings them together and threatens to drive them apart." Booklist

Jacobson, Howard

The **Finkler** question. Bloomsbury 2010 307p pa $15

ISBN 978-1-608-19611-1; 1-608-19611-9

"The book follows Julian Treslove, a nebbishy British gentile who, after years of service at the BBC and a slew of failed relationships, finds himself middle-aged, unmoored and unmarried. Tellingly, his primary romantic fantasy involves a woman expiring in his arms. Treslove's defining quality is being bizarrely tabula rasa: His work is impersonating disparate celebrities at parties; a lover sums him up, 'There's something missing from you.' But Treslove is content with himself and his life until the day he is violently robbed by a woman. In the aftermath, Treslove in memory whittles the robber's commands from 'Your jewels' to 'You're Jules' to 'You Jew.' He comes to the shocking realization that he's been the victim of anti-Semitism and spends the rest of the book obsessively trying to fill that 'something missing' in him with a Jewish identity much to the bafflement of friends and family." San Francisco Chron

Jacobson, Howard

Kalooki nights. Simon & Schuster 2007 450p $26

ISBN 978-1-4165-4342-8; 1-4165-4342-2

LC 2006-50183

First published 2006 in the United Kingdom

"Jacobson spins a loose yarn around Max's inquiry into his old friend's crime, leaving plenty of opportunities for caustic insights and hilarious detours, as when the teen-aged Max, on his first double date, embarrasses himself in front of Isaiah Berlin." New Yorker

Jacobson, Howard

The **mighty** Walzer; Howard Jacobson. St. Martins Press 2011 400 p.

ISBN 9780099274728; 9781608196852

LC 99490230

This "coming-of-age story . . . follows Oliver Walzer, member of an extended Jewish family in 1950s Manchester, England. Surrounded by aunts and steeped in the culture brought over from eastern Europe, Oliver starts as a shy and observant youth who begins to discover himself and the world through his natural gift as a Ping-Pong player. As the years progress, Oliver and his mates also discover girls, and the novel follows his sexual awakening and maturing, as told from the perspective of a painfully self-conscious, perspicacious, and somewhat cynical teenager. Oliver moves beyond his local roots and attends Cambridge but later in life returns to Manchester for a visit." (Libr J)

Jaeggy, Fleur

★ **I** am the brother of XX; Fleur Jaeggy ; translated by Gini Alhadeff. New Directions 2017 125 p. (paperback) $14.95

ISBN 9780811225984; 9780811225991

LC 2017000508

This book, by Fleur Jaeggy, translated by Gini Alhadeff, presents a collection of short stories. "In the gloomy title story, a man describes his love-hate relationship with his entrancing older sister. . . . In 'The Heir,' an old woman collapses in a fire that may have been set by her servant. . . . The wealthy, death-obsessed family in 'The Last of the Line' lives out a fable of decadence in decay, where lakes dream and haunting portraits portend murder." (Kirkus Reviews)

"In prismatic translation from the Italian, these tiny tales sparkle with wit and worldly wisdom." Kirkus

Jaffe, Rona

Class reunion; a novel. Delacorte Press 1979 338p

LC 78-25838

"In the Fifties, when rules were rules, college campuses were husband-hunting grounds, and 'going all the way' could ruin a girl's reputation, four Radcliffe students pursue the dream of Mr. Right, Marriage, and Living Happily Ever After. Jaffe builds this book around their 20th reunion, using alternate chapters to flash back through the tales of beautiful Annabel, witty Chris, golden girl Daphne, and insecure Emily. {The author focuses on these women's lives} from college romances to crises which rock them—loveless marriage, divorce, adultery both homosexual and heterosexual, murder, nervous breakdown, birth of a mongoloid child." Libr J

Jakeman, Jane

In the Kingdom of mists. Berley Prime Crime 2004 355p $23.95

ISBN 0-425-19512-0

LC 2003-62800

"The novel tells a dramatic story about crime and perception, art and reality through the eyes of the famous painter, the policeman and a young diplomat. Multilayered and voiced, this is a fascinating attempt to add an extra dimension to this historical crime novel." Guardian

Jakes, John

The **best** western stories of John Jakes; edited by Bill Pronzini and Martin H. Greenberg. Ohio Univ. Press 1991 275p

LC 90-49427

"This collection combines new material with several of Jakes's better efforts published earlier in the pulp magazines of the 1950s." Libr J

Jakes, John

Great stories of the American West; stories by John Jakes {et al.}; edited by Martin H. Greenberg. Fine, D.I. 1994 290p il

LC 94-071113

"This excellent collection of 19 short stories is a suitable introduction to western fiction or a marvelous way to rekindle one's enthusiasm for the genre." Booklist

Jakes, John

Love and war. Harcourt Brace Jovanovich 1984 1019p

LC 84-12895

This sequel to North and South "carries forward the entwined sagas of the Hazards of Pennsylvania, industrialists, and the Mains of South Carolina, plantation owners. . . . The story moves from action on the battlefield to the corridors of Washington to the shipyards of Liverpool. It encompasses deeds heroic and dastardly; passions licit and illicit; spying, assassination plotting and cynical profiteering; and the trying out of new military interventions." Publ Wkly

Followed by Heaven and hell

Jakes, John

★ **North** and South. Harcourt Brace Jovanovich 1982 740p

LC 81-47898

In this first novel of a trilogy the author "introduces two families: The Main family of South Carolina, and the Hazard family of Pennsylvania. The families are basically different. The Mains from the South grow rice and represent the old ways while the Hazards of the North produce iron and are examples of the Industrial Revolution. Their paths converge however, when Orry Main meets George Hazard as the two are entering West Point in 1842. Their friendship is immediate and strong. Orry's family owns slaves, and George, while loving his friend, cannot understand it. As the years pass each grows more entrenched in his beliefs. . . . George's sister Virgilia, an avowed abolitionist, seeks to pry the friendship apart and nearly succeeds. George and Orry's struggles are representative of that which plague the nation." West Coast Rev Books

Followed by Love and war

Jakes, John

On secret service; a novel. Dutton 2000 448p

ISBN 0-525-94544-X

LC 99-47951

"Numerous historical figures are represented accurately and plausibly, and lesser-known events like the horrific Draft Riots in New York are vividly portrayed." Libr J

Jakes, John

Savannah; or, A gift for Mr. Lincoln. Dutton 2004 288p il $23.95

ISBN 0-525-94803-1

LC 2004-49417

This "historical novel recounts the taking of Savannah by Gen. William Tecumseh Sherman's Union Army during Christmas 1864. Fundamentally, it is the story of Sara Lester and her precocious 12-year-old daughter, Hattie, who has an aversion to General Sherman until she finds herself in need of his help. The novel includes a rich cast of characters who, as Union forces move north, are ultimately left to their own devices. The narrative offers adventure, romance, humor, and crime along with the trials of an American city living under what is, to its citizens, occupation by a foreign army." Libr J

James, Eloisa

Four Nights With the Duke; Eloisa James. HarperCollins 2015 384 p. $7.99

ISBN 0062223917; 9780062223913

In this book, "when her fiancé abruptly jilts her . . . Mia Carrington blackmails Evander Brody, the Duke of Pindar and the source of her most cruel teenage humiliation, into marriage. Mia has no choice; she must marry soon or lose the guardianship of her eight-year-old nephew to his greedy, tyrannical uncle. A temporary marriage to a man who can't possibly love her seems like the perfect solution--until Vander decides he wants the real thing, and Mia finds him hard to resist." (Library Journal)

"With peeks at Thorn and India from Lady X, as well as other secondary characters and storylines that enhance and add texture to an already complex plot, James gives readers a welcome opportunity to revisit a popular community and flexes her powerful romantic storytelling muscles, somehow getting even stronger. Historical romance at its smart, poignant best." Kirkus

James, Eloisa

★ The **Lady** Most Willing; A Novel in Three Parts. Julia Quinn, Eloisa James, Connie Brockway. Avon 2012 384 p. $7.99

ISBN 0062107380; 9780062107381

This historical romance is "set in 1819 Scotland. Laird Taran Ferguson goes to great drunken lengths to kidnap four young women—and John Shevington, duke of Bretton, by accident—in hope of finding brides for his nephews, Byron (an English earl) and Robin (improbably, a French count). No one takes Taran seriously or feels at all endangered or coerced, but while they're all stuck in his castle waiting out a storm, romance blossoms of its own accord." (Publishers Weekly)

"Clever, engaging, funny, and guaranteed to keep the pages turning, this well-written Regency 'novel in three parts' by popular authors Quinn, Eloisa James, and Connie Brockway is a pure delight." LJ

James, Eloisa

My American Duchess; by Eloisa James. HarperCollins 2016 400 p. $25.99

ISBN 0062465805; 9780062465801

LC 2016299657

In this book, by Eloisa James, "the arrogant Duke of Trent intends to marry a well-bred Englishwoman. The last woman he would ever consider marrying is the adventuresome Merry Pelford—an American heiress who has infamously jilted two fiancés. But after one provocative encounter with the captivating Merry, Trent desires her more than any woman he has ever met. He is determined to have her as his wife, no matter what it takes. And Trent is a man who always gets what he wants." (Publisher's note)

James, Eloisa

★ **Seven** minutes in heaven; Eloisa James. Avon Books 2017 420 p. (Desperate duchesses by the numbers) (paperback) $7.99

ISBN 9780062660121; 9780062389459; 9780062389466; 0062389459

In this book in the Desperate Duchesses by the Numbers series, by Eloisa James, "witty and elusive Eugenia Snowe has all society begging for one of her premiere governesses-except the powerful Edward Reeve, who bursts into her office with his arrogant demands. . . . He wants Eugenia, and he'll stop at nothing to have her-including kidnapping. Will Eugenia lose her heart in the most reckless gamble of her life, or will she discover the sweetest pleasure she's ever known?" (Publisher's note)

"Another bright, delightful read from a queen of historical romance." Kirkus

James, Eloisa

★ **Three** Weeks With Lady X; by Eloisa James. HarperCollins 2014 400 p. (Desperate Duchesses) $7.99

ISBN 0062223895; 9780062223890

In this book, by Eloisa James, "Thorn Dautry, the powerful bastard son of a duke, decides that he needs a wife. But to marry a lady, Thorn must acquire a gleaming, civilized façade, the specialty of Lady Xenobia India. Exquisite, headstrong, and independent, India vows to make Thorn marriageable in just three weeks. But neither Thorn nor India anticipate the forbidden passion that explodes between them." (Publisher's note)

"Emotionally rewarding and elegantly written, with textured characters and a captivating plot." Kirkus

James, Eloisa

★ The **ugly** duchess; Eloisa James. HarperCollins 2012 366 p. (paperback) $7.99; (ebook) $7.99

ISBN 0062021737; 9780062021731; 9780062197962

LC 2012451739

In this book by Eloisa James, "James Ryburn . . . is forced by his father . . . to marry his best friend, the sweet but notoriously unattractive Theodora Saxby, so her dowry can cover [his] gambling debts. When Theo . . . realizes all they wanted was her money, she demands that Islay leave her--and leave England. . . . When Islay returns to England, he is a very different man, and Theo must decide whether to let him into her heart." (Publishers Weekly)

James, Eloisa

When beauty tamed the beast; [by] Eloisa James. Avon 2011 374p pa $7.99

ISBN 0062021273; 9780062021274; 978-0-06-202127-4

LC 2011658844

"Her vivacious beauty, a rejection by her current princely flirt, and a series of false assumptions have the entire ton gleefully thinking Linnet Berry Thrynne is carrying a royal bastard—and, therefore, is now unmarriageable. So she finds herself accompanying the Duke of Windebank to the wilds of Wales as the perfect bride for his son, a brilliant physician and impotent nobleman with a beastly reputation, in order to ensure the succession. But Linnet is not pregnant, and Piers Yelverton, Earl of Marchant, is not impotent. He is, however, in possession of a rather beastly temper, rude manners, and a determination not to marry or fall in love—a challenge that Linnet is more than willing to accept. . . . Graced with sly humor, addictive dialog, elegant prose, and a skillfully woven subtext, this smart, deliciously sensual twist on a fairy tale classic is a breathtaking addition to James's series of reimagined fairy tales. Readers will be clambering for more." Libr J

James, Henry

Complete stories, 1864-1874. Library of Am. 1999 972p $40

ISBN 1-883011-70-1

LC 98-53919

James, Henry

Complete stories, 1874-1884. Library of Am. 1999 941p $35

ISBN 1-883011-63-9

LC 98-19252

Includes bibliographical references

James, Henry

Complete stories, 1884-1891. Library of Am. 1999 904p $35

ISBN 1-883011-64-7

LC 98-19250

Includes bibliographical references

James, Henry

Complete stories, 1892-1898. Library of Am. 1996 948p

ISBN 1-883011-09-4

LC 95-23463

James, Henry

Complete stories, 1898-1910. Library of Am. 1996 946p $35

ISBN 1-883011-10-8

LC 95-23462

James, Henry

Daisy Miller; introduction by Elizabeth Hardwick; notes by James Danly. Modern Library 2002 xxiv, 80p pa $14.50

ISBN 0-375-75966-2

LC 2001-44626

First published 1878

"The book's title character is a young American woman traveling in Europe with her mother. There she is courted by Frederick Forsyth Winterbourne, an American living abroad. In her innocence, Daisy is compromised by her friendship with an Italian man. Her behavior shocks Winterbourne and the other Americans living in Italy, and they shun her. Only after she dies does Winterbourne recognize that her actions reflected her spontaneous, genuine, and unaffected nature and that his suspicions of her were unwarranted." Merriam-Webster's Ency of Lit

James, Henry

The **golden** bowl. Knopf 1992 596p $22

ISBN 0-679-41733-8

LC 92-52927

First published 1904 by Scribner

Maggie Verver, daughter of an American millionaire living in London, marries an indigent "Italian prince who has had a love affair with Maggie's closest friend, Charlotte Stant. Charlotte visits the pair and continues her intimacy. Then she marries Maggie's father. Everybody tries to keep secret from the others that he or she knows all that has happened or is happening. The complications are solved when Maggie's father goes back to America with Charlotte. James depicts with all the subtlety of his late style the cultural and moral involvements that follow on international marriage and irregular sex relationships." Benet's Reader's Ency of Am Lit

James, Henry

★ The **portrait** of a lady. Knopf 1991 xxv, 626p $20

ISBN 0-679-40562-3

LC 91-52999

First published 1881 by Houghton

"This is one of the best James's early works, in which he presents various types of American character transplanted into a European environment. The story centres in Isabel Archer, the 'Lady,' an attractive American girl. Around her we have the placid old American banker, Mr. Touchett; his hard repellent wife; his ugly, invalid, witty, charming son Ralph, whom England has thoroughly assimilated; and the outspoken, brilliant, indomitably American journalist Henrietta Stackpole. Isabel refuses the offer of marriage of a typical English peer, the excellent Lord Warburton, and of a bulldog-like New Englander, Casper Goodwood, to fall a victim, under the influence of the slightly sinister Madame Merle (another cosmopolitan American), to a worthless and spiteful dilettante, Gilbert Osmond, who marries her for her fortune and ruins her life; but to whom she remains loyal in spite of her realization of his vileness." Oxford Companion to Engl Lit. 6th edition

James, Henry

The **turn** of the screw; edited by Allan Lloyd Smith. J.M. Dent 1993 xxxii, 139p pa $8.95

ISBN 0-460-87299-0

LC 94-125860

First published 1898

This novella "is told from the viewpoint of the leading character, a governess in love with her employer, who goes to an isolated English estate to take charge of Miles and Flora, two attractive and precocious children. She gradually realizes that her young charges are under the evil influence of two ghosts, Peter Quint, the ex-steward, and Miss Jessel, their former governess. At the climax of the story, she enters into open conflict with the children, as a result of which Flora is alienated and Miles dies of fright." Reader's Ency. 4th edition

James, Henry

★ The **wings** of the dove. Modern Lib. 1993 711p

ISBN 0-679-60067-1

LC 93-15338

First published 1902 by Scribner

"The story is set in London and Venice. Kate Croy is a Londoner who encourages her secret fiancé, Merton Densher, to woo and marry Milly Theale, a wealthy young American who is dying of a mysterious malady. This, Kate reasons, although Milly will die soon, she will at least be happily in love, Merton will inherit her fortune, and Kate and Merton can marry and be rich. Shortly after Milly learns of Merton's and Kate's motives, she dies, leaving Merton a legacy that he is too guilt-ridden to accept. Kate is unwilling to forgo the inheritance, and she and Merton part forever, their relationship destroyed by Milly's unwittingly prescient gift." Merriam-Webster's Ency of Lit

James, Marlon, 1970-

The **book** of night women. Riverhead Books 2009 417p $26.95

ISBN 1-59448-857-6; 978-1-59448-857-3

LC 2008-46309

This "is the story of Lilith, born into slavery on a Jamaican sugar plantation at the end of the eighteenth century. Even at her birth, the slave women around her recognize a . . . power that they—and she—will come to both revere and fear. The Night Women, as they call themselves, have long been plotting a slave revolt, and as Lilith comes of age and reveals the extent of her power, they see her as the key to their plans." (Publisher's note)

This novel "is both beautifully written and devastating. While the gruesome history of slavery in the Americas is a story we may dare to think we already know, every page of 'The Book of Night Women' reminds us that we don't know nearly enough. . . . While his cast includes sadistic plantation owners and vicious overseers, 'house Negroes' and field slaves, James deftly avoids the clichéd melodrama such characters all too often inspire." N Y Times Book Rev

James, Marlon, 1970-

★ A **brief** history of seven killings; a novel. Marlon James. Riverhead Books 2014 560 p. (hardback) $28.95

ISBN 159448600X; 9781594486005

LC 2014018475

Man Booker Prize (2015)

In this novel, by Marlon James, "an assassination attempt on Bob Marley stokes this . . . portrait of Jamaica, encompassing a host of gangsters, CIA agents, journalists and businessmen. . . . The opening chapters, set in late 1976, evoke an attempt on his life sparked by tensions between gangs representing rival political parties." (Kirkus Reviews)

"This is a breakthrough novel not only for the author but also for Caribbean and world literature. The Kingston milieu (and its extensions, including New York) is made horrifyingly believable; the patois is rhythmic, slangy, and often quite funny." Booklist

Includes bibliographical references and index

James, P. D.

The **black** tower. Scribner 1975 271p

"Adam Dalgliesh, convalescing after a severe illness, arrives at Toynton Grange (Dorset coast), the rest home for the young disabled, just too late to find out why his old friend Father Baddeley had sent for him. The monk-robed Wilfred Anstey and his staff are an odd lot, as are the few patients, all in wheelchairs. There's already been a suspicious suicide, and Dalgliesh is not satisfied that the old priest's death was caused by myocarditis alone. Handicapped by poor health, he finally manages to unearth the secret of the grange." Barzun. Cat of Crime. Rev and enl edition

James, P. D.

A **certain** justice. Knopf 1997 364p $25

ISBN 0-375-40109-1

LC 97-36889

"In obedience to the classic crime-writing genre, James finally offers up the guilty party, resolving a complicated plot with impeccable logic. But there the symmetry ends, for the moral and emotional questions she asks do not admit of such neatness." N Y Times Book Rev

James, P. D.

Death comes to Pemberley; [a novel] / P. D. James. 1st United States ed. Alfred A. Knopf 2011 291p

ISBN 0571283578; 9780307959850; 9780571283576

LC 2011941315

This book "draws the characters of Jane Austen's . . . novel 'Pride and Prejudice' into a tale of murder and emotional mayhem. Six years since Elizabeth and Darcy embarked on their life together at Pemberley, Darcy's magnificent estate. . . . Elizabeth has found her footing as the chatelaine of the great house. They have two fine sons . . . [and] there is optimistic talk about the prospects of marriage for Darcy's sister Georgiana. And preparations are under way for their much-anticipated annual autumn ball. Then, on the eve of the ball . . . a coach careens up the drive carrying Lydia, Elizabeth's disgraced sister, who with her husband, the very dubious Wickham, has been banned from Pemberley. She stumbles out of the carriage, hysterical, shrieking that Wickham has been murdered." (Publisher's note)

James, P. D.

Death in holy orders. Knopf 2001 415p

ISBN 0-375-41255-7

LC 2001-88108

In this mystery "almost everything happens behind the closed doors of St. Anselm's, a small Anglican theological college set on a windy cliff abutting the sea. Commander Adam Dalgliesh, as always both wistful and stern, returns to St. Anselm's, where he spent a few blissful boyhood summers, to investigate the death of a student, but the case quickly expands as bodies begin to fall like so many dominoes. It's a pleasure to read James at the top of her form, as she often is here." New Yorker

James, P. D.

★ **Death** of an expert witness. Scribner 1977 322p

LC 77-21530

"Basically James is a novelist who happens to put her character into mystery stories. She is just as much interested in people and their relationships as she is in the conventions of the genre. And being the perceptive and sensitive writer she is, she constructs books that can be read on several levels." N Y Times Book Rev

James, P. D.

Devices and desires. Knopf 1990 433p

LC 89-45305

First published 1989 in the United Kingdom

"As always with P. D. James, the whodunit element is the lagniappe, so interesting are her characters, so absorbing her depiction of time and place, so rich the texture of the tale she tells." N Y Times Book Rev

James, P. D.

Innocent blood. Scribner 1980 311p

LC 79-28699

"What starts things moving in the tale is a young (adopted) woman's determination to find her real parents. This headstrong wish is gratified, creating social difficulties, deep changes in personal relations, the plotting of a murder, the experience of jail, and miscellaneous sexual activity. The diverse characters are admirably drawn and the author's fingerwork in tying and untying threads is as deft as her touches of sordid life and as nimble as her prose." Barzun. Cat of Crime. Rev and enl edition

James, P. D.

The **lighthouse**. Knopf 2005 335p $25.95

ISBN 0-307-26291-X

LC 2005-51039

This novel "is too rooted in genre conventions to count originality as its strong suit. But it has deviousness to burn, and it also offers other enticements. It's the kind of book that boasts a wryly humorous Scrabble scene, not to mention a Scrabble-lover's vocabulary." N Y Times Book Rev

James, P. D.

Original sin. Knopf 1995 416p

LC 94-26094

First published 1994 in the United Kingdom

A mystery featuring Commander Adam Dalgliesh of Scotland Yard. "Innocent House, a nineteenth-century pile on the Thames that accommodates the Peverell Press, presides over this novel of revenge. After Gerard Etienne, the new chairman of the press, announces his plan to sell the house, he ends up dead, with the head of a toy snake stuffed in his mouth. In this elaborate novel, the author . . . does what she does best: shows that guilt and blame have no single address." New Yorker

James, P. D.

The **private** patient. Alfred A. Knopf 2008 416p $25.95

ISBN 978-0-307-27077-1; 0-307-27077-7

LC 2008-27137

"The book begins by introducing investigative journalist Rhoda Gradwyn, whose face is marked by a disfiguring scar. She chooses prominent plastic surgeon George Chandler-Powell to remove it at his private clinic in Cheverell Manor. . . . It's a place where the comfortably situated can have their cosmetic work done in privacy — and not everyone welcomes the arrival of a professional snoop. The evening after her surgery, Gradwyn is murdered. Dalgleish and his team are called in to solve the mystery, then have to deal with a second murder. . . . The investigation disrupts lives and disturbs secrets far beyond the little group at the manor. James is in excellent form in 'Patient.' She engages the brain as she entertains with apt descriptions and wry asides, and sets the reader to thinking beyond the obvious." St. Louis Post-Dispatch

James, P. D.

The **skull** beneath the skin. Scribner 1982 328p

LC 82-5981

"Fading actress Clarissa Lisle has been receiving frightening notes and is terrified of failing in her comeback performance, a revival of 'The Duchess of Malfi', held on a small private island off Dorset. Her husband hires detective Cordelia Gray to stop the notes. Once on the island, Cordelia discovers that nearly everyone there has a good reason to hate Clarissa, who is soon found gruesomely battered to death. The isolated group of suspects, hidden clues, and macabre atmosphere of an island castle complete with skulls and underground passageways make a pleasant traditional mystery. But James is never superficial, and her in-depth characterizations and excellent writing reveal complex relationships, motives, and human frailties." Libr J

James, P. D.

A **taste** for death. Knopf 1986 459p

LC 86-45273

Sir Paul Berowne, a minister of the Crown, is found with his throat cut in the vestry of St. Matthew's church in London. A tramp has also been killed. Dalgliesh and his assistant Kate Miskin seek the solution to the mystery in the victims' past. All the family members and witnesses have something to conceal

This "book is about murder and the way murder changes everything. . . . It is also about the human condition in London today, enlarged by a sense of the British past that stretches back like a rich and barely dwindling perspective." N Y Times Book Rev

James, P. D.

★ An **unsuitable** job for a woman. Scribner 1973 216p

First published 1972 in the United Kingdom

"In this book James's usual investigator, Chief Superintendent Dalgliesh, plays only a minor part. It is Cordelia Gray, the young, intelligent, and clear-thinking owner of an unsuccessful detective agency, who solves the case. She is hired by Sir Ronald Callender to investigate the death by suicide of his son, Mark. Miss Gray's meticulous research leads her to suspect that Mark was murdered and makes her a prime target for murder. There are suspenseful moments, close calls, and a very surprising encounter, at last, between Cordelia and Supt. Dalgliesh." Shapiro. Fic for Youth. 3d edition

Jamison, Leslie

The **gin** closet. Free Press 2010 274p $25

ISBN 1-4391-5321-3; 978-1-4391-5321-5

LC 2009-20264

"Stella, in her 20s, is struggling to make ends meet in New York, working for a demanding writer and sleeping with a married man, when she learns that her mother had a runaway sister named Tilly. She tracks her down and finds an aging alcoholic, living in a trailer in Nevada. Tilly tells Stella that she has a son named Abe, a banker in San Francisco, who has offered her a place to stay, if she cleans up. So Stella helps her aunt to detox and they hit the road, moving into Abe's South of Market loft, where the three form a fragile new family, all hoping to make a better story out of their lives. . . . [This] is no escapist fantasy but a slow and steady heartbreak. It is also exquisitely beautiful. Jamison writes like a poet, her imagery breathtaking, her sentences unfurling unpredictably, to the novel's devastating end." San Francisco Chron

Jance, Judith A.

Birds of prey; a novel of suspense. [by] J.A. Lance. Morrow 2001 390p

ISBN 0-380-97407-X

LC 00-59445

"Retired Seattle cop J. P. Beaumont accompanies his newlywed, eightysomething grandmother and her crusty hubby, Lars Jenssen, on an Alaskan cruise to act as a chaperone of sorts. The jaded protagonist is inadvertently forced to masquerade as an FBI agent when Dr. Harrison Featherman's shrill blonde wife Margaret is tossed overboard, and the crime is captured on ship security cameras." Libr J

Jance, Judith A.

Devil's claw; a Joanna Brady mystery. [by] J.A. Jance. Morrow 2000 374p

ISBN 0-380-97501-7

LC 00-25805

"The Arizona desert, as usual in Jance's mysteries, plays an unforgettable part in this atmospheric tale." Publ Wkly

Jance, Judith A.

Queen of the night; [by] J. A. Jance. William Morrow 2010 358p $25.99

ISBN 978-0-06-123924-3; 0-06-123924-0

LC 2009-38976

This "suspense novel featuring former homicide detective Brandon Walker and his wife, novelist Diana Ladd . . . , spans some 50 years, from a murder in 1959 in San Diego to a rash of killings in Thousand Oaks, Calif., and Tucson, Ariz., in 2009. Interwoven with these crimes are legends of the Tohono O'odham Indians (aka the Desert People) and the lives of such contemporary Native people as Lani Walker, Brandon and Diana's adopted daughter. Jance's masterful handling of a complex cast of characters makes it easy for the reader to appreciate the intricate web of relationships that bind them across generations." Publ Wkly

Jance, Judith A.

Skeleton canyon; a Joanna Brady mystery. {by} J. A. Jance. Avon Bks. 1997 373p

LC 97-3217

"When high-school valedictorian Bree O'Brien is found dead in the southeastern Arizona mountains, suspicion falls on her boyfriend, Ignacio Ybarra, who refuses to explain his fresh cuts and bruises. But the case isn't that simple, as Coshise County Sheriff Joanna Brady learns. . . . Jance's regional knowledge runs deep, whether she writes about troubled Anglo-Hispanic relations along the border or the surprising power of Arizona thunderstorms." Publ Wkly

Jarvis, Stephen

★ **Death** and Mr. Pickwick; a novel. Stephen Jarvis. Farrar, Straus & Giroux 2015 816 p. illustrations (hardback) $30

ISBN 0374139660; 9780374139667

LC 2015002954

This novel by Stephen Jarvis looks at "the writing and publication of Charles Dickens's first novel, 'The Posthumous Papers of the Pickwick Club,' in 1836. Written under the pen name Boz, Pickwick made Dickens perhaps the first literary celebrity. But who deserves credit for creating Pickwick, the book's protagonist: Dickens, the man who created the text, or Robert Seymour, the caricaturist who came up with the name and the graphic image of the rotund Englishman?" (Publishers Weekly)

"Readers don't have to buy Jarvis' argument to appreciate his teeming chronicle. Packed with interesting characters and tall tales, and ranging in setting from sporting clubs (read drinking clubs) to the theater to a factory floor to a debtors prison, this is fiction writ large." Booklist

Jaswal, Balli Kaur

Erotic stories for Punjabi widows; a novel. Balli Kaur Jaswal. HarperCollins 2017 304 p. $26.99

ISBN 0062645129; 9780062645128

In this book, by Balli Kaur Jaswall, "Nikki, a law school dropout, impulsively takes a job teaching a 'creative writing' course at the community center in . . . London's close-knit Punjabi community. . . . [T]he proper Sikh widows who show up are expecting to learn basic English literacy . . . When one of the widows finds a book of sexy stories in English and shares it with the class, Nikki realizes that . . . her students have a wealth of fantasies and memories." (Publisher's note)

"Jaswal's charming debut features an engaging protagonist who longs to break free from her more traditional mother's expectations and who is still smarting from her father's death, but it's the portrayal of the women in Nikki's class that is the highlight: these women are considered invisible, but through their writing they can be seen and their desires and dreams can be acknowledged." Publishers' Weekly

Jeffries, Sabrina

'Twas the night after Christmas; Sabrina Jeffries. Gallery Books 2012 368 p. (hardcover) $19.99

ISBN 1451642466; 1451642504; 9781451642469; 9781451642506

LC 2012015020

In this book by Sabrina Jeffries, "when a meddling but warmhearted lady's companion tries to force a reconciliation between a dowager countess and her son, no one can guess at the resentment and betrayals that will be unearthed. . . . Meanwhile, Camilla and the earl grow ever closer, and for the first time, Devonmont considers marriage, though Camilla knows a match between them is unacceptable." (Kirkus Reviews)

Jemc, Jac

★ The **grip** of it; Jac Jemc. Farrar, Straus & Giroux 2017 276 p. (paperback) $15

ISBN 9780374716073; 9780374536916

LC 2016041347

This novel, by Jac Jemc, "is a chilling literary horror novel about a young couple haunted by their newly purchased home. . . . This house, which sits between a lake and a forest, has its own plans for the unsuspecting couple. As Julie and James try to establish a sense of normalcy, the home and its surrounding terrain become the locus of increasingly strange happenings." (Publisher's note)

"Shivery and smart. A book that brings the legacy of Henry James into the modern world with great effect." Kirkus

Jemisin, N. K., 1972-

★ The **fifth** season; N. K. Jemisin. Orbit 2015 512 p. map (The broken earth) (trade pbk.) $15.99

ISBN 0316229296; 9780316229296

LC 2015002138

Hugo Award: Best Novel (2016)

"In a world plagued by cataclysmic tectonic activity, the only way to survive is to constantly prepare for the next fifth season. But no one is ready for the scope of the disaster that strikes when the capital city of a continent-wide empire is subsumed in a massive rift that spreads hundreds of miles. Using alternating points of view, Jemisin explores the lives of several characters in the years leading up to the cataclysmic disaster." (Library Journal)

"Jemisin's graceful prose and gritty setting provide the perfect backdrop for this fascinating tale of determined characters fighting to save a doomed world." Pub Wkly

Other titles in this series are:
The obelisk gate (2016)
The stone sky (2017)

Jemisin, N. K., 1972-

The **hundred** thousand kingdoms. Orbit 2010 427p (Inheritance trilogy) pa $13.99

ISBN 9780316043915

LC 2009-02075

The first volume of the projected Inheritance Trilogy. "When her mother dies mysteriously, outcast barbarian Yeine Darr answers a summons to the grand city of Sky from her grandfather, King Dekarta Arameri. Proclaimed one of three heirs to the throne of the Hundred Thousand Kingdoms, Yeine must learn the customs of the skyborne capital and its ruling elite before she succumbs to their treachery. Debut author Jemisin creates a mesmerizingly exotic world where fallen gods serve as slaves to the ruling class and murder and ambition go hand in hand." Libr J

Other titles in this series are:
The broken kingdoms (2010)
The kingdom of gods (2011)

Jemisin, N. K., 1972-

The **killing** moon; N.K. Jemisin. Orbit 2012 440 p.

ISBN 0316187283; 9780316187282

LC 2011028110

This fantasy novel by N. K. Jemisin takes place in "the ancient city-state of Gujaareh, [where] peace is the only law. Upon its rooftops and amongst the shadows of its cobbled streets wait the Gatherers - the keepers of this peace. Priests of the dream-goddess, their duty is to harvest the magic of the sleeping mind and use it to heal, soothe . . . and kill those judged corrupt. But when a conspiracy blooms within Gujaareh's great temple, Ehiru—the most famous of the city's Gatherers—must question everything he knows. Someone, or something, is murdering dreamers in the goddess' name, stalking its prey both in Gujaareh's alleys and the realm of dreams. Ehiru must now protect the woman he was sent to kill—or watch the city be devoured by war and forbidden magic." (Publisher's note)

Jemisin, N. K., 1972-

★ The **obelisk** gate; N. K. Jemisin. Orbit 2016 448 p. map (The broken earth) (ebook) $48; (paperback) $15.99

ISBN 9780316388511; 9780316229265

LC 2016016502

Hugo Award: Best Novel (2017)

In this book, by N. K. Jemisin, "this is the way the world ends, for the last time. The season of endings grows darker, as civilization fades into the long cold night. Essun—once Damaya, once Syenite, now avenger—has found shelter, but not her daughter. Instead there is Alabaster Tenring, destroyer of the world, with a request. But if Essun does what he asks, it would seal the fate of the Stillness forever." (Publisher's note)

"The Stillness and those who dwell there are vividly drawn, and the threats they face are both timely and tangible. Once again Jemisin immerses readers in a complex and intricate world of warring powers, tangled morals, and twisting motivations." Pub Wkly

Jemisin, N. K., 1972-

★ The **stone** sky; N.K. Jemisin. Orbit 2017 445 p. map (The broken earth) (paperback) $16.99

ISBN 9780316229241; 9780316402699

LC 2017017064

Hugo Finalist: Best Novel (2018)

Nebula Finalist: Best Novel (2017)

In this book in The Broken Earth series, by N. K. Jemisin, "the Moon will soon return. Whether this heralds the destruction of humankind or something worse will depend on two women. Essun has inherited the power of Alabaster Tenring. With it, she hopes to find her daughter Nassun. . . . For Nassun, her mother's mastery of the Obelisk Gate comes too late. She has seen the evil of the world, and accepted what her mother will not admit." (Publisher's note)

"Vivid characters, a tautly constructed plot, and outstanding world-building meld into an impressive and timely story of abused, grieving survivors fighting to fix themselves and save the remnants of their shattered home." Pub Wkly

Jen, Gish

The **love** wife. Knopf 2004 379p $24.95

ISBN 1-400-04213-5

LC 2004-40917

"In a story told from multiple points of view, Jen turns stereotypes upside down by giving each character an issue, label or characteristic you might not expect." USA Today

Jen, Gish

Mona in the promised land. Knopf 1996 303p

LC 95-44447

This work "has a wide-ranging exuberance that's unusual in what is still—to its credit—a realistic novel. Ms. Jen doesn't sacrifice her characters to satire. And her story can take the broad view even while it focuses on smaller, more personal matters because she works in so many voices and because she includes so many perfectly timed set pieces." N Y Times Book Rev

Jen, Gish

Typical American. Plume 1992 296p (Plume contemporary fiction) pa $13.95

ISBN 0-452-26774-9

LC 91-33814

First published 1991 by Houghton Mifflin

"Yefing Chang becomes Ralph Chang in America and begins a hard struggle to achieve the American dream—a career, a family and a home of his own. In poverty, he succeeds finally to win a doctoral degree, a college position, a happy marriage to Helen, two delightful daughters and a close reunion with his older sister, Theresa. The dream becomes a nightmare when he meets Grover Ding whose corrupt influence over Ralph and Helen begins to unravel all that the Changs have managed to achieve. This is an honest novel that does not promise happy endings and recognizes the human weaknesses that can destroy a family's stability." Shapiro. Fic for Youth. 3d edition

Followed by Mona in the promised land (1996)

Jen, Gish

Who's Irish? stories. Knopf 1999 207p

ISBN 0-375-40621-2

LC 98-42801

"Jen's characters, Chinese immigrants and their American-born children, find themselves commuting between two cultures, between familial expectations and their own yearnings for self-definition, between remembered traditions and shiny, new dreams." N Y Times Book Rev

Jen, Gish

★ **World** and town; a novel. Alfred A. Knopf 2010 386p $26.95

ISBN 978-0-307-27219-5; 0-307-27219-2

LC 2010-07057

Gish sets this novel in "an idyllic New England town, the kind of place we like to carelessly fetishize as the real America. At the center is 68-year-old Hattie Kong, a descendant of Confucius who's still reeling from the back-to-back deaths of her husband and her best friend. Her life, flattened by grief, is shaken up when a former lover moves to town and a family of Cambodian immigrants takes up in the trailer down the hill. Everybody in these pages, it seems, is in desperate need of a fresh start and a sense of belonging. It's into this mix that Jen gracefully introduces some of the great issues of our time: how the shock of 9/11 reverberated from city to town; how lost souls can cling meanly to fundamentalism; how it feels when a chain store bulldozes into a mom-and-pop community, or a family farm finally collapses." Entertainment Wkly

Jenkins, Beverly

★ **Breathless**; Beverly Jenkins. HarperCollins 2017 376 p. (ebook) $7.99; $7.99

ISBN 9780062389039; 0062389025; 9780062389022

In this book, by Beverly Jenkins, "as manager of one of the finest hotels in Arizona Territory, Portia Carmichael has respect and stability—qualities sorely missing from her harsh childhood. She refuses to jeopardize that by hitching herself to the wrong man. Suitors are plentiful, but none of them has ever looked quite as tempting as the family friend who just rode into town…and none has looked at her with such intensity and heat." (Publisher's note)

"Her writing is both sexy and smart, and her characters come to life as real people the reader will want to know better. A thrilling and enjoyable read." Kirkus

Jenkins, Beverly

Forbidden; Beverly Jenkins. HarperCollins 2016 384 p. (paperback) $7.99

ISBN 0062389009; 9780062389008

In this Western romance novel, by Beverly Jenkins, "Rhine Fontaine is building the successful life he's always dreamed of—one that depends upon him passing for White. But for the first time in years, he wishes he could step out from behind the façade. The reason: Eddy Carmichael, the young woman he rescued in the desert. Outspoken, defiant, and beautiful, Eddy tempts Rhine in ways that could cost him everything . . . and the price seems worth paying." (Publisher's note)

"The characters are strong and appealing in this excellent western historical romance, with its fascinating background and modern implications." Booklist

Jenkins, Victoria

An **unattended** death; Victoria Jenkins. The Permanent Press 2012 214 p. $28

ISBN 1579622844; 9781579622848

LC 2012016405

In this mystery novel by Victoria Jenkins "Anne Paris is found dead, her body floating in the slough at the bottom of her family's remote summer property on an island in Puget Sound, the apparent victim of a sailing accident. Irene Chavez, the lone female detective in a rural Washington State sheriff's department, is assigned to investigate the death of this privileged young psychiatrist." (Publisher's note)

Jenoff, Pam

★ The **Ambassador's** Daughter; by Pam Jenoff. Harlequin Books 2013 336 p. (paperback) $14.95

ISBN 0778315096; 9780778315094

In this historical romance by Pam Jenoff, "conflicted Margot accompanies her German diplomat father to Paris for the treaty negotiations following WWI. . . . Margot deliberately delays . . . the impending union with her injured fiancé Stefan. . . . Her world changes when she meets Krysia--a pianist from Poland with radical political affiliations, an ethereal appearance, and an affinity for forthright speech--and then Georg, the striking but troubled German naval officer." (Publishers Weekly)

Jensen, Jane

Dante's equation; Jane Jensen. Ballantine Books 2003 484p ill. $15.95

ISBN 0345430379; 9780345430373

LC 2003273636

In this book, "physics professor Jill Talcott is experimenting with energy waves that somehow directly influence matter and living things. Journalist Denton Wyle . . . track[s] down the scattered fragments of a manuscript written in 1944 in Auschwitz by Yosef Kobinski. A kabbalist and physicist of genius, Kobinski mathematically described a dimension of good and evil. . . . In Jerusalem, rigid, self-absorbed Rabbi Aharon Handalman studies the Bible for coded messages supposedly buried in the text. Astonishingly, he finds dozens of menacing references to Kobinski and weapons. . . . Jill's experiment . . . causes an explosion that kills dozens of innocents. This attracts Handalman's attention—and also that of Calder Farris, part of a secret Defense Department group whose purpose is to acquire possible new weapons technology and either co-opt or silence the inventors. Ambitious Jill is minded to accept Farris's job offer, until Handalman shows up and tells her about Kobinski." (Kirkus)

Jensen, Liz

The **uninvited**; Liz Jensen. Bloomsbury Publishing PLC 2012 307 p. (hardcover) $25

ISBN 1608199924; 9781608199921

LC 2012451595

In this horror novel, by Liz Jensen, "across the world, children are killing their families. . . . As chilling murders by children grip the country, anthropologist Hesketh Lock has his own mystery to solve: a bizarre scandal in the Taiwan timber industry. . . . Nothing obvious connects Hesketh's Asian case with the atrocities back home. . . . But when Hesketh's Taiwan contact dies shockingly . . . he is forced to acknowledge possibilities that defy . . . rational principles." (Publisher's note)

Jensen, Nancy

The **sisters**; Nancy Jensen. 1st ed. St. Martin's Press 2011 viii, 324 p.p

ISBN 9780312542702; 0312542704

LC 2011025854

This book is set in "hardscrabble Kentucky in the 1920s, . . . [and tells the story of] Bertie Fischer and her older sister Mabel [who] have no one but each other--with perhaps a sweetheart for Bertie waiting in the wings. But on the day that Bertie receives her eighth-grade diploma, good intentions go terribly wrong. A choice made in desperate haste sets off a chain of misunderstandings that will divide the sisters and reverberate through three generations of women. . . . From the Depression through World War II and Vietnam, and smaller events both tragic and joyful, Bertie and Mabel forge unexpected identities that are shaped by unspeakable secrets. As the sisters have daughters and granddaughters of their own, they discover that both love and betrayal are even more complicated than they seem." (Publisher's note)

Includes bibliographical references and index.

Jerkins, Grant

The **ninth** step; Grant Jerkins. 1st ed. Berkley Prime Crime 2012 p. cm. (paperback) $15.00

ISBN 9780425255988

LC 2012014770

This novel, by Grant Jerkins, follows "Helen, . . . a recovering alcoholic struggling through a twelve-step program. Now it's time to make amends for . . . a hit and run accident that killed the wife of school teacher Edgar Woolrich. . . . [T]he ninth step begins with a lie--the first of many as their relationship grows, and Helen knows it's far too late to reveal the truth to a man she's come to love. Then one day, she receives an anonymous note: Does he know you killed his wife?" (Publisher's note)

Jewell, Lisa

The **making** of us; a novel. by Lisa Jewell. 1st Atria paperback ed. Atria Books 2012 403 p. (paperback) $16.00

ISBN 9781451609110; 9781451609134

LC 2012009042

This novel, by Lisa Jewell, is "about three strangers who are brought together by the father they never knew. . . . Lydia, Dean and Robyn live very different lives, but each of them . . . has always felt that something was missing. . . . [A] letter is about to arrive that will turn their lives upside down. It is a letter containing a secret . . . that will bind them together and show them what love and family and friendship really mean." (Publisher's note)

Jewett, Sarah Orne

The **country** of the pointed firs and other stories. Modern Lib. 1995 247p

ISBN 0-679-60173-2

LC 95-2831

In addition to the title story, this volume also includes the following: The queen's twin; A Dunnet shepherdess; The foreigner; William's wedding

Jhabvala, Ruth Prawer

East into Upper East; plain tales from New York and New Delhi. Counterpoint 1998 314p

ISBN 1-88717-850-3

LC 98-34881

"Jhabvala is a connoisseur of divided souls, conceiving characters whose inner longings are at odds with their outer protective coloration—Indians who covet and achieve more tidy, 'modernized' existences, then feel as if someone had stolen their life force; Westerners who eagerly hand themselves over to India's chaotic bliss, then find it too rigorous to endure." N Y Times Book Rev

Jhabvala, Ruth Prawer

★ **Heat** and dust. Harper & Row 1976 181p

First published 1975 in the United Kingdom

"The juxtaposition of past and present India is explored in this novel. The 1923 storyline tells of Olivia, who, though married to a British officer stationed in India, falls madly in love with an Indian prince. It is also about Olivia's husband's granddaughter by a second marriage, who has come to India to discover the details of Olivia's life but finds that, although India and women have become modernized, she must face many of the same choices as Olivia. The intrusion of British culture on India's own traditions and values is a second theme in the novel." Shapiro. Fic for Youth. 3d edition

Jhabvala, Ruth Prawer

My nine lives. Shoemaker & Hoard 2004 277p $25

ISBN 1-59376-028-0

"Jhabvala name-drops Chekhov, and this is no pretension given the grace of her spiraling plots, the depth of her psychology, the elegance of her humor, the subtly of her eroticism, and her masterfully concise descriptions of imperiled households, eccentric personalities, sexual enthrallment, unexpected alliances, and transcendent love." Booklist

Jhabvala, Ruth Prawer

Out of India; selected stories. Morrow 1986 288p

LC 85-25961

"Out of a web of subtle but not precious ironies, couched in a limpid style, arises a sense of the author's obvious love-hate attitude toward this land that is so difficult to live in, for foreigner and native alike. Jhabvala sensitively explores the tense juncture between Western and Indian cultures; plots and characters glow with realism and energy." Booklist

Jiang Rong

Wolf totem; a novel. translated by Howard Goldblatt. Penguin Press 2008 527p $26.95

ISBN 978-1-59420-156-1; 1-59420-156-0

LC 2007-37554

Original Chinese edition, 2004

"The novel's literary claims are shaky; and Jiang Rong's apparent wish to transform China's national character through a benign conservationism is compromised by his boy-scoutish arguments for toughness. Yet few books about today's China can match Wolf Totem as a guide to the troubled self-images of so many of its people as they stumble, grappling with some inconvenient truths of their own, into modernity." N Y Times Book Rev

Jiles, Paulette

The **color** of lightning; a novel. William Morrow 2009 349p $25.99

ISBN 978-0-06-169044-0; 0-06-169044-9

LC 2008-46339

"It is 1863, and Britt Johnson saddles up with a few other men from his North Texas settlement to ride to a nearby town for supplies. Johnson, a free African American, has brought his beautiful wife and three small children to this desolate, dangerous country to build a life he hopes will be freer of racism than it would have been in Kentucky. While he is gone, a war party of 700 Comanche and Kiowa descend into the valley, killing the men and kidnapping women and children. His wife and two younger children are taken as captives. . . . Based on the true story of an African American who was legendary for his ability to bargain with Native Americans for the return of captives, the novel also tells the fictional tale of a well-meaning, but naive young Quaker from Philadelphia, Samuel Hammond, who is sent to run a regional Bureau of Indian Affairs. The contrast between Johnson, a pragmatic man of action, and Hammond, an idealist who struggles with the ambiguities of reality, echoes the history of a period when government programs and westward expansion collided, ruinously, with Native cultures. Jiles' spare and melancholy prose is the perfect language for this tale in which survival necessitates brutality." Seattle Times

Jiles, Paulette

Enemy women. Morrow 2002 321p

ISBN 0-06-621444-0

LC 2001-40200

"For Adair Randolph Colley, at 18 the eldest daughter of a widowed Missouri Ozarks schoolmaster and justice of the peace, the Civil War becomes personal when her father, who has remained neutral in the conflict, is arrested by the Union militia, their home is nearly burned and their possessions stolen. At the start of this . . . novel, Adair and her two younger sisters try to follow their father's captors, but Adair is falsely denounced as a Confederate spy. At the prison in St. Louis, upright commandant Maj. William Neumann is . . . touched by Adair's beauty and spirit and asks her to give him some information so she can be released. Instead, she writes the story of her life, augmented by folk tales and fables, and he finds himself falling in love. When he gets his reassignment orders, he proposes marriage and asks her to escape, promising to find her after the war. Thus begins a long and terrible journey for each of them." Publ Wkly

Jiles, Paulette

★ **News** of the world; A Novel. Paulette Jiles. William Morrow 2016 224 p. maps (hardback) $22.99

ISBN 0062409204 ; 9780062409201

LC 2015041173

National Book Award Finalist: Fiction (2016)

In the winter of 1970, Captain Jefferson Kyle Kidd has made a fairly comfortable living in northern Texas. . . . When he's asked to deliver a 10-year-old German girl back to her relatives in San Antonio in exchange for $50 in gold, he agrees. Johanna's parents had been killed by the Kiowa, but she was spared and was raised as one of their own for four years. Captain Kidd finds that Johanna, now in his care, has lost nearly all memory of her language, comportment, and upbringing. Facing a 400-mile journey filled with threats of ambush and an uncooperative charge, Captain Kidd wonders if his choice to deliver the girl was the right one." (Booklist)

"Lyrical and affecting, the novel succeeds in skirting cliches through its empathy and through the depth of its major characters." Kirkus

Jin, Ha, 1956-

★ The **boat** rocker; Ha Jin. Pantheon Books 2016 240 p. (ebook) $65; (hardback) $25.95

ISBN 9780307911636; 9780307911629

LC 2016007449

This novel, by Ha Jin, is set in "New York, 2005. Chinese expatriate Feng Danlin is a fiercely principled reporter at a small news agency that produces a website read by the Chinese diaspora around the world. . . . But his newest assignment may be his undoing: investigating his ex-wife, Yan Haili, an unscrupulous novelist who has willingly become a pawn of the Chinese government in order to realize her dreams of literary stardom." (Publisher's note)

"Ha Jin's prose is always pleasurable to read." Pub Wkly

Jin, Ha, 1956-

The **bridegroom**; stories. Pantheon Bks. 2000 225p

ISBN 0-375-42067-3

LC 00-28405

"In this dazzling collection of stories, set in provincial China in the fairly recent past, most of the protagonists are emerging from the numbing predictability of totalitarianism, realizing that they must abandon the passivity that has insured their survival in the past." New Yorker

Jin, Ha, 1956-

The **crazed**. Pantheon Bks. 2002 323p

ISBN 0-375-42181-5

LC 2002-22427

"Writing with a searing restraint born of long-brewing grief over the Chinese government's surreal savageness, Ha Jin depicts a warped society in which everyone is driven mad by viciousness and injustice. But Ha Jin's dramatic indictment does not preclude love, or the ancient power of story to memorialize, awaken compassion, and shore up hope." Booklist

Jin, Ha, 1956-

A **free** life. Pantheon Books 2007 660p $26

ISBN 978-0-375-42465-6; 0-375-42465-2

LC 2007-6177

"Jin's main character, Nan Wu, is a graduate student in political science studying at Brandeis. He is married to a pretty, resourceful Chinese woman named Pingping. The Wus have a young son, Taotao, who has just been reunited with his parents after four years living with Nan's parents in China. . . . The Tiananmen riots mark a change in Nan's fortunes. Disillusioned about China's future, he drops out of school, determined to make a life in America any way he can. The events of 'A Free Life' move from Boston to New York, where Wu, frustrated in his literary pursuits, learns to be a chef the old-fashioned way by starting as a busboy; and then to the outskirts of Atlanta where Nan and Pingping become the new owners of a local Chinese restaurant named the Gold Wok. At each location Jin creates a rich community of characters — writers, artists, political dissidents, waiters, shopkeepers, even the Dalai Lama makes an appearance — that give this quiet story of modest triumph a universal dimension." Seattle Times

Jin, Ha, 1956-

A **good** fall. Pantheon Books 2009 240p

ISBN 0-307-37868-3; 978-0-307-37868-2

LC 2009-08638

This is a collection of twelve stories by the author of Waiting (1999), The Bridegroom (2000), and A Free Life (2007).

"It's an uneven collection in the best sense of the word, combining superfluous vignettes with moments of stark insight into an amalgamation that itself resembles a melting pot. . . . A few missteps don't spoil a collection of sublime moments, not the least of which occurs in the title story, its plot capturing the entire arc of the immigrant experience." Denver Post

Jin, Ha, 1956-

★ A **map** of betrayal; a novel. Ha Jin. Pantheon Books 2014 304 p. (hardback) $26.95

ISBN 0307911608; 9780307911605

LC 2014008892

In this book, by Ha Jin, "when Lilian Shang, born and raised in America, discovers her father's diary after the death of her parents, she is shocked by the secrets it contains. She knew that her father, Gary, convicted decades ago of being a mole in the CIA, was the most important Chinese spy ever caught. But his diary, an astonishing chronicle of his journey as a Communist intelligence agent, reveals the pain and longing that his double life entailed." (Publisher's note)

"A sharply ironic, stealthily devastating tale of the tragic cost of 'blind' patriotism, told by a master of clarifying fiction, that unites the personal and the geopolitical." Booklist

Jin, Ha, 1956-

Nanjing requiem. Pantheon Books 2011 303p $26.95

ISBN 978-0-307-37976-4; 0-307-37976-0

LC 2010-47608

This novel "focuses on the atrocities committed by the Japanese occupiers in 1937 Nanjing. Jin describes horrible acts in a style bordering on reportage, lending bitter realism to his chronicle of violence and privation. While much will be familiar to readers of Iris Chang's The Rape of Nanjing, Jin anchors his tale on two characters: the middle-aged narrator, Anling Gao, and real-life American missionary Minnie Vautrin, dean of Jinling Women's College. Anling assists Minnie, and through her eyes we follow the missionary's heroic decision to open the college to homeless refugees, creating a safety zone that the Japanese can't penetrate. . . . Jin paints a convincing, harrowing portrait of heroism in the face of brutality." Publ Wkly

Jin, Ha, 1956-

Waiting. Pantheon Bks. 1999 308p $24

ISBN 0-375-40653-0

LC 99-21334

This novel "provides a dual education: a crash course in Chinese society during and since the Cultural Revolution, and more leisurely but nonetheless compelling exploration of the less exotic terrain that is the human heart." N Y Times Book Rev

Jin, Ha, 1956-

War trash. Pantheon Books 2004 352p $25

ISBN 0-375-42276-5

LC 2004-43428

"Written in the modest, uninflected prose of a soldier's letter home, Ha Jin's story, a mixture of authentic historical detail and realistic invention, is a powerful work of the imagination whose psychic territory is not the hunger and humiliation of the prison camp but the haunted past that was the old, lost China and the mysterious future that is in the process of becoming Mao Zedong's chimerical new China." Washington Post

Includes bibliographical references

Jio, Sarah

The **last** camellia; a novel. Sarah Jio. Plume 2013 320 p. $15

ISBN 0452298393; 9780452298392

LC 2012049474

In this novel by Sarah Jio set "on the eve of the Second World War, the last surviving specimen of a camellia plant known as the Middlebury Pink lies secreted away on an English country estate. Flora, an amateur American botanist, is contracted by an international ring of flower thieves to infiltrate the household and acquire the coveted bloom. Her search is at once brightened by new love and threatened by her discovery of a series of ghastly crimes." (Publisher's note)

Jio, Sarah

The **violets** of March; Sarah Jio. Plume 2011 296p.

ISBN 9780452297036 pa; 0452297036

LC 2010037282

This book tells the "story of a woman rebuilding after romantic and professional setbacks. A few years ago, Emily Wilson was a bestselling writer married to a loving and handsome man. Now her husband has ditched her and she's unable to string four words together. Looking for rejuvenation and inspiration, Emily leaves New York City for a month at her great-aunt Bee's Bainbridge Island home, but soon after she arrives, she discovers a mysterious diary from 1943 and becomes fascinated by the love story captured by the unknown diarist. Emily's attempts to ferret out the story behind the diary bring her into contact with the island's . . . locals; as Emily enjoys a simmering romance with an artist, answers prove hard to come by, and even Bee is reluctant to share the truth." (Publishers Weekly)

Johansen, Iris

And then you die-- Bantam Bks. 1998 344p

ISBN 0-553-10616-3

LC 97-40073

"When photojournalist Bess Grady is sent on assignment to a small town in Mexico, she unwittingly finds herself in the midst of a horrific nightmare. Every citizen of the town has died of anthrax poisoning as a result of a terrorist germ-warfare attack. Because she survived, Bess is sought by both the terrorists and a hard-hearted CIA man. The plot is filled with clever detours that twist and turn and cast suspicion on all of the main players until Bess doesn't know who to trust." Booklist

Johansen, Iris

Blind alley. Bantam Books 2004 344p $25

ISBN 0-553-80341-7

LC 2004-54410

In this thriller featuring "Atlanta detective Joe Quinn and the love of his life, forensic sculptor Eve Duncan, Joe gives Eve a skull to reconstruct. Eerily enough, the face resembles 17-year-old Jane MacGuire, who has been offered sanctuary by Eve and Joe after surviving a rough-and-tumble life on the streets. . . . Several look-alikes have already been killed in Europe, and Scotland Yard sends in hunky Mark Trevor to help. Eve mistrusts him, but Jane, who has had recurring nightmares related to the killings, believes that he's there to help her. Eve and Joe want to protect Jane, but the intrepid teenager knows that unless she confronts the killer, she will live the rest of her life in fear. Johansen has become adept at mixing supernatural elements with intriguing suspense." Booklist

Johansen, Iris

Final target. Bantam Bks. 2001 340p $24.95

ISBN 0-553-80094-9

LC 00-65124

At the center of this thriller "is the Wind Dancer, a priceless gold statue of the winged horse Pegasus. The statue has been in the Andreas family since the fall of Troy and now, centuries later, U.S. President Jonathan Andreas is in Paris to lend the family heirloom to a museum. On the night of the ceremony, his daughter, seven-year-old Cassie, is awakened at the family's farmhouse in the south of France by masked men who murder her nanny and her nurse, intent on kidnapping Cassie and ransoming her in exchange for the Wind Dancer. Cassie is saved in the nick of time by the arrival of Michael Travis, international underworld information dealer, but eight months later, the child is being treated in the Virginia home of psychiatrist Dr. Jessica Riley and Jessica's psychically extrasensitive sister, Melissa, for severe catatonic trauma. . . . Michael Travis then reappears and lures Cassie and the Riley sisters into a web of intrigue." Publ Wkly

Johansen, Iris

Long after midnight. Bantam Bks. 1997 371p

LC 96-24957

"Johansen knows how to take the formula and run with it, and readers will be won over by her flesh-and-blood characters, crackling dialogue and lean, suspenseful plotting." Publ Wkly

Johansen, Iris, 1938-

No easy target; Iris Johansen. St. Martin's Press 2017 340 p. (hardcover) $27.99

ISBN 9781466887220; 9781250075840

LC 2016046601

In this novel, by Iris Johansen, "Margaret Douglas has . . . a strange gift: the ability to understand animals and to communicate with them. . . . [And] every time someone gets too close, Margaret uproots her life and outruns them. When John Lassiter breaks into Margaret's apartment, she vanishes again, but Lassiter has good reason to be persistent. . . . Turning from the hunted to the hunter, Margaret must use everything she has ever learned . . . to defeat a great evil." (Publisher's note)

"Loyal Johansen fans will welcome yet another strong female hero to her prolific body of work." Booklist

Johansen, Iris, 1938-

The **perfect** witness; Iris Johansen. St. Martin's Press 2014 342 p. (hardcover) $27.99

ISBN 1250020050; 9781250020055

LC 2014025167

In Iris Johansen's novel "when Teresa Casali was young she discovered she had a strange gift: the ability to read people's memories. But the gift seemed more like a curse as her mob boss father used her to gain the upper hand in his world of corruption and violence. Exposed by her own family to the darkest impulses of mankind, Teresa is alone and unprotected. She realizes that if she is to survive, she has to run." (Publisher's note)

"Johansen creates an intriguing world that revolves around a psychic underground and is peppered with some really diabolical bad guys. Readers will likely feel engaged by the story, though a few plot points seem slightly contrived, and the sexual tension between Mandak and Allie begins when she's 16, which makes sense contextually but feels slightly unwholesome. An enticing hook and compelling storytelling overcome some small flaws." Kirkus

Johansen, Iris, 1938-

Taking Eve; Iris Johansen. St. Martin's Press 2013 352 p. (hardcover) $27.99

ISBN 1250019982; 9781250019981

LC 2013002635

This is Iris Johansen's 15th novel featuring forensic sculptor Eve Duncan and begins a new trilogy. "A gunman taking a shot at Eve's adopted daughter, Jane, interrupts the quiet life that Eve and her longtime lover, police detective Joe Quinn, have been leading at their lakeside cottage outside Atlanta, Ga. To add to their woes, a madman, Jim Doane, kidnaps Eve and orders her to reconstruct the face of his late son, Kevin, from what he claims is Kevin's skull." (Publishers Weekly)

John, Elnathan

Born on a Tuesday; a novel. Elnathan John. Grove Press, Black Cat 2016 256 p. (ebook) $16; $16

ISBN 9780802189905; 9780802124821; 0802124828

LC 2016021939

In this novel, by Elnathan John, "in far northwestern Nigeria, Dantala lives among a gang of street boys who . . . are paid by the Small Party to cause trouble. When their attempt to burn down the opposition's local headquarters ends in disaster, Dantala . . . makes his way to a mosque that provides him with food, shelter, and guidance. . . . When bloodshed erupts in the city around him, Dantala must decide what kind of Muslim—and what kind of man—he wants to be." (Publisher's note)

"Nigerian author John's story is an absorbing and sometimes disquieting look inside the contemporary Muslim world." Booklist

Johnson, Adam

★ **Fortune** smiles; stories. Adam Johnson. Random House Inc. 2015 320 p. (hardcover : acid-free paper) $27

ISBN 0812997476; 9780812997477

LC 2015023455

National Book Award: Fiction (2015)

This collection of short stories, by Adam Johnson, "delves deep into love and loss, natural disasters, the influence of technology, and how the political shapes the personal. 'Nirvana' . . . portrays a programmer whose wife has a rare disease. . . . In 'Hurricanes Anonymous' . . . a young man searches for the mother of his son in a Louisiana devastated by Hurricanes Katrina and Rita. 'George Orwell Was a Friend of Mine' follows a former warden of a Stasi prison in East Germany." (Publisher's note)

"Often funny, even when they're wrenchingly sad, the stories provide one of the truest satisfactions of reading: the opportunity to sink into worlds we otherwise would know little or nothing about, ones we might even cross the street to avoid." Pub Wkly

Johnson, Adam, 1967-

★ The **orphan** master's son; Adam Johnson. Random House 2012 443p. hbk $26

ISBN 9780679643999 ebook; 9780812992793

LC 2011013410

Pulitzer Prize: Fiction (2013)

The novel is "set within the highest levels of the North Korean dictatorship. . . . The orphan master's son is Pak Jun Do, and he has perhaps the most valuable skill possible for advancement in North Korea -- the gift of saying a lie while speaking the truth. His bravery and fearlessness leading Army orphan brigades through dangerous mines is quickly noted, and Jun Do is selected for even more difficult missions - kidnapping Japanese citizens and repatriating them to North Korea, then language school and back to a fishing boat to spy on American submarines. . . . The Americans have confused Jun Do with a government minister who often is at dangerous odds with Kim Jong Il. . . . So the . . . Leader simply replaces the commander with Jun Do -- sending the once-powerful man into the mines and Do to live with his beautiful actress-wife and kids." (USA Today)

Johnson, Adam, 1967-

Parasites like us; a novel. Viking 2003 341p $24.95

ISBN 0-670-03240-9

LC 2002-41181

"Johnson relates all of this with great ingenuity and bravado—as well as a good deal of unfocused energy. . . . The most daring element in this heterogeneous mix, however, may well be the vein of earnest solemnity that Johnson adds to it. Unlike most satirists, he's not afraid to let the mask of irony fall occasionally." N Y Times Book Rev

Johnson, Alaya Dawn

Moonshine; [by] Alaya Johnson. Thomas Dunne Books/St. Martin's Press 2010 278p pa $14.99

ISBN 978-0-312-56547-3; 0-312-64806-5

LC 2009-39261

"The author imagines jazz-age New York as a city in which vampires and other supernatural denizens stalk the same streets as entertainers like Josephine Baker or the corrupt politicians of Tammany Hall. Our narrator is feisty Zephyr Hollis, daughter of a famous monster-hunter, who has reinvented herself in the city as a social organizer and teacher. Zephyr preaches tolerance of nonhumans but carries a silver switchblade to protect herself from the nightlife, despite a natural immunity to vampires. Among her interesting companions are ambitious tabloid reporter Lily Harding, progressive activist Iris Tomkins and, most dangerously, Amir the Djinn. . . . A bit jumbled, but entertaining and potentially a good start for a series offering a different take on the undead craze." Kirkus

Johnson, Barb

More of this world or maybe another; Barb Johnson. Harper Perennial 2009 188, 12p (pbk.) $13.99

ISBN 9780061732270

LC 2010277106

Stonewall Book Awards: Barbara Gittings Literature Award (2011)

In this collection of interconnected short stories, author Barb "Johnson maps the lives of several New Orleanians who orbit Delia Delahoussaye's Laundromat on Palmyra Street, where 'saying hello and fighting can sound just alike.' The title story finds a stoned teenage Delia longing to kiss a girl named Chuck in the belly of an empty oil tank, a makeshift sense-deprivation chamber that Delia thinks 'shakes you loose from yourself.' By the end of the second story, 'Keeping Her Difficult Balance,' it's unclear whether Delia will ever escape her childhood identity. 'If the Holy Spirit Comes for You' finds her brother, Dooley, nursing a pig his uncles want to slaughter, and the story's moral nuance and consequences echo through 'Killer Heart,' where an older Dooley's good deeds lead to tragedy." (Publishers Weekly)

Johnson, Charles Richard

★ **Middle** passage; [by] Charles Johnson. Atheneum Pubs. 1990 209p

LC 90-32713

"Johnson's exciting sea narrative provides an unusual historical look at the horrifying Middle Passage experience. . . . Like Moby-Dick's Ahab, the captain of the Republic is on his own special quest (in this case, the capture of the African trickster god). . . . Above all, the book is valuable in offering a rare perspective of the shocking experience of the slave trade and the consequences of that event for American blacks." Choice

Johnson, Craig, 1961-

✓ **Another** man's moccasins; Craig Johnson. Viking 2008 290 p.

ISBN 0670018619; 9780670018611

LC 2007029979

Spur Awards: Best Western Novel, Short Novel (2009)

In Craig Johnson's "fourth mystery to feature Wyoming sheriff Walt Longmire, . . . Walt responds to a call that leads to the discovery of the body of a young Vietnamese woman, Ho Thi Paquet, along an Absaroka County highway. Squatting nearby with Paquet's purse is a massive Crow Indian later identified as Virgil White Buffalo. When Walt finds a photograph of himself and a Vietnamese barmaid taken in 1968 among the victim's belongings, Walt realizes that the murder isn't as clear-cut as it appears. With the help of his longtime friend, Cheyenne Indian Henry Standing Bear, Walt retraces Paquet's steps and uncovers disturbing links to a California human trafficking ring as well as to his own past as a military inspector in Vietnam." (Publishers Weekly)

Johnson, Craig

✓ The **dark** horse. Viking 2009 318p

ISBN 0-670-02087-7; 978-0-670-02087-4

LC 2008-54093

In this outing, "Sheriff Walt Longmire goes undercover to prove that Mary Barsad, confessed murderer, did not kill her husband after he shot her horses and set the barn on fire. Walt finds that there is a lot more going on in Wyoming's remote Powder River area, as he meets a cast of characters with much to hide. . . . Johnson's deft, twisty storytelling immediately grips the reader. His latest has a heart as big as a Wyoming sky." Libr J

Johnson, Craig

✓ **Death** without company; Craig Johnson. Viking 2006 xii, 271 p.p

ISBN 9780670034673; 0670034673

LC 2005042357

In this book, part of the Walt Longmire mystery series, "Mari Baroja is found poisoned at the Durant Home for Assisted Living" so "Sheriff Longmire is drawn into an investigation that reaches fifty years into the mysterious woman's dramatic Basque past. Aided by his friend Henry Standing Bear, Deputy Victoria Moretti, and newcomer Santiago Saizarbitoria, Sheriff Longmire must connect the specter of the past to the present to find the killer among them." (Amazon.com)

"Johnson combines a vivid sense of the dailiness of life--and the way human relationships take root in that dailiness--with a sure--handed touch for jolting both his characters and his readers out of their comfort zones and deep into harm's way." Booklist

Johnson, Craig, 1961-

✓ **Hell** is empty. Viking 2011 viii, 312p

ISBN 9780670022779; 0670022772

LC 2010048021

This book tells the story of "Sheriff Walt Longmire of Absaroka County, Wyo., a self-deprecating and experienced lawman . . . [whose assignment to] a seemingly simple prisoner transport evolves into a grueling physical and mental trial where Walt doggedly pursues an escaped psychotic murderer." (denverpost.com)

Johnson, Craig, 1961-

✓ **Spirit** of steamboat; a Walt Longmire story. by Craig Johnson. Viking 2013 160 p. (Longmire) (hardback) $20

ISBN 0670015784; 9780670015788

LC 2013017053

This book, by Craig Johnson, "offers the earliest glimpse yet of Walt Longmire's tenure as sheriff of Wyoming's Absaroka County. Longmire is reading Dickens in his office when an unexpected visitor arrives bearing a mysterious gift, triggering memories of an eventful night long past . . . when, with a huge storm blowing in and the highways closed, the only way to transport a burn victim to the hospital in Denver was via a WWII bomber gathering dust in the hangar of Durant's tiny airport. The only person who could fly it? Lucian Connally, Longmire's crusty predecessor." (Booklist)

Johnson, D. E.

Detroit shuffle; D.E. Johnson. Minotaur Books 2013 336 p. (hardcover) $25.99

ISBN 1250006767; 9781250006769

LC 2013013935

In author D.E. Johnson's book, "Will Anderson inadvertently breaks up a key suffrage rally when he thwarts a gunman set on killing his lover, Elizabeth Hume. No one else saw the man, and Elizabeth believes he hallucinated the entire incident, a side effect of the radium 'treatment' he received at Eloise Hospital. She asks him to sit on the sidelines while she and her companions try to get the women's suffrage amendment passed by Michigan voters. Instead, Will sets out to protect Elizabeth and prove his sanity." (Publisher's note)

Johnson, Dana

Elsewhere, California; Dana Johnson. Counterpoint 2012 276 p. $15.95

ISBN 158243784X; 9781582437842

This novel tells the story of Avery Arlington, an African-American girl who "is nine when her family escapes L.A.'s gang violence and moves to the suburbs, becoming the only black people in the neighborhood. Feeling alienated, but impressionable, Avery adjusts . . . . At 40, Avery has become a visual artist, her rich and sensual Italian boyfriend clearly instrumental in helping her find the self-acceptance that eluded her for so long." The story shifts between Avery's past and present. (Publishers Weekly)

Johnson, Denis, 1949-2017

Jesus' son; stories. Farrar, Straus & Giroux 1992 160p $19

ISBN 0-374-17892-5

LC 92-16880

This is a collection of eleven short stories "linked by a common narrator—a young, nameless substance abuser of unspecified background and education. Like the other marginal and directionless individuals who populate these tales, he is locked into a downward spiral of booze, drugs, and petty crime, the squalor of his life emblematic of a more profound spiritual malaise." (Libr J)

In this is "masterfully bleak sequence of short stories narrated by a young heartland lowlife, brutality is unpredictable and unremarkable: shootings, stabbings, guns held to heads, heroin overdoses, gruesome car wrecks—and confrontations that don't turn violent only because the antagonists can't stay focused. . . . As grunge sociology, 'Jesus' Son' is claustrophobic; as art, it's exhilarating." Newsweek

Johnson, Denis, 1949-2017

The **largesse** of the sea maiden; stories. Denis Johnson. Random House 2018 207 p. (hardcover) $27

ISBN 9780812988635; 9780812988642

LC 2017027298

This book "is the long-awaited new story collection from Denis Johnson. Written in the luminous prose that made him one of the most beloved and important writers of his generation, this collection finds Johnson . . . contemplating the ghosts of the past and the elusive and unexpected ways the mysteries of the universe assert themselves. Finished shortly before Johnson's death, this collection is the last word from a writer whose work will live on for many years to come." (Publisher's note)

"The second story collection from the late Johnson (Jesus' Son) is a masterpiece of deep humanity and astonishing prose." Pub Wkly

Johnson, Denis

Nobody move; a novel. Farrar, Straus and Giroux 2009 196p $23

ISBN 978-0-374-22290-1; 0-374-22290-8

LC 2008-43420

Originally serialized, in slightly different form, in Playboy

"Johnson's sympathies seem to be with Gambol, a bad man who isn't so much seeking redemption as having redemption thrust on him. When offered an exit out of this seedy underworld, he takes it with Mary, a 'heavyset blonde' and former Army medic who brings him back to health. Gambol may deal in death, and sometimes even take pleasure in it, but he is distinguished by a lack of human hatred for others and himself. In the brutal world of Nobody Move, that makes all the difference." Pittsburgh City Paper

Johnson, Denis, 1949-2017

★ **Train** dreams. Farrar, Straus and Giroux 2011 116p $18

ISBN 978-0-374-28114-4; 0-374-28114-9

LC 2011007505

First published, in slightly different form, 2002 in The Paris Review

"The story concerns the life of Robert Grainier, a fictional orphan shipped by train in 1893 into the woods of the Idaho panhandle. He grows up, works on logging gangs, falls in love, and loses his wife and baby daughter to a particularly pernicious wildfire. What Johnson builds from the ashes of Grainier's life is a tender, lonesome and riveting story, an American epic writ small, in which Grainier drives a horse cart, flies in a biplane, takes part in occasionally hilarious exchanges and goes maybe 42 percent crazy. It's a love story, a hermit's story and a refashioning of age-old wolf-based folklore like 'Little Red Cap.' It's also a small masterpiece. You look up from the thing dazed, slightly changed." N Y Times Book Rev

Johnson, Denis, 1949-2017

Tree of smoke. Farrar, Straus & Giroux 2007 614p $27

ISBN 0-374-27912-8; 978-0-374-27912-7

LC 2007-06562

National Book Award: Fiction (2007)

This novel is set during the Vietnam War. It is "the story of Skip Sands-spy-in-training, engaged in Psychological Operations against the Vietcong—and the disasters that befall him thanks to his famous uncle, a war hero known in intelligence circles simply as the Colonel. This is also the story of the Houston brothers, Bill and James, young men who drift out of the Arizona desert into a war in which the line between disinformation and delusion has blurred away." (Publisher's note)

"Mr. Johnson not only succeeds in conjuring the anomalous, hallucinatory aura of the Vietnam War as authoritatively as Stephen Wright or Francis Ford Coppola, but he also shows its fallout on his characters with harrowing emotional precision. He has written a flawed but deeply resonant novel that is bound to become one of the classic works of literature produced by that tragic and uncannily familiar war." N Y Times (Late N Y Ed)

Johnson, Diane

Le divorce. Dutton 1997 309p

LC 96-9644

"The author pokes fun at the Americans for moralizing, and at the French for being amoral; and she manages to be even-handed because she displays admiration for French elegance of behavior, and affection for American earnest good will." N Y Rev Books

Johnson, Diane

Le mariage; a novel. Dutton 2000 322p $23.95

ISBN 0-525-94518-0

LC 99-89849

This companion to Le divorce is "set again in Paris with a few overlapping characters, the plot revolves around two couples—Tim Nolinger, a Belgian American journalist engaged to the very French Anne-Sophie, a dealer in equine collectibles; and the very beautiful American Clara, a former actress married to the reclusive film director Serge Clay. Thrown into the entertaining mix is a stolen illuminated manuscript, a murdered flea market dealer, Y2K cults, an adulterous liaison, and of course Johnson's perceptive and witty insights on love, marriage, and Anglo-French relations." Libr J

Johnson, Kij

★ The **Dream**-Quest of Vellitt Boe; by Kij Johnson. St. Martin's Press 2016 169 p. (paperback) $14.99

ISBN 9780765386519; 9780765391414; 0765391414

Hugo Finalist ; Nebula Finalist

This book, by Kij Johnson, "is both a commentary on a classic H.P. Lovecraft tale and a profound reflection on a woman's life. Vellitt's quest to find a former student who may be the only person who can save her community takes her through a world governed by a seemingly arbitrary dream logic in which she occasionally glimpses an underlying but mysterious order, a world ruled by capricious gods and populated by the creatures of dreams and nightmares." (Publisher's note)

"Superb worldbuilding and gorgeous prose will hold readers rapt." Pub Wkly

Johnson, Lindsey Lee

The **most** dangerous place on earth; A Novel. Lindsey Lee Johnson. Random House Inc 2016 288 p. (ebook) $65; $27

ISBN 9780812997286; 9780812997279

LC 2015035537

This novel, by Lindsey Lee Johnson, "exposes at every turn the real human beings beneath the high school stereotypes. Abigail Cress is ticking off the boxes toward the Ivy League when she . . . [enters] into an inappropriate relationship with a teacher. Dave Chu, who . . . [is] a typical B student, takes desperate measures to live up to his parents' crushing expectations. [And] Emma Fleed, a gifted dancer, balances rigorous rehearsals with wild weekends." (Publisher's note)

"Readers may find themselves so swept up in this enthralling novel that they finish it in a single sitting." Pub Wkly

Johnson, Mat

Pym; a novel. Spiegel & Grau 2010 322p $24

ISBN 978-0-8129-8158-2; 0-8129-8158-8

LC 2010-29331

"Recently canned professor of American literature Chris Jaynes is obsessed with The Narrative of Arthur Gordon Pym of Nantucket, Edgar Allan Poe's strange and only novel. When he discovers the manuscript of a crude slave narrative that seems to confirm the reality of Poe's fiction, he resolves to seek out Tsalal, the remote island of pure and utter blackness that Poe describes with horror. Jaynes imagines it to be the last untouched bastion of the African Diaspora and the key to his personal salvation. He convenes an all-black crew of six to follow Pym's trail to the South Pole in search of adventure, natural resources to exploit, and, for Jaynes at least, the mythical world of the novel." Publisher's note

Johnson, T. Geronimo

Welcome to Braggsville; a novel. T. Geronimo Johnson. William Morrow 2015 384 p. (hardcover) $25.99

ISBN 0062302124; 9780062302120; 9780062302137

LC 2014021045

This novel, by T. Geronimo Johnson, is a "comedy about four UC Berkeley students who stage a dramatic protest during a Civil War reenactment. . . . Born and raised in the heart of old Dixie, Daron Davenport finds himself in unfamiliar territory his freshman year at UC Berkeley. Two thousand miles and a world away from his childhood, he is a small-town fish floundering in the depths of a large, hyper-liberal pond." (Publisher's note)

"Though the reader might occasionally feel whipsawed by Johnson's shifts in tone from comedy to tragedy, the swerving seems appropriate to the complexity of its theme. A rambunctious, irreverent yet still serious study of the long reach of American institutional racism." Kirkus

Includes bibliographical references

Johnston, Wayne

The **colony** of unrequited dreams. Anchor Bks. (NY) 1999 562p

ISBN 0-385-49542-0

LC 99-19144

"The very human story of Smallwood and Fielding and its historical counterpoint may both appear inauspicious, even contrived, at first, but as the book proceeds they and their pairing gather momentum to achieve a mesmerizing inevitability." N Y Times Book Rev

Joinson, Suzanne

A **lady** cyclist's guide to Kashgar; Suzanne Joinson. Bloomsbury 2012 374 p.

ISBN 9781608198115

LC 2011046720

Part of this book is set in "1923 . . . [as] Evangeline English, keen lady cyclist, arrives with her sister Lizzie at the ancient Silk Route city of Kashgar to help establish a Christian mission. Lizzie is in thrall to their forceful and unyielding leader Millicent, but Eva's motivations for leaving her bourgeois life back at home are less clear-cut. . . . In present-day London, . . . Frieda, a young woman adrift in her own life, opens her front door one night to find a man sleeping on the landing. . . . Tayeb, who has fled to England from Yemen, has arrived on Frieda's doorstep just as she learns that she is the next-of-kin to a dead woman she has never heard of. . . . The two wanderers begin an unlikely friendship as their worlds collide." (Publisher's note)

Joinson, Suzanne

The **Photographer's** Wife; by Suzanne Joinson. St. Martin's Press 2016 320 p. $26

ISBN 9781620408322; 1620408309; 9781620408308

In this historical novel, by Suzanne Joinson, "Palestine has been a surprisingly harmonious mix of British colonials, exiled Armenians, and Greek, Arab, and Jewish officials rubbing elbows, but there are simmers of trouble ahead. When Harrington learns that Eleanora's husband is part of an underground group intent on removing the British, a dangerous game begins." (Publisher's note)

"Atmospheric, romantic, yet refreshingly acerbic—Joinson's timely portrayal of the difficult relationships between different cultures is rivaled by her heartbreaking delineation of the fragile relationships between individuals." Kirkus

Jones, Darynda

Second grave on the left. St. Martin's Press 2011 307p $21.99

ISBN 978-0-312-36081-8

LC 2011-11243

Sequel to First grave on the right (2011)

"The fiery relationship between Charley and Reyes will satisfy paranormal romance fans, but it's the distinctive characters, dead and alive, and the almost constant laughs that will leave readers eager for the next installment." Publ Wkly

Jones, Diana Wynne

A **sudden** wild magic. Morrow 1992 412p

LC 92-10860

"Jones's sly sense of humor and her accurate, affectionate depiction of relations between women and men give an extra kick to this effervescent tale." Publ Wkly

Jones, Douglas C.

★ The **court**-martial of George Armstrong Custer. Scribner 1976 291p

"Slowly building the cases for the prosecution and defense, Jones does well by mixing the drama of courtroom proceedings with the color of a controversial incident." Booklist

Followed by Arrest Sitting Bull

Jones, Edward P.

The **known** world. Amistad 2003 388p $24.95

ISBN 0-06-055754-0

LC 2003-40389

This work of historical fiction explores "the world of blacks who owned blacks in the antebellum South." The book "starts with the dying 31-year-old Henry Townsend, a former slave -- now master of 33 slaves of his own and more than 50 acres of land . . . worried about the fate of his holdings upon his early death." (Publishers Weekly)

"Henry Townsend, born a slave, is purchased and freed by his father, yet he remains attached to his former owner, even taking lessons in slave owning when he eventually buys his own slaves. Townsend is part of a small enclave of free blacks who own slaves, thus offering another angle on the complexities of slavery and social relations in a Virginia town just before the Civil War." Booklist

Jones, Edward, 1951-

All Aunt Hagar's children. Amistad 2006 399p $25.95
ISBN 0060557567; 9780060557560

LC 2006-42746

"This collection of 14 short stories" by Edward P. Jones depicts "black life in America. His stories span the 20th century in Washington, DC. Jones's Washington is not as much the center of international power as a place offering hope for rural descendants of slaves. Several characters have made it to the middle class, often through government employment, but economic success doesn't exempt one from suffering." (Library Journal)

"In 14 short stories, Jones . . . demonstrates his skill at drawing complex and nuanced characters and predicaments. Washington, D.C., is the setting for this collection of stories in assorted time frames with assorted characters, most of whom come from the rural South, and all of whom are coping with the transformation of their lives and their adjustments to a new way of life. . . . Jones' stories are rich in detail and emotions as he plumbs the intricacies of people's relationships with one another and with spiritual forces at work in urban as well as natural environments." Booklist

Jones, J. Sydney

The **silence**; J. Sydney Jones. Severn House 2011 240p.
ISBN 9780727880840

This book tells the story of "[y]oung lawyer Karl Werthen [who] loves taking on private investigations . . . [and] is eager to pursue the disappearance of a member of the illustrious Wittgenstein family. Concurrently, a Vienna councilman is found shot in his office, an apparent suicide. Working his missing-person case, Werthen interviews a gay freelance journalist who knows young Wittgenstein and, interestingly, has also been writing inflammatory articles about council activities. The missing man is soon found, but the journalist is murdered. Afraid that his interview triggered the man's death, Werthen feels morally compelled to identify the killer." (Libr J)

Jones, James, 1921-1977

★ **From** here to eternity. Scribner 1951 861p

This book by James Jones follows two American soldiers in the months before the bonbing of Pearl Harbor, Hawaii. " Pvt. Robert E. Lee Prewitt is a champion welterweight and a fine bugler. But when he refuses to join the company's boxing team, he gets "the treatment" that may break him or kill him. First Sgt. Milton Anthony Warden knows how to soldier better than almost anyone, yet he's risking his career to have an affair with the commanding officer's wife." (Publisher's note)

"Mr. Jones has grappled with a variety of materials and handles some of them less successfully than others. There is a good deal of weak stuff in the two love affairs and the characterizations of the women, and the sorties into the field of general ideas are unimpressive. The book as a whole, however, is a spectacular achievement; it has tremendous vitality and driving power and graphic authenticity." Atlantic

Jones, James

★ The **thin** red line. Scribner 1962 495p

"This novel will surely offend some readers, lavishly bespattered as it is with Anglo-Saxon words and physiological detail. Nevertheless, it bears the Jones stamp of authenticity and is a major combat novel of World War II." Ont Libr Rev

Followed by Whistle

Jones, Luanne

The **Dixie** Belle's Guide to Love; Luanne Jones . Avon Books 2002 374p (pbk.) $5.99
ISBN 9780380819348

In this book, "when her two-timing husband leaves her with nothing but ownership of the local Pig Rib Palace, Rita Stark decides to get her life back into high gear and turn the rib joint into a cash cow. But her best girlfriends are sure the former Miss Dixie Belle Duchess needs help getting the eatery—and her recently broken heart—back into shape. So they've hired the sexiest man ever to hit Hellon, Tennessee, Will 'Wild Billy' West, to lend a hand. Will's suddenly relighting a fire that Rita was sure went out long ago. What could a sexy prize like him possibly see in a small-town gal like her, especially when he's planning to skip town at summer's end?" (Publisher's note)

Jones, Sadie

Outcast. Harper 2008 347p $24.95
ISBN 978-0-06-137403-6; 0-06-137403-2

"An explosive drama, fuelled by the repression of 1950s Britain. Troubled 19-year-old Lewis Aldridge has never recovered from the death of his mother. After a stint in prison, he heads home and attempts to convince his father of his worth. But his good intentions crumble in the face of his father's disapproval, and Lewis reveals the horrifying realities that lie under the seemingly sedate rural community. Devastatingly good." Marie Claire

Jones, Sadie

Small wars; a novel. Harper 2010 376p $24.99
ISBN 978-0-06-192988-5; 0-06-192988-3

LC 2009-45485

First published 2009 in the United Kingdom

"Hal Treherne graduated from the Royal Military Academy Sandhurst six months too late to see action in World War II. So the third-generation Army scion, now a popular major with a reputation for fair play, is rather chuffed when he gets his chance on British-occupied Cyprus 10 years later. His wife, Clara, and two baby daughters follow him out to the rocky island, where Clara is faced with the unenviable task of trying to maintain the home front in the face of guerrilla warfare. . . . Jones toggles back and forth between Clara's fear and boredom at home, and Hal's days of house-to-house searches for terrorists and firefights in the mountains. Jones is excellent at evoking fraught moments in both halves of the Trehernes' lives." Christ Sci Monit

Jones, Sadie

The **uninvited** guests; Sadie Jones. HarperCollins 2012 262 p.
ISBN 0062116509; 9780062116505

LC 2012372210

This novel by Sadie Jones begins "[o]ne late spring evening in 1912, in the kitchens at Sterne, preparations begin for an elegant supper party in honor of Emerald Torrington's twentieth birthday. But only a few miles away, a dreadful accident propels a crowd of mysterious and not altogether savory survivors to seek shelter at the ramshackle manor—and the household is thrown into confusion and mischief. . . . As the passengers wearily search for rest, the house undergoes a strange transformation. One of their number (who is most definitely not a gentleman) makes it his business to join the birthday revels. Evening turns to stormy night, and a most unpleasant parlor game threatens to blow respectability to smithereens." (Publisher's note)

Jones, Sherry

Four sisters, all queens; Sherry Jones. 1st Gallery Books trade pbk ed Gallery Books 2012 434 p. ill., map (paperback) $15.99
ISBN 1451633246; 9781451633245; 9781451633252

LC 2011044484

In this historical novel, by Sherry Jones, "[a]mid the lush valleys and fragrant wildflowers of Provence, . . . Marguerite's illustrious match with the young King Louis IX makes her Queen of France. Soon Eleonore . . . is betrothed to Henry III of England. In turn, . . . Sanchia and . . . Beatrice wed noblemen who will also make them queens. . . . [L]oyalty succumbs to bitter sibling rivalry, and sister is pitted against sister for . . . Provence itself." (Publisher's note)

Jones, Tayari

★ An **American** marriage; a novel. Tayari Jones. Algonquin Books of Chapel Hill 2018 320 p. (hardcover : alk. paper) $26.95

ISBN 9781616201340

LC 2017030582

In this novel by Tayari Jones, "newlyweds Celestial and Roy are the embodiment of both the American Dream and the New South. He is a young executive, and she is an artist on the brink of an exciting career. But as they settle into the routine of their life together, they are ripped apart by circumstances neither could have imagined." (Publisher's note)

Jones "crafts an affecting tale that explores marriage, family, regret, and other feelings made all the more resonant by her well-drawn characters and their intricate conflicts of heart and mind." Booklist

Jones, Tayari

Silver sparrow; a novel. Algonquin Books of Chapel Hill 2011 340p

ISBN 1-56512-990-3; 978-1-56512-990-0

LC 2010-48098

"A tense, layered and evocative tale. . . . Jones explores the rivalry and connection of siblings, the meaning of beauty, the perils of young womanhood, the complexities of romantic relationships and the contemporary African-American experience." Minneapolis Star Trib

Jong, Erica

★ **Fear** of Dying; A Novel. by Erica Jong. St. Martin's Press 2015 288 p. $26.99

ISBN 1250065917; 9781250065919

LC 2015017627

In this novel, by Erica Jong, "Vanessa Wonderman . . . watches her parents age, attends doctor appointments with her pregnant daughter, and sits by the hospital bed of her husband, Asher, fifteen years her senior. With her best years as an actress behind her, she's discovering that beginnings are easy, but endings can be hard. Could her fountain of youth fantasies be fulfilled on zipless.com?" (Publisher's note)

"Jong's first novel since Sappho's Leap (2003)... Jong does have interesting—even arresting—things to say about age and dying. They're just hard to find in this overlong and self-satisfied novel. Not without its moments." Kirkus

Jong, Erica

★ **Fear** of flying; a novel. Holt, Rinehart & Winston 1973 340p

"At times, Jong gets caught in clichés about women, men, sex, and Jewish mothers, all {of} which she could do without. However, when she takes herself more seriously, the language is penetrating, paying tribute to her worth as a poet." Libr J

Followed by How to save your own life (1977) and Parachutes and kisses (1984 paper only)

Jordan, Hillary

Mudbound; a novel. Algonquin Books of Chapel Hill 2008 328p $22.95

ISBN 978-1-56512-569-8; 1-56512-569-X

LC 2007-44471

"With authentic, earthy prose . . . Jordan picks at the scabs of racial inequality that will perhaps never fully heal and brings just enough heartbreak to this intimate, universal tale, just enough suspense, to leave us contemplating how the lives and motives of these vivid characters might have been different." San Antonio Express-News

Jordan, Hillary, 1963-

When she woke; a novel. Algonquin Books of Chapel Hill 2011 344p

ISBN 1565126297; 9781565126299; 1-56512-629-7; 978-1-56512-629-9

LC 201122799

This book tells the story of "Hannah Payne . . . [whose] life has been devoted to church and family, but after her arrest, she awakens to a nightmare: she is lying on a table in a bare room, covered only by a paper gown, and cameras are broadcasting her every move to millions at home, for home observing new Chromes—criminals whose skin color has been genetically altered to match the class of their crime--is a new and sinister form of entertainment. Hannah is a Red; her crime is murder. The victim, says the state of Texas, was her unborn child, and Hannah is determined to protect the identity of the father—a public figure with whom she's shared a fierce and forbidden love." (Publisher's note)

"Jordan manages to open up powerful feminist and political themes without becoming overly preachy—and the parallels with Hawthorne are fun to trace." Kirkus

Jordan, Robert, 1948-2007

The **eye** of the world; Robert Jordan. Tor Books 1990 670p il maps (The Wheel of Time) pbk $8.99; hbk $34.99

ISBN 9780812511819; 9780312850098; 0812511816; 0312850093

"The peaceful villagers of Emond's Field pay little heed to rumors of war in the western lands until a savage attack by troll-like minions of the Dark One forces three young men to confront a destiny which has its origins in the time known as The Breaking of the World." (Library Journal)

Other titles in this series are:
The great hunt (1990)
The dragon reborn (1991)
The shadow rising (1992)
The fires of heaven (1993)
Lord of chaos (1994)
A crown of swords (1996)
The path of daggers (1998)
Winter's heart (2000)
Crossroads of twilight (2003)
Knife of dreams (2005)
The gathering storm (2009)
Towers of midnight (2010)
A memory of light (2013)

Joseph, Manu

★ **Serious** men. W.W. Norton & Co. 2010 310p pa $14.95

ISBN 978-0-393-33859-1; 0-393-33859-2

LC 2010-09298

Joseph's "novel elegantly describes collisions with an unyielding status quo, ably counterpointing the frustrations of the powerless with the unfulfilling realities of power. With this astute comedy of manners he makes a convincing bid for his own recognition as a novelist of serious talent, the latest addition to a roster of Indian writers who are creating fine literary art from their country's fearsome contradictions." Independent

Joshi, S. T., 1958-

The **white** people and other weird stories; edited with an introduction and notes by S.T. Joshi; foreword by Guillermo del Toro. Penguin Books 2011 xxviii, 377p (Penguin classics)

ISBN 0143105590; 9780143105596

LC 2011027590

This book presents a collection of fantasy stories. "In 'The Inmost Light' . . . a scientist constructs a gem that can contain a human soul, leaving the soul's owner a demonic empty husk. . . . In the gory 'Novel of the White Powder'. . . a woman watches as her husband slowly turns into a malevolent creature from the ingestion of a curative prescribed for depression." (Times Literary Supplement)

"At the turn of the 20th century, Welsh author Machen (The Hill of Dreams) wrote tales about evil and 'ecstasy' (his term for supernatural experience) that made a significant impact on horror fiction. For this volume, weird fiction scholar S.T. Joshi collects 11 key works that typify Machen's vision of the uncanny and the veil that keeps 'the Beyond' mercifully concealed from mortal eyes. Included are his masterpieces 'The White People,' about an innocent's unwitting indoctrination into foul rites of sorcery; 'Novel of the Black Seal,' which uncovers the survival of a malignant race of 'little people' in present times; and 'Novel of the White Powder,' in which a drug brings on a terrifying transformation in a victim who abuses it. Though the volume doesn't include Machen's best-known tale, 'The Great God Pan,' it features an insightful foreword by horror movie director Guillermo del Toro." Publ Wkly

Includes bibliographical references.

Joss, Morag

Among the missing; a novel. Delacorte Press 2011 255p $25

ISBN 978-0-385-34274-2; 0-385-34274-8

LC 2010-52989

"Ron, Annabel and Silva are all in their different ways among the missing. Ron, who's just completed a prison term for inadvertently causing the disastrous bus accident that killed a pregnant teacher and six schoolchildren, is working a job for which he has no credentials. Annabel ran away from her 50-year-old bridegroom Colin after he refused to accept any responsibility for the baby she was carrying. Silva has always felt that she was merely the substitute for the baby of her mother's friend, who died while Silva's mother was pregnant. Now, in the aftermath of the catastrophic wreck of the bridge near Netherloch that brought them together to make an ad hoc household in an out-of-the-way trailer, each of them is keeping a secret. . . . [Joss] builds the relationships among her sad trio slowly, through excruciatingly subtle modulations of tone. But the ending fully justifies every intimation of imminent doom." Kirkus

Joss, Morag

Half broken things; Morag Joss. Delacorte Press 2005 303 p. (pbk.) $15.00; (hbk.) o.p.

ISBN 9780440242444; 0385339402

LC 2005048487

Dagger Awards: Silver Dagger (2003)

This book offers "a novel that peers into the lives of three dangerously lost people . . . and the ominous haven they find when they find each other. Jean is a house sitter at the end of a dreary career. Steph is nine months pregnant and on the run. And Michael is a thief. Through a mixture of deceit, good luck, and misfortune, these three damaged loners have come together at a secluded country home called Walden Manor. Now all three have found what they needed most: a new beginning, a little kindness, a little love. Living off the manor's riches, tending its grounds and gardens, they leave the outside world far behind and build a happiness so long denied them. That is, until the first unexpected visitor arrives." (Publisher's note)

Joss, Morag

The **night** following. Delacorte Press 2008 354p $22

ISBN 978-0-385-34118-9; 0-385-34118-0

LC 2007034711

"While shopping for groceries, a middle-aged woman discovers her husband's infidelity — there's a condom wrapper in the glove compartment of their car. Driving home minutes later, she strikes and kills a bicyclist, then leaves the body by the side of the road. In The Night Following, a bleak, exquisitely written novel, Morag Joss braids together three stories of shattering loneliness that intersect in surprising, haunting ways." Entertainment Wkly

Joyce, Graham, 1954-2014

The **limits** of enchantment. Atria 2005 263p $22

ISBN 0-575-07231-8

"Generally the prose is economical, hurrying along a plot which engages as a whole, despite the weight of Fern's introspection." Times Lit Suppl

Joyce, Graham, 1954-2014

Some kind of fairy tale; a novel. Graham Joyce. 1st ed. Doubleday 2012 310 p. (hardcover) $24.95; (paperback) $15.95; (downloadable audio) $47.95

ISBN 0385535783; 9780385535786; 9780307949073; 9781455162642

LC 2012001946

In this novel by Graham Joyce, "[w]hen 35-year-old Tara Martin shows up on her parents' doorstep two decades after she disappeared, unkempt and looking oddly as if she's barely aged, her older brother, Peter, a farrier married with four kids, can't hide his hurt, angry feelings--but they grow even stronger when Tara offers a preposterous story about riding away with a man on a white horse as an explanation for her disappearance." (Publishers Weekly)

Joyce, James

★ **Dubliners**. Knopf 1991 lxvii, 287p $19

ISBN 0-679-40574-7

LC 91-53001

First published 1914 in the United Kingdom; first United States edition published 1916 by Huebsch

"This collection of 15 stories provides an introduction to the style and motifs found in Joyce's writing. The stories stand alone as individual scenes of Dublin society and are intertwined by the use of autobiography and symbolism." Shapiro. Fic for Youth. 3d edition

Joyce, James

★ **Finnegans** wake. Viking 1939 628p

This novel is "written in a unique and extremely difficult style, making use of puns and portmanteau words, (using at least 40 languages besides English) and a very wide range of allusion. The central theme of the work is a cyclical pattern of history, of fall and resurrection inspired by Vico's Scienza nuova. This is presented in the story of Humphrey Chimpden Earwicker, a Dublin tavern-keeper, and the book is apparently a dream-sequence representing the stream of his unconscious mind through the course of one night. Other characters are his wife Anna Livia Plurabelle, their sons Shem and Shaun, and their daughter Isabel." Oxford Companion to Engl Lit. 6th edition

Joyce, James

★ A **portrait** of the artist as a young man; with an introduction by Richard Brown. Knopf 1991 xli, 318p $18

ISBN 0-679-40575-5

LC 91-52979

First appeared serially, 1914-1915 in the United Kingdom; first United States edition published 1916 by Huebsch

This autobiographical novel "portrays the childhood, school days, adolescence, and early manhood of Stephen Dedalus, later one of the leading characters in Ulysses. Stephen's growing self-awareness as an artist forces him to reject the whole narrow world in which he has been brought up, including family ties, nationalism, and the Catholic religion. The novel ends when, having decided to become a writer, he is about to leave Dublin for Paris. Rather than following a clear narrative progression, the book revolves around experiences that are crucial to Stephen's development as an artist; at the end of each chapter Stephen makes some assertion of identity. Through his use of the stream-of-consciousness technique, Joyce reveals the actual materials of his hero's world, the components of his thought processes." Reader's Ency. 4th edition

Joyce, James

★ **Ulysses**; with an introduction by Craig Raine. Knopf 1997 xlv, 1076p $25

ISBN 0-679-45513-2

First published 1922

"The novel is constructed as a modern parallel to Homer's Odyssey. All of the action of the novel takes place in Dublin on a single day (June 16, 1904). The three central characters—Stephen Dedalus (the hero of Joyce's earlier Portrait of the Artist as a Young Man), Leopold Bloom, a Jewish advertising canvasser, and his wife Molly Bloom—are intended to be modern counterparts of Telemachus, Ulysses, and Penelope, and the events of the novel parallel the major events in Odysseus' journey home. The main stream of Ulysses lies in its depth of character portrayal and its breadth of humor." Merriam-Webster's Ency of Lit

Joyce, Rachel, 1962-

The **Love** Song of Miss Queenie Hennessy; a novel. Rachel Joyce. Random House Inc 2015 384 p. illustration (hardback : acid-free paper) $25

ISBN 0812996674; 9780812996678

LC 2014024364

This novel, by Rachel Joyce, is a parallel story retelling the events of the author's previous novel "The Unlikely Pilgrimage of Harold Fry." "Setting pen to paper, Queenie makes a journey of her own. . . . One word after another, she promises to confess long-buried truths--about her modest childhood, . . . the heartbreak that brought her to Kingsbridge and to loving Harold. . . . And, finally, the devastating secret she has kept from Harold for all these years." (Publisher's note)

"Sequels are often slippery things, books readers welcome a bit hesitantly, fearful that the second installment won't hold a candle to the first. In telling Queenie's side of the story, Joyce accomplishes the rare feat of endowing her continuing narrative with as much pathos and warmth, wisdom and poignancy as her debut. Harold was beloved by millions; Queenie will be, too." Booklist

Joyce, Rachel, 1962-

The **unlikely** pilgrimage of Harold Fry; a novel. Rachel Joyce. 1st ed. Random House 2012 320 p. map (ebook) $25.00; (hardcover : acid-free paper) $25.00; (downloadable audiobook) $30.32

ISBN 0812993292; 9780679645115; 9780812993295; 9781448123148

LC 2011052581

In this book by Rachel Joyce, "Harold Fry receives a surprising letter . . . from beloved friend and colleague Queenie Hennessy, whom he hasn't heard from in 20 years, writing from a distant terminal cancer ward to say good-bye. This letter returns Harold to a . . . painful part of his past, [and] threatens his already troubled marriage. . . . He decides to embark on a 600-mile walk to say goodbye to Queenie in person." (Library Journal)

Julavits, Heidi

The **uses** of enchantment; a novel. Doubleday 2006 356p $24.95

ISBN 0-385-51323-2

LC 2006-45434

"A spooky coming-of-age tale set in West Salem, Massachusetts, a town whose witch-hanging history both captivates and circumscribes the lives of the teenage girls who reside there. One afternoon in 1985, sixteen-year-old Mary Veal disappears from field-hockey practice at the austere Semmering Academy; she reappears a few weeks later claiming to have been abducted. The truth of what happened is only hinted at in Mary's sexually charged experiences with her supposed captor and in her provocative exchanges with the therapist assigned to her case. He decides that Mary is lying—aspects of her story seem taken from a previous student's faked abduction, itself inspired by a centuries-old fable involving a kidnapped girl and witchcraft—but, it turns out, he is not without his own agenda. Julavits expertly keeps the reader baffled until the end, but beneath the mystery is a sophisticated meditation on truth and bias." New Yorker

July, Miranda

No one belongs here more than you; stories. Scribner 2007 205p $23

ISBN 978-0-7432-9939-8; 0-7432-9939-6

LC 2006-51156

"July writes about desire — to be understood, to be part of another person. . . . The engine that drives these stories is July's voice — the book is full of wistful, wonderful observations about the limits of connection, about the hopes and disappointments of intimacy." Los Angeles Times

Jungstedt, Mari

The **inner** circle; English translation by Tiina Nunnally. St. Martin's Minotaur 2008 280p map $24.95

ISBN 978-0-312-36378-9; 0-312-36378-8

LC 2008-24761

Original Swedish edition, 2005

"In summer the Baltic island of Gotland, Beowulf's old stomping ground, offers stunning scenery for tourists and white nights for love and lust, all of which shape the backdrop of Det. Supt. Anders Knutas's investigation into one horrifying crime after another. . . . The decapitation of a harmless pony is followed by the 'threefold' Viking ritual murder of a female archeology student, who's been carrying on a torrid affair with a secret lover, then two more grisly executions, all punctuated by chilling glimpses into a psychopathic mind. The fluid translation evokes the stark economy of the ancient sagas, where all that mattered was how one fought and died. A little of that old warrior spirit still inhabits Jungstedt's tired, frustrated Swedish policemen and journalists, facing monsters within and without and, like Beowulf, never giving in." Publ Wkly

Just, Ward S.

American romantic; a novel. Ward Just. Houghton Mifflin Harcourt 2014 272 p. $26

ISBN 0544196376; 9780544196377

LC 2013026310

This book, by Ward Just, tells the story of an "American foreign service officer and the two women who love him. Harry Sanders is a low-level diplomat with the U.S. embassy in Saigon in the early 1960s. . . . Harry's budding career, however, takes a fatal turn when he is duped into a secret, unsanctioned negotiation with the North Vietnamese and his actions come back to haunt him." (Publishers Weekly)

"Just's clever plot reveals a man conflicted by duty and loyalty, adroitly playing the State Department career game, but always wondering what might have happened if he had just made one or two different choices in his life." Pub Wkly

Just, Ward S.

Exiles in the garden; [by] Ward Just. Houghton Mifflin Harcourt 2009 279p $25

ISBN 978-0-547-19558-2; 0-547-19558-3

LC 2008-49572

"Wars and their consequences make exiles of all involved. The commando, the senator and Alec the observer form an triangle, but not an equilateral triangle. Ward Just is too astute for that. And he leaves us pondering that ageless question of where the personal becomes the political or if it is possible to maintain a distinction at all." Miami Herald

Just, Ward S.

Forgetfulness; [by] Ward Just. Houghton Mifflin Co. 2006 258p $25

ISBN 978-0-618-63463-7; 0-618-63463-0

LC 2006-13906

"Just makes no easy declarations in this often arduously analytical novel. . . . Thomas knows that forgetfulness is not a reasonable response to assault, either personal or national. But he also knows the utter futility of vengeance. This is the paradox that wrenches him in this mature meditation on the personal, private grief that's cultivated in a global war on terror, the search for subtle moral truths in a climate of slogans and curses." Washington Post Book World

Just, Ward S.

Rodin's debutante; [by] Ward Just. Houghton Mifflin Harcourt 2011 263p $26

ISBN 978-0-547-50419-3; 0-547-50419-5

LC 2010-42695

This novel "begins early in the 20th century with Tommy Ogden, a rich, enigmatic Chicagoan who drunkenly decides one day to endow a boys' prep school. Flash forward a few decades to Lee Goodell, who attends Ogden Hall School for Boys and privately wants to become a sculptor. We follow his life, witnessing the two acts of violence that change him. Rodin's Debutante is a surprising story, never going where you expect it to, and Just's spare prose packs a solid emotional punch." Entertainment Wkly

Just, Ward S.

★ An **unfinished** season; [by] Ward Just. Houghton Mifflin 2004 256p $24

ISBN 0-618-03669-5

LC 2004-42722

"Set in 1950's Chicago during a single summer, this novel recounts the story of the owner of a printing company, the narrator's father, who is on the management side of a vicious union dispute and begins to carry a gun. Wilson Raven, his son, takes a summer job at a scandal rag, where no amount of ink on his sleeves lives down the day he arrives at work wearing his bowed dancing shoes from debutante balls on the ritzy North Shore." Economist

Just, Ward S.

The **weather** in Berlin; {by} Ward Just. Houghton Mifflin 2002 305p $24

ISBN 0-618-03668-7

LC 2001-51885

This novel "follows a burned-out American movie director on a three-month stay at an artists-and-intellectuals institute in the capital of the new Germany. At 64, Dix Greenwood is remembered for a film made decades ago, an art-house favorite set in a German lake village just after World War I. . . . Ailing physically, tantalized by a fading memory of artistic inspiration, resenting his actress wife for her still-active career, Greenwood repairs to the city Willy Brandt once called Germany's Schicksalstadt, city of destiny. Berlin is experiencing a rebirth; perhaps Dix will too." N Y Times Book Rev

K

K'wan (Author)

Animal; K'wan. Cash Money Content 2012 407 p. (trade paper) $14.99

ISBN 1936399253; 9781936399253; 9781936399260

LC 2011943461

This book, part of author K'wan's "Hood Rat" series, focuses on "Animal, a rapper-turned-killer whom everyone thought had been murdered. The streets are tense as the crews of King James and Shai Clark sense a major gang war is set to erupt. Cruising on the perimeter is Animal, the vicious killer who is waiting to take revenge on the shooter who tried to kill his woman, Gucci." (Library Journal)

K'wan (Author)

Section 8; a hood rat novel. K'wan. St. Martin's Griffin 2009 ix, 358 p.p

ISBN 0312536968; 9780312536961

LC 2009012530

In this ninth novel of K'wan's 'Hood Rat' series, the author depicts 'action, murder, betrayal, sex, more action, familiar faces and a few surprises. Readers are first introduced to Tionna, a single mom of two, desperate to recover her footing after her man gets arrested for his involvement in drug and gun dealing. Moving back to her old neighborhood in shame, Tionna devises a plan with her girlfriends--Gucci, Boots and Tracy--to con local record label mogul Don B. Meanwhile, Gucci meets and falls for Animal, a notorious criminal who's on the fence about going legitimate as a rapper. As their pursuits intertwine, Tionna and friends find much to learn about unintended consequences." (Publishers Weekly)

K'wan (Author)

Welfare wifeys; K'wan. St. Martin's Griffin 2010 337 p. (Hood rat novel.) (paperback) $14.99

ISBN 0312536976; 9780312536978

LC 2010030122

Street Literature Book Award Medal Honoree (2011)

In this novel by K'wan, part of the Hood Rat series, "the man known on the streets as Animal relocates to Texas and finds fame and stardom as the newest act signed to the notorious Big Dawg Entertainment. His girlfriend, Gucci, is thrilled when she gets the news that he's coming back to New York on a promotional tour, but when she discovers the hidden agenda behind his homecoming nothing can prepare her for the life-altering consequences that will come of it." (Publisher's note)

Kadare, Ismail

The **general** of the dead army; a novel. [translated from the French of Jusuf Vrioni by Derek Coltman] Arcade Pub. 2008 264p $24.95

ISBN 978-1-55970-790-9

LC 2008-06946

Original Albanian edition, 1963; this translation first published 1971 in the United Kingdom and 1991 in the United States by New Amsterdam Books

"The book's protagonist is an Italian army officer who has come to Albania to recover the bodies of soldiers who died twenty years earlier in World War II. The General and his team carry crudely drawn maps and directions to burial sites supplied by aging war veterans. At first, the General fantasizes about returning home in triumph with his army of dead soldiers, but his optimism quickly fades. Rain and cold weather make recovery difficult, and the sullen Albanians continue to treat the Italians as invaders. . . . Before long, the General is haunted by terrifying dreams and hallucinations. He starts to see living people as skeletal remains and, fatally, begins to feel sympathy for the Albanians. This gloomy but powerful antiwar novel provides an excellent introduction to Albania's best-known author." Libr J

Kadare, Ismail

The **ghost** rider; translated from the French of Jusuf Vrioni by Jon Rothschild; updated, with new sections added, by Ismail Kadare and David Bellos; introduction by David Bellos. Canongate 2010 208p pa $13.95

ISBN 978-1-84767-341-1

Originally published in Albanian; this edition translated from French

The author "takes an ancient Albanian tale, 'The Ballad of Constantine and Doruntine,' as the starting point for this compelling if enigmatic novel set in medieval Albania. The deaths of the nine Vranaj brothers, all soldiers, many felled by a plague carried by their battlefield adversaries, have devastated a small Albanian community. Their mother's loss is only compounded by the absence at the time of her daughter, Doruntine, who was married three years earlier and moved far away from home. When Doruntine suddenly appears at her mother's door, claiming that one of her brothers, Kostandin, was her traveling companion, the news that Kostandin has been dead for years sends both mother and daughter to their deathbeds, leaving the local police captain to try to explain the inexplicable. Kadare excels at depicting the ever-expanding repercussions of what could have been a tragedy limited just to the Vranaj family." Publ Wkly

Kadare, Ismail

The **Successor**; a novel. translated from the French of Tedi Papavrami by David Bellos. Arcade Publishing 2005 207p $24

ISBN 1-55970-773-9

LC 2005-10311

Original Albanian edition, 2003

This novel "depicts an Albania governed by the whim and vanity of the aging Guide when the Successor, second in command, is found dead in his bedroom. The international intelligence community and the citizens of Albania contemplate the questions of how the Successor fell from grace and whether he died through murder or suicide. From day to day, the official word varies as the Guide decides whether the Successor is an enemy of the state or a martyr for the party. Drawing on real events–Mehmet Shehu was poised to succeed Albanian dictator Enver Hoxha in 1981 when he mysteriously died–Kadare successfully builds suspense by portraying multiple suspects with the motivation to commit murder; all believe they are guilty of the crime in some small or large way." Libr J

Kadare, Ismail

★ The **three**-arched bridge; translated from the Albanian by John Hodgson. Arcade Pub. 1997 184p

ISBN 1-55970-368-7

LC 96-41236

Originally written 1976-1978; published in French translation 1993

In this "matter-of-fact parable, a fourteenth-century Albanian monk attempts to 'record the lie we saw and the truth we did not see' about the building of a stone bridge that is a threatening wonder to the local people. The lie is the myths and legends exploited by the foreign builders to destroy their competitors; the truth is the mercenary nature of their crime. Kadare manages to appeal to a sense of outrage and hunger for evidence even as he suggests the outlines of today's Balkans." New Yorker

Kafka, Franz, 1883-1924

★ The **castle**. Knopf 1992 xxxviii, 378p $17

ISBN 0-679-41735-4

LC 92-52904

Original German edition, 1926; this translation first published 1930

In this unfinished novel, the hero, "known only as K., is constantly frustrated in his efforts to gain entrance into a mysterious castle to which he believes he has been summoned to work as a land surveyor. The castle is administered by an extraordinarily complicated and incompetent bureaucratic hierarchy that refuses to either recognize or reject K.'s claim. He is put to work instead as a school janitor and is denied his right to practice his craft. According to Brod, Kafka intended K., an ailing man throughout the novel, to die of exhaustion at the end of the novel." Reader's Ency. 4th edition

Kafka, Franz, 1883-1924

★ **Collected** stories; edited and introduced by Gabriel Josipvici. Knopf 1993 lv, 503p $21

ISBN 0-679-42303-6

LC 93-1858

Contents: Children on a country road; Unmasking a confidence trickster; The sudden walk; Resolutions; Excursion into the mountains; Bachelor's ill luck; The tradesman; Absent-minded window-gazing; The way home; Passers-by; On the tram; Clothes; Rejection; Reflections for gentlemen-jockeys; The street window; The wish to be a red Indian; The trees; Unhappiness; The judgment; The stoker; The metamorphosis; In the penal colony; The new advocate; A country doctor; Up in the gallery; An old manuscript; Before the law; Jackals and Arabs; A visit to a mine; The next village; An imperial message; The cares of a family man; Eleven sons; A fratricide; A dream; A report to an Academy; The bucket rider; First sorrow; A little woman; A hunger artist; Josephine the singer; Description of a struggle; Wedding preparations in the country; The student; The angel; The village schoolmaster {the giant mole}; Blumfeld, an elderly bachelor; The Hunter Gracchus; The proclamation; The bridge; The Great Wall of China; The knock at the manor gate; An ancient sword; New lamps; My neighbor; A crossbreed {a sport}; A splendid beast; The watchman; A common confusion; The truth about Sancho Panza; The silence of the sirens; Prometheus; The city coat of arms; Poseidon; Fellowship; At night; The problem of our laws; The conscription of troops; The test; The vulture; The helmsman; The top; Hands; A little fable; Isabella; Home-coming; A Chinese puzzle; The departure; Advocates; Investigations of a dog; The married couple; Give it up!; On parables; The burrow

Kafka, Franz, 1883-1924

★ **Metamorphosis**. Vanguard Press 1945 98p il

Written in 1915 this is "often regarded as Kafka's most perfectly finished work. 'The Metamorphosis' begins as its hero, Gregor Samsa, awakens one morning to find himself changed into a huge insect; the story proceeds to develop the effects of this change upon Samsa's business and family life and ends with his death. It has been read as everything from a religious allegory to a psychoanalytic case history; it is notable for its clarity of depiction and attention to significant detail, which give its completely fantastic occurrences an aura of indisputable truth, so that no allegorical interpretation is necessary to demonstrate its greatness." Reader's Ency. 4th edition

Kafka, Franz, 1883-1924

The **penal** colony: stories and short pieces; translated by Willa and Edwin Muir. Schocken Bks. 1948 320p il

Stories included are: The judgment; The metamorphosis; A country doctor; In the penal colony; A hunger artist

Kafka, Franz, 1883-1924

★ The **trial**; translated from the German by Willa and Edwin Muir; revised, with additional notes, by E. M. Butler. Knopf 1992 299p $19

ISBN 0-679-40994-7

Original edition 1924; first Everyman's Library edition, 1922

"Joseph K., a respected bank assessor, is arrested and spends his remaining years fighting charges about which he has no knowledge. The helplessness of an insignificant individual within a mysterious bureaucracy where answers are never accessible is described in this provocative and disturbing book." Shapiro. Fic for Youth. 3d edition

Kallos, Stephanie

Broken for you. Grove Press 2004 371p $24

ISBN 0-8021-1779-1

LC 2004-40631

"The novel itself is a mosaic of eccentric characters and their interlocking storylines, which sometimes border on the fantastic. . . . So lovely is the world Kallos has created that it seems more reparative to curl up on the couch with this book and suspend belief than to deconstruct the plot." Washington Post Book World

Kalotay, Daphne

Sight Reading; Daphne Kalotay. HarperCollins 2013 336 p. (hardcover) $25.99

ISBN 0062246933; 9780062246936

This novel, by Daphne Kalotay, begins "on a warm spring day after a long New England winter, Hazel and Remy spot each other for the first time in years. . . . Remy, a gifted violinist, is married to the Scottish composer Nicholas Elko--once the love of Hazel's life. . . . In the twenty years since Hazel's world was tipped on its axis, these three artists have faced unexpected joys, mysterious afflictions and other puzzles of life, their fates irrevocably interlaced." (Publisher's note)

Kaminsky, Stuart M.

Dancing in the dark. Mysterious Press 1996 228p

LC 95-13095

The author "effortlessly choreographs Hollywood history, colorful cast and dirty doings." Publ Wkly

Kaminsky, Stuart M.

A **fatal** glass of beer. Mysterious Press 1997 246p

LC 96-49494

The author "balances one-liners from Fields with headlines about the war effort in this amiable adventure that delivers a nicely twisted plot with fully dimensioned characters, including the usually caricatured misanthropic comedian." Publ Wkly

Kaminsky, Stuart M.

Murder on the Trans-Siberian Express. Mysterious Press 2001 277p

ISBN 0-89296-747-1

LC 2001-26218

"The action reaches back to Siberia in 1894, when one man in a band of starving, disease-ridden convicts, sentenced to work on constructing the great rail line from Moscow to Vladivostok, buries his treasure—a leather pouch containing a tiny gold box with a letter inside. More than a century later, Inspector Porfiry of the Moscow Police is sent on the 6,000-mile rail line to find this box. Porfiry leaves behind two other investigations: the kidnapping of a skinhead rock star and a series of murders in the Moscow Metro. How Kaminsky weaves these tangled plot lines into a taut suspense fabric, while providing fascinating, sad-funny commentary on his characters and the tensions inherent in the new Russian social order, is a matter of wonder." Booklist

Kaminsky, Stuart M.

To catch a spy; a Toby Peters mystery. Carroll & Graf Pubs. 2002 230p $24

ISBN 0-7867-1023-3

LC 2002-67254

In this installment the author supposes Cary Grant "to have been a British intelligence agent, his job to detect the activities of Nazi sympathizers in Hollywood. Married to Woolworth heiress Barbara Hutton at the time, he finds more pro-Nazis among his wife's rich friends than among the acting community. Grant hires Toby, who packs a .38 with which he's unable to hit the broad side of a sound stage, to deliver a satchel of money in the dark of night to a man who'll give him an envelope in return." Publ Wkly

Kaminsky, Stuart M.

Tomorrow is another day. Mysterious Press 1995 201p

LC 94-18987

"Set during World War II, when Hollywood was at its most glamorous, the plot involves the mysterious stabbing death of an extra on the set of Selznick International's Gone with the Wind. Five years after the murder, the debonair Clark Gable approaches Toby {Peters} to ask for help—seems Gable's been receiving bizarre death threats in the form of poems. . . . Nostalgic readers with a yen for the good old days—when men were men and movies were movies—will find Kaminsky's story entertaining, clever, eminently readable, and chock-full of snippets from Hollywood's Golden Age." Booklist

Kane, Ben

★ **Spartacus**; the gladiator. Ben Kane. 1st U.S. ed. St. Martins Press 2012 466 p. maps (trade) $26.99; (paperback) $15.99; (downloadable audio) $34.42

ISBN 1250001161; 9781250001160; 9781250021564; 9781466802667; 9781448115976

LC 2011279125

Author Ben Kane tells the story of Spartacus and the Roman Army. "Betrayed to the Romans by his jealous king, Spartacus--and with him Ariadne--are taken in captivity to the gladiator school at Capua. It is from here--against the unbelievable brutality of gladiatorial life--that Spartacus and Crixus the Gaul plan their escape to Vesuvius, where they recruit and train a huge slave army. An army which will keep the might of Rome at bay for two years." (benkane.net)

Kanon, Joseph

Istanbul passage; a novel. Joseph Kanon. Atria Books 2012 404 p.

ISBN 1439156417; 9781439156414

LC 2011045510

This espionage novel is set in "1945 Istanbul, [as] Allied veteran Leon Bauer is running spy missions under the cover of a U.S. tobacco-importing business. With the war over, U.S. operations are closing up shop in the neutral capital, but Leon has one last big job: to take possession of a Romanian defector in possession of important Russian secrets and get him flown to safety. The rub is the defector, Alexei, was involved in a heinous massacre of Jews four years earlier." (Kirkus)

Kanon, Joseph

Los Alamos; a novel. Broadway Bks. 1997 403p

LC 96-44055

"'Los Alamos,' besides being a terrific mystery, wonderfully evokes the Southwest in the '40s, reminding us in a dozen subtle ways that life goes on even while history is being made." Newsweek

Kantor, MacKinlay

★ **Andersonville**. World Pub. 1955 767p il

"After twenty-five years of research Kantor wrote this novel, which realistically portrays the atrocities of Andersonville Prison, home of many Yankee soldiers during the Civil War. Ira Claffey, Georgia planter and owner of the property on which Andersonville is built, serves as a humane central character whose sorrows and frustrations serve to point up the brutality of war. The primitive, indeed horrible, existence of the prisoners is described in detail." Shapiro. Fic for Youth. 3d edition

Kardos, Michael

The **Three**-Day Affair; Michael Kardos. Pgw 2012 256 p. $24.00

ISBN 0802120261; 9780802120267

This crime novel by Michael Kardos follows a group of reunited college friends. "While the three are out for a drive, just after Will has persuaded the other two to invest in his plan to start a record label, Jeffrey emerges from a convenience store with a hostage in tow--for no good reason." (Publishers Weekly)

Karinthy, Ferenc

Metropole; translated from the Hungarian by George Szirtes. Telegram 2008 236p pa $14.95

ISBN 978-1-84659-034-4; 1-84659-034-5

Original Hungarian edition, 1970

"Budai, a linguist en route to a conference, steps off of a plane and finds himself not in Helsinki but in a land with an impenetrable language and a massive population swarming the streets and sidewalks. Every morning, he sets out to find his way home, or at least to find someone who speaks Hungarian, and every night, he finds himself back at the hotel with his dwindling supply of money, bewildered by the world in which he is trapped. Karinthy's story is anxious and claustrophobic, but it's shot through with humor and surprising believability. Budai is relentless and resourceful, and Karinthy is a skilled enough writer that his protagonist's failed attempts to make headway never become monotonous. Metropole invites comparisons to Kafka, and manages to live up to them." NPR

Karlsson, Jonas

The **room**; a novel. Jonas Karlsson. Hogarth 2014 192 p. $14

ISBN 0804139989; 9780804139984

LC 2014014601

In this novel by Jonas Karlsson "Bjorn . . . discovers a secret room at the government office where he works--a secret room that no one else in his office will acknowledge. When Bjorn is in his room, what his co-workers see is him standing by the wall and staring off into space looking dazed, relaxed, and decidedly creepy. Bjorn's bizarre behavior eventually leads his co-workers to try and have him fired, but Bjorn will turn the tables on them with help from his secret room." (Publisher's note)

"Part psychological drama documenting a disturbed man's possible descent into madness and part satirical take on corporate culture and the alienated workers it produces, Karlsson succeeds admirably in creating the perfect combination of funny, surreal, and disturbing." Booklist

Karnezis, Panos

The **maze**. Farrar, Straus and Giroux 2004 376p $24

ISBN 0-374-20480-2

LC 2003-60261

"As with many an imperial expedition, the soldiers seem to be lost without honor; they massacre civilians on their fool's errand undertaken for worthless ends. Karnezis dramatizes their plight with remorseless clarity and dry humor." N Y Times Book Rev

Karon, Jan, 1937-

At home in Mitford; Jan Karon. G.P. Putnam's Sons 2015 540 p. (hardcover) $27.95

ISBN 0399183566; 9780399183560

LC 2015025082

Originally published 1994

"It's easy to feel at home in Mitford. In these high, green hills, the air is pure, the village is charming, and the people are generally lovable. Yet, Father Tim, the bachelor rector, wants something more. Enter a dog the size of a sofa who moves in and won't go away. Add an attractive neighbor who begins wearing a path through the hedge. Now, stir in a lovable but unloved boy, a mystifying jewel theft, and a secret that's sixty years old." (Publisher's note)

Other Mitford novels are:

A light in the window (1995)
These high, green hills (1996)
Out to Canaan (1997)
A new song (1999)
A common life (2001)
In this mountain (2002)
Shepherds abiding (2003)
Light from heaven (2005)
Somewhere safe with somebody good (2014)
Come rain or come shine (2015)
To be where you say (2017)

Karpyshyn, Drew

Children of fire; Drew Karpyshyn. Del Rey 2013 512 p. (hardback) $26

ISBN 0345542231; 9780345542236

LC 2013020337

In this book, "decades after the tyrannical Order of the Crown suppresses magic with the violent 'Purging,' the Legacy, a barrier protecting the mortal realm from ancient Gods, is weakened. Lucifer-like Daemron transports four pieces of enchanted stone into the mortal world through the birth of four children. Each child is destined to wreak destruction with chaotic powers, thrust into a cruel and desperate war among gods, mages, and kings where the prize is reality itself." (Publishers Weekly)

Karunatilaka, Shehan

The **legend** of Pradeep Mathew; a novel. Shehan Karunatilaka. Graywolf Press 2011 397 p. (pbk.) $16

ISBN 1555976115; 9781555976118

LC 2012931911

This novel follows "Sri Lankan . . . sportswriter Wijedasa Gamini Karunasena (Wije to his friends) [who] fits in well with the American stereotype of the journalist as a cigarette-smoking boozer. . . . After years of abusing his liver, and after the Cricket World Cup matches in 1996, he begins to track down the enigmatic Pradeep Mathew, a 'spinner' and the best Sri Lankan cricketer ever." (Kirkus Reviews)

Kashua, Sayed

Second person singular; Sayed Kashua ; translated from the Hebrew by Mitch Ginsburg. Grove Press 2012 346 p.

ISBN 0802120199; 9780802120199

2011 Bernstein Award

This Bernstein Award-winning Israeli psychological novel by Sayed Kashua, "centers on an ambitious lawyer who is considered one of the best Arab criminal attorneys in Jerusalem. He has a thriving practice in the Jewish part of town, a large house, speaks perfect Hebrew, and is in love with his wife and two young children. One day at a used bookstore, he picks up a copy of Tolstoy's The Kreutzer Sonata, and inside finds a love letter, in Arabic, in his wife's handwriting. Consumed with suspicion and jealousy, the lawyer hunts for the book's previous owner—a man named Yonatan—pulling at the strings that hold all their lives together. . . . Kashua spins a tale of love and betrayal, honesty and artifice, and questions whether it is possible to truly reinvent ourselves." (Publisher's note)

Kasischke, Laura, 1961-

The **raising**; a novel. Harper Perennial 2011 461p pa $14.99

ISBN 978-0-06-200478-9; 0-06-204478-6

LC 2010-21605

"Kasischke excels at depicting the psychology of the young and the traumatized even as she delivers a scathing indictment of the siege mentality of college administrators. In this literary page-turner, reminiscent of Donna Tartt's Secret History (1992), the talented author inlays her academic novel with a touch of the supernatural and a deep sense of foreboding." Booklist

Katzenbach, John

The **analyst**. Ballantine Bks. 2002 424p

ISBN 0-345-42626-6

LC 2001-43841

The author has "potently chronicled a long journey of revenge and redemption. Some of his psychological plot points . . . are a stretch, but the novel's fine sense of pacing, sudden switchbacks and chilling characterizations far overshadow its minor faults." Publ Wkly

Katzenbach, John

Hart's war; a novel. Ballantine Pub. Group 1999 490p

ISBN 0-345-42624-X

LC 98-29890

"Katzenbach's setting is flawlessly grim, and his characters chillingly reveal the divisive bigotry of soldiers ostensibly fighting for the same values, as well as some unexpected sources of redemption." Publ Wkly

Katzenbach, John

Just cause. Putnam 1992 431p

ISBN 0-399-13626-6

LC 91-15135

"Despite some extraneous subplots, the story generally proceeds at a breakneck pace, enhanced by ear-perfect dialogue and complex characterization." Publ Wkly

Katzenbach, John

★ **What** comes next; John Katzenbach. Mysterious Press 2012 448 p. $27.00

ISBN 0802126111; 9780802126115

In this book, "Adrian Thomas, a retired professor," recently diagnosed with degenerative dementia, "witnesses a man and a woman in an unmarked van kidnap 16-year-old Jennifer Riggins, who's running away from home. The couple have seized Jennifer to star in Whatcomesnext.com, a Web site where viewers watch the girl's torture in real time. Despite his failing mind, Adrian is able to use the psychological insights he gleaned as a professor to hunt for Jennifer." (Publishers Weekly)

Kaufman, Bel

★ **Up** the down staircase. Prentice-Hall 1964 340p il

"Fresh from graduate study in English and crammed with pedagogy courses, young Sylvia Barrett begins her first year as a teacher in Calvin Coolidge High School. The experiences of this first year teacher, determined to remain true to her ideals despite the administrative confusion and organizational chaos of a New York City high school, form the core of Up the Down Staircase. . . . It tells its story through a series of letters, administrative memoranda, student compositions, suggestion box contributions, and intraschool communications." Best Sellers

Kaufman, Millard

Bowl of cherries; a novel. McSweeney's Books 2007 326p $22

ISBN 9781932416831; 1-932416-83-8

"Kaufman's rapier-sharp prose and keen instinct for finding the absurd in everyday life makes this a social satire of the first order." LA Wkly

Kaufman, Sue

★ **Diary** of a mad housewife. Random House 1967 311p

"Bettina Balser, in her mid-thirties, with a husband, two daughters ages nine and seven, and a bright apartment on Central Park West, (New York City), has arrived at a point in her life where she has completely lost her way, her purpose, her identity. She is literally terrified of so many things . . . that she is also afraid she is losing her mind. She decides to write out the things that so alarm her, as a form of therapy." Best Sellers

Kaufmann, Nicholas

★ **Dying** Is My Business; Nicholas Kaufmann. St Martins Pr 2013 384 p. $15.99

ISBN 1250036100; 9781250036100

LC 2013025227

In this book, by Nicholas Kaufmann, "an amnesiac discovers he can't stay dead. . . . Trent, a man who has no last name and no past that he can remember, dies often but fails to remain dead. Every time someone murders Trent, he pops back to life. . . . Trent meets Thornton, the undead werewolf, and Bethany Savory. . . . They lead Trent to others who are on the same quest, including magicians, vampires and various magical creatures." (Kirkus Reviews)

Kava, Alex

Hotwire. Doubleday 2011 291p $25.95

ISBN 978-0-385-53201-3

LC 2010-52991

"A sizzling plot, achingly real characters, and government officials working their backsides off to save their backsides, all strike as lethally as lightning." Publ Wkly

Kawabata, Yasunari

Snow country, and Thousand cranes; the Nobel Prize edition of two novels. translated from the Japanese by Edward G. Seidensticker. Knopf 1969 2v in 1

First United States editions published 1957 and 1959, respectively

Snow country "describes the three visits of Shimamura, a rich Tokyo dilettante, to a hotspring in the west of Japan, the snowiest region in the world. Here a young geisha, Komako, becomes his mistress and falls in love with him. . . . Komako's sparkling freshness stirs him, and he is touched by the 'irresistible sadness' she makes him feel, a sense of beauty going to waste and of immanent decay. But he cannot return her love; and their strange relationship, to which she gives so much, is doomed from the start." Atlantic

Kawabata, Yasunari

The **sound** of the mountain; translated from the Japanese by Edward M. Seidensticker. Knopf 1970 276p

"The language is delicate, allusive, intensely Japanese; and, since plot and character development count for little, the style is all-important. We are fortunate that it should have been a writer with Mr. Seidensticker's gifts who ventured to convey {Kawabata's} rarefied novels into English." N Y Times Book Rev

Kay, Guy Gavriel

★ **Children** of earth and sky; Guy Gavriel Kay. New American Library 2016 560 p. map (hardcover) $27

ISBN 9780451472960; 9780698183278; 0698183274; 0451472969

LC 2015047832

This book by Guy Gavriel Kay is "set in a world inspired by the conflicts and dramas of Renaissance Europe. Against this tumultuous backdrop the lives of men and women unfold on the borderlands—where empires and faiths collide. . . . As these lives entwine, their fates—and those of many others—will hang in the balance, when the khalif sends out his massive army to take the great fortress that is the gateway to the western world." (Publisher's note)

"This intricately plotted literary novel will appeal to Kay's many fans as well as readers who enjoy character-driven historical fiction with just a touch of fantasy." Booklist

Kay, Guy Gavriel

★ **River** of Stars; Guy Gavriel Kay. Penguin Group USA 2013 656 p. (hardcover) $26.95

ISBN 0451464974; 9780451464972

LC 2013002317

This is the second in Guy Gavriel Kay's alternate historical fantasy series about the fictional country of Kitai. "Several hundred years after the events of 'Under Heaven' (which was set in the equivalent of the Tang Dynasty), teen Ren Daiyan demonstrates legend-level archery prowess and becomes a marsh outlaw. Years later, when a cloistered emperor's hobby begins destroying lives, Daiyan tries to redeem his honor by joining the imperial army to halt the empire's decline." (Publishers Weekly)

"An elegant, imaginative inhabitation of Song-dynasty China of 1,000 years ago." Kirkus

Kay, Guy Gavriel

Under heaven. Roc-New American Library 2010 573p $26.95

ISBN 978-0-451-46330-2

LC 2010-4833

"Virtually everything a reader could want in a book: a thrilling adventure, a love story, a coming-of-age tale, a military chronicle, a court-intrigue drama, a tragedy and on and on. It is a sumptuous feast of storytelling." Globe and Mail

Kay, Guy Gavriel

★ **Ysabel**. Roc 2007 421p

ISBN 978-0-451-46129-2; 0-451-46129-0

LC 2006-28326

"The author's historical detail, evocative writing and fascinating characters—both ancient and modern—will enthrall mainstream as well as fantasy readers." Publ Wkly

Kaye, M. M.

The **far** pavilions. St. Martin's Press 1978 957p

LC 78-3975

"It's a leisurely, panoramic, enjoyable tale, convincing and varied in characterization, rich in adventure, heroism, cruelty and love, rich in India." Publ Wkly

Kazantzakis, Nikos

The **last** temptation of Christ; translated from the Greek by P. A. Bien. Simon & Schuster 1960 506p

"The Christ created here by Kazantzakis is definitely not the Christ of the Gospels. . . . Far from it. Kazantzakis has composed a fictional biography of Jesus that is written with passion, a colorful, lyric testimony of his, Kazantzakis' own anguished search for God." Best Sellers

Kazantzakis, Nikos

★ **Zorba** the Greek; translated by Carl Wildman. Simon & Schuster 1952 311p

"The spirit of Zorba, full of energy and peasant philosophy, is contrasted with that of the narrator, a learned but staid Englishman who comes to Crete for adventure. The relationship between the two men deepens despite Zorba's mismanagement of the narrator's mining business, and despite Zorba's attempts to change his friend's behavior to a more zestful one. Kazantzakis creates in Zorba a character that represents the vitality sapped by the inhibitions civilization has created." Shapiro. Fic for Youth. 3d edition

Kazinski, A. J.

The **last** good man; a novel. by A.J. Kazinski ; translated from the Danish by Tiina Nunnally. Scribner 2012 469 p. (hardcover) $26.99

ISBN 9781451640755; 9781451640762; 9781451640779

LC 2011044179

In this book, "[t]he Jewish legend that the world is kept from destruction by 36 just people, who are unaware of their status, underpins . . . [the plot by author A. J.] Kazinski, the pseudonym of filmmaker Anders Rønnow Klarlund and Jacob Weinreich. When Italian police officer Tommaso di Barbara becomes aware that good people have been dying all over the world, he concludes that the victims are 34 of the 36, and contacts a Danish colleague, hostage negotiator Niels Bentzon, to assist him in saving the last two members of the group. Bentzon, in turn, finds unexpected help in the form of scientist Hannah Lund, who uses the inquiry to re-engage with the world after her son's suicide." (Publishers Weekly)

Keane, Mary Beth

Fever; Mary Beth Keane. Simon & Schuster 2013 320 p. $26

ISBN 1451693419; 9781451693416

LC 2013409090

This historical novel focuses on Typhoid Mary. "Apprehended by the New York Department of Health in 1907, following the deaths of the family for whom she cooks, Mary Mallon is turned into a guinea pig on an East River island with little to comfort her aside from rare letters from her lover Alfred. Slowly she builds a case to win her freedom and returns to a changed New York of Chinese laundries, tenement fires, and Alfred, now-destitute," surviving by getting another cook position. (Publishers Weekly)

Kearsley, Susanna

The **Firebird**; Susanna Kearsley. Sourcebooks Inc 2013 544 p. (paperback) $16.99

ISBN 140227663X; 9781402276637

LC 2013010359

In this book by Susanna Kearsley, protagonist "Nicola Marter works for a London gallery. . . . She also has the secret ability to hold an object and see past events.When a woman comes in with a small carved bird, Nicola has a vision of the Empress Catherine giving it to a young woman named Anna. With no documented provenance, the carving is worthless to collectors, and Nicola feels impelled to authenticate it." (Booklist)

Keating, H. R. F.

The **soft** detective. St. Martin's Press 1998 268p

ISBN 0-312-19335-1

LC 98-8817

First published 1997 in the United Kingdom

"When Detective Chief Inspector Phil Benholme begins investigating the murder of a Nobel Prize-winning physiologist, he can scarcely believe what he discovers: his own teenage son may be involved. Keating's latest is a gripping examination of one of a police officer's worst nightmares—a portrait of a man faced with the choice between defending his son and helping to prove he's a killer." Booklist

Keene, John

Counternarratives; John Keene. New Directions 2015 320 p. (hardcover : acid-free paper) $24.95

ISBN 0811224341; 9780811224345

LC 2015001269

This book by John Keene presents "a collection of complex, genre-defying stories, focusing primarily on the range and variety of the black experience. Unrolling chronologically across three sections--the first set in earlier eras, such as 17th-century Brazil and revolutionary America; the second set mostly in mid-19th- to early-20th century America; and the third in modern-day Africa--these stories interrogate the meanings of identity, agency, duty, and freedom within each period." (Publishers Weekly)

"The occasional piece gets heavy-handed, but these are mostly concise, arresting stories that will attract smart readers." LJ

Keesey, Anna

★ **Little** century; a novel. Anna Keesey. 1st ed. Farrar, Straus and Giroux 2012 322 p. (hardcover) $26

ISBN 0374192049; 9780374192044

LC 2011046308

In this historical novel, "newly orphaned Esther Chambers leaves Chicago for the high desert of Oregon," and claims "a homestead adjoining" the land of her cattle rancher cousin Pick. Slowly Esther learns to feel at home in the small town, learning "to ride a horse and tak[ing] up typewriting and typesetting." Pick wants to marry her, but she loves a sheep farmer. "Then a murder turns the town inside out." (Library Journal)

Kehlmann, Daniel

Fame; a novel in nine episodes. translated from the German by Carol Brown Janeway. Pantheon Books 2010 175p $24

ISBN 978-0-307-37871-2; 0-307-37871-3

LC 2009-52380

Original German edition, 2009

"The sly humor of this book is indebted to an excellent translation by Carol Brown Janeway. . . . Clearly divided and purposefully connected, the stories in 'Fame' make a terrific case for the way fiction enables us to lead double lives—and then, at the stories' end, to go home." Boston Globe

Keilson, Hans

Comedy in a minor key; translated from the German by Damion Searls. Farrar, Straus and Giroux 2010 135p $22

ISBN 978-0-374-12675-9; 0-374-12675-5

LC 2010-01482

Original German edition, 1947

"Not once does the author mention Hitler. Not once does he mention death camps. Not once does he put the word Nazi on paper. Rather, in 'Comedy in a Minor Key,' author Hans Keilson reveals the horrors of the Holocaust in an eerie, intense way. He takes readers inside the minds of three main characters and provides a gripping psychoanalysis of what it was like both for a Jew in hiding and the couple who gave him sanctuary. . . . The novel, a dark comedy, is semi-autobiographical. A Dutch couple, Marie and Wim, agree to hide a Jewish man during World War II. The fugitive, who gives his name as Nico rather than his Jewish-sounding name, dies after a prolonged illness. Dead, the man is more dangerous to the couple than alive." Boston Globe

Keilson, Hans

Life goes on; Hans Keilson ; translated from the German by Damion Searls. Farrar, Straus and Giroux 2012 272 p.

ISBN 0374191956; 9780374191955

LC 2012012326

Originally published as Leben geht weiter: Berlin : S. Fischer, 1933.

This book by Hans Keilson is "an autobiographical novel that paints a dark yet illuminating portrait of Germany between the world wars. It is the story of Herr Seldersen -- a Jewish store owner modeled on Keilson's father, a textile merchant and decorated World War I veteran -- along with his wife and son, Albrecht, and the troubles they encounter as the German economy collapses and politics turn rancid." (Publisher's note)

Keller, Julia ✓

★ A **killing** in the hills; Julia Keller. Minotaur Books 2012 384 p. (hardcover) $24.99

ISBN 9781250003485; 9781250018069

LC 2012016583

In this book, "the shooting of three old men having coffee in a diner on a Saturday morning rattles the people of Acker's Gap, West Virginia, . . . in the Appalachians. Next on the hired shooter's list is county prosecutor Belfa (Bell) Elkins, whose return to poverty-plagued Acker's Gap after a dreadful childhood led to her divorce. . . . Bell remains dogged in her war against the drugs that she sees as the single biggest threat to the future of the state." (Booklist)

Other books about Bell Elkins are:

Bitter river (2013)

Summer of the dead (2014)

Last ragged breath (2015)
Sorrow road (2016)
Fast falls the night (2017)

Keller, Julia ✓

Last Ragged Breath; Julia Keller. Minotaur Books 2015 384 p. $25.99

ISBN 125004474X; 9781250044747

LC 2015017000

In this novel, by Julia Keller, "Royce Dillard doesn't remember much about the day his parents-and one hundred and twenty-three other souls-died in the 1972 Buffalo Creek disaster. But now Dillard, who lives off the grid with only a passel of dogs for company, is fighting for his life one more time: He's on trial for murder. Prosecutor Bell Elkins faces her toughest challenge yet in this haunting story of vengeance, greed and the fierce struggle for social justice." (Publisher's note)

"With bits of her backstory still being revealed, Elkins is certainly among the best-drawn characters in crime fiction today." Booklist

Kellerman, Faye ✓

The **forgotten**. Morrow 2001 374p (Peter Decker/Rina Lazarus Series)

ISBN 0-688-15614-2

"The depiction of how teens and parents push and pull at one another's emotions is dead on." Booklist

Kellerman, Faye ✓

Jupiter's bones; a novel. Morrow 1999 375p (Peter Decker/Rina Lazarus Series)

ISBN 0-688-15612-6

LC 99-33356

"Kellerman has pulled together elements of suspense, violence, humor, pathos, and love and wrapped them into a potent plot certain to captivate genre fans." Booklist

Kellerman, Faye ✓

Milk and honey; a novel. Morrow 1990 384p (Peter Decker/Rina Lazarus Series)

LC 89-39592

"On a summer night in a housing development near Los Angeles, police sergeant Peter Decker finds a winsome two-year-old girl playing on a swing set—and wearing blood-soaked pajamas. Unclaimed, 'Sally' is placed in a foster home while Decker and partner Marge Dunn try to learn her identity. Bee stings on her arms lead them days later to the scene of a bloody multiple murder at a honey farm. While piecing together a bizarre puzzle of betrayal and revenge . . . Peter is also investigating rape and assualt charges brought against an old army buddy from Vietnam. The pressures of the murder case and doubts about his friend's innocence compound Peter's anxiety as he waits for young Orthodox Jewish widow Rina Lazarus to decide if she will marry him." Publ Wkly

Kellerman, Faye

Prayers for the dead. Morrow 1996 406p (Peter Decker/Rina Lazarus Series)

ISBN 0688143679; 9780688143671

LC 96-7494

This novel "continues the story of Peter Decker and Rina Lazarus, an L.A. detective and his beautiful wife. Someone has murdered Azor Sparks, noted heart surgeon, and Peter must discover the motive and the murderer. Was the motive greed, ambition, random violence, or love gone wrong? Was the murderer one of Spark's colleagues, or one of his family? And what is the connection between Rina and Sparks's son Abram?" (Libr J)

This "mystery begins with the brutal murder and mutilation of renowned heart surgeon, researcher and fundamentalist Christian Azor Sparks. LAPD Lieutenant Decker gets the call. He also gets an abundance of suspects. . . . Religion and morality are integral to Kellerman's mysteries—built on the bedrock of the Deckers' orthodox Judaism. Here she deftly casts her net around the commanding victim, whose shadow lay equally over family and colleagues, and his son, the theologian Father Abram, whose past connection with Rina may force Decker off the case." Publ Wkly

Kellerman, Faye ✓

Serpent's tooth; a Peter Decker/Rina Lazarus novel. Morrow 1997 400p

ISBN 0-688-14368-7

LC 97-10685

"The scope of the investigation is broad and the moralizing is kept to a minimum, giving Decker a rare chance to do some solid police work."' N Y Times Book Rev

Kellerman, Jesse

The **genius**. G.P. Putnam's Sons 2008 374p $24.95

ISBN 978-0-399-15459-1; 0-399-15459-0

LC 2008-5810

"When Manhattan art dealer Ethan Muller is shown a dingy rent-controlled apartment bursting with fabulous work, he jumps on it, soon mounting a show—even though the artist, Victor Cracke, has vanished. Who was Cracke, and why do some of the faces in his drawings look like young boys murdered years ago, the crimes unsolved? Prodded by a retired cop, Ethan begins to investigate—first unwillingly, then compulsively—and it becomes clear that Cracke's story is intertwined with that of Ethan's own family. Despite some cumbersome flashbacks, Jesse Kellerman's The Genius boasts a masterful plot and dead-on pacing." Entertainment Wkly

Kellerman, Jonathan

✓ **Billy** Straight; a novel. Random House 1999 467p

ISBN 0-679-45959-6

LC 98-19583

Hollywood homicide detective Petra Connor "frantically scours the city in search of a runaway 12-year-old boy who witnessed the vicious stabbing of a woman in Griffith Park. This case quickly draws the media carrion crows when it comes out that the victim was recently divorced from the popular star of a television series. Like Connor, the investigation is competent but strictly by the book—and not the reason you're turning the pages so fast. That distinction goes to the winsome title character and frequent narrator, a self-taught street kid with an artless affection for books." N Y Times Book Rev

Kellerman, Jonathan

✓ **Bones**; an Alex Delaware novel. Ballantine Books 2008 353p $27

ISBN 978-0-345-49513-6; 0-345-49513-6

LC 2008-35125

"Kellerman's strength is that he can set up an intriguing situation and keep things moving at a breakneck pace. He can also, when he wants to, write well. He's good at short, vivid descriptions. . . . I don't think the plot of "Bones" will withstand scrutiny, but most readers probably won't care. The story sweeps them along, offering plenty of snappy dialogue and cheap thrills, plus a fair amount of suspense that is relieved by the final unveiling of the killer." Washington Post Book World

Kellerman, Jonathan

The **clinic**. Bantam Bks. 1997 370p

LC 96-24626

The author "has crafted another masterly, darkly psychological tale, drawing upon timely issues ranging from abortion to organ harvesting." Libr J

Kellerman, Jonathan

Devil's waltz. Bantam Bks. 1993 416p

ISBN 0553092057; 9780553092059

LC 92-18089

"This psychological mystery centers on a disorder called Munchausen Syndrome {by proxy}, in which a primary care-giver—usually the mother—inflicts harm upon her child in order to focus attention on herself as a concerned parent. The suspicion of this crime alerts Dr. Stephanie Eves to consult with her long-time friend and colleague, Dr. Alex Delaware, a retired child psychologist. . . . {Twenty-one-month-old Cassie Jones} suffers from a variety of medical symptoms, made all the more alarming by the earlier SIDS death of her brother. As Dr. Delaware begins to unravel the mystery of Cassie's continuing medical traumas, he uncovers two related murders and a web of hospital intrigue." (SLJ)

"Alex Delaware, the child psychologist and amateur sleuth . . . returns to the beleaguered Los Angeles pediatrics hospital where he was trained. Called in to consult on the baffling case of a 2-year-old girl with phantom ailments, Alex performs his clinical chores with his customary tenderness, while bearing the details of the child's extraordinary medical history. Despite Mr. Kellerman's overelaborate approach, he maintains the harrowing suspense of a medical mystery too horrid to be anything but real." N Y Times Book Rev

Kellerman, Jonathan

Gone; an Alex Delaware novel. Ballantine Books 2006 365p $26.95

ISBN 0-345-45261-5

LC 2006-296289

"Delaware joins forces with his sometimes official partner in crime, LAPD detective Milo Sturgis, and together they pursue an investigative trail littered with corpses leading to an unconventional acting school and the family of the eccentric woman who runs it. While the murderer's identity may not be that surprising, the author's ability to convey the unrelenting sadness of his characters' lives and his deep psychological insights will satisfy those looking for more than mere thrills." Publ Wkly

Kellerman, Jonathan

Monster; a novel. Random House 1999 396p

ISBN 0-679-45960-X

LC 99-20098

"A handsome young actor is found murdered and mutilated, a female psychologist meets a similar fate, and twin brothers are gruesomely dispatched—all in separate events, on the same evening. The murders, though different, seem to be the work of the same killer. As Dr. Alex Delaware, psychologist and consultant to the LAPD, and detective Milo Sturgis unravel the mystery of the killer's identity, it becomes clear that Ardis Peake (a.k.a. 'Monster'), incarcerated in a psychiatric hospital for the criminally insane for the past 16 years, is somehow involved." Libr J

Kellerman, Jonathan

Private eyes. Bantam Bks. 1992 475p

LC 91-17314

"Harvard-bound, 18-year-old heiress Melissa Dickinson, whom child psychologist Alex Delaware had successfully treated for anxiety 10 years earlier, calls him with concerns about leaving her wealthy mother, an agoraphobe. Years before Melissa's birth, Gina Dickinson Ramp had been disfigured by acid thrown for never-revealed reasons by a former lover, now out of prison and back in town. Widowed for many years, recently remarried and making progress in her own intensive therapy with a noted husband-and-wife team of behaviorial psychologists, Gina is still fragile. When she disappears, Melissa enlists Delaware's help and that of his friend, Milo Sturgis, on leave from the LAPD. . . . Kellerman deftly handles the strings of his plot." Publ Wkly

Kellerman, Jonathan

Self-defense. Bantam Bks. 1995 390p

LC 94-26175

Psychologist Alex Delaware "is treating 25-year-old Lucy Lowell for a recurring nightmare that she has been having ever since serving on the hanging jury that convicted a serial killer. . . . When Lucy's terrifying dream is complicated by incidents of sleepwalking, bed-wetting, narcolepsy and a possible suicide attempt, Alex suspects a repressed childhood memory. After putting his patient through hypnotic regression, he is convinced that she witnessed a murder and he sets out to prove it. . . . An exciting story that is loaded with tension and packed with titillating insights into abnormal psychology." N Y Times Book Rev

Kellerman, Jonathan

Therapy. Ballantine Bks. 2004 387p $26.95

ISBN 0-345-45259-3

The author "manages to take the story of a lovers' lane double murder near Mulholland Drive to the point where it involves human rights atrocities in Rwanda. Along the way Mr. Kellerman packs in the descriptive detail that is one of his hallmarks and one of the incidental attractions in his fiction." N Y Times (Late N Y Ed)

Kellerman, Jonathan

Time bomb; a novel. Bantam Bks. 1990 468p

LC 90-349

This novel featuring "child psychologist and private detective Alex Delaware begins when Delaware is called upon to deal with the potential trauma to elementary school children of a sniper killed in their midst during lunch recess. He quickly learns that the sniper's target may not have been the children at all, but either a right-wing politician holding a news conference at the school or his liberal counterpart, a publicity-hungry, former 1960's radical who had appeared unexpectedly for an impromptu debate and whose bodyguard shot the sniper to death." N Y Times Book Rev

Kelly, Erin

Broadchurch; Erin Kelly; based on the TV series by Chris Chibnall. 1st U.S. ed. Minotaur Books 2014 448 p. map (hardback) $25.99

ISBN 1250055504; 9781250055507

LC 2014019562

"Detective Ellie Miller has just returned from vacation, only to learn that she's been passed over for a promotion at work in favor of outsider Alec Hardy. He, escaping the spectacular failure of his last case, is having trouble finding his way into this tight-knit community wary of new faces. But professional rivalry aside, both detectives are about to receive some terrible news: 11-year-old Danny Latimer has been found murdered on the beach." (Publisher's note)

"Kelly's novelization of the eponymous British TV series . . . works as both a classic puzzle and an unnerving portrait of a little English town wracked by a young boy's murder." Kirkus

Kelly, Erin

★ The **burning** air; a novel. Erin Kelly. Pamela Dorman Books 2013 336p. (hardback) $26.95

ISBN 0670026727; 9780670026722

LC 2012029302

In this suspense novel, the MacBride family gather to lay matriarch Lydia to rest, and "it becomes clear that all is not well. The usually sober father—retired headmaster Rowan—is unaccountably drunk; daughter Sophie and son-in-law Will may have reached an impasse because of an affair and a breakdown; mixed-race grandson Jake has been in trouble with the law; and disfigured son Felix has a beautiful new girlfriend whose initial silence unsettles everyone." (Publishers Weekly)

Kelly, Erin

The **poison** tree; a novel. Pamela Dorman Books/Viking 2011 322p $26.95

ISBN 978-0-670-02240-3

LC 2010-24260

First published 2009 in the United Kingdom

"Veteran mystery fans looking for nail-biting thrills will find plenty that is fresh and surprising about The Poison Tree, and Kelly's masterful plotting and intricately crafted story make the comparisons to Tana French and Donna Tartt well-deserved." BookPage

Kelly, James Patrick

The **wreck** of the Godspeed; with a foreword by Bob Eggleton. Golden Gryphon Press 2008 358p $24.95

ISBN 978-1-930846-51-7

LC 2007-48662

"Kelly's stories depend on future technologies based on physics, information theory, genetics, and other au courant disciplines, but they're about love, friendship, and loyalty." Booklist

Kelly, Jim

The **fire** baby; Jim Kelly. St. Martin's Minotaur 2004 322 p. (Philip Dryden Series) 9780312321451 $26

ISBN 0312321457

LC 2004048691

Sequel to: The Water Clock (2003)

This book is a sequel to Jim Kelly's novel, "The Water Clock." "When his mother's old caretaker makes a startling deathbed confession, Cambridgeshire reporter Philip Dryden finds himself revisiting a decades-old tragedy—a fatal U.S. Air Force crash that claimed many lives, including a weeks-old infant. That probe may be intertwined with several others—into an illegal immigrant smuggling ring, a pornography and date-rape racket, and several murders. Assisted by a motley assortment of friends and allies, and, surprisingly, by his wife, who's been in a coma but has begun to communicate haltingly by spelling out words letter by letter, Dryden . . . uncovers the dark truths behind the crimes." (Publishers Weekly)

Kelly, Jim

The **moon** tunnel; Jim Kelly. St. Martin's Minotaur 2005 viii, 322 p.p

ISBN 031234922X; 9780312349226

LC 2005049449

In Jim Kelly's "third mystery to feature Cambridgeshire journalist Philip Dryden . . . an archeological team discovers human remains in the remnants of what appears to have been an escape tunnel from a WWII-era POW camp in England's fen country. That the victim was shot heading toward the camp piques Philip's interest. When forensic evidence dates the victim's death to well after the war, Philip sets out to find the corpse's identity. His search leads to the local Italian community, academics at Cambridge University, the proprietress of a nearby landfill--and to his intellectual and emotional reawakening after a period of feeling half alive." (Publishers Weekly)

Kelly, Martha Hall

Lilac girls; a novel. Martha Hall Kelly. Ballantine Books 2016 496 p. (hardback) $26; (ebook) $65

ISBN 9781101883075; 9781101883068

LC 2015048417

"Kelly's compelling first novel follows three women through the course of World War II and beyond. Caroline, a wealthy New Yorker, volunteers at the French consulate in New York, assisting refugees and raising funds. She meets Paul, a charming, married French actor, and sparks fly. Kasia, a young woman living in Poland during the Nazi invasion, works for the resistance until she is captured and sent to Ravensbruck, the women's concentration camp. There, she encounters Herta, a doctor hired to help execute inmates and perform experiments." (Publishers Weekly)

Kelman, James

Mo said she was quirky; by James Kelman. Other Press 2013 303 p. (pbk.) $15.95

ISBN 1590516001; 9781590516003; 9781590516010

LC 2012036336

This novel by James Kelman "tells the story of Helen . . . a very ordinary young woman. Her boyfriend said she was quirky but she is much more than that. Trust, love, relationships; parents, children: these are the ordinary parts of the everyday that become extraordinary when you think of them as Helen does. On Helen's way home from work . . . man crosses the road [who] appears to be her lost brother. What follows [the] story of twenty-four hours in the life of a young woman." (Publisher's note)

Kelton, Elmer

Badger boy. Forge 2001 286p

ISBN 0-312-87319-0

LC 00-48457

Sequel to The buckskin line

As the Texas Rangers disband, Badger Boy, a white boy whose parents were murdered by Comanches and who was himself captured and raised by a Comanche warrior, falls prisoner to David "Rusty" Shannon

Kelton, Elmer

Texas sunrise; two novels of the Texas Republic. Forge 2008 363p $24.95

ISBN 978-0-7653-2064-3; 0-7653-2064-9

LC 2008-34735

"Two novels, both concerning the Texas revolution against Mexico as witnessed by two young brothers, Joshua and Thomas Buckalew. In the first book, 'Massacre at Goliad,' the Buckalews' dream of adventure and free land is dispelled by the harsh reality of the West: hard work, Indians, bandits and the simmering cultural, racial and political animosity between Americans and Mexicans. When violence finally breaks out, the boys miss the slaughter at the Alamo only to be caught up in the massacre of Texan prisoners at Goliad. Only one brother survives, going on to avenge Goliad at the Battle of San Jacinto. In 'After the Bugles,' the surviving brother returns home to rebuild his ranch and his life, but must contend with cheating opportunists, murderous outlaws and deadly Comanche attacks, as well as growing Texan racism against his Mexican friends and neighbors. As with all of Kelton's westerns, characters are colorful and well drawn, the action is fast and bloody, and the plotting carefully thought out." Publ Wkly

Kelton, Elmer

Texas vendetta. Forge 2004 301p $24.95

ISBN 0-7653-0572-0

LC 2003-17352

"Within the exciting context of a western adventure, [Kelton] explores paternal relationships-good and bad-and the crippling consequences of hanging on too tightly to a painful past." Booklist

Kelton, Elmer

★ The **way** of the coyote. Forge 2001 283p

ISBN 0-312-87318-2

LC 2001-40482

"Kelton covers a wide swath of history with aplomb, illuminating a little-known period in Western history. California is still Mexican, Indians are a real threat and outlaws rule the land in this rough-riding adventure tale." Publ Wkly

Kemelman, Harry

Monday the rabbi took off. Putnam 1972 316p

"This is not so much a novel of mystery and detection as it is a beautifully conceived and executed novel of conditions in Israel and a rabbi's dilemma." Best Sellers

Kemelman, Harry

One fine day the rabbi bought a cross. Morrow 1987 234p

LC 86-23571

"Central to the plot is a Palestine Liberation Organization arms cache that Druse fighters would dearly love to steal. An American professor unwittingly delivers a letter with a map of the cache to a Druse agent in Jerusalem. The American is promptly murdered. Rabbi Small is in Jerusalem and solves the case." N Y Times Book Rev

Kemelman, Harry

Thursday the rabbi walked out. Morrow 1978 250p

LC 78-8466

"Kemelman's famous town, Barnard's Crossing, is in a turmoil after the murder of mean, anti-Semitic Ellsworth Jordan. Again Police Chief Lanigan asks Rabbi Small for help with the case, complicated by too many suspects. Those with motive and opportunity include members of Small's flock. Maltzman, president of the Temple, is one. So are the head of the local bank and his secretary as well as the dead man's illegitimate son by a Jewish mother." Publ Wkly

Kendrick, Beth

New uses for old boyfriends; Beth Kendrick. New American Library 2015 336 p. illustrations (softcover) $15

ISBN 0451465865; 9780451465863

LC 2014028502

In this novel by Beth Kendrick "when her happily-ever-after implodes, Lila must return to Black Dog Bay, the tiny seaside town where she grew up. She's desperate for a safe haven, but everything has changed over the past ten years. Her family's fortune is gone--and her mother is in total denial. She's lost everything she thought she needed but found something--someone--she desperately wants. A boy she hardly noticed has grown up into a man she can't forget." (Publisher's note)

"Kendrick has a light, breezy writing style that manages to take readers on unexpectedly poignant journeys with some startling twists and turns on the road. An astute and charming look at friendship, love and self-discovery." Kirkus

Keneally, Thomas, 1935-

★ The **Daughters** of Mars; Tom Keneally. Pocket Books 2013 544 p. (hardcover) $28

ISBN 1476734615; 9781476734613

LC 2012427270

In this book by Thomas Keneally, "[d]uring World War I, sisters Naomi and Sally Durance leave Australia to serve as nurses, first at Gallipoli and then on the western front, where their training hardly prepares them for the carnage they witness. In a French hospital, they both have the chance at love they never thought they'd take." (Library Journal)

"Keneally must have done copious research, but historical details and information about wartime medical treatment are presented organically, without the weight of historical retrospection... Highly recommended." LJ

Includes bibliographical references (p. 592)

Keneally, Thomas, 1935-

A **family** madness. Simon & Schuster 1986 336p

LC 85-26121

"Keneally brilliantly combines three diverse narrative techniques, and while the book is not light or easy reading, it is enormously rewarding." Publ Wkly

Keneally, Thomas, 1935-

Flying hero class. Warner Bks. 1991 289p

ISBN 0-446-51582-5

LC 90-50524

This is "despite some problems, a good book. Unlike many suspense novels, it never deadens our sensibilities with predictable characters, simpleminded politics or slick prose. Mr. Keneally's people are always fascinating, and so are the ideas his plot generates, making the hijacking a metaphor for the complex relationship between the West and third world peoples deprived of land and dignity." N Y Times Book Rev

Keneally, Thomas, 1935-

★ **Schindler's** list. Simon & Schuster 1982 400p $25; pa $14

ISBN 0-671-51688-4; 0-671-88031-4 pa

LC 82-10489

"An actual occurrence during the Nazi regime in Germany forms the basis for this story. Oskar Schindler, a Catholic German industrialist, chose to act differently from those Germans who closed their eyes to what was happening to the Jews. By spending enormous sums on bribes to the SS and on food and drugs for the Jewish prisoners whom he housed in his own camp-factory in Cracow, he succeeded in sheltering thousands of Jews, finally transferring them to a safe place in Czechoslovakia. Fifty Schindler survivors from seven nations helped the author with information." Shapiro. Fic for Youth. 3d edition

Keneally, Thomas, 1935-

Shame and the Captives; a novel. Thomas Keneally. Pocket Books/Atria Books 2015 400 p. $26

ISBN 147673464X; 9781476734644

LC 2014034535

This novel by Thomas Keneallev "explores a World War II prison camp, where Japanese prisoners resolve to take drastic action to wipe away their shame. Alice is a young woman living [in] an Australian country town, while her husband is held prisoner in Europe. When Giancarlo, an Italian anarchist at the prisoner-of-war camp down the road, is assigned to work on the farm, she hopes that being kind to him will somehow influence her husband's treatment. What she doesn't anticipate is how dramatically Giancarlo will expand her outlook and self-knowledge." (Publisher's note)

"Keneally explores multiple and multifaceted themes of courage, loyalty, empathy, and cultural dissonance." Booklist

Keneally, Thomas, 1935-

★ **Woman** of the inner sea. Doubleday 1993 277p

LC 92-28554

First published 1992 in the United Kingdom

This novel "succeeds on many fronts. It is a picaresque and often hilarious adventure story, recounting one woman's unforgettable if improbable travels. It is a series of love stories, as Kate meets the man who is appropriate for her at each stage of her life, and it is a mystery story as well. But the novel is also very much an exploration of ethics." N Y Times Book Rev

Kennedy, A. L.

What becomes; stories. Alfred A. Knopf 2010 208p $24.95

ISBN 978-0-307-27354-3; 0-307-27354-7

LC 2009-46507

First published 2009 in the United Kingdom

In this collection "Kennedy is familiarly off-kilter ('Story of My Life' revolves around the protagonist's deadpan, excruciating recounting of her successive dental traumas); unwelcoming ('Sympathy,' a tour de force that could easily be a disaster, recounts entirely in dialogue an episode of anonymous sex in a hotel room); and desolate (most of these stories involve marriages unhappy or unraveling; violence animates several and lurks in most). A preternaturally refined stylist, Kennedy leaves the reader shaken but not depressed: these are stories of endurance, not despair. And humor, albeit of a particularly hard-won variety, suggests Kennedy (a sometime stand-up comic), is vital to fortitude, even if that humor is sidelong and, though humane, unrelentingly cheerless." Atlantic

Kennedy, Douglas, 1955-

The **big** picture. Hyperion 1997 374p

ISBN 0-7868-6298-X

LC 96-44446

"The book is more than just a compelling read: it also has poignant and moving things to say about lost opportunities and wasted lives in America, the cynical quality of sudden fame, the awfulness of willed seperation from deeply loved children." Publ Wkly

Kennedy, Douglas, 1955-

The **moment**; a novel. Atria Books 2011 535p $26.99

ISBN 978-1-4391-8079-2; 1-4391-8079-2

LC 2010-48577

"Despite his rambling pace, Kennedy's evocative prose makes the eventual spellbinding finish worth the trip." Kirkus

Kennedy, Kathryne

★ **Everlasting** Enchantment; by Kathryne Kennedy. Sourcebooks Inc 2013 384 p. $7.99

ISBN 1402269919; 9781402269912

In this book, by Kathryne Kennedy, "Millicent Pantere has lived her entire life in the . . . London Underground. . . . Millicent is coerced into tracking down the rumors of a mysterious man. . . . [Her] search leads her to one of Merlin's legendary relics and the . . . knight whose fate is bound up with it. Centuries ago, Sir Gareth Solimere made the mistake of seducing the wrong woman, and he has been trapped ever since by a diabolical curse." (Publisher's note)

Kennedy, William

Chango's beads and two-tone shoes. Viking 2011 328p $26.95

ISBN 978-0-670-02297-7; 0-670-02297-7

LC 2011-19764

The book "is a two-part invention. In the first part, newspaper reporter Daniel Quinn travels to Havana in March 1957 to meet two of his heroes—Ernest Hemingway and Fidel Castro. In the second part, Quinn is back home in Albany 11 years later to cover the race riots that break out after Robert F. Kennedy is gunned down in Los Angeles. What holds the two parts together is the figure of Quinn, the author's alter ego. As a journalist he is a 'failed witness to history.' And so, at the end of the novel, he turns to fiction as the more effective method to 'reveal history in language graceful but hip, simple but sly, exfoliating with the essential stories he had tracked down and wanted to tell the world.'" (Commentary)

"Kennedy's prose hangs on every deft noirish turn, never succumbing to lazy pastiche. Best of all is his Castro, an impressively human rendering of the Commandante who falls halfway between Brando and Marcus Aurelius." Bookforum

Kennedy, William

★ **Ironweed**. Viking 1983 227p hardcover o.p. pa $14

ISBN 0-14-007020-6 pa

LC 82-40370

With this "tale of skid-row life in the Depression, Kennedy adds another chapter to his 'Albany cycle'—a group of novels set in the Albany, New York, underworld from the 1920s onward. Following 'Legs' and 'Billy Phelan's Greatest Game,' 'Ironweed' tells the story of Francis Phelan, a 58-year-old bum with muscatel on his breath and hallucinations on his mind. Chief among the latter is a vision of his infant son, who died after falling out of Francis' arms. It is the desire to reconcile himself to the memory of his dead son that brings Francis home to Albany, ultimately opening the door to a possible reconciliation with his family." Booklist

Kenney, John

★ **Truth** in advertising; John Kenney. Simon & Schuster 2013 308 p. (hardcover) $24.99

ISBN 1451675542; 9781451675542

LC 2012009173

This book by John Kenney follows "Finbar Dolan, [who] has a successful career in commercials. . . . Fin's life is a mess: he broke up with his fiancée a month before their wedding, is infatuated with his office assistant, Phoebe, and is estranged from his entire family. When his workaholic boss drags him into the office over Christmas to craft a Super Bowl commercial . . . and his abusive, long-lost father turns up in the hospital Fin's universe is tipped on its ear." (Publishers Weekly)

Kent, Christobel

The **loving** husband; Christobel Kent. Farrar, Straus & Giroux 2017 408 p. (hardcover) $27

ISBN 9780374716011; 9780374194123

LC 2016025969

In this novel, by Christobel Kent, "Fran awakes groggily to her baby's cries one February night and finds the bed empty beside her. Her husband, Nathan, is gone. . . . Fran soon makes a devastating discovery that upends her marriage and any semblance of safety. . . . Increasingly isolated, [Fran] grows paranoid—but Nathan isn't the only one hiding something. Though she can't tell a soul, Fran is shielding a damning secret of her own." (Publisher's note)

"There is something about Fran's complexity that sets this one apart and makes for a truly chilling, absorbing read." Kirkus

Kent, Hannah

★ **Burial** rites; a novel. Hannah Kent. Little, Brown and Co. 2013 336 p. (hardcover) $26

ISBN 0316243914; 9780316239806; 9780316243919

LC 2013014305

This book presents "a retelling of real-life events from 1828, Iceland, when Agnes Magnusdottir and two others are convicted and sentenced to death in a brutal double murder. . . . The murderers were servants, assistants, and sometime lovers to one of the victims . . . herbalist and healer Natan Ketilsson. As Iceland's primitive prison system is ill equipped to house death row inmates, a local farm family is prevailed upon to board Agnes until the date of her execution." (Library Journal)

Kent, Kathleen

The **Dime**; Kathleen Kent. Mulholland Books 2017 343 p. (hardcover) $26

ISBN 0316311030; 9780316311038; 9780316466288

In this book, by Kathleen Kent, "Dallas, Texas is not for the faint of heart. Good thing for Betty Rhyzyk she's from a family of take-no-prisoners Brooklyn police detectives. But her Big Apple wisdom will only get her so far when she relocates to The Big D, where Mexican drug cartels and cult leaders, deadbeat skells and society wives all battle for sunbaked turf. Betty is as tough as the best of them, but she's deeply shaken when her first investigation goes sideways." (Publisher's note)

"A worthy addition to the ranks of strong female detectives." Booklist

Kent, Kathleen

The **heretic's** daughter; a novel. Little, Brown and Co. 2008 332p $24.99

ISBN 978-0-316-02448-8; 0-316-02448-1

LC 2008-01887

"After a bout of smallpox, 10-year-old Sarah Carrier resumes life with her mother on their family farm in Andover, Mass., dimly aware of a festering dispute between her mother, Martha, and her uncle about the plot of land where they live. The fight takes on a terrifying dimension when reports of supernatural activity in nearby Salem give way to mass hysteria, and Sarah's uncle is the first person to point the finger at Martha. Soon, neighbors struggling to eke out a living and a former indentured servant step forward to name Martha as the source of their woes. Sarah is forced to shoulder an even heavier burden as her mother and brothers are taken to prison to face a jury of young women who claim to have felt their bewitching presence. Sarah's front-row view of the trials and the mayhem that sweeps the close-knit community provides a fresh, bracing and unconventional take on a much-covered episode." Publ Wkly

Kent, Kathleen

The **outcasts**; a novel. Kathleen Kent. Little, Brown and Co. 2013 336 p. (hardback) $26

ISBN 0316206121; 9780316206129

LC 2013017705

In this book, "Lucinda Carter, a prostitute given to epileptic episodes, is making plans to escape her brothel and meet her lover in Middle Bayou, TX. They've heard rumors of a pile of gold buried in the area and are looking to strike it rich, even if it means swindling the locals out of everything dear to them. Across the state, the governor has appointed Nate Cannon to bring a savage killer to justice with the help of two seasoned rangers, Dr. Tom and Deerling." (Library Journal)

Kepler, Lars

The **hypnotist**; translated from the Swedish by Ann Long. Farrar, Straus and Giroux 2011 503p $27

ISBN 978-0-374-17395-1; 0-374-17395-8

LC 2010-44603

Original Swedish edition, 2009

As this novel opens, "a schoolteacher and his librarian wife, pillars of their small Stockholm-area community, have been savagely butchered, and their young daughter, too, with a teenage son sliced to ribbons and left for dead. Enter Erik Maria Bark, a therapist and hypnotist called onto the scene by the supervising physician and a world-weary (naturally) police investigator, Joona Linna, who theorizes that the killer had waited for the father, a soccer referee in his off hours, hacked him into pieces, then headed to his house to dispatch the rest of the family, suggesting at least some acquaintance. . . .Linna and Bark make a great crime-solving pair precisely because they puzzle each other so thoroughly—says Bark, for instance, 'The patient always speaks the truth under hypnosis. But it's only a matter of what he himself perceives as the truth.' To which Linna responds, 'What is it you're trying to say?' Indeed. What Bark is trying to say is that there are monsters hiding everywhere beneath the reasonable and rational, and Kepler's book makes for a satisfying and scary testimonial." Kirkus

Kerangal, Maylis de, 1967-

The **heart**; a novel. Maylis de Kerangal ; translated by Sam Taylor. Farrar, Straus & Giroux 2016 256 p. (hardback) $25

ISBN 9780374240905; 9780374713287; 0374240906

LC 2015023340

This novel, by Maylis de Kerangal and translated by Sam Taylor, "takes place over the twenty-four hours surrounding a fatal accident and a resulting heart transplant as life is taken from a young man and given to a woman close to death. Three teenage boys go surfing. Returning home, exhausted, the driver lets the car drift off the road into a tree. Two of the boys are wearing seat belts; one is . . . declared brain-dead shortly after arriving at the hospital. His heart is still beating." (Publisher's note)

"It's clear de Kerangal has done extensive research, and the novel contains a wealth of medical knowledge. But her prose is more than just technical; the writing is uncommonly beautiful and never lacking humanity." Pub Wkly

Kerley, Jack

★ The **death** collectors; Jack Kerley. Dutton 2005 320p.

ISBN 0525948775

LC 2004028816

This book is "the second [volume] in the series featuring Mobile, Ala., PD detectives Carson Ryder and Harry Nautilus. Carson and Harry are the department's psychopathological and sociopathological investigative team. . . . When a naked female body buried beneath flowers and surrounded by candles is found in a seedy motel, the crime is weird enough to be assigned to them. More bodies turn up, each accompanied by a tiny but beautiful oil painting. Retired police detective Jacob C. Willow hears of the murder/painting connection and tells Carson he thinks it has something to do with a serial killer case he worked early in his career." (Publishers Weekly)

Kerouac, Jack

The **Dharma** bums. Viking 1958 244p

"This novel deals with Zen Buddhism. It's about two young men who are seeking to find themselves through meditation, voluntary poverty, separation from society, and intimate contact with nature, especially the Western mountains. . . . Sometimes Kerouac seems a little foolish, often he is extreme, but he is genuine, he is alive, and he is native." Libr J

Kerouac, Jack, 1922-1969

★ **On** the road. Viking 1957 310p

"Sal Paradise (a self-portrait of Kerouac), a struggling author in his mid-twenties, tells of his meeting Dean Moriarty (based on Neal Cassady), a fast-living teenager just out of a New Mexico reform school, whose soul is 'wrapped up in a fast car, a coast to reach, and a woman at the end of the road.' During the next five years they travel coast to coast, either with each other or to each other. Five trips are described." Oxford Companion to Am Lit. 6th edition

Kerouac, Jack, 1922-1969

★ **Road** novels 1957-1960; [edited by Douglas Brinkley] Library of America 2007 864p $35

ISBN 978-1-59853-012-4

LC 2007-924522

Kerouac's work "marked the articulation of a new voice far more interesting for what the author had to say and the way in which he said it than for the technical breakthroughs that it was heralded—and scorned—for at the time." San Francisco Chron

Kerr, Philip

Field gray. G. P. Putnam's Sons 2011 435p

ISBN 978-0-399-15741-7

LC 2010-45006

Bernie Gunther "is living the lazy life in Cuba in 1954, doing this and that for the gangster Meyer Lansky, when a chance run-in with the American Navy sends him first to Guantánamo and then to Landsberg Prison in West Germany, where he's roughed up by American interrogators and grilled about his wartime relationship with Erich Mielke, soon to take charge of the East German Stasi. Anxious to distance himself from the war criminals stockpiled at Landsberg, Bernie takes his interrogators back to 1930, when a humanitarian impulse led him to save Mielke's life in Berlin. But the young Communist repaid the favor by killing two policemen, sending Bernie on a vengeance mission that lasted throughout the war. Thanks to his examiners, Bernie is forced to reflect on horrific events that Kerr seems to have culled from historical sources. But Bernie's cynical, completely twisted idea of payback is brilliantly in character." N Y Times Book Rev

Kerr, Philip, 1956-

Hitler's peace; a novel of the Second World War. Philip Kerr. G.P. Putnam's Sons 2005 448p (pbk.) $15.00; (acid-free paper) o.p.

ISBN 9780143036951; 0399152695

LC 2004043170

This book takes place in "Autumn 1943. Since Stalingrad, Hitler has known that Germany cannot win the war. . . . Realizing that the unconditional surrender FDR has demanded will leave Germany in ruins, Hitler has put out peace feelers. . . . FDR and Stalin are willing to negotiate. Only Churchill refuses to listen. At the center . . . is Willard Mayer, an OSS operative who has been chosen by FDR to serve as his envoy. He is the perfect foil for the steamy world of deception, betrayals, and assassinations that make up the moral universe of realpolitik. . . . Mayer has embraced the stylish philosophy of the day, in which no values are fixed. In the course of the novel, his beliefs will be put to the ultimate test." (Publisher's note)

Kerr, Philip, 1956-

★ The **lady** from Zagreb; Philip Kerr. G. P. Putnam's Sons 2015 432 p. (Bernie Gunther) (hardcover) $26.95

ISBN 0399167641; 9780399167645

LC 2015002935

"Kerr sets his tenth Bernie Gunther novel . . . in 1942 Zagreb, Croatia, and Zurich, Switzerland. Joseph Goebells, the ambitious and manipulative Nazi propaganda minister, forces Bernie to track down the estranged father of a glamorous German actress, Dalia Dresner . . . . Bernie finally locates Antun Dragun Djurkovic, who has become a fanatical Croatian fascist and the sadistic commandant of a notorious concentration camp, killing countless Serbs and Jews. While returning to Berlin, our hero is ensnared by American, Swiss, and German intelligence operatives owing to his connections with powerful people in the Reich.

"Kerr unspools a whopping good historical thriller here, brilliantly evoking not only wartime Berlin, but also Switzerland and Croatia, as well as portraying the German cinema in a time of peril. And, of course, there is the ever-fascinating Bernie, neither as tough nor as cynical as he pretends to be." Booklist

Kerr, Philip, 1956-

A **Man** Without Breath; a Bernie Gunther novel. Philip Kerr. Penguin Group USA 2013 448 p. (hardcover) $26.95

ISBN 0399160795; 9780399160790

LC 2012050227

In this latest "in [Philip] Kerr's Bernie Gunther series, set during World War II and featuring a German police detective, Bernie is asked to investigate a mass grave site in the Katyn Forest that contains the bodies of Polish army officers." The book's authenticity was boosted by Kerr's discovery, while researching the book, of "a map of Smolensk made by SS cartographers in 1942, with all the streets renamed by Germany after it conquered Poland." (Library Journal)

Kerr, Philip, 1956-

March violets; Philip Kerr. Penguin Books 1990 245 p.

ISBN 0142004146; 9780142004142

LC 2004044275

This book features "Bernhard Gunther, a . . . private eye who solves a case of theft, murder, and corruption among the Nazis and their new supporters . . . in 1936 Berlin. When the daughter of Herr Doktor Hermann Six, . . . and his son-in-law, Paul Pfarr, are shot together in bed, their safe robbed of a fabulous Cartier diamond necklace, and their house torched, Six engages . . . Gunther to recover the necklace without nosing into the family's private affairs. It's a hopeless charge, for Bernie soon finds that both Pfarr and his wife were cheating on each other; that the safe contained . . . evidence that Pfarr, secretly a storm trooper, had been gathering against Six; and that Six's young second wife . . . is worried that Bernie's really looking for evidence of her infidelity." (Kirkus)

Other books about Bernie Gunther are:
The pale criminal (1990)
A German requiem (1991)
The one from the other (2006)
A quiet flame (2009)
If the dead rise not (2009)
Field gray (2011)
Prague fatale (2012)
A man without breath (2013)
The lady from Zagreb (2015)
The other side of silence (2016)
Prussian blue (2017)
Greeks bearing gifts (2018)

Kerr, Philip, 1956-

★ **Prussian** blue; a Bernie Gunther novel. Philip Kerr. G.P. Putnam's Sons 2017 528 p. (A Bernie Gunther novel) (hardcover : alk. paper) $27

ISBN 9780399177057; 9780698413139

LC 2016046341

In this Bernie Gunther Novel, by Philip Kerr, "when his cover is blown, former Berlin bull and unwilling SS officer Bernie Gunther must re-enter a cat-and-mouse game that continues to shadow his life a decade after Germany's defeat in World War 2. . . . Bernie's old and dangerous adversary Erich Mielke . . . is calling in a debt and wants Bernie to travel to London to poison a female agent they've both had dealings with. But Bernie isn't keen on assassinating anyone." (Publisher's note)

"As always, Kerr lets Bernie have fun with genre conventions without losing sight of the horror behind the tough talk. At the top of everyone's WWII mystery list." Booklist

Kerstan, Lynn

The **golden** leopard; Lynn Kerstan. Onyx 2002 370p.
ISBN 0451410572

LC 2003611039

Romantic Times Reviewers' Choice Award: Historical (2002)

In this book, "[i]n 1821 India, charming con artist Lord Hugo Duran stands trial for stealing the Heart of Alanbad. Needing a lie when he knows the truth of innocence will not work, Hugo insists a dream brought him here and that he is to go home to England to find the Golden Leopard and return it to its rightful owner. The court rules if he fails to restore the jewel within a year, he will die. Hugo needs help to succeed and at the same time he sees this as an opportunity to finish his business with Jessica Carville, who he once hurt badly. . . . Jessie, tempted by his quest, agrees to accompany him, but does not relish the idea of marrying him to keep her reputation intact. As the excursion turns dangerous, both realizes they still love one another." (thebestreviews.com)

Kerstan, Lynn

Heart of the tiger; Lynn Kerstan. New American Library 2003 375 p. (pbk.) o.p.
ISBN 0451410858

LC 2004573017

This book, chosen by "Library Journal" as a Top Ten Best Romance Novel of 2003, follows the story of "Michael Keynes, mercenary adventurer, [who] returns to England to destroy his evil brother. . . . But someone else gets there first. Suspicion falls on Michael, the duke's own daughter, and a soft-voiced young woman with a heart of steel. Now he must find a way to exonerate both of them, even if it means confessing to a crime he didn't commit. . . . Then the real murderer and an enemy from Michael's past resurface, and survival itself becomes the only game in town." (lynnkerstan.com)

Kesey, Ken

★ **One** flew over the cuckoo's nest; a novel. Viking 1962 311p hardcover o.p. pa $7.99
ISBN 0-670-03058-9; 0-451-16396-6 pa

"Life in a mental institution is predictable and suffocating under the iron rule of Nurse Ratched, who tolerates no disruption of routine on her all-male ward. Half-Indian Chief Bromden, almost invisible on the ward because he is thought to be deaf and dumb, describes the arrival of rowdy Randle Patrick McMurphy. McMurphy takes on the nurse as an adversary in his attempt to organize his fellow inmates and breathe some self-esteem and joy into their lives. The battle is vicious on the part of the nurse, who is relentless in her efforts to break McMurphy, but a spark of human will brings an element of hope to counter the despotic institutional power." Shapiro. Fic for Youth. 3d edition

Keyes, Daniel

★ **Flowers** for Algernon. Harcourt Brace Jovanovich 1966 274p

"Charlie Gordon, aged thirty-two, is mentally retarded and enrolls in a class to 'become smart.' He keeps a journal of his progress after an experimental operation that increases his I.Q. Although Charlie becomes brilliant, he is unhappy because he cannot shed his former personality and is tormented by his memories. In the end he begins to lose the mental powers he has gained." Shapiro. Fic for Youth. 3d edition

Keyes, Marian

Last Chance Saloon. Morrow 2001 370p $25
ISBN 0-688-18072-8

LC 00-67891

First published 1999 in the United Kingdom

This novel's "protagonists are two London women who grew up together in the small, repressive Irish town of Knockavoy. Tara, a computer analyst, lives with Thomas, a bitter and miserly high school geography teacher. . . . Katherine Casey, an accountant for an advertising agency, wears boring suits, has a hyperorganized underwear drawer and brushes off all advances, including those of attractive advertising account executive Joe Roth. As they turn 31, each woman is full of suggestions for improving the other's life and full of excuses for doing nothing about her own. That begins to change when Fintan O'Grady, their gay pal and fellow Knockavoy refugee, falls ill with a mysterious disease." Publ Wkly

Khadivi, Laleh

★ A **good** country; Laleh Khadivi. Bloomsbury USA 2017 239 p. (hardback) $27
ISBN 9781632865847; 9781632865861

LC 2016050042

This novel, by Laleh Khadivi, tells the story of "Alireza Courdee, a fourteen-year-old straight-A student and chemistry whiz, [who] takes his first hit of pot. . . . He loses his virginity, takes up surfing, and sneaks away to all-night raves. . . . But then he changes again, falling out with the bad boy surfers and in with a group of kids more awake to the world around them, who share his background, and whose ideas fill him with a very different sense of purpose." (Publisher's note)

"The story unfolds deftly, beautifully capturing the psychology of an American teen who goes down the path of radicalization; readers will understand what would motivate a sheltered, shortsighted young person to run away to join extremists." SLJ

Khan, Ausma Zehanat

✓ **Among** the ruins; Ausma Zehanat Khan. Minotaur Books 2017 viii, 357 p.p (Rachel Getty and Esa Khattak novels) (hardcover) $25.99
ISBN 9781250096739; 9781250096753

LC 2016044900

In this novel, by Ausma Zehanat Khan, "Esa Khattak is traveling in Iran, reconnecting with his cultural heritage . . . when he's approached by a Canadian government agent in Iran, asking him to look into the death of renowned Canadian-Iranian filmmaker Zahra Sobhani. . . . Khattak calls on his partner, Detective Rachel Getty, for help. Rachel uncovers a conspiracy linked to the Shah of Iran and the decades-old murders of a group of Iran's most famous dissidents." (Publisher's note)

"Khan uses an involving mystery in a vividly portrayed setting to illustrate unspeakable violations undertaken by governments in religious and political chaos. In Khan's hands, mysteries carry powerful messages." Booklist

Khan, Ausma Zehanat

✓ The **unquiet** dead; A Novel. Ausma Zehanat Khan. Minotaur Books 2015 352 p. (Rachel Getty and Esa Khattak Novels) (hardback) $25.99
ISBN 1250055113; 9781250055118

LC 2014032396

In this novel, by Ausma Zehanat Khan, "Detective Rachel Getty trusts her boss, Esa Khattak, implicitly. But she's still uneasy at Khattak's tight-lipped secrecy when he asks her to look into Christopher Drayton's death. Drayton's apparently accidental fall from a cliff doesn't seem to warrant a police investigation . . . But . . . [it] soon comes to light that Drayton may have been a war criminal with ties to the Srebrenica massacre of 1995." (Publisher's note)

"Khan's stunning debut is a poignant, elegantly written mystery laced with complex characters who force readers to join them in dealing with ugly truths." Kirkus

Another title in this series is:

The language of secrets (2016)

Khoury, Elias

Gate of the sun; translated from the Arabic by Humphrey Davies. Archipelago Books 2006 539p (Rainmaker translations) $26

ISBN 0-976395-02-9

LC 2005-21036

Original Arabic edition, 1998

"This is a challenging novel that demands from us an imagination potent enough to link its many loose threads. The good news is that Khoury's language is derived from everyday colloquial Arabic, rather than the formal language of intellectuals and the media. Humphrey Davies's translation is masterful, allowing us to appreciate Gate of the Sun's short, clear sentences and crisp metaphors afresh." New Statesman

Kibler, Julie

Calling Me Home; a novel. Julie Kibler. 1st ed. St Martins Pr 2013 325 p. (hardcover) $24.99

ISBN 1250014522; 9781250014528

LC 2012041949

This novel, set in 1930s Kentucky, centers on a forbidden romance between a teenage white girl, Isabelle McAllister, and Robert Prewitt, the black son of the McAllister's maid. Chafing under her mother's restrictive notions of female propriety, Isabelle finds a kindred spirit in Robert. The two begin to meet clandestinely, but any hope of a future together is threatened by the overwhelming racism of the era. Against impossible odds, the pair elopes to neighboring Cincinnati." (Booklist)

Kidd, Sue Monk

★ The **invention** of wings; a novel. Sue Monk Kidd. Viking 2014 384 p. (hardback) $27.95

ISBN 0670024783; 9780670024780

LC 2013028185

In this novel, by Sue Monk Kidd , "Hetty 'Handful' Grimke, an urban slave in early nineteenth century Charleston, yearns for life beyond the . . . Grimke household. The Grimke's daughter, Sarah, has known from an early age she is meant to do something large in the world, but she is hemmed in by the limits imposed on women. . . . On Sarah's eleventh birthday, . . . she is given ownership of ten year old Handful, who is to be her handmaid." (Publisher's note)

Kidd, Sue Monk

★ The **secret** life of bees. Viking 2002 301p hardcover o.p. pa $14

ISBN 0-14-200174-0 pa; 0-670-89460-5

LC 2001-26310

"It is 1964, in small-town Georgia peach country. Lily . . . {is the} daughter of T. Ray, a man of implacable rage. . . . He mocks her, he beats her. . . . On the day of Lily's fourteenth birthday, . . . Lily and {her black housekeeper} Rosaleen take a fateful walk into town so that Lily can buy herself a present and Rosaleen can register to vote. . . . Rosaleen, challenged, gets herself jailed for spitting on a white man's shoes. . . . The feisty Lily springs her and, loosed from their assorted prisons, they take off. . . . {They find themselves at} the idosyncratic compound of three black women bee-keepers, May, June, and August {Boatwright}." (Women's Rev Books)

"Lily is a wonderfully petulant and self-absorbed adolescent, and Kidd deftly portrays her sense of injustice as it expands to accommodate broader social evils." N Y Times Book Rev

Kiefer, Christian

★ The **infinite** tides; a novel. Christian Kiefer. Bloomsbury USA 2012 393 p. $26.00

ISBN 1608198103; 9781608198108

LC 2011045534

"Keith Corcoran has spent his entire life preparing to be an astronaut. At the moment of his greatness, finally aboard the International Space Station, hundreds of miles above the earth's swirling blue surface, he receives word that his sixteen-year-old daughter has died in a car accident, and that his wife has left him. Returning to earth, and to his now empty suburban home, he is alone with the ghosts, the memories and feelings he can barely acknowledge, let alone process." (Publisher's note)

Kienzle, William X.

The **rosary** murders. Andrews & McMeel 1979 257p

LC 78-31833

"From Ash Wednesday, when the murderer first struck Detroit's Catholic community, the police seemed helpless to solve the string of senseless murders. The weeks that followed became a nightmare for the crack homicide team of investigators headed by Lieutenant Walter Koznicki, until Father Koesler broke the madman's code." Publisher's note

Kiernan, Caitlin R.

Blood oranges; Caitlín R. Kiernan. Roc 2013 288 p. (pbk.) $16

ISBN 0451465016; 9780451465016

LC 2012032442

This book is the first in Kathleen Tierney's supernatural horror series featuring Siobhan Quinn. Here, heroin-addicted Quinn has "a steady supply of good dope and an apartment thanks to her benefactor, the mysterious fixer and manipulator she calls Mean Mr. B. . . . She goes werewolf hunting in Rhode Island. Instead of staying alert, however, Quinn shoots up and gets bitten by the werewolf—just as a vampire shows up! When she regains consciousness, . . . she finds she's now a werewolf and a vampire." (Kirkus)

Kiernan, Caitlin R.

The **red** tree. Roc 2009 385p pa $16

ISBN 978-0-451-46276-3; 0-451-46276-9

LC 2009-15105

"Author Sarah Crowe leaves Atlanta after her girlfriend commits suicide, settling at a homestead in rural Rhode Island in order to finish her latest book, which is well past deadline. There's something sinister about the house, and Sarah quickly learns that the previous tenant, a professor and folklorist named Charles Harvey, killed himself while researching a book about the supernatural folklore of New England. Exploring the basement, Sarah discovers Harvey's manuscript, and she quickly finds herself in the middle of a living nightmare centered on a mysterious red oak tree in the house's yard. . . . [An] intelligent blend of folklore, horror, and dark fantasy." Libr J

Kiernan, Stephen P.

The **Curiosity**; by Stephen Kiernan. HarperCollins 2013 320 p. $25.99

ISBN 006222106X; 9780062221063

In this novel by Stephen Kiernan "Dr. Kate Philo and her scientific exploration team make a . . . discovery in the Arctic: the body of a man buried deep in the ice. Remarkably, the frozen man is brought back to the lab and successfully reanimated. The team learns that he was—is—a judge, Jeremiah Rice. Kate and Jeremiah grow closer. But the clock is ticking and Jeremiah's new life is slipping away...and . . . Kate must decide how far she is willing to go to protect the man she has come to love." (Publisher's note)

Kilpack, Josi S.

A **heart** revealed; a proper romance. Josi S. Kilpack. Shadow Mountain 2015 336 p. (paperbound) $15.99

ISBN 1609079906; 9781609079901

LC 2014033807

In this Regency romance novel, by Josi S. Kilpack, part of the "Proper Romance" series, "Amber Marie Sterlington . . . has her pick of men and she knows what she wants most in a husband: a title and a fortune. . . . But Amber's social standing is shattered by a rare disorder. . . . Publicly humiliated and estranged from her shamed family, . . . Amber wonders if isolation is for the best and questions what real love means until she finds a romantic path to a man who offers unconditional love." (Publisher's note)

"In spite of the heroine and the hero both being totally unlikable at the beginning of the book, the unusually well-crafted prose draws the reader along, and Amber's personal evolution makes the book more literary than other romances. Readers of this gentle story won't miss the steamy scenes it lacks. A very compelling read." Kirkus

Kilpack, Josi S.

The **vicar's** daughter; Josi S. Kilpack. Shadow Mountain 2017 317 p. (Proper romance) (paperback) $15.99

ISBN 9781629722801

LC 2016029521

In this book in the Proper Romance series, by Josi S. Kilpack, ''Cassie hatches a plan to kindle a love affair between Lenora and handsome Mr. Glenside, a newcomer to their small village. Circumventing decorum . . . , Cassie begins a secret correspondence with Mr. Glenside, pretending to be Lenora, explaining her sister's terrible social shyness. Before long, Cassie falls for Mr. Glenside herself, only to be dismayed by her plan's unexpected success." (Publishers Weekly)

"Themes of betrayal and reconciliation, forgiveness and redemption, and the high value of integrity and kindness in all relationships make for a sweet and satisfying tale." Pub Wkly

Kimani, Peter

Dance of the Jakaranda; Peter Kimani. Akashic Books 2017 342 p. (trade pbk. original) $15.95

ISBN 9781617755033; 9781617754968

LC 2016935080

This novel, by Peter Kimani, "traces the lives and loves of three men--preacher Richard Turnbull, the colonial administrator Ian McDonald, and Indian technician Babu Salim--whose lives intersect when they are implicated in the controversial birth of a child. Years later, when Babu's grandson Rajan . . . accidentally kisses a mysterious stranger in a dark nightclub, the encounter provides the spark to illuminate the three men's shared, murky past." (Publisher's note)

"Kimani's complex novel will leave readers questioning the meanings of citizenship and belonging during an era of significant social upheaval in Kenya's history." Booklist

Kincaid, Jamaica

★ **Annie** John. Farrar, Straus & Giroux 1985 148p hardcover o.p. pa $12

ISBN 0-374-10521-9; 0-374-52510-2 pa

"Episodes from the young life of Annie John, aged 10 to 17, as she grows up on the Caribbean island of Antigua. This is a magical coming-of-age tale, ripe with the special ambience of its tropical setting and sustained by Annie's far from naive awareness of the world around her. Death, illness, and poverty intrude on the narrator's perceptive sensibility from time to time, but even these experiences instruct her and expand her understanding of life and its shifting reality. . . . A poetic and intensely moving work." Booklist

Kincaid, Jamaica

Autobiography of my mother. Farrar, Straus & Giroux 1995 228p

ISBN 0-374-10731-9

LC 94-24580

In Kincaid's "poised and crystalline prose, precise and serene as a knife drawn through water, she now gives us this starkly memorable 'self-portrait' of a calm, thoughtful, utterly alienated woman who has learned to lead a life devoid of love, but not devoid of dignity." Christ Sci Monit

Kincaid, Jamaica

★ **Lucy**. Farrar, Straus & Giroux 1990 163p

LC 90-83987

The narrator, Lucy Potter, a nineteen year old from Antigua, tells of her experiences as an au pair for a wealthy family in a large North American city

"The great motifs of Western literature, like goodness and evil, innocence and experience, resonate in Kincaid's novel in a completely updated and unselfconscious way. In other hands, this story of a West Indian au pair would just be sociology. In Kincaid's recasting, it is both art and argument." Christ Sci Monit

Kinder, Chuck

Honeymooners; a cautionary tale. Farrar, Straus & Giroux 2001 357p $24

ISBN 0-374-17258-7

LC 00-63616

"Both wives emerge as major characters, reflecting the humor and anguish of living with men who, despite their successes, seem headed for rock bottom. Kinder's speedy, wry prose transports the reader to a time when drug use and personal freedom were unquestioned." Libr J

Kinder, R. M.

An **absolute** gentleman; a novel. Counterpoint 2007 288p pa $14

ISBN 978-1-58243-388-2; 1-58243-388-7

LC 2007-17932

"Taciturn English professor Arthur Blume launches his narrative by boldly stating that he is believed to have murdered as many as 17 women. Yet what most outrages him, now that he has been incarcerated, is that journalists are depicting him as a monster. He pens a memoir to correct this impression. In it, he describes in lavish detail the outfitting of his newly rented rooms in the small university town of Mason, Missouri; demurs over particulars of his illicit love affair with a fellow professor; and shares self-deprecating anecdotes about his gallant championing of a maligned colleague. Tucked among these decorous tidbits, however, are tantalizing clues to the demon within, one Kinder allows to emerge as stealthily as a cobra sliding from its bamboo basket. The addition of a self-explanatory epilogue regarding her personal experience detracts only slightly from Kinder's otherwise spellbinding debut novel, a pitch-perfect rendition of the cunning malevolence that can lie hidden beneath the guise of refined civility." Booklist

King, Laurie R.

The **beekeeper's** apprentice, or, on the segregation of the queen; Laurie R. King. Picador/Thomas Dunne Books 2007 xxi, 346p (Mary Russell and Sherlock Holmes mysteries) pa $14

"In 1915, Sherlock Holmes is retired and quietly engaged in the study of honeybees in Sussex when a young woman literally stumbles onto him on the Sussex Downs. Fifteen years old, gawky, egotistical, and recently orphaned, the young Mary Russell displays an intellect to impress even Sherlock Holmes. Under his reluctant tutelage, this very modern, twentieth-century woman proves a deft protégée and a fitting partner for the Victorian detective." (Publisher's note)

ISBN 978-0-312-42736-8

Other titles in this series are:
A monstrous regiment of women (1995)
A letter of Mary (1997)
The moor (1998)
O Jerusalem (1999)
Justice Hall (2002)
The game (2004)
Locked rooms (2005)
The language of bees (2009)
The god of the hive (2010)
Pirate king (2011)
Garment of shadows (2012)
Dreaming spies (2015)
The murder of Mary Russell (2016)

King, Laurie R.

A **darker** place. Bantam Bks. 1999 384p
ISBN 0-553-10711-9

LC 98-29835

"King's solid research into alternative religious sects makes the desert commune feel like a real place, while her taut pacing insures that an air of menace hangs over the strange rituals that go on there. But the strongest appeal of the story lies in its superb characters, especially the children who become Anne's charges." N Y Times Book Rev

King, Laurie R.

★ The **game**; a Mary Russell novel. Bantam Books 2004 368p map $23.95
ISBN 0-553-80194-5

LC 2003-55684

"Whatever this grueling land journey lacks in urgency, it repays in scenes of vibrant local color, described by Russell in the droll tongue of a woman with the wit to realize that, while she may be dirty and tired and in constant danger, she is having the time of her life." N Y Times Book Rev

King, Laurie R.

Keeping watch. Bantam Bks. 2003 383p $23.95
ISBN 0-553-80191-0

LC 2002-34266

"At its simplest, this is the story of a man who helps rescue women and/or children from dangerously abusive men. King's lengthy, brillantly executed backstory of Allen Carmichael's experiences in Vietnam, his disastrously unhappy return home and his eventual discovery of his 'calling' showcase some of her finest writing. Now in his early 50s, Allen is ready to retire from his dangerous vocation, to settle on his remote island and perhaps serve as a consultant to those who continue the struggle. But his last rescue, that of a 12-year-old boy trapped in a horrible situation, continues to haunt him." Publ Wkly

King, Lily, 1963-

★ **Euphoria**; a novel. Lily King. Pgw 2014 256 p. $25
ISBN 9780802122551; 0802122558

In this novel by Lily King, "English anthropologist Andrew Bankson has been alone in the field for several years, studying the Kiona river tribe in the Territory of New Guinea. . . . Set between two World Wars and inspired by events in the life of revolutionary anthropologist Margaret Mead, Euphoria is [a] . . . story of passion, possession, exploration, and sacrifice." (Publisher's note)

"King does not shy from showing the uncomfortable relationship among all three anthropologists and those they study. . . . A small gem, disturbing and haunting." Kirkus

King, Lily, 1963-

★ The **father** of the rain. Atlantic Monthly Press 2010 354p $24
ISBN 978-0-8021-1949-0; 0-8021-1949-2

"There's something so raw and affecting about Daley's love for her damaged father that the book will linger in your mind long after you've finished it." Entertainment Wkly

King, Ross

Domino. Walker & Co. 2002 435p $26
ISBN 0-8027-3378-6

LC 2002-29620

"Replete with mystery and suspense and immersed in vivid historical details, this work is also a sharp, philosophical musing on the disguises of the world and the search for the truth that lies beneath." Libr J

King, Stephen, 1947-

★ **11** /22/63; a novel. Stephen King. Scribner 2011 ix, 849 p.p
ISBN 1451627289; 1451627297; 1451627300; 9781451627282; 9781451627299; 9781451627305

LC 2011025874

"King's protagonists, Al Templeton, the owner of a diner, and Jake Epping, his loyal customer and friend, take a dispassionate and calculated view of the assassinadon. At the back of his pantry in a small town in present-day Maine, Al finds a wormhole which comes out in September 1958 . . . Al then decides to use his access to the portal to further the public good, and to stay in the past until 1963 so that he can prevent Oswald from killing Kennedy. But Al is not quite sure, from his observadon of Oswald, that he was acting alone when he unsuccessfully attempted to assassinate General Edwin Walker in April 1963." (London Review of Books)

"Though his scenarios aren't always plausible in strictest terms, King's imagination, as always, yields a most satisfying yarn." Kirkus

King, Stephen, 1947-

The **bazaar** of bad dreams; stories. Stephen King. Scribner 2015 512 p. (hardcover) $30
ISBN 9781501111679

LC 2015022286

This horror short story collection, by Stephen King, "delivers a generous collection of stories, several of them brand-new, featuring revelatory autobiographical comments on when, why, and how he came to write (or rewrite) each story. . . . There are thrilling connections between stories; themes of morality, the afterlife, guilt, what we would do differently if we could see into the future or correct the mistakes of the past." (Publisher's note)

"Best of all, lifting the curtain, King prefaces the stories with notes about how they came about ("This one had to be told, because I knew exactly what kind of language I wanted to use"). Those notes alone make this a must for aspiring writers. Readers seeking a tale well told will take pleasure in King's sometimes-scary, sometimes merely gloomy pages." Kirkus

King, Stephen, 1947-

Black house; a novel. [by] Stephen King [and] Peter Straub. Random House 2001 624p

ISBN 0-375-50439-7

LC 2001-31657

Sequel to The talisman (1984)

"In French Landing, Wis., a serial killer called the Fisherman is doing unspeakable things to local children. But a retired Los Angeles homicide detective named Jack Sawyer, who has done a mighty job of repressing his boyhood trials in an alternate world called the Territories, knows that there's more to these crimes than mere banal human cruelty. . . . What elevates 'Black House' beyond ordinary horror novels is the richness of its cast, from a bunch of philosophy-reading bikers to a sleazy journalist to a grieving mother on the brink of madness." N Y Times Book Rev

King, Stephen, 1947-

★ **Carrie**. Doubleday 1974 199p $32.50

ISBN 0-385-08695-4

"A terrifying treat for both horror and parapsychology fans." SLJ

King, Stephen, 1947-

Cujo. Viking 1981 319p

ISBN 0-670-45193-2

LC 81-50265

"Carefully plotted, the novel throbs with the malignant evil that permeates all of King's fiction." Saturday Rev

King, Stephen, 1947-

Different seasons. Viking 1982 527p pa $7.99; $37.95

ISBN 0-451-16753-8 pa; 0-670-27266-3

LC 82-70145

This is a collection of four novellas. "In 'Rita Hayworth and Shawshank Redemption,' a man wrongly convicted of the murder of his wife and her lover spends 27 years secretly chipping away the wall of his cell until he reaches freedom. . . . A 13-year-old boy's obsession with the Nazi Party is the subject of 'Apt Pupil.'. . . 'The Body' is a . . . tale of a young boy who, overhearing his big brother describe where the body of a missing boy lies undiscovered, takes his pals on an expedition to find it. . . . In a men's club in New York City tales are told before a fire late at night. One Christmas season a doctor tells of a pregnant unwed woman to whom he teaches 'The Breathing Method' and of what he observes when she is decapitated just prior to giving birth." (SLJ)

This "is a collection of four novellas. . . . The first tale is about how one self-contained individual coped with life in a Maine jail. The second is not so much about Nazism today as it is about how victim and victimizer can develop a symbiotic relationship. In the third a search by 12-year-olds for a body in the woods has implications for their innocence. The last is a good old-fashioned horror story." Libr J

King, Stephen, 1947-

Doctor Sleep; a novel. Stephen King. Scribner 2013 544 p. (hardcover : alk. paper) $30

ISBN 1476727651; 9781451698855; 9781451698862; 9781476727653

LC 2013000431

This sequel to Stephen King's "The Shining," follows "Dan Torrence, the alcoholic son of the very dangerously alcoholic father." Dan's substance abuse problems "all trace back to the bad doings at the Overlook Hotel . . . and all those voices in poor Dan's head, which speak to (and because of) a very special talent he has. That 'shining' is a matter of more than passing interest for a gang of . . . torture-loving, soul-sucking folks who aren't quite folks at all--the True Knot." (Kirkus Reviews)

King, Stephen, 1947-

★ **Dolores** Claiborne. Viking 1993 305p

ISBN 0-670-84452-7

LC 92-15467

"What drives Dolores Claiborne is a powerful characterization of the title figure, a cranky old Maine islander who takes no guff from life or death. . . . King's mimicry is startlingly good." Time

King, Stephen, 1947-

End of watch; a novel. by Stephen King. Scribner 2016 496 p. (The Bill Hodges trilogy) (hardback) $30

ISBN 9781501129742; 9781501134142

LC 2015039639

In this book by Stephen King, published as part of The Bill Hodges Trilogy series, "the diabolical 'Mercedes Killer' drives his enemies to suicide, and if Bill Hodges and Holly Gibney don't figure out a way to stop him, they'll be victims themselves. . . . When Bill and Holly are called to a suicide scene with ties to the Mercedes Massacre, they find themselves pulled into their most dangerous case yet." (Publisher's note)

"King's mystery experiment has been page-flipping fun from the start, and no one's going to want to miss seeing how it all pans out." Booklist

King, Stephen, 1947-

Finders Keepers; a novel. Stephen King. Simon & Schuster 2015 448 p. $30

ISBN 1501100076; 9781501100079

LC 2015295899

This suspense novel, by Stephen King, part of "The Bill Hodges trilogy," is "about a reader whose obsession with a reclusive writer goes far too far. . . . John Rothstein [is] an iconic author who created a famous character, Jimmy Gold, but . . . hasn't published a book for decades. Morris Bellamy is livid . . . Morris kills Rothstein and empties his safe of cash, yes, but the real treasure is a trove of notebooks containing at least one more Gold novel." (Publisher's note)

"This being a King novel, the narrative hums and roars along like a high-performance vehicle, even though there are times when its readers may find themselves several tics ahead of the book's plot developments. But such qualms are overcome by the plainspoken, deceptively simple King style, which has once again fashioned a rip-snorting entertainment; one that also works as a sneaky-smart satire of literary criticism and how even the most attentive readers can often miss the whole point behind making up characters and situations. Reading a King novel as engrossing as this is a little like backing in a car with parking assist: after a while, you just take your hands off the wheel and the pages practically turn themselves." Kirkus

King, Stephen, 1947-

Firestarter. Viking 1980 428p hardcover o.p. pa $7.99

ISBN 0-670-31541-9; 0-451-16780-5 pa

LC 80-14793

"This is your advanced post-Watergate cynical American thriller with some eerie parapsychological twists, and it's been done so distinctively well that we'd better talk about genius rather than genre." Quill Quire

King, Stephen, 1947-

Four past midnight. Viking 1990 763p hardcover o.p. pa $7.99

ISBN 0-451-17038-5 pa

LC 90-50046

This volume contains four novellas: The Langoliers; Secret window, secret garden; The library policeman; The sun dog.

This book "is hard to put down, truly chilling, and sure to be enjoyed by YA horror afficionados everywhere." SLJ

King, Stephen, 1947-

Full dark, no stars. Scribner 2010 368p $27.99

ISBN 978-1-4391-9256-6; 1-4391-9256-1

LC 2010-32866

"Returning to the novella—possibly his brightest canvas—King provides four raw looks at the limits of greed, revenge, and self-deception. The first, '1922,' is an outright masterpiece and takes the form of the written confession of one Wilf James. Back in 1922, see, Wilf killed his wife to prevent her selling off part of the farm, but tossing her corpse down the well didn't exactly stop her. It's Poe meets Creepshow by way of Steinbeck and carries the bleak, nearly romantic doom of an old folk ballad about murderin' done wrong. A pair of the remaining tales feature female protagonists considering hiding others' crimes: 'Big Driver' is a rape-revenge tale about a writer of cozy mysteries who ends up in the uncoziest of situations, while 'A Good Marriage' stars a wife whose husband of 27 years turns out to be hiding an unimaginable secret. Though the shortest story by far, 'Fair Extension' is no slouch, submitting for your approval one Mr. Elvid (get it?), who is out to shine a little light on our blackest urges. Rarely has King gone this dark." Booklist

King, Stephen, 1947-

★ The **girl** who loved Tom Gordon; a novel. Scribner 1999 224p $16.95

ISBN 0-684-86762-1

LC 99-13109

"Nine-year-old Trisha McFarland is hopelessly lost in the woods. Out for a morning hike with her bickering mother and brother, she runs off to relieve herself and discovers she can't find her way back to the path. . . . Trisha wanders for a week in the mosquito-infested forest with nothing but her wits, her Walkman and the pitching prowess of her hero, the dreamy Red Sox reliever Tom Gordon, to guide her. As Trisha fights to stay alive, King demonstrates his empathy for the inner lives of children and an outdoorsman's knowledge of the edible wild flora of Maine." N Y Times Book Rev

King, Stephen, 1947-

It. Viking 1986 1138p

ISBN 0-670-81302-8

LC 85-41062

"Six adults, living separately in a blessed fog of forgetfulness, are summoned back to their hometown to complete the destruction of a horrific, shape-changing entity who breakfasts on the city's children. This same group first encountered the menace more than a quarter century before, as schoolchildren in the 1950s. Their quest breeds some riveting chase scenes as adults and children alike flee from an assortment of menacing humans and slavering monsters—most of which are manifestations of an evil so vile its true nature can never be known. King's considerable talent for grounding this supernatural stuff in the minutiae of everyday life is evident." Booklist

King, Stephen, 1947-

★ **Misery**. Viking 1987 310p

LC 86-40504

"Even if 'Misery' is less terrifying than his usual work—no demons, no witchcraft, no nether-world horrors—it creates strengths out of its realities. Its excitements are more subtle. And, as such, it is an intriguing work." N Y Times Book Rev

King, Stephen, 1947-

Mr. Mercedes; a novel. Stephen King. Scribner 2014 448 p. (hardback) $30

ISBN 1476754454; 9781476754451; 9781476754475

LC 2013046172

Edgar Award: Best Novel (2015)

In this suspense novel by Stephen King, "Brady Hartsfield lives with his alcoholic mother in the house where he was born. He loved the feel of death under the wheels of the Mercedes, and he wants that rush again. Only Bill Hodges, with a couple of highly unlikely allies, can apprehend the killer before he strikes again. And they have no time to lose, because Brady's next mission, if it succeeds, will kill or maim thousands." (Publisher's note)

"This exists outside of the usual Kingverse (Pennywise the Clown is referred to as fictive); add that to the atypical present-tense prose, and this feels pretty darn fresh. Big, smashing climax, too." Booklist

King, Stephen, 1947-

Night shift. Doubleday 1978 xxii, 336p hardcover o.p. pa $7.99

ISBN 0-385-12991-2; 0-307-74364-0 pa

LC 77-75146

The stories "all begin in our normal world, where everything is safe and warm. But in almost every instance, something slips, and we find ourselves in the nightmare world of the not-quite real. . . . Such stories require a willing suspension of disbelief, of course, but they also require an author who is an expert manipulator. . . . King is an expert." Best Sellers

King, Stephen, 1947-

Nightmares & dreamscapes. Viking 1993 816p

LC 92-46881

"There's certainly nothing skimpy about this collection of large, leisurely short stories. . . . Fans of Mr. King's work will find here his usual menu: wild conspiracies; repellent, zestful monsters; scenes speckled and splashed with gore." N Y Times Book Rev

King, Stephen, 1947-

Pet sematary. Doubleday 1983 373p

ISBN 0-385-18244-9

LC 82-45360

"King's characters are so solid and next-door neighborly that we are drawn quite naturally and trustingly into their lives. And then, a single note at a time, the eerie music begins and we are entranced." Best Sellers

King, Stephen, 1947-

★ **Salem's** Lot. Doubleday 1975 439p $35

ISBN 0-385-00751-5

"It is to Stephen King's credit as a stylist that he has charmed us into such familiar territory. Sparing the endless atmospheric creaks and cobwebs and cupolas of this New England landscape, he thrusts us into the private terror of his characters." Best Sellers

King, Stephen, 1947-

★ The **shining**. Doubleday 1977 447p $35

ISBN 0-385-12167-9

LC 76-24212

"In a fast-paced and gory denouement, the terror comes to a violent end. King is a masterful technician of suspense whose readers as well as characters are the victims of his relentless heightening of horror." Libr J

King, Stephen, 1947-

Skeleton crew. Putnam 1985 512p hardcover o.p. pa $7.99

ISBN 0-451-16861-5 pa

LC 84-15947

This "collection of King's shorter work is a hefty sampler from all stages of his career, and demonstrates the range of his abilities. . . . There are several stories here that must rank among King's best." Publ Wkly

King, Stephen, 1947-

The **stand**. Doubleday 1978 823 p.

ISBN 9780385199575; 9780307743688; 9780606256155

LC 77016928

"A flu-like plague escapes from an experimental lab. Within days it devastates the country, leaving only a few thousand immune people. Besides their immunity, the survivors have in common a terrible dream pitting a faceless man of evil against a woman of goodness. The survivors make their choices and head west, gathering for the confrontation between the satanic Randall Flagg and the God-anointed Mother Abigail." Libr J

King, Stephen, 1947-

Thinner; {by} Richard Bachman. New Am. Lib. 1984 309p

LC 84-11462

"Bachman blends extraordinary events so cleanly and credibly into the fabric of his characters' lives that we are compelled to read on to the story's chilling conclusion. A superbly crafted drama." Booklist

Kingsolver, Barbara

★ The **bean** trees; a novel. 10th anniversary ed; Harper-Flamingo 1997 261p $19.95; pa $7.99

ISBN 0-06-017579-6; 0-06-109731-4 pa

LC 97-2691

A reissue of the title first published 1988

This book "gives readers something that's increasingly hard to find today—a character to believe in and laugh with and admire." Christ Sci Monit

Followed by Pigs in heaven (1993)

Kingsolver, Barbara

★ **Flight** behavior; a novel. by Barbara Kingsolver. HarperCollins 2012 448 p. (hardback) $28.99

ISBN 0062124269; 9780062124265

LC 2012025321

Author Barbara Kingsolver's book "tells the story of Dellarobia Turnbow, a petite, razor-sharp 29-year-old who nurtured worldly ambitions before becoming pregnant and marrying at seventeen. Now, after more than a decade of tending to small children on a failing farm, oppressed by poverty, isolation and her husband's antagonistic family, she has mitigated her boredom by surrendering to an obsessive flirtation with a handsome younger man." (Publisher's note)

Kingsolver, Barbara

Pigs in heaven; a novel. HarperCollins Pubs. 1993 343p

ISBN 9780060922535; 9780061436680

LC 92054739

In this sequel to The bean trees, Taylor Greer and her adopted Cherokee Indian daughter Turtle "are on a trip to the Hoover Dam, where Turtle is the only person to see a man fall over the side. . . . The rescue makes Turtle a heroine. But becoming a heroine, which culminates in an appearance on 'Oprah,' engenders a new disaster. Annawake Fourkiller, an Indian-rights lawyer, sees the white mother with her Cherokee daughter on TV and decides the child must be returned to the Cherokee Nation. . . . But Taylor isn't about to let go of the little girl. . . . They pack up and run." Newsweek

Kingsolver, Barbara

★ The **poisonwood** Bible; a novel. HarperFlamingo 1998 546p $26; pa $16.99

ISBN 0-06-017540-0; 0-06-157707-3 pa

LC 98-19901

"Buttressing her suspenseful chronicle with authentic background detail, Kingsolver's narrative is at once a compelling family saga and an astute look at Western imperialism in Africa." Publ Wkly

Kinsella, Sophie

I've got your number; Sophie Kinsella. Dial Press 2012 433 p.

ISBN 9780385342063; 9780679644682

LC 2011031146

In this book, "Poppy Wyatt . . . is about to marry her ideal man, Magnus Tavish, but in one afternoon . . . [n]ot only has she lost her engagement ring in a hotel fire drill but in the panic that follows, her phone is stolen. As she paces shakily around the lobby, she spots an abandoned phone in a trash can. . . . Now she can leave a number for the hotel to contact her when they find her ring. . . . [But] the phone's owner, businessman Sam Roxton, . . . wants his phone back and doesn't appreciate Poppy reading his messages and wading into his personal life. What ensues is a hilarious and unpredictable turn of events as Poppy and Sam increasingly upend each other's lives through emails and text messages." (Publisher's note)

Kinsella, Sophie

My not so perfect life; Sophie Kinsella. Dial Press 2017 448 p. (ebook) $65; (hardback) $28

ISBN 9780812998276; 9780812998269

LC 2016025629

In this novel, by Sophie Kinsella, "everywhere Katie Brenner looks, someone else is living the life she longs for, particularly her boss, Demeter. Katie's life, meanwhile, is a daily struggle. Then, just as she's finding her feet . . . Demeter fires Katie. Shattered but determined to stay positive, Katie retreats to her family's farm in Somerset to help them set up a vacation business. London has never seemed so far away—until Demeter unexpectedly turns up as a guest." (Publisher's note)

"A perfect combination of fun, laughable moments rounded out with some deep-seated family and relationship issues." Booklist

Kipling, Rudyard, 1865-1936

★ **Collected** stories; selected and introduced by Robert Gottlieb. Knopf 1994 xxxvii, 911p $25

ISBN 0-679-43592-1

LC 94-5854

"There is an enormous range of subject matter, genre, styles, and tones in Kipling's prose work. . . . {He} is undoubtedly one of the great short-story writers in English and the subtlety of his early narrative technique has led some to claim him as a proto-Modernist." Oxford Companion to 20th Cent Lit in Engl

Includes bibliographical references

Kirk, David

★ **Sword** of honor; or Hours of the dog. by David Kirk. Doubleday 2015 464 p. (hardcover) $26.95

ISBN 0385536658; 9780385536653

LC 2015002270

In this book, by David Kirk, "Musashi Miyamoto travels through Japan determined to proclaim his revolutionary epiphany that the 'way of the samurai,' the ancient code that binds warriors to their masters, needs to be abolished. . . . Musashi will learn, however, that the capital of the nation is rife with intrigue and potential rebellion against the newly established government, a struggle into which he unwittingly enters." (Publisher's note)

"Kirk doesn't shrink from the violence these warriors mete out to each other and even finds both poetic and excruciatingly exact ways to describe the many duels that take place." Kirkus

Kirkpatrick, Jane

This road we traveled; Jane Kirkpatrick. Revell 2016 352 p. (softcover) $14.99

ISBN 9780800722333

LC 2016018462

In this book, by Jane Kirkpatrick, "when Tabitha Brown's son makes the fateful decision to leave Missouri and strike out for Oregon, she refuses to be left behind. . . . The trials they face along the way will severely test Tabitha's faith, courage, and ability to hope. . . . What she couldn't know was how this frightening journey would impact how she understood her own life--and the greater part she had to play in history." (Publisher's note)

"This is more than one woman's story of courage and faith; it is the story of a family that journeys, grows, and heals together. Kirkpatrick's vivid, rich prose will keep readers in awe and on the edges of their seats." Pub Wkly

Includes bibliographical references (pages 333-334).

Kirshenbaum, Binnie

An **almost** perfect moment. Ecco 2004 321p $23.95

ISBN 0-06-052086-8

LC 2003-54961

The protagonist of this novel is Valentine Kessler. "A nice Jewish girl growing up in late-1970s Brooklyn, she becomes infatuated with her Polish American math teacher and with the Virgin Mary, for she mysteriously resembles the vision of Mary seen by Bernadette of Lourdes. Valentine's father left when she was a baby, and ever since her mother, Miriam, indulges her beautiful, newly withdrawn daughter while eating herself into obesity and playing mah-jongg every afternoon with her buddies. The so-called Girls are like a Greek chorus, commenting on life around them and wondering at Valentine's inspired silence. . . . Bursting with hyperbole, this is a hilarious and uncanny snapshot of a bygone era." Libr J

Kitamura, Katie

A **separation**; a novel. Katie Kitamura. Riverhead Books 2017 240 p. (ebook) $65; (hardcover) $25

ISBN 9780399576126; 9780399576102

LC 2016026580

In this novel, by Katie Kitamura, "a young woman has agreed with her faithless husband: it's time for them to separate. . . . As she begins her new life, she gets word that Christopher has gone missing . . . [and] she reluctantly agrees to go look for him, still keeping their split to herself. . . . As her search comes to a shocking breaking point, she discovers she understands less than she thought she did about her relationship and the man she used to love." (Publisher's note)

"A minutely observed novel of infidelity unsettles its characters and readers." Kirkus

Kittredge, William

The **Willow** Field. Knopf 2006 342p $25.95

ISBN 1-4000-4097-3

LC 2006-45157

This "multigenerational saga begins with a stunning set piece—a classic horse drive, more than 200 head, from Nevada to Calgary. Rossie, a veteran ranch hand but still barely 20, signs on for the drive as a way of breaking ties with a girl and winds up forging even stronger ties with another girl, Eliza Stevenson, the unmarried but pregnant daughter of a rancher in Montana's Bitterroot Mountains. 'We could be it, entirely it,' Eliza says shortly after she meets Rossie, and as we watch their lives unfold, from the Depression through World War II and on into the 1960s, we realize that this strong-willed woman was both right and wrong. . . . Rossie and Eliza are 'entirely it,' but—fiery individuals both—they are also in perpetual conflict, cherishing their union just as they struggle not to be consumed by the other. This transcendent love story is at the heart of Kittredge's novel, but it is set against not one but two imposing landscapes—the Bitterroot and the Nevada desert, both of which demand their own allegiance from the characters' minds and hearts." Booklist

Klaussmann, Liza

Tigers in red weather; a novel. Liza Klaussmann. Little, Brown & Co. 2012 356 p. (hardcover) $25.99; (paperback) $14.99

ISBN 0316211338; 9780316211338; 9780316211321

LC 2011050204

This book by Liza Klaussmann, "set in . . . post-WWIII Martha's Vineyard . . . finds a family unmoored by an unsolved murder. . . . Once carefree girls, now jaded women . . . [Nick and Helena have] returned to Tiger House with their families, but their lives have lost much of the rosy glow they had before the murder. Selfish and aloof, Nick can't stay faithful to her husband. . . . Helena . . . prefers pills and booze to dealing with her poor excuse for a relationship." (Publishers Weekly)

Klay, Phil, 1983-

★ **Redeployment**; Phil Klay. The Penguin Press 2014 304 p. (hardback) $26.95; (pbk.) $16.00

ISBN 9781594204999; 9781594204999; 0143126822; 1594204993

LC 2013028125

National Book Award: Fiction (2014)

This short story collection, by Phil Klay, "takes readers to the frontlines of the wars in Iraq and Afghanistan, asking us to understand what happened there, and what happened to the soldiers who returned. Interwoven with themes of brutality and faith, guilt and fear, helplessness and survival, the characters in these stories struggle to make meaning out of chaos." (Publisher's note)

"Klay is a Marine veteran who served in Iraq, and the 12 stories reveal a deep understanding of the tedium, chaos and bloodshed of war, as well as the emotional disorientation that comes with returning home from it." Kirkus

Klein, Joe

Primary colors; a novel of politics. [by] Anonymous. Random House 1996 366p

ISBN 0-679-44859-4

LC 95-39823

"This is, in short, a quite outstanding novel of political process and motive that reads like a slightly hipper version of Gore Vidal." New Statesman (1913)

Klein, Matthew

Con ed. Warner Books 2007 285p $23.99

ISBN 978-0-446-57955-1; 0-446-57955-6

LC 2006-18438

"Once-rich con-man Kip Largo is going straight, living small, and making $10 per hour in a dry-cleaning store after doing eight years for wire fraud. Life is dull, but Kip wants it that way, until his son Toby shows up, on the run from the Russian Mob. Kip needs a big score to save Toby, and a timely proposal from the stunning young wife of a dangerous Las Vegas casino owner provides him with a target for a grand scam. Con Ed is a brisk, clever, and charming page-turner." Booklist

Klein, Rachel

The **moth** diaries; a novel. Counterpoint 2002 249p $24

ISBN 1-58243-205-8

LC 2001-7226

"The unnamed narrator of Klein's first novel is a studious, thoughtful 16-year-old at an elite boarding school in the late '60s. Her closest friend is her sweet, friendly roommate, Lucy, who navigates the school's social system with ease. The arrival of quiet, mysterious Ernessa upsets the balance between the friends when Ernessa befriends and seemingly takes Lucy away from the narrator. . . . Thanks to reading LeFanu's vampire story 'Carmilla' and other tales, and to Ernessa's odd behavior and Lucy's mysterious wasting illness, the narrator begins to suspect that Ernessa is a vampire. . . . The diary format of Klein's story gives it immediacy, and a menacing atmosphere permeates it." Booklist

Kleypas, Lisa

Brown-Eyed Girl; A Novel. by Lisa Kleypas. St. Martin's Press 2015 304 p. $25.99

ISBN 0312605374; 9780312605377

LC 2015017165

In this novel, by Lisa Kleypas, "[w]edding planner Avery Crosslin may be a rising star in Houston society, but she doesn't believe in love-at least not for herself. When she meets wealthy bachelor Joe Travis and mistakes him for a wedding photographer, she has no intention of letting him sweep her off her feet. But Joe is a man who goes after what he wants, and Avery can't resist the temptation of a sexy southern charmer and a hot summer evening." (Publisher's note)

"When it comes to delivering a pair of perfectly matched protagonists whose heart-melting romance is fueled by an abundance of smoldering sexual chemistry, RITA award-winning Kleypas (Blue-Eyed Devil, 2015) is a class by herself, and the conclusion to her Travis Brothers quartet deserves an A+." Booklist

Kleypas, Lisa

★ **Cold**-hearted Rake; by Lisa Kleypas. HarperCollins 2015 416 p. (The Ravenels) $7.99

ISBN 0062371819; 9780062371812

"Devon Ravenel, London's most wickedly charming rake, has just inherited an earldom. But his powerful new rank in society comes with unwanted responsibilities . . . and more than a few surprises. His estate is saddled with debt, and the late earl's three innocent sisters are still occupying the house . . . along with Kathleen, Lady Trenear, a beautiful young widow whose sharp wit and determination are a match for Devon's own." (Publisher's note)

"Kleypas begins a new historical romance series with two damaged characters who might find happiness if they can ever learn to trust themselves and one another. Intricately and elegantly crafted, intensely romantic, and with secondary characters and an epilogue that will leave readers anxiously awaiting more." Kirkus

Other titles in this series include:

Marrying Winterborne (2016)

Devil in Spring (2017)

Hello Stranger (2018)

Kleypas, Lisa

Crystal Cove. St. Martin's Griffin 2013 316 p. (paperback) $14.99; (hardcover) $26.99

ISBN 1250011752; 1250032075; 9781250011756; 9781250032072

LC 2012532398

This book follows Justin Hoffman, "born shortly before her father died. Losing the great love of her life was so hard on Justine's mother, Marigold, that Marigold cast a spell on her daughter to protect her from the pain of finding and then losing that kind of love. What her mother did based on a loving desire to protect her child, grown-up Justine views as a curse that needs to be lifted." (Kirkus)

Kleypas, Lisa

Rainshadow road; a novel. Lisa Kleypas. 1st ed. St. Martin's Griffin 2012 viii, 324 p.p (hardcover) $34.99; (trade pbk.) $14.99

ISBN 9781410446640 large print; 0312605889; 9780312605889; 9781429938372

LC 2011041081

This book follows "Lucy Marinn . . . [who] is stunned and blindsided . . . [when she is left by] her fiance Kevin. . . . His new lover is Lucy's own sister. . . . Facing the severe disapproval of Lucy's parents, Kevin asks his friend Sam Nolan, a local vineyard owner . . . to 'romance' Lucy and hopefully loosen her up. . . . Complications ensue when Sam and Lucy begin to fall in love . . . and Lucy discovers that the new relationship in her life began under false pretenses." (Publisher's note)

Kline, Christina Baker

Orphan train; a novel. Christina Baker Kline. William Morrow 2012 288 p. (pbk.) $14.99

ISBN 9780061950728; 9780062101204; 0061950726

LC 2012027409

"Penobscot Indian Molly Ayer is close to 'aging out' out of the foster care system. A community service position helping an elderly woman clean out her home is the only thing keeping Molly out of juvie and worse. . . . As she helps Vivian sort through her possessions and memories, Molly learns that she and Vivian aren't as different as they seem to be. A young Irish immigrant orphaned in New York City, Vivian was put on a train to the Midwest with hundreds of other children whose destinies would be determined by luck and chance. Molly discovers that she has the power to help Vivian find answers to mysteries that have haunted her for her entire life--answers that will ultimately free them both." (Publisher's note)

Klosterman, Chuck

Downtown Owl; a novel. Scribner 2008 275p $24

ISBN 978-1-4165-4418-0; 1-4165-4418-6

LC 2007-47088

This novel focuses on the lives of "the football-playing teenager Mitch, the 20-something Julia, and the elderly Horace. The three have little in common—they all live in the small town of Owl, North Dakota, but otherwise have little interaction—but by weaving their three stories around each other, Klosterman constructs a touching, incisive, and (of course) funny snapshot of small-town America circa 1984. And if the story occasionally falters or takes off on tangents, who cares? It's all tremendously fun to read." PopMatters

Klosterman, Chuck

The **visible** man; a novel. Scribner 2011 230p $25

ISBN 978-1-4391-8446-2; 1-4391-8446-1

"Klosterman has conjured up a novel that manages to be both wildly experimental and accessible, while making perceptive observations about privacy, human nature, and of course, the author's forte, pop culture." Entertainment Wkly

Knausgaard, Karl Ove

My struggle; Karl Ove Knausgaard ; translated from Norwegian by Don Bartlett. 1st Archipelago Books ed. Archipelago Books 2012 430 p. (alk. paper) $18.00

ISBN 1935744186; 9781935744184

LC 2011048978

Author Karl Ove Knausgaard offers "a coming of age story--told in fits and starts--and a philosophical exploration of what it means to be a son, brother, and writer. The first in a series of six, this work . . . [looks at] how to survive in a world too minutely examined to trust or love: on the first page, the narrator's focus shifts in a moment from a sentimental note on the life of the heart to an outline of the physical processes of bodily decomposition. . . . Karl's attention is constantly drawn toward the vanishing point of his late estranged, alcoholic father." (Publishers Weekly)

Volume 1 of 6

Knausgård, Karl Ove, 1968-

My struggle; Book five Karl Ove Knausgaard ; translated from the Norwegian by Don Bartlett. Archipelago Books 2016 624 p. (hardcover) $27

ISBN 0914671391; 9780914671398

LC 2015049328

This book is the "fifth book of [Karl Ove] Knausgaard's . . . My Struggle series. . . . As a nineteen-year-old, Karl Ove moves to Bergen and invests all of himself in his writing. But his efforts get the opposite effect - he wants it so much that he gets writer's block. At the same time, he sees his friends, one-by-one, publish their debuts. He suspects that he will never get anything published." (Publisher's note)

"It will be fascinating to see how Knausgaard weds his intensely personal narrative with events of such national and historical significance." Booklist

Kneale, Matthew, 1960-

English passengers; Matthew Kneale. Nan A. Talese 2000 446 p. facsim. (pbk.) $9.99

ISBN 0385497431; 9780385497442

LC 99016402

Whitbread Award for Novel and Book of the Year (2000)

This book takes place "[i]n 1857 when Captain Illiam Quillian Kewley and his band of rum smugglers from the Isle of Man have most of their contraband confiscated by British Customs . . . [and] are forced to put their ship up for charter. The only takers are two eccentric Englishmen. . . . The Reverend Geoffrey Wilson believes the Garden of Eden was on the island of Tasmania. His traveling partner, Dr. Thomas Potter, unbeknownst to Wilson, is developing a sinister thesis about the races of men. Meanwhile, an aboriginal in Tasmania named Peevay recounts his people's struggles against the invading British, a story that begins in 1824, moves into the present with approach of the English passengers in 1857, and extends into the future in 1870." (Publisher's note)

Kneale, Matthew, 1960-

★ **When** we were Romans; a novel. Nan A. Talese 2008 224p $23.95

ISBN 978-0-385-52625-8; 0-385-52625-3

LC 2007-45523

First published 2007 in the United Kingdom

"We, the adult readers of 'When We Were Romans,' learn to peer through the screen of Lawrence's limited point of view to see what's really going on even as our narrator begins to guess at what lies behind his mother's version of events and even to catch a glimpse of the mysteries of his own heart. In life as well as in books, there are some truths that it's much better to sneak up on." Salon.com

Knight, Michael, 1969-

Eveningland; stories. Michael Knight. Atlantic Monthly Press 2017 277 p. (hardback) $25

ISBN 9780802125972

LC 2016030180

This collection of stories, by Michael Knight, captures the authenticity of place and "the ways in which ordinary life astounds us with its complexity. A teenage girl with a taste for violence holds a burglar hostage in her house on New Year's Eve; a middle aged couple examines the intricacies of their marriage as they prepare to throw a party; and a real estate mogul in the throes of grief buys up all the property on an island only to be accused of madness by his daughters." (Publisher's note)

"A quiet, beautifully modulated group of six short stories and a novella set in or near Mobile, Alabama." Kirkus.

Knopf, Chris, 1951-

✓★ **Dead** anyway; Chris Knopf. The Permanent Press 2012 248 p. $28.00

ISBN 1579622836; 9781579622831

LC 2012016404

Followed by: Cries of the Lost (2013)

In this book, a hitman shoots Arthur Cathcart, leaving him for dead, after killing Mrs. Cathcart. When Cathcart awakes from the subsequent coma, he "succeeds, with the connivance of his physician sister, in having himself declared dead. As he begins the tortuous rehabilitation process and looks into establishing new identities, Cathcart realizes that it's almost impossible to go off the grid totally and still be able to function effectively, so he has to compromise in inventive ways." (Publishers Weekly)

Knopf, Chris

✓The **last** refuge; Chris Knopf. Permanent Press 2005 287p (Sam Acquillo mysteries) $26

ISBN 1-57962-118-X

LC 2004-65314

"While [Sam's] low-key investigation is only minimally suspenseful, the characters he chats up are such original oddballs and their conversation so bracing that you want to kick off your shoes and spend some time on the porch with them, just taking in the view and enjoying the talk." N Y Times Book Rev

Other titles in this series are:
Two time (2006)
Head wounds (2008)
Hard stop (2009)
Black swan (2011)
Cop job (2015)
Back lash (2016)
Tango down (2017)

Knowles, John

★ A **separate** peace; a novel. Macmillan 1960 186p
ISBN 0-02-564850-0

First published 1959 in the United Kingdom

"Gene Forrester looks back on his school days, spent in a New England town just before World War II. He both admires and envies his close friend and roommate, Finny, who is a natural athlete, in contrast to Gene's special competence as a scholar. When Finny suffers a crippling accident, Gene must face his own involvement in it." Shapiro. Fic for Youth. 3d edition

Ko, Lisa

★ The **leavers**; A novel. Lisa Ko. First edition. Algonquin Books of Chapel Hill 2017 338 p. $25.95
ISBN 9781616206888

LC 2016043934

Pen/Bellwether Prize (2017)
National Book Award Finalist: Fiction (2017)

This book by Lisa Ko, "gives us one of fiction's most singular mothers. Loving and selfish, determined and frightened, Polly is forced to make one heartwrenching choice after another. 'The Leavers' is a vivid examination of borders and belonging. It's a moving story of how a boy comes into his own when everything he loves is taken away, and how a mother learns to live with the mistakes of the past." (Publisher's note)

"Ko's stunning tale of love and loyalty—to family, to country—is a fresh and moving look at the immigrant experience in America, and is as timely as ever." Pub Wkly

Koch, Herman, 1953-

★ The **dinner**; a novel. Herman Koch; translated from the Dutch by Sam Garrett. Crown Publishers 2013 304 p. $24
ISBN 0770437850; 9780770437855

LC 2012025626

This book by Herman Koch, which won the Publieksprijs prize, "starts out as a witty look at contemporary manners . . . before turning into a take-no-prisoners psychological thriller. The Lohman brothers . . . meet at an expensive Amsterdam restaurant . . . to discuss a situation involving their respective 15-year-old sons, Michel and Rick. . . . During this five-course dinner, from aperitif to digestif, secrets come out that threaten relations between the two families." (Publishers Weekly)

"In a single setting, Koch successfully deploys multiple narratives of a single event to effectively show that our construction of history, and constant attempts at overdetermining the future, is problematic. A shocking, humorous, and entertaining novel." LJ

Koen, Karleen

Before Versailles. Crown 2011 xii, 460p
ISBN 9780307716576; 0307716570

LC 2010035562

The book offers a historical fiction of young King of France Louis XVI. "After the death of his prime minister, Cardinal Mazarin, twenty-two-year-old Louis steps into governing France. He's still a young man, but one who, as king, . . . takes everything he can get--including his brother's wife. As the love affair between Louis and Princess Henriette burns, it sets the kingdom on the road toward unmistakable scandal and conflict with the Vatican. . . . But there are other problems lurking outside the chateau of Fontainebleau: a boy in an iron mask has been seen in the woods, and the king's finance minister, Nicolas Fouquet, has proven to be more powerful than Louis ever thought—a man who could make a great ally or become a dangerous foe." (Publisher's note)

Koen, Karleen

Through a glass darkly. Random House 1986 743p

LC 86-422

"Expertly paced, the novel blends quaint historical romance with a sharp-edged, contemporary psychodramatic style. Its characters are memorable and full-bodied, maturing through a series of rapidly escalating tragedies that bring the sweetly naive heroine into full womanhood and force her to make a decision that will forever change her life. A sophisticated, atmospheric work." Booklist

Koenig, Minerva

Nine days; a mystery. Minerva Koenig. Minotaur Books 2014 293 p. (hardback) $24.99
ISBN 1250051940; 9781250051943

LC 2014016747

In this book, by Minerva Koenig, "Julia Kalas is a damned good criminal. For 17 years she renovated historic California buildings as a laundry front for her husband's illegal arms business. Then the Aryan Brotherhood made her a widow, and witness protection shipped her off to the tiny town of Azula, Texas. . . . Julia figures she'll pick up where she left off, but she's got a federal watchdog now: police chief Teresa Hallstedt." (Publisher's note)

"Small-town Texas is vividly brought to life in this atmospheric and entertaining debut that also introduces a memorable and unusual protagonist. It's bound to delight fans of Tricia Fields, Lori G. Armstrong, or James Lee Burke's "Hackberry Holland" books." LJ

Koestler, Arthur

★ **Darkness** at noon; translated by Daphne Hardy. Macmillan 1987 267p
ISBN 0-02-565210-9

LC 86-31273

First published 1940 in the United Kingdom; this is a reissue of the 1941 edition

This novel "deals with the arrest, imprisonment, trial, and execution of N. S. Rubashov in an unnamed dictatorship over which 'No. 1' presides. Koestler describes Rubashov as 'a synthesis of the lives of a number of men who were victims of the so-called Moscow trials,' and the novel did much to draw attention to the nature of Stalin's regime." Oxford Companion to Engl Lit. 6th edition

Kolpan, Gerald

Magic words; The Tale of a Jewish Boy-Interpreter, the Frontier's Most Estimable Magician, a Murderous Harlot, and America's Greatest Indian Chief. Gerald Kolpan. Pegasus Books 2012 400 p.
ISBN 1605983691; 9781605983691

In this novel, "young Julius Meyer comes to the New World to find himself acting as translator for the famed Indian chief Standing Bear. Young Jewish immigrant Julius comes of age surrounded by the wild world of 1867 Nebraska. He . . . [is] captured by the Ponca Indian tribe. . . . Julius meets the noble chief Standing Bear and his young daughter, Prairie Flower, with whom he falls in love. . . . [Then] his older cousin, Alexander—who, as the Great Herrmann, is the most famous young magician in America [arrives]. . . . [Julius]does . . . [not] suspect the ultimate consequences of Alex's affair with Lady-Jane Little Feather. . . .

[The book] is [an] . . . adventure about the nature of prejudice, the horror of genocide, and a courageous young man who straddles two worlds to fight for love and freedom." (Publisher's note)

Konar, Affinity

★ **Mischling**; a novel. Affinity Konar. Little, Brown & Co. 2016 344 p. illustrations (hardcover) $27

ISBN 9780316269414; 9780316308106

LC 2015958011

In this novel, by Affinity Konar, "Pearl is in charge of: the sad, the good, the past. Stasha must care for: the funny, the future, the bad. It's 1944 when the twin sisters arrive at Auschwitz. . . . As part of the experimental population of twins known as Mengele's Zoo, the girls experience privileges and horrors unknown to others, and they find themselves changed, stripped of the personalities they once shared, their identities altered by the burdens of guilt and pain." (Publisher's note)

"Konar makes every sentence count; it's to her credit that the girls never come across as simply victims: they're flawed, memorable characters trying to stay alive. This is a brutally beautiful novel." Pub Wkly

Koontz, Dean R. (Dean Ray), 1945-

The **bad** place. Putnam 1990 382 p.

ISBN 9780399134982 out of print; 9780425195482

LC 89010861

"Married detectives Julie and Bobby Dakota agree to help frightened amnesiac Frank Pollard figure out what he does when he's asleep. . . . In due course, Frank and the Dakotas join forces against murderer Candy Pollard and his weird sisters, who want to kill Frank—evidently the sole human in the monstrous family. Candy extends psychic feelers toward potential victims, emanations that are sensed by Julie's younger brother Thomas. A Down's syndrome child, Thomas is telepathically gifted and able to warn Bobby of the demons who threaten Julie." Publ Wkly

Koontz, Dean R. (Dean Ray), 1945-

Brother Odd; [by] Dean Koontz. Bantam Books 2006 364p (Odd Thomas series) $27

ISBN 978-0-553-80480-5; 0-553-80480-4

LC 2006-32253

"Odd is the kind of instantly and persistently likable narrator that Fredric Brown used in such detective classics as the Ed and Am mysteries . . . though the pace of a Brown novel is relaxed in comparison. Also like Brown, Koontz employs dry, goofy humor, often in daring counterpoint to the story's spikes in tension and horror. Koontz also waxes as honorably sentimental as Ray Bradbury, and writes in breathy, two-line paragraphs, recalling the punchy manner of Robert Bloch. Obviously, then, this is a book worthy of any of the great three Bs of pop fiction." Booklist

Other titles in this series include:
Odd Thomas (2003)
Forever Odd (2005)
Odd Hours (2008)
Odd Interlude (2012)
Odd Apocalypse (2012)
Deeply Odd (2013)
Odd Thomas (2014)
Saint Odd (2015)

Koontz, Dean R. (Dean Ray), 1945-

The **darkest** evening of the year; [by] Dean Koontz. Bantam Books 2007 354p $27

ISBN 978-0-55380-482-9; 0-55380-482-0

LC 2007-40255

"Amy Redwing, the survivor of a horrifying marriage, establishes Golden Heart to rescue golden retrievers. . . . A supernatural chain of events ensues after Amy and her architect boyfriend, Brian McCarthy, rescue Nickie during a violent intervention in a family dispute. Soon the pair are on a mission that leads to a transformative confrontation with a number of ugly characters—Gunther Schloss, a frustrated aspiring novelist turned killer-for-hire; Moonglow, a psychobitch in the Mommie Dearest league; and Moonglow's lover, Harrow, a self-obsessed sicko. This is the perfect book for thriller addicts who know the darkest hour is just before dawn and for canine lovers who remember 'dog' spelled backwards is 'god.'" Publ Wkly

Koontz, Dean R. (Dean Ray), 1945-

The **husband**; [by] Dean Koontz. Bantam Books 2006 400p $27.95

ISBN 978-0-553-80479-9; 0-553-80479-0

LC 2006-42696

"Koontz focuses relentlessly on Mitch and, in chapters scattered judiciously throughout the latter 230 pages, Holly. Not for him the flirtation with evil thinking that an Elmore Leonard does so well or the temptation to sympathize with evildoers that an Alfred Hitchcock offers. And yet Koontz is no less an artist for his championing of the good and his determination to have readers identify with it, as this hair-raising thriller attests." Booklist

Koontz, Dean R. (Dean Ray), 1945-

Innocence; a novel. Dean Koontz. Bantam Books 2013 352 p. $28

ISBN 0553808036; 9780553808032

LC 2013014516

"Addison Goodheart, a 26-year-old man so 'exceedingly ugly' that his appearance causes 'the most terrible rage' in regular people, lives alone in a hidden part of an American metropolis. . . . An unexpected encounter in a deserted library with Gwyneth, an 18-year-old Goth girl who's the target of the rare-book curator's lust, throws him for a loop. Addison bonds with Gwyneth, who suspects her nemesis, J. Ryan Telford, of murdering her father by sending him poisoned honey." (Publishers Weekly)

"The narrative is intense, with an old-fashioned ominousness and artistically crafted descriptions. . . . Koontz's allegory on morality and love (agape rather than sensual) probes the idea that evil is woven through humankind." Kirkus

Koontz, Dean R. (Dean Ray), 1945-

★ **Intensity**; a novel. by Dean Koontz. Knopf 1995 307p

ISBN 0-679-42525-X

LC 95-33591

"The velocity of the plot is the book's true pleasure; the story does not move so much as rocket up the portentously gloomy highway with the reader in violent pursuit." N Y Times Book Rev

Koontz, Dean R. (Dean Ray), 1945-

Velocity; [by] Dean Koontz. Bantam Books 2005 400p $27

ISBN 0-55380-415-4

"Billy Wiles, a 30-something bartender and former writer, is content with his solitary Napa County existence listening to 'beer-based psychoanalysis' from tavern regulars; visiting his hospitalized, comatose fiancée, Barbara; and carving wood sculptures. But the simple life gets mighty complicated when he finds a note with a deadly, time-sensitive ultimatum: he must choose between the death of a young schoolteacher or an elderly humanitarian in six hours. Reluctant local sheriff Lanny Olsen dismisses it as a joke until a comely teacher is found strangled and another threatening note appears—offering even less time for Billy to decide the fate of two more people. Who would have guessed that one of those people would be Olsen? After his friend's murder, Billy finds that the cunning killer has gained access to every aspect of his life as the ultimatums grow increasingly more personal. . . . Graphic, fast-paced action, well-developed characters and relentless, nail-biting scenes show Koontz at the top of his game." Publ Wkly

Koontz, Dean R. (Dean Ray), 1945-

Watchers. Putnam 1987 352p hardcover o.p. pa $7.99

ISBN 0-399-13263-5; 0-425-18880-9 pa

LC 86-22687

"When the Russians sabotage a genetic research project in California, two mutated creatures escape from the lab. One is a golden retriever with high enough intelligence to think and communicate with humans; the other is the Outsider, a vicious monster created from a baboon and bred to kill. Both the man who befriends and adopts the dog and his new bride find themselves stalked by government agents anxious to find the dog, a particularly repulsive Mafia hit man intent on stealing him, and the Outsider, with whom the dog is linked telepathically." Libr J

Koryta, Michael

The **Cypress** House. Little, Brown and Co. 2011 426p $24.99

ISBN 978-0-316-05372-3; 0-316-05372-4

LC 2010-11405

"Though Koryta's evocation of the Depression could be stronger, the novel builds to a richly satisfying climax in which Arlen is guided by the spirit of his father and voices of the recently departed. A commanding performance in the field of supernatural noir. " Kirkus

Includes bibliographical references (p. 417).

Koryta, Michael

★ The **prophet**; Michael Koryta. Little, Brown and Co. 2012 416 p. $25.99

ISBN 0316122610; 9780316122610

LC 2012014690

In this book, "Adam Austin, a . . . bail bondsman and sometime private investigator in the small town of Chambers, Ohio, has never gotten past the guilt of letting his little sister Marie walk home from a football game alone" which led to her murder. "After Adam unknowingly sends a 17-year-old client to her death by telling her where she can find a letter-writing ex-con she thinks is her father, the past eerily collides with the present." (Kirkus)

Koryta, Michael

The **ridge**; Michael Koryta. Little, Brown and Co. 2011 357p. $24.99

ISBN 978-0-316-05366-2; 031605366X

LC 201111377

"When local drunk Wyatt French, who inexplicably built a wooden lighthouse far from any large body of water, calls Kevin Kimble, the county's chief deputy, and asks whether he'd investigate a suicide, Kimble, who's driving in his car to visit a prison inmate, refers French to a suicide hotline. Soon after, reporter Roy Darmus, whose newspaper has just folded, receives an unsettling call from French that prompts Darmus to go to the lighthouse, where he finds the man has apparently shot himself in the mouth. French's death may be connected with an eerie blue light seen in the vicinity of Blade Ridge, a phenomenon that riles the big cats residing in a wildlife refuge that's just set up shop on property adjoining French's. Koryta . . . matches an original and complex plot line with prose full of understated menace." Publ Wkly

Koryta, Michael

So cold the river. Little, Brown and Co. 2010 508p $24.99

ISBN 9780316053631; 0-316-05363-5

LC 2009-32414

"Koryta spins a spellbinding tale of an unholy lust for power that reaches from beyond the grave and suspends disbelief through the believable interactions of fully developed characters. A cataclysmic finale will put readers in mind of some of the best recent works of supernatural horror, among which this book ranks." Publ Wkly

Koryta, Michael

★ **Those** who wish me dead; Michael Koryta. Little, Brown and Co. 2014 400 p. (hardcover) $26

ISBN 0316122556; 9780316122559

LC 2014934962

Alex Award (2015)

"When fourteen-year-old Jace Wilson witnesses a brutal murder, he's plunged into a new life, issued a false identity and hidden in a wilderness skills program for troubled teens. The plan is to get Jace off the grid while police find the two killers. . . known as the Blackwell Brothers, [who] are slaughtering anyone who gets in their way in a methodical quest to reach him." (Publisher's note)

"Koryta . . . has upped his game with this stand-alone's seamless blend of western-wilderness thriller and mainstream crime fiction, with a prickly dab of horror." Booklist

Koryta, Michael

Tonight I said goodbye; Michael Koryta. 1st ed; Thomas Dunne Books\St. Martin's Minotaur 2004 290p (Lincoln Perry series) $21.95

ISBN 0-312-33245-9

LC 2004-46781

"The Cleveland police would charge private investigator Wayne Weston with murdering his wife and daughter except that their bodies can't be found and he's dead, apparently a suicide. Weston's father isn't buying it, however, and he hires private investigators Lincoln Perry and Joe Pritchard to clear his son's name and find his family. Perry is a former cop whose cheating ex-fiancée set him off on a bender that cost him his job. Pritchard, his old partner, is ready to retire and become what all retired cops become, a P.I. The hardboiled cliché works beautifully here as these two men find themselves chasing Russian Mafiya, a real estate mogul, and an ex-Marine while dodging bullets, cops, and the FBI. The Cleveland setting is a nice change from the usual East Coast/West Coast locales." Libr J

Other titles in this series are:
Sorrow's anthem (2006)
A welcome grave (2007)
The silent hour (2009)

Kosinski, Jerzy N.

★ **Being** there; [by] Jerzy Kosinski. Harcourt Brace Jovanovich 1971 142p

ISBN 0-15-111700-4

"An illiterate gardener, Chance, knows the world only through his gardening and by watching television, to which he is addicted. Without education or any identifiable background, he is evicted into the outside world when his employer dies. He makes horticultural analogies to current events, which give him a reputation for wisdom that he really does not have, and which catapult him into national prominence. Chance's simple statements are interpreted by his listeners to be profound observations, and we see him being considered for positions of great importance. This is a satire on human behavior in the worlds of power, government, and the media." Shapiro. Fic for Youth. 3d edition

Kosinski, Jerzy N.

The **devil** tree; {by} Jerzy Kosinski. Harcourt Brace Jovanovich 1973 208p

This novel "confronts the disintegration of the American dream as seen through the eyes of Jonathan James Whalen, the man-who-has-everything. For Whalen and many of the people who surround him, the American dream has become the American nightmare. Their efforts to escape their roots become a frenetic search to find their roots, until, like the devil tree, they get turned upside down and confirm the fact of their own extinction. Jonathan Whalen is as empty as the life he leads, although on the surface he is a man who can be and do anything he wants." Publ Wkly

Kosinski, Jerzy N.

★ The **painted** bird; [by] Jerzy Kosinski. 2nd Modern Library ed; Modern Lib. 1983 234p

ISBN 0-394-60433-4

LC 82-42869

First published 1965 by Houghton Mifflin

"In Eastern Europe during World War II a ten-year-old boy is separated from his parents and struggles to survive in primitive villages where he is viewed as an unwanted outsider. Dark-haired and dark-eyed, he is unlike the Polish villagers among whom he tries to find refuge. He is the gypsy, the 'painted bird,' and savage abuse is heaped upon him time after time. He has, nevertheless, the will to transcend the sadism and superstition of these ignorant people." Shapiro. Fic for Youth. 3d edition

Kosmatka, Ted

★ The **games**; Ted Kosmatka. Del Rey 2012 360 p. (hardback) $25

ISBN 9780345526618; 9780345526632

LC 2011042718

In this science fiction novel, a "new gladiatorial contest between genetically engineered monsters has proven to be a popular Olympic sport. For this year's games, the U.S. Olympic Committee (USOC) uses its most sophisticated AI computer to design the latest combatant. . . . Despite disturbing signs that the program's reclusive creator is losing touch with reality, the USOC clears Felix for competition. The stage is set for a catastrophic finale, with international repercussions." (Library Journal)

Kostova, Elizabeth

★ The **historian**; a novel. Little, Brown and Co 2005 642p $25.95

ISBN 0-316-01177-0

LC 2004-22563

"Kostova's vampire is no campy Lugosi knockoff but a blend of the cunning, powerful count who debuts in Bram Stoker's 1897 classic novel and the actual Dracula, Vlad the Impaler, a 15th-century Romanian prince who was both a nationalist hero and a sadistic torturer. Blending history and myth, Kostova has fashioned a version so fresh that when a stake is finally driven through a heart, it inspires the tragic shock of something happening for the very first time." Newsweek

Kostova, Elizabeth

The **swan** thieves; a novel. Little, Brown and Co. 2009 564p $26.99

ISBN 978-0-316-06578-8; 0-316-06578-1

LC 2009-31954

"The troubled, enigmatic artist about whom [Kostova] writes in The Swan Thieves is Robert Oliver, whose story begins with his confinement at a sanitarium after he attempts to slash a 19th-century painting of Leda, the mortal ravished by Zeus, who comes to her in the form of a swan. Psychiatrist Andrew Marlow, himself a painter, can't get Oliver to talk about the incident or anything else. Determined to unlock the mystery of Oliver's motivations, Marlow seeks out Oliver's ex-wife, Kate, and his ex-lover Mary, and investigates a mysterious trove of 19th-century letters that Oliver reads repeatedly. Through these sources, Marlow pieces together Oliver's story. There's much to like in The Swan Thieves. Kostova's painterly descriptions of artwork are luscious. . . . And the 19th-century love story which runs parallel to Oliver's story is exquisitely told." USA Today

Kotzwinkle, William

The **bear** went over the mountain. Doubleday 1996 306p

ISBN 0-385-48428-3

LC 96-2296

"This genuine parable for our time is as full of truth as it is of humor." Nation

Kowal, Mary Robinette

Shades of milk and honey. Tor 2010 304p (Glamourist histories) $24.99

ISBN 978-0-7653-2556-3; 0-7653-2556-X

LC 2010-32725

"A tale of romance in Regency England with just a sprinkling of fantasy. . . . In the Ellsworth family, it is pretty and flirtatious Melodie who attracts the most attention from would-be suitors, but her older sister Jane is the one who knows how to work magic. Able to pull 'glamour' out of the ether and create intricate tableaux that trick the eye and delight the mind, Jane yearns for true love but believes herself to be too old and too plain to catch any bachelor's eye. While two eligible young men, Captain Livingston and Mr. Dunkirk, hover around Melodie, Jane finds herself intrigued by the older, taciturn and somewhat sullen Mr. Vincent, a professional glamourist creating a complicated mural at a neighboring estate. When Melodie's dalliances threaten to stain the Ellsworths' honor, it is up to Jane to set things right, perhaps at the expense of her own happiness. . . . A low-key and witty debut novel, one that succeeds through understated humor and sprightly prose, rather than through absurd juxtapositions of the historical and the supernatural." San Francisco Chron

Other titles in this series are:

Glamour in glass (2012)

Without a summer (2013)

Valour and vanity (2014)

Of noble family (2015)

Kowal, Mary Robinette

Without a summer; Mary Robinette Kowal. 1st ed. Tor 2013 368 p. (hardcover) $24.99

ISBN 0765334151; 9780765334152

LC 2012043342

This is the third book in Mary Robinette Kowal's Glamorist Histories. Here, Sir David and Lady Jane Vincent "invite Melody, Jane's younger sister, to join them [in London], hoping to brighten her mood and provide better opportunities for making a good match. But the couple must also fend off demands from Vincent's estranged family, protect misunderstood coldmongers, determine the truth from lies told, and still work their artistry." (Library Journal)

Kracht, Christian, 1966-

Imperium; a fiction of the South Seas. Christian Kracht ; translated from the German by Daniel Bowles. Farrar, Straus & Giroux 2015 192 p. (hardcover) $23

ISBN 0374175241; 9780374175245

LC 2014039370

Author "Christian Kracht's [novel] uses the outlandish details of [August] Engelhardt's life to craft a fable about the allure of extremism and its fundamental foolishness. Engelhardt is at once a pitiable, misunderstood outsider and a rigid ideologue, and his misguided notions of purity and his spiral into madness presage the horrors of the mid-twentieth century." (Publisher's note)

"Comparable to the adventure stories of Robert Louis Stevenson, Jack London, and Daniel Defoe, albeit with a definite philosophical inclination, this amusing, fantastical tale features fabulous language, delightfully concocted descriptions, and an excellent translation by Bowles." LJ

Krall, Hanna

Chasing the king of hearts; Hanna Krall ; translated from the Polish by Philip Boehm ; afterword by Mariusz Szczygiel. Feminist Press at the City University of New York 2017 193 p. illustrations (paperback) $15.95

ISBN 1558619445; 9781558619449; 9781908670137

LC 2016034906

This book, by Hanna Krall, translated by Philip Boehm, "is a terse, unexpected human lesson born of an occupation-era love story. Based on a true story, the raw interplay of history and fictionalization spans the Warsaw Ghetto, the war-torn countryside, and the nightmare of Auschwitz." (Publisher's note)

"A quirky but exceptional story of infinite love and life-sustaining commitment." Kirkus

Kramer, Larry, 1935-

Search for My Heart; A Novel. by Larry Kramer. Farrar, Straus & Giroux 2015 800 p. $40

ISBN 0374104395; 9780374104399

LC 2014023449

In the first part of Larry Kramer's "American People" series, "which runs up to the 1950s, we meet prehistoric monkeys who spread a peculiar virus, a Native American shaman whose sexual explorations mutate into occult visions, and early English settlers who live as loving same-sex couples only to fall victim to the forces of bigotry. . . . In the twentieth century . . . a religious sect conspires with eugenicists, McCarthyites, and Ivy Leaguers to exterminate homosexuals." (Publisher's note)

"There is nary a dog in these pages that is not supremely shaggy, never a missed opportunity to offend someone. Kramer ranges among voices, eras and styles, the dominant ones being steely anger shading into Pynchon-esque goofiness but always with serious intent. Breathtakingly well-written. And how could one not keep reading, no matter how endless, a book with a line such as 'You don't just drop a penis like Tibby's into the narrative and let it go'?" Kirkus

Krantz, Judith

Mistral's daughter. Crown 1983 531p

ISBN 0-517-54906-9

LC 82-17966

The author "possesses an undeniable talent for plot-weaving and descriptive detail." Best Sellers

Krasikov, Sana

The **patriots**; a novel. Sana Krasikov. Spiegel & Grau 2017 560 p. (acid-free paper) $28; (ebook) $65

ISBN 9780385524414; 9780399588846

LC 2015045869

This novel, by Sana Krasikov, "is a riveting evocation of the Cold War years. . . . Alternating between Florence's and Julian's perspectives, it is at once a mother-son story and a tale of two countries bound in a dialectic dance; a love story and a spy story; both a grand, old-fashioned epic and a contemporary novel of ideas. . . . [This] is a poignant tale of the power of love, the rewards and risks of friendship, and the secrets parents and children keep from one another." (Publisher's note)

"We do the best we can in an imperfect world, Krasikov reminds us in a dark tale brightened by tender compassion for human frailty." Kirkus

Krauss, Nicole

Forest dark; a novel. Nicole Krauss. HarperCollins 2017 290 p. (hardcover) $27.99

ISBN 0062430998; 9780062431011; 9780062430991

In this novel, by Nicole Krauss, "Jules Epstein, a man whose drive, avidity, and outsized personality have . . . been a force to be reckoned with, is undergoing a metamorphosis. In the wake of his parent' deaths, his divorce from his wife of more than thirty years, and his retirement from the New York legal firm where he was a partner, he's felt an irresistible need to give away his possessions, alarming his children and perplexing the executor of his estate." (Publisher's note)

"Krauss's elegant, provocative, and mesmerizing novel is her best yet. Rich in profound insights and emotional resonance, it follows two characters on their paths to self-realization." Pub Wkly

Krauss, Nicole

Great house. W. W. Norton & Co. 2010 289p $24.95

ISBN 978-0-393-07998-2; 0-393-07998-8

LC 2010-29946

National Book Award Finalist: Fiction (2010)

Connected solely by a desk of enormous dimension and many drawers that exerts a power over those who possess it or give it away, three people-a lonely American novelist clinging to the memory of a poet who has mysteriously vanished in Chile, an old man in Israel facing the imminent death of his wife of 51 years, and an esteemed antiques dealer tracking down the things stolen from his father by the Nazis-struggle to create a meaningful permanence in the face of inevitable loss.

"For most of the novel, it's unclear what the desk represents or whether the book's far-flung characters will ever meet. But Krauss has a unique way of assembling novels—baroque, complex, and with a stunning tidiness that isn't clear until the very last page. All the parts do fit together in the end. The shape they form is a ghostly Great House, and its walls are ideas that leave the reader reverberating." Atlantic

Krauss, Nicole

The **history** of love. Norton 2005 252p $23.95

ISBN 0-393-06034-9

LC 2005-00936

"Beyond the vigorous whiplash that keeps Ms. Krauss's [book] moving (and keeps its reader off-balance until a stunning finale), this novel is tightly packed with ingenious asides. They range from parodying various publications' characteristic obituaries of a very famous writer, a man who was best known for a single, ecstatic five-page paragraph (Ms. Krauss perfectly mimics the syntax of both The Times and The New Republic) to skewering the kind of editor whom all writers dread." N Y Times (Late N Y Ed)

Krentz, Jayne Ann, 1948-

Dream eyes; Jayne Ann Krentz. G. P. Putnam's Sons 2013 336 p. $26.95

ISBN 0399158952; 9780399158957

LC 2012027313

This book is Jayne Ann Krentz's sequel to "Copper Beach." "When Gwen Frazier returns to Wilby, Ore., to investigate the death of her mentor, she knows she's opening up psychic wounds she'd rather forget, and when her best friend sends in investigator Judson Coppersmith to help, she realizes she's met her match, romantically and psychically. Will their attraction, skills and talent be enough, in time, to solve the mystery and save them both?" (Kirkus)

Krentz, Jayne Ann, 1948-

Promise not to tell; Jayne Ann Krentz. Berkley 2018 325 p. (hardcover) $27

ISBN 9780399585272; 9780399585265

LC 2017025348

In this book, by Jayne Ann Krentz, "Seattle gallery owner Virginia Troy has spent years battling the demons that stem from her childhood time in a cult and the night a fire burned through the compound, killing her mother. And now one of her artists has taken her own life, but not before sending Virginia a last picture: a painting that makes Virginia doubt everything about the so-called suicide--and her own past." (Publisher's note)

"Another complex, compelling romantic suspense novel from a queen of the genre." Kirkus

Krentz, Jayne Ann, 1948-

River road; Jayne Ann Krentz. G. P. Putnam's Sons 2014 352 p. $26.95

ISBN 9780399165122

LC 2013036136

In this book, by Jayne Ann Krentz, "thirteen years ago, . . . Mason Fletcher rescued 16-year-old Lucy Sheridan from becoming the victim of sociopathic classmate Tristan Brinker. Now Lucy is back in Summer River, CA, to fix up the . . . home she inherited from her Aunt Sara. Mason . . . is also back in town, to help out his uncle. When he and Lucy open up the old fireplace in her house, a body falls out, and things take an ominous turn." (Library Journal)

An "irresistible mix of scintillating humor, stunning suspense, and sexy romance." Booklist

Krentz, Jayne Ann, 1948-

Running hot. G.P. Putnam's Sons 2008 337p $25.95

ISBN 978-0-399-15521-5; 0-399-15521-X

LC 2008-28340

Reluctantly paired for a murder investigation by the paranormal Arcane Society, former cop Luther Malone and aura-reading librarian Grace Renquist find their mutual disgust dissolving into a powerful attraction, during a case that is further complicated by operatives for a ruthless underground psychic group.

"This arresting tale combines witty humor with clever plotting to weave an exceptionally memorable romance." Libr J

Krentz, Jayne Ann, 1948-

Secret sisters; Jayne Ann Krentz. Berkley Books 2015 368 p. (ebook) $65; (hardcover) $26.95

ISBN 9780698193666; 9780399174483

LC 2015016234

In this suspense novel by Jayne Ann Krentz, "Madeline and Daphne were once as close as sisters—until a secret tore them apart. . . . Madeline has returned to Washington after her grandmother's mysterious death. And at the old, abandoned hotel, . . . a dying man's last words convey a warning: the secrets she and Daphne believed buried forever have been discovered. . . . Unable to trust the local police, Madeline summons Jack Rayner, the hotel chain's new security expert." (Publisher's note)

"Krentz scores another winner with complex characters and seamless plotting." Pub Wkly

Krentz, Jayne Ann, 1948-

Trust no one; Jayne Ann Krentz. Putnam Adult 2015 352 p. (hardback) $26.95

ISBN 0399165134; 9780399165139

LC 2014023348

In this book by Jayne Ann Krentz, "when Grace Elland finds her murdered boss's body, she comes to the attention of the police, a sexy new neighbor and an apparent stalker who seems linked to both this crime and a violent event from Grace's past. After years of searching for the right professional fit, Grace has fallen into her dream job as the behind-the-scenes inspiration for self-help guru Sprague Witherspoon. Discovering his body throws her life into chaos." (Kirkus Reviews)

"Clever plotting, complex pacing, and a compelling cast of characters propel Trust No One to its dynamite finish. Factor Krentz's (River Road, 2014) deliciously dry sense of wit into the story and you have another flawlessly executed novel of romantic suspense from one of the genre's most reliable literary stars." Booklist

Krentz, Jayne Ann, 1948-

When all the girls have gone; Jayne Ann Krentz. Berkley 2016 352 p. (ebook) $65.00; (hardcover) $27.00

ISBN 9780698193673; 9780399174490

LC 2016026198

In this book, by Jayne Ann Krentz, "when Charlotte Sawyer is unable to contact her stepsister, Jocelyn, to tell her that one of her closest friends was found dead, she discovers that Jocelyn has vanished. . . . Jocelyn has gone off the grid before, but never like this. In a desperate effort to find her, Charlotte joins forces with Max Cutler, a struggling PI who recently moved to Seattle after his previous career as a criminal profiler went down in flames—literally." (Publisher's note)

"Krentz returns with an intricately plotted romantic suspense novel that satisfies on every level, includes some clever twists with the senior community, and may open the door for a sequel. A terrific read by a stellar author." Kirkus

Krentz, Jayne Ann, 1948-

White lies; Jayne Ann Krentz. G. P. Putnam's Sons 2007 371p o.p.; o.p.; (pbk.) $9.99

ISBN 039915373X; 9780399153730; 9780515143997

LC 2006044829

This book follows "Clare Lancaster, . . . a member of the clandestine Arcane Society, an association of parasensitives who are dedicated to the study of the paranormal. Clare's . . . abilities as a human lie detector make even other paranormals uneasy, with the exception of her half-sister Elizabeth. Elizabeth's troubled marriage brings Clare to Arizona. . . . There, Clare finally meets Archer Glazebrook, her biological father, but she also meets Jake Salter, another highly talented parasensitive who turns out to be on assignment . . . to track down a possible plot to take over the society. The cabal he's after has some connection to the still-unsolved murder of Clare's . . . brother-in-law months before. More murders follow, and Jake and Clare have to work together to save themselves and the society." (Publishers Weekly)

Kress, Nancy, 1948-

After the Fall, Before the Fall, During the Fall. Independent Pub Group 2012 189 p. (paperback) $14.95

ISBN 1616960655; 9781616960650

In this novel from Nebula- and Hugo-winner Nancy Kress, teenager "Pete makes brief runs back in time from the . . . year 2035, using alien technology that can only transport children, to pick up fresh supplies and recruits. Julie, a mathematician in 2013, finds a pattern in a series of kidnappings. They are . . . Pete's expeditions, and as the two head towards their inevitable collision, the clock ticks down on the catastrophe that will turn Julie's orderly world into Pete's devastated landscape." (Publishers Weekly)

Kress, Nancy, 1948-

Dogs; a novel. Tachyon Publications 2008 280p pa $14.95

ISBN 978-1-892391-78-0; 1-892391-78-3

"The best scenes . . . have a straight-ahead, disaster novel feel to them, full of suspense and creepy details." San Francisco Chron

Kristoff, Jay

Nevernight; Jay Kristoff. Thomas Dunne Books 2016 427 p. illustrations (hardcover) $25.99

ISBN 9781250073020; 9781466885035; 1250073022

LC 2016003323

In this book, by Jay Kristoff, "in a land where three suns almost never set, a fledgling killer joins a school of assassins, seeking vengeance against the powers who destroyed her family. Daughter of an executed traitor, Mia Corvere is barely able to escape her father's failed rebellion with her life. Alone and friendless, she hides. . . . But her gift for speaking with the shadows leads her to the door of a retired killer, and a future she never imagined." (Publisher's note)

"A sensuous, shades-of-moral-gray world; a compelling, passionate heroine; a high-stakes quest for revenge—this is a fantasy fans won't be able to put down." Kirkus

Krivak, Andrew

★ The **signal** flame; a novel. Andrew Krivak. Scribner 2017 254 p. (hardcover) $26

ISBN 1501126377; 9781501126376; 9781501126406

LC 2016046415

In this novel, by Andrew Krivak, "Hannah and her son Bo mourn the loss of the family patriarch, Jozef Vinich. . . . They are a war-haunted family in a war-torn century. . . . Vinich journeyed to America and built a life for his family. His daughter married the Hungarian-born Bexhet Konar, who enlisted to fight with the Americans in the Second World War but . . .[was] killed in a hunting accident. . . . In 1971, Hannah's . . . son, Sam, was reported MIA in Vietnam." (Publisher's note)

"This family saga is quiet at its core, but it's Kriväk's gorgeous prose and deep grasp of the relationship between longing and loss that make the book such a stunner." Pub Wkly

Includes bibliographical references.

Krivak, Andrew

The **sojourn**. Bellevue Literary Press 2011 191p pa $14.95

ISBN 978-1-934137-34-5; 1-934137-34-0

LC 2010-53027

"After Jozef Vinich's mother dies while saving his life as an infant, Jozef and his widowed father relocate from a small Colorado mining town back to their Austrian homeland. Though Jozef's boyhood is marred by lingering feelings of abandonment, resentment, ingrained sadness, and two bullying stepbrothers, his life is enhanced by frequent dreams of his mother and a close friendship with troubled distant cousin Zlee. Both boys revel in the family hunting trips, which hone their sharpshooting abilities, expertise put to use when both go off to fight in WWI as marksmen, over Jozef's father's objections. Krivak dexterously exposes the stark, brutal realities of trench warfare, the horror of a POW camp, and the months of violent bloodshed that stole the boys' innocence. Once home from war, the author's depiction of Jozef's arduous return to life, love, and family is charged with emotion and longing." Publ Wkly

Krueger, William Kent

✓ **Ordinary** grace; a novel. by William Kent Krueger. Atria Books 2013 320 p. (hardcover) $24.99

ISBN 1451645821; 9781451645828; 9781451645859; 9781451645866

LC 2012034884

This novel, by William Kent Krueger, is set in "New Bremen, Minnesota, 1961. . . . Frank begins the season preoccupied with the concerns of any teenage boy, but when tragedy unexpectedly strikes his family . . . he finds himself thrust into an adult world full of secrets, lies, adultery, and betrayal, suddenly called upon to demonstrate a maturity and gumption beyond his years . . . discovering the terrible price of wisdom and the enduring grace of God." (Publisher's note)

Krueger, William Kent

✓ **Vermilion** drift; a novel. Atria Books 2010 304p $25

ISBN 978-1-4391-5384-0

LC 2010-13258

"For someone who writes such muscular prose, Krueger has a light touch that humanizes his characters." N Y Times Book Rev

Kubica, Mary

Pretty Baby; Mary Kubica. Harlequin Books 2015 384 p. $24.95

ISBN 0778317706; 9780778317708

In this novel by Mary Kubica "Heidi Wood has always been a charitable woman. Still, her husband and daughter are horrified when Heidi returns home one day with a young woman named Willow and her four-month-old baby in tow. Disheveled and apparently homeless, this girl could be a criminal--or worse. As clues into Willow's past begin to surface, Heidi is forced to decide how far she's willing to go to help a stranger. " (Publisher's note)

"Kubica's debut novel, The Good Girl (2014), also employed multiple points of view and timelines, but Kubica serves up a much more cohesive tale this time around—the story is almost hypnotic and anything but predictable. The writing is compelling, but Kubica's strong point is being able to juggle a complicated plot and holding the reader's interest without dropping any of the balls she has in the air. This book will give insomniacs a compelling reason to sit up all night." Kirkus

Kundera, Milan

★ **Immortality**; translated from the Czech by Peter Kussi. Grove Weidenfeld 1991 345p

LC 90-28628

"Immortality swings easily, almost imperceptibly, from narrative to rumination and back again, collapsing the distinction between action and concepts. . . . Out of a story about contemporary neuroses, Kundera has fabricated a context in which everything, literally, can be claimed to matter. What is more, the author indulges this obsessiveness without ever droning or turning out a dull page. In its inventiveness and its dazzling display of what written words can convey, Immortality gives fiction back its good name." Time

Kundera, Milan

★ The **unbearable** lightness of being; translated from the Czech by Michael Henry Heim. Harper & Row 1984 314p

LC 83-48363

"Set against the background of Czechoslovakia in the 1960s, the novel concerns a young Czech physician who substitutes a series of erotic adventures over which he thinks he can maintain control for becoming involved in his country's politics, where he feels he can have no power or freedom. Inevitably, he is drawn into Czechoslovakia's political unrest. In a parallel vein, he is forced to choose among the women with whom he is involved." Merriam-Webster's Ency of Lit

Kunkel, Benjamin

Indecision; a novel. Random House 2005 241p $21.95

ISBN 1-4000-6345-0

LC 2004-62894

"Ever the clever chef, Kunkel reduces the sprawling, indigestible postmodern novel to an amiable pop confection that goes down like a milkshake. The result is a stylistic triumph of sorts. The half-serious pastiche is the ideal vehicle for bright apercus, capers, riffs, and dreamy ruminations." New Leader

Kunzru, Hari

★ **Gods** without men. Alfred A. Knopf 2012 369 p.

ISBN 024114311X pa; 9780241143117 pa; 9780307957115; 030795711X

LC 2011488728

"Jaz and Lisa Matharu, a young couple from New York City, are plunged into a surreal public hell after their autistic son, Raj, disappears during a vacation to the California desert. But the desert is inexplicable and miraculous, and the fates of the Matharus are bound up with those of others, all converging at an odd, remote town near a rock formation called The Pinnacles; among them are a debauched British rock star, a former member of an extraterrestrial-worshipping cult, and a teenage Iraqi refugee who befriends a young black Marine while playing the role of 'Iraqi villager' in a military simulation exercise." (Publisher's note)

Kunzru, Hari

The **impressionist**. Dutton 2002 383p

ISBN 0-525-94642-X

LC 2001-47137

This novel "includes a multitude of richly imagined characters. A bold, unfashionably omniscient voice narrates the story as it tackles such subjects as race, class, colonialism, and the roots of personal identity" New Leader

Kunzru, Hari

My revolutions. Dutton 2008 280p $25.95

ISBN 978-0-525-94932-9; 0-525-94932-1

LC 2007-39459

First published 2007 in the United Kingdom

This novel "is, as Virginia Woolf said of George Eliot's Middlemarch, a book for grownup people (although that shouldn't imply it is at all ponderous or worthy) and it is very much a book about the process of growing up. My Revolutions is impassioned, intelligent and profoundly serious literature." Sydney Morning Herald

Kunzru, Hari

White tears; Hari Kunzru. Alfred A. Knopf 2017 271 p. (hardcover) $26.95

ISBN 9780451493699

LC 2016011904

Kirkus Prize Finalist: Fiction (2017)

In this novel, by Hari Kunzru, "when Seth accidentally records an unknown singer in a park, Carter sends it out over the Internet, claiming it's a long lost 1920s blues recording by a musician called Charlie Shaw. When an old collector contacts them to say that their fake record and their fake bluesman are actually real, the two young white men . . . spiral down into the heart of the nation's darkness, encountering a suppressed history of greed, envy, . . . and exploitation." (Publisher's note)

"Record collecting turns dangerous in a smart, time-bending tale about cultural appropriation." Kirkus.

Kushner, Dale M.

The **conditions** of love; Dale Kushner. Grand Central Pub. 2013 384 p. (hardcover) $24.99

ISBN 1455519758; 9781455519750

LC 2012040786

This novel, by Dale M. Kushner, "traces the journey of a girl from childhood to adulthood as she reckons with her parents' abandonment . . . and her overwhelming desire for spiritual and erotic love. . . . Eunice lives in the backwaters of Wisconsin. . . . A freak storm sends Eunice away from all things familiar. Rescued by the shaman-like Rose, Eunice's odyssey continues with a stay in a hermit's shack and ends with a passionate love affair with an older man." (Publisher's note)

Kushner, Ellen

Swordspoint; a novel. by Ellen Kushner. Arbor House 2003 269 p. (ebook) $23.97; $15.95; $7.99

ISBN 9780307418357; 0553585495; 0877959234; 9780553585490

LC 87011483

Originally published 1987

"On the treacherous streets of Riverside, a man lives and dies by the sword. Even the nobles on the Hill turn to duels to settle their disputes. Within this elite, dangerous world, Richard St. Vier is the undisputed master, as skilled as he is ruthless--until a death by the sword is met with outrage instead of awe, and the city discovers that the line between hero and villain can be altered in the blink of an eye." (Publisher's note)

Other titles in this series are:

The privilege of the sword (2006)

The fall of kings (2002)

Thomas the rhymer (1990)

Kushner, Rachel

★ The **flamethrowers**; a novel. Rachel Kushner. Scribner 2013 400 p. ill. (hardcover) $26.99

ISBN 1439142009; 9781439142004; 9781439142011; 9781439154175

LC 2012027350

National Book Award: Fiction: Finalist (2013)

This novel, by Rachel Kushner, begins in 1975 in New York. "Reno . . . begins an affair with an artist named Sandro Valera, the semi-estranged scion of an Italian tire and motorcycle empire. When they visit . . . Italy, Reno falls in with members of the radical movement that overtook Italy in the seventies. Betrayal sends her reeling into a clandestine undertow." (Publisher's note)

Includes bibliographical references (p. 387)

Kutsukake, Lynne

★ The **translation** of love; a novel. Lynne Kutsukake. Doubleday 2016 336 p. (ebook) $65; (hardcover) $25.95

ISBN 9780385540681; 9780385540674

LC 2015024191

In this book, by Lynne Kutsukake, "after spending the war years in a Canadian internment camp, thirteen-year-old Aya Shimamura and her father are faced with a gut-wrenching choice: Move east of the Rocky Mountains or go 'back' to Japan. Barred from returning home to the west coast and bitterly grieving the loss of Aya's mother during internment, Aya's father signs a form that enables the government to deport them." (Publisher's note)

"A vivid delight chronicling a fascinating—and little-discussed—chapter in world history." Kirkus

Kwan, Kevin

China rich girlfriend; a novel. Kevin Kwan. Doubleday 2015 400 p. (hardcover) $26.95

ISBN 0385539088; 9780385539081

LC 2015003996

Sequel to: Crazy rich Asians

This novel, by Kevin Kwan, describes a world "of social climbing, secret e-mails, art-world scandal, lovesick billionaires, and . . . what happens when Rachel Chu, engaged to marry Asia's most eligible bachelor, discovers her birthfather. . . . On the eve of her wedding to Nicholas Young, heir to one of the greatest fortunes in Asia, Rachel should be over the moon. . . . Until: a shocking revelation draws Rachel into a world . . . beyond anything she has ever imagined." (Publisher's note)

"Lovers of clothes, cuisine, and cars will find themselves at home in Kwan's second smart and snarky send-up of the Chinese jet set." Booklist

Kwan, Kevin

★ **Crazy** rich Asians; Kevin Kwan. Doubleday 2013 416 p. (hardcover : alk. paper) $25.95

ISBN 0385536976; 9780385536974; 9780385536981

LC 2012032395

This book by Kevin Kwan is a "novel about three super-rich, pedigreed Chinese families and the gossip, backbiting, and scheming that occurs when the heir to one of the most massive fortunes in Asia brings home his ABC (American-born Chinese) girlfriend to the wedding of the season. . . . Initiated into a world of dynastic splendor beyond imagination, Rachel meets Astrid, the It Girl of Singapore society . . . [and] Eleanor, Nick's formidable mother." (Publisher's note)

Kwan, Kevin

Rich people problems; a novel. Kevin Kwan. Doubleday 2017 397 p. (hardcover) $27.95

ISBN 9780385542241; 9780385542234

LC 2017930108

This novel, by Kevin Kwan, "takes us from the elegantly appointed mansions of Manila to the secluded private islands in the Sulu Sea, from a kidnapping at Hong Kong's most elite private school to a surprise marriage proposal at an Indian palace, caught on camera by the telephoto lenses of paparazzi. . . . [It] reveals the long-buried secrets of Asia's most privileged families and their rich people problems." (Publisher's note)

"The fairy tale/soap opera/lux-a-thon that began with Crazy Rich Asians (2013) and China Rich Girlfriend (2015) comes to a fittingly majestic and hilarious end in Kwan's third novel." Kirkus

Kwok, Jean

Girl in translation; Jean Kwok. Riverhead Books 2010 293 p. $25.95

ISBN 9781594487569; 1594487561

LC 2009041041

Alex Award (2011)

"Along with her widowed mother, 11-year-old Kimberly (Ah-Kim) Chang is transported from the balmy familiarity of her native Hong Kong to the icy, inhospitable projects of 1980s Brooklyn — a girl with little grasp of the language and cultural mores of her newly adopted homeland, and even less financial means. How Kimberly fights through almost obscene marginalization to forge her own version of the American dream is consistently compelling, even if Girl's needlessly soapy conclusion seems unworthy of what came before." Entertainment Wkly

L

L'Amour, Louis

★ **Bendigo** Shafter. Dutton 1979 324p

LC 78-15280

"This book's hero is 18-year-old Bendigo Shafter. He is part of a small band of migrants that breaks off its westward trek and builds a small community. The group increases with the coming of other members. It has to fight off the dangers of the frontier both within and outside its confines. Among the main influences on Ben's life are the Widow Macken, who inspires him to read Locke, Rousseau, and Blackstone; Uruwishi, an old Indian brave; and Ethan Sackett, woodsman nonpareil. There are heroes and villains, both white and red, and shooting from the hip in old Western style as Ben demonstrates all the traditional values of courage, honesty, loyalty, and stamina." Shapiro. Fic for Youth. 3d edition

L'Amour, Louis

The **Californios**. Saturday Review Press 1974 188p

"An expert blend of the fascinating settling of California in the 1840's; strong, self-reliant characters . . . and a plot of evil doings but triumphant good. The theme of mysticism and the legends of The Old Ones is what lifts this book above the typical western. Intriguing even for those who aren't westerns fans." Libr J

L'Amour, Louis

End of the drive. Bantam Bks. 1997 257p

LC 96-36872

Contents: Caprock rancher; Elisha comes to Red Horse; Desperate men; The courting of Griselda; End of the drive; The lonesome gods; Rustler roundup; The skull and the arrow

L'Amour, Louis

★ **Last** of the breed. Bantam Bks. 1986 358p

LC 86-3622

"Joe Mack is a classic American hero, thrown back into the wilderness and forced to rely on his wits and his ancestral skills to survive the deadly cold and elude his Soviet pursuers, including his nemesis, a Siberian tracker. L'Amour brings the same colorful realism to this sweeping adventure that has made his Westerns so beloved." Publ Wkly

L'Amour, Louis

May there be a road. Bantam Bks. 2001 276p

ISBN 0-553-80213-5

LC 2001-18127

In this collection of 10 previously uncollected stories with settings ranging from the coasts of Brazil to the border of Tibet to the very heartland of America . . . [the author] takes us into those sudden moments when lives and futures are altered forever, when men and women face a deadly enemy, meet a kindred spirit, or confront their own mortality." Publisher's note

L'Amour, Louis

To the far blue mountains. Saturday Review Press 1976 287p

In this Sackett novel Barnabas returns from America with a cargo of goods. He "is in Lincolnshire on business when he learns that there is a queen's warrant out for him because he is suspected of stealing the crown jewels. He is thrown in prison but manages to escape and make his way to Bristol and a ship back to Raleigh's Land. In Virginia, he recruits a band of brave settlers and strong women and they take boats up the James River in the direction of the blue mountains until they find rich land to farm. There Barnabas's children are born and the community flourishes even though there is ever-present danger from hostile Indians. This tale is much more leisurely and nonviolent than the usual L'Amour story, but it has its share of suspense and gives us a different kind of look at colonial America." Publ Wkly

L'Engle, Madeleine

Certain women. Farrar, Straus & Giroux 1992 351p

ISBN 0-374-12025-0

LC 91-34048

In this novel, "terminally ill David Wheaton, a prominent and much-married American actor, obsessively recalls an unfinished play about King David, a role he coveted. L'Engle explores Christian faith, love, and the nature of God by framing the delayed-maturation story of Emma, Wheaton's daughter, within three subplots: the Wheaton family saga, the story of King David, and the history of the play's development. The characterizations of both Davids are compelling, but the primary interest here is the community of women which surrounds each man. L'Engle describes complex truths very simply. . . . Because she also details the emotional cost of discovering and accepting such concepts, many readers will find these observations memorable but never simplistic." Libr J

Lackberg, Camilla

The **hidden** child; Camilla Lackberg; translated by Tiina Nunnally. Harper 2014 506 p. $25.95

ISBN 000741949X; 1605985538; 9780007419494; 9781605985534

LC 2011535392

In this murder mystery, author "Camilla Lackberg weaves together [a] . . . contemporary psychological thriller with the chilling struggle of a young woman facing the darkest chapter of Europe's past. . . . Crime writer Erica Falck is shocked to discover a Nazi medal among her late mother's possessions. . . . Detective Patrik Hedstrom, Erica's husband, . . . soon becomes embroiled in the murder investigation. Who would kill so ruthlessly to bury secrets so old?" (Publisher's note)

"Though the flashbacks to the 1940s can be distracting, this secondary plot is just as intriguing as the main story line. Though dealing with the serious subjects of extremist groups and prisoners of war, the novel has its humorous moments." LJ

Lackberg, Camilla

The **ice** princess; Camilla Läckberg; translated [from the Swedish] by Steven T. Murray. Free Press 2011 391 p.

ISBN 1451621744; 9781451621747; 9781451621754

LC 2010032941

"Erica Falck returns to her tiny, remote hometown of Fjällbacka, Sweden, after her parents' deaths only to encounter another tragedy: the suicide of her childhood best friend, Alex. It's Erica herself who finds Alex's body suspended in a bathtub of frozen water, her wrists slashed. Erica is bewildered: Why would a beautiful woman who had it all take her own life? Teaming up with police detective Patrik Hedström, Erica begins to uncover shocking events from Alex's childhood. As one horrifying fact after another comes to light, Erica and Patrik's curiosity gives way to obsession" and their flirtation grows into uncontrollable attraction." (Publisher's note)

Other titles in this series are:

The preacher

The stonecutter

The stranger

The hidden child

The drowning

The lost boy

Buried angels

The ice child

Lackberg, Camilla

The **lost** boy; Camilla Lackberg ; translated by Tiina Nunnally. W. W. Norton & Co. Inc. 2016 493 p. (hardcover) $25.95

ISBN 1681772043; 9781681772042; 9780007419586

LC 2016035757

In this novel, by Camilla Lackberg, translated by Tiina Nunnally, "Detective Patrik Hedstrom is no stranger to tragedy. A murder case concerning Fjällbacka's dead financial director, Mats Sverin, is a grim but useful distraction from his recent family misfortunes. . . . His high school sweetheart, Nathalie, has just returned to Fjällbacka with her five-year-old son. . . . However, Nathalie has her own secret. If it's discovered, she will lose her only child." (Publisher's note)

"Läckberg weaves fine lines through this multilayered thriller, connecting a ghostly historic backstory, tragic portrayals of domestic violence, shady business dealings, and series regulars' various personal dramas." Booklist

Lackberg, Camilla

The **preacher**; translated by Steven T. Murray. Pegasus Crime 2011 419p $25.95

ISBN 978-1-60598-173-4; 1-60598-173-7

Original Swedish edition, 2004; this translation first published 2008 in the United Kingdom

This mystery featuring detective Patrik Hedstrom "is again set in the small Swedish village of Fjällbacka. The story opens with the discovery of the skeletons of two women who disappeared more than 20 years ago, along with a fresh victim killed in a similar manner. In researching the decades-old murders, the police are led to the dysfunctional family of a religious fanatic, Ephraim Hult, who was known as a preacher and healer. Hedstrom must find the key to connect the old crimes with the new. In addition, Patrik's girlfriend, Erica, is about to give birth, and he must come to terms with his feelings about becoming a father. Erica, in turn, is deeply troubled by her sister's increasingly serious marriage problems. Läckberg's many-layered story features plot twists and turns galore." Libr J

Lackberg, Camilla

The **stonecutter**; Camilla Lackberg ; translated by Steven T. Murray. Pegasus Books 2012 473 p.

ISBN 1605983306; 9780007305933; 9780007253982; 9781605983301; 0007253982; 0007305931

LC 2010533249

In this mystery novel, "Patrik Hedström['s] . . . sympathies as both father and cop are demanded by the murder of Sara Klinga. . . . [Camilla] Läckberg . . . parcels out hints of the tragedy's roots in the loveless marriage some 75 years ago between flirtatious heiress Agnes Stjernkvist and Anders Andersson, the stonecutter she'd captivated and planned to leave before her father discovered her pregnancy and forced the couple to wed. . . . Patrik and his . . . colleagues on the Tanumshede police force focus their suspicions on imperious Lilian . . . ; Kaj Wiberg, the neighbor with whom she's long feuded over every pretext she can find; and Kaj's son Morgan, a computer game designer with Asperger's Syndrome who'd be poorly equipped to take the air even in a much sunnier spot than Fjällbacka." (Kirkus)

"A perfectly plotted and paced mystery bolstered by strong, realistic characters." Booklist

Lackey, Mercedes

The **fairy** godmother. Harlequin 2004 432p $24.95

ISBN 0-373-80202-1

This fantasy is "set in a world where The Tradition tries its magical—and surreptitious-best to force the characters into their 'legendary' roles. But things sometimes go awry, and when Elena is denied her predestined Cinderella role because her kingdom's prince is too young, she is chosen as an apprentice by the local Fairy Godmother and ends up creating a legend of her own. A spirited, resourceful, though somewhat impulsive heroine, a prince who needs to learn a lesson in manners, humility, and compassion, and a host of magical creatures—including some delightful house elves and besotted unicorns—result in a lively, humorous fantasy romance." Libr J

Lackey, Mercedes

Joust. DAW Bks. 2003 373p il $24.95; pa $7.99

ISBN 0-7564-0122-4; 0-7564-0153-4 pa

LC 2003-544990

Vetch, an Altan serf, must learn the secret of the Tian jousters and their dragons in order to save his people

"This uplifting tale, which contains a valuable lesson or two on the virtues of hard work, is a must-read for dragon lovers in particular and for fantasy fans in general." Publ Wkly

Lackey, Mercedes

Winds of fate. DAW Bks. 1991 385p il (Mage winds)

ISBN 0-88677-489-6

This first volume of a trilogy is set in the "imperiled land of Valdemar, encountered earlier in Lackey's Heralds of Valdemar series. The heir to the throne, Herald Elspeth, sets out with Gwena, her Companion (a Guardian Spirit embodied as a horse), to find an Adept who can teach her people both to use and to deflect the power of magic. . . . Lackey's delightful world of magic is inhabited by strong and believable men, women and creatures." Publ Wkly

Followed by Winds of change (1992)

Lafferty, Mur

The **shambling** guide to New York City; Mur Lafferty. Orbit 2013 368 p. (paperback) $14.99

ISBN 0316221171; 9780316221160; 9780316221177

LC 2012032172

In this novel, by Mur Lafferty, "a travel writer takes a job with a shady publishing company in New York, only to find that she must write a guide to the city--for the undead! . . . Not to be put off by anything . . . , Zoe delves deep into the monster world. But her job turns deadly when the careful balance between human and monsters starts to crumble." (Publisher's note)

Lafferty, Mur

★ **Six** wakes; Mur Lafferty. Orbit 2017 391 p. (trade paperback) $15.99

ISBN 9780316389693; 9780316389686

LC 2016040517

Nebula Finalist: Best Novel (2017)

Hugo Finalist: Best Novel (2018)

In this science fiction novel, by Mur Lafferty, "Maria Arena had . . . no memory of how she died. That was . . . new; before, when she had awakened as a new clone, her first memory was of how she died. Maria's vat was in the front of six vats, each one holding the clone of a crew member of the starship Dormire, each clone waiting for its previous incarnation to die so it could awaken. And Maria isn't the only one to die recently." (Publisher's note)

"Lafferty delivers a tense nail-biter of a story fueled by memorable characters and thoughtful worldbuilding. This space-based locked-room murder mystery explores complex technological and moral issues . . ." Pub Wkly

Lagercrantz, David

The **Girl** in the Spider's Web; by David Lagercrantz. Random House Inc. 2015 400 p. (Millennium) $27.95

ISBN 0385354282; 9780385354288

In this book, by David Lagercrantz, "Lisbeth Salander and Mikael Blomkvist return. She is the girl with the dragon tattoo--a genius hacker and uncompromising misfit. He is a crusading journalist whose championing of the truth often brings him to the brink of prosecution. Late one night, Blomkvist receives a phone call from a source claiming to have information vital to the United States. The source has been in contact with a young female superhacker." (Publisher's note)

A "very fine thriller, true to the characters and the world Larsson created but also taking the ongoing story in some new and exciting directions. Wisely, Lagercrantz begins with a set of new characters, principally Swedish computer genius Frans Bader; his autistic savant son, August; and the bulldog head of security at the NSA, Ed Needham." Booklist

Lagercrantz, David

The **girl** who takes an eye for an eye; David Lagercrantz ; translated from the Swedish by George Goulding. Alfred A. Knopf 2017 vii, 347 p.p (Millennium series) (hardcover) $27.95

ISBN 0451494326; 9780451494320; 9780451494337

LC 2016288478

Sequel to: The Girl in the Spider's Web (2015)

In this novel in the Millennium Series, by David Lagercrantz, "Lisbeth Salander--obstinate outsider, volatile seeker of justice for herself and others--seizes on a chance to unearth her mysterious past once and for all. And she will let nothing stop her--not the Islamists she enrages by rescuing a young woman from their brutality; . . . and not the people who will do anything to keep buried knowledge of a sinister pseudoscientific experiment known only as The Registry." (Publisher's note)

"Once again, Lagercrantz succeeds in carefully staying true to the framework created by the late Stieg Larsson in his original trilogy, and fans can continue to follow their favorite hacker heroine from obscurity to notoriety to unsought fame and unwanted attention." Booklist

Lagerkvist, Par

Barabbas; translated by Alan Blair; with a preface by Lucien Maury and a letter by André Gide. Random House 1951 180p

Original Swedish edition, 1950

This "is a psychological study of the spiritual journey of Barabbas, the criminal in the New Testament who was offered to the mob in place of Jesus but was spared from execution. The widely translated work was noted for its economical writing style, and it brought Lagerkvist international fame." Merriam-Webster's Ency of Lit

Lahiri, Jhumpa

Interpreter of maladies; stories. Houghton Mifflin 1999 198p $23

ISBN 0-618-10136-5

LC 98-50895

First published in paperback

"The rituals of traditional Indian domesticity—curry-making, hair-vermilioning—both buttress the characters of Lahiri's elegant first collection and mark the measure of these fragile people's dissolution. . . . Lahiri's touch in these nine tales is delicate, but her observations remain damningly accurate, and her bittersweet stories are unhampered by nostalgia." Publ Wkly

Lahiri, Jhumpa

★ The **lowland**; a novel. by Jhumpa Lahiri. Alfred A. Knopf 2013 352 p. (hardcover) $27.95

ISBN 0307265749; 9780307265746; 9780385350402

LC 2012043878

National Book Awards: Fiction: Finalist (2013)

Man Booker Prize: Shortlist (2013)

In this book, by Jhumpa Lahiri, "Subhash and Udayan Mitra are inseparable brothers, one often mistaken for the other in the Calcutta neighborhood where they grow up. It is the 1960s, and Udayan . . . finds himself drawn to the Naxalite movement, a rebellion waged to eradicate inequity and poverty. Subhash . . . leaves home to pursue a life of scientific research in . . . America. When Subhash learns what happened to his brother . . . he goes back to India." (Publisher's note)

Lahiri, Jhumpa

The **namesake**. Houghton Mifflin 2003 291p $24; pa $14

ISBN 0-395-92721-8; 0-618-48522-8 pa

LC 2003-41718

"Its incorrigible mildness and its ungilded lilies aside, Lahiri's novel is unfailingly lovely in its treatment of Gogol's relationship with his father. This is the classic American parent-child bond." N Y Times Book Rev

Lake, Jay

Endurance. Tor 2011 319p $26.99

ISBN 978-0-7653-2676-8

LC 2011-21613

Sequel to Green (2009)

Courtesan and trained assassin Green returns to Copper Downs where she must defend the gods from the Godslayers, magicians dedicated to the destruction of all deities, by tracking them down and removing the threat.

"Lake deftly weaves complicated, stubborn characters into a plot that reaches the grandest and most personal scales without ever straining credulity." Publ Wkly

Laker, Rosalind

To dance with kings. Doubleday 1988 564p

LC 88-3698

"Set during the reigns of Louis XIV and Louis XVI, the sweeping saga takes place mainly in the Chateau of Versailles and the surrounding town from which the magnificent edifice took its name. . . . Spanning four generations, the protagonists are the women of one family, named, in turn, Marguerite, Jasmin, Violette and Rose, all of whose destinies are entwined with those of their monarchs as well as the dashing men who bring them love and heartache." Publ Wkly

Lalami, Laila

★ The **Moor's** account; a novel. Laila Lalami. Pantheon Books 2014 336 p. (hardcover : alk. paper) $26.95

ISBN 0307911667; 9780307911667

LC 2013045255

Pulitzer Prize Finalist: Fiction (2015)

This historical novel, by Laila Lalami, "brings us the imagined memoirs of the first black explorer of America--a Moroccan slave whose testimony was left out of the official record. In 1527, the conquistador Pánfilo de Narváez sailed from the port of Sanlúcar de Barrameda. . . . But from the moment the Narváez expedition landed in Florida, it faced peril--navigational errors, disease, starvation, as well as resistance from indigenous tribes." (Publisher's note)

"Estebanico's account alternates between this disastrous mission and his past as a merchant, with the two threads combining to create a deeply layered, complex portrait of all-too-familiar characters in an unfamiliar world. The result is a totally engrossing and captivating novel that reconsiders the overlooked roles of Africans in New World exploration." Booklist

Includes bibliographical references

Lally, Caitriona

Eggshells; a novel. Catriona Lally. Melville House 2017 256 p. (ebook) $12.99; (hardcover) $16.99

ISBN 9781612195988; 9781612195971

LC 2016024545

In this novel, by Catriona Lally, "Vivian doesn't feel like she fits in - and never has. . . . Now, living alone in Dublin, the neighbors treat her like she's crazy, her older sister condescends to her, social workers seem to have registered her as troubled, and she hasn't a friend in the world. So, she decides it's time to change her life: She begins by advertising for a friend. . . . Then one day someone named Penelope answers her ad for a friend." (Publisher's note)

"Absent the dramatic character arcs or plot twists readers would expect from an American novel, this urban fairy tale delivers something that is both subtle and profound in its examination of the human soul. Magically delicious." Kirkus

Lam, Vincent

The **headmaster's** wager; a novel. Vincent Lam. 1st U.S. ed. Random House Inc. 2012 423 p. (hardcover) $25.00; (audiobook) $76.00; (ebook) $25.00

ISBN 0307986462; 9780307986467; 9780449808306; 9780307986474

LC 2012462250

This "novel centres on the life of Percival Chen, the titular headmaster whose father, like others before him, left China . . . [for] a small town just outside Saigon. . . . Once there, Chen becomes headmaster of the Percival Chen English Academy. . . . Despite his best attempts to achieve some measure of stability, his idea of family keeps fracturing, and his belief in his Chinese superiority results in unexpected repercussions for his son." (Quill & Quire)

Lamb, Alex

Roboteer; Alex Lamb. Victor Gollancz 2017 439 p. (paperback) $13.99

ISBN 9781473206090; 147320609X

In this science fiction novel, by Alex Lamb, "the starship Ariel is on a mission of the utmost secrecy. . . . Though the ship is a mile long, its six crew are crammed into a space barely large enough for them to stand. Five are officers, geniuses in their field. The other is Will Kuno-Monet, the man responsible for single-handedly running a ship comprised of the most dangerous and delicate technology that mankind has ever devised. He is the Roboteer." (Publisher's note)

"Lamb's excellent first novel is an exciting and fast-paced, fresh take on space warfare and the future of humankind." Booklist

Lamb, Wally

We Are Water; a novel. by Wally Lamb. HarperCollins 2013 576 p. $29.99

ISBN 0061941026; 9780061941023

LC 2013431133

Lambda Literary Awards Finalist (2014)

This book, by Wally Lamb, is a "novel about a marriage, a family, and human resilience in the face of tragedy. . . . After 27 years of marriage and three children, Anna Oh—wife, mother, outsider artist—has fallen in love with Viveca, the wealthy Manhattan art dealer who orchestrated her success. They plan to wed in the Oh family's hometown of Three Rivers in Connecticut. But the wedding provokes some very mixed reactions and opens a Pandora's Box of . . . secrets." (Publisher's note)

"A searching novel of contemporary manners . . . Lamb turns in a satisfyingly grown-up story, elegantly written." Kirkus

Includes bibliographical references (page 564)

Lambdin, Dewey

Hostile Shores; An Alan Lewrie Naval Adventure. Dewey Lambdin. St Martins Pr 2013 368 p. $25.99

ISBN 0312595727; 9780312595722

This book is part of Dewey Lambdin's Capt. Sir Alan Lewrie series. After his ship Reliant is refitted, Lewrie sails to Cape Town. There, "Lewrie talks his way into a naval brigade sent ashore with the troops and sees some action on land. But once the British secure the Cape, the admiral in charge sends the entire fleet to South America for a poorly planned invasion of the Argentine. Lewrie has no choice but to follow orders and does his best to make the best of a potentially bad situation." (Kirkus)

Lambdin, Dewey

King's captain; an Alan Lewrie naval adventure. St. Martin's Press 2000 358p

ISBN 0-312-26885-8

LC 00-31764

Fresh from a stunning victory against the formidable Spanish Armada in the Battle of St. Vincent's Cape, Lewrie is promoted and rewarded with the command of an enviable new warship. Shortly after being installed as the captain of the H.M.S. Proteus, he must contend with a treasonable mass mutiny, a bitter enemy bent on revenge, and several rather complicated romantic entanglements. A rip-roaring sea yarn brimming with riveting action and lusty diversions." Booklist

Lamberson, Gregory

The **frenzy** way. Medallion 2010 356p pa $15.95

ISBN 978-1-605421-07-0; 1-605421-07-3

"Possessing spirited action scenes and distinctive dialogue, the novel penetrates the psyche of a terrorist and comprehends the psychology of terror. It's like taking a savagely wild walk—in animal form." Hellnotes.com

Lambert, Charles

The **children's** home; a novel. Charles Lambert. Scribner 2016 224 p. (hardback) $24

ISBN 1501117394; 9781501117398; 9781501117404

LC 2015027042

This novel, by Charles Lambert, is "about a mysterious group of children who appear to a disfigured recluse . . . and the startling revelations their behavior evokes. Morgan takes them in, giving them free reign of the mansion he shares with his housekeeper Engel. Then more children begin to show up. They show a prescient understanding of Morgan's past, and their bizarre discoveries in the mansion attics grow increasingly disturbing." (Publisher's note)

"Despite the strangeness of the novel's world, the story retains its subtlety, and though it is profoundly symbolic--and not always easy to decode--it remains compulsively readable." Kirkus

Lamott, Anne

Blue shoe. Riverhead Bks. 2002 291p

ISBN 1-57322-226-7

LC 2002-22824

"The acceptence of one's imperfections is a pillar of wisdom in Lamott's New Age Christianity. Mattie is an embodiment of that philosophy, but she's better written than that makes her sound. She and her family are hilariously specific." NY Times Book Rev

Lamott, Anne

Imperfect birds; a novel. Riverhead Books 2010 278p $25.95

ISBN 978-1-59448-751-4; 1-59448-751-0

LC 2009-36107

A novel "about Elizabeth and James, liberal do-gooders from Marin County, California (and the subjects of [Lamott's] previous novels Rosie and Crooked Little Heart), and their daughter Rosie. At 17, Rosie is 'black-haired, strapping and fabulous' and an academic high achiever, but she does every drug under the sun, including her peers' parentally dispensed Adderall. The book is a stark illustration of deception, denial and parents' desperate desire to stay loved." Time

Lanagan, Margo

The **brides** of Rollrock Island; Margo Lanagan. Alfred A. Knopf 2012 305 p. (hardback) $17.99

ISBN 0375869190; 9780375869198; 9780375969195; 9780375989308

LC 2011047466

This novel, by Margo Lenagan, takes place around "remote Rollrock Island, [where] men go to sea to make their livings--and to catch their wives. The witch Misskaella knows the way of drawing a girl from the heart of a seal . . . [a]nd for a price a man may buy himself a lovely sea-wife. . . . But from his first look into [her] . . . eyes, he will be just as transformed as she. He will be equally ensnared. And the witch will have her true payment." (Publisher's note)

Lancaster, Jen

Here I go again; Jen Lancaster. New American Library 2012 320 p. $25.95

ISBN 0451236726; 9780451236722

LC 2012021417

This book is the story of Lissy Ryder. A bully during high school, Lissy "may finally be getting her karmic payback: her husband asks for a divorce, and she loses her PR job and moves back in with her parents. Mix in one hellish 20th high school reunion and a New Age classmate with a special potion . . . , and suddenly Lissy's back to 1991," where she tries to right her wrongs. "But in so doing, will she . . . mess up the future—not only for herself but for others?" (Publishers Weekly)

Lanchester, John

The **debt** to pleasure; a novel. Holt & Co. 1996 251p il

ISBN 0-8050-4388-8

LC 95-34658

The author "has written a novel masquerading as an essay masquerading as a cookbook, and it somehow manages to combine the virtues of all three. The narrator, Tarquin Winot, is the brother of a famous sculptor, but his own talent—as emerges in the course of his endlessly digressive, enormously erudite disquisitions on food—is for the art of murder. Tarquin's marvellously perverse intelligence never falters, and, fortunately, neither do his lapidary sentences." New Yorker

Lanchester, John

Fragrant Harbor. Putnam 2002 342p
ISBN 0-399-14866-3

LC 2001-57876

This "is not an enormous novel, but it feels like one—it is bursting with ideas. Lanchester takes on almost every major theme and succeeds with most of them: race, class, love, war, the fall of rulers and the rise of the ruled." N Y Times Book Rev

Land, Jon

Strong at the break; Jon Land. Forge 2011 348p.
ISBN 9780765323378; 0765323370

LC 2011011542

This book tells the story of "fifth-generation Texas Ranger Caitlin Strong," set "two decades" after "her father shot down the cult-like leader of a separatist church . . . That man's son, Malcolm Arno, has become head of a militia movement bent on unleashing chaos and anarchy across the country. . . . Already mired in one investigation of drug smuggling over the U.S.-Canadian border and another involving an Iraqi war veteran who claims the army is trying to kill him, Caitlin finds herself embroiled in the search for the kidnapped son of former outlaw Cort Wesley Masters. When the missing boy's trail leads to Malcolm Arno's Texas compound, the three cases converge". (Publisher's note)

Landay, William, 1963- ✓

★ **Defending** Jacob; William Landay. Delacorte Books 2012 421p.
ISBN 9780345527592; 9780385344227

LC 2011011623

This book offers a novel about "Andy Barber [who] has been an assistant district attorney in his suburban Massachusetts county for more than twenty years. He is respected in his community, tenacious in the courtroom, and happy at home with his wife, Laurie, and son, Jacob. But when a shocking crime shatters their New England town, Andy is blindsided by what happens next: His fourteen-year-old son is charged with the murder of a fellow student. Every parental instinct Andy has rallies to protect his boy. . . . But as damning facts and shocking revelations surface, as a marriage threatens to crumble and the trial intensifies, as the crisis reveals how little a father knows about his son, Andy will face a trial of his own—between loyalty and justice, between truth and allegation, between a past he's tried to bury and a future he cannot conceive." (Publisher's note)

Lane, Harriet

Alys, always; a novel. Harriet Lane. Scribner 2012 209 p. $24.00
ISBN 1451673167; 9781451673166; 9781451673180

LC 2011040905

In this book, "a young woman named Frances Thorpe comes upon an overturned car in a ditch. She calls for help and speaks to the dying driver, Alys, offering sympathy, comfort, and support. Later, the family requests a meeting with Frances to thank her . . . . On meeting the bereaved husband, a noted English novelist who enjoys a life of culture and privilege, Frances is struck with the glimmer of an idea that grows and flourishes as her connection with the family deepens." (Library Journal)

Lange, Richard

Angel baby; a novel. Richard Lange. Mulholland Books / Little, Brown and Co. 2013 304 p. (hardcover) $25.99
ISBN 0316219827; 9780316219822

LC 2012037350

In this novel, by Richard Lange, "to escape the awful life she has descended into, Luz plans carefully. She takes only the clothes on her back, a Colt .45, and all the money in her husband's safe. . . . Luz needs to find the daughter she left behind years earlier, but she knows she may die trying. Her husband is . . . a key player in a high-powered drug cartel, a business he runs with the same violence he has used to keep Luz his perfect, obedient wife." (Publisher's note)

Langton, Jane

The **deserter**; murder at Gettysburg. St. Martin's Minotaur 2003 322p il $23.95
ISBN 0-312-30186-3

LC 2002-191961

"The suspense builds as the author adroitly shifts between past and present. Period photos, an 1860 playbill for the Hasty Pudding show, quotations from Walt Whitman and loads of Harvard lore add historical weight." Publ Wkly

Langton, Jane

Murder at Monticello; a Homer Kelly mystery. illustrations by the author. Viking 2001 256p il $22.95
ISBN 0-670-89462-1

LC 00-43369

"It's the bicentennial of Jefferson's election to the presidency, and Homer and his wife, Mary, are invited to a Fourth of July celebration at Monticello, Jefferson's Virginia home, where, incidentally, a serial killer has been murdering young women. Like the previous Kelly novels, this one features a smart mystery, delightful characters, and vastly entertaining dialogue." Booklist

Langton, Jane

The **thief** of Venice. Viking 1999 247p il
ISBN 0-670-88210-0

LC 98-54894

Homer Kelly, "a policeman-turned-scholar, and his professor wife, Mary, have ventured to Venice to attend a scholarly conference on rare books. Homer is intoxicated by the riches afforded in the Biblioteca Marciana, while Mary prowls the streets of the Italian city, camera in hand. An expatriate English doctor, Richard Henchard, seeking an apartment for his demanding mistress, stumbles upon a cache of golden artifacts. He kills twice to protect his secret, and his path soon intersects Mary's. . . . With a master hand, Langton develops the various subplots into a sophisticated, elegantly constructed thriller." Publ Wkly

Lansdale, Joe R.

✓★ The **bottoms**. Mysterious Press 2000 328p $30
ISBN 0-89296-704-8

LC 00-32886

"An emotionally charged tale very reminiscent of To Kill a Mockingbird. Effectively combining mystery and family history, it offers a vivid, multifaceted glimpse back to a simpler, but not necessarily better, time." Booklist

Lansdale, Joe R.

The **complete** Drive-in; three novels of anarchy, aliens & the Popcorn King. Underland Press 2010 376p il pa $16.95
ISBN 978-0-9802260-4-1

"The festivities get started with The Drive-In, the story of Jack and his friends Bob, Willard, and Randy, and the trip they take to the All Night Horror Show at the Orbit, a drive-in movie theater with six screens full of murder, mayhem, and madness. One special Friday, a comet comes out of the sky, grins at the crowd, and takes the rest of the outside world away. Without an exit, the Orbit's audience turns into a small country of starving psychotics, and whoever's running the show keeps throwing in plot twists to keep life interesting. Twists like the Popcorn King, a crazed despot made of twisted flesh, lightning, and concession-stand treats. Lansdale followed the original novel with The Drive-In: Not Just One Of Them Sequels and The Drive-In: The Bus Tour. In both, things continue to go downhill. It's no surprise that Lansdale's story loses some steam by the end. Given how much power he's able to wring out of the premise's stark simplicity, the real wonder is that the sequels work as well as they do." A V Club

Lansdale, Joe R.

Devil red. Alfred A. Knopf 2011 206p $24

ISBN 978-0-307-27098-6

LC 2010-47476

This Hap and Leonard mystery "opens with the duo investigating a series of murders in their patch of east Texas. Each murder site is signed with a drawing of a red devil's head . . . , and suspects are as thick on the ground as pine needles before the adrenaline-stoked shoot-out of a conclusion. Nobody's better at smacking us with the look, feel, and smell of derring-do. Along the way, there is the usual camaraderie, banter, and sex." Libr J

Lansdale, Joe R., 1951-

Edge of dark water; Joe R. Lansdale. Mulholland Books/ Little, Brown and Co. 2012 292 p.

ISBN 0316188433; 9780316188432

LC 2011030557

This book features characters, who "paddling a makeshift raft down the Sabine River, . . . flee East Texas, a New York minute ahead of their pursuers. There are four of them: tough-minded Sue Ellen Wilson . . . ; Jinx, Sue Ellen's lifelong black friend who . . . knows she's better than the bigotry she's endured all her life; angry, resentful Terry, not wholly reconciled to the fact that he's gay; and Sue Ellen's alcoholic mom Helen. . . . They've been brought together by a murder." (Kirkus Reviews)

Lansdale, Joe R.

A **fine** dark line. Mysterious Press 2003 307p $24.95

ISBN 0-89296-729-3

LC 2002-71387

"Stanley doesn't unravel everything, but race and power, and what people do to each other in the name of desire and religion, coalesce to a mighty climax." Booklist

Lansdale, Joe R., 1951-

★ **Honky** tonk samurai; Joe R. Lansdale. Mulholland Books/Little, Brown & Co. 2016 352 p. (A Hap and Leonard novel) (ebook) $78; (hc) $26.00

ISBN 9780316268608; 9780316329408

LC 2015021762

This Hap and Leonard novel, by Joe R. Lansdale, starts "when Hap, a former 60s activist and self-proclaimed white trash rebel, and Leonard, a tough black, gay Vietnam vet and Republican with an addiction to Dr. Pepper, are working a freelance surveillance job in East Texas. The uneventful stakeout is coming to an end when the pair witness a man abusing his dog. Leonard takes matters into his own fists, and now the bruised dog abuser wants to press charges." (Publisher's note)

"This shambolic, action-packed novel will ensnare new readers and satisfy devoted fans alike." Pub Wkly

Lansdale, Joe R., 1951-

★ **Paradise** sky; Joe R. Lansdale. Little, Brown & Co. 2015 416 p. $26

ISBN 0316329371; 9780316329378

LC 2014954932

"In Deadwood, South Dakota Territory, Nat becomes a Buffalo Soldier and is befriended by Wild Bill Hickok. After winning a famous shooting match, Nat's peerless marksmanship and charm earn him the nickname Deadwood Dick, as well as a beautiful woman. But the hellhounds are still on his trail, and they brutally attack. Pursuing the men who have driven his wife mad, Nat heads south for a final, deadly showdown." (Publisher's note)

"Loosely based on the true story of African American cowboy Nat Love (1854-1921), this fast-paced Western with its multicultural cast of characters is a winner." LJ

Lansdale, Joe R.

★ **Sunset** and sawdust. Alfred A. Knopf 2004 321p $22

ISBN 0-375-41453-3

LC 2003-60478

"The mystery is only mildly engrossing here; the great pleasure of Lansdale's work lies in his pitch-perfect vernacular prose. . . . The book opens with a cyclone, ends with a plague of grasshoppers and in between there's insanity, extreme violence, sex, grotesques aplenty and an excellent dog. What's not to like?" Publ Wkly

Lansdale, Joe R., 1951-

The **thicket**; by Joe R. Lansdale. Mulholland Books 2013 352 p. (hardback) $26

ISBN 031618845X; 9780316188456

LC 2013016949

Author Joe R. Lansdale presents the "turn-of-the-twentieth-century coming-of-age tale of 16-year-old Jack Parker and his . . . sister, Lula. Still shocked by the sudden deaths of their parents from smallpox, they see their grandfather murdered by outlaws, who then abduct Lula. Jack must turn to bounty hunters Eustace Cox and Shorty. Their bond is the discrimination they face, and they are willing to chase the outlaws into the primordial and lawless deep woods of East Texas' Big Thicket." (Booklist)

Lansdale, Joe R.

Vanilla Ride. Alfred A. Knopf 2009 243p $24.95

ISBN 978-0-307-27097-9; 0-307-27097-1

LC 2009-08821

In this "outing, the unlikely partners—Hap's a white, horny heterosexual good ol' boy, and Leonard's a black homosexual Vietnam vet—rescue a friend's daughter from the clutches of drug dealers. Unbeknownst to our heroes, the dealers are part of the Dixie Mafia, which proceeds to send waves of assassins in retaliation, each worse than the last. Joking as they go, Hap and Leonard dispose of each with their usual brand of brutality. Then, the mafia sends its weapon of last resort, Vanilla Ride, a beautiful hit woman. . . . Lansdale's storytelling skills are as sharp as ever." Publ Wkly

Lansens, Lori

The **wife's** tale; a novel. Little, Brown 2010 356p $24.99

ISBN 978-0-316-06931-1; 0-316-06931-0

LC 2009-22062

The novel contains "loving reflections on marriage and family in small-town Ontario, hilarious travelogues about American obsessions like McMansions and vanity license plates, and a tender documentary of the improbable compassion of strangers for fellow travelers. Of course, there's plenty of self-discovery too. . . . Mary is no Wife of Bath, but Lansens has more than a few tales worth telling." N Y Times Book Rev

Lapierre, Alexandra

Between love and honor; Alexandra Lapierre ; translated by Jane Lizop. AmazonCrossing 2012 xix, 514 p.p $14.95

ISBN 1611091454; 9781611091458

LC 2011963463

Author Alexandra Lapierre tells "a historical love story based on the facts of Czar Nicholas I of Russia's 25-year struggle to contain the Muslims of the Caucasus Mountains. The book follows Jamal Eddin, son of the Jihadist warrior Imam Shamil, as he's taken hostage by the Czar. . . . [After falling in love with a girl,] Jamal Eddin could have her hand only if he agreed to convert to Christianity. . . . 17 years after his kidnapping, Jamal's father makes his move [to rescue his son], but leaves the choice to his son: will he return to his village or remain with his love?" (Publisher's note)

Laplante, Alice

A **Circle** of Wives; by Alice LaPlante. Pgw 2014 325 p. $25

ISBN 0802122345; 9780802122346

LC 2013497763

In this book, by Alice Laplante, "Dr. John Taylor is found dead in a hotel room. . . . The local police find enough incriminating evidence to suspect foul play. Detective Samantha Adams, whose Palo Alto beat usually covers small-town crimes, is innocently thrown into a high-profile murder case that is more intricately intertwined than she could ever imagine. . . . A closeted polygamist, Dr. Taylor was married to three very different women in three separate cities." (Publisher's note)

"The narration alternates from chapter to chapter and from woman to woman. An investigation of a crime becomes an exploration of the choices these women made and the resulting impact." LJ

Laplante, Alice

Turn of mind. Atlantic Monthly 2011 307p $24

ISBN 978-0-8021-1977-3; 0-8021-1977-8

"The story is told from the perspective of Dr. Jennifer White, once an intellectually commanding orthopedic surgeon, now . . . a fast-deteriorating Alzheimer's patient. . . . As she's narrating the story, White often has no idea what's going on, or she's buried in her past, carrying on dementia-muddled conversations with loved ones now departed. Turn of Mind is part mystery novel, part family drama, and it's no small feat that LaPlante manages to spin a coherent tale despite her main character's profound disorientation. White's best friend, Amanda, has been murdered, her fingers sliced off with suspiciously surgical precision. Did White kill Amanda? The cops think so, but she's continually betrayed by her decaying brain: She just can't remember. Her two grown kids, meanwhile, are alternately protective and manipulative as they grapple with their mother's degeneration and some difficult family history. LaPlante has a gift for rhythm, crafting rat-a-tat passages that are their own pleasures." Entertainment Wkly

Lardner, Ring

Ring around the bases; the complete baseball stories of Ring Lardner. edited and with an introduction by Matthew J. Bruccoli; foreword by Ring Lardner, Jr. Scribner 1992 609p il $35

ISBN 0-684-19374-4

LC 91-38363

"This volume collects all {of Lardner's baseball} tales, including the famous Jack Keefe epistolary stories that made up the well-known volume You Know Me Al (1914), plus some prime journalistic pieces. . . They all display the writer's excellence in capturing the idiom and nuances of baseball talk." Libr J

Includes bibliographic references

Larsen, Nella

Passing; introduction by Ntozake Shange; critical foreword and notes by Mae Henderson. Modern Lib. 2002 lxxxv, 206p (Modern Library classics) pa $10.95

ISBN 0-375-75813-5

LC 2001-45037

First published 1929 by Knopf

This "is a shrewdly conceived and finely executed novella that raises questions not only of racial identity in a realistically rendered middle and upper-middle-class Negro society (in Harlem and Chicago, 1927) but of the murderous rage one woman might feel for another who has 'passed' beyond her." N Y Rev Books

Larsen, Reif

I Am Radar; Reif Larsen. Penguin Group USA 2015 656 p. illustrations, maps $29.95

ISBN 1594206163; 9781594206160

LC 2014036655

This novel by Reif Larsen, "A kaleidoscopic novel both heartbreaking and dazzling, Reif Larsen's 'I Am Radar' begins with Radar's perplexing birth but rapidly explodes outward, carrying readers across the globe and throughout history, as well as to unknown regions where radio waves and subatomic particles dance to their own design. Spanning this extraordinary range with grace and empathy, humor and courage, 'I Am Radar' is the vessel where a century of conflict and art unite." (Publisher's note)

"If Larsen's story makes demands of its readers, it also offers plenty of rewards. Imaginative, original, nicely surreal—and hyperpigmentarily so." Kirkus

Larsen, Reif

The **selected** works of T. S. Spivet. Penguin Press 2009 374p il map $27.95

ISBN 978-1-59420-217-9; 1-59420-217-6

LC 2009-06277

"Only at the end does Larsen lose control of the already outlandish plot, but that's to be forgiven. His debut is oddly affecting, and T.S. Spivet is a character to root for." Dallas Morning News

Larson, Nathan

The **Dewey** Decimal system; a novel. Akashic Books 2011 251p pa $15.95

ISBN 978-1-61775-010-6; 1-61775-010-7

"Proof positive that the private detective will remain a serious and seriously enjoyable literary archetype." PopMatters

Larsson, Asa ✓

Until thy wrath be past; translated by Laurie Thompson. Silver Oak 2011 250p $24.95

ISBN 978-1-4027-8716-4; 1-4027-8716-2

Original Swedish edition, 2008

"Corporate lawyer Rebecka Martinsson is working as a prosecutor in Kiruna when the spring thaw reveals the body of a woman in the river. Rebecka's sleep has been troubled by a threatening spectre: what do these dreams have to do with the dead woman? Rebecka becomes part of an investigation into the disappearance of a plane carrying supplies for the wartime Wehrmacht, but there are those who believe that aspects of the country's past must remain hidden – among them, a ruthless killer. The novel shows that Larsson is ready to confront unpalatable truths. Among the current batch of Nordic writers, the new Larsson is one to be followed with the most minute attention." Independent (UK)

Larsson, Stieg

★ The **girl** who kicked the hornets' nest; translated from the Swedish by Reg Keeland. Alfred A. Knopf 2010 563p $27.95

ISBN 978-0-307-26999-7; 0-307-26999-X

LC 2010-06361

Original Swedish edition, 2007; this translation first published 2009 in the United Kingdom

"The Millennium Trilogy is a fantastically exciting and original set of books, admittedly with flaws, but with a great breadth and intelligence — of the characters as well as of the story — and with an ability to draw the reader into an exciting narrative so that one is lost in the book, not knowing whether to turn the pages rapidly to find out what happens next, or to turn them slowly to prolong the totally mesmerising read, so ably conveyed to English readers by the translator, Reg Keeland." Euro Crime

Larsson, Stieg

The **girl** who played with fire; translated from the Swedish by Reg Keeland. Alfred A. Knopf 2009 503p $25.95

ISBN 978-0-307-26998-0; 0-307-26998-1

LC 2009-14053

Original Swedish edition, 2006

"For all the complications of the melodramatic story, which advances at a brisk, violently cinematic clip in Reg Keeland's translation, it's clear where Larsson's strongest interests lie—in his heroine and the ill-concealed attitudes she brings out in men." N Y Times Book Rev

Larsson, Stieg, 1954-2004

The **girl** with the dragon tattoo; by Stieg Larsson ; translated from the Swedish by Reg Keeland. Alfred A. Knopf 2008 532p $24.95

ISBN 978-0-307-26975-1; 0-307-26975-2

LC 20080411003

Origina Swedish edition, 2005

This novel is "about the disappearnce forty years ago of Harriet Vanger, a young scion of one of the wealthiest families in Sweden . . . and about her octogenarian uncle, determined to know the truth about what he believes was her murder. It's about Mikael Nlomkvist, . . . hired to get to the bottom of Harriet's disappearance . . . and about Lisbeth Salander, a twenty-four-year-old . . . [hacker] who assists Blomkvist with the investigation." (Publisher's note)

First title in the author's Millennium trilogy. "Convicted of libeling a prominent businessman and awaiting imprisonment, financial journalist Mikael Blomkvist agrees to industrialist Henrik Vanger's request to investigate the 40-year-old disappearance of Vanger's 16-year-old niece, Harriet. In return, Vanger will help Blomkvist dig up dirt on the corrupt businessman. Assisting in Blomkvist's investigation is 24-year-old Lisbeth Salander, a brilliant but enigmatic computer hacker." Libr J

Lasdun, James

The **fall** guy; A Novel. James Lasdun. W.W. Norton & Co Inc. 2016 224 p. (hardcover) $25.95; (ebook) $50

ISBN 9780393292329; 9780393292336

LC 2016018259

In this novel, by James Lasdun, "it is summer, 2012. Charlie, a wealthy banker with an uneasy conscience, invites his troubled cousin Matthew to visit him and his wife in their idyllic mountaintop house. As the days grow hotter, the friendship between the three begins to reveal its fault lines, and with the arrival of a fourth character, the household finds itself suddenly in the grip of uncontrollable passions." (Publisher's note)

"An undercurrent of menace and threat finally erupts, and Lasdun presents the inexorable turnings of fate in a subtle and disconcerting way." Pub Wkly

Lasdun, James

The **horned** man. Norton 2002 193p $24.95

ISBN 0-393-00336-1

LC 2002-539

"This arch, assured satire is a psychological thriller, too, and it races cleanly and hungrily to unexpected (and expected) revelations; the academic and sexual politics that ground it are familiar, but this almost doesn't matter, since Lasdun is interested in the inevitability of error when we mistake trendiness for truth." New Yorker

Lasdun, James

It's beginning to hurt. Farrar, Straus and Giroux 2009 227p $23

ISBN 978-0-374-29902-6; 0-374-29902-1

LC 2008-54251

"Reading Lasdun is like reading a sly collaboration between Kafka and Updike: elegant, acutely observed and utterly unflinching . . . . This is a collection that examines the most inward mechanisms of rage, fear and desire with astonishing skill and strangely lyric power." Times (London)

Lashner, William

A **killer's** kiss. William Morrow 2007 327p $24.95

ISBN 978-0-06-114346-5; 0-06-114346-4

LC 2007-61202

In this crime thriller featuring Philadelphia DA Victor Carl, "two police detectives pay Carl a late-night call to inform him that Dr. Wren Denniston, the husband of Carl's former fiancée, Julia, was found shot to death in his Chestnut Hill mansion earlier that evening. Since Carl, known for his malleable ethics, had been entertaining Julia at his apartment shortly before the detectives' arrival in an effort to revive their relationship, he becomes a prime suspect in the doctor's murder. Unsure whether his lover is setting him up, Carl must dodge a rogue's gallery of villains who had their own reasons for wanting Denniston out of the way before he can uncover the real culprit and figure out Julia's true feelings for him. Chandler and Hammett fans looking for a fix will be well rewarded." Publ Wkly

Lashner, William

Kockroach; [by] Tyler Knox. William Morrow 2007 356p il $23.95

ISBN 978-0-06-114333-5; 0-06-114333-2

LC 2006-48138

"Literary fiction is not often this wildly funny. . . . Knox shifts voices and perspective, from hard-boiled to modern-hip, dropping allusions to people as varied as Richard Nixon and the Ramones. You can tell when an author is having a good time, and Knox has a ball." Seattle Times

Lasser, Scott

Say nice things about Detroit; Scott Lasser. W.W. Norton & Co. 2012 267 p.

ISBN 0393082997; 9780393082999

LC 2012006784

In this book, it's 25 "years after his high school graduation, [and] David Halpert returns to a place that most people flee--his hometown of Detroit. But David is making his own escape--from his divorce and the death of his son. In Detroit, David learns about the double shooting of his high school girlfriend Natalie and her black half-brother, Dirk. As David becomes involved with Natalie's sister, he will discover that both he and his hometown have reasons to hope." (Publisher's note)

Lathen, Emma

Brewing up a storm; a John Thatcher mystery. St. Martin's Press 1996 248p

LC 96-22116

In this novel "a protest organization sues a local brewery, claiming that the firm's new nonalcoholic beer contributed to the alcohol-related death of a teenager. When someone murders the protest leader, the brewery calls on series sleuth John Thatcher, a Wall Street banker." Libr J

Lathen, Emma

East is east. Simon & Schuster 1991 268p

LC 91-32789

Ms. Lathen "has a wonderful knack for turning the driest, most complicated corporate maneuvers into high drama, and occasionally burlesque." N Y Times Book Rev

Lathen, Emma

Something in the air. Simon & Schuster 1988 270p

LC 88-4491

This mystery featuring "John Thatcher of New York's Sloan Guaranty Trust is set mainly in Boston, headquarters of the commuter airline Sparrow Flyways. A product of airline deregulation, Sparrow is a nonunion operation surviving on horizontal management and project development teams. Mitchell Scovil, CEO and guiding figure of the founders, dreams of expansion, but a group of lower-level employees (and shareholders) is worried about their investment. When their arrogant spokesperson is murdered, the Sloan, holding 20% of unsalable Sparrow stock in a trust, becomes involved." Publ Wkly

Latin@ rising; an anthology of latin@ science fiction and fantasy. edited by Matthew David Goodwin. Wings Press 2017 xx, 250 p.p (pbk. : alk. paper) $16.95

ISBN 9781609405243; 9781609405250

LC 2016027239

This book, edited by Matthew David Goodwin, "is the first anthology of science fiction and fantasy written by Latinos/as living in the United States. The book gives an overview to the field of Latino/a speculative literature, showing the great variety of stories being told by Latino/a writers. . . . The 21st century writers and artists of 'Latin@ Rising' help us to imagine a Latino/a past, present, and future which have not been whitewashed by mainstream perspectives." (Publisher's note)

"Sloughing off the worn veil of magical realism, Goodwin's anthology amplifies a new generation of Latin@ speculative fiction voices." Booklist

Includes bibliographical references

Latour, Jose

The **Havana** World Series; José Latour. 1st ed; Grove Press 2003 320p $23

ISBN 0-8021-1754-6

LC 2003-60716

The author "tells the story of a gang of Cuban crooks, funded by New York Mob boss Joe Bonanno, who sets out to rob Meyer Lansky's Capri casino on the last day of the 1958 World Series (when the coffers are overflowing). The portraits of Lansky, Bonnano, and the other gangsters are full-bodied, but it's the fictional blue-collar crooks, led by mastermind Ox Contreras, who give the novel its appeal and afford the best view of Cuban life. Although the documentary style occasionally seems flat, it contrasts nicely with the richness of detail and quirkiness of character." Booklist

Laukkanen, Owen

Criminal enterprise; Owen Laukkanen. G. P. Putnam's Sons 2013 416 p. $26.95

ISBN 0399157905; 9780399157905

LC 2012028673

This book, by Owen Laukkanen, is the second in the "Stevens and Windermere" series. "Carter [Tomlin] . . . robs a bank. Then he robs another. As the red flags start to go up, FBI Special Agent Carla Windermere homes in on Tomlin from one direction, while Minnesota state investigator Kirk Stevens picks up the trail from another. The two cops haven't talked since their first case together, but that's all going to change very quickly." (Publisher's note)

Laukkanen, Owen

The **professionals**; a novel. Owen Laukkanen. Putnam 2012 372 p.

ISBN 9780399157899

LC 2012000907

In this crime novel, "[f]our college friends . . . decide to make money by kidnapping bankers and other extremely wealthy men around the U.S. . . . The group's luck runs out on a Michigan job when their target turns out to be connected to the Mafia, a mistake that starts an avalanche of violence. Their crime spree leads to the involvement of FBI agent Carla Windermere and Minnesota state investigator Kirk Stevens, who race the mob to catch the kidnappers." (Publishers Weekly)

Other titles in this series are:
Criminal enterprise (2013)
Kill fee (2014)
The stolen ones (2015)
The watcher in the wall (2016)
The forgotten girls (2017)

LaValle, Victor D.

Big machine; a novel. [by] Victor LaValle. Spiegel & Grau 2009 352p $25

ISBN 978-0-385-52798-9; 0-385-52798-5

LC 2009-00381

"Despite its steady pulse of dark humor, its supernatural Voice and the presence of some creepy entities known as the Devils of the Marsh, Big Machine is a novel about faith and the ways in which religion can create monsters far more terrifying than anything dreamed up by H.P. Lovecraft." Washington Post Book World

LaValle, Victor D.

The **devil** in silver; a novel. Victor LaValle. 1st ed. Spiegel & Grau 2012 412 p. (ebook) $81.00; (hardcover : acid-free paper) $27.00

ISBN 0679604863; 1400069866; 9780679604860; 9781400069866

LC 2011034970

This horror novel, by Victor LaValle, follows "Pepper, . . . [a] minor-league troublemaker, working-class hero (in his own mind), and, suddenly, the surprised inmate of a . . . mental institution. . . . [H]e's visited by a terrifying creature with the body of an old man and the head of a bison who nearly kills him. . . . It's no delusion: The other patients confirm that a hungry devil roams the hallways. . . . Pepper rallies three other inmates in a plot to fight back." (Publisher's note)

Lavender, Will

Dominance. Simon & Schuster 2011 353p $25
ISBN 978-1-4516-1729-0; 978-1-4516-1731-3 ebook
LC 2010046118

"Back in 1994, Alex Shipley was one of the elite chosen for a special night class at Jasper College, 'Unraveling a Literary Mystery,' taught by genius professor Richard Aldiss from his prison cell where he was serving a life term for the brutal slayings of two of his female students. Alex became one of Aldiss's favorites and was able to prove his innocence. Seventeen years later, Alex is a literature professor at Harvard, but she is called back to her old stomping ground because someone is killing her former classmates. . . . Well-drawn characters, excellent plot, good use of flashbacks, and many red herrings will keep the pages turning to the very end." Libr J

Law, Susan Kay

The **paper** marriage; Susan Kay Law. Berkley Books 2008 362 p. (pbk.) $19
ISBN 9780425219355
LC 2007046576

This book tells the story of Ann McCrary, whose "marriage came to a standstill when a car crash nearly ended her husband's life and put him into a deep coma. That was 12 years ago, and ever since, her life has been on hold. . . . Then former baseball star Tom Nash moves in, clueless as to how to deal with his rebellious teenage daughter, and Ann's world expands in a totally unexpected way." (Library Journal)

"[O]ne night a few days before Ann's wedding anniversary she . . . realiz[es] that after this anniversary she . . . would officially have spent more of [her] relationship with him in a coma than when he was really alive. Tom comes over to comfort her. . . . She ends up getting pregnant after this one night. . . . 5 years after the baby is born Ann's husband finally succumbs to an infection and passes away and the book ends with Ann and Tom getting married." (debbiesworldofbooks.com)

Lawrence, D. H.

Collected stories; with an introduction by Craig Raine. Knopf 1994 xxxv, 1397p
LC 94-2493

Contents: A modern lover; The old Adam; Her turn; Strike-pay; The witch à la mode; New Eve and old Adam; A prelude; Love among the haystacks; A chapel and a hay hut among the mountains; Once; A fly in the ointment; Lessford's rabbits; A lesson on a tortoise; The Prussian officer; The thorn in the flesh; Daughters of the vicar; A fragment of stained glass; The shades of spring; Second best; The shadow in the rose garden; Goose fair; The white stocking; A sick collier; The christening; Odour of chrysanthemums; England, my England; Tickets, please; The blind man; Monkey nuts; Wintry peacock; You touched me; Samson and Delilah; The thimble; The mortal coil; The primrose path; The horse dealer's daughter; Delilah and Mr. Bircumshaw; Fanny and Annie; The ladybird; The fox; The captain's doll; St. Mawr; The princess; Two blue birds; Sun; The woman who rode away; Smile; The border line; Jimmy and the desperate woman; The last laugh; In love; Glad ghosts; None of that; The man who loved islands; The lovely lady; Rawdon's roof; The rocking-horse winner; Mother and daughter; The blue moccasins; Things; The virgin and the gipsy; The man who died

Lawrence, D. H.

★ **Lady** Chatterley's lover; the historic unexpurgated Grove Press edition. with Archibald MacLeish's letter to Barney Rosset, an introduction by Mark Schorer, and Judge Bryan's decision in the obscenity case. Modern Lib. 1993 liii, 491p
ISBN 0-679-60065-5
LC 93-15337

First published 1928 in a limited edition in Florence

A novel "presenting the author's mystical theories of sex in the story of Constance, or Connie, the wife of an English aristocrat, who runs away with her gamekeeper. Her husband, Sir Clifford, has been rendered impotent by a war wound and is also an emotional cripple. The gamekeeper, Mellors, is a forthright individualistic man, uncontaminated by industrial society." Reader's Ency. 4th edition

Lawrence, D. H.

The **rainbow**; with an introduction by Barbara Hardy. Knopf 1993 xxxv, 460p $20
ISBN 0-679-42305-2
LC 93-1860

First published 1915

"The story line traces three generations of the Brangwen family in the Midlands of England from 1840 to 1905. The marriage of farmer Tom Brangwen and foreigner Lydia Lensky eventually breaks down. Likewise, the marriage of Lydia's daughter Anna to Tom's nephew Will gradually fails. The novel is largely devoted to Will and Anna's oldest child, the schoolteacher Ursula, who stops short of marriage when she is unsatisfied by her love affair with the conventional soldier Anton Skrebensky. The appearance of a rainbow at the end of the novel is a sign of hope for Ursula, whose story is continued in Lawrence's Women in Love." Merriam-Webster's Ency of Lit

Followed by Women in love

Lawrence, D. H.

★ **Sons** and lovers. Knopf 1991 xxvii, 403p $17
ISBN 0-679-40572-0
LC 91-53002

First published 1913

"Paul Morel, adored youngest son of a middle-class mother who feels that her coal-miner husband was unworthy of her, has difficulty in breaking away from her. Mrs. Morel has given her son all her warmth and love for so long a time that Paul finds it impossible to establish a relationship with another women. Miriam is supportive and understanding of his artistic nature but appeals mainly to his higher nature; Clara Dawes becomes his mistress but she is married and will not divorce her husband. After the death of his mother, Paul arranges a reconciliation between Clara and her husband and, after months of grieving for his mother, at last finds the strength to strike out on his own." Shapiro. Fic For Youth. 3d edition

Lawrence, D. H.

★ **Women** in love. Knopf 1992 475p
ISBN 0-679-40995-5
LC 91-53191

Sequel to The rainbow

First published 1920

This novel "examines the ill effects of industrialization on the human psyche, resolving that individual and collective rebirth is possible only through human intensity and passion. Women in Love contrasts the love affair of Rupert Birkin and Ursula Brangwen with that of Gudrun, Ursula's artistic sister, and Gerald Crich, a domineering industrialist. Birkin, an introspective misanthrope, struggles to reconcile his metaphysical drive for self-fulfillment with Ursula's practical view of sentimental passion. Their love affair and eventual marriage are set as a positive antithesis to the destructive relationship of Gudrun and Crich." Merriam-Webster's Ency of Lit

Lawrence, David

The **dead** sit round in a ring. Thomas Dunne Books 2004 435p $24.95

ISBN 0-312-32710-2

LC 2004-41878

This mystery offers a "perspective on London that is darker and grittier than in conventional treatments. But the writing is the thing. Whether he's describing a bizarre death scene . . . or observing a group of streetwalkers plying their night trade . . . Lawrence, a published poet, writes with a delicacy and restraint rare in the genre." N Y Times Book Rev

Lawrence, Margaret K.

Hearts and bones; {by} Margaret Lawrence. Avon Bks. 1996 307p il

LC 96-2394

"Through a combination of diary entries, trial records, autopsy reports, and engrossing narrative, Lawrence reveals the story of a witness and a participant in a brutal war crime and their decade-long silence." Booklist

Lawson, Mary

Crow Lake. Dial Press (NY) 2002 291p hardcover o.p. pa $14

ISBN 0-385-33611-X; 0-385-33763-9 pa

LC 2001-53779

"Lawson achieves a breathless anticipatory quality in her surprisingly adept first novel, in which a child tells the story, but tells it very well indeed." Booklist

Lawton, John

Old flames. Atlantic Monthly Press 2003 416p $24

ISBN 0-87113-864-6

LC 2002-28025

"Lawton has created an effective genre-bending novel that is at once a cerebral thriller and an uproarious, deliciously English spoof." Publ Wkly

Lawton, John

Then We Take Berlin. Pgw 2013 400 p. $26

ISBN 0802121969; 9780802121967

This book is the first in a series from John Lawton. It "opens on the eve of President Kennedy's 1963 Berlin visit, but the real meat lies in the . . . backstory of John Wilford Holderness, an East London Cockney who joins the RAF in 1946. Aircraftman Wilderness . . . is cheeky to the point of risking court-martial, but an RAF colonel spots Joe's potential, sends him to Cambridge, and makes him a spy." He's posted to Berlin to identify former Nazis. (Publishers Weekly)

Layton, Edith

To wed a stranger; Edith Layton. Avon Books 2003 375 p. (pbk.) $5.99

ISBN 0060502177

LC 2003611531

This book tells the story of "Lady Annabelle Wylde, [who] has had many flirtations but has never found love. Nevertheless, she knows she must wed; resigned to a loveless relationship, she dutifully agrees to an arranged marriage with Miles Croft, Viscount Pelham, a man she hardly knows. Disaster strikes on the couple's honeymoon as virulent influenza robs Annabelle of her beauty and vitality, and their relationship takes on a deeper dimension as they learn to know each other and discover what is really important to them." (Library Journal)

Lazar, Zachary

Sway; a novel. Little, Brown and Co. 2008 255p $23.99

ISBN 978-0-316-11309-0; 0-316-11309-3

LC 2007-9920

"It is not the now-historic acts of violence that make Sway so riveting, but its vivid character portraits and decadent, muzzy atmosphere, all rendered with the heightened sensory awareness associated with drugs and paranoia. The near miniaturist precision with which he describes Keith Richards's attempts to master his guitar, Brian Jones's acid trips and Anger's obsessive desire for Beausoleil bring this large-scale tableau into stunning relief." Time Out N Y

Le Carre, John

Absolute friends. Little, Brown 2004 455p $26.95

ISBN 0-316-00064-7

LC 2003-61196

"If le Carre's symbols are a little obvious and his rhetoric a little heated, his technical skill is pure joy." New Leader

Le Carre, John

★ The **constant** gardener; a novel. Scribner 2001 492p

ISBN 0-7432-1505-2

LC 00-53340

"Globalization in its uglier aspects . . . has replaced the Cold War as the moral backdrop in Le Carre's work. His Cold War novels did not spare the conscience even of citizens on the 'right' side, confronting them with crimes committed in their names, and the globalization novels do not spare the stockholder." Atl Mon

Le Carré, John, 1931-

★ A **Delicate** Truth; A Novel. by John Le Carre. Viking Adult 2013 309 p. (hardcover) $28.95

ISBN 0670014893; 9780670014897

LC 2013001536

In this book by John Le Carre, a "plot to capture an arms dealer in Gibraltar under the mantle of counterterrorism goes awry. . . . Toby Bell, who was kept out of the loop, has incriminating information about the mission and the chance to use it three years later when one of the soldiers involved ends up dead and a retired British diplomat, roped into participating against his will, tries to salve his conscience about some nasty pieces of collateral damage." (Publishers Weekly)

Le Carre, John

★ The **honourable** schoolboy. Knopf 1977 533p

LC 77-75001

Jerry Westerby is the honorable schoolboy of the title. He works with George Smiley of the British Secret Service, described by the author as The Circus, to discover why the Russian Secret Service is paying $25,000 a month into the bank account of the prosperous Hong Kong business man, Drake Ko. The action takes place in London and Southeast Asia. The story opens in the Hong Kong press club

This "is superbly well-organized, combining a grandiose sweep with an intricate pattern. It has hard-edged reality instead of fuzzy near-fantasy, a host of sharply etched characters instead of a few eccentric caricatures, and a style which, subtle and flexible . . . never obtrudes, yet never goes unnoticed." Times Lit Suppl

Le Carre, John

The **little** drummer girl. Knopf 1983 429p

LC 82-48733

"Mr. le Carré's novel is certainly the most mature, inventive and powerful book about terrorists-come-to-life this reader has experienced. It transcends the genre." NY Times Book Rev

Le Carre, John

A **most** wanted man; a novel. Scribner 2008 323p $28

ISBN 978-1-4165-9488-8; 1-4165-9488-4

LC 2008-30704

"Le Carré's dialogue has snap, rhythm and wit, particularly in those passages where intelligence chiefs maneuver to gain an edge on each other. Too, his immaculate timing helps him fold in different plot lines without smudging narrative pace and tone. Ever the spymaster, he also differentiates the challenges faced by spies today from those of their Cold War counterparts." St. Louis Post-Dispatch

Le Carre, John

★ **Our** kind of traitor; a novel. Viking 2010 305p $27.95

ISBN 978-0-670-02224-3; 0-670-02224-1

LC 2010-19513

Le Carre "seems positively re-invigorated in a retro sort of way. The story carries on with an extra spring in the step that harkens back, both in the manner of plotting and the style, to le Carré's earliest and still greatest novels. That's due in large part to how he engages with current events: the teetering economy, Britain (and Europe's) austerity-oriented response, and the rise of state surveillance even as the events of September 11 grow more distant." Daily Beast

Le Carre, John

A **perfect** spy. Knopf 1986 475p

LC 85-45587

"Not a spy novel in the usual sense . . . but a skillfully manipulated, complex, and probingly written study spiced with lively anecdotes. To be savored." Libr J

Le Carre, John

The **secret** pilgrim. Knopf 1990 335p

LC 90-52944

"There's always been a didatic quality to le Carré's work that has been part of his novels' charm, but in no other book has he said so much about the ravages that the spying profession works upon the agent." Newsweek

Le Carre, John

Smiley's people. Knopf 1980 374p

LC 79-2299

First published 1979 in the United Kingdom

This novel "is a complete winner, exciting, well-paced, and convincing. . . . There is a lot of the Le Carré gloom, but now it seems almost elegiac and touching. Absolutely not to be missed." Libr J

Le Carre, John

The **spy** who came in from the cold. Walker & Company 2005 223p $19

ISBN 0-8027-1454-4

First published 1963 in the United kingdom; first United States edition published 1964 by Coward-McCann

"The story of Alec Leamas, 50-year-old professional secret agent who has grown stale in espionage, who longs to 'come in from the cold' and how he undertakes one last assignment before that hoped-for retirement. Over the years Leamas has grown unsure where his workday carapace ends and his real self begins. . . . Recalled from Berlin after the death of his last East German contact at the Wall, Leamas lets himself be seduced into a pretended defection-thereby providing the East Germans with data from which they can deduce that the head of their own spy apparatus is a double agent." N Y Times Book Rev

Le Carre, John

The **tailor** of Panama. Knopf 1996 331p

ISBN 0-679-45446-2

LC 96-34802

Le Carré "reveals in the contortions of British diplomats, aghast at the arriviste spy masters whom they pretend to accept, all the while struggling to extricate themselves from absurd but inevitable catastrophe. Readers who wonder whether Graham Greene was not here 40 years ago are right, and Mr le Carré acknowledges his debt to 'Our Man in Havana'. This tale, told with wit and ingenuity, is a splendid homage from one master of political thrillers to another." Economist

Le Carre, John

★ **Tinker,** tailor, soldier, spy. Knopf 1974 355p

Smiley "instinctively realises from the outset who the traitor is but refuses to confront the embarrassing truth. A perceptive reader will sense the secret too, but one goes on reading entranced not so much by the ramifications of the plot, beautifully engineered though it is, as by concern for the characters, a rare thing in thrillers." New Statesman (1913)

Le Guin, Ursula K.

The **beginning** place. Harper & Row 1980 183p

LC 79-2653

"The style is fluent, concise and elegant, and the story that is told is easily understood by anyone who has ever found himself at a loss to deal with the realities of modern life." Best Sellers

Le Guin, Ursula K.

The **birthday** of the world and other stories. HarperCollins Pubs. 2002 362p $24.95

ISBN 0-06-621253-7

LC 2001-39508

"Le Guin appears to have the most fun with her investigations of sex and gender . . . but the costs of revolution, religious bliss, and technology are also provicatively explored, and one returns to the current headlines with a fresh awareness of the exotic providional nature of human arrangements." New Yorker

Le Guin, Ursula K.

★ The **dispossessed**; an ambiguous Utopia. Harper & Row 1974 341p il

ISBN 9780060512750; 9781451783964; 9780060504007

"Shevek, a brilliant physicist, is caught between the prejudices and hatreds of two worlds. His quest to bridge the gap between Ararres, an anarchist, egalitarian society, and Varas, a structured, capitalistic world, unleashes a storm of intrigue and drama. The two distinct cultures provide insights into the role of women in society, the issue of free will versus obligation to the state, human rights, and ecomonic systems." Shapiro. Fic for Youth. 3d edition

Le Guin, Ursula K.

Four ways to forgiveness. HarperPrism 1995 228p

LC 95-11459

"Four interrelated novellas deal with the Hainish culture on the twin planets of Werel and Yeowe and examine the relationship between love, freedom and forgiveness." Publ Wkly

Le Guin, Ursula K.

The **lathe** of heaven; a novel. Scribner 2008 184p pa $15

ISBN 978-1-4165-5696-1; 1-4165-5696-6

LC 2007047222

Le Guin, Ursula K.

★ The **left** hand of darkness; with a new afterword and appendixes by the author. 25th Anniversary ed; Walker & Co. 1994 345p

ISBN 0-8027-1302-5

LC 94-27147

A reissue of the title first published 1969 by Walker & Company

"This is a tale of political intrigue and danger on the world of Gethen, the Winter planet. Genly Ai, high official of the Eukeman—the commonwealth of worlds—is on Gethen to convince the royalty to join the Federation. He soon becomes a pawn in Gethen's power struggles, set against the elaborate mores of the Gethenians, a unisex hermaphroditic people whose intricate sexual physiology plays a key role in the conflict. Allied with Estraven, fallen lord, Genly is forced to cross the savage and impassable Gobrin Ice." Shapiro. Fic for Youth. 3d edition

Le Guin, Ursula K.

Orsinian tales. Harper & Row 1976 179p

This is a cycle of interrelated short stories. "Set in a vaguely Middle-European country, Le Guin's tales deal with love, freedom, and tyranny in a society which over a series of historical periods appears to be perpetually in the last stages preceding cataclysm." Booklist

Le Guin, Ursula K.

The **other** wind. Harcourt 2001 246p

ISBN 0151006849

LC 2001-24632

In this novel, Alder the sorcerer is troubled by dreams of the dead, who may gain enough strength to invade Earthsea.

"The Earthsea saga, begun in 1968 as a young adults' series, has evolved into one of Le Guin's, and modern science fiction's, signature achievements." N Y Times Book Rev

Le Guin, Ursula K.

The **telling**. Harcourt 2000 264p

ISBN 0-15-100567-2

LC 00-29574

A title in the authors Hainish cycle. "As a member of the Ekumen's embassy on the planet Aka, Sutty undertakes a delicate mission that leads her to a mountain village reported to contain the last remnants of a dying culture. Following a trail of subtle clues concealed in stories and folk sayings, Sutty discovers the suppressed history of a planet willing to abandon its old ways in the name of progress. . . . This parable of the modern world's headlong rush toward monocultural sterility exemplifies the author's elegant simplicity and keen insight." Libr J

Le, Thi Diem Thuy

The **gangster** we are all looking for. Knopf 2003 160p $18

ISBN 0-375-40018-4

LC 2002-33999

"The story opens slowly but gathers strength, and though it remains somewhat muted, Le's lyrical writing and skill with the telling vigette will reward patient readers." Libr J

Leavitt, David

★ The **Two** Hotels Francfort; a novel. David Leavitt. Bloomsbury 2013 272 p. (hc : alk. paper) $25

ISBN 1596910429; 9781596910423

LC 2013015952

Lambda Literary Awards Finalist (2014)

Stonewall Honor Book - Literature (2015)

In this book, by David Leavitt, "it is the summer of 1940, and Lisbon, Portugal, is the only neutral port left in Europe. . . . Awaiting safe passage to New York on the SS Manhattan, two couples meet: Pete and Julia Winters, expatriate Americans fleeing their sedate life in Paris; and Edward and Iris Freleng, sophisticated, independently wealthy, bohemian, and beset by the social and sexual anxieties of their class. . . . This journey will change their lives irrevocably." (Publisher's note)

Lebbon, Tim

Fallen. Bantam Spectra 2008 413p il pa $12

ISBN 978-0-553-38467-3; 0-553-38467-8

LC 2008-10401

"Some 4,000 years before the events of Dusk (2006), the people of Noreela are just beginning an era of expansion, with explorers going constantly further into unknown territory for profit and glory. Blocking the voyagers' southward journeys, however, is the Great Divide, a cliff that reaches into the clouds. Ramus Rheel, an aging explorer battling cancer, and Nomi Hyden, whose wealth has not diminished her craving for adventure, are friendly enemies who set out to scale the Divide and earn recognition as the greatest voyagers of all. When they find the lair of one of the ancient Sleeping Gods, they get considerably more excitement—and terror—than they bargained for. Lebbon creates vivid and convincing major and minor characters, places and creatures, blending wonder and nightmare in this dark and memorable novel." Publ Wkly

Lebedev, Sergei

The **Year** of the Comet; by Sergei Lebedev, translated by Antonia W. Bouis. New Vessel Press 2017 245 p. (paperback) $17.95

ISBN 9781939931429; 9781939931412; 193993141X

LC 2016915499

This book, by Sergei Lebedev, translated by Antonia W. Bouis, is a "story of . . . Russian boyhood and coming of age as the Soviet Union is on the brink of collapse. An idyllic childhood takes a sinister turn. Rumors of a serial killer haunt the neighborhood, families pack up and leave town without a word of warning, and the country begins to unravel." (Publisher's note)

"This gorgeously written, unsettling novel—a rare work about the fall of the Soviet Union as told through the eyes of a child—leaves us with a fresh understanding of that towering moment in recent history." Kirkus

Lebrecht, Norman

The **song** of names. Anchor Bks. 2004 311p pa $14

ISBN 1-4000-3489-2 pa

LC 2003-67451

"Lebrecht's story delves into the horrors of the Holocaust and the Blitz, as well as the quiet communities of Hasidic Judaism that developed in Britain after the flight of so many refugees. What emerges is a vivid and outstanding story that sings about artistry, genius, music, love, envy, friendship, and revenge." Booklist

Leckie, Ann

★ **Ancillary** justice; Ann Leckie. Orbit 2013 416 p. (trade pbk.) $15

ISBN 031624662X; 9780316246620

LC 2012051135

Philip K. Dick Award Nominee (2013)

Hugo Award: Best Novel (2014)

Nebula Award: Best Novel (2013)

In this space opera, by Ann Leckie, "the soldier known as Breq is drawing closer to completing her quest. . . . Years ago, she was the Justice of Toren--a colossal starship with an artificial intelligence linking thousands of corpse soldiers in the service of the Radch, the empire that conquered the galaxy. An act of treachery has ripped it all away, leaving her with only one fragile human body." (Publisher's note)

"Using the format of sf military adventure blended with hints of space opera, Leckie explores the expanded meaning of human nature and the uneasy balance between individuality and membership in a group identity." LJ

Leckie, Ann

Ancillary mercy; Ann Leckie. Orbit 2015 368 p. (Imperial Radch) (trade pbk.) $15.99

ISBN 0316246689; 9780316246682

LC 2015020915

This science fiction novel, by Ann Leckie, is the "conclusion to the trilogy that began with the Hugo, Nebula, and Arthur C. Clarke award-winning 'Ancillary Justice.' . . . For a moment, things seemed to be under control for Breq, the soldier who used to be a warship. Then a search of Athoek Station's slums turns up someone who shouldn't exist, and a messenger from the mysterious Presger empire arrives, as does Breq's enemy, the divided and quite possibly insane Anaander Mianaai--ruler of an empire at war with itself." (Publisher's note)

"Leckie creates a grand backdrop to tell an intimate, cerebral story about identity and empowerment. She devotes as much attention to the characters' personal relationships and their mental and emotional difficulties as she does to the wider conflict." Kirkus

Leckie, Ann

Ancillary sword; Ann Leckie. Orbit 2014 400 p. (Imperial Radch) (paperback) $16

ISBN 0316246654; 9780316246651

LC 2014018730

Locus Award: Science Fiction Novel (2015)

In this science fiction novel, by Ann Leckie, "sequel to 'Ancillary Justice,' winner of the Hugo, Nebula, British Science Fiction, Locus and Arthur C. Clarke Awards . . . , Breq is a soldier who used to be a warship. Once a weapon of conquest controlling thousands of minds, now she has only a single body and serves the emperor. . . . Breq is ordered to . . . Athoek Station to protect the family of a lieutenant she once knew--a lieutenant she murdered in cold blood." (Publisher's note)

"Breq's struggle for meaningful justice in a society designed to favor the strong is as engaging as ever." Pub Wkly

Leckie, Ann

Provenance; Ann Leckie. Orbit 2017 439 p. (hardback) $26

ISBN 031638867X; 9780316388658; 9780316388672

LC 2017018846

Hugo Finalist: Best Novel (2018)

In this book, by Ann Leckie, "a power-driven young woman has just one chance to secure the status she craves and regain priceless lost artifacts prized by her people. She must free their thief from a prison planet from which no one has ever returned. Ingray and her charge will return to her home world to find their planet in political turmoil, at the heart of an escalating interstellar conflict. Together, they must make a new plan to salvage Ingray's future, her family, and her world, before they are lost to her for good." (Publisher's note)

"Leckie again uses large-scale worldbuilding to tell a deeply personal story--in this case, to explore what binds children to their families. As always, she impels the reader to consider the power language, and specifically names, has to shape perception and reality." Kirkus

LeCraw, Holly

The **swimming** pool. Doubleday 2010 307p $25.95

ISBN 978-0-385-53193-1; 0-385-53193-1

LC 2009-08314

"This novel about Cape Cod's social circles reveals the upper-middle-class miseries hiding beneath its sanitized and highly chlorinated surface. When Jed, a moody lawyer in his mid-20s, finds an old, crumpled bathing suit in a closet at the family vacation home, it leads him to Marcella, a divorcé who, years earlier, conducted an affair with his father. Jed and Marcella then embark on their own liasion. In The Swimming Pool, Holly LeCraw wades slowly into her narrative instead of diving straight in, so the story takes a while to pick up. But once it does, the suburban afflictions that are drowning these characters make it difficult to put down." Entertainment Wkly

Ledgard, J. M.

Submergence; a novel. by J. M. Ledgard. Coffee House Press 2013 209 p. (pbk.) $15.95

ISBN 1566893194; 9781566893190

LC 2012036524

In this novel, "James More is held captive by jihadist fighters. Posing as a water expert to report on al-Qaeda activity in the area, he now faces extreme privation. . . . On the Greenland Sea, Danielle Flinders, a biomathematician, half-French, half-Australian, prepares to dive in a submersible to the ocean floor. Both are drawn back . . . to a French hotel on the Atlantic coast, where a chance encounter on the beach led to an intense and enduring romance." (Publisher's note)

Lee, C. Y.

The **flower** drum song. Farrar, Straus & Cudahy 1957 244p

A story of family life in San Francisco's Chinatown. The principal characters are the elderly Mr. Wang and his oldest son, Wang Ta, torn between Chinese tradition and western custom

"A first novel that is always fascinating, and by turns amusing and pathetic—a novel written with grace and decorum in the even, unimpassioned narrative style that is characteristic of classical Chinese fiction." Chicago Sunday Trib

Lee, Chang-Rae

Aloft. Riverhead Books 2004 343p $24.95

ISBN 1-573-22263-1

LC 2003-58630

Set on affluent Long Island, {this novel} follows the life of a suburban, upper-middle-class man during a time of family crisis. Jerry Battle's favorite diversion is to fly his small plane over the neighboring towns and villages. When his daughter and her fiance arrive from Oregon to announce their marriage plans, he looks back on his life and faces his disengagement with it . . . and the people he loves." Publisher's note

Lee, Chang-Rae

A **gesture** life. Riverhead Bks. 1999 356p

ISBN 1-573-22146-5

LC 99-28382

"This is a wise, humane, fully rounded story, deeply but unsentimentally moving, and permeated with insights about the nature of human relationships." Publ Wkly

Lee, Chang-rae, 1965-

★ **On** such a full sea; Chang-rae Lee. First edition Riverhead Books 2014 368 p. $27.95

ISBN 1594486107; 9781594486104

LC 2013036600

Carnegie Medal Shortlist: Fiction (2015)

This book "tells the mythic story of young, small, yet mighty Fan, a breath-held diver preternaturally at home among the farmed fish she tends to. When her boyfriend inexplicably disappears, Fan escapes from B-Mor to search for him, embarking on a daring, often surreal quest in a violent, blighted world. She encounters a taciturn healer bereft of all that he cherished, a troupe of backwoods acrobats, and a disturbing cloister of girls creating an intricate mural of their muffled lives." (Booklist)

"A harrowing and fully imagined vision of dystopian America. . . . Welcome and surprising proof that there's plenty of life in end-of-the-world storytelling." Kirkus

Lee, Chang-rae, 1965-

★ The **surrendered**. Riverhead Books 2010 469p $26.95

ISBN 9781594489761; 1-59448-976-9

LC 2009-30887

This is a novel by the author of Aloft (2004) and The Drama of Consciousness (2006). "The lasting memory of the Korean War changes the lives of two of its survivors—a Korean girl and an American vet—as well as the lives of those who come to know them. Hector Brennan was a handsome GI stationed in Korea during the war. June Han was a girl orphaned by the fighting. For a season of wartime existence, their lives overlapped at a missionary-run orphanage. Now, thirty years later, they are reunited in the United States in an unusual mission that will force them to come to terms with their individual experiences of that time, but also the secret they share." (Publisher's note)

"In its ineffably quiet way, there really is something Tolstoyan in this searching fiction's determination to understand the characters specifically as members of families and products of other people's influences. The characterizations of Hector and Sylvie are astonishingly rich and complex, and the risktaken in depicting the adult June as the woman readers will hope she would not become is triumphantly vindicated." Kirkus

Lee, Don

Country of origin. W.W. Norton & Co 2004 315p $24.95

ISBN 0-393-05812-3

LC 2004-4722

"Issues of race, class, and national identity drive this clear-eyed story of closure, redemption, and carving out a place in the world." Booklist

Lee, Gus

China boy; a novel. Dutton 1991 322p hardcover o.p. pa $14

ISBN 0-525-24994-X; 0-452-27158-4 pa

LC 90-21687

"Based on events in his own childhood, Mr. Lee's depiction of Kai's efforts to reconcile his Chinese heritage with the several equally bewildering worlds of American culture he is simultaneously exposed to . . . is vivid and moving." N Y Times Book Rev

Followed by Honor & duty (1994)

Lee, Harper, 1926-2016

Go set a watchman; a novel. Harper Lee. HarperCollins 2015 278 p. (hardcover) $27.99

ISBN 0062409859; 9780062409850; 9780062433657

This novel, by Harper Lee, "is set during the mid-1950s and features many of the characters from 'To Kill a Mockingbird' some twenty years later. Scout (Jean Louise Finch) has returned to Maycomb from New York to visit her father Atticus. She is forced to grapple with issues both personal and political as she tries to understand both her father's attitude toward society, and her own feelings about the place where she was born and spent her childhood." (Publisher's note)

Lee, Harper, 1926-2016

★ **To** kill a mockingbird; Harper Lee. 50th anniversary ed; Harper 2010 323p $25.00

ISBN 9780061743528

A reissue of the title first published 1960 by Lippincott

"Scout, as Jean Louise is called, is a precocious child. She relates her impressions of the time when her lawyer father, Atticus Finch, is defending a black man accused of raping a white woman in a small Alabama town during the 1930's. Atticus's courageous act brings the violence and injustice that exists in their world sharply into focus as it intrudes into the lighthearted life that Scout and her brother Jem have enjoyed until that time." Shapiro. Fic for Youth. 3d edition

Lee, J. M.

The **investigation**; a novel. J.M. Lee; translated by Chi-Young Kim. W W Norton & Co Inc 2015 325 p. $24.95

ISBN 1605988464; 9781605988467

This novel by J.M. Lee is set in "Fukuoka Prison, 1944. Watanbe Yuichi, a young guard with a passion for reading, is ordered to investigate a murder. The victim, Sugiyama, also a guard, was feared and despised throughout the prison and inquiries have barely begun when a powerful inmate confesses. But Watanbe is unconvinced; and as he interrogates both the suspect and Yun Dong-ju, a talented Korean poet, he starts to realize that the fearsome guard was not all he appeared to be." (Publisher's note)

"Based on the true story of one of Korea's most revered poets, Lee's U.S. debut is a breathtakingly beautiful novel that boasts a cerebral murder mystery and a rare look at the human impact of Japan's colonialism in Korea. David Guterson's Snow Falling on Cedars (1994) makes an excellent pairing, providing a contrasting but also beautifully portrayed exploration of the impact of Japan's role in WWII." Booklist

Lee, Janice Y. K.

The **piano** teacher. Viking 2009 336p $25.95

ISBN 978-0-670-02048-5

LC 2008-27449

"This cinematic tale of two love affairs in mid-century Hong Kong shows colonial pretensions tainted by wartime truths. Will Truesdale, a rootless, handsome Briton, arrives in the colony in 1941, and is swept up by Trudy Liang, the blithe and glamorous daughter of a Shanghai millionaire and a Portuguese beauty. They quickly become inseparable, their days spent in a whirl of parties and champagne, but when the Japanese invade, Will is interned and Trudy resorts to increasingly Faustian methods to survive. After the war, Claire Pendleton, the naïve wife of a British civil servant, arrives. She begins giving piano lessons to the daughter of a rich Chinese couple, and falls in love with their wounded and inscrutable driver: Will. Lee unfolds each story, and flits between them, with the brisk grace and discretion of the society she describes—a world in which horrors are adumbrated but seldom told." New Yorker

Lee, Krys

★ **Drifting** house; Krys Lee. Viking 2012 210 p.

ISBN 9780670023257

LC 2011036188

This book presents short stories "about the conflicts between Korean and American culture. [Krys] Lee tends to focus on domestic relationships, the tensions--sometimes unbridgeable--between husband and wife, between parent and child. In the opening story, 'A Temporary

Marriage,' Mrs. Shin saves money to travel from Seoul to southern California to find her daughter Yuri, who she feels has been 'kidnapped' and spirited away to America by her ex-husband." (Kirkus Reviews)

Lee, Marie G., 1964-

Somebody's daughter; Marie Myung-Ok Lee. Beacon Press 2005 x, 264 p.p (cloth : acid-free paper) o.p.; (pbk.) $16

ISBN 0807083887; 0807083895

LC 2004025757

This novel tells the "story of Sarah Thorson, who discovers the truth about her birth when she is nineteen. Sarah's story begins when she drops out of the University of Minnesota and, more by happenstance than design, decides to study in Korea. As the summer progresses, Sarah becomes more and more intrigued by her Korean heritage, eventually discovering the truth about her adoption: her birth mother did not die in a car crash. With the help of two remarkable men, Jun-Ho Kim, a Korean hoping to befriend Americans, and Doug Henderson, a Korean American struggling with his mixed heritage, Sarah embarks on a crusade to find her birth mother that leads her to a deepening involvement with the culture, language, and people of Korea." (Publisher's note)

Lee, Min Jin

Pachinko; Min Jin Lee. Grand Central Publishing 2017 496 p. (ebook) $81; (hardcover) $27

ISBN 9781455569656; 9781455563937

LC 2016023353

National Book Award Finalist: Fiction (2017)

In this book, by Min Jin Lee, "four generations of a poor, proud immigrant family fight to control their destinies, exiled from a homeland they never knew. . . . Sunja, the adored daughter of a crippled fisherman, falls for a wealthy stranger at the seashore near her home in Korea. He promises her the world, but when she discovers she is pregnant-and that her lover is married-she refuses to be bought. Instead, she accepts an offer of marriage from a gentle, sickly minister." (Publisher's note)

"Those who enjoy historical fiction with strong characterizations will not be disappointed as they ride along on the emotional journeys offered in the author's latest page-turner." LJ

Lee, Patrick

★ **Runner**; by Patrick Lee. Minotaur Books 2014 336 p. (A Sam Dryden Novel) (hardback) $24.99

ISBN 1250030730; 9781250030733

LC 2013032586

In this book, by Patrick Lee, "ex-soldier Sam Dryden is easing into a midnight run when a young girl darts from the shadows, fleeing a shadowy group of men following close behind. She's desperate but begs Sam to trust that she has a good reason not to go to the police. . . . Rachel's memory has been clouded by interrogation drugs, so she doesn't know exactly whom her pursuers are, but it's soon evident that their motives are connected to Rachel's powerful ability to read minds." (Booklist)

"Tension mounts right from the start in this nonstop action-packed narrative and seldom flags, as Lee . . . continually blurs the lines between the good guys and the bad guys." LJ

Another title in this series is:

Signal (2015)

Lee, Patrick

★ **Signal**; Patrick Lee. Minotaur Books 2015 320 p. (Sam Dryden novels) (hardcover) $25.99

ISBN 1250030781; 9781250030788

LC 2015016970

In this suspense novel by Patrick Lee, featuring the character Sam Dryden, "through their actions, Dryden and Calvert have unknowingly placed themselves in the cross-hairs of a frightening and dangerous enemy, the result of a generations-long conspiracy finally coming to fruition. What these people have is a technology that allows them to affect events before they even happen. How they are planning to use it, however, will result in the death of millions." (Publisher's note)

"A credible hero and a plot filled with nonstop cinematic action will leave thriller fans eager for the next installment." Pub Wkly

Lee, Yoon Ha

Ninefox gambit; by Yoon Ha Lee. Pocket Books 2016 317 p. $9.99

ISBN 1781084491; 9781781084496

LC 2016023834

Nebula Award Nominee: Best Novel (2017)

Hugo Nominee: Best Novel (2017)

In this book, by Yoon Ha Lee, "Captain Kel Cheris of the hexarchate is disgraced for using unconventional methods in a battle against heretics. Kel Command gives her the opportunity to redeem herself by retaking the Fortress of Scattered Needles, a star fortress that has recently been captured by heretics. Cheris's career isn't the only thing at stake. If the fortress falls, the hexarchate itself might be next." (Publisher's note)

Other titles in this series are:

Raven stratagem (2017)

Revenant Gun (2018)

Lee, Yoon Ha

Raven Stratagem; Yoon Ha Lee. Solaris 2017 355 p. (Machineries of empire) (paperback) $9.99

ISBN 1781085374; 9781781085370

Sequel to: Ninefox Gambit (2016)

Hugo Finalist: Best Novel (2018)

In this book, by Yoon Ha Lee, "when the hexarchate's gifted young captain Kel Cheris summoned the ghost of the long-dead General Shuos Jedao to help her put down a rebellion, she didn't reckon on his breaking free of centuries of imprisonment—and possessing her. Even worse, the enemy Hafn are invading, and Jedao takes over General Kel Khiruev's fleet, which was tasked with stopping them." (Publisher's note)

"This follow up to the Nebula- and Hugo-nominated Ninefox Gambit combines exciting space opera action with dazzling, imaginative worldbuilding." LJ

Lehane, Dennis

The **given** day; a novel. William Morrow 2008 704p $27.95

ISBN 978-0-688-16318-1; 0-688-16318-1

LC 2008-35137

This novel is set at the "end of the First World War, as waves of immigration, uneasy race relations, and agitation over labor issues culminate in a police strike in Boston. Danny, a patrolman and the son of a powerful captain, pursues a pair of anarchists determined to create chaos but also finds himself drawn to the growing police union; Luther, a talented black baseball player, flees to Boston after killing a drug lord in Tulsa. Lehane laces his narrative with melodrama—two brothers in love with the same woman, who harbors a secret past; a viciously racist cop out to destroy Luther and frame the burgeoning N.A.A.C.P.—and a subplot, involving Babe Ruth, feels stale and unnecessary. But he brings vividly to life the struggles that the working classes faced in pursuit of decent working conditions and a fair wage." New Yorker

Lehane, Dennis ✓

★ **Live** by night; Dennis Lehane. William Morrow 2012 401 p.

ISBN 0060004878; 9780060004873

LC 2012462328

This novel by Dennis Lehane tells the story of "Joe Coughlin, . . . [who has] graduated from a childhood of petty theft to a career in the pay of [Boston's]most fearsome mobsters. . . . Joe embarks on a dizzying journey up the ladder of organized crime that takes him from the flash of Jazz Age Boston to the sensual shimmer of Tampa's Latin Quarter to the sizzling streets of Cuba." (Publisher's note)

Lehane, Dennis ✓

★ **Mystic** river. Morrow 2001 401p il $25

ISBN 0-688-16316-5

LC 2001-273012

"Lehane identifies that turning point in the life and spiritual death of a working-class Boston neighborhood as the day in 1975 when 11-year-old Dave Boyle climbed into a car with two strange men—and his best friends, Sean Devine and Jimmy Marcus, did not. A quarter-century later, when the murder of Jimmy's 19-year-old daughter forces the three of them into a heart-scorching reunion, they still carry the scars of that childhood trauma. 'Maybe they had gotten in that car. All three of them,' Sean thinks. 'And what they now thought of as their life was just a dream state.' Lehane spares nothing in his wrenching descriptions of how a crime in the neighborhood kills the neighborhood, taking it down house by house, family by family." N Y Times Book Rev

Lehane, Dennis ✓

Prayers for rain; a novel. Morrow 1999 337p $25

ISBN 0-688-15333-X

LC 99-22048

"In what he thinks is an open-and-shut case, Boston private investigator Patrick Kenzie and his sidekick Bubba Rowgoski convince Cody Falk, a stalker with a nasty record of rape and sexual assault, to cease his harassment of Patrick's client, Karen Nichols. But six months later, a naked Karen leaps to her death off the observation deck of the Custom House tower. . . . Aided by Bubba and ex-partner/ex-lover Angie Gennaro, Patrick decides to investigate Karen's death. . . . Lehane's love of Boston, its neighborhoods, and its people shines through his hard-edged prose." Libr J

Lehane, Dennis ✓

Sacred. Morrow 1997 288p

ISBN 0-688-14381-4

LC 96-53115

"When detectives Patrick Kenzie and Angela Gennaro are kidnapped by dying billionaire Trevor Stone and forced to find his lost daughter, they become entwined in a vicious whodunit in which 'up is down and north is south.' The case takes them to Grief Release Inc., a Boston-area church/cult whose members purge their sins, secrets, and financial records; then, accompanied by Stone's henchmen, to Tampa, Florida, where a top-of-the-line sports car and all the money they can spend are put at their disposal. . . . When the detectives finally find their prize, the perfecto, leggy Desiree Stone, she turns out to be much more than they bargained for." Libr J

Lehane, Dennis ✓

Shutter Island. Morrow 2003 325p $25.95

ISBN 0-688-16317-3

LC 2003-48744

"From the 1993 perspective of the prologue, Shutter Island is one of those unpopulated islands in Boston's outer harbor that always look so mysterious from a distance and so scruffy up close. But in 1954, when the United States marshall Teddy Daniels and his partner, Chuck Aule, alight on its rocky shores to hunt for an escaped murderess, this bleak spot is home to Ashecliffe Hospital, a maximum-security institution for the criminally insane. . . . The atmosphere is properly dark and moody, and so long as Teddy and Chuck stick to the manhunt and their investigation of Ashecliffe's creepy medical staff, they play their roles with muscle and grace." N Y Times Book Rev

Lehane, Dennis ✓

Since we fell; a novel. Dennis Lehane. First edition HarperCollins 2017 418 p. $27.99

ISBN 0062129384; 9780062129383

LC bl2017011981

This novel, by Dennis Lehane, "follows Rachel Childs, a former journalist who, after an on-air mental breakdown, now lives as a virtual shut-in. In all other respects, however, she enjoys an ideal life with an ideal husband. Until a chance encounter on a rainy afternoon causes that ideal life to fray. . . . Sucked into a conspiracy thick with deception, violence, and possibly madness, Rachel must find the strength . . . to conquer unimaginable fears and mind-altering truths." (Publisher's note)

"He produces one of crime fiction's most exciting and well-orchestrated finales-rife with dramatic tension and buttressed by rich psychological interplay between the characters." Booklist

Lehane, Dennis ✓

★ **World** gone by; a novel. Dennis Lehane. 1st edition William Morrow 2015 416 p. (hardcover) $27.99

ISBN 0060004908; 9780060004903; 9780062351814

LC 2014027026

Sequel to: Live By Night (2012)

"Ten years have passed since Joe Coughlin's enemies killed his wife and destroyed his empire, and much has changed. Prohibition is dead, the world is at war again, and Joe's son, Tomás, is growing up. Now, the former crime kingpin works as a consigliore to the Bartolo crime family, traveling between Tampa and Cuba, his wife's homeland. . . . He has everything--money, power, a beautiful mistress, and anonymity. But success cannot protect him from the dark truth of his past." (Publisher's note)

"A multilayered, morally ambiguous novel of family, blood and betrayal." Kirkus

Lehmann, Stephanie

Astor Place Vintage; Stephanie Lehmann. Simon & Schuster 2013 416 p. (paperback) $16

ISBN 1451682050; 9781451682052; 9781451682069

LC 2012031168

This novel "tells the stories of two New York women a century apart." The "present-day timeline involves Amanda Rosenbloom, who owns the eponymous Astor Place Vintage clothing store and has a strong attachment to the past. . . . Amanda discovers the 1907 diary of Olive Westcott, an upper-class woman who dreamed of becoming a department store buyer. The story switches to the past, with Olive, after her father's death, facing widespread prejudices" against women working. (Publishers Weekly)

Lehrer, Jim

The **special** prisoner; a novel. Random House 2000 227p

ISBN 0-375-50371-4

LC 00-701284

"A chance airport encounter sends retired Methodist bishop John Quincy Watson to San Diego, following a man whose too-familiar eyes drag Watson 50 years into the past, to a Japanese prisoner of war camp, where the then youthful, red-haired B29 pilot became a 'special prisoner' when captured after parachuting from his dying plane. His pursuit of the interrogator he knew as Tashimoto, the Hyena, alternates with the minister's memories of the horrors of Camp Sengei 4." Booklist

Leigh, Eva

Forever Your Earl; Eva Leigh. HarperCollins 2015 384 p. (The wicked quills of London) $7.99

ISBN 0062358626; 9780062358622

In this novel, by Eva Leigh, "Eleanor Hawke loves a good scandal. And readers of her successful gossip rag live for the exploits of her favorite subject: Daniel Balfour, the notorious Earl of Ashford. So when the earl himself marches into her office and invites her to experience his illicit pursuits firsthand, Eleanor is stunned. Daniel has secrets, and if 'The Hawk's Eye' gets wind of them, a man's life could be at stake. But . . . their desire for each other threatens even his best-laid plans." (Publisher's note)

"Leigh (the pseudonym of best-selling romance author Zoe Archer) launches the Wicked Quills of London series on a high note with this fabulously fun Regency-set historical that superbly showcases the author's flair for mixing sharp wit and sexy romance." Booklist

Leigh, Eva

Temptations of a Wallflower; by Eva Leigh. HarperCollins 2016 384 p. (The wicked quills of London) (ebook) $7.99; $7.99

ISBN 9780062358677; 0062358669; 9780062358660

LC 2016017516

In this book, by Eva Leigh, "she's known as the Watching Wallflower-shy, quiet, and certainly never scandalous. Yet beneath Lady Sarah Frampton's demure façade hides the mind of The Lady of Dubious Quality, author of the most titillating erotic fiction the ton has ever seen. Sarah knows discovery would lead to her ruin, but marriage—to a vicar, no less—could help protect her from slander." (Publisher's note)

"Leigh's latest is a thoughtful and sensuous romance." Pub Wkly

Leimbach, Marti

Daniel isn't talking. Nan A. Talese 2006 275p $22.95

ISBN 0-385-51751-3

LC 2005-52890

"Watching a handicapped child rend the fragile seams of a woman's personality and her marriage exposes us to some of the more honest and guilty realities of being a parent, and with it a mother's very human pursuit of a livable, if not perfect, ending." N Y Times Book Rev

Leimbach, Marti

The **man** from Saigon; a novel. Nan A. Talese/Doubleday 2010 342p $25.95

ISBN 978-0385-52986-0; 0-385-52986-4

LC 2009-30332

First published 2009 in the United Kingdom

"Sent by a women's magazine to find human-interest stories in 1967 Saigon, journalist Susan Gifford forms a fateful alliance with Son, a Vietnamese photographer. Traveling with U.S. troops, Gifford and Son survive an ambush only to be captured by the Vietcong. What follows is harrowing, as Leimbach vividly recreates the chemical strafing of the countryside, the misery of the refugee camps and the suffocating humidity of the jungle. This impressive novel finds a new way of illuminating the horrors of an old war." People

Leine, Kim

The **prophets** of eternal fjord; Kim Leine ; translated from the Danish by Martin Aitken. Liveright Publishing Corp 2015 576 p. (hardcover) $29.95

ISBN 0871406713; 9780871406712

LC 2015013260

In this novel by Kim Leine "Morten Falck . . . is a newly ordained priest sailing to Greenland in 1787 to convert the Inuit to the Danish church. He's . . . departs for the forsaken Sukkertoppen colony, where he will endeavor to convert the locals. A town battered by unremittingly harsh winters and simmering with the threat of dissent, it is a far cry from the parish he envisioned; natives from neighboring villages have unified to reject colonial rule and establish their own settlement atop Eternal Fjord." (Publisher's note)

"Epic in sweep and noteworthy for its large cast of skillfully drawn characters, this is a lush, brave book about idealism and faith." LJ

Leithauser, Brad

The **art** student's war. Alfred A. Knopf 2009 495p il $28.95

ISBN 978-0-307-27111-2; 0-307-27111-0

LC 2009-19468

This novel "is, at its core, a traditional American wartime love story. As such, it is timely and engrossing." Boston Globe

Lelic, Simon

The **child** who; a novel. Simon Lelic. Penguin Books 2012 303 p.

ISBN 0143120913; 9780143120919

LC 2011045210

In this book, "Felicity was a bright, bouncy, much-liked preteen. Adults doted on her, schoolmates clustered around her, and her future seemed unlimited--until Daniel Blake, barely a year older, assaulted her, tortured her, bound her hands with wire and left her to drown. County solicitor Leo Curtice happens to answer the phone call requesting representation for Daniel. From the moment he agrees, his life spirals out of control. . . . Leo needs to understand why Daniel became Daniel. The boy has nothing to say. . . . But Leo keeps asking why: why did this happen, what's in Daniel's past? When menacing letters arrive threatening Leo's family, he downplays the danger. . . . Then Leo's daughter goes missing, and he and his wife suffer the anguish of Felicity's family." (Kirkus)

Lelic, Simon

The **facility**; [a novel] Simon Lelic. Penguin Books 2011 339 p. (paperback) $15.00

ISBN 0143120689; 9780143120681

LC 2012023398

In this novel, by Simon Lelic, set "[i]n a near-future dystopian Britain, . . . [e]mboldened by new anti-terrorism laws, police start to 'disappear' people from the streets. . . . But when . . . Arthur Priestley is . . . held prisoner at a top-secret facility, his estranged wife, Julia, and a brave but naive journalist named Tom Clarke embark on a harrowing quest for the truth. Following a trail that leads to the very top of government, they soon find themselves fighting for their lives." (Publisher's note)

Lem, Stanislaw

★ **Eden**; translated by Marc E. Heine. Harcourt Brace Jovanovich 1989 262p

LC 89-1963

"No one writes sf more intellectually challenging or of greater literary distinction than Lem." Booklist

Lem, Stanislaw

★ **Fiasco**; translated from the Polish by Michael Kandel. Harcourt Brace Jovanovich 1987 322p

LC 86-31816

Original Polish edition, 1986

"The crew's dense, challenging discussions—of physics, philosophy, military tactics, morality, cybernetics, psychology, game theory, etc.—are punctuated by bursts of action whose initial release only serves to increase the tension, as new data disproves old theses and one fiasco follows another. Brilliant and demanding, this is one of Lem's best novels, putting the reader through an intellectual and emotional wringer." Publ Wkly

Lem, Stanislaw

His Master's Voice; translated from the Polish by Michael Kandel. Harcourt Brace Jovanovich 1983 199p

LC 82-15765

Original Polish edition, 1968

"A stream of 'signals' from outer space is the subject of various attempted decodings and an excuse for all kinds of wild hypotheses about who might have sent the message and why, in which are reflected various human hopes and fears. Good satire." Anatomy of Wonder 4

Lem, Stanislaw

★ **Solaris**; translated from the French by Joanna Kilmartin and Steve Cox; afterword by Darko Suvin. Walker & Co. 1970 216p

LC 75-123267

Original Polish edition, 1962

"This novel combines profound philosophic speculation with the structure of action-adventure SF, embodied in a clear, vivid writing style that somehow survived two translations. A planet under study by Earth scientists is swathed in a world-girdling ocean, which the scientists conclude is sentient. For unknown reasons, the ocean 'reads' the deepest memories of the four men and sends each a double of a woman in his past. The mysterious world-ocean, constantly flinging up strange shapes that defy the savants' efforts at classification, may be the first, infantile phase of an emerging 'imperfect God.' A major work by any measure." Anatomy of Wonder 5

Lemaitre, Pierre

★ **Irene**; Pierre Lemaitre ; translated by Frank Wynne. MacLehose Press 2014 416 p. (The Commandant Camille Verhoeven Trilogy) (hardcover) $26.99

ISBN 1623658004; 9781623658007

LC 2014951595

In this novel by Pierre Lemaitre "Camille Verhoeven . . . has reached an unusually content (for him) place in life. But when a new murder case hits his desk . . . Verhoeven is overcome with a sense of foreboding. As links emerge between the bloody set-piece and at least one past unsolved murder, it becomes clear that a calculating serial killer is at work. Then Verhoeven makes a breakthrough discovery: the murders are modeled after the exploits of serial killers from classic works of crime fiction." (Publisher's note)

"Verhoeven is a one-of-a-kind detective, and Lemaitre does an excellent job surrounding him with characters who demand their share of the limelight." Booklist

Lennon, J. Robert

Castle; a novel. Graywolf Press 2009 229p $22

ISBN 978-1-55597-522-7; 1-55597-522-4

LC 2008-935603

"Like two other powerful novels of recent years—James Lasdun's Horned Man and Peter Cameron's Andorra—Castle is told by an egomaniacal, unlikable man with a precarious grasp on reality, especially his own. . . . Castle tells a terrific story, dire and confusing and convincing." N Y Times Book Rev

Lennon, J. Robert

Familiar; J. Robert Lennon. Farrar Straus & Giroux 2012 224 p. $15.00

ISBN 1555976255; 9781555976255

LC 2012936386

Author J. Robert Lennon tells the story of "a parallel universe. At some random midtrip interval, with Elisa wending her way homeward from her annual pilgrimage to the grave of her son, Silas, dead in an auto accident at age 15, she morphs into a different version of the same person. No longer a spare, contained woman . . . Elisa becomes more voluptuous . . . [and] on her way home from a professional conference. And Silas isn't dead, which she'll soon learn. But there is this: All that has been a barrier to peace and contentment remains." (Kirkus)

Lent, Jeffrey

Lost nation. Atlantic Monthly Press 2002 370p $25

ISBN 0-87113-843-3

LC 2001-56495

"In 1838, a man called Blood opens a tavern and one-girl brothel in an ungoverned area on the New Hampshire—Canada border. His prostitute, Sally, is a teenager he won in a game of cards. While the territory is already home to a number of society's escapees, Blood's presence introduces a new volatility. Blood and Sally's relationship grows in unpredictable ways, the law threatens to descend, and Blood's secret past returns in a surprising manner. . . . The author has tremendous literary gifts: a fine ear for speech, a keen eye for period detail, the ability to craft a well-turned phrase and create rich interior lives for his characters." Booklist

Lent, Jeffrey

A **slant** of light; a novel. Jeffrey Lent. Bloomsbury USA 2015 368 p. (hardcover : acid-free paper) $27

ISBN 1620404966; 9781620404966

LC 2014021632

In this book by Jeffrey Lent, "at the close of the Civil War, weary veteran Malcolm Hopeton returns to his home in western New York State to find his wife and hired man missing and his farm in disrepair. A double murder ensues, the repercussions of which ripple through a community with spiritual roots in the Second Great Awakening." (Publisher's note)

"There's an overabundance of detail on farming, but many sentences demand rereading for their sheer beauty, and each love story—some tragic, others newly born—has a poignant emotional charge. Lent offers eloquent insight into what makes his characters tick, yet enough unknowns remain to keep the novel unpredictable through the final pages." Booklist

Leon, Donna ✓

About face. Atlantic Monthly Press 2009 278p $24

ISBN 978-0-8021-1896-7; 0-8021-1896-8

LC 2009-12211

"It would be easy to punch holes in a contrived subplot, thick with symbolism, about a beautiful young woman whose face was ruined by cosmetic surgery. But who would want to, when Leon is being so generous with the humanizing details that make this series special? There are long walks in Brunetti's warm company and lively talks with his clever wife and even more engaging father-inlaw. . . . As detective work goes, it's a tiny masterpiece of analysis." N Y Times Book Rev

Leon, Donna

✓**Beastly** Things; Donna Leon. Atlantic Monthly 304 p.
ISBN 9780802120236

This detective novel, a volume of the Guido Brunetti series, offers a "tale of the murder of a quiet veterinarian. . . . One painfully human mistake, a simple act of hubris, draws an ordinary man into an inescapable trap that leaves him dead in a Venetian canal, carrying no identification and wearing only one shoe. Gradually, Commissario Brunetti and his colleague Inspector Vianello follow the trail to the town of Mestre, on the mainland near Venice, and to a slaughterhouse, where the animals that provide the meat which adorns the plates of the finest Venetian restaurants (and Brunetti's own table) are killed and "dressed" in . . . [a] barbaric manner." (Booklist)

Leon, Donna

✓★ **Blood** from a stone; Donna Leon. Atlantic Monthly Press 2005 276p. o.p.; (pbk.) $14.95; (hbk.) o.p.
ISBN 0871138875; 9780143117094; 9780871138873

LC 2005040961

This crime novel "brings Commissario Brunetti . . . [to] the [crime] scene: On a cold Venetian night shortly before Christmas, a street vendor is killed in a scuffle in Campo Santo Stefano. The closest witnesses to the event are the American tourists who had been browsing the man's wares . . . before his death. The dead man had been working as a 'vu cumpra,' one of the many African immigrants peddling goods outside normal shop hours and trading without work permits. . . . Because these workers have few social connections and little money, infighting seems to be the answer. And yet the killings have all the markings of a professional operation. Once Brunetti begins to investigate, . . . he discovers that matters of great value are at stake within the secretive society." (Publisher's note)

Leon, Donna

✓ **Drawing** conclusions. Atlantic Monthly 2011 260p $24
ISBN 978-0-8021-1979-7; 0-8021-1979-4

This installment "epitomizes what we treasure most about this series: a feeling for the life of a sublimely beautiful city and a sensitivity to the forces that are reshaping it. Not to mention the pleasure of being in Brunetti's company when this shrewd but scrupulously honest man is having a crisis of ethics at the flower market or trying to pry information from a hostile nun." N Y Times Book Rev

Leon, Donna

✓ **Falling** in Love; A Commissario Guido Brunetti Mystery. by Donna Leon. Atlantic Monthly Press 2015 256 p. map $26
ISBN 0802123538; 9780802123534

In this suspense novel, by Donna Leon, a sequel to "Death at La Fenice," "when a talented young Venetian singer who has caught Flavia's attention is savagely attacked, Brunetti begins to think that Flavia's fears are justified in ways neither of them imagined. He must enter in the psyche of an obsessive fan before Flavia, or anyone else, comes to harm." (Publisher's note)

"This is a dark novel with an ironic title that resonates on multiple levels. In particular, it explores the nature of love—and hate—in a manner that will haunt readers well after they have finished the book. Another provocative addition to a fine series, certain to appeal to aficionados of profound literary mysteries such as Louise Penny's How the Light Gets In." LJ

Leon, Donna

✓ The **girl** of his dreams. Atlantic Monthly Press 2008 276p $24
ISBN 978-0-87113-980-1; 0-87113-980-4

"Political reality prevails over justice, and a child's death goes unpunished despite the best efforts of Commissario Guido Brunetti in Leon's . . . Venetian mystery. When 11-year-old Ariana Rocich drowns in a canal and goes unidentified for days, she begins to haunt Brunetti's dreams. But Ariana is a Rom, or gypsy, found with stolen jewelry items secreted in and on her person, a discovery that makes Brunetti's investigation particularly sensitive in the face of new departmental directives regarding multicultural issues. The book opens with the funeral of Brunetti's mother before segueing into a subplot about a religious charlatan; so religion, as well as politics, becomes a topic around the family table for Brunetti, wife Paola, daughter Chiara, and son Raffi." Libr J

Leon, Donna

✓The **Golden** Egg. Pgw 2013 256 p. (hardcover) $26
ISBN 0802121012; 9780802121011

In this, the 22nd entry in Donna Leon's Guido Brunetti mystery series, Commissario Guido Brunetti "investigates the suspicious death of a disabled man, Davide Cavanella. . . . Davide's mother is unwilling to discuss his death. Worse, there's no official evidence of Davide's existence: he apparently was never born and never went to school, saw a doctor, or received a passport. The colorful locals are uncooperative." (Publishers Weekly)

Leon, Donna

✓ A **question** of belief; a Commissario Guido Brunetti mystery. Donna Leon. Atlantic Monthly Press Distributed by Publishers Group West 2010 262 p. (Commissario Guido Brunetti mystery.)
ISBN 0802119425; 9780802119421

LC 2011281197

In this book, "[s]et during an oppressive Venetian August, [author Donna] Leon's . . . 19th Commisario Guido Brunetti mystery . . . presents Brunetti with two puzzles that impinge on his most intimate beliefs. Close associate Ispettore Vianello, who's worried about his elderly aunt's involvement with an astrologer, nudges Brunetti toward ruminations on the differences in male and female evidences of affection. Meanwhile, Toni Brusca, head of employment records at the Commune, who's perplexed by a female judge's erratic court case postponements, surprises Brunetti by implying that a woman could be more criminal than a man. Brunetti patiently untangles a sordid skein of desires warped, trusts abused, and loves distorted into depravity." (Publishers Weekly)

Leon, Donna

✓ **Uniform** justice. Atlantic Monthly Press 2003 259p $24
ISBN 0-87113-903-0

LC 2003-44326

"As a thinking man, Brunetti reads Cicero for moral direction, looks to his wife for doses of cynical realism and humbly consults his secretary, the terrifyingly efficient Signorina Elettra, on practical matters. But it is as a man of sensibility that this endearing detective most engages us." N Y Times Book Rev

Leonard, Elmore

★ **Be** cool. Delacorte Press 1999 292p
ISBN 0-385-33391-9

LC 98-36601

Sequel to Get Shorty

"Aside from the wit, the fun and the colorful figures that populate Elmore Leonard's novels, the real magic of his work is in the language. . . . This is Elmore Leonard at his best, the sweeping synaptic prose effortlessly echoing the argot of the gutter." N Y Times Book Rev

Leonard, Elmore

Charlie Martz and other stories; the unpublished stories. Elmore Leonard. William Morrow 2015 256 p. (hardcover) $25.99

ISBN 0062364928; 0062364936; 9780062364920; 9780062364937

LC 2015008625

This book, by Elmore Leonard, offers "a collection of fifteen [crime] stories, eleven of which have never been previously published. . . . Marked by his unmistakable grit and humor, the stories . . . reveal a writer in transition, exploring new voices and locations, from the bars of small-town New Mexico and Michigan to a film set in Hollywood, a hotel in Southern Spain, even a military base in Kuala Lumpur." (Publisher's note)

"[T]his posthumous collection showcases the early writing of the author of westerns and crime stories, revealing his particular genius in embryonic, pulpish form." Pub Wkly

Leonard, Elmore

★ The **complete** Western stories of Elmore Leonard. William Morrow 2004 528p $27.95

ISBN 0-06-072425-0

LC 2004-55969

Leonard, Elmore

Djibouti. William Morrow 2010 279p $26.99

ISBN 978-0-06-173517-2; 0-06-173517-5

LC 2010-02111

"Leonard, as his many readers will attest, writes a wonderfully effective straightforward sentence that pushes the drama along. But the heart of this deliciously made novel — which is, geographically a stretch for the usually U.S.-bound novelist — comes in the dialogue." San Francisco Chron

Leonard, Elmore

Freaky Deaky. Arbor House 1988 341p

LC 87-19466

Leonard "excels here with his trademark menace and his deadpan, throwaway humor. His superlative ear for the vernacular makes all the characters spring to life; Woody, 'always in low with his dims on,' is a brilliant creation." Publ Wkly

Leonard, Elmore

★ **Get** Shorty. Delacorte Press 1990 292p

LC 89-25816

"Leonard's strongest books make you stand up and sit down a lot during their tight moments, but 'Get Shorty,' despite its occasional white-knuckle passages, belongs to that vast vinegary canon known as the Hollywood novel. . . . Best of all is the portrait Leonard gives us of a seven-million-dollar-a-picture star named Michael Weir." New Yorker

Followed by Be cool

Leonard, Elmore

Glitz. Arbor House 1985 228p

LC 84-16794

"There is a steady flow of intrigue and action set just outside the law in a world both dirty and glamorous. Several characters develop into complex personalities, but Mora is never quite clear." Libr J

Leonard, Elmore

The **hot** kid. William Morrow 2005 312p $25.95

ISBN 00-6072422-6

"Where so much of Leonard's recent fiction has a sharp, almost hyperrealistic quality, 'The Hot Kid' is noirish and even a little pulpy at times, in the fashion of 30's movies and detective magazines. . . . Tony Antonelli isn't a portrait of the artist as young man, exactly, but rather a fond wink at the tradition of potboilers and genre writing that gave rise to Leonard himself and from which, for all his success, he has never cut himself off." N Y Times Book Rev

Leonard, Elmore

★ **Killshot**. Arbor House 1989 287p

LC 88-31532

"Mr. Leonard has either done his homework or he's been there—up on the high beams in Detroit, on the Mississippi towing barges from Baton Rouge to Hickman, Ky., looking into the flat stare of an irritated cop, and somehow, improbably, inside the head of a woman who has had it with being treated like 'the wife.' 'Killshot' is pure, distilled, vintage Leonard." N Y Times Book Rev

Leonard, Elmore

LaBrava. Arbor House 1983 283p

ISBN 0-87795-527-1

LC 83-72676

"What makes the author's work memorable is his uncompromisingly direct prose, his affectionately crafted yet very real characters, and, of course, the fact that Leonard knows that providing entertainment is the novelist's first commandment. Nobody brings the illogic of crime and criminals to life better." Christ Sci Monit

Leonard, Elmore

Mr. Paradise. Morrow 2004 291p $25.95

ISBN 0-06-008395-6

LC 2003-64867

"Leonard addresses those who think they hear the same music he does, but who are open to questioning the familiar, to listening carefully and seeing when something has a different emphasis. . . . 'Mr. Paradise' is about deception. People deceive through false identity (appropriating, dissembling), just as they, themselves, have been deceived whether by the implied promise of collapsed dot-coms or by positive, false assumptions about family." N Y Times Book Rev

Leonard, Elmore

Pagan babies. Delacorte Press 2000 263p

ISBN 0-385-33392-7

LC 00-29506

This "is one of Mr. Leonard's funniest books, with a typically colourful cast of oddballs. The dialogue, too, is snappy. . . . Mr. Leonard steers the reader effortlessly through a maze of plots and counterplots, then brings the whole thing in with a bravura flourish and stops on a dime." Economist

Leonard, Elmore

★ **Raylan**; Elmore Leonard. William Morrow 2012 263 p.

ISBN 006211946X; 0062119478; 0062132326 (B&N ed.); 9780062119469; 9780062119476; 9780062132321 (B&N ed.)

LC 2011024392

In this novel, "Raylan Givens, the U.S. Marshal . . . is back in a series of three interlinked stories. . . . The first . . . of the stories complicates Raylan's apprehension of marijuana trader Angel Arenas with the discovery that the dealers with whom Angel was meeting left with his money, his grass and his kidneys, which they propose to sell back to him. . . . Their encounter ends with a sizable body count. . . . Raylan's second adventure pits him against Carol Conlan, a law-school-trained vice president of M-T Mining, whose skills in dealing with the problems that beset her employer extend far beyond the courtroom. . . . The villain of th[e] third piece, Delroy Lewis, forces three of his female acquaintances to rob banks and then gets mighty annoyed when one of them ends up with an exploding dye packet." (Kirkus)

Leonard, Elmore

Rum punch. Delacorte Press 1992 297p

ISBN 0-385-30143-X

LC 91-38738

"Mr. Leonard never tells you; he shows you. The story is all action, a scam within a scam. . . . His style is the absence of style, stripped of fancy baggage . . . the absence, as far as it's possible, of an authorial ego." NY Times Book Rev

Leonard, Elmore

Tishomingo blues; a novel. Morrow 2002 308p

ISBN 0-06-000872-5

LC 2001-44405

"Dennis Lenahan, an itinerant high diver setting up for a Mississippi casino show, watches a Dixie drug-ring murder from his eighty-foot diving platform. Various factions—a smooth-talking Detroit con man, a mob-backed explosives expert, redneck crank dealers, local police on either side of the law—try to badger or buy his silence or coöperation, but Lenahan stays cool and uncommitted, until a @Shane'-like showdown at a local Civil War re-enactment. Lenahan's composure and his easy acrobatics feel like a stand-in for the author's; both seem to play it by ear even after the guns start firing. And the hurtling plot twists keep coming, right up to the perfect rip of a finish." New Yorker

Leonard, Elmore

When the women come out to dance, and other stories. Morrow 2003 228p $24.95

ISBN 0-06-008397-2

LC 2002-26426

"Reading the clipped, unfailingly accurate dialogue that comes out of the mouths of Leonard's characters can make you feel as if you're in the presence of a writer who is both ventriloquist and psychic. It's not just that Leonard captures the cadences and elisions of each character's speech, it's that he has an uncanny sense of knowing what each will say next." N Y Times Book Rev

Lerner, Ben

★ **Leaving** the Atocha Station; a novel. Coffee House Press 2011 181p il pa $15

ISBN 978-1-56689-274-2; 1-56689-274-0

LC 2011-24105

The novel "has a beguiling mixture of lightness and weight. There are wonderful sentences and jokes on almost every page. Lerner is attempting to capture something that most conventional novels, with their cumbersome caravans of plot and scene and 'conflict,' fail to do: the drift of thought, the unmomentous passage of undramatic life." New Yorker

Leroy, Margaret

Postcards from Berlin; a novel. Little, Brown 2003 391p $22.95

ISBN 0-316-73813-1

LC 2003-40069

"The resolution of Leroy's novel has a fairy-tale aspect, but fairy tales can nevertheless be very absorbing. Despite the occasional straining of her plot, Leroy succeeded in making me care about these characters; even at my most incredulous." N Y Times Book Rev

Les Becquets, Diane

★ **Breaking** wild; Diane Les Becquets. Berkley Books 2016 320 p. (hardback) $26

ISBN 9780425283783; 042528378X

LC 2015015383

In this novel, by Diane Les Becquets, "when Amy Raye doesn't return to camp, ranger Pru Hathaway and her dog respond to the missing person's call. After an unexpected snowfall and few leads, the operation turns into a search and recovery. . . . The more she learns about the woman for whom she is searching, and about Amy Raye's past, the more she suspects that Amy Raye might yet be alive." (Publisher's note)

"The reimagining of a romantic West through the experiences of two strong women both challenges the dominant stereotype of 'cowboy country' and simultaneously offers the comment that gender has no place when it comes to matters of survival." Kirkus

Lescroart, John T.

The **first** law; a novel. by John Lescroart. Dutton 2003 403p $25.95

ISBN 0-525-94705-1

LC 2002-37902

"The popular lawyer-cop team of Dismas 'Diz' Hardy (lawyer) and Abe Glitzky (cop) returns for another episode of legal maneuvering on the streets of San Francisco. The bullet wound sustained by Abe in Lescroart's last adventure. . . confines him to a desk job, so he's no help to Diz when he goes up against the Patrol Special, a private-enterprise neighborhood security system supervised by the SFPD. It seems that Diz's good friend, John Holliday, a bar owner in one of the patrolled areas, is fingered as a murder suspect; however, John contends the corrupt beat 'cops' framed him. . . . Lescroart's expert crafting turns this legal thriller into quite a wild ride." Booklist

Lescroart, John T.

Guilt; [by] John Lescroart. Delacorte Press 1997 462p

ISBN 0-385-31655-0

LC 96-43756

"Lescroart effectively dramatizes the many moral dilemmas that emerge in this case, not the least of which is posed by the role of the Catholic Church." Booklist

Lescroart, John T.

The **hearing**; {by} John Lescroart. Dutton 2001 451p $25.95

ISBN 0-525-94575-X

LC 00-34119

In this legal thriller "attorney Dismas Hardy not only defends confessed murderer Cole Burgess but is forced to confront the fallibility of his friend, Abe Glitsky, chief of the San Francis Police Department's homicide division. Burgess, a heroin addict, is found near the lifeless body of a prominent female attorney, unable to remember the events that brought him there. Lescroart tantalizes readers with a tightly constructed plot in which Hardy and Glitsky track crime and political corruption to an unexpected source." Libr J

Lescroart, John T.

Nothing but the truth; [by] John Lescroart. Delacorte Press 1999 435p

ISBN 0-385-33353-6

LC 99-32584

"Lescroart orchestrates a cadre of multi-dimensional characters through a plot full of political subterfuge and action without losing track of the subtlety of modern personal relationships." Libr J

Lescroart, John T.

The **oath**; [by] John Lescroart. Dutton 2002 408p

ISBN 0-525-94576-8

LC 2001-47055

San Francisco attorney Dismas Hardy "finds himself representing Dr. Eric Kensing, who stands accused of murdering his boss, Tim Markham, the CEO of the Parnassus Medical Group, a struggling HMO providing health services to all the city's employees. An autopsy shows that Markham, hospitalized in critical condition following a hit-and-run, died not of his injuries but of a potassium overdose. . . . The author wisely steers clear of taking cheap shots at the HMO industry, yet manages to direct a sharp beam into some of its darker crevices." Publ Wkly

Leshem, Ron

Beaufort; translated from the Hebrew by Evan Fallenberg. Delacorte Press 2008 360p $24

ISBN 978-0-553-80682-3

LC 2007-30292

Original Hebrew edition, 2006

"In order to limit Hezbollah's attacks on Israeli settlements, Israel maintained a security force in southern Lebanon for close to 20 years. Leshem's . . . novel chronicles the lives of the last group of Israeli soldiers to man the outpost at Beaufort, a crusader-castle ruin of questionable military significance. Written as the diary of Liraz 'Erez' Liberti, the hotheaded twentysomething leader of a 13-man commando unit stationed in an outpost prior to the Israeli withdrawal in 2000, the novel brings to life the situation of very young men on a dangerous mission. This is a picture of war from a soldier's point of view. Its language is crude, the body count rises, and yet the tenderness of the bonds among the men is extraordinary." Libr J

Leskov, N. S. (Nikolai Semenovich), 1831-1895

The **enchanted** wanderer and other stories; by Nikolai Leskov ; translated by Richard Pevear and Larissa Volokhonsky. Alfred A. Knopf 2013 608 p. (hardcover) $35

ISBN 0307268829; 9780307268822

LC 2012025416

This book is a new translation of several short stories by Nikolai Leskov. The stories gathered here are "all lightly linked in the way that those of the 'Canterbury Tales' are." The "opener is a stern study in the dangers of adultery; then come other pieces set in 'Wooden Russia,' the old heartland south of Moscow, with all its elaborate prejudices against Gypsies, Jews, Ukrainians and the other outsiders who so often figure in Leskov's pages." (Kirkus Reviews)

Includes bibliographical references

Lessing, Doris May

African stories; {by} Doris Lessing. Simon & Schuster 1965 636p hardcover o.p.

A collection of "tales which taken together reflect myriad aspects of African existence. Vivid personality delineation, narrative integrity, and artistry dominate each story whatever its subject or theme." Booklist

Lessing, Doris May

Children of violence; [by] Doris Lessing. v1-5

v1-4 published by Simon & Schuster; v5 published 1969 by Knopf with title: The four-gated city

This "is an account of the life of Martha Quest and of her search for self-definition, which for her is to be achieved through total commitment to a person or a cause. We follow her from her beginnings as a wayward but intelligent child on a Rhodesian farm, through two unsuccessful marriages and active involvement in the Communist party in Salisbury during World War II. After the war Martha goes to London and becomes an increasingly disenchanted observer of London life and behavior in the 1950s; the last volume of the sequence anticipates an apocalyptic, science-fiction future, as Martha dies in a devastated, radioactive world at the end of the twentieth century." Wakeman. World Authors, 1950-1970

Lessing, Doris May

★ The **fifth** child; [by] Doris Lessing. Knopf 1988 133p

ISBN 0-394-57105-3

LC 88-2680

"Acting as a social moralist, Lessing exposes the division between the warm and comfortable domestic scene and the harsh reality of the outside world, piercing the boundary between the two as human desires clash with a more brutal vision of existence. A psychologically probing and emotionally powerful performance." Booklist

Followed by Ben, in the world

Lessing, Doris May

★ The **golden** notebook; [by] Doris Lessing. Simon & Schuster 1962 567p

"Regarded as one of the key texts of the Women's movement of the 1960s, it opens in London in 1957 with a section ironically entitled 'Free Women', a realistic account of a conversation between two old friends, writer Anna Wulf, mother of Janet, and Molly, divorced from Richard, and mother of disturbed son Tommy, who will later attempt suicide. The novel then fragments into the four sections of Anna's 'Notebooks.' . . . This pattern of five non chronological overlapping sections is repeated four times, as it tracks both the past and the present, and although one of Lessing's concerns is to expose the dangers of fragmentation, she also builds up through pastiche and parody, and through many refractions and mergings, a remarkably coherent and detailed account of her protagonists and the world they inhabit." Oxford Companion to Engl Lit. 6th edition

Lessing, Doris May

The **good** terrorist; {by} Doris Lessing. Knopf 1985 375p

LC 85-40214

"Unsparingly, fiercely, often satirically, Lessing is writing a narrative about death: the death of the heart when ideology tyrannizes over just, kindly human relations, abstractions over common sense." Ms

Lessing, Doris May

The **grass** is singing; [by]Doris Lessing. Crowell 1950 245p

The novel begins with the newspaper notice of the death of Mary Turner, wife of an unsuccessful South African farmer. There seems to be some reluctance among the other whites about discussing the case. The author then turns back to the story of Mary Turner's life, showing her gradual disintegration as a person, and ending with her murder by a Kaffir houseboy

This novel "besides being very well-written is an extremely mature psychological study. It is full of those terrifying touches of truth, seldom mentioned but instantly recognized. By any standards, this book shows remarkable powers and imagination." New Statesman (1913)

Lessing, Doris May

Love, again; a novel. {by} Doris Lessing. HarperCollins Pubs. 1996 352p

LC 95-53317

"Sarah Durham was widowed young; now in her mid-60s, she is manager of and playwright for a London fringe theater group. A production of a play based on the journals and music of a 19th-century quadroon from Martinique, Julie Vairon, inflames Sarah's dormant sexual impulses. And she is not the only one: all of the actors, the director and a rich patron, Stephen Ellington-Smith, are also sublimely seduced by Julie's words, music and the few portraits of her that survive. . . . Although the book is long and rambling, asking much of a reader's patience and willingness to spend so much time inside Sarah's head, Lessing, wields a formidable analytic intelligence that makes this work provocative and often astonishingly beautiful." Publ Wkly

Lessing, Doris May

★ The **memoirs** of a survivor; [by] Doris Lessing. Knopf 1975 213p

First published 1974 in the United Kingdom

This is "an extraordinary and compelling meditation about the enduring need for loyalty, love and responsibility in an unprecedented time that places unbearable demands upon people." Time

Lessing, Doris May

★ **Shikasta**; re: colonised planet 5; personal, psychological, historical documents relating to visit by Johor (George Sherban) emissary (grade 9) 87th of the period of the last days. [by] Doris Lessing. Knopf 1979 364p (Canopus in Argos: archives)

LC 79-11295

"First of the Canopus in Argos: Archives five-volume series. Shikasta is Earth, whose history—extending over millions of years—is here put into the cosmic perspective, observed by Canopeans who seem to be in charge of galactic history although responsible to some higher, impersonal authority. The sequels follow the exploits of various human cultures whose affairs are subtly influenced by the Canopeans; all share the remotely detached perspective that transforms the way in which individual endeavors are seen. Thoughtful and painstaking." Anatomy of Wonder 4

Followed by The marriages between zones three, four, and five (1980); The Sirian experiments (1981); The making of the representative for Planet 8 (1982); Documents relating to the sentimental agents in the Volyen Empire (1983)

Lessing, Doris May

The **sweetest** dream; [by] Doris Lessing. HarperCollins Pubs. 2002 478p hardcover o.p. pa $13.95

ISBN 0-06-621334-7; 0-06-093755-6 pa

LC 2002-279950

"Lessing's understanding of relationships-both personal and political-has always been keen; now . . . it is unparalleled. This novel is warm and heartfelt, old-fashioned and ambitious in its historical sweep." New Statesman

Lester, Julius

Do Lord remember me; a novel. Holt & Co. 1985 210p

LC 84-3845

"Smith's memories link with those of older people in his past, whose stories take him back to slavery times. What emerges is a picture of black experience covering more than 150 years, with memory and storytelling providing continuity between present and past. A rich and moving reading experience." Booklist

Lethem, Jonathan

Chronic city. Doubleday 2009 467p $27.95

ISBN 978-0-385-51863-5; 0-385-51863-3

LC 2009-07587

"Lethem's vision of New York can approach the Swiftian. It is impressively observant in its detail and scourging in its mocking satire." Boston Globe

Lethem, Jonathan

★ **Dissident** Gardens. Random House Inc. 2013 384 p. (hardcover) $27.95

ISBN 0385534930; 9780385534932

This book "begins with the case of Rose Zimmer, in Queens, New York, who was officially ousted from the [American Communist] party in 1955 for sleeping with a black cop. Rose's daughter, Miriam, is a teenager at the time, and she soon discovers the pull of Greenwich Village bohemians. Rose's and Miriam's stories are interwoven, as the narrative moves back and forth in time." (Publishers Weekly)

"The cast makes for a heady, swirly mix of fascinating, lonely people. Lethem's writing, as always, packs a witty punch." Pub Wkly

Lethem, Jonathan

The **fortress** of solitude; a novel. Doubleday 2003 511p $26

ISBN 0-385-50069-6

LC 2003-43535

"Dylan Ebdus is a white kid on a black-and-brown street. As he struggles through public school in 1970s Brooklyn, he is 'yoked'-put in a headlock-and frisked for change on a daily basis. Testing into a good Manhattan school, he steps into a long-lasting role: vulnerable among street kids, he's street-smart compared to his new, privileged pals, and loathes himself as a poseur with both crowds. When he finds a ring that grants the power of flight, he's afraid to use it, but his black friend, Mingus, is not." Booklist

Lethem, Jonathan

Motherless Brooklyn. Doubleday 1999 311p

ISBN 0-385-49183-2

LC 99018194

In this novel, Lionel Essrog, a Brooklyn private detective with Tourette's syndrome, investigates the murder of his boss, Frank Minna.

"The short and shady life of Frank Minna ends in murder, shocking the four young men employed by his dysfunctional Brooklyn detective agency/limo service. The 'Minna Men' have centered their lives around Frank. . . . Tourette's-afflicted Lionel has found security as a Minna Man and is shattered by Frank's death. Lionel determines to become a genuine sleuth and find the killer. The ensuing plot twists are marked by clever wordplay, fast-paced dialog, and nonstop irony." Libr J

Letts, Billie

Shoot the moon; Billie Letts. Warner Books 2004 333p $24

ISBN 0-446-52900-1

LC 2004-3447

"No one in sleepy DeClare, Oklahoma, has forgotten the 1972 murder of pretty Cherokee Gaylene Harjo and the abduction of her infant son, Nicky Jack. Hard-nosed deputy sheriff Oliver 'O Boy' Daniels pinned the blame on local preacher Joe Dawson, but few in town believed the kindly Joe was capable of such an act. Powerful emotions resurface 30 years later, when Nicky Jack, adopted and raised by a rich couple in Beverly Hills, mysteriously reappears, determined to learn about his mother and the circumstances surrounding her death. . . . Letts peppers her prose with a cast of quirky characters." Booklist

Leung, Brian

World famous love acts; stories. Sarabande Books 2004 202p $14.95

ISBN 1-88933-016-7

LC 2003-11923

"As diverse as they are similar, Leung's characters and their conditions run the gamut from elderly widower to precocious youngsters, porn star to AIDS victim, serial killer to estranged sisters, and all are lucidly portrayed in prose that is achingly lyrical and elegantly refined." Booklist

Levack, Simon

Demon of the air; Simon Levack. Thomas Dunne Books/ St. Martin's Minotaur 2005 xiv, 296p maps o.p.; o.p.

ISBN 9780312348342; 0312348347

LC 2005043976

This book takes place in "Mexico, 1517. Emperor Montezuma rules the known world . . . [but he] is troubled. Mysterious strangers have appeared in the East. . . . The soothsayers he turns to for guidance give him only enigmatic answers, and he knows he cannot trust his advisers--especially his chief minister . . . Lord Feathered in Black. Yaotl, the chief minister's slave, is troubled, too. He was ordered to escort a sacrificial victim up the steps of the Great Pyramid, but the victim ran amok, uttering a bizarre and sinister prophecy and leaping to his death before the War-God's priests could cut out his heart. Then Yaotl learns that the emperor's soothsayers have vanished. The emperor senses a connection between these two events and orders Yaotl to find it." (Publisher's note)

Leveen, Lois

The **secrets** of Mary Bowser; a novel. Lois Leveen. William Morrow 2012 453 p. $15.99

ISBN 006210702X; 0062107909; 9780062107022; 9780062107909

LC 2011038111

This book follows "Mary . . . a slave. . . When [her master's daughter] decides to send Mary to Philadelphia to be educated, she must leave her family to seize her freedom. Life in the North brings . . . a far different education than Mary ever expected, one that leads her into the heart of the abolition movement. . . . Posing as a slave in the Confederate White House in order to spy on President Jefferson Davis, Mary deceives even those who are closest to her to aid the Union command." (Publisher's note)

"Deftly balancing history, romance and adventure, Leveen honors the life and historical importance of a brave, resourceful woman." Kirkus

Levi, Primo

If not now, when? translated from the Italian by William Weaver; introduction by Irving Howe. Summit Bks. 1985 349p

LC 85-2526

Original Italian edition, 1982

"The author, himself a victim of Nazi atrocities, has based his novel on true events. A band of Jewish partisans makes its way from Russia to Italy waging their personal war against the Nazis. They blow up trains, rescue concentration camp inmates, and face incredible dangers in their efforts to strike back against a ruthless, seemingly invincible enemy. The story is a testament to human endurance and courage." Shapiro. Fic for Youth. 3d edition

Levi, Primo

The **monkey's** wrench; translated from the Italian by William Weaver. Summit Bks. 1986 171p

LC 86-5803

Original Italian edition, 1978

"Among other things, The Monkey's Wrench is a model of the interplay between storytellers and listeners. For their part, readers can envy Levi's sixth sense about building bridges between what can be seen and what must be imagined." Time

Levien, David

City of the sun; a novel. Doubleday 2008 310p $24.95

ISBN 978-0-385-52366-0; 0-385-52366-1

LC 2007-28002

"While it deals with the practical mechanics of how a private detective tracks down a boy who has been missing for more than a year, this relentless novel is really about how parents suffer the loss of a child. As such, the story conveys a piercing sense of honesty, even when the investigation itself seems implausibly free of complications." N Y Times Book Rev

Levin, Ira

★ The **boys** from Brazil; a novel. Random House 1976 312p

"Ninety-four potential Hitlers are created through the technique of cloning by Dr. Mengele, infamous doctor of Auschwitz. Striving to recreate the early environment of the original Hitler, Mengele plots the murder of the fathers of these ninety-four children. Yakov Liebermann, a pursuer of Nazis, tries to stop the murders at the cost of great, almost mortal, danger to himself." Shapiro. Fic for Youth. 3d edition

Levin, Ira

A **kiss** before dying. Simon & Schuster 1953 244p

"The plot has to do with a remarkably ingenious, subtle, and relentless murderer, who does away with a pregnant college girl, goes on from there to kill her sister and a more or less innocent bystander, and is cheated of the fortune that has driven him to these desperate measures only by a couple of tiny oversights that might easily have escaped Sherlock Holmes. The book is a succession of solid and quite legitimate surprises, the suspense is admirably sustained, the detail is thorough and convincing, and the writing is considerably above the level usually associated with fictional crime and passion." New Yorker

Levin, Ira

★ **Rosemary's** baby; a novel. Random House 1967 245p

ISBN 9780451194008

LC 68136323

"Guy and Rosemary Woodhouse dismiss the warnings of friends and move into a luxurious Manhattan apartment building where, supposedly, rites of witchcraft and suicides have occurred. Rosemary's instincts warn her to beware of their neighbors, the Castevets, but her husband is not convinced and they become a dominant influence on Guy when Rosemary becomes pregnant. She is alone in her fear and becomes a helpless victim." Shapiro. Fic for Youth. 3d edition

Followed by: Son of Rosemary (1998)

Levin, Ira

The **Stepford** wives. Random House 1972 145p

ISBN 0-394-48199-2

"Attractive, talented Joanna moves with her husband and kids to a suburb, where she comes to suspect that the village housewives have all been murdered and replaced by robots, the suspected villain being a chauvinistic Men's Association . . . and so Joanna begins to fear for her life." Libr J

Levin, Meyer

Compulsion. Simon & Schuster 1956 495p

Using fictionalized names and probing deeply into the psychological aspects of the crime, this is a retelling of the Loeb-Leopold murder case

"The writing shows the hand of a master. Despite the fact that the reader who is familiar with the history of the case knows the outcome, Mr. Levin manages to fill this book with sustained suspense." N Y Times Book Rev

Levine, David D., 1961-

★ **Arabella** of Mars; David D. Levine. St. Martin's Press 2016 352 p. (Adventures of Arabella Ashby) $25.99; (ebook) $49.99

ISBN 0765382814; 9780765382818; 9781427280763

LC 2016028453

In this novel in the "Adventures of Arabella Ashby" series by David D. Levine, a "British colony on Mars is home to Arabella Ashby, a young woman who is perfectly content growing up in the untamed frontier. But . . . her mother [has] plans to . . . move to an exotic world Arabella has never seen: London, England. However, when events transpire that threaten her home on Mars, Arabella decides that sometimes doing the right thing is far more important than behaving as expected." (Publisher's note)

"The alternate-world science is novel, the plot thrilling, and the romance appropriately chaste, but with her wits, resourcefulness, and courage, Arabella cuts a dashing figure as the heroine of this story." Booklist

Levine, James A.

Bingo's Run; a novel. James A. Levine. First edition Spiegel & Grau 2013 287 p. (acid-free paper) $24

ISBN 1400068835; 9781400068838

LC 2013002647

Alex Award (2015)

This novel, by James A. Levine, is a story of "morality and the redemptive powers of art. . . . Meet Bingo, the greatest drug runner in the slums of Kibera, Nairobi, and maybe the world. A teenage grifter, often mistaken for a younger boy, he faithfully serves Wolf, the drug lord of Kibera. . . . Bingo earns his keep by running 'white' to a host of clients, including Thomas Hunsa, a reclusive artist whose paintings, rooted in African tradition, move him." (Publisher's note)

"As Bingo asserts many times throughout Levine's second novel (after The Blue Notebook), "I am the greatest runner in Kibera, Nairobi, and probably the world."... Bingo is a fascinating and inimitably likable character. Levine, a Mayo clinic professor of medicine and well-known child advocate, excels at telling his adventurous, comic, and realistically gritty story with humor but not with pathos, successfully addressing the harsh and sometimes tragic story of a child at risk." LJ

Levine, Sara

Treasure Island!!! Europa Editions 2011 172 p. (paperback) $15.00

ISBN 1609450612; 9781609450618

This book offers a "comedy about a young woman obsessed with Robert Louis Stevenson's classic pirate tale. . . . The narrator . . . is an unnamed twenty-five-year-old living in her home town a few years after completing an English degree. We gather that her life since graduation has amounted to not much more than 'a history of low-paying jobs and hapless boyfriends,' and that she has no . . . plans to better herself. . . . The story begins motion when the narrator picks up her sister's copy of 'Treasure Island' and becomes enraptured with its hero, Jim Hawkins. . . . So begins the quest to transform the dross of her everyday life into a carnival of derring-do. . . . In practice, this means a series of reckless decisions that lead to wounded feelings and property damage." (TLS)

Levithan, David

The **lover's** dictionary. Farrar, Straus, and Giroux 2011 240p. $18

ISBN 978-0-374-19368-3

LC 201014392

Alex Award (2012)

"Levithan takes a hoary narrative—sexual electricity, domesticity, familiarity, tensions, betrayal—and recasts it in a fresh, modern way. The first person narrative is so intimate as to make the reader feel voyeuristic, like reading the diary of a logophile stranger. Entries echo the roller coaster of love, by turns wry, insecure, funny, coy, poetical, philosophical, bitter and even mawkishly sentimental." Maclean's

Levitt, Paul M.

Come with me to Babylon. University of New Mexico Press 2008 232p $24.95

ISBN 978-0-8263-4178-5; 0-8263-4178-0

LC 2007-39410

This historical novel "follows the Cohen family from their village in Russia to the United States, led by strong-willed Esther Cohen. Under the auspices of the Baron de Hirsch Fund, an agency focused on emigration, the Cohens are supposed to become farmers in rural New Jersey. But the bucolic occupation doesn't interest her husband, the gently raised Meyer Cohen. . . . All too soon, the Cohens have become a tenement family. Daughter Fanny is disabled in the Triangle Shirtwaist Co. fire, which killed more than 100 garment workers in a locked building. Son Ben begins dating a whore and running errands for a strikebreaking criminal. . . . Levitt hooks and plays his readers well. One influential character never appears directly: Jacob, Meyer and Esther's estranged son. The story of how he left the family, and how it grieves both parents, is a subtle but unmistakable undercurrent to Babylon." Rocky Mountain News

Levy, Andrea

★ The **long** song. Farrar, Straus and Giroux 2010 313p $26

ISBN 978-0-374-19217-4; 0-374-19217-0

LC 2009-43181

"For all its power to disturb, this is a beautifully written and cleverly constructed novel that projects convincing personal relationships on to the feral backdrop of the Jamaican plantations." Times (London)

Levy, Andrea

Small island. Picador 2005 441p pa $14

ISBN 0-312-42467-1

LC 2005-298527

First published 2004 in the United Kingdom

"In the shabby remnants of post-blitz London, three near-strangers find themselves in a single house. Queenie Bligh is a spirited Yorkshirewoman waiting for her husband to return from the war and taking in tenants to make ends meet. Gilbert Joseph, a Jamaican R.A.F. veteran, is struggling to establish himself in England, a country that he'd been taught was his motherland but which regards him as an interloper; his bride, Hortense, has just arrived in London and is bewildered that her education and class can't transcend the color of her skin. The narrative voice jumps between the characters, a technique that embeds familiar cultural observations in closely observed and surprising lives. If the plot sometimes verges on the operatic, Levy's writing deftly illuminates the complex and contradictory motives behind each character's behavior." New Yorker

Levy, Deborah, 1959-

Hot Milk; Deborah Levy. St. Martin's Press 2016 240 p. $26

ISBN 1620406691; 9781620406694

LC 2016001369

Man Booker Prize Shortlist (2016)

In this novel, by Deborah Levy, "Sofia . . . has spent much of her life trying to solve the mystery of her mother's unexplainable illness. [They] travel to . . . Spain to see a famous consultant--their very last chance--in the hope that he might cure her unpredictable limb paralysis. But Dr. Gomez has strange methods that seem to have little to do with physical medicine. Sofia's role as detective . . . deepens as she discovers her own desires in this transient desert community." (Publisher's note)

"Levy has crafted a great character in Sofia, and witnessing a pivotal point in her life is a pleasure." Pub Wkly

Levy, Deborah, 1959-

Swimming home; a novel. Deborah Levy ; with an introduction by Tom McCarthy. Bloomsbury USA 2012 157 p. (alk. paper) $14

ISBN 162040169X; 9781620401699

This novel, by Deborah Levy, begins at a "villa in the hills above Nice, [where] Joe sees a body in the swimming pool. But the girl is very much alive. She is Kitty Finch: a self-proclaimed botanist with green-painted fingernails, walking naked out of the water and into the heart of their holiday. Why is she there? What does she want from them all? And why does Joe's enigmatic wife allow her to remain?" (Publisher's note)

Includes bibliographical references and index

Lewis, Beverly

The **brethren**; Beverly Lewis. Bethany House 2006 349p.

ISBN 0764201077; 0764202316; 0764202324; 9780764201073; 9780764202315; 9780764202322

LC 2006019314

This book, winner of the 2007 Christy Award, tells "the story of an Amish girl torn between her family's way of life and her artistic dreams. Annie Zook has been wrestling with the decision of whether to commit her life to the church even though it would mean giving up her art for good. Also complicating her life is Ben Martin, the non-Amish boy she fell in love with but sent away. Ben's own life and identity are tested when he learns a secret that his parents have kept from him for his entire life." (Library Journal)

Lewis, Beverly

The **missing**; Beverly Lewis. Bethany House 2009 332p (pbk.) $14.99

ISBN 9780764205729

LC 2009025139

In this book, "Grace Byler longs to uncover the secret that drove her mother to leave the family weeks ago. When all hopes are dashed for such a search, an unlikely friendship leads to a surprising invitation. Meanwhile, the young Amishman Grace thought was courting her best friend takes a sudden interest in her, and Grace's decision to remain single is challenged." (Publisher's note)

Lewis, Beverly

The **preacher's** daughter; Beverly Lewis. Bethany House Publishers 2005 349p (Annie's people) $19.99

ISBN 0764201204 (alk. paper); 0764201050 (pbk. : alk. paper); 0764201212 (lg print pbk. : alk. paper)

LC 2005018581

This book follows 20-year-old Annie Zook, "a budding artist . . . [whose] conservative Amish community forbids its members to draw or paint pictures. . . . How will she choose between family and vocation? The disappearance of a small child years ago has left scars on various characters, and new developments in the case threaten to open old wounds. Annie's best friend in the community, Esther Hochstetler, finds that her marriage to an abusive man has become a nightmare, while Annie's pen pal, the wealthy Colorado 'Englisher' Louisa Stratford, . . . visits Annie in Paradise to heal from a broken engagement. Both women explore the possibilities of change." (Publishers Weekly)

Lewis, C. S.

★ **Out** of the silent planet. Scribner Classics 1996 158p $22; pa $13

ISBN 0-684-83364-6; 0-7432-3490-1 pa

LC 96-30110

A reissue of the title first published 1938 in the United Kingdom; first United States edition published 1943 by Macmillan

"The trilogy can be read on two levels: first for its exciting plot and second as a theological allegory, although Lewis denied this interpretation. The stories are about temptation. They concern the classic battle between good, as represented by Ransom, the philologist, and evil, as represented by Weston, the physicist. The battle is played out on the planets of Malacondra (Mars), Perelandra (Venus), and Earth." Shapiro. Fic for Youth. 3d edition

Followed by Perelandra (1943) and That hideous strength (1945)

Lewis, C. S.

Perelandra; a novel. Scribner Classics 1996 190p $22

ISBN 0-684-83365-4

LC 96-20724

A reissue of the title first published 1944 by Macmillan

In the second volume of the fantasy trilogy Dr. Ransom "is ordered to Perelandra (Venus) by the supreme being and finds there a paradise threatened by the villainous scientist Weston, who becomes the devil incarnate." Booklist

Followed by That hideous strength

Lewis, C. S.

That hideous strength; a modern fairy-tale for grown-ups. Scribner Classics 1996 380p $23

ISBN 0-684-83367-0

LC 96-20722

A reissue of the title first published 1946 by Macmillan

In the final volume of the fantasy trilogy Ransom and Weston again represent the struggle between good and evil, this time in a college community on Earth. Mark Studdock learns the error of his attempts to play faculty politics, and his wife discovers the footlessness of modern theories of love and life

Lewis, C. S.

Till we have faces; a myth retold. Harcourt Brace & Co. 1957 313p il

First published 1956 in the United Kingdom

"The religious allegory is plain to read. In Mr. Lewis's sensitive hands the ancient myth retains its fascination, while being endowed with new meanings, new depths, new terrors." Saturday Rev

Lewis, M. G. (Matthew Gregory), 1775-1818

★ The **monk**; by Matthew Lewis, with an introduction by Stephen King. Oxford Univ. Press 2002 442p (Oxford world's classics) $20

ISBN 0-19-515136-4

LC 2002-25111

First published 1796 in the United Kingdom

This is a reissue of Matthew Lewis's 1796 Gothic novel. It tells "a lurid tale of sex and murder involving a Roman Catholic priest: Ambrosio, the revered head of a Capuchin monastery in Madrid, rapes and stabs Antonia, a local beauty of noble descent, in the crypt of the convent next door. The priest drugs her with an opiate so powerful that she is presumed dead and carted off in a coffin to the crypt, where, as soon as she revives, he forces himself on her and then finishes her off with two dagger blows to the heart. In an earlier fit of lustful frenzy, he also strangles her mother." (N Y Times (Late N Y Ed))

"Ambrosio, the worthy superior of the Capuchins of Madrid, falls to the temptations of Matilda, a fiend-inspired wanton who, disguised as a boy, has entered his monastery as a novice. Now utterly depraved, Ambrosio falls in love with one of his penitents, pursues the girl with the help of magic and murder, and finally kills her in and effort to escape detection. But he is discovered, tortured by the Inquisition, and sentenced to death, finally compounding with the devil for escape from burning, only to be hurled by him to destruction and damnation. Although extravagant in its mixture of the supernatural, the terrible, and the indecent, the book contains scenes of great effect. It enjoyed a considerable contemporary vogue." Oxford Companion to Engl Lit. 6th edition

Lewis, Sinclair

Arrowsmith; Elmer Gantry; Dodsworth. Library of America, Distributed to the trade in the U.S. by Penguin Putnam 2002 1346p $40

ISBN 1-931082-08-1

LC 2002-19451

Lewis, Sinclair

★ **Babbitt**; with an introduction and notes by James M. Hutchisson. Penguin Books 1996 xxxii, 365p il pa $9.95

ISBN 0-14-018902-5

LC 95-36188

First published 1922 by Harcourt, Brace

Satire on American middle-class life in a good-sized city. George F. Babbitt is a successful real estate man, a regular fellow, booster, Rotarian, Elk, Republican, who uses all the current catchwords, molds his opinions on those of the Zenith Advocate-Times and believes in "a sound business administration in Washington"

"The novel's scathing indictment of middle-class American values made Babbittry a synonym for adherence to a conformist, materialistic, anti-intellectual way of life." Merriam-Webster's Ency of Lit

Lewis, Sinclair

Dodsworth; a novel. Harcourt Brace & Co. 1929 377p

"The book's protagonist, Sam Dodsworth, is an American automobile manufacturer who sells his company and takes an extended European vacation with his wife, Fran. Dodsworth recounts their reactions to Europeans and European values, their various relationships with others, their estrangement, and their brief reconciliation." Merriam-Webster's Ency of Lit

Lewis, Sinclair

★ **Elmer** Gantry. Harcourt Brace 1927 432p

This novel "deals with a brazen ex-football player who enters the ministry and, through his half-plagiarized sermons, his physical attractiveness, and his unerring instinct for promotion, becomes a successful evangelist and later the leader of a large Middle Western church. Carefully researched, the novel was realistic enough to shock both the faithful and unfaithful." Reader's Ency. 3d edition

Lewis, Sinclair

★ **Main** Street. Harcourt, Brace 1920 451p

"Carol Milford, a girl of quick intelligence but no particular talent, after graduation from college meets and marries Will Kennicott, a sober, kindly, unimaginative physician of Gopher Prairie, Minn., who tells her that the town needs her abilities. She finds the village to be a smug, intolerant, unimaginatively standardized place, where the people will not accept her efforts to create more sightly homes, organize a dramatic association, and otherwise improve the village life." Oxford Companion to Am Lit. 6th edition

Lewis, Sinclair, 1885-1951

It can't happen here; Sinclair Lewis. reprint Signet Classics 2005 xv, 384 p.p MM $9.99; Tr Pa $15.00

ISBN 0451529294; 9780451216588

LC 2004061606

"Written in 1935, this political satire depicts the United States ruled by a President who slowly morphs into a dictator. It astonishingly mimics developments in Nazi Germany before they happened." (Library Journal)

"In an enigmatic election year, Sinclair Lewis's 1935 political satire It Can't Happen Here holds unexpectedly fresh warnings." Chronicle of Higher Education

Lewis, Ted

★ **GBH**; Ted Lewis. Soho Crime 2015 320 p. (hardback) $26.95

ISBN 1616955503; 9781616955502

LC 2014033183

Originally published 1980 in the U.K.

In this book, by Ted Lewis, "George Fowler heads a lucrative criminal syndicate that specializes in the production and distribution of 'blue films'--nasty illegal pornography. Fowler is king, with a beautiful girl at his side and a swanky penthouse office, but his entire world is in jeopardy. Someone is undermining his empire from within, and Fowler becomes increasingly ruthless in his pursuit of the unknown traitor. " (Publisher's note)

"Though he narrates his own story, Fowler's lack of self-awareness makes this book about a bad man a great one." Booklist

Lianke, Yan

★ **Dream** of Ding Village; translated by Cindy Carter. Grove 2011 341p $24

ISBN 978-0-8021-1932-2

"Ding Village, a town of 800 people located in the Henan province, finds a quick fix to its dire needs in the form of a plasma-selling scheme promoted by county officials. Money flows the way the Yellow River once did before changing course and leaving the village parched. But exposed to dirty syringes and tainted cotton, and eager to give blood more frequently than their bodies can tolerate, townspeople in increasing numbers come down with 'the fever' and face certain death. Told from the grave by a 12-year-old boy whose grandfather is the deposed town leader and conscience, and whose father buys blood and resells it for a profit, the novel details the contamination of the town's moral as well as physical being. . . . A sorrowful but captivating novel about the price of progress in modern China. The book, which was censored in that country, builds to an act of violence that resonates with the impact of Greek tragedy or Shakespearean drama." Kirkus

Lichtenstein, Alice

Lost; a novel. Scribner 2010 242p $24

ISBN 978-1-4391-5982-8; 1-4391-5982-3

LC 2009-37973

The "characters are believable and fully drawn by Lichtenstein and well matched to share the stage of 'Lost.' They deploy impassioned subject matter with balance and control, never allowing the material to become maudlin. . . . [The novel] is a remarkable feat in technical craftsmanship that is nonetheless shot through with much raw feeling." St. Louis Post-Dispatch

Lightman, Alan P.

The **diagnosis**; [by] Alan Lightman. Pantheon Bks. 2000 369p

ISBN 0-679-43615-4

LC 00-24543

National Book Award Finalist: Fiction (2000)

"Bill Chalmers is an executive at an 'information company' in Boston who on his way to work one day forgets completely who he is, what he does or where he is supposed to be going. After a number of nightmarish experiences, in which he rapidly becomes a homeless bum, he awakens in a hospital, more or less his old self—except that his body is beginning to turn numb." Publ Wkly

Lightman, Alan P.

★ **Einstein's** dreams; [by] Alan Lightman. Pantheon Bks. 1993 179p il

LC 92-50465

"Lightman starts out with commonplaces, neurological conditions or abstractions of our personal experience of time. Then, with one or two exceptions, he embodies the concept in brilliant, folkloric tales with extraordinary assurance." New Statesman Soc

Lightman, Alan P.

Reunion; [by] Alan Lightman. Pantheon Bks. 2003 231p $23

ISBN 0-375-42167-X

LC 2002-34575

"Lightman infuses even the simplest scenes with quiet menace as he explores the cataclysmic power of both erotic love and shocking betrayal." Booklist

Lijia Zhang

Lotus; Lijia Zhang. Henry Holt & Co. 2016 x, 370 p.p (hardcover) $28

ISBN 9781250138668; 9781627795678; 9781627795661

LC 2016010682

This novel, by Lijia Zhang, "follows a young woman torn between past traditions and modern desires--as she carves out a life for herself in China's 'City of Sins.' . . . Inspired by the deathbed revelation that the author's grandmother had been sold to a brothel in her youth, 'Lotus' offers compelling insight into China's bustling underground world and reveals the surprising strength found in those confronted with impossible choices." (Publisher's note)

"Easy to read and containing fully drawn characters and story lines, Zhang's first foray into fiction does not disappoint." LJ

Limón, Martin

Mr. Kill; Martin Limón. Soho Crime 2011 375p.

ISBN 1569479348; 9781569479346

LC 2011024936

'This book offers a military mystery story in which "the brutal rape of a young mother sparks rage on the powder-keg peninsula of Korea, pitting Koreans against Americans and the 8th Army brass against the truth. Eyewitness accounts indicate the culprit was most likely a U.S. serviceman, but by the time Sergeants George Sueno and Ernie Bascom, U.S. Army investigators, are called in, the rapist has disappeared and anti-American fervor in this proud Asian country is threatening to explode. George and Ernie search in vain for the culprit, all the while becoming entangled in the web of military apologists who deny that any Americans were involved, and the designs of a beautiful blonde musician who fronts an all-female country western band--a woman who is out to entertain the troops in more ways than one." (Publisher's note)

Lin Yutang

Moment in Peking; a novel of contemporary Chinese life. Day 1939 815p

A story of family life among the upper middle class of China, covering forty years from the time of the Boxer Rebellion to the Japanese invasion

"There are many scenes and passages of great beauty in the book, excerpts from the classics, poetry and philosophy. There are also incidents of humor, delicate and subtle. Equally skillful is the author in depicting scenes of dramatic intensity, stark tragedy of war and acts of heroism" Springfield Repub

Lin, Jeannie

The **Dragon** and the Pearl; Jeannie Lin. Harlequin Books 2011 288p.

ISBN 9780373296620 pa

This book tells the story of "Lady Ling Suyin, former consort of the late Emperor, [who] is grateful but wary when fierce warlord Li Tao saves her from the assassins of powerful military governor Gao Shiming. With the kingdom in turmoil, Suyin trusts no one, especially not Li Tao, whose loyalty to Emperor Shen is in question and the reason for her rescue unclear. Li Tao has no idea why Gao Shiming would want the legendary beauty dead, but he wasn't about to let that happen. Despite their mutual distrust, Tao and Suyin can't resist the attraction that arcs between them or the star-crossed love that develops." (Libr J)

Linden, Caroline

Love and other scandals; Caroline Linden. Avon 2013 374 p. $5.99

ISBN 0062244876; 9780062244871

In this book, "Joan Bennet is a respectable young lady worried that she'll never find a husband. She's also addicted to a not-so-respectable publication called 50 Ways To Sin. When her brother's cheerfully disreputable friend Tristan Burke becomes his houseguest, Tristan and Joan strike up a flirtation that neither of them expects to go anywhere." (Publishers Weekly)

Lindgren, Torgny

Hash; a novel. translated from the Swedish by Tom Geddes. Overlook Press 2004 236p $23.95

ISBN 1-585-67408-7

LC 2003-63976

Original Swedish edition, 2002

"Lindgren delivers a story that's a clever sendup of the conceits of storytellers and a bittersweet meditation on life and the pleasures that bind us to it." N Y Times Book Rev

Lindqvist, John Ajvide, 1968-

Little star; John Ajvide Lindqvist ; translated by Marlaine Delargy. Thomas Dunne Books 2012 533 p.

ISBN 0312620519; 9780312620516; 9781250012821

LC 2012028223

This novel by John Ajvide Lindqvist is a "portrait of adolescence . . . for the age of internet bullies, offensive reality television, and overnight You Tube sensations. . . . A man finds a baby in the woods. . . . He brings the baby home, . . . [but] [w]hen a shocking and catastrophic incident occurs, the couple's son Jerry whisks the girl away to Stockholm, . . . [where] he enters her in a nationwide singing competition. Another young girl who's never fit in sees the performance on TV, and a spark is struck." (Publisher's note)

Lindsay, Jeffry P.

Darkly dreaming Dexter. Doubleday 2004 288p $22.95

ISBN 0-385-51123-X

LC 2004-45460

Dexter Morgan is a "Miami police-department blood-spatter analyst with a weakness for bowling shirts and batidos, who, when the moon is full, carves up villains in a careful ritual, keeping a single drop of blood on a slide as a souvenir. (He's collected thirty-six so far.) When other victims start popping up, dispatched with the same creativity as Dexter's, he pursues the copycat murderer with acute professional self-interest. Like other charismatic killers—Hannibal Lecter, say, or Tom Ripley—Dexter has a set of motives that are tough to untangle. But his quest proves weirdly convincing as he ponders whether to turn his doppelgänger over to the cops or take care of the problem himself." New Yorker

Other titles in this series are:
Dearly devoted Dexter (2005)
Dexter in the dark (2007)
Dexter by design (2009)
Dexter is delicious (2010)
Double Dexter (2011)
Dexter's final cut (2013)
Dexter is dead (2015)

Lindsay, Jeffry P.

Dearly devoted Dexter; [by] Jeff Lindsay. Doubleday 2005 292p

ISBN 0-385-51124-8

This is the second book in the Dexter series. "Dexter Morgan, a Miami P.D. blood splatter analyst and ethical serial killer, is in a funk: his police department arch-nemesis, Captain Doakes, who rightly believes that Dexter is guilty of illegal behavior, is shadowing him. . . . So when a new serial killer with Doakes on his list arrives in Miami, Dexter is excited. Not only does he get to hunt a fellow hunter, but he also sees the opportunity to be rid of Doakes. The only thing worrying him is the involvement of his sister, since she's the only person for whom Dexter has feelings. . . . There's plenty of graphic violence and dark humor, but Lindsay manages to retain a light edge." Libr J

Link, Charlotte

The **other** child; Charlotte Link; translated from the German by Stefan Tobler. Orion Books 2012 416 p. (hardcover) $25.95

ISBN 1605984302; 9781605984308

LC 2012398355

In this crime thriller, "when two murders occur in the small English village of Scarborough, the second one a copycat killing that takes place months after the first, Det. Valerie Almond is at a loss. Then she learns that the murders may be connected to the evacuation of children from the area during World War II." (Library Journal)

Link, Charlotte

The **Watcher**; A Novel of Crime. by Charlotte Link. W W Norton & Co Inc 2014 400 p. $25.95

ISBN 1605985597; 9781605985596

LC 2013497684

In this crime novel, by Charlotte Link, "Samson Segal, an unemployed thirty-something, has taken to spying on his neighbors, particularly beautiful and successful Gillian Ward. When Gillian's daughter comes home to an empty, locked house, Samson takes her in but finds himself venting his anger in his diary when his good Samaritan actions go unappreciated, unaware that his suspicious sister-in-law cracked his password long ago." (Publisher's note)

"In Link's skilled hands, seemingly disparate story lines come together in a nail-biting climax. This is the second novel (following The Other Child, 2013) by a best-selling author in her native Germany to be released in the U.S. Fans of Tana French's twisty crime novels will devour this suspenseful read." Booklist

Link, Kelly

Get in trouble; stories. Kelly Link. Random House Inc 2015 352 p. $25

ISBN 0804179689; 9780804179683

LC 2014011170

Pulitzer Prize Finalist: Fiction (2016)

This short story collection, by Kelly Link, "may begin in familiar territory--a birthday party, a theme park, a bar, a spaceship--but they quickly draw readers into an imaginative, disturbingly ominous world of realistic fantasy and unreal reality. Like Kafka hosting Saturday Night Live, [author Kelly] Link mixes humor with existential dread. . . . Link's characters, driven by yearning and obsession, not only get in trouble but seek trouble out." (Publishers Weekly)

"In short, the tales are imaginatively bizarre yet can be seen as allegorical representations of our own crazy modern world. Most of the protagonists here are female and resourceful." LJ

Link, Kelly

Magic for beginners; illustrated by Shelley Jackson. Small Beer Press 2005 272p il $24

ISBN 978-1-931520-15-7; 1-931520-15-1

LC 2005-5394

"Link's second collection has a McSweeney's-like tendency to digress, but does so without irony. Whether describing witches filled with ants that carry pieces of time, or an orange-juice-colored corduroy couch that looks as if it 'has just escaped from a maximum security prison for criminally insane furniture,' these stories examine American middle and lower-middle-class life from unexpected angles that mix fairy tale, science fiction, and zaniness. . . . Reading Link, one has a sense that sometimes a person needs to wander off for a better perspective, and sometimes a person simply needs to wander off." New Yorker

Link, Teresa

Denting the Bosch; a novel of marriage, friendship, and expensive household appliances. Teresa Link. 1st ed. Thomas Dunne Books 2012 276 p. (hardcover) $25.99

ISBN 0312643411; 9780312643416; 9781250010506

LC 2012011014

In author Teresa Link's book, "three couples in San Diego--best friends, empty nesters living the California dream--have reached a tipping point. With the blurry years of child rearing and corporate ladder-climbing over, each pair is finally free to enjoy the golden years together. Until two of the husbands suddenly announce they want a divorce. . . . Marriages and friendships unravel and the prosperity of the last few decades spins toward financial meltdown." (Publisher's note)

Lipman, Elinor

The **dearly** departed; a novel. Random House 2001 269p $23.95

ISBN 0-679-46312-7

LC 00-67368

The novel "entertains the reader with quirky details and amusing dialogue, but most nourishing is its picture of small-town life, in which everyone knows everyone else's business but they love one another just the same." Atl Mon

Lipman, Elinor

The **family** man. Houghton Mifflin Harcourt 2009 305p $25

ISBN 978-0-618-64466-7; 0-618-64466-0

LC 2008-46222

"Hilarious, literate and unnervingly accurate in its observations of the quirks of human nature, 'The Family Man' proclaims that whatever bizarre sort of family you have, you're better off with it than without." PopMatters

Lipman, Elinor

The **Inn** at Lake Devine. Random House 1998 253p

ISBN 0-679-45693-7

LC 97-1307

"Skillfully interweaving the bittersweet narrative with threads of both tragedy and comedy, Lipman displays a healthy amount of empathy and affection for her flawed and slightly eccentric cast of characters." Booklist

Lipman, Elinor

The **pursuit** of Alice Thrift; a novel. Random House 2003 269p $23.95

ISBN 0-679-46313-5

LC 2002-31864

"The eponymous Alice is a sleep-deprived surgical intern at a Boston hospital. A graduate of MIT and Harvard and a congenital workaholic, she's also devoid of social skills, a sense of humor or elementary tact. Though miserably unequipped with self-esteem, Alice is an intelligent, well-brought-up offspring of upper-middle-class parents. Why, then, does she fall prey to the romantic blandishments of Ray Russo, a vulgar loudmouth and con artist who—it turns out—lies every time he opens his mouth? That Lipman can make this story plausible, and tell it with humor, pschological insight and rising suspense, is a triumph." Publ Wkly

Lippman, Laura ✓

★ **After** I'm gone; Laura Lippman. William Morrow, An Imprint of HarperCollinsPublishers 2014 352 p. (hbk.) $26.99; (pbk. Large Print) $26.99

ISBN 0062083392; 0062298496; 9780062083395; 9780062298492

LC 2013018550

Written by Laura Lippman, this book tells a "story that explores how one man's disappearance echoes through the lives of the wife, mistress, and daughters he left behind. When Julie disappears . . . everyone assumes she's left to join her old lover--until her remains are eventually found. Now, twenty-six years after Julie went missing, Roberto 'Sandy' Sanchez, a retired Baltimore detective working cold cases for some extra cash, is investigating her murder." (Publisher's note)

"Lippman incisively explores marriage, Jewish family life, class distinctions, and the power and liability of physical beauty, thus creating an involving and elegant novel of the psychological ravages of crime." Booklist

Lippman, Laura ✓

★ **And** when she was good; by Laura Lippman. 1st ed. William Morrow 2012 314 p. (hardcover) $26.99; (ebook) $21.99; (paperback) $14.99

ISBN 0061706876; 9780061706875; 9780062201614; 9780062197733

LC 2011279905

Author Laura Lippman's protagonist "Heloise Lewis is a survivor who rose from the ashes of her past to run a profitable call-girl service, occasionally meeting special clients herself. To her neighbors, she's a young widow and a devoted mother . . . [and] to the IRS, she's a lobbyist with several women on her payroll and a medical plan . . . [Her] carefully constructed life is falling apart because Val Deluca, her son's father . . . may be released from prison . . . [without knowing that] he's Scott's father or that Heloise's betrayal put him behind bars for murder." (Publishers Weekiy)

Lippman, Laura

Hardly knew her; stories. William Morrow 2008 292p $23.95

ISBN 978-0-06-158499-2; 0-06-158499-1

Lippman "clearly agrees with Kipling that the female of the species is deadlier than the male. Women's victims here include a female friend, boyfriends (both current and ex), a husband, and one-night stands and strangers; their murders are all the more chilling. The novella 'Scratch A Woman,' featuring a single suburban Maryland soccer mom who works as a prostitute, and one of several stories featuring Tess [Monaghan] are the only entries not published previously. But those that have been published are scattered in a variety of anthologies over the last seven years, including Baltimore Noir. Here are nearly all of the short stories Lippman has ever written in one volume; read them fast, like a glutton, or slowly to savor each one. Either way, this is a treasure." Libr J

Lippman, Laura

✓★ **Hush** hush; Laura Lippman. William Morrow/HarperCollins 2015 384 p. (A Tess Monaghan Novel) (hardcover) $26.99

ISBN 0062083422; 9780062083425

In this novel, by Laura Lippman, "Melisandre Harris Dawes . . . left her two-month-old daughter locked in a car while she sat nearby on the shores of the Patapsco River. Melisandre was found not guilty by reason of criminal insanity, although there was much skepticism. . . . Tess Monaghan wants nothing to do with a woman crazy enough to have killed her own child. But her mentor and close friend Tyner Gray, Melisandre's lawyer, has asked Tess . . . to assess Melisandre's security needs." (Publisher's note)

"With an intriguing cast of characters, stinging dialogue, hilarious moments, and a superbly convoluted and suspenseful plot, Lippman has created an incisive and provocative tale about parents good and evil." Booklist

Lippman, Laura

I'd know you anywhere. Morrow 2010 374p $25.99

ISBN 978-0-06-170655-4; 0-06-170655-8

"Eliza Benedict is an easygoing wife and mother of two living in suburban Maryland. The family recently returned to America after five years in England, which would seem to account for Eliza's lack of friends. Her biggest problem appears to be her argumentative 13-year-old daughter, Iso, who traded in kindness for popularity when the family crossed the ocean. Then Eliza receives a letter from Walter Bowman, the man who kidnapped her and held her hostage for nearly six weeks when she was 15. Walter wants a favor: He wants to talk to Elizabeth (the name that she used in her life 'before'), and, despite his residency on death row, he still holds sway over her. I'd Know You Anywhere is a crime story, but it's not a whodunit. Rather, it's an exquisitely sensitive story about the psychological impact of crime on its victims. It's a story about shame, about anger, about survivor's guilt." Ft. Worth Star-Telegram

Lippman, Laura

The **most** dangerous thing. Morrow 2011 344p $25.99

ISBN 978-0-06-170651-6; 0-06-170651-5

"No one explores the delicate interplay between children and the adults they grow into better than Lippman." Kirkus

Lippman, Laura

No good deeds. William Morrow 2006 343p $24.95

ISBN 978-0-06-057072-9; 0-06-057072-5

LC 2005-58358

"Lippman has pulled off the near-impossible: writing a conventional procedural that still feels fresh. It's impossible not to like the complex, all-too-real Monaghan, a strong, wry detective prone to 'derailing my own gravy train.'" Washington Post Book World

Lippman, Laura

What the dead know. William Morrow 2007 376p $24.95

ISBN 978-0-06-112885-1; 0-06-112885-6

LC 2006-52495

"As artful as she is at interweaving disarming scenes of two spirited girls on the day they vanished with painful moments in the lives of their parents—maintaining all the while a thread of continuity in the current-day police investigation—Lippman pulls off something more ambitious than a high-wire act of technical virtuosity. With great thought and compassion, she uses her fractured narrative style to delve into the ways in which every serious crime tears to shreds the lives of its victims." N Y Times Book Rev

Lippman, Laura

Wilde Lake; A Novel. Laura Lippman. William Morrow & Co 2016 384 p. (hardcover) $26.99

ISBN 9780062083456; 9780062083463; 0062083457

In this novel, by Laura Lippman, "Luisa 'Lu' Brant is the newly elected . . . state's attorney of Howard County, Maryland. . . . Fiercely intelligent and ambitious, she sees an opportunity to make her name by trying a mentally disturbed drifter accused of beating a woman to death in her home. It's not the kind of case that makes headlines, but peaceful Howard county doesn't see many homicides. As Lu prepares for the trial, the case dredges up painful memories." (Publisher's note)

"As shocking secrets are revealed, the reader realizes that nothing and no one can be taken at face value in Lippman's brainy, witty, socially conscious, and all-consuming inquiry into human nature and our slowly evolving sense of justice and equality." Booklist

Lipsyte, Sam

★ The **ask**. Farrar, Straus and Giroux 2010 296p $25

ISBN 0-374-29891-2; 978-0-374-29891-3

LC 2009-29508

After he loses his job as a development officer at a university, family man Milo Burke is given a chance to regain his position, but only if he can reel in a potential donor, one who has requested his involvement and turns out to be his sinister college classmate.

"Milo Burke, a recently fired donations officer at a third-tier university, is a paragon of failure: a horny, bile-filled chunk of a man, veering into middle age with nothing to show for his youthful dreams of artistic glory. The Ask's narrative heft comes from the reappearance of a wealthy friend from Milo's college days and the tragicomic scenarios that follow — the plight of socialist daycare workers and legless Iraq-war vets among them. But the gift is Sam Lipsyte's writing: a chewy, corrosive, and syntactically dazzling prose style that doesn't so much run across the page as pick it up and throttle it. You may want to throttle Milo yourself frequently, but you won't stop reading." Entertainment Wkly

Lish, Atticus

Preparation for the Next Life; Atticus Lish. Tyrant Books 2014 250 p. pbk $15

ISBN 9780988518339; 0988518333

PEN/Faulkner Award for Fiction: Shortlist (2015)

In this novel by Atticus Lish, "Zou Lei, orphan of the desert, migrates to work in America and finds herself slaving in New York's kitchens. She falls in love with a young man whose heart has been broken in another desert. A new life may be possible if together they can survive homelessness, lockup, and the young man's nightmares, which may be more prophecy than madness." (Publisher's note)

"Zou Lei and Skinner have their budding relationship tested by insurmountable odds, and their own foibles and peculiarities are rendered with vivid detail. Lish's prose is at once raw and disciplined, and every word feels necessary." Pub Wkly

Lispector, Clarice, 1920-1977

The **complete** stories; Clarice Lispector; translated by Katrina Dodson; edited and with an introduction by Benjamin Moser. New Directions 2015 645 p. $28.95

ISBN 9780811219631; 0811219631

LC 2015013285

This short story collection, by Clarice Lispector, translated by Katrina Dodson, and edited by Benjamin Moser, features several characters and events "from teenagers coming into awareness of their sexual and artistic powers to humdrum housewives whose lives are shattered by unexpected epiphanies to old people who don't know what to do with themselves." (Publisher's note)

"Lispector's stories are surreal, modernist, and laced with magic realism, and she has been compared to Franz Kafka and Virginia Woolf. But Lispector's tales are distinctly her own--sharp, swift, and dangerous in their stinging humor and burning illuminations of the paradoxical human condition." Booklist

Includes bibliographical references

Liss, David

A **spectacle** of corruption. Random House 2004 381p $24.95

ISBN 0-375-50855-4

LC 2003-54806

Weaver "turns out to be the hard-outside, soft-inside private investigator of the noir thrillers inserted into 1720s London: Philip Marlowe done up in a wig and buckles." Washington Post Book World

Liss, David

The **whiskey** rebels; a novel. Random House 2008 525p $26

ISBN 1-4000-6420-1; 978-1-4000-6420-5

LC 2008-00075

"Ethan Saunders, once among George Washington's most valued spies, now lives in disgrace, haunting the taverns of Philadelphia. An accusation of treason has long since cost him his reputation and his beloved fiancee, Cynthia Pearson, but at his most desperate moment he is recruited for an unlikely task—finding Cynthia's missing husband. To help her, Saunders must serve his old enemy, Treasury Secretary Alexander Hamilton." (Publisher's note)

The author "delivers a portrait of postcolonial Philadelphia and New York, as well as the western frontier, that is convincing and acutely detailed." Houston Chron

Littell, Robert

★ The **company**; a novel of the CIA. Overlook Press 2002 894p $27.95

ISBN 1-58567-197-5

LC 2001-51383

"There is plenty here to amuse anyone with even a network news interest in current events—and a gold mine for true conspiracy theorists." N Y Times Book Rev

Littell, Robert

The **Stalin** epigram; a novel. Simon & Schuster 2009 366p $26

ISBN 9781416598640; 1-4165-9864-2

LC 2008-52277

"This is a timeless story of courage and truth confronting the madness of absolute power. It's a brilliant work, always readable, sometimes funny and often heartbreaking. There are many books about Stalin's terror, but there cannot be many that bring its truths more vividly, painfully to life." Washington Post Book World

Littell, Robert

Vicious circle; a novel of complicity. Overlook 2006 300p $24.95

ISBN 1-58567-855-4

This novel "takes place in the volatile Holy Land of the near future. When the Arab leader of a terrorist faction kidnaps a rabbi who heads an ultraconservative settlers' group, Israeli security services go on red alert. In adding a smart-alecky American reporter to the mix, Littell . . . ratchets up the action to a heart-bursting sprint that stops only for big gulps of violence and torture. What makes this book unforgettable is the extraordinary relationship between kidnapper and victim. Extremists both, they joust with vehement hatred yet are strangely drawn together. Littell's acute portrayal of their inflamed psychological states illuminates an understanding that goes far beyond the day's headlines." Libr J

Little, Terra

Where there's smoke; Terra Little. Urban Books 2009 326 p.

ISBN 1933967781; 9781933967783

LC 2008924560

In this novel, "Father's Day is an occasion for celebration--unless, that is, you don't know you're a father. So it goes for Alec 'Smoke' Avery, who learns that he has a 16-year-old son. Now a respectable teacher, Alec . . . used to deal down in the 'hood, and one of his best customers, Breanne, now Anne, similarly reformed, is the mother. 'I'd sampled some of the ladies,' admits Alec, 'but I hadn't left any babies behind that I knew of. . . .' But young Isaiah looks like dad. . . . He's also headed down a path that may not have such a happy ending. . . . It's up to Alec to offer some role modeling and save the son he didn't know he had--easier said than done, since down at the projects, the competition is fierce and the temptations many." (Kirkus)

Liu Cixin, 1963-

The **dark** forest; by Liu Cixin ; translated by Joel Martinsen. Tor Books 2015 512 p. (hardback) $25.99

ISBN 9780765377081

LC 2015016174

In this book, by Cixin Liu, translated by Joel Martinsen, "Earth is reeling from the revelation of a coming alien invasion-in just four centuries' time. The aliens' human collaborators may have been defeated, but the presence of the sophons, the subatomic particles that allow Trisolaris instant access to all human information, means that Earth's defense plans are totally exposed to the enemy. Only the human mind remains a secret." (Publisher's note)

"The book's large cast of characters form a latticework of precisely placed focal points around which the story weaves and connects to wonderful moments of revelation." Booklist

Includes bibliographical references and index

Liu Cixin, 1963-

Death's End; Cixin Liu. St. Martin's Press 2016 608 p. (Three-body trilogy) (hardcover) $26.99; (ebook) $60

ISBN 9780765377104; 0765377101; 9781466853454

LC 2016295859

Hugo Nominee: Best Novel (2017)

In this conclusion to the Remembrance of Earth's Past series by Cixin Liu, "half a century after the Doomsday Battle, the uneasy balance of Dark Forest Deterrence keeps the Trisolaran invaders at bay. Earth enjoys unprecedented prosperity. . . . Cheng Xin, an aerospace engineer from the early 21st century, awakens from hibernation. . . . She brings with her knowledge of a long-forgotten program, . . . and her very presence may upset the delicate balance between two worlds." (Publisher's note)

"The time scale is an obstacle to emotional engagement, but there are emotionally moving moments that ground the intriguing speculations about science and human nature." Pub Wkly

Liu Cixin, 1963-

★ The **three**-body problem; Cixin Liu ; translated by Ken Liu. Tor Books 2014 400 p. (hardback) $25.99

ISBN 0765377063; 9780765377067

LC 2014033729

Hugo Award: Best Novel (2015)

In this novel by Cixin Liu "set against the backdrop of China's Cultural Revolution, a secret military project sends signals into space to establish contact with aliens. An alien civilization on the brink of destruction captures the signal and plans to invade Earth. Meanwhile, on Earth, different camps start forming, planning to either welcome the superior beings and help them take over a world seen as corrupt, or to fight against the invasion." (Publisher's note)

"The narrative will grab readers' attention with its passionate and fascinating critique of early Communist China, augmented by translator Liu's lean but informative footnotes for the likely uninformed English readers. But the high-minded premise is really just a vessel for a collection of surreal and hauntingly beautiful scenes that will hook you deep and drag you relentlessly across every page." Booklist

Followed by The Dark Forest and Death's End

Liu, Ken

The **grace** of kings; Ken Liu. Saga Press 2015 800 p. color map (hardcover) $27.99

ISBN 1481424270; 9781481424271

LC 2014019957

"Wily, charming Kuni Garu, a bandit, and stern, fearless Mata Zyndu, the son of a deposed duke, seem like polar opposites. Yet, in the uprising against the emperor, the two quickly become the best of friends after a series of adventures fighting against vast conscripted armies, silk-draped airships, and shapeshifting gods. Once the emperor has been overthrown, however, they each find themselves the leader of separate factions." (Publisher's note)

Liu, Ken

The **wall** of storms; Ken Liu. Saga Press 2016 880 p. (ebook) $13.99; (hardback) $29.99

ISBN 9781481424325; 9781481424301; 9781481485210

LC 2016034254

This novel, by Ken Liu, follows "Kuni Garu, now known as Emperor Ragin, [who] runs the archipelago kingdom of Dara, . . . an unexpected invading force from the Lyucu empire in the far distant west comes to the shores of Dara--and chaos results. . . . he sends the only people he trusts to be Dara's savvy and cunning hopes against the invincible invaders: his children, now grown and ready to make their mark on history." (Publisher's Note)

"This tale of divided loyalties, deadly ambition, and 'silkpunk' technology delivers enough excitement and sense of wonder to enchant any fan of epic fantasy." Pub Wkly

Lively, Penelope

Cleopatra's sister. HarperCollins Pubs. 1993 281p

LC 92-54424

In alternating chapters, the author "depicts the lives of paleontologist Howard Beamish and crusading journalist Lucy Faulkner, both successful in their careers but unfulfilled because they have not established enduring relationships. They meet when the plane they are taking to Cairo makes a forced landing in Callimbia, a fictional country in the throes of a bloody revolution led by a lunatic dictator. Lively's . . . construction of Callimbia's history ranges from its establishment by Cleopatra's sister Berenice through the rise of the 'moral renegade' who orders the plane's British passengers taken hostage. Through the eyes of Howard and Lucy, and in counterpoint to their growing love for each other, Lively depicts the passengers' responses to their plight." Publ Wkly

Lively, Penelope

Consequences. Viking 2007 258p $24.95

ISBN 978-0-670-03856-5; 0-670-03856-3

LC 2007-297882

"A keen perception of the meanings of time and space joins the three generations of women . . . . as much as their shared blood does; it also allows author Penelope Lively to observe the worlds of change that occur during their lifetimes. She remains a heartbreakingly human and elegant writer." BookPage

Lively, Penelope, 1933-

How it all began; Penelope Lively. Viking 2012 229p.

ISBN 9780143122647; 9780670023448

LC 2011032994

In this novel, "[w]hen Charlotte Rainsford, a retired schoolteacher, is accosted by a petty thief on a London street, the consequences ripple across the lives of acquaintances and strangers alike. A marriage unravels after an illicit love affair is revealed through an errant cell phone message; a posh yet financially strapped interior designer meets a business partner who might prove too good to be true; an old-guard historian tries to recapture his youthful vigor with an ill-conceived idea for a TV miniseries; and a middle-aged central European immigrant learns to speak English and reinvents his life with the assistance of some new friends." (Publisher's note)

Lively, Penelope

★ **Moon** tiger. Grove Press 1988 208p

ISBN 0-8021-3533-1

LC 87-23798

First published 1987 in the United Kingdom

"Moon Tiger is an extremely accomplished novel which tells an interesting story with an impressive variety of fictional techniques." Quill Quire

Lively, Penelope

★ **Passing** on. Grove Weidenfeld 1990 210p

ISBN 0-8021-1155-6

LC 89-7459

First published 1989 in the United Kingdom

"Penelope Lively is blessed with the gift of being able to render matters of great import with a breath, a barely audible sigh, a touch. The result is wonderful writing, and a marvelous book." N Y Times Book Rev

Livesey, Margot

Banishing Verona; a novel. Henry Holt 2004 321p $24

ISBN 0-8050-7462-7

LC 2004-52383

"Both Zeke and Verona have just enough quirks to be endearing without being implausible; the supporting characters are similarly well realized. As Livesey . . . probes the depths of longing, betrayal and forgiveness, her gift for creating sublimely unexpected sentences is abundantly on display." Publ Wkly

Livesey, Margot

Criminals; a novel. Knopf 1996 271p

ISBN 0-679-44487-4

LC 95-31512

The reader becomes "enmeshed in the complex windings of Ms. Livesey's plot, a web of criminal circumstance and moral consequence that conveys the awful randomness of life even as it offers the abiding pleasures of artfully constructed fiction." N Y Times Book Rev

Livesey, Margot

Eva moves the furniture. Holt & Co. 2001 232p

ISBN 0-8050-6801-5

LC 00-143895

"Eva McEwen grows up engulfed by a vast and hopeful loneliness. She lives in a small Scottish town with her father and an overprotective aunt, her mother having died of the flu at her birth, in 1920. After Eva turns six, her solitary play is interrupted at unpredictable moments by a girl and a woman who, more than once, come to her aid. Only when she starts school does she realize that these two are invisible to everyone else-and, moreover, jealous of new acquaintances. At eighteen, Eva is desperate to escape the emotional tyrannies of her upbringing, but she eventually comes to feel the fullness of her love for both the real and the imaginary companions of her childhood. Livesey has written a ghost story, of sorts, minus the theremin musiclike 'Our Town,' with its speakers from the grave-and, if it moves you, the end will send you back to the beginning again." New Yorker

Livesey, Margot

The **flight** of Gemma Hardy; Margot Livesey. HarperCollins 2012 447p.

ISBN 9780062064226; 9780062064233

LC 2012371565

This book tells the story of "Gemma Hardy. Orphaned by the age of ten, neglected by a bitter and cruel aunt, sent to a boarding school where she is both servant and student, young Gemma seems destined for a life of hardship and loneliness. . . . Fiercely intelligent, singularly determined, Gemma overcomes each challenge and setback. . . . Now an independent young woman with dreams of the future, she accepts a position as an au pair on the remote and beautiful Orkney Islands. But Gemma's biggest trial is about to begin . . . a journey of passion and betrayal that will lead her to a life she's never dreamed of." (Publisher's note)

Livesey, Margot

The **house** on Fortune Street. Harper 2008 311p $24.95

ISBN 978-0-06-145152-2; 0-06-145152-5

LC 2007-29611

"That people with the closest of bonds—lovers, family members, best friends—can be strangers to one another is a familiar literary motif, but it has seldom been more affectingly dramatized than in this extraordinary book." Entertainment Wkly

Livesey, Margot

The **missing** world; a novel. Knopf 2000 325p

ISBN 0-375-40581-X

LC 99-35785

"Adroitly paced, meticulously plotted and increasingly suspenseful, the novel transcends its genre as psychological thriller." Publ Wkly

The **living** dead; edited by John Joseph Adams. Night Shade Books 2008 487p pa $15.95

ISBN 978-1-59780-143-0; 1-59780-143-7

"These stories range from the truly disgusting (Poppy Z. Brite's 'Calcutta: Lord of Nerves') to the nearly wistful ('Followed' by Will McIntosh) and even one with no supernatural elements at all (Joe Hill's 'Bobby Conroy Comes Back from the Dead'). Included are pieces by big names in horror like Stephen King and Clive Barker but also contributions by less obvious suspects like Harlan Ellison, Sherman Alexie, and George R.R. Martin. The final treat is John Langan's 'How the Day Runs Down,' a nasty little play best described as Our Town with zombies. Highly recommended for all horror fiction collections." Libr J

Llewellyn, Richard

★ **How** green was my valley. Macmillan 1940 495p

"A remarkably beautiful novel of Wales. And although it follows stirringly in the romantic traditions, there is the resonance of a profound and noble realism in its evocation, its intensity and reach of truth." N Y Times Book Rev

Llywelyn, Morgan

1916. Forge 1998 447p

ISBN 0-312-86101-X

LC 97-29838

Followed by: 1921 (2001); 1949 (2003); 1972 (2005)

"Battle scenes are both accurate and compelling. The betrayals, slaughters and passions of the day are all splendidly depicted as Llywelyn delivers a blow-by-blow account of the rebellion and its immediate aftermath. The novel's abundant footnotes should satisfy history buffs; its easy, gripping style will enthrall casual readers." Publ Wkly

Llywelyn, Morgan

1921. Forge 2001 445p $25.95

ISBN 0-312-86754-9

LC 00-49021

Sequel to 1916

"Incessantly haunted by the rather passive role he played in the doomed Easter Rebellion, Henry Mooney, a journalist struggling for objectivity in the midst of controversy and mayhem, reevaluates his own convictions and commitment to the cause of a free Ireland. When Henry falls in love with an Anglo-Irish woman, simmering tensions wrought by centuries of domination and repression are reflected in a microcosm of passion and agony. The lucid narrative and the compelling subject matter will enthrall both Irish history buffs and fans of sweeping historical fiction." Booklist

Includes bibliographical references (p. {437}-445)

Llywelyn, Morgan

1949; a novel of the Irish Free State. Forge 2003 414p $25.95

ISBN 0-312-86753-0

LC 2002-32525

Sequel to: 1921

"Llywelyn's great strength is her ability to communicate sweeping historical events through the eyes of both passive bystanders and active participants." Booklist

Includes bibliographical references (p. {409}-414)

Llywelyn, Morgan

After Rome; a novel of Celtic Britain. Morgan Llywelyn. 1st ed. Forge 2013 332 p. map (hardcover) $24.99

ISBN 0765331233; 9780765331236

LC 2012027562

This historical novel by Morgan Llywelyn, set in Great Britain, "focuses on two cousins, Dinas and Cadogan, who develop different survival strategies in the arduous time after the fall of the Roman Empire. Dinas is a schemer with dreams of political power who, it seems, will always land on his feet, while Cadogan is more of a drifter and dreamer who eventually begins to stake out a new community to escape the chaos swirling about." (Kirkus Reviews)

Includes bibliographical references (p. 335).

Lochen, Andrea

The **repeat** year; Andrea Lochen. Berkley Books 2013 vi, 393 p.p (paperback) $16

ISBN 0425263134; 9780425263136

LC 2012045918

In this novel, by Andrea Lochen, "after a year of hardships, . . . Olive is ready to start fresh. But when she wakes up in her ex-boyfriend's bed on New Year's Day 2011--a day she has already lived--Olive's world is turned upside down. . . . Olive learns that she has the chance to rewrite her future. Given the opportunity of a lifetime, Olive has to decide what she really wants." (Publisher's note)

Lock, Norman

American meteor; by Norman Lock. First edition Bellevue Literary Press 2015 208 p. (pbk.) $15.95

ISBN 1934137944; 9781934137949

LC 2014036638

In this book, by Norman Lock, "Stephen Moran comes of age with the young country that he crosses on the Union Pacific, just as the railroad unites the continent. Propelled westward from his Brooklyn neighborhood, . . . he befriends Walt Whitman, receives a medal from General

Grant, becomes a bugler on President Lincoln's funeral train, goes to work for railroad mogul Thomas Durant, apprentices with frontier photographer William Henry Jackson, and stalks General George Custer." (Publisher's note)

Lock, Norman

Love among the particles & other stories; Norman Lock. Bellevue Literary Press 2013 224 p. (alk. paper) $14.95

ISBN 1934137642; 9781934137642

LC 2012046160

This short story collection, written by Norman Lock, is "at once a . . . critique of our romance with technology and a love letter to language. In a whirlwind tour of space, time, and history, Norman Lock creates worlds that veer wildly from the natural to the supernatural via the premodern, mechanical, and digital ages." (Publisher's note)

Includes bibliographical references and index

Locke, Attica

Bluebird, bluebird; Attica Locke. Mulholland Books 2017 307 p. (hardcover) $26

ISBN 9780316363297; 9780316511179; 0316363294

LC 2017941350

In this book, by Attica Locke, "East Texas plays by its own rules--a fact that Darren Mathews, a black Texas Ranger, knows all too well. . . . When his allegiance to his roots puts his job in jeopardy, he travels up Highway 59 to the small town of Lark, where two murders . . . have stirred up a hornet's nest of resentment. Darren must solve the crimes--and save himself in the process--before Lark's long-simmering racial fault lines erupt." (Publisher's note)

"Locke . . . deserves a career breakthrough for this deftly plotted whodunit whose writing pulses throughout with a raw, blues-inflected lyricism." Kirkus

Locke, Attica

The **cutting** season. Harper 2012 374 p. $25.99

ISBN 0061802050; 9780061802058

2013 BCALA Literary Award: Honor Book for Fiction

In this novel, by Attica Locke, "Caren Gray manages . . . a[n] . . . antebellum plantation. . . . Outside the gates, a corporation . . . has been . . . replacing local employees with illegal laborers. . . . [T]he body of a female migrant worker is found . . . on the edge of the property. . . . [Caren] ventures into dangerous territory as she unearths startling new facts about . . . the long-ago disappearance of a former slave . . . that has unsettling ties to the current murder." (Publisher's note)

Locke, Thomas

★ **Emissary**; Thomas Locke. Revell 2015 394 p. map (Legends of the realm) (pbk.) $14.99

ISBN 0800723856; 9780800723859; 9780800724474

LC 2014029802

In this fantasy, by Thomas Locke, part of the Legends of the Realm series, "a reluctant hero undertakes a dangerous and heroic quest to discover his destiny and fight against the dark forces seeking to control The Realm." (Publisher's note)

"Locke (a pseudonym for Christy-winning inspirational thriller author Davis Bunn) launches the Legends of the Realm fantasy series with this competent story that owes more to the Lord of the Rings trilogy than the Bible . . . Even if fans of Bunn's international thrillers don't follow him over to the fantasy realm, readers of inspirational fantasy will enjoy his foray into a new genre." Pub Wkly

Lockridge, Ross

★ **Raintree** County. Houghton Mifflin 1948 1066p il

An epic novel describing a day, the Fourth of July of 1892, in the life of school teacher Johnny Shawnessy in which he participates in the holiday ceremonies of his small Indiana town and meets two old boyhood friends. These events set off a series of flashbacks in his mind and he relives his schooldays, his Civil war experiences, his brief political life, his two marriages, and a love affair that ends badly

"The book is full-blooded, it has gusto, ribaldry, vision, beauty, and narrative skill. It is also repetitious, overly 'organized,' reminiscent of a variety of predecessors, 'literary' in the wrong sense, and too dependent upon source material. But the breath of life sweeps through its voluminous pages." Saturday Rev

Lodato, Victor

Edgar and Lucy; by Victor Lodato. St. Martin's Press 2017 533 p. $27.99

ISBN 1250096987; 9781250096982

LC 2016044041

In this book, by Victor Lodato, "eight-year-old Edgar Fini remembers nothing of the accident people still whisper about. He only knows that his father is gone, his mother has a limp, and his grandmother believes in ghosts. When Edgar meets a man with his own tragic story, the boy begins a journey into a secret wilderness where nothing is clear--not even the line between the living and the dead." (Publisher's note)

"Lodato's remarkable novel traces a broken family's spiritual journey toward healing in moving, magical prose." Booklist.

Lodato, Victor

Mathilda Savitch. Farrar, Straus and Giroux 2009 292p $24

ISBN 978-0-374-20400-6; 0-374-20400-4

LC 2009-04719

A novel about "a preteen whose older sister has died, pushed off a train platform. Logging in to her sister's e-mail, Mathilda eventually adopts her sister's life, contacting her old boyfriends and trying to retrace the footsteps of her last days. . . . Trying to provoke her parents, Mathilda dresses up in her dead sister's birthday dress. Numb, in search of deeper numbness, her mother downs the vodka, and crawls on the kitchen floor, howling, in search of another bottle. Mathilda's original observations carry these incidents—blending imagination, intelligence and kookily beautiful imagery. . . . For the most part, this is a delight and a devil of a book, a tale that fills you with despair and pleasure—often at the same time." Time Out N Y

Lodge, David

Deaf sentence. Viking 2008 294p $25.95

ISBN 978-0-670-01992-2; 0-670-01992-5

LC 2008-1772

"This is a brave novel, which puts a brave face on everything we'd rather not know about ageing, without ducking the atrocity of it all." London Rev Books

Lodge, David, 1935-

Nice work. Viking 1989 277p

ISBN 0-670-82806-8

LC 88-40480

"Robyn Penrose is a lecturer in 19-century literature at a university located in the fictitious English Midlands city of Rummidge. Vic Wilcox is managing director of Pringle's, an industrial casting company located in a grimy suburb. They are thrown together as part of a 'shadow scheme' concocted by their superiors in response to a governmentally ordained 'Industry Year.' Entering into the arrangement with considerable skepticism and lack of appreciation for the other's mode of life, they get off to a rocky start, but then slowly develop a mutual respect and even liking for each other." (Libr J)

A satirical look at "Thatcher's England. Two representatives from different worlds–the groves of academe and the dark satanic mills–meet and fall in (a semblance of) love as they aim to satisfy their physical passions and also open their emotions to new experiences. The academic is a young female professor of literature, and her industrial counterpart is a middle-aged factory manager. Their initial meeting does set off sparks but only to fan the flames of mutual antagonism before an attraction of sorts takes place." Booklist

Lodge, David

★ **Paradise** news; a novel. Viking 1992 293p

ISBN 0-670-84228-1

LC 91-32128

First published 1991 in the United Kingdom

"Mr. Lodge is a serious author who bravely uses coincidence and contrivance to tie up loose ends. And just under the surface of the spirited and often comic adventures of his travelers he runs an undercurrent of understanding about their longings for the perfection of paradise. This comes to us in graceful and disciplined prose that offers vivid glimpses of what lies beyond the tourist hotels of Waikiki–the natural and imperfect world." N Y Times Book Rev

Lodge, David

Thinks-- a novel. Viking 2001 341p

ISBN 0-670-89984-4

LC 2001-17555

"This is the first Lodge novel set in the world of science, and it paints an utterly persuasive portrait of it. The story is a cracking tale, but read it, too, for the ideas. It's obvious that Lodge has become fascinated by the science of thought. Reading this is, so will you." New Sci

Lofts, Norah

Gad's Hall. Doubleday 1978 282p

LC 77-92220

First published 1977 in the United Kingdom

"Dismissing Mrs. Spender's claims that Gad's Hall is haunted, her son Bob and daughter-in-law Jill buy the grand English country estate. . . . With this setup, Lofts deserts her modern family to describe the lives of the Thorleys who founded Gad's Hall in the 1800s. The widowed Mrs. Thorley of that era exerts firm control over the affairs of her children and stepchildren. When unwed Lavinia becomes pregnant, Mrs. Thorley hides the girl until the baby is born. The tragedy that results creates the ghosts that haunt the manor, to affect the Spenders, more than 100 years later." Publ Wkly

Followed by The haunting of Gad's Hall

Logan, Chuck

South of Shiloh; a thriller. HarperCollins Publishers 2008 402p $24.95

ISBN 978-0-06-113669-6; 0-06-113669-7

LC 2007-25672

"When Minnesotan Paul Edin is killed during a re-enactment of the battle of Kirby Creek near Corinth, Miss., local law enforcement quickly declares his death a tragic accident. But when Paul's widow, Jenny, learns that the bullet may have been meant for deputy Kenny Beeman, she's determined to uncover the truth. Reconnecting with John Rane—her ex-lover and the biological father of the child she raised with Paul—Jenny persuades John to go to Corinth and investigate. A photographer and former cop known for taking risks, John joins forces with Kenny in Mississippi and attempts to unravel a complex web of family feuds. John soon realizes that the upcoming re-enactment of the battle of Shiloh could end up as bloody as the original. Despite a few plot holes, Logan skillfully immerses the reader in the traditions and eccentricities of the men who meticulously recreate every aspect of the Civil War." Publ Wkly

Logan, Kirsty

The **gracekeepers**; a novel. Kirsty Logan. Crown Publishers 2015 320 p. (hardcover) $25

ISBN 9780553446616

LC 2014041691

Lambda Literary Awards: LGBT SF/F/Horror (2016)

In this novel, by Kirsty Logan, is "set in a world covered by water. . . . In a world divided between those inhabiting the mainland ('landlockers') and those who float on the sea ('damplings'), loneliness has become a way of life for North and Callanish, until a sudden storm offshore brings change to both their lives--offering them a new understanding of the world they live in and the consequences of the past, while restoring hope in an unexpected future." (Publisher's note)

"Into this forbidding realm, Logan mixes the traditional folklore of Scotland, creating a new mythic tale that is as beautiful and enchanting as it is dark. Lyrical descriptions vividly portray a fantasy world that seems at once futuristic and ancient and evokes the magical tone of Mark Helprin's Winter's Tale (1983)." Booklist

Loh, Vyvyane

Breaking the tongue; a novel. W.W. Norton 2004 407p map $24.95

ISBN 0-393-05792-5

LC 2003-15870

The author "explores such concepts as loyalty to one's family and country, the place of language in culture, and the roles of race, racism and ethnicity in how we perceive ourselves and others. In doing so, she has skillfully touched on questions at the very heart of politics, culture and global relations today." Washington Post Book World

Includes bibliographical references (p. [409]

Lohmann, Jennifer

Winning Ruby Heart; Jennifer Lohmann. Harlequin Books 2014 380 p. $6.75

ISBN 0373608691; 9780373608690

In this novel by Jennifer Lohmann, "exposing world-class athlete Ruby Heart's cheating scandal five years ago made reporter Micah Blackwell's career. Falling in love with her now could end it. Working with Ruby to tell America her story, Micah falls deeper under her spell. But at a crucial moment, his feelings for her conflict with his job--the very thing that once saved him." (Publisher's note)

"Librarian and author Lohmann, a Romance Writers of America Librarian of the Year, has written a remarkable story of a heroine who refuses to let her past mistakes define her future. Lohmann's realistically flawed characters and emotionally compelling plot will resonate with readers who cherish such groundbreaking contemporary romances as Rio Grande Wedding by Ruth Wind (2011), Barefoot in the Grass by Judith Arnold (2010), and Kathleen Korbel's A Soldier's Heart (1994)." Booklist

Loigman, Lynda Cohen ✓

The **two**-family house; Lynda Cohen Loigman. St. Martin's Press 2016 viii, 290 p.p (hardcover) $25.99

ISBN 9781250076922; 9781466888883

LC 2015042915

In this novel, by Lynda Cohen Loigman, "[in] Brooklyn, 1947: in the midst of a blizzard, in a two-family brownstone, two babies are born, minutes apart. The mothers are sisters by marriage: dutiful, quiet Rose,

. . . and warm, generous Helen. . . . Raising their families side by side, supporting one another, Rose and Helen share an impenetrable bond forged before and during that dramatic winter night." (Publisher's note)

"In her first novel, Loigman uses complex characters to deconstruct the anatomy of family relationships and expose deep-rooted emotions, delivering a moving story of love, loss, and sacrifice." Booklist

London, Jack

★ The **call** of the wild; pictures by Wendell Minor. Atheneum Books for Young Readers 1999 112p il $24; pa $4.95

ISBN 0-689-81836-X; 1-4165-0019-7 pa

LC 97-45019

First published 1903 by Macmillan

"Buck, half-St. Bernard, half-Scottish sheepdog, is stolen from his comfortable home in California and pressed into service as a sledge dog in the Klondike. At first he is abused by both man and dog, but he learns to fight ruthlessly. He becomes lead dog on a sledge team, after bettering Spitz, the vicious old leader, in a brutal fight to the death. In John Thornton, he finally finds a master whom he can respect and love. When Thornton is killed by Indians, Buck breaks away to the wilds and becomes the leader of a wolf pack, returning each year to the site of Thornton's death." Reader's Ency. 4th edition

London, Jack

The **complete** short stories of Jack London; edited by Earle Labor, Robert C. Leitz, III, and I. Milo Shepard. Stanford Univ. Press 1993 3v $195

ISBN 0-8047-2058-4

LC 92-44856

"The London scholar and enthusiast will find this collection of Jack London's short fiction invaluable for the 5 previously unpublished stories it contains and for the 28 others it collects for the first time since their original publication in magazines." Choice

London, Jack

Martin Eden. Macmillan 1909 411p

A semi-autobiographical novel. "Eden has had a knock-about life as a sailor, and falling in love with a girl used to middle-class refinement and luxuries, tries to write. He is rejected by editors, and the girl jilts him. The abysmal contrast between the genius of this man, his vital ideals and the big realities of life, and on the other hand, the narrow, unintelligent mediocrity of the 'cultured classes' is brought out with characteristic force." Baker. Guide to Hist Fic

London, Jack

The **Sea**-Wolf; with illustrations by W.J. Aylward. Macmillan 1904 366p

"Wolf Larsen, ruthless captain of the tramp steamer 'Ghost,' receives an unexpected passenger on the high seas, Humphrey Van Weyden, a wealthy ne'er-do-well. In spite of his selfish brutality, Larsen becomes an instrument for good. The treatment he gives to the dilettante Van Weyden teaches the latter to stand on his own legs. He and the poet Maude Brewster, whom the 'Sea-Wolf' loves also, escape to an island as the 'Ghost' sinks and Larsen, mortally sick, is deserted. The lovers later return to civilization." Haydn. Thesaurus of Book Dig

London, Jack

South Sea tales. Macmillan 1911 327p

Contents: The house of Mapuki; The whale tooth; Mauki; "Yah! Yah! Yah"; The heathen; The terrible Solomons; The inevitable white man; The seed of McCoy

London, Jack

The **star** rover. Macmillan 1915 329p

In this science fiction novel about transmigration of the soul, Darrell Standing is condemned to solitary confinement in a corrupt prison. He discovers how to free his soul from his body and escapes through time and space to relive the experiences of his past lives, which include being a caveman, a Danish soldier in the Roman legions, a French swordsman, and an American pioneer boy

London, Jack

★ **White** Fang; Jack London. Scholastic 2001 252p. hardcover o.p. rpt $5.99

ISBN 9780439236195 rpt

LC 98-19241

First published 1906

White Fang "is about a dog, a cross-breed, sold to Beauty Smith. This owner tortures the dog to increase his ferocity and value as a fighter. A new owner Weedom Scott, brings the dog to California, and, by kind treatment, domesticates him. White Fang later sacrifices his life to save Scott." Haydn. Thesaurus of Book Dig

London, Joan, 1948-

The **Golden** Age; Joan London. Penguin Group USA 2016 224 p. (ebook) $9.99; $17

ISBN 9781609453268; 1609453328; 9781609453329

LC 2016033831

In this book, by Joan London, "thirteen-year-old Frank Gold's family, Hungarian Jews, escape the perils of World War II to the safety of Australia in the 1940s. But not long after their arrival Frank is diagnosed with polio. He is sent to a sprawling children's hospital called The Golden Age, where he meets Elsa, the most beautiful girl he has ever seen, a girl who radiates pure light. Frank and Elsa fall in love, fueling one another's rehabilitation." (Publisher's note)

"Like Sister Penny, London sees past people's exteriors to their complex and desirous interiors, and she generously offers those people to us in all their fullness. The novel was a recipient of multiple awards in London's native Australia, and deservedly so: it is pretty much perfect." Pub Wkly

London, Julia

Wild Wicked Scot; Julia London. Harlequin Books 2016 384 p. (The Highland grooms) (ebook) $7.99; $7.99

ISBN 9781459294066; 0373789661; 9780373789665

LC 2016056649

In this Highland Grooms novel, by Julia London, "Margot Armstrong didn't belong in a Scottish chieftain's devil-may-care world. Three years ago she fled their marriage of convenience and hasn't looked back—except to relive the moments spent in wild, rugged Arran McKenzie's passionate embrace. But as their respective countries' fragile unity threatens to unravel, Margot must return to her husband to uncover his role in the treachery before her family can be accused of it." (Publisher's note)

"This absorbing and passionate romance bodes well for future Highland Grooms titles." Booklist

London, Laura

The **windflower**; by Laura London. Grand Central Pub 2014 544 p. $8

ISBN 1455573280; 9781455573288

Originally published 1984

In this historical romance novel, by Laura London, "Merry Wilding is a lady of breeding, of innocence, and of breathtaking beauty. . . . She sets sail from New York . . . [and after being] mistakenly swept aboard an infamous pirate ship, Merry finds herself at the mercy of a wicked crew . . . and one sinfully handsome pirate. Soon she's spending her days yearning for escape, and her nights learning the pleasures of captivity." (Publisher's note)

"A young American on her way to England ends up aboard a pirate ship and in the arms of a dashing buccaneer in this classic romance that is one of the genre's most memorable . . . with exquisite writing, beautifully rendered characters, and perfectly nuanced sexual tension, it's a keeper for fans and libraries alike." LJ

Long, Jeff

The **reckoning**. Atria Books 2004 278p $25

ISBN 0-7434-6300-5

LC 2004-43657

A "journey into the dark past-and present-of Cambodia's former killing fields. Molly Drake, a would-be photojournalist, accompanies a U.S. Army-led search for the bones of a pilot shot down during the war. She meets Duncan O'Brian, an archeologist at a local dig, and John Kleat, who has come back to the country repeatedly, seeking his brother's remains. When bones unexpectedly turn up, Molly photographs them, breaking her agreement with the army not to take pictures of bodies. The captain in charge dismisses her along with O'Brian and Kleat, and the trio make their way to an ancient, fog-enshrouded Angkor-like city where they have evidence an army patrol went missing years ago. . . . Long's considerable knowledge of Cambodian folklore and history is put to good use as he superbly depicts the war-scarred country, its people and its beautiful, hazardous landscape." Publ Wkly

Long, Julie Anne

Hot in Hellcat Canyon; Julie Anne Long. HarperCollins 2016 384 p. (Hellcat Canyon series) (ebook) $7.99; $7.99

ISBN 9780062397621; 0062397613; 9780062397614

LC 2016017408

In this novel, by Julie Anne Long, "a broken truck, a broken career, and a breakup heard around the world land superstar John Tennessee McCord in Hellcat Canyon. Legend has it that hearts come in two colors there: gold or black. And that you can find whatever you're looking for, whether it's love . . . or trouble. JT may have found both in waitress Britt Langley. . . . It's up to the people of Hellcat Canyon to help make sure their future includes a happily ever after." (Publisher's note)

"This laugh-out-loud treat is warmly emotional and richly satisfying." Pub Wkly

Other titles in this series are:
Wild at Whiskey Creek (2016)
Dirty dancing at Devil's Leap (2017)
The first time at Firelight Falls (2018)

Long, Julie Anne

Wild at Whiskey Creek; A Hellcat Canyon Novel. Julie Anne Long. HarperCollins 2016 384 p. (ebook) $7.99; $7.99

ISBN 9780062397645; 006239763X; 9780062397638

LC 2016053087

In this Hot in Hellcat Canyon novel, by Julie Anne Long, "everyone knows the Greenleaf family puts the 'Hell' in Hellcat Canyon—legend has it the only way they ever leave is in a cop car or a casket. But Glory Greenleaf has a different getaway vehicle in mind: her guitar. She has a Texas-sized talent and the ambition (and attitude) to match, but only two people have ever believed in her: her brother, who's in jail, and his best friend . . . who put him there." (Publisher's note)

"A splendid, delectable romance." Kirkus

Longworth, M. L.

Death at the Chateau Bremont; a Verlaque and Bonnet mystery. by M. L. Longworth. Penguin 2011 320p

ISBN 9780143119524

LC 2011007573

In author M. L. Longworth's book, Marine Bonnet "and best friend Sylvie console each other over their affairs, most recently Marine's breakup with Antoine Verlaque . . . So Marine has big butterflies in her stomach as she climbs the stairs to . . . Verlaque's apartment to help him in his latest case: the death of Étienne de Bremont, who supposedly fell from the window of his family's chateau. Marine, a childhood friend of Etienne and his brother François, confirms that a fall by the sure-footed young count is unlikely . . . Verlaque and Bonnet want answers—but is that all they want?" (Kirkus)

Longworth, M. L.

Murder in the Rue Dumas; a Verlaque and Bonnet provençal mystery. M.L. Longworth. Penguin Books 2012 296 p.

ISBN 0143121545; 9780143121541

LC 2012023725

This novel by M. L. Longworth "finds Verlaque stumped. The director of theology at the Université d'Aix was just about to name the recipient of an elite fellowship, as well as his own successor, when his lips were sealed permanently. Yet Verlaque isn't convinced that any of the academics are capable of murder. Aided by Bonnet, Verlaque turns Provence upside down, uncovering a world far more complicated than university politics." (Author's note)

Longworth, M. L.

Murder on the Île Sordou; a Verlaque and Bonnet Provençal mystery. M.L. Longworth. Penguin Books 2014 320 p. (paperback) $15

ISBN 0143125540; 9780143125549

LC 2014010451

In this novel by M.L. Longworth "Judge Antoine Verlaque and his girlfriend, law professor Marine Bonnet, are hoping to enjoy a relaxing holiday at the Locanda Sordou, an opulent hotel. The murder of one of the guests casts a shadow over everyone's vacation, and Verlaque and Bonnet are once again called to investigate. But things go from bad to worse when a violent storm cuts off all communication with the mainland." (Publisher's note)

"Longworth once again immerses readers in French culture with this whodunit, which will delight Francophiles and fans of Donna Leon and Andrea Camilleri. The setting will also appeal to readers who enjoy trapped-on-the-island mysteries in the tradition of Agatha Christie's And Then There Were None." LJ

López Barrio, Cristina

The **House** of Impossible Loves; Cristina Lopez Barrio ; translated from the Spanish by Lisa Carter. Houghton Mifflin Harcourt 2013 336 p. (hardcover) $25

ISBN 0547661193; 9780547661193

In this novel, by Cristina Lopez Barrio, "the Laguna women suffer from an odd affliction: each generation is condemned to tragic love affairs and to give birth only to girls who are unable to escape the cruel fate of their mothers. . . . Clara Laguna, the latest in the family line, . . . [is] pregnant with yet another daughter, but the seeds of change are sown. Eventually the long-awaited son--Santiago, the great-great grandson of Clara--is born." (Publisher's note)

Lopez, Barry Holstun

Resistance; [by] Barry Lopez. Alfred A. Knopf 2004 163p il $18

ISBN 1-400-04220-8

LC 2003-65986

"If it's true the author's erudite, well-meaning characters all sound very much alike, it's also true that one of his goals is to underscore the responsibility of artists to speak as one when speaking truth to power. To his credit, Lopez never sacrifices craft to politics." N Y Times Book Rev

Lopez, Robert

All back full; a novel in three acts. Robert Lopez. Dzanc Books 2017 202 p. (paperback) $16.95

ISBN 9781941088678

LC 2016017549

"Told in a genre-defying style that melds the depth of the novel with the honesty of the stage, 'All Back Full,' [by Robert Lopez] charts one day in a marriage at once usual and unusual, exploring what we say to each other when we say nothing, and the ways we speak to each other without words." (Publisher's note)

" The result is a provocative portrait of domesticity, made curiously more realistic by its unexpected strangeness." Booklist

Lopez, Robert

Good People; Robert Lopez. Bellevue Literary Press 2016 192 p. $16.95

ISBN 1942658028; 9781942658023

In this short story collection, Robert Lopez, "a motley cast of obsessive, self-deluded outsiders narrate their darker moments, which include kidnapping, voyeurism, and psychic masochism. As their struggles give way to the black humor of life's unreason, the bleak merges with the oddly poetic, in a style as lean and resolute as Carver or Hemingway." (Publisher's note)

Lord, Bette Bao

The **middle** heart; a novel. Knopf 1996 370p $25

ISBN 0-394-53432-8

LC 95-36165

The story begins in early 1930s China, "when three young people forge an unlikely alliance that survives five decades of loss and love. There's Steele Hope, the second son of the head of the once noble and powerful Li family; Mountain Pine, his 'bookmate' and retainer; and a destitute girl posing as a boy named Firecrackers. The novel's early sections sparkle with hope and joy as the three devoted friends romp and grow, but personal tragedy and war soon intrude." Booklist

Lord, Karen

Redemption in indigo; a novel. Small Beer Press 2010 188p pa $16

ISBN 9781931520669 pa; 1931520666 pa

LC 2009-54298

Based on a Senegalese folktale, Lord "recounts the fantastical adventures of Paama, who escapes her unfortunate marriage only to be placed in unwitting charge of awesome universal powers. An enchanted kitchen implement allows Paama to bring the slightest probabilities to pass. At first unconscious of this ability, she rescues a drowning boy and resurrects a plague victim from the dead. Gradually the 'undying ones' . . . teach her how the branching implications of her interference lead to consequences a mere human woman could never foresee. Full of sharp insights and humorous asides. . . , 'Redemption' extends the Caribbean Island storyteller's art into the 21st century and hopefully, beyond." Seattle Times

Lordan, Beth

But come ye back; a novel in stories. Morrow 2004 278p $23.95

ISBN 0-06-053036-7

LC 2003-56217

"Lordan's muted prose and fluting Irishisms ('Right, so,' 'Grand') are pleasant if rather selfconscious, and her characters are human, breathing people, forthrightly crafted. The novel-in-stories structure produces some inconsistencies and redundancies, but this is a quietly engaging effort." Publ Wkly

Louis, Édouard

The **end** of Eddy; Édouard Louis ; translated from the French by Michael Lucey. First American edition Farrar, Straus & Giroux 2017 192 p. (hardback) $23

ISBN 9780374716394; 9780374266653

LC 2016041340

"'The End of Eddy' captures the violence and desperation of life in a French factory town. It is also a sensitive, universal portrait of boyhood and sexual awakening. Like Karl Ove Knausgaard or Edmund White, Édouard Louis writes from his own undisguised experience, but he writes with an openness and a compassionate intelligence that are all his own." (Publisher's note)

"In this excellent autobiographical novel, a middle school boy struggles to forge an identity in a French industrial town hostile in every way to his homosexuality." Pub Wkly

Lourey, Jess ✓

★ **January** thaw; a Murder-by-Month Mystery. Jess Lourey. Midnight Ink 2014 288 p. (A Murder-by-Month mystery) $14.99

ISBN 0738738751; 9780738738758

LC 2013027483

In this book, by Jess Lourey, "private-eye-in-training Mira James loves Minnesota's crisp January days. . . . But when Mrs. Berns's erratic Zamboni driving uncovers an icebound dead man, Mira's cold-weather tranquility threatens to melt away. . . . There's big trouble brewing in Battle Lake. And if Mira can't figure out who's behind it, the next time she feels sub-zero temperatures, she may be sporting a toe tag in the town morgue." (Publisher's note)

Lourie, Richard

A **hatred** for tulips. Thomas Dunne Books 2007 182p $22.95

ISBN 978-0-312-34933-2; 0-312-34933-5

LC 2006-48862

"Lourie's novel is more than a mystery: at its heart is not only Anne Frank's history, but all of Holland's. Joop derides the Dutch for indulging what, until recently, was a very real Anne Frank amnesia. . . . Ironically, the book is best where it has little to say about Anne Frank. The connection allows Lourie to pose interesting questions about collaboration and guilt during the war, but it rings truest as a story about a boy, in a difficult family, in a difficult time, and the unintended consequences of trying to do what looks like the right thing." Christ Sci Monit

Lovecraft, H. P.

At the mountains of madness, and other novels; selected by August Derleth; with texts edited by S.T. Joshi and introduction by James Turner. Arkham House Pubs. 1985 458p

ISBN 0-87054-038-6

LC 85-1254

A reissue of the title first published 1964 and analyzed in Short story index

Lovecraft, H. P.

The **Dunwich** horror, and others; selected by August Derleth, with texts edited by S.T. Joshi and an introduction by Robert Block. Arkham House Pubs. 1985 433p

ISBN 0-87054-037-8

A reissue of the title first published 1963 and analyzed in Short story index

Lovecraft, H. P.

★ **H.** P. Lovecraft; tales. edited by Peter Straub. Library of America 2005 838p $35

ISBN 1-93108-272-3

LC 2004-48979

"If you spend enough time in Lovecraft's lonely landscapes, fear really does develop: not the fear that you will come across unearthly creatures, but the fear that you will come across little else. And what first seems horridly overdone accumulates a creepy minimalism. Taken as a whole, Lovecraft's work exhibits a hopeless isolation not unlike that of Samuel Beckett: lonely man after lonely man, wandering aimlessly through a shadowy city or holing up in rural emptiness, pursuing unspeakable secrets or being pursued by secret unspeakables, all to little avail and to no comfort. There is something funny about this—in small doses. But by the end of this collection, one does not hear giggling so much as the echoes of those giggles as they vanish into the ether lonely, desperate and, yes, very, very scary." N Y Times Book Rev

Lovecraft, H. P.

The **horror** in the museum, and other revisions; with texts edited by S. T. Joshi, and an introduction by August Derleth. Arkham House Pubs. 1989 450p

LC 88-7921

"The volume is divided into 'Primary Revisions,' those stories that are all Lovecraft but for an idea, and 'Secondary Revisions,' clients' manuscripts heavily edited and revised." Publ Wkly

Lovesey, Peter

Bertie and the seven bodies. Mysterious Press 1990 196p

LC 89-12405

"Narrated by Bertie himself, the voice here is perfectly accurate; Lovesey gives his main character just the right tone of sophistication, charm, anti-intellectualism, and savoir faire—mixed in with ennui. A wonderfully put together puzzle." Booklist

Lovesey, Peter

★ **Diamond** dust. Soho Press 2002 343p $24

ISBN 1-56947-291-2

LC 2002-17567

"In a bold display of virtuosity, Lovesey takes his hero to emotional places he's never been before while constructing a plot of infernal ingenuity." N Y Times Book Rev

Lovesey, Peter

Diamond solitaire. Mysterious Press 1993 343p

ISBN 0-89296-535-5

LC 92-50660

First published 1992 in the United Kingdom

"Peter Diamond is plagued by bad karma. Formerly detective superintendent of police in Bath, he's sunk to being a security guard at Harrod's—until a small Asian child is found in the area of the store Peter patrols. Out of a job once again (security breaches are no laughing matter at terrorist-obsessed Harrod's), Diamond becomes intrigued by the Asian child, who is autistic and who remains unclaimed despite massive publicity. What starts out as a kindly effort to restore the child to her parents turns into an international adventure as Diamond travels from London to New York to Japan and confronts millionaire sumo wrestlers, unethical drug researchers, and corrupt businessmen." Booklist

Lovesey, Peter

The **house** sitter. Soho Press 2003 346p $25

ISBN 1-56947-326-9

LC 2002-42626

"The identity of the killer, when finally revealed, is genuinely startling, and not because of authorial obfuscation. The writing is as smooth as polished steel." Publ Wkly

Lovesey, Peter

The **last** detective. Doubleday 1991 331p

LC 91-11859

"An intricate, many-tiered examination of police work, especially modern forensic technology, complete with computers and genetic fingerprinting. Everything meshes perfectly in this airtight tale." Booklist

Other titles about Peter Diamond are:
Diamond solitaire (1992)
The summons (1995)
Bloodhounds (1996)
Upon a dark night (1997)
The vault (2000)
Diamond dust (2002)
The house sitter (2003)
The secret hangman (2007)
Skeleton hill (2009)
Stagestruck (2011)
Cop to corpse (2012)
The tooth tattoo (2013)
The stone wife (2014)
Down among the dead men (2015)
Another one goes tonight (2016)
Beau death (2017)

Lovesey, Peter

Skeleton Hill. Soho Press 2009 326p $24

ISBN 978-1-56947-598-0; 1-56947-598-9

LC 2009-11128

Another of Lovesey's "convoluted plots, layered with historical lore and teeming with comic characters up to their necks in no good. Diamond is a classic—better catch him while you can." N Y Times Book Rev

Lovesey, Peter

The **tooth** tattoo; Peter Lovesey. Soho Press, Inc. 2013 348 p. (hardcover) $25.95

ISBN 161695230X; 9781616952303

LC 2012043412

This is Peter Lovesey's 13th Peter Diamond mystery. Violist Mel Farran is robbed of his viola. "Seven years later, an acclaimed string quartet, whose previous violist disappeared in Budapest in 2008, recruits Farran. Meanwhile, Bath CID's Diamond, who's having some trouble with his significant other, looks into the suspicious death of a woman found in a canal. The only clue to her identity is the tattoo of a musical note on one of her teeth." (Publishers Weekly)

Lovesey, Peter

Upon a dark night. Mysterious Press 1998 374p

LC 97-48922

First published 1997 in the United Kingdom

A "triumph of plotting from this master of the classic puzzle form." N Y Times Book Rev

Lovesey, Peter

The **vault**. Soho Press 2000 331p $23

ISBN 1-56947-208-4

LC 00-41010

First published 1999 in the United Kingdom

"A wealth of good things fills this novel: Lovesey's deft plotting, his hilarious send-ups of the Brits through the perspective of the American professor, and his intriguing allusions to the architecture and literary history of Bath." Booklist

Lovesey, Peter

Waxwork. Pantheon Bks. 1978 239p

LC 77-90420

"There is certainly enough here to warrant the praise given this tale by more than one highly regarded colleague in crime. Set in the London and Kew of 1888, a case of KCN poisoning following upon blackmail taxes the abilities of the police, but in the end Sgt. Cribb really does distinguish himself. The title alludes to Tussaud's Waxwork Exhibition." Barzun. Cat of Crime. Rev and enl edition

Lovett, Andrew

Everlasting Lane; Andrew Lovett. Melville House 2015 368 p. (hardback) $25.95

ISBN 1612193803; 9781612193809

LC 2014012463

This book by Andrwe Lovett "follows 10-year-old Peter Lambert, who is uprooted by his mother to go live in a 'dusty and undisturbed' cottage in the Amberley countryside in the mid-1970s after his WWII veteran father's untimely death. Even more confounding than his new environment are his mother's decision to change her name to Kat; her reference to the fact that he'd lived in the town before; and the plucky, dominating behavior of Anna-Marie, the girl next door." (Publishers Weekly)

"The narrative is driven by images, connecting and unfolding like the mysteries beneath the surface: mirrors, clocks, butterflies and a storybook rambling through the physical Everlasting Lane, lush and green and seemingly unending. Deeper still is the reminder that the narrative itself is connected to the realm of imagination, as Peter muses on the idea that like stories, real life can be amended for happy endings and a second chance to make the right decision. Beautifully written, and as charming as it is dark, the novel unwraps the endless secrets that elude a child." Kirkus

Lovett, Charlie

The **bookman's** tale; a novel of obsession. Charlie Lovett. Viking 2013 352 p. (hardcover) $27.95

ISBN 0670026476; 9780670026470

LC 2013001559

In this novel, by Charlie Lovett, "nine months earlier, the death of his beloved wife, Amanda, had left him shattered. The young antiquarian bookseller relocated from North Carolina to the English countryside. . . . But upon opening an eighteenth-century study of Shakespeare forgeries, . . . a portrait of Amanda tumbles out of its pages. Of course, it isn't really her. . . . Yet the resemblance is uncanny, and Peter becomes obsessed with learning the picture's origins." (Publisher's note)

Lovett, Charlie

The **lost** book of the Grail; or, a visitor's guide to Barchester Cathedral. Charlie Lovett. Viking 2017 320 p. (hardcover : alk. paper) $26

ISBN 0399562516; 9780399562518; 9780399562525

LC 2016056682

This book, by Charlie Lovett, is "about an obsessive bibliophile's quest through time to discover a missing manuscript, the unknown history of an English Cathedral, and the secret of the Holy Grail. . . . Lovett's unique work combines literary and historical research with classic elements of cozy mysteries, classic love stories, and exciting adventure tales." (Publisher's note)

"A solidly built, innocently bookish diversion with a distinct Masterpiece Theater flavor." Kirkus

Lowell, Elizabeth

Pearl Cove. Avon Bks. 1999 376p

ISBN 0-380-97404-5

LC 99-21639

This is the author's "third book featuring the Donovan clan. . . . Archer, the oldest son, is plunged into the past with a call for help from the only woman he has ever loved, Hannah McGarry, his half-brother Len's wife. After an injury paralyzes Len, he focuses on developing a unique strain of black pearls and mentally torturing his wife. When a cyclone hits their Australian pearl farm, Hannah finds her husband dead and the pearls missing. Archer comes to protect her and avenge Len's death. . . . This is a riveting mix of suspense and romance." Booklist

Lowenthal, Michael

Charity girl. Houghton Mifflin 2007 323p $24

ISBN 978-0-618-54629-9; 0-618-54629-4

LC 2005-37775

"Lowenthal's narrative style is perfect for a heroine who suffers but remains a survivor, striking just the right mix of dark and light, worldly and innocent. Providing Frieda with flickers of humor and joy, he guarantees her our sympathy." N Y Times Book Rev

Lowry, Malcolm

★ **Under** the volcano. Reynal & Hitchcock 1947 375p

This novel "presents in detail the events of {a} single day in a single place—the Day of the Dead in a town in Mexico, with Popocatepetl and Ixtaccihuatl looking down. It is the last day on earth of the British Consul, Geoffrey Firmin, and he is dying of alcoholism. Like any tragic hero, he is fully aware of the choice he has made: he clings to his sloth, he needs salvation through love but will not utter the word which will bring it, he lets his morbid lust for drink drag him from bar to bar. In other words, he has made a deliberate choice of damnation. . . . We don't despise or even dislike Firmin, despite his weaknesses and his self-destructive urge. As with all tragic heroes (and this novel is a genuine tragedy) he sums up the flaws which are latent or actual in all of us." Burgess. 99 Novels

Ludlum, Robert, 1927-2001

★ The **Bourne** identity. Marek, R. 1980 523p

ISBN 9780553593549; 9781417618101

LC 79023638

"Jason Bourne is shot and left for dead. He survives, but without a memory. Slowly, painstakingly, he retraces his past, only to find himself hunted by assassins of several governments, including his own. He fights against seemingly insurmountable odds—especially his very limited knowledge of his past—to discover his identity and stop his enemies before it is too late." Libr J

Followed by The Bourne supremacy

Ludlum, Robert, 1927-2001

The **Bourne** supremacy. Random House 1986 597p

ISBN 9781442081284; 9780345538208

LC 85018318

"In this sequel to The Bourne Identity David Webb, still suffering flashbacks to his Jason Bourne persona, is forced to undertake a final, possibly fatal mission after his wife is kidnapped. He must find and capture an assassin who is posing as Bourne in Hong Kong. By so doing he'll foil a plot that could plunge the Far East and then the world into war." Libr J

Followed by The Bourne ultimatum

Ludlum, Robert, 1927-2001

The **Bourne** ultimatum. Random House 1990 611p

ISBN 9780345538215; 9780679400431

LC 89043201

"When the international terrorist known as Carlos the Jackal penetrates his civilian identity, Webb must again assume the Bourne persona to protect his wife and small children. In their renewed struggle, the two master assassins uncover the revived existence of Medusa, the sinister alliance that originally led to the establishment of the Bourne identity." Publ Wkly

Ludlum, Robert, 1927-2001

The **Gemini** contenders. Dial Press (NY) 1976 402p

Ludlum is "at the top of his form here as he tells a suspenseful story that gives fresh slants to old themes." Publ Wkly

Ludlum, Robert, 1927-2001

The **Janson** directive. St. Martin's Press 2002 547p $27.95

ISBN 0-312-25348-6

LC 2002-5136

"The hero is Paul Janson, a private security consultant who retired a few years ago after a notorious career as the U.S. government's go-to guy for nasty jobs no one else was willing to take. Against his better judgment, Janson accepts an assignment to rescue Peter Novak, a Nobel Peace Prize-winning philanthropist and international troubleshooter held captive by Islamic extremists on an island in the Indian Ocean. . . . Extremely engaging and agonizingly suspenseful, Ludlum's plot bolts from scene to scene and locale to locale—Hungary, Amsterdam, London, New York City—never settling for one bombshell when it can drop four or five." Publ Wkly

Ludlum, Robert, 1927-2001

The **Matlock** paper. Dial Press (NY) 1973 312p

"James Matlock, instructor in Elizabethan literature at Carlyle University in Connecticut, formerly an Army officer in Vietnam, is drawn into the most personally dangerous and violent struggle of his life when he is requested to cooperate with a government narcotic agent in exploring Carlyle's connection with the expanding drug traffic in New England." Publ Wkly

Ludlum, Robert, 1927-2001

The **Prometheus** deception. St. Martin's Press 2000 509p

ISBN 0-312-25346-X

LC 00-62585

"Nick Bryson works for an ultrasecret intelligence organization; after making a mistake during a mission, he's put out to pasture. Later, he's brought back into the game by a different intelligence group, and he learns that everything he believed about his former bosses was a lie—until, that is, he discovers that everything the second organization has told him is also a lie. Bryson winds up trying single-handedly to save the world from a shadowy terrorist group, while simultaneously trying to figure out which of the various @good guys' he should believe. . . . The pace is fast, the action plentiful, and the story confusing enough to keep us turning the pages." Booklist

Ludlum, Robert, 1927-2001

The **Rhinemann** exchange. Dial Press (NY) 1974 460p

"A World War II espionage novel detailing an attempted treasonous exchange between the Germans and the Americans—the technological secret of a gyroscopic guidance system in return for industrial diamonds. This is to be brought off by a disenfranchised German Jew in Buenos Aires, tracked by an American agent not quite in the know and thus in jeopardy." Booklist

Ludlum, Robert, 1927-2001

The **Sigma** protocol. St. Martin's Press 2001 535p

ISBN 0-312-27688-5

LC 2001-48240

"Ludlum keeps things moving with plenty of gunplay and running about. Uncharacteristically, he also lets things slow down from time to time, long enough for us to get to know the players in this complicated story." Booklist

Ludwig, Benjamin

★ **Ginny** Moon; a novel. by Benjamin Ludwig. Park Row Books 2017 360 p. $26.99

ISBN 0778330168; 9780778330165

In this novel, by Benjamin Ludwig, "Ginny Moon is exceptional. Everyone knows it--her friends at school . . . and especially her new adoptive parents. They all love her, even if they don't quite understand her. They want her to feel like she belongs. What they don't know is that Ginny has no intention of belonging. She's found her birth-mother on Facebook, and is determined to get back to her--even if it means going back to a place that was extremely dangerous." (Publisher's note)

"Ludwig's excellent debut is both a unique coming-of-age tale and a powerful affirmation of the fragility and strength of families." Pub Wkly.

Luiselli, Valeria

The **story** of my teeth; Valeria Luiselli ; translation, Christina MacSweeney. Coffee House Press 2015 195 p. illustrations (paperback) $16.95

ISBN 1566894093; 9781566894098

LC 2015009759

Los Angeles Times Book Prize: Fiction (2015)

National Book Critics Circle Award Finalist: Fiction (2015)

"Highway is a late-in-life world traveler, yarn spinner, collector, and legendary auctioneer. His most precious possessions are the teeth of the 'notorious infamous' like Plato, Petrarch, and Virginia Woolf. Written in collaboration with the workers at a Jumex juice factory, 'Teeth' is [a] . . . romp through the industrial suburbs of Mexico City and . . . Luiselli's own literary influences." (Publisher's note)

"Reminiscent of the serialized novels used to entertain and educate Cuban cigar-rollers, Luiselli marvelously redefines the relationship between author and audience." Booklist

Lukas, Michael David

The **Oracle** of Stamboul; a novel. Harper 2011 294p $24.99

ISBN 978-0-06-201209-8; 0-06-201209-6

LC 2010-14810

"Lukas' book is an appealing blend of magical and historical realism. Its story line is as loosely drawn, and as purposeful, as that flock of hoopoes that accompany the protagonist everywhere she goes. Lukas, too, is a graceful and inventive writer, and reflects his travels across Turkey and his love especially for Istanbul in dozens of polished and elegant passages scattered through the narrative. . . . And while it might seem a novel for young readers, this is a polished literary work that will appeal to a wide readership." Cleveland Plain Dealer

Lundrigan, Nicole

Glass boys; a novel. Douglas & McIntyre 2011 300 p. (paperback) $18.95

ISBN 1553657977; 9781553657972

In this book by Nicole Lundrigan, "when Roy Trench is killed in a drunken prank gone wrong, his brother Lewis sees blood on the hands of the man responsible: the abusive alcoholic, Eli Fagan. Though the courts rule the death an accident, the event opens a seam of hate between the two families of Knife's Point, Newfoundland." (Publisher's note)

Lupton, Rosamund

Afterwards; a novel. Rosamund Lupton. Crown 2012 386 p.

ISBN 9780307716545

LC 2011041524

In this book, "Grace Covey and her teenaged daughter Jenny are badly injured in an arson fire, and both lie unconscious in the hospital. Despite outside appearances, both are well aware of what's going on around them and are taking steps to understand what happened. Grace, suffering from a head injury that leaves her in a coma, and Jenny, badly burned, are both able to leave their damaged bodies. They can speak to each other, hear all the conversations going on around them, and can even hitch rides in cars as police and family members inspect the scene and question those involved. . . . [T]hey realize the danger isn't over. They are the only ones who have all the pieces of the mystery but they can only communicate with each other." (Libr J)

Lupton, Rosamund

Sister; a novel. Crown Publishers 2011 319p $24

ISBN 978-0-307-71651-4

LC 2010-25327

"Written in the form of a letter from Beatrice, the older, more substantial sister, to her younger, bohemian sibling, Tess, the narrative reveals within the first few pages that Tess has gone missing and is found dead. Bea and Tess, even with a big age difference and an ocean between them, were incredibly close, so when Bea receives the 'phone call,' she drops everything and races from New York City to London. Although Tess's death is ruled a suicide, Bea knows her sister would never kill herself. As Bea frantically tries to find the murderer, in the process losing pieces of herself, the reader is catapulted into the search." Libr J

Lurie, Alison

Foreign affairs. Random House 1984 291p

LC 84-42657

"Lurie portrays these entanglements with her customary astute wit and deft characterization, but also with unexpected warmth and generosity. A wry, wonderful book." Libr J

Lustbader, Eric

Floating city; a Nicholas Linnear novel. by Eric Lustbader. Pocket Bks. 1994 404p

LC 93-49360

"Nicholas Linnear and his private-eye buddy, Lew Croaker, dash around the globe attempting to thwart the murder of the Yakuza boss of bosses and stop the development of a terrible new weapon and a super-cartel bent on world domination." Booklist

Lustbader, Eric

Mistress of the pearl. Tor Bks. 2004 588p map $27.95

ISBN 0-312-87237-2

LC 2003-60698

This novel "builds powerfully upon its predecessors, thanks to characters of uncommon depth and complexity, lots of perplexing dilemmas for them to wrestle with, and plenty of exciting swordplay and gore." Booklist

Lutz, John

Burn. Holt & Co. 1995 278p

ISBN 0-8050-3480-3

LC 94-32187

This mystery, "in which the motive isn't greed or passion but rather grief and loss, is one of the best in a fine series." Booklist

Lutz, John

Final seconds; by John Lutz and David August. Kensington Bks. 1998 316p

ISBN 1-57566-259-0

LC 97-75929

"The most welcome realism in the book comes from the authors' resistance to the far-fetched elements that creep into many thrillers. Their seamless collaboration is notable for the efficiency of the plotting and for the unusual credibility of the story, its characters and the methodical way they do their work." Publ Wkly

Lutz, John

Lightning. Holt & Co. 1996 296p

ISBN 0-8050-4379-9

LC 95-43273

"Behind the intransigent and hackneyed rhetoric of both sides, Carver finds venality aplenty as he and Beth attempt to come to terms with their loss. Veteran novelist Lutz ties some nifty twists into his plot, which moves quickly towards a final deadly confrontation." Publ Wkly

Lutz, Lisa

Curse of the Spellmans. Simon & Schuster 2008 409p $25

ISBN 978-1-4165-3241-5; 1-4165-3241-2

LC 2007-21152

"Licensed P.I. Isabel 'Izzy' Spellman has been arrested for the fourth time in two months, and no one from her oddball family of fellow investigators will bail her out. Her sister, Rae, has run over Izzy's 'fiancé,' Inspector Henry Stone, during a driving lesson. The senior Spellmans have staged a 'disappearance,' their term for a vacation where no one can reach them. To complicate Izzy's life further, a man with the suspiciously ordinary name of John Brown has moved next door, and she's absolutely positive he's up to no good. . . . Once again, Lutz treats readers to a madcap roller-coaster ride." Libr J

Lutz, Lisa

How to start a fire; Lisa Lutz. Houghton Mifflin Harcourt 2015 352 p. (hardcover) $25

ISBN 0544411633; 9780544411630

LC 2014033603

In this book, by Lisa Lutz, "[t]hree friends try to muddle through their complicated lives. Kate Smirnoff, Anna Fury, and Georgianna 'George' Leoni become friends at UC Santa Cruz in the early 1990s. . . . Over the next two decades, the women will find opportunities to reconnect as their lives, and the nature of their friendship, carry on in a constant state of flux. They fall in and out of marriages, careers, cities, and winning or losing sides of battles with their personal demons." (Kirkus Reviews)

"Although the ending is a bit flat in comparison to the narrative drive of the story, this is an absorbing tale that will satisfy Spellman fans as well as women's-fiction readers who like a good ensemble story." Booklist

Lutz, Lisa

The **last** word; a Spellman novel. Lisa Lutz. Simon & Schuster 2013 352 p. $25

ISBN 1451686668; 9781451686661

LC 2013005096

This is Lisa Lutz's sixth Spellman novel. Here, everyone "in the Spellman clan is in an uproar because of Isabel's hostile takeover of the firm. . . . Meanwhile, Izzy is helping client Edward Slayter hide his Alzheimer's, but it's clear someone is determined to get him kicked out as CEO of a very profitable venture capital firm, and that someone is willing to sic the FBI on Izzy for embezzlement as part of the scheme." (Publishers Weekly)

Lutz, Lisa

The **Passenger**; by Lisa Lutz. Simon & Schuster 2016 320 p. $25.99

ISBN 1451686633; 9781451686630

In this book, by Lisa Lutz, "Forty-eight hours after leaving her husband's body at the base of the stairs, Tanya Dubois cashes in her credit cards, dyes her hair brown, demands a new name from a shadowy voice over the phone, and flees town. It's not the first time. She meets Blue, a female bartender who recognizes the hunted look in a fugitive's eyes and offers her a place to stay. With dwindling choices, Tanya-now-Amelia accepts. An uneasy—and dangerous—alliance is born." (Publisher's note)

"Lutz develops riveting suspense by slowly revealing the events that first sent Tanya/Amelia on the run, while pouring threats on her gritty heroine's increasingly tenuous bids at survival. Binge-worthy fare, especially for those drawn to strong female protagonists." Booklist

Lutz, Lisa

Revenge of the Spellmans. Simon & Schuster 2009 375p $25

ISBN 978-1-4165-9338-6

LC 2009-2281

"Those in the market for mayhem and mirth will revel in Lutz's irresistible blend of suspense, irony, and wit." Booklist

Lutz, Lisa

The **Spellman** files; a novel. Simon & Schuster 2007 352p $25

ISBN 978-1-4165-3239-2; 1-4165-3239-0

LC 2006-49161

"Isabel 'Izzy' Spellman, a San Francisco PI who began working for Spellman Investigations at age 12, could easily pass as Buffy or Veronica Mars's wiser but funnier older sister. Izzy digs TV, too, especially Get Smart (an ex-boyfriend's ownership of the complete bootlegged DVD set is his major selling point). Now 28, Izzy thinks she wants out, but elects to take on a cold case while dealing with 14-year-old sister Rae, a nightmarish Nancy Drew, and parents who have no qualms about bugging their children's bedrooms. At times the dialogue-heavy text reads like a script and the action flags, but these are quibbles. When Rae suddenly disappears, Izzy and her family must learn some serious lessons in order to find her." Publ Wkly

Lychack, William

The **wasp** eater. Houghton Mifflin 2004 164p $21

ISBN 0-618-30244-1

LC 2004-42728

"Just when the dysfunctional family drama seems entirely wrung out, along comes a book so freshly original that it seems to have invented the genre. What's so remarkable here is the understatedness, the quietly intense writing carefully containing more emotion than many louder novels have to show. Original, too, is the impulse to heal rather than break away-however mixed the outcome." Libr J

Lynch, Jim

Border songs. Alfred A. Knopf 2009 291p $25.95

ISBN 978-0-307-27117-4; 0-307-27117-X

LC 2008-53514

"Six foot eight and dyslexic, Brandon Vanderkool has trouble relating to people, but he's supremely knowledgeable about birds. His dad doesn't think he's cut out for dairy farming, so Brandon ends up in the Border Patrol ruling the divide between Washington and Canada. Though he spends most of his time bird watching, smugglers and illegals keep falling his way, and he soon has a reputation as the patrol's top man. Meanwhile, his father struggles with the farm, his mother struggles with incipient Alzheimer's, a Canadian girl that Brandon's sweet on struggles with her decision to cultivate pot to smuggle across the border, and a new neighbor delights in interviewing everyone." Libr J

Lynch, Jim

Truth like the sun; Jim Lynch. Alfred A. Knopf 2012 253 p. $25.95

ISBN 030795868X; 9780307958686; 9781408830314

LC 2011050564

This novel, set in Seattle, Washington, follows "Roger Morgan . . . the mastermind behind the fair that made the city famous and . . . a backstage power forty years later, when at the age of seventy he runs for mayor in hopes of restoring all of Seattle's former glory. Helen Gulanos, a reporter . . . sees her assignment to investigate the events of 1962 become front-page news with Morgan's candidacy, and resolves to find out who he really is and where his power comes from." (Publisher's note)

"A briskly paced novel that gives us an insider's view into both the politics of culture and the culture of politics." Kirkus

Lynch, Katie

Confucius Jane; A Novel. Katie Lynch. Forge Books 2016 352 p. (hardback) $26.99; (ebook) $60

ISBN 9780765381682; 9780765383792; 9781466883529

LC 2015033356

This novel by Katie Lynch "depicts New York City's Chinatown while taking the reader on a touching journey of family, community, and love. . . . Jane Morrow has a new job, helping out in her uncle's fortune cookie factory. . . . When Jane meets medical student Sutton St. James, . . . sparks fly. . . . Sutton inspires Jane to . . . dream again—and challenges her to have faith in herself. But can Sutton and Jane overcome a scandalous secret that threatens to keep them apart?" (Publisher's note)

"Lynch's new adult debut is a solid modern romance that expresses the gamut of emotions involved at the start of a new relationship." LJ

Lynch, Scott

The **lies** of Locke Lamora. Bantam 2006 499p map (Gentleman Bastard) hardcover o.p. pa $7.99

ISBN 0-553-80467-7; 978-0-553-80467-6; 0-553-58894-x; 9780553588941

LC 2006-42653

"Fans of lavishly appointed fantasy will be in seventh heaven here, but it will be nearly as popular with readers of literary crime fiction. This is a true genre bender, at home on almost any kind of fiction shelf." Booklist

Lynch, Scott

Red seas under red skies; Scott Lynch. Bantam Books 2007 558 p. maps (Gentlemen Bastard) $23

ISBN 0553804685; 9780553804683

LC 2007018597

This fantasy novel, by Scott Lynch, continues the adventures of "a band of daring thieves led by con artist extraordinaire Locke Lamora. . . . After a brutal battle with the underworld . . . , Locke and his trusted sidekick, Jean, . . . are soon back to . . . stealing from the undeserving rich and pocketing the proceeds for themselves. . . . This time, however, they have targeted the grandest prize of all: the Sinspire, the most exclusive and heavily guarded gambling house in the world." (Publisher's note)

"[F]ast paced, colorful, funny, with a fiendishly intricate plot containing plenty of right-angle turns." Booklist

Lynch, Scott

The **Republic** of Thieves; by Scott Lynch. Del Rey 2013 672 p. (hardcover : acid-free paper) $28

ISBN 0553804693; 9780553804690

LC 2013024809

In this book by Scott Lynch, "with what should have been the greatest heist of their career gone spectacularly sour, Locke and his trusted partner, Jean, have barely escaped with their lives. Or at least Jean has. But Locke is slowly succumbing to a deadly poison that no alchemist or physiker can cure. Yet just as the end is near, a mysterious Bondsmage offers Locke an opportunity that will either save him or finish him off once and for all." (Publisher's note)

Lyndon, Robert

Hawk quest; Robert Lyndon. 1st U.S. ed. Sphere 2012 658 p. map (hardcover) $25.99

ISBN 0316219568; 0748128441; 9780316219563; 9780748128440

LC 2012429363

This book is set in 1072, when "the known world is at war, hunger and disease are widespread, Viking raids are still common, and explorers are just beginning to investigate beyond the confines of Europe. Into this turbulence Vallon, a minor nobleman, escapes from a Moorish prison, becoming the leader of a motley crew of adventurers who travel thousands of miles from continental Europe to Iceland, across the steppes of Russia, to ransom Sir Walter, captive of the Turkish leader Süleyman." (Library Journal)

Lynn, Allison

Now you see it; a novel. Touchstone 2004 281p $13

ISBN 0-7432-5026-5 pa

LC 2003-70450

In this "novel, a Manhattan couple decides to infuse their lives with meaning by having a child. David hangs out in the middle of the masthead at a middlebrow magazine while Jessica teaches school, but after several failed fertility treatments, they focus on clearing hurdles in the adoption process. And then one day, Jessica vanishes, her keys left on the counter, a bedroom window ajar. . . . So without evidence of a crime, the detached David and Jessica's increasingly desperate mother must come to grips with the jarring disappearance in their own way and time. David does so by revisiting the story of a U.S. businessman gone missing in Peru—the one real scoop of his career, which he landed on his honeymoon. Although Jessica is more plot device than compelling character, Lynn deftly employs David's journey to explore how someone might rediscover his internal compass when he no longer has any reason to lie to himself." Booklist

Lyon, Annabel

The **sweet** girl; by Annabel Lyon. Alfred A. Knopf 2013 235 p. $24.95

ISBN 0307962555; 9780307962553

LC 2012049210

This novel by Annabel Lyon "follows Aristotle's . . . daughter as she shapes her own destiny. Aristotle has never been able to resist a keen mind, and Pythias is certainly her father's daughter. With the death of Alexander the Great, her fortunes suddenly change. Aristotle's family is forced to flee Athens for a small town, where the great philosopher soon dies. Pythias quickly discovers that the world is not a place of logic after all, but one of superstition." (Publisher's note)

Lytal, Benjamin

A **map** of Tulsa; Benjamin Lytal. Penguin Books 2013 272 p. (paperback) $15

ISBN 0142422592; 9780142422595

LC 2012036711

In this novel, by Benjamin Lytal, "Jim Praley is home from college, ready to unlock Tulsa's secrets. He drives the highways. . . . He's invited to a party. And . . . he meets Adrienne Booker; Adrienne rules Tulsa, in her way. A high-school dropout with a penthouse apartment, she takes a curious interest in Jim. Through her eyes, he will rediscover his hometown: its wasted sprawl, the beauty of its late nights, and . . . the unsleeping light of its skyscrapers." (Publisher's note)

"Although [Adrienne] is the focus of Jim's obsession, the strength of this debut novel is Lytal's evocation of place: Tulsa through Jim's eyes is tenderly revealed. There is magic here if the reader has experienced any such provincial city, for the prose provokes remembered images, acutely vivid." Pub Wkly

Lytton, Edward Bulwer Lytton

The **last** days of Pompeii. Harper 1834 2v

The setting is Pompeii just before and during the famous eruption of Vesuvius, A.D. 79. "The simple story relates principally to two young people of Grecian origin, Glaucus and Ione, who are deeply attached to each other. The former is a handsome young Athenian, impetuous, high-minded, and brilliant, while Ione is a pure and lofty-minded woman. Arbaces, her guardian, the villain of the story, under a cloak of sanctity and religion, indulges in low and criminal designs. His character is strongly drawn; and his passion for Ione, and the struggle between him and Glaucus, form the chief part of the plot. . . . The book, full of learning and spirit, is not only a charming novel, but contains many minute and interesting descriptions of ancient customs; among which, those relating to the gladiatorial combat, the banquet, the bath, are most noteworthy." Keller. Reader's Dig of Books

M

Ma Jian, 1953-

Beijing coma; translated from the Chinese by Flora Drew. Farrar, Straus & Giroux 2008 586p

ISBN 0374110174; 9780374110178

LC 2008-925628

Awakening after a decade in a coma, former Tiananmen Square protester Dai Wei learns that his mother had sold one of his kidneys to finance his care, and that the China he knew has undergone radical change.

"A valuable work. Ma's writing can be lively, and his use of dialogue that embraces everyday chitchat gives the book a sense of reality. The idealism of youth is ably captured. Indeed, the students' frequently lofty and at times naive emotions are touching." New Leader

Ma Jian, 1953-

Stick out your tongue; translated from the Chinese by Flora Drew. Farrar, Straus and Giroux 2006 93p $16

ISBN 0-374-26988-2

LC 2006-4282

Original Chinese edition, 1998

In these five loosely connected stories "a Chinese writer whose marriage has fallen apart travels to Tibet. As he wanders through the countryside, he witnesses the sky burial of a Tibetan woman who died during childbirth, shares a tent with a nomad who is walking to a sacred mountain to seek forgiveness for sleeping with his daughter, meets a silversmith who has hung the wind-dried corpse of his lover on the wall of his cave, and hears the story of a young female incarnate lama who died during a Buddhist initiation rite. In the thin air of the high plateau, the divide between dream and reality becomes confused." Publisher's note

Maalouf, Amin

Balthasar's odyssey; a novel. translated from the French by Barbara Bray. Arcade Pub. 2002 391p $25.95

ISBN 1-55970-666-X

LC 2002-74630

Original French editon, 2000

The author " sets this historical novel mostly in the Mediterranean of the mid-1600s. Balthasar Embriaco, an exiled Italian merchant, becomes fixated on retrieving a mysterious religious text called The Hundreth Name that he mistakenly sold to a traveler who stopped in his shop in the Levant. He thus sets out on a long journey, accompanied by his two nearly grown nephews, his manservant, and a woman seeking her estranged husband." Libr J

Maalouf, Amin

Leo Africanus; translated by Peter Sluglett. New Amsterdam 1992 360p pa $16.95

ISBN 1-561-31022-0

LC 91-36145

Original French edition, 1986; this translation first published 1988 in England with title: Leo the African

This "historical novel recreates the era when the Moors were expelled from Spain, and much of North Africa and southern Europe was in turmoil. Hassan al-Wazzan was just a child the year Columbus sailed to the New World. . . . The gradual exile of Hassan's family from Spain is developed through recollections of his proud, erring father, his badly treated mother and her diplomat brother. As a merchant and emissary, Hassan travels from Fez to Cairo to Mecca and—by misadventure—to Rome and the Vatican, where he is later renamed Leo Africanus." Publ Wkly

MacBride, Stuart

Blind eye; Stuart MacBride. 1st U.S. ed. Minotaur Books 2009 517 p. (hardcover) $26.99

ISBN 0312382642; 9780312382643

LC 2009021058

This is Stuart MacBride's fifth Logan McRae thriller. Here, "Aberdeen's growing Polish community is under attack from a serial offender who leaves mutilated victims to be discovered on building sites—eyes gouged out and the sockets burned. Detective Sergeant Logan McRae is assigned to the investigation, code-named Operation Oedipus, but with the victims too scared to talk, it's going nowhere fast." (Publisher's note)

MacBride, Stuart

Close to the Bone; Stuart Macbride. HarperCollins Publishers 2013 viii, 511 p.p (hardcover) $24.99

ISBN 0007344260; 9780007344260

In this installment of Stuart MacBride's Logan MacRae series, the detective inspector "is working under Acting Detective Chief Inspector Steel, who is dumping cases and more paperwork on Logan than he can handle. Among his cases are rival drug gangs fighting over the cannabis trade in Aberdeen, a pair of missing teens, and a jewelry store robbery. Logan also has a new detective sergeant assigned to him who is efficient but very ambitious and eager to make a name for herself." (Library Journal)

MacBride, Stuart

★ **Cold** granite; Stuart MacBride. St. Martin's Minotaur 2005 458p (pbk.) $6.99; o.p.

ISBN 9780312940591; 9780312339951; 031233995X

LC 2005042780

"Det. Sgt. Logan MacRae, back from a lengthy convalescence caused by a crazed suspect's knife attack, is plunged straightaway into the investigation of a brutally murdered child. To make matters worse, the victim's family learns of the death from a reporter before the police have a chance to inform them. Angered and embarrassed by the press leak, Logan, aided by WPC Jackie Watson, vows to expose the source within the precinct. . . . More children go missing, and soon the populace of Aberdeen is screaming for blood. Further inciting the rabble, a notorious defense attorney earns acquittal for a habitual child molester. As a result, a hapless, ruined scholar-turned-street sweeper becomes a scapegoat for the chilling fear that grips the community." (Publishers Weekly)

Other titles about Logan McRae are:
Dying light (2006)
Bloodshot (2007)
Flesh house (2008)
Blind eye (2009)
Dark blood (2010)
Shatter the bones (2011)
Close to the bone (2013)
The missing and the dead (2015)
In the cold dark ground (2016)

MacBride, Stuart

Dying Light; Stuart MacBride. 1st St. Martin's Minotaur ed. St. Martin's 2006 424 p. (hardcover) $24.95

ISBN 0312339976; 9780312339975

LC 2006043700

This is Stuart MacBride's second Logan MacRae novel. Here, "a madman has sealed up a squatter's apartment and set it—and the six people partying inside—afire. That same evening, a prostitute is found beaten to death, and Det. Sgt. Logan MacRae . . . is on the case. But his star has fallen; after a botched raid, MacRae has been demoted to the 'Screw-Up Squad,' led with a droll lack of enthusiasm by one Inspector Steel." (Publishers Weekly)

MacBride, Stuart

Flesh house. St. Martin's Minotaur 2008 467p il $24.95

ISBN 978-0-312-38263-6; 0-312-38263-4

LC 2008-23605

Det. Sgt. Logan McRae "is on the hunt for a serial killer called the Flesher who butchers his victims and then feeds their meat to their family members. The first murders occurred 20 years ago, and Ken Wiseman was convicted but later released on a technicality. Now the Flesher is again terrorizing Aberdeen, and McRae is working to find Wiseman and stop the murders. To add to the pressure, a BBC documentary on the Grampian police force is being filmed during the investigation, so every move the officers make is being recorded. McRae, a very human hero, is juggling the investigation along with his superior officers' eccentricities and a breakup with his girlfriend, even as he ferries around a visiting police chief who was involved in the investigation of the first murders." Libr J

MacBride, Stuart

Shatter the bones; Stuart MacBride. HarperCollins 2011 438 p. (hardcover) $24.95; (paperback) $16.95; (paperback) $12.99

ISBN 000734421X; 0007344228; 0007344244; 9780007344215; 9780007344222 reprint; 9780007344246 reprint

LC 2012371203

This is Stuart MacBride's seventh Logan McRae novel. Here, the Aberdeen, Scotland detective "finds himself working two kidnapping cases . . . . In the first, a mother-daughter singing duo, made famous on the TV show 'Britain's Next Big Star,' is being held for ransom . . . . In the other, a junkie has gone missing, presumably due to her boyfriend's role in a drug deal." (Booklist)

MacDonald, Ann-Marie

Fall on your knees; a novel. Simon & Schuster 1997 508p il

ISBN 9780743237185

LC 96-34186

"James Piper and {Materia}, his Lebanese child bride, raise their four daughters on Cape Breton Island in the early 1900s. . . . Kathleen finds her way to New York City, studying opera by day and sneaking into the smoky world of Harlem jazz by night. Her sister Mercedes, cursed with imperfect religious fervor, tries to keep the two youngest sisters safe from the dark forces that threaten the family left behind. Frances, with her own destructive secrets, seeks solace in sleazy back alleys and raunchy speakeasies. And little Lily, damaged by polio, whose ethereal innocence protects her from nothing, proves toughest of all." (Libr J)

In this novel "James Piper and his Lebanese child bride raise their four daughters on Cape Breton Island in the early 1900s. Gorgeous, talented, and aloof, Kathleen finds her way to New York City, studying opera by day and sneaking into the smoky world of Harlem jazz by night. Her sister Mercedes, cursed with imperfect religious fervor, tries to keep the two youngest sisters safe from the dark forces that threaten the family left behind. Frances, with her own destructive secrets, seeks solace in sleazy back alleys and raunchy speakeasies. And little Lily, damaged by polio, whose ethereal innocence protects her from nothing, proves toughest of all." Libr J

MacDonald, Ann-Marie

The **way** the crow flies; a novel. HarperCollins Publishers 2003 722p $26.95

ISBN 0-06-057895-5

LC 2003-61076

This is "a brilliant portrayal of child abuse and its consequences, but it is much more than that. It is a fiercely intelligent look at childhood, marriage, families, the 1960s, the Cold War and the fear and isolation that are part of the human condition." Washington Post Book World

MacDonald, John D.

Cinnamon skin; the twentieth adventure of Travis McGee. Harper & Row 1982 275p

LC 81-48159

"Travis McGee and his friend Meyer search for Meyer's niece's new husband, who has killed his wife and faked his own death in an explosion. The search is plodding and long, but MacDonald makes it interesting through the diverse and lively characters involved. The showdown, on Mexico's Yucatán Peninsula, is a bit slow but colorful and original." Libr J

MacDonald, John D.

The **green** ripper. Lippincott 1979 221p

LC 79-12063

"MacDonald is unsurpassed at showing the American brand of loneliness. He catches foibles in a phrase and gives us many-sided, wounded but courageous, characters." Booklist

MacDonald, John D.

★ The **lonely** silver rain. Knopf 1985 232p

LC 84-23373

"Travis McGee is growing older, and here he has good reason to feel his age. Besides combating a drug-smuggling potentate out to kill him, he finds himself the father of a young woman, all of which make the sleuth-philosopher reflect even more somberly on his life, his friends, his lonely job. One of the last MacDonald stories, it is also one of the best." Barzun. Cat of Crime. Rev and enl edition

MacDonald, John D.

The **long** lavender look. Lippincott 1972 264p

First published in paperback 1970 by Fawcett Books

When McGee avoids running his Rolls Royce into a young girl, he finds himself embroiled in intrigue

MacDonald, John D.

A **purple** place for dying. Lippincott 1976 204p

First published 1964 in paperback by Fawcett Books

"Travis McGee is pondering whether to take on the beautiful Mona Yeoman as a client when someone decides for him by shooting her in the back and hiding the body. Mona's husband soon dies of poison, and the killers might have been in the clear if they had not tried to add McGee (and one of those lovely women he always attracts) to their list. The usual literate and fast-paced stuff expected from MacDonald." Booklist

MacDonald, John D.

The **scarlet** ruse. Lippincott 1980 262p

LC 79-24843

First published 1973 in paperback by Fawcett Books

Private detective Travis McGee, "who lives on a houseboat, is told that the owner is planning on cleaning up the waterfront so he's going to lose his mooring place. McGee is bothered by this but to take his mind off this impending disaster, he takes on a case wherein a dealer of rare stamps is being made the victim of a stamp collector who is substituting 'junk' stamps—worthless stamps for valuable one-of-a-kind stamps. MacDonald keeps the pot boiling as McGee conducts his investigation and, as tradition would have it, runs into all kinds of unforeseen difficulties in settling this case, up to and including murder." West Coast Rev Books

MacDonald, John D.

The **turquoise** lament. Lippincott 1973 287p

McGee goes to the rescue of the daughter of a man who saved his life

"One of the best McGee adventures." Publ Wkly

MacDonald, Philip

The **list** of Adrian Messenger. Doubleday 1959 224p

"If some readers find Mr. MacDonald's style a bit stiff and old-fashioned, they will also find that he provides such other old-fashioned elements as honest clues, characters who stick in the mind from page to page, an original idea, and, in Anthony Gethryn, a detective who inspires utter confidence." New Yorker

Macdonald, Ross

★ The **drowning** pool. Knopf 1950 244p

"Admirers of the later Ross Macdonald will detect in this early book the capacities subsequently so well exploited. Lew Archer started as he continued: tough and straight; clever and informed, but not omniscient; full of love and hostility toward Southern California. This story, of a woman who has made a bad marriage to a mother-dominated husband of ambivalent sexual character, has a bit too much violence, but the character-drawing shows a sure hand, and the tangle is so capably manipulated that it does not annoy." Barzun. Cat of Crime. Rev and enl edition

Macdonald, Ross

★ The **far** side of the dollar. Vintage Books 1996 247p pa $12

ISBN 0-679-76865-3

LC 97-120671

First published 1965 by Knopf

This mystery "begins with Lew Archer's visit to a school for troubled boys, in search of a lead on Tommy Hillman, who has just escaped. . . . It turns out that Hillman had borrowed and wrecked a neighbor's car, and was put in the school by his father to teach him a lesson. Next, Archer learns that a ransom of $25,000 has been demanded for the return of Tommy Hillman. The Hillmans are a typically horrifying wealthy couple whose life has become unmoored through too much lying. The investigation of their past at one point brings up a connection to Archer's, showing that he has more in common with these people than he at first supposed." Murphy. Ency of Murder and Mystery

Macdonald, Ross

★ The **Galton** case. Vintage Books 1996 242p pa $12

ISBN 0-679-76864-5

LC 97-118474

First published 1959 by Knopf

"Archer is hired by Lawyer Gordon Sable on a hopeless case: to search for the elderly Mrs. Galton's son and heir, Anthony Galton. What he quickly turns up is a decapitated corpse buried on the spot where Anthony had lived twenty years before, and a young man working in a gas station who looks exactly like Anthony and may be his son. . . . The Galton trail leads to a bleak provincial town in Canada, and Macdonald's wry and funny glance at the beatnik poetry scene in San Francisco enriches the early part of the novel, putting on display the strength and flexibility of Macdonald's mature style. With The Galton case, Macdonald had 'arrived' precisely by finding a mythical form for his own beginnings." Murphy. Ency of Murder and Mystery

Macdonald, Ross

The **goodbye** look. Knopf 1969 243p

Private detective Lew Archer is brought "into the affairs of the Chalmers family because their lawyer thinks they are worried about a theft from their safe. But the Chalmers have other problems, and Lew becomes involved with murders old and new." Libr J

Macdonald, Ross

Sleeping beauty. Knopf 1973 271p

The scene "is California and the concern is with what power and money can do to wreck a family. Lew {Archer} befriends a lost lady who is running away from fears and responsibilities and from her young husband. Before very long word comes that the girl has been kidnapped and a ransom is demanded of her oil rich family. Bit by bit, as Archer probes deeper into the family relationships, he begins to see that nothing is what it seems and the key to the present lies deep in the past." Publ Wkly

Macdonald, Ross

★ The **underground** man. Knopf 1971 272p

"With his customary skill and economy of means, the author gets us, through Archer, into a tangle of passions about runaway spouses, disaffected and drug-taking children, amateur blackmail, and, of course, murder." Barzun. Cat of Crime. Rev and enl edition

Machado, Carmen Maria

★ **Her** body and other parties; stories. Carmen Maria Machado. Graywolf Press 2017 245 p. (alk. paper) $16

ISBN 9781555977887; 155597788X

LC 2017930115

Kirkus Prize Finalist: Fiction (2017)

National Book Award Finalist: Fiction (2017)

In this collection of stories, author Carmen Maria Machado "blithely demolishes the arbitrary borders between psychological realism and science fiction, comedy and horror, fantasy and fabulism. . . . A wife refuses her husband's entreaties to remove the green ribbon from around her neck. A woman recounts her sexual encounters as a plague slowly consumes humanity. A salesclerk in a mall makes a horrifying discovery within the seams of the store's prom dresses." (Publisher's note)

"Machado creates eerie, inventive worlds shimmering with supernatural swerves in this engrossing debut collection. Her stories make strikingly feminist moves by combining elements of horror and speculative fiction with women's everyday crises." Pub Wkly

Machart, Bruce

The **wake** of forgiveness. Houghton Mifflin Harcourt 2010 309p $26

ISBN 978-0-15-101443-9; 0-15-101443-4

LC 2009-47459

"A historical tale set at the end of the 19th century up to the mid-1920s, The Wake of Forgiveness is a tragic family saga in the Faulknerian tradition of sins long simmering and revenge gone wrong. Set in a mythical South Texas town, full of dark deeds and troubled townsfolk, it details a somber world marked by flashes of romance. At the outset, in 1895, the bitter figure of Vaclav Skala commands the stage, ruing the death of his wife in childbirth to his last son, Karel, and treating all three of his sons as either livestock or his curse and cross to bear. Karel emerges as the central figure of the novel, and although he inherits some of his father's tendencies, he's certainly more complex. It's his role to stand up to and stand by his difficult father, to inherit his curse of anger and see it through to the end. Into this mix of personalities ride the Knedlik twins, local orphans and ne'er-do-wells. Both eloquent and fast-paced, the novel only bogs down in extremely detailed action scenes." Dallas Morning News

MacInnes, Helen

Prelude to terror. Harcourt Brace Jovanovich 1978 368p

"Colin Grant, art consultant, is asked by a wealthy art collector to purchase a specific seventeenth-century painting at an art auction in Vienna. The owner of the painting needs money to escape from Hungary, and the transaction must be kept secret. When Colin arrives in Vienna, he finds that the auction conceals a conspiracy for laundering money that is used to buy weapons for terrorist groups. In spite of great personal danger Colin searches for the key piece of information that will stop this source of financing." Shapiro. Fic for Youth. 2d edition

MacInnes, Helen

Ride a pale horse. Harcourt Brace Jovanovich 1984 355p
LC 84-9037

"The device of dual protagonists moves the plot along smartly, and the demonstration of the insidious uses of disinformation could hardly be more timely." Booklist

MacInnes, Helen

The **Venetian** affair. Harcourt, Brace & World 1963 405p

This "suspense novel is set in Paris and Venice in 1961. An American newspaperman on vacation picks up the wrong raincoat on arrival at Orly airport, and finds himself involved in a communist plot to assassinate De Gaulle and implicate the United States. American agents enlist his help to thwart the plotters and to unmask the mysterious and ruthless spymaster." Publ Wkly

MacKall, Dandi Daley, 1949-

With love, wherever you are; Dandi Daley Mackall. Tyndale House Publishers, Inc. 2017 473 p. illustrations (hardcover) $22.99

ISBN 9781496421258; 9781496421210; 9781496421227
LC 2016040796

In this novel, by Dandi Daley Mackall, "after a whirlwind romance and wedding, Helen Eberhart Daley, an army nurse, and Lieutenant Frank Daley, M.D. are sent to the front lines of Europe with only letters to connect them for months at a time. Surrounded by danger and desperately wounded patients, they soon find that only the war seems real--and their marriage more and more like a distant dream. If they make it through the war, will their marriage survive?" (Publisher's note)

"The no-holds-barred depictions of war, in-depth characterizations, and suspense make Mackall's historical novel an excellent choice for libraries of all types." Booklist

MacKenzie, Sally

Bedding Lord Ned; Sally MacKenzie. Zebra Books 2012 426 p. $7.99

ISBN 1420123211; 9781420123210

This historical romance novel by Sally MacKenzie follows "Nell Bowman, [who] can't remember when she fell in love with Ned Valentine. . . .[B]ut instead he proposes to their mutual friend, Cecily. . . . [S]he dies during childbirth, leaving Ned bitter and guilt-ridden. Some years later, . . . Lady 'Venus' Valentine . . . hosts a party to celebrate Ned's thirtieth birthday. However, the clever duchess' real plans involve her most important matchmaking coup to date." (Booklist)

Mackintosh, Clare

I let you go; Clare Mackintosh. Penguin Group USA 2016 384 p. (hardcover) $26

ISBN 1101987499; 9781101987490
LC 2015025112

This book, by Clare Mackintosh, "follows Jenna Gray as she moves to a ramshackle cottage on the remote Welsh coast, trying to escape the memory of the car accident that plays again and again in her mind and desperate to heal from the loss of her child and the rest of her painful past. At the same time, the novel tracks the pair of Bristol police investigators trying to get to the bottom of this hit-and-run." (Publisher's note)

"Mackintosh's excellent writing features both memorable characters and a compelling portrayal of the eccentricities of small-town life in a close-knit community. But the author's real skill is in the way she incorporates jaw-dropping, yet plausible, plot twists into the already complex storyline." Kirkus

Mackintosh, Clare

I see you; Clare Mackintosh. Berkley 2017 384 p. (ebook) $65; (hardback) $26

ISBN 9781101988312; 1101988290; 9781101988299
LC 2016032022

In this book, by Clare Mackintosh, "every morning and evening, Zoe Walker takes the same route to the train station, waits at a certain place on the platform, finds her favorite spot in the car, never suspecting that someone is watching her... It all starts with a classified ad. During her commute home one night, while glancing through her local paper, Zoe sees her own face staring back at her; a grainy photo along with a phone number and a listing for a website called FindTheOne.com." (Publisher's note)

"The author's meticulous detail to investigative accuracy and talent in weaving a thrilling tale set her work apart from others in the field." Kirkus

MacLean, Sarah

★ **Never** Judge a Lady by Her Cover; Sarah MacLean. Avon 2014 384 p. (Rules of Scoundrels) $7.99

ISBN 0062068512; 9780062068514

"Duncan West is intrigued by the beautiful, ruined woman who is somehow connected to a world of darkness and sin. He knows she is more than she seems, and he vows to uncover all of Georgiana's secrets, laying bare her past, threatening her present, and risking all she holds dear." (Publisher's note)

"Brilliant, seductive, and intensely engaging, this addictive story pairs powerful, driven protagonists with a seemingly unsolvable dilemma in an ingenious, wonderfully satisfying conclusion to MacLean's remarkable quartet." LJ

MacLean, Sarah

No Good Duke Goes Unpunished; By Sarah MacLean. Avon Books 2013 400 p. (The Rules of Scoundrels) $7.99

ISBN 0062068547; 9780062068545
LC 2014657923

Written by Sarah MacLean and part of the Rule of Scoundrels series, this book describes how Temple "is the Killer Duke, accused of murdering Mara Lowe on the eve of her wedding. . . . Mara planned never to return to the world from which she'd run, but when her brother falls deep into debt at Temple's exclusive casino, she has no choice but to offer Temple a trade that ends in her returning to society and proving to the world what only she knows . . . that he is no killer." (Publisher's note)

"MacLean once again creates compelling and complex characters and sets them on a path toward love and reconciliation that begins with seemingly impossible odds and ends with exquisite fulfillment." Kirkus

MacLean, Sarah

One Good Earl Deserves a Lover; Sarah MacLean. HarperCollins 2013 384 p. (Rules of scoundrels) $7.99

ISBN 0062068539; 9780062068538

Sequel to: A rogue by any other name (2012)

In this novel by Sarah MacLean, Pippa Marbury is "looking forward to marrying her simple fiancé and living out her days quietly with her dogs and her scientific experiments. But before that, Pippa has two weeks to experience all the rest -- fourteen days to research the exciting parts of life. . . .She needs Cross, the clever, controlled partner in London's most exclusive gaming hell, with a carefully crafted reputation for wickedness." (Publisher's note)

MacLean, Sarah

The **Rogue** Not Taken; Scandal & Scoundrel, Book I. Sarah MacLean. HarperCollins 2015 432 p. (Scandal & scoundrel) (ebook) $5.59; $7.99

ISBN 9780062379399; 0062379410; 9780062379412

In this book, by Sarah MacLean, "when Sophie, the least interesting of the Talbot sisters, lands her philandering brother-in-law backside-first in a goldfish pond in front of all society, she becomes the target of very public aristocratic scorn. Her only choice is to flee London, vowing to start a new life far from the aristocracy. Unfortunately, the carriage in which she stows away isn't saving her from ruin . . . it's filled with it." (Publisher's note)

"Readers will be intoxicated by the emotional connection between the lovers, which makes their banter that much more amusing and their eventual physical passion that much more satisfying. Sophie's delightful family will leave readers eager for future installments in the series." Pub Wkly

MacLean, Sarah

A **Scot** in the dark; Scandal & Scoundrel, Book II. by Sarah MacLean. HarperCollins 2016 352 p. (Scandal & scoundrel) $7.99; (ebook) $7.99

ISBN 0062379429; 0062465848; 9780062379429; 9780062465849; 9780062379443

In this book, by Sarah MacLean, "Miss Lillian Hargrove has lived much of her life alone in a gilded cage, longing for love and companionship. When an artist offers her pretty promises and begs her to pose for a scandalous portrait, Lily doesn't hesitate . . . until the lying libertine leaves her in disgrace. With the painting now public, Lily has no choice but to turn to the one man who might save her from ruin." (Publisher's note)

"After wowing readers with the first in her Scandal & Scoundrel series, MacLean is on target to do so again with another brilliantly written, sensual, arch, and nuanced love story that is simply too good to miss." Booklist

Macmillan, Gilly

The **perfect** girl; Gilly Macmillan. William Morrow & Co 2016 439, 12 p.p (hardcover) $25.99

ISBN 9780062476753; 9780062567482; 0062567489

LC 2016590507

In this novel, by Gilly Macmillan, "Zoe Maisey is a seventeen-year-old musical prodigy with a genius IQ. Three years ago, she was involved in a tragic incident that left three classmates dead. She served her time, and now . . . Zoe is giving a recital that [her mother] Maria has been planning for months. . . . But instead, by the end of the evening, Maria is dead. In the aftermath, everyone . . . . tries to piece together what happened." (Publisher's note)

Includes bibliographical references (second pagination, pages 8-12).

Maguire, Gregory, 1954-

After Alice; A Novel. by Gregory Maguire. HarperCollins 2015 256 p. $26.99

ISBN 0060548959; 9780060548957

This novel, by Gregory Maguire, is "a magical new twist on 'Alice's Adventures in Wonderland,' published to coincide with the 150th anniversary of Lewis's Carroll's beloved classic. When Alice toppled down the rabbit-hole 150 years ago, she found a Wonderland as rife with inconsistent rules and abrasive egos as the world she left behind. But what of that world? How did 1860s Oxford react to Alice's disappearance?" (Publisher's note)

"... Maguire firmly sets Wonderland in time and place and weaves an intricate web of symbolism and allegory, asking readers to consider issues of humanity that are as timeless as the original tale itself. The novel is full of the magic, wonder, and fresh twists that his fans have come to expect, and Maguire- and Wonderland-lovers alike will enjoy this fantastic return." Booklist

Maguire, Gregory, 1954-

Hiddensee; a tale of the once and future Nutcracker. Gregory Maguire. William Morrow 2017 xi, 287 p.p (hardcover) $26.99

ISBN 0062684388; 9780062684400; 9780062684387

This book, by Gregory Maguire, "imagines the backstory of the 'Nutcracker,' revealing how this entrancing creature came to be carved and how he guided an ailing girl named Klara through a dreamy paradise on a Christmas Eve. At the heart of Hoffmann's mysterious tale hovers Godfather Drosselmeier-- the ominous, canny, one-eyed toy maker made immortal by Petipa and Tchaikovsky's fairy tale ballet--who presents the once and future Nutcracker to Klara, his goddaughter." (Publisher's note)

"A splendid revisitation of folklore that takes us to and from familiar cultural touchstones into realms to make Freud blanch." Kirkus

Maguire, Gregory, 1954-

Son of a witch; a novel. ReganBooks 2005 337p il $26.95

ISBN 0-06-054893-2

LC 2005-46232

"This sequel to the adult fairy tale Wicked (1995) . . . begins ten years after the destruction of Elphaba, a.k.a. the Wicked Witch of the West. In Maguire's dark version of the Land of Oz, there's not much to ring the bells for in the Emerald City, despite the tyrannical Wizard's departure. Corruption is rife, political factions compete for power, and radicals proclaim 'Elphaba lives!' Elsewhere, a horribly injured young man called Liir wakes in the religious House of Saint Glinda to many puzzles. . . . Above all, was Elphaba his mother? These and other questions drive a tale that adroitly mixes drama, humor, and political satire into a well-knit examination of good and evil-and leaves several doors open for future journeys over the rainbow into this cleverly constructed dystopia." Libr J

Maguire, Gregory, 1954-

Wicked; the life and times of the wicked witch of the West : a novel. Gregory Maguire ; illustrations by Douglas Smith. ReganBooks 1995 406 p. ill. $26.99

ISBN 0060391448

LC 950669

This book tells the story of "Elphaba, the future Wicked Witch of the West. . . . Her mother is embarrassed and repulsed by her bright-green baby with shark's teeth and an aversion to water. At college, the coed experiences disapproval and rejection by her roommate, Glinda, a silly girl interested only in clothes, money, and popularity. Elphaba is a serious and inquisitive student. When she learns that the Wizard of Oz is politically corrupt and causing economic ruin, Elphaba finds a sense of purpose to her life -- to stop him and to restore harmony and prosperity to the land. . . . The conclusion, however, is the same as L. Frank Baum's." (School Library Journal)

"Born with green skin and huge teeth, like a dragon, the free-spirited Elphaba grows up to be an anti-totalitarian agitator, an animal-rights activist, a nun, then a nurse who tends the dying—and, ultimately, the headstrong Wicked Witch of the West in the land of Oz. Maguire's strange and imaginative postmodernist fable uses L. Frank Baum's Wonderful Wizard of Oz as a springboard to create a tense realm inhabited by humans, talking animals (a rhino librarian, a goat physician), Munchkinlanders, dwarves and various tribes." Publ Wkly

Mahajan, Karan, 1984-

The **association** of small bombs; a novel. by Karan Mahajan. Penguin Group USA 2016 288 p. (ebook) $48; (hardcover) $26

ISBN 9780698407060; 0525429638; 9780525429630

National Book Award Finalist: Fiction (2016)

In this book, by Karan Mahajan, "when brothers Tushar and Nakul Khurana, two Delhi schoolboys, pick up their family's television set at a repair shop with their friend Mansoor Ahmed one day in 1996, disaster strikes without warning. A bomb . . . detonates in the Delhi marketplace, instantly claiming the lives of the Khurana boys, to the devastation of their parents. Mansoor survives, bearing the physical and psychological effects of the bomb." (Publisher's note)

"Mahajan's talent is in conveying the sense that the world is gray, not black-and-white, and he accomplishes this by weaving together the evolving motives and passions of his characters so intricately that in the end we see each as culpable, and human." Pub Wkly

Mahfouz, Naguib, 1911-2006

Children of the alley; by Naguib Mahfouz; translated by Peter Theroux. Doubleday 1996 448 p.

ISBN 9780385264730; 9780385420945

LC 95015510

Original Arabic version serialized 1959 in Cairo newspaper; previous English translation with title: Children of Gebelaawi, published 1981 in paperback by Three Continents Press

"Gabalawi's mansion sits at the desert's edge, surrounded by high-walled gardens. His sons, however, quarrel over his estate, and the omnipotent gangster banishes them from his earthly paradise. Their descendants settle outside the wall, desperately poor but always praying to Gabalawi for salvation. As each succeeding generation spawns its messiah, the people rise up against the ruling gangsters, seizing their portion of the estate, but greed and ignorance prove their ultimate undoing, poverty and suffering their inescapable fate." Libr J

Mahfouz, Naguib, 1911-2006

Midaq Alley; {by} Naguib Mahfouz; translated by Trevor Le Gassick. Anchor Bks. (NY) 1992 286p

LC 91-27459

"Written in the 1940s, this novel . . . deals with the plight of impoverished classes in an old quarter of Cairo. The lives and situations depicted create an atmosphere of sadness and tragic realism. Indeed, few of the characters are happy or successful. Protagonist Hamida, an orphan raised by a foster mother, is drawn into prostitution. Kirsha, the owner of a café in the alley, is a drug addict and a lustful homosexual. Zaita makes a living by disfiguring people so that they can become successful beggars. Transcending time and place, the social issues treated here are relevant to many Arab countries today." Libr J

Mahfouz, Naguib, 1911-2006

★ **Palace** of desire; translated by William M. Hutchins and Olive E. Kenny. Doubleday 1991 422p

LC 90-3753

Original Arabic edition, 1957

"Mr. Mahfouz excels at fusing deep emotion and soap opera. Fortunately, the translators . . . are equal to the task of animating rather than embalming Mr. Mahfouz's elegant and often explosive text." N Y Times Book Rev

Followed by Sugar Street

Mahfouz, Naguib, 1911-2006

★ **Palace** walk; translated from the Arabic by William M. Hutchins with Olive E. Kenny. Doubleday 1990 498p

LC 89-23348

Originally published in Arabic

This is the first volume in the author's trilogy "dealing with three generations of a Cairo family in the first half of the twentieth century. The emotional and physical struggles of these middle-class people are depicted with a great deal of sympathy and honesty, from the torments of adolescent love through the banked passions of an established marriage. The novel begins with a series of domestic scenes featuring the five children of a merchant and his wife; later, the setting shifts to Cairo nightclubs, coffee shops, and stores as Mahfouz re-creates the everyday existence of his characters in almost Dickensian detail." Booklist

Followed by Palace of desire

Mahfouz, Naguib, 1911-2006

Sugar Street; translated by William Maynard Hutchins and Angele Botros Samaan. Doubleday 1992 308p

LC 91-12938

Original Arabic edition, 1957

"The ordinary nature of Mr. Mahfouz's world, with its willingness to confront the complexities of human intentions, makes it an extraordinary exception in a marketplace of manufactured ideas and is, for that, all the more admirable." N Y Times Book Rev

Mailer, Norman

Ancient evenings. Little, Brown 1983 709p

LC 82-22839

"Set in the span between the reigns of Ramses II and Ramses IX, Mailer's . . . novel is narrated by the remnant spirits of Menenhetet I and his great-grandson as they join mutuality to survive the land of the Dead and to ascend to Ra. The story is largely the account of Menenhetet's first life (he has had four) as he rises from peasant stock to become first charioteer to Ramses II, then general, then overseer of the harem." Libr J

Mailer, Norman

The **castle** in the forest; a novel. Random House 2007 477p $27.95

ISBN 978-0-394-53649-1; 0-394-53649-5

LC 2006-49389

"Over the course of the novel a complex demonology is posited, clearly based on Dante and medieval scholasticism, and the narrator's chatty tone and Jesuitical logic are strangely reminiscent of C.S. Lewis' persuasive devil, Screwtape. All of this takes Hitler's life out of the realm of moral choice and into that of the supernatural, making it irrelevant to the novel's stated theme-unless one is an Augustinian Catholic, which as everyone knows the author is not. . . . . Occasionally a real insight slips in, almost by accident." New Leader

Mailer, Norman

★ The **executioner's** song. Modern Lib. 1993 1002p

ISBN 0-679-42471-7

LC 92-51066

A reissue of the title first published 1979 by Little, Brown

"In this study of a condemned murderer Mailer not only vividly portrays the character in a real-life drama but also invokes the whole history of westward migration of the Mormons of Utah." Reader's Ency. 3d edition

Mailer, Norman

The **Gospel** according to the Son. Random House 1997 242p

LC 96-48018

Mailer's "gospel is written in a direct, rather relaxed English that yet has an eerie, neo-Biblical dignity." New Yorker

Mailer, Norman

★ The **naked** and the dead. Holt & Co. 1948 721p

ISBN 9781439571606; 9780312265052

"In 1944 an American platoon takes part in the invasion and occupation of a Japanese-held island. The action is divided into three parts: the landing on the island, the counter-attack by night, and a daring patrol by the platoon behind enemy lines. The style is simple realism and therefore the language is rough, in keeping with the army setting." Shapiro. Fic for Youth. 3d edition

Maine, David

Fallen. St. Martin's Press 2005 244p $23.95

ISBN 0-312-32849-4

LC 2005-46588

"The first recorded murder takes barely 26 lines in Genesis. What Maine does with those few facts is masterfully creative. The story is told in reverse, beginning with Cain as an old man waiting to die and mourning the fact that the ghost of his murdered brother has left him. It deftly moves backward to the murder and God's punishment, where the point of view shifts to Abel just a few days before the murder. Finally, the point of view is shared by Adam and Eve alternately as they deal with aging and their burgeoning family, back to their first moments outside of the garden. Maine's explanations of Cain's hatred, God's dismissal of his sacrifice, and the real forbidden fruit are fascinating and often wildly funny. Once again he has turned his focus on the family dynamics and come away with a divinely passionate tale." Booklist

Maine, David

The **preservationist**. St. Martin's Press 2004 230p $24.95

ISBN 0-312-32847-8

LC 2003-70881

This is an "elegant, inventive book and in no way a cynical one, despite the author's keen appreciation of the incongruous. . . . The book resounds with the gravity of Noe's mission even as it invents the quotidian details of his story." N Y Times Book Rev

Majmudar, Amit

Partitions; Amit Majmudar. 1st ed.; Metropolitan Books 2011 xii, 211p.p

ISBN 9780805093957; 0805093958; 9781250007629

LC 2010045159

This book takes place "[a]s India is rent into two nations, [and] communal violence breaks out on both sides of the new border and streaming hordes of refugees flee from blood and chaos. At an overrun train station, Shankar and Keshav, twin Hindu boys, lose sight of their mother and join the human mass to go in search of her. A young Sikh girl, Simran Kaur, has run away from her father, who would rather poison his daughter than see her defiled. And Ibrahim Masud, an elderly Muslim doctor driven from the town of his birth, limps toward the new Muslim state of Pakistan, rediscovering on the way his role as a healer." (Publisher's note)

Majors, Inman

Love's winning plays; Inman Majors. 1st ed. W. W. Norton & Company 2012 256 p. (hardcover) $25.95

ISBN 0393062805; 9780393062809

LC 2012020171

This novel by Inman Majors is "about the sublimely ridiculous world of college football. . . . Raymond Love, a young coach unfamiliar with the banquet circuit of big-shot boosters and chat-room gurus, will go along as . . . head coach Von Driver's . . . wide-eyed errand boy . . . on a Pigskin Cavalcade to the small towns in the state. . . . Also on the trip is the athletic director's daughter, whom Love has tried to win by joining her book club -- a dubious strategy at best." (Publisher's note)

Makine, Andreï, 1957-

★ **Dreams** of my Russian summers. Arcade Pub. 1997 241p

ISBN 1-55970-383-0

LC 97-2720

Original French edition, 1995

This is the story "of Charlotte Lemonnier, born in France at the turn of the century, who as a child moved to Russia, where her father practiced medicine. Traveling back and forth over the years, she found herself in France on the eve of World War I, only to return to Russia with a Red Cross mission during the Revolution. There she remained to see the horrors of civil war and famine, and later witnessed the Stalinist purges, the war with Germany, the dehumanizing industrialization of the country and ultimately the fall of Communism's idols. By the time her grandson, the novel's narrator, begins visiting her for his summer holidays, she has been long settled in the sleepy Siberian town where her Russian husband lies buried." N Y Times Book Rev

Makine, Andrï, 1957-

The **life** of an unknown man; Andrei Makine ; translated by Geoffrey Strachan. Sceptre 2010 vi, 250 p.p (hardcover) $29.80; (paperback) $15.00

ISBN 155597614X; 9780340998786; 9781555976149

LC 2010467995

This novel, by Andrei Makine, tells of how "a disenchanted writer, revisits St. Petersburg after twenty years. . . . Instead, he meets Volsky, an old man who tells him . . . of surviving the siege of Leningrad, the march on Berlin, and Stalin's purges, and of a transcendent love affair. Volsky's life is an inspiration to Shutov. . . . This depth of feeling stands in sharp contrast to the empty lives Shutov encounters in the new Russia, and to his own life." (Publisher's note)

Makine, Andreï, 1957-

Music of a life; translated from the French by Geoffrey Strachan. Arcade Pub. 2002 109p $21.95

ISBN 1-55970-637-6

LC 2002-25854

Original French edition, 2001. Published in the United Kingdom with title: A life's music

"It is 1941, and Alexei, a budding concert pianist, is returning to his Moscow apartment two days before his first public recital when a neighbor warns his off: his parents are being arrested. Knowing that he will be sent to the Gulag, too, Alexei flees to the home of relatives in the countryside. Then the Germans invade, decimating his family's village but providing a plethora of bodies from which he can pillage an identity. . . . Stalin's atrocities are made visceral in this wisp of a book." New Yorker

Makine, Andrei, 1957-

The **woman** who waited; translated from the French by Geoffrey Strachan. Arcade Publishing 2006 182p $24

ISBN 1-559-70774-7

LC 2005-10314

Original French edition, 2004

"The Woman Who Waited quite deliberately avoids breaking your heart. It just comes very, very close. Vera is perceived only through the eyes of the narrator, but she is clearly more than just the woman who waits: only a fool would fail to understand that she's also the kind of woman worth waiting for, and far kinder and wiser than any romantic fiction." Washington Post Book World

Makkai, Rebecca

The **borrower**; a novel. Viking 2011 324p $25.95

ISBN 978-0-670-02281-6; 0-670-02281-0

LC 2010-52432

A "crime farce about a hapless librarian–cum–accidental kidnapper. Lucy Hull is a 26-year-old whose rebellion against her wealthy Russian mafia parents has taken the form of her accepting a children's librarian job in smalltown Missouri. After an unnecessarily long-winded first act, the novel picks up when Lucy discovers her favorite library regular, 10-year-old Ian Drake, hiding out in the stacks one morning after having run away from his evangelical Christian parents, who censor his book choices and are pre-emptively sending him to SSAD (Same-Sex Attraction Disorder) rehab, and Lucy soon aids and abets his escape. The tale of their subsequent jaunt across several state lines dodging cops, a persistent suitor of Lucy's, and a suspicious black-haired pursuer is fast-paced, suspenseful, and thoroughly enjoyable." Publ Wkly

Makkai, Rebecca

The **hundred**-year house; Rebecca Makkai. Viking 2014 352 p. (hardback) $26.95

ISBN 052542668X; 9780525426684

LC 2013047855

In this book, by Rebecca Makkai, "[h]usband to the heir of an estate that once sponsored an arts colony, Doug is eager to jump-start his academic career by plumbing the colony's files. But the secrets he discovers about the colony, the house, and the family make his hair stand on end." (Library Journal)

"The book is exceptionally well constructed, with engaging characters busy reinventing themselves throughout, and delightful twists that surprise and satisfy." Pub Wkly

Maksik, Alexander

A **marker** to measure drift; by Alexander Maksik. Alfred A. Knopf 2013 240 p. (hardcover) $24.95; (ebook) $74.85

ISBN 0307962571; 9780307962577; 9780307962584; 9780345803863

LC 2012038249

This novel, written by Alexander Maksik, focuses on Jacquelin, a young Liberian woman living alone in a cave on a remote island in the Aegean Sea. She experiences "the euphoric obliteration of memory and, with it, the unspeakable violence she has seen and from which she has miraculously escaped. Slowly, irrepressibly, images from a life before this violence begin to resurface. Jacqueline must find the strength to contend with what she has survived or tip forward into . . . madness." (Publisher's note)

Makumbi, Jennifer Nansubuga

Kintu; Jennifer Nansubuga Makumbi; with introduction by Aaron Bady. Transit Books 2017 viii, 443 p.p (paperback) $16.95

ISBN 9781945492013; 9781945492037; 9781945492037

LC 2016961684

This book, by Jennifer Nansubuga Makumbi, was "first published in Kenya in 2014 to critical and popular acclaim, 'Kintu' is a modern classic, a multilayered narrative that reimagines the history of Uganda through the cursed bloodline of the Kintu clan. Divided into six sections, the novel begins in 1750, when Kintu Kidda sets out for the capital to pledge allegiance to the new leader of the Buganda Kingdom." (Publisher's note)

"Makumbi's debut novel is a sprawling family chronicle that explores Uganda's national identity through a brilliant interlacing of history, politics, and myth." Pub Wkly

Malae, Peter Nathaniel

What we are. Grove Press 2010 383p $24

ISBN 978-0-8021-1907-0; 0-8021-1907-7

"Predictably, Paul doesn't take to conformity all that well, and gives it up. But he does grow more empathetic for the exercise. Even so, in testament to how hostile this novel is to empathy, much of its climactic dialogue is in Spanish. You can get the gist of it without knowing the language, but you miss out on the exact voice of our hero at his most generous and self-affirming. It's a wasted moment that makes it hard for us to care about Paul's future. And yet we have to care, since his is the voice of the Me Generation, which needs a lot of help." N Y Times Book Rev

Malamud, Bernard

The **assistant**; a novel. Farrar, Straus & Giroux 1957 246p hardcover o.p. pa $13

ISBN 0-374-50484-9 pa

This novel is "set in the prison of a failing grocery store, where Morris Bober, its elderly, long-suffering Jewish owner, teaches his assistant, Frankie Alpine, what it means to be a Jew, and what it means to be a man. After decades in which Jewish protagonists struggled to assimilate to the non-Jewish world around them, The Assistant is a tale about reverse assimilation, one in which Frankie takes over the store on Morris's death and undergoes a painful conversion to Judaism." Benet's Reader's Ency of Am Lit

Malamud, Bernard

★ The **complete** stories; introduction by Robert Giroux. Farrar, Straus & Giroux 1997 634p hardcover o.p. pa $18

ISBN 0-374-12639-9; 0-374-52575-7 pa

LC 97-12394

"Whether, stark, comic or fanciful, Malamud's stories give us immigrant Jews and their descendants pondering moral questions and experiencing moments of magical intervention while enduring life's ridiculous situations. Yet the stories transcend their ethnic settings and achieve a universal resonance." Publ Wkly

Malamud, Bernard

★ The **fixer**. Farrar, Straus & Giroux 1966 355p hardcover o.p. pa $14

ISBN 0-374-52938-8 pa

"Yakov Bok, a handyman, is arrested and charged with the killing of a Christian boy. Innocent of the crime, he is only guilty of being a Jew in Czarist Russia. In jail he is mentally and physically tortured as a scapegoat for a crime he insists he did not commit. Although his suffering and degradation are unrelenting, Bok emerges a hero as he maintains his innocence. Malamud has fashioned a powerful story of injustice and endurance based on a true incident." Shapiro. Fic for Youth. 3d edition

Malamud, Bernard

★ The **natural**. Harcourt Brace & Co. 1952 237p
ISBN 9780374502003

LC 93241037

"The fanaticism and seriousness of baseball to both players and fans are vividly pictured in this novel about a man whose sole ambition was to be 'the greatest ever.' Roy Hobbs, who has made his own bat, Wonderboy, starts off at nineteen years of age to a possible spot on a big team. That promising beginning is blasted when he has an encounter with an erratic, seductive woman. When we next meet Roy fifteen years later, he is trying again to realize his dream as the best baseball player. His wrong-headed decisions and the exciting descriptions of the games played by his team, The Knights, make this a tense story up to the last out." Shapiro. Fic for Youth. 3d edition

Malerman, Josh

Bird Box; by Josh Malerman. HarperCollins 2014 272 p. $25.99
ISBN 0062259652; 9780062259653

This book, by Josh Malerman, is a "horror thriller, set in an apocalyptic near-future world. . . . Something is out there . . . that must not be seen. One glimpse and a person is driven to deadly violence. . . . Five years after it began, a handful of scattered survivors remain, including Malorie and her two young children. Living in an abandoned house near the river, she has dreamed of fleeing to a place where they might be safe." (Publisher's note)

"The author uses understatement and allusion to create a lean, spellbinding thriller." Pub Wkly

Malik, Tania

Three bargains; a novel. Tania Malik. W W Norton & Co Inc 2014 368 p. (hardcover) $25.95
ISBN 0393063402; 9780393063400

LC 2014011419

In this novel, by Tania Malik, "twelve-year-old Madan lives with his impoverished family in the town of Gorapur, [India]. Madan's father works for Avtaar Singh, a powerful and controlling man who owns the largest factory in town and much of the land around it. Madan's sharp mind and hardened determination catch Avtaar Singh's attention. When Madan's father's misdeeds jeopardize his sister's life, Madan strikes his first bargain with Avtaar Singh to save her." (Publisher's note)

"Malik's first outing is an absorbing bildungsroman, a lovely and multifaceted tribute to the enduring bonds of family, blood or otherwise." Booklist

Malliet, G. M. ✓

A **Demon** Summer; a Max Tudor Novel. G.M. Malliet. Minotaur Books 2014 400 p. (A Max Tudor Mystery) (hardback) $25.99
ISBN 1250021413; 9781250021410

LC 2014019884

In G.M. Maillet's novel "omeone has been trying to poison the 15th Earl of Lislelivet. Since Lord Lislelivet has a gift for making enemies, no one--particularly his wife--finds this too surprising. What is surprising is that the poison was discovered in a fruitcake made and sold by the Handmaids of St. Lucy of Monkbury Abbey. Max Tudor, vicar of Nether Monkslip and former MI5 agent, is asked to investigate. But just as Max comes to believe the poisoning was accidental, a body is discovered in the cloister well." (Publisher's note)

"The fourth fun entry (after Pagan Spring) in this charming English cozy series is delightful in tone. Think Agatha Christie meets Ian Fleming." LJ

Malliet, G. M. ✓

A **fatal** winter; a Max Tudor novel. G.M. Malliet. Minotaur Books 2012 384 p. (hardcover) $24.99
ISBN 0312647972; 9780312647971; 9781250018250

LC 2012035879

Sequel to: Wicked Autumn (2011)

Author G.M. Malliet features a murder mystery. "Traveling back to his home in Nether Monkslip, Anglican priest Max Tudor . . . [is] summoned to Chedrow Castle by DCI Cotton, of the Monkslip-super-Mare police, who eagerly seeks Max's MI5 experience to investigate at the castle when Lady Baynard's brother and titleholder, Lord Footrustle, is murdered . . . Soon after his arrival, Lady Baynard's body is found. Now, the pressure is on Max to determine who most profited from the deaths of the brother and sister." (Kirkus)

Malliet, G. M. ✓

Pagan spring; a mystery. by G.M. Malliet. Minotaur Books 2013 304 p. (Max Tudor) (hardcover) $24.99
ISBN 1250021405; 9781250021403

LC 2013016676

In this book, by G.M. Malliet, "Vicar Max Tudor, reveling in his new-found personal happiness with Awena Owen, feels that life at the moment holds no greater challenge than writing his Easter sermon. But when one of the dinner guests is found dead in the pre-dawn hours, Max knows a poisonous atmosphere has once again enveloped his perfect village of Nether Monkslip. Connections to long-ago crimes . . . help Max unravel the clues—but can he restore peace to Nether Monkslip and still manage to finish his sermon?" (Publisher's note)

Malliet, G. M. ✓

Wicked autumn. Minotaur Books 2011 297p map (Max Tudor mysteries) $23.99
ISBN 978-0-312-64697-4

LC 2011-19523

His tranquility as the established vicar of a New Age village shattered by the murder of an unpopular woman, former MI5 agent Max Tudor struggles with past demons while trying to identify a killer in his peaceful community.

"Malliet has mastered the delights of the cozy mystery so completely that she seems to be channeling Agatha Christie, albeit with a hero who adds sex appeal to the mix. She also includes snippets of ironic humor that contribute a little spice to the village charm, making the story even more delicious. Religion, espionage, tea, and crumpets: a winning menu." Booklist

Other titles in this series are:
A fatal winter (2012)
Pagan spring (2013)
A demon summer (2014)
The haunted season (2015)
Devil's breath (2017)
In prior's wood (2018)

Mallinson, Allan

A **close** run thing; a novel of Wellington's army of 1815. Bantam Bks. 1999 306p
ISBN 0-553-11114-0

LC 98-52512

"An exciting historical adventure steeped in authentic military detail." Booklist

Mallon, Thomas

Bandbox. Pantheon Books 2004 305p $24.95

ISBN 0-375-42116-5

LC 2003-54861

"Mallon, in his other books, has gravitated toward previous eras out of an affinity for something like reticence. 'Bandbox,' then, is a real departure: antic, stylized, and up-tempo. The dialogue has a Kaufman-and-Hart crackle, and the story boasts more lotharios, floozies, mobsters, and wised-up dames than an MG-M double feature." New Yorker

Mallon, Thomas

Fellow travelers. Pantheon Books 2007 353p $25

ISBN 978-0-375-42348-2; 0-375-42348-6

LC 2006-24586

"The author keeps his own political convictions to himself. . . . Mallon is not an ideologically driven writer; political issues are his springboard for questions of individual integrity. We might take Mary, the novel's most adult character, as his stand-in. She quietly uses her affluent father's connections to help a State Department coworker fired for "lavender" inclinations and works behind the scenes in Congress to stymie McCarthyite legislation. . . . . Rueful maturity and large-minded sympathy are not qualities that help you navigate a city gripped by political hysteria. They are, however, among the salient qualities of 'Fellow Travelers,' a work of art that tempers judgment with compassion." Los Angeles Times Book Rev

Mallon, Thomas

Finale; A Novel of the Reagan Years. by Thomas Mallon. Pantheon Books 2015 480 p. hbk $27.95

ISBN 0307907929; 9780307907929

LC 2014044333

This novel, by Thomas Mallon, "captures the crusading ideologies, blunders, and glamour of the still-hotly-debated Reagan years, taking readers to the political gridiron of Washington, the wealthiest enclaves of Southern California, and the volcanic landscape of Iceland, where the president engages in two almost apocalyptic days of negotiation with Mikhail Gorbachev." (Publisher's note)

"Despite all the scene-jumping, the transitions are seamless; there's a whirlwind of activity and abundant snappy dialogue." Booklist

Mallon, Thomas

Watergate. Pantheon Books 2012 x, 432 p.p

ISBN 0307378721; 9780307378729

LC 2011017393

This book offers a "retelling of the Watergate scandal, as seen through a kaleidoscope of its . . . perpetrators and investigators. . . . [It covers] the Nixon presidency through the . . . perspectives of seven characters, . . . moving readers from the private cabins of Camp David to the klieg lights of the Senate Caucus Room, from the District of Columbia jail to the Dupont Circle mansion of Theodore Roosevelt's sharp-tongued ninety-year-old daughter, . . . and into the hive of the Watergate complex itself, home not only to the Democratic National Committee but also to the president's attorney general, his . . . loyal secretary, and the shadowy man from Mississippi who pays out hush money to the burglars." (Publisher's note)

Malone, Michael

The **four** corners of the sky; a novel. Sourcebooks Landmark 2009 560p $24.99

ISBN 978-1-570717-44-4; 1-570717-44-3

LC 2008-38938

"Malone delivers a tale that takes a little long to tell but that pays off nicely in the end. Secrets and intrigues among the honeysuckle: a sun-washed yarn of the New South, affectionately told." Kirkus

Malouf, David

The **complete** stories. Pantheon Books 2007 508p $27.50

ISBN 978-0-375-42497-7; 0-375-42497-0

LC 2006-37694

"Malouf is a master of the art of the short story in its most elusive, Chekhovian form, and he uses the genre, it seems to me, for three delicate purposes in particular: the exploration of the ordinary; the evocation of moments of change, often seemingly slight; and the interrogation of loss." Slate

Malouf, David

Ransom. Pantheon Books 2010 224p $24

ISBN 978-0-307-37877-4; 0-307-37877-2

LC 2009-20669

First published 2009 in Australia

A "retelling of Achilles' desecration of Hector's corpse and his capitulation to Priam's appeal for proper rites and burial for the Trojan hero. Malouf's prose is triumphantly sure, and his characterizations of the subtle and complex bonds between Priam and Achilles, gods and mortals, wives and husbands, parents and children, nobles and commoners, and beasts and men resonate with authority." Libr J

Malouf, David

Remembering Babylon. Pantheon Bks. 1993 200p

LC 93-7888

"The book is more reflective than polemic. Without excusing the actions of the townsfolk, . . . Malouf shows how difficult original thought is for members of a community that perceives itself as surrounded by danger. The book is a joy to read: richly layered, complex, and dense." Christ Sci Monit

Maloy, Kate

Every last cuckoo; a novel. Algonquin Books of Chapel Hill 2008 277p $22.95

ISBN 978-1-56512-541-4; 1-56512-541-X

LC 2007-16641

Maloy "has created a truly engrossing novel, with situations at times both joyful and horribly sad and an entirely likable protagonist surrounded by an eclectic cast of friends and family. An excellent book club selection." Libr J

Malraux, Andre

Man's fate (La condition humaine) translated by Haakon M. Chevalier. Smith & Hass 1934 360p

Original French edition, 1933; published in the United Kingdom with title: Storm in Shanghai

"The time is 1927, during the unsuccessful Communist uprising in China. The author focuses on three types of revolutionaries. Ch'en, a Chinese terrorist, believes that Chiang Kai-shek must be killed to start a revolution and is willing to sacrifice himself to bring this about. Kyo, half-French, half-Japanese, is drawn to the revolution because of his belief in human dignity. He finds it difficult to reconcile the idealistic theories of Marx with the political realities of the revolution. Katov, a Russian who has had experience in the revolution in his own country, feels there is strength in the solidarity of his comrades. Though their attempts at revolution fail, each man dies feeling he has given meaning to his life trying to bring change to China." Shapiro. Fic for Youth. 3d edition

Malraux, Andre

Man's hope; translated from the French by Stuart Gilbert and Alastair Macdonald. Random House 1938 511p

Original French edition, 1937; published in the United Kingdom with title: Days of hope

The story of the first eight months of the Civil War in Spain based on the author's experiences as commander of the Loyalist government's international air force

"Vividly realistic as it is, the book is remarkably free from the senseless dwelling upon physical injuries which often weakens the effect of war novels. M. Malraux has concentrated upon the essential rather than the incidental horrors of war, of civil war in particular." Manchester Guardian

The **mammoth** book of steampunk; edited by Sean Wallace. Perseus Books Group 2012 vii, 498 p.p

ISBN 0762444681; 9780762444687

LC 2011930509

This anthology of steampunk short stories edited by Sean Wallace "focus[es] on newer elements of steampunk, one which deconstructs the staples of the genre and expands on them, rather than simply repeating them, with a greater spread both in terms of location and character. This is steampunk with a modern, post-colonial sensibility." (Publisher's note)

Manchette, Jean-Patrick

Fatale; translated from the French by Donald Nicholson-Smith; afterword by Jean Echenoz. New York Review Books 2011 98p pa $12.95

ISBN 1590173813; 9781590173817

LC 2010-34848

Original French edition, 1977

The MO of the murderer Aimée Joubert "involves insinuating herself into the financial elite of a new locale, most recently the obscure coastal industrial town of Bléville." (Bookforum)

"'For her stay in Bléville, the young woman had chosen to call herself Aimée Joubert, and that is what I shall call her from now on,' Manchette says of his female assassin, who 'aside from her husband,' as French author Jean Echenoz mentions in the afterword, 'has already killed seven men, among them a factory owner, a stock breeder, and a doctor.' Told in tight behaviorist language and laced with deadly black humor, this compact neo-noir follows Joubert as she steps much too far into her self-made career toward a showdown worthy of any action film." Publ Wkly

Mandel, Emily St. John, 1979-

★ **Station** eleven; a novel. Emily St. John Mandel. Knopf 2014 352 p. (hardback) $24.95

ISBN 0385353308; 9780385353304

LC 2014003560

Arthur C. Clarke Award (2015)

PEN/Faulkner Award for Fiction: Shortlist (2015)

National Book Award Shortlist: Fiction (2014)

This novel, by Emily St. John Mandel, is "set in the eerie days of civilization's collapse . . . [and] tells the spellbinding story of a Hollywood star, his would-be savior, and a nomadic group of actors roaming the scattered outposts of the Great Lakes region, risking everything for art and humanity." (Publisher's note)

"In this unforgettable, haunting, and almost hallucinatory portrait of life at the edge, those who remain struggle to retain their basic humanity and make connections with the vanished world through art, memory, and remnants of popular culture." LJ

Manfredi, Valerio Massimo

A **Winter's** Night; by Valerio Manfredi. Penguin Group USA 2012 368 p. (paperback) $18.00

ISBN 1609450760; 9781609450762

Author Valerio Manfredi tells "the story of the Brunis, a family of farmers from the Italian Padan Plain who have worked the land since time immemorial. And it is a story about the homeless multitudes, travelers, and tinkers, roaming Europe during the hardscrabble nineteen-twenties and thirties . . . [T]hese two worlds meet when the Brunis open their great barn and offer it as a refuge for those in need of a warm, dry, and safe place to sleep and eat, [and] the barn becomes font and inspiration for a series of vivid stories involving sundry strangers." (Amazon)

Manicka, Rani

The **rice** mother. Viking 2003 432p $24.95

ISBN 0-670-03192-5

LC 2002-32421

"When 14-year-old Lakshmi marries a widower of 37, she believes that she is leaving her Sri Lankan village for a life of luxury in Malaysia. Instead, she endures hardship and poverty, giving birth to six children in the years before the Japanese invasion of World War II. In this gripping multigenerational saga, the tumultuous history of Malaysia becomes the backdrop for Lakshmi's indomitable spirit. The barbarity of the Japanese, postwar prosperity, the bursting of the Southeast Asian financial bubble, the vice trades of opium, gambling, and sex—all take their toll on Lakshmi's children and grandchildren." Libr J

Mankell, Henning ✓

Dogs of Riga; a Kurt Wallander mystery. translated by Laurie Thompson. Norton 2003 326p $24.95

ISBN 1-56584-787-2

LC 2002-30503

Original Swedish edition, 1992

"Set against the chaotic backdrop of eastern Europe after the fall of the Berlin Wall, Mankell's intense, accomplished mystery, the last in his Kurt Wallander series. . . explores one man's struggle to find truth and justice in a society increasingly bereft of either. Here the provincial Swedish detective takes on a probably fruitless task: investigating the murders of two unidentified men washed up on the Swedish coast in an inflatable dinghy." Publ Wkly

Mankell, Henning

The **eye** of the leopard; translated from the Swedish by Steven T. Murray. New Press 2008 315p $26.95

ISBN 978-1-59558-077-1; 1-59558-077-8

LC 2008-299522

Original Swedish edition, 1990

"The story revolves around a young Swede, Hans Olofson, who flies to Zambia in the 1970s in search of himself and to fulfil the quest of a dead friend. For lack of anything better to do, Olofson finds himself taking over the running of an upcountry egg farm. Intending to stay weeks, 20 years pass before he finally manages to extricate himself. . . . Where his white farmer neighbours only speak to blacks when giving orders, he tries to befriend them, provides materials to improve their homes, builds a school, takes a woman called Joyce and her daughters under his care and tries a number of other ways to break down the barriers that stand between himself and the people around him. But in a tense tale whose violence and uneasiness contrast to great effect with Olofson's deadpan narrative tone and Mankell's spare prose, it is made clear that there are no easy fixes, no quick ways to remedy the situation. Olofson escapes the gruesome fate of his neighbours, whose butchered corpses he finds, but he cannot escape his own despair." Spectator

Mankell, Henning

Firewall; translated by Ebba Segerberg. New Press (NY) 2002 405p $25.95

ISBN 1-56584-767-9

LC 2002-25543

Original Swedish editon, 1998

A mystery featuring Swedish police inspector Kurt Wallander. A "criminal mastermind is about to press the button and send the global financial network into free fall when his partner is murdered, giving Wallander a window of opportunity to scotch this mischief and let us use our A.T.M.'s again. Although things get pretty tense at the end in Ebba Segerberg's well-paced translation, this a thinking man's thriller bearing the messsage that no infernal machine is a match for a decent man with a sense of good and evil." N Y Times Book Rev

Mankell, Henning

The **man** from Beijing; translated from the Swedish by Laurie Thompson. Alfred A. Knopf 2010 366p $25.95

ISBN 0-307-27186-2; 978-0-307-27186-0

LC 2009-45198

Original Swedish edition, 2008

This novel "opens with the discovery of 19 dead and disfigured bodies in the fictional town of Hesjovallen. . . . The local police uncover exactly two clues: The victims appear to be distantly related, and someone dropped a red ribbon in the adjoining woods." (N Y Times Book Rev)

"A sweepingly ambitious tale of corruption, injustice and revenge that ranges over three continents and 140 years. . . . Breathtakingly bold in its scope. If Mankell never links his far-flung, multigenerational horrors closely together, that's an important part of his point." Kirkus

Mankell, Henning

The **man** who smiled; a Kurt Wallander mystery. translated from the Swedish by Laurie Thompson. New Press 2006 325p $24.95

ISBN 978-1-56584-993-8; 1-56584-993-0

LC 2006-21925

Original Swedish edition, 1994; this translation first published 2005 in the United Kingdom

"When the bleak landscapes of Henning Mankell's Swedish police procedurals start to look like home, it's time to head for the hills. Either that, or confront the grim truths about modern society that give weight to this author's absorbing but disquieting existential mysteries." N Y Times Book Rev

Mankell, Henning

★ **One** step behind; translated by Ebba Segerberg. New Press (NY) 2002 408p $24.95

ISBN 1-56584-652-4

LC 2001-34254

Original Swedish edition, 1997

This is a "Swedish police prodedural which features a conscience-driven detective named Kurt Wallander who works out of the port city of Ystad. . . . {The case is} the meticulously staged homicide of three friends who costumed themselves as 18th-century bacchants and went into the woods on Midsummer's Eve to party. When a murdered police officer is implicated in the widening investigation, Wallander suspects internal corruption." (N Y Times Book Rev)

This mystery, featuring chief Inspector Kurt Wallander of the Ystad, Sweden police turns on the "meticulously staged homicide of three friends who costumed themselves as 18th-century bacchants and went into the woods on Midsummer's Eve to party. When a murdered police officer is implicated in the widening investigation, Wallander suspects internal corruption. . . . The sweep and complexity of Mankell's plot are reason enough for tackling this dense book, thoughtfully translated by Ebba Segerberg. But his meditations on surprising subjects like time travel and 'man's relationship to monsters' make him something special." N Y Times Book Rev

Mankell, Henning

★ The **return** of the dancing master; translated by Laurie Thompson. New Press 2004 391p $24.95

ISBN 1-56584-860-8

Original Swedish edition, 2000

"With its expansive time frame and meticulous procedural details, the story (as translated by Laurie Thompson) has a density that demands–and rewards–intellectual involvement." N Y Times Book Rev

Mankell, Henning

The **troubled** man; translated from the Swedish by Laurie Thompson. Knopf 2011 367p $26.95

ISBN 978-0-307-59349-8; 0-307-59349-5

LC 2010-49169

Original Swedish edition, 2009

Not only does this novel "widen the scope of the detective's investigations into the world of international geopolitics and the relationship of Sweden to the United States and Russia, it is a work of genuine heft and substance, a melancholy, elegiac book that is thoughtful and perceptive about memory, regret and the unfathomability of human nature." PopMatters

Mann, Thomas, 1875-1955

The **black** swan; translated from the German by Willard R. Trask. Knopf 1954 141p

LC 90-38617

Original German edition, 1953; this is a reissue of the 1954 Knopf edition

Tragic psychological tale of a middle-aged German widow's passion for the young American tutor of her son

In this novelette Mann "returns to the compact dimensions and to the subject matter of Death in Venice (transposed into heterosexual terms)—the infatuation of an aging person for a young one. The current novella—though it is not nearly as memorable a piece of storytelling as the masterpiece of 1913—is a provocative addition to Mann's writings." Atlantic

Mann, Thomas, 1875-1955

★ **Buddenbrooks**; the decline of a family. translated from the German by John E. Woods. Knopf 1993 648p

ISBN 0-679-41994-2

LC 92-18990

Original German edition, 1901. First United States edition translated by H. T. Lowe-Potter published 1924 in two volumes

This is a new translation of Thomas Mann's earliest novel. "Mann portrays several generations of a merchant family who belong to the bourgeois aristocracy in Lübeck, tracking them from high point to decline." (Libr J) For the first American edition, translated by H.T. Lowe-Porter, see BRD 1924.

"Mann's first novel, it expressed the ambivalence of his feelings about the value of the life of the artist as opposed to ordinary, bourgeois life. The novel is the saga of the fall of the Buddenbrooks, a family of merchants, from the pinnacle of their material wealth in 1835 to their extinction in 1877." Merriam-Webster's Ency of Lit

Mann, Thomas, 1875-1955

★ **Death** in Venice; translated from the German by Kenneth Burke. Knopf 1965 118p

Original German edition, 1913; this translation first published 1925 as the title novella of a collection

"Gustav von Aschenbach, the hero, is a successful author, proud of the self-discipline with which he has ordered his life and work. On a trip to Venice, however, he becomes aware of mysterious decadent potentialities in himself, and he finally succumbs to a consuming love for a frail but beautiful Polish boy named Tadzio. Though he learns that there is danger of a cholera epidemic in Venice, he finds he cannot leave the city, and eventually dies of the disease. The story is permeated by a rich and varied symbolism with frequent overtones from Greek literature and mythology." Reader's Ency. 4th edition

Mann, Thomas, 1875-1955

Doctor Faustus; translated from the German by John E. Woods. Knopf 1997 534p

ISBN 0-375-40054-0

LC 97-2818

A new translation of the novel originally published 1947 in German; first English translation by H. T. Lowe-Parker published 1948

In this novel "the intense and tragic career of the hero Adrian Leverkühn, a composer, is made to parallel the collapse of Germany in World War II. To achieve this end, Mann employs the device of having another character, Serenus Zeitblom, narrate Leverkühn's story from memory, while the war is going on, and intersperse his narrative with remarks about the present situation. In this way, it is implied that it is the same demonic and always potentially destructive energy inherent in Leverkühn's music that is also, on a larger scale, behind the outburst of Nazism. Mann thus suggests that the violent 'Faustian' drive, when it is not diverted into art, or when there is no single artistic genius to harness it into creative process, will be perverted and result in grossly sub-human degradation." Reader's Ency. 4th edition

Mann, Thomas, 1875-1955

★ The **magic** mountain; a novel. translated from the German by John E. Woods. Knopf 1995 706p

ISBN 0-679-44183-2

LC 94-42885

Original German edition, 1924

This novel "tells the story of Hans Castorp, a young German engineer, who goes to visit a cousin in a tuberculosis sanatorium in the mountains of Davos, Switz. Castorp discovers that he has symptoms of the disease and remains at the sanatorium for seven years, until the outbreak of World War I. During this time, he abandons his normal life to submit to the rich seductions of disease, introspection, and death. Through talking with other patients, he gradually becomes aware of and absorbs the predominant political, cultural, and scientific ideas of 20th-century Europe. The sanatorium comes to be the spiritual reflection of the possibilities and dangers of the actual world away from the magic mountain" Merriam-Webster's Ency of Lit

Mann, Thomas, 1875-1955

Six early stories; translated from the German with a note by Peter Constantine; edited with an introduction by Burton Pike. Sun & Moon Press 1997 128p

ISBN 1-55713-298-4

"These newly translated stories give insight into the still-forming mind of the Nobel laureate, revealing his philosophical and literary influences as well as demonstrating the uninhibited experimentation of a young, romantic writer." Publ Wkly

Manning, Kate

My notorious life; a novel. Kate Manning. Scribner 2013 448 p. (hardcover) $26.99

ISBN 9781451698084; 1451698062; 1451698070; 1451698089; 9781451698060; 9781451698077

LC 2012031031

This book is "loosely based on the life of Ann Trow Lohman (aka Madame Restell), the infamous abortionist who became known as 'the Wickedest Woman in New York.'" In Kate Manning's fictional version, "Axie Muldoon endured a scrappy childhood as the . . . daughter of Irish immigrants living amidst the filth of lower Manhattan. She began her midwifery apprenticeship at 14, . . . before becoming the renowned Madame X with a thriving business." (Publishers Weekly)

Mansbach, Adam

Rage is back; Adam Mansbach. Viking 2012 304 p. $26.95

ISBN 0670026123; 9780670026128

LC 2012019123

In this novel by Adam Mansbach "Dondi Vance is the son of two famous graffiti artists from New York City's 'golden era' of subway bombing. . . . [and is] immune to rumors that his long-lost father, Billy Rage, has returned after sixteen years on the lam. . . . Anastacio Bracken, the transit cop who ruined Billy's life and shattered his crew back in 1987, is running for mayor. Only by rallying the forgotten writers of the eighties . . . can Billy and Dondi bring Bracken down." (Publisher's note)

Manseau, Peter

Songs for the butcher's daughter; a novel. Free Press 2008 370p $25

ISBN 978-1-4165-3870-7; 1-4165-3870-4

LC 2007-49787

This is "the story of fictional Yiddish poet Itsik Malpesh, born in the Moldovan city of Kishinev in 1903. Itsik's story is told through his Yiddish memoirs, which he helps a young American Catholic . . . translate. Inspired by the image of Sasha, the brave butcher's daughter who was present at his birth, Itsik reaches America in young adulthood through haphazard luck, a taste for troublemaking and the inventiveness of a printer. Sasha continually inspires and confounds Itsik throughout his life, becoming an apt symbol for Yiddish humor, sorrow and idealism. As Itsik's darkly picaresque immigrant narrative unfolds, it competes with the translator's modern romance and with insights into the art of translation and the history of Yiddish. Occasional narrative missteps are not enough to undercut this rich, often ironic homage to Yiddish culture and language." Publ Wkly

Mantel, Hilary, 1952-

The **assassination** of Margaret Thatcher; stories. Hilary Mantel. Henry, Holt & Co. 2015 242 p. (hardback) $27

ISBN 9781627792103; 9781250074720

LC 2014015900

This book, by Hilary Mantel, is a "collection of contemporary stories. . . . Stories of dislocation and family fracture, of whimsical infidelities and sudden deaths with sinister causes. . . . Cutting to the core of human experience, Mantel . . . writes about marriage, class, family, and sex. " (Publisher's note)

The "atmosphere throughout is creepy, alarming, and unsettling. . . . Mood and plot merge into incredible scenarios that ultimately and disturbingly end up seeming to be perfectly natural." Booklist

Mantel, Hilary, 1952-

★ **Bring** up the bodies; a novel. Hilary Mantel. Henry Holt and Co. 2012 xvii, 410 p.p $28

ISBN 0805090037; 9780805090031

LC 2012006335

Sequel to: Wolf Hall

Costa Novel Award Winner 2012

This biographical historical novel by Hilary Mantel, winner of the 2012 Man Booker Prize, tells how "[Thomas] Cromwell helped Henry annul his marriage to his wife of 20 years, Catherine, so he could marry the younger Anne Boleyn. But three years later, Anne has committed two fatal errors: she hasn't given the king a son, and she has become outspoken. Henry's eyes are on a younger, more placid woman, Jane Seymour. He wants to be rid of Anne, and it is up to Cromwell to see that Henry gets what he wants." (Library Journal)

Mantel, Hilary, 1952-

★ **Wolf** Hall; a novel. Henry Holt and Co. 2009 532p $27

ISBN 978-0-8050-8068-1; 0-8050-8068-6

LC 2009-19912

This novel depicts the world of Henry VIII. "England in the 1520s is a heartbeat from disaster. If the king dies without a male heir, the country could be destroyed by civil war. Henry VIII wants to annul his marriage of twenty years, and marry Anne Boleyn. The pope and most of Europe opposes him. The quest for the king's freedom destroys his adviser, the brilliant Cardinal Wolsey, and leaves a power vacuum. Into this impasse steps Thomas Cromwell. Cromwell is a . . . consummate politician, hardened by his personal losses, implacable in his ambition. But Henry is volatile: one day tender, one day murderous. Cromwell helps him break the opposition, but what will be the price of his triumph?" (Publisher's note)

"Set in 16th-century Tudor England, Wolf Hall thrusts the reader into Henry VIII's seething court, where the players include Anne Boleyn, her sister Mary, Cardinal Wolsey, Thomas More and Jane Seymour. At the book's center: Thomas Cromwell, the ruthless blacksmith's son who rose to power under Henry VIII because of his intelligence, cunning and work ethic. . . . Mantel's novel is less about Henry's sex life and more about power: how to get it, wield it, keep it, particularly if you — like the lowborn Cromwell — lived in a merciless world ruled by the rich and titled. Cromwell usually is presented as a bully utterly lacking scruples, but Mantel's Cromwell is a sympathetic character modern readers will understand." USA Today

Mapson, Jo-Ann

Bad Girl Creek; a novel. Simon & Schuster 2001 381p

ISBN 0-7432-0256-2

LC 2001-27006

"Phoebe DeThomas has lived carefully all her life. Thirty-eight years old and in a wheelchair because of a bad heart, she's always felt dwarfed by her flamboyant aunt Sadie and her successful brother James. Now Sadie has died, bequeathing her a flower farm on California's Central Coast. In order to make a go of it, Phoebe takes in three women as boarder/farmhands. Each of the three is 'homeless,' having recently undergone traumatic life changes: Ness, a black cowgirl with a horse and a secret fear that she has AIDS, has lost her job; Nance, a down-on-her-luck Southern belle, has broken up with ber boyfriend; and Beryl, a former kindergarten aide with a prison record, has been evicted from her apartment. . . . Mapson combines poignancy with the good-natured banter of girlfriends in her tale of women in transition, waiting to be reborn." Publ Wkly

Mapson, Jo-Ann

Solomon's oak; a novel. Bloomsbury 2010 374p $25

ISBN 978-1-608-19330-1; 1-608-19330-6

LC 2010-09792

"Mapson's three damaged souls, and the ghosts in their lives, are able to find in each other just the thing to make life worth living. A tender portrayal of those left behind in the wake of tragedy." Kirkus

March, William

The **bad** seed. Rinehart 1954 247p

"Rhoda Penmark at 8 years of age had a mind of her own and a will to match. Aged people doted on her splendid manners, but rogues knew her as one of themselves while older children were afraid of her. Christine, her mother suddenly discovers her daughter's horrible tendencies and also finds out that she is the murderess of two people who stood in her way. Christine resolves to check back and finds that she had been adopted and that the mother she had never known had also been a successful killer. Christine tries to stop the pattern in her daughter, but in the process dies herself." Libr J

Marcus, Ben, 1967-

The **flame** alphabet; Ben Marcus. Alfred A. Knopf 2012 289 p. $25.95

ISBN 9780307739971; 030737937X; 9780307379375

LC 2011936249

In this book, "a terrible epidemic has descended: whenever children speak, adults sicken and eventually die. At first, only Jewish families are stricken, stirring echoes of history's uglier sentiments. But soon every adult is affected. Near death . . . Claire still longs for daughter Esther, a standard-issue obnoxious teenager who's hardened with the knowledge of her power. . . . But what terrifies Esther's . . . father, Sam, is that soon Esther will be an adult." (Library Journal)

Margolin, Phillip

Wild justice. HarperCollins Pubs. 2000 332p

ISBN 0-06-019624-6

LC 00-24351

"The plot is straightforward enough: a serial killer is torturing and murdering people seemingly at random, and investigators scramble to stop the psychopath. . . . There are not one but two prime suspects—Dr. Vincent Cardoni, a prominent surgeon, and Dr. Justine Castle, Cardoni's estranged wife. Each accuses the other of a frame-up, and Amanda Jaffe, a rather inexperienced young attorney, has to figure out which of her clients may be a murderer. A very clever thriller indeed." Booklist

Marias, Javier, 1951-

All souls; translated by Margaret Jull Costa. New Directions 2000 210p pa $14.95

ISBN 978-0-8112-1453-7; 0-8112-1453-2

LC 00-55026

Original Spanish edition, 1989; this translation first published 1992 by HarperCollins

"'Oxford is, without a doubt, one of the cities of the world where the least work gets done.' So opens this arch portrait of a university town, marked by languid ennui and gossipy, semifossilized dons. The point of view is that of an unnamed visiting Spaniard scholar, whose memory flits among several eccentric people and events. Thus the recollection doesn't unfold chronologically. The reader learns early on that the Spaniard carried on a desultory affair with a don's wife, whom he met at 'High Table,' a stylized Oxfordian dinner that Marias spoofs to good effect. The personality of that wife, Clare, emerges in a discrete fashion, with dots of conversations and digressions of personal revelations that say, verily, this will not be an affair to remember. The Spaniard seems better acquainted with Cromer-Blake, a sickly professor, closet gay, and guide to Oxford's picayune atmosphere of bored superiority. Though nothing eventful occurs, Marias' refined prose achieves an appealing characterization of place." Booklist

Marias, Javier, 1951-

A **heart** so white; translated from the Spanish by Margaret Jull Costa. New Directions 2000 278p $24.95; pa $14.95

ISBN 978-0-8112-1505-9; 0-8112-1452-4; 978-0-8112-1505-3 pa; 0-8112-1505-9 pa

LC 00-55021

Original Spanish edition, 1992; this translation first published 1995 in the United Kingdom

Marias is "the most subtle and gifted writer in contemporary Spanish literature." Boston Globe

Marías, Javier, 1951-

The **Infatuations**; by Javier Marias and translated by Margaret Jull Costa. Knopf 2013 352 p. $26.95

ISBN 0307960722; 9780307960726

LC 2013016429

In this book by javier Marias, "the narrator, María Dolz, eavesdrops on a conversation that undoes all she thinks she knows about Javier, her lover, and his dear friend, the victim of an apparently brutal and senseless murder. What she believed was a tragedy may be the result of a conspiracy." (Booklist)

Marías, Javier, 1951-

★ The **man** of feeling; translated from the Spanish by Margaret Jull Costa. New Directions 2003 182p $22.95

ISBN 0-8112-1531-8

LC 2002-153935

Original Spanish edition, 1986

"Narrated by the young opera singer, the novel opens as he recalls traveling on a train from Milan to Venice, silently absorbed for hours by the woman asleep in the seat opposite his. . . . The Man of Feeling turns on the poles of anticipation and recollection." (Publisher's note)

"While in Madrid to perform the role of Cassio in Verdi's 'Otello,' a Spanish tenor meets a man whose job is to amuse the neglected wife of a powerful Brussels banker. The paid companion invites the singer on his outings with the woman, setting the stage for an affair. . . . (This). . . would seem to offer little more than banal melodrama. Everything depends, however, on how the plot unfolds. Marias avoids a straightforward delivery in favor of a digressive narrative that moves back and forth in time. . . . This suggestive indirection perfectly suits Marias's preoccupation: the erotic imagination." N Y Times Book Rev

Marías, Javier, 1951-

★ **Thus** bad begins; by Javier Marías; translated from the Spanish by Margaret Jull Costa. Alfred A. Knopf 2016 443 p. (hardcover : alk. paper) $27.95

ISBN 9781101911914; 9781101946084; 9781101946091

LC 2015049902

This novel, by Javier Marías, translated by Margaret Jull Costa, is set in "Madrid, 1980. Juan de Vere . . . takes a job as personal assistant to Eduardo Muriel, an eccentric, once-successful film director. . . . But Muriel's voluptuous wife, Beatriz, inhabits their home like an unwanted ghost; and on the periphery of their lives is Dr. Jorge Van Vechten, a family friend implicated in unsavory rumors that Muriel now asks Juan to investigate." (Publisher's note)

"Another challenging, boundary-stretching work from Marías, complete with a jaw-dropping last-chapter revelation." Kirkus

Marías, Javier, 1951-

While the women are sleeping; translated by Margaret Jull Costa. New Directions 2010 128p

ISBN 978-0-8112-1663-0; 0-8112-1663-2; 9780811219143

LC 2010-21110

Original Spanish edition, 1990

This collection of short stories, by Javier Marías, translated by Margaret Jull Costa, features "slippery figures in anomalous situations -- ghosts, spies, bodyguards, criminals. . . . The characters come bearing their strange and special secrets. . . . In one story, a man obsessed with his much younger lover endlessly videotapes her every move,and then confides his surprising plans for her; in another, a ghost can't stop resigning from his job." (Publisher's note)

"Having sneaked out of the hotel bed where his wife is sleeping to sit by a pool where a stranger relates a plan to kill his girlfriend before she grows old, the narrator of the title story in Marías's collection glances nervously back to his own balcony, as if half-suspecting himself of murder. In another story, a soldier returns from war to see his wife strangled by a man who looks exactly like him. Like many of Marías's narrators, these men are observers whose instinct when confronted with mortal danger is to stand and ruminate. In much of his short fiction, Marías . . . relies on occult devices like doppelgängers and ghosts to remind us of the life-or-death stakes. Other stories, including one in which a butler must dispose of an infant's corpse, cast their own spells. Few of these tales rise to the level of Marías's longer works (most of them also adeptly translated by Costa), which build up suspense by punctuating long passages of erudition with moments of brutal violence. But some are quite good on their own terms." N Y Times Book Rev

Marias, Javier, 1951-

Your face tomorrow: volume one: Fever and spear; translated from the Spanish by Margaret Jull Costa. New Directions 2005 387p $24.95

ISBN 0-8112-1612-8

LC 2005-992

Original Spanish edition, 2002

The book uses "spy novel elements in order to frame certain far-ranging meditations on history, memory, and identity. The resultant effect is reminiscent of the cerebral play of Borges, the dark humor of Pynchon, and the meditative lyricism of Proust." Review of Contemporary Fiction

Marias, Javier, 1951-

Your face tomorrow: volume three: Poison, shadow and farewell; translated from the Spanish by Margaret Jull Costa. New Directions 2009 546p $24.95

ISBN 978-0-8112-1812-2; 0-811-21812-0

Original Spanish edition, 2007

"Marías has concluded one of the most striking works in recent memory, giving us the cap to a philosophical espionage trilogy that could have been written by Henry James or Marcel Proust. . . . [He] weaves multi-page disquisitions on the Nationalist takeover of Spain, the collapse of the Cold War spy state and 16th century Italian art with moments of revelry involving Ian Fleming, hairnets, armpits, sex and swordplay. With an elegant, nimble translation by Margaret Jull Costa, the trilogy's 1,273 pages move right along." Los Angeles Times Book Rev

Marias, Javier

Your face tomorrow: volume two: Dance and dream; translated from the Spanish by Margaret Jull Costa. New Directions 2006 341p $24.95

ISBN 0-8112-1656-x

LC 2006-15589

Oiginal Spanish edition, 2004

"Marias's is a style of thinking more than writing. In 'Your Face Tomorrow' it is faithfully rendered by Margaret Jull Costa, his principal English translator, who achieves a rare feat: presence and near invisibility." N Y Times Book Rev

Marillier, Juliet

Daughter of the forest. TOR Bks. 2000 400p (Sevenwaters trilogy) hardcover o.p. pa $15.95

ISBN 0-312-84879-X; 0-312-87530-4 pa

LC 00-25216

"As the only daughter and youngest child of Lord Colum of Sevenwaters, Sorcha grows up protected and pampered by her six older brothers. When a sorceress's evil magic ensorcels Colum's sons, transforming them into swans, only Sorcha's efforts can break the curse. . . . The author's keen understanding of Celtic paganism and early Irish Christianity adds texture to a rich and vibrant novel that belongs in most fantasy collections." Libr J

Other titles in the Sevenwaters trilogy are:
Child of the prophecy (2002)
Son of the shadows (2001)

Marion, Isaac

Warm bodies; a novel. Atria Books 2011 241p pa $15

ISBN 978-1-4391-9231-3; 1-4391-9232-6

LC 2010-48583

"R, as he calls himself (the rest of his name has rotted away), is a zombie. He can't remember his former existence, can't read, can't speak more than four syllables at a time. . . . Life among the undead is meaningless for him until he kills a suicidal teen leading a scavenging party and eats his brain. Zombies, in Marion's gruesome yet poetic vision, eat brains to get high on memories like those they've lost. When R consumes the teen's gray matter, he becomes infused with that boy's love for Julie Grigio, the feisty blonde accompanying him. R saves Julie from being killed by the rest of his pack and takes her back with him to their airport lair. . . . Absurd as its premise could be called, 'Warm Bodies' works on lots of levels. It's a moving romance that makes obvious allusions to Shakespeare: R is a stand-in for Romeo, and Julie for Juliet. It's a metaphor for the battle between the forces of hope and despair. And it's a paean to the power of storytelling." Seattle Times

Mark, David ✓

Cruel mercy; David Mark. Blue Rider Press 2017 354 p. (Detective Sergeant McAvoy) (hardcover) $28

ISBN 9780399185113; 9780399185137; 0399185119

LC 2016052098

In this book in the Detective Sergeant McAvoy series, by David Mark, "Detective Ronny Alto is investigating a crime that's left one man dead and the other in a medically induced coma. . . . McAvoy is flown in to assist with the case, but he has his own motives. . . : find . . . Valentine Teague. . . . But every step toward locating Valentine is a step deeper into a sinister underground network of misguided loyalty, faith, and honor that pulses beneath the streets of New York." (Publisher's note)

"Beautifully crafted, filled with flashbacks, horror, angst, and chilling detail, this one is his most complex and best yet." Kirkus

Mark, David

The **dark** winter; David Mark. Blue Rider Press 2012 304 p. (alk. paper) $25.95

ISBN 0399158642; 9780399158643

LC 2012024256

In this book by David Mark, "a series of suspicious deaths has rocked Hull, a port city in England. . . . Detective Sergeant Aector McAvoy is sure there is a connection between these crimes, but his fellow officers are not convinced -- they would rather get a quick arrest than bother themselves with finding the true killer. . . . Compelled by his keen sense of justice, McAvoy decides to strike out alone."(Publisher's note)

Includes bibliographical references and index

Other titles about Aector McAvoy are:
Original skin (2013)
Sorrow bound (2014)
Taking pity (2015)
Cruel mercy (2017)
Dead pretty (2018)

Mark, David ✓

Original skin; David Mark. Blue Rider Press 2013 448 p. (DS Aector McAvoy) (hardcover) $26.95

ISBN 0399158650; 9780399158650

LC 2013001237

In this book, part of author David Mark's Aector McAvoy series, "Det. Supt. Trish Pharaoh and her detectives look into the escalating attacks on Vietnamese cannabis farmers by brutal rival gangs. Meanwhile, McAvoy is distracted by the year-old apparent suicide of Simon Appleyard, a gay man who had been frequenting sex parties with his self-loathing best friend, Suzie Devlin. McAvoy believes that Suzie may be a murderer's next target, and her unique tattoos are a clue." (Publishers Weekly)

Mark, David

Sorrow bound; David Mark. Blue Rider Press 2014 352 p. (Detective Sergeant McAvoy) (hardback) $26.95

ISBN 0399168206; 9780399168208

LC 2013050353

In this book, by David Mark, "it's a sweltering summer in Hull. . . . Detective Sergeant Aector McAvoy and the rest of the Serious and Organized Crime Unit are being pushed to the brink by the local drug trade as a sadistic new boss takes over and violent crime escalates. But it's not long before McAvoy and DS Trish Pharaoh are distracted by something deadlier: a serial murderer with a taste for the grisly and macabre." (Publisher's note)

"The physically imposing Aector, a terrific lead, hews closely to the rules. Well-fleshed out supporting characters round out the cast." Pub Wkly

Markandaya, Kamala

Nectar in a sieve; with a new introduction by Indira Ganesan. Signet Classic 2002 190p pa $6.95

ISBN 0-451-52823-9

LC 2001-49544

First published 1954 in the United Kingdom; first United States edition published 1955 by Day

"This realistic novel of peasant life in a southern Indian village portrays the struggle that Nathan and Rukmani must make to survive. Their first child is a daughter, Irawaddy, and there follow five other children, all sons, after an interval of seven years. Hardships are innumerable and insurmountable, whether they are disasters of nature such as drought, or such manmade catastrophes as the coming of a tannery to their village and a subsequent labor conflict. After many crises, Nathan and Rukmani come to the city to seek help from one of their sons, but he has disappeared. Nathan, finally destroyed by privation, dies, believing to the end that his life with Rukmani has been a happy one." Shapiro. Fic for Youth. 3d edition

Markovits, Anouk

I am forbidden; a novel. Anouk Markovits. Hogarth 2012 302 p.

ISBN 9780307984739

LC 2011041305

2013 Sophie Brody Medal Honor Book

In this book, "[o]rphaned during the Holocaust, two ultra-orthodox Jews bound by love and faith are driven apart by the same forces. . . . French-raised [Anouk] Markovits' . . . debut opens in Manhattan in 2005 with the meeting of two women: Atara, who . . . fled her Hasidic family to avoid an arranged marriage; and Judith, the granddaughter of Atara's adopted sister, burdened by a cataclysmic secret. Then the clock turns back to Transylvania in 1939" to trace Atara's family history. (Kirkus)

Marks, John

Fangland. Penguin Press 2007 385p $25.95

ISBN 1-59420-117-X; 978-1-59420-117-2

LC 2006-49809

Marks has "written an electrifying modern tale of horror that pays homage to Bram Stoker's Dracula. He goes much further, however, creating a hideous vampire more horrifying than anything that ever came from Stoker's imagination." Libr J

Marks, Laurie J.

Fire logic. Tor Bks. 2002 335p $25.95

ISBN 0-312-87887-7

LC 2001-58352

"Marks is an absolute master of fantasy in this book. Her characters are beautifully drawn, showing tremendous emotional depth and strength as they endure the unendurable and strive always to do the right thing." Booklist

Markson, David

The **last** novel. Shoemaker & Hoard 2007 190p pa $15

ISBN 978-1-59376-143-1; 1-59376-143-0

LC 2006-38793

"Just when one had started mourning the demise of avant-garde and postmodern fiction, buried under the avalanche of historical novels, chick lit and just plain old traditional stories, here comes David Markson's latest 'novel,' 'The Last Novel,' which is anything but a novel in any conventional sense of the term. Yet it manages to keep us enthralled during the length of its short 190-page span, and even moved to tears at the end. And what a thrill it is to witness the performance, a real tour de force." N Y Times Book Rev

Markson, David

Vanishing point; a novel. Shoemaker & Hoard 2004 191p pa $15

ISBN 1-59376-010-8 pa

"The premise is that 'The Author' as the narrator refers to himself, is assembling a box of note cards full of information he has gathered over the years with the hope of forging a novel. Life then imitates art as Markson literally accomplishes what his narrator hopes to: he creates a novel out of fragments of ideas and information. Vanishing Point feels a little like a literary Trivial Pursuit, or the associative stream of consciousness produced by a surrealist party game, and it's just as entertaining." Booklist

Marlantes, Karl

★ **Matterhorn**; a novel of the Vietnam War. Atlantic Monthly Press; El Len Literary Arts 2010 598p il map $24.95

ISBN 978-0-8021-1928-5; 0-8021-1928-X

"Matterhorn is one of those countless hills in Vietnam that makes young men's lives so cheap. In this case, it's the Marines of Bravo Company and the hardened NVA (North Vietnamese Army) soldiers. The story revolves around a young Marine lieutenant, Waino Mellas, who must quickly learn the difference between officer candidate school and the reality of life in the bush. Lt. Mellas tries to straddle the line between being one of the guys and a platoon commander. This division between the troops and a low-ranking officer like Mellas (who is only a few years older than his men) can become too vague if he is overly friendly. In combat, that can be disastrous. The delicate balance between life and death resonates throughout Matterhorn, as it does in real combat. What is so fresh and fascinating about this novel is Marlantes' depiction of the specific activities and conflicting motivations that take place in a war zone." BookPage

Marlette, Doug

Magic time. Farrar, Straus and Giroux 2006 480p $25

ISBN 978-0-374-20001-5; 0-374-20001-7

LC 2005-36396

"Magic Time presents a realistic portrait of the collective amnesia of the South and the generational tensions that the civil rights movement stirred up, then and now. It's a real Mississippi story, not merely a faded imitation." Washington Post Book World

Marley, Louise

The **child** goddess; Louise Marley. Ace Books 2004 324p $23.95

ISBN 0441011365

LC 2003063836

This book is "set on 23rd-century Earth and the oceanic world Virimund. . . . The Magdalenes, a celibate Roman Catholic order of women priests known as Enquirers, travel the galaxy as anthropological investigators. . . . Assigned to probe Oa, a mysterious child discovered on Virimund, empathetic Isabel soon learns that Oa represents one of humanity's deepest yearnings, for the fountain of eternal youth. Torn between her forbidden love for Dr. Simon Edwards, like herself a healer, and her sacred vow of celibacy, Isabel asks Simon to help Oa escape the megaworld ExtraSolar Corporation, whose general administrator, Gretchen Boreson, has her own devious reasons to claim Oa and her few fellow 'anchens,' the abandoned children of Virimund." (Publishers Weekly)

Maron, Margaret

Bootlegger's daughter. Mysterious Press 1992 261p

LC 91-58021

This mystery takes place in "Cotton Grove, N.C., a close-knit rural community on the outskirts of Raleigh, and introduces savvy Deborah Knott, a lawyer whose singular upbringing as a child of a bootlegging power broker has prepared her well for the county race for district court judge. But just as she begins her campaign . . . Deborah is asked to turn over the dead leaves of an 18-year-old murder case. It seems that the daughter of an old flame can't start her life until she finds out who killed her mother as she watched with uncomprehending infant eyes." N Y Times Book Rev

Maron, Margaret

High country fall. Mysterious Press 2004 303p $24

ISBN 0-89296-808-7

LC 2004-1953

"Deborah's narrative voice, with its engaging tone of amusement at the human foibles she witnesses in her travels, is just the ticket for this dramatic view of the spectacular Blue Ridge Mountains." N Y Times Book Rev

Maron, Margaret

Shooting at loons. Mysterious Press 1994 229p

LC 93-47141

"District Court Judge Deborah Knott, a native North Carolinian, looks forward to filling in for a sick colleague at the Harker's Island courthouse. But on her first fishing trip after arriving on the island, she discovers the body of an old fisherman known to her since childhood. . . . The down-home prose flows well, spiced by Judge Knott's wit, charm, and extended family as well as by references to the local food and drink." Libr J

Maron, Margaret

Storm track. Mysterious Press 2000 260p $28

ISBN 0-89296-656-4

LC 99-51761

"Deborah Knott, the district court judge who presides over this enchanting regional series, guides us through these crises with her customary good sense. . . . Deborah is the voice of sanity and the soul of wit." N Y Times Book Rev

Maron, Margaret

Uncommon clay. Warner Bks. 2001 288p $28

ISBN 0-89296-720-X

LC 00-66266

This mystery "does more than honor local folk art and the generations of artisans who carry on the regional heritage. It shows us how deeply these homespun crafts are rooted in the collective artistry of individual families—and what a devastating loss it is when these families die out." N Y Times Book Rev

Maron, Margaret

Up jumps the Devil. Mysterious Press 1996 278p

LC 96-7715

"The droll characters and their lilting regional humor seem ever more endearing because we sense their days are numbered." N Y Times Book Rev

Marr, Andrew

Head of State; Andrew Marr. Penguin Group USA 2015 384 p. $27.95

ISBN 1468310569; 9781468310566

LC 2014504557

In this political satire by Andrew Marr, "It's September 2017, and the United Kingdom is on the verge of a crucial referendum that will determine, once and for all, if the country remains a member of the European Union or goes its own way. But . . . there is a shocking secret at the very heart of government that could change everything in an instant. A group of ruthlessly determined individuals will stop at nothing--including murder--to prevent that from happening." (Publisher's note)

"This is a very British satire, with inside jokes for the most devoted Anglophiles, but skewering a dysfunctional political system is, unfortunately, universal." Booklist

Marra, Anthony

★ A **constellation** of vital phenomena; a novel. Anthony Marra. Hogarth 2013 400 p. $26

ISBN 0770436404; 9780770436407

LC 2012017444

This novel "intertwines the stories of a handful of characters at the end of the second, war in bleak, apocalyptic Chechnya. Though the novel spans 11 years, the story traces five days in 2004 following the arrest of Dokka, a villager from the small Muslim village of Eldar. His eight-year-old daughter escapes, and is rescued by Dokka's friend Akhmed, the village doctor, who entrusts her to the care of Sonja, the lone remaining doctor at a nearby hospital." (Publishers Weekly)

Marra, Anthony

★ The **tsar** of love and techno; stories. Anthony Marra. Hogarth 2015 352 p. (hardcover) $25

ISBN 0770436439; 9780770436438

LC 2015010773

National Book Critics Circle Award Finalist: Fiction (2015)

This book, by Anthony Marra, presents "interwoven stories about family, sacrifice, the legacy of war, and the redemptive power of art. A 1930s Soviet censor. . . . A chorus of women recount their stories and those of their grandmothers, former gulag prisoners who settled their Siberian mining town. . . . Young men across the former USSR face violence at home and in the military. And great sacrifices are made in the name of an oil landscape." (Publisher's note)

"As in his previous novel, Marra is deft at managing different characters at different points in time, but the book's brilliance and humor are laced with the somber feeling that the country is allergic to evolution: KGB thugs then, drug dealers and Internet scammers now, with a few stray moments of compassion in between. A powerful and melancholy vision of a nation with long memories and relentless turmoil." Kirkus

Marsh, Ngaio

Dead water. Little, Brown 1963 244p

Scotland Yard's Superintendent "Roderick Alleyn finds himself involved unofficially in magic and faith healing when his former French teacher, now a formidable lady of 80, inherits an island off the coast of Cornwall which has, as its chief claim to fame and source of income, a Pixie Well supposed to cure warts, asthma and other ills. . . . Skillful writing, convincing atmosphere, and sharply etched characterization will please Ngaio Marsh fans, but the plot is less complex than some of her others." Publ Wkly

Marsh, Ngaio

False scent. Little, Brown 1959 273p

This mystery "takes place in the opulent London home of a famous—and temperamental—actress on her 50th birthday anniversary. The flamboyant people surrounding Mary Bellamy are properly subdued only when the polished Roderick Alleyn of Scotland Yard and his capable assistant, Inspector Fox, enter the scene and uncover the ugly secrets that led to murder." Libr J

Marsh, Ngaio

Grave mistake. Little, Brown 1978 252p

LC 78-16910

"When a rich eccentric old lady in a rest home suddenly dies, friends and the police suspect murder. {Inspector} Alleyn's trail leads him to the old lady's daughter, her fiance, his father, a close friend, and a few assorted others including a Scots gardener—named Gardener! When a will turns up leaving all her money to the doctor who runs the rest home, the supposed case of suicide really becomes murder." West Coast Rev Books

Marsh, Ngaio

Last ditch. Little, Brown 1977 265p

LC 76-52287

The novel takes place on one of the Channel Islands, to which Ricky, Superintendent Roderick Alleyn's son, "has come during the Easter vacation to write a novel. Here he meets Jasper and Julia Pharamond, friends of his parents, and falls in love with the magnolia-skinned Julia. . . . A riding expedition ends in a fatal accident, attended by suspicious circumstances; at the same time Ricky stumbles, he thinks, across the tracks of a gang of drug smugglers. But Scotland Yard's attention has already been called to the island, and Chief Superintendent Alleyn and Inspector Fox are soon on their way there." Times Lit Suppl

Marsh, Ngaio

Light thickens. Little, Brown 1982 232p ✓

LC 82-13085

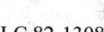

"A production of Macbeth, directed by Peregrine Jay at the Dolphin Theatre, is beset with macabre incidents. During rehearsals, realistic-looking dummy heads turn up in dark corners and on banquet trays, and a rat's head is found in the witch's effects. But the incidents cease, and reviews call the production 'the flawless Macbeth'—until the night when the actor playing Macbeth is decapitated during the play. Roderick Alleyn is, of course, in the audience." Libr J

Marsh, Ngaio

When in Rome. Little, Brown 1971 260p

First published 1970 in the United Kingdom

Set in Italy, "much of the action takes place in an ancient church which reproduces three levels of civilization. . . . The mystery centers on a sinister blackmailing tour entrepreneur who gathers together a motley group of people, some innocent, some with good reason to want him out of the way. Drugs, sex orgies, even more delicate scandals are all grist to his mill and when he meets a very nasty demise the field of suspects is wide open. Not the least of the pleasures here is a charming love affair, and the slightly comic opera encounters between English Inspector Roderick Alleyn and the Rome police." Publ Wkly

Marshall, Alex

★ A **crown** for cold silver; Alex Marshall. Orbit 2015 656 p. (hardback) $26

ISBN 0316277983; 9780316277983

LC 2014037807

In this fantasy novel, by Alex Marshall, "twenty years ago, feared general Cobalt Zosia led her five villainous captains and mercenary army into battle, wrestling monsters and toppling an empire. When there were no more titles to win and no more worlds to conquer, she retired and gave up her legend to history. Now the peace she carved for herself has been shattered by the unprovoked slaughter of her village. Seeking bloody vengeance, Zosia heads for battle once more." (Publisher's note)

"This brawny revenge fantasy feels like a Tarantino movie: a hugely entertaining mix of adventure and comedy, punctuated by moments of darkness, with clever dialogue and explosive set pieces." Booklist

Other titles in this series are:

A blade of black steel (2016)

A war in crimson embers (2017)

Marshall, Catherine

★ **Christy**. Avon Books 2006 576p pa $6.99

ISBN 0-380-00141-1

A reissue of the title first published 1967 by McGraw-Hill

"A spirited young woman leaves the security of her home to become a teacher in Cutter Gap, Kentucky. It is 1912 and the needs of the Appalachian people are great. Christy learns much from the poverty and superstition of the mountain folk. Marshall's Christian faith and ideals are intertwined in the plot, which includes a love story." Shapiro. Fic for Youth. 3d edition

Marshall, Paule

Brown girl, brownstones; with a foreword by Edwidge Danticat; afterword by Mary Helen Washington. 2nd Feminist Press ed.; Feminist Press at the City University of New York 2006 319p pa $16.95

ISBN 1-55861-498-2; 978-1-55861-498-7

LC 2005-29191

First published 1959 by Random House

"Set in Depression-era Brooklyn, NY, this 1959 coming-of-age novel finds Selina Boyce caught in the middle of her immigrant parents. Mom wants Selina to get an American education, while dad dreams of returning to Barbados. Along with her parental woes, our heroine must deal with the poverty and racism that surrounds her." Libr J

Marshall, Paule

The **fisher** king; a novel. Scribner 2000 222p $23

ISBN 0-684-87283-8

LC 00-28470

"Marshall's prose is full of expert dialogue, mellifluous rhythms and sharply drawn portraits of Sonny-Rett's loved ones." N Y Times Book Rev

Marshall, Paule

Praisesong for the widow. Putnam 1983 256p

LC 82-13215

This novel "tells of a sixtyish widow, Avey Johnson, refined, well-to-do, and complacent. Troubled by strange dreams and symptoms, she cuts short her annual Caribbean cruise and disembarks on a small island. An old man recognizes her as one of the 'people who can't call their nation,' and persuades her to join him and others on their yearly ritual visit to a neighboring island they call home. There, purged of her old self, Avey rediscovers her roots." Libr J

Marston, Edward

The **Bawdy** basket. St. Martin's Minotaur 2002 262p

ISBN 0-312-28501-9

LC 2002-2510944

An Elizabethan mystery featuring "Nicholas Bracewell, stage manager of Lord Westfield's Men. . . . When a young actor's father is tried, convicted, and hung for a brutal murder he claims he did not commit, his sins are unfortunately visited upon his loyal son. Nicholas agrees to investigate the matter in an effort to clear the unlucky man's name and to restore a promising young thespian to the ranks of his beloved theater company." Booklist

Marston, Edward

The **Devil's** apprentice; a novel. St. Martin's Minotaur 2001 273p

ISBN 0-312-26574-3

LC 2001-19259

Elizabethan stage manager Nicholas Bracewell "fends off accusations of witchcraft and worse after the troupe performs at a manor house in Essex. A new apprentice taken on there seems to be at the root of the trouble. Lively and entertaining: for fans of Elizabethan historicals." Libr J

Marston, Edward

The **roaring** boy; a novel. St. Martin's Press 1995 260p

LC 95-8568

"Marston's colorful (and convincing) characterizations shine as Nicholas chases the secrets of the murder in order to save the company. The plot, except for one transparently finagled episode, is expertly wrought, with the suspense building steadily to breathtaking climax and some surprises saved for the very end." Publ Wkly

Marston, Edward

The **vagabond** clown. St. Martin's Minotaur 2003 292p $24.95

ISBN 0-312-30789-6

LC 2002-191950

"Lord Westfield's Men, the actors' troupe for which Bracewell works as stage manager, are forced to leave their theater after a violent act of sabotage trashes the place. Worse, someone has killed one of Westfield's friends during the melee. Bracewell struggles to save the troupe and its reputation. An outstanding historical." Libr J

Marston, Edward

The **wanton** angel; a novel. St. Martin's Press 1999 279p

ISBN 0-312-20391-8

LC 99-22062

This mystery, set in Elizabethan England, finds Nicholas Bracewell's "acting troupe ejected from its theater at the Queen's Head when one of the actors impregnates the landlord's daughter and is then murdered." N Y Times Book Rev

Martel, Yann

Beatrice and Virgil; a novel. Spiegel & Grau 2010 197p $24

ISBN 978-1-4000-6926-2; 1-4000-6926-2

LC 2009-48995

"Whimsy takes a deadly serious turn in a novel that will enchant some readers and exasperate others." Kirkus

Martel, Yann

The **high** mountains of Portugal; a novel. Yann Martel. Spiegel & Grau 2016 352 p. ("Author of Life of Pi"--Jacket.) (alk. paper) $27

ISBN 9780812997170

LC 2015022883

This book, by Yann Martel, "part quest, part ghost story, part contemporary fable--offers a haunting exploration of great love and great loss. Filled with tenderness, humor, and endless surprise, it takes the reader on a road trip through Portugal in the last century--and through the human soul." (Publisher's note)

"Nevertheless, this allegorical tale drives home the ephemeral nature of beauty and joy and the thin line we all walk between normalcy and madness, especially in the wake of loss." Booklist

Martel, Yann

★ **Life** of Pi; a novel. Harcourt 2001 319p $25

ISBN 0-15-100811-6

LC 2001-39737

"An impassioned defense of zoos, a death-defying trans-Pacific sea adventure à la 'Kon-Tiki,' and a hilarious shaggy-dog story starring a four-hundred-and-fifty-pound Bengal tiger named Richard Parker: this audacious novel manages to be all of these. . . . This breezily aphoristic, unapologetically twee saga of man and cat is a convincing hands-on, how-to guide for dealing with what Pi calls, with typically understated brio, 'major lifeboat pests.'" New Yorker

Martin, Clancy W.

How to sell; [by] Clancy Martin. Farrar, Straus & Giroux 2009 296p $24

ISBN 978-0-374-17335-7; 0-374-17335-4

LC 2008-55450

This novel is, "with memorably dark comedy, a virtual handbook on fraud. The world the Clark boys build for themselves and teeter precariously upon . . . is a compelling setting for Martin's propulsive storytelling. His narration feels cinematic, the sets and scenery popping off the page. With remarkable skill as the story spools out, Martin omits just enough exposition and interior insights to keep his characters shrouded in mystery, as if constantly reminding us that we'll always be the customer, never the insider." Elle

Martin, George R. R.

A **clash** of kings. Bantam Bks. 1999 761p (Song of ice and fire) $26.95

ISBN 0-553-10803-4

LC 98-37954

"The novel is notable particularly for the lived-in quality of its world, created through abundant detail that dramatically increases narrative length even as it aids suspension of disbelief; for the comparatively modest role of magic . . . and for its magnificent action-filled climax." Publ Wkly

Followed by Storm of swords

Martin, George R. R.

A **dance** with dragons. Bantam Books 2011 1016p map (Song of ice and fire) $35

ISBN 978-0-553-80147-7

LC 2011-15508

This is the fifth book in a series begun with A game of thrones (1996). New threats emerge to endanger the future of the Seven Kingdoms, as Daenerys Targaryen, ruling in the East, fights off a multitude of enemies, while Jon Snow, Lord Commander of the Night's Watch, faces his foes both in the Watch and beyond the great Wallof ice and stone.

"The heart-hammering conclusion hints that the next installment will see a return to the fiery battles and icy terror that earned the series its fanatic following. Even ostensibly disillusioned fans will be caught up in the interweaving stories, especially when Martin drops little hints around long-debated questions such as Jon's parentage." Publ Wkly

Followed by Winds of Winter

Martin, George R. R.

A **feast** for crows. Bantam Books 2005 753p maps (Song of ice and fire) $30

ISBN 0-553-80150-3

LC 2005-53034

The author introduces "plot twists and characters that continue to flesh out one of the genre's most detailed and intriguing worlds. A must-purchase for libraries owning the series, this panoramic fantasy adventure is highly recommended." Libr J

Followed by A Dance with Dragons

Martin, George R. R.

★ A **game** of thrones. Bantam Bks. 1996 694p il (Song of ice and fire) $18.00

ISBN 9780553381689

LC 95-43936

The first volume in A Song of Ice and Fire saga, "combines intrigue, action, romance, and mystery in a family saga. The family is the Starks of Winterfell, a society in crisis due to climatic change that has created decades-long seasons, and a society almost without magic but with human perversity abundant and active. Martin reaches a new plateau in terms of narrative technique, action scenes, and integrating . . . his political views into the story." Booklist

Followed by A Clash of Kings

Martin, George R. R.

Hunter's run; [by] George R.R. Martin, Gardner Dozois, and Daniel Abraham. Eos 2008 303p $25.95

ISBN 978-0-06-137329-9; 0-06-137329-X

LC 2007-29817

"The first item of business to get out of the way is the tripartite authorship of this book. At first it seems a rather circuslike distraction that, however, has actually resulted in a superb fusion of talents. . . . The book reads like the work of one melded intelligence, seamless and organic. In Ramón, the authors have created an appallingly attractive antihero straight out of Leigh Brackett's canon. His rough-and-tumble progress from unknowingness to self-awareness is handled deftly all the way." SciFi Wkly

Martin, George R. R.

A **storm** of swords; George R.R. Martin. Bantam Books 2000 973 p. ill., maps (Song of ice and fire)

ISBN 0553106635; 9780553106633

LC 00060827

"The third volume of the high fantasy saga that began with A Game of Thrones and continued in A Clash of Kings . . . Martin's richly imagined world slides closer to its 10-year winter, both the weather and the warfare worsen. In the north, King Joffrey of House Lannister sits uneasily on the Iron Throne. . . . Jaime Lannister, the Kingslayer, escapes from jail in Riverrun. . . . Meanwhile, . . . Queen Daenarys tries to assert her claim to the various thrones with an army of eunuchs, but discovers that she must choose between conquering more and ruling well what she has already taken." Pub Wkly

"The author's ability to interweave dozens of plot lines and to create memorable characters makes this a rousing saga that should appeal to most fans of grand-scale fantasy. Recommended for most libraries, along with its predecessors, A Game of Thrones and A Clash of Kings." LJ

Followed by A Feast for Crows

Martin, Lee

The **bright** forever; a novel. Lee Martin. Shaye Areheart Books 2005 269p. o.p.; (pbk.) $14.00

ISBN 1400097916; 9780307209863

LC 2004023758

In this book, "Katie Mackey is nine and lives with older brother Gilley and her parents in the small town of Tower Hill, Ind[iana]. . . . On the other side of the tracks is Henry Dees, a lonely bachelor and math teacher, who is Katie's private tutor this summer of 1972. His neighbor is the equally lonely widow, Clare Mains, who has taken up with the self-styled Raymond R., a new arrival and, like Dees, victim of a grim childhood. . . . Then, on a perfect summer evening, Katie disappears. . . . The searchers for Katie feel burdened by 'the weight of all their sins.' Small wonder, then, that in time Katie's murder will lead to vigilante justice and another missing body." (Kirkus)

Martin, Steve

An **object** of beauty; a novel. Grand Central Pub. 2010 295p il $26.99

ISBN 978-0-446-57364-1; 0-446-57364-7

LC 2010-07885

"For all her charisma, the ruthlessly self-serving Lacey is not inherently a creature of much emotional heft or warmth. Still, Martin has a gift for rendering an esoteric scene accessible, piercing its sillier pretensions while making a case for art\'s real aesthetic (if not monetary) value. It takes a certain nimbleness to play the dual roles of proxy art-history professor and compelling storyteller without falling off the literary balance beam. Martin, wry, wise, and keenly observant, rarely misses a step." Entertainment Wkly

Martin, Steve

The **pleasure** of my company; a novella. Hyperion 2003 163p $19.95

ISBN 0-7868-6921-6

LC 2003-49954

This work features "one of the odder yet more charming protagonists in recent fiction, Daniel Pecan Cambridge, a gentle soul suffering from a mild mix of autism and obsessive-compulsive disorder. Daniel, 33, lives in a rundown Santa Monica apartment, his life constricted by an armor of defensive habit. . . his dull days punctuated only by imagined romances and visits by his student social worker, lovely and kind Clarissa. Daniel's ways (a product of child abuse, Martin shows with subtlety) are challenged when Clarissa and her infant son, Teddy, move in to escape an abusive husband. . . . This novella is a delight, embodying a satisfying story arc, a jeweler's eye for detail, intelligent pacing and a clean, sturdy prose style." Publ Wkly

Martin, Steve

★ **Shopgirl**; a novella. Hyperion 2000 130p

ISBN 0-7868-6658-6

LC 00-38874

The main characters in this novella are Mirabelle Butterfield, "a 28-year-old woman behind the glove counter at the Neiman Marcus department store in Beverly Hills . . . {and} Ray Porter, the fiftysomething man Mirabelle admits into her solitary life." Time

Martin, Valerie

Italian fever; a novel. Knopf 1999 259p $22

ISBN 0-375-40542-9

LC 98-31824

"When Lucy Stark's employer falls inelegantly down a well in Tuscany, Lucy must travel there to see that he's given a decent burial. Not surprisingly, within a day she has contracted the kind of gruesome fever that makes you revel in your own health, and she has encountered the kind of Italian lover that makes you book the next flight over. What lingers in the mind, though, is the novel's final touching twist, which slyly dismantles its own satire and casts a long and mysterious shadow over everything that has come before." New Yorker

Martin, Valerie

★ **Mary** Reilly. Doubleday 1990 263p

LC 89-38313

"Whereas the atmosphere of Robert Louis Stevenson's tale was all foggy nights and sinister uncertainties, Mary Reilly weaves a somewhat more ambiguous but equally gripping web of mystery around the same riveting events. In both cases the end product is a fascinating story." Quill Quire

Martin, Valerie

Property. Talese 2003 196p $23.95

ISBN 0-385-50408-X

LC 2002-66846

This work "presents itself as a novel about the abuse of power within the loveless marriage between an antebellum plantation owner and his wife, their private suffering amplified by the social context of slavery. Bondage and its invitation to brutality are not unexplored terrain, but embedded within what might be mistaken as a morality play is a more subtle and compelling story—a contest of wills between two women, Manon Gaudet and Sarah, the slave she received from her aunt as a wedding gift." N Y Times Book Rev

Martin, Valerie

Trespass; a novel. Nan A. Talese/Doubleday 2007 288p $25

ISBN 0-385-51545-6; 978-0-385-51545-0

LC 2006-101676

"Chloe Dale's life is in good order. Her only child, Toby, has started his junior year at New York University; her husband, an academic on sabbatical, is working at home on his book about the Crusades; and Chloe is busy creating illustrations for a special edition of Emily Brontë's Wuthering Heights. Yet Chloe is disturbed—by the aggression of her government's foreign policy, by the poacher who roams the land behind her studio punctuating her solitude with rifle fire, and finally, by Toby's new girlfriend, a Croatian refugee named Salome Drago." (Publisher's note)

The novel "provides a searing commentary on the human desire to set boundary lines against threats, perceived and real. It's a testament to Martin's skill as both storyteller and writer that her complex characters defy separation into two camps those who accept and those who judge. Nothing in 'Trespass' is quite as it seems, and that is precisely the point." San Francisco Chronicle

Martin, William

Cape Cod. Warner Bks. 1991 652p

LC 90-50534

"Martin embraces the entire sweep of American history with unflagging relish for authentic detail and private moments. He creates generation after generation of feisty Hilyards and cruel Bigelows, pitting them against one another in religious and political skirmishes and joining them in risky love. They endure hardships and shipwrecks, scandal and imprisonment, shame and anger, and contribute their bit to the making of America." Booklist

Martinez, A. Lee

Gil's All Fright Diner; A. Lee Martinez. Tor 2005 268p o.p.; (pbk.) $6.99

ISBN 9780765311436; 0765311437; 9780765350015

LC 2004063791

In this book, author A. Lee "Martinez leads us into the lives of Earl the Vampire and Duke the Wolf Man, who met on the night that Duke first changed from human to werewolf, attacked Earl in the woods and began eating his guts. We meet these two . . . in their ratty pickup truck as they pull into Gil's All Night Diner in Rockwood County in the middle of nowhere. . . . Loretta . . . run[s the] . . . diner. Over the years she's shotgunned about 185 zombies, but they continue to attack the eatery in small groups. Duke and Earl decide to stick around and help Loretta ward off these unwelcome walking dead. It turns out that Rockwood County has been pestered in recent years by various occult disturbances, thanks to Tammy, a high-schooler intent on becoming Lilith, Queen of the Universe." (Kirkus)

Martinez, Nina Marie

Caramba! a tale told in turns of the card. Knopf, distributed by Random House 2004 359p il $24.95

ISBN 0-375-41375-8

LC 2003-56192

"At times, ¡Caramba! transcends kitschiness and absurdity to evoke something more authentic. Natalie and Consuelo's relationship, for instance, conveys genuine intimacy, particularly in their unique brand of shorthand-speak." Washington Post Book World

Martini, Steven Paul

Compelling evidence; {by} Steve Martini. Putnam 1992 379p

LC 91-30253

"Besides giving us the scoop on ballistics analysis and post-mortem blood distribution, the author answers just about every cynical question you've ever had about the games lawyers play." N Y Times Book Rev

Martinusen-Coloma, Cindy

The **salt** garden; Cindy McCormick Martinusen. Tyndale House Publishers 2004 313p o.p.; (pbk.) $14.99

ISBN 0842373640; 9781595542922

LC 2003024485

In this book, set in "a small town on the Pacific coast, a shipwreck is being salvaged that will disclose secrets from the past. [Cindy] Martinusen . . . tells her story from the viewpoints of three women. Claire O'Rourke is a San Francisco reporter recently returned to her small hometown. . . . Her path soon intersects with that of Sophia Fleming, a 70-something reclusive author whom Claire has admired since childhood. When a salt-damaged book washes ashore, some long-buried secrets are illuminated through the journal entries of Josephine Vanderook, a passenger on an ill-fated ship." (Publishers Weekly)

Marwood, Alex

The **killer** next door; Alex Marwood. Penguin Books 2014 400 p. (paperback) $16

ISBN 0143126695; 9780143126690

LC 2014012901

In this thriller, by Alex Marwood, "everyone who lives at 23 Beulah Grove has a secret. If they didn't, they wouldn't be renting rooms in a dodgy old building. . . . It's the kind of place you end up when you you've run out of other options. The six residents mostly keep to themselves, but one unbearably hot summer night, a terrible accident pushes them into an uneasy alliance. What they don't know is that one of them is a killer." (Publisher's note)

"Marwood, a British journalist writing under a pseudonym, not only creates a cast of memorable characters, but also ratchets up the suspense, leaving readers to dread what might be around the next corner. Many writers shine at characterization or at creating tension; the trick is in successfully combining the two. In this case, readers will care what happens to Collette and the rest of the boarders while simultaneously waiting for the literary axe to fall. Marwood—whose first novel, The Wicked Girls (2013), won an Edgar Award—proves she's got staying power in this addictive tale." Kirkus

Masello, Robert

The **Romanov** cross; a novel. Robert Masello. Bantam Books 2013 512 p. (acid-free paper) $26

ISBN 0553807803; 9780345533593; 9780553807806

LC 2012015943

In this supernatural thriller, Robert Masello "weaves together the story of the deaths of the Russian royal family with the possibility of a new worldwide influenza pandemic. St. Peter's, a small island . . . , was once the home of a tiny community of followers of Rasputin, the notorious Russian monk. St. Peter's sole living inhabitant, if living is the right word, is a Romanov—the recipient of a blessing from Rasputin, or maybe it was a curse." (Publishers Weekly)

Mason, Bobbie Ann

In country; a novel. Harper Perennial 2005 245, 16p pa $14.99

ISBN 978-0-06-083517-0; 0-06-083517-6

LC 2006-273518

First published 1985

"Sam, 17, is obsessed with the Vietnam War and the effect it has had on her life—losing a father she never knew and now living with Uncle Emmett, who seems to be suffering from the effects of Agent Orange. In her own forthright way, she tries to sort out why and how Vietnam has altered the lives of the vets of Hopewell, Kentucky. . . . A harshly realistic, well-written look at the Vietnam War as well as the story of a young woman maturing." SLJ

Mason, Bobbie Ann

Shiloh and other stories; with a foreword by George Ella Lyon. University Press of Ky. 1995 247p $19.95

ISBN 0-8131-1948-0

LC 95-16581

A reissue of the title first published 1982 by Harper & Row

"Capturing in vivid detail the emotional frustrations of her characters and the unsettling ambience of her small-town Kentucky settings, Mason portrays the uneasy feelings of people who don't know what they want out of life but who do know that what they have isn't it." Booklist

Mason, Daniel

The **piano** tuner. Knopf 2002 317p $24

ISBN 0-375-41465-7

LC 2002-19069

"Mason proves himself equally adept at scenes of wry humor and moments of rapture; most remarkable, he has written a profound adventure story with an unexpected climax, as the mild piano tuner finally becomes the hero of his own life." New Yorker

Mason, Jamie

★ **Three** graves full; by Jamie Mason. Gallery Books 2013 307 p. (alk. paper) $24.99

ISBN 1451685033; 9781451685039

LC 2012014974

In this book by Jamie Mason, "more than a year ago, mild-mannered Jason Getty killed a man he wished he'd never met. Then he planted the problem a little too close to home. But just as he's learning to live with the undeniable reality of what he's done, police unearth two bodies on his property--neither of which is the one Jason buried. Jason races to stay ahead of the consequences of his crime, and while chaos reigns on his lawn, his sanity unravels." (Publisher's note)

Includes bibliographical references and index

Mason, Richard, 1978-

Who killed Piet Barol? Richard Mason. First American edition Alfred A. Knopf 2017 367 p. (hardcover) $27.95

ISBN 9780385352888; 9780385352901

LC 2016008860

In this novel, by Richard Mason, "Piet Barol was a tutor before he came to South Africa, his wife, Stacey, an opera singer. In Cape Town they are living the high life, impersonating French aristocrats--but their lies are catching up with them. The Barols' furniture business is on the verge of collapse. They need top-quality wood, and they need it cheap. Piet enlists two Xhosa [pron. KO-sa] men to lead him into a vast forest, in search of a fabled tree." (Publisher's note)

"Luminously reminiscent of Chinua Achebe's Things Fall Apart (1958) and recalling the disastrous culture clash of Barbara Kingsolver's Poisonwood Bible (1998)." Booklist

Massey, Sujata

★ The **widows** of Malabar Hill; Sujata Massey. Soho Crime 2018 385 p. maps (hardcover) $26.95

ISBN 9781616957780; 9781616957797

LC 2017021391

In this book in the Mystery of 1920s Bombay series, by Sujata Massey, "Perveen Mistry, the daughter of a respected Zoroastrian family, has just joined her father's law firm. . . . Mistry Law has been appointed to execute the will of Mr. Omar Farid, a wealthy Muslim mill owner who has left three widows behind. But as Perveen examines the paperwork, she notices something strange: all three . . . wives have signed over their full inheritance to a charity. What will they live on?" (Publisher's note)

"The period detail and thoughtful characterizations, especially of the capable, fiercely independent lead, bode well for future installments." Pub Wkly

Includes bibliographical references.

Mastai, Elan

All our wrong todays; a novel. Elan Mastai. Dutton 2017 384 p. (ebook) $65; (hardback) $26

ISBN 9781101985144; 1101985135; 9781101985137; 9781101985151

LC 2016013073

In this novel, by Elan Mastai, "Tom Barren's 2016 . . . thrives in a techno-utopian paradise of flying cars, moving sidewalks, and moon bases. . . . Except Tom just can't seem to find his place in this dazzling, idealistic world, and that's before his life gets turned upside down. Utterly blindsided by an accident of fate, Tom makes a rash decision that drastically changes not only his own life but the very fabric of the universe itself." (Publisher's note)

"A potent mixture of sincere introspection and a riveting examination of time travel and alternate realities, this highly recommended novel is reminiscent of Jo Walton's My Real Children with the breeziness of Robin Sloan's Mr. Penumbra's 24-Hour Bookstore." LJ

Matar, Hisham

Anatomy of a disappearance; a novel. Dial Press 2011 224p $22

ISBN 978-0-385-34044-1; 0-385-34044-3

LC 2011-01561

"Part of what makes 'Anatomy of a Disappearance' worth reading is that its ambiguous and slightly cruel ending does not yield easy transcendence. In fact, it entirely recasts the meaning of the title. There are many disappearances that haunt the narrator not least his own. Though politics take a back seat, they shadow its margins, like the unknown men who kidnap Kamal. . . . For Americans attempting to understand the Middle East, this book provides a poignant picture of grief at the hands of political forces much larger than the individual lives they rupture." Cleveland Plain Dealer

Matar, Hisham

★ **In** the country of men. Dial Press 2007 246p $22

ISBN 978-0-385-34042-7; 0-385-34042-7

LC 2006-50649

First published 2006 in the United Kingdom

"A remarkably perceptive and affecting portrait of a young boy's premature political awakening. . . . [Matar] expertly builds an atmosphere of palpable tension, and though this novel never delves directly into politics, the menacing pall cast by political tyranny looms over the proceedings." Miami Herald

Matheson, Richard

Hunted past reason. Forge 2002 335p $24.95

ISBN 0-7653-0271-3

LC 2001-50768

"Two old friends, Bob (a novelist) and Doug (an actor), head off into the woods for a short hiking trip. Bob wants some hands-on experience for a novel he's working on; Doug is an expert in woodsmanship. From the get-go, there is tension between them: Doug seems excessively demanding; Bob reacts a little too sharply to his friend's criticisms of his stamina and abilities. Soon the mood turns dark, transforming the story into a psychological thriller." Booklist

Matheson, Richard

★ **I** am legend. Tom Doherty Associates 2007 317p pa $14.95

ISBN 0-7653-1874-1; 978-0-7653-1874-9

First published 1954

A pandemic devastates the human population, turning its victims into vampires. Robert Neville, the only man who escapes from the disease, must try to survive in a world in which he is now considered the monster.

Mathews, Brendan

The **world** of tomorrow; Brendan Mathews. Little, Brown & Co. 2017 552 p. illustrations (hardcover) $28

ISBN 9780316382199; 9780316382175

LC 2017932052

In this book, by Brendan Mathews "Francis Dempsey and his . . . brother Michael are on an ocean liner from Ireland bound for their brother Martin's home in New York City, having stolen a small fortune from the IRA. . . . The lives of these three brothers collide spectacularly with big-band jazz musicians, a talented but fragile heiress, a Jewish street photographer facing a return to Nazi-occupied Prague, a vengeful mob boss, and the ghosts of their own family's revolutionary past." (Publisher's note)

"With the wit of a "30s screwball comedy and the depth of a thoroughly researched historical novel, this one grabs the reader from the beginning to its suspenseful climax." Pub Wkly

Mathis, Ayana

The **twelve** tribes of Hattie; by Ayana Mathis. Alfred A. Knopf 2013 p. cm.

ISBN 9780307959423

LC 2012010779

2013 BCALA Literary Award: 1st Novelist Award

In this book, "Ayana Mathis tells the story of the children of the Great Migration through the trials of one . . . family. In 1923, fifteen-year-old Hattie Shepherd flees Georgia and settles n Philadelphia, hoping for a chance at a better life. . . . Hattie gives birth to nine . . . children. . . . Captured here in twelve . . . narrative threads, their lives tell the story of a mother's . . . courage and the journey of a nation." (Publisher's note)

Matthews, Jason

★ **Palace** of treason; a novel. Jason Matthews. Scribner 2015 480 p. (hardback) $26.99

ISBN 1476793743; 9781476793740; 9781476793764

LC 2015017172

In this spy novel by Jason Matthews, "Captain Dominika Egorova of the Russian Intelligence Service (SVR) has returned from the West to Moscow. She despises the men she serves, the oligarchs, and crooks, and thugs of Putin's Russia. What no one knows is that Dominika is working for the CIA as Washington's most sensitive penetration of SVR and the Kremlin." (Publisher's note)

"Authentic tradecraft, a complex plot that steadily builds tension, and credible heroes and villains on both sides make this a standout. Recipes at the end of each chapter provide some welcome relief from some brutal violence." Pub Wkly

Matthews, Jason

Red sparrow; a novel. Jason Matthews. 1st Scribner hardcover ed. Scribner 2013 448 p. (hardcover) $26.99

ISBN 1476706123; 1476706131; 147670614X; 9781476706122; 9781476706139; 9781476706146

LC 2012031933

In this book, the "malicious injuring of a ballerina starts a train wreck that ends in the unmasking of highly placed moles in the United States and Russia. The dancer is inveigled into service as an agent but must first attend a graphically described 'Sparrow School' where recruits are taught the art of sexual seduction. Her target is an American agent whose defeat obsesses Russian leader Vladimir Putin himself." (Library Journal)

Matthiessen, Peter

Bone by bone. Random House 1999 410p $26.95

ISBN 0-375-50102-9

LC 98-46180

In this final volume in the trilogy about E.J. Watson, "Matthiessen has given us Watson's own story in Watson's own words. . . . That story goes right back to Civil War days in South Carolina, and the terrible childhood E.J. endured at the hands of his drunken, brutal and rascally father and his remote and vindictive mother. Thus were laid the seeds of the later outbursts of violence and rage that so frequently punctuated what should have been a promising life. For Watson, as he portrays himself, is ambitious, hardworking and ever ingenious at figuring ways to make the remote Florida Everglades shores yield riches—a true pioneer spirit." Publ Wkly

Matthiessen, Peter

★ **Far** Tortuga. Random House 1975 408p il

"Almost casually, we have been given a full measure of suspense, adventure, and first-rate descriptive writing; and along with and underneath these things, a group of characters who come fully alive with a complexity and even depth that the usual, traditional story of men at sea never gives us." Choice

Matthiessen, Peter, 1927-2014

In Paradise; A Novel. by Peter Matthiessen. Riverhead Books 2014 240 p. $27.95

ISBN 1594633177; 9781594633171

LC 2013046176

In this novel, author Peter Matthiessen "leaps into the big questions raised by the horrors of the Holocaust. What is the nature of good and evil? Can we bear to bear witness? Can beauty endure after the smokestacks of Auschwitz? These questions are pondered by a group gathering for a weeklong meditation retreat at the site of a World War II concentration camp." (Library Journal)

"The strongest sections relate to these more concrete missions—passages about Olin's family history, in particular, stand out. But the novel focuses mainly on the abstract: what it feels like to spend days on end at the death camp—the frustration, alienation, and otherworldliness of it." Pub Wkly

Matthiessen, Peter

Killing Mister Watson. Random House 1990 372p

LC 89-43424

"By the time he was murdered, Watson was one of the most successful sugar-cane farmers between Tampa and Key West. Everyone liked and admired him, but no one trusted him. Proof was always scant but people wound up dead when Watson was around. . . . Matthiessen tells his story through the voice of Watson's family and neighbors in a series of oral histories, diary entries and old newspaper accounts, all of it fiction. By turns droll, rambunctious, foolish and wise, this collective narration mounts into a carefully orchestrated cacophony of contradictory testimony in which suspicion and mistrust are gradually revealed as the base elements of mystery." Newsweek

Followed by Lost Man's River

Matthiessen, Peter

★ **Shadow** country; a new rendering of the Watson legend. Modern Library 2008 892p $40; pa $16

ISBN 978-0-679-64019-6; 0-679-64019-3; 978-0-8129-8062-2 pa; 0-8129-8062-X pa

LC 2007-25117

National Book Award: Fiction (2008)

Matthiessen is meticulous in creating characters, lyrical in describing landscapes, and resolute in dissecting the values and costs that accompanied the development of this nation. Seattle Times

Maturin, Charles Robert

★ **Melmoth** the wanderer; edited with and introduction and notes by Victor Sage. Penguin Books 2000 xxxi, 659p pa $12

ISBN 0-14-044761-x

LC 2001-265474

First published 1820 in the United Kingdom

This novel "was in effect the last, and also one of the most effective, of the 'Gothic' school. The tale rushes energetically through every kind of horror and iniquity, and has moments of genuine power. Melmoth, who has sold his soul for the promise of prolonged life, offers relief from suffering to each of the characters, whose terrible stories succeed one another, if they will take over his bargain with the Devil. But Stanton, imprisoned in the cell of a raving lunatic; Moncada in the hands of the Inquisition; Walberg, who sees his children dying of hunger; and many other sufferers, all reject the proposed bargain." Oxford Companion to Engl Lit. 6th edition

Maugham, W. Somerset

The **best** short stories of W. Somerset Maugham; selected, and with an introduction by John Beecroft. Modern Lib. 1957 489p

Maugham, W. Somerset

Cakes and ale; or, The skeleton in the cupboard. Doubleday, Doran 1930 308p

This novel, Maugham's "most genial book, is a comedy about the good-natured Rosie Driffield, the wife of a Grand Old Man of Letters; whom most took to be based on Hardy; Alroy Kear, a self-promoting writer, was recognized as Hugh Walpole." Oxford Companion to Engl Lit. 5th edition

Maugham, W. Somerset

★ **Complete** short stories. Doubleday 1952 2v

Maugham, W. Somerset

The **moon** and sixpence. Doran, G.H. 1919 314p

"Based closely on the life of Paul Gauguin it tells of Charles Strickland, a conventional London stockbroker, who in middle life suddenly decides to desert his wife, family, and business in order to become a painter. He goes to paint in Tahiti, where he takes a native mistress. Eventually Strickland dies of leprosy." Reader's Ency. 4th edition

Maugham, W. Somerset

★ **Of** human bondage; introduction by Gore Vidal. Modern Library 1999 xxxix, 611p pa $11.95

ISBN 0-375-75315-X

LC 98-46169

First published 1915

This novel's "hero is Philip Carey, a sensitive, talented, club-footed orphan who is brought up by an unsympathetic aunt and uncle. It is a study of his struggle for independence, his intellectual development, and his attempt to become an artist. Philip gets entangled and obsessed by his love affair with Mildred, a waitress. After years of struggle as a medical student, he marries a nice woman, gives up his aspirations, and becomes a country doctor. The first part of the novel is partly autobiographical, and the book is regarded as Maugham's best work." Reader's Ency. 4th edition

Maugham, W. Somerset

★ The **razor's** edge. Doubleday 1944 343p hardcover o.p. pa $14

ISBN 1-4000-3420-5 pa

"The novel is concerned in large part with the search for the meaning of life and with the dichotomy between materialism and spirituality. The main focus of the story is on Larry Darrell, who has returned from service as an aviator in World War I utterly rejecting his prewar values. He is concerned chiefly with discovering the meaning of human existence and eliminating evil in the world. To that end, he spends five years in India seeking—but not finding—answers." Merriam-Webster's Ency of Lit

Maupin, Armistead

Mary Ann in autumn; a Tales of the city novel. Harper 2010 287p $25.99

ISBN 978-0-06-147088-2; 0-06-147088-0

LC 2010-24322

"Twenty years have passed since Mary Ann Singleton left her husband and child in San Francisco to pursue her dream of a television career in New York. Now a pair of personal calamities has driven her back to the city of her youth and into the arms of her oldest friend, Michael 'Mouse' Tolliver, a gardener happily ensconced with his much-younger husband. Mary Ann finds temporary refuge in the couple's backyard cottage, where, at the unnerving age of fifty-seven, she licks her wounds and takes stock of her mistakes. Soon, with the help of Facebook and a few old friends, she begins to reengage with life, only to confront fresh terrors when her checkered past comes back to haunt her in a way she could never have imagined." Publisher's note

Maupin, Armistead

Michael Tolliver lives. HarperCollins Publishers 2007 277p $25.95

ISBN 978-0-06-076135-6; 0-06-076135-0

LC 2006-52979

This is a "novel only in the loosest sense of the term. The chapters are independent yet interdependent, flowing into one another gracefully while remaining very much singular entities. . . . The book is great fun to read. Maupin is a master at sustained and sustaining comic turns." N Y Times Book Rev

Maurois, André, 1885-1967

Climates; by André Maurois ; translated by Adriana Hunter. Other Press 2012 400 p. (trade pbk.) $15.95

ISBN 1590515382; 9781590515389; 9781590515396

LC 2012008856

In a new translation of the 20th-century French classic, wealthy Philippe Marcenat makes two attempts to find the perfect partner and fails both times. . . . Stripped of its period shading, this is a sad and timeless tale of women on pedestals and the pain of loving not wisely, but too well." Kirkus

Maurois, André, 1885-1967

★ The **collected** stories of Andre Maurois; translated by Adrienne Foulke. Washington Sq. Press 1967 396p

Contents: Reality transposed; Darling, good evening; Lord of the shadows; Ariane, my sister . . . ; Home port; Myrrhine; Biography; Thanatos Palace Hotel; Friends; Dinner under the chestnut trees; Bodies and souls; The curse of gold; For piano alone; The departure; The fault of M. Balzac; Love in exile; Wednesday's violets; A career; Ten years later; Tidal wave; Transference; Flowers in season; The will; The campaign; The life of man; The Corinthian porch; The Cathedral; The ants; The postcard; Poor Maman; The green belt; The Neuilly Fair; The birth of a master; Black masks; Irene; The letters; The cuckoo; The house

Mawer, Simon

The **fall**; a novel. Little, Brown 2002 370p $24.95

ISBN 0-316-09780-2

LC 2002-73193

"Intricately weaving time and place, from the bombed-out ruins of World War II London to isolated Alpine mountain peaks, Mawer crafts a sinuously devastating tale of foridden love and faithless betrayal. A haunting and mesmerizing novel from an expert storyteller." Booklist

Mawer, Simon, 1948-

The **glass** room. Other Press 2009 405p il pa $14.95

ISBN 1-59051-396-7; 978-1-59051-396-5

LC 2009-39912

Mawer "has written this novel as though it were a translation, endowing his prose with a patina of Old World formality that sounds all the more romantic. He claims he doesn't know Czech or German, but his characters speak both fluently, and his attention to foreign languages enriches every episode." Washington Post Book World

Maxwell, Robin

The **Queen's** bastard; a novel. Arcade Pub. 1999 436p $24.95

ISBN 1-55970-475-6

LC 98-50502

Sequel to The secret diary of Anne Boleyn

"Arthur's first person narration is cleverly juxtaposed with third-person dramatization of significant events in the queen's life. . . . Maxwell's research examines the biographical gaps in, and documented facts about, the queen's life, making this incredible tale plausible, and the author aptly embellishes her story with rich period details and the epic dramas of the late 16th century." Publ Wkly

Maxwell, Robin

The **secret** diary of Anne Boleyn. Arcade Pub. 1997 281p

ISBN 1-55970-375-X

LC 96-49275

"Painting vicious court intrigue, national and international politics and the role of the Reformation, Maxwell brings not only the two queens but all of bloody Tudor England vividly to life." Publ Wkly

Followed by The Queen's bastard

Maxwell, Robin

The **wild** Irish. William Morrow 2003 393p $24.95

ISBN 0-06-009142-8

LC 2003-42184

"When Grace O'Mally, passionate clan chieftain and legendary Irish pirate, visits the court of Elizabeth I to plead for the release of her imprisoned son, the two most extraordinary women of their time find they have much in common. As Grace relates her incredible life and times to Elizabeth, the aging Bess also revisits her own often tragic past. Caught between these two powerful and magnetic females, Elizabeth's favorite courtier and onetime lover, Robert Devereaux, earl of Essex, is inexorably drawn into the tangled web of the Irish rebellion. . . . Superbly crafted, this dynamic tale brings a host of historical characters vividly to life." Booklist

Maxwell, William

All the days and nights; the collected stories of William Maxwell. Knopf 1995 415p

LC 94-27509

May, Peter

✓ The **Blackhouse**; Peter May. SilverOak 2012 432 p. (hardcover) $24.95

ISBN 1454901276; 9781454901273; 9781454901280

LC 2012016939

In this book by Peter May, "Edinburgh-based DI Fin Macleod is dispatched to Scotland's remote Isle of Lewis to compare two deaths. Two hangings, one in Edinburgh and one in Fin's childhood home of Crobost, share the same traits. Is a serial killer or a copycat at work? Since the Crobost victim was the village bully, Fin must sift through multiple motives and his own memories to tease out the killer." (Library Journal)

Mayle, Peter

Hotel Pastis; a novel of Provence. Knopf 1993 389p

LC 93-14641

The author "displays his satiric eye for social foibles by skewering advertising execs in England and the U.S.; he is equally adept at evoking typical Provencal villagers. Wickedly sharp and sympathetic at the same time, his characterizations are accurate down to nuances of class differences, voice, accent and vocabulary." Publ Wkly

Maynard, Joyce

Labor Day; a novel. William Morrow 2009 244p $24.99

ISBN 978-0-06-184340-2; 0-06-184340-7

LC 2009-13167

"During a trip to the local discount department store, 13-year-old Henry, worldly well beyond the limits of his New Hampshire town, meets the mysterious, middle-aged Frank. Bleeding and limping, Frank asks Henry's lonely, single mom, Adele, to take him to their house. She wordlessly assents. Soon, over coffee, Frank reveals the root of his injury: an escape from the state penitentiary. What follows is the tale of a mid-1980s weekend that's physically imprisoning (with Frank on the lam, the house becomes a hideout) but emotionally freeing, for everyone. Frank and Adele, both broken in multiple ways, find comfort in each other, and Adele and Henry quickly turn from Frank's captives to his confidants. . . . Maynard writes from the point of view of the angsty adolescent, and compellingly so." USA Today

Maynard, Joyce

The **usual** rules. St. Martin's Press 2003 390p $24.95

ISBN 0-312-24261-1

LC 2002-36754

"The novel is about a thirteen-year-old girl whose mother dies in the World Trade Center on September 11. . . . Not long after that, {her} ne'er-do-well biological dad (Peter Pan) shows up and whisks Wendy off with him to California." Women's Rev Books

Mayor, Archer

Red herring; a Joe Gunther novel. Minotaur Books 2010 291p $24.99

ISBN 978-0-312-38193-6; 0-312-38193-X

LC 2010-30458

"Three people are dead in Vermont. There is a dearth of clues, except for a single drop of blood left at the scene of each death. The Vermont Bureau of Investigation is called in, and Joe Gunther's . . . team must use every new investigation technique available (this even involves a trip to Long Island's Brookhaven National Laboratory) as well plain, old-fashioned legwork to catch the guilty. With cool forensic details for CSI fans, Mayor's heart-racing tale ends in a dramatic finish that will leave readers gasping." Libr J

Mayor, Archer

The **sniper's** wife. Mysterious Press 2002 312p $23.95

ISBN 0-89296-767-6

LC 2002-67183

"Mayor writes a tough story for his tortured protagonist, and the unfamiliar setting brings out a new, edge-of-the-knife side of his incisive descriptive powers." N Y Times Book Rev

Mayor, Archer

Tag man; a Joe Gunther novel. Minotaur Books 2011 290p

ISBN 9780312681944; 978-0-312-68194-4

LC 2011018779

A mystery featuring Joe Gunther, "head of the Vermont Bureau of Investigation, and VBI staffers Willy Kunkle, Sammie Martens, and Lester Spinney as well as their Brattleboro police colleague, Ron Klesczewski. The action centers on the person known as 'Tag Man,' who breaks into supposedly secure, occupied houses, explores them, takes nothing of value, but leaves a Post-it as his calling card. The Tag Man enjoys the challenge and the risk, until he makes a grisly discovery and is identified by one of his victims, who sends a hit man after him. Gunther, though on medical leave following a grievous personal loss, volunteers to help Klesczewski unmask the Tag Man. Multiple games of cat-and-mouse ensue as the Tag Man tries to elude both police and a determined killer. Vermont's history and geography again serve Mayor well in this deadly and highly entertaining entry." Publ Wkly

Mazzarella, Nicole

This heavy silence; a novel. Nicole Mazzarella. Paraclete Press 2005 255 p. o.p.; (pbk.) $14.95

ISBN 1557254257; 9781557255082

LC 69248687

Christy Award: First Novel (2006)

This book, a finalist for the Paraclete Press Fiction Award of 2004, tells the story of "[s]tubborn, independent Dottie Connell, [whose] greatest desire is to won the 300 acres of farmland that her family has worked all her life. Then childhood friend Zela Brubaker dies unexpectedly, naming Dottie as the guardian of her young daughter, Mattie. Although Dottie is not sure she wants to raise the girl, she finally has her chance to purchase her beloved land, but the cost requires Mattie's total inheritance, which is more than the property will ever be worth." (Library Journal)

Mbue, Imbolo

Behold the Dreamers; a novel. Imbolo Mbue. Random House 2015 400 p. (ebook) $65; (hardback : alk. paper) $28

ISBN 9780812998498; 9780812998481

LC 2015011560

In this novel by Imbolo Mbue, "Jende Jonga, a Cameroonian immigrant living in Harlem, has come to the United States to provide a better life for himself, his wife, Neni, and their six-year-old son. . . . Jende . . . lands a job as a chauffeur for . . . a senior executive at Lehman Brothers. . . . When the financial world is rocked by the collapse of Lehman Brothers, the Jongas are desperate to keep Jende's job—even as their marriage threatens to fall apart." (Publisher's note)

"Realistic, tragic, and still remarkably kind to all its characters, this is a special book." Kirkus

McBain, Ed

Alice in jeopardy. Simon & Schuster 2005 292p $25

ISBN 0-7432-6250-6

LC 2004-52478

"Alice Glendenning has been surviving, just barely. When her husband, Eddie, died in a boating accident nearly a year ago, she was left a widow with two very young children and a life insurance policy with a fly-by-night company that has delayed payment because the body was lost at sea. But things can always get worse, much worse. The ransom call comes not long after her two kids don't return home on the bus after school. The instructions are simple: the money from the insurance policy or the kids are dead–plus the standard 'Don't call the cops.' Alice doesn't call the cops, but the baby-sitter does, and soon Alice is mired in a jurisdictional jihad among local, state, and federal law-enforcement agencies of varying levels of competence." Booklist

McBain, Ed

The **big** bad city; a novel of the 87th Precinct. Simon & Schuster 1999 271p

ISBN 0-684-85512-7

LC 98-40890

"A young woman is murdered in a city park across town from her home. She has no identification except a wedding ring with the inscription IHS. Detetctive Steve Carella of the NYPD's 87th Precinct recognizes the inscription from his Catholic schoolboy days as a Latin monogram for 'Jesus, Savior of Men.' Jane Doe is a nun, Sister Mary Vincent, once known as Kate Cochrane. . . . Meanwhile, the man who killed Carella's father and walked because of an incompetent prosecution, Samson Wilber 'Sonny' Cole, has revenge on his mind." Booklist

McBain, Ed

Fat Ollie's book; a novel of the 87th Precinct. Simon & Schuster 2002 271p $25

ISBN 0-7432-0270-8

LC 2002-75830

"In McBain's howlingly funny sendup, the novel is pure drivel; but Ollie loved it, and darned if we don't like him for that." N Y Times Book Rev

McBain, Ed

The **frumious** Bandersnatch; a novel of the 87th Precinct. Simon & Schuster 2004 287p $25

ISBN 0-7432-5034-6

LC 2003-57258

"Tamar Valparaiso, a hot young singer on the verge of superstardom, is set to launch her debut CD and video Bandersnatch when she is kidnapped in the middle of a performance for a record industry party and the press. The whole episode is caught on camera, but the masked abductors flee, leaving behind few clues. Steve Carella and Cotton Hawes of the 87th Precinct are called in and are soon joined by a Joint Task Force and FBI agents. Detective Ollie Weeks, resident racist, homophobe, and misogynist, is also back on the scene, this time romancing a fellow officer. McBain displays his usual mastery of the police procedural along with an astute grasp of the music industry, the news media, and publicity, as well as political ramifications within the force." Libr J

McBain, Ed

Hark! a novel of the 87th Precinct. Simon & Schuster 2004 293p il $24.95

ISBN 0-7432-5035-4

LC 2004-49102

"Vintage McBain, complete with pitch-perfect dialogue, subplots that thrust various precinct cops into the spotlight, a pace that encourages the reader to forget about dinner or a good night's rest, and a plot that teases and tantalizes from start to finish." Publ Wkly

McBain, Ed

The **last** dance; a novel of the 87th Precinct. Simon & Schuster 2000 269p il

ISBN 0-684-85513-5

LC 99-53534

An "accomplished mix of police procedure, characterization, social commentary and tight plotting that has long distinguished this landmark series." Booklist

McBain, Ed

Nocturne. Warner Bks. 1997 291p

LC 96-42030

In this 87th precinct novel "detectives Carella and Hawes catch the first call on the night shift: the shooting death of a destitute woman who was once a renowned concert pianist. . . . Right away we're hooked, because these cops not only know their procedures, they also value a human life. Before this long, dark night is through, Mr. McBain will make us care abot a 19-year-old hooker who is savagely killed in a gang rape, a pimp and a drug dealer who also die hard and 25 roosters torn up in a cockfight." N Y Times Book Rev

McBride, Eimear, 1976-

A **girl** is a half-formed thing; Eimear McBride. Coffee House Press 2014 240 p. hardcover $24

ISBN 1101903430; 1566893682; 9781101903438; 9781566893688

LC 2014006994

In this novel, author "Eimear McBride tells the story of a young girl's devastating adolescence as she and her brother, who suffers from a brain tumor, struggle for a semblance of normalcy in the shadow of sexual abuse, denial, and chaos at home. Plunging readers inside the psyche of a girl isolated by her own dangerously confusing sexuality, pervading guilt, and unrelenting trauma, McBride's writing carries echoes of Joyce, O'Brien, and Woolf." (Publisher's note)

"In an uncomfortable but always eye-opening tale, McBride investigates the tensions among family, love, sex and religion.Lovers of straightforward storytelling will shirk, but open-minded readers(specifically those not put off by the unusual language structure) will be surprised, moved and awed by this original novel." Kirkus

McBride, James, 1957-

★ **Five**-carat soul; James McBride. Riverhead Books 2017 308 p. (hardcover) $27

ISBN 9780735216716; 9780735216693; 9780525533252

LC 2017007480

This book, by James McBride, presents stories that "spring from the place where identity, humanity, and history converge. . . . An antiques dealer discovers that a . . . toy commissioned by Civil War General Robert E. Lee now sits in the home of a black minister in Queens. . . . An American president draws inspiration from a conversation he overhears in a stable. And members of The Five-Carat Soul Bottom Bone Band recount stories from their own messy and hilarious lives." (Publisher's note)

"A versatile, illustrious author brings out his first short-fiction buffet for sampling, and the results are provocatively varied in taste and texture; sometimes piquant, other times zesty." Kirkus

McBride, James, 1957-

The **good** lord bird; by James McBride. Riverhead Books 2013 432 p. $27.95

ISBN 1594486344; 9781594486340

LC 2013004014

National Book Award: Fiction (2013)

In this novel, by James McBride, "Henry Shackleford is a young slave living in the Kansas Territory in 1857, when the region is a battleground between anti- and pro-slavery forces. When John Brown, the legendary abolitionist, arrives in the area, an argument between Brown and Henry's master quickly turns violent. Henry is forced to leave town--with Brown, who believes he's a girl. Eventually [Henry] finds himself with Brown at the historic raid on Harpers Ferry in 1859." (Publisher's note)

McBride, James, 1957-

Song yet sung. Riverhead Books 2008 359p $25.95

ISBN 978-1-59448-972-3; 1-59448-972-6

LC 2007-35969

"McBride borrows liberally from actual historical events and figures to fabricate this engrossing tale, and then emphasizes the implications of past actions by interspersing them with Liz's recurring nightmares of the future. . . . [His] characters evoke an extraordinary time that spawned ghosts that haunt us still." Seattle Times

McCabe, Erin Lindsay

I shall be near to you; a novel. Erin Lindsay McCabe. Crown 2014 320 p. (hardback) $24

ISBN 0804137722; 9780804137720

LC 2013028670

This book, by Erin Lindsay McCabe, is a "novel about a strong-willed woman who disguises herself as a man in order to fight beside her husband, inspired by the letters of a . . . female soldier who fought in the Civil War. . . . With the army desperate for recruits, Rosetta has no trouble volunteering, although she faces an incredulous husband. She drills with the men, proves she can be as good a soldier as anyone, and deals with the tension as her husband comes to grips with having a fighting wife." (Publisher's note)

"[A] narrative full of authentic dialogue, historical realism, and great feeling. Loosely based on true events, including the letters of the more than 200 women who are known to have served as men in the Civil War." Booklist

McCaffrey, Anne

★ **Acorna**; the unicorn girl. [by] Anne McCaffrey and Margaret Ball. HarperPrism 1997 291p

LC 97-11099

"Found in a survival pod in space by prospectors, the infant Acorna soon exhibits the ability to analyze deficiencies in plants by taste, purify water and air, and heal. Taken to the planet Kezdet to avoid scientists who want to study her, Acorna discovers barbaric child-labor practices and vows to rescue the children. McCaffrey and Ball have created a magical alien in this fantasy/science fiction story." Libr J

Followed by Acorna's quest

McCaffrey, Anne

Dragon's Kin; [by] Anne McCaffrey [and] Todd McCaffrey. Del Rey/Ballantine Bks. 2003 304p $24.95

ISBN 0-345-46198-3

The action in this Dragonriders of Pern tale "takes place during an unexplored period in the history of Pern, before the coming of the Thread. The watch-whers are already playing a prominent role, however, keeping watch at night at the holds and weyrs and helping in the mines. The protagonists are Kindin and Nuella, young people living in a mining camp. A cave-in wipes out Kindin's father and brothers as well as the old watch-wher, and Kindin moves in with camp Harper. There he learns the skills of being a Harper, including discretion and mediation. Eventually, he and Nuella learn the secret of how watch-whers see in the dark, and about their communication with dragons, which opens a wholly new range of capabilities for the dragon-riders." Booklist

McCaffrey, Anne

★ **Dragonflight**; volume 1 of The Dragonriders of Pern. Ballantine Bks. 1978 337p il (Dragonriders of Pern) hardcover o.p. pa $12.95

ISBN 0-345-27749-X; 0-345-48426-6 pa

LC 78-16707

First published 1968 in paperback. Based on two award winning stories entitled: Weyr search and Dragonrider. Many titles co-written by Todd McCaffrey

ALA YALSA Margaret A. Edwards Award (1999)

The planet Pern, originally colonized from Earth but long out of contact with it, has been periodically threatened by the deadly silver Threads which fall from the wandering Red Star. To combat them a life form on the planet was developed into winged, fire-breathing dragons. Humans with a high degree of empathy and telepathic power are needed to train and preserve these creatures. As the story begins, Pern has fallen into decay, the threat of the Red Star has been forgotten, the Dragonriders and dragons are reduced in number and in disrepute, and the evil Lord Fax has begun conquering neighboring holds.

Fantasy titles set on Pern include:
All the Weyrs of Pern (1991)
The chronicles of Pern: first fall (1993)
Dragon Harper (2007)
Dragon's fire (2006)
Dragon's kin (2003)
Dragon's time (2011)
Dragondrums (1979)
Dragonquest (1971)
Dragonsdawn (1988)
Dragonseye (1997)
Dragonsinger (1977)
Dragonsong (1976)
The masterharper of Pern (1998)
Morets: Dragonlady of Pern (1983)
Nerilka's story (1986)
The Renegades of Pern (1989)
The skies of Pern (2001)
White dragon (1978)

McCaffrey, Anne

★ **Freedom's** landing. Putnam 1995 342p

LC 94-43820

"With her customary talent for imaginative storytelling, the author skillfully portrays the environmental and personal challenges faced by the new colonists." Libr J

Followed by Freedom's choice (1997) and Freedom's challenge (1998)

McCaffrey, Anne

The **white** dragon; volume 3 of The Dragonriders of Pern. Ballantine Bks. 1978 497p il (Dragonriders of Pern)

LC 77-18913

Sequel to Dragonquest

"A prologue summarizes the first two volumes of the saga. . . . Young Jaxom and his white dragon Ruth (a male), previously encountered, mature, fight the deadly Threads from the Red Planet, help open the largely unexplored continent and discover in an ancient spaceship a map, key to major changes for Pern. Once all the necessary background is assimilated, it's a rousing adventure and colorful portrayal of a unique and carefully-worked-out culture." Publ Wkly

McCaffrey, Todd

Dragonsblood; Todd McCaffrey. Ballantine Books 2005 viii, 438p map (hbk.) o.p.; (hbk.) o.p.; (pbk.) $7.99

ISBN 0345441249; 9780345441249; 9780345441256

LC 2004051086

This fantasy novel of the Pern saga follows "Wind Blossom, one of the original colonists of Pern, who's struggling to create a legacy for future generations before she dies, and Lorana, a young dragonrider born 450 years later with unusual talents for healing and telepathy. A . . . set of time travel puzzles and paradoxes is set against the . . . backdrop of two populations struggling to survive: the children of the colonists, learning to live in a new world as they lose the technology of the old one, and the dragons of Lorana's time, who are dying of a mysterious plague just when they're needed to protect Pern. The strength of the two women and the mysterious connection between them is gradually revealed through a number of . . . parallel occurrences." (Publishers Weekly)

McCall Smith, Alexander

Blue shoes and happiness. Pantheon Books 2006 227p $21.95

ISBN 0-375-42272-2

LC 2005-52122

In this installment "Botswana detective Precious Ramotswe faces one of her toughest challenges: losing weight. Luckily, there are plenty of dilemmas to keep her mind off her girth: a nearby village that seems under the influence of witchcraft, a cook suspected of filching food for her increasingly portly spouse, and a newspaper advice columnist who's doing more damage than good. Readers become better acquainted with assistant detective Mma Grace Makutsi, best known for earning a stellar 97 percent grade at the Botswana Secretarial College. . . . McCall Smith renders brisk, seamless tales that are both wry and profound. Amidst the mayhem (like the cobra that slithers its way into the detective agency's headquarters) are eloquent descriptions of the serene African country that holds a special place in his heart." Booklist

McCall Smith, Alexander

The **comforts** of a muddy Saturday. Pantheon Books 2008 240p $23.95

ISBN 978-0-375-42513-4; 0-375-42513-6

LC 2008-18573

Philosophical sleuth Isabel Dalhousie, "who's recently assumed ownership of the obscure journal she's edited for many years, the Review of Applied Ethics, applies her deductive gifts to the case of a disgraced doctor. When a patient dies after taking a new antibiotic that Marcus Moncrieff deemed safe in clinical trials, the doctor's original report turns out to contain falsified data. Did Moncrieff skew the data to please the drug manufacturers? Moncrieff's wife turns to Isabel for help in lifting her husband out of his despondency. While the truth isn't straightforward, the motives of the guilty party prove to be both plausible and rational. The strengths of the book . . . lie in its protagonist's determination to treat others without judgment—and in the author's revealing glimpses into the human soul." Publ Wkly

McCall Smith, Alexander, 1948-

A **conspiracy** of friends; Alexander McCall Smith. Pantheon Books 2011 261 p. $24.95

ISBN 0307907236; 9780307907233

LC 2011051041

This novel "visits the self-contained fictional world encompassing the residents of Corduroy Mansions in London's Pimlico neighborhood. The book opens by introducing an immense ensemble cast, which includes Oedipus Snark, 'the only truly nasty Liberal Democrat Member of Parliament'; his mother, Berthea, at work on a 'hostile biography' of her son; . . . as well as the hapless, affable wine merchant William French and his dog, Freddie de la Hay. Each has his or her own tale: a conflict at work, a longing for love, the search for new smells." (Publishers Weekly)

McCall Smith, Alexander

Corduroy mansions; illustrations by Iain McIntosh. Pantheon Books 2010 353p il $24.95

ISBN 978-0-307-37908-5; 0-307-37908-6

LC 2009-47155

First published 2009 in the United Kingdom

First title in a "new series set among a collection of flats in London's lively Pimlico neighborhood. Residents here run the gamut from the very likable to the much loathed. There's William, a well-meaning, widowed wine merchant determined to oust his lazy twentysomething son from his house. . . . Then there's the thoroughly despicable Oedipus Snark, a Parliament member devoid of scruples, conscience, and class. Even his own mother despises him; she's writing his biography, with the aim of exposing every one of his faults. Four young women share a flat as well. Among them is Dee, a health-food devotee who can't understand a male coworker's resistance to her offer of a high-colonic, and art history student Caroline, who has designs on a friend unsure whether he wants to date women or men. Also afoot throughout the book is the astonishingly astute Freddie de la Hay, a canine inclined to paws and reflect." Booklist

McCall Smith, Alexander

The **Double** Comfort Safari Club. Pantheon Books 2010 211p $24.95

ISBN 978-0-375-42450-2; 0-375-42450-4

LC 2009-49060

"It's not in the stories themselves, but in the telling of them, that the secret of McCall Smith's appeal lies. His Botswana may indeed be a kindly place, but he has an ability – a very rare one – to write with kindness too. This world, he says, is only ours for a short time, and we realise that more and more with age. And when we cry, he'll point out, how odd it is that we rock forward and back, as our mothers comforted us, as if we were trying to comfort ourselves. Such aperçus are, of themselves, not original. What is, is the way McCall Smith effortlessly weaves them into stories of fun and laughter and heartfelt love of place and character." Scotsman

McCall Smith, Alexander, 1948-

The **forgotten** affairs of youth; Alexander McCall Smith. Pantheon Books 2011 261 p. (hardcover) $24.95

ISBN 9780307379184; 0307379183

LC 2011023394

This book tells the story of "Isabel Dalhousie, . . . a philosopher . . . [and an] Edinburgh-based heroine[, who] is a professional in the field, the editor of a journal, the Review of Applied Ethics. . . . But by this point in the series, Isabel's issues have been put more or less straight: . . . She is . . . engaged to . . . Jamie, who is helping raise their toddler son, Charlie. . . . Only Isabel's jealous niece Cat, Jamie's former lover, is still a loose cannon, and when mysterious mushrooms from Cat's delicatessen land Isabel in the emergency room, high drama seems about to be let loose. . . . Before long, Isabel is back on her feet and involved in the main mystery of the book. This time, that means helping a colleague, Jane Cooper, a philosopher who has returned on sabbatical to the land of her birth from Australia. Alone and somewhat isolated, Jane, who was adopted, hopes to track her birth father in the hope of gaining some semblance of belonging, and Isabel has both the contacts and the character to act as an amateur sleuth on her behalf." (Boston.com)

McCall Smith, Alexander, 1948-

The **full** cupboard of life; Alexander McCall Smith. Pantheon Books 2003 198 p.

ISBN 0375422188; 9780375422188

LC 2003062379

In this book, "Mma Ramotswe and Mr. J.L.B. Matekoni are still engaged, but with no immediate plans to get married. . . . For indeed he has other things on his mind--particularly a frightening request (involving a parachute jump) made by Mma Potokwani, the persuasive matron of the orphan farm. Mma Ramotswe herself has weighty matters on her mind, including a case in which a wealthy woman wonders whether her suitors are interested in her or just her money. Meanwhile, Mma Makutsi--plucky assistant detective and deputy manager of the Tlokweng Road Speedy Motors garage--is moving. Her entrepreneurial venture, the Kalahari Typing School for Men, is thriving and with this new income she has rented two rooms in a house." (Publisher's note)

McCall Smith, Alexander

The **good** husband of Zebra Drive. Pantheon Books 2007 213p (No. 1 Ladies Detective Agency) $21.95

ISBN 978-0-375-42273-7; 0-375-42273-0

LC 2006-39047

In this mystery, set in Botswana, "Dr. Cronje, who's half Xhosa and half Afrikaner, consults . . . Precious Ramotswe, because patients at his hospital who have occupied a particular bed have been dying mysteriously at the same time of day. Meanwhile, Mma Ramotswe's recently engaged assistant, Grace Makutsi, threatens to break their longstanding association. Mma Ramotswe must adjust their relationship in order to retain Mma Makutsi's services. The author's subtlety of touch and humane portrayal of figures at all levels of society will continue to win him new readers even as his deepening of the ties binding the main figures will satisfy those who have followed the lady detectives from their first recorded case." Publ Wkly

McCall Smith, Alexander ✓

★ **In** the company of cheerful ladies. Pantheon Books 2005 233p $19.95

ISBN 0-375-42271-4

LC 2004-56827

In this installment, "Botswana detective Precious Ramotswe, the traditionally built-and newly married-owner of the No. 1 Ladies' Detective Agency, is saddled with a surfeit of challenging cases and personal crises. There has been an intruder in her home (he managed to escape, but left a telltale pair of trousers in his wake). And the levelheaded sleuth is flustered by an encounter with a man from her past. Meanwhile, Mma Ramotswe's husband, master mechanic Mr. J.L.B. Matekoni, is neck-deep in work after the resignation of one of his apprentices, who has become romantically entangled with a married woman (Mma Ramotswe and assistant detective Grace Makutsi slyly gather the scurrilous details). . . . [The author] renders colorful characters with names that trip off the tongue." Publ Wkly

McCall Smith, Alexander, 1948- ✓

The **Kalahari** typing school for men; Alexander McCall Smith. Pantheon Books 2003 186 p.

ISBN 037542217X; 9780375422171

LC 2002030709

In this book, "Mma Precious Ramotswe is content. Her business is well established with many satisfied customers, and in her mid-thirties . . . she has a house, two adopted children, a fine fiancé. But, as always, there are troubles. Mr. J.L.B. Matekoni has not set the date for their marriage. Her able assistant, Mma Makutsi, wants a husband. And worse, a rival detective agency has opened in town--an agency that does not have the gentle approach to business that Mma Ramotswe's does." (Publisher's note)

McCall Smith, Alexander, 1948- ✓

The **Limpopo** Academy of Private Detection; Alexander McCall Smith. Pantheon Books 2012 257 p. (No. 1 Ladies Detective Agency)

ISBN 9780307378408

LC 2011050788

This book is the 13th in Alexander McCall Smith's No. 1 Ladies' Detective Agency series featuring detective Precious Ramotswe. In it, "an unknown tall man appears in a dream to Mma Ramotswe, and before long, one shows up for real, in the person of American Clovis Andersen. . . . Anderson ends up assisting his biggest fan in looking into the dirty laundry of a businessman whose plans to make the local orphanage more efficient threaten the role of its matron and its successful operation." (Publishers Weekly)

McCall Smith, Alexander ✓

The **lost** art of gratitude. Pantheon Books 2009 262p $23.95

ISBN 978-0-375-42514-1; 0-375-42514-4

LC 2009-22618

A mystery featuring Scottish philosopher Isabel Dalhousie. "Minty Auchterlonie, who once alerted Isabel to some insider trading, fears someone is out to get her. The tax authorities have suddenly investigated Minty, and an unknown party has sent her a funeral wreath. When Isabel looks into these provocative acts, she draws on lessons learned from the journal she edits, the Review of Applied Ethics, to arrive at the complex truth behind them. Meanwhile, the father of Isabel's young son proposes marriage, and a defeated academic rival accuses her of knowingly publishing plagiarism. Smith's trademark humor and telling observations about people heighten the appeal." Publ Wkly

McCall Smith, Alexander ✓

Love over Scotland. Anchor Books 2007 357p pa $13.95

ISBN 978-0-307-27598-1

LC 2007-22072

First published 2006 in the United Kingdom; originally serialized in The Scotsman

In this installment "anthropologist Domenica has flown off to the Straits of Malacca to study modern-day pirates. Back in Edinburgh, Pat moves from 44 Scotland Street and develops a crush on fellow art student Wolf, whose strange ways hint at a darker subplot that involves Pat's flatmate. Pat moves in with gallery owner Matthew, who struggles with both a sudden fortune and a yearning for Pat. Meanwhile, child prodigy saxophonist Bertie becomes a reluctant member of the Edinburgh Teenage Orchestra at age six and later, on a trip to Paris, finds himself wonderfully unsupervised. Poet/portrait painter Angus is tormented by the theft of his beloved dog Cyrus. The proceedings sparkle with McCall Smith's trademark wit (It was not always fun being a child, just as it had not always been fun being a medieval Scottish saint), proving once again, he's a true treasure. Illustrations by Iain McIntosh enliven the text." Publ Wkly

McCall Smith, Alexander, 1948- ✓

The **No.** 1 Ladies' Detective Agency; Alexander McCall Smith. Pantheon Books 2005 235 p. (No. 1 Ladies' Detective Agency) (hardcover) $21.95

ISBN 9780375423871; 0375423877

LC 2005047587

Originally published 1998

"This first novel in Alexander McCall Smith's . . . The No. 1 Ladies Detective Agency series[, which was voted one of the International Books of the Year and the Millennium by the "Times Literary Supplement,"] tells the story of . . . Precious Ramotswe, who is drawn to her profession to "help people with problems in their lives." Immediately upon setting up shop in a small storefront in Gaborone, she is hired to track down a missing husband, uncover a con man, and follow a wayward daughter. But the case that tugs at her heart, and lands her in danger, is a missing eleven-year-old boy, who may have been snatched by witchdoctors." (Publisher's note)

Other titles in this series are:
Tears of the giraffe (2000)
Morality for beautiful girls (2002)
The Kalahari typing school for men (2003)
The full cupboard of life (2004)
In the company of cheerful ladies (2005)
Blue shoes and happiness (2006)
The good husband of Zebra Drive (2007)
The miracle at Speedy Motors (2008)
Tea time for the traditionally built (2009)
The Double Comfort Safari Club (2010)
The Saturday big tent wedding party (2011)
The Limpopo Academy of Private Detection (2012)
The minor adjustment beauty salon (2013)
The Handsome man's de luxe cafe (2014)
The woman who walked in sunshine (2015)
Precious and Grace (2016)
The house of unexpected sisters (2017)

McCall Smith, Alexander, 1948- ✓

The **Saturday** big tent wedding party; The New No. 1 Ladies' Detective Agency Novel. Alexander McCall Smith. Recorded Books 2011 213 p. $24.95

ISBN 9781456116224 lib bdg

LC 2010054099

In this book, "Mma Precious Ramotswe's latest client, Botsalo Moeti, made no enemies working for a mining company, and he's hardly had the opportunity to make any as a farmer. So why has someone killed two of his cattle by cutting their Achilles tendons? Although a trip to his farm persuades Mma Ramotswe that he may have more enemies than he realizes, it doesn't tell her which of them is responsible. . . . Charlie, the eternal apprentice mechanic at Tlokweng Road Speedy Motors, the establishment owned by Mma Ramotswe's husband, Mr. J.L.B. Matekoni, seems so determined to avoid Prudence Ramkhwane after she bears his twins that he runs away when he's taxed with his responsibilities." (Kirkus)

McCall Smith, Alexander, 1948-

Tea time for the traditionally built; Alexander McCall Smith. Pantheon Books 2009 212 p.

ISBN 9780375424496

LC 2009000774

This book is the 10th in Alexander McCall Smith's series featuring detective Precious Ramotswe. Here, she is asked by "Leungo Molofololo, the owner of the Kalahari Swoopers, a local soccer team with a lot of athletic talent," to explore a possible "traitor on the squad [who] is deliberately sabotaging games for an unknown reason. Despite her complete ignorance of the sport, Mma Ramotswe agrees to look into the matter. She and her prickly assistant, Grace Makutsi, attend a match and begin interviewing the players in an effort to solve what amounts to the book's main mystery. The soccer inquiry, though, is secondary to a major event in Mma Ramotswe's life--the impending demise of the little white van she's used for many years that's much more than a machine to her." (Publishers Wkly)

McCall Smith, Alexander, 1948-

Trains and Lovers; Alexander McCall Smith. Pantheon Books 2013 256 p. $22

ISBN 0307908542; 9780307908544

LC 2012042073

In this novel by Alexander McCall Smith "four travelers pass the time by sharing tales of trains that have changed their lives. A . . . Scotsman recounts how he turned a friendship with a female coworker into a romance. An Australian woman shares how her parents . . . spent their life together running a railroad siding. A[n] . . . American . . . recalls his own youthful crush on another man. A young Englishman describes how exiting his train at the wrong station [le] him to meet [a] . . . woman." (Publisher's note)

McCall Smith, Alexander

The **world** according to Bertie. Anchor Books 2008 343p il pa $13.95

ISBN 978-0-307-38706-6; 0-307-38706-2

LC 2008-28140

First published 2007 in the United Kingdom

"It is clear even to an outsider that someone who knows Edinburgh would recognize many people and places in '44 Scotland Street.' But an outsider can still relish McCall Smith's depiction of this place 'of angled streets and northern light,' and enjoy his tolerant, good-humored company." N Y Times Book Rev

McCammon, Robert R.

Boy's life. Pocket Bks. 1991 440p

LC 91-2813

"In 1964, 12-year-old Cory Mackenson lives with his parents in Zephyr, Alabama. It is a sleepy, comfortable town. Cory is helping with his father's milk route one morning when a car plunges into the lake before their eyes. His father dives in after the car and finds a dead man handcuffed to the steering wheel. Their world no longer seems so innocent: a vicious killer hides among apparently friendly neighbors." Libr J

McCann, Colum

Let the great world spin; a novel. Random House 2009 349p $25

ISBN 978-1-4000-6373-4; 1-4000-6373-6

LC 2008-46963

National Book Award: Fiction (2009)

This "begins on August 7, 1974, when New Yorkers are stopped in their tracks by the sight of a man walking between the towers of the World Trade Center. Yes, it's Philippe Petit, the subject of the Academy Award–winning documentary Man on Wire and one of McCann's many intense and valiant characters. The cast also includes two Irish brothers: Corrigan, a radical monk, and Ciaran, who follows him to the blasted Bronx, where he encounters resilient prostitute Tillie and her spirited daughter Jazzlyn. Gloria lives in the same housing project, and she befriends Claire of Park Avenue as they mourn the deaths of their sons in Vietnam. McCann's hallucinatory descriptions of a great city tattooed and besmirched with graffiti, blood, and drugs in the midst of a financial freefall are eerie in their edgy beauty, chilling reminders of how quickly civilization unravels. Here, too, are portals onto war, the justice system, and the dawning of the cyber age." Booklist

McCann, Colum, 1965-

★ **Thirteen** ways of looking; fiction. Colum McCann. Random House 2015 256 p. $26

ISBN 0812996720; 9780812996722

LC 2015011762

In this collection of short stories, author Colum McCann "charts the territory of chance. . . . In the . . . title novella, a retired judge reflects on his life's work. . . . In 'Sh'khol,' a mother . . . confronts the unthinkable when [her son] disappears while swimming. . . . In 'Treaty,' an elderly nun . . . [learns] the man who once kidnapped and brutalized her is alive. . . . And in 'What Time Is It Now, Where You Are?' a writer constructs a story about a Marine in Afghanistan." (Publisher's note)

"McCann's first story collection in 12 years marks his triumphant return to the genre. Luminescent prose and finely rendered characters create a spell readers will be reluctant to shake." LJ

McCann, Colum, 1965-

★ **Transatlantic**; a novel. Colum McCann. Random House Inc 2013 320 p. (acid-free paper) $27

ISBN 1400069599; 9781400069590

LC 2012043294

Man Booker Prize: Shortlist (2013)

This is a historical fiction novel from Colum McCann. "In the first half, four men--fugitive slave Frederick Douglass, diplomat George Mitchell, and the two war-scarred aviators responsible for the first nonstop transatlantic flight--travel from the New World back to Ireland on missions of historical import; in the second, the women, who at first seem to figure as historical backwash, show how those disparate missions are stitched together." (Esquire Magazine)

McCann, Colum

Zoli; a novel. Random House 2007 333p $24.95

ISBN 978-1-4000-6372-7; 1-400-06372-8

LC 2006-42922

First published 2006 in the United Kingdom

"Zoli becomes a flash point for her tribe while raising an important question: In a world driven by conformity and (more lately) consumerism, how can the outsider survive? . . . . McCann's story feels like an important reminder of one dimension that has gladly been left behind:

the soul-deadening totalitarianism that snuffs out dissent and difference with the force of its bureaucracy." Seattle Times

McCarry, Charles

The **Mulberry** Bush; by Charles McCarry. Mysterious Press 2015 320 p. $26

ISBN 0802124100; 9780802124104

This book, by Charles McCarry, "burns with the fury of the wronged, as personal vendetta and political idealism collide. In a rose garden in Buenos Aires, an unnamed American spy meets the beautiful daughter of a famous Argentinean revolutionary. . . . But he is no ordinary spy—he is a . . . lone wolf who spent his first five years working for 'Headquarters' hunting terrorists in the Middle East. Unbeknownst to his lenient handlers, he is loyal to a hidden agenda: to avenge his father." (Publisher's note)

"McCarry (The Shanghai Factor, 2013) again creates a richly engaging world of spooks, double agents, terrorists, and Company characters and culture, all delivered in prose that is variously concise, discursive, amusing, insightful, and often gorgeous. The Mulberry Bush is outrageously entertaining." Booklist

McCarry, Charles

Old boys. Overlook Press 2004 476p $25.95

ISBN 1-58567-545-8

LC 2004-48320

American spy novelist "McCarry returns to the world of his character Paul Christopher--who has mysteriously disappeared. Led by Christopher's cousin Horace, a group of his retired colleagues--the "Old Boys' from the Outfit--embark on a . . . worldwide search for the master spy and an ancient scroll that may reveal an unspeakably dangerous truth." (Publisher's note)

"When Paul Christopher, the enigmatic hero of several earlier McCarry novels, disappears while on a quest for his nonagenarian mother, Lori, his black-sheep cousin, Horace Hubbard, convenes a discreet cadre of over-the-hill spies to find their confrere-and to save the world from Ib'n Awad, an aging Islamic terrorist in possession of 12 nuclear suitcase bombs. In a beguiling twist . . . . , all parties also seek a fabled ancient scroll that unmasks Jesus as an agent provocateur, handled by Judas for Roman spymaster Paul. The nonstop peregrinations of this league of extraordinary spooks take them to a score of exotic locales, pitting them against Chechen thugs, Chinese secret police, Nazi doctors, and a case of acute myocardial fibrillation. McCarry's commitment to this fanciful premise is absolute, and the resulting yarn combines the intrepid exploits of John Buchan, the cagey intrigue of Eric Ambler, and the clipped cadences of Dashiell Hammett. Tremendous fun." Booklist

McCarthy, Cormac

★ **All** the pretty horses. Knopf 1992 301p $27.50; pa $14.95

ISBN 0-394-57474-5; 0-679-74439-8 pa

LC 91-58560

"Though some readers may grow impatient with the wild prairie rhythms of McCarthy's language, others will find his voice completely transporting." Publ Wkly

Other titles in the Border trilogy are:
Cities of the Plain (1998)
The crossing (1994)

McCarthy, Cormac

★ **Blood** meridian; or, The evening redness in the West. Random House 1985 337p

ISBN 0-394-40027-5

"This book is set in the south-west borderland between the United States and Mexico, and follows the experiences of the (unnamed) kid, as he gets involved with a gang of mercenaries called the Glantons, and meets one of the most menacing figures in modern literature, Judge Holden, a huge, pale, manic individual who seems to know every aspect of human culture and to conduct a single-handed and satanic campaign to destroy it all. This is a savage book, full of rape and pillage, with more scalpings described in more detail–the Indians are just as savage as the whites–than (surely) in any other book. It is also beautifully written, a great poetic exploration of nature and the myth of the West." Good Fiction Guide

McCarthy, Cormac

Cities of the plain. Knopf 1998 291p $27.50

ISBN 0-679-42390-7

LC 98-11583

"McCarthy's language carries a brooding, evolutionary sense of time and labor—in his hands the changing of a tire on an old truck becomes a mythic deed. The weight of history rests on the shoulders of John Grady, too, and he's doomed to learn that 'when things are gone they're gone. They aint comin back.'" New Yorker

McCarthy, Cormac

The **crossing**. Knopf 1994 425p

ISBN 0-394-57475-3

LC 94-4281

The author "is a great and inventive storyteller, and he writes brilliantly and knowledgeably about animals and landscapes—but . . . the power and delight of the book derive from the fact that he seems incapable of writing a boring sentence. Reading him, one is very much in the hands of a stylist. . . . The style comes from Joyce and Hemingway out of Gertrude Stein. It is a matter of straight-on writing, a veering accumulation of compound sentences, stinginess with commas and a witching repetition of words." N Y Times Book Rev

McCarthy, Cormac

No country for old men. Knopf 2005 309p $24.95

ISBN 0-37540-677-8

"As devised and refined by James M. Cain, Jim Thompson and their gloomy paperback peers, the crime novel aimed its cheap handgun at the heart of America's most prized beliefs about its destiny: that the loot we've scooped up will belong to us forever and that history allows clean getaways. Cormac McCarthy's 'No Country for Old Men' is as bracing a variation on these noir orthodoxies as any fan of the genre could expect." N Y Times Book Rev

McCarthy, Cormac

The **road**. Knopf 2006 241p $24.00

ISBN 0307265439; 9780307265432

LC 2006-23629

"A father and his son walk alone through burned America. Nothing moves in the ravaged landscape save the ash on the wind. It is cold enough to crack stones, and when the snow falls it is gray. They sky is dark. Their destination is the coast, although they don't know what, if anything, awaits them there. They have nothing; just a pistol to defend themselves against the lawless bands that stalk the road, the clothes they are wearing, a cart of scavenged food—and each other." (Publisher's note)

"A nuclear holocaust has reduced everything to ash, mummifying all but a few unlucky souls, who must kill or be killed (and eaten). The main characters are a father and his son, who was born a few nights after the bombs fell. 'We're still the good guys,' the man repeatedly assures the boy as they scavenge their way south for the winter, trying to avoid 'bad guy' survival techniques. . . . The horrors here—an infant 'headless and gutted and blackening on the spit'—are extreme, and, deprived of historical context, . . . [the author's] brutality can seem willful. But McCarthy's prose retains its ability to seduce . . . and there are nods to the gentler aspects of the human spirit." New Yorker

McCarthy, Mary

★ **Birds** of America. Harcourt Brace Jovanovich 1971 344p

"Miss McCarthy is astringent and sharp in all the right places, gentle where she should be. What she has written is an honest and appropriate love letter to an essentially decent young American." Publ Wkly

McCarthy, Mary

A **charmed** life. Harcourt Brace & Co. 1955 313p

"John and Martha Sinnott encounter an amazing assortment of would-be bohemians when, in the hope of gaining a new lease on their marriage, they move to the artistic community of New Leeds. They long for privacy but cocktail parties, drama groups, and Martha's first husband Miles keep breaking in. Even Martha's pregnancy brings unforeseen problems for due to one after-the-party interlude the question of fatherhood broadens to two possibilities: John or Miles. The author is at her brilliant best in this comic tragedy of modern man's dilemma: the fluctuation between belief and unbelief, courage and despair." Booklist

McCarthy, Mary

★ The **group**. Harcourt Brace & Co. 1963 378p

"It is perhaps as social history that the novel will chiefly be remembered; but over and above its sensitive observations it has a quality that one has not come to expect from this particular author, and that is compassion." Saturday Rev

McCarthy, Mary

The **groves** of Academe. Harcourt Brace & Co. 1952 302p

"An intelligent and sophisticated dissection of faculty life at Jocelyn, a small progressive college in Pennsylvania. The impending dismissal of self-styled liberal, Henry Mulcahy, Joycean scholar and instructor in literature, and the spring Poetry Conference are the main incidents in the narrative; but woven around them and even tying them together quite neatly is the probing, satirical and often deadly accurate account of college administration and personalities. A few of America's leading poets seem to appear pseudonymously during the conference." Libr J

McCarthy, Tom

C. Alfred A. Knopf 2010 310p $25.95

ISBN 978-0-307-59333-7; 0-307-59333-9

LC 2010-04071

"Opening in England at the turn of the twentieth century, C is the story of a boy named Serge Carrefax, whose father spends his time experimenting with wireless communication while running a school for deaf children. Serge grows up amid the noise and silence with his brilliant but troubled older sister, Sophie: an intense sibling relationship that stays with him as he heads off into an equally troubled larger world. After a fling with a nurse at a Bohemian spa, Serge serves in World War I as a radio operator for reconnaissance planes. When his plane is shot down, Serge is taken to a German prison camp, from which he escapes. Back in London, he's recruited for a mission to Cairo on behalf of the shadowy Empire Wireless Chain." Publisher's note

McCarthy, Tom

Satin Island; a novel. Tom McCarthy. Alfred A. Knopf 2015 192 p. (hardback) $24

ISBN 0307593959; 9780307593955; 9780307739629

LC 2014023461

Man Booker Prize Shortlist (2015)

In this novel by Tom McCarthy, "U., a 'corporate anthropologist,' is tasked with writing the Great Report, an all-encompassing ethnographic document that would sum up our era. Yet at every turn, he feels himself overwhelmed by the ubiquity of data, lost in buffer zones, wandering through crowds of apparitions. As he begins to wonder if the Great Report might remain a shapeless, oozing plasma, his senses are startled awake by a dream of an apocalyptic cityscape." (Publisher's note)

"The book itself subtly takes the form of his Great Report, with U. often addressing the reader, and is marked by fascinating philosophical tangents that justify the apparent lack of a story." Pub Wkly

McClellan, Brian

Promise of blood; Brian McClellan. Orbit 2013 548 p. maps (The powder mage) (hardcover) $23.99; (paperback) $16

ISBN 0316219037; 9780316219037; 9780316219044

LC 2012032171

This novel, by Brian McClellan, is the first entry in "The Powder Mage" Trilogy. "Field Marshal Tamas' coup against his king . . . brought bread to the starving. But it also provoked war . . . , internal attacks by royalist fanatics, and the greedy to scramble for money and power by Tamas's supposed allies. . . . Tamas is relying heavily on his few remaining powder mages, including . . . his estranged son, and . . . a retired police inspector whose loyalty is being tested by blackmail." (Publisher's note)

McClure, James

The **steam** pig. Harper & Row 1972 247p

First published 1971 in the United Kingdom

White Lieutenant Kramer and his Zulu sergeant Zondi investigate the grisly murder of a beautiful white girl in a small South African town

"An absolutely scathing look at contemporary South Africa is provided in {this} . . . novel that is uncanny in its multi-leveled perceptions. It is a grostesquely vivid picture of life under apartheid. But it is also a first-rate mystery with a solution that is a shocker." Saturday Rev

McCorkle, Jill, 1958-

Life after life; a novel. by Jill McCorkle. 1st ed. Algonquin Books of Chapel Hill 2013 352 p. (hardcover) $24.95

ISBN 1565122550; 9781565122550

LC 2012023445

In this novel, "single mother C.J. is desperate not to repeat her mother's cycle of prostitution and suicide but knows she faces long odds. Stanley enters a nursing home and feigns dementia to keep his son Ned at a distance . . . . Mired in a hopeless marriage, Ben tries to reach out to his daughter Abby with magic tricks. . . . Hospice volunteer Joanna, Ben's childhood friend and former assistant, is the point of connection among many storylines." (Publishers Weekly)

McCormack, Mike

Forensic songs; stories. by Mike McCormack. Random House, LLC Soho Press 2014 194 p. $15

ISBN 1616954140; 9781616954147

LC 2014006293

"Amid much hollow laughter a prisoner is drawn from his cell in the middle of the night to play a video game; two rural guards ponder the security threat posed by the only man in Ireland not to have written his memoirs; a child tries to offset his destiny as a serial killer by petitioning his father for a beating; a late night American cop show becomes a savage analysis of a faltering marriage in the west of Ireland; two men turn up at the door of a slacker to give him news of his death and recruit him to some mysterious surveillance mission; an older brother worries about the health of his younger sibling; the prodigal son returns to reveal the fear and hypocrisy which lies at the heart of his brothers life. In twelve stories McCormack's characters find themselves trying to hold onto their identities in a world where love is too often and too easily obscured." (Publisher's Note)

"McCormack's consummate craftsmanship and equal facility with black humor, sober realism, and speculative fiction distinguish him as one of Ireland's leading literary talents." Booklist

McCormack, Mike

★ **Solar** bones; Mike McCormack. Soho Press 2017 217 p. (hardcover) $25

ISBN 9781616958541; 1616958537; 9781616958534

LC 2017007611

This book, by Mike McCormack, winner of the 2016 Goldsmiths Prize, tells the story of "Marcus Conway, a middle-aged engineer, [who] turns up one afternoon at his kitchen table and considers the events that took him away and then brought him home again. . . . [It is a] story of order and chaos, love and loss [which] captures how minor decisions ripple into waves and test our integrity every day." (Publisher's note)

"Deserving a readership far larger than Irish-literature devotees, this is a work of bold risks and luminous creativity." Booklist

McCormick, Chris

Desert boys; Chris McCormick. Picador 2016 240 p. (hbk.) $25

ISBN 9781250075505; 1250075505

LC 2015044337

Stonewall Book Award, Literature (2017)

This short story collection, by Chris McCormick, follows "the life of a young man growing up, leaving home, and coming back again, marked by the stark beauty of California's Mojave Desert and the various fates of those who leave and those who stay behind. . . . McCormick traces the development of towns into cities, of boys into men, and the haunting effects produced when the two transformations overlap." (Publisher's note)

"The linked stories that make up McCormick's debut loosely trace Daley Kushner's coming of age in the Antelope Valley, a small community near California's Mojave Desert. The question everyone from Antelope Valley faces is whether to stay or go, and even after Daley leaves to pursue a writing career in San Francisco, he can't quite escape his memories—the discovery of his homosexuality as a teenager, the loss of his Armenian mother to cancer and his best friend to war, and the haunting desert landscape, home to unforgettable characters. . . Bold and intoxicating, McCormick's stories redefine manhood in the face of war, longing, and escape." Booklist

McCracken, Elizabeth

The **giant's** house; a romance. Dial Press (NY) 1996 259p

ISBN 0-385-31433-7

LC 95-52433

"The reader is mesmerized by this low-key narrative, first lured by Peggy's alternately acerbic and tender voice, then captivated by James's situation and intrigued by his family, later engulfed by pathos as James's body begins to fail and, finally, amazed by a turn of events that ends the novel with a major surprise. McCracken also invests the narrative with humor, sometimes through Peggy's astringent comments and more often through the use of minor characters who add vivid color and their own distinctive voices." Publ Wkly

McCracken, Elizabeth

Niagara Falls all over again. Dial Press (NY) 2001 308p

ISBN 0-385-31837-5

LC 2001-28314

This novel chronicles the ups and downs in the relationship between two vaudeville entertainers. It is narrated by an aging Moses Sharensky, who as Mose Sharp was the straight man to his more exuberant partner Rocky Carter

"McCracken understands the ambiguous relationship between comedy and tragedy as well as she understands the relationship between these two funny men. Even a fictional celebrity memoir risks being maudlin, but McCracken knows when to pull back. . . . {She} has a wonderful ear for the way a line or a friendship breaks." Christ Sci Monit

McCrea, Gavin

Mrs. Engels; Gavin McCrea. Catapult 2015 368 p. $16.95

ISBN 1936787296; 9781936787296

LC 2015933696

In this biographical novel, by Gavin McCrea, "Lizzie is a poor worker in the Manchester, England, mill that Frederick owns. When they move to London to be closer to Karl Marx and family, she must learn to navigate the complex landscapes of Victorian society. . . . Yet despite their profound differences, Lizzie and Frederick are drawn together in this high-spirited love story." (Publisher's note)

"Moving, finely detailed, rife with full-bodied, humanizing portraits of historical icons, and told in striking prose, this is a novel to be savored." Booklist

McCrumb, Sharyn

★ The **ballad** of Frankie Silver. Dutton 1998 386p

ISBN 0-525-93969-5

LC 97-24867

"By working in two time frames and alternating the narrative voice, McCrumb threads both stories into a single pattern, a dense and lovely but very dark design that illustrates the social hypocrisy of the legal system as much as the harshness of mountain justice—then and now." N Y Times Book Rev

Includes bibliographical references (p. {385}-386)

McCrumb, Sharyn

The **ballad** of Tom Dooley; a ballad novel. Thomas Dunne Books 2011 311p

ISBN 0-312-55817-1; 978-0-312-55817-8

LC 2011-19929

A novel "based on actual events that happened in Wilkes County, N.C. in 1866, the year after the end of the Civil War. The real Tom Dula (Dooley was the local pronunciation of his name) was the prime suspect when Laura Foster, a young girl, was found murdered and buried in a shallow grave. Dula was her lover, and as the prime suspect, was hanged for the crime. He was also involved in a longtime affair with a married woman, Ann Melton, who was jailed as a possible accomplice after her cousin, Pauline Foster, reported that Ann had showed her where Laura's body was buried. . . . The sensational elements in this love-triangle case attracted national attention. Even former North Carolina Governor Zeb Vance boosted his political career by leading the defense team. Add to this mix Dula's confession on the eve of his execution, saving Ann Melton, the woman he really loved. . . . McCrumb has written a compelling work of fiction, coming up with a new version of the intricacies of relationships that led to murder. In the process of sorting out the mystery, she may have developed the most villainous Appalachian woman character ever written." A! Magazine for the arts

McCrumb, Sharyn

Foggy Mountain breakdown and other stories. Ballantine Bks. 1997 326p

ISBN 0-345-41493-4

LC 97-18787

The author "has an uncanny knack for picking up the subtle nuances of dialogue, place, and personality that make her characters and settings sparkle with life. She can perfectly mimic the hillbilly twang of an Appalachian healer or the dulcet, pearshaped tones of an upper-class Briton; she can create the excitement of teenagers in lust, mirror the evil that lurks in a serial killer's heart, or convey the quiet desperation of a woman trapped in a miserable marriage. But most of all, McCrumb can make her readers believe what she writes." Booklist

McCrumb, Sharyn

★ **If** ever I return, pretty Peggy-O. Scribner 1990 312p

ISBN 0-684-19104-0

LC 89-24337

The author's "strongly individualized characters give serious and intelligent thought to the ghosts raised by the reunion—including the tangible spector of a murderer." N Y Times Book Rev

McCrumb, Sharyn

If I'd killed him when I met him; an Elizabeth MacPherson novel. Ballantine Bks. 1995 277p

LC 94-23701

"Buoyed by intriguing characters, a wry—sometimes macabre—wit, and lush Virginia atmosphere, McCrumb's mystery spins merrily along on its own momentum, concluding that justice will triumph . . . but in surprising ways." Publ Wkly

McCrumb, Sharyn

She walks these hills. Scribner 1994 336p

ISBN 0-684-19556-9

LC 94-9458

"In 1779, Katie Wyler, 18, was captured by the Shawnee in North Carolina. The story of her escape and arduous journey home through hundreds of miles of Appalachian wilderness is the topic of ethno-historian Jeremy Cobb's thesis. . . . As Cobb begins to retrace Katie's return journey, 63-year-old convicted murderer Hiram (Harm) Sorley escapes from a nearby prison. Suffering from Korsakoff's syndrome, he has no recent memory. . . . Hamelin, Tenn., police dispatcher Martha Ayers uses the opportunity to convince the sheriff to assign her as a deputy. . . . Deftly building suspense, McCrumb weaves these colorful elements into her satisfying conclusion." Publ Wkly

McCullers, Carson

Collected stories; including The member of the wedding and The ballad of the sad cafe. introduction by Virginia Spencer Carr. Houghton Mifflin 1987 392p

LC 87-3944

"McCullers often wrote about grotesques, people afflicted physically and emotionally. Her themes include loneliness and the mental anguish that stems from love gone awry. Her style is unadorned, quietly rigorous. She's both charming and disquieting—an absorbing challenge to readers of serious fiction." Booklist

McCullers, Carson

★ **Complete** novels. Library of America, Distributed to the trade in the United States by Penguin Putnam 2001 827p $35

ISBN 1-931082-03-0

LC 2001-29049

Includes bibliographical references

Contents: The heart is a lonely hunter; Reflections in a golden eye; The ballad of the sad café; The member of the wedding; Clock without hands

McCullers, Carson

The **heart** is a lonely hunter. Modern Lib. 1993 430p $14.95

ISBN 0-679-42474-1

LC 92-51062

A reissue of the title first published 1940 by Houghton Mifflin

"After his friend is committed to a hospital for the insane, John Singer, a deaf mute, finds himself alone. He becomes the pivotal figure in a strange circle of four other lonely individuals: Biff Brannon, the owner of a cafe; Mick Kelly, a young girl; Jake Blount, a radical; and Benedict Copeland, the town's black doctor. Although Singer provides companionship for others, he remains outside the warmth of close relationships." Shapiro. Fic for Youth. 3d edition

McCullers, Carson

The **member** of the wedding. Houghton Mifflin 1946 195p hardcover o.p. pa $7.95

ISBN 0-395-07981-0; 0-618-49239-9 pa

"Twelve-year-old Frankie is experiencing a boring summer until news arrives that her older brother will soon be returning to Georgia from his Alaska home in order to marry. Plotting to accompany the newlyweds on their honeymoon occupies much of Frankie's waking hours, while at the same time she is coping with the pressures of puberty and its effects on her body and mind. Particularly revealing are her conversations with her six-year-old cousin and the nurturing black family cook, Bernice." Shapiro. Fic for Youth. 3d edition

McCullers, Carson

Reflections in a golden eye. Houghton Mifflin 1941 182p

"Set in the 1930s on a Southern army base, the novel concerns the relationships between self-destructive misfits whose lives end in tragedy and murder. The cast of characters includes Captain Penderton, a sadomasochistic, latent homosexual officer; his wife, who is having an affair with Major Langdon; the major's wife, who responds to the trauma of her son's death with self-mutilation; Anacleto, a homosexual servant who is befriended by the major's wife, and an army private who engages in voyeurism." Merriam-Webster's Ency of Lit

McCullough, Colleen

★ The **first** man in Rome. Morrow 1990 896p il

LC 90-37080

The first installment in the Masters of Rome series "outlining the demise of the Roman republic and tracing the origins of the Roman Empire, this volume commences in 110 B.C.E. and revolves around the smoldering political ambitions of two seemingly unsuitable statesmen. Lacking the requisite patrician pedigree, stolid and wealthy Gaius Marius, a brilliant general, acquires respectability by marrying into the irreproachable Julian dynasty. Deprived of his noble birthright by a dissolute and profligate father, the impoverished and curiously amoral Lucius Cornelius Sulla resorts to murder in order to claim an inheritance and purchase his way into the senate. Branded as outsiders, Marius and Sulla forge a formidable alliance, culminating in a succession of unparalled military and political triumphs." Booklist

Followed by The grass crown

McCullough, Colleen

An **indecent** obsession. Harper & Row 1981 317p

LC 81-47547

This novel is "set in the psychiatric ward of a small military hospital in the South Pacific soon after the end of the Second World War. A novel about duty (the 'indecent obsession'), it has the prescribed mix of best-selling ingredients, romance, sex, violence and paranoia." Oxford Companion to Australian Lit

McCullough, Colleen

★ The **thorn** birds. Harper & Row 1977 533p

"The backdrop to this congested, sensational and often bizarre plot, is the Australian outback, with its dramatic landscapes, vast distances, isolation, bush camaraderie, and natural hazards. The novel aroused lively literary controversy. It was labelled by its critics as a 'potboiler': crudely crafted, sensationally exaggerated, devised to cater to the florid expectations of the mass of undiscriminating readers of modern popular fiction. Its supporters see it as a vigorously-written and racy narrative." Oxford Companion to Australian Lit

McDermid, Val ✓

The **distant** echo. St. Martin's Minotaur 2003 404p $24.95

ISBN 0-312-30199-5

LC 2003-52902

"Individually, the characters are sensitively drawn. Collectively, they present the inscrutable face of closed-off communities so terrified of change they would kill for peace." N Y Times Book Rev

McDermid, Val ✓

A **place** of execution. St. Martin's Minotaur 2000 403p

ISBN 0-312-26632-4

LC 00-59145

First published 1999 in the United Kingdom

"When a 13-year-old English schoolgirl goes missing from her Derbyshire village in the winter of 1963, George Bennett, the police inspector in charge of the case, quickly realizes that the secrets of the child's life and possible death are locked in the collective mind of Scardale, an isolated hamlet of inbred families united by their common surnames and their hostility to strangers. Through Bennett's exhaustive efforts, the likely villain is caught and hanged—or so it seems, until the story reaches 35 years into the future for its chilling resolution." N Y Times Book Rev

McDermott, Alice

After this. Farrar, Straus and Giroux 2006 279p $24

ISBN 0-374-16809-1; 978-0-374-16809-4

LC 2006-5598

This novel is set on Long Island. It "spans several decades, from the post-World War II years through the . . . Vietnam era, and [relates] . . . the story of Mary and John Keane and their four children." (N Y Times (Late N Y Ed))

McDermott's "easy authority with this material, combined with her clear-eyed sympathy for her characters, results in a moving, old-fashioned story about longing and loss and sorrow." N Y Times (Late N Y Ed)

McDermott, Alice

At weddings and wakes. Farrar, Straus & Giroux 1992 213p

ISBN 0374106746; 9780374106744

LC 91-42070

Set in Brooklyn during the sixties, this novel "tells the story of an extended Irish-American family observed primarily through the eyes of the children, son and two daughters. Time circles backwards and forwards around a variety of family rituals: holiday meals, vacations at the shore, the wedding of a favorite aunt. The poignant middle-aged romance that develops between the aunt, a former nun, and her suitor, a shy mailman, exacerbates already pronounced family tensions. As they listen to oft-repeated stories about poverty, disease, and early deaths, the children are solemn witnesses to the Irish immigrant experience in America." Libr J

McDermott, Alice

★ **Charming** Billy; a novel. Farrar, Straus & Giroux 1998 280p

ISBN 0-374-12080-3

LC 97-77089

This "novel is set in a close-knit Irish American neighborhood, taking place between the end of World War II and the present. Billy Lynch's friends and family have gathered in a bar-and-grill . . . to mourn him. They recall Billy's charm and his troubles, including an addiction to alcohol and 'that Irish girl.' Eva, the Irish girl whom Billy met following the war, . . . went home to Ireland engaged to Billy. However, as Billy learns from Dennis, his oldest friend, Eva died from tuberculosis before she could return to Billy and be married. The narrator of the story {is} Dennis' daughter." (Booklist)

This "novel opens at the wake of the debonair Billy Lynch—gifted talker, abandoned suitor, faithful husband, devout Catholic, raging alcoholic. It then ranges back and forth through dozens of family theories and anecdotes to answer the question of what did or didn't make him who he was. At once a love story, a portrait of Irish Catholic Queens, and an ode to an edenic postwar East Hampton, this novel honors the consequences of everyday decisions, both sacred and profane, burnishing them in the retelling to a high shine." New Yorker

McDermott, Alice

Child of my heart. Farrar, Straus & Giroux 2002 242p $23

ISBN 0-374-12123-0

LC 2002-69764

This is a "summer idyll in which a cat is hit by a car, a dog is shot, the heroine loses her virginity, and her fairy-like cousin succumbs to a fatal disease and want of parental love. All this loss—of innocence, of dearly loved creatures—and yet, there is not a word of sentimentality or taste of treacle. On the contrary, Child of My Heart is a golden and luminous memory retrieved by a narrator who has achieved a cool and slightly ironic distance from one of those summers in the late fifties or early sixties." Commonweal

McDermott, Alice

★ The **ninth** hour; a novel. Alice McDermott. Farrar, Straus & Giroux 2017 247 p. (hardcover) $26

ISBN 9780374712174; 9780374280147

LC 2017011508

National Book Critics Circle Award Finalist: Fiction (2017)

Kirkus Prize Finalist: Fiction (2017)

In this book, by Alice McDermott, in "Catholic Brooklyn in the early part of the twentieth century, decorum, superstition, and shame collude to erase [a] man's brief existence, and yet his suicide, though never spoken of, reverberates through many lives--testing the limits and the demands of love and sacrifice, of forgiveness and forgetfulness, even through multiple generations." (Publisher's note)

"National Book Award winner McDermott (Someone) delivers an immense, brilliant novel about the limits of faith, the power of sacrifice, and the cost of forgiveness." Pub Wkly

McDermott, Alice

Someone; A Novel. Alice McDermott. 1st ed. Farrar, Straus and Giroux 2013 224 p. (hardcover) $25

ISBN 0374281092; 9780374281090

LC 2013014938

This historical novel, by Alice McDermott, follows "Marie's first heartbreak and her eventual marriage; her brother's brief stint as a Catholic priest, subsequent loss of faith, and eventual breakdown; the Second World War; her parents' deaths; the births and lives of Marie's children; [and] the changing world of her Irish-American enclave in Brooklyn." (Publisher's note)

McDermott, Alice

★ **That** night. Farrar, Straus & Giroux 1987 183p $14.95

ISBN 0-374-27361-8

LC 84-45765

"In spite of its brevity, 'That Night' is a wonderfully unfettered, ample novel, one that celebrates voice, personality and feeling when so much fiction avoids those rewarding characteristics. Ms. McDermott has invested her novel with a strong sense of historical authority, rendering with sure clarity a time and place marked by both a cultural innocence and the premonition of its inevitable loss." N Y Times Book Rev

McDevitt, Jack

The **Cassandra** project; Jack McDevitt and Mike Resnick. Ace Books 2012 387 p. (hardcover) $25.95

ISBN 1937008711; 9781937008710

LC 2012021236

This book by Jack McDevitt and Mike Resnick follows "Jerry Culpepper, a NASA press agent, [who] is caught between his hopes for a better future for the space program and puzzling clues that suggest Neil Armstrong was the fifth man to walk on the Moon. Adding in a libertarian entrepreneur with his own Moon rocket and a president anxious to learn what may be hiding on the far side of the moon, Jerry is caught in a race to discover [the] truth." (Publishers Weekly)

McDevitt, Jack

Odyssey; Jack McDevitt. Ace Books 2006 410p. o.p.; (pbk.) $7.99; o.p.

ISBN 044101433X; 9780441015405; 9780441014330

LC 2006019259

This science fiction book is "[s]et in the 23rd century . . . [and] explores the immorality of big business and the short-sightedness of the American government in minimizing support for space travel. These destructive forces are held off by . . . Gregory MacAllister, editor of a nonpartisan journal, The Nation, and Priscilla 'Hutch' Hutchins, manager of a government-sponsored space-research agency, the Academy. While often on opposite sides of support for the Academy's research budget, MacAllister and Hutch together uncover and react to evidence that Orion Tours' CEO, Charles Dryden, is engaged in a massive conspiracy to jump-start his intergalactic tour business. MacAllister unmasks the others supporting Dryden's faked alien attacks, targeting a physicist who colluded in the hoax. His skepticism about space travel, however, prevents him from seeing the existence of real aliens, something Hutch must pursue at risk to her career." (Publishers Weekly)

Mcdonald, Gregory

Fletch. Bobbs-Merrill 1974 179p

"A rich young California industrialist, Stanwyck, who is apparently dying of cancer, offers someone he takes to be a beach bum a rich reward if he'll murder him on a particular date. The 'bum' chosen is Fletch, ace journalist, ace philanderer, who accepts the proposition. However, Fletch, who is already investigating the beach drug scene for his newspaper, now investigates Stanwyck—his marital and extramarital life, his relationship with his parents, his obsession with piloting experimental planes. The two strands of the story come together in one deft twist as Fletch . . . both gets the drop on the doublecrossing Stanwyck and uncovers the source of the beach's drugs." Publ Wkly

McDonald, Ian

The **Dervish** House. Pyr 2010 357p $26

ISBN 978-1-61614-204-9

LC 2010-12843

McDonald "brilliantly [imagines] what a world of functional, consumer nano would mean for business, culture, faith, play and terrorism; painting a vivid picture of Istanbul as a gem of human society; and delighting with details of the marvels to be found there." Boing Boing

McDonald, Ian

★ **River** of gods. Pyr 2006 597p $25

ISBN 1-59102-436-6; 978-1-59102-436-1

LC 2005-35110

"It's 2047, and the centennial of India's nationhood approaches. Amid the turmoil and vigor of a nation teeming with people and clogged with information, the lives of nine individuals, including a policeman, a journalist, a scientist, a politician, and a standup comic, intersect in an unanticipated union with the fate of their country at stake. . . . [The author] provides a kaleidoscopic, freewheeling encounter with the near future in one of the most exotic—and impoverished—parts of the world. . . . Every library should purchase this multitextured tale of future perils and possibilities in the land of a thousand gods." Libr J

McDonald, Roger

Mr. Darwin's shooter. Atlantic Monthly Press 1999 365p

ISBN 0-87113-733-X

LC 98-36819

"Mr. MacDonald is a generous, leisurely author who gives the reader a large cast of quirky characters, much peripheral detail, lively action, and a view of nineteenth-century social patterns. Covington, moreover, is no plaster saint, and the Beagle's long voyage offers opportunities for adventure. One need not be pro or anti either Darwin or Genesis to enjoy this well-written tale." Atl Mon

McEwan, Ian

Amsterdam. Doubleday 1999 193p

ISBN 0-385-49423-8

LC 98-41401

McEwan "has written a tastily vicious tale in his usual polished prose." Libr J

McEwan, Ian

Atonement; a novel. Doubleday 2002 351p $26

ISBN 0-385-50395-4

LC 2001-44291

First published 2001 in the United Kingdom

This is a "work of astonishing depth and humanity. . . . The upper-class milieu, the sense of place and time, are rendered with an exactitude worthy of Elizabeth Bowen. . . . Mr McEwan has achieved the difficult task of combining literary sophistication with moral gravity." Economist

McEwan, Ian

Black dogs. Putnam 1992 xxii, 149p

LC 92-7418

This novel is "compassionate without resorting to sentimentality, clever without ever losing its honesty, an undisguised novel of ideas which is also Ian McEwan's most human work." Times Lit Suppl

McEwan, Ian, 1942-

★ The **child** in time. Houghton Mifflin 1987 263p
ISBN 0-395-42912-9

LC 87-8603

This novel deals with the effects upon Stephen and Julie Lewis of the disappearance of their child from a supermarket.

"Many of the plot turns in the novel may seem improbable and even fanciful, but the feelings expressed by the characters and their sense of time (running up, running down and running out) are, without exception, genuine. . . . [This is an] astonishing book." Time

McEwan, Ian, 1942-

★ The **children** act; a novel. Ian McEwan. 1st American ed. Nan A. Talese/Doubleday 2014 240 p. (hardback) $25
ISBN 0385539703; 9780385539708

LC 2014018448

In this novel by Ian McEwan, "Fiona Maye is a leading High Court judge who presides over cases in the family court. . . . But her professional success belies private sorrow and domestic strife. There is the lingering regret of her childlessness, and now her marriage of thirty years is in crisis. At the same time, she is called on to try an urgent case: Adam, a beautiful seventeen-year-old boy, is refusing for religious reasons the medical treatment that could save his life." (Publisher's note)

In "a tranquil mix of exacting word choice and easily flowing sentences, McEwan once again observes with depth and wisdom the universal truth in the uncommon situation." Booklist

McEwan, Ian

The **innocent**. Doubleday 1990 270p
LC 89-25669

"There is . . . a point to all this, which is to display the astonishing deeds that human beings can perpetrate and yet retain a measure of innocence. . . . In spite of what has happened, Leonard is able to live with himself. This is far and away Ian McEwan's most mature work." New Statesman Soc

McEwan, Ian

On Chesil Beach. Nan A. Talese/Doubleday 2007 176p $22.95
ISBN 978-0-385-52240-3; 0-385-52240-1

LC 2006-100720

McEwan's brief novel is as "tautly constructed as anything he has written, though sprawling in imagination. It's emblematic of a generation, a semi-scornful elegy for a repressed age, sarcastic about mores and unrelentingly honest about psychological and sexual intimacy. It's a big book in a little space. You can feel the author at times wishing to burst the bounds of his limited span, to go crashing past these tightly constrained boundaries and begin sweeping up the host of other generational topics available to him. McEwan resists the urge, which is for the best, this is a book better suited for the sprint than the marathon." PopMatters

McEwan, Ian, 1942-

Nutshell; Ian McEwan. Nan A. Talese/Doubleday 2016 197 p. (hardcover : acid-free paper) $24.95
ISBN 9780385542081; 9780385542074

LC 2016026696

In this novel, by Ian McEwan, "Trudy has betrayed her husband, John. She's still in the marital home, . . . but John's not there. Instead, she's with his brother, the profoundly banal Claude, and the two of them have a plan. But there is a witness to their plot: the inquisitive, nine-month-old resident of Trudy's womb. Told from a perspective unlike any other, 'Nutshell' is a classic tale of murder and deceit from one of the world's master storytellers." (Publisher's note)

"Packed with humor and tinged with suspense, this gem resembles a sonnet the narrator recalls hearing his father recite: brief, dense, bitter, suggestive of unrequited and unmanageable longing, surprising, and surprisingly affecting." Pub Wkly

McEwan, Ian

Saturday. Nan A. Talese/Doubleday 2005 289p $26
ISBN 0-385-51180-9

"It's clear that with this volume, Mr. McEwan has not only produced one of the most powerful pieces of post-9/11 fiction yet published, but also fulfilled that very primal mission of the novel: to show how we—a privileged few of us, anyway—live today." NY Times (Late NY Ed)

McEwan, Ian, 1942-

Sweet tooth; a novel. Ian McEwan. Nan A. Talese/Doubleday 2012 301 p. (hbk. : alk. paper) $26.95
ISBN 0385536828; 9780385536820

LC 2012013932

In this novel by Ian McEwan "Serena Frome's beauty and intelligence make her the ideal recruit for MI5. The year is 1972. The Cold War is far from over. England's legendary intelligence agency is determined to manipulate the cultural conversation by funding writers whose politics align with those of the government. . . . [Serena is assigned to] infiltrate the literary circle of a promising young writer named Tom Haley. At first, she loves his stories. Then she begins to love the man." (Publisher's note)

McFadden, Bernice L.

The **Book** of Harlan; by Bernice L. McFadden. Akashic Books 2016 341 p. (paperback) $16.95
ISBN 9781617754463; 9781617754456; 9781617754548; 1617754455; 1617754463

LC 2015953875

NAACP Image Award: Outstanding Literary Work - Fiction (2017)

This book, by Bernice L. McFadden, "opens with the courtship of Harlan's parents and his 1917 birth in Macon, Georgia. After his prominent minister grandfather dies, Harlan and his parents move to Harlem, where he eventually becomes a professional musician. When Harlan and his best friend, trumpeter Lizard Robbins, are invited to perform at a popular cabaret in the Parisian enclave of Montmartre . . . Harlan jumps at the opportunity, convincing Lizard to join him." (Publisher's note)

"Playing with themes of divine justice and the suffering of the righteous, McFadden presents a remarkably crisp portrait of one average man's extraordinary bravery in the face of pure evil." Booklist

Includes bibliographical references.

McFadden, Bernice L.

Gathering of waters; by Bernice L. McFadden. Akashic Books 2012 252 p. (pbk.) $15.95
ISBN 161775031X; 9781617750311; 9781617750328

LC 2011923109

In this book, NAACP Image Award and Hurston/Wright Legacy Award finalist Bernice McFadden "reimagines the summer Emmett Till spent in Mississippi in 1955 and the events leading up to his murder. The story chronicles the young love between Emmett and Tass Hilton, which finally transcends death. Having left Mississippi for Detroit after Emmett dies, Tass returns 40 years later as a widow to reawaken his spirit, trapped in the dank waters of the Tallahatchie River." (Library Journal)

McFarlane, Fiona

★ The **night** guest; a novel. Fiona McFarlane. Farrar Straus & Giroux 2013 256 p. $26

ISBN 0865477736; 9780865477735

LC 2013022511

This novel, by Fiona McFarlane, is "about trust, dependence, and fear. . . . Ruth is widowed, her sons are grown, and she lives in an isolated beach house outside of town. . . . One day a stranger arrives at her door, looking as if she has been blown in from the sea. This woman—Frida—claims to be a care worker sent by the government. Ruth lets her in. . . . How far can she trust this mysterious woman, Frida, who seems to carry with her own troubled past? And how far can Ruth trust herself?" (Publisher's note)

McGahan, Andrew

The **white** earth. Soho 2006 376p $25

ISBN 1-56947-417-6

LC 2005-50415

"Set in Australia's Queensland province, the novel begins with the blaze of 70 acres of wheat, a conflagration that consumes nine-year-old William's father and sends the boy and his mother packing to his great-uncle John McIvor's rotting mansion on the arid plains of what was once a vast sheep ranch. Chapters alternate between William settling into his new existence (action set in the early 1990s), and the story of John's youth on the ranch, where as the son of the ranch manager he nurtured ambitions to one day own the estate. John recruits William's help in organizing a rally for his right-wing group, which opposes the proposed Native Title laws that would return Aboriginal-claimed land to the original inhabitants. The novel's first half is a slow build, the second half, a well-wrought, meditative reflection on Australia's colonialist demons, brings the book's gothic intimations home to roost." Publ Wkly

McGahern, John

By the lake; a novel. Knopf 2002 335p

ISBN 0-679-41914-4

LC 2001-50258

"The story is an old one: in search of a quieter way of life, Joe and Kate Ruttledge have traded their careers in London for a farm near a small Irish village, where they learn how to raise sheep and are steadily drawn into the lives of their neighbors. There's the Shah, a rich bachelor in search of an heir for his business; John Quinn, a weaselly sexual predator, and a danger to women throughout the county; and Jimmy Joe McKiernan, an I.R.A. leader whose exploits periodically stir up high feeling. McGahern is never sentimental, and the novel's greatest pleasures come from the unflinching probity of his observations." New Yorker

McGarrity, Michael

Everyone dies; a Kevin Kerney novel. Dutton 2003 273p $23.95

ISBN 0-525-94761-2

LC 2003-9208

"Michael McGarrity is one of those low-key pros who keep the genre honest with realistic crime stories and plain-talking cops who know the procedures." N Y Times Book Rev

McGowan, Heather

Duchess of nothing; a novel. Bloomsbury Pub. 2006 215p $23.95

ISBN 1-59691-066-6

LC 2005-18197

McGowan reveals her "narrator's character slowly, with delicacy and precision. 'Duchess of Nothing' is the kind of book that relies entirely on the power of its voice. McGowan is no ironist, smirking at the world and going for cheap laughs. There's plenty of comedy here, but its function turns out to be solace." N Y Times Book Rev

McGown, Jill

Murder at the old vicarage. St. Martin's Press 1989 256p

LC 88-30603

First published 1988 in the United Kingdom with title: Redemption

"McGown's complex plot is masterful and her sleuths and their predicament are enthralling." Publ Wkly

McGown, Jill

Verdict unsafe. Fawcett Columbine 1997 327p

LC 97-4949

"The pace is methodical and the cast cheerless, but McGown wraps her grim tale in a complex, satisfying solution." Publ Wkly

McGrath, Patrick

Asylum. Random House 1997 254p

ISBN 0-679-45228-1

LC 96-24849

"It is part of McGrath's bemusing artfulness in Asylum that he can make the reader suffer the fate of all his characters. Everyone in the novel, that is to say, is deranged by their own, and other people's, plausibility. When anyone speaks in Asylum–and McGrath has an extraordinary ear for the hollows in conversation, for the lurking soliloquies–we seem to see through them in the full knowledge that they never see through themselves." London Rev Books

McGrath, Patrick

★ The **grotesque**. Poseidon Press 1989 186p

ISBN 0-671-66509-X

LC 89-3486

"Part of the fun of reading 'The Grotesque' is recognizing the literary allusions and watching as one after another the subgenres of murder mystery, Gothic horror, social satire, black comedy and stories of the double are invoked and skillfully woven together." N Y Times Book Rev

McGrath, Patrick

Spider. Poseidon Press 1990 221p

ISBN 0-671-66510-3

LC 90-7492

"Despite a less pungent second half, Spider confirms McGrath's mastery of the terrain he's staked out for himself: a twisted place where the most rank, hideous experiences are conveyed in a prose so tight, assured, and essentially self-mocking that he maintains a fine balance between high gothic horror and fussy stylization." Voice Lit Suppl

McGregor, Jon

Even the dogs; a novel. Bloomsbury USA 2010 195p pa $14

ISBN 978-1-59691-348-6; 1-59691-348-7

LC 2009-49556

"The book is narrated by a group of urban ghosts, victims of drug overdoses who look on as someone they know, Robert Radcliffe, is found dead in his shabby apartment. Other friends, family members and acquaintances, most of whom were part of Robert's life, come in and out of focus as they move around the city looking for their next fixes and, along with the police and investigators, respond to Robert's death. As a novel about the consequences of addiction — particularly heroin addiction — 'Even the Dogs' is harrowing. . . . But McGregor's devotion to craft comes at a significant cost to a reader's emotional engagement with his characters and story. His technique intrudes, becomes showy." N Y Times Book Rev

McGuane, Thomas

★ The **cadence** of grass. Knopf 2002 238p

ISBN 0-679-44674-5

LC 2001-50623

"The real engine of the book is not plot . . . but language: McGuane's sentences are like no one else's, crisp and spare, yet some how baroque, and he perpetually balances the picaresque against the sublime." New Yorker

McGuane, Thomas, 1939-

★ **Crow** fair; stories. Thomas McGuane. Alfred A. Knopf 2015 288 p. (hardcover) $25.95

ISBN 0385350198; 9780385350198

LC 2014018360

This short story collection, by Thomas McGuane, is "set in . . . Big Sky country, with its mesmeric powers. . . . The ties of family make for uncomfortable binds: A devoted son is horrified to discover his mother's antics before she slipped into dementia. A father's outdoor skills are no match for an ominous change in the weather. But complications arise equally in the absence of blood, as when lifelong friends on a fishing trip finally confront their deep dislike for each other." (Publisher's note)

"The conflicts throughout this book are age-old--indeed, the title story evokes 'Oedipus'--but McGuane's clean writing and psychological acuity enliven them all. A slyly cutting batch of tales." Kirkus

McGuane, Thomas

Gallatin Canyon; stories. Knopf 2006 220p $24

ISBN 1-4000-4156-2

LC 2005-44680

"McGuane has become our poet-philosopher of the arm's length, of the prudently aborted intimacy that keeps both isolation and commitment equally at bay." N Y Times Book Rev

McGuane, Thomas

Nothing but blue skies. Houghton Mifflin 1992 349p

ISBN 0-395-54540-4

LC 92-23623

"The author's underlying theme is the unimportance of money by comparison with love, an old point that he makes with novel means and without sentimental sugar." Christ Sci Monit

McGuire, Ian

The **North** water; a novel. by Ian McGuire. Henry Holt & Co. 2016 272 p. $27

ISBN 1627795944; 9781627795944

LC 2015023830

In this book, by Ian McGuire, "Henry Drax is a harpooner on the Volunteer, a Yorkshire whaler bound for the rich hunting waters of the arctic circle. Also aboard for the first time is Patrick Sumner, an ex-army surgeon with a shattered reputation, no money, and no better option than to sail as the ship's medic on this violent, filthy, and ill-fated voyage." (Publisher's note)

"There is no light, no letup in this gruesome tale, so there is great significance in the rare but moving acts of kindness and camaraderie between these men in peril. An amazing journey." Pub Wkly

McHugh, Laura

Arrowood; a novel. by Laura McHugh. Spiegel & Grau 2016 288 p. (hardcover : acid-free paper) $27; (ebook) $65

ISBN 9780812996395; 9780812996401

LC 2015039961

In this novel by Laura McHugh, the Arrowood house in southern Iowa "has a mystery it has never revealed: It's where Arden Arrowood's younger twin sisters vanished on her watch twenty years ago—never to be seen again. . . . [Now] Arden returns to her childhood home determined to discover what really happened to her sisters that traumatic summer. . . . With the help of a young amateur investigator, Arden tracks down the man who was the prime suspect in the kidnapping." (Publisher's note)

"Lyrical prose and in-depth character studies examine the reliability of memory, punctuated by believable suspense and aided by a careful look at a small town." Pub Wkly

McHugh, Maureen F.

After the apocalypse; Maureen F. McHugh. Small Beer Press 2011 188p.

ISBN 9781931520294 (trade pbk. : alk. paper); 9781931520355 (ebook); 978-1-931520-29-4; 978-1-931520-35-5

LC 20116769

Each short story in this collection "takes place in the near future, and usually in the aftermath of some global disaster." (Washington Post) It was the author's intent to explore "what the fall of civilization might actually feel like. The cataclysms . . . range from flu epidemics to dirty bombs to water shortages to good old-fashioned economic depression. . . . One of the persistent themes in this book is that when the world as we know it collapses, certain groups are far more likely to end up crushed in the rubble." (salon.com)

McHugh, Maureen F.

Nekropolis. Eos 2001 257p

ISBN 0-380-97457-6

LC 2001-33525

"As a @jessed' or bonded servant, Hariba possesses a chemically induced sense of loyalty to her master until her growing affection for an artificial construct drives her to an act of desperation and changes her life forever. . . . This luminous tale of forbidden love in a near-future Morocco explores the evolution of human nature in a world where technology has redefined the meaning of the word human." Libr J

McInerney, Jay

Bright lights, big city; a novel. Vintage Bks. 1984 182p pa $15

ISBN 0-394-72641-3

LC 84-40074

This "is a very funny, oddly touching book, and something of a tour de force as well. McInerney employs an unusual and challenging narrative device; he tells his tale through the second person in the historical present tense and fashions a coherent and engaging voice with it, one that is totally believable at almost every moment in the novel." New Repub

McInerney, Jay

The **good** life. Knopf 2006 353p $25

ISBN 0-375-41140-2

LC 2005-44370

This is a novel "about 9/11's effects on four privileged Manhattanites: a retired corporate raider, a would-be screenwriter, a former model, and a book editor. . . . This is really the story of two of the above, part of a cast meaningfully reassembled from Brightness Falls (1992), who meet as volunteers at a soup kitchen for rescue workers at Ground

Zero. Both of them are in miserable marriages, and they're left shaken when the nation's worst day leads to the best days of their lives. McInerney probes the human response to tragedy, and the complexity of human desire, with both precision and empathy." Booklist

McInerney, Lisa

The **Glorious** Heresies; by Lisa McInerney. John Murray Publishers Ltd 2016 384 p. $27

ISBN 0804189064; 144479888X; 9780804189064; 9781444798883

LC 2015043597

Baileys Women's Prize for Fiction (2016)

This book, by Lisa McInerney, is "about life on the fringes of Ireland's post-crash society. When grandmother Maureen Phelan is surprised in her home by a stranger, she clubs the intruder with a Holy Stone. The consequences of this unplanned murder connect four misfits struggling against their meager circumstances." (Publisher's note)

"This gritty, urban character study will be perfect for readers favoring strong blends of literary and crime fiction, overlaid with striking dark comedy." Booklist

McInerny, Ralph M.

Celt and pepper; {by} Ralph McInerny. St. Martin's Minotaur 2002 210p $22.95

ISBN 0-312-29117-5

LC 2002-69938

"After a young Notre Dame professor/Poet dies unexpectedly, Professor Roger Knight. . . suspects murder. His erudition, coupled with assistance from his brother Philip, a private investigator, ultimately leads to a killer. Solid plotting from a practiced hand." Libr J

McInerny, Ralph M.

Irish coffee; [by] Ralph McInerny. St. Martin's Minotaur 2003 247p $23.95

ISBN 0-312-30901-5

LC 2003-50620

"Everybody likes Fred Neville, who works in Notre Dame's sports information office. Everybody but one person-the person who killed him. A different side of unassuming Fred surfaces when two women arrive at his funeral, each claiming Fred as their fiance. Because South Bend, home of Notre Dame, is always deferential to the university, the locals have no objection when the Knight brothers become unofficial consultants on the case. Phillip Knight is a streetwise PI, and his immensely rotund brother, Roger, is an amateur sleuth and a revered professor of Catholic studies. . . . A fine effort by a deservedly respected genre veteran." Booklist

McInerny, Ralph M.

Requiem for a realtor; a Father Dowling mystery. [by] Ralph McInerny. St. Martin's Minotaur 2004 263p $23.95

ISBN 0-312-32417-0

LC 2004-41858

"Stanley Collins is Fox River's most notorious philandering realtor. His wife, Phyllis, wants to divorce him but is afraid to lose her claim on an impending inheritance. She is stringing along her dentist, love-struck Dave Jameson, who's also a devout Catholic. Jameson is a prominent member of St. Hilary's parish and, as an emissary for Phyllis Collins, asks Father Dowling's advice regarding a divorce and her standing in the church. Circumstances change when Stanley Collins is run down by his own car a couple of blocks from the apartment of a local nightclub torch singer, with whom he is having an affair. Dowling closely watches as the investigation–directed by his closest friend, Phil Keegan, of the Fox River PD–unfolds. . . . McInerny adds a moral catch-22 for Dowling as he struggles to choose between helping solve a murder and betraying the sanctity of a parishioner's confidences." Booklist

McIntosh, Will

Hitchers; Will McIntosh. Night Shade Books 2012 283 p.

ISBN 1597803359; 9781597803359

The author, Hugo Award winner Will McIntosh, "delivers a . . . tale of individual grief and recovery against the backdrop of a devastated world. When an anthrax attack on Atlanta devastates the population, widower Finn Darby loses two of his few remaining friends . . . [and] finds himself . . . uttering sentences that have no meaning to him. They seem to be connected to his late grandfather, . . . who created the comic strip that Darby now writes against his grandfather's dying wishes. . . . Darby discovers other sufferers, including . . . a waitress who might be possessed by Darby's dead wife. Darby, with his . . . grief serving as synecdoche for the entire city, is forced to confront his guilt over his wife's death and his co-opting of his grandfather's work." (Publishers Weekly)

McIntyre, Vonda N.

Dreamsnake. Houghton Mifflin 1978 313p

LC 77-18891

"This is based on McIntyre's Nebula Award-winning novelette, 'Of Mist, and Grass, and Sand,' which is also the first chapter of the book. Snake, the healer, and her three healing serpents attend a young boy ill with a tumor. His fearful parents kill Grass, the dreamsnake, who can ease the dying by removing their pain. Without Grass, Snake is incomplete as a healer, and since the dreamsnakes come from off-world, she cannot get a replacement. To atone for her carelessness in losing Grass, Snake sets off for the city where off-worlders trade, hoping to get more dreamsnakes. She has many heart-stopping adventures, and the reader is engrossed every step of the way." Libr J

McKenzie, Elizabeth

★ The **portable** Veblen; a novel. Elizabeth McKenzie. Penguin Group USA 2016 448 p. (hardback) $26

ISBN 9781594206856; 1594206856

LC 2015043056

This novel, by Elizabeth McKenzie, is "set in and around Palo Alto, amid the culture clash of new money and old (antiestablishment) values, and with the specter of our current wars looming across its pages. . . . A young couple . . . find their engagement in danger of collapse. Along the way they weather everything from each other's dysfunctional families, to the attentions of a seductive pharmaceutical heiress, to an intimate tête-à-tête with a very charismatic squirrel." (Publisher's note)

"McKenzie's idiosyncratic love story scampers along on a wonderfully zig-zaggy path, dashing and darting in delightfully unexpected directions as it progresses toward its satisfying end and scattering tasty literary passages like nuts along the way." Kirkus

McKillip, Patricia A.

Alphabet of thorn. Ace Books 2004 314p $22.95

ISBN 0-441-01130-6

LC 2003-62912

"The day that the new queen of Raine is crowned, a translator working in the palace receives a book written in a strange language of thorn-like characters. As Nepenthe, the translator, unlocks the language's secret, she learns of a legend from the ancient past that involves her and the queen in an intrigue that threatens the kingdom itself. McKillip . . . creates the atmosphere of a fairy tale with her elegantly lyrical prose and attention to nuance. Her characters are at once intimately personal and larger than life." Libr J

McKillip, Patricia A., 1948-

Ombria in shadow; Patricia A. McKillip. Ace Books 2002 298p. (pbk.) $16

ISBN 044100895X; 9780441010165

LC 2001046388

Mythopoeic Award: Adult Literature (2003), World Fantasy Awards: Novel (2003)

In this fantasy novel, the winner of the 2003 World Fantasy Award and Mythopoeic Award, "[g]reed, despair, grief and avarice have all taken their toll on the once-beautiful city of Ombria, but it is the death of its prince that pushes it over the edge into darkness and shadow. Several key players participate in this particular procession of dying and rebirth: Kyel Greve, the new prince-to-be who is too young to rule but old enough to feel the despair of those around him; Lydea, the dying prince's lover who feels the weight of the city resting on her shoulders; Ducon Greve, the bastard prince who sees and feels the change happening but is in no position to alter the coming darkness; Domina Pearl, the sorceress who is pushing the city even further on its path of destruction; and Mag and Faey, two mysterious women who hold some of the past, present and future of Ombria inside them." (Publishers Weekly)

McKinney-Whetstone, Diane

Leaving Cecil Street; a novel. Diane McKinney-Whetstone. 1st ed; Morrow 2004 297p $24.95

ISBN 0-688-16385-8

LC 2003-55845

"Cecil Street is a quiet, tree-lined haven in West Philadelphia, a place where everyone knows everyone else, a place removed from the turmoil and violence of the late 1960s. Yet the residents of Cecil Street have their problems. Joe and Louise's marriage is strained; Johnetta's sexy niece has arrived, ripe for trouble; and teenaged Shay tries to help best friend Neet deal with an unwanted pregnancy. When Neet's abortion goes tragically wrong, everyone on the street must rally around her, while Joe, Louise, and Neet's mother, Alberta, discover how their pasts have now drawn them together. McKinney-Whetstone's portrayal of African American family life is sensitive and compassionate, with characters who love, work, live, and die without veering into soap opera." Libr J

McKinty, Adrian ✓

The **cold** cold ground; a Detective Sean Duffy novel / by Adrian McKinty. Seventh Street Books 2012 p. cm.

ISBN 9781616147167

LC 2012023528

In this book by Adrian McKinty, book one of the Troubles Trilogy, "a Catholic cop tracks a killer operating amidst the sectarian violence of the conflict in Northern Ireland. The Thatcher government has flooded the area with soldiers but nightly there are riots, bombings, and sectarian attacks. In the midst of the chaos, Sean Duffy, a young, witty, Catholic detective in the almost entirely Protestant Royal Ulster Constabulary, is trying to track down a serial killer who is targeting gay men." (Publisher's note)

McKinty, Adrian ✓

In the Morning I'll Be Gone; a Detective Sean Duffy novel. by Adrian McKinty. Seventh Street Books 2014 300 p. (The Troubles Trilogy) (pbk.) $15.95

ISBN 1616148772; 9781616148775

LC 2013037740

In this book, by Adrian McKinty, "Sean Duffy, a conflicted Catholic cop in the Protestant RUC (Royal Ulster Constabulary), is recruited by MI5 to hunt down Dermot McCann, an IRA master bomber who has made a daring escape from the notorious Maze Prison. In the course of his investigations Sean discovers a woman who may hold the key to Dermot's whereabouts; she herself wants justice for her daughter who died in mysterious circumstances in a pub locked from the inside." (Publisher's note)

"The explosive conclusion to McKinty's Troubles trilogy . . . combines an IRA thriller with a locked-room mystery." Pub Wkly

McLain, Paula

★ **Circling** the Sun; A Novel. by Paula McLain. Random House Inc. 2015 368 p. $28

ISBN 0345534182; 9780345534187

LC 2015011091

This novel, by Paula McLain, "brings to life a fearless and captivating woman--Beryl Markham. . . . Brought to Kenya from England as a child and then abandoned by her mother, Beryl is raised by both her father and the native Kipsigis tribe who share his estate. . . . Beryl forges her own path as a horse trainer, and her uncommon style attracts the eye of the Happy Valley set, a decadent, bohemian community of European expats who also live and love by their own set of rules." (Publisher's note)

"McLain's . . . latest showcases her immersive command of setting and character, fictionalizing the exploits of real-life aviator and author Beryl Markham in British Kenya in the early 20th century. . . . Markham's true life was incredibly adventurous, and it's easy for readers to identify with this woman who refused to be pigeonholed by her gender." Pub Wkly

Includes bibliographical references

McLain, Paula

The **Paris** wife; a novel. Ballantine Books 2011 320p $25

ISBN 978-0-345-52130-9; 0-345-52130-7

LC 2010-37878

"McLain's vivid, clear-voiced novel is a conjecture, an act of imaginary autobiography on the part of the author. Yet her biographical and geographical research is so deep, and her empathy for the real Hadley Richardson so forthright (without being intrusively femme partisan), that the account reads as very real indeed. Big things happen: Hadley is there as Hemingway meets Gertrude Stein and Scott Fitzgerald, as he writes The Sun Also Rises, as he falls in love with bullfighting. But a thousand less glamorous, more quotidian things happen too, as Hadley tries to find a way to live her own life (she's a fine pianist) and support her moody husband, and keep up with hard-drinking company, and run a household in a country not her own. By making the ordinary come to life, McLain has written a beautiful portrait of being in Paris in the glittering 1920s — as a wife and one's own woman." Entertaiment Wkly

McLaren, Kaya

The **road** to enchantment; Kaya McLaren. St. Martin's Griffin 2017 ix, 342 p.p (paperback) $15.99

ISBN 9781250058225; 9781466862272

LC 2016043106

In this novel, by Kaya McLaren, "Willow [and her mother] set off to New Mexico, . . . [as] her eccentric mother believed in this new life and set about starting a winery and goat ranch. But for Willow, it meant initially being bullied and feeling like an outsider. Today, as a grown woman, Willow much prefers Los Angeles and her job as a studio musician. But things tend to happen in threes: her mother dies, her boyfriend dumps her, and Willow discovers she is pregnant." (Publisher's note)

'Despite its relatively somber tone, this touching novel of homecoming will draw apt comparisons to early Barbara Kingsolver." Booklist

McLarty, Ron

Art in America. Viking 2008 366p $25.95
ISBN 978-0-670-01895-6; 0-670-01895-3

LC 2007-40454

"In Creedemore, Colo., a land-rights dispute pitches locals against one another and attracts national media attention. Into the fray arrives Steven Kearney, a prolific New York author of unpublished novels, poems and plays, who has been invited by the Creedemore Historical Society to write and direct a play dramatizing the town's history. Steven's relocation sparks a colorful fish-out-of-water story populated with cowboys, environmental activists, hordes of reporters, performance artists, ecoterrorists and bona fide outlaws. Keeping the peace is sheriff Petey Myers, whose recollections of (and occasional conversations with) his slain partner provide some of the novel's finest moments." Publ Wkly

McLaughlin, Emma

The **nanny** diaries; a novel. [by] Emma McLaughlin and Nicola Kraus. St. Martin's Press 2002 305p
ISBN 0-312-27858-6

LC 2001-48652

This is "a diabolically funny New York story. . . . [Nanny] is a vastly entertaining narrator and impromptu social critic. . . . Not surprisingly, 'The Nanny Diaries' fades slightly when the X's are out of sight, despite the boyfriend and family matters that are meant to fill out Nanny's story. The heart of the matter remains perfectly pitched social satire. . . . This book is saved from self-righteousness not only by the authors' cleverness but also by their compassion. For oblivious parents, lonely offspring and overworked, underpaid employees alike, they're out to fix something that's broken." N Y Times (Late N Y Ed)

McMahon, Jennifer

The **One** I Left Behind; Jennifer McMahon. HarperCollins 2013 432 p. $14.99
ISBN 006212255X; 9780062122551

In this book by Jennifer McMahon, "a serial killer called Neptune begins kidnapping women. He leaves their severed hands on the police department steps and . . . displays their bodies around town. Just when Reggie needs her mother, Vera, the most, Vera's hand is found on the steps. But after five days, there's no body and Neptune disappears. Now, twenty-five years later, Reggie . . . gets a call revealing that her mother has been found alive." (Publisher's note)

McMillan, Terry, 1951-

A **day** late and a dollar short. Viking 2001 448p
ISBN 0-670-89676-4

LC 00-46232

McMillan "takes a multiperspective view of dysfunctional families with each member of the Price clan giving his or her own version of how screwed up they all are. . . . Their heavy load—incest, substance abuse, poverty, infidelity, death—makes this a soap opera, but it is leavened with a big dollop of sass." Time

McMillan, Terry, 1951-

★ **How** Stella got her groove back. Viking 1996 368p
ISBN 0140865063; 9780140865066

LC 96-15374

This novel's protagonist, Stella Payne, "is a successful 42-year-old investment analyst and divorced mother of an 11-year-old son, Quincy. But Stella has begun to feel that her life needs some 'groove.' On the spur of the moment, she plans a trip to Jamaica to relax and escape from her routine. She meets a man, half her age, whose honesty and physical charm challenge her perceptions of what is acceptable and force her to rethink . . . her image of herself and her life." (Booklist)

"Readers who have been yearning for a Judith Krantz of the black bourgeoisie—albeit one with a dirty mouth and a more ebullient spirit—will be pleased with this fantasy of sexual fulfillment." Publ Wkly

McMillan, Terry, 1951-

I Almost Forgot About You; Terry McMillan. Random House Inc 2016 368 p. $27
ISBN 1101902574; 9781101902578

LC 2015373336

In this book by Terry McMillan, "Dr. Georgia Young's wonderful life--great friends, family, and successful career--aren't enough to keep her from feeling stuck and restless. When she decides to make some major changes in her life, including quitting her job as an optometrist and moving house, she finds herself on a wild journey that may or may not include a second chance at love." (Publisher's note)

"Here is McMillan's trademark style in full, feisty effect: strong, complicated female characters, energetic prose, and an entertaining, seductive narrative. A heartwarming story that reminds us of the pure joy of believing in love." Kirkus

McMillan, Terry, 1951-

★ **Waiting** to exhale. Viking 1992 409p $22.95
ISBN 0-670-83980-9

LC 91-46564

"Terry McMillan's heroines are so well drawn that by the end of the novel, the reader is completely at home with the four of them. They observe men—and contemporary America—with bawdy humor, occasional melancholy and great affection. But the novel is about more than four lives; the bonds among the women are so alive and so appealing they almost seem a character in their own right." N Y Times Book Rev

McMullen, Sean

Souls in the great machine. Tor Bks. 1999 448p
ISBN 0-312-87055-8

LC 99-21934

"In the fortieth century, librarians rule the world. Through a byzantine system of political favor, mathematical expertise, civil service testing, and dueling, the librarians strive for power in the 'mayoralty' of Rochester, the most powerful of several Australian fiefdoms that emerged long ago from a nuclear winter. The highliber is the scheming yet honorable Zarvora. She has ruthlessly assembled scores of mathematicians, who make the Calculor, a bizarre flesh-and-machine supercomputer that Zarvora needs to unify this quasi-medieval world and save it from the impending doom implicit in the Call. . . . Decidedly original, sometimes whimsical, and captivating, this is a genuine tour de force." Booklist

McMurtry, Larry

Boone's Lick; a novel. Simon & Schuster 2000 287p
ISBN 0-684-86886-5

LC 00-56342

"McMurtry's historical novel, told with humor and candor from the perspective of Mary Margaret's oldest son, Shay, is highly recommended for adults and adolescents alike." Libr J

McMurtry, Larry

Buffalo girls; a novel. Simon & Schuster 1990 351p

LC 90-42486

"This is a nostalgic, funny, and sad novel about the Old West when cowboys and Buffalo girls whooped it up. Their behavior was amoral rather than immoral, and they lived by their own special code of behavior. Friendship was often life-saving as well as comforting, and the women of the bawdy houses called their clients 'sweethearts' even if their encounter was only for one night. Jim Ragg and Bartle Bone had become almost a dying breed and Custer, in their opinion, was a stupid old man at Little Big Horn to think that he could fight 3,000 Indians with 200 of his men. Highlights of the book are Bill Cody's (Buffalo Bill's) Wild West show and Calamity Jane's (whose drunkenness was calamitous) letters to a daughter. Fact and fiction are entwined in an enjoyable story that is mythic and memorable." Shapiro. Fic for Youth. 3d edition

McMurtry, Larry

Comanche moon; a novel. Simon & Schuster 1997 752p
ISBN 0-684-80754-8

LC 97-29609

"McMurtry has created a sprawling, picaresque novel that, like the history of the West itself, leaves more than a few loose ends. . . . The characters are the novel's strength. McMurtry's rangers are heroic because of their vulnerabilities, not despite them." N Y Times Book Rev

McMurtry, Larry

Dead man's walk; a novel. Simon & Schuster 1995 477p
ISBN 0-684-80753-X

LC 95-21011

"If Dead Man's Walk were not a prequel, it would be worth only glancing notice. As things are, it is a satisfactory foothill, with the grand old mountain in view. There are no heroics, though there is plenty of calamity. . . . McMurty has a fine time with youthful damnfoolishness, and so does the reader." Time

McMurtry, Larry

The **evening** star. Simon & Schuster 1992 637p
LC 92-2596

Sequel to Terms of endearment

"The success of a book like this one depends on the tone the author manages to muster up. Mr. McMurtry's is sentimentality laced with comic irony, and it works very well. . . . And if, in the end, Aurora Greenway and her extended and highly dysfunctional family turn out to be more entertaining than genuinely moving, it's reassuring to know that they—and the reader—are in the hands of a real pro." N Y Times Book Rev

McMurtry, Larry

★ **Lonesome** dove; a novel. Simon & Schuster 1985 843p hardcover o.p. pa $18
ISBN 0-671-50420-7; 1-4391-9526-9 pa

LC 85-2192

"'Lonesome Dove' shows, early on, just about every symptom of American Epic except pretentiousness. McMurtry has laconic Texas talk and leathery, slim-hipped machismo down pat, and he's able to refresh heroic clichés with exact observations about cowboy prudery, ignorance and fear of losing face." Newsweek

Other titles in the Lonesome dove trilogy are:
Dead man's walk (1995)
Streets of Laredo (1993)

McMurtry, Larry

Rhino Ranch; a novel. Simon & Schuster 2009 278p $26
ISBN 978-1-4391-5639-1; 1-4391-5639-5

LC 2009-19648

With this novel "McMurtry ends the west Texas saga of Duane Moore, begun in 1966 with The Last Picture Show. . . . Duane, now in his late 60s, is a prosperous and retired widower, lonely in his hometown of Thalia, Tex. Then billionaire heiress K.K. Slater moves in and opens the Rhino Ranch, a sanctuary intended to rescue the nearly extinct African black rhinoceros. Slater is a strong-willed, independent woman whose mere presence upsets parochial Thalia, and Duane can't quite figure her out. His two best buddies, Boyd Cotton and Bobby Lee Baxter, both work for Slater, and the three friends schmooze with the rich, talk about geezer sex, rat out local meth heads and try to keep track of a herd of rhinos." Publ Wkly

McMurtry, Larry

Sin killer. Simon & Schuster 2002 300p (Berrybender narratives) $25
ISBN 0-7432-3302-6

LC 2002-17616

"McMurtry's prose is plain and exact, exhibiting the kind of clarity that appears simple yet is anything but." N Y Times Book Rev

McMurtry, Larry

★ **Streets** of Laredo; a novel. Simon & Schuster 1993 589p
LC 93-19279

"As in some great 19th-century saga, the story has more than its share of improbable coincidences—but these seem only mild contrivances to shape a story packed with action, terror, humor and pathos. Laredo is a fitting conclusion to a remarkable feat of reconstruction and sheer storytelling genius." Publ Wkly

McMurtry, Larry

★ **Terms** of endearment; a novel. Simon & Schuster 1975 410p

"Suddenly, just when we are enjoying ourselves the most, McMurtry changes his style, and we are plunged into a moving but agonizing realistic account of daughter Emma's death from cancer at 37 and the way in which her family and old friends react. . . . The shift of pace may throw some readers off stride badly. McMurtry certainly remains, however, one of our most exciting novelists." Publ Wkly

Followed by The evening star

McMurtry, Larry

Zeke and Ned; a novel. by Larry McMurtry and Diana Ossana. Simon & Schuster 1997 478p
LC 96-44906

"What gives this well-wrought tale its depth is how McMurtry and Ossana convey the era's various moral shades of gray." Publ Wkly

McNally, T. M.

The **goat** bridge; a novel. T. M. McNally. University of Michigan Press 2005 310p $29
ISBN 0472115111; 9780472115112

LC 2005008513

This book "follows Stephen Brings, a burnt-out American photographer who is reeling from the unexplained disappearance of his son in Rome, and who finds an unlikely measure of understanding and acceptance in the wartorn Sarajevo of the early '90s. Brings, pointedly not 'covering' the war in any conventional sense, drifts through the city, helping where he can, taking the occasional photograph and forming attachments with a . . . group of locals, diplomats and journalists, including the German journalist Elise, with whom he begins a tentative affair." (Publishers Weekly)

McNeal, Tom

To be sung underwater; 1st ed.; Little, Brown and Company 2011 436 p.
ISBN 9780316127394; 0316127396

LC 2010041554

In this novel, "Judith Whitman, a film editor in California, doesn't seem to like her life, which includes teenage daughter, Camilla, and husband, Malcolm, and so, as she says, she came up with a swerve. 'My life had utterly settled into itself and then this little swerve occurred, or maybe I meant it to occur, maybe I'd actually plotted it out in one of those corners of your brain or heart you access only in dreams.' That swerve took her back to Nebraska and her first love, Willie Blunt. . . . One of them is really in love, and one of them just thinks so. That tempers the underlying structure." (JournalStar.com)

McPhee, Jenny

No ordinary matter; a novel. Free Press 2004 259p $23

ISBN 0-7432-6072-4

LC 2004-43246

"For more than a decade, thirtysomething sisters Lillian and Veronica have met at a Manhattan Hungarian bakery the first Monday of the month. Stunningly beautiful but ice-cold Lillian is a brilliant neurologist. Her lovely younger sister, warmhearted, insecure Veronica, is a scriptwriter for the wildly popular soap opera Ordinary Matters. Veronica has spent a lifetime worshiping her older sister, who unfailingly swats back at Veronica's overtures. In a series of coincidences that would give Victor Hugo pause, the sisters' already complicated and deeply entwined lives become even more so. A dysfunctional childhood (a dead father and a neglectful mother), a pregnancy, a new lover, a psychiatrist with Tourette's syndrome, several independent private investigations into secret second families, a long-lost brother, and other delicious surprises draw the reader in for the fun." Libr J

McPhee, Martha

Gorgeous lies. Harcourt 2002 326p $31

ISBN 0-15-100613-X

LC 2002-7213

Sequel to Bright angel time (1997)

National Book Award Finalist: Fiction (2002)

"In 20 years, many things have changed in the lives of the large Furey-Cooper clan. Once the members were widely known as exemplars of a new kind of blended family, living out the utopian visions of patriarch Anton. Now Anton lies virtually helpless, dying slowly with many dreams unrealized and his magnum opus on human sexuality unwritten. The siblings gather at the family farm, linked painfully not only by grief but also by longtime resentments, disappointments, and misunderstandings that fester as Anton's end approaches." Libr J

McPhee, Martha

L'America. Harcourt 2006 294p $25

ISBN 0-15-101171-1

LC 2005-20986

McPhee "is a brilliant stylist, and here she creates characters so palpably real, they seem to ache on the page. . . . L'America is dizzyingly hypnotic, roaming back and forth across time, telling the story through Cesare, Beth and, later, through Beth's grown daughter, Valeria. The shadow of 9/11 is subtly referenced throughout the story, and its power becomes almost unbearable." Washington Post Book World

McPherson, Catriona

The **child** garden; a novel. by Catriona McPherson. Midnight Ink 2015 312 p. $24.99

ISBN 9780738745497

LC 2014050106

In this novel, by Catriona McPherson, "Eden was its name. 'An alternative school for happy children.' But it closed in disgrace after a student's suicide. Now it's a care home. . . . Gloria Harkness is its only neighbor, staying close to her son who lives in the home. . . . When a childhood friend turns up at her door, . . . [he] claims a girl from Eden is stalking him and has goaded him into meeting near the site of the suicide. Only then, the dead begin to speak—it was murder, they say." (Publisher's note)

"Better known for her "Dandy Gilver" cozies, McPherson has written a terrific stand-alone that is complex, haunting, and magical. Readers who appreciate Kate Atkinson or Audrey Niffeneger for their intricate plotting and character development will be sure to pounce on this stunning title." LJ

McPherson, Catriona

★ **Quiet** neighbors; a novel. Catriona McPherson. Midnight Ink 2016 360 p. $24.99

ISBN 9780738747620; 9780738747811

LC 2015044401

In this novel, by Catriona McPherson, "the oldest bookshop in a town full of bookshops . . . [is] full of treasures if you look hard. Jude found one of the treasures when she visited last summer, the high point of a miserable vacation. Now, in the depths of winter, when she has to run away, Lowell's chaotic bookshop in that backwater of a town is the safe place she runs to." (Publisher's note)

"McPherson's literary observations are delightful, her quirky collection of characters intriguing, and the unfolding mystery highly satisfying." Pub Wkly

Mda, Zakes

★ The **Madonna** of Excelsior. Farrar, Straus and Giroux 2004 258p $23

ISBN 0-374-20008-4

LC 2003-54728

"The voice that emerges suggests not just a writer who can seduce us through beautiful language and unfailing humor. We also encounter a writer who has the power to shock and frighten us, to astound and anger and unsettle us. The Madonna of Excelsior suggests, in short, that his is a voice for which one should feel not only affection but admiration." N Y Times Book Rev

Mda, Zakes

The **whale** caller. Farrar, Straus and Giroux 2005 230p $23

ISBN 0-374-28785-6

LC 2005-14196

"Despite the lighthearted and often hilarious antics, this love triangle, like so many others, is tragically unsustainable. Perhaps this is where The Whale Caller defies expectation: If it is a morality play, these are unusually funny, richly developed characters. If it is a quirky, romantic comedy, it's dispensed with a heaping helping of human frailty, tragic behavior and self-destruction. With an offhanded mastery of lyrical language, this gifted storyteller's prose shimmers without extravagance." Washington Post Book World

Meadows, Rae

★ **I** will send rain; A Novel. Rae Meadows. Henry Holt & Co. 2016 272 p. (ebook) $60; (hardcover) $26

ISBN 9781627794275; 9781627794268

LC 2015046689

In this novel by Rae Meadows, "Annie Bell can't escape the dust. . . . It's 1934 and the Bell farm in Mulehead, Oklahoma is struggling as the earliest storms of The Dust Bowl descend. . . . As the Bells wait for the rains to come, . . . Annie's fragile young son, Fred, suffers from dust pneumonia; her headstrong daughter, Birdie, flush with first love, is choosing a dangerous path out of Mulehead; and Samuel, her husband, is plagued by disturbing dreams of rain." (Publisher's note)

"When tragedy strikes or hope emerges, it makes sense and comes to fruition organically. This makes for a vibrant, absorbing novel that stays with the reader." Pub Wkly

Means, David

★ **Hystopia**; A Novel. David Means. Farrar, Straus & Giroux 2016 352 p. (hardcover) $26

ISBN 9780865479135; 0865479135

LC 2015035421

This alternate history novel by David Means is set at the end of the 1960s, when "President John F. Kennedy is entering his third term in office. The Vietnam War rages on, and the president has created . . . the Psych Corps, dedicated to maintaining the nation's mental hygiene by any means. . . . Soldiers returning from the war have their battlefield traumas 'enfolded'—wiped from their memories through drugs and therapy—while veterans too damaged to be enfolded roam at will." (Publisher's note)

"Means' first novel is a compelling portrait of an imagined counterhistory that feels entirely real." Kirkus

Means, David

The **secret** goldfish; stories. Fourth Estate 2004 211p

ISBN 0-00-716489-0

LC 2004-50617

"With stunning simplicity, Means offers 15 stirring portraits of tragedy, loss, and love." Esquire

Medeiros, Teresa

The **Temptation** of Your Touch. Pocket Books 2013 432 p. (paperback) $7.99

ISBN 1439157901; 9781439157909

In this book, "after his fiancée abandons him at the altar to marry his brother, Max Burke flees London for the isolation of a ramshackle, reputedly haunted castle in Cornwall, where he'll contend with a surly, secretive staff, a mesmerizing portrait of a woman-turned-ghost and a housekeeper he's tempted to strangle—or seduce." (Kirkus)

Medlicott, Joan A.

The **ladies** of Covington send their love; [by] Joan Medlicott. St. Martin's Press 2000 326p

ISBN 0-312-25329-X

LC 99-89922

"The women grow in self-confidence until one publishes a book, one finds love, and one runs a physically demanding business. The ending is pure fantasy, but readers will enjoy the ride." Libr J

Meek, James

The **heart** broke in; James Meek. Farrar, Straus and Giroux 2012 401 p. (hardcover : alk. paper) $28.00

ISBN 0374168717; 9780374168711

LC 2012012377

This novel, by James Meek, is "about everything that matters to us now: children, celebrity, secrets and shame, the quest for youth, loyalty and betrayal, falls from grace, acts of terror, and the wonderful, terrible inescapability of family." It follows the family dynamics of "an aging pop star and a producer of a reality show for teen talent, . . . the editor of a powerful tabloid newspaper, . . . a gene therapist, . . ." and a just-released prison convict." (Publisher's note)

Meek, James

The **people's** act of love. Canongate 2005 391p $24

ISBN 1-841-95706-2

LC 2005-363497

"Thrown together in a remote Siberian village during the civil war that followed the Russian Revolution, the leader of a sect of Christian castrates and an escaped convict who aspires to be a terrorist revolutionary play out the fatal logic of, respectively, religious and political extremism. Meek expertly renders each man's devotion to the task of securing paradise on earth, and exposes the unsettling affinity between the devout servant of God and the cold, calculating murderer. The higher purpose assumed by Meek's tormented believers is mocked by the novel's subsidiary characters, a lusty village woman and the Jewish lieutenant of an occupying Czech legion." New Yorker

Mehta, Gita

Raj; a novel. Simon & Schuster 1989 479p

LC 88-38504

"Grounded in details of ancient royal tradition and Hindu ritual, Jaya's story counterpoints a vanished way of life against the complex political realities involved in the passing of the Raj and the birth of the modern nations of India and Pakistan." Publ Wkly

Mehta, Gita

A **river** Sutra. Doubleday 1993 291p

LC 92-35779

"This is an idealized India, free of political and religious violence. 'A River Sutra' takes place in a fabled land of the romantic imagination, drawing on timeless literary traditions. Told with skill and sensitivity, Gita Mehta's tales are a delight to read, bringing to Western readers the mystery and drama of a rich cultural heritage." N Y Times Book Rev

Mehta, Rahul

Quarantine; stories. Rahul Mehta. Harper Perennial 2011 214 p.

ISBN 0062020455; 9780062020451

LC 2010053604

This collection of "stories . . . revolve[s] around artsy, educated protagonists trying to navigate young adulthood as gay Indian-American men. In the title story, a young Indian-American man takes his boyfriend, Jeremy, home to West Virginia to meet his parents. . . . The narrator resents having to hide the fact that he is in a gay relationship from his grandfather, and has conflicted feelings when the old man hits it off with Jeremy. . . . While the older generation struggles to adjust to life in the States, the first- or second-generation protagonists encounter their own identity crises as well. In 'Floating,' Darnell and his boyfriend, Sid, take a trip to India, where they juggle the pain of homophobia and the guilt of privilege after having been scammed." (Publishers Weekly)

Melamed, Jennie

★ **Gather** the daughters; a novel. Jennie Melamed. Little, Brown & Co. 2017 341 p. (hardcover) $26

ISBN 9780316463652; 9780316501408

LC 2016950142

In this book, by Jennie Melamed, "years ago, just before the country was incinerated to wasteland, ten men and their families colonized an island off the coast. They built a radical society of ancestor worship, controlled breeding, and the strict rationing of knowledge and history. Only the Wanderers--chosen male descendants of the original ten--are allowed to cross to the wastelands. . . . The daughters of these men are wives-in-training." (Publisher's note)

"Melamed's haunting and powerful debut blazes a fresh path in the tradition of classic dystopian works." Pub Wkly

Meloy, Maile

Do not become alarmed; a novel. Maile Meloy. Riverhead Books 2017 342 p. (hardback) $27

ISBN 0735216525; 9780735216525

LC 2016051263

In this novel by Maile Meloy "when Liv and Nora decide to take their husbands and children on a holiday cruise, everyone is thrilled. The four children--ages six to eleven--love the nonstop buffet and their newfound independence. But when they all go ashore for an adventure in Central America, a series of minor misfortunes and miscalculations leads the families farther from the safety of the ship. One minute the children are there, and the next they're gone." (Publisher's note)

"This writer can apparently do it all--New Yorker stories, children's books, award-winning literary novels, and now, a tautly plotted and culturally savvy emotional thriller. Do not start this book after dinner or you will almost certainly be up all night." Kirkus

Meloy, Maile

A **family** daughter; a novel. Scribner 2006 325p $24

ISBN 0-7432-7766-X

LC 2005-51574

"It's 1979, and seven-year-old Abby, the youngest member of the close-knit Santerre family, is trapped indoors with the chicken pox during a heat wave. The events set in motion that summer will span decades and contents [and] change the Santerres forever." (Publisher's note)

"Continuing the family saga of her first novel, 'Liars and Saints.' Meloy's second follows Abby Collins from the age of seven, when her feckless mother and sober father separate, to her success as a young novelist. The kernel of the story is a melodrama involving her uncle Jamie, who rescues her first from the boredom of her childhood illness and then, later, from grief after the sudden death of her father. When a mutual sexual attraction develops, though, Abby must learn to rescue herself, which she does mainly by recasting the dilemmas of her extended family as a work of fiction. All this might easily come off as soap opera were Meloy not a wise and astonishing conjurer of convincing realities." New Yorker

Meloy, Maile

Liars and saints; a novel. Scribner 2003 260p $24

ISBN 0-7432-4435-4

LC 2002-30852

"Meloy's unerring mastery of narrative is remarkable. The disciplined economy and resonant clarity of her prose allow her to present a complex story in swift, lean chapters. The alternating points of view of eight main characters shine with authenticity and illuminate the moral complexities felt by each generation." Publ Wkly

Meltzer, Brad

The **inner** circle. Grand Central Pub. 2011 449p $26.99

ISBN 978-0-446-57789-2

LC 2010-36506

"Beecher White is an archivist with the National Archives, who stumbles upon an old book hidden away in a room used exclusively by the president. But did the president know that the book (a spelling dictionary that once belonged to George Washington) was there? And—almost impossible for Beecher to imagine—could it be that the president or someone close to him is willing to kill to regain possession of the book? . . . Meltzer expertly develops the story, throwing in twists and turns at appropriate intervals, and he does an excellent job of putting us in Beecher's corner and making us care about what happens to him." Booklist

Other titles in this series are:

The fifth assassin (2013)

The President's shadow (2015)

Meltzer, Brad

The **tenth** justice. Morrow 1997 389p

ISBN 0-688-15089-6

LC 96-44815

"Just out of Yale Law School, . . . {Ben Addison's} already landed the highly desirable top job of clerk to a Supreme Court justice, experiences instant chemistry with his new co-clerk Lisa, and shares an apartment with three lifelong friends. Then a misplaced trust leads Ben to reveal a confidential court decision. . . . With Ben's career in jeopardy and a blackmailer on his trail, his friends use their job connections at the State Department, a Washington newspaper, and a senator's office to aid Ben and Lisa in a plot to apprehend Ben's blackmailer." (Libr J)

"Meltzer moves the story along at a crisp pace, spicing the action and legalese with lively banter and intriguing D.C. arcana." Publ Wkly

Meltzer, Brad

The **zero** game. Warner Bks. 2004 460p $25.95

ISBN 0-446-53098-0

LC 2003-15157

This thriller is "packed with plenty of backroom D.C. ambience and lots of action." Booklist

Melville, Herman

★ **Billy** Budd, sailor; supplementary material written by Kathleen Helal. Pocket Books 2006 xxi, 166p pa $4.99

ISBN 978-1-416-52372-7; 1-416-52372-3

LC 2006-299200

Written in 1891 but in a still unfinished manuscript stage when Melville died. First publication 1924 in the United Kingdom, as part of the Standard edition of Melville's complete works

'Narrates the hatred of petty officer Claggart by Billy, handsome Spanish sailor. Billy strikes and kills Claggart, and is condemned by Captain Vere even though the latter senses Billy's spiritual innocence.' Haydn. Thesaurus of Book Dig

Includes bibliographical references

Melville, Herman

The **complete** shorter fiction; with an introduction by John Updike. Knopf 1997 478p $20

ISBN 0-375-40068-0

Contents: The piazza; Bartleby, the scrivener; Benito Cereno; The lightning-rod man; The encantadas; or, Enchanted isles; The bell-tower; Fragments from a writing desk; Authentic anecdotes of ¿Old Zack¿; Hawthorne and his mosses; The happy failure; The fiddler; Cock-a-doodle-doo!; Poor man's pudding; Rich man's crumbs; The two temples: Temple second; The paradise of bachelors; The tartarus of maids; Jimmy Rose; The 'gees; I and my chimney; The apple-tree table; Billy Budd, sailor; The two temples: Temple first

Melville, Herman

The **confidence**-man: his masquerade; edited, with an introduction and notes by John Bryant. Modern Library 2003 xlix, 331p pa $11.95

ISBN 0-375-75802-X

LC 2003-44561

First published 1857

"The scene is a Mississippi River boat, ironically named the 'Fidele.' A plotless satire taking place on April Fool's Day, the book is filled with characters difficult to distinguish from one another; most of them are different manifestations of the confidence man. A sign hanging on the door of the 'Fidele's' barbershop expresses the theme: 'No Trust.' The confidence man, king of a world without principle, succeeds in gulling men by capitalizing on false hopes and offering false pity. At the end of the book, the flickering light hanging above the table where an old man reads the Bible goes out completely." Reader's Ency. 4th edition

Melville, Herman

★ **Moby**-Dick; or, The whale; illustrated by Rockwell Kent. Modern Library 1992 xxxv, 822p il $21

ISBN 0-679-60010-8

LC 92-50222

First published 1851

"'Moby-Dick' had some initial critical appreciation, particularly in Britain, but only since the 1920s has it been recognized as a masterpiece, an epic tragedy of tremendous dramatic power and narrative drive." Oxford Companion to Engl Lit. 5th edition

Melville, Herman

Omoo: a narrative of adventures in the South Seas; edited by Harrison Hayford, Hershel Parker, G. Thomas Tanselle. Northwestern University Press 1999 316p pa $16.95

ISBN 0-8101-1765-7

LC 99-41391

First published 1847 by Harper

"Based on Melville's own experiences in the South Pacific, this episodic novel, in a more comical vein than that of Typee, tells of the narrator's participation in a mutiny on a whale ship and his subsequent wanderings in Tahiti with the former doctor of the ship." Merriam-Webster's Ency of Lit

Melville, Herman

Pierre; or, The ambiquities, Israel Potter: his fifty years of exile, The piazza tales, The confidence-man: his masquerade, Uncollected prose, Billy Budd, Sailor: (an inside narrative) Library of America 1984 1478p $45

ISBN 0-940450-24-0

LC 84-11249

Pierre; or, The Ambiguities (1852) "moves between the idyllic Berkshire countryside and the nightmare landscape of early New York City. Its hero, a young American patrician trying to redeem the secret sins of his father, elopes to the city, discovers Bohemian life, attempts a literary epic, and struggles his way through incest, murder, and madness. . . . Israel Potter [1855, is] the story of a veteran of the Revolution, victim of a thousand mischances, and a long-suffering exile in England. . . . The Piazza Tales [1856, is a collection of six stories], including 'The Encantadas,' about nature's two faces—enchanting and horrific; the famous 'Bartleby the Scrivener,' about a Wall Street copyist who 'would prefer not to'; and the enigmatic 'Benito Cereno,' about a credulous Yankee sea captain who stumbles into an intricately plotted mutiny aboard a disabled slave ship. The Confidence-Man [1857], Melville's last published novel, is in many ways a forerunner of modernist American fiction. . . . Many pieces never before collected are also included. . . . Finally, there is the posthumously published masterpiece Billy Budd, Sailor, the haunting story of a beautiful, innocent sailor who is pressed into naval service, slandered, provoked to murder, and sacrificed to military justice." Publisher's note

Melville, Herman

Redburn, his first voyage; White-jacket, or, The world in a man-of-war; Moby-Dick, or, The whale. Literary Classics of the United States, Inc, Distributed to the trade by the Viking Press 1983 1437p $35

ISBN 0-940450-09-7

LC 82-18677

Redburn (1849) is a semiautobiographical novel about a young man's ill-fortuned trip across the Atlantic. White-jacket (1850), another semi-autobiographical novel, centers around a young sailor nicknamed for the white jacket that he buys in Peru and wears throughout the novel. It also features an appearance by Jack Chase, a character who appears in several of Melville's works and who is here the first captain of the top, and a vivid description of the floggings and other punishments suffered by the crew for often minor infractions. Moby-Dick is entered separately.

Includes bibliographical references

Melville, Herman

Typee: a peep at Polynesian life. Northwestern Univ. Press 1968 374p il $75

ISBN 0-8101-0161-0

First published 1846

"Based on Melville's own experiences, the story tells of the hero and his friend Toby, who jump ship in the Marquesas Islands and wander mistakenly into the valley of Typee, which is inhabited by cannibals. The Typees become their benevolent captors, refusing to allow them to leave. Toby escapes, while the hero, suffering from a leg wound, remains to be nursed by the lovely Fayaway. Tempted to enjoy a somnolent, vegetative existence, the moral American chooses, with regret, to return to civilization." Reader's Ency. 4th edition

Melville, Herman

Typee: a peep at Polynesian life; Omoo: a narrative of adventures in the South Seas; Mardi: and a voyager thither. Library of Am. 1982 1333p $40

ISBN 0-940450-00-3

LC 81-18600

Omnibus edition of the author's first three novels. The first two titles are entered separately. In Mardi, first published 1849, Melville "entertained questions of ethics and metaphysics, politics and culture, sin and guilt, innocence and experience. The complexity of the novel's content, in fact, destroys all pretensions to literary form. Originally a narrative of adventure, 'Mardi' became an allegory of mind." Benet's Reader's Ency of Am Lit

Mengestu, Dinaw, 1978-

★ **All** our names; by Dinaw Mengestu. Alfred A. Knopf 2014 272 p. (hardcover) $25.95

ISBN 038534998X; 9780345805669; 9780385349987

LC 2013031632

Author Dinaw Mengestu presents a "love story about a searing affair between an American woman and an African man in 1970s America and an unflinching novel about the fragmentation of lives that straddle countries and histories. Yet this idyll is inescapably darkened by the secrets of his past: the acts he committed and the work he left unfinished. Most of all, he is haunted by the beloved friend he left behind, the charismatic leader who first guided him to revolution." (Publisher's note)

"Mengestu . . . portrays the intersection of cultures experienced by the immigrant with unsettling perception." Pub Wkly

Mengestu, Dinaw, 1978-

The **beautiful** things that heaven bears. Riverhead Books 2006 228p $22.95

ISBN 1-59448-940-8; 978-1-59448-940-2

LC 2006-25058

"Seventeen years ago, Sepha Stephanos fled the Ethiopian Revolution after witnessing soldiers beat his father to the point of certain death, selling off his parents' jewelry to pay for passage to the United States. Now he finds himself running a grocery store in a poor African-American neighborhood in Washington, D.C." (Publisher's note)

"A tender, thoughtful novel that quietly takes on serious themes: the meaning of home and family, of nationality and exile, of isolation and connection." People

Mengestu, Dinaw, 1978-

How to read the air. Riverhead Books 2010 305p $25.95

ISBN 1-59448-770-7; 978-1-59448-770-5

LC 2010-03045

"One early September afternoon, Yosef and Mariam, young Ethiopian immigrants who have spent all but their first year of marriage apart, set off on a road trip from their new home in Peoria, Illinois, to Nashville, Tennessee, in search of a new identity as an American couple. Soon, their son, Jonas, will be born in Illinois. Thirty years later, Yosef has died, and Jonas needs to make sense of the volatile generational and cultural ties that have forged him. How can he envision his future without knowing what has come before? Leaving behind his marriage and job in New York, Jonas sets out to retrace his mother and father's trip and weave together a family history that will take him from the war-torn Ethiopia of his parents' youth to his life in the America of today, a story—real or invented—that holds the possibility of reconciliation and redemption." (Publisher's note)

"Mengestu's lyrical prose makes each layer upon layer of story a satisfying read, despite the book's sometimes unbearable sense of foreboding. It's hard not to root for Jonas, even during his most misguided attempts to engage. It's hard not to ache for Jonas, wondering if he'll ever find his place." Seattle Times

Meno, Joe

The **boy** detective fails. Akashic 2006 320p pa $14.95

ISBN 1-933354-10-0

LC 2006-923114

"In their youth, Billy Argo, his kid sister Caroline, and their friend Fenton solved a series of puzzling crimes with only a cheap detective kit and their imaginations. After Billy goes to college to study criminology, Caroline commits suicide and guilt-ridden Billy attempts it, ending up heavily sedated in a mental hospital. Ten years later, he connects with two other outcast, nerdy sorts to help solve the mysteries going on in their lives and in that of a kleptomaniac widow who is as fragile and traumatized as he is. The one mystery he can't solve is Caroline's death. This is postmodern fiction with a head and a heart, addressing such depressing issues as suicide, death, loneliness, failure, anomie, and guilt with compassion, humor, and even whimsy." Libr J

Meno, Joe

Marvel and a wonder; Joe Meno. Akashic Books 2015 336 p. (hardcover) $29.95

ISBN 1617753939; 9781617753930

LC 2015934078

This novel, by Joe Meno, awarded Booklist Editors' Choice for 2015 and longlisted for the American Library Association's 2016 Andrew Carnegie Medal for Excellence in Fiction, is "set at the end of the twentieth century. In summer 1995, Jim Falls, a Korean War vet, struggles to raise his sixteen-year-old grandson, Quentin, on a farm in southern Indiana. In July, they receive a mysterious gift--a beautiful quarter horse--which upends the balance of their difficult lives." (Publisher's note)

"Narrating with piercing empathy in the indelible voices of his characters, Meno parallels the frantic search for the racehorse, an embodiment of nature's pure glory, with the complicated troubles of a coltish young woman on the run. Evoking William Faulkner and Cormac McCarthy, Meno's suspenseful, mordantly incisive, many-layered tale can also be read as an equine Moby-Dick." Booklist

Merey, Ilike

A + e 4ever; a graphic novel. Lethe Press 2011 214 p.

ISBN 1590213904; 9781590213902

This book tells the story of "Asher Machnik [who] is a teenage boy cursed with a beautiful androgynous face. Guys punch him, girls slag him and by high school he's developed an intense fear of being touched. Art remains his only escape from an otherwise emotionally empty life. Eulalie Mason is the lonely, tough-talking . . . [lesbian] from school who befriends Ash. The only one to see and accept all of his sides as a loner, a fellow artist and a best friend, she's starting to wonder if Ash is ever going to see all of her. . . . [The book] is a graphic novel set in that ambiguous crossroads where love and friendship, boy and girl, straight and gay meet." (Publisher's note)

Merimee, Prosper

★ **Carmen**; translated from the French and illustrated by Edmund H. Garrett, with a memoir of the author by Louise Imogen Guiney. Little, Brown 1896 xxx, 117p il

Original French edition, 1845

"Georges Bizet's opera Carmen is based on the story. As a hot-blooded young corporal in the Spanish cavalry stationed near Seville, Don José is ordered to arrest Carmen, a young, flirtatious Gypsy woman, for assaulting a coworker. Greatly charmed by her, José allows her to escape. He deserts the army, kills two men on Carmen's account, and takes up a life as a robber and smuggler. He is insanely jealous of Carmen, who is unfaithful to him, and when she refuses to change on his behalf, he kills her and surrenders himself to the authorities." Merriam-Webster's Ency of Lit

Merullo, Roland

Breakfast with Buddha; a novel. Algonquin Books of Chapel Hill 2007 323p $23.95

ISBN 978-1-56512-552-0; 1-56512-552-5

LC 2007-7978

"Somewhere between bowling and yoga class, Rinpoche teaches Otto to examine himself, and readers will be rooting for the success of this unlikely pair. Merullo's clear writing ensures that readers will master Rinpoche's sometimes cryptic reflections as well." BookPage

Followed by Lunch with Buddha (2012) and Dinner with Buddha (2015)

Merullo, Roland

The **talk**-funny girl; Roland Merullo. Crown Publishers 2011 x, 304p.p

ISBN 9780307452924; 0307452921

LC 2011003328

Alex Award (2012)

This book tells the story of "seventeen-year-old- Marjorie Richards . . . [who] has been raised by parents so intentionally isolated from normal society that they have developed their own dialect . . . as the nearby factory town sinks deeper into economic ruin and as her parents fall more completely under the influence of a sadistic cult leader, her options for escape dwindle. But then, thanks to a loving aunt, Marjorie is hired by a man . . . who is building what he calls 'a cathedral,' right in the center of town. . . . Gradually, through exposure to the world beyond her parents' wood cabin thanks to the kindness of her aunt and her boss, and an almost superhuman determination, she discovers what is loveable within herself." (Publisher's note)

Merullo, Roland

Vatican waltz; Roland Merullo. Crown Publishing Group 2013 304 p. (hardcover) $24

ISBN 0307452956; 9780307452955

LC 2013003075

In this novel, by Roland Merullo, "Cynthia Piantedosi lives a quiet, unassuming life . . . guided by her Catholic faith. When she . . . begins experiencing 'spells' of such intense spiritual intimacy . . . , she wonders about her sanity. . . . A message begins to emerge from Cynthia's prayers: God is calling her to be the first female Catholic priest. . . . Unable to tune out the divine messages, she lets the power of unswerving faith drive her all the way to the Vatican." (Publisher's note)

"A fresh, moving portrait of religion as it could and should be." Kirkus

Messud, Claire

The **emperor's** children. Alfred A. Knopf 2006 431p $25

ISBN 0-307-26419-X

LC 2005-57783

The author "writes with the archness of a Muriel Spark, only more subtly and sympathetically wielded. . . . Ultimately, most impressive is the way Messud relates 9/11 to her characters' lives: The public tragedy doesn't eclipse but rather seeps into and amplifies their private sorrows." Nation

Messud, Claire

★ The **woman** upstairs; a novel. Claire Messud. 1st ed. Alfred A. Knopf 2013 253 p. (hardcover) $25.95; (ebook) $77.85

ISBN 0307596907; 9780307596901; 9780307962409

LC 2012017806

In this book by Claire Messud, "elementary school teacher Nora Eldridge . . . [has] sold out her artistic dreams for success and stability, and become angry and full of self-loathing somewhere along the way. But when a young student, Reza Shahid, and his family enter her life, Nora finds herself changing as she is drawn into the Shahids' world." (Publishers Weekly)

Meyer, Deon

Devil's peak; a novel. translated by K.L. Seegers. Little, Brown 2008 409p $24.99

ISBN 0-316-01785-X; 978-0-316-01785-5

LC 2007-30129

Original Afrikaans edition, 2004; this translation first published 2007 in the United Kingdom

"Former mercenary Thobela Mpayipheli is trying to live a peaceful life, but these plans are shattered when his eight-year-old son, Pakamile, is shot dead. The two gunmen responsible escape before sentencing, and the grieving father decides to take matters into his own hands. As he pursues his son's killers, Mpayipheli begins to target pedophiles and other perpetrators of violence against children, meting out justice with a Xhosa tribal sword called an assegai. Dubbed 'Artemis' by the papers as the killings increase, Mpayipheli becomes a kind of folk hero to the people of Capetown. Insp. Benny Griessel, an aging alcoholic whose struggles with the bottle have all but cost him his family and his life, works the case with a desperate intensity." Publ Wkly

Other titles about Benny Griessel are:

Thirteen hours (2010)

Seven days (2012)

Cobra (2014)

Icarus (2015)

Meyer, Deon

Heart of the hunter; translated by K. L. Seegers. Little, Brown 2004 374p $23.95

ISBN 0-316-93549-2

LC 2003-25683

"Despite the complexity of its tightly woven plot-skillfully revealed through newspaper articles and intelligence reports-Meyer's U.S. debut moves at a breathtaking pace that will carry readers away. A sympathetic protagonist and the landscape of South Africa add color to the story." Libr J

Meyer, Deon

Trackers; translanted from Afrikaans by K.L. Seegers. Atlantic Monthly Press 2011 488 p. map

ISBN 080211993X; 9780802119933; 9781444723656

LC 2012358359

In this book, "Lemmer, a freelance bodyguard, goes against his rule to not get involved when a wealthy farmer asks for his help smuggling a pair of rare black rhinos out of Zimbabwe, where the animals are murdered for their horns. Before he knows it, Lemmer is in a small airplane, zipping across the border with an airsickness bag in his hand and a military-grade shotgun at his feet. . . . Back in Cape Town, Milla Strachan, the emotionally abused wife of a philandering husband and the mother of a cruel teenage son, . . . start[s] a new life . . . [and] find[s] work as a journalist and Milla takes what she can get--in this case, a classified job writing intelligence reports. . . . Connecting Milla and Lemmer is Mat Joubert, a former detective working on his first case as a private eye." (Publisher's note)

Meyer, Nicholas

The **seven**-per-cent solution; being a reprint from the reminiscences of John H. Watson, M.D., as edited by Nicholas Meyer. Dutton 1974 253p

"In a field replete with pastiche Meyer succeeds because of a superior ear for Conan Doyle's style, a gentle sense of fun, and a talent for plot that few of the imitators have possessed." Libr J

Meyer, Philipp

American rust. Spiegel & Grau 2009 368p $24.95

ISBN 978-0-385-52751-4; 0-385-52751-9

LC 2008-22461

The author "conjures up this blue-collar Rust Belt town with the same sort of social detail and emotional verisimilitude that Richard Russo has brought to his depictions of upstate New York and Russell Banks has brought to downstate New Hampshire. He writes about his characters' lives in Buell with sympathy and unsentimental clarity." N Y Times (Late N Y Ed)

Meyer, Philipp

★ The **Son**; Philipp Meyer. HarperCollins 2013 viii, 561 p.p (hardcover) $27.99

ISBN 0062120395; 9780062120397

This historical family novel, by Philipp Meyer, presents "an epic of the American West and a multigenerational saga of power, blood, land, and oil that follows the rise of one [prominent] . . . Texas family, from the Comanche raids of the 1800s to the to the oil booms of the 20th century." (Publisher's note)

Meyers, Kent

The **work** of wolves. Harcourt 2004 416p $24

ISBN 0-15-101057-9

LC 2003-26365

Meyer's "spare dialogue is brilliantly and often comically expressive, and Carson, his taciturn, rational hero, is an original and compelling character. Strong themes of generational responsibility and family history add resonance to this gratifying, very American novel." Publ Wkly

Miasha, 1981-

Chaser; Miasha. Simon & Schuster 2009 211 p.

ISBN 1416589864; 9781416589860

LC 2009011380

In this novel, "Leah Baker is in trouble. Her boyfriend, Kenny, is . . . determined to kill her . . . [then] the novel flashes back five months earlier as Leah, whose toxic relationship with Kenny is all about being draped in money, is angry at Kenny's lack of attention. She [meets] one of Kenny's helpers, Nasir, who is a chaser running a scam on accident victims by towing their cars to a shady repair shop." (Libr J)

"[Leah and Nasir] quickly become lovers and soon business partners. She helps him discover his inner hustler and he shows her the way to independence. Together they work every angle and scheme of the wreck-chasing business, regardless of the law, until they find themselves at the top. But they've angered many on their way up and there are many who want to see them fall." (Publisher's note)

Michaels, Anne

Fugitive pieces. Knopf 1997 294p

ISBN 0-679-45439-X

LC 96-36678

First publishd 1996 in Canada

Michaels "offers a richly imagined portrait of Jakob's slow progress from reticence to poetic eloquence and of the complex blend of memories, feelings, insights, and experiences that makes him the man he becomes. She even tackles the perpetually troubling question of how so many seemingly ordinary, 'civilized' people could have eagerly committed such monstrous crimes against defenseless children and civilians." Christ Sci Monit

Michaels, Barbara

Houses of stone. Simon & Schuster 1993 334p

LC 93-27926

"Michaels sets her heroine, Professor Karen Holloway, to the task of discovering the provenance of a remnant from an old manuscript. Holloway is convinced that it is a thinly disguised autobiographical novel by an obscure feminist poet whose verses have already helped Holloway carve a niche in the cutthroat business of academia. The professor's archenemies, two fellow literature experts, are equally convinced of the work's value and attempt desperate measures to gain access of the manuscript. Michaels has composed a mystery that is brimming with suspense yet revolves around authorial research rather than money and multiple murders." Booklist

Michaels, Barbara

Stitches in time. HarperCollins Pubs. 1995 307p

ISBN 0-06-017763-2

LC 95-4286

A "mystery based on a haunted quilt. Rachel Grant is a doctoral student working on her thesis—an investigation of women's garments designed for important rites of passage—when she takes a part-time job at a chic vintage clothing shop run by two women, Kara and her sister-in-law Cheryl. When Cheryl's police officer husband is shot, Rachel is drawn into the family because she moves into Cheryl's home, which is connected to the shop. Meanwhile, the message from the quilt lures Rachel into dangerous misdeeds. The unraveling of the mystery proves fascinating." Booklist

Michaels, Leonard

The **collected** stories. Farrar, Straus and Giroux 2007 403p $26

ISBN 978-0-374-12654-4; 0-374-12654-2

LC 2006-102556

"Michaels never stopped reflecting on the condition of being Jewish. Now that he is gone, it is easier to place him in a broader context, as part of that astonishing flowering of American Jewish writing that included Bellow, Malamud, Mailer and Roth, toward which he can be seen as both filial heir and mischievous critic." Nation

Michels, Elizabeth

The **rebel** heir; Elizabeth Michels. Sourcebooks Casablanca 2016 411 p. (Spare heirs) (paperback) $7.99

ISBN 9781492621386; 9781492621362; 1492621366

In this novel, by Elizabeth Michels, "to please her family, . . . [Lady Evangeline Green] masquerades as the perfect debutante...until she meets . . . Lord Crosby. . . . Ash is not Lord Crosby. He's a con artist, a noble Spare Heir living off his silver tongue. When the Green family ruined his, he swore he'd make them pay . . . until he met Evangeline. . . . [W]hat's a con to do but deceive all of London and steal the one lady who dared match wits with the devil himself?" (Publisher's note)

"Michels expertly delivers a heart-wrenching romance that will leave the reader eagerly anticipating future installments." Pub Wkly

Michener, James A.

★ The **bridges** at Toko-ri. Random House 1953 146p

"In this hard-hitting novel of the Korean conflict, Admiral George Tarrant commands the Naval Task Force, whose carrier-based jets are to knock out strategic points throughout Korea. The focal point of the novel is Harry Brubaker, a lawyer who goes reluctantly to war after being called up as a jet pilot. The reader will remember also Beer Barrel, the landing officer who can get the jets back on the carrier's decks, no matter how rough the seas; and Mike Forney, helicopter rescue pilot who gets pilots out of the freezing waters if they are downed." Shapiro. Fic for Youth. 3d edition

Michener, James A.

Caravans; a novel. Random House 1963 341p

The story, set in Afghanistan in the year 1946, "focuses on Ellen Jasper, an American bored with her native land, who flees to Afghanistan to become the second wife of a man named Nazrullah. Her parents haven't heard from her in 13 months and Mark Miller, of the U.S. Embassy in that country, is sent to investigate. The search takes Miller into unknown territory. He joins a nomad tribe and experiences a love affair of rare beauty with Mira, daughter of the Great Zulfiqar, chieftain of all the nomadic peoples scattered around Afghanistan. {The novel describes} Ellen's degeneration into a sensualist, {and} the encounter of Miller (a Jew) with an ex-Nazi who tortured Jews." America

Michener, James A.

Caribbean. Random House 1989 672p

LC 89-42785

A novel about the "Caribbean islands from the days when the peace-loving Arawak Indians were overpowered by cannibalistic Caribs, to a ship's tour of today's still lush, but troubled, paradise. Sir Francis Drake, pirate Henry Morgan, Horatio Nelson, Haitian General Toussaint L'Ouverture, Fidel Castro march across the pages, and while the pace is sometimes achingly slow, the dialogue stilted and the characterization skimpy, Michener laces the whole with fiery Caribbean drama." Publ Wkly

Michener, James A.

★ **Centennial**. Random House 1974 909p

"Written to celebrate the United States centennial, the book centers on a fictional town in Colorado. It begins with an examination of the geological formation of the land and a discussion of the first animals to live there. It continues with the arrival of the Indians, the coming of the first settlers, the traders, the search for gold, the building of the railroads, and the start of cattle ranching—virtually all the activities that made this country develop as it did. The conclusion brings us to the social and ecological problems of the 1970s." Shapiro. Fic for Youth. 3d edition

Michener, James A.

Chesapeake. Random House 1978 865p

LC 78-2892

"Through the interwoven stories of three families and the Indians, Blacks, and Irish immigrants with whom they interact, Michener chronicles four centuries of life on Maryland's Eastern Shore. . . . Michener elaborates . . . variations on his themes of personal accountability for social change, man's self-expulsion from paradise, and the interrelated ecological network of all things." Libr J

Michener, James A.

The **covenant**. Random House 1980 887p

LC 80-5315

This novel spans 500 years of South African history. Three families mingle "with the outstanding historic figures of their times. They are the Nxumalos, the Van Doorns, and the Saltwoods, representing respectively the African, Afrikaans, and English. . . . Over several hundred years their descendants make contact, and thrive through the contact, only to become adversaries as contact subsequently gives way to conflict. Finally they find themselves irretrievably stuck in the hard concrete of South Africa's racial policies." Christ Sci Monit

Michener, James A.

Hawaii. Random House 1959 937p

"High-domed, long-haired littérateurs may argue that Michener's characters are often as paper-thin as the colored image in which Hawaii is held by mainland tourists, but 'Hawaii,' is still a masterful job of research, an absorbing performance of storytelling, and a monumental account of the islands from geologic birth to sociological emergence as the newest, and perhaps the most interesting of the United States." Saturday Rev

Michener, James A.

Mexico. Random House 1992 625p

LC 92-50151

"There are splendid and authentic scenes in the plaza de toros that are as dramatic as any written by Ernest Hemingway or Barnaby Conrad, and one chapter, where the bulls' horns are shaved by the father of a torero, is James Michener the storyteller and parabolist at his finest." N Y Times Book Rev

Michener, James A.

Space. Random House 1982 622p

LC 82-40127

"Michener has caught the essence of what motivated and then enfeebled our space program. . . . As usual, Michener has done his homework, this time with affection and excitement as well—his pro-space enthusiasm is the book's driving force, and he has deftly woven an incredible amount of information into the tale." Natl Rev

Mieville, China

The **city** & the city. Del Rey Ballantine Books 2009 312p $26

ISBN 978-0-345-49751-2; 0-345-49751-1

LC 2009-13775

"A murder mystery set in two cities, Ul Qoma and Beszel, one rich and one poor, where residents have been trained to 'unsee' each other in order to coexist. . . . The story takes the form of a police procedural as the protagonist, Inspector Tyador Borlú of the Extreme Crime Squad, tries to crack the murder case. There are no elves or UFOs. Instead, the story focuses on the lengths to which people will go to enforce borders and maintain separate cultural identities. Evoking such writers as Franz Kafka and Mikhail Bulgakov, Mr. Miéville asks readers to make conceptual leaps and not to simply take flights of fancy." Wall Street J

Mieville, China

Embassytown. Ballantine Books 2011 345p $26

ISBN 978-0-345-52449-2

LC 2011-02854

"It's a joy to find this young author coming into his own, and bringing the craft of science fiction out of the backwaters where it's been caught lately between the regressive drag of publishers marketing to a 'safe' readership and the bewildering promises of change and growth offered by postmodernism in all its forms and formlessness. Embassytown is a fully achieved work of art. Only the trash forms of science fiction are undemanding and predictable; the good stuff, like all good fiction, is not for lazy minds. Where the complexity of realistic novels is moral and psychological, in science fiction it's moral and intellectual; individual character is seldom the key. But Miéville's characters are deftly sketched, and his narrator-protagonist, Avice, is a subtler portrait than she seems at first." Guardian (UK)

Mieville, China

Kraken; an anatomy. Del Rey/Ballantine Books 2010 509p $26

ISBN 978-0-345-49749-9; 0-345-49749-X

LC 2010-13893

"With his tale of a giant-squid corpse, Miéville, never predictable, lobs a grenade into the urban-fantasy genre, remaking it into wild comedy. To wit: A perfectly preserved Architeuthis dux specimen — percolating in the bowels of London's Natural History Museum — vanishes, plunging curator Billy Harrow into a bizarre shadow world of vampires, criminals, and cults. Miéville tears through the story with an almost manic energy, bulldozing past the few places where the plot falters. (It's saying something about his imagination that the gigantic tentacled creature is one of the least odd things in Kraken.) Anyone who reads this is never going to think about natural-history museums — or aquariums — in the same way again." Entertainment Wkly

Mieville, China

Perdido Street Station. Del Rey 2001 710p map pa $18.95

ISBN 0-345-44302-0

LC 00-67474

"Scientist Isaac Dan der Grimnebulin and his lover, an insectlike creature named Lin, discover the risks of meddling in the affairs of mobsters, renegades, and revolutionaries when they fall afoul of the powers that rule the sprawling city of New Crobuzon. The author . . . delivers a powerful tale about the power of love and the will to survive in a dystopian universe that combines Victorian elements with a fantasy version of cyberpunk." Libr J

Miéville, China, 1972-

Three moments of an explosion; stories. China Miéville. Del Rey 2015 400 p. (hardcover) $27

ISBN 9781101884720; 110188472X

LC 2015014298

This book, by China Miéville, presents several short stories, which are "by turns speculative, satirical, and heart-wrenching, fresh in form and language, and featuring a cast of damaged yet hopeful seekers who come face-to-face with the deep weirdness of the world--and at times the deeper weirdness of themselves." (Publisher's note)

"Though these stories can be enjoyed by any reader with a taste for thought experiments (including fans of Jonathan Lethem and George Saunders), Miéville would have been better served by a more ruthlessly edited selection." Booklist

Milan, Courtney

The **Duchess** War; by Courtney Milan. Femtopress 2013 264 p. (The Brothers Sinister) (pbk.) $12.99

ISBN 1937248283; 9781937248284; 9781937248093

"Miss Minerva Lane is a quiet, bespectacled wallflower, and she wants to keep it that way. After all, the last time she was the center of attention, it ended badly--so badly that she changed her name to escape her scandalous past. . . . So when a handsome duke comes to town, the last thing she wants is his attention. But that is precisely what she gets. Because Robert Blaisdell, the Duke of Clermont, is not fooled." (Publisher's note)

Other titles in this series are:
The heiress effect (2013);
The countess conspiracy (2013);
The suffragette scandal (2014)

Miles, Jonathan

Dear American Airlines. Houghton Mifflin 2008 180p $22

ISBN 978-0-54705-401-8; 0-54705-401-7

LC 2007-52150

In this novel, "Benny Ford, a 53-year-old recovering alcoholic and failed poet, has been stranded at Chicago's O'Hare International Airport for most of a day. He is about to miss his long-lost daughter's wedding. While he waits, Benny decides to give the airline a piece of his mind in writing. The letter he writes turns into his life story. Rage and a rambling self-narrative is a brutal barroom combination, best avoided on the page, too. But Miles is such a clever, amusing writer that he turns what should be a shtick into a terrifically fun read." Boston Globe

Miles, Valerie

A **thousand** forests in one acorn; an anthology of Spanish-language fiction. [edited by] Valerie Miles. Open Letter 2014 717 p. (pbk. : acid-free paper) $19.95

ISBN 1934824917; 9781934824917

LC 2014040025

This anthology, edited by Valerie Miles, offers an "introduction to twenty-eight of the most influential Spanish-language authors of the twentieth century. . . . [The book] combines interviews with these authors about their influences, about what they're trying to accomplish with their writing . . . with each author's 'favorite piece ever written.'" (Publisher's note)

"...the editor has succeeded in assembling an exceptional anthology that provides invaluable context in the form of biographical snapshots and brief interviews with each author." Booklist

Millay, Katja

The **Sea** of Tranquility; a novel. by Katja Millay. Atria Books 2013 448 p. $15

ISBN 1476730946; 9781476730943

LC 2013012207

Alex Award Winner (2014)

"Two and a half years after an unspeakable tragedy left her a shadow of the girl she once was, Nastya Kashnikov moves to a new town determined to keep her dark past hidden and hold everyone at a distance. But her plans only last so long before she finds herself inexplicably drawn to the one person as isolated as herself: Josh Bennett. Josh's story is no secret. Every person he loves has been taken from his life until, at seventeen years old, there is no one left. . . . [A]s the undeniable pull between them intensifies, he starts to wonder if he will ever learn the secrets she's been hiding--or if he even wants to." (Publisher's note)

"[F]ans of character-driven fiction will find much to admire in this deeply felt novel that is an excellent example of crossover fiction." LJ

Miller, Andrew

Oxygen. Harcourt 2002 323p $30

ISBN 0-15-100721-7

LC 2001-51459

First published 2001 in the United Kingdom

"Written in elegant, resonant prose, this book breathes with compassion and honesty, and with the rare quality called hope." Publ Wkly

Miller, Andrew

Pure. Europa Editions 2012 331 p.

ISBN 1609450671; 9781609450670

Costa Book of the Year (2011); Costa Novel Award Winner (2011).

In this book, the 2012 winner of the Costa Book of the Year, a "young man of humble background, Jean-Baptiste Baratte is ordered to exhume the vast and ancient cemetery of Les Innocents in the poor Parisian quarter of Les Halles and demolish its church. No one knows how many bodies are buried there . . . but it has recently begun to burst its banks, poisoning the city and spreading 'moral disturbance.' . . . As Baratte's story unfolds, the impending [French] revolution hangs over the narrative. . . . Jean-Baptiste Baratte, or John the Baptist the Churn, is in Paris to prepare the people for the coming of the true messiah. It is his duty to rip away the filth of the past, to lay the foundations for a new, better world." (The Guardian)

Miller, Derek B.

★ The **girl** in green; Derek B. Miller. Houghton Mifflin Harcourt 2017 336 p. (ebook) $26; (hardcover) $26

ISBN 9780544706279; 9780544706255

LC 2016005409

In this novel, by Derek B. Miller, as two men "near Checkpoint Zulu, one hundred miles from the Kuwaiti border, . . . argue about whether it makes sense to cross the nearest border in search of an ice cream, they become embroiled in a horrific attack in which a young local girl in a green dress is killed as they are trying to protect her. . . . Twenty-two years later, . . . they meet again and are offered an unlikely opportunity to redeem themselves." (Publisher's note)

"A penetrating, poetic, and unexpectedly disarming book about the ageless conflict in the Middle East by a writer who has made that topic his specialty." Kirkus

Miller, Derek B.

Norwegian by night; a novel. Derek B. Miller. Houghton Mifflin Harcourt 2013 304 p. $26

ISBN 0547934874; 9780547934877

LC 2012018089

In this novel by Derek Miller "Sheldon Horowitz . . . a former Marine . . . who failed his only son by sending him to Vietnam to die . . . move[s] in with his granddaughter . . . in Norway. Sheldon witnesses a dispute between [a] woman . . . and a . . . stranger. When events turn dire, Sheldon . . . shields the neighbor's young son from the violence, and they flee the scene. As Sheldon and the boy look for a haven . . . reality and fantasy, past and present, weave together." (Publisher's note)

Miller, Henry

★ **Tropic** of Cancer. Grove Press 1961 318p

First published 1934 in France

Miller "uses themes—cadging for food, shelter, and sex; attacks on such bourgeois values as work and marriage; denunciations of traditional art and literature—and imagery—wild, exuberant, often shockingly frank—that together represent a savage, nihilistic (and at times enormously funny) revulsion against a world of stupidity and ugliness." Ency of World Lit in the 20th Century

Followed by Tropic of Capricorn

Miller, Henry

★ **Tropic** of Capricorn. Grove Press 1962 348p

First published 1939 in France

"In a form like that of Tropic of Cancer the autobiographical account describes the writer's boyhood in Brooklyn, his quest to discover himself by sexual experiences and by other means, and his fury at the faults he finds in many of the values and ways of life in the U.S." Oxford Companion to Am Lit. 6th edition

Miller, Karen E. Quinones

An **angry**-ass black woman; Karen E. Quinones Miller. Gallery Books Karen Hunter Publishing 2012 272 p. $15

ISBN 1451607822; 9781451607826; 9781451608991

LC 2011047077

In this autobiographical novel by Karen E. Quinones Miller, Ke-Ke Quinones "grew up poorer than poor in Harlem in the 1960s and '70s, a place of unrelenting violence, racism, crime, rape, scamming, drinking, and drugging. . . . [But she] was whip smart and sassy, a voracious reader of everything from poetry to the classics. . . . Decades later, comatose in a hospital bed after a medical crisis, she reflects on her life." (Publisher's note)

Miller, Kei

★ **Augustown**; Kei Miller. First American edition Pantheon Books 2017 239 p. (hardback) $25.95

ISBN 9781101871621; 9781101871614

LC 2016042414

This book tells "the story of Bedward, an Augustown preacher and forerunner of the rastafari. Sixty years earlier, Bedward's miraculous attempt '"to rise up into de skies like Elijah"'was halted by the 'Babylon boys' pulling him down 'with a long hooker stick.' Like Bedward, Kaia's mother believes she might escape . . . after the local college accepts her application, 'a certain lightness of being' takes her over, 'as if she could close her eyes right now and begin to rise.'" (Publisher's Weekly)

"Fusing facts with what-could-have-well-been, Augustown is a gorgeously plotted, sharply convincing, achingly urgent novel deserving widespread attention." Booklist

Miller, Madeline

The **song** of Achilles; Madeline Miller. Ecco 2012 378 p. $25.99

ISBN 0062060619; 0062060627; 9780062060617; 9780062060624

LC 2011275637

Orange Prize for Fiction (2012)

This novel is a "romantic retelling of the Trojan War as a story of longtime companions narrated by Patroclus. . . . The future lovers meet as 5-year-olds at a footrace and are reunited when Patroclus is banished to Achilles' father's kingdom. By the time they are 13, there are the first of many 'stirrings' . . . followed some years later by couplings." (Time)

"With language both evocative of her predecessors and fresh, and through familiar scenes that explore new territory, this first-time novelist masterfully brings to life an imaginative yet informed vision of ancient Greece featuring divinely human gods and larger-than-life mortals." Pub Wkly

Miller, Mary

Always happy hour; stories. Mary Miller. W W Norton & Co Inc 2017 256 p. (hardcover) $24.95; (ebook) $50

ISBN 9781631492181; 9781631492198; 1631492187

LC 2016032939

This book, by Mary Miller, "weaves tales of young women—deeply flawed and intensely real—who struggle to get out of their own way. They love to drink and have sex; they make bad decisions with men who either love them too much or too little; and they haunt a Southern terrain of gas stations, public pools, and dive bars. Though each character shoulders the weight of her own baggage . . . , they are united in their unrelenting suspicion that they deserve better." (Publisher's note)

"Like a two-for-one drink special or a boxful of beer, this bracingly strong collection may prove intoxicating." Kirkus

Miller, Rebecca

★ **Jacob's** folly; a novel. Rebecca Miller. 1st ed. Farrar, Straus and Giroux 2013 384 p. (hardcover) $26

ISBN 0374178542; 9780374178543

LC 2012022882

National Jewish Book Awards: Fiction Finalist (2013)

The protagonist of this book is "an 18th-century Jewish peddler reincarnated as a fly on contemporary Long Island, NY. At first devastated to discover that he is not an angel, as he first presumed, Jacob Cerf nonetheless exerts a mysterious influence on two individuals: Leslie Senzatimore, a saintly boat remodeler, and Masha, a young Orthodox Jewish woman. Jacob feels compelled to pull Masha away from her religion and to knock Leslie off his do-gooder pedestal." (Library Journal)

Miller, Risa

Welcome to Heavenly Heights. St. Martin's Press 2003 230p $23.95

ISBN 0-312-30180-4

LC 2002-31876

The author "has peered inside Tova's life to show us the search for joy that lies at the heart of her religious ritual and the beauty of people like her who devote themselves to that search. And then Miller has broken our hearts—with Tova's—byshowing us how horrible it is when the poetic liturgical metaphors of Judaism become the terrible realities of nationalism, when holiness tries to reconcile itself with the inevitable human corruption of statehood." N Y Times Book Rev

Miller, Sue

For love. HarperCollins Pubs. 1993 301p

LC 92-54422

"Fortyish freelance writer Lottie leaves her new husband in Chicago to spend part of the summer in Cambridge, Massachusetts, getting the family house ready to sell now that her brother Cameron has placed their alcoholic mother in a nursing home. While she and her son Ryan paint and clean, Lottie examines the concept of love in an article she is writing, studying her own troubled marriage and Cameron's resumption of a love affair with childhood sweetheart Elizabeth. For Elizabeth, who is staying with her mother after leaving her philandering husband, this romance is just a fling. But Cameron's obsessive love for the golden girl of his youth leads to {an accident}." Libr J

Miller, Sue

The **good** mother. Harper & Row 1986 310p

LC 85-45475

"The fulcrum on which the novel's plot pivots is the allegation by Anna's ex-husband that Anna's lover has molested Molly, and the ensuing custody trial. Miller's treatment of this high point of tension in the novel is dramatic, discreet, compassionate. Each development in the legal process increases the tension. The drama heightens, the suspense builds, character is further developed, and the latitude for choice logically narrowed. Like a final judgment, the custody decision breaks over reader and character alike." Christ Sci Monit

Miller, Sue

The **Lake** Shore Limited. Alfred A. Knopf 2010 269p $25.95

ISBN 978-0-307-26421-3; 0-307-26421-1

LC 2009-46504

The novel is "craftily plotted, too good for a reviewer to give much of it away. Also, as with her previous novels, Miller resists allowing her characters the resources of eloquence; nor does she — in Henry James's words — 'go behind' them to offer us deeper truths about their behavior." Boston Globe

Miller, Sue

Lost in the forest. Knopf 2005 247p $24.95

ISBN 1-400-04226-7

LC 2004-48963

"Miller has always been adept at rendering the complexities of family life, the way even well-intentioned, decent people can't walk across a room without wounding at least one person they love. But while some of her plots . . . can be cluttered and occasionally clumsy, Lost in the Forest has a seemingly effortless grace; Miller quickly captures and never loses our attention." N Y Times Book Rev

Miller, Sue

The **senator's** wife. Alfred A. Knopf 2008 306p $24.95

ISBN 978-0-307-26420-6

LC 2007-14659

"No one captures the domestic landscape with language as lush as Miller's. She is the Martha Stewart of fictional space. From peeling an orange to laying out Christmas dinner to arranging lilies on a table, her prose is almost erotic. Moreover, her writerly gift extends beyond graceful imagery. She describes sexual encounters with graphic intensity and brings to Meri's labor and delivery a verisimilitude that will flatten you." Houston Chron

Miller, Sue

While I was gone. Knopf 1999 265p

ISBN 0-375-40112-1

LC 98-14211

"Miller's narrative is a beautifully textured picture of the psychological tug of war between finding integrity as an individual and satisfying the demands of spouse, children and community." Publ Wkly

Miller, Walter M.

★ A **canticle** for Leibowitz; a novel. by Walter M. Miller, Jr. Lippincott 1960 320p hardcover o.p. pa $13.95

ISBN 0-06-089299-4

"Here is science fiction of the highest literary excellence and thematic intelligence. A monastery founded by the scientist Leibowitz is discovered decades after an atomic war. In the first part of the book a young novice in the monastery is the protagonist; in the second part we see scholars in a new period of enlightenment; and in the final section we observe man's proclivity for repeating mistakes and the apparent inevitability of history's repeating itself." Shapiro. Fic for Youth. 3d edition

Millet, Lydia

Ghost lights; a novel. Lydia Millet. W. W. Norton & Co. 2011 255p $24.95

ISBN 978-0-393-08171-8; 0-393-08171-0

LC 2011026502

"Picking up in the vicinity of where her last novel, How the Dead Dream, left off, Ghost Lights finds new protagonist Hal flying to Belize to find the previous novel's main man T., who disappeared there months before. Hal's wife is T.'s executive assistant, and when she contemplates hiring a private investigator to root out her boss, Hal volunteers, claiming his experience at the IRS qualifies him to track a person down. The truth is Hal suspects his wife of cheating on him, and his decision to embark on a hero's quest is as much fueled by booze and insecurity as it is by any sense of righteousness. . . . A much more contemplative novel—where T. is led by action and bravado, Hal prefers to ruminate and be led—Ghost Lights puts together a clearer vision of the previous book's themes of the way identity is tied up with social purpose." Time Out Chicago

Millet, Lydia

How the dead dream; a novel. Counterpoint 2008 244p $24

ISBN 978-1-59376-184-4; 1-59376-184-8

LC 2007-35242

"For the reader, T.'s adventures with animals carry more emotional impact than any of the human encounters. They prompt the serious , sometimes convoluted but always moving meditations that are the spine if this strange, lovely novel." Chicago Sun-Times

Millet, Lydia

★ **Magnificence**; a novel. Lydia Millet. W.W. Norton & Co. 2012 255 p. $25.95

ISBN 0393081702; 9780393081701

LC 2012015145

This novel by Lydia Millet "introduces Susan Lindley, a woman adrift after her husband's death. Suddenly gifted her great uncle's Pasadena mansion, Susan decides to restore his extensive collection of preserved animals. . . . Meanwhile, a menagerie of uniquely damaged humans--including a cheating husband and a chorus of eccentric elderly women--joins her in residence." (Publisher's note)

Millet, Lydia

Oh pure and radiant heart; Lydia Millet. Soft Skull Press 2005 489p (hbk.) $25

ISBN 1932360859; 9781932360851

LC 2005001028

This novel is framed around the questions "What if Robert Oppenheimer, Enrico Fermi and Leo Szilard, the primary physicists from the Manhattan Project, returned to contemporary America to survey their atomic legacy? . . . [In this book,] the souls of the three take earthly form in the present-day Southwest. Ann, a New Mexico librarian, spots the reincarnated Oppenheimer and Fermi at a restaurant near her home; Szilard soon joins them; Ann persuades her garden-designer husband, Ben, to take them all in. Subsequent trips to Los Alamos and . . . Japan to view the monuments at Hiroshima persuade the three to work for disarmament. Army surveillance ensues; at one rally, shots are fired; and Christian Fundamentalists" also find their way into the narrative. (Publishers Weekly)

Millet, Lydia

Sweet Lamb of Heaven; Lydia Millet. W W Norton & Co Inc 2016 256 p. (hardcover) $25.95

ISBN 0393285545; 9780393285543

LC 2016000554

This novel, by Lydia Millet, "is the first-person account of a young mother, Anna, escaping her cold and unfaithful husband, a businessman who's just launched his first campaign for political office. When Ned chases Anna and their six-year-old daughter from Alaska to Maine, the two go into hiding. . . . As his pursuit of Anna and their child moves from threatening to criminal, Ned begins to alter his wife's world in ways she never could have imagined." (Publisher's note)

"A top-notch tale of domestic paranoia that owes a debt to spooky psychological page-turners like Rosemary's Baby yet is driven by Millet's particular offbeat thinking." Kirkus

Millhauser, Steven

★ **Dangerous** laughter; thirteen stories. Alfred A. Knopf 2008 244p $24

ISBN 978-0-307-26756-6; 0-307-26756-3

LC 2007-22929

"While most short-story writers in the past three decades joined the realist rebellion against the fabulism of the '70s, Steven Millhauser has stayed true to the fantastic tradition that extends from Scheherazade to Poe, to Kafka and Barth. He rejects the ordinary world of the merely real, and playfully and powerfully explores the incredible world of purely aesthetic creation. . . . Millhauser's stories are not mere ingenuity, although they are devilishly clever. Millhauser is motivated by the desire to see a world in a grain of sand, to affirm that the road of excess leads to the palace of wisdom. He is our most brilliant practicing romantic, for whom surface reality is merely an uninteresting illusion." San Francisco Chron

Millhauser, Steven

★ **Martin** Dressler; the tale of an American dreamer. Crown 1996 294p

ISBN 0-517-70319-X

LC 96-683

This novel tells the "story of a 19th-century New York entrepreneur. . . . {Martin} Dressler starts out in his family's cigar store but gets into the hotel industry at an early age and moves up rapidly, thanks to his energy and vision. His ambition leads him to take on increasingly extravagant projects, from lunch rooms to larger and larger hotels to the Grand Cosmo, his vision of a world unto itself." (Libr J)

The author "again examines the American imagination in terms of cosmology. This time, his world-creator is young Martin Dressler, an entrepreneurial wunderkind who starts out at his father's cigar store. What ensues is an expertly woven fable of Victorian Manhattan, as Martin transforms his hunger for 'something else' into a series of colossal hotels. Martin's sights are firmly set on tomorrow, but he's cursed to be forever premodern: the skycraper always seems to lurk around the next turn of the page, but he can envision only period eclecticism. As the new century dawns, Martin's crowning achievement, the Grand Cosmo, begins to look like the ultimate castle in the air, and he ponders—without regret—the consequences of having 'dreamed the wrong dream.'" New Yorker

Millhauser, Steven

Voices in the night; stories. Steven Millhauser. Alfred A. Knopf 2015 304 p. (hardback) $25.95

ISBN 0385351593; 9780385351591; 9780385351607

LC 2014025425

This book presents short stories by Steven Millhauser. "In 'Miracle Polish,' a man buys a mirror-cleaning chemical that makes his reflection slightly but meaningfully more upbeat and glimmering; a sly riff on the myth of Narcissus ensues. 'A Report on Our Recent Troubles' describes a community wrecked by a spate of suicides, some seemingly done as perverse pleas for attention." (Kirkus Reviews)

"Millhauser intuits modes of storytelling like nobody else, and even his satire of sports-announcer-speak in "Home Run" elevates the quotidian to the cosmic. A superb testament to America's quirkiest short story writer, still on his game." Kirkus

Mills, Mark

Amagansett; Mark Mills. Putnam 2004 394p $24.95

ISBN 0-399-15184-2

LC 2004-44394

"The novel combines a touching love story, told in flashback, with a nicely detailed procedural starring an unlikely investigative duo: the taciturn Basque and the Amagansett assistant police chief, who hopes to resurrect his career in the wake of scandal. . . . This is a novel to savor, both for its portrait of roughhewn individuals finding selfhood beyond the breakers and for its snapshot of the postwar world not yet locked in the death grip of modernity." Booklist

Min, Anchee

Becoming Madame Mao. Houghton Mifflin 2000 337p $25

ISBN 0-618-00407-6

LC 99-58520

"Min reveals the complexities of love, betrayal, and ambition in this lyrical and thrilling depiction of a once-powerless woman in the jaws of power, giving us an all-too-rare glimpse into the life of a woman within the machine." Ms

Includes bibliographical references (p. {340})

Min, Anchee

Empress Orchid. Hougton Mifflin 2004 336p $24

ISBN 0-618-06887-2

LC 2003-56891

The author "has done a prodigious amount of on-site research to capture the glorious, hopeless last days of the Ching dynasty. . . . Readers will be enthralled by the gorgeously woven cultural tapestry and the psychologically astute portrait of the empress a talented girl from the provinces who married (way) up." Publ Wkly

Mina, Denise ✓

The **dead** hour; a novel. Little, Brown and Co. 2006 341p $24.99

ISBN 978-0-316-73594-0; 0-316-73594-9

LC 2006-01610

"Surely Paddy Meehan is the most unlikely, and most relistic, investigator in recent crime fiction. . . . The Dead Hour is some kind of magnificent." Wall Street Journal

Mina, Denise, 1966-

The **end** of the wasp season; a novel. Little, Brown and Company 2011 390p $25.99

ISBN 978-0-316-06933-5; 0-316-06933-7

LC 2011-18242

A procedural "set in Glasgow and featuring a gutsy cop named Alex Morrow. Since Morrow is pregnant with twins, her mates on the Strathclyde police force try to shield her from the savagery done to the victim of a home invasion in the exclusive suburb of Thorntonhall. But when she realizes the prudish cops are actually revolted by the dead woman's provocatively exposed body, Morrow feels 'sheer, suffocating pity' for the victim, whose battered face and halfÐnaked corpse have nullified both her identity and her dignity. This is the sort of insightful observation that makes Mina's novels so extraordinarily rich and unpredictable. There are the usual rewards in following the evidence that leads the police to the teenage sons of Kay Murray, who cleaned house for the murdered woman and the invalid mother she had only recently buried. But there's greater satisfaction in watching Mina transform this seemingly simple cleaning woman into a complex character, possessed of great depths of feeling." N Y Times Book Rev

Mina, Denise, 1966-

Field of blood; a novel. Denise Mina. Little, Brown 2005 360p (pbk.) $7.50; (hbk.) $35

ISBN 0316735930; 9780316154581; 9780316735933

LC 2004023408

In this novel, "Patricia 'Paddy' Meehan, a copygirl at Glasgow's 'Daily News,' has struggled with issues of goodness since childhood. 'I knew I was lying when I made my first communion,' she confesses to fiancé Sean Ogilvy the night she delivers other shockers. She won't marry him. And she wants his help interviewing his 10-year-old cousin, Callum, who's been charged with murdering a toddler. . . . Paddy, who shares a nickname with a career criminal wrongfully imprisoned for murder, can't tolerate injustice. At the heart of the plot is her decision pose as colleague Heather Allen when she makes dangerous inquiries, a choice that spells death for the real Heather, who's everything Paddy isn't: slim blonde whistle bait—and ambitious enough to steal a story from Paddy." (Publishers Weekly)

Mina, Denise, 1966-

Gods and beasts; a novel. Denise Mina. Reagan Arthur Books/Little, Brown and Co. 2013 320 p. (hardback) $25.99

ISBN 0316188522; 9780316188524

LC 2012022241

This book is the third in Denise Mina's Det. Sgt. Alex Morrow series. Here, Morrow tries to figure out why a bank robber guns down an elderly gentleman who apparently tried to assist during his robbery. "Meanwhile, looming budget cuts and police layoffs lure two of Morrow's subordinates into stealing a pile of dirty drug money. Finally, a former labor hero turned politician is caught up in a sex scandal with a 17-year-old female staffer." (Publishers Weekly)

Mina, Denise, 1966-

The **long** drop; a novel. Denise Mina. Little, Brown & Co. 2017 236 p. (hardcover) $26

ISBN 9780316269735; 9780316380577; 0316380571

LC 2016954169

In this book, by Denise Mina, "William Watt's wife, daughter, and sister-in-law are dead, slaughtered in their own home in a brutal crime that scandalized Glasgow. Despite an ironclad alibi, police zero in on Watt as the primary suspect, but he maintains his innocence. Distraught and desperate to clear his name, Watt puts out a bounty for information that will lead him to the real killer." (Publisher's note)

"A terrific exploration of crime and oppression." Kirkus

Mina, Denise, 1966-

The **red** road; A Novel. Denise Mina. Little, Brown and Co. 2014 304 p. (Alex Morrow) (hardcover) $26

ISBN 0316188514; 9780316188517

LC 2013956654

"Police detective Alex Morrow has met plenty of unsavory characters in her line of work, but arms dealer Michael Brown ranks among the most brutal and damaged of the criminals she's known. Morrow is serving as a witness in Brown's trial, where the case hinges on his fingerprints found on the guns he sells." (Publisher's note)

"Mina's at the top of her game here, deftly unveiling the sad truths of the past and present to create a gritty must-read for fans of complex, psychological police procedurals." Booklist

Mina, Denise

Slip of the knife; a novel. Little, Brown and Co. 2008 340p $24.99

ISBN 978-0-316-01558-5; 0-316-01558-X

LC 2007-42881

First published 2007 in the United Kingdom

"Mina excels at this kind of writing, the back-and-forth of competitors and colleagues, the way tension and love bind people uneasily. She's a leisurely writer; although Terry's murder opens the book, the action plays out slowly, and she lets us soak up the abundant ambience and personality." Boston Globe

Mina, Denise

Still midnight; a novel. Denise Mina. Little, Brown and Co. 2010 342p (Alex Morrow novels) $24.99

ISBN 9780-316015639; 0316015636

LC 2009-22061

First published 2009 in the United Kingdom

Other titles in this series are: The end of the wasp season (2011); Gods and beasts (2013); The red road (2014); Blood, salt, water (2015)

"Mina's strength has always been her depiction of her characters' inner lives. With a background in health care, law, and criminology, she knows — and can show readers — the small choices, the subtle moral nuances that make one sibling a cop, another a gangster. In 'Still Midnight,' she concentrates on such character studies, keeping the action — the home invasion and kidnapping, their cause and resolution — on a smaller scale than in previous works." Boston Globe

Minato, Kanae

Confessions; a novel. Kanae Minato, Stephen Snyder. First edition Little, Brown & Co. 2014 240 p. $15

ISBN 0316200921; 9780316200929

LC 2014937563

Alex Award (2015)

In this novel by Minato Kanai, "All Yuko Moriguchi had to live for was her four-year-old child, Manami. Now, after a heartbreaking accident on the grounds of the middle school where she teaches, Yuko has given up and tendered her resignation. But first, she has one last lecture to deliver. She tells a story that will upend everything her students ever thought they knew about two of their peers, and sets in motion a maniacal plot for revenge." (Publisher's note)

"Yuko Moriguchi leads a relatively simple life, teaching middle school and raising her four-year-old daughter, Manami, on her own. But when Manami is murdered in a sick act of hatred, Yuko decides the legal system is unreliable and plans her own revenge...This award-winning debut novel is a creepy and mesmerizing psychological thriller that challenges the conventions of right vs. wrong, good vs. evil, and law vs.

justice. There are no happy endings here, but Minato has pieced together an intriguing puzzle that will keep readers glued to their seats." LJ

Minot, Susan

Evening. Knopf 1998 264p

ISBN 0-375-40037-0

LC 98-15437

"Ann Lord's life has been shaped by the men who have married her. As she lies on her deathbed, trying to make some sense of that life, a rediscovered balsam pillow evokes a Maine wedding, in 1954, where she fell in love for the first—and perhaps the last—time. This almost crude conceit produces a narrative of considerable ambition and complexity. . . . For heroine and reader alike, death's painful confusions are tempered by the spirited directness of Ann's younger self, as yet unscathed by time and experience." New Yorker

Minot, Susan

Rapture. Knopf 2002 115p $18

ISBN 0-375-41327-8

LC 2001-38377

"This novella takes place during a single act of oral sex. . . . Benjamin is a handsome and hapless film director with a moneyed and supportive fiancée; Kay is his former production designer, with whom he had a fling on a shoot in Mexico. After three years of agonized liaisons and enforced partings, Benjamin and Kay fall into bed once more, but they seem to bring the rest of their lives along with them, and Minot's saucy conceit evolves into a disconcerting examination of love and war between the sexes." New Yorker

Mirvis, Tova

The **outside** world. Alfred A. Knopf 2004 283p $24

ISBN 1-400-04161-9

LC 2003-58923

"Beneath the women's wigs and the men's black fedoras, Mirvis finds reservoirs of belief, doubt, ambition, folly, lust and the rest of the human equation." Washington Post Book World

Mishima, Yukio, 1925-1970

★ The **decay** of the angel; translated from the Japanese by Edward G. Seidensticker. Knopf 1974 236p (Sea of fertility)

ISBN 0-394-46613-6

Original Japanese edition, 1971

"The novel concludes with a superbly written scene that casts doubt on the reality of the events described in the four volumes. In the end we discover that the 'sea of fertility' may be as arid as the region of that name on the moon, although it seems to suggest infinite richness." Ency of World Lit in the 20th Century

Mishima, Yukio, 1925-1970

Runaway horses; translated from the Japanese by Michael Gallagher. Knopf 1973 421p (Sea of fertility)

ISBN 0-394-46618-7

Original Japanese edition, 1969

"Mishima uses the same literary artistry in this novel as in the first but changes the gently romantic tone to one of martial ideology with a weirdly beautiful emphasis on ritual suicide. In the interplay of entanglements between the two novels, each self-contained, the author experiments with the Buddhist doctrine of reincarnation." Booklist

Followed by The Temple of Dawn

Mishima, Yukio, 1925-1970

★ **Spring** snow; translated from the Japanese by Michael Gallagher. Knopf 1972 389p (Sea of fertility)

ISBN 0-394-44239-3

Original Japanese edition, 1968

"Kiyoaki Matsugae, a young Japanese, comes from a wealthy family whose attention to the most formal aspects of Japanese life has changed because of their attraction to Western culture. His best friend, Shigekuna Honda, is not so handsome or affluent but is a more serious scholar. The story emphasizes the difference in the character of the two young men as the plot describes the passionate, although ambivalent, love that Kiyoaki feels for the beautiful Satoko. When she concludes that Kiyoaki does not return her love, despite the fact that their affair has been serious and intimate, she allows herself to be betrothed to someone else. As always, what is forbidden becomes more desirable and Kiyoaki tries desperately to regain his loved one. Japanese customs and rituals intervene to bring a tragic ending to this love story." Shapiro. Fic for Youth. 3d edition

Followed by Runaway horses

Mishima, Yukio, 1925-1970

★ The **Temple** of Dawn; translated from the Japanese by E. Dale Saunders and Cecilia Segawa Seigle. Knopf 1973 334p (Sea of fertility)

ISBN 0-394-46614-4

Original Japanese edition, 1970

The third volume in the Sea of fertility series is "divided into two parts: the first is set in southeast Asia, where we first see the Thai princess who is the reincarnation of Isao; the second takes place in Japan after World War II, when the old values of society have been corrupted." Ency of World Lit in the 20th Century

Followed by The decay of the angel

Mistry, Rohinton

A **fine** balance; a novel. Knopf 1996 603p

ISBN 0-679-44608-7

LC 95-49317

"It is impossible not to seethe at the injustices of the police state, and impossible not to take these characters passionately to heart: this is a novel that can stand with the best of Dickens." New Yorker

Mitcham, Judson

Sabbath Creek; a novel. University of Georgia Press 2004 169p $22.95

ISBN 0-8203-2577-5

LC 2003-15704

"Lewis observes everything with the alertness of someone who does not yet take common experiences, such as kissing and drunkenness, for granted; he never resorts to shorthand to convey them, but describes them with a scrupulous fidelity to his own perceptions." N Y Times Book Rev

Mitchard, Jacquelyn

★ The **deep** end of the ocean. Viking 1996 434p

ISBN 0-670-86579-6

LC 95-26234

"One of the most remarkable things about this rich, moving and altogether stunning first novel is Mitchard's assured command of narrative structure and stylistic resources. Her story about a child's kidnapping and its enduring effects upon his parents, siblings, and extended family is a blockbuster read." Publ Wkly

Mitchard, Jacquelyn

No time to wave goodbye; a novel. Random House 2009 228p $25

ISBN 978-1-4000-6774-9; 1-4000-6774-X

LC 2009-12905

"Mitchard charts a tormented family dynamic with shocking ease. This action-packed and emotionally rich drama is every bit as satisfying as its predecessor." Publ Wkly

Mitchard, Jacquelyn

A **theory** of relativity. HarperCollins Pubs. 2001 351p $26

ISBN 0-06-621023-2

LC 00-54261

"Keefer Nye, only a year old when her parents die in a car crash near Madison, Wis., is the focal point of a bitter, protracted and precedent-setting custody battle. Keefer's bachelor uncle, 24-year-old science teacher Gordon McKenna, seems the most appropriate custodian for his tiny niece, since he helped his elderly parents care for Keefer while his sister (Keefer's mother, Georgia) battled cancer. Challenging his claim, the affluent Nye grandparents, country-club Floridians, believe that their niece and her husband, born-again Christians, should get custody. Mitchard's nuanced character portrayals are her strong suit; no one is without frailties." Publ Wkly

Mitchell, David

Black swan green; a novel. Random House 2006 294p hardcover o.p.

ISBN 0-8129-7401-8 pa; 1-4000-6379-5; 978-0-8129-7401-0 pa; 978-1-4000-6379-6

LC 2005052914

This is a novel by the author of Cloud Atlas (2004). "Black Swan Green tracks a single year in what is, for thirteen-year-old Jason Taylor, the sleepiest village in muddiest Worcestershire in a dying Cold War England, 1982." (Publisher's note)

This is a "portrait of a thirteen-year-old boy, growing up in Worcestershire in 1982, who is afflicted with a stammer, unhappy parents, and a snide older sister. Mitchell hasn't abandoned his fascination with the chapter: his meditation on being thirteen has thirteen sections, each featuring a self-contained story. This time, however, his approach has the subtlety of a watermark. . . . By settling into a single narrative voice, and skipping the pyrotechnics, Mitchell has come by something that eluded him before: a sense of earned emotion." New Yorker

Mitchell, David

★ The **bone** clocks; a novel. David Mitchell. Random House Inc 2014 640 p. (hardback) $30

ISBN 1400065674; 9781400065677

LC 2014008517

In this novel by David Mitchell, "following a scalding row with her mother, fifteen-year-old Holly Sykes slams the door on her old life. But Holly is . . . a lightning rod for psychic phenomena. . . . A Cambridge scholarship boy grooming himself for wealth and influence, a conflicted father who feels alive only while reporting on the war in Iraq, a middle-aged writer mourning his exile from the bestseller list--all have a part . . . in this surreal, invisible war." (Publisher's note)

"From gritty realism to far-out fantasy, each section has its own charm and surprises." Pub Wkly

Mitchell, David

★ **Cloud** atlas; a novel. Random House Trade Paperbacks 2004 509p pa $14.95

ISBN 0-375-50725-6 pa

LC 2003-69314

The author "presents six narratives that evoke an array of genres, from Melvillean high-seas drama to California noir and dystopian fantasy. There is a naïve clerk on a nineteenth-century Polynesian voyage; an aspiring composer who insinuates himself into the home of a syphilitic genius; a journalist investigating a nuclear plant; a publisher with a dangerous bestseller on his hands; and a cloned human being created for slave labor. These five stories are bisected and arranged around a sixth, the oral history of a post-apocalyptic island, which forms the heart of the novel. Only after this do the second halves of the stories fall into place, pulling the novel's themes into focus: the ease with which one group enslaves another, and the constant rewriting of the past by those who control the present. Against such forces, Mitchell's characters reveal a quiet tenacity." New Yorker

Mitchell, David

★ The **thousand** autumns of Jacob de Zoet; a novel. Random House 2010 479p il $26

ISBN 978-1-4000-6545-5; 1-4000-6545-3

LC 2009-47296

"Mitchell's meticulously reconstructed the lost world of Edo-era Japan, and in doing so he's created his most conventional but most emotionally engaging novel yet: it's as if an acrobatic but show-offy performance artist, adept at mimicry, ventriloquism and cerebral literary gymnastics, had decided to do an old-fashioned play and, in the process, proved his chops as an actor." N Y Times (Late N Y Ed)

Mitchell, Judith Claire

A **reunion** of ghosts; Judith Claire Mitchell. Harper 2015 400 p. (hardcover : acid-free paper) $26.99

ISBN 0062355880; 9780062355881; 9780062355898

LC 2014026485

In Judith Claire Mitchell's novel, readers "meet the Alter sisters. These three mordantly witty, complex women share their family's apartment on Manhattan's Upper West Side. They love each other fiercely, but being an Alter isn't easy. Bad luck is in their genes. n the waning days of 1999, the trio decides it's time to close the circle of the Alter curse. But first, as the world counts down to the dawn of a new millennium, Lady, Vee, and Delph must write the final chapter of a saga lifetimes in the making." (Publisher's note)

"Inspired in part by the life of German chemist Fritz Haber, this novel is a carefully crafted, thought-provoking examination of history past and present as seen through the eyes of a complex yet humble family." Booklist

Mitchell, Margaret

★ **Gone** with the wind; with a new preface by Pat Conroy and an introduction by James A. Michener. 60th Anniversary ed; Scribner 1996 959p il

ISBN 0-684-82625-9

LC 95-52609

A reissue of the title first published 1936 by Macmillan

"The proud people of the South have been subjugated in the Civil War, the dreadful period of Reconstruction has followed, and Scarlett O'Hara, beautiful and headstrong, has been reduced to poverty and near-starvation. No longer the belle of the ball, she must do whatever possible to feed herself and her family, and she does not hesitate to use feminine wiles to accomplish her ends. When she finds a man she can respect, she discovers her real feelings too late and loses him. Scarlett and her plantation home, Tara, are among the most memorable names in fiction." Shapiro. Fic for Youth. 3d edition

Mitford, Nancy

★ The **pursuit** of love & Love in a cold climate; two novels. Modern Lib. 1994 617p $19.95

ISBN 0-679-60090-6

LC 93-43632

A combined edition of two titles about the Radlett family originally published 1945 and 1949 respectively. Subsequent works about the family and its associates are The blessing (1951) and Don't tell Alfred (1960)

These quasi-autobiographical novels take a satiric look at the various social and amatory trials and triumphs of an eccentric upper-class English family following World War I

Miyamoto, Teru

Kinshu: Autumn brocade. New Directions 2005 196p $22.95

ISBN 0-8112-1633-0

LC 2005-20111

Original Japanese edition, 1982

This novel "features letters exchanged over the course of about a year between Aki Katsunuma and her ex-husband, Yasuaki Arima. Aki's initial letter stems from a chance encounter with Yasuaki over a decade after their divorce. Through their correspondence, readers discover Aki's grief in having to raise her eight-year-old mentally challenged son with her unfaithful second husband, Soichiro Katsunuma. Aki herself learns the true motives behind the suicide/murder that Yasuaki's then lover attempted, which, in an ironic twist of fate, ends her life only to save his. After Yasuaki recovers from his attack, his life is no picnic either as he learns to confront his own share of demons while striving to forge ahead. As the story progresses, the former husband and wife come to realize the cathartic properties of their letters; by learning to forgive and respect each other, they bring about a sense of closure to their relationship once and for all. Though brief, this novel features a distinctly compelling narrative; credit Thomas's effective translation." Libr J

Mizushima, Margaret ✓

★ **Killing** Trail; Margaret Mizushima. Crooked Lane Books 2015 320 p. (Timber Creek K-9 Mysteries) (hardcover) $24.99

ISBN 9781629533810; 1629533815

"When a young girl is found dead in the mountains outside Timber Creek, life-long resident Officer Mattie Cobb and her partner, K-9 police dog Robo, are assigned to the case that has rocked the small Colorado town. With the help of Cole Walker, local veterinarian and a single father, Mattie and Robo must track down the truth before it claims another victim." (Publisher's note)

"The operational details about the K-9 unit are fascinating, and the interactions between Mattie and Robo will tug atthe heartstrings of every dog lover. There are also very well realized scenes between Cole and his daughter as they struggle with grief over Grace's death and the absence of Cole's ex-wife." Booklist

Mizushima, Margaret ✓

Stalking Ground; by Margaret Mizushima. Crooked Lane Books 2016 310 p. (Timber Creek K-9 mysteries) (hardcover) $25.99

ISBN 1629538337; 9781629538358; 9781629538334

Colorado Book Award finalist (Mystery 2017); International Book Awards finalist (Fiction: Mystery/Suspense 2017)

In this book, by Margaret Mizushima, "when Deputy Ken Brody's sweetheart goes missing in the mountains outside Timber Creek, Mattie Cobb and Robo are called to search. But it's mid-October and a dark snow storm is brewing. . . . By the time they find her body, the storm has broken and the snow is coming down hard. While Brody hikes down to bring back the forensics team and veterinarian Cole Walker gathers supplies to protect them from the storm, Mattie and Robo find themselves alone." (Publisher's note)

"Realistic characters and believable plot twists distinguish Mizushima's brisk sequel to 2015's Killing Trail." Pub Wkly

Mo Yan, 1955-

Frog; a novel. Mo Yan ; [translated by Howard Goldblatt] Viking Adult 2015 387 p. hardcover $27.95

ISBN 0525427988; 9780241972366; 9780525427988

LC 2014038473

Author Mo Yan won the Nobel Prize in Literature in 2012.

This novel by Mo Yan, translated by Howard Goldblatt, "a celebrated midwife, skilled at delivering babies in difficult rural circumstances, finds herself at the blunt end of enforcement of the country's controversial one-child policy. Through a complex family story told through letters and narrative forms, Mo explores the emotional and moral toll of state-controlled family planning on a traditional community that places a high value on a large family." (Publisher's note)

"Heavily laced with ardent social criticism, mystical symbolism, and historical realism, Mo Yan's potent exploration of China's most personal and intrusive social control programs probes the horrors and pain such policies inflict." Booklist

Mo Yan, 1955-

Life and death are wearing me out; translated from the Chinese by Howard Goldblatt. Arcade Pub. 2008 540p $29.95

ISBN 1559708530; 9781559708531

LC 2007-22843

Original Chinese edition, 2006

This novel's protagonist is "Ximen Nao, a landowner known for his generosity and kindness and benevolence to his peasants, but who in Mao's Land Reform Movement of 1948 was . . . cruelly executed, despite his protestations of innocence. The novel opens in Hell, where Lord Yama, king of the underworld, has Ximen Nao tortured endlessly. . . . He is reborn not, alas, as a human but first as a donkey, then a horse, a pig, a monkey, and finally the big-headed boy Lan Qiansui." (Publisher's note)

"Yan's hero and chief narrator, Ximen Nao, is a former rich landowner who falls victim to Mao Zedong's Land Reform Movement. Although known as a fair and decent man, Nao loses both his land and his life to the Communist regime. Relegated to Hell, Nao is forced by Lord Yama, King of the Underworld, to be reborn, again and again, until his anger with his perceived injustice is purged from his soul. First, he reenters the world as a donkey, then, in succession, as an ox, pig, dog, and monkey, until he finally returns as a human. From the unique vantage point as an animal with some lingering human thoughts, Nao relates the life of his peasant village and its people through 50 years of economic and personal struggle. Inventing a large cast of believable people is one thing. (Yan's list of principle characters numbers 17.) To bring them vividly to mind while simultaneously fashioning a counter world of animal intelligence—the smells, sights, fears and violence implicit in the daily life of creatures—is a spectacular achievement." Seattle Times

Modesitt, L. E.

Archform; beauty. TOR Bks. 2002 330p $25.95

ISBN 0-7653-0433-3

LC 2001-59655

"Set against a background of biological terrorism, Modesitt's tale explores social issues . . . sure to resonate with many readers. This brilliant novel is as thought provoking as it is entertaining." Publ Wkly

Modesitt, L. E.

Imager's battalion; L.E. Modesitt, Jr. 1st ed. Tor 2013 512 p. (hardcover) $27.99

ISBN 0765332833; 9780765332837

LC 2012027589

This book is the "third part of a prequel fantasy series . . . wherein wizards are known as 'imagers,' since the work involves the intense, precise and accurate visualization of the magic's objective. Previously, scholar, imager and now soldier Quaeryt almost single-handedly defeated the invasion of Telaryn by the megalomaniac Rex Kharst of Bovaria. Recognizing that the only way to bring peace is to annihilate Rex Kharst, Lord Bhayar of Telaryn orders his armies to invade Bovaria." (Kirkus)

Modesitt, L. E.

Imager's challenge; the second book of the Imager portfolio. by L.E. Modesitt, Jr. 1st ed. Tor 2009 460 p. (hardcover) $27.99

ISBN 0765321262; 9780765321268

LC 2009019454

This is the second book in L.E. Modesitt's Imager Portfolio series. Here, "still recovering from injuries received in foiling the plots of the Ferran envoy, Rhenn is preparing to take up his new duties as imager liaison to the Civic Patrol of L'Excelsis." He finds that "the Commander of the Civic Patrol doesn't want a liaison from the infamous Collegium." Further, "Rhenn receives formal notice that one of the High Holders . . . has declared his intention to destroy Rhenn and his family." (Publisher's note)

Modesitt, L. E.

Imager's intrigue; L.E. Modesitt, Jr. 1st ed. Tor 2010 495 p. map (hardcover) $27.99

ISBN 0765325624; 9780765325624

LC 2010030209

In this third installment of J.R. Modesitt's Imager series, "Rhennthyl, a powerful 'imager' (as wizards are known here) and security operative is also a captain of police, and only a little distracted by his beautiful wife Seliora and their three-year-old daughter Diestrya. But several ominous developments are stirring great unease at the Collegium Imago and among the Civil Patrol and the Council of Solidar." (Kirkus Reviews)

Modesitt, L. E.

The **one**-eyed man; a fugue, with winds and accompaniment. L. E. Modesitt, Jr. Tor Books 2013 352 p. (hardback) $25.99

ISBN 0765335441; 9780765335449

LC 2013022128

In this book, "Paulo Verano is an ecologist sent to survey the far-flung planet of Stittara, the sole source of life-extending 'cosmetic and physiological anagathics' and home to the mysterious and possibly intelligent skytubes." (Publishers Weekly) Verano "finds that many facts [about the skytubes] are being concealed or deliberately ignored." (Kirkus Reviews)

Modesitt, L. E.

Scholar; L.E. Modesitt, Jr. Tor 2011 508p. map

ISBN 9780765329554; 0765329557

LC 2011021610

This book is "set on the world of Terahnar . . . where a handful of people have the power to create objects through visualization. . . . Telaryn's young, talented ruler, Bhayar . . . suggests to Quaeryt, a young scholar whose advice he values, that troops might be withdrawn from the occupation of Tilbor for redeployment. . . . Quaeyrt allows Bhayar to persuade him to travel to Tilbor and report. Quaeryt is secretly an imager, or wizard, as well as a scholar. . . . Quaeryt arrives in Tilbor, where he finds that the governor, Rescalyn, has quietly accreted and trained an army vastly larger than anybody suspected. . . . After combing through the records, Quaeryt realizes he might need to risk his own life to uncover the truth." (Kirkus)

Modiano, Patrick, 1945-

Suspended sentences; three novellas. Patrick Modiano, translated by Mark Polizzotti. Yale University Press 2014 213 p. (The Margellos World Republic of Letters) paperback $16

ISBN 0300198051; 9780300198058

LC 2014026824

Author Patrick Modiano won the Nobel Prize in Literature in 2014.

This story collection, by Patrick Modiano, translated by Mark Polizzotti, is a "trilogy of novellas by the winner of the 2014 Nobel Prize in Literature. . . . Although originally published separately, Modiano's three novellas form a single, compelling whole, haunted by the same gauzy sense of place and characters. . . . Orphaned children, mysterious parents, forgotten friends, enigmatic strangers--each appears in this three-part love song to a Paris that no longer exists." (Publisher's note)

"Even Modiano's style, plain but elliptical and carefully wrought, keeps much of the action from view, as Modiano considers the modernization of Paris as a means of forgetting. It's as if all the characters are minor, so little can be known about them. But it is just as likely they have something to hide, even from themselves. Unforgettable." Booklist

Moehringer, J. R.

Sutton; J. R. Moehringer. Hyperion 2012 334 p.

ISBN 1401323146; 9781401323141

LC 2011052473

This biographical novel, by J. R. Moehringer, tells the story of the bank robber Willie Sutton. "[I]n the first year of the twentieth century, Willie Sutton came of age at a time when banks were out of control. . . . Sutton saw only one way out, only one way to win the girl of his dreams. So began the career of America's most successful bank robber. . . . In Moehringer's retelling, it was more than need or rage at society that drove Sutton. It was one unforgettable woman." (Publisher's note)

Mogford, Thomas

Shadow of the rock; Thomas Mogford. Walker & Co. 2012 261 p. (hardcover) $25

ISBN 0802779999; 9780802779991

LC 2011038765

This is the first in Thomas Mogford's series with "Spike Sanguinetti, a tax lawyer turned detective. One night in Gibraltar's Old Town, Spike runs into an old school friend, Sephardic Jew Solomon Hassan, who needs his help . . . fighting extradition to Morocco, where Solomon is wanted for the murder of Esperanza Castillo, the tattooed, multipierced, promiscuous stepdaughter of Ángel Castillo, cofounder of a new solar energy venture that promises billions of euros in potential revenues." (Publishers Weekly)

Moggach, Deborah

Tulip fever. Delacorte Press 2000 281p

ISBN 0-385-33489-3

LC 99-42048

First published 1999 in the United Kingdom

A novel set in 17th-century Amsterdam. "Moggach introduces us to the elderly Cornelis Sandvoort; his beautiful young bride, Sophia, . . . her lover, Jan, who is hired to paint the Sandvoorts' portrait; and Sophia's maid, Maria. As 'Tulip Fever' unfolds, Sophia's tentative romance with Jan gradually becomes so reckless that it is analogous to Amsterdam's obsession with tulips. Made ruthless by love, the couple plan to escape the city. . . . Moggach's book reads like a thriller: it's a novel that ponders what it means to push things too far, and keenly examines what the consequences might be." N Y Times Book Rev

Mohamed, Nadifa

★ The **orchard** of lost souls; a novel. Nadifa Mohamed. Farrar Straus & Giroux 2014 352 p. (hardback) $26

ISBN 0374209146; 9780374209148

LC 2013034411

In this book, "a brutal confrontation in pre-civil war Somalia intertwines three women's lives. . . . The story opens in 1987 in the city of Hargeisa, as the widow Kawsar and the orphan Deqo prepare for a pro-government rally that all locals are required to attend. . . . When Kawsar saves Deqo from a beating for forgetting her dance steps, a female soldier, Filsan, arrests Kawsar and beats her so severely that she can never walk again." (Publishers Weekly)

"Mohamed evokes the burgeoning unrest of a city on the brink of chaos with vibrant, evocative language and imagery, crafting a story that will stay with readers long after the final page is turned." Booklist

Includes bibliographical references

Mohr, Joshua

Damascus; a novel. Two Dollar Radio 2011 206p pa $16

ISBN 978-0-9826848-9-4

LC 2011-925179

"It's 2003, and Mohr's Damascus is not the Syrian capital but a dingy Mission District bar decorated with shards of broken glass and cotton-ball clouds. Its lovable and lonely owner, Owen, feels less proud of his bar than imprisoned by it. After 18 years, he's still barely scraping by, partly because he's too generous toward his patrons. Haunting Damascus is a man called No Eyebrows, who is dying of cancer, his skin 'gray like toxic oatmeal,' and Shambles, a commitment-phobic woman who eschews intimacy by performing sexual favors in the bar's bathroom. Joining them is Byron Settles, a bitter Iraq veteran 'missing in inaction' after a parachute accident forced him to come home the moment he touched down in Bashur. Driving the story to its violent but cathartic climax is Syl, an artist who honors the fallen soldiers of the wars in Iraq and Afghanistan with an exhibition in Damascus that involves a fish slaughter." San Francisco Chron

Momaday, N. Scott

The **ancient** child; a novel. Doubleday 1989 313p

LC 89-31304

"Locke Setman, a highly successful Bay Area painter, fears that he has lost touch with his 'inner child' in the process of making it big. Then, during a brief trip to Oklahoma, he meets a beautiful American Indian woman named Grey who dresses in beaded buckskin, speaks Kiowa and Nanajo like one of the elders, and has elaborate visionary conversations with the ghost of Billy the Kid. Armed with a medicine bundle and a bag of peyote buttons, Grey slowly draws Setman into a magical world of ritual that both revitalizes and transforms him. . . . A fascinating and hypnotically beautiful book that belongs in every collection of Western Americana." Libr J

Momaday, N. Scott

House made of dawn. Harper & Row 1968 212p

"Abel, a young American Indian, lives with his grandfather, observing Indian customs, until he is drafted into the army. The story covers the years 1945 to 1952, during which time Abel seems unable to find his place either in the white world, where he is driven to violence, or on the Indian reservation where he was born. The pain of being caught between two cultures is keenly felt and can be comprehended as a problem that has affected other ethnic groups." Shapiro. Fic for Youth. 3d edition

Monaghan, Nicola

The **killing** jar; a novel. Scribner 2007 288p $24

ISBN 978-0-7432-9968-8; 0-7432-9968-X

LC 2006-48679

First published 2006 in the United Kingdom

"The violence of The Killing Jar is often difficult, the inhumanity often unbearable, but the book rewards a reader who wants an unsparing-really, really unsparing-account of a disastrous childhood, an account that is nonetheless sensitively rendered and deceptively simple." City Paper (Baltimore)

Monette, Paul

Afterlife. Crown 1990 278p

LC 89-48754

"Despite its comic flourishes, this is a tough, painful book about gay sex and love, pursued in the valley of the shadow of AIDS. And its unrelenting descriptions of the ravages of the disease, along with its sexual details and 'talking dirty,' are surely going to make some readers uncomfortable." N Y Times Book Rev

Monsarrat, Nicholas

The **cruel** sea. Knopf 1951 509p

"The Compass Rose is a British corvette commissioned to convoy duty and to the hunting of German U-boats during World War II. First Mate Lockhart and Skipper Erikson develop a close relationship. When their ship is sunk and few of the crew survive, Lockhart and Erikson team up again on a new ship, undaunted by the experiences visited upon them by the cruel sea." Shapiro. Fic for Youth. 3d edition

Moody, David

Hater. Thomas Dunne Books 2009 281p $21.95

ISBN 978-0-312-38483-8; 0-312-38483-1

LC 2008-36519

First published 2006 in the United Kingdom

"The novel moves at a deliberate, relentless pace, feeding readers just enough information to keep them perplexed and paranoid, and the depiction of a society being rent at the seams by violence rings true. Moody creates some truly chilling scenes, but there are also flashes of black comedy. At times savagely brutal—the moments of outrageous violence may be considered over-the-top by some readers—but engrossing and effective." Kirkus

Moody, Rick

Right livelihoods; three novellas. Little, Brown 2007 223p $23.99

ISBN 978-0-316-16634-8; 0-316-16634-0

LC 2006-26937

"In 'The Omega Force,' a tale rife with satirical meaning, the patriotic doctor defending the security of his domain against people who are 'dark-complected' turns out to be a lunatic. Paranoia is also evident in 'K&K' as an office manager finds some dissident messages in the company's suggestion box and suspects a conspiracy. The third, 'The Albertine Notes,' introduces an amateur journalist who, while researching the drug issue for a porno magazine, falls victim to drug culture and suffers from hallucinations that New York City is being obliterated. The unreliable and eccentric characters that so often populate Moody's novels again effectively remind us of the nation's collective hysteria. His convoluted narrative may challenge the patience of some readers, but those who persist will find it rewarding." Libr J

Moon, Elizabeth

Once a hero. Baen Pub. Enterprises 1997 400p

ISBN 0-671-87769-0

LC 96-48176

"Moon's mastery of contemporary science fiction is evident in every line. The characters spring to life on the page, the intricacies of societies are astutely explored, and the pace never flags." Booklist

Moon, Elizabeth

The **speed** of dark. Del Rey Bks. 2002 340p $23.95

ISBN 0-345-44755-7

LC 2002-20771

"Moon is effective at putting the reader inside Lou's mind, and it is both fascinating and painful to see the behavior and qualities of so-called normals through his eyes." Booklist

Moor, Margriet de

The **storm**; a novel. translated by Carol Brown Janeway. Alfred A. Knopf 2010 257p $25.95

ISBN 978-0-307-26494-7

LC 2009-37578

Original Dutch edition, 2005

"In the winter of 1953, hurricane-driven flood waters rushing in from the North Sea destroyed dikes and obliterated an entire province in the southwestern Netherlands. . . . De Moor observes this disaster from the juxtaposed viewpoints of two sisters—young wife and mother Lidy and her virginal younger sibling Armanda. When Armanda offers to take Lidy's two-year-old daughter Nadja to a party, in exchange for Lidy's appearance at a similar event held for Armanda's godchild—for the sisters resemble each other so closely, few people can tell them apart—they also exchange destinies. Lidy travels to the imminently endangered seaside town of Zierkezee, while Armanda becomes companion for the day to Nadja and her father (and Lidy's husband) Sjoerd. . . . It's hard to resist using the word 'symphonic' to describe this exquisitely composed, piercingly moving story. De Moor continues to scale increasingly impressive heights." Kirkus

Moorcock, Michael

An **alien** heat; volume one of a trilogy The dancers at the end of time. Harper & Row 1973 158p (Dancers at the end of time)

First published 1972 in the United Kingdom

This novel "is set near the end of the world, when Earth is populated by hedonistic immortals who restructure continents and their own bodies at whim. A young man named Jhereck becomes unfashionably obsessed with Mrs. Amelia Underwood, a time traveler from the 19th century, his favorite period. He follows her to London of 1896, where he is tried for murder and hanged, which somehow returns him to the future, sans Amelia but with insights into love and the true human condition. This tale could be called an Art Nouveau morality play or a science fiction comedy of manners. The humor is genuine, the style lush but controlled." Libr J

Followed by The hollow lands

Moorcock, Michael

The **dreamthief's** daughter; a tale of the albino. Warner Bks. 2001 343p $35

ISBN 0-446-52618-5

LC 00-43836

"In this latest installment in his multivolume saga of the Eternal Champion, Moorcock . . . teams his favorite hero, the melancholy albino swordsman Elric of Melniboné, with Count Ulric von Bek, the last in a line of German noblemen. . . . War is in the offing, and Hitler, having learned that the von Bek family may own both an enchanted sword and the Holy Grail itself, sends SS Major Gaynor von Minct to take possession of these mystical relics so they may be used to further the cause of the Third Reich. Von Bek and Gaynor, however, are merely the current earthly avatars of the Eternal Champion and one of his greatest foes; they are knights fighting in the causes, respectively, of Chaos and Law, in innumerable, gorgeously described, alternate realities." Publ Wkly

Moore, Alan, 1953-

Jerusalem; a novel. Alan Moore. Liveright Publishing Corp. 2016 1280 p. illustrations, map (hardcover) $35

ISBN 9781631491344; 9781631492433

LC 2016014957

In this epic novel by Alan Moore, the "rich cast of characters includes the living, the dead, the celestial, and the infernal. . . . In these pages lurk demons from the second-century Book of Tobit and angels with golden blood who reduce fate to a snooker tournament. Vagrants, prostitutes, and ghosts rub shoulders with Oliver Cromwell, Samuel Beckett, James Joyce's tragic daughter Lucia, and Buffalo Bill, among many others." (Publisher's note)

Moore "bundles all his ruminations about space, time, life, and death into an immense interconnected narrative that spans all human existence within the streets of his native Northampton, U.K. Reading this sprawling collection of words and ideas isn't an activity; it's an experience." Pub Wkly

Moore, Alison

The **Lighthouse**; Alison Moore. Salt Publishing 2012 183 p. (paperback) $9.17; (ebook) $15.82

ISBN 1907773177; 9781907773174; 9780857869968

Man Booker Prize Shortlist (2012)

This book by Alison Moore was longlisted for the Man Booker prize. "Its Anglo-German protagonist, Futh, takes a walking holiday on the continent to recover from the break-up of his marriage. But as his story unfolds -- a series of memories nested like Russian dolls -- we soon see that what's really under his skin is his mother's decision to leave him and his father some 30 years earlier." (Guardian)

Moore, Brian

The **lonely** passion of Judith Hearne. Little, Brown 1956 223p

First published 1955 in the United Kingdom with title: Judith Hearne

"Judith Hearne is a middle-aged spinster whose plain looks and loneliness make her depressed and increasingly isolated from any social contact. The other renters in her Belfast boarding house disdain her. Only Mrs. O'Neill, an old school friend, treats her kindly. When her landlady's brother, Jim Madden, returns from America, he pays some attention to Judith, thinking she has money. Jim's bad character is revealed in many ways, including a sexual attack on a young housemaid, and Judith finds more and more solace in drinking. Her pathetic world falls apart completely when even her religious faith deserts her. This sad novel presents a portrait of despair that is almost unbearable." Shapiro. Fic for Youth. 3d edition

Moore, Christopher

A **dirty** job; a novel. Morrow 2006 387p il $24.95

ISBN 0-06-059027-0

LC 2005-57501

"Much of the pleasure of Moore's tale resides not only in the ingeniously unpredictable events but also in the prickly vitality of his language. Striking figures of speech . . . and aphorisms grace the text." Washington Post Book World

Moore, Christopher, 1957-

Sacre bleu; a comedy d'art. Christopher Moore. HarperCollins 2012

ISBN 006177975X; 0061779741; 9780061779756; 9780061779749

LC 2012009804

In this novel, "[a]n aspiring painter and unabashed romantic joins the greatest artists of the age in chasing his muse across fin de siècle-era France. . . . The story surrounds the mysterious suicide of Vincent van Gogh, who famously shot himself in a French wheat field only to walk a mile to a doctor's house. The mystery . . . is blue: specifically the exclusive ultramarine pigment that accents pictures created by the likes of Michelangelo and van Gogh. To find the origin of the hue, [Christopher] Moore brings on Lucien Lessard, a baker, aspiring artist and lover of Juliette, the brunette beauty who breaks his heart. After van Gogh's death, Lucien joins up with the diminutive force of nature Henri Toulouse-Lautrec to track down the inspiration behind the Sacré Bleu." (Kirkus)

Moore, Christopher, 1957-

The **Serpent** of Venice; a novel. Christopher Moore. William Morrow 2014 336 p. map $26.99

ISBN 0061779768; 9780061779763

LC 2014002826

Sequel to: Fool (2009)

This book, [Christopher] Moore's mash-up of Othello and The Merchant of Venice with [Edgar Allan] Poe's 'The Cask of Amontillado' is a . . . sequel to 'Fool,' his twisted retelling of King Lear. . . . After a dastardly trio of Venetians (including Iago) plot to bury alive Pocket the fool for thwarting an attempt to cook up a new Crusade from which they'd hoped to profit. . . . He washes up in Venice's Jewish ghetto and is rescued by Shylock's lovably abrasive daughter, Jessica." (Publishers Weekly)

"Pocket fumbles his way through a complicated adventure buoyed by Moore's half-cocked Shakespearean dialogue, puerile humor and ceaseless banter. The setting helps the author's cause, lending a rich historical backdrop that includes trade disputes, political intrigue and Shakespearean spectacle." Kirkus

Moore, Christopher

You suck; a love story. Morrow 2007 208p $21.95

ISBN 978-0-06-059029-1; 0-06-059029-7

Moore "manages, despite figures like a blue-painted prostitute who prompts visions of sex with a Smurf, to keep the book's eccentricity in check and its screwball antics from becoming insufferable. As with his best work, there's a fundamental sweetness beneath the antics." N Y Times (Late N Y Ed)

Moore, Edward Kelsey

The **Supremes** at Earl's all-you-can-eat; by Edward Kelsey Moore. 1st ed. Alfred A. Knopf 2013 320 p. (hardcover) $24.95

ISBN 0307959929; 9780307959928

LC 2012028743

Followed by: The Supremes at Earl's All-You-Can-Eat (2017)

This debut novel from Edward Kelsey Moore tells the "story of a trio of women nicknamed the Supremes in smalltown Indiana—Odette, Clarice, and Barbara Jean. . . . From high school on, through marriages and children, the three friends regularly get together with their husbands at Earl's All-You-Can-Eat (the first black-owned business in Plainview) to see and be seen, share gossip, and help each other through bad times." (Library Journal)

Moore, Edward Kelsey

The **Supremes** sing the happy heartache blues; a novel. Edward Kelsey Moore. Henry Holt & Co. 2017 299 p. (hardcover) $28

ISBN 9781250107923; 9781250107947

LC 2016048172

Sequel to: The Supremes at Earl's All-You-Can-Eat (2013)

In this novel, by Edward Kelsey Moore, "when a late life love affair blooms between Mr. Forrest Payne, the owner of the Pink Slipper Gentleman's Club, and Miss Beatrice Jordan, famous for . . . yelling warnings of eternal damnation at the [club's] departing patrons, their wedding summons a legend to town. Mr. El Walker, the great guitar bluesman, comes home to give a command performance in Plainview, Indiana, a place he'd sworn . . . he'd never set foot in again." (Publisher's note)

Moore, Graham, 1981-

The **last** days of night; a novel. Graham Moore. Random House 2016 368 p. (hardcover) $28

ISBN 9780812988918; 9780812988901

LC 2015050362

This novel, by Graham Moore, is "based on actual events . . . [and is] about the nature of genius, the cost of ambition, and the battle to electrify America. New York, 1888. . . . A young untested lawyer named Paul Cravath . . . takes a case that seems impossible to win. Paul's client, George Westinghouse, has been sued by Thomas Edison over a billion-dollar question: Who invented the light bulb and holds the right to power the country?" (Publisher's note)

"Moore's extensive research is apparent, and readers are likely to walk away from the book feeling as informed as they are entertained." Pub Wkly

Moore, Graham, 1981-

The **Sherlockian**. Twelve 2010 350p $24.95

ISBN 978-0-446-57259-0; 0-446-57259-4

LC 2010-09554

"Thanks to the sly self-awareness that keeps "The Sherlockian" smart and agile, it's possible to enjoy this book's laughable affectations and still be seduced by them. This is a novel by, for and about Holmes-quoting mystery nuts, and it understands what makes them happy." N Y Times (Late N Y Ed)

Moore, Jonathan

The **night** market; Jonathan Moore. Houghton Mifflin Harcourt 2018 304 p. (San Francisco novels) (hardcover) $24

ISBN 9780544671898

LC 2017044907

In this thriller, by Jonathan Moore, "it's late Thursday night, and Inspector Ross Carver is at a crime scene. . . . The dead man on the floor is covered by an unknown substance that's eating through his skin. Before Carver can identify it, six FBI agents burst in and remove him from the premises. . . . On Sunday he wakes in his bed to find his neighbor, Mia . . . reading aloud to him. He can't remember the crime scene or how he got home; he has no idea two days have passed." (Publisher's note)

"A sharp and scary near-future thriller that delivers a dark message about society's love affair with technology." Kirkus

Moore, Kathleen Dean

Piano tide; a novel. Kathleen Dean Moore. Counterpoint 2016 xiii, 269 p.p (hardcover) $25

ISBN 9781619028708; 9781619027916

LC 2016020230

In this novel, by Kathleen Dean Moore, "Axel Hagerman . . . has made a killing in . . . [a] remote Alaskan harbor by selling off the spruce, the cedar, the herring and halibut. But when he decides to export the water from a salmon stream, he runs head-long into young Nora Montgomery, just arrived on the ferry with her piano and her dog. . . . But when Axel's next business proposition, a bear pit, turns lethal, Nora has to act." (Publisher's note)

"Moore writes so eloquently and with such passion about the natural world, from tiny tide-pool inhabitants to giant grizzlies and towering hemlocks, that she leaves the reader in wonder and awe." Booklist

Moore, Lisa

February. Black Cat 2010 310p pa $14.95

ISBN 978-0-8021-7070-5; 0-8021-7070-6

First published 2009 in Canada

This is the account "account of how one ordinary Newfoundland family carries on after the Ocean Ranger disaster, the infamous sinking of the offshore oil rig on Valentine's Day, 1982, that killed all 84 men aboard, including the fictional Cal O'Mara. Cal leaves behind his wife, Helen, and four children, one of whom is just a twinkle in her dead father's eye that night. (Not even Helen knows she's pregnant yet.) How Helen manages on her own, and doesn't, and the effect the loss of his father has on John, Cal and Helen's firstborn, 10 in 1982, amounts to a meditation on grief. . . . Moore offers us, elegantly, exultantly, the very consciousness of her characters." Globe and Mail

Moore, Liz ✓

★ The **Unseen** World; A Novel. Liz Moore. W W Norton & Co Inc 2016 448 p. $26.95

ISBN 0393241688; 9780393241686

In this book by Liz Moore, "Ada Sibelius is raised by David, her brilliant, eccentric, socially inept single father, who directs a computer science lab in 1980s-era Boston. . . . Ada accompanies David to work every day; by twelve, she is a painfully shy prodigy. The lab begins to gain acclaim at the same time that David's mysterious history comes into question. When his mind begins to falter, leaving Ada virtually an orphan, she is taken in by one of David's colleagues." (Publisher's note)

Moore, Lorrie, 1957-

Bark; stories. by Lorrie Moore. Alfred A. Knopf 2014 208 p. (hardcover : alk. paper) $24.95

ISBN 0307594130; 9780307594136

LC 2013014777

This book presents eight short stories by Lorrie Moore. "Here are people beset, burdened, buoyed; protected by raising teenage children; dating after divorce; facing the serious illness of a longtime friend; setting forth on a romantic assignation abroad, having it interrupted midtrip, and coming to understand the larger ramifications and the impossibility of the connection." (Publisher's note)

"Smart, funny, and overlaid with surprising metaphor, these stories depict absurd situations that are at the same time strikingly familiar." LJ

Moore, Lorrie, 1957-

A **gate** at the stairs; a novel. Alfred A. Knopf 2009 321p $25.95

ISBN 0-375-40928-9; 978-0-375-40928-8

LC 2009-03091

"Set just after the events of September 2001, [this novel is] about a twenty-year-old woman from a small midwestern farm." (Publisher's note)

"The novel concludes in a tone of wan hope, with Tassie wiser and stronger, though forever sadder. . . . This book is—not above all, but in the service of all—funny. Moore is not shy about the bad joke, and never pushes a great one too far. Her humor, always pointed at insight and elaboration, strikes the perfect balance between taste and feeling." PopMatters

Moore, Meg Mitchell

So far away; a novel. Meg Mitchell Moore. Reagan Arthur Books 2012 322 p.

ISBN 0316097691; 9780316097697

LC 2011051322

This novel by Meg Mitchell Moore follows "thirteen-year-old Natalie Gallagher [who] is trying to escape. . . . Adrift, confused, she is a girl trying to find her way in a world that seems to either neglect or despise her. Her salvation arrives in an unlikely form: Bridget O'Connell, an Irish maid working for a wealthy Boston family. The catch? Bridget lives only in the pages of a dusty old 1920s diary Natalie unearthed in her mother's basement." (Publisher's note)

Moore, Susanna

The **big** girls. Alfred A. Knopf 2007 224p $24

ISBN 978-1-4000-4190-9; 1-4000-4190-2

LC 2006-48819

"Set in a women's prison on the Hudson River, Moore's sixth novel chronicles the aftermath of a highly publicized murder and its impact on four intertwined lives. The story is told in the alternating voices of Helen, who has long suffered terrifying schizophrenic hallucinations and is serving a life sentence for killing her two small children; Helen's psychiatrist, a single mother who came to work at the prison out of guilt over a patient's suicide; a corrections officer who becomes involved with the psychiatrist; and an ambitious Hollywood star whom Helen believes to be her sister. Moore gradually probes Helen's psychosis to its horrifying origins, while also delivering a nuanced and devastating account of the fights, rapes, and alliances built from necessity that constitute prison life." New Yorker

Moore, Susanna, 1948-

The **life** of objects; Susanna Moore. Alfred A. Knopf 2012 239 p.

ISBN 0307268438; 9780307268433

LC 2012019890

This novel, by Susanna Moore, takes place "in 1938. . . . Seventeen-year-old Beatrice, . . . finds herself . . . whisked away . . . to join the Berlin household of Felix and Dorothea Metzenburg. . . . But Germany has launched its campaign of aggression across Europe, and . . . the conflict reaches the Metzenburgs' threshold. . . . Beatrice, . . . bears heartrending witness to the atrocities of the age and to the human capacity for strength in the face of irrevocable loss." (Publisher's note)

Mootoo, Shani

Moving forward sideways like a crab; Shani Mootoo. Akashic Books 2017 304 p. (hardcover) $27.95

ISBN 9781617755545; 9781617755774; 1617755346; 9781617755347; 161775577X

LC 2016953891

Lambda Literary Award Shortlist (2014); Scotiabank Giller Prize Longlist (2014)

In this novel, by Shani Mootoo, "Jonathan Lewis-Adey was nine when his parents separated, and his mother, Sid, vanished entirely from his life. It is not until he is a grown man that Jonathan finally reconnects with his beloved lost parent, only to find, to his shock and dismay, that the woman he knew as 'Sid' in Toronto has become an elegant man named Sydney living in his native Trinidad." (Publisher's note)

"A finalist for the Lambda Award, Mootoo's character-driven novel is rich in setting and slow in pace, inviting the reader to linger over its closely observed details." Booklist

Morais, Richard C.

The **hundred**-foot journey; a novel. Scribner 2010 245p $23

ISBN 1-4391-6564-5; 978-1-4391-6564-5

LC 2009-50619

An earlier edition of this work was originally published in India in 2008

In this novel, Hassan Haji, a boy from Mumbai, becomes a world-class chef in Paris.

"A lovely little book, something sweet, savory, if not dense, agreeable to all, ambitious about food, if not necessarily about plot or character. Sometimes readers yearn for a feast of a book. Other times, a tasty morsel will do." Philadelphia Inquirer

Moran, Michelle

Rebel queen; a novel. Michelle Moran. Touchstone 2015 368 p. (hardcover) $26

ISBN 1476716358; 9781476716350; 9781476716367

LC 2014026037

This novel by Michelle Moran tells the "story of Queen Lakshmi--India's Joan of Arc--who against all odds defied the mighty British invasion to defend her beloved kingdom. Instead of surrendering, Queen Lakshmi raises two armies--one male and one female--and rides into battle, determined to protect her country and her people." (Publisher's note)

"This often deeply moving novel focuses on its characters, allowing history to play out as a backdrop to the personal story of a young woman who would risk everything, including her own life, for her people. Fans of the author's earlier novels will almost certainly greet this one with enthusiasm, but, because it's not tied to Moran's earlier books, it's perfect for new historical-fiction readers, too." Booklist

Morgan Jones, Chris, 1971-

The **jackal's** share; Chris Morgan Jones. The Penguin Press 2013 336 p. $25.95

ISBN 1594205353; 9781594205354

LC 2012039511

Sequel to: The silent oligarch (2012)

This book is part of Chris Morgan Jones's Ben Webster series. Here, Webster works for the corporate investigation company, Ikertu Consulting. Darius Qazai, London-based refugee Iranian owner of Tabriz Asset Management, needs their services" to determine why a business deal fell through. "A . . . phone call unearths the rat: rumors circulate that Qazai was responsible for the theft of the Sargon relief, a half-ton eighth-century Assyrian stone art object looted from Baghdad post-invasion." (Kirkus)

Morgan Jones, Chris, 1971-

The **silent** oligarch; Chris Morgan Jones. Penguin Press 2012 312 p.

ISBN 9781594203190

LC 2011044536

In this book "[m]ysterious men, cryptic of speech and beautifully tailored, move through glittery settings-seacoasts, grand hotels, swank neighborhoods. . . . Rows of massive buildings 'bullied all the leaves off the bare limes and left the trees cowering in the middle of the road.' Ben Webster is a snoop employed by a London corporate espionage firm. His boss' client has hired the company to bring down a Kremlin functionary, the toadlike Malin, whose manipulation of Russia's oil industry is making him a trillionaire. Webster attempts to get at the toad through his dithering money launderer, Richard Lock. . . . Men are betrayed. Drugged. Kidnapped. Tossed off buildings. Downed by snipers. If the good guys win, it's at such a cost they're left wondering if they accomplished anything. They did." (Booklist)

Morgan, C. E., 1976-

All the living. Farrar, Straus and Giroux 2008 208p $23

ISBN 0-374-10362-3; 978-0-374-10362-0

LC 2008-13854

"One summer, a young woman travels with her lover to the isolated tobacco farm he has inherited after his family dies in a terrible accident. As Orren works to save his family farm from drought, Aloma struggles with the loneliness of farm life." (Publisher's note)

"Aloma, the 21-year-old protagonist of C.E. Morgan's debut novel, doesn't appear to have a whole lot going for her. An orphan whose guardians farmed her out to a mission school before her 12th birthday, she's never lived in a house, is poorly educated and has no family to speak of. Romanced by a young tobacco farmer from Kentucky hill country, Aloma falls in love as only a young woman with so little life experience can. When Orren invites her to quit her job teaching piano at the mission school and live with him on his family's broken-down farm after his widowed mother and brother are killed in a car accident, she packs up what little she has and moves in. Thus sets the stage for a quiet but undeniably moving story about loss and desire, and how to reconcile the two." Edmonton J

Morgan, C. E., 1976-

★ The **sport** of kings; A Novel. C. E. Morgan. Farrar, Straus & Giroux 2016 560 p. (hardback) $27

ISBN 9780374281083; 0374281084

LC 2015038512

Kirkus Prize: Fiction (2016)

Pulitzer Prize Finalist: Fiction (2017)

Baileys Women's Prize for Fiction: Shortlist (2017)

In this book, by C. E. Morgan, "Hellsmouth, an indomitable Thoroughbred with the blood of Triple Crown winners in her veins, runs for the glory of the Forge family, one of Kentucky's oldest and most powerful dynasties. Henry Forge has partnered with his daughter, Henrietta, . . . to breed the next superhorse. . . . But when Allmon Shaughnessy, an ambitious young black man, comes to work on their farm, the violence of the Forges' history . . . are brought starkly into view." (Publisher's note)

"A dense meditation on the ugliness that undergirds much of the sublime we as humans strive for and admire in life." LJ

Morgan, Jessica

The **royal** we; Heather Cocks, Jessica Morgan. Grand Central Publishing 2015 464 p. (hardcover) $26

ISBN 1455557102; 9781455557103

LC 2014049047

This novel, by Heather Cocks and Jessica Morgan, "debunk[s] the princess fantasy in a fictional tell-all inspired by the courtship of Kate Middleton and Prince William. On the night before her wedding, Rebecca Porter admits that she wasn't an obvious match for Prince Nicholas of Wales when they first met in the dorms at Oxford. . . . The question is not whether she loves Nick but whether his love is worth a lifetime of public scrutiny." (Kirkus Reviews)

"Parallels to the love story of Prince William and Kate Middleton are obvious, but the authors create their own unique and endearing characters with Bex and Nick--along with an entertaining cast of characters including lovable rogue Prince Freddie, Nick's younger brother; Bex's twin, Lacey; and a bunch of colorful school chums." Pub Wkly

Morgan, Jude

The **Secret** Life of William Shakespeare; Jude Morgan. St. Martin's Press 2014 448 p. (hardback) $26.99

ISBN 1250025036; 9781250025036; 9781250054838

LC 2013045690

"There are so few established facts about how the son of a glove maker from Warwickshire became one of the greatest writers of all time that some people doubt he could really have written so many astonishing plays." This novel, by Jude Morgan, "pulls back the curtain to imagine what it might have really been like to be Shakespeare before a seemingly ordinary man became a legend." (Publisher's note)

Morgan "takes liberties with the Bard's words, motivations, and personality while staying true to the spirit of the Shakespeare we all know and love. An entertaining read." Booklist

Morgan, Richard K.

Altered carbon. Del Rey Bks. 2003 375p pa $13.95

ISBN 0-345-45768-4

LC 2002-31165

First published 2002 in the United Kingdom

A "seamless marriage of hardcore cyberpunk and hard-boiled detective tale." Times (London, England)

Morgan, Richard K.

Broken angels. Del Rey Bks. 2004 366p pa $14.95

ISBN 0-345-45771-4 pa

LC 2003-62515

This novel "is clearly the work of a gifted, ambitious storyteller. Morgan's prose is clean and direct, his characters almost uniformly hard-edged, his future convincing, well conceived and decked out with an almost limitless array of technological marvels." Washington Post Book World

Morgan, Richard K.

Thirteen. Del Rey 2007 544p $24.95

ISBN 978-0-345-48525-0; 0-345-48525-4

LC 2007-10617

Published in the United Kingdom with title: Black man

"For all that Morgan steps outside some of the usual conventions he is still recognisably working in the format and [Thirteen] comes with some of its bad habits. . . . Morgan's approach is problematic but at the same time it is so utterly different to anything else ou there that it is almost impossible not to admire it." Strange Horizons

Morgan, Robert, 1944-

The **road** from Gap Creek; a novel. Robert Morgan. Algonquin Books of Chapel Hill 2013 336 p. $25.95

ISBN 1616201614; 9781616201616

LC 2013008906

This book is Robert Morgan's sequel to "Gap Creek." Here, "Annie, the daughter of Gap Creek's Julie and Hank, is married to Muir Peace, but her younger brother Troy and his dog, Old Pat, are closest to her affections. . . . While Troy's work produces admiration and opportunity, Muir's work often leads to humiliation; he lays the foundation for an ill-fated stone church on a mountaintop that mirrors his dream of becoming a preacher." (Publishers Weekly)

Morgenstern, Erin

The **night** circus. Doubleday 2010 387 p. $26.95

ISBN 978-0-385-53463-5; 0-385-53463-9; 9780385534635

LC 2010050546

Alex Award (2012), RUSA Reading List: Fantasy (2012)

In this book "two magicians of indefinite but certainly magically long lifespan - one a public performer named Prospero the Enchanter, aka Hector Bowen; the other known only as 'the man in the grey suit' or 'Mr. A. H---' - are engaged in a profound rivalry, played out over many generations by appointed pupils. In the late 19th century, Bowen elects his six-year-old daughter Celia, while his counterpart chooses a nameless nine-year-old orphan who will be called Marco Alisdair. These two are bound into a lifelong challenge, the parameters of which are never fully explained to them; and for years they do not know their adversaries. The circus . . . is also the creation of Marco and Celia, both of who, over the years, become passionately embroiled in its performances and acts, as well as, inevitably, with each other." (The Guardian)

"The plot follows the separate and then intertwining lives of Celia and Marco, both forced to spend their lives pitting their unusual talents against each other in a cruel competition. But their world is Morgenstern's most vivid creation, a fantastical circus featuring illusionists whose powers transcend mere sleight of hand; like those performers, the author entices her audience to suspend disbelief and rewards its members with captivating pleasure." People

Moriarty, Laura

The **center** of everything. Hyperion 2003 291p $22.95; pa $14

ISBN 1-401-30031-6; 0-7868-8845-8 pa

LC 2002-32898

"Any map clearly shows that Kansas is the center of everything. Ten-year-old Evelyn Bucknow notices it on every map that she sees and truly believes that is where she belongs—in the center. Unfortunately, Evelyn is forced to parent her mother, a flighty, unrealistically romantic woman who is having an affair with her married boss. . . . Fortunately, Evelyn takes the events of her life and her mother's life and learns her lessons, with a few glitches along the way. Young people will find Evelyn appealing and real despite the book's setting in the age of Ronald Reagan and big hair, and they will respond positively to her determination." Voice Youth Advocates

Moriarty, Liane, 1966-

★ **Big** little lies; Liane Moriarty. Penguin Group USA 2014 480 p. $26.95

ISBN 0399167064; 9780399167065

LC 2015300007

Written by Liane Moriarty, "'Big Little Lies' follows three women, each at a crossroads: Madeline's teenage daughter seems to be choosing Madeline's ex-husband over her. . . . Celeste is the kind of beautiful woman who makes the world stop and stare. While she may seem a bit flustered at times, who wouldn't be, with those rambunctious twin boys? . . . New to town, single mom Jane is so young that another mother mistakes her for the nanny." (Publisher's note)

"Moriarty demonstrates an excellent talent for exposing the dark, seedy side of the otherwise 'perfect' family unit while keeping the characters believable enough to be someone you might know." LJ

Moriarty, Liane, 1966-

The **husband's** secret; by Liane Moriarty. Amy Einhorn Books 2013 416 p. $25.95

ISBN 0399159347; 9780399159343

LC 2013009340

In this book by Liane Moriarty "Cecilia Fitzpatrick . . . finds a letter from her husband, John-Paul, to be opened only in the event of his death. She opens it anyway, and everything she believed is thrown into doubt. Meanwhile, Tess O'Leary's husband, Will, and her cousin and best friend, Felicity, confess they've fallen in love, so Tess takes her young son, Liam, and goes to Sydney to live with her mother." (Publishers Weekly)

"There is real darkness here, but it is offset by the author's natural wit . . . and irrepressible goodwill toward her characters. " Kirkus

Moriarty, Liane, 1966-

Truly madly guilty; Liane Moriarty. Flatiron Books 2016 432 p. (ebook) $60; (hardcover) $26.99

ISBN 9781250069818; 9781250069795

LC 2016014386

In this book, by Liane Moriarty, "Sam and Clementine have a wonderful, albeit, busy life: they have two little girls, Sam has just started a new dream job, and Clementine, a cellist, is busy preparing for the audition of a lifetime. . . . Clementine and Erika are each other's oldest friends. . . . But theirs is a complicated relationship, so when Erika mentions a last minute invitation to a barbecue with her neighbors, Tiffany and Vid, Clementine and Sam don't hesitate." (Publisher's note)

"This novel sheds light on the truths that we all fear as parents, spouses, and friends. It's perfect for those long summer days, but readers will have to pace themselves to not devour it in one sitting." LJ

Moriarty, Liane

What Alice forgot. Amy Einhorn Books 2011 426p $24.95

ISBN 978-0-399-15718-9; 0-399-15718-2

LC 2011002904

First published 2009 in Australia

"Alice's journey of reconciling herself to how her life came to be what it is, and her slowly building understanding of how the threads of her marriage began to unravel, is moving, well-paced, and thoroughly pleasurable." Publ Wkly

Morley, Isla

Come Sunday. Sarah Crichton Books/Farrar, Straus and Giroux 2008 322p $25

ISBN 978-0-374-12687-2; 0-374-12687-9

LC 2008-38829

"Although true resolution is far from sure, Come Sunday, organized by portions of the liturgical year, ends with Ascension Day. It's a hopeful note that promises redemption." Christianity Today

Morrell, David, 1943-

Murder as a fine art; David Morrell. Mulholland Books/ Little, Brown and Co. 2013 368 p. $25.99

ISBN 0316216798; 9780316216791

LC 2012020034

Author David Morrell tells a mystery story about a serial killer in London, England. "Thomas De Quincey . . . is the prime suspect in a series of horrific murders that paralyze London. The killer seems to be imitating De Quincey's true-crime essay 'On Murder Considered as One of the Fine Arts.' Desperate to prevent more atrocities but crippled by opium addiction, De Quincey is aided by his brilliant daughter, Emily, as well as two determined Scotland Yard detectives." (Publisher's note)

Morris, Keith Lee

The **dart** league king. Tin House Books 2008 270p pa $14.95

ISBN 978-0-9794198-8-1; 0-9794198-8-3

LC 2008-20391

"A dark and deeply involving novel with a haunting moment on just about every page. Suspenseful, gritty, great." McSweeney's

Morris, Mary McGarry

Songs in ordinary time. Viking 1995 740p

ISBN 0-670-87907-X

LC 94-44071

"The novel is frequently perceptive about the bitter pathos bred by the feeling that you've always lived on someone else's leftovers. . . . The novel is also insightful and frightening on the unshakable resilience of family grudges." N Y Times Book Rev

Morris, Michael

Man in the blue moon; Michael Morris. Tyndale 2012 400 p. (hc) $19.99

ISBN 1414373309; 9781414368429; 9781414373300

LC 2012016147

"Single mother Ella Wallace fights to keep a banker from buying the Florida land that has been in her family for generations when a mysterious stranger shows up and convices Ella he can help her, until his past comes to light." (Publisher's note)

"A magical and mesmerizing page-turner..." Pub Wkly

Morris, Willie

Taps; a novel. Houghton Mifflin 2001 340p $26

ISBN 0-618-09859-3

LC 00-68250

"Over the course of a year, in intervals framed by a dozen graveside ceremonies for men shipped back from Korea to the summer-baked or winter-frozen cemetery outside town, Swayze tells the story of a passing Southern world and his own troubled growing up. . . . Funerals are its talismans and 'Taps' is at it strongest when it describes them." N Y Times Book Rev

Morrison, Toni, 1931-

★ **Beloved**; a novel. by Toni Morrison ; [with a new foreword by the author] Vintage International 2004 xix, 321 p.p

ISBN 1400033411; 9781400033416

LC 2004555136

Pulitzer Prize for Fiction (1988)

"Before the war, Sethe, pregnant, sent her children away to their grandmother in Ohio, whose freedom had been paid for by their father. Sethe runs too, but when her 'owners' come to recapture her, she attempts to murder the children, succeeding with one, named Beloved. This murder will (literally) haunt Sethe for the rest of her life and affect everyone around her." (Library Journal)

This novel, "set in the third quarter of the 19th century, focuses on the life of the runaway slave woman Sethe and her struggle with the unspeakable pain of her past. Like Morrison's earlier novels, Beloved is marked by rich and lyrical language, narratives shot through with exotic and magical elements, and a fragmented structure that requires readers to participate in the telling." Benet's Reader's Ency of Am Lit

Morrison, Toni, 1931-

★ The **bluest** eye; with a new afterword by the author. Knopf 2005 215p $19.95

ISBN 0-375-41155-0

LC 93-43124

A reissue of the title first published 1970 by Holt, Rinehart & Winston

"This tragic study of a black adolescent girl's struggle to achieve white ideals of beauty and her consequent descent into madness was acclaimed as an eloquent indictment of some of the more subtle forms of racism in American society. Pecola Breedlove longs to have 'the bluest eye' and thus to be acceptable to her family, schoolmates, and neighbors, all of whom have convinced her that she is ugly."

"This tragic study of a black adolescent girl's struggle to achieve white ideals of beauty and her consequent descent into madness was acclaimed as an eloquent indictment of some of the more subtle forms of racism in American society. Pecola Breedlove longs to have 'the bluest eye' and thus to be acceptable to her family, schoolmates, and neighbors, all of whom have convinced her that she is ugly." Merriam-Webster's Ency of Lit

Morrison, Toni, 1931-

★ **God** help the child; Toni Morrison. Alfred A. Knopf 2015 192 p. (hardcover : acid-free paper) $24.95

ISBN 0307594173; 9780307594174; 9780307740922

LC 2014034972

This novel by Toni Morrison centers on "a young woman who calls herself Bride, whose stunning blue-black skin is only one element of her beauty, her boldness and confidence, her success in life, but which caused her light-skinned mother to deny her even the simplest forms of love. There is Booker, the man Bride loves, and loses to anger. Rain, the mysterious white child with whom she crosses paths. And finally, Bride's mother herself, Sweetness." (Publisher's note)

"There are some moves here that may seem obvious, but the pieces all fit together seamlessly in a story about beating back the past, confronting the present, and understanding one's worth." LJ

Morrison, Toni, 1931-

★ **Home**; Toni Morrison. Random House Inc 2013 145 p. (pbk.) $14

ISBN 0307740919; 9780307740915

LC 2012462661

In this book, the "Korean conflict is over, and soldier Frank Money has returned to the States with a disturbed psyche that sends him beyond anger into actually acting out his rage. From the mental ward in which he has been incarcerated for an incident he can't even remember, he determines that he must escape. He needs to get to Atlanta to attend to his gravely ill sister and take her back to their Georgia hometown of Lotus." (Booklist)

Morrison, Toni

Jazz. Knopf 1992 229p $26.95

ISBN 0-679-41167-4

LC 91-58555

"As the story unfolds, we come to understand, if not excuse, what happened. The characters themselves cannot excuse their own behavior, which baffles them. Violet is obsessed by the memory of the dead girl whose face she slashed: What was it about her that Joe found so special? She is driven to visit the girl's aunt Alice, who is understandably frightened. . . . Some of the most interesting scenes in the book are the subsequent meetings of these two very different women who come to respect each other, even before they learn to understand each other." Christ Sci Monit

Morrison, Toni

Love. Knopf 2003 201p $23.95

ISBN 0-375-40944-0

LC 2003-52737

"Like all of Morrison's best fiction, this is a village novel. Race and racism, ancillary concerns in 'Love' for the most part, throw the small groups she writes about upon one another, steeping their passions. Even when the setting is contemporary, Morrison's books feel old fashioned, set in a world where the perpetual distraction of the media hasn't diluted people's fascination with their neighbors." N Y Times Book Rev

Morrison, Toni

A **mercy**; a novel. Knopf 2008 167p $23.95

ISBN 978-0-307-26423-7; 0-307-26423-8

LC 2008-21067

The fate of a slave child abandoned by her mother animates this allusive novel part Faulknerian puzzle, part dream-song about orphaned women who form an eccentric household in late-17th-century America. Morrison's farmers and rum traders, masters and slaves, indentured whites and captive Native Americans live side by side, often in violent conflict, in a lawless, ripe American Eden that is both a haven and a prison an emerging nation whose identity is rooted equally in Old World superstitions and New World appetites and fears. N Y Times Book Rev

Morrison, Toni

Paradise. Knopf 1998 318p $25

ISBN 0-679-43374-0

LC 97-80913

"In 1950, a core group of nine old families leaves the increasingly corrupted African American community of Haven, Okla., to found in that same state a new, purer community they call Ruby. But in the early 1970s, the outside world begins to intrude on Ruby's isolation, forcing a tragic confrontation. It's about this time, too, that the first of five damaged women finds solace in a decrepit former convent near Ruby. . . . The individual stories of both the women and the townspeople reveal Morrison at her best." Publ Wkly

Morrison, Toni

★ **Song** of Solomon. Knopf 1977 337p $27.50

ISBN 0-394-49784-8

LC 77-874

"Chaos marked the world into which Macon (known as Milkman) Dead was born. Each member of his family was haunted by some wild obsession—his father's desire for money, land, and social status, his mother's need for love, his sisters' silence, and his Aunt Pilate's madness. To these was added Macon's desire to unearth the family's buried past. This is a novel of mystery and revelation as it unfolds the lives of four generations of blacks in America." Shapiro. Fic for Youth. 3d edition

Morrison, Toni

Sula. Knopf 1974 174p hardcover o.p. pa $14

ISBN 0-394-48044-9; 1-4000-3343-8 pa

This "is the story of two black women friends and of their community of Medallion, Ohio. The community has been stunted and turned inward by the racism of the larger society. The rage and disordered lives of the townspeople are seen as a reaction to their stifled hopes. The novel follows the lives of Sula and Nel from childhood to maturity to death." Merriam-Webster's Ency of Lit

Morrison, Toni

Tar baby. Knopf 1981 305p $26.95

ISBN 0-394-42329-1

LC 80-22821

"Each of the characters in Toni Morrison's Tar Baby comes with a history, quite a complete history that is given to us in a series of stunning performances." New Repub

Morrow, James

The **last** witchfinder; a novel. William Morrow 2006 526p il $25.95

ISBN 0-06-082179-5

LC 2005-47177

"Although steeped in period language and scholarship, the narrative never falters. Morrow's panoramic vision of the Enlightenment encompasses the ideology of that turbulent, transformative era, and his wry commentary–related through the sprightly voice of Newton's Principia Mathematica, speaking for itself–lightens the novel's tone without softening its message. This impeccably researched, highly ambitious novel. . . is a triumph of historical fiction." Booklist

Morrow, James

The **philosopher's** apprentice. William Morrow 2008 411p $25.95

ISBN 978-0-06-135144-0; 0-06-135144-X

LC 2007-29815

This novel " begins with Mason Ambrose walking out on his Ph.D. defense, disgusted by what he perceives as the innate hypocrisy in the process. He stumbles into a job for which he seems ideal. Edwina Sabacthani, world-renowned geneticist, hires him to teach her 17-year-old daughter, Londa, about morality. According to Edwina, Londa suffered an accident that caused not only profound amnesia but a complete loss of her moral sense. . . . A satirist of the first water, Morrow gives us a novel by turns poignant, piquant and potent. From his initial premise—part 'Frankenstein,' part 'Emile,' with a dash of 'The Island of Dr. Moreau' thrown in—he backs away from none of the implications of the technology or the ideologies of the main characters, taking us down a rabbit hole that is both haunting and exhilarating. He confronts the reader with the ramifications of choice and action, offering a harrowing tour of cause and consequence." St. Louis Post-Dispatch

Mortimer, John

Felix in the underworld. Viking 1997 246p

LC 97-16562

"This novel is actually about the characters of literary and legal London, and we soon realize that the point is not just to allow these people to circulate in the pages of narrative but, more importantly, to turn character into caricature. . . . John Mortimer's writing is fluent, gently humorous, and possesses the comic's virtue, tact." Times Lit Suppl

Mortimer, John

Quite honestly. Viking 2006 206p $24.95

ISBN 0-670-03483-5

LC 2005-53157

First published 2005 in the United Kingdom

"Good intentions pave Lucy Purefoy's way into all kinds of misadventures in this engaging satire. . . . Mortimer clearly enjoys poking fun at middle-class do-gooders-especially Lucy's dad, a bishop so tolerant that he probably puts a 'pretty please' at the end of the Sixth Commandment. The end result is a tad slight, but fine for readers who enjoy light satire with a little larceny on the side." Christ Sci Monit

Mortimer, John

Rumpole's return. Armchair Detective Lib. 1992 159p

LC 91-29415

First published 1980 in paperback in the United Kingdom

"After losing in Judge Bullingham's court for the tenth straight time, Rumpole finds the beaches of Florida a welcome change from the dampness of home. Basking in the sun, he comes across an account of the Notting Hill Gate murder in a back copy of The Times which sparks a nerve. This is the sort of case he enjoyed. The evidence is stacked against the accused. . . . Rumpole's uncanny assessment of the situation is that the facts are out of synch." Publisher's note

Morton, Brian, 1955-

Florence Gordon; Brian Morton. Houghton Mifflin Harcourt 2014 320 p. (hardback) $25

ISBN 0544309863; 9780544309869

LC 2014011676

In this novel by Brian Morton, "At seventy-five, Florence has earned her right to set down the burdens of family and work and shape her legacy at long last. But just as she is beginning to write her long-deferred memoir, her son Daniel returns to New York from Seattle with his wife and daughter, and they embroil Florence in their dramas, clouding the clarity of her days and threatening her well-defended solitude. And then there is her left foot, which is starting to drag." (Publisher's note)

"Morton's characters are sharply drawn, vivid in temperament and behavior, and his prose smartly reveals Florence's strength and dignity." Pub Wkly

Morton, Carson

Stealing Mona Lisa; Carson Morton. 1st ed.; Minotaur Books 2011 340p.

ISBN 9780312621711; 9781250015730

LC 2011009099

This book, which was named "Library Journal"'s Best Mystery of 2011, tells the story of Eduardo de Valfierno, an art forger who "makes a very respectable living in Argentina fleecing the nouveau rich. . . . But when Eduardo meets the beautiful Mrs. Hart on his latest con, he takes a risk that forces him back to the city he loved and left behind—Paris. There he assembles his team of con artists for their final and most ambitious theft, one that will enable them to leave the game forever: The Mona Lisa. But when a member of the team turns up missing, and Mr. Hart shows up in Paris, Valfierno and his crew must stay one step ahead of a relentless police inspector, endure a devastating flood, and conquer their own doubts to keep the priceless painting in play—and survive." (Publisher's note)

Includes bibliographical references [339]-340).

Morton, Kate

The **distant** hours; a novel. Kate Morton. Atria Books 2010 562 p. $26

ISBN 1439152780; 9781439152782

LC 2010033472

This book by Kate Morton is an "intergenerational story . . . centering on two families: the Blythes of Milderhurst Castle and the Burchills, from working-class London. While researching a children's novel, Edie Burchill is led to the idiosyncratic Blythe sisters, now quite elderly, who had resided at Milderhurst when her mother, Meredith, was sent there to escape the blitz during World War II." (Library Journal)

Morton, Kate

The **house** at Riverton; a novel. Atria Books 2008 473p $24.95

ISBN 978-1-4165-5051-8; 1-4165-5051-8

LC 2008-7023

First published 2006 in Australia with title: The shifting fog

"For decades, Grace Reeves has kept secret the truth of a poet's violent death by the lake at Riverton House in Oxfordshire. Now at the end of her life, 98-year-old Grace's memory is swept back, after interviews for a film about the tragic incident, to those years of her service for the Hartford family. At 15, Grace begins her adult life as a housemaid in the grand Riverton House, quickly learning her place in the servant hierarchy. Her loyalty and attachment to Hannah and Emmeline Hartford grow over the years, as the Hartford family is affected by war, death, financial failings, and illicit love. . . . A suspenseful and beautifully atmospheric novel capturing the transitional time from the end of the Edwardian era through World War I into the Roaring Twenties." Libr J

Moses, Kate

Wintering; a novel of Sylvia Plath. St. Martin's Press 2003 292p $23.95

ISBN 0-312-28375-X

LC 2002-36753

"A fictionalization of the grueling months following the dissolution of Plath's marriage to Ted Hughes and leading up to her suicide at the age of 30 in 1963. 'Wintering' is beautiful and moving. The narrative voice is a distillation of Plath's diaries, letters and poems; with lyrical dexterity and great economy, Moses portrays a demanding, pitiless woman struggling against the stark fact of her husband's infidelity and her own inner demons." N Y Times Book Rev

Mosher, Howard Frank

On Kingdom Mountain. Houghton Mifflin Co. 2007 276p $24

ISBN 978-0-618-19723-1; 0-618-19723-0

LC 2006-23568

"Mosher's passionate geographical hyperbole is both justifiable and charming, producing a wonderfully intriguing sense of place." Washington Post Book World

Moshfegh, Ottessa, 1981-

Eileen; A Novel. by Ottessa Moshfegh. Penguin Group USA 2015 272 p. $25.95

ISBN 1594206627; 9781594206627

LC 2015297387

Man Booker Prize Shortlist (2016)

National Book Critics Circle Award Finalist: Fiction (2015)

In this novel, by Ottessa Moshfegh, "the title character is a plain-Jane type stuck in a miserable job (secretary at a boys' prison) and an even worse home life (she minds her desperately alcoholic father in an unkempt house). . . . The sole shaft of light arrives in the form of Rebecca Saint John, a new education director at the prison who rapidly becomes an unhealthy source of emotional solace." (Kirkus Reviews)

"Moshfegh keeps all options on the table while keeping her heroine coherent. A shadowy and superbly told story of how inner turmoil morphs into outer chaos." Kirkus

Mosley, Walter, 1952-

All I did was shoot my man; Walter Mosley. Riverhead Books/Penguin Group 2012 326p $26.95

ISBN 9781594488245

LC 2011046844

In this book, "author Walter Mosley takes readers back into the world of private investigator Leonid McGill. The novel is Mosley's fourth thriller featuring the New York City PI, and this time, he's wrapped up with the case of a woman named Zella Grisham. Grisham has just served eight years on a 16-year prison term for grand larceny. Though McGill played a key role in her arrest, he is convinced that Grisham is innocent. . . . The novel follows McGill's journey to atone for his corrupt past, as he helps Grisham get her life back on track." (NPR)

Mosley, Walter, 1952-

And sometimes I wonder about you; a Leonid McGill mystery. Walter Mosley. Doubleday, an imprint of Penguin Random House 2015 288 p. (hardcover) $26.95

ISBN 0385539185; 9780385539180; 9780804172097

LC 2014044246

In this mystery novel, by Walter Mosley, New York private eye "Leonid finds himself in an unusual pickle of trying to balance his cases with his chaotic personal life. . . . Meanwhile, Leonid is approached by an unemployed office manager named Hiram Stent to track down the whereabouts of his cousin, Celia. . . . Leonid declines the case, but after his office is broken into and Hiram is found dead, he gets reeled into the underbelly of Celia's wealthy old-money family." (Publisher's note)

"While Mosley is best known for his Easy Rawlins novels, set in the post-WWII and later twentieth-century era, this gritty, present-day series deserves serious attention from all fans of mainstream hard-boiled detective fiction." Booklist

Mosley, Walter

Bad Boy Brawly Brown. Little, Brown 2002 311p

ISBN 0-316-07301-6

LC 2002-16232

"As Easy persists in his investigation, he is dismissed by black radicals and rousted by racist cops. . . . So he can't really be blamed for spending more time than he should in places like Sam's Hambones soul food diner, engaging in invigorating of often aimless conversations with characters who have little to offer on Brawly's whereabouts but lots to say about whatever is on their minds. Aside from their appealing hero, Mosley's crime novels take their vitality from the racy language and boisterous humanity of his characters, so these neighborhood encounters provide their own joy." N Y Times Book Rev

Mosley, Walter

Black Betty. Norton 1994 255p

ISBN 0-393-03644-8

LC 94-6839

"Mosley gives us a recognizable moment in American history viewed through the eyes of a single black man. This perspective, rare in crime fiction, vivifies not only the black experience but the larger event as well. Here we feel the hot winds that would eventually ignite the Watts riots not as abstract issues in race relations, but as emotions in the hearts of individuals we have come to know and care about." Booklist

Mosley, Walter

Cinnamon kiss. Little Brown 2005 312p $24.95

ISBN 0-316-07302-4

LC 2005-5739

"As ever, Mosley is able to capture the era–hippies, Watts, communes–in brief strokes that provide a brilliant background to Easy's search for solutions to both a convoluted mystery and complex personal problems." Publ Wkly

Mosley, Walter, 1952-

★ **Devil** in a blue dress. Norton 1990 219p $19.95

ISBN 0-393-02854-2

LC 89-25503

"Ezekiel 'Easy' Rawlins, a young, tough black veteran living in 1948 Los Angeles, only wants respect and enough money to pay his mortgage. When fired from his factory job, however, he undertakes some paid errands for a shady white mobster. . . . As Easy plumbs his usual hangouts for clues, he relays information to the mobster, runs afoul of the police, meets the mysterious woman, discovers a murder, then investigates in self-defense." (Library Journal)

"Mosley's prose is a little stiff and his plot is far too complicated. But he has a keen eye for period details. . . . And his lowdown humor never deserts him." Newsweek

Other titles about Easy Rawlins are:

A red death (1991)
White butterfly (1992)
Black Betty (1994)
A little yellow dog (1996)
Gone fishin' (1997)
Bad boy Brawly Brown (2002)
Six Easy pieces (2003)
Little Scarlet (2004)
Cinnamon kiss (2005)
Blonde faith (2008)
Little green (2014)
Rose gold (2014)
Charcoal Joe (2016)

Mosley, Walter

Fearless Jones; a novel. Little, Brown 2001 312p

ISBN 0-316-59238-2

LC 00-53502

This "mystery is narrated by Paris Minton, a black man who sells used books in nineteen-fifties L.A. Paris's life is perfect—he reads all day without interruption—until a bewitching young woman named Elana Love walks through his door. She's looking for a religious group called the Messenger of the Divine, but the thug who bursts in after her is looking for a bond worth thousands of dollars. Mayhem and seduction ensue, and when Paris's bookstore is burned to the ground, he knows it's time to seek the aid of the incomparable Fearless Jones. The unlikely friendship of these men—Fearless is all fists and testosterone, Paris is a gun-shy truth-seeker—is the source of the novel's humor, and propels the reader through the plot's knottier moments." New Yorker

Mosley, Walter ✓

Fortunate son. Little, Brown and Co. 2006 313p hardcover o.p. pa $13.99

ISBN 978-0-316-11471-4; 0-316-11471-5; 978-0-316-06628-0 pa; 0-316-06628-1 pa

LC 2005-24477

"Tommy was born out of wedlock with a hole in his heart; he's also lame and black. Eric, on the other hand, glows with health; he is so beautiful that people want to touch him—and he's white. For a few years, the boys live together after Tommy's mother and Eric's widowed doctor father fall in love after meeting in the hospital ward. Then Tommy's mother dies, and Tommy is wrested from the only family he's known. Eric grows up leading a life that appears blessed, but with Tommy gone, he's lost all that is important to him. Tommy, meanwhile, ends up on the street but feels lucky simply to be alive. . . . The writing is crisp and the plotting impeccable." Libr J

Mosley, Walter

Gone fishin' an Easy Rawlins novel. Black Classic Press 1997 244p

LC 97-124077

This novel marks the first appearance of Mosley's detective-hero, Easy Rawlins. "Written before the other Rawlins novels but never published, it takes Easy and his lethal friend Mouse back to Texas before World War II and their subsequent move to Los Angeles. The 19-year-old Easy . . . knows little of the larger world. His journey to awareness begins with a soul-changing road trip to the bayous of Pariah, Texas, where Mouse hopes to settle a score with his hated stepfather." (Booklist)

This is "in some respects, the best of Mosley's novels. . . . It firmly establishes Mosley as a writer whose work transcends the thriller category and qualifies as serious literature." Time

Mosley, Walter ✓

Known to evil. Riverhead Books 2010 325p $25.95

ISBN 978-1-59448-752-1; 1-59448-752-9

LC 2009-42643

"This second installment of Walter Mosley's new detective series opens at the dinner table. He gives you a quick look around the room — walnut cabinet, Blue Danube china, old quart pickle jar doing duty as a flower vase — then takes you inside the protagonist's head. That's how a great portion of the story unfolds: through private detective Leonid McGill's inner musings. If you thought Easy Rawlins was a complicated character, spend a little time with McGill as he tries to find a missing woman, avoid police determined to jail him, deal with his imploding marriage, protect his sons from themselves, fend off a move to evict him from his offices and heal from a broken heart administered by an ex-lover." NPR

Mosley, Walter

✓The **last** days of Ptolemy Grey. Riverhead Books 2010 277p $25.95

ISBN 978-1-59448-772-9; 1-59448-772-3

LC 2010-12317

"Physically fragile and mentally lost, 91-year-old Ptolemy Grey . . . [is] dependent on his great-grandnephew Reggie for the basic necessities of life. . . . When Reggie is killed in a drive-by shooting, his caregiver duties are assumed by 17-year-old Robyn Small." (N Y Times Book Rev)

"Narrated in an intimate whisper, the story draws us deep into the mind of an old man wandering through the remnants of his memories, searching for the key to an old mystery. Physically fragile and mentally lost, 91-year-old Ptolemy Grey lives alone in shocking squalor, dependent on his great-grandnephew Reggie for the basic necessities of life. Ptolemy is still capable of holding a conversation — but mostly with people from long ago, like Coy McCann, the charismatic friend and mentor who entrusted the young Ptolemy with a stolen fortune. . . . When Reggie is killed in a drive-by shooting, his caregiver duties are assumed by 17-year-old Robyn Small, a 'wild and violent' but 'sweet and loving' family friend who cleans and fumigates Ptolemy's pestilential apartment and takes him to a clinic where the old man's dementia is temporarily reversed with a miraculous but toxic experimental drug. . . . His wits restored, Ptolemy takes action, in the short time he has left to live, to unearth Coy's lost 'pirate's treasure,' avenge Reggie's murder and ensure the future well-being of his family. The tale of an aged superhero who performs valiant deeds with the aid of a devoted young sidekick (pointedly named Robyn) may sound like the charming stuff of myth. But Mosley invests his wish-fulfillment fantasy with deeper meaning and higher purpose." N Y Times Book Rev

Mosley, Walter, 1952-

Little green; an Easy Rawlins mystery. Walter Mosley. Doubleday 2013 304 p. (hardcover) $25.95

ISBN 0385535988; 9780385535984; 9780385535991

LC 2012036464

This novel, by Walter Mosley, is part of the "Easy Rawlins Mystery" series. "We last saw Easy . . . fighting for his life after his car plunges over a cliff. True to form, the tough WWII veteran survives, and soon his murderous sidekick Mouse has him back cruising the mean streets of L.A., in all their psychedelic 1967 glory, to look for a young black man, Evander 'Little Green' Noon, who disappeared during an acid trip." (Publisher's note)

Mosley, Walter, 1952-

Little Scarlet; Walter Mosley. 1st ed. Little, Brown and Co. 2004 306 p. (hardcover) $24.95

ISBN 0316073032; 9780316073035

LC 2003023002

In this book by Walter Mosley, private investigator "Easy Rawlins returns to solve a mystery. . . . Just after devastating riots tear through Los Angeles in 1965 . . . the police turn up at Easy Rawlins's doorstep. . . . [T]hey've come to ask for his help. A man was wrenched from his car by a mob at the riots' peak and escaped into a nearby apartment building. Soon afterward, a woman known as Little Scarlet was found dead in that building . . . but the man has vanished." (Publisher's note)

"This is Mosley's best novel to date: the plot is streamlined and the language simple yet strong, allowing the serpentine story line to support Easy's amazingly complex character and hypnotic narration as Mosley plunges us into his world and, by extension, the world of all blacks in white-run America. Fierce, provocative, expertly entertaining, this is genre writing at its finest." Pub Wkly

Mosley, Walter

A **little** yellow dog; an Easy Rawlins mystery. Norton 1996 300p

ISBN 0-393-03924-2

LC 96-4231

This mystery, set in the early 1960s, finds Easy Rawlins "working in a high school as head custodian for the Board of Education two years after giving up drinking and the 'street life.' When a corpse turns up on school grounds, Easy finds himself reluctantly caught up in the investigation—between the rock and the hard place of the cops and the killers. Mosley writes in the grand tradition of the American hard-boiled private investigator. His dialog is sharp and his characters vivid—the reader can almost feel the mean L.A. streets." Libr J

Mosley, Walter

The **long** fall. Riverhead Books 2009 305p $25.95

ISBN 978-1-59448-858-0; 1-59448-858-4

LC 2008-46238

The novel "accomplishes most of what an inaugural installment of a mystery series should. The three major plot strands are solidly developed and neatly resolved. McGill's quest for redemption, however, is far from over, but it will be interesting to watch it play out across a number of subsequent volumes. If 'The Long Fall' is overstuffed with incidental characters whose importance may not be obvious until later installments, that's a minor flaw. Having retired Easy Rawlins, Mosley has devised a worthy successor in Leonid McGill." San Francisco Chron

Mosley, Walter

The **man** in my basement; a novel. Little, Brown 2004 249p $22.95

ISBN 0-316-57082-6

LC 2003-56317

"In this successful and intriguing departure from his usual work, Mr. Mosley creates a substantial subplot about heritage and history. . . . In the end this audacious novel is about facing up to such brutal realities. But it is also about seeking refuge." N Y Times (Late N Y Ed)

Mosley, Walter

A **red** death. Norton 1991 284p

ISBN 0-393-02998-0

LC 90-23660

"In this second installment in the series, the calendar has moved ahead to the early 1950s, and the good-natured (and aptly named) Easy is in a pickle. The IRS is after him for hiding income from the apartment buildings he secretly owns; a Red-hating FBI agent strong-arms him into investigating a labor agitator; and the local police suspect him in two murders." Booklist

Mosley, Walter

RL's dream. Norton 1995 267p

ISBN 0-393-03802-5

LC 95-8695

"A mesmerizing and redemptive tale of friendship, love, and forgiveness. . . . {This} is, without doubt, the author's finest achievement to date, a rich literary gumbo with blue-stinged rhythms that make it a joy to read and a book to remember." San Francisco Rev Books

Mosley, Walter

Six easy pieces. Atria Bks. 2003 278p $24

ISBN 0-7434-4252-0

"Mosley is as fine as ever, offering compelling commentary on black-white relations in 1964, writing in a style so simple that it deceives us into thinking wwriting great fiction is as easy as putting one foot in front of the other. It's not, but turning these pages is." Booklist

Mosley, Walter, 1952-

When the thrill is gone. Riverhead Books 2011 359p $26.95

ISBN 978-1-59448-781-1; 1-59448-781-2

LC 2010-39098

This installment finds Leonid McGill still "unable to shake his underworld connections — as a personal favor he['s undertaking a search for the lost friend of a powerful crime boss. But there are other pressing matters to be taken care of: a man who has been like a father to him lies dying in McGill's apartment, McGill's wife is sleeping with a man half her age and if McGill doesn't get a paying job he won't be able to pay the rent on his office. . . . For a healthy retainer, McGill takes the case of a nervous wife who suspects her billionaire husband of having an affair and planning to murder her to avoid a messy divorce. . . . Unlike the flamboyant criminals who swagger through Mosley's Easy Rawlins novels, the characters who catch your eye here are people who are normally invisible: old folks living on the edges of society and young black men with 'no notion of their history and no hope for a future except what they were told by the TV.' The qualities that make McGill fit to be their hero are the same ones that make him the quintessential New Yorker: he sees it all and knows it all and somehow feels responsible for it all." N Y Times Book Rev

Mosley, Walter ✓

White butterfly. Norton 1992 272p $19.95

ISBN 0-393-03366-X

LC 91-44700

"Standard stuff, to be sure—the makings of your typical made-for-television movie. But what elevates it is the character. It is not just that Rawlins is such an engaging fellow. He is a man who both ages and evolves." N Y Times Book Rev

Motion, Andrew

Silver; return to Treasure Island. Andrew Motion. Crown 2012 viii, 403 p.p (alk. paper) $24

ISBN 0307884872; 9780307884879; 9780307884893

LC 2012023773

This book by Andrew Motion is a sequel to Robert Louis Stevenson's book "Treasure Island." "Jim Hawkins now runs an inn . . . with his son, Jim, and Long John Silver has returned to England to live in obscurity with his daughter, Natty. . . . But for Jim and Natty, the adventure is just beginning. One night, Natty approaches young Jim with a proposition: return to Treasure Island and find the remaining treasure that their fathers left behind so many years before." (Publisher's note)

Followed by: The new world (2015)

Mott, Jason

The **Returned**. Harlequin Books 2013 400 p. $24.95

ISBN 0778315339; 9780778315339

In this book, all "are confused and disconcerted when people who have died inexplicably come back, including [an elderly] couple's 8-year-old son, whom they lost nearly 50 years ago. No one understands why people who died are coming back. . . . Considered by some the work of the devil, by others a miracle, the confounding reality is that an already struggling planet must abruptly support a staggering influx of beings who have typical human needs: food, water, shelter, sanitation." (Publishers Weekly)

Moulessehoul, Mohammed

The **swallows** of Kabul; translated from the French by John Cullen. Nan A. Talese\Doubleday 2004 195p $18.95

ISBN 0-385-51001-2

LC 2003-50769

The author is "intimately familiar with the consequences that war and religious extremism have on people's daily lives, and in this book he gives the reader a tactile sense of what life under the Taliban might have been like." N Y Times (Late N Y Ed)

Mowat, Farley

The **Snow** Walker. Little, Brown 1975 222p

The stories range "from the ancient to the overwhelmingly modern. . . . There are tales of starvation, cannibalism out of love, the giving of one body to another with the poignancy of the Eucharist. There are tales so simple and strong you read them again to make sure you haven't been tricked into feeling a story in your stomach for a change." N Y Times Book Rev

Moya, Horacio Castellanos

The **dream** of my return; by Horacio Castellanos Moya ; translated from the Spanish by Katherine Silver. New Directions Books 2015 160 p. (New Directions paperbook) (alk. paper) $15.95

ISBN 0811223434; 9780811223430

LC 2014027200

In this novel, by Horacio Castellanos Moya, "[d]rinking way too much and breaking up with his wife, an exiled journalist in Mexico City dreams of returning home to El Salvador. . . . When he decides to treat his liver pain with hypnosis, his few impulse-control mechanisms rapidly dissolve. Hair-brained schemes, half-mad arguments, unraveling murder plots, hysterical rants: everything escalates at a maniacal pace, especially the crazy humor." (Publisher's note)

"Moya has written a tight little novel that is wickedly witty and built on the idea of memory as a never-ending cause of inspiration and turmoil." Kirkus

Moyes, Jojo, 1969-

The **girl** you left behind; Jojo Moyes. Pamela Dorman Books/Viking 2013 384 p. $27.95

ISBN 0670026611; 9780670026616

LC 2013016795

This book "entwines two love stories set 90 years apart, connected by a painting called The Girl You Left Behind. In 1916, 22-year-old Sophie Lefevre struggles against a new German commandant in her occupied village in northern France," a man with a deep interest in a painting of Sophie her husband made. "Jumping ahead to London in 2006, the story turns to 32-year-old Liv Halston, whose architect husband David bought Sophie's painting for Liv shortly before he died in an accident." (Publishers Weekly)

Moyes, Jojo, 1969-

Me before you; a novel. Jojo Moyes. Pamela Dorman Books 2012 384 p. (hardback) 27.95

ISBN 0670026603; 9780670026609

LC 2012029301

In this book, 26-year-old Louisa "lives with her working-class family . . . and works at a local cafe. Then, the cafe closes, and she must find a job fast to ease her family's financial stress. Enter Will Traynor, a former world traveler, ladies' man and business tycoon who's been a quadriplegic since a traffic accident two years ago." To prevent Will's suicide, Louisa "decides to convince him to stay alive with a series of adventures." (Kirkus Reviews)

Followed by After you (2015)

Moyes, Jojo, 1969-

One Plus One; a Novel. Jojo Moyes. Pamela Dorman Books/Viking 2014 384 p. (hardback) $27.95

ISBN 0525426582; 9780525426585

LC 2013048524

In this book by Jojo Moyes, "Jess, barely able to make ends meet as a house cleaner after her husband, Marty, walks out, enlists the help of rich client Ed to drive her math-genius daughter Tanzie to a competition. If Tanzie wins, the prize will be enough to pay for her to attend a top-notch school." (Publishers Weekly)

"There's never anything predictable about stubbornly optimistic and protective Jess and her oddball kids, or the distracted Ed and his disjointed work-family relationships. It's exactly that quality that makes this offbeat journey so satisfying." Pub Wkly

Mrazek, Robert J.

Unholy fire; a novel of the Civil War. Thomas Dunne Bks. 2003 299p $24.95

ISBN 0-312-30673-3

LC 2002-32512

"Mrazek's portrayal of Civil War battle is stark, graphic, bloody and exciting, and is only exceeded by his memorable description of Washington, D. C. as a Gomorrah on the Potomac." Publ Wkly

Mueenuddin, Daniyal

In other rooms, other wonders. W. W. Norton & Company 2009 247p $23.95

ISBN 0-393-06800-5; 978-0-393-06800-9

LC 2008-40632

National Book Award Finalist: Fiction (2009)

This collection of linked stories describes the lives of landowners and their retainers on the Gurmani family farm in Pakistan.

"In eight beautifully crafted, interconnected stories, Mueenuddin explores the cutthroat feudal society in which a rich Lahore landowner is entrenched. . . . An elegant stylist with a light touch, Mueenuddin invites the reader to a richly human, wondrous experience." Publ Wkly

Mukherjee, Abir

A **Rising** Man; Abir Mukherjee. Pegasus Books 2017 386 p. (hardcover) $25.95

ISBN 168177416X; 9781681774770; 9781681774169

In this novel, by Abir Mukherjee, "Captain Sam Wyndham, former Scotland Yard detective, is a new arrival to Calcutta. Desperately seeking a fresh start after his experiences during the Great War, Wyndham has been recruited to head up a new post in the police force. He is immediately overwhelmed by the heady vibrancy of the tropical city, but with barely a moment to acclimatize or to deal with the ghosts that still haunt him, Wyndham is caught up in a murder investigation." (Publisher's note)

"Mukherjee's outstanding debut and series launch combines a cleverly constructed whodunit with an unusual locale—Calcutta in 1919—portrayed with convincing detail." Pub Wkly

Mukherjee, Bharati

Miss New India. Houghton Mifflin Harcourt 2011 328p $25

ISBN 978-0-618-64653-1; 0-618-64653-1

LC 2010-25569

"Mukherjee subtly continues the stories of the sisters from Desirable Daughters (2002) and The Tree Bride (2004) as she introduces Anjali Bose, a smart, rebellious 19-year-old who flees her provincial town after her father's attempt to arrange her marriage goes catastrophically wrong. With the help of her scholarly, covertly gay, expat American teacher, Anjali finds refuge in a decaying mansion, a remnant of the Raj, in Bangalore, the booming capital of call centers and electronic startups. There the brave country girl undergoes a crash course in urban life and the fizzing world of outsourcing, avatars, and social networks. Each character fascinates, and every detail glints with irony and intent, as Mukherjee brilliantly choreographs her compelling protagonist's struggles against betrayal, violence, and corruption in a dazzling plot that cunningly considers forms of tyranny blatant and insidious in a metamorphosing society." Booklist

Mukherjee, Neel

A **life** apart; A Novel. Neel Mukherjee. W W Norton & Co Inc 2016 371 p. (pbk.) $16.95

ISBN 0393352102; 9780393352108

In this novel, by Neel Mukherjee, "Ritwik Ghosh, twenty-two and recently orphaned, finds the chance to start a new life when he arrives in England from Calcutta. But Oxford holds little of the salvation Ritwik is looking for. Instead, he moves to London, where he drops out of official existence into a shadowy hinterland of illegal immigrants. The story that Ritwik writes to stave off his loneliness begins to find ghostly echoes in his own life." (Publisher's note)

"Historical and contemporary, lit with flashes of magic and violence, this intriguing novel offers multifaceted portraits of India and England as seen from the perspective of a clever, burdened misfit." Kirkus

Mukherjee, Neel

★ The **Lives** of Others; by Neel Mukherjee. W. W. Norton & Company 2014 416 p. $26.95

ISBN 0393247902; 9780393247909

LC 2014034302

Man Booker Prize Shortlist (2014)

This book, by Neel Mukherjee, is the "story of a family and a nation. The aging patriarch and matriarch of the Ghosh family preside over their large household, made up of their five adult children and their respective children. . . . Each set of family members occupies a floor of the home. . . . Poisonous rivalries between sisters-in-law, destructive secrets, and the implosion of the family business threaten to unravel bonds of kinship as social unrest brews in greater Indian society." (Publisher's note)

"This is an immensely accomplished, steady-handed achievement, Victorian in its solidity, quietly enthralling in its insightful observation of the ties that bind." Kirkus

Mukherjee, Neel

★ A **state** of freedom; a novel. Neel Mukherjee. W W Norton & Co Inc 2018 278 p. (hardcover) $25.95

ISBN 0393292908; 9780393292909; 9780393292916

LC 2017050182

"In this stunning novel, prize-winning author Neel Mukherjee wrests open the central, defining events of our century: displacement and migration. Five characters, in very different circumstances--from a domestic cook in Mumbai, to a vagrant and his dancing bear, to a girl who escapes terror in her home village for a new life in the city--find out the meanings of dislocation and the desire for more." (Publisher's note)

"Mukherjee's diverse perspectives and narrative treatments offer an honest, uncompromising look at the realities of his characters' circumstances and, most pointedly, their lack of control over them, as well as a compelling exploration of disparity and identity." Booklist

Mullen, Thomas

Darktown; A Novel. Thomas Mullen. 37 Ink/Atria 2016 384 p. (ebook) $19.99; (hardcover : acid-free paper) $26

ISBN 9781501133886; 9781501133862; 9781501133879

LC 2015041687

In this novel, by Thomas Mullen, that is set in the postwar, pre-civil rights South, "the Atlanta Police Department is forced to hire its first black officers, including war veterans Lucius Boggs and Tommy Smith, . . . [who] are met with deep hostility by their white peers. . . . When a black woman who was last seen in a car driven by a white man turns up dead, Boggs and Smith suspect white cops are behind it." (Publisher's note)

"Mullen's writing is extremely evocative in bringing the pre-civil rights South to life." Booklist

Mullen, Thomas

Lightning men; a novel. Thomas Mullen. 37 INK/Atria Books 2017 374 p. (the Darktown series) (hardcover) $26

ISBN 9781501138799; 9781501138805; 9781501138812

LC 2017004468

Sequel to: Darktown (2016)

In this novel in The Darktown Series, by Thomas Mullen, "officer Denny Rakestraw and 'Negro Officers' Lucius Boggs and Tommy Smith have their hands full in an overcrowded and rapidly changing Atlanta. . . . When Rake's brother-in-law launches a scheme to rally the Ku Klux Klan to 'save' their neighborhood, his efforts spiral out of control, forcing Rake to choose between loyalty to family or the law." (Publisher's note)

"Mullen effectively uses the police-procedural format to shine a light on the daily indignities and violence blacks suffered in the pre-civil rights South, while delivering a plot that never lets up on suspense." Booklist

Müller, Herta, 1953-

The **hunger** angel; a novel. Herta Müller; translated by Philip Boehm. Henry Holt and Co. 2012 p. cm. $26

ISBN 9780805093018

LC 2011050952

"This novel of the Gulag" follows "17-year-old Leo Auberg, [who] has just started having sex with men in the park, fearfully, risking jail; when the soldiers come calling, he's glad to escape his watchful small town. That gladness disappears on the cattle cars. . . . What follows are dozens of short sections as Leo riffs on conditions in the camp." (Kirkus Reviews)

"Under Müller's influence, the subject matter not only begs a reader's sympathy, but deftly illuminates the complex psychological state of starvation and displacement." Pub Wkly

Muller, Marcia ✓

Both ends of the night. Mysterious Press 1997 353p

LC 97-10129

Sharon McCone "sets out to help a friend and former flying instructor find her missing lover, but soon the friend has been murdered, and a missing-persons case has been transformed into a grudge match. With the help of her own lover and fellow flyer Hy Ripinsky, McCone ventures into the depths of the federal witness protection program, finding first the missing lover and then the killer in the wilds of Minnesota. There's plenty of nicely paced action here, and the flying lore provides effective ballast. Best of all, though, there is McCone at work, both as day-to-day professional detective and as aggrieved friend out for justice." Booklist

Muller, Marcia ✓

City of whispers. Grand Central Pub. 2011 262p $25.99

ISBN 978-0-446-57333-7

LC 2010051674

Private eye Sharon McCone receives an e-mail asking for help from her emotionally disturbed half-brother, Darcy Blackhawk, but he fails to reply to her response. As her search widens, Sharon uncovers a connection to an unsolved murder of a young woman who was heiress to a multimillion dollar fortune.

"Alternating chapters narrated by different characters add to the suspense of the intricate plot, which propels readers through a San Francisco few tourists see—from Colma, the city's necropolis, to the exclusive mansions of Sea Cliff—and to a harrowing, haunting denouement." Publ Wkly

Muller, Marcia

Cyanide Wells. Mysterious Press 2003 292p map $24.95

ISBN 0-89296-781-1

LC 2002-45516

"Matt Lindstrom leaves the life he has rebuilt in British Columbia to search for his ex-wife, Gwen. After she vanished from their California home, innuendo that he had murdered her ruined him, forcing his relocation. He discovers that she's in a Soledad County town called Cyanide Wells, living with a lesbian lover and an adopted child. When he goes there—For revenge? for solace?—he discovers she has taken off again, this time with the child. He and Carly McGuire, publisher of the county newspaper and Gwen's partner, perform an uneasy dance as they try to bring her back." Booklist

Muller, Marcia

★ **Dead** midnight. Mysterious Press 2002 289p

ISBN 0-89296-765-X

LC 2002-20097

This mystery has Sharon McCone "gathering evidence for a wrongful-death suit brought by the family of a sensitive young man driven to kill himself by the deplorable working conditions at a trendy online magazine. But events never advance in a straight line in Muller's complicated narratives, and the job that McCone took on because she thought it would help her come to grips with her own brother's suicide turns into a lethal game of industrial sabotage." N Y Times Book Rev

Muller, Marcia ✓

A **walk** through the fire. Mysterious Press 1999 293p $23

ISBN 0-89296-688-2

LC 98-51314

In this adventure, "Sharon McCone is seduced by the legends of Hawaii and nearly by one particular Hawaiian. Brought to Kauai initially to investigate 'accidents' on the set of her filmmaker friend's documentary, McCone finds herself dealing with murder, Hawaiian militants, and drug dealers." Libr J

Muller, Marcia ✓

Where echoes live. Mysterious Press 1991 326p

LC 90-84898

"Private eye Sharon McCone is on the ecological beat, as a renovated gold mine that could lead to environment destruction also leads to several deaths. A good mystery as fresh as today's headlines." Booklist

Muller, Marcia ✓

While other people sleep. Mysterious Press 1998 344p

ISBN 0-89296-650-5

LC 98-13394

"Muller's straightforward, no-nonsense writing and fully dimensioned characterizations lend credibility and color to her deftly plotted tale." Publ Wkly

Muller, Marcia ✓

A **wild** and lonely place. Mysterious Press 1995 386p

LC 94-48255

"A mellow, engaging and determined Sharon here heads a diverse and intriguing supporting cast." Publ Wkly

Muller, Marcia ✓

Wolf in the shadows. Mysterious Press 1993 356p

LC 92-50536

"San Francisco private eye Sharon McCone is understandably concerned about the disappearance of her mysterious lover, Hy Ripinsky. When she finds out that he had gone to Mexico to deliver $2 million in ransom, she really gets worried." Libr J

Munoz Molina, Antonio

In her absence; translated by Esther Allen. Other Press 2007 134p $13.95

ISBN 978-1-59051-253-1; 1-59051-253-7 pa

LC 2006-38139

Original Spanish edition, 2001

"Mario's limited yet intensely focused world does not let the reader take a breath for even a paragraph. Perhaps that is why the novel is so short. Neither the writer nor the reader could sustain such a pitch of living inside the head of an increasingly disturbed human being. But how can a short novel, a mere 134 pages, with little action and a mystery left unsolved, take hold of the reader in this way? The power is in the writing—preserved masterfully in Esther Allen's translation—the ability to slice away the exterior of a character like Mario and to offer a simple, naked view of his small joys and great sufferings." Washington Post Book World

Munoz Molina, Antonio

A **manuscript** of ashes; translated from the Spanish by Edith Grossman. Harcourt 2008 305p $25

ISBN 978-0-15-101410-1; 0-15-101410-8

LC 2007-36557

Original Spanish edition, 1986

"The most piercing moments arrive as the narrative edges toward Minaya's own voice. It may be that the author was still discovering how to experiment with the limitations and possibilities of third-person narration. Regardless, the release of this first novel not only provides insight into Munoz Molina's development as a writer but also ably introduces readers to one of his favorite themes: that the essence of a story lies in the mechanics of its telling." Bookforum

Munro, Alice

★ **Dear** life; stories. Alice Munro. Alfred A. Knopf 2012 319 p. (hardcover) $26.95

ISBN 0307596885; 9780307596888

LC 2012020455

Author Alice Munro won the Nobel Prize in Literature in 2013.

This collection of short stories by Alice Munro "illumines the moment a life is forever altered by a chance encounter or an action not taken, or by a simple twist of fate that turns a person out of his or her accustomed path and into a new way of being or thinking. While most of these stories take place in Munro's home territory--the small Canadian towns around Lake Huron--the characters sometimes venture to the cities." (Publisher's note)

Munro, Alice

Family furnishings; selected stories, 1995-2014. Alice Munro. Alfred A. Knopf 2014 640 p. (hardback) $30

ISBN 1101874104; 9781101872352; 9781101874103

LC 2014023046

Author Alice Munro won the Nobel Prize in Literature in 2013.

This book presents short stories by Alice Munro written between 1995 and 2014. The "stories illuminate the quotidian yet extraordinary particularity in the lives of men and women, parents and children, friends and lovers as they discover sex, fall in love, part, quarrel, suffer defeat, set off into the unknown, or find a way to be in the world." (Publisher's note)

"Top-shelf collection by Canadian Nobelist Munro, perhaps the best writer of short stories in English today.Certainly few, if any, narrators are less trustworthy than Munro's; among many other things, she is the ascended master of quiet betrayals, withheld information and unforeseeable reversals of fortune... As is true of so many of Munro's tales, taken straight from the pages of quotidian life, its end is heartbreaking, tragic, not a little mysterious—and entirely unexpected. In fact, all that can be expected from these economical, expertly told stories is that they're near peerless, modern literary fiction at its very best." Kirkus

Munro, Alice

Friend of my youth; stories. Knopf 1990 273p

LC 89-43295

"Ms. Munro, who has deepened the channels of realism, is a writer of extraordinarily rich texture; her imagery stuns or wounds and her sentences stick to the rough surfaces of our world." N Y Times Book Rev

Munro, Alice

Hateship, friendship, courtship, loveship, marriage; stories. Knopf 2001 320p

ISBN 0-375-41300-6

LC 2001-29870

"Opulent in their beauty and gem-bright psychology, the extraordinary stories in {this} collection span the spectrum from romance to tales of manners to deep meditations on love and mortality, and all evince Munro's profound understanding of the power of memories and the stories we tell ourselves." Booklist

Munro, Alice

Lives of girls & women. McGraw-Hill 1971 250p

ISBN 0-07-044043-3

"Although the locale is Canada, Del Jordan's story could take place in the United States as well. She lives among hard-working, lower-middle-class people in a family that includes her parents and a brother, Owen. The mother seeks independence from the traditional role of women and even goes 'out on the road,' as her disapproving sisters-in-law term it, to sell encyclopedias. For Del's mother the pursuit of knowledge is an ideal. For Del and her best friend Naomi more interest lies in their maturing and curiosity about sex as a vital part of growing up. There is humor and recognizable adolescent self-questioning. While sexual scenes are explicit, they are also sensitive and real and avoid both vulgarity and titillation. In spite of the experiences that Naomi and Del have, it becomes clear that the paths they will follow will diverge greatly." Shapiro. Fic for Youth. 3d edition

Munro, Alice

The **love** of a good woman; stories. Knopf 1998 339p

ISBN 0-375-40395-7

LC 98-36721

"Munro knows her characters intimately, yet she is at peace with the fact that their lives will, and should, retain a fundamental mysterious quality. This paradox, which originates in a knowledge of life, is not often so knowledgeably conveyed in fiction." Yale Rev

Munro, Alice

Open secrets; stories. Knopf 1994 293p

ISBN 0-679-43575-1

LC 94-2099

The author "peoples these exquisite tales with sad, lonely eccentrics leading lives of quiet self-deception. Her heroines are often troubled souls with the unforgiving task of fitting into the rigorously confining community that spawned them. . . . Munro expertly captures the vagaries of history and geography in this satisfying and immensely pleasurable collection." Booklist

Munro, Alice

Runaway; stories. Knopf 2004 337p $25

ISBN 1-400-04281-X

LC 2004-46539

"Munro's spare style belies the psychological depth of the stories, which feature characters running away from someone or something (often representative of the past) or telling a lie by commission or omission (another form of running away)." Libr J

Munro, Alice

Selected stories. Knopf 1996 545p $30

ISBN 0-679-44627-3

LC 96-4145

"Little gems from one of Canada's best writers, drawn from seven collections." Libr J

Munro, Alice

★ **Too** much happiness; stories. Alfred A. Knopf 2009 303p $25.95

ISBN 978-0-307-26976-8

LC 2009-200010

"The collection's 10 stories take on some sensational subjects. In fact, a quick tally yields all the elements of pulp fiction: violence, adultery, extreme cruelty, duplicity, theft, suicide, murder. But while in pulp fiction the emotional climax coincides with the height of external drama, a Munro story works according to a different scheme. Here the nominally momentous event is little more than an anteroom to an echo chamber filled with subtle and far-reaching thematic reverberations." N Y Times Book Rev

Munro, Alice

The **view** from Castle Rock; stories. Knopf 2006 349p

ISBN 1-4000-4282-8

LC 2006-45261

This collection differs from Munro's "usual examinations of women in rural Canada leaving home to remake their possibilities. She draws instead on family documents, historical records, and what feels like memoir to piece together, in 12 parts, a fictionalized chronicle of how her tough-minded clan got from the Ettrick Valley near Edinburgh, Scotland, to America. The book shows how much can be done in a simple short story but breaks every rule ever taught in a writing seminar, setting up a writing master class along the way." Time

Murakami, Haruki

★ **1Q84**; translated from the Japanese by Jay Rubin and Philip Gabriel. Alfred A. Knopf 2011 924p $30.50

ISBN 978-0-307-59331-3; 0-307-59331-2

LC 2011-14274

Original Japanese edition, 2009

This novel "follows two people who find themselves in an alternate world (dubbed 1Q84 by one character) where dual moons hang in the sky and small differences start to have big implications. Several characters spend extended periods sitting by themselves in small rooms. A mysterious band of 'Little People' crawl out of a dead goat's mouth. Religious cults, menacing bill collectors, expert assassins, and questions about the nature of time and space all figure prominently. 'It's like the rules that govern the world have begun to loosen up around us,' says one of the book's lost souls. In typical Murakami fashion, the result is deeply weird—and surprisingly convincing." Entertainment Wkly

Murakami, Haruki

After dark; translated from the Japanese by Jay Rubin. Knopf 2007 191p $22.95

ISBN 978-0-307-26583-8; 0-307-26583-8

LC 2007-4828

"The narrative flows like a jazz ballad, excruciatingly slow yet hypnotically entrancing . . . . Each character is unique in his or her form of loneliness, yet each possesses a capacity for momentary empathy that is both sweet and heartbreaking. Murakami's genius, on both large and small canvases, is to create worlds both utterly alien and disconcertingly familiar." Booklist

Murakami, Haruki

After the earthquake; stories. translated from the Japanese by Jay Rubin. Knopf 2002 181p $22

ISBN 0-375-41390-1

LC 2001-38829

Original Japanese edition, 2000

"These six stories, all loosely connected to the disastrous 1995 earthquake in Kobe, are Murakami. . . at his best. The writer, who returned to live in Japan after the Kobe earthquake, measures his country's suffering and finds reassurance in the inevitability that love will surmount tragedy, mustering his casually elegant prose and keen sense of the absurd in the service of healing." Publ Wkly

Murakami, Haruki

Blind willow, sleeping woman; twenty-four stories. translated from the Japanese by Philip Gabriel and Jay Rubin. Knopf 2006 333p

ISBN 1-4000-4461-8

LC 2005-44544

"Murakami's first collection of short stories in more than a decade again demonstrates his fabulous talent for transporting readers and making 'the world fade away' with a few short strokes of his pen. . . . Murakami's characters are as alienated as any in Albert Camus, and as lost as any in J.D. Salinger. . . . What shines in all of [the stories] is Murakami's love for the open-ended mystery at the core of existence and his willingness to give himself up 'to the flow' in order to capture some of the magic in the mundane." Christ Sci Monit

Murakami, Haruki, 1949-

★ **Colorless** Tsukuru Tazaki and his years of pilgrimage; a novel. Haruki Murakami ; translated by Philip Gabriel. Knopf 2014 400 p. (hardback) $25.95

ISBN 0385352107; 9780385352109; 9780385352116; 9780804170123

LC 2014010404

In this novel, author Haruki Murakami "gives us the remarkable story of Tsukuru Tazaki, a young man haunted by a great loss; of dreams and nightmares that have unintended consequences for the world around us; and of a journey into the past that is necessary to mend the present. It is a story of love, friendship, and heartbreak for the ages." (Publisher's note)

A "a trademark [Murakami] story that blends the commonplace with the nightmarish in a Japan full of hollow men." Kirkus

Murakami, Haruki, 1949-

Kafka on the shore; Haruki Murakami ; translated from the Japanese by Philip Gabriel. Alfred A. Knopf 2005 436 p. (pbk.) $15.95; o.p.

ISBN 9781400079278; 1400043662

LC 2004048907

World Fantasy Awards: Novel (2006)

This book tells the story of "Kafka Tamura [who] is a 15-year-old boy . . . [and] runs away from home to escape an Oedipal curse: he will murder his father, a famed sculptor with whom he lives alone, and sleep with both his sister and his mother, who abandoned him as a small boy. He runs off to a city where no one will know him and finds work and shelter at a library under the watchful tutelage of a hermaphroditic librarian, Oshima, and his mysterious and elegant employer, Miss Saeki, a middle-aged woman that may be Kafka's mother, and who lives in mourning following the death of her lover years before. No sooner does Kafka leave than his father is found murdered, and Kafka wakes up in a city miles away, covered in blood." (January Magazine)

"Like his characters' quests, Murakami's expeditions off the worn path of literature can be both rewarding and terrifying. Finishing 'Kafka on the Shore' is like waking from a great dream. Nothing has changed, but everything about the world looks different." Newsweek

Murakami, Haruki

South of the border, west of the sun; translated from the Japanese by Philip Gabriel. Knopf 1999 213p

ISBN 0-375-40251-9

LC 97-49459

"The narrative unfolds as an introspective ghost story in which Hajime must exorcise his past in the person of the enigmatic Shimamoto before he can affirm the new direction of his life. The ending, at once tender and hopeful, shows Murakami in a more mellow aspect than his work has exhibited before." Publ Wkly

Murakami, Haruki, 1949-

★ The **wind**-up bird chronicle; translated from the Japanese by Jay Rubin. Knopf 1997 610p

ISBN 0-679-44669-9

LC 97-2813

Original Japanese edition, 1995

The narrator, Toru Okada, an unemployed man in his thirties trying to find his way in life "loses his cat and then his wife. He devotes himself to finding the latter but spends much of his time in the bottom of a well, hoping to pass through the well and into an alternate world where the secrets lie. Meanwhile, he encounters a series of ever more puzzling characters, including a World War II veteran who recounts the . . . story of the battle of Nomonhan, during which thousands of Japanese died meaninglessly in conflict with Russians and Mongolians." (Booklist) Bibliography.

Murakami's "protagonist is a harmless fellow who merely wants to recover his cat and his wife. The troubles, real and delusional, that he encounters can be seen as extravagant metaphors for every ill from personal isolation to mass murder. The novel is a deliberately confusing, illogical image of a confusing, illogical world. It is not easy reading, but it is never less than absorbing." Atl Mon

Murakami, Ryu

In the miso soup; translated by Ralph McCarthy. Kodansha International 2004 180p $22.95

ISBN 4-7700-2957-8

Original Japanese edition, 1997

"Beyond one terribly shocking scene, Miso is a thoughtful novel about loneliness, lack of identity and cultural and moral corruption. Through simple yet chilling language, Murakami doesn't condemn his characters. Instead he takes aim at rampant consumerism and the dumbing-down of Japanese and American culture. No one, Murakami seems to say, is completely guilty because we are shaped by the world around us." USA Today

Murasaki Shikibu

The **tale** of Genji; a novel in six parts. {by} Lady Murasaki; translated from the Japanese by Arthur Waley. Modern Lib. 1960 1135p

"A Japanese romance of the Heian period (794-1185). . . . This vast chronicle, often considered the world's first novel for its psychological depth, centers on the career of Prince Genji, his progeny, and the women with whom they associate. While delineating the elaborate rituals of courtly life, this work reflects the melancholy beauty of a world in constant flux and the vulnerability of women dependent upon the instability of human affection. Rich in poetry and elaborate wordplay, this work has had tremendous impact on the subsequent literary tradition." Reader's Ency. 4th edition

Murdoch, Iris

★ An **accidental** man. Viking 1971 442p

ISBN 0-670-10208-3

"The central figure of this novel is one of those accident-prone figures whose . . . misfortune becomes a substitute source of strength. . . . Ever since his brother injured his hand in a childhood incident, the world owes Austin a blank cheque to cover subsequent reverses—which do not fail to arrive. But someone is always sorry for him, always getting him out of trouble even at the price of their own. His self-pity destroys others in accordance with what Miss Murdoch . . . calls 'whatever deep mythological forces control the destinies of men.'" New Statesman (1913)

Murdoch, Iris

The **bell**; a novel. Viking 1958 342p

"The setting is an Anglican lay community attached to an abbey on one of the great estates of England. . . . The members of this community and its temporary residents are on the whole an odd, and certainly an oddly assorted, bunch. And their high-minded leader is a homosexual who was once involved in a scandal that ended his plans for entering the church. The story concerns itself with the relationships between various members of this hothouse world, with the arrival of a new bell for the abbey and the simultaneous discovery in the lake of the lost fourteenth-century bell about which there is a sinister legend. The climax is an eruption of scandal and disaster." Atlantic

Murdoch, Iris

The **book** and the brotherhood. Viking 1988 607p

ISBN 0670819123; 9780670819126

LC 87-40294

First published 1987 in the United Kingdom

This novel, the author's twenty-third, is set in England in the 1980s. "A group of idealistic men and women, who met as students {at Oxford}, later formed a society to support one of their number, a brilliant radical named David Crimond, in his efforts to write a major work tackling the big questions of history, politics, philosophy, art, and ethics. As the story opens, the group members, now middle-aged, are having qualms about Crimond and the enterprise they once agreed to fund." (Christ Sci Monit)

"Despite its excessive length and passages that can seem almost as self-indulgent as the characters they represent, The Book and The Brotherhood demonstrates again and again that Iris Murdoch is among the most gifted descriptive and narrative writers in English—and certainly one of the most consistently entertaining." NY Rev Books

Murdoch, Iris

A **fairly** honourable defeat. Viking 1970 436p

"As is usual with a Murdoch novel, the action in summary seems preposterous. But given her inventiveness, her Gothic imagination, her gift for melodrama and suspense, she creates a world that becomes an effective vehicle for her moral vision." Choice

Murdoch, Iris

The **good** apprentice. Viking 1986 522p

LC 85-40635

"The esthetic puzzle is whether the comic story and the spiritual kernel can be held together by Miss Murdoch's archaic stance as an authorial will. And yet no other contemporary British novelist seems to me of her eminence." N Y Times Book Rev

Murdoch, Iris

★ The **green** knight. Viking 1994 472p

LC 93-30618

First published 1993 in the United Kingdom

"That a cold, dark, evil act should open up a gap through which warmth and light can flood into the world is a paradox characteristic of Iris Murdoch's deeply meditated insight into the nature of the good." London Rev Books

Murdoch, Iris

The **nice** and the good. Viking 1968 378p

The action "begins with a violent death in the chambers of Whitehall faintly suggestive of a Le Carré thriller. . . . At times hilariously funny, slightly shivery (intimations of blackmail, suicide, dabblings in black magic) 'The Nice and the Good' is first and foremost a delightful love story. The friends, relatives, hanger-ons, whose lives revolve around the happily married Octavian and Kate Gray are all seeking after love in their own ways. They find it, too, and sometimes in the most amazing places. The characterizations are superb, the mood that of a happy fairy tale crossed with highly sophisticated sexual comedy." Publ Wkly

Murdoch, Iris

Nuns and soldiers. Viking 1981 505p

LC 80-16935

First published 1980 in the United Kingdom

This novel explores the tangled lives of recently widowed Gertrude; Tim, a painter; Anne, a former nun; and "Count" Peter who is in love with Gertrude

"The glory of Iris Murdoch at her best—as she almost always is in Nuns and Soldiers—is that she can convey with total respect the awareness, readjusting and hunger, and at the same time 'place' it, with a severe but not savage irony, in a world which hints at quite different forces and priorities." New Statesman (1913)

Murdoch, Iris

★ The **philosopher's** pupil. Viking 1983 576p

LC 82-45901

This "collaboration between Murdoch and her imagination is both challenging and irresistible: a combination of gossip and profundity, modern times and ancient edicts." Time

Murdoch, Iris

The **sea,** the sea. Viking 1978 502p

LC 78-13516

The narrator of this "novel is Charles Arrowby, a former actor and director who has retired from the theater to take up solitary residence in a remote house on a northern coast. His tale begins as a mixture of diary and memoir: alternately he records his first impressions of his new home and reviews his past life as though the better to understand the man he has become. . . . His recollections largely concern a succession of love-affairs with actresses; but before all these, and dwarfing them in its importance to his development, was an unconsummated but passionate childhood relationship with a girl named Hartley, who disappeared abruptly and woundingly from his life before he was twenty and married another man." Times Lit Suppl

Murphy, Sara Flannery

★ The **possessions**; a novel. Sara Flannery Murphy. HarperCollins 2017 354 p. (hardcover) $26.99

ISBN 0062458329; 9780062458339; 9780062458322

In this novel, by Sara Flannery Murphy, "Eurydice works for the Elysian Society, a private service that allows grieving clients to reconnect with lost loved ones. . . . But when Edie channels Sylvia, the dead wife of . . . Patrick Braddock, she becomes obsessed with the . . . couple. Despite the murky circumstances surrounding Sylvia's drowning, Edie breaks her own rules and pursues Patrick, moving deeper into his life and summoning Sylvia outside the Elysian Society's walls." (Publisher's note)

"This poignant tale is a study of grief and obsession told by a person who will do anything to forget while surrounded by those who refuse to move on." LJ

Murphy, Yannick

The **call**; Yannick Murphy. Harper Perennial 2011 220p. pa $14.99

ISBN 0-06-202314-4; 978-0-06-202314-8

LC 2010051661

L. L. Winship/PEN New England Award: Fiction category (2012)

"An extraneous plot twist at the end tests the family and the reader's suspension of disbelief, and the emotional resonance seems to recede. But throughout, the most delicate and satisfying snippets answer questions like what the house says at night—'I'm closing you in, and buttoning you tight,' which quietly and brilliantly speaks to both comfort and threat. In the quotidian details of farm life, Murphy demonstrates how crucial it is to focus on the small, real tasks in the face of something too big and too dark to understand." Time Out N Y

Murphy, Yannick

Signed, Mata Hari; a novel. Little, Brown 2007 278p $23.99

ISBN 978-0-316-11264-2; 0-316-11264-X

LC 2006-102966

"Weaving back and forth in time between Mata Hari's prison cell in Paris and her prior life in its many manifestations, the seductive narrative spins an irresistible tale of a woman whose legendary exploits are still a matter of historical debate. Was she or was she not a victim of time and circumstance? Did she really deserve to be executed as a spy? In the end, it doesn't really matter, but what does matter is that Murphy has fashioned a mesmerizing novel that creatively reimagines the life of one of the most notorious, and perhaps overvilified, women of all time." Booklist

Murr, Naeem

★ The **perfect** man; a novel. Random House Trade Paperbacks 2007 451p pa $13.95

ISBN 978-0-8129-7701-1; 0-8129-7701-7

LC 2006-43088

This novel "succeeds in recreating an entire world with a full spectrum of human emotions in a small Missouri town, as Faulkner did in the imaginary Yoknapatawpha County in Mississippi." Times Lit Suppl

Murray, Paul

The **mark** and the void; A Novel. Paul Murray. Farrar, Straus & Giroux 2015 480 p. (hardcover) $27

ISBN 9780865477551; 0865477558

LC 2015015136

In this book, author Paul Murray tells "a darkly comic, lightly meta-fictional tale about a banker seeking love and a novelist seeking wealth amid the fallout from the financial boom and bust in Ireland." (Kirkus Reviews)

"Here, again, the author displays much of the quick wit of his popular previous novel, but this effort also boasts a more modernist slant, with ever-blurring lines between art imitating life and life imitating art for the characters. The result is another page-turner with smarts, an absurdist riff on our economic follies, one that leaves the impression that it's all not so far-fetched, after all." Pub Wkly

Murray, Paul

Skippy dies. Faber & Faber 2010 661p $28; pa 3v boxed set $30

ISBN 978-0-86547-943-2; 0-8654-7943-7; 978-0-8654-7948-7 pa; 0-8654-7948-8 pa

LC 2010-926173

"First off, the title of Skippy Dies should come with a spoiler alert, because Skippy does in fact die. And oh, the humanity! He dies like a fish on the floor of Ed's Doughnut House, where he's been locked in a doughnut-eating contest with his tubby, brilliant, but unhinged prep-school buddy Ruprecht. . . . Essentially, though, the novel's about a fusty old Catholic school trying to cope and connive after the Skippy Doughnut Tragedy, while dealing with the more commonplace tragedy that being an adolescent sucks, as do being middle-aged and being old. Murray's humor and inventiveness never flag. And despite a serious theme—what happens to boys and men when they realize the world isn't the sparkly planetarium they had hoped for—Skippy Dies leaves you feeling hopeful and hungry for life. Just not for doughnuts." Entertainment Wkly

Murray, Sabina

Forgery. Grove Press 2007 248p $24

ISBN 978-0-8021-1844-8; 0-8021-1844-5

LC 2006-52645

The author "juxtaposes the subject of fake antiquities with both fake and real portraits of characters. Lacking rhythm, the restrained prose does not effectively create flowing dialog, but with just a few words Murray conjures images that stay with the reader for days." Libr J

Musil, Robert, 1880-1942

★ The **man** without qualities; translated from the German by Sophie Wilkins. Knopf 1995 1774p 2v

ISBN 0-394-51052-6

LC 92-37943

Musil "worked on this . . . unfinished novel, which he began in the early 1920s, until he died in 1942. Set on the verge of World War I, the novel revolves around the efforts of Ulrich, the man without qualities, to find meaning in a society in which convention stifles a new era struggling to be born." (Libr J)

"The first two volumes of this monumental work were published in 1930 and 1932; a fragmentary third was published posthumously in 1942, and in 1952 the novel appeared, with additional chapters, in one volume. Apart from providing a brilliant, existential portrait of Ulrich, the scholarly, purposeless 'man without qualities' the book is a vivid depiction of Austrian decadence before the outbreak of World War I. This single remarkable work established Musil as one of the most influential German-language novelists in the first half of the 20th century." Reader's Ency. 4th edition

My mistress's sparrow is dead; great love stories, from Chekhov to Munro. edited by Jeffrey Eugenides. HarperCollins 2008 587p $24.95; pa $15.99

ISBN 978-0-06-124037-9; 0-06-124037-0; 978-0-06-124038-6 pa; 0-06-124038-9 pa

LC 2007-35989

Eugenides "has assembled something quite extraordinary here: a fascinating, consistently compelling, and superbly edited collection of short stories about romantic love. Part of the collection's appeal is its range and depth: at 600 pages, it offers gems and new discoveries at every turn." Libr J

Myśliwski, Wiesław, 1932-

Stone upon stone; Wiesław Myśliwski; translated from the Polish by Bill Johnston. Archipelago Books Distributed by Consortium Book Sales and Distribution 2010 534 p.

ISBN 098262462X; 9780982624623

LC 2010038451

This book, a winner of Three Percent's 2012 Best Translated Book Award, offers an "epic in the rural tradition" a . . . stream of memory cutting through the rich and varied terrain of one man's connection to the land, to his family and community, to women, to tradition, to God, to death, and to what it means to be alive. Wise and impetuous, plain-spoken and compassionate Szymek, recalls his youth in their village, his time as a guerrilla soldier, as a wedding official, barber, policeman, lover, drinker, and caretaker for his invalid brother. Filled with interwoven stories and voices, . . . Szymek's narrative . . . [presents the] wisdom of one who has suffered, yet who loves life to the very core." (Publisher's note)

The **Mysterious** West; edited by Tony Hillerman. HarperCollins Pubs. 1994 392p

LC 94-25842

"This stunning collection . . . offers readers some wonderful choices in fiction. Each story is strikingly different in tempo, plot, and setting, yet each is part of and contributes to the diversified world of the mysterious West." SLJ

N

Nabb, Magdalen

Some bitter taste. Soho Press 2002 247p $24

ISBN 1-569-47317-X

LC 2002-70579

The author "has Simenon's knack of unlocking the deeper mysteries of ordinary people's pedestrian lives. . . . In Nabb's world, nothing is simple and no life, after all, is ordinary." N Y Times Book Rev

Nabokov, Vladimir Vladimirovich

★ **Ada**; or, Ardor: a family chronicle. [by] Vladimir Nabokov. McGraw-Hill 1969 589p

"In its prodigious length and with the family tree on its frontispiece the book recalls the great 19th-century novels of the author's native Russia, but Ada boldly turns its predecessors on their heads. For his rich, sweeping saga of the Veen-Durmanov clan, Nabokov invented an incestuous pair of 'cousins' (actually siblings, Van and Ada), a hybrid country (Amerussia), a familiar but strange planet (Antiterra), and a dimension of malleable time. The novel follows the lovers from their childhood idylls through impassioned estrangements and reunions to a tenderly shared old age. The work's rich narrative style incorporates untranslated foreign phrases, esoteric data, and countless literary allusions." Merriam-Webster's Ency of Lit

Nabokov, Vladimir Vladimirovich

★ **King,** queen, knave; a novel. [by] Vladimir Nabokov; translated by Dmitri Nabokov in collaboration with the author. McGraw-Hill 1968 272p

Original Russian edition, 1928

"The image of a deck of playing cards is used throughout the novel. Franz, an unsophisticated young man, works in the department store of his rich uncle Dreyer. Out of boredom Martha, the uncle's young wife, seduces Franz. The lovers subsequently plot to drown Dreyer and marry each other. Martha changes her mind abruptly when she learns that an invention by Dreyer stands to increase his wealth, but she then dies suddenly from pneumonia. Her husband never discovers his wife's duplicity." Merriam-Webster's Ency of Lit

Nabokov, Vladimir Vladimirovich

★ **Lolita**; [by] Vladimir Nabokov. Knopf 1992 335p $19

ISBN 0-679-41043-0

LC 92-52931

First published 1955 in France

"Humbert Humbert is a middle-aged intellectual who has a passion for girls between the ages of nine and fourteen. He falls in love with the twelve-year-old Dolores Haze, whom he calls Lolita. In his plot to seduce her, he marries Dolores's mother, whose accidental death then allows Lolita and Humbert to take off on an odyssey across the U.S. Humbert is surprised when, contrary to his schemes, Lolita seduces him and again when she leaves him for Clare Quilty, whom Humbert later murders. Lolita eventually marries Richard F. Schiller. The book presents a quest for eternal innocence, albeit in satirical terms. . . . It combines parody, fanciful imaginative flights, literary puzzles, and a brilliant satirical overview of American culture." Reader's Ency. 4th edition

Nabokov, Vladimir Vladimirovich

Look at the harlequins! {by} Vladimir Nabokov. McGraw-Hill 1974 253p

In this pseudo-autobiographical novel, the narrator, a Russian émigré novelist and college professor who has lived in London, Paris and the United States, recalls his life, loves (including four marriages) and work in a manner which often parodies Nabokov's own life and writings

This is a book "to enchant Nabokov fans and irritate everybody else. . . . {It} is part roman a clef, part fantasy, a tale of 'wives and books interlaced monogrammatically.' It is full of erudite allusions, Russian words in various stages of translation and absurd mistranslation, puns, anagrams, acronyms. Also opinions. . . . Comic, polished, international, {Nabokov} offers sophisticated entertainment, a concoction of romantic and literary matters." Christ Sci Monit

Nabokov, Vladimir Vladimirovich

Novels and memoirs, 1941-1951; . Literary Classics of the U.S. 1996 710p il (Library of America) $35

ISBN 1-883011-18-3

LC 96-15257

The real life of Sebastian Knight (1941) is about a Russian living in Paris who learns about his half-brother, a famous English novelist, by writing his biography. Bend sinister (1947) is about a professor's attempts to maintain his integrity in a totalitarian state.

Nabokov, Vladimir Vladimirovich

Novels, 1955-1962. Library of Am. 1996 904p $35

ISBN 1-883011-19-1

LC 96-15256

Contents: Lolita; Pnin; Pale fire; Lolita, a screenplay

Nabokov, Vladimir Vladimirovich

Novels, 1969-1974. Library of Am. 1996 824p il $35

ISBN 1-883011-20-5

LC 96-15255

Transparent things (1972) is a novella about a rootless American who murders his wife

Nabokov, Vladimir Vladimirovich

★ **Pale** fire; a novel. [by] Vladimir Nabokov. Putnam 1962 315p

This novel is "both pedantry and a satire on pedantry. The core of the novel is a 999-line poem by an American author, John Shade—a sort of Robert Frost—which consists mainly of a rather moving meditation on the tragic end of the poet's daughter. After Shade's death, a foolish scholar named Kinbote—an exile from the mythical country of Zembla and a visiting professor of Zemblan at Wordsmith College, New Wye, Appalachia—edits this work, providing a preface and a detailed corpus of notes. But Kinbote has an 'idée fixe'—the history of his own country—and he believes that Shade's poem is an allegory of this history, with Kinbote himself—fantasized into the deposed King Charles Xavier II—as the hero. The humour—and Nabokov's humour is subtle as well as occasionally brutal—lies in the disparity between the simple truth of the poem and the gross self-exalting hallucinations of its editor." Burgess. 99 Novels

Nabokov, Vladimir Vladimirovich

Pnin; {by} Vladimir Nabokov. Doubleday 1957 191p

"Not a novel, not really a collection of short stories, but rather a series of sketches, all of them dealing with Timofey Pnin, professor of Russian in a small American university. Each one finds Pnin valiantly trying to cope with the daily crises of American society—Pnin on the wrong train, Pnin learning to drive, Pnin giving a party, Pnin and the washing machine. They are all gently amusing, affectionate portraits of a Russian expatriate of the old school caught up in the inexplicable complexities of daily life." Libr J

Nabokov, Vladimir Vladimirovich

The **stories** of Vladimir Nabokov. Knopf 1996 659p

ISBN 0-394-58615-8

LC 95-23466

For this chronologically-arranged collection, "Nabokov's son Dmitri has assembled the 52 stories published in English before Nabokov died in 1977, and translated another 13 written in Russian between 1920 or '21 and 1924." Newsweek

Nadel, Barbara

The **Ottoman** cage; a novel of Istanbul. Barbara Nadel. Thomas Dunne Books/St. Martins Minotaur 2005 312 p. $14.95

ISBN 0312337698; 9781933397849

LC 2004061875

In this book, "[w]hen a brutal murder shocks Istanbul's rundown Jewish quarter, the Turkish police force unleashes their best weapon - the chain-smoking, brandy-swilling Inspector Cetin Ikmen, husband to a strict Muslim woman (who disapproves of his drinking) and loving father of eight (with another on the way)." (Publisher's note)

Nadler, Stuart

The **inseparables**; A Novel. Stuart Nadler. Little, Brown & Co. 2016 352 p. (hardcover : acid-free paper) $27

ISBN 9780316335256

LC 2015028889

In this novel, by Stuart Nadler, "Henrietta has lost her husband and nearly all of her money, and is about to lose her hard-won anonymity. After a lifetime spent trying to outrun the humiliation her own book caused her, Henrietta has reluctantly agreed to a reissue of The Inseparables. . . . At the same time, her daughter, Oona, has moved back home . . . And Oona's teenage daughter, Lydia, away at boarding school, is facing . . . scrutiny and shame when a nude photo of her goes viral." (Publisher's note)

"The characters share humiliations, yet also find the resilience to move on. This novel contains plenty of romance, tension, and tenderness to make for a rich and compelling read." Pub Wkly

Nadler, Stuart

Wise men; a novel. Stuart Nadler. Reagan Arthur Book 2013 335 p. (hardcover) $25.99

ISBN 0316126489; 9780316126489

LC 2012020020

This novel, by Stuart Nadler, begins in Cape Cod "during the summer of 1952. . . . Arthur's teenage son, Hilly, makes friends with Lem Dawson, a black man whose job it is to take care of the house. . . . When Hilly finds himself falling for Lem's niece, Savannah, . . . the results shatter his family, and hers. Years later, haunted by his memories of that summer, Hilly sets out to find Savannah, in an attempt to right the wrongs he helped set in motion." (Publisher's note)

Nadol, Jen

This is how it ends; Jen Nadol. Simon Pulse 2014 310 p. (hardcover) $18.99

ISBN 1481402110; 9781481402101; 9781481402118

LC 2014030160

In this book, by Jen Nadol "Riley and his friends . . . find a mysterious pair of binoculars. Those who dare to look through them see strange visions, which they brush off as hallucinations. . . . In the weeks that follow, the visions begin to come true...including a gruesome murder. One of Riley's closest friends is now the prime suspect. But who is the murderer? Have Riley and his friends really seen the future through those mysterious binoculars?" (Publisher's note)

Nadzam, Bonnie

Lamb; a novel. Other Press 2011 275p pa $15.95

ISBN 978-1-59051-437-5; 1-59051-437-8

"People can tell about Lamb, a man whose wife has left him and who finds so little control left in his own life he decides to exert some on Tommie, a seventh-grade girl. Tommie's friends put her up to bumming a cigarette off Lamb just after his dad's funeral. Lamb takes it as an opportunity to teach her and her friends a lesson, pretending to kidnap her (in a manner convincing enough that Tommie's not sure if it's real). The two strike up what could charitably be called an uneasy friendship, with Lamb convincing himself he's finally doing right by guiding Tommie, and Tommie happy for the attention and the wealthier Lamb's gifts. They both make the very bad decision to road trip to the Rockies together, where pretty much everything goes wrong. Nadzam oversaturates every inch of Lamb's pages. The title character's unacknowledged grief for his father and his own misdirected life floods the subtext, and the writing is both beautiful and unabashedly indulgent. . . . But Nadzam earns that excess. As Lamb always sits on the flinty side of combustion, so does the reader." Time Out Chicago

Nahai, Gina B.

The **luminous** heart of Jonah S. Gina B. Nahai. Akashic Books 2014 380 p. (hardcover) $29.95

ISBN 1617753211; 9781617753206; 9781617753213; 9781617753299

LC 2014938697

National Jewish Book Award Finalist: Fiction (2014)

This book, by Gina B. Nahai, "is a sweeping saga that tells the story of the Soleymans, an Iranian Jewish family tormented for decades by Raphael's Son, a crafty and unscrupulous financier who has futilely claimed to be an heir to the family's fortune. Forty years later in contemporary Los Angeles, Raphael's Son has nearly achieved his goal--until he suddenly disappears, presumed by many to have been murdered." (Publisher's note)

"With touches of magic realism, extraordinary characters, and a spiraling, multigenerational plot involving fraud, a murder mystery, epic suffering, heroic generosity, women's struggle for freedom, and the clash between East and West, Nahai's mythic, tragic, often beautiful immigrant family saga illuminates timeless questions of prejudice, trauma, inheritance, loyalty, and love." Booklist.

Naipaul, V. S.

★ A **bend** in the river. Knopf 1979 278p

LC 78-21591

"This is a beautifully composed book, with an almost Conradian power of description. Aesthetically most satisfying, it is also profoundly depressing. But depression is sometimes a stone on the road to literary exaltation." Burgess. 99 Novels

Naipaul, V. S.

★ **Guerrillas**. Knopf 1975 248p

"This is a novel without a villain, and there is not a character for whom the reader does not at some point feel deep sympathy and keen understanding, no matter how villainous or futile he may seem." N Y Times Book Rev

Naipaul, V. S.

Half a life. Knopf 2001 211p $24

ISBN 0-375-40737-5

LC 2001-33730

"In the book's last moments a narrative that has seemed to meander pulls suddenly tight, giving 'Half a Life' an interest that lies beyond its relation to Naipaul's other work. . . . The very fissures in its structure, its change from voice to voice, transform 'Half a Life' into a meditation on the difficulties of building a coherent self." N Y Times Book Rev

Naipaul, V. S.

★ A **house** for Mr. Biswas; with an introduction by Karl Miller. Knopf 1995 xxi, 564p $20

ISBN 0-679-44458-0

A reissue of the title first published 1961 by McGraw-Hill

"Trinidad, West Indies, is the setting for the story of lonely Mr. Mohun Biswas, a Hindu of high caste but low economic status. Throughout the book he longs for independence from his wife's large family and a house of his own. In a portrait that is both funny and compassionate, West Indian life is vividly described, especially the relationships among members of Mr. Biswas's family." Shapiro. Fic for Youth. 3d edition

Naipaul, V. S.

Magic seeds. Knopf 2004 280p $25

ISBN 0-375-40736-7

LC 2004-48964

The author "has written a calculated polemic. . . . Naipaul is suggesting that our racial and ethnic fate is sealed; we can never escape who we are, and must learn to live with our unchosen identities whether we like them or not. It's not a consoling vision; neither is it despairing. It simply is." N Y Times Book Rev

Naipaul, V. S.

A **way** in the world; a novel. Knopf 1994 380p

ISBN 0-394-56478-2

LC 93-44680

In this autobiographical fiction, Naipaul examines "feelings of rootlessness, the realities of the colonial experience, the impact of cultural displacement, and our need to belong. He does so through a series of linked historical narratives. Among them is an imagined vision of Raleigh's desperate but futile search for El Dorado. We are also introduced to Francisco de Miranda, one of the precursors to Bolivar's revolution. We are witness to the irony inherent in the life of Lebrun, a Trinidadian/Panamanian Communist of the 1930s. And then there is Blair, a former co-worker of the narrator in Trinidad, whose African roots prove no help when he becomes an adviser to an East African despot. These are tales of lost souls desperate to find a place at the table but who never quite succeed, leaving them doomed to remain on the fringes of history." Libr J

Narayan, R. K.

The **grandmother's** tale and selected stories. Viking 1994 312p

LC 94-4581

Set in India these stories "emphasize perceptively drawn characters and situations rather than their colorful foreign backdrops. All the tales display a wry, gentle humor." Publ Wkly

Narayan, R. K.

★ **Malgudi** days. Viking 1982 246p

LC 81-52204

"This selection distills, magically, Malgudi's vibrancy, its mythological-animistic throb, the large and small corruptions of its citizens—from bureaucrats to back-street people—and the reassuring backdrop of its cyclical rhythms. Distinguished writing; rewarding reading." Booklist

Narayan, R. K.

Mr. Sampath--the printer of Malgudi, The financial expert, Waiting for the Mahatma; with an introduction by Alexander McCall Smith. Everyman's Library 2006 xxxviii, 578p $25

ISBN 0-4000-4477-4

LC 2006-279228

An omnibus edition of three novels first published 1949, 1952 and 1955, respectively

"Mr. Sampath—The Printer of Malgudi is the story of a businessman who adapts to the collapse of his weekly newspaper by shifting to screenplays, only to have the glamour of it all go to his head. In The Financial Expert, a man of many hopes but few resources spends his time under a banyan tree dispensing financial advice to those willing to pay for his knowledge. In Waiting for the Mahatma, a young drifter meets the most beautiful girl he has ever seen—an adherent of Mahatma Gandhi—and commits himself to Gandhi's Quit India campaign, a decision that will test the integrity of his ideals against the strength of his passions." Publisher's note

Narayan, R. K.

Swami and friends, The bachelor of arts, The dark room, The English teacher; with an introduction by Alexander McCall Smith. Everyman's Library 2006 xxxvii, 609p $25

ISBN 1-4000-4476-6

LC 2006-279229

An omnibus edition of four titles first published 1935, 1937, 1938 and 1945, respectively

"Swami and Friends introduces us to Narayan's beloved fictional town of Malgudi, where ten-year-old Swaminathan's excitement about his country's initial stirrings for independence competes with his ardor for cricket and all other things British. The Bachelor of Arts is a poignant coming-of-age novel about a young man flush with first love, but whose freedom to pursue it is hindered by the fixed ideas of his traditional Hindu family. In The Dark Room, Narayan's portrait of aggrieved domesticity, the docile and obedient Savitri, like many Malgudi women, is torn between submitting to her husband's humiliations and trying to escape them. The title character in The English Teacher, Narayan's most autobiographical novel, searches for meaning when the death of his young wife deprives him of his greatest source of happiness." Publisher's note

Narayan, R. K.

Under the banyan tree and other stories. Viking 1985 193p

LC 85-3234

"Narayan's clarity, his mastery of technique, his respect for the spectrum of human predicament, his absence of malice and his freedom from a single philosophy that explains everything away put him in the unique position of being able to turn a teeming cultural life into lucid and enjoyable stories." New Statesman

Naslund, Sena Jeter

Abundance; a novel of Marie Antoinette. William Morrow 2006 545p $26.95

ISBN 978-0-06-082539-3; 0-06-082539-1

LC 2006-43817

"With vivid detail and exquisite narrative technique, Naslund exemplifies the best of historical fiction, finding the woman beneath the pose, a queen facing history as it rises up against her." Publ Wkly

Naslund, Sena Jeter

Ahab's wife; or, The star-gazer; a novel. Morrow 1999 668p $28

ISBN 0-688-17187-7

LC 99-22135

"At age 12, Una escapes her religiously obsessed father in rural Kentucky to live with relatives in a lighthouse off New Bedford, Mass. When she is 16—disguised as a boy—she runs off to sea aboard a whaler, which sinks after being rammed by its quarry. Una and two young men who love her are the only survivors of a group set adrift in an open boat, but the dark secret of their cannibalism will leave its mark. Rescued, Una is wed to one of the young men by the captain of the Pequod, handsome, commanding Ahab, who has not as yet met the white whale that will be his destiny. . . . Una's later marriage to Ahab—a passionate and intellectually satisfying relationship—the loss of her mother and her newborn son in one night, and her life as a rich woman in Nantucket are further developments in a plot teeming with arresting events and provocative ideas." Publ Wkly

Naslund, Sena Jeter

The **Fountain** of St. James Court; or, Portrait of the Artist as an Old Woman: A Novel. Sena Jeter Naslund. William Morrow 2013 400 p. $26.99

ISBN 0061579327; 9780061579325

This book offers a novel-within-a-novel, following two women: "French painter Elisabeth Vigée-LeBrun, who barely survived the revolution, and Kathryn Callaghan, who has written a fictional account of Vigée-LeBrun. Kathryn, who is standing meditatively by the fountain of Venus Rising from the Sea as the novel opens, has spent too much time in the past and must reckon with her life in contemporary America." (Library Journal)

Naslund, Sena Jeter

Four spirits; a novel. Morrow 2003 524p $26.95

ISBN 0-06-621238-3

LC 2003-51170

"Naslund has done something unusually fine—she's written a drifting collective portrait of a city in distress. The characters of 'Four Spirits' are deeply entwined, sometimes without knowing it." N Y Times Book Rev

Nathan, Robert

Portrait of Jennie. Knopf 1940 212p

"Eban Adams, a struggling artist who is unable to sell his art work, meets an unusual child named Jennie in the park and immediately begins to prosper. He knows little about her except that she belongs in the past and that every few months, when their paths cross, she has aged by years. His finest painting is a portrait of her, a token of his love, which ends in predestined tragedy." Shapiro. Fic for Youth. 3d edition

Nathanson, E. M.

The **dirty** dozen. Random House 1965 498p

This "is not an ordinary war book. The fight here is not so much against the Wehrmacht as it is against self, society, and 'the system.' . . . If the situation seems impossible, if Reisman seems a superman, no matter, for the insights into good and evil are richly rewarding in this exciting and highly compelling novel." Libr J

Naylor, Gloria

Bailey's Cafe. Harcourt Brace Jovanovich 1992 229p

LC 91-42089

The author "takes us many keys down, and sometimes back up, in this virtuoso orchestration of survival, suffering, courage and humor, sounding through the stories of these lives." N Y Times Book Rev

Naylor, Gloria

Linden Hills. Ticknor & Fields 1985 304 p.

ISBN 9780140088298; 9780899193571 out of print

LC 84016222

The author "sketches the development of the community of Linden Hills through its founder, Luther Nedeed, and successive generations of Nedeeds, showing in the decline of the family the corrosive effect of ambition, arrogance and the abuse of power. The residents of Linden Hills are similarly subverted by the accommodations, sacrifices and perversions of soul blacks must endure to live in an affluent community, even, as in this case, an all-black one." Publ Wkly

Naylor, Gloria, 1950-2016

★ **Mama** Day. Ticknor & Fields 1988 311p

ISBN 0899197167; 9780899197166

LC 87-18157

"Willow Springs is a sparsely populated sea island just off America's southeastern coast whose small black community is dominated by the elderly matriarch, Miranda 'Mama' Day. When Mama Day's great-niece, Cocoa, marries, she returns to Willow Springs with her husband {George} for an extended visit. Once there, strange forces—both natural and supernatural—work to separate the couple. After visiting the menacing Ruby, a local root doctor, Cocoa becomes dangerously ill." (Libr J)

"When she is not didactically fostering our spiritual instruction, Gloria Naylor serves another worthy purpose beautifully: she invites us to imagine the lives of complex characters at work and play, and gives us a faithfully rendered community in all its seasons." Ms

Naylor, Gloria

The **men** of Brewster Place. Hyperion 1998 173p

ISBN 0-7868-6421-4

LC 97-45987

"Ben, a neighborhood janitor (and chorus) resurrected from the previous Brewster Place novel, narrates seven tales of neighborhood men and the women who love them. Their travails feature the familiar ills of the inner city, yet Naylor lends these archetypal situations complexity and depth: Basil yearns to be the kind of father he never had but chooses a path that leads to heartbreak; Eugene's restlessness in his marriage and friendship with a transsexual force him to face a difficult fact about himself; Reverend Moreland T. Woods rehearses his political aspirations with maneuvers on his church's board; and C.C. Baker, involved in local drug trafficking, keeps a startling truth from the police." Publ Wkly

Naylor, Gloria

The **women** of Brewster Place. Viking 1982 192p

LC 81-69969

This "novel is set, as the title indicates, in Brewster Place, a block-long dead-end street of run-down apartment buildings in a northern city. In an interrelated series of vignettes, Naylor focuses on seven black women, residents of Brewster Place. She is concerned with the distance between their dreams and realities, problems and solutions; these women are of different ages, come from different backgrounds, react differently to their blackness and to men, and have different notions of personal accomplishment, but all are burdened by being both black and female. Naylor is not angry; she writes with conviction and beautiful language, but spares the reader any bitterness. Characters are not puppets but exist and function as well-rounded personalities." Booklist

Ndiaye, Marie

Ladivine; Marie NDiaye ; translated from the French by Jordan Stump. Alfred A. Knopf 2016 273 p. (hardcover) $26.95

ISBN 0385351887; 9780385351898; 9780385351881

LC 2015016260

In this novel, by Marie NDiaye, translated from the French by Jordan Stump, "every month, Clarisse Rivière leaves her husband and young daughter and secretly takes the train to Bordeaux to visit her mother, Ladivine. . . . When her husband, Richard, finally leaves her, Clarisse finds comfort in the embrace of a volatile local man, Freddy Moliger. With Freddy, she finally feels reconciled to, or at least at ease with, her true self. But this peace comes at a terrible price." (Publisher's note)

"NDiaye reveals only as much reality as she wants to at any given moment, though—and therein lies her magic. Come for the promise of a big reveal; stay for the beauty of small moments. " Kirkus

Ndiaye, Marie

Three strong women; a novel. by Marie NDiaye ; translated by John Fletcher. Alfred A. Knopf 2012 293 p.

ISBN 0307594696; 9780307594693

LC 2012003533

This novel, by Marie NDiaye winner of the Prix Concourt award, "is the story of three women: . . . Norah, a French-born lawyer who finds herself in Senegal, summoned by her estranged, tyrannical father; . . . Fanta, who leaves a modest but contented life as a teacher in Dakar to follow her white boyfriend back to France; . . . and Khady, a penniless widow put out by her husband's family with nothing but the name of a distant cousin . . . who lives in France." (Publisher's note)

Negron, Luis

Mundo cruel; stories. by Luis Negron and translated by Suzanne Jill Levine. Seven Stories Press 2013 91 p. $13.95

ISBN 160980418X; 9781609804183

LC 2012046128

Lambda Literary Award: Gay General Fiction (2014)

"Slender but never slight, and often extremely funny, the nine stories in this debut collection offer insight into both gay life in Puerto Rico and the human condition in general. 'The Chosen One' deals with the intermixing of religion and sexuality. . . . 'La Edwin' reaches the conclusion, with far more delight than resignation, that 'the world has been the world for a long time,' and it is this ratio of delight to resignation that sets the tone of the book." Pub Wkly

Nehme, Farran Smith

Missing reels; Farran Smith Nehme. Overlook Hardcover 2014 352 p. (hardback) $26.95

ISBN 1468309277; 9781468309270

LC 2014034174

This book by Farran Smith Nehme "follows young Ceinwen Reilly, who is working in a vintage clothing store, dressing like a '40s film star, and obsessing over older films. While on the job, she encounters the affable Matthew, an Englishman and professor of mathematics at NYU. He introduces her to the quirky yet endearing world of silent film aficianados, and she soon discovers that her neighbor, Miriam Gibson . . . may have had no small part to play in a long-lost silent film." (Publishers Weekly)

"With breakneck, back-and-forth dialogue that recalls such movie classics as His Girl Friday and The Philadelphia Story, this debut novel by prominent film blogger Nehme is a joyful insider tale of cinematic obsession and a celebration of the ways in which fandom brings us closer to one another." Booklist

Nelson, Antonya

Bound; a novel. Bloomsbury 2010 231p $25

ISBN 978-1-59691-575-6; 1-59691-575-7

LC 2010-09791

"Nelson wields words with breathtaking precision. . . . This is no heartwarming makeshift-family-bonding story; Nelson has something truer in mind. Turning tiny moments into revelations, she brilliantly exposes the fears and delusions that drive people to rationalize destructive choices. . . . [A] wise exploration of the war between our worst impulses and our better selves." O Magazine

Nelson, Antonya

Funny once; stories. Antonya Nelson. Bloomsbury USA 2014 304 p. $26

ISBN 1620408619; 9781596915763; 9781620408612

LC 2013044001

In this collection of short stories by Antonya Nelson, "a couple held together by bad behavior fall into a lie with their more responsible friends. . . . A woman visits her father at a nursing home, recalling his equanimity at her teenage misdeeds and gaining a new understanding of his own past indiscretions. . . . [And] siblings muddle through in the aftermath of their elder brother's too-early departure from the world." (Publisher's note)

Nelson's "particular wizardry in the short form . . . is found in her exceptional melding of pristine prose with a rampaging imagination and a comic's perfect timing." Booklist

Nemirovsky, Irene, 1903-1942

Fire in the blood; translated by Sandra Smith. Alfred A. Knopf 2007 137p $22

ISBN 978-0-307-26748-1; 0-307-26748-2

LC 2007-28730

"In a book fuelled with images of fire and embers, Némirovsky brilliantly depicts a closed-in, inward-looking community, then gives what happens in it universal resonance by exhibiting not only what people do to each other but what the passing of time does to us all." London Times

Nemirovsky, Irene, 1903-1942

Suite Francaise. Knopf 2006 401p $25

ISBN 1-4000-4473-1

LC 2006-3461

Original French edition, 2004

"Nemirovsky, a young Russian Jewish emigre, became a celebrated novelist in Paris at age 26 in 1929. She wrote eight more novels; then, even though she was certain that she wouldn't survive Germany's occupation of France, she embarked on a . . . work about France's collaboration with the Nazis. She completed two of five planned movements before she was sent to Auschwitz, a heart-wrenching story meticulously documented in a supplemental section. As for Nemirovsky's masterpiece, it begins with the tumultuous 'Storm in June,' in which diverse Parisians frantically evacuate Paris during the June 1940 German invasion. Nemirovsky's gift for combining the panoramic with the intimate, high emotion with stinging wit, is reminiscent of Turgenev, Babel, and Berberova. Acutely sensitive to class differences, and mordantly scornful of hypocrisy, she orchestrates a veritable carnival of cowardice, lies, larceny, and murder as a panicked populace drops all pretense of civilization. The second movement, 'Dolce,' evokes the eye of the storm in the village of Bussy, where German officers are billeted in French homes, and life and love resume. Suite Francaise is a magnificent novel of the insidious devastation of occupation, and Nemirovsky is brilliant and heroic, summoning up profound empathy for all, including regretful German soldiers." Booklist

Nesbit, TaraShea

The **wives** of Los Alamos; a novel. by TaraShea Nesbit. Bloomsbury USA 2014 240 p. (hardback) $25

ISBN 1620405032; 9781620405031

LC 2013036239

This book, by TaraShea Nesbit, describes the lives of Los Alamos scientists' wives during the creation of the atomic bomb. "Hope quickly turned to hardship as they were forced to adapt to a rugged military town where everything was a secret, including what their husbands were doing at the lab. They lived in barely finished houses with P.O. box addresses in a town wreathed with barbed wire, all for the benefit of a project that didn't exist as far as the public knew." (Publisher's note)

"Nesbit uses a collective 'we' to narrate her story, allowing her to explore contradictory points of view among the women. . . . [A] well-researched and fast-paced novel." LJ

Nesbø, Jo ✓

The **Bat**; Jo Nesbø ; translated from the Norwegian by Don Bartlett. Random House Inc 2013 384 p. (Harry Hole) pbk $15.95

ISBN 034580709X; 9780345807090

Originally published 1997 in Norway

"Inspector Harry Hole of the Oslo Crime Squad is dispatched to Sydney to observe a murder case. Harry is free to offer assistance, but he has firm instructions to stay out of trouble. The victim is a twenty-three year old Norwegian woman who is a minor celebrity back home. Never one to sit on the sidelines, Harry befriends one of the lead detectives, and one of the witnesses, as he is drawn deeper into the case. Together, they discover that this is only the latest in a string of unsolved murders, and the pattern points toward a psychopath working his way across the country. As they circle closer and closer to the killer, Harry begins to fear that no one is safe, least of all those investigating the case." (Publisher's note)

"Inspector Harry Hole's 1997 debut finally follows its seven successors into English translation. . . . Fans of Harry's later adventures (The Redeemer, 2013, etc.) will wait with bated breath to see how long it takes him to break every rule in the book." Kirkus

Other titles about Harry Hole are:
Cockroaches
The redbreast
Nemesis
The devil's star
The redeemer
The snowman

The leopard
Phantom
Police
The thirst

Nesbø, Jo

Blood on snow; a novel. Jo Nesbo; translated by Neil Smith. Alfred A. Knopf 2015 224 p. (hardback) $23.95

ISBN 0385354193; 9780385354196

LC 2014047050

This novel by Jo Nesbo, translated by Neil Smith, "is the story of Olav: an extremely talented 'fixer' for one of Oslo's most powerful crime bosses. He has a capacity for love that is as far-reaching as is his gift for murder. He is our straightforward, calm-in-the-face-of-crisis narrator with a storyteller's hypnotic knack for fantasy. And while his latest job puts him at the pinnacle of his trade, it may be mutating into his greatest mistake. . . ." (Publisher's note)

"Nesbø tells this small but razor-sharp story with precision and understated eloquence, even generating suspense despite the inevitability built into the plot: we know there will be blood on snow, but we're not quite sure whose and how much... A 60,000 first printing isn't that high for Nesbø, but expect this small plate to draw a big audience all the same."

Nesbo, Jo, 1960-

The **devil's** star; translated from the Norwegian by Don Bartlett. Harper 2010 452p $25.99

ISBN 978-0-06-113397-8; 0-06-113397-3

LC 2009-17819

Original Norwegian edition, 2003

"Devastated by his inability to convince his superiors that fellow detective Tom Waaler is both guilty of his former partner Ellen's murder . . . and an arms dealer, Harry Hole goes on a four-week bender. Dragged back to work by his loyal boss, Harry is partnered with Waaler to investigate what quickly looks like a serial killer on the loose in Oslo who leaves star-shaped red diamonds with his victims. . . . Scandinavian noir is alive and well, and Nesbø is one of its best authors." Libr J

Nesbo, Jo, 1960-

The **headhunters**; translated from the Norwegian by Don Bartlett. Vintage Crime/Black Lizard 2011 265, 21p pa $14.95

ISBN 978-0-307-94868-7; 0-307-94868-4

Original Norwegian edition, 2008

"Roger Brown, a British expat comfortably ensconced in Oslo, has developed a reputation as one of the best corporate headhunters in the business, but money problems lead him to use information he gleans from job applicants about valuable art they own. Brown arranges to steal their art works and replace them with clever fakes. When Clas Greve, the former CEO of a major European GPS company, lets slip that he accidentally discovered a long-lost Rubens painting in the apartment he inherited from his aunt, Brown anticipates making his biggest score. Of course, the heist doesn't go smoothly, and the dizzying reversals of fortune and situations that would be over-the-top in lesser hands make for a delightful roller-coaster ride." Publ Wkly

Nesbø, Jo

★ The **leopard**; Jo Nesbo ; translated from the Norwegian by Don Bartlett. Alfred A. Knopf 2012 517 p. map (alk. paper) $26.95

ISBN 0307595870; 9780307595874

LC 2011041049

In this book by Jo Nesbo, "Inspector Harry Hole has literally and figuratively run away from home. Harry hides in Hong Kong's underbelly, drowning his sorrows and painful memories. He only reluctantly returns home to Oslo after two women are violently killed and his father lay on his deathbed, both events demanding Harry's attention and singular expertise." (Library Journal)

Nesbø, Jo

★ **Phantom**; Jo Nesbo; ; translated from the Norwegian by Don Bartlett. Alfred A. Knopf 2012 377 p.

ISBN 0307960471; 9780307960474

LC 2012019892

In this novel by Jo Nesbo "Former Police Detective Harry Hole returns to Oslo after three years abroad. . . . to request permission to investigate a homicide. But the case is already closed; a young junkie, Gusto, was in all likelihood shot by a pal in a conflict over drugs. Harry is granted permission to visit the accused boy in prison. There, he meets himself and his own history. It's the start of a solitary investigation of the most impossible case in Harry Hole's life." (Author's note)

Nesbø, Jo

The **redbreast**; translated from the Norwegian by Don Bartlett. HarperCollins 2007 521p $24.95

ISBN 0-06-113399-X; 978-0-06-113399-2

Original Norwegian edition, 2006

"This is a fine novel, ambitious in concept, skillful in execution and grownup in its view of people and events. In important ways it's also a political novel, one concerned with the threat of fascism, in Norway and by implication everywhere. All in all, The Redbreast certainly ranks with the best of current American crime fiction." Washington Post Book World

Nesbø, Jo

The **redeemer**; 1st U.S. ed. Alfred A. Knopf 2013 416 p. (hardcover) $25.95

ISBN 0307595854; 9780307595850

This book, the sixth in author Jo Nesbo's Harry Hole series, "introduces 17-year-old Robert Karlsen and his year older brother, Jon, who in 1991 are cadets at a Salvation Army retreat in the Norwegian countryside, where a 14-year-old girl is sexually assaulted. . . . 22 years later, detective Hole is winding up the investigation of a drug-related murder in Oslo. The main action begins when a Serbian hit man, Cristo Stankic, shoots Robert on a crowded city street." (Publishers Weekly)

Nesbø, Jo

The **snowman**; translated from the Norwegian by Don Bartlett. Alfred A. Knopf 2011 383p $25.95

ISBN 978-0-307-59586-7; 0-307-59586-2

LC 2010049170

Original Norwegian edition, 2007; this translation originally published 2010 in the United Kingdom

This book follows "antihero police investigator, Harry Hole, . . . [through a murder investigation] that will take Hole to the brink of insanity. . . . A boy named Jonas wakes in the night to find his mother gone. Out his window, in the cold moonlight, he sees the snowman that inexplicably appeared in the yard earlier in the day. Around its neck is his mother's pink scarf. Hole suspects a link between a menacing letter he's received and the disappearance of Jonas's mother—and of perhaps a dozen other women, all of whom went missing on the day of a first snowfall. As his investigation deepens, something else emerges: he is becoming a pawn in an increasingly terrifying game whose rules are devised—and constantly revised—by the killer." (Publisher's note)

This mystery featuring Oslo's Inspector Harry Hole is "about a psychopath who waits for the year's first snowfall to build menacing snowmen outside the homes of his victims, all married women cheating on their spouses. Nesbo has a horrormeister's flair for transforming natural scenes into ominous situations, so those recurring images of beady-eyed snowmen can ruin a walk in the woods or a stolen hour of sexual pleasure. The atmosphere of guilt and gloom is also a reflection of Harry's moody thoughts about his own troubled relationships, his obsessive work ethic and his unhealthy preoccupation with the nature of evil. . . . Harry is a cool hero, but whenever his musings get a bit sticky it's worth remembering that he's afraid of the dark" N Y Times Book Rev

Nesbø, Jo ✓

★ The **son**; A Novel. Jo Nesbo. Alfred A. Knopf 2014 416 p. $25.95

ISBN 0385351372; 9780385351379

LC 2014934518

In this novel, by Jo Nesbo, "Sonny Lofthus is a strangely charismatic and complacent young man. Sonny's been in prison for a dozen years, nearly half his life. The inmates who seek out his uncanny abilities to soothe leave his cell feeling absolved. They don't know or care that Sonny has a serious heroin habit--or where or how he gets his uninterrupted supply of the drug. Or that he's serving time for other peoples' crimes." (Publisher's note)

"A terrific thriller but also a tragic, very moving story of intertwined characters swerving desperately to avoid the dead ends in their paths." Booklist

Nesbø, Jo ✓

The **thirst**; Jo Nesbo. First United States edition Random House Inc 2017 461 p. Map (Harry Hole) $26.95

ISBN 0385352166; 9780385352161

LC 2017008487

In this book in the Harry Hole Series, by Jo Nesbo, "Inspector Harry Hole hunts down a serial murderer who targets his victims . . . on Tinder. . . . There's something about these murders that catches his attention, something in the details that the investigators have missed. . . . Harry throws himself back into the hunt for a figure who haunts him, the monster who got away." (Publisher's note)

"This 11th entry (after Police) in Nesbo's Scandinoir series features thoroughly developed characters, an intricate plot, and suspenseful twists, all hallmarks of a master storyteller." LJ

Netzer, Lydia

Shine shine shine; Lydia Netzer. 1st ed. St. Martin's Press 2012 312 p.

ISBN 1250007070; 9781250007070; 9781250015075

LC 2012007426

In this novel by Lydia Netzer "[Sunny has] got the housewife thing down perfectly, but Maxon, a genius engineer, is on a NASA mission to the moon. . . . Once they were two outcasts who found unlikely love in each other . . . now they're parents to an autistic son . . . [and] [t]heir marriage is on the brink of imploding. . . . When an accident in space puts the mission in peril . . . [d]ark secrets, long-forgotten murders, and a blond wig all come tumbling to the light." (Publisher's note)

Neugeboren, Jay

1940; a novel. Two Dollar Radio 2008 274p pa $15

ISBN 978-0-9763895-6-9

LC 2008-900720

"Neugeboren traverses the Hitlerian tightrope with all the skill and formal daring that have made him one of our most honored writers of literary fiction and masterful nonfiction. This new book is, at once, a beautifully realized work of imagined history, a rich and varied character study and a subtly layered novel of ideas, all wrapped in a propulsively readable story." Los Angeles Times Book Rev

Neuhaus, Nele

Snow White must die; Nele Neuhaus ; translated by Steven T. Murray. Minotaur Books 2013 384 p. (hardback) $24.99

ISBN 0312604254; 9780312604257

LC 2012038365

In this mystery novel, by Nele Neuhaus, "A woman has fallen from a pedestrian bridge onto a car driving underneath. . . . The investigation leads [detectives] Pia and Oliver to a small village, and the home of the victim, Rita Cramer. . . . In the village, Pia and Oliver encounter a wall of silence. When another young girl disappears, the events of the past seem to be repeating themselves in a disastrous manner." (Publisher's note)

Neuman, Andres, 1977-

Traveler of the century; Andrés Neuman ; translated from the Spanish by Nick Caistor and Lorenza Garcia. Farrar, Straus and Giroux 2012 564 p.

ISBN 0374119392; 9780374119393

LC 2011047016

This Alfaguara Prize and National Critics Prize-winning Spanish novel by Andrés Neuman begins when "the enigmatic traveler Hans stops in a small city on the border between Saxony and Prussia. . . . [H] e begins to meet the various characters who populate the town, including a young freethinker named Sophie. Though she is engaged to be married, Sophie and Hans begin a relationship that defies contemporary mores about female sexuality and what can and cannot be said about it." (Publisher's note)

Nevill, Adam

The **house** of small shadows; Adam Nevill. St. Martin's Press 2014 384 p. (hardback) $25.99

ISBN 1250041279; 9781250041272

LC 2014003160

In this horror novel by Adam Nevill, "Catherine can't believe her luck when Mason's elderly niece invites her to stay at Red House itself, where she maintains the collection until his niece exposes her to the dark message behind her uncle's 'Art.' Catherine tries to concentrate on the job, but Mason's damaged visions begin to raise dark shadows from her own past." (Publisher's note)

"This is largely a haunted-house story, though Nevill's merciless assault upon primordial fears—darkness, disfigurement, and disablement—does not so much recall the slow, seeping insanity of Stephen King's The Shining (1977) as it does Stanley Kubrick's treatment of the novel, single-minded in its determination to terrorize regardless of which rational concerns are dropped by the wayside." Booklist

Includes filmography and bibliographical references

Nevill, Adam

The **ritual**; Adam Nevill. St. Martin's Griffin 2012 432p.

ISBN 9780312641849

LC 2011036132

This book tells the story of "four old University friends [who] set off into the Scandinavian wilderness of the Arctic Circle . . . to briefly escape the problems of their lives and reconnect with one another. But when Luke . . . finds he has little left in common with his well-heeled friends, tensions rise. With limited experience between them, a shortcut meant to ease their hike turns into a nightmare scenario. . . . But then they stumble across an old habitation. Ancient artefacts decorate the walls and there are bones scattered upon the dry floors. The residue of old rites and pagan sacrifice for something that still exists in the forest. Something responsible for the bestial presence that follows their every step." (Publisher's note)

Neville, Katherine

The **eight**; a novel. Ballantine Bks. 1989 550p

LC 87-91363

"Involving Napoleon, Talleyrand, Casanova, Voltaire, Rousseau, Robespierre and Catherine the Great in the quest, Neville has great fun rewriting history and making it all ring true." Publ Wkly

Neville, Katherine

The **fire**; a novel. Ballantine Books 2008 451p il $26

ISBN 978-0-345-50067-0; 0-345-50067-9

LC 2008-26624

"Alexandra Solarin, child chess prodigy now grown, finds herself immersed in the Game, searching for a legendary chess set, the Montglane Service, which when assembled spells out the formula for the secret of immortality. The quest for the set ranges from the harem of Ali Pasha in 19th-century Albania to present-day Baghdad and Washington, D.C., and involves such historic figures as Charlemagne, Isaac Newton, Lord Byron and Napoleon. Despite the staggering amount and quality of the research, nothing feels shoehorned or extraneous. The story's relentless pace is matched by characters both sympathetic and real." Publ Wkly

Neville, Stuart

The **ghosts** of Belfast. Soho 2009 326p $25

ISBN 978-1-56947-600-0; 1-56947-600-4

LC 2009-11312

Published in the United Kingdom with title: The twelve

"Neville's debut is as unrelenting as Fegan's ghosts, pulling no punches as it describes the brutality of Ireland's 'troubles' and the crime that has followed, as violent men find new outlets for their skills. Sharp prose places readers in this pitiless place and holds them there. Harsh and unrelenting crime fiction, masterfully done." Kirkus

New Cthulhu; edited by Paula Guran. Prime Books 2011 520p.

ISBN 9781607012894

This book collects short speculative fiction inspired by the creations of horror writer H. P. Lovecraft. "Both Laird Barron in 'Old Virginia' and Charles Stross in 'A Colder War' speculate on the horrors that might ensue if government research teams were allowed to explore Lovecraftian monsters as potential weapons. In Cherie Priest's 'Bad Sushi,' a chef uncovers a cosmic conspiracy involving supernaturally corrupted seafood. Sherlock Holmes foils worshipers of Lovecraft's Great Old Ones in Neil Gaiman's 'A Study in Emerald,' while in Elizabeth Bear's 'Shoggoths in Bloom,' an African-American scientist finds himself sympathizing with enslaved creations of those eldritch entities." (Publishers Weekly)

The **new** space opera; edited by Gardner Dozois and Jonathan Strahan. Eos 2007 517p pa $15.95

ISBN 978-0-06-084675-6; 0-06-084675-5

"An exceedingly fine set of stories written specifically for this collection by some of the best sf authors writing today. These 18 tales run the gamut from technologically centered hard science (think exploding comets and artificial intelligence) to character-driven soft science (settling on new worlds). Alien perspectives are balanced by humanistic introspection. Many of the stories mine the genre's favorite nuggets by exploring political and ethical questions from varied and unusual points of view." Libr J

New stories from the South: the year's best [date] edited by Shannon Ravenel. Algonquin Books of Chapel Hill

Annual. First published 1986

An annual collection of short stories culled from a wide variety of magazines. Among the authors represented are Frederick Barthelme, George Singleton, Chris Offutt, Tony Earley, Janice Daugharty, and Elizabeth Spencer

Newitz, Annalee

Autonomous; Annalee Newitz. Tor Books 2017 301 p. (hardcover) $25.99

ISBN 0765392070; 9780765392091; 9780765392077

Nebula Finalist: Best Novel (2017)

In this book, by Annalee Newitz, "Earth, 2144. Jack is an anti-patent scientist turned drug pirate, . . . fabricating cheap scrips for poor people. . . . But her latest drug hack has left a trail of lethal overdoses. . . . Hot on her trail . . . [are] Eliasz . . . and his robotic partner, Paladin. As they race to stop information about the sinister origins of Jack's drug from getting out, they begin to form . . . [a] bond that neither of them fully understand." (Publisher's note)

"In a phenomenal debut that's sure to garner significant awards attention, Newitz, cofounder of io9, sends three fascinating characters on an action-packed race against time through a strange yet familiar futuristic landscape." Pub Wkly

Newman, Janis Cooke

Mary; a novel. MacAdam/Cage Pub. 2006 707p $26

ISBN 978-1-93156-163-1; 1-93156-163-X

LC 2006-15591

A "portrait of Mary Todd Lincoln. Writing in her journal while confined to Bellvue asylum, Mary alternates between recalling her past life as First Lady and detailing her current experiences in that institution. The first-person narrative and liberal use of descriptive details, perfected perhaps by Newman's extensive experience writing nonfiction, enlist the reader's sympathy for the mentally unstable Mrs. Lincoln. At the same time, we can become dismayed at her seeming lack of common sense. Her obsessions are chronicled, from compulsive shopping and fears for the safety of her loved ones, to her sexual needs. Mary's hopes, dreams, feelings, and thoughts are conveyed with depth and subtlety." Libr J

Newman, Sandra, 1965-

The **Country** of Ice Cream Star; Sandra Newman. ECCO, an imprint of HarperCollinsPublishers 2015 581 p. (hbk.) $26.99

ISBN 0062227092; 9780062227096

LC 2015301791

In this novel by Sandra Newman, set "in the ruins of a future America, fifteen-year-old Ice Cream Star and her nomadic tribe live off of the detritus of a crumbled civilization. Theirs is a world of children; before reaching the age of twenty, they all die of a mysterious disease. When her brother begins showing signs of the disease, Ice Cream Star sets off on a bold journey to find this cure. Led by a stranger, . . . Ice Cream Star plunges into the unknown, risking her . . . life." (Publisher's note)

"This suspenseful, provocative tale is The Hunger Games meets Lord of the Flies and The Walking Dead, only much, much better... Could this be the next big book to capture readers all across the age spectrum? Don't bet against it." Booklist

Newman, Sharan

Strong as death. Forge 1996 384p

LC 96-1410

"Colorful characters and thoroughly researched culture add up to wonderful historical fiction." Libr J

Newton, Charlie

Calumet City. Touchstone/Simon & Schuster 2008 388p pa $14

ISBN 978-1-4165-3322-1; 1-4165-3322-2

LC 2007-16112

"An atmospheric shocker. . . . Newton certainly has all the hallmarks and above all the classic noir tone — urban and nocturnal, stealthy and smoky, grim determination doing its two-step with gallows humor." Chicago Sun Times

Newton, Charlie

Start shooting; Charlie Newton. Doubleday 2012 305 p.

ISBN 9780385534697; 9780385534703

LC 2011002844

In this book, set "thirty years after the rape-murder of his childhood girlfriend Coleen Brennan in his West Side Chicago neighborhood—a crime for which a retarded African-American man was executed—young Latino cop Bobby Vargas finds himself accused of the killing. Meanwhile, Coleen's twin sister Arleen, an actress, is targeted by criminal elements after fatally shooting a member of the Korean mafia on a police sting she was forced into by Bobby's older brother Ruben, also a cop. . . . Chicago is re-bidding for the 2016 Olympics . . . meaning the City Hall will do anything to protect its image. With star crime reporter Tracy Moens on the prowl for juicy exposes for the fictional Chicago Herald, that's going to take some doing." (Kirkus)

Newton, Mark Charan

Nights of Villjamur; Mark Charan Newton. Spectra/Ballantine Books 2009 437 p. (alk. paper) o.p.; (pbk.) $16; (alk. paper) o.p.

ISBN 9780345520845; 9780345520852; 034552084X

LC 2010009845

This fantasy novel, the first volume of the Legends of the Red Sun series, takes place in "Villjamur [which] is under siege from the encroaching ice age. Refugees threaten to overwhelm the city and stability is undermined from within by scheming chancellors. After the suicide of the emperor, Captain Brynd Lathraea is charged with bringing back the emperor's daughter from self-imposed exile, to be installed as a puppet empress. Meanwhile Randur Estevu, a country lad with vaunting ambitions, comes to Villjamur seeking immortality." (The Guardian)

Followed by: City of ruin (2011)

Ng, Celeste

★ **Everything** I never told you; a novel. Celeste Ng. Penguin Press HC 2014 304 p. (hardback) $26.95

ISBN 159420571X; 9781594205712

LC 2013039961

Alex Award (2015)

This novel, by Celeste Ng, is "about a Chinese American family living in 1970s small-town Ohio. Lydia is the favorite child of Marilyn and James Lee. . . . Her parents are determined that Lydia will fulfill the dreams they were unable to pursue. . . . When Lydia's body is found in the local lake, the delicate balancing act that has been keeping the Lee family together tumbles into chaos, forcing them to confront the long-kept secrets that have been slowly pulling them apart." (Publisher's note)

"Ng constructs a mesmerizing narrative that shrinks enormous issues of race, prejudice, identity, and gender into the miniaturist dynamics of a single family." LJ

Ng, Celeste

★ **Little** fires everywhere; by Celeste Ng, narrated by Jennifer Lim. Penguin Press 2017 338 p. (hardcover) $27

ISBN 9780735224308; 9780735224292

LC 2016056762

This audiobook, by Celeste Ng, narrated by Jennifer Lim, is set "in Shaker Heights, a . . . progressive suburb of Cleveland, [where] everything is planned--from the layout of the winding roads, . . . to the successful lives its residents will go on to lead. . . . Enter Mia Warren--an enigmatic artist and single mother--who. . . . carries with her a mysterious past and a disregard for the status quo that threatens to upend this carefully ordered community." (Publisher's note)

"The characters she creates here are wonderfully appealing, and watching their paths connect . . . is mesmerizing, casting into new light ideas about creativity and consumerism, parenthood and privilege." Kirkus

Ng, Fae Myenne

Bone. Hyperion 1993 193p

ISBN 1-56282-944-0

LC 92-6028

"Ng is a master storyteller. Her gift for observation and language make Bone truly extraordinary." Women's Rev Books

Nguyen, Viet Thanh, 1971-

★ The **Refugees**; by Viet Thanh Nguyen. Pgw 2017 224 p. $25; (ebook) $25

ISBN 0802126391; 9780802126399; 9780802189356

LC 2016058763

This book, by Viet Thanh Nguyen, "is a collection of perfectly formed stories written over a period of twenty years, exploring questions of immigration, identity, love, and family. . . . From a young Vietnamese refugee who suffers profound culture shock when he comes to live with two gay men in San Francisco, to a woman whose husband is suffering from dementia and starts to confuse her for a former lover, . . . the stories are a captivating testament to the dreams and hardships of immigration." (Publisher's note)

"Nguyen is the foremost literary interpreter of the Vietnamese experience in America, to be sure. But his stories, excellent from start to finish, transcend ethnic boundaries to speak to human universals." Kirkus

Nguyen, Viet Thanh, 1971-

★ The **Sympathizer**; Viet Thanh Nguyen. Grove Press 2015 384 p. $26

ISBN 0802123457; 9780802123459

LC 2015375327

PEN/Faulkner Award for Fiction: Shortlist (2016)

Carnegie Medal: Fiction (2016)

Pulitzer Prize: Fiction (2016)

This novel by Viet Thanh Nguyen "begins with its nameless protagonist, a highly placed young aide to a general in the South Vietnamese army, recalling how he finalized the details of escape before the fall of Saigon. But our hero is a double agent, a communist sympathizer who will continue to feed information to the North even after he makes the harrowing escape . . . on the last plane out, and becomes part of the Vietnamese refugee community in Southern California." (Library Journal)

"Nguyen's probing literary art illuminates how Americans failed in their political and military attempt to remake Vietnam--but then succeeded spectacularly in shrouding their failure in Hollywood distortions. Compelling--and profoundly unsettling." Booklist

Nicholas, Douglas

Something red; a novel. Douglas Nicholas. Atria Books 2012 336 p.

ISBN 1451660073; 9781451660074; 9781451660227; 9781451660234

LC 2011044435

This book is set "[d]uring the thirteenth century in northwest England." An "Irish healer, Molly, and the troupe she leads are driving their three wagons, hoping to cross the Pennine Mountains before the heavy snows set in." The group becomes "aware that they are being stalked by something terrible. As danger continues to rise, it becomes clear that the creature must be faced and defeated—or else they will all surely die." (Publisher's note)

Includes bibliographical references and index

Other titles in this series are:

The wicked (2013)

Throne of darkness (2015)

Nicholas, Douglas

The **wicked**; by Douglas Nicholas. Atria Books 2014 368 p. hbk $16

ISBN 1451660243; 9781451660241

LC 2013004311

Sequel to: Something Red

"Something evil has come to reside in a castle by the chill waters of the North Sea: men disappear and are found as horribly wizened corpses, knights ride out and return under an enchantment that dulls their minds. Both the townspeople and the court under Sir Odinell's protection live in fear, terrorized by forces beyond human understanding." (Publisher's note)

"The 13th-century traveling troupe of players from Nicholas's debut, Something Red, returns in another meticulously plotted and researched blend of horror and historical fantasy. . . . The players, especially point-of-view character Hob, are nuanced and interesting, but it is the setting and tense action that make this a gripping read." LJ

Nicholls, David

One day. Vintage Books 2010 437p pa $14.95

ISBN 978-0-307-47471-1; 0-307-47471-2

First published 2009 in the United Kingdom

"On July 15, 1988, the night they graduate from the University of Edinburgh, brainy, working-class Emma Morley and posh hottie Dexter Mayhew share a bed, and almost recognize the powerful chemistry in their unlikely pairing. Almost. The point is they don't, because Emma and Dexter haven't lived enough yet to know who they really are, as opposed to who they fancy themselves to be. That part takes time—20 years—during which Dex wastes most of the opportunities the universe showers on him (the women who desire him, the shallow TV career) and Emma, a writer in the making, clings to her belief that she deserves only the universe's castoffs (the dingy waitressing jobs, the dull boyfriend). Nicholls charts the maturing of these two Gen-X specimens by the calendar, marking July 15 as the day to check in on Emma and Dex, year after year. Along the way, the author is alert not only to how it feels to be in one's twenties and thirties in the '80s and '90s, but in a larger sense, of how it feels to age. Loss lurks in the wings—don't expect sunshine and cute quirks. But even as he explores sadness, Nicholls creates new poignancy from the old truth that a life is just a stack of days, one after another, stretching into years. One day can truly make a difference." Entertainment Wkly

Nicholls, David

A **question** of attraction. Villard Books 2004 338p $23.95; pa $13.95

ISBN 1-400-06181-4; 0-8129-7140-X pa

LC 2003-59627

"Recounted in the first person with good-natured, self-deprecating humor, this first novel tells a delightful coming-of-age story." Libr J

Nicholls, David

★ **Us**; a novel. David Nicholls. HarperCollins 2014 416 p. (hardcover) $26.99

ISBN 0062365584; 9780062365583

LC 2014015360

"Douglas Petersen may be mild-mannered, but behind his reserve lies a sense of humor that, against all odds, seduces beautiful Connie into a second date . . . and eventually into marriage. Now, almost three decades after their relationship first blossomed in London, they live more or less happily in the suburbs with their moody seventeen year-old son, Albie. Then Connie tells him she thinks she wants a divorce." (Publisher's note)

"This is Nicholls's most ambitious work to date, and his realistically flawed characters are somehow endearing despite the many bruises they inflict upon each other." Pub Wkly

Nichols, John Treadwell

★ The **Milagro** beanfield war; by John Nichols; illus. by Rini Templeton. Holt, Rinehart & Winston 1974 445p

"Nichols has written a bawdy, slangy, modern proletarian novel that is—if finally perhaps excessively sentimental—still a consistently entertaining film scenario while at the same time it manages to make funny-serious sense out of a contemporary situation enduring injustice and imminent violence." Choice

Nichols, John Treadwell

On top of Spoon Mountain; John Nichols. University of New Mexico Press 2012 223 p.

ISBN 0826352707; 9780826352705; 9780826352729

LC 2012012396

In this novel by John Nichols "Jonathan Kepler wants to climb Spoon Mountain with his grown son and daughter on his sixty-fifth birthday. . . . Still reeling from his third, nearly fatal, divorce, he has a rotten heart, serious asthma, and a fed-up girlfriend. . . .Once a celebrated novelist, Hollywood screenwriter, and environmental activist, Jonathan is now tottering at the ragged end of his career and yearning to make amends to his children for his past sins." (Publisher's note)

Nichols, John Treadwell

The **sterile** cuckoo; by John Nichols. McKay, D. 1965 210p

When the heroine, Pookie Adams "first stumbles on the hero, Jerry Payne, waiting at a cross-country bus stop, he sees only a skinny, scrub-by-haired girl, balancing a toothpick on her tongue. Then she bursts into speech and Jerry . . . remains bewitched until the last syllable. Her pursuit of Jerry is launched with . . . determination. . . . When fate places the couple at neighboring Eastern colleges, Jerry succumbs to his first frantic affair. . . . As their romance plunges into its second year, they make a final attempt to slow to a more normal pace, but on a New York weekend, somewhat the worse for an over indulgence in Tiki Puka Pukas, their affair staggers to a close." Publisher's note

Nichols, Peter, 1950-

★ The **rocks**; Peter Nichols. Riverhead Books 2015 432 p. $27.95

ISBN 1594633312; 9781594633317

LC 2014022801

This novel by Peter Nichols "opens with a confrontation and a secret: What was the mysterious, catastrophic event that drove two honeymooners apart so suddenly and absolutely in 1948 that they never spoke again despite living on the same island for sixty more years? And how did their history shape the Romeo and Juliet—like romance of their (unrelated) children decades later?" (Publisher's note)

"The proceedings are enriched by a sharply drawn cast of secondary players. Nichols deftly melds comedy and compassion." Booklist

Nicholson, Christopher

The **elephant** keeper. William Morrow 2009 298p $24.99

ISBN 978-0-06-165160-1; 0-06-165160-5

LC 2009-00852

"Tom Page is the plain-spoken narrator who begins his working life as a stable boy to Mr. John Harrington, sugar merchant of Bristol, and who later finds his vocation as the elephant keeper to Lord Bidborough of Sussex. In 1773, Tom's master, in the cause of science, instructs Tom to write a full description of the elephant in his care. The elephant's story, as related by Tom, is of course his own story. In Nicholson's hands, however, it is also a lively portrait of 18th-century manners and ideas." Boston Globe

Nicholson, William

Motherland; William Nicholson. Simon & Schuster 2013 448 p. (trade pbk.) $15.99

ISBN 1476706069; 9781451687132; 9781476706061

LC 2013000433

"Summer, 1942. Kitty, an army driver stationed in Sussex, meets Ed, a Royal Marine commando, and Larry, a liaison officer with Combined Ops. She falls instantly in love with Ed, who falls in love with her. So does Larry. Both men go off to war, and Ed wins the highest military honor for his bravery. But sometimes heroes don't make the best husbands." (Publisher's note)

"it's the book's quieter moments, infused with realistic dialogue and fastidious attention to historical detail, that will make true romantics swoon and should win over a wide mainstream audience." Booklist

Nickson, Chris, 1954- ✓

Cold cruel winter. Creme de la Crime 2011 224p

ISBN 9781780290058

In this crime fiction novel, "[s]et in 1732, . . . [the reader] finds Richard Nottingham, constable of the city of Leeds, fearful that he will lose more loved ones after his older daughter falls ill and dies. An especially hard winter is making things tough for the entire community. Then a savage murder—that of wool merchant Samuel Graves, whose throat was cut and the skin flayed from his back—tests Nottingham and his men to their utmost. While the motive for the mutilation murder of the respectable Graves isn't obvious, the constable soon learns the grisly reason for the trophy taking. Other victims will follow, he realizes, if he doesn't manage to stop the butcher first." (Publishers Weekly)

Niffenegger, Audrey

Her fearful symmetry; a novel. Scribner 2009 406p il $26.99

ISBN 978-1-4391-6539-3; 1-4391-6539-4

LC 2009018771

The novel is "at its best in its early pages, when Niffenegger gives herself room to present her cast of characters; there are some charming descriptions, particularly of these odd, wan mirror twins. The author's love for and deep research into Highgate is also apparent. . . . Not a deep meditation, the novel requires its readers to thoroughly suspend their disbelief and to go along for the haunted ride." Chicago Trib

Niffenegger, Audrey

The **time** traveler's wife; a novel. MacAdam\Cage 2003 518p $25

ISBN 1-931561-64-8

LC 2003-10159

Niffenegger "writes with the unflinching yet detached clarity of a war correspondent standing at the sidelines of an unfolding battle. She possesses a historian's eye for contextual detail. This is no romantic idyll." USA Today

Nightmares; a new decade of modern horror. edited by Ellen Datlow. Tachyon Publications 2016 427 p. (paperback) $16.95

ISBN 1616962321; 9781616962333; 9781616962326; 9781616962357

In this collection of horror stories, by Ellen Datlow, "unlucky thieves invade a house where 'Home Alone' seems like a playground romp. An antique bookseller and a mob enforcer join forces to retrieve the Atlas of Hell. Postapocalyptic survivors cannot decide which is worse: demon women haunting the skies or maddened extremists patrolling the earth." (Publisher's note)

"This volume is not only the perfect discovery tool for readers looking for the very best of modern horror, it should also be used as a collection-development tool by library staff." Booklist

Nin, Anais

Cities of the interior; introduction by Sharon Spencer. Swallow Press 1974 xx, 589p

First one-volume version published 1959 by the author. Although intended as a connected work exploring the lives of women, it was originally published as five separate novelettes. This edition contains the expanded and retitled version of the fifth novelette

In Ladders to fire (1946), which concerns a largely American group of characters in Paris, Lillian's hunger for life and love leave her unsatisfied with her seemingly changeless marriage to Larry. She develops an increasingly possessive relationship with Djuna, whose inner clarity and control, concealed beneath a delicate feminine exterior, offer a comforting contrast to her own emotional turbulence. Lillian's love affair with the painter Jay is complicated by the love-hate relationship which they both establish with Sabina

Nissenson, Hugh, 1933-2013

The **pilgrim**. Sourcebooks Landmark 2011 356p $24.99

ISBN 978-1-4022-0924-6

LC 2011-17815

"A marvelously intimate look back through time. Charles' fears and desires are made quite believable as he recalls the everyday horrors of the time—and the bits of Scripture that both justified and aggravated them. And while the young protagonist earnestly seeks salvation, his all-too-human failings—such as when he and the pretty Abigail Winslow flirt on the Sabbath—make him as sympathetic as any young striver since Holden Caulfield. The author's return to historical fiction raises human questions with immediacy and flair." Kirkus

Niven, Larry

The **Best** of Larry Niven; edited by Jonathan Strahan. Subterranean 2010 616p $40

ISBN 978-1-59606-331-0; 1-59606-331-9

"These 27 short stories, originally published from 1965 to 2000, demonstrate Niven's tremendous range and literary prowess in the fields of SF (Hugo winners 'Neutron Star' and 'The Borderland of Sol,' featuring clever pilot Beowulf Shaeffer), fantasy ('Not Long Before the End'), nonfiction (the famously footnote-heavy 'Man of Steel, Woman of Kleenex'), and mystery ('The Deadlier Weapon'). . . . An introduction by frequent Niven collaborator Jerry Pournelle (Escape from Hell) focuses on Niven's attraction to hard SF, and brief headnotes by Niven himself provide context and color. This spellbinding collection is a must for fans of classic SF." Publ Wkly

Niven, Larry

Lucifer's hammer; by Larry Niven & Jerry Pournelle. Playboy Press 1977 494p

LC 77-8074

"The hammer of the title is an eons-old comet that strikes earth with devastating physical and psychological consequences that are meticulously dramatized in the lives of dozens of major and minor characters. The second and more powerful part details the immense task of rebuilding civilization or preserving what remains of it. The authors excel in their suspenseful and thought-provoking hypothesis about the nature of civilized man and the ethics of survival when the future of their fragile community is at stake." Booklist

Niven, Larry

★ The **Mote** in God's Eye; by Larry Niven & Jerry Pournelle. Simon & Schuster 1974 537p hardcover o.p. pa $7.99

ISBN 0-671-74192-6

"Superior space opera in which Earth's interstellar navy contacts and does battle with an enormously hostile alien race. The scenes of space warfare are well handled, and the alien Moties are fascinating." Anatomy of Wonder 4

Another title about the war between humans and the Moties is:
The gripping hand (1993)

Niven, Larry

★ **Ringworld**. Ballantine Bks. 1970 342p pa $7.99

ISBN 0-345-33392-6

"The Ringworld, a world shaped like a wheel so huge that it surrounds a sun, is almost too fantastic to conceive of. With a radius of 90 million miles and a length of 600 million miles, the Ringworld's mystery is compounded by the discovery that it is artificial. What phenomenal intelligence can be behind such a creation? Four unlikely explorers, two humans and two aliens, set out for the Ringworld, bound by mutual distrust and unsure of each other's motives." Shapiro. Fic for Youth. 3d edition

Other available titles in this series are:
The Ringworld engineers (1980)
The Ringworld throne (1996)
Ringworld's children (2004)

Niven, Larry

The **Ringworld** engineers. Holt & Co. 1980

"Twenty-three years after their original journey, Louis Wu and Speaker-to-Animals once more find themselves kidnapped companions of a mad Puppeteer who returns with them to Ringworld to steal a transmutation device. The Puppeteer encounters unexpected obstacles to this goal, however: Louis has become a wirehead addicted to the electric current fed almost constantly to his brain; Speaker-to-Animals is now a kzinti Patriarch and resents his enforced participation in the venture; the Ringworld has developed an unstable orbit and is about to desintegrate into its sun." SLJ

"This is a good example of the kind of novel where the basic idea—the Ringworld itself—is the true 'hero.'" Booklist

Followed by The Ringworld throne

Niven, Larry

The **Ringworld** throne. Ballantine Bks. 1996 424p

LC 95-47882

The third title in the author's Ringworld series "offers two stories crowded into one. A motley array of hominid inhabitants are seeking to defeat a plague of vampires. Meanwhile, returning hero Louis Wu is battling what effectively is a plague of Protectors . . . whose rivalries threaten Ringworld's existence. The battle against the vampires is the more exciting of the two stories, filled with action, scenes of the Ringworld and explorations of ritualistic interspecies sex. Wu's pursuit of the Protectors displays Niven's deft hand at portraying aliens." Publ Wkly

Niven, Larry

Ringworld's children. Tor Bks. 2004 $24.95

ISBN 0-7653-0167-9

LC 2003-26581

"Action and clever world building should captivate newcomers to Ringworld, while returners will appreciate picking up loose ends from previous Ringworld volumes." Booklist

Niven, Larry

Saturn's race; [by] Larry Niven & Steven Barnes. TOR Bks. 2000 317p

ISBN 0-312-86726-3

LC 00-28646

"Brilliantly weaving high-tech internets, augmentation technologies and social issues into a fast-paced cloak-and-dagger action adventure, this novel effortlessly moves from the depths of the ocean to the heights of VR to create a dazzling, seamless whole." Publ Wkly

Noble, Kate

The **Game** and the Governess; Kate Noble. Pocket Books 2014 432 p. $7.99

ISBN 1476749388; 9781476749389

"When the Earl of Ashby, Ned Granville, and his secretary, John Turner, travel to the small town of Hollyhock to examine Ned's deceased mother's property, they wager that if Ned poses as John he'll be unable to seduce a lady within two weeks. While staying at the home of Sir Nathan and Lady Widcoate, the deceivers meet a houseful of marriageable women, and Ned quickly learns how unimportant he appears as a mere secretary. He becomes intrigued by the governess, Phoebe Baker, initially seeing her as a means to win the bet but soon realizing that he is completely enamored of her." (Publishers Weekly)

"Noble's buoyant sense of wit gracefully propels the plot of her latest Regency-set historical to its immensely entertaining and eminently satisfying conclusion." Booklist

Noel, Katharine

Halfway house. Atlantic Monthly Press 2006 367p $23

ISBN 0-871-13934-0

LC 2005-53636

"There are moments when the author could have allowed feel-good plot turns to transform the story into a sentimental domestic drama, but instead she tenaciously adheres to the realistic trajectory of mental illness. While reading [the novel], a reader can't help considering the classic protagonist of this literary genre: Esther Greenwood in 'The Bell Jar,' by Sylvia Plath. . . . Thankfully, Ms. Noel doesn't attempt to reinvent Plath's masterpiece; she steers clear of the first-person voice and instead relies on her third-person tapestry. That said, Ms. Noel offers her own contemporary, insightful chronicle of a young woman trying to define herself through the miasma of mental illness." N Y Times (Late N Y Ed)

Noire (Author)

Natural born liar; Misadventures of Mink LaRue. Noire. Dafina Books/Kensington Pub. Corp. 2012 275 p. (pbk.) $15.00

ISBN 0758266081; 9780758266088

LC 2011279554

This novel, by Noire, follows "what happens when beautiful, twenty-year-old petty thief and ex-stripper Mink LaRue finds out she's a dead ringer for the age-progressed photo of the missing oil heiress Sable Dominion. Harlem-born Mink LaRue makes a beeline to Dallas, Texas, pretending to be the Dominion's long-lost daughter, Sable. . . . But it's not long before Mink's newfound siblings grow suspicious of the ghetto princess, who has a rap sheet a mile long." (Publisher's note)

Noon, Jeff

Vurt. Crown 1995 342p

LC 94-25544

First published 1993 in the United Kingdom

This "fluorescent and phantasmagorical novel . . . isn't quite the equal of Anthony Burgess's A Clockwork Orange, with which it is being compared, but in some ways it comes close. It's good enough in its first 50 or 60 pages of atmosphere setting, all smoke machines and flashing strobes, that the reader blinks, shakes his head and wonders whether Noon can sustain the weirdness." Time

Nordan, Lewis

★ **Wolf** whistle; a novel. Algonquin Bks. 1993 290p

ISBN 1-56512-028-0

LC 93-1011

"Propelled by Nordan's musical prose, much of this narrative soars above the commonplace into the realm of myth." Publ Wkly

Nordhoff, Charles, 1887-1947

Botany Bay; by Charles Nordhoff and James Norman Hall. Little, Brown 1941 374p

"The story of the Australian penal colony at Botany Bay, and especially of Hugh Tallant, an American, who had been stranded in England, turned highwayman, and was one of the first criminals shipped to Botany Bay, where life was bitterly hard and adventurous." Ont Libr Rev

Nordhoff, Charles, 1887-1947

The **Bounty** trilogy; by Charles Nordhoff and James Norman Hall; illustrated by N. C. Wyeth. Little, Brown 1982 691p il hardcover o.p.

A reissue of the combined volume first published 1936

Based on actual events stemming from a mutiny on a British war vessel in 1787, "this great trilogy begins with the story of the men who mutinied against the now famous Captain Bligh—'Mutiny on the Bounty.' In 'Men Against the Sea' Bligh and his supporters, set adrift in a small boat, made an incredible journey to safety. 'Pitcairn's Island' is the story of the mutineers who found refuge on a remote Pacific island." Books for you

Nordhoff, Charles, 1887-1947

Men against the sea; by Charles Nordhoff and James Norman Hall. Little, Brown 1934 251p

ISBN 9780316738880; 9780891905646

Sequel to Mutiny on the Bounty

This volume tells the story of Captain Bligh and the eighteen loyal men, who under his leadership sailed in an open boat thirty-six hundred miles from the Friendly Islands in the South Pacific to the Dutch colony of Timor in the East Indies. The story is told as if by Ledward, the surgeon, but the events, the wind and the weather of the narrative are those recorded in Captain Bligh's log

Followed by Pitcairn's Island

Nordhoff, Charles, 1887-1947

Mutiny on the Bounty; by Charles Nordhoff and James Norman Hall. Little, Brown 1932 396p hardcover o.p. pa $13.95

ISBN 0-316-61157-3; 0-316-61168-9 pa

Also available from other publishers

This narrative is "based on the famous mutiny that members of the crew of the 'Bounty', a British war vessel, carried out in 1787 against their cruel commander, Captain William Bligh. The authors kept the actual historical characters and background, using as narrator an elderly man, Captain Roger Byam, who had been a midshipman on the 'Bounty.' The story tells how the mate of the ship, Fletcher Christian, and a number of the crew rebel and set Captain Bligh adrift in an open boat with the loyal members of the crew." Reader's Ency. 4th edition

Other titles in the Bounty trilogy are:

Men against the sea (1934)

Pitcairn's Island (1934)

Nordhoff, Charles, 1887-1947

Pitcairn's Island; by Charles Nordhoff and James Norman Hall. Little, Brown 1934 333p

ISBN 9780316611602 out of print; 9780316738873

LC 88008520

Sequel to Men against the sea

"This final volume {of the trilogy} is the history of those mutineers who, with eighteen Polynesian men and women, reached Pitcairn's Island and there destroyed the 'Bounty.' Unvisited for eighteen years, the community fought over women and possession, and all but one of the men died violent deaths. A blood-curdling story, not for the squeamish reader." Booklist

Norfolk, Lawrence

John Saturnall's feast; Lawrence Norfolk. Grove Press 2012 416 p. (hardcover) $26.00

ISBN 0802120512; 9780802120519

This novel by Lawrence Norfolk is "the story of a cook and his eponymous cookbook and an allegory of service and human purpose. . . . [When] the Reformation asserts itself, . . . John [Saturnall] and his mother are victimized. Their lives appear heretical. Exiled from home, John . . . grows into his calling as a cook in the clattering kitchens of Master Scovell; into his consciousness of class and the wages of factional warfare; and into his awareness of the importance of his mother's holy book." (Kirkus Reviews)

Norman, Howard

★ The **bird** artist. Farrar, Straus & Giroux 1994 289p

LC 94-70542

This work evokes "a way of life, a distinctive community and a fatalistic view of human behavior. The novel sings with tension and sparkles with antic humor." Publ Wkly

Norman, Howard

The **haunting** of L. Farrar, Straus & Giroux 2002 326p $24

ISBN 0-374-16825-3

LC 2001-51120

"This is a mesmerizing melodrama rendered magical thanks to lyrical evocations of fog and storm, sexual bliss and fear, a conflation of atmospheric conditions and states of mind that makes of the human heart a realm as treacherous and exquisite as the Arctic." Booklist

Norman, Howard

The **museum** guard; a novel. Farrar, Straus & Giroux 1998 310p

ISBN 0-374-21649-5

LC 98-8413

The author "fills this enigmatic novel with elements of fable and fairy tale blended with memorable characterizations and subtle narrative probings into the nature of self and the consequences of actions." Libr J

Norman, Howard

Next life might be kinder; Howard Norman. Houghton Mifflin Harcourt 2014 272 p. (hardback) $26

ISBN 054771212X; 9780547712123

LC 2013045635

In this book, by Howard Norman, "Sam Lattimore meets Elizabeth Church in 1970s Halifax, in an art gallery. The sparks are immediate, leading quickly to a marriage. . . . [T]he circumstances of Elizabeth's murder are revealed in . . . increments. Sam's life afterward is complicated. For one thing, in a moment of desperate confusion, he sells his life story to a Norwegian filmmaker named Istvakson, known for the stylized violence of his films." (Publisher's note)

"The book blends macabre elements, including murder, with an absurdity and humor out of Kafka or Pirandello (a film is in fact being made about the murder). It also includes utterly convincing depictions of human love and compassion." LJ

Norman, Howard

What is left the daughter. Houghton Mifflin Harcourt 2010 243p $25

ISBN 978-0-618-73543-3; 0-618-73543-7

LC 2009-44460

A novel "set in the gray majesty of Nova Scotia, where 17-year-old orphan Wyatt Hillyer moves in with his devoted aunt and uncle and their adopted daughter, Tilda, the love of stoic Wyatt's life. The ravages of Hitler and his dastardly German U-boats lurking beneath Canadian waters hit their home hard. . . . Norman writes with spare elegance and dry humor, and the extraordinary emotional power of his slim new novel is earned with authentic grace." Entertainment Wkly

Norris, Frank

★ **McTeague**; a story of San Francisco. edited with an introduction by Kevin Starr. Penguin Books 1994 xlviii, 442p pa $10.95

ISBN 0-14-018769-3

First published 1899 by Doubleday

"A prime example of the American naturalistic novel, McTeague treats the gradual degeneration of a stupid, but initially harmless, giant of a man whose instincts are nearer brute than human. McTeague practices dentistry without a license in a poor section of San Francisco's Polk Street and marries Trina, who has just won $5,000 in a lottery. He soon loses his job and takes to drink. Trina becomes a miser, and McTeague murders her in a fit of rage and steals her money but is tracked down and killed by her cousin." Benet's Reader's Ency of Am Lit

Norris, Frank

Novels and essays. Library of America 1986 1232p $40

ISBN 0-940450-40-2

Vandover and the brute (1914) depicts the degeneration of a once affable and talented young man after he is afflicted with the psychological condition lycanthropy. McTeague and The octopus are entered separately.

Norris, Frank

★ The **octopus**; a story of California. Doubleday 1901 652p

First volume of an unfinished trilogy The epic of wheat

"The battle waged between the wheat growers and the railroad men in California is the theme of this novel. Concerned with social injustice, man's inhumanity to man, and the relentlessness of power struggles, Norris is able to combine these themes with a love interest." Shapiro. Fic for Youth. 3d edition

Followed by The pit

Norris, Frank

★ The **pit**; a story of Chicago. Doubleday 1903

The second volume of the author's unfinished The epic of wheat trilogy "is a story of manipulations in the Chicago Exchange. Curtis Jadwin, a stock speculator, is so absorbed in making money that he neglects his emotionally starved wife Laura. Into this situation steps Sheldon Corthell, dilettante artist, to console her. Laura loves her husband, and postpones for awhile going away with the aesthete. Meanwhile, Jadwin engages in a struggle with the Crookes gang of speculators. He beats them, but is crushed by fluctuations in wheat production. He and Laura effect a reconciliation." Haydn. Thesaurus of Book Dig

Nors, Dorthe

Karate chop; Dorthe Nors, Martin Aitken. Graywolf Press 2014 112 p. (alk. paper) $14

ISBN 1555976654; 9781555976651

LC 2013946921

This short story collection, by Dorthe Nors and translated by Martin Airken, features "fifteen compact stories . . . [with] meticulously observed glimpses of everyday life that expose the ominous lurking under the ordinary. . . . Shifting between moments of violence (real and imagined) and mundane contemporary life." (Publisher's note)

"These stories are swift and unexpected and bruising. Nors' insight into the strange nuances of human interactions, especially those rooted in violence or sorrow, is keen to the point of vivisection." Booklist

North, Anna

The **Life** and Death of Sophie Stark; by Anna North. Blue Rider Press 2015 288 p. $26.95

ISBN 0399173390; 9780399173394

Lambda Literary Award: Bisexual Fiction (2016)

This book, by Anna North, "is a haunting story of fame, love, and legacy told through the propulsive rise of an iconoclastic artist. Sophie Stark begins her filmmaking career by creating a documentary about her obsession, Daniel, a college basketball star. But when she becomes too invasive, she finds herself the victim of a cruel retribution. The humiliation doesn't stop her. . . . Sophie begins to use stories from the lives of those around her to create movies." (Publisher's note)

"As taut and artistically ambitious as its title character, North's novel upends the trope of the lone, tortured genius, considering instead the deeply human consequences of one person's uncompromising vision." Booklist

North, Claire

The **Sudden** Appearance of Hope; by Claire North. Little, Brown & Co. 2016 432 p. $27

ISBN 9780316335980; 0316335991; 9780316335997

World Fantasy Award (2017)

"When she was 16, Hope Arden began to notice that people were forgetting her; her friends suddenly behaved as though they didn't know who she was, and her parents seemed surprised when she came home, as though they weren't aware they had a daughter. Soon the truth became apparent: the world was forgetting Hope. Hope turns to a life of crime--thievery, after all, is a natural career path for someone who is almost immediately forgotten by everyone she comes into contact with—until the death of another woman shows Hope that there may be a way to cure herself and become ordinary again." (Booklist)

North, Ryan

Romeo And/Or Juliet; A Chooseable-Path Adventure. Ryan North. Penguin Group USA 2016 400 p. illustrations (some color) (paperback) $20

ISBN 1101983302; 9781101983300

LC 2016438671

Alex Award (2017)

In this choose-your-own-path version of Romeo and Juliet by Ryan North, "you choose where the story goes every time you read! What if Romeo never met Juliet? What if Juliet got really buff instead of moping around the castle all day? What if they teamed up to take over Verona with robot suits? Whatever your adventure, you're guaranteed to find lots of romance, lots of epic fight scenes, and plenty of questionable decision-making by very emotional teens." (Publisher's note)

"North has turned Shakespeare's play about star-crossed lovers into a seemingly endless game of choices, with the ability to play as either Romeo or Juliet and a guarantee that any path taken will turn into an outrageously silly adventure. For some threads, North cleverly inserts original passages from Shakespeare's work to heighten the comic effect." SLJ

The **Norton** book of science fiction; North American science fiction, 1960-1990. edited by Ursula K. Le Guin and Brian Attebery; Karen Joy Fowler, consultant. Norton 1993 869p hardcover o.p. pa $38.13

ISBN 0-393-03546-8; 0-393-97241-0 pa

LC 93-16130

Damon Knight, Robert Silverberg, Connie Willis and Harlan Ellison are among the authors represented in this anthology of more than 60 stories.

A "compilation of intelligent and entertaining sf that belongs in virtually every fiction collection." Booklist

Norton, Andre

Beast Master's ark; [by] Andre Norton and Lyn McConchie. TOR Bks. 2002 318p

ISBN 0-7653-0041-9

LC 2002-67249

Third volume in the author's Beast Master series begun with the Beast Master (1959) and Lord of Thunder (1962)

"A mysterious killer, referred to as 'Death-which-come-in-the-night' by the planet Arzor's indigenous inhabitants, threatens to eradicate sentient life on the desertlike world. Beast Master Storm Hosteen discovers that the only chance of saving his adopted home lies with a young woman name Tani, who has learned to deny her own Beast Master heritage." Libr J

Norton, Andre

The **elvenbane**; an epic high fantasy of the Halfblood chronicles. [by] Andre Norton, Mercedes Lackey. Doherty Assocs. 1991 390p (Halfblood chronicles)

LC 91-21177

"In a world ruled by some of the most brutal and tyrannical elves ever encountered, the most persecuted are the part-human, part-elven halfbloods. After her human mother is cast into the desert, {Shana} the bastard daughter of the powerful Lord Dyran survives and is raised by dragons to seek her destiny as the Elvenbane." Booklist

Followed by Elvenblood

Norton, Andre

Elvenblood; an epic high fantasy. [by] Andre Norton and Mercedes Lackey. Doherty Assocs. 1995 348p (Halfblood chronicles)

LC 95-5797

"Following rumors of the existence of a tribe of humans immune to the enslaving magics of the land's elven overlords, halfelven rebel Shana and her dragon companion encounter unexpected complications in their struggle for freedom. The talents of collaborators Norton and Lackey blend seamlessly as they expand the background to their epic fantasy to include an exotic desert culture, which provides a rich contrast to the stifling atmosphere of elven society." Libr J

Norton, Andre

Golden Trillium. Bantam Bks. 1993 296p (Trillium)

ISBN 0-553-09507-2

LC 92-43875

Third in the fantasy series that includes Black Trillium by Marion Zimmer Bradley, Julian May, and Andre Norton, and Blood Trillium by Julian May

"Having aided her sisters in establishing peace in the land of Ruwenda, the warrior-maiden Kadiya journeys through the swamps to return the Three-Orbed Sword to the place of its origin only to find that her fight against evil is not yet done. The grande dame of sf and fantasy returns to a favorite theme—the discovery of an ancient and highly advanced lost civilization—in this heroic adventure." Libr J

Norton, Andre

Redline the stars; [by] Andre Norton, P.M. Griffin. Tor Bks. 1993 304p

LC 92-43708

The authors "recreate the flavor of Norton's four Solar Queen books . . . while updating some concepts and quite a bit of technology. The crew of the Free Trader vessel Solar Queen, flying under Capt. Miceál Jellico, has mixed reactions to new crewmate Rael Cofort, who is plying the space lanes as a jack-of-all-trades despite her position as a physician and status as sister of the successful rival Free Trader, Teague Cofort. Upon arriving at Canuche of Halio, the most advanced planet of the sector, the Queen's crew is endangered when Rael picks up the odor of man-eating rodents used in a gruesome gem-stealing scheme." Publ Wkly

Norton, Carla

What doesn't kill her; a novel. Carla Norton. Minotaur Books 2015 313 p. (Reeve LeClaire series) (hardcover) $25.99

ISBN 1250032806; 9781250032805

LC 2015013519

"Reeve is finally recovering a life of her own after four years of captivity. Flint is safely locked up in Olshaker Psychiatric Hospital, where he belongs. It seems that he is still suffering the effects of the head injury he suffered in the car crash that freed Reeve seven years ago. Reeve is shocked out of her new life by her worst nightmare: Her kidnapper has escaped. When Flint evades capture . . ., Reeve suddenly realizes that she is the only one who can stop him." (Publisher's note)

Nova, Craig

All the dead Yale men; a novel. Craig Nova. Counterpoint Press 2013 352 p. (hard cover) $26

ISBN 1582438285; 9781582438283

LC 2013001213

In this sequel to author Craig Nova's book "The Good Son," Nova features the consequences of his character Chip's decision to marry to secure his future through "the story of Frank Mackinnon, son of Chip, a prosecutor in Boston with a happy marriage and a daughter set to follow his footsteps into law school. Chip's death throws Frank into his family's legacy. . . . And when Frank's daughter Pia falls under the sway of local bad boy Aurlon Miller, his grief over his father's death triggers the family legacy of social standing and manipulation." (Publisher's note)

Novak, Chase

Breed; Chase Novak. Mulholland Books 2012 310 p. $25.99

ISBN 0316198560; 9780316198561

LC 2012014689

In author Chase Novak's book, "Alex and Leslie have everything--luxurious Manhattan domicile, fine jobs, each other--except a baby. Leslie seems more willing to adopt, but Alex is desperate to try anything. If he weren't, he might have had second thoughts after they traveled to see the mysterious doctor in Slovenia . . . Bad choice . . . [T]hey proceed at Alex's insistence, subsequently indulge in some spectacularly animalistic sex, have twins . . . and develop a taste for rodents, household pets, fellow human beings and perhaps even their offspring." (Kirkus)

Followed by Brood (2014)

Nović, Sara

Girl at war; a novel. Sara Nović. Random House Inc 2015 336 p. maps $26

ISBN 9780812996340; 0812996348

LC 2014027466

Alex Award (2016)

Author Sara Nović presents this "novel about a girl's coming of age--and how her sense of family, friendship, love, and belonging is profoundly shaped by war. Zagreb, 1991. Ana Jurić is a carefree ten-year-old. But that year, civil war breaks out across Yugoslavia. Ana must find her way in a dangerous world. New York, 2001. Ana is now a college student. She can't escape her memories of war. Haunted by the events that forever changed her family, Ana returns to Croatia after a decade away." (Publisher's note)

"Elegiac, and understandably if unrelievedly so, with a matter-of-factness about death and uprootedness. A promising start." Kirkus

Novik, Naomi

Blood of tyrants; Naomi Novik. Ballantine Books 2013 448 p. (The Temeraire series) $26

ISBN 0345522893; 9780345522894

LC 2013020334

Author "[Naomi] Novik's eighth and penultimate alternate history novel" in the Temeraire series "opens with series hero Laurence shipwrecked and taken prisoner in Japan. . . . His reunion with Temeraire, his dragon companion, is awkward, as Laurence has suffered a head injury and entirely forgotten the past several years. . . . They journey to Temeraire's native China for some court intrigue, then fly to Russia to confront Napoleon's invading army." (Publishers Weekly)

Novik, Naomi

His majesty's dragon. Del Rey 2006 356p (Temeraire series) pa $7.50

ISBN 0-345-48128-3

LC 2005-46342

Published in Great Britain with title: Temeraire

In this novel, the opening salvo of the Temeraire series, Novik "blends fantasy into the history of the Napoleonic wars. Here be dragons, beasts that can speak and reason, bred for strength and speed and used for aerial support in battle. Each nation has its own breeds, but none are so jealously guarded as the mysterious dragons of China. Veteran Capt. Will Laurence of the British Navy is therefore taken aback after his crew captures an egg from a French ship and it hatches a Chinese dragon, which Laurence names Temeraire. When Temeraire bonds with the captain, the two leave the navy to sign on with His Majesty's sadly understaffed Aerial Corps." Publ Wkly

Other titles in this series are:
Throne of jade (2006)
Black powder war (2006)
Empire of ivory (2007)
Victory of eagles (2009)
Tongues of serpents (2010)
Crucible of gold (2012)
Blood of tyrants (2013)
League of dragons (2016)

Novik, Naomi

★ **League** of Dragons; Naomi Novik. Random House Inc 2016 352 p. map (Temeraire) hbk $28

ISBN 9780345522924; 9780345522931; 0345522931; 0345522923

In the final book in the Temeraire series by Naomi Novik, "Napoleon's invasion of Russia has been roundly thwarted. But even as Capt. William Laurence and the dragon Temeraire pursue the retreating enemy through an unforgiving winter, Napoleon is raising a new force, and . . . has promised the dragons of every country—and the ferals, loyal only to themselves—vast new rights and powers if they fight under his banner." (Publisher's note)

"Thrilling scenes of aerial combat are interspersed with detailed character work, moral complexities, and political maneuvering. Novik expertly balances a myriad of plotlines and characters and offers an extremely satisfying resolution." Booklist

Novik, Naomi

Uprooted; Naomi Novik. Del Rey 2015 448 p. (hardcover) $25

ISBN 0804179034; 9780804179034

LC 2014032606

Nebula Award: Best Novel (2016)

In this novel by Naomi Novik, "Agnieszka loves her valley home, her quiet village, the forests and the bright shining river. But the corrupted Wood stands on the border. Her people rely on the cold, driven wizard known only as the Dragon to keep its powers at bay. But he demands a terrible price for his help: one young woman handed over to serve him for ten years. Agnieszka . . . knows . . . that the Dragon will take Kasia . . . and her dearest friend in the world." (Publisher's note)

"Novik's use of language is supremely skillful as she weaves a tale that is both elegantly grand and earthily humble, familiar as a Grimm fairy tale yet fresh, original, and totally irresistible." Pub Wkly

Nunez, Elizabeth

Anna in-between. Akashic Books 2009 347p $22.95

ISBN 978-1-933354-84-2; 1-933354-84-4

LC 2009-922936

"The title of her latest novel suggests a sitcom, or the upbeat identity lit marketed to teenagers. But Elizabeth Nunez layers Anna In-Between, a psychologically and emotionally astute family portrait, with dark themes like racism, cancer and the bittersweet longing of the immigrant. Foremost, she explores the late innings of a successful marriage, in which husband and wife cling together in the shadow of mortality." N Y Times Book Rev

Nunez, Elizabeth

Grace. Ballantine Bks. 2003 294p $23.95

ISBN 0-345-45533-9

LC 2002-26260

"This is a tender, graceful novel of personal amd material struggle that also explores the power of literature and poetry in everyday life." Booklist

Nunez, Sigrid

The **last** of her kind. Farrar, Straus and Giroux 2006 375p $25

ISBN 0-374-18381-3

LC 2005-40098

This "portrait of countercultural America in the sixties and seventies opens in 1968, when two girls meet as roommates at Barnard College. Ann is rich and white and wants to be neither, confiding, 'I wish I had been born poor'; Georgette has no illusions about poverty, having just escaped her depressed home town, where 'whole families drank themselves to disgrace.' Georgette finds Ann at once despicable and mesmerizing, and she's stunned—if not entirely surprised—when, years after the end of their friendship, Ann is arrested for killing a cop. In previous works, Nunez has proved herself a master of psychological acuity. Here her ambitions are grander, and the result is a remarkable and disconcerting vision of a troubled time in American history, and of its repercussions for national and individual identity." New Yorker

Nunez, Sigrid

Salvation city. Riverhead Books 2010 280p $25.95

ISBN 978-1-59448-766-8; 1-59448-766-9

LC 2010-01989

"The great success of Nunez's book is that the end of the world is filtered through Cole's imperfect perspective, so that the collapse of society is no more devastating than first love, and deeply felt conflict rages as a young man tries to find something worth preserving in a place determined to obliterate the past." Publ Wkly

Nussbaum, Susan

★ **Good** kings bad kings; a novel. by Susan Nussbaum. Algonquin Books of Chapel Hill 2013 336 p. $23.95

ISBN 1616202637; 9781616202637

LC 2013001350

PEN/Bellwether Prize for Socially Engaged Fiction (2012)

This book by Susan Nussbaum "takes readers behind the scenes at a facility for disabled teens." It is "woven from short individual chapters in first-person narrative. . . . As the book progresses . . . the darker side of the facility's management and desire for profit emerges." Characters include "Yessenia (transferred from Juvie) . . . Mia (keeping a horrifying secret) . . . [and] Michelle (working for the management company and slowly growing aware of what her job entails)." (Publishers Weekly)

"Nussbaum charms, outrages, and enlightens readers as she cycles among these and other characters, boldly contrasting the transcendence of love with the harsh realities of a negligent for-profit nursing home." Booklist

O

O'Brian, Patrick

Blue at the mizzen. Norton 1999 261p il $24

ISBN 0-393-04844-6

LC 99-42043

"There is nothing in this century that rivals Patrick O'Brian's achievement in his chosen genre. His novels embrace with loving clarity the full richness of the 18th-century world." N Y Times Book Rev

O'Brian, Patrick

★ The **commodore**. Norton 1995 281p $22.50

ISBN 0-393-03760-6

LC 95-2653

First published 1994 in the United Kingdom

Another "novel in O'Brian's series following Captain (now Commodore) Jack Aubrey and his surgeon friend, Stephen Maturin, through the naval side of the Napoleonic Wars. Although O'Brian is ingenious at devising new adventures, it is the richness of his characters which justifies his readers' continuing enthusiasm. The most arresting moments in this installment come not in battle but in dramas of parenthood and marriage far from the sea. O'Brian acknowledges Jane Austen as one of his inspirations, and she need not be ashamed of the affiliation." New Yorker

O'Brian, Patrick

The **golden** ocean; a novel. Day, J. 1957 316p il

First published 1956 in the United Kingdom

"This novel is based on the exploits of Commodore George Anson, who set out in 1740 with five men-of-war to circle the globe and returned four years later with one ship and a small but very wealthy crew. The expedition is seen through the eyes of Peter Palafox, a young midshipman who blossoms into an able-bodied seaman. . . . As always, the author's erudition and humor are on display. . . . The attention to period speech and detail is uncompromising, and while the cascades of nautical lore can be dizzying, both aficionados and newcomers will be swept up by the richness of Mr. O'Brian's prodigious imagination." N Y Times Book Rev

O'Brian, Patrick

The **hundred** days. Norton 1998 280p $24

ISBN 0-393-04674-5

LC 98-35866

"Battles there are aplenty, and O'Brian matches Forester in the excitement, detail and bloody realism of his reconstructions. But these naval tales are blended into a larger panorama of Georgian society and politics, science, medicine, botany and the whole conspectus of contemporary Enlightenment knowledge about the natural world." N Y Times Book Rev

O'Brian, Patrick, 1914-2000

The **unknown** shore. Norton 1995 313p $23

ISBN 0-393-03859-9

LC 95-32887

First published 1959 in the United Kingdom

"Based on British Commodore Anson's 1740 circumnavigation of the world . . . this is the story of HMS Wager, a ship separated from Anson's squadron while sailing around Cape Horn. The Wager is shipwrecked off Patagonia, and the largest part of the narrative details the hardships of the diminishing band of survivors on that inhospitable shore. . . . Though this novel isn't quite as polished or stylish as the author's later work, it's a most honorable ancestor." Publ Wkly

O'Brian, Patrick

★ The **wine**-dark sea. Norton 1993 261p $22.50

ISBN 0-393-03558-1

LC 93-1521

"The naval actions are bang-on and bang-up—fast, furious and bloody—and the Andean milieu is as vivid as the shipboard scenes." Publ Wkly

O'Brian, Patrick

The **yellow** admiral. Norton 1996 261p $24

ISBN 0-393-04044-5

LC 96-24149

"As their careers have advanced and their children have grown, Captain Jack Aubrey and Stephen Maturin have battered Napoleon's ships and thwarted his spies, but here, at last, the Emperor is Elba-bound, and our heroes are left high and dry. Aubrey, ashore at half pay and with scant hope of promotion, prays that peace may not last long—a sentiment doubtless shared by O'Brian's readers. Still, Elba is not St. Helena, so war will surely return, if only for a short finale." New Yorker

O'Brien, Dan

The **contract** surgeon; a novel. Lyons Press 1999 316p $24.95

ISBN 1-55821-932-3

LC 99-35243

This novel is "based on the true story of the unusual friendship between Crazy Horse and Dr. Valentine McGillicuddy, a civilian surgeon contracted to serve with the army during the Indian wars on the Great Plains. McGillicuddy relates the tale as an old man. . . . He faces his greatest moral test when Crazy Horse is bayoneted in the back by a soldier, and McGillicuddy is pressured by the army to keep the famous warrior alive, because his death would spur on the Indians to renewed battle. . . . This powerful story is a thinking man's western, in which action is secondary to O'Brien's nuanced exploration of character and the tragic dimensions of a morally fraught conflict." Publ Wkly

O'Brien, Edna

★ The **country** girls trilogy and epilogue. Farrar, Straus & Giroux 1986 531p

LC 85-32113

Omnibus edition of three titles originally published separately in 1960, 1962 and 1964 respectively, with an epilogue added by the author

The country girls portrays two friends, Kate and Baba, growing up in Ireland. They are sent to a convent school they despise and they contrive to get expelled and move to Dublin. In The lonely girl, Kate, now 21, becomes involved first with an older married man, then with a filmmaker. Eugene encourages and pampers her, but she is unresponsive. The relationship disintegrates and she moves to London. In Girls in their married bliss, Kate has married Eugene and has a son, but the marriage is destroyed when Eugene's indifference pushes Kate into a love affair. Meanwhile, Baba settles into marriage and financial security with an architect, and pulls through the crisis of a pregnancy brought on by a one-night stand. The Epilogue contains Baba's reflections, twenty years later

"O'Brien's particular appeal is that she can be tender yet merciless, romantic yet grittily sexual. She resides admirably where quality and popular writing intersect." Booklist

O'Brien, Edna

A **fanatic** heart; selected stories of Edna O'Brien. Farrar, Straus & Giroux 1984 461p

LC 84-13762

"Each story is superbly written and, despite the overall seriousness, graced by humor." Publ Wkly

O'Brien, Edna

House of splendid isolation. Farrar, Straus & Giroux 1994 232p $21

ISBN 0-374-17309-5

LC 93-42602

The author "manages to sum up a century of Irish sorrow in this taut, lyrical novel, filled with scenes so vividly rendered they seem captured in a flash of lightning. Not the least of O'Brien's accomplishments is her ability to present both sides of the Irish problem in all their complexity without settling heavily on either side." Libr J

O'Brien, Edna

In the forest. Houghton Mifflin 2002 262p $24

ISBN 0-618-19730-3

LC 2001-51883

A novel about "how a community can be collectively paralyzed by fear. The result is a brilliant illumination of human nature." Booklist

O'Brien, Edna

Lantern slides; stories. Farrar, Straus & Giroux 1990 223p

ISBN 0-374-18332-5

LC 90-33594

"O'Brien's short stories expand on the anguish and brutality endemic to modern Irish lives, and her characters have more than their own secret problems to brood and moon about. . . . O'Brien mines her home territory to splendid effect with her glinting looks at what the Irish have made of their struggle and what Ireland has made of their unhappy lives." Booklist

O'Brien, Edna, 1930-

The **love** object; selected stories. Edna O'Brien. Little, Brown & Co. 2015 544 p. (hardcover) $30

ISBN 0316378267; 9780316378260

LC 2014955118

In this short story collection, by Edna O'Brien, "coming of age, the impact of class, and familial and romantic love are the prevalent motifs, along with the instinct toward escape and subsequent nostalgia for home. Some of the stories are linked and some carry O'Brien's distinct sense of the comical." (Publisher's note)

"O'Brien's reputation as one of the greatest storytellers in modern literature is only strengthened by this volume's publication. Highly recommended." LJ

O'Brien, Edna, 1930-

Saints and sinners; stories. Back Bay Books/Little, Brown and Co. 2011 245p pa $13.99

ISBN 978-0-316-12272-6; 0-316-12272-6

LC 2010-31577

"The world, if viewed in clichéd terms, is indeed populated by the two types of individuals cited in the title of this new collection of short stories by the doyenne of contemporary Irish literature, an acknowledged master of the form. But that is all that is clichéd about this splendid book. . . . Eleven stories in total bring literary lovers' rapt attention to this author's clear, immaculate style and her brilliant selection of detail, nimble plot construction, and astute character delineation. Recommend O'Brien along with William Trevor and Alice Munro." Booklist

O'Brien, Edna

Time and tide. Farrar, Straus & Giroux 1992 325p

LC 92-3962

This novel is O'Brien's "harshest yet most beautiful work. She has a touchy, rich theme: the sexuality of the bond between mothers and sons. . . . O'Brien brings together the earthy and the delicately poetic: she has the soul of Molly Bloom and the skills of Virginia Woolf." Newsweek

O'Brien, Edna

Wild Decembers. Houghton Mifflin 2000 259p $24

ISBN 0-618-04567-8

LC 99-56110

First published 1999 in the United Kingdom

"The novel is a dirge that keens and lulls by turns. The entrancing rhythms and refrains, the density and chant-like, drumming fragmentation work on the reader like magic. . . . O'Brien combines this lyricism with a masterly storytelling instinct, so that {the novel} reads at once like an intricate poem and a taut, suspenseful page-turner." Commonweal

O'Brien, Flann, 1911-1966

★ The **complete** novels; with an introduction by Keith Donohue. Everyman's Library 2007 xxxiii, 787p $25

ISBN 978-0-307-26749-8; 0-307-26749-0

"Truth is an odd number, even numerals are the province of the devil class, and there is safety in a triad. These are some of the essential wisdoms in the world of Flann O'Brien, the Irish writer who is often said to form, along with Samuel Beckett and James Joyce, 'the holy trinity of modern Irish literature.' . . . There may be safety in a triad, but to lump O'Brien with Joyce and Beckett is to miss the playfulness, black humor, and deranged whimsy that characterize his style." Slate

O'Brien, Flann, 1911-1966

The **Short** Fiction of Flann O'Brien; by Flann O'Brien, edited by Neil Murphy and Keith Hopper, and translated by Jack Fennell. Dalkey Archive Press 2013 157 p. (pbk. : acid-free paper) $14.50

ISBN 156478889X; 9781564788894

LC 2013012011

This book, edited by Neil Murphy and Keith Hopper, "gathers together an expansive selection of [author] Flann O'Brien's shorter fiction in a single volume, as well as O'Brien's last and unfinished novel, 'Slattery's Sago Saga.' Also included are new translations of several stories originally published in Irish, and other rare pieces. With some of these stories appearing here in book form for the very first time, and others previously unavailable for decades." (Publisher's note)

O'Brien, Tim

★ **Going** after Cacciato; a novel. Lawrence, S. 1978 338p hardcover o.p. pa $14.95

ISBN 0-440-02948-1; 0-7679-0442-7 pa

LC 77-11723

"Paul Berlin's squad is sent to retrieve Cacciato, a young deserter from the Vietnam War. Fantasy colors the progress of the squad as a dream of peace and the possibility of forsaking war follow them through many adventures. The horror and destruction of war is vividly conveyed and the language is rough, as would be expected. Cacciato becomes a kind of symbol for resisting bureaucratic militarism and an enviable model for Berlin himself." Shapiro. Fic for Youth. 3d edition

O'Brien, Tim

In the Lake of the Woods. Houghton Mifflin 1994 306p

ISBN 0-395-48889-3

LC 94-5395

"What O'Brien really offers is a portrait of one man and woman at the most critical juncture of their relationship. It's a dark portrait, taking issue with a stock notion of commercial fiction: that after suffering comes redemption. Maybe not. Maybe there's only oblivion. A beautifully written, haunting novel that evokes lives in deep crisis." Booklist

O'Brien, Tim, 1946-

★ The **things** they carried; a work of fiction. Houghton Mifflin 1990 273p

LC 89-39871

This book presents "a series of stories about the Vietnam experience, based on the author's recollections. [Tim] O'Brien begins by sharing the talismans and treasures his select small band of young soldiers carry into battle. The tales, ranging from a paragraph to 20 or so pages, reveal one truth after another. Sometimes the author tells the same story from different points of view, revealing the lingering, sometimes consuming, effect war leaves on the soul." (School Library Journal)

"This book may be self-conscious . . . but through its determination to treat these men with dignity and decency it proves immensely affecting." Newsweek

O'Brien, Timothy L.

The **Lincoln** conspiracy; a novel. Timothy L. O'Brien. Ballantine Books 2012 349 p. (hardcover) $26.00

ISBN 0345496779; 9780345496775; 9780345535597

LC 2012022133

This historical thriller novel, by Timothy L. O'Brien, asks, "What if the plot to assassinate President Lincoln was wider and more sinister? . . . In late spring of 1865, . . . Washington, D.C., police detective Temple McFadden makes a startling discovery: . . . [T]wo diaries . . . that together reveal the true depth of the Lincoln conspiracy. Securing the diaries will put Temple's life in jeopardy--and will endanger the fragile peace of a nation still torn by war." (Publisher's note)

O'Connell, Carol

The **chalk** girl; Carol O'Connell. G. P. Putnam's Sons 2012 384p.

ISBN 9780399157745

LC 2011027853

This murder mystery book tells the story of a "little girl [who] appeared in Central Park: red-haired, blue-eyed, smiling, perfect-except for the blood on her shoulder. It fell from the sky, she said, while she was looking for her uncle, who turned into a tree. . . . For Mallory, newly returned to the Special Crimes Unit after three months' lost time, there is something about the girl that she understands. Mallory is damaged, they say, but she can tell a kindred spirit. And this one will lead her to a story of extraordinary crimes: murders stretching back fifteen years, blackmail and complicity and a particular cruelty that only someone with Mallory's history could fully recognize." (Publisher's note)

O'Connell, Carol

✓ **Crime** school. Putnam 2002 352p
ISBN 0-399-14928-7

LC 2002-22860

Detective Kathy Mallory, "of the Special Crimes Unit, comes face to face with her past when she and her partner are called to a crime scene in which a call girl has been ritualistically murdered. The call girl, Sparrow, offered Mallory protection when she was a child but later betrayed her. Before Mallory has time to call up her knowledge of Sparrow's past in finding the killer, she and her partner are thrown into a morass of spree killings on the streets of New York. O'Connell's crime-scene investigations techniques ring true, her plotting is breathtaking, and her psychology acute. Searing suspense." Booklist

O'Connell, Carol

✓ **Judas** child. Putnam 1998 340p $24.95
ISBN 0-399-14380-7

LC 97-46504

"O'Connell thoughtfully tackles material that in other hands would be merely sensational. Dark in tone, gripping suspense, and tempered with the hope of redemption, this is highly recommended." Libr J

O'Connell, Carol

✓ **Killing** critics. Putnam 1996 308p

LC 95-43894

"As mesmerizing as the murder case is, it's heartless, soulless Mallory herself—computer genius, street fighter, provocative waif, peerless investigator, manipulative beauty—who's absolutely the star of this brilliant thriller." Booklist

O'Connell, Carol

✓ **Mallory's** oracle. Putnam 1994 286p

LC 94-2234

The author's "writing is stunning in its luminosity, originality, simplicity, and power. Her plot is ingenious, inventive, and enigmatic, and her characters sparkle with originality and charm." Booklist

O'Connell, Carol

✓ **Stone** angel. Putnam 1997 341p

LC 96-44504

How the author "manages to imbue what's basically a who-was-that-masked-man tall tale of revenge with Molierian elegance is as great a mystery as who killed Mallory's mother nearly two decades ago." New Yorker

O'Connor, Flannery

★ **Collected** works. Library of Am. 1988 1281p $35
ISBN 0-940450-37-2

LC 87-37829

Contents: Wise blood; A good man is hard to find; The violent bear it away; Everything that rises must converge; Stories and occasional prose; Letters

O'Connor, Flannery

The **complete** stories. Farrar, Straus & Giroux 1971 555p hardcover o.p. pa $17
ISBN 0-374-51536-0

This collection is "arranged in chronological order from the story she wrote for her master's thesis at the University of Iowa to 'Judgement Day.' . . . The stories here include the original openings and other chapters of her two novels 'Wise Blood' and 'The Violent Bear It Away.'" N Y Times Book Rev

O'Connor, Flannery

Everything that rises must converge. Farrar, Straus & Giroux 1965 xxxiv, 269p

Contents: Everything that rises must converge; Greenleaf; A view of the woods; The enduring chill; The comforts of home; The lame shall enter first; Revelation; Parker's back; Judgement Day

O'Connor, Flannery

The **violent** bear it away. Farrar, Straus & Cudahy 1960 243p

"A macabre tale set in the backwoods of Georgia and presenting the fanatical mission of a boy intent on baptizing a still younger boy." Oxford Companion to Am Lit. 6th edition

O'Connor, Flannery

Wise blood. Harcourt Brace & Co. 1952 232p

This novel "centers on Hazel Motes, a discharged serviceman who abandons his fundamentalist faith to become a preacher of anti-religion in a Tennessee city, establishing the 'Church Without Christ.' Motes is a ludicrous and tragic hero who meets a collection of equally grotesque characters. One of his young followers, Enoch Emery, worships a museum mummy. Hoover Shoats is a competing evangelist who creates the 'Holy Church of Christ Without Christ.' Asa Hawks is an itinerant preacher who pretends to have blinded himself to show his faith in redemption." Merriam-Webster's Ency of Lit

O'Connor, Frank

Collected stories; introduction by Richard Ellmann. Knopf 1981 701p hardcover o.p.
ISBN 0-394-51602-8

LC 81-1253

The author "grew up with 'the troubles,' but the Ireland he evokes in these 72 stories . . . is the provincial life of his Cork boyhood." Libr J

O'Connor, Joseph

Ghost light. Farrar, Straus and Giroux 2011 246p $25
ISBN 978-0-374-16187-3; 0-374-16187-9

LC 2010-22672

First published 2010 in the United Kingdom

"O'Connor's impressionistic, intense style delivers a mismatched love story and a social landscape dominated by forceful characters such as W.B. Yeats and Synge's formidable mother, but it is Molly's perspective which prevails, the voice of a comical, intuitive, irrepressible life force. An empathetic act of literary homage offering nuggets of emotional intensity." Kirkus

O'Connor, Robert

Buffalo soldiers. Knopf 1993 323p

LC 92-54278

"O'Connor writes bitter, funny prose and creates bureaucratic snafus of the first order. Alternating scenes of Army idiocy and clinically realistic drug addiction are far more compelling than O'Connor's attempt to attribute his hero's bracing nihilism to his tragic past. Toward its end the book falters, as Elwood flirts with maudlin self-pity. But O'Connor misfires now and then only because he aims high." Publ Wkly

O'Dell, Tawni

Back roads. Viking 1999 338p $24.95

ISBN 0-670-88760-9

LC 99-20649

"Harley's first-person account of the deterioration of his family and his own slow-motion meltdown is harrowing. O'Dell, a native of western Pennsylvania, renders finely detailed characters and settings in a desperate and failed mining town. This is a riveting first novel of violence, incest, murder, and madness." Booklist

O'Dell, Tawni

Coal Run. Viking 2004 354p $24.95

ISBN 0-670-89995-X

LC 2003-62645

"After more than 15 years living in Florida, Ivan Zoschenko returns to his home in western Pennsylvania, his arrival coinciding with the release from prison of his highschool alter ego, Reese Raynor. Ivan is not thrilled to return home: he had gladly left behind memories of the explosion at the mine that killed his father and nearly 100 other miners when he was six, and he doesn't look forward to hearing the locals' reaction to the bizarre injury that brought his career as a pro football player to an abrupt end. But here he is, sleeping on his sister's couch and working temporarily as deputy for the sheriff's office. The novel takes place over the course of only one week, yet O'Dell manages to give the story an epic dimension through masterful intercutting of past and present. Reese's pending release drives the plot, and as the day nears, Ivan confronts his own demons and secrets with true-to-life reluctance." Booklist

O'Dell, Tawni

Fragile beasts; a novel. Shaye Areheart Books 2010 401p $25

ISBN 978-0-307-35168-5; 0-307-35168-8

LC 2009-34352

"O'Dell's eye for class conflict remains as sharp as ever, but she's broadened the reach of her sympathies, tamed her taste for lurid plotting and found new depths in her subject matter and her human understanding." Kirkus

O'Dell, Tawni

Sister mine; a novel. Shaye Areheart Books 2007 416p $23

ISBN 978-0-307-35126-5; 0-307-35126-2

LC 2006-15355

"At 40, Shae-Lynn Penrose has overcome a mostly motherless, abusive childhood and a teenage pregnancy to finish college, work for the D.C. Capitol Police, raise her son alone, and return to her coal-mining hometown of Jolly Mount, Pennsylvania. Here she runs a one-vehicle cab company; her father died in a mine; her best friend, E. J., was one of the Jolly Mount 5, whose survival after a mine explosion made headlines; and her son, Clay, is a deputy for Sheriff Ivan Zoschenko . . . . Then Shannon, the younger sister Shae-Lynn thought long dead, shows up and reveals an unorthodox means of making money that's causing a ruckus. Dealing with a burgeoning love affair and revelation of parentage, plus the surviving miners' intent to sue the coal company, O'Dell also examines such issues as abuse, betrayal, abandonment, perseverance, and reconciliation, with love at the heart of it all, in crisp, insightful prose that sweeps the reader along. A knockout." Booklist

O'Donnell, Lisa

Closed Doors; by Lisa O'Donnell. William Heinemann Ltd 2013 256 p. $26.99

ISBN 006227189X; 0434022551; 9780062271891; 9780434022557

LC 2013497809

This book, by Lisa O'Donnell, is set "on the island of Rothesay in Scotland . . . during the early 1980s" and narrated "by an eleven-year old boy, Michael. . . . Michael 'listen[s] at doors now. It's the only way to find out stuff,' and he obsessively spies on his neighbour Mrs Connor ('I only watch her dance because her windows are so low'). What begins as childish curiosity tums into unpleasant, adult reality." (Times Literary Supplement)

"The novel asks (and possibly answers) two important questions—to what extent should children be protected from the truth, and does silence do more harm than good? While it deals with disturbing subject matter, this is an engaging page-turner that effectively explores the trials and tribulations of childhood with warmth and humor." Booklist

O'Donnell, Lisa

★ The **death** of bees; a novel. Lisa O'Donnell. Harper 2013 311 p. $25.99

ISBN 0062209841; 9780062209849

LC 2012031882

Alex Award (2014)

This novel, by Lisa O'Donnell, is "a coming-of-age story in which two young sisters attempt to hold the world at bay after the mysterious death of their parents. Marnie and Nelly, left on their own in Glasgow's Hazlehurst housing estate, attempt to avoid suspicion until Marnie can become a legal guardian for her younger sister." (Publisher's note)

O'Donovan, Gerard

Dublin dead; a novel. Gerard O'Donovan. Scribner 2012 280 p.

ISBN 9781451610635

LC 2011031170

In this book, "it seems eminently logical that Cormac Horgan, the millionaire head of his family's chain of estate agents, would have completed his financial ruin by topping himself at a spot favored by dozens of other suicides. Nor is anyone shedding tears over the demise of Declan (Bingo) Begley in sunny Spain--except for accountant Gemma Kearney's mother. . . . Gemma was Begley's girlfriend, she tells . . . reporter Siobhan Fallon . . . [DI Mike] Mulcahy follows a tip from veteran informant Eddie McTiernan that seems to link still another death . . . to an epic consignment of drugs by sea and a well-traveled Colombian assassin. . . . Siobhan and Mulcahy realize that they're pulling opposite ends of the same tangled skein and reluctantly join forces." (Kirkus)

O'Donovan, Gerard

The **priest**; a novel. Scribner 2011 323p $25

ISBN 978-1-4516-1060-4; 1-4516-1060-2

LC 2010-33448

"Although it's clear early on who the psycho is . . . Mr. O'Donovan builds suspense carefully and cleverly, leading us to a pulse-raising climax at a huge cross in a Dublin park." Pittsburgh Post-Gazette

O'Faolain, Sean

★ The **collected** stories of Sean O'Faolain. Little, Brown 1983 1304p il

LC 83-205346

O'Farrell, Maggie

The **hand** that first held mine. Houghton Mifflin Harcourt 2010 341p $25

ISBN 978-0-547-33079-2; 0-547-33079-0

LC 2009-42058

"Lexie Sinclair moves from the Cornwall area to post-World War II London and begins a thrilling new life under the tutelage of her lover, Innes Kent, an editor and art collector. Even the eventual knowledge that he is legally married doesn't alter her allegiance to him, and she becomes the mother of his son, as well as a respected art critic. In between chapters about Lexie and Innes, readers meet contemporary London artist Elina, who lives with her boyfriend Ted. They have just had a son together, and Elina, who almost died in childbirth, is housebound during her recovery. Growing into his new role as a father, Ted suffers confusing flashbacks about his own childhood." Libr J

O'Farrell, Maggie

Instructions for a heat wave; Maggie O'Farrell. Alfred A. Knopf 2013 304 p. (Hardcover) $25.95

ISBN 0385349408; 9780385349406

LC 2013004580

In this book, "when Gretta Riordan's husband . . . disappears during the 1976 London heatwave, her three grown children return home. . . . All are dealing with personal crises that inform their relationships with each other and are tied back to their family history. The oldest, Michael Francis, is trying to keep his marriage together . . . and his two sisters, Monica and Aoife, have been estranged for years over a bitter secret that led Aoife across the ocean to New York." (Publishers Weekly)

O'Farrell, Maggie

★ **This** must be the place; by Maggie O'Farrell. Alfred A. Knopf 2016 400 p. illustrations (ebook) $65; (hardback) $26.95

ISBN 9780385349437; 9780385349420

LC 2015044361

In this book, by Maggie O'Farrell, "Daniel Sullivan [is] a man with a complicated life. A New Yorker living in the wilds of Ireland, he has children he never sees in California, a father he loathes in Brooklyn, and a wife, Claudette, who is a reclusive ex-film star. . . . But the life Daniel and Claudette have so carefully constructed is about to be disrupted by an unexpected discovery about a woman Daniel lost touch with twenty years ago." (Publisher's note)

"There is enough possibility and randomness for three books, yet the story never feels overstuffed, and when it ends, the reader is stunned and grateful, relieved that in the face of all that can go (and have gone) wrong, some things have come right." Pub Wkly

O'Farrell, Maggie

The **vanishing** act of Esme Lennox. Harcourt 2007 245p $23

ISBN 978-0-15-101411-8; 0-15-101411-6

LC 2007-6079

First published 2006 in the United Kingdom

"At the heart of this fantastic new novel is a mystery you want to solve until you start to suspect the truth, and then you read on in a panic, horrified that you may be right." Washington Post Book World

O'Flynn, Catherine

Mr. Lynch's holiday; a novel. Catherine O'Flynn. Henry Holt and Company 2013 272 p. $26

ISBN 0805091815; 9780805091816

LC 2012050500

This novel, by Catherine O'Flynn, tells the story of "a father and son reconnecting in a foreign place . . . Retired bus driver and recent widower Dermot Lynch grabs his bags . . . and begins to climb the hill to his son's house. It is Dermot's first time in Spain. . . . When he finally arrives . . . Dermot learns that Eamonn, only one of a handful of settlers in the half-finished ghost town of Lomaverde, has fallen prey to an alluring vision and is upside down in a dream that is slipping away." (Publisher's note)

"O'Flynn offers trenchant commentary on capitalism even as she balances the comic and tragic aspects of disillusionment. Overflowing with warmth and compassion as well as a sly humor." Booklist

O'Flynn, Catherine

The **news** where you are; a novel. Henry Holt and Co. 2010 252p pa $15

ISBN 978-0-8050-9180-9; 0-8050-9180-7

LC 2009-45217

This is "a funny, moving, acutely observed story about family and loss, getting old and being alone. That it also manages to take in British architecture and urban space and the problems of celebrity culture, while being disarmingly easy to read, is testament to Catherine O'Flynn's comic timing and lightness of touch." Scotland on Sunday

O'Hagan, Andrew

Be near me. Harcourt, Inc. 2007 305p $24

ISBN 978-0-15-101303-6; 0-15-101303-9

LC 2006-30402

First published 2006 in the United Kingdom

"A distinctive voice resonates clearly through the first-person narrative, clerically portentous at times, a shade trite or unabashedly sentimental at others, yet in all its registers convincing. What it tells us is a story compounded from passion and resurrection as opposed to professional failure or spiritual collapse." Times Lit Suppl

O'Hara, John, 1905-1970

★ **Appointment** in Samarra. Modern Lib. 1994 xxi, 269p $14.95

ISBN 0679601104

LC 94-4340

A reissue of the title first published 1934 by Harcourt Brace & Co.

"The novel is written episodically, but achieves integration by its hard-boiled theme of the destructive effects of fast living." Haydn. Thesaurus of Book Dig

O'Hara, John

★ **Butterfield** 8; a novel. Harcourt Brace & Co. 1935 310p

"A novelization of the sensational lives of the night-club set involved in an actual New York murder case. Young Gloria Wandrous is found drowned on a beach near New York. The problem is to find the murderer and his motive. The investigation, described in machine-gun reportage, reveals that Gloria had had a good education, but owing to an adolescent sexual experience had become a 'party girl' in the unsavory life of New York speakeasies and luxurious Long Island clubs. Under the sleekness of Park Avenue sophistication, O'Hara reveals New York's hard soullessness." Haydn. Thesaurus of Book Dig

O'Hara, John

Collected stories of John O'Hara; selected and with an introduction by Frank MacShane. Random House 1984 414p

LC 84-42661

Contents: The doctor's son; It must have been spring; Over the river and through the woods; Price's always open; Are we leaving tomorrow; Pal Joey; The gentleman in the tan suit; Good-by, Herman; Olive; Do you like it here; Now we know; Free; Too young; Bread alone; Graven image; Common-sense should tell you; Drawing room B; The pretty daughters; The moccasins; Imagine kissing Pete; The girl from California; In the silence; Exactly eight thousand dollars exactly; Winter dance; The flatted saxophone; The friends of Miss Julia; How can I tell you?; Ninety minutes away; Our friend the sea; Can I stay here?; The hardware man; The pig; Zero; Fatimas and kisses; Natica Jackson; We'll have fun

O'Hara, John

From the terrace; a novel. Random House 1958 897p

"Alfred Eaton, the younger son of Samuel Eaton, steel magnate of Port Johnson, Pennsylvania, had a tolerably happy childhood until the death of his older brother William, when Alfred was twelve. After the death of his favorite son, Samuel Eaton retreated into an obsessive grief. Alfred's mother, neglected, turned elsewhere for affection and Alfred was left to grow up as best as he could, closer to the servants than to his parents. The rest of his life though rewarded with business success and filled with a variety of amorous adventures, was basically barren and loveless." Booklist

O'Hara, John

Ten North Frederick. Random House 1955 408p

A character study of one of the 'first citizens' of a Pennsylvania town, Gibbsville. "In the first quarter of a crowded, eventful narrative, Joe Chapin is seen only through the eyes of some of those at {his} funeral. Then {O'Hara} . . . switches back to Joe's parents, who established the home at Ten North Frederick Street, where Joe lived all his life. He tells Joe's story from the beginning, and the stories of those whose lives have touched Joe's at some significant point." N Y Times Book Rev

O'Loughlin, Ed

Minds of winter; Ed O'Loughlin. Quercus 2017 497 p. maps (hardcover) $26.99

ISBN 9781681442426; 9781681442440; 9781681442457

LC 2016033791

In this novel, by Ed O'Loughlin, "Sir John Franklin's 1845 campaign in search of the Northwest Passage ended in tragedy. All 129 men were lost to the ice, . . . including two rare and valuable Greenwich chronometers. When one of the chronometers appears a century and a half later in London, in pristine condition and crudely disguised as a Victorian carriage clock, new questions arise about what really happened on that expedition--and the fates of the men involved." (Publisher's note)

"A massive, complex novel about a long-lost chronometer." Kirkus

O'Malley, Daniel

The **rook**; a novel. Daniel O'Malley. Little, Brown and Co. 2012 486p.

ISBN 9780316098793

LC 2011019741

"Myfanwy Thomas wakes in a London park surrounded by bodies, unable to remember her identity. However, she quickly learns she's a Rook: a mid-level member of the Chequy, an intelligence agency of superpowered operatives. So Myfanwy begins investigating clues to fill in the gaps of her lost memory and determine the cause of her amnesia." (Publishers Weekly)

"O'Malley's narrative is peppered with sly humor, referential social commentary and the ironic, double-layered self-awareness that will have genre fans believing Buffy the Vampire Slayer has joined Ghostbusters." Kirkus

Followed by:

Stiletto (2016)

O'Malley, Thomas

This magnificent desolation; a novel. Thomas O'Malley. Bloomsbury 2013 416 p. (hardcover) $26

ISBN 1608192792; 9781608192793

LC 2012025659

In this novel, by Thomas O'Malley, "Duncan's entire world is the orphanage where he lives. . . . Aged ten in 1980, he has no memories of his life before now. . . . Duncan is sure that his mother is dead until the day she turns up to claim him. . . . Thrown into [a] mysterious adult world, Duncan finds comfort in an ancient radio, from which tumble the voices of Apollo mission astronauts who never came home, and dreams of finding his real father." (Publisher's note)

O'Mara, Tim

Crooked Numbers; Tim O'Mara. Minotaur Books 2013 320 p. (Raymond Donne mysteries) (hardcover) $25.99

ISBN 1250009006; 9781250009005

LC 2013024554

This book is the second in Tim O'Mara's series featuring former detective-turned-school dean Raymond Donne. Here, one of Donne's former students, Douglas Lee, is found stabbed to death after earning a private school scholarship. "Donne attends the funeral home wake, where Dougie's mother beseeches him to do what he can to pressure the police to dig deeper into her son's murder." (Publishers Weekly)

O'Nan, Stewart

Emily, alone. Viking 2011 255p $25.95

ISBN 978-0-670-02235-9; 0-670-02237-7

LC 2010-35333

This "novel revisits the Emily Maxwell of Wish You Were Here [2002] as a widow and traces the course of three-quarters of a year near the end—but decidedly not at the end—of her long life. Born in small-town Appalachia to a building inspector and a teacher, Emily achieved the cultured and refined life for which she yearned by marrying into a gracious Pittsburgh family. She appreciates classical music, visits the library regularly, reserves a table at 'the club' for special occasions, pines for the heyday of Masterpiece Theatre and Mystery! (although not the gritty, Helen Mirren era, much as she admires the actress herself). O'Nan cannot write without nuance, and Emily contains the contradictions and failings of a real person. Her second-guessing of, frustration with, and love for her adult children and grandchildren; her observations concerning her comparatively young neighbors; her dependence on and resentment toward her sister-in-law are all a voyeuristic pleasure." Atlantic

O'Nan, Stewart

The **good** wife. Farrar, Straus and Giroux 2005 312p $24

ISBN 0-374-28139-4

LC 2004-53247

"From the trial, through the various appeals process, the visits to the prison, the waiting, the hoping, the struggle to make ends meet, and the gradual resilience and self-sufficiency, O'Nan, with seldom a false beat, perceptively and compassionately depicts the bureaucratic insanities of the penal system and the hardships, fears, and frustrations of those left behind." Booklist

O'Nan, Stewart, 1961-

Last night at the Lobster; a novel. Viking 2007 146p

ISBN 0-670-01827-9; 978-0-670-01827-7

LC 2006-102825

Managing a failed seafood restaurant in a New England mall just before Christmas, Manny DeLeon coordinates a final shift of mutinous staff members, an effort that is complicated by his love for a waitress.

"O'Nan's empathy for his characters is one of his great gifts as a novelist, and it is an impressive achievement that Manny's misplaced affection for Red Lobster is not risible, but tragic." N Y Times Book Rev

O'Nan, Stewart

★ The **names** of the dead. Doubleday 1996 399p

LC 95-36745

"O'Nan's language is powerfully restrained; his word pictures of the war and its effect on the men who fought there are fresh and vivid. He rightfully refuses to pander to our desire for easy answers and happy endings." Booklist

O'Nan, Stewart

The **night** country; or, The darkness on the edge of town. Farrar, Straus & Giroux 2003 229p $23

ISBN 0-374-22215-0

LC 2002-44765

"O'Nan is wonderful at describing teenage ritual, the simultaneous desire for the comforting familiarity of friends and the lust for speed and novelty and excitement that will lift teenagers out of the confines of their suburban town, the routine of school, out of their own restless bodies." N Y Times Book Rev

O'Nan, Stewart, 1961-

The **odds**; a love story. Stewart O'Nan. Viking 2012 179p.

ISBN 9780670023165; 0670023167

LC 2011033330

The novel "examines the quotidian sore spots and the comforting core of a realistic 30-year marriage against the . . . background of Niagara Falls. Marion and Art Fowler, middle-class victims of the 2008 crash, revisit the site of their honeymoon to gamble what remains of their liquid assets in a last-ditch attempt to skirt bankruptcy. Even more than solvency is at stake, however, since their marriage is foundering along with their finances, and the weekend, at least from Art's point of view, is also a chance to win big in love and reclaim his wife." (Atlantic Monthly)

O'Nan, Stewart

★ **Snow** angels. Doubleday 1994 305p

ISBN 0-385-47574-8

LC 94-12037

The author "weaves together these seemingly disparate small-town tragedies–one narrated in the first person, the other in the third–with consummate skill, seamlessly shifting the focus among characters he wishes to make the reader care about." Libr J

O'Nan, Stewart

Songs for the missing. Viking 2008 287p $25.95

ISBN 978-0-670-02032-4; 0-670-02032-X

LC 2008-22274

The author's "greatest literary talent lies with his characters. It's as if he has lived each of the lives he creates, and nothing is too mundane nor too overblown. . . . O'Nan has honed his ability to tap into the most basic components of small town life and ordinary people. His latest is both an intriguing page-turner and a sometimes agonizing look at human emotion in the face of inexplicable loss." Rocky Mountain News

O'Neill, Heather

★ The **Lonely** Hearts Hotel; by Heather O'Neill. Penguin Group USA 2017 400 p. (ebook) $65; $27

ISBN 9780735213753; 0735213739; 9780735213739

LC 2016036295

In this book, by Heather O'Neill, "two babies are abandoned in a Montreal orphanage in the winter of 1914. Before long, their talents emerge: Pierrot is a piano prodigy; Rose lights up even the dreariest room with her dancing and comedy. As they travel around the city performing clown routines, the children fall in love with each other and dream up a plan for the most extraordinary and seductive circus show the world has ever seen." (Publisher's note)

"O'Neill's prose is crisp and strange, arresting in its frankness; much like the novel itself, her writing is both gleefully playful and devastatingly sad. Big and lush and extremely satisfying; a rare treat." Kirkus

O'Neill, Jamie

At swim, two boys; a novel. Scribner 2002 572p $27

ISBN 0-7432-2294-6

LC 2001-57694

First published 2001 in the United Kingdom

"In this novel the cause of Ireland and the cause of gay people fuse with a complete lack of apology or embarrassment. . . . O'Neill is not, however, being patly outrageous; the closeness and exactness of his vision prove that." N Y Times Book Rev

O'Neill, Joseph

Netherland. Pantheon Books 2008 256p $23.95

ISBN 978-0-307-37704-3; 0-307-37704-0

LC 2007033711

This novel is "narrated by a Dutch financier whose privileged Manhattan existence is upended by the events of Sept. 11, 2001. When his wife departs for London with their small son, he stays behind, finding camaraderie in the unexpectedly buoyant world of immigrant cricket players, most of them West Indians and South Asians, including an entrepreneur with Gatsby-size aspirations." N Y Times Book Rev

O'Reilly, Brian

Angelina's bachelors; a novel, with food. recipes by Virginia O'Reilly. Gallery Books 2011 359p pa $15

ISBN 978-1-4516-2056-6; 1-4516-2056-X

LC 2011-13170

Managing sudden widowhood and joblessness by cooking bounteous and sumptuous feasts that she shares with her neighbors, Angelina D'Angelo is offered a job as cook for a retiree and his elderly sister and finds her culinary talents winning her a circle of friends and protectors.

"Filled with more than 20 (fairly complicated) recipes for Angelina's gourmet fare, the food is only half of the novel's winning ingredient—O'Reilly's keen ear for the neighborhood swells lends a charming, timeless quality to the tale. Light comedy and good food make a winning combination." Kirkus

O'Shaughnessy, Perri

Breach of promise. Delacorte Press 1998 435p $23.95

ISBN 0-385-31872-3

LC 98-5519

"O'Shaughnessy offers up a gripping courtroom drama, throws in pithy ethical and moral dilemmas and some surprising plot twists, and adds plenty of heart-stopping action." Booklist

O'Shaughnessy, Perri

Invasion of privacy. Delacorte Press 1996 419p

LC 96-1251

"Tahoe-area attorney Nina Reilly was shot at the end of Motion to Suppress. As the increasingly alarming facts of her latest case pile up, she is haunted by memories of that wounding. No less haunting are certain details of her personal past, which Nina's new client, Terry London, an energetically spiteful documentary filmmaker, seems to know as much about as Nina does. Out of that past and into Tahoe comes Kurt Scott, the father of Nina's son, Bob. Almost immediately, Terry is murdered, Kurt is accused of the crime and Nina must assemble his murder defense. . . . Fans of the genre will luxuriate in this deft, multileveled tale of legal and criminal treachery, whose pleasures include elegant courtroom sleight-of-hand and the eerily wintry backdrop of Lake Tahoe." Publ Wkly

O'Shaughnessy, Perri

Motion to suppress. Delacorte Press 1995 420p

LC 95-5615

"Although the characterizations are a bit uncertain (the luscious Misty is unbelievably prim and proper), the plot is a real puzzler, with twists diabolical enough to take to court." N Y Times Book Rev

O'Shaughnessy, Perri

Obstruction of justice. Delacorte Press 1997 392p

LC 96-48585

In this thriller, attorney Nina Reilly is "a witness to the death by lightning of a construction mogul in the Tahoe Mountains. When his father returns from a business trip, he wants Nina to have the body exhumed and autopsied for signs of murder, setting off a family furor. Suddenly, the grave is empty, the bodies of both father and son turn up in a smoldering mountain cabin, and the grandson is charged with murder. Nina is then asked to clear the grandson amid an increasingly complex series of interrelationships involving the D.A., his dead wife, a not-so-grieving widow, and, of course, the gardener. . . . A compelling story with some great courtroom drama and a likable heroine." Libr J

O'Shaughnessy, Perri

Unlucky in law. Delacorte Press 2004 376p $25

ISBN 0-385-33646-2

LC 2004-47840

In this legal thriller California lawyer Nina Reilly has "moved herself and 14-year-old son Bob from their usual Tahoe turf to the Monterey Peninsula to spend time with her lover, PI Paul van Wagoner. Paul has asked Nina to marry him, offering a big diamond to seal the deal. Nina puts him off while she prepares for a big trial: she's newly employed at Pohlmann, Cunningham, and Turk, and her first case, working with Klaus Pohlmann, is defending 28-year-old Stefan Wyatt, charged with murder and grave robbing. O'Shaughnessy has been accused of sloppy plotting in the past, but not so here." Publ Wkly

O'Shaughnessy, Perri

Writ of execution. Delacorte Press 2001 403p

ISBN 0-385-33483-4

LC 2001-28468

"Readers will relish the myriad plot details and the procedural drama, and enjoy the cast of offbeat characters." Publ Wkly

Oates, Joyce Carol, 1938-

★ The **Accursed.** HarperCollins 2013 688 p. $27.99

ISBN 0062231707; 9780062231703

In this book by Joyce Carol Oates, "strange things start happening in peaceful, polished Princeton, NJ. Folks dream about vampires, the daughters of the town's classiest families start vanishing, and a bride-to-be runs away with a vaguely menacing European, presumably a prince and possibly the Devil. As her brother gives chase, he encounters characters from former President Grover Cleveland and future President Woodrow Wilson to authors like Upton Sinclair." (Library Journal)

Oates, Joyce Carol

American appetites. Dutton 1989 340p

LC 88-18904

"A zippy story about successful lives dramatically altered by one sudden and inexplicable lapse of judgment." Publ Wkly

Oates, Joyce Carol, 1938-

★ **Carthage**; a novel. by Joyce Carol Oates. HarperCollins 2014 384 p. $26.99

ISBN 0062208128; 9780062208125

In this book by Joyce Carol Oates, "Zeno Mayfield's daughter has disappeared into the night, gone missing in the wilds of the Adirondacks. But when the community of Carthage joins a father's frantic search for the girl, they discover the unlikeliest of suspects--a decorated Iraq War veteran with close ties to the Mayfield family." (Publisher's note)

"Once again, Oates's gift for exposing the frailty--and selfishness--of humans is on display." Pub Wkly

Oates, Joyce Carol

★ **Because** it is bitter, and because it is my heart. Dutton 1990 405p

LC 89-25965

"At its best, the novel awakens the reader to something like the unexpected new comprehensions of the universe that Iris experiences." N Y Rev Books

Oates, Joyce Carol

★ **Bellefleur**. Dutton 1980 558p

ISBN 0-525-06302-1

LC 79-28193

"In this Gothic novel, Oates weaves a shimmering tapestry made of odd and contradictory threads: a hermaphroditic birth, a vulture that devours an infant, a dwarf with 'powers,' a vampire, a cannibal, religious mystics and clairvoyants. Such are the Gothic trappings of this epic about the Bellefleurs, an old and powerful American family whose estate is located in the Adirondacks and whose history is an interpretation of American history from pioneer days to the present." Benet's Reader's Ency of Am Lit

Oates, Joyce Carol

Black girl/White girl. Ecco 2006 272p $25.95

ISBN 0-06-112564-4

LC 2006-48306

"Oates has never been shy about peering into the darkest corners of American culture. Her best books . . . showcase her fascination with violence, her almost vampiric ability to tap into the subconscious of her troubled characters and her taste for appropriating real-life tragedy. Oates's latest offering is no exception." N Y Times Book Rev

Oates, Joyce Carol, 1938-

Black dahlia & white rose; stories. Joyce Carol Oates. Ecco 2012 274 p. $24.99

ISBN 0062195697; 9780062195692

LC 2012462476

This collection of short stories by Joyce Carol Oates "explores the menace that lurks at the edges of and intrudes upon even the seemingly safest of lives. . . . Oates takes readers deep into dangerous territory, from a maximum-security prison . . . to the inner landscapes of two beautiful and mysteriously doomed young women in 1940s Los Angeles: Elizabeth Short, otherwise known as the Black Dahlia, . . . and her roommate Norma Jeane Baker, soon to become Marilyn Monroe." (Publisher's note)

Oates, Joyce Carol

Black water. Dutton 1992 154p

LC 91-40463

"Those who remember Chappaquiddick can predict Kelly's ultimate fate, but certainly not the horrors she must have suffered strapped to the seat of a car that would become an aqueous death chamber. Immense courage shines through the tangled streams of her thoughts, memories, and hallucinations. As witnesses to her plight, we can only keep vigil as she drifts in and out of consciousness, waiting for the reprieve that surely must be hers. Oates brilliantly redefines the meanings of guilt and innocence, vengeance and reward in this thought-provoking allegory of our life and times." Libr J

Oates, Joyce Carol

Blonde. Ecco Press 2000 738p

ISBN 0-06-019607-6

National Book Award Finalist: Fiction (2000)

"Joyce Carol Oates takes the boldest path to comprehending 'the riddle, the curse of Monroe' by proceeding directly and frankly to fiction. Her novel 'Blonde' is fat, messy and fierce. It's part Gothic, part kaleidoscopic novel of ideas, part lurid celebrity potboiler, and it is seldom less than engrossing." N Y Times Book Rev

Oates, Joyce Carol

A **Bloodsmoor** romance. Dutton 1982 615p

LC 82-2416

The novel "details the bizarre goings-on in a 19th-century inventor's family. One daughter becomes a medium, another an actress and Mark Twain's mistress, a third runs away on her wedding night. Even Octavia, the perfect wife, is secretly subversive. . . . The narrator misunderstands and misinterprets much that happens; the reader, therefore, enters into collusion with the characters who use the period's conventions to subvert prescribed female roles." Libr J

Oates, Joyce Carol

Broke heart blues. Dutton 1999 369p $24.95

ISBN 0-525-94451-6

LC 98-51570

Oates "dramatizes how wanting and memory compete. It's about how lonely, unhappy people mythologize their adolescence. . . . This is not a bashful or subtle book. It doesn't woo you so much as run you down." N Y Times Book Rev

Oates, Joyce Carol, 1938-

Daddy Love; Joyce Carol Oates. Pgw 2013 240 p. $24

ISBN 0802120997; 9780802120991

In Joyce Carol Oates' book, "Dinah Whitcomb is playing . . . with her five-year-old son, Robbie . . . when a stranger seizes the boy. . . . Robbie is renamed Gideon by Daddy Love, his abductor, who has kidnapped several little boys through the years, killing them when they're adolescents. . . . Spanning six years, the action shifts between Gideon and Daddy Love, who's quick to mete out cruel punishments, and Dinah and her husband, bonded by guilt in a crumbling marriage." (Publishers Weekly)

Oates, Joyce Carol

Dear husband, Ecco 2009 326p $24.99

ISBN 978-0-06-170431-4; 0-06-170431-8

"Oates' characters are masterfully rendered, but she is particularly gifted at creating a certain type: The appallingly egocentric, sometimes to the point of (usually) unwitting hostility. . . . Oates' characters are all self-absorbed to some extent. They all regard themselves as more real than their bystanders, with needs that always take precedence. They appear to exist for their own benefit, certainly not the reader's. While it may seem obvious that any worthwhile fiction will feature such characters, some authors are more skilled at delivering them than others. In this regard, Oates is one of the best." Idaho Statesman

Oates, Joyce Carol, 1938-

The **Doll**-Master and Other Tales of Terror; Joyce Carol Oates. Mysterious Press 2016 304 p. (hardcover) $24

ISBN 9780802124883; 0802124887

This short story collection, by Joyce Carol Oates, offers six horror tales. "In the title story, a young boy becomes obsessed with his cousin's doll after she tragically passes away from leukemia. . . . In 'Gun Accident,' . . . an intruder forces his way into the house while the girl is there, [and] the fate of more than one life is changed forever. In 'Equatorial,' set in the exotic Galapagos, an affluent American wife experiences disorienting assaults upon her sense of who her charismatic husband really is." (Publisher's note)

"This devil's half-dozen of dread and suspense is a must read." Pub Wkly

Oates, Joyce Carol, 1938-

★ **Evil** Eye; Four Novellas of Love Gone Wrong. by Joyce Carol Oates. Pgw 2013 224 p. $23

ISBN 0802120474; 9780802120472

This book, by Joyce Carol Oates, presents "four . . . tales of love gone horribly wrong, showing the lengths people will go to find love, keep it, and sometimes end it. In 'Evil Eye,' we meet Mariana, the young 4th wife of a prominent intellectual. . . . In 'So Near, Anytime, Always,' shy teenager Lizbeth meets Desmond, a charming boy who offers this introverted girl the first sparks of young romance." (Publisher's note)

Oates, Joyce Carol

Faithless; tales of transgression. Ecco Press 2001 386p

ISBN 0-06-018525-2

LC 00-60007

"As the subtitle suggests, the book's preoccupation is sin, but otherwise the stories are richly various. They range from quiet, intimate tales—such as the chilling opening effort, @Au Sable,' about a man let in on a suicide he cannot prevent—to the satiric fantasia on TV journalism and police brutality that closes the volume." Publ Wkly

Oates, Joyce Carol

★ The **falls**; a novel. Ecco 2004 481p $26.95

ISBN 0-06-072228-2

LC 2004-43310

"Set around Niagara, the story reflects all the romance, mystery, and terror of that spectacular waterfall. It's a great confluence of tones-grotesque and domestic, tragic and comic. The currents of various styles and points of view blend together in a way that can't possibly work, but does." Christ Sci Monit

Oates, Joyce Carol

Foxfire; confessions of a girl gang. Dutton 1993 328p

ISBN 0-525-93632-7

LC 92-43858

"Legs Sadovsky is a brilliant creation—wholly heroic, wholly convincing, racing for her tragic consummation impelled by a finer sensibility and a more thoughtful daring than is usually granted to the tragic male outlaws we love and need. . . . 'Foxfire' burns brightly; it is completely assured and occasionally exhilarating." N Y Times Book Rev

Oates, Joyce Carol

A **garden** of earthly delights. Vanguard Press 1967 440p

The book describes the early life of Clara Walpole, the daughter of a migrant farm worker; her life after she leaves her father; her romance with a rum-runner; and her marriage to a rich man, whom she convinces is the father of her illegitimate baby. The final part of the novel deals with the childhood and adolescence of Swan, the son

"The book has much to say of society's indifference to the plight of the disadvantaged, and of the shallowness of a way of life based entirely on getting and spending." Libr J

Oates, Joyce Carol

The **gravedigger's** daughter; a novel. Ecco 2007 582p $26.95

ISBN 978-0-06-123682-2; 0-061-23682-9

LC 2006-48546

"This is neither a depressing story nor an uplifting one. Oates succeeds here, as she often does, in making such judgments feel simple-minded. What it all seems is true and therefore moving and somewhat terrible, but in an exhilarating way. Every aspect of the ungainly plot feels right, including its ungainliness." Washington Post Book World

Oates, Joyce Carol

Haunted; tales of the grotesque. Dutton 1994 310p

LC 93-25223

"All the pieces here have a redeeming literary bent, although some are transparent in their motives. Undoubtedly a master of this form, Oates plies her craft like a skilled seducer, setting the mood and moving in for the conquest night after night after night." Publ Wkly

Oates, Joyce Carol

High lonesome; new & selected stories, 1966-2006. Ecco 2006 664p $34.95

ISBN 0-06-050119-7; 978-0-06-050119-8

LC 2005-51147

This "collection, which includes classic stories like "In the Region of Ice," which won the O. Henry prize in 1967, and the much anthologized "Where Are You Going, Where Have You Been?" as well as 11 new stories, spans Oates's career and gives a remarkably coherent picture of her work." N Y Times Book Rev

Oates, Joyce Carol

I am no one you know; stories. Ecco 2004 290p $24.95

ISBN 0-06-059288-5

LC 2003-61283

"Oates is vitally concerned, even obsessed, with the most primal and disturbing encounters between females and males, and her new searing short stories explore the malevolent aspects of human sexuality with unflinching authenticity and a cathartic fascination." Booklist

Oates, Joyce Carol

★ **I** lock my door upon myself. Ecco Press 1990 98p

ISBN 0-88001-260-9

LC 90-31878

Is this "all a parable of the artist's position as an observer and interpreter of society? Is it an illustration of how a writer constructs a coherent story out of disjointed events? Either way, it provokes thought." Atlantic

Oates, Joyce Carol, 1938-

Jack of Spades; A Tale of Suspense. Joyce Carol Oates. Mysterious Press 2015 208 p. $24

ISBN 0802123945; 9780802123947

In this novel by Joyce Carol Oates, "Andrew J. Rush has achieved the kind of critical and commercial success most authors only dream about. . . . But Rush is hiding a dark secret. Under the pseudonym 'Jack of Spades,' he writes . . . dark potboilers that are violent. Rush [is] accused . . . of plagiarizing [a woman's] self-published fiction. Rush's reputation, career, and family life all come under threat—and unbidden . . . the Jack of Spades starts thinking ever more evil thoughts." (Publisher's note)

"As this tour de force reveals, Oates is a master of bleak literary fiction and its (sometimes) poor relation, crime/noir fiction. Examining and delineating insanity, obsession, paranoia, alcoholism, manipulation, and murder, not to mention book collecting and writer's block, this tale of suspense makes for another high-caliber Oatesian outing, displaying flair, noir sophistication, and King-like flourishes." LJ

Oates, Joyce Carol

Little bird of heaven; a novel. Ecco Press 2009 442p $25.99

ISBN 978-0-06-182983-3; 0-06-182983-8

The narrators of this novel, set in upstate New York, are "an angry young man whose mother is murdered and a shy, introspective young woman whose father is a suspect. But the character who leaps most off the page is the victim, Zoe Kruller. . . . She abandons her son, Aaron, and her husband, Delray. She has an affair with Eddy Diehl, whose daughter Krista finds life in their small town of Sparta almost impossible to bear. And singing with her band, the Black River Breakdown, she wears spangly outfits, enchants the townspeople and belts out the song that gives the novel its title. . . . Krista and Aaron meet as teenagers. He's a gruff, rough, half-Indian guy with tattoos and little use for school. She is a blond waif, trying to tough it out on the basketball court to win the affection of her daddy and the respect of her peers. But it is her longing for Aaron that rules her life, particularly after Zoe Kruller is found murdered. Her death seals their connection forever, even though they rarely speak and, when they are together, the conditions are as far from romantic as you can get. . . . Oates deftly merges the personalities of Zoe, Eddy, Krista and Aaron into what is essentially a mystery." St. Louis Post-Dispatch

Oates, Joyce Carol, 1938-

Lovely, Dark, Deep; stories. Joyce Carol Oates. Ecco 2014 432 p. $25.99

ISBN 0062356941; 9780062356949

LC 2015296686

This short story collection, by Joyce Carol Oates, offers "stories that maps the eerie darkness within us all. . . . A woman and a man are joined in an erotic bond forged out of terror and gratitude. . . . A sixteen-year-old boy realizes the depth of his love for his grandmother--and how vulnerable those feelings make him. . . . And in the title story, the elderly Robert Frost is visited by an interviewer . . . who seems to know a good deal more about his life than she should." (Publisher's note)

"Oates is at her caustically splendorous best in the title story, a brilliantly choreographed, diabolically brutal pas de deux between the aging poet Robert Frost and a seemingly timid graduate writing student with the Edgar Allan Poe name of Evangeline Fife. Oates' stories seethe and blaze." Booklist

Oates, Joyce Carol

Marya; a life. Dutton 1986 310p

LC 85-16283

"Marya's development and her innermost fears and insecurities are revealed in a very personal, almost autobiographical manner. A major work by an important writer." Libr J

Oates, Joyce Carol

Middle age; a romance. Ecco Press 2001 464p

ISBN 0-06-620946-3

LC 2001-23062

"Adam Berendt, an eccentric sculptor, goes sailing on the Hudson River one Fourth of July. A nearby boat capsizes, and Adam leaps in to save a drowning child. He gets to her in time, but is struck by a heart attack as he holds her afloat, and dies. Adam's death is the engendering mistake, the accidental firecracker that sets off the rest of the book. In 'Middle Age,' the people affected are those left behind: Adam Berendt's neighbors in Salthill-on-Hudson." N Y Times Book Rev

Oates, Joyce Carol

Missing mom. Ecco 2005 434p $25.95

ISBN 0-06-081621-X

LC 2005-40002

"Oates's grip on crime, violence and the long-buried is sure, but Missing Mom is actually more disturbing in its relentless, dead-on accretion of small-time, small-town, middle-class details. Oates piles them on with pitiless virtuosity." N Y Times Book Rev

Oates, Joyce Carol, 1938-

Mudwoman; Joyce Carol Oates. Ecco 2012 448 p.

ISBN 9780062095626

LC 2012376456

In this book, "Mudgirl is a child abandoned by her mother." After being adopted she grows up to be the "first woman president of an Ivy League university. . . . Involved with a secret lover whose feelings for her are teasingly undefined, and concerned with the intensifying crisis of the American political climate as the United States edges toward war with Iraq, M.R. is confronted with challenges to her leadership that test her in ways she could not have anticipated." (Publisher's note)

Oates, Joyce Carol

Rape; a love story. Carroll & Graf 2004 154p $16

ISBN 0-7867-1294-5

A novel "about the nearly fatal beating and gang rape of Teena MacGuire on the Fourth of July in the small town of Niagara Falls. Teena and her 12-year-old daughter, Bethel, are walking home from a party when the vicious attack takes place, and Bethel only narrowly escapes her mother's terrible fate. Terrorized but valiant, Bethel identifies their assailants and is determined to testify, but the townspeople close ranks behind the indicted brutes, their sons and brothers, and Teena is assaulted all over again in court. But there is one man on the case who possesses a clear and unshakable sense of justice, and his empathic connection with Bethel is at the heart of this lean and potent tale." Booklist

Oates, Joyce Carol

Sourland; stories. Ecco/HarperCollins 2010 373p $25.99

ISBN 978-0-06-199652-8; 0-06-199652-1

"This collection could be used as a master class in the art of pure, suspenseful storytelling. There are real plots here, fascinating psychological and domestic mysteries we need to solve, portraying people we want to understand...Oates is a dangerous writer in the best sense of the word, one who takes risks almost obsessively, with energy and relish. For a writer in her early 70s, she continues to be wonderfully, unnervingly anarchic, experimental, angry. As if her aim were not to satisfy or entertain—though she always does both—but to do the vandalistic prose equivalent of spray-painting or setting fire to bins in public parks." N Y Times Book Rev

Oates, Joyce Carol

Them; introduction by Greg Johnson; afterword by the author. 2000 Modern Library ed; Modern Lib. 2000 xxiv, 546p $21.95

ISBN 0-679-64025-8

LC 99-54471

A reissue of the title first published 1969 by Vanguard Press

"Violent and explosive in both incident and tone, the work is set in urban Detroit from 1937 to 1967 and chronicles the efforts of the Wendell family to break away from their destructive, crime-ridden background. Critics praised the novel for its detailed social observation and its bitter indictment of American society." Merriam-Webster's Ency of Lit

Oates, Joyce Carol

We were the Mulvaneys. Dutton 1996 454p

ISBN 0-525-94223-8

LC 96-17267

"Oates has written an uncharacteristically cathartic book with a provocatively happy ending. . . . Oates eloquently employs daily details, cataloguing Corinne's antiques, mapping Patrick's Ithaca jogging route, calculating the number of paint gallons required to spruce up High Point Farm. She is a vivid storyteller, and the occupations, names and places are rich in allusive imagery. . . . Oates is fascinated by the markings of kinship. Particularly impressive is her shaping of siblings' passions, allegiances and resentments." Nation

Oates, Joyce Carol

Wild nights! stories about the last days of Poe, Dickinson, Twain, James, and Hemingway. Ecco 2008 238p $24.95

ISBN 978-0-06-143479-2; 0-06-143479-5

LC 2008-273051

"The classic authors who appear as fictionalized characters in 'Wild Nights!' aren't the ones most of us met in Intro to American Literature. Edgar Allan Poe copulating with a one-eyed amphibian? Mark Twain pursuing pubescent girls? Henry James clubbing a cat to death? Joyce Carol Oates may cause a few elderly professors to keel over, but the rest of us can take perverse delight in her five surreal tales. In each, Oates imagines the final days of a famous author, drawing from biographical fact but freely embroidering with Gothic excess. " Buffalo News

Oates, Joyce Carol

Will you always love me? and other stories. Dutton 1996 326p

LC 94-43865

"Joyce Carol Oates's readers have come to expect from her a sensationalistic terrain of accident, suicide, rape, murder and madness, all of which are well represented in this collection, which includes none of the small, too-precious moments that can vitiate the short story." N Y Times Book Rev

Obioma, Chigozie

★ The **fishermen**; a novel. Chigozie Obioma. Little, Brown & Co. 2015 304 p. illustrations, map (hardcover) $26

ISBN 9780316338370; 9780992918248; 0316338370

LC 2014959603

Los Angeles Times Book Prize: Art Seidenbaum Award for First Fiction (2015)

NAACP Image Award: Outstanding Literary Work--Debut Author (2016)

Man Booker Prize Shortlist (2015)

Written by Chigozie Obioma, this novel is "told from the point of view of nine year old Benjamin, the youngest of four brothers. . . . 'The Fishermen' is the Cain and Abel-esque story of an unforgettable childhood in 1990's Nigeria, in the small town of Akure. . . . At the ominous, forbidden nearby river, they meet a dangerous local madman who persuades the oldest of the boys that he is destined to be killed by one of his siblings." (Publisher's note)

"Obioma excels at juxtaposing sharp observation, rich images of the natural world, and motifs from biblical and tribal lore; his novel succeeds as a convincing modern narrative and as a majestic reimagining of timeless folklore." Pub Wkly

Object lessons; the Paris Review presents the art of the short story. edited by Lorin Stein and Sadie Stein. Picador 2012 358 p. (trade pbk.) $16

ISBN 1250005981; 9781250005984; 9781250016188

LC 2012026322

In this book, edited by Lorin Stein and Sadie Stein, "twenty contemporary authors introduce twenty . . . examples of the short story from the pages of 'The Paris Review.' Over the course of the last half century, the Review has launched hundreds of careers while publishing some of the most inventive and best-loved stories of our time. This anthology. . . [is a] resource for writers, students, and anyone else who wants to understand fiction from a writer's point of view." (Publisher's note)

Obregon, Nicolas ✓

Blue light Yokohama; Nicolas Obregon. Minotaur Books 2017 408 p. (hardcover) $25.99

ISBN 1250110483; 9781250110497; 9781250110480

LC 2016053844

In this book, by Nicolas Obregon, "Inspector Iwata . . . [and his] partner, Noriko Sakai are assigned to investigate the slaughter of an entire family. . . . As Iwata investigates, it becomes clear that these murders by the Black Sun Killer are not the first, nor the last. . . . As he tries to track down the history of black sun symbol, puzzle out the motive for the crime, and connect this to other murders, Iwata finds himself racing another clock." (Publisher's note)

"Obregon's full-bodied prose is by turns gritty and poetic, and it's consistently energetic. Given the terrific chemistry between the two lead detectives, here's hoping this debut novel kicks off a new series." Kirkus

Obreht, Tea

The **tiger's** wife; a novel. 1st ed. Random House 2011 337 p. (hbk. : acid-free paper) $25

ISBN 0385343833; 9780385343831

LC 2010-09612

Orange Broadband Prize for Fiction (2011)

National Book Award Finalist: Fiction (2011)

"The evolving story of the tiger's wife . . . forms one of three strands that sustain the novel, the other two being Natalia's efforts to care for orphans and a wayward family who, to lift a curse, are searching for the bones of a long-dead relative; and several of her grandfather's stories about Gavran Gailé, the deathless man, whose appearances coincide with catastrophe and who may hold the key to all the stories that ensnare Natalia." Publ Wkly

"Every word, every scene, every thought is blazingly alive in this many-faceted, spellbinding, and rending novel of death, succor, and remembrance. " Booklist

Odell, Jonathan

The **healing**; Jonathan Odell. 1st ed. Nan A. Talese/Doubleday 2012 340p.

ISBN 978-0-385-53467-3; 0385534671

LC 2011005998

This book tells the story of "Mississippi plantation mistress Amanda Satterfield [who] loses her daughter to cholera after her husband refuses to treat her for what he considers a 'slave disease.' Insane with grief, Amanda takes a newborn slave child as her own and names her Granada, much to the outrage of her husband and the amusement of their white neighbors. Troubled by his wife's disturbing mental state and concerned about a mysterious plague sweeping through his slave population, Master Satterfield purchases Polly Shine, a slavewoman reputed to be a healer. But Polly's sharp tongue and troubling predictions cause unrest across the plantation. Complicating matters further, Polly recognizes "the gift" in Granada, the Mistress's pet, and a domestic battle of wills ensues." (Publisher's note)

Oe, Kenzaburo

★ The **changeling**; translated from the Japanese by Deborah Boliver Boehm. Grove Press 2010 468p $26

ISBN 978-0-8021-1936-0; 0-8021-1936-0

Original Japanese edition, 2000

"Oe's deft mix of high intellectual reflection and absurd slapstick scenarios is polished to a high gloss, giving this book a tone that may remind American readers of Saul Bellow's Humboldt's Gift." Publ Wkly

Oe, Kenzaburo

★ **Death** by Water; by Kenzaburo Oe. Grove Press 2015 432 p. $28

ISBN 0802124011; 9780802124012

In this book, author Kenzaburo Oe's "literary alter-ego returns to his hometown village in search of a red suitcase fabled to hold documents revealing the details of his father's death during WWII. . . . Kogito Choko planned to fictionalize his father's fatal drowning in order to fully process the loss. Stricken with guilt and regret over his failure to rescue his father, Choko has long been driven to discover why his father was boating on the river in a torrential storm." (Publisher's note)

"This novel, teeming with crises and disclosures, proceeds almost exclusively via conversation made up of intricate, literarily and dramaturgically knowledgeable, politically progressive, long speeches. And it is enchanting." Booklist

Oe, Kenzaburo

Nip the buds, shoot the kids; translated and introduced by Paul St. John Mackintosh and Maki Sugiyama. Boyars, M. 1995 189p $22.95

ISBN 0-7145-2997-4

LC 94-40897

Original Japanese edition, 1958

"In the waning days of WW II, a group of Japanese reformschool boys are evacuated to a remote village in a densely wooded valley. The villagers treat the teenagers horribly, making them bury a mountain of animal corpses, locking them into a shed for the night and feeding them raw potatoes. The unnamed narrator—one of the group's leaders—discovers that a plague is ravaging the valley. When a couple of people are infected by the disease, the villagers panic. Believing the boys to be infected, the villagers remove themselves to the other side of the valley and block the only road out of town. At first, the boys can think only of escape, but then . . . they start to make the village their own. . . . But each pleasant turn, every apparently liberating step away from unremitting brutality, serves to make the characters' inevitable future suffering even more painful." Publ Wkly

Oe, Kenzaburo

★ A **quiet** life; translated from the Japanese by Kunioki Yanagishita with William Wetherall. Grove Press 1996 240p

LC 96-25795

Original Japanese edition, 1990

"A famous Japanese writer whose first name begins with K takes off with his wife for a year to become writer in residence at 'one of the several campuses of the University of Carolina,' leaving their almost equally famous son, an idiot savant who is a remarkable composer, in the care of their daughter, Ma-chan. It is Ma-chan, a conscientious young woman acutely aware of the responsibility that devolves on her during her parents' absence, who tells the story related in Kenzaburo Oe's novel 'A Quiet Life,' and the translators, Kunioki Yanagishita and William Wetherall, admirably succeed in conveying a certian archness of style that infuses the work with Ma-chan's personality." N Y Times Book Rev

Oe, Kenzaburo

Somersault; a novel. translated from the Japanese by Philip Gabriel. Grove Press 2003 570p $29.95

ISBN 0-8021-1738-4

LC 2002-29746

Original Japanese edition, 1999

This novel "takes place against the background of a religious cult's terrorist plan (even more drastic than Aum Shinrikyo's 1995 gas attack on the Tokyo subway), which is thwarted when the cult's leaders appear on television to renounce their creed—the 'smersault' of the title. Now, ten years later, the cult's charismatic guru is planning to reestablish his church. . . . Through the believers' motivations for joining the cult, Oe explores the struggle of contemporary Japanese to situate themselves between a traditional culture and the bullet-train pace of the boom years." New Yorker

Offill, Jenny

Dept. of speculation; Jenny Offill. Knopf 2014 192 p. (hardback) $22.95

ISBN 0385350813; 9780345806871; 9780385350815

LC 2013019367

PEN/Faulkner Award for Fiction: Shortlist (2015)

In this novel, author Jenny Offill presents a "portrait of a marriage. It is also a beguiling rumination on the mysteries of intimacy, trust, faith, knowledge, and the condition of universal shipwreck that unites us all. Offill's heroine . . . once exchanged love letters with her husband postmarked Dept. of Speculation, their code name for all the uncertainty that inheres in life and in the strangely fluid confines of a long relationship." (Publisher's note)

"The 46 short chapters are told mostly in brief fragments and fly through the life of the nameless heroine. Her mind wanders from everyday tasks and struggles, the beginnings of her marriage, the highs and lows with her husband, the joys of having a daughter." Pub Wkly

Ogilvie, Elisabeth

When the music stopped. McGraw-Hill 1989 326p

ISBN 0-07-047792-2

LC 88-28636

"Author Eden Winters, finds herself in the midst of local scandal and terrifying deaths. Set in a small town along the Maine coast, the plot turns on the return to town of two aging sisters who had left on the wings of scandal decades earlier. While there are plenty of people with reason to despise the returning ladies—who audaciously take up residence in the area's most elegant house—there are just as many people, such as Eden and her family, who are delighted to see them. When the women are found brutally murdered, suspects abound, including a stranger who alternately captures Eden's suspicions and heart. Well-crafted fiction that holds the reader's attention and avoids contrivance." Booklist

Ohanesian, Aline

Orhan's inheritance; a novel. by Aline Ohanesian. Algonquin Books of Chapel Hill 2015 352 p. map $25.95

ISBN 1616203749; 9781616203740

LC 2014031970

In this book, by Aline Ohanesian, "[w]hen Orhan's brilliant and eccentric grandfather, who built a dynasty out of making kilim rugs, is found dead in a vat of dye, Orhan inherits the decades-old business. But his grandfather's will raises more questions than it answers. Kemal has left the family estate to a stranger thousands of miles away, an aging woman in a retirement home in Los Angeles." (Publisher's note)

"Ohanesian does a remarkable job of conveying the weight and the influence of time and place without excusing or excluding the human dimension that necessarily factors into the unfolding cataclysm." Booklist

Ohlsson, Kristina

The **Disappeared**; a novel. Kristina Ohlsson; translation, Marlaine Delargy. Pocket Books 2014 416 p. $25

ISBN 1476734003; 9781476734002

In this book, by Kristina Ohlsson, "Fredrika, a Stockholm detective who has returned from maternity leave too soon, lives with an emotionally fragile, much older partner, who's being targeted by a vengeful student. Recently widowed Alex Recht, a colleague of Fredrika's who became obsessed with the disappearance of Rebecca Trolle two years earlier, must contend with the discovery of Rebecca's dismembered body." (Publishers Weekly)

"This is a complicated yet fast-moving story, and the detectives all find themselves with personal connections to the case. Ohlsson excels at creating multilayered stories with substantive characters." Booklist

Ohlsson, Kristina

Unwanted; a novel. Kristina Ohlsson. Atria Books 2012 357 p.

ISBN 9781439198896; 9781439198919; 9781439198933

LC 2011031787

Stabilo Prize for Best Crime Writer of Southern Sweden (2010)

"When a young girl is abducted off a train in Stockholm, it seems like a classic custody crime, as the parents are divorced and hostile. But Frederika Bergman isn't willing to accept the easy answer, even though she's only a civilian researcher working for one of the most revered detectives in Sweden, Alex Recht. Then the girl's body appears in a remote town in the north with the word 'Unwanted' written across it. Bergman is the only one who isn't surprised, but that still doesn't make the investigation any easier. Realizing that he is up against a highly intelligent serial killer, Recht acknowledges that it's going to take a combination of his experience and Bergman's research skills to track down the sociopath." (Booklist)

Other titles in this series are:

Silenced (2013)

The disappeared (2014)

Hostage (2015)

The chosen (2016)

Okorafor, Nnedi

Binti; home. Nnedi Okorafor. St. Martin's Press 2017 176 p. paperback $14.99

ISBN 9780765393111; 0765393115

Hugo Finalist: Best Novella (2018)

In this book in the Binti series, by Nnedi Okorafor, "it's been a year since Binti and Okwu enrolled at Oomza University. A year since Binti was declared a hero for uniting two warring planets. . . . And now she must return home to her people, with her friend Okwu by her side, to face her family and face her elders. But Okwu will be the first of his race to set foot on Earth in over a hundred years, and the first ever to come in peace." (Publisher's note)

Okorafor, Nnedi

★ **Who** fears death; Nnedi Okorafor. Daw Books Inc. 2010 386 p. $24.95

ISBN 9780756406172

LC 2011389634

Romantic Times Reviewers' Choice Award: Best Science Fiction & Fantasy (2010), World Fantasy Awards: Novel (2011)

This book is set in "a desolate, postapocalyptic Africa of endless desert, failing technology, superstition, and magic. . . . Prophesy speaks of a sorcerer who will change the future, end the wars and slavery, and reunite the people. Onyesonwu is a child of rare talent. Conceived by rape, physically different from her peers, Onyesonwu has the light skin, fair hair, and freckles that traditionally mark her as unworthy, frightening, ugly, and evil. But rather than accepting her outcast role, a defiant Onyesonwu uses her magic to prove herself, avenge her mother's rape, and lead her people." (Library Journal)

"There's a lot of grim, painful stuff in this book: it starts with an horrific gang rape scene (be forewarned), then progresses through violence, torture, prejudice, bullying, female genital cutting, colorism, child soldiering, and more. Yet these are all treated in a nuanced fashion. . . . This is a horrifying, inspiring, painful, joyous book." io9

Okparanta, Chinelo

Happiness, Like Water; stories. Chinelo Okparanta. Houghton Mifflin Harcourt 2013 208 p.

ISBN 0544003454; 9780544003453

LC 2013026349

Lambda Award for Lesbian General Fiction Winner (2014)

This debut short story collection, by Nigerian-American author Chinelo Okparanta, presents multiple tales "centered on Nigerian women, as they build lives out of longing and hope, faith and doubt, the struggle to stay and the mandate to leave, and the burden and strength of love." (Publisher's note)

"In her first collection of stories, Nigerian-born Okparanta focuses primarily on African women and their relationships with family, lovers, colleagues, and the community at large. Okparanta draws on her experience as a Jehovah's Witness growing up in Port Harcout and immigrating to the U.S. These are fierce, unflinching stories of the complicated knotting of close ties and the strange behaviors of language...Named one of Granta's New Voices, Okparanta joins the good company of young writers like NoViolet Bulawayo (We Need New Names, 2013) and Téa Obreht (The Tiger's Wife, 2011)." (Booklist)

Okparanta, Chinelo

★ **Under** the udala trees; Chinelo Okparanta. Houghton Mifflin Harcourt 2015 352 p. (hardcover) $26

ISBN 9780544003361; 9780544003446

LC 2014044506

NAACP Image Award Nominee: Outstanding Literary Work - Fiction (2016)

Lambda Literary Award: Lesbian Fiction (2016)

In this book, by Chinelo Okparanta, "Ijeoma comes of age as her nation does; born before independence, she is eleven when civil war breaks out in the young republic of Nigeria. Sent away to safety, she meets another displaced child and they, star-crossed, fall in love. They are from different ethnic communities. They are also both girls. When their love is discovered, Ijeoma learns that she will have to hide this part of herself. But there is a cost to living inside a lie." (Publisher's note)

"The fact that Nigeria criminalized same-sex marriages in 2014 makes Okparanta's tale that much more sobering and urgent. It is especially gratifying that one of the defining tag lines of the feminist movement, 'a woman without a man,' just might be co-opted here in another time and place." Booklist

Oksanen, Sofi

When the doves disappeared; a novel. Sofi Oksanen. Alfred A. Knopf 2015 304 p. map (hardback) $25.95

ISBN 0385350171; 9780345805904; 9780385350174

LC 2014034970

In this novel by Sofi Oksanen, set "in Communist-ruled, war-ravaged Estonia, two men are fleeing from the Red Army--Roland, a . . . freedom fighter, and his . . . cousin Edgar. When the Germans arrive, Roland goes into hiding; Edgar abandons his unhappy wife, Juudit, and takes on a new identity as a loyal supporter of the Nazi regime. 1963: Estonia is again under Communist control. Edgar is . . . desperate to hide the secrets of his past life. But his fate remains entangled with Roland's, and with Juudit." (Publisher's note)

"Oksanen captures both the futility of the citizens of a tiny country who yearn for freedom and the dark heart of an opportunist who would sell out his own family in order to survive. This is powerful fiction that stirs history, war crimes, and psychology into a compelling mix." Booklist

Okuizumi, Hikaru

The **stones** cry out; translated from the Japanese by James Westerhoven. Harcourt Brace & Co. 1999 138p $20

ISBN 0-15-100365-3

LC 98-14434

Original Japanese edition, 1993

"A monstrous tale, The Stones Cry Out is written with a lyrical beauty that only underscores the horror Manase's life becomes. As Okuizumi elegantly plays Manase's nightmare out, Manase is compelled to reenact the real atrocities he has tried so desperately to forget." Booklist

Olmstead, Robert

★ **Coal** black horse. Algonquin Books of Chapel Hill 2007 218p $23.95

ISBN 978-1-56512-521-6; 1-56512-521-5

LC 2006-42914

This novel "is mostly memorable as an exquisite corpse, a fictive vision of war so vivid and gruesome that it remains in the memory—grotesque, stiff and gape-mouthed—after every other detail of Olmstead's tale fades away." Paste

Olmstead, Robert

The **coldest** night; a novel. by Robert Olmstead. Algonquin Books 2012

ISBN 9781616200435

LC 2011045515

In this book, "Henry Childs grew up in the mountains of West Virginia, raised by his grandfather and his sweet-natured mother Clemmie. . . . He helps out at some stables where he meets Mercy. She comes from money and is university-bound, while Henry seems headed for a factory. . . . Henry is warned off by her father and brother. The lovers elope to New Orleans, where an apartment is waiting for them, courtesy of Mercy's accommodating aunt. They make it their Eden. Father and brother come to expel them, abducting Mercy, giving Henry a final warning. Though underage, he enlists as a Marine and is sent to Korea. He does recon with Lew, a gruff World War II vet. . . . The cold is arctic. The Chinese come at night, waves of them. It's kill or be killed; answer atrocity with atrocity." (Kirkus)

Olmstead, Robert

Far bright star; a novel. Algonquin Books of Chapel Hill 2009 207p $23.95; pa $13.95

ISBN 978-1-56512-592-6; 1-56512-592-4; 978-156512-980-1 pa; 1-56512-980-6 pa

LC 2008-41858

"Gleaming, spellbinding fiction . . . . Terrifying and abruptly beautiful, the new novel gleams with a masculine intensity; it is hard to read and hard to put down." Cleveland Plain Dealer

Olsen, Tillie

Tell me a riddle; a collection. Lippincott 1961 156p

"In writing which is individualized but not eccentric, experimental but not obscure, Mrs. Olsen has created imagined experience which has the authenticity of autobiography or memoir. With a faultless accuracy, her stories treat the very young, the mature, the dying—poor people without the means to buy or invent lies about their situations—and yet her writing never succumbs to mere naturalism." Commonweal

Olsson, Linda

Astrid & Veronika. Penguin Books 2007 259p pa $14

ISBN 978-0-14-303807-8; 0-14-303807-9

LC 2006-50660

First published 2005 in New Zealand with title: Let me sing you gentle songs

"Unlike the voice of the novel's omniscient narrator, [Veronika and Astrid's] are natural and vivid, utterly convincing. And unlike the nove's flatly depicted present, the physical world of the past, in which their stories take place, generously opens to admit us." N Y Times Book Rev

Omarsdottir, Kristin

Children in Reindeer Woods; Kristín Ómarsdóttir ; translated from the Icelandic by Lytton Smith. Open Letter 2012 198 p. (pbk. : acid-free paper) $14.95

ISBN 1934824356; 9781934824351

LC 2011043995

In this book, "[t]hree soldiers arrive at a farm that is also a 'temporary home for children' named Children in Reindeer Woods. Without apparent motive, they murder everyone except an 11-year-old girl, Billie. Then the soldier named Rafael murders his comrades. Now he wants to stop killing and become a farmer. Billie is oddly unmoved by the killings and becomes his (platonic) companion as he tries to remake himself into a peaceful human being." (Kirkus Reviews)

Ondaatje, Michael

Anil's ghost. Knopf 2000 307p $25

ISBN 0-375-41053-8

LC 99-59208

"Anil comes with Western-bred investigative passion: the certainty that facts are there to be unearthed and that truth is to be constructed out of them. Sarath, a polymorphous spirit and the book's most memorable figure, cautions that the real truth of his country is ambiguous and unobtainable. . . . It is Ondaatje's extraordinary achievement to use magic in order to make the blood of his own country real." N Y Times Book Rev

Includes bibliographical references (p. {310}-311)

Ondaatje, Michael, 1943-

★ The **cat's** table. Alfred A. Knopf 2011 269p $26

ISBN 978-0-307-70011-7; 0-307-70011-9

LC 2011-20820

This novel takes place on "a cruise ship sailing from Ceylon to England in 1954. The tale opens with the narrator, who shares with the author the name Michael, recalling how, as an 11-year-old, he left his aunt and uncle for a 21-day ocean voyage to be reunited with his mother, who had left the family home some years previously. . . . [Michael] Ondaatje presents . . . the daily shipboard lives of the 11-yearold boy, his cousin Emily and his two companions, Cassius and Ramadhin. . . . Years after his arrival in England, the narrator returns to the voyage as he retells the story to his own children. . . . He also wrestles with mid-life questions as to whether . . . he has a cold heart, whether he loved his friends enough and whether he has become a distracted, superficial person." (America)

"The book tells the tale of an 11-year-old boy named Michael who is on a boat trip from Colombo, Sri Lanka, to England in 1954. In the sections that take place on the boat, we are entirely in a boy's head and feverish point of view. It is also told by a Michael 50 years later, when he has become a celebrated writer and lives in Canada. His long past is behind him, but emigration has marked him. He has never truly felt at home anywhere in the world. . . . [The novel] expertly strums these cords of autobiography without overdoing it. As a result this small, and beautifully minor book, vibrates with the borrowed intimacy of real life. It also never force-feeds its young hero with wisdom he could not have acquired or stolen at such an age." Boston Globe

Ondaatje, Michael, 1943-

★ The **English** patient; a novel. Knopf 1992 307p

ISBN 0-679-41678-1

LC 92053089

This novel "begins in 1945, in a bomb-damaged Italian villa near Florence, recently used as a war hospital. Abandoned as the Allied front moved north, it now shelters one last casualty, an Englishman slowly dying of burns. . . . Hana, a young Canadian nurse, stays on devotedly, supplying him with morphine and foraged food. They are joined by David Caravaggio, a friend of Hana's family from Toronto who is a professional thief turned military spy, and by Kirpal Singh {Kip}, a Sikh soldier, charged with defusing bombs and mines in the area." (N Y Times Book Rev)

"This is a poetic and solemn narrative of the horrible process of war, the discipline, displacement, loss, and sudden, desperate love. Ondaatje seems to whisper, even confess each scene to his readers, handling them gingerly like shards of shattered glass." Booklist

Ondaatje, Michael

In the skin of a lion; a novel. Knopf 1987 243p

LC 87-45340

Ondaatje is a "beautiful writer. What he writes about most beautifully is work. Mr. Ondaatje is passionate about process, the way work, particularly construction of all kinds, is done and how it feels to do it. This is, of course, a rarity in fiction at any time, and one can only be grateful for a man who is not focused on the classroom, the bedroom and the bar." N Y Times Book Rev

Onstad, Katrina

Everybody Has Everything. Emblem Editions 2012 323 p. $14

ISBN 0771068980; 1455522929; 9780771068980; 9781455522927

In this book, married couple Ana, a career-oriented lawyer, and James, an unemployed writer, have been unsuccessful in having a child despite fertility treatments. "Things change when they become guardians of 2-year-old Finn. Little Finn's mother, Sarah, is in a coma . . . . James takes pleasure in being a loving, attentive father to Finn. Ana, on the other hand, . . . realizes she doesn't really want to be a mother but also that such a sentiment is not one a woman can easily express." (Kirkus Reviews)

Orczy, Emmuska

★ The **Scarlet** Pimpernel; [by] Baroness Orczy. Alfred A. Knopf 1999 299p (Everyman's library children's classics) $14.95

ISBN 0-375-40658-1

LC 2001-272396

First published 1905 by Putnam

"An adventure story of the French Revolution. The apparently foppish young Englishman, Sir Percy Blakeney, is found to be the daring Scarlet Pimpernel, rescuer of distressed aristocrats." Reader's Ency. 4th edition

Orner, Peter

Love and shame and love; a novel. Little, Brown and Co. 2011 439p il $24.99

ISBN 978-0-316-12939-8

LC 2011-22547

"Orner anatomizes family relationships with precision in a novel that spans three—and touches on four—generations. At the center of the author's examination is Alexander Popper, a fiction writer manqué (he tries in vain to write a 'good, sad story') and reluctant law-school graduate who winds up handling misdemeanor cases for the Cook County Public Defender. . . . [This] is a masterful, multifaceted novel. Readers will find both love and shame in abundance in Orner's teeming fictional world." Kirkus

Orringer, Julie

★ The **invisible** bridge. Alfred A. Knopf 2010 602p $26.95

ISBN 978-1-4000-4116-9; 1-4000-4116-3

LC 2009-46498

"Andras is a Hungarian Jew studying in Paris as Hitler's influence begins to spread across a continent already riddled with anti-Semitism and bloodlust. He falls for fellow émigré Klara, and their world is soon rocked by war. Other characters weave in and out of the story line, but it's the love tethering Andras and Klara that powers the narrative's massive machinery. The Invisible Bridge is without a doubt an ambitious slice of literature, but Orringer fulfills her ambitions with crisp writing that never wanders far from the story's path. World War II is hardly undiscovered literary territory. Still, this stunning work manages to feel both original and part and parcel of the well-blazed tradition of historical novels that came before it." Entertainment Wkly

Orullian, Peter Vance

The **unremembered**; Peter Orullian. Tor 2011 669p. $27.99

ISBN 9780765325716

LC 2010036105

This book tells the story of "Tahn, Wendra, and Sutter," orphans who are recruited for "a perilous and mysterious quest . . . by a wizardly stranger and an elven Far." (Publishers Weekly) The danger which threatens their world is "the god Quietus" who has been "bound behind a magical barrier, along with the horrific monsters of his making . . . [and now] seeks to escape his prison." (Libr J)

As the barrier begins to weaken, and "the most remote cities are laid waste by fell, nightmarish troops . . . some people dismiss the attacks as mere rumor. Instead of standing against the real threat, they persecute those with the knowledge, magic and power to fight these abominations, denying the inevitability of war and annihilation." (Publisher's note)

Another title in this series is:

Trial of intentions (2015)

Orwell, George, 1903-1950

★ **Animal** farm; with an introduction by Julian Symons. Knopf 1993 xl, 113p $16

ISBN 0-679-42039-8

LC 92-54299

First published 1945 in the United Kingdom; first United States edition 1946

"The animals on Farmer Jones's farm revolt in a move led by the pigs, and drive out the humans. The pigs become the leaders, in spite of the fact that their government was meant to be 'classless.' The other animals soon find that they are suffering varying degrees of slavery. A totalitarian state slowly evolves in which 'all animals are equal but some animals are more equal than others.' This is a biting satire aimed at communism." Shapiro. Fic for Youth. 3d edition

Orwell, George, 1903-1950

Burmese days; Keep the aspidistra flying; Coming up for air; with an introduction by John Carey. Alfred A. Knopf 2011 xxxiii, 677p (Everyman's Library) $28

ISBN 978-0-307-59504-1; 0-307-59504-8

Burmese days (1934) is an indictment of British colonial rule, based on Orwell's own experience while serving in the Indian Imperial Police. Keep the aspidistra flying (1936) recounts the literary aspirations, financial humiliations, and shot-gun wedding of a bookseller's assistant. Coming up for air (1939) is about the suburban frustration and Edwardian nostalgia of an insurance agent on the eve of the Second World War.

Orwell, George, 1903-1950

★ **Nineteen** eighty-four; with an introduction by Julian Symonds. Knopf 1992 xlii, 325p $19

ISBN 0-679-41739-7

LC 92-52906

First published 1949 by Harcourt, Brace

"A dictatorship called Big Brother rules the people in a collectivist society where Winston Smith works in the Ministry of Truth. The Thought Police persuade the people that ignorance is strength and war is peace. Winston becomes involved in a forbidden love affair and joins the underground to resist this mind control." Shapiro. Fic for Youth. 3d edition

Osborne, Lawrence

The **forgiven**; a novel. Lawrence Osborne. 1st ed. Hogarth 2012 272 p. (hardcover) $25.00; (ebook) $25.00

ISBN 0307889033; 9780307889034; 9780307889058

LC 2011025942

This book by Lawrence Osborne "follows British couple David and Jo Henniger into the Moroccan desert for a debauched weekend at their friends' palatial ksar. Driving to the estate, David is distracted while arguing with Jo, and consequently hits and kills a young Moroccan. . . .

The next morning, the dead boy's father, Abdellah, arrives and demands that David return with him to help bury his son." (Publishers Weekly)

Osondu, E. C.

This house is not for sale; a novel. E.C. Osondu. HarperCollins 2015 208 p. $25.99

ISBN 0061990884; 9780061990885

LC 2014013856

This novle by E. C. Osondu, "brings to life an African neighborhood and one remarkable house, seen through the eyes of a young member of the household. The house lies in a town seemingly lost in time, full of colorful, larger-than-life characters; at the narrative's heart are Grandpa . . . and the house itself, which becomes a character in its own right and takes on the scale of legend." (Publisher's note)

Osondu, E. C.

Voice of America; stories. HarperCollins Publishers 2010 215p $19.99

ISBN 9780061990861; 0-06-199086-8

LC 2010-05729

"Osondu's excellent short stories, set in both Nigeria and the U.S., reveal the vast cultural chasm that persists between our countries. . . . These richly shaded tales explore old ways and new, wealth and poverty, myth and misapprehension. Though there is sadness here, the tone is deadpan, and the reader can imagine the storyteller's eyes crinkled in a smile." Booklist

Ostermiller, Dori

Outside the ordinary world. Mira 2010 374p pa $14.95

ISBN 978-0-7783-2889-6; 0-7783-2889-9

"Traumatized as a child by her mother's affair, Sylvia Sandon has vowed never to repeat her mother's infidelities. But at 42, Sylvia is facing a moment of uncomfortable truth. Her marriage to Nate, a kind city planner obsessed with renovating their antique farmhouse, is faltering, and her own creative life as a painter is stalled. Her two daughters, 4-year-old Emmie and sulky, teenage Hannah, are exhaustively demanding and she's fraying at the seams. When she meets Tai, an affable landscape artist whose son is one of her art students, passion sparks in a way that's frighteningly familiar. . . . Partly set against the fire-shocked California coast in the 1970s, the age of 'The Joy of Sex' and Helen Reddy songs about female empowerment, Ostermiller captures what it's like to be a child caught in a sticky web of family drama." Boston Globe

Ostlund, Lori

After the Parade; by Lori Ostlund. Simon & Schuster 2015 352 p. $25

ISBN 1476790108; 9781476790107

In this book, by Lori Ostlund, "grand-hearted and bumbling, 40-year-old Aaron feels a need to take charge of his own life and splits from Walter, his controlling partner of 20 years, moving to San Francisco and teaching English as a Second Language. But he soon realizes that what he really needs is to reconcile with his youth spent feeling like an outsider in little Morton, MN." (Library Journal)

"An example of realism in its most potent iteration: not a neatly arranged plot orchestrated by an authorial god but an authentic, empathetic representation of life as it truly is." Kirkus

Otsuka, Julie, 1962-

The **Buddha** in the attic. Alfred A. Knopf 2011 129p

ISBN 0307700003 Alfred A. Knopf; 9780307700001 Alfred A. Knopf; 9781905490875 Fig Tree

LC 20110013568

National Book Award Finalist: Fiction (2011)

"The novel revolves around a group of mail-order brides who leave Japan in the early 1900s. They're on their way to meet husbands in San Francisco who emigrated years earlier and have written of their many successes in America. When the travelers — some as young as 14 — disembark, they discover that the photographs the men sent are outdated, their successes are a fantasy, and a hard life awaits. We also know the snare that history has set for them. Decades after they establish themselves, they will be sent to internment camps. . . . . [The tale unfolds in a] daring first-person plural narrative. Even as the women step off the boat and their paths diverge, the novel proceeds in a flow of we and us, with the occasional individual voice raised from the whole. Knowing what will come, plot is not what urges the reader on. Rather, it is the details of the women's lives that fascinate as they spread throughout California like fireflies released from a jar." Cleveland Plain Dealer

Otsuka, Julie

When the emperor was divine; a novel. Knopf 2002 141p hardcover o.p. pa $10.95

ISBN 0-375-41429-0; 0-385-72181-1 pa

LC 2002-20814

Otsuka "demonstrates a breathtaking restraint and delicacy throughout this supple and devastating first novel." Booklist

Otto, Whitney

Eight girls taking pictures; a novel. Whitney Otto. Scribner 2012 342 p. (hardback) $25

ISBN 1451682697; 9781451682694; 9781451682724; 9781451682731

LC 2012009167

Author Whitney Otto "explores the ambitions, passions, conflicts and desires of eight female photographers throughout the twentieth century. . . . From San Francisco to New York, London, Berlin, Buenos Aires, and Rome, Otto . . . [offers a] portrait of the history of feminism and of photography. While their circumstances may differ, the tensions these women experience--from wanting a private life or a public life; passion or security; art or domesticity; children or creative freedom--are universal." (Publisher's note)

Includes bibliographical references.

Otto, Whitney

How to make an American quilt. Villard Bks. 1991 179p $20

ISBN 0-679-40070-2

LC 90-48233

"Otto has tremendous insight and compassion, understanding the rareness of a perfect marriage, the anger of thwarted lives, and the vagaries of love and motherhood." Booklist

Overholser, Wayne D.

Death of a cattle king; a western story. Five Star 2011 188p $25.95

ISBN 978-1-43282-517-1; 1-43282-517-8

LC 2011-15379

"The Holt family traveled the Oregon Trail from Pennsylvania to the Northwest, where they established the modest Rainbow Ranch. Even after Sam's wife, Helen, dies, leaving him with two kids, Mary and Bruce, the ranch continues to prosper. But trouble arrives in the form of Morgan Drew, son of Sam's late best friend. Drew's ambition and greed become plain as he allies himself with the valley's biggest rancher. Now he intends to absorb the Holt ranch as well as all the other small claims in the valley. If Sam doesn't accept Drew's offer, the implied threat is that the Rainbow will be taken by force. An Indian uprising puts a temporary hold on the land grab as the ranchers form an uneasy alliance to ward off the threat . . . . Like most of [Overholser's] work, this novel is driven less by violence and more by the timeless human emotions of greed, jealousy, and love." Booklist

Overholser, Wayne D.

Law at Angel's Landing; a western story. Five Star 2010 164p $25.95

ISBN 978-1-59414-907-8; 1-59414-907-0

LC 2010-08448

"Mark Girard moved to Angel's Landing in the Colorado foothills as a young boy with his mother and father, who was a chase-the-rainbow gold miner. When the strike played out and the town was destined to be abandoned, the elder Girard wanted to pick up stakes and move to the next big strike. Mark's mother refused, opting for stability in the soon to be very tiny village. Mother, son, and the town all survived, with Mark becoming county sheriff. Overholser tells two stories here: the melancholy saga of a broken family reunited too late and the pendulum-swinging life of a boom-and-bust gold town. . . . Overholser, a consummate western storyteller with an eye for character and dialogue, delivers another solid effort." Booklist

The **Oxford** book of American detective stories; edited by Tony Hillerman, Rosemary Herbert. Oxford Univ. Press 1996 686p $35; pa $18.95

ISBN 0-19-508581-7; 0-19-511792-1 pa

LC 95-4504

This collection includes stories by B. Pronzini, E. A. Poe, E. S. Gardner, E. Queen and M. Muller

The **Oxford** book of American short stories; edited by Joyce Carol Oates. Oxford Univ. Press 1992 768p $40; pa $18.95

ISBN 0-19-507065-8; 0-19-509262-7 pa

LC 92-1353

This anthology of American short stories includes selections from writers such as Henry James, Edith Wharton, Zora Neale Hurston, Ralph Ellison, Kurt Vonnegut, Louise Erdrich, David Leavitt, Sandra Cisneros, and Pinckney Benedict. Index.

"Fifty-six short stories showcase this ever-vital and challenging art form's suppleness and power from Washington Irving's classic, 'Rip Van Winkle,' to the work of Sandra Cisneros. While Oates couldn't resist masterpieces such as Ernest Hemingway's 'A Clean, Well-Lighted Place,' her goal was 'familiar names, unfamiliar titles,' and her intention was to call our attention to works by the likes of Edgar Allan Poe, Harriet Beecher Stowe, Henry James, Kate Chopin, William Carlos Williams, and Saul Bellow that aren't anthologized to death. . . . Her standards of excellence are consistent throughout." Booklist

The **Oxford** book of English ghost stories; chosen by Michael Cox and R. A. Gilbert. Oxford Univ. Press 1987 xvii, 504 p.p hardcover o.p.

ISBN 9780199556304; 9780192141637 out of print

LC 86008690

First published 1986 in the United Kingdom

Arranged chronologically, the forty-two stories gathered here "date from the 1820s . . . to the 1980s. . . . In addition to featuring those writers one would expect to find here—Sheridan Le Fanu, M. R. James, and Walter de la Mare, for example—there is also a bounty of wonderful authors with whom U.S. audiences may not be familiar." Booklist

The **Oxford** book of English short stories; edited by A.S. Byatt. Oxford Univ. Press 1998 xxx, 439p hardcover o.p. pa $19.95

ISBN 0-19-214238-0; 0-19-956160-5 pa

LC 97-44998

In this anthology Byatt "includes necessary masters—Rudyard Kipling, Saki, D. H. Lawrence, and V. S. Pritchett, to name a few. But . . . she draws into the fold the work of several extremely talented writers of which few readers on this side of the Atlantic will have heard. Falling into this category are such writers as Malachi Whitaker, H. E. Bates, Sylvia Townsend Warner, and Charlotte Mew." Booklist

The **Oxford** book of gothic tales; edited by Chris Baldick. Oxford Univ. Press 1992 xxiii, 533p hardcover o.p. pa $19.95

ISBN 0-19-286219-7 pa

LC 91-27290

This chronologically arranged anthology contains thirty-seven stories dating from the 18th to 20th century. Among the authors are Hawthorne, Poe, Stevenson, Hardy, Faulkner, Welty, Borges, Angela Carter and Isabel Allende.

The **Oxford** book of Irish short stories; edited by William Trevor. Oxford Univ. Press 1989 567p $40; pa $17.95

ISBN 0-19-214180-5; 0-19-280193-7 pa

LC 88-28147

"The great Irish writers—from Oliver Goldsmith and Oscar Wilde to James Joyce and Edna O'Brien—are represented in a collection for older advanced readers." Booklist

The **Oxford** book of Latin American short stories; edited by Roberto González Echevarria. Oxford Univ. Press 1997 xiv, 481 p.p

ISBN 9780195095906 out of print; 9780195130850

LC 97005395

"The 53 stories in {this anthology} are grouped together in three chapters—the 'Colonial Period,' 'New Nations,' and the 'Contemporary Period.' . . . Classic writers such as Gabriel García Márquez, Carlos Fuentes, and Jorge Luis Borges are included, as well as lesser-known authors like José Balza and Horacio Quiroga." (Libr J) Index.

The **Oxford** book of modern fairy tales; edited by Alison Lurie. Oxford Univ. Press 1993 455p $30; pa $14.95

ISBN 0-19-214218-6; 0-19-282385-X pa

LC 92-28007

This volume is "full of old favorites and some priceless new gems, with a wonderful chronological arrangement that allows readers to absorb information on literary developments and trends, or simply to enjoy the well-told tales. . . . The whole collection is first rate and demonstrates beautifully that modern fairy tales are not just for kids." SLJ

The **Oxford** book of science fiction stories; edited by Tom Shippey. Oxford Univ. Press 1992 xxvi, 587p (paperback) $19.95

ISBN 9780192142047 out of print; 9780192803818

LC 92009512

The **Oxford** book of short stories; chosen by V.S. Pritchett. Oxford Univ. Press 1981 547p hardcover o.p. pa $19.95

ISBN 0-19-214116-3; 0-19-958313-7 pa

LC 81-156872

In addition to one of his own short stories, Pritchett has selected 40 others, written in English during the 19th and 20th centuries. Most of the authors are English, Irish or American and include Somerset Maugham, D. H. Lawrence, Faulkner, Twain, and Eudora Welty.

The **Oxford** book of spy stories; edited by Michael Cox. Oxford Univ. Press 1996 356p $30
ISBN 0-19-214242-9
LC 95-15519

The **Oxford** book of twentieth-century ghost stories; edited by Michael Cox. Oxford Univ. Press 1996 xix, 425 p
ISBN 9780192142603 out of print
LC 96004913

Oyeyemi, Helen

Boy, snow, bird; a novel. Helen Oyeyemi. Riverhead Hardcover 2014 320 p. (hardback) $27.95
ISBN 1594631395; 9781594631399
LC 2013025053

This novel, by Helen Oyeyemi, retells the "Snow White fairy tale . . . as a story of family secrets, race, beauty, and vanity. In the winter of 1953, Boy Novak arrives by chance in a small town in Massachusetts, . . . marries a local widower and becomes stepmother to his . . . daughter, Snow Whitman. . . . The birth of Boy's daughter, Bird, who is dark-skinned, exposes the Whitmans as light-skinned African Americans passing for white." (Publisher's note)

"Dense with fully realized characters, startling images, original observations and revelatory truths, this masterpiece engages the reader's heart and mind as it captures both the complexities of racial and gender identity in the 20th century and the more intimate complexities of love in all its guises." Kirkus

Oyeyemi, Helen

Mr. Fox. Riverhead Books 2011 324p $25.95
ISBN 978-1-59448-807-8; 1-59448-807-X
LC 2011-13747

"St. John Fox is a writer famous for killing off women in his stories; Mary Fox is a creation he uses as a tool to scold and inform himself of his motivations and to act as moxie gatekeeper of his most closely held secrets. His wife, Daphne Fox, is the writer's loving, lighthearted companion — until she wises up to the existence of Mary Fox, whom she at first believes to be her husband's mistress. She finds out otherwise, and then both Fox women go out to lunch. Each character is so superbly formed, and they are believable people whose habits of thought and language are so perfectly pitched and entertaining that they become instantly lovable, that is until we learn more about them. The combination of intensity and changeability in all three characters reflect many of the archetypal baddies from myth and batty old fairy-fables, the most prominent of which is Bluebeard, with his many bloodbaths, and the Furies, with their readiness to punish crime." Chicago Sun-Times

Oyeyemi, Helen

The **opposite** house. Nan A. Talese/Doubleday 2007 257p $23.95
ISBN 978-0-385-51384-5; 0-385-51384-4
LC 2006-36812

The novel is "insightful, urgently and sometimes painfully so. What Oyeyemi shows us about cultural alienation, about what makes and marks a migrant, needs to be seen. . . . At times, it's true, Maja's skin feels thin, stretched, raw. We can feel Oyeyemi writing through her character. But those times are rare; on most of the pages in this novel Maja lives, and it matters that she lives. This is her life." Strange Horizons

Oz, Amos

Don't call it night; translated from the Hebrew by Nicholas de Lange. Harcourt Brace & Co. 1996 199p
LC 96-14587

Original Hebrew edition, 1994

"This novel is a piece of sweet but melancholy chamber music—light but not necessarily insubstantial. It belongs to a genre of restful novel that is ruled by an esthetic of peace and a yearning for peace. If one is looking for politics, there is that—clearly, if quietly." N Y Times Book Rev

Oz, Amos

★ **Fima**; translated from the Hebrew by Nicholas de Lange. Harcourt Brace & Co. 1993 322p
LC 92-44200

Original Hebrew edition, 1991

"Not only does Mr. Oz strive toward a Chekhovian compassion for his characters, but his novel depends . . . on making us believe in the possibility of last-minute grace. When tragedy strikes, we watch Fima rise to the occasion and begin to tap his own resources of generosity, humility, common sense, and his sense of purpose." N Y Times Book Rev

Oz, Amos

Panther in the basement; translated from the Hebrew by Nicholas de Lange. Harcourt Brace & Co. 1997 147p $21
ISBN 0-15-100287-8
LC 97-20577

Original Hebrew edition, 1995

"It is Jerusalem in 1947, during the final days of the British mandate in Palestine, and Proffy, a twelve-and-a-quarter-year-old Jewish boy, is leading a double life. In his parents' eyes, Proffy (short for Professor) is a word savant. By his own definition, he is second-in-command of the underground organization F. O. D. (Freedom or Death), for whose noble cause he scatters bent nails and composes war slogans like 'Perfidious Albion, hands off Zion!' Proffy's identity as an eloquent militant is threatened, however, when his compatriots charge him with treason for befriending a British policeman, and he is forced to reevaluate the implications of word 'enemy.'" New Yorker

Oz, Amos

The **same** sea; translated from the Hebrew by Nicholas de Lange in collaboration with the author. Harcourt 2001 201p $30
ISBN 0-15-100572-9
LC 2001-24121

Original Hebrew edition, 1999

"Never has the author's writing been more controlled and polished. . . . His depictions of his characters' lives are tableaux vivants, succint and visual." Times Lit Suppl

Oz, Amos

Scenes from village life; [translated from the Hebrew by Nicholas de Lange] Houghton Mifflin Harcourt 2011 182p.
ISBN 978-0-547-48336-8 Houghton Mifflin Harcourt; 978-0-701-18550-3 Chatto and Windus; 9780547483368; 0547483368
LC 2011016055

"This . . . volume of eight stories with recurring characters (which Mr Oz has referred to as a novel) is alive with individuals who are less preoccupied with 'The Situation'--as Israelis call the regional conflict--than with other more universal concerns. In one chapter Kobi, a 17-year-old with a crush on the 30-year-old postmistress and librarian of the town, decides to act on his feelings, which leads to an awkward confrontation. In another a middle-aged doctor reflects on her relationship with a nephew, who has failed to materialise from the bus he was meant to have arrived on. . . . Tel Ilan is the small fictional town where these stories take place." (Economist)

Ozeki, Ruth L., 1956-

★ A **tale** for the time being; Ruth Ozeki. Viking 2013 432 p. (hardcover) $28.95

ISBN 0670026638; 9780670026630

LC 2012039878

Man Booker Prize Shortlist (2013)

This novel, by Ruth Ozeki, begins in "Tokyo, [where] sixteen-year-old . . . Nao . . . plans to document the life of her great grandmother. . . . A diary is Nao's only solace. . . . Across the Pacific, we meet Ruth, a novelist living on a remote island who discovers a collection of artifacts washed ashore in a Hello Kitty lunchbox. . . . As the mystery of its contents unfolds, Ruth is pulled into the past, into Nao's drama and her unknown fate, and forward into her own future." (Publisher's note)

"The novel's seamless web of language, metaphor and meaning can't be disentangled from its powerful emotional impact: These are characters we care for deeply, imparting vital life lessons through the magic of storytelling. A masterpiece, pure and simple." (Kirkus)

Includes bibliographical references

Ozick, Cynthia

Dictation; a quartet. Houghton Mifflin 2008 179p $24

ISBN 978-0-547-05400-1; 0-547-05400-9

LC 2007-52331

"In the wonderfully witty and biting opening novella, 'Dictation,' Miss Bosanquet and Miss Hallowes, the respective amanuenses of Henry James and Jospeh Conrad at the height of their careers, concoct a marvelous scheme to write themselves into posterity. . . . 'Actors' follows the fortunes of Matt Sorley as he searches for work in New York and eventually is tapped to play Lear in an adaptation of the play that features Lear as a Jewish emigrant. Sorley's production is interrupted by a real Lear—an elderly and quite mad Jewish actor who had performed this role originally many years ago. In 'At Fumicaro,' an art critic attempts to marry his Italian maid only to realize that she has strung him along to rob him. Finally, in 'What Happened to the Baby?' a young girl rehearses the story of her uncle's infidelity and her aunt's Medea-like revenge. Ozick is at the top of her form in these splendid stories." Libr J

Ozick, Cynthia

★ **Foreign** bodies. Houghton Mifflin Harcourt 2010 255p $26

ISBN 978-0-547-43557-2; 0-547-43557-6

LC 2010-05757

"Ozick is a craggy writer, with strenuous climbs, momentary slides and startling views. Some of Bea's confrontations, feeling out her new independence back in the United States, seem contrived, even stagy. But her vision of Europe and its tragic history is profound; and Lili is a creation of stunning depth. It is not Jamesian, it is Ozickian." Boston Globe

Ozick, Cynthia

★ **Heir** to the glimmering world. Houghton Mifflin 2004 310p $24

ISBN 0-618-47049-2

LC 2004-42723

"In 1933, the Mitwissers, a family of German Jews, arrive in America after a narrow and eccentric escape from Berlin. . . . After landing somewhat haphazardly in New York, they place an ad for help in a local paper. The only applicant for the job is an eighteen-year-old orphan, Rose Meadows, who narrates the story, and who observes the Mitwissers with the dry neutrality of an invisible servant. Her duties are vaguely defined—part nanny, part secretary—and her salary comes intermittently, the family's sole source of income being the whimsy of a troubled benefactor. Ozick portrays this ramshackle household to dazzling effect, as it adjusts to its many states of exile—from a sense of security, from cherished ideas, and from the consolations of each other." New Yorker

Ozick, Cynthia

★ The **Puttermesser** papers. Knopf 1997 235p $23

ISBN 0-679-45476-4

LC 96-39155

"This entertaining fable is a social commentary as well as a comic tour de force, and it bristles with Ozick's formidable intelligence and wit." Publ Wkly

Ozick, Cynthia

The **shawl**. Knopf 1989 69p $12.95

ISBN 0-394-57976-3

LC 89-2652

"Rosa is brilliantly realized. Her dark night of the soul is lit by flashes of insight about memory, culture, old age, a welcome meditation on the euphemistic inadequacy of the word 'survivor.'" N Y Times Book Rev

P

Packer, Ann

★ The **Children's** Crusade; A Novel. by Ann Packer. Simon & Schuster 2015 448 p. $26.99

ISBN 1476710457; 9781476710457

LC 2015301766

This novel, by Ann Packer, "explores the secrets and desires, the remnant wounds and saving graces of one California family, over the course of five decades. . . . One by one, the siblings take turns telling the story--Robert, a doctor like their father; Rebecca, a psychiatrist; Ryan, a schoolteacher; and James, the malcontent, the problem child, the only one who hasn't settled down--their narratives interwoven with portraits of the family at crucial points in their history." (Publisher's note)

"Packer fully captures the intimacy of this family's life and, by extension, the way the children's interactions impact their adult lives. A masterful portrait of indelible family bonds." Booklist

Packer, Ann

★ The **dive** from Clausen's pier; a novel. Knopf 2002 369p hardcover o.p. pa $14

ISBN 0-375-41282-4; 0-375-72713-2 pa

LC 2001-42522

"A reckless attempt to impress Carrie, Mike's dive off Clausen's Pier rendered him paralyzed. Now Carrie finds herself torn between the loyalty she's expected to feel toward Mike and her need to transform herself. She takes a dive of her own—into adulthood—when she escapes to New York." Booklist

Packer, Ann

Songs without words. Knopf 2007 321p $24.95

ISBN 978-0-375-41281-3

LC 2006-100512

This "novel examines the bonds of female friendship and how the connections formed by a childhood tragedy develop with age. Liz, married to a Bay Area technology executive and the mother of two teenagers, is preoccupied with yoga and creating a pleasurable environment for her children. Sarabeth, who was absorbed into Liz's family when her mother committed suicide, lives a makeshift existence in Berkeley. When Liz's daughter attempts to kill herself, a rift opens between the two women. . . . [Packer] shows a deft touch in framing emotional dilemmas, such as whether it is the duty of those who have been raised with affection to compensate those who have gone without." New Yorker

Packer, Ann

Swim back to me. Alfred A. Knopf 2011 225p $24.95
ISBN 978-1-4000-4404-7; 1-4000-4404-9

LC 2010-51792

This book is a collection of short stories by Ann Packer. "In the opener, 'Walk for Mankind,' teenager Richard Appleby describes his bittersweet relationship with Sasha Horowitz, a rebellious, risk-taking 14-year-old, who has a clandestine affair with a drug dealer. . . . 'Molten' conveys a mother's grief over her adolescent son's senseless death; 'Dwell Time' features a protagonist's happy second marriage—until her husband disappears." (Publisher's note)

"Packer's sterling collection is framed by two novellas. In the opener, 'Walk for Mankind,' teenager Richard Appleby describes his bittersweet relationship with Sasha Horowitz, a rebellious, risk-taking 14-year-old, who has a clandestine affair with a drug dealer. . . . 'Things Said or Done' is set three decades later, when Sasha, now 51 and divorced, has become Richard's caretaker, forced to deal with his self-destructive, narcissistic personality while recognizing the ways in which they are alike. Packer's talents are evident in these psychologically astute novellas, and also in the stories in between. . . . [She] presents complex human relationships with unsentimental compassion." Publ Wkly

Packer, ZZ

Drinking coffee elsewhere. Riverhead Bks. 2003 238p hardcover o.p. pa $14
ISBN 1-57322-378-6 pa; 1-57322-234-8

LC 2002-73971

"The predominantly African American characters in Packer's first collection of short fiction struggle to maintain their sense of self while they confront unexpected life events." Booklist

Page, Katherine Hall

✓The **body** in the Big Apple. Morrow 1999 239p $22
ISBN 0-688-15748-3

LC 99-33511

This prequel to the Faith Fairchild series "catches the amateur sleuth at the start of her career. . . . It's winter in Manhattan and 23-year-old Faith is darting from one holiday party to the next, bearing hearty comfort foods to a chic clientele of East Side socialites and yuppies. . . . At one of these soirees Faith runs into an old school chum, now married to an up-and-coming politician, who confides that she is being blackmailed." N Y Times Book Rev

Page, Katherine Hall

✓The **body** in the bog. Morrow 1996 276p

LC 96-3468

"Sleuth Faith Fairchild occupies her time in small-town Massachusetts with her husband, Tom, a preacher; their two small children; Have Faith, her catering business; and an occasional murder. When wetlands are converted into a chi-chi housing development, poison pen letters fly, one of the houses burns, and police discover murder. Faith's persistent quest for clues exposes many secrets, but the ultimate confrontation occurs in Have Faith's kitchen. Well-delineated action and characters mix easily with Faith's attendant domesticity." Libr J

Page, Katherine Hall

✓The **body** in the bookcase. Morrow 1998 244p $22
ISBN 0-688-15747-5

LC 98-36708

A mystery featuring Faith Fairchild, "the Aleford, Mass., caterer, wife and mother of two. Faith, like everybody else in town, is appalled when 80-year-old Sarah Winslow is found dead after her house is burglarized. After her own home is broken into, Faith decides to solve the crimes. . . . Page's tale is tightly written, with strong characterizations and delightful descriptions of its New England setting." Publ Wkly

Pajer, Bernadette

Capacity for murder; Bernadette Pajer. 1st ed. Poisoned Pen Press 2013 250 p. (hardcover) $24.95; (paperback) $14.95
ISBN 1464201285; 9781464201264; 9781464201288

LC 2012952569

This is Bernadette Pajer's third Professor Bradshaw mystery. This installment takes the professor-detective "to the Healing Sands Sanitarium in the remote coastal town of Ocean Springs, Wash. Dr. Arnold Hornsby, Healing Sands' owner, wants Bradshaw to investigate the electrocution death of his son-in-law, David Hollister, in an electrotherapy machine." The professor quickly determines the death was not accidental. (Publishers Weekly)

Pajer, Bernadette

Fatal induction; Bernadette Pajer. 1st ed. Poisoned Pen Press 2012 225 p. (hardcover) $24.95; (paperback) $14.95
ISBN 1590586123; 9781590586129; 9781590586143

LC 2011942724

This is Bernadette Pajer's second Professor Bradshaw mystery. Here, "people in 1901 Seattle are quick to dismiss the death of a gypsy peddler as not important, but Professor Bradshaw knows the dead man's young daughter is desperately in need of protection. At the same time, Bradshaw has entered a 'musical telephone' contest that just might generate a tool (wiretapping comes to mind) he and the police can use for spying on the suspected bad guys." (Library Journal)

Pajer, Bernadette

A **spark** of death. Poisoned Pen 2011 210p pa $14.95
ISBN 978-1-59058-907-6

"Ever since his mentally unstable wife committed suicide at a dinner party, Prof. Benjamin Bradshaw has devoted himself to bringing up his son Justin. He's moved to Seattle, settled at the University of Washington and hired the competent Mrs. Prouty as a housekeeper. Now his life may be ruined by the murder of his colleague Prof. Oglethorpe, a man he had no cause to like. Oglethorpe was found electrocuted, apparently by a machine built in a university lab that was soon to be used in a demonstration for President McKinley. Bradshaw is certain that he must solve the murder to save his own life. . . . [This book] presents a good mystery, a clever detective and a fascinating look at the early days of electrical power." Kirkus

Palahniuk, Chuck, 1962-

Beautiful you; A Novel. By Chuck Palahniuk. Doubleday 2014 240 p. (hardcover) $25.95
ISBN 0385538030; 9780345807113; 9780385538039

LC 2013033379

This novel, by Chuck Palahniuk, is "about the apocalyptic marketing possibilities of female pleasure. . . . Penny Harrigan is a low-level associate in a big Manhattan law firm with an apartment in Queens and no love life at all. So it comes as a great shock when she finds herself invited to dinner by one C. Linus Maxwell, aka 'Climax-Well,' a software mega-billionaire and lover of the most gorgeous and accomplished women on earth." (Publisher's note)

"Palahniuk's newest is an unsubtle, often hilarious, over-the-top satire about rampant consumerism and man's attempts to (literally) control women's sexuality." Booklist

Palahniuk, Chuck, 1962-

Choke; a novel. Chuck Palahniuk. Doubleday 2001 293p (pbk.) $15; o.p.; o.p.

ISBN 9780385720922; 9780307388926; 0385501560; 9780385501569

LC 00063905

This book tells the story of "Victor Mancini [who] plays a colonial servant by day and reveals his true sex-addicted con artist self by night. All for the purpose of trying to cope with and fix a withered relationship with his ailing mother. Mancini purposely chokes on food at restaurants to gain the attention of other diners and force someone to save his life. . . . As if Victor couldn't get any more pathetic, his raging sex addiction sends him to sex addicts anonymous meetings to troll for sexual partners. Although his Alzheimer's-suffering mother has no idea who he is, she tells him--through a diary written completely in Italian—that he is a direct descendent of Jesus Christ himself." (Publisher's note)

Palahniuk, Chuck

Diary; a novel. Doubleday 2003 260p $24.95

ISBN 0-385-50947-2

LC 2003-43900

"Catchy, jarring prose, cryptic pronouncements and baroque flights of imagination are instantly recognizable, and {the author's} sharp, bizarre meditations on the artistic process make this twisted tale one of his most memorable works to date." Publ Wkly

Palahniuk, Chuck, 1962-

Fight Club; by Chuck Palahniuk. W. W. Norton & Company 1996 208p $25.95

ISBN 0393039765; 9780393039764

LC 95047591

Oregon Book Awards: Ken Kesey Award for Fiction (1997)

In this book, "[e]very weekend, in the basements and parking lots of bars across the country, young men with white-collar jobs and failed lives take off their shoes and shirts and fight each other barehanded just as long as they have to. Then they go back to those jobs with blackened eyes and loosened teeth and the sense that they can handle anything. Fight club is the invention of Tyler Durden, projectionist, waiter, and dark, anarchic genius, and it's only the beginning of his plans for violent revenge on an empty consumer-culture world." (Publisher's note)

Palahniuk, Chuck

Lullaby; a novel. Doubleday 2002 260p

ISBN 0-385-50447-0

LC 2001-52979

"This is vintage Palahniuk: weird, creepy, twisted, upsetting, and ultimately a great read for anyone who wants to be scared for pleasure." Libr J

Palahniuk, Chuck

Pygmy. Doubleday 2009 241p $24.95

ISBN 978-0-385-52634-0; 0-385-52634-2

LC 2009-06507

A "novel about an unlikely terrorist cell: foreign-exchange students who arrive at a midwestern city, bent on unleashing 'Operation Havoc.' The story unfolds in a series of dispatches from an unnamed 13-year-old agent, dubbed 'Pygmy' by the locals. . . . Despite Pygmy's command of the deadly arts, he is still a 13-year-old, prone to unwanted erections, and he is not the coolest kid in the cadre, either. The frisson around his internal, target-acquiring narrative, the locals' unwitting perception of him, and his outsider's view of the routine humiliations inflicted upon high-school youth is so spot-on it produces a sense of déjà vu: surely someone would have thought of this before." Booklist

Palahniuk, Chuck

Rant; an oral biography of Buster Casey. Doubleday 2007 320p $24.95

ISBN 978-0-385-51787-4; 0-385-51787-4

LC 2006-28918

"In telling this utterly bizarre tale, a story that only gets heavier as it goes on, Rant's friends and family give their recollections of the twisted things he did as a kid and young adult before his violent death, stories as improbable as the all-American tall tale, only really gross. Gross, but fiercely smart, and in Palahniuk's signature way of raging against the deadening sterility of modern life." PopMatters

Palaia, Marian

The **given** world; A Novel. Marian Palaia. Simon & Schuster 2015 224 p. $25

ISBN 1476777934; 9781476777931

LC 2014017676

In this book, by Marian Palaia, "Riley is thirteen, and her brother Mick has gone missing in Vietnam. . . . At sixteen, she meets a boy from the reservation. He becomes her first love and perhaps her deliverance, except that he, too, is sent to fight, unaware that Riley is carrying his child. Riley sets off then, in search of answers, of clues, of a way to be in the world. She travels from her family's Montana farm to San Francisco, and from there to Saigon." (Publisher's note)

"The plot of The Given World is troublesome, both in concept (the author doesn't fully comes to grips with the cruelty of Riley's abandonment of her parents and son) and execution (the many men who are instantly charmed by Riley, eager to help her over the years). But there is no denying Palaia's immense writing talent. She is able to convey three pieces of information in one elegant sentence, and she writes paragraphs that build meaning upon metaphorical meaning that leave your highlighter used up and dry—and you anticipating her next novel." Booklist

Paley, Grace

★ The **collected** stories. Farrar, Straus & Giroux 1994 386p $27.50

ISBN 0-374-12636-4

LC 93-42230

This volume includes stories from three previously published collections

Palin, Michael, 1943-

The **truth**; Michael Palin. St. Martin's Press 2013 272 p. (hardcover) $24.99

ISBN 1250028248; 9781250028242

LC 2013010537

This book "details a journalist's quest to discover the truth about a reclusive environmental activist. Once, London journalist Keith Mabbut was an award-winning crusader, exposing chemical polluters, but now he's just another hack, . . . mourning his separation from his Polish wife, Krystyna, who's just announced she wants a divorce . . . . The good news is that a top publisher wants him to do a book on Hamish Melville, the elderly, widely admired environmentalist," if Keith can find him. (Kirkus Reviews)

Palliser, Charles

★ The **quincunx**. Ballantine Bks. 1990 788p

LC 89-91787

"This is not an ironic parody à la Barth, not an echo of Eco, but a genuine reproduction of a full-bodied 19th-century page-turner of a novel, set in late Regency England, thick with characters of all classes, with plots, counterplots, fore-bodings, reversals and interpolated tales. . . . Mr. Palliser's re-creation of this period is absolutely convincing, his dialogue never jars, his command of details never falters." N Y Times Book Rev

Palliser, Charles

Rustication; a novel. by Charles Palliser. W W Norton & Co Inc 2013 336 p. $25.95

ISBN 0393088723; 9780393088724

LC 2013031249

In this book by Charles Palliser, "it is winter 1863, and Richard Shenstone, aged seventeen, has been sent down" "rusticated"—from Cambridge under a cloud of suspicion. Addicted to opium and tormented by sexual desire, he finds temporary refuge in a dilapidated old mansion on the southern English coast inhabited by his newly impoverished mother and his sister. Soon . . .Richard finds himself the leading suspect in a series of crimes and misdemeanors ranging from vivisection to murder." (Publisher's note)

Palliser, Charles

The **unburied**. Farrar, Straus & Giroux 1999 403p $25

ISBN 0-374-28035-5

LC 99-14740

"All the murders are puzzles, and Palliser constructs his plot like a maze and lures his readers into it. The book's ruthless consistency of style and the somewhat bleak view of humankind set it apart from the usual thriller." New Yorker

Palma, Felix J.

The **map** of time; Félix J. Palma ; translated by Nick Caistor. Atria Books 2011 611p. (Map of time) (hbk.) $26.00

ISBN 9781439167397; 1439167397; 143916746X; 9781439167465

LC 2010047304

Originally published in Spain in 2008

"In 1896 England, aristocratic Andrew Harrington plans to take his own life, despondent over the death years earlier of his lover, the last victim of Jack the Ripper. Meanwhile, 21-year-old Claire Haggerty plots to escape her restrictive role as a woman in Victorian society by journeying to the year 2000. A new commercial concern, Murray's Time Travel, offers such a trip for a hefty fee. Finally, Scotland Yarder Colin Garrett believes that the fatal wound on a murder victim could only have been caused by a weapon from the future. Linking all three stories is H.G. Wells, the author of The Time Machine." (Publishers Weekly)

Other titles in this series are:

The map of the sky (2012)

The map of chaos (2015)

Palmer, Daniel, 1969-

Helpless; Daniel Palmer. Kensington 2012 409 p.

ISBN 9780758246653

LC 2011937865

In this novel, "[f]ollowing his ex-wife's murder, things go from terrible to worse for New Hampshire high-school soccer coach Tom Hawkins, who is falsely implicated in a child-pornography ring, accused of sleeping with his 16-year-old daughter Jill's best friend and targeted by an old military pal who was involved in smuggling heroin from Germany with the dead wife. . . . [Tom's] daughter was already mad enough at him thanks to all the terrible things her mother told her about him. . . . Now their long-unheard-from third wheel overseas appears on the scene. . . . [Tom's] old high school nemesis [is] the cop assigned to the case and other town folk [want] bad things to happen to this good person." (Kirkus)

Palmer, Dexter

The **dream** of perpetual motion; [by] Dexter Palmer. St. Martin's Press 2010 340p $24.99

ISBN 978-0-312-55815-4; 0-312-55815-5

LC 2009-40231

"Palmer takes elements from Nabokov, Neal Stephenson, Steven Millhauser and 'The Tempest,' tosses them into a retro-futuristic blender and hits 'purée.' The result is a singular riff on steampunk—sophisticated, subversive entertainment that never settles for escapism." N Y Times Book Rev

Palmer, Dexter

★ **Version** control; A Novel. Dexter Palmer. Pantheon Books 2016 512 p. $27.95

ISBN 0307907597; 9780307907592

LC 2015018879

This book, by Dexter Palmer, is "about the effects of science and technology on our friendships, our love lives, and our sense of self. Rebecca Wright has reclaimed her life, finding her way out of her grief and depression following a personal tragedy years ago. She spends her days working in customer support for the internet dating site where she first met her husband. But she has a strange, persistent sense that everything around her is somewhat off-kilter." (Publisher's note)

"A Mobius strip of a novel in which time is more a loop than a path and various possibilities seem to exist simultaneously." Kirkus

Palmer, Liza

Nowhere but home; Liza Palmer. HarperCollins 2013 384 p. (paperback) $14.99

ISBN 0062007475; 9780062007476

In this novel, by Liza Palmer, "after Queenie Wake is dismissed from her restaurant job, she returns to North Star. . . . Hopeful that the bad memories of her late mother and promiscuous sister . . . have been forgotten by the locals, Queenie discovers that some people can't be forgotten--heartbreaker Everett Coburn--her old high-school sweetheart. When secrets from the past emerge, will Queenie be able to stick by her family or will she leave home again?" (Publisher's note)

Palmer, Michael

The **fifth** vial. St. Martin's Press 2007 372p $25.95

ISBN 0-312-34351-5; 978-0-312-34351-4

LC 2006-50971

"Palmer is adept at tapping into people's natural fear of disease, doctors, and hospitals and converting that fear into unnerving suspense. In this . . . medical thriller, Palmer plays with the phenomenon of organ donation, forcing the reader to ask nervously, 'Where do donated organs come from?' The answer comes slowly, in the best medical-thriller tradition." Booklist

Palmer, Michael

The **last** surgeon. St. Martin's Press 2010 373p $26.99

ISBN 978-0-312-58749-9; 0-312-58749-X

LC 2009-39234

"Palmer's latest has an appealing couple at its center, plus good pacing and gritty action to keep the pages turning." Libr J

Palmer, Michael

Miracle cure. Bantam Bks. 1998 399p $23.95

ISBN 0-553-10523-X

LC 98-4884

A medical thriller revolving around a new drug "called Vasclear, a heart medication being developed at the Boston Heart Institute by Newbury Pharmaceuticals. The FDA is being pressured by a Massachusetts senator (who, it turns out, is secretly taking Vasclear himself) to approve the release of the drug. And Vasclear may be the magic wand that can save the life of Jack 'Coach' Holbrook, whose health is declining after a quintuple bypass. Coach's son, Brian . . . not only faces the ethical dilemma of stealing the drug if he can't place his father as a test patient but also finds evidence of potentially dangerous side effects—evidence that could derail the drug's release to the public." Publ Wkly

Palmer, Michael

The **patient**. Bantam Bks. 2000 324p $24.95

ISBN 0-553-10983-9

LC 99-57838

This medical thriller features "Dr. Jessie Copeland, a neurosurgeon in her 40s with a combined under-graduate degree in biology and mechanical engineering. Now working under egomaniacal chief surgeon Carl Gilbride at a top Boston hospital, Jessie gets to try out ARTIE (Assisted Robotic Tissue Incision and Extraction) on cadavers, while Gilbride coaxes foundations to cough up millions for the revolutionary new procedure. Attracted by the media attention, . . . shadowy terrorist Claude Malloche, known as 'the Mist,' who also has a brain tumor, comes to the hospital for treatment—and winds up holding patients and staff hostage in case the operation fails. It's finally up to Jessie and a rogue CIA agent to keep everyone healthy." Publ Wkly

Includes bibliographical references (p. 324)

Palmer, Michael

The **society**. Bantam Bks. 2004 351p $25

ISBN 0-553-90057-9

LC 2004-303038

This thriller begins "with the murder of several loathsome CEOs of HMOs in Massachusetts. Dr. Will Grant is a talented and caring physician in the Boston area who works long hours and hates the unfair and obstructive practices of the big insurance companies. Patty Moriarity is a rookie state cop whose first big case is investigating the deaths of the health care vultures. After some early research, Patty suspects Will, but soon enough that's all straightened out and they're smooching on the couch. After Will is drugged and collapses during a delicate operation, things get rough: he's kicked out of his hospital for drug abuse and sued. Next he's being tortured, while Patty, shot after attempting to save the boorish chauvinist detective who has taken over her case, lies in a coma. The action is a bit preachy in the beginning, but once Palmer gets all his characters in place, the suspense builds." Publ Wkly

Palwick, Susan

Mending the moon; Susan Palwick. Tor 2013 336 p. (hardcover) $24.99

ISBN 0765327589; 9780765327581

LC 2012043362

In this novel by Susan Palwick, "Melinda Soto . . ., vacationing in Mexico, is murdered by a fellow American tourist. She leaves behind her adopted son, Jeremy [and] a circle of friends: Veronique, the academic stuck in a teaching job from which she can't retire; Rosemary, who's losing her husband to Alzheimer's; Henrietta, the priest at Rosemary's and Melinda's church. An invitation to them all, from the murderer's mother, to come to Seattle for his memorial [brings] a chance to heal." (Publisher's note)

Palwick, Susan

★ The **necessary** beggar; Susan Palwick. Tor 2005 316p $24.95

ISBN 076531097X ; 9780765310972

LC 2005041919

Alex Award (2006)

This book follows a family from "Gandiffri, a world of peace and abundance," who are exiled to Earth. "Twenty-something Darroti and a devout young noblewoman, Gallicina, fall in love. . . . Darroti comes to be accused of murdering her and his sentenced to exile in another dimension. . . . Darroti's father, brothers, and the latter's wives and children accompany him. Taking only what they can carry, they walk through a strange blue door and into a refugee camp in Nevada. There Darroti . . . commits suicide, which marks each remaining family member differently. . . . Yet the magic of Gandiffri isn't lost to them. It lives in a tiny, undying pet beetle; in the unbreakable bond of Darroti and Gallicina; in a ghost seeking redemption; and in the healing power of love." (Booklist)

Palwick, Susan

Shelter. Tor 2007 576p pa $15.95

ISBN 978-0-312-86602-0; 0-312-86602-X

LC 2007-7316

"Palwick has built a rich and complex possible future, complete with political and religious systems, rapid and extraordinary technological advancement, and all the moral polarization that naturally follows such developments." Strange Horizons

Pamuk, Orhan

The **museum** of innocence; translated from the Turkish by Maureen Freely. Alfred A. Knopf 2009 535p il map $28.95

ISBN 0-307-26676-1; 978-0-307-26676-7

LC 2009-19475

Original Turkish edition, 2008

In this novel "a privileged Istanbul resident named Kemal tells of his obsession with Fusun, a beautiful shopgirl." (N Y Times Book Rev) Index.

"Pamuk is brilliant at the human parade, and especially at humiliation in its masculine forms, frequently played out in Istanbul along East-West tensions." Cleveland Plain Dealer

Pamuk, Orhan, 1952-

★ **My** name is Red; translated from the Turkish by Erdag Göknar. Knopf 2001 417p

ISBN 0-375-40695-6

LC 2001-29866

Original Turkish edition, 1998

This is a novel by the author of The Black Book, The New Life and The White Castle. It "is set in the late 16th century, during the reign of {the Turkish} Sultan Murat III, a patron of the miniaturists whose art had come over from Persia. . . . {The story} tells of two murders among Murat's court artists; one of Elegant, a master miniaturist, the other of Enishte, a . . . figure commissioned by the sultan to produce a book by his four finest artists. . . . The style the sultan's artists are surreptitiously instructed to adopt . . . is that of the Italian Renaissance." (N Y Times Book Rev)

"The Ottoman Istanbul, which Mr. Pahmuk depicts with skill and linguistic energy, is a rich, cruel and claustrophobic world where art leads, through dark alleyways to murder. The novel is also about the conflicts of Turkishness, about . . . a society caught between religious zealotry and an authoritarian state—themes as relevant to Turkey now as they were 400 years ago." Economist

Pamuk, Orhan, 1952-

The **red**-haired woman; Orhan Pamuk ; translated from the Turkish by Ekin Oklap. Alfred A. Knopf 2017 253 p. (hardcover) $26.95

ISBN 9780451494429; 9780451494436

LC 2016057733

In this novel, by Orhan Pamuk, "on the outskirts of a town thirty miles from Istanbul, a master well digger and his young apprentice are hired to find water on a barren plain. . . . The pair will come to depend on each other and exchange stories reflecting disparate views of the world. But in the nearby town, where they buy provisions and take their evening break, the boy will find an irresistible diversion. The Red-Haired Woman, an alluring member of a travelling theatre company." (Publisher's note)

"As usual, Pamuk handles weighty material deftly, and the result is both puzzling and beautiful." Booklist

Pamuk, Orhan, 1952-

Silent house; by Orhan Pamuk ; translated from the Turkish by Robert Finn. Alfred A. Knopf 2012 334 p. $26.95

ISBN 0307700283; 9780307700285

LC 2012005468

This novel by Orhan Pamuk, translated by Robert Finn, "is the story of a Turkish family gathering in the shadow of the impending military coup of 1980. . . . A widow, Fatma, awaits the annual summer visit of her grandchildren. . . . The eldest, Faruk, a dissipated historian, wallows in alcohol. . . . His sensitive leftist sister, Nilgün, has yet to discover the real-life consequences of highminded politics; and Metin, a high school nerd . . . fantasizes about going to America." (Publisher's note)

Pamuk, Orhan, 1952-

★ **Snow**; translated by Maureen Freely. Knopf 2004 426p

ISBN 0375406972

Original Turkish edition, 2002

This novel concerns the conflict between Islamism and secularism (the legacy of Ataturk) in contemporary Turkey. Ka, the protagonist, "a blocked poet and one time radical, . . . returns from Germany after 12 years' exile to get back in touch with his country. A newspaper assignment takes him to {Kars}, a town near the Georgian border, to investigate a rumor . . . about a wave of schoolgirls who killed themselves when ordered to remove their head scarves. . . . There is an old Communist who tolerates a daughter's head scarf as a rebellion against the establishment, and a newspaper editor who publishes as past events those that are still to take place. . . . {Ka} is chilled and infuriated by Blue, a lethal yet childlike underground activist. . . . He becomes involved with Sunay, a theater impresario and former leftist who . . . glories in having achieved a supreme work of art, one whose dramatic culmination will be his own death onstage." (N Y Times (Late N Y Ed))

"Upon returning to his home in secular Turkey, a poet named Ka discovers two things that will change his life: Ipek, the girl he loved as a child, still lives in the city of Kars, and the community has been stunned by a rash of suicides of zealously religious girls who refused to remove their head scarves while in public. With an investigator's eye, Ka seeks out information about the tragedies from all sources, eventually leading to the man at the eye of the storm "Blue," a charismatic Islamite who will not let the message that these girls carried be silenced." Libr J

Pamuk, Orhan, 1952-

★ A **strangeness** in my mind; Orhan Pamuk. Alfred A. Knopf 2015 624 p. illustration; gen. table $28.95

ISBN 9780307700292

LC 2015006769

This novel, by Orhan Pamuk, is "the unforgettable tale of an Istanbul street vendor and the love of his life. Since his boyhood in a poor village in Central Anatolia, Mevlut Karataş has fantasized about what his life would become. . . . But luck never seems to be on Mevlut's side. As he watches his relations settle down and make their fortunes, he spends three years writing love letters to a girl he saw just once at a wedding, only to elope by mistake with her sister." (Publisher's note)

"If anything, Pamuk recalls the great Victorian novelists as he ranges confidently from near-documentary passages on real estate machinations and the privatization of electrical service to pensive meditations on the gap between people's public posturing and private beliefs. The oppression of women is quietly but angrily depicted as endemic... As Pamuk follows his believably flawed protagonist and a teeming cast of supporting players across five decades, Turkey's turbulent politics provide a thrumming undercurrent of unease. Rich, complex, and pulsing with urban life: one of this gifted writer's best." Kirkus

Pancake, Ann

Strange as this weather has been; a novel. Shoemaker & Hoard 2007 360p pa $15.95

ISBN 978-1-59376-166-0; 1-59376-166-X

LC 2007-11838

"With her beloved West Virginia hollows and valleys under constant onslaught by a savage coal-mining industry whose raping of the land threatens her home with devastating floods, Lace Ricker finds herself battling callous forces both without and within her own family. As thunderous blasts weaken their home's foundation and poisoned wastewater infiltrates their well, Lace and her daughter, Bant, secretly become more determined to find a way to stop the mines, while Lace's husband pragmatically refuses to fight the union bosses, and her sons tentatively, then calamitously, accept the challenges and adventure of life lived in the shadow of imminent danger. By tracing the devastating impact of coal mining through the eyes of Lace and her four children, Pancake's powerful debut novel evinces a poetic pathos and authentic respect for the land and the people who love it." Booklist

Parameswaran, Rajesh

I am an executioner; love stories. Rajesh Parameswaran. Knopf 2012 259 p.

ISBN 0307595927; 9780307595928

LC 2011033754

The infamous Bengal Ming -- The strange career of Dr. Raju Gopalarajan -- Four Rajeshes -- I am an executioner -- Demons -- Narrative of Agent 97-4702 -- Bebhutibhushhan Mallik's final storyboard -- Elephants in captivity (part one) -- On the banks of the Table River (Planet Lucinda, Andromeda Galaxy, AD 2319).

This book is a collection of love stories from author Rajesh Parameswaran. In one story, "although the executioner takes pride in doing his job well, he hid the true nature of his work from his new, now deeply depressed wife and is, therefore, exiled to the couch. . . . A thoughtful zoo tiger is only trying to express love when he inadvertently goes on a killing spree. . . . [Another is a] story about an aging art director helplessly in love with the wife of a world-famous filmmaker." (Booklist)

Paretsky, Sara

Bitter medicine. Morrow 1987 321p

LC 86-33238

"A young Hispanic woman and her premature infant die in a wealthy suburban hospital. Her doctor is found beaten to death the next day. As a favor to Lottie Herschel, her long-time friend and mentor, Chicago private investigator and lawyer V. I. Warshawski agrees to look into the case. Abortion and medical ethics are the backdrop for this powerful and moving novel." Libr J

Paretsky, Sara

Blacklist; a V.I. Warshawski novel. Putnam 2003 415p $24.95

ISBN 0-399-15085-4

LC 2003-43157

"A dead reporter, a missing Egyptian boy wanted in connection with terrorist activities, and an elderly woman convinced that an intruder is in her family manse are all elements of Paretsky's . . . novel featuring Chicago private investigator V. I. Warshawski. As V. I. looks into these peoples' lives, she discovers connections among them. She uncovers a story of betrayal and secrets that spans several generations and involves Chicago's wealthiest families, the Red Scare, and the House Un-American Activities Committee hearings of the 1950s. As always, V. I.'s determined pursuit of the truth ensures at least a few heart-stopping moments." Libr J

Paretsky, Sara

Bleeding Kansas. G.P. Putnam's Sons 2008 431p $25.95; pa $9.99

ISBN 978-0-399-15405-8; 978-0-451-22448-4 pa

LC 2007-35962

"Set in the rural Kaw River Valley, where the author grew up, and sparked by a feud between two families that pioneered this farm region during the 1850s, the multigenerational narrative bristles with the kind of prickly social issues that give substance to Paretsky's detective stories. . . . The blood-boiling issue in Bleeding Kansas is religious intolerance. Bigotry comes naturally to the members of the Schapen clan, who worship at the Salvation Through the Blood of Jesus Full Bible Church and become apoplectic when Gina Haring, a New York lesbian and New Age Wiccan, moves into an old farmhouse and attempts to practice her beliefs. . . . Any inclination on the part of the reader to sympathize with the Schapens (for being born and bred stupid) in this barnyard feud are wiped out when Chip Grellier, who joins the Army after being suspended from school for a fight started by his Schapen tormentors, is killed in Iraq. But the Schapens do provide much black humor by breeding the 'perfect red heifer' referred to in the Old Testament, creating an international storm that ensnares both fundamentalist Christians and ultraorthodox Jews." N Y Times Book Rev

Paretsky, Sara, 1947-

★ **Breakdown**; Sara Paretsky. G. P. Putnam's Sons 2012 431p

ISBN 9780399157837

LC 2011047676

This book tells the fictional story of "pre-teens who are crazy about a series of books featuring 'Carmilla,' a shapeshifter who can turn into a raven. In the Carmilla books, there's a lot of werewolf and vampire activity too. . . . In 'Breakdown,' V.I. (which is short for Victoria Iphigenia . . .), stumbles across the girls doing some sort of initiation ceremony in a dark cemetery in the rain. All the girls are out after curfew and V.I.'s cousin Petra has been frantic to know where they are. After V.I. rounds them up, they turn to leave, only to find that a man has been laid out on a tomb perilously close to where the girls were frolicking, and he's been pierced through the heart with a large hunk of steel. Instead of leaving in the orderly way planned, everyone goes screaming through the night, and it's V.I. who has to explain everything to the police. . . . V.I. (or Vic, as some call her) dashes from the homes of the rich girls' parents to the bleak mental hospital to the right-wing news station, all trying to make the facts fit together." (Technorati.com)

Paretsky, Sara, 1947-

★ **Brush** back; by Sara Paretsky. G. P. Putnam's Sons 2015 480 p. $27.95

ISBN 9780399160578

LC 2015005018

In this book, by Sara Paretsky, "back in high school, V.I. thought she was in love with Frank. He broke up with her, she went off to college, he started driving trucks for Bagby Haulage. She forgot about him until the day his mother was convicted of bludgeoning his kid sister, Annie, to death. Stella Guzzo . . . did a full twenty-five years for her daughter's murder. Newly released from prison, Stella is looking for exoneration, so Frank asks V.I. for help." (Publisher's note)

"Paretsky, who plots more conscientiously than anyone else in the field, digs deep, then deeper, into past and present until all is revealed. The results will be especially appealing to baseball fans, who'll appreciate the punning chapter titles and learn more than they ever imagined about Wrigley Field." Kirkus

Paretsky, Sara, 1947-

Fallout; a V.I. Warshawski novel. Sara Paretsky. William Morrow 2017 x, 433 p.p (V.I. Warshawski) (hardcover) $27.99

ISBN 9780062435835; 9780062435842; 0062435841

LC 2017296649

This book, by Sara Paretsky, features "V. I. Warshawski. To her parents, she's Victoria Iphigenia. To her friends, she's Vic. But to clients seeking her talents as a detective, she's V.I. And her new case will lead her from her native Chicago and into Kansas, on the trail of a vanished film student and a faded Hollywood star. . . . V.I. tracks her quarry through a university town, across fields where missile silos once flourished—and into a past riven by long-simmering racial tensions." (Publisher's note)

"Paretsky is at the top of her game here, evidenced by the satisfying, layered puzzle peopled by a vividly described and intriguing cast." Booklist

Paretsky, Sara

Fire sale. Putnam 2005 402p $25.95

ISBN 0-399-15279-2

LC 2005-47601

This entry draws V. I. Warshawski "back to her South Chicago roots when she reluctantly agrees to coach the girls basketball team at her former high school, which is struggling with poverty, teen pregnancy, a lack of equipment, and gang influence. The old neighborhood has declined, too, and when a small local factory is sabotaged, V.I. is persuaded to investigate. Meanwhile, she hopes to gain financial support for the basketball team from By-Smart, a megadiscount chain whose founder also grew up in South Chicago. In a series of events that includes an explosion at the local factory, a horrifying murder, and the disappearance of a basketball player, V.I. is drawn into a deadly conflict between By-Smart and South Chicago's residents. Fast-paced and as entertaining." Libr J

Paretsky, Sara

Ghost country. Delacorte Press 1998 386p $24.95

ISBN 0-385-29933-8

LC 98-12294

Chicagoans "Harriet and Mara Stonds have been raised in luxury by their grandfather, famous neurosurgeon Abraham Stonds. Harriet is the apple of her grandfather's eye—tall, blond, successful at everything she does, always the good girl. Mara plays the role of ugly stepsister, at least to her grandfather, who has told her for years that she's lazy, stupid, and ungrateful. But things are about to change for the Stonds family. A drunken opera singer, a softhearted psychotherapist, a group of homeless women, and a mysterious visitor who performs miracles will each play a key role in opening the eyes of Harriet and Mara to a world they've never imagined. This book is rich, astonishing, and affecting." Booklist

Paretsky, Sara

√**Guardian** angel. Delacorte Press 1992 370p

LC 91-24976

While investigating a local manufacturer Chicago private eye V.I. Warshawski uncovers a bond-parking scheme that reaches into her ex-husband's law firm and ties into the bizarre behavior of her neighbors

"The plot serves nicely to bring V.I. into contact with tough, down-and-out types, whom Ms. Paretsky draws extremely well. . . . Bits and pieces of V.I.'s background are worked into the narrative unobtrusively, so that we come to know her as the story progresses, the way we come to know people in real life." N Y Times Book Rev

Paretsky, Sara

√**Hard** time; a V.I. Warshawski novel. Delacorte Press 1999 384p $24.95

ISBN 0-385-31363-2

LC 99-22214

When V. I. Warshawski "swerves to avoid a body lying in the middle of the road, she never imagines that her search for the reasons behind the vicious beating death of Nicola Aguinaldo will take her from the upper classes of Chicago society to a long stint behind bars at a private women's prison overrun with sadistic guards and almost equally threatening inmates." Libr J

Paretsky, Sara

√**Hardball**. G.P. Putnam's Sons 2009 446p $26.95

ISBN 978-0-399-15593-2; 0-399-15593-7

LC 2009-20700

"The thing about Sara Paretsky is, she's tough—not because she observes the bonebreaker conventions of the private-eye genre but because she doesn't flinch from examining old social injustices others might find too shameful (and too painful) to dig up." N Y Times Book Rev

Paretsky, Sara

★ **Total** recall; a V.I. Warshawski novel. Delacorte Press 2001 414p

ISBN 0-385-31366-7

LC 2001-28801

This mystery "is written with the stylistic verve and intellectual energy of a writer just coming into her own." N Y Times Book Rev

Paretsky, Sara

Tunnel vision. Delacorte Press 1994 432p

LC 94-6050

Chicago private detective V.I. Warshawski uncovers a "cynical swindle when she tries to help a wretched family she finds living in the basement of her office building. After getting the bum's rush from an advocacy group for the homeless and from feminist friends protecting their own grants, V.I. sticks out her jaw and goes it alone on this dirty, complicated fraud case. Mustn't feel sorry for V.I., though, because her outrage gives her the strength to take on the whole corrupt establishment. This principled private eye intimidates people because she doesn't know the meaning of compromise and won't tolerate moral slackers." N Y Times Book Rev

Paretsky, Sara

Windy City blues; V. I. Warshawski stories. Delacorte Press 1995 258p

LC 95-8302

"Although V.I.'s just as feisty and tough-talking as ever, she presents a somewhat softer side in this series of stories that gives a nostalgic nod to Vic's friends, family, and past." Booklist

Parini, Jay

The **passages** of H.M. a novel of Herman Melville. Doubleday 2010 454p $26.95

ISBN 978-0-385-52277-9; 0-385-52277-0

LC 2010-06291

"Most intriguing . . . is the way Parini weaves elements from Melville's writings into his account of the author's life and travels. . . . Even if you've read none of Melville, or remember only echoes from readings long ago, the narrative is complete, the literary facts clear enough to sustain its powerful drama. And for those who know Melville well, 'The Passages of H.M.' is a labor of love and inspiration." Cleveland Plain Dealer

Park, Patricia

Re Jane; Patricia Park. Penguin Group USA 2015 352 p. (hbk.) $27.95

ISBN 0525427406; 9780525427407

LC 2015288096

In this novel, by Patricia Park, "Jane Re . . . [is] thrilled to become the au pair for the Mazer-Farleys, two Brooklyn English professors and their adopted Chinese daughter. . . . Jane is the recipient of . . . Ed Farley's very male attention. But when a family death interrupts Jane and Ed's blossoming affair, she flies off to Seoul, leaving New York far behind. . . . [When] Jane returns to Queens, where she must find a balance between two cultures and accept who she really is." (Publisher's note)

"This brightly written and engrossing read takes Jane Eyre and turns it into a lesson about self-acceptance. It will appeal to readers who enjoy modern retellings of classic literature, as well as fans of Jean Kwok and Ha Jin." LJ

Park, Samuel

This burns my heart; Samuel Park. Simon & Schuster 2011 288p.

ISBN 9781439199619

LC 2010043441

This book presents a "love story set in the . . . landscape of postwar South Korea. On the eve of marriage to her weak, timid fiancé, Soo-Ja falls in love with a young medical student. But out of duty to her family and her culture she turns him away, choosing instead a world that leaves her trapped by suffocating customs. In a country torn between past and present, Soo-Ja struggles to find happiness in a loveless marriage and to carve out a successful future for her only daughter. Forced by tradition to move in with her in-laws, she must navigate the dangers of a cruel household and pay the price of choosing the wrong husband." (Publisher's note)

Parker, Barbara

Criminal justice. Dutton 1997 304p

LC 96-44143

The author "has written a brutal commentary on the Miami music scene, offering unforgettable characters and some hilarious potshots at suburbia." Libr J

Parker, Barbara

Suspicion of betrayal; a novel. Dutton 1999 347p $23.95

ISBN 0-525-94468-0

LC 98-52080

This suspense novel features Miami "attorney Gail Connon, whose love affair with high-powered defense attorney Anthony Quintana is going full-speed ahead. Gail's plate is way too full as she tries to save her struggling solo practice while addressing a custody dispute with her ex over their 10-year-old daughter, Karen. Just when Gail thinks everything's under control, the bottom falls out when Karen starts receiving anonymous death threats." Booklist

Parker, Barbara

Suspicion of deceit. Dutton 1998 358p $23.95

ISBN 0-525-94401-X

LC 97-38429

"The narrative triumphs, . . . thanks to Parker's rich mix of tropical politics, edgy romance and secrets from the past." Publ Wkly

Parker, Barbara

Suspicion of vengeance. Dutton 2001 359p $23.95

ISBN 0-525-94601-2

LC 2001-33521

Gail Connor "is asked to take on the case of an old family friend's grandson, Kenny Ray Clark, who was convicted of the stabbing death of a housewife over a decade earlier, indirectly causing the death of her infant son. Now, after 11 years on death row, his appeals are about to run out. Anthony, Gail's on-again, off-again fiancé, himself a high-powered Florida attorney, warns her of the futility of trying to save Clark. But Gail digs into the records and finds, among other things, a drunk defense attorney, a bogus confession and a witness who would have provided an alibi but was threatened by police." Publ Wkly

Parker, K. J.

The **company**. Orbit 2008 419p $24.99

ISBN 978-0-316-03853-9; 0-316-03853-9

LC 2008-35282

The author "blends gritty military fantasy with the 18th-century 'island story' tradition. Seven years after the end of a war between unnamed countries, four friends who fought together have settled back into civilian life. Then their former leader, Kunessin, now a celebrated and embittered general, turns up and reminds them of their old pledge to retire together to a peaceful island. Better yet, he's found a suitable place and will fund the venture. A local matchmaker finds women smart and desperate enough to be colonists, and they marry the ex-soldiers in a group wedding that sets the tone of the book: humorous, grim and utterly unromantic. The would-be republicans soon reach the island and settle in, but the discovery of gold in a stream changes everything." Publ Wkly

Parker, K. J.

Devices and desires. Little, Brown 2007 635p (Engineer trilogy) pa $12.99

ISBN 978-0-316-00338-4; 0-316-00338-7

LC 2007-9926

First published 2005 in the United Kingdom

"When engineer Ziani Vaatzes is sentenced to death for building a device that differs from the official standards, he manages to flee from his home in the Guild-controlled Republic of Mezentia and find refuge in the enemy country of Eremia. To ensure his safety, he offers to teach Mezentine engineering techniques to the technologically ignorant Eremians, so that they can build weapons equal to those of their Mezentine enemies. Eremia's Duke Orsea reluctantly gives his approval, unwittingly laying himself and those he loves open to the machinations of a man out for vengeance against the country that condemned his work as well as the enemy who gave him succor. . . . [A] richly textured and emotionally complex fantasy." Libr J

Parker, K. J.

Sharps; K.J. Parker. Orbit 2012 471 p. (paperback) $15.99

ISBN 031617775X; 9780316177757

LC 2011944517

In this novel by K. J. Parker "an uneasy truce has been called between two neighbouring kingdoms. The war has been long and brutal, fought over the usual things: resources, land, money. . . . Now, there is a chance for peace. Diplomatic talks have begun and with them, the games. Two teams of fencers represent their nations at this pivotal moment. When the future of the world lies balanced on the point of a rapier, one misstep could mean ruin for all." (Publisher's note)

Parker, Robert B.

★ **Appaloosa**. Putnam 2005 276p $24.95

ISBN 0-399-15277-6

LC 2004-58745

In this western, "deputy Everett Hitch recounts the struggle between lawman Virgil Cole and outlaw rancher Randall Bragg for control of the little town of Appaloosa. Modeled on Wyatt Earp, Cole is the kind of man who never loses a fight, and he comes close to taking down the murderous Bragg with ease, until Bragg's hired guns rescue him by abducting Cole's romantic interest and using her as a hostage. This precipitates a long chase, a struggle with wandering Kiowa, and a gunfight reminiscent of the OK Corral. The story gallops along to a surprise ending, but beneath the trappings of this gunfighter novel, Parker really has something to say about the nature of men and women in the Old West." Libr J

Parker, Robert B.

Back story. Putnam 2003 291p $24.95

ISBN 0-399-14977-5

LC 2002-36901

"The repartee between Spenser and Hawk is fast and funny; the sentiment between Spenser and Susan and the musings about Spenser's code are only occasionally cloying; and there's a scattering of remarkable action scenes including a tense shootout in Harvard Stadium." Publ Wkly

Parker, Robert B.

Blue-eyed devil. G.P. Putnam's Sons 2010 276p $25.95

ISBN 978-0-399-15648-9; 0-399-15648-8

LC 2010-03109

"More shifting allegiances, moral dilemmas and characters capable of change than Virgil and Everett's fans may be used to. It's a shame that this youngest of the late Parker's franchises has to end so soon." Kirkus

Parker, Robert B.

Brimstone. G.P. Putnam's Sons 2009 293p $25.95

ISBN 978-0-399-15571-0; 0-399-15571-6

LC 2009-08107

"Parker's gunslinging saddle pals Virgil Cole and Everett Hitch return for their third adventure. . . . Here, Virgil and Everett rescue Allie French, Virgil's former sweetie who ran off to become a prostitute, and head to Brimstone, where the two gunmen sign on as deputy sheriffs. Brimstone, however, doesn't exactly provide a quiet respite for this trio. Virgil and Allie have a hard time getting over his hurt and her shame, a mysterious Indian is killing local folks and leaving taunting messages, and brutal saloon owner Pike and corrupt preacher Brother Percival are headed for a showdown. . . . The result is classic Parker—exciting, suspenseful, fast-moving and entertaining." Publ Wkly

Parker, Robert B.
Chance. Putnam 1996 307p
LC 95-49950

"Parker's stouthearted hero proves that he is still as tough and manly as they come, and more principled than ever in this punchy private-eye caper." N Y Times Book Rev

Parker, Robert B.
Cold service. Putnam 2005 305p $24.95
ISBN 0-399-15240-7
LC 2004-56608

"As the tale begins, the heretofore-indestructible Hawk is recovering from a near-death experience: shot in the back while protecting a bookie from the upstart Ukrainian Mob. It's payback time, of course, but not before Hawk nurses himself back to psychic and physical health. Meanwhile, Spenser does a bit of sleuthing on his own, determining that Hawk's assailants are the tip of a Ukrainian iceberg that has stuck its tentacles deep into Boston's underworld. Payback, Hawk style, requires eliminating not just the shooters but also the entire Mob. The action comes in a rush near the end, but the satisfying part here is watching Parker dig deeply into the remarkable friendship between two tough guys constitutionally averse to the whole touchy-feely side of life." Booklist

Parker, Robert B.
Death in paradise. Putnam 2001 294p
ISBN 0-399-14779-9
LC 2001-31874

"Given his raw nerves, bursts of violence and unhealthy devotion to his ex-wife, Jesse is still unpredictable and a little scary. Let's trust Parker to keep him on the edge." N Y Times Book Rev

Parker, Robert B.
Double Deuce. Putnam 1992 224p
LC 91-29594

In this novel Spenser "finds himself, at the behest of his pal Hawk, defending the residents of a gang-terrorized Boston housing project known as Double Deuce. The drive-by shooting of a teenage mother and her child brings the duo into a confrontation with gangleader Major Johnson and his posse." Publ Wkly

Parker, Robert B.
Double play. Putnam 2004 288p $24.95
ISBN 0-399-15188-5
LC 2004-40029

"Parker pretty much defies category altogether in this deeply felt and intimately told memory tale, which takes place during the historic baseball season of 1947, when Jackie Robinson broke the color bar in major-league baseball by playing first base for the Brooklyn Dodgers. Fusing this chapter of sports history with a hardboiled gangster plot and haunting recollections of his own Boston boyhood, Parker fashions a hugely entertaining fiction that also serves as a blueprint for the themes that preoccupy him as a writer and the code of values that sustains his work." N Y Times Book Rev

Parker, Robert B.
Family honor. Putnam 1999 322p $22.95
ISBN 0-399-14566-4
LC 99-27488

Private detective Sunny Randall "is hired by a powerful family to find their runaway daughter, Millicent, who, it transpires, is hooking and needs rescuing. . . . Millicent, it happens, witnessed a conspiracy to murder arising from her cold, ambitious parents—her father aims to be governor—and the Italian mobsters who control them. The mobsters now want her dead, and Sunny, too, if need be. . . . The high suspense is equaled by the emotional power of Sunny's bonding with the damaged girl. A bravura performance." Publ Wkly

Parker, Robert B.
Gunman's rhapsody. Putnam 2001 289p
ISBN 0-399-14762-4
LC 00-53327

The novel "shows surprising fidelity to most of the known facts without letting them get in the way of a good story. Parker's strengths here, as in his crime novels, are plot and dialogue." N Y Times Book Rev

Parker, Robert B.
Hugger mugger. Putnam 2000 307p
ISBN 0-399-14587-7
LC 99-56105

"Culture shock brings out a certain waggishness in Spenser, who is fascinated by the elaborately staged lives of the horsy set and more amused than appalled by the character flaws he uncovers beneath all the polite gentility. Without compromising his expert sleuthing techniques . . . he manages to pick up enough regional skills to communicate with the devious natives in their own idiom—and catch them at their own wicked games." N Y Times Book Rev

Parker, Robert B.
Hush money. Putnam 1999 309p $22.95
ISBN 0-399-14458-7
LC 98-37344

In this mystery Boston private eye Spenser "is thrown by the lethal combination of sex (straight, gay, kinky) and politics (racial, sexual, academic) that erupts at a certain university in Cambridge when an African-American professor is implicated in the suicide of a militantly gay graduate student. In a situation that adds to his discomposure, Spenser finds himself being sexually hounded by a woman whom he has just rescued from the similarly unhealthy attentions of a former boyfriend." NY Times Book Rev

Parker, Robert B.
Melancholy baby. Putnam 2004 296p $24.95
ISBN 0-399-15218-0
LC 2004-50377

"Boston P.I. Sunny Randall is unhappy to learn that the ex-husband she still loves is getting married to someone else. Her life seemingly a mess, Sunny seeks the help of psychiatrist Susan Silverman. In between sessions that probe her relationship with her insufferable mother and beloved father, Sunny works on the case of Sarah Markham, a distraught 21-year-old woman who wants to track down her biological parents. The only trouble is that the couple who raised her claim she's theirs but refuse to take a DNA test to prove it. Sunny soon learns that Sarah's parents have lied about their past. . . . Parker, as always, leavens his story with sly wit while relying on dialog to advance the plot and develop character." Libr J

Parker, Robert B.
Now and then. G. P. Putnam's Sons 2007 296p $25.95
ISBN 978-0-399-15441-6; 0-399-15441-8
LC 2007-23056

In this "addition to the series, the troubled client is a husband who feels his wife has been behaving bizarrely. Spenser thinks she's probably having an affair, and through the magic of a planted listening device, he presents the worried husband with the damning evidence. The device has also picked up that the wife's lover is involved in a group called Last Hope, which turns out to be a kind of brokerage outlet for terrorists looking for equipment and other terrorists. The case has moved from the kind of private-eye work that Spenser finds sleazy to one with horrific ramifications. The story itself makes compelling reading on its own, but Parker, as usual, spikes it with caustic wit and the interplay between Spenser and his longtime love, Susan. And here he ups the ante by calling on Spenser to use all his brain and brawn to protect Susan. Terrific." Booklist

Parker, Robert B. ✓

Painted ladies. G.P. Putnam's Sons 2010 291p $26.95

ISBN 978-0-399-15685-4; 0-399-15685-2

LC 2010-20027

"The focus on Susan comes at the expense of the plot, which, as Spenser novels go, is fairly pedestrian. . . . The story gives us extended looks at two of the most-beloved Spenser side characters, homicide Capt. Martin Quirk and Sgt. Frank Belson, as well as brief nods to many of the others who have stood at Spenser's side in the past — Hawk, Vinnie, Chollo, Lee Farrell, Epstein, Tedy Sapp, the Grey Man. Mostly, though, what Painted Ladies gives us is Spenser being Spenser. And he couldn't do that without Susan." Chicago Sun-Times

Parker, Robert B. ✓

Potshot. Putnam 2001 294p

ISBN 0-399-14710-1

LC 00-68342

"Spenser takes on the job of clearing out a gang of @mountain trash' who are intimidating the residents of Potshot, Arizona. Even the supremely resourceful Spenser needs a little help with this one, so he drafts six of his compadres from previous adventures." Booklist

Parker, Robert B. ✓

Rough weather. G.P. Putnam's Sons 2008 294p $26.95

ISBN 978-0-399-15519-2; 0-399-15519-8

LC 2008-33702

"The familiar elements here include the child in distress, the wealthy with their own agenda, the killer with a code of honour, and an almost interminable repetition of the Spenser-Susan-Hawk mutual self-appreciation society. I'm not sure if Parker figures he's got to reprise the psychology between this triangle, . . . but he does and they do at great length here, to the detriment of what is otherwise a pretty interestingly plotted book. . . . Parker remains the master of the easy-reading, compelling, thriller." Crime Time

Parker, Robert B. ✓

School days. Putnam 2005 295p $24.95

ISBN 0-399-15323-3

LC 2005-74690

"A wealthy grandmother hires Spenser to clear her 17-year-old grandson of being the coconspirator and co-killer in a school shooting at a private school that has left five students, a teacher, and an administrator dead. The boy's buddy has named him, and he has confessed to the crime. Everyone–police, school officials, the defense lawyer, and the immediate family–has given up on the kid, but Spenser has never seen a slammed door he didn't long to break down. Soon he's questioning everyone in the kid's circle, looking for the chink in that slammed door. Along the way, he rummages through all sorts of closets in the privileged world of the private school, turning up links to the underworld." Booklist

Parker, Robert B. ✓

Sea change. Putnam 2006 295p $24.95

ISBN 0-399-15267-9

LC 2004-43150

"The body of an unidentified woman is found in a cove off the Massachusetts village of Paradise, where Jesse Stone, former L.A. homicide detective, is now chief of police. With no clues and a bevy of nonlocals in town for the annual sailboat competition, Stone must use every resource at his disposal to find out who the woman was, what happened to her, and why no one has reported her missing. . . . Parker is a master at creating memorable characters and crime stories that are inevitably tied to social issues of some importance." Libr J

Parker, Robert B. ✓

Shrink rap. Putnam 2002 304p $24.95

ISBN 0-399-14930-9

LC 2002-24826

The Sunny Randall novel "has the Boston private eye on a national book tour with a best-selling author who is being stalked by her former husband, an unethical and possibly unhinged psychiatrist. The situation proves ideal for Parker's patented brand of knowing humor, yielding glossary snapshots of dithering book dealers, dollar-driven publishers and awe-struck fans." N Y Times Book Rev

Parker, Robert B. ✓

Sixkill. G. P. Putnam's Sons 2011 293p map $26.95

ISBN 978-0-399-15726-4; 0-399-15726-3

LC 2010-48041

In this mystery, "a young woman is found dead in a Hollywood star's Boston hotel room. Looks like murder, smells like murder, but something doesn't sit right with police captain Quirk — he prefers surety, so he asks Spenser to nose around. The star, Jumbo Nelson, a self-absorbed pig, rubs everyone the wrong way but insists he didn't kill her. Jumbo's bodyguard, a Cree Indian named Zebulon Sixkill, first gets thumped by Spenser and then adopted by him like a big puppy. Spenser helps him turn his life around and gets a new temporary sidekick. . . . The ending is typical A-Grade Parker. Things gleaned earlier in the book coalesce when another piece of info triggers a connection, and when that happens, Spenser sets into motion a trap that nets the truth. Plus he has a word or two with the story's true villain. The story has the depth of a puddle, but it's a well-designed puddle, so when it ripples, the clean, steady rolling of the waves is like a shimmering poem." Chicago Sun-Times

Parker, Robert B.

Small vices. Putnam 1997 308p $21.95

ISBN 0-399-14244-4

LC 96-9827

"Mr. Parker has written a powerful piece about the defeat and reclamation of a hero, but I wouldn't say that Spenser's dance with death teaches the old knight to act his age. . . . By virtue of his mythic death and rebirth, he has defied mortality altogether and become like some fertility god who lowers himself into the ground each winter and comes roaring back to life each spring." N Y Times Book Rev

Parker, Robert B. ✓

Thin air. Putnam 1995 293p

LC 94-39046

Spenser's "friend and ultradeadly ally, Hawk, is off in Burma, leaving Spenser on his own when longtime pal Frank Belson of Boston Homicide needs help. Belson's beautiful young bride, Lisa St. Claire, has disappeared. When Belson is wounded in an ambush that may be related to Lisa's disappearance, Spenser undertakes the search." Booklist

Parker, Robert B.

Trouble in Paradise. Putnam 1998 324p $22.95
ISBN 0-399-14433-1

LC 98-7354

This novel finds Jesse Stone, "the chief of police of modest Paradise, Mass., battling a ruthless gang of thieves even as he jousts with personal demons. Two parallel plotlines tell the story. One follows career criminal James Macklin and his moll, Faye, and their planning and subsequent execution of the heist of all the money and valuables on super-rich Stiles Island, which is connected by bridge to Paradise. Meanwhile, there's Stone, a cool customer who's not afraid to step on wealthy toes but who can't get his love life in order and can barely control his taste for booze. . . . Stone's romantic entanglements, particularly his troubled relationship with his ex-wife, add texture to the novel." Publ Wkly

Parker, Robert B.

Walking shadow. Putnam 1994 270p

LC 94-5127

Boston PI Spenser "encounters danger, venality and plenty of comic material in this . . . tale spanning the worlds of experimental theater and illegal immigration. While he'd rather be at work renovating the old farmhouse that he and his lover, psychiatrist Susan, have bought in nearby Concord, Spenser agrees to find out who is following the Artistic Director of the Port City Theater Company, on whose board of directors Susan sits." Publ Wkly

Parker, Robert B.

Widow's walk. Putnam 2002 294p
ISBN 0-399-14845-0

LC 2001-48771

"Attorney Rita Fiore, who's worked with the Boston PI before, hires Spenser to find out if her new client, Mary Smith, . . . indeed shot to death her husband, banker and Mayflower descendant Nathan Smith, as the evidence indicates. . . . The writing is as clean as fresh ice, and from the opening sentence ('I think she's probably guilty,' Rita Fiore said to me), it's clear that readers are in the hands of a vet who knows what he's doing." Publ Wkly

Parker, T. Jefferson

Black water. Hyperion 2002 338p
ISBN 0-7868-6804-X

LC 2001-51903

"Merci Rayborn, homicide detective for the Orange County, California, sheriff's department, has a crime scene that's a puzzler. And it's going to be very high profile—it's in an upscale enclave of million-dollar estates, and one of the victims is a cop. Gwen Wildcraft is dead, and her husband, Archie, is unconscious with a severe head wound. Wildcraft is a patrol officer with the department, and his gun appears to be the murder weapon. Merci's superiors would prefer a quick call of murder-suicide, but her instincts tell her that's the wrong conclusion. . . . A thoughtful, multilayered tale in which crime is a catalyst rather than the centerpiece." Booklist

Parker, T. Jefferson

The **blue** hour. Hyperion 1999 359p $23.95
ISBN 0-7868-6288-2

LC 98-43135

"Solid police work, beefed up with some ingenious devices from Parker's bottomless bag of tricks, makes it all come out right—but not before the wondrously weird characters have taken this lurid plot to its outer limits." N Y Times Book Rev

Parker, T. Jefferson

California girl. Morrow 2004 370p $24.95
ISBN 0-060-56236-6

A mystery set in 1960s Southern California. "The Becker boys (Andy the homicide reporter, Nick the cop, and David the minister; Clay was killed in Vietnam) grew up near the Vonns, a troubled, abusive family burdened with more than its share of tragedy. When 19-year-old beauty queen Janell Vonn, the essence of a California girl, is found beheaded in the abandoned SunBlesst packing house, the Becker brothers begin their separate quests to find her killer, finally bringing him to justice while realizing redemption for themselves. But 40 years after a conviction, it becomes apparent that the Beckers were wrong, very wrong. Drenched in lust, love, betrayal, and unfulfilled promise, California Girl features masterly plotting, smart prose, and memorable characters." Libr J

Parker, T. Jefferson

Cold pursuit. Hyperion 2003 360p $23.95
ISBN 0-7868-6805-8

LC 2002-32940

"The murder of retired San Diego Port Commissioner and local politician Pete Braga falls in the lap of homicide detective Tom McMichael, whose family has a multigenerational feud going with the Bragas. Parker makes the most of a standard mystery device here—murder driven by a motive from the distant past—but the real joy of the novel is its remarably evocative prose, which flows seamlessly from lyrical descriptions of rainy San Diego to crisp, no-nonsense dialogue." Booklist

Parker, T. Jefferson

The **fallen**; a novel. William Morrow 2006 323p $24.95
ISBN 0060562382

LC 2005047934

"This stand-alone classic police procedural, replete with its portrait of big-city crime and power-hungry politicians, follows a recognizable storyline. However, its lively writing, well-paced plot, rounded characters (from call girls to shady politicians), and twists stand out." Bookmarks Magazine

Parker, T. Jefferson

L.A. outlaws; a novel. Dutton 2008 372p $25.95
ISBN 978-0-525-95055-4; 0-525-95055-9

LC 2007-33722

"Parker writes with an understanding of the West's essential character: in Outlaws, he casts Los Angeles as an eternally sprawling, brawling camp town, populated by bandits and bigots, the quick and the dead, where the poor who once rendered tallow now work the deep fryer at KFC. . . . His concise prose, at once low-key and lyrical, plays almost like cowboy poetry." Los Angeles Times

Parker, T. Jefferson

Little Saigon. St. Martin's Press 1988 354p

LC 88-11586

"Chuck Frye, a surf bum who has recently failed at journalism, business and marriage, lives in the shadow of his war-hero brother Bennett, and their father, a wealthy real-estate tycoon. Bennett's Vietnamese wife is a singer whose protest music has made her a heroine among anticommunists and Asian expatriates. When she is kidnapped during a performance, Chuck joins the search for her, hoping to end his estrangement from the Frye clan. But the more he learns about the crime's motive—politics, gang warfare or revenge are all possibilities—the more intently his family tries to shut him out of the investigation." Publ Wkly

Parker, T. Jefferson

Pacific beat. St. Martin's Press 1991 364p

LC 90-27411

"John Weir, an ex-sheriff's department employee, and brother-in-law Raymond battle corrupt police, development-at-all-cost advocates, and a known sex offender when they try to find the murderer of John's beloved sister. Splayed against the coastal community of Newport Beach, California, where oldtime residents hope to elect a 'slow-growth' candidate, their investigation reveals ever-deeper layers of deception. This exciting, multidimensional plot should grab even the most demanding mystery reader." Libr J

Parker, T. Jefferson

Silent Joe. Hyperion 2001 341p

ISBN 0-7868-6728-0

LC 00-53938

"A complex mix of seemingly unconnected plot lines, vivid characterization, and real mystery merge to form a truly satisfying thriller." Libr J

Parker, T. Jefferson

Storm runners. HarperCollins 2007 370p $25.95

ISBN 978-0-06-085423-2; 0-06-085423-2

"In Southern California, as San Diego weather lady Frankie Hatfield puts it, 'Rain is life!' Rain is also raw power in the land of avocadoes and sod farms. When Hatfield stumbles upon a family secret that allows her to control the rain, that discovery brings her unfathomable power with potentially deadly consequences. P.I. Matt Stromsoe is battling with his own demons—his wife and child have been murdered, and he's seeking redemption—and he willingly accepts an assignment to protect Hatfield. The case takes him from fragrant orange groves in the San Diego hills to the cold cement of Pelican Bay State Prison. Parker's trademark is the ability to create real characters—tangible, flawed, and heroic—and Stromsoe follows the tradition." Libr J

Parker, T. Jefferson

Where serpents lie. Hyperion 1998 432p $23.95

ISBN 0-7868-6287-4

LC 97-2633

A thriller set in "Orange County, California, where cop Terry Naughton, head of Crimes Against Youth, a division he helped create, is fiercely trying to track down a creepy pedophile who calls himself Horridus . . . before he kills one of the young girls that he has kidnapped. It seems that besides child pornography and rape, Horridus is also into snakes—really big, hungry snakes—and there's evidence that he has used these 'pets' to dispose of victims in the past. . . . This taut police procedural mixes high supense with believable characters; it's a real page-turner." Libr J

Parkhurst, Carolyn

★ The **dogs** of Babel. Little, Brown 2003 264p $21.95

ISBN 0-316-16868-8

LC 2002-43644

"As Paul slips into ever more desperate behavior, we hear an account of his and Lexy's courtship and marriage—the tender, tentative union of two damaged people. But then Paul contacts a man convicted of operating on dogs to install vocal chords, and what had been a poignant, affecting tale turns truly frightening . . . . Parkhurst delivers a remarkable debut in quiet, authoritative prose." Libr J

Parkhurst, Carolyn

Lost and found. Little, Brown and Co. 2006 292p hardcover o.p. pa $13.99

ISBN 978-0-316-15638-7; 0-316-15638-8; 978-0-316-06639-6 pa; 0-316-06639-7 pa

LC 2005-029741

"Older teens may find that this book presses just the right buttons." SLJ

Parkhurst, Carolyn

The **nobodies** album; a novel. Doubleday 2010 313p $25.95

ISBN 978-0-385-52769-9; 0-385-52769-1

LC 2009-41886

"Novelist Octavia Frost is used to inventing unlikely plots, but when her famous rocker son is accused of bludgeoning his girlfriend to death, she finds her life is turning into one of her own books. A previously dormant maternal instinct drives her to attempt to prove her son's innocence and, in the process, close the wounds that have kept them from speaking to each other for four years. Excerpts from Frost's novels punctuate the low-key, introspective murder-mystery narrative, offering a pinhole glimpse into the mind of a fascinating woman for whom life and fiction are stitched tightly together." Entertainment Wkly

Parks, Brad

The **girl** next door; a mystery. Brad Parks. Minotaur Books 2012 326 p. (Carter Ross mysteries) (hbk.) $24.99

ISBN 1429949996; 031266768X; 9780312667689; 9781429949996

LC 2011040880

In this book by Brad Parks, "Carter Ross's insignificant decision to write a feature obit about hit-and-run victim Nancy Marino, a hard-working waitress and deliverer of the very newspaper for which he works, plunges him into a far more sinister . . . story. . . . Quickly discovering there was more to the middle-aged everywoman than met the eye, including her role as a leader in her union's acrimonious labor dispute at the paper, Ross starts to suspect her death was no accident." (Publishers Weekly)

Parks, Brad

Say nothing; a novel. Brad Parks. Dutton 2017 448 p. (ebook) $65; (hardcover) $26

ISBN 9781101985618; 1101985593; 9781101985595

LC 2016018767

In this novel, by Brad Parks, "Judge Scott Sampson doesn't brag about having a perfect life, but the evidence is clear: A prestigious job. A beloved family. On an ordinary Wednesday afternoon, he is about to pick up his six-year-old twins to go swimming when his wife, Alison, texts him that she'll get the kids from school instead. It's not until she gets home later that Scott realizes she doesn't have the children. And she never sent the text." (Publisher's note)

"The nerve-shredding never lets up for a minute as Parks picks you up by the scruff of the neck, shakes you vigorously, and repeats over and over again till a climax so harrowing that you'll be shaking with gratitude that it's finally over." Kirkus

Parks, Gordon

★ The **learning** tree. Harper & Row 1963 303p

"At 12 years of age Newt is awakening to the world around him in his small town of Cherokee Flats, Kansas, in the 1920s. There is the impact of a first sexual experience and a first love, and because he is a Negro, special responsibility of behavior when one individual may represent an entire group in the eyes of the community." Shapiro. Fic for Youth. 3d edition

Parks, Suzan-Lori

Getting mother's body; a novel. {by} Suzanne Lori. Random House 2003 257p $23.95

ISBN 1-400-06022-2

LC 2002-31762

"Set in the summer of 1963, and recounted in a slow, Southern drawl befitting the mood, the story unravels from a myriad of viewpoints, including the no-good custom coffin salesman who's fathered Billy's unborn baby, the one-legged neighbor in love with Billy, and her deceased mother's feisty lesbian lover." Publ Wkly

Parmar, Priya

Vanessa and her sister; a novel. Priya Parmar. Ballantine Books 2014 368 p. (hardcover : acid-free paper) $26

ISBN 080417637X; 9780804176378

LC 2014030434

This novel by Priya Parmar is the story "of the inseparable bond between Virginia [Woolf] and her sister, the gifted painter Vanessa Bell, and the real-life betrayal that threatened to destroy their family. Virginia has always lived in the shelter of Vanessa's constant attention and encouragement. Without it, she careens toward self-destruction and madness. As tragedy and betrayal threaten to destroy the family, Vanessa must decide if it is finally time to protect her own happiness above all else." (Publisher's note)

"Parmar's novel sparkles, intrigues, and attracts, just as the Stephen sisters must have done in their time. It should inspired readers to revisit the works of the Bloomsbury crowd in a new light, especially Virginia Woolf's." Booklist

Parris, S. J.

Sacrilege; a novel. S.J. Parris. Doubleday 2012 423 p.

ISBN 0385535473; 9780385535472

LC 2011047763

This historical thriller by S. J. Parris is "set in sixteenth-century England and centered on the highly secretive cult of Saint Thomas Becket. . . . London, summer of 1584: Radical philosopher, ex-monk, and spy Giordano Bruno suspects he is being followed by an old enemy. He is shocked to discover that his pursuer is in fact Sophia Underhill, a young woman with whom he was once in love. When Bruno learns that Sophia has been accused of murdering her husband, a prominent magistrate in Canterbury, he agrees to do anything he can to help clear her name. . . . Bruno begins to uncover unsuspected secrets that point to the dead man being part of a larger and more dangerous plot in the making." (Publisher's note)

Parshall, Sandra

Bleeding through; Sandra Parshall. 1st ed. Poisoned Pen Press 2012 250 p. (ebook) $6.99; (hardcover : alk. paper) $24.95; (trade pbk. : alk. paper) $14.95

ISBN 9781615954124; 1464200297; 9781464200274; 9781464200298

LC 2012936476

Author Sandra Parshall tells the story of Rachel Goddard, "the northern Virginia veterinarian living with her beau, Deputy Sheriff Tom Bridger, and dealing with a case that literally hits too close to home. Shortly before her sister, Michelle, [comes to visit] . . . Rachel and Tom come across the body of missing law school student Shelley Beecher along a highway in rural Mason County . . . Meanwhile, Rachel struggles to rescue Michelle from a breakdown brought on by . . . a stalker who appears to have followed her from her Maryland home." (Publishers Weekly

Parshall, Sandra

Poisoned ground; Sandra Parshall. Poisoned Pen Press 2014 250 p. (Rachel Goddard Mysteries) hc $24.95

ISBN 9781464202261; 9781464202247; 1464202249

LC 2013941231

In this book, by Sandra Parshall, "a powerful development company sets its sights on Mason Country, Virginia, as the location for a sprawling resort for the rich. . . . Few oppose the development more vocally than veterinarian Rachel Goddard. She sides with locals reluctant to sell their land and, in the process, complicates the life of her new husband, Sheriff Tom Bridger." (Publisher's note)

"Rachel is a likable amateur sleuth who displays genuine affection for her neighbors and the animals she treats. Readers will enjoy seeing series regulars appear throughout the story and appreciate a peek at how Rachel and Tom are getting along as newlyweds." Booklist

Parsons, Kelly

★ **Doing** harm; Kelly Parsons. St. Martin's Press 2014 368 p. (hardback) $25.99

ISBN 1250033470; 9781250033475

LC 2013030121

This book, by Kelly Parsons, is "about a med student . . . and the evil game in which she engages at a major medical school and teaching hospital. Chief resident Steve Mitchell . . . meets medical student Gigi, nicknamed "GG." . . . After sabotaging one of Mitchell's patients and then seducing the young doctor, GG lets Mitchell in on what is happening and tells him that unless he tries to figure out whom she is going to kill next, she'll proceed with her next victim." (Kirkus Reviews)

Pasternak, Boris Leonidovich

★ **Doctor** Zhivago; [by] Boris Pasternak. Pantheon Bks. 1958 558p hardcover o.p.

First published 1957 in Italy

"The account of the life of a Russian intellectual, Yurii Zhivago, a doctor and a poet, during the first three decades of the 20th c. A broad epic picture of Russia is developed as the background to Zhivago's family life, his creative ecstasies, his love for Lara (another man's wife), his emotional upheavals, wanderings, and moments of happiness. Though the novel ends with Zhivago's decline and death as a result of what the author saw as the dehumanization of life that prevailed in the postrevolution years, the epilogue is full of expectations of the freedom that is to come." Ency of World Lit in the 20th Century

Patchett, Ann, 1963-

Bel canto; a novel. HarperCollins Pubs. 2001 318p $25

ISBN 0-06-018873-1

LC 00-53671

Loosely based on the 1996 events in Lima, Peru, when members of the guerrilla group Tupac Amaru seized hostages at the residence of the Japanese ambassador, "Patchett's fourth novel is set in the vice-presidential mansion of an unnamed South American capital, where some 200 foreign diplomats, government officials and businessmen have gathered to celebrate the birthday of a Japanese electronics mogul and opera buff named Katsumi Hosokawa." (N Y Times Book Rev)

"An impoverished South American country hosts a birthday extravaganza for a Japanese industrialist in the hope of securing new foreign investment. The lure? An internationally renowned lyric soprano. Indeed, when Roxane Coss sings, even the ragtag terrorists who are about to flood through the air-conditioning vents and take the guests hostage hold their breath, transported by the beauty of her voice. Patchett's tragicomic novel—a fantasia of guns and Puccini and Red Cross negotiations—invokes the glorious, unreliable promises of art, politics, and love." New Yorker

Patchett, Ann, 1963-

★ **Commonwealth**; a novel. Ann Patchett. Harper, an imprint of HarperCollinsPublishersCollins 2016 336 p. (hardcover) $27.99

ISBN 0062491792; 9780062491794

LC 2016028804

In this novel by Ann Patchett, "Bert Cousins shows up at Franny Keating's christening party uninvited. Before evening falls, he has kissed Franny's mother, Beverly--thus setting in motion the dissolution of their marriages and the joining of two families. Spanning five decades, Commonwealth explores how this chance encounter reverberates through the lives of the four parents and six children involved." (Publisher's note)

"A satisfying meat-and-potatoes domestic novel from one of our finest writers." Kirkus

Patchett, Ann

Run. HarperCollins Publishers 2007 295p $25.95

ISBN 978-0-06-134063-5; 0-06-134063-4

LC 2006-41297

"Ms. Patchett gives her readers much to contemplate when genetics, privilege, opportunity and nurture come into play. And to her credit she is neither vague nor reductive about any of these things; she creates a genuinely rich landscape of human possibility." N Y Times (Late N Y Ed)

Patchett, Ann, 1963-

★ **State** of wonder. Harper 2011 353p $26.99

ISBN 978-0-06-204980-3; 0-06-204980-1

LC 2010-29229

"Dr. Marina Singh, a scientist with a Minnesota pharmaceutical company, is dispatched to the Amazon to investigate a colleague's death. Anders Eckman had been her research partner charged with finally confronting the elderly and elusive head of the Amazonian project, Dr. Annick Swenson. The women of the Lakashi tribe can bear babies throughout their lives. By scraping the bark from a grove of isolated trees with their teeth they are fertile unto death. Families of five generations are the norm. If a viable fertility drug can be synthesized and marketed, billions are to be made. But Swenson is so secretive as to make a paranoid seem transparent. An abrupt note informs the head office that Eck man died of a fever. That's all she wrote, not bothering to fill in any details of the enterprise in which the company is so heavily invested." N Y Daily News

Paton, Alan

Ah, but your land is beautiful. Scribner 1982 271p

ISBN 0-684-17336-0

LC 81-13547

First published 1981 in the United Kingdom

"Alan Paton's considerable practical life in South Africa aside, his place in the literature of social protest has been secured by his steady devotion to the ideal of the empathetic imagination in fiction." N Y Times Book Rev

Paton, Alan

★ **Cry,** the beloved country. Scribner Classics 2003 316p $28; pa $15

ISBN 0-7432-6195-X; 0-7432-6217-4 pa

First published 1948

"Reverend Kumalo, a black South African preacher, is called to Johannesburg to rescue his sister. There he learns that his son Absalom has been accused of murdering a young white attorney whose interests and sympathies had been with the natives. Despite this, the attorney's father comes to the aid of the minister to help the natives in their struggle to survive a drought." Shapiro. Fic for Youth. 3d edition

Paton, Alan

Tales from a troubled land. Scribner 1961 128p

"Most of the tales are told from the point of view of a compassionate white director of a boy's reformatory; however, one of the most moving concerns a native shepherd who, though innocent, becomes a victim when his employer is robbed." Booklist

Paton, Alan

Too late the phalarope. Scribner 1953 276p

"The book is written with superb simplicity. It is cadenced but unaffected; it will inevitably be called Biblical and yet there is no conscious parodying of scriptual prose. It flows relentlessly to its crisis, and sometimes we cry out at its power. The people are all clear and real, the South African backgrounds are colorfully and deeply etched. The conflicts are diverse but they all contribute to the basic struggle; father and son, races, languages, prejudices." Christ Sci Monit

Patterson, James

1st to die; a novel. Little, Brown 2001 424p $32

ISBN 0-316-66600-9

LC 00-61123

"The story opens in San Francisco with the gruesome murder of a bride and groom on their wedding night. Detective Lindsay Boxer is called to the scene, just after learning she is suffering from a rare and potentially life-threatening blood disease. For help with the case, she calls on her best friend, Claire, a medical examiner, and, reluctantly at first, Cindy, a newspaper reporter who is covering the story. . . . Patterson keeps up the suspense until the very last page." Booklist

Patterson, James

★ **Along** came a spider; a novel. Little, Brown 1993 435p

ISBN 0-316-69364-2

LC 92-24581

This novel opens with a "multiple murder in the projects southeast of Capitol Hill in Washington, D.C. and the kidnapping of two famous children—the son of the Treasury secretary and the daughter of a movie star—from Georgetown Day School by the school's math and computer teacher. Is the teacher (whose ransom bid is signed 'Son of Lindbergh') a victim of a rare multiple personality disorder, or a psychopath who feigns multiple personalities to prove his brilliance and escape punishment? African-American psychologist Alex Cross, a widowed district police detective with two children and a very wise grandmother, seek the answer in tense collaboration with FBI and Secret Service agents." (Booklist)

"Alex Cross, a black Washington, D.C., police detective with a Ph.D. in psychology, and Jezzie Flanagan, a white motorcycling Secret Service agent, become lovers as they work together to apprehend a chilling psychopath who has kidnapped two children from a posh private school. . . . Patterson's storytelling talent is in top form in this grisly escapist yarn." Libr J

Patterson, James

★ **Cat** & mouse; a novel. Little, Brown 1997 399p

ISBN 0-316-69329-4

LC 97-20277

Black Washington, D.C. detective/psychologist Alex Cross' "old nemesis, psychopath Gary Soneji, is dead set on killing Alex in the ugliest, most terrifying way he can devise, but first, he's decided to play a game of cat and mouse with his intended victim. In Europe, a sadistic torturer dubbed 'Mr. Smith' is on the loose, and if Soneji is the king of cat and mouse, Mr. Smith is the grand high emperor. Elusive and terrifying, he performs autopsies on his living victims. FBI Agent Thomas Pierce has been assigned to the Smith case, but he's come back to America especially to help Alex track down Soneji." Booklist

Patterson, James

Cross. Little, Brown and Co. 2006 393p $27.99
ISBN 978-0-316-15979-1; 0-316-15979-4

LC 2006-12929

"Even as the story whips by with incredible speed, Patterson manages to pack it full of suspense, emotion, and a resolution that, while perfectly satisfying, carries the author's trademark teaser hinting at the 'more' that surely will come." Booklist

Patterson, James

Four blind mice; a novel. Little, Brown 2002 387p $27.95
ISBN 0-316-69300-6

LC 2002-67540

"The action leads, as is Patterson's custom, to a fire-cracker string of climaxes; the finale finds Cross handcuffed and stripped naked in deep woods, about to be killed. Throughout, Patterson expertly balances the conspiratorial action with intriguing developments in Cross's domestic life." Publ Wkly

Patterson, James

Hide & seek; a novel. Little, Brown 1996 356p

LC 95-35928

"Beautiful Maggie Bradford seems to have it all: a successful career as a singer/songwriter, fame, money, and two precious children. However, she killed her first husband in self-defense and now she's in jail awaiting trial for the murder of her second husband, Will Shepherd, a charming, psychotic professional soccer player. At first, Maggie's marriage seems fine, but soon Will begins to act irrationally. The increasing tension comes to a head when Maggie comes to believe that Will has been sexually abusing her daughter, the resulting confrontation ends in Will's death and Maggie's arrest. Climaxing in Maggie's celebrity trial, this page-turner delivers a solid punch, complete with a surprise ending." Libr J

Patterson, James

I, Alex Cross. Little, Brown and Co. 2009 374p $27.99
ISBN 978-0-316-01878-4; 0-316-01878-3

LC 2009-15513

In this installment Alex Cross takes on a serial killer known as Zeus. "Word that an estranged 24-year-old niece, Caroline Cross, has been murdered disturbs Cross's birthday party. To make that horror even worse, the killer fed Caroline's body through a wood chipper. Cross soon discovers that Caroline supported herself as a high-price escort for Washington, D.C.'s elite, and that other women who served similar clients have turned up missing. Cross's investigation soon attracts the attention of the feds, and he concludes that Zeus is better connected than most of the psychopaths he's brought to justice." Publ Wkly

Patterson, James

Jack and Jill; a novel. Little, Brown 1996 432p
ISBN 0-316-69371-5

LC 96-8037

This novel features "African American psychologist-turned-detective Alex Cross. . . . Alex is troubled when a young child is murdered near the school his son attends and frightened when the murderer strikes again. On the other side of town, away from the scary inner-city D.C. streets, a pair of killers who call themselves Jack and Jill are terrorizing the movers and shakers by murdering a series of high-profile people. . . . A fast-paced, electric story that is utterly believable." Booklist

Patterson, James

Kiss the girls; a novel. Little, Brown 1995 451p
ISBN 0-316-69370-7

LC 94-14177

"'Casanova' works the East Coast, 'The Gentleman Caller' works the West Coast, and these two serial killers might just be working together. Washed-up Washington, D.C., police detective Alex Cross gets involved when his niece is abducted." Libr J

Patterson, James

London bridges; a novel. Little, Brown and Co 2004 391p $27.95
ISBN 0-316-71059-8

LC 2004-16752

"The book is a model of economy, delivering a full package of suspense, emotion and characterization in a minimum number of words." Publ Wkly

Patterson, James

Roses are red; a novel. Little, Brown 2000 400p
ISBN 0-316-69325-1

LC 00-28192

In this Alex Cross thriller set in Washington, D.C. a sociopath calling himself "the Mastermind" orchestrates a series of bank robberies, but he "isn't content to relieve the banks of their cash. He also has to torment the bankers by massacring their families when the mood strikes him. Having captured people's attention with these acts of cunning cruelty, the Mastermind pulls off a coup de théâtre when he hijacks a tour bus carrying the wives and children of insurance company executives and demands $30 million in ransom." N Y Times Book Rev

Patterson, Kevin

Consumption; a novel. Nan A. Talese 2007 384p $25
ISBN 978-0-385-52074-4

LC 2006-36573

First published 2006 in Canada

"In the early sixties, the 'anachronistic malady' of tuberculosis haunts a small Inuit community in the Canadian Arctic. A child is taken from her family for treatment in Montreal and returns six years later, forever marked as unique by her hunger for the outside world and the scars of a brutal surgery. Meanwhile, an influx of white men—and modernity—has estranged the natives from the land and the traditions that enabled them to survive there. Sweeping in scale but microscopic in its portrait of dislocated lives, this début novel finds its most compelling voice in the rueful meditations of a blundering, morphine-addicted American doctor, marooned by his own volition at the edge of the world." New Yorker

Patterson, Richard North

Balance of power. Ballantine Bks. 2003 611p $27.95
ISBN 0-345-45017-5

LC 2003-51848

"This complex novel has a fascinating debate at its heart. To his credit, Patterson has done his research, and though it's clear which side he's on, he does a good job of presenting all the arguments." Booklist

Patterson, Richard North

Conviction; a novel. Random House 2005 465p $25.95

ISBN 0-345-45019-1

LC 2004-51175

"Fifteen years ago, brothers Rennell and Payton Price were sentenced to death for the brutal murder of nine-year-old Thuy Sen. Now, as Rennell's scheduled execution approaches, pro bono lawyer Theresa Peralta Page (also seen in Eyes of a Child), along with her attorney husband and attorney stepson, takes his final appeal all the way to the Supreme Court. At the same time, Theresa deals with her troubled teenage daughter and her own guilt. While it is apparent that the author opposes the death penalty, Patterson nevertheless provides compelling evidence for both sides of the argument." Libr J

Patterson, Richard North

Dark lady; a novel. Knopf 1999 384p $25.95

ISBN 0-679-45043-2

LC 99-23565

"Patterson is familiar with the civic shenanigans that can destroy a community, and he draws wisely on the history and geography of Cleveland to portray a city struggling to escape its bondage to organized crime, racial conflict and the entrenched corruption of its elected officials." N Y Times Book Rev

Patterson, Richard North

Eclipse; a novel. Henry Holt and Company 2009 369p $26

ISBN 978-0-8050-8772-7; 0-8050-8772-9

LC 2008-17386

"Eclipse aspires to be any number of books: a novel of political intrigue, an international conspiracy thriller, a courtroom drama, a romance, even a straightforward murder mystery. . . . To Patterson's credit, the novel succeeds on all counts." Washington Post Book World

Patterson, Richard North

No safe place. Knopf 1998 497p

LC 98-14573

"The main character, Kerry Kilcannon, is an Irish Catholic U.S. senator, reminiscent of the Kennedy brothers. Embroiled in a close campaign with the vice president for the Democratic presidential nomination, Kilcannon struggles to maintain his honesty and upright values in a sleazy world where everything depends on image and the proper spin. At the same time, a militant right-to-lifer vows to kill Kilcannon for his pro-choice stance on abortion. Throughout the constant twists and turns of the plot, Patterson builds realistic supporting characters and brings to life the surrealistic world of a presidential campaign." Libr J

Patterson, Richard North

Protect and defend; a novel. Knopf 2000 549p il

ISBN 0-679-45044-0

LC 00-712975

"When the Chief Justice drops dead at the inauguration of Kerry Kilcannon, the charismatic new president appoints federal judge Caroline Masters to the high court and begins assembling a strategy to get her approved by a contentious Congress. Meanwhile, a pregnant teen with a damaged fetus goes to court to challenge her parents, who helped to pass a new parental-consent law that prevents her from having an abortion. The two events become intertwined. . . . Patterson skillfully juggles a large cast of characters and controversies." SLJ

Patterson, Richard North

Silent witness. Knopf 1997 493p

ISBN 0-679-45040-8

LC 96-36672

"Silent Witness is more than a typical legal thriller; it is a story about the growth of two men and how each one deals with and subsequently changes after experiencing the anguish and the introspection that come from being accused of murder." Booklist

Pattison, Eliot

The **lord** of death; Eliot Pattison. Soho 2009 314 p. (alk. paper) $24

ISBN 1569475792; 9781569475799

LC 2009005421

In this book by Eliot Pattison, part of the Inspector Shan series, "two women -- a Chinese minister and an outspoken American hiker -- have been shot and left for dead at the side of the road. . . . Shan questions revered soothsayers and surly colonels in search of answers, ever aware that the survival of his son Ko -- currently imprisoned in a Chinese asylum -- depends on his success." (Booklist)

Pattison, Eliot

The **skull** mantra. St. Martin's Minotaur 1999 403p $24.95

ISBN 0-312-20478-7

LC 99-23847

"Set against a background that is alternately bleak and blazingly beautiful, this is at once a topnotch thriller and a substantive look at Tibet under siege." Publ Wkly

Paul, Bart

Under Tower Peak; by Bart Paul. 1st ed. Arcade Publishing 2013 288 p. (hardcover) $23.95

ISBN 1611458366; 9781611458367

LC 2012043982

In this novel, by Bart Paul, "Tommy Smith has returned to his former life as a cowboy and wilderness guide in California's Sierra Nevada, hoping to reclaim the simplicity of his youth and heal the wounds the world can't see. When, high on a mountain pass, he and his partner find the wrecked plane of a billionaire adventurer who disappeared months earlier, a seemingly innocent act triggers a breathtaking cycle of violence that threatens Tommy's world." (Publisher's note)

Pavone, Chris

★ The **expats**; a novel. Chris Pavone. Crown Publishers 2012 327 p. (hardback) $26

ISBN 0307956350; 9780307956354; 9780307956378

LC 2011046207

This book tells the story of "Kate Moore [who] is a working mother, struggling to make ends meet, to raise children, to keep a spark in her marriage . . . and to maintain an increasingly unbearable life-defining secret. So when her husband is offered a lucrative job in Luxembourg, she jumps at the chance to leave behind her double-life, to start anew. She begins to reinvent herself as an expat." (Publisher's note)

Pawel, Rebecca

Death of a nationalist. Soho Press 2003 262p $24

ISBN 1-56947-304-8

LC 2002-26921

"Madrid in 1939 is filled with bomb craters, desecrated churches and nearly abandoned streets, while black markets are just about the only markets with anything to sell. The hatreds and atrocities shared by the Nationalists (supported by the Communists) still simmer and erupt in sporadic violence. The Guardia Civil has the responsibility to maintain authority—and their enthusiasm and ruthlessnesss for enforcing order terrorizes the citizens. The intertwined fates of Sergeant Tejada Alonzo Leon of the Guardia Civil and that of Gonzalo Llorente, a wounded

Republican in hiding are handled with unusual skill and subtlety." Publ Wkly

Peace, David

Occupied city. Alfred A. Knopf 2010 275p $25.95

ISBN 978-0-307-23675-9; 0-307-26375-4

LC 2009-43254

First published 2009 in the United Kingdom

"Powerful and ambitious, this British import is deepened by a multiperspective, Rashomon-like approach. But reader be warned: The immensely talented Peace . . . is not in the business of making his work easy." Kirkus

Peace, David

Tokyo year zero. Alfred A. Knopf 2007 $24

ISBN 978-0-307-26374-2; 0-307-26374-6

LC 2007-23813

This novel is based "on a real-life serial-killer case in post-WWII Japan. When the nude body of a young woman turns up in a local park, Inspector Minami of the Tokyo police and his squad of detectives investigate. At the crime scene, Minami finds another woman's body nearby and begins to suspect there will be more to come. Minami, married and a father of two, is smart, tenacious and experienced; he's also addicted to sedatives, keeps a mistress, is in the pocket of a local crime lord and not above sampling the wares of prostitutes he encounters while roaming the city at night. . . . Peace, whose complex style feels like a cross between Haruki Murakami and James Ellroy, delivers an expressionistic portrait of a harrowing, devastated time and place." Publ Wkly

Pearl, Matthew

The **Dante** Club; a novel. Random House 2003 372p $24.95

ISBN 0-375-50529-6

LC 2002-17886

A literary thriller about a "serial murderer who draws gory inspiration from the torments of Dante's Inferno. . . . The author sets this novel in Boston in 1865, when Henry Wadsworth Longfellow, James Russell Lowell, and Oliver Wendell Holmes were translating Dante into English. As they work through the cantos, the Dante-inspired corpses arrive on cue, and the versifiers must turn detective." New Yorker

Pearl, Matthew

The **last** Dickens; a novel. Random House 2009 386p $25

ISBN 978-1-4000-6656-8; 1-4000-6656-5

LC 2008-46962

"Pearl is too smart to hinge his plot on mere publishing rights. Like Dickens, he finds compelling stories in every social stratum, viewing the downtrodden with sympathy and the upper crust with a gimlet eye." N Y Daily News

Pearl, Matthew

The **Poe** shadow; a novel. Matthew Pearl. Random House 2006 370p o.p.; (pbk.) $15

ISBN 1400061032 ; 9780812970128

LC 2005057998

This book follows "[y]oung Baltimore lawyer Quentin Clark, [who,] already obsessed with his favorite writer, Edgar Allan Poe, becomes outraged when newspapers write off Poe's mysterious death as an alcoholic breakdown. So outraged in fact that he abandons his practice and fiancée to visit France to locate the detective whom Poe's character Auguste Dupin is based upon, in an attempt to solve the mystery and clear Poe's name. Instead, Clark finds two such men--one a flamboyant charlatan, the other an eccentric genius--both of whom come to Baltimore and compete to explain Poe's demise." (Library Journal)

Pearl, Matthew

The **technologists**; Matthew Pearl. 1st ed. Random House 2012 480 p. ill.

ISBN 9780679605072; 9781400066575

LC 2011014628

This book takes place in "Spring 1868, and the population of Boston is being terrorised by technological attacks: first a magnetic storm causes ships in the harbour to collide in flames, then in another bizarre catastrophe every piece of glass in the financial district spontaneously melts - clocks, windows, eyeglasses. Nothing in nature can do this: these are man-made disasters. . . . The city's fate relies on four young students of the recently founded Massachusetts Institute of Technology: Marcus Mansfield, a Civil War veteran determined to repay MIT's founder for taking a chance on him, brash Bob Richards, meticulous Edwin Hoyt and the eccentric but brilliant Ellen Swallow, the first woman at MIT, who experiments secretly in a basement laboratory. . . . In a climate of rising hysteria, these four courageous individuals must unite against the forces of darkness to uncover the mastermind before he can stage his greatest outrage." (Publisher's note)

Pearlman, Edith

Binocular vision; new & selected stories. Edith Pearlman. Lookout Books/University of North Carolina Wilmington 2011 xiii, 373p

ISBN 0-9823382-9-5; 978-0-9823382-9-2

LC 2010033376

National Book Critics Circle Award for Fiction (2011)

Edward Lewis Wallant Award (2011)

This is a collection of 34 stories by the author of Vaquita and Other Stories (1996), Love Among the Greats and Other Stories (2002), and How to Fall (2005).

"Short stories are like miniatures: A delicate touch makes all the difference. In Edith Pearlman's world, that light hand means choosing the perfect phrase to capture a moment or a mood. Often it leaves the reader breathless. In 'Binocular Vision,' a hefty collection of 34 stories, including 13 new ones, . . . Pearlman shows her unerring sense for the right words. . . . Set all over the world, in different times during the last hundred years, and involving characters of all ages, these tales focus on the precise pivotal moments when life changes — often for the worse. Death and dying are common themes, while ill-fated liaisons, frequently involving incest, occur with regularity." Boston Globe

Pearlman, Edith

★ **Honeydew**; stories. Edith Pearlman. Little, Brown & Co. 2015 272 p. $25

ISBN 0316297224; 9780316297226

LC 2014028880

In this short story collection, Edith Pearlman "shines a light on small, devastatingly precise moments to reflect the beauty and grace found in everyday life. . . . Whether the characters we encounter are a special child with pentachromatic vision, a group of displaced Somali women adjusting to life in suburban Boston, or a staid professor of Latin unsettled by a random invitation to lecture on the mystery of life and death." (Publisher's note)

"Ovid is a subtle influence throughout, as Pearlman imagines gentle metamorphoses catalyzed by longing, as in the ravishing title story about the headmistress of a private girls' day school and an anorexic, ant-loving student. Pearlman not only writes with bewitching clarity, she also fathoms much about our inner lives and relationships that is unexpectedly wondrous." Booklist

Pears, Iain ✓

Death and restoration; a Jonathan Argyll mystery. Scribner 1998 223p $22

ISBN 0-684-81461-7

LC 97-39932

This mystery features "esthete-sleuth, Jonathan Argyll, and his companion, Flavia di Stefano, a senior, investigator for Italy's Art Theft Squad. Most of the legwork falls to Flavia when an icon is stolen from a rundown monastery in Rome and a French dealer is discovered floating in the Tiber. This frees up Jonathan to sprinkle his acidic wit on art experts and thieves like Dan Menzies, . . . who has been engaged by the monastery to apply his savage artistry to its dubious Caravaggio." N Y Times Book Rev

Pears, Iain

The **dream** of Scipio. Riverhead Bks. 2002 398p ✓

ISBN 1-57322-202-X

LC 2001-58916

"Pears builds a multilayered tale of moral choice, love, danger and loss. Like an archaeologist, he uncovers worlds beneath worlds in a few square miles of Provencal earth." N Y Times Book Rev

Pears, Iain

The **immaculate** deception. Scribner 2000 221p

ISBN 0-7432-1257-6

LC 2001-267391

In this Jonathan Argyll "mystery, set in Rome and Tuscany, the police investigator Flavia di Stefano is called in to find a painting that has been stolen by a radical performance artist; meanwhile, her husband, an art historian, is trying to track down the provenance of a beguiling little fifteenth-century Virgin that belongs to Flavia's former boss. Like those classic Nick and Nora whodunits, this book is really a comedy in disguise: the plot twists are finely turned, our heroes flirt harmlessly with danger, and in the end everyone gets what he may not have known he wanted all along." New Yorker

Pears, Iain ✓

An **instance** of the fingerpost. Riverhead Bks. 1998 691p $27

ISBN 1-57322-082-5

LC 97-23899

First published 1997 in the United Kingdom

"Robert Boyle, the devout chemist, and John Thurloe, Cromwell's inscrutable spymaster, are among the historical characters who figure in this richly imagined mystery set in Oxford in the sixteen-sixties, after Charles II has been restored to the throne. A Fellow of New College is found dead, and a woman accused of whoring and witchcraft is sentenced to hang for the murder. Three narrators—all unreliable and all self-interested—tell their versions of the story, which unfolds in a turbulent atmosphere of scientific, political, and religious dissent. Not until a fourth, and final, narrator speaks are the mysteries, including the meaning of the book's title, revealed." New Yorker

Pears, Iain

The **last** judgment. Scribner 1996 224p

LC 95-38120

First published 1993 in the United Kingdom

"Jonathan Argyll, British art dealer, and his amour, Flavia de Stefano, a member of Rome's art-theft squad, have decided to marry after happy months of living together. But first, there's business to tend to. On a buying trip to Paris, Jonathan is asked by a colleague to deliver a valuable painting to a client in Rome. He soon discovers that whoever is interested in this picture seems to wind up dead. . . . A sophisticated, adventurous, and gripping story that is sure to hold wide appeal." Booklist

Pears, Iain ✓

The **portrait**; Iain Pears. Riverhead Books 2005 211 p. (alk. paper) o.p.; (pbk.) $15

ISBN 1573222984; 9781594481758

LC 2004051204

This book presents a "monolog, delivered by an unnamed artist painting the portrait of an old friend . . . [which] reveals . . . the characters" shared past and the sitter's irredeemable sins. As a callow Scottish boy, the artist had been in thrall to his sitter, a monstrously powerful critic who helped his career. At its height, however, the artist fled early 20th-century London for a rough and rocky little island off the coast of France, and the critic has evidently come to discover why, with the request to have his portrait painted serving as pretext. As the artist unleashes his ever-darker discourse, we learn just how carelessly the critic has treated others, including the artist's model Jacky and a colleague named Evelyn." (Library Journal)

Pears, Iain

Stone's fall; a novel. Spiegel & Grau 2009 594p $27.95

ISBN 978-0-385-52284-7; 0-385-52284-3

LC 2009-00472

"Pears manages his complicated structure with a confidence and dexterity possible only to a master of the craft of fiction. It is a novel which frequently and daringly challenges credibility, skating on the thinnest of ice, and yet meets that challenge successfully every time." Scotsman

Pearson, Allison

I think I love you. Alfred A. Knopf 2011 331p $24.95

ISBN 978-1-4000-4235-7; 1-4000-4235-6

LC 2010-36710

The author "does a winning job of making Petra and Bill, and Petra's best friend and fellow David worshipper — the sunny, goodhearted and slightly ditsy Sharon — as funny and incisive as characters created by, say, Nick Hornby or Stephen Fry, though with considerably more tenderness and felt emotion. Her portraits somehow manage to combine effervescence with earnestness, a finely tuned sense of absurdity with nostalgia, satiric wit with genuine warmth. . . . Ms. Pearson has written a groovy little novel whose charms easily erase any objections the reader might have to the prepackaged and heavily borrowed plot." N Y Times (Late N Y Ed)

Pearson, Ridley

The **angel** maker; a novel. Delacorte Press 1993 341p

LC 92-36573

"Pearson's engaging forensic detail . . . and brisk prose will have readers racing to the cliffhanger climax." Publ Wkly

Pearson, Ridley

The **art** of deception. Hyperion 2002 451p

ISBN 0-7868-6724-8

LC 2002-69055

This Lou Boldt-Daphne Matthews suspense novel "finds the Seattle police lieutenant and his forensic psychologist colleague investigating two cases that ultimately become one. Boldt is tracking a serial killer, and Matthews is investigating the death of a woman who was thrown from Seattle's Aurora Bridge. . . . Pearson makes particularly good use of his Seattle setting this time; the legendary Underground (created when the city was rebuilt after its great fire of 1889) has often appeared in mysteries, but Pearson's detail-rich treatment goes well beyond the typical clichés of dark passages and abandoned storefronts. On every level, this series remains one of the mystery genre's great pleasures." Booklist

Pearson, Ridley

Beyond recognition. Hyperion 1997 480p

LC 96-21125

"A rag and a bone are literally all the Seattle PD has to work with after a violent fire consumes a home and its helpless female occupant, a divorced mother. When a second victim dies the same way, detective Lou Boldt and police psychologist Daphne Matthews begin the process of profiling a serial killer who uses rocket fuel to torch women because they resemble his mother. Elsewhere, a young boy named Ben, whose abusive stepfather has all but driven him into the street, has been befriended by a fraudulent 'psychic' named Emily Richland, who hires Ben to scout her clients' vehicles while they're meeting with her. This task leads, . . . to Ben witnessing an exchange of cash for rocket fuel, a sighting that in turn eventually takes the police to their killer." Publ Wkly

Pearson, Ridley

★ The **body** of David Hayes. Hyperion 2004 344p $23.95

ISBN 0-7868-6725-6

LC 2003-56575

In this "Detective Lou Boldt thriller, computer whiz David Hayes has embezzled $17 million from the bank where he worked and hidden it within the computer system. Now paroled for the crime, he wants to get the money and be free of all competing parties, including some utterly ruthless Russian Mafia types who will stop at nothing to get the loot. Years before, Hayes had an affair with Boldt's wife—now VP of systems at the bank—and he blackmails her into helping him recover the money. Though dedicated and skilled, Boldt and his team are human and fallible; Boldt must balance his jealousy as a husband with his professionalism as a detective. Pearson's novels are always well written, and he takes special care with richly drawn subordinate characters." Libr J

Pearson, Ridley

The **first** victim. Hyperion 1999 381p $23.95

ISBN 0-7868-6440-0

LC 98-49992

"Boldt's usual partner, forensic psychologist Daphne Matthews, plays a lesser role this time, but in her place Pearson substitutes television news anchor Stevie McNeal, who mounts her own investigation, thus introducing a meaty subplot involving media excesses. As always, Pearson builds suspense incrementally, brilliantly amassing details until his plot reaches critical mass at just the right moment." Booklist

Pearson, Ridley

Killer summer. G. P. Putnam's Sons 2009 367p $24.95

ISBN 978-0-399-15572-7; 0-399-15572-4

LC 2009-12998

"Although his ending is a bit flat, seasoned thriller writer Pearson serves up steady suspense and a compelling setting in which members of society's underbelly prey on those living above it all." Booklist

Pearson, Ridley

Middle of nowhere; a novel. Hyperion 2000 375p

ISBN 0-7868-6563-6

LC 99-51670

This thriller "boasts simmering suspense, a plot with a level of detail that comes only from painstaking research, and dynamic chemistry between Boldt and his colleagues and family." Publ Wkly

Pearson, Ridley

Undercurrents. St. Martin's Press 1988 386p

LC 88-1014

"A killer is on the loose—a brutal, terrifying murderer who was himself supposed to be dead. Seattle Police Sergeant Lou Boldt, haunted by the deaths of the man he believed to have been the Cross Killer (so called because of the crosses he slashes onto his victims) and of the real criminal's new victims, is in charge of the case and determined to solve it. . . . Undercurrents is not for the squeamish; it is grittily detailed and no punches pulled. But Pearson clearly understands what makes a good mystery move, and this one sprints breathlessly along, taking the reader with it to a surprising, and satisfying, conclusion." West Coast Rev Books

Pearson, T. R., 1956-

Beluga; Rick Gavin. Minotaur Books 2012 304 p. (hardback) $24.99

ISBN 9781250015228; 9781250015990; 1250015227

LC 2012030068

In this novel by Rick Gavin "Nick Reid and his compadre Desmond liberated some money from a nasty meth dealer, and now they need to launder it. The brother of Desmond's ex-wife wants a small sum to set up a scheme involving a trailer full of stolen tires. . . . [and] Shawnica insists that Nick and Desmond help her brother out. In the next few days, they're set upon by a ninja schoolgirl assassin and a couple of Delta gangsters." (Publisher's note)

Pearson, T. R.

A **short** history of a small place; a novel. Linden Press/ Simon & Schuster 1985 381p

ISBN 0-671-54352-0

LC 84-29720

"Pearson handles the interlinked strands of these stories with a truly wonderful offhand comic style that doesn't dismiss the reality of his characters' lives." Booklist

Peebles, Frances de Pontes

The **seamstress**; a novel. HarperCollins 2008 646p map $25.95

ISBN 978-0-06-073887-7; 0-06-073887-1

This "historical saga of Brazil in the 1920s and 1930s follows sisters Emília and Luzia dos Santos from their impoverished childhoods as village seamstresses to their unimaginable futures: Emília marries the scion of an upper-class family in Recife, while Luzia marries The Hawk, an infamous bandit-cum-Robin Hood who terrorizes provincial landowners. Using as backdrop the populist revolt of 1930 and the push to develop Brazil's enormous resources at the expense of the subsistence farmers, Peebles creates a vast and diverse cast of characters. . . . However, the novel's true beauty is the exquisitely realized relationship between Emília and Luzia, two strong women who, despite the separate paths their lives take, remain connected and committed to each other." Libr J

Peet, Mal, 1947-2015

The **Murdstone** trilogy; Mal Peet. Candlewick Press 2015 320 p. $18.99

ISBN 9780763681845

LC 2014957054

In this book, by Mal Peet, "YA author Philip Murdstone is in trouble. His star has waned. The world is leaving him behind. His agent, the ruthless Minerva Cinch, convinces him that his only hope is to write a sword-and-sorcery blockbuster. Unfortunately, Philip—allergic to the faintest trace of Tolkien—is utterly unsuited to the task. In a dark hour, a dwarfish stranger comes to his rescue. But the deal he makes with Pocket Wellfair turns out to have Faustian consequences." (Publisher's note)

"The resulting novel, which Philip calls Dark Entropy, is brilliant but incomplete.. Bitter and frothy as a pint of stout, this formula-thwarting satire will intoxicate fantasy fans with strong stomachs." Kirkus

Pekearo, Nicholas T.

The **wolfman**; [by] Nicholas Pekearo. Tor 2008 286p $23.95

ISBN 978-0-7653-2026-1; 0-7653-2026-6

LC 2008-3984

"At first glance, Marlowe Higgins seems like a typically flawed noir protagonist: He's an ill-tempered Vietnam War veteran who has drifted from job to job since returning to the U.S. a changed man. He has a propensity for razor-sharp sarcasm, jaw-dropping profanity, binge drinking and sudden outbursts of psychotic violence . . . . Although he has never had a lasting relationship (he's currently involved with a prostitute named Alice), Higgins is a diehard romantic with a heroic code of honor. He also happens to be a werewolf, and when transformed into the beast he is nothing short of 'the wrath of God.' Having slaughtered more than 300 people since returning from the war, and now settled down in the small town of Evelyn, Higgins, who retains the memories and mannerisms of all those he has killed, has vowed to use his torturous affliction for the greater good. Every full moon when he becomes a primeval 'boogeyman,' he tracks down criminals in the region with the help of information from Danny Pearce, a detective with the local police who is the closest thing Higgins has to a friend. . . . Crime-fiction, paranormal-fantasy and horror fans alike should cherish this outstanding debut." Chicago Tribune

Pelecanos, George P.

★ The **big** blowdown. St. Martin's Press 1996 313p

ISBN 0-312-14284-6

LC 95-53148

"Pelecanos lovingly recreates old Washington with small details about soft-drink brands, finned cars and cherished smokes. The ending is a haze of gunsmoke that drifts away to leave a mixed tableau of heroism and futility. With stylistic panache and forceful conviction, Pelecanos delivers a darkly powerful story of the American city." Publ Wkly

Pelecanos, George P.

The **cut**; a novel. Little, Brown and Co. 2011 292p $25.99

ISBN 978-0-316-07842-9; 0-316-07842-5

LC 2010-44937

"At 29, Spero Lucas, an unlicensed investigator for a criminal defense attorney (and anyone else who'll give him a cut of the action), is considerably younger and friskier than the heavy-lidded private eyes who have imprinted their world-weary stamp on this genre. His values are also different, shaped by the street culture of his tough neighborhood and by his experiences as a Marine in Iraq. . . . Moonlighting for an imprisoned mobster who agrees to his hefty cut for retrieving some stolen shipments of marijuana, Lucas becomes trapped in a gang war that quickly turns brutal and bloody. Before he knows it, he's aiming to kill. The novel's story is O.K., but nowhere near as heart-racing as the storytelling." N Y Times Book Rev

Pelecanos, George P.

Drama city; a novel. [by] George Pelecanos. Little, Brown and Co 2005 291p $24.95

ISBN 0-316-60821-1

LC 2004-16757

"There is a fierce inevitability to the way George Pelecanos's new book unfolds. Drama City is unleashed, not simply set in motion. In the tough, imperiled parts of Washington, where his earlier books have been set, Mr. Pelecanos puts the forces of good and evil on a collision course, igniting the kind of suspense that hinges on heartbreak. As this lean, stirring, knife-edged novel escalates, the question is not whether one of its principals will become a casualty. The question is when." N Y Times (Late N Y Ed)

Pelecanos, George P. ✓

Hard revolution; a novel. [by] George Pelecanos. Little, Brown 2004 376p $24.95

ISBN 0-316-60897-1

LC 2003-54501

"Pelecanos's foray into Strange's past does not in the end diminish, but rather adds to, our sense of his complexity and humanity. In narrating Derek's buried crime story, Pelecanos has further tapped into an archetypal vein of family experience in the black community since the 1950's, as drugs, murder and prison cut a swath through three generations of young men." N Y Times Book Rev

Pelecanos, George P. ✓

Hell to pay; a novel. Little, Brown 2002 344p $24.95

ISBN 0-316-69506-8

LC 2001-38111

This mystery, set in Washington, D.C., features ex-cop detectives Derek Strange and Terry Quinn. "As a black man with plenty of miles behind him, Strange has access to neighborhoods where his Irish partner would be handed his head; but both of them take big chances when they cross Worldwide Wilson, a menacing pimp who breaks in teenage runaways, and then go after the wild street kids who shot the 9-year-old quarterback of the Petworth Panthers, the Pee-Wee team Strange coaches. Pelecanos's style is one of total-shock immersion in the sights, sounds and cultural codes of the dangerous world he roams." N Y Times Book Rev

Pelecanos, George P.

The **night** gardener; a novel. Little, Brown 2006 377p $24.99

ISBN 978-0-316-15650-9; 0-316-15650-7

LC 2006-1286

A "disturbingly gritty excavation of racism and social politics in modern Washington." Christ Sci Monit

Pelecanos, George P.

Right as rain; a novel. Little, Brown 2001 332p

ISBN 0-316-69526-2

LC 00-34886

"What is perhaps most remarkable about this outstanding novel . . . is the way his plot-rich, extremely violent stories parallel the turbulence of his characters' inner lives. We care about these characters passionately, and we savor their tentative moments of tranquility as we do our own." Booklist

Pelecanos, George P.

Shame the devil; a novel. Little, Brown 2000 299p $24.95

ISBN 0-316-69523-8

LC 99-29854

"Pelecanos is one of those dangerous writers who aren't afraid to take risks, so there's a merciless reality to his characters and a cold clarity about the way they talk, think and feel. Whatever their flaws, none of the people in this writer's world are ashamed to tell the truth." N Y Times Book Rev

Pelecanos, George P.

Soul circus; a novel. Little, Brown 2003 341p $24.95

ISBN 0-316-60843-2

LC 2002-16207

"Pelecanos is fascinated with the way things work, and he takes apart the gun trade like an urban anthropologist, fitting the pieces into the drug business and the gang culture with an exactness that is breathtaking—and depressing. At the same time, he treats his criminals like human beings, talking their talk, driving their cars, listening to their music, getting into their world with something that can only be called sympathy." N Y Times Book Rev

Pelecanos, George P.

★ The **sweet** forever; a novel. Little, Brown 1998 298p $23.95

ISBN 0-316-69109-7

LC 97-41963

Sequel to King Suckerman (1997)

"Pelecanos's kickback style works just as well when his characters put down their weapons to watch a ball game or to hit the music clubs on a Friday night. This may be a battleground, but it's also Pelecanos's home ground, and he knows the territory as well as any crime writer alive." N Y Times Book Rev

Followed by Shame the devil

Pelecanos, George P.

The **turnaround**; a novel. [by] George Pelecanos. Little, Brown, and Co. 2008 294p $24.99

ISBN 978-0-316-15647-9; 0-316-15647-7

LC 2007-33276

"Pelecanos does what few, if any, American writers do: He tells the truth. Twain told the truth; Faulkner toyed with the truth; Hemingway told his version of the truth and Chandler certainly told a cold, cynical truth. Pelecanos' truth is from deep in the heart, from places where red blood cells know more than all the sweet, heady words truth usually hides behind." Chicago Sun-Times

Pelecanos, George P.

The **way** home; a novel. [by] George Pelecanos. Little, Brown and Co. 2009 323p $24.99

ISBN 978-0-316-15649-3

LC 2008-54837

This novel "examines a generational battle between working-class Thomas Flynn, owner of a Washington, D.C., carpet business, and his son Chris, who is more concerned with the rules of the urban streets than with his future. . . . [Chris eventually lands] in the Pine Ridge facility for juveniles, where punishment, not redemption, is the order of the day. Chris survives the system, but the jailhouse code of standing tall, staring down authority and avenging wrongs dogs him as he tries to build a new, adult life in the face of temptation. In a sense, 'The Way Home' is a coming-of-age story, as Chris tries to find his place in the world. More fortunate than most of the boys who share his past, he can succeed, Pelecanos tells us — but not everybody is quite so lucky." PopMatters

Pelevin, Victor

The **hall** of singing caryatids; translated by Andrew Bromfield. New Directions 2011 pa $9.95

ISBN 978-0-8112-1942-6 pa

"After auditioning for the part as a singing geisha at a dubious bar, Lena and eleven other 'lucky' girls are sent to work at a posh underground nightclub reserved exclusively for Russias upper-crust elite. They are to be a sideshow attraction to the rest of the club's entertainment, and are billed as the 'famous singing caryatids.' Things only get weirder from there. Secret ointments, praying mantises, sexual escapades, and grotesque murder are quickly ushered into the plot." Publisher's note

Penguin book of gay short fiction; edited by David Leavitt and Mark Mitchell; introduction by David Leavitt. Viking 1994 655p

LC 93-1390

The **Penguin** book of lesbian short stories; edited by Margaret Reynolds. Viking 1994 429p

LC 93-34061

First published 1993 in the United Kingdom

Penman, Sharon Kay

Cruel as the grave; a medieval mystery. Holt & Co. 1998 242p $22

ISBN 0-8050-5608-4

LC 98-13085

"Penman's clear prose and engrossing plot, the skill with which she brings the politics, people, and ambience of medieval England alive, and her engaging characters make this a must-read, must-have mystery." Booklist

Penman, Sharon Kay

Devil's brood. G. P. Putnam's Sons 2008 734p $28.95

ISBN 978-0-399-15526-0

LC 2008-29451

Final volume in the author's trilogy based on the lives of Henry II and Eleanor of Aquitaine; earlier titles: When Christ and his saints slept; Time and chance

"As the novel opens, [Eleanor and Henry's] four sons are beginning to chafe under the heavy hand of their father, who has crowned the eldest, Hal, as a coregent but gives him little authority or power. Egged on by their mother, the young king and his brothers mount a decadelong crusade of rebellion and treachery against their father and each other as they vie for land, money, and power. The empathetic reader can't help but be both horrified by the machinations of this grievously dysfunctional family and filled with pity for the pain they inflict upon one another. Penman does a remarkable job of depicting passionate, dramatic characters and the perilous times in which they live. For those who like their historical fiction as complex and tightly woven as a medieval tapestry, this book cannot fail to please." Libr J

Penman, Sharon Kay

Dragon's lair; a medieval mystery. Sharon Kay Penman. G.P. Putnam's Sons 2003 322p $23.95

ISBN 0-399-15077-3

LC 2003-46745

In this mystery, "Justin de Quincy, tries to recover, quite literally, a king's ransom in coffers of precious metals and bales of wool, which are as valuable as gold, that have been stolen in northern Wales. It's 1193, and Queen Eleanor of Aquitaine fervently needs to ransom her eldest son, Richard Lionheart, from the Holy Roman Emperor before King Philippe of France can interfere and her younger son, John, can seize the crown. Justin proceeds into the thickets and wild forests of Wales, where he's deeply mistrusted both as an Englishman and an outsider. He must penetrate abundant Welsh intrigues and deceptions in order to discover the treasure as well as solve murders and comfort bereaved lovers. Despite a large cast of characters from every social class, Penman keeps them all clearly distinguishable." Publ Wkly

Penman, Sharon Kay

Falls the shadow. Holt & Co. 1988 580p

LC 87-32255

In this second volume of the trilogy begun with Here be dragons "Penman focuses on the mid-13th-century reign of England's Henry III and stories of those who opposed that inept king. A main detractor is French-born Simon de Montfort, Earl of Leicester, who leads the fight for parliamentary restrictions on the monarch, and later becomes Henry's brother-in-law through marriage to Eleanor, Countess of Pembroke. She emerges as a major figure, as does a distant relative by marriage, Llewelyn ap Gruffydd, who fights for supremacy in Wales." Libr J

Followed by The reckoning

Penman, Sharon Kay

Here be dragons. Holt, Rinehart & Winston 1985 704p

LC 84-23480

This first title in the author's historical trilogy about 13th century England "is the story of one man, a Welsh prince called Llewelyn the Great, who dares to dream of peace and who will spend a lifetime trying to wrest his country away from feudal England. Standing in his way is King John, who marries his daughter, Joanna, to Llewelyn in hopes of taming the rebellious prince. Penman focuses her novel on the tempestuous emotional and political battles that Joanna is forced to endure as both the daughter and wife of warring kings." Booklist

Followed by Falls the shadow

Penman, Sharon Kay

A **King's** Ransom; by Sharon Kay Penman. Penguin Group USA 2014 448 p. maps $35

ISBN 0399159223; 9780399159220

LC 2013042663

Sequel to: Lionheart (2011)

This book, by Sharon Kay Penman, is the "story of the last event-filled years in the life of Richard, Coeur de Lion. Taken captive by the Holy Roman Emperor while en route home--in violation of the papal decree protecting all crusaders--he was to spend fifteen months imprisoned, much of it in the notorious fortress at Trefils, from which few men ever left alive, while Eleanor of Aquitaine moved heaven and earth to raise the exorbitant ransom." (Publisher's note)

Penman "gives readers a well-researched and impressively detailed narrative displaying a strong commitment to historical accuracy and richly drawn, sympathetic characters." LJ

Penman, Sharon Kay

Lionheart. G. P. Putnam's Sons 2011 594p map $28.95

ISBN 978-0-399-15785-1

LC 2011-13731

Richard, the second surviving son of Henry Plantagenet and Eleanor of Aquitaine, inherits the throne from his brother, before embarking on the Third Crusade, a conflict that is complicated by the schemes of his usurping brother, John.

"Penman expertly weaves well-researched historical events into her fast-paced revisionist story. Certain to appeal to historical fiction fans interested in the medieval era." Libr J

Penman, Sharon Kay

The **queen's** man; a medical mystery. H. Holt 1996 291p $20

ISBN 0-8050-3885-X

LC 96-15027

"Penman's authentic period details, larger-than-life characters, and fast-paced plot add up to great reading for both mystery fans and history buffs." Booklist

Penman, Sharon Kay

The **reckoning**. Holt & Co. 1991 592p

LC 90-27099

"The action involves religious and political intrigue, battles and plots. The players include well-researched historical personages and fictional characters. As with Penman's other historical novels, this one is both informative and enjoyable. Settings, events, and individuals are well drawn." Libr J

Penman, Sharon Kay

The **sunne** in splendour. Holt, Rinehart & Winston 1982 936p

LC 81-20149

"The novel covers a great deal of ground, tracing the shifting alliances and the battles between the noble houses of York and Lancaster from 1459, when Richard was seven to 1492, seven years after his death on Bosworth Field. . . . A historical novel of the first rank." Publ Wkly

Penman, Sharon Kay

Time and chance. Putnam 2002 515p

ISBN 0-399-14785-3

LC 2001-48255

Sequel to: When Christ and his saints slept

This second volume of the author's medieval trilogy "re-creates the drama, the intrigue, and the passion that distinguished the lives of Henry Plantagenet, Eleanor of Aquitaine, and Thomas Becket. Though the subject has been exhaustively chronicled in both history and literature, this fictionalized account of the trials and tribulations of this prominent trio of historical figures manages to breathe new life into a familiar story." Booklist

Penman, Sharon Kay

When Christ and his saints slept. Holt & Co. 1995 746p il

LC 94-22593

The author "showcases her mastery of the historical novel in this long and thoroughly engrossing study of pragmatic politics, idealism, and the role of women during the 12th century. She brings to life a vast array of unforgettable characters, both historical and invented, all of whose loyalties are being constantly tested by the chaos of the times." Libr J

Penney, Stef

The **invisible** ones; by Stef Penney. G.P. Putnam's Sons 2012 400p

ISBN 9780399157714; 9780425253212

LC 2011046797

This book tells the story of "private eye Ray Lovell [who] wakes up in an English hospital with little memory and partial paralysis. . . . Ray, who is half-Gypsy himself, is offered a job by a fellow Gypsy, Leon Wood, who wants Ray to find his daughter, Rose, who he hasn't seen or spoken to in seven years, ever since she married Ivo Janko, another Gypsy. . . . Why Leon wants to find Rose after so much time begins the mystery. He tells Ray it's because her mother has died and she should know, but Leon suspects foul play." (Publishers Weekly)

Penney, Stef

The **tenderness** of wolves; a novel. Simon & Schuster 2007 371p $25

ISBN 978-1-4165-4074-8; 1-4165-4074-1

LC 2006-100796

First published 2006 in the United Kingdom

A "confident and complex portrait of 1860s Ontario. . . . Between twists and turns of plot, Penney evokes the land—its shades of light and changes of weather, its marshes and treacherous waters. Rarely has winter seemed so febrile." Books of Canada

Penny, Louise

★ The **beautiful** mystery; a Chief Inspector Gamache novel. Louise Penny. St. Martin's Minotaur 2012 373 p. (hardcover : alk. paper) $25.99

ISBN 0312655460; 9780312655464; 9781250015273

LC 2012024186

This book by Louise Penny presents "a locked-room mystery set in a remote monastery deep in the wilderness of northern Québec. There are 24 cloistered monks. One is dead. There are only 23 suspects. The monks have taken a vow of silence, except that they made the most beautiful recording of Gregorian chant ever heard. And it caused a schism. And then a murder. Chief Inspector Gamache and Jean-Guy Beauvoir of the Sûreté du Québec come to investigate." (Library Journal)

Includes bibliographical references and index

Penny, Louise

Bury your dead; Louise Penny. Minotaur Books 2010 ix, 371 p.p $24.99

ISBN 0312377045 (alk. paper); 9780312377045 (alk. paper)

LC 2010026415

"An obsessive historian's quest for the remains of the founder of Quebec, Samuel de Champlain, ends in murder." (Publisher's note)

"Front and center are the travails of Gamache, chief inspector of the Sûreté du Quebec, who is visiting an old friend in Quebec City and hoping to recover from a case gone wrong. Soon, however, he is involved with a new case: the murder of an archaeologist who was devoted to finding the missing remains of Samuel de Champlain, founder of Quebec. As Gamache is drawn into this history-drenched investigation—the victim's body was found in an English-language library, calling up the full range of animosity between Quebec's French majority and dwindling English minority—he is also concerned that he might have jailed the wrong man in his last case (The Brutal Telling, 2009) and orders his colleague, Jean Guy Beauvoir, back to the village of Three Pines to find what they missed the first time. Hovering over both these present investigations is the case gone wrong in the past, the details of which are gradually revealed in perfectly placed flashbacks. Penny brilliantly juggles the three stories, which are connected only by a kind of psychological membrane." Booklist

Penny, Louise

The **cruelest** month; a Three Pines mystery. St. Martin's Minotaur 2008 311p $23.95

ISBN 978-0-312-35257-8; 0-312-35257-3

LC 2007-42422

Chief Inspector Armand Gamache of the Surete du Quebec is called to investigate the death of a villager at an Easter seance that was held at the Old Hadley House.

"Penny paints a vivid picture of the French-Canadian village, its inhabitants and a determined detective who will strike many Agatha Christie fans as a 21st-century version of Hercule Poirot." Publ Wkly

Penny, Louise

★ **Glass** houses; Louise Penny. Minotaur Books 2017 391 p. (A Chief Inspector Gamache novel) (hardcover) $28.99

ISBN 9781466873681; 1250066190; 9781250066190

LC 2017021224

In this book, by Louise Penny, "a mysterious figure appears in Three Pines one cold November day. . . . From the moment its shadow falls over the village, Gamache, now Chief Superintendent of the Sûreté du Québec, suspects the creature has deep roots and a dark purpose. Yet he does nothing. What can he do? Only watch and wait. And hope his mounting fears are not realized." (Publisher's note)

"A meticulously built mystery that follows a careful ascent toward a breaking point that will leave you breathless." Kirkus

Penny, Louise

★ A **great** reckoning; A Novel. Louise Penny. Minotaur Books 2016 400 p. (Inspector Armand Gamache) (hardback) $28.99

ISBN 9781250022134

LC 2016019580

This book by Louise Penny in the "Chief Inspector Gamache Novel" series begins when an old map "given to Armand Gamache as a gift [on] the first day of his new job . . . eventually leads him to shattering secrets. To an old friend and older adversary . . . [and] to places even he is afraid to go. . . . And there he finds four young cadets in the Sûreté academy, and a dead professor. And, with the body, a copy of the old, odd map." (Publisher's note)

"Young, learning minds are precious things, and Penny is here to make us aware of the evil out there, eager for a chance to mold—and poison—them. A chilling story that's also filled with hope—a beloved Penny trademark." Kirkus

Penny, Louise

★ **How** the light gets in; Chief Inspector Gamache novel. Louise Penny. 1st Minotaur Books ed. Minotaur Books 2013 416 p. (hardcover) $25.99

ISBN 0312655479; 9780312655471

LC 2013013622

This book is part of Louise Penny's Chief Inspector Armand Gamache series. Here, Inspector Gamache heads to "Three Pines to help therapist-turned-bookseller Myrna find out why her friend Constance Pineault didn't turn up for Christmas. . . . En route to Three Pines, Gamache happens upon a fatality at the Champlain Bridge and agrees to handle the details. But this case takes a back seat to the disappearance of Constance when she turns up dead in her home." (Kirkus Reviews)

Penny, Louise

The **long** way home; Louise Penny. Minotaur Books 2014 384 p. (Chief Inspector Gamache) (hardback) $27.99

ISBN 1250022061; 9781250022066

LC 2014016727

"After the explosive events in the previous book, Gamache and his wife have retired to Three Pines for peace and recuperation. But Gamache feels obligated to leave his refuge as one of his best friends, Clara Morrow, requires his expertise when her husband Peter goes missing. After Clara became a more famous artist than her spouse, Peter left to find himself, promising to be back in a year. But he has not returned. Retracing Peter's journey, Gamache, hoping to find his friend, instead encounters murder and madness." (Library Journal)

"Over the course of the intriguing search, Penny offers real insight into the evolution of artistic style as well as the envy that artists feel about each other's success." Pub Wkly

Penny, Louise

★ The **nature** of the beast; a Chief Inspector Gamache novel. Louise Penny. Minotaur Books 2015 384 p. (hardcover) $27.99

ISBN 1250022088; 9781250022080

LC 2015017153

In this mystery, by Louise Penny, "[h]ardly a day goes by when nine year old Laurent Lepage doesn't cry wolf. . . . But when the boy disappears, the villagers are faced with the possibility that one of his tall tales might have been true. And so begins a frantic search for the boy and the truth. What they uncover deep in the forest sets off a sequence of events that leads to murder, leads to an old crime, leads to an old betrayal. Leads right to the door of an old poet." (Publisher's note)

"Penny is an expert at pulling away the surface of her characters to expose their deeper—and often ugly—layers, always doing so with a direct but compassionate hand." Kirkus

Penny, Louise ✓

Still life. St. Martin's Minotaur 2006 312p $22.95
ISBN 978-0-312-35255-4; 0-312-35255-7

LC 2006-41992

First published 2005 in the United Kingdom

"The residents of a tiny Canadian village called Three Pines are shocked when the body of Miss Jane Neal is found in the woods. Miss Neal, the village's retired schoolteacher and a talented amateur artist, has been a good friend to most of the townsfolk, so her loss is keenly felt. At first, her death appears to be a tragic accident—it's deer-hunting season, and it looks a stray hunter's arrow killed her. But some folks are suspicious, and Chief Inspector Armand Gamache of the Montreal Surete is called in to investigate." Booklist

Other titles about Chief Inspector Gamache are:
A fatal grace (2006)
The cruelest month (2008)
A rule against murder (2009)
The brutal telling (2009)
Bury your dead (2010)
A trick of the light (2011)
The beautiful mystery (2012)
How the light gets in (2013)
The long way home (2014)
The nature of the beast (2015)
A great reckoning (2016)
Glass houses (2017)

Penny, Louise ✓

A **trick** of the light. Minotaur Boooks 2011 339p $25.99
ISBN 978-0-312-65545-7; 0-312-65545-2

LC 2011020256

"Penny, elevating herself to the pantheon that houses P.D. James, Ruth Rendell and Minette Walters, demonstrates an exquisite touch with characterization, plotting and artistic sensitivity. And there could be no better explanation of A.A. than you will find here." Kirkus

Percy, Benjamin

The **dead** lands; a novel. Benjamin Percy. Grand Central Publishing 2014 403 p. (hardcover) $26
ISBN 1455528242; 9781455528240; 9781455582044

LC 2014008658

In this novel by Benjamin Percy, "a post-apocalyptic reimagining of the Lewis and Clark saga, a super flu and nuclear fallout have made a husk of the world we know. A few humans carry on, living in outposts such as the Sanctuary. Then a rider . . . reports on the outside world: west of the Cascades, rain falls, crops grow, civilization thrives. But there is danger too: . . . an army that pillages and enslaves every community they happen upon. Against the wishes of the Sanctuary, a small group sets out in secrecy." (Publisher's note)

"Short chapters shift from character history to fast-paced action, and Percy uses his gift for literary horror, as seen in Red Moon (2013), to create a compelling and at times disturbing story that will leave readers wanting more." Booklist

Percy, Benjamin

Red moon; Benjamin Percy. Grand Central Pub. 2013 544 p. (hardcover) $25.99
ISBN 1455501662; 9781455501663

LC 2012016127

In this werewolf novel, a "lycan rights group launches a terrorist attack on an airliner that shocks the nation, and the main characters deal with the aftereffects. Claire is a lycan who lives an uneventful suburban life with her parents when a post-attack government raid sends her on the run. The lone passenger who survived the attack is Patrick, whose father's National Guard unit has just shipped out as part of the U.S. peacekeeping mission in the werewolf homeland." (Library Journal)

Percy, Benjamin

The **wilding**; a novel. Graywolf Press 2010 258p $23
ISBN 978-1-55597-569-2; 1-55597-569-0

LC 2010-922923

"The plot concerns a hunting trip taken by Justin Caves and his sixth-grade son, Graham, with Justin's bullying father, Paul, a passionate outdoorsman in failing health who's determined to spend one last weekend in the Echo Canyon before real estate developer Bobby Fremont turns the sublime pocket of wilderness into a golfing resort. Justin, a high school English teacher, has hit an almost terminally rough patch in his marriage to Karen, who, while the boys camp, contemplates an affair with Bobby, though she may have bigger problems with wounded Iraq war vet Brian, a case study in creepy stalker. The men, meanwhile, are being tracked by a beast and must contend with a vengeful roughneck roaming the woods. A taut plot and cast of deeply flawed characters—Justin is a masterwork of pitiable wretchedness—will keep readers rapt as peril descends and split-second decisions come to have lifelong repercussions. It's as close as you can get to a contemporary Deliverance." Publ Wkly

Percy, Walker

★ **Lancelot**. Farrar, Straus & Giroux 1977 257p

In this novel the author "knowledgeably fingers what he perceives as the rotting fabric of Southern aristocratic life, and describes it with vividness and a kind of affection, even as he starts to shred it." Christ Sci Monit

Percy, Walker

★ The **last** gentleman. Modern Lib. 1997 442p $18.50
ISBN 0-679-60272-0

LC 97-15381

"The plot is less important than the delineation of character, the preoccupation with the way people speak and define themselves geographically and historically . . . and the rendering of a composite South." Burgess. 99 Novels

Followed by The second coming

Percy, Walker

Love in the ruins; the adventures of a bad Catholic at a time near the end of the world. Farrar, Straus & Giroux 1971 403p

"A beautifully comic and humane work, the satirist's projection of a grotesque future world based on the realities of the present and stimulus to thought and evaluation and, hopefully, to improvement. Percy's style shows mastery of language." Choice

Percy, Walker

★ The **moviegoer**. Knopf 1961 241p $26

ISBN 0-394-43703-9

"A philosophical exploration of the problem of personal identity, the story is narrated by Binx Bolling, a successful but alienated businessman. Bolling undertakes a search for meaning in his life, first through an obsession with the movies and later through an affair." Merriam-Webster's Ency of Lit

Percy, Walker

The **second** coming. Farrar, Straus & Giroux 1980 359p

ISBN 0-374-25674-8

LC 80-12899

"A beautiful . . . exploration of Percy's recurrent theme—an individual man's search for the hand of God in the meaningless muddle of contemporary life." Booklist

Perec, Georges, 1936-1982

★ **Life**; a user's manual. translated by David Bellos. Godine 1987 581p

ISBN 0-87923-700-7

LC 87-8782

Original French edition, 1978

The author of this novel, set in a Paris apartment house on a single day, was a member of OuLiPo, Ouvroir de littérature potentielle (Workshop of potential literature), a group devoted to experiments with puns, acrostics, palindromes and other literary devices. In 99 chapters and an epilogue, the author describes the building's 100 rooms and the life stories of past and present occupants as a painting in progress, the work of one of the tenants. The book also tells of Percival Bartlebooth, an Englishman who has spent his life learning to paint. The paintings when complete are transformed into jigsaw puzzles, reassembled and then dipped into detergent, leaving blank sheets of paper. Originally published in France in 1978 under the title La vie: mode d'emploi.

"The inextricable incoherence of things is presumably the basic theme of the late Georges Perec's work, but this pessimistic view of life is dramatized with inventiveness, audacity, and even humor." Atlantic

Perec, Georges

★ A **void**; translated by Gilbert Adair. HarperCollins Pubs. 1994 285p

ISBN 0-00-271119-2

Original French edition, 1969

"Gilbert Adair has now shown quite brilliantly that a lipogrammatic text in one language can be more than adequately done into another, retaining not only the alphabetical constraint but much of the virtuosity of the original." London Rev Books

Perez-Reverte, Arturo

★ **Captain** Alatriste; translated from the Spanish by Margaret Sayers Peden. Putnam 2005 253p $23.95

ISBN 0-399-15275-X

LC 2004-60210

"Equipped with a quick-witted, charismatic hero and much to provoke and goad him, Mr. Pérez-Reverte has the makings of a flamboyantly entertaining series. Captain Alatriste ends with a wicked flourish, an evil laugh and a strong likelihood that the best is yet to come." N Y Times (Late N Y Ed)

Perez-Reverte, Arturo

★ The **Club** Dumas; translated from the Spanish by Sonia Soto. Harcourt Brace & Co. 1996 362p il $23

ISBN 0-15-100182-0

LC 96-11962

Original Spanish edition, 1993

"Corso, a tough-guy bibliophile living in Madrid, is hired by a wealthy client to track down a rare seventeenth-century book on how to summon the Devil. He soon finds himself in noir metafiction in which he's been cast as D'Artagnan and is threatened by characters suspiciously like Richelieu's agents—a menacing man with a scar and a blonde with a fleur-de-lis tattoo. Even a reader armed with a Latin dictionary and a copy of 'The Three Musketeers' cannot anticipate the thrilling twists of this stylish, Escher-like mystery." New Yorker

Perez-Reverte, Arturo

The **fencing** master; translated from the Spanish by Margaret Jull Costa. Harcourt Brace & Co. 1999 245p $24

ISBN 0-15-100181-2

LC 98-35536

Original Spanish edition, 1988

"In lieu of snappy pater, Pérez-Reverte provides artful, intricate conversation. Rather than send his characters on a relentless search, he provides them with an inexorable unfolding of revelation, increasingly ghastly. And instead of the clever puzzle that lies at the heart of many a lesser crime novel, he substitutes a subtle meditation on the deeper mysteries of fate and choice." N Y Times Book Rev

Perez-Reverte, Arturo

The **nautical** chart; translated from the Spanish by Margaret Sayers Peden. Harcourt 2001 466p

ISBN 0-15-100534-6

LC 2001-39446

Original Spanish edition, 2000

"This is the story of a down-and-out sailor (@We could call him Ishmael, but in truth his name is Coy') who washes up in modern-day Barcelona, where he is recruited to join in the treasure hunt for a cargo of emeralds . . . that went down with a merchant ship that sank off the Spanish coast in 1767." N Y Times Book Rev

Pérez-Reverte, Arturo, 1951-

The **painter** of battles; a novel. translated from the Spanish by Margaret Sayers Peden. Random House 2008 211p $25

ISBN 1-4000-6598-4; 978-1-4000-6598-1

LC 2007-16997

Original Spanish edition, 2006

Andrés Faulques, "a contemporary war photographer exchanges his . . . [camera] for a paintbrush as he . . . embarks on a pictorial representation of suffering, all '26 centuries of the iconography of war.'" (N Y Times Book Rev)

"The character of the title is Andrés Faulques, a hermit who spends his time painting a colossal battle scene on the interior of a watchtower. Faulques was once a war photographer, famed for his ability to capture in a single image horror, beauty and geometry. One day he has a visitor, the subject of one of Faulques's most celebrated shots: a weary Croatian soldier in the hour of dejected defeat. The photograph helped to change Faulques's life, winning an award. It also changed the soldier's: its publication and his identification as the husband of a young woman sheltering in a Serbian village saw her raped and then, along with his son, tortured and murdered. Now he has come to pay Faulques back. What follows is a game of mental chess, an excursion into art, history and imagination, and both men's lives as Faulques realises that only the continuation of their discourse, and his painting, is keeping him alive." London Times

Perez-Reverte, Arturo

Purity of blood; translated from the Spanish by Margaret Sayers Peden. G.P. Putnam's Sons 2006 267p $23.95

ISBN 0-399-15320-9

LC 2005-50984

Original Spanish edition, 1997

In this installment featuring the 17th-century swordsman, Alatriste "is contracted to help a man from a Jewish-turned-Catholic family rescue his daughter from behind the thick walls of a Madrid convent, which the chaplain 'has turned . . . into his private seraglio.' This novel is written in the mold of Dumas' musketeer novels and excitingly upholds the tradition." Booklist

Pérez-Reverte, Arturo, 1951-

The **siege**; a novel. Arturo Pérez-Reverte; translated from the Spanish by Frank Wynne. Random House Inc 2014 624 p. maps $28

ISBN 1400069688; 9781400069682

LC 2014004597

This novel, by Arturo Perez-Reverte, is a "thriller filled with history, adventure, suspense, and . . . love. Cádiz, 1811: The Spanish port city has been surrounded by Napoleon's army for a year. . . . And now the bodies of random women have begun to turn up throughout the city--victims of a shadowy killer. Police Comisario Rogelio Tizón has been assigned the case. Known for his razor-sharp investigation skills . . . Tizón has seen everything. Or so he thought." (Publisher's note)

"There may be a little too much going on here—the density of both the prose and the story lines can seem almost suffocating at times—but there is no denying the author's ability to build character, evoke landscape, and communicate the crush of history on individual lives... Pérez-Reverte, an international best-seller and a favorite among booksellers and librarians, has not had a new book since 2010 and will attract plenty of attention with this one." Booklist

Perez-Reverte, Arturo

★ **What** we become; A novel. Arturo Perez-Reverte ; translated by Nick Caistor and Lorenza Garcia. Atria Books 2016 464 p. (hardback) $28

ISBN 9781476751986

LC 2015037715

In this novel, by Arturo Perez-Reverte, "en route from Lisbon to Buenos Aires in 1928, Max and Mecha meet aboard a luxurious transatlantic cruise ship. There Max teaches the stunning stranger and her erudite husband to dance the tango. A steamy affair ignites at sea and continues as the seedy decadence of Buenos Aires envelops the secret lovers." (Publisher's note)

"Pérez-Reverte summons the romantic spirit of an old black-and-white movie: impossibly glamorous, undeniably wistful." Kirkus

Perillo, Lucia, 1958-2016

★ **Happiness** is a chemical in the brain; stories. Lucia Perillo. W.W. Norton & Co. 2012 211 p.

ISBN 0393083535; 9780393083538

LC 2012001613

This book, by the Kingsley Tufts Prize-winning author Lucia Perillo, presents a series of short stories in "a small town in the Pacific Northwest. . . . An addict trapped in a country house becomes obsessed with vacuum cleaners. . . . An accidental mother struggles to answer her daughter's badgering about her paternity. And . . . a woman with Down syndrome . . . serves as an accomplice to her younger sister's sexual exploits and her aging mother's fantasies of revenge." (Publisher's note)

Perkins-Valdez, Dolen

Wench; a novel. Dolen Perkins-Valdez. 1st ed.; Amistad 2010 293 p. $24.99

ISBN 006170654X; 9780061706547

LC 2010277174

This book, by Dolen Perkins-Valdez, chronicles "the lives of four slave women—Lizzie, Reenie, Sweet and Mawu—who are their masters' mistresses. The women meet when their owners vacation at the same summer resort in Ohio. There, they see free blacks for the first time and hear rumors of abolition, sparking their own desires to be free. For everyone but Lizzie, that is, who believes she is really in love with her master, and he with her." (Publishers Weekly)

"Readers of historical fiction centering on Southern women's stories like Lalita Tademy's Cane River or Lee Smith's On Agate Hill will be moved by the skillful portrayal of Lizzie's precarious situation and the tragic stories of her fellow slaves." LJ

Perlman, Elliot

★ The **street** sweeper; Elliot Perlman. Riverhead Books 2012 600p.

ISBN 9781594488474

LC 2011046366

This book is "is a . . . tale that spans decades and bridges generations while chronicling the predominant chapters of racial persecution perpetrated in the darkest hours of the 20th century. . . . Lamont Williams, a janitor on probationary period at New York's Memorial Sloan-Kettering Cancer Center, wants to start afresh after a spell in prison, and locate the estranged daughter he hasn't seen for years. Adam Zignelik, a Columbia history professor, is raw after casting off his girlfriend, a feeling exacerbated when the university denies him tenure for his lack of ambition. Both characters get their second chances from unimagined collisions with history [and the Holocaust in particular]." (SFGate)

Perrotta, Tom

★ The **abstinence** teacher. St. Martin's Press 2007 358p $24.95

ISBN 978-0-312-35833-4; 0-312-35833-4

LC 2007-21961

"Perrotta, an accomplished satirist who has made the suburbs his personal stomping ground, turns Stonewood Heights . . . into a battleground for the hearts and minds (and, need I add, souls) of his characters. While Perrotta does do more than give lip service to both sides, it's pretty clear where his allegiance lies. . . . What keeps the book from getting too heavy-handed, besides the sharply written humor, is the fact that Perrotta makes his evangelical Christian protagonist less of a zealot than the atheist." Christ Sci Monit

Perrotta, Tom

Joe College. St. Martin's Press 2000 306p

ISBN 0-312-26184-5

LC 00-31722

"Perrotta's genius is his ability to depict student culture with dead-on accuracy. His satiric touch is like a light, but killing frost." Christ Sci Monit

Perrotta, Tom

The **leftovers**. St. Martin's Press 2011 355p $25.99

ISBN 978-0-312-35834-1; 0-312-35834-2

LC 2011-19509

In this novel, "the catalyst to the plot is the Sudden Departure, a 'Rapture-like event' in which millions of people suddenly vanished from the face of the earth. . . . The nuclear family that [Tom] Perrotta takes as his focus survives the Sudden Departure intact, only to splinter under the weight of its implications. It is left to the father, Kevin, the mayor of their small town . . . and the daughter, Jill, to keep calm and carry on." (Times Literary Supplement)

"When the 'Sudden Departure' occurs, millions of people around the world—true believers and nonbelievers alike—simply disappear in an 'indiscriminate Rapture.' In the town of Mapleton, the young and old struggle through their daily lives as they come to grips with losing family members and childhood friends, while cults such as the Healing Hug Movement, the Barefoot People and the Guilty Remnant (also known as the Watchers) prey upon the vulnerable and the grieving survivors. . . . Kevin Garvey's wife, Laurie, leaves him for the Guilty Remnant, while his son chooses to seek a father figure in the charismatic leader of the Healing Hug Movement. Kevin's teenage daughter lives at home, but spends her time drinking and playing a more adventurous version of 'Spin the Bottle' with other bored teenagers. Meanwhile, Kevin takes on the role of Mapleton's new mayor, with no real agenda except to try to bring together a town that is about to fall apart. Perrotta has a gifted ear for dialogue and a distinct appreciation for the particularities of suburban life." Minneapolis Star Tribune

Perrotta, Tom

★ **Little** children. St. Martin's Press 2004 355p $24.95
ISBN 0-312-31571-6

LC 2003-15947

"The eponymous children in this satirical novel are actually adults who, chafing at the burdens of parenthood, try to recreate their unencumbered youth. Sarah, an overeducated young homemaker, likens her tantrum-prone daughter to a 'brooding Russian epileptic' out of Dostoevsky, and pines for lost college days of feminism and bisexuality. While her husband orders used panties online, she has furtive sex with a stay-at-home dad whose repeated failure to pass the bar has earned him the contempt of his gorgeous wife. The humor is sometimes cruel, but Perrotta never betrays the complexity of his characters." New Yorker

Perry, Anne

Bedford Square. Fawcett Columbine 1999 330p $24.95
ISBN 0-449-90633-7

LC 98-29854

"Through a campaign of 'whisper, suspicion and innuendo,' someone is slandering men of high position in 1891 London society, and it is up to Thomas Pitt, commander of the Bow Street police station, to scotch these poisonous rumors of dishonorable behavior before reputations are destroyed and lives ruined. Through his discreet investigations, the sympathetic Pitt exposes the subtle cruelty of the anonymous letters that bring disgrace to one man and death to another." N Y Times Book Rev

Perry, Anne ✓

Belgrave Square. Fawcett Columbine 1992 361p

LC 91-73144

The author "paints handsome portraits of . . . {Victorian} aristocratic society and provides luxurious details of the gala balls and garden parties, the fashionable outings at Covent Garden and the Royal Academy of Arts, where they congregate to preen themselves. But it isn't all done for show. The author has the eyes of a hawk for character nuance and her claws out for signs of the criminal injustices rampant among the privileged classes during this gilded historical period." N Y Times Book Rev

Perry, Anne

Bluegate Fields. St. Martin's Press 1984 308p

LC 84-11769

"Inspector Pitt and his splendid wife, Charlotte, pursue {a} murder investigation that takes them from the squalor of the slums to the hypocrisy of high-society drawing rooms in Victorian London. Pitt is uncomfortable with a case built against a humorless tutor by a zealous young policeman who possesses a potentially obstructive reverence for the upper class. However the witnesses appear irrefutable . . . and Pitt's superior is adamant about not reopening so embarrassing a case—a teenager from a wealthy family was murdered in a bathtub and shoved down a London sewer. Charlotte, impelled by the tutor's wife, launches her own campaign to prove that the wrong man has been arrested." Booklist

Perry, Anne

A **breach** of promise. Fawcett Columbine 1998 374p $25
ISBN 0-449-90849-6

LC 98-21212

"Aside from the jarring coincidence that sets up the resolution, the story is full of feeling and weighted with intelligent thought about the status of women in mid-Victorian society." N Y Times Book Rev

Perry, Anne

Buckingham Palace gardens; a novel. Ballantine Books 2008 312p $26
ISBN 978-0-345-46931-1; 0-345-46931-3

LC 2007-42767

A mystery featuring Perry's 19th-century police inspector, Thomas Pitt. "Unlike so many detective series gliding on cruise control, this mature work provides a fine introduction to Perry's alluring world of Victorian crime and intrigue. Ever the master of her milieu, she delivers sumptuous descriptions of life among the gentry when England still basked in its imperial glory. And in an intricate plot about a murder at the palace while the Prince and Princess of Wales are in residence, she also marshals the series's major themes: the way crime reverberates throughout the social classes; the precarious status of women of every rank; and the need for honorable heroes to preserve and protect the Empire, sometimes from itself." N Y Times Book Rev

Perry, Anne

Cain his brother. Fawcett Columbine 1995 390p

LC 95-8680

"This one deserves high marks for superb plotting, fine writing, intriguing characters, and outstanding historical detail." Booklist

Perry, Anne

Cardington Crescent. St. Martin's Press 1987 314p

LC 86-27942

A Victorian "mystery featuring the stalwart Inspector Thomas Pitt of Scotland Yard and his inquisitive wife, Charlotte. When Charlotte's beloved sister is suspected of poisoning her philandering husband, the Pitts undertake the investigation of the unfortunate victim's seemingly irreproachable, upper-crust family. Amid the luxurious splendor of an elegant town house and the hideous squalor of a London slum, they uncover a scandalous web of depravity and corruption that has inevitably culminated in the murder. A detailed period puzzler suffused with atmosphere, emotion, and suspense." Booklist

Perry, Anne

A **dangerous** mourning. Fawcett Columbine 1991 330p

LC 91-70655

"Murder in an aristocratic London household pits Inspector William Monk . . . against the Victorian sense of propriety, a bootlicking superior officer and a family's fierce determination to protect its reputation. Octavia Haslett, widowed daughter of Sir Basil Moidore, is found stabbed to death in her bedroom dressed only in nightclothes; when Monk proves no outsider could have entered the house that night, the family and servants remain sole suspects. As tension mounts in the household and a handsome and disliked footman becomes a scapegoat, Monk covertly arranges to introduce Hester Latterly, who served with Florence Nightingale in the Crimea and has helped Monk before, as a nurse in the Moidore home." Publ Wkly

Perry, Anne

Death of a stranger. Ballantine Bks. 2002 337p
ISBN 0-345-44005-6

LC 2002-66735

This Monk mystery "opens with the murder of a wealthy railroad businessman in a brothel. Outraged by the crime, high society pressures the police into cracking down on prostitution. But a police presence is bad for business, and the pimps take out their frustration on the call girls. These battered women seek medical assistance at a Coldbath Square clinic rum by Monk's wife, Hester. . . . Meanwhile, a mysterious young socialite asks Monk to investigate her fiancé, a partner in a successful railroad company that, she fears, is involved in fraud and corruption." Libr J

Perry, Anne

Defend and betray. Fawcett Columbine 1992 385p

LC 92-52665

"The climactic trial, and its ugly disclosures, are well wrought. . . . Throughout, the plight of the intelligent, educated woman who is not rich—her need for a meaningful independence, her culture's resistance to her fulfillment—is, while not deeply explored, frequently touched upon." N Y Times Book Rev

Perry, Anne

The **face** of a stranger. Fawcett Columbine 1990 328p

LC 90-34169

The author "understands her amnesiac sleuth so intimately that she knows he can rediscover himself only in moments of inspiration along the trail of his quarry. This, and the fact that Monk has more to learn about himself even as the story concludes, are brilliant touches that effectively blend contemporary understanding of character with a Victorian sensibility." N Y Times Book Rev

Perry, Anne

Farriers' Lane. Fawcett Columbine 1993 374p

LC 92-54390

"In the wave of anti-Semitic hysteria in 1884 that follows the crucifixion of an English gentleman, a young Jewish actor is hastily tried and executed for the crime. Five years later, a justice of the appeals court is murdered when he attempts to reopen the sensational case. Only a man of discretion, intelligence and integrity—a man like Inspector Thomas Pitt of the Bow Street police division—can solve the devious affair of passion and political intrigue in Victorian London." N Y Times Book Rev

Perry, Anne

Funeral in blue. Ballantine Bks. 2001 344p
ISBN 0-345-44001-3

LC 2001-37481

A mystery featuring Hester and William Monk. "In the studio of a London artist, two women have been murdered, one of them the wife of Dr. Kristian Beck, a physician from Vienna with whom Hester's dear friend, Lady Callandra, is secretly in love. When Beck is charged with the murder, Callandra enlists the aid of Hester and William. . . . The author excels at re-creating the ambience of 1860s London streets." Publ Wkly

Perry, Anne

Half Moon Street. Ballantine Bks. 2000 312p
ISBN 0-449-00655-7

LC 99-55232

"Perry sinks inspector Pitt knee-deep in the morally suspect world of the theater and the completely subterranean culture of pornography. . . . Cameos from Oscar Wilde and W.B. Yeats add to the sense of artistic turmoil set against middle-class timidity." Booklist

Perry, Anne

Highgate rise. Fawcett Columbine 1991 330p

LC 90-85131

"Inspector Thomas Pitt, is appalled by the callousness of an arsonist who torches a physician's town house, burning his wife to death. Pitt's highborn wife, Charlotte, shares his horror when she learns that the dead woman was a quiet crusader on behalf of poor slum tenants. . . . Ms. Perry gives Pitt a breather from his customary gutter research by confining his investigation to the victim's upper-class social circle. Following her own conscience, Charlotte insinuates her way into elegant drawing rooms where the author's satirical wit is free to spread its rather showy skirts." N Y Times Book Rev

Perry, Anne

The **Hyde** Park headsman. Fawcett Columbine 1994 392p

LC 93-22124

Inspector Thomas Pitt "struggles to solve the brutal and confounding murder of Captain the Honorable Oakley Winthrop, R.N., who's been found beheaded in Hyde Park. Pitt suspects the victim knew his killer, but it's only after three more deadly murders take place that enough evidence can be mustered to accuse the real killer." Booklist

Perry, Anne

No graves as yet; a novel of World War I. Ballantine Bks. 2003 642p $25.95
ISBN 0-345-45652-1

LC 2003-52233

"Perry's melancholy evocation of the 'eternal afternoon' that would soon turn to night all over England is lovely." N Y Times Book Rev

Perry, Anne

Paragon Walk. St. Martin's Press 1981 204p

"A psychopathic killer stalks the fashionable London neighborhood called Paragon Walk—the rapist's atrocities are as incredible, and terrifying to the Paragon Walk aristocrats as a sudden outbreak of the bubonic plague. Inspector Pitt's investigation of one brutal slaying, that of 17-year-old Fanny Nash, leads him to his own family—and himself." Booklist

Perry, Anne

Pentecost Alley. Fawcett Columbine 1996 405p

LC 95-43557

"Perry has created a superbly plotted, grippingly suspenseful period piece filled with intriguing characters and fascinating descriptions of the manners and customs of Victorian London." Booklist

Perry, Anne

Resurrection row. St. Martin's Press 1981 204p

LC 81-8846

"For no discernible reason, someone digs up the corpses of recently buried citizens and sets them up in public places. With these crimes demanding Pitt's concentration, he also has to investigate the murder of Godolphin Jones—an artist, pornographer and blackmailer. The detective's efforts to gather evidence against Jones's clients, obvious suspects, are fruitless until (as always) his quick-witted wife Charlotte drops a startling hint." Publ Wkly

Perry, Anne

Seven dials. Ballantine Bks. 2003 345p $25.95
ISBN 0-345-44007-2

LC 2002-35605

"When the Egyptian mistress of a senior cabinet minister is discovered in her garden in the middle of the night, using a wheelbarrow to dispose of the body of a junior diplomat, the apparent crime of passion turns into an international incident. Thomas Pitt. . . chafes at the order from Special Branch to extricate the government official, Saville Ryerson, from the affair; but he sees the gravity of the political situation. . . . Although the focus of the plot tends to drift, the visual panorama is voluptuous to behold." N Y Times Book Rev

Perry, Anne

Shoulder the sky. Ballantine Bks. 2004 338p $25.95
ISBN 0-345-45654-8

"Questions about the morality of war resonate throughout this harrowing novel, which Perry has constructed with hallmark attention to period detail and sense of place. Her vivid evocations of the battlefield . . . are unforgettable." Booklist

Perry, Anne

The **silent** cry. Fawcett Columbine 1997 361p $24.95
ISBN 0-449-90848-8

LC 97-16848

"With her grimly detailed descriptions of the match factories, sweatshops, paupers hospitals and tenement 'rookeries' crowded into these slums, Perry brings a rank sense of reality to the wretched living conditions of the working poor." N Y Times Book Rev

Perry, Anne

The **sins** of the wolf. Fawcett Columbine 1994 374p

LC 94-12099

"Nurse Hester Latterly, who served courageously in the Crimean War and has assisted former policeman William Monk in many of his investigations . . . is charged with murdering a patient for personal gain. Hester hires on to accompany aging but lively Mary Farraline by train from Edinburgh to London and to administer the proper dose of heart medication. But Mary dies enroute—and her pearl brooch is discovered in Hester's bag. The dead woman's family, the police and most of Edinburgh are convinced that Hester killed her to obtain the pin. Coming to her aid are former policeman Monk, barrister Oliver Rathbone and Lady Callandra Daviot." Publ Wkly

Perry, Anne

Slaves of obsession. Ballantine Bks. 2000 344p
ISBN 0-345-43326-2

LC 00-40375

"Perry's images of the carnage and confusion of battle are relentless in their intensity, unflinching in their truth-telling detail." N Y Times Book Rev

Perry, Anne

★ **Southampton** Row. Ballantine Bks. 2002 326p
ISBN 0-345-44003-X

LC 2001-52664

Thomas Pitt "ventures into the world of spiritualism when, on the eve of a critical parliamentary election, the wife of the Liberal candidate is implicated in the murder of a clairvoyant. As she has done increasingly in recent books, Perry links the crime to a secret political cabal known as the Inner Circle and draws everyone into its machinations. . . . Perry's proto-feminists have the kind of intellectual radiance that eludes their spouses." N Y Times Book Rev

Perry, Anne

A **sunless** sea; a William Monk novel. Anne Perry. Ballantine Books 2012 372 p. (hardcover : alk. paper) $26.00
ISBN 034551064X; 9780345510648; 9780345535931

LC 2012022484

This book is part of the William Monk Victorian mystery series. Here, Monk investigates the death of Zenia Gadney, found mutilated on Limehouse Pier. "While the public cries out for blood, Monk, his spirited wife, Hester, and their brilliant barrister friend, Oliver Rathbone, search for answers. From dank waterfront alleys to London's fabulously wealthy West End, the three trail an ice-blooded murderer." (Publisher's note)

Perry, Anne

Traitor's gate. Fawcett Columbine 1995 411p

LC 94-27624

"In combination with her meticulous research, Ms. Perry's infallible feeling for the historical moment yields animated political debate over the colonization of Africa, glittering views of Victorian society at play and tantalizing glimpses of a confident, assertive creature known as the 'new woman.'" N Y Times Book Rev

Perry, Anne

The **twisted** root. Ballantine Bks. 1999 346p $25
ISBN 0-345-43325-4

LC 99-34689

"A beautiful widow named Miriam Gardiner has disappeared, leaving behind a distraught fiancé and a dead coachman. Monk is called in to find Gardiner and then must uncover the truth when she is charged with murdering the coachman." Libr J

Perry, Anne

★ **Weighed** in the balance. Fawcett Columbine 1996 355p

LC 96-34824

William Monk "a Victorian-era 'agent of inquiry,' is still haunted by a baffling amnesia, and he feels that his associates—the rigidly proper barrister Sir Oliver Rathbone and the uncompromising and outspoken nurse Hester Latterly—have taken on more than they can handle when Sir Oliver decides to defend Countess Zorah Rostova against a slander charge. The patriotic Zorah has accused Princess Gisela of Felzburg of murdering her husband, Prince Friedrich, heir to the throne, who presumably had died as a result of a fall from a horse. Gisela is suing. " Publ Wkly

Perry, Anne

The **Whitechapel** conspiracy. Ballantine Bks. 2001 341p
ISBN 0-345-43328-9

LC 00-64206

"When Pitt delivers the testimony that condemns a prominent man for murder, he is 'rewarded' by being shuffled off to the Special Branch, which operates in London's risky East End." Libr J

Perry, Drew

This is just exactly like you. Viking 2010 320p $25.95
ISBN 978-0-670-02154-3; 0-670-02154-7

LC 2009-42562

"If the novel's world sounds a little circumspect, Perry brings it all to life in such remarkably pinpoint, hilarious, and convincing fashion that you revel in spending more than 300 pages here. It's difficult to come across a sentence, let alone a word, that doesn't smack tone-perfect and also refreshingly colloquial, candid, real. His quietly comic touch is equally consistent." Boston Globe

Perry, Sarah, 1979-

The **Essex** Serpent; a novel. Sarah Perry. Custom House 2017 416 p. (hardback) $26.99
ISBN 9780062666376; 0062666371; 9780062666390

LC 2016056531

In this novel by Sarah Perry, "a keen amateur naturalist with no patience for religion or superstition, Cora is immediately enthralled, and certain that what the local people think is a magical sea beast may be a previously undiscovered species. Eager to investigate, she is introduced to local vicar William Ransome. Will, too, is suspicious of the rumors. But unlike Cora, this man of faith is convinced the rumors are caused by moral panic, a flight from true belief." (Publisher's note)

"Stuffed with smarts and storytelling sorcery, this is a work of astonishing breadth and brilliance." Kirkus

Perry, Thomas

Blood money; a novel. Random House 2000 351p $24.95
ISBN 0-679-45304-0

LC 99-18340

"Perry's inventive ways of keeping Jane and her charges one step ahead of the mob squad are downright dazzling—all the more so because they pass up coldblooded technology and go for good old human wit and ingenuity." N Y Times Book Rev

Perry, Thomas

The **boyfriend**. Grove Press 2013 288 p. (hardcover) $25
ISBN 0802126065; 9780802126061

In this mystery, "private investigator Jack Till is hired by the parents of Catherine Hamilton to find her killer. . . . He relentlessly pursues leads to find Catherine's killer, stepping into the sordid territory of high--priced call girls . . . . Before long, he discovers that it isn't just a case of call girls being murdered by their clients. The pattern is in the girls' looks, all beautiful strawberry blondes, and in a custom-made necklace and anklet each of the dead girls was wearing." (Library Journal)

Perry, Thomas

Dance for the dead. Random House 1996 324p
ISBN 0-679-44911-6

LC 95-32716

In this thriller, Native American private agent Jane Whitefield, "appoints herself the guardian angel of Timmy Phillips, a little boy with a big trust fund. The master criminal who had Timmy's foster parents murdered has an ingenious scheme for plundering his inheritance; but, since 'none of this works if the heir is alive,' Jane takes aggressive action to save his life." N Y Times Book Rev

Perry, Thomas

Death benefits; a novel. Random House 2001 383p $24.95
ISBN 0-679-45305-9

LC 00-41476

San Francisco insurance data analyst John Walker is "sleepwalking through his young life when the boss assigns him to assist a private detective on an inside job involving Walker's ex-girlfriend, a claims adjuster who disappeared after being implicated in a $12 million scheme to defraud the company. Judicious applications of Perry's knowing wit energize the tutor-pupil dynamics between Walker and Max Stillman, the crafty and somewhat sinister P.I. who calls the shots on this case." N Y Times Book Rev

Perry, Thomas

The **face**-changers; a novel. Random House 1998 372p $24
ISBN 0-679-45303-2

LC 97-34078

Seneca Indian guide Jane Whitefield "is asked by her surgeon husband to help his old mentor, Dr. Richard Dahlman, who has been accused of murdering his research partner. In her attempts to keep Dahlman out of the hands of the law and far away from the two men who want to kill him, she finds that someone is using her name to make people disappear permanently, and Dahlman has gotten caught in the backlash. . . . The plot is full of heart-stopping suspense, Native American lore, and engaging characters, but the real pull is how Jane will surmount adversity and still keep her honor and ethics intact." Libr J

Perry, Thomas

Fidelity. Harcourt 2008 357p $25
ISBN 978-0-15-101292-3; 0-15-101292-X

LC 2007-26507

Perry's "characters are uncannily good at sizing one another up and anticipating what the next moves will be. Though he briefly equates Hobart's tactics to the ways a coyote slinks through a neighborhood, Mr. Perry need not even articulate this. It's always built into his storytelling, and it's already on the page." N Y Times (Late N Y Ed)

Perry, Thomas

The **informant**. Houghton Mifflin Harcourt 2011 325p $27
ISBN 978-0-547-56933-8; 0-547-56933-5

LC 2010-43566

"Perry's immaculate style—clean, polished, uncluttered by messy emotions—suits the Butcher's Boy, who executes his kills with the same cool, dispassionate skill." N Y Times Book Rev

Perry, Thomas

Nightlife; a novel. Random House 2006 373p $24.95
ISBN 1-4000-6004-4

LC 2005-46449

"This novel's intensity comes from the skillful way in which Perry lets readers in on the secrets of the serial killer: we see her change disguises and identities; we see her pick up and destroy men. We see more than the police and the private eye do, as they try to find the woman they suspect killed the Portland man, and as we see her leave that old identity far, far behind. Perry also offers a complex character in detective Catherine Hobbes as she races against the private eye to catch a protean killer." Booklist

Perry, Thomas

Poison flower; a Jane Whitefield novel. Thomas Perry. Mysterious Pr: Grove/Atlantic 2012 274 p. $24
ISBN 9780802126054

In this book, "Jane Whitefield's latest attempt to hide someone other people are looking for puts her in even more danger than usual, and that's not easy. Jane has . . . little trouble breaking James Shelby, framed for murdering his wife, out of police custody at the Clara Shortridge Foltz Criminal Courts Building in Los Angeles. . . . Three hard types who've been tracking Shelby go after Jane instead. Driving her to a remote desert location, they . . . seek . . . information about her client, then realize that they can make a queen's ransom by auctioning her off to one of the many criminals she's outwitted. . . . Jane manages to escape and takes refuge in a battered women's shelter in Las Vegas, where she acquires yet another fugitive who must be hidden away." (Kirkus)

Perry, Thomas

Pursuit; a novel. Random House 2002 370p $24.95

ISBN 0-679-45306-7

LC 2001-40365

The key players in this thriller "are James Varney, a sociopathic hit man whose handiwork has left 13 people dead in a Louisville, Ky., restaurant, and Roy Prescott, the professional manhunter hired to track him down by the father of one of the victims. . . . Although Prescott initiates most of the fiendish maneuvers, he is checkmated at every turn by his opponent's ability to anticipate or recover from each trap. When this brilliant game is finally called, it isn't advanced weaponary or high-tech skills that determine the victor; it's one player's greater insights into the other's twisted mind—a mind very much like his own." N Y Times Book Rev

Perry, Thomas

Runner. Houghton Mifflin Harcourt 2009 441p $26

ISBN 978-0-15-101528-3; 0-15-101528-7

LC 2008-7119

"Never melodramatic and always masterful at creating conflicted characters . . . , Perry offers a highly enjoyable tale in which the roles of hunter and hunted are reversed with devastating effect." Libr J

Perry, Thomas

Shadow woman. Random House 1997 350p $22

ISBN 0-679-45302-4

"Although the frantic pace allows no time for sight-seeing, Perry lingers long enough over Pete's amiable character to make him worth all this excruciating suspense." N Y Times Book Rev

Perry, Thomas

Vanishing act. Random House 1995 289p

ISBN 0-679-43536-0

LC 94-17413

"Jane Whitefield is a Seneca Indian from upstate New York who has set herself up as a one-woman underground railroad to help worthy fugitives disappear. . . . A desperate man like John Felker is right up her alley. A burned-out cop who quit the job to become an accountant, Felker was set up on an embezzlement rap. But he grabbed the dough anyway, and now he has a contract on his head. Drawing on her clan contacts, Jane guides Felker on a trip into oblivion, via a rugged route across the Canadian border. This is all very satisfying and quite scenic—until certain deadly reversals tip off Jane that her operation has been compromised." N Y Times Book Rev

Persson, Leif G. W.

Another time, another life; the story of a crime. Leif GW Persson ; translated from the Swedish by Paul Norlen. Pantheon Books 2011 404 p.

ISBN 9780307377463

LC 2011017394

In this book, "[t]he story, based on real events linked to the still-unsolved assassination of Swedish prime minister Olof Palme, picks up in 1989, as the seemingly unrelated stabbing death of a civil servant is investigated by officers Bo Jarnebring and Anna Holt. . . . [T]he case gets surreptitiously swept under the rug, and the victim is tied to a string of sex-related crimes, despite evidence to the contrary. Another ten years pass before the confounding truth about the murder victim is unearthed. Just as Lars Martin Johansson, a friend of Jarnebring's, begins his tenure as the head of the Swedish Security Police, . . . [r]evealed . . . are not only the identities of the other collaborators but also the identity of the murderer: an intelligent, capable lawyer a heartbeat away from the top position in Sweden's Ministry of Defense." (Publisher's note)

Persson, Leif G. W.

Between summer's longing and winter's end; the story of a crime. Leif G.W. Persson ; translated from the Swedish by Paul Norlen. Pantheon Books 2010 551 p.

ISBN 0307377458; 9780307377456

LC 2010004678

This book begins when a "young man falls to his death from a window in a student dorm in Stockholm, his loose shoe striking and killing the little dog being taken for his evening walk by an old man. . . . [T] he young man is American, not Swedish, and there are a couple of odd things about his room when . . . [the police] search it. . . . [Author] Leif GW Persson . . . begins to unravel . . . a web of international espionage, backroom politics, greed, sheer incompetence, and the shoddy work of Sweden's intelligence force that leads to the murder of the prime minister. [This book is t]he first novel in a . . . trilogy . . . [that offers a] fictional account of the unsolved 1986 assassination of Swedish Prime Minister Olof Palme." (Publisher's note)

Persson, Leif G. W.

Free falling, as if in a dream; the story of a crime. Leif GW Persson ; translated from the Swedish by Paul Norlen. 1st American ed. Pantheon Books 2014 608 p. $27.95

ISBN 0307377474; 9780307377470

LC 2012050987

This book, by Leif G.W. Persson and translated by Paul Norlen, is "centered on the assassination of Olof Palme in 1986. It's August 2007, and Lars Martin Johansson, chief of the National Bureau of Criminal Investigation in Sweden, is determined once again to reopen the dusty files on the unsolved murder of Prime Minister Palme. . . . But the closer the group gets to the truth, the more Johansson compromises the greater good for personal gain, becoming a pawn in the private vendetta of a shady political spin doctor." (Publisher's note)

"Strong characterization, a solid grasp of investigatory complexities, and an appreciation of the elusive, chimerical nature of "truth" make this a fine example of a conspiracy thriller." Pub Wkly

Pesci, David

Amistad; the thunder of freedom. Marlowe & Co. 1997 292p hardcover o.p. pa $12.95

ISBN 1-56924-748-X; 1-56924-703-X pa

LC 96-54050

"In August 1839, Singbe-Pleh, a Mende tribesman, led his fellow African captives aboard the Spanish ship Amistad in successful revolt. The Africans took over the ship but could not sail it back to Africa. They were captured and put on trial in Connecticut. . . . The case was politically charged, with pro-slavery President Van Buren's administration wanting to give the Africans to Spain, abolitionists rallying for their freedom, and former President John Quincy Adams eventually defending them before the Supreme Court. Pesci deftly blends the facts of this fascinating historical episode with story." SLJ

Pessl, Marisha

★ **Night** Film; A Novel. Marisha Pessl. Random House Inc. 2013 624 p.

ISBN 9781400067886

LC 2012041163

In this book, "when Scott McGrath hears that the young woman found dead in an abandoned Chinatown warehouse is Ashley Cordova, his investigative journalist genes begin to percolate. He knows Ashley as the gorgeous daughter of the legendary cult horror film director Stanislas Cordova. . . . The reporter has his own previous history with the elder Cordova and almost from the first, he suspects that, whatever the coroner said, Ashley's death was no suicide." (Publishers Weekly)

Includes bibliographical references and index

Pessl, Marisha

Special topics in calamity physics. Viking 2006 514p il $25.95

ISBN 0-670-03777-X

LC 2005-58474

"Even the physics equation on the book's back cover has outsized verve. And what begins as a dubious proposition, in a world wholly without need for additions to its Prep School Confidential bibliography, becomes a whirling, glittering, multifaceted marvel, delivered in an irrepressibly smart and flamboyant new voice." N Y Times (Late N Y Ed)

Peters, Elizabeth

The **deeds** of the disturber; an Amelia Peabody mystery. Atheneum Pubs. 1988 289p

LC 87-33457

"Determined Victorian feminist Peabody refuses to be intimidated by a phenomenon reported at the British Museum, where a sem priest is supposedly working a curse in revenge for the desecration of an ancient mummy. The priest's supernatural figure is momentarily glimpsed at the exhibit, before a murderer strikes. Disobeying Emerson, of course, Peabody lays her life on the line and unmasks the decidedly human villain." Publ Wkly

Peters, Elizabeth

The **golden** one. Morrow 2002 429p

ISBN 0-380-97885-7

LC 2001-52169

"On arriving in Luxor for a season of archaeological investigation, Amelia {Peabody Emerson} and her family discover that war (it's 1917) has taken its toll on their beloved Egypt. Before too long, the conflict intrudes on their plans and embroils them in an adventure, complete with double agents, Turkish spies, derring-do, and the ever-puzzling Sethos. At the same time, they must reckon with tomb robbers, killers, and antiquities fraud." Booklist

Peters, Elizabeth

★ **Guardian** of the horizon. Morrow 2004 416p $24.95

ISBN 0-06-621471-8

LC 2003-67665

"Peters' writing works on several levels. She maintains a fast-paced mystery story, her characters are complex, and the fictional cast interacts with historical figures convincingly." Archaeology

Peters, Elizabeth

He shall thunder in the sky; an Amelia Peabody mystery. Morrow 2000 400p

ISBN 0-380-97659-5

LC 00-25807

In this episode, set in 1915, Amelia Peabody's family's "annual excavations in Egypt are overshadowed by the specter of world war. An invasion of Egypt by the Turks seems imminent, the climate is ripe for spies, and it isn't long before the Emerson clan is up to its eyebrows in intrigue. Then there's Emerson's discovery of a beautiful gold statue: Has the ardent archvillain Sethos returned with more tricks? Peters works in drama galore, plus the usual shots of wry humor and local color." Booklist

Peters, Elizabeth

The **hippopotamus** pool. Warner Bks. 1996 384p

LC 95-31886

In this mystery set in 19th century Egypt, Amelia Peabody "is celebrating the turn of the century at a New Year's Eve ball at Shepheard's Hotel in Cairo when she and her husband, the sexy Egyptologist Radcliffe Emerson, are approached by a mysterious stranger who hands over a scarab ring that he claims was recovered from the lost tomb of Queen Tetisheri. 'Oh, good Gad!' Emerson explodes. 'Are we to have another of these melodramatic distractions?' Indeed we are—and it's a dandy one too. Such romantic nonsense. Such fun." N Y Times Book Rev

Peters, Elizabeth

The **last** camel died at noon. Warner Bks. 1991 352p il

LC 90-26759

"The Emersons are decidedly unstodgy Victorians—feminist, democratic, egalitarian, respectful of other cultures—and charming, witty, entertaining sleuths." Booklist

Peters, Elizabeth

Lion in the valley; an Amelia Peabody mystery. Atheneum Pubs. 1986 291p

LC 85-48126

"The stouthearted Victorian Englishwoman, Amelia Peabody Emerson, and her lusty, irascible husband are back in Egypt (with their precocious eight-year-old son, Ramses in tow). . . . The master criminal whom they thwarted but did not bring to justice in 'The Mummy Case' is once again up to nefarious deeds, which include kidnapping Amelia in order to woo her. Murder, mayhem . . . and a pair of distressed young lovers, not to mention a modicum of archaeological pursuits, round out a decided treat for fans of the indomitable duo—or, perhaps, with Ramses, it is now a trio." Booklist

Peters, Elizabeth

The **mummy** case. Congdon & Weed 1985 313p

LC 84-21500

"Victorian Amelia Peabody with her virile husband Emerson and precocious son Ramses embarks on a . . . archaeological dig in Egypt—but not before the death of a dealer in stolen antiquities. A disappearing mummy case and missing Coptic Papyri are the clues in this slapstick comedy-mystery. The ample archaeological detail is vivid, albeit a bit confusing. The irresistable attraction of this story: the heroine's droll tone and intrepid spirit." Libr J

Peters, Elizabeth

Night train to Memphis. Warner Bks. 1994 353p

LC 94-3967

Vicky Bliss, "a curator at Munich's National Museum, is asked to go undercover on a cruise down the Nile. Her mission: to spot who among her fellow passengers might be the master criminal about to carry out a major theft of valuable antiquities. Vicky has a sneaking suspicion that the thief the police are after is the mysterious man she knows as John, who's perfectly capable of illegal activities and who's been both her sworn enemy and her sometime lover. When John shows up on the cruise and a crew member is murdered, Vicky begins to fear her suspicions are correct—but she doesn't have enough evidence to rule out the other passengers. This one is vintage Peters at her entertaining best." Booklist

Peters, Elizabeth

Seeing a large cat. Warner Bks. 1997 386p il

LC 96-37998

"Amelia's unquenchable joie de l'aventure continues to define the exuberant style of these mysteries, but Peters doesn't leave it at that. There are always grand views of Egyptian antiquities in her stories, as well as acidic caricatures of globe-trotting tourists and the endlessly entertaining spectacle of busy professional parents confounded by their own progeny." N Y Times Book Rev

Peters, Elizabeth

The **snake,** the crocodile, and the dog. Warner Bks. 1992 340p

LC 92-54096

In this mystery novel, archaeologist Amelia Peabody Emerson and her husband leave their son Ramses in England to excavate in Egypt. "Amelia anticipates time alone with Emerson, but the Master Criminal devises otherwise: In his quest for directions to the . . . Lost Oasis, he attempts abduction, subterfuge, and espionage." Libr J

Peters, Ellis

The **benediction** of Brother Cadfael. Mysterious Press 1992 348p il maps

LC 91-50965

A combined edition of A morbid taste for bones and One corpse too many, both entered separately. This volume also includes a description of Cadfael country by Rob Talbot and Robin Whiteman

Peters, Ellis

Brother Cadfael's penance; the twentieth chronicle of Brother Cadfael. Mysterious Press 1994 292p

LC 94-27140

This Brother Cadfael mystery "has the gentle monk leaving his cloister on a journey that will prove both dangerous and wrenching. In twelfth-century Britain, a rebellion has arisen, with factional fighting between the knights supporting Empress Maud and those swearing allegiance to her cousin Stephen. Philip FitzRobert, a traitor to the empress, has taken 30 hostages, among them a young man named Olivier de Bretagne, who is Cadfael's son from a chance encounter years earlier. Although Cadfael has lost tract of the boy's mother, he's never forgotten his son, and once he finds out that Olivier has been spirited away and imprisoned, nothing . . . can keep him from setting out to find the young man who has never known his true father." Booklist

Peters, Ellis

Dead man's ransom; the ninth chronicle of Brother Cadfael. Morrow 1985 189p

LC 84-22668

First published 1984 in the United Kingdom

This "novel focuses on the brutality of civil war between England and Wales in the early twelfth century, as the Benedictine monk is pulled into a hostage drama that turns into a politically repercussive murder. A young Welshman is exchanged for the sheriff of Shropshire and taken to Cadfael's abbey, where he falls in love with the sheriff's daughter. The sheriff's subsequent murder leaves rampant speculation that the young lovers are the perpetrators of the crime. Cadfael, as ever, is patient and insightful. A wonderfully atmospheric whodunit." Booklist

Peters, Ellis

Death to the landlords! Morrow 1972 221p

The setting is "southern India, and the landlords are wealthy landholders who are the objectives of a terrorist murder gang. Dominic Felse . . . is at the center of the action, touring with a casual American acquaintance. The two young men meet up again and again with some of the same people as they travel India's Cape Comorin, among them a very intense English girl and a shy Indian nurse. Although the setting seems idyllic and the young people most attractive there is an undercurrent of brutal violence that hits home hard. The deaths are achieved by bombing. . . . Most effective of all is the interesting, perceptive, intuitive portrait of . . . problem-ridden India that emerges." Publ Wkly

Peters, Ellis

Fallen into the pit. Mysterious Press 1994 324p

LC 92-50656

First published 1951 in the United Kingdom

"This mystery launched Peters's Inspector Felse series. Set in Britain just after WW II, the main sleuth here is not actually George Felse but his 13-year-old son Dominic. He and his best friend, Pussy Hart, are playing when Dom finds the body of Helmut Schauffler, an ex-P.O.W. who had stayed on after the war in the Comerford area. An autopsy indicates that Schauffler's skull was fractured by blows that were 'precise, neat and of murderous intention.' Helmut, a loathsome blend of cruelty, cowardice and anti-Semitism, is hardly mourned, but his death so rends the village's social fabric that solving the case is imperative. In his first murder investigation, George has difficulty viewing his neighbors as suspects." Publ Wkly

Peters, Ellis

★ The **hermit** of Eyton Forest. Mysterious Press 1988 224p

LC 87-40398

"A 10-year-old boy in school at the abbey suddenly finds himself Lord of Eaton when his father dies. His grandmother has plans for him; she wants him to marry a neighboring heiress. The abbot refuses to let him go. The grandmother takes steps to get him back. During all this, a mysterious monk living as a hermit and an equally mysterious young man who runs errands for him make their presence strongly felt. A nobleman is murdered, and the sharp eyes of Brother Cadfael notice things that are not apparent to all." N Y Times Book Rev

Peters, Ellis

Monk's-hood; the third chronicle of Brother Cadfael. Morrow 1981 223p il

LC 80-26326

First published 1980 in United Kingdom

In this novel Brother "Cadfael investigates the murder by monkshood of Gervase Bonel, a wealthy man who was about to donate his lands to the monastery. Along the way, Cadfael becomes swept up in the monastery's internecine power plays. Peters' language has a full, rich cadence, and her story is wonderfully vivid." Booklist

Peters, Ellis

The **potter's** field; the seventeenth chronicle of Brother Cadfael, of the Benedictine Abbey of Saint Peter and Saint Paul, at Shrewsbury. Mysterious Press 1990 230p

LC 90-6340

"In place of the pretty romances with which the author often lightens her historically plausible fictions, Ms. Peters provides darker characters and a more somber view of Shrewsbury life. More than the brilliant detection of a crime, the true subject of her wintry tale is human misery, as it extends from the meanest peasant cottage to the grandest manor house." N Y Times Book Rev

Peters, Ellis ✓

A **rare** Benedictine. Mysterious Press 1989 118p il $19.95
ISBN 0-89296-397-2

LC 89-42603

First published 1988 in the United Kingdom

The author "reveals for the first time how her medieval sleuth, Brother Cadfael, came to his calling at Shrewsbury Abbey. . . . For all his spirituality, mild Brother Cadfael once again impresses us with his practical grasp of the criminal side of human nature." N Y Times Book Rev

Peters, Ellis ✓

The **rose** rent; the thirteenth chronicle of Brother Cadfael. Morrow 1986 190p

LC 87-5733

"When Judith Perle, a most generous benefactor of the abbey, vanishes without a trace, Cadfael immediately connects her disappearance with the vicious murder of a pious young monk and the seemingly senseless destruction of a rose bush. An accomplished whodunit meticulously wrought with a wealth of medieval detail." Booklist

Peters, Ellis ✓

Saint Peter's Fair; the fourth chronicle of Brother Cadfael. Morrow 1981 219p il

LC 81-11020

Brother Cadfael, "who led an adventurous life in the world before becoming a monk, is on the side of young love, honor and truth as he investigates deaths taking place while a local fair is in full swing. A well-respected merchant is found murdered, and his lovely daughter takes it upon herself to keep secrets so she involves two young men, both of whom fancy her. Another death occurs. Peters has an authentic eye and ear for her 12th century way of life and death, and engages our interest all the way." Publ Wkly

Peters, Ellis

The **sanctuary** sparrow; the seventh chronicle of Brother Cadfael. Morrow 1983 221p

LC 83-5389

Brother Cadfael "undertakes the problems of young Liliwin, a juggler and acrobat of Shrewsbury who stands accused of pilfering the valuables of one Master Walter Aurifaber, the townships's goldsmith, while Liliwin was amusing Aurifaber and the assembled patrons who were at the wedding feast of Aurifaber's son, Daniel." West Coast Rev Books

Peters, Ellis ✓

The **summer** of the Danes. Mysterious Press 1991 251p

LC 91-11621

In this novel Brother Cadfael "must pilgrimage deep into Wales on an errand of Church diplomacy. He is accompanied by young Brother Mark and the passionate Heledd, a young woman fleeing an arranged marriage. The three become pawns in the battle between two Welsh princes and the mercenary Danes whom one prince has hired to help vanquish his brother. There is a murder to be considered when Bledri ap Rhys—who has offended everyone from Heledd's father, Canon Meirion, to countless common soldiers—is found in his bed, stabbed through the heart." Publ Wkly

Peters, Ellis ✓

The **virgin** in the ice; the sixth chronicle of Brother Cadfael. Morrow 1983 220p il

LC 82-14500

First published 1982 in the United Kingdom

"The setting is England during the winter of 1139, A.D. Brother Cadfael, who has taken a vow against war and arms, finds himself in a country torn by civil war. Brother Elyas, a fellow monk of a nearby town, is sent to deliver two orphans, Ermina and Yves Hugonin, and their chaperone Sister Hilaria, to Laurence d'Angers, the childrens' uncle. During the journey Ermina sees her chance to escape and marry her lover. . . . Brother Elyas is attacked by a brutal band of marauders and left for dead. Brother Cadfael, sent on a medical errand to look after Brother Elyas, takes over his responsibility to bring the three safely to Laurence d'Angers. During his journey, Brother Cadfael discovers a murder and feels morally obliged to solve it." Best Sellers

Peters, Ralph

Hell or Richmond; Ralph Peters. Forge 2013 542 p. (hardback) $25.99
ISBN 0765330482; 9780765330482

LC 2012049720

This book by Ralph Peters presents a " fictional reconstruction of the terrible Overland Campaign of 1864. . . . Peters picks up the story that properly begins with Lee's rout and George Meade's failure to pursue and destroy the Army of Northern Virginia. Instead, it was up to a different commander a year later, as Ulysses S. Grant moved in from the west to assume command of the Union Army and pursue that goal." (Kirkus Reviews)

Peterson, Paula W.

Women in the grove. Beacon Press 2004 205p $20
ISBN 0-8070-8352-6

LC 2003-14314

"Each of the stories in this beautiful collection focuses on a woman living with HIV/AIDS. . . . [Peterson] clearly knows her subject, and she challenges the reader to put an individual face and story on the HIV/AIDS epidemic. Rich with emotion, this book is too good to be categorized as any one genre of fiction but should be celebrated and read widely." Libr J

Petrushevskaya, Ludmila

There once lived a woman who tried to kill her neighbor's baby; scary fairy tales. selected and translated with an introduction by Keith Gessen and Anna Summers. Penguin Books 2009 206p pa $15
ISBN 978-0-14-311466-6; 0-14-311466-2

LC 2009-29419

Petrushevskaya "is so disquieting that long after Solzhenitsyn had been published in the Soviet Union, her fiction was banned—even though nothing about it screams 'political' or 'dissident' or anything else. It just screams. These stories work the boundary states of consciousness—between sleep and waking, hallucination and realization, life and death—like a tongue works an aching tooth. You never know where you are or where you're going, because the ground beneath the narratives is constantly shifting. You know only that the world you are in is as bleak as Beckett, as astringent as witch hazel, as poetic as your finest private passing moments." Elle

Petterson, Per

I curse the river of time; translated from the Norwegian by Charlotte Barslund with Per Petterson. Graywolf 2010 233p (Lannan translation series) $23

ISBN 978-1-55597-556-2; 1-55597-556-9

LC 2010-920770

Original Norwegian edition, 2008

This novel "concerns thirtysomething Arvid Jansen, who's reeling from a divorce just as his mother is dying of stomach cancer. Needless to say, it's a sad book, and at times it'll feel alien to readers who've never been young Communists or hung out in, say, Nittedal or Eidsvoll. (The translation can also be quite a rickety bridge.) But there's no denying the novel's Raymond Carver-like power as Arvid and his mother come to terms with how life hands you hope just before it hands you disappointment and tragedy." Entertainment Wkly

Petterson, Per

I refuse; Per Petterson, Don Bartlett. Graywolf Press 2015 224 p. (alk. paper) $25

ISBN 1555976999; 9781555976996

LC 2014950984

"In his signature spare style, [author Per] Petterson weaves a tale of two men whose accidental meeting one morning recalls their boyhood thirty-five years ago. . . . Now Jim fishes alone on a bridge as Tommy drives by in a new Mercedes, and it's clear their fortunes have reversed. Over the course of the day, the life of each man will be irrevocably altered." (Publisher's note)

"Without pyrotechnics, Petterson brings his characters and working-class Norway vividly, even passionately, to life; days after they finish the novel , readers may still have dreams of ice cracking." Kirkus

Petterson, Per

In the wake; translated from the Norwegian by Anne Born. Thomas Dunne Books 2006 202p $22.95

ISBN 0-312-34383-3

LC 2006-40196

Original Norwegian edition, 2002

This novel is, "among other things, a story about literature itself. . . . Arvid, amid his struggles, reads and rereads the works of favorite writers and poets. Ultimately, moving between literature, with its ability to confer meaning on life, and his growing willingness to re-engage with life, Arvid cautiously rejoins the world. In 'In the Wake' Mr. Petterson demonstrates, through his own commanding art, the solace of the written word as well as the necessity of human connection. It is understandable why European readers have long admired his work." N Y Times Book Rev

Petterson, Per

It's fine by me; Per Petterson, Don Bartlett. Graywolf Press 2012 208 p. (alk. paper) $22.00

ISBN 1555976263; 9781555976262

LC 2012936227

This book, by Per Petterson, follows the character "Arvid Jansen in his youth. . . . Arvid befriends a boy named Audun. On Audun's first day of school he refuses to talk or take off his sunglasses. . . . Audun lives with his mother in a working-class district of Oslo. He delivers newspapers and talks for hours about Jack London and Ernest Hemingway with Arvid. But he's not sure that school is the right path for him and feels that life holds other possibilities." (Publisher's note)

Petterson, Per

★ **Out** stealing horses; translated by Anne Born. Graywolf Press 2007 258p (Lannen translation series selection) $22

ISBN 978-1-55597-470-1; 1-55597-470-8

LC 2006-938263

Original Norwegian edition, 2003; this translation first published 2005 in the United Kingdom

In this "novel, Trond Sander, a widower nearing seventy, moves to a bare house in remote eastern Norway, seeking the life of quiet contemplation that he has always longed for. A chance encounter with a neighbor—the brother, as it happens, of his childhood friend Jon—causes him to ruminate on the summer of 1948, the last he spent with his adored father, who abandoned the family soon afterward. Trond's recollections center on a single afternoon, when he and Jon set out to take some horses from a nearby farm; what began as an exhilarating adventure ended abruptly and traumatically in an act of unexpected cruelty. Petterson's spare and deliberate prose has astonishing force, and the narrative gains further power from the artful interplay of Trond's childhood and adult perspectives." New Yorker

Pettersson, Vicki

The **taken**; Vicki Pettersson. Harpercollins 2012 417 p.

ISBN 0062064649; 9780062064646

This supernatural suspense romance novel by Vicki Petterson follows "Griffin Shaw [who] used to be a PI, . . . Fifty years later, he's an angel. . . . One small mistake has altered fate, and now he's been dumped back onto the mortal mudflat to collect another soul—Katherine 'Kit' Craig, a journalist whose latest investigation is about to get her clipped. . . . Grif refuses to let [her] come to harm. Besides, protecting her offers a chance to solve the mystery of his own unsolved murder. . . . But a ruthless killer determined to destroy them isn't Grif's biggest threat. His growing attraction to Kit could cost them both their lives, along with the answer to the haunting question of his long afterlife." (Publisher's note)

Phillips, Arthur, 1969-

Prague; a novel. Random House 2002 367p

ISBN 0-375-50787-6

LC 2001-48975

"In Phillips's wry and skillful telling, a sexual tryst or the renting of an apartment can become a tragicomic pantomime about East and West. . . . As @Prague' progresses, each of the five foreigners at the cafe table becomes less and less attractive, and the satiric edge to Phillips's portrayal sharpens into something close to anger: at their solipsism, their savage cynicism, their detachment from their surrounding and from one another." N Y Times Book Rev

Phillips, Arthur, 1969-

The **song** is you; a novel. Random House 2009 254p $25

ISBN 978-1-4000-6646-9; 1-4000-6646-8

LC 2008-28845

This novel "takes on loneliness, alienation, middle age and what it means to feel passé and weighted down by your past. . . . Yet despite these sober concerns, Phillips' sparkling prose makes for a seriously fun read." San Francisco Chron

Phillips, Arthur, 1969-

★ The **tragedy** of Arthur. Random House 2011 368p $25.95

ISBN 978-1-4000-6647-6

LC 2010-21192

This novel "turns on the discovery of a lost Shakespearean drama, 'The Most Excellent and Tragical Historie of Arthur, King of Britain,' purportedly written in 1596. The play spreads across the final 107 pages of this book in strict iambic pentameter and five acts. The drama centers on King Arthur, without his famous sword in the stone, mired in 5th century lust, doubt and battle. The novel's narrator, Arthur Phillips, believes the play a hideous fraud, perpetrated by his con-artist father, a forger also called Arthur Phillips. If you are counting, we're up to five Arthurs — the mythical king, the pivotal character in the new play, the writer of this novel, the narrator of the book (himself a novelist) and the narrator's father. But instead of sinking into an annoying bog of meta-fiction; the story is light, the tone often diabolically merry. Random House, the publisher of both actual novelist and fictional narrator, is hungry to capitalize, drawing up contracts and recruiting a vetting panel of scholars." Cleveland Plain Dealer

Phillips, Caryl

Dancing in the dark. Knopf 2005 209p $23.95

ISBN 1-4000-4396-4

LC 2005-44106

"As subjects for historical novels go, Bert Williams is an inspired choice; his strange career exemplified all the ironies and paradoxes that confronted the African-American performers of his time. . . . Dancing in the Dark is riveting when it recreates mores and social conventions our culture has done its best to forget." N Y Times Book Rev

Phillips, Caryl

A **distant** shore. Knopf 2003 277p $23.95

ISBN 1-400-04109-0

"This muted, sad novel breaks down the distinction between the placed and the displaced, dissolving our sense of security, if we had one, about safely belonging in the world, dispelling our illusion of being at home. We are all adrift, Phillips says, whether we know it or not: a fact not of race or nationality, but of the human condition." N Y Times Book Rev

Phillips, Caryl

Foreigners. Alfred A. Knopf 2007 235p $24.95

ISBN 978-1-4000-4397-2

LC 2007-29219

"With great empathy, and through a collage of voices, Phillips has created three distinct portraits. All are superbly crafted and utterly absorbing . . . . As Phillips suggests, Englishness, like foreignness, is a complex and changeable thing. An important and sobering book, highly relevant today." Daily Mail

Phillips, Gin

Fierce kingdom; a novel. Gin Phillips. Viking 2017 275 p. (hardcover : acid-free paper) $25

ISBN 9780735224285; 9780735224278

LC 2016057138

In this novel, by Gin Phillips, "the zoo is nearly empty as Joan and her four-year-old son soak up the last few moments of playtime. . . . But what Joan sees as she hustles her son toward the exit gate minutes before closing time sends her sprinting back into the zoo, her child in her arms. And for the next three hours . . . she keeps on running. Joan's intimate knowledge of her son and of the zoo itself . . . is all that keeps them a step ahead of danger." (Publisher's note)

"A searing exploration of motherhood at its most basic, this all-too-plausible horror story may haunt even readers with steely nerves and strong stomachs." Pub Wkly

Phillips, Helen

The **beautiful** bureaucrat; a novel. by Helen Phillips. Henry Holt & Co. 2015 192 p. (hardcover) $25

ISBN 9781627793766

LC 2014045386

In this novel, by Helen Phillips, "Josephine inputs an endless string of numbers into something known only as The Database. After a long period of joblessness, she's not inclined to question her fortune, but as the days inch by and the files stack up, Josephine feels increasingly anxious in her surroundings. . . . When one evening her husband Joseph disappears and then returns, offering no explanation as to his whereabouts, her creeping unease shifts decidedly to dread." (Publisher's note)

"Phillips takes situations and sentiments that will be all too familiar to many readers—a soul-crushingly dull job that callously steals our youth and beauty, the desperate yearning to be free of it, the restoring power of love and food and intimacy and of shared language and laughter—and uses them to explore bigger universal themes of life and death and the choices and compromises they demand. Intense and enigmatic, tense and tender, this novel offers no easy answers—its deeper meanings may mystify—but it grabs you up, propels you along, and leaves you gasping, grasping, and ready to read it again." Kirkus

Phillips, Jayne Anne

Lark and Termite; a novel. Alfred A. Knopf 2009 254p $24

ISBN 978-0-375-40195-4; 0-375-40195-4

LC 2008-33453

National Book Award Finalist: Fiction (2009)

Phillips "has done in Lark and Termite what she did in previous novels such as Machine Dreams (1984) and Shelter (1994), which is to take a relatively simple, straightforward tale and twist it into something luminous and haunting and singular. This is Phillips' first novel in almost a decade, but it doesn't feel tardy or excessively fussed over. It feels fresh. It feels as if it has been taken straight from the griddle and is still too hot to touch. And because it deals with issues over which people have been arguing for centuries—family and war—the novel's raw immediacy is really quite spectacular." PopMatters

Phillips, Jayne Anne

MotherKind; a novel. Knopf 2000 295p $24

ISBN 0-375-40194-6

LC 99-49256

"Over the course of a year, Kate, a resolutely independent poet and editor, becomes enmeshed in domesticity: she has a baby, acquires two stepchildren, and discovers that her mother is dying of cancer. Kate has always resisted her mother's desire to care for others perfectly, but she's now preoccupied with making crisp French fries, turning down beds, ironing out problems; frequently overwhelmed, she must also rely on nurses and efficient neighbors. Phillips, an abundantly talented writer, never lapses into sentimentality while describing this woman." New Yorker

Phillips, Jayne Anne

★ **Quiet** dell; a novel. by Jayne Anne Phillips. Scribner 2013 480 p. (Hardcover : alk. paper) $28

ISBN 1439172536; 9781439172537

LC 2013016013

Author Jayne Anne Phillips presents a "novel based on a real-life multiple murder by a con man who preyed on widows. Asta Eicher, mother of three, is lonely and despairing, pressed for money after the sudden death of her husband. She begins to receive seductive letters from a chivalrous, elegant man [and] weeks later, all four Eichers are dead. Emily Thornhill, one of the few women journalists in the Chicago press, becomes deeply invested in understanding what happened to this beautiful family." (Publisher's note)

Phillips, Susan Elizabeth

Ain't she sweet. Morrow 2004 383p $24.95

ISBN 0-06-621124-7

LC 2003-59297

This "light, contemporary, and enjoyable love story is filled with alluring plot lines." Libr J

Phillips, Susan Elizabeth

Call me irresistible. Morrow 2011 400p

ISBN 9780061351525; 0061351520; 0062064215; 9780062064219

LC 2010526285

This book tells the story of a young woman named Meg Koranda, whose best friend "is about to Marry Mr. Irresistible -- Ted Beaudine -- the favorite son of Wynette, Texas. . . . [Meg] is determined to save her friend from a mess of heartache. Even though Meg knows that breaking up her best friend's wedding is the right thing to do, no one else seems to agree. . . . [S]tuck . . . with a dead car, an empty wallet, and a very angry bridegroom," (Publisher's note) "Meg earns the animosity of the town, and gradually she and Ted fall in love." (Publishers Weekly)

Phillips, Susan Elizabeth

First lady; Susan Elizabeth Phil[l]ips. Avon Books 2000 376 p. (pbk.) $7.99

ISBN 0380808072; 9780380808076

LC 99095329

RITA Awards: Top Ten Favorite Books (2000)

In this novel, "[t]he beautiful young widow of the President of the United States thought she was free of the White House, but circumstances have forced her back into the role of First Lady. Not for long, however, because she's made up her mind to escape -- if only for a few days -- so she can live the life of an ordinary person. All she needs is the perfect disguise . . . and she's just found it. An entire nation is searching for her, but the First Lady is in the last place anybody would think to look: in the company of a man, an infuriatingly secretive and quietly seductive stranger whose charm, good looks, and sensuous appeal are awakening the forgotten woman within the dignitary." (Publisher's note)

Phillips, Susan Elizabeth

★ **First** Star I See Tonight; A Novel. by Susan Elizabeth Phillips. HarperCollins 2016 384 p. (ebook) $25.99; $26.99

ISBN 9780062405630; 0062405616; 9780062405616

In this novel by Susan Elizabeth Phillips, part of the "Chicago Stars" series, "Piper Dove is a woman with a dream—to become the best detective in the city. . . . And . . . Cooper Graham, a legendary sports hero who always gets what he wants—even if what he wants just might be an intrepid detective hell bent on proving she's as tough as he is. From the . . . streets of Chicago to . . . Biscayne Bay, two people . . . will test . . . each other to discover what matters most." (Publisher's note)

"This thoroughly enjoyable novel delivers a swift kick to the heart—an essential summer read." Kirkus

Phillips, Susan Elizabeth

The **great** escape; Susan Elizabeth Phillips. 1st ed. HarperCollins 2012 432 p. (hardcover) $25.99; (paperback) $14.99; (ebook) $20.99

ISBN 0062106066; 9780062106063; 9780062106186; 9780062106100

This book by Susan Elizabeth Phillips follows "Lucy Jorik . . . saved as a young teen by the woman who would become the first female President of the United States, Lucy has spent her life . . . [in] the perfect First Family. But on the day she's supposed to marry . . . she bolts from a life she feels she has fallen into, rather than one she really wants. Accepting a ride from the church on the back of a motorcycle . . . Lucy embarks on a journey of self-discovery." (Kirkus Reviews)

Phillips, Susan Elizabeth

★ **Heroes** are my weakness; Susan Elizabeth Phillips. William Morrow 2014 384 p. (hardback) $26.99

ISBN 0062106074; 9780062106070; 9780062106193

LC 2014007547

"He's a reclusive writer whose imagination creates chilling horror novels. She's a down-on-her-luck actress reduced to staging kids' puppet shows. He knows a dozen ways to kill his characters with his bare hands. She knows a dozen ways to kill an audience with laughs. But she's not laughing now. Annie Hewitt has arrived on Peregrine Island in the middle of a snowstorm and at the end of her resources." (Publisher's note)

Phillips "takes all the iconic elements of those classic gothic novels of the 1960s and '70s and deftly combines them with her own signature literary calling cards of realistically quirky yet all too relatable characters, polished writing, tart humor, and an abundance of potent sexual chemistry." Booklist

Phillips, Susan Elizabeth

It had to be you. Avon 2008 381p pa $12.95

ISBN 978-0-06-155581-7; 0-06-155581-9

First published 1994

"The Windy City isn't quite ready for Phoebe Somerville—the outrageous, curvaceous New York knockout who has just inherited the Chicago Stars football team. And Phoebe is definitely not prepared for the Stars' head coach Dan Celebow, a sexist jock taskmaster with a one-track mind. Celebow is everything Phoebe abhors. And the sexy new boss is everything Dan despises—a meddling bimbo who doesn't know a pigskin from a pitcher's mound." Publisher's note

Phillips, Susan Elizabeth

Match me if you can; Susan Elizabeth Phillips. William Morrow 2005 386p (pbk.) $7.99; o.p.

ISBN 9780060734565; 0060734558

LC 2004065644

This book tells the story of sports "agent, Heath Champion, and Annabelle Granger, the girl least likely to succeed. Annabelle's endured dead-end jobs, a broken engagement . . . even her hair's a mess! But that's going to change now that she's taken over her late grandmother's matchmaking business. All Annabelle has to do is land the Windy City's hottest bachelor as her client, and she'll be the most sought-after matchmaker in town. Why does the wealthy, driven, and gorgeous sports agent Heath Champion need a matchmaker, especially a red-haired screw-up like Annabelle Granger? True, she's entertaining, and she does have a certain quirky appeal. But Heath is searching for the ultimate symbol of success—the perfect wife." (Publisher's note)

Phillips, Susan Elizabeth

Natural born charmer. William Morrow 2007 394p $24.95

ISBN 978-0-06-073457-2; 0-06-073457-4

LC 2006-49173

"While the verbal sparring in this textbook case of opposites attracting feels stagy at first, the rough edges come together in an alluring way." Publ Wkly

Piazza, Tom

City of refuge; a novel. HarperCollins Publishers 2008 403p $24.95

ISBN 978-0-06-123861-1; 0-06-123861-9

LC 2008-13673

"Piazza describes the families' experience with a journalist's eye for detail and a New Orleanian's fury over the mismanagement that led to the breach of the levees and the government's lackadaisical approach to helping the survivors. . . . Righteous anger propels 'City of Refuge' forward, but occasionally it can overwhelm the story line." Christ Sci Monit

Picoult, Jodi

Change of heart; a novel. Atria Books 2008 447p $26.95; pa $16

ISBN 978-0-7434-9674-2; 0-7434-9674-4; 978-0-7434-9675-9 pa; 0-7434-9675-2 pa

LC 2007-35721

"Freelance carpenter Shay Bourne was sentenced to death for killing a little girl, Elizabeth Nealon, and her cop stepfather. Eleven years after the murders, Elizabeth's sister, Claire, needs a heart transplant, and Shay volunteers, which complicates the state's execution plans. Meanwhile, death row has been the scene of some odd events since Shay's arrival—an AIDS victim goes into remission, an inmate's pet bird dies and is brought back to life, wine flows from the water faucets. The author brings other compelling elements to an already complex plot line: the priest who serves as Shay's spiritual adviser was on the jury that sentenced him; Shay's ACLU representative, Maggie Bloom, balances her professional moxie with her negative self-image and difficult relationship with her mother. Picoult moves the story along with lively debates about prisoner rights and religion." Publ Wkly

Picoult, Jodi

House rules; a novel. Atria Books 2010 529p $28

ISBN 978-0-7432-9643-4; 0-7432-9643-5

LC 2009-26381

"Emma, a single mother, copes just fine with her teenage sons — until the day Jacob is arrested for the murder of his tutor. Jacob has Asperger's, and the cops confuse his symptoms — such as avoiding eye contact — with guilt. Jodi Picoult loses points for ruining what could have been a riveting mystery by establishing Jacob's innocence at the outset. (The real story behind the tutor's death is obvious to the careful reader.) The author has delivered a sweet family drama that doubles as a handbook on Asperger's — not exactly a thrill, but hardly a bad thing." Entertainment Wkly

Picoult, Jodi

Keeping Faith; a novel. Morrow 1999 422p $24

ISBN 0-688-16825-6

LC 98-43953

"When seven-year-old Faith White and her mother, Mariah, swing by the house on the way to ballet class, they find that Daddy is home and he's brought a playmate. This is not the first time he's been caught cheating. After the fuss and feathers have settled and Dad has moved out, Faith begins talking to an imaginary friend who, it seems, is God. And God is not male but female. Faith is able to effect miraculous cures and is also occasionally afflicted with stigmata. When the media gets wind of this, the circus begins. . . . If you can suspend disbelief on one or two points, this is an entrancing novel." Libr J

Picoult, Jodi

Nineteen minutes; a novel. Atria Books 2007 455p $26.95; pa $15

ISBN 978-0-7434-9672-8; 0-7434-9672-8; 978-0-7434-9673-5 pa; 0-7434-9673-6 pa

LC 2006-49276

"Picoult's adept character development and intelligent plot twists make for a story that runs deeper than mere voyeurism of titillation. [The novel] is both a page turner and a thoughtful exploration of popularity, power, and the social ruts that can define us in ways we may not wish to be defined." Rocky Mountain News

Picoult, Jodi, 1966-

Leaving Time; a novel. Jodi Picoult. Random House Inc/ Ballantine Books 2014 416 p. $28

ISBN 0345544927; 9780345544926

LC 2014023994

"For more than a decade, Jenna Metcalf has never stopped thinking about her mother, Alice, who mysteriously disappeared in the wake of a tragic accident. Refusing to believe she was abandoned, Jenna searches for her mother regularly online and pores over . . . Alice's old journals. A scientist who studied grief among elephants, Alice wrote mostly of her research . . . , yet Jenna hopes the entries will provide a clue to her mother's whereabouts." (Publisher's note)

"A truly engaging read that crosses through the genres of mystery and the supernatural. The interspersing of elephant behavior information and Alice's journal entries about her subjects provide just the right amount of parallelism." LJ

Picoult, Jodi, 1966-

Lone wolf; a novel. Jodi Picoult. 1st Atria Books hardcover ed. Atria Books 2012 vi, 421 p.p ill. (paperback) $16.00; (hardcover) $28.00

ISBN 9781439149690; 9781439102756; 1439102740; 9781439102749

LC 2011039017

This book is the story of "Luke Warren [who] has spent decades learning the inner workings of wolf packs. Yet his relationship with his own family is strained. Divorced from his wife and estranged from his son, Edward, Luke remains close to his daughter, Cara. When the two are involved in a car accident that leaves Luke in a coma, Edward must return home to make important medical decisions regarding life-sustaining measures." (Library Journal)

Picoult, Jodi, 1966-

My sister's keeper; a novel. Atria 2004 423p $25; pa $15

ISBN 0-7434-5452-9; 0-7434-5453-7 pa

LC 2004-300043

"Picoult's timely and compelling novel will appeal to anyone who has thought about the morality of medical decision making and any parent who must balance the needs of different children." Libr J

Picoult, Jodi

Sing you home; a novel. Atria Books 2011 466p $28

ISBN 978-1-4391-0272-5; 1-4391-0273-4

LC 2010-41180

Picoult "may have an agenda, but she has written an immensely entertaining melodrama with crackerjack dialogue." USA Today

Picoult, Jodi, 1966-

The **Storyteller**; a novel. Jodi Picoult. 1st Emily Bestler/ Atria hc.ed. Atria/Emily Bestler Books 2013 ix, 460 p.p (hardcover) $28.99

ISBN 1439102767; 9781439102763

LC 2012048982

In this book, "twenty-five-year-old reclusive baker Sage Singer befriends the elderly Josef Weber, who shares something shocking from his past and asks her to help him die, a request that pins Sage between morality and retribution. Sage, a Jew who now considers herself an atheist, begins to think more deeply about faith. [Author Jodi] Picoult examines the links between family identity, religion, humanity, and how it all figures in difficult decisions." (Publishers Weekly)

Picoult, Jodi

Vanishing acts; a novel. Atria Books 2005 418p $25

ISBN 0-7434-5454-5

LC 2004-59454

"Picoult weaves together plot and characterization in a landscape that is fleshed out in rich, journalistic detail, so that readers will come away with intriguing questions rather than pat answers." Publ Wkly

Piercy, Marge

Gone to soldiers; a novel. Summit Bks. 1987 703p

LC 86-30118

"In many male war novels character development is sacrificed; the 'woman's touch' here is excellent. The battlefront is not all blood and guts—there is also the grief of separation from family and the mitigating solace of friendship. On the home front there are race riots as well as ration books, and the heartbreak of shattered families." N Y Times Book Rev

Piercy, Marge

Sex wars; a novel of the turbulent post-Civil War period. Morrow 2005 411p $14.99

ISBN 9780060789879

LC 2005-41499

This novel, "set in post-Civil War New York stars a true-life cast of characters that includes Victoria Woodhull, the spiritualist turned first woman to run for the U.S. presidency; passionate suffragette Elizabeth Cady Stanton; the aged Cornelius Vanderbilt, who sits atop a $100-million fortune as he tries to make contact with his dead son; and Anthony Comstock, a crusading moralist who dedicates his life to outlawing pornography and 'obscene objects made of rubber.' . . . Most poignant among the invented characters is Freydeh Leibowitz, a young Russian-Jewish widow, who, far from the scandalous headlines and saloon gossip of the times, makes a living for herself and her adopted children, penny by penny, as a manufacturer of reliable condoms." Publ Wkly

Piercy, Marge

★ **Vida**. Summit Bks. 1979 412p

ISBN 0-671-40110-6

LC 79-19298

This novel "is not 'simply' a novel but a political brief. I have my differences with 'Vida,' but I think they are substantive rather than literary. It is an interesting—and challenging—book. . . . Marge Piercy has written about movement people before but never, I think, as lovingly as here." N Y Times Book Rev

Piercy, Marge

★ **Woman** on the edge of time. Knopf 1976 369p

"A Hispanic-American mother undergoes experimental psychosurgery. She makes psychic contact with the 22nd-century world that has resulted from a feminist revolution whose success may depend on the subversion of the experiments in which she is involved. Outstanding for the elaborate description of the future utopia and the graphic representation of the inhumanity inherent in the way that contemporary people can and do treat one another." Anatomy of Wonder 4

Pierpont, Julia

Among the ten thousand things; a novel. Julia Pierpont. Random House Inc 2015 336 p. (hardcover : acid-free paper) $26

ISBN 0812995228; 9780812995220

LC 2014024453

This novel, by Julia Pierpont, is "a portrait of an American family on the cusp of irrevocable change, and a . . . story of love and time lost. . . . As the Shanleys spin apart into separate orbits, leaving New York in an attempt to regain their bearings, fifteen-year-old Simon feels the allure of adult freedoms for the first time, while eleven-year-old Kay wanders precariously into a grown-up world she can't possibly understand." (Publisher's note)

"With acid wit and thoughtful melancholy, Pierpont catalogs the wreckage, mourns the death of innocence, and measures varying degrees of recovery, achieving a Salingeresque ambience." Booklist

Pierson, D. C., 1984-

The **boy** who couldn't sleep and never had to; a novel. DC Pierson. Vintage Books 2010 226 p. ill. $14.95

ISBN 9780307474612

LC 2009021984

Alex Award (2011)

In this book, the recipient of a 2010 ALA Alex Award, "[w]hen [high-school student] Darren Bennett meets [classmate] Eric Lederer, there's an instant connection. They share a love of drawing, the bottom rung on the cruel high school social ladder and a pathological fear of girls. Then Eric reveals a secret: He doesn't sleep. Ever. When word leaks out about Eric's condition, he and Darren find themselves on the run. Is it the government trying to tap into Eric's mind, or something far darker? It could be that not sleeping is only part of what Eric's capable of, and the truth is both better and worse than they could ever imagine." (Publisher's note)

Pietroni, Anna Lawrence

Ruby's spoon; a novel. Spiegel & Grau 2010 366p $26

ISBN 978-1-4000-6868-5; 1-4000-6868-1

LC 2009-34841

The author "knows her territory as thoroughly as Ruby, and she has created an evocative fairy tale that slowly pulls a reader under as surely as one of the mermaids the locals tell legends about. . . . The Black Country English dialect her characters speak takes some getting used to, but it's more than showboating. Lawrence Pietroni is able to conjure an entire lost world through their words, and the writing of 'Ruby's Spoon' is one of its chief pleasures." Christ Sci Monit

Pilcher, Robin

A **risk** worth taking. Thomas Dunne Bks. 2004 308p $24.95

ISBN 0-312-27002-X

LC 2003-58564

"Dan Porter had it all: the nice house in suburban London, three children, a beautiful wife, and a great job in finance until the dot-com crash and 9/11 changed his outlook about life and making money. Dan lost a good friend in the tragedy, and is now content being a househusband focusing on his family, while his wife, Jackie, pursues her high-level job with a fashion designer, but changes in income have caused strife. His wife and daughters want their old life back, and Jackie perceives Dan and their son, Josh, as loafers because they seem content with less. Recognizing his wife's discontent, Dan takes action after reading an article in a women's magazine about a woman who started a clothing company in a remote area of Scotland and now wants to sell. Dan travels to Scotland with the hope of buying the company and expanding the business, but he finds something much more valuable. Pilcher offers a charming story about life in the new millennium and one man's pursuit of happiness." Booklist

Pilcher, Rosamunde

Coming home. St. Martin's Press 1995 728p $25.95

ISBN 0-312-13451-7

LC 95-21656

"The book's heroine is Judith Dunbar, who is a schoolgirl of 13 when the tale begins in 1935. Sent to boarding school in Cornwall because her parents are posted to Singapore, Judith becomes friends with Loveday Carey-Lewis, who introduces her to a family and an estate, Nancherrow, that is to influence her for the rest of her life. Pilcher does a marvelous job of describing life in England before World War II." Booklist

Pilcher, Rosamunde

Flowers in the rain & other stories. St. Martin's Press 1991 277p

LC 91-18237

"Throughout this collection of stories, Pilcher maintains a pervasive gentility along with an abiding wisdom. Filled with poignant scenes, romantic and bittersweet, these stories, many written earlier in the author's career, will appeal to readers of Pilcher's very successful novels." Booklist

Pilcher, Rosamunde

September. St. Martin's Press 1990 536p

ISBN 0-312-04419-4

LC 89-70340

"Character is at the heart of a story, and this fine tale has plenty of that." N Y Times Book Rev

Pilcher, Rosamunde

★ The **shell** seekers. St. Martin's Press 1987 530p

LC 87-28345

"It is a measure of this story's strength and success that a reader can be carried for more than 500 pages in total involvement with Penelope, her children, her past and the painting that hangs in her country cottage. 'The Shell Seekers' is a deeply satisfying story, written with love and confidence." N Y Times Book Rev

Pilcher, Rosamunde

Winter solstice. Thomas Dunne Bks. 2000 454p $27.95

ISBN 0-312-24426-6

LC 00-31713

A novel set in "northern Scotland, where five vaguely connected people find themselves together at Christmas in a large Victorian house. . . . Elfrida, a lonely retired actress, befriends Oscar, who is barely surviving the grief of the deaths of his wife and daughter in a car crash. Carrie, bereft after an aborted love affair, takes over the holiday care of her 14-year-old niece, Lucy, who is unwanted by her mother, grandmother, and indifferent father, Sam, in town to take charge of the old woolen mill, is reeling because his wife left him for another man. What lifts this saga above melodrama is the author's skill at creating believable, multifaceted characters." Libr J

Pinborough, Sarah

A **matter** of blood; Sarah Pinborough. Ace Books 2013 352 p. (The forgotten gods) (paperback) $16

ISBN 0425258467; 9780425258460

LC 2012049588

This novel, by Sarah Pinborough, is the first entry in "The Forgotten Gods" trilogy. "London's ruined economy has pushed everyone to the breaking point. . . . Detective Inspector Cass Jones struggles to keep integrity in the police force, but now, two gory cases will test his mettle. A gang hit goes wrong, leaving two schoolboys dead, and a serial killer calling himself the Man of Flies leaves a message on his victims saying 'nothing is sacred.'" (Publisher's note)

"Nuanced characters, evocative settings, tricky plot connections and a spin on genre conventions mark what appears to be the start of a distinctive series." Kirkus

Pineiro, Claudia

A **Crack** in the Wall; Claudia Pineiro. Bitter Lemon Press 2013 230 p. $14.95

ISBN 1908524081; 9781908524089

In author Claudia Pineiro's book, "Pablo Simo's life is a mess. His career as an architect is at a dead-end; reduced to designing soulless office buildings desecrating the heart of Buenos Aires. His marriage seems to be one endless argument with his wife over the theatrics of their rebellious teenage daughter. . . . Everything changes with the unexpected appearance of Leonor, a beautiful young woman who brings to light a crime that happened years before, a crime that everyone in the office wants forgotten, at all costs." (Publisher's note)

Pintoff, Stefanie

Hostage taker; a novel. Stefanie Pintoff. Bantam Books 2015 432 p. (hardcover) $26

ISBN 034553140X; 9780345531407

LC 2015001375

This thriller novel, by Stefanie Pintoff, features "Eve Rossi, head of a secret division of the FBI. . . . As Eve manages a taut hostage situation, she relies on the combined skills of her team--a secret unit inspired by France's most notorious criminal and made up of ex-convicts with extraordinary talents, oversized egos, and contempt for the rules." (Publisher's note)

"Strong writing, a well-paced plot, and intriguing characters make this one of the best thrillers of the year." LJ

Pintoff, Stefanie

In the shadow of Gotham. Minotaur Books 2009 385p $24.99; pa $14.99

ISBN 978-0-312-54490-4; 0-312-54490-1; 978-0-312-62812-3 pa; 0-312-62812-9 pa

LC 2008-45676

"Detective Simon Ziele lost his fiancée in the General Slocum ferry disaster—a thousand perished on that summer day in 1904 when an onboard fire burned the boat down in the waters of the East River. Still reeling from the tragedy, Ziele transferred to a police department north of New York, to escape the city and all the memories it conjured. But only a few months into his new life in a quiet country town, he's faced with the most shocking homicide of his career to date: Young Sarah Wingate has been brutally murdered in her own bedroom in the middle of an otherwise calm and quiet winter afternoon. After just one day of investigation, Simon's contacted by Columbia University's noted criminologist Alistair Sinclair, who offers a startling claim about one of his patients, Michael Fromley—that the facts of the murder bear an uncanny resemblance to Fromley's deranged mutterings." Publisher's note

Pipkin, John

Woodsburner; a novel. Nan A. Talese 2009 365p $24.95

ISBN 978-0-385-52865-8; 0-385-52865-5

LC 2008-33233

"Pipkin doesn't underplay Thoreau's horror at what he's done (or overplay the inherent irony of the author of 'Walden' burning down the woods). Instead, he concentrates on the ability of a natural disaster to act as a catalyst in people's minds and lives. The result is, well, transcendent." Christ Sci Monit

Pirandello, Luigi

Short stories; selected, translated and introduced by Frederick May. Oxford Univ. Press 1965 xxxvi, 260p

Contents: The little hut; The cooper's cockerels; A dream of Christmas; Twelve letters; Fear; The best of friends; Bitter waters; The jar; The tragedy of a character; A call to duty; In the abyss; The black kid; Signora Frola and her son-in-law, Signor Ponga; The man with the flower in his mouth; Destruction of the man; Puberty; Cinci; All passion spent; The visit; The tortoise; A day goes by

Pirie, David

The **patient's** eyes; the dark beginnings of Sherlock Holmes. St. Martin's Minotaur 2002 244p il

ISBN 0-312-29095-0

"A 'fictional' account of Arthur Conan Doyle's early life that relates how his association with Edinburgh physician Joseph Bell was the inspiration for his Holmes character. Pirie vividly evokes the dark ambience of Victorian England, his prose is elegant, and his gift for mimicking the slightly haughty tone of Doyle's writing is uncanny." Booklist

Pistalo, Vladimir

Tesla; a portrait with masks. Vladimir Pistalo, Bogdan Rakic, John Jeffries. Graywolf Press 2015 384 p. (alk. paper) $18

ISBN 1555976972; 9781555976972

LC 2014948533

Author Vladimir Pistalo's book on Nikola Tesla is a "novel of the extraordinary life of one of the twentieth century's most prodigious and colorful inventors. [It] captures the whirlwind years of the dawn of the electrical age, when his flair for showmanship kept him in the public eye. For every successful invention--the alternating current electrical system and wireless communication among them--there were hundreds of others. But what of the man behind the image?" (Publisher's note)

"This is the great empathetic work that fiction can do: taking a life from the past and making it relatable. A moving, inventive and poetic work of biographical fiction." Kirkus

Pittard, Hannah

The **fates** will find their way; a novel. Ecco 2011 243p $22.99

ISBN 978-0-06-199605-4; 0-06-199605-X

LC 2010-09129

"Nora Lindell, a 16-year-old private schoolgirl in a suburban town, disappears one Halloween night. The boys in the town collectively narrate this haunted tale of Nora's imagined fate and their own lives, from their teens until they are adults with families. Nora lives on in their imagination—there are sightings and multiple theories about where she ended up, the boys fantasize about and date her younger sister, and they continue to think of her when they are with their own wives and children." Libr J

Pitts, Leonard

Freeman; a novel. Leonard Pitts. Agate 2012 404 p. (paperback) $16

ISBN 1932841644; 9781572846999; 9781932841640

LC 2012009592

Pulitzer Prize winner Leonard Pitts, Jr.'s second novel "begins in the first few months after President Lincoln has died. By that time Philadelphian Sam Freeman has already taken to the road to return to the brutal Mississippi plantation he fled 15 years earlier. His mission: to find Tilda, the wife he left behind. Unbeknownst to Sam, Tilda is traveling west with a gun pointed at her head by her former master, who has a scheme to start plantations in territories that will uphold enslavement." (Essence)

Plaidy, Jean

The **captive** Queen of Scots. Putnam 1970 410p

Sequel to Royal road to Fotheringay (1968)

First published 1963 in the United Kingdom

"The story of the last 18 years of Queen Mary's life, during which she was first a prisoner of her Scottish enemies and later, after a dramatic escape and flight to England, the captive of her archenemy, Queen Elizabeth. Treated with at least some respect due a queen, Mary is pictured with her retinue of loyal friends and servants, living in varying degrees of discomfort and confinement as she moved from one castle to another at the whim of Elizabeth. She emerges as a generous, overly trustful, emotional victim, attractive even as she grew older though not wise, who met her tragic fate because she could not cope with the treachery and intrigue of both friends and enemies." Booklist

Plaidy, Jean

Murder most royal. Putnam 1972 542p

First published 1949 in the United Kingdom

"Concentrating on Anne Boleyn and her younger cousin Catherine Howard, the author follows the two from childhood to death on the block, with her usual thoroughness, sentimentality, and overdramatization, sparing the reader few details of torture, violence, intrigue, or thwarted love affairs." Booklist

Plaidy, Jean

The **pleasures** of love; the story of Catherine of Braganza. Putnam 1992 329p

ISBN 0-399-13731-9

LC 91-34593

First published 1991 in the United Kingdom

When Catherine, daughter of King John IV of Portugal, finally married Charles II her "happiness as the new Queen of England was short-lived. The Merry Monarch's notorious affairs amused the public but devastated Catherine, who longed for the love only a husband and children could provide. When it became clear that Catherine was barren, the people verged on rebellion and court intimates intrigued against her, hoping that Charles would divorce his queen, marry one of his mistresses, and beget an heir. But while Charles would never be faithful to Catherine, he loved her and was her fiercest protector. And in the end, their struggle against their enemies only drew the king and queen closer together." Publisher's note

Plaidy, Jean

William's wife. Putnam 1993 276p

LC 92-32588

In this historical novel about the "struggle for power between Catholic and Protestant, England's heir to the throne, the lovely and bright Princess Mary, is forced to marry William of Orange in order to prevent the kingdom from falling under Catholic rule. Despite Mary's attempts to win her husband's love, the dour, power-hungry William won't even feign affection for her; instead, he continues a blatant affair with Elizabeth Villiers. As the inevitable power struggle ensues between her husband and her father, James II, Mary finds herself torn between marital and filial loyalties. But with the crown of England the ultimate prize, Mary discovers that while she is James's daughter, she is first and foremost William's wife." Publisher's note

Plain, Belva

Crescent City; a novel. Delacorte Press 1984 429p

LC 84-5045

A novel "set against the backdrop of America's South during the Civil War. At the story's center is Miriam Raphael, a European Jew transplanted as a child to New Orleans, the 'Crescent City' nestled at the mouth of the Mississippi. Both she and her older brother, David, must adjust to what seems a bright, promising new land filled with languid days and lavish feasts. But all too quickly their eyes are opened to the grimmer features of their landscape—the slaves whom David vows to set free and the southern tradition of youthful marriage, which Miriam, herself no better off than a slave, must gracefully endure." Booklist

Plain, Belva

Evergreen; a novel. Delacorte Press 1978 593p

LC 77-20778

"This warm and sympathetic family saga gives life and meaning to the commonplace events of unspectacular lives." Publ Wkly

Followed by The golden cup

Plain, Belva

The **golden** cup. Doubleday 1986 399p

LC 86-8851

The author "invests her story with dignity and historical relevance while insightfully depicting the class consciousness of Progressive Era Americans." Publ Wkly

Followed by Tapestry

Plain, Belva

Harvest. Delacorte Press 1990 409p

LC 90-34417

This novel continues the "saga of the Werners and their extended clan as they reaffirm their Jewish heritage during the stormy 1960s. Dark, sensitive Iris, daughter of the glowing, russet-haired Anna (by urbane banker Paul Werner—unbeknownst to Iris) is married to wealthy, improvident Dr. Theo Stern, whose European glamour excites other women. Iris's jealousy goads her to play at her own romance with a sinister partner. Her four children are growing up, but rebel Steve balks at his bar mitzvah, already anticipating the anarchist/bomb expert he will be at college, radicalized by cynical professor Tim Powers, whom he doesn't know is his distant cousin. When Paul's wife dies and his mistress leaves to fulfill her mission as a doctor in Israel, Paul hovers protectively over Iris's, troubled family." Publ Wkly

Plain, Belva

Looking back. Delacorte Press 2001 340p $25.95

ISBN 0-385-33471-0

LC 00-65691

A "story about three college roommates—brainy Norma, lovely Amanda, preppy Cecile. . . . When the three women graduate, Amanda, desperate to escape her lower-class background, marries Larry Balsan, Norma's brother, who is in the family real estate business. As Mrs. Balsan, she can shop to her heart's content, but she soon realizes she is not as happy as Cecile, who marries her college sweetheart, or even Norma, who is biding her time until she meets Mr. Right." Publ Wkly

Plain, Belva

Random winds. Delacorte Press 1980 496p

LC 79-26845

The author "knows how to sweep from one dramatic scene to another, often evoking poignancy, and the irony underlying Martin's daughter's romance with Fern's stepson produces a bittersweet ending." Publ Wkly

Plain, Belva

Tapestry. Delacorte Press 1988 440p

LC 87-22346

"Paul Werner, the key figure of a powerful New York banking family, is the protagonist in this saga of one man's concerns with the impending doom of World War II and the plight of his German-Jewish relatives and friends. Paul is caught in a passionless, childless marriage, and he struggles for years with the memory and reality of his first love and subsequent affairs of the heart." Libr J

Followed by Harvest

Plath, Sylvia

★ The **bell** jar; with an introduction by Diane Wood Middlebrook. Knopf 1998 xxv, 229p $17

ISBN 0-375-40463-5

LC 98-27309

First published 1963 in the United Kingdom; first United States edition published 1971 by Harper & Row

"Esther Greenwood, having spent what should have been a glorious summer as guest editor for a young woman's magazine, came home from New York, had a nervous breakdown, and tried to commit suicide. Through months of therapy, Esther kept her rationality, if not her sanity. In telling the story of Esther, Plath thinly disguised her own experience with attempted suicide and time spent in an institution. Like Esther, she was rehabilitated and finished college. She went to London, married poet Ted Hughes, had three children and published some poetry and this novel. When she felt the world slipping away from her again, she did commit suicide." Shapiro. Fic for Youth. 3d edition

Includes bibliographical references (p. xix)

Pochoda, Ivy

★ **Visitation** Street; Ivy Pochoda. HarperCollins Publishers 2013 320 p. (hardcover) $25.99

ISBN 0062249894; 9780062249890

This novel, by Ivy Pochoda, is a "literary mystery set against the rough-hewn backdrop of the New York waterfront in Red Hook. . . . June and Val, two fifteen-year-olds, take a raft out onto the bay at night to see what they can see. And then they disappear. Only Val will survive, washed ashore; semi-conscious in the weeds. . . . Val contends with the shadow of her missing friend and a truth she buries deep inside." (Publisher's note)

Poe's children; the new horror: an anthology. [edited by] Peter Straub. Doubleday 2008 534p $24.95

ISBN 978-0-385-52283-0; 0-385-52283-5

LC 2008-3013

"An impressive, highly personal assortment of perspectives and techniques. The result is a remarkably consistent, frequently unsettling book that does as much to blur the artificial boundary between genre fiction and 'literature' as any anthology in living memory. . . . [The anthology] transcends genre labels and deserves to be recognized for what it is: first-rate fiction." Washington Post Book World

Poe, Edgar Allan

The **collected** tales and poems of Edgar Allan Poe. Modern Lib. 1992 1026p $20

ISBN 0-679-60007-8

LC 92-50231

A reissue of The complete tales and poems of Edgar Allan Poe published 1938

This volume contains short stories, poems, and a sampling of Poe's essays, criticism and journalistic writings

Poe, Edgar Allan

★ **Complete** stories and poems of Edgar Allan Poe. Doubleday 1966 819p $21.95

ISBN 0-385-07407-7

Poe, Edgar Allan

The **imaginary** voyages: The narrative of Arthur Gordon Pym; The unparalleled adventure of one Hans Pfaall; The journal of Julius Rodman. Twayne Pubs. 1981 667p

LC 81-2915

Omnibus edition of three titles, the first of which is entered separately under variant form: The narrative of Arthur Gordon Pym of Nantucket, The unparalleled adventure of one Hans Pfaall, first published 1835 describes a voyage to the moon and The journal of Julius Rodman, an unfinished novel first published anonymously in 1840 deals with exploration of the Missouri River Basin

Pohl, Frederik

All the lives he led. Tor 2011 347p $25.99

ISBN 978-0-7653-2176-3; 0-7653-2176-9

LC 2010-36667

"An entertaining futuristic thriller with several thought-provoking threads ranging from the ethics of biotechnology to the fragility of the global economy." Libr J

Pohl, Frederik

Beyond the blue event horizon. Ballantine Bks. 1980 327p

LC 79-21757

Sequel to Gateway

"Multimillionaire Robinette Broadhead, still mourning the loss of his great love from the first book, backs an expedition to investigate one of the alien Heechee's 'food factories.' Earth is overpopulated, and the ship's resources are desperately needed to prevent mass starvation. The members of the expedition are all from the same family: Lurvey, a veteran space pilot and her engineer husband; Lurvey's money hungry father, and her precocious 14-year-old sister. Despite the tensions which surface during their three and a half year voyage, the family manages to successfully make contact with the factory and its innocent, human occupant. They begin to explore the marvels of the alien technology, but events on Earth and the inhabitants of another Heechee spaceship threatens to end the expedition in disaster." Voice Youth Advocates

Followed by Heechee rendezvous

Pohl, Frederik

The **boy** who would live forever; a novel of Gateway. Tor Bks. 2004 380p $25.95

ISBN 0-7653-1049-X

LC 2004-49579

A title set in the author's Heechee universe. "When recently orphaned Stan Avery inherits enough money to buy a trip to Gateway, the alien Heechee waystation that allows travel to all parts of space, he doesn't realize that his voyage has effectively cut him off forever from the world he left behind. Pohl's first Gateway novel in 15 years (the 1977 original Gateway won the Hugo and Nebula Awards) revitalizes a favorite far-future setting as it tells the tale of a young man's journey to self-realization amid the stars." Libr J

Pohl, Frederik

Chernobyl; a novel. Bantam Bks. 1987 355p

ISBN 0-553-05210-1

LC 86-47896

The author "re-creates in fiction the massive 1986 Ukrainian nuclear power plant disaster. The book opens during normal days just before the accident; suspense builds, as the reader expects the worst. Characters that would actually have been on the scene are seen being overwhelmed by berserk technology, their lives shattered. The tale is gripping, and the locale well established." Libr J

Pohl, Frederik

★ **Gateway**. St. Martin's Press 1977 313p

First volume in the author's Heechee saga

"The novel's protagonist, Robinette Broadhead, suffers from tremendous feelings of guilt: for the death of his parents, for his wealth (a stroke of luck he feels he does not deserve), and for the living death of his girl friend and fellow crew members. Gateway presents Broadhead's story in chapters that alternately describe his life before the novel opens and record present conversations between Broadhead and his computer psychiatrist, Sigfrid von Shrink. With a sensitive mixture of humor and sympathy, Pohl explores Broadhead's condition and ends with one of the finest affirmations of humanity in any literary work." New Ency of Sci Fic

Followed by Beyond the blue event horizon

Pohl, Frederik

Heechee rendezvous; a novel. Ballantine Bks. 1984 311p

LC 83-15637

Sequel to Beyond the blue event horizon

In this novel "the elusive, benevolent aliens called Heechee are forced to come out of hiding because the future not only of humankind but of the universe itself is at stake. Compelled by personal reasons, tycoon Robinette Broadhead takes part in another dangerous venture into space, moving inexorably toward his surprising yet fitting destiny." Booklist

Followed by The annals of the Heechee

Pohl, Frederik

★ **Man** Plus. Random House 1976 215p

"The novel describes the transformation of a human astronaut into a cyborg capable of living on Mars and confronts the question of human dignity: as the central character, Roger Torraway, becomes less 'human,' the people who were once so important to him are unable to cope with what he is, and Roger must also learn to handle the new thing he has become. Moreover, Roger's reflections on his growing inability to control his own life parallel the thoughts of people throughout the country who believe the world has gone out of control. The result is a remarkably readable novel that succeeds in presenting a fully rounded character in an SF setting." New Ency of Sci Fic

Pohl, Frederik

★ The **space** merchants; by Frederik Pohl and C. M. Kornbluth. Ballantine Bks. 1953 179p

"Kornbluth later stated that he and Pohl packed into this story everything they hated about advertising, and it came out with Swiftian savagery. One of the first novels by writers with primary roots in the pulps to make an impact in mainstream circles." Anatomy of Wonder 4

Followed by The merchants' war (1984)

Pohl, Frederik

The **world** at the end of time. Ballantine Bks. 1990 393p
LC 89-18462

"As vast intelligences play deadly power games using stars for pawns, the fledgling colonists on the planet Home fight to maintain their existence while 'unknown forces' wreak havoc with the laws of physics and the universe. Pohl's sparkling wit attaches itself to macro- and microcosmic themes in a novel which pits a luckless human hero against a childlike being of inordinate power and extraordinary paranoia. Grand in scope, poignant in delivery." Libr J

Polansky, Daniel

Low Town; a novel. Doubleday 2011 341p $25.95
ISBN 978-0-385-53446-8; 0-385-53446-9
LC 2010-49587

"Polansky's writing is confident and punchy from the offset. The action rips along at a brilliant pace allowing us to experience this gritty world through the eyes of a thrilling, dangerous, flawed, yet strangely endearing protagonist. This is modern, dark fantasy at its best and a debut to be envied." British Fantasy Society

Pollen, Bella

The **summer** of the bear. Atlantic Monthly 2011 441p $24
ISBN 978-0-8021-1974-2; 0-8021-1974-3
First published 2010 in the United Kingdom

"When Nicky Fleming, a British diplomat working in East Germany in 1979 dies, he leaves behind his wife, Letty, and children, Georgie, 17, Alba, 14, and Jamie, 8. Jamie has some kind of learning disability and some kind of gift. On the way to the family's summer house in the Outer Hebrides after his father's death, Jamie leaves hand-drawn maps to the house so that his father can find him. He remembers a grizzly bear he and his father saw at the zoo; he knows that bear has something to do with his father's death and something to do with his young life. The 800-pound bear, in the meantime, has escaped from a cargo boat in the North Atlantic and swum to shore. It lives in a cave in the Outer Hebrides. The novel has a bit of the style of Lemony Snicket and a smidgeon of 'The Secret of Roan Inish.' Pollen's writing is clean and clear enough that you can really smell the peat smoke and feel the wind. As for the question of Jamie's father's unexpected death — was it truly suicide? Was he a traitor?" L A Times Book Rev

Pollock, Donald Ray

The **devil** all the time; a novel. Doubleday 2011 261p $26.95
ISBN 978-0-385-53504-5; 0-385-53504-X
LC 2010-53322

"The flawless cadence of Pollock's gorgeous shadow-and-light prose plays against the heinous acts of his sorrowful and sometimes just sorry characters." Elle

Pollock, Donald Ray

Knockemstiff. Doubleday 2008 206p
ISBN 978-0-385-52382-0
LC 2007-39806

"Knockemstiff—real name, real town—is full of the sorriest group of people imaginable, a bunch of damaged souls with crass manners, greasy hair, sour breath, addictions galore and savage tendencies. Some can sense the possibilities of a better life, but their longing for escape just might lead them to do something crazy. Others are simply rotting away, trapped by self-defeating habits impossible to shake. Pollock underscores their struggles with vivid imagery and, at times, a tender touch. . . . Pollock's writing has been compared to that of Flannery O'Connor, Raymond Carver and Cormac McCarthy. He draws his readers in slowly, tangling them in the mundane toil of small-town life, before smacking them upside the head with something unexpected and primal. Small moments yield big surprises." Oregonian

Pomerantz, Sharon

★ **Rich** boy. Twelve 2010 517p $24.99
ISBN 978-0-446-56318-5; 0-446-56318-8
LC 2009-32386

The novel's protagonist is "Robert Vishniak, the golden-boy progeny of a working-class Jewish family in 1950s Philadelphia whose singular drive to transcend his circumstances is—almost—matched by his abilities. As a boy, he craves the security and social acceptance that comes with money; as a young man, he is ushered into the rarefied, sweet-smelling world of those who possess it in staggering amounts. There's more than a little of Saul Bellow's Augie March in Robert, too, especially in Rich Boy's opening chapters, populated by a colorful cast of neighbors, extended family, and schoolmates (his romantic education begins early). Soon enough, though, he finds escape via admission to a top-tier Northeastern University, where his charm and good looks garner him a new class of friends. . . . It would spoil Pomerantz's pleasingly soapy narrative to detail too much of Robert's subsequent journey, first in 1960s Boston and then in the go-go Manhattan of the '70s and '80s. But while his tale often feels allegorical . . . Rich Boy is told with such page-turning skill that its pleasures, if not deep, feel rich indeed." Entertainment Wkly

Poole, Sara

The **Borgia** mistress; a novel. Sara Poole. St. Martin's Press 2012 406 p. $14.99
ISBN 031260985X; 9780312609856; 9781250010926
LC 2012007569

In this book, part of the Poisoner Mysteries series, "Francesca Giordano—court poisoner to the House of Borgia—returns to confront an ancient atrocity that threatens to extinguish the light of the Renaissance. . . . As the enemies of Pope Alexander VI close in and the papal court is forced to flee from Rome, Francesca joins forces with her lover, the brilliant and ruthless Cesare Borgia to unravel a conspiracy that strikes at the heart of Christendom." (Publisher's note)

"True to its characters and historical facts, Poole's novel immerses readers in a seductive Renaissance environment, full of danger and passion." Pub Wkly

Poore, Michael

Reincarnation Blues; Michael Poore. Del Rey 2017 374 p. (hardcover) $27
ISBN 0399178481; 9780399178498; 9780399178481
LC 2017030780

In this book, by Michael Poore, "Milo has had 9,995 chances so far and has just five more lives to earn a place in the cosmic soul. If he doesn't make the cut, oblivion awaits. But all Milo really wants is to fall forever into the arms of Death. Or Suzie, as he calls her. More than just Milo's lover throughout his countless layovers in the Afterlife, Suzie is literally his reason for living." (Publisher's note)

"Poore (Up Jumps the Devil) addresses humans' relationship to the universe through a clever, personal story filled with gentle humor, wry sweetness, and perhaps even some wisdom." Pub Wkly

Pope, Barbara Corrado

The **blood** of Lorraine. Pegasus Books 2010 367p $25
ISBN 978-1-60598-098-0; 1-60598-098-6

A "look at the rise of anti-Semitism in France after the arrest of Capt. Alfred Dreyfus for treason in 1894. Now transferred to Nancy, the capital of Alsace, [magistrate Bernard]Martin doesn't relish investigating a politically sensitive case—the murder of seven-month-old Marc-Antoine Thomas, whose parents claim that a Jew killed and mutilated their son—that Martin's Jewish colleague, David Singer, insists that Martin take over. When a prominent member of the Jewish community, Victor Ullmann, is later bludgeoned to death, the magistrate fears that it was a revenge killing. Martin must also deal with a devastating personal tragedy as pressure to solve the Ullmann case mounts. Pope, a historian, more than compensates for a not fully satisfying ending with a complex lead and the skill with which she makes the anti-Semitic atmosphere of the times both palpable and tragically prophetic." Publ Wkly

Includes bibliographical references

Porter, Henry

The **bell** ringers. Atlantic Monthly Press 2010 402p $24

ISBN 978-0-8021-1931-5; 0-8021-1931-X

"The tale is set in England, where cameras identify license plates and faces, computers catalog phone and financial records, and submitting an incomplete form can be a felony. What's to prevent a prime minister from abusing these powers? Just a few committed (if sometimes cliched) characters, some intricately complex plotting and gobs of local color. The world of 'The Bell Ringers' isn't as dystopian as '1984,' but it's not that far off." Cleveland Plain Dealer

Porter, Katherine Anne

★ The **collected** stories of Katherine Anne Porter. Harcourt Brace & World 1965 495p hardcover o.p. pa $16

ISBN 0-15-618876-7

Contains three collections of short stories: Flowering Judas, and other stories (1935); The leaning tower, and other stories (1944); Pale horse, pale rider (1939); and four additional short stories: Virgin Violeta; The martyr; The fig tree; and Holiday.

"These are perfect examples of the short story and are representative not only of the best American writing but of the best in the world." SLJ

Porter, Katherine Anne

Flowering Judas and other stories. Harcourt Brace Jovanovich 1935 285p

First published 1930. This edition adds four additional stories

Porter, Katherine Anne

The **leaning** tower, and other stories. Harcourt Brace & Co. 1944 246p

Contents: The source; The witness; The circus; The old order; The last leaf; The grave; The downward path to wisdom; A day's work; The leaning tower

Porter, Katherine Anne

★ **Pale** horse, pale rider: three short novels; Modern Library ed; Modern Lib. 1998 205p $18.95

ISBN 0-679-60303-4

LC 98-12008

A reissue of the title first published 1939 by Harcourt, Brace

In the title story "Miranda, a young journalist, is caught in a personal dilemma. She must choose between a career and a commitment to Adam, a soldier on leave during World War I. Porter's simple tale becomes more complex as Miranda's anxieties and fears about war, death, and personal loss are revealed. She hovers close to death during the terrbile flu epidemic of 1918. Miranda survives and the war ends, but it brings her no happiness because the epidemic has claimed Adam as a victim." Shapiro. Fic for Youth. 3d edition

Porter, Katherine Anne

Ship of fools. Little, Brown 1962 497p

"A satire in which the world is likened to a ship whose passengers, fools and deranged people all, are sailing toward eternity. Porter's novel is set in 1931 aboard a German passenger ship returning to Bremerhaven, Germany, from Veracruz, Mexico. The ship carries a microcosm of peoples, including Germans, Americans, Spaniards, Gypsies, and Mexicans, Jews, anti-Semites, political reactionaries, revolutionaries, and neutrals coexist aboard ship, at the same time that jeaolusy, cruelty and duplicity pervade their lives." Merriam-Webster's Ency of Lit

Porter, Max

★ **Grief** Is the Thing With Feathers; A Novel. Max Porter. Farrar, Straus & Giroux 2016 128 p. $14

ISBN 1555977413; 9781555977412

LC 2015953714

This novel by Max Porter tells the story of "a man adrift in the wake of his wife's sudden, accidental death. And there are his two sons who like him struggle in their London apartment to face the unbearable sadness that has engulfed them. . . . In this moment of violent despair they are visited by Crow--antagonist, trickster, goad, [and] protector. . . . This self-described 'sentimental bird,' . . . threatens to stay with the wounded family until they no longer need him." (Publisher's note)

"Porter's daringly strange story skirts disbelief to speak, engagingly and effectively, of the pain this world inflicts, of where the ghosts go, and of how we are left to press on and endure it all." Kirkus

Portis, Charles

★ The **dog** of the South. Knopf 1979 245p

ISBN 0-394-4506146

LC 78-65780

"Simultaneously hilarious and heart breakingly odd. . . you find yourself laughing so hard in sections that tears run down your face." Baltimore Sun

Portis, Charles

★ **Gringos**; a novel. Simon & Schuster 1991 269p

ISBN 0-671-72457-6

LC 90-42476

"'Gringos,' by far, is Portis's most inward-turning book, a story of a grownup trying to grow up, to keep it together with some dignity. Watching him pull it off is one of the finest pleasures afforded by any novel in a long time." Newsweek

Portis, Charles

★ **Masters** of Atlantis; a novel. Knopf 1985 247p

ISBN 0-394-54683-0

LC 85-40212

This novel "concerns the establishment of the order of Gnomons, a secret society purporting to teach the hidden knowledge of Atlantis. The action begins in 1917, when soldier Lamar is relieved of $200 by a fast-talking stranger in exchange for the key to Gnomonism. The plot spins dizzily along as sly Sydney Hen and antic Austin Popper are drawn into the society, engineer a farcical schism, and espouse assorted crackpot causes. . . . Those who enjoy deadpan comedy should get a good laugh here." Libr J

Portis, Charles

True grit; a novel. Simon & Schuster 1968 215p

"Mattie Ross, a fourteen-year-old living in Yell County, Arkansas, is determined to get justice when her father is killed by a hired hand. She is joined in her quest by Rooster Cogburn, a U.S. marshal, and by a Texas

Ranger. This strange trio faces a series of perilous encounters requiring true grit to confront them." Shapiro. Fic for Youth. 3d edition

Potok, Chaim

The **gift** of Asher Lev. Knopf 1990 369p

LC 89-43401

Sequel to My name is Asher Lev

"Following the death of his beloved uncle, Asher, who is now middle-aged and settled in France, finds he must return with his family to the Brooklyn Hasidic Jewish community from which he has been exiled 20 years. Greeted there with suspicion and anger by many who still insist that his art is anathema to Hasidim—a sentiment that continues to haunt his relationship with his father, a tireless, well-respected ambassador for the religious community's Rebbe—Asher finds himself struggling once again to balance art and faith, this time in a difficult emotional coming-to-terms that involves the future of his five-year-old son, Avrumel." Booklist

Potok, Chaim

★ **My** name is Asher Lev. Knopf 1972 369p

"Young Asher Lev is an obedient son of strict Jewish parents. When his artistic endeavors are discovered, he is sent to a religious leader for consultation because artists are not viewed favorably by the Hasidim. Asher's struggle for fulfillment and his ultimate rejection by his parents are poignantly drawn." Shapiro. Fic for Youth. 3d edition

Followed by The gift of Asher Lev

Pottinger, Stanley

The **last** Nazi. St. Martin's Press 2003 324p $24.95

ISBN 0-312-27676-1

LC 2003-53852

"Be prepared to feel horror for a villain who is not only the last Nazi but also one of the most terrifying." Libr J

Pötzsch, Oliver ✓

The **beggar** king; a hangman's daughter tale. Oliver Pötzsch; translated by Lee Chadeayne. 1st Mariner Books ed. Houghton Mifflin Harcourt 2013 512 p. (paperback) $18.00

ISBN 054799219X; 9780547992198

LC 2012038023

This book is the third historical mystery in Oliver Pötzsch's Hangman's Daughter Tale series. Here, hangman and garbage collector Jakob Kuisl is "accused of murder in the Free City of Regensburg, where he has gone to visit his ailing sister. Meanwhile, Kuisl's fiercely independent daughter, Magdalena, an apprentice midwife, accuses master baker Michael Berchtholdt of both impregnating his maid and fatally poisoning her with ergot in an attempt to induce an abortion." (Publishers Weekly)

Pötzsch, Oliver ✓

The **Ludwig** Conspiracy; a historical thriller. Oliver Pötzsch; [translated by Anthea Bell] Houghton Mifflin Harcourt 2013 464 p. $26

ISBN 0547740107; 9780547740102

LC 2013026948

In this book, "Steven, a bookseller with a curious past, and Sara, an art detective, are caught up in the hunt for the last letter of a 19th-century ruler. King Ludwig II, the fairy tale king of Bavaria known for his magnificent castles, died under mysterious circumstances after being declared insane. . . . Throw in a coded diary, a madman, and an assassin, and the treasure hunt takes a deadly turn." (Library Journal)

✓

Pötzsch, Oliver

The **play** of death; a hangman's daughter tale. Oliver Pötzsch; translated by Lee Chadeayne. Mariner Books 2017 xvi, 493 p.p maps (Hangman's daughter tales) (paperback) $18

ISBN 9781328663078; 9781328662088

LC 2016051868

In this novel, the sixth entry in the Hangman's Daughter series, by Oliver Pötzsch, "it is 1670 and Simon Fronwieser is in the town of Oberammergau to bring his . . . son to boarding school. . . . [when] news comes of a . . . murder: the man who was to play the part of Christ in the town's Passion Play has been found dead. . . . Soon he is joined by his father-in-law, Jakob Kuisl, the Schongau hangman, and the two begin piecing together the puzzle of the actor's death." (Publisher's note)

"A veritable Series of Unfortunate Events for adults and perfect for fans of bleak, folktale-laden landscapes and bogeyman heroes . . . ." Booklist

Pötzsch, Oliver ✓

The **Poisoned** Pilgrim; A Hangman's Daughter Tale. Oliver Pötzsch ; translated by Lee Chadeayne. Houghton Mifflin Harcourt 2013 512 p. $18

ISBN 0544114604; 9780544114609

LC 2013026783

This book is part of Oliver Pötzsch's Hangman's Daughter series. Here, "Magdalena Kuisl and her husband, Simon, have embarked on a religious pilgrimage to the Bavarian Holy Mountain. . . . This trip goes awry when the duo encounters violence, including a bell tower attack on Magdalena, and three apparent murders. When a monk is wrongfully jailed for the murders, he confides in Magdalena that he's a former hangman and begs her to get her father, Jakob, to come help." (Library Journal)

Powell, Anthony, 1905-2000

★ A **dance** to the music of time; All Four Movements. by Anthony Powell. University of Chicago Press 1995 2,978 p. 12v in 4 (pbk.) $72.80

ISBN 0226677192 4 vol. set; 9780226677194 4 vol. set

LC 94-47228

An omnibus reissue of the twelve titles comprising The Music of time series, which were originally published separately

This is a republication of Powell's twelve-novel chronicle of the experiences of Nicholas Jenkins. "Roughly speaking, the first three books (A Question of Upbringing, A Buyer's Market, and The Acceptance World), which make up the first volume of this set, cover Jenkins's school days and the period just after; the next three (At Lady Molly's, Casanova's Chinese Restaurant, and The Kindly Ones) his young manhood; the third (The Valley of Bones, The Soldier's Art, and The Military Philosophers) the {World War II} years; and the final three (Books Do Furnish a Room, Temporary Kings, and Hearing Secret Harmonies) everything after that, concluding in the 1970s." (Atl Mon)

"The novels, spanning a period of over fifty years, from the early 1920s, describe the school days, youth, and maturity of the narrator-hero, Nicholas Jenkins, and his upper-class cohorts, especially the egregious Widmerpool. Though primarily satiric in tone, they express an underlying melancholy about life and time reminiscent of Marcel Proust." Reader's Ency. 4th edition

Powell, Jim

The **breaking** of eggs. Penguin Books 2010 342p pa $15

ISBN 978-0-14-311726-1; 0-14-311726-2

LC 2010-07716

"That Powell succeeds in placing the conflicted and evolving Feliks at the center of a profound tale encapsulating Europe's 20th-century travails makes 'The Breaking of Eggs' that rare and remarkable achievement: a novel that meshes storytelling potency with historical erudition." Boston Globe

Powell, Padgett

★ **Edisto**; a novel. Farrar, Straus & Giroux 1984 183p
ISBN 0-374-14651-9

LC 83-25334

This is "distinctly a tour de force. . . . Powell's ear is acute: one of the pleasures of the book is his ability to catch the nuances of Southern speech, whether it is the malicious conversation of the Doctor's academic colleagues at a cocktail party or the genial banter of country Negroes at the fishing pier." N Y Times Book Rev

Powell, Padgett

Edisto revisited; a novel. Holt & Co. 1996 145p
ISBN 0-8050-4237-7

LC 95-34071

This novel, set in South Carolina, "begins with Simons {Manigault} having a short but steamy affair with first-cousin Patricia. . . . This proves too much for poor recent college graduate Simons, who escapes for a series of adventures deeper south. He tries his hand at fishing in Corpus Christi, quits, and again flees, this time to visit with Taurus, Simons's alcoholic mother's former lover, who is a game warden in the deepest bayou in Louisiana. All the while he debates accepting the responsibility concomitant with adulthood." (Libr J)

"'Edisto Revisited' is a puzzling work of high style, a rendering of haplessness that seems to poeticize passivity. While his novel may make you wonder if it has much of what is called meaning, Mr. Powell finally overpowers such doubts with his countless quotable passages, his humor and his seductive evocation of the romance of giving up." N Y Times Book Rev

Powell, Padgett

The **interrogative** mood; a novel? Ecco 2009 176p $21.99
ISBN 978-0-06-185941-0; 0-06-185941-9

"Our inquisitor, by turns cantankerous and plaintive, mourns the decline of butter churns and wonders under what circumstances—impending death, perhaps—it might be acceptable to molest a candy striper. There's not a whisper of a plot, but the torrent of queries is hypnotic, and the cumulative effect is of a latter-day Scheherazade, desperately staving off the final answer." New Yorker

Powell, Sophie

The **Mushroom** Man. Putnam 2003 196p $23.95
ISBN 0-399-14963-5

LC 2002-21355

At the heart of this novel is a "child's invented fairy tale, set in a Welsh forest, about an amiable hermit who fashions umbrellas from wild mushrooms to protect the local fairy population from the rain. . . . Eleven-year-old Amy—a triplet who lives on a farm in the Welsh countryside with her identical sisters; her older brother, Joseph; and her widowed mother, Beth—is the creator of the tale. One night she tells it to her 6-year-old cousin, Lily, who's so enchanted that she sets out to find the mushroom man and goes missing in the process, thus setting the novel's plot in motion. . . . The Welsh countryside has never seemed so alluring, or the existence of simple magic, despite the nasty disappointments of adult life, so probable." N Y Times Book Rev

Power, Susan

The **grass** dancer. Putnam 1994 300p hardcover o.p. pa $7.99
ISBN 0-399-13911-7; 0-425-14962-5 pa

LC 93-47199

This "is a passionate portrayal of universal human emotions and a vivid account of Native American history and culture." SLJ

Powers, J. F.

★ **Wheat** that springeth green. Knopf 1988 335p
LC 87-46104

"The beauty of Mr. Powers's writing lies in its art's being almost invisible. The craft and balance of the novel's literary achievement are discernible in every sentence, but only on second thought, so thoroughly has the author subordinated form to function." N Y Times Book Rev

Powers, Kevin

★ The **yellow** birds; a novel. Kevin Powers. 1st ed. Little, Brown & Company 2012 226 p. (hardcover) $32.99; (paperback) $14.99; (hardcover) $24.99
ISBN 9781410452566 large print; 9780316219341; 0316219363; 9780316219365

LC 2012019435

New York Times Notable Books - Fiction and Poetry: 2012
Guardian First Book Award (2012)
National Book Awards Finalist: (2012)

This book by Kevin Powers follows "twenty-one-year old Private Bartle and eighteen-year-old Private Murphy. . . . Bound together since basic training when Bartle makes a promise to bring Murphy safely home, the two have been dropped into a war neither is prepared for. . . . The two young soldiers do everything to protect each other. . . . Murphy becomes increasingly unmoored from the world around him and Bartle takes actions he could never have imagined." (Publisher's note)

Powers, Kim

Capote in Kansas; a ghost story. Carroll & Graf 2007 254p $25
ISBN 978-0-7867-2033-0; 0-7867-2033-6

In the last year of his life Truman Capote is "plagued by the ghosts of the people whose deaths he chronicled in his greatest book, In Cold Blood. The now-old Harper Lee, or Nelle as she calls herself, is the only one who has a shot at understanding Truman—his childhood friend, she served as companion and researcher on the trip to Kansas that produced In Cold Blood. But Nelle has her own ghosts to exorcise having to do with why she never wrote a second book. In Kansas, Powers speculates, Truman exposed Nelle to her own sexuality, which she continues to suppress. And at his famous 1966 Black and White Ball, green with envy over Nelle's having won the Pulitzer Prize for fiction, Truman spreads the rumor that it was he who wrote To Kill a Mockingbird, not she. Powers . . . succeeds brilliantly in blending fact and fiction to produce a sensitive portrait of two lost souls." Libr J

Powers, Richard

The **echo** maker. Farrar, Straus and Giroux 2006 451p $25
ISBN 978-0-374-14635-1; 0-374-14635-7

LC 2006-00093

National Book Award: Fiction (2006)

This "novel—a kind of neuro-cosmological adventure—is an exhilarating narrative feat. The ease with which the author controls his frequently complex material is sometimes as thrilling to watch as the unfolding of the story itself." Washington Post Book World

Powers, Richard

★ **Galatea** 2.2. Farrar, Straus & Giroux 1995 329p
ISBN 0-374-19948-5

LC 94-44319

In this novel, protagonist Richard Powers is a "humanist-in-residence at the Center for the Study of Advanced Science, where he uses his literary expertise to help Dr. Philip Lentz, a cognitive neurologist, win a bet that he can create a thinking machine capable of passing a comprehensive master's exam in English. As the computer, Helen, learns the fundamentals of language and literature, she develops a sense of her own identity and self-worth. Paralleling Powers' growing attachment to Helen is a reassessment of the year he spent living in Holland writing his novels and the demise of his longtime relationship with {C.}, a former student." (Booklist)

Powers, Richard

Generosity; an enhancement. Farrar, Straus and Giroux 2009 296p $25
ISBN 978-0-374-16114-9; 0-374-16114-3

LC 2008-54249

"Depending on personal philosophy, readers will disagree as to whether Generosity has a happy ending. But few will fail to be moved by Thassadit's joyful vision of human life." Dallas Morning News

Powers, Richard

The **gold** bug variations. Morrow 1991 639p
ISBN 0-688-09891-6

LC 90-20267

"The novel jumps back and forth between the late '50s, when brilliant scientists Stuart Ressler is involved with an Illinois research team trying to break the mysteries of DNA coding, and the '80s, when librarian Jan O'Deigh and computer programmer Franklin Todd get to know Ressler, now holding an insignificant night job at a massive computer database operation in Brooklyn, N.Y., and try to figure what derailed his promising career." Publ Wkly

Powers, Richard

★ **Orfeo**; a novel. Richard Powers. W.W. Norton & Company 2014 393 p. (hardcover) $26.95
ISBN 0393240827; 9780393240825

LC 2013031952

In this novel, author Richard Powers "tells the story of a man journeying into his past as he desperately flees the present. Composer Peter Els opens the door one evening to find the police on his doorstep. His home microbiology lab . . . has aroused the suspicions of Homeland Security. Panicked by the raid, Els turns fugitive. Through . . . help . . . Els hatches a plan to turn this disastrous collision with the security state into a work of art." (Publisher's note)

Powers, Richard

★ **Plowing** the dark. Farrar, Straus & Giroux 2000 415p $25
ISBN 0-374-23461-2

LC 99-45084

"In Seattle, a woman painter joins a team of software engineers who are devising a virtual-reality module; at the same time, an American hostage, moldering in a bare cell in Beirut, tries to mentally reconstruct his Stateside existence. Powers's intellectual dexterity is dazzling, especially in the descriptions of virtual-realty programming, and he has plenty to say about the intersections of art, war, commerce, and literature." New Yorker

Powers, Tim, 1952-

Declare; Tim Powers. William Morrow 2001 517p (alk. paper) o.p.
ISBN 0380976528

LC 2001267560

International Horror Guild Awards: Best Novel (2000); World Fantasy Awards: Novel (2001)

This book offers a "spy story involving rivalries between . . . four intelligence services: British, French, Russian and American. In 1963, Andrew Hale is summoned to reenter the secret service. He has a past [which includes] . . . a[n] . . . unsuccessful mission on Mount Ararat in 1948. . . . [Author Tim] Powers posits that the mountain . . . is . . . the dwelling place of many djinns, supernatural beings that often take the form of rocks in the Arabian deserts. . . . [I]t seems that a supernatural power, manifesting itself as an old woman, is safeguarding the Soviet Union, and if fragments of a destroyed djinn can be introduced into Moscow, they could destroy her protection and make the Soviet Union susceptible to normal human laws. This is Hale's mission." (Publishers Weekly)

Powers, Tim

Hide me among the graves; Tim Powers. William Morrow 2012
ISBN 9780061231544

LC 2011049629

This book takes place in "London, winter of 1862, [when] Adelaide McKee, a former prostitute, arrives on the doorstep of veterinarian John Crawford, a man she met once seven years earlier. Their brief meeting produced a child who, until now, had been presumed dead. McKee has learned that the girl lives--but that her life and soul are in mortal peril from a vampiric ghost. But this is no ordinary spirit; the bloodthirsty wraith is none other than John Polidori, the onetime physician to the mad, bad, and dangerous Romantic poet Lord Byron. . . . Determined to save their daughter, McKee and Crawford join forces . . . and soon . . . are plunged into a supernatural London underworld whose existence goes beyond their wildest imaginings." (Publisher's note)

Powers, Tim

Three days to never; a novel. William Morrow 2006 420p $25.95
ISBN 978-0-380-97653-9

LC 2006-41900

"Imagine a world where time travel is possible. Now imagine a world where the mummified head of an Einstein clone is helping a secret sect, led by a quasi-hermaphroditic ghost who speaks in iambic pentameter, track down and locate the time machine, an integral component of which is Charlie Chaplin's footprints in a cement slab, and you'll begin to get a grasp on just how bizarrely populated Powers' world is. Almost despite its wonderful weirdness, this thriller maneuvers at a frantic clip as Frank Marrity, Einstein's great-grandson, must pit his wits against not only the malicious secret society bent on attaining immortality but also a specialized paranormal branch of Israel's Mossad, who'd like to use the time machine to avert the Six Days' War of 1967, a stunning psychic assassin who can only see out of other people's eyes, and none other than his own bitter, alcoholic future Frank Marrity self to save his daughter, Daphne, from not merely death but from never having been." Booklist

Powning, Beth

The **sea** captain's wife; Beth Powning. Plume 2011 374p map (pbk.) $15
ISBN 9780452296954

LC 2010030032

This book tells the "19th-century tale of a young woman desperate to live at sea with her captain husband. . . . When Azuba married Nathaniel, she thought that as husband and wife they would exploring the world together on his boat. . . . But when Carrie is born, Nathaniel insists Azuba stay safely ashore at home in Whelan's Cove, New Brunswick, Canada, to raise their daughter. During Nathaniel's long absences, Azuba befriends Rev. Simon Walton, and their companionship sparks rumors of an affair that even reach Nathaniel, who returns to Whelan's Cove in a jealous rage. But Azuba persuades him to finally bring her and Carrie aboard ship, turning a long-held dream into bittersweet reality." (Publishers Weekly)

Poyer, David

Black storm. St. Martin's Press 2002 292p

ISBN 0-312-26969-2

LC 2001-58562

In this "Dan Lenson adventure, Poyer injects the special ops ace into the heart of Operation Desert Storm and confrontation with the menace of Iraqi biological warfare. Attached, along with Major Maddox, a female army doctor, to a marine recon team aiming to infiltrate Baghdad and target a suspected bioweapons site, Lenson survives claustrophobic rides in a milk truck's tank, mad SAS men, and capture and torture by the Iraqis. . . . The remarkably vivid portraits he draws of the variety of men and women drawn to serve their country merit high praise, too." Booklist

Poyer, David

A **country** of our own; a novel of the Civil War at sea. Simon & Schuster 2003 429p $24

ISBN 0-684-87134-3

LC 2003-45435

"Lt. Ker Claiborne has reluctantly relinquished his commission in the U.S. Navy and joined the Confederacy. He's an anomaly—a Virginian who opposes slavery. The plot follows Claiborne throughout the South and then across the Atlantic as captain of a highly successful and feared rebel commerce raider. There are enough spies, plots, battles, storms, and shipwrecks to satisfy any reader." Libr J

Poyer, David

Down to a sunless sea; a Tiller Galloway thriller. St. Martin's Press 1996 306p

ISBN 0-312-14589-6

LC 96-3120

"The cave-diving scenes are riveting, claustrophobic, terrifying, and beautiful, and Tiller has grown into one of the most spectacularly flawed and failed characters ever to seek redemption in popular fiction." Booklist

Poyer, David

Fire on the waters; a novel of the Civil War at sea. Simon & Schuster 2001 445p

ISBN 0-684-87133-5

LC 2001-20307

"An interesting character study of a young man's coming of age as well as an accurate historical novel." Libr J

Poyer, David

The **gulf**. St. Martin's Press 1990 xx, 442p

LC 90-36140

"Dan Lenson, is the executive officer on a frigate in the Persian Gulf, assigned to convoy a succession of oil tankers through perilous waters. Lenson's shipmates include hard-living helicopter pilots, minor crooks, and idealistic young officers. Not far away, a group of divers, naval reservists, must battle the hostility of 'real' sailors as they undertake a dangerous mission of their own. Lenson's physical and mental courage are sorely tried in the climactic scenes, where he battles enemies and the ocean itself." Libr J

Poyer, David

Thunder on the mountain. Forge 1999 382p $25.95

ISBN 0-312-86494-9

LC 98-43454

Poyer's "pitch-perfect dialogue and explosive imagery capture both sides of the bloody battle that gave birth to the unions. This is a stunning period tale in which the oft-forgotten essence of the American dream is visible in every chapter." Publ Wkly

Poyer, David

The **Whiteness** of the Whale; David Poyer. St Martins Pr 2013 336 p. (hardcover) $26.99

ISBN 1250020565; 9781250020567

LC 2013002630

In this novel, "Dr. Sara Pollard joins the antiwhaling activists aboard the Black Anemone, a high-tech yacht. . . . The crew battles snow, ice, frigid temperatures, storms, and each other before encountering the whalers in the midst of slaughtering hundreds of whales. The appearance of a mysterious rogue whale, however, introduces an even more deadly hazard than the crew's human enemies." (Publishers Weekly)

Pratchett, Terry

★ The **color** of magic; a novel of Discworld. Harper 2005 224p pa $13.95

ISBN 0-06-085592-4

LC 2005-46289

First published 1983 by St. Martin's Press with title: The colour of magic

This first book of Discworld features the tourist Twoflower, the wizard Rincewind, and several other unusual characters as they travel together on a flat planet.

Pratchett, Terry

The **fifth** elephant; a novel of Discworld. HarperPrism 2000 321p

ISBN 0-06-105157-8

LC 99-43960

"Pratchett cheerfully takes readers on an exuberant tale of mystery and invention. . . . Along the way, he skewers everything from monarchy to fascism, as well as communism and capitalism, oil wealth and ethnic identities, Russian plays, immigration, condoms and evangelical Christianity—in short, most everything worth talking about." Publ Wkly

Pratchett, Terry

Going postal; a novel of Discworld. HarperCollins 2004 377p $24.95

ISBN 0-06-001313-3

LC 2004-47391

"When petty con man Moist von Lipwig is hung for his crimes . . . it appears to be the end. But this is Discworld after all, a world 'a lot like our own but different.' Moist awakes from the shock of his hanging to find that the city's Patrician, Lord Vetinari, has assigned him a government job (a fate worse than death?) restoring the defunct postal system. Of course, there is much more to restore than the flow of letters and packages. Justice as well as communication has been poorly served by a hostile takeover of the 'clacks' a unique messaging system that is part semaphore, part digital, and under the monopoly of the Grand Trunk

Company. Before Moist can get very far into the job, he encounters ghosts, the voices of unsent letters, and a ruthless corporate conspiracy. . . . The author's inventiveness seems to know no end, his playful and irreverent use of language is a delight, and there is food for thought in his parody of fantasyland." SLJ

Pratchett, Terry

Monstrous regiment; a novel of Discworld. HarperCollins Pubs. 2003 353p hardcover o.p. pa $7.99

ISBN 0-06-001315-X; 0-06-001316-8 pa

LC 2003-50800

"Pratchett revels in pricking pomp and assurance, but it isn't going too far to say that of late his real subject, like Wilfred Owen's, is the pit of war. Pratchett's approach may be less lyrical, but he can move from farce to sadness in seconds." N Y Times Book Rev

Pratchett, Terry

Thief of time; a novel of Discworld. HarperCollins Pubs. 2001 324p

ISBN 0-06-019956-3

LC 00-65347

"This is Discworld, an adolescent Oz in which far fewer folks are immortal, but long life doesn't entail decrepitude; magic works; and politics and culture are fluid, far off, and mostly for old guys. Spun out of words and wit, it is as light and curiously tasty as cotton candy." Booklist

Pratchett, Terry

Thud! a novel of Discworld. HarperCollins 2005 384p $24.95

ISBN 0-06-081522-6

LC 2005-46271

"Commander Sam Vines of Ankh-Morpork's City Watch finds a 'perfect day' going downhill quickly. Not only is there a murderer loose in the city but Sam also faces pressure to add a vampire to a police force that already contains trolls and werewolves and an old rivalry that threatens to break out into overt warfare. It's all in a day's work for the City Watch in the latest novel set in the author's hilariously surreal Disc World." Libr J

Pratchett, Terry

The **truth**; a novel of Discworld. HarperCollins Pubs. 2000 324p il

ISBN 0-380-97895-4

LC 00-31928

"When he stumbles upon the dwarven secret of movable type, young scribe William de Word discovers a new career and starts a newspaper—the first of its kind in the city of Ankh-Morpork. Pratchett's . . . @Discworld' novel takes on the press and investigative journalism in a hilarious romp that examines the fleeting nature of truth and lies." Libr J

Prcic, Ismet

Shards. Black Cat 2011 392p pa $14.95

ISBN 978-0-8021-7081-1

The author's "debut is about a young Bosnian, also named Ismet Prcic, who has fled his wartorn homeland and is now struggling to reconcile his past with his present life in California. He is advised that in order to make peace with the corrosive guilt he harbors over leaving behind his family behind, he must 'write everything.' The result is a great rattlebag of memories, confessions, and fictions: sweetly humorous recollections of Ismet's childhood in Tuzla appear alongside anguished letters to his mother about the challenges of life in this new world. As Ismet's foothold in the present falls away, his writings are further complicated by stories from the point of view of another young man real or imagined named Mustafa, who joined a troop of elite soldiers and stayed in Bosnia to fight. When Mustafa's story begins to overshadow Ismet's new-world identity, the reader is charged with piecing together the fragments of a life that has become eerily unrecognizable, even to the one living it." Bookreporter

Prentiss, Molly

Tuesday nights in 1980; a novel. by Molly Prentiss. Scout Press 2016 336 p. (hardcover : alk. paper) $26

ISBN 9781501121043; 9781501121050; 9781501121067

LC 2015027259

This book, by Molly Prentiss, "follows a critic, an artist, and a desirous, determined young woman as they find their way—and ultimately collide—amid the ever-evolving New York City art scene of the 1980s. . . . [It] renders a complex moment when the meaning and nature of art is being all but upended, and New York City as a whole is reinventing itself." (Publisher's note)

"Prentiss' characters—rich, nuanced, satisfyingly complicated—are informed not only by their emotional lives, but also by their intellectual and artistic ones; their relationships to art are as lively and essential as their relationships to each other. But while the novel is elegantly infused with an ambient sense of impending loss—this is New York on the cusp of drastic gentrification—it miraculously manages to dodge the trap of easy nostalgia, thanks in large part to Prentiss' wry humor. As affecting as it is absorbing. A thrilling debut." Kirkus

Preston, Caroline

The **scrapbook** of Frankie Pratt; Caroline Preston. Ecco Press 2011 228p. ill. (some col.)

ISBN 0061966908; 9780061966903

LC 2012372952

Alex Award (2012)

In this book, "Frankie receives a blank scrapbook and her deceased father's typewriter as high-school graduation gifts and begins to record her adventures with the keepsakes she collects. Although Vassar offers Frankie a scholarship, Frankie still can't afford to attend college. Instead she takes a job caring for elderly Mrs. Pingree. . . . The dowager's visiting nephew Jamie, a dashing, emotionally damaged World War I vet in his 30s, emotionally seduces 17-year-old Frankie. . . . When the not-yet-sexual affair is discovered, Mrs. Pingree gives Frankie a $1,000 check. . . . Soon Frankie heads off to Vassar. . . . After graduation, Frankie moves to Greenwich Village and finds a job at 'True Story.' . . . When Frankie realizes why [her boyfriend doesn't propose], she goes to Paris, . . . where the past catches up with her and a whole new chapter of life starts." (Kirkus)

Preston, Douglas

Blasphemy; [by] Douglas J. Preston. Forge Books 2008 414p il $25.95

ISBN 978-0-7653-1105-4; 0-7653-1105-4

LC 2007-31811

This suspense novel centers around "Isabella, a giant superconducting supercollider particle accelerator. . . . The ostensible goal of Isabella's creator, physicist Gregory North Hazelius, is to discover new forms of energy, but what he really wants is to talk to God. The project, located inside Red Mesa (a five-hundred-square-mile tableland on the Navajo Indian Reservation), is behind schedule, so presidential science adviser Stanton Lockwood hires ex-CIA man Wyman Ford to go to Red Mesa and find out what's causing the holdup. Meanwhile, a Navajo medicine man, a televangelist and a pastor who runs a failed mission on the reservation are gearing up to pull the plug on Isabella before she destroys the earth. Science has often tangled with religion in this genre, but Preston puts his own philosophical spin on the usual proceedings, and when he gets his irate villagers with their burning torches headed for the castle, the pages simply fly." Publ Wkly

Preston, Douglas

Brimstone; [by] Douglas Preston and Lincoln Child. Warner Bks. 2004 497p $25.95

ISBN 0-446-53143-X

LC 2004-1968

"Erudite, swiftly paced, brimming (occasionally overbrimming) with memorable personae and tense set pieces, this is the perfect thriller." Publ Wkly

Preston, Douglas

The **cabinet** of curiosities; {by} Douglas Preston and Lincoln Child. Warner Bks. 2002 466p

ISBN 0-446-53022-0

LC 2001-39580

This novel features "fabulous locales, colorful characters, pointed riffs on city and museum politics, cool forensic and paleontological speculation and several gripping set pieces including an extended white-knuckle climax." Publ Wkly

Preston, Douglas

The **codex**. Forge 2004 396p $24.95

ISBN 0-7653-0700-6

LC 2003-49427

"A treasure hunter and tomb raider, Maxwell Broadbent is one of the wealthiest men on the planet owing to his extensive art collection. Dying of cancer, he decides to force his three estranged sons to work together for their inheritance. Leaving them a videotape of his plan, Max takes everything of value and buries himself and the goods somewhere in the world. To claim their inheritance, his sons have to find the tomb. Others are watching and rooting them on so that they can claim the rewards for themselves. One item of significance is a Mayan codex that contains the secret instructions to create medicine from the native jungle plants. This discovery would revolutionize the pharmaceutical industry. Fascinating characters, exotic jungle scenery, and surprising twists make this nonstop thrill ride well worth deciphering." Libr J

Preston, Douglas

Impact. Forge 2010 364p $25.99

ISBN 978-0-7653-1768-1; 0-7653-1768-0

"The thriller elements mix well with the science aspects of the story, and the author makes even the hard-to-grasp concepts easy to understand." Libr J

Preston, Douglas

Reliquary; [by] Douglas Preston, Lincoln Child. Forge 1997 382p $24.95

ISBN 0-312-86095-1

LC 96-53533

"Although Reliquary is a sequel, its exposition carries us easily into the new plot and excites interest in seeing what Preston and Child come up with next, after this yarn's all-loose-ends-tied finale." Booklist

Preston, Douglas

Still life with crows; {by} Douglas Preston and Lincoln Child. Warner Bks. 2003 435p $24.95

ISBN 0-446-53142-1

LC 2002-192401

FBI Agent Pendergast arrives "in tiny Medicine Creek, KS, just in time to investigate a series of gruesome murders. Life in rural Medicine Creek usually revolves around the local turkey-processing plant and growing corn, but all hell breaks loose when a female corpse is found in a clearing in a cornfield, surrounded by a ring of dead crows impaled on arrows." Libr J

Preston, Douglas

Tyrannosaur Canyon. Forge 2005 368p $24.95

ISBN 0-765-31104-6

LC 2005-5171

"A prospector discovers the treasure of his lifetime and takes bullets in the back for his effort. With his dying breath, he gives a journal to innocent bystander Tom Broadbent (the hero of Preston's . . . The Codex) and asks Tom to deliver the information to his daughter. The prospector's killer, of course, wants the ledger, so now Tom and his wife are in mortal danger. Why is the journal so valuable? It contains information leading to the fossilized remains of a complete Tyrannosaurus rex, a scientific discovery worth millions and a lifetime of accolades to the finder. In addition, a mysterious black ops agency wants the skeleton to hide a deadly secret originally discovered on the moon over 30 years ago by the crew of Apollo 17. The truth will shake the foundation of paleontology to its core. Preston's exhilarating and absorbing science-based effort will thrill readers from the first page to the last." Libr J

Preston, Douglas

The **wheel** of darkness; [by] Douglas Preston & Lincoln Child. Warner Books 2007 388p $25.99

ISBN 978-0-446-58028-1; 0-446-58028-7

LC 2007-20551

In this supernatural thriller, "FBI agent Aloysius Pendergast and his ward, Constance Greene, seek peace of mind at a remote Tibetan monastery, only to fall into yet another perilous, potentially earthshaking assignment. The monastery's abbot asks them to recover a stolen relic, the cryptic Agozyen, which could, in the wrong hands, wipe out humanity. The pair follow the trail to a luxury cruise ship, where a series of brutal murders suggests the relic's evil spirit might already have been invoked. . . . While not as frightening as others in the series, this entry still shows why the authors stand head and shoulders above their rivals in this subgenre." Publ Wkly

Price, Nancy

Night woman. Pocket Bks. 1992 314p

ISBN 0-671-74993-5

LC 92-50164

"Gritty, wry characterization, chilling images of insanity, and a long, ultimately satisfying tease which ends with Mary at last getting her due will keep readers flipping pages." Publ Wkly

Price, Nancy

Sleeping with the enemy. Simon & Schuster 1987 332p

LC 86-29778

"Battered women don't usually have the courage of Sara Burney. Desperate and bruised physically and emotionally, she evolves a plan to flee her obsessive husband. She knows he will come after her and kill her eventually, so that mere flight will offer only temporary reprieve. So she decides to 'get lost.' She assumes a new identity, a new look, and seeks respite and a new life hundreds of miles from their home in Massachusetts. . . . Price has written an absorbing tale and her language has a sensual quality that transports the reader into her panoramas that affect all the senses." West Coast Rev Books

Price, Reynolds

★ The **good** priest's son. Scribner 2005 278p $26

ISBN 0-7432-5400-7

LC 2004-65383

This novel is "thematically rich—indeed, it is rather bowed by its meanings—and features many pleasing Southern voices, along with an impeccable depiction of the region's deep-rooted traditions." N Y Times Book Rev

Price, Reynolds

Roxanna Slade. Scribner 1998 301p $25

ISBN 0-684-83292-5

LC 97-39167

"Many of the virtues that have endeared Price . . . to readers are present in this story of a North Carolina woman and several generations of her family. Price's musically cadenced, nostalgia-washed prose, plangent with portent and loss and vibrant with imagery, is as beguiling as ever. His picture of life in the South a century ago is imbued with candor about customs and attitudes—especially those concerning women and race." Publ Wkly

Price, Richard

★ **Clockers**. Houghton Mifflin 1992 599p

ISBN 0-395-53761-4

LC 91-43318

This is "an incredible course in urban street life, particularly the crack culture." Booklist

Price, Richard

Freedomland. Broadway Bks. 1998 546p $25

ISBN 0-7679-0024-3

LC 98-10527

"Price's characters are, as usual, dead-on, and his eye for unflinchingly capturing humans at their very best—and very worst—is unrivaled." Libr J

Price, Richard

Lush life. Farrar, Straus & Giroux 2008 455p $26

ISBN 978-0-374-29925-5; 0-374-29925-0; 0374299250; 9780374299255

LC 200808437

This novel is set in New York City. Eric Cash is "thirty-five years old and he's still living on the Lower East Side, still in the restaurant business, still serving the people he wanted to be. What does Eric do? He manages. Not like Ike Marcus. Ike was young, good-looking, people liked him. Ask him what he did, he wouldn't say tending bar. He was going places—until two street kids stepped up to him and Eric one night and pulled a gun. At least, that's Eric's version." (Publisher's note)

"Price has been around for what seems like forever, but there's a reason we still read him. Because every sentence is a pleasure. Because he never puts a foot wrong, and never lingers. He takes just enough time to make you care." Esquire

Price, Richard

Samaritan. Knopf 2003 377p $25

ISBN 0-375-41115-1

"Ray Mitchell, an Emmy-nominated TV writer who returned to teach pro bono at his old high school amid the projects of Dempsy, New Jersey, has had his head bashed in. Nerese Ammons, a cop 10 weeks from retirement, takes the case personally because of a good turn Ray did her when they were children. But Ray, deteriorating in the hospital, doesn't want to tell her who attacked him." Booklist

Price, Steven

By Gaslight; A Novel. Steven Price. Farrar, Straus & Giroux 2016 752 p. (ebook) $60; $28

ISBN 9780374714116; 0374160538; 9780374160531

LC 2016032498

In this novel by Steven Price, "William Pinkerton is already famous, the son of the most notorious detective of all time, when he descends into the underworld of Victorian London in pursuit of a new lead on the fabled con Edward Shade. William's father died without ever finding Shade, but William is determined to drag the thief out of the shadows. . . . A fog-enshrouded hunt . . . [will create] the most unlikely of bonds . . . [in] finding Edward Shade." (Publisher's note)

"Yet Price's novel is entirely contemporary, and assuredly his own: a sweeping tale of hunter and hunted in which the most-dangerous pursuer is always the human heart." Pub Wkly

Priest, Cherie

Boneshaker. Tor 2009 416p pa $15.99

ISBN 978-0-7653-1841-1

LC 2009-18700

"Intelligent, exceptionally well written and showcasing a phenomenal strong female protagonist who embodies the complexities inherent in motherhood, this yarn is a must-read for the discerning steampunk fan." Publ Wkly

Priest, Cherie

Clementine; Cherie Priest. Subterranean Press 2010 201 p. $25

ISBN 1596063084; 9781596063082

"In this steampunk thriller" by Cherie Priest "Maria Isabella Boyd, a notorious former actress and Confederate spy, is on her first mission for the renowned Pinkerton Detective Agency. The airship Clementine must deliver its cargo unimpeded, but its former owner, escaped slave-turned-air pirate Croggon Hainey, is determined to recover the ship he stole fair and square. A simple pursuit quickly evolves, and soon Maria and Croggon are forced to fight on the same side." (Publishers Weekly)

Priest, Cherie

Dreadnought; Cherie Priest. Tor 2010 400 p. (pbk.) $14.99

ISBN 0765325780; 9780765325785

LC 2010032571

In this "Civil War steampunk thriller"by Cherie Priest, "Mercy Lynch, recently widowed and taxed to exhaustion by caring for Confederate wounded in Richmond, must cross the war-torn nation to reach her estranged father, who lies dying in the Washington territories. After her dirigible is shot out of the air, Mercy joins Horatio Korman, a Texas Ranger with an agenda, on the Union's famous steam engine, the Dreadnought." (Publishers Weekly)

Priest, Cherie

The **Family** Plot; Cherie Priest. Tor Books 2016 365 p. (hardcover) $25.99

ISBN 9781466860650; 9780765378248; 9780765396075; 0765378248

LC 2016288284

In this novel, by Cherie Priest, "business is lean and times are tight, so [Chuck's] thrilled when the aged and esteemed Augusta Withrow appears in his office, bearing an offer. She has a massive family estate to unload. For a check and a handshake, it's all his. He assigns his daughter Dahlia to personally oversee the project. It's empty, but it isn't abandoned. Something in the Withrow mansion is angry and lost. This is its last chance to raise hell before the house is gone forever." (Publisher's note)

"Priest has written an excellent modern house story from start to finish." Pub Wkly

Priest, Cherie

Fiddlehead; Cherie Priest. Tor Books 2013 368 p. illustrations (pbk.) $14.99

ISBN 0765334070; 9780765334077

LC 2013018477

In this novel by Cherie Priest, part of the Clockwork Century series, "Gideon Bardsley is a brilliant inventor, but the job is less glamorous than one might think, especially since the assassination attempts started. They're trying to destroy his greatest achievement: a calculating engine called Fiddlehead. Bardsley has no choice but to ask his patron, former president Abraham Lincoln, for help. [Lincoln] calls on his old private security staff to protect Gideon." (Publisher's note)

"Priest's final Clockwork Century novel . . . wraps things up nicely, once again turning a mash-up of too-worn genre tropes (steampunk, alternate Civil War, zombies) into a work of entertainment laced with social criticism." Pub Wkly

Priest, Christopher

The **islanders**; Christopher Priest. Gollancz 2011 339 p.

ISBN 0575070048; 9780575070042

LC 2012379979

This book "presents itself as a [fictional] gazetteer for the Dream Archipelago, a vast array of islands situated between two warring continents to the north and south, [but] becomes, instead, a study of some of the islands' most interesting inhabitants. As the stories of a reclusive novelist, a simple young man accused of murder, a social theorist and author, a celebrated mime, and other significant individuals unfold, another tale—of a very public murder . . . --evolves." (Library Journal)

Pritchett, Laura

The **blue** hour; a novel. Laura Pritchett. Counterpoint Press 2017 240 p. (hardcover) $25

ISBN 9781619028487; 9781619028890; 1619028484

LC 2016040253

In this book, by Laura Pritchett, "the residents of Blue Moon Mountain form a tight-knit community of those living off the land, stunned by the beauty and isolation all around them. So when, at the onset of winter, the town veterinarian commits a violent act, the repercussions of that tragedy are felt all across the mountainside, upending their lives and causing their paths to twist and collide in unexpected ways." (Publisher's note)

"A richly sensual, tenderly proffered portrait of the most vulnerable yet appealing aspects of the human condition." Booklist

Pronzini, Bill

★ **Crazybone**; a nameless detective novel. Carroll & Graf Pubs. 2000 197p

ISBN 0-7867-0730-5

Pronzini's nameless detective "lumbers down the San Francisco Peninsula to a private enclave of wooded estates and walled country clubs to find out why a grieving widow has refused a $50,000 insurance settlement for the accidental death of her husband. The look of 'raw terror' on the woman's face when he confronts her . . . suggests that she might have something to hide, and the nameless hero does a good job of ferreting out her secret. But the real fun comes from watching the old war horse plod through a hostile social environment, observing the swells at their selfish pursuits and making them regret every condescending sneer they threw in his face." N Y Times Book Rev

Pronzini, Bill

The **crimes** of Jordan Wise. Walker & Co. 2006 233p $23.95

ISBN 0-8027-1493-5

LC 2006-46115

"Like an expert fisherman, Pronzini spins out his yarn to its inevitable conclusion; there's only one way to end the old story of a lovesick sap and a dame whose appetites can never be satisfied. The Crimes of Jordan Wise is a neat piece of writing: James M. Cain by way of Jimmy Buffett." Washington Post Book World

Pronzini, Bill

Fever; a Nameless Detective novel. Forge 2008 288p $24.95

ISBN 978-0-7653-1818-3; 0-7653-1818-0

LC 2008-5228

"Mitchell Krochek, who's worried about the gambling addiction of his wife, Janice, hires Nameless to trace Janice, who's disappeared for the fourth time in four years. When Jake Runyon, Nameless's associate, traces Janice to an apartment hotel near their San Francisco office, Nameless and Jake decide to honor Janice's request not to reveal her location to her husband. Later, a battered Janice shows up at the detective agency's office, where she agrees to go home, only to vanish again amid circumstances strongly indicating foul play. . . . This insightful novel will appeal to those who like the mean streets portrayed with understatement and subtlety rather than gory violence." Publ Wkly

Pronzini, Bill

The **hidden**; a novel of suspense. Walker & Co. 2010 210p $24

ISBN 978-0-8027-1800-6; 0-8027-1800-0

LC 2010-30153

This "is a fairly short novel in these days of bloated best sellers, tightly written and tightly plotted, but never mechanical or obvious. It is strongly cinematic, but the pleasures, as always with Pronzini, are in the writing and not merely his visual sense. His characters are recognizable people, not merely pawns to the suspense element." Mystery Scene

Pronzini, Bill

In an evil time. Walker & Co. 2001 266p $23.95

ISBN 0-8027-3353-0

LC 00-49996

"Jack Hollis, a family man and law-abiding citizen, is ready to cross the line. His daughter, Angela, is being stalked by her abusive second husband, David Rakubian, a successful personal-injury lawyer in San Francisco. In fact, it's Rakubian's knowledge of the law's limitations that makes him so dangerous to Angela and her toddler son. Jack has weighed the options and sees Rakubian's death as the only way out for his daughter. . . . {Pronzini} has fashioned a nail-biter out of the issue of domestic abuse and the law's inability to deal with it effectively." Booklist

Pronzini, Bill

Mourners; a nameless detective novel. Forge 2006 285p $24.95

ISBN 0-7653-0932-7

LC 2005-43510

"When Nameless made his assistant, Tamara, a partner in his detective agency and hired Jake, a new operative, he genuinely felt he was moving toward retirement. But business has increased, and Nameless finds himself reluctant to give up the work that has defined him for so long, even though he has recently become a husband and father. His current case involves a wealthy financial planner who attends the funerals of strangers, walks deserted beaches at night, and makes solitary visits to a secret rental apartment. His wife is worried and hires the firm to investigate. . . . Pronzini's series becomes more layered and complex with each entry. This time the primary characters are all in one stage or another of mourning, but the only one who recognizes it is the initial subject of the investigation. He is also the only one who understands the timeless omnipresence of grief. . . . A dark, foreboding entry in a classic series." Booklist

Pronzini, Bill

Nightcrawlers; a nameless detective novel. Forge 2005 301p $24.95

ISBN 0-7653-0931-9

LC 2004-56323

"The 'Nameless' detective is doing his best to settle into semiretirement after making his longtime assistant, Tamara Corbin, a partner in the agency and adding Jake Runyon, a former cop, as a field operative. However, some cases require Nameless' attention. Thugs are roaming the streets of San Francisco's Castro district, attacking gay men. Runyon's son's lover is one of the thug's victims, prompting Runyon and Nameless to investigate. Meanwhile Tamara, on a routine surveillance of a credit deadbeat, sees her subject carry something into his house that raises the hair on the back of her neck. The long-running Nameless series continues to evolve. With the novels no longer exclusively first-person narratives by Nameless, parallel plotlines have been introduced from multiple points of view, giving readers a chance to view Nameless as others see him. And, as always, the novels are never just about crime." Booklist

Pronzini, Bill

Savages; a nameless detective novel. Forge 2007 300p $24.95

ISBN 978-7653-0933-4; 0-7653-0933-5

"San Francisco detective Nameless is asked by a former client to look into the death of her sister, who was trapped in an unhappy marriage. Althought the death had been ruled an accident, Nameless soon finds himself stymied by ethical questions and lack of evidence. Meanwhile, Jake Runyon, a partner in Nameless's agency, is trying to serve a subpoena and gets caught in a case of serial arson and murder. It is hard to find a better crime writer than Pronzini, and his understanding of feminine angst as well as male motivations has made this one of the best detective series ever." Libr J

Pronzini, Bill

Spook; a nameless detective novel. Carroll & Graf Pubs. 2003 233p $25

ISBN 0-7867-1086-1

"The case seems simple enough. Spook, a homeless street person, becomes a fixture at a local business; its employees provide assistance as needed for the obviously mentally disturbed individual. He is murdered in an especially heinous assault. His unofficial 'family' wants San Francisco private investigator 'Nameless' to learn his real identity. Nameless hands the case over to his newly hired field operative, Jake Runyon, a former Seattle cop. . . . A fascinating entry in a series that continues to redefine noir fiction even as it honors its roots." Booklist

Pronzini, Bill

★ **Step** to the graveyard easy. Walker & Co. 2002 165p $21.95

ISBN 0-8027-3375-1

LC 2001-55914

"Compelling modern noir with a thought-provoking conclusion." Booklist

Pronzini, Bill ✓

The **violated**; Bill Pronzini. Bloomsbury USA 2017 xiv, 252 p.p (hardcover : alk. paper) $26

ISBN 9781632866608; 9781632866615; 9781632866622

LC 2016025590

In this novel, by Bill Pronzini, "in the small town of Santa Rita, California, the mutilated body of Martin Torrey is found by two passersby. A registered sex offender, Torrey has been a suspect in a string of recent rapes, and instant suspicion for his murder falls on the relatives and friends of the women attacked. Police chief Griffin Kells and detective Robert Ortiz are under increasing pressure . . . [for] results in a case that has no easy solution." (Publisher's note)

"This is a psychological novel dressed up in a thriller suit, which means the teeth are showing, and Pronzini's skill keeps things moving. Another satisfying tale from a crime master." Booklist

Prose, Francine

★ **Blue** angel; a novel. HarperCollins Pubs. 2000 314p $25

ISBN 0-06-019541-X

LC 99-40564

National Book Award Finalist: Fiction (2000)

An "ironic gloss on Von Sternberg's tragedy of erotic abasement. . . . Prose's retelling focuses less on the ridiculous and self-destructive behavior of the professor . . . than on the far more laughable (and hazardous) rigidity of the politically correct behavior codes governing his tiny Vermont campus." New Yorker

Prose, Francine

A **changed** man; a novel. Francine Prose. HarperCollins Publishers 2005 421p $24.95

ISBN 0-06-019674-2

LC 2004-47448

A "satire of liberal pieties, the radical right and the fund-raising world. The 'changed man' of the title is Vincent Nolan, a 32-year-old tattooed ex-skinhead who appears one morning in the New York offices of World Brotherhood Watch, a foundation headed by Meyer Maslow, a Holocaust survivor. Vincent declares that he has had a personal conversion (never mind that it was triggered by a heavy dose of Ecstasy) and wants to work with the foundation to 'save guys like me from becoming guys like me.' Meyer takes Vincent on faith—and convinces Bonnie Kalen, the foundation's fundraiser, to put Vincent up in the suburban home she shares with her two sons, Max, 12, and Danny, 16. Prose tears into this unusual premise with the piercing wit that has become her trademark." Publ Wkly

Prose, Francine

Goldengrove; a novel. HarperCollins Publishers 2008 275p $24.95

ISBN 978-0-06-621411-5; 0-06-621411-4

LC 2008-02112

A young girl faces the consequences of sudden loss after the death of her sister. As her parents drift toward their own risky consolations, thirteen-year-old Nico is left alone to grope toward understanding and clarity, falling into a seductive, dangerous relationship with her sister's enigmatic boyfriend. Over one haunted summer, Nico must face that life-changing moment when children realize their parents can no longer help them. She learns about the power of art, of time and place, the mystery of loss and recovery. But for all the darkness at the novel's heart, the narrative itself is radiant with the lightness of summer and charged by the restless sexual tension of teenage life.

"Nico's introduction into adult situations is accelerated and scary, and Prose doesn't handle the topic with kid gloves. As Nico's relationship with Aaron progresses, her thoughts about physical intimacy run rampant. Prose expertly conveys the newfound sexual desires teenagers experience as they grow into adults." Deseret News

Prose, Francine

Household saints. St. Martin's Press 1981 227p

LC 80-29116

"When Joseph Santangelo, the sausagemaker, wins the bride, Catherine, in a pinochle game, he sets in motion a pattern of events laced with ancient Mediterranean customs, superstition and religion that affect the women in his life. In addition to Catherine, there is his mother, a nonstop oracle of doom, and his Americanized daughter who seeks and perhaps finds Jesus in obsessive domesticity. A skillful fabulist, {the author} . . . not only captures the domestic scenes and smells of Little Italy but allows her 'naifs' to unfold in recognizable earthiness and warmth as they confront life's mysteries." Publ Wkly

Prose, Francine

Hunters and gatherers. Farrar, Straus & Giroux 1995 247p

LC 95-3569

This is a "delightful satire, . . . irreverent, funny, critical, compassionate. . . . Prose brilliantly captures the absurdities and hypocrisies inherent in such groups. The women obsess about wombs, menstrual periods and the glories of being female. Yet separatism does not remove the worst dynamics between women." Women's Rev Books

Prose, Francine

Mister monkey; Francine Prose. Harper 2016 304 p. (ebook) $25.99; (hardcover) $26.99

ISBN 9780062397850; 9780062397836

LC 2016013864

This book, by Francine Prose, "follows the exploits and intrigue of a constellation of characters affiliated with an off-off-off-off Broadway children's musical. Mister Monkey--a screwball children's musical about a playfully larcenous pet chimpanzee--is the kind of family favorite that survives far past its prime." (Publisher's Note)

"Wickedly funny and sharply observant, in the author's vintage manner, with a warmth that softens the satire just enough." Kirkus

Prose, Francine

My new American life. Harper 2011 306p $25.99

ISBN 978-0-06-171376-7

LC 2010-43012

"Lula is 26 and restless, an Albanian immigrant whiling away her days in suburban New Jersey as a spectacularly lax caretaker to sullen teenager Zeke (her ''nannying' largely consists of mixing up afterschool mojitos and heating frozen pizzas) while his single father works long hours in finance. Soon enough, intrigue arrives in the form of three leather-jacketed comrades from the old country on her doorstep, asking Lula — though, really, it's not a request — to stash a gun for them, and Prose . . . is in her sweet spot as a nimble chronicler of contemporary culture. Though satirical fiction can often leave a sour aftertaste, her deft comic touch rarely falters." Entertainment Wkly

Prose, Francine

★ **Primitive** people. Farrar, Straus & Giroux 1992 227p

ISBN 0-374-23722-0

LC 91-28692

This "comedy of manners has a serious purpose but it is never earnest and provides a lot of shrewd and malicious fun. . . . The author finds it hard to write a dull sentence. Her gargoyles are sometimes gruesome. They are also witty and she has a perfect ear for the chatter of this particular set of rich Americans." Economist

Proulx, Annie

Accordion crimes; [by] E. Annie Proulx. Scribner 1996 381p

ISBN 0-684-19548-8

LC 96-16299

"Following successive owners of an accordion—from its creator, an Italian immigrant, who was lynched in Louisiana in 1891, to some fatherless black children living on the edge of a noxious landfill in 1991—this twelve-car pileup of a book brims with the sort of disasters you read about on the inside pages of the paper." New Yorker

Proulx, Annie

Bad dirt; Wyoming stories 2. Scribner 2004 219p $25

ISBN 0-7432-5799-5

LC 2004-56530

"This poignant and often humorous collection is packed with well-drawn characters that linger in the mind and heart. As expected, the Wyoming landscape is the enduring character in each story, silently wielding its magical and brutal power." Libr J

Proulx, Annie, 1935-

Barkskins; a novel. Annie Proulx. Scribner 2016 800 p. genealogical tables (hardback) $32

ISBN 9780743288781; 9780743288798

LC 2015030152

This novel by Annie Proulx is "about the taking down of the world's forests. In the late seventeenth century two penniless young Frenchmen, René Sel and Charles Duquet, arrive in New France . . . [and] become wood-cutters-barkskins. . . . Proulx tells the stories of the descendants of Sel and Duquet over three hundred years—their travels, . . . the revenge of rivals, accidents, pestilence, Indian attacks, and cultural annihilation." (Publisher's note)

"Despite the length, nothing seems extraneous, and not once does the reader sense the story slipping from Proulx's grasp, resulting in the kind of immersive reading experience that only comes along every few years." Pub Wkly

Proulx, Annie

Close range; Wyoming stories. watercolors by William Matthews. Scribner 1999 283p il $23.50

ISBN 0-684-85221-7

LC 98-56066

"Geography, splendid and terrible, is a tutelary deity to the characters in 'Close Range': hardpan ranchers, battered cowpokes and bull riders, bar girls and bar brawlers. Their lives are a futile uphill struggle conducted as a downhill, out-of-control tearaway. Proulx writes of them in a prose that is violent and impacted and mastered just at the point where, having gone all the way to the edge, it is about to go over." N Y Times Book Rev

Proulx, Annie

Fine just the way it is; Wyoming stories 3. Scribner 2008 221p $25

ISBN 978-1-4165-7166-7; 1-4165-7166-3

LC 2008-13682

This "collection of Wyoming tales, continues [Proulx's] Dickensian delight in memorable nomenclature. So, prepare to meet: Duck Slaver, Harp Daft, the Grainblewer twins, Wacky Lipe, Fenk Fipps, Tug Diceheart and more. Like Dickens, Proulx has a keen eye for the eccentricity of the individual, admitting that 'everyone in the sparsely settled country' is noted for a 'salty dog quirk or talent' that their names might suggest. . . . Proulx's writing can be as fine as anything being produced in America today." Times Lit Suppl

Proulx, Annie

Postcards; by E. Annie Proulx. Scribner 1992 308p il
ISBN 0-684-18718-3

LC 91-25089

"Ms. Proulx's expansion of the concept of postcards is what transforms a rambling tale into a minimalist saga. . . . Story makes this novel compelling; technique makes it beautiful. What makes 'Postcards' significant is that Ms. Proulx uses both story and technique to make real the history of post-World War II America." N Y Times Book Rev

Proulx, Annie

★ The **shipping** news. Scribner 1993 337p

LC 92-30315

The author "blends Newfoundland argot, savage history, impressively diverse characters, fine descriptions of weather and scenery, and comic horseplay without ever lessening the reader's interest in Quoyle's progress from bumbling outsider to capable journalist." Atlantic

Proulx, Annie

That old ace in the hole; a novel. Scribner 2002 361p $26
ISBN 0-684-81307-6

LC 2002-30462

This novel's "hero, Bob Dollar, a decent sort who was abandoned at 8, is sent by his company to Woolybucket, Tex., to scout locations for factory hog farms, but is soon smitten with the high, flat country, the locals and their tales of stubborn ranchers, plagues of locusts and family farms undone by corporate greed." N Y Times Book Rev

Proust, Marcel

The **captive** [and] The fugitive; translated by C.K. Scott Moncrieff & Terence Kilmartin; revised by D.J. Enright. Modern Lib. 1993 957p (In search of lost time) $24.95
ISBN 0-679-42477-6

LC 93-15168

Sequel to Sodom and Gomorrah
Original French edition, 1923

In The captive "Albertine is living in the narrator's Paris home, where he attempts to keep complete watch on her activities. The Verdurins provoke a scandalous rupture between Morel and Charlus. Albertine suddenly flees, just as the narrator is ready to dismiss her. {In the fugitive} the narrator seeks the return of Albertine, but after her death he observes the gradual encroachment of oblivion on grief until, on a trip to Venice, he finds his pain completely cured. Gilberte has become the social-climbing Mlle de Forcheville; she marries Saint-Loup, who is now Morel's lover." Merriam-Webster's Ency of Lit

Followed by Time regained

Proust, Marcel

The **complete** short stories of Marcel Proust; compiled and translated by Joachim Neugroschel; foreword by Roger Shattuck. Cooper Sq. Pubs. 2001 201p $25.95
ISBN 0-8154-1136-7

LC 00-65739

This collection contains Proust's "first literary endeavor, 'Pleasures and Days,' translated into English for the first time in 50 years, along with six additional stories, never before seen in English. . . . Delicately translated by Neugroschel . . . these early musings are priceless, insightful venturing into the mind of a maturing virtuoso." Booklist

Proust, Marcel

The **Guermantes** way; translated by C.K. Scott Moncrieff and Terence Kilmartin; revised by D.J. Enright. Modern Lib. 1993 834p (In search of lost time) $23.95
ISBN 0-679-60028-0

LC 92-33975

Sequel to Within a budding grove
Original French edition published 1920-1921

"The narrator, whose family have been tenants in the large Guermantes home in Paris, conducts his laborious ascent to the summit of high society, finally attending the duchesse de Guermantes's reception. He also describes Saint-Loup's passion for the actress and prostitute Rachel, and the death of his own beloved grandmother." Reader's Ency. 4th edition

Followed by Sodom and Gomorrah

Proust, Marcel

★ **Remembrance** of things past. Random House 1981 3v
ISBN 0-394-50643-X set

LC 79-5542

Includes the seven volumes, published separately and entered in this catalog. Volume one and two translated by C. K. Scott Moncrieff and Terence Kilmartin; volume three by C. K. Scott Moncrieff, Terence Kilmartin and Andreas Mayor

This "is the first complete English version of Proust's masterpiece, translated from the definitive 1954 Pléiade edition, Terence Kilmartin has checked the Scott Moncrieff translation (which comprised the first 11 volumes of the English language version and was made from the uneven first French edition) against the impeccable Clarac-Ferre Pléiade edition. The 12th volume, Andreas Mayor's 1970 translation of 'Time Regained' was the only English translation based on the Pléiade edition prior to this one and has been incorporated into it with only minor changes." Libr J

Proust, Marcel

Sodom and Gomorrah; translated by C.K. Scott Moncrieff and Terence Kilmartin; revised by D.J. Enright. Modern Lib. 1993 747p (In search of lost time) $22.95
ISBN 0-679-60029-9

LC 92-27272

Sequel to The Guermantes way
Original French edition published 1921-1922. Variant title: Cities of the plain

"Marcel again meets Swann at a reception given by the Princesse de Guermantes, a cousin of the Duchesse. Swann is now suffering from a deadly ailment. He is an ardent adherent of Alfred Dreyfus. Swann urges Marcel to write to Gilberte, since she speaks of him frequently. But Gilberte, no longer has any enchantment for Marcel; Albertine again holds his affections. She offers herself to him, but distracted by physical attachments for other owmen, he desires her company only at intervals to titillate his jaded senses. Eventually he is drawn closer to her, but now his suspicion that she is a Lesbian causes him jealousy and endless torment." Haydn. Thesaurus of Book Dig

Followed by The captive

Proust, Marcel

Swann's way; translated by C.K. Scott Moncrieff and Terence Kilmartin; revised by D.J. Enright. Modern Lib. 1992 xx, 615p (In search of lost time) $21.95
ISBN 0-679-60005-1

LC 92-25657

Original French edition, 1913

The first volume of the In search of lost time series "describes in an involved parenthetical style, with a multitude of details, the brilliant society in which the author moved. The 'Marcel' of the story is Proust's own counterpart, and it is through his hypersensitive and critical eye that we examine the tastes, feelings, motives and actions of the characters, most of whom can be identified as real people." Enoch Pratt Free Libr

Followed by Within a budding grove

Proust, Marcel

Time regained; translated by Andreas Mayor and Terence Kilmartin; revised by D.J. Enright. Modern Lib. 1993 749p (In search of lost time) $24.95

ISBN 0-679-42476-8

LC 93-3628

Sequel to The fugitive

Original French edition, 1927

In this final volume of the series "World War I accelerates the kaleidoscopic changes in society. The narrator attends a reception of the new princesse de Guermantes, actually the former Mme Verdurin, and finds most of his acquaintances almost unrecognizable. He has enjoyed three 'privileged moments' of memory, and in contemplating them discovers that his vocation is to be the shaping of his experiences into a literary work of art." Reader's Ency. 4th edition

Proust, Marcel

Within a budding grove; translated by C.K. Scott Moncrieff and Terence Kilmartin; revised by D.J. Enright. Modern Lib. 1992 749p (In search of lost time) $24

ISBN 0-679-60006-X

LC 92-25656

Sequel to Swann's way

Original French edition, 1918

"As he grows up, Marcel falls in love with Swann's daughter, Gilberte. It is a deep and poetic attachment, but she gradually tires of him; his ardent nature and his attentions begin to irritate her. Out of wounded pride he avoids her, although he continues his friendly relations with the Swanns. Two years later he feels he is thoroughly cured of his hopeless passion, when he becomes involved with Albertine, a beautiful brunette he meets in Balbec. But he eventually discovers that she is interested only in platonic relations with men, and so he suffers another disappointment." Haydn. Thesaurus of Book Dig

Followed by The Guermantes way

Puchner, Eric

Model home; a novel. Scribner 2010 360p $26

ISBN 978-0-7432-7048-9; 0-7432-7049-7

LC 2009-38051

"Family love flickers capriciously throughout this fine domestic drama, which runs the gamut from hilarious to harrowing." Kirkus

Puenzo, Lucía, 1976-

The **fish** child; Lucía Puenzo ; translated by David William Foster. Texas Tech University Press 2010 161 p.

ISBN 0896727149; 9780896727144

LC 2010024465

In this novel, "[a]ffluent Lala and impoverished Guayi, her Paraguayan maid, are determined to pursue their romance despite overwhelming disparities in class and status. Although they have plotted a future together near Paraguay's Ypacaraí Lake, Guayi's native region, a shocking discovery and an even more shocking reaction lead Lala to depart without her disappeared lover. As she ventures by bus far from her privileged Buenos Aires home, Lala delves into Guayi's past, in due time encountering the disturbing legend of the fish boy who is said to guide drowning victims to the bottom of the lake. . . . [Lucia] Puenzo's debut novel explores the character and choices of two strong-willed young women through the vehicle of the economic and social circumstances of two South American nations where archaic elements coexist with shrill modernity." (Publisher's note)

Puig, Manuel

★ **Kiss** of the spider woman; translated from the Spanish by Thomas Colchie. Knopf 1979 281p

LC 78-14307

Original Spanish edition, 1976

"Mostly consisting of dialogue between two men in an Argentine jail cell, the novel traces the development of their unlikely friendship. Molina is a middle-aged homosexual who passes the long hours in prison by acting out scenes from his favorite movies. Valentin is a young socialist revolutionary, who initially berates Molina for his effeminacy and his lack of political conviction. Sharing the hardships of a six-month prison term, the two eventally forge a strong relationship that becomes sexual. In an ironic role reversal at the end of the novel, Molina dies as a result of his involvement in politics while Valentin escapes the pain of torture by retreating into a dream world." Merriam-Webster's Ency of Lit

Pulley, Natasha

The **Bedlam** Stacks; by Natasha Pulley. Bloomsbury USA 2017 337 p. (hardcover) $26

ISBN 1620409674; 9781620409688; 9781620409671

In this book, by Natasha Pulley, "in 1859, ex-East India Company smuggler Merrick Tremayne is trapped at home in Cornwall after sustaining an injury that almost cost him his leg. On the sprawling, crumbling grounds of the old house, something is wrong; a statue moves, his grandfather's pines explode, and his brother accuses him of madness. When the India Office recruits Merrick for an expedition to fetch quinine . . . from deep within Peru, he knows it's a terrible idea." (Publisher's note)

"Pulley"s beautifully descriptive language sets the stage for a mysterious and dangerous journey reminiscent of the grand scientific expeditions of the nineteenth century." Booklist

Pulley, Natasha

★ The **watchmaker** of Filigree Street; Natasha Pulley. Bloomsbury 2015 336 p. (hardcover) $26

ISBN 9781620408346; 9781620408339; 1620408333

This novel, by Natasha Pulley, is set in "1883. Thaniel Steepleton returns home to his tiny London apartment to find a gold pocket watch on his pillow. Six months later, the mysterious timepiece saves his life, drawing him away from a blast that destroys Scotland Yard. At last, he goes in search of its maker, Keita Mori, a kind, lonely immigrant from Japan. Although Mori seems harmless, a chain of unexplainable events soon suggests he must be hiding something." (Publisher's note)

"The story thwarts expectations; whenever an outcome looks as predetermined as clockwork, it might well go another way. Clever and engaging, this impressive first novel will reward both casual readers looking for a fun period adventure and those fascinated by the tension between free will and fate." Kirkus

Pushkin, Aleksandr Sergeevich

★ **Alexander** Pushkin: complete prose fiction; translated with an introduction and notes, by Paul Debreczeny; verse passages translated by Walter Arndt. Stanford Univ. Press 1983 545p $60

ISBN 0-8047-1142-9

LC 81-85450

This collection also contains the non-fictional History of Pugachev (which furnishes historical background for The captain's daughter) and Appendices which contain minor fictional fragments and outlines

"The translations are accurate and graceful and well supported by an ample array of footnotes." Libr J

Putney, Mary Jo

The **burning** point; Mary Jo Putney. Berkley Books 2000 335 p.

ISBN 042517428X

LC 2003576658

In this book, "Kate Corsi and Patrick Donovan, divorced 10 years ago, are reunited by the death of Kate's father, Sam, who was killed in an explosion at work. The Corsi family company, Phoenix Demolition, takes pride in its spotless accident record, and Sam's death is suspicious. His will leaves the business to his former son-in-law, on the condition that Donovan and Kate live under the same roof for one year. If Kate refuses, the company will be sold. Forbidden by her father to work for the company, Kate now has her chance to work at Phoenix. But can she work and live in such close proximity to the ex-husband she seems to both love and fear?" (Publishers Weekly)

Putney, Mary Jo

A **kiss** of fate. Ballantine Bks. 2004 340p $23.95

ISBN 0-345-44916-9

"Born into a legendary family of mages known as the Guardians, Gwyneth Owens believes that she has little inherited power. She does, however, have a destiny to fulfill. When the Guardian elders seek to forestall a coming disaster by invoking her Guardian oath and asking her to marry Duncan Macrae, Lord Ballister, the most powerful weather mage in the realm, she cannot honorably refuse. Although they are already attracted to each other, Gwyneth can't forget the single kiss from him that sent alarming visions of destruction flaming through her mind—or the sword that he held in his hand. Intelligent, compelling characters that appeal to both heart and mind, a brilliant blending of history and fantasy, and a beautifully unfolding love relationship combine to produce a magical tale." Libr J

Putney, Mary Jo

Loving a lost lord; Mary Jo Putney. Kensington Publishing Corp. 2009 340 p.

ISBN 1420103288; 9781420103281

LC 2010398215

Romantic Times Reviewers' Choice Awards: Best Historical (2009)

This historical romance novel, the first volume of the Lost Lords series, is set in "[t]he year . . . 1812. Westerfield [Academy]'s first student, Adam Lawford, Duke of Ashton, who is now a respected member of the peerage despite his Anglo-Indian heritage, has lost his memory in a steamboat accident. When Adam awakes he is relieved to find that he was dragged ashore near his own home, in Cumberland, and is safe in the delectable arms of his wife. There is just one problem: Mariah Clarke falsely claimed her injured guest as her husband in order to rid herself of an obnoxious suitor. Mariah wishes to end the deception but fears that, if she acknowledges the truth, her patient may never recover his wits." (Historical Novel Series)

Putney, Mary Jo

The **marriage** spell; a novel. Mary Jo Putney.. Ballantine Books 2006 322p o.p.; (pbk.) $6.99

ISBN 0345449185 (acid-free paper); 9780345449191

LC 2005057087

This book is set "in an alternate Regency England, where magic flourishes but is despised, and practicing it may lead to death. . . . As a daredevil officer in Wellington's army, Jack [Langdon] breaks his neck and is treated by Abigail Barton, a talented healer, who states that her price will be marriage. After a grueling healing process, Abby discovers that Jack possesses untapped magical powers. . . . Jack marries Abby, even though his injuries prevent him from consummating the marriage. Abby suspects that Jack's reckless ways and reluctance to return to his home may be the result of an evil spell. Together they must discover the cause of the blight and use their love to save their lands and tenants." (Booklist)

Putney, Mary Jo

No longer a gentleman; Mary Jo Putney. Zebra Books 2012 368 p.

ISBN 1420117238; 9781420117233

This romance novel is the fourth in Mary Jo Putney's "Lost Lords Regency" series. "Experienced secret agent Cassie Fox is sent to France at the height of the Napoleonic wars in search of the long-missing Grey Sommers, Lord Wyndham, illegally imprisoned by the corrupt and vengeful official Claude Durand after a tryst with Durand's wife. Even a successful rescue and the pair's passionate encounters cannot heal the trauma of Grey's decade-long ordeal or bridge the social gap between the dedicated spy with a mysterious past and the heir to an earldom." (Publishers Weekly)

Putney, Mary Jo

Not quite a wife; by Mary Jo Putney. Kensington Pub Corp 2014 321 p. $7.99

ISBN 1420127160; 1617733091; 9781420127164; 9781617733093

In this book, by Mary Jo Putney, "James, Lord Kirkland, . . . is a ruthlessly effective spymaster. . . . Laurel Herbert gave James her heart as an innocent young girl - until she saw him perform an act of shocking violence before her very eyes. That night she left her husband, and he let her go without a word of protest. Now, ten years later, a chance encounter turns passionate, with consequences that cannot be ignored." (Publisher's note)

"RITA Award-winning Putney (Sometimes a Rogue, 2013) continues her Lost Lords series with a superbly written historical Regency that borrows a classic romance story line and imbues it with all the elements her readers love: simmering sensuality, subtle wit, a surfeit of danger, and a sophisticated flair for characterization." Booklist

Putney, Mary Jo

Nowhere near respectable; Mary Jo Putney. Zebra Books 2011 352p.

ISBN 9781420117226 pa; 9781611730760

LC 2011008371

This book tells the story of "Anglo-Hindu Lady Kiri Lawford, [who] is about to accept a proposal from an English gentleman when she learns that his racist, fortune-hunting relatives secretly despise her. Stealing a horse, Kiri rides for Dover and right into a den of smugglers. Gambling club owner Damian Mackenzie aids her escape and passion instantly flares between them, but they resist, knowing the daughter of a duke and an Indian princess could never wed an actress's bastard son. When Kiri visits Damian's club, foils a kidnapping, and gets involved in a covert investigation, their romance sizzles out of control." (Publishers Weekly)

Putney, Mary Jo

Stolen magic; M.J. Putney. Del Rey Books 2005 337p (pbk.) $7.99

ISBN 0345476891; 9780345476906

LC 2004063400

This fantasy novel tells the story of "Earl of Falconer, Simon Malmain, chief enforcer of the Guardian Council, which oversees the use of magic in 18th-century Britain, [who] has been turned into a unicorn by Lord Drayton, a renegade mage whom Simon charges with encouraging the Jacobite uprising; only a virgin can transform Simon back into human form. Luckily for Simon, animal-loving 'Mad Meggie,' Drayton's 'servant,' succeeds in doing so, while Simon breaks the spell that's kept Meg in the dark sorcerer's thrall. Allied in a 'pretend' marriage, the pair pool their unusual talents in an effort to ruin Lord Drayton's plan to prevent the Industrial Age from revolutionizing England." (Publishers Weekly)

Puzo, Mario

The **family**; a novel. completed by Carol Gino. ReganBooks 2001 373p il

ISBN 0-06-039445-5

LC 2001-31876

"In his final novel, @The Family'—Puzo died in 1999, and this book was completed by his companion, the novelist Carol Gino—he has dipped back into 15th-century Italy to tell the tale of the Borgia family, led by Cardinal Rodrigo Borgia, who became Pope Alexander VI." N Y Times Book Rev

Puzo, Mario

★ The **godfather**. Putnam 1969 446p $24.95

ISBN 0-399-10342-2

This novel focuses on "Vito (Don) Corleone, boss of an important New York City Mafia family. Names, places, crimes have been changed, but the Mafia world remains true to fact. Here is Cosa Nostra: the wars of the competing families; their changing 'business enterprises'; their struggle for power and money; their weapons—graft, guns, spies, violence, murder. A wide variety of characters are colorfully drawn. The Don comes though as a person you will remember." Libr J

Puzo, Mario

The **last** Don. Random House 1996 482p

LC 96-3401

"Mr. Puzo wraps up his intricate plot with the same ingenuity he exhibits throughout this satisfying novel." N Y Times Book Rev

Puzo, Mario

The **Sicilian**. Linden Press 1984 410p

LC 84-17087

"Perhaps only an American writer with deep Sicilian roots and passions could have succeeded as Mr. Puzo has in symbolizing a desperate society through the deeds of a desperado, and in revealing how thin is the line that often separates a freedom-fighter from a terrorist." N Y Times Book Rev

Pym, Barbara

Civil to strangers and other writings. Dutton 1988 388p

LC 87-30341

First published 1987 in the United Kingdom

This is a volume of selections from Pym's unpublished writings. It contains a complete novel, Civil to strangers, written in 1936, sections of three others: Gervase and Flora, Home front novel, and So very secret, written between 1937 and 1941, four short stories (So, some tempestuous morn; Goodbye Balkan capital; The Christmas visit; Across a crowded room) and a radio talk

"We are not often given the chance to witness a writer's struggle to find a voice. But this 'last sheaf,' blemishes and all, shows us how very hard Barbara Pym worked for the voice she eventually found." N Y Times Book Rev

Pym, Barbara

Excellent women. Dutton 1978 256p

LC 78-19877

First published 1952 in the United Kingdom

"Mildred Lathbury, 30ish, a spinster, a clergyman's daughter, is an excellent woman, one who, with no life of her own to speak of, finds herself somewhat unwillingly a part of the lives of others. Her days are made up of small things—church, flowers, dinner with the bachelor vicar and his sister, brief encounters with neighbors. . . . Pym's singular world is a lonely, bittersweet familiar place. She travels it with rueful wit, views the human landscape with a wise, sharp, compassionate eye." Publ Wkly

Pym, Barbara

Jane and Prudence. Dutton 1981 222p

LC 81-68399

First published 1953 in the United Kingdom

"Jane is the somewhat scatterbrained wife of a country vicar; Prudence, once her student at Oxford, works at a 'vague cultural organization' in London, where she alternately revels in and despairs over her unrequited passion for the rather dreary little man who is her employer. As she goes about doing 'those tasks in the parish that seem within her powers,' Jane knows she really is unsuited to be a clergyman's wife—she somehow never seems to have the right money for the collection plate—but she does love Nicholas. And in her good-hearted, if usually ineffectual, way she tries to look after Prudence too, hoping to supply a suitable man for her younger friend." Libr J

Pym, Barbara

Quartet in autumn. Dutton 1978 218p

LC 78-58498

First published 1977 in the United Kingdom

This novel "follows the lives and thoughts of four elderly single people on the verge of retirement, in a society that has no time for them but relegates them to the impersonal care of the Welfare State. Here Pym achieves something of a tour de force, showing, with wit and compassion, how ordinary quirky acts of impulsive kindness and human feeling make the difference between despair and hope." Libr J

Pym, Barbara

The **sweet** dove died. Dutton 1979 208p

LC 78-74024

First published 1978 in the United Kingdom

"Pym's extraordinary vision of an ordinary world wherein she details the intricacies of loneliness, the ditherings of hesitating souls, the comedies of errors, sexual and asexual makes this a little masterpiece." Publ Wkly

Pym, Barbara

★ An **unsuitable** attachment. Dutton 1982 256p

ISBN 0-525-24117-5

LC 82-70741

"The bygone mysteries of the Church of England and the lost snobberies of empire return as ghostly and gently comic echoes of themselves in the habits and pretensions of Barbara Pym's people, who, like the good antiques that furnish their rented bed-sitters . . . are no longer quite appropriate to the present day." N Y Times Book Rev

Pynchon, Thomas

Against the day. Penguin Press 2006 1085p $35

ISBN 1-59420-120-X

LC 2006-50714

"For all its brilliant passages, this is the book that makes you wonder whether even Pynchon knows what lies behind all those veils he's always urging us to part. But wouldn't you know it? Even when he jumps the shark, he does it with an agility that can take your breath away." Time

Pynchon, Thomas

★ **Bleeding** edge; Thomas Pynchon. The Penguin Press 2013 496 p. $28.95

ISBN 1594204233; 9781594204234

LC 2013017173

National Book Award: Fiction: Finalist (2013)

In this book, "Maxine Tarnow is, on the face of it, just another working mom in the city, but in reality, after she's packed her kids' lunches and delivered them at school, she's ferreting around with data cowboys and code monkeys, looking into various sorts of electronic fraud. . . . One track she follows leads to a genius billionaire and electronic concoctions that can scarcely be believed--but also . . . to organized crime, terrorism, big data and the U.S. government." (Kirkus Reviews)

Pynchon, Thomas

★ The **crying** of lot 49. Lippincott 1966 183p

"Oedipa Maas becomes a coexecutor of the estate of her former multi-millionaire lover, Pierce Inverarity. She becomes involved in tracking down the significance of a geometric symbol that appears to have some connection with the existence of an ancient, revolutionary mail service. In this search, she meets a strange assortment of characters, loses her husband, her psychiatrist (named Hilarious!), and her lover. The author aims his arrows at many of those phenomena that have turned people into things. Among his targets are rock 'n' roll (a group called 'The Paranoids'), right-wing extremists, and a strange group called Inamorati Anonymous." Shapiro. Fic for Youth. 3d edition

Pynchon, Thomas

★ **Gravity's** rainbow. Viking 1973 760p

ISBN 0-670-34832-5

"Fiction allows at last what was forbidden to the original suffering poets and novelists of 1914-18—the utmost in obscene description, the limit of masochistic pornography. If 'Gravity's Rainbow' is often nauseating it is in a good cause. This is the war book to end them all." Burgess. 99 Novels

Pynchon, Thomas

Inherent vice. Penguin Press 2009 369p $27.95

ISBN 978-1-59420-224-7; 1-59420-224-9

LC 2009-07705

"An account of the adventures of a hippie private eye pursuing assorted nonlucrative commissions in a Southern California beach town around 1970, 'Inherent Vice' is a sun-struck, pot-addled shaggy dog story that fuses the sulky skepticism of Raymond Chandler with the good-natured scrappiness of 'The Big Lebowski.' It's an inspired formula; the mystery plot supplies the novel with a minimum of structure (as well as confidence that there's some point to the enterprise) and the genre provides ample cover for Pynchon's literary weaknesses." Salon

Pynchon, Thomas

Mason & Dixon. Holt & Co. 1997 773p $27.50

ISBN 0-8050-3758-6

LC 97-6467

"From historical odds and ends and the Field Journal they left behind, Pynchon re-imagines Mason and Dixon before, during and after the four-plus years, 1763-1767, they took to draw their 244-mile-long line through the American wilderness, dividing the proprietorships of the Penns of Pennsylvania and the Calverts of Maryland, ordaining our North and South. From his omnivorous reading, with his diabolical genius for mimicry, he also re-creates their tumultuous era." Nation

Pynchon, Thomas

★ **V.** a novel. Lippincott 1963 492p

This novel is a "parody of the 'Black Humor' techniques it employs. The multiple plots involve the schlemiel Benny Profane, a hunter of alligators in New York's sewers, and Herbert Stencil, who becomes obsessed by his pursuit of V., an initial he found in his dead father's notebooks. V.'s various manifestations include a femme fatale, a spy, and a hag who happened to be present at every significant event in Europe from 1890 to World War II." Reader's Ency. 4th edition

Pynchon, Thomas

Vineland. Little, Brown 1990 385p

LC 89-13025

This is "manifestly the work of a man of quick intelligence and quirky invention. Many of its episodes flicker with an appealingly far-flung humor. And Pynchon displays throughout Vineland what might be called an internal loyalty: he keeps the faith with the generally feckless and almost invariably inarticulate misfits he assembles, tracking their looping thoughts and indecisive actions with a patience that seems grounded in affection." N Y Rev Books

Pyne, Daniel

★ **Twentynine** Palms; a novel. Counterpoint 2010 229p pa $14.95

ISBN 978-1-58243-573-2; 1-58243-573-1

LC 2010-05454

"Marginal Hollywood actor Jack Baylor ends an affair with the wife of his best friend, Tory, and knowing Tory's anger-management issues, he retreats to the California desert town of Twentynine Palms to let the metaphorical dust settle. There he promptly begins an affair with Mona, a young mother of two. But Tory arrives in the town bent on revenge, Mona and her kids disappear, and Jack's motel room is awash with blood. Jack is promptly arrested and must escape to clear himself. Character is everything in this desert-noir debut, and Jack is the embodiment of fecklessness; without a script, he's simply lost. Rachel, a clever 14-year-old runaway, saves him repeatedly. . . . Great fun" Booklist

Pyper, Andrew

The **damned**; a novel. Andrew Pyper. Simon & Schuster 2015 304 p. (hardback) $25

ISBN 1476755116; 9781476755113; 9781476755120

LC 2014016217

This book, by Andrew Pyper, is a "supernatural thriller about a survivor of a near-death experience haunted by his beautiful, vindictive twin sister. Most people who have a near-death experience come back alone--After he survived a fire that claimed the life of his twin sister, Ashleigh, Danny Orchard wrote a bestselling memoir about going to Heaven and back. But despite the resulting fame and fortune, he's never been able to enjoy his second chance at life. Ash won't let him." (Publisher's note)

"Pyper's pacing, as well as the novel's length, is perfect, and his evocative description of Detroit, a city desolate in its decline, comes off as both sad and poetic at the same time. A treat for fans of intelligent treatments of the supernatural and rock-solid writing." Kirkus

Pyper, Andrew

The **killing** circle. St. Martin's Minotaur 2008 321p $24.95

ISBN 978-0-312-38476-0; 0-312-38476-9

LC 2008-20635

The novel is "gorgeously written and thoroughly unnerving. . . . Taken as either a classy ghost story or the chronicle of one man's mental breakdown, this is a terrific yarn." N Y Times Book Rev

Pywell, Sharon L.

What happened to Henry; [by] Sharon Pywell. G.P. Putnam's Sons 2004 292p $19.95

ISBN 0-399-15168-0

LC 2003-62239

The plot of this novel revolves around a "tightly knit family. Henry, Lauren, and Winston Cooper are 10, 7, and 5 in 1960, when their newborn sister dies of SIDS. Henry pulls his younger siblings through their grief while their mother is barely functioning and their father is lost in his work. But four years later, Henry begins to crack, becoming obsessed with a picture of a man near Hiroshima's firestorm. . . . A powerful novel full of surprises, unbreakable sibling bonds, and insightful reflection on the power of love to overcome grief." Booklist

Q

Qashu, Sayed

Dancing Arabs; Sayed Qashu; translated from the Hebrew by Miriam Shlesinger. Grove Press 2004 227p $24

ISBN 0-8021-4126-9

LC 2003-67765

Original Hebrew edition, 2002

"After solving a quiz-show riddle, the young Palestinian protagonist earns the rare opportunity to study at a Jewish university in Jerusalem. There is hope for him, so we suspect, and for his village and people. In Jerusalem, though, he feels the truth of his father's pessimism ('once an Arab, always an Arab, and you don't stand a chance') and finds and forfeits forbidden love with Naomi. Yet nationalism, optimism, and his family's hope that his intelligence will lead to the first Arab atom bomb fizzle out and leave a headachy and resentful middle-aged man, unhappily married to an Arab wife back in the borderlands." Booklist

Qiu Xiaolong ✓

Death of a red heroine; Qiu Xiaolong. Soho Press 2000 463p (Inspector Chen Cao mysteries) hbk $25

ISBN 9781569471937; 1-569-47193-2

LC 00-20362

"Inspector Chen Cao of the Shanghai Police Bureau faces a difficult choice. For the first time he is in charge of a homicide investigation. The victim, National Model Worker Guan Hongying, anointed as a role model by the Party, is a celebrity of utmost probity. But perhaps her personal life was not so pristine? Chen, a published poet and T.S. Eliot translator who has been assigned to head the Shanghai Police Bureau's Special Case Squad, is urged by his superiors to consider the political implications. Commissar Zhang, an old bureaucrat, doesn't want him to peer under any stones. Does he dare to continue his investigation?" (Publisher's note)

"An engrossing first novel set in China during the 1990s that begins as a simple police procedural and then just keeps on getting more complex. . . . Chen is an irresistible protagonist, likable and determined to make the honorable choices, no matter how dangerous." Kirkus

Other titles in this series are:
A loyal character dancer (2002)
When red is black (2004)
A case of two cities (2006)
Red mandarin dress (2007)
The Mao case (2009)
Don't cry, Tai Lake (2011)
Enigma of China (2013)
Shanghai redemption (2015)

Qiu Xiaolong

Red mandarin dress. St. Martin's Minotaur 2007 320p

ISBN 978-0-312-37107-4; 0-312-37107-1

LC 2007-44109

In this mystery featuring Shanghai's Chief Inspector Chen, "young women, clad in torn, red mandarin dresses—hose with slits on the sides to show attractive legs—start turning up dead in public places. Chen is away, pursuing his love of literature, and the case bumps along, murder victim after murder victim, and the Shanghai police department looks incompetent in its duty of protecting the public. Then Chen becomes re-engaged halfway through the book, and the story takes off at a brisk pace. The suspense, and the way Qiu weaves in the human wreckage caused by Mao Zedong's Cultural Revolution, gives one of contemporary fiction's best pictures yet of the wrenching changes facing China as it struggles with its recent, wretched past." St. Louis Post-Dispatch

Qiu Xiaolong

✓★ **Shanghai** redemption; an Inspector Chen novel. Qiu Xiaolong. Minotaur 2015 320 p. (Inspector Chen Cao) (hardcover) $25.99

ISBN 9781250065278; 1250065275

LC 2015016967

"Removed from his prestigious job in the Shanghai police department, Inspector Chen has been 'promoted' to director of the Shanghai Legal Reform Committee. This is a familiar Communist Party trick, a demotion in the guise of a promotion; the committee has no power and is decorative at best. . . . Hiding out and keeping his head down, Chen is trying to figure out why he is suddenly an enemy of the people and who might want him dead." (Library Journal)

"Chen's 10th outing is another complex, methodical police procedural as well as a multifaceted look at a powerful society in flux." Kirkus

Qiu Xiaolong

When red is black. Soho Press 2004 309p $25

ISBN 1-569-47369-2

LC 2003-23436

This mystry "offers a complex and riveting portrait of Shanghai, a city in transition from a proletarian dictatorship to a capitalist playground." Washington Post Book World

Qiu Xiaolong

Years of Red Dust; stories of Shanghai. St. Martin's Press 2010 227p $24.99

ISBN 978-0-312-62809-3; 0-312-62809-9

LC 2010-29209

"Qiu's witty, evocative book of interrelated short stories . . . focuses more on the moral compromises wrought by China's growing materialism than on the government's resistance to political change. He portrays—without sentimentality—the ordinary man adrift in a freer market, not the hero fighting for free expression." Washington Post Book Rev

Quade, Kirstin Valdez

Night at the Fiestas; stories. Kirstin Valdez Quade. W.W. Norton & Co. 2015 288 p. (hardcover) $25.95

ISBN 9780393242980

LC 2014038352

This book by Kirstin Valdez Quade presents a collection of short stories "set in northern New Mexico. . . . The deadbeat father of a pregnant teenager tries to transform his life by playing the role of Jesus in a bloody penitential Passion. A young man discovers that his estranged father and a boa constrictor have been squatting in his grandmother's empty house. A lonely retiree new to Santa Fe becomes obsessed with her housekeeper." (Publisher's note)

"A piercingly perfect debut collection from a young writer who's already arrived; highly recommended." LJ

Quick, Amanda

Garden of Lies; Amanda Quick. Penguin Group USA 2015 352 p. (cloth) $26.95

ISBN 0399165150; 9780399165153

LC 2014049767

In this book, by Amanda Quick, "unwilling to believe that the death of Anne Clifton, one of her best employees, was suicide, secretarial agency owner Ursula Kern sets out to get some answers. Her plan is to take Anne's place in her last position, as Lady Fulbrook's secretary, and do some snooping, but when archaeologist and sleuth Slater Roxton, one of Ursula's current clients, gets wind of her scheme, he senses danger and isn't about to let her go alone." (Library Journal)

"The end result is another top-drawer historical romance that delivers the perfect fusion of witty dialogue, intriguing characters, and seductive passion." Booklist

Quick, Amanda

★ The **girl** who knew too much; Amanda Quick. First edition. Berkley 2017 355 p. (hardback) $27

ISBN 9780399174476

LC 2016050066

This novel, by Amanda Quick, is set in 1930s California. "When Hollywood moguls and stars want privacy, they head to an idyllic small town on the coast, where the exclusive Burning Cove Hotel caters to their every need. It's where reporter Irene Glasson finds herself staring down at a beautiful actress at the bottom of a pool The dead woman had a red-hot secret about up-and-coming leading man Nick Tremayne, a scoop that Irene couldn't resist." (Publisher's note)

"Quick (Jayne Ann Krentz, who also writes as Jayne Castle) transports readers back to the 1930s, showing the grimy truth behind Hollywood's glamorous facades and proving that she is a titan of historical romantic thrillers." Pub Wkly

Quick, Amanda

I thee wed. Bantam Bks. 1999 341p $23.95

ISBN 0-553-10084-X

LC 98-37168

"Strong-willed, and with a redhead's combustible temper, paid companion Emma Greyson finds herself embroiled in a dangerous adventure with the dashing Edison Stokes. A wealthy member of Regency England's 'Polite World,' Stokes follows the clue in a dying man's last words to arrive at Ware Castle, where he suspects a dark plot is underway. At the castle he encounters Emma, who stands out among the era's decadent and depraved society as a woman of sharp intelligence. . . . Attractive protagonists, loose bodices, thwarted love and odds overcome prove themselves once again the ingredients for success in this genre." Publ Wkly

Quick, Amanda

Late for the wedding. Bantam Bks. 2003 322p $24.95

ISBN 0-553-80271-2

LC 2002-34254

"As this engaging effort demonstrates, Quick has the Regency-murder mystery mix down to a fine science." Publ Wkly

Quick, Amanda

The **paid** companion. Putnam 2004 418p $24.95

ISBN 0-399-15174-5

LC 2003-62348

"Elenora Lodge is in quite a fix. Her stepfather lost her farm and all of her possessions in a mining venture, and her fiance dumps her faster than the proverbial hot potato. But Elenora is practical and pragmatic. So when Arthur Lancaster, earl of St. Merryn, offers her a position as a paid companion, she accepts. St. Merryn is in a bit of a fix himself. His favorite uncle has been murdered, and he's sworn vengeance on the killer, a mad alchemist intent on perfecting the ultimate weapon of mass destruction. Unfortunately, St. Merryn's fiancee has also dumped him, and his renewed status as one of London's most eligible bachelors is interfering with his quest for justice, hence his paying Elenora to pose as his new fiancee. . . . {Quick} mixes humor, suspense, and tantalizing historical detail with all the savory ingredients her fans have come to expect: a feisty, resourceful heroine; a hero with a decidedly dangerous edge; witty repartee; and strongly appealing secondary characters." Booklist

Quick, Amanda

Slightly shady. Bantam Bks. 2001 343p

ISBN 0-553-80188-0

LC 00-58528

"Arch humor and the expert removal of bodices are Quick's stock in trade, and the old formula still works splendidly." Publ Wkly

Quick, Amanda

★ **'Til** death do us part; Amanda Quick. Berkley Books 2016 352 p. (hardcover) $27

ISBN 9780399174469; 039917446X

LC 2015037168

In this book, by Amanda Quick, "Calista Langley operates an exclusive 'introduction' agency in Victorian London, catering to respectable ladies and gentlemen who find themselves alone in the world. But now, a dangerously obsessed individual has begun sending her trinkets and gifts suitable only for those in deepest mourning. . . . Desperate for help and fearing that the police will be of no assistance, Calista turns to Trent Hastings, a reclusive author of popular crime novels." (Publisher's note)

"The plot is smart and tight and the characters complex, while the subtle wink of humor toward a successful mystery author's plight and romance subplots will make fans smile. Quick's appealing new direction somehow balances Gothic intensity and lighthearted wit." Kirkus

Quick, Amanda

Wicked widow. Bantam Bks. 2000 297p

ISBN 0-553-10087-4

LC 99-59194

"Regency-era historical romance features Madeline Deveridge, a misunderstood London widow with a reputation for murder, and the strapping Artemis Hunt, a secret owner of the Dream Pavilions, a popular pleasure garden. When one of Madeline's maids is abducted outside the Dream Pavilions, she blackmails Artemis into helping her in the rescue. . . . A delicious combination of adventure and romance, this lively tale keeps the reader enthralled from start to finish." Booklist

Quindlen, Anna

Black and blue. Random House 1998 293p $23

ISBN 0-679-43539-5

LC 97-25208

"Following fault lines of power, dependence, and love, Quindlen takes her heroine to a bereaved country where there are no answers, only choices; in Brooklyn-born Frannie, she has created an utterly believable, flinty character." New Yorker

Quindlen, Anna

Every last one; a novel. Random House 2010 299p $26

ISBN 978-1-4000-6574-5; 1-4000-6574-7

LC 2010-292390

Quindlen "has a talent for gently, almost imperceptibly, setting the stage for what happens. The narrative of life with the Lathams is subtly prophetic regarding the impending doom. All the while, we come to love this family, because Quindlen makes their ordinary lives so fascinating, their mundane interactions engaging and important. Every Last One is about excruciating grief. It's about how people treat victims of violence, survivors' guilt, random blame and figuring out how to go on living." USA Today

Quindlen, Anna

Object lessons. Random House 1991 262p

ISBN 0-394-56965-2

LC 90-48656

This novel describes a summer in the life of an Irish American family in suburban New York in the 1960s. The central figure is twelve-year-old Maggie, daughter of Tommy Scanlan and Connie, an Italian American whose father is a cemetery caretaker in the Bronx. Tommy's father John, who made a fortune in religious goods and construction, is dying after a stroke, but still seeks to control the lives of his children and grandchildren, especially Tommy, the rebel

"Quindlen's social antennae are acute: she conveys the fierce ethnic pride that distinguishes Irish and Italian communities, their rivalry and mutual disdain. Her character portrayal is empathetic and beautifully dimensional, not only of Maggie but of her mother, who experiences her own wrenching rite of passage." Publ Wkly

Quindlen, Anna, 1953-

Still life with bread crumbs; a novel. by Anna Quindlen. Random House 2014 272 p. $26

ISBN 1400065755; 9781400065752

LC 2013015992

This novel, by Anna Quindlen, "begins with an imagined gunshot and ends with a new tin roof. Between the two is . . . Rebecca Winter, a photographer. . . . Her career is now descendent, her bank balance shaky, and she has fled the city for the middle of nowhere. There she discovers, in a tree stand with a roofer named Jim Bates, that what she sees through a camera lens is not all there is to life." (Publisher's note)

Quindlen "crafts a poignant glimpse into the inner life of an aging woman who discovers that reality contains much more color than her own celebrated black-and-white images." Booklist

Quinn, Julia

An **offer** from a gentleman; Julia Quinn. Avon Books 2001 377 p. (pbk.) $7.99

ISBN 0380815583; 9780380815586

LC 2002568860

This book tells the story of "Sophie Beckett [who] never dreamed she'd be able to sneak into Lady Bridgerton's famed masquerade ball - or that 'Prince Charming' would be waiting there for her! Though the daughter of an earl, Sophie has been relegated to the role of servant by her disdainful stepmother. But now, spinning in the strong arms of . . . Benedict Bridgerton, she feels like royalty. Alas, she knows all enchantments must end when the clock strikes midnight. Who was that extraordinary woman? Ever since that magical night . . . [h]e has sworn to find and wed his mystery miss, but this breathtaking maid makes him weak with wanting her. Yet, if he offers her his heart, will Benedict sacrifice his only chance for a fairy tale love?" (Publisher's note)

Quinn, Peter

★ **Dry** bones; Peter Quinn. Overlook Hardcover 2013 352 p. (hardback) $25.95

ISBN 1468307363; 9781468307368

LC 2013022334

This book, by Peter Quinn, is the "story of an ill-fated OSS mission into the heart of the Eastern front and its consequences more than a decade after the war's end. As the Red Army continues its unstoppable march toward Berlin in the winter of 1945, [Fintan] Dunne and his fellow soldier Dick Van Hull volunteer for a dangerous drop behind enemy lines to rescue a team of OSS officers trying to abet the Czech resistance." (Publisher's note)

Quirk, Matthew

Cold barrel zero; Matthew Quirk. Mulholland Books/ Little, Brown & Co. 2016 384 p. (hc) $26.00; (ebook) $78

ISBN 9780316259217; 9780316268615

LC 2015024562

In this novel, by Matthew Quirk, "John Hayes is a Special Operations legend who went rogue on a deep-cover mission and betrayed his own soldiers. . . . Only one man can stop him: Thomas Byrne. He once fought alongside Hayes as a combat medic, but he gave up the gun. . . . Hayes and Byrne were once as close as brothers, but with the fate of the nation hanging in the balance and nothing as it seems, both men must decide whom to trust--and whom to betray." (Publisher's note)

"Characters, most known only by their last names, are well drawn and motivated, and their exploits are hair raising. Another hard-to-put-down adventure from Quirk, this is even more chilling for its air of plausibility. A fine thriller." Booklist

R

Raban, Jonathan

Surveillance. Pantheon Books 2007 257p $24

ISBN 978-0-375-42244-7; 0-375-42244-7

LC 2006-50332

"In a near-future Seattle, a police state, replete with imagined disaster scenarios, spy cameras, and intelligence gathering, is in effect, and everyone is under a surveillance of some kind.Aspiring actor Tad Zachary performs in emergency drills while his friend Lucy Bengstrom, a freelance journalist and single mom, tries to support her 11-year-old daughter. Lucy hits pay dirt when GQ hires her to write about August Vanags, a reclusive author of a memoir describing his World War II childhood. But as she delves into his life, Lucy starts to suspect literary fraud," Bookmarks

Raban, Jonathan

Waxwings; a novel. Pantheon Bks. 2003 281p $24

ISBN 0-375-41008-2

LC 2003-42997

This novel "succeeds as a sharply observed satire of the Internet boom and as a bittersweet meditation the American dream." Libr J

Rabb, Jonathan

Among the living; Jonathan Rabb. Other Press 2016 303 p. (hardcover) $25.95

ISBN 9781590518045; 9781590518038

LC 2016008314

This novel, by Jonathan Rabb, is "about a Holocaust survivor's unconventional journey back to a new normal in 1940s Savannah, Georgia. . . . [The book] grapples with questions of identity and belonging, and steps beyond the Jewish experience as it situates . . . [Yitzhak Goldah's] story within the last gasp of the Jim Crow era." (Publisher's note)

"This stirring, powerful novel never sugarcoats its themes or characters; what emerges is a hard-won realism and a compelling look at one corner of the postwar world." Booklist

Rabb, Jonathan

The **book** of Q; a novel. Crown 2001 375p

ISBN 0-609-60483-X

LC 00-47550

"A solid, hard-edged tale set in a climate of Catholic intrigue and social controversy." Publ Wkly

Racculia, Kate

★ **Bellweather** rhapsody; Kate Racculia. Houghton Mifflin Harcourt 2014 352 p. $25

ISBN 0544129911; 9780544129917

LC 2013026339

Alex Award (2015)

In this book, by Kate Racculia, "a high school music festival goes awry when a young prodigy disappears from a hotel room that was the site of a famous crime. . . . Fifteen years ago, a murder/suicide . . . rocked the grand old Bellweather Hotel. . . . Now hundreds of high school musicians . . . have gathered in its . . . halls for the annual Statewide festival. . . . Then one of the orchestra's stars disappears. . . . Is it a prank, or has murder struck the Bellweather once again?" (Publisher's note)

"[A] novel of dueling wills, marked by textured characterization and an ebullient storytelling style." Pub Wkly

Racculia, Kate

This must be the place; a novel. Henry Holt and Co. 2010 350p $25

ISBN 978-0-8050-9230-1; 0-8050-9230-7

LC 2010-01434

"The story opens with Arthur Rook, a Hollywood photographer besotted by love for his quirky wife, Amy, who then dies—electrocuted at her job, building monsters for movies. Armed with a box of her baffling memorabilia and her enormous, cranky cat, Arthur makes his way back East to Amy's hometown, where he rents a room in a boardinghouse run by her high school friend Mona. And the book simply explodes from there. Plot, characters, secrets, back story, subplots and sub-subplots there's much to keep track of in this rich and overstuffed book, but it's all well worth it." Minneapolis Star Tribune

Rachman, Tom, 1974-

★ The **imperfectionists**. Dial Press 2010 272p

ISBN 0-385-34366-3; 978-0-385-34366-4

LC 2009-33148

This novel traces the history of a struggling English-language newspaper in Rome. Each of the eleven chapters is devoted to one of the newspaper's staff members.

"A flagging international newspaper in Rome is about to fold. Unsurprising, considering the 1950s-founded paper doesn't even have a website. Circulation, like the readership, is slowly dying off. But the staff are so caught up in their own lives that they barely notice. Rachman takes us by the hand and introduces us to the paper's staff, with each chapter of the book dedicated to one character. Lloyd Burko, the ageing and down-on-his luck reporter in France who doesn't own a computer and still sends pitches by fax is desperate and without work. Ruby Zaga, the spinster copy editor whose office chair is always amiss, has a life that is both amusing and heartbreaking. Rachman's strength lies in his rendering of the characters – all 11 are believable, flawed and loveable. The narrative works and forms a coherent whole." Scotsman

Radcliffe, Ann Ward

★ The **mysteries** of Udolpho; [by] Ann Radcliffe; edited with an introduction and notes by Jacqueline Howard. Penguin Books 2001 xxxix, 653p (Penguin classics) pa $13

ISBN 0-14-043759-2

LC 2001-277143

First published 1794 in the United Kingdom

"The orphaned Emily St Aubert is carried off by her aunt's villanous husband Montoni to a remote castle in the Apennines, where her life, honour, and fortune are threatened and she is surrounded by apparently supernatural terrors. These are later explained as due to human agency and Emily escapes, returns to France and, after further mysteries and misunderstandings, is reuinted with her lover Valancourt." Oxford Companion to Engl Lit. 6th edition

Rader-Day, Lori

The **black** hour; Lori Rader-Day. Seventh Street Books 2014 331 p. (paperback) $15.95

ISBN 1616148853; 9781616148850; 9781616148867

LC 2014003653

In this book, by Lori Rader-Day, "after 10 months spent recovering from a gunshot wound, sociology professor Amelia Emmet returns to the classroom. . . . Nathaniel, a new graduate student hoping to share Amelia's dark area of study, snags his dream job as her graduate assistant. Amelia's erratic behavior and battle to manage her pain make her a challenging boss, but he's dedicated to her, especially since he secretly plans to study her shooting for his graduate thesis." (Booklist)

"Chapters that alternate between Amelia and Nath's viewpoints provide an irresistible combination of menace, betrayal, and self-discovery." Pub Wkly

Rader-Day, Lori

The **day** I died; a novel. Lori Rader-Day. William Morrow, an imprint of HarperCollins Publishers 2017 408, 10 p.p (paperback) $14.99

ISBN 9780062560292; 9780062560285; 0062560298

This book, by Lori Rader-Day, is an "Anna Winger can know people better than they know themselves with only a glance--at their handwriting. . . . [W]hen she is called to use her expertise on a note left behind at a murder scene . . . , the crime gets under Anna's skin and rips open her narrow life for all to see. To save her son--and herself--once and for all, Anna will face her every fear, her every mistake, and the past she thought she'd rewritten." (Publisher's note)

"Beautiful prose and tack-sharp observations round out this slow-burning but thought-provoking meditation on the ravages of domestic violence." Pub Wkly

Raeder, Leah

Black iris; Leah Raeder. Atria Paperback 2015 384 p. (softcover) $15

ISBN 9781476786421; 1476786429

LC 2014041873

"It only took one moment of weakness for Laney Keating's world to fall apart. One stupid gesture for a hopeless crush. Then the rumors began. If Laney could erase that whole year, she would. College is her chance to start with a clean slate. She's not looking for new friends, but they find her. When . . . the bully who broke her down completely [resurfaces] she decides it's time to live up to her own legend." (Publisher's note)

"Told through flashbacks over the past two years that are interwoven with present-day events, Raeder's compelling and unnerving dysfunctional love story is about revenge and survival." Booklist

Raeder, Leah

Cam girl; Leah Raeder. Atria Paperback 2015 422 p. (paperback) $16

ISBN 1501114999; 9781501114991

LC 2015028559

"Vada Bergen is broke, the black sheep of her family, and moving a thousand miles away from home for grad school, but she's got the two things she loves most: her art and her best friend—and sometimes more—Ellis Carraway. Ellis and Vada have a friendship so consuming it's hard to tell where one girl ends and the other begins. . . . And nothing can tear them apart. Until an accident on an icy winter road changes everything." (Publisher's note)

"Readers who have grappled with their sexual identities will particularly be drawn to Vada and her story, but it's a must-read for anyone wanting a sexy deep dive into a tangled psyche and a difficult life." Pub Wkly

Rahimi, Atiq

A **thousand** rooms of dream and fear; a novel. translated from Dari by Sarah Maguire and Yama Yari. Other Press 2011 155p $15.95

ISBN 978-1-59051-361-3

LC 2010-38973

First edition in English published 2006 in the United Kingdom

"In prose that is spare and incisive, poetic and searing, prizewinning Afghani author Rahimi, who fled his native land in 1984, captures the distress of his people." Booklist

Raimondo, Lynne

Dante's wood; by Lynne Raimondo. Seventh Street Books 2012 350 p. (Mark Angelotti novels) (pbk.) $15.95

ISBN 1616147180; 9781616147181

LC 2012031725

"Chicago psychiatrist Mark Angelotti receives a visit from the parents of 18-year-old Charlie Dickerson, who has the mental age of a grade schooler and has been crying in the middle of the night at his care facility, the New Horizons Center. . . . The psychiatrist . . . doubts abuse, but he soon faces a bigger problem after Charlie confesses to the murder of the center's art teacher, Shannon Sparrow." (Publishers Weekly)

Other titles in this series are:
Dante's poison (2014)
Dante's dilemma (2015)

Rajaniemi, Hannu

The **fractal** prince; Hannu Rajaniemi. Tor 2012 320 p. $25.99

ISBN 0765329506; 9780765329509

LC 2012037360

In this book by Hannu Rajaniemi, "when Mieli, the winged Hunter . . . encounters quantum thief Jean de Flambeur for the second time, the thief is in the process of experimenting with Schrödinger's box for his current patron. . . . At the same time, two sisters in the haunted city of Sirr, one of the last cities on a broken Earth, plan a revolution to free their city from the might of the Sobornost's virtual control of the solar system." (Library Journal)

Rajaniemi, Hannu

The **quantum** thief. Tor 2011 329p $24.99

ISBN 978-0-7653-2949-3

LC 2011-07399

"Liberated from the infamous Dilemma Prison run by the Archons of the Sobernost collective of the Inner Solar System, master thief Jean le Flambeur agrees to accompany his rescuer, a mysterious woman named Mieli who owns a sentient spaceship with a taste for flirtation, to the Oubliette, a moving city of Mars that traffics in time as currency. Flambeur's tale intersects with that of detective Isidore Beautrelet in an intricately woven, highly charged pas de deux that brings both men to a startling discovery that reinvents the story of their experiences." Libr J

Ramirez Mercado, Sergio

A **thousand** deaths plus one; a novel. by Sergio Ramirez; translated from the Spanish by Leland H. Chambers. McPherson & Co. 2009 295p $25

ISBN 978-0-929701-87-5

LC 2009-02415

Original Spanish edition, 2004

"In 1987 Warsaw, an unnamed narrator becomes obsessed with a photographer named Castellón when he stumbles upon an exhibit showing the same scenes before and during the Nazi occupation. He learns that Castellón was Nicaraguan and took the photos while traveling with the Nazis, who had murdered his daughter and son-inlaw. From here, the book shifts to Castellón's own voice as the story moves back and forth in time, connecting Castellón to luminaries such as Chopin, George Sand, Turgenev and Flaubert." Publ Wkly

Ramsland, Morten

Doghead; translated from the Danish by Tiina Nunnally. St. Martin's Press 2009 383p $24.95

ISBN 978-0-312-37654-3; 0-312-37654-5

LC 2008-35410

Original Danish edition, 2005; this translation first published 2007 in the United Kingdom

This "quirky novel follows three generations of a Scandinavian family with enough dysfunction to make Augusten Burroughs squirm: There's Askild, the alcoholic grandfather who survived a Nazi concentration camp; Jug Ears, the father forced to wear an armor-plated corset as a youngster so that he'd stop touching his ears; and narrator Asger, who as a child felt a certain satisfaction in wrestling his obese, mentally challenged aunt. Sound bizarre? It is, but the absurd scenes are infused with enough playful emotion to make their outlandishness forgivable, and even enjoyable. Though intricate shifts in time make for a complex read, Doghead—which has plenty of bite—is definitely worth the effort." Entertainment Wkly

Rand, Ayn

Anthem; 50th anniversary ed; Dutton 1995 253p $23.95

ISBN 0-525-94015-4

LC 95-9854

First published 1946 by Pamphleteers

"A short novel about a heroic dissenter in a future monolithic and collectivized state." Oxford Companion to Am Lit. 6th edition

Rand, Ayn

★ **Atlas** shrugged. Random House 1957 1168p

"In a technological civilization Rand's characters remain insecure and look to the government for protection. In exchange they sacrifice their creativity and independence. The heroes, a copper tycoon and an inventor, reject this philosophy and fight for the individualist." Shapiro. Fic for Youth. 3d edition

Rand, Ayn

★ The **fountainhead**. Macmillan 1943 754p

First published by Bobbs-Merrill

This novel "celebrates the achievements of an architect (presumably suggested by Frank Lloyd Wright) who is fiercely independent in pursuing his own ideas of design and who is therefore an example of the author's concept of Objectivism, which lauds individualism and 'rational self-interest.'" Oxford Companion to Am Lit. 5th edition

Rand, Ayn

We the living. Random House 1959 433p

Originally published in 1936 by Macmillan, this edition of Rand's first novel contains a foreword describing the plight of the individual in the Soviet Union since then. It is the story of post-revolutionary Russia, and of a woman torn between two men who love her, one a Communist, the other an aristocrat

Randel, Weina Dai

The **empress** of bright moon; Weina Dai Randel. Sourcebooks Landmark 2016 368 p. (Novel of Empress Wu) (pbk. : alk. paper) $15.99; (ebook) $15.99

ISBN 9781492613596; 9781492613602

LC 2015022864

In this book, by Weina Dai Randel, "at the moment of the Emperor's death, everything changes in the palace. Mei, his former concubine, is free, and Pheasant, the heir and Mei's lover, is proclaimed as the new Emperor, heralding a new era in China. But just when Mei believes she's closer to her dream, Pheasant's chief wife, Lady Wang, powerful and unpredictable, turns against Mei and takes unthinkable measures to stop her." (Publisher's note)

"A must-read for fans of historical fiction set in ancient China, this novel offers a compelling look at a woman's unprecedented rise to power and a fresh take on the often vilified Empress Wu." LJ

Rankin, Ian ✓

★ **Black** and blue; an Inspector Rebus mystery. St. Martin's Press 1997 394p

LC 97-25381

"Rankin has a point to make about the corrosive effects of human wickedness that, if left unchecked, seeps into the bloodstream and poisons the national body—a point well made in his blunt and bruising style." N Y Times Book Rev

Rankin, Ian ✓

The **complaints**. Little, Brown and Company 2011 438p $24.99

ISBN 978-0-316-03974-1; 0-316-03974-8

LC 2010-12792

First published 2009 in the United Kingdom

This novel is "part mystery, part buddy story, part morality essay. Mr. Rankin never lets the reader down for a single page." Pittsburgh Post-Gazette

Rankin, Ian ✓

Exit music. Little, Brown and Co. 2008 421p $24.99

ISBN 978-0-316-05758-5; 0-316-05758-4

LC 2008-1888

First published 2007 in the United Kingdom

The "final novel in Rankin's Inspector Rebus series is set during the Edinburgh detective's final week at work. (He is nearing the mandatory retirement age of sixty.) The novel begins with a dissident Russian poet beaten to death, and expands to take in smalltime drug dealers, cloak-wearing women who act in walking mystery tours of the city, international oligarchs, and Scottish bank executives. A contemporary artist who makes sound installations may be in league with politicians agitating for Scotland's independence. Rebus is as gruffly mischievous as ever, and the novel ends in a cliffhanger scene with his archenemy that will have readers gasping into the blank space that follows. Rankin's work is crime fiction at its most consuming, cerebral best." New Yorker

Rankin, Ian ✓

The **falls**; an Inspector Rebus novel. St. Martin's Minotaur 2001 399p $24.95

ISBN 0-312-20610-0

LC 2001-41946

First published 2000 in the United Kingdom

Rankin combines "complicated multiple plot lines with finely drawn characters and fascinating Scottish lore and settings." Libr J

Rankin, Ian, 1960- ✓

The **impossible** dead. Little, Brown and Company 2011 391p $25.99

ISBN 978-0-316-03977-2

LC 2011-34256

Edinburgh Internal Affairs cop Malcolm Fox and his "two colleagues receive a frosty reception in Kirkcaldy, where they must decide whether a disgraced officer's three fellow cops helped cover up his misdeeds. Det. Constable Paul Carter, found guilty of sexual misconduct, intrigues Fox because it was Carter's ex-copper uncle, Alan, who turned him in. Since interviewing the belligerent Carter and his mates leads nowhere, Fox turns to Alan for insight. He discovers the elder Carter was hired by a prestigious lawyer to look into the 1985 'suicide'—or possible murder—of Francis Vernal, a fellow attorney, well-known orator, and vocal supporter of the fringe Scottish separatist movement. Soon Fox's attention is divided between following up scant leads in the Carter investigation and unearthing decades-old secrets about Vernal's life and associates. Rankin elegantly weaves together the two story lines without forcing a connection." Publ Wkly

Rankin, Ian ✓

The **naming** of the dead; an Inspector Rebus novel. Little, Brown and Co. 2007 425p $24.99

ISBN 978-0-316-05757-8; 0-316-05757-6

LC 2006-31495

First published 2006 in the United Kingdom

"In his backhanded, reluctant way Rebus winds up uniting all the book's loose ends, and seeing how he accomplishes this is a pleasure. Besides, 'The Naming of the Dead' isn't really about its detective plot. It's about Rebus's taking stock, not only of his own past but also of the world around him." N Y Times (Late N Y Ed)

Rankin, Ian ✓

★ A **question** of blood; an Inspector Rebus novel. Little, Brown and Co. 2004 406p $22.95

ISBN 0-316-09564-8

LC 2003-59549

First published 2003 in the United Kingdom

"This series's strength starts with Rebus himself, who . . . has emerged as the baddest of the bad boys of modern crime fiction. He is fiftyish, overweight, alcoholic, a chain smoker, surly, short-tempered, divorced, estranged from his family, a loner, a nut about obscure rock-and-roll groups, hostile to all authority and possibly psychotic. Needless to say, women love him—ladies love outlaws—and his police colleagues tolerate him because he's an ace detective." Washington Post Book World

Rankin, Ian, 1960-

Rather be the devil; Ian Rankin. Little Brown & Co 2017 310 p. (Inspector Rebus novel series) (hardcover) $27

ISBN 0316342572; 9780316466271; 9780316342575
LC 2016959691

In this Rebus Novel, by Ian Rankin, "as he settles into an uneasy retirement, Rebus has given up his favorite vices. There's just one habit he can't shake: he can't let go of an unsolved case. It's the only pastime he has left and up until now, it's the only one that wasn't threatening to kill him. But when Rebus starts reexamining the facts behind the long-ago murder of a glamorous woman . . . , the past comes roaring back to life with a vengeance." (Publisher's note)

"The ongoing pas de deux between these two aging antiheroes has been one of the best things in crime fiction for years, but Rankin kicks it up several notches here, with both men facing mortality and screaming in two-part harmony against the dying of the light." Booklist

Rankin, Ian

Resurrection men; an Inspector Rebus novel. Little, Brown 2003 436p $23.95

ISBN 0-316-76684-4
LC 2002-16271

"We are well and truly in Rankin country—a shady world where good and evil are relative terms and truth is an arbitrary concept." N Y Times Book Rev

Rankin, Ian

Set in darkness. St. Martin's Press 2000 415p

ISBN 0-312-20609-7

"Rebus has been assigned to a bogus task force called the Policing of Parliament Liaison Committee. Things liven up, though, when a body is found inside a bricked-up fireplace in one of the buildings under construction for the new Scottish Parliament. That's a tantalizing enough mystery, but when a top politico is found dead at the construction site, Rebus has something he can sink his teeth into—a decades-old crime whose tentacles touch the present and lead to a new confrontation with Rebus' longtime nemesis, Edinburgh crime boss Big Ger Cafferty. . . . Nobody writes darker than Rankin." Booklist

Rankin, Ian

Watchman. Little, Brown and Co. 2007 258p $24.99

ISBN 978-0-316-00913-3; 0-316-00913-X
LC 2007-19761

First published 1988 in the United Kingdom; first American edition published 1991 for the Crime Club by Doubleday

This thriller "features British spy Miles Flint, a markedly different sort of agent than, say, James Bond. Flint is a watcher from behind darkened windows, a listener to tapped phone lines. When a lapse in judgment results in the death of a valued source, his shot at redemption comes in the form of a seemingly routine mission to Belfast. . . . The mission quickly turns deadly, and Flint realizes that he has been set up by someone in his organization. Watchman keeps the reader on pins and needles from page one." BookPage

Rao, Shobha

An **Unrestored** Woman; Shobha Rao. St. Martin's Press 2016 256 p. (hardcover) $24.99; (ebook) $60

ISBN 9781250073822; 9781250118721; 1250073820; 9781250073839

This book of linked stories, by Shobha Rao, "recounts the untold human costs of one of the largest migrations in history. 1947: the Indian subcontinent is partitioned into two separate countries, India and Pakistan. . . . A new mother is trapped on the wrong side of the border; a soldier finds the love of his life but is powerless to act on it; . . . a young prostitute quietly, inexorably plots revenge on the madam who holds her hostage." (Publisher's note)

"Exquisite turns of phrase and editing with a fine-edged scalpel only add to an outstanding and memorable debut." Booklist

Rash, Ron

Burning bright; stories. Ecco 2010 205p $22.99

ISBN 978-0-06-180411-3; 0-06-180411-8; 0061804118; 9780061804113

This collection of short stories by Ron Rash "begins with 'Hard Times,' in which a struggling farmer in the midst of the Great Depression tries to discover who's stealing eggs from his henhouse without offending the volatile pride of his impoverished neighbors. The present-day stories are also situated in poverty-plagued small towns whose young citizens are being lost to meth addictions." (Publishers Weekly)

The stories in this collection "are set in the rural, meth-addled hills of North Carolina. Pervaded with desperation—pawn shops, gravediggers, arson and a sense of impending death—these are not uplifting stories. . . . 'Burning Bright' is a collection to be read for the quality of the prose, which reflects Rash's intimate knowledge of this region and its history. His heart is clearly in this place—the dialect is pitch-perfect and he is a skillful translator of the inner worlds and difficult lifestyles of the unique, hardened-by-necessity breed of people who have populated the area, past and present." Portland Oregonian

Rash, Ron

★ The **cove**; Ron Rash. Ecco Press 2012 255p.

ISBN 9780061804199; 9780061804205; 9781410448583

This book, set in "North Carolina during WWI" tells the story of "the alienated Laurel Shelton [who] lives with her wounded war veteran brother in an isolated cabin. While out doing laundry by the creek one day, Laurel discovers Walter Smith, an illiterate, mute flutist en route to New York City, who has been incapacitated by hornet stings. As she nurses the mysterious Walter back to health, Laurel begins to fall in love. . . . However, local Army recruiter Chauncey Feith threatens to ruin all that Laurel and Walter hope for. A rabid anti-German agitator, he begins to suspect that Walter is not who he claims to be. Driven by fear, patriotism, and bloodlust, Chauncey progresses from arrogant drunk to a craven yet dangerous force." (Publishers Weekly)

Rash, Ron

Serena; a novel. Ecco 2008 371p $24.95

ISBN 978-0-06-147085-1; 0-06-147085-6
LC 2008-00712

"Set in 1929, in the rugged mountains of North Carolina, Rash's novel is a tightly knit tale of industrial development, greed, and betrayal. George Pemberton and his new bride, Serena, maintain a close watch over a burgeoning logging empire, dealing with their workers while fighting off the efforts of environmental activists to expand the country's network of national parks. As the title character—a Depression-era Lady Macbeth wholly comfortable in the wilderness—drives her husband to commit increasingly malevolent acts, he must also contend with the reemergence of a woman with whom he had an illegitimate child years earlier. Rash's evocative rendering of the blighted landscape and the tough characters who inhabit it recalls both John Steinbeck and Cormac McCarthy, while the malignant character of Serena, who projects a 'stark unflinching certainty' about her actions, propels his finely paced story." New Yorker

Rash, Ron

Something rich and strange; selected stories. Ron Rash. HarperCollins 2014 448 p. $27.99

ISBN 0062349341; 9780062349347

LC 2015301756

A collection of short stories by author Ron Rash, "'Something Rich and Strange' showcases this revered master's artistry and craftsmanship in thirty stories culled from his previously published collections 'Nothing Gold Can Stay,' 'Burning Bright,' 'Chemistry,' and 'The Night New Jesus Fell to Earth.'" (Publisher's note)

"These superbly suspenseful stories evoke a world of hurt, but what makes them so deeply satisfying is that they enlarge our capacity for empathy." Booklist

Ratner, Vaddey

In the shadow of the banyan; Vaddey Ratner. Simon & Schuster 2012 336 p.

ISBN 1451657706; 9781451657708; 9781451657715; 9781451657722

LC 2011033320

This novel explores "the atrocities committed by the Khmer Rouge regime in Cambodia between 1975 and 1979, when an estimated two million people lost their lives. . . . For seven-year-old Raami, the shattering end of childhood begins with the footsteps of her father returning home in the early dawn hours, bringing details of the civil war that has overwhelmed the streets of Phnom Penh, Cambodia's capital. Soon the family's world of carefully guarded royal privilege is swept up in the chaos of revolution and forced exodus. Over the next four years, as the Khmer Rouge attempts to strip the population of every shred of individual identity, Raami clings to the only remaining vestige of her childhood—the mythical legends and poems told to her by her father." (Publisher's note)

Rawles, Nancy

My Jim; a novel. Nancy Rawles. Crown Publishers 2005 174p hardcover o.p. (paperback) $12.95; (hardcover) $19.95

ISBN 9781400054015; 1400054001

LC 2004011606

Alex Award (2006)

This book "is the story of Sadie Watson, the wife of 'N##ger Jim,' as he was referred to in the Mark Twain classic 'Huckleberry Finn.' Jim was the escaped slave who took the journey down the Mississippi . . . with runaway Huck. [Author Nancy] Rawles says that Jim mentions his family at least twice in Twain's book, but that the classic divulges no details about who this woman was. Starting from that point, Rawles created Sadie, a woman who never resigned herself to involuntary servitude, and who was Jim's lifelong love. Rawles relied upon new research revealing more about the daily lives of slaves to show how Jim and Sadie—like real-life slaves in the South—created family in the midst of chaos, and, . . . sought stability in an environment that offered none." (National Public Radio)

Rawn, Melanie

The **diviner**. DAW Books 2011 374p $25.95

ISBN 978-0-7564-0681-3; 0-7564-0681-1

Prequel to: The golden key (1996)

"The Sheyqa Nizzira, despotic ruler of a Middle East–flavored land in the year 611, has meticulously planned to wipe out a large family of her rivals, murdering them down to the smallest child. When young wastrel Azzad alMa'alique misses his date with doom and flees, he sets in motion a complex revenge plot that will change the future of many lands and generations of both families. . . . Rawn at her best remains a mesmerizing writer, and there is some of her best here." Publ Wkly

Rawn, Melanie

Touchstone; Melanie Rawn. Tor 2012 363 p. $25.99

ISBN 9780765323620

LC 2011025175

In this fantasy novel, "Cayden Silversun, a blend of Elven, Fae, and Wizard bloodlines, defies his noble family to pursue a life in the theater, forming the four-person troupe Touchstone with the goal of making it to the highest echelons of the performing circuit. Given the talents of troupe member Mieka Windthistle, a brilliant 'glisker' whose job is to enhance with magic both the crowd's emotions and the performances' special effects, their goal seems reachable. Yet Cayden's prophetic dreams indicate something sinister about Mieka's presence and tempt him to try to change fate without incurring a larger doom." (Libr J)

Ray, Kalyan

No country; a novel. Kalyan Ray. Simon & Schuster 2014 560 p. (hardcover) $27

ISBN 1451635990; 9781451635997; 9781451636383

LC 2013027167

This novel by Kalyan Ray "[spans] two centuries and three continents. . . . In rural Ireland in 1843, Padraig Aherne leaves behind his best friend, Brendan, and girlfriend, Brigid, and sets off to Dublin to rally for his country's independence, unaware that Brigid is pregnant with his child. But once he reaches the big city, a dangerous mistake forces him on a ship destined for Calcutta. As the potato famine devastates their home, Brendan escapes with Padraig's young daughter across the ocean." (Publisher's note)

"Told from multiple perspectives, this thoughtful novel offers a panoramic view of the way personal and national destinies collide, sometimes ending in tragedy, sometimes in triumph." Booklist

Ray, Shann

American masculine; stories. Graywolf 2011 185p pa $15

ISBN 978-1-55597-588-3; 1-55597-588-7

LC 2011-923187

"Set almost exclusively in Montana, Ray's stories depict broken families from every possible angle. A dead brother, abusive or absent fathers, unfaithful spouses, separating parents: The collection runs the whole gamut. This isn't the American West of Annie Proulx or Cormac McCarthy; it's less centered on landscapes and overarching narrative, and more closely focused on relatives drawing blood with words, fists, or mere looks." AV Club

Raybourn, Deanna ✓

A **perilous** undertaking; a Veronica Speedwell mystery. Deanna Raybourn. Berkley Books 2017 338 p. (Veronica Speedwell mystery) (hardback) $26

ISBN 9780698198456; 9780451476159

LC 2016019601

Sequel to: A Curious Beginning (2015)

In this novel in the Veronica Speedwell Mystery series, by Deanna Raybourn, "London, 1887. Victorian adventuress and butterfly hunter Veronica Speedwell receives an invitation to visit the Curiosity Club. . . . There she meets . . . Lady Sundridge, who begs her to . . . [save] society art patron Miles Ramsforth from execution. . . . Together with her natural historian colleague Stoker, Veronica races against time to find the true murderer." (Publisher's note)

"Another exciting installment in Raybourn's promising historical-mystery series, starring a fun heroine who defies convention and embraces intrigue." Booklist

Rayfiel, Thomas

★ **In** pinelight; a novel. Thomas Rayfiel. TriQuarterly Books/Northwestern University Press 2013 278 p. (pbk. : alk. paper) $18.95

ISBN 0810152363; 9780810152366

LC 2013002127

In this novel, author Thomas Rayfiel, "has created a poetic world through William, his narrator, who answers questions put to him by a real or imagined, but unseen, questioner about his life and those around him in Conklingville, a town now buried beneath the deep waters of a hydroelectric dam. . . . There is no linear storyline; it jumps and stutters . . . William tries to connect the dots of wayward clues and memories for the man who is asking him questions offstage." (Kirkus Reviews)

Raymond, Jonathan

The **half**-life; a novel. Bloomsbury 2004 355p $23.95

ISBN 1-582-34448-5

LC 2003-22602

"In the early nineteenth century, a half-starved band of fur trappers struggles through the Oregon woods. Their young, diffident cook is intimidated by the rougher members of the group. When another young man, fleeing from some vengeful Russians, stumbles into camp, a friendship blossoms. Move ahead to the Reagan era. A teenager is dragged by her mother to live in an Oregon commune. Lonely and resentful while living among slightly absurd, aging counterculturists, she is drawn to the only other young woman in the settlement, and as their bond grows, they work together on a film project. The discovery of a pair of skeletons buried on the commune provides the link between these pairs of friendships. Raymond, in his first novel, seamlessly links the two narratives with elegant and often haunting prose. The characters are finely drawn, and Raymond poses them against a seductively beautiful landscape." Booklist

Rayne, Sarah

Property of a lady. Severn House 2011 252p $28.95

ISBN 978-0-7278-8028-4

"Rayne's crisp and fast-paced writing deftly combines sharp characters, obscure legend, the panorama of 20th-century history, subtle romance, and even subtler melancholy, turning the picked-over bones of the haunted house story into something fresh and frequently terrifying." Publ Wkly

Read

Affairs at Thrush Green; illustrations by J. S. Goodall. Houghton Mifflin 1984 256p il

LC 84-6702

First published 1983 in the United Kingdom

"The catastrophic fire that destroyed Thrush Green rectory in Gossip from Thrush Green, has caused Charles Henstock and his wife, Dimity, to move into the luxurious, large rectory in Lulling, thus drawing the adventures of the residents of these two towns even closer. . . . Henstock tends to his new duties with gracious vigor despite his own doubts and those expressed by several parishioners." Booklist

Read

At home in Thrush Green; illustrated by J.S. Goodall. Houghton Mifflin 1986 261p il

LC 86-20864

First published 1985 in the United Kingdom

The author describes "a year of bustling and visiting at Thrush Green. The creation of eight homes for elderly residents on the site of the old vicarage takes up much of the novel's action, absorbing the interests of the villagers as the recipients must be decided upon and settled in. School life under the stern Miss Watson and the more amiable Miss Fogarty also receives a share of attention. Readers familiar with Thrush Green's inhabitants will be delighted to note the changes in the lives of their favorite characters and will be pleased as always by the book's emphasis on familiar annual patterns." Booklist

Read

Farewell to Fairacre; illustrations by John S. Goodall. Houghton Mifflin 1994 213p il

LC 94-25628

"With an influx of new students, Miss Read's worries about the future of her beloved school can finally be set aside. In their wake, however, come concerns about the head mistress' own health. Two small strokes spur her decision to retire, and she spends her final months in her usual busy fashion, tending to her students at Fairacre, fending off the surprising attentions of two suitors, and becoming ever more comfortable with thoughts of a new life ahead. Nostalgic without being sentimental, this is a fitting conclusion to a delightful series, recalling old friends and pleasant times in a tranquil English village." Booklist

Read

Thrush Green; illustrated by J.S. Goodall. Houghton Mifflin 1960 226p il

First published 1959 in the United Kingdom

"Confined to the events of May 1, the day when Mrs. Curdle's traveling carnival brings its special magic to Thrush Green, the story tells what takes place in the lives of a small boy, a lonely girl, an elderly doctor and his young assistant, and various other people, including the redoubtable Mrs. Curdle herself." Booklist

Read, Cornelia

Invisible boy. Grand Central Pub. 2010 418p $24.99

ISBN 978-0-446-51134-6; 0-446-51134-X

LC 2009-17205

"Read expertly evokes the New York City of the period, from the nearly palpable grime of Chelsea to disturbing undertones of racism and classism in the justice system. Equal parts toughness and vulnerability, Madeline is always a bracing heroine." Publ Wkly

Read, Piers Paul

Alice in exile. St. Martin's Press 2002 344p $24.95

ISBN 0-312-30398-X

"As striking in her beauty as she is shocking in her behavior, Alice Fry has an uninhibited sexuality that makes her attractive to two very different men. Pregnant with fiance Edward Cobb's child, Alice is abandoned by him when her father becomes embroiled in a sexual scandal that threatens Cobb's political ambition. With no one to turn to and nowhere to go, Alice is rescued by Baron von Rettenberg, a womanizing Russian nobleman who hires her as his children's governess. . . .To read Read is to be caught up in an epic wonder of passion, scandal, adn international intrigue." Booklist

Read, Piers Paul

The **professor's** daughter. Lippincott 1971 276p

Henry Rutledge, "the professor is a middle-aged old-line liberal who has dabbled in politics behind the scenes in the Kennedy era. In . . . flashbacks we learn how and why he and his wife have become the kind of people they are, and what has gone wrong with their marriage. The professor's daughter is something else again, desperate, attempting suicide, all but destroyed sexually and every other way by traps she has drifted into without ever understanding what was happening to her. When father and daughter strike up an incongruous but ultimately quite believable alliance with a group of campus radical activists who believe assassination is a valid revolutionary tool, tension mounts to a keen pitch." Publ Wkly

Reay, Katherine

The **Brontë** plot; Katherine Reay. Thomas Nelson 2015 352 p. (softcover) $15.99

ISBN 9781401689759

LC 2015022374

In this book, by Katherine Reay, "Lucy Alling makes a living selling rare books, often taking suspicious liberties to reach her goals. When her unorthodox methods are discovered, Lucy's secret ruins her relationship with her boss and her boyfriend, James—leaving Lucy in a heap of hurt and trouble. Something has to change; she has to change. In a sudden turn of events, James's wealthy grandmother, Helen, hires Lucy as a consultant for a London literary and antiques excursion." (Publisher's note)

"The moral ambiguity makes the story more modern than its premise would suggest—and proves how well its source material holds up over time." Kirkus

Red Spectres; Russian Gothic tales from the twentieth century. selected, translated from the Russian, and with an introduction by Muireann Maguire. Penguin Group USA 2013 224 p. $25.95

ISBN 1468303481; 9781468303483

This collection of 20th century Russian gothic fiction "includes eleven vintage tales by seven writers of the period: Valery Bryusov, Mikhail Bulgakov, Aleksandr Grin and Sigizmund Krzhizhanovsky;. . . Aleksandr Chayanov, . . . and the emigres Georgy Peskov and Pavel Perov. Through the traditional gothic repertoire of ghosts, insanity, obsession, retribution and terror, Red Spectres conveys the turbulence and dissonance of life in Russia in these years." (Publisher's note)

Redfern, Elizabeth

Auriel rising. G.P. Putnam's Sons 2004 386p $24.95

ISBN 0-399-15105-2

LC 2003-58507

"Redfern sets a blistering pace and never breaks stride or tone. Resisting the standard static historical tableau, she gives us a troubled city constantly reinventing itself, peopled by souls no less changeable." N Y Times Book Rev

Redfield, James

The **celestine** prophecy; an adventure. Warner Bks. 1994 246p $19.95

ISBN 0-446-51862-X

LC 93-61754

"The saga begins when the unnamed middle-aged male narrator whimsically quits his nondescript life to track down an ancient Peruvian manuscript (pretentiously called the Manuscript) containing nine Insights that supposedly prophesy the modern emergence of New Age spirituality. South of the border, he encounters resistance from the Peruvian government and church authorities, who believe the document will undermine traditional family values. While dodging evil soldiers, paranoid priests and pseudoscientific researchers, our hero sequentially discovers all nine Insights during a series of chance encounters. Redfield has a real talent for page-turning action." Publ Wkly

Followed by The tenth insight (1996)

Redhill, Michael

Bellevue Square; Michael Redhill. Doubleday Canada 2017 262 p. (hardcover) $27

ISBN 9780385684835; 9780385684842; 0385684835

Scotiabank Giller Prize (2017)

In this novel, by Michael Redhill, "Jean Mason has a doppelganger. . . . Apparently, her identical twin hangs out in Kensington Market, where she sometimes buys churros. . . . Jean's a grown woman with a husband and two kids, as well as a thriving bookstore in downtown Toronto, and she doesn't rattle easily--not like she used to. But after two customers insist they've seen her double, Jean decides to investigate." (Publisher's note)

Redhill, Michael

Consolation; a novel. Little, Brown and Co. 2007 340p $24.99

ISBN 978-0-316-73498-1; 0-316-73498-5

LC 2006-934104

First published 2006 in the Canada

"A gentle but unfaltering cadence, a well-tempered voice, and a highly resolved sense of detail bring readers back and forth smoothly between these two eras." Quill & Quire

Reed, Ishmael, 1938-

★ **Flight** to Canada; Ishmael Reed. Atheneum 1989 179 p. $8.95; (ebook) $29.99; (paperback) $15

ISBN 0684847507; 0689707339; 9781453287989; 9780684847504

LC 89014875

This book by Ishmael Reed spins "the tale of three runaway slaves and the master determined to catch them. His . . . parody of fugitive slave narratives and other literary forms includes a hero who boards a jet bound for Canada; Abraham Lincoln waltzing through slave quarters to the tune of 'Hello, Dolly'; and a plantation mistress entranced by TV's 'Beecher Hour'. [The book is] filled with insights into the political consciences (or lack thereof) of both blacks and whites." (Publisher's note)

Reed, Ishmael, 1938-

★ **Mumbo** jumbo; Ishmael Reed. Atheneum 1989 223 p. illustrations (ebook) $29.99; (paperback) $16

ISBN 9781453287972; 0684824779; 0689707304; 9780684824772

LC 88016628

This novel on race relations by Ishmael Reed offers a "satiric deconstruction of Western civilization, a racy and uproarious commentary on our society. In it, Reed, one of our preeminent African-American authors, mixes portraits of historical figures and fictional characters with sound bites on subjects ranging from ragtime to Greek philosophy." (Publisher's note)

Bibliography: p. [219]-223

Reich, Christopher

Rules of deception. Doubleday 2008 390p $24.95

ISBN 978-0-385-52406-3; 0-385-52406-4

LC 2007-36368

"Reich's everyman hero, Jonathan Ransom, is plunged into a world of intrigue when his wife dies in an accident. Growing questions about her true identity dig him deeper into trouble. Ransom is unaware that he is interrupting the endgame of an enormous and long-running conspiracy that he—and the Swiss cop tracking him—could derail. Reich . . . throws readers off the scent but never loses control of the plot. He skillfully handles the pacing, and this results in a suspenseful story balanced by cinematic action scenes. . . . Fans of early Ludlum will particularly enjoy it." Libr J

Reich, Tova

My Holocaust; a novel. HarperCollins 2007 326p $24.95
ISBN 978-0-06-117345-5; 0-06-117345-2
LC 2007-297195

"Tova Reich is fearless, in the best possible way, and her take on the culture of victimization spares no captives in the gulag of self-anointed martyrdomÐ. Reich's gift for satire is impeccable, her ear for absurdity pitch perfect." Philadelphia Inquirer

Reichs, Kathleen J.

★ **Bare** bones; [by[Kathy Reichs. Scribner 2003 306p $23.95
ISBN 0-7432-3346-8
LC 2003-40725

"Tempe, a forensic anthropologist, is back home in Charlotte, N.C., anticipating a nice, long vacation from the county medical examiner's office, when a series of unnatural disasters drags her back to the lab. . . . Whether she's examining the pulverized remains of the victims of a suspicious plane crash or reassembling the bones of an illegally slaughtered bear, Tempe is a pro's pro at her job, but also a compassionate woman who isn't afraid to show her outrage at the cruelty done to man and beast for the sake of a dirty dollar." N Y Times Book Rev

Reichs, Kathleen J.

Break no bones; [by] Kathy Reichs. Scribner 2006 339p $25.95
ISBN 978-0-7432-3349-1; 0-7432-3349-2
LC 2006-45038

"While supervising a dig of Native American burial grounds in Charleston, S.C., Brennan finds more recent remains. Soon, her ex-husband, who's a lawyer, appears in town, pursuing leads in a missing persons case connected with a local church. Bodies start piling up at an alarming rate, and Brennan begins to suspect that the deaths are linked to each other—and her ex-husband's inquiry. Reichs's down-to-earth heroine is an appealing creation, who deftly juggles personal problems with professional challenges." Publ Wkly

Reichs, Kathleen J.

Deja dead; [by] Kathy Reichs. Scribner 1997 411p
LC 97-2990

"Dr. Tempe Brennan, a trowel-packing forensic anthropologist from North Carolina, works in Montreal's Laboratoire de Médecine Légale examining recovered bodies to help police solve missing-persons cases and murders. It's clear to Tempe that the remains of several women killed and savagely mutilated point to a sadistic serial killer, but she can't convince the police. Determined to prevent more brutal deaths, she sleuths solo, tracking her quarry through Montreal's seedy underworld of hookers, where her anthropologist friend Gabby, doing her own scary research, is being stalked by a creep. . . . Except for imparting an excess of lab information, Reichs, also a forensic anthropologist, drives the pace at a heady clip. A first-class writer, she dazzles readers with sensory imagery that is apt, fresh, and funny." Libr J

Reichs, Kathleen J.

Grave secrets; [by] Kathy Reichs. Scribner 2002 317p $25
ISBN 0-684-85973-4
LC 2002-22695

"While in Guatemala to assist in the exhumation of an old mass grave, forensic specialist Temperance Brennan is called upon to determine whether a body found in a septic tank is that of the missing daughter of the Canadian ambassador to Guatemala. The gruesome search, vividly described, leaves even the toughened Tempe aghast." Booklist

Reid, Iain, 1981-

★ **I'm** thinking of ending things; Iain Reid. Scout Press 2016 224 p. (hardcover) $22.95
ISBN 9781501126925; 9781501126949
LC 2015031094

In this suspense novel, by Iain Reid, "the narrator, known only as the girlfriend, is driving with her beau, Jake . . . to meet his parents at the family farm. The relationship is new, but, as the title implies, she's already thinking of calling it quits. . . . Reid intercuts the couple's increasingly tense journey with short interstitial chapters that imply a crime has been committed. . . . On the drive back, Jake makes a detour to an empty high school." (Kirkus Reviews)

"Reid's tightly crafted tale toys with the nature of identity and comes by its terror honestly, building a wall of intricately layered psychological torment." Kirkus

Reid, Taylor Jenkins

Forever, interrupted; a novel. by Taylor Jenkins Reid. 1st Washington Square pbk ed. Washington Square Press 2013 352 p. (paperback) $15
ISBN 1476712824; 9781476712826; 9781476712833
LC 2012035073

In this book, written by Taylor Jenkins Reid, "Elsie Porter is an average twentysomething [who meets] the adorable and charming Ben Ross. Within weeks, the two are head over heels in love. By May, they've eloped. Only nine days later, Ben is out riding his bike when he is hit by a truck and killed on impact. At the hospital, she must face Susan, the mother-in-law she has never met—and who doesn't even know Elsie exists." It Interweav[es] Elsie and Ben's . . . romance with Elsie and Susan's healing process." (Publisher's note)

Reiken, Frederick

Day for night. Little, Brown and Co. 2010 326p $24.99
ISBN 978-0-316-07756-9
LC 2009-38597

"During a 1984 trip to Florida, a widowed marine biologist swims among tolerant manatees with his pediatrician girlfriend, a Polish Jew who fled the Nazis. Their young-dude guide, Tim, of German descent, accompanies his bandmate Dee, whose wealthy Utah family is part of a violent cult, on a clandestine visit to see her brother, who is in a coma after surviving a motorcycle accident in Israel. On the plane, Tim sits next to a tall, reserved woman, who may be a 1960s radical turned fugitive from justice with mystical powers. A Massachusetts veterinarian suffering from severe allergies ends up in Israel, where a man working at a nature reserve . . . . Well, it's an entrancing and profoundly complicated tale Reiken tells as he slowly reveals the submerged connections among his intriguing characters while sustaining psychological sophistication, suspense, shrewd humor, and many-tiered compassion." Booklist

Reimringer, John

★ **Vestments**. Milkweed Editions 2010 407 p.
ISBN 1-57131-080-0; 1571310800; 978-1-57131-080-4; 9781571310804
LC 2010007143

In this book, "[j]ust a few years after his ordination and his first assignment as a parish priest, James Dressler is placed on leave. His housekeeper found some letters from a woman and turned them in to the archdiocese. For little more than a kiss, he is relegated to a parish in a backwater burg. He opts instead to live back home with his mother in St. Paul until he can come up with a better game plan. But his gritty hometown has its own temptations, and broke and in need of work, James finds himself renovating apartments and butting heads with his tough, bad-tempered father and attracted once again to his old high-school lover, Betty Garcia." (Booklist)

Reisman, Nancy

The **first** desire. Pantheon Books 2004 310p $24
ISBN 0-375-42308-7

LC 2004-44665

The novel is "both lovely and heartbreaking in its vision of family ties at their most inevitable." N Y Times (Late N Y Ed)

Remarque, Erich Maria

★ **All** quiet on the western front; translated from the German by A.W. Wheen. Ballantine Books 1996 295p $15.00
ISBN 0449911497; 9780449911495

LC 96096745

First published 1929 by Little, Brown

"This is the testament of Paul Bäumer, who enlists with his classmates in the German army during World War I. They become soldiers with youthful enthusiasm. But the world of duty, culture, and progress they had been taught breaks in pieces under the first bombardment in the trenches. Through years of vivid horror, Paul holds fast to a single vow: to fight against the principle of hate that meaninglessly pits young men of the same generation but different uniforms against one another . . . if only he can come out of the war alive." (Publisher's note)

Remarque, Erich Maria

Arch of triumph; translated from the German by Walter Sorell and Denver Lindley. Appleton-Century 1945 455p

"A story of Paris in the period preceding the {Second World} war. The central character is a German doctor who, having escaped from the Nazis, is living illegally in France, subject to deportation if the police discover his presence. Without a passport and identification papers he is not allowed to practice, but in secret performs difficult operations for a well-known society doctor. Other refugees, figures from the underworld, outcasts and derelicts are the characters in a book which pictures a society nearing its doom." Wis Libr Bull

Remarque, Erich Maria

The **night** in Lisbon; translated by Ralph Manheim. Harcourt, Brace & World 1964 244p

Original German edition, 1962

"One night in Lisbon in 1942 a German refugee offers passage to the U.S. and his passport to another refugee on condition that he be kept company through the night and that he be permitted to tell his story. The narration reveals the first refugee's flight from Germany in the 1930's, his hazardous return after five years to see his wife, his second escape in which his wife joins him, and their subsequent flight from place to place in Europe during which, in spite of dangers, they achieved moments of intense happiness because of their mutual love and understanding." Booklist

Remarque, Erich Maria

The **road** back; translated from the German by A. W. Wheen. Little, Brown 1931 343p

Sequel to All quiet on the western front

"A profoundly moving, a painfully moving, document. Unlike tragedy, it has no katharsis, but, like a tragedy, it has to be looked at open-eyed, honestly, courageously." Spectator

Remarque, Erich Maria

A **time** to love and a time to die; translated from the German by Denver Lindley. Harcourt Brace & Co. 1954 378p

"The whole story is told with great restraint, with little sentimentality for those in misery and with little open rage at those who caused it." Chicago Sunday Trib

Renault, Mary

★ The **bull** from the sea. Pantheon Bks. 1962 343p

"A sequel to The King Must Die, this mythological novel begins with Theseus, King of Athens, returning in triumph from Crete, where he has killed the Minotaur. On a subsequent adventure he captures and falls in love with the warrior princess, Hippolyta. Although married to Phaedra of Crete, Theseus continues his relationship with Hippolyta and both women bear him sons. Tragedy occurs when Phaedra is attracted to and spurned by Hippolyta's youthful son." Shapiro. Fic for Youth. 3d edition

Renault, Mary

Funeral games. Pantheon Bks. 1981 335p
ISBN 9780394520681 out of print; 9780375714191

LC 81047273

This concludes the story of Alexander the Great that began in Fire from heaven and The Persian boy. 'At 32 Alexander is dying in Babylon. The generals, two pregnant wives and a covey of conspirators keep a jackal-like vigil, anticipating the fight for possession of the empire, extending from Europe to India, that will break out when the godlike leader dies. At his death, the murderous power struggle ensues'Alexander's mother and his brain-injured half-brother, Philip, vie with the Regent and other extrafamilial seekers of the throne." Publ Wkly

Renault, Mary

The **king** must die. Pantheon Bks. 1958 338p hardcover o.p. pa $14
ISBN 0-394-75104-3

"Retold by its hero, the legend of Theseus becomes a logical sequence of adventures that befell a slight, wiry, quick-witted youth impelled to prove his manhood in a semibarbaric society that put a premium on size and brawn. Although, at seventeen, he was already a king and a seasoned warrior, Theseus obeyed his patron god's prompting and voluntarily joined a company of young people conscripted for the bull-dances in Crete, became a renowned bull-leaper, and took advantage of an earthquake to overthrow the Cretan kingdom." Booklist

Followed by The bull from the sea (1962)

Renault, Mary

★ The **last** of the wine. Pantheon Bks. 1956 389p

"This is a fictionalized account of Athens during the years of the Peloponnesian War told by Alexias, a young Athenian of good family background. We learn the details of daily life within the Greek city state, including the literary, cultural, recreational, and political texture of the time. One very memorable account is that of a wrestling match at the Isthmian Games." Shapiro. Fic for Youth. 3d edition

Renault, Mary

The **Persian** boy. Pantheon Bks. 1972 432p

This sequel to Fire from heaven continues the "story of Alexander the Great, focusing upon his momentous expedition into Asia. This time we observe events through the eyes of Bagoas, a beautiful Persian eunuch who was loved by King Darius and then by Alexander himself. The multiple facets of Renault's art, familiar to a host of admirer's, are once again apparent: a particularly sensitive depiction of boyhood and youth; an astounding grasp of the facts and the spirit of the ancient world; an unerring sense of the dramatic which, along with her superb descriptive powers, brings to life a great historical period." Libr J

Followed by Funeral games

Rendell, Ruth

Adam and Eve and Pinch me; a novel. Crown 2002 356p pa $13.95

ISBN 0-609-61025-2; 1-4000-3118-4 pa

LC 2001-32539

First published 2001 in the United Kingdom

"Part ghost story, part serial-killer hunt, part excoriation of the wicked ways of Westminster and Fleet Street, this tale tightens the noose of suspense through the build-up of vivid domestic and social detail." Booklist

Rendell, Ruth

Blood lines; long and short stories. Crown 1996 215p

LC 96-852

"In this collection of short stories, Rendell is at her best, using her own quixotic brand of dark humor and an often heartwrenching poignancy to produce 11 minimasterpieces." Booklist

Rendell, Ruth

★ The **bridesmaid**. Mysterious Press 1989 259p

ISBN 0-89296-388-3

LC 88-43471

"Ms. Rendell is a diabolically subtle writer. For much of this claustrophobic study of mutual obsession, she has us peering into Senta's mind through Philip's eyes, suspiciously analyzing her bizarre statements and mysterious behavior. But, like a cunning old spider, the author has caught two flies in her web; and in the end, Philip proves the more interesting study, with his phobia about violence and his fanaticism for propriety." N Y Times Book Rev

Rendell, Ruth

★ The **crocodile** bird. Crown 1993 361p

LC 93-14734

"A kind of fairy-tale unreality informs this narrative, for all its present-day accoutrements; it is written in careful, straightforward, almost childlike prose; and it keeps you on tenterhooks, once you've surrendered to the atmosphere." Times Lit Suppl

Rendell, Ruth

The **face** of trespass. Doubleday 1974 184p

The author "conveys the derelict half-dream, half-nightmare life Gray is leading in an Essex hovel far better than a crime-writer need, and through this . . . makes credible the blindness that allows him to be led to total disaster." Times Lit Suppl

Rendell, Ruth

Going wrong. Mysterious Press 1990 260p

LC 90-40421

"Rendell is a master of depicting the long, slow slide into madness, making each tiny step toward the abyss resound with chilling logic." Publ Wkly

Rendell, Ruth

Harm done; an Inspector Wexford mystery. Crown 1999 346p $24

ISBN 0-609-60547-X

LC 99-20432

Three of the cases Wexford is involved in "have to do with the abuse of women or children. The crimes range from the ridiculous (a petulant university girl and a mentally challenged girl from a low-income housing project are each kidnapped to do housework and returned for ineptitude) to the monstrous (Wexford and his men must protect a child molester who was released from prison while a rich man tortures his wife in the comfort of his spacious home." Publ Wkly

Rendell, Ruth

Heartstones; illustrations by George Underwood. Harper & Row 1987 80p il

LC 86-46098

"Such is Rendell's mastery of psychological suspense that throughout we remain unsure of the seriousness of Elvira's intentions." Libr J

Rendell, Ruth

★ A **judgment** in stone. Doubleday 1978 188p

LC 77-76961

"Despite our knowing on p.2 who will die, and at whose hand, we are carried along by the powerful suspense of events in one upper-middle-class English family. The sense of impending doom amply takes the place of detective work, of which there is a little in the last three short chapters. The depiction of the 'perfect servant' is masterly and the whole thing a tour de force." Barzun. Cat of Crime. Rev and enl edition

Rendell, Ruth

The **keys** to the street; a novel of suspense. Crown 1996 326p $24

ISBN 0-517-70685-7

LC 96-3114

A novel about the "homeless denizens who haunt Regent's Park in London. Residents of the exclusive neighborhoods abutting the park make a point of not even noticing wretches like Effie and Dill and Pharaoh and Roman. Only Mary Jago, a frail, sensitive young woman who has recently moved into the neighborhood as a housesitter, pays any attention to these street people—until someone starts killing them and impaling their bodies on the spiked railings that surround the park. . . . All the characters are drawn with psychological insight, but it takes a visionary author to see the bonds that connect them all." N Y Times Book Rev

Rendell, Ruth

Kissing the gunner's daughter. Mysterious Press 1992 378p

LC 91-50615

This is an "intricate story that hinges on vanity and self-deception, a story in which the most minor and seemingly innocent relationships are charged with meaning and malice." N Y Times Book Rev

Rendell, Ruth

Live flesh. Pantheon Bks. 1986 272p

LC 86-4922

"The obvious way to write this novel would have been to tell it through the eyes of the crippled policeman; Rendell takes the bolder path of getting inside the mind of Jenner. . . . {This} is a frightening, resonant novel—an extraordinary achievement." New Statesman (1913)

Rendell, Ruth

Not in the flesh; a Wexford novel. Crown 2008 303p $25.95

ISBN 978-0-307-40681-1; 0-307-40681-4

LC 2007-40945

First published 2007 in the United Kingdom

"Rendell has been documenting change in her imaginary Kingsmarkham for 44 years; 'Not in the Flesh' continues to hold a mirror to British society. . . . [She] also weaves into the story Wexford's heartbreaking attempts to address the tradition of female genital mutilation within the Somali community of Kingsmarkham." Los Angeles Times Book Rev

Rendell, Ruth ✓

A **sight** for sore eyes. Crown 1999 327p $24

ISBN 0-609-60417-1

LC 98-27654

"Rendell charts a harrowing collision course for two preternaturally beautiful teen-agers: Teddy Brex, an unloved child who grows up to be a sociopath, and Francine Hill, an overprotected child who grows up to be his ideal victim. . . . Reaching back a generation to get more traction for her macabre love story, Rendell takes a ruthless probe to every person (from Teddy's emotionally arrested parents to the faceless stranger who murdered Francine's mother) who had a hand in shaping the psyches of this ill-met pair. Spare and unforgiving, these incisive character studies illuminate the darker corners of Teddy's and Francine's family histories without dimming the originality of their bizarre lives." N Y Times Book Rev

Rendell, Ruth

Simisola. Crown 1995 327p

LC 95-8428

"Rendell's long acquaintance with her characters has not diminished the freshness of her work, nor her consummate storytelling. Rather, in Simisola, she offers a finely tuned moral tale that raises questions as it solves crimes." Times Lit Suppl

Rendell, Ruth

A **sleeping** life. Doubleday 1978 180p

LC 77-27716

When Chief Inspector Wexford is "called in to investigate the murder of one Rhoda Comfrey he is baffled to be unable to learn anything at all about her private life, friends, or means of supporting herself. His only clue, an expensive leather wallet, leads him up and down blind alleys until a chance remark by his own daughter, whose marriage is in jeopardy, leads him to Webster's International Dictionary and a brilliant deduction about the motive of the murderer." Shapiro. Fic for Youth. 3d edition

Rendell, Ruth

Tigerlily's orchids; a novel. Scribner 2011 257p $26

ISBN 978-1-4391-5034-4; 1-4391-5034-6

LC 2011-18103

First published 2010 in the United Kingdom

"Aside from the wretched woman in Flat No. 6 who is systematically drinking herself to death, the residents of Lichfield House take their sweet time in revealing themselves through the secret vices and obsessions that will bring several of them to grief. But that doesn't inhibit Duncan Yeardon, the lonely widower and self-acknowledged 'people watcher' who lives across the street, from speculating wildly (and mistakenly) on the intimate details of their lives. Stuart Font, the conspicuously beautiful narcissist who has recently moved into the building, gives everyone something to gossip about when the ragingÐbull husband of his mistress crashes his housewarming party. And both Stuart and Duncan spin romantic fantasies about an elusive Asian woman they call Tigerlily. But it takes a murder to accelerate the destructive actions of ostensibly civilized strangers when they're suddenly involved in their neighbors' private lives. Rendell builds her characters with such subtle strokes that it's impossible to catch the moment when she begins to tear them down." N Y Times Book Rev

Rendell, Ruth

The **tree** of hands. Pantheon Bks. 1985 271p

LC 84-19002

First published 1984 in the United Kingdom

"Benet, successful author and unwed mother, is visited by her mentally unstable mother, Mopsa. When the baby dies, Mopsa snatches another child to give to Benet. Substitute-baby Jason is the offspring of child abuser, larcenous Carol. The child's putative father is a gigolo intent on defrauding his current patroness. The story explores spectrum of parental feeling against a background of pervasive anxiety and impending doom. This is not a mystery, really, but rather an engrossing psychological thriller." Libr J

Rendell, Ruth

The **water's** lovely; a novel. Crown Publishers 2007 340p $25.95

ISBN 978-0-307-38136-1; 0-307-738136-6

LC 2006-29492

First published 2006 in the United Kingdom

"Rendell is in absolute top form here. The Water's Lovely is as suspenseful as any crime novel she has written, but it also has the generous humanity of her best Inspector Wexford cases. . . . Rendell provides the reader with many pleasures: her intelligence and humanity, her sculpted sentences, her jokeless wit, her refusal to join her colleagues in the torture-porn business to spice up her plots. Oh, yes—those plots. What a sneaky mind the woman has." Washington Post Book Rev

Resnick, Mike

The **return** of Santiago. TOR Bks. 2003 464p $25.95

ISBN 0-7653-0224-1

LC 2002-75660

Sequel to: Santiago (1986)

"An eminently satisfying space western, with just the right mixture of fast-drawing gunmen and talented women to keep the action going." Booklist

Restrepo, Laura

No place for heroes; a novel. translated from the Spanish by Ernesto Mestre-Reed. Nan A. Talese/Doubleday 2010 272p $25.95

ISBN 978-0-385-51991-5

LC 2009-47858

Original Spanish edition, 2009

"Lorenza, a Colombian woman who spent her youth as a leftist activist under the Argentine dictatorship of the '70s and '80s, has returned to Buenos Aires with her 18-year-old son, Mateo. They have come in search of Mateo's father, Ramón, whom Lorenza met when they were both clandestine organizers against the regime. Locating this mysterious, lost father is almost absurdly easy: After much conjecture about what sophisticated guerrilla tactics they might have to use, they find his name in the phone book. He is not, after all, one of the 'disappeared.' He split up with Lorenza after a harrowing incident she calls the 'dark episode,' during which he abducted their infant son across national borders. The more complicated challenge lies in deciding how to approach Ramón, and, even more important, coming to understand him by shedding light on the convoluted past. It is this quixotic endeavor that occupies the protagonists for most of the book. . . . Ultimately, this coming-of-age dance, the winding stories of Lorenza's past and the search for Ramón all converge in a climax as unexpected as it is moving." San Francisco Chron

Reuland, Rob

Semiautomatic; a novel. Random House 2004 242p $24.95

ISBN 0-375-50502-4

LC 2003-46806

This thriller is "notable not for violence but for subtle characterizations, moral ambiguities and exceptional writing." Washington Post Book World

Reuss, Frederick

Mohr; a novel. Unbridled Books 2006 312p il $25.95

ISBN 1-932961-17-8

LC 2005-37958

"Reuss's prose rarely if ever impresses through sheer imagery or wordplay or beauty, but it's concise and solidly-constructed, and it conveys his meaning well. The strength of Reuss's writing is more in his observations, the way he builds emotions out of little details like the objects in the clutter of a room or the way a certain person moves. The writing and the photographs play off of one another, illustrating each other. And the images seem to perfectly capture the mood of the story as it goes on." PopMatters

Reuss, Frederick

The **wasties**. Pantheon Bks. 2002 229p $23

ISBN 0-375-42071-1

LC 2001-55450

"This should appeal to sophisticated readers who like darkly humorous, cerebral fiction." Booklist

Revoyr, Nina

Wingshooters. Akashic Books 2011 250p

ISBN 978-1-936070-71-8 pa; 978-1-936070-86-2

LC 2010-928792

"The racism [Revoyr] depicts is disheartening; the loss of innocence she chronicles is shattering; the love shared between a fallible man and his granddaughter is remarkable, and the best thing about this novel." Milkwaukee J Sentinel

Reyn, Irina

What happened to Anna K. a novel. Simon & Schuster 2008 244p $24

ISBN 978-1-4165-5893-4; 1-4165-5893-4

LC 2007-39332

"It takes a lot of self-confidence to suggest that your first novel is a modern-day retelling of Anna Karenina. But once you're finished marveling at Reyn's audacity, her formidable storytelling gift sweeps you along and keeps you turning the pages in rapt anticipation, even as you're aware that the sound in the distance is the rumble of that inevitable approaching train." N Y Times Book Rev

Reynolds, Alastair

The **prefect**. Ace Books 2008 410p $25.95

ISBN 978-0-441-01591-7; 0-441-01591-3

LC 2008-60017

"As a prefect working for the Panoply, Tom Dreyfus enforces the law in the utopian society of the Glitter Band, a collection of space habitats that orbit the planet Yellowstone. When an attack on one of the habitats leaves nearly 1000 people dead, Dreyfus uncovers a plot that threatens the freedom of the entire Glitter Band. Reynolds . . . returns to the universe of Revelation Space as he demonstrates his powerful ability to blend futuristic suspense/intrigue with personal drama in a tale of one man's search for truth, however unpleasant or demanding it may be. . . . Action-packed hard sf." Libr J

Reynolds, Alastair

Revenger; Alastair Reynolds. Orbit 2017 427 p. (paperback) $15.99

ISBN 9780316555562; 9780316555630

LC 2016037813

Locus Award (2017)

In this book, by Alastair Reynolds, "Adrana and Fura Ness are the newest crew members of the legendary Captain Rackamore's ship, using their mysterious powers as Bone Readers to find clues about their next score. But there might be more waiting for them in space than adventure and fortune: the fabled and feared Bosa Sennen, in particular." (Publisher's note)

"The award-winning Reynolds' newest action-packed science fiction novel is a tale of sisterly devotion, heartbreaking loss, and brutal vengeance." Booklist

Reynolds, Marjorie

The **Starlite** Drive-in; a novel. Morrow 1997 282p $23

ISBN 0-688-15389-5

LC 97-728

"When developers find a body in a well at the old Starlite Drive-In, Callie Ann Benton knows whose body it is. It takes her back to when she was 12; her father ran the drive-in, and her mother, Teal, had become completely trapped inside her house by agoraphobia. It traps her father, too, forcing him to give up dreams, and his resentment comes out in nasty sniping, continuous put-downs that drain her—until a drifter named Charlie Memphis arrives, falls in love with Teal, and plans to take her and Callie away. This stunning novel is told by 12-year-old Callie, torn between her crush on Memphis, her love for her father, and her resentment of her mother's sexuality and personhood." Libr J

Reynolds, Sheri

A **gracious** plenty; a novel. Harmony Bks. 1997 205p $21

ISBN 0-609-60225-X

LC 97-21544

"Lyricism and the gentle voice of her heroine carry this poignant but redemptive story of an emotionally and physically scarred woman who finds her way out of the land of the dead and into the land of the living." Publ Wkly

Reznikoff, Charles

By the waters of Manhattan; introduction by Philip Lopate. David R. Godine 2009 170p pa $17.95

ISBN 978-1-57423-214-1; 1-57423-214-2

LC 2009-03263

First published 1930 by C. Boni

Reznikoff "writes prose like a poet, indeed he is one, with his rock-hard choice of words styled into deceptively simple sentences. Deceptive because when juxtaposed, each sentence accelerating into the next, they relay condensed lives, jammed with emotion, kin, and striving. Lopate's tender and eloquent introduction sets the record straight for this under-acknowledged literary master." BOMB

Rhodes, David

Driftless. Milkweed Editions 2008 429p $24

ISBN 978-1-57131-059-0; 1-57131-059-2

LC 2008-20881

"Set in a rural Wisconsin town, the book presents a series of portraits that resemble Edgar Lee Masters's 'Spoon River Anthology' in their vividness and in the cumulative picture they create of village life. There's a drifter trying to put down roots, a hardworking dairy farmer being taken advantage of by a corrupt milk coöperative, a female pastor who hears heavenly voices, and a cranky retiree who discovers a cougar living in his haymow." New Yorker

Rhodes, David

Jewelweed; a novel. David Rhodes. Milkweed Editions 2013 448 p. (hardcover : acid-free paper) $26

ISBN 1571311009; 9781571311009; 9781571311061; 9781571318831

LC 2012027827

This book by David Rhodes "introduces a cast of characters who must overcome the burdens left by the past. After serving time for a dubious conviction, Blake Bookchester is paroled. As Blake attempts to adjust, he reconnects with Danielle Workhouse, a single mother whose son, Ivan, explores the woods with his precocious friend, August. Ivan and August befriend Lester Mortal, a recluse who lives in a melon field. These characters . . .approach the future with . . . hope and trepidation." (Publisher's note)

Rhodes, Jewell Parker

Voodoo dreams; a novel of Marie Laveau. St. Martin's Press 1993 436p

LC 93-24283

This novel is about "Marie Laveau, New Orleans' legendary nineteenth-century voodoo queen. Although few biographical facts are known about Marie, Rhodes has parlayed them into a character of vast dimension and feminine power. Like her grandmother and mother before her, Marie is a voodooienne, a woman visited and possessed by the African god Damballah, and the third Marie Laveau to suffer the consequences of this terrifying blessing in a world poisoned by the sin of slavery. As Rhodes imagines Marie's strange and painful life, from her protected childhood deep in the bayou to her reign as healer in New Orleans, she evokes all the lust, tumult, and cruelty of that race-obsessed city." Booklist

Rhodes, Jewell Parker

Yellow moon. Atria Books 2008 293p $24

ISBN 978-1-4165-3710-6; 1-4165-3710-4

LC 2008-15221

This sequel to Voodoo season (2006) is the second title in the author's New Orleans trilogy

In this thriller, "a wazimamoto, or African vampire, stalks Dr. Marie Laveau, a 21st-century doctor, modern voodoo practitioner and descendant of the legendary Voodoo Queen of New Orleans. Haunted by the unquiet spirits of people killed by the wazimamoto, the young doctor vows to stop it with the help of new boyfriend NOPD Det. Daniel Parks; her Creole boss, Dr. Louis DuLac; and others devoted to Marie and her young adopted daughter, Marie-Claire. . . . Rhodes includes an informative author's note about the evolution of the African vampire as a 'response and a warning about racist brutality' and 'cultural vampirism,' giving some cultural weight to this hypnotic thriller." Publ Wkly

Rhys, Jean

Quartet. Simon & Schuster 1929 228p

First published 1928 in the United Kingdom with title Postures

"The ingredients: an English girl in Paris, married to a Polish adventurer, who is imprisoned for theft and leaves her penniless, a stranger except for casual acquaintances in the foreign colony, to become the guest of an English couple, a man who desires her and can arouse her passion, and his wife, who keeps the girl in the home where she has her always under observation, always at a disadvantage, until she can finally crush her. The attitudes of the three are exposed with pitiless precision—the utter helplessness of the victim, the diabolic ingenuity of the wife, the social cowardice of the husband which makes a peculiarly disgusting setting for his lust. The background of Paris, in its cold hostility, with its tedious round of mechanical pleasures, throws the episode into harsh relief." Bookman (NY)

Rhys, Jean

★ **Wide** Sargasso Sea; introduction by Francis Wyndham. Norton 1967 189p

First published 1966 in the United Kingdom

This novel, "set in Dominica and Jamaica during the 1830s, presents the life of the mad Mrs. Rochester from 'Jane Eyre,' a Creole heiress here called Antoinette Cosway; in the brief last section she is imprisoned in the attic in Thornfield Hall." Oxford Companion to Engl Lit. 6th edition

Ricci, Nino

The **origin** of species; a novel. Other Press 2010 472p pa $16.95

ISBN 978-1-59051-349-1; 1-59051-349-5

LC 2009-41070

First published 2008 in Canada

"A profoundly moving novel that lovingly creates a world of flawed but very real characters." Winnipeg Free Press

Rice, Anne

Angel time; a novel. Alfred A. Knopf 2009 267p (The songs of the seraphim) $25.95

ISBN 978-1-4000-4353-8; 1-4000-4353-0

LC 2009-15470

"Angelically inspiring. Devilishly clever." Kirkus

Rice, Anne

Blood canticle. Knopf 2003 305p (Vampire chronicles) $25.95

ISBN 0-375-41200-X

LC 2002-192475

This tenth volume of the Vampire chronicles takes up where "Blackwood Farm ended, the now-doppelganger-free Quinn Blackwood and Lestat save Quinn's true love, the witch Mona Mayfair, from certain death by making her an immortal. In his effort to attain sainthood, Lestat must deal with a lot of metaphysical angst. The opulent Blackwood estate and its spooky swamps, as well as New Orleans and a Caribbean isle, provide the settings for many elegant costume changes as the exquisite vampiric triumvirate gleefully suck several deserving victims dry and lay waste to dozens of a drug lord's minions." Publ Wkly

Rice, Anne

Christ the Lord: out of Egypt. Knopf 2005 336p $25.95

ISBN 0-375-41201-8

LC 2005-44077

"Rice is a first-rate writer. There are no purple patches in this narrative, and no attempts to sermonize. There is a story to tell, and since we know the story on which it is based, Rice adroitly forces us to think about how she is going to weave in the gospel stories without sounding contrived or forced." Commonweal

Rice, Anne, 1941-

Christ the Lord: the road to Cana. Knopf 2008 242p $25.95

ISBN 1-400-04352-2; 978-1-4000-4352-1

Following Christ the Lord: Out of Egypt (2005), Rice's second book in her "life of Christ begins during his last winter before his baptism in the Jordan and concludes with the miracle at Cana. It is a novel in which we see Jesus—he is called Yeshua bar Joseph—during a winter of no rain, endless dust, and talk of trouble in Judea. Legends of a Virgin birth have long surrounded Yeshua, yet for decades he has lived as one among many who come to the synagogue on the Sabbath. All who know and love him find themselves waiting for some sign of the path he will eventually take. And at last we see him emerge from his baptism to confront his destiny—and the Devil. We see what happens when he takes the water of six great limestone jars, transforms it into cool red wine, is recognized as the anointed one, and urged to call all Israel to take up arms against Rome and follow him as the prophets have foretold." (Publisher's note)

The second title in the author's projected four-volume life of Christ "opens with Jesus, known as Yeshua, as a young man, now more than 30, living with his extended family in the village of Nazareth. He knows who he is, or rather what he is, to be sure, but the path of this book takes him through his 40 days in the desert to the first great miracle of his ministry, the changing of water into wine. The story of Christ is the most famous story in the world; what revelations are there for the novelist? One of the great achievements of Rice's undertaking, thus far, is to reveal Christ's Jewish roots in all their strength and complexity. . . . Rice has achieved a prose style that is much simpler, much more straightforward, than that of her earlier works. Yet, in moments of revelation, her old breathless rapture serves her well." New Orleans Times-Picayune

Rice, Anne

The **Feast** of All Saints. Simon & Schuster 1979 571p

LC 79-16680

"The world of the Free People of Color (the 'gens de couleur libre') in antebellum New Orleans (the old French city) is the background for this romantic historical novel that brings to life an era and a place. . . . Quadroon Marcel Ste. Maria and his lovely sister Marie, children of a white plantation owner, and the lovely Cecile, his dusky mistress, grow up in the demimonde, housed and supported and educated as gentility by their father, but destined to be separated from his world by virtue of their mixed blood. . . . {The story} pits passion and principle and love against the hard realities of class and color in old New Orleans." Publ Wkly

Rice, Anne

★ **Interview** with the vampire; Reset for anniversary ed; Knopf 1996 340p $27.95; pa $7.99

ISBN 0-394-49821-6; 0-345-33766-2 pa

LC 96-232882

First published 1976

"In contemporary New Orleans a young reporter listens as Louis, a vampire, unfolds his tale. His story spans several hundred years . . . of a Faustian search for some meaning to his life-in-death existence, an existence complicated by his relationship to three other vampires. Lestat, the vampire who made him, is hated by Claudia, the five-year-old extraordinarily beautiful child-vampire Louis loves. . . . After Claudia attempts to kill Lestat she and Louis go to Europe in search of other vampires. In Paris they find Armand, Master Vampire, and he and Louis fall in love, remaining together for a time after Claudia's death in a state of meaningless immortality." Libr J

Followed by The vampire Lestat (1985); The queen of the damned (1988); The tale of the body thief (1992); Memnoch the Devil (1995); The vampire Armand (1998); Merrick (2000); Blood and gold; or, The story of Marius (2001)

Rice, Anne

Of love and evil; the songs of the seraphim: a novel. Alfred A. Knopf 2010 171p $24.95

ISBN 978-1-4000-4354-5; 1-4000-4354-9

LC 2010-28267

"If this kinder, gentler Rice has you rattled, fear not, for the scenes in the seething cesspool of sin that typify Pope Leo X's Rome prove the author hasn't lost her verve for the seamier side of life." Minneapolis Star Tribune

Rice, Anne, 1941-

Prince Lestat; Anne Rice. Alfred A. Knopf 2014 480 p. (The vampire chronicles) (hardback) $28.95

ISBN 0307962520; 9780307962522

LC 2014009319

This novel by Anne Rice "opens with the vampire world in crisis—vampires have been proliferating out of control; burnings have commenced all over the world. Old vampires, roused from slumber in the earth are doing the bidding of a Voice commanding that they indiscriminately burn vampire-mavericks in cities from Paris and Mumbai to Hong Kong, Kyoto, and San Francisco." (Publisher's note)

"Featuring beloved characters from previous installments and spanning continents and centuries, Rice's exciting return to the Vampire Chronicles is bound to please her legions of fans.HIGH-DEMAND BACKSTORY: Rice's return to her vampire series is big book news, and an author tour and initial 300,000 print run are set to meet reader enthusiasm." Booklist

Rice, Anne, 1941-

★ The **queen** of the damned; the third book in the vampire chronicles. Knopf 1988 448p (Vampire chronicles) $27.50

ISBN 0-394-55823-5

LC 88-45311

This is a sequel to Interview with the Vampire and The Vampire Lestat (1985). "The plot revolves around an internecine struggle in vampiredom. On one side is 6000-year-old Akasha, who has concluded that the world would be a safer, more peaceful and equitable place if women ran it. Her plan is to set herself up as the reigning Goddess of Earth; then to kill off all human males except a few breeders, until {the} time when female values are firmly in place and males can be allowed to flourish again. Her opponents argue that you can't make a peaceful world through violence." (Ms)

"Don't let the title or the subject matter fool you; this is quality fiction written with care and intelligence. There are no false steps or wasted words in the multilayered plot, and the many characters each have a distinct voice. It's not absolutely necessary to have read the other 'Chronicles' to understand this one, but it would add greatly to the richness of the whole." Libr J

Followed by The tale of the body thief

Rice, Anne

The **tale** of the body thief. Knopf 1992 430p (Vampire chronicles) $30

ISBN 0-679-40528-3

LC 92-53085

"Readers who crave a happy ending, a justice and a moral coherence that transcend the muddle they really live in, may feel {the author} has broken faith with them. After all, isn't that what escapist fiction is supposed to provide? Grown-ups, on the other hand, will be intelligently entertained, and no more disquieted than usual." Newsweek

Followed by Memnoch the Devil

Rice, Anne

The **vampire** Armand. Knopf 1998 387p (Vampire chronicles) $26.95

ISBN 0-679-45447-0

LC 98-14579

The sixth volume of the Vampire chronicles follows the vampire Armand "from his boyhood in Kiev Rus, a conquered city under the rule of the Mongols, to ancient Constantinople, where he is sold into slavery by vicious Tartars, to the palazzo in Renaissance Venice, where he meets the great vampire Marius, who gives him the gift of the vampire blood and shows him how to be an 'ethical' vampire. . . . As always, Rice paints a fascinating and dazzling historical tapestry, providing a beautifully written and incredibly absorbing tale." Booklist

Rice, Anne, 1941-

The **vampire** Lestat; the second book in the chronicles of the vampires. Alfred A. Knopf 1985 481p (Vampire chronicles) $27.50

ISBN 0-394-53443-3

LC 85-40123

This novel "is ornate and pungently witty. In the classic tradition of Gothic fiction, it teases and tantalizes us into accepting its kaleidoscopic world. Even when they annoy us or tell us more than we want to know, its undead characters are utterly alive. Their adventures and frustrations are funny, frightening and surprising at once." N Y Times Book Rev

Followed by The queen of the damned

Rice, Anne

★ The **witching** hour; a novel. Knopf 1990 965p $29.95

ISBN 0-394-58786-3

LC 90-53103

Rice "tells the story of the prominent and wealthy Mayfair family who, for five centuries, has cavorted with a supernatural entity that has brought them both great bounty as well as abject misery. Neurosurgeon Rowan Mayfair inherits the family fortune, along with the sinister attentions of this entity. When Rowan saves the life of Michael Curry their fates become entwined, and together they seek to understand and destroy the terrible force that holds her family in its power. Helping them in this dangerous task is occult investigator Aaron Lightner. . . . Although a bit long-winded at times, this is still a compelling novel." Libr J

Followed by Lasher

Rice, Luanne

★ **Blue** moon. Viking 1993 305p

LC 92-50732

"Such a rare combination of realism and romance comes along well, once in a blue moon. You don't have to be a sucker for happy endings to love this book, but it helps." N Y Times Book Rev

Rice, Luanne

The **deep** blue sea for beginners; a novel. Bantam Books 2009 302p $26

ISBN 978-0-553-80514-7; 0-553-80514-2

LC 2009-13277

This sequel to Geometry of sisters is "about a reunion of a mother and her two daughters who've been separated for 10 years due to a disturbing secret. Set on the picturesque isle of Capri, Rice's touching tale reflects on how families can survive and thrive despite tragedies. Lyra Nicholson is a lonely heiress living in Italy while her equally lonely daughters, 16-year-old Pell and Lucy, a 14-year-old math whiz, live in Newport, R.I. with their grandmother. Lucy's already tried to contact (via equations) the ghost of her dead father with Beck, her BFF and the sister of Pell's boyfriend, Travis. Pell travels to Italy, wanting Lyra, who abandoned her and Lucy, to finally take responsibility for them. . . . Rice gives Pell an old-beyond-her-years stability that Lyra lacks in this beguiling beach read." Publ Wkly

Rice, Luanne

The **geometry** of sisters. Bantam Books 2009 319p $25

ISBN 978-0-553-80513-0; 0-553-80513-4

LC 2008-55703

"Maggie Shaw second-guesses herself all the way from Columbus, Ohio, to Newport, Rhode Island, after two tragedies threaten to tear her family apart. While on vacation, her husband drowned, and her oldest daughter Carrie ran away after surviving the accident. Maggie is uprooting her son Travis, the football star, and her fragile daughter Beck, who mourns the loss of her beloved sister, so she can support the family as a teacher at a unique private high school. Maggie's past is anchored to Newport, with her estranged sister and J. D., the man who drove a wedge between them, living nearby. . . . The always insightful and engaging Rice explores the mystical bond between sisters as she portrays families learning what it means to love and forgive." Booklist

Rice, Luanne

Home fires. Bantam Bks. 1995 312p

LC 94-23911

In this novel, "privileged New Yorker Anne Davis returns to her New England island childhood home after the death of her four-year-old daughter and the breakup of her marriage. Seeking solitude from her sister, who has never left the island, she finds kinship—and love—with a scarred fireman who understands tragedy, having survived it himself. At the same time she reconnects with her teenaged niece, whose high school days are in danger of becoming a haze of alcohol and lust. . . . A strikingly real story of family feelings and grief." Libr J

Rice, Luanne

Last kiss. Bantam Books 2008 339p $25

ISBN 978-0-553-80512-3; 0-553-80512-6

LC 2007-52179

"Rice makes a . . . return visit to the Hubbard's Point, Conn., setting of Beach Girls (2004). As the book opens, a year soaked in Wild Turkey has passed since singer/songwriter Sheridan Rosslare lost her son, Charlie, in a random New York mugging. While Sheridan drowns her sorrows, Charlie's girlfriend, Nell Kilvert, is more assiduous; she hires private investigator Gavin Dawson to prove there was nothing random about Charlie's death. For his part, Hubbard's Point native Gavin, a New York transplant, had pretty much written off Hubbard's Point after Sheridan, once the love of his life, dumped him for his wild and reckless ways years before. Now, older and wiser, he's still in love with Sheridan and wants to start over, but Sheridan's grief soon proves a formidable obstacle. An element of supernatural whimsy, a dark secret involving a trust fund and a disturbing question related to Charlie's estranged father, Randy, add complexity, while cameos from other Beach Girls characters contribute an engaging, homey touch." Publ Wkly

Rice, Luanne

The **lemon** orchard; Luanne Rice. Pamela Dorman Books 2013 304 p. $27.95

ISBN 0670025275; 9780670025275

LC 2013009690

In this novel from Luanne Rice, "five years after the death of her daughter, Julia comes to Malibu to house-sit and is drawn to the overseer of the orchard property, [Roberto], an illegal immigrant who has his own tragic past." Roberto lost his daughter "during their arduous and dangerous trek from Mexico into the U.S." (Kirkus Reviews)

Rice, Luanne

The **letters**; [by] Luanne Rice & Joseph Monninger. Bantam Books 2008 199p $22

ISBN 978-0-553-80741-7; 0-553-80741-2

LC 2008-25627

"With each character–and each author–providing vivid descriptions of his and her surroundings and intense emotions, it's hard for the reader to remember that she is reading fiction and not eavesdropping on personal correspondence saturated with sadness and love." Booklist

Rice, Luanne

Little night; Luanne Rice. Pamela Dorman Books/Viking 2012 321 p.

ISBN 0670023566; 9780670023561

LC 2011049237

In this novel, "Clare Burke's life took a devastating turn when she tried to protect her sister, Anne, from an abusive and controlling husband and ended up serving prison time for assault. The verdict largely hinged on Anne's defense of her spouse—all lies—and the sisters have been estranged ever since. Nearly twenty years later, Clare is living a quiet life in Manhattan as an urban birder and nature blogger, when her niece, Grit, turns up on her doorstep. . . . Together they face the wounds inflicted by Anne and find in their new connection a place of healing. When Clare begins to suspect her sister might be in New York, she and her niece hold out hope for a long-awaited reunion with her." (Publisher's note)

Rice, Luanne

Summer light. Bantam Bks. 2001 372p

ISBN 0-553-80122-8

LC 2001-25475

A novel about wedding planner May Taylor and her "daughter, Kylie, a special child who seems to feel things more deeply than others and who sees angels. It's Kylie who brings her mother and Bruins hockey star, Martin Cartier, together. For Martin, its love at first sight, but May is leery of relationships. She finally agrees to marriage, but life is complicated as their careers require that they live alternately in Connecticut, Canada, and Boston. . . . With her gift, Kylie tries to unite the family in the face of tragedy, and the prolific Rice skillfully blends romance with magic." Booklist

Rich, David

Caravan of thieves; David Rich. Dutton 2012 295 p. $25.95

ISBN 0525952888; 9780525952886

LC 2012001870

In author David Rich's book, Rollie is "assigned undercover in Afghanistan to stop black-market weapons thefts . . . Recalled to Camp Pendleton when his undercover connection is killed, Rollie learns he's being tailed . . . Rollie soon learns he's being followed because the feds are tracing [stolen] military caskets full of money . . . Now word is circulating that [his con man father] Dan dug up one casket from a veteran's gravesite, and with Dan nowhere to be found, good guys and bad suspect devious Dan has the millions, and they want Rollie to find him." (Kirkus)

Rich, Nathaniel

The **mayor's** tongue. Riverhead Books 2008 310p $24.95

ISBN 978-1-594-48990-7; 1-594-48990-4

LC 2008-06832

"Both Eugene Brentani and Mr. Schmitz are on quests to the enchanted hinterlands of Italy's mountainous North—one for his disappeared lady love, the other for his inexplicably deteriorating best friend. Their journeys are distinct but complementary, not overlapping so much as being similarly mired in a fantastical domain ruled by the words and rumored presence of Constance Eakins, a celebrated lothario, philosopher king and profligate poet. The novel's foremost delight is its measured, nearly imperceptible descent into the realm of fairy-tale. There is no rabbit hole to fall through—reality and fairy-tale coexist, sharing the same borders, the same characters, and the same heartbreak for jilted lovers." Paste

Rich, Nathaniel

Odds against tomorrow; [a novel] Nathaniel Rich. 1st ed. Farrar, Straus and Giroux 2013 320 p. ill. (hardcover) $26

ISBN 0374224242; 9780374224240

LC 2012028928

In this novel, by Nathaniel Rich, "Mitchell Zukor, a gifted young mathematician, is hired by a mysterious new financial consulting firm, FutureWorld. . . . He is asked to calculate worst-case scenarios in the most intricate detail. . . . As Mitchell immerses himself in the mathematics of catastrophe. . . . Then, . . . an actual worst-case scenario overtakes Manhattan. Mitchell realizes he is uniquely prepared to profit. But at what cost?" (Publisher's note)

Richards, David Adams

The **bay** of love and sorrows; a novel. Arcade Pub. 2003 307p $24.95

ISBN 1-55970-650-3

LC 2002-38348

"Michael is as naive as the other downtrodden individuals Everette has chosen as pawns to carry out his darkly laid plans, and the tragic events that ensue will forever be ingrained in the minds of the townpeople residing in The Bay of Love and Sorrows. Richards' story falls into place with the ease of a domino rally, providing all of the elements for a riveting story." Booklist

Richardson, C. S.

The **end** of the alphabet. Doubleday 2007 119p $16.95

ISBN 978-0-385-52255-7; 0-385-52255-X

LC 2006-36823

"The surprise of this little book is not that it is poignant but that it is delightful: graceful, stylish, humorous, intelligent and lacking even the faintest whiff of sanctimony." Washington Post Book World

Richardson, Kat

Greywalker. Roc 2006 341p pa $14

ISBN 0-451-46107-X

LC 2006-11233

"Recovering from a brutal assault that had left her clinically dead for two minutes, private investigator Harper Blaine finds her perceptions have changed. Now she sees people that others can't and often struggles against a grayish mist that seems to permeate her world. A friendly couple with experience in the paranormal explain to her that she is a Greywalker, someone with the ability to cross between the living and the ghostly worlds. Suddenly, her life—and her business—grow a lot more interesting and much more dangerous. Richardson's first novel features a genuinely likable and independent heroine with a unique view of reality." Libr J

Richardson, Samuel

★ **Clarissa**; or, The history of a young lady. edited with an introd. and notes by Angus Ross. Penguin Books 1985 1533p

ISBN 0-14-043215-9

First published 1749

In this epistolary novel Clarissa Harlowe "has been coldly commanded by her tyrannical family to marry Mr. Solmes, a man she despises. She refuses, even though it pains her to defy her parents. Locked in her room, isolated from family and friends, Clarissa corresponds secretly with Robert Lovelace, a suitor disapproved of by her family; she finally throws herself upon his protection and flees with him. It soon becomes clear to her, however, that Lovelace's sole aim is to seduce her. Her virtue is so great that Lovelace becomes obsessively absorbed in breaking it down." Reader's Ency. 4th edition

Richardson, Samuel

★ **Pamela**; or, Virtue rewarded. edited with explanatory notes by Thomas Keymer and Alice Wakely; with an introduction by Thomas Keymer. 2008 xxlv, 546p (Oxford world's classics) pa $9.95

ISBN 978-0-19-953649-8; 0-19-953649-X

First published 1740-1741

"On the death of Pamela Andrews' mistress, her mistress's son, Mr. B, begins a series of mild stratagems designed to end in Pamela's seduction. These failing, he abducts her and renews his siege in earnest. Pamela spurns his advances, and halfway through the novel Mr. B offers marriage. In the second half of the novel, Pamela wins over those who had disapproved of the misalliance." Merriam-Webster's Ency of Lit

Richler, Mordecai

★ **Barney's** version; a novel, with footnotes and an afterword by Michael Panofsky. Knopf 1997 355p $25

ISBN 0-679-40418-X

LC 97-37033

"What entertains and affects us in 'Barney's Version' is the headlong, spendthrift passage of a life, redeemed from oblivion in the unbridled telling. The edge of the grave makes a lively point vantage." New Yorker

Richler, Mordecai

★ **Solomon** Gursky was here; a novel. Knopf 1990 413p

LC 89-43393

Richler is a "ringmaster, making his performers do dazzling backflips without missing a beat. At the same time he is a moralist, recoiling from those who would sentimentalize the Holocaust or make power a sacrament." Time

Richler, Nancy

Your mouth is lovely; a novel. Ecco Press 2002 357p $25.95

ISBN 0-06-009677-2

LC 2002-23521

This "novel summons up the lost world of the Russian shtetls around the Pripet marshes in Ukraine, and shows how those communities were first changed and then annihilated by the events that led, ultimately, to the Russian Revolution. At the center of Richler's tale is Miriam Lev, whose mother drowned herself when she was a day old, and who at age six is taken in hand by her father's new wife, Tsila, a harsh, beautiful seamstress who teaches Miriam the alphabet and dreams of another life. After an ill-starred and and painful series of events, Miriam ends up, at nineteen, in Siberia, having shot an officer of the Tsar at point-blank range. Miriam's hegira is told here as a letter to her own daughter, whom she hasn't seen since she gave birth to her, in prison. Richler's work recalls the stories of Isaac Babel, in which the knowable is charged with mystery." New Yorker

Richmond, Michelle

No one you know; a novel. Delacorte Press 2008 306p pa $15

ISBN 978-0-385-34013-7; 0-385-34013-3; 978-0-385-34014-4 pa; 0-385-34014-1 pa

LC 2008-13508

"As complex and beautiful as a mathematical proof, this gripping, thought-provoking novel will keep you thinking long after the last page has been turned." Family Circle

Richter, Conrad

★ The **awakening** land. Knopf 1966 3v in 1

This trilogy depicts " a pioneer family and settlement's slow evolution from virgin wilderness to an organized community." Reader's Ency. 4th edition

Richter, Conrad

★ The **light** in the forest. Knopf 1953 179p

Companion volume to A country of strangers (1966)

"John Butler is kidnapped at the age of four and raised by Delaware Indians. Eleven years later, under a truce agreement between the Indians and the colonials, he is forcibly returned to his family. Irrevocably divided in his heart, he escapes and goes back to the Indians but is sent away after the failure of an Indian ambush." Shapiro. Fic for Youth. 3d edition

Richter, Conrad

★ The **sea** of grass. Knopf 1937 149p

"Set in New Mexico in the late 19th century, the novel concerns the often violent clashes between the pioneering ranchers, whose cattle range freely through the vast sea of grass, and the farmers, or 'nesters,' who build fences and turn the sod. Against this background is set the triangle of rancher Colonel Jim Brewton, his unstable Eastern wife Lutie, and the ambitious Brice Chamberlain. Richter casts the story in Homeric terms, with the children caught up in the conflicts of their parents." Merriam-Webster's Ency of Lit

Rickards, John

Winter's end; John Rickards. 1st U.S. ed; Thomas Dunne Books 2003 297p $23.95

ISBN 0-312-31097-8

LC 2003-46874

"Sheriff Dale Townsend asks for an old friend's help in interrogating a very slippery and clever murder suspect in small-town Maine. Dale himself found the suspect standing over the victim clutching the alleged murder weapon, but the guy refuses to give his name or answer any questions. When Dale's PI friend Alex Rourke, an ex-FBI agent good at interrogation, appears, he bores a few chinks in the guy's armor. Strangely, the suspect knows about Alex and seemed to expect him. An attention-getting plot, riveting prose, calculated suspense, and tense, human-interest subplotting mark this noteworthy first novel." Libr J

Ricks, Thomas E.

A **soldier's** duty; a novel. Random House 2000 250p $24.95

ISBN 0-375-50544-X

LC 2001-18601

"One would have to look far for a novel that touches so deftly on the complexities and challenges of leadership of military organizations at the highest levels." Parameters

Ridgway, Bee

The **river** of no return; by Bee Ridgway. Dutton 2013 464 p. $27.95

ISBN 0525953868; 9780525953869

LC 2012043510

In this novel, by Bee Ridgway, "a man and a woman travel through time in a quest to bring down [the Guild,] a secret society that controls the past and, thus, the future. When Nick returns home as if from the dead, older than he should be and battle scarred, Julia begins to suspect that her very life depends upon the secrets Grandfather never told her. As their knowledge of the Guild and their feelings for each other grow, the fate of the future itself is hanging in the balance." (Publisher's note)

Ridgway, Keith

★ **Hawthorn** & child; By Keith Ridgway. New Directions Publishing Corporation 2013 247 p. (alk. paper) $15.95

ISBN 0811221660; 9780811221665

LC 2013021075

This detective novel by Keith Ridgway is "part noir, part London snapshot. . . . Hawthorn and Child are mid-ranking detectives tasked with finding significance in the scattered facts. They appear and disappear in the fragments of this book along with a ghost car, a crime boss, a pick-pocket, a dead racing driver and a pack of wolves." (Publisher's note)

Rigosi, Giampiero

Night bus; translated from the Italian by Ann Goldstein. Bitter Lemon Press 2006 348p pa $14.95

ISBN 1-904738-11-7

LC 2006-386274

Original Italian edition, 2000

"Francesco is a gambling-addicted bus driver in Bologna, with a thuggish debt collector on his trail; Leila is a smart dame with a great pair of legs, who each night looks for a man to bed, drug, and rob. In perfect noir fashion, the two become uneasy allies, trying to escape a pair of vicious intelligence agents after Leila unknowingly swipes a mysterious document from a victim's apartment. Rigosi somewhat overdoes character quirks—one agent has a condition that leads him to constantly leak tears as he slices apart his victims—but an ever-expanding cast of creeps and criminals keeps the plot accelerating, and he describes the dripping of blood and the angle of a broken neck as lovingly as the preparation of a nice eggplant parmigiana." New Yorker

Riley, Judith Merkle

In pursuit of the green lion. Delacorte Press 1990 440p

LC 90-32498

"In this non-stop picaresque adventure quips fly as thickly as a barrage of arrows; a steady stream of drunken noblemen, corrupt priests, scheming ladies and truculent ghosts keep the action white-hot." Booklist

Riley, Judith Merkle

The **serpent** garden. Viking 1996 467p

LC 95-36067

"Susanna Dallet is determined to support herself after the untimely death of her spouse and turns to the art of miniature portraiture, a profession she learned from her enlightened father. After Susanna becomes enmeshed in the political intrigue of the court of Henry VIII, she is sought after by a heretical religious sect, a minor demon, and a free-spririted archangel, all of whom believe she is the key to their success. Riley . . . creates a stunning period fantasy that combines historical detail with magical realism." Libr J

Riley, Judith Merkle

A **vision** of light. Delacorte Press 1989 442p

LC 88-17514

This "is a chronicle rich with the ambience and flavor of the Middle Ages, but it is a 14th-century story told with a 20th-century sensibility." N Y Times Book Rev

Followed by In pursuit of the green lion

Riley, Lucinda

The **girl** on the cliff; a novel. Lucinda Riley. Atria Books 2012 407 p. (trade paper) $15

ISBN 1451655827; 9781451655827; 9781451655858

LC 2012027861

In this book Lucinda Riley, "after a heartbreaking miscarriage, Grania Ryan abandons New York . . . to return to her rural Irish roots in a wind-swept coastal village. There, she befriends a motherless red-haired child, despite her own mother's cryptic warnings, and becomes involved with the rich, reclusive Lisle family. Only after she has given her heart to the girl, Aurora, does Grania's mother hand over a packet of letters that explains the long-standing family feud." (Kirkus Reviews)

Rindell, Suzanne

The **Other** Typist; Suzanne Rindell. Amy Einhorn Books/Putnam 2013 368 p. (hardcover) $25.95

ISBN 0399161465; 9780399161469

LC 2013000995

In this novel, by Suzanne Rindell, "Rose Baker [is] . . . a typist in a New York City Police Department precinct. . . . It is 1923, . . . a new era for women, and New York is a confusing place for Rose. . . . Prudish Rose is stuck in the fading light of yesteryear. . . . When glamorous Odalie, a new girl, joins the typing pool, . . . the two women navigate between the sparkling underworld of speakeasies by night and their work at the station by day." (Publisher's note)

Rinehart, Mary Roberts

The **circular** staircase; with illustrations by Lester Ralph. Bobbs-Merrill 1908 362p il

Featuring the detective talents of Mr. Jamieson, this novel concerns a maiden aunt and her nephew and niece who take a country house for the summer and are plunged into a series of mysterious crimes

Rinehart, Mary Roberts

Miss Pinkerton: adventures of a nurse detective. Rinehart 1959 403p

Two short stories and two novels featuring the exploits of nurse Hilda Adams

Rinehart, Steven

Built in a day; a novel. Doubleday 2003 241p $23.95

ISBN 0-385-49855-1

LC 2003-41968

"The charm of the protagonist, clearly, is not the primary appeal of this novel. The charms of Rinehart's writing, however, more than countervail; though stripped-down and deadpan, his sentences pack a lot of raw, juicy comic power." N Y Times Book Rev

Riordan, Rick, 1964-

Cold Springs. Bantam Bks. 2003 340p $23.95

ISBN 0-553-80236-4

LC 2003-40365

Riordan's "voice is fresh yet sure, with insights so trenchant they nearly provoke tears. And Riordan's characters, even the minor ones, are achingly believable." Booklist

Rivas, Manuel

In the wilderness; Manuel Rivas; translated from the Galician by Jonathan Dunne. Overlook Press 2005 170 p.

ISBN 1585674672; 9781585674671

LC 2005040603

This book is set in "the village of Aran, in Galicia, [where] a young girl (Rosa) notices a fresco that has suddenly appeared on a church wall, depicting gorgeously arrayed females whom she presumes to be saints. Aran's priest, Don Xil, however, assures his parishioners that the figures are embodiments of the Seven Deadly Sins. This accusation was perhaps unwise, for Don Xil dies—and is reincarnated as a mouse . . . . As years pass, Rosa grows up and marries, bears her brutal husband Cholo three children, befriends the wealthy old woman (Misia) . . . , and takes a lover: 'Spiderman,' recently returned from working on a construction gang in New York City. These events' and others are observed by several people, including Don Xil, who have transmigrated into the bodies of animals after dying. (Kirkus)

Rivers, Francine, 1947-

Bridge to haven; Francine Rivers. Tyndale House Publishers, Inc. 2014 480 p. (hc) $25.99

ISBN 1414368186; 9781414368184

LC 2013040115

In this novel by Francine Rivers, "Hollywood feels like a million miles from Haven, and naive Abra quickly learns what's expected of an ambitious girl with stars in her eyes. But fame comes at an awful price. She has burned every bridge to get exactly what she thought she wanted. Now, all she wants is a way back home." (Publisher's note)

"Rivers nicely evokes 1950s Hollywood, with its gossip columnists, high-wattage movie stars, and ladder-climbing aspirants; Elvis Presley and Lana Turner put in cameos. This story arc will be particularly resonant for Christian readers, but Rivers has the writing ability to reel in others who enjoy a well-told tale of redemption." Pub Wkly

★ The **road** ahead; fiction from the forever war. edited by Adrian Bonenberger & Brian Castner; foreword by Roxana Robinson. Pegasus Books 2017 xvii, 349 p.p illustrations (hardcover) $24.95

ISBN 9781681773728; 9781681773070; 1681773074

In this book, edited by Adrian Bonenberger and Brian Castner, "twenty-five diverse veteran voices reflect the changing face of combat and reflect the haunting realities and truths only fiction can reveal. These masterfully crafted stories from writers who have served reflect the entire breadth of human emotion—loss, anger, joy, love, fear, and courage--and the evolving nature of what has become America's 'Forever War.'" (Publisher's note)

"Bonenberger and Castner's treasury captures the contemporary American soldier's experience in intimate and harrowing detail, touching on everything from loneliness to pride, death to brotherhood, and paranoia to compassion." Booklist

Robards, Karen

Ghost moon. Delacorte Press 2000 313p $24.95

ISBN 0-385-31972-X

LC 99-47420

Robards "has crafted a mossy modern gothic drenched in gore. . . . {She} conveys the dusty heat of the Louisiana summer, and has an ear for the nuances of dialogue." Publ Wkly

Robards, Karen

Shiver; Karen Robards. Gallery Books 2012 400 p. (hardcover : alk. paper) $25

ISBN 1451678673; 9781451678673; 9781451678680; 9781451678697

LC 2012037437

In this suspense romance novel, by Karen Robards, Daniel Panterro is rescued by tow truck driver Samantha. "Danny knows he hasn't seen the last of the vicious drug runners who kidnapped him from protective custody. His only recourse is to take his pretty savior hostage and force her to help him. . . . With ruthless killers stalking their trail, Sam's only choice is to trust this handsome, menacing stranger. But as she relinquishes control, Sam feels an unmistakable desire." (Publisher's note)

Includes bibliographical references and index

Robb, J. D.

Naked in death. G.P. Putnam's Sons 2004 294p

ISBN 0-399-15157-5

LC 2003-54813

This is the first volume in the author's futurisitic police procedural At death series. Over thirty titles have followed

"Naked in Death features Lt. Eve Dallas of the NYPD as she searches for a serial killer of prostitutes. It hints at the isolation, neglect, and sexual abuse that Eve suffered as a child, memories that she tries to suppress. The adult Eve is slow to trust and awkward when faced with affection and kindness. Yet over the course of this series, she acquires a husband, Roark; a partner, Peabody; and a varied host of friends—hard-boiled reporter Nadine, humanitarian doctor Louise, and worldly wise, bursting with life, rock star Mavis." Libr J

Robbins, Charles

The **accomplice**; a novel. Charles Robbins. 1st ed. Thomas Dunne Books 2012 viii, 356 p.p (hardcover) $24.99

ISBN 1250010519; 9781250010513; 9781250018359

LC 2012026602

This book by Charles Robbins presents a "look at how love, lust, and murder can derail a presidential campaign. Press secretary Henry Hatten . . . accepts a top spot in the presidential campaign of Sen. Tom Peele, a moderate Nebraska Republican. . . . Peele has a decent shot at the upcoming nomination. Unfortunately, he also has . . . a tendency to skirt and often cross lines that are at least unethical and sometimes illegal." (Publishers Weekly)

Robbins, David L.

The **last** citadel; a novel of the Battle of Kursk. Bantam Bks. 2003 421p $24.95

ISBN 0-553-80177-5

LC 2003-44304

"The battle for the Soviet city of Kursk in July 1943 during World War II involved two million soldiers. Code-named Citadel, it was Hitler's frenzied—and final—attempt to defeat Russia on the eastern front and was the largest buildup of German armed power of the war. Robbins re-creates the battle in this rousing novel: its characters being Hitler; his generals and advisers; Russian, German, and Spanish foot soldiers and tank drivers; fighter pilots (both men and women); partisans; and even elderly men and women digging trenches." Booklist

Includes bibliographical references (p. {420}-421)

Robbins, David L.

War of the rats; a novel. Bantam Bks. 1999 392p $23.95

ISBN 0-553-10817-4

LC 98-43918

"The final confrontation takes a while to play out, but once Robbins . . . gets to the heart of the matter, he presents a riveting account of a battle within a battle, and the sniper motif proves an ideal vehicle to analyze the strengths and weaknesses of both sides." Publ Wkly

Includes bibliographical references (p. {391}-392)

Robbins, Tom

Fierce invalids home from hot climates. Bantam Bks. 2000 415p

ISBN 0-553-10775-5

LC 99-51683

The hero of this novel, Switters, "is a pistol-packing C.I.A. operative. . . . Dispatched to release his kooky grandmother's pet parrot into the South American jungle, {he} encounters a shaman who takes him on a mind-expanding hallucinogenic trip . . . and reveals that the secret to transcendence is laughter, . . . a message {Switters} carries to America, the Middle East and even the Vatican." (N Y Times Book Rev)

"Switters, the protagonist, is an errand boy for the CIA, a secret lover of Broadway show tunes and a pedophile. On assignment in Peru . . . Switters encounters a Kandakandero medicine man who gives him mind-altering drugs and wisdom, but in exchange inflicts a curse: if Switters's feet ever touch the ground, he will be struck dead instantly. So Switters spends the rest of the novel in a wheelchair, although this in no way slows him down. He returns to Seattle, chases after his 16-year-old stepsister and numerous art students, then embarks on a mission to Syria to sell gas masks to Kurds; there, he beds a nun who even so remains a virgin. In true Robbins style, the writing throughout is lush and sexy, containing a great deal of witty social and political commentary." Publ Wkly

Robbins, Tom

Half asleep in frog pajamas. Bantam Bks. 1994 386p

LC 94-11549

"The yarn has a genuineness, a warmth, a humor, and an incredibly compelling plot, which hold our attention to the end." Booklist

Robbins, Tom

Jitterbug perfume. Bantam Bks. 1984 342p

LC 84-45233

"Priscilla Partido, a Seattle member of Daughters of the Daily Special (waitresses with college degrees), gets a beet tossed in her window; Madame Devalier and V'lu Jackson, New Orleans purveyors of fine perfume, get a beet too; so do the owners of LeFever Odeurs in Paris. What does it all mean? . . . The real theme here is immortality, in the person of Alobar, a 1000-year-old Nordic imp who sports across the globe (ending up as Einstein's janitor) with the secrets to olfactory wisdom and eternal life and love. Also at large is a Leary-esque philanderer, Wiggs Dannyboy, who as founder of an immortalist sect, the Last Laugh Foundation, accompanies Priscilla on her quest for happiness and the perfect (beet-based) scent. Robbins is still in top form, still mixing the lunatic and the thoughtful—or rather, doing a literary watusi up every page and jitterbugging back down." Publ Wkly

Robbins, Tom

Skinny legs and all. Bantam Bks. 1990 422p il

LC 89-18309

"A painter's struggle with her art, a restaurant opened as an experiment in brotherhood, the journey of several inanimate objects to Jerusalem, a preacher's scheme to hasten Armageddon, and a performance of a legendary dance: these are the diverse elements around which Robbins has built this wild, controversial novel. Ellen Cherry Charles, one of the 'Daughters of the Daily Special' in Jitterbug Perfume, takes center stage. She has married Boomer Petway and moved to New York, hoping to make it as a painter. Instead, she winds up a waitress at the Isaac and Ishmael, a restaurant co-owned by an Arab and a Jew. . . . Few contemporary novelists mix tomfoolery and philosophy so well." Libr J

Robbins, Tom

★ **Still** life with Woodpecker. Bantam Bks. 1980 277p

LC 81-103498

The author's "prose, as spasmodic as his heroine's sex life, is marbled with limping puns heavily splattered with recurrent motifs and a boyish zeal for the scatalogical." SLJ

Robbins, Tom

Villa incognito. Bantam Bks. 2003 241p $27.50

ISBN 0-553-80332-8

LC 2003-40353

"The novel begins with the story of Tanuki, a badgerlike Asian creature with a reputation as a changeling and trickster and a fondness for sake. Also part of the cast is a beautiful young woman who may or may not have Tanuki's blood in her veins. . . and three American MIAs who have chosen to remain in Laos long after the Vietnam War. Events are set in motion when one of the MIAs, dressed as a priest, is arrested with a cache of heroin taped to his body. In vintage Robbins style, the plot whirls every which way, as the author, writing with unrestrained glee, takes potshots at societal pillars: the military, big business and religions of all ilks. The language is eccentric, electrifying and true to the mark." Publ Wkly

Robert, Katee

The **devil's** daughter; Katee Robert. Montlake Romance 2017 304 p. (paperback) $12.95

ISBN 1503940918; 9781503940918

LC 2017296178

In this book in the Hidden Sins series, by Katee Robert, "ten years ago, Eden Collins left Clear Springs, Montana, and never once looked back. But when the bodies of murdered young women surface, their corpses violated and marked with tattoos worn by her mother's followers, Eden, now an FBI agent, can't turn a blind eye. To catch the killer, she's going to have to return to the fold." (Publisher's note)

"From veteran romance writer Robert (An Indecent Proposal, 2016, etc.), this is a great addition to Montlake Romance's innovative mixed-genre repertoire." Kirkus

Roberts, Michele

Ignorance; Michele Roberts. Bloomsbury USA 2012 240 p. $25

ISBN 9781608197712; 1608197719

LC 2011042283

This book, "set in a small French town during the Second World War, centers on the lives of two girls: Jeanne, the daughter of a widowed Jew who converted to Catholicism, and Marie-Angèle, whose family owns the village store. When Jeanne's mother falls ill, Jeanne is sent to the local convent. There she makes mischief with Marie-Angèle, tolerates the nuns' cruelties, and meets a Jewish outcast who teaches her to draw and takes advantage of her innocence." (New Yorker)

Roberts, Michele

Reader, I married him. Pegasus Books 2006 229p pa $13.95

ISBN 1-933648-02-3

First published 2004 in the United Kingdom

"To say that Aurora has been unlucky in love is an understatement. Husbands one, two, and three all met untimely deaths, but now Aurora is ready to move on with her life. A trip to the Italian countryside, ostensibly to scout out new tempting tidbits for her London delicatessen and visit with her old friend, the feisty feminist turned convent abbess Leonora, seems just the ticket, and would have been, had not Aurora's domineering stepmother, Maude, arrived along with her parish priest, the oh-so-attractive and oh-so-mysterious Father Michael. Unable to stay at the convent for more than one night, Aurora is offered lodging in the museum apartment owned by another old friend, Frederico, a man whose sexual orientation Aurora has evidently mistaken. As Aurora succumbs to her passion for the erstwhile priest, Frederico expresses more than just friendship for the vulnerable Aurora. Roberts whimsically indulges her passion for favored themes of religion, sex, and food in this riotous and ribald tale that packs a didn't-see-that-one-coming ending." Booklist

Roberts, Nora, 1950-

Angel's fall. G. P. Putnam's Sons 2006 439p $25.95

ISBN 0-399-15372-1

LC 2006-40902

"After suffering a horrific shock, Reece Gilmore is slowly starting to put her life back together. Leaving her home in Boston, Reece travels around the country, but when she arrives in Angel's Fist, Wyoming, her car refuses to go any further. Planning on staying only until she earns enough money to fix her car, Reece takes a job as a cook in the Angel Food Cafe. Then, as she gets to know her new boss, her coworkers, and the other residents of the little town, including Brody, an annoyingly stubborn yet mysteriously sexy writer, she starts to believe that for the first time in a very long time, she may have found a place she might actually want to call home. Reece's hard-won happiness and sense of security is threatened, however, when she becomes not only the sole witness to a murder but also the next target of the killer, who is determined to drive her crazy. . . . Roberts deftly imbues a deliciously subtle sense of menace into a chilling and thrilling plot." Booklist

Roberts, Nora, 1950-

Dance upon the air; Nora Roberts. Jove Books 2001 386p (pbk.) $7.99

ISBN 0515131229; 9780515131222

LC 2002554345

RITA Awards: Top Ten Favorite Books (2001)

In this book, "[w]hen Nell Channing arrives on charming Three Sisters Island, she believes that she's finally found refuge from her abusive husband—and from the terrifying life she fled so desperately eight months ago. . . . [I]n this quiet, peaceful place, Nell never feels entirely at ease. Careful to conceal her true identity, she takes a job as a cook at the local bookstore café—and begins to explore her feelings for the island sheriff, Zack Todd. . . . Just as Nell starts to wonder if she'll ever be able to break free of her fear, she realizes that the island suffers under a terrible curse—one that can only be broken by the descendants of the Three Sisters, the witches who settled the island back in 1692." (Publisher's note)

Sequel: Heaven and earth.

Roberts, Nora, 1950-

Midnight Bayou. Putnam 2001 352p

ISBN 0-399-14824-8

LC 2001-41643

"When wealthy Boston attorney Declan Fitzgerald discovers that Manet Hall, a dilapidated mansion on the bayou just outside New Orleans, is for sale, he leaves his practice and moves in to renovate, restore, and redecorate. Independent and tough, bar owner Lena fascinates him from the minute he lays eyes on her. Believing that he's incapable of romance, he's amazed by how quickly and overwhelmingly he falls head over heels in love with her. But he worries about his own sanity when he experiences fugue states that leave him with memories of events and people who lived in the mansion more than 100 years earlier. . . . Roberts has cleverly crafted an enticing tangle of times and relationship." Booklist

Roberts, Nora, 1950-

The **obsession**; Nora Roberts. Berkley Books 2016 464 p. (hardcover) $28

ISBN 9780399175169

LC 2015025894

In this book, by Nora Roberts, "Naomi Bowes lost her innocence the night she followed her father into the woods. In freeing the girl trapped in the root cellar, Naomi revealed the horrible extent of her father's crimes and made him infamous. No matter how close she gets to happiness, she can't outrun the sins of Thomas David Bowes. Now a successful photographer living under the name Naomi Carson, she has found a place that calls to her, a rambling old house in need of repair." (Publisher's note)

"Roberts retains her impeccably high standards in this excellently executed tale, once again dazzling readers with a sophisticated blend of edge-of-your-seat suspense and sexy romance." Booklist

Roberts, Nora, 1950-

Whiskey Beach; Nora Roberts. G. P. Putnam's Sons 2013 496 p. (hardcover) $27.95

ISBN 0399159894; 9780399159893

LC 2012047883

In this novel, by Nora Roberts, "a Boston lawyer, Eli has weathered an intense year . . . after being accused of . . . the murder of his soon-to-be-ex wife. He finds sanctuary at Bluff House. . . . Abra Walsh is always there, though. Whiskey Beach's resident housekeeper, yoga instructor, jewelry maker, and massage therapist, Abra is a woman of many talents--including helping Eli take control of his life and clear his name." (Publisher's note)

Roberts, Victoria

After the fall; an illustrated novel. by Victoria Roberts. W. W. Norton & Company 2012 184 p. (hardcover) $24.95

ISBN 0393073556; 9780393073553

LC 2012023516

This novel by Victoria Roberts "introduces us to a brilliantly eccentric family from New York's Upper East Side. . . . One fateful day, Alan returns home to find that the family has gone bust, not even a penny to be found. The next morning, to the children's surprise, the family wakes up in Central Park along with the entire contents of their penthouse arranged just as before--art, furniture, pugs, and all. . . . the family makes Central Park into a comfortable and creative home." (Publisher's note)

Robertson, Imogen

Anatomy of murder; Imogen Robertson. Pamela Dorman Books 2012 382 p. map

ISBN 0670023175; 9780670023172

LC 2011036291

In this novel, "[s]pies, corpses, tarot cards and countertenors combine in this . . . adventure featuring a pair of amateur sleuths in 18th-century London. . . . Mrs. Harriet Westerman, one half of the detective duo, is preoccupied with the mental health of her naval captain husband James, wounded after capturing a French ship carrying a spy during the war with the American Rebels. Now Harriet and her forensic scientist friend Gabriel Crowther are invited by the British authorities to help trace the espionage links to London, starting with the examination of a body found floating in the Thames. These investigations, and the dark fears of a slum-dwelling fortune-teller[, are depicted]." (Kirkus)

Robertson, Imogen

Circle of shadows; Imogen Robertson. Viking 2013 384 p. (hardcover) $27.95

ISBN 9780670026289

LC 2013009688

This book by Jenny Robertson "takes widow Harriet Westerman and her investigative partner, anatomist Gabriel Crowther, to Germany's Duchy of Maulberg, where her brother-in-law, Daniel Clode, has been charged with murder. Clode, disoriented and bleeding from an apparent suicide attempt, was found behind a locked door near the smothered corpse of Maria Martesen. . . . Westerman and Crowther, having doubts about Clode's guilt, soon find evidence suggesting someone else was the killer." (Publishers Weekly)

Robertson, Imogen

Instruments of darkness. Pamela Dorman Books/Viking 2011 373p $26.95

ISBN 978-0-670-02242-7; 0-670-02242-X

LC 2010-33777

First published 2009 in the United Kingdom

"The plot is a little loopy, but the dialogue crackles along, and Robertson's enjoyment of the period and her characters is infectious. One begins not to mind the incongruity of it all—in the 18th century, could Harriet really befriend a single gentleman like Crowther without scandal?—not to mention Harriet's surprisingly modern ruminations on subjects like breastfeeding. Even the appearance of characters who seem to have been recycled from other books—the enigmatic manservant, the kindly guardian—becomes part of the fun." N Y Times Book Rev

Robertson, Imogen

Island of bones; Imogen Robertson. Pamela Dorman Books 2012 384 p.

ISBN 0670026271; 9780670026272

LC 2012003378

Sequel to: Anatomy of murder (2012) and Instruments of darkness (2011)

This novel by Imogen Robertson features "the forthright Mrs. Harriet Westerman and reclusive anatomist Gabriel Crowther. . . . In 'Island of Bones,' Crowther's haunting past is at last revealed. For years he has pursued his forensic studies -- and the occasional murder investigation -- far from his family estate. But an ancient tomb there will reveal a wealth of secrets. When laborers discover an extra body inside, the lure of the mystery brings Crowther home at last." (Publisher's note)

Robertson, Imogen

The **Paris** winter; a novel. Imogen Robertson. St. Martin's Press 2014 368 p. (hardcover : acid-free paper) $25.99

ISBN 1250051835; 9781250051837

LC 2014026998

In Imogen Robertson's novel "while her fellow students enjoy the dazzling decadence of the Belle Epoque, Maud slips into poverty. Quietly starving, and dreading another cold Paris winter, she stumbles upon an opportunity when Christian Morel engages her as a live-in companion to his . . . sister, Sylvie. But all is not as it seems. Christian and Sylvie, Maud soon discovers, are not quite the darlings they pretend to be. Sylvie has a secret addiction to opium and Christian has an ominous air of intrigue." (Publisher's note)

"For readers of historical fiction looking for a complex story, this is a sure bet and most likely the next big hit of any book discussion group." LJ

Robertson, Michael

The **brothers** of Baker Street. Minotaur Books 2011 274p $24.99

ISBN 978-0-312-53813-2; 0-312-53813-8

LC 2010-42020

"According to the terms of their lease, . . . Reggie and Nigel Heath were able to set up their modern-day law practice in the desirable 200 block of Baker Street by agreeing to answer all correspondence addressed to Sherlock Holmes at 221B. Reggie, the less whimsical of the pair, has been neglecting that responsibility, so . . . that task falls to Nigel, freeing up Reggie to concentrate on defending a young cab driver accused of robbing and killing two American tourists. An anonymous letter to Holmes gives Reggie a valuable tip, but the communications from a certain Professor Moriarty add a more sinister twist to this breezy and entertaining legal mystery." N Y Times Book Rev

Robinson, Elisabeth

The **true** and outstanding adventures of the Hunt sisters; a novel. Little, Brown 2004 327p $23.95

ISBN 0-316-73502-7

LC 2003-47713

"Over the course of about 200 letters (and a few e-mails), Robinson succinctly shows the full range of Olivia's emotions and relationships, from the optimism she tries to instill in her shocked family to the admiration she holds for Maddie's spouse. She poignantly portrays the frustration of trying to sustain a relationship while engaged in a consuming profession." USA Today

Robinson, Kim Stanley

2312; Kim Stanley Robinson. Orbit 2012 561 p.

ISBN 9780316098120

LC 2011044805

This science fiction novel takes place "In the year 2312, [when] humans have developed the technology to colonize most of the solar system, including Mercury, which boasts a single city that travels on rails around the planet just ahead of the rising sun. When Swan Er Hong arrives to mourn her recently deceased grandmother Alex, one of Mercury's movers and shakers, Swan realizes how little she knew about the woman who raised her. Meeting some of Alex's scientific friends reveals to Swan that mysterious projects were in the works and that she must uncover her grandmother's secrets before they destroy not only Mercury but the entire solar system." Kim Stanley Robinson presents a "portrait of a solar system economy based on the mining of the asteroid belt." (Libr J)

Robinson, Kim Stanley

★ **Antarctica**. Bantam Bks. 1998 511p $24.95

ISBN 0-553-10063-7

LC 97-41701

This is "an exhilarating addition to a body of work distinguished by two elements all too rare in modern science fiction: a sense of character and a sense of place. Robinson brings the two together by writing about people who are in love with where they are." N Y Times Book Rev

Robinson, Kim Stanley

Aurora; Kim Stanley Robinson. Orbit 2015 466 p. (hardback) $26

ISBN 0316098108; 9780316098106

LC 2014046162

In this science fiction novel, by Kim Stanley Robinson, "in the 26th century, a ship departs our solar system, bound for the Tau Ceti system and carrying 2,000 humans who live within a series of miniecosystems. Nearly 200 years later, the descendants of the original crew are preparing to reach their destination. . . . Unfortunately, it soon becomes apparent that the planets and satellites of Tau Ceti may not be suitable for colonization." (Kirkus Reviews)

"Robinson's latest well-researched novel exposes the fundamental flaws in one of science fiction's most beloved tropes: the multigenerational space ark traveling at sub-light speed to colonize a planet around a distant star." Kirkus

Robinson, Kim Stanley

Blue Mars. Bantam Bks. 1996 609p

ISBN 9780553101447 out of print; 9780553573350; 9780553898293

LC 95046700

In this concluding volume of the trilogy "colonists almost succeed in terraforming Mars. While they fight for independence from Earth and attempt to avert a civil war, they find their new civilization threatened by an ice age." Libr J

Robinson, Kim Stanley

Galileo's dream. Ballantine Books 2010 532p $26

ISBN 978-0-553-80659-5; 0-553-80659-9

LC 2009-42729

"Kim Stanley Robinson is one of the great 'hard science fiction' authors and this novel is no exception, with fantastic theories of the evolution of science, quantum theory and the true nature of time. Galileo's Dream is a little slow paced in the beginning but unfolds to a very thought-provoking and fresh science fiction novel with a very engrossing story challenging preconceptions about time, reality and history itself." Sciencefictionandfantasy.co.uk

Robinson, Kim Stanley

The **Martians**. Bantam Bks. 1999 336p hardcover o.p. pa $7.50

ISBN 0-553-80117-1; 0-553-57401-9 pa

LC 99-13115

Set in the universe of the author's Mars trilogy this volume includes vignettes, essays, fables, poems, and the following short stories: Michel in Antarctica; Exploring Fossil Canyon; Maya and Desmond; Four teleological trails; Coyote makes trouble; Michel in provence; Arthur Sternbach brings the curveball to Mars; Jackie on Zo; Keeping the flame; Big Man in love; Sexual dimorphism; What matters; Sax moments; A Martian romance; Purple Mars

"Also included is 'Green Mars,' a previously published novella about climbing Olympus Mons, the highest mountain in the solar system. . . . Some of the pieces here will be of interest only to those who have already read the trilogy, but the finest of the short fiction stands firmly on its own. As is the norm with Robinson's work, the stories are beautifully written, the characters are well developed and the author's passion for ecology manifests on every page." Publ Wkly

Robinson, Kim Stanley

New York 2140; Kim Stanley Robinson. Orbit 2017 613 p. (Science in the Capital) (hardback) $28

ISBN 9780316262347

LC 2016039922

Hugo Finalist: Best Novel (2018)

In this novel, by Kim Stanley Robinson, "as the sea levels rose, every street became a canal. . . . For the residents of one apartment building in Madison Square, however, New York in the year 2140 is far from a drowned city. There is the market trader, who finds opportunities where others find trouble. There is the detective, whose work will never disappear. . . . There is the internet star, . . . and the building's manager, quietly respected for his attention to detail." (Publisher's note)

"A post-disaster fairy tale that's light on plot...but a thoroughly enjoyable exercise in worldbuilding, written with a cleareyed love for the city's past, present, and future." Kirkus.

Robinson, Kim Stanley

★ **Red** Mars. Bantam Books 1993 519p il hardcover o.p. pa $7.99

ISBN 0-553-09204-9; 0-553-56073-5 pa

LC 92-21607

This book "concerns the first permanent settlement on Mars, a multinational band of 100 hardy experts, and their mission [of terraforming it]--to begin making Mars habitable for humans by releasing underground water and oxygen into the atmosphere. Unfortunately, they are divided over whether this is a desirable step in human evolution or an ecological crime." (Booklist)

"A novel fully inhabited both by detailed technical processes and by people whose careers those processes are; it is also a novel with a complex sense of political reality. . . . This is one of the finest works of American SF because it is one of the few that aspire to the dignity of the genuinely tragic." Times Lit Suppl

Other titles in the Mars trilogy are:

Blue Mars (1996)

Green Mars (1994)

Robinson, Kim Stanley

★ The **years** of rice and salt. Bantam Bks. 2002 658p

ISBN 0-553-10920-0

LC 2001-43492

"Because this alternate history is set in the same lawful universe as ours, its science must be the same. Because its people have the same basic human needs, their societies resemble ours. However, as events march toward the alternative year of 2002, some of his characters come to believe, despite much evidence to the contrary, that they can change the way they live. The reader is left to ponder whether this is an illusion." N Y Times Book Rev

Robinson, Lewis

Water dogs; a novel. Random House 2009 244p $25

ISBN 978-1-4000-6217-1; 1-4000-6217-9

LC 2008-16564

"Bennie knows that the details of his life don't show well. A twenty-seven-year-old college dropout with stalled ambitions, he works at an animal shelter and lives with his bullheaded older brother, Littlefield, in their old family home on Meadow Island, Maine. . . When a massive blizzard hits the state one Saturday afternoon, Bennie, Littlefield, and a crew of roughneck war-game enthusiasts decide to play paintball at the local granite quarry. Bennie accidentally falls into a gully, landing in the hospital, and wonders if his life can get any worse. But when one of the players disappears during the storm and Littlefield becomes the main suspect in the disappearance, Bennie realizes that the game might have had much higher stakes. Then Littlefield takes off without a word of explanation, forcing Bennie to seriously question his loyalty to his enigmatic brother. With the guidance of his intrepid girlfriend, Helen, and his twin sister, Gwen, Bennie goes looking for answers. . . . Written in prose as arresting and spare as the novel's rural Maine setting, Lewis Robinson's Water Dogs is a marvel of modern fiction, a book rich in empathy that follows one man's path through the uncertainties of youth and loss toward self-discovery." Bookmarks

Robinson, Lynda Suzanne

Murder at the feast of rejoicing; a Lord Meren mystery. {by} Lynda S. Robinson. Walker & Co. 1996 229p $20.95

ISBN 0-8027-3274-7

LC 95-33190

"Good scholarship authenticates the historical setting; imagination provides the sense of danger and romance to make it come alive." N Y Times Book Rev

Robinson, Lynda Suzanne

Murder at the God's gate; a Lord Meren mystery. {by} Lynda S. Robinson. Walker & Co. 1995 236p $19.95

ISBN 0-8027-3198-8

LC 94-28806

"Young King Tutankhamun's chief adviser/agent Lord Meren, known to some as the Falcon, investigates the murder of a priest in a temple dedicated to the teenaged Tut. Robinson . . . surrounds Meren with palace and temple intrigue, authentic details of daily life, and frequent mention of a wide assortment of indigenous animals." Libr J

Robinson, Marilynne, 1943-

★ **Gilead**. Farrar, Straus and Giroux 2004 247p $23

ISBN 0-374-15389-2

LC 2004-47063

Pulitzer Prize: Fiction (2005)

"Gilead possesses the quiet ineluctable perfection of Flaubert's A Simple Heart as well as the moral and emotional complexity of Robert Frost's deepest poetry. There's nothing flashy in these pages, and yet one regularly pauses to reread sentences, sometimes for their beauty, sometimes for their truth." Washington Post Book World

Robinson, Marilynne, 1943-

Home. Farrar, Straus & Giroux 2008 325p $25

ISBN 978-0-374-29910-1; 0-374-29910-2

LC 2008-18301

National Book Award Finalist: Fiction (2008)

This book is the second in Marilynne Robinson's "Gilead" trilogy. "Glory Boughton, aged thirty-eight, has returned to Gilead to care for her dying father. Soon her brother, Jack--the prodigal son of the family, gone for twenty years--comes home too, looking for refuge and trying to make peace with a past littered with tormenting trouble and pain." (Publisher's note)

"There is almost no first-rate American fiction about what happens in a household where religion is the family business, but if you ever wondered what it's like to be a preacher's kid, you can't do better than 'Home.' Robinson's greatest achievement is that she manages to introduce the notions of belief and religious mystery without ever seeming vague. She never shies from uncomfortable truths." Newsweek

Robinson, Marilynne, 1943-

★ **Lila**; Marilynne Robinson. Farrar Straus & Giroux 2014 272 p. (hardcover) $26

ISBN 0374187614; 9780374187613

LC 2013038776

National Book Award Shortlist: Fiction (2014)

National Book Critics Circle Award: Fiction (2014)

In this novel, by Marilynne Robinson, "Lila, homeless and alone after years of roaming the countryside, steps inside a small-town Iowa church--the only available shelter from the rain--and ignites a romance and a debate that will reshape her life. She becomes the wife of a minister, John Ames, and begins a new existence while trying to make sense of the life that preceded her newfound security." (Publisher's note)

A "passionate and learned moral and spiritual inquiry, a paean to the earth, and a witty and transcendent love story." Booklist

Robinson, Patrick

Kilo class. HarperCollins Pubs. 1998 442p $25

ISBN 0-06-019129-5

LC 97-51172

In this sequel to Nimitz class, "the plot concerns 10 formidable Soviet-built Kilo Class patrol submarines, which can run submerged at speeds up to 17 knots without being detected, travel 6,000 miles before refueling, and fire nuclear-tipped torpedoes. An insolvent Russian military has agreed to sell them to China. With the subs, China could control the Taiwan Strait, blocking Western trade routes. The Chinese could then attack and conquer Taiwan. The U.S. Navy must stop delivery of the subs without starting World War III." Booklist

Robinson, Patrick

Nimitz class. HarperCollins Pubs. 1997 411p il

LC 96-46872

"Military fiction fans will admire {the author's} authoritative exploitation of weaponry and tactics, however, and most readers will be engaged, despite some sluggish passages, by his persuasive cautionary tale about the perils of military downsizing at a time when rogue nations are amassing weapons of great and terrible destructiveness." Publ Wkly

Followed by Kilo class

Robinson, Peter

Cold is the grave. Morrow 2000 369p

ISBN 0-380-97808-3

LC 00-37231

"Banks discovers the precariousness of Emily's position in her new life and, more disturbingly, the grotesque truth behind a facade of perfect family life. A cunningly constructed plot, enhanced by Robinson's engaging descriptions and insights." Booklist

Robinson, Peter

The **first** cut. Dark Alley 2004 310p $13.95

ISBN 0-06-073535-X pa

LC 2003-67660

Published in the UK as Caedmon's Song

"Recent university graduate Kirsten survives a brutal Jack the Ripper-style attack of which she has no memory. As Kirsten recovers, she becomes fixated on finding the man who nearly killed her. Miles away, Martha has come to the coastal town of Whitby, where she is doing research for a book. Or is she? Carefully surveying her surroundings, Martha grows more obsessed with the object of her trip. The women's stories are told in alternate chapters until the unsettling end. This atmospheric tale of suspense will keep readers wondering what's really going on." Libr J

Robinson, Peter ✓

★ **Innocent** grave; an Inspector Banks mystery. Berkley Prime Crime 1996 346p

LC 95-38218

"Although the story follows the classical form of a whodunit, the characters have complexity and the issues range broad and deep, raising interesting moral questions about bigotry, class privilege and the terrible crime of being different." N Y Times Book Rev

Robinson, Peter ✓

Piece of my heart. William Morrow 2006 336p $24.95

ISBN 978-0-06-054435-5; 0-06-054435-X

LC 2005-58363

The author "invokes the most disturbing aspects of the 60's—to the point at which even the Manson murders have repercussions in Yorkshire—to sustain the book's ominous mood. There is pathos too, as Banks winds up revisiting characters who were young and energetic in 1969 but are now tea-sipping retirees." N Y Times (Late N Y Ed)

Robinson, Roxana

Cost. Farrar, Straus & Giroux 2008 420p $25

ISBN 978-0-374-27187-9; 0-374-27187-9

LC 2007-47954

"It's a nice touch that no one much likes Carpenter, the bossy and authoritative purveyor of unwelcome information. One of Robinson's most impressive achievements is to show that even in extreme situations, individual personalities come into play, and people respond in characteristic ways. . . . Bleak though it undeniably is, 'Cost' is also a warmly human and deeply satisfying book, marking a new level of ambition and achievement for this talented author." Chicago Tribune

Robinson, Roxana

A **perfect** stranger; and other stories. Random House 2005 235p $23.95

ISBN 0-375-50918-6

LC 2004-59537

Robinson's "finely tuned realism, as well as her settings and characters—New York, its bedroom communities, the Eastern seaboard and the comfortable upper-middle-class living there—recall Cheever and Updike. . . . The collection's most affecting stories touch on the chasm between parents and children, husbands and wives. Robinson's ear is wonderful, her graceful prose a real pleasure." Publ Wkly

Robinson, Roxana

Sparta; Roxana Robinson. Sarah Crichton Books/Farrar, Straus and Giroux 2013 400 p. (hardcover : alk. paper) $27

ISBN 0374267707; 9780374267704

LC 2012034611

In this novel, "Conrad entered the Marines shortly before 9/11 with an ambition to do something big: He studied Greek military history in college, admiring the discipline of city-states like Sparta (hence the title) but neglecting that place's undercurrent of hubris. Returning home after two tours in Iraq to his sturdily middle-class family outside New York, Conrad is incapable of shaking off his experience." (Kirkus Reviews)

Robinson, Roxana

Sweetwater; a novel. Random House 2003 319p $24.95

ISBN 0-375-50916-X

LC 2002-31830

"Robinson writes big solid scenes bubbling with tension, that hold the reader's interest. She has always shown her characters' flaws, and the dark emotions stirred up by divorce and parenthood; here she has reached farther to relate her characteristic predicaments to the larger world outside." N Y Times Book Rev

Robinson, Spider

Callahan's con. Tor Bks. 2003 286p $23.95

ISBN 0-7653-0270-5

LC 2003-40285

"When Jake Stonebender and his wife, Zoey, move to Florida and open up the Place, the latest incarnation of the unusual bar once known as Callahan's Place, he acquires a collection of strange friends, including a talking German shepherd, a merman, and a foul-mouthed parrot. An encounter with the Florida bureaucracy over the homeschooling of his hyperintelligent daughter, Erin, and the intrusion of the local Mafia result in a grand scheme to outwit both intrusions and rescue Jake's missing wife in the process. Robinson's latest entry in his Callahan series features more zaniness, good humor, and bad jokes." Libr J

Robotham, Michael, 1960- ✓

Say you're sorry; Michael Robotham. Mulholland Books 2012 433 p. $24.99

ISBN 0316221244; 9780316221245

LC 2012020772

In this novel by Michael Robotham, part of the Joe O'Loughlin series, "pretty and popular teenagers Piper Hadley and Tash McBain disappear one Sunday morning. . . . Three years later, during the worst blizzard in a century, a husband and wife are brutally killed in the farmhouse where Tash McBain once lived. A suspect is in custody, a troubled young man who can hear voices and claims that he saw a girl that night being chased by a snowman." (Publisher's note)

Robotham, Michael, 1960- ✓

★ **Suspect**; Michael Robotham. Doubleday 2005 360p. $24.95; (pbk.) $13.95

ISBN 0385508611; 9788496940277

LC 2004050156

This mystery thriller tells the story of "Joe O'Loughlin, a London psychologist, [who] loves his job and loves his family. . . . O'Loughlin's life takes two disastrous turns: first, he's diagnosed with Parkinson's disease; second, while helping Det. Insp. Vincent Ruiz on the case of a murdered nurse, Catherine Mary McBride, he becomes the primary suspect in the killing. The crime occurred close to O'Loughlin's London home, giving him opportunity, and it turns out that McBride had been his patient and had accused him of harassment, giving him plenty of motive." (Publishers Weekly)

Robotham, Michael

The **wreckage**. Mulholland Books/Little, Brown and Co. 2011 439p $24.99

ISBN 978-0-316-12640-3; 0-316-12640-3

LC 2011-12657

After being robbed of his briefcase, ex-cop Vincent Ruiz tracks down the thieves, who had mistaken him for someone else, and becomes unwittingly involved in unraveling plots surrounding bank bombings in Baghdad and a missing VP at an international finance powerhouse.

"This fast-paced, gritty, and violent tale of international crime and investigation, with a sharp political edge, will appeal to readers seeking summer fiction with depth." Libr J

Robson, Justina

Keeping it real. Pyr 2007 337p pa $15

ISBN 978-1-59102-539-9; 1-59102-539-7

LC 2007-483

First title in the author's Quantam gravity series

First published 2006 in the United Kingdom

"Life is anything but real in this entertaining fusion of SF and fantasy spiced with sex, rockin' elves and drunk faeries. . . . Deft prose helps the reader accept what in lesser hands would be merely absurd." Publ Wkly

Robson, Justina

Living next door to the god of love. Bantam Books 2006 453p pa $13

ISBN 0-553-58742-0

LC 2005-56271

Robson "handles her characters' voices with confidence and wit, weaving together multiple stories to produce an elaborate whole that's somehow, finally, compacted into a simple seed, a timeless myth of death and resurrection." Strange Horizons.com

Rock, Peter

My abandonment. Houghton Mifflin Harcourt 2008 240p $22

ISBN 978-0-15-101414-9; 0-15-101414-0

LC 2007-44412

"The narrative unfolds as a meditative interior monologue, with some of the plot developing beyond Caroline's immature comprehension, leaving tantalizing gaps for the reader to fill. Gaps that may be filled with crime and sex. Yet bit by bit steady as water dripping on limestone reality carves a groove in Caroline's consciousness, turning her childhood trust into a sense of betrayal. . . . If this is a Bildungsroman, it's one for grownups. Caroline comes of age in circumstances so harsh yet so tender that her redemption will be tempered by loss and uncommon learning." Newsday

Rock, Peter

The **Shelter** Cycle; Peter Rock. Houghton Mifflin Harcourt 2013 224 p. (hardcover) $23

ISBN 0547859082; 9780547859088

LC 2012040363

In this book, "Francine and Colville are friends who grew up in the Church Universal and Triumphant, adherents of the Violet Flame. Members believed in the coming apocalypse and the possibility of Soviet air strikes, building underground bunkers to protect themselves. But nothing happened, and the community broke up, leaving the two friends to negotiate the larger world on their own. Now married and pregnant, Francine is searching for a girl gone missing from her Idaho town when Colville shows up." (Library Journal)

Rodriguez, Linda

Every broken trust; Linda Rodriguez. 1st ed. Thomas Dunne Books/Minotaur Books 2013 304 p. (hardcover) $25.99

ISBN 1250030358; 9781250030351

LC 2013006992

In this novel, by Linda Rodriguez, "a party to celebrate the arrival of George 'Mel' Melvin, a Kansas City politician . . . , rapidly turns into disaster when Skeet's best friend, Karen Wise, stumbles on a body in Chouteau University's storage caves and is attacked herself. . . . Skeet . . . serving as chief of campus police . . . must struggle against the clock to solve a series of linked murders before . . . her best friend winds up in jail--or worse." (Publisher's note)

Rodriguez, Linda

Every hidden fear; a Skeet Bannion mystery. Linda Rodriguez. Minotaur Books 2014 304 p. (hardback) $26.99

ISBN 1250049156; 9781250049155

LC 2014008152

In this book, by Linda Rodriguez, "Ash Mowbray, a bad boy from the wrong side of the tracks, comes back to Brewster as a wealthy developer, pushing plans to build a shopping mall on the outskirts of town. . . . Mowbray makes things worse by announcing that he is the real father of the high school athlete Noah Steen. . . . It's not long before Mowbray turns up murdered with Noah as the prime suspect. . . . Noah's girlfriend Angie turn[s] to Skeet to find the murderer." (Publisher's note)

"This is a strong series featuring a multidimensional heroine." Booklist.

Rodriguez, Linda

Every last secret; a mystery. Linda Rodriguez. Minotaur Books 2012 289 p. (hardcover) $24.99

ISBN 1250005450; 9781250005458; 9781466802285

LC 2012005484

In this book, "former Kansas City police officer Marquitta 'Skeet' Bannion now heads a small college's police force in a nearby Missouri town. Things fire up pretty quickly when the college newspaper's student editor, Andrew, is murdered at his desk. Not well liked, the victim had a number of enemies on campus. . . . When Skeet figures out that Andrew was blackmailing several individuals," she realizes the murderer isn't done yet. (Library Journal)

Rogan, Charlotte

The **lifeboat**; a novel. Charlotte Rogan. Little, Brown and Co. 2012 278 p.

ISBN 0316185906; 9780316185905

LC 2011032492

This book, "[s]et at the beginning of WWI," is "[Charlotte] Rogan's debut" and "follows 22-year-old Grace Winter, a newlywed, newly minted heiress who survives . . . three weeks at sea following the sinking of her ocean liner and the disappearance of her husband, Henry. Safe at home in the U.S., Grace and two other survivors are put on trial for their actions aboard the under-built, overloaded lifeboat. At sea, as food and water ran out, and passengers realized that some among them would die, questions of sacrifice and duty arose. Rogan interweaves the trial with a . . . day-by-day story of Grace's time aboard the lifeboat, and circles around society's ideas about what it means to be human, what responsibilities we have to each other, and whether we can be blamed for choices made in order to survive." (Publishers Wkly)

Rogers, Rob

Devil's Cape. Wizards of the Coast Discoveries 2008 409p il pa $14.95

ISBN 978-0-786949-01-4; 0-786949-01-5

LC 2007-21311

"Devil's Cape is a town in Louisiana, just a few miles away from New Orleans. The town was founded by pirates and, today, the bad guys rule in Devil's Cape. Pity any superhero who dares try to fight them. If they can't kill you, they'll kill your family. If you don't have a family, they'll find someone close to you to kill, whatever it takes for them to keep their power over you – and the city. Rogers creates a vivid and vibrant world from whole cloth which seems like it truly can exist right outside your window. And that is what makes this book so successful. Devil's Cape is a quick read in the best sense of the word. It is truly difficult to put down. It proudly deserves a place next to Tom Clancy and Stephen King as a sterling example of the best of genre fiction. Even if you don't like superheroes, you are bound to be captivated by Devil's Cape." PopMatters

Rogues; edited by George R.R. Martin and Gardner Dozois. Bantam Books 2014 832 p. (hardback) $30

ISBN 0345537262; 9780345537263; 9780804179607

LC 2014010317

Edgar Award: Best Short Story for "What Do You Do?" by Gillian Flynn (2015)

Edited by George R. R. martin and Gardner Dozois, this fantasy fiction short story collection includes stories by "Gillian Flynn, Joe Abercrombie, Neil Gaiman, Patrick Rothfuss, Scott Lynch, Cherie Priest, Garth Nix, and Connie Willis, as well as other masters of literary sleight-of-hand. . . . And George R. R. Martin himself offers a brand-new A Game of Thrones tale chronicling one of the biggest rogues in the entire history of Ice and Fire." (Publisher's note)

"The wide array of styles and genres mean that this is easiest to dip in and out of rather than read cover to cover, but there is not a single bad story in the bunch. Perhaps inevitable owing to Martin's coediting (with skilled anthologist Dozois), some of the most exquisitely written are the fantasy descriptions." LJ

Includes bibliographical references

Roiphe, Anne Richardson

An **imperfect** lens; a novel. [by] Anne Roiphe. Shaye Areheart Books 2006 296p $25

ISBN 1-4000-8211-0

LC 2005-11250

"Commissioned by an aging Louis Pasteur to identify and isolate the cholera microbe and 'bring glory to France,' an eclectic band of young researchers arrive in plague-stricken Alexandria in 1883. Set loose in this exotic locale, these novice scientists face a daunting task as pestilence and disease ravage the city. In addition to racing against time and famed German scientist Dr. Robert Koch, the team members face multiple political, cultural, and romantic distractions. Roiphe does an incredible job of painting paradoxical portraits of collective fear and coolheaded reason as she painstakingly reconstructs the life cycle of a deadly epidemic. This authentically detailed blend of fact and fiction gift wraps the history of an astonishing medical and scientific breakthrough inside an irresistible love story, providing a little something for everyone across a wide spectrum of readers." Booklist

Roiphe, Anne Richardson

★ **Lovingkindness**; a novel. by Anne Roiphe. Summit Bks. 1987 279p

LC 87-6448

"Annie Johnson, widowed before the birth of her daughter Andrea, is a modern, successful, professional woman. Her relations with Andrea has been marked with alienation on her daughter's part, as she appears to be intent on destroying her life as a drop-out from schools, an abuser of drugs, and a young woman who has already experienced three abortions. Annie Johnson seeks psychiatric help for Andrea with no success. It is not until Andrea, finding herself a visitor in Israel, is taken into a yeshiva community that some change in her behavior comes about. The rigorous, although warm, Jewish orthodox discipline appears to change Andrea into a submissive young woman living a life completely foreign to anything her mother understands. The destruction inherent in some parent-child conflicts is painfully described here." Shapiro. Fic for Youth. 3d edition

Rojstaczer, Stuart

The **Mathematician's** Shiva; a novel. Stuart Rojstaczer. Penguin Books 2014 384 p. (paperback) $16

ISBN 0143126318; 9780143126317

LC 2014012521

National Jewish Book Awards Winner: Debut Fiction (2014)

In Stuart Rojstaczer's novel "when the greatest female mathematician . . . passes away, her son, [Sasha], just wants to mourn. But rumor has it [she] has solved one of the most difficult problems in all of mathematics, and has spitefully taken the solution to her grave. As a ragtag group of mathematicians from around the world descends upon Rachela's shiva, determined to find the proof or solve it for themselves . . . Sasha must come to terms with his mother's outsized influence on his life." (Publisher's note)

"Though Rojstaczer doesn't have the spikey wit of Gary Shteyngart or the inventiveness of Michael Chabon, his steadiness and empathy are appealing in their own ways. A geophysicist, he brings an added dimension to the book's discussions of scientific matters. He's very good at exploring the apparent divide between genius and happiness as well as the intersection of cultures. An enjoyable debut, the book is distinguished by a fluid, lyrical style that is equally at home with serious and comic matters." Kirkus

Rollins, James

The **blood** Gospel; James Rollins and Rebecca Cantrell. William Morrow 2013 496 p. (hardcover) $27.99

ISBN 006199104X; 9780061991042

LC 2012031044

In this novel, by James Rollins and Rebecca Cantrell, "a military forensic expert, . . . a Vatican priest[,] and . . . a brilliant but disillusioned archaeologist" explore a recently discovered tomb. "But a brutal attack at the site sets the three on the run, thrusting them into a race to recover what was once preserved in the tomb's sarcophagus: a book rumored to have been written by Christ's own hand, a tome that is said to hold the secrets to His divinity." (Publisher's note)

Rollins, James

The **devil** colony. William Morrow 2011 480p map $27.99

ISBN 978-0-06-178478-1

LC 2011-15981

This is the seventh novel in the author's Sigma Force series. "While exploring a mysterious cavern full of desiccated human bodies in the Rocky Mountains of Utah, two teenage boys discover the gold-coated skull of a saber-toothed tiger atop a granite plinth. Later, after others bring this prehistoric artifact to the surface, it triggers a blast that creates a strange force that dissolves rock and eats its way into the ground, eventually unleashing a volcano. When the members of the special forces unit known as Sigma, led by Painter Crowe, investigate, they uncover a massive conspiracy that has its roots in Mormonism, Native American legends, Thomas Jefferson, and explorer Meriwether Lewis, to name just a few of the fascinating characters and scientific threads that stitch this intricate action thriller together." Publ Wkly

Rollins, James

The **eye** of God; a Sigma Force novel. James Rollins. William Morrow, An Imprint of HarperCollinsPublishers 2013 432 p. (A Sigma Force novel) (alk. paper) $27.99

ISBN 006178480X; 9780061784804

LC 2013016685

This book is part of James Rollins's Sigma Force series. Here, a "satellite crashes in Mongolia, but before it does, it transmits what appears to be an image of Boston, New York City, and Washington, D.C. in ruins. The image, it turns out, is time-shifted from the very near future by about 90 hours. . . . As Painter Crowe, head of Sigma, tries to understand the situation, operative Gray Pierce learns of an ancient relic that seems to predict the imminent disaster." Can Sigma Force prevent it? (Booklist)

Includes bibliographical references and index

Rolvaag, Ole Edvart

★ **Giants** in the earth; a saga of the prairie. by O. E. Rölvaag; translated from the Norwegian. Harper 1927 465p

This novel "chronicles the struggles of Norwegian immigrant settlers in the Dakota territory in the 1870s. . . . The book's indomitable protagonist, Per Hansa, his wife Beret, their children, and three other Norwegian immigrant families settle at Spring Creek, living in makeshift sod huts. Surviving the winters' fierce blizzards, they see their crops destroyed by locusts in summer. They nonetheless persist; new settlers arrive, and the community grows." Merriam-Webster's Ency of Lit

Followed by Peder Victorious

Rolvaag, Ole Edvart

Peder Victorious; a novel. by O. E. Rölvaag; translated from the Norwegian; English text by Nora O. Solum and the author. Harper 1929 350p

"Carries on the characters of 'Giants in the earth,' the interest centering in Peder Victorious and Beret, the boy's mother, against the background of a community no longer intensely struggling with the soil, but adapting itself to the ways of the new country, or resisting adaptation as Beret continues to do. The boy Peder, with his changing ideas and his ardent pursuit of girls is a foil for the character of Beret, perhaps the most finely conceived personality in the book." N Y Libr

Followed by Their father's God (1931)

Romano, Stephen

Resurrection Express; Stephen Romano. 1st Gallery Books hc. ed. Gallery Books 2012 437 p. (hardcover) $25.00; (trade paperback) $7.99

ISBN 1451668643; 9781451668643; 9781451668650; 9781451668667

LC 2012015053

In this mystery novel, "[t]wo years after . . . Elroy Coffin survived a gunshot to the head that's affected his memory," he's in prison. "Wealthy and well-connected Jayne Jenison [visits and] tells him his . . . wife, Toni, whom he believed dead, is still alive. Jenison promises to get Coffin released . . . if he'll agree to help track down her grown daughter, who's being held . . . along with Toni." (Publishers Weekly)

Romano-Lax, Andromeda

The **Spanish** bow. Harcourt 2007 554p $25

ISBN 978-0-15-101542-9; 0-15-101542-2

LC 2006-100937

"Expertly woven throughout the book are cameo appearances by Pablo Picasso, Adolf Hitler, Francisco Franco, Bertolt Brecht, and others, but it is the fictional Feliu, Justo, and Aviva who will keep you mesmerized to the last page." Christ Sci Monit

Roncagliolo, Santiago

Red April; translated from Spanish by Edith Grossman. Pantheon Books 2009 271p $24.95

ISBN 978-0-375-42544-8; 0-375-42544-6

LC 2008-36654

Original Spanish edition, 2006

"In 2000, associate district prosecutor Félix Chacaltana Saldívar, who's returned to the province of Ayacucho from Lima, clashes with his superiors after the discovery of a charred and mutilated corpse. Rigidly adhering to bureaucratic procedure, Saldívar demands that an official police report on the crime be filed, despite the active resistance of the police and the local military commander. The prosecutor's refusal to abort his inquiry threatens the official line that the Shining Path terrorists are a thing of the past. Eventually, he's reassigned to help monitor elections, only to encounter more corruption." Publ Wkly

Rooney, Kathleen

★ **Lillian** Boxfish Takes a Walk; by Kathleen Rooney. St. Martin's Press 2017 304 p. (ebook) $60; $25.99

ISBN 9781250113337; 1250113326; 9781250113320

LC 2016036418

In this novel, by Kathleen Rooney, "it's the last night of 1984 and Lillian, 85 years old but just as sharp and savvy as ever, is on her way to a party. It's chilly enough out for her mink coat and Manhattan is grittier now—her son keeps warning her about a subway vigilante on the prowl—but the quick-tongued poetess has never been one to scare easily." (Publisher's note)

"Elegantly written, Rooney creates a glorious paean to a distant literary life and time—and an unabashed celebration of human connections that bridge the past and future." Pub Wkly

Includes bibliographical references (pages 286-287).

Roorbach, Bill

Life among giants; a novel. by Bill Roorbach. Algonquin Books of Chapel Hill 2012 331 p. $24.95

ISBN 1616200766; 9781616200763

LC 2012016965

In this novel by Bill Roorbach "David 'Lizard' Hochmeyer is nearly seven feet tall, a star quarterback, and Princeton-bound. His future seems all but assured until his parents are mysteriously murdered, leaving Lizard and his older sister, Kate, adrift and alone. Sylphide, the world's greatest ballerina, lives across the pond from their Connecticut home, . . . and it turns out that her rock star husband's own disasters have intersected with Lizard's--and Kate's." (Publisher's note)

Roosevelt, Elliott

The **Hyde** Park murder. St. Martin's Press 1985 231p

LC 85-1752

"The author's fascinating glimpses into history, into the Roosevelts at home, and into corrupt politics are delivered in a measured and surefooted manner." Booklist

Roosevelt, Elliott

Murder and the First Lady. St. Martin's Press 1984 227p

LC 83-24659

"This historical mystery is set just before World War II, when international tensions are at a peak. Philip Garber, a lowly bookkeeper and assistant to the chief usher at the White House, is found murdered. Eleanor Roosevelt turns sleuth when it's discovered that Garber was found dead in the room of her British secretary, Pamela Rush-Hodgeborne." Booklist

Roosevelt, Elliott

Murder at midnight; an Eleanor Roosevelt mystery. St. Martin's Press 1997 216p $20.95

ISBN 0-312-15596-4

LC 96-53530

"Judge Horace Blackwell, friend and adviser to the president, is stabbed to death in his White House suite, and Sara Carter, a black maid, is arrested after finding the body. After promising the girl a fair hearing and gaining the confidence of lead investigator Lawrence Pickering, Eleanor takes an active role. Her doubts about Sara's guilt lead to some disturbing discoveries, not least of which is that the judge appears to have been a sadistic womanizer. . . . Peopled with famous lights of 1933, including Babe Ruth, William Faulkner and Gertrude Stein, Washington, D.C., is bought to life in the mirror of the White House." Publ Wkly

Roosevelt, Elliott

Murder in the map room; an Eleanor Roosevelt mystery. St. Martin's Press 1998 251p il $21.95

ISBN 0-312-18168-X

LC 97-37243

"When Mrs. Roosevelt discovers a murder in the White House during the state visit of Madame Chiang Kai-shek in 1943, her investigation is hampered by both diplomatic protocol and the fact that the U.S. is deeply involved in a war raging on two fronts. . . . As usual, Elliot Roosevelt's respectfully playful portrayal of his down-to-earth mother as a clever sleuth is enough to keep the pages turning." Booklist

Roosevelt, Elliott

Murder in the Oval Office; an Eleanor Roosevelt mystery. St. Martin's Press 1989 247p

LC 88-18848

"Her sense of justice (not to mention her curiosity) sparked by the murder of a Southern Congressman during a White House soiree, the resourceful First Lady shows spunk and wit, and also considerable charm, in her investigation of the locked room puzzle." N Y Times Book Rev

Roosevelt, Kermit

In the shadow of the law. Farrar, Straus and Giroux 2005 370p $24

ISBN 0-374-26187-3

LC 2004-24222

This novel "portrays life inside a cutthroat corporate firm in Washington." (N Y Times Book Rev)

This novel "goes behind the scenes at Morgan Siler, one of Washington, D.C.'s most powerful K Street law firms, as several lawyers become embroiled in two difficult cases: a pro bono death penalty case in Virginia and a class action suit brought against a Texas chemical corporation after an explosion kills dozens of workers. . . . Though the novel features plenty of satisfying twists and turns, the book transcends the legal thriller genre. Roosevelt . . . offers a fascinating insider's look into the culture of a high-stakes firm, while also presenting a considered meditation on the law itself and its potential to compromise those driven to practice it." Publ Wkly

Rosales, Guillermo

The **halfway** house; introduction by Jose Manuel Prieto; translated by Anna Kushner. New Directions 2009 121p pa $14.95

ISBN 978-0-8112-1802-3

LC 2009-05947

Written 1987; original Spanish edition, 2003

A "story set in a Miami home for the mentally ill. William Figueras, a 38-year-old [exiled schizophrenic Cuban writer] . . . , is deposited in a boarding house by his aunt, because nothing more can be done. His writing was deemed morose, pornographic, and also irrelevant by the Cuban government, and now he has grown as hopeless and abandoned as the other desperate outcasts who inhabit the shabby home owned by the miserly Mr. Curbelo and run by a beer-guzzling flunky named Arsenio. Figueras despises the other residents and clearly recognizes how they are being exploited by Mr. Curbelo and Arsenio, yet out of his own state of self-debasement, he joins in the cruelty. Briefly, hope inspires him in the form of a new female inmate, and together they plan an escape. However, life outside promises to be more treacherous than staying in the ward. It's a frightening, nihilistic cousin of One Flew Over the Cuckoo's Nest." Publ Wkly

Rose, Joel

Blackest bird; a novel of murder in nineteenth-century New York. W.W. Norton 2007 479p $24.95

ISBN 978-0-393-06231-1; 0-393-06231-7

LC 2006-31703

"Rose does a scrupulous and impressive job of mustering the pace and mood of the rapidly expanding city, its still pastoral fringes and its customs." PopMatters

Rose, M. J.

Seduction; a novel of suspense. by M.J. Rose. Atria Books 2013 372 p. (hardcover) $24.00

ISBN 1451621507; 9781451621501

LC 2013005582

This book follows "Jac L'Etoile . . . a mythologist by trade and perfumer by pedigree. . . . Jac has been dodging her painful past for years. . . . [M. J.] Rose's time-shifting narrative recounts French novelist Victor Hugo's exile on the Isle of Jersey and his participation in hundreds of séances. In the present day, Jac is lured by the island's Celtic history and becomes enmeshed in a family drama that seems to stem back to ancient times." (Library Journal)

Includes bibliographical references and index

Rose-Innes, Henrietta

Nineveh; Henrietta Rose-Innes. Unnamed Press 2016 201 p. (paperback) $16

ISBN 9781939419972; 9781944700270; 1939419972

LC 2016954665

In this book, by Henrietta Rose-Innes, "Katya Grubbs is Cape Town's only ethical pest removal specialist . . . with the help of her unwitting nephew, Toby. When she is hired to remove the exotic beetles that have overrun Nineveh, a new luxury housing development on the coast, Katya finds that bugs aren't the only unwelcome creatures. . . . As she investigates further, it becomes clear that Nineveh is fast becoming an environmental, not to mention architectural, blunder." (Publisher's note)

"A persuasive, witty exploration of a tough and unconventional young woman—and a consistently lively account of the entanglements of cultural politics, class, and architecture in contemporary South Africa." Kirkus

Rosen, Jonathan

Joy comes in the morning. Farrar, Straus and Giroux 2004 389p $25

ISBN 0-374-18026-1

LC 2004-1742

"In her work as a hospital volunteer, Deborah Green, a Manhattan rabbi, encounters an ailing Holocaust survivor—recovering from a debilitating stroke and a suicide attempt—and his skeptical son. To complicate matters, she is beautiful and single, while the skeptical son is a shy bachelor; the romance causes crises of faith for both, as they negotiate their divergent attitudes toward their religion. As the story moves from wedding to funeral and back again, and Deborah officiates at the momentous changes in other people's lives, she increasingly finds her own life empty of the things that she has always counselled her congregation to treasure. Served with the merest teaspoon of schmaltz, Rosen's touching novel of Jewish manners thoughtfully addresses the question of whether piety can teach us faith." New Yorker

Includes bibliographical references and index

Rosen, Renée

★ **Dollface**; a novel of the roaring twenties. Renee Rosen. New American Library 2013 416 p. $15

ISBN 0451419200; 9780451419200

LC 2012051794

This novel, by Renee Rosen, tells the story of "America in the 1920s. . . . Vera Abramowitz is determined to . . . live a more exciting life. . . . As the ultimate flapper, Vera captures the attention of two high rollers. . . . She thinks her biggest problem is choosing between them until the truth comes out. Her two lovers are really mobsters from rival gangs during Chicago's infamous Beer Wars, a battle Al Capone refuses to lose." (Publisher's note)

Rosenberg, Joel C.

Damascus Countdown; Joel C. Rosenberg. Tyndale House Publishers, Inc. 2013 470 p. (hardcover) $26.99

ISBN 1414319703; 9781414319704

LC 2012040475

This is Joel C. Rosenberg's third David Shirazi novel. Here, the Iranian-born agent "has infiltrated the jihadist regime in Iran. Although Israel has successfully launched a first strike, destroying Iran's nuclear sites, two Iranian warheads have survived. David moves quickly to find the surviving warheads before the Twelfth Imam can launch a retaliation and bring about full-scale war." (Library Journal)

Rosenberg, Joel C.

The **Tehran** initiative; Joel C. Rosenberg. Tyndale House Publishers, Inc. 2011 xiii, 462 p.p (hardcover) $26.99

ISBN 1414319355; 9781414319353

LC 2011026051

This book is in Joel C. Rosenberg's David Shirazi series. Here, he "continues to work undercover to glean information about Iran's plan to eradicate Israel and the United States through a nuclear attack. In Tehran, the Twelfth Imam has emerged, attracting those Muslims who believe him to be the messiah and call for the destruction of those who would oppose them." (Library Journal)

Rosenberg, Joel C.

The **twelfth** Imam; Joel C. Rosenberg. Tyndale House Publishers 2010 viii, 490p o.p.; o.p.; (pbk.) $14.99

ISBN 141431163X; 9781414311630; 9781414311647

LC 2010030082

In this book, the 2011 Retailers Choice Award winner, "[a]s the apocalyptic leaders of Iran call for the annihilation of Israel and the U.S., CIA operative David Shirazi is sent into Tehran with one objective: use all means necessary to disrupt Iran's nuclear weapons program—without . . . triggering a regional war. . . . [N]one of his training has prepared Shirazi for what will happen next. An obscure religious cleric is suddenly hailed throughout the region as the Islamic messiah known as the Mahdi or the Twelfth Imam. News of his miracles, healings, signs, and wonders, spread like wildfire, as do rumors of a new and horrific war. With the prophecy of the Twelfth Imam seemingly fulfilled, Iran's leaders prepare to strike Israel and bring about the End of Days." (Publisher's note)

Rosenberg, Nancy Taylor

Abuse of power. Dutton 1997 326p $23.95

ISBN 0-525-93768-4

LC 96-44141

In this novel, "policewoman Rachel Simmons takes on a corruption-riddled police force. Molested as a child, she is filled with a fiery purpose and uncompromising honesty. These scruples act against her when she witnesses an abuse of police authority and reports it. The duel between Rachel's conscience and her own family's safety forms the basis of the plot line. The novel moves rapidly to a powerful conclusion." Libr J

Rosenberg, Nancy Taylor

First offense. Dutton 1994 338p

LC 94-550

"Just when readers will have figured all the angles, savvy Rosenberg unveils the villain and flips the plot into an exciting manhunt, with Ann as bait." Publ Wkly

Rosenberg, Nancy Taylor

Interest of justice; a novel. Dutton 1993 368p

LC 93-13005

"Lara Sanderstone is such an intelligent, finely detailed character that even the unlikeliest plot twists work in this absorbing legal thriller." Publ Wkly

Rosenberg, Nancy Taylor

Mitigating circumstances. Dutton 1993 362p

LC 92-23035

"For all the adrenaline that the author pumps into her story, her writing is far more persuasive when it isn't so feverish—during intimate mother-daughter exchanges, for example, and in the realistically mundane procedures of ordinary, hard-working cops and lawyers." N Y Times Book Rev

Rosenberg, Nancy Taylor

Sullivan's law. Kensington Bks. 2004 314p $24

ISBN 0-7582-0618-6

Carolyn Sullivan is a "probation officer attending night school to become an attorney. Juggling her coursework and her job is hard enough, let alone having to worry about how she'll handle single parenthood with her preteen daughter and college-bound son. Carolyn's pressures only mount when one of her probationary charges, convicted killer and paranoid schizophrenic Daniel Metroix, is arrested for rape. . . . Rosenberg puts it all together here with another thoroughly believable heroine dealing with corruption, greed, deceit, and danger." Booklist

Rosenberg, Robert

This is not civilization. Houghton Mifflin 2004 293p $24

ISBN 0-618-38601-7

"This is risky comedy that in less deft hands would clunk into condescension, but Rosenberg keeps it aloft with a sweet sense of appreciation. . . . What a generous, bighearted book this is, perceptive enough to catch the goodness in all these well-intentioned people." Christ Sci Monit

Rosenblatt, Roger

Lapham rising. Ecco 2006 243p $23.95

ISBN 0-06-083361-0

LC 2005-48835

"This is a zany tale. It is a comic novel perfectly conjugated, moving the reader with delight through a three-act plot featuring a hero who is slightly mad, not quite prevailing over the antagonist, who is slightly mad; all of this with appropriate commentary from Hector, a talking dog who is pious and insolent." National Rev

Rosenfeld, Lucinda

I'm so happy for you; a novel about best friends. Little, Brown 2009 268p pa $13.99

ISBN 978-0-316-04450-9 pa; 0-316-04450-4 pa

LC 2008-45124

"The hapless, too-eager-to-please heroine of Rosenfeld's new novel is an ill-paid editor at an obscure leftist journal who secretly resents her husband for abandoning his job to write a sci-fi screenplay and for failing to get her pregnant. No wonder she thrills to the travails of her best friend, a suicidal beauty who has always overshadowed her but is now languishing in a dead-end affair. Then, to her chagrin, her friend meets Mr. Right. The book's confectionery veneer belies a heart of poison, as Rosenfeld tartly dispels the cherished chick-lit notion that female friendship conquers all. Equally ruthless is her sendup of overachieving New York women in feral pursuit of have-it-all motherhood without having first ascertained if they even like children." New Yorker

Rosenfelt, David

Don't tell a soul. St. Martin's Minotaur 2008 306p $24.95
ISBN 978-0-312-37395-5; 0-312-37395-3

LC 2008-14777

"Rosenfelt keeps the plot hopping and popping as he reveals a complex frameup of major proportions with profound political ramifications both terrifying and enlightening." Publ Wkly

Rosero Diago, Evelio

★ The **armies**; [by] Evelio Rosero; translated from the Spanish by Anne McLean. New Directions 2009 199p pa $14.95
ISBN 978-0-8112-1864-1; 0-8112-1864-3

LC 2009-19620

Original Spanish edition, 2007

"The novel begins idyllically with a rural scene saturated in color and lust: Ismail, retired teacher, spends his days picking oranges and stealing glimpses of his neighbor's naked, sunbathing wife. Mortified, Otilia, Ismail's wife of 40 years, urges her husband to confess his misdeed. But Ismail never seeks out the priest. Instead, he wanders through San Jose, meeting up with old friends. Through their beautifully written conversations, San Jose's troubled past emerges: kidnappings, murders and violent incursions that rocked the town only four years ago and threaten it once more. When Ismail returns home, Otilia is missing, and as he searches for her, armed forces begin to sack the town." Time Out N Y

Rosero Diago, Evelio

Good offices. New Directions 2011 119p pa $13.95
ISBN 978-0-8112-1930-3

LC 2011-12524

Original Spanish edition, 2009

"Tancredo, a young hunchback, observes and participates in the rites at the Catholic church where he lives under the care of Father Almida. Also in residence are the sexton Celeste Machado, his goddaughter Sabina Cruz, and three widows known collectively as the Lilias, who do the cooking and cleaning and provide charity meals for the local poor and needy. One Thursday, Father Almida and the sexton must rush off to meet the parish's principal benefactor, Don Justiniano. It will be the first time in forty years Father Almida has not said mass. Eventually they find a replacement: Father Matamoros, a drunkard with a beautiful voice whose sung mass is spellbinding to all. The Lilias prepare a sumptuous meal for Father Matamoros, who persuades them to drink with him. Over the course of the long night the women and Tancredo lose their inhibitions and confess their sins and stories to this strange priest, and in the process reveal lives crippled by hypocrisy." Publisher's note

Ross, A.

Mr. Peanut; Adam Ross. Alfred A. Knopf 2010 335 p. $25.95
ISBN 978-0-307-27070-2; 0-307-27070-X; 030727070X; 9780307270702

LC 2009041693

"This story of a marriage, played out in flashbacks, . . . is told in alternating chapters by David Pepin and by Ward Hastroll, the police detective assigned to investigate Pepin after his wife, Alice, is found slumped on the kitchen floor, dead of anaphylactic shock (an offending peanut still wedged in her throat). Though Pepin argues that Alice who long battled obesity and depression took her own life, Hastroll isn't buying it, especially once he finds a link to a notorious hitman." Entertainment Wkly

Ross, Adam

Ladies and gentlemen. Alfred A. Knopf 2011 243p
ISBN 0-307-27071-8; 978-0-307-27071-9

LC 2011-6960

This book presents a "short-story collection [entitled] 'Ladies and Gentlemen,' . . . by [author Adam] Ross. . . . 'Futures,' the first and longest of the set, follows David Applebow . . . as he tries to find employment after losing his job as manager of a theater company. . . . 'When in Rome,' [is] about the disastrous relationship between two boys grown to manhood. . . . In another story, 'The Suicide Room,' Ross presents a college sophomore in a foursome slowly getting stoned in a dorm room, ending in a game of 'Can you top that?' and its repercussions. . . .The title story, 'Ladies and Gentlemen,' . . . packs the . . . life of Sara, a successful freelance writer on an interview assignment in Nashville when the past catches up to her, or she catches up with it." (Yale Review)

"Truly funny, original, acerbic [and] surprising. . . . Ross deftly dissects how our best efforts to establish intimacy or better ourselves in the economy can result in excruciating, if hilarious, humiliations. Amusing morality at its compulsive, can't-wait-to-pick-it-up-again best." AM N Y

Ross-Macdonald, Malcolm

For they shall inherit; a novel. {by} Malcolm Macdonald. St. Martin's Press 1985 591p

LC 84-52352

First published 1984 in the United Kingdom with title: In love and war

"MacDonald skillfully depicts the English class system and the struggles inherent in it. The characters are multifaceted and solidly drawn, and the writing is smooth. An absorbing portrayal of human emotion and an individual's will to prevail." Libr J

Ross-Macdonald, Malcolm

The **rich** are with you always; [by] Malcolm Macdonald. Knopf 1976 483p

"In this sequel to 'The World From Rough Stones' Macdonald continues the interlocking family dramas of John and Nora Stevenson, born dirt poor, driving hard for money and power in Victorian England, and Walter and Arabella Thornton, aristocratic, unhappy, the Stevensons' opposites in every way. It is Nora and John who dominate this part of the saga in the fierce get-rich-quick era of railroad schemes and bonanzas and bankruptcies." Publ Wkly

Followed by Sons of fortune (1978)

Ross-Macdonald, Malcolm

Tamsin Harte; [by] Malcolm Macdonald. St. Martin's Press 2000 345p il $24.95
ISBN 0-312-20628-3

LC 99-88104

"Set in a Cornish fishing village at the turn of the last century. . . . Tamsin Harte and her mother, Harriet, fall from the upper echelon of society when Tamsin's father dies and his shipping firm goes bankrupt. They open a boarding house to get by. Energetic, enterprising and ambitious, Tamsin discovers that she has a mind suited to business enterprises. (Her secret ambition is to build 'the best hotel in Cornwall.') When it comes to romance, however, she is still bound by tradition." Publ Wkly

Ross-Macdonald, Malcolm

The **Trevarton** inheritance; {by} Malcolm Macdonald. St. Martin's Press 1996 395p $24.95
ISBN 0-312-14748-1

LC 96-20035

"Macdonald always maintains a brisk narrative pace, and his sound social commentary adds to the reader's enjoyment." Publ Wkly

Ross-Macdonald, Malcolm

The **world** from rough stones; [by] Malcolm Macdonald. Knopf 1975 535p il

"This saga of England in 1839-40 and the start of a great railroad building dynasty opens fast and never once lets up its pace and drama. Above all, its people are believable human beings, caught up in the tumultuous movement of beginning social change." Publ Wkly

Followed by The rich are with you always

Rossner, Judith

Emmeline. Simon & Schuster 1980 331p

LC 80-15553

The author "handles her material so meticulously that she inspires a renewed respect for the complexities of skillful story-telling. Instead of propagandizing, she evinces complete respect for the period and setting of her story." Books of the Times

Rossner, Judith

★ **Looking** for Mr. Goodbar. Simon & Schuster 1975 284p

"The tale is stark, capably told, believable; Rossner's prose is a delight, and her sense of the inner life of her characters, all tortured, is deft and sure. This is a very good novel." Booklist

Rossner, Judith

Perfidia; a novel. Talese 1997 308p

LC 97-10882

"Rossner reveals a gritty new style, stripped down to the clean bones of feeling. 'Perfidia' is an unsparing close-up of the seductive attachment and growing repulsion of a mother and daughter who mean far too much to each other." N Y Times Book Rev

Rosten, Leo

Captain Newman, M.D. Harper 1962 331p

First published 1961 in the United Kingdom

"A book of great insight, warmth and humor. . . . It is a tremendously impressive piece of verbal tight-rope walking. There are the expected flashes of GI humor, the much-documented war of rank, there are also moments of great tenderness and understanding in this chronicle of that most delicate of explorations, the exploration into the shattered minds that are the common responsibilities of all of us." N Y Her Trib Books

Rotert, Rebecca

Last night at the blue angel; a novel. Rebecca Rotert. William Morrow 2014 320 p. (hardback) $25.99

ISBN 0062315285; 9780062315281; 9780062315298

LC 2013036555

This novel, by Rebecca Rotert, is "set against the backdrop of the early 1960s Chicago jazz scene. . . . Naomi Hill, a singer at the Blue Angel club, has been poised on the brink of stardom for nearly ten years. Finally, her big break arrives--the cover of 'Look' magazine. But success has come at enormous personal cost. . . . No one knows this better than Sophia, her clever ten-year-old daughter." (Publisher's note)

"Though the characters are very different, the author's interpretation of both emerges spot-on. And, while Naomi's journey is interesting, Sophia's story hooks the reader from the beginning and dominates." Kirkus

Roth, Gabriel

The **unknowns**; a novel. Gabriel Roth. Reagan Arthur Books 2013 224 p. $25

ISBN 031622328X; 9780316223287

LC 2012027289

In this book, a "dot-com millionaire with an analytical mind and crippled maturity clumsily negotiates the minefields of adult relationships. . . . Our nominal hero is Eric Muller, a tense, gifted programmer who hit it big with a bit of popular software. He has the serious hots for Maya Marcom, a journalist who's just old enough not to buy into Eric's bullshit moves." Painful childhood incidents from both Eric and Maya's pasts emerge. (Kirkus Reviews)

Roth, Henry

★ **Call** it sleep. Ballou, R.O. 1934 599p

"The years between the sixth and ninth birthdays of a young boy are described in this vivid, sensitive portrayal of a Jewish childhood in the ghettos of Brownsville, and the Lower East Side in New York. Because David's father is a violent and bitter man, the child always turns to his mother, with whom he is very close. Her love protects him from the terrors of street gangs, poverty, the sexual conflicts between his parents, and his own initiation into sex by a lame girl. A literary technique that distinguishes between the language used by members of this family when they are speaking their native tongue (Yiddish) and when they speak broken English they have learned as immigrants in the United States is an unusual feature in this remarkable book." Shapiro. Fic for Youth. 3d edition

Roth, Henry

A **diving** rock on the Hudson. St. Martin's Press 1995 418p (Mercy of a rude stream)

ISBN 0-312-11777-9

This second volume of the author's autobiographical cycle "continues the saga of Ira Stigman, teenage son of Orthodox Jewish immigrant parents, as he struggles to find his way in the larger world. Narrated by the now elderly Ira, it effectively evokes both life in 1920s New York and the angst of adolescent existence. In Ira's case, this angst results not only from the growing distance that separates his and his parents' views of the world but from uncontrollable urges that drive him to violate one of society's strongest taboos."

"Simultaneously, we are inside the mind of a troubled adolsecent and that of an aged but still mentally vital man, a man engaged with words, with concepts, obsessively reconsidering the role of the artist and in particular his own responsibility in portraying events truthfully." Booklist

Followed by From bondage

Roth, Henry

From bondage. St. Martin's Press 1996 397p (Mercy of a rude stream) $25.95

ISBN 0-312-14341-9

This third volume of Roth's autobiographical cycle "continues the story of Ira Stigman, son of East European Jewish immigrant parents and now college aged, as he struggles to find his way in 1920s New York. But, like the previous volumes, it is also the story of Ira the octogenarian writer who, nearing the end of his life, is trying to come to terms with both the forces and the choices that shaped it. Paralleling Roth's own experience, this volume focuses on the beginnings of what was to become a decade-long affair between Ira and NYU professor Edith Welles." Libr J

Followed by Requiem for Harlem

Roth, Henry

Requiem for Harlem. St. Martin's Press 1997 291p il (Mercy of a rude stream) $24.95

ISBN 0-312-16980-9

LC 97-17824

"Even as we see the older writer commenting ruefully on all that has come to pass, we see the young artist taking in every detail of the world. . . . And if it is hard to sympathize with either the egocentric youth or the rueful old man, taken together they meld into a living whole. This is Roth's achievement, this double vision of the artist as both young and old man, hungry and regretful, flawed and penitent." N Y Times Book Rev

Roth, Henry

★ A **star** shines over Mt. Morris Park. St. Martin's Press 1994 290p (Mercy of a rude stream)

LC 93-37270

"Mr. Roth remains an admirable craftsman, and the scenes of immigrant life in the second decade of the century are evoked with persuasive concreteness." N Y Times Book Rev

Followed by A diving rock on the Hudson

Roth, Joseph

★ The **collected** stories of Joseph Roth; translated with an introduction by Michael Hofmann. Norton 2002 400p $27.95

ISBN 0-393-04320-7

LC 2001-44747

The triumph of beauty explores the impact of a fickle hypochondriac on her husband. In the bust of the emperor an elderly nobleman continues to perform dutifully even after the state renders his commitment obsolete. The leviathan portrays a coral merchant preoccupied with the mystery of the exotic life forms that provide his livelihood

"Combining a shrewd reportorial eye with a taste for the fantastic and droll, Roth portrays characters living materially and spiritually impoverished lives in isolated Eastern European villages and those left homeless in their own homes in the tumultuous aftermath of World War I." Booklist

Roth, Philip

★ **American** pastoral. Houghton Mifflin 1997 423p

ISBN 0-395-86021-0

LC 96-49368

"This cultural horror story is deepened by Roth's genius for blending humor, pathos, sympathy and rage. . . . You will search the shelf of contemporary fiction long and hard to find a parental nightmare projected with the emotional force and verbal energy that Roth brings to American Pastoral." Time

Roth, Philip

The **American** trilogy, 1997-2000. Library of America 2011 1094p $40

ISBN 978-1-59853-103-9; 1-59853-103-4

LC 2011-923051

"The tragic hero of American Pastoral (1997) is Seymour 'Swede' Levov—a legendary high school athlete, a devoted family man, a hard worker, the prosperous inheritor of his father's Newark glove factory—who comes of age in thriving, triumphant postwar America. But everything he loves is lost when the country goes to war in Vietnam, and the family of this strong, confident master of social equilibrium is overwhelmed by the forces of disorder unleashed by the turbulent 1960s. I Married a Communist (1998) is set in America's anti-Communist 1940s. Radio actor Iron Rinn (born Ira Ringold) is a big Newark roughneck blighted by a brutal personal secret from which he is perpetually in flight. A self-educated ditchdigger turned popular performer, a six-foot six-inch Abe Lincoln look-alike, he emerges from serving in World War II a clandestine and formidable Communist. His passionate commitment to Marxist revolution in America will lead him to ruin in the era of the blacklist. The Human Stain (2000) concludes Roth's . . . trilogy of postwar American lives. . . . The time is 1998, the year of the presidential impeachment; the location is a small New England town, where an aging classics professor, Coleman Silk, is forced to retire when his colleagues declare him a racist. The charge is a lie, but the real truth about Silk would astonish his most virulent accuser." Publisher's note

Roth, Philip

★ The **anatomy** lesson. Farrar, Straus & Giroux 1983 291p

LC 83-11645

"A ferocious, heartfelt book. . . . One might venture to say that, like a goodly number of Roth's previous works, 'The Anatomy Lesson' revolves around the paradox of incarnation—the astonishing coexistence in one life of infantilism and intelligence, of selfishness and altruism, of sexual appetite and social conscience—and has the form and manner of a monologue conducted under psychoanalysis." New Yorker

Roth, Philip

The **dying** animal. Houghton Mifflin 2001 156p $22

ISBN 0-618-13587-1

LC 00-54225

"Like many works of modern literature, The Dying Animal ends on a note of radical ambiguity and indeterminacy. What is rather unusual about it is the way it challenges the reader at every point to define and defend his own ethical position toward the issues raised by the story. It is a small, disturbing masterpiece." N Y Rev Books

Roth, Philip

Everyman. Houghton Mifflin 2006 182p $24

ISBN 0-618-73516-X

LC 2005-31538

"From a distance, Everyman looks like a shaggy dog story—a long, quotidian story whose meaning resides in its final pointlessness. Up close, though, it is a parable that captures, as few works of fiction have, the pathos of Being, as it's manifested even in the favored precincts of affluent America." Washington Post Book World

Roth, Philip

Exit ghost. Houghton Mifflin 2007 292p $26

ISBN 0-618-91547-8; 978-0-618-91547-7

LC 2006-102467

According to the author, this is the final novel about his fictional surrogate, Nathan Zuckerman, the protagonist of The Ghost Writer (1979). "Zuckerman comes back to New York, the city he left eleven years before. Alone on his New England mountain, Zuckerman has been nothing but a writer: . . . no women, no news, no tasks other than his work and the enduring of old age. Walking the streets like a revenant, he quickly makes three connections that explode his carefully protected solitude. One is with a young couple with whom, in a rash moment, he offers to swap homes. . . . From the time he meets them, Zuckerman also wants to swap his solitude for the erotic challenge of the young woman, Jamie. . . . The second connection is with a figure from Zuckerman's youth, Amy Bellette, companion and muse to Zuckerman's first literary hero, E. I. Lonoff. . . . Amy is now an old woman depleted by illness. . . . The third connection is with Lonoff's would-be biographer, . . . who will do and say nearly anything to get to Lonoff's 'great secret.'" (Publisher's note)

"Mr. Roth has created a melancholy, if occasionally funny, meditation on aging, mortality, loneliness and the losses that come with the passage of time. . . . For fans of the Zuckerman books, it provides a poignant coda to Nathan's story, putting a punctuation point to his journey from youthful idealism and passion through midlife confusion and angst toward elderly renunciation." N Y Times (Late N Y Ed)

Roth, Philip

The **ghost** writer. Farrar, Straus & Giroux 1979 179p

LC 79-13146

"A brief but intricate tale about a young writer {Nathan Zuckerman} who, when accused of travestying his fellow Jews, seeks counsel from a respected older Jewish author and finds this distinguished figure ambiguously involved with a girl whom the young writer fantasizes to be Anne Frank." Oxford Companion to Am Lit. 6th edition

Followed by Zuckerman unbound

Roth, Philip

★ **Goodbye,** Columbus, and five short stories. Modern Lib. 1995 298p hardcover o.p. pa $14

ISBN 0-679-60159-7; 0-679-74826-1 pa

LC 94-44528

A reissue of the title first published 1959 by Houghton Mifflin

"The title story in this collection is about a young Radcliffe girl and a Rutgers boy who learn that there is more to love than exuberance and passion. All of the stories dramatize the dilemma of modern American Jews, torn between two worlds." Publ Wkly

Roth, Philip

The **great** American novel. Holt, Rinehart & Winston 1973 382p

ISBN 0-8050-1734-8

This novel is "at once a burlesque and an allegory, its telling of the downfall of a great baseball team serving as a satirical parallel to contemporary American political and social events." Oxford Companion to Am Lit. 6th edition

Roth, Philip

The **human** stain. Houghton Mifflin 2000 361p $26

ISBN 0-618-05945-8

LC 99-89867

"Roth is clearly enjoyed himself. The Human Stain is as fresh, as angry and as bitterly amused as his early fiction. It vibrates with mockery, disapproval, poetry, and a healthy dose of personal vindictiveness that one would be tempted to dismiss as unworthy if it weren't so funny." New Leader

Roth, Philip

I married a communist. Houghton Mifflin 1998 323p $26

ISBN 0-395-93346-3

LC 98-16797

"What Zuckerman/Roth does with this imagined material is constantly mesmerizing. Library shelves groan under the weight of books published about the witch hunts and blacklistings during the Truman and Eisenhower presidencies, but it would be hard to find one among them that presents as nuanced, as humanly complex an account of those years as I Married a Communist." Time

Roth, Philip

Indignation. Houghton Mifflin Company 2008 233p $26

ISBN 0-54705-484-X; 978-0-54705-484-1

LC 2008-11431

The narrator recalls his short life. "Against the backdrop of the Korean War, a young man faces life's unimagined chances and terrifying consequences. It is 1951 in America, the second year of the Korean War. A studious, law-abiding, intense youngster from Newark, New Jersey, Marcus Messner, is beginning his sophomore year on the pastoral, conservative campus of Ohio's Winesburg College." (Publisher's note)

"We are back in nineteen-fifties Newark, and nineteen-year-old Marcus Messner, the son of a kosher butcher, attempts to escape his father's stifling influence by enrolling at a college in Ohio farm country. Messner is a scholarly type, while his new classmates are an unfriendly bunch of churchgoing, beer-swilling louts. Stubbornly disregarding overtures of friendship from members of the school's only Jewish fraternity, Messner devotes his attentions to a troubled Gentile named Olivia Hutton. There's something of Portnoy in the masturbation-filled high jinks that follow, but Messner, fearful that he might 'wind up a rifleman in Korea,' is a far darker creation." New Yorker

Roth, Philip

Letting go. Random House 1962 630p $12.50

ISBN 0-394-43305-X

Gabe Wallach is "a young university instructor who is literally unable to let go in his personal relationships. This is true with his father, a well-to-do Jewish dentist who suffers because his wife is dead and his only child lives in Chicago instead of New York; with Martha Reganhart, a divorcée, mother of two small children, a woman Gabe loves enough to make his mistress but not his wife; and with Paul and Libby Herz, a young couple suffering the difficulties arising from a mixed marriage, no money, inability to have children, and a host of other problems real and imagined." Libr J

Roth, Philip

My life as a man. Holt, Rinehart & Winston 1974 330p

The "novel consists of three stories: a long autobiographical narrative told by the novelist Peter Tarnopol, preceded by two of Peter's stories, 'useful fictions' in which elements of his 'true story' are metamorphosed. Peter's alter ego, Nathan Zuckerman, is, like his author, a highly self-conscious intellectual urban Jew, adept at eliciting astonishing sexual performances from teen-age girls, but fatally drawn into a disastrous marriage with an older, damaged woman who is incapable of sexual response." Newsweek

Roth, Philip

★ **Nemesis**. Houghton Mifflin Harcourt 2010 280p

ISBN 978-0-547-31835-6

LC 2010026217

"In a book set in 1944 Newark, devoted playground director Bucky Cantor, sidelined from the war due to his poor eyesight, watches in horror as the city's polio epidemic begins to ravage the children on his playground." (Publisher's note)

In this novel Roth "evokes his native Newark amid a raging [polio] epidemic in 1944. . . . Popular young athlete and high school physical education teacher Eugene 'Bucky' Cantor has been hired to manage a playground for the summer in the city's Jewish Weequahic section. Soon, some of the adolescent boys who spend the long summer days playing baseball there are stricken, and panic spreads in the community as parents blame the outbreak on everything from Italian toughs spitting on the sidewalk to overly vigorous physical activity. Despairing of any hope of stemming the outbreak, Bucky flees . . . to a place of apparent safety: a summer camp in Pennsylvania's Pocono Mountains where his fiancée works as a counselor." BookPage

Roth, Philip

Novels, 1993-1995. Library of America 2010 842p $35

ISBN 978-1-59853-078-0; 1-59853-078-X

Operation Shylock (1993) "presents the author in face-to-face confrontation with his double, a look-alike impostor—and perfect stranger—who has usurped his biography and whose self-appointed task is to lead the Jews out of Israel and back to Europe, a Moses in reverse and a monstrous nemesis to the real Philip Roth. . . . [The novel] is at once spy story, political thriller, meditation on identity, confession, and unfathomable journey through a volatile, frightening Middle East. Sabbath's Theater (1995) is a comic creation of epic proportions. . . . Once a scandalously inventive puppeteer, [Mickey] Sabbath at sixty-four is still defiantly antagonistic and exceedingly libidinous. But ghost-ridden and grief-stricken after the death of his longtime Croatian mistress, the unsurpassable Drenka, he contrives a succession of farcical disasters that take him to the brink of madness and extinction." Publisher's note

Roth, Philip

The **plot** against America. Houghton Mifflin 2004 391p $26

ISBN 0-618-50928-3

LC 2004-47490

"When the renowned aviation hero . . . Charles A. Lindbergh defeated Franklin Roosevelt by a landslide in the 1940 presidential election, fear invaded every Jewish household in America. Not only had Lindbergh, in a nationwide radio address, publicly blamed the Jews for selfishly pushing America toward a pointless war with Nazi Germany, he negotiated a cordial 'understanding' with Adolf Hitler, whose conquest of Europe and virulent antiSemitic policies he appeared to accept with difficulty. . . . [The protagonist Philip Roth] recounts what it was like for his Newark family . . . during the menacing years of the Lindbergh presidency." Publisher's note

Roth, Philip

★ **Portnoy's** complaint. Random House 1969 274p

"Roth has the courage to wish to show things as he has experienced them, but the exaggerations of Portnoy's Complaint have a shrillness which could be considered unwholesome if the book were not so funny. It is very funny." Burgess. 99 Novels

Roth, Philip

The **professor** of desire. Farrar, Straus & Giroux 1977 263p

ISBN 0-374-23756-5

LC 77-24032

This novel concerns "David Kepesh, professor of comparative literature. . . . Kepesh becomes involved with a series of women: the coeds at Syracuse University, whom he affronts with his outrageous candor; two Swedish girls in London, who join him, one with self-loathing and the other with zest, in various sexual adventures; a disorganized California beauty, with whom he takes up at the end of his graduate studies at Stanford University; and a well-organized New York beauty, who rescues him from the wreckage of his marriage to the Californian." New Yorker

Roth, Philip

Sabbath's theater. Houghton Mifflin 1995 451p

ISBN 0395739829; 9780395739822

LC 95-914

This novel's protagonist, "Morris (Mickey) Sabbath, a 64-year-old ex-puppeteer, . . . has lived for decades in a rural New England village, Madamaska Falls, teaching drama at a local college until forced to resign over a scandal involving a phone-sex tape and a student. Sabbath is married to a recovering alcoholic, Roseanna. . . . The great erotic love of his life, his Croatian mistress, Drenka Balich, . . . has recently died of ovarian cancer, leaving Sabbath grief-stricken and desperate. . . . News of yet another death, that of a former friend, . . . precipitates his decision to leave Roseanna and drive to the city for the funeral, then arrange for his own death." (N Y Times Book Rev)

"There is plenty of the nasty in this virtuoso performance by our best literary stand-up comic. . . . The verbal play is almost tactile, like slaps, as the narrative moves from third-person comic to first-person perverse confession, but there is a polemical energy that lifts it beyond verbal playfulness; at times the message is painful." N Y Times Book Rev

Roth, Philip

When she was good. Random House 1967 306p

"Roth knows exactly what he's doing. With unerring fidelity, he records the flat surface of provincial American life, the look and feel and sound of it—and then penetrates it to the cesspool of its invisible dynamisms. Beneath the 'good,' and impelling it, he says, lies the horrid." Newsweek

Roth, Philip

Zuckerman bound; a trilogy and epilogue, 1979-1985. Library of America 645p $35

ISBN 978-1-59853-011-7; 1-59853-011-9

LC 2007-926533

"The Ghost Writer (1979) introduces Nathan Zuckerman in the 1950s, a budding writer infatuated with the Great Books, discovering the contradictory claims of literature and experience while an overnight guest in the secluded New England farmhouse of his literary idol, E. I. Lonoff. Zuckerman Unbound (1981) finds him far from Lonoff's domain—the scene is Manhattan as the sensationalizing 1960s are coming to an end. Zuckerman, in his mid-thirties, is suffering the immediate aftershock of literary celebrity. The high-minded protégé of E. I. Lonoff has become a notorious superstar. The Anatomy Lesson (1984) takes place largely in the hospital isolation ward that Zuckerman has made of his Upper East Side apartment. It is Watergate time, 1973, and to Zuckerman the only other American who seems to be in as much trouble as himself is Richard Nixon. Zuckerman, at forty, is beset with crippling and unexplained physical pain; he wonders if the cause might not be his own inflammatory work. In The Prague Orgy (1985), entries from Zuckerman's notebooks describing his 1976 sojourn among the outcast artists of Soviet-occupied Czechoslovakia." Publisher's note

Roth, Philip

★ **Zuckerman** unbound. Farrar, Straus & Giroux 1981 225p

LC 81-4640

"After three marriages and a respected body of fiction, Nathan Zuckerman has suddenly struck free with the scandalous and subversive success of a book about a Portnoyish complainer called Carnovsky. The promising apprentice of The Ghost Writer who engaged in biographical fantasy, has himself become a creature of public fantasy who cannot cope comfortably even with material success. The consequences range from bizarre comedy (the plague of a ruined quiz show contestant who claims his life has been plagiarized) to the distortion of family relations." Libr J

Followed by The anatomy lesson

Rothfuss, Pat

The **name** of the wind; the Kingkiller chronicle, day one. by Patrick Rothfuss. DAW Books 2007 661p $24.95

ISBN 978-0-7564-0407-9; 0-7564-0407-X

This is "quite simply the best fantasy novel of the past 10 years, although attaching a genre qualification threatens to damn it with faint praise. Say instead that The Name of the Wind is one of the best stories told in any medium in a decade." Onion

Rothfuss, Pat

The **wise** man's fear; the Kingkiller chronicle, day two. [by] Patrick Rothfuss. DAW Books 2011 993p $29.95

ISBN 978-0-75640-473-4; 0-75640-473-8

Sequel to: The name of the wind

"As Kvothe, now the unassuming keeper of the Waystone Inn, continues to share his astounding life story—a history that includes saving an influential lord from treachery, defeating a band of dangerous bandits, and surviving an encounter with a legendary Fae seductress—he also offers glimpses into his life's true pursuit: figuring out how to vanquish the mythical Chandrian, a group of seven godlike destroyers that brutally murdered his family and left him an orphan. But while Kvothe recalls the events of his past, his future is conspiring just outside the inn's doors. This breathtakingly epic story is heartrending in its intimacy and masterful in its narrative essence, and will leave fans waiting on tenterhooks for the final installment." Publ Wkly

Rothschild, Hannah, 1962-

The **improbability** of love; a novel. Hannah Rothschild. Knopf 2015 416 p. (hardback) $27.95

ISBN 9781101874141

LC 2014047753

In this novel, by Hannah Rothschild, "we meet Annie McDee. . . . Recovering from the end of a long-term relationship, she is searching in a . . . shop for a birthday present for her . . . new lover . . . [and a] painting catches her eye. After spending her meager savings on the picture, Annie prepares an elaborate birthday dinner for two, only to be stood up. The painting becomes hers, and as it turns out, Annie has stumbled across a lost masterpiece." (Publisher's note)

"For readers anticipating the next irresistible blend of art, mystery, and intrigue along the lines of Donna Tartt's The Goldfinch, the wait is over. This compulsively readable, immensely enjoyable novel will deeply satisfy that craving." LJ

Includes bibliographical references and index

Rourke, Lee

★ The **canal**. Melville House 2010 199p pa $14.95

ISBN 978-1-935554-01-1; 1-935554-01-8

LC 2010-11960

"You have to salute Rourke—he has written a novel about boredom and how it saturates modernity, which is a ballsy thing to do. But The Canal also takes in urban renewal, technology and violence as it questions the manner in which we live our lives in the 21st century. . . . For a book about urban ennui it's one hell of a page-turner." GQ (UK)

Roussel, Raymond

Locus solus; Raymond Roussel; translated by Rupert Copeland Cuningham. New Directions 2017 251 p. (softcover : alk. paper) $15.95

ISBN 9780811226455; 9780811226462; 081122645X

LC 2016048024

In this book, by Raymond Roussel, translated by Rupert Copeland Cuningham, "wealthy scientist Martial Canterel guides a group of visitors through his expansive estate, Locus Solus, where he displays his various deranged inventions, . . . like a machine propelled by the weather, which constructs a mosaic out of varying hues of human teeth . . . and a bizarre theater in which corpses are reanimated with a special serum to enact the most important movements of their past lives." (Publisher's note)

"Both a guide to a deranged scientist's estate and a prism for refracting Roussel's diverse stories, this incredible novel is somehow both Gothic and modern at the same time." Pub Wkly

Row, Jess

Your face in mine; a novel. Jess Row. Riverhead Hardcover 2014 384 p. (hardback) $27.95

ISBN 1594488347; 9781594488344

LC 2013038938

In this novel, by Jess Row, "Kelly Thorndike has moved back to his hometown of Baltimore [and] an African American man he doesn't recognize calls out to him. To Kelly's shock, the man identifies himself as Martin, who was one of Kelly's closest friends in high school—and, before his disappearance nearly twenty years before, skinny, white, and Jewish. . . . After years of immersing himself in black culture, he's had a plastic surgeon perform 'racial reassignment surgery,'" (Publisher's note)

"Row has outdone himself in a first novel that offers great quantities of food for thought and discussion involving, for starters, questions of race and identity. Plunging deeper than common notions of the self and racial distinctions, Row presents wholly credible, if not thoroughly trustworthy, characters and complicated circumstances that will inspire serious reflection." Booklist

Rowell, Rainbow, 1973-

Landline; Rainbow Rowell. St. Martin's Press 2014 320 p. (hardback) $24.99

ISBN 1250049377; 9781250049377

LC 2014008538

"TV writer Georgie McCool is trying to have it all, but it becomes clear that she's failing when her husband, Neal, heads to Nebraska for a family Christmas with their kids--without her. The career opportunity of a lifetime has appeared, but now her marriage may be ending as a result. . . . Georgie finds a way to talk to Neal, but he's not the Neal who's just left her. Instead, she's talking to him in the past, right before they got engaged." (Kirkus Reviews)

"Rowell knows romance writing and executes many conventions well: Christmastime setting, romantic triangle, and barriers to vital communication. Yet her tinkering with genre to explore love already in progress is the true gem." Booklist

Rowling, J. K., 1965-

The **casual** vacancy; J.K. Rowling. Little, Brown and Co. 2012 503 p. $35

ISBN 1451696191; 9780316228534; 9780316228541

LC 2012943788

In this novel by J. K. Rowling "Barry Fairbrother dies unexpectedly in his early forties, [and] the little town of Pagford is left in shock. Pagford is, seemingly, an English idyll, with a cobbled market square and an ancient abbey, but what lies behind the pretty façade is a town at war. And the empty seat left by Barry on the town's council soon becomes the catalyst for the biggest war the town has yet seen." (Publisher's note)

Rowling, J. K., 1965-

The **cuckoo's** calling; Robert Galbraith. 1st north American ed. Mulholland Books / Little, Brown and Co. 2013 464 p. (hardcover) $25.99

ISBN 0316206849; 9780316206846

LC 2013933193

In this mystery novel, by Robert Galbraith, "Cormoran Strike is barely scraping by as a private investigator. . . . He has also just broken up with his longtime girlfriend and is living in his office. Then John Bristow walks through his door with an amazing story: His sister, the legendary supermodel Lula Landry, known to her friends as the Cuckoo, famously fell to her death a few months earlier. The police ruled it a suicide, but John refuses to believe that." (Publisher's note)

Roy, Anuradha

An **atlas** of impossible longing. Free Press 2010 319p
ISBN 1-4516-0862-4; 978-1-4516-0862-5

LC 2010-19362

First published 2008 in the United Kingdom

This novel "covers multiple generations of an Indian family from the turn of the 20th century to India's partition. Three distinct sections revolve around Amulya, who runs an herbal medicine and fragrance business; his mentally ill wife, Kananbala, who spies on the goings-on of her English neighbors from the room Amulya keeps her locked in; their sons, Kamal and Nirmal; their wives; Nirmal's daughter Bakul, whose mother died in childbirth; and finally Mukunda, an orphan that Amulya helps support, at which point Nirmal brings Mukunda home as a companion for Bakul." Pub Wkly

"Roy's prose is luscious yet economical. Capturing the rhythms of life in rural backwater and big city alike, she strings together jewellike episodes, skipping across decades and defining historical events in mere sentences, and giving her story the quality of something remembered. Incidental characters are conjured with an almost Dickensian alacrity." National Newspaper

Roy, Arundhati, 1946-

★ The **god** of small things. Random House 1997 321p
ISBN 0679457313; 9780679457312

LC 96-39190

This novel "begins with a return and a death: first, the reappearance of the twins, Esha and Rahel, at the house in Kerala, {India}, after twenty-three years of exile and separation; and, second, the funeral, back in December 1969, of their cousin Sophie Mol. The motivating force behind Roy's narrative is the search for answers to the tragic events which occurred that long-ago December. . . . As memory returns, . . . the twins learn to see themselves once more as 'joint identities', and to remember Sophie Mol's drowning, as well as another death, the brutal killing by the police of Velutha, the untouchable, whom they had loved and whom they had betrayed." (Times Lit Suppl)

"If the symbolism is a trifle overdone, the lush local color and the incisive characterizations give the narrative power and drama." Publ Wkly

Roy, Arundhati, 1946-

★ The **ministry** of utmost happiness; a novel. Arundhati Roy. First United States edition Alfred A. Knopf 2017 449 p. (hardcover : acid-free paper) $28.95
ISBN 1524733156; 9781524733155; 9781524733162

LC 2017002124

Women's Prize for Fiction Longlist (2018)

National Book Critics Circle Award Finalist: Fiction (2017)

This book, by Arundhati Roy, "takes us on an intimate journey of many years across the Indian subcontinent--from the cramped neighborhoods of Old Delhi and the roads of the new city to the mountains and valleys of Kashmir and beyond, where war is peace and peace is war. It is an aching love story and a decisive remonstration, a story told in a whisper, in a shout, through unsentimental tears and sometimes with a bitter laugh." (Publisher's note)

"Roy joins Dickens, Naipaul, García Márquez, and Rushdie in her abiding compassion, storytelling magic, and piquant wit as she questions our perceptions of gender, family, home, country, war, freedom, love, and death in this righteous and tender illumination of humankind's paradoxical capacities for cruelty and kindness." Booklist

Roy, Lori

Bent Road. Dutton 2011 355p $25.95
ISBN 978-0-525-95183-4; 0-525-95183-0

LC 2010-37239

"Like Michael Chabon's work, which sometimes crosses genres, Roy's novel could be called literary fiction or mystery. Whatever the label, 'Bent Road' is written with the care and craft of standout storytelling. There's inevitability to the novel's crisis and denouement but plenty of surprise. Psychological acuity, tight plot and in-depth character development keep the reader trying to resist the urge to read ahead." Kansas City Star

Roy, Lori

Let me die in his footsteps; Lori Roy. Dutton 2015 336 p. (hardcover) $26.95
ISBN 0525955070; 9780525955078

LC 2014035841

In this novel by Lori Roy, "on a dark Kentucky night in 1952 exactly halfway between her fifteenth and sixteenth birthdays, Annie Holleran crosses into forbidden territory. . . . As . . . she comes of age as Aunt Juna did in her own time, Annie's dread mounts. Juna will come home now, to finish what she started. If Annie is to save herself, her family, and this small Kentucky town, she must prepare for Juna's return, and the revelation of what really happened all those years ago." (Publisher's note)

"As three generations struggle with deception and death, there's much ado about lavender--in kitchens, in sachets, in bread and tea, symbolizing devotion--in this tale driven by something stranger. A sure winner with fans of backwoods country noir." Kirkus

Roy, Lori

Until she comes home; Lori Roy. Dutton 2013 352 p. (hardcover) $26.95
ISBN 0525953965; 9780525953968

LC 2012031919

In this book, "the placid lives of Malina Herze, Julia Wagner, Grace Richardson, and the other women of Alder Avenue are upended, first by the murder of a 'colored' woman near the factory where their husbands work, then by the disappearance of Elizabeth Symanski, a mentally challenged young adult who lives with her widowed father." (Publishers Weekly)

Roy-Bhattacharya, Joydeep

The **watch**; a novel. Joydeep Roy-Bhattacharya. Hogarth 2012 290 p.
ISBN 0307955893; 9780307955890

LC 2011037317

This novel by Joydeep Roy-Bhattacharya takes place in the U.S.-led Afghan War. "Following a desperate night-long battle, a group of beleaguered soldiers in an isolated base in Kandahar are faced with a lone woman demanding the return of her brother's body. Is she a spy, a black widow, a lunatic, or is she what she claims to be: a grieving young sister intent on burying her brother according to local rites? Single-minded in her mission, she refuses to move from her spot on the field in full view of every soldier in the stark outpost. Her presence quickly proves dangerous as the camp's tense, claustrophobic atmosphere comes to a boil when the men begin arguing about what to do next." (Publisher's note)

Rubenfeld, Jed

The **death** instinct. Riverhead Books 2011 464p $26.95
ISBN 978-1-59448-782-8; 1-59448-782-0

LC 2010-16609

"The novel has many stellar set pieces: life in post-World War I America as it roars into the 1920s, shady Washington politics, the radium craze in which the element was credited with everything from reviving male virility to curing cancer, and the early days of Prohibition. Rubenfeld's novel is brilliantly concocted and more than just a little eerie. The fictional and actual events surrounding the 1920 bombing are as relevant today as they were nearly a century ago." USA Today

Ruby, Ilie

The **salt** god's daughter; Ilie Ruby. Soft Skull Press 2012 338 p. (hard cover) $25

ISBN 1619020025; 9781619020023

LC 2012040919

This novel, by Ilie Ruby, uses the folk mythology of selkies, or Celtic mermaids. "Young Naida yearns for her mysterious father. But to understand his role in her life, she must first understand the stories of the women who came before her. The story swirls back to begin with her mother's tale. . . . [Later,] Ruthie meets Graham, a Scottish fisherman whose soul calls to hers. Graham's love for Ruthie is intense, yet his presence ebbs and flows like the tide." (Publisher's note)

Rucker, Rudy von Bitter

Hylozoic; [by] Rudy Rucker. Tor 2009 334p $25.95

ISBN 978-0-765-32074-2; 0-765-32074-6

LC 2008-53399

"Serious, uproarious fun, with brain-teasers and brilliant ideas tossed about like confetti." Kirkus

Rucker, Rudy von Bitter

★ **Mathematicians** in love; [by] Rudy Rucker. Tor 2006 364p $24.95

ISBN 978-0-7653-1584-7; 0-7653-1584-X

LC 2006-5725

Rucker "is palpably and quiveringly tuned in to the zeitgeist and can offer cultural and scientific commentary and satire better than almost any other SF author practicing today. . . . But aside from all the glories of the speculative science and math and interdimensional jaunts . . . , what we have here is a rollicking, roisterous, (ir-)reverent campus novel." Sci Fi Wkly

Rucker, Rudy von Bitter

Postsingular; [by] Rudy Rucker. Tor 2007 320p $25.95

ISBN 978-0-7653-1741-4; 0-7653-1741-9

LC 2007-20210

"In the very near future, two influential and maladjusted individuals initiate a radical transformation of the world through the use of sentient nanotechnology-only to have their plans foiled by Chu, the autistic son of two scientists engaged in nanotechnology research. The persistence of money and politics, however, creates a strange new world in which humans become telepaths and can travel to other worlds in the quantum universe; finally, gigantic visitors from another place entirely arrive to sort things out. Rucker . . . excels in mind-bending premises and thought-stretching stories peopled with appealingly flawed characters that resonate with familiarity despite their eccentricities." Libr J

Ruiz Zafon, Carlos

The **angel's** game; translated into English by Lucia Graves. Doubleday 2009 531p $26.95

ISBN 978-0-385-52870-2; 0-385-52870-1

LC 2008-53650

A prequel to: The shadow of the wind

Original Spanish edition, 2008

"As the book opens in 1917, David Martín is 17, a down-on-his-luck Barcelona writer and budding journalist. An orphan since his father was murdered, David is forced by necessity to subvert his lofty literary ambitions in the service of writing a series of pulp novels in the macabre Grand Guignol tradition. Then a mysterious stranger named Andreas Corelli, a close relative of the stranger in Mark Twain's book of the same name and every other deal-with-the-devil tale you've ever read, presents a proposal to Martín—write a book that will create a perfect narrative for a religion. In essence, his assignment is to create a mythical story that will seduce the masses into belief. The mortal medical condition Martín suffers from goes into remission, and a fortune is placed in his bank account. And off we go. This novel operates on so many levels, a brief review can't quite do justice to its many layers." Seattle Times

Ruiz Zafon, Carlos, 1964-

The **prisoner** of heaven; a novel. Harper 2012 288 p. (hardcover) $25.99

ISBN 0062206281; 9780062206282; 0062207261 Large Print; 9780062207265 Large Print

This novel, by Carlos Ruiz Zafon, is set in "Barcelona, 1957. . . . Daniel Sempere and his wife . . . have a beautiful new baby son, . . . and their close friend Fermin Romero de Torres is about to be wed. But their joy is eclipsed when a mysterious stranger visits the Sempere bookshop and threatens to divulge a terrible secret that has been buried for two decades in the city's dark past." (Publisher's note)

Ruiz Zafon, Carlos

The **shadow** of the wind; translated by Lucia Graves. Penguin Press 2004 486p $24.95

ISBN 1-59420-010-6

LC 2003-062376

Original Spanish edition, 2001

"In post-World War II Barcelona, young Daniel is taken by his bookseller father to the Cemetery of Forgotten Books, a massive sanctuary where books are guarded from oblivion. Told to choose one book to protect, he selects The Shadow of the Wind, by Julian Carax. He reads it, loves it, and soon learns it is both very valuable and very much in danger because someone is determinedly burning every copy of every book written by the obscure Carax. . . . Daniel's initiation into the mysteries of adulthood is given the same weight as the mystery of the book-burner. And the setting—Spain under Franco—injects an air of sobriety into some plot elements that might otherwise seem soap operatic. Part detective story, part boy's adventure, part romance, fantasy, and gothic horror, the intricate plot is urged on by extravagant foreshadowing and nail-nibbling tension." Booklist

Ruiz-Camacho, Antonio

Barefoot dogs; stories. Antonio Ruiz-Camacho. Scribner 2015 160 p. (hardback) $23

ISBN 1476784965; 9781476784960; 9781476784977

LC 2014018416

This collection of linked short stories, by Antonio Ruiz-Camacho, "follow[s] the members and retinue of a wealthy Mexican family forced into exile after the patriarch is kidnapped. . . . José Victoriano Arteaga . . . vanishes on his way home from work. The Arteagas find few answers; the full truth of what happened to Arteaga is lost to the shadows of Mexico's vast and desperate underworld, a place of rampant violence and kidnappings, and government corruption." (Publisher's note)

"Energetic and colloquially written, this engaging collection shows what it's like to live in a world that isn't quite yours." LJ

Runcie, James

Canvey Island; a novel. Other Press 2008 301p pa $13.95

ISBN 978-1-59051-293-7; 1-59051-293-6

LC 2007-52431

First published 2006 in the United Kingdom

"In 1953 Canvey Island, off the coast of Britain, suffered the ill effects of a storm surge, which flooded the island. In this fictionalized account of the tragedy, nine-year-old Martin and his mother, Lily, fight to stay above water, but Lily is unable to free herself from the debris, and she is swept under. Her death becomes the defining moment of Martin's life; he grows up obsessed with water and becomes an engineer, forever trying to figure out the best way to hold back the sea. He never quite forgives his father, Len, for failing to save his wife and for taking up with her sister, the flamboyant Violet. Martin himself gives up his free-spirited girlfriend, in part because he loves her too much, opting instead to marry Claire, a vicar's daughter with a rebellious streak. In highly readable chapters narrated by each family member, the book manages to address class and generational conflict as it travels through the decades." Booklist

Runcie, James ✓

Sidney Chambers and the Forgiveness of Sins; James Runcie. St. Martin's Press 2015 416 p. $18

ISBN 1632861038; 9781632861030

In this short story collection by James Runcie "the loveable full-time priest and part-time detective, Canon Sidney Chambers, continues his sleuthing adventures in 1960's Cambridge. A stranger seeks sanctuary in Grantchester's church, convinced he has murdered his wife. Sidney and his wife . . . go for a shooting weekend in the country and find their hostess has a sinister burn on her neck. Sidney's friend Amanda receives poison pen letters when . . . approaching matrimony." (Publisher's note)

"Chambers is a winning protagonist, fervid in his faith yet prone to human frailty, and his exploits provide multiple pleasures for readers of cozies and beyond. The full Grantchester mystery series, projected to include six novels, will have a new entry in each of the next two years, and readers, as well as fans of the PBS show based on this series, should treasure them." Booklist

Rush, Norman

★ **Mating**. Knopf 1991 480p

LC 90-25752

"Mr. Rush has created one of the wiser and wittier fictive meditations on the subject of mating. His novel illuminates why we yield when we don't have to. It seeks to illuminate the nature of true intimacy—how to define it, how to know when one has achieved it. And few books evoke so eloquently that state of love at its apogee." N Y Times Book Rev

Rush, Norman

Mortals; a novel. Knopf 2003 715p $26.95

ISBN 0-679-40622-0

LC 2002-43289

"The richness of Rush's vision, and its stringent moral clarity, sweep the reader into his brilliantly observed world." Publ Wkly

Rush, Norman

Subtle bodies; By Norman Rush. Alfred A. Knopf 2013 256 p. (hardcover) $26.95

ISBN 140004250X; 9781400042500; 9781400077137

LC 2013013813

Author Norman Rush presents "a . . . romp through the particular joys and tribulations of marriage, and the dilemmas of friendship, as a group of college friends reunites in upstate New York twenty-some years after graduation. When Douglas, the ringleader of a clique of self-styled wits of 'superior sensibility' dies suddenly, his four remaining friends are summoned to his luxe estate high in the Catskills to memorialize his life and mourn his passing." (Publisher's note)

Rushdie, Salman

East, west; stories. Pantheon Bks. 1995 214p

LC 94-28277

First publishd 1994 in the United Kingdom

"Rushdie's brilliant style reinforces his stories' marvelous combination of dignity and poignancy. Though these stories were originally published in such periodicals as the New Yorker and the Atlantic, the collection will serve for many readers as an introduction to Rushdie's talent in the short story form." Booklist

Rushdie, Salman

The **enchantress** of Florence; a novel. Random House 2008 355p $26

ISBN 978-0-375-50433-4; 0-375-50433-8

LC 2008-70

"A tall, yellow-haired, young European traveler calling himself 'Mogor dell'Amore,' the Mughal of Love, arrives at the court of the Emperor Akbar, lord of the great Mughal empire, with a tale to tell that begins to obsess the imperial capital, a tale about a mysterious woman, a great beauty believed to possess powers of enchantment and sorcery, and her impossible journey to the far-off city of Florence." Publisher's note

Rushdie, Salman

★ The **golden** house; a novel. Salman Rushdie. Random House 2017 380 p. (hardback) $28.99

ISBN 9780399592812; 9780399592805; 0399592806

LC 2017031173

In this novel, by Salman Rushdie, "on the day of Barack Obama's inauguration, an enigmatic billionaire from foreign shores takes up residence in . . . 'the Gardens,' a cloistered community in New York's Greenwich Village. . . . Along with his . . . unmistakable whiff of danger, Nero Golden has brought along his three adult sons. . . . There is no mother, no wife; at least not until Vasilisa . . . snags . . . Nero, becoming the queen to his king--a queen in want of an heir." (Publisher's note)

"A sort of Great Gatsby for our time: everyone is implicated, no one is innocent, and no one comes out unscathed, no matter how well padded with cash." Kirkus

Rushdie, Salman

The **ground** beneath her feet; a novel. Holt & Co. 1999 575p $26

ISBN 0-8050-5308-5

LC 98-42407

"Vina and Ormus are icons, not fully formed characters. But that's the point. And Rai . . . is the most moving character Rushdie's ever created." Newsweek

Rushdie, Salman, 1947-

Haroun and the sea of stories. Granta Books in association with Viking 1990 219p hardcover o.p. pa $14

ISBN 0-14-015737-9 pa

LC 90-45496

"Rashid Khalifa, a famous storyteller, loses the gift of gab when his wife leaves him. His saddened son, Haroun, wants to get daddy's talent back. To reconnect Rashid's supply of Story Water—without which he cannot tell tales—Haroun journeys to the Land of Gup ('gossip' in Hindustani), on earth's second moon. When he arrives there, with the help of Iff, water genie, and Butt, a mechanical bird, Haroun finds the Guppees preparing for war. The denizens of Chup ('quiet'), led by Khattam-Shud, a/k/a the Prince of Silence, have begun polluting the Sea of Stories." (Voice Lit Suppl)

"This delightful fantasy is filled with adventures, amusing characters with names like Iff and Butt, and villains to fight against and defeat. Rushdie's puns and rhymes will be enjoyed by young and old—the catchy tunes by the younger readers and the political allegory by the adults. Rashid is a professional story-teller whose son, Haroun, delights in hearing them. When Rashid's source of stories seems to have disappeared Haroun faces many dangerous opponents to help his father regain his Gift of Gab." Shapiro. Fic for Youth. 3d edition

Rushdie, Salman

★ **Midnight's** children; with an introduction by Anita Desai. Knopf 1995 xxxi, 589p $20

ISBN 0-679-44462-9

LC 90-38447

A reissue of the title first published 1980 in the United Kingdom; 1981 in the United States

"The novel is about Shiva and Saleem, two of the 1,001 babies born in the hour following independence at midnight on August 15, 1947. It is notable as much for its portrayal of contemporary politics in India as for the brilliance of its style and insights into human nature and mind." Reader's Ency. 4th edition

Rushdie, Salman

The **Moor's** last sigh. Pantheon Bks. 1996 435p

LC 95-24392

First published 1995 in the United Kingdom

This is a "marvellously inventive display of verbal dexterity; an exuberant, entertaining, zestful novel which proves, if proof were needed, that Mr Rushdie's spirit remains undiminshed." Economist

Rushdie, Salman, 1947-

★ The **satanic** verses. Viking 1989 546p $27.95

ISBN 0670825379

LC 88-40266

"When a terrorist's bomb destroys a jumbo jet high above the English Channel, two passengers fall safely to earth: Gibreel {Farishta}, an Indian movie actor, and Saladin {Chamcha}, star of the controversial British television program, The Alien Show. The near-death experience changes them into living symbols of good and evil—Saladin grows horns, Gibreel a halo." (Libr J)

A "panoramic novel which moves with dizzying speed from the streets and film studios of Bombay to multicultural Britain, from Argentina to Mount Everest, as Rushdie questions illusion, reality, and the power of faith and tradition in a world of hijackers, religious pilgrimages and warfare, and celluloid fantasy." Oxford Companion to Engl Lit. 6th edition

Rushdie, Salman

Shalimar the clown. Random House 2005 398p $25.95

ISBN 0-679-46335-6

LC 2005-42796

"Rushdie has written an intensely political novel, infused with recent events, but its emotional scope reaches so far beyond our current crisis and its vision into the vagaries of the heart is so perceptive that one can imagine Shalimar the Clown being read long after this age of sacred terror has faded into history." Washington Post Book World

Rushdie, Salman, 1947-

★ **Two** years eight months and twenty-eight nights; a novel. Salman Rushdie. Random House Inc. 2015 304 p. (hardcover) $28

ISBN 081299891X; 9780812998917

LC 2015008158

In this book by Salman Rushdie, set "in the near future, after a storm strikes New York City, the strangenesses begin. . . . Centuries ago, Dunia, a princess of the jinn, fell in love with a mortal man of reason. . . . Once the line between worlds is breached on a grand scale, Dunia's children and others will play a role in an epic war between light and dark spanning a thousand and one nights--or two years, eight months, and twenty-eight nights." (Publisher's note)

"Rushdie scatters intriguing allusions (Beckett, Magritte, Gogol, Obama) about like fairy dust and coins of the realm while sustaining swiftly flowing, incisive, piercingly funny commentary on everything from religious extremists to reality TV, anti-Semitism and racism, and economic injustice." Booklist

Ruskovich, Emily

Idaho; a novel. Emily Ruskovich. Random House 2017 308 p. (ebook) $65; (acid-free paper) $27

ISBN 9780812994056; 0812994043; 9780812994049

LC 2016006621

In this novel, by Emily Ruskovich, "Ann and Wade have carved out a life for themselves from a rugged landscape in northern Idaho, where they are bound together by more than love. With her husband's memory fading, Ann attempts to piece together the truth of what happened to Wade's first wife, Jenny, and to their daughters." (Publisher's note)

"Shocking and heartbreaking, Ruskovich has crafted a remarkable love story and a narrative that will stay with readers." Pub Wkly

Russell, Karen

St. Lucy's home for girls raised by wolves. Knopf 2006 246p

ISBN 0-307-26398-3

LC 2006-45156

"A series of upbeat, sentimental fables, the 10 stories of Russell's debut are set in an enchanted version of North America and narrated by articulate, emotionally precocious children from dysfunctional households. Each merges the satirical spirit of George Saunders with the sophisticated whimsy of recent animated Hollywood film." Publ Wkly

Russell, Karen

★ **Swamplandia!** Karen Russell. Alfred A. Knopf 2011 315p. $24.95

ISBN 0307263991; 9780307263995

LC 201036708

This book tells the story of "Swamplandia!, [which] is a shabby tourist attraction deep in the Everglades, owned by the Bigtree clan of alligator wrestlers. When Hilola, their star performer, dies, her husband and children lose their moorings, and Swamplandia! itself is endangered as audiences dwindle. The Chief leaves. Brother Kiwi, 17, sneaks off to work at the World of Darkness, a new mainland amusement park featuring the 'rings of hell.' Otherworldly sister Osceola, 16, vanishes after falling in love with the ghost of a young man who died while working for the ill-fated Dredge and Fill Campaign in the 1930s. It's up to Ava, 13, to find her sister." (Booklist)

"When Hilola Bigtree, professional alligator wrestler and star attraction at a Florida venue that calls itself "the Number One Gator-Themed Park and Swamp Café in the area," dies in the vise grip not of some prehistoric behemoth but of unglamorous cancer, the family-owned tourist destination shrivels into insolvency. Likewise, the remaining Bigtree clan unspools in her absence, and Ava, the youngest of three children, can only watch as they drift apart. Her sister, Ossie, obsessed with the afterlife, carries out furtive relationships with the spirits of dead boys she claims possess her. Her brother, Kiwi, runs off to work for the World of Darkness, an amusement park designed to resemble hell. The plot of Swamplandia! tilts toward the odd. Kiwi toils in his ersatz inferno; Ava goes on a quest to save Ossie after she elopes into the otherworldly wetlands with one of her phantom paramours. But Russell isn't a magic realist. In fact, the only truly magical things about this book are its effortless prose and its small, beautifully drawn cast of characters." Entertainment Wkly

Russell, Karen

★ **Vampires** in the lemon grove; stories. by Karen Russell. Alfred A. Knopf 2013 243 p. (paperback) $15.00; (hardcover) $24.95; (ebook) $74.85

ISBN 0307957233; 9780307947475; 9780307957238; 9780307961082

LC 2012027415

Author Karen Russell presents a collection of short stories, with plots including a "teenager [who] discovers that the universe is communicating with him through talismanic objects left behind in a seagull's nest. A community of girls held captive in a silk factory slowly transmute into human silkworms, . . . a massage therapist discovers she has the power to heal by manipulating the tattoos on a war veteran [and] a group of boys [find a] scarecrow [resembling a] missing classmate." (Publisher's note)

Russell, Mary Doria

Children of God; a novel. Villard Bks. 1998 438p $23.95

ISBN 0-679-45635-X

LC 97-42160

"Russell succeeds in painting an alien culture with remarkably detailed verisimilitude." N Y Times Book Rev

Russell, Mary Doria, 1950-

★ **Doc**. Random House 2011 394p $26

ISBN 978-1-4000-6804-3; 1-4000-6804-5

LC 2010-15062

"An engaging bit of de-mythology, a vivid re-imagining of a more authentic, slightly less 'wild' West than the one we've come to know through dime-store novels." Cleveland Plain Dealer

Russell, Mary Doria

Dreamers of the day; a novel. Random House 2008 251p il

ISBN 978-1-40006471-7; 1-400-06471-6

LC 2007-24665

"Russell perfectly captures the political and social milieus of the 1920s, driving home how important it is to consider history when dealing with present-day issues. . . . The fact that Agnes is telling her story after she has—yes—already died does not come across as a literary conceit but as perfectly fitting for this perfectly enchanting tale." BookPage

Russell, Mary Doria, 1950-

Epitaph; A Novel of the O.K. Corral. Mary Doria Russell. HarperCollins 2015 592 p. $27.99

ISBN 0062198769; 9780062198761

Author Mary Doria Russell's "historical novel continues the story she began in 'Doc,' following Wyatt Earp and Doc Holliday to Tombstone, Arizona, and to the gunfight at the O.K. Corral. [It] tells Wyatt's real story, unearthing the Homeric tragedy buried under 130 years of mythology, misrepresentation, and sheer indifference to fact. Epic and intimate, this novel gives voice to the real men and women whose lives were changed forever by those fatal thirty seconds in Tombstone." (Publisher's note)

"The multitude of points of view exemplifies the best of third-person omniscience, revealing innermost secrets, hopes, and fears. Readers of Lyndsay Faye's Gods of Gotham are sure to enjoy this novel, and fans of Westerns ready to branch out beyond Louis L'Amour and Max Brand might see it as a breath of fresh air." LJ.

Russell, Mary Doria

★ The **sparrow**. Villard Bks. 1996 408p

LC 96-11180

This novel about first contact with an extraterrestrial civilization features "Father Emilio Sandoz, a Jesuit linguist whose messianic virtues hide his occasional doubt about his calling. . . . The narrative ping-pongs between the years 2016, when Sandoz begins assembling the team that first detects signs of intelligent extraterrestrial life, and 2060, when a Vatican inquest is convened to coax an explanation from the physically mutilated and emotionally devastated priest." Publ Wkly

Followed by Children of God

Russell, Mary Doria

A **thread** of grace; a novel. Mary Doria Russell. 1st ed; Random House 2005 430p $25.95

ISBN 0-375-50184-3

LC 2004-50942

"This is a morality play that at times uses black humor, and then shifts to solemn reflection or moving portraiture. A Thread of Grace is deft, sensate, ruthless in its moral incisiveness, and affirming in that even in the worst of times, the lamp of humanity cannot be completely extinguished." Hudson Rev

Russell, Sheldon

This insane train. Minotaur Books 2010 312p $25.99

ISBN 978-0-312-56671-5; 0-312-56671-9

LC 2010-32672

The author "imbues even bit characters with personality, and presents a rough-edged view of the world that will be familiar to fans of classic hardboiled writers such as Chandler and Hammett." Publ Wkly

Russo, Richard

Bridge of sighs. Alfred A. Knopf 2007 528p $26.95

ISBN 978-0-375-41495-4

LC 2007-27970

"Whatever the scale of their lives, Russo's characters—the stars and the walk-ons are gorgeously drawn. The writing is always in service of illuminating them—with one exception. The black characters speak in a corny-sounding dialect, which can make the reader stop to decode sentences. In this case, the reach for authenticity doesn't work. But everything else works brilliantly. . . . That Russo manages to juggle so many characters, themes, places, and time periods through 528 delicious pages is an astounding achievement. From its lovely beginning to its exquisite, perfect end, Russo has written a masterpiece." Boston Globe

Russo, Richard

★ **Empire** Falls. Knopf 2001 483p $29.95

ISBN 0-679-43247-7

LC 2001-88568

"Miles Roby is a typical Russo hero: wry, unlucky in love and money; and just a little bit smarter than the people who populate his run-down industrial town. In this case, the town is Empire Falls, Maine, where Miles manages a restaurant that serves as a kind of meeting hall for the novel's large cast of characters. There's David, Miles's recovering-alcoholic brother; Walt, the health-club entrepreneur who has stolen Miles's estranged wife; Tick, Miles's precocious, befuddled teen-age daughter; and Francine Whiting, the rich widow who runs everything. Russo is preoccupied with the death of a certain version of the American dream, but his belief in the power of comedy—sometimes low, sometimes high—rescues his work from bathos and elvates it into the realm of literature." New Yorker

Russo, Richard, 1949-

★ **Everybody's** fool; A Novel. Richard Russo. Alfred A. Knopf 2016 496 p. (hardback) $27.95

ISBN 9780307270641; 0307270645

LC 2015043451

Sequel to: Nobody's fool

This novel, by Richard Russo, "picks up roughly a decade since we were last with Miss Beryl and Sully on New Year's Eve 1984. The irresistible Sully, who in the intervening years has come by some unexpected good fortune, is staring down a VA cardiologist's estimate that he has only a year or two left, and it's hard work trying to keep this news from the most important people in his life." (Publisher's note)

"Russo's reunion with these beloved characters is genius: silly slapstick and sardonic humor play out in a rambling, rambunctious story that poignantly emphasizes that particular brand of loyalty and acceptance that is synonymous with small-town living." Booklist

Russo, Richard

★ **Nobody's** fool. Random House 1993 549p

ISBN 0-394-57778-7

LC 92-56844

"A grand read sparkling with witty dialogue and memorable characters, Russo's novel is a rollicking tale of a born loser on a downward slide. An economically depressed upper New York State community is the setting, and its lower-middle-class and blue-collar inhabitants are portrayed with empathy and a shrewd understanding of human nature." Publ Wkly

Russo, Richard

The **risk** pool. Random House 1988 479p

ISBN 0-394-56527-4

LC 88-42666

"A superbly original, maliciously funny book, peopled by characters that most of us would back away from plenty fast if they ever lurched toward our barstool. It is Mr. Russo's brilliant, deadpan writing that gives their wasted lives and miserable little town such haunting power and insidious charm." N Y Times Book Rev

Russo, Richard

The **straight** man. Random House 1997 391p

ISBN 0-679-43246-9

LC 96-48578

"The novel's greatest pleasures derive not from any blazing impatience to see what happens next, but from pitch-perfect dialogue, persuasive characterization and a rich progression of scenes, most of them crackling with an impudent, screwball energy reminiscent of Howard Hawks's movies." N Y Times Book Rev

Russo, Richard

That old Cape magic; a novel. Alfred A. Knopf 2009 261p $25.95

ISBN 978-0-375-41496-1; 0-375-41496-7

LC 2009-20311

"Suffused with Russo's signature comic sensibility, and with insights, by turns tender and tough, about human frailty, forbearance, fortitude, and fervor." Boston Globe

Russo, Richard

The **whore's** child; and other stories. Knopf 2002 225p

ISBN 0-375-41168-2

LC 2002-19023

"Russo's rueful understanding of the twisted skein of human relationships is as sharp as ever, and the dialogue throughout is barbed, pointed and wryly humorous." Publ Wkly

Rutherford, Ethan

The **Peripatetic** Coffin and other stories; by Ethan Rutherford. HarperCollins 2013 240 p. $13.99

ISBN 0062203835; 9780062203830

This collection of short stories by Ethan Rutherford offers "eight tales that ponder the methods in which humans achieve isolation. While many of these methods take the form of physical vessels—the Civil War-era submarine in the title story, the Russian ship headed toward the North Pole in 'The Saint Anna,' a futuristic shipper-tank named Halcyon roaming the desert for dying prey in 'Dirwhals!'—the author also fashions narratives focusing on psychological, corporeal seclusion." (Publishers Weekly)

Rutherfurd, Edward

The **forest**; a novel. Crown 2000 598p il

ISBN 0-609-60382-5

LC 00-22219

This historical saga focuses on "the New Forest, part of the southern coast of England bounded by the English Channel. Rutherfurd traces the lives of peasants, smugglers, churchmen, woodsmen, and upper-class families from the 11th to the 20th centuries. These assorted men and women take part in the events surrounding the death of King Rufus (William the Conqueror's son), the failure of the Spanish Armada, England's Civil War, and more." Libr J

Rutherfurd, Edward

London. Crown 1997 829p $25.95

ISBN 0-517-59181-2

LC 97-10176

First published 1995 in the United Kingdom

This "fictional history of London is told through the experiences of a group of diverse families who, over the generations, meet, mingle, intermarry, and feud. Beginning with prehistory and continuing to the present, Rutherfurd combines geological details, historical events, real people, and his fictional characters to bring London to life." Libr J

Rutherfurd, Edward

Paris; the novel. Edward Rutherfurd. 1st ed. Random House Inc 2013 x, 809 p.p (hardcover) $32.50

ISBN 0385535309; 9780385535304

LC 2013005884

This novel by Edward Rutherfurd explores the history of Paris, "recounting all the most significant transformative events as the City of Light evolves from its humble origins as a Roman trading post to the cultural epicenter of Western civilization. Utilizing . . . real-life and fictional characters, he stitches their individual stories and experiences together in order to humanize and personalize the emergence of a mighty metropolis over a period of 2,000 years." (Booklist)

Rutherfurd, Edward

★ The **princes** of Ireland; the Dublin saga. Doubleday 2004 776p $27.95

ISBN 0-385-50286-9

LC 2003-70005

"Beginning in the tribal, pre-Christian times of the warrior kings at Tara, this first book in a two-part novelized history of Ireland sweeps readers through the early centuries of Druids, chieftains, monks, Vikings, noblemen, merchants, and mercenaries, ending with the disastrous invasion of England that tragically changed the course of Irish history. Through the eyes of the men and women who built the mighty city that became Dublin, the unfolding of a colorful and turbulent history is told with energy and a meticulous attention to historical detail." Libr J

Rutherfurd, Edward

The **rebels** of Ireland; the Dublin Saga. Doubleday 2006 xxv, 863p $28.95

ISBN 0-385-51289-9

LC 2006-273953

"Beginning with Elizabeth's ascendancy to the English throne and the 'plantation' period of the English conquest of Ireland and ending with the founding of the Irish republic in 1922, this sequel to Princes of Ireland vividly tells the history of Irish suppression through the lives of ordinary people on both sides of the turmoil. It is a story of bitter and tragic contrast. Rutherfurd casts the Irish, thought to be savages by England's Protestant elite, against a backdrop of a vibrant, intellectual Dublin, deeply divided by religion and politics yet aglow with the literary renaissance of Yeats, Shaw, and Joyce." Libr J

Rutherfurd, Edward

Russka; the novel of Russia. Crown 1991 760p

LC 90-34457

The book "does provide a sweeping overview of the land whose very vastness and complexity make it overwhelming and fascinating." Christ Sci Monit

Rutherfurd, Edward

Sarum; the novel of England. Crown 1987 897p

LC 87-6710

This novel, set in Salisbury, England, aims to trace English history from the last Ice Age to the present through the lives of five fictional families

"Rutherfurd is strong on the explication of trends and the narration of events. But he relies heavily on the repetition of character types. Nevertheless, 'Sarum' is fascinating and will appeal to Anglophiles, history buffs, and fans of epic-style novels." Christ Sci Monit

Rutland, Eva

No crystal stair; Eva Rutland. Mira 2000 474p.

ISBN 9781551666624; 9781551665191; 1551665190

LC 2003576586

The story follows "the lives of privileged Ann Elizabeth Carter and Army Air Corps pilot Robert Metcalf--their romance, their struggles, and their ultimate happiness--as it sweeps its characters from the genteel, segregated world of Atlanta's black elite through the rough realities of war, prejudice, and civil rights activism and into the present." (Libr J)

Ryan, Hank Phillippi

The **other** woman; Hank Phillippi Ryan. 1st ed. Forge 2012 416 p. (Jane Ryland mysteries) (hardcover) $24.99

ISBN 0765332574; 9780765332578; 9781466800861

LC 2012019932

"When several young women are found murdered near bridges in Boston, the media incite panic by suggesting a serial killer is at work. Det. Jake Brogan must handle the fallout. Meanwhile, Jane Ryland, a recently discredited investigative TV journalist-turned-newspaper reporter, uncovers a possible scandal involving a Senate contender. The plot thickens as story lines entwine and Jane's career and life are endangered." (Library Journal)

Other titles in this series are:

The wrong girl (2013)

Truth be told (2014)

What you see (2015)

Say no more (2016)

Ryan, Jennifer

His cowboy heart; Jennifer Ryan. Avon Books 2017 407 p. (Montana men) (paperback) $7.99

ISBN 9780062435415; 9780062435408; 006243540X

In this novel in the Montana Men series, by Jennifer Ryan, "Ford Kendrick has often dreamed of the day that Jamie Keller would come home to Montana. After high school, she needed to leave--and he, duty-bound to rescue his family's ranch, pushed her to go. . . . Every day since she left, Jamie has longed for Ford. One glimpse confirms it: the sexy, dangerous-looking cowboy left a hole in her heart that nothing else can fill." (Publisher's note)

"Unconditional love and a cast of memorable characters make this tearjerker novel a winner." Pub Wkly

Ryman, Geoff

Paradise tales. Small Beer Press 2011 313p pa $9.99

ISBN 978-1-931520-64-5; 1-931520-64-X

LC 2010-48947

"Often contemplative and subtly ironic, the 16 stories in this outstanding collection work imaginative riffs on a variety of fantasy and SF themes. 'Pol Pot's Beautiful Daughter,' a Cambodian ghost story, and 'The Last Ten Years in the Life of Hero Kai,' a samurai-style narrative, have the delicacy of Asian folktales or lyrical fantasies. By contrast, 'V.A.O.,' about a future society destabilized by prohibitively expensive health care, and 'The Film-makers of Mars,' which suggests that Edgar Rice Burroughs's John Carter stories were drawn from life, are set in futures that credibly extrapolate current scientific and cultural trends. Ryman . . . frequently explores human emotional needs in heartless environments, as in 'Warmth,' which poignantly portrays a young boy's bond with his robot surrogate mother. Readers of all stripes will appreciate these thoughtful tales." Publ Wkly

S

Saadawi, Ahmed

Frankenstein in Baghdad; a novel. Ahmed Saadawi; translated from the Arabic by Jonathan Wright. Penguin Books 2017 281 p. (paperback) $16

ISBN 9780143128809; 9780143128793

LC 2017008182

Man Booker International Prize Longlist (2018)

In this novel, by Ahmed Saadawi, translated by Jonathan Wright, "Hadi--a scavenger . . . --collects human body parts and stitches them together to create a corpse. His goal, he claims, is for the government to recognize the parts as people and to give them proper burial. But when the corpse goes missing, a wave of eerie murders sweeps the city. . . . Hadi soon realizes he's created a monster, one that needs human flesh to survive." (Publisher's note)

"A haunting and startling mix of horror, mystery, and tragedy." Booklist

Sabatini, Rafael

Captain Blood; his odyssey. Houghton Mifflin 1922 356p

"Peter Blood was many things in his time—soldier, country doctor, slave, pirate, and finally Governor of Jamaica. Incidentally, he was an Irishman. Round his humorous-heroic figure Mr. Sabatini has written an exciting romance of the Spanish Main, the facts of which he alleges to have been found in the diary and log books of one Jeremiah Pitt, a follower of Monmouth in 1685 and Blood's faithful companion in adventure." Times Lit Suppl

Sabatini, Rafael

Scaramouche; a romance of the French revolution. Houghton Mifflin 1921 392p

"The story, primarily of love and adventure, is woven around a hero who devoted himself to furthering the republican cause during the first years of the French Revolution (1788-1792). The title character, successively a lawyer, politician, swordsman, and buffoon, crosses paths repeatedly with his sworn enemy, in the end attaining love and happiness." Lenrow. Reader's Guide to Prose Fic

Followed by Scaramouche, the king-maker (1931)

Saberhagen, Fred

Berserker's star. TOR Bks. 2003 368p $24.95

ISBN 0-7653-0423-6

LC 2003-41016

"Wanted in parts of the galaxy for his theft of a powerful space cannon, pilot Harry Silver accepts a business proposition from a mysterious woman who claims she wants to rescue her husband from cultists on Maracanda, a pseudo-planet wedged between a black hole and a neutron star. En route, Silver discovers that his passenger's agenda is not quite what it seems and, after making planefall, he finds that Maracanda holds secrets and terrors beyond his worst fears. . . . Witty dialog, clever plot twists, and a likeably roguish protagonist make this a good selection for most sf collections." Libr J

Saberhagen, Fred

The **fifth** book of lost swords: Coinspinner's story. Doherty Assocs. 1989 244p

LC 89-39878

"When the legendary sword Woundheale disappears from its resting place in the White Temple of Sarykam, investigations reveal that the Sword of Chance, Coinspinner, is once again loose in the world." Libr J

Saberhagen, Fred

The **first** book of lost swords: Woundhealer's story. Doherty Assocs. 1986 281p

LC 86-50319

This book begins a new sequence in the author's fantasy series about mythical swords

A "pleasant adventure that benefits greatly from Saberhagen's narrative gifts as the various strands leapfrog forward, keeping the reader off balance but constantly intrigued." Publ Wkly

Saberhagen, Fred

The **fourth** book of lost swords: Farslayer's story. Doherty Assocs. 1989 252p

LC 89-11638

"Two rival families wage a war of attrition and vengeance for possession of 'Farslayer,' one of the 12 Lost Swords made by the gods and imbued with unearthly powers. A grim sense of fatality underlies the deceptive simplicity of the author's style." Libr J

Saberhagen, Fred

The **last** book of swords: Shieldbreaker's story. TOR Bks. 1994 255p

LC 93-43232

In this concluding book of the saga, "battle extends from palace to peasant hut—indeed, all the way to the moon—and is loaded with remnants of premagical technology as well as the secret of why the Old World fell and magic came to rule. Key to the battle against Vikata the Dark King is Prince Mark's second son, Prince Stephen, who turns out to be a formidable wielder of swords. By the time journeys and battles are done, the only one of the twelve swords that survives is Woundhealer, for even the terrifying Shieldbreaker has perished." Booklist

Saberhagen, Fred

The **second** book of lost swords: Sightblinder's story. Doherty Assocs. 1987 248p

LC 87-50477

"The present story limits itself to a single locale, the island castle of the wizard Honan-Fu, where Prince Mark is imprisoned in ice alongside the wizard by the usurper called the Ancient One. Mark's friends find themselves the temporary allies of Honan-Fu's traitorous daughter, Ninazu, and of the magician emperor, currently incognito with a traveling show. . . . An entertainment of high order." Publ Wkly

Saberhagen, Fred

The **seventh** book of lost swords: Wayfinder's story. TOR Bks. 1992 251p

LC 92-858

"One of 12 magical swords forged by the Gods, Wayfinder has the power to guide its possessor to whatever the seeker wants. Chance brings Wayfinder to Ben of Purkinje, who uses it to find Woundhealer, the sword with powers to cure the injured wife of Prince Mar of Sarykam. The evil magician Wood also wants the swords; his attack on Ben brings Mark, and even more swords, into the fray. . . . Saberhagen keeps the plot moving, providing a pleasurable light reading experience." Publ Wkly

Saberhagen, Fred

The **sixth** book of lost swords: Mindsword's story. TOR Bks. 1990 250p

LC 90-38899

"Intended as a peace offering from Prince Murat to the Princess Kristin, the Mindsword—one of the legendary weapons used in the war that brought about the death of the gods—plunges two countries into near-war as the well-meaning Murat falls victim to the sword's seductive powers. Saberhagen treads a fine line between fantasy and moral fable in his latest addition to a popular series." Libr J

Saberhagen, Fred

The **third** book of lost swords: Stonecutter's story. Doherty Assocs. 1988 247p

LC 87-51397

This novel "deals with the search of Prince al-Farabi and Magistrate Wen Chang for the lost sword Stonecutter. The book's virtues include a cast of well-drawn characters and some vividly realized societies, as well as Saberhagen's usual spare prose and sound narrative technique." Booklist

Sackville-West, V.

All passion spent. Doubleday, Doran 1931 294p

"When Lady Slane, after the death of her famous husband, shocks her family by going to live by herself in a little house in Hempstead, she is for the first time in her eighty-eight years asserting her right to live her own life. The year of quiet reminiscences there is not without exciting moments, for a man who has loved her silently for sixty years renews his friendship, tells her of his love, then suddenly dies, and leaves her his enormous fortune. What she does with this fortune is another instance of her self-assertion. Gentle, charming Lady Slane, her family, and her friends, drawn with wit and skill in this tale of graceful old age, create an impression of subtlety and beauty." Booklist

Sackville-West, V.

The **Edwardians**. Doubleday, Doran 1930 314p

The setting of this story of Edwardian England is the beautiful old manor-house of Chevron. The characters are grouped around Sebastian, the young heir to the dukedom, and his mother, a famous hostess of the day. Individuals count for less in the novel—a decadent but decorative society. The close of the story, marked by King George's coronation, finds the young duke breaking with the traditions that have bound him, not unwillingly, and starting a new era for himself

"'The Edwardians' is of undoubted excellence from two points of view. First, it is a magnificent portrait of a class and an era. Secondly, it is remarkable for its excellent prose style." Springfield Repub

Sada, Daniel

Almost never; Daniel Sada; translated by Katherine Silver. Graywolf Press 2012 330 p. (alk. paper) $16

ISBN 1555976093; 9781555976095

LC 2011944859

This book by Daniel Sada presents a "Rabelaisian tale of lust and longing in the drier precincts of postwar Mexico. . . . One day, more bored than usual, Demetrio visits a bordello. . . . There he begins an all-consuming . . . relationship with a prostitute named Mireya. . . . He meets the beautiful and virginal Renata and quickly falls in love. . . . Naturally he tries to maintain both relationships." (Publisher's note)

Sáenz, Benjamin Alire, 1954-

Everything Begins and Ends at the Kentucky Club; Benjamin Alire Sáenz. Cinco Puntos Press 2012 222 p. $16.95

ISBN 1935955322; 9781935955320

LC 2012004532

Stonewall Book Awards: Literature Honor Book (2012)

PEN/Faulkner Award for Fiction (2013)

This collection of short stories by Benjamin Alire Saenz "have even more to do with boundaries--the boundaries people set to protect themselves from physical or emotional harm, the ones that people cross in order to survive, or the ones they cross to intrude or intervene in someone else's life. Sàenz's tales are about the arbitrary boundaries that society sets and the ones children build against a world they don't understand." (Booklist)

"Sáenz's moving collection of short stories hinges on the intergenerational clientele of the titular borderland watering hole just south of the U.S.-Mexican divide on Avenida Juárez. . . . [T]here's much to enjoy in these gritty, heartfelt stories." Pub Wkly

Saer, Juan Jose

The **sixty**-five years of Washington; translated from the Spanish by Steve Dolph. Open Letter 2010 203p pa $14.95

ISBN 978-1-934824-20-7; 1-934824-20-8

LC 2010-29041

Original Spanish edition, 1986

In this novel, "the Argentine writer Saer packs several decades of his country's history into a single hour. The premise is deceptively simple. On a fall morning in 1961 a pair of young men take a stroll in the city of Santa Fe. Ángel Leto, a skinny man who lives with his mother, skips work and runs into a tall, white-clad acquaintance known among friends as 'the Mathematician,' a chemical engineer distributing press releases about a recent trip to Europe. In three sections covering seven blocks each, Saer flits between his protagonists' minds, relating their fleeting sensations, memories, epiphanies and distractions in exquisite detail. As they speculate about the events of a recent party that neither attended (for the 65th birthday of Jorge Washington Noriega, the 'Washington' of the title) the reader begins to grasp the web of relationships that bind their circle of intellectuals and activists. . . . With meticulous prose, rendered by Dolph's translation into propulsive English, Saer's novel captures the wilderness of human experience in all its variety." N Y Times Book Rev

Sagan, Carl

Contact; a novel. Simon & Schuster 1985 432p

LC 85-14645

"A serious blend of science fact and speculation with a fast-paced and well-crafted story . . . suggesting that Sagan is more interested in illustrating human relations and human response than depicting alien creatures. . . . Sagan has provided a novel of ideas, and finds drama in how people interact with them in a situation of challenge and discovery." Christ Sci Monit

Sagan, Francoise

★ **Bonjour** tristesse; translated from the French by Irene Ash. Dutton 1955 128p

Original French edition, 1954

"The story of a jealous, sophisticated 17-year-old girl whose meddling in her father's impending remarriage leads to tragic consequences, it was written with 'classical' restraint and a tone of cynical disillusionment. The book showed the persistence of traditional form during a period of experimentation in French fiction." Merriam-Webster's Ency of Lit

Sager, Riley

Final girls; Riley Sager. Dutton, an imprint of Penguin Random House 2017 342 p. (hardcover) $26

ISBN 9781101985373; 9781101985366

LC 2016034340

In this novel, by Riley Sager, "ten years ago, college student Quincy Carpenter went on vacation with five friends and came back alone, the only survivor of a horror movie–scale massacre. In an instant, she became a member of a club no one wants to belong to—a group of similar survivors known in the press as the Final Girls. . . . Now, Quincy is doing well—maybe even great, thanks to her Xanax prescription. . . . That is, until Lisa, the first Final Girl, is found dead in her bathtub." (Publisher's note)

"Sager does an excellent job throughout of keeping the audience guessing until the final twist. A fresh voice in psychological suspense." Kirkus

Sahota, Sunjeev, 1981-

The **year** of the runaways; Sunjeev Sahota. Alfred A. Knopf 2016 496 p. (hardcover) $27.95

ISBN 1101946105; 9781101946107

LC 2015005197

Man Booker Prize Shortlist (2015)

In this novel by Sunjeev Sahota, "three young men, and one unforgettable woman, come together in a journey from India to England, where they hope to begin something new—to support their families; to build their futures; to show their worth; to escape the past. . . . [It] unfolds over the course of one shattering year . . . in which their hopes

. . . are decimated by the punishing realities of immigrant life." (Publisher's note)

"Quarrelling, parting, and finding solace in one another in unexpected ways, Sahota's characters are wonderfully drawn, and imbued with depth and feeling." Pub Wkly

Saint James, Simone

The **haunting** of Maddy Clare; Simone St. James. New American Library 2012 330 p.

ISBN 0451235681; 9780451235688

LC 2011033391

This novel, by Simone St. James, begins when "Sarah Piper's . . . temporary agency sends her to assist a ghost hunter. Alistair Gellis . . . has been summoned to investigate the spirit of nineteen-year-old maid Maddy Clare, who is haunting the barn where she committed suicide. . . . Maddy's ghost is real [and] she's angry. . . . Can Sarah and Alistair's assistant . . . discover who Maddy was, where she came from, and what is driving her desire for vengeance-before she destroys them all?" (Publisher's note)

Saint, H. F.

Memoirs of an invisible man. Atheneum Pubs. 1987 396p

ISBN 0-689-11735-3

LC 85-48144

"The CIA agents, always just one step behind, are deliciously funny Keystone Cops, ridiculous in their attempts to capture a non-entity. This delightful first novel updates a common childhood fantasy with the excitement of a spy story and a hilarious adult portrayal of life and love under the most peculiar conditions." Libr J

Saint-Exupery, Antoine de

★ The **little** prince; written and illustrated by Antoine de Saint-Exupery; translated from the French by Richard Howard. Harcourt 2000 83p il $18; pa $12

ISBN 0-15-202398-4; 0-15-601219-7 pa

LC 99-50439

A new translation of the title first published 1943 by Reynal & Hitchcock

"This many-dimensional fable of an airplane pilot who has crashed in the desert is for readers of all ages. The pilot comes upon the little prince soon after the crash. The prince tells of his adventures on different planets and on Earth as he attempts to learn about the universe in order to live peacefully on his own small planet. A spiritual quality enhances the seemingly simple observations of the little prince." Shapiro. Fic for Youth. 3d edition

Saint-Exupery, Antoine de

Night flight; preface by André Gide; translated by Stuart Gilbert. Century 1932 198p

"In a story that captures the adventures of early aviation, Rivière, chief of the airport at Buenos Aires, supervises the night flights of airmail in South America. He challenges his crew to meet any and all obstacles. When one of his three mail planes crashes over the Andes, he dispatches the European mail plane on schedule anyway." Shapiro. Fic for Youth. 3d edition

Saintcrow, Lilith

Trailer park fae; Lilith Saintcrow. Orbit 2015 352 p. (series: Gallow and Ragged) (softcover) $15

ISBN 9780316277853

LC 2014046001

In this fantasy novel, by Lilith Saintcrow, part of the Gallow and Ragged series, "Jeremiah Gallow is just another construction worker, and that's the way he likes it. He's left his past behind, but some things cannot be erased. Like the tattoos on his arms that transform into a weapon, or that he was once closer to the Queen of Summer than any half-human should be." (Publisher's note)

"Saintcrow's excellent tale will immerse readers in a complex and eerily familiar world of fae-inhabited trailer parks and diners and find definite appeal among fans of Seanan Maguire's "October Daye" series. Try this for Charles de Lint aficionados who want something a touch lighter but still with profound worldbuilding and characters." LJ

Sakey, Marcus

A **Better** World; by Marcus Sakey. Thomas & Mercer 2014 390 p. (The Brilliance Saga) pbk $14.95

ISBN 9781477823941; 1477823948

"U.S. President Lionel Clay, a man temperamentally and intellectually better suited to the classroom than to national leadership, desperately needs the help of Nick Cooper, one of the "brilliants" born since 1980 with special gifts that outstrip 99% of humanity. The members of a shadowy group, the Children of Darwin, are burning truckers alive, starving three American cities, and threatening all-out civil war." (Publishers Weekly)

"Sakey's series has been taken as an allegory of America devouring its own. Could be. But recommend it, too, as a first-rate actioner forever pulsing forward, told in vivid, even poetic prose." Booklist

Sakey, Marcus

The **blade** itself. St. Martin's Minotaur 2007 307p $22.95

ISBN 978-0-312-36031-3; 0-312-36031-2

LC 2006-50562

As the author "takes Danny apart and looks to see what the man is really worth, the novel delivers some implicit social commentary about the shaky foundation on which Danny's new life has been built. . . . Not until the very end of the story is it clear who Danny is or where he stands. His ability to churn these questions so vigorously will bring Mr. Sakey attention." N Y Times (Late N Y Ed)

Sakey, Marcus

Brilliance; by Marcus Sakey. Amazon Pub 2013 452 p. (paperback) $14.95

ISBN 1611099692; 9781611099690

In his novel, author Macus Sakey focuses his plot on individuals with extraordinary psychological abilities "called 'brilliants,' and since 1980, one percent of people have been born this way. Nick Cooper is among them; a federal agent, Cooper has gifts rendering him exceptional at hunting terrorists. His latest target may be the most dangerous man alive, a brilliant drenched in blood and intent on provoking civil war. But to catch him, Cooper will have to violate everything he believes in--and betray his own kind."

Other titles in this series are:
A better world (2014)
Written in fire (2016)

Sakey, Marcus

The **two** deaths of Daniel Hayes; a novel. Dutton 2011 390p $25.95

ISBN 978-0-525-95211-4

LC 2011-04280

This book "begins with Daniel Hayes, naked and nearly drowned, lying in the surf off the coast of Maine. Suffering from amnesia and a vague feeling of guilt, he believes the answers to his current state lie in Los Angeles and heads there trying to find his identity. He discovers that he is a successful screenwriter and that his glamorous TV star wife has just been murdered in a car accident. The cops are after him as a suspect, and a blackmailing hard guy is also pursuing him. . . . The action is fast-paced, the tension is nearly constant, and there are more twists in the plot than in a double helix." Libr

Saki

★ The **short** stories of Saki; with an introduction by Christopher Morley. Modern Lib. 1983 $12.95

ISBN 0-394-60428-8

LC 83-5468

First published 1930 by Viking; first Modern Library edition 1951

Salak, Kira

The **white** Mary; a novel. Henry Holt and Co. 2008 351p $25

ISBN 978-0-8050-8847-2; 0-8050-8847-4

LC 2008-7278

"Salak's descriptions of the jungle passage are compelling and dreamlike. Even stronger are flashbacks of Marika in Bodo and a wrenching, horrific account of Lewis's capture and torture in East Timor. Salak's own journalistic experiences—she covered the Rwandan genocide and the 2003 war in the Congo, among other conflicts—have armed her with heartfelt, if indelibly grim, insights into man's capacity for 'an endless stream of the worst, most inconceivable acts of inhumanity'. . . . In The White Mary, Salak shows the courage of facing down that darkness and the inescapable price it exacts upon one's soul." Washington Post Book World

Salinger, J. D.

★ The **catcher** in the rye. Little, Brown 1951 277p $24.95; pa $5.99

ISBN 0-316-76953-3; 0-316-76948-7 pa

"The story of adolescent Holden Caulfield who runs away from boarding-school in Pennsylvania to New York where he preserves his innocence despite various attempts to lose it. The colloquial, lively, first-person narration, with its attacks on the 'phoniness' of the adult world and its clinging to family sentiment in the form of Holden's affection for his sister Phoebe, made the novel accessible to and popular with a wide readership, particularly with the young." Oxford Companion to Engl Lit. 5th edition

Salinger, J. D.

★ **Franny** & Zooey. Little, Brown 1961 201p $24.95; pa $5.99

ISBN 0-316-76954-1; 0-316-76949-5 pa

"At 20, Franny Glass is experiencing desperate dissatisfaction with her life and seems to be looking for help via a religious awakening. Her brother Zooey tries to help her out of this depression. He recalls the influence on their growth and development of their appearance as young radio performers on a network program called 'It's a Wise Child.' An older brother, Buddy, is also an important component of the interrelationships in the Glass family." Shapiro. Fic for Youth. 3d edition

Salinger, J. D.

★ **Nine** stories. Little, Brown 1953 302p $24.95; pa $5.99

ISBN 0-316-76956-8; 0-316-76950-9 pa

This collection "introduced various members of the Glass family who would dominate the remainder of Salinger's work. Critical response divided itself between high praise and cult worship. Most of the stories deal with precocious, troubled children, whose religious yearnings—often tilting toward the East—are in vivid contrast to the materialistic and spiritually empty world of their parents. The result was a perfect literary formula for the 1950s." Benet's Reader's Ency of Am Lit

Salinger, J. D.

★ **Raise** high the roof beam, carpenters, and Seymour: an introduction. Little, Brown 1963 248p $24.95

ISBN 0-316-76957-6

This volume "reprints stories from The New Yorker (1955, 1959), in which Buddy Glass tells, first, of his return to New York during the war to attend his brother Seymour's wedding and of Seymour's jilting of the bride and then of their later elopement; and, second, after Seymour's suicide, of Buddy's own brooding, to the point of breakdown, upon Seymour's virtues, human and literary." Oxford Companion to Am Lit. 6th edition

Sallis, James ✓

Cripple Creek; a novel. Walker & Co. 2006 193p $23

ISBN 978-0-8027-3382-5; 0-8027-3382-4

LC 2005-28095

"As this tale opens, Turner, ex-cop, ex-con, and ex-psychotherapist, remains on the lam in rural Cypress Grove, Tennessee, escaping the demons of past lives in Memphis, but he is starting to mend. There's a developing relationship with Val Bjorn, teacher and country musician; there's the appearance of his daughter from Seattle; and there's the fact that he has come out of hibernation to accept the job as deputy sheriff of Cypress Grove. Then his boss, the kindly sheriff, is assaulted by a gang of mobbed-up toughs in the act of breaking one of their own out of the small-town jail. Turner pursues the thugs to Memphis, confronting his past and giving vent to his suppressed blood lust. Every action prompts a reaction, however, and soon the thugs return to Cypress Grove looking for some blood of their own. Sallis tells the violent tale quietly, effectively using jump cuts, flashbacks, and flashforwards to generate both suspense and, simultaneously, a sense of inevitability. The stunning finale makes clear that Turner has a lot more healing to do." Booklist

Sallis, James

✓ **Cypress** Grove. Walker & Co. 2003 255p $24

ISBN 0-8027-3380-8

LC 2002-41480

"Turner ('just Turner'), a former Memphis cop who went to prison for something he'd like to forget, has dropped out of human circulation and buried himself in a cabin in the deep woods. Because Turner's communication skills are rusty, Sallis gives him a constrained narrative voice, the guarded speech of a man so wary of emotion that the very act of speaking seems to leave his throat raw. When the sheriff of this rural backwater asks for his help with a murdered drifter who was found with a wooden stake in his chest, Turner crawls out of hibernation." N Y Times Book Rev

Sallis, James

Drive. Poisoned Pen Press 2005 Book $18.95

ISBN 1590581814; 9781590581902

LC 2005925325

This noir fiction novel, adapted into a 2011 motion picture, centers on "amoral Driver, who is what he does—a man who drives stunt cars in Hollywood for a day job, and getaway cars in his spare time. The novel opens with the aftermath of a shoot-out, the result of the gang Driver is with robbing someone too powerful for them. Driver continues to kill in order to stay alive and, as he does so, the novel asks just how much we are tied to our fates; whether we can ever escape our backgrounds." (The Independent)

"Sallis gives us his most tightly written mystery to date, worthy of comparison to the compact, exciting oeuvre of French noir giant Jean-Patrick Manchette." Pub Wkly

Sallis, James

★ **Driven**. Poisoned Pen Press 2012 158p

ISBN 9781464200113; 9781464200120

LC 2011944604

This noir fiction novel, a sequel to the author's novel "Drive," continues with "[t]he enigmatic loner known as Driver, introduced in 2005's Drive, [who] takes to the road again after two thugs assault him and his fiancée on a Phoenix, Ariz., street. . . . Maybe Driver is paranoid, but is it really paranoia when one team of hit men after another track you down and try to put you on ice? 'Two cars this time, and they'd waited for an isolated stretch of road. Chevy Caprice and a high-end Toyota.'" (Publishers Weekly)

"The language is plain, the action is brutal, and the characters are memorably and briefly etched... This gritty, gristly tale will rivet Sallis's growing audience." LJ

Sallis, James

The **killer** is dying; a novel. Walker Pub. Co. 2011 232p $24

ISBN 978-0-8027-7945-8; 0-8027-7945-X

LC 2010-38548

Sallis "takes his time weaving together the lives of these lost souls, each apparently as aimless as the bugs and birds they can't help noticing. The payoff is a moment of well-nigh miraculous consolation." Kirkus

Sallis, James

Salt River; a novel. Walker & Company 2007 146p $21.95

ISBN 978-0-8027-1617-0; 0-8027-1617-2

In this mystery featuring John "Turner—Vietnam veteran, former cop, ex-con, retired psychiatrist, and interim sheriff of a rural county south of Memphis—Sallis's story meanders through a summer and fall, chronicling Turner's professional and private lives as they merge into one. Turner's tranquillity is shattered when the son of his predecessor drives what might be a stolen car through the front of the city hall, seriously injuring himself and launching a case that escalates into breaking and entering, elder abuse, kidnapping, and murder. Meanwhile, Turner deals with the return of a friend who is wanted by the police in Texas and a less-than-welcome report from his physician. Sallis has created a laid-back, small-town setting in which understanding motives sometimes takes precedence over punishing crimes." Libr J

Salter, James, 1925-2015

All that is; a novel. James Salter. 1st ed. Alfred A. Knopf 2013 304 p. (ebook) $80.85; (hardcover) $26.95

ISBN 1400043131; 9780307961099; 9781400043132

LC 2012020914

In this book, World War II veteran "Philip Bowman returns to America and finds a position as a book editor" while struggling with his love life. "One marriage goes bad; another fails to happen; and, finally, he meets a woman who enthralls, then betrays him, setting him on a course he could never have imagined for himself." (Publisher's note)

Salter, James

Last night. Knopf 2005 132p $20

ISBN 1-4000-4312-3

LC 2004-57793

"All of the stories in 'Last Night' are superb, but the title story is the tautest and most memorable. . . . This story about the consequences of adultery gives new meaning to the phrase 'the morning after.' Despite its shocking plot twist, the story maintains the exacting, calm narrative voice that has distinguished all of Salter's work. His characters may be haunted by death and disappointment, but Salter never judges them, never even pretends to have them neatly pegged. He lets them stay elliptical, in shadow." N Y Times Book Rev

Samarasan, Preeta

Evening is the whole day. Houghton Mifflin 2008 340p $24

ISBN 0-618-87447-X; 978-0-618-87447-7

LC 2008-4729

"This first novel, set in Malaysia, revolves around the secrets of an Indian family." (N Y Times Book Rev)

This "novel revolves around a wealthy Indian family living in modern-day Malaysia. What seems like a simple act—the firing of the servant girl—has greater implications for the family than it could ever have imagined, especially for six-year-old Aasha. Aasha has a secret, one that could devastate not only her family but also the entire community. Samarasan wisely withholds this secret and others, pulling readers in. Because the description of Malaysia and its diverse population is so achingly lyrical, readers will want to slow down to absorb each word; at other times, as when they get caught up in the family drama, they will want to quicken their pace." Libr J

Sams, Ferrol

Down town; the journal of James Aloysius Holcombe, Jr. for Ephraim Holcombe Mookinfoos. Mercer University Press 2007 309p $25

ISBN 978-0-8814-6072-8; 0-8814-6072-9

LC 2007-12030

"For poetry-spouting bachelor lawyer James 'Buster' Aloysius Holcombe Jr., even the finest Southern woman is no competition for his beloved Georgia hometown. . . . [This novel is] crafted as a folksy journal tracing the paths of the good people of Fayette County, Georgia, from the Civil War right up to the prosperous present. . . . Despite Buster's penchant for quoting Edna St. Vincent Millay as a means of seduction, in advancing years he ambles on blissfully single. After all, who needs romance when the folks in your hometown are so utterly charming—the wise doctor, the wealthy and eccentrically frugal banker and his blithering albeit loveable wife all keep Buster plenty busy with their conceits and confidences. Like the best road trips, Down Town is not intent upon reaching any particular destination, but rather savoring the journey along the way." BookPage

Samuel, Barbara

No place like home; Barbara Samuel. Ballantine Books 2002 298p (pbk.) $19

ISBN 0345445651 (alk. paper); 9780345460370

LC 2001052666

RITA Awards: Best Contemporary Single Title (2002), Romantic Time Reviewers' Choice Award: Mainstream (2002)

RITA Awards: Top Ten Favorite Books (2002)

This book tells the story of "Jewel Sabatino [who] lives in New York and has a gay best friend dying of AIDS, rancid memories of a nonmarriage to a nonstarter, a teen musician son, an estrangement from her father, . . . and an unrelieved case of low self-esteem. When she learns . . . that she's inherited her great-aunt's house and that her apartment building in Greenwich Village is going condo, Sabatino knows it's time to go home. She, 17-year-old son Shane and ill best friend Michael Shaunnessey head for her third-generation Italian-American enclave in Pueblo, Colo. There she comes to terms with who she is, helped considerably by Malachi Shaunnessey, a 'big, alligator-blood-drinking tough guy' who shows up to ease his dying brother Michael's last days, bringing more than just comfort to Jewel in the process." (Publishers Weekly)

Sanchez, Thomas

King Bongo; a novel of Havana. Knopf 2003 309p $25

ISBN 0-679-40696-4

LC 2002-40770

"The byzantine plot is neatly constructed and thoroughly involving but never an end in itself. Sanchez shows us a city and a people on the eve of revolution but filters it all through the emotions of a conflicted hero, sympathetic to the cause but loyal only to himself and those he loves. Havana is both setting and soul in this pulsing bolero of a novel." Booklist

Sand, George

★ **Lelia**; translated, with an introduction by Maria Espinosa. Indiana Univ. Press 1978 xxi, 234p

LC 77-23639

Original French edition, 1833

"Independent and sensual Lélia has had many lovers. Now repelled by physical passion, which represents the means by which men dominate women, Lélia tells her sister Pulchérie, a courtesan, that neither celibacy nor love affairs satisfy her. Pulchérie suggests that Lélia become a courtesan; she may find fulfillment by giving pleasure to others. Lélia tries to seduce Sténio, a young poet who is in love with her; she cannot continue, however, and sends Pulchérie in her stead. As a result of this betrayal, Sténio falls into utter debauchery, and despite attempts to rescue him, he comes to a tragic end." Merriam-Webster's Ency of Lit

Sand, George

Marianne. Carroll & Graf Pubs. 1988 171p

LC 88-7308

Original French edition, 1876

"Marianne Chevreuse, the 25-year-old heroine of this romantic tale set in 1825 . . . is independent yet intensely female, and she breaks many conventions of society while living by her own deeply held moral beliefs. Pierre André is an older man who has known her since her childhood. When asked to introduce her to a prospective suitor, he discovers his own love for Marianne. The plot twists and turns until the unsuitable Philippe Gaucher—who is indeed gauche—is sent packing and Pierre and Marianne are betrothed. While very much a period piece, this last scrap of Sand's tremendous oeuvre is a charming bit of entertainment." Publ Wkly

Sanders, Dori

★ **Clover**; a novel. Algonquin Bks. 1990 183p $17.95

ISBN 0-945575-26-2

LC 89-39072

After her father dies within hours of being married to a white woman, Clover Hill, a ten-year-old black girl, learns with her new stepmother to overcome grief and to adjust to a new place in their rural Black South Carolina community

The author "has staked out an impressive new territory here, replete with peach farmers, textile workers, drunks and crazy people, with the newly middle class as well as the terminally poor. As a specimen of the new realism in regional fiction, 'Clover' is very much the genuine item." N Y Times Book Rev

Sanders, Lawrence

★ The **first** deadly sin. Putnam 1973 566p

This novel "pits a psychopathic killer loose in New York against a tough, dedicated police officer who is not without his own hangups. Telling his story alternately from the psychopath's point of view and that of the detective, Mr. Sanders draws the two men closer and closer together on an inevitable collision course. Probing the dark side of the killer's mind, his sexual conflicts and involvement with a strange trio of brother, sister and valet who are as kinky as they come, he shows the man's accelerating descent into total madness. Meanwhile, Captain Edward X. Delaney, in whose upper East Side precinct a series of random murders is taking place, accepts an undercover assignment to track down the man responsible." Publ Wkly

Sanders, Lawrence

The **fourth** deadly sin. Putnam 1985 380p

LC 84-24789

"Delaney displays that combination of computerlike efficiency and human touch that make him such an appealing detective. It's a masterly performace, not only chilling, but thought-provoking and often touching." Publ Wkly

Sanders, Lawrence

McNally's dilemma. Putnam 1999 309p $24.95

ISBN 0-399-14490-0

LC 99-20988

"McNally is a Palm Beach gumshoe who, with his attorney father, makes up the firm of McNally and Son's Department of Discreet Inquiries. . . . This time, the action begins with a late-night call from wealthy Melva Ashton Manning Williams, who has just blown away her second husband, Geoff Williams, née Wolinsky, after finding him in the arms of another woman. Things quickly shift from murder to blackmail and puzzles within puzzles, all of which Archy sorts out in his usual stylish fashion." Booklist

Sanders, Lawrence

★ **McNally's** gamble. Putnam 1997 307p $24.95

ISBN 0-399-14248-7

LC 96-50369

A "comic whodunit featuring Archy McNally, the foppish but likable head of 'discreet inquiries' at his father's law firm in Palm Beach, Fla. This time Archy's task is to investigate the credentials of a suspicious investment adviser, Frederick Clemens, and his secretary, Felix Katz. . . . Mr. Sanders clearly delights in playing up the bumbling, spoof aspects of this detective yarn, especially during its climactic but unavoidably funny denouement." NY Times Book Rev

Sanders, Lawrence

McNally's puzzle. Putnam 1996 311p

LC 95-45703

In this mystery, playboy/sleuth Archy McNally "must dig into the gruesome death of a millionaire parrot-shop owner named Hiram Gottschalk in an attempt to unravel the circumstances of his passing and the tangled mess of the family he leaves behind. . . . The real focus is on Archy's prancing and preening and so-called life of the mind as he tools around south Florida entertaining the millionaire's twin daughters, fencing with his housekeeper and tracking the bizarre activities—parrot smuggling is one, perhaps—of Gottschalk's troubled stepson." N Y Times Book Rev

Sanders, Lawrence

The **second** deadly sin. Putnam 1977 412p

LC 77-3652

A "police procedural in which Edward X. Delaney, recently retired as Manhattan's chief of detectives, returns by invitation of the department to work on the mystery-murder of a thoroughly unlikable genius, painter Victor Maitland. Delaney, a curious mixture of force and sensitivity, is teamed with a young sergeant, whose drinking has brought him to the edge of dismissal. The two, with an accidentally added starter, Jason T. Jason (black, smart, and very big), by a combination of hard work, intuition, and some luck finally track down the killer." Booklist

Sanders, Lawrence

The **sixth** commandment; a novel. Putnam 1979 350p

ISBN 0-399-12305-9

LC 78-13158

"This gloomy escapade about a hard-drinking, chain-smoking, world-pitying investigator . . . is brimful of juice and excitement, with some insight and much foolishness—a genuinely riveting diversion." New Yorker

Sanders, Lawrence

Sullivan's sting. Putnam 1990 348p

ISBN 0-399-13542-1

LC 89-70046

This novel "profiles the slimy underbelly of south Florida, where con men posing as financial wizards bilk greedy, unsuspecting investors out of their money (aging widows are a prime mark). The main player here is sexy David Rathbone, a man who apparently could sell igloos to Eskimos. Equally sexy undercover cop Rita Angela Sullivan is on a mission from the SEC to 'sting' Rathbone. She traps her prey, starts to play house, and moves in for the kill—then finds herself falling in love with the guy." Booklist

Sanders, Lawrence

The **third** deadly sin. Putnam 1981 444p

LC 80-26325

"Sergeant Boone of Manhattan's Homicide Squad persuades former Chief of Detectives Delaney to help find what police fear most, a random killer. The two men . . . begin the slow, almost hopeless, scrupulously painstaking chore of tracking down and piecing together the tiniest clues. The detecting account alternates with vivid, step-by-step descriptions of drab Zoe Kohler, who tarts herself up periodically and ritually murders men she picks up in convention-crowded hotels. In the telling, Sander's characters discuss facets of feminism and crime provocatively, and not at all simplistically, adding to the dimensions of a superior mystery." Publ Wkly

Sanders, Lawrence

Timothy's game. Putnam 1988 382p

LC 87-29073

This novel is "set on Wall Street, where clever detective Timothy Cone dresses in Salvation Army chic, chain-smokes Camels, and drinks too much. Cone has a cat named Cleo who eats ham hocks, potato salad, and garlic salami, and a girlfriend named Samantha who sports long, auburn hair. Throw in a foul-mouthed woman who owns a garbage-hauling firm controlled by the mob, an insider-trading leak, murder, and a tong war in Chinatown, and you have the usual brand of Sanders' readable fiction." Booklist

Sanderson, Brandon

Elantris. Tor 2005 492p il $27.95

ISBN 978-0-765-31177-1

LC 2004-63765

This fantasy is "refreshingly complete unto itself and free of the usual genre clichés, offers something for everyone: mystery, magic, romance, political wrangling, religious conflict, fights for equality, sharp writing and wonderful, robust characters." Publ Wkly

Sanderson, Brandon

The **final** empire; Brandon Sanderson. Tor 2006 541p il (Mistborn) $27.95

ISBN 978-0-765-31178-8; 0-765-31178-X

LC 2005-34496

"The Sliver of Infinity, the Lord Ruler, is the locus of religious and temporal order in a world in which the skaa are slaves or worse. Half-skaa erstwhile thief Kelsior is the only person to survive and escape the Lord Ruler's most brutal prison, in which, however, he discovered he has the powers of the Mistborn, which are based on the internal 'burning' of certain metals, all of which the Mistborn can use, while most others can burn only one. Now Kelsior plans his most daring raid ever, into the center of the palace to discover the secret of the Lord Ruler's power. . . . Intrigue, politics, and conspiracies mesh complexly in a world Sanderson realizes in satisfying depth and peoples with impressive characters." Booklist

Other titles in this series are:
The well of ascension (2007)
The hero of ages (2008)
The alloy of law (2011)
Shadows of self (2015)
The bands of mourning (2016)

Sandford, John

Broken prey. Putnam 2005 390p $26.95

ISBN 0-399-15272-5

LC 2005-42981

Lucas Davenport, a "Minnesota State Bureau of Criminal Apprehension investigator, had lately been doing political fix-it jobs for the governor, but this time he's got a psychopathic serial killer on his hands. . . . The first victim, a young woman, was 'scourged' with a wire whip; number two, a young man, had his penis cut off. Evidence first points to recently released sex offender Charlie Pope. Though Charlie is pretty dumb and the killer is extremely smart, it takes Davenport and his series partner, Detective Sloan, a while to realize they're chasing the wrong guy. Sandford introduces some lighter moments, the most entertaining about Davenport's new iPod and his quest to compile a list of the 100 best rock songs ever recorded, which every cop on the force gives him suggestions for. These moments allow readers to catch their breath amid the otherwise nonstop tension." Publ Wkly

Sandford, John

Buried prey. G. P. Putnam's Sons 2011 390p $27.95

ISBN 978-0-399-15738-7

LC 2011-04990

"The bodies of two teenage sisters are discovered in a plastic bag beneath the concrete-floor basement of a house being razed in Minneapolis. City police are called, but Davenport, an investigator with a state law enforcement agency, also arrives quickly at the scene. To his anguish, Davenport readily recognizes their clothing. Two-anda-half decades earlier, he had been the lead investigator on the Minneapolis police force that probed their 1985 disappearance. Sandford . . . flashes back to 1985, when a suspect died during a manhunt. Davenport never believed the suspect killed the girls because the homeless drifter didn't seem mentally capable. Also, Minneapolis police were never able to identify the caller of two tips that made the drifter the top suspect. Flashing forward to the present, Davenport takes on the reopened case." San Antonio Express-News

Sandford, John

Certain prey. Putnam 1999 339p $24.95

ISBN 0-399-14496-X

LC 99-19048

"Trying to avoid facing his empty personal life, enigmatic Minneapolis Deputy Police Chief Lucus Davenport is jolted out of the doldrums by the handiwork of professional hitwoman Clara Rinker, in town to do what she does best. Adding to his problems is glamorous defense attorney Carmel Loan, a clever and intimidating lawyer. When Davenport suspects an alliance between the two women, he soon faces two deadly enemies. Sandford keeps the level of suspense dizzyingly high as he shifts viewpoints between the women and Davenport." Booklist

Sandford, John, 1944-

Deadline; John Sandford. Putnam Adult 2014 400 p. (hardcover) $27.95

ISBN 9780399162374

LC 2014026891

In this book, by John Sandford, "a school board meeting is coming to an end. The board chairman announces that the rest of the meeting will be closed, due to personnel issues. . . . The proposal up for a vote before them is whether to authorize the killing of a local reporter. . . . Meanwhile, not far away, Virgil Flowers is helping out a friend by looking into a dognapping, which seems to be turning into something much bigger and uglier." (Publisher's note)

"Sanford balances straight-talking Virgil Flowers' often hilariously folksy tone and Trippton's dark core of methamphetamine manufacturers and sociopaths; the result is pure reading pleasure for thriller fans." Booklist

Sandford, John

Mind prey. Putnam 1995 323p

LC 95-3790

"When psychiatrist Andi Manette and her two young daughters are kidnapped, {Davenport} must discover whether it's a ransom snatch, the work of one of Andi's ex-patients or the ruse of someone in her life who might benefit from her death. . . . Readers know the kidnapper is John Mail, a scary ex-patient who's entertained nasty dreams of Andi for years. . . . Sandford expertly ratchets up the suspense from beginning to the brutal finish." Publ Wkly

Sandford, John

★ **Naked** prey. Putnam 2003 359p $26.95

ISBN 0-399-15043-9

LC 2003-41364

Lucas Davenport "is now Director of Regional Studies in the Minnesota Bureau of Criminal Apprehension, which is a fancy name for the job of investigating difficult crimes as quickly as possible and answering to the governor of the state. Known for his ability to solve the unsolvable, he goes to a remote area of the state to discover why a black man and a white woman were hanged in a groove of trees. . . . Fast paced and full of surprises, this may be Sandford's best novel yet." Libr J

Sandford, John

Night prey. Putnam 1994 336p

LC 94-7564

"Despite its length, Night Prey is a tight, fast-moving thriller with appealing good guys and a suitably evil villain. Especially fascinating among the characters is Policewoman Connell." Libr J

Sandford, John

Rules of prey. Putnam 1989 316p

LC 89-4040

"A killer who calls himself the 'maddog' has been murdering Minneapolis women, seemingly without pattern or motive. The crimes are linked only by their brutality and by the slayer's 'signature': at each scene, he leaves a written rule of crime, such as 'Never kill anyone you know,' or, 'Never carry a weapon after it has been used.' Into the case comes Lucas Davenport, a policeman with five kills in the line of duty, a surefire sense of how to handle the thirsty media and strong instincts about the killer's psyche." Publ Wkly

Sandford, John

Shock wave. G.P. Putnam's Sons 2011 388p $27.95

ISBN 978-0-399-15769-1; 0-399-15769-7

LC 2011-27848

"Virgil Flowers is a pretty mellow guy. If he isn't casting off in some quiet trout stream, John Sandford's Minnesota crimeÐstopper might be found behind Bob's Bad Boy Barbeque & Bar, watching some well-nourished farm girls playing a cutthroat game of beach volleyball. But when Virgil's troubleshooting skills are called for, as they are . . . when a bomb-maker initiates a wave of industrial terrorism against the small-town incursions of a big-box chain store, he can move as fast as the next action hero. For someone who casually saunters onto a crime scene in a pink T-shirt, jeans and cowboy boots, Virgil can think on his feet, a valuable asset when the bomber steps up his deadly campaign against Willard Pye's PyeMart empire, which threatens to destroy the small-town character of Butternut Falls." N Y Times Book Rev

Sandford, John, 1944-

Silken prey; John Sandford. G.P. Putnam's Sons 2013 416 p. (Prey) (hardcover) $27.95

ISBN 0399159312; 9780399159312

LC 2013003703

This novel, by John Sandford, is an episode in the author's "Prey" thriller series. "Murder, scandal, political espionage, and an extremely dangerous woman. Lucas Davenport's going to be lucky to get out of this one alive. . . . Davenport is investigating another case when the trail leads to the man's disappearance, then . . . to the Minneapolis police department, then . . . to a woman who could give Machiavelli lessons." (Publisher's note)

Sandford, John, 1944-

Storm Front; by John Sandford. G. P. Putnam's Sons 2013 376 p. (A Virgil Flowers Novel) $27.95

ISBN 0399159304; 9780399159305

LC 2013024514

In this book by John Sandford, "when an archeological dig in Israel turns up a stele--an inscribed piece of stone--with the potential to shake the roots of Biblical faith, Elijah Jones . . . steals the precious artifact and flees. Virgil, a Minnesota Bureau of Criminal Investigation agent, at first simply attempts to recover the stolen object, but soon finds himself trying to outwit mercenary Turks as well as agents of the Mossad, Hezbollah, and Texas gazillionares, all of whom want the artifact." (Publishers Weekly)

Sandford, John

★ **Winter** prey. Putnam 1993 336p

LC 92-42072

"Davenport, a cool, cynical man of action, is entirely in his element in this harsh terrain—so bitter that it turns animals against men, so brutal that it turns men into beasts." N Y Times Book Rev

Sandlin, Lisa

The **do**-right; by Lisa Sandlin. Cinco Puntos Press 2015 306 p. pbk $16.95

ISBN 1941026192; 9781941026199

LC 2015024949

"1959. Delpha Wade killed a man who was raping her. Wanted to kill the other one too, but he got away. Now, after fourteen years in prison, she's out. It's 1973, and nobody's rushing to hire a parolee. Persistence and smarts land her a secretarial job with Tom Phelan, an ex-roughneck turned neophyte private eye. Together these two pry into the dark corners of Beaumont, a blue-collar, Cajun-influenced town dominated by Big Oil." (Publisher's note)

Sanghera, Sathnam

Marriage Material; by Sathnam Sanghera. William Heinemann 2013 320 p. $18

ISBN 0434021903; 1609453077; 9780434021901; 9781609453077

This novel, by Sathnam Sanghera, "is a luminous exploration of the life of an immigrant family in the UK, layering the contemporary story of a young man caught between British and Punjabi culture, the history of his family, and the new life he's made for himself. In a fresh narrative voice that wryly observes, questions, and reflects, Sanghera confronts the complexities of tradition, culture, love, and family." (Publisher's note)

"Sanghera's precise, hilarious rendition of voices and cultural details is the signal pleasure of a novel rich in humor, history, and heart." Kirkus

Sankaran, Lavanya

The **hope** factory; a novel. Lavanya Sankaran. 1st ed. Dial Press 2013 384 p. (hardcover) $26

ISBN 0385338198; 9780385338196; 9780812984620

LC 2012023483

This novel, "set in Bangalore, traces the disparate yet intersecting lives of Anand Murthy, principal at Cauvery Auto, and Kamala, his family's maid, who is struggling to provide for her 12-year-old son. . . . While Anand and Kamala are both desperately working for what they want, the distance between their worlds is further emphasized by the chasm between their goals." (Publishers Weekly)

Sansom, C. J.

Winter in Madrid. Viking 2008 537p $25.95

ISBN 978-0-670-01848-2; 0-670-01848-1

LC 2007-42552

First published 2006 in the United Kingdom

"Sansom deftly plots his politically charged tale for maximal suspense, all the way up to its stunning conclusion. . . . This moving opus leaves the reader mourning for the Spain that might have been—and the England that maybe never was." Publ Wkly

Santiago, Esmeralda

Conquistadora; a novel. Alfred A. Knopf 2011 416p

ISBN 9780307268327

LC 2010051324

"The book's greatest strength lies in its dissection of the systematic enslavement and oppression of people without which the large-scale planting, harvesting, processing, and transporting of sugar was impossible. Santiago's language is most animated in her depiction of slavery. . . . In Ana, Santiago creates a woman consciously at odds with her culture, chafing at her own oppression, and reluctant but willing to oppress others in order to achieve her own freedom. Though the plot of 'Conquistadora' is thin and the characterizations are flat, in Ana's uneasy rationalization of the brutal, unsustainable system on which these dreams depend, Santiago fleetingly achieves the hallmark of great historical fiction—she makes her protagonist a woman of her times." Boston Globe

Sapienza, Goliarda, 1924-1996

The **art** of joy; Goliarda Sapienza; Translated from the Italian by Anne Milano Appel; With a foreword by Angelo Pellegrino. Farrar Straus & Giroux 2013 704 p. (hardcover) $30

ISBN 0374106142; 9780374106140

LC 2013005477

This book by Goliarda Sapienza follows "a Sicilian woman born on January 1, 1900, whose strength and character are an affront to conventional morality. Impoverished as a child, Modesta believes she is destined for a better life. She is able, through grace and intelligence, to secure marriage to an aristocrat--without compromising her own deeply felt values. Friend, mother, lover--Modesta revels in upsetting the rules of her fascist, patriarchal society." (Publisher's note)

Saramago, Jose

All the names; translated by Margaret Jull Costa. Harcourt 2000 238p $24

ISBN 0-15-100421-8

Original Portuguese edition 1997; this translation first published 1999 in the United Kingdom

"Modest, self-mocking, mildly ironic, yet magisterial, Saramago's gentle voice rings with the unmistakable authority of the true artist." Christ Sci Monit

Saramago, Jose

★ **Blindness**; a novel. translated from the Portuguese by Giovanni Pontiero. Harcourt Brace & Co. 1998 294p $22

ISBN 0-15-100251-7

LC 98-12009

Original Portuguese edition, 1995; this translation first published 1997 in the United Kingdom

"A man waiting in his car for a red light to turn green is the first of an entire city's population—with one exception—to be blinded by a 'milky sea' of dazzling whiteness. The inexplicably disabled victims grope and stumble their way through nightmarish landscapes—first an asylum where those initially afflicted are quarantined, and then the chaotic, squalid streets to which they return. Saramago's surreal allegory explores the ability of the human spirit to prevail in even the most absurdly unjust of conditions, yet he reinvents this familiar struggle with the stylistic eccentricity of a master." New Yorker

Saramago, José, 1922-2010

Cain; translated from the Portuguese by Margaret Jull Costa. Houghton Mifflin Harcourt 2011 159p

ISBN 978-0-547-41989-3

LC 2011-28600

Original Portuguese edition, 2009

This book follows "Cain, the firstborn son of Adam and Eve . . . Cain's travels across a barren landscape lead him to a lusty tryst with Lilith and the witnessing, or altering, of many key events of the Old Testament (the building of the Tower of Babel; the destruction of Sodom and Gomorrah). God appears often and is defined less by his perfection than his faults; He is morally ambiguous . . . and doesn't understand his powerlessness in preventing Cain's meddling. Rounding out the narrative are angels who circumvent God's will, visions of the urban modernity that the future holds, an ironic description of Darwinian evolution, and God himself touting the heliocentric theory that will cause something of a ruckus five centuries on." (Publishers Weekly)

This is the author's "final novel, but the story it tells is among the world's first. In this version of several biblical tales, characters lose their initial capitals, and readers follow the adventures and misadventures of adam and eve, cain and abel, lilith and joshua and job—plus those of 'the lord, also known as god' with new eyes. Typographical diminution is the first of many wonderful acts of estrangement. Like a postmodern Creator of sorts, Saramago crafts a new world by recycling a series of well-known episodes and interpreting them from the viewpoint of a common reader." San francisco Chron

Saramago, Jose

★ The **cave**; translated from the Portuguese by Margaret Jull Costa. Harcourt 2002 307p $25

ISBN 0-15-100414-5

LC 2002-2355

Original Portuguese edition, 2000

"As a further warning against the urge to seek safety on common ground—moving to the center, as it were—the writer highlights the menaces of cliche by parodying the worldly-wise narrative interventions of an earlier era. . . . Such deft manipulations in Saramago's style are brilliantly rendered in Margaret Jull Costa's agile English version of his Portuguese." N Y Times Book Rev

Saramago, Jose

Death with interruptions; translated from the Portuguese by Margaret Jull Costa. Harcourt 2008 238p $24

ISBN 978-0-15-101274-9; 0-15-101274-1

LC 2008-10088

Original Portuguese edition, 2005

"Starting at the stroke of midnight on New Year's, in an unidentified country in an undetermined year, in Jose Saramago's new novel, death goes on strike. Nobody dies from illness or suicide or, Mr. Saramago writes, 'from a car accident, so frequent on festive occasions, when blithe irresponsibility and an excess of alcohol jockey for position on the roads to decide who will reach death first.' Thus the Saramago sentence: conversational but a conversation with oneself; portentous yet ludicrous, like a solemn address delivered by someone who has forgotten to wear pants. Thus too the Saramago plot: an impossible event like universal blindness, or Portugal's history altered because of a proofreader's error in a history book. Or, as here, death feeling unappreciated and refusing to oblige. . . . Mr. Saramago, one of the last of the old-line Communists, has written an atheist's religious parable; a story abounding in sentiment and purged of it." N Y Times (Late NY Ed)

Saramago, José, 1922-2010

★ The **elephant's** journey; translated from the Portuguese by Margaret Jull Costa. Houghton Mifflin Harcourt 2010 205p $24

ISBN 978-0-547-35258-9; 0-547-35258-1

LC 2010-19044

Original Portuguese edition, 2008

This novel "begins in 1551, when Portugal's Catholic King João III and his wife, Caterina of Austria, send the elephant Solomon as a wedding gift to her cousin, the Lutheran-sympathetic Archduke Maximilian of Austria. Saramago conjures up a cast of fictional characters to flesh out those based on historic record. First among them is Subhro, Solomon's mahout or keeper. . . . Subhro is a canny man who would be near the bottom of the rigid hierarchy were he not outside it. To keep his job and preserve Solomon's health and safety, he must be prepared to match wits with everyone he encounters, including the Portuguese captain leading the retinue and the Austrian archduke. . . . [This] is a tale rich in irony and empathy, regularly interrupted by witty reflections on human nature and arch commentary on the powerful who insult human dignity." Los Angeles Times

Saramago, Jose

The **history** of the siege of Lisbon; translated from the Portuguese by Giovanni Pontiero. Harcourt Brace & Co. 1997 314p

LC 96-46826

Original Portuguese edition 1989; this translation first published 1996 in the United Kingdom

"Although the novel's stream-of-consciousness technique, baroque prose and paragraphs that run on for pages may daunt some readers, this hypnotic tale is a great comic romp through history, language and the imagination." Publ Wkly

Saramago, José, 1922-2010

Manual of painting & calligraphy; a novel. Jose Saramago; translated from the Portuguese by Giovanni Pontiero. Mariner Books/Houghton Mifflin Harcourt 2012 243 p. $13.95

ISBN 1857540433 Carcanet Press; 1994; 0547640226 Houghton Mifflin; 2012; 9780547640228 Houghton Mifflin; 2012

LC 2012005375

This novel is the story of "a portrait painter . . . known only as 'H.' While H. is introspective and speculative, he's also self-critically aware of his limitations as an artist. At the moment he's working on a portrait of 'S.,' a successful industrialist." He has an affair with S.'s "secretary, Olga. . . . Dissatisfied with his original portrait, H. works on a second portrait and, still dissatisfied, tries to capture a 'portrait' of S. in words." Additionally, "H. makes a brief but serene visit to Italy, where he embarks on a pilgrimage to see the works of truly great artists like Cimabue and Piero della Francesca, but he's quickly pulled back to life in Portugal, where his friend Antonio has been arrested by the secret police in Salazar's regime." (Kirkus)

Sargent, Colin

Museum of human beings. McBooks Press 2008 337p map $23.95

ISBN 978-1-59013-167-1; 1-59013-167-3

LC 2008-37492

"Sargent sends the youthful Baptiste on a multi-leveled grand tour of discovery that never lets up or disappoints . . . With wit, humor, detailed understanding of the time, imagination and uncomplicated storytelling, Sargent opens a door on an era." Maine Sunday Telegram

Saroyan, William

★ The **human** comedy; Rev by the author; Dell 1971 192p pa $7.50

ISBN 0-440-33933-2

First published 1944 by Harcourt, Brace and Company

"Homer, the narrator, identifies himself in this novel as a night messenger for the Postal Telegraph office. He creates a view of family life in the 1940s in a small town in California. His mother, Ma Macauley, presides over the family and takes care of four children after her husband dies. Besides Homer, there is Marcus, the oldest, who is in the army; Bess; and Ulysses, the youngest, who describes the world from his perspective as a solemn four-year-old." Shapiro. Fic for Youth. 3d edition

Sarton, May

Anger; a novel. Norton 1982 223p

ISBN 0-393-01643-9

LC 82-7843

"Successful Boston banker Ned Fraser finds himself captivated by an unexpected encounter with mezzo-soprano Anna Lindstrom. He pursues the gifted, determined-to-be-famous performer without success until, at a chance meeting, he wins her—somewhat to the surprise of them both. They marry within a short time, no starry-eyed youngsters, but two mature adults. Both are settled in their emotional patterns: she given to outspoken and tempestuous outbursts of joy and despair, he to internalizing his feelings and maintaining the proper facade. This results in a lack of communication that threatens their marriage until Anna penetrates Ned's reserve. A romantic, yet realistic portrait." Libr J

Sarton, May

As we are now; a novel. Norton 1973 133p $10.95

ISBN 0-393-08372-1

"It is a bitter book, more a tract than a novel, and an utterly desolating experience, as it is meant to be. There are complexities that unwind themselves now and then, which preserve the concerns of the novel; but on the whole, the work is a piece of rhetoric, and very good rhetoric, too. . . . For the book satisfies in the way that cold anger can when it is pure, despairing, and written with no aim but the impulse to record the way things are." Saturday Rev/World

Sarton, May

Kinds of love; a novel. Norton 1970 464p

ISBN 0-393-08620-8

"The touching friendship of two elderly women, the love/hate relationship of the permanent residents and the summer people, and a young girl's discovery of the magic and the pain of love are some of the threads in this quiet tale." Booklist

Sarton, May

★ A **reckoning**; a novel. Norton 1978 254p

LC 78-9691

"Sarton incorporates . . . the issues of mother/daughter relationships, what it is to be a woman (and a man), and the conflict of art and life." Libr J

Sarton, May

A **small** room; a novel. Norton 1961 249p

Sarton "presents her cast of faculty types with scrupulous respect. There is no villain among them. . . . The essence of this novel is not so much in the conflict of characters as in the conflict in ideas—and ideas about teaching." N Y Her Trib Books

Sartre, Jean Paul

★ The **age** of reason; translated from the French by Eric Sutton. Knopf 1947 397p (Roads to freedom)

Original French edition, 1945

First of a series of three novels by the French philosopher, exponent of existentialism. The scene of this novel is Paris in 1938. A fourth title was never completed

"The central character is Mathieu, a professor of philosophy who writes one short story a year. . . . The problem that obsesses Mathieu, that of freedom, how to remain free, is worked out in the story and exemplified in the lives of the characters. . . . Mathieu differs from your ordinary character of fiction in that he is motivated by this abstract ethical ideal to keep his freedom. It is assailed as soon as the novel opens, for he learns that his mistress is pregnant; the action consists largely of his attempts to raise by borrowing—in the end, by stealing—the five thousand francs required to procure an abortion; unnecessarily, as it turns out, for Marcelle decides to marry someone else and have the child." Spectator

Followed by The reprieve

Sartre, Jean Paul

Intimacy, and other stories; translated by Lloyd Alexander. New Directions 1952 270p

First published 1948 in a limited edition with title: The wall, and other stories

"The most impressive thing about the book, rising from it like a stench, is a disgust for life, a sense of universal defilement. The insistence on the physical in the stories is indistinguishable from an aversion to it." New Repub

Sartre, Jean Paul

★ **Nausea**; translated from the French by Lloyd Alexander. New Directions 1949 238p

Original French edition, 1938

"Nausea is written in the form of a diary that narrates the recurring feelings of revulsion that overcome Roquentin, a young historian, as he comes to realize the banality and emptiness of existence. As the attacks of nausea occur more frequently, Roquentin abandons his research and loses his few friends. In an indifferent world, without work, love, or friendship to sustain him, he must discover value and meaning within himself." Merriam-Webster's Ency of Lit

Sartre, Jean Paul

The **reprieve**; translated from the French by Eric Sutton. Knopf 1947 445p (Roads to freedom)

Original French edition, 1945

This sequel to The age of reason "confines itself to the eight frenetic days that led to the Munich Pact and the rape of Czechoslovakia. The original characters reappear merging now with many others as a shocked France mobilizes for war. Sartre, the leading exponent of Existentialism manages in this kaleidoscope novel to re-create the confusion, even the odor of the fear that gripped Europe in September, 1938." Libr J

Followed by Troubled sleep

Sartre, Jean Paul

Troubled sleep; translated from the French by Gerald Hopkins. Knopf 1950 421p (Roads to freedom)

Sequel to The reprieve

Original French edition, 1949; published in the United Kingdom with title: Iron in the soul

"No other book gives such insight into the anguished feelings of the French as they passed from apathy to consciousness of their dignity as men revolting against fate, accepting their solidarity with other men—wretched, but lucid and free fighters." Saturday Rev

Satyal, Rakesh

No one can pronounce my name; Rakesh Satyal. First edition. Picador 2017 384 p. (hardcover) $26

ISBN 9781250112118

LC 2016058277

In this novel, by Rakesh Satyal, "in a suburb outside Cleveland, a community of Indian Americans has settled into lives that straddle the divide between Eastern and Western cultures. For some, America is a bewildering and alienating place where coworkers can't pronounce your name but will eagerly repeat the Sanskrit phrases from their yoga class. Harit, a lonely Indian immigrant in his mid forties, lives with his mother who can no longer function after the death of Harit's sister, Swati." (Publisher's note)

"Satyal captures his characters' experiences within a close-knit Indian community, rounded out with excellent supporting characters like Harit's mother and Ranjana's husband, who have their own stories to tell, resulting in a vivid, complex tale." Pub Wkly

Saul, John

The **homing**. Fawcett Columbine 1994 389p $21.50

ISBN 0-449-90863-1

LC 93-50606

The author provides "splendidly creepy bug-infested house of horrors and a fitting revenge for the villain." Libr J

Saul, John

Midnight voices. Ballantine Bks. 2002 341p

ISBN 0-345-43331-9

LC 2002-283839

"This is good, drafty atmospheric horror stuff unafraid to indulge in not-at-all subtle gory bits." Booklist

Saul, John

Second child. Bantam Bks. 1990 341p

LC 89-77149

Melissa "doesn't fit into the snooty social life of the exclusive East Coast beach community of Secret Cove, and her cruel mother hates her for this failing. The arrival of Melissa's beautiful half-sister, Teri, exacerbates the situation. Melissa escapes her mother's punishments by entering a trance state where her imaginary friend D'Arcy protects her. And who is D'Arcy? Apparently, the ghost of a spurned servant girl who returned an engagement ring still attached to her severed hand. Murderous Teri tries to manipulate Melissa's apparent psychosis, but D'Arcy intercedes. Mother and half-sister are evil incarnate." Booklist

Saunders, George

In persuasion nation; stories. Riverhead Books 2006 228p $23.95

ISBN 1-59448-922-X

LC 2005-57715

"The most unnerving fiction boldly envisions the dire consequences of our most hubristic tendencies: our bottomless greed, maniacal competitiveness, hyper-materialism, environmental obliviousness, spiritual callousness, and fear of being different. Following in the footsteps of Orwell, Bradbury, and Atwood, Saunders writes shrewd, off-the-charts speculative fiction. . . . In his third savagely imaginative collection, his most riveting to date, he considers various forms of diabolical persuasion in a techno-colonized world in which advertising governs every aspect of life." Booklist

Saunders, George

★ **Lincoln** in the bardo; a novel. George Saunders. Random House Inc. 2017 368 p. (ebook) $65; (hardcover) $28

ISBN 9780812995350; 9780812995343

LC 2016004993

Carnegie Medal Finalist: Fiction (2018)

Man Booker Prize (2017)

In this book, author George Saunders "spins an unforgettable story of familial love and loss that breaks free of its realistic, historical framework into a supernatural realm both hilarious and terrifying. Willie Lincoln finds himself in a strange purgatory where ghosts mingle, gripe, commiserate, quarrel, and enact bizarre acts of penance. Within this transitional state--called, in the Tibetan tradition, the bardo--a monumental struggle erupts over young Willie's soul." (Publisher's note)

"With this book, Saunders asserts a complex and disturbing vision in which society and cosmos blur." Kirkus

Saunders, George

★ **Tenth** of December; stories. George Saunders. Random House 2013 272 p. $26

ISBN 0812993802; 9780812993806 (acid-free paper); 9780812993813

LC 2012013782

National Book Award: Fiction: Finalist (2013)

This fiction collection, by George Saunders, presents multiple short stories. "In 'Victory Lap,' a boy witnesses the attempted abduction of the girl next door. . . . In 'Home,' a . . . soldier moves back in with his mother and struggles to reconcile the world . . . to which he has returned. And in the title story, . . . a . . . cancer patient walks into the woods to commit suicide, only to encounter a troubled young boy who . . . gives the dying man a final chance." (Publisher's note)

Saunders, Kate ✓

The **Secrets** of Wishtide; by Kate Saunders. St. Martin's Press 2016 352 p. (ebook) $48; $26

ISBN 9781632864505; 1632864495; 9781632864499

In this book, by Kate Saunders, "Mrs. Laetitia Rodd, aged fifty-two, is the widow of an archdeacon. Living in Hampstead with her confidante and landlady, Mrs. Bentley, . . . Laetitia makes her living as a highly discreet private investigator. Her brother, Frederick Tyson, is a criminal barrister living in the neighboring village of Highgate with his wife and ten children. Frederick finds the cases, and Laetitia solves them." (Publisher's note)

"The book is a sheer delight, with its deliciously intricate puzzle and well-drawn characters whom readers are sure to continue to enjoy in volumes to come." Booklist

Savage, Sam

The **cry** of the sloth; the mostly tragic story of Andrew Whittaker being his collected, final, and absolutely complete writings. Coffee House Press 2009 224p pa $14.95

ISBN 978-1-56689-231-5; 1-56689-231-7

LC 2009-20904

"Success, sex and sense all elude Whittaker as he halfheartedly tries to keep his life together . . . . Savage's sense of humor is true to his name, but The Cry of the Sloth reminds us of the great Russian satirist Ivan Goncharov, who also saw the tragedy in pretending to be productive." Time Out Chicago

Savage, Sam

Firmin; adventures of a metropolitan lowlife: a novel. Coffee House Press 2006 151p pa $14.95

ISBN 978-1-566-89181-3; 1-566-89181-7

LC 2005-35803

In this dark comedy, "the titular metropolitan lowlife is a rat, albeit one with lofty literary ambitions. The runt of 13 siblings spawned in the basement of a shambolic Boston bookshop, Firmin survives his lean first weeks by munching on the edges of books. He quickly develops a predilection for actually reading them, too. Soon he's perusing everything from Joyce to compendiums of dirty jokes and even developing a secret fondness for the bookshop's owner, Norman. Tutored by a sign-language book, Firmin tries to communicate with Norman and his human brethren with predictably disastrous results until an obscure science fiction author, who writes about rats and lives above the bookshop, takes him in as a pet. There Firmin enjoys a brief respite of security, writing odes in his head and dreaming of glory, until the wrecking ball threatens the decaying neighborhood. Blending philosophy and abundant literary references with originality, Savage crafts a small comic gem about the costs and rewards of literary illusions." Booklist

Savage, Sam

Glass; a novel. Coffee House Press 2011 223p pa $15

ISBN 978-1-56689-273-5; 1-56689-273-2

LC 2011-24104

"should be a tedious read and the first pages feel like the beginning of a long, high-fiber slog, but Savage's uncanny control over his material soon has the story pulling the reader in." Minneapolis Star Tribune

Savage, Sam

The **way** of the dog; a novel. by Sam Savage. Coffee House Press 2013 153 p. (paperback) $14.95

ISBN 1566893127; 9781566893121

LC 2011046604

This novel, by Sam Savage, "follows Harold Nivenson, a decrepit, aging man who was once a painter and arts patron. The death of . . . his friend turned romantic and intellectual rival, prompts him to ruminate on his own career as a minor artist and collector and make sense of a lifetime of gnawing doubt. Over time, his bitterness toward his family, his gentrifying neighborhood, and the decline of intelligent artistic discourse gives way to a kind of peace within himself." (Publisher's note)

Saville, Laurel

★ **Henry** and Rachel; Laurel Saville. Amazon Pub 2013 284 p. $14.95

ISBN 1611099668; 9781611099669

In this novel, by Laurel Saville, "Henry never expected to fall in love again after his wife died in childbirth. . . . It wasn't until he laid eyes on Rachel, the mysterious girl employed by Mr. George, that he believed his heart could be full again. Years later, when Rachel and their children flee the home they shared, Henry is forced to pick up the pieces of his life and finally discover the truth about Rachel." (Booklist)

Sayers, Dorothy L.

★ **Busman's** honeymoon; a love story with detective interruptions. Harper & Row 1986 381p $17.95

ISBN 0-06-055021-X

LC 86-45139

First published 1937 by Harcourt, Brace

"Not near the top of her form, but remarkable as a treatment of the newly wedded and bedded pair of eccentrics, Peter Wimsey and Harriet Vane, with Bunter in the offing and three local characters, chiefly comic. Peter's mother—dowager duchess of Denver—Peter's sister, John Donne, a case of vintage port, and the handling of 'corroded sut' provide plenty of garnishing for an indifferent murder, even if we weren't also given an idea of Lord Peter's sexual tastes and powers under trying circumstances." Barzun. Cat of Crime. Rev and enl edition

Sayers, Dorothy L.

The **Dawson** pedigree. Dial Press (NY) 1928 299p

First published 1927 in the United Kingdom; reissued 1987 by Harper & Row with title: Unnatural death

A chance remark overheard in a restaurant starts a long inquiry and an apparently natural death is proved to have been a murder. But Lord Peter Wimsey, aided by his friends, Parker from Headquarters, and that garrulous and delightful maiden lady, Miss Climpson, has a very difficult time to catch the murderer

Sayers, Dorothy L.

★ The **documents** in the case; by Dorothy L. Sayers and Robert Eustace. Brewer & Warren 1930 304p

A reissue of the title first published 1930 by Brewer & Warren

An "account, largely in letter form, of a case of poisoning by synthetic muscarine alkaloid made to look like mushroom poisoning. Evidence of optical activity and what it means beautifully handled, although the authors are said to have made a mistake in their choice of the particular mushroom to which the 'accidental' death should be attributed. Characters outstanding." Barzun. Cat of Crime. Rev and enl edition

Sayers, Dorothy L.

★ The **five** red herrings; (Suspicious characters) Harper & Row 1958 306p il

First published 1931. Variant title: Suspicious characters

Lord Peter Wimsey had always found himself welcome in the proud Scottish village of Kirkcudbright, although the villagers were not ordinarily tolerant of outsiders. But one day the body of an artist was found on the pointed rocks. The artist might have fallen, but there were too many suspicious elements in his death, especially when six suspects had wished him dead. Lord Peter uses all his ingenuity to unravel the tangles of this crime

"A work that grows on rereading and remains in the mind as one of the richest, most colorful of her group studies. The Scottish setting, the artists in the colony, the train-ticket puzzle, and the final chase place this triumph among the four or five chefs d'oeuvre from her hand." Barzun. Cat of Crime. Rev and enl edition

Sayers, Dorothy L. ✓

Gaudy Night. Harcourt Brace & Co. 1936 469p

First published 1935 in the United Kingdom

Harriet's return to Oxford for the Gaudy Dinner is welcomed by poison-pen letters and attempted blackmail. Lord Peter, of course, summons all his skill to detect the blackmailer and win Harriet

"Harriet Vance and the grown-up nephew of Lord Peter help give variety, and the college scene justifies good intellectual talk. The motive is magnificently orated on by the culprit, a scene that in itself is a unique bit of work. And though the don-esses are sometimes hard to keep apart, the architecture is very good." Barzun. Cat of Crime. Rev and enl edition

Sayers, Dorothy L.

Lord Peter; a collection of all the Lord Peter Wimsey stories. compiled and with an introduction by James Sandoe; coda by Carolyn Heilburn; codetta by E.C. Bentley. Harper & Row 1972 464p

Analyzed in Short story index

Sayers, Dorothy L.

Murder must advertise; a detective story. Harcourt Brace & Co. 1933 344p

Lord Peter Wimsey, less whimsical and more interesting than usual, enters the advertising profession in order to solve the possible murder by catapult of an advertising copywriter

"A superb example of Sayers' ability to set a group of people going. The advertising agency is inimitable, and hence better than the De Momerie crowd that goes with it." Barzun. Cat of Crime. Rev and enl edition

Sayers, Dorothy L. ✓

The **nine** tailors. Harcourt Brace Jovanovich 1989 397p il $15.95

ISBN 0-15-165897-8

LC 89-38102

A reissue of the title first published 1934

"One New Year's Eve, Lord Peter Wimsey, driving through a snowstorm, goes off the road near Fenchurch, St Paul, and is the chance guest of the rector. A providential visit all around, for Peter, acquainted with the ancient art of bellringing, acts that night as a substitute, but further than that, he finds use for his versatile mind later, upon the shocking discovery of a mutilated corpse in another man's grave. The unusual plot is developed with dexterity and ingenuity." N Y Libr

Sayers, Dorothy L.

Strong poison. Brewer & Warren 1930 344p

Because Harriet Vane's lover died of arsenic poisoning, and because Harriet was writing a book on the subject of poisons, everybody—except Lord Peter Wimsey—was convinced of her guilt. Lord Peter, with the aid of the inimitable Miss Climpson, gets to work on the business of clearing Harriet

Sayers, Dorothy L.

Thrones, dominations; {by} Dorothy L. Sayers and Jill Paton Walsh. St. Martin's Press 1998 312p $23.95

ISBN 0-312-18196-5

LC 97-42585

Paton Walsh "has made a valiant and resourceful stab at mimicry. No devotee of Lord Peter and his novelist wife Harriet Vane will want to miss it." New Stateman (Engl)

Sayers, Dorothy L.

The **unpleasantness** at the Bellona Club. Harper & Row 1986 345p $17.95

ISBN 0-06-055026-0

LC 86-45145

A reissue of the title first published 1928 by Payson & Clarke

Lord Peter Wimsey investigates the murder of an elderly member of a staid men's club

Sayers, Dorothy L.

Whose body? Boni & Liveright 1923 278p

When a nude corpse, wearing a golden pince-nez only, is found in the bathtub of the flat of a timid little architect, and the discovery coincides with the disappearance of a wealthy financier, Sir Reuben Levy, whom the body resembled, Sir Peter's sporting blood is aroused. Together with a friend from Scotland Yard he unofficially, playfully, as it were, conducts a roundabout inquiry under the jealous eye of the bungling official Scotland Yard investigators and finally tracks down the murderer

Sayers, Valerie

The **powers**; a novel. Valerie Sayers. Northwestern University Press 2013 ix, 297 p.p ill. (hardcover) $24.95

ISBN 0810152290; 9780810152298

LC 2012036262

This novel, by Valerie Sayers, is set in "1941 . . . , Joe DiMaggio's record-breaking hitting streak enlivens the summer, and winter begins with the shock and horror of the Japanese attack on Pearl Harbor. . . . Joltin' Joe, possessing a sweet swing and range in center, also has another gift: he can see the future. And he sees dark times ahead. . . . At once magical and familiar, [the novel] is a story of witness and moral responsibility." (Publisher's note)

Sayles, John

A **moment** in the sun; a novel. McSweeney's 2011 955p $29

ISBN 978-1-936365-18-0; 1-936365-18-9

"At times, Sayles' research for A Moment in the Sun makes the writing absolutely vivid: His description of a difficult childbirth is so precise that it will have you flinching. But at other times, the historical trivia overcrowds the book: The novel's world can be so cluttered with exterior detail that it feels as though there is insufficient space for its characters' interior lives. This might seem a natural pitfall for a filmmaker writing a novel. Persnickety fans and critics point out any accidental anachronism that slips into a film's frames, and, so, perhaps, he transfers this anxiety to his fiction. But it is wrongheaded to look at Sayles as just a filmmaker writing a book. If anything, his career has been so interesting because it has demonstrated the opposite: how a novelist would think about and make films." Daily Beast

Saylor, Steven

The **house** of the Vestals; the investigations of Gordianus the Finder. St. Martin's Press 1997 260p $22.95

ISBN 0-312-15444-5

LC 97-7597

"Saylor serves up a collection of short stories designed to fill in some of the gaps that have piqued the curiosity of devoted fans of his popular Roma Sub Rosa series. Set between the years 80 and 72 B.C., these nine tales document some of the early adventures of Gordianus the Finder. . . . While each brief mystery presented is a gem in and of itself, readers will delight in the informational overview provided by the collection as a whole. As usual, Saylor does a superb job of seamlessly incorporating the tumultuous history of the Roman Republic into the narrative flow." Booklist

Saylor, Steven

The **judgment** of Caesar; a novel of Ancient Rome. St. Martin's Minotaur 2004 290p maps $24.95

ISBN 0-312-27119-0

LC 2003-69548

"Readers will be equally absorbed by the bloody history unfolding (Saylor's description of the beheading of Pompey is both suspenseful and wrenching); by the historical figures depicted (Ptolemy listening to his flute player with the head of Pompey in a clay jar at his feet is a miniature study in royal pathology); and by the mysteries Gordianus must solve to keep his own head. Wonderful reading." Booklist

Saylor, Steven

A **mist** of prophecies. St. Martin's Press 2002 270p

ISBN 0-312-27121-2

LC 2001-58901

A mystery set in "Rome during the Civil War. A beautiful young woman, given the street name Cassandra for her habit of delivering prophesies, is found murdered. Gordianus is disturbed that no one claims her body—even though, he reflects, someone cared enough to murder her. Yet, at Cassandra's funeral pyre, seven of the most powerful women in Rome, including the wives of Caesar, Cicero, and Marc Antony, attend. Gordianus sorts out the tangled motives of the women who watched Cassandra burn, believing one of them to be her murderer. Saylor brings a wealth of historical information lightly to bear on a chilling mystery." Booklist

Saylor, Steven

Raiders of the Nile; a novel of the ancient world. Steven Saylor. Minotaur Books 2014 352 p. maps (Novels of ancient Rome) (hardback) $26.99

ISBN 1250015979; 9781250015976

LC 2013032463

This is author Steven Saylor's "14th novel featuring ancient Roman sleuth Gordianus the Finder. . . . In 88 B.C.E. Alexandria, Gordianus celebrates his turning 22 with his lover—and slave—Bethesda, who disappears after they take in a satiric play mocking King Ptolemy that's broken up by the monarch's soldiers. . . . Finding his sweetheart's whereabouts is complicated, and sets Gordianus on the trail of brigands known as the Cuckoo's Gang." (Publishers Weekly)

"Gordianus leaps from the pages as a modern trope—a wisecracking, good-hearted charmer—and Saylor frames him against an entrancing interpretation of ancient Egypt." Kirkus

Saylor, Steven

Roma; the novel of ancient Rome. St. Martin's Press 2007 555p map $25.95

ISBN 978-0-312-32831-3; 0-312-32831-1

LC 2006-51179

"Livy's Early History of Rome offers fertile material for a crime writer. The body count is high, and Saylor adds plenty more along the way. Even Livy smelt a 'whodunit' in the sudden apotheosis of Romulus in a thunderclap in the middle of a Senatorial meeting. Saylor illuminates the mystery in gory detail as, with unfailing efficiency, he unravels the enigmas. There is plenty of instruction here for students of classical civilization but sometimes the period detail founders in bathos when characters explain to each other facts they must already know, for the reader's benefit. Sometimes, though, with the scalpel-like deftness of a Hollywood director, Saylor puts his finger on the very essence of Roman history." Times Lit Suppl

Saylor, Steven

Rubicon; a novel of ancient Rome. St. Martin's Press 1999 276p $23.95

ISBN 0-312-20576-7

LC 99-18090

In this mystery "Gordianus the Finder attempts to solve the murder of Pompey's cousin Numerius. The civilized world of 49 B.C.E. is in turmoil at the onset of the Roman Civil War. Julius Caesar has crossed the Rubicon River into Italy with his hand-picked troops. Pompey, his chief rival for control of Rome, has fled Rome with his followers from the Senate, and all is chaos as the people leave the city. . . . This novel is an excellent blending of mystery and history." Libr J

Saylor, Steven

The **seven** wonders; a novel of the ancient world. Steven Saylor. Minotaur Books 2012 321 p.

ISBN 0312359845; 9781466801967; 9780312359843

LC 2012005475

This historical adventure novel by Steven Saylor is set in '92 B.C. Gordianus has just turned eighteen and is about to embark on the adventure of a lifetime: a far-flung journey to see the Seven Wonders of the World. . . . Accompanying Gordianus on his travels is his tutor, Antipater of Sidon, the world's most celebrated poet. . . . Teacher and pupil journey to the fabled cities of Greece and Asia Minor, and then to Babylon and Egypt. . . . Along the way they encounter murder, witchcraft and ghostly hauntings. . . . Gordianus discovers that amorous exploration goes hand-in-hand with crime-solving. . . . and at the end of the journey, an Eighth Wonder awaits him in Alexandria. Her name is Bethesda." (Publisher's note)

Saylor, Steven

The **triumph** of Caesar; a novel of ancient Rome. St. Martin's Minotaur 2008 311p $24.95

ISBN 978-0-312-35983-6; 0-312-35983-7

LC 2008-3668

"Julius Caesar, the dictator of Rome, and Cleopatra, the queen of Egypt, have followed the Gordianus clan back to Rome, and Caesar is planning to celebrate not one but four triumphs in recognition of his many military victories around the Mediterranean. Hieronymus, an old friend of Gordianus . . . has become a spy for Calpurnia, Caesar's wife, and gotten himself stabbed in the heart for his pains. Calpurnia is obsessed with the idea that Caesar's life is in danger, and Gordianus reluctantly agrees to investigate Hieronymus' death. . . . Saylor's vivid character sketches of historical figures are just as strong as always, with bright cameos by Arsinoë (Cleopatra's younger sister) and, for the first time in this series, the aloof, reserved Octavius (the future emperor Augustus). But Saylor's acute historical sensibility is aware that his readers already know how the story ends." January

Saylor, Steven

Wrath of the furies; by Steven Saylor. Minotaur Books 2015 320 p. illustrations, maps (Novels of ancient Rome) (hardcover) $26.99

ISBN 1250015987; 9781250015983

LC 2015022081

In this novel, by Steven Saylor, "it seems as if the entire ancient world is at war. In the west, the Italian states are rebelling against Rome; in the east, Mithridates is marching through and conquering the Roman Asian provinces. Even in the relatively calm Alexandria, a coup has brought a new Pharaoh to power. . . . The young Gordianus has been waiting out the chaos in Alexandria, with Bethesda, when he gets a cryptic message from his former tutor and friend, Antipater." (Publisher's note)

"Those who have read Saylor's Roma Sub Rosa novels, about Gordianus the Finder as a mature 'detective' years later, should especially enjoy seeing him as a clever but still green young man." Booklist

Scalzi, John

The **android's** dream. Tor 2006 396p $24.95

ISBN 978-0-765-30941-9; 0-765-30941-6

LC 2006-10480

"When a human diplomat causes the death of an alien counterpart, the aliens threaten war unless Earth's government can present them with a particular kind of sheep used in their race's coronation ceremony. War hero and superhacker Harry Creek, along with his friend Brian Javna (now an artificial intelligence), tracks down the sheep, only to discover that it is, in fact, Robin Baker, a pet store owner whose DNA contains remnants of sheep genetic material. While Creek and Javna attempt to find a way around their dilemma, other forces are searching for Baker—and they don't care whether she's dead or alive. . . . . A tongue-in-cheek sf adventure that delivers serious action and intrigue as well as clever comedic barbs aimed at diplomatic airs, sf cults, and other foibles of the modern era." Libr J

Scalzi, John

The **collapsing** empire; John Scalzi. Tor Books 2017 336 p. $25.99

ISBN 076538888X; 9780765388889

Hugo Finalist: Best Novel (2018)

In this novel, by John Scalzi, "The Flow, [is] an extradimensional field available at certain points in space-time, which can take us to other planets around other stars. Riding The Flow, humanity spreads to innumerable other worlds. Earth is forgotten. A new empire arises, the Interdependency, based on the doctrine that no one human outpost can survive without the others. It's a hedge against interstellar war--and, for the empire's rulers, a system of control." (Publisher's note)

"Fans of Game of Thrones and Dune will enjoy this bawdy, brutal, and brilliant political adventure..." Booklist

Scalzi, John

The **End** of All Things; John Scalzi. St. Martin's Press 2015 432 p. $24.99

ISBN 0765376075; 9780765376077

LC 2015016175

In this novel by John Scalzi "humans expanded into space...only to find a universe populated with multiple alien species bent on their destruction. Thus was the Colonial Union formed, to help protect us from a hostile universe. In this collapsing universe, CDF Lieutenant Harry Wilson and the Colonial Union diplomats he works with race against the clock to discover who is behind attacks on the Union and on alien races, to seek peace with a suspicious, angry Earth, and keep humanity's union intact." (Publisher's note)

"This novel—actually four connected novellas—provides a conclusion to the latest plotline while remaining open to new stories in the universe. It's classic crowd-pleasing Scalzi, offering thrilling adventure scenes (space battles, daring military actions, parachute jumps through a planet's atmosphere), high-stakes politics, snarky commentary, and food for thought. Delightful, compulsively readable, and even somewhat nutritious brain candy." Kirkus

Scalzi, John

The **ghost** brigades. Tor 2006 317p $23.95

ISBN 0-765-31502-5

LC 2005-27330

"The premise of a schizophrenic soldier allows Scalzi to explore the essence of conciousness and the ways in which it is shaped and influenced by memory, experience, and the individual's intrinsic personality. Combine that with good battle scenes, clever storytelling, and the ability to juggle abstruse scientific principles without breaking a sweat, and it makes for an impressive piece of work." Philadelphia Inquirer

Scalzi, John

The **human** division; John Scalzi. 1st ed. Tor 2013 432 p. (hardcover) $25.99

ISBN 0765333511; 9780765333513

LC 2012049551

This science fiction novel, by John Scalzi, "tells the story of the fight to maintain the unity of the human race. The people of Earth now know that the human Colonial Union has kept them ignorant of the dangerous universe around them. . . . Now the CU's secrets are known to all. Other alien races have come on the scene and formed a new alliance. . . . And they've invited the people of Earth to join them. For a shaken and betrayed Earth, the choice isn't obvious or easy." (Publisher's note)

Scalzi, John

★ **Lock** in; John Scalzi. Tor Books 2014 336 p. (hardback) $24.99

ISBN 0765334712; 0765375869; 9780765375865

LC 2014015247

Alex Award (2015)

In this science fiction novel by John Scalzi, a disease leaves "[v]ictims fully awake and aware, but unable to move or respond to stimulus. . . . A quarter of a century later, in a world shaped by what's now known as 'Haden's syndrome,' rookie FBI agent Chris Shane is paired with veteran agent Leslie Vann. The two of them are assigned what appears to be a Haden-related murder at the Watergate Hotel, with a suspect who . . . can let the locked in borrow their bodies for a time." (Publisher's note)

"[C]ontains plenty of action, great character development, vivid and believable worldbuilding and a thought-provoking examination of disability culture and politics." Kirkus

Scalzi, John

Old man's war. Tor 2005 316p

ISBN 0-765-30940-8

LC 2004-57953

"With his wife dead and buried, and life nearly over at 75, John Perry takes the only logical course of action left him: he joins the army. Now better known as the Colonial Defense Force (CDF), Perry's service-of-choice has extended its reach into interstellar space to pave the way for human colonization of other planets while fending off marauding aliens. The CDF has a trick up its sleeve that makes enlistment especially enticing for seniors: the promise of restoring youth. After bonding with a group of fellow recruits who dub their clique the Old Farts, Perry finds himself in a new body crafted from his original DNA and upgraded for battle, including fast-clotting 'smartblood' and a brain-implanted personal computer." Booklist

Scalzi, John

Redshirts; John Scalzi. Tor 2012 317 p.

ISBN 0765316994; 1429963603; 9780765316998; 9781429963602

LC 2012009383

Hugo Award: Best Novel (2013)

This science fiction novel by John Scalzi follows "Ensign Andrew Dahl [as he] has just been assigned to the Universal Union Capital Ship Intrepid, flagship of the Universal Union since the year 2456. . . . Life couldn't be better . . . until Andrew begins to pick up on the fact that (1) every Away Mission involves some kind of lethal confrontation with alien forces, (2) the ship's captain, its chief science officer, and the handsome Lieutenant Kerensky always survive these confrontations, and (3) at least one low-ranked crew member is, sadly, always killed." (Publisher's note)

Scapellato, Joseph

Big Lonesome; stories. Joseph Scapellato. Mariner Books 2017 182 p. (paperback) $13.95

ISBN 9780544769809; 9780544770546

LC 2016029360

In this book, author Joseph Scapellato uses "twenty-five stories to conjure worlds, themes, and characters who are at once unquestionably familiar and undeniably strange. 'Big Lonesome' navigates through the American West--from the Old West to the modern-day West to the Midwest, from cowboys to mythical creatures to everything in between--exploring place, myth, masculinity, and what it means to be whole or to be broken." (Publisher's note)

"Scapellato's debut is unpredictable, witty, and self-aware while remaining heartfelt in the most unexpected ways." Kirkus

Schaefer, Jack Warner

The **collected** stories of Jack Schaefer; with an introduction by Winfield Townley Scott. Houghton Mifflin 1966 520p

"The author's mastery of narrative technique, his excellent character development, and his consistently concise description combine in avoiding the unfortunate aspects of typical 'Western' fiction and melodrama." Libr J

Schaefer, Jack Warner

Monte Walsh. Houghton Mifflin 1963 501p

This novel of the old West follows Monte from runaway boy to trail hand, to topnotch cowhand and bronc buster, to aging saddle bum and encompasses the rise, the peak and the eventual collapse of the open range

"His characters seem real, and, according to the author, the characters and the episodes are based upon historical accounts. This is not just another 'Western.' It is worthy of a place alongside the writing of Will James and Eugene Manlove Rhodes." Libr J

Schaefer, Jack Warner

★ **Shane**; [by] Jack Schaefer; illustrated by John McCormack. Houghton Mifflin 1954 214p il $18

ISBN 0-395-07090-2

Illustrated edition of the title first published 1949

"Wyoming in 1889 is the scene of conflict between cattlemen and homesteaders when Shane mysteriously disappears. He works hard as a hired hand for the Starrett family, and young Bob Starrett grows to love him, unaware that he is a feared gunfighter escaping his past." Shapiro. Fic for Youth. 3d edition

Schaffert, Timothy

The **coffins** of Little Hope; a novel. Unbridled Books 2011 262p

ISBN 1609530403; 9781609530402

LC 2010043201

This novel's narrator, Essie, is an eighty-three-year-old obituary writer for a small-town Nebraska newspaper. When Lenore, "a young country girl, is reported to be missing, perhaps whisked away by an itinerant aerial photographer, Essie stumbles onto the story of her life. Or, it all could be simply a hoax, or a delusion, the child and child-thief invented from the desperate imagination of a lonely, lovelorn woman. Either way, the story of the girl reaches far and wide, igniting controversy, attracting curiosity-seekers and cult worshippers from all over the country to this dying rural town. And then it is revealed that the long awaited final book of a . . . series of YA gothic novels, [the Miranda-and-Desiree books], is being secretly printed on the newspaper's presses." (Publisher's note)

"Schaffert's protagonist is Esther Myles, an 83-year-old obituary writer for the County Paragraph, a small Nebraska newspaper. . . . Myles does not normally specialize in scoops, but when she hears that an 11-year-old girl named Lenore might have been abducted, she cannot ignore the story, for personal and professional reasons. As Myles investigates, however, the truth becomes more, not less, murky. Was the abduction real, or a hoax perpetrated by Daisy, the alleged mother? Does Lenore even exist in the flesh, or is she a figment of Daisy's imagination? In a parallel narrative, Schaffert spins a sendup of book publishing. The newspaper employing Myles has been chosen as a contract printer by a New York City publisher for the final book of a bestselling young adult series. The printing is supposed to be confidential, because the publisher wants to avoid leaks before the official release date of the book. The confidentiality disintegrates, though, when somebody reveals portions of the manuscript. The formerly lazy, peaceful Nebraska town is now a center of attention, with amusing and not-so-amusing consequences." Minneapolis Star Trib

Schanbacher, Gary

Crossing Purgatory; by Gary Schanbacher. 1st ed. W W Norton & Co Inc 2013 336 p. (hardcover) $25.95

ISBN 1605984434; 9781605984438

In this novel by Gary Schanbacher, Thompson Grey, a young farmer, travels to his father's estate seeking funds to expand his holdings. He returns home to find that his absence has contributed to a devastating family tragedy. Thompson abandons his farm and begins a westward exile in the attempt to outpace his grief. Set against the backdrop of the frontier during the years just preceding the Civil War, [it] tells a story of unprincipled ambition, guilt, and the price one man is willing to pay for atonement." (Publisher's note)

Schappell, Elissa

Blueprints for building better girls; fiction. Simon & Schuster 2011 288p $24

ISBN 978-0-7432-7670-2; 0-7432-7670-1

LC 2011-28068

"A sequence of eight darkly comic, interlinked tales explores the common experiences that shape early adulthood, marriage and motherhood and features an eclectic cast of archetypal female characters who navigate the pitfalls of the cultural landscape between the 1970s and the present." (Publisher's note)

"Schappell's stories read like snapshots—capturing precise moments from a woman's life from a distinct perspective. Considered together, Blueprints for Building Better Girls is a treasured photo album." BookPage

Schickler, David

Sweet and vicious. Dial Press 2004 242p $23

ISBN 0-385-33568-7

LC 2004-47830

"Schickler is a rare find; with straightforward and yet deeply insightful writing, he mixes love, violence, ardor, and humor in this funny and heartbreaking modern-day fable." Booklist

Schine, Cathleen

The **love** letter. Houghton Mifflin 1995 257p

LC 95-5202

"As light, and as risky, as a soufflé, The Love Letter indulges an enchanting fantasy, while invoking the powerful interplay of language and love. Literature, Schine suggests, can make booksellers glamorous, can ignite passion in the most unlikely of settings, and can even allow doomed love to live on." N Y Rev Books

Schine, Cathleen

The **New** Yorkers; with drawings by Leanne Shapton. Farrar, Straus and Giroux 2007 290p il $24

ISBN 978-0-374-22183-6; 0-374-22183-9

LC 2006-32711

"A swift-moving, gently poignant romantic comedy of manners. . . . The breezy storytelling in The New Yorkers is deceptive: the novel offers more than a sweet story of puppy love. Schine strikes a rare, deeply personal, and very loving chord as she portrays the way these devoted pets elicit joy from the depressed (except once, when it's already too late) and humanity from the merciless, and inspire flirtations and encounters between the shy and monastic." Village Voice

Schine, Cathleen

The **three** Weissmanns of Westport. Farrar, Straus & Giroux 2010 292p $25

ISBN 978-0-374-29904-0; 0-374-29904-8

LC 2009-25425

"When Joseph Weissmann divorces Betty, his wife of forty-eight years, she takes refuge in her cousin's cottage in Connecticut, with her two daughters. Annie, the elder, is a sober worrywart, while Miranda, the younger, is self-involved, inclined to melodrama, and on the verge of bankruptcy after her literary agency represented too many fraudulent memoirs. The sisters become involved in a shifting game of romantic entanglements that include a celebrated reclusive writer, a semi-retired lawyer, a Hollywood-bound schemer, an epidemiologist, and a couple of vacuous hangers-on. The ironic title—the three are anything but wise men—does little justice to Schine's real wit, which playfully probes the lies, self-deceptions, and honorable hearts of her characters." New Yorker

Schlink, Bernhard

Homecoming; translated from the German by Michael Henry Heim. Pantheon Books 2008 260p $24; pa $14.95

ISBN 978-0-375-42091-7; 0-375-42091-6; 978-0-375-72557-9 pa; 0-375-72557-1 pa

LC 2007-16121

Original German edition, 2006

This is "an exceedingly delicate meditation on the German past that refuses to moralize. Decent people can be driven to do the devil's work, just as truly moral verdicts can result in unimaginable collateral damage: Debauer witnesses both of these." N Y Sun

Schlink, Bernhard

★ The **reader**; translated from the German by Carol Brown Janeway. Pantheon Bks. 1997 218p $20

ISBN 0-679-44279-0

LC 97-1511

Original German edition, 1995

"In post WW II Germany, a teenage boy is seduced by a streetcar conductor twice his age who insists that he read to her before they make love. Years later, when he is a law student, she appears as a defendant on trial for war crimes during the Nazi era. This novel raises provocative questions about guilt and responsibility, as well as the power of literature to heal and bind." Publ Wkly

Schlink, Bernhard

Self's punishment; [by] Bernhard Schlink and Walter Popp; translated from the German by Rebecca Morrison. Vintage Books 2005 248p pa $14

ISBN 0-375-70907-X

LC 2004-57166

This mystery features former Nazi prosecutor turned investigator Gerhard Self. "It's the early 1980s, and Self has been hired by a boyhood friend to smoke out a hacker who's playing havoc with the computers at Rhineland Chemical Works. But after Self springs a trap that gets the troublemaker murdered, he gradually faces the guilt he still carries for his youthful embrace of National Socialism. His simple refusal to let himself off the hook and step back into his old public prosecutor's role after the war doesn't seem like penance enough anymore. . . . Self's unwitting participation in the new crime drives him to pursue the path of justice wherever it may lead. A fascinating exploration of how people often manage to carve out normal lives even after being complicit in terrible acts." Booklist

Schlink, Bernhard

Summer lies; stories. Bernhard Schlink; translated from the German by Carol Brown Janeway. Pantheon Books 2012 229 p. (hardcover) $25.95

ISBN 0307907260; 9780307907264

LC 2012005994

This fiction collection, by Bernhard Schlink, translated by Carol Janeway, features seven short stories "brim[ming] with the delusions, the passions, the outbursts, and the sometimes irrational justifications people make within a melange of . . . relationships." Stories include "After the Season," "Johann Sebastian Bach on Ruegen," and "The Night in Baden-Baden." (Publisher's note)

Schlink, Bernhard

The **weekend**; translated from the German by Shaun Whiteside. Pantheon Books 2010 215p $24.95

ISBN 978-0-307-37815-6; 0-307-37815-2

LC 2010-05396

Original German edition, 2008

"The narrative style can sometimes be confusing. We spend a little time inside each guest's head—learning how they feel about Jorg and why they think they were invited for the weekend. Credit must be given to the English translator, Shaun Whiteside, who distills the often-difficult German into relatively simple sentences that add to the pace of Schlink's plot." Deseret News

Schmidt, Sarah

See what I have done; Sarah Schmidt. 1st Grove Atlantic hdcvr. ed. Atlantic Monthly Press 2017 328 p. $26

ISBN 0802126596; 9780802126597

LC 2017003331

Women's Prize for Fiction Longlist (2018)

In this book, author Sarah Schmidt "recasts one of the most fascinating murder cases of all time into an intimate story of a volatile household and a family devoid of love. . . . The brutal ax-murder of Andrew and Abby Borden in their home in Fall River, Massachusetts, leaves little evidence and many unanswered questions. While neighbors struggle to understand why anyone would want to harm the respected Bordens, those close to the family have a different tale to tell." (Publisher's note)

"Equally compelling as a whodunit, 'whydunit,' and historical novel, the book honors known facts yet fearlessly claims its own striking vision." Pub Wkly

Scholz, Carter

The **amount** to carry; stories. Picador 2003 208p $23

ISBN 0-312-26901-3

LC 2002-192667

"In each keenly meta-physical fable Scholz, a connoisseur of the imagination, parses the language of science, literature, art, and music as he ponders the quintessentially human habit of telling stories, a valiant attempt to render sense out of the delirium of existence." Booklist

Scholz, Carter

★ **Radiance**. Picador 2002 388p $24

ISBN 0-312-26893-9

LC 2001-56018

"Wickedly satiric and eggheaded in its level of scientific detail, 'Radiance' is a serious, engrossing novel." N Y Times Book Rev

Schulberg, Budd

★ **Waterfront**; a novel. Random House 1955 320p

"The prize-winning screen play 'On the waterfront' has been expanded into a novel which differs on several counts from the film. It remains an angry indictment of racketeering in the labor unions along the New Jersey waterfront, but the happy ending of the screen play has been supplanted by a tragic one, in which the hero Terry Malloy is murdered by the henchmen of Johnny Friendly, the labor racketeer, and the terrorism along the waterfront continues. The more leisurely framework of the novel form permits the author to document to the full the abuses in longshoremen's unions, without sacrificing the explosive force of the film." Booklist

Schulberg, Budd

★ **What** makes Sammy run? Modern Lib. 1941 303p

"The protagonist, Sammy Glick, is a tough New York youth who works his way into a position of power in the motion-picture industry, where his harshness and crude manners are not out of place." Benet's Reader's Ency of Am Lit

Schulman, Helen

This beautiful life; a novel. HarperCollins 2011 222p $24.99

ISBN 978-0-06-202438-1; 0-06-202438-8

This novel tells the story "of the four Bergamots, who have moved from a college town . . . to the Upper West Side of Manhattan." (N Y Times (Late N Y Ed))

In this novel "15-year-old Jake Bergamot is newly arrived at a competitive private school on the Upper East Side when a younger girl, hoping to be taken seriously as girlfriend material, emails him a video of herself stripping for the camera in her messy bedroom. . . . Shocked, confused, and unsure whether he finds the video sexy or horrifying, Jake forwards the email to his best friend for advice. Overnight, [the video] has made Gawker and the teens and families involved are devastated. . . . Because this is a story about kids, sex, and the Internet, we expect it also to be a story about the irreconcilable generation gap between today's teens and their parents. Instead, This Beautiful Life illuminates the common ground, or maybe more aptly, the common void between the generations. Shulman knows her characters well, and her prose comes alive when she's rendering a character's thorniest, most intimate moments." Slate

Schultz, Emily

The **Blondes**; Emily Schultz. Doubleday Canada 2012 400 p. $25.99

ISBN 0385671059; 1250043352; 9780385671057; 9781250043351

LC 2014042873

In this novel by Emily Schultz "Hazel Hayes . . . learns she is pregnant . . . at an apocalyptically bad time: random but deadly attacks on passers-by, all by blonde women, are terrorizing New Yorkers. Soon it becomes clear that the attacks are symptoms of a strange illness that is transforming blondes . . . into rabid killers. Hazel . . . sets out on a trip across a paralyzed America to find the one woman--perhaps blonde, perhaps not--who might be able to help her." (Publisher's note)

"Schultz sharply addresses a slew of social failings, from gender stereotypes and racial profiling to inane media frenzy, mass hysteria, and the tyranny of a declared state of emergency in this ferociously clever, exceedingly well written variation on the pandemic novel, which is now so prevalent that it's time, given the advent of climate fiction, or cli-fi, to coin vi-fi for virus fiction. The pandemic and its ripple effects make for a gripping, darkly bemusing read. But there's more. This canny, suspenseful, acidly observant satire cradles an intimate, poignant, and hilarious story of one lonely, stoic, young mother-to-be caught up in surreal and terrifying situations. Schultz gives readers a lot to think about in this rampaging yet sensitive tale about the true depths of womanhood." Booklist

Schulze, Ingo

New lives; the youth of Enrico Turmer in letters and prose. edited and with commentary and foreword by Ingo Schulze; translated from the German by John E. Woods. Alfred A. Knopf 2008 570p $28.95

ISBN 978-0-307-26559-3; 0-307-26559-5

LC 2008-19615

Original German edition, 2005

"All his life Türmer has wanted nothing so much as to write a novel, to pour experience onto the page and make it ripple. . . . But he never manages to create a shaped and formed work. The only writing he produces is a series of long letters about his agonies to his sister, friends, and love interests. As it happens, all of Türmer's letters are all composed in the first half of 1990, in the months between the fall of the Berlin Wall and the reunification of East and West Germany – a strange era, at once a kind of twilight and a dawn. Despite his failure to write a novel, when Türmer rereads these letters, he finds his literary aspirations renewed. . . . He believes he now has the material for an epistolary novel in his hands, a work that will 'essentially write itself.' It is these letters, with their mixture of ambition and naiveté, that are presented to us in 'New Lives' as collected and annotated by a skeptical but fastidious literary scholar named Ingo Schulze." Christ Sci Monit

Schumacher, Julie, 1958-

Dear Committee Members; Julie Schumacher. Doubleday 2014 192 p. (hardcover) $22.95

ISBN 0385538138; 9780345807335; 9780385538138

LC 2013043014

In this satirical novel by Julie Schumacher, "Jason Fitger is a beleaguered professor of creative writing and literature at Payne University, a small and not very distinguished liberal arts college in the midwest. His department is facing draconian cuts and squalid quarters, while one floor above them the Economics Department is getting lavishly remodeled offices. . . . In short, his life is a tale of woe, and the vehicle this droll and inventive novel uses to tell that tale is a series of hilarious letters of recommendation that Fitger is endlessly called upon by his students and colleagues to produce." (Publisher's note)

"Schumacher's warm satire of the peculiarities of the Ivory Tower will be recognizable to anyone who has encountered the bureaucracy and internal politics of higher education." Booklist

Schupack, Deborah

The **boy** on the bus; a novel. Free Press 2003 215p $23

ISBN 0-7432-4220-3

LC 2002-32179

"Motherhood with all its contradictions has rarely been shown so nakedly. Schupack gives us Meg's view and everyone else's in overlapping layers. . . . From beginning to end in this novel, nothing is ordinary, while at the same time everything is." N Y Times Book Rev

Schwab, V. E.

A **Darker** Shade of Magic; Victoria Schwab. St. Martin's Press 2015 400 p. (Shades of Magic) $25.99

ISBN 0765376458; 9780765376459

LC 2015004143

In this novel by Victoria Schwab, "Kell is one of the last Travelers - magicians with a rare ability to travel between parallel Londons. There's Grey London, dirty and crowded and without magic, home to the mad king George III. There's Red London, where life and magic are revered. Then, White London, ruled by whoever has murdered their way to the throne. But once upon a time, there was Black London..." (Publisher's note)

"The brisk plot makes this a page-turner that confronts darkness but is never overwhelmed by it. Fantasy fans will love this fast-paced adventure, with its complex magic system, thoughtful hero and bold heroine." Kirkus

Other titles in this series are:
A Gathering of Shadows (2016)
A Conjuring of Light (2017)

Schwab, V. E.

A **gathering** of shadows; A Novel. V. E. Schwab. Tom Doherty Associates, LLC 2016 512 p. (Shades of magic) (hardback) $25.99

ISBN 9780765376473; 9781427277046

LC 2015031510

In this book in the Shades of Magic series, by V. E. Schwab, "Red London is about to host the Essen Tasch, or Element Games, pitting the most talented magicians against one another. . . . In White London, a new king rises, and he will do anything, and sacrifice anyone, to make his London great again. Lila, Kell, and Rhy are complex, fully realized creations who challenge conventional ideas of what a hero should be made of, and the supporting characters feel just as real." (Publisher's note)

"New touches such as a bustling magical market enliven already-rich worldbuilding. Tensions rise steadily, culminating with the exciting Element Games, and the finale will leave readers breathless" Pub Wkly

Schwartz, John Burnham

The **commoner**; a novel. Nan A. Talese 2008 351p $24.95

ISBN 978-0-385-51571-9; 0-385-51571-5

LC 2007-15391

"An American taking on a fictional memoir about a living Japanese empress is a gutsy move, but Schwartz makes it work. . . . While the external details of life in the palace remain stunning, it's Schwartz's grasp of [Haruko's] internal struggle that resonates after the last page is turned." Denver Post

Schwartz, John Burnham

Northwest corner; a novel. Random House 2011 285p $26.00

ISBN 1400068452; 9781400068456

LC 2010045784

"Twelve years after a tragic accident and a cover-up that led to prison time, Dwight Arno, now fifty, is a man who has started over. . . . Dwight manages a sporting goods store and dates a woman to whom he hasn't revealed the truth about his past." (Publisher's note)

Schwartz, John Burnham

Reservation Road; a novel. Knopf 1998 292p

LC 98-14580

"The story is told in the alternating voices of father, mother and murderer, which overlap and swell to a crescendo in an operatic chorus of pain." Economist

In Reservation Road (1998), Dwight Arno "accidentally hit and killed a child while driving; now, his prison time served, he plods through his days as manager of a dreary sporting-goods store, haunted by memories of his past life. . . . Then his son Sam, whom he has not seen in 12 years, lands on Dwight's doorstep, on the run after clobbering someone with a metal bat in a bar fight. 'I wanted to hurt him,' Sam admits to his dad. And that is the bitter, awful truth that father and son must work through as they struggle to patch their tattered relationship: Deep down, they harbor the same dark impulses. They can succumb to them, or they can take a shot at redemption. The choice is theirs. The story emerges, slowly at first, not just from their viewpoints but from those of their girlfriends as well as Sam's mother. Multiple viewpoints are usually jarring, interrupting the flow of a novel, but not here: In Schwartz's hands, the narrative unfolds delicately, each chapter a puzzle piece that fits seamlessly into the whole. It's painful to watch the two men confront their lives—but it's also exhilarating." Entertainment Wkly

Schwartz, Leslie

Angels Crest; a novel. Doubleday 2004 303p $23.95

ISBN 0-385-51185-X

LC 2003-64635

"Ethan Denton is out for a drive with his three-year-old son, Nate, in the woods of Northern California, when he decides to stop to follow several bucks he spots just off the road. When he returns 15 minutes later, his son is gone, and his own personal hell, as well as that of the small town of Angels Crest, is just beginning. Ethan's alcoholic ex-wife, Cindy, who lost custody of Nate; his former best friend, Glick, who slept with Cindy; Rocksan and Jane, a settled lesbian couple; and Jack, a lonely judge from outside the town are among those who help Ethan search for his son. . . . This beautiful, moving novel works brilliantly as a study of a tragedy and the various characters' reactions to the tragedy itself, as well as how it causes them to reexamine their own lives." Booklist

Schwartz, Lynne Sharon

The **writing** on the wall; a novel. Counterpoint 2005 297p $24

ISBN 1-582-43299-6

LC 2004-24877

This novel "would have been excellent already without its 9/11 ballast. It is full of intuitive dread, as if Joan Didion had written Play It As It Lays in the same Brooklyn boarding house where Norman Mailer was writing Barbary Shore." Harper's

Schwartzman, Adam

Eddie Signwriter. Pantheon Books 2010 293p $25.95

ISBN 978-0-307-37873-6; 0-307-37873-X

LC 2009-19509

"Themes and scenes from multiple other works poke through the lattice of Schwartzman's prose, including the Book of Genesis itself. . . . Resonating with allusions, this book features literary rediscovery too. If 'Eddie Signwriter' is about the struggle to recover from the flip-flops of fate, it's also about the problem of recovering oneself, about remaining who one is in a world prone to terrifying transformation." Los Angeles Times

Schwarz, Christina

All is vanity; a novel. Doubleday 2002 368p $24.95

ISBN 0-385-49972-8

LC 2002-67583

"Schwarz's portrait of the talentless, self-absorbed Margaret is surgically accurate. . . . Anyone who has ever tried to write and been blocked will howl with recognition at the indignities that befall the novelist. . . . The novel is both a page turner and a cautionary tale of consumerism run amok." N Y Times Book Rev

Schwarz, Christina

Drowning Ruth. Doubleday 2000 338p $23.95

ISBN 0-385-50253-2

LC 00-29523

"The vivid realism of the novel's setting adds depth to an already gripping plot. . . . Schwarz maintains her mystery with an expert hand, arriving at far more than a simple determination of guilt." N Y Times Book Rev

Schwarz, Christina

The **Edge** of the Earth; a novel. by Christina Schwarz. 1st Atria Books hardcover ed. Pocket Books 2013 275 p. (hardcover) $25

ISBN 1451683677; 9781451683677

LC 2013000480

In this novel by Christina Schwarz "[Trudy] falls in love with enigmatic and ambitious Oskar, [and] she believes she's found her escape from the banality of her pre-ordained life. . . . The couple moves across the country to take a job at a lighthouse in the eerily isolated Point Lucia, California. Upon arriving they meet the light station's only inhabitants--the Crawleys, a family whose plain appearance is no indication of what lies below the surface." (Publisher's note)

Schwarz-Bart, Andre

The **last** of the just; translated from the French by Stephen Becker. Atheneum Pubs. 1960 374p

Original French edition, 1959

"The thread that runs through the narration is the ancient Jewish tradition of the Lamed-Vov, according to which the world reposes upon 36 Just Men, who often are not aware themselves of the position they hold. . . . Harrowing as the book is, it is a valuable addition to the titles on the Holocaust, lest we forget how inhumane man can be." Shapiro. Fic for Youth. 3d edition

Schweblin, Samanta

Fever dream; Samanta Schweblin; translated by Megan McDowell. Riverhead Books 2017 192 p. (hardback) $25; (ebook) $65

ISBN 0399184597; 9780399184598; 9780399184611

LC 2016026585

In this book, by Samanta Schweblin, translated by Megan McDowell, "a young woman named Amanda lies dying in a rural hospital clinic. A boy named David sits beside her. She's not his mother. He's not her child. Together, they tell a haunting story of broken souls, toxins, and the power and desperation of family." (Publisher's note)

"A taut, exquisite page-turner vibrating with existential distress and cumulative dread." Kirkus

Scott, Anne

Calpurnia. Knopf 2003 293p $24

ISBN 0-375-41380-4

LC 2002-30096

"Scott sets the book in the 1980's, before online antique auctions and the advent of dot-com billionaires who might have competed fiercely to buy a flashy old pile like Calpurnia. Her central theme, however, the impulse to make and live with art, is timeless." N Y Times Book Rev

Scott, James

★ The **kept**; James Scott. Harper 2014 368 p. (hardback) $25.99

ISBN 0062236733; 9780062236654; 9780062236739

LC 2013027875

"Elspeth Howell is a midwife returning home after a months-long absence. She trudges through falling snow to their remote farmhouse only to find husband Jorah and four of their children shot dead. The sole survivor is 12-year-old Caleb, who had watched the three killers from the barn." (Kirkus Reviews)

"Scott writes with sustained intensity and strong descriptive powers, whether evoking the pair's dangerous trudge through high snowdrifts, the rough lake town where many answers lie, or his characters' complex lives and motivations." Booklist

Scott, Joanna

Everybody loves somebody; stories. Back Bay Books/ Little, Brown and Co. 2006 260p $13.99

ISBN 978-0-316-01345-1; 0-316-01345-5

LC 2006-12310

A "collection of 10 stories that stalk across the 20th century to document love and its consequences. . . . Scott's craft can be breathtaking—and her perceptions uncanny." Publ Wkly

Scott, Joanna

Follow me; a novel. Little, Brown and Company 2009 420p $24.99

ISBN 978-0-316-05165-1; 0-316-05165-9

LC 2008-42643

Scott "traces the meandering path of a runaway girl from place to place, name to name, starting as 16-year-old Sally Werner in 1947 rural Pennsylvania. Her saga begins with an innocent motorcycle ride with an older cousin at a church picnic, which results in a baby son and rejection by her fundamentalist parents. She decides her only option is escape, following the Tuskee River that snakes across the Werners' back fields. . . . Over the next four decades, she washes up in towns farther along the Tuskee, surviving on the kindness of strangers. . . . Her many reincarnations are pieced together years later by her granddaughter and a man who believes he is the infant that Sally abandoned. Scott . . . excels in her stream-of-consciousness descriptions of the mysterious Tuskee that provides Sally's true north." Washington Post Book World

Scott, Joanna

★ **Tourmaline**; a novel. Little, Brown 2002 279p $23.95

ISBN 0-316-77618-1

LC 2002-67111

"Book reviewers are fond of calling belletristic novels 'poetic.' 'Tourmaline' isn't poetic because of its pretty writing but because of its sympathetic ordering and reordering of ideas, its philosophical probing." N Y Times Book Rev

Scott, Kim

That deadman dance; Kim Scott. 1st U.S. ed; Bloomsbury 2011 368p.

ISBN 9781608197057; 1608197050

LC 2011014163

Australian Literature Society Gold Medal (2011)

Miles Franklin Award (Australia) (2011)

Commonwealth Writers' Prize: Regional Award: South East Asia & Pacific: Best Book (2011)

Adelaide Festival Awards (Australia): Fiction (2012)

Adelaide Festival Awards (Australia): Premier's Award (2012)

This book, which won the Miles Franklin Award in 2011, tells the story of "the early contact between the Aboriginal Noongar people and the first European settlers [of Western Australia]. . . . Clever, resourceful and eager to please, Bobby [Wabalaginy, a young Aborigine] befriends the new arrivals . . . [and] is even welcomed into a prosperous local white family. . . . But slowly—by design and by accident—things begin to change. . . . Stock mysteriously start to disappear; crops are destroyed; there are 'accidents' and injuries on both sides. As the Europeans impose ever stricter rules and regulations in order to keep the peace, Bobby's Elders decide they must respond in kind. . . . Bobby is forced to take sides: he must choose between the old world and the new." (Publisher's note)

Scott, Kirstin

Motherlunge; Kirstin Scott; [edited by] William Olsen, Kimberly Kolbe. 1st American ed. New Issues Poetry & Prose 2013 252 p. (Awp award series in the novel) (paperback) $15

ISBN 1936970112; 9781936970117

LC 2012936333

In this debut novel from Kirstin Scott, winner of the 2011 Association of Writers & Writing Programs Prize, motherhood, sisterhood, and making decisions is explored. Readers hear "Thea tell her unborn daughter about sex and love and sorrow, and what happened when she left her small Montana town to go to the big city and help out the pregnant Pavia." (Publishers Weekly)

Scott, Paul, 1920-1978

The **Raj** quartet; introduction by Hilary Spurling. Alfred A. Knopf 2007 1032p 2v ea $32.50

ISBN 0-307-26396-7 v1; 0-307-26397-5 v2; 978-0-307-26396-4 v1; 978-0-307-26397-1 v2

LC 2007-277260

This collection of the author's four novels on British India comprises: The Jewel in the Crown (1966), The Day of the Scorpion (1968), The Towers of Silence (1971), and A Division of the Spoils (1975).

Scott, Paul

★ **Staying** on; a novel. Morrow 1977 215p

LC 77-1491

"After India succeeds in obtaining independence from Britain, Tusker and Lucy Smalley, part of the British colonial army, stay on in the country where almost all their married life has been spent. The book describes their relationships with the Indians who, at this point, constitute all of their daily and social contacts. . . . There is humor in the informative portrayals of the relationships between the British and the Indians, and the final scene is as simple and moving a description of loss as has ever been written." Shapiro. Fic for Youth. 3d edition

Scott, Walter

The **bride** of Lammermoor; edited by J.H. Alexander. Columbia Univ. Press 1995 398p $44.50

ISBN 0-231-10572-X

LC 96-143055

First published 1819

"The most tragic of Scott's romances, on which Donizetti's opera 'Lucia di Lammermoor' is based. The last scion of a ruined family and the daughter of his ancestral enemy in possession of the estates fall in love. For a while there is a glimpse of hope and happiness; but the ambitious mother opposes the match, prophecies and apparitions prognosticate tragedy, and the romance closes in death and sorrow. . . . Caleb Balderstone, the faithful retainer, is one of Scott's humorous creations, whose obstinate care for his unhappy master relieves the overpowering tragedy." Baker. Guide to the Best Fic

Scott, Walter

★ **Ivanhoe**; a romance. Modern Lib. 1997 xxxvii, 535p $16

ISBN 0-679-60263-1

LC 96-48579

First published 1819

"The action occurs in the period following the Norman Conquest. The titular hero is Wilfred, knight of Ivanhoe, the son of Cedric the Saxon, in love with his father's ward Rowena. Cedric, however, wishes her to marry Athelstane, who is descended from the Saxon royal line and may restore the Saxon supremacy. The real heroine is Rebecca the Jewess, daughter of the wealthy Isaac of York, and a person of much more character and charm than the mild Rowena. Richard the Lion-Hearted in the guise of the Black Knight and Robin Hood as Locksley play prominent roles." Reader's Ency. 4th edition

Scott, Walter

★ **Rob** Roy; with an introduction by Eric Anderson. Knopf 1995 xliii, 494p $20

ISBN 0-679-44362-2

First published 1817; first Everyman's library edition 1906

"Full of intrigue with political overtones, it is set in northern England just before the Jacobite rebellion of 1715, and it is considered one of the author's masterpieces. Francis Obaldistone, the novel's hero, contends with his jealous, unscrupulous cousin Rashleigh for the hand of the beautiful Diana Vernon. Aided by the Scottish outlaw Rob Roy (based on a historical Jacobite outlaw), Francis succeeds in exposing Rashleigh's villainy." Merriam-Webster's Ency of Lit

Scottoline, Lisa

Accused; A Rosato & Associates Novel. Lisa Scottoline. St. Martin's Press 2013 368 p. (hardcover) $27.99

ISBN 1250027659; 9781250027658

LC 2013024428

This is Lisa Scottoline's 12th Rosato & Associates novel. Here, partner Mary DiNunzio's "first client as a partner is 13-year-old Allegra Gardner, who wants to retain the firm to prove that Lonnie Stall, imprisoned for the murder of Allegra's older sister, Fiona, six years earlier, is innocent and to find the real killer. Allegra may be precocious, and she has her own funds, but her wealthy parents oppose her actions directly and forcibly." (Publishers Weekly)

Scottoline, Lisa

★ **Come** home; Lisa Scottoline. St. Martin's Press 2012 371 p.

ISBN 9780312380823; 9781429942324

LC 2011046492

This book tells the story of "Jill Farrow [who] is a typical suburban mom . . . [and] has finally gotten her and her daughter's lives back on track after a divorce. She is about to remarry, her job as a pediatrician fulfills her . . . and her daughter, Megan, is . . . happily . . . juggling homework and the swim team. But Jill's life is turned upside down when her ex-stepdaughter, Abby, shows up on her doorstep . . . and delivers shocking news: Jill's ex-husband is dead. Abby insists that he was murdered and pleads with Jill to help find his killer. Jill reluctantly agrees to make a few inquiries and discovers that things don't add up. As she digs deeper, her actions threaten to rip apart her new family, destroy their hard-earned happiness, and even endanger her own life." (Publisher's note)

Scottoline, Lisa

Dead ringer. HarperCollins Pubs. 2003 339p $25.95

ISBN 0-06-051493-0

LC 2002-191931

A "legal caper featuring the lady lawyers of series heroine Bennie Rosato's Philadelphia law firm Rosato and Associates. This time out it's Bennie playing the lead role, as she fights to save her financially sinking firm; mother her lovable partners, Mary DiNunzio and Judy Carrier; solve the murder of a valuable client; and battle her evil twin, Alice. . . . Bennie grows on you, and soon enough you're rooting for the home team and laughing at her corny jokes." Publ Wkly

Scottoline, Lisa

Don't Go; Lisa Scottoline. 1st ed. St Martins Pr 2013 384 p. (hardcover) $27.99

ISBN 1250010071; 9781250010070

LC 2013002622

In this mystery novel, "Mike Scanlon, a reservist in the Army Medical Corps serving in Afghanistan, is allowed to return for one week to his suburban Philadelphia home to bury his wife, Chloe, who apparently died in an odd household accident. Overcome with grief, Mike realizes that . . . Chloe was hiding a shocking secret." He "begins an out-of-control campaign to uncover Chloe's secret life, risking the loss of custody of his daughter, his health, and his own freedom." (Publishers Weekly)

Scottoline, Lisa

★ **Every** fifteen minutes; Lisa Scottoline. St. Martin's Press 2015 352 p. (hardcover) $27.99

ISBN 9781250010124; 9781250010117; 125001011X

LC 2014042835

In this novel, by Lisa Scottoline, when "Dr. Eric Parrish . . . takes on a new patient, Eric's entire world begins to crumble. Seventeen-year-old Max has . . . OCD and violent thoughts about a girl he likes. . . . Max can't turn off the mental rituals he needs to perform every fifteen minutes that keep him calm. With the pressure mounting, Max just might reach the breaking point. When the girl is found murdered, Max is nowhere to be found." (Publisher's note)

Scottoline "casts an unflinching eye on the damaged world of sociopaths in this exciting page-turner. . . . Many characters who seem to be gunning for Eric are likely candidates for a sociopathic diagnosis. Once the red herrings are dispatched, the identity of the culprit who plots his downfall is a genuine surprise." Pub Wkly

Scottoline, Lisa ✓

Killer smile. HarperCollins 2004 358p $25.95

ISBN 0-06-051495-7

LC 2003-67650

In this installment in the "series starring the all-female Philadelphia law firm of Rosato & Associates, young Mary DiNunzio takes center stage. Mary has taken on a pro bono case representing her 'peeps' an Italian American business group (the circolo) working on behalf of the estate of Amadeo Brandolini, who committed suicide while interned during World War II. The estate seeks reparations, and Mary feels drawn to the case, so much so that others fear she's obsessed with it. Under the guise of taking a vacation, Mary visits the site of the internment camp in Montana where Amadeo killed himself and finds herself with still more unanswered questions. Interesting author's notes at the end of this engaging drama disclose Scottoline's own discovery of her grandparents' internment, lending this unusual story a welcome authenticity." Booklist

Scottoline, Lisa

Legal tender. HarperCollins Pubs. 1996 291p

LC 96-7165

The protagonist of this legal thriller is Philadelphian Bennie Rosato "a ravishing six-foot blonde, one of two partners in a thriving law firm. In quick order, the foundations of her world come crashing down. Her partner and ex-lover, Mark, turns up murdered shortly after he tells Bennie that he is planning to dissolve the partnership. It's not surprising that she then becomes the cops' prime suspect. When the murder weapon is found in her apartment, Bennie goes underground. Then a drug company CEO is killed, and she is falsely accused of that death, too." Publ Wkly

Scottoline, Lisa

Mistaken identity. HarperCollins Pubs. 1999 480p $24

ISBN 0-06-018747-6

LC 98-43200

Scottoline "succeeds in creating a brisk, multilayered thriller that plunges Rosato & Associates into a maelstrom of legal, ethical and familial conundrums, culminating in an intricate, dramatic and intense courtroom finale." Publ Wkly

Scottoline, Lisa

Moment of truth. HarperCollins Pubs. 2000 358p

ISBN 0-06-019609-2

LC 99-89325

"Sharp, funny characters, crafty plot twists, and a flavorful depiction of high- and lower-middle Philadelphia society will keep readers riveted to this tense, often mischievous page-turner." Publ Wkly

Scottoline, Lisa

One perfect lie; Lisa Scottoline. St. Martin's Press 2017 355 p. (hardcover) $27.99

ISBN 9781250099587; 9781250099563

LC 2016053892

This book, by Lisa Scottoline, "is an emotional thriller and a suburban crime story that will have readers riveted up to the shocking end. . . . On paper, Chris Brennan looks perfect. . . . He's ready to step in as an assistant baseball coach . . . , but everything about . . . [him] is a lie. . . . Susan Sematov is proud of her son Raz, a high school pitcher so athletically talented that he's being recruited for a full-ride scholarship to a Division I college." (Publisher's note)

"Scottoline keeps the pace relentless as she drops a looming threat into the heart of an idyllic suburban community, causing readers to hold their breath in anticipation." Booklist

Scottoline, Lisa

Rough justice. HarperCollins Pubs. 1997 344p

LC 97-5810

"Scottoline deftly balances the varied personalities of the women and manages a large cast, including judge and jury, with precision. She skillfully depicts personal quirks that give her characters dimension." Publ Wkly

Scotton, Christopher

The **secret** wisdom of the earth; Chris Scotton. Grand Central Publishing 2015 480 p. (hardback) $26

ISBN 1455551929; 9781455551927

LC 2014012917

Author Christopher Scotton presents a "novel about an act of violence in a small, Southern town and the repercussions that will forever change a young man's view of human cruelty and compassion. When Buzzy witnesses a brutal hate crime, a sequence is set in play that tests Buzzy and Kevin to their absolute limits in an epic struggle for survival in the Kentucky mountains." (Publisher's note)

"Scotton offers literary observation—"a storm was filling the trees with bursting light"—and a thoughtful appreciation of Appalachia's hard-used people and fragile landscape. A powerful epic of people and place, loss and love, reconciliation and redemption." Kirkus

Searles, John

Boy still missing. Morrow 2001 292p

ISBN 0-688-17570-8

LC 00-40758

"Searles builds suspense and excitement with surprising turns of plot weaving back into one another, and while many of the secondary characters lack depth, Dominic Pindle will resonate with readers." Booklist

Searles, John

★ **Help** for the Haunted; A Novel. John Searles. William Morrow 2013 368 p. $26.99

ISBN 0060779632; 9780060779634

Alex Award (2014)

In this book, "Sylvie Mason's parents are--or were--'demonologists.' Devoutly Christian, her dad zealously worked the lecture circuit while her mom had the talent to soothe the haunted humans who came to them for help. When they are both murdered in a church on a snowy night, 14-year-old Sylvie is the sole witness but doesn't fully remember what happened. . . . Sylvie struggles to reconcile her bleak new life with her slightly less-bleak former life. " (Kirkus Reviews)

Sears, Michael

Black Fridays; Michael Sears. G. P. Putnam's Sons 2012 341 p. (hardcover) $25.95

ISBN 0399158669; 9780399158667

LC 2012011085

Author Michael Sears's protagonist "disgraced executive Jason Stafford lands a new job in record time . . . fresh from two years in jail . . . He's called in to tidy up records that were left in disarray after junior trader Brian Sanders died in an apparent boating accident. It doesn't take long to figure out that the death wasn't accidental . . . [and] the trail leads Sanders through the Wall Street world he once frequented and leads to a colorful FBI showdown." (Kirkus)

Seay, Martin

The **mirror** thief; Martin Seay. Melville House 2016 592 p. (hardback) $27.95

ISBN 9781612195148

LC 2015038526

In this book, by Martin Seay, "the core story is set in Venice in the sixteenth century, when the famed makers of Venetian glass were perfecting one of the old world's most wondrous inventions: the mirror. . . . Meanwhile, in two other Venices—Venice Beach, California, circa 1958, and the Venice casino in Las Vegas, circa today—two . . . schemers launch . . . dangerous plans to get away with a secret." (Publisher's note)

"In sum, this is a splendid masterpiece, to be loved like a long-lost friend, an epic with near-universal appeal." Pub Wkly

Sebald, Winfried Georg, 1944-2001

★ **Austerlitz**; [by] W.G. Sebald; translated by Anthea Bell. Random House 2001 298p il $25.95

ISBN 0-375-50483-4

LC 2001-19785

"The eponymous subject of 'Austerlitz' . . . is a veteran of one of the Kindertransport that came to Britain just before the second world war. An unnamed narrator recalls how he met the mysterious Jacques Austerlitz in Belgium, where they talked about architecture—in particular the hubristic grandiosity of public buildings, and the extravagant but useless defensive fortifications once beloved of European rulers. . . . Conversations they will have decades later . . . touch on the frenzied elaborations of Nazism and describe the ultimately futile defences Austerlitz himself erected against the awareness of his lost origins." (Economist)

"As so often in Sebald's fiction, direct connections are never highlighted in the vast loops and sudden knottings of his rhetoric, but the reader cannot escape the inference that in the long sweep of history the Nazis were not alone, but that an inquirer searching for meaning is." NY Times Book Rev

Sebald, Winfried Georg, 1944-2001

★ The **emigrants**; [by] W.G. Sebald; translated by Michael Hulse. New Directions 1996 237p il $22.95

ISBN 0-8112-1338-2

LC 96-22223

Original German edition, 1995

The four fictional "accounts/reports/reminiscences tell of . . . people who left Germany in the 20th century. Three are about Jews who went to England or Switzerland—either in the 1930s or before WW I—die or commit suicide long after WW II, but who, nonetheless, are victims of the Holocaust. One is about the narrator's non-Jewish great uncle, who went to America at the turn of the century, led an adventuresome life, and died a horrible death in the 1950s." (Choice)

"A profound and original work . . . . W. G. Sebald has created an end-of-century meditation that explores the most delicate, most painful, most nervously repressed and carefully concealed lesions of the last hundred years. Illuminatingly engaged with the history and literature of the modern era, Mr. Sebald's book gains power through its poetic obsessions with the past." N Y Times Book Rev

Sebald, Winfried Georg

★ **Vertigo**; [by] W.G. Sebald; translated by Michael Hulse. New Directions 2000 263p il $23.95

ISBN 0-8112-1430-3

LC 99-58955

Original German edition published 1990; this translation first published 1999 in the United Kingdom

"W.G. Sebald is unusual for a literary star. He fuses genres (travelogue, biography, the novel, meditation, myth), confounding the categories most readers are used to. The narrator of 'Vertigo' offers a fair account of Mr. Sebald's intricate methods. . . . This is poetic or philosophical fiction for readers content to follow the path of a remarkable author's thoughts without the guard-rail of an overarching story." Economist

Sebold, Alice

The **almost** moon; a novel. Little, Brown and Co. 2007 291p $24.99

ISBN 978-0-316-67746-2; 0-316-67746-9

LC 2007-09917

This novel is "brilliantly paced, it's brutally honest, and the Gordian knot at its core—an abusive mother and her traumatically attached daughter— is depicted with such generous intelligence that the fineness of the novel more than surpasses its own horror show of circumstance. Sebold has managed to give us a sympathetic protagonist who smothers her mother in the opening pages, and yet the decades that led up to this black moment are delivered without a shred of sentimentality or melodramatic overkill. It's a tightrope walk of character building." Boston Globe

Sebold, Alice

★ The **lovely** bones. Little, Brown 2002 328p $21.95; pa $13.95

ISBN 0-316-66634-3; 0-316-16881-5 pa

LC 2001-50622

"As pleasant as Susie's heaven is, there's no God there, and certainly no Jesus. This is spirituality for an age that's ecumenical to a fault. But emotionally, it's faultless. Sebold never slips as she follows this family. The risks she walks are enough to give you vertigo." Christ Sci Monit

Sedaris, David

Holidays on ice; by David Sedaris. 2nd ed; Little, Brown and Co. 2008 166p $16.99

ISBN 978-0-316-03590-3; 0-316-03590-4

LC 2008-925927

First published 1997

"David Sedaris's beloved holiday collection is new again with six more pieces, including a never before published story. Along with such favorites as the diaries of a Macy's elf and the annals of two very competitive families, are Sedaris's tales of tardy trick-or-treaters ("Us and Them"); the difficulties of explaining the Easter Bunny to the French ("Jesus Shaves"); what to do when you've been locked out in a snowstorm ("Let It Snow"); the puzzling Christmas traditions of other nations ("Six to Eight Black Men"); what Halloween at the medical examiner's looks like ("The Monster Mash"); and a barnyard secret Santa scheme gone awry ("Cow and Turkey")." (Publisher's note)

"For those dreading the holiday season, bestseller Sedaris (When You Are Engulfed In Flames) makes life a little easier with this re-release of his uproarious essay collection, newly expanded from the original 1997 edition." (Publishers Weekly)

Sedgwick, Marcus

A **love** like blood; a novel. by Marcus Sedgwick. W W Norton & Co Inc. 2015 310 p. (hardcover) $25.95

ISBN 1605986836; 9781605986838

This novel, by Marcus Sedgwick, offers a "saga of love, revenge, and obsession--and vampires. In 1944, just days after the liberation of Paris, Charles Jackson sees something horrific: a man in a dark tunnel, apparently drinking the blood of a murdered woman. . . . Seven years later he returns to the city--and sees the same man dining in the company of a fascinating, beautiful young woman. When they leave the restaurant, Charles decides to follow." (Publisher's note)

"In this macabre psychological thriller, Sedgwick offers atmospheric settings and a relentless, chilling plot that gives a whole new meaning to the idea of 'blood feud.'" Kirkus

Sedgwick, Marcus

Mister Memory; a novel. Marcus Sedgwick. Pegasus Crime 2017 327 p. (hardcover) $25.95

ISBN 9781681773407; 9781681773919; 1681773406

In this novel, by Marcus Sedgwick, "in Paris in the year 1899, Marcel Després is arrested for the murder of his wife and transferred to the famous Salpetriere Asylum. . . . But the doctor assigned to his care soon realizes this is no ordinary patient: Marcel Després, Mister Memory, is a man who cannot forget. And the policeman assigned to his case soon realizes that something else is at stake: For . . . why are his superiors so keen for the whole affair to be closed?" (Publisher's note)

"Marvelously imagined and sure to appeal to readers who enjoy an intelligent thriller." Kirkus

Sedia, Ekaterina

Alchemy of stone. Prime 301p pa $12.95

ISBN 978-0-8095-7284-7; 0-8095-7284-2

This "steampunk fable about the price of industrial development, follows Mattie, an emancipated automaton, as her home city is rent by conflict between alchemists and the mechanics whose clanking, steaming inventions are changing society. Though created by a leader of the mechanics, Mattie chose to join the alchemists, but her creator still holds the key that winds her up. When a terrorist bombing and an assassination touch off all-out war between the two factions, she discovers the ugly secrets and exploitation that keep the city supplied with food and coal. Sedia's exquisitely bleak vision deliberately skewers familiar ideas from know-it-all computers to talking statues desperate for souls." Publ Wkly

See, Carolyn

★ The **handyman**. Random House 1999 220p $22.95

ISBN 0-375-50155-X

LC 98-21098

"Bob Hampton, a future great artist, leads a quintessentially California life as a freelance handyman before he answers his true calling; in the course of a hot Los Angeles summer, he worries about his lack of aesthetic sophistication, comforts lonely housewives in the time-honored way, and rescues a drowning child and an AIDS patient. Despite a confusing start, the novel quickly takes on the brightness of a sun-dazzled swimming pool and makes a case for shadowless living—a state its hero achieves through an unlikely combination of application and hedonism." New Yorker

See, Carolyn

There will never be another you; a novel. Random 2006 242p $24.95

ISBN 0-679-46317-8

LC 2005-44932

"Among the most potent and poignant new novels to address post-9/11 America. . . . It is potent because the sense of dread and unease that mark almost every moment in the book is palpable; it is poignant because See, who in previous books has proven eminently capable of skewering her characters when they misbehave, has such compassion for the largely villain-less ensemble that populates this tale." Washington Post Book World

See, Lisa

Dragon bones; a novel. Random House 2003 348p $24.95

ISBN 0-679-46320-8

LC 2002-24871

"Hulan and David must overcome their estrangement and work together to solve the crimes. In a land where bribery and corruption are the norm, there are many suspects. The novel flows beautifully, engaging readers in the mystery while gently introducing them to China's rich cultural history." Libr J

See, Lisa

Dreams of joy; a novel. Random House 2011 354p $26

ISBN 978-1-4000-6712-1; 1-4000-6712-X

LC 2011-03891

Sequel to: Shanghai girls

"Although the ending betrays See's roots in genre fiction, this is a riveting, meticulously researched depiction of one of the world's worst human-engineered catastrophes." Kirkus

See, Lisa

Peony in love; a novel. Random House 2007 284p $23.95

ISBN 978-1-4000-6466-3; 1-4000-6466-X

LC 2007-01623

This novel, "is—for the reader willing to venture a crucial suspension of disbelief—a complex period tapestry inscribed with the age-old tragedy of love and death and bordered round with vignettes from Chinese metaphysics, dynastic history and the intimate chamber tales of women's friendship and rivalry. . . . See is gifted with a lucid, graceful style and a solid command of her many motifs." N Y Times Book Rev

See, Lisa

Shanghai girls; a novel. Random House 2009 314p $25

ISBN 978-1-4000-6711-4; 1-4000-6711-1

LC 2008-49245

"Pearl and May Chin are 'Beautiful Girls,' models in 1930s Shanghai whose images grace calendars and ads and who party with the young and restless in the Paris of Asia. But the party is soon over. . . . Their father sells them into arranged marriages with the sons of a Chinese family that emigrated to Los Angeles. The daughters rebel and literally miss the boat—until the Japanese attack on Shanghai in 1937 forces them on an Odyssean journey to America. In this moving historical novel, Lisa See explores her Chinese-American roots and those of the Chinese who headed to California in the early 20th century in hopes of a better life, only to find hardship and discrimination." USA Today

See, Lisa

The **tea** girl of hummingbird lane; by Lisa See. Simon & Schuster 2017 384 p. (ebook) $18.99; $27

ISBN 9781501154843; 1501154826; 9781501154829

LC 2016055462

In this book, by Lisa See, "Li-yan and her family align their lives around the seasons and the farming of tea. There is ritual and routine, and it has been ever thus for generations. Then one day a jeep appears at the village gate—the first automobile any of them have seen—and a stranger arrives. In this remote Yunnan village, the stranger finds the rare tea he has been seeking and a reticent Akha people." (Publisher's note)

"With vivid and precise details about tea and life in rural China, Li-Yan's gripping journey to find her daughter comes alive." Pub Wkly

Segal, Erich

★ **Love** story. Harper & Row 1970 131p

"A very professionally crafted short first novel. The author makes no great claims of insight for his work. Indeed, the story is all on the surface. But it is funny and sad and generally recommended." Libr J

Followed by Oliver's story (1977)

Segal, Francesca

The **awkward** age; Francesca Segal. Riverhead Books 2017 358 p. (hardcover) $27

ISBN 9780399576478; 9780399576454

LC 2016048993

This book, by Francesca Segal, examines Julia who has "fallen deeply, unexpectedly in love. American obstetrician James is everything she didn't know she wanted--if only her teenage daughter, Gwen, didn't hate him so much. Uniting two households is never easy, but when Gwen turns for comfort to James's seventeen-year-old son, Nathan, the consequences will test her mother's loyalty and threaten all their fragile new happiness." (Publisher's note)

"In finely wrought prose, with characters who seem to walk beside us and speak aloud, Segal's latest novel is a sympathetic portrait of the difficulties in finding love and raising teenagers." Kirkus

Segal, Lore Groszmann

Shakespeare's kitchen; stories. [by] Lore Segal. The New Press 2007 225p $22.95

ISBN 978-1-59558-151-8; 1-59558-151-0

LC 2006-30107

"In Segal's world, a world where domestic tragedies occur against the backdrop of historic human cruelties, people tend to behave badly not out of a perverted sense of ambition or power but from a deep need for attachment and belonging. And so it's crucial that the book doesn't move in a straight line. The same people who are good are not good. The bad guys sometimes do decent things. The truth—surprise!—is nuanced, and so is the story, which doesn't end the way it seems to be heading." N Y Times Book Rev

Seiffert, Rachel

Field study. Pantheon Books 2004 215p $19.95

ISBN 0-375-42259-5

LC 2003-66364

In this collection of stories, "all set primarily in Europe, we meet a variety of characters, among them an architect losing his grip on his profession and on reality, a British soldier AWOL in World War II Italy, a teenaged couple struggling with the reality of becoming parents, and an American woman driving her elderly father-in-law to his former street in East Berlin. . . . This is a fine collection from a young writer who displays a modern Europe with its particular social and political issues amid universal human themes." Libr J

Seitz, Nicole

Trouble the water; Nicole Seitz. Thomas Nelson 2007 v, 296 p.p (softcover) $15.99

ISBN 1595544003; 9781595544001

LC 2007051520

This book follows a woman named "Honor, in her mid-40s, [who] escapes to St. Anne's Isle off the South Carolina coast with her life in tatters. She's unemployed and broke, and feels unworthy of love after a divorce and a failed relationship. Her attempted suicide is thwarted by a group of Gullah nannies who rescue her and love her back to health, introducing her to Duchess, a quirky woman with a penchant for nudity. Honor lives with Duchess for a while as they help each other heal, and eventually Honor reclaims her love for life and painting, and reconnects with her sister Alice. The narration switches regularly among the three women (Honor, Duchess and Alice) and the story jumps back and forth over an eight-year span." (Publishers Weekly)

Sekaran, Shanthi

★ **Lucky** boy; Shanthi Sekaran. G.P. Putnam's Sons 2017 472 p. (ebook) $65; (hardcover) $27

ISBN 9781101982259; 1101982241; 9781101982242

LC 2016008418

In this book, by Shanthi Sekaran, "Solimar Castro-Valdez embarks on a perilous journey across the Mexican border. Weeks later, she arrives in Berkeley, California, dazed by first love found then lost, and pregnant. This was not the plan. Undocumented and unmoored, Soli discovers that her son, Ignacio, can become her touchstone, and motherhood her identity in a world where she's otherwise invisible." (Publisher's note)

"Sekaran is a master of drawing detailed, richly layered characters and relationships; here are the subtly nuanced lines of love and expectation between parents and children; here, too are moments of great depth and insight. A superbly crafted and engrossing novel." Kirkus

Self, Will

The **Book** of Dave; a revelation of the recent past and the distant future. Bloomsbury Pub. 2006 495p $24.95

ISBN 0-670-91443-6

LC 2006-4750

"In this tale of an embittered taxi-driver whose psychotic rantings become the creed of a blighted people hundreds of years after his death, Self unleashes his apparently boundless misanthropy on modern London, the origins of religion, and the postapocalyptic future. Dave Rudman, driven mad by divorce and ill-prescribed antidepressants, thinks he is God and writes a vitriolic screed, which he has printed on metal plates and buries in a garden. Discovered by the survivors of a catastrophic flood and adopted as a gospel, it demands the complete separation of mothers and fathers (children to spend exactly half the week with each). Switching between a narrative of Dave's unlucky life and the phonetically rendered 'Mokni' speech of his wretched followers, Self achieves an elaborate vision of vicious superstition and hopeless struggle." New Yorker

Self, Will

Dorian; an imitation. Grove Press 2002 277p $23

ISBN 0-8021-1729-5

LC 2002-29962

"In this retelling of Oscar Wilde's The Picture of Dorian Gray, most of the original's characters are cleverly transmuted into their late-20th-century counterparts: dissolute Henry Wotton, now openly homosexual with a nasty heroin habit; his protege, eager young video artist 'Baz' Hallward; and the title character, the quintessential amoral narcissist. . . . Self uses Wilde's plot to examine post-Stonewall gay life, from its drug-fueled hedonistic excesses to the reckoning of the AIDs epidemic. The novel skewers every layer of British society—street hustlers, members of Parliament and the idle rich." Publ Wkly

Self, Will

Shark; Will Self. Grove Press 2014 400 p. $26

ISBN 0802123104; 9780802123107

LC 2015410962

In this novel by Will Self, a prequel to his novel "Umbrella," "maverick psychiatrist Dr Zack Busner has been tricked into joining a decidedly ill advised LSD trip with several of its disturbed residents. Five years later, sitting in a nearby cinema watching Steven Spielberg's Jaws, Busner realizes the true nature of the events that transpired on that dread-soaked day." (Publisher's note)

"This jumbled structure is the platform from which Self explores society's judgments of and effects on sanity and mental health. Self's style pays homage to the modernism of writers such as Joyce and Céline and the black humor of Vonnegut and Heller in this challenging but exceptional read." Booklist

Self, Will

Umbrella; Will Self. Pgw 2013 397 p. $25

ISBN 0802120725; 9780802120724

Man Booker Prize Shortlist (2012)

This novel, by Will Self, follows "maverick psychiatrist Zachary Busner" and his encounters with his patient "Audrey Dearth, an elderly woman born in the slums of West London in 1890. Audrey's memories of a bygone Edwardian London, her lovers, involvement with early feminist and socialist movements, and, in particular, her time working in an umbrella shop, alternate with Busner's attempts to treat her condition and bring light to her clouded world." (Publisher's note)

Selgin, Peter

Drowning lessons; stories. University of Georgia Press 2008 235p $24.95

ISBN 978-0-8203-3210-9; 0-8203-3210-0

LC 2008-20377

Flannery O'Connor Award for Short Fiction

"Whether as a force for life or one of destruction, water in all its forms is the unifying theme in writer and artist Peter Selgin's powerful collection, Drowning Lessons. Selgin is never heavyhanded in his use of metaphor, and it's rewarding to trace the skill with which he employs it in many of these 13 stories." BookPage

Sem-Sandberg, Steve

★ The **chosen** ones; a novel. Steve Sem-Sandberg; translated by Anna Paterson. Farrar, Straus & Giroux 2016 592 p. (hardback) $28; (ebook) $60

ISBN 9780374122805; 9780374711269

LC 2015042554

In this novel, by Steve Sem-Sandberg, translated by Anna Paterson, "the Am Spiegelgrund clinic, in glittering Vienna, masqueraded as a well-intentioned reform school. . . . The reality, however, was very different: in the wake of Germany's annexation of Austria on the eve of World War II, . . . the Nazi regime's euthanasia program would come to determine the fate of many of the clinic's inhabitants." (Publisher's note)

"With a gift for finding humanity in even the darkest of stories, Sem-Sanberg has written an indelible, moving novel." Pub Wkly

Semple, Maria

Where'd you go, Bernadette; a novel. Maria Semple. Little, Brown and Company 2012 336 p. $25.99

ISBN 0316204277; 9780316204279

LC 2011040639

Alex Award (2013)

This novel, by Maria Semple, is an "Internet-age domestic comedy about a wife/mother/genius architect who goes a little nuts from living in . . . Seattle." Bernadette lives with her genius husband Elgie and her daughter Bee in Seattle, where she "hates everything" and everyone, "especially the other mothers at Bee's" school. She disappears days before a "planned family trip to Antarctica," leaving Elgie and Bee to search for her. (Kirkus Reviews)

Senna, Danzy

New People; by Danzy Senna. Penguin Group USA 2017 229 p. $26

ISBN 159448709X; 9781594487095

LC 2016045954

In this book, by Danzy Senna, "Maria is at the start of a life she never thought possible. She and Khalil, her college sweetheart, are planning their wedding. . . . They live together in a black bohemian enclave in Brooklyn, where Khalil is riding the wave of the first dot-com boom and Maria is plugging away at her dissertation, on the Jonestown massacre. . . . Everything Maria knows she should want lies before her--yet she can't stop daydreaming about another man, a poet she barely knows." (Publisher's note)

"Senna combines the clued-in status details you'd find in a New York magazine article with the narrative invention of big-league fiction. Every detail and subplot, including Maria's dissertation on the Jonestown massacre and her buried secret about a college prank gone awry, is resonant." Kirkus

Seth, Vikram

An **equal** music. Broadway Bks. 1999 380p $25

ISBN 0-7679-0291-2

LC 99-20421

Seth's "writing is a throwback, freely romantic, wondrously out of date, totally unhedged. His book attempts no cool, contains not a single pose. He can be playful with language, though not distractingly so. . . . The book is also stocked with humor, which appears when it is most needed, as the story grows almost suffocatingly sad." Natl Rev

Seth, Vikram

★ A **suitable** boy; a novel. HarperCollins Pubs. 1993 1349p

LC 92-54744

This novel is, "at its heart an elegy as well as a comedy of manners, about a traditional society in a time of change, and about a leisurely world of graces giving way to a new, more democratic time." Times Lit Suppl

Seton, Anya

Avalon. Houghton Mifflin 1965 440p

"Late tenth- and early eleventh-century life in England and in the lands colonized by the Norsemen {i.e. Iceland} is re-created from early Anglo-Saxon chronicles, French manuscripts, and secondary sources. . . . The action and milieu are vivid and though the characterization is not strong the psychological and historical motivations are believable. An honest historical novel for enthusiasts of the genre." Booklist

Seton, Anya

★ **Dragonwyck**. Houghton Mifflin 1944 336p

An American "Gothic" novel. The time is the 1830's and 1840's; the place, New York City and the great Van Ryn estate, Dragonwyck, on the Hudson. A young farm girl, a distant cousin of the Van Ryn's goes to live at Dragonwyck as governess to the Van Ryns' small daughter. At the death of the child's mother, Miranda becomes the second Mrs. Van Ryn. The story of Miranda's gradual horrified awakening follows

"For all its trappings and devices—and they are good, spine-chilling trappings, handled with considerable skill—the novel manages to have life and substance." NY Her Trib Books

Seton, Anya

Green darkness. Houghton Mifflin 1973 591p

First published 1972 in the United Kingdom

"Reincarnation is the theme of {this} . . . novel. A 16th-century Benedictine monk, Stephen Marsdon, falls prey to a consuming passion for alluring Celia de Bohun and forsakes his vows. The tragic end of the lovers, involving murder and suicide, brings, nearly 400 years later, madness and near death to their reincarnations, newlyweds Celia and Richard Marsdon. Fortunately, a Hindu doctor (himself a reincarnated Italian physician in Tudor England who longed for warmer climates) hovers nearby to monitor the proceedings and brings the souls to rest." Libr J

Seton, Anya

Katherine. Houghton Mifflin 1954 588p

Historical romance about the life of Katherine Swynford, sister-in-law of Geoffrey Chaucer, and mistress and later wife of John Gaunt

"It is a story that demands no intellectual or emotional effort from the reader. . . . But Miss Seton presents her facts accurately. Her research extends as far as visiting what remains of any of John of Gaunt's 30 castles and her zest for her subject communicates itself to the reader." San Francisco Chron

Seton, Anya

★ The **Winthrop** woman. Houghton Mifflin 1958 586p

"The novel is noteworthy for its insights into the Puritan 'Bible Commonwealth.'" Saturday Rev

Settle, Mary Lee

★ **Charley** Bland. Farrar, Straus & Giroux 1989 207p il

ISBN 0-374-12078-1

LC 89-207125

"Having fled the suffocating small-town environment of her West Virginia home and recreated herself as a writer in postwar Paris, the heroine of this condensed, lyric novel returns to discover that having dreams come true is sometimes disastrous. For there she again meets Charley Bland, the golden boy she worshiped as a child, now the town's most eligible–and elusive–bachelor. . . . The affair they begin quickly demolishes everything this woman had made of herself in the years she had been away." Libr J

Settle, Mary Lee

★ The **killing** ground. Farrar, Straus & Giroux 1982 385p

ISBN 0-374-18107-1

LC 82-2477

"In this novel, the last of the Beulah Quintet, Settle describes the various homecomings of Hannah McKarkle, a woman from an affluent West Virginia coal-mining family who has pursued a writing career in New York. In 1960, Hannah returns to find that her brother Johnny has been killed by a man who turns out to be a poor distant relative. The brother's death, the intricate interplay among classes in the closed rural society of West Virginia, and the inevitable pull of one's native home on the heart and soul are central to her subsequent visits in 1978 and 1980." Libr J

Settle, Mary Lee

★ **O** Beulah Land; a novel. Viking 1956 368p

First published volume of the author's Beulah Quintet, set in rural West Virginia. Chronologically follows Prisons (1973). Subsequent titles in the series: Know nothing (1960); The scapegoat (1980) and The killing ground

Historical novel of the Virginia frontier from 1754 to 1775. "Jonathan Lacey is a strong man, as only a gentleman is strong. And he is a gentleman, by the standards of the Virginia wilderness country in the years preceding the American Revolution. After his service at the Battle of Little Meadows in 1775, Johnny scouts and surveys far into the mountains, and leads a heterogeneous group of early Americans westward with him, to claim and clear his bounty land in the undefended King's Part of the colony, beyond the Proclamation Line. It is on this land, called Beulah by Jeremiah the New Light preacher, that Johnny proves his strength." N Y Times Book Rev

Sexton, Margaret Wilkerson

A **kind** of freedom; a novel. Margaret Wilkerson Sexton. Counterpoint Press 2017 256 p. $26; $25.99

ISBN 9781619029224; 9781640090026

LC 2017015331

In this novel, by Margaret Wilkerson Sexton, "Evelyn is a Creole woman who comes of age in New Orleans at the height of World War II. Her family inhabits the upper echelon of Black society, and when she falls for no-account Renard, she is forced to choose between her life of privilege and the man she loves." (Publisher's note)

"This novel sparked a competition among literary agents, and for good reason. This family is worth every minute of a reader's time." (Booklist)

Seymour, Gerald

The **heart** of danger. HarperCollins Pubs. 1995 358p

ISBN 0-06-100968-7

LC 95-4808

"Using this wheels-within-wheels frame, Seymour constructs a harshly detailed novel about a dirty little war, peopled with a wide variety of deeply etched characters and suffused with a nearly palpable sense of despair and weariness." Publ Wkly

Seymour, Gerald

Killing ground. HarperCollins Pubs. 1997 390p

LC 96-51178

"Twenty-three-year-old Charlotte 'Charlie' Parsons is suffocating. Living at home with her parents in a small village in Cornwall, she sees no future except teaching snotty first-formers in the village primary. But excitement enters her life twice in one day. First, she receives a letter from Giuseppe and Angela Ruggerio, the Italian family Charlie worked for one wonderful summer. Will she come back to Italy and take care of the three Ruggerio children? To Charlie, it's a heaven-sent opportunity to escape. Later that day, she's visited by a coldly sinister American DEA agent named Axel Moen, who plans to use Charlie to reel in Mario Ruggerio, brother of Giuseppe and capo of the Sicilian Mafia. . . . A gripping thriller that leads to a shattering climax." Booklist

Seymour, Gerald

Rat run. Overlook Press 2007 240p $24.95

ISBN 978-1-58567-894-5; 1-58567-894-5

LC 2006-51533

"Seymour gives us two stories to follow: Malachy's pursuit of drug lord Ricky Capel and the saga of his gradual personal redemption. The pursuit story is intricate and suspenseful, as Seymour's many fans have come to expect; in the redemption story, he nimbly avoids most of the cliches associated with the type (it's probably not possible to avoid them all). A thriller with a human side." Booklist

Shaara, Jeff

Gods and generals. Ballantine Bks. 1996 498p $25

ISBN 0-345-40492-0

LC 95-53360

This novel "focuses simultaneously on the lives of four men who played significant roles in the military side of the Civil War in battles leading up to the great one at Gettysburg. The novel follows Stonewall Jackson, Winfield Scott Hancock, Joshua Chamberlain, and Robert E. Lee from 1858 to 1863, giving the reader splendidly detailed witness to how the war drew them into commanding positions. As should be the case with good historical fiction, Shaara, in taking actual figures from the past, rekindles them; he uses the personal experiences of these four men to meaningfully explore the political and military issues of the day." Booklist

Shaara, Jeff

Gone for soldiers. Ballantine Bks. 2000 424p il

ISBN 0-345-42750-5

LC 00-22745

"The book is simply wonderful, populated with eminently human heroes who are called upon to perform Herculean tasks in a war muddied beyond redemption by the ambitions of back-home and battlefield politicians." Libr J

Shaara, Jeff

The **last** full measure. Ballantine Bks. 1998 560p map $25

ISBN 0-345-40491-2

LC 97-49383

This volume follows "the course of the war in Virginia from Lee's retreat from Gettysburg to his surrender at Appomattox Court House. Ulysses S. Grant has come East to assume command of all Federal forces and to confront Lee, and the war they make is marked by such horrendous battles as The Wilderness and Spotsylvania. As characters, Grant and Lee dominate this book. . . . Civil War buffs will find Shaara nodding on some small details, but they generally will be delighted with this book." Libr J

Shaara, Jeff

The **rising** tide; a novel of the World War II. Ballantine Books 2006 xxxvi, 536p $27.95

ISBN 978-0-345-46141-4; 0-345-46141-X

LC 2006-42936

Shaara opens this first volume of a projected trilogy "in the deserts of North Africa, where Allied troops attempt to match wits and forces with the Desert Fox, wily German commander Field Marshall Erwin Rommel, and his formidable Afrika Korps. After Hitler overruns France, solidifying his position in Western Europe, he turns his attention eastward toward the vast Russian expanse. With the German focus split, the Allies sense the time is right to launch a united second front in North Africa, setting their sights on an eventual invasion of southern Italy. As plans for Operation Torch become a reality, Shaara vividly recreates a cast of military and political heroes and villains, including General Dwight D. Eisenhower, General George Marshall, General George Patton, British general Bernard Montgomery, German field marshal Erwin Rommel, Adolf Hitler, Winston Churchill, and Franklin Roosevelt." Booklist

Shaara, Jeff

The **steel** wave; a novel of World War II. Ballantine Books 2008 xxvi, 493p map $28

ISBN 978-0-345-46142-1; 0-345-46142-8

LC 2008-4813

Sequel to The rising tide; this is the second volume of Shaara's World War II trilogy

This "epic-scale novel opens on January 25, 1944, with British commandos gathering soil samples on Omaha Beach to assess landing sites. Shaara gives the Americans, called the great waves of steel by the Germans, their due portion in the grisly, brutal Allied invasion, and the experiences of the grunt soldiers—most notably the indefatigable U.S. Army Sgt. Jesse Adams—offers a field-level view of D-Day and afterward, generating more suspenseful reading than the matter-of-fact accounts of the big-brass dealings of Eisenhower and Churchill. The Allied leaders' personalities emerge with agile clarity, while German Field Marshal Erwin Rommel embodies the good soldier laboring under a delusional Hitler and German High Command ensconced in cozy Berlin. Rommel's ambivalent complicity in the assassination plot on Hitler is convincingly rendered and paves the way for the final act. The muscular prose, deft sense of military drama and relentless pacing are well suited for this crackerjack saga." Publ Wkly

Shaara, Michael

★ The **killer** angels; a novel. Random House 1993 374p il $24

ISBN 0-679-42541-1

LC 92-38365

This is a fictionalized account of four days in July, 1863 at the Battle of Gettysburg. The point of view of the Southern forces is represented by Generals Robert E. Lee and James Longstreet, while Colonel Joshua Chamberlain and General John Buford are the focus for the North

"Shaara's version of private reflections and conversations are based on his reading of documents and letters. Although some of his judgments are not necessarily substantiated by historians, he demonstrates a knowledge of both the battle and the area. The writing is vivid and fast moving." Libr J

Shabtai, Yaakov

Uncle Peretz takes off; short stories. translated from the Hebrew by Dalya Bilu. Overlook Press 2004 239p $24.95

ISBN 1-585-67340-4

LC 2004-58316

"At their best, the stories in this collection . . . are masterful, ironically drawn character studies evoking the Israeli frontier spirit under the British mandate while capturing the shift from old world religiosity to new world secularism. Originally published in Hebrew in 1972, the collection is bookended by two linked stories chronicling the deaths of the narrator's grandparents and with them the loss of Jewish traditions." Publ Wkly

Shacochis, Bob

★ The **Woman** Who Lost Her Soul; by Bob Shacochis. Atlantic Monthly Press 2013 640 p. $28

ISBN 0802119824; 9780802119827

Author Bob Shacochis presents a "novel of sex, lies, and American foreign policy, [where] 1990s Haiti, Nazi-occupied Croatia, and Cold War–era Istanbul are shown as places where people are pulled into a vortex of personal and political destruction. Shacochis details how espionage not only reflects a nation's character but can also endanger its soul." (Publishers Weekly)

Shafak, Elif

The **bastard** of Istanbul. Viking 2007 360p $24.95

ISBN 978-0-670-03834-3; 0-670-03834-2

LC 2006-42116

"Shafak's writing is seductive; each chapter of her novel is named for a food, and the warmth of the Turkish kitchen lies at the center of its wide-ranging plot. The Bastard of Istanbul portrays family as more than merely a function of genetics and fate, folding together history and fiction, the personal and the political into a thing of beauty." Elle

Shafak, Elif

Honor; Elif Shafak. Viking 2013 352 p. (hardcover) $26.95

ISBN 0670784834; 9780670784837

LC 2012039761

In this novel, by Elif Shafak, "an honor killing shatters and transforms the lives of Turkish immigrants in 1970s London. . . . While Jamila stays to become a midwife, Pembe follows her Turkish husband, Adem, to London, where they hope to make new lives for themselves and their children. . . . When Pembe begins a chaste affair with a man named Elias, Iskender, [the eldest son,] . . . will discover that you could love someone with all your heart and yet be ready to hurt them." (Publisher's note)

Shakar, Alex

Luminarium; a novel. Soho Press 2011 432p il $25

ISBN 978-1-56947-975-9; 1-56947-975-5

LC 2011013331

The novel's "most impressive aspect is that it always seems to be grounded. It's about the possibility of life after death, spiritualism through technology, Lord Of The Rings, 9/11, and the societal potential of videogames, and yet it mostly doesn't feel like it's overreaching." A.V. Club

Shalev, Meir

Two she-bears; Meir Shalev; translated from the Hebrew by Stuart Schoffman. Schocken Books 2016 301 p. (hardcover : alk. paper) $26.95

ISBN 9780805243291; 9780805243307

LC 2016001663

This book, by Meir Shalev, translated by Stuart Schoffman, "gives us a story of village love and vengeance in the early days of British Palestine that is still being played out two generations later. . . . Ruta [Tavori] weaves a tale of friendship between men, and of love and betrayal, which carries us from British Palestine to present-day Israel, where forgiveness, atonement, and understanding can finally happen." (Publisher's note)

"This tale of love and bloodshed resonates with the primal passions of the biblical texts it invokes, while opening provocative new perspectives on modern questions about Israeli politics and gender identity." Booklist

Shalvis, Jill

Sweet little lies; Jill Shalvis. HarperCollins 2016 384 p. $7.99; (ebook) $7.99

ISBN 0062448021; 9780062448026; 9780062448033

LC 2016022994

In this novel in the Heartbreaker Bay series, by Jill Shalvis, tour boat captain Pru is "in danger of stumbling into love with Mr. Right for Anybody But Her. . . . Pub owner Finn O'Riley is . . . [a] hard-working hottie who always makes time for his friends. When Pru becomes one of them, she discovers how amazing it feels to be on the receiving end of that deep green gaze. But when a freak accident . . . leads to shirtless first aid, things rush way past the friend zone." (Publisher's note)

"Shalvis has created a love story romance fans can't help but root for and grounds it in an affable community they'll adore." Kirkus

Shamsie, Kamila

Home fire; Kamila Shamsie. Riverhead Books 2017 276 p. (hardcover) $26

ISBN 9780735217683; 9780735217706

LC 2017003238

Women's Prize for Fiction Longlist (2018)

In this novel, by Kamila Shamsie, "Isma is free. After years of watching out for her younger siblings in the wake of their mother's death, she's accepted an invitation from a mentor in America that allows her to resume a dream long deferred. But she can't stop worrying about Aneeka, her . . . sister . . . or their brother, Parvaiz. . . . Then Eamonn enters the sisters' lives. Son of a powerful political figure, he has his own birthright to live up to--or defy." (Publisher's note)

"In accessible, unwavering prose and without any heavy-handedness, Shamsie addresses an impressive mix of contemporary issues . . ." Booklist

Shan, Sa

The **girl** who played go; translated from the French by Adriana Hunter. Knopf 2003 312p $22.95

ISBN 0-4000-4025-6

Original French edition, 2001

"The alternating parallel tales add an extra spark of energy to this swift-moving novel, as Sa portrays tenderness and brutality with equal clarity." Publ Wkly

Shanbhag, Vivek

Ghachar ghochar; Vivek Shanbhag; translated from the Kannada by Srinath Perur. Penguin Books 2017 128 p. (ebook) $45; (paperback) $15

ISBN 9781101992944; 9780143111689

LC 2016027137

In this book, by Vivek Shanbhag, "a young man's close-knit family is nearly destitute when his uncle founds a successful spice company, changing their fortunes overnight. As they move from a cramped, ant-infested shack to a larger house on the other side of Bangalore, and try to adjust to a new way of life, allegiances realign; marriages are arranged and begin to falter; and conflict brews ominously in the background." (Publisher's note)

"Absorbing, insightful, and altogether a wonderful read." Pub Wkly

Shange, Ntozake

Betsey Brown; a novel. St. Martin's Press 1985 207p

LC 85-2663

"Miss Shange is a superb storyteller who keeps her eye on what brings her characters together rather than what separates them: courage and love, innocence and the loss of it, home and homelessness. Miss Shange understands backyards, houses, schools and churches. {This novel} rejoices in—but never sentimentalizes—those places on earth where you are accepted, where you are comfortable with yourself." N Y Times Book Rev

Shange, Ntozake

Sassafrass, Cypress & Indigo; a novel. St. Martin's Press 1982 224p

LC 82-5565

"Poetry, magical spells, recipes, and choreographs are woven into the narrative providing a vital interplay between the sisters and their creations. The setting of much of the story, Charleston, South Carolina, becomes a place of magic and joy for the reader." Libr J

Shannon, Samantha

The **bone** season; Samantha Shannon. Bloomsbury Press 2013 480 p. (alk. paper) $24

ISBN 1620401398; 9781620401392

LC 2012038358

In this novel by Samantha Shannon "it is the year 2059. Cities are under the control of a security force called Scion. Paige Mahoney works [for] secret cell known as the Seven Seals. Paige is a dreamwalker, a rare kind of clairvoyant. When Paige is captured and arrested . . . the voyant prison is a separate city. Paige is assigned to . . ., Warden, who will be in charge of her. If she wants to regain her freedom, Paige will have to learn something of his mind and his own mysterious motives." (Publisher's note)

Other titles in this series are:
The mime order (2015)
The song rising (2017)

Shannon, Samantha

The **mime** order; a novel. by Samantha Shannon. St. Martin's Press 2015 528 p. map $25

ISBN 1620408937; 9781620408933

This book, by Samantha Shannon, is the "second volume of a projected seven-volume fantasy/science-fiction epic. The novel begins with Paige's escape to London as she eludes pursuers of all stripes and becomes public enemy No. 1. On the plus side, she's with a gang of clairvoyants, and her cohort is headed by Jaxon Hall, one of the mime-lords of the title. . . .The prime mover of action here is Paige's relentless pursuit by Scion, a governmental organization." (Kirkus Reviews)

"Shannon creates vividly dilapidated, macabre, and mysterious worlds both urban and within the dreamscapes Paige valiantly enters. The motley, elaborately costumed characters are compelling; the non-stop, often eerie action is riveting." Booklist

Shapiro, B. A.

The **muralist**; a novel. by B. A. Shapiro. Algonquin Books of Chapel Hill 2015 352 p. (hardcover) $26.95

ISBN 9781616203573

LC 2015016909

In this novel, by B. A. Shapiro, when "Alizée Benoit, a young American painter working for the Works Progress Administration (WPA), vanishes in New York City in 1940, no one knows what happened to her. . . . Not her close-knit group of friends and fellow WPA painters, including Mark Rothko, Jackson Pollock, and Lee Krasner. And, some seventy years later, not her great-niece, Danielle Abrams, who . . . uncovers enigmatic paintings hidden behind works by those . . . artists." (Publisher's note)

"Mystery and historical fiction lovers who can accept that many lives and tragic histories can indeed intersect and converge around works of art in New York and France will find this a riveting read." LJ

Sharfeddin, Heather

Mineral spirits; a novel. Bridge Works 2006 250p $21.95

ISBN 978-1-882593-98-9; 1-882593-98-7

LC 2006-762

"Freshly elected as the sheriff in a one-lawman town in Montana, Kip Edelson is immediately put to task when 10-year-old Gray Dausman discovers a rotting corpse down by the river. As Edelson attempts to discern the identity of the victim, he becomes increasingly convinced that it is none other than the boy's missing mother, and he reluctantly takes Gray under his wing even as his own marriage evaporates before him. When Edelson stumbles upon an illicit drug ring involving the local tavern owner and various other shady locals, the identity of the corpse takes on a new, unexpected significance." Booklist

The author "blends Western and mystery genres into a fine, heady concoction." Libr J

Sharma, Akhil

Family Life; a novel. Akhil Sharma. W W Norton & Co Inc 2014 224 p. $23.95

ISBN 0393060055; 9780393060058

LC 2013041222

In this novel by Akhil Sharma, readers "meet the Mishra family in Delhi in 1978, where eight-year-old Ajay and his older brother Birju [are] waiting for the day when their plane tickets will arrive and they and their mother can fly across the world and join their father in America. Life is extraordinary until tragedy strikes, leaving one brother severely brain-damaged and the other lost and virtually orphaned in a strange land." (Publisher's note)

"A moving story of displacement and of the inevitable adjustments one must make when life circumstances change." Kirkus

Sharp, Zoë

Die easy; A Charlie Fox Thriller. W W Norton & Co Inc 2013 336 p. $25.95

ISBN 1605984000; 9781605984001

This is Zoë Sharp's 10th Charlie Fox thriller. Here, professional bodyguard Charlie takes on an assignment in post-Katrina New Orleans—the first job with her lover and partner, Sean Meyer, since he recovered from being shot in the head. . . . Tasked with protecting wealthy businessman Blake Dyer during the After Katrina Foundation fundraising event, Charlie is grateful for what appears to be a straight-forward task." Things inevitably go wrong. (Publishers Weekly)

Sharp, Zoë

Fourth Day. Pegasus 2011 447 p. (hardcover) $25

ISBN 1605981214; 9781605981215

In this, Zoë Sharp's fourth Charlie Fox novel, Charlie, "now working for a Manhattan company, seeks to extricate schoolteacher Thomas Witney from Fourth Day, a cult in the desert near Los Angeles. . . . While Charlie and her lover, Sean Meyer, manage to get Thomas out, they're unprepared for either his complete about-face on [cult leader] Bane or the intense interest that Homeland Security suddenly has in the cult and Thomas's insider knowledge." (Publishers Weekly)

Sharratt, Mary

Daughters of the Witching Hill. Houghton Mifflin Harcourt 2009 333p $24

ISBN 978-0-547-06967-8; 0-547-06967-7

LC 2009-42057

"Based on the infamous 1612 Lancashire witch trials, Sharratt's . . . novel vividly portrays the religious turmoil and hardscrabble life of 17th-century rural England. It's a familiar premise: an old beggar woman accused of witchcraft is sentenced to hang, along with others of her ilk. What makes this story stand out are the strong voices of the two main characters, stalwart Bess Southerns (aka Demdike) and her feisty granddaughter Alizon Device. Demdike is a cunning woman, able to heal animals and people with herbal folk magic. She strives to do only good, but when she teaches her dear friend the craft, she releases a Pandora's box of resentment, revenge, and evil." Libr J

Sharratt, Mary

Illuminations; a novel of Hildegard von Bingen. Mary Sharratt. Houghton Mifflin Harcourt 2012 xiv, 274 p.p (hardcover) $25

ISBN 0547567847; 9780547567846

LC 2012014252

This novel by Mary Sharratt "reveals the . . . story of how . . . [Benedictine abbess and polymath] Hildegard [of Bingen], offered as a tithe to the Church at the age of eight, triumphed against impossible odds to become the greatest woman of her age." The book presents a "portrait of a woman of faith and power -- a visionary in every sense of the word." (marysharratt.com)

Shattuck, Jessica

Perfect life; a novel. W.W. Norton & Co. 2009 315p $24.95

ISBN 978-0-393-06950-1; 0-393-06950-8

LC 2009-15080

"Jenny, a former prom queen climbing the corporate ladder in the pharmaceutical industry, has gone to great lengths to keep her ex, the underachieving Neil, at a distance. When he returns to Boston after a long L.A. exile, however, he quickly draws in another old friend, the vulnerable Laura, just as the sharp-minded scientist Elise gets tangled in the ropes of familial obligation. The four main characters are pulled together and spun apart by various dramas (sperm-donor babies, corporate espionage) that could come off as soap-opera-ish in lesser hands, but Perfect is too nuanced to slide into broad archetypes or easy resolutions. With her elegant prose, Shattuck manages to make her characters' stories feel both engrossing and utterly real." Entertainment Wkly

Shaw, Irwin

Beggarman, thief. Delacorte Press 1977 436p

ISBN 0-440-00673-2

LC 77-24523

Sequel to Rich man, poor man

"Wayward brother Tom Jordache has been murdered, leaving his son Wesley with a legacy of violence and revenge that is echoed in his nephew Billy, who becomes involved in a terrorist group in Brussels while serving in the U.S. Army. The story does not focus entirely on the second generation—the tangled lives of the older Jordaches are also featured. . . . Scenes from the earlier novel are interwoven allowing the unfamiliar reader to complete enjoyment and understanding." Booklist

Shaw, Irwin

★ **Rich** man, poor man. Delacorte Press 1970 723p

"Each member of the clan is doomed in one way or another. They fight, love, live hard and their fortunes are inevitably intertwined. Mr. Shaw has juxtaposed their rise and fall against a panoramic picture of the times. . . . This may not be great literature but it certainly has popular appeal." Publ Wkly

Followed by Beggarman, thief

Shaw, Irwin

Short stories: five decades. Delacorte Press 1978 756p

LC 78-16020

"Among these sixty-three stories are iconic works such as 'The Eighty-Yard Run,' a tale of an American dream crippled on Black Monday, and 'Main Currents in American Thought,' in which a hack radio copywriter is tormented by the glitz of show business." (Publisher's note)

Shearn, Amy

How far is the ocean from here; a novel. Shaye Areheart Books 2008 307p $23

ISBN 978-0-307-40534-0

LC 2007-33956

"Ms. Shearn's shifting points of view are a bit tricky. The book is told mostly through Susannah's eyes, but every now and then we're suddenly in Frankie's head or Tim's or Kit's for a paragraph or two. She also has a glorious way with description, conjuring vivid images with brevity and wit." Dallas News

Sheck, Laurie

A **monster's** notes. Alfred A. Knopf 2009 544p $30

ISBN 978-0-307-27105-1; 0-307-27105-6

LC 2008-55081

"The book's conceit is high-concept: that Shelley's literary monster was inspired by a mysterious being who visited her as a young girl during visits to her mother's grave. (That would be author and proto-feminist Mary Wollstonecraft, who died days after giving birth to Shelley.) But this 'real' creature, who has survived into the 21st century, is gripped by a profound identity crisis; his understanding of self is limited to the backstory Shelley devised. He attempts to glean further enlightenment by—and here's where this gets tricky—envisioning correspondence written by Shelley, her stepsisters, and Wollstonecraft, as well as (and here's where it gets really tricky) two fictional characters, Henry Clerval from Frankenstein and a leper dying in an Italian sanitarium. These letters are presented as part of the monster's journal, which also contains articles on subjects—robotics, genetic privacy, the nature of time, John Zorn's experimental music, medieval philosophers—that speak to the creature's existential plight. Yep: This is a heady, hard read, at times repetitive and ponderous. Nonetheless, A Monster's Notes is a thrilling feat of literary scholarship, beautiful wordsmithing, and deep empathy." Entertaiment Wkly

Includes bibliographical references.

Sheehan, Aurelie

The **anxiety** of everyday objects; a novel. Penguin Books 2004 278p pa $14

ISBN 0-14-200370-0 pa

LC 2003-49873

This novel is "set at the law firm of Grecko Mauster Crill, where Winona Bartlett toils as a secretary. She has the potential to be much more and, indeed, aspires to be a filmmaker. Her would-be film, entitled The Anxiety of Everyday Objects, centers on the theme of how people misreading something as simple as a street sign can gain significant insight into their lives. The only one who seems to see Winona's potential (other than Rex, the cute lawyer who has a crush on her) is the firm's new associate, Sandy Spires, who has been hired in conjunction with a case involving the beauty makeover consulting firm Lisa Box. Sandy–beautiful, glamorous, and blind–befriends Winona, treating her to a day at a spa and introducing her to a filmmaker. But as Winona becomes interested in Sandy as a subject for her film, she gradually realizes Sandy may be as manipulative as she is charming. A quirky, introspective novel about a creative woman finding her footing in a very corporate world." Booklist

Sheehy, Hugh

The **invisibles**; stories. by Hugh Sheehy. University of Georgia Press 2012 208 p. (cloth : alk. paper) $24.95

ISBN 0820343293; 9780820343297

LC 2011050391

This collection of short stories by Hugh Sheehy, which won the Flannery O'Connor Award for Short Fiction, "shine[s] a spotlight on the bleak fringes of America. . . . A dismal assistant teacher spiking her coffee after school is suddenly locked in a basement with a student who has just witnessed his father's murder. A seventeen-year-old girl at a skate rink whose name no one can remember is motherless, friendless, and sure she will be the next to go." (Publisher's note)

Sheers, Owen

Resistance; a novel. Nan A. Talese/Doubleday 2008 306p $23.95

ISBN 978-0-385-52210-6; 0-385-52210-X

LC 2007-15068

First published 2007 in the United Kingdom

"Sheers is at his best describing the everyday rituals of rural life amid the rocky and unforgiving Welsh countryside, and in particular the tenderness exerted by the women in caring for their livestock in a strangely childless community. The novel's most memorable image is of an orphaned lamb sewn into the skin of a larger, dead lamb to lure the bereaved ewe into accepting the orphan as her own. That mixture of brutality and kindness—the bloody exigencies carried out not only in wartime, but in everyday rural life—is the great insight of Resistance." N Y Times Book Rev

Shelley, Mary Wollstonecraft

★ **Frankenstein;** or, The modern Prometheus; with an introduction by Wendy Lesser. Knopf 1992 xxxiii, 231p $15

ISBN 0-679-40999-8

LC 91-53195

First published 1818

"The tale relates the exploits of Frankenstein, an idealistic Genevan student of natural philosophy, who discovers at the university of Ingolstadt the secret of imparting life to inanimate matter. Collecting bones from charnel-houses, he constructs the semblance of a human being and gives it life. The creature, endowed with supernatural strength and size and terrible in appearance, inspires loathing in whoever sees it." Oxford Companion to Engl Lit. 5th edition

Shepard, Jim

★ The **book** of Aron; Jim Shepard. Alfred A. Knopf 2015 272 p. (hardcover) $23.95

ISBN 1101874317; 9781101872741; 9781101874318

LC 2014014402

Carnegie Medal Shortlist: Fiction (2016)

In this novel, by Jim Shepard, "Aron, the narrator, is an engaging if peculiar and unhappy young boy whose family is driven by the German onslaught from the Polish countryside into Warsaw and slowly battered by deprivation, disease, and persecution. He and a handful of boys and girls risk their lives by scuttling around the ghetto to smuggle and trade contraband through the quarantine walls in hopes of keeping their fathers, mothers, brothers, and sisters alive." (Publisher's note)

"Aron proves to be engaging company as he describes the selfishness that will help him survive as the world becomes increasingly hellish. The horrors are so incremental that Aron--and the reader--might be compared to the lobster dropped into the pot as the temperature keeps rising past the boiling point." Kirkus

Includes bibliographical references

Shepard, Jim

Like you'd understand, anyway; stories. Alfred A. Knopf 2007 211p $23

ISBN 978-0-307-26521-0

LC 2007-3639

"Each of the 11 stories is presided over by a different narrator, and they're as diverse as can be: Chernobyl engineers, Roman centurions, high school football stars, Victorian Australian explorers, Russian cosmonauts and the chief executioner of Paris' age of terror all tell their tales, shoving the reader from continent to continent, and from past to present like a pinball. . . . Despite the variety of voices in these stories, they are sewn deftly together with a dark and ominous thread; in all their diversity, the characters share troubled fates, with many of the pieces ending either on the very edge of impending disaster or with a foreboding abruptness that hits the reader like a power outage." St. Louis Post-Dispatch

Shepard, Jim

★ The **world** to come; stories. Jim Shepard. Alfred A. Knopf 2017 258 p. (hardcover) $25.95

ISBN 9781524731816; 9781524731809

LC 2016038353

Written by Jim Shepard, "these ten stories ring with voices belonging to--among others--English Arctic explorers in one of history's most nightmarish expeditions, a young contemporary American negotiating the shockingly underreported hazards of our crude-oil trains, eighteenth-century French balloonists inventing manned flight, and two mid-nineteenth-century housewives trying to forge a connection despite their isolation on the frontier of settlement." (Publisher's note)

"With the release of his fifth story collection, Shepard . . . continues to weave interlacing narrative threads that imaginatively evoke time and place." LJ

Shepard, Jim

You think that's bad; stories. Alfred A. Knopf 2011 225p $24.95

ISBN 978-0-307-59482-2; 0-307-59482-3

LC 2010-35998

This collection "focuses on characters whose love for a wild, demanding task leads to some very messy relationships. Selfishness is the centripetal force at work in these eleven stories. A woman explores uncharted terrain by following a map Marco Polo left behind in 'The Track of the Assassins.' In 'Poland Is Watching,' winter mountaineers embrace risk. Other pieces feature 15th-century French cultists, 'black ops' spies and beleaguered Dutch engineers. Throughout, a common element is extruded: an addictive impulse to isolate and sacrifice closeness with other people. . . . Shepard has plenty of technique he makes sharp, tightly constructed stories. Their sharp and shiny edges, which may attract some, will warn away others. It's hard to find a way inside or to reach a comfortable place. Which may be the point, if you find humanity that way." Cleveland Plain Dealer

Shepard, Karen

The **Celestials**; a novel. by Karen Shepard. Tin House Books 2013 320 p. $15.95

ISBN 1935639552; 9781935639558

LC 2012050808

In this book, industrialist "Calvin Sampson manages a successful shoe factory in North Adams, MA, in 1870 but is troubled by union demands. To break a strike, he takes the unusual step of importing workers from San Francisco—young Chinese men, most of them teenagers. Thus begins North Adams's decade-long experiment with the Celestials, as the workers are called, since China was then known as the Celestial Kingdom." (Library Journal)

Shepard, Sam

Day out of days; stories. Alfred A. Knopf 2010 282p $25.95; pa $15

ISBN 978-0-307-26540-1; 0-307-26540-4; 978-0-307-27782-4 pa; 0-307-27782-8 pa

LC 2009-19578

"Highways, rundown motels, Muzak-plagued franchises, bars, and beaches, snowstorms and blistering heat, these are the settings and circumstances in Shepard's hypnotic new book of entwined short stories. . . . Strands of autobiography infuse Shepard's magnetic and beautifully tooled stories with their potent intimacy, wry humor, and tightrope tension. Shepard's central narrator is a restless man with a thousand-mile stare who prowls America's interstates and back roads with no particular purpose except to catch the buzz of forward motion through scrolling landscapes. As much as he roams, he can't escape his past, even as age plays havoc with his memories, and the ordinary collides with the inexplicable." Booklist

Shepard, Sam

Great dream of heaven; stories. Knopf 2002 142p $20

ISBN 0-375-40505-4

LC 2002-70054

"Each involving story is psychologically loaded, but what lassoes the reader is the tension between Shephard's acuity and tenderness, his high regard for the recklessness of life." Booklist

Shepherd, Lynn

A **fatal** likeness; a novel. by Lynn Shepherd. 1st ed. Delacorte Press 2013 384 p. (hardcover) $26.00; (ebook) $78.00

ISBN 0345532449; 9780345532442; 9780345538673

LC 2012038988

In this book, a "note from Sir Percy Shelley, son of the late Romantic poet, causes elderly Charles Maddox to have a fit of apoplexy," so "Maddox's great-nephew and namesake, who's a private detective, responds to Sir Percy instead. The Shelley family hires the younger Maddox to prevent the poet's former lover, Claire Clairmont, from tarnishing his posthumous reputation." (Publishers Weekly)

Shepherd, Lynn

★ The **solitary** house; a novel. Lynn Shepherd. Delacorte Press 2012 340 p.

ISBN 0345532422; 9780345532428; 9780345533555

LC 2011029728

This novel by Lynn Shepherd presents a "detective story . . . that borrows characters from Charles Dickens' "Bleak House" and Wilkie Collins' "The Woman in White." Ever since Metropolitan police officer Charles Maddox was dismissed for insubordination, he's eked out a living as a private detective. He currently has two cases. The first is finding the grandchild of a man who had cast out his pregnant daughter years before. The second is identifying the writer of threatening scrawls for Edward Tulkinghorn, a powerful attorney who represents the interests of the wealthy and high-born. . . . At length he realizes that his work for Tulkinghorn is leaving in its wake a string of corpses, many of them evidently connected to the horrific murder of several women." (Kirkus Reviews)

Sher, Ira

Gentlemen of space. Free Press 2003 291p $23

ISBN 0-7432-4218-1

LC 2002-192807

"Sher's affection for his characters is clear, and they shine with softly absurd humor. . .and a DeLillo-like nostalgia for Americana and belief. This is beautiful, eloquent first novel." Booklist

Sherrill, Steven

The **minotaur** takes his own sweet time; Steven Sherrill. John F. Blair 2016 261 p. (hardcover : acid-free paper) $26.95

ISBN 9780895876737; 9780895876744

LC 2016026939

In this novel, by Steven Sherrill, "sixteen years have passed since Steven Sherrill first introduced us to 'M,' the selfsame Minotaur from Greek mythology, transplanted to the modern American South. . . . M has moved north, from a life of kitchens and trailer parks, to that of Civil War re-enactor at a run-down living history park in the dying blue-collar rustbelt of central Pennsylvania." (Publisher's note)

"This novel's juxtaposition of magical realism and the mundane allows for a number of haunting and contemplative moments." Kirkus

Sherwood, Frances

The **book** of splendor. Norton 2002 348p $25.95

ISBN 0-393-02138-6

LC 2002-520

This is a "provocative, gripping novel that's part farce, historical adventure, theological meditation, and bodice-ripping romance. Fans of magic realism will love this." Booklist

Sherwood, Frances

Night of sorrows. Norton 2006 425p map $24.95

ISBN 978-0-393-05825-3; 0-393-05825-5

LC 2006-420

"An account of conquest and dehumanization, [this novel] is also a story of survival in the midst of a harsh cultural clash. The linguistic and narrative riches of the book enhance its moral complexity: Sherwood has refused to settle for the black-and-white thinking that so often mars this sort of historical fiction." N Y Times Book Rev

Shields, Carol

The **republic** of love. Viking 1992 366p

LC 91-16154

"Not only are Fay and Tom exceptionally likable and capable of arresting insights, their worlds are complete and organic. Secondary characters are respectfully but economically drawn via short monologues, and the city of Winnipeg bustles in the background." Publ Wkly

Shields, Carol

★ The **stone** diaries. Viking 1994 361p il

LC 93-30239

This "novel provides, glancingly, a panorama of 20th-century life in North America. Written in a diary format, it traces the life of one seemingly unremarkable woman: Daisy Goodwill Flett, who is born in 1905 and lives into the 1990's." N Y Times Book Rev

Shields, Carol, 1935-2003

Unless; a novel. Fourth Estate/HarperCollins Pubs. 2002 213p

ISBN 0-00-714107-6

LC 2002-19923

The protagonist of this novel, Reta Winters (née Summers), a writer, is facing a family crisis. "Reta's eldest daughter, the intelligent and beautiful Norah, has opted out of life and is sitting on a street corner, blank-eyed and begging, in downtown Toronto. Around her neck hangs a sign saying 'goodness.'" (N Y Times Book Rev)

Reta Winters—loving helpmate "to a doctor, mother of three cheerful daughters, and author of a successful comic novel—has always considered herself happy, even blessed. Then her eldest child, nineteen-year-old Norah, briefly disappears and resurfaces as a panhandling mute on a Toronto street corner, holding up a homemade placard that says @Goodness.' Shields's ability to use Reta's darkest fears to reveal the order lurking in chaos, without ever losing her light touch . . . is nothing short of astonishing." New Yorker

Shinn, Sharon

Jenna Starborn; Sharon Shinn. Ace Books 2002 381 p. (pbk.) $25.00

ISBN 044100900X; 9780441009008

LC 2001056051

This book tells the story of "Jenna Starborn [who] was created out of frozen embryonic tissue, a child unloved and unwanted." (Publisher's note) "Jenna accepts a job as a nuclear reactor maintenance technician at remote Thorrastone Park, owned by the wealthy Everett Ravenbeck.

She becomes indispensable to the household—and to Everett. Despite their difference in stations—Jenna is only a half-citizen—they fall in love. After a long, difficult courtship, . . . the two plan to marry. But at the wedding, Jenna receives a terrible shock: Everett has another wife. Unable to live with him as his wife without being married, Jenna flees to a remote planet, where she falls in with a family that provides help and aid to travelers. She's on the verge of deciding whether to marry another and go with him to colonize a new planet when she hears Everett's voice, impossibly calling from afar." (Publishers Weekly)

Sholem Aleichem

The **adventures** of Menahem-Mendl; translated from the Yiddish by Tamara Kahana. Putnam 1969 222p

Original Yiddish edition published 1909 in Russia

This book "consists of an exchange of letters between the hero and his . . . wife Sheineh-Sheindl, whom he has left behind looking after the children in their . . . native town of Kasrilevka while he tries to make his fortune in the big city—first Odessa, then Kiev. Menahem-Mendl is . . . {an} over-optimistic schemer who somehow contrives to make a living out of thin air; at one moment he is a currency speculator . . . then next a dabbler in commodities, after that a would-be broker, a journalist, a matchmaker, an insurance agent." N Y Rev of Books

Sholem Aleichem

The **adventures** of Mottel, the cantor's son; translated by Tamara Kahana; illustrated by Ilya Schor. Abelard-Schuman 1953 342p il

"The lighthearted humor of young Mottel, the narrator, adds a touch of pathos to the stories of an impoverished Jewish family in a European village, its wanderings in Europe en route to America, and finally its arrival and settlement in the U.S." Booklist

Sholem Aleichem

The **nightingale**; or, The Saga of Yosele Solovey the cantor. translated by Aliza Shevrin. Putnam 1985 240p

LC 85-12073

Originally written in Yiddish and copyrighted 1917

This "is more than a popular novel; it is a social document, a study of a failed artist and, in its way, an early feminist work." N Y Times Book Rev

Sholem Aleichem

Tevye the dairyman and The railroad stories; [by] Sholom Aleichem; translated from the Yiddish and with an introduction by Hillel Halkin. Schocken Bks. 1987 xli, 309p hardcover o.p. pa $15

ISBN 0-8052-1069-5 pa

LC 86-24835

"In the first eight stories of this collection, Tevye, the Russian Jew so familiar from Fiddler on the Roof, bemoans his fate. In these as well as the following 21 tales, the author displays his splendid storytelling skills." Booklist

Sholem Aleichem

★ **Tevye's** daughters; translated by Frances Butwin. Crown 1949 302p

Translated from the Yiddish, many of these stories are "about the seven daughters of Tevye the Dairyman and the life each chooses as she comes of age in Russia during the years preceding the first World War." Publ Wkly

Sholokhov, Mikhail Aleksandrovich

★ **And** quiet flows the Don; [by] Mikhail Sholokhov; translated from the Russian by Stephen Garry. Knopf 1934 755p

"Set in the Don River basin of southwestern Russia at the end of the czarist period, the novel traces the progress of the Cossack Gregor Melekhov from youthful lover to Red Army soldier and finally to Cossack nationalist. War—in the form of both international conflict and civil revolution—provides the epic backdrop for the narrative and determines its tone of moral ambiguity." Merriam-Webster's Ency of Lit

Followed by The Don flows home to the sea

Sholokhov, Mikhail Aleksandrovich

The **Don** flows home to the sea; {by} Mikhail Sholokhov; translated from the Russian by Stephen Garry. Knopf 1941 777p

This translation first published 1940 in the United Kingdom

This sequel to And quiet flows the Don, covers the period following the Revolution of 1917 to the end of the civil war in 1921. The narrative traces the fortunes of a group of Cossacks as they fight alternately with the Reds and the Whites

"It is a tale of misfortunes multiplied, yet a broad and earthy humor and the hearty Cossack gaiety break continuously over the grim surface. At the end the Cossack, with his intense individualism, his passionate love of the land, and his primitive pride, stands revealed." Nation

Followed by Seeds of tomorrow (1959)

Shonk, Katherine

Happy now? Farrar, Straus and Giroux 2010 262p $25

ISBN 978-0-374-28143-4; 0-374-28143-2

LC 2009-29509

"On the surface, such a story might seem like fodder for a Lifetime television network drama or a women's magazine story. But Shonk (the sort of writer Saul Bellow might have dubbed 'a first-class noticer') makes gold of it—invariably stripping away sentimentality and replacing it with the mix of caustic intelligence and biting wit of someone who feels things deeply but never loses the ability to step back a bit and see the dysfunctional theater of it all." Chicago Sun-Times

Shreve, Anita

★ **Eden** Close; a novel. Harcourt Brace Jovanovich 1989 265p $17.95

ISBN 0-15-127582-3

LC 89-34712

"'Eden Close' is not a novel of suspense but one of sensibility. Its insights are keen, its language measured and haunting. In it, a sense of loss and then of rupture is everywhere." N Y Times Book Rev

Shreve, Anita

Fortune's Rocks; a novel. Little, Brown 2000 453p $24.95

ISBN 0-316-78101-0

LC 99-42665

"The level of suspense never falters, but becomes breathtaking during a custody court battle. . . . The astounding denouement of cascading events will leave no reader unmoved." Publ Wkly

Shreve, Anita

★ The **last** time they met; a novel. Little, Brown 2001 313p $28

ISBN 0-316-78114-2

LC 00-53496

"Romantic regret is Anita Shreve's subject in this instantly captivating novel. . . . Fiction writers could go to school on Shreve's command of scene." Atl Mon

Shreve, Anita

The **pilot's** wife; a novel. Little, Brown 1998 293p $23.95

ISBN 0-316-78908-9

LC 97-51647

"The climax, less dramatic than meditative, may strike some readers as too muted: understatement is one of this novel's strengths. What haunts us is the way Jack's secret life gradually weakens its hold on Kathryn's imagination and ours." Publ Wkly

Shreve, Anita

Sea glass; a novel. Little, Brown 2002 378p

ISBN 0-316-78081-2

LC 2002-20897

"Shreve does not use her characters frivolously. They reveal who they are through their actions, with the author—who writes with admirable economy—rarely having to point a finger or underline the obvious. The true power of her novel comes from the appalling social conditions she describes so vividly, the grim but heroic lives her characters live." N Y Times Book Rev

Shreve, Anita

Testimony; a novel. Little, Brown 2008 307p $25.99

ISBN 9780316059862; 0-316-05986-2

LC 2008-5027

"Shreve arrows in on many targets—underage drinking, instant exposure via the Internet, familial expectations, youthful insecurities, and peer pressure, among them—as she flawlessly weaves a tale that is mesmerizing, hypnotic, and compulsive." Libr J

Shreve, Anita

The **weight** of water. Little, Brown 1997 246p $22.95

ISBN 0-316-78997-6

LC 96-21326

"Deftly moving among almost as many plot lines as there are islands and employing at least two distinct voices, Ms. Shreve unravels themes of adultery, jealousy, crimes of passion, incest, negligence, loss and guilt, and then manages somehow to knit them all together into an engrossing tale." N Y Times Book Rev

Shriver, Lionel

The **post**-birthday world. HarperCollins Publishers 2007 517p $25.95

ISBN 978-0-06-118784-1; 0-06-118784-4

LC 2006-49233

"Lawrence often verges on being a parody of a judgmental, snobbish prig, while Ramsey often verges on being a parody of a hard-living, irresponsible celebrity. . . . That we're able to overlook the flaws of Ramsey and Lawrence is, in the end, a testament to Ms. Shriver's ability to make Irina into a thoroughly compelling character, an idiosyncratic yet recognizable heroine about whom it's impossible not to care." N Y Times (Late N Y Ed)

Shriver, Lionel

So much for that; a novel. Harper 2010 436p $25.99

ISBN 978-0-06-145858-3; 0-06-145858-9

LC 2009-28815

National Book Award Finalist: Fiction (2010)

"Though there is one farcical plot development that is poorly woven into the emotional fabric of the story, and though some of the asides about health care feel shoehorned into the narrative, the author's understanding of her people is so intimate, so unsentimental that it lofts the novel over such bumpy passages, insinuating these characters permanently into the reader's imagination." N Y Times (Late N Y Ed)

Shriver, Lionel

We need to talk about Kevin. Counterpoint 2003 400p

ISBN 1-58243-267-8

LC 20020152753

This is a novel by the author of The Bleeding Heart (1990). "That neither nature nor nurture bears exclusive responsibility for a child's character is self-evident. But such generalizations provide cold comfort when it's your own son who's just opened fire on his fellow students and whose class photograph—with its unseemly grin—is blown up on the national news. The question of who's to blame for teenage atrocity tortures our narrator, Eva Khatchadourian. Two years ago, her son, Kevin, murdered seven of his fellow high school students, a cafeteria worker, and a popular algebra teacher. Because he was only fifteen at the time of the killings, he received a lenient sentence and is now in a prison for young offenders in upstate New York. Telling the story of Kevin's upbringing, Eva addresses herself to her estranged husband through a series of letters." (Publisher's note)

"It's a harrowing, psychologically astute, sometimes even darkly humorous novel, with a clear-eyed, hard-won ending and a tough-minded sense of the difficult, often painful human enterprise." Publ Wkly

Shteyngart, Gary

The **Russian** debutante's handbook. Riverhead Bks. 2002 452p

ISBN 1-57322-213-5

LC 2001-47676

"Failurchka-Mother's Little Failure-is what Vladimir Girshkin's overweening Russian immigrant mother calls her 25-year-old son at the beginning of this picaresque . . . first novel. Vladimir is stuck in a dead-end job and saddled with girlfriend Challah, 'queen of everything musky and mammal-like.' Then through a series of chance encounters, he is catapulted to the eastern European city of 'Prava' to find himself welcomed into the fold of powerful Mafiosi." Libr J

Shteyngart, Gary

★ **Super** sad true love story; a novel. Random House 2010 334p

ISBN 1-4000-6640-9; 978-1-4000-6640-7

LC 2009-37971

On his last night of a year's stay in Rome, Lenny meets Eunice Park, a Korean American "who traveled to Europe to escape her abusive father. Soon, she follows Lenny to New York." (Bookforum)

"Full-tilt and fulminating satirist Shteyngart . . . is mordant, gleeful, and embracive as he funnels today's follies and atrocities into a devilishly hilarious, soul-shriveling, and all-too plausible vision of a ruthless and crass digital dystopia in which techno-addled humans are still humbled by love and death." Booklist

Shulman, Alix Kates

Memoirs of an ex-prom queen; a novel. Knopf 1972 274p

"In the third grade, tomboy Sasha realizes that 'there's only one thing worth bothering about: becoming beautiful,' and begins to apply herself to that end. At 15 she has succeeded: she is elected queen of the high school prom and loses her virginity the same evening, an occurrence not at all coincidental, since she measures beauty in terms of sex appeal. By her 25th birthday, she's had 25 lovers. Although she's intelligent (a Columbia Ph.D. candidate) and ambitious, she is unable to escape the trap she has set for herself. Her identity is determined only in terms of her femininity and her relationships with men. Her ideas and ambitions must be sacrificed to theirs, if necessary, and it always seems to 'be' necessary. Her decline from potential philosopher to typical housewife appears completed by the birth of her children, but age and fading looks finally prove to be her salvation." Publ Wkly

Shumway, Charity

Ten girls to watch; a novel. Charity Shumway. 1st ed. Washington Square Press 2012 356 p. (paperback) $15.00

ISBN 1451673418; 9781451673418; 9781451673425

LC 2011048888

In this book by Charity Shumway, "recent graduate Dawn West . . . lands a job tracking down the past winners of 'Charm' magazine's 'Ten Girls to Watch' contest. . . . As Dawn gets to know their life stories, she'll discover that success, love, and friendship can be found in the most unexpected of places. Most importantly, she'll learn that while those who came before us can be role models, ultimately, we each have to create our own happy ending." (Publishers Weekly)

Shute, Nevil

★ **On** the beach. Morrow 1957 320p

"A nuclear war annihilates the world's Northern Hemisphere, and as atomic wastes are spreading southward, residents of Australia try to come to grips with their mortality. In spite of the inevitability of death, these people face their end with courage and live from day to day. They even plant trees they may never see mature." Shapiro. Fic for Youth. 3d edition

Siddons, Anne Rivers

Heartbreak Hotel. Simon & Schuster 1976 252p

ISBN 0-671-22315-1

"Maggie Deloach, a Southern beauty of the 50s, seems well on the way to success Dixie-style. Sorority girl, well-born, a leader, she is pinned to Boots Claiborne, scion of an old land-owning Delta family. It would seem that marriage and a happy-ever-after life are ahead of her. But Randolph University exposes her to more that frat parties and frivolity. A professor, a reporter and a student from New Jersey sow the seeds of questions. A visit to Boot's family and an ugly incident there make Maggie's questions more insistent and, for her, unnerving since they not only challenge her carefully planned future, but reveal stirring in the South she had never anticipated." Publ Wkly

Sidhu, Ranbir Singh

★ **Good** Indian Girls; Stories. Ranbir Singh Sidhu. Soft Skull Press 2013 240 p. (alk. paper) $15.95

ISBN 1593765312; 9781593765316

LC 2013017908

This collection of short stories, by Ranbir Singh Sidhu, follows "the lives of ordinary Indians living in America. . . . A woman attends a de-cluttering class in search of love. A low-level, drunkard diplomat finds himself mysteriously transferred to the Consulate in San Francisco, where everyone believes he is a great, lost poet. An . . . expedition searching for early human fossils goes disastrously wrong." (Publisher's note)

Includes bibliographical references and index

Sidor, Steven

Pitch dark. St. Martin's Griffin 2011 305p pa $14.99

ISBN 978-0-312-35414-5; 0-312-35414-2

LC 2010-43574

"It's Christmas Eve, and what should be a peaceful night in the small town of American Rapids, Minn., turns out to be a living hell when satanic followers and their leader, The Pitch, invade the town in search of the Tartarus Stone, described in the book as the fallen angel's equivalent of the Holy Grail. A small town is the perfect setting for such a story, an arena that germinates suspicion, where people point fingers and oddities are the norm. Sidor has a gift for blending misfit characters and perverse situations with the right dose of intrigue and suspense that will keep readers glued until the book's end." Chicago Sun-times

Siegel, Jan

Prospero's children; Jan Siegel. Ballantine Pub. Group 2000 xviii, 350p (pbk.) $6.99; o.p.

ISBN 9780345441430; 0345439015

LC 000190160

In this fantasy novel, "[t]he sunken island is the former homeland of the mystically minded kind that 16-year-old Fern Capel and her younger brother, Will, encounter when they move to an inherited family house in the Yorkshire countryside. . . . [T]hey soon discover that their home is a magnet for sorceresses, shapeshifters, unicorns and god-possessed vessels, all of whom survived the island's cataclysmic collapse into the sea eons before and are drawn by a potent Atlantean talisman--a magic key that unlocks the door between life and death--kept hidden on the premises. When a scheming opportunist misuses the key and accidentally ruptures the barrier separating past and present, feisty Fern . . . must retrieve it from the antediluvian past it has disappeared into." (Publishers Weekly)

Sienkiewicz, Henryk

★ **Quo** Vadis; a narrative of the time of Nero. translated from the Polish by Jeremiah Curtin. Little, Brown 1896 541p

A historical novel dealing with the "Rome of Nero and the early Christian martyrs. The Roman noble, Petronius, a worthy representative of the dying paganism, is perhaps the most interesting figure, and the struggle between Christianity and paganism supplies the central plot, but the canvas is large. A succession of characters and episodes and, above all, the richly colorful, decadent life of ancient Rome give the novel its chief interest. The beautiful Christian Lygia is the object of unwelcome attentions from Vinicius, one of the Emperor's guards, and when she refuses to yield to his importunities, she is denounced and thrown to the wild beasts of the arena. She escapes and eventually marries Vinicius, whom Peter and Paul have converted to Christianity." Reader's Ency. 4th edition

Sigurdardottir, Yrsa

★ The **silence** of the sea; Yrsa Sigurdardóttir; translated from the Icelandic by Victoria Cribb. Minotaur Books 2016 325 p. (hardback) $25.99

ISBN 1250051487; 9781250051486

LC 2015040619

In this book, by Yrsa Sigurdardottir, "a luxury yacht crashes into a Reykjavik pier. But the boat is empty; no one is on board. What has happened to the crew? And what has happened to the family who were very much present when the yacht left Lisbon? What should Thora Gudmundsdottir . . . make of the rumors that the vessel was cursed? She is spooked even more when she boards the yacht and thinks she sees one of the missing children." (Publisher's note)

"The trick of alternating chapters between the present and the very recent past shouldn't work, but it does, producing a tour de force capped by a haunting final scene." Kirkus

Sigurosson, Sigurjon Birgir

The **blue** fox; Sjón; translated from the Icelandic by Victoria Cribb. Farrar Straus & Giroux 2013 128 p. $10

ISBN 0374114455; 9780374114459

LC 2012039701

In this novel by Sjón, winner of the 2005 Nordic council Literature Prize, "set against the . . . backdrop of the Icelandic winter, an elusive, enigmatic fox leads a hunter on a transformative quest. At the edge of the hunter's territory, a naturalist struggles to build a life for his charge, a young woman with Down syndrome . By the end . . . none of their lives will be the same." (Publisher's note)

Silber, Joan

★ **Fools**; Joan Silber. W W Norton & Co Inc 2013 256 p. (hardcover) $25.95

ISBN 0393088707; 9780393088700

LC 2013000342

PEN/Faulkner Award for Fiction: Shortlist (2014)

In this short story collection by Joan Silber, "a sequence of six linked stories explores the lives of those who risk something for their ideals. . . . In 'Fools,' a merry band of political idealists lives a bohemian life in New York in the '20s. In the background looms the incarceration and execution of Sacco and Vanzetti. The characters make love, marry, cheat on their spouses and scatter. . . .'Two Opinions' follows Louise . . . in jail as a conscientious objector." (Kirkus Reviews)

Silber, Joan

Ideas of heaven; a ring of stories. W.W. Norton 2004 250p $23.95

ISBN 0-393-05908-1

LC 2003-24324

National Book Award Finalist: Fiction (2004)

"Six elegantly connected stories explore, through first-person narratives, the conflicts and commonalities of love, faith and sex. A minor character in the first story becomes the narrator in the second, and so on, with each story building on its predecessor until they come full circle. . . . Silber uses the device of interwoven narratives beautifully; these lengthy stories can stand alone, but the subtle connections and emotional resonances help create a satisfying structural unity." Publ Wkly

Silber, Joan

The **size** of the world; a novel. W.W. Norton 2008 288p $23.95

ISBN 978-0-393-05909-0; 0-393-05909-X

LC 2008-01342

This "work of fiction consists of interlinked stories where minor or passing characters in one piece become the narrators of others, roaming from WWII Sicily to roaring '20s Siam, and from Vietnam-era Mexico to 9/11-era Bloomington, Ind. All six stories turn on the tensions between home, exile and otherness, but to follow any of the threads would be to give away the subtle connections among the characters, from a male Sicilian-American postcolonialist professor from Hoboken to a Florida woman named Kit who can sum up an old boyfriend as the sort of boy who seemed startled when having sex. At the time his awe and confusion were endearing. The frankness of Silber's characters is deliciously at odds with the delicacy of their observations as they absorb children, affairs, fractured and repaired families and early death in environments familiar and alien to them." Publ Wkly

Silko, Leslie, 1948-

Almanac of the dead; a novel. by Leslie Marmon Silko. Penguin Books 1992 763 p. $22

ISBN 0140173196; 9780140173192

LC 9119978

In this novel by Leslie Marmon Silko,"when the ex-mistress of a sinister cocaine wholesaler takes a job as secretary to a Native American clairvoyant . . . she begins transcribing an ancient manuscript that foretells the second coming of Quetzalcoatl and the violent end of white rule in the Americas. Witches and shamans across the country are working to fulfill this prophecy, but the capitalist elite is mounting a dirty war of its own, with weapons such as heroin and cocaine." (Library Journal)

Silko, Leslie, 1948-

★ **Ceremony**; Leslie Marmon Silko; introduction by Larry McMurtry; with a new preface by the author. Penguin Books 2006 xxiii, 243 p.p (paperback) $17; (ebook) $51

ISBN 0143104918; 9780143104919; 9781440621826

LC 2006050705

This novel by Leslie Marmon Silko, focuses on a "young World War II veteran, Tayo, born of a promiscuous Navajo mother and a nameless white father. He has retreated into mental illness . . . and is kept for a while in a Veterans hospital. . . . The novel traces his efforts to become whole again . . . in an arid land where the ex-GIs . . . [try] to forget what the whites have taken from them. " (Kirkus Reviews)

Silko, Leslie, 1948-

Gardens in the dunes; a novel. {by} Leslie Marmon Silko. Simon & Schuster 1999 479p $25

ISBN 0-684-81154-5

LC 98-51987

Set in the 19th century this is the "tale of two sisters, the last remaining members of the ancient Sand Lizard tribe. Sister Salt, so called for her light skin, and her younger sister, Indigo, learn all about the hidden, life-sustaining plants of the desert from Grandma Fleet, who teaches them how to live happily with a minimum of material goods and a wealth of knowledge. Such self-sufficiency is essential if they are to stay free from the misery of reservation life, but even so their liberty is put at risk when they travel to the mean little town of Needles, Arizona, where hundreds of Indians gather to dance in anticipation of the arrival of the Messiah. In the chaotic aftermath of the miraculous visitation, the girls lose their mother and grandmother and then are cruelly separated by the authorities." Booklist

Sillitoe, Alan

★ The **loneliness** of the long-distance runner. Knopf 1960 176p

First published 1959 in the United Kingdom

"This collection of short stories portrays life from the point of view of the English working class. The unnamed narrator in the title story, which is probably the best known in the book, is a roguish young man who has been in trouble with authority all his life. He is told by the head of a Borstal institution where he is an inmate that he can reform himself by training to be a long-distance runner. He enters into training, and during practice runs, his thoughts go back to the circumstances that led to his detention. The climax of the story is in a track meet between his penal institution and a private school. The boy easily outruns his competitors but pulls up at the finish line and refuses to cross it, thus revenging himself against the head of the institution and spoiling the victory of the other school." Shapiro. Fic for Youth. 3d edition

Sillitoe, Alan

★ **Saturday** night and Sunday morning. Knopf 1959 239p

First published 1958 in the United Kingdom

This novel's "protagonist, anarchic young Arthur Seaton, lathe operator in a Nottingham bicycle factory, provided a new prototype of the working class Angry Young Man; rebellious, contemptuous towards authority in the form of management, government, the army, and neighbourhood spies, he unleashes his energy on drink and women, with quieter interludes spent fishing in the canal. . . . A landmark in the development of the post-war novel." Oxford Companion to Engl Lit. 6th edition

Silone, Ignazio

★ **Bread** and wine; a new version translated from the Italian by Harvey Fergusson II; with a new preface by the author. Atheneum Pubs. 1962 331p

First published 1937 in the United States by Harper

"The hero, Pietro Spina, returns to his native Abruzzi after fifteen years of exile to continue his antifascist agitation. As he travels through the country, disguised as a priest, he sees the inroads made upon the Italian character by Mussolini's rule. Finding that the underground movement is in chaos and doubting the validity of his old revolutionary slogans, he eventually flees to avoid certain arrest." Reader's Ency. 4d edition

Followed by The seed beneath the snow (1942)

Silva, Daniel

★ The **black** widow; by Daniel Silva. HarperCollins 2016 528 p. illustrations (ebook) $26.99; (hbk.) $27.99; (pbk.) $9.99

ISBN 9780062320247; 006232022X; 9780062320223; 0062320238; 9780062320230

In this book, by Daniel Silva, "Gabriel Allon, the art restorer, spy, and assassin, . . . is poised to become the chief of Israel's secret intelligence service. But on the eve of his promotion, events conspire to lure him into the field for one final operation. ISIS has detonated a massive bomb in the Marais district of Paris, and a desperate French government wants Gabriel to eliminate the man responsible before he can strike again." (Publisher's note)

"Silva proves once again that he can rework familiar genre material and bring it to new life." Pub Wkly

Silva, Daniel

The **English** Girl; Daniel Silva. HarperCollins 2013 482 p. $27.99

ISBN 0062073168; 9780062073167; 9780062277787

LC 2013026041

This is part of Daniel Silva's Gabriel Allon series. Here, "Ari Shamron, former head of the 'Office,' Israel's secret spy agency, wants Allon to aid the Brits. The British prime minister's lover, Madeline Hart, has been kidnapped while vacationing in Corsica. Allon, working with Graham Seymour, MI5 deputy director, soon drops into a rabbit hole of double-dealing and sleeper agents, greed and revenge." (Kirkus Reviews)

Silva, Daniel

The **mark** of the assassin; a novel. Villard Bks. 1998 465p $25

ISBN 0-679-45563-9

LC 98-5268

"With concise, vivid character sketches, Silva weaves a swiftly paced, internationally tangled plot." Libr J

Silva, Daniel

The **messenger**. Putnam 2006 388p $25.95

ISBN 0-399-15335-7

LC 2006-367534

"An engrossing and beautifully written contemporary spy thriller." Booklist

Silva, Daniel

Prince of Fire. Putnam 2005 369p $25.95

ISBN 0-399-15243-1

LC 2004-60066

"Not long after an explosion in Rome destroys the Israeli embassy compound, a file linked to the terrorists behind the bombing surfaces; it contains a remarkably comprehensive account of the career of Gabriel Allon, including the date of his recruitment by the Israeli secret service. Living in Venice and about to embark upon the restoration of a priceless Rubens painting, Gabriel, a talented art restorer and a reluctant spy, must return to Israel and the auspices of the agency bureaucrats. He is assigned the task of identifying the bombers, which eventually results in a face-to-face meeting with Yassar Arafat, the man responsible for the death of Gabriel's child and the maiming of his wife some 10 years earlier. He suspects that Arafat is deeply connected to the Rome bomber, whom Gabriel believes is a third-generation terrorist who has been protected and schooled as a mastermind by Arafat himself. Along with the meticulously detailed plot, Silva . . . provides a clear-eyed chronicle of the endless warfare between the Israelis and the Palestinians." Booklist

Silva, Daniel

The **secret** servant. G.P. Putnam's Sons 2007 385p $25.95

ISBN 978-0-399-15422-5; 0-399-15422-1

LC 2007-17548

"Daniel Silva is a craftsmanlike writer of international thrillers. He has a nice, no-nonsense style; he plots simply, directly and suspensefully; and in Gabriel Allon he has a reliable protagonist." Los Angeles Times Book Rev

Silver, Elizabeth L.

★ The **execution** of Noa P. Singleton; a novel. by Elizabeth L. Silver. Crown Publishers 2013 320 p. $25

ISBN 038534743X; 9780385347433

LC 2012040204

In this novel by Elizabeth L. Silver "Noa P. Singleton never spoke a word . . . throughout a brief trial that ended with a jury finding her guilty of first-degree murder. Ten years later, having accepted her fate, she sits on death row. She is visited by Marlene Dixon, . . . attorney [and] the mother of the woman Noa was imprisoned for killing. Marlene tells Noa that she . . . will do everything . . . to convince the governor to commute the sentence to life in prison, in return for [Noa's story]." (Publisher's note)

Silver, Marisa

The **god** of war. Simon & Schuster 2008 271p $23

ISBN 978-1-4165-6316-7; 1-4165-6316-4

LC 2007-25424

"Finely wrought characters and an illuminating portrait of the secret world of autism makes for a powerful, often tragic tale." Kirkus

Silver, Marisa

Mary Coin; A Novel. Marisa Silver. Blue Rider Press 2013 336 p. $26.95

ISBN 0399160701; 9780399160707

LC 2012039861

This novel from Marisa Silver is "inspired by Dorothea Lange's most emblematic Depression-era photo. Her characters are Mary Coin, a struggling migrant mother; Vera Dare, an ambitious young photographer compelled to abandon her own children to work; and Walker Dodge, a contemporary professor of cultural history with a surprising personal connection to Vera's photo of Mary." (Library Journal)

Includes bibliographical references and index

Silverberg, Robert

★ **Lord** Valentine's castle. Harper & Row 1980 449p

ISBN 9780060780456; 9780451464613; 9780060140267 out of print

LC 79002658

"Majipoor is an enormous planet inhabited by intelligent beings and ruled by a benevolent lord. . . . The story begins as Valentine, a young amnesiac, wanders into the city of Pidruid in time for a festival celebrating a once-in-a-lifetime visit of another Valentine, Lord Valentine, the supreme ruler of the planet. Early in the book readers know what Valentine is slow to understand; he is the real Lord Valentine and the one in power is an imposter. On a coming-of-age journey to Lord Valentine's Castle, gathering friends, supporters, and ultimately troops en route, Valentine discovers his true identity and gains a better understanding of the people and place he is destined to rule. A good story, inventively told, which abounds with adventure and curious characters." SLJ

Followed by Majipoor chronicles

Silverberg, Robert

A **Robert** Silverberg omnibus; The man in the maze; Nightwings; Downward to the Earth. Harper & Row 1981 544p

LC 80-8232

An omnibus edition of three titles first published separately 1969, 1969, and 1970 respectively

In the novel Nightwings Earth is taken over by aliens; the man in the maze dramatizes aspects of alienation and Downward to the Earth employs religious imagery in a story of repentence and rebirth

All three novels in this collection "feature strong but psychologically wounded male protagonists, descriptions of bizarre beings and far-away worlds and imaginative, if sometimes unrealistic plots. . . . For readers who appreciate swiftly-paced action." Voice Youth Advocates

Silverberg, Robert

★ **Roma** eterna. Eos 2003 396p $25.95

ISBN 0-380-97859-8

LC 2002-35416

This is "a what-if history of the world, starting from the premise that the Roman Empire never fell. Spaning 1,500 years, the narrative unfolds in a world without Christianity. It seems that the failure of the ancient Hebrews to escape Pharaonic oppression prevented the rise of mystical religious cults in the province of Syria Palaestina, thereby guaranteeing the survival of Roman hegemony down to the beginning of space travel. Silverberg, who has written numerous popular works of history and archaeology, brings his alternate Rome to life by blending invention with a dazzling array of details borrowed from the annals of the real Rome." N Y Times Book Rev

Simenon, Georges

Maigret and the madwoman; translated from the French by Eileen Ellenbogen. Harcourt Brace Jovanovich 1972 176p

Original French edition, 1970

"Maigret exerts himself to make up for his failure to prevent the murder of a nice old lady who had told him of her fears. He goes to Toulon to interview a suspect and generally behaves as a chief superintendent should. Madame Maigret plays a larger part than usual." Barzun. Cat of Crime. Rev and enl edition

Simenon, Georges

Maigret and the Saturday caller; translated by Tony White. Harcourt Brace Jovanovich 1991 124p

LC 90-46032

Original French edition, 1962

"Maigret is visited by a harelipped man who confesses that he wants to murder his wife and her lover but hasn't yet done so. Needless to say, Maigret cannot dismiss the man's plans as the fantasy of a harmless lunatic and begins to probe around the edges, irritated by the handicaps imposed by the public prosecutor's recent restrictions on police powers." Booklist

Simenon, Georges

Maigret goes home; translated by Robert Baldick. Harcourt Brace Jovanovich 1989 139p

LC 89-2011

Original French edition, 1931; this translation first published 1940 in the United Kingdom

"The countess of the estate where Maigret grew up drops dead during early mass on All Souls' Day, shocked to death by a fake newspaper report falsely reporting the suicide of her son. Although the estate had been heavily mortgaged to pay for the son's debts and the countess' young lovers, the inheritance is still not inconsiderable, and, of course, there are at least three likely suspects." Booklist

Simmons, Dan

The **abominable**; by Dan Simmons. Little, Brown and Co. 2013 672 p. (hardback) $29

ISBN 0316198838; 9780316198837

LC 2013017754

This book by Dan Simmons, set in 1924, focuses on three climbers on Mount Everest. "The three climbers--joined by [a] missing boy's female cousin--find themselves being pursued through the night by someone . . . or something. This nightmare becomes a matter of life and death at 28,000 feet - but what is pursuing them? And what is the truth behind the 1924 disappearances on Everest?" (Publisher's note)

Simmons, Dan

Endymion. Bantam Bks. 1996 486p

ISBN 9780553572940; 9780553100204 out of print

LC 95033191

"The protagonist, a good-hearted soldier named Raul Endymion, sets off on a quest with historic consequences: he must keep from harm a young girl who holds the key to a rebirth of human civilization. Arrayed against him is the power of the Pax, a militarized Catholic Church that offers its adherents a literal resurrection of the body. It is Mr. Simmons's inspiration to embody the Pax in the person of Father Captain Federico de Soya, a starship commander who pursues Endymion and the young girl from one exotic planet to the next." N Y Times Book Rev

Followed by The rise of Endymion (1997)

Simmons, Dan

The **fall** of Hyperion. Doubleday 1990 517p

ISBN 0-385-24950-0

LC 89-37438

"While the worlds of the Hegemony fight a desperate war in space against the Ouster rebels who threaten galactic unity, a group of seven pilgrims on the planet Hyperion wage their own war within the Tombs of Time, a mysterious artifact which conceals a hideous creature whose freedom means death for humanity. In this sequel to Hyperion, Simmons weaves together many strands of a complex plot with lucidity and poetic imagination." Libr J

Simmons, Dan

★ **Hyperion**. Doubleday 1989 481p

ISBN 0-385-24949-7

LC 88-33407

"On the world called Hyperion, beyond the law of the Hegemony of Man, there waits the creature called the Shrike. There are those who worship it. There are those who fear it. And there are those who have vowed to destroy it. In the Valley of the Time Tombs, where huge, brooding structures move backward through time, the Shrike waits for them all. On the eve of Armageddon, with the entire galaxy at war, seven pilgrims set forth on a final voyage to Hyperion seeking the answers to the unsolved riddles of their lives. Each carries a desperate hope-and a terrible secret. And one may hold the fate of humanity in his hands." Publisher's note

Followed by The fall of Hyperion

Simmons, Dan

The **rise** of Endymion; a novel. Bantam Bks. 1997 579p

ISBN 9780553106527 out of print; 9780553572988

LC 97005658

Sequel to Endymion (1996)

"In 3131, most of the galaxy is populated by born-again Christians and ruled by the Catholic pope. Nonbelievers are persecuted and forced to accept the cruciform parasite, which allows people to be resurrected. The biggest threat to the establishment is Aenea, a young female architectural apprentice who teaches peace and the way to immense knowledge of the heart and mind. Aided by her lover, Raul Endymion, Aenea exposes organized religion as a parasite of the Core—the sentient evolution of the World Wide Web." (Libr J)

In this concluding volume of the author's series about a far-future interstellar society, "most of the galaxy is populated by born-again Christians and ruled by the Catholic pope. Nonbelievers are persecuted and forced to accept the cruciform parasite, which allows people to be resurrected. The biggest threat to the establishment is Aenea, a young female architectural apprentice who teaches peace and the way to immense knowledge of the heart and mind. Aided by her lover, Raul Endymion, Aenea exposes organized religion as a parasite of the Core—the sentient evolution of the World Wide Web." Libr J

Simmons, Dan

★ The **terror**; a novel. Little, Brown and Co. 2007 769p $25.99

ISBN 978-0-316-01744-2; 0-316-01744-2

LC 2006-14608

"A deeply absorbing story that combines awe-inspiring myth, grinding horror and historically accurate adventure." Seattle Times

Simonson, Helen

Major Pettigrew's last stand; a novel. Random House 2010 358p

ISBN 1-4000-6893-2; 978-1-4000-6893-7

LC 2009-22231

This novel is set in an English village. Major Pettigrew, a widower, "leads a quiet life valuing the proper things that Englishmen have lived by for generations: honor, duty, decorum, and a properly brewed cup of tea. But then his brother's death sparks an unexpected friendship with Mrs. Jasmina Ali, the . . . shopkeeper from the village. Drawn together by their shared love of literature and the loss of their respective spouses, the Major and Mrs. Ali soon find their friendship blossoming into something more. But village society insists on embracing him as the quintessential local and her as the permanent foreigner. Can their relationship survive the risks one takes when pursuing happiness in the face of culture and tradition?" (Publisher's note)

"As with the polished work of Alexander McCall Smith, there is never a dull moment but never a discordant note either. Still, this book feels fresh despite its conventional blueprint. Its main characters are especially well drawn, and Ms. Simonson makes them as admirable as they are entertaining." N Y Times (Late N Y Ed)

Simonson, Helen

The **summer** before the war; a novel. Helen Simonson. Random House Inc 2016 496 p. (acid-free paper) $28

ISBN 9780812993103

LC 2015016554

In this novel, by Helen Simonson, it is "1914. It is the end of England's brief Edwardian summer. . . . Hugh Grange, down from his medical studies, is visiting his Aunt Agatha, who lives with her husband in the small, idyllic coastal town of Rye. . . . When Beatrice Nash arrives with one trunk and several large crates of books, it is clear she is significantly more freethinking—and attractive—than anyone believes a Latin teacher should be." (Publisher's note)

"The novel starts slowly—it takes until Page 282 for Beatrice to reach the classroom—and a few bromides clutter the denouement, but this book is beautifully plotted and morally astute. Even the callow American has his part to play. Aficionados of Downton Abbey and The Guernsey Literary and Potato Peel Pie Society will sigh with pleasure." Kirkus

Simpson, Mona

Anywhere but here. Knopf 1987 406p

LC 86-45282

"Any single episode could stand on its own, but Simpson keeps piling them on, building with strength and grace." Booklist

Simsion, Graeme

The **Rosie** effect; a novel. Graeme Simsion. Simon & Schuster 2014 352 p. (hardcover) $25.99

ISBN 1476767319; 9781476767314; 9781476767321

LC 2014034569

In this sequel to "The Rosie Project," Graeme Simsion "throws the life-altering complication of fatherhood at Don Tillman. Although the genetics professor has not formally been diagnosed with Asperger's syndrome, he is extremely driven by logic, [and] finds it difficult to read people. . . . He is now married to his ideal woman, but when Rosie announces she's pregnant, it touches off a series of events that leads Don to the brink of losing his freedom, his job, and his new life." (Booklist)

Simsion, Graeme

★ The **Rosie** project; a novel. Graeme Simsion. Simon & Schuster 2013 295 p. (hardcover) $24

ISBN 1476729085; 9781476729084; 9781476729091

LC 2013000364

This book focuses on genetics professor Don Tillman's search for a wife. His "devised solution is the Wife Project: dating only those who 'match' his idiosyncratic standards as determined by an exacting questionnaire. His plans take a backseat when he meets Rosie, a bartender who wants him to help her determine her birth father's identity. His rigidity and myopic worldview prevents him from seeing her as a possible love interest, but he nonetheless agrees to help." (Publishers Weekly)

"The story lurches from one set piece of deadpan nudge-nudge, wink-wink humor to another: We laugh at, and with, Don as he tries to navigate our hopelessly emotional, nonliteral world, learning as he goes." Kirkus

Sinclair, Upton

★ The **jungle**; introduction by Jane Jacobs; afterword by Anthony Arthur. Modern Library pbk. ed., Centennial ed.; Modern Library 2006 xxii, 388p pa $9.95

ISBN 978-0-8129-7623-6; 0-8129-7623-1

LC 2007-279794

First published 1906 by Doubleday, Page

"Jurgis Rudkus, an immigrant from Lithuania, arrives in Chicago with his father, his fiancée, and her family. He is determined to make a life for his bride in the new country. The deplorable conditions in the stockyards and the harrowing experiences of impoverished workers are vividly described by the author." Shapiro. Fic for Youth. 3d edition

Includes bibliographical references

Singer, Isaac Bashevis

★ **Collected** stories: A friend of Kafka to Passions. Library of America 2004 856p $35

ISBN 1-931082-62-6

LC 2003-66057

The sixty-five short stories in this volume have appeared in the three books: A friend of Kafka and other stories (1970); A crown of feathers and other stories (1973); Passions and other stories (1975).

Singer, Isaac Bashevis

★ **Collected** stories: Gimpel the fool to The letter writer; [Ilan Stavans is the editor of this volume] Library of America 2004 789p $35

ISBN 1-931082-61-8

LC 2003-66055

The fifty-four short stories in this volume have appeared in the four books: Gimpel the fool & other stories (1955); The Spinoza of Market Street (1966); Short Friday & other stories (1964); and The séance & other stories (1968). Gimpel the fool & other stories is entered separately.

Singer, Isaac Bashevis

Collected stories: One night in Brazil to The death of Methuselah. Library of America 2004 899p $35

ISBN 1-931082-63-4

LC 2003-66081

Most of the short stories in this volume have appeared in the six books: Old love (1979); The collected stories of Isaac Bashevis Singer (1982); Image & other stories (1985); Gifts (1985); and The death of Methuselah & other stories (1988). Also included are thirteen uncollected stories at the end of the volume. The collected stories of Isaac Bashevis Singer and The death of Methuselah are entered separately.

Singer, Isaac Bashevis

Enemies, a love story. Farrar, Straus & Giroux 1972 280p

ISBN 0-374-14830-9

Originally written in Yiddish, 1966

"The book has the surface gaiety, ribaldry and surprise of a medieval fabliau. Yet the New York subways, telephone calls, Bronx Zoo, bus trip to the Adirondacks are solidly, meticulously real. Herman's three women expand into mythic dimension. . . . Whether or not you accept its ending, {this} is a brilliant, unsettling novel." Newsweek

Singer, Isaac Bashevis

The **family** Moskat; translated from the Yiddish by A.H. Gross. Knopf 1950 611p

"Panoramic in sweep, the novel follows many characters and story lines in depicting Jewish life in Warsaw from 1911 to the late 1930s. Singer examines Hasidism, Orthodoxy, the rise of secularism, the breakdown of 19th-century traditions, assimilation, Marxism, and Zionism." Merriam-Webster's Ency of Lit

Singer, Isaac Bashevis

★ The **magician** of Lublin; translated from the Yiddish by Elaine Gottlieb and Joseph Singer. Farrar, Straus & Giroux 2010 246p

ISBN 978-0-374-53254-3; 0-374-53254-0

Originally serialized 1959 in Yiddish newspaper; first published in book form 1960 by Noonday Press

"The novel is set in late 19th-century Poland. It concerns Yasha Mazur, an itinerant professional conjurer, tightrope walker, and hypnotist. He loves five women, including his barren and pious wife. To support himself, his assorted women, and his future plans to escape to Italy, he attempts a robbery and fails. Yasha has a crisis of conscience and returns to his wife, becoming a recluse. People begin to refer to him as Jacob the Penitent, and they flock to him as if to a holy man." Merriam-Webster's Ency of Lit

Singer, Israel Joshua

★ The **brothers** Ashkenazi; [by] I. J. Singer; translated from the Yiddish by Maurice Samuel. Knopf 1936 642p

"Deals with the rise and decay of the textile city of Lodz, Poland, and with the fortunes of the Polish-Jewish brothers, Max and Jacob Ashkenazi, whose personalities gradually come to dominate the life of the town. . . . What gives the book its significance is not the picture of nineteenth-century Jewish family life, and not the characterizations of the two brothers, but the clear exposition of the class struggle of which Max and Jacob form unconscious parts." New Yorker

Singh, Nalini

★ **Shield** of winter; by Nalini Singh. Berkley Books 2014 448 p. (Psy-Changeling) $25.95

ISBN 0425264017; 9780425264010

LC 2014000522

"Trained from childhood to feel no emotions under the rigid Silence Protocol, the Psy race is plunged into violent, often insane chaos when the Silence falls and feeling things is no longer forbidden. Now, a deadly disease has infected the network that mentally links the race, and the long-suppressed Psy empaths (E-Psys) are the only ones who can save it—. . . . Ivy Jane joins an experimental project to unlock her abilities and ends up attracted to Vasic, the lethal Arrow assassin sworn to protect her at all costs." (Booklist)

"Singh shines with elaborate, compelling worldbuilding and scorching sexual and emotional tension." Kirkus

Sinha, Indra

★ **Animal's** people. Simon & Schuster 2008 374p $25

ISBN 978-1-4165-7878-9; 1-4165-7878-1

LC 2007-42118

"Animal is a teenage boy who lives on the streets of the Indian city of Khaufpur. He goes around on all fours since his spine is badly damaged; he cannot walk normally. As an infant, he was one of the thousands of victims of a poison gas leak at an American-owned company, here just called 'the Kampani.' Animal also lost his parents 'that night' (as the local people refer to the horrible event). Animal has a lively mind and a way with words, some of them angry and profane, some of them bitterly funny, as he gets caught up in the struggle of those in Khaufpur who seek long-delayed justice from the Kampani. Sinha . . . has clearly based his story on the human and environmental disaster at the Union Carbide factory in Bhopal in 1984. The result is a gripping novel that also reminds us of a continuing real-life tragedy." Libr J

Sinisalo, Johanna

The **Blood** of Angels; Johanna Sinisalo; translated by Lola Rogers. Peter Owen Publishers 2014 240 p. $16.95

ISBN 0720610044; 9780720610048

In this book by Johanna Sinisalo, "symptoms of catastrophic ecological damage, including the sudden and inexplicable disappearance of bees, spread until they reach Orvo's own small hives in Finland. When Orvo's teenage son, Eero, a fervent animal rights activist, gets killed during an idealistic stunt, Orvo's grief over his son and the loss of his bees leads him to discover a portal to an unspoiled parallel world where he hopes to find both." (Kirkus Reviews)

"The story is told with a quiet, literary precision and is a welcome addition to the sometimes raucous and violent nature of dystopian literature. Sinisalo won the James A. Tiptree award for her novel Troll: A Love Story in 2003" Booklist

Sisters of the Revolution; a feminist speculative fiction anthology. edited by Ann VanderMeer and Jeff VanderMeer. Palgrave Macmillan Ltd. 2015 352 p. (paperback) $15.95

ISBN 9781629630359; 1629630357

LC 2014908072

This anthology, edited by Ann VanderMeer and Jeff VanderMeer, "gathers a highly curated selection of feminist speculative fiction (science fiction, fantasy, horror, and more) chosen by one of the most respected editorial teams in speculative literature today, the award-winning Ann and Jeff VanderMeer. Including stories from the 1970s to the present day, the collection seeks to expand the conversation about feminism while engaging the reader in a wealth of imaginative ideas." (Publisher's note)

"This fascinating collection illustrates how writing trends from new-wave sf and feminist speculative fiction reflect changes in culture and in perspectives on women and feminism. It also provides a valuable primer on women writers in the sf, fantasy, and horror genres." Booklist

Sittenfeld, Curtis

Eligible; a novel. Curtis Sittenfeld. Random House Inc 2016 512 p. (acid-free paper) $28

ISBN 9781400068326; 1400068320

LC 2015027778

This novel, by Curtis Sittenfeld, "honors and updates Jane Austen's 'Pride and Prejudice.' Liz is a magazine writer in her late thirties who, like her yoga instructor older sister, Jane, lives in New York City. When their father has a health scare, they return to their childhood home in Cincinnati to help. . . . And Mrs. Bennet has one thing on her mind: how to marry off her daughters, especially as Jane's fortieth birthday fast approaches." (Publisher's note)

"Sittenfeld's style is endlessly amusing and, at times, gut-wrenchingly painful. Her take on Austen's iconic characters is skillful, her pacing excellent, and her dialog highly entertaining." LJ

Sittenfeld, Curtis

Prep; a novel. Random House 2005 406p hardcover o.p. pa $13.95

ISBN 1-4000-6231-4; 0-8129-7235-X pa

LC 2004-46858

During the late 1980s, a fourteen-year-old leaves her middle-class Indiana family to enroll in an elite New England boarding school, becoming a shrewd observer of the rituals and mores of upper-class Easterners.

"Lee Fiora, a scholarship student at the prestigious Ault School (not Ault Academy, as her parents embarrassingly refer to it), negotiates her days there in a blaze of self-consciousness that is, by turns, hilarious and excruciating: 'I believed then that if you had a good encounter with a person, it was best not to see them again for as long as possible.' And yet she becomes an expert on the rituals that govern the rarefied micro-environment in which she finds herself: the students' fondness for catch-phrases like 'therein lies the paradox' and 'LMC' (lower middle class); the taboo against enthusiasm for anything other than sports; the fact that the school always sings 'God be with you till we meet again' at chapel before breaks. In the end, Lee's incisive vision of herself and others is her downfall but also—as this richly textured narrative suggests—her greatest gift." New Yorker

Sittenfeld, Curtis

★ **Sisterland**; a novel. Curtis Sittenfeld. 1st ed. Random House Inc. 2013 416 p. (hardcover) $27

ISBN 1400068312; 9781400068319

LC 2012043726

In this novel, by Curtis Sittenfeld, "Kate and her identical twin sister, Violet, knew that they were unlike everyone else. Kate and Vi were born with . . . innate psychic abilities concerning future events and other people's secrets. Though Vi embraced her visions, Kate did her best to hide them. Now, years later, their different paths have led them both back to their hometown of St. Louis." (Publisher's note)

"The author turns conventions on their collective head and creates a world that is familiar, maddening, alluring, and, ultimately, guardedly hopeful." LJ

Sjowall, Maj

★ The **laughing** policeman; [by] Maj Sjöwall and Per Wahlöö; translated from the Swedish by Alan Blair. Pantheon Bks. 1970 211p

Original Swedish edition, 1968

In this Martin Beck mystery "a Stockholm city bus is found one rainy night with a cargo of bullet-riddled corpses. Nothing unites the passengers that could explain the mass murder, but one of the victims is a young colleague from the homicide division. . . . The gloomy weather of the Swedish winter, the commercialization of Christmas, Vietnam War protests, and the low morale of the much-criticized police leave Beck and his harassed colleagues with not much to laugh about. The atmosphere and ingenious plotting of the novel make it one of the best in the series." Murphy. Ency of Murder and Mystery

Skibell, Joseph

A **curable** romantic; a novel. Algonquin Books of Chapel Hill 2010 593p $26.95

ISBN 978-1-56512-929-0

LC 2010-18605

Skibell "Skibell plays fast and loose with the intermingling of historical fact and fiction, giving Sigmund Freud his own resurrection, as well as Esperanto founder Dr. L.L. Zamenhof, and others. The past here is bathed in a soft-focus filter, cloaked in gaslights and cigar smoke, brought to life with stylistic flair and linguistic pizazz, complete with multilingual translations and breathless enthusiasm. Sammelsohn, like Zelig, is there to see it all." Dallas Morning News

Skyhorse, Brando

The **Madonnas** of Echo Park; a novel. Free Press 2010 199p $23

ISBN 978-1-4391-7080-9; 1-4391-7080-0

LC 2009-34403

"By having each chapter introduce a fresh story and a new perspective, Skyhorse propels the reader through the novel at a breakneck pace. And in each section, readers are rewarded with a deeper layer, and a new connection, that enriches the plot. While the novel pivots around Mexican-Americans in L.A., Skyhorse uses elegant prose and vivid storytelling to tackle questions surrounding culture, belonging, and identity that haunt every immigrant community." Christ Sci Monit

Slaughter, Karin

Pretty Girls; Karin Slaughter. HarperCollins 2015 400 p. (hardcover) $27.99

ISBN 9780062429056; 0062429051

In this novel, by Karin Slaughter, "more than twenty years ago, Claire and Lydia's teenaged sister Julia vanished without a trace. The two women have not spoken since, and now their lives could not be more different. . . . But neither has recovered from . . . their shared loss—a devastating wound that's cruelly ripped open when Claire's husband is killed. . . . What could connect them? Forming a wary truce, the surviving sisters look to the past to find the truth." (Publisher's note)

"Slaughter (Cop Town, 2014, etc.) is so uncompromising in following her blood trails to the darkest places imaginable that she makes most of her high-wire competition look pallid, formulaic, or just plain fake." Kirkus

The **Sleeper** wakes; Harlem Renaissance stories by women. edited and with an introduction by Marcy Knopf; foreword by Nellie Y. McKay. Rutgers Univ. Press 1993 xxxix, 277p

LC 92-30446

"This anthology rescues short stories written by the women writers of the Harlem Renaissance from archival obscurity. . . . While these writers share some common themes . . . each has her own distinctive voice, and none sacrifices the art of storytelling for polemics. A passionate, dynamic, and invaluable collection." Booklist

Sloan, Robin, 1979-

Mr. Penumbra's 24-hour bookstore; Robin Sloan. Farrar, Straus and Giroux 2012 288 p.

ISBN 0374214913; 9780374214913

LC 2012012357

Alex Award (2013)

This novel by Robin Sloan "follows Clay Jannon, a young San Franciscan with a background in the tech industry, as he starts work at the titular bookstore . . . Most of the store's customers don't buy books at all; they borrow a series of beautiful, cryptic volumes that contain nothing but grids of numbers. Clay recruits some fellow high-tech friends to try to figure out the secret behind the store and its curious proprietor." (NPR)

Sloin, Hilary

Art on fire; by Hilary Sloin. Bywater Books 2012 289 p. $14.95

ISBN 1612940315; 9781612940311

Stonewall Book Awards: Barbara Gittings Literature Award (2014)

This book, by Hilary Sloin, "is the apparent biography of subversive painter Francesca deSilva, the founding foremother of 'pseudorealism,' who lived hard and died young. But . . . it's a fiction from start to finish. . . . Interspersed with Francesca's narrative are thirteen critical 'essays' on the paintings of Francesca deSilva by critics, academics, and psychologists--essays that are . . . satires on art, lesbian life, and the academic world." (Publisher's note)

Slouka, Mark

Brewster; a novel. Mark Slouka. W.W. Norton & Co. Inc. 2013 256 p. (hardcover) $25.95

ISBN 0393239756; 9780393239751

LC 2013009415

Alex Award winner (2014)

Author Mark Slouka's book takes place in "1968, a year after the summer of love and the peak of the Vietnam War. The world is changing, and sixteen-year-old Jon Mosher is determined to change with it. Racked by guilt over his older brother's childhood death, Jon turns his rage into victories running track. When he meets Ray Cappicciano, a local legend in the making, a rebel as gifted with his fists as Jon is with his feet, he recognizes a friendship with the potential to save him." (Publisher's note)

"The setup is familiar: bright Jewish track star Jon is befriended by long-coat, wrong-side-of-the-tracks loner Ray as they both fall for smart, empathetic beauty Karen, but she loves only one of them (guess which?). What separates Slouka's coming-of-age story from most others are dead-on characters, the small-town setting in downstate New York, and the 1968-71 time frame." (Library Journal)

Slouka, Mark

God's fool. Knopf 2002 271p $24

ISBN 0-375-40216-0

LC 2001-53975

"Slouka, a gifted stylist, eschews much of the freak-show energy that thrust Chang and Eng onto the stage of world history, in favor of an alluring balance between the elegiac and the ironic." Publ Wkly

Smiley, Jane, 1949-

Early warning; a novel. Jane Smiley. Alfred A. Knopf 2015 496 p. (Last Hundred Years) (hardcover) $26.95

ISBN 0307700321; 9780307700322

LC 2014041395

Sequel to Some Luck

This novel, by Jane Smiley, "opens in 1953 with the Langdon family at a crossroads. Their stalwart patriarch, Walter, who with his wife, Rosanna, sustained their farm for three decades, has suddenly died, leaving their five children, now adults, looking to the future. Only one will remain in Iowa to work the land, while the others scatter to Washington, D.C., California, and everywhere in between." (Publisher's note)

"Each of the large cast of characters has sharply individualized traits, and though we're seldom emotionally wrapped up in their experiences . . . they are unfailingly interesting." Kirkus

Smiley, Jane, 1949-

Golden age; a novel. Jane Smiley. Alfred A. Knopf 2015 464 p. (Last hundred years trilogy) (hardcover) $26.95

ISBN 0307700348; 9780307700346

LC 2015016461

This novel, by Jane Smiley, the final entry of the "Last hundred years trilogy" series, "opens in 1987, the next generation of Langdons face economic, social, political and personal challenges unlike anything their ancestors have encountered before. . . . [This book] brings to a magnificent conclusion the century-spanning portrait of this unforgettable family and the dynamic times in which they've loved, lived, and died." (Publisher's note)

"As for Smiley's cantering, far-reaching, yet intimate trilogy, it is both timely in the issues it so astutely raises, especially as Iowa is once again in the presidential election spotlight, and timeless in the rapture of its storytelling and the humanness of its insights into family, self, and our connection to the land. Readers will be reading and rereading Smiley's Last Hundred Years far into the next." Booklist

Smiley, Jane

Horse heaven. Knopf 2000 561p

ISBN 0-375-40600-X

LC 99-52728

"What's remarkable about Smiley's handling of horses as characters is that she manages to bring it off at all—and more, she does it brilliantly." N Y Times Book Rev

Smiley, Jane, 1949-

★ **Some** luck; Jane Smiley. Alfred A. Knopf 2014 416 p. (Last hundred years trilogy) (hardcover : alk. paper) $26.95

ISBN 0307700313; 9780307700315; 9780385350396

LC 2013041010

This novel, by Jane Smiley, focuses on the "life and times of a remarkable family over three transformative decades in America. On their farm in Denby, Iowa, Rosanna and Walter Langdon abide by time-honored values that they pass on to their five wildly different children: from Frank, the handsome, willful first born, and Joe, whose love of animals and the land sustains him, to Claire, who earns a special place in her father's heart." (Publisher's note)

"An expansive, episodic tale showing this generally flinty author in a mellow mood: surprising, but engaging." Kirkus

Followed by Early Warning (2015) and Golden Age (2015)

Smiley, Jane, 1949-

★ A **thousand** acres. Knopf 1991 371p $25

ISBN 0-394-57773-6

LC 91-52720

This is a novel by the author of Duplicate Keys and The Greenlanders. "It is May of 1979, and when a neighbor, Harold Clark, holds a community pig roast to announce the return of his prodigal son, Jess, Larry Cook uses the occasion to announce—surprisingly—that he is giving his {Iowa} farm to his daughters: Ginny, Rose and Caroline. At the last minute, angered by her seeming hesitance, he cuts Caroline, the youngest, out of the grant. . . . Ginny Cook narrates the book from her position as the oldest daughter, 36, that year." (N Y Times Book Rev)

"What makes this novel such a triumph is Smiley's brilliant twist on the Lear story: she tells it not from Larry's point of view but from his eldest daughter's. . . . In the end Smiley does what Shakespeare himself never did: she creates a female heroine who grows through her own anguish until she towers over the hero and conquers him." Newsweek

Smith, Ali

The **accidental**. Pantheon Bks. 2006 305p $22.95

ISBN 0-375-42225-0

LC 2005-51031

First published 2005 in the United Kingdom

Smith "is a wonderful ventriloquist, adept at throwing her voice into an astonishing array of characters. . . . [She] can do suicidal teenage angst and middle-aged ennui, a 12-year-old's sardonic innocence and an aging Lothario's randy daydreams with equal aplomb. And in riffing on the stream of consciousness form, pioneered by such highbrow litterateurs as Joyce and Woolf, she manages to make it as accessible and up to the minute (if vastly more entertaining) as talk radio or an Internet chat room." N Y Times (Late N Y Ed)

Smith, Ali, 1962-

★ **Autumn**; a novel. Ali Smith. Pantheon Books 2017 264 p. (ebook) $65; (hardcover) $24.95

ISBN 1101870737; 9781101870747; 9781101870730

LC 2016036972

Man Booker Prize Shortlist (2017)

In this novel, by Ali Smith, "Daniel is a century old. Elisabeth, born in 1984, has her eye on the future. The United Kingdom is in pieces, divided by a historic, once-in-a-generation summer. Love is won, love is lost. Hope is hand-in-hand with hopelessness. The seasons roll round, as ever. Ali Smith's new novel is a meditation on a world growing ever more bordered and exclusive, on what richness and worth are, on what harvest means." (Publisher's note)

"Smith's book is a kaleidoscope whose suggestive fragments and insights don't easily render a pleasing pattern, yet it's compelling in its emotional and historical freight, its humor, and keen sense of creativity and loss." Kirkus

Winter (2018)

Smith, Ali, 1962-

★ **How** to be Both; by Ali Smith. Pantheon Books 2014 384 p. (hardcover) $25.95

ISBN 0375424105; 9780375424106

LC 2014032965

Man Booker Prize Shortlist (2014)

"One half of this . . . novel" follows "a precocious teen struggling with the death of her arty, brilliant mother. George, née Georgia . . . is mostly helped by her first crush, the alluring H, who starts to pull her out of her shell. The other half of the novel is narrated by the disembodied voice of a fifteenth-century painter caught in the wave-laden air of twentieth-century Britain. . . . She casts back to her own life disguised as a boy in order to practice her art." (Booklist)

"The narratives are captivating, challenging, and often puzzling, as the prose varies among contemporary vernacular English, archaic 15th-century rhetoric interposed with fragments of poetry, and unpunctuated stream-of-consciousness narration. . . . Smith's two-in-one novel is a provocative reevaluation of the form." Pub Wkly

Smith, Ali

There but for the. Pantheon Books 2011 236p $25

ISBN 978-0-375-42409-0; 0-375-42409-1

LC 2010-51377

The novel is "ostensibly about a dinner-party guest who locks himself in a spare bedroom and refuses to come out, inadvertently sparking a media frenzy. But the book—packed with jokes and random facts—is really about small stuff like life and death and the meaning of human existence, all told with sharp humor and real insight. The novel itself is a riddle with no solution, which is exactly the point: When you reluctantly come to the end, you can't help going back to the beginning, trying to unravel this beautifully elusive book's mysterious spell." Entertainment Wkly

Smith, Ali

★ **Winter;** Ali Smith. First United States edition Pantheon Books 2018 322 p. (Seasonal (Ali Smith)) eBook $65.00; hardcover $25.95

ISBN 9781101870761; 9781101870754

LC 2017043695

The second novel in the Man Booker Prize-nominated author's Seasonal cycle; the much-anticipated follow-up to Autumn (a New York Times, Washington Post, NPR, Financial Times, The Guardian, Southern Living, and Kirkus Reviews best book of the year). Winter. Bleak. Frosty wind, earth as iron, water as stone, so the old song goes. And now Art's mother is seeing things. Come to think of it, Art's seeing things himself. When four people, strangers and family, converge on a fifteen-bedroom house in Cornwall for Christmas, will there be enough room for everyone?

"In the solid second entry in Smith's seasonally themed quartet of novels, three estranged relatives and a charming stranger argue their way through Christmas in a manor house in the English countryside." Publishers Weekly

Smith, April ✓

Judas horse; an FBI special agent Ana Grey mystery. Alfred A. Knopf 2008 318p $23.95

ISBN 978-1-4000-4205-0; 1-4000-4205-4

LC 2007-42863

Smith "writes too well to settle for the mindless shootouts of a plot geared to summon armed-to-the-teeth SWAT teams at the least provocation. With every dynamic scene, including a wild mustang roundup that thunders right off the page, the reader, like Ana, is reminded of the lost ideals and divided loyalties that make these mortal conflicts so bloody—and so sad." N Y Times Book Rev

Smith, Betty

★ **Joy** in the morning. Harper & Row 1963 308p

LC 62-14560

"When their families find out that Annie McGairy and Carl Brown have married, the two are cut off without a cent. Carl, a law student, takes a full-time job and goes to law school at night. Annie, who had dropped out of school to help her family, longs to be at college. She is given a chance to audit a course in literature because of her abiding interest in it. Her pregnancy, however, increases the pressure on their lives, and only their deep love sees them through their difficulties." Shapiro. Fic for Youth. 3d edition

Smith, Betty

★ A **tree** grows in Brooklyn; with a foreward by Anna Quindlen. HarperCollins Pubs. 2001 493p $23.95; pa $16.95

ISBN 0-06-000194-1; 0-06-112007-3 pa

LC 2001-39509

A reissue of the title first published 1943

"Life in the Williamsburg section of Brooklyn during the early 1900s is rough, but the childhood and youth of Francie Nolan is far from somber. Nurtured by a loving mother, Francie blossoms and reaches out for happiness despite poverty and the alcoholism of a father whose weakness is somewhat compensated for by his lovable disposition." Shapiro. Fic for Youth 3d edition

Smith, Dodie

I capture the castle. Little, Brown 1948 343p il

LC 48-4880

"From its memorable opening line, 'I write this sitting in the kitchen sink', the 17-year-old narrator, Cassandra Mortmain, captivates the reader as she describes a life of penury in a gloomy Gothic castle with her oddball family. Wise beyond her years, romantic and lyrical, yet beadily perceptive . . . , Cassandra is wonderfully engaging and believable." Good Fiction Guide

Smith, Dominic

Bright and distant shores. Washington Square 2011 470p map

ISBN 9781439198865

Chicago, 1897. An obsessive collector and insurance magnate commissions the world's tallest building. Determined to compete with Marshall Field's recent donation of $1 million to found the Field Museum, the tycoon funds a private collecting voyage into the Pacific.

"Beautifully researched and ripe with symbolism—an enthralling narrative peopled by characters both exotic and real." Kirkus

Smith, Dominic

★ The **last** painting of Sara De Vos; a novel. Dominic Smith. Sarah Crichton Books 2016 304 p. (hardback) $26

ISBN 0374106681; 9780374106683

LC 2015033152

In this novel, by Dominic Smith, beginning in Amsterdam in 1631, "Sara de Vos becomes the first woman to be admitted as a master painter to the city's Guild of St. Luke. . . . The only known surviving work of Sara de Vos, 'At the Edge of a Wood,' hangs in the bedroom of a wealthy Manhattan lawyer, Marty de Groot, a descendant of the original owner. . . . Now a celebrated art historian and curator, Ellie Shipley is mounting an exhibition in her field of specialization." (Publisher's note)

"Rich in historical detail, the novel explores the immense challenges faced by women in the arts (past and present), provides a glimpse into the seedy underbelly of the art world across the centuries, and illustrates the transformative power and influence of great art." Booklist

Smith, Gregory Blake

★ The **maze** at Windermere; Gregory Blake Smith. Viking 2018 339 p. (hardcover : alk. paper) $27

ISBN 9780735221925; 9780735221949

LC 2017025390

In this novel, by Gregory Blake Smith, "a reckless wager between a tennis pro with a fading career and a drunken party guest . . . launches a narrative odyssey that braids together three centuries of aspiration and adversity. A witty and urbane bachelor of the Gilded Age embarks on a high-risk scheme to marry into a fortune; [and] a young writer soon to make his mark turns himself to his craft with harrowing social consequences." (Publisher's note)

"Taken individually, each story is dramatic and captivating, but as the author makes ever-increasing connections among the stories and shuffles them all into one unbroken narrative, the novel becomes a moving meditation on love, race, class, and self-fulfillment in America across the centuries." Pub Wkly

Smith, Julie

82 Desire; a Skip Langdon novel. Ballantine Pub. Group 1998 309p $24

ISBN 0-449-00060-5

LC 98-22259

"Russell Fortier, a prominent businessman, has vanished. His wife asks Langdon, a New Orleans detective, to look into his disappearance. Later, a private detective who was investigating Fortier turns up dead, and one of his employees, a poet and freelance computer expert, wants to know how Fortier's disappearance is connected with the murder. . . . The novel is intricately constructed, and while Smith keeps nothing important unfairly hidden from her readers, she manages to spring some nice little surprises." Booklist

Smith, Lee

The **devil's** dream. Putnam 1992 315p

LC 92-1027

"It is ultimately the writer's sensibility that gives 'The Devil's Dream' its charm and power. If there's weeping to be done, Ms. Smith allows her reader to weep, but she never descends to sentimentality." N Y Times Book Rev

Smith, Lee

★ **Fair** and tender ladies. Putnam 1988 316p

ISBN 0-399-13382-8

LC 88-10915

An "exquisite novel. . . . Through Ivy's curiously spelled and situated letters, we see the growth not only of her own family, but also of wider Appalachia." Christ Sci Monit

Smith, Lee

Family linen. Putnam 1985 272p

ISBN 0-399-13080-2

LC 85-3664

"This is a companionable, chatty book populated by people who tell us about themselves in a rambling style and with good humor." N Y Times Book Rev

Smith, Lee

Mrs. Darcy and the blue-eyed stranger; new and selected stories. Algonquin Books of Chapel Hill 2010 352p $23.95

ISBN 978-1-56512-915-3; 1-56512-915-6

LC 2009-27915

"A Southern writer with characteristic wry wit and a keen eye for tragic humor, Smith is often compared to Katherine Anne Porter, Eudora Welty, and Flannery O'Connor. . . . As the characters face the changes that upend them, Smith turns ordinary struggles of love, health, and faith into believable and entertaining moments of meaning—even, occasionally, transcendence." Providence J

Smith, Lee

On Agate Hill; a novel. Algonquin Books of Chapel Hill 2006 367p $24.95

ISBN 1-56512-452-9

LC 2006-45859

"Molly is like a grown-up, Southern version of Louisa May Alcott's Jo, only she is thrown into circumstances that test her essentially wholesome nature. For the most part, she battles back not with sass—which modern novels seem to think is universally charming—but pluck. As this is Smith's first historical novel, she deserves credit for understanding this subtle, but essential period point." Denver Post

Smith, Lee

Oral history. Putnam 1983 286p

ISBN 0-399-12794-1

LC 82-18081

"Smith is excellent at making the separate voices distinctive. . . . Serious fiction readers will be interested in Smith's techniques and will appreciate her decision to utilize this 'oral history' format to best achieve her intentions." Booklist

Smith, Lillian Eugenia

★ **Strange** fruit; a novel. [by] Lillian Smith. Reynal & Hitchcock 1944 371p

This novel, set in a small town in Georgia, is about the love of an educated black girl for a white man. The reaction to this affair results in murder and a lynching

This is a "regional novel, in the finest sense. As such, it offers a magnificently detailed picture of the small-town South, lashed by an urge for self-destruction as old as time. The author has suggested no cure for that urge: you will find no black messiahs here, no white devils." N Y Times Book Rev

Smith, Mark Allen

★ The **Inquisitor**; Mark Allen Smith. 1st ed. Henry Holt and Co. 2012 336 p. $27

ISBN 0805094261; 9780805094268; 9780805095920

LC 2011026552

This book tells the story of "Geiger, [who] . . . knows a lie the instant he hears it. . . . [W]hen his partner, former journalist Harry Boddicker, unwittingly brings in a client who demands that Geiger interrogate a twelve-year-old boy, Geiger . . . rescues the boy from his captor. . . . But if Geiger and Harry cannot quickly discover why the client is so desperate to learn the boy's secret, they themselves will become the victims of an utterly ruthless adversary." (Publisher's note)

Followed by The Confessor (2015)

Smith, Martin Cruz

December 6; a novel. Simon & Schuster 2002 339p

ISBN 0-684-87253-6

LC 2002-29437

This "thriller is set in Tokyo in the last days of 1941, just before the bombing of Pearl Harbor; its central character, the American Harry Niles, grew up in Japan, where his missionary parents were preaching the Word. Harry isn't very holy, however: he owns a night club called the Happy Paris, dabbles in assorted short cons, and spends much of his time with various mistresses. . . . As the rumors of war heat up, Harry finds that he has become too Japanese, and the Japanese suspect him of being a spy. Smith's plot is more than slightly reminiscent of 'Casablanca' and the spectre of the Second World War seems, at this distance, almost quaint, but the characters are so well drawn and the local color so colorful that these quibbles hardly interfere with the novel's pleasures." New Yorker

Smith, Martin Cruz

★ **Gorky** Park. Random House 1981 365p

LC 80-6022

The author "has succeeded in rendering very believable, realistic, and gripping portrayals of certain segments of Soviet society and of one man's search for meaning." Christ Sci Monit

Smith, Martin Cruz

Havana Bay; a novel. Random House 1999 329p $25.95

ISBN 0-679-42662-0

LC 99-235977

"His earnest unsentimentality and calm tenaciousness on the hunt are what make Renko one of the most interesting detectives in modern fiction. What a clever stroke for Smith to dispatch him to Havana, where sentimentality and passion are in rare abundance." N Y Times Book Rev

Smith, Martin Cruz

Rose. Random House 1996 364p

LC 95-37914

"Rose has everthing a compelling novel needs: Blair is a fascinating protagonist, by turns a hero and a boor; other significant characters are complex and as multifaceted as a chunk of coal; the mystery is gripping. But it is the horrific, mesmerizing portrayal of the dark, hellish Wigan, the mines themselves, and the lives of miners that makes this novel much more than a good read." Booklist

Smith, Martin Cruz

Stalin's ghost; an Arkady Renko novel. Simon & Schuster 2007 333p $26.95

ISBN 978-0-07432-7672-6; 0-7432-7672-8

LC 2006-100963

"Every page reeks of Moscow: dirty snow, the stink of cigarette and vodka fumes, the cynicism and tasteless opulence of the mafia, the all-pervasive corruption. . . . Like the Red Army facing the Nazis, Renko refuses to give up, surrendering neither his investigation nor those he loves. In this subtle, moving book, he is an everyman, whose loyalty and courage speak to all of us." Economist

Smith, Martin Cruz

★ **Tatiana**; An Arkady Renko Novel. by Martin Cruz Smith. Simon & Schuster 2013 304 p. $25.99

ISBN 1439140219; 9781439140215

In this novel by Martin Cruz Smith "Tatiana Petrovna falls to her death from a sixth-floor window in Moscow the same week that a mob billionaire, Grisha Grigorenko, is shot. No one makes the connection, but Arkady [Renko] is transfixed by the tapes he discovers of Tatiana's voice. His only link is a notebook written in the personal code of a translator whose body is found in the dunes. Arkady's only hope of decoding the symbols lies in Zhenya, a teenage chess hustler." (Publisher's note)

Smith, Martin Cruz

Wolves eat dogs; a novel. Simon & Schuster 2004 337p $25.95

ISBN 0-684-87254-4

LC 2004-52585

Senior Investigator Arkady Renko "must determine whether the defenestration death of a Russian tycoon was suicide or murder. The discovery of radioactive salt in the dead man's apartment leads Renko to the abandoned Ukrainian towns of Chernobyl and Pripyat, still dangerously contaminated 18 years after the world's deadliest nuclear accident. There he finds a ghostly world inhabited by scavengers, elderly villagers, and a small group of Russian militia and scientists. As Renko pursues his investigation, he uncovers a greater crime, the sad legacy of Soviet ineptitude and corruption." Libr J

Smith, Roger

Wake up dead; a thriller. Henry Holt and Co. 2010 290p $26

ISBN 978-0-8050-8876-2; 0-8050-8876-8

LC 2009-21779

"The backdrop for Smith's urban nightmare is both fantastic and hyperrealistic, somewhat in the manner of graphic novels or urban fantasy. . . . [His] Cape Town slums are as grim as any steampunk Victorian hellhole, and none of his characters rich, poor, colored, white, or black has anything better than a bleak present and an infernal past. The novel's flashbacks, narrative asides, and occasional political jabs, even the inflection of the characters' speech, contribute to a vivid sense of place. " Philadelphia Inquirer

Smith, Scott, 1965-

★ A **simple** plan; a novel. Knopf 1993 335p

ISBN 0-679-41985-3

LC 92-42478

This novel is so "cunningly imagined that for the most part Mr. Smith drags us willingly through what in less deft hands could be a morally repugnant story." N Y Times Book Rev

Smith, Tom Rob

★ **Agent** 6. Grand Central Pub. 2012 448p

ISBN 978-1-84737-567-4; 1-84737-567-7; 9781847375681; 9780446550765

LC 2011505662

"Leo Demidov is no longer a member of Moscow's secret police. But when his wife, Raisa, and daughters Zoya and Elena are invited on a 'Peace Tour' to New York City, he is immediately suspicious." (Publisher's note)

Smith, Tom Rob

Child 44. Grand Central Pub. 2008 439p $24.99

ISBN 978-0-446-40238-5; 0-446-40238-9

LC 2007-28272

"Smith captures the rhythm of day-today paranoia in Stalinist Russia and the ways that personal jealousies can balloon into ruthless vendettas. It's hard to fathom which is more grisly, the descriptions of the serial murders or the scenes of torture perpetrated by Leo's colleagues in the MGB. Throughout, Smith's prose is propulsive but plain; his real genius is his careful plotting." Entertainment Wkly

Smith, Tom Rob

The **secret** speech. Grand Central Pub. 2009 407p $24.99

ISBN 978-0-446-40240-8; 0-446-40240-0

LC 2008-48329

"Former state security officer Leo Demidov, eyes now wide open to Soviet excess, is struggling to forge a new life. His heroism in 'Child 44' earned him a job in the newly formed Moscow homicide bureau, but his efforts to create a family with his wife Raisa and two orphaned girls are a struggle, mainly because the elder, Zoya, rightly blames Leo for her parents' deaths. Other things have changed as well: Stalin is dead, and a widely distributed, once-secret letter denouncing his actions—from his successor Khrushchev—acts as a catalyst for those seeking revenge against Stalin's oppressors. Like Leo. Based on real events, 'The Secret Speech' is jam-packed with action—the near-sinking of a prison ship, a violent takeover at a Kolyma gulag, and a rebellion in Hungary—and Smith explores pertinent questions of revenge, morality and responsibility." PopMatters

Smith, Wilbur A.

Birds of prey; a novel. {by} Wilbur Smith. St. Martin's Press 1997 554p

LC 97-8192

"Smith's depiction of the African coast, and of life aboard ship, is vivid and believable. He handles the action sequences well, opting for short, trenchant paragraphs to sustain momentum. . . . Smith knows what his readers want, and once again he delivers the goods." Publ Wkly

Followed by Monsoon

Smith, Wilbur A.

Monsoon; {by} Wilbur Smith. St. Martin's Press 1999 613p $26.95

ISBN 0-312-20339-X

LC 99-24554

This sequel to Birds of Prey "finds Sir Hal Courtney and his sons up to their bloody sword arms in piracy, intrigue, treachery and civil war in late 17th and early 18th century East Africa and Arabia. . . . Wealthy English landowner Sir Hal earned his fortune as a sea captain with the East India Company. To protect his overseas investments, he becomes a privateer to combat Arab pirates attacking company ships from bases in Zanzibar and Madagascar. Accompanied by three of his four sons, Sir Hal embarks on a desperate voyage that will bring either glory and treasure or ruin. . . . Clever plot twists and lavish historical detail attend the siblings' adventures." Publ Wkly

Smith, Zadie, 1975-

The **autograph** man; a novel. Random House 2002 347p

ISBN 0-375-50186-X

LC 2002-69705

"Smith's pen portraits of the shabby, yobbish autograph trading circle are intermittently funny, but her prose is so busy being clever that the laughter never builds. This is disappointing but, even with its faults, the novel points to a literary talent of a high order." Publ Wkly

Smith, Zadie, 1975-

★ **NW**; a novel. Zadie Smith. Penguin Press 2012 401 p. $26.95

ISBN 1594203970; 9781594203978

LC 2012015114

This novel by Zadie Smith "is the story of a city. . . .[The] novel follows four Londoners--Leah, Natalie, Felix and Nathan--as they try to make adult lives outside of Caldwell, the council estate of their childhood. From private houses to public parks, at work and at play, their London is a complicated place, as beautiful as it is brutal, where the thoroughfares hide the back alleys and taking the high road can sometimes lead you to a dead end." (Publisher's note)

Smith, Zadie, 1975-

On beauty. Penguin Press 2005 445p $25.95

ISBN 1-59420-0637

"Ms Smith has her shortcomings. The novel's first half is under-edited; surely we do not need to meet every guest at an anniversary party. . . . Nevertheless, the book gathers momentum, and the second half gallops along." Economist

Smith, Zadie, 1975-

★ **Swing** time; by Zadie Smith, read by Pippa Bennett-Warner. Penguin Group USA 2016 416 p. $27

ISBN 1594203989; 9781594203985

LC 2016040560

Carnegie Medal Finalist: Fiction (2017)

In this book, by Zadie Smith, "two brown girls dream of being dancers--but only one, Tracey, has talent. The other has ideas: about rhythm and time, about black bodies and black music, what constitutes a tribe, or makes a person truly free. It's a close but complicated childhood friendship that ends abruptly in their early twenties, never to be revisited, but never quite forgotten, either." (Publisher's note)

"Moving, funny, and grave, this novel parses race and global politics with Fred Astaire's or Michael Jackson's grace." Kirkus

Smith, Zadie, 1975-

★ **White** teeth; a novel. Random House 2000 448p $24.95

ISBN 0-375-50185-1

LC 99-43658

"Hopscotching through several continents and 150 years of history, 'White Teeth' encompasses a teeming family saga, a sly inquiry into race and identity and a tender-hearted satire on religious antagonism and cultural bemusement. . . . Smith holds it all together with a raucous energy and confidence." N Y Times Book Rev

Snow, C. P.

★ **Strangers** and brothers. Scribner 1960 309p (Strangers and brothers)

First published 1940 in the United Kingdom

George Passant, a solicitor in an English provincial town, exerts a crucial influence on his group of young protegés, Lewis Eliot among them. An idealist, courageous and high-principled Passant seems destined for great things yet the story ends in his trial for fraud. The reasons for this are revealed

"Essentially the tragedy of a good man defeated by the mediocrity of his world, the story of George Passant is completed in the novel 'Homecoming.' . . . Like all the novels in the series, 'Strangers and Brothers' is distinguished by virtue of its analysis of motive and character and its anatomization of a world in which a smooth mediocrity is the greatest virtue." Libr J

Sofer, Dalia

The **Septembers** of Shiraz. Ecco/HarperCollins Publishers 2007 340p $24.95

ISBN 978-0-06-113040-3; 0-06-113040-0

LC 2007-299587

"Sofer paints a complicated picture of postrevolutionary Iran: The Amins (and especially their relatives) aren't entirely innocent, having shut their eyes to brutality and corruption under the shah, but [the author] recoils from the idea of justice by 'collective retribution' voiced by Farnaz's formerly docile housekeeper. While the dialogue can feel overly formal at times, the impression the reader is left with at the end is that of a powerful story honestly told." Christ Sci Monit

Soli, Tatjana

The **lotus** eaters. St. Martin's Press 2010 389p $24.99

ISBN 978-0-312-61157-6; 0-312-61157-9

LC 2009045697

This is Soli's debut novel. "On a stifling day in 1975, the North Vietnamese army is poised to roll into Saigon. As the fall of the city begins, two lovers make their way through the streets to escape to a new life. Helen Adams, an American photojournalist, must take leave of a war she is addicted to and a devastated country she has come to love. Linh, the Vietnamese man who loves her, must grapple with his own conflicted loyalties of heart and homeland. As they race to leave, they play out a drama of devotion and betrayal that spins them back through twelve war-torn years, beginning in the splendor of Angkor Wat, with their mentor, larger-than-life war correspondent Sam Darrow, once Helen's infuriating love and fiercest competitor, and Linh's secret keeper, boss and truest friend." (Publisher's note)

"Soli is at her best in conveying the day-to-day mix of adventure, tedium, and violence in wartime. Her descriptions are visceral, almost cinematic. . . . And she captures the camaraderie and tension among soldiers in a way that seems authentic." Boston Globe

Solomon, Anna

Leaving Lucy Pear; by Anna Solomon. Penguin Group USA 2016 336 p. map $26

ISBN 1594632650; 9781594632655

LC 2016021048

This novel by Anna Solomon, set in 1920's New England tells "the story of two women who are both mothers to the same unforgettable girl. . . Solomon weaves together an unforgettable group of characters as their lives collide on the New England coast. Set against one of America's most turbulent decades, [the book] delves into questions of class, freedom, and the meaning of family." (Publisher's note)

"A beautifully rendered tale of discovering one's true nature." LJ

Solomon, Asali

Disgruntled; a novel. Asali Solomon. Farrar, Straus & Giroux 2015 304 p. (hardcover) $26

ISBN 0374140340; 9780374140342

LC 2014027442

This novel by Asali Solomon is a "coming-of-age tale, a portrait of Philadelphia in the late eighties and early nineties, an examination of the impossible double-binds of race. [It] follows Kenya from West Philadelphia to the suburbs, from public school to private, from childhood through adolescence, as she grows increasingly disgruntled by her inability to find any place or thing or person that feels like home." (Publisher's note)

"Solomon's cultural references resound, her dialogue stings, and the intricate and surprising relationships she choreographs are saturated with racial, sexual, and political quandaries of intimate and epochal repercussions. A deft, knowing, bold, and witty debut." Booklist

Solomon, Rivers

An **unkindness** of ghosts; Rivers Solomon. Akashic Books 2017 349 p. (paperback) $15.95

ISBN 9781617755996; 9781617755880; 1617755885

LC 2017936119

In this book, by Rivers Solomon, "Aster has little to offer folks in the way of rebuttal when they call her ogre and freak. . . . [S]he only wishes there was more truth to them. If she were truly a monster, as they accuse, she'd be powerful enough to tear down the walls of the brutal ship where she and her ancestors have lived for generations. The lowdeck slums of HSS Matilda [is] an antiquated space vessel ferrying the last of humanity to a mythical Promised Land." (Publisher's note)

"Infused with the spirit of Octavia Butler . . . an Unkindness of Ghosts will appeal to a wide variety of readers. Solomon's impassioned, speculative, literary book is sorely needed on library shelves." Booklist

Solzhenitsyn, Aleksandr

★ **Cancer** ward; translated from the Russian by Nicholas Bethell and David Burg. Farrar, Straus & Giroux 1969 560p

"Set mostly in a provincial cancer ward, the novel traces the ways in which a number of moribund patients come to terms with their death, centering on an investigation of the moral and psychological development of the exiled hero, Kostoglotov. This novel, in which the cancer ward has been widely interpreted as symbolizing the Soviet state, was typeset for publication in the Soviet Union but never published there until after Perestroika began." Reader's Ency. 4th edition

Solzhenitsyn, Aleksandr

In the first circle; a novel. [by] Aleksandr I. Solzhenitsyn; translated by Harry T. Willetts. the restored text; Harper Perennial 2009 xxx,741 pa $18.99

ISBN 978-0-06-147901-4 pa

LC 2008-39336

First English version, translated by Thomas P. Whitney, published 1968 by Harper & Row with title: The first circle

"It has taken a half-century for English-language readers to receive the definitive text of 'In the First Circle,' the best novel by one of the greatest authors of our time. Such is the fate of art created under a totalitarian regime. But now it is finally available in the West as the author envisioned it. The English translator is Harry T. Willetts, renowned for combining fidelity to Aleksandr Solzhenitsyn's rich, complex Russian with supple equivalents in English prose and the only person Solzhenitsyn fully trusted to render his fiction into English." Wall Street J

Solzhenitsyn, Aleksandr

One day in the life of Ivan Denisovich; translated from the Russian by H. T. Willets; with an introduction by John Bayley. Knopf 1995 xxvii, 159p $15

ISBN 0-679-44464-5

Original Russian edition, 1962; this is a reissue of the translation published 1991 by Farrar, Straus & Giroux

"Drawing on his own experiences, the author writes of one day, from reveille to lights-out, in the prison existence of Ivan Denisovich Shukhov. Innocent of any crime, he has been convicted of treason and sentenced to ten years in one of Stalin's notorious slave-labor compounds. The protagonist is a simple man trying to survive the brutality of a totalitarian system." Shapiro. Fic for Youth. 3d edition

Sontag, Susan

★ **In** America; a novel. Farrar, Straus & Giroux 2000 387p $26

ISBN 0-374-17540-3

LC 99-54641

National Book Award: Fiction (2000)

This novel "displays Sontag in a relaxed, pleasure-seeking mode, guiding her characters through a long travelogue in time, specifically the beginnings of the gilded age in the brave new world." Time

Sontag, Susan

The **volcano** lover; a romance. Farrar, Straus & Giroux 1992 419p il $22

ISBN 0-374-28516-0

LC 92-71738

Sontag's "narrative deftly blends the magnetism of personality and the suspense of event with shrewd commentary and sly mockery as she contrasts the habits of thought in that age with ours and reflects on the meaning of mercy and vengeance, self-invention and praise, love and obsession. In all, a memorable group portrait and a brilliant, fresh improvisation on classically grand themes." Booklist

Sorokin, Vladimir

Ice; translated from the Russian by Jamey Gambrell. New York Review Books 2007 321p $23.95

ISBN 978-1-59017-195-0

LC 2006-21077

Original Russian edition, 2002

"The ice of the title is from a giant comet that landed in Tungus, Siberia, in 1908 and transformed 23,000 alien beings of light into human form, all blue-eyed blonds. Only a few are aware of their true selves, and they must locate the others to awaken their hearts by bashing them in the chest with axes made from the cosmic ice. For every new Brother or Sister of Light so transformed, many humans must die. Sorokin builds the suspense by incrementally telling the story from the perspectives of three beings in the process of reawakening, their spiritual leader, and a variety of beings who are transformed in their version of the Rapture. Ice succeeds brilliantly as both a thriller and a cautionary tale about totalitarianism, bigotry, elitism, and fundamentalism." Libr J

Sosin, Danielle

The **long**-shining waters. Milkweed Editions 2011 270p $24

ISBN 978-1-57131-083-5

LC 2011-02077

"Lake Superior proves to be more than a bucolic backdrop for Sosin's debut novel. It swallows fishing nets, boats, and even men, and shapes the lives of three women from different eras: Grey Rabbit, an Ojibwe woman following seasonal routes with her family in 1622 and struggling to feed her children; Berit Kleiven, who lives in a lonely cove with her husband, Gunnar, in 1902; and Nora Truneau, a Duluth bar owner who explores the lake in 2000 after a crisis. . . . Sosin writes sensuously detailed prose and distills the emotions of her characters into a profound and universal need for acceptance and love." Publ Wkly

Southgate, Martha

The **fall** of Rome; a novel. Scribner 2002 223p hardcover o.p. pa $13

ISBN 0-684-86500-9; 0-7432-2721-2 pa

LC 2001-34225

The author "delves deeply into the social and emotional elements that unite and divide us. Issues of race, identity, and integrity are intensely explored through a tragic human triangle." Booklist

Southgate, Martha

The **taste** of salt; a novel. Algonquin Books of Chapel Hill 2011 281p pa $13.95

ISBN 978-1-56512-925-2; 1-56512-925-3

LC 2011-24615

"Growing up in shabby, landlocked Cleveland in a household ravaged by alcoholism, Josie Henderson finds escape in 'the pure blue pleasure' of water. Her fascination with the life aquatic eventually leads to an esteemed position as a research scientist, making her one of few black women in the cloistered field of marine biology. Still, the tidal pull of her troubled family—and the sad legacy of her father's addiction, revisited upon her beloved baby brother, Tick—laps at the edges of her orderly life. . . . Southgate writes with a minor-key melancholy that comes on softly, but lingers long after." Entertainment Wkly

Spark, Muriel

Aiding and abetting. Doubleday 2000 166p

ISBN 0-385-50153-6

LC 00-55559

"The unsettling wit of @Aiding and Abetting' hits the funny bone as hard it pricks the conscience. . . . It's kiln-dried wit that never cracks, with a smile that dares you to laugh. As always {Spark is} breathtakingly deft with the anxieties of well-bred people, people who know how to dress, where to eat, and how to commit the most heinous cruelty. If satire is your cup of tea, . . . {this is a} perfectly seeped book to be savored." Christ Sci Monit

Spark, Muriel

The **driver's** seat. Knopf 1970 117p

"The author's perspective is cosmically cool and fantastic: she knows no more about her protagonist, Lise, than does the reader. . . . She follows this woman, another of her slightly bizarre lunatics, through a day's grotesque project, narrating only its circumstances, leaving all motive, all emotion, all inner plan to be inferred. The result is a long, elusive joke that casts as deep an irony on life's arbitrariness as do the more 'compassionate' ironies of, say, E. M. Forster." Nation

Spark, Muriel

★ A **far** cry from Kensington. Houghton Mifflin 1988 189p

ISBN 0-395-47694-1

LC 88-5904

"Spark balances devastatingly eccentric characters and funny situations with darker elements, even pathos. Her well-constructed novel has no loose ends and few contrived situations." Libr J

Spark, Muriel

★ The **girls** of slender means. Knopf 1963 176p

"The novel, set primarily in London during World War II, focuses on the inhabitants of a residential club for unmarried women and on the friendship of several of them with a young man named Nicholas Farringdon. When tragedy strikes and 13 of the women are killed, Nicholas realizes that there is no safety anywhere, especially for those on whom fortune had once seemed to smile. This epiphany stimulates his conversion to Roman Catholicism. Years later, he dies in Haiti, where he has gone as a missionary." Merriam-Webster's Ency of Lit

Spark, Muriel

Loitering with intent. Coward, McCann & Geoghegan 1981 217p

ISBN 0-698-11047-1

LC 80-26049

"Would-be novelist Fleur Talbot works for the snooty, irascible Sir Quentin Oliver at the Autobiographical Association, whose members are all at work on their memoirs. When her employer gets his hands on Fleur's novel-in-progress, mayhem ensues when its scenes begin coming true. Generating hilarious turns of phrase and larger-than-life characters (especially Sir Quentin's batty mother), Sparks's inimitable style make this literary joyride thoroughly appealing." Publ Wkly

Spark, Muriel

★ The **Mandelbaum** Gate. Knopf 1965 369p

"The changing shape of any identity, be it of person or of situation, is the theme of this novel, typified by the Mandelbaum Gate of the title, 'hardly a gate at all, but a piece of street between Jerusalem and Jerusalem' . . . The narrative goes and returns piecemeal between the two parts of the Holy Land, focusing on two English characters–Barbara Vaughan, a spinster, half Jewish by birth and Roman Catholic by conviction, come to Israel to be near her archeologist fiance (and lover) in Jordan and to make a pilgrimage to the Holy sites; and Freddy Hamilton, proper foreign officer, moved by an unexpected impulse to change his personal pattern of responsibility and by kindness to keep Barbara from the danger of being apprehended by Jordan authorities because of her background." Libr J

Spark, Muriel

★ **Memento** mori. Lippincott 1959 224p

"Several elderly London friends receive anonymous telephone calls with a single message: 'Remember you must die.' Each hears and interprets the words differently. Old rivalries and romances still color the friends' relations, and Spark makes clear that their personalities in old age are but a continuation of their earlier lives." Merriam-Webster's Ency of Lit

Spark, Muriel

★ **Open** to the public; new & collected stories. New Directions 1997 376p $24.95

ISBN 0-8112-1367-6

LC 97-20607

"With 10 tales new to American readers, Open to the Public brings Spark's stories up to date with the rest of her prolific output." Publ Wkly

Spark, Muriel

★ The **prime** of Miss Jean Brodie. Lippincott 1962 187p

First published 1961 in the United Kingdom

"Miss Jean Brodie, teacher at the Marcia Blaine School for Girls in Edinburgh in the 1930s, gathers around herself a group of young girls who are set apart from other students as the Brodie set: Monica Douglas, who will be famous for her mathematical ability; Rose Stanley, who will be famous for her sex appeal; Eunice Gardiner, of great swimming and gymnastic ability; Sandy Stranger, of the small eyes and outstanding vowel sounds; and Mary MacGregor, who is considered a silent lump. Miss Brodie will make these girls the 'crème de la crème,' especially if they will follow her advice to recognize their prime. Her teaching is unorthodox and her relationship with the students most informal, so that they are privy to her affair with the school's music teacher. We get glimpses into the future of these young girls and are made aware that students are capable of treachery as well as teacher-worship." Shapiro. Fic for Youth. 3d edition

Sparks, Nicholas, 1965-

★ The **notebook**. Warner Bks. 1996 214p

ISBN 0446520802

LC 96-33815

This is Sparks' first novel. "At 80, Noah Calhoun reads daily from a notebook containing the love story of Noah and Allie. We learn of the teenaged lovers, their 14-year separation and reunion in New Bern, North Carolina, just weeks before Allie is to marry another man. Back in the present, we learn that Noah and Allie did marry and were happy for more than 40 years. Now, they are residents of a nursing home, separated both by rooms and, more profoundly, by Allie's Alzheimer's. Noah's daily reading from the notebook is not to himself; he reads aloud to Allie, hoping that the power of their love story will reach her." (Libr J)

"At 80, Noah Calhoun reads daily from a notebook containing the love story of Noah and Allie. We learn of the teenaged lovers, their 14-year separation and reunion in New Bern, North Carolina, just weeks before Allie is to marry another man. Back in the present, we learn that Noah and Allie did marry and were happy for more than 40 years. Now, they are residents of a nursing home, separated both by rooms and, more profoundly, by Allie's Alzheimer's. Noah's daily reading from the notebook is not to himself; he reads aloud to Allie, hoping that the power of their love story will reach her." Libr J

Sparks, Nicholas

A **walk** to remember. Warner Bks. 1999 240p $19.95

ISBN 0-446-52553-7

LC 99-12079

In Beaufort, North Carolina in 1958, 17-year-old high school senior Landon Carter takes Jamie Sullivan, the minister's daughter, to the homecoming dance, stars with her in the Christmas play, and falls in love with her, only to discover her sad secret

The author "is a master at pulling heartstrings and bringing a tear to his readers' eyes. . . . Told in Landon's down-home voice, this bittersweet tale will enthrall Sparks' numerous fans." Booklist

Speller, Elizabeth

The **strange** fate of Kitty Easton; Elizabeth Speller. Houghton Mifflin Harcourt 2012 407 p.

ISBN 0547547528; 9780547547527

LC 2011036972

This historical mystery novel by Elizabeth Speller begins "[w]hen Great War veteran Laurence Bartram arrives in Easton Deadall. . . . Now peace prevails, and the rest of England is newly alight with hope, but Easton Deadall remains haunted by tragedy - as does the Easton family. In 1911, five-year-old Kitty disappeared from her bed and has not been seen in thirteen years; only her fragile mother still believes she is alive. While Laurence is a guest of the manor, a young maid vanishes in a sinister echo of Kitty's disappearance. And when a body is discovered in the manor's ancient church, Laurence is drawn into the grounds' forgotten places, where deadly secrets lie in wait". (Publisher's note)

Spencer, Elizabeth

★ The **southern** woman; new and selected fiction. Modern Lib. 2001 448p $23.95

ISBN 0-679-64218-8

LC 00-54612

"This collection offers selections from the Mississippi native's earlier short fiction together with several new stories. Best known of the earlier fiction is her stunning novella, The Light in the Piazza (1960), the deceptively simple tale of an American mother and daughter in Florence." Libr J

Spencer, Elizabeth

The **stories** of Elizabeth Spencer; with a foreword by Eudora Welty. Doubleday 1981 429p

ISBN 0-385-15697-9

LC 79-6601

The stories included in this collection were written between 1944 and 1977 and were originally published in various periodicals. The novelette Knights & dragons was published separately in 1965 by McGraw-Hill. It concerns an American divorcee living in Rome. Other stories in the collection are: The little brown child; The eclipse; First dark; A southern landscape; Moon rocket; The white azalea; The visit; Ship Island; The fishing lake; The adult holiday; The Pincian gate; The absence; The day before; The Bufords; Judith Kane; Wisteria; A bad cold; Presents; On the Gulf; Sharon; The finder; Instrument of destruction; Go South in the winter; A kiss at the door; A Christian education; Mr. McMillan; I, Maureen; Prelude to a parking lot; Indian summer; The search; Port of embarkation: The girl who loved horses

Spencer, LaVyrle

Bitter sweet. Putnam 1990 382p

ISBN 0-399-13508-1

LC 89-38089

"Readers who can accept the plausibility of Maggie's original separation from Eric will enjoy following her journey of self-discovery and reawakening." Booklist

Spencer, LaVyrle

Morning glory. Putnam 1989 384p

ISBN 0-399-13413-1

LC 88-28166

"Tall, dark and handsome Will Parker has served time for the killing of a Texas prostitute, but keeps losing jobs as his reputation becomes known. In the small town of Whitney, Ga., at the beginning of WW II, he answers the advertisement of a pregnant widow and mother of two, the abused and reclusive Eleanor Dinsmore, who is looking for a husband. Soon in love with ostensibly plain, bedraggled Ellie, Parker dotes on her two boys, and works to support the family. Fittingly for this sort of bucolic idyll, Will and Ellie, despite their rudimentary educations, love books and develop a special friendship with wise old Miss Beasley, the local librarian. Alas, brazen and rapacious Lula Peak, the town floozie, sets her sights on Will, waylaying him in the library; meantimes, Lula is blackmailing her lover, the cowardly Harley Overmire, who is no friend of Will. The clearly drawn characters fulfill their imperatives—including Will, who becomes a war hero—and all is neatly and pleasingly resolved." Publ Wkly

Spencer, LaVyrle

Small town girl. Putnam 1997 364p

ISBN 0-399-14249-5

LC 96-24317

"When small-town girl Tess McPhail followed the pull of Nashville's glittering lights, she placed her dreams on becoming a country singer. Eighteen years later, she is a megastar and is caught in a whirlwind of tours, recording sessions, and financial meetings—a whirlwind that crashes to a stop when her sister demands her help in caring for their mother. Angered at her sister's orders, Tess breezes in to town for a month and crashes straight into the past in the form of Kenny Kronek, the boy-next-door 'dork' from high school who has been helping her mother." Booklist

Spencer, LaVyrle

That Camden summer. Putnam 1996 368p
ISBN 0-399-14120-0

LC 95-20055

In 1916, divorceé Roberta Jewett, "returns to her provincial hometown of Camden, Maine, in order to build a new life for herself and her three daughters. Braving adversaries such as her lecherous brother-in-law, condemning mother, and a community that considers a divorced woman little better than a prostitute, Roberta Jewett behaves 'scandalously,' securing a job as a country nurse to support her children, learning to drive, and buying a 'Model-T car.' Roberta is embittered by her humiliating marriage to an outrageous philanderer, but not surprisingly she 'finds love' with Gabriel Farley, the gruff yet inwardly sensitive widowered carpenter retained to renovate her home. Although predictable and somewhat belabored, Spencer's latest novel is overall an enjoyable read." Libr J

Spencer, Sally

The **dead** hand of history. Severn House Pub Ltd 2009 235 p. (Monika Paniatowski mysteries) (hardcover) $27.95
ISBN 0727868055; 9780727868053

In this Monika Paniatowski mystery from Sally Spencer, set in 1973, it is Monika's "first case as a newly promoted DCI" since her boss Charlie Woodend retired and she "must prove herself to those she works with and solve a particularly difficult crime involving a pair of severed hands." (Library Journal)

Other titles in this series are:
The ring of death (2010)
Echoes of the dead (2011)
Backlash (2011)
Lambs to the slaughter (2012)
A walk with the dead (2013)
Death's dark shadow (2014)
Supping with the devil (2014)
Best served cold (2015)
Thicker than water (2016)
Death in disguise (2016)
The hidden (2017)

Spencer, Sally

★ **Echoes** of the dead. Severn House Pub Ltd 2011 224 p. (Monika Paniatowski mysteries) $28.95
ISBN 0727869809; 9780727869807

In this DCI Monika Paniatowski mystery, a "dying man who served 20 years for a young girl's murder reveals that he was coerced by the police to confess. DCI Monika Paniatowski is ordered to lead an unofficial investigation, but the man in charge of the original case was her old mentor, Scotland Yard DI Charlie Woodend. Moving between the two time periods," the reader sees both Woodend's and Paniatowski's investigations. (Library Journal)

Spencer, Scott

★ **Endless** love. Knopf 1979 417p
LC 79-2089

The author "has achieved something quite remarkable in this unabashedly romantic and often harrowing novel. He has created an adolescent love that is believably endless. . . . Mr. Spencer has an acute grasp of character and situation. He gives us details that make these often tormented people uncommonly convincing." N Y Times Book Rev

Spencer, Scott

Man in the woods; a novel. Ecco 2010 307p $24.99
ISBN 978-0-06-146655-7; 0-06-146655-7

A "novel about what happens to a couple when the man, Paul Phillips, impulsively decides to stop a stranger from beating his dog. . . . Paul's partner, Kate Ellis, is successful, sober and blissfully happy in love, a hard-won trifecta. Her collection of essays, 'Prays Well With Others,' chronicling her years as an alcoholic and wayward mother, has become a best seller; Kate's brand of honesty, humor and religion has found a wide audience. She and her young daughter Ruby (both characters from Spencer's novel, 'A Ship Made of Paper') are living with Paul, a carpenter. . . . After a stressful meeting with a Manhattan client one day, Paul stops off at a state park to clear his head before driving on to Kate's home in rural New York. He spots the man and the dog. One life-altering moment isn't new in fiction, of course, but Spencer makes it fresh, and compelling." Cleveland Plain Dealer

Spencer-Fleming, Julia

All mortal flesh. St. Martin's 2006 336p $22.95
ISBN 0-312-31264-4

While the "setup might sound conventional, Spencer-Fleming's handling of it is far from mechanical. Her unusual heroine has brains and wit and the fearless spirit of an ex-Army chaplain and helicopter pilot who saw action in Kuwait. If anyone can clear Russ and find the real murderer, Clare can do it—if she can only escape from Elizabeth de Groot, the 'frighteningly competent deacon' who has been sent by the bishop to monitor her unorthodox behavior. In a story as unpredictable as its characters, the resolution takes this series in a direction that should give the good bishop heart palpitations." N Y Times Book Rev

Spencer-Fleming, Julia

In the bleak midwinter. Thomas Dunne Bks. 2002 308p $23.95
ISBN 0-312-28847-6

LC 2001-51303

A mystery set in the "upstate New York town of Millers Kill. As the new (and first female) priest of St. Alban's Episcopal Church, Clare {Fergusson} faces her first test when an infant is left on the rectory doorstep by an unwed teenage mother who is found frozen to death by the river. More crises follow in this freshly conceived and meticulously plotted whodunit when a police investigation raises suspicions about two parishioners who are frantic to adopt the child, and when Clare's own inquiries within her conservative flock turn up troubling evidence of domestic abuse." N Y Times Book Rev

Spiegelman, Peter

Black maps. Knopf 2003 285p $22.95
ISBN 1-4000-4075-2

LC 2003-273218

This mystery introduces John March, "a Manhattan P.I. who walks the mean streets of Beaver and Broad. As the rebel son in four generations of merchant bankers, who turned his back on the family business to become a cop . . . he's quick enough to grasp the byzantine forensic accounting procedures that fire up this technically accomplished financial mystery." N Y Times Book Rev

Spiegelman, Peter

Thick as thieves. Alfred A. Knopf 2011 295p $24.95
ISBN 978-0-307-26317-9; 0-307-26317-7

LC 2011-17855

"Though the end has perhaps one too many surprise! moments, Spiegelman's sharp prose and deft plotting elevate this Ocean's Eleven-style caper story." Entertainment Wkly

Spillane, Mickey ✓

The **Consummata**; by Mickey Spillane and Max Allan Collins. Hard Case Crime 2011 255p pa $9.95

ISBN 978-0-85768-288-8; 0-85768-288-1

Spillane "decided to introduce a new series featuring a master criminal called Morgan the Raider. The first entry, The Delta Factor, came out in '67. So far, so good. Then the business intervened in the form of Hollywood, which decided to make a movie out of the first Morgan book. But the experience left Spillane so upset that he stopped work on the already announced second installment. . . . Collins finishes this project seamlessly. It is impossible to tell where one great writer left off and another begins." Bookreporter

Spillane, Mickey

The **Goliath** bone; [by] Mickey Spillane with Max Allan Collins. Harcourt 2008 274p $23

ISBN 978-0-15-101454-5; 0-15-101454-X

LC 2008-10091

"Much of the jargon is vintage, as is the indomitable Hammer as he strives to protect the kids and prevent the Goliath bone from setting off the next big war. While not on a par with early Spillane classics, this is a fitting capstone to Hammer's career." Publ Wkly

Spillane, Mickey

★ The **Mike** Hammer collection [v1] [introduction by Max Allan Collins] New Am. Lib. 2001 513p pa $16

ISBN 0-451-20352-6

LC 00-52728

Omnibus edition of the author's first three Mike Hammer mysteries. Includes I, the jury (1947), My gun is quick (1950), and Vengeance is mine (1950). "Hammer is a foul-mouthed, violent vigilante and a sucker for beautiful damsels in distress, some of whom pull the wool over his eyes. With his trusty, sexy assistant Velda keeping him honest (sort of), he exacts revenge on racketeers, cheats and murderers." Publ Wkly

Spillane, Mickey

★ The **Mike** Hammer collection [v2] [introduction by Lawrence Block] New Am. Lib. 2001 517p pa $17

ISBN 0-451-20425-5

Omnibus edition of three Mike Hammer mysteries. Includes One lonely night (1951), The big kill (1951), and Kiss me, deadly (1952).

Spiotta, Dana

Eat the document. Scribner 2006 291p $24

ISBN 0-7432-7298-6

LC 2005-54050

National Book Award Finalist: Fiction (2006)

"Spiotta has written a glorious sendup of contemporary social and ecological activists with all their preening idealism and absurdity—especially the intelligent—sounding nonsense people spew at one another, even as they rarely connect on any meaningful level." N Y Times Book Rev

Spiotta, Dana

Innocents and others; a novel. Dana Spiotta. Scribner 2016 288 p. (hardback) $25

ISBN 9781501122729; 9781501122736

LC 2015022360

This novel, by Dana Spiotta, "is about two women, best friends, who . . . become filmmakers. Meadow and Carrie have everything in common—except their views on sex, power, movie-making, and morality. Their lives collide with Jelly, a loner whose most intimate experience is on the phone. Jelly is older, erotic, and mysterious. She cold calls powerful men and seduces them not through sex but through listening. She invites them to reveal themselves, and they do." (Publisher's note)

"A novel for readers thrilled by Jennifer Egan, Siri Hustvedt, Rachel Kushner, and Claire Messud, Spiotta's deeply inquiring tale is about looking and listening, freedom and obligation, our dire hunger for illusion, and our profound need for friendship." Booklist

Spiotta, Dana

Stone Arabia; a novel. Scribner 2011 239p $24

ISBN 978-1-4516-1796-2; 1-4516-1796-8

LC 2011-17816

The "story of rock musician Nik Worth, a fictional almost-pop star in the '80s. He has withdrawn from public life but continues to make music, releasing handcrafted CDs only to those closest to him and writing fake, intricate reviews and self-interviews. Is he a genius madman, or a sane artist unsullied by 21st-century American idolatry? The tale is told by his sister, who is equal parts ambivalent enabler and ultimate fan. . . . [A] movingly fab narrative; it's as though Nabokov had written a rock novel." Entertainment Wkly

Spufford, Francis, 1964-

★ **Golden** Hill; a novel of old New York. Francis Spufford. Scribner 2017 302 p. (hardcover) $26

ISBN 9781501163876; 9781501163890; 1501163876

LC 2017022622

This novel, winner of the Costa First Novel Award 2016, the RSL Ondaatje Prize 2017 and the Desmond Elliott Prize 2017, by Francis Spufford, "follows the adventures of a mysterious young man in mid-eighteenth century Manhattan, thirty years before the American Revolution. . . . Spufford paints an irresistible picture of a New York . . . a place where a young man with a fast tongue can invent himself afresh, fall in love--and find a world of trouble." (Publisher's note)

"Spufford's . . . spirited 'novel of Old New York,' playfully rendered in simulated eighteenth-century prose, pays homage to the literature of the colonial era." Booklist

St. Aubyn, Edward, 1960-

At last; Edward St. Aubyn. Farrar, Straus and Giroux 2012 266 p. $15

ISBN 0374298890; 1250023904; 9780374298890; 9781250023902

LC 2011034964

This book follows "Patrick Melrose as he . . . attends the funeral of his mother, who died after a lingering illness—and after giving her home and fortune not to Patrick but to a New Age spiritual center. Eleanor was often absent in Patrick's life, somehow oblivious as he was raped by his sadistic father. Highly intelligent Patrick, now divorced with two sons and sober after years of drug and alcohol abuse, is always analyzing those around him but never fully participates in life." (Library Journal)

St. Aubyn, Edward, 1960-

The **complete** Patrick Melrose novels; Edward St. Aubyn. Picador 2015 857 p. (ebook) $40; (pbk.) $30

ISBN 9781250069627; 1250069602; 1250069610; 9781250069603; 9781250069610

LC 2015295911

In this book, author Edward St. Aubyn "offers his reader the often darkly funny and self-loathing world of privilege as we follow Patrick Melrose's story of abuse, addiction, and recovery from the age of five into early middle age." (Publisher's note)

St. John Mandel, Emily

★ The **singer's** gun. Unbridled Books 2010 287p $24.95

ISBN 978-1-93607-164-7; 1-93607-164-9

LC 2009-53826

"This is a gripping story, full of moral ambiguities, where deception and betrayal become the norm, and where the expression, 'a riddle wrapped in a mystery, inside an enigma,' is lifted to new heights." St. Louis Post-Dispatch

Stabenow, Dana

★ **Hunter's** moon; a Kate Shugak mystery. Putnam 1999 260p $23.95

ISBN 0-399-14468-4

LC 98-33465

Aleut sleuth Kate Shugak "and her boyfriend sign on here as wilderness guides for the management team of a German software company whose arrogant C.E.O. fancies himself a big-game hunter. . . . His cowed employees would have been better advised to bone up on 'The Most Dangerous Game,' because the first big catch is one moose, a few salmon and two junior executives." NY Times Book Rev

Stabenow, Dana

Killing grounds. Putnam 1998 273p $22.95

ISBN 0-399-14356-4

LC 97-23900

"Alaskan private investigator Kate Shugak . . . who practically wallows in the surrounding wild beauty of nature, spars with an abusive, strikebreaking fisherman who later winds up dead. Kate's recently returned lover, enigmatic kin, and eccentric acquaintances make this a delightful read." Libr J

Stabenow, Dana

Less than a treason; Dana Stabenow. Head of Zeus 2017 309 p. maps (Kate Shugak series) (hardcover) $26.95

ISBN 9781786695697; 1786695693

Sequel to: Bad Blood (2013)

In this book, in the Kate Shugak series, by Dana Stabenow, "Kate Shugak is a native Aleut working as a private investigator in Alaska. . . . [She] carries a scar that runs from ear to ear across her throat, and owns a half-wolf, half-husky dog named Mutt. Resourceful, strong-willed, defiant, Kate is tougher than your average heroine--and she needs to be, to survive the worst the Alaskan wilds can throw at her." (Publisher's note)

"The book is sprinkled with wit, studded with exquisite descriptions of the rugged landscape, and filled with opinionated and endearing characters, including reality TV show producers, park rangers, geologists, and barkeeps." Pub Wkly

Stabenow, Dana

Restless in the grave; Dana Stabenow. Minotaur Books 2012 371 p. (Kate Shugak series.)

ISBN 9780312559137; 9781429950381

LC 2011037662

In this book, "Finn Grant's death in the crash of his small plane in an apparent act of sabotage raises the question: who would want the self-made billionaire dead? About half the population of southwest Alaska, as Kate Shugak discovers when she goes undercover as a barmaid. . . . Kate's . . . prying reveals that the unsavory Grant was involved in blackmail, mail fraud, and embezzlement, all connected to Alaska's many small airlines. Kate has a casual approach to evidence gathering, and her skill at breaking and entering finds her eventually thrown into a chest freezer, tossed into a Dumpster, and locked inside a freight container while her stalwart and highly intelligent companion, Mutt, who's half-wolf, half-husky, provides assistance." (Publishers Weekly)

Stabenow, Dana

Though not dead; Dana Stabenow. Minotaur Books 2011 446 p. (Kate Shugak series.)

ISBN 0312559119; 9780312559113

LC 2010039080

This book tells the story of "Alaskan native Kate Shugak, . . . former investigator for the Anchorage DA, [who] investigates her own family's past. When he dies, Kate's uncle and foster father, Old Sam, leaves everything to Kate. . . . While packing up Sam's extensive book collection, she finds an old diary. But before she's read very much of it, someone bashes her in the head and steals it. The theft is only the first in a series of dangerous encounters. After she's run off the road, attacked and shot at while checking out Sam's property in the remote Canyon Hot Springs area, she realizes that Sam had something someone badly wants, and that Sam's life must hold the clues to what she needs to know. So she travels around Alaska digging up information." (Kirkus)

Stabenow, Dana

Whisper to the blood. Minotaur Books 2009 354p map $24.95

ISBN 978-0-312-36974-3; 0-312-36974-3

LC 2008-33959

Between two suspicious murders and a series of attacks on snow mobilers up the Kanuyaq River, part-time P.I. and newly elected chairman of the Niniltna Native Association Kate Shugak has her hands full.

"A dynamite combination of atmosphere, action, and character." Booklist

Stachniak, Eva

The **chosen** maiden; Eva Stachniak. Doubleday Canada 2017 412 p. (paperback) $18

ISBN 9780385678568; 9780385678551; 0385678568

This novel, by Eva Stachniak, presents the story of ballet dancer Bronislava Ninjinska "who charts her own course through the tumultuous years of early twentieth-century Europe. Beautifully blending fiction with fact, 'The Chosen Maiden' plunges readers into an artistic world upended by modernity, immersing them in the experiences of the era's giants, from Anna Pavlova and Serge Diaghilev to Coco Chanel and Pablo Picasso." (Publisher's note)

"A memorable literary rendering of a remarkable woman's life." Booklist

Stachniak, Eva

The **Winter** Palace; Eva Stachniak. Bantam Books 2011 444p.

ISBN 9780553808124; 9780553908046 ebook

LC 2011004928

This book takes place "[i]n 1745, [when] 16-year-old Vavara, the orphaned daughter of a bookbinder, enters the Russian court as a servant. She soon catches the attention of the Chancellor, who teaches her to spy for him. Trained to listen and report, Vavara is tasked to befriend the young Princess Sophia, who is to marry the Empress Elizabeth's nephew, and then disclose all her secrets to the Chancellor and the Empress. But Sophia and Vavara become confidants and friends and Vavara switches sides, assisting Sophia in her transformation into Catherine and her subsequent rise to power. Narrated by Vavara, this historical novel takes readers on a grand tour of the 18th-century Russian Court. . . . Catherine and Vavara each navigate the palace intrigue in their own way according to their stations, but Vavara, loyal to Catherine, uses her influence . . . to help Catherine gain power." (School Libr J)

Stafford, Jean

The **collected** stories of Jean Stafford. Farrar, Straus & Giroux 1969 463p

Contents: Maggie Meriwether's rich experience; The children's game; The echo and the nemesis; The maiden; A modest proposal; Caveat emptor; Life is no abyss; The hope chest; Polite conversation; A country love story; The bleeding heart; The lippia lawn; The interior castle; The healthiest girl in town; The tea time of stouthearted ladies; The mountain day; The darkening moon; Bad characters; In the zoo; The liberation; A reading problem; A summer day; The philosophy lesson; Children are bored on Sunday; Beatrice Trueblood's story; Between the porch and the altar; I love someone; Cops and robbers; The captain's gift; The end of a career

Stamm, Peter, 1963-

We're flying; stories. Peter Stamm; translated from the German by Michael Hofmann. Other Press 2012 vi, 370 p.p (pbk. : acid-free paper) $15.95

ISBN 159051324X; 9781590513248; 9781590514191

LC 2012001180

This book presents a short story collection by Peter Stamm. "Some of these stories deal with the awkwardness of adolescence and sexual initiation, but the protagonists of many more are innocents as well. In 'Children of God' . . . a minister navigates between sin and divinity as he falls in love with a young girl who insists that her pregnancy is an immaculate conception. . . . Another protagonist, a young girl who lives 'In the Forest,' survives through 'alert indifference.'" (Kirkus Reviews)

Standiford, Les

Deal with the dead; a novel. Putnam 2001 302p

ISBN 0-399-14704-7

LC 00-55938

In this John Deal novel, "the independent building contractor working in South Florida is still marinating in his guilt over how his wife was nearly killed during his last caper and his agony over the splintering apart of their marriage. A blast from Deal's late father's checkered past, in the form of a visit from one of Dad's cronies just after Deal has been awarded a lucrative waterfront project, theatens to annihiliate his carefully pieced together recovery. . . . The action is nonstop, the setting of volatile South Florida from the 1950s to the present is fascinating, and the characterization of a man forced to defend what he loves because of the greed of others is compelling." Booklist

Stanisic, Sasa

How the soldier repairs the gramophone; translated from the German by Anthea Bell. Grove Press 2008 304p $24

ISBN 978-0-8021-1866-0; 0-8021-1866-6

"Through the eyes of the fourteen-year-old narrator, Aleksandar Krsmanovi, we witness a massacre perpetrated by Bosnian Serbs against their Muslim neighbors in the town of Vĭsegrad in 1992. The outlines of the plot are autobiographical: The protagonist's escape to Germany from the attack on Vĭsegrad parallels the author's own at the same age. But rather than rendering a direct account, Stanisic refracts these events through his young narrator's wildly imaginative storytelling. A hyperactive fabulist, Aleksandar embarks on madcap flights of invention and comic exaggeration, which clash movingly with the painfully real chronicle of terror, loss, and exile at the story's heart." Bookforum

Stanley, Michael ✓

A **carrion** death; introducing Detective Kubu. HarperCollins 2008 467p map (Detective Kubu mysteries) $23.95

ISBN 978-0-06-125240-2; 0-06-125240-9

LC 2008-299326

"Readers may be lured to Africa by the landscape, but it takes a great character like Kubu to win our loyalty." N Y Times Book Rev

Other titles in this series are:

The second death of Goodluck Tinubu (2009)
Death of the mantis (2011)
Deadly harvest (2013)
A death in the family (2015)
Dying to live (2017)

Stanley, Michael

Deadly Harvest. HarperCollins 2013 xiv, 477 p.p (paperback) $14.99

ISBN 0062221523; 9780062221520

This is the fourth in Michael Stanley's Detective Kubu series. Here, "newcomer Det. Samantha Khama helps Det. David 'Kubu' Bengu when a serial killer targets girls in Botswana, possibly to use their bodies in a potion called muti. A father, devastated by loss, seeks revenge by murdering a politician in this complicated case." (Library Journal)

Stanley, Michael ✓

Death of the mantis; Michael Stanley. 1st ed.; Harper Paperbacks 2011 448p map

ISBN 9780062000378 pa

LC 2011022154

This book tells the story of "A dedicated Botswana detective [who] finds himself in the middle of simmering tensions between police and nomadic Bushmen." (Kirkus) "A fractious ranger named Monzo is found dying from a severe head wound in a dry ravine. . . . Detective David 'Kubu' Bengu is on the case, an investigation that his old school friend Khumanego claims is motivated by racist antagonism on the part of local police. But when a second bizarre murder, and then a third, seem to point also to the nomadic tribe, the intrepid Kubu must journey into the depths of the Kalahari to uncover the truth." (Publisher's note)

Stansberry, Domenic

The **ancient** rain. St. Martin's Minotaur 2008 293p $24.95

ISBN 978-0-312-36453-3; 0-312-36453-9

LC 2007-49768

In this Dante Mancuso mystery "the former San Francisco cop becomes entangled in a cold case surrounding the unintentional shooting death of a woman during a bank robbery involving a group of militant political anarchists in 1976. In a paranoia-fueled post 9/11 America with new antiterror laws, a federal prosecutor with a deep-rooted grudge arrests Bill Owens, an acquaintance of Mancuso's who was the prime suspect in the 1976 murder. Hired to help exonerate Owens, Mancuso tracks down individuals linked to the original case. . . . Equal parts contemporary crime fiction and dark, existential poetry, this novel should win Stansberry new fans." Publ Wkly

Stark, Richard ✓

Ask the parrot. Mysterious Press 2006 279p $23.99

ISBN 0-89296-068-X

LC 2006-927625

"Unconscious in front of the TV is the fate awaiting most in this corner of purgatory, and Parker's assistance in helping Tom Lindahl escape its confines with a decent stash is the closest he's come to an act of mercy in his entire bullet-ridden career. As for what happens to the parrot—don't ask." N Y Times Book Rev

Stark, Richard

Breakout. Mysterious Press 2002 299p $23.95
ISBN 0-89296-779-X

LC 2002-23492

"Richard Stark (the name that Donald E. Westlake uses when he lets Parker off the leash) writes with ruthless efficiency. His bad guys are polished pros who think hard, move fast and turn on a dime in moments of crisis. And because talk doesn't come cheap, every bit of dialogue counts." N Y Times Book Rev

Stark, Richard

Comeback. Mysterious Press 1997 292p

LC 97-7019

"The plot for this caper is a cunningly engineered sequence of catastrophes, each one set in motion by some seemingly minor miscalculation that escalates into disaster. Oiling the machinery is the author's biting irony toward characters who talk the big talk about love and trust and loyalty but ditch their Christian values for a hot babe or a cool buck. In a world of warped values, an honest crook like Parker is a true treasure." N Y Times Book Rev

Stark, Richard

Dirty money. Grand Central Pub. 2008 276p $23.99
ISBN 978-0-446-17858-7; 0-446-17858-6

LC 2007-931314

"Lots went wrong after Parker and two partners robbed an armored car in rural Massachusetts of $2.2 million in 2004's Nobody Runs Forever. The money was 'poisoned' (i.e., marked); one of his partners was captured before killing a marshal and escaping; and bounty-hunter Sandra Loscalzo wants to cut herself in on the take. The pragmatic, quick-thinking Parker must find a way to retrieve the stashed haul he and his confederates left in Massachusetts without getting caught by the law or nibbled to death by other crooks." Publ Wkly

Stark, Richard

The **hunter**; University of Chicago Press ed.; University of Chicago Press 2008 198p
ISBN 0-226-77099-0; 978-0-226-77099-4

LC 2008-11226

First published 1963 by Pocket Bks.

In this first novel of the author's Parker series, "Parker roars into New York City, seeking revenge on the woman who betrayed him and on the man who took his money, stealing and scamming his way to redemption." Publisher's note

Stark, Richard

The **jugger**; with a new foreword by John Banville. The University of Chicago Press 2009 211p pa $14
ISBN 978-0-226-77102-1; 0-226-77102-4

LC 2008-42432

First published 1965 by Pocket Bks.

This novel in the author's Parker series has the main character in Sagamore, Nebraska, at the request of Joe Sheer, a retired safe cracker who carries many of Parker's criminal secrets.

Starnone, Domenico

Ties; Domenico Starnone; translated from the Italian by Jhumpa Lahiri. Europa Editions 2017 150 p. (paperback) $16
ISBN 1609453859; 9781609453855; 9781609453862

In this novel, by Domenico Starnone, translated by Jhumpa Lahiri, "like many marriages, Vanda and Aldo's has been subject to strain, to attrition, to the burden of routine. Yet it has survived intact. Or so things appear. The rupture in their marriage lies years in the past, but if one looks closely enough, the fissures and fault lines are evident. It is a cracked vase that may shatter at the slightest touch. Or perhaps it has already shattered." (Publisher's note)

"A slim, stunning meditation on marriage, fidelity, honesty, and truth." Kirkus

Stead, Christina

★ The **man** who loved children; with an introduction by Doris Lessing. Knopf 1995 xxxvii, 529p $22
ISBN 0-679-44364-9

A reissue of the title first published 1940 by Simon & Schuster

"Unfolding a harrowing portrait of a disintegrating family, Stead examines the hostility between a husband and wife: Sam Pollit, revealed to be a tyrannical crank far removed from the civilized man he thinks he is, whose claim to love his children lends the ironic title; and Henny, who has become a bitter virago." Merriam-Webster's Ency of Lit

Stedman, M. L.

★ The **light** between oceans; a novel. M.L. Stedman. Scribner 2012 352 p. (hardback) $25.00
ISBN 9781451681734; 9781451681758; 9781451681765

LC 2011050244

In this debut novel, WWI veteran "Tom Sherbourne . . . takes a lighthouse keeper's post on an Australian island," and marries a woman named Isabel. Their "love grows, [b]ut four years on the island and several miscarriages" dampen their spirits "until a boat washes ashore with a dead man and a living child. Isabel convinces herself--and Tom--that the baby is a gift from God." Two years later, they must confront the child's still-alive real mother. (Publishers Weekly)

Steel, Danielle, 1947-

First sight; by Danielle Steel. Delacorte Press 2006 373 p. (hardcover) $28.00
ISBN 0385338309; 9780385338301

LC 2006042666

This novel by Danielle Steel focuses on "Timmie O'Neill, whose renowned [fashion] line, Timmie O, is the embodiment of casual chic, in fashion and for the home. She has created a business that . . . consumes her life. During Paris Fashion Week, [a] Frenchman comes into her life. First, Timmie and Jean-Charles Vernier are only patient and physician. They become confidants. But neither can deny their growing friendship and the electricity that sparks whenever they meet." (Publisher's note)

Steel, Danielle

The **kiss**. Delacorte Press 2001 347p $26.95
ISBN 0-385-33540-7

LC 00-66009

"Isabelle Forrester is the unhappy wife of a coldhearted and distant Parisian banker. . . . Unable to bear the strain of her lonely, unhappy life, Isabelle strikes up an innocent friendship—conversing mostly by phone or mail—with American Bill Robinson. A Washington power broker, Robinson is also trapped in an unhappy marriage. The pair's relationship intensifies steadily until they finally agree to meet in London for a few passionate days. There they are involved in a serious car accident, which leaves them both in a coma, fighting for their lives." Booklist

Steel, Danielle

Sunset in St. Tropez. Delacorte Press 2002 230p $19.95
ISBN 0-385-33546-6

LC 2001-47517

Three pairs of friends in their 50s and 60s decide to vacation together in St. Tropez

"Shortly before the vacation begins, one of the women dies of a heart attack, and the other women are scandalized when her supposedly grieving husband brings along a hot, young movie star in his wife's stead. Another scandal soon unfolds as another husband is revealed to be having an affair with a much younger woman. In addition, the house the group has rented (sight unseen) turns out to be a dump and comes complete with two very strange caretakers, who lend a bit of comic relief to the high drama all around them." Booklist

Steele, Allen M.

Coyote; a novel of interstellar exploration. Ace Bks. 2002 390p $23.95

ISBN 0-441-00974-3

LC 2002-74517

"A much-foreshadowed 'surprise' ending is by far the least of the surprises in Steele's bag of tricks. But each page of this novel bears evidence of fresh thought about the opportunities inherent in science fiction to take the familiar and make it new." N Y Times Book Rev

Steele, Jon

The **watchers**; Jon Steele. Blue Rider Press 2012 592 p. $26.95

ISBN 039915874X; 9780399158742

LC 2012001267

This book, set at the Lausanne cathedral in Switzerland, tells the story of "Marc Rochat, who's served for years as the cathedral's 'watcher,'" "American expatriate Katherine Taylor, who through her work as a highly paid escort has recently run afoul of vicious Russian criminals," and "Jay Harper, an amnesiac operative for the International Olympic Committee who's been investigating a former Olympian's bizarre death." Events bring the three together to defend the cathedral. (Publishers Weekly)

Stegner, Wallace Earle

★ **Angle** of repose; {by} Wallace Stegner. Doubleday 1971 569p

This novel "is set mainly in the West in the late 1800's; but the central characters cannot be confined to the West nor to the 19th Century. They have a healing effect on the narrator, their grandson and biographer. . . . The beautiful, talented, charming Susan and her inarticulate engineer husband Oliver Ward rough it in mining camps and desolate, unfinished irrigation project camps. Their lives are hard and their marriage is strained past redemption. Yet their suffering and their strength do redeem." Libr J

Stegner, Wallace Earle

★ The **Big** Rock Candy Mountain; [by] Wallace Stegner. Duell, Sloan & Pearce 1943 515p

"A well-written study of the footloose family. . . . The life of the household is a misery of continual cruelty and often crushing poverty, alternating with occasional scenes of simple family happiness which stand out beautifully and unforgettably." New Yorker

Stegner, Wallace Earle

Crossing to safety; [by] Wallace Stegner. Random House 1987 277p

LC 87-20482

"The Langs and the Morgans, young couples who meet when their husbands begin teaching at a Wisconsin university, forge bonds of wonderful, lasting friendship. Charity Lang and Sally Morgan are unlike in personality but see each other through devastating crises because of that friendship. Sid Lang is a frustrated poet whose life is over-directed by his wife; Larry Morgan, much less financially secure than Sid, realizes a slow but successful climb to a position of noted writer. This novel has no violence, explicit sex or ugliness. Instead it is a hymn to solid marriages and loyalty in friendship. The dramatic events are those that occur in the lives of ordinary people." Shapiro. Fic for Youth. 3d edition

Stein, Garth

The **art** of racing in the rain; a novel. Harper 2008 321p $23.95

ISBN 978-0-06-153793-6; 0-06-153793-4

LC 2007-33890

"Enzo narrates his life story, beginning with his impending death. Enzo's not afraid of dying, as he's seen a television documentary on the Mongolian belief that a good dog will reincarnate as a man. Yes, Enzo is a dog. And he belongs to Denny: husband, father, customer service technician. Denny's dream is to be a professional race-car driver, and Enzo recounts the triumphs and tragedies-medical, financial, and legal-they share in this quest, the dangers of the racetrack being the least of their obstacles. . . . [Stein] creates a patient, wise, and doggish narrator that is more than just fluff and collar." Libr J

Stein, Gertrude

★ **Three** lives; stories of the good Anna, Melanctha, and the gentle Lena. Grafton Press 1909 279p

"Written in a clear and masterly style, free from any of its author's later stylistic mannerisms, this book consists of three character studies of women. 'The Good Anna' deals with a kindly but domineering German servingwoman; 'Melanctha' is concerned with an uneducated but sensitive black girl; and 'The Gentle Lena' is about a pathetically feeble-minded young German maid." Reader's Ency. 4th edition

Steinbeck, John

★ **Cannery** Row. Viking 1945 208p hardcover o.p.

"In this episodic work Steinbeck returned to the manner of Tortilla Flat (1935) and produced a rambling account of the adventures and misadventures of workers in a California cannery and their friends." Herzberg. Reader's Ency of Am Lit

Followed by Sweet Thursday (1954)

Steinbeck, John

★ **East** of Eden. Viking 1952 602p

Steinbeck's "most ambitious post-war novel is . . . a parable of the fall of man, of Cain and Abel, and of human possibility, showing many of the virtues of his best books, but touched with sentimentality, melodrama and intrusive commentary." Penguin Companion to Am Lit

Steinbeck, John

★ The **grapes** of wrath. Viking 1939 619p

"In this moving book, Steinbeck wrote a classic novel of a family's battle with starvation and economic desperation. The story also tells in vivid terms the story of the westward movement and the frontier. The Joads, Steinbeck's central figures, are 'Okies,' farmers moving west from a land of drought and bankruptcy to seek work as migrant fruit-pickers in California. They are beset by the police, participate in strike violence, and are harried by death." Benet's Reader's Ency of Am Lit

Steinbeck, John

In dubious battle. Covici-Friede 1936 349p

"One of the more important books to come out of the proletarian movement. This was Steinbeck's first successful novel. 'In Dubious Battle' deals with a fruit strike in a California valley and the attempts of the radical leaders to organize, lead, and provide for the striking pickers. Perhaps the most important, although not the central, character is

Doc Burton, who helps the strikers and is concerned with seeing things as they exist, without labels of good and bad attached. The strike fails, and Jim, one of the two leaders, is senselessly killed." Benet's Reader's Ency of Am Lit

Steinbeck, John

The **long** valley. Viking 1938 304p

This volume "includes the four magnificent 'Red Pony' stories, and could serve as an admirable introduction to Steinbeck, showing his characteristic interests—the tensions of the town and country, of past and present, of labour and ownership, as well as the objectivity of biological observation and a sort of Lawrencean mystic concept of personal power." Penguin Companion to Am Lit

Steinbeck, John

★ **Of** mice and men. Covici-Friede 1937 186p

"Two uneducated laborers dream of a time when they can share the ownership of a rabbit farm in California. George is a plotter and a schemer, while Lennie is a mentally deficient hulk of a man who has no concept of his physical strength. As a team they are not particularly successful, but their friendship is enduring." Shapiro. Fic for Youth. 3d edition

Steinbeck, John

The **pearl**; with drawings by José Clemente Orozco. Viking 1947 122p il

"Kino, a poor pearl-fisher, lives a happy albeit spartan life with his wife and their child. When he finds a magnificent pearl, the Pearl of the World, he is besieged by dishonest pearl merchants and envious neighbors. Even a greedy doctor ties his professional treatment of their baby when it is bitten by a scorpion to the possible acquisition of the pearl. After a series of disasters, Kino throws the pearl away since it has brought him only unhappiness." Shapiro. Fic for Youth. 3d edition

Steinbeck, John

Sweet Thursday. Viking 1954 273p

Sequel to Cannery Row

After World War II the "Palace Flophouse passed into new hands, the Bear Flag Café got a new madam named Fauna (nee Flora), and Doc lost his old pleasure in women, liturgical music, and the Western Biological Laboratories. Then Suzy came to Cannery Row . . . {and} egged on by the others, she brought Doc back to his prewar contentment." Booklist

Steinbeck, John

Tortilla Flat; illustrated by Ruth Gannett. Covici-Friede 1935 316p

"This episodic tale concerns the poor but carefree 'paisano' Danny and his friends Pillon, Pablo, Big Joe Portagee, Jesus Maria Corcoran, and the old Pirate, all of whom gather in Danny's house, which Steinbeck tells us 'was not unlike the Round Table.' The novel (accepted after nine publishers had turned it down) contrasts the complexities of modern civilization with the simple life of the 'paisanos.'" Benet's Reader's Ency of Am Lit

Steinbeck, John

Travels with Charley and later novels, 1947-1962. Library of America 2007 990p $40

ISBN 978-1-59853-004-9; 1-59853-004-6

LC 2006-48757

First published 1950, Burning bright, "an allegory set against shifting backgrounds (circus, sea, farm) and revolving around the fear of sterility and the desire for self-perpetuation, marks Steinbeck's involvement with the drama in its fusion of the forms of novel and play." Publisher's note

Steinbeck, John

The **winter** of our discontent. Viking 1961 311p

Ethan Allen Hawley, the impoverished heir to an upright New England tradition is the focus of this story. Ethan, under pressure from his restless wife and discontented children who want more of this world's goods than his grocery store job provides, decides to take a holiday from his scrupulous standards to achieve wealth and success. What happens as he compromises with his integrity makes up this story

In this novel Steinbeck "continues his exploration of the moral dilemmas involved in being fully human, this time in contemporary America, where choices between genteel poverty and corrupt comfort press in upon the protagonist with a force and reality that suggest no easy resolution." Ency of World Lit in the 20th Century

Steiner, Peter

The **resistance**; a thriller. Peter Steiner. 1st ed. Minotaur Books 2012 p. cm. (hardcover) $26.99

ISBN 9781250003713; 9781250011305

LC 2012013572

This mystery thriller novel, by Peter Steiner, is part of his ex-CIA operative Louis Morgon series. "When Louis purchases a rundown house in Saint-Leon-sur-Deme, . . . he discovers evidence of a long forgotten crime hidden beneath the floorboards. Unable to leave a good mystery unsolved, he enlists the help of his friend Renard, a French cop, and sets out to discover exactly what happened in this small French village during the Nazi occupation." (Publisher's note)

Steiner, Peter

The **terrorist**. Minotaur Books 2010 216p $23.99

ISBN 978-0-312-37344-3; 0-312-37344-9

LC 2009-47489

Louis Morgon, "the hero of this improbable and charming spy novel, the third in a series, is a kind of septuagenarian Jason Bourne: a former intelligence operative, he was drummed out of the C.I.A. decades ago, and is now lying low in a sleepy French village. When the agency comes calling, wanting him to reactivate his contacts in the Middle East as part of the war on terror, he refuses. Only when an Algerian boy he has taken under his wing is arrested does he decide to plunge back into his old life. Few men of any age could so nimbly chase down Taliban leaders and Al Qaeda sleepers—all while undergoing chemotherapy for prostate cancer. Steiner has a light touch, and what the story may lack in verisimilitude it makes up for in wit and an appreciation, amid the action, for the gentler pleasures." New Yorker

Steinhauer, Olen

★ **All** the Old Knives; Olen Steinhauer. First edition Minotaur Books 2015 294 p. hc $23.99

ISBN 9781250045423; 1250045428

LC 2014040117

In Olen Steinhauer's novel, "six years ago in Vienna, terrorists took over a hundred hostages, and the rescue attempt went terribly wrong. Two of the CIA's case officers in Vienna, Henry Pelham and Celia Harrison, were lovers at the time, and on the night of the hostage crisis Celia decided she'd had enough. But neither of them can forget that long-ago question: Had their agent been compromised? If so, how?" (Publisher's note)

"It's an understatement to say that nothing is as it seems, but even readers well-versed in espionage fiction will be pleasantly surprised by Steinhauer's plot twists and double backs." Kirkus

Steinhauer, Olen

An **American** spy; Olen Steinhauer. Minotaur Books 2012 416 p

ISBN 9780312622909; 9780312622893; 9781429950442

LC 2011040874

This book tells the story of "Milo Weaver . . . [who is] no longer a member of the CIA's deeply clandestine Department of Tourism, which was shut down after Chinese spy Xin Zhu, motivated more by personal vengeance than allegiance to his government, orchestrated the assassination of 33 of its agents one by one around the world. When Alan Drummond, Weaver's boss at the now defunct department, disappears from his London hotel. Weaver gets on his trail--a matter that becomes much more urgent after Drummond's wife and daughter are kidnapped." (Publishers Weekly)

Steinhauer, Olen

The **Bridge** of Sighs. St. Martin's Minotaur 2003 278p $23.95

ISBN 0-312-30245-2

LC 2002-68127

"This is an intelligent, finely polished debut, loaded with atmospheric detail that effortlessly re-creates the rubble-strewn streets of the postwar period in an Eastern state 'liberated' from German occupation by the Russians." Libr J

Steinhauer, Olen

The **Cairo** affair; Olen Steinhauer. Minotaur Books 2014 416 p. (hardback) $26.99

ISBN 1250036135; 9781250036131

LC 2013033452

In this suspense novel, by Olen Steinhauer, "minutes after [a woman] confesses to her husband, a mid-level diplomat at the American embassy in Hungary, that she had an affair while they were in Cairo, he is shot in the head and killed. . . . Omar Halawi has worked in Egyptian intelligence for years, and he knows how to play the game. . . . But the murder of a diplomat in Hungary has ripples all the way to Cairo, and Omar must follow the fall-out wherever it leads." (Publisher's note)

"A complex tale of the Arab Spring, WikiLeaks, the CIA, and a marriage, this leaves us with the unsettling feeling that, despite all the information won, lost, hoarded, and put to use, the world of intelligence is no stronger than the fragile, fallible humans who navigate it." Booklist

Steinhauer, Olen

The **nearest** exit. Minotaur Books 2010 404p $25.99

ISBN 978-0-312-62287-9; 0-312-62287-2

LC 2009-47486

Sequel to: The tourist (2009)

"Like le Carré's George Smiley, Weaver is a richly imagined creation with a scarred psyche and a complex back story that elevates him above the status of run-of-the-mill world-weary spook." N Y Times Book Rev

Steinhauer, Olen

The **tourist**. Minotaur Books 2009 408p $24.95

ISBN 978-0-312-36972-9; 0-312-36972-7

LC 2008-33958

"As rich and intriguing as the best of Le Carré, Deighton or Graham Greene, Steinhauer's complex, moving spy novel is perfect for our uncertain, emotionally fraught times." Los Angeles Times Book Rev

Steinke, Rene

Holy skirts. Morrow 2005 360p $24.95

ISBN 0-688-17694-1

LC 2004-52783

National Book Award Finalist: Fiction (2005)

"Steinke's writing is vivid and wonderful, and she can make even a sorrowful story entertaining because she never allows the character's melancholy to infect the prose. The baroness might have been sad, but not tragic. The heroism of her spirit is expressed in a way that transcends the shroud of misfortune." Hudson Rev

Stendhal

The **charterhouse** of Parma; translated from the French by Richard Howard; illustrations by Robert Andrew Parker. Modern Lib. 1999 507p il maps $24.95

ISBN 0-679-60245-3

LC 98-36417

Original French edition, 1839. Variant title: The chartreuse of Parma

"The scene is a little Italian Court, whither the young adventurer Fabrice has found his way, and in dramatic importance plays second fiddle to the fascinating Duchess Sanseverina and her jealous lover, the astute minister, Count Mosca. The book opens with a famous narrative of the battle of Waterloo. It is a novel that set a standard of flawless technique, of the lucid unfolding of character and motive, of accurate comprehension of the inherent disorder of life, that has rarely been approached in dramatic narration." Baker. Guide to the Best Fic

Stendhal

★ The **red** and the black; a chronicle of 1830. a new translation by Burton Raffel; introduction by Diane Johnson; notes by James Madden. Modern Library 2003 xxii, 524p

ISBN 0-679-64284-6

LC 2002-40798

Original French edition, 1830; first United States edition published 1898 by G.H. Richmond

"The author's most celebrated work, it is equally acclaimed for its psychological study of its protagonist—the provincial young romantic Julien Sorel—and as a satiric analysis of the French social order under the Bourbon restoration. Its intensely dramatic plot is purposively romantic in nature, while Stendhal's careful portraiture of Sorel's inner states is the work of a master realist, foreshadowing new developments in the form of the novel." Reader's Ency. 4th edition

Stephenson, Neal

Anathem. William Morrow 2008 937p $29.95

ISBN 978-0-06-147409-5; 0-06-147409-6

LC 2008-13175

"Set on an Earthlike planet called Arbre and narrated by Fraa Erasmus, a young scholar, the story begins within the walls of Saunt Edhar, a 3,400-year-old monastery. A home to cloistered philosophers, scientists and mathematicians, Edhar opens its gates to the 'saecular' world at Apert, a celebration that happens every one, ten, hundred or thousand years. This rite allows visitors to enter and residents to experience a taste of an 'extramuros' society steeped in religion, obsessed with technology and diverted by movies, shopping and legalized gambling. While he does provide a glossary and a timeline, Stephenson isn't interested in quickly explicating Arbre's history and language for the casual reader. . . . Readers who persevere, however, will be rewarded by a slight acceleration in the plot when Erasmus, along with some of his peers and teachers, is expelled from Saunt Edhar and sent on a mission in which the fate of the entire planet hangs in the balance." San Francisco Chron

Stephenson, Neal

Cryptonomicon. Avon Bks. 1999 918p $27.50

ISBN 0-380-97346-4

LC 99-11685

"This fast-paced, genre-transcending novel is full of absorbing action, witty dialogue and well-drawn characters. Amazingly, it is also, even at its tremendous length, only the first volume in what promises to be one of the most extravagant literary creations of the turn of the millennium—and beyond." Publ Wkly

Stephenson, Neal

The **diamond** age; or, Young lady's illustrated primer. Bantam Bks. 1995 455p

ISBN 0-553-09609-5

LC 94-30486

"With breathtaking vision and insight, Stephenson establishes himself as not only a major voice in contemporary sf but also a prophet of technology's future." Booklist

Stephenson, Neal

Reamde. Morrow 2011 1044p $35

ISBN 978-0-06-197796-1; 0-06-197796-9

LC 2011-20573

"Stephenson's novels have always been a little nuts, but thoughtfully nuts. That he is even able to keep this big, careening, recreational-vehicular novel on the road during its hairpin narrative turns says a lot about him as a plot juggler and information wrangler." N Y Times Book Rev

Stephenson, Neal

The **rise** and fall of D.O.D.O. a novel. Neal Stephenson and Nicole Galland. William Morrow 2017 752 p. (hardcover : alk. paper) $35

ISBN 9780062409171; 9780062409157; 9780062409164; 9780062670663

LC 2016043352

In this novel, by Neal Stephenson and Nicole Galland, "Melisande Stokes, an expert in linguistics and languages, accidentally meets military intelligence operator Tristan Lyons. . . . [who] needs Mel to translate some very old documents, which,. . . . prove that magic actually existed and was practiced for centuries. . . . And so the Department of Diachronic Operations--D.O.D.O. --gets cracking on its real mission: to develop a device that can bring magic back. . . ." (Publisher's note)

"A departure for both authors and a pleasing combination of much appeal to fans of speculative fiction." Kirkus

Stephenson, Neal

Seveneves; a novel. Neal Stephenson. HarperCollins 2015 880 p. color illustrations (hardcover) $35

ISBN 0062190377; 9780062190376

In this novel, by Neal Stephenson, "in a feverish race against the inevitable, nations around the globe band together to devise an ambitious plan to ensure the survival of humanity far beyond our atmosphere, in outer space. . . . Five thousand years later, their progeny--seven distinct races now three billion strong--embark on yet another audacious journey into the unknown . . . to an alien world utterly transformed by cataclysm and time: Earth." (Publisher's note)

"Stephenson's remarkable novel is deceptively complex, a disaster story and transhumanism tale that serves as the delivery mechanism for a series of technical and sociological visions. . . . There's a ton to digest, but Stephenson's lucid prose makes it worth the while." Pub Wkly

Stephenson, Neal

★ **Snow** Crash; Neal Stephenson. Bantam Books 2000 470 p. (pbk.) $16

ISBN 9780553380958; 0553380958

LC 9145453

Originally published 1992

In this science fiction novel, by Neal Stephenson, named one of Time magazine's 100 all-time best English-language novels, "Hiro Protagonist delivers pizza for Uncle Enzo's CosoNostra Pizza Inc., but in the Metaverse he's a warrior prince. Plunging headlong into the enigma of a new computer virus that's striking down hackers everywhere, he races along the neon-lit streets on a search-and-destroy mission for the shadowy virtual villain threatening to bring about infocalypse." (Publisher's note)

Sterling, Bruce

Holy fire; a novel. Viking 1996 326p

LC 96-15139

The author "understands that salvation in a posthuman world can only be a process, not a prize. He has written a book in praise of ambiguity that manages to find consoling moments of joy in the most unlikely places." N Y Times Book Rev

Sterling, Bruce

Schismatrix plus. Ace Books 1996 319p pa $16

ISBN 0-441-00370-2

LC 97-106127

This compilation of short stories in the author's Shapers-Mechanists universe includes Schismatrix (1985), which focuses on the life and political struggles of Shaper-trained renegade Abélard Lindsay.

Stern, Steve, 1947-

The **pinch**; A Novel. by Steve Stern. Graywolf Press 2015 368 p. (alk. paper) $26

ISBN 1555977154; 9781555977153

LC 2014960045

In this book, by Steve Stern, "it's the late 1960s. The Pinch, once a thriving Jewish community centered on North Main Street in Memphis, has been reduced to a single tenant. Lenny Sklarew awaits the draft by peddling drugs and shelving books--until he learns he is a character in a book about the rise and fall of this very Pinch." (Publisher's note)

"With a motley cast, including blues musicians, a folklorist, an ogre, levitating Hasidim, and a limping tightrope walker, Stern, an ebullient maestro of words and mayhem, wonder and conscience, orchestrates a cacophonous, whirling, gritty, tender, time-warping saga that encompasses a cavalcade of horror, stubborn love, cosmic slapstick, burlesque humor, and a scattering of miracles." Booklist

Sternbergh, Adam

Shovel ready; a novel. by Adam Sternbergh. Crown Publishers 2014 240 p. $24

ISBN 0385348991; 9780385348997

LC 2013012901

This book, by Adam Sternbergh, is "about a garbage man turned kill-for-hire. Spademan used to be a garbage man . . . before the dirty bomb hit Times Square, before his wife was killed, and before the city became a blown-out shell of its former self. Now he's a hitman. In a near-future New York City split between those who are wealthy enough to 'tap in' to a sophisticated virtual reality, and those who are left to fend for themselves in the ravaged streets, Spademan chose the streets." (Publisher's note)

The author "combines stunning narrative sleight-of-hand with an ability to create flesh-and-blood characters who bring humor and a resilient humanity to their torn-asunder world." Booklist

Sterne, Laurence

★ The **life** and opinions of Tristram Shandy, gentleman and A sentimental journey through France and Italy. Modern Lib. 1995 832p $19.50

ISBN 0-679-60091-4

A combined edition of two titles first published 1759-67 and 1768 respectively

A sentimental journey is a "combination of autobiography, fiction, and observations made by Sterne on his own travels, chronicles the journey through France of a charming and sensitive young man named Yorick and his servant LaFleur. (Though the title mentions Italy, the book ends before they reach that country.)" Merriam-Webster's Ency of Lit

Stevens, Chevy

Always watching; Chevy Stevens. St. Martin's Press 2013 352 p. (hardcover) $25.99

ISBN 0312595697; 9780312595692

LC 2013011251

In this thriller, psychiatrist Nadine Lavoie "has largely managed to repress traumatic memories of the time she spent as a teen in a commune . . . led by charismatic self-styled guru Aaron Quinn. Then she hears his name for the first time in years--from new patient Heather Simeon, a suicidal, terrified young woman who has just left Quinn's River of Life Spiritual Center." Her investigation into Quinn, for Heather's sake, leads to strange events and distressing flashbacks. (Publishers Weekly)

Stevens, Chevy

Never let you go; a novel. Chevy Stevens. St. Martin's Press 2017 406 p. (hardcover) $26.99

ISBN 1250034566; 9781250034571; 9781250034564

LC 2016043109

In this novel, by Chevy Stevens, "eleven years ago, Lindsey Nash escaped . . . with her young daughter and left an abusive relationship. Her ex-husband, Andrew, was sent to jail. . . . Now, Lindsey is older and wiser, with her own business and a teenage daughter. . . . When Andrew is finally released from prison, Lindsey believes she has cut all ties and left the past behind her. But she gets the sense that someone is watching her, tracking her every move." (Publisher's note)

"Stevens's taut writing and chilling depiction of love twisted beyond recognition make this a compelling read from the first page to the last." Pub Wkly

Stevens, Chevy

Still missing. St. Martin's Press 2010 342p $24.99

ISBN 978-0-312-59567-8; 0-312-59567-0

LC 2009-47037

"As Annie's experience as an abductee prompts her to explore hidden corners of her former life and dredge up old secrets, 'Still Missing' risks sounding extremely generic. This, after all, is the template for countless current novels in which a single shattering event leads to shocking revelations about the past. But 'Still Missing' runs deeper than that in the chills it delivers, the surprises it holds and the resilience of its main character." N Y Times (Late N Y Ed)

Stevens, Taylor

The **informationist**; a novel. Taylor Stevens. 1st ed. Shaye Areheart Books 2011 307 p. (paperback) $23.00

ISBN 0307717097; 9780307717092

LC 2009045523

In this novel, by Taylor Stevens, "Vanessa 'Michael' Munroe deals in information. . . . Born . . . in lawless central Africa, Munroe took up with an infamous gunrunner and his mercenary crew when she was just fourteen. . . . A Texas oil billionaire has hired her to find his daughter who vanished in Africa four years ago. . . . Munroe finds herself back in the lands of her childhood, betrayed, cut off from civilization, and left for dead." (Publisher's note)

Other titles in this series are:

The innocent (2011)

The doll (2013)

The catch (2014)

The mask (2015)

Stevenson, Robert Louis

★ The **complete** short stories; edited and introduced by Ian Bell. Holt & Co. 1994 2v set $50

ISBN 0-8050-3203-7

LC 93-79628

Stevenson, Robert Louis

★ The **strange** case of Dr. Jekyll and Mr. Hyde; with an introduction by Joyce Carol Oates. Vintage Books 1991 97p pa $8.95

ISBN 0-679-73476-7

LC 90-50600

First published 1886. Variant title: Dr. Jekyll and Mr. Hyde

"The work is known for its vivid portrayal of the psychopathology of a 'split personality.' The calm, respectable Dr. Jekyll develops a potion that will allow him to separate his good and evil aspects for scientific study. At first Jekyll has no difficulty abandoning the drug induced persona of the repulsive Mr. Hyde, but as the experiments continue the evil personality wrests control from Jekyll and commits murder. Afraid of being discovered, he takes his life; Hyde's body is found, together with a confession written in Jekyll's hand." Merriam-Webster's Ency of Lit

Stewart, Amy

★ **Girl** waits with gun; Amy Stewart. Houghton Mifflin Harcourt 2015 416 p. (hardcover) $27

ISBN 0544409914; 9780544409910

LC 2014045223

In Amy Stewart's novel, "Constance Kopp . . . has been isolated from the world since a family secret sent her and her sisters into hiding fifteen years ago. One day a belligerent and powerful silk factory owner runs down their buggy, and a dispute over damages turns into a war of bricks, bullets, and threats as he unleashes his gang on their family farm. When the sheriff enlists her help in convicting the men, Constance is forced to confront her past and defend her family." (Publisher's note)

"A sheer delight to read and based on actual events, this debut historical mystery packs the unexpected, the unconventional, and a serendipitous humor into every chapter." Booklist

Includes bibliographical references

Other titles in this series are:

Lady cop makes trouble (2016)

Miss Kopp's midnight confessions (2017)

Stewart, George Rippey

Earth abides. Random House 1949 373p

LC 49-11267

"In a near future, a plague devastates humankind, leaving isolated pockets of survivors. . . . One group in the San Francisco Bay area subsists for some time on the bounties of civilization that have remained intact. But the subtler social fabric, formerly held together by the cooperation of large numbers of people, is too much for this handful to sustain. With a mournful backward look at the millions of now-doomed volumes in the University of California library, the protagonist teaches the new children how to make bows and arrows. He lives long enough to see society forming itself anew at the tribal level. He himself is fated to be misremembered as a legendary culture hero. A major work." Anatomy of Wonder. 5th edition

Stewart, Mary

Airs above the ground. Mill, M.S. 1965 286p

Vanessa, a young English veterinarian, "after inadvertently discovering that her husband is not just a traveling salesman but doubles as a secret agent, helps him solve a case involving the Lipizzan horses, a medieval Austrian castle, a circus, a murder, and a narcotics ring." Booklist

Stewart, Mary

★ The **crystal** cave. Morrow 1970 521p

First title in the author's Merlin trilogy. "Presumed to be the offspring of the daughter of the King of Wales and the devil himself, Merlin spends a difficult childhood in the court of the king. He learns much that is mystical under the tutelage of a learned wizard and gains a knowledge of several languages. Escaping to 'Less Britain,' Merlin becomes an important element in the struggle to unite all Britain. The book is rich in descriptions of fifth-century Britain and Brittany, the Druids and their fearful rites, and the superstitions surrounding pagan worship." Shapiro. Fic for Youth. 3d edition

Followed by The hollow hills

Stewart, Mary

★ The **hollow** hills. Morrow 1973 499p

This second novel in the author's Merlin trilogy begins with "Merlin's dismissal by Uther, Arthur's father, who has nonetheless promised to deliver the babe, when born, to Merlin's care. The book traces Merlin's travels to the east, during which time he monitors, through his second sight, Arthur's growth in Brittany and in England. Merlin returns to finish Arthur's education, and the book concludes with Arthur being proclaimed king. With this Merlin epic Mary Stewart has rightly won an honorable place among the modern writers of Arthurian legend." Tymn. Fantasy Lit

Followed by The last enchantment

Stewart, Mary

The **ivy** tree. Mill, M.S. 1961 320p

A Canadian girl visiting England is mistaken for a missing and supposedly dead heiress to an estate "by handsome Connor Winslow, a cousin of the runaway, and now manager of Whitescar. Finally convinced that she is Mary Grey, he and his dour sister Lisa persuade her to masquerade as the long-gone Annabel, promising her the opportunity to claim the considerable legacy left to Annabel by her mother on condition that she surrender her share in Whitescar to Connor upon the death of Uncle Matthew. Reluctantly, Mary enters into the scheme, but soon repents but finds herself too deeply involved." Best Sellers

Stewart, Mary

The **last** enchantment. Morrow 1979 538p

LC 79-12937

This is the concluding volume of a trilogy about "Merlin the Enchanter, set amidst the turbulent events of fifth-century Britain when Arthur became High King. . . . This novel tells of the early years of Arthur's reign: the battles with the Saxons, building of Camelot, marriages with two successive Guiniveres, and birth of Mordred" Libr J

Stewart, Mary

The **moon**-spinners. Mill, M.S. 1963 303p

First published 1962 in the United Kingdom

"Nicola Ferris, an English girl on vacation in Crete, decides to walk the last mile over a rough track to the tiny village where she is expected the next day. She walks into a mystery. She stumbles upon a shepherd's hut guarded by a Greek who threatens to kill her if she makes a sound. Inside the hut, she finds a young Englishman seriously wounded and much upset by her intrusion. In her determination to help him, she is drawn into his dangerous situation." Horn Book

Stewart, Mary

Nine coaches waiting. Mill, M.S. 1959 342p

First published 1958 in the United Kingdom

"Intelligent, spirited Linda Martin comes to Valmy, an isolated château in the French Alps, as English governess to nine-year-old Philippe, the orphaned Comte de Valmy. After several frightening 'accidents' Linda discovers that her pupil is the object of a murder plot which apparently involves his crippled uncle and the latter's handsome son Raoul, with whom she is in love." Booklist

Stewart, Mary

Touch not the cat. Morrow 1976 336p

A "tale set on a family estate in England. Garbled words of warning uttered by her dying father lead Bryony Ashley into danger as she investigates the intricacies of past and present intrigues within the Ashley family. Bryony's inherited extrasensory abilities add to the suspenseful story." Booklist

Stewart, Mary

Wildfire at midnight. Appleton-Century-Crofts 1956 214p

Gianetta Brooke comes to the Isle of Skye to forget the husband she has painfully divorced and finds herself in danger as a series of murders takes place

Stibbe, Nina

Man at the helm; a novel. Nina Stibbe. Little, Brown & Co. 2015 320 p. (hardback) $25

ISBN 0316286672; 9780316286671

LC 2014020467

In this novel by Nina Stibbe "Lizzie Vogel moves with her siblings and newly single mother to a tiny village in the English countryside, where the new neighbors are horrified by their unorthodox ways and fatherless household. Lizzie's theatrical mother only invites more gossip by spending her days drinking whiskey, popping pills, and writing plays. The one way to fit in, the children decide, will be to find themselves a new man at the helm." (Publisher's note)

"Stibbe gives her and her siblings a sense of self well beyond their years and the dialogue to accompany it. This is an impressive first novel, a combination of P. G. Wodehouse pacing and the eccentricity of Gerald Durrell's My Family and Other Animals (1956). An extraordinarily well-written, deeply satisfying read about an unusual, highly entertaining group of people." Booklist

Another title in this series is:
Paradise Lodge (2016)

Stirling, S. M.

The **city** who fought; [by] Anne McCaffrey, S.M. Stirling. Baen Pub. Enterprises 1993 435p

ISBN 0-671-72166-6

LC 93-2651

Previous titles in this series published in paperback are: The ship who sang (1969); Partnership (1992); and The ship who searched (1992)

"Within the fabric of McCaffrey's universe, she and Stirling merge seamlessly, sporting wit, action galore, superior characterization, and plausible hardware." Booklist

Followed by The ship who won (1994)

Stirling, S. M.

Dies the fire; S.M. Stirling. New American Library 2004 483p (hbk.) o.p.; (pbk.) $7.99

ISBN 0451459792; 9780451460417

LC 2004004363

This book takes place after "a mysterious event that caused electricity, internal combustion engines, and gunpowder to fail, [and takes place in] the Pacific Northwest [which] furnishes enough land to support subsistence existence in a future that belongs . . . to people who know older ways. Musician Juniper takes refuge on her family's land with a growing group of friends that becomes 'Clan MacKenzie.' Reenactors know useful things, . . . such as how to build log houses and craft bows for hunting. Meanwhile, Mike Havel, a pilot who was flying when the Change happened, and his passengers, having survived . . . [and t]hanks to a former Society for Creative Anachronism . . . fencer, and after hard work and the accident that gives their group the name 'Bearkillers,' they have the knowledge to sell their protective services." (Booklist)

Stockett, Kathryn

★ The **help**. Amy Einhorn Books 2009 451p $24.95

ISBN 0-399-15534-1; 978-0-399-15534-5

LC 2008-30185

Twenty-two-year-old Skeeter has just returned home after graduating from Ole Miss. She may have a degree, but it is 1962, Mississippi, and her mother will not be happy till Skeeter has a ring on her finger. Skeeter would normally find solace with her beloved maid Constantine, the woman who raised her, but Constantine has disappeared and no one will tell Skeeter where she has gone.

Stoker, Bram

★ **Dracula**; edited with an introduction and notes by Maurice Hindle; preface by Christopher Frayling. Penguin Books 2003 xlvii, 454p pa $11

ISBN 0-14-143984-X

LC 2003-269578

First published 1897

"Count Dracula, an 'undead' villain from Transylvania, uses his supernatural powers to lure and prey upon innocent victims from whom he gains the blood on which he lives. The novel is written chiefly in the form of journals kept by the principal characters—Jonathan Harker, who contacts the vampire in his Transylvanian castle; Harker's fiancee (later his wife), Mina, adored by the Count; the well-meaning Dr. Seward; and Lucy Westenra, a victim who herself becomes a vampire. The doctor and friends destroy Dracula in the end, but only after they drive a stake through Lucy's heart to save her soul." Merriam-Webster's Ency of Lit

Stoker, Bram

The **new** annotated Dracula; Bram Stoker; edited with a foreword and notes by Leslie S. Klinger; additional research by Janet Byrne; introduction by Neil Gaiman. W W Norton & Co Inc 2008 613 p. illustrations (some color) (hardcover) $39.95

ISBN 9780393064506; 0393064506

LC 2008025919

In this book, author Leslie S. Klinger, "accepts [Bram] Stoker's contention that the Dracula tale is based on historical fact. Traveling through two hundred years of popular culture and myth as well as graveyards and the wilds of Transylvania, Klinger's notes illuminate every aspect of this haunting narrative. . . . Klinger investigates the many subtexts of the original narrative." (Publisher's note)

"An introduction by Neil Gaiman, numerous illustrations, essays on topics ranging from Dracula in the movies to the academic response, and much more enhance the package." Pub Wkly

Includes bibliographical references.

Stone, Irving

★ The **agony** and the ecstasy. New American Library 2004 776p pa $16

ISBN 0-451-21323-8

First published 1961 by Doubleday

"Stone's Michelangelo is an idealized version, purged not only of ambisexuality, but of the egotism, faultfinding, harsh irony, and ill temper that we know were characteristic of Michelangelo." Saturday Rev

Stone, Irving

Lust for life; a novel of Vincent van Gogh. illustrated with 150 reproductions of Vincent van Gogh's pictures arranged by J. B. Neumann. Twentieth anniversary ed.; Doubleday 1954 507p il

First published 1934 by Longmans, Green and Co.

"Vincent Van Gogh lived a turbulent life but throughout it he was loved and supported by his brother, Theo. Sons of a Dutch Protestant minister, Vincent and Theo were raised rather strictly, but Vincent's love of color and movement led him into the life of an artist. He always felt challenged to fill a blank canvas with light and color. Vincent's search for meaning and fulfillment in his life took him over Europe but only toward the end of his life did he meet other artists who shared his artistic views, and it was not until after his death that his work began to be appreciated." Shapiro. Fic for Youth. 3d edition

Stone, Michel

Border child; Michel Stone. Nan A. Talese/Doubleday 2017 254 p. (hardcover : alk. paper) $26.95

ISBN 9780385541640; 9780385541657

LC 2016012857

In this novel, by Michel Stone, "for Héctor and Lilia, pursuit of the American Dream became every parent's worst fear when their infant daughter [Alejandra] vanished as they crossed from Mexico to the United States. . . . Now, four years later, . . . back in . . . Oaxaca, the couple enjoys a semblance of normal life. . . . Then they receive an unexpected tip that might lead them to Alejandra, and both agree they must seize this chance, whatever the cost." (Publisher's note)

"A gripping and politically savvy look at the human impact of current immigration policy and an honest examination of the perils facing desperate immigrants as they travel north." Kirkus

Stone, Nick ✓

The **king** of swords; a novel. Harper 2008 559p $24.95; pa $14.99

ISBN 978-0-06-089731-4; 0-06-089731-7; 978-0-06-089732-1 pa; 0-06-089732-5 pa

LC 2008-33704

"The Miami of the early 1980s has become an almost mythical place, an era steeped in the lore of Miami Vice and Scarface and seen as the epicenter for drugs and the glamour of a new South Beach. Nick Stone captures that reality in his gritty, brutal and expertly plotted The King of Swords, offering an authentic vision of South Florida along with plenty of hardboiled action." Miami Herald

Stone, Nick

The **Verdict**; A Novel. Nick Stone. Pegasus Crime 2015 499 p. (ebook) $50; $25.95

ISBN 9781605989242; 1605989231; 9781605989235

LC 2015298646

In this crime novel, by Nick Stone, "Terry Flynt is a struggling legal clerk, desperately trying to get promoted. And then he is given the biggest opportunity of his career: to help defend a millionaire accused of murdering a woman in his hotel suite. The only problem is that the accused man, Vernon James, turns out to be not only someone he knows, but someone he loathes." (Publisher's note)

"The suspense never lets up in this terrific courtroom drama. Fans of John Grisham will love it. It's definitely movie material." Kirkus

Stone, Robert

★ **Bay** of souls. Houghton Mifflin 2003 249p $25

ISBN 0-395-96349-4

LC 2002-192171

"Unusual (for Stone) in is brevity, this is a highly concentrated work, probably the least violent yet most unnerving of his novels. And the philosophical conflict dramatized in it ends surprisingly, in a way that provokes new questions about what Stone is up to in his writing." N Y Times Book Rev

Stone, Robert

Damascus Gate. Houghton Mifflin 1998 500p $26

ISBN 0-395-66569-8

LC 97-49615

Stone "is so comprehending of Israel's convoluted workings and its bifurcated culture—where the Biblical fervor of Jerusalem coexists with the disco fever of Tel Aviv—that he makes other writers on the subject seem like the breeziest of literary tourists." New Yorker

Stone, Robert

★ **Dog** soldiers; a novel. Houghton Mifflin 1974 342p

"Part melodrama, part morality play, 'Dog Soldiers' offers a vision of a predatory, insensate society from which all moral authority has fled. It is a world in which innocence or vestigial remnants of decent behavior prove fatal to their owners; Hicks . . . is nearly violent enough to survive, but he is done in by his own loyalty to Marge. All of this corruption and vulnerability, this savagery and stoned withdrawal, this combination of passion and cynicism works convincingly, for Stone is a very good storyteller indeed." Newsweek

Stone, Robert

Fun with problems; stories. Houghton Mifflin Harcourt 2010 195p $24

ISBN 978-0-618-38625-3; 0-618-38625-4

LC 2009-13748

"The stories in Fun With Problems, Stone's 11th book of fiction and his second collection of short stories, are as spare and razor-edged as any of Stone's early work, and for the uninitiated reader, every bit as unnerving. Stone's title comes from a 1999 rehab video: 'Overcoming difficulties can present spiritual opportunities. It is actually possible to have fun with problems.' Used as an epigraph, it defines Stone's temperament and his approach: in its derived meaning earned from hard experience, in its balance of elements sacred and profane, and in its sly, deadpan humor." Dallas Morning News

Stone, Robert

★ **Outerbridge** Reach. Ticknor & Fields 1992 409p

LC 91-34875

"Robert Stone's blend of heroic aspiration and mordantly deflationary irony results in something like tragicomedy. . . . But whatever you call it, 'Outerbridge Reach' seems to me a triumph—a beautifully and painstakingly composed piece of literary art." N Y Times Book Rev

Stonich, Sarah

Vacationland; a novel. Sarah Stonich. University of Minnesota Press 2013 288 p. (pb : acid-free paper) $16.95

ISBN 0816687668; 9780816687664

LC 2012048343

In this novel by Sarah Stonich "on a lake in northernmost Minnesota, you might find Naledi Lodge—only two cabins still standing. And there you might meet Meg, or the ghost of the girl she was, growing up under her grandfather's care in a world apart and a lifetime ago. Now an artist, Meg paints images 'reflected across the mirrors of memory and water,' much as the linked stories of 'Vacationland.' Those whose paths have crossed at Naledi inhabit 'Vacationland.' (Publisher's note)

Stories; all-new tales. edited by Neil Gaiman and Al Sarrantonio. William Morrow 2010 428p $27.99

ISBN 978-0-06-123092-9; 0-06-123092-8

LC 2010-20363

"An ambitious anthology with a pleasing mix of modes and moods. 'Stories' has a little something for everyone who appreciates the possibilities of short fiction." San Francisco Chron

Stott, Rebecca

The **coral** thief; a novel. Spiegel & Grau 2009 286p il map $25

ISBN 978-0-385-53146-7; 0-385-53146-X

LC 2009-12846

"Aside from her graceful writing style and believable characters, Stott also delights with her grasp of history. Romantic, full of twists and turns and glimpses of the past, The Coral Thief is an unlikely page-turner." BookPage

Stott, Rebecca

Ghostwalk; a novel. Spiegel & Grau 2007 304p il $24.95

ISBN 978-0-385-52106-2; 0-385-52106-5

LC 2006-22326

"Stott brings a nervy intelligence to her work, skillfully linking the war on terror, quantum physics, alchemy, serial murder, ghosts, and thwarted romance." Miami Herald

Stout, Rex

Black orchids; &, the silent speaker; introduction to Black orchids by Lawrence Block; introduction to The silent speaker by Walter Mosley. Bantam Books 2009 various paging il pa $16

ISBN 978-0-553-38655-4; 0-553-38655-7

LC 2009-464755

Black orchids first published 1942 by Farrar & Reinhart; The silent speaker first published 1946 by Viking Press

Contains two titles in the author's Nero Wolfe series. In The black orchids, Wolfe goes to a flower show to see a rare black orchid; "unfortunately, the much-anticipated event is soon overshadowed by a murder as daring as it is sudden. . . . [In The silent speaker,] a government power broker scheduled to speak before an influential group of millionaires turns up dead. . . . Soon a second victim is discovered, a missing stenographer's tape causes a panic, and a dead man speaks, after a fashion." Publisher's note

Stout, Rex

The **doorbell** rang; a Nero Wolfe novel. Viking 1965 186p

"Nero Wolfe tangles with the FBI, on behalf of a wealthy woman who has sent as gifts to prominent people 10,000 copies of Fred Cook's book criticizing the FBI. . . . She is being shadowed and spied on by the FBI. To the surprise of Wolfe and of Archie Goodwin, they have the good will of the New York Police Department. The New York Police believe that FBI agents have murdered a magazine writer who was doing an article on the FBI. The police are powerless to prove anything or to prosecute. Clever and ingenious, this ranks among the best Rex Stout mysteries." Publ Wkly

Stout, Rex

Fer-de-lance; &, The league of frightened men; introduction to Fer-de-lance by Loren D. Estleman; introduction to The league of frightened men by Robert Goldsborough. Bantam Books 2008 285, 302p il pa $16

ISBN 978-0-553-38545-8; 0-553-38545-3

LC 2008-299738

Combined edition of two titles first published 1934 and 1935 respectively by Farrar & Rinehart

Contains two titles in the author's Nero Wolfe series. "The fer-de-lance is among the most deadly snakes known to man. When someone makes a present of one to Nero Wolfe, his partner, Archie Goodwin, suspects it means Wolfe is getting close to solving the devilishly clever murders of an immigrant and a college president. . . . [In The league of frightened men,] Paul Chapin's Harvard cronies never forgave themselves for the hazing prank that left their friend a cripple. Yet they believed that Paul himself had forgiven them—until a class reunion ends in death and a series of poems promising more of the same. Now this league of frightened men is desperate for Nero Wolfe's help." Publisher's note

Stout, Rex

★ **Gambit**; a Nero Wolfe novel. Viking 1962 188p

"There is more detection in this story than in any other of the mulling-and-quizzing sort; here we really see N.W.'s thoughts whirring. Moreover, Archie is in excellent form, and although a chess tournament is a feature, the game itself is not. The great scene is that in which Nero reads and burns the pages of Webster's Dictionary, Third Edition." Barzun. Cat of Crime. Rev and enl edition

Stout, Rex

The **rubber** band & The red box; introduction to The red box by Carolyn G. Hart. Bantam Books 2009 189, 257p pa $15

ISBN 978-0-553-38603-5; 0-553-38603-4

LC 2009-455172

Combined edition of two titles first published 1936 and 1937 respectively by Farrar & Rinehart

Contains two titles in the author's Nero Wolfe series. In The rubber band, "a forty-year-old pact, a five-thousand-mile search, and a million-dollar murder are all linked to an international scandal that could rebound on the great detective and his partner, Archie, with fatal abruptness. . . . [In The red box] a beautiful woman is poisoned after indulging in a box of candy." Publisher's note

Stout, Rex

Some buried Caesar & The golden spiders; introduction to Some Buried Caesar by Diane Mott Davidson; introduction to the Golden Spiders by Linda Barnes. Bantam Books 2008 206p pa $15

ISBN 978-0-553-38567-0

LC 2008-301309

Some buried Caesar first published 1939 by Farrar & Rinehart; The golden spiders first published 1953 by Viking Press

Contains two titles in the author's Nero Wolfe series. In Some buried Caesar "a prize bull destined for the barbecue is found pawing the corpse of a late restaurateur. Wolfe is certain that Hickory Caesar Grindon, the soon-to-be-beefsteak bull, isn't the murderer. But who among a veritable stampede of suspects—including a young woman who's caught Archie's eye—turned the tables on Hickory's would-be butcher? . . . [In The golden spiders] a twelve-year-old boy shows up at Wolfe's brownstone with an incredible story. Soon the great detective finds himself hired for the grand sum of $4.30 and faced with the question of why the last two people to hire him were murdered. To keep it from becoming three, Wolfe must discover the unlikely connection between a gray Cadillac, a mysterious woman, and a pair of earrings shaped like spiders dipped in gold." Publisher's note

Stout, Rex

Too many cooks; & champagne for one; introduction to Champagne for One by Lena Horne. Bantam Dell/Random House, Inc. 2009 179, 205p pa $15

ISBN 978-0-553-38629-5; 0-553-38629-8

LC 2009-464724

Too many cooks first published 1938 by Farrar & Rinehart; Champagne for one first published 1958 by Viking Press

Contains two titles in the author's Nero Wolfe series. Too many cooks involves a poisoning at a gathering of great chefs in which Wolfe is a guest of honor. In Champagne for one, "Faith Usher talked about taking her own life and even kept cyanide in her purse. So when she died from a lethal champagne cocktail in the middle of a high society dinner party, everyone called it suicide—including the police. But Nero Wolfe isn't convinced—and neither is Archie. Especially when Wolfe is warned by four men against taking the case." Publisher's note

Stowe, Harriet Beecher

★ **Uncle** Tom's cabin; with an introduction by Alfred Kazin. Knopf 1995 xxix, 494p $20

ISBN 0-679-44365-7

"The book relates the trials, suffering, and human dignity of Uncle Tom, an old slave. Cruelly treated by a Yankee plantation owner, Simon Legree, Tom dies as the result of a beating. Uncle Tom is devoted to Little Eva, the daughter of his white owner, Augustine St. Clare. Other important characters are the mulatto girl Eliza; the impish black child Topsy; Miss Ophelia St. Clare, a New England spinster; and Marks, the slave catcher. The setting is Kentucky and Louisiana." Reader's Ency. 4th edition

Straight, Susan

Between heaven and here; Susan Straight. McSweeney's Books 2012 234 p. $24

ISBN 1936365758; 9781936365753

In this novel by Susan Straight "Glorette Picard is dead, and across the canal, out in the orange groves, they'll gather shovels and pickaxes and soak the dirt until they can lay her coffin down. As the residents of [Rio Seco, California] prepare to bury their own, it becomes clear that Glorette's life and death are deeply entangled with the dark history of the city and the untouchable beauty that, finally, killed her." (Publisher's note)

Straight, Susan

The **gettin** place. Hyperion 1996 488p $22.95

ISBN 0-7868-6086-3

LC 95-50065

"Against the backdrop of the under-acknowledged race riots of 1920s Tulsa and the contrastingly media-saturated 1992 L.A. riots, Straight realizes the chillingly natural, almost blithe cynicism and violence of teenagers, the profound weight of hard history on the old, and the bewilderment of those in-between. A lyrical and unflinching stunner." Libr J

Straight, Susan

Highwire moon; a novel. Houghton Mifflin 2001 306p map $24

ISBN 0-618-05614-9

LC 00-53878

National Book Award Finalist: Fiction (2001)

"Susan Straight's Rio Seco is a microcosm of suspicious, segregated America, a place where racism often boils down to fear, ignorance and willful obliviousness." N Y Times Book Rev

Straight, Susan

A **million** nightingales. Pantheon Books 2006 340p $24.95

ISBN 0-375-42364-8

LC 2005-50052

"Straight's book is a deep consideration of the servitude all women experienced then—and, in some ways and some places, continue to experience even now. . . . But her novel is, besides, a powerful and moving story, written in language so beautiful you can almost believe the words themselves are capable of salving history's wounds." N Y Times Book Rev

Straight, Susan

Take one candle light a room; Susan Straight. Pantheon Books 2010 320 p. $25.95

ISBN 0307379140; 9780307379146

LC 2010012683

This novel, by Susan Straight, follows the charater of "Fantine Antoine. . . . When she returns to mark the fifth anniversary of the murder of her . . . friend, Glorette, she finds herself pulled into the tumultuous life of Glorette's twenty-two-year-old son . . . Victor. After getting involved in a shooting, Victor has fled to New Orleans. Together with her father, Fantine follows Victor, determined to help him avoid the criminal future that he suddenly seems destined for." (Publisher's note)

Straub, Emma, 1980-

★ **Modern** lovers; Emma Straub. Riverhead Books 2016 368 p. (hardcover) $26

ISBN 9781594634673; 159463467X

LC 2016002756

In this novel, by Emma Staub, "friends and former college bandmates Elizabeth and Andrew and Zoe have watched one another marry, buy real estate, and start businesses and families, all while trying to hold on to the identities of their youth. . . . Now nearing fifty, they all live within shouting distance in the same neighborhood. . . . But the summer that their children reach maturity (and start sleeping together), the fabric of the adult lives suddenly begins to unravel." (Publisher's note)

"Straub's handful of characters, followed with alternating close third-person narratives, are honestly and devilishly observed with clarity and kindness." Booklist

Straub, Emma, 1980-

The **vacationers**; Emma Straub. Riverhead Books 2014 304 p. hc $26.95

ISBN 9781594631573; 1594631573

LC 2013037110

Written by Emma Straub, this is a "novel about the secrets, joys, and jealousies that rise to the surface over the course of an American family's two-week stay in Mallorca. . . . This is a story of the sides of ourselves that we choose to show and those we try to conceal, of the ways we tear each other down and build each other up again, and the bonds that ultimately hold us together." (Publisher's note)

"Spongy and dear, sharply observed and funny, Straub's domestic-drama-goes-abroad is a delightful study of the complexities of family and love, and the many distractions from both." Booklist

Straub, Peter

★ A **dark** matter; a novel. Doubleday 2010 397p $26.95

ISBN 978-0-385-51638-9; 0-385-51638-X

LC 2009-20028

A "multiple-perspective take on a murky collegiate misadventure in 1966. Spencer Mallon, campus-flitting intellectual and seducer of coeds, is compared in the early pages to a host of flattering figures: a god, a hero, a guru. What Mallon feels most like to us, though, is a Manson-like charmer who lures several young people out to a field, where one of them dies. How, though? Straub expertly weaves a Rashômon-crazy quilt of varying and sometimes conflicting recollections of the incident, left purposefully vague, as we shuttle through the intervening years—unkind ones in which his characters are struck by blindness, become criminals and, in an especially sad case, go insane. A slight slackness in the story's middle game will have some readers exhorting, 'Get over it already!'—whatever it is. But ambitiously, the author mounts his referendum on a wild, unpredictable moment of the 1960s, saluting the era's competing urges of decadence and justice." Time Out N Y

Straub, Peter

★ **Ghost** story. Coward, McCann & Geoghegan 1979 483p

ISBN 0-698-10959-7

LC 78-27120

"With considerable technical skill, Peter Straub has constructed an extravagant entertainment which, though flawed, achieves in its second half some awesome effects." Newsweek

Straub, Peter

In the night room; a novel. Random House 2004 330p $21.95

ISBN 1-400-06252-7

LC 2004-51425

In this sequel to Lost boy lost girl, horror novelist Tim Underhill receives "an e-mail sent to him by the spirit of an ancient Byzantine, who explains that the daughter of one of the serial killers in Lost boy lost girl wasn't murdered by her father, as Tim supposed; that the exceedingly strange fan who cornered Tim in his local breakfast hangout is an embodiment of the wronged murderer's spirit; and that, yes, that was an angel Tim saw fly away over Manhattan while he walked home. Meanwhile, over in New Jersey, YA novelist Willy Patrick is about to marry mysterious Mitchell Faber when she comes upon evidence that he is responsible for her husband's violent, gangland-like killing. She flees Faber's estate, pursued by his minions, to New York and into a reading-signing appearance by Tim. There is a catch to this, for Willy's plot is that of the new novel Tim has been writing; that is, a character Tim created has emerged in his reality. As Tim and Willy repair to their hometown, Millhaven, Illinois, to slake the murderer's spirit, his real and her fictive worlds converge toward an ending that promises, like that of Lost boy lost girl, the transcendent redemption of violated souls. Inventive and moving." Booklist

Straub, Peter

Lost boy lost girl; a novel. Farrar, Straus & Giroux 2003 281p $24.95

ISBN 1-4000-6092-3

LC 2003-046689

"Inquisitive and open-minded as Tim is, he makes it easy for Mr. Straub to move from conventionally hair-raising effects . . . to the more happening teenage world of cyberscares. Strongly visual without resorting to secondhand cinematic imagery, the book is equally well equipped to play both kinds of tricks." N Y Times (Late N Y Ed)

Straub, Peter

Mr. X; a novel. Random House 1999 482p $25.95

ISBN 0-679-40138-5

LC 98-47688

"From childhood, Ned Dunstan has experienced precognitive visions. . . . Summoned home to Edgerton, Ill., by a premonition of his mother's death on the eve of his 35th birthday, Ned finds himself implicated in a tangle of felonies and murders, all of which point to someone strenuously manipulating events to frame him. Digging into local history, he finds reason to believe that the mysterious father he never knew, or possibly a malignant doppelgänger, are pulling the strings. . . . {Straub's} evocative prose, a seamless splice of clipped hard-boiled banter and poetic reflection, contributes to the thick atmosphere of apprehension that makes this one of the most invigorating horror reads of the year." Publ Wkly

Straub, Peter

★ **Mystery**. Dutton 1990 548p il

LC 89-7734

Second title in the author's Blue rose trilogy. "When a traffic accident nearly ends his young life, Tom Pasmore experiences all the usual near-death sensations: warm lights at the end of tunnels and friendly faces beckoning him onward. But by cheating death, his life is forever changed. Tom becomes obsessed with murder, with detection, and especially with a recent killing on Mill Walk, the fictional Caribbean island where his family lives. Tom's sleuthing mania is fed by an eccentric neighbor, Lamont von Heilitz, a famous retired detective. . . . The remarkable depth of characterization make apparent the fact that Mystery is meant to be much more than a conventional shocker. For the most part, Straub delivers the goods." Booklist

Strayed, Cheryl

Torch. Houghton 2005 322p $24

ISBN 0-618-47217-7

LC 2005-10333

"A beautiful book, expansive in its treatment of tragedy and grief, but equally attentive to all of the most telling details. The language is lovely, offering delicious, compelling imagery without being heavy-handed." Providence Journal

Strieber, Whitley

The **hunger**. Pocket Books 1981 357p pa $24.95

ISBN 978-1-416-58374-5

First published 1981 by Morrow

Miriam Blaylock, an ancient vampire, sets out to find a new human companion when her current one begins to age rapidly.

Followed by The last vampire

Stroby, Wallace

Cold shot to the heart. Minotaur Books 2011 289p $24.99

ISBN 978-0-312-56025-6; 0-312-56025-7

LC 2010-37538

"Crissa Stone is a robber for hire, now employed by a mobster who wants her and two cronies to break into a Fort Lauderdale hotel and bust up a card game that has a million bucks on the table. The three miscreants decide to rappel down the side of the building. The scenes of preparation and execution are chilling. But the heist goes wrong. A man is killed because, we're told, one of the gunmen spooked. But maybe not. Could the caper be disguised murder for hire? Why else does Crissa suddenly find herself pursued by a reptile called Eddie the Saint? Their clashes are cinematic: hurtling cars and bloodstained snow. Stroby has been called a nascent Crumley or Pelecanos. He shares their sense that cynicism is the last pose left to a romantic." Booklist

Stroby, Wallace

Shoot the woman first; Wallace Stroby. Minotaur Books 2013 288 p. (Crissa Stone) (hardback) $25.99

ISBN 1250000386; 9781250000385

LC 2013029818

This book, by Wallace Stroby, centers on "professional thief Crissa Stone. . . . When [a] split goes awry in a blaze of gunfire, Crissa finds herself on the run with a duffel bag of stolen cash. . . . In pursuit are the drug kingpin's lethal lieutenants and a former Detroit cop with his own deadly agenda. They think the money's there for the taking, for whoever finds her first. But Crissa doesn't plan to give it up without a fight." (Publisher's note)

"Stroby transports readers through his spare, believable dialog—making the story race by like a runaway train." LJ

Stross, Charles

Accelerando. Ace Books 2005 390p

ISBN 0-441-01284-1

LC 2005-42815

"Expanded from several stories originally published in Asimov's Science Fiction, . . . [this] novel follows several generations of the Macx family through the rapidly transforming, Internet-enabled global economy of the early twenty-first century to the human and transhuman populated worlds of the outer solar system a half century later. . . . Stross has his thumb squarely on the pulse of technology's leading edge and exults in extrapolating mere glimmers of ideas out to their mind-bending limits." Booklist

Stross, Charles

Empire games; Charles Stross. Tom Doherty Associates 2017 331 p. (Empire games) (hardcover : alk. paper) $25.99

ISBN 9780765337566; 9781466835160

LC 2016043537

In this book in the Empire Games series, by Charles Stross, "the year is 2020. It's seventeen years since the Revolution overthrew the last king of the New British Empire, and the newly-reconstituted North American Commonwealth is developing rapidly. . . . But Miriam Burgeson, commissioner in charge of the shadowy Ministry of Intertemporal Research and Intelligence--the paratime espionage agency tasked with catalyzing the Commonwealth's great leap forward--has a problem." (Publisher's note)

"Stross handles the story well enough that you don't need to have read the previous six books. Of course, those who have will be overjoyed to renew their acquaintance with Miriam and her associates . . ." Booklist

Stross, Charles

Glasshouse. Ace Books 2006 335p $24.95

ISBN 0-44101-403-8

LC 2006-4358

The novel "gives in a little to convention near the end, as the story inevitably progresses toward a rebellion plot, but even here, Stross keeps the sweet little surprises coming. . . . Mostly, Glasshouse is an incisive look into societies that allow themselves, for whatever reason, to be guided not by cooperation and the greater good but by fear and mistrust." SF Reviews.net

Stross, Charles

The **Jennifer** morgue; plus bonus story Pimpf and afterword: The golden age of spying. Golden Gryphon Press 2006 313p $25.95

ISBN 1-930846-45-2

LC 2006-11154

"Bob Howard is a computer übergeek employed by the Laundry, a secret British agency assigned to clean up incursions from other realities caused by the inadvertent manipulation of complex mathematical equations: in other words, magic. In 1975, the CIA used Howard Hughes's Glomar Explorer in a bungled attempt to raise a sunken Soviet submarine in order to access the Jennifer Morgue, an occult device that allows communication with the dead. Now a ruthless billionaire intends to try again, even if by doing so he awakens the Great Old Ones, who thwarted the earlier expedition. It's up to Bob and a collection of British eccentrics even Monty Python would consider odd to stop the bad guy and save the world, while getting receipts for all expenditures or else face the most dreaded menace of all: the Laundry's own auditors. Stross has a marvelous time making eldritch horror appear commonplace in the face of bureaucracy." Publ Wkly

Stross, Charles

Neptune's brood; by Charles Stross. Ace Hardcover 2013 336 p. (hardcover) $25.95

ISBN 9780425256770; 0425256774

LC 2013002384

In this novel by Charles Stross "the year is AD 7000. The human species is extinct—for the fourth time—due to its fragile nature. Krina Alizond-114 is metahuman, descended from the robots that once served humanity. She's on a journey to the water-world of Shin-Tethys to find her sister Ana. But her trip is interrupted when pirates capture her ship. Their leader, the enigmatic Count Rudi, suspects that there's more to Krina's search than meets the eye." (Publisher's note)

Stross, Charles

Saturn's children; a space opera. Ace Books 2008 323p $24.95

ISBN 978-0-441-01594-8

LC 2008-8228

"Stross tosses out ideas aplenty. Since his robots know they were created by humans, for example, they consider evolution heretical. It isn't a relaxing bedtime read, but it is the sort of mind-expanding adventure that made 'hard' science fiction famous." New Scientist

Strout, Elizabeth

Amy and Isabelle. Random House 1999 303p $22.95

ISBN 0-375-50134-7

LC 98-19995

"As the cacophony of disaster grows ever louder in contemporary culture, Strout has written an excellent novel about enduring the banalities of ordinary life." New Yorker

Strout, Elizabeth

★ **Anything** is possible; a novel. Elizabeth Strout. Random House Inc. 2017 254 p. $27

ISBN 0812989406; 9780812989403

LC 2016020620

This book, by Elizabeth Strout, "explores the whole range of human emotion through the intimate dramas of people struggling to understand themselves and others. . . . Reverberating with the deep bonds of family, and the hope that comes with reconciliation, 'Anything Is Possible' again underscores . . . Strout's place as one of America's most respected and cherished authors." (Publisher's note)

"A radiant collection of stories linked to Strout's previous novel, My Name Is Lucy Barton...but moving beyond its first-person narration to limn small-town life from multiple perspectives." Kirkus.

Strout, Elizabeth

★ The **Burgess** boys; a novel. Elizabeth Strout. 1st ed. Random House Inc. 2013 336 p. (ebook) $78.00; (hardcover) $26.00

ISBN 1400067685; 9780812984613; 9781400067688

LC 2012035132

In this book, "haunted by the freak accident that killed their father when they were children, Jim and Bob Burgess escaped from their Maine hometown . . . as soon as they possibly could. . . . Their long-standing dynamic is upended when their sister, Susan . . . urgently calls them home. Her lonely teenage son, Zach, has gotten himself into a world of trouble, and Susan desperately needs their help. And so the Burgess brothers return to the landscape of their childhood." (Publisher's note)

Strout, Elizabeth

My name is Lucy Barton; a novel. Elizabeth Strout. Random House 2016 208 p. $26

ISBN 9780812989076; 9781400067695

LC 2015018930

"Lucy Barton is recovering slowly from what should have been a simple operation. Her mother, to whom she hasn't spoken for many years, comes to see her. Gentle gossip about people from Lucy's childhood in Amgash, Illinois, seems to reconnect them, but just below the surface lie the tension and longing that have informed every aspect of Lucy's life: her escape from her troubled family, her desire to become a writer, her marriage, her love for her two daughters." (Publisher's note)

"In a compact novel brimming with insight and emotion, Strout relays with great tenderness and sadness the way family relationships can both make and break us." Booklist

Strout, Elizabeth

Olive Kitteridge. Random House 2008 270p $25

ISBN 1-4000-6208-X; 978-1-4000-6208-9

LC 2007-16999

Olive Kitteridge, a retired schoolteacher, deplores the changes in her little town [in Maine] and in the world at large, but she doesn't always recognize the changes in those around her. (Publisher's note)

These linked stories introduce the inhabitants of Crosby, Maine, where the pull of domestic tragedy is stronger for rarely being spoken of. Angela doesn't mention the bruises shes noticed on her mother's arm at the nursing home; Marlene learns of her husband's infidelity only after his funeral; Kevin plans to shoot himself, like his mother before him. And there in every story, like a tree thats been blackened by lightning but still leafs in the spring, stands Olive Kitteridge, a retired math teacher who loves her tulips, bullies her husband, and barks at anyone foolish enough to irritate her. You loathe this woman at the book's beginning; you long for her at its finish. Strout makes us experience not only the terrors of change but also the terrifying hope that change can bring: she plunges us into these churning waters and we come up gasping for air. New Yorker

Strugatsky, Arkady Natanovich, 1925-1991

Roadside picnic; Arkady and Boris Strugatsky; translated by Olena Bormashenko. Chicago Review Press 2012 ix, 209 pagesp

ISBN 1613743416; 9781613743416

LC 2012001294

This book is a re-release of a 1972 Russian science fiction novel by Arkady Natanovich Strugatsky and Boris Natanovich Strugatsky. "Red Schuhart is a stalker, one of those young rebels who are compelled, in spite of extreme danger, to venture illegally into the Zone to collect the mysterious artifacts that the alien visitors left scattered around. His life is dominated by the place and the thriving black market in the alien products." (Publisher's note)

Stuckey-French, Elizabeth

Revenge of the radioactive lady; a novel. Doubleday 2010 333p $25.95

ISBN 978-0-385-51064-6; 0-385-51064-0

LC 2010-14724

"Stuckey-French's desire to keep the action moving makes some connections feel hastily drawn. Characters occasionally come to realizations that seem delivered by the author rather than organic to who they are. But the author's insistence on rendering her characters as complex human beings with conflicting desires keeps the novel from reading like mere farce. While the plot may hinge on revenge, the unpredictability of love is the true subject. It turns out to be the best kind of page-turner—one with heart ." Boston Globe

Styron, William

The **confessions** of Nat Turner. Modern Lib. 1994 xliv, 428p hardcover o.p. pa $14

ISBN 0-679-60101-5; 0-679-73663-8 pa

LC 94-9393

A reissue of the title first published 1967 by Random House

This "account of an actual person and event is based on the brief contemporary pamphlet of the same title presented to a trial court as evidence and published in Virginia a year after the revolt of fellow slaves led by Turner in 1831. Imagining much of Turner's youth and early manhood before the rebellion that he headed at the age of 31, Styron in frequently rhetorical and pseudo-Biblical style has Turner recall his religious faith and his power of preaching to other slaves." Oxford Companion to Am Lit. 5th edition

Styron, William

Lie down in darkness. Bobbs-Merrill 1951 400p

"The book is not bleakly written. On the contrary, it is richly and even (in the best sense) poetically written. . . . If the parts seem to succeed each other with no apparent logic or dialectic, each part is brilliantly made and lovingly accomplished." Atlantic

Styron, William

★ **Sophie's** choice. Modern Lib. 1998 599p $22; pa $14

ISBN 0-679-60289-5; 0-679-73637-9 pa

LC 97-36895

A reissue of the title first published 1979

"It was a daring act for Styron, whose sensibilities are wholly Southern, to venture into the territory of the American Jew, to say nothing of his plunge into European history. The book is powerfully moving." Burgess. 99 Novels

Suárez, Daniel

Change agent; a novel. Daniel Suarez. Dutton 2017 398 p. (hardcover) $27

ISBN 9781101984680; 9781101984666

LC 2016030244

In this novel, by Daniel Suarez, "in 2045 Kenneth Durand leads Interpol's most effective team against genetic crime, hunting down black market labs that perform 'vanity edits' on human embryos for a price. . . . With the worlds of genetic crime and human trafficking converging, Durand and his fellow Interpol agents discover that one figure looms behind it all: Marcus Demang Wyckes, leader of a powerful and sophisticated cartel known as the Huli jing." (Publisher's note)

"This outstanding speculative thriller from bestseller Suarez (Kill Decision) imagines a future of 'living technology—a fourth industrial revolution of synthetic biology and genetic editing,' as the author puts it in an opening note to the reader." Pub Wkly

Includes bibliographical references.

Sullivan, Michael J.

Theft of swords; Michael J. Sullivan. 1st ed. Orbit 2011 691p.

ISBN 9780316187749

LC 2011008814

In this fantasy book, "Royce Melborn, a skilled thief, and his mercenary partner, Hadrian Blackwater, make a profitable living carrying out dangerous assignments for conspiring nobles--until they are hired to pilfer a famed sword. What appears to be just a simple job finds them framed for the murder of the king and trapped in a conspiracy that uncovers a plot far greater than the mere overthrow of a tiny kingdom. Can a self-serving thief and an idealistic swordsman survive long enough to unravel the first part of an ancient mystery that has toppled kings and destroyed empires in order to keep a secret too terrible for the world to know? And so begins the first tale of treachery and adventure, sword fighting and magic, myth and legend." (Publisher's note)

Sundaresan, Indu

In the Convent of Little Flowers; stories. Atria Books 2008 216p $22

ISBN 978-1-4165-8609-8; 1-4165-8609-1

LC 2008-34437

Sundaresan "bluntly questions how evolved the globalized world truly is in these stories of individuals trapped between India's archaic traditions and blitz into modernity. . . . Sundaresan (The Twentieth Wife) bluntly questions how evolved the globalized world truly is in these stories of individuals trapped between India's archaic traditions and blitz into modernity." Publ Wkly

Sundaresan, Indu

The **splendor** of silence; a novel. Atria Books 2006 403p $25

ISBN 978-0-7432-8367-0; 0-7432-8367-8

LC 2006-48364

"Flashbacks to 1940s India occur when Olivia receives a mysterious trunk that promises to explain who she is. The trunk arrives on the same day that her father, Sam, dies and contains information about her biological mother, Mila. Through a letter hidden among the keepsakes in the box, Olivia learns that her father spent time in India searching for his missing brother. While there, he fell in love with Mila, the daughter of the local political agent and fiancée of a prince. It was also there that he got to know Mila's brothers, who knew the whereabouts of his own brother. A series of events leads to the arrival of the trunk for Olivia years later. Sundaresan's descriptive writing style makes for a colorful, engrossing read, and while the story does hop between time periods and locations, the reader is never lost along the way." Libr J

Sundin, Sarah

Through waters deep; a novel. Sarah Sundin. Revell, a division of Baker Publishing Group 2015 384 p. (softcover) $14.99

ISBN 9780800723422

LC 2015000435

In this book, by Sarah Sundin, "It is 1941 and America teeters on the brink of war. Outgoing naval officer Ensign Jim Avery escorts British convoys across the North Atlantic in a brand-new destroyer, the USS Atwood. Back on shore, Boston Navy Yard secretary Mary Stirling does her work quietly and efficiently, happy to be out of the limelight. . . . When evidence of sabotage on the Atwood is found, Jim and Mary must work together to uncover the culprit." (Publisher's note)

"Providing readers with an immersive experience, Sundin (In Perfect Time) vividly re-creates the atmosphere of a country on the brink of entering World War II. The tender romance at the story's center keeps readers rooting for Jim and Mary to realize their true feelings for each other. In the wake of the popularity of Anita Diamant's The Boston Girl, this book holds local interest for those who have lived in or loved the city. Fans of Rachel Hauck and Melody Carlson will be delighted." LJ

Sundstøl, Vidar

★ The **Land** of Dreams; Vidar Sundstøl; translated by Tiina Nunnally. University of Minnesota Press 2013 344 p. (Minnesota trilogy) $24.95

ISBN 0816689407; 9780816689408

LC 2013027215

This book, the first in a trilogy, follows "Lance Hansen . . . a police officer with the U.S. Forest Service. . . . His real passion is local history. While making his morning rounds, he finds the body of a young man who has been bludgeoned to death. . . . Hansen is just as intrigued by the story of a murdered Native American in the 1800s as he is in the current murder, and finds some ominous ties to his own family." (Booklist)

"The landscape is a big part of the story, as is the history of the area, making this a fascinating look at Minnesota as well as a suspenseful thriller." Booklist

Followed by Only the Dead (2014) and The Ravens (2015)

Suri, Manil

The **age** of Shiva; a novel. W. W. Norton 2008 455p $24.95

ISBN 978-0-393-06569-5; 0-393-06569-3

LC 2007-37322

"Coming of age in Delhi in the fifties, Meera takes her father's atheism and progressive attitudes for granted, but she keenly resents the tyrannies of her favored older sister, who forces Meera to play the go-between in her romance with the handsome Dev. When Dev is dumped for a more suitable fiancé, Meera rashly attempts to console him; soon she is stuck with yet another of her sister's hand-me-downs—this time, forever. Dev drinks too much, and his family lives in a one-bedroom flat by the railroad tracks. Only when Meera conceives a child will she truly have something to call her own. Suri's . . . novel is a sensuous, nuanced portrait of motherhood, but it also sparks with the frictions of being female in an India where television soaps and political slogans compete noisily with Hindu myth." New Yorker

Suri, Manil

The **city** of Devi; Manil Suri. W.W. Norton & Co. Inc. 2013 400 p. map (hardcover) $26.95

ISBN 0393088758; 9780393088755

LC 2012041805

Lambda Literary Award Finalist: Gay General Fiction (2014)

In this book by Manil Suri, "Sarita, recently married, is desperate to find her husband, Karun, before the promised nuclear holocaust some days hence. She sets out from Mumbai toward the suburb where he went before the worst of the violence began. On her way she encounters militant Hindu and Muslim groups, a fantastical cult that worships a would-be deity named Devi, and a Muslim man named Jaz whose attentions she can't seem to shake." (Publishers Weekly)

"The strong plot and character development make the novel a page-turner, while insight into the taboos of interfaith and same-gender relationships in India and commentary on what true love really is add substance." LJ

Suri, Manil

The **death** of Vishnu. Norton 2001 295p $24.95

ISBN 0-393-05042-4

LC 00-58414

"Its clever structure allows {this book} to display a manageable cross-section of contemporary Indian life, including class and religious frictions. But Suri . . . has more to offer here than gentle social comedy. During the course of the novel, Vishnu's soul disentangles itself from his earthly remains and begins ascending the apartment house stairs. As this spirit looks back on the life just ending, Suri's novel achieves an eerie and memorable transcendence." Time

Suskind, Patrick

★ **Perfume**: the story of a murderer; translated from the German by John E. Woods. Knopf 1986 255p

LC 86-45419

Original German edition, 1985

"Those readers who feel they are wasting their time with novels unless they are picking up facts will welcome Süskind's encyclopedic overview of the methods of making perfume. Like the best scents, there is something fundamentally formulaic about this novel, but its effects will linger long after it has been stoppered." Time

Sutcliff, Rosemary

Sword at sunset. Coward-McCann 1963 495p

A novel based on historical facts about the legendary Arthur. "The time is the century after the last Roman legions leave Britain, and Arthur is desperately striving to hold Britain against the Saxons, Picts, and other invading savage tribes. {This is} the story of his tragic fate, his good times and bad." Publ Wkly

Svevo, Italo

★ **Zeno's** conscience; translated from the Italian by William Weaver with an introduction by Elizabeth Hardwick. Knopf 2001 xlix, 437p $20

ISBN 0-375-41330-8

LC 2001-40821

Original Italian edition, 1923; previous English translations had title: The confessions of Zeno

This is "a highly human story and its material is fundamentally as sound as its method. . . . The work of a man who wrote to please himself, it has an individuality and originality you cannot escape noticing, and it has, too, a fine and comprehensive knowledge of its character." N Y Times Book Rev

Swann, Maxine

The **foreigners**. Riverhead Books 2011 258p $25.95

ISBN 978-1-59448-830-6; 1-59448-830-4

"Daisy, 35, arrives in Argentina from the United States in 2002, just a year after her nine-year marriage has dissolved and disenchantment with her work in the theater has led her to explore other job possibilities. A bout with a mysterious illness has left her frustrated, confused, and very disillusioned—estranged, in fact, from her own life. . . . A friend decides what Daisy needs is to travel and offers her an urban studies grant to study public water works in Buenos Aires. Though the project is out of her comfort zone, Daisy jumps at the trip as a kind of 'renegade expedition.' The fashionable Isolde, also 35, is from a small village in Austria. Good-natured, innocent, hopeful, she is 'someone to whom life happened, one thing led to the next, with minimal forethought on her part.' Her one surprising move is to quit her safe, predictable job at a bank and set off with her savings to travel, reinventing herself as a darling of the cocktail party crowd in Buenos Aires, where being European conveys instant status. She dreams of becoming an ambassador to the European art world, but constantly skirts the edges of desperation with dwindling finances, no real job, and a pervasive loneliness. . . . [Swann] vividly evokes the city and its lively, diverse, and conflicted social landscape, from the denizens of posh hotels to the unfortunate poor living in the city's slums." Boston Globe

Swanson, Peter

Her every fear; A Novel. Peter Swanson. William Morrow, an imprint of HarperCollinsPublishers 2017 352 p. (ebook) $25.99; (hardcover) $26.99

ISBN 9780062427045; 0062427024; 0062427032; 9780062427021; 9780062427038

LC 2016007758

In this novel, by Peter Swanson, "Kate Priddy was always a bit neurotic, experiencing momentary bouts of anxiety that exploded into full blown panic attacks after an ex-boyfriend kidnapped her. . . . When Corbin Dell, a distant cousin in Boston, suggests the two temporarily swap apartments, Kate . . . agrees. . . . But soon after her arrival at Corbin's grand apartment on Beacon Hill, Kate makes a shocking discovery: his next-door neighbor . . . has been murdered." (Publisher's note)

"Psychological thriller devotees should block time to read Swanson's (The Kind Worth Killing) novel in one sitting, preferably in the daylight. Readers can expect the hairs on their necks to stand straight up as they are consumed with a full-blown case of heebie-jeebies." LJ

Swanwick, Michael

Bones of the earth. HarperCollins Pubs. 2002 335p

ISBN 0-380-97836-9

LC 2001-40196

"Swanwick writes about paleontologists who travel back to the Mesozoic to study dinosaurs firsthand, with a technology supplied by enigmatic aliens. . . . His focus never strays far from the two reluctant collaborators, Griffin and the Old Man, who have transformed paleontology into an experimental science. The air of competence they adopt in their day-to-day operations cannot mask their anxiety over who ultimately are the experimenters and who are the subjects." N Y Times Book Rev

Swanwick, Michael

The **dog** said bow-wow. Tachyon Publications 2007 296p pa $14.95

ISBN 978-1-892391-52-0; 1-892391-52-X

"There is a camaraderie about the stories Michael Swanwick has assembled in The Dog Said Bow-Wow, a willingness to share their deepest ingenuities with the reader, that makes the book almost tingle in the mind: wagging its tale to tell more. What the stories in this collection are so good at doing, to put it another way, is being stories. They wear their hearts on their sleeves. This is not exactly to say that Michael Swanwick does the same. The other side of the exuberance of The Dog Said Bow-Wow is a severe chastity of reticence. Michael Swanwick is a teller, but he does not tell himself. But we cannot fault a writer for selecting his remit. And the polished variousness of Swanwick's gift is in itself gift enough." Sci Fi Wkly

Swanwick, Michael

Not So Much, Said the Cat; Michael Swanwick. Tachyon Publications 2016 288 p. (ebook) $9.99; (ebook) $9.99; (paperback) $15.95

ISBN 9781616962296; 9781616962319; 9781616962289; 1616962283

This short story collection, by Michael Swanwick, "takes us on a whirlwind journey across the globe and across time and space, where magic and science exist in possibilities that are not of this world. These tales are intimate in their telling, galactic in their scope, and delightfully sesquipedalian in their verbiage." (Publisher's note)

"This is as good as short speculative fiction gets." Pub Wkly

Swarthout, Glendon Fred

Bless the beasts and children; [by] Glendon Swarthout. Doubleday 1970 205p

"Six rich teenagers, rejected by their parents and avoided by their peers, group together at Box Canyon Summer Boys' Camp. Fragile egos and self-destructive personalities begin to heal under the leadership of Cotton, who gently pokes fun at their soft spots while building up their self-esteem. An effort on the part of the group to stop the wanton slaughter of buffalo provides a high point of suspense." Shapiro. Fic for Youth. 3d edition

Swarthout, Glendon Fred

The **shootist**; {by} Glendon Swarthout. Doubleday 1975 186p

"This is definitely more than a Western; the characterization is flawless, the plot absorbing and convincing." Libr J

Sweeney, Cynthia D'Aprix

The **Nest**; by Cynthia D'Aprix Sweeney. HarperCollins 2016 368 p. $26.99

ISBN 0062414216; 9780062414212

In this book, by Cynthia D'Aprix Sweeney, "the Plumb family stands out as spectacularly dysfunctional. Years of simmering tensions finally reach a breaking point . . . as Melody, Beatrice, and Jack Plumb gather to confront their . . . older brother, Leo, freshly released from rehab. Months earlier, an inebriated Leo got behind the wheel of a car. . . . The ensuing accident has endangered the Plumbs' joint trust fund, 'The Nest,' which they are months away from finally receiving." (Publisher's note)

"D'Aprix gives each of the characters a distinct and true personality, and she has a flair for realistic and funny dialogue—readers will feel as though they're sitting right next to the clan as they bicker and barter. Fans of Jonathan Tropper will adore D'Aprix's debut." Booklist

Swerling, Beverly

Shadowbrook; a novel of love and war. Beverly Swerling. Simon & Schuster 2004 490p il $24.95

ISBN 0-7432-2812-X

LC 2003-64127

"Covering the years 1754-1760, with the British, French and Indians slaughtering each other for king and empire, Swerling tells of two men who straddle the white and red man's worlds, desperate to preserve the best of each culture, but fearful they will lose everything they love. Quentin Hale is a gentleman turned scout whose family owns a prosperous New York plantation called Shadowbrook. He is white, but also follows the Indian ways of his adopted tribe, the Potawatomi. Cormac Shea is part-Irish and part-Indian, nearly a brother to Hale, but he wants all whites driven from Canada. Together these men find themselves caught up in a bloody war neither wants, but they must fight to save the plantation and create a homeland for the Indians. . . . Surrounding them are colorful historical figures like the young George Washington, the hapless General Braddock and the powerful Ottawa chief, Pontiac." Publ Wkly

Swierczynski, Duane

Fun and games. Mulholland Books 2011 286p pa $14.99

ISBN 978-0-316-13328-9; 0-316-13328-0

LC 2010-44951

"After second-tier movie actress Lane Madden survives multiple attempts by aggressive fellow drivers to run her off some treacherous Los Angeles roads, she has the good fortune to meet Charlie Hardie, a peripatetic house-sitter with a violent past, at the house in the Hollywood Hills where she takes refuge. Hardie, a former police consultant who's haunted by the deaths of several innocents, is skeptical of the actress's claim that she's being pursued by the Accident People, a shadowy group of killers who stage their homicides to appear as accidents. An escalating series of violent encounters builds to an unforgettable climax." Publ Wkly

Swift, Graham, 1949-

★ **England** and other stories; Graham Swift. Alfred A. Knopf 2015 237 p. (hardcover) $25.95

ISBN 110187418X; 9781101874189

LC 2014028381

In this short story collection by Graham Swift, readers will "meet Dr. Shah who has never been to India, and Mrs. Kaminski, on her way to Poland; meet Holly and Polly, who have come to their own Anglo-Irish understanding, and Charlie and Don, who have seen the docks turn into Docklands; Daisy Baker, who is terrified of Yorkshire; and Johnny Dewhurst, stranded on Exmoor." (Publisher's note)

"Few stories are longer than ten pages, and some are only four or five pages, but within the confines of brevity Swift manages to create lives and invest them with drama and import. Although war and death are sometimes featured, the impact and dramatic force is usually focused on the personal, the emotional, and the slighter nuances of character, memory, and regret, which is what makes them memorable." LJ

Swift, Graham, 1949-

★ **Last** orders. Knopf 1996 294p

LC 96-13726

"On a bleak spring day, four men meet in their favorite pub in a working-class London neighborhood. They are about to begin a pilgrimage to scatter the ashes of a fifth man, Jack Dodds, friend since WWII of three of them, adoptive father to the fourth. By the time they reach the seaside town where Jack's 'last orders' have sent them, the tangled relationship among the men, their wives and their children has obliquely been revealed." Publ Wkly

Swift, Graham, 1949-

★ **Mothering** Sunday; a romance. Graham Swift. Alfred A. Knopf 2016 192 p. (ebook) $65; (hardback) $22.95

ISBN 9781101947531; 9781101947524

LC 2015033402

In this novel by Graham Swift, "Jane Fairchild, [who] has worked as a maid at an English country house, . . . has [also] been the clandestine lover to Paul Sheringham, young heir of a neighboring house. The two now meet on an unseasonably warm March day—Mothering Sunday—a day that will change Jane's life forever. As the narrative moves back and forth from 1924 to the end of the century, what we know and understand about Jane . . . expands with every vividly captured moment." (Publisher's note)

"Swift has fun with language, with class conventions, and with narrative expectations in a novel where nothing is as simple or obvious as it seems at first." Kirkus

Swift, Graham, 1949-

Tomorrow. Alfred A. Knopf 2007 255p $23.95

ISBN 978-0-307-26690-3

LC 2007-18684

"The need to hold our interest is more than adequately covered by Paula's poignant account of what was required of her and Mike when she resolved to become pregnant, and the psychological adjustments subsequently required of both of them; this is Graham Swift at his impressive best in entering the minds of people with whom he can have little genuine connection or affinity." Times Lit Suppl

Swift, Graham, 1949-

★ **Waterland**. Poseidon Press 1984 309p il

ISBN 0-671-49863-0

LC 83-21248

This novel concerns "Tom Crick, an English history teacher in his mid-50s who, as the novel opens, has just been forced to accept early retirement. In response to his students' belief that history is a 'fairy-tale' and only the 'here and now' matters, Crick has abandoned the formal curriculum to tell stories about his childhood in East England's Fens. The headmaster, a physicist, shares the students' opinion of the past, and Crick's 'trying to put himself into history' is the last straw. But Crick won't go—his students are for once interested in his 'crazy yarns'—until one day his wife goes mad and steals a baby from a supermarket shopping cart. The prospect of retirement gives Crick the freedom to tell his pupils the lurid story that lies behind his wife's theft." (Nation)

"The novel exceeds credibility and attenuates our tolerance in exactly the same degree as it creates, through [Swift's] own words, the portrait of a man who is deeply disturbed, and who is vainly attempting to build a structure from these words which will protect him from his childlessness, from his failure to create the future." Times Lit Suppl

Swift, Graham, 1949-

Wish you were here; Graham Swift. Alfred A. Knopf 2012 319p.

ISBN 0307700127; 9780307700124

LC 2011050296

"This . . . novel is about longing for the people in our lives who have died. Taking place over just a few days, it focuses on Jack Luxton's journey to retrieve the remains of his brother Tom, a soldier who died in Iraq. The brothers grew up on a farm in the British countryside, and hovering over the story is the specter of mad cow disease on one end and terror (both political and personal) on the other." (Library Journal)

Swift, Jonathan

★ **Gulliver's** travels; with an introduction by Pat Rogers. Knopf 1991 xlv, 318p map $20

ISBN 0-679-40545-3

LC 91-53011

First published 1726

"In the account of his four wonder-countries Swift satirizes contemporary manners and morals, art and politics—in fact the whole social scheme—from four different points of view. The huge Brobdingnagians reduce man to his natural insignificance, the little people of Lilliput parody Europe and its petty broils, in Laputa philosophers are ridiculed, and finally all Swift's hatred and contempt find their satisfaction in degrading humanity to a bestial condition." Baker. Guide to the Best Fic

Swinson, Kiki

Playing dirty; Kiki Swinson. Dafina Books 2009 281 p.

ISBN 075822835X; 9780758228352

In this novel, "Miami defense attorney Yoshi Lomax bribes, manipulates, blackmails and uses her body to win cases and a promotion at her firm, but her physical assets and flexible morals end up doing her more harm than good. . . . Yoshi's singular . . . motivation is money, and it drives her to, among other things, sleep with her boss, betray her DEA agent best friend and make some questionable calls about what clients she takes on. Then her lucky streak ends: she gets demoted at work, loses her bid to get a case dismissed, gets arrested for drug possession, gets abandoned by her best friend and is framed for murder." (Publishers Weekly)

Syjuco, Miguel

Ilustrado. Farrar, Straus and Giroux 2010 306p $26

ISBN 0-374-17478-4; 978-374-17478-1

LC 2009-43083

On a winter's day, "the battered corpse of Crispin Salvador is pulled from the Hudson River—taken from the world is the controversial lion of Philippine literature. Gone, too, is the only manuscript of his final book, a work meant to rescue him from obscurity by exposing the crimes of the Filipino ruling families. Miguel, his student and only remaining friend, sets out for Manila to investigate. To understand the death, Miguel scours the life, piecing together Salvador's story through his poetry, interviews, novels, polemics, and memoirs. The result is a . . . family saga of four generations, tracing 150 years of Philippine history." (Publisher's note)

"This début novel begins as a murder mystery and develops into an ambitious exploration of cultural identity, ambition, and artistic purpose. When the Filipino writer Crispin Salvador is found dead, his protégé, Miguel, resolves to investigate and to resurrect Salvador's precarious reputation as the Philippines' quintessential intellectual export. The narrative of Miguel's quest is intercut with e-mails, fragments of manuscripts, interviews, poems, and blog entries; real people mingle with fictional characters. The result is a self-referential collage encompassing both sociopolitical polemic and lighter fare, such as a memorable thread of bawdy jokes." New Yorker

Sykes, S. D. ✓

Plague Land; A Murder Mystery. by S. D. Sykes. W.W. Norton & Co. Inc. 2015 336 p. map $25.95

ISBN 1605986739; 9781605986739

In this historical mystery novel, by S. D. Sykes, "Oswald de Lacy was never meant to be the Lord of Somerhill Manor. Despatched to a monastery at the age of seven, sent back at seventeen when his father and two older brothers are killed by the Plague, Oswald has no experience of running an estate. He finds the years of pestilence and neglect have changed the old place dramatically, not to mention the attitude of the surviving peasants." (Publisher's note)

"With political intrigue and the social barriers of the Middle Ages in play, Sykes adds an intricate and intriguing debut to the ever-widening pool of medieval-era mysteries. Thrilling plot twists and layered characters abound in this rich tale of murder and mystery in 14th-century Kent." LJ

Another title in this series is:
The Butcher Bird (2016)

Szalay, David, 1974-

All that man is; A Novel. David Szalay. Graywolf Press 2016 272 p. (alk. paper) $25

ISBN 9781555977535

LC 2016931139

Man Booker Prize Shortlist (2016)

This book by David Szalay focuses on the lives of "nine men. Each of them at a different stage in life, each of them away from home, and each of them striving--in the suburbs of Prague, in an overdeveloped Alpine village, beside a Belgian motorway, in a dingy Cyprus hotel--to understand what it means to be alive, here and now." (Publisher's note)

"A grim but compelling composite portrait by a talented writer." Kirkus

T

Tabucchi, Antonio

It's getting later all the time; a novel in the form of letters. translated from the Italian by Alastair McEwen. New Directions 2006 232p pa $15.95

ISBN 978-0-8112-1546-6; 0-8112-1546-6

LC 2006-7369

Original Italian edition, 2001

"This epistolary novel is composed of 18 love letters; the fictional authors are 17 men and one woman, whose sweeping, summative voice closes the collection abruptly. . . . Written from places all over Europe, the letters are intimate and often exquisite, lingering over transcendent details of landscape, or ruefully soliloquizing on memory. One rancorous letter, 'A Good Man Like You,' recalls a betrayal seven years in the past, while another contemplates a journey never taken: 'Do you remember when we didn't go to Samarkand?' The whole makes for delicious voyeurism, leavened with pointed bafflement at these partially rendered relationships: just as the reader wishes for all the gaps to be filled in, the letter writers wish to recompose fractured relationships." Publ Wkly

Tademy, Lalita

Cane River. Warner Bks. 2001 418p il

ISBN 0-446-53052-2

LC 00-43682

"Five generations and a hundred years in the life of a matriarchal black Louisiana family are encapsulated in this . . . novel that is based in part upon the lives, as preserved in both historical record and oral tradition, of the author's ancestors. . . . Her frank observations about black racism add depth to the tale, and she demonstrates that although the practice of slavery fell most harshly upon blacks, and especially women, it also constricted the lives and choices of white men. Photos of and documents relating to Tademy's ancestors add authenticity to a fascinating story." Publ Wkly

Tallis, Frank

Fatal lies; a novel. Frank Tallis. Random House Trade Paperbacks 2009 439 p. (trade pbk.) $15.00

ISBN 0812977777; 9780812977776

LC 2008023474

In this book by Frank Tallis, "a dogged police inspector and an insightful young psychiatrist match wits with depraved criminal minds," investigating "the mysterious and savage death of a young cadet in the most elite of military academies." Psychiatrist Max Liebermann is also dealing with "a crisis of his own: handling his conflicted and forbidden feelings for two different women, one a former patient." (Publisher's note)

Tallis, Frank

★ **Vienna** blood; a novel. Frank Tallis. Random House Trade Paperbacks 2007 485 p. ill.

ISBN 0812977769; 9780812977769

LC 2007019605

Sequel to: A death in Vienna (2006)

In the sequel to "A Death in Vienna," 1902 Vienna is terrorized by a serial killer targeting prostitutes and leaving strange crosslike symbols in his wake, and Detective Oscar Rheinhardt and Dr. Max Liebermann reunite to find a murderer. (Publisher's note)

Includes bibliographical references (p. 485)

Tallis, Frank

Vienna Twilight; Frank Tallis. Random 2011 368 p. $15.00

ISBN 0812981006; 9780812981001

LC 2011284360

In this novel, by Frank Tallis, set "[i]n . . . Vienna of 1903, a brilliant psychoanalyst and a brave detective battle to catch criminals. . . . Detective Inspector Oskar Reinhardt finds that young women are being slain . . . with a small, almost undetectable, hat pin. . . . [T]he killer . . . murders in the midst of consensual love. . . . As danger mounts, Liebermann must find the answer while struggling with his own forbidden desire for a female patient." (Publisher's note)

Tan, Amy

The **bonesetter's** daughter. Putnam 2001 353p

ISBN 0-399-14643-1

LC 00-62673

"A fine and highly readable novel, The Bonesetter's Daughter is essentially about writing and the act of writing, what fuels it and how it is created. More specifically still, it is about how we, as women creatively express ourselves via language." Women's Rev Books

Tan, Amy

The **hundred** secret senses. Putnam 1995 358p

LC 95-31791

"Nearing divorce from her husband, Simon, Olivia Yee is guided by her elder half-sister, the irrepressible Kwan, into the heart of China. Olivia was five when 18-year-old Kwan first joined her family in the United States, and though always irritated by Kwan's oddities, Olivia was entranced by her eerie dreams of the ghost World of Yin. Only when visiting Kwan's home in Changmian does Olivia realize the dreams are, in Kwan's mind, memories from past lives. . . . Tan tells a mysterious, believable story and delivers Kwan's clipped, immigrant voice and engaging personality with charming clarity." Libr J

Tan, Amy, 1952-

★ The **Joy** Luck Club. Putnam 1989 288p $24.95

ISBN 0-399-13420-4

LC 88-26492

Chapters in this novel alternate "between the lives of four Chinese women in pre-1949 China and the lives of their American-born daughters in California. . . . The members of the Joy Luck Club are four aging 'aunties' who gather regularly in San Francisco to play mah-jongg, eat Chinese food and gossip about their children. When one of the women dies, her daughter, Jing-mei (June) Woo, is drafted to sit in for her at the game. But she feels uncomfortably out of place in this unassimilated environment. . . . Slowly she begins to comprehend how, after all they have endured, {the aunties} might well be anxious and concerned lest all cultural continuity between their pasts and their children's futures be lost." (N Y Times Book Rev)

"Four aging Chinese women who knew life in China before 1949 and now live in San Francisco meet regularly to play mah-jongg and share thoughts about their American-born children. In alternating sections we learn about the cultural differences between the elderly 'aunties' and the younger generation. When one of the older women dies, her daughter is pressed to take her place in the Joy Luck Club. Her feeling of being out of place gradually gives way to an understanding of the need to retain cultural continuity and an appreciation for the strength and endurance of the older women." Shapiro. Fic for Youth. 3d edition

Tan, Amy, 1952-

★ The **kitchen** god's wife. Putnam 1991 415p

ISBN 0399138560; 9780399138560

LC 91-7828

The novel "relates the story of Jiang Weili (Weiwei) from the time she was 6 years old in the China of 1925 through the present, in which she is Winnie Louie, the widowed matriarch of an extended Chinese family living in San Francisco." (N Y Times Book Rev)

"Within the peculiar construction of Amy Tan's second novel is a harrowing, compelling and at times bitterly humorous tale in which an entire world unfolds in a Tolstoyan tide of event and detail." N Y Times Book Rev

Tan, Amy

Saving fish from drowning. Putnam 2005 474p $26.95

ISBN 0-399-15301-2

LC 2005-48724

"Amy Tan has created a meta-fable of Orwellian stature, where Americans abroad think they know best, yet follow others blindly; where illusions and assumptions meet self-righteousness and arrogance." Ms.

Tan, Amy, 1952-

★ The **Valley** of Amazement; Amy Tan. HarperCollins 2013 608 p. $29.99

ISBN 0062107313; 9780062107312

In this novel, Amy Tan "explores the complex relationships between mothers and daughters, control and submission, tradition and new beginnings. Jumping from bustling Shanghai to an isolated village in rural China to San Francisco at the turn of the 19th century, the epic story follows three generations of women pulled apart by outside forces. The main focus is Violet, once a virgin courtesan in one of the most reputable houses in Shanghai, who faces a series of crippling setbacks." (Publishers Weekly)

Tan, Twan Eng, 1972-

★ The **Garden** of Evening Mists; a novel. Tan Twan Eng. 1st U.S. ed. Weinstein Books 2012 335 p. (paperback) $15.99; (ebook) $15.99

ISBN 1602861803; 9781602861800; 9781602861817

LC 2012462473

Man Booker Prize Shortlist (2012)

"Malaya, 1949. . . . Yun Ling Teoh, herself the scarred lone survivor of a brutal Japanese wartime camp, seeks solace among the jungle fringed plantations of Northern Malaya. . . . There she discovers . . . the only Japanese garden in Malaya, and its owner and creator, the enigmatic Aritomo, exiled former gardener of the Emperor of Japan." (Publisher's note)

Includes bibliographical references (p. 333-334).

Tanenbaum, Robert

Act of revenge; a novel. [by] Robert K. Tannenbaum. HarperCollins Pubs. 1999 402p $25

ISBN 0-06-019218-6

LC 98-54268

"Tanenbaum has crafted a believably twisted gem of a gangster tale with visceral action and smooth comic relief in a technicolor, Big Apple setting that waxes nostalgic for the 'gentleman' killers of yesteryear." Publ Wkly

Tanenbaum, Robert K.

Tragic; Robert K. Tanenbaum. Gallery Books 2013 390 p. $26

ISBN 1451635559; 1451635567; 9781451635553; 9781451635560

LC 2013005283

In this, the 25th entry in Robert K. Tanenbaum's Roger "Butch" Karp series, Karp takes on organized crime. "Recently deceased union leader Leo Corcione left two prospective heirs: ruthless Charlie Vitteli and upstanding Vince Carlotta. Vitteli's thugs, led by brutal Joey Barros, set out to . . . [put] a bullet through Carlotta's head. Karp works to pin Vitteli to the crime, but when Karp's wife, ADA Marlene Campi, provides crucial testimony, the personal connection threatens to discredit" them. (Publishers Weekly)

Tanizaki, Jun'ichiro

★ The **Makioka** sisters; translated and introduced by Edward G. Seidensticker. Knopf 1993 xxxv,498 $20

ISBN 0-679-943452-0

LC 92-55051

Original Japanese edition, 1949; this translation first published 1957

"The narrative is very quiet, very leisurely. At times it seems interminable, but it is like the pigment used by a Renaissance painter to build up his picture. It is done with utmost skill and results in a dignified masterpiece of great beauty and quality." Chicago Sunday Trib

Tanner, Haley

Vaclav and Lena; a novel. Dial Press 2011 292p $25

ISBN 978-1-4000-6931-6; 1-4000-6931-9

LC 2010023907

"This debut starts off cute but slight, with 10-year-olds Vaclav and Lena exploring a proto-romance to the odor of borscht and the lilt of mangled syntax in Russian-immigrant Brooklyn. Then Lena suddenly leaves under murky circumstances and the book heads for something darker and deeper, especially after the story jumps forward seven years and the couple reunite to grapple with the past and, possibly, feel their way toward a future. Vaclav and especially Lena never quite cohere into threedimensional characters, but Tanner is a gifted-enough storyteller to bring some real emotional heft to Vaclav & Lena." Entertainment Wkly

Tao Lin

Taipei; a novel. Tao Lin. Random House Inc 2013 272 p. $14.95

ISBN 0307950174; 9780307950178

LC 2013005675

In this book, "protagonist Paul is still prowling Brooklyn parties and bars. He's made a quick trip home to Taiwan, but little happened there either. Back in the borough, Paul has moved from one maybe-a-girlfriend to another, met dealer friends who trade in recreational pharmaceuticals--Xanax, Adderall, cocaine, 'shrooms and MDMA--and ruminated a bit about his novel, soon to be released." (Kirkus Reviews)

Tapply, William G.

Dead winter; a Brady Coyne novel. Delacorte Press 1989 230p

LC 88-13867

"The plot takes some gothic turns—bastardy, incest, and earlier violent death—but Tapply never neglects his nicely defined characterizations or loses his cool control over narrative tension in this very satisfying caper." Publ Wkly

Tarkington, Booth

★ **Alice** Adams; illustrated by Arthur William Brown. Doubleday, Page 1921 434p il

"A social climber, the title character is ashamed of her unsuccessful family. Hoping to attract a wealthy husband, she lies about her background, but she is found out and is shunned by those whom she sought to attract. At the novel's end, she knows her chances for happiness and a successful marriage are bleak, but she remains unbowed." Merriam-Webster's Ency of Lit

Tarkington, Booth

★ The **magnificent** Ambersons. Modern Library 1998 268p pa $12.95

ISBN 0-375-75250-1

LC 98-19552

First published 1918 by Doubleday, Page

"The novel traces the growth of the United States through the decline of the once-powerful, socially prominent Amberson family. Their fall is contrasted with the rise of new industrial tycoons and land developers, whose power comes not through family connections but through financial dealings and modern manufacturing." Merriam-Webster's Ency of Lit

Tartt, Donna, 1963-

★ The **goldfinch**; Donna Tartt. Little Brown & Co 2013 784 p. (hardback) $30

ISBN 0316055433; 9780316055437; 9780316242370

LC 2013028907

Carnegie Medal: Fiction (2014)

Pulitzer Prize: Fiction (2014)

In this Pulitzer-Prize-winning book by Donna Tartt, "Theo Decker . . . miraculously survives an accident that kills his mother. Abandoned by his father, Theo is taken in by the family of a wealthy friend. . . . Disturbed by schoolmates who don't know how to talk to him, and tormented above all by his unbearable longing for his mother, he clings to one thing that reminds him of her: a small, mysteriously captivating painting that ultimately draws Theo into the underworld of art." (Publisher's note)

"The novel is slow to build but eloquent and assured, with memorable characters. . . . A standout." Kirkus

Tartt, Donna

The **little** friend. Knopf 2002 555p $26

ISBN 0-679-43938-2

LC 2002-66878

Tartt's "book is a ruthlessly precise reckoning of the world as it is—drab, ugly, scary, inconclusive—filtered through the bright colors and impossible demands of childhood perception. It grips you like a fairy tale, but denies you the consoling assurance that it's all just make-believe." N Y Times Book Rev

Tartt, Donna, 1963-

★ The **secret** history. Knopf 1992 523p

ISBN 0-679-41032-5

LC 92-53053

In this book by Donna Tartt, "under the influence of their charismatic classics professor, a group of clever, eccentric misfits at an elite New England college discover a way of thinking and living that is a world away from the humdrum existence of their contemporaries. But when they go beyond the boundaries of normal morality their lives are changed profoundly and forever, and they discover how hard it can be to truly live and how easy it is to kill." (Publisher's note)

This novel "is set on a small college campus in Vermont. Dissatisfied with the crass values of their fellow students, a small corps of undergraduates groups itself around a favored professor of classics, who nurtures both their sense of moral elevation and an insularity from conventional college life that ultimately proves fatal. Among Prof. Julian Morrow's followers are Henry Winter, a tall scion of a wealthy St. Louis family, . . . the twins Charles and Camilla Macaulay, both intellectually gifted and eccentric only in their excessive mutual devotion; Francis Abernathy, a dandyish homosexual slowly awakening to his sexuality; and Edmund (Bunny) Corcoran, . . . [who] becomes the group's victim." N Y Times Book Rev

Taseer, Aatish

The **way** things were; a novel. Aatish Taseer. Faber & Faber 2015 576 p. (hardcover) $30

ISBN 0865478244; 9780865478244

LC 2014049064

This novel, by Aatish Taseer, "opens with the death of Toby, the Maharaja of Kalasuryaketu, a Sanskritist who has not set foot in India for two decades. It falls to his son, Skanda, to return Toby's body to his birthplace. . . . This journey takes him halfway around the world and returns him to his family, the drawing-room elite of Delhi, whose narcissism and infighting he has worked hard to escape." (Publisher's note)

"Authors often attempt to frame a given period of a country's history through a single family's story, but Taseer's book is a cut above the rest. Colonialism, racism, sectarian violence, class tension, and the rise of the Indian nouveau riche are all handled with a delicate touch. This is a difficult book to put down, and readers will enjoy every minute of it, as well as learning about contemporary Indian culture." Pub Wkly

Tatlock, Ann

Things we once held dear; Ann Tatlock. Bethany House 2006 396p o.p.

ISBN 0764200046 (pbk.)

LC 2005028048

In this book, "artist Neil Sadler's wife dies suddenly in New York City, [and] he is drawn back to Mason, Ohio, the hometown that he fled almost three decades before. He spends the summer helping remodel an old 'Gothic Horror' farmhouse into a bed-and-breakfast, trying to reconnect with his past and his cousin Mary Beeken. After a childhood spent caring for an invalid mother, Mary is trapped in a 23-year-old marriage to a troubled, alcoholic cop and feels her life has never quite gotten started. Mary's mother's murder years earlier . . . cast shadows on the lives of several Mason families. As Neil and Mary try to make sense of what has happened to their lives, they both discover that '[y]ou don't have to understand something completely to know it's true.'" (Publishers Weekly)

Taylor, Alex

The **marble** orchard; Alex Taylor. Ig Publishing 2015 304 p. (softcover) $16.95

ISBN 1935439995; 9781935439998

LC 2014045522

This book by Alex Taylor "tells the story of Beam, the black sheep of the Sheetmire family, a large and entrenched rural Kentucky clan. Beam finds himself on the run after killing a man who was trying to rob him, a man who turns out to be the son of Loat Duncan, a powerful local businessman and cold-blooded killer. With Loat . . . and Elvis, the local sheriff, hot on his trail, Beam leads a nomadic existence as he descends deeper into his own heart of darkness." (Publisher's note)

"Taylor's understanding of place, 'ancient beyond all measure and remote beyond all reckoning,' and the hard people who 'walk around with the dark all their lives until they are the dark' echoes the cultural dissections of Daniel Woodrell and James Lee Burke. A brilliant debut." Pub Wkly

Taylor, Elizabeth

★ **Mrs.** Palfrey at the Claremont. Viking 1971 178p

"A tale about an elderly British widow who takes up residence in one of those shabby, genteel hotels along London's Cromwell Road. She is at a desperate loss for what to do with herself to fill in the time and try to make her fellow lodgers believe she still has some semblance of a personal life. The portraits of the elderly and crotchety residents are drawn with a pen only lightly tipped in acid, and Mrs. Palfrey herself is very human and endearing. She finds her real hope for the future in pretending that a rather callow but not unkind casual acquaintance is really her grandson." Publ Wkly

Taylor, M. Glenn

The **ballad** of Trenchmouth Taggart. Vandalia Press 2008 276p pa $16.50

ISBN 978-1-933202-31-0; 1-933202-31-9

LC 2008-927388

"Taylor's prose is so fluid and seemingly effortless that The Ballad of Trenchmouth Taggart bridges the usually irreconcilable gap between popular fiction and literary fiction. It's that rare creature—a literary page-turner—and it will please both the casual reader and the college professor . . . . [This] is a stunning, fully realized, unique and ambitious book that proves there's still passion, fire and brilliance in the American novel." Houston Chron

Taylor, M. Glenn

The **Marrowbone** Marble Company; a novel. [by] Glenn Taylor. Ecco 2010 360p $24.99

ISBN 978-0-06-192393-7; 0-06-192393-1

"Each chapter of 'The Marrowbone Marble Company' stands as a self-contained bit. Each could be taken, individually, as a short story; puzzled together as a whole, they paint a picture composed of sideways glances. The resulting work is nuanced, with characters and conflicts emerging as three-dimensional creations. It's a rich stew, one well-worth savoring." Denver Post

Taylor, Peter Hillsman

★ A **summons** to Memphis; [by] Peter Taylor. Knopf 1986 209p

LC 86-45417

"A son, now a grown man, recounts the family's subservience to a strong-willed father. Against a background of Southern manners in Memphis and Nashville, the Carver daughters and sons experience frustration of their hopes to marry and enjoy family lives of their own. The mother, soon after her marriage to George Carver, withdraws from resisting his authority. The daughters never find suitors who suit their father. One brother, escaping to war, is killed and the narrator, Philip, a bachelor still at 49, is summoned home by his sisters to prevent their father, at 81, from remarrying. The seemingly selfless care given by the daughters might stem from self-interest rather than filial devotion." Shapiro. Fic for Youth. 3d edition

Tea, Michelle

Rose of no man's land; a novel. MacAdam/Cage Pub. 2006 306p $22

ISBN 1-59692-160-9

LC 2005-224876

This novel is "both a riotously funny coming-of-age story and a poignant cautionary tale that smacks of 'there but for the grace of God' heartbreak. . . . But Trisha's cynical, wisecracking descriptions are almost too brilliantly evocative, too clever as she illuminates the story's small cast of characters with vivid, telling details." Boston Globe

Tearne, Roma

Mosquito. Europa Editions 2008 299p pa $16.95

ISBN 978-1-933372-57-0; 1-933372-57-5

First published 2007 in the United Kingdom

"Flashes of true beauty, along with an impressively sustained forward drive, are enough to make Mosquito an engaging and thought-provoking novel." Times Lit Suppl

Temple, Peter

The **broken** shore. Farrar, Straus and Giroux 2007 357p $25

ISBN 978-0-374-11693-4; 0-374-11693-8

LC 2006-32983

First published 2005 in Australia

"Flinty, funny, subtle, and smart, The Broken Shore sags under the burden of a few too many narrative complications and, like many a top-drawer mystery, collapses toward the end, as the haunting questions, so elegantly posed, are suddenly and a little awkwardly answered. But this is a hazard of the genre, and Temple ranks among its very best practitioners." Entertainment Wkly

Templeton, Edith

Gordon. Pantheon Bks. 2001 226p $22

ISBN 0-375-42194-7

LC 2002-70427

First published 1966 in the United Kingdom under the pseudonym Louise Walbrook

"This eerie tale of sexual obsession is narrated by a young woman adrift in London just after the Second World War. She meets a 'frightening, sinister, implacable' psychiatrist who, over all protest, invades her, body and mind, arousing previously unsuspected tastes for submission and humiliation. One part 'Story of O' to two parts Muriel Spark, the book beautifully evokes the tightened belts and loose morals of postwar London." New Yorker

Tepper, Sheri S.

★ The **gate** to Women's Country. Doubleday 1988 278p

LC 88-387

"A feminist fable set somewhere in the Pacific Northwest 300 years after a nuclear holocaust. Men and women now live in separate but adjacent communities. Although the men are organized into military garrisons, the women appear to have the upper hand in government, deciding matters of trade and law and, most important, reproduction. . . . The elaborate society that the author takes such pains to describe is based on a big lie; the story she tells is part of the deception. Some will find this narrative strategy as distasteful as the secret it conceals. But Ms. Tepper is not afraid to ask hard questions, beginning with this: If biology is destiny, how can society hope to control its self-destructive tendencies without controlling biology as well?" N Y Times Book Rev

Tepper, Sheri S.

★ **Grass**. Doubleday 1989 426p

LC 89-30105

In this first volume of a trilogy "diplomats are dispatched to the planet Grass in search of the cure for a deadly disease that is spreading throughout inhabited space. The human settlers, xenophobic and conservative landed gentry, lead an existence tightly structured around the Hunt, a complex and violent ritual involving the use of alien mounts that seem nearly demonic in their malevolence. The presence of a number of not particularly sympathetic religious groups adds complexity to the situation. This is a beautifully written novel with well-developed characters and a number of very interesting aliens." Anatomy of Wonder 4

Followed by Raising the stones

Tepper, Sheri S.

The **Margarets**. Eos 2007 508p il $26.95

ISBN 978-0-06-117065-2; 0-06-117065-8

LC 2006-47079

"Margaret is the only kid on a research colony orbiting Mars. Smart, bored and profoundly lonely, she begins to create alter egos for fun. . . . As Margaret grows into a smart and lonely teenager her family must return to the grim, environmentally ravished Earth, where the only economically viable product for interplanetary export is human slaves. Facing a series of blind choices that pull her in two directions, she begins to shed the imaginary Margarets. The Margarets scatter off to other settled worlds, unaware of their other selves. Each Margaret struggles to survive by her (or his) wits, and to understand the growing threats to Earth and humanity. . . . [This novel] incorporates a grab bag of creatures, cultures, psychological metaphors, characters, commentaries and predicaments. The result is a delightful variation on the kind of novel with disparate characters and plot threads that somehow come together at the end. In this tale, they are together in the mind of a child at the beginning." Salon.com

Tepper, Sheri S.

Singer from the sea. Avon Eos 1999 426p $24

ISBN 0-380-97480-0

LC 99-10231

"Despite her status as a young noblewoman of the planet Haven, Genevieve rebels against the strict regulations concerning highborn women. Defying her father's wishes, she seeks her own forbidden destiny and discovers the dark secrets that lie at the heart of her world and its forgotten history. Tepper . . . continues to explore the intricacies of human societal structures and the complex connections between humans and their environment, combining stylistic grace with imaginative insight." Libr J

Tepper, Sheri S.

The **visitor**; a novel. Eos 2002 407p

ISBN 0-380-97905-5

LC 2001-40197

"Tepper has created a mesmerizing story full of intriguing characters, resonant images and powerful themes." Publ Wkly

Teran, Andi

Ana of California; a novel. Andi Teran. Penguin Books 2015 368 p. (paperback) $16

ISBN 0143126490; 9780143126492

LC 2014042525

"Fifteen-year-old orphan Ana Cortez has just blown her last chance with a foster family. She agrees to leave East Los Angeles for a farm trainee program in Northern California. Emmett Garber is skeptical that this slight city girl can be any help on his farm. His sister Abbie, however, thinks Ana might be just what they need. Ana comes to love Garber Farm. But when she inadvertently stirs up trouble in town, Ana is afraid she might have ruined her last chance." (Publisher's note)

"Teran presents a modern riff on the beloved classic Anne of Green Gables . . . [and] populates her novel with modern bugbears--drugs, gang violence, and hipsters. Newcomers will find a smart-mouthed heroine, a small town populated by a cast of lovable characters, and zippy dialogue that keeps the plot trotting along." Kirkus

Tevis, Walter S.

★ The **queen's** gambit; [by] Walter Tevis. Random House 1983 243p

LC 82-15058

"Familiarity with chess is not needed in order to enjoy this book though aficionados will delight in its evocation of their esoteric freemasonry." Times Lit Suppl

Texier, Catherine

Victorine. Pantheon Books 2004 324p $24

ISBN 0-375-42124-6

LC 2003-54860

"With lush, vivid description, Texier brings to life both the world around Victorine and the woman herself." Libr J

Tey, Josephine

Brat Farrar. Macmillan 1950 219p

First published 1949 in the United Kingdom

"The scene is an English country home owned by the orphaned Ashby children and managed for them by their aunt, who has made a success of the horses she bred and exhibited. Simon, charming and spoiled, is about to take over as he comes of age, when a well-coached imposter arrives and claims to be the elder brother who had disappeared eight years before, leaving a suicide note." Booklist

Tey, Josephine

The **daughter** of time. Macmillan 1952 204p

First published 1951 in England

The author "not only reconstructs the probably historical truth, she re-creates the intense dramatic excitement of the scholarly research necessary to unveil it." N Y Times Book Rev

Tey, Josephine

The **Franchise** affair. Macmillan 1948 238p

"A lawyer in an English country town answers an appeal for help from two women who, having only recently inherited a home, were still outsiders to the townspeople and, being independent, reserved, and unusual, were called witches. When a girl in another town accused them of imprisoning, starving, and beating her in their attic, they were helpless, for the circumstantial evidence seemed indisputable. Good characterization, good writing, and to the lawyer's surprise, an emotional involvement for him." Booklist

Tey, Josephine

The **man** in the queue. Macmillan 1953 213p

First published 1929 by Dutton under the pseudonym Gordon Daviot

A man is stabbed to death waiting in the ticket line of a popular London musical, and Inspector Grant of the C.I.D. is assigned to the case

"Every detail of the discovery of first the identity and then the murderer of the knifed man is admirably invented, and the story, at first sight a simple build-up . . . turns out to be a serious inductive exercise." Springfield Repub

Thackeray, William Makepeace

★ **Vanity** fair; [by] W.M. Thackeray; edited with an introduction by John Sutherland; with 193 illustrations by the author. Oxford University Press 2008 lviii, 949p il (Oxford world's classics) pa $8.95

ISBN 978-0-19-953762-4; 0-19-953762-3

First published 1848

"The book is a densely populated, multi-layered panorama of manners and human frailties. . . . The novel deals mainly with the interwoven fortunes of two women, the wellborn, passive Amelia Sedley and the ambitious, essentially amoral Becky Sharp, the latter perhaps the most memorable character Thackeray created. The adventuress Becky is the character around whom all the men play their parts." Merriam-Webster's Ency of Lit

Thackeray, William Makepeace

The **Virginians**; introduction by M. R. Ridley. Dutton 1965 2v

First published 1857; first United States edition published 1869 by Fields, Osgood & Co.

"A sequel to 'Henry Esmond', it relates the story of George and Harry Warrington, the twin grandsons of Colonel Henry Esmond. The novel follows the brothers from boyhood in America, through various experiences in England, and finally through the American Revolution, in which George fights on the British side and Harry on the side of his friend George Washington." Reader's Ency. 4th edition

Thayer, Nancy

Island girls; a novel. Nancy Thayer. 1st ed. Random House Inc. 2013 320 p. (hardcover) $26.00

ISBN 0345528735; 9780345528735

LC 2013010417

In this novel, "thrice-married Rory Randall dies and in his will leaves his expensive home in Nantucket to his three daughters on the condition that they all live in it together for a summer. Arden and Meg are half sisters. Jenny is the daughter of Rory's third wife, Justine, whom Rory legally adopted." The formerly estranged women "embark upon the requisite summer together. After a rocky start, the reunion results in a life-changing summer for all." (Kirkus Reviews)

Thelen, Albert Vigoleis, 1903-1989

★ The **island** of second sight; from the applied recollections of Vigoleis. Albert Vigoleis Thelen; translated from the

German by Donald O. White. Penguin Group USA 2012 816 p. $29.95

ISBN 1468301160; 1903385067; 9781468301168; 9781903385067

LC 2011379493

First published in German as Die Insel des zweiten Gesichts: Dusseldorf : Diederichs, 1953.

This novel by Albert Vigoleis Thelen is "set on Mallorca in the 1930s in the years leading up to World War II. . . . Pursued by both the Nazis and Spanish Francoists, Vigoleis and Beatrice embark on a series of the most unpredictable and surreal adventures in order to survive. Low on money, the couple seeks shelter in a brothel for the military, serves as tour guides to groups of German tourists, and befriends such literary figures as Robert Graves and Harry Kessler." (Publisher's note)

Theorin, Johan

Echoes from the dead. Delacorte Press 2008 388p pa $12

ISBN 978-0-385-34221-6; 0-385-34221-7

LC 2008-6631

Original Swedish edition, 2007

This novel "set on the desolate Baltic island of Öland, a 'summer place' which is almost uninhabited for the rest of the year. Julia Davidsson has never come to terms with the disappearance of her five-year-old son 20 years previously. No trace of the child has ever been found; until Julia's father, a retired sea captain who lives on the island, receives one of the boy's shoes in the post. Together, father and daughter begin to piece together fragments of the past. Yes, there's plenty of etiolated Nordic gloom, but Theorin's prose is wonderfully descriptive and he writes so well about the natural world that the island is as much a character as the people who live there. The exposition of history and the nature of memory is haunting and lyrical, but never impedes a cracking good plot." Guardian

Theroux, Alexander

★ **Darconville's** cat. Doubleday 1981 704p

ISBN 0-385-15951-X

LC 80-00629

"The hero works as English lecturer in an American Southern women's college and falls in love with a student. Marriage is proposed and arranged, but the false hilding falls for another man. Revenge is planned and curses are articulated, but Darconville meets natural death in Venice. This simple tale easily fills 704 pages, for, in the Rabelaisian manner, it is decorated with monstrous catalogues, liturgies, baroque pastiches, diaries–anything, in fact, to prevent the story from moving fast" Burgess. 99 Novels

Theroux, Marcel

Far north. Farrar, Straus and Giroux 2009 314p $25

ISBN 978-0-374-15353-3; 0-374-15353-1

LC 2008-49224

National Book Award Finalist: Fiction (2009)

"In a postapocalyptic world where civilization is a thing barely remembered, one man in Siberia sees a plane overhead and sets off in search of the place where planes still have the fuel to fly. Theroux's haunting meditation on annihilation gives his novel the power of grief-stricken mourning." Booklist

Theroux, Marcel

★ **Strange** bodies; a novel. Marcel Theroux. Farrar, Straus and Giroux 2014 292 p. $26

ISBN 0374270651; 9780374270650

LC 2013034018

This book follows an inmate of a psychiatric hospital "who insists that he is Dr. Nicholas Slopen, failed husband and impoverished Samuel Johnson scholar. Slopen has been dead for months. Yet nothing can make this man change his story. What begins as a tale of apparent forgery, involving unseen letters by the great Dr. Johnson, grows to encompass a conspiracy between a Silicon Valley mogul and his Russian allies to exploit the darkest secret of Soviet technology: the Malevin Procedure." (Publisher's note)

"Observations about science, medicine, psychology, love, madness, and literature result in a thought-provoking and engaging fusion of comedy and horror, irony and insight." Pub Wkly

Theroux, Paul

Kowloon Tong. Houghton Mifflin 1997 243p

LC 96-29717

"Neville 'Bunt' Mullard is a quintessential Englishman: he likes eating at Fatty's Chophouse, going to the races, and having tea and oaties with Mum. Only Bunt was born and bred in Hong Kong, where he now runs a factory that his father established with Mr. Chuck, who has just died and left his shares to the Mullard family. Bunt is trying to ignore the imminent Chinese takeover of Hong Kong, but then Mr. Hung arrives from the mainland, demanding to buy the well-situated factory—and backing up his demands with some ugly tactics." Libr J

Theroux, Paul

★ The **Mosquito** Coast; a novel. with woodcuts by David Frampton. Houghton Mifflin 1982 374p

LC 81-6787

"The physical impact of the style, the exact observation, the occasional intrusion of the hallucinatory make this a remarkable work of art; its philosophical content is profound." Burgess. 99 Novels

Theroux, Paul

★ **My** secret history. Putnam 1989 511p

LC 88-32182

"'My secret history' is about the permanence of marriage in the face of mistrust and infidelity; it's about the wisdom of women and the foolishness of men; and it's about mature love as the necessary and sometimes successful antidote to youthful selfishness." N Y Times Book Rev

Theroux, Paul

★ **Picture** palace; a novel. Houghton Mifflin 1978 359p

ISBN 0-395-26475-8

LC 77-18725

Picture palace "is an elaborate visual conceit, a sublime meditation on seeing and knowing. Confident and commanding, the author displays his narrative gifts which range from the laconic to the lyrical, the telescopic to the microscopic. This is a novel which, like a photograph, one will return to again and again." Christ Sci Monit

Thien, Madeleine, 1974-

★ **Do** not say we have nothing; a novel. Madeleine Thien. W W Norton & Co. 2016 480 p. (hardcover) $26.95; (ebook) $50

ISBN 039360988X; 9780393609882; 9780393609899

LC 2016040336

Scotiabank Giller Prize (2016)

Man Booker Prize Shortlist (2016)

Baileys Women's Prize for Fiction: Shortlist (2017)

This novel, by Madeleine Thien, "takes us inside an extended family in China, showing us the lives of two successive generations--those who lived through Mao's Cultural Revolution and their children, who became the students protesting in Tiananmen Square. At the center of this epic story are two young women, Marie and Ai-Ming." (Publisher's note)

"Mythic yet realistic, panoramic yet intimate, intellectual yet romantic--Thien has written a concerto dauntingly complex and deeply haunting." Kirkus

Includes bibliographical references

Thilliez, Franck

Syndrome E; Franck Thilliez; translated by Mark Polizzotti. Viking 2012 384 p. $26.95

ISBN 9780670025787

LC 2012004718

In this "French thriller, a veteran Paris profiler struggling with paranoid schizophrenia and a lonely female police detective are brought together by a series of . . . murders" related to "an old experimental film containing disturbing subliminal images." Detective Lucie Hennebelle and Chief Inspector Franck Sharko meet in Canada, where they "learn about the . . . phenomenon of Syndrome E--the inducement of hysteria and violence through sensory control--and its possible role in mass killings." (Kirkus Reviews)

★ **This** way to the end times; classic tales of the apocalypse. edited by Robert Silverberg. Three Rooms Press 2016 xvii, 452 p.p (paperback) $19.95

ISBN 9781941110485; 9781941110478

LC 2016936893

This book, edited by Robert Silverberg, presents "twenty-one exceptional tales of Earth's devastation and humans' inventive, and often ironically self-destructive, ways of surviving . . . These stunning stories contemplate survival while question whether life is worth saving, and many have such rich ideas and settings that they could easily spark full-length novels." (Publishers Weekly)

"With its range of contributors, this is a much-needed volume that will both satisfy the high demand for apocalyptic tales and remind readers of the actual breadth and depth of this literature of the end of the world." Booklist

Thom, James Alexander

Panther in the sky. Ballantine Bks. 1989 655p il

LC 88-48012

The "portrait of Tecumseh, the renowned Shawnee chief and warrior who established a confederacy of tribes in order to resist U.S. encroachment into the Ohio valley, is suitably suffused with fascinating elements of native American lore, legend, and culture. . . . Action and reflection are juxtaposed in a riveting narrative that animates a remarkable cast of celebrated characters and vivifies recorded events. This respectful version of the life of a heroic and courageous native American represents historical fiction at its finest." Booklist

Thom, James Alexander

The **red** heart. Ballantine Bks. 1997 454p map $25

ISBN 0-345-41719-4

LC 97-18577

A "novel based on the well-known true life story of Frances Slocum. The five-year-old daughter of a Pennsylvania Quaker family, Slocum was kidnapped by Delaware Indians in 1778 and adopted by an Indian woman who raised the child as her own. In Thom's telling of her story, we see Slocum grow into a respected figure among the Miamis, becoming Maconakwa—Little Bear Woman—and raising a family on her own. The events of her life are set against the gradual destruction of Indian life on the early U.S. frontier. . . . Thom's research is exhaustive, his eye for detail impressive." Publ Wkly

Thomas, D. M.

★ The **white** hotel. Viking 1981 274p

LC 80-52004

"Repetition, stunningly enacted in imagery that continually circles in on itself, is the method by which Thomas binds us to his prose. The white hotel is the leitmotif. . . . The richness of this book is reminiscent of a painstakingly woven tapestry; one can focus on the details but must be absorbed by the whole." New Repub

Thomas, Dylan

★ The **collected** stories. New Directions 1984 362p

LC 84-6822

Contents: After the fair; The tree; The true story; The enemies; The dress; The visitor; The vest; The burning baby; The orchards; The end of the river; The lemon; The horse's ha; The school for witches; The mouse and the woman; A prospect of the sea; The holy six; Prologue to an adventure; The map of love; In the direction of the beginning; An adventure from a work in progress; A fine beginning; Plenty of furniture; Four lost souls; Quite early one morning; A child's Christmas in Wales; Holiday memory; The crumbs of one man's year; Return journey; The followers; A story; Brember; Jarley's; In the garden; Gasper, Melchior, Balthasar; Portrait of the artist as a young dog: The peaches; A visit to grandpa's; Patricia, Edith, and Arnold; The fight; Extraordinary little cough; Just like little dogs; Where Tawe flows; Who do you wish was with us; Old Garbo; One warm Saturday

Thomas, Matthew

We are not ourselves; a novel. Matthew Thomas. Simon & Schuster 2014 640 p. (hardback) $28

ISBN 147675666X; 9781476756660; 9781476756677

LC 2013044414

In this novel, by Matthew Thomas, "Eileen encourages her husband to want more: a better job, better friends, a better house, but as years pass it becomes clear that his growing reluctance is part of a deeper psychological shift. An inescapable darkness enters their lives, and Eileen and Ed and their son Connell try desperately to hold together a semblance of the reality they have known, and to preserve, against long odds, an idea they have cherished of the future." (Publisher's note)

"Thomas works on a large canvas to create a memorable depiction of Eileen's vibrant spirit, the intimacy of her love for Ed, and the desperate stoicism she exhibits as reality narrows her dreams." Pub Wkly

Thomas, Rosie

All my sins remembered. Bantam Bks. 1992 548p

LC 92-8547

First published 1991 in the United Kingdom

This "tale revolves around interviews biographer Elizabeth Ainger records with her grandmother's elderly cousin, Clio, an accomplished novelist. Once three generations of family history are reconstructed, Elizabeth's project has revealed much more than girlish crushes and failed love affairs. This rousing, thoroughly engaging read moves from Victorian drawing rooms to bohemian Bloomsbury and Nazi Germany, with painful secrets and bittersweet betrayals revealed at every turn." Booklist

Thomas, Rosie

Other people's marriages. Morrow 1994 425p

LC 93-8885

First published 1993 in the United Kingdom

"Effective, precise details vivify physical settings (various homes are as acutely rendered as the cathedral, the novel's central symbol), and the characters, some unappealing but all understandable, are well drawn." Libr J

Thomas, Ross

Ah, treachery! Mysterious Press 1994 274p

LC 94-15118

"In 1989, army major Edd 'Twodees' Partain took part in an illegal operation in El Salvador that his former comrades now want expunged from the record. Meanwhile, top political fund-raiser Millicent Altford needs to recover $1.2 million in stolen under-the-table contributions. These two scenarios dovetail as Altford engineers to have Partain, who was drummed out of the service for assaulting a superior officer, fired from his job in a Wyoming gun store in order to hire him to 'ride shotgun' as she goes after the loot. . . . Thomas's yarn reaffirms his expertise at the black-humored political thriller." Publ Wkly

Thomas, Ross

The **fourth** Durango. Mysterious Press 1989 312p

LC 89-3091

Durango, California is "the ideal hideout for a man with a price on his life. For a fee, the shrewd mayor and her loyal chief of police offer sanctuary to a judge who has just done time on a cooked-up bribery charge. The judge and his son-in-law, a disbarred lawyer, move into 'the only money-losing Holiday Inn west of Beirut' and devise a plan for smoking out the person with the vendetta against the judge. For an even bigger fee, the mayor and her top cop are game to conspire in the scheme—until an extremely ugly man comes to town and starts shooting up the citizenry." N Y Times Book Rev

Thomas, Sherry

Beguiling the beauty; Sherry Thomas. Berkley Sensation 2012 296 p.

ISBN 0425246965; 9780425246962

In this late Victorian historical novel, "Venetia Easterbrook is blindsided when Christian de Montfort, the Duke of Lexington, recklessly states during a Harvard lecture that all beautiful women are untrustworthy and then twists the events of her past marriages to illustrate his point. The twice-widowed beauty gathers her wits and plots the perfect revenge--she will disguise herself during their transatlantic crossing, make him fall in love with her, and then drop him. But her bold plan has unexpected consequences when their passionate, soul-searing affair flares into something more. Venetia realizes too late that she has fallen in love and into her own trap--and Christian will never forgive her deception." (Libr J)

Thomas, Sherry

Delicious; Sherry Thomas. Bantam Books 2008 viii, 404p $6.99

ISBN 9780440244325; 0440244323

LC 2008577558

This romance novel tells the story of "Madame Verity Durant [who] works for Bertram 'Bertie' Somerset at his estate, Fairleigh Park—after serving as the mistress he failed to marry (due to a questionable background that includes an illegitimate child). When Bertie dies unexpectedly at 38, Verity worries as Bertie's 'bastard-born' brother, Stuart—now London's foremost barrister—takes over the estate. Verity had shared a secret, mouthwatering affair with Stuart 10 years earlier, and she doesn't expect him to keep her on, especially since he's affianced to the very proper Miss Lizzy Bessler." (Publishers Weekly)

Thomas, Sherry

★ The **Luckiest** Lady in London; Sherry Thomas. Berkley Pub Group 2013 304 p. (Berkley Sensation historical romance) $7.99

ISBN 0425268888; 9780425268889

In this book, by Sherry Thomas, "Felix Rivendale, the Marquess of Wrenworth, is . . . a man all men want to be and all women want to possess. . . . But underneath is a damaged soul soothed only by public adulation. Louisa Cantwell needs to marry well to support her sisters. She does not, however, want Lord Wrenworth—though he seems inexplicably interested in her. . . . Still, when he is the only man to propose at the end of the London season, she reluctantly accepts." (Publisher's note)

Thomas, Sherry

My Beautiful Enemy; Sherry Thomas. Berkley 2014 304 p. $7.99

ISBN 0425268896; 9780425268896

In this novel by Sherry Thomas "Catherine Blade's [has] a daring that matches any man's. She still doesn't have the one thing she craves: the freedom to live life as she chooses. Finally given the chance to earn her independence, who should be standing in her way but the only man she's ever loved. Their reunion, however, plunges them into a web of espionage, treachery, and deadly foes. With everything at stake, Leighton and Catherine are forced to work together to find a way out." (Publisher's note)

"A thought-provoking exploration of gender roles in the East and West and in the historical romance genre. It's also a darn good read." Kirkus

Thomas, Sherry

Private arrangements. Bantam Books 2008 351p pa $6.99

ISBN 978-0-440-24431-8; 0-440-24431-5

LC 2008-577025

"Camden Saybrook, Lord Tremaine, returns to late 19th-century England to confront his wife, Gigi, about her petition for divorce. Still bitter from Gigi's machinations to snare him as her husband, Camden will grant the divorce under one condition—Gigi must give him an heir within a year. Sparks fly as the two embark on heated attempts to put the bun in the oven, despite Gigi's fear that her next conquest, the insipid Lord Frederick, will discover her duplicitously lusty reunion. A captivating subplot emerges when Gigi's mother, Mrs. Rowland, sets her own plan in motion for Gigi's next nuptials. Thomas propels the plot forward with revealing repartee and gives the leads real nuance." Publ Wkly

Thomas, Sherry

Ravishing the heiress; Sherry Thomas. Berkley Sensation 2012 304 p. $7.99

ISBN 0425250873; 9780425250877

This book is the "second in [Sherry] Thomas's Fitzhugh romance trilogy [and] is set against the realism of 19th-century English arranged marriages. To fill the empty coffers of his family's estate, Lord Fitzhugh must marry Millie Graves, a prosperous manufacturer's daughter" despite wanting to marry his childhood love Isabelle. "Millie . . . proposes a marriage of convenience for a term of eight years. . . . Fitz and Millie's romantic tension grows as they renegotiate their marriage terms." (Publishers Weekly)

Thomas, Sherry

A **study** in scarlet women; Sherry Thomas. Berkley Books 2016 336 p. $15; (ebook) $45

ISBN 9780425281406; 9780698196353

LC 2016019090

In this first book in the Lady Sherlock Series by Sherry Thomas, "Charlotte Holmes has never felt comfortable with the demureness expected of the fairer sex in upper class society. . . . [When London] is struck by a trio of unexpected deaths and suspicion falls on her sister and her father, Charlotte is desperate to find the true culprits and clear the family name. She'll have help from . . . a kind-hearted widow, a police inspector, and a man who has long loved her." (Publisher's note)

"A must-read for fans of historical mysteries and a solid suggestion for classic British mystery lovers." LJ

Another title in this series is:

A conspiracy in Belgravia (2017)

Thomas, Sherry

Tempting the bride; Sherry Thomas. Berkley Sensation 2012 296 p.

ISBN 0425251020; 9780425251027

In this historical romance novel, by Sherry Thomas, "Helena Fitzhugh understands perfectly well that she would be ruined should her secret love affair be discovered. So . . . it is with the greatest reluctance that she accepts help from David Hillsborough, Viscount Hastings, and elopes with him to save her reputation. . . . Helena has despised David since they were children. . . . David, on the other hand, has always loved Helena, but his pride will never let him admit the secrets of his heart." (Publisher's note)

Thompson, James

Lucifer's tears; James Thompson. G.P. Putnam's Sons 2011 323p.

ISBN 9780399157004; 039915700X

LC 2010037041

This book tells the story of Inspector Kari Vaara, a detective who "is pushed into investigating a ninety-year-old national hero for war crimes committed during World War II. The Interior Minister demands a conclusion of innocence, preserving Finland's heroic perception about itself and its role in the war, but Germany wants extradition. In a seeming coincidence, Kari is drawn into the murder-by-torture case of Iisa Filippov, the philandering wife of a Russian businessman. Her lover is clearly being framed for the crime -- and Ivan Filippov's arrogance and nonchalance point the finger at him. But he's being protected from above, leading Kari to the corrupt corridors of power." (Publisher's note)

Thompson, Jean, 1950-

The **humanity** project; Jean Thompson. Blue Rider Press 2013 352 p. (hardcover) $26.95

ISBN 0399158715; 9780399158711

LC 2012028041

"This novel follows two single fathers and their teenage kids. Sean is struggling to find construction work as his house goes into foreclosure. His son, Conner, should be looking forward to college, but, instead, he, too, is scrambling for a job. Art, a pot-smoking, part-time college teacher smitten with his neighbor, Christie, a worldly-wise nurse . . . , has played no role in his now 15-year-old daughter's life," but must after she moves in with him following a school shooting. (Booklist)

Thompson, Jean, 1950-

Wide blue yonder; a novel. Simon & Schuster 2002 367p $24

ISBN 0-7432-0512-X

LC 2001-34157

"It's summer 1999 in Springfield, IL, and Harvey Sloan's sole interest in life continues to be the Weather Channel. His great-niece, Josie, possessed by a hopeless teenage love, confides in Abe Lincoln. Her divorced mother, Elaine, starts to believe that a good or bad day is indicated by her car's service engine light. Meanwhile, Rolando Gottschalk, armed with a gun and an unknown agenda, seems to be headed to Springfield from Los Angeles, leaving a wake of random destruction. Add Mitch, a gorgeous cop, and Rosa, a Mexican cleaning woman, to the mix and you have a novel with characters both memorable and believable." Libr J

Thompson, Jean, 1950-

★ The **year** we left home. Simon & Schuster 2011 325p $25

ISBN 978-1-4391-7588-0; 1-4391-7588-8

LC 2010-47553

"even minor characters receive the full attention of the author's prodigious talents; each one is drawn so vividly that they never feel less than utterly real. To say too much more would ruin the slow, lovely unfurling of Home, a string of largely unremarkable moments told with extraordinary grace." Entertainment Wkly

Thompson, Jim

The **killer** inside me; Jim Thompson; foreword by Stephen King. Mulholland Books/Little, Brown and Company 2014 256 p. (paperback) $15; (ebook) $45

ISBN 9780316404068; 9780316203739

LC 2014015143

In this book, by Jim Thompson, "everyone in the small town of Central City, Texas loves Lou Ford. A deputy sheriff, Lou's known to the small-time criminals, the real-estate entrepreneurs, and all of his coworkers . . . as the nicest guy around. He may not be the brightest or the most interesting man in town, but nevertheless, he's the kind of officer you're happy to have keeping your streets safe. The sort of man you might even wish your daughter would end up with someday." (Publisher's note)

Thompson, Victoria

Murder in Chinatown; a gaslight mystery. Victoria Thompson. Berkley Prime Crime 2007 305 p. (hardcover) $23.95

ISBN 0425215318; 9780425215319

LC 2006052669

This book by Victoria Thompson is part of the Gaslight Mystery series "featuring midwife Sarah Brandt and Detective Sergeant Malloy in turn-of-the-century New York City. Sarah Brandt has made her uneasy way to Chinatown to deliver a baby. . . . When the new mother's half-Chinese, half-Irish niece goes missing, Sarah knows that alerting the police will accomplish nothing, and seeks the one person she can turn to--Detective Sergeant Malloy." (Publisher's note)

Thompson, Victoria

Murder on Fifth Avenue; Victoria Thompson. 1st ed. Berkley Prime Crime 2012 296 p. (A gaslight mystery) (hardcover) $24.95

ISBN 0425247414; 9780425247419

LC 2011052355

This novel, by Victoria Thompson, is part of the Edgar Award-nominated "Gaslight Mystery" series. "From the tenements to the town houses of nineteenth-century New York, midwife Sarah Brandt and Detective Sergeant Frank Malloy never waiver in their mission to aid the innocent and apprehend the guilty. Now, the latest novel . . . finds Sarah and Malloy investigating the murder of a Knickerbocker club member who was made to pay his dues." (Publisher's note)

Thompson, Victoria

Murder on Lenox Hill; a gaslight mystery. Victoria Thompson. 1st ed. Berkley Prime Crime 2005 291 p. (paperback) $23.95

ISBN 0425202607; 9780425202609

LC 2004062759

In this book, part of author Victoria Thompson's Gaslight Mystery series, "[w]hen the affluent Lintons of Lenox Hill summon Sarah Brandt to examine their teenage daughter, their worst fear is confirmed: she is with child. The pregnancy is a mystery, however, as the young woman--mentally still a child herself--is never left on her own. . . . It's a delicate situation, casting suspicion on those close to the Lintons, including their beloved minister." (Publisher's note)

Thomson, E. S. ✓

Beloved poison; E. S. Thomson. Pegasus Crime 2016 390 p. (Jem Flockhart mystery) (hardcover) $25.95

ISBN 9781681772141; 9781681772684; 9781681775388; 1681772140

LC 2017296035

In this novel by E.S. Thomson, "set in . . . 1850s London . . . , St. Saviour's Infirmary awaits demolition. Within its stinking wards and cramped corridors, the doctors bicker and backstab. Ambition, jealousy, and loathing seethe beneath the veneer of professional courtesy. Always an outsider, and with a secret of her own to hide, apothecary Jem Flockhart observes everything but says nothing." (Publisher's note)

"A debut mystery chock full of mysterious doings, riveting historical detail, and so many horrifying anecdotes about the state of medicine in the mid-1800s that you can almost feel the evil miasma rising from the pages." Kirkus

Thon, Melanie Rae

In this light; new and selected stories. Graywolf Press 2011 270p pa $16

ISBN 978-1-55597-585-2

"Two of the book's nine stories center on men. In the other stories in this fine, edgy, often bleak collection, young women crash parties on Indian reservations, break into homes, or live in the woods or in broken-down trailers at the end of desolate Montana roads. Sexually and physically abused as children, the characters experience more in their frequent journeys from home than most adults experience in a lifetime. . . . The book's epigraph reads 'within the pain of living and the tragedy of dying there is ... a luminous mystery that redeems the human adventure in the world.' Luminous mysteries comfort the suffering in Thon's luminous book." Minneapolis Star Tribune

Thu Huong Duong

The **zenith**; Duong Thu Huong; translated by Stephen B. Young and Hoa Pham Young. Viking 2012 509 p.

ISBN 0670023752; 9780670023752

LC 2011046011

This novel, by Duong Thu Huong, "offers an . . . imagined account of the final months in the life of President Ho Chi Minh at an isolated mountaintop compound where he is imprisoned both physically and emotionally, weaving his story in with those of his wife's brother-in-law, an elder in a small village town, and a close friend and political ally, to explore how we reconcile the struggles of the human heart with the external world." (Publisher's note)

Tidhar, Lavie

Central Station; by Lavie Tidhar. Tachyon Publications 2016 288 p. map $15.95

ISBN 1616962143; 9781616962142

In this book, by Lavie Tidhar, "when Boris Chong returns to Tel Aviv from Mars, much has changed. Boris's ex-lover is raising a strangely familiar child who can tap into the datastream of a mind with the touch of a finger. His cousin is infatuated with a robotnik—a damaged cyborg soldier who might as well be begging for parts. His father is terminally-ill with a multigenerational mind-plague. And a hunted data-vampire has followed Boris to where she is forbidden to return." (Publisher's note)

"Tidhar (A Man Lies Dreaming; The Violent Century) changes genres with every outing, but his astounding talents guarantee something new and compelling no matter the story he tells." LJ

Tidhar, Lavie

★ A **man** lies dreaming; a novel. Lavie Tidhar. Melville House 2016 320 p. (hardback) $25.95

ISBN 9781612195049; 1612195040

LC 2015031072

In this novel, by Lavie Tidhar, "Wolf, a low-rent private detective, roams London's gloomy, grimy streets, haunted by dark visions of a future that could have been--and a dangerous present populated by British Fascists and Nazis escaping Germany. Shomer, a pulp fiction writer, lies in a concentration camp, imagining another world. And when Wolf and Shomer's stories converge, we find ourselves drawn into a novel both shocking and profoundly haunting." (Publisher's note)

"Everything in this genre-bender works; intriguing historical characters are worked into expertly managed plots, and the visceral noir atmosphere is juxtaposed nicely against the drawing-room world of London's political scene." Booklist

Tie Ning, 1957-

The **bathing** women; a novel. Tie Ning; translated by Hongling Zhang and Jason Sommer. Scribner 2012 361 p. $26.99

ISBN 1451694849; 9781451694840

LC 2012372350

This book by Tie Ning "follows the lives of four women -- Tiao, a children's book editor; Fan, her sister, who thinks escaping to America might solve her problems; Fei, a hedonistic and self-destructive young woman; and Youyou, a chef -- from childhood during the Cultural Revolution to adulthood in the new market economy. This . . . novel charts the journey of these women as they grapple with love, sibling rivalry, and, ultimately, redemption." (Publisher's note)

The **time** traveler's almanac; edited by Ann and Jeff VanderMeer. Tor Books 2014 948 p. (hardback) $37.99

ISBN 0765374218; 9780765374219; 9780765374240

LC 2014009954

This science fiction anthology, edited by Ann and Jeff VanderMeer, "compiles more than a century's worth of literary travels into the past and the future that will serve to reacquaint readers with beloved classics of the time travel genre and introduce them to thrilling contemporary innovations. This . . . volume includes . . . authors such as Douglas Adams, Isaac Asimov, Ray Bradbury, William Gibson, Ursula K. Le Guin, George R. R. Martin, . . . and Connie Willis." (Publisher's note)

"The VanderMeers, claiming with a wink to have written their preface in 2150 under the watchful eye of the Preservationist Guild, offer these more than 70 stories as proof that fiction is one of the most effective time travel machines in the universe. Organized into four categories--Experiments, Reactionaries & Revolutionaries, Mazes & Traps, and Communiqués--this extensive survey traces literary time travel from its earliest published example, in 1881, to 2012." Booklist

Tinti, Hannah

Animal crackers. Dial Press 2004 197p $22.95

ISBN 0-385-33743-4

LC 2003-70125

"Tinti boldly parses primal emotions in her stealthy short stories, which, like cats' paws, conceal weapons of great precision. Each tale posits interaction between animals and humans, which, rather than offering cuddly moments, lead to vicious or spooky confrontations. Zoos make perfect theaters for Tinti's creepy and caustic satires. . . . Tinti's fables are dark and wily, grim yet morbidly fascinating exposures of both our animal selves and our uniquely human psychoses." Booklist

Tinti, Hannah

The **good** thief. Dial Press 2008 327p $25

ISBN 978-0-385-33745-8

LC 2008-13507

Alex Awards (2009)

This "novel is an homage to old-fashioned boy's-own adventure stories, and unfolds like a Robert Louis Stevenson tale retold amid the hardscrabble squalor of Colonial New England. The sheer strangeness of the story is beguiling: a one-handed boy, tainted by his upbringing in a Catholic orphanage and with little to offer but a head full of lice, is adopted by a con artist, and enters an underworld of ruthless mousetrap-manufacturing barons, feisty chimney-dwelling dwarves, and, perhaps most terrifying of all, black-market dentists. In keeping with the gothic tradition, Tinti writes with an arch, almost camp sensibility. While on a nocturnal grave-digging excursion to procure bodies for a crazy scientist, for instance, the pair encounter an assassin, who tells the twelve-year-old hero that he was 'made for killing.' Will the boy ever discover the truth of his past? It's good fun watching him find out." New Yorker

Tinti, Hannah

The **twelve** lives of Samuel Hawley; Hannah Tinti. The Dial Press 2017 400 p. (ebook) $65; (hardcover) $27

ISBN 9780812989892; 9780812989885

LC 2016021409

In this novel, by Hannah Tinti, "Samuel Hawley isn't like the other fathers in Olympus, Massachusetts. A loner who spent years living on the run, he raised his beloved daughter, Loo, on the road, moving from motel to motel, always watching his back. Now that Loo's a teenager, Hawley wants only to give her a normal life. In his late wife's hometown, he finds work as a fisherman, while Loo struggles to fit in at the local high school." (Publisher's note)

"An accomplished if overstuffed merger of coming-of-age tale and literary thriller." Kirkus

Tobar, Héctor

The **barbarian** nurseries. Farrar, Straus and Giroux 2011 422p il $27

ISBN 978-0-374-10899-1; 0-374-10899-4

LC 2011-10703

This book by Hétor Tobar, set in Orange County, California, follows the "Torres-Thompson household. . . . "Scott, a programmer, . . . lives in the shadow of his own faded glory as a start-up wizard. . . . Maureen is a creative and driven mother. . . . Araceli, the aloof housekeeper and cook . . . is thrust into serving as nanny when Scott dismisses the other Mexican employees because of finances." (World Literature Today)

"Maureen and Scott Torres-Thompson live with their children in upscale Laguna Rancho Estates. Despite Scott's income as a computer game company vice president, bad investments and extravagant spending have forced them to fire their Mexican gardener and nanny. Housekeeper Araceli Ramirez must now do double duty. Though she's a dazzling cook, she's not up for child care, but her undocumented status forces her to accept the situation. Meanwhile, a disconnect is growing between Scott and Maureen. Without communicating to each other or to Araceli, they separately escape the pressures at home, and neither returns for four days. Araceli, alone and worried, has to do something, so she takes off with the two boys to Grandpa John's, with only a vague idea where he lives in central Los Angeles." Libr J

Todd, Charles

A **duty** to the dead; Charles Todd. William Morrow 2009 329 p. (Bess Crawford mysteries) (pbk.) $14.99; o.p.; (hbk.) o.p.

ISBN 9780061791772; 0061791768; 9780061791765

LC 2008055909

"Dedicated to helping the many wounded during the Great War, Bess Crawford receives a desperate request from a dying lieutenant while serving as a nurse aboard a hospital ship. 'Tell my brother Jonathan that I lied,' the young man says. 'I did it for Mother's sake. But it has to be set right.' Back home in England, Bess receives an unexpected response from the dead soldier's family, for neither Jonathan Graham—his mother—nor his younger brother admit to understanding what the message means. But the Grahams are harboring a grim secret, and Bess must, somehow, get to the bottom of it." (Publisher's note)

Other titles in this series are:
An impartial witness (2010)
A bitter truth (2011)
An unmarked grave (2012)
A question of honor (2014)
An unwilling accomplice (2014)
A pattern of lies (2015)
The shattered tree (2016)
A casualty of war (2017)

Todd, Charles

A **question** of honor; a Bess Crawford Mystery. Charles Todd. William Morrow, An Imprint of HarperCollinsPublishers 2013 320 p. (acid-free paper) $25.99

ISBN 0062237152; 9780062237156

LC 2013001604

In this book by Charles Todd, "World War I nurse and amateur sleuth Bess Crawford investigates an old murder that occurred during her childhood in India. . . . The locals are certain that the British soldier was innocent. Yet the present owner of the house where the crime was committed believes otherwise, and is convinced that Bess's father helped Wade flee. To settle the matter once and for all, Bess sets out to find Wade and let the courts decide." (Publisher's note)

Todd, Charles

The **red** door. William Morrow 2010 344p $24.99

ISBN 978-0-06-172616-3; 0-06-172616-8

LC 2009-24160

In post-World War I England, Scotland Yard detective Ian Rutledge faces a wall of silence as he attempts to bring a ruthless killer to justice for the bludgeoning death of a Lancashire woman and the murder of a man who never came home from the Great War

"Twelve books into a series of mysteries set in England in the aftermath of World War I, the mother and son who team-write under the name of Charles Todd keep finding new ways to gauge the emotional effects of war on the living and the half-dead." N Y Times Book Rev

Todd, Charles

An **unmarked** grave; a Bess Crawford mystery. by Charles Todd. William Morrow 2012 262 p. $24.99

ISBN 9780062015723

LC 2011050979

"Gripping, powerful, and evocative, this superb mystery masterwork unfolds during the deadly Spanish Influenza pandemic of 1918, as Bess [Crawford] discovers the body of a murdered British officer among the many dead and sets out to unmask a craven killer." (Publisher's note)

Toer, Pramoedya Ananta

All that is gone; translated from the Indonesian by Willem Samuels. Hyperion East 2004 255p $23.95

ISBN 1-401-36663-5

LC 2003-56675

"A sense of duty is perhaps natural for a writer who spent nearly two decades as a political prisoner under three different regimes. But the striking achievement of these stories is an unshakable innocence of voice and a willingness to leave judgment to the reader. Pramoedya's art is made more of sadness than of anger, and he is particularly adept at narrating from a child's perspective—as when a six-year-old boy sees his best friend, a girl of eight, married off, beaten by her husband, and, after she flees, made a social outcast." New Yorker

Toer, Pramoedya Ananta

The **girl** from the coast; translated by Willem Samuels. Hyperion 2002 280p $22.95

ISBN 0-7868-6820-1

LC 2002-69063

Original Indonesian edition, 1987

In this "tale of feudal Java, a beautiful young woman from a poor fishing village has the misfortune of catching the eye of a Muslim aristocrat who asks to marry her, but who, after a brief ceremony in which a dagger takes the place of the groom, merely installs her in his bleak residence as a lowly concubine. . . . As Toer unfurls this entrancing, indelible tale based on his grandmother's hard life, he deftly dissects the conventions that enable a brutal few to oppress the suffering many." Booklist

Toews, Miriam

A **complicated** kindness; a novel. Miriam Toews. Counterpoint 2004 246p $23

ISBN 1-582-43321-6

LC 2004-7960

"Nomi's hunger for life prevents the novel from being as bleak as her situation might suggest; her account of her trials is veined with a dark humor that glints with the glee of payback." N Y Times Book Rev

Tóibín, Colm, 1955-

The **blackwater** lightship; a novel. Scribner 2000 273p

ISBN 0-684-87389-3

LC 00-21036

First published 1999 in the United Kingdom

"The novel shows us discreetly what a practical, complicated matter dying is, how much logistics and paraphernalia it requires, and its unflinchingly exact style is a kind of respect paid to this. The commonplce and the catastropic lie cheek-by-jowl." London Rev Books

Tóibín, Colm, 1955-

Brooklyn; a novel. Scribner 2009 262p $25

ISBN 978-1-4391-3831-1

LC 2009-10753

This novel "is set in Brooklyn and Ireland in the early 1950s, when one young woman crosses the ocean to make a new life for herself. Eilis Lacey has come of age in small-town Ireland in the years following World War Two. Though skilled at bookkeeping, she cannot find a job in the miserable Irish economy. . . . [In New York], Eilis finds work in a department store on Fulton Street, and when she least expects it, finds love. Tony, a blond Italian from a big family, slowly wins her over with patient charm. . . . But just as Eilis begins to fall in love with Tony, devastating news from Ireland threatens the promise of her future." (Publisher's note)

"A diligent young woman with few opportunities in nineteen-fifties Ireland is packed off by her family to Brooklyn, where she works in a department store, goes to church and night school, and acquires a boyfriend, before a family crisis presents her with a stark choice between her new life and her old one. Within these confines, Tóibín creates a narrative of remarkable power, writing with a spareness and intensity that give the minutest shades of feeling immense emotional impact. Seen through his protagonist's cautious eyes, even hackneyed tropes of Brooklyn life, such as trips to Ebbets Field and Coney Island, take on a subtle strangeness. Purging the immigrant novel of all swagger and sentimentality, Tóibín leaves us with a renewed understanding that to emigrate is to become a foreigner in two places at once." New Yorker

Tóibín, Colm, 1955-

★ The **empty** family; stories. Scribner 2010 275p $24

ISBN 978-1-4391-3832-8; 1-4391-3832-X

LC 2010-32931

The "slow deletion of personal relationships is at the core of the nine stories in this collection, as Tóibín projects a slideshow of reclusive figures, many of whom have found that a life well-hid is a life sufficient. With a spare, eloquent style, he guides us through hotel lobbies and pensiónes from Dublin to Barcelona. He directs our attention to estranged family members, divorcées and Muslim immigrants, catching each of them at the moment in which they are forced to reckon with their pasts." Los Angeles Times Book Rev

Tóibín, Colm, 1955-

★ The **heather** blazing. Viking 1993 245p

ISBN 0-670-84789-5

LC 92-50350

First published 1992 in the United Kingdom

The novel "explores the rigidly controlled mind and soul of a high court Dublin judge, Eamon Redmond. Tóibin . . . {presents the} particulars of Redmond's life: his devotion to the law, his daughter's out-of-wedlock pregnancy, his controversial decision in a case concerning the expulsion of a pregnant high school student, and his wrenching memories of his motherless childhood and his father's debilitation after a stroke." Booklist

Tóibín, Colm, 1955-

House of Names; A Novel. by Colm Toibin. First Scribner hardcover ed. Simon & Schuster 2017 275 p. $26

ISBN 1501140213; 9781501140211

LC 2016478481

This book, by Colm Toibin, presents "Clytemnestra's tale of her own life in ancient Mycenae, the legendary Greek city from which her husband King Agamemnon left when he set sail with his army for Troy. Clytemnestra rules Mycenae now, along with her new lover Aegisthus, and together they plot the bloody murder of Agamemnon on the day of his return after nine years at war." (Publisher's note)

"This extraordinary book reads like a pristine translation rather than a retelling, conveying both confounded strangeness and timeless truths about love's sometimes terrible and always exhilarating energies." LJ

Tóibín, Colm, 1955-

★ The **master**. Scribner 2004 338p $25

ISBN 0-7432-5040-0

LC 2003-67376

This novel depicts the writer Henry James during his middle years.

"What Tóibín has so boldly done-and so brilliantly and successfully-is forge a sympathetic imagining of James' interior lifeÐ.Even the reader who knows little about Henry James or his work can enjoy this marvelously intelligent and engaging novel, which presents not on a silver platter but in tender, opened hands a beautifully nuanced psychological portrait." Booklist

Tóibín, Colm, 1955-

Mothers and sons; stories. Scribner 2007 271p $24

ISBN 978-1-4165-3465-5; 1-4165-3465-2

LC 2006-47181

First published 2006 in the United Kingdom

"So flawless and unshowy is the language in Mothers and Sons that only on reflection does it sink in how varied the tone is among these stories. Yes, they're nearly all melancholic, but every shade in the rainbow of melancholy is represented, and the perspective shifts from mother to son to omniscient with no discernible change in authority." Montreal Gazette

Tóibín, Colm, 1955-

Nora Webster; a novel. Colm Tóibín. Simon & Schuster 2014 384 p. $27

ISBN 1439138338; 9781439138335

LC 2014008519

Carnegie Medal Shortlist: Fiction (2015)

"Set in Wexford, Ireland, [author] Colm Tóibín's . . . seventh novel introduces the formidable, memorable and deeply moving Nora Webster. Widowed at forty, with four children and not enough money, Nora has lost the love of her life, Maurice, the man who rescued her from the stifling world to which she was born. And now she fears she may be drawn back into it." (Publisher's note)

"A novel of mourning, healing and awakening; its plainspoken eloquence never succumbs to the sentimentality its heroine would reject." Kirkus

Tóibín, Colm, 1955-

The **testament** of Mary; Colm Tóibín. Scribner 2012 81 p. $19.99

ISBN 1451688385; 9781442354944; 9781451688382; 9781451690750; 9781451692389

LC 2012007578

Man Booker Prize: Shortlist (2013)

This novel, by Colm Tóibín, portrays the Virgin Mary "as a solitary older woman still seeking to understand the events that become the narrative of the New Testament and the foundation of Christianity. In the ancient town of Ephesus, Mary lives alone, years after her son's crucifixion. She has no interest in collaborating with the authors of the Gospel. . . . She does not agree that her son is the Son of God; nor that his death was 'worth it.'" (Publisher's note)

"A stunning interpretation that is as beautiful in its presentation as it is provocative in its intention." (Booklist)

Tolkien, J. R. R.

★ The **fellowship** of the ring; being the first part of The lord of the rings. 2nd ed.; Houghton Mifflin 1986 423p il $21.95

ISBN 0-395-48931-8

LC 88-120282

First published 1954

"Frodo, a home-loving young hobbit, inherits the magic ring which his uncle Bilbo brought back from the adventures described in the juvenile fantasy 'The hobbit'. This sequel, expressly addressed to adults, is the first of a three-part saga that tells of Frodo's valiant journey undertaken to prevent the ring from falling into the hands of the powers of darkness. Elves, dwarfs, hobbits, men, and sundry evil beings, each as real as the other, populate an allegorical tale that shows how power corrupts." Booklist

Followed by The two towers

Tolkien, J. R. R.

★ The **hobbit,** or, There and back again. Houghton Mifflin 2001 330p il $18; pa $10

ISBN 0-618-16221-6; 0-618-26030-7 pa

LC 2001276594

"Bilbo Baggins is a hobbit who enjoys a comfortable, unambitious life, rarely traveling any farther than his pantry or cellar. But his contentment is disturbed when the wizard Gandalf and a company of dwarves arrive on his doorstep one day to whisk him away on an adventure. They have launched a plot to raid the treasure hoard guarded by Smaug the Magnificent, a large and very dangerous dragon. Bilbo reluctantly joins their quest, unaware that on his journey to the Lonely Mountain he will encounter both a magic ring and a frightening creature known as Gollum." (Publisher's note)

Tolkien, J. R. R.

★ The **lord** of the rings; 50th Anniversary ed; Houghton Mifflin 2004 xxv, 1157p il map slip case $100

ISBN 0-618-51765-0

LC 2004-275215

First published 1954 in the United Kingdom

"This is a tale of imaginary gnomelike creatures who battle against evil. Led by Frodo, the hobbits embark on a journey to prevent a magic ring from falling into the grasp of the powers of darkness. The forces of good succeed in their fight against the Dark Lord of evil, and Frodo and Sam bring the Ring to Mount Doom, where it is destroyed." Shapiro. Fic for Youth. 3d edition

Tolkien, J. R. R.

★ The **return** of the king; being the third part of The lord of the rings. 2nd ed; Houghton Mifflin 1986 440p $21.95

ISBN 0-395-48930-X

LC 88-195987

First published 1955 in the United Kingdom

In the concluding volume of the trilogy "The dark lord of evil is overthrown, the rightful king comes into his own, and the Age of Men begins." Booklist

Tolkien, J. R. R.

The **Silmarillion**; edited by Christopher Tolkien. Houghton Mifflin 1977 365p hardcover o.p.

LC 77-8025

"Tolkien began writing these introductory legends in 1917 and, sporadically throughout his life, continued adding to them; his son Christopher has edited and compiled the various versions into a single cohesive work. Two brief tales, which outline the origin of the world and describe the gods who create and rule, precede the title story about the Silmarils—three brilliant, jewel-like creatures who are desired and fought over, setting up a clash between good and evil." Booklist

Tolkien, J. R. R.

★ The **two** towers; being the second part of The lord of the rings. 2nd ed; Houghton Mifflin 1986 352p $21.95

ISBN 0-395-48933-4

LC 88-195969

First published 1954

"Here the Companions of the Ring, separated, meet Saruman the wizard, cross the Dead Marshes, and prepare for the Great War in which the power of the Ring will be undone." Libr J

Followed by The return of the king

Tolkien, Simon ✓

The **king** of diamonds; Simon Tolkien. 1st ed.; Minotaur Books 2011 324p.

ISBN 9780312539085; 9781250002006; 0312539088

LC 2010040567

This book tells the story of "Oxford police inspector Bill Trave, [who] wasn't fully convinced that David Swain was guilty of murder" when his testimony led to Swain serving a life sentence for the murder of his ex-girlfriend Katya's lover. (Booklist) "Two years later, Trave's marriage has fallen apart. His wife, Vanessa, finds support in the unlikely person of Titus Osman, Katya's uncle, unaware that Titus is keeping Katya a virtual prisoner in her own home. Meanwhile, an embittered Swain plots an escape from prison to get his revenge on his former girlfriend, a plan that results in yet another murder." (Publishers Weekly) "Trave's suspicions lead him to . . . Osman . . . and his sinister brother-in-law, Franz Claes who will go to any lengths to conceal his past connections to the Nazis. . . . Once David is captured, Trave is willing to risk everything . . . to pursue his obsessive belief in Osman's guilt." (Publisher's note)

Tolkien, Simon ✓

Orders from Berlin; Simon Tolkien. Minotaur Books 2012 320 p. $25.99

ISBN 0312632142; 9780312632144

In this World War II novel by Simon Tolkein, "Albert Morrison, ex-chief of MI6, is pushed over the banister outside his London apartment. . . .Scotland Yard detective . . . Trave discovers that Morrison was visited by Alec Thorn, deputy head of MI6, on the day of his death. Could Thorn . . . be involved in a plot to betray his country that Morrison tried to halt?" (Publisher's note)

Tolstaia, Tatiana, 1951 May 3-

The **slynx**; {by} Tatyana Tolstaya; translated by Jamey Gambrell. Houghton Mifflin 2003 278p $24

ISBN 0618124977

LC 2002-27627

Original Russian edition, 2000

This is a first novel by the author of the short story collections "On the Golden Porch" (1989) and "Sleepwalker in a Fog" (1992) and the nonfiction collection "Pushkin's Children: Writings on Russia and Russians." "The novel takes place some 200 years after 'the Blast'—an apparently catastrophic event that left many of the inhabitants of what was once known as Moscow with terrible physical mutations—and concerns the adventures of a numbskull named Benedikt: a foolish, self-centered dolt, thoroughly ignorant of history and thoroughly devoid of moral intelligence." (N Y Times (Late N Y Ed))

"It takes some time for a plot to develop, but Tolstaya sketches a vivid picture of life in this permanent winter. . . . In this extended fable, she captures the Russian yearning for culture, even in desperate circumstances. Gambrell ably translates the mix of neologisms and plain speech with which Tolstaya describes this devastated world." Publ Wkly

Tolstoy, Leo

★ **Anna** Karenina; edited and introduced by Leonard J. Kent and Nina Berberova. Modern Lib. 1993 xxvii, 927p $22.95

ISBN 0-679-60079-5

LC 93-43634

Written in 1873-1876

This novel "is the story of a tragic, adulterous love. Anna meets and falls in love with Aleksei Vronski, a handsome young officer. She abandons her child and husband in order to be with Vronski. When she thinks Vronski has tired of her, she kills herself by leaping under a train. The idea for the story reputedly came to Tolstoy after he had viewed the body of a young woman who committed a similar suicide. A subplot concerns the contrasting happy marriage of Konstantin Levin and his young wife Kitty. Levin's search for meaning in his life and his love for a natural, simple existence on his estate are reflections of Tolstoy's own moods and thoughts of the time." Reader's Ency. 4th edition

Tolstoy, Leo

Childhood, Boyhood and Youth; translated from the Russian by C. J. Hogarth. Knopf 1991 314p $17

ISBN 0-679-40578-X

LC 91-52984

Originally published separately, 1852, 1854 and 1857 respectively; this edition first published 1912

"An autobiographical trilogy. . . . 'Childhood' was the first of Tolstoy's works to receive wide attention. The descriptions of life on a provincial estate are among the best depictions of nature in Russian literature." Reader's Ency. 4th edition

Tolstoy, Leo

The **death** of Ivan Ilyich and Confession; by Leo Tolstoy and translated by Peter Carson. Liveright Publishing Corporation 2013 224 p. (hardcover) $23.95

ISBN 0871404265; 9780871404268

LC 2013018533

In this book, translator Peter Carson presents English versions of fiction and nonfiction works by Leo Tolstoy. "Unlike so many previous translations that have tried to smooth out Tolstoy's rough edges, Carson presents a translation that captures the verisimilitude and psychological realism of the original Russian text." (Publisher's note)

Includes bibliographical references

Tolstoy, Leo

Divine and human and other stories; new translations by Peter Sekirin. Zondervan 2000 211p $19.99

ISBN 0-310-22367-9

LC 00-20791

"These 16 selections from Tolstoy's final eclectic collection of tales titled The Sunday Reading Stories represent the Russian novelist's turn away from the troubling human condition in Anna Karenina toward a growing preoccupation with moral issues." Publ Wkly

Tolstoy, Leo

Resurrection; a new translation, with an introduction, by Anthony Briggs. Penguin Books 2009 xxxiv, 520p (Penguin classics) pa $16

ISBN 978-0-14-042463-8; 0-14-042463-6

Original Russian edition, 1899

"The story deals with the spiritual regeneration of a young nobleman, Prince Nekhlyudov. In his earlier years, he seduced a young girl, Katyusha Maslova. She became a prostitute and later became involved with a man she is accused of poisoning. Nekhlyudov, serving on the jury, recognizes her and decides that he is morally guilty for her predicament. He decides to marry her, and when she is convicted he follows her to Siberia to accomplish his aim. Maslova is repelled by his reforming zeal. She marries another prisoner, but is finally convinced of Nekhlyudov's sincerity and accepts his friendship." Reader's Ency. 4th edition

Tolstoy, Leo

Short stories; selected and introduced by Ernest J. Simmons. Modern Lib. 1964 2v

Contents: v 1: A history of yesterday; The raid; A billiard-markers' notes; The wood-felling; Sevastopol in December 1854; Sevastopol in May 1855; Sevastopol in August 1855; Meeting a Moscow acquaintance in the detachment; The snow storm; Lucerne; Albert; Three deaths; Strider; The porcelain doll; v2: God sees the truth, but waits; A prisoner in the Caucasus; The bearhunt; What men live by; A spark neglected burns the house; Two old men; Where love is, God is; Evil allures, but good endures; Little girls wiser than men; Elias; The story of Iván, the Fool; The repentant sinner; The three hermits; The imp and the crust; How much land does a man need; A grain as big as a hen's egg; The godson; The empty drum; Esarhaddon, King of Assyria; Work, death and sickness; Three questions; The memoirs of a madman; After the ball; Fëdor Kuzmich; Alyósha

Tolstoy, Leo

★ **War** and peace; translated by Constance Garnett. Modern Lib. 1994 1386p $25.95

ISBN 0-679-60084-1

LC 93-38836

Original Russian edition, 1864-1869

"The story covers roughly the years between 1805 and 1820, centering on the invasion of Russia by Napoleon's army in 1812 and the Russian resistance to the invader. Over five hundred characters, all carefully rendered, populate the pages of the novel. Every social level, from Napoleon himself to the peasant Platon Karatayev, is represented. Interwoven with the story of the war are narrations of the lives of several main characters, especially those of Natasha Rostova, Prince Andrey Bolkonsky, and Pierre Bezukhov. These people are shown as they progress from youthful uncertainties and searchings toward a more mature understanding of life." Reader's Ency. 4th edition

Toole, F. X.

Pound for pound; a novel. Ecco 2006 366p $25.95

ISBN 978-0-06-088133-7

LC 2005-49508

This is the "story of Eduardo 'Chicky' Garza, a young San Antonio fighter and grandson of onetime contender Eloy 'Texas Wolf' Garza. When Chicky is cheated out of a shot at the Olympic team, his grandfather encourages him to move to Los Angeles and find trainer Dan Cooley, a former boxer who lost to the grandfather 40 years earlier in a fixed fight. Though struggling with a deep depression brought on by the accidental death of his young grandson, Cooley decides to take Chicky on, paving the way for him to face the fighter who cheated him. The result is powerful and very readable, if somewhat sentimental, and Toole's deep love of boxing's rituals, traditions, and code of honor shines through." Libr J

Toole, John Kennedy

★ A **confederacy** of dunces; foreword by Walker Percy. Louisiana State Univ. Press 1980 338p $24.95

ISBN 0-8071-0657-7

LC 79-20190

"At the heart of this splendid mock-heroic with its blundering and canniness, its falstaffian excesses and 'Alice in Wonderland' wit, lies a profound sense of solitude. Like everything else in Ignatuis J. Reilly's world, the absence of love is larger than life." Newsweek

Torday, Daniel

The **Last** Flight of Poxl West; a novel. Daniel Torday. St. Martin's Press 2015 304 p. $25.99

ISBN 1250051681; 9781250051684

LC 2014036360

In this book, Daniel Torday "introduces readers to Poxl West, whose bestselling 1980s memoir 'Skylock' is the book within this . . . debut novel. Eighteen-year-old Poxl fled his native Czechoslovakia for Rotterdam when Hitler rolled into Austria. . . . He made his way to London, eventually flying bombers in the RAF. Those impossibly difficult war years unfold over five acts . . . which alternate with the narrative of Elijah Goldstein, Poxl's young nephew." (Publishers Weekly)

"After each section of the memoir, Eli returns to fill us in on reviews in the Times and the Economist, the book signings and the things we will not be discussing in this review. A richly layered, beautifully told and somehow lovable story about war, revenge and loss." Kirkus

Torres, Justin

★ **We** the animals. Houghton Mifflin Harcourt 2011 128p $18

ISBN 978-0-547-57672-5; 0-547-57672-2

LC 2011-09159

"An unnamed narrator—the youngest of three boys—grows up dirt poor in upstate New York with a fragile white mother and an unpredictable Puerto Rican father. From flying kites made of trash bags to pounding tomatoes with a mallet until juice runs down their kitchen walls, these boys are out of control and vividly alive. Though partially autobiographical, the novel evokes the exhilaration and violence of boyhood with such authenticity, the reader wonders how the author accessed his memories with such accuracy. Torres . . . brings a poet's attention to the placement and rhythm of words. His lyrical language sustains an almost trancelike reading experience—that is, until an abrupt chronological leap late in the novel finds the narrator transformed from boy to adolescent. Despite this jarring effect, the picture of the narrator's messy upbringing feels complete. His relationships with his brothers and his parents veer off in unexpected, often unwanted, directions, and the force of the book's final emotional punch surprises." Time Out N Y

Tournier, Michel

★ **Friday**; translated from the French by Norman Denny. Johns Hopkins University Press 1997 235p pa $25

ISBN 0-8018-5592-6

LC 96-45295

Original French edition, 1967; this translation first published 1969 by Doubleday

"M. Tournier is a cultivated and disciplined writer, and his Robinson, the son of a Yorkshire draper, is most likable. . . . The castaway has that quaint and peculiarly English stolidity that seems to exist only in the imagination of the French." New Yorker

Tournier, Michel

★ The **ogre**; translated from the French by Barbara Bray. Johns Hopkins University Press 1997 373p pa $19.95

ISBN 0-8018-5590-x

LC 96-46778

Original French edition, 1970; this translation first published 1972 by Doubleday and in the United Kingdom by Collins with title: The Erl-king

A work that "bears patently the marks of greatness. It relentlessly pushes individual idiosyncrasy to–and even beyond–the point of universality. It covers simultaneously the events inside one head and one continent. It uses documentary knowledge–minute and encyclopedic knowledge of photography, history, zoology, anthropometry, weaponry–to illustrate the otherwise undocumentable progress of a human obsession." New Yorker

Towles, Amor

★ A **Gentleman** in Moscow; A Novel. Amor Towles. Penguin Group USA 2016 480 p. map (ebook) $65; $27.00
ISBN 9780399564048; 0670026190; 9780670026197

LC 2016030082

In this novel, by Amor Towles, it is 1922 and "Count Alexander Rostov is deemed an unrepentant aristocrat by a Bolshevik tribunal, and is sentenced to house arrest in the Metropol, a grand hotel across the street from the Kremlin. Rostov, an indomitable man of erudition and wit, has never worked a day in his life, and must now live in an attic room while some of the most tumultuous decades in Russian history are unfolding outside the hotel's doors." (Publisher's note)

"Count Rostov's long transformation occurs against a lightly sketched background of upheaval, repression, and war. Gently but dauntlessly, like his protagonist, Towles is determined to chart the course of the individual." Pub Wkly

Towles, Amor

Rules of civility; a novel. Viking 2011 335 p.
ISBN 9780670022694

LC 2011004118

This novel, which takes place in "1930s New York, . . . [opens with] Katey and her roommate Eve [who are] . . . too besotted with the dashing young banker Tinker to see any signs of trouble. . . . [The book pursues] this love triangle. . . . Katey winds up on Fifth Avenue at the end of her book." (Commonweal)

The book features "New York's wealthy class . . . [with] an unmistakable sense of who belongs and who does not. . . . Towles . . . depict[s] . . . how the upper class can use its money and influence to manipulate others' lives in profoundly unsavory ways." (Publishers Weekly)

"On New Year's Eve 1937, at a jazz bar in New York's Greenwich Village, Katey and Eve are charmed by the handsome and successful Tinker Grey. The three become fast friends and spend early 1938 exploring the town together, until a car accident permanently injures Eve. Feeling guilty, Tinker, the driver, takes care of Eve and unsuccessfully tries to love her. Despite the presence and initial impact of Tinker and Eve, though, this first novel is about Katey's 1938." Libr J

Townsend, Sue

Adrian Mole; the Cappucino years. Soho Press 2000 390p
ISBN 1-56947-204-1

LC 99-87241

First published 1999 in the United Kingdom

"Adrian is a comic Job in a world gone mad with irony and greed. But his confused heart brims with love and good intentions, and Townsend skewers end-of-the millennium Britain with acumen and glee." Booklist

Townsend, Sue

★ The **Adrian** Mole diaries. Grove Press 1986 342p
ISBN 0-394-55298-9

LC 86-226

First published 1985 in the United Kingdom; A combined edition of two titles: The secret diary of Adrian Mole, age 13 ¾ (1982); and Growing pains (1984)

"The messy, inconsistent world of adulthood is seen through the eyes of a 14-year-old aspiring intellectual and poet. Adrian Mole begins his diary when spots appear on his face and his parents' marriage dissolves. By the diary's end he has been in love, become helpmate to a feisty 89-year-old, and held his mother's hand during the birth of his sister. Adrian's pithy commentary records the ludicrousness of school and state bureaucracy and the aberrations of the nuclear age." Booklist

Followed by Adrian Mole: the lost years

Townsend, Sue

Adrian Mole: the lost years. Soho Press 1994 309p $22
ISBN 1-56947-014-6

LC 94-11276

"Portions of this text appeared in The True Confessions of Adrian Albert Mole, while @Adrian Mole and the Small Amphibians' appeared in Adrian Mole, From Minor to Major. Adrian Mole, The Wilderness Years appears in its entirety. All were first published in Great Britain." Verso of title page

"Adrian's latest diaries chronicle his mighty struggle to survive the adolescent and postpubescent years. His outrageous clothes and strong views about everything from the government to unwed mothers can't disguise the angst he suffers: he's still trying to find a niche for his unrecognized genius. . . . Townsend is a satirist of the first order, offering brilliantly witty humor peppered with sobering insights into the troubles and traumas of working-class Brits." Booklist

Townsend, Sue

Number 10; Sue Townsend. Soho 2003 277p $24
ISBN 1-569-47349-8

LC 2003-50562

This novel combines "social satire with an odd-couple road trip. The buddy team includes Jack, a policeman who grew up on the edge of squalor but manages to emerge a decent and levelheaded man. The other half is Edward, reared in privilege to take his all-but-predestined place as prime minister. Struck with the realization that he has no idea what life is like for ordinary citizens, Edward sets off, incognito, for a week-long safari into the land of the common folk, with Jack as his escort. Because it's hard for the prime minister to travel unnoticed, he does what any sensible man would do—slips into a wig and high heels and becomes 'Edwina.' The book doesn't lack for skewering observations of the upper and lower classes, but Edward and Jack are both such well-meaning characters, the book comes off ultimately as more affirming than biting." Booklist

Toyne, Simon

Sanctus. William Morrow 2011 486p $25.99
ISBN 978-0-06-203830-2; 0-06-203830-3

LC 2010-47233

In this first volume of a projected trilogy, "an ancient sect of monks who live in the Citadel, a church carved out of a mountain near the fictional Turkish city of Ruin, have been protecting a secret, 'the Sacrament,' since before the Christian era. A monk who knows the secret, Brother Samuel, escapes from the Citadel and throws himself off the mountain in full view of spectators and news crews. Later, American newspaper reporter Liv Adamsen learns that her phone number, carved into a small leather strap, has been found inside Samuel's stomach. The monk turns out to be her brother, whom she hasn't seen in years, so Liv travels to Ruin to try to solve the puzzle of his mysterious death. She and several other groups battle the deadly monks, who will stop at nothing to thwart their efforts to discover the Sacrament's secret. The truly mind-boggling revelation will leave astounded readers eager for the next installment." Publ Wkly

Tracy, P. J.

Monkeewrench. Putnam 2003 373p $23.95
ISBN 0-399-14978-3

LC 2002-68139

"Unlike the conventionally dimwitted cops and hick sheriff's deputies, Grace and her four geek partners in the software company . . . add real flavor to the proceedings with their colorful jargon and quirky personas. These techno-nerds may be freaks—and one of them may even be a killer—but they have style." N Y Times Book Rev

Tran, Vu, 1975-

Dragonfish; a novel. Vu Tran. W W Norton & Co Inc 2015 320 p. (hardcover) $26.95

ISBN 9780393077803; 0393077802

LC 2015005764

In Vu Tran's novel "Robert, an Oakland cop, still can't let go of Suzy, the enigmatic Vietnamese wife who left him two years ago. Now she's disappeared from her new husband, Sonny, a violent Vietnamese smuggler and gambler who's blackmailing Robert into finding her for him. As he pursues her through the sleek and seamy gambling dens of Las Vegas, . . . Robert learns more about his ex-wife than he ever did during their marriage." (Publisher's note)

"This haunting and mesmerizing debut is filled with all the noir elements—a dark and seedy underworld, damsels in distress, tarnished heroes, and a blurring of moral boundaries. It examines such themes as culture, desperation, memory, mental illness, love, loss, and redemption. Highly recommended for mystery fans." LJ

★ **Transgressions**; edited by Ed McBain. Forge 2005 783 p. (hdbk. : acid-free paper) $27.95

ISBN 0765308517

LC 2004061960

This book presents an anthology of novellas in the "crime and suspense" genre. Donald E. Westlake's "Walking Around Money" follows a "humorous burglar hero." Anne Perry's "Hostages" is a "portrait of a woman caught up in the current Irish troubles who tries to keep her sanity by doing household chores." (Publishers Weekly)

Other stories include "The Corn Maiden" by Joyce Carol Oates, a "tabloid thriller about a mean girl who abducts a slow classmate for ritual sacrifice" and Lawrence Block's "Keller's Adjustment," which tells the story of an "assassin [who] finds himself having existential thoughts about golf communities after 9/11." (Booklist)

Traven, B.

★ The **treasure** of the Sierra Madre. Knopf 1935 366p

Original German edition, 1927

This novel analyzes the "psychology of greed in telling of three Americans searching for a lost gold mine in Mexican mountains." Oxford Companion to Am Lit. 6th edition

Tregillis, Ian

★ The **Mechanical**; Ian Tregillis. Orbit 2015 480 p. (The Alchemy Wars) (paperback) $17

ISBN 0316248002; 9780316248006

LC 2014018728

This speculative fiction novel by Ian Tregillis presents an alternative history where the Dutch created self-aware robotic slaves and have an empire that spans the known world. In it, one mechanical man becomes self-aware and seeks his freedom on a journey to New Amsterdam.

"Although he keeps the pace moving at a brisk clip, the author is able to work in some Big Ideas, asking us to think about what we mean when we speak about souls and free will." Booklist

Another title in this series is:
The Rising (2015)

Tremain, Rose, 1943-

★ The **American** Lover; and other stories. Rose Tremain. W W Norton & Co Inc 2015 256 p. (hardcover) $25.95

ISBN 9780393246711; 039324671X

LC 2014033773

In this short story collection author Rose Tremain "lays bare the soul of her characters--the admirable, the embarrassing, the unfulfilled, the sexy, and the adorable--to uncover a dazzling range of human emotions and desires." (Publisher's note)

"The title story is an extremely well-expressed, profoundly felt look at a done-with affair that spurred the woman to write a novel that becomes famous—but the draw of the story is that the usual affair tropes are given fresh life. The most rewarding story is 'The Housekeeper,' breathtaking in its ingenuity as Tremain imagines the real housekeeper behind Daphne Du Maurier's character Mrs. Danvers, in Rebecca." Booklist

Tremain, Rose

The **color**. Farrar, Straus & Giroux 2003 382p $25

ISBN 0-374-12605-4

LC 2002-192528

"As the story gathers momentum, it widens . . . . Tremain's excursions into the minds of her Maori and Chinese characters are written with a blend of sympathy and irony that sabotages our expectations of things exotic and inscrutable." N Y Times Book Rev

Tremain, Rose

Music & silence. Farrar, Straus & Giroux 2000 485p

ISBN 0-374-19989-2

LC 99-42880

First published 1999 in the United Kingdom

"So hypnotic are Rose Tremain's seductive paragraphs that we are borne along without effort in a world which is neither fact nor fiction but has the strengths of both, with a uniquely sensitive imagination at work." N Y Rev Books

Tremain, Rose

The **road** home. Little, Brown 2008 432p $24.99

ISBN 978-0-316-00261-5; 0-316-00261-5

LC 2008-921700

First published 2007 in the United Kingdom

"Lev has left his mother and child in his village in Eastern Europe to seek work in London, bringing with him an E.U. passport, a handful of English phrases, and a small stash of cash and vodka. At first, he is repelled by what he finds: the shaved heads, the greasy food in disposable packaging, the women thrusting their breasts at him from the pages of the daily paper. But opportunities also push themselves forward in this cold new world; soon he is scheming for a way to unite his future and his past. At once timeless and bitingly contemporary, this novel explores the life now lived by millions—when one's hope lies in one country and one's heart in another." New Yorker

Tremain, Rose

Sacred country. Atheneum Pubs. 1993 323p $21

ISBN 0-689-12170-9

LC 92-21457

First published 1992 in the United Kingdom

The author "gives us a precisely imagined landscape and a complicated group of characters that we come to care deeply about." N Y Times Book Rev

Tremain, Rose

Trespass. W. W. Norton & Co. 2010 253p $24.95

ISBN 978-0-393-07956-2

LC 2010-20934

This novel's first chapter "delivers a minute study of the dissatisfactions of a young girl on a field trip on a hot day. The insights into psychology are penetrating; the aggressive quality of nature is forcefully and believably evoked; the prose itself is luminous. The reader finds much to admire and enjoy, even though the stakes don't seem terribly high. And then the girl starts screaming. Set in the Cévennes region of

France (known for its relentless mistrals and wild mountains), written in an unfaltering style, and peopled by robust characters with shameful, life-altering secrets and unbreakable emotional bonds, this is both a page-turning thriller packed with betrayal, murder, and love, and a gorgeous, meaty literary novel. Perhaps real life cannot unfold as neatly as this plot, but in fiction, such clarity satisfies." Atlantic

Tremayne, Peter, 1943- ✓

Chalice of blood; a mystery of ancient Ireland. Minotaur Books 2011 368p map $25.99

ISBN 978-0-312-55121-6

Investigating the murder of an eminent scholar who was robbed of mysterious manuscripts, Sister Fidelma and her companion, Brother Eadulf, are quickly targeted by the same killer in a case that is complicated by divisive personal problems.

"Tremayne delves deep beneath the surface puzzle, peeling back layer upon layer of fascinating medieval Irish history." Booklist

Tremblay, Paul

Disappearance at Devil's Rock; a novel. Paul Tremblay. William Morrow 2016 288 p. (hardcover) $25.99

ISBN 9780062363268

LC 2015042759

In this book by Paul Tremblay "a family is shaken to its core after the mysterious disappearance of a teenage boy. . . As the search grows more desperate, and the implications of what happened become more haunting and sinister, no one is prepared for the shocking truth about that night and Tommy's disappearance at Devil's Rock." (Publisher's note)

"This tense, quick-moving story, part mystery and part folktale with a dash of police procedural, moves between points of view that offer tantalizing clues and moments of discomfort. The result is a satisfying piece of fiction that shifts genres underneath the reader. " Booklist

Tremblay, Paul

A **Head** Full of Ghosts; Paul Tremblay. William Morrow 2015 304 p. $25.99

ISBN 0062363239; 9780062363237

Bram Stoker Award: Superior Achievement in a Novel (2016)

In this novel, by Paul G. Tremblay, "when 14-year-old Marjorie Barrett begins behaving as though she's demonically possessed, her Massachusetts family starts a reality-based television show, The Possession, to earn the money they desperately need to keep their household together. But is Marjorie really channeling a creature of supernatural evil, or is she just good at Internet research, which keeps her one step ahead of her gullible parents and doctors? " (Publishers Weekly)

"The novel is stylishly written and well-conceived, with lifelike characters and an air of plausibility about it, as if all this really could happen." Booklist

Treuer, David

Prudence; a novel. by David Treuer. Riverhead Books 2015 272 p. $27.95

ISBN 1594633088; 9781594633089

LC 2014028541

This novel, by David Treuer, "about love, loss, race, and desire in World War II-era America. . . . Frankie Washburn returns to his family's rustic Minnesota resort for one last visit before he joins the war as a bombardier. . . . Awaiting him at the Pines are those he's about to leave behind. . . . But before the homecoming can be celebrated, the search for a German soldier, escaped from the POW camp across the river, explodes in a shocking act of violence." (Publisher's note)

"Clearness and precision are what Ojibwa writer Treuer (The Translation of Dr Apelles, 2006) so evocatively attains in this magnetizing and richly original novel. As he cycles in and out of his extraordinarily affecting characters' lives of deprivation and stoicism, he elucidates stygian emotions and annihilating psychological traumas incited by brutal, even genocidal conflicts over sexuality, race, and religion. Treuer's trenchant and compassionate novel glimmers with nature's potent beauty, fresh historical detail, and scrupulous insight." Booklist

Treuer, David

The **translation** of Dr Apelles; a love story. Graywolf 2006 344p $23

ISBN 978-1-55597-451-0; 1-55597-451-1

LC 2006-924339

This "novel is a metaphysical blending of two love stories, one mythological, the other very much in the urban present. Dr Apelles is a Native American translator of ancient Native American texts—every other Friday. The rest of his time is spent in a vast library, sorting an endless succession of obscure books. He feels that no one would notice if he disappeared, and knows that he takes too much comfort in 'the bouquet of languages he holds so dear.' Then a new translation he is working on sends him into a tailspin. It's a mythological tale of two orphaned Native Americans from different tribes who fall in love, suffer hardships, and eventually marry. Dr Apelles becomes immersed in his translation, seeing his own life as pale and loveless in comparison. As he becomes romantically involved with a coworker, the translation becomes the story he tells her of his own life. Treuer's novel comprises an intricate and provocative labyrinth that challenges the reader at every turn." Booklist

Trevanian

★ The **Eiger** sanction. Crown 1972 316p

"American art professor-mountain climber Dr. Jonathan Hemlock moonlights as an assassin in the employ of the Search and Sanction Division of the mythical counter-assassination bureau known as C-11. In his last mission before retirement, he is sent along on a top-flight mountain climbing expedition in Switzerland with orders to liquidate one of three companions known to have killed an unlucky C-11 agent in Montreal. Not knowing the identity of the assassin Hemlock ruthlessly plans to bump off all three." Smith. Cloak and Dagger Fic

Trevanian

Incident at Twenty Mile. St. Martin's Press 1998 308p $24.95

ISBN 0-312-19233-9

LC 98-19401

"Matthew Dubcheck wanders into the dying silver-mining town of Twenty-Mile, Wyoming, and declares himself the Ringo Kid, after the hero of his favorite dime novels. The romanticized West clashes with the real West when an escaped con comes to town, befriends Matthew, and the wheels begin to turn toward an inevitably tragic conclusion. The anti-western is also a staple of the genre, and this tragicomic tale takes its place alongside such similar efforts as True Git and poet David Waggoner's delightful Where Is My Wandering Boy Tonight?" Booklist

Trevanian

The **Loo** sanction; a novel. Three Rivers Press 2005 294p pa $13.95

ISBN 1-4000-9828-9; 978-1-4000-9828-6

LC 2004-29743

First published 1973

"The plot, though fast-moving, is not the most sophisticated, yet there is a certain excitement in this descendant of James Bond, and it works despite one's better judgment." Libr J

Trevanian

Shibumi. Crown 1979 374p

LC 78-20950

This novel relates the "feats of Hel, the world's highest-paid assassin. Hel guns down political terrorists of the CIA, PLO, and various other organizations, then takes on the superpower of espionage agencies, the Mother Company." Publ Wkly

Trevanian

★ The **summer** of Katya. Crown 1983 242p

LC 83-1790

"The time is 1914 and the story takes place in a small French Basque village. Dr. Jean-Marc Montjean, young and newly graduated from medical school, meets and falls in love with Katya, a beautiful young girl. Their encounter comes by way of an accident that befalls Katya's brother Paul, to whom she is very attached. Jean-Marc becomes involved with their family and begins to pay court to Katya. He is warned that any romantic attachment is out of the question because of her delicate health. A mystery in the background of the family hangs over all their relationships, and in a final meeting there is a shocking climax that leaves the reader stunned." Shapiro. Fic for Youth. 3d edition

Trevor, William

A **bit** on the side. Viking 2004 244p $24.95

ISBN 0-670-91507-6

LC 2004-42035

The author "reveals his native Ireland as a world sandwiched between modernity and its accompanying wealth, secularism and vulgarity, and a past that was more soulful and pious but also more restrictive. . . . Trevor . . . explores the many sources and shadings of regret with his usual delicate but brilliant psychological nuance, brightened occasionally by nostalgia for the lost love that once impelled his characters forward. " Pub Wkly

Trevor, William

★ **Death** in summer. Viking 1998 214p $23.95

ISBN 0-670-88202-X

LC 98-21569

"A sudden death brings together a rootless, shifty young woman named Pettie and the recently widowed Thaddeus Davenant, who is trying to find a nanny for his baby daughter. With a badly typed letter of reference and threadbare clothing, Pettie is quickly turned away, but not before she has formed an irresistible (if deceived) impression of the life she could share with Thaddeus. Trevor inhabits his characters so fully that they seem present before us, and his exploration of their accidental connections demonstrates, yet again, his ability to imbue the most casual actions with unsettling significance." New Yorker

Trevor, William

★ **Felicia's** journey. Viking 1995 212p

ISBN 0-670-85745-9

LC 94-32413

First published 1994 in the United Kingdom

"Trevor is chilling and precise in his evocation of the loss of innocence, loss of heart, while he highlights the dismal features of contemporary society. Felicia's journey proceeds in an inimical atmosphere in which disquiet and corruption are the order of the day." New Statesman Soc

Trevor, William, 1928-2016

Fools of fortune. Viking 1983 238p

ISBN 0-670-32355-1

LC 83-47867

"Willie Quinton tells of an idyllic childhood on his family's small estate, an ordered life shattered by the uprising, by the division of Irish society and, finally, by murder and destruction of their home. Uprooted to Cork, Willie lives with his widowed, alcoholic mother; goes to school; and eventually meets Marianne, a distant cousin from England. Their brief love is eclipsed by Willie's vengeance on his family's destroyer, shattering all their lives until his gentle daughter, Imelda, resumes the thread." (Libr J)

Trevor, William

Love and summer. Viking 2009 211p $25.95

ISBN 978-0-670-02123-9; 0-670-02123-7

LC 2009-18184

"The speech in this novel, bare and unvarnished, is a constant joy, partly because [Trevor's] characters tend to reticence, to a reluctance to reveal themselves in what they say, and yet do so time and again, even in conversations in which nothing is said openly, but only obliquely, indeed especially in such conversations. His sympathy extends, with rare art, to them all." Scotsman

Trigiani, Adriana

Big Cherry Holler; a Big Stone Gap novel. Random House 2001 272p

ISBN 0-375-50617-9

LC 2001-18599

"Although readers of Big Stone Gap are going to find this novel more serious, they should rest assured that most of the old favorite small town characters are still there. Catching an earful, usually unsolicited, of their views and advice on life, marriage, and love is a part of the charm of both the predecessor and this follow-up." Booklist

Trigiani, Adriana

Big Stone Gap; a novel. Random House 2000 272p

ISBN 0-375-50403-6

LC 99-43306

"One chapter, which is based on a real-life campaign visit from John Warner and his then-wife Elizabeth Taylor is a hoot. And you don't want to miss Ave Maria's friend, the sexy Iva Lou Wade, one of the best fictional librarians to come along in years." Libr J

Trigiani, Adriana

Very Valentine. HarperCollins Publishers 2009 371p $25.95

ISBN 978-0-06-125705-6; 0-06-125705-2

LC 2008-34314

In this first book in a projected trilogy, Valentine Roncalli struggles to save her decades-old family business, finding love and the life she wants along the way.

"Food, shoes and romance feature prominently in this zesty novel of an Italian-American family. . . . Rich descriptions of beautiful things—a Greenwich Village rooftop garden, the Blue Grotto of Capri, a bounty of well-made meals, sexy men in sweaters—create a (not quite) fairy tale of guilty pleasures." Kirkus

Trollope, Anthony

★ **Barchester** Towers. Knopf 1992 xxxiii, 277p (Chronicles of Barsetshire) $20

ISBN 0-679-40587-9

LC 91-53197

First published 1857. Second of the Chronicles of Barsetshire

"Continues the picture of clerical society with its peculiar humors and foibles. The chief incidents are connected with the appointment of a new bishop, the troubles and disappointments this involves, and the intrigues and jealousies of the clergy: the henpecked bishop, the ambitious archdeacon, and the dean, canons, and others, with their wives. The picture of the eccentric Stanhope family is particularly delicious." Lenrow. Reader's Guide to Prose Fic

Followed by Doctor Thorne

Trollope, Anthony

Doctor Thorne; with an introduction by N. John Hall. Knopf 1993 xxxi, 319p (Chronicles of Barsetshire) $20

ISBN 0-679-42304-4

LC 93-1853

First published 1858. Third of the Chronicles of Barsetshire

"A story of quiet country life; and the interest of the book lies in the character studies rather than in the plot. The scene is laid in the west of England about 1854. The heroine, Mary Thorne, is a sweet, modest girl, living with her kind uncle Doctor Thorne, in the village of Greshambury, where Frank Gresham, the young heir of Greshambury Park, falls in love with her." Keller. Reader's Dig of Books

Followed by Framley parsonage

Trollope, Anthony

★ The **Eustace** diamonds. Knopf 1992 xxxi, 249p $20

ISBN 0-679-41745-1

LC 92-52910

First published 1872

The third Palliser novel. "The story follows two contrasting women and their courtships. Lizzie Eustace and Lucy Morris are both hampered in their love affairs by their lack of money. Lizzie's trickery and deceit, however, contrast with Lucy's constancy. Trollope was understood to be commenting on the malaise in Victorian England that allowed a character like Lizzie, who marries for money, steals the family diamonds, and behaves despicably throughout, to rise unscathed in society." Merriam-Webster's Ency of Lit

Trollope, Anthony

Framley parsonage; with an introduction by Graham Handley. Knopf 1994 xxxi, 587p (Chronicles of Barsetshire) $20

ISBN 0-679-43133-0

First published 1861. Fourth of the Chronicles of Barsetshire

"The vicar of Framley, a weak but honest young man, is led astray and into debt by a spendthrift M. P., and finds himself in a false position. The other branch of the story deals with his sister's chequered love affair and marriage to young Lord Lufton. A great crowd of characters are engaged in the social functions, the intrigues and the match making, the general effect of which is comic, though graver interest is never far off, and there are situations of deepest pathos." Baker. Guide to the Best Fic

Followed by The small house at Allington

Trollope, Anthony

The **last** chronicle of Barset; with an introduction by Graham Handley. Knopf 1995 xxix, 983p (Chronicles of Barsetshire) $24

ISBN 0-679-44366-5

LC 95-75205

First published 1867. Sixth in the Chronicles of Barsetshire

"The ecclesiastical society of 'The Warden,' Mr. Harding, Mrs. Proudie, and the rest make their last appearance. The dominant situation is one of intense anguish. A poor country clergyman, proud, learned, sternly conscientious is accused of a felony, and the pressure of family want makes his guilt seem only too probable." Baker. Guide to the Best Fic

Trollope, Anthony

★ The **prime** minister. Oxford University Press 2009 xxiv, 438p il (Oxford world's classics) pa $14.95

ISBN 978-0-19-953775-4; 0-19-953775-5

First published 1876

"Considered by modern critics to represent the apex of the 'Palliser novels', it is the fifth in the series and sustains two plot lines. One records the clash between the Duke of Omnium, now prime minister of a coalition government, and his high-spirited wife, Lady Glencora, whose drive to become the most brilliant hostess in society causes embarrassment for her husband and eventually contributes to his downfall. The second plot reveals the machinations of Ferdinand Lopez, an ambitious social climber who wins the support of Lady Glencora—but not her husband—for an election campaign. The novel brilliantly dissects the politics of both marriage and government." Merriam-Webster's Ency of Lit

Trollope, Anthony

The **warden**; introduction by Louis Auchincloss; notes by Andrew Maunder. Modern Library 2003 230p (Chronicles of Barsetshire) pa $11

ISBN 0-8129-6704-6

LC 2002-24533

First published 1855. First of the Chronicles of Barsetshire

"The Reverend Septimus Harding, the conscientious warden of a charitable retirement home for men, resigns after being accused of making too much profit from the sinecure." Merriam-Webster's Ency of Lit

Includes bibliographical references

Followed by Barchester Towers

Trollope, Joanna

The **best** of friends. Viking 1998 293p $23.95

ISBN 0-670-87973-8

LC 97-49162

First published 1995 in the United Kingdom

"Trollope's facility at spinning an intricate story is enhanced by light-fingered dialogue, and the lesson she spins in this tale of easy pleasure and its complicated aftermath is both sobering and hopeful." Publ Wkly

Trollope, Joanna

Brother and sister. Bloomsbury 2004 311p $23.95

ISBN 1-582-34400-0

LC 2003-62649

"Trollope is a pointillist of domestic relationships, and she has built an impressive body of work addressing powerful tensions like those that animate Brother and Sister. With well-placed strokes, she brings to life all of her characters, including the complex lives of the birth mothers. She's especially accomplished in her portrayals of children by turns humorous, frustrating or heartbreaking, but never precious." Washington Post Book World

Trollope, Joanna

Friday nights; a novel. Bloomsbury 2008 330p $24.99

ISBN 978-1-59691-407-0; 1-59691-407-6

LC 2007-37579

"Retiree Eleanor often sees Paula and Lindsay, two harried young mothers, passing on the street and decides they should have time to relax. Paula and Lindsay, who have never met each other before, turn down Eleanor's offer of babysitting but are flustered enough to accept her invitation to visit her one Friday evening. The group soon expands to include Blaise, Eleanor's neighbor; Karen, Blaise's coworker; and Jules, Lindsay's younger sister. Trollope outlines each woman's history, deftly interweaving their individual stories with those of the new connections growing among them. When Paula begins dating Jackson Miller, the equilibrium of the group is altered, and as Jackson becomes a part of all of their lives, events occur that will change the group forever. Trollope's novel rings true, portraying the complexities of contemporary women's lives without sentimentality or melodrama." Libr J

Trollope, Joanna

Marrying the mistress. Viking 2000 293p

ISBN 0-670-89150-9

LC 99-462175

"None of the themes here . . . are terribly unusual, but Trollope's proven ability to present them intelligently, as moral and emotional tangles faced by thinking, interesting people, satisfyingly combines the universally recognizable and the intellectually engaging." Publ Wkly

Trollope, Joanna

The **men** and the girls. Random House 1993 248p

LC 93-18421

First published 1992 in the United Kingdom

"One of the pleasures in good contemporary British fiction like 'The Men and the Girls' is the writing itself—deft, fluid, perceptive and concise. Another is the wonderfully wry humor, particularly when its objects are sacred cows. Like Muriel Spark, Joanna Trollope is hilarious about old people, for instance." N Y Times Book Rev

Trollope, Joanna

Next of kin. Viking 2001 289p $23.95

ISBN 0-670-89999-2

LC 2001-17743

"In addition to crafting an absorbing narrative, Trollope charms with her depiction of several young children, whose speech and behavior are captured with clarity and endearing fidelity." Publ Wkly

Trollope, Joanna

The **other** family. Simon & Schuster 2010 321p pa $15

ISBN 978-1-4391-2983-8

LC 2010-00529

"Richie Rossiter is an aging crooner with a shrinking yet substantial fan base. He lives in London with Chrissie, his beautiful, common-law wife, 20 years his junior. Chrissie has been managing his career for 25 years, ever since they embarked on the affair that demolished his marriage. Only Richie never legally ended his marriage. Even after raising three daughters with Chrissie, he has refused to propose. Chrissie has been comforting herself with the knowledge that he hardly thinks of his wife and their son. But when Richie dies suddenly of a heart attack, she learns the truth. Richie has left his first family the lion's share of his musical estate, which includes a beautiful Steinway piano, his prized possession. The novel brilliantly explores the fallout of Richie's will." Globe and Mail

Trollope, Joanna

★ **Other** people's children. Viking 1999 294p $23.95

ISBN 0-670-88513-4

LC 98-40004

"Falling in love with a man does not mean falling in love with his children: that is the premise of this story of linked and sundered families. Josie's second marriage includes three stepchildren, whose loyalty to their inadequate mother makes them hate Josie for her very competence; Elizabeth's beloved fiancé comes with a son she adores and a grown daughter determined to oust her. Trollope may not aim high, but she aims for the heart, and she hits it." New Yorker

Trollope, Joanna

Second honeymoon; a novel. Bloomsbury 2006 323p $23.95

ISBN 978-1-59691-038-6; 1-59691-038-0

LC 2005-57011

The author "excels at middle-class family dramas, and [this] is a welcome entry in her canon. Like an overzealous housewife who just can't step away from the vacuum, she succumbs to the impulse to tidy up all the subplots. But Edie, Russell, and their brood are winning enough that fans will want to move in right along with the kids." Christ Sci Monit

Trollope, Joanna

A **Spanish** lover. Random House 1996 334p

LC 96-24846

First published 1993 in the United Kingdom

"Lizzie has been rather smug about her thriving marriage, her four children, her successful shop, and her big house, but she becomes unconscionably jealous when Frances, her quiet, devoted twin, finds love with the sexy, supportive, but married—and foreign—Luis. This British author excels at setting up the stuff of female fantasy and, from those worn materials, making something that draws you in and slams you with a thud of emotion so authentic it becomes your own." New Yorker

Tropper, Jonathan

How to talk to a widower. Delacorte Press 2007 341p $20

ISBN 978-0-385-33890-5; 0-385-33890-2

LC 2006-28678

"Since magazine columnist Doug Parker's wife died in a plane crash one year ago, he's been caught in the whirlpool of his grief. The bigger world, though, is trying to pull him back out. Doug's teen stepson is getting into trouble at school, and his little sister is getting married soon. Meanwhile, his other sister is trying to set him up with every woman in town. What ensues is equal parts hilarity and despair—often, both at once. As always, Jonathan Tropper cares deeply for his characters, warts and all, and writes very sweetly about the fragile yet resilient world they inhabit." PopMatters

Tropper, Jonathan

One last thing before I go; a novel. Jonathan Tropper. Dutton 2012 324 p.

ISBN 0525952365; 9780525952367

LC 2012019370

In this novel by John Tropper "Drew Silver is dying in many ways: his marriage has been over for seven years, his ex-wife is getting remarried, his career as a rock drummer is long past, his 18-year-old daughter is pregnant, and he has a life-threatening heart condition. . . . [T]he awareness of his precarious health causes him to rethink his pathetic life, and he's able to come up with a to-do list. . . . By the end of the novel he's able to cross almost everything off." (Kirkus)

Trueblood, Valerie

Seven loves; a novel. Little, Brown and Co. 2006 232p $23.95

ISBN 978-0-316-05893-3

LC 2005-26604

This "novel follows the story of 74-year-old May Nilsson, a retired English teacher and widow, who finds herself belonging to the country of old women and reminiscing on a past defined by love. May remembers the difficult and pleasurable years of her marriage to a doctor as well as the excitement and pain of an extramarital affair. She reflects on a young coworker's elementary nature, her son's capriciousness, and her mother's political convictions. Each chapter presents an impressionistic view of May's family, friends, and lovers and their varying degrees of longing and happiness. Gently told, Trueblood's first work is poetic, contemplative, and tender." Booklist

Truman, Margaret ✓

Murder at Ford's Theatre. Ballantine Bks. 2002 326p $24.95

ISBN 0-345-44489-2

LC 2002-74748

"When the body of congressional intern Nadia Zarinski turns up outside the stage door of Ford's Theatre, D.C. police detectives Mo Johnson and Rick Klayman, who happens to be a Lincoln buff, are assigned the case. Nadia worked in the office of Senator Bruce Lerner, ex-husband of Clarise Emerson, head of Ford's Theatre and nominee for chair of the National Endowment for the Arts. Once Clarise determines with Klayman's help that her son, Jeremiah, was the last to see Nadia alive, she appeals to former attorney Mackensie 'Mac' Smith to represent him." Publ Wkly

Truman, Margaret

Murder at the Library of Congress. Random House 1999 322p $25

ISBN 0-375-50068-5

LC 99-14953

"Pre-Columbian art expert Annabel Smith has been asked to write an article on a second diary of Columbus' voyage—if such an artifact really exists. Her research takes her into the inner workings of LC and leads to the discovery of illicit payoffs and the solutions to a pair of murders, one old, one new." Booklist

Truman, Margaret ✓

Murder in the White House; a novel. Arbor House 1980 235p

LC 79-54004

"When Secretary of State Blaine is murdered in the Lincoln Sitting Room of the White House, President Webster orders Special Counsel Fairchild to coordinate efforts to solve the case with the authorities. The lawyer turned detective begins investigating everyone with access to the White House, including Webster, the First Lady and her daughter Lynne." Publ Wkly

Truman, Margaret

Murder on Capitol Hill; a novel. Arbor House 1981 255p

LC 80-70223

"Lawyer Lydia James agrees to the request of Veronica Caldwell to act as counsel for the senatorial committee investigating the killing of her husband, Senate Majority leader Cale Caldwell. He has been stabbed at a reception honoring him, where his black-sheep son Mark, member of a fanatical cult, is among the 200 or more guests. Mark is arrested for the murder, and also on suspicion of having killed Jimmye, Veronica's niece, years earlier, an unsolved crime. His mother and brother, Cale Jr., sorrowfully agree that Mark is guilty, but Lydia believes the charges are trumped up. She gets herself into dicey situations, chasing clues." Publ Wkly

Trumbo, Dalton

★ **Johnny** got his gun. Lippincott 1939 309p

"Far more than an antiwar polemic, this compassionate description of the effects of war on one soldier is a poignant tribute to the human instinct to survive. Badly mutilated, blind, and deaf, Johnny fights to communicate with an uncomprehending medical world debating his fate." Shapiro. Fic for Youth. 3d edition

Truong, Monique

Bitter in the mouth; a novel. [by] Monique Truong. Random House 2010 282p $25

ISBN 978-1-4000-6908-8; 1-4000-6908-4

LC 2009051674

A personal tragedy compels Linda to return to Boiling Springs, North Carolina, and spend time with her family.

"Linda, a young woman coming of age in small-town North Carolina, has a fascinating condition—one that causes her to 'taste' the words she hears. It forces her to struggle through a distracting bombardment of flavors like canned green beans, sour cream, parsnips and Fruit Stripe gum. But Linda's relationship with food and language soon becomes quirky background music when compared with the relationships she has with the people in her life, including her overweight childhood best friend, her doting gay uncle, her first secret affair and her oddly distant mother. . . . Truong's narrative yanks the reader through Linda's world swiftly and with impressive command." Time Out N Y

Truong, Monique

The **book** of salt; [by] Monique Truong. Houghton Mifflin 2003 261p $24

ISBN 0-618-30400-2

LC 2002-192152

"Truong is tapping some trendy territory here: the postcolonial perspective; the book derived from a minor character in another well-known book. . .; the gay novel; the novel of exile. And Truong's central character, the gay Asian houseboy, is something of a stereotype in itself. But nothing in this distinctive novel feels secondhand." N Y Times Book Rev

Truscott, Lucian K.

Heart of war. Dutton 1997 370p

LC 96-29876

"Despite some occasionally breathy prose, Truscott's novel provides a fascinating peek behind the olive drab curtain, blending a solid plot with a piercing critique of hypocrisy, power politics and sexual misconduct in today's armed forces." N Y Times Book Rev

Trussoni, Danielle

Angelology. Viking 2010 451p $27.95

ISBN 978-0-670-02147-5; 0-570-2147-4

LC 2009-41430

"An ambitious adventure story with enough literary heft and religious fervor to satisfy anyone able to embrace its imaginative conceits and Byzantine plot." Kirkus

Trussoni, Danielle

Angelopolis; Danielle Trussoni. Penguin Group USA 2013 320 p. (hardcover) $27.95

ISBN 0670025542; 9780670025541

LC 2013001515

In this novel, by Danielle Trussoni, "now an elite angel hunter for the Society of Angelology, [Verlaine] pursues his mission with single-minded devotion: to capture, imprison, and eliminate . . . [half-angels]. But when Evangeline suddenly appears on a twilit Paris street, Verlaine finds her nature to be unlike any of the other creatures he so mercilessly pursues, casting him into a spiral of doubt and confusion." (Publisher's note)

"Trussoni's unevenly paced second offering is not quite up to the standards set by her debut novel. Exciting skirmishes and conflicts are dragged down by extensive historical explanations, and the introduction of a new major character falls flat. Despite the inconsistencies, devotees of Trussoni's first novel will enjoy this continuation of the crusade to save humankind." LJ

Tryon, Thomas

In the fire of spring. Knopf 1991 609p

LC 91-414

In this sequel to The wings of the morning "a runaway slave, Rose Mills, is helped to safety by the abolitionist Appleton Talcott and two of his daughters as they return home to Pequot Landing. . . . The Talcotts and the slave-owning Grimes family are still feuding, but it's now 1841, and fuel has been added to the fire. First of all, the Talcotts open a school for young black women, which gives the Grimeses something new to holler about. Second, Appleton's wife, Mabel Talcott, is secretly dying. As she ponders her mortality and worries about her children, her dying wish is granted: daughter Aurora, abroad for years with husband and child, returns home. Mab's heart breaks as she learns of her daughter's travails and of her undying love for the true father of her child—none other than the swashbuckling, lady-killing Sinjin Grimes." Booklist

Tryon, Thomas

★ The **other**. Knopf 1971 280p

"Bizarre events occur in and around the once-prosperous Perry family in Connecticut during the 1930s. The men have all died mysteriously and brutally. Niles and Holland, 12-year-old twins, seem to be linked to the ghastly deaths and disasters. A compassionate Russian grandmother plays along with Niles's deception and tries to protect him." Shapiro. Fic for Youth. 3d edition

Tryon, Thomas

The **wings** of the morning. Knopf 1990 567p

LC 89-39513

"Unalloyed pleasure for fans of this genre, Tryon's literate 19th-century soap opera is steeped in the rhythms of Trollope and Scott." Publ Wkly

Followed by In the fire of spring

Tsan-hsueh

Blue light in the sky & other stories; [by] Can Xue; translated by Karen Gernant and Chen Zeping. New Directions 2006 212p pa $14.95

ISBN 978-0-8112-1648-7; 0-8112-1648-9

LC 2006-9091

Can Xue "writes in the artless prose of fairy tales and employs a curious dreamlike logic in her narratives. Characters witness grotesque illnesses, dodge natural catastrophes and endlessly wander through dark labyrinths of misunderstanding. . . . [One of her narrator's] says of fishing nets, 'Only a random string is needed-the less related, the better,' and it's a deft description of Can Xue's eccentric storytelling." Publ Wkly

Tsukiyama, Gail

Dreaming water. St. Martin's Press 2002 288p $23.95

ISBN 0-312-20607-0

LC 2001-58896

"At 38, Hana Murayama is dying of Werner's syndrome, a genetic defect that causes premature aging. Hana is almost totally dependent on her mother, Cata, who at 62 is still recovering from the sudden death of her husband, Max. . . . Over the course of two days, Hana and Cate retrace in memory their lives and Max's. Their scattered and sometimes conflicting expectations are brought into sharp focus when Hana's best friend, Laura, now a successful East Coast lawyer, arrives with her two daughters, Hana's godchildren, allowing Hana and Cate to find a measure of the reconciliation that has eluded them." Publ Wkly

Tsukiyama, Gail

The **street** of a thousand blossoms. St. Martin's Press 2007 422p $24.95

ISBN 978-0-312-27482-5; 0-312-27482-3

LC 2007-21012

"Set in Japan and spanning over 25 years (1939-66), the novel unravels the hardships and triumphs of two brothers raised by their loving maternal grandparents following the loss of their parents in a tragic accident. The dreams of older brother Hiroshi of becoming a sumotori (a sumo wrestler) and younger brother Kenji of becoming a Noh theater mask artisan are quelled by the onset of World War II. Passages describing the devastation wrought by the atomic bombings upon their lives and of those close to them, particularly the family of sisters Haru and Aki, who later becomes Hiroshi's wife, are well written and emotionally gripping." Libr J

Tsypkin, Leonid

★ **Summer** in Baden-Baden; a novel. translated from the Russian by Roger and Angela Keys; introduction by Susan Sontag. New Directions 2001 xxi, 146p $23.95

ISBN 0-8112-1484-2

LC 2001-32658

Originally serialized 1982 in Russian emigré weekly; this translation first published 1987 in the United Kingdom

"Tsypkin's stream-of-consciousness prose style is associative, inclusive, allusive, detached and yet humane." N Y Times Book Rev

Tuck, Lily

The **Double** Life of Liliane; by Lily Tuck. Atlantic Monthly Press 2015 256 p. illustrations $26

ISBN 080212402X; 9780802124029

In this book, by Lily Tuck, "[a]s the child of a German movie producer father who lives in Italy and a beautiful, artistically talented mother who resides in New York, Liliane's life is divided between those two very different worlds. A shy and observant only child with a vivid imagination, Liliane uncovers the stories of family members as diverse as Moses Mendelssohn, Mary Queen of Scots and an early Mexican adventurer, and pieces together their vivid histories." (Publisher's note)

"Tuck remains one of America's most brilliant novelists and short story writers, and this distinctive work, penned with a masterly eye for details that speak volumes and illustrated throughout with intriguing uncaptioned photos, allows her literary gifts to come full circle." LJ

Tuck, Lily

I married you for happiness. Atlantic Monthly Press 2011 193p $24

ISBN 978-0-8021-1991-9; 0-8021-1991-3

"This slim, magnificent novel is rarefied by its heartbreaking immediacy, and the moving, aching stream of consciousness chronicles not only the psychology of shock and mourning, but also the minute-by-minute way in which Nine begins to put life as she knows it in the past tense." BookPage

Tucker, Neely

★ The **ways** of the dead; a novel. Neely Tucker. Viking Adult 2014 288 p. (hardback) $27.95

ISBN 0670016586; 9780670016587

LC 2013047847

In this novel, by Neely Tucker, "Sarah Reese, the teenage daughter of a powerful Washington, D.C. judge, is dead. . . . Though the police promptly arrest three local black kids, newspaper reporter Sully Carter suspects there's more to the case. Reese's slaying might be related to a string of cold cases the police barely investigated, among them the recent disappearance of a gorgeous university student." (Publisher's note)

"Rich yet taut description, edgy storytelling, rock-and-rolling dialogue, and a deeply flawed but compelling hero add up to a luminous first novel." Kirkus

Another title in this series is:
Murder, D.C. (2015)

Tucker, Todd

Over and under. Thomas Dunne Books/St. Martin's Press 2008 275p $23.95

ISBN 978-0-312-37990-2; 0-312-37990-0

LC 2008-12472

Alex Award (2009)

"A bitter 1979 labor strike at southern Indiana's Borden Casket Company serves as the volatile backdrop for this haunting coming-of-age novel. . . . With their fathers on opposite sides of the dispute, Andrew Jackson Gray and Thomas Jefferson Kruer, both 14, learn there is more to life than exploring caves, shooting targets with their prized M-6 Scout rifles and sneaking out on starry nights to run through the woods. . . . Tucker convincingly makes Andy's voice at once eloquent and gritty, and makes the rural Indiana landscape palpable." Publ Wkly

Tuomainen, Antti

The **healer**; Antti Tuomainen; translated from the Finnish by Lola Rogers. 1st ed. Henry Holt and Co. 2013 224 p. (hardcover) $26

ISBN 0802777511; 9780805095548

LC 2012027372

In this novel, by Antti Tuomainen, "Helsinki is battling a ruthless climate catastrophe. . . . The authorities have issued warnings about malaria, tuberculosis, Ebola, and the plague. . . . When Tapani's beloved wife, Johanna, a newspaper journalist, goes missing, he embarks on a frantic hunt for her. Johanna's disappearance seems to be connected to a story she was researching about a politically motivated serial killer known as 'The Healer.'" (Publisher's note)

Turgenev, Ivan Sergeevich

★ **Fathers** and sons; a new translation by Michael R. Katz. Norton 1994 157p $25

ISBN 0-393-03559-X

LC 92-40010

Original Russian edition, 1862. Variant title: Fathers and children

This novel "concerns the inevitable conflict between generations and between the values of traditionalists and intellectuals. The physician Bazarov, the novel's protagonist, is the most powerful of Turgenev's creations. He is a nihilist, denying the validity of all laws save those of the natural sciences. Uncouth and forthright in his opinions, he is nonetheless susceptible to love and by that fact doomed to unhappiness. In sociopolitical terms he represents the victory of the revolutionary nongentry intelligentsia over the gentry intelligentsia to which Turgenev belonged." Merriam-Webster's Ency of Lit

Turgenev, Ivan Sergeevich

First love and other stories; {by} Ivan Turgenev; translated by Isaiah Berlin and Leonard Schapiro; introduced by V.S. Pritcett. Knopf 1994 xxxvii, 253p $17

ISBN 0-679-43594-8

LC 94-6233

Contents: First love; Spring torrents; A fire at sea

Turgenev, Ivan Sergeevich

★ The **torrents** of spring; [by] Ivan Turgenev; illustrated by Valentin Popov; translated by Ivy and Tatiana Litvonov. Grove Press 1996 174p il $25

ISBN 0-8021-1594-2

LC 96-14697

Original Russian edition, 1872. Variant title: Spring torrents

This classic Russian novel "is a love story beautifully and simply told: a young Russian nobleman, Dimitry Sanin, falls in love with a pure and sweet girl, Gemma, but through unforeseen circumstances and his own weakness he forsakes her for a sensual woman of the world, Maria Nikolayevna, for whom men are mere playthings of the moment. He does so in spite of being fully aware that this liaison will bring him nothing but ruin and humiliation. . . . This short novel has no political overtones and deals only with the emotional experiences of the characters." Libr J

Turner, Frederick W.

★ **1929**; [by] Frederick Turner. Counterpoint Bks. 2003 390p $25

ISBN 1-58243-265-1

LC 2002-154007

"Written in a period-appropriate overheated, romantic prose, and incorporating memorable appearances by Capone, Bing Crosby, Maurice Ravel, Paul Whiteman, and Clara Bow, the book is by turns corny, intoxicating, and ineffably sad, like the 'hot' music it is designed to evoke." New Yorker

Turner, Nancy E., 1953-

My name is Resolute; a novel. Nancy E. Turner. Thomas Dunne Books/St. Martin's Press 2014 608 p. (hardback) $27.99

ISBN 1250036593; 9781250036599

LC 2013031729

Author Nancy E. Turner presents a novel about "a woman struggling to find herself during the tumultuous years preceding the American Revolution.The year is 1729, and Resolute Talbot and her siblings are . . . brought to the New World. Resolute and her sister are sold into slavery in colonial New England. When Resolute finds herself alone in Lexington, Massachusetts, she struggles to find her way." (Publisher's note)

"Throughout the narrative, Turner skillfully keeps her main characters in the forefront and reveals historical events through their eyes and actions rather than by means of long, explanatory passages that stall the plot. The novel is lengthy and somewhat repetitious as so many characters are introduced, disappear and then are reunited multiple times, but the author convincingly conveys a pivotal time in American history and provides a rewarding reading experience. A fitting story about resiliency, ingenuity and heroism." Kirkus

Includes bibliographical references (pages 591-593)

Turner, Nancy E.

These is my words; the diary of Sarah Agnes Prine, 1881-1901. ReganBooks 1998 384p $23

ISBN 0-06-039225-8

LC 97-37622

"The language is rich and fine, sounding true to its time without being precious." Booklist

Turner, Nikki

Heartbreak of a hustler's wife; a novel. Nikki Turner. One World Trade Paperbacks 2011 x, 212 p.p

ISBN 0345511085; 9780345511089; 9780345526403

LC 2011001780

In his novel, "the fourth installment of [Nikki] Turner's . . . series (after 'Forever a Hustler's Wife'), hustler Desmond 'Des' Taylor has found a new gig raking in the money as head of the Good Life Ministry, to the dismay of his wife, Yarni. Not only does the once-wild hustler's wife have moral qualms, but as an attorney, she's gaining a new respect for the consequences of crime. Then masked men hold up a church service, gun down one of Des's closest associates, and force his accountant to wire them $10 million. Threats also mount against Yarni, their young daughter, and Des's mother, in violation of the gangsta code. Meanwhile, his previously unsuspected 18-year-old daughter turns up and announces she needs to move in with them." (Publishers Weekly)

Turner, Nikki

Natural born hustler; a novel. Nikki Turner. One World Trade Paperbacks/Ballantine Books 2010 xi, 114 p.p

ISBN 9780345523600

LC 2010022021

In this novel, "Desember Day is beautiful, confident, and smart. . . . But . . . her love for [her boyfriend] Fame can't stand in the way of Desember selling anything and everything . . . so that she never has to depend on a man. The only thing Desember feels she's lacking is a father to call her own. And her mother refuses to tell Desember who he is. When Fame finds himself at the wrong end of a gun . . . Desember wants nothing more than to stand by her man, but Fame warns her . . . that she isn't safe. Desember wonders if she was the real target. Her mother . . . arranges for her daughter to travel to Richmond, Virginia, to live with Desember's father and his wife. And when her father's identity is finally revealed, Desember learns that she is a Natural Born Hustler." (Publisher's note)

Turow, Scott

The **burden** of proof. Farrar, Straus & Giroux 1990 515p $22.95

ISBN 0-374-11734-9

LC 90-33593

"The plotting is clear and clean, spun out with Greek inevitability and the niceties of law and finance are lucidly, smoothly, explained. Stern's complex character is well-drawn . . . and the members of his family are individualized and believable. The Federal judges and prosecutors have unique backgrounds and prejudices. Even the minor characters are given faces and personalities." America

Turow, Scott

★ **Innocent**. Grand Central Pub. 2010 406p $27.99

ISBN 978-0-446-56242-3; 0-446-56242-4

LC 2009-49544

Sequel to: Presumed innocent (1987)

"The writing is elegant, the characters lived-in, and the legal and trial details expertly rendered. It's the suspense, though, that will keep you reading. The narrative perspective and timeline jump around—first person for Rusty, his mistress, and his adult son; third person for Molto. None is perfectly reliable. They all have their prejudices and agendas. Turow's neatest trick is to plant small inconsistencies or omissions in their accounts. These pockets of doubt allow readers the satisfaction of detecting weaknesses and contradictions in the case before the characters do." Philadelphia Inquirer

Turow, Scott

The **laws** of our fathers. Farrar, Straus & Giroux 1996 533p $26.95

ISBN 0-374-18423-2

LC 96-16104

In this legal thriller, "the wife of a state senator has been killed in a drive-by shooting, and Judge Sonia Klonsky is presiding over the trial of the victim's son, who has been accused of masterminding the murder. Most of the protagonists have crossed paths decades before, when they were campus radicals, and there are some distinctly unconvincing flashbacks to the apocalptic days of '69. Still, as the novel gathers momentum it reveals a complex portrait, in which children are forced to live in the shadow of their parents, and chastened middle-aged idealists must reckon with the enthusiasms and sins of their youth." New Yorker

Turow, Scott

Limitations. Picador 2006 197p pa $13

ISBN 978-0-312-42645-3; 0-312-42645-3

LC 2006-50345

First published in serial form in the New York Times Magazine

"The action centers on the fictional Kindle County in Illinois, and [Turow] revives some familiar characters, including George Mason from Personal Injuries and Rusty Sabich, the hero of . . . Presumed Innocent. Mason is now an appellate judge, faced with the challenge of crafting the decision in a high-profile case involving a sexual assault that reawakens his long-suppressed guilt over his role in a similar incident decades before. To compound his inner turmoil, Mason finds himself the object of threatening e-mails from an unknown source. . . . Turow's writing is assured as ever." Publ Wkly

Turow, Scott

Ordinary heroes. Farrar, Straus & Giroux 2005 384p $25

ISBN 0-374-18421-6

LC 2005-11824

"Stewart Dubinsky is not especially close to his father, David Dubin. Even their names are different, yet David's death prompts Stewart to try and find out more about this enigmatic man. He uncovers some startling information: that his father was engaged to another woman before his mother, and that he was court-martialed during the Battle of the Bulge. Dubinsky decides to write a family history, starts digging, and uncovers a manuscript his father wrote about his war experiences that is alternately moving and horrifying, vindicating, and vilifying and shines light on a side of his parents that he never knew. While some of the historical facts presented are not 100 percent accurate, the book's emotional wallop more than justifies the literary license and should secure its place in the canon of World War II literature." Libr J

Turow, Scott

Personal injuries. Farrar, Straus & Giroux 1999 403p $27

ISBN 0-374-28194-7

LC 99-30829

"U.S. Attorney Stan Sennett has set his sights on a powerful group of corrupt judges, vowing to prosecute them at any cost. With the help of the FBI, he devises a set of legal traps designed to produce the evidence he needs to convict. The centerpiece of this subversion is Robbie Feaver, a Kindle County personal injury lawyer nabbed for tax evasion by Sennett. . . . Densely packed and tightly constructed, this tangle of human relationships and legal machinations will have Turow fans burning the midnight oil." SLJ

Turow, Scott

★ **Reversible** errors. Farrar, Straus & Giroux 2002 433p il $28

ISBN 0-374-28160-2

LC 2002-70891

"What Turow has done, in book after book, is to give us page turners that are also pleasing literary artifacts, mysteries that are also investigations into coomplex human emotions." N Y Times Book Rev

Turow, Scott, 1949-

★ **Presumed** innocent. Farrar, Straus & Giroux 1987 431p

ISBN 0-374-23713-1

LC 87-368

This is a "courtroom novel about a prosecuting attorney who is charged with the murder of a female colleague with whom he once had an affair." (Christ Sci Monit)

"Rusty Sabich, the chief deputy prosecuting attorney assigned to investigate the murder of his co-worker and former lover, Carolyn Polhemus, is the narrator who draws us into the world of big-city crime and law enforcement as seen through a lawyer's eyes. Because his boss, Raymond Horgan, the Prosecuting Attorney in this unnamed Midwestern city, is up for re-election, Carolyn's murder has become a political issue, and the heat is on Rusty to bring in the killer as soon as he can." N Y Times Book Rev

Tursten, Helene, 1954- ✓

Night rounds; Helene Tursten; translation by Laura A. Wideburg. Soho Press 2012 326p.

ISBN 1616950064; 9781616950064

LC 2011034073

This "Scandinavian crime novel . . . [begins when] a nurse, Marianne Svärd, is found strangled at a small hospital in Göteborg after a blackout that also claimed the life of a patient who was on a respirator, [and] the night nurse on duty, Siv Persson, tells the police an incredible story. While the power was out, Persson claims she saw the ghost of a nurse who committed suicide in the hospital 50 years earlier after having an affair with a surgeon. While Huss and her team instantly dismiss a supernatural explanation, she becomes convinced that the motive for Svärd's slaying stems from the hospital's past." (Publishers Weekly)

Turtledove, Harry

Into the darkness. Doherty Assocs. 1999 540p

ISBN 0-312-86895-2

LC 98-43610

First title in the author's Alternate world fantasy series. "In the beginning, militarily efficient Algarve occupies the Duchy of Bari . . . and is quickly followed by one of Algarve's traditional foes, Unkerlant. . . . Throughout, World War II buffs will search for further reflections in Turtledove's fantastic mirror, but they will also, like other readers, be quickly caught up in the sheer ingenuity of the tale, in which dragons provide airpower, behemoths (think rhinoceroses the size of elephants) are tanks, magic wands take the place of rifles, and submarine warfare is in the hands of leviathan-riders." Booklist

Turtledove, Harry

Rulers of the darkness. TOR Bks. 2002 576p il $27.95

ISBN 0-7653-0036-2

LC 2001-58465

Sequel to : Through the darkness

"The fourth volume of the alternate-history saga Darkness deals with the fourth year of a World War II. . . . Kuusamo's sorcerous Manhattan Project has the potential to generate destructive energy by drawing on the past and the future, which is the same way the Algarvians use the life energy of murdered Kaunians. Meanwhile, more conventional counteroffensives against Algarve are in progress, with Unkerlant and Algarve reaching a gigantic confrontation in a battle recognizable as a re-imagining of the Battle of Kursk. One need not, however, be able to run down all of Turtledove's real-world parallels to appreciate how well he presents the human dilemmas of global warfare." Booklist

Tussing, Justin

The **best** people in the world. HarperCollins 2006 336p $24.95

ISBN 0-06-081533-7

LC 2005-46064

"The scenes between Alice and Thomas are almost absurdly lyrical and chaste. . . . But Tussing's indexes and inventories of Actual Things, circa 1972, are mercifully never more than a page or two away. At his best, Tussing is a kind of Wacko-Thoreau, and 'The Best People in the World' is one bright book of exuberant American life." N Y Times Book Rev

Twain, Mark, 1835-1910

The **adventures** of Tom Sawyer, Tom Sawyer abroad, Tom Sawyer, detective; edited by John C. Gerber, Paul Baender, and Terry Firkins. University of Calif. Press 1980 717p il

LC 76-47974

A combined edition of three Tom Sawyer titles first published 1876, 1894 and 1896, respectively

Twain, Mark, 1835-1910

The **complete** short stories of Mark Twain; now collected for the first time. edited with an introduction by Charles Neider. Doubleday 1957 xxiv, 676p hardcover o.p. pa $6.95

ISBN 0-553-21195-1 pa

"The sixty pieces which are here hospitably called short stories illustrate both the weaknesses and the strengths of Mark Twain as a writer of fiction." N Y Times Book Rev

Twain, Mark, 1835-1910

★ A **Connecticut** Yankee in King Arthur's court; edited by Bernard L. Stein; with an introd. by Henry Nash Smith. Published for the Iowa Center for Textual Studies by the University of California Press 1979 827p il $75

ISBN 0-520-03621-2

LC 77-91761

First published 1889; published in the United Kingdom with title: Yankee at the court of King Arthur

This satiric novel is a "tale of a commonsensical Yankee who is carried back in time to Britain in the Dark Ages, and it celebrates homespun ingenuity and democratic values in contrast to the superstitious ineptitude of a feudal monarchy." Merriam-Webster's Ency of Lit

Twain, Mark, 1835-1910

The **gilded** age and later novels. Library of America 2002 1053p $40

ISBN 1-931082-10-3

LC 2001-38053

The gilded age (1873), written with Charles Dudley Warner, is a panorama of an age in which the nation's capital teemed with would-be power brokers and vast fortunes piled up amid thriving corruption. In The American claimant (1892), an English viscount travels to America in search of an heir to his father's earldom. There he meets the primary claimant to the title, an eccentric yet good natured inventor, Colonel Mulberry Sanders. In Tom Sawyer abroad (1994), Tom, Huck Finn, and

Jim take a trip via balloon across the Atlantic to the Sahara desert. In Tom Sawyer, detective (1896), Tom and Huck solve a complex murder mystery involving a diamond theft and Tom's Uncle Silas. No. 44, the mysterious stranger (1969) is a different version of the posthumously published The mysterious stranger, based on Twain's final manuscript. This version, set in Eseldorf, Austria in 1490, features "a likable young printer's devil, called only No. 44, who is possessed of satanic powers that allow him to master the craft of printing in a few hours. Singlehandedly he speedily produces a Bible and magically summons up phantasmagoric people to print innumerable copies." Oxford Companion to Am Lit. 6th edition

Includes bibliographical references

Twain, Mark, 1835-1910

Historical romances; The prince and the pauper, A Connecticut Yankee in King Arthur's court, Personal recollections of Joan of Arc. [notes by Susan K. Harris] Library of Am. 1994 1029p maps (Library of America) $35

ISBN 0-940450-82-8

LC 93-40246

In The prince and the pauper (1882), a prince, Edward VI, switches clothes with Tom Canty, a poor boy who looks exactly like him. When the two are discovered, Edward is mistakenly driven from the castle and forced to endure Tom's harsh, impoverished life while Tom experiences Edward's life as royalty. A Connecticut Yankee in King Arthur's court and Personal recollections of Joan of Arc are entered separately.

Twain, Mark, 1835-1910

Mississippi writings. Literary Classics of the United States 1982 1084p $30

ISBN 0-940450-07-0

LC 82-9917

The adventures of Tom Sawyer, The adventures of Huckleberry Finn, and Pudd'nhead Wilson are entered separately. Life on the Mississippi (1883) is an autobiographical narrative that focuses on the author's childhood near the river.

Twain, Mark, 1835-1910

Personal recollections of Joan of Arc; by the Sieur Louis de Conte (her page and secretary); illustrated by G. B. Cutts. Harper 1926 596p il

First published 1896

"De Conte, who tells the story in the first person, has been reared in the same village with its subject, has been her daily playmate there, and has followed her fortunes in later life, serving her to the end, his being the friendly hand that she touches last. After her death, he comes to understand her greatness; he calls hers 'the most noble life that was ever born into this world save only One.' Beginning with a scene in her childhood that shows her innate sense of justice, goodness of heart, and unselfishness, the story follows her throughout her stormy career. We have her audiences with the king; her marches with her army; her entry into Orleans; her fighting; her trial; her execution; all simply and naturally and yet vividly told. The historical facts are closely followed." Keller. Reader's Dig of Books

Twain, Mark, 1835-1910

Pudd'nhead Wilson; and, Those extraordinary twins. introduction by Ron Powers; illustrations by F.M. Senior and C.H. Warren. Modern Library 2002 xvi, 263p il (Modern Library classics)

ISBN 0-81296-622-8

LC 2002-66002

Pudd'nhead Wilson was first published 1894 with title: The tragedy of Pudd'nhead Wilson. The short story Those extraordinary twins is about conjoined twins of completely opposite philosophy and temperament

"David Wilson is called 'Pudd'nhead' by the townspeople, who fail to understand his combination of wisdom and eccentricity. He redeems himself by simultaneously solving a murder mystery and a case of transposed identities. The mystery revolves around two children, a white boy and a mulatto, who are born on the same day. . . . The book is an implicit condemnation of a society that allows slavery. It also includes a series of brilliant epigrams which are distillations of Twain's wit and wisdom." Reader's Ency. 4th edition

Tyler, Anne

★ The **accidental** tourist. Knopf 1985 355p

LC 85-40161

"Thanks to her inimitable mix of an extraordinary inventiveness with characters and a profound humanity, Tyler makes this book a joy to read." Wilson Libr Bull

Tyler, Anne

★ The **amateur** marriage; a novel. Knopf 2004 306p $24.95

ISBN 1-400-04207-0

LC 2003-59536

This novel presents a portrait of the six-decade marriage of a Baltimore couple, Michael and Pauline Anton. Älthough acquaintances like to think of them as a perfect couple, Pauline and Michael are constantly bickering, sulking and fighting at home. . . . {Yet} Pauline and Michael are also tied to each other by their children, by shared adventures and, as the years pass, by bonds of memory and inertia. Caring for aging parents, witnessing the illnesses and travails of friends, adapting to a move to the suburbs-these are all experiences that bind Pauline and Michael to each other, even as their very different temperaments and interests increasingly pull them apart." N Y Times (Late N Y Ed)

Tyler, Anne

Back when we were grownups; a novel. Knopf 2001 273p $25

ISBN 0-375-41253-0

LC 2001-88107

This "is as perceptive, as full of gentle comedy and human warmth as any of Ms Tyler's previous novels. She manages her quirky, engagingly named characters (Patch, Biddy, NoNo, Jeep, Zeb) beautifully, spinning a web of family tensions with a wonderful lightness of touch—in this, Ms Tyler is matchless." Economist

Tyler, Anne, 1941-

The **beginner's** goodbye; a novel. by Anne Tyler. Alfred A. Knopf 2012 197 p.

ISBN 9780307957276

LC 2011033507

This novel by Anne Tyler focuses on "Aaron, who works for a small-family publishing firm that specializes in its Beginners series. . . . Aaron is in the beginning stages of mourning, after a tree crashed through his house and crushed his slightly older wife. . . . Early on, Aaron receives visits from his dead wife, whom no one else can see, and whom he admits might well be a projection or an apparition. . . . Mourning is both a rite of passage and a process of discovery for Aaron." (Kirkus Reviews)

Tyler, Anne

★ **Breathing** lessons. Knopf 1988 327p

LC 88-45260

This novel has "irresistibly funny passages you want to read out loud and poignant insights that illuminate the serious business of sharing lives in an unsettling world." Publ Wkly

Tyler, Anne

Celestial navigation. Knopf 1974 273p

Set in Baltimore, this novel tells of artist Jeremy Pauling's attempts to overcome his comfortable isolation and make contact with others

The author "is especially gifted in the art of freeing her characters and then keeping track of them as they move in their unique and often solitary orbits. . . . She has a way of transcribing their peculiarities with such loving wholeness that when we examine them we keep finding more and more pieces of ourselves." N Y Times Book Rev

Tyler, Anne

The **clock** winder. Knopf 1972 312p

The author has a "remarkable understanding of the intricacies of family life, a sympathy for odd-ball characters who never become merely southern grotesques . . . but are observed so gently that the term 'neurotic' seems equally inappropriate for them." New Repub

Tyler, Anne

Digging to America; a novel. Knopf 2006 277p $24.95

ISBN 0-307-26394-0

LC 2005-52963

With this novel, "Tyler has delivered something startlingly fresh while retaining everything we love about her work . . . . Her success at portraying culture clash and the complex longings and resentments of those new to America confirms what we knew, or should have known, all along: There's nothing small about Tyler's world, nothing precious about her attention to the hopes and fears of ordinary people." Washington Post Book World

Tyler, Anne

★ **Dinner** at the Homesick Restaurant. Knopf 1982 303p hardcover o.p. pa $14.95

ISBN 0-394-52381-4; 0-449-91159-4 pa

LC 81-13694

"Pearl Tull, an angry woman who vacillates between excesses of maternal energy and spurts of terrifying rage, has been deserted by her husband and has brought up her three children alone. Cody, the eldest, is handsome, wild, and in a lifelong battle of jealousy with his young brother, the sweet-tempered and patient Ezra. Their sister Jenny tries, through three marriages, to find a stability which was never present in Pearl's home. Ezra also tries to achieve a permanence through his homey Homesick Restaurant in Baltimore, but he is cruelly tricked by his brother and is unable to establish any unity in the family." Shapiro. Fic for Youth. 3d edition

Tyler, Anne

Earthly possessions. Knopf 1977 197p

ISBN 0-394-4114-7

LC 76-41222

This "novel concerns Charlotte Emory, a 35-year-old woman who goes to her bank in Clarion, Md., one morning to withdraw enough cash to leave her husband. Instead, she is hustled off as hostage to a bank robber and peripatetic demolition-derby rider named Jake Simms. Simms needs funds to get to Florida and take his girlfriend out of a home for unwed mothers. All that he and Charlotte share, apart from the stolen car they are riding in, is a distrust of 'closed-in spaces'—for him, the prison he has just escaped; for her, a household that includes a gaunt preacher husband, two children, three brothers-in-law and a procession of itinerant sinners, soldiers and salesmen." Newsweek

Tyler, Anne

Ladder of years. Knopf 1995 325p $24

ISBN 0-679-43941-2

LC 94-38909

"'Ladder of Years' feels, indeed, like the story of a woman who thought she could prune her life down to a short story, only to find it blooming, unexpectedly, into an Anne Tyler novel. There can be few more delightful revelations." New Yorker

Tyler, Anne

Morgan's passing. Knopf 1980 311p

LC 79-20272

"A young girl-wife goes into labor while she and her boy-husband are putting on a puppet-show of Cinderella at a church fair in Baltimore in 1967. Her baby is delivered en route to the hospital by a member of the audience who claims to be a doctor. . . . The fake doctor—who lives in a tumultuous . . . cluttered house with an imperturbable wife, seven daughters, his half-senile mother, and crackpot sister—attaches himself to the young couple and their child, following them, popping up at odd moments. Later, after they have all become friends, this attachment, narrows, focusing upon the young wife, with unsettling consequences for everyone." New Repub

Tyler, Anne

Noah's compass; a novel. Alfred A. Knopf 2009 277p $25.95

ISBN 978-0-307-27240-9; 0-307-27240-0

LC 2009-14925

"When Liam Pennywell is nearly 61, he loses his job teaching fifth grade at St. Dyfrig, a 'second-rate' boys' school in Baltimore. He's been downsized, not fired, he's quick to point out to inquisitive family members, and he never really liked being a teacher anyway. . . . Within the week, Liam moves to a one-bedroom apartment near the Baltimore Beltway and begins his own systematic downsizing. . . . The first night in his sparse new home Liam is attacked by an intruder—an event he can't remember when he wakes up the next day in the hospital, bandaged and bruised. And so unfolds the next stage in Liam's quiet life, in which he reopens himself to the possibility of love, while finally accepting the fact that his relationships with his father and daughters are fixed, whatever their flaws may be. Tyler's acutely perceptive observations of family interactions are dead on." BookPage

Tyler, Anne

A **patchwork** planet. Knopf 1998 287p $24

ISBN 0-375-40256-X

LC 98-84431

This novel, set in Baltimore, "tells the story of a year in the life of 30-year-old Barnaby Gaitlin who, despite coming from a wealthy family, works as an odd-job man. Barnaby is an ordinary and somewhat bewildered man whose life turns on a chance encounter with a woman who may represent the angel that brings change and gives direction to his life." Libr J

Tyler, Anne

★ **Saint** maybe. Knopf 1991 337p $22

ISBN 0-679-40361-2

LC 91-52704

"Tyler's remarkable novel pulls at the heart strings and jogs the memories of forgotten youth. . . . While the majority of YA readers lack enough life experiences to appreciate the pure joy of Tyler's descriptions and thoughts, not to steer them in her direction would be a shame." SLJ

Tyler, Anne

Searching for Caleb. Knopf 1976 309p

ISBN 0-394-49848-8

"Anne Tyler's tone is understated, ironic, and elliptical, which suits her characters well. Searching for Caleb rarely gives us heights and depths of emotion or the excitement of discovery, but it does offer the very welcome old-fashioned virtues of a patient, thoughtful chronicle." Saturday Rev

Tyler, Anne

A **slipping**-down life. Knopf 1970 214p

"Evie Decker, unattractive and unpopular, and Drumsticks Casey, an unknown rock musician, are misfits living in a small Southern town. They are drawn together in a union which is more bizarre than romantic. It is a union, however, that seems to fulfill the needs of each and makes for a marriage that is marked by quiet desperation." Shapiro. Fic for Youth. 3d edition

Tyler, Anne, 1941-

★ A **spool** of blue thread; a novel. Anne Tyler. Random House Inc 2015 368 p. (hardcover) $25.95

ISBN 1101874279; 9781101874271

LC 2014045502

Man Booker Prize Shortlist (2015)

"Abby and Red and their four grown children have accumulated not only tender moments, laughter, and celebrations, but also jealousies, disappointments, and carefully guarded secrets. . . . Here are four generations of Whitshanks, their lives unfolding in and around the sprawling, lovingly worn Baltimore house that has always been their anchor." (Publisher's note)

"Using her signature gifts for brilliant dialog and for intricately framing the complex messiness of parental and spousal relationships, Tyler beautifully untangles the threads that bind and sometimes choke all of them." LJ

Tyler, Anne

The **tin** can tree. Knopf 1965 273p

"Six-year-old Janie Rose Pike was killed in a fall from a tractor, an accident which shook but does not really change the little world in which she lived. Mrs. Pike, left stunned and silent by her daughter's death, is too apathetic to pay attention to her 10-year-old son, Simon. Her grown-up niece, who lives with the family, tries to take care of Simon and at the same time to cope with her own problems. It is Simon himself . . . who finally awakens his mother to the need for life to continue." Libr J

Tyler, Anne, 1941-

Vinegar girl; The taming of the shrew retold. Anne Tyler. Hogarth Shakespeare 2016 224 p. (hardcover) $25; (ebook) $65

ISBN 9780804141260; 9780804141277

LC 2015040137

This book, by Anne Tyler, is a "contemporary take on one of Shakespeare's most beloved comedies. Kate Battista feels stuck. How did she end up running house and home for her eccentric scientist father and uppity, pretty younger sister Bunny? Plus, she's always in trouble at work—her pre-school charges adore her, but their parents don't always appreciate her unusual opinions and forthright manner." (Publisher's note)

"The Taming of the Shrew meets Green Card in this delightful reinvention that owes as much to Tyler's quirky sensibilities as it does to its literary forebear. Come for the Shakespeare, stay for the wonderful Tyler." LJ

U

Uchida, Yoshiko

Picture bride; a novel. University of Washington pa. ed; University of Washington Press 1997 216p pa $14.95

ISBN 0-295-97616-0

LC 97-3

"Carrying a photograph of the man she is to marry but has yet to meet, young Hana Omiya arrives in San Francisco, California, in 1917, one of several hundred Japanese 'picture brides' whose arranged marriages brought them to America in the early 1900s. Her story is intertwined with others: her husband, Taro Takeda, an Oakland shopkeeper; Kiku and her husband Henry, who reject demeaning city work to become farmers; Dr. Kaneda, a respected community leader who is destroyed by the adopted land he loves. All are caught up in the cruel turmoil of World War II, when West Coast Japanese Americans are uprooted from their homes and imprisoned in desert detention camps." Publisher's note

Udall, Brady

The **lonely** polygamist; a novel. W. W. Norton 2010 602p $26.95

ISBN 978-0-393-06262-5; 0-393-06262-7

LC 2009-52226

"Udall's control over his complex plot, and his psychological insight into his characters, are admirable and impressive. But perhaps the most pleasing thing about 'The Lonely Polygamist' is the way it avoids giving in to the prurient interests that could easily have dominated a novel about polygamy." Chicago Tribune

Ulfelder, Steve

Purgatory chasm; Steve Ulfelder. Minotaur Books 2011 292p.

ISBN 9780312672928; 0312672926; 9781250007025

LC 2011001265

This book tells the story of "Conway Sax, a recovering alcoholic, ex-con, and car mechanic who lives in Massachusetts, fulfills his moral obligations to the Barnburners, the AA group that got him clean and sober, by doing odd jobs for them. Tander Phigg, a Barnburner whose 1980 Mercedes-Benz 450SEL Sax once worked on, persuades him to help retrieve the classic car--and the $3,500 deposit--from Das Motorenwerk, a garage in New Hampshire that's had the vehicle for 18 months and done nothing. When Sax visits the garage, someone he doesn't see coldcocks him. The assault heightens Sax's suspicions about Das Motorenwerk, and his later discovery of a dead body confirms them." (Publishers Weekly)

Ulinich, Anya

Petropolis. Viking 2007 324p $24.95

ISBN 978-0-670-03819-0; 0-670-03819-9

LC 2006-41356

"In the end, [the author] ties a neat bow around Sasha's serious coming-of-age problems, but bittersweetness lingers. Petropolis bursts with artful details of an immigrant's peripatetic youth and quest for home-the grappling for the strong woman inside of the lost girl." Ms.

Ulitskaya, Ludmila

The **big** green tent; A Novel. Ludmila Ulitskaya; translated from the Russian by Bela Shayevich. Farrar, Straus & Giroux 2014 544 p. (hardcover) $35

ISBN 0374166676; 9780374166670

LC 2014016972

This novel, by Ludmila Ulitskaya, "tells the story of three school friends who meet in Moscow in the 1950s and go on to embody the heroism, folly, compromise, and hope of the Soviet dissident experience. These three boys--an orphaned poet; a gifted, fragile pianist; and a budding photographer with a talent for collecting secrets--struggle to reach adulthood in a society where their heroes have been censored and exiled." (Publisher's note)

"The book is as much a collection of stories, several of which can stand on their own, as it is a sustained narrative. Taken as a whole, it loops back on itself, using a bendable approach to chronology to reveal characters and flesh out events. The stark realities of life under a repressive regime are vividly portrayed, as are life's daily joys and satisfactions. Give this to readers who like Russian literature and big, realistic fiction." Booklist

Ullman, Ellen

By blood; Ellen Ullman. Farrar, Straus and Giroux 2012 378p.

ISBN 0374117551; 9780374117559

LC 2011041626

This book follows a "disgraced professor [who] takes an office in a downtown tower to plot his return. But the walls are thin and he's distracted by voices from next door—his neighbor is a psychologist, and one of her patients dislikes the hum of the white-noise machine. And so he begins to hear about the patient's troubles with her female lover, her conflicts with her adoptive, avowedly WASP family, and her quest to track down her birth mother. . . . Armed with the few details he's gleaned, the professor takes up the quest and quickly finds the patient's mother in records from a German displaced-persons camp. . . . His research leads them deep into the history of displaced-persons camps, of postwar Zionism, and—most troubling of all—of the Nazi Lebensborn program." (Publisher's note)

Umrigar, Thrity N.

The **space** between us; a novel. [by] Thrity Umrigar. William Morrow 2005 321p

ISBN 0-06-07915-5-1

LC 2005-50510

"The life of the privileged is harshly measured against the life of the powerless, but empathy and compassion are evoked by both strong women, each of whom is forced to make a separate choice. Umrigar is a skilled storyteller, and her memorable characters will live on for a long time." Washington Post Book World

Umrigar, Thrity N.

★ The **weight** of heaven; a novel. [by] Thrity Umrigar. Harper 2009 365p $25.99

ISBN 978-0-06-147254-1

LC 2008-32950

This is "is a bold, beautifully rendered tale of cultures that clash and coalesce." Booklist

Umrigar, Thrity

The **world** we found; Thrity Umrigar. HarperCollins 2012 320 p.

ISBN 9780062107138; 0061938343; 9780061938344

This book tells the "story of four women and the unbreakable ties they share. As university students in late 1970s Bombay, Armaiti, Laleh, Kavita, and Nishta were inseparable. . . . But much has changed over the past thirty years. Following different paths, the quartet drifted apart. . . . Then comes devastating news: Armaiti, who moved to America, is gravely ill and wants to see the old friends she left behind. . . . In the course of their journey to reconnect, Armaiti, Laleh, Kavita, and Nishta must confront the truths of their lives--acknowledge long-held regrets, face painful secrets and hidden desires, and reconcile their idealistic past and their compromised present." (Publisher's note)

Under African skies; modern African stories. edited and with an introduction by Charles R. Larson. Farrar, Straus & Giroux 1997 315p $25

ISBN 0-374-21178-7

LC 96-48601

An "impressive collection of short stories from sub-Saharan Africa. Published between 1952 and 1996, some translated from French, Portuguese, and Arabic, these stories share a common outrage against Africa's decay, whether from oppressive colonialism and corruption or the repression of tradition and ignorance. These are not folk tales about great chiefs but heart-rending stories about ordinary people . . . trying to make a life for their families, caught up in the political and spiritual struggle for Africa." Libr J

Undset, Sigrid

★ **Kristin** Lavransdatter; translated from the Norwegian. Knopf 1935 3v in 1 $50

ISBN 0-394-43262-2

Contains three novels originally published separately in Norway in 1920, 1921, and 1922 respectively; first United States publication with titles: The bridal wreath (1923); The mistress of Husaby (1925); The cross (1927)

Although the "action takes place in the fourteenth century, the lives of the characters are marked by almost the same problems depicted in modern novels: passion, adultery, premarital pregnancy, ambition, conflict. Kristin, daughter of Lavrans and Ragnfrid, is betrothed to Simon Andressön but falls in love with Erlend Nikulassön and finally wins her father's approval to marry him. Her father realizes on their wedding night that they are already lovers. The book follows Kristin's life as she tries to manage her estate and as her husband loses his lands and leaves her after a bitter quarrel. After several attempts at reconciliation, Erlend returns, only to be killed in a fight. The six sons of Kristin follow different paths. Two die during the Black Plague, which was so dreadful a scourge in that era. The portrayal of this Norwegian woman is vivid and human." Shapiro. Fic for Youth. 3d edition

Unferth, Deb Olin

Vacation. McSweeney's 2008 215p $22

ISBN 978-1-93478-109-8; 1-93478-109-6

"The novel follows a woman who finds out her husband's deepest secret: he once jumped out of a window in pursuit of a bird who flew into the room. The deadpan humor continues as the woman decides to harbor her own secret: she has an affair, which consists entirely of trailing of a random man whom she never seeks to meet. The prose is highly stylized and full of devastating wit. Each sentence springs from an almost visual idiom. . . . Funny, bleak, often brilliant, Vacation once again proves that Unferth can preform a linguistic high-wire act all her own." Esquire

The **Unforgetting** heart: an anthology of short stories by African American women (1859-1993) edited by Asha Kanwar. Aunt Lute Bks. 1993 xxi, 292p

ISBN 1-879960-31-1

LC 93-3240

Features unknown tales from the nineteenth century as well as works by contemporary authors

Unger, Lisa

Heartbroken; a novel. Lisa Unger. Crown 2012 370 p.
ISBN 0307465209; 9780307465207

LC 2011050497

In this psychological thriller, "[a]n island on an Adirondack lake becomes both a haven and a hell for three women. . . . Kate Burke's annual visits to Heart Island, owned by her wealthy parents, never go smoothly, mainly because of the uneasy relationship she has with her imperious 75-year-old mother, Birdie, Kate expects the next visit will be even more upsetting because she's written a novel based on journals kept by her aunt and grandmother that's a thinly veiled story of a love affair that ended in tragedy on the remote island. Meanwhile, Birdie has visions of a dark intruder prowling Heart Island at all hours. Finally, Emily, a waitress drifting through life, feels powerless to resist as her boyfriend pulls her into schemes that will betray the people closest to her." (Publishers Weekly)

Unger, Lisa

The **red** hunter; Lisa Unger. Touchstone 2017 358 p. (hardcover) $25.99
ISBN 9781501101670; 9781501101687; 9781501101694

LC 2016029518

This book, by Lisa Unger, "Claudia Bishop's perfect life fell apart when the aftermath of a brutal assault left her with a crumbling marriage. . . . For Zoey Drake the defining moment of her childhood was the horrific murder of her parents. . . . Strangers to each other, and walking very different paths in the wake of trauma, these two women are on a collision course. . . . As Zoey seeks justice, and Claudia seeks peace, both will confront the terrifying monsters at the door." (Publisher's note)

"Unger's knack for blending encroaching danger with complex relationship themes is as sharp as ever here, as she creates characters facing the tangle of betrayals and mistakes that have shaped their identities." Booklist

Unnikrishnan, Deepak

Temporary people; Deepak Unnikrishnan. Restless Books 2017 251 p. illustrations (paperback) $17.99
ISBN 1632061422; 9781632061423

LC 2017934293

In this book, author Deepak "Unnikrishnan presents twenty-eight linked stories that careen from construction workers who shapeshift into luggage and escape a labor camp, to a woman who stitches back together the bodies of those who've fallen from buildings in progress, to a man who grows ideal workers designed to live twelve years and then perish--until they don't, and found a rebel community in the desert." (Publisher's note)

"The author's crisp, imaginative prose packs a punch, and his whimsical depiction of characters who oscillate between two lands on either side of the Arabian Sea unspools the kind of immigrant narratives that are rarely told." Kirkus

Unsworth, Barry

★ **After** Hannibal. Talese 1997 250p il
ISBN 0-385-48651-0

LC 96-20856

First published 1996 in the United Kingdom

In this novel "five sets of outsiders invade Umbria by renovating houses along a country track. Trouble is made for them by local peasants and by an exploitative speculating Brit, but the real story is the way their various hopes and intrigues retrace ingrained historical patterns. Recognizing these patterns and, in a sense, presiding over them is an Italian lawyer so shrewd and wizardly that he seems supernatural." New Yorker

Unsworth, Barry

Land of marvels; a novel. Nan A. Talese 2009 287p $26
ISBN 978-0-385-52007-2

LC 2008-09201

"It is 1914, and, after three years in the deserts of Mesopotamia, the British archeologist John Somerville believes he is on the brink of a great discovery. Before he can uncover what he thinks was the residence of the last Assyrian king, Somerville must fight off plans for a railway that will encroach on his dig site, and thwart the efforts of Elliot, a charismatic, straight-talking American (in British historical novels there is rarely any other kind) who is bent on finding oil and on destroying what remains of Somerville's marriage. There is something of E. M. Forster in Unsworth's knowing depiction of a decaying empire run by upper-class incompetents, and in his generous and sympathetic portrayal of women caught between cultures." New Yorker

Unsworth, Barry

Losing Nelson; a novel. Talese 1999 338p $23.95
ISBN 0-385-48652-9

LC 99-28757

"Unsworth is in complete control of his material, effortlessly sustaining an almost unbearable level of tension that is suddenly resolved in an unusually effective surprise ending." Libr J

Unsworth, Barry

Morality play. Talese 1995 192p

LC 95-4106

This novel, set in 14th century England, is narrated by "Nicholas Barber, a young monk who has forsaken his calling and joined an itinerant troupe of players that gets caught up in the real-life drama of a small-town murder. The crime presents Barber and his fellows with an opportunity to attract a larger-than-usual audience, and they turn sleuths, weaving the bits of information yielded by their investigation into an improvised play that eventually reveals the surprising, sordid truth. Rich in historical detail, Unsworth's well-told tale explores some timeless moral dilemmas and reads like a modern page-turner." Libr J

Unsworth, Barry, 1930-2012

The **quality** of mercy; a novel. Barry Unsworth. Nan A. Talese/Doubleday 2011 319 p. $26.95
ISBN 0091937124 Hutchinson; 0385534779 Nan A. Talese; 9780091937126 Hutchinson; 9780307948045; 9780385534772 Nan A. Talese

LC 2011010110

Sequel to: Sacred hunger.

In this historical novel, "Erasmus Kemp has tracked down the crew members who absconded to Florida with his late father's slave ship and has hauled them back to Newgate Prison [in England]. But the long-delayed satisfaction he hopes to exact from these sailors is being challenged. . . . A wealthy abolitionist has taken up the crew members' defense, arguing that when they killed their captain, they weren't committing mutiny; they were protecting innocent Africans from drowning." (Washington Post)

"Unsworth's finely crafted plot brings together a vivid cast of seamen, miners, and landowners at a moment in history when crimes of property were considered more serious than crimes against persons and a more enlightened future lay just around the corner." LJ

Unsworth, Barry

The **ruby** in her navel; a novel of love and intrigue in the twelfth century. Nan A. Talese 2006 399p $26
ISBN 0-385-50963-4

LC 2006-40370

"Like the best historical fiction writers, Unsworth tells his story while also fleshing out the backdrop with details that ground us in the moment and make it tangibly real. He makes his characters' individual experiences representative of larger concerns." Washington Post Book World

Unsworth, Barry

Sacred hunger. Doubleday 1992 629p

LC 91-33237

"Deftly utilizing a flood of period detail, Unsworth has written a book whose stately pace, like the scope of its meditations, seems accurately to evoke the age. Tackling here a central perversity of our history—the keeping of slaves in a land where 'all men are created equal'—Unsworth illuminates the barbaric cruelty of slavery, as well as the subtler habits of politics and character that it creates." Publ Wkly

Unsworth, Barry

★ The **songs** of the kings; a novel. Doubleday 2003 338p $26

ISBN 0-385-50114-5

LC 2002-66845

"A stubborn wind from the northeast ushers in rough times for the House of Atreus, and the Greek ships, en route to Troy, remain trapped in the straits at Aulis. Unsworths' retelling of the story, familiar from Euripides, of the sacrifice of Iphigeneia to appease the gods so that the boats can sail is a bold, modern tale with cynical riffs on the themes of duty and power, truth and fiction. His Greek warriors are schemers and media-savvy self-promoters who are desperate to look good in the sung reports that are their equivalent of the news media—songs that are, we realize, the seeds of the Homeric tradition." New Yorker

Upadhyay, Samrat

The **guru** of love. Houghton Mifflin 2003 290p $23

ISBN 0-618-24727-0

LC 2002-32234

The author "excels at depicting the thousand small cuts that afflict a middle-class married man having an affair. . . . The writing is emotionally restrained and doesn't call attention to itself. There are no lyrical bursts of exuberance over the country's beauty or the torments of love. At points the novel is excessively terse; when three words would have sufficed, Upadhyay uses two. In spite of that it is gripping, because you like the characters so much, and wish them well." N Y Times Book Rev

Updike, John

The **afterlife** and other stories. Knopf 1994 316p $24

ISBN 0-679-43583-2

LC 94-9818

"In these mellow, reflective stories, where parents die and grandchildren are born, Updike's heroes are acutely aware of lost glory yet discover the strength to persevere." Libr J

Updike, John

Brazil. Knopf 1994 260p $23

ISBN 0-679-43071-7

LC 93-28632

This novel, "for all its political incorrectness, seems good-natured and bent on self-parody. . . . If the book's surface is sometimes a little sticky, its allegorical underpinnings are graceful and firm." N Y Times Book Rev

Updike, John

★ The **centaur**. Knopf 1963 302p $24.95

ISBN 0-394-41881-6

"Utilizing a contemporay setting in Olinger, Pennsylvania, Updike attempts to retell the myth of Chiron, wisest of the centaurs, a creature who gave up his immortality on behalf of Prometheus. In this modern version, Chiron is a high-school science teacher, George Caldwell, and Prometheus is his 15-year-old son, Peter. The story revolves around three critical days in their lives." Shapiro. Fic for Youth. 3d edition

Updike, John

Gertrude and Claudius. Knopf 2000 212p $23

ISBN 0-375-40908-4

LC 99-57601

"Updike turns to Shakespeare's 'Hamlet,' exploring the origin of Gertrude and Claudius' 'reechy kisses.' When the sixteen-year-old Gertrude is unwillingly betrothed to the elder Hamlet, Horwendil, by her father . . . she quickly falls for his brother, Claudius. The two honorably resist their feelings until they are beset by the anxieties of aging; as it turns out, the murder of Horwendil is an act of emotional (and political) desperation rather than cold calculation. Likewise, Updike's portrayal of Gertrude and Claudius' thwarted affections is not just a deft literary exercise but an affecting—and funny—invocation of the abundant desires of what Hamlet called 'this too too solid flesh." New Yorker

Updike, John

In the beauty of the lilies. Knopf 1996 491p $25.95

ISBN 0-679-44640-0

LC 95-23467

The novel "opens in Paterson, New Jersey, in 1910. 'At the moment Mary Pickford fainted' while making a movie close by, Presbyterian minister Clarence Wilmot loses his faith. That loss precipitates another loss: his job. Since 'now he was free—free to sink,' he turns to selling encyclopedias door to door and to an addictive habit of watching the fabulous new medium, moving pictures. Updike then tells of the following three generations of Clarence's family. . . . Updike's soaring novel becomes an extended yet taut metaphor for the secularization of religion and the concomitant infatuation with movies as a substitute for religion." Booklist

Updike, John

Licks of love; short stories and a sequel. Knopf 2000 359p $25

ISBN 0-375-41113-5

LC 00-34906

"This book of stories, mostly about old wives and girlfriends recollected in middle-aged tranquillity, also includes a novella—a return to the world of Harry Angstrom, Updike's unlikely alter ego. In 'Rabbit Remembered,' it turns out that Rabbit's untimely demise has not diminished his ability to shake up the lives of those around him. His family may not miss him, exactly, but, like the rest of us, they still can't get over him." New Yorker

Updike, John

Memories of the Ford Administration; a novel. Knopf 1992 371p

ISBN 0-679-41681-1

LC 92-52955

"Updike's elegant, yet slangy portrait of the Ford era demonstrates considerable finesse. Even more impressive is his authentic, yet unstilted, evocation of Buchanan's era." Christ Sci Monit

Updike, John

My father's tears and other stories. Alfred A. Knopf 2009 292p $25.95

ISBN 978-0-307-27156-3; 0-307-27156-0

LC 2008-54376

"A perfect bookend to Pigeon Feathers, the precocious collection of stories that nearly five decades ago announced their 30-year-old writer's discovery of his own inimitable voice. . . . Mr. Updike writes in these stories . . . with the quiet assurance of someone in complete control of his craft." N Y Times (Late N Y Ed)

Updike, John

Pigeon feathers, and other stories. Knopf 1962 278p hardcover o.p. pa $14

ISBN 0-394-44056-0; 0-449-91225-6 pa

These stories "are filled with gentle humor and irony. Youth, marriage, and family life provide most of the themes." Cincinnati Public Libr

Updike, John

The **poorhouse** fair. Knopf 1959 185p

A reissue with a new introduction of the title first published 1959

This novel concerns the lives of a handful of marvelously eccentric and understandable people in a poorhouse on the undulating plains of central New Jersey. It begins on the morning of the annual Fair, an innovation of Conner, the new and very ambitious prefect. Conner's struggle to institutionalize old age inevitably meets the stiff opposition of those who want to individualize it

"This is a wise book with much to say on individualism and conformity, mechanization and craftsmanship, the 'welfare state' and the 'old days'—and, foremost, on 'death' as it is looked upon by the aged and the young. Updike's old people are memorable." Libr J

Updike, John

Rabbit Angstrom; a tetralogy. with an introduction by author. Knopf 1995 xxxi, 1519p $30

ISBN 0-679-44459-9

Contents: Rabbit, run (1960); Rabbit redux (1971); Rabbit is rich (1981); Rabbit at rest (1990)

Updike, John

★ **Roger's** version. Knopf 1986 328p

ISBN 0-394-55435-3

LC 86-45298

This novel "succeeds in spite of its symbolic structure. Its power and charm lie in the terrific appeal it makes to our capacity for intellectual wonderment. It's rather thrilling to watch Updike assimilate the new vocabularies of particle physics and computer technology—and then fuse them with the ancient vocabulary of religious belief." Newsweek

Updike, John

S. Knopf 1988 279p

LC 87-40496

This "is an acid comedy of illusions and delusions told entirely in the words of a woman who is both deceived and deceiver." Atlantic

Updike, John

Seek my face. Knopf 2002 276p $23

ISBN 0-375-41490-8

LC 2002-18442

"Despite its uncomplicated premise, the novel achieves a remarkable depth of characterization and a glowing beauty in its articulation of the artistic sensibility." Booklist

Updike, John

Terrorist. Alfred A. Knopf 2006 320p $24.95

ISBN 0-307-26465-3

LC 2005-57985

"The last part of the novel is suspenseful. It brings together a serviceable plot, which leans a little heavily on coincidental connections, a questionable provocation and some broadly motivated acts of heroism. It seems meant as a fable, and any good fable requires some derring-do. The most satisfactory elements in 'Terrorist' are those that remind us that no amount of special pleading can set us free of history, no matter how oblivious and unresponsive to it we may be." N Y Times Book Rev

Updike, John

Toward the end of time. Knopf 1997 334p $25

ISBN 0-375-40006-0

LC 97-5167

"Like Updike, Ben can write elegant sentences. Although his temporal excursions (and Updike's researched inventions) at first seem random, they fit together into a paranoid structure by novel's end. Ben's report from the body front and reflections on his failures . . . are simultaneously sad and comic, often worthy of that old endgamer Beckett." Nation

Updike, John

Trust me; short stories. Knopf 1987 302p

LC 86-46018

Contents: Trust me; Killing; Still of some use; The city; The lovely troubled daughters of our old crowd; Unstuck; A constellation of events; Deaths of distant friends; Pygmalion; More stately mansions; Learn a trade; The ideal village; One more interview; The other; Slippage; Poker night; Made in heaven; Getting into the set; The wallet; Leaf season; Beautiful husbands; The other woman

Updike, John

The **widows** of Eastwick. Knopf 2008 308p $24.95

ISBN 978-0-307-26960-7; 0-307-26960-4

LC 2008-18513

"One wonders whether anybody has ever described the small physical indignities of the aging process with as much tenderness and good humor as Updike. . . . Now the witches' sex lives are over, but their lives aren't, and you sense Updike's twinkly eyes peering cautiously into the darkness, beyond the glow of the merely fleshly, trying to make out what the world beyond might look like." Time

Updike, John

★ The **witches** of Eastwick. Knopf 1984 307p

LC 83-49048

"While not a typical Updike narrative, the author's glittering wit, pungent observations, and fabled legerdemain at tabulating mundane particulars reach their peaks in the first half of the novel. Only in the last sections does the reader's attention flag." Booklist

Upson, Nicola

An **expert** in murder; a new mystery featuring Josephine Tey. Nicola Upson. Harper 2008 292p (Josephine Tey mysteries) pbk $13.99; hbk o.p.

ISBN 0061451533; 9780061451553; 006145155X; 9780061451539

LC 2008276250

"March 1934. Revered mystery writer Josephine Tey is traveling from Scotland to London for the final week of her celebrated play Richard of Bordeaux. But joy turns to horror when her arrival coincides with the murder of a young woman she had befriended on the train ride, and Tey quickly finds herself plunged into a mystery as puzzling as any of those in her own works. Detective Inspector Archie Penrose is convinced that the killing is connected to her play. Richard of Bordeaux has been the surprise hit of the season, with pacifist themes that strike a chord in a world still haunted by war. Now, however, it seems that Tey could become the victim of her own success, as her reputation--and even her life--is put at risk." (Publisher's note)

Other titles in this series are:
Angel with two faces (2010)
Two for sorrow (2011)
Fear in the sunlight (2013)
The death of Lucy Kyte (2014)
London rain (2015)
Nine lessons (2017)

Upson, Nicola ✓

London rain; a new mystery featuring Josephine Tey. Nicola Upson. Bourbon Street Books 2016 336 p. (Josephine Tey) (paperback) $15.99

ISBN 9780062418159

LC 2015026889

This novel, by Nicola Upson, part of the "Josephine Tey" mystery series, is set in "London, 1937. . . . [Playwright] Josephine gets wrapped up in another sort of drama. . . . Britain's most venerable newsman, Anthony Beresford . . . is shot to death in his broadcasting booth at the deafening height of the [King's] coronation ceremony. . . . After two more murders, it falls to Josephine to unravel a web of betrayal, jealousy, and long-held secrets." (Publisher's note)

"Although Upson (The Death of Lucy Kyte, 2014, etc.) keeps her readers anticipating action nearly as long as British subjects wait for the crowning of their king, the complexity of the overlapping relationships and a burst of momentum make her fictionalized heroine's sixth case a worthy sequel to its predecessors." Kirkus

Upson, Nicola ✓

Two for sorrow. HarperCollins 2011 488 p.

ISBN 9780571246335; 9780061451584

LC 2010497725

This book is a mystery novel based on "the murders of newborn innocents for which two British women were hanged at Holloway Prison in 1903. Decades later, mystery writer Josephine Tey has decided to write a novel based on Amelia Sach and Annie Walters, the notorious 'Finchley baby farmers,' unaware that her research will entangle her in the desperate hunt for a modern-day killer. A young seamstress . . . has been found brutally slain in the studio of Tey's friends, the Motley sisters, amid preparations for a star-studded charity gala. Despite initial appearances, Inspector Archie Penrose is not convinced this murder is the result of a long-standing domestic feud--and a horrific accident involving a second young woman soon after supports his convictions. Now he and his friend Josephine must unmask a sadistic killer before more blood flows." (Publisher's note)

Ure, Louise

The **fault** tree. St. Martin's Minotaur 2008 336p $24.95

ISBN 978-0-312-37585-0; 0-312-37585-9

LC 2007-38730

Ure "makes a convincing case for a woman who overcomes her overwhelming sense of inadequacy to become a heroine. Heart-stopping suspense that builds to a crescendo and well-defined characters make this a topnotch mystery." Libr J

Uris, Leon

Armageddon; a novel of Berlin. Doubleday 1964 632p

Berlin from the close of World War II to the end of the airlift is the setting of this novel. Sean O'Sullivan, an American captain responsible for the military government of the city of Rombaden, nurses a fierce hatred of the Germans, and is faced with a dilemma when he falls in love with a German girl

The author "provides a broad and moving panorama of the rebuilding of post-war Germany at the time when the Allies and the Russians first came to clash over Berlin and its routes of access." Atlantic

Uris, Leon

Battle cry. Putnam 1953 505p

"Taking an average group of American boys from their home environment through the ordeal of boot camp, to the battlefields of Guadalcanal, Tarawa, and Saipan, the author fills in a detailed picture of Marine training and traditions." Booklist

Uris, Leon

★ **Exodus**. Doubleday 1958 626p il hardcover o.p. pa $7.99

ISBN 0-385-05082-8; 0-553-25847-8 pa

"Following World War II the British forbade immigration of the Jews to Israel. European Jewish underground groups, aided by Palestinian agent Ari Ben Canaan, made every effort to aid these unfortunate victims of Nazi persecution. The novel provides insight into the heritage of the Jews and understanding of the danger involved in helping them reach a safe haven. It also includes the warm love story of Ari and a gentile nurse, Kitty Fremont, who cared very much for the welfare of the Jewish children caught in this nightmare." Shapiro. Fic for Youth. 3d edition

Uris, Leon

Mila 18. Doubleday 1961 539p $19.95

ISBN 0-385-02076-7

"Uris' major talent is that he is a master storyteller. And in 'Mila 18' he uses this talent fully and unhampered, in a straight narrative that generates an almost unbelievable dramatic intensity." San Francisco Chron

Uris, Leon

QB VII. Doubleday 1970 504p

"Two thirds of this jumbo novel are concerned with the trial, Kelna versus Cady. The judge allows this and overrules that. Dramatic, impassioned confrontations before the Queen's Bench alternate with contributory scenes: the two principals surrounded by worried families, mistresses and friends, the police pressing their search for missing witnesses, the speculation about who's guilty and who's innocent." N Y Times Book Rev

Uris, Leon

Redemption; a novel. HarperCollins Pubs. 1995 827p

ISBN 0-06-018333-0

LC 95-10834

The focus of this sequel is "the conflict between two of the three dominant families of Trinity, the tempestuous Larkins and their staid British counterparts, the Hubbles. . . . Uris begins by tracing the Larkin legacy from patriarch Liam's exile to New Zealand, where he becomes squire of a sheep farm; his brother, Conor, becomes a legendary Irish revolutionary. Another Larkin progeny, Liam's son Rory, is acclaimed as a war hero after fighting with the British at Gallipoli, while Rory's brother Dary takes Catholic clerical vows, only to have a powerful love drive him to question both celibacy and his calling. Uris balances the struggles of the Larkins with the more repressed travails of Caroline Hubble, who battles the efforts of her husband to oppress the Irish after losing a pair of sons in the disastrous British battle against the Turks." Publ Wkly

Uris, Leon

★ **Trinity**. Doubleday 1976 751p il $21.95

ISBN 0-385-03458-X

"The story has a kind of relentless power, based on the real tragedy of Ireland, and Uris's achievement is that he has neither cheapened nor trivialized that tragedy." N Y Times Book Rev

Urquhart, Jane

Away; a novel. Viking 1994 356p

LC 94-178660

"Urquhart's blending of the spiritual and political sides of the Irish makes an amazing story told in a language that is melodious and laden with complex imagery." Booklist

Urquhart, Jane

A **map** of glass. MacAdam/Cage Pub. 2006 371p $25

ISBN 1-596921-70-6

LC 2006-360

First published 2005 in Canada

"Set in present-day Toronto and in the 19th-century world of rural Ontario timber barons, [this novel] opens with the wintry death of Alzheimer's sufferer Andrew, whose body, borne by an ice floe, runs aground on the small Lake Ontario island where artist Jerome McNaughton is seeking inspiration. The story steps back a century, to when Andrew's ancestors, owners of the same island, razed forests to build ships, then it jumps forward a year from the opening scene of Andrew's death, to when Sylvia, Andrew's married lover of 20 years, sets out to meet with Jerome, who discovered Andrew's body, and, through Jerome, to reconnect one last time with Andrew. Meanwhile, Jerome, the relationship-shy adult child of an abusive, alcoholic father, is slowly coming to trust that girlfriend Mira's love for him is real. Urquhart reveals all of their haunted personal histories in the lyrical first and third parts of the novel. But it's in the compact family-saga middle, where a slew of Andrew's memorable forebears take the stage, that this novel's luminous heart truly lies." Publ Wkly

Urquhart, Jane

The **Night** Stages. Farrar, Straus & Giroux 2015 416 p. $27

ISBN 0374222193; 9780374222192

LC 2015010123

In this novel by Jane Urquhart, Tam is "leaving her lover, Niall. The airliner she is traveling on becomes grounded . . . in Newfoundland. As she waits for the fog to clear, she notices an enigmatic mural that moves her to revisit . . . the circumstances that brought her to Ireland [and] her . . . relationship with Niall and his growing despondency over the disappearance of his younger brother, Kieran. We learn of Kieran's troubled childhood and of the tragedy that caused him as a boy to be separated from his family." (Publisher's note)

"Canadian author Urquhart's (Sanctuary Line, 2013) elegiac prose evokes metaphors of arrivals and departures as she weaves together Tam and Niall's love story, Kieran's history, and a fictionalized account of Lochhead's creation of the enigmatic mural that serves as the narrative centerpiece." Booklist

Urquhart, Rachel

The **Visionist**; A Novel. by Rachel Urquhart. Simon & Schuster Ltd 2014 400 p. $26

ISBN 0316228117; 1471113329; 9780316228114; 9781471113321

LC 2013940557

In this novel, by Rachel Urquhart, "[a]fter 15-year-old Polly Kimball sets fire to the family farm, killing her abusive father, she and her young brother find shelter in a Massachusetts Shaker community called the City of Hope. It is the Era of Manifestations, when young girls in Shaker enclaves all across the Northeast are experiencing extraordinary mystical visions, earning them the honorific of 'Visionist' and bringing renown to their settlements." (Publisher's note)

"For historical fiction fans wanting to immerse themselves in a setting they may know little about, this novel fits the bill." LJ

Urrea, Luis Alberto

The **hummingbird's** daughter; a novel. Luis Alberto Urrea. Little, Brown, and Co. 2005 499p $24.95; $14.99

ISBN 0316745464; 9780316154529

LC 2004027849

Kiriyama Prize: Fiction category (2005)

This work of historical fiction "is based on the first 19 years in the life of the author's Mexican great aunt, Teresa Urrea, or Saint Teresa of Cabora (1873-1906). The illegitimate daughter of a poor Indian woman and a wealthy landowner, Teresa is raised on a farm and taught the healing arts by a curandera (female healer) until a near-death experience endows her with the divine gift of healing. Teresa's popularity soars, and she serves as the battle cry for an antigovernment insurrection, after which she and her father are exiled to the United States, where she is not officially recognized as a saint owing to the somewhat unorthodox nature of her work." (Library Journal)

Urrea, Luis Alberto

Into the beautiful North; a novel. Little, Brown and Company 2009 342p $24.99

ISBN 978-0-316-02527-0; 0-316-02527-5

LC 2008-39962

This novel is "about Nayeli, who is 19 years old and working in a taco shop in what would conventionally be referred to as a 'sleepy Mexican village.' The town is not as sleepy as the residents would like. Bandidos—drug dealers—have appeared and are threatening their way of life. There aren't enough men left in town to defend the women, children and old people from their incursions. Nayeli comes up with a solution after seeing 'The Magnificent Seven' at the local cinema. . . . She decides to go to the United States and find seven men to bring back home. They will marry, start families and be the salvation of the village. Their mere presence will deter bandidos. Her Tia Irma won't let her go alone, so she takes Irma's American Express card; Tacho, the gay owner of the taco shop; and her two best friends, Yolo, the reader, and Veronica, the goth girl. So begins their picaresque adventure. The escapades of these four and the people they meet, who help or hinder them, are alternately hilarious, poignant, scary and sad." Seattle Times

Urrea, Luis Alberto

Queen of America; Luis Alberto Urrea. Little, Brown 2011 491p.

ISBN 9780316154864; 0316154865

LC 2011023065

Sequel to: The Hummingbird's Daughter.

This novel takes place "[a]fter the bloody Tomochic rebellion, [when] Teresita Urrea, beloved healer and 'Saint of Cabora,' flees with her father to Arizona. But their plans are derailed when she once again is claimed as the spiritual leader of the Mexican Revolution. Besieged by pilgrims and pursued by assassins, Teresita embarks on a journey through turn-of-the-century industrial America-New York, San Francisco, St. Louis. She meets immigrants and tycoons, European royalty and Cuban poets, all waking to the new American century." (Publisher's note)

Urrea, Luis Alberto

The **Water** museum; stories. Luis Alberto Urrea. Little, Brown & Co. 2015 272 p. (hardcover) $25

ISBN 9780316334372; 9780316334396; 0316334375

LC 2014958990

PEN/Faulkner Award for Fiction: Shortlist (2016)

This short story collection, by Luis Alberto Urrea, "examin[es] the borders between one nation and another, between one person and another. . . . This collection includes the Edgar-award winning 'Amapola' and his now-classic 'Bid Farewell to Her Many Horses,' which had the honor of being chosen for NPR's 'Selected Shorts'" radio program. (Publisher's note)

"Urrea's well-recommended collection leads readers to feel empathy for each character, deserving or not, and provides a gut-wrenching view of life along the sidelines." LJ

Urza, Gabriel

All that followed; a novel. Gabriel Urza. Henry Holt & Co. 2015 272 p. (hardback) $25

ISBN 1627792430; 9781627792431

LC 2014041150

This novel, by Gabriel Urza, is "about a politically-charged act of violence that echoes through a small Spanish town. . . . Five years have passed since the kidnapping and murder of a young local politician--a family man and father--and the town's rhythms have almost returned to normal. But in the aftermath of the Atocha train bombings in Madrid, an act of terrorism that rocked a nation and a world, the townspeople want a reckoning of Muriga's own troubled past." (Publisher's note)

"Urza, who has Basque roots, provides an intimate perspective on how communities ripped apart by ill-conceived acts of violence can be slowly stitched back together and given a second life. This thoughtful novel will draw some literary-thriller readers, but its real strength is what it contributes to the modern-day conversation on terrorist extremism, particularly as it pertains to how youth from small, long-oppressed towns can get pulled into the fray." Booklist

V

Vachss, Andrew H.

Another life; a Burke novel. Pantheon Books 2008 271p $24.95

ISBN 978-0-307-37741-8; 0-307-37741-5

LC 2008-00213

"When a sniper shoots Burke's father, the Prof, the Prof's uneasy relationship with the law means that his life-threatening wounds can't be treated at a hospital. While his father's fate remains uncertain, a shadowy figure connected with U.S. intelligence draws Burke, an ex-con turned avenging angel for hire, into a kidnapping case. Early one morning, somebody removed the infant son of a Saudi prince from his father's custom Rolls, parked near an abandoned pier near the Hudson River, after the prince was serviced by a prostitute, who didn't realize the child was in the back seat. Burke visits his usual seamy corners of New York City in the ensuing investigation." Publ Wkly

Vachss, Andrew H.

Choice of evil; {by} Andrew Vachss. Knopf 1999 305p $23

ISBN 0-375-40647-6

LC 99-61596

"At a gay rally in New York City, Burke's friend Crystal Beth is killed in a drive-by shooting. Burke and his tribe of shadowy, semicriminal associates set out to track down the killer, but their investigation is soon impeded by a retaliatory series of murders perpetrated against known gay bashers. . . . Vachss creates a gun-metal gray, paranoid milieu where few can be trusted, where to be mainstream is to be compromised, and where children and women are always—yes, always—at risk." Booklist

Vachss, Andrew H.

Dead and gone; [by] Andrew Vachss. Knopf 2000 333p

ISBN 0-375-41121-6

LC 00-40565

"The left-for-dead-but-back-for-revenge plot is an old one, but Vachss manages to give it new life. Burke isn't quite as dark as he's been in the past, finding time to wax poetic on Chicago bluesman Son Seals and to discuss hot cars with other gear heads. But the message is the same: no mercy for the exploiters of children." Booklist

Vachss, Andrew H.

Down here; [by] Andrew Vachss. Knopf 2004 289p $19.95

ISBN 1-400-04173-2

LC 2003-58860

"This is yet another carefully crafted descent into a hellish environment in which sexual predators roam virtually unchecked, at least until targeted by Burke. One would think the same revenge plot would get old when recast again and again, but, amazingly, Vachss adds enough subtle differences to keep each novel unique and engaging." Booklist

Vachss, Andrew H.

Down in the zero; a novel. by Andrew Vachss. Knopf 1994 259p

LC 94-12312

In this mystery Burke is "confronted with young adult suicides and sexual blackmail in an affluent Connecticut suburb. Hired to watch the young son of a former lover, Burke is drawn into a bizarre situation populated by characters almost as strange as his friends. The suicides and the sadomasochistic sex, which are weirdly connected, force Burke to enlist his usual cohorts. Fans will want this crisply written work." Libr J

Vachss, Andrew H.

Footsteps of the hawk; {by} Andrew Vachss. Knopf 1995 237p

LC 95-17596

"The action begins when Burke is approached by a female police officer, Belinda, who wants him to exonerate her lover, now serving time as a serial killer. Belinda contends that the real killer is still on the loose; her lover is a connected guy who probably deserves to be in prison, but he's no killer. So she says. She also pins the cover-up on Morales, a psycho cop with a desire to send Burke to prison for his role in the violent breakup of a child pornography ring. Burke employs his familiar Fagin's army of street types to discover the real killer and the real motives behind the crime. As always in Vachss' work, New York's underbelly is vividly evoked." Booklist

Vachss, Andrew H.

Hard candy; a novel. by Andrew Vachss. Knopf 1989 241p

LC 89-45272

In this "novel featuring unlicensed New York private eye Burke, word is out that the ex-con PI has become a gun-for-hire. Besides coping with this crazy rumor, Burke contends with two figures from his youth who suddenly turn up. One of them, Candy, now a miniskirted call girl fond of whips and leashes, wants Burke to rescue her teenaged daughter from a cult in Brooklyn; the other, Wesley, an Uzi-toting hit man, already has the cult's leader, Train, in his sights. When Burke learns that the cult safehouse is a baby-breeding operation, vigilante-style justice ensues." Publ Wkly

Vachss, Andrew H.

Pain management; [by] Andrew Vachss. Knopf 2001 307p

ISBN 0-375-41322-7

LC 2001-29868

"Vachss finally lets his secondary characters speak for themselves, as opposed to being wholly defined by Burke's inner growl." Publ Wkly

Vachss, Andrew H.

★ **Sacrifice**; a novel. by Andrew Vachss. Knopf 1991 271p

LC 90-53582

"Vachss' clipped, blunt, ocassionally overly melodramatic sentences may, in some way, be ripe for parody (à la Mickey Spillane), but they also convey the frightening impact of the somber, shocking, emotionally deadening hellholes that Burke, breaking every civilized rule, battles gamely through." Booklist

Vachss, Andrew H.

Safe house; {by} Andrew Vachss. Knopf 1998 291p

LC 97-50557

"At the request of Crystal Beth, operator of a Manhattan safe house, Burke agrees to take the case of a mother being stalked by her estranged husband, the leader of a neo-Nazi cell. As Burke untangles the web that connects the white supremacists to protectors in the federal government, he helps foil a terrorist plot that echoes the real Oklahoma City bombing. As always, Burke's exploits are an occasion to provide updates on Max the Silent, Michelle the transsexual and other veterans of his guerrilla underground—and to offer a quick study of the ways in which the justice system fails victims of crime." Publ Wkly

Vachss, Andrew

That's how I roll; Andrew Vachss. Pantheon Books 2011 213 p.

ISBN 9780307379948

LC 2011013503

In this book, "Esau, who's crippled by spina bifida, recounts a horrific childhood of parental abuse. He finds purpose in protecting his strapping little brother, Tory-boy, whose only defect is being a little 'slow'. Esau later becomes a bomb maker and assassin, carving out a precariously balanced life plying his deadly trade for both of the two crime bosses who share his unnamed community. When the authorities finally catch up with him, Esau continues to plan to protect Tory-boy whether Esau is dead or alive by cleverly playing both sides of the law." (Publishers Weekly)

Vachss, Andrew H.

★ **Two** trains running; [by] Andrew Vachss. Pantheon Books 2005 447p $25

ISBN 0-4000-4381-6

LC 2004-60127

"Locke City, a Southern mill town turned tourist mecca, is controlled by the firm but benevolent hand of local crime tsar Royal Beaumont. When the New York mafia arrives, he hires former undercover FBI agent Walker Dett to protect his interests. In short snippets of action and dialog, Vachss . . . creates a broad picture of crime in Locke City, from teenage street gangs to crooked national politicians, with the Ku Klux Klan, militant African Americans, and other factions woven into a shocking climax. A riveting page-turner that marks a definite change of direction from the author's dark Burke thrillers." Libr J

Valdes-Rodriguez, Alisa

Dirty girls on top. St. Martin's Press 2008 324p $24.95

ISBN 978-0-312-34967-7; 0-312-34967-X

LC 2008-12930

Sequel to: The Dirty Girls Social Club (2003)

"The six sucias (dirty girls) return with hilarious and raunchy tales of Latina-tinged love, marriage, and sex told from each character's point of view. Pop star Cuicatl likens the touch of one of her groupie lovers to 'uncooked tofu from the refrigerator,' while man-izer Usnavys describes her husband's wardrobe style as 'like a college student on welfare cheese.' Despite a plot full of guilty-pleasure material, Dirty Girls admirably dives into darker areas like infidelity, mortality, addiction, and abuse. Hey, life can't be a fiesta 24/7." Entertainment Wkly

Valente, Catherynne M.

Radiance; Catherynne M. Valente. Tom Doherty Associates, LLC 2015 432 p. (hardcover : alk. paper) $24.99

ISBN 0765335298; 9780765335296

LC 2015016177

In Catherine M. Valente's novel "Severin Unck's father is a famous director . . . in an alternate 1986 in which talking movies are still a daring innovation. Rebelling against her father's films of passion . . ., Severin starts making documentaries. But her latest film, which investigates the disappearance of a diving colony on a watery Venus populated by island-sized alien creatures, will be her last. Though her crew limps home to earth and her story is preserved by the colony's last survivor, Severin will never return." (Publisher's note)

"The splendiferous prose swirls and twirls in a manic, vocabulary-enhancing dance in a world where silent black-and-white movies have never gone out of vogue. Expect Valente's hugely imaginative, retro adventure on multiple science-fiction- and fantasy-award short lists." Booklist

Valentine, Genevieve

Mechanique; a tale of Circus Tresaulti. Prime Books 2011 284p il pa $14.95

ISBN 978-1-60701-253-5

The author "raises the novel above the ordinary through her ability to convey the richness of the circus performers' emotional lives, coupled with impressive writing—as in a description of Alec's surgically attached wings, every bone-and-brass feather 'jigsawed and hammered and smoothed so thin that when it strikes another feather it rings out a clear note.'" N Y Times Book Rev

Vallgren, Carl-Johan

The **horrific** sufferings of the mind-reading monster Hercules Barefoot; his wonderful love and his terrible hatred. HarperCollins 2006 288p $23.95

ISBN 0-06-084199-0

LC 2005-52695

Original Swedish edition, 2002

"Overflowing with engrossing drama and superlative characterizations, Vallgren's novel is a masterful meditation on the triumph of love over human degradation." Booklist

Vamos, Miklos

The **book** of fathers; a novel. translated from the Hungarian by Peter Sherwood. Other Press 2009 474p pa $15.95

ISBN 978-1-59051-339-2; 1-59051-339-8

LC 2009-02614

Original Hungarian edition, 2000; this translation first published 2006 in the United Kingdom

"Vámos's novel chronicles a Hungarian family from 1705 until the present, as its members pass down their recollections of joy and hardship in the carefully preserved manuscript of the title. The novel proceeds via discrete episodes, each focussing on the life and death of a male progenitor with the ability to see into the past and, often, into the future. Steadily, a portrait emerges of an artistic, emotional group of men with a tendency toward violent death. . . . Vámos's fatalistic narrative follows in the tradition of 'One Hundred Years of Solitude,' but it stands as a unique and affecting illustration of the vicissitudes of Hungarian history." New Yorker

Van Booy, Simon

Everything beautiful began after; a novel. Harper Perennial 2011 404p pa $14.99

ISBN 978-0-06-166148-8; 0-06-166148-1

In this novel, "flight attendant Rebecca Baptiste moves to Athens, Greece, where she meets George Cavendish, an American with a passion for languages and drinking. Their romance blooms quickly, but when Rebecca falls for a Welsh archeologist named Henry, George drinks so much that he stumbles in front of a car—Henry's car. Without knowing what they share, Henry tends to George's injuries, cementing an immediate and long-lasting alliance. But some time later, George sees Rebecca with Henry, and the shock of recognition leaves these three sensitive souls shaken, snapping George into sobriety and sending Henry adrift. When Henry finally returns two years later, after a devastating earthquake, both he and Athens have changed dramatically. Finally, his discovery of a journal that may have belonged to Rebecca makes him wonder how well he knew her. The rhythms of Henry's tender, damaged heart propel the narrative, and Van Booy wisely resists romanticizing torment, instead suggesting that grief—tied as it is to fate and faith—can give way to promise." Publ Wkly

Van Booy, Simon

The **illusion** of separateness; a novel. Simon Van Booy. Harper 2013 224 p. $23.99

ISBN 0062112244; 9780062112248

LC 2012031842

This novel's story "opens in 2010 as Martin, an employee at a retirement home, awaits a Mr. Hugo, who dies upon his arrival. From there, the story branches out, with chapters dedicated to Hugo, who obscured his Nazi past to become a successful filmmaker in England; John, a U.S. World War II bomber pilot who crashes in France in 1944; his blind granddaughter, Amelia, who works at the Museum of Modern Art in the present day; and more." (Kirkus Reviews)

Van de Wetering, Janwillem

The **Amsterdam** cops; collected stories. Soho Crime 1999 254p $22

ISBN 1-56947-171-1

LC 99-23243

"Written during the past 16 years, the stories feature the Amsterdam Murder Brigade's cynical, jowly Detective-Adjutant Henk Grijpstra and his handsome assistant Detective-Sergeant Rinus de Gier." Publ Wkly

Van de Wetering, Janwillem

The **blond** baboon; a novel. Houghton Mifflin 1978 194p

LC 77-17338

"Elaine Carnet, one-time chanteuse, is found by her daughter at the bottom of the stairs leading to the garden. Elaine, retired from the cabaret world, has run a profitable furniture business for some years now. It is not clear who might wish her dead, if anyone did. But . . . {detectives Grijpstra and de Gier} feel Carnet's daughter and her explanation of the events don't ring true." Publ Wkly

Van de Wetering, Janwillem

★ The **hollow**-eyed angel. Soho Press 1996 282p $22

ISBN 1-56947-056-1

LC 95-26296

"A young gay reserve policeman asks the commissaris, who happens to be going to a conference in New York, to investigate the mysterious death of his uncle in Central Park. Rinus de Gier follows the commissaris, who is now very old and nods off during lectures. Meanwhile, Henk Grijpstra investigates the death of a baron on a golf course as a possible homicide." Murphy. Ency of Murder and Mystery

Van de Wetering, Janwillem

Just a corpse at twilight. Soho Press 1994 265p $20

ISBN 1-56947-016-2

LC 94-9499

"Responding to de Gier's trans-Atlantic call for help, Grijpstra leaves the cozy embrace of his mistress, Nellie, for a daunting journey to a small coastal island in Maine where his former partner has gone to seek solitude and wisdom . . . and is being blackmailed for having pushed a local woman, his sometime lover, over a cliff to her death. . . . More than one drug-running operation, a money-making scam of lesser proportion, gratuitous cruelty, venality, a Papuan rite of revenge and intelligent, unpredictable humor wrap up this narrative delight." Publ Wkly

Van de Wetering, Janwillem

★ The **perfidious** parrot. Soho Press 1997 280p $22

ISBN 1-56947-102-9

LC 97-2548

In this novel "Grijpstra and de Gier have retired and started a private detective agency. A sleazy character named Carl Ambagt twists their arms into investigating piracy on the high seas—the theft of a chartered oil tanker in the Caribbean. The case takes them to Key West and The Perfidious Parrot, a lap dancing bar, then on to St. Eustatius. Van de Wetering's ribald streak is getting stronger and stronger, his writing looser and looser; in The Perfidious Parrot, he writes like a Dutch Carl Hiaasen." Murphy. Ency of Murder and Mystery

Van Dyken, Rachel

Cheater; Rachel Van Dyken. Skyscape 2017 308 p. (Curious liaisons) (paperback) $9.99

ISBN 1503942090; 9781503942097

LC 2017299573

In this book in the Curious Liaisons series, by Rachel Van Dyken, "Lucas Thorn wasn't born a cheater. All it took was a single moment . . . and boom. Reputation destroyed forever and always. So now he owns it. He has a lady friend for every night of the week . . . , and his rules are simple: No commitments. No exceptions. But a certain smart-mouthed, strawberry blonde vixen is about to blow that all to hell." (Publisher's note)

"Told in the alternating voices of Avery and Lucas, Van Dyken's diverting cat and mouse matchup is pure starry-eyed escapist fun." Pub Wkly

Van Eekhout, Greg

California bones; Greg van Eekhout. Tor Books 2014 304 p. (hardcover) $24.99

ISBN 0765328550; 9780765328557; 9781429946858

LC 2013029670

In this book, by Greg van Eekhout, "[w]hen Daniel Blackland was six, he ingested his first bone fragment, a bit of kraken spine plucked out of the sand during a visit with his demanding, brilliant, and powerful magician father, Sebastian. When Daniel was twelve, he watched Sebastian die at the hands of the Hierarch of Southern California, devoured for the heightened magic layered deep within his bones. Now, years later, Daniel is a petty thief with a forged identity." (Publisher's note)

"The story is structured like a caper novel, and fans of stories about heists will enjoy it, but its fantastical elements make it an absolute must for urban-fantasy readers, too." Booklist

Other titles in this series are:
Pacific fire (2015)
Dragon coast (2015)

Van Essen, Thomas

The **Center** of the World; by Thomas Van Essen. Random House Inc. 2013 384 p. (paperback) $15.95

ISBN 9781590515495

LC 2013003848

This novel, by Thomas Van Essen, "is the story of renowned British painter J. M. W. Turner and his circle of patrons and lovers. It is also the story of Henry Leiden, a middle-aged family man with a troubled marriage and a dead-end job, who finds his life transformed by his discovery of Turner's 'The Center of the World', a mesmerizing and unsettling painting of Helen of Troy that was thought to have been lost forever." (Publisher's note)

Van Niekerk, Marlene

Agaat; translated by Michiel Heyns. Tin House Books 2010 581p pa $19.95

ISBN 978-0-98250-309-6; 0-98250-309-1

LC 2009-39476

First published 2006 in South Africa with title: The way of the women

"In 1947, Milla Redelinghuys is determined to turn her wealthy new husband, Jak, into the latest salt-of-the-earth farmer in her family's line. But her demands and manipulative personality cause an early marital rift that only worsens with time. As Van Niekerk follows young Milla through the decades, the author parallels it with the last days of an elderly Milla in 1996—miserable, afflicted with ALS, and reliant on her black maid, Agaat, for survival. Slowly, Milla's story—her abandonment and her masochistic relationship with Agaat—is revealed in all its ugliness. Clearly an allegory for race relations in South Africa, the novel succeeds on numerous other grounds: a rich evocation of family dynamics; a chilling portrait of bodily and mental decay; and a successful experiment in combining diaries, the second-person, and stream of consciousness." Publ Wkly

Van Rooy, Michael

An **ordinary** decent criminal. Minotaur Books 2010 278p

ISBN 978-0-312-60628-2

LC 2010-12889

First published 2005 in Canada

This "novel tracks the travails of an ex-con whose plan to settle down, go straight, and put his past behind him is rather rudely interrupted by a trio of home invaders, a vindictive mid-level crime lord, and a cop who has such a big chip on his shoulder, you're surprised he can even stand up. Monty Haaviko, the well-meaning ex-con who defends his home and winds up fighting for his life, is a very engaging protagonist and narrator with a story arc that takes him in one direction and then another, back and forth, until the tale reaches its rewarding and appropriate conclusion. . . . Van Rooy is not merely a capable writer but a quite gifted one; he draws us into the story pretty much immediately and never really gives us an opportunity to turn away." Booklist

Van Rooy, Michael

Your friendly neighborhood criminal. Minotaur Books 2011 325p $24.99

ISBN 978-0-312-60630-5; 0-312-60630-3

LC 2011-08786

"In this superb follow-up to An Ordinary Decent Criminal from the late Canadian author Van Rooy, ex-con Monty Haaviko, who's been a thief, a burglar, an armed robber, a smuggler, and a drug dealer, continues to try to put his past behind him and live quietly with his wife and son in Winnipeg. But Haaviko falls back into his old ways after Marie Blue Duck, a do-gooder seeking to smuggle refugees into the U.S. and Canada who can't enter legally despite their desperate situations, seeks to enlist his professional experience on the side of the angels. Of course, things don't go smoothly, and Haaviko must resort to violence to protect both Blue Duck's operation and his family." Publ Wkly

Van Vogt, A. E.

★ **Slan**; An Orb ed.; Orb 1998 255p pa $13.95

ISBN 0-312-85236-3

LC 97-38438

First published 1940

"One of the landmark novels of the genre, Van Vogt's 1940 tale follows the 'Slan,' a new breed of telepathic humans and their search for a society free from persecution. Essential for all libraries." Libr J

Followed by Slan hunter

Vanderbes, Jennifer

Easter Island; a novel. Dial Press (NY) 2003 304p $24.95

ISBN 0-385-33673-X

LC 2002-31588

This novel "parallels two stories: that of Elsa Pendleton, who travels to Easter Island in 1913 with her much older husband and her mentally impaired sister to study the toppled moai statues, and of Dr. Greer Faraday, who in the 1970s escapes grief after the death of her famed scientist husband, accused of fraud, by studying ancient pollen on the island. Both women have been suppressed by circumstance—Elsa, always her sister's caretaker, has made a bid for security by marrying a colleague of her father after his death, and Greer battles prejudice against women scientists." Libr J

Vanderbes, Jennifer

Strangers at the feast; a novel. Scribner 2010 334p $26

ISBN 978-1-4391-6695-6; 1-4391-6695-1

LC 2009-49756

"A Thanksgiving Day showdown between a well-to-do family and the impoverished residents of a housing project. Anthropology professor and new mother Ginny Olson is hosting the Thanksgiving Day festivities for the first time. She has just returned from India, where she adopted a mute seven-year-old girl. . . . The guests include her taciturn dad, her well-meaning but clueless mom, and her wealthy brother, whose over-investment in an office project just as the real-estate downturn hit has made his wife one angry lady (her cold-eyed pragmatism provides much of the book's entertainment value). A stove malfunction forces the family to move houses and sets them on an inevitable collision course with two young black men. Vanderbes lays on the cultural ironies a little too thickly in what is otherwise an inventively plotted, highly readable novel about white Americans' overweening sense of entitlement." Booklist

Vanderhaeghe, Guy

The **last** crossing. Alantic Monthly Press 2004 393p $24

ISBN 0-87113-912-X

LC 2003-60152

"Centered on three English brothers who venture to the American West—one as a missionary, the two others in pursuit when he disappears—this saga encompasses a wide range of characters through alternating narrative voices. In a panorama of late-nineteenth-century Montana and western Canada, Vanderhaeghe details the lawlessness of the early frontier towns and the desperate ferocity of the dying indigenous tribes. He dwells with particular pathos on the children of white traders and Native American women, who are caught between two cultures. The prose can be overripe, particularly in the opening chapters, and moments of historical exposition are clumsily inserted. However, the sweep of the narrative gradually overcomes these missteps, and as the various searches for revenge or redemption get under way the writing achieves unforced grace and power." New Yorker

VanderMeer, Jeff

Acceptance; Jeff VanderMeer. Farrar, Straus & Giroux 2014 341 p. (Southern Reach Trilogy) (pbk.) $15

ISBN 0374104115; 9780374104115

LC 2014016962

In this novel, by Jeff VanderMeer, "[it] is winter in Area X, the mysterious wilderness that has defied explanation for thirty years, rebuffing expedition after expedition, refusing to reveal its secrets. As Area X expands, the agency tasked with investigating and overseeing it--the Southern Reach--has collapsed on itself in confusion. Now one last, desperate team crosses the border, determined to reach a remote island that may hold the answers they've been seeking." (Publisher's note)

"The series is less about a straight throughline of plot and more about constructing a fully realized portrait of peculiar, often alienated people and the odd landscapes they inhabit, both inside and outside of their skulls; and this the author has decidedly achieved." Kirkus

VanderMeer, Jeff

★ **Annihilation**; Jeff VanderMeer. Farrar Straus & Giroux 2014 208 p. (Southern Reach Trilogy) $13

ISBN 0374104093; 9780374104092

LC 2013038709

Nebula Award: Best Novel (2015)

In this book by Jeff VanderMeer, "Area X has been cut off from the rest of the continent for decades. The first expedition returned with reports of a pristine . . . landscape [and] the second expedition committed suicide; the third expedition died in a hail of gunfire. This is the twelfth expedition. They arrive expecting the unexpected . . . but it's . . . the secrets the expedition members are keeping from one another, that change everything." (Publisher's note)

"A gripping fantasy thriller. . . . VanderMeer weaves together an otherworldly tale of the supernatural and the half-human." Booklist

VanderMeer, Jeff

Authority; Jeff VanderMeer. 1st ed. Farrar Straus & Giroux 2014 352 p. (Southern Reach trilogy) (pbk.) $15

ISBN 0374104107; 9780374104108

LC 2013041337

This second book in The Southern Reach trilogy, by Jeff VanderMeer, "continues to investigate the secrets of Area X, a mysterious zone somewhere in the United States, isolated from the rest of the world through (as-yet) inexplicable processes, and from which participants of multiple expeditions have returned enormously, changed--if they return at all." (Publishers Weekly)

"The new director of the Southern Reach is in over his head. His predecessor disappeared on the last mission that the agency sent across the border into Area X, and all that John Rodriguez, aka 'Control,' has to go on to understand the mysterious zone are cryptic notes, disturbing videos, unreliable colleagues, and the interviews he conducts with one of the survivors who made it out. . . . [VanderMeer] carefully ladles out just enough information to keep readers hooked and the truth shadowed." LJ

VanderMeer, Jeff

★ **Borne**; Jeff VanderMeer. First edition MCD/Farrar, Straus & Giroux 2017 323 p. (hardcover) $26

ISBN 9780374115241

LC 2016033244

In this novel, by Jeff VanderMeer, "Rachel survives as a scavenger in a ruined city half destroyed by drought and conflict. . . . One day, Rachel finds Borne during a scavenging mission and takes him home. Borne as salvage is little more than a green lump--plant or animal?--but exudes a strange charisma. . . . As Borne grows, he begins to threaten the balance of power in the city and to put the security of her sanctuary with [her partner,] Wick[,] at risk." (Publisher's note)

"VanderMeer marries bildungsroman, domestic drama, love story, and survival thriller into one compelling, intelligent story centered not around the gee-whiz novelty of a flying bear but around complex, vulnerable characters struggling with what it means to be a person." Booklist

VanderMeer, Jeff

Finch. Underland Press 2009 339p pa $14.95

ISBN 978-0-98022-601-0; 0-98022601-5

"Surreal and at times intoxicating, Finch is ambitious in a way that few genre novels ever are. VanderMeer has tried and, often, succeeded in blending fantasy, science fiction, and crime fiction into something delightfully evil and strange. He's converted the traditional hard edges of noir fiction into the foggy, fungal shapes of magical science realism." io9

VanderMeer, Jeff

The **third** bear. Tachyon 2010 273p pa $14.95

ISBN 978-1-892391-98-8

"These 15 elegantly crafted stories ably demonstrate VanderMeer's skill at telling tales of wonder in language that enhances the reading experience. Fans of imaginative literature and true speculative fiction should appreciate this groundbreaking collection by a World Fantasy Award winner that calls to mind the works of Borges, Kafka, and Stanislaw Lem." Libr J

Vann, David

★ **Aquarium**; David Vann. Atlantic Monthly Press 2015 272 p. color illustrations $24

ISBN 080212352X; 9780802123527

In this novel by David Vann, "twelve year old Caitlin lives alone with her mother . . . in subsidized housing next to an airport in Seattle. Each day, while she waits to be picked up after school, Caitlin visits the local aquarium to study the fish. Gazing at the creatures within the watery depths, Caitlin accesses a shimmering universe. . . . When she befriends an old man at the tanks one day, who seems as enamored of the fish as she, Caitlin cracks open a dark family secret." (Publisher's note)

"By pulling no punches in this explicit exploration of family, forgiveness, duty, acceptance, parent-child relationships, and what constitutes abuse, Vann has outdone himself." Booklist

Vann, David

Caribou Island; a novel. Harper 2011 293p $25.99

ISBN 978-0-06-187572-4; 0-06-187572-4

LC 2010-15703

"Vann locates his characters in an utterly convincing Alaska, but the natural world provides no ease for human anguish—nor is nature anything except a mirror in which these characters see what they wish to see. . . . [His] writing is confident—concrete and efficient. His characters' emotions and experiences bleed directly into the reader." Los Angeles Times Book Rev

Vann, David

Goat Mountain; A Novel. David Vann. Harper 2013 256 p. $25.99

ISBN 006212109X; 9780062121097

In author David Vann's book, "an 11-year-old boy at his family's annual deer hunt is eager to make his first kill [in the fall of 1978]. His father discovers a poacher on the land, a 640-acre ranch in Northern California, and shows him to the boy through the scope of his rifle. With this simple gesture, tragedy erupts, shattering lives irrevocably." (Publisher's note)

Vann, David

Legend of a suicide. University of Massachusetts Press 2008 172p $24.95

ISBN 978-1-55849-672-9; 1-55849-672-6

LC 2008-35381

This "collection, five stories and a novella, . . . revolves obsessively around the suicide of an Alaskan father. Hopscotching through time, each tale examines the father's death from the perspective of his young son, Roy. . . . Vann uses startling powers of observation to create strong characters, tense scenes and genuine surprises, leading to a ghastly conclusion that's sure to linger." Publ Wkly

Vantrease, Brenda Rickman

The **illuminator**; Brenda Rickman Vantrease. St. Martin's Press 2005 406p $24.95; (pbk.) $13.95

ISBN 0312331916; 9780312331924

LC 2004030095

In this book, "a medieval illuminator with radical views finds himself sharing quarters with a widow struggling to preserve her independence. . . . Lady Kathryn . . . must be practical to ensure the future of her 15-year-old twin sons. Little as she cares for . . . the local abbey, she is happy to do them a favor by taking in a master illuminator as lodger. . . . Their subsequent passionate affair blinds them to the romance developing between Finn's innocent daughter, Rose, and Kathryn's pious son, Colin. Meanwhile, the unsolved murder of an unscrupulous priest on the manor grounds puts everyone in jeopardy, and Finn's secret sympathy with John Wycliffe and his Lollard followers, who champion an English translation of the Scriptures, endangers his livelihood, not to mention his life." (Publishers Weekly)

Vapnyar, Lara

Broccoli and other tales of food and love. Pantheon Books 2008 148p $20

ISBN 978-0-375-42487-8; 0-375-42487-3

LC 2007-41537

"This slim collection of six short stories (plus recipes) focuses on Russian and Eastern European immigrants to the US. They are lonely, they are disoriented, and they hope dinner will assuage their longings. Food is the slender thread that connects their pasts to their presents. Vapynar's characters are funny, vulnerable, somewhat deluded, but also courageous. . . . [They] drift wistfully through landscapes they have not yet learned how to embrace. Yet Vapnyar's sly humor keeps her narratives light along with their poignance." Christ Sci Monit

Vargas Llosa, Mario

★ **Aunt** Julia and the scriptwriter; translated by Helen R. Lane. Farrar, Straus & Giroux 1982 374p

LC 82-5159

Original Spanish edition, 1977

In this novel Vargas Llosa "draws on memories of his youth during the mid-1950s, namely his marriage to an aunt despite strong family opposition, and the action-packed soap operas penned by a mad colleague at a Lima radio station where Vargas Llosa was employed. The work's overriding irony stems from the juxtaposition of the two plot lines, the first based on fact and the second on imaginary events. The end result is a kind of metanovel in which the author sees the objective account of his courtship and marriage gradually assume the characteristics of melodrama." Ency of World Lit in the 20th Century

Vargas Llosa, Mario

The **bad** girl; translated from the Spanish by Edith Grossman. Farrar, Straus & Giroux 2007 276p $25

ISBN 978-0-374-18243-4

LC 2007-04941

Original Spanish edition, 2006

"Each chapter in Ricardo's life, in Edith Grossman's tart, fluent translation, is a small novel unto itself with its own amiable or striking protagonists, offering a whole fabric of reality waiting to be shredded to pieces by the reappearance of the bad girl. In this way, Vargas Llosa lures us into the world of Latin American revolutionaries; the tony equestrian crowd of Norfolk, England; the denizens of sex clubs in Tokyo; and much more. . . . Vargas Llosa, pulling back one illusory screen after another, eventually reveals the bad girl's true story in a manner that couldn't be more satisfying." Seattle Times

Vargas Llosa, Mario

Captain Pantoja and the Special Service; translated from the Spanish by Gregory Kolovakos and Ronald Christ. Harper & Row 1978 244p

ISBN 0-06-014494-7

LC 76-26280

Original Spanish edition, 1973

"Pantoja is a diligent young army officer who is sent to the Peruvian tropics to organize a squadron of prostitutes and thus make life more bearable for lonely soldiers stationed in remote out-posts. Because of his puritanical nature and zealously analytical approach to his assignment, Pantoja elicits the reader's guffaws from the beginning, but ultimately he comes to typify the absurd hero who continues to struggle against overwhelming odds. The theme of absurdity is underscored, moreover, by the hilarious parodies of military procedures, the clashing montage of incompatible episodes, and generous doses of irony and the grotesque." Ency of World Lit in the 20th Century

Vargas Llosa, Mario

Conversation in the cathedral; a novel. translated by Gregory Rabassa. Rayo 2005 601p pa $15.99

ISBN 978-0-06-073280-6

LC 2004-63263

Original Spanish edition, 1969; this translation first published 1975 by Harper & Row

This novel "takes place in 1950s Peru during the dictatorship of Manuel A. Odría. Over beers and a sea of freely spoken words, the conversation flows between two individuals, Santiago and Ambrosia, who talk of their tormented lives and of the overall degradation and frustration that has slowly taken over their town." Publisher's note

Vargas Llosa, Mario

Death in the Andes; translated by Edith Grossman. Farrar, Straus & Giroux 1996 275p

LC 95-40883

Original Spanish edition, 1993

This novel "begins with a mystery. . . . It concludes with an enigma: How slender is the boundary between civilization and tenebrous horror? The novel's indecipherable mystery is exquisitely attractive to the clear, transparent country that is a genial reader's mind." Atl Mon

Vargas Llosa, Mario, 1936-

★ The **Discreet** Hero; Mario Vargas Llosa; translated from the Spanish by Edith Grossman. Farrar, Straus & Giroux 2015 336 p. $26

ISBN 0374146748; 9780374146740

LC 2014031209

Mario Vargas Llosa's novel "follows two fascinating characters whose lives are destined to intersect: neat, endearing Felícito Yanaqué, a small businessman in Piura, Peru, who finds himself the victim of blackmail; and Ismael Carrera, a successful owner of an insurance company in Lima, who cooks up a plan to avenge himself against the two lazy sons who want him dead." (Publisher's note)

"Vargas Llosa, a soaring storyteller, mixes humor with solemnity, farce with seriousness, to arrive at novels that maintain a perfect balance between rigorous literary standards and free-for-all fun." Booklist

Vargas Llosa, Mario, 1936-

The **dream** of the Celt; Mario Vargas Llosa; translated from the Spanish by Edith Grossman. Farrar, Straus and Giroux 2012 358 p.

ISBN 0374143463; 9780374143466

LC 2011052181

In this book, "Nobel Prize for Literature winner (in 2010) and one-time Peruvian presidential candidate, [Mario] Vargas Llosa chronicles the life of Roger Casement, an Irish patriot and human rights activist, or 'specialist in atrocities,' who was executed by the British in 1916 after the Easter Rising, which heralded the beginning of Irish independence." (Publishers Weekly)

Vargas Llosa, Mario, 1936-

The **Feast** of the Goat; translated from the Spanish by Edith Grossman. Farrar, Straus & Giroux 2001 404p pa $14; $25

ISBN 0-312-42027-7 pa; 0-374-15476-7

LC 2001-33480

Original Spanish edition, 2000

"Based on events that took place during and immediately after the three-decade-long rule (1930-1961) of Rafael Trujillo over the Dominican Republic, 'The Goat' creates a . . . fictional portrait of a dictator, described by one character as 'the devil.' . . . {The} story is related in three overlapping narratives, tracing the respective experiences of Trujillo in the days before his assassination; the band of conspirators who are planning to kill him; and a woman named Urania Cabral, who is the daughter of one of the dictator's disgraced ministers." (N Y Times (Late N Y Ed))

"This fictional portrait of ruthless Dominican Republic dictator Rafael Trujillo focuses on the end of the old 'goat's' life. . . . Vargas Llosa relates Trujillo's story from the perspective of Urania Cabral, a successful New York lawyer who has spent a lifetime in exile but returns to her homeland when the tyrant is finally murdered. Urania hopes to rid herself of the demons that have possessed her since 1961, when as a teenager she was battered and humiliated by the impotent and vindictive old dictator." Libr J

Vargas Llosa, Mario

The **Green** House; a novel. translated by Gregory Rabassa. Rayo 2005 405p pa $14.99

ISBN 978-0-06-073279-0; 0-06-073279-2

LC 2004-63259

Original Spanish edition, 1965; this translation first published 1968 by Harper & Row

This "novel takes place in a Peruvian town, situated between desert and jungle, which is torn by boredom and lust. Don Anselmo, a stranger in a black coat, builds a brothel on the outskirts of the town while he charms its innocent people, setting in motion a chain reaction with extraordinary consequences. This brothel, called the Green House, brings together the innocent and the corrupt: Bonificia, a young Indian girl saved by the nuns only to become a prostitute; Father Garcia, struggling for the church; and four best friends drawn to both excitement and escape." Publisher's note

Vargas Llosa, Mario

★ The **notebooks** of Don Rigoberto; translated by Edith Grossman. Farrar, Straus & Giroux 1998 259p il $23

ISBN 0-374-22327-0

LC 98-70961

Original Spanish edition, 1997

"Vargas Llosa's complex, gorgeous prose, heroically translated by Edith Grossman, sweeps the reader into a rich confusion of art and fact, fiction and reality, fantasy and deed, where there are no vices and the only virtue is imagination." N Y Times Book Rev

Vargas Llosa, Mario

The **time** of the hero; translated by Lysander Kemp. Farrar, Strauss & Giroux 1986 409p pa $18

ISBN 978-0-374-52021-2; 0-374-52021-6

Original Spanish edition, 1962; this translation first published 1966 by Grove Press

This "novel is a remarkably mature (and, one imagines, highly autobiographical) account. . . . In a sense Llosa is too clever a writer, for his novel gets swamped in places with unnecessary attempts at literary sophistication, repeated flashbacks, multiple viewpoints, and so on. The first hundred pages or so are inordinately prolix, but it is worth making an effort. . . . If [the] novel had been severely edited at an early stage its dramatic core would, I think, have emerged more effectively: despite its prolixity, it is still a harsh and honest piece of fiction." N Y Rev of Books

Vargas Llosa, Mario

The **war** of the end of the world; translated by Helen R. Lane. Picador; Farrar, Strauss and Giroux 2008 568p pa $17

ISBN 978-0-312-43798-6; 0-312-42798-0

Original Spanish edition, 1981; this translation first published 1984 by Farrar, Straus and Giroux

"Vargas Llosa depicts a clash not only between two opposing factions but also between two societies inhabiting the same nation, who share only one thing in common: their ignorance of one another. This work represents his most ambitious novel to date in terms of the vastness of the world it portrays and the intensity of its epic action. Helen R. Lane's superb translation now makes this novel available to the English-speaking reader who will find the book to be a memorable literary experience." Choice

Vargas Llosa, Mario

★ The **way** to paradise; translated by Natasha Wimmer. Farrar, Straus & Giroux 2003 373p $25

ISBN 0-374-22803-5

LC 2003-56379

"A whiff of the lecture hall is detectable all through this book. (Some passages have more dates than an almanac.) But the juxtaposition of Tristan's and Gauguin's stories is fascinating all the same. In their different ways, both were moralists and proselytizers." N Y Time Book Rev

Vargas, Fred, 1957-

The **Ghost** Riders of Ordebec; a commissaire adamsberg mystery. Fred Vargas; translated from the French by Siân Reynolds. Penguin Books 2013 368 p. $15

ISBN 0143123122; 9780143123125

LC 2012042668

In this novel by Fred Vargas "Commissaire Adamsberg has no jurisdiction in Ordebec. Yet, he cannot ignore a widow's plea. Her daughter Lina has seen a vision of the Ghost Riders with four nefarious men. According to the thousand-year-old legend, the vision means that the men will soon die a grisly death. When one of them disappears, Adamsberg races to Ordebec, where he becomes entranced by the gorgeous Lina—and embroiled in the small Normandy town's ancient feud." (Publisher's note)

Varley, John, 1947-

Dark lightning; John Varley. Ace Books 2014 352 p. (Thunder and lightning) (hardback) $26.95

ISBN 0425274071; 9780425274071

LC 2014009515

In this novel, by John Varley, "the starship Rolling Thunder is powered by an energy no one understands, except for its eccentric inventor Jubal Broussard. Like many of the ship's inhabitants, Jubal rests in a state of suspended animation for years at a time. . . . The moments when Jubal emerges from suspended animation are usually a cause for celebration for his family. . . . But this time, Jubal makes a shocking announcement: The ship must stop, or everyone will die." (Publisher's note)

Varley, John

Demon. Putnam 1984 464p

LC 84-4814

The author "concludes his trilogy about Gaea, the sentient asteroid circling Titan. Cirocco Jones and her allies, including various Titanides and a Terran bodybuilder, struggle to provide the last refuge for fugitives from an Earth devastated by nuclear war." Booklist

Varley, John

The **golden** globe. Ace Bks. 1998 425p $22.95

ISBN 0-441-00558-6

LC 98-14612

"Galactic actor and con man Sparky Valentine runs afoul of the Charonese Mafia on Pluto and takes on the most important role of his long and illustrious career—that of a desperate survivor. Varley . . . artfully combines a rousing sf adventure with generous doses of Shakespearean lore and theater history, all of which serve as an elaborate backdrop for a moving portrait of a child actor who never quite grew up." Libr J

Varley, John

Red lightning. Ace Books 2006 330p $24.95

ISBN 0-441-01364-3

LC 2005-34226

"Drawing unabashedly on current events from 9/11 to Hurricane Katrina, the author mixes space opera-esque adventure and merriment with uncensored images of disaster areas and teenage sex. At his Heinlein-channeling best, Varley preaches the gospel of individual responsibility with all the fervor of a space-age libertarian revival preacher." Publ Wkly

Varley, John

Red thunder. Ace Bks. 2003 411p $23.95

ISBN 0-441-01015-6

LC 2002-38231

"When a Chinese spacecraft, Heavenly Harmony, threatens to land on Mars a few days before the U.S. shuttle vehicle Ares Seven, washed-up ex-astronaut Travis Broussard, his brilliant but uncoventional cousin, Jubal, and four kids from Florida decide to build their own private spaceship, Red Thunder, and get there first in this riveting SF thriller. . . . With hilarious, well-drawn characters, extraordinary situations presented plausibly, plus exciting action and adventure, this book should do thunderously well." Publ Wkly

Varley, John

Rolling thunder. Ace Books 2008 344p $24.95

ISBN 978-0-441-01563-4; 0-441-01563-8

LC 2007-46581

"In the distant future, Mars is a colony of Earth, and Lt. Patricia Podkayne is a third-generation Martian with something to prove. As a member of the Music, Arts, and Drama Division of the Martian Navy, she accepts an assignment as an entertainer on the planet Europa, not realizing that trouble is brewing on that world. . . . Varley's style of future sf is immediate and gritty, filled with realistic details and believable characters. His conclusion to a trilogy begun with Red Lightning and Red Thunder demonstrates his skill as both raconteur and master of science-based fiction." Libr J

Varley, John

★ **Titan**; illustrated by Freff. Berkley Pub. Corp. 1979 302p il

LC 78-23865

The first volume of a trilogy that includes Wizard and Demon

"The heroine finds an artificial world among the satellites of Saturn and becomes an agent of its resident intelligence, the godlike Gaea, before being forced to turn against 'her.' Conscientiously nonsexist action-adventure SF." Anatomy of Wonder. 3d edition

Followed by Wizard

Varley, John

Wizard; illustrated by Freff. Berkley Pub. Corp. 1980 354p il

LC 79-24871

"In this sequel to . . . 'Titan,' Varley continues his exploration of the sentient, wheel-shaped world called Gaea. Twenty years have passed, and now that Earth is aware of her, Gaea has tried to protect herself by becoming valuable to humanity—offering us 'miracles' based on her immense scientific knowledge. Two supplicants for such boons are the central characters: Chris, a man from Earth, and Robin, a woman from the Coven, an all-female orbital colony. To earn their miracles, Gaea requires them to become heroes. To achieve this, they accompany Rocky and Gaby (heroines of the first book, back in supporting roles) on a dangerous odyssey through Gaea's rebellious regions and learn that Gaea herself is the real enemy." Publ Wkly

Followed by Demon

Vásquez, Juan Gabriel, 1973-

★ The **sound** of things falling; Juan Gabriel Vasquez; Translated from the Spanish by Anne McLean. Riverhead Books, a member of Penguin Group (USA) Inc. 2013 288 p. $27.95

ISBN 1594487480; 9781594487484

LC 2013009330

In this book by Juan Gabriel Vasquez, set "around 1996, when murder and bloody mayhem fueled by the drug trade were commonplace in Bogotá, the young law professor Antonio Yammara befriends enigmatic stranger Ricardo Laverde. One night, assassins on motorbikes open fire on the two, killing Laverde and seriously wounding Yammara. Conflicted and at a loss to understand the damage Laverde has wrought, Yammara looks into his life story." (Publishers Weekly)

Vassanji, M. G.

The **assassin's** song. Alfred A. Knopf 2007 313p $25

ISBN 978-1-4000-4217-3; 1-400-04217-8

LC 2007-8562

"Karsan Dargawalla is destined from boyhood to succeed his father and his father's father as avatar of Pirbaag, a 13th-century Sufi shrine. As the novel unfolds in fits and starts, Karsan rejects his spiritual inheritance and decamps for Harvard in 1970, against his chagrined father's wishes. The three decades of stubborn self-exile that follow represent a sorrowful generational rift between father and son that ends when Karsan returns home after his ascetic father's death." Publ Wkly

Vassanji, M. G.

The **in**-between world of Vikram Lall. Knopf 2004 369p $25

ISBN 1-400-04216-X

LC 2004-48967

"In this novel set among Kenya's Indian diaspora, two ill-fated loves—Vikram Lall's for a young English girl, his sister's for a young African man—symbolize their family's tenuous social position as neither privileged oppressor nor righteous oppressed. Vikram, now in exile in Canada, recounts Kenya's painful process of decolonization and his own role laundering money for government officials, an activity that he justifies as the survival tactic of one considered 'inherently disloyal' because of his race. . . . The book admirably captures the tenor of the postcolonial period: the predicament of the Asian minority, the corruption that marred Kenya's fledgling independence, and the individual tragedies that were the cost of revolution." New Yorker

Vassanji, M. G., 1950-

★ The **Magic** of Saida; A novel. M.G. Vassanji. 1st U.S. ed. Knopf 2013 303 p. (hardcover) $25.95

ISBN 0307961508; 9780307961501

LC 2012041081

This novel, by M. G. Vassanji, is a story of "an African/Indian man who returns to the town of his birth in search of the girl he once loved--and the sense of self that has always eluded him. . . . Kamal [Punja] had reached a stage of both undreamed-of material success and disintegrating personal ties. Then, suddenly, he . . . 'allowed an old regret to awaken,' and set off to find the girl he had known as a child, to finally keep his promise to her that he would return." (Publisher's note)

Verdon, John

Shut your eyes tight. Crown Publishers 2011 509p $24

ISBN 978-0-307-71789-4

LC 2010-53589

Sequel to: Think of a number (2010)

Superstar detective Dave Gurney's renewed efforts to retire are halted by the brutal murder of a young bride at her wedding reception, a crime subsequently linked to a brilliant criminal who targets Gurney's family to further his agendas.

"Red herrings come thick and fast in the labyrinthine plot, and the suspense builds until the violent denouement. But it is the nature of the criminal conspiracy—utterly vile, fantastic, and yet curiously plausible—that will have crime readers willingly losing sleep." Booklist

Verdon, John

Think of a number; a novel. Crown Publishers 2010 418p $22

ISBN 978-0-307-58892-0; 0-307-58892-0

LC 2009-28512

"Verdon is a master at controlling pace, illustrating the story of a rich but complicated marriage, pondering what it means to be sucked back into your life's work even if it might kill you, and demanding that the reader use his or her brain to figure out what comes next. When you're finished, you may not trust silly parlor games ever again." Salon

Verghese, Abraham

Cutting for stone; a novel. Alfred A. Knopf 2009 541p $26.95

ISBN 978-0-375-41449-7; 0-375-41449-5

LC 2008-28252

A "novel about identical twin boys born in Addis Ababa in 1954 and instantly orphaned—their mother dies, their father flees. Raised by doctors at the hospital, Shiva and Marion soon begin practicing medicine themselves, but their lives unhappily diverge. . . . Verghese, a doctor, has an affinity for unstinting detail and unscientific intuition. The exhaustive gore of the medical procedures is matched by a poetic perception of the outside world—arriving in New York, Marion misses the cacophony of Addis Ababa's roads, observing that in America 'the cars were near silent, like a school of fish.' Verghese bends history and coincidence to his narrative needs—characters cross paths when they should and find the information they seek—creating a story much like the human bodies Marion painstakingly describes: beautiful, amazing, and a bit of a mess." New Yorker

Verissimo, Luis Fernando

Borges and the eternal orangutans; translated from the Portuguese by Margaret Jull Costa. New Directions 2005 135p pa $13.95

ISBN 0-8112-1592-x

LC 2004-28203

Original Portuguese edition, 2000

"Most writers feel passionate about Borges, but few would have the temerity to put the enigmatic sage into their fiction. That's because evoking Borges's presence would likely overwhelm any meager thoughts of their own. Yet Brazilian novelist Luis Fernando Verissimo has such temerity, as well as the talent to pull it off." Washington Post Book World

Verne, Jules

★ **Around** the world in eighty days; translated with an introduction and notes by William Butcher. Oxford University Press 2008 xlv, 247p (Oxford world's classics) pa $9.95

ISBN 978-0-19-955251-1

LC 2008-482138

Original French edition, 1873

"The hero, Phileas Fogg, undertakes his hasty world tour as the result of a bet made at his London club. He and his French valet Passepartout, meet with some fantastic adventures, but these are overcome by the loyal servant and the endlessy inventive Fogg. The feat they perform is incredible for its day; Fogg wins his bet, having circled the world in only eighty days." Reader's Ency. 4th edition

Includes bibliographical references

Verne, Jules

★ The **extraordinary** journeys: Twenty thousand leagues under the sea; translated with an introduction and notes by William Butcher. Oxford University Press 2009 xlviii, 445p pa $11.95

ISBN 978-0-19-953927-7

LC 2009-464589

Original French edition, 1870; This translation first published 1998

"The voyage of the Nautilus permitted Verne to describe the wonders of an undersea world almost totally unknown to the general public of the period. Indebted to literary tradition for his Atlantis, he made his major innovation in having the submarine completely powered by electricity, although the interest in electrical forces goes back to Poe and Shelley. So far as the enigmatic ending is concerned, his readers had to wait for the three-part The Mysterious Island (1874-1875) to learn that Nemo had been the Indian warrior-prince Dakkar, who had been involved in the Sepoy Mutiny of 1857." Anatomy of Wonder 4

Includes bibliographical references

Verne, Jules

From the earth to the moon, and Round the moon; With pictures of the author and his environment and illus. of the setting of the book, together with an introd. by Arthur C. Clarke. Dodd, Mead 1962 308p il (Great illustrated classics)

LC 63-07412

The two books comprising this volume were first published 1865 and 1872 respectively

These titles provide a "striking example of early hard SF, detailing with great precision the preparations and scientific premises (still mostly correct, apart from the deadly effect of acceleration on the passengers) for a voyage to the moon." New Ency of Sci Fic

Verne, Jules

★ A **journey** to the centre of the earth; introduction by David Brin. Modern Library 2003 195p pa $8.95

ISBN 0-8129-7009-8

LC 2003-59947

Original French edition, 1864. Variant title: A trip to the center of the earth

"More than half the book is given to the preliminaries before the actual descent begins, the first two chapters relying on a standard point of departure, the discovery of a manuscript giving the location of the caverns in Iceland. The narrative shows Verne's intense care in presenting the latest scientific thought of his age, while the sighting of the plesiosaurus and the giant humanoid shepherding mammoths indicates how well he incorporated lengthy imaginary episodes to flesh out the factual report." Anatomy of Wonder 4

Verne, Jules

The **mysterious** island; pictures by N. C. Wyeth. Scribner 1988 493p il $25.95

ISBN 0-684-18957-7

LC 88-3167

Sequel to Twenty thousand leagues under the sea

Original French edition, 1874; first United States edition published 1883 by J. W. Lovell; this is a reissue of the 1918 edition

A story of adventure in three parts: Dropped from the clouds; Abandoned; and The secret of the island

"Five men and a dog are carried out to sea in a balloon and drop from the clouds on the mysterious island. Their Crusoe-like resourcefulness and adventures are the theme of the book." Toronto Public Libr

Vernon, Olympia

Eden. Grove Press 2003 272p $23

ISBN 0-8021-1728-7

LC 2002-33863

"Fourteen-year-old Maddy Dangerfield is called upon to help her cancer-afflicted aunt Pip live out her last days. Maddy's mother, Faye, can't forgive her sister's betrayal of her with her own husband. Maddy is caught in the vortex of unresolved conflicts among the adults: a stoic, overworked mother who can't make peace with a dying sister; an alcoholic husband addicted to gambling; and a fiery aunt who has lived her life on her own terms. The small black community of Pyke County, Mississippi, is also saturated with unresolved conflicts, seething resentments, and violence. . . .Vernon's writing is lyrical and emotionally powerful." Booklist

Vernon, Olympia

A **killing** in this town. Grove Press 2006 246p $22

ISBN 0-8021-1813-5

LC 2005-52547

"The novel shows the debilitating cancer of hatred and prejudice and the beauty of the effort to stop the violence. In language reminiscent of Toni Morrison and William Faulkner, Vernon weaves a powerful yet dreamlike story of our not-too-distant past." Booklist

Veselka, Vanessa

Zazen. Red Lemonade 2011 264p pa $15.95

ISBN 978-1-935869-05-4

"The deeply disaffected young woman narrator of Veselka's . . . [novel] must decide whether to flee a dystopian America or try to endure it, and, in the process maybe help save it a little. Della is a waitress with an obsessive interest in self-immolation, a sharp wit, and a dwindling hope in humanity. When a bomb goes off in an office building in her faceless industrial city's downtown, Della finds that the distant wars the country's been fighting are coming closer to home. At first she considers leaving like many others, but then the chaos becomes attractive to Della and she calls in a series of phony bomb threats around town, taking big delight in watching people scramble from, for instance, a mall-church complex. But when someone starts setting off bombs at places from her list of 'targets,' Della realizes that she might be part of something bigger than her own absurd protest. Veselka's prose is chiseled and laced with arsenic observations, and though she unleashes some savage social satire, her focus is more on the hypocrisy, heartache, and confusion that drive Della and those around her." Publ Wkly

Vestal, Shawn

Daredevils; Shawn Vestal. Penguin Press 2016 320 p. $27

ISBN 1101979895; 9781101979891

This novel, by Shawn Vestal, is "set in Arizona and Idaho in the mid-1970s. . . . Fifteen-year-old Loretta . . . slips out of her bedroom every evening to meet her so-called gentile boyfriend. Her strict Mormon parents catch her returning one night, and promptly marry her off to Dean Harder, a devout yet materialistic fundamentalist who already has a wife and a brood of kids. The Harders relocate to his native Idaho, where Dean's teenage nephew Jason falls hard for Loretta." (Publisher's Note)

"Vestal has created a riveting, rollicking thrill ride about throwing caution to the wind." Pub Wkly

The **vicious** circle; mystery and crime stories by members of the Algonquin Round Table. edited by Otto Penzler. Pegasus Books 2007 205p $25; pa $13.95

ISBN 978-1-933648-67-5; 1-933648-67-8; 978-1-605980-24-9 pa; 1-605980-24-2 pa

"As mystery expert Penzler admits in his introduction, this volume contains 'little classic detection . . . and less nail-biting suspense' than the usual crime fiction anthology, but those curious about the legendary figures of the Algonquin Round Table—a group of New York City writers and critics from the 1920s, many affiliated with the New Yorker—will get at least a taste of the wit and sophistication for which they were known." Publ Wkly

Vida, Vendela

Let the Northern Lights erase your name; a novel. Ecco 2007 226p $23.95

ISBN 978-0-06-082837-0; 0-06-082837-4

LC 2006-45030

In this novel, "a twenty-eight-year-old editor of film subtitles discovers on her father's death that he is not her biological parent: her mother, who abandoned her as a teenager, had been married to another man. Feeling betrayed by her fiancé, who has known about the deception for years, she abruptly leaves him to search for her real father in the northern reaches of Finland. Vida gives the icy landscape an eerie, forbidding beauty, and her writing has moments of great emotional acuity. Her heroine is inexplicable and often unlikable, but Vida skillfully draws a parallel between her harsh and thoughtless behavior and that of her mother." New Yorker

Vidal, Gore

1876; a novel. Modern Lib. 1998 524p $22.95

ISBN 0-679-60294-1

LC 98-21216

A volume in the author's American chronicle series

A reissue of the title first published 1976 by Random House

"As in 'Burr,' Charles Schuyler, hinted-at as the illegitimate son of Aaron Burr, again narrates. Now a respected and popular journalist-historian, Schuyler at 63 has returned, after years abroad, to the U.S. in the company of his widowed daughter, the Princess d'Agrigente, who is in need of a well-connected husband—thereby giving Vidal another occasion to crash society's party as he follows Schuyler on his journalistic assignments through New York, the city of Washington, later to Philadelphia for the Centennial, then Cincinnati for the Republican Convention." Publ Wkly

Vidal, Gore

Burr. Modern Lib. 1998 697p $20

ISBN 0-679-60285-2

LC 97-39825

A volume in the author's American chronicle series

"Burr is a novel in the form of a memoir told in part by Burr and in part by the young journalist Charles Schuyler, a fictional creation and Vidal's strongest character." Choice

Vidal, Gore, 1925-2012

The **city** and the pillar. Vintage 2003 207p pa $15

ISBN 1-4000-3037-4; 978-1-4000-3037-8

First published 1948 by Dutton

"Jim, a handsome, all-American athlete, has always been shy around girls. But when he and his best friend, Bob, partake in 'awful kid stuff,' the experience forms Jim's ideal of spiritual completion. Defying his parents' expectations, Jim strikes out on his own, hoping to find Bob and rekindle their amorous friendship. Along the way he struggles with what he feels is his unique bond with Bob and with his persistent attraction to other men." Publisher's note

Vidal, Gore

Clouds and eclipses; the collected short stories. Carroll & Graf 2006 166p pa $13.95

ISBN 0-78671-810-2

"This volume collects the short fiction of Vidal . . . , including the recently rediscovered story from which the book takes its title. All eight pieces date to the author's early career and, with the exception of the title story, were previously published in 1956. Diverse, engaging, and full of surprising twists and turns, the stories take the general theme of homosexual encounter from various points of view. The writing is crisp; the images, crystal clear and often breathtaking." Libr J

Vidal, Gore

Creation; a novel. Random House 1981 510p il

LC 79-5528

"The narrator, old and blind and finishing out his days as Persian ambassador to Pericles' Athens, is recounting his life's experiences, mostly as acquired in the service of Darius the Great and his son Xerxes. . . . In particular, he describes his special missions to India, where, as well as meeting a variety of world princes, he converses with the Buddha, and to what is now China, where he becomes a friend and admirer of Confucius." Publ Wkly

Vidal, Gore

★ **Empire**; a novel. Modern Lib. 1998 651p $23.95

ISBN 0-679-60293-3

LC 98-21224

A volume in the author's American chronicle series

A reissue of the title first published 1987 by Random House

"Interesting and well-developed real-life characters abound, including, most memorably, Secretary of State and Lincoln's old friend John Hay. Intermixed with the well-researched backdrop of historical characters and events is Caroline's personal story." Libr J

Vidal, Gore

The **golden** age; a novel. Doubleday 2000 467p $27.50

ISBN 0-385-50075-0

LC 00-43071

Seventh and final volume in the author's American chronicle series. Set chronologically after Washington, D.C.

"Vidal is best on the surface. His account of the 1940 conventions is a real romp. He depicts F.D.R. with irreverent skill. . . . It's good to know how badly Wendell Willkie could give a public speech; and there are some wonderful scenes in which Eleanor Roosevelt skillfully manipulates her husband and the bosses of the old Democratic Party." N Y Times Book Rev

Vidal, Gore

Hollywood; a novel of America in the 1920s. Modern Lib. 1999 558p $24.95

ISBN 0-679-60292-5

LC 98-46174

A volume in the author's American chronicle series

A reissue of the title first published 1990 by Random House

Vidal's "highly polished prose style, in part the fruit of his classical training, is a constant delight." N Y Times Book Rev

Vidal, Gore

★ **Lincoln**. Modern Lib. 1993 712p hardcover o.p.

LC 92-27273

A reissue of the title first published 1984 by Random House

This novel "is not so much an imaginative reconstruction of an era as an intelligent, lucid and highly informative transcript of it, never less than workmanlike in its blocking out of scenes and often extremely compelling." N Y Times Book Rev

Vidal, Gore

★ **Myra** Breckinridge [and] Myron. Random House 1986 417p $19.95

ISBN 0-394-55376-4

LC 86-11423

Combined edition of two titles first published 1968 and 1974 respectively

In the first novel, Myra who was once Myron seduces both Rusty Godowsky and his girlfriend Mary-Ann Pringle. The sequel is set in 1973. Myron Breckinridge, the alter ego of the transsexual heroine, is pushed through his television screen and onto the set of a 1948 film "Siren of Babylon" starring Maria Montez. He has difficulty in getting out. Myra periodically takes command of Myron's body. She attempts to save the world from overpopulation by altering the male sex

Vidal, Gore

Washington, D.C. a novel. Modern Lib. 1999 422p $24.95

ISBN 0-679-60291-7

LC 98-46173

A volume in the author's American chronicle series

Set from the New Deal to the McCarthy years this "political novel features the ambitions of both a senator and his young secretary for the Presidency. The senator loses his chance for the Democratic nomination when Roosevelt decides to run for a third term. The secretary, mapping his course to the top, with the help of a journalist invents a non-happening which makes him a national hero. He then blackmails the senator into withdrawing from the race and wins the senatorial seat for himself." Booklist

Vila-Matas, Enrique

★ **Montano's** malady; translated from the Spanish by Jonathan Dunne. New Directions 2007 $14.95 pa $14.95

ISBN 978-0-8112-1628-9; 0-8112-1628-4

LC 2006-102330

Original Spanish edition, 2002

"Written in the form of a journal, which becomes a novel, then a dictionary of writers' journals, then a lecture on the writing of such journals, Montano tells of its narrator's obsession with literature. Middle-aged and married to Rosa, he has become 'a walking dictionary of quotations', unable to do anything without it triggering a memory of something he's read or, worse, something remembered by a writer that he's read, which in turn recalls a thought from the head of yet another writer. Following him and his overactive brain from his native Barcelona to Nantes, Chile, the Azores, Lisbon and Budapest—via Walter Benjamin, Kafka, W. G. Sebald, Pessoa and Robert Walser among others—is like playing a mental version of Twister. . . . Shunning narrative, the book continues to seduce with writerly observations—both the narrator's, and quotations from other writers." Telegraph (London)

Vila-Matas, Enrique

Never any end to Paris; translated from the Spanish by Anne McLean. New Directions Books 2011 197p $15.95

ISBN 978-0-8112-1813-9

LC 2011-02601

Original Spanish edition, 2003

This novel is "is told in the form of a lecture delivered by a novelist clearly a version of the author himself. The 'lecturer' tells of his two-year stint living in Marguerite Duras's garret during the seventies, spending time with writers, intellectuals, and eccentrics, and trying to make it as a creator of literature. . . . Encountering such luminaries as Duras, Roland Barthes, Georges Perec, Sergio Pitol, Samuel Beckett, and Juan Marsé, our narrator embarks on a novel whose text will 'kill' its readers and put him on a footing with his beloved Hemingway." Publisher's note

Villarreal, José Antonio, 1924-2010

Pocho; José Antonio Villarreal. Anchor Books 1989 187 p. (paperback) $15; ($9.95 Can.)

ISBN 9780385061186; 0385061188 $7.95

LC 89018204

This novel by José Antonio Villarreal is set in Depression-era California and "focuses on Richard, a young pocho who experiences the intense conflict between loyalty to the traditions of his family's past and attraction to new ideas. Richard's struggle to achieve adulthood as a young man influenced by two worlds reveals both the uniqueness of the Mexican-American experiences and its common ties with the struggles of all Americans -- whatever their past." (Publisher's note)

Villars, Elizabeth

The **Normandie** affair. Doubleday 1982 319p

LC 81-43727

This novel is "set aboard an opulent cruise liner, the 'Normandie,' in the days when luxury and sumptuousness were taken for granted. Villars' story covers six days of irrevocable change in the lives of several passengers crossing from New York to France in 1936. At the center of this drama is mysterious Anson Sherwood, a wealthy Bostonian with a passion for and inordinate knowledge of the 'Normandie.' Sherwood turns out to be a dedicated meddler who interferes in the lives of his fellow passengers, involving himself in both romantic entanglements and political intrigues, usually with fortuitous results. Neatly bundling drama and romance, Villars has captured the dichotomous nature of shipboard life." Booklist

Vine, Barbara

Anna's book; [by] Ruth Rendell writing as Barbara Vine. Harmony Bks. 1993 394p

LC 92-34309

"Vine's story is utterly riveting, rich and multifaceted in its complexity. Her characters are wonderfully real and fascinatingly unconventional." Booklist

Vine, Barbara

The **brimstone** wedding. Harmony Bks. 1996 330p $24

ISBN 0-517-70339-4

LC 95-30280

"Both Jenny and Stella embrace their pain with the sense of fatalism that has always been Ms. Vine's literary hallmark. The wonder is that they can speak their hearts in such clear and distinctive voices and yet retain their interior mystery." N Y Times Book Rev

Vine, Barbara

★ The **chimney** sweeper's boy; a novel. Harmony Bks. 1998 344p $24

ISBN 0-609-60287-X

LC 98-10567

This novel revolves around the "sudden death of Gerald Candless, a celebrated English novelist who lived on the Devon coast with his wife, Ursula, and two daughters to whom he was conspicuously devoted. When one daughter, Sarah, starts researching her father's early history for the biography she has been asked to write, she discovers that he was living under a false identity for most of his life. As more facts emerge from Sarah's research, they both illuminate and contradict the dark views of Gerald's personality supplied by his bitter wife and the deep, if ambiguous, insights contained in his own novels." N Y Times Book Rev

Vine, Barbara

★ **Gallowglass**. Harmony Bks. 1990 272p $19.95

ISBN 0-517-57744-5

LC 89-29026

"Miss Vine's most penetrating foray yet into the dark mysteries of the heart's obsessions, this haunting novel examines love in many guises—romantic, parental, idolatrous, possessive, selfless, erotic, platonic and sick. The scope of observation is dazzling; the tone, remarkably nonjudgmental." N Y Times Book Rev

Vine, Barbara

Grasshopper; a novel. Harmony Bks. 2000 392p $25

ISBN 0-609-60789-8

LC 00-38281

"Only a handful of writers, in any genre, can match Barbara Vine for imaginative originality and ingenuity. . . . Grasshopper is about good intentions gone wrong, violence, innocence and an encounter with true evil. . . . To say that a book can open your eyes to a different world is a cliché, but rarely has it been more apt than in describing this novel." New Statesman (Engl)

Vine, Barbara

The **house** of stairs; [by] Ruth Rendell writing as Barbara Vine. Harmony Bks. 1989 277p

LC 88-38303

First published 1988 in the United Kingdom

"Elizabeth Vetch, a writer, recalls her adolescence and young womanhood living with her cousin Cosette in a big, eccentric house in the Notting Hill section of London. Lots of people besides Elizabeth and Cosette lived in the House of Stairs, though; it was nest to many of their friends as well. Cosette is intent on recovering her lost youth, and because of her vulnerability in that direction, two residents conspire against her to gain her money. The consequence is violent death, with Elizabeth losing the one person she truly loved. A complex, eloquent novel—sure to retain Vine's large readership and undoubtedly gain her even more followers." Booklist

Vine, Barbara

King Solomon's carpet. Harmony Bks. 1992 355p

LC 91-43668

First published 1991 in the United Kingdom

The author "displays her remarkable ability to spot and dissect the terrifying beneath the ordinary, to imbue a setting with its own, almost palpable terror, and to construct in the process a narrative maze filled with constant, fearful surprise." Booklist

Vine, Barbara

The **minotaur**; a novel. Shaye Areheart Books 2005 341p $25

ISBN 0-307-23760-5

LC 2005-10837

"This is very satisfying reading, a sort of blend of Edgar Allan Poe and Anthony Trollope." Booklist

Vine, Barbara

★ **No** night is too long. Harmony Bks. 1995 315p $23

ISBN 0-517-79964-2

LC 94-13064

First published 1994 in the United Kingdom

"This is a novel about the effects of passion in which the mood is as bleak as the cold North Sea; a murder mystery in which the crucial killing is imaginary, and the actual killing arbitrary. . . . Nevertheless—the novel does grip and its scheme is impressive; it is hard to withhold applause from an author so lavishly endowed with the capacity to invent interlocking segments of plot." Times Lit Suppl

Vinge, Joan D.

★ The **Snow** Queen. Dial Press (NY) 1980 536p

LC 79-20555

"An amalgam of SF and heroic fantasy borrowing the structure of Hans Christian Andersen's famous story, set on a barbarian world exploited by technologically superior outworlders, against the background of a fallen galactic empire." Anatomy of Wonder 4

Followed by World's end

Vinge, Joan D.

The **Summer** Queen. Warner Bks. 1991 670p

LC 90-50521

Sequel to World's end

"Plots and subplots proliferate, and although the prose is sometimes florid and the romance and sex scenes overly sentimental, the book is so full of drama, conflict and tragedy that it justifies its length." Publ Wkly

Vinge, Joan D.

World's end. Bluejay Bks. 1984 230p

LC 83-21374

In this novel "BZ Gundhalinu, a police inspector who played a minor role in . . . {The Snow Queen} is the central character. Having left Carbuncle at the time of the Change he has traveled to World's End in search of his two irresponsible older brothers. World's End, a barely habitable frontier planet, is center of a 'Company' mining operation but also contains Fire Lake, an unexplained anomaly that appears to drive those who approach it insane." Voice Youth Advocates

Followed by: The Summer Queen

Vinge, Vernor

The **children** of the sky. Tor Books 2011 444p il (Zones of thought) $25.99

ISBN 978-0-312-87562-6

LC 2011024210

Sequel to A fire upon the deep (1992)

'Ten years have passed on Tines World, where Ravna Bergnsdot and a number of human children ended up after a disaster that nearly obliterated humankind throughout the galaxy. Ravna and the pack animals for which the planet is named have survived a war, and Ravna has saved more than one hundred children who were in cold-sleep aboard the vessel that brought them. While there is peace among the Tines, there are those among them--and among the humans--who seek power...and no matter the cost, these malcontents are determined to overturn the fledgling civilization that has taken root since the humans landed. On a world of fascinating wonders and terrifying dangers, Vernor Vinge has created a powerful novel of adventure and discovery that will entrance the many readers of A Fire Upon the Deep. Filled with the inventiveness, excitement, and human drama that have become hallmarks of his work, this new novel is sure to become another great milestone in Vinge's already stellar career. '--

"It has been ten years since Ravna Bergnsdot brought 150 children to the primitive planet Tines World and, with the assistance of the native species, caninelike creatures with a pack mind, formed the last stronghold of humanity in the galaxy. Residing in the universe's 'slow zone,' in which faster-than-light travel is impossible and technological developments are limited, Ravna hopes to keep her colony safe from the alien Blight, which has already destroyed high-tech worlds. Not all the children brought to safety, however, believe in Ravna's tale of technology gone wrong or in the existence of the Blight, and their actions might bring about the cataclysmic disaster Ravna and her Tinish partner, Woodcarver, hoped to avoid. . . . Vinge has crafted a tale that should captivate his fans and win for him a larger and well-deserved audience. Libraries should anticipate demand." Libr J

Vinge, Vernor

A **deepness** in the sky. TOR Bks. 1999 606p

ISBN 0-312-85683-0

LC 98-43457

Prequel to A fire upon the deep

Vinge "is among the very best of the current crop of hard SF writers, producing work that is not only fast-paced and intellectually challenging, but also stylishly written and centered on carefully drawn characters." Publ Wkly

Vinge, Vernor

★ A **fire** upon the deep. TOR Bks. 1992 391p

LC 91-39020

"Thoughtful space opera at its best, this book delivers everything it promises in terms of galactic scope, audacious concepts and believable characters both human and nonhuman." N Y Times Book Rev

Vinge, Vernor

Rainbows end. Tor 2006 364p $25.95

ISBN 0-312-85684-9

LC 2006-278136

"Vinge's world is saturated with the logical extensions of current R&D. He has thought long and hard about how pervasive and ubiquitous information technology will transform our lives." Sci Fic Wkly

Viswanathan, Padma

The **toss** of a lemon. Harcourt 2008 619p il $26

ISBN 978-0-15-101533-7; 0-15-101533-3

LC 2008-13369

This "novel spans 66 years-from 1896 to 1962—in the life of one Tamil family. The matriarch of the clan, Sivakami, a Brahmin, was married at ten and widowed at 18. Already a mother of two, Sivakami was determined to set a pious example. This meant that she shaved her head, wore only white, and touched no one, not even her children or grandchildren, between dusk and dawn. What's more, she obeyed the custom of staying inside her home, venturing outdoors only three times in the many decades before her death. Sivakami's proscribed world is portrayed in amazing detail, and the life of the Brahmin elite is vividly captured. . . . Gender rules, class relations, and the political castes of late 19th- and early to mid-20th-century India are well presented, making this an important work of historical fiction." Libr J

Vlautin, Willy

Lean on Pete; a novel. Harper Perennial 2010 277, 16p pa $13.99

ISBN 978-0-06-145653-4; 0-06-145653-5

LC 2009-20460

"Charley Thompson is a 15-year-old boy who dreams of a normal home and the chance to play high-school football. Newly arrived in Portland with a mostly absent father, Charley hopes for the best and gets the worst. Suddenly homeless, he hangs out on the backstretch at Portland Meadows racetrack and finds a friend—an aging Thoroughbred named Lean on Pete. That's exactly what Charley does, at least for a while, until Pete, bound for the slaughterhouse, needs to lean on Charley. The perilous journey on which Charley and Pete embark must end badly—think of Kirk Douglas and another loyal horse on the run from civilization in Lonely Are the Brave—but on the road Charley tells Pete the story of his life, and in this young boy's flatly descriptive but heartbreaking words, reprising a lifetime of barely getting by . . . , Vlautin transforms what might have been a weepy, unbelievable TV-movie of a novel into a tough-and-tender account of a boy, a big-hearted horse, and a mostly unforgiving world." Booklist

Vlautin, Willy

Northline; a novel. Harper Perennial 2008 192, 18p pa $14.95

ISBN 978-0-06-145652-7; 0-06-145652-7

LC 2008-297989

"Vlautin's writing style is perfectly suited to his material: Things happen the way they happen, slowly but inexorably, with the significance of any moment rarely evident until after the fact, or maybe never evident at all. There are no epiphanies here; new lives are built one unassuming sentence at a time." Portland Mercury

Vollmann, William T.

Argall. Viking 2001 746p il $40

ISBN 0-670-91030-9

LC 2001-17744

"The eponymous Captain Argall edges into the foreground in the second part, succeeding Smith as Jamestown's leading spirit; he has the sinister bearing of some Jacobean theater devil—like Iago, there's menace in his meanings. He kidnaps Pokahuntas and manipulates her assimilation into settler culture. Vollman's ability to write in Smith's English and endow it with a contemporary snap is an extraordinary feat." Publ Wkly

Includes bibliographical references

Vollmann, William T., 1959-

The **Dying** Grass; A Novel of the Nez Perce War. by William T Vollmann. Penguin Group USA 2015 1408 p. illustrations, maps $55

ISBN 0670015989; 9780670015986

"In this new installment in his acclaimed series of novels examining the collisions between Native Americans and European colonizers, William T. Vollmann tells the story of the Nez Perce War, with flashbacks to the Civil War. Defrauded and intimidated at every turn, the Nez Perces finally went on the warpath in 1877, subjecting the U.S. Army to its greatest defeat since Little Big Horn." (Publisher's note)

"Telegraphic and episodic—so much so that it recalls the later work of Eduardo Galeano—Vollmann's saga is a note-perfect incantation. Stunning." Kirkus

Vollmann, William T.

★ **Europe** central. Viking 2005 832p il $39.95

ISBN 0-670-03392-8

LC 2004-61170

National Book Award: Fiction (2005)

"What sets 'Europe Central' apart from Vollmann's other large-scale historical productions is its strong narrative lines. The pieces are dated and arranged chronologically to give the book a plot that arcs from pre-war political machinations to Germany's surge east to Russia's counter-offensive, and that ends with cold war politics in divided Berlin." N Y Times Book Rev

Vollmann, William T.

★ **Fathers** and crows. Viking 1992 990p

ISBN 0-670-84333-4

LC 92-18315

The language "moves interestingly between contemporary colloquial, Hollywood historical, Middle High Tolkientalk, and a quirky and enjoyable poetry: never less than vigorous and inventive. . . . Despite nudges, the narrative grips." Times Lit Suppl

Includes bibliographical references

Vollmann, William T.

The **ice**-shirt. Viking 1990 415p il maps

ISBN 0-670-83239-1

LC 90-50051

"Without apparent strain, the story interweaves numerous characters, sea voyages, murders and supernatural horrors, digressing with relish. . . . 'The Ice-Shirt' impresses mightily in its scope, its scene-painting and its enciphered social messages." N Y Times Book Rev

Vollmann, William T., 1959-

★ **Last** stories and other stories; William T. Vollmann. Viking 2014 704 p. $36

ISBN 0670015970; 9780670015979

LC 2013047856

In this book, author William T. Vollmann "offers a collection of ghost stories linked by themes of love, death, and the erotic. A Bohemian farmer's dead wife returns to him, and their love endures, but at a gruesome price. A geisha prolongs her life by turning into a cherry tree. A journalist, haunted by the half-forgotten killing of a Bosnian couple, watches their story, and his own wartime tragedy, slip away from him. A dying American romances the ghost of his high school sweetheart." (Publisher's note)

"The writing is atmospheric, otherworldly, and highly accessible." LJ

Includes bibliographical references

Vollmann, William T.

The **rifles**. Viking 1994 411p il maps

ISBN 0-670-84856-5

LC 93-31577

"What The Rifles demonstrates, and what magnetizes the narrative's scattered contexts is the real and binding continuity between nineteenth and twentieth-century patterns of mind-above all, this terrible insistence on our will to power over the world." Yale Rev

Vollmann, William T.

The **royal** family. Viking 2000 780p $40

ISBN 0-670-89167-3

LC 99-56587

"Vollmann is after large-scale social chronicle; he includes characters from nearly every walk of life, and trains his attentions on processes not often seen by the faint of heart. . . . But this hypperrealistic novelist also aims to present a metaphysics: the two brothers stand for two kinds of human being, the chosen and the outcast. As in all Vollmann's novels, the author's encylopedic ambition sometimes overwhelms the human scale; some supporting characters, though, do stay vivid. Vollmann avoids simply glamorizing the outcasts but remains, deep down, a Blakean romantic: prostitution is for him not only the universal indictment of the human race but also, paradoxically, the only paradise we can actually visit." Publ Wkly

Volpi, Jorge

In search of Klingsor; translated by Kristina Cordero. Scribner 2002 414p $26

ISBN 0-7432-0118-3

LC 2002-17582

Original Spanish edition published 1999 in Mexico

The author "delivers a novel that manages to function as a crackling spy thriller while delivering a thoughtful treatist on the nature of love and deception." Booklist

Voltaire

Candide and other stories; translated from the French, with an introduction and notes, by Roger Pearson. Knopf 1992 307p $17

ISBN 0-679-41746-X

Contents: Candide; Micromegas; Zadig; The ingenu; The white bull

Voltaire

Voltaire's Candide, Zadig, and selected stories; translated with an introduction by Donald M. Frame. Candide illustrations by Paul Klee. Indiana Univ. Press 1961 351p il

Contains 14 satiric tales in addition to Candide (1759) and Zadig (1748)

Vonnegut, Kurt

Armageddon in retrospect; and other new and unpublished writings on war and peace. [illustrations by the author; introduction by Mark Vonnegut] G. P. Putnam's Sons 2008 232p il $24.95

ISBN 978-0-399-15508-6; 0-399-15508-2

Twelve previously unpublished writings on war and peace include such pieces as an essay on the destruction of Dresden, a story about the first-meal fantasies of three soldiers, and a meditation on the impossibility of shielding children from the temptations of violence.

"Only a few of the . . . stories rely on the twists of reality and narrative present in Vonnegut's novels; the majority are carried by the characters' struggle with the absurdities of war and peace. Vonnegut's World War II experience as a prisoner of war in Dresden haunts the work, with multiple stories featuring American POWs in Germany. . . . Readers of Vonnegut's books won't find any surprises here, but because he is at his sardonic best when working in short form, they won't be let down by his humor and poignancy, either." Libr J

Vonnegut, Kurt

Bagombo snuff box: uncollected short fiction. Putnam 1999 295p hardcover o.p. pa $13.95

ISBN 0-399-14505-2; 0-425-17446-8 pa

LC 99-13665

"The 23 stories in this collection were published in magazines . . . during the Fifties and are collected here for the first time. The topics covered include space travel ('Thanasphere'), which describes the first manned orbit of Earth; finding the American dream ('The package'), about a new home full of the latest accessories; and an attempt to impress an old girlfriend (the title story). . . . Although many of the stories are topically dated, the ironic insights and illumination of character are timeless, and no one does it better than Vonnegut." Libr J

Vonnegut, Kurt

★ **Breakfast** of champions; or, Goodbye blue Monday! by Kurt Vonnegut, Jr; with drawings by the author. Delacorte Press 1973 295p il

"In this novel Vonnegut is . . . clearing his head by throwing out acquired ideas, and also liberating some of the characters from his previous books. . . . This explosive meditation ranks with Vonnegut's best." N Y Times Book Rev

Vonnegut, Kurt

★ **Cat's** cradle; by Kurt Vonnegut, Jr. Holt, Rinehart & Winston 1963 233p

"In this mordant satire on religion, research, government, and human nature, a free-lance writer becomes the catalyst in a chain of events that unearths the secret of ice-nine. This is an element potentially more lethal than that produced by nuclear fission. The search leads to a mythical island, San Lorenzo, where the writer also discovers the leader of a new religion, Bokonon." Shapiro. Fic for Youth. 3d edition

Vonnegut, Kurt

Deadeye Dick. Delacorte Press/Seymour Lawrence 1982 240p

ISBN 0-440-01780-7

LC 82-13024

"In Midland City, Ohio, the {Waltz} family is isolated and scorned by the community for patriarch Otto's ersatz career as an artist and his strident support for Nazi policies. Their wealth and what's left of their social position is decimated when younger son Rudy (Deadeye Dick) accidently shoots a pregnant woman. Father pleads guilty to the crime, Rudy becomes a night-shift pharmacist, author of the prize-winning but unsuccessful play 'Katmandu' and cook and maid for his useless mother. Brother Felix becomes the president of NBC, and mother dies of radiation emitted from the fireplace of their 'shitbox' home. The entire populace is eventually exterminated . . . by the inadvertent dropping of a neutron bomb." SLJ

Vonnegut, Kurt

★ **Galapagos**; a novel. Delacorte Press/Seymour Lawrence 1985 295p

LC 85-4581

"A group of tourists on a cruise survive the end of the world, settling on a small Galapagos Island and beginning a new evolutionary sequence. The ghostly narrator looks back on things from a perspective one million years later." Anatomy of Wonder 4

Vonnegut, Kurt

God bless you, Mr. Rosewater; or, Pearls before swine. by Kurt Vonnegut, Jr. Holt, Rinehart & Winston 1965 217p

"With a satirist's eye for the meanness of man, especially his greed, Vonnegut tells the story of Eliot Rosewater, president of the Rosewater Foundation, who uses his position to help all petitioners. Discovering a plot to remove him from authority Rosewater gives all his money to over 50 children he is falsely accused of fathering." Booklist

Vonnegut, Kurt

Hocus pocus. Putnam 1990 302p

LC 90-34535

"Vonnegut remains an effectual stylist, combining deadpan irony and faux naiveté. As usual, his central narrative winds through a mosaic of aphorisms, verbal tics, digressions, homilies, obscure facts. . . . This compendium of devices and concerns may have hardened into a formula, but it has not yet ceased to be a diverting one." Times Lit Suppl

Vonnegut, Kurt

Jailbird; a novel. by Kurt Vonnegut, Jr. Delacorte Press/Seymour Lawrence 1979 246p

ISBN 0-440-05449-4

LC 79-12881

This novel "opens with Walter F. Starbuck, a 64-year-old victim of Watergate, about to be released from a Georgia prison for white-collar workers. Bereft of fortune and family (his wife is dead, his son is ungrateful) Starbuck retreats to the past via flashbacks of World War II, old love affairs, and past occupations. Eventually he regains respectability in the ubiquitous RAMJAC Corporation . . . which owns 19% of America and continues to swallow every major enterprise in its path." Libr J

Vonnegut, Kurt

Look at the birdie; unpublished short fiction. Delacorte Press 2009 251p il $27

ISBN 978-0-385-34371-8; 0-385-34371-X

LC 2009-34612

"Vonnegut is hardly an American Kafka, but more in the vein of Twain and Swift. He delivers kicks to the sacred cows of the era (psychoanalysis, big corporations, money, success, the dawn of sexual liberation) with such hilarity that readers forget we have just witnessed a body blow. Vonnegut's power to work that magic is already on display in these early stories." Boston Globe

Vonnegut, Kurt

★ **Novels** & stories, 1963-1979; Sidney Offit, editor. Library of America 2011 851p $35

ISBN 978-1-59853-098-8; 1-59853-098-4

This volume opens with Cat's Cradle (1963), "in which a would-be historian of the bombing of Hiroshima finds himself a privileged witness to the icy end of the world. God Bless You, Mr. Rosewater (1965) chronicles the alcoholic unraveling and spiritual rebirth of a goodhearted dreamer tormented by the question 'What are people for?' Slaughterhouse-Five (1969) . . . is the jump-cutting saga of Billy Pilgrim, who, having come unstuck in time, is doomed to relive continually both the destruction of Dresden and his abduction by space aliens. And in a text enhanced by the author's spirited line drawings, Breakfast of Champions (1973) describes the fateful meeting of a luckless science-fiction writer and an unhinged Pontiac dealer who disastrously believes that everyone but himself is a robot." Publisher's note

Vonnegut, Kurt

★ **Player** piano; by Kurt Vonnegut, Jr. Scribner 1952 295p

"Paul Proteus, engineer, leads revolt against machine-computer conformist civilization, only to find that when it succeeds, people wish for the machines again. In order or in chaos, mob psychology is stupid. Modern civilization has hate-love affinity for machines. Incisive satire; a classic modern dystopia." Anatomy of Wonder. 3d edition

Vonnegut, Kurt

★ The **sirens** of Titan; by Kurt Vonnegut, Jr. Houghton Mifflin 1961 319p

First published 1959 in paperback by Dell

This novel "attacks the concept of causality and the confusion of luck with God's will {and} reveals human history as a trivial incident manipulated by the alien Tralfamadorians to further an equally trivial scheme." New Ency of Sci Fic

Vonnegut, Kurt

Slapstick; or, Lonesome no more! a novel. Delacorte Press/ Seymour Lawrence 1976 243p

In this satirical fantasy, President of the United States Dr. Wilbur Daffodil-11 Swain sits in the ruins of Manhattan's Skycraper National Park writing his memoirs. As deformed children, he and his twin sister were separately regarded as idiots but discovered that together they were super-intelligent and went on to write a best-selling child-rearing manual. As president, Wilbur instituted a program to combat loneliness by forming artificial extended families

"Slapstick is a deceptively short and simple book. Its readability should not distract one from the fact that Vonnegut has found a fictional situation which considers serious human problems." New Repub

Vonnegut, Kurt

★ **Slaughterhouse**-five; or, The children's crusade: a duty-dance with death. 25th anniversary ed; Delacorte Press 1994 205p il $22.50; pa $6.99

ISBN 0-385-31208-3; 0-440-18029-5 pa

LC 94-171120

A reissue of the title first published 1969

"A masterpiece, in which Vonnegut penetrated to the heart of the issues developed in his earlier absurdist fabulations. A key work of modern SF." Anatomy of Wonder 4

Vonnegut, Kurt

Timequake. Putnam 1997 219p il $23.95

ISBN 0-399-13737-8

LC 97-14508

"The cataclysm of the title—in 2001, time undergoes a tremor, and everyone must relive the nineties—provides an excuse for Vonnegut and his longtime alter ego, Kilgore Trout, to trade rants: on desert camouflage, thirties socialism, the joys of waiting in line at the post office, the traitorousness of Dillinger's Hungarian girlfriend, semicolons. The resulting quilt of snippets is equal parts memoir, literary charm, self-congratulation, humanist sermon, randy geriatric fantasy, and toastmasterly jokefest." New Yorker

Vonnegut, Kurt

Welcome to the monkey house; a collection of short works. by Kurt Vonnegut, Jr. Delacorte Press 1968 298p

Contents: Where I live; Harrison Bergeron; Who am I this time?; Welcome to the monkey house; Long walk to forever; The Foster portfolio; Miss Temptation; All the king's horses; Tom Edison's shaggy dog; New dictionary; Next door; More stately mansions; The Hyannis Port story; D.P.; Report on the Barnhouse Effect; The euphio question; Go back to your precious wife and son; Deer in the works; The lie; Unready to wear; The kid nobody could handle; The manned missiles; EPICAC; Adam; Tomorrow and tomorrow and tomorrow

Vonnegut, Kurt

While mortals sleep; unpublished short fiction. Delacorte Press 2011 253p il $27

ISBN 978-0-385-34373-2

LC 2010-33817

"In well over a dozen novels and hundreds of short stories, Vonnegut wrote about the madness of war and about alienation in the modern machine age. When he died in 2007, he was acclaimed as a great American writer with a signature style. [This] is the second collection of his previously unpublished short stories. Written early in his career, they are concerned less with war and corporate malfeasance than with the pursuit of success, happiness and love. Vintage Vonnegut, for better and worse, they put characters, settings and stories in the service of moral messages. At their best, these messages achieve a simple and powerful eloquence." Pittsburgh Post-Gazette

Vreeland, Susan, 1946-2017

Clara and Mr. Tiffany; a novel. Random House 2011 405p $26

ISBN 978-1-4000-6816-6

LC 2010-07758

"Vreeland traces the secret history of an objet d'art— . . . the iconic Tiffany lamp. Her heroine is Clara Driscoll, head of the all-female glass-cutting department at Tiffany Studios, who designed many of the fanciful, nature-inspired leaded-glass lamps for which Louis Comfort Tiffany earned fame. . . . Through Driscoll's life, Vreeland offers a fascinating look at turn-of-the-century New York City." People

Includes bibliographical references

Vreeland, Susan

Girl in hyacinth blue. MacMurray & Beck 1999 242p $17.50

ISBN 1-87844-890-0

LC 99-27405

"Vreeland strikes a pleasing balance between the timeless world of the painting as a work of art and the finite worlds of its possessors and admirers—not to mention the world of its subject and its creator. Intelligent, searching and unusual, the novel is filled with luminous moments; like the painting it describes so well, it has a way of lingering in the reader's mind." N Y Times Book Rev

Vreeland, Susan

Luncheon of The Boating Party. Viking 2007 434p il map

ISBN 978-0-670-03854-1; 0-670-03854-7

LC 2006-35324

In this novel Vreeland turns "to French impressionist master Auguste Renoir's famous painting Luncheon of the Boating Party , which depicts a group of people (in 1880) enjoying leisure time on the terrace of a riverside restaurant. The current conditions in the life of the painter himself launch the author on an amazingly engrossing reinvigoration of the lives of the individuals who modeled for Renoir for that work, all of whom were actual people, and all are given a third dimension in Vreeland's lovely prose." Booklist

Vreeland, Susan

The **passion** of Artemesia. Viking 2002 288p

ISBN 0-670-89449-4

LC 2001-26119

"Vreeland palpably captures Artemisia's joy as she blends colors and watches her artistic imaginings take shape. . . . Although her final confrontation with her father, artist Orazio Gentileschi, feels forced, the novel brilliantly captures the life of an extraordinary artist." Libr J

Vyleta, Dan

★ **Smoke**; a novel. Dan Vyleta. Doubleday 2016 448 p. (hardcover) $27.95

ISBN 0385540167; 9780385540162

LC 2015037301

This novel, by Dan Vyleta, takes place in "a Victorian England unlike any other. . . . Thomas Argyle, a son of aristocracy, has been sent to an elite boarding school. Here he will be purged of Wickedness, for the wealthy do not Smoke. When he resists a sadistic headboy's temptations to Smoke, a much larger struggle beyond the school walls is revealed." (Publisher's note)

Vyleta "imagines an alternative turn-of-the-century England where the proletariat and aristocratic classes are further divided by the relationship to Smoke, the manifestation of sin that flows from the body as blackened breath or ashen sweat whenever someone thinks or acts immorally." Booklist

W

Waite, Urban

Sometimes the wolf; a novel. Urban Waite. William Morrow 2014 352 p. (hardcover) $26.99

ISBN 0062216910; 9780062216915; 9780062216922

LC 2014005706

This novel, by Urban Waite, is "set in the Pacific Northwest, a . . . story of family, violence, and unintended consequences. . . . Patrick is on parole under the watchful eye of his son Bobby, who just happens to be a deputy sheriff in his father's old department. Bobby hasn't had it easy, either. He's carried the weight of his father's guilt, forsaking his own dreams, and put off the knowledge that his own marriage could be stronger and more hopeful." (Publisher's note)

"It's not uncommon for novels set in the contemporary West to find humanity in the interplay between the stiff-jawed determination of rugged individualists and their suppressed vulnerability, but Waite goes even further. His characters are determined, yes, but they are more than vulnerable; their lives are suffused with 'guilt and disappointment, hope for something better that never comes, and a desire for relief that always seemed just beyond.' It's a rare thing to balance a thriller plot on characters with such stooped shoulders, but Waite manages the feat with surprising dexterity. Another emotionally rich novel from a very special writer." Booklist

Waite, Urban

The **terror** of living; a novel. Little, Brown and Co. 2011 306p $24.99

ISBN 978-0-316-09789-5; 0-316-09789-6

LC 2010021840

"Waite brings a nimble touch to the material. Throwaway lines are rendered with surprising delicacy, and Living's knife-fetishist villain makes for an oddly endearing sociopath." Entertainment Wkly

Wakefield, Dan

★ **Starting** over. Delacorte Press/Seymour Lawrence 1973 290p

"A powerful, naturalistic depiction of the agony suffered by a man whose affluence merely conceals an utter absence of value and direction." Libr J

Walbert, Kate

The **gardens** of Kyoto; a novel. Scribner 2001 288p

ISBN 0-684-86948-9

LC 2001-18876

"Ellen, the self-effacing narrator, mourns the disappearance of her cousin on Iwo Jima during the Second World War, and tries to decipher a book he has left her about the Kyoto gardens. The beauty of these landscapes lies in their impenetrability: one, made up entirely of shadows, must be viewed at night; another may be seen only through a window whose blind is forever drawn. Similarly, Ellen stands on the fringes of other, more dramatic lives, first befriending a fellow-coed whose affair with a married professor ends in an illegal abortion, then falling in love with a traumatized veteran of the Korean War. In precise, delicate prose, the author renders with equal power the quiet desperation of a girl growing up in nineteen-fifies America . . . and the ethereal." New Yorker

Waldman, Amy

The **submission**. Farrar, Straus and Giroux 2011 299p

ISBN 0-374-27156-9; 9780374271565

LC 2011007509

"A jury gathers in Manhattan to select a memorial for the victims of a devastating terrorist attack. Their fraught deliberations complete, the jurors open the envelope containing the anonymous winner's name—and discover he is an American Muslim." (Publisher's note)

"It's two years after the events of 9/11, and a (fictional) high-profile committee has convened in Manhattan to select a monument that will transform the still-raw wound at Ground Zero into a safe haven of healing and remembrance. The winner, chosen from a pool of anonymously submitted blueprints, is a beauty: a walled garden whose spare geometry poetically echoes the fallen towers. And its designer? A brilliant young architect, Virginia-born and Yale-educated, named Mohammad Khan. Or as one dismayed committee member exclaims behind the doors of Gracie Mansion, "'It's a goddamn Muslim!'" Within hours, a tabloid reporter has sniffed out the story, and so begins the ugly political do-si-do of a national scandal, one pushed along as much by personal agendas as by genuine outrage. Among the players: the hapless, overmatched committee head; two grieving widows, one wealthy and white, the other poor and Bangladeshi; and the black-sheep brother of a fallen firefighter. And at its center, of course, 'Mo' Khan himself: Wary and increasingly weary, he refuses all easy outs, even as he is tried and convicted in the kangaroo court of public opinion." Entertainment Wkly

Waldman, Ayelet

Love and treasure; a novel. Ayelet Waldman. Alfred A. Knopf 2014 368 p. (hardcover) $26.95

ISBN 0385533543; 9780385533546

LC 2012049781

This novel by Ayelet Waldman "weaves a tale around the fascinating, true history of the Hungarian Gold Train in the Second World War. In 1945 on the outskirts of Salzburg, victorious American soldiers capture a train filled with unspeakable riches: piles of fine gold watches; mountains of fur coats; crates filled with wedding rings, silver picture frames, family heirlooms, and Shabbat candlesticks passed down through generations." (Publisher's note)

"[A] sensitive and heartbreaking portrayal of love, politics, and family secrets. . . . The story line forges a connection among a roguish young American soldier . . . ; Nina, a young suffragist in 1913; and Natalie, the soldier's granddaughter, in search of the descendants of the owner of a treasured peacock pendant that the soldier had plundered from the train." LJ

Waldman, Ayelet

Red Hook Road. Doubleday 2010 343p $25.95

ISBN 978-0-385-51786-7; 0-385-51786-6

LC 2009-20023

The book "begins with a prelude, appropriately, since so much of this novel involves music. The wedding of a young couple, Becca Copaken and John Tetherly, has just taken place in a small town on the Maine coast. The setting is described gloriously. Then, in a moment of breathtaking horror, a speeding driver crashes into the bridal couple's limousine and kills them. . . . [The novel] follows the relatives of the bride and groom over the four summers following the tragedy, revealing how they cope with grief and loss, and how they don't. Waldman writes with practiced skill. She's familiar with her subject matter: Maine, classical music, yacht building, violins, lobster molting." Boston Globe

Walker, Alice

By the light of my father's smile; a novel. Random House 1998 222p $22.95

ISBN 0-375-50152-5

LC 98-5464

"Walker has created a romantic but propagandistic fairy tale that veers disconcertingly from the facile to the heartfelt." Booklist

Walker, Alice

★ The **color** purple; 10th anniversary ed; Harcourt Brace Jovanovich 1992 290p il $24; pa $14

ISBN 0-15-119154-9; 0-15-602835-2 pa

LC 91-47202

A reissue of the title first published 1982

"A feminist novel about an abused and uneducated black woman's struggle for empowerment, the novel was praised for the depth of its female characters and for its eloquent use of black English vernacular." Merriam-Webster's Ency of Lit

Walker, Alice

Now is the time to open your heart; a novel. Random House 2004 240p $24.95

ISBN 1-400-06173-3

LC 2003-54766

"Walker's dreamlike novel incorporates the political and spiritual consciousness and emotional style for which she is known and appreciated." Booklist

Walker, Alice

Possessing the secret of joy. Harcourt Brace Jovanovich 1992 286p $25

ISBN 0-15-173152-7

LC 92-6883

"The people in Ms. Walker's book are archetypes rather than characters as we have come to expect them in the 20th-century novel, and this is by defiant intention. . . . When the novel is operating genuinely on this archetypal level, it has a mythic strength. Its many voices are not rendered as stream-of-consciousness monologues, nor are they made to belong to distinct individuals. Instead, they are highly stylized, operatic, prophetic—and powerfully poetic." N Y Times Book Rev

Walker, Alice, 1944-

The **temple** of my familiar. Harcourt Brace Jovanovich 1989 416p $19.95

ISBN 0-15-188533-8

LC 88-7995

"Alice Walker describes her new novel as 'a romance of the last 500,000 years.' . . . At the center of the story are {three} marriages. . . . {Suwelo}, a guerrilla history professor and {Fanny}, a teacher of women's studies turned masseuse try to draw closer while remaining free. {Arveyda}, a rock star and his Latin American refugee wife {Carlotta} are parted by an unlikely 'other woman.' And {Mr. Hal}, a gentle artist and {Miss Lissie}, a silverhaired goddess . . . have been companions for so many years they are virtually interchangeable. As they talk about themselves and reconnect with missing pieces of the past, they uncover disquieting truths about relations between the sexes, the races, and the species during our tenure on the planet." (Publisher's note)

This is a "novel only in a loose sense. Rather, it is a mixture of mythic fantasy, revisionary history, exemplary biography and sermon. It is short on narrative tension, long on inspirational message." N Y Times Book Rev

Walker, Alice, 1944-

★ The **third** life of Grange Copeland; Alice Walker. Harcourt 2003 318 p. (paperback) $16.95; (ebook) $29.99

ISBN 9780156028363; 9781453223949; 0156028360

LC 2003005923

In this novel in the Harvest Book series by Alice Walker, "black tenant farmer Grange Copeland leaves his wife and son in Georgia to head North. After meeting an equally humiliating existence there, he returns to Georgia, years later, to find his son, Brownfield, imprisoned for the murder of his wife. As the guardian of the couple's youngest daughter, Grange Copeland is looking at his third -- and final -- chance to free himself from spiritual and social enslavement." (Publisher's note)

Walker, Alice

The **way** forward is with a broken heart. Random House 2000 200p $23.95

ISBN 0-679-45587-6

LC 00-27172

"In seven beautifully written and astoundingly perceptive short stories—admittedly based in fact, then fictionalized—{Walker} homes in on the problems endemic to interracial romance and offers a near stream-of-consciousness reflection on her own ten-year marriage to a white civil rights attorney." Libr J

Walker, Alice

You can't keep a good woman down; stories. Harcourt Brace Jovanovich 1981 167p

LC 80-8761

Contents: Nineteen fifty-five; How did I get away with killing one of the biggest lawyers in the States? It was easy; Elethia; The lover; Petunias; Coming apart Fame; The abortion; Porn; Advancing Luna¿and Ida B. Wells; Laurel; A letter of the times; or, Should this sado-masochism be saved; A sudden trip home in the spring; Source

Walker, Karen Thompson, 1980-

★ The **age** of miracles; a novel. Karen Thompson Walker. Random House 2012 272 p.

ISBN 0812992970; 9780812992977; 9780679644385

LC 2011040664

This novel, by Karen Thompson Walker, is a story of "coming of age set against the backdrop of an utterly altered world. On a seemingly ordinary Saturday in a California suburb, Julia and her family awake to discover, along with the rest of the world, that the rotation of the earth has suddenly begun to slow. . . . Yet as she struggles to navigate an ever-shifting landscape, Julia is also coping with the normal disasters of everyday life." (Publisher's note)

Walker, Margaret

★ **Jubilee**. Houghton Mifflin 1966 497p

"Vyry was a slave and the daughter of a slave. She suffered slavery's tribulations and looked forward to the time of freedom to bring her a home of her own and provide an education for her children. The Civil War and the Reconstruction period brought the possibility of that day of jubilation, but the attainment of her two desires still seemed remote. The author gives a clear picture of the everyday life of slaves, their modes of behavior, and the patterns and rhythms of their speech." Shapiro. Fic for Youth. 3d edition

Walker, Martin

Bruno, chief of police; Martin Walker. Alfred A. Knopf 2008 262p

ISBN 0307270173; 9780307270177

"Bruno is a former soldier who has embraced the pleasures and slow rhythms of country life--living in his restored shepherd's cottage; patronizing the weekly market; sparring with, and basically ignoring, the European Union bureaucrats from Brussels. He has a gun but never wears it; he has the power to arrest but never uses it. But then the murder of an elderly North African who fought in the French army changes everything and galvanizes Bruno's attention: the man was found with a swastika carved into his chest." (Publisher's note)

Other titles in this series are:
The dark vineyard (2009)
Black diamond (2010)
The crowded grave (2011)
The devil's cave (2013)
The resistance man (2014)
The children return (2015)
The patriarch (2015)
Fatal pursuit (2016)

Walker, Martin

The **crowded** grave; Martin Walker. 1st U.S. ed. Alfred A. Knopf 2011 313 [1] p. map (hardcover) $24.95

ISBN 0307700194; 9780307700193

LC 2011050746

This mystery novel, by Martin Walker, begins in "spring in . . . St. Denis, [France] and for Chief of Police Bruno Courreges that means . . . a new string of regional crimes and international capers. When a local archaeological team . . . turns up a corpse with a watch on its wrist and a bullet in its head, it's up to Bruno to solve the case. . . . Complicating events, . . . the professor in charge of the dig is soon reported missing." (Publisher's note)

Walker, Martin

The **dark** vineyard. Alfred A. Knopf 2010 303p $23.95

ISBN 978-0-307-27018-4; 0-307-27018-1

LC 2009-45814

First published 2009 in the United Kingdom

"Bruno handles both cases with great discretion, circulating so quietly and tactfully among his neighbors that his interviews are more like friendly visits. Its a wonderful detection method and an even cannier literary strategy, allowing Walker to pursue the plot of his mystery while beguiling the reader with extended scenes of village market days, old-fashioned wine harvests and some exceptionally congenial dinner parties." N Y Times Book Rev

Walker, Martin

The **Patriarch**; Martin Walker. Alfred A. Knopf 2015 336 p. map (Bruno, chief of police) (hardcover) $24.95

ISBN 9780385354172; 9780804173513

LC 2015001516

In this mystery, by Martin Walker, "Bruno is invited to the lavish birthday celebration of World War II flying ace and national icon Marco 'the Patriarch' Desaix. . . . But when the party ends in the death of Gilbert, Marco's longtime friend, it's another day on the job for the chef de police. All signs point to a tragic accident, but Bruno isn't so sure." (Publisher's note)

"This entry is sure to delight readers who relish a skillful blend of complex international political nuance and pastoral intrigue mixed with a soupcon of fine French wine and cuisine." Pub Wkly

Walker, Mary Willis

All the dead lie down. Doubleday 1998 308p $22.95

ISBN 0-385-47858-5

LC 97-24131

"Several topics concern magazine writer Molly Cates: the upcoming concealed handgun bill in the Texas legislature, the plight of homeless women in Austin, and her refusal to believe her father's suicide some 28 years earlier. So Molly learns how to shoot, interviews bag ladies, and pursues a new source of material about her father. Literate prose, in-depth characterization, and a cleverly manipulated plot." Libr J

Walker, Mary Willis

Under the beetle's cellar. Doubleday 1995 311p

ISBN 0-385-46859-8

LC 95-10708

"If there can be such a thing as a heartwarming suspense thriller, then Mary Willis Walker has written a nifty one. . . . The real drama is played underground, where the heroic bus driver draws on his war experiences in Vietnam and every bit of his strength to comfort the children and prepare them for what may well be the end of their world." N Y Times Book Rev

Walker, Sarai

Dietland; Sarai Walker. Houghton Mifflin Harcourt 2015 320 p. (hardback) $26

ISBN 054437343X; 9780544373433

LC 2014026803

In Sarai Walker's novel "Plum Kettle does her best not to be noticed, because when you're fat, to be noticed is to be judged. When Plum notices she's being followed by a mysterious woman . . . she finds herself [in] . . . a community of women who live life on their own terms. At the same time, a dangerous guerilla group begins to terrorize a world that mistreats women, and as Plum grapples with her own personal struggles, she becomes entangled in a sinister plot." (Publisher's note)

"Through her protagonist, debut novelist Walker gives a plaintive yet powerful voice to anyone who has struggled with body image, feelings of marginalization, and sexual manipulation. Her robust satire also vibrantly redefines what it means to be a woman in contemporary society." Booklist

Walker, Walter

Crime of Privilege; a novel. Walter Walker. Random House Inc. 2013 432 p. (hardcover) $26

ISBN 0345541537; 9780345541536

LC 2013004332

This novel, by Walter Walker, begins with "a murder on Cape Cod . . . [and] a rape in Palm Beach. All they have in common is the presence of one of America's most . . . influential families. But nobody is asking questions. . . . Certainly not George Becket . . . of the Cape & Islands district attorney's office. . . . Now, an investigation brings him deep inside the world of the truly wealthy--and shows him what a perilous place it is." (Publisher's note)

Wall, Kathryn R.

The **Mercy** Oak. St. Martin's Minotaur 2008 310p $24.95

ISBN 978-0-312-37534-8; 0-312-37534-4

LC 2008-3304

In this episode, South Carolina Lowcountry PI Bay Tanner "must tackle two cases that hit close to home. Her housekeeper's son disappears after the suspicious hit-and-run death of a young Hispanic woman who had been advocating for the rights of illegal immigrants. Then, during a bank robbery, Lavinia, the woman who raised Bay and still lives with her father, tries to help an old man who has recognized one of the robbers. At the risk of her own life, Bay is desperate to keep those she cares about safe. Sue Grafton, Sara Paretsky, and Marcia Muller come to mind as the quintessential writers of the modern female private eye novel. Wall, in a quiet and unassuming way, has produced a body of work of equal quality as she tackles complex modern issues that trouble her very human characters." Libr J

Wall, P. S.

The **Wilde** women; a novel. [by] Paula Wall. Atria Books 2007 310p

ISBN 978-0-7434-9621-6; 0-7434-9621-3

LC 2006-48023

Having left her southern hometown of Five Points five years earlier after discovering that her sister and fiancé had been having an affair, unpredictable Pearl Wilde returns home to exact revenge.

"Each and every character in Wall's tall tale has a uniquely flawed personality, and Wall has a wonderful sense of place and an adept way with words, adding up to an enthralling novel." Booklist

Wallace, Carey

The **blind** contessa's new machine. Pamela Dorman Books/ Viking 2010 207p $23.95

ISBN 978-0-670-02189-5; 0-670-02189-X

LC 2010-03332

"The time is the late 19th century, the place the northern Italian countryside, where minor aristocrats flourish as abundantly as grapevines. A blooming rose, Contessa Carolina Fantoni is about to marry Pietro, a neighboring landowner. Neither Pietro nor her parents take her seriously, however, when Carolina tells them she is going blind. With a love deeper than Pietro's fickle infatuation, Carolina's devoted admirer, Turri, a local eccentric and amateur inventor, gives her a precious gift, the ability to communicate with an outside world locked out by her blindness and her overprotective husband. He invents a machine, the typewriter, which Carolina uses to arrange their increasingly indiscreet—and ill-fated—assignations. A small gem of sensuality." Boston Globe

Wallace, Daniel

★ **Big** fish; a novel of mythic proportions. Algonquin Bks. 1998 180p

ISBN 1-56512-217-8

LC 98-26216

"William Bloom's father, Edward, is dying. He dies in fact in four different takes, all of which have William and his mother waiting outside a bedroom door as the family doctor tells them it's time to say their goodbyes. He intersperses the four takes with stories (all filtered through William's mind and voice) about the elusive Edward. . . . In a plainspoken style dotted with transcendent passages, Wallace mixes the mundane and the mythical. His chapters have the transformative quality of fable and fairy tale, and the novel's roomy structure allows the mystery and lyricism of the story to coalesce." Publ Wkly

Wallace, Daniel

Mr. Sebastian and the Negro magician; a novel. Doubleday 2007 257p

ISBN 978-0-385-52109-3; 0-385-52109-X

LC 2006-28103

"The unraveling of a man's myth to illuminate the essence of his life is the charm of this accomplished and inventive novel." Paste

Wallace, Daniel

The **Watermelon** King. Houghton Mifflin 2003 226p $23

ISBN 0-618-22138-7

LC 2002-75941

"This is a unique and spellbinding novel, an unforgettable southern tall tale with extraordinary characters." Booklist

Wallace, David Foster, 1962-2008

★ **Brief** interviews with hideous men; David Foster Wallace. Back Bay Books 2000 288 p. (pbk) $16.00; (hbk.) $24.00

ISBN 9780316925198; 0316925411; 0316925195; 978-0316925419

LC 98050944

This collection of stories by David Foster Wallace "is a sequence of imagined interviews with men on the subject of their relations with women. These portraits of men at their most self-justifying, loquacious, and benighted explore poignantly and hilariously the agonies of sexual connections." (Publisher's note)

Wallace, David Foster

★ **Infinite** jest; a novel. Little, Brown 1996 1079p $29.95

ISBN 0-316-92004-5

LC 95-30619

This novel is "set sometime in the next century, on the grounds of a New England tennis academy and in a rehab clinic. Among other things, the book contains perhaps the most moving and hypnotic writing on the psychology of addiction and recovery to be found in modern fiction. There are obsessive riffs on sports, on drugs, and on the hidden horrors of entertainment: the title of the novel refers to the title of a movie that is said to be so 'terminally compelling' that viewers will watch it passively and repeatedly to the point of death. Comparisons with Pynchon are inevitable, and in this case they are fully justified." New Yorker

Wallace, David Foster

Oblivion; stories. Little, Brown 2004 329p $25.95

ISBN 0-316-91981-0

"Unpacking our inner lives with empathy and care, Oblivion showcases the incredibly rich textures and crystalline clarity of Wallace's prose, confirming the singular genius of his expansive imagination and resonating with the complexities of minds in motion." American Book Review

Wallace, David Foster

★ The **pale** king; an unfinished novel. Little, Brown and Co. 2011 548p $27.99

ISBN 978-0-316-07423-0; 0-316-07423-3

LC 2010-45489

The novel "treats its central subject—boredom itself—not as a texture (as in Fernando Pessoa), or a symptom (as in Thomas Mann), or an attitude (as in Bret Easton Ellis), but as the leading edge of truths we're desperate to avoid. It is the mirror beneath entertainment's smiley mask, and The Pale King aims to do for it what Moby-Dick did for the whale. . . . In the end, Wallace's body of work amounts to an extended philosophical experiment. Can 'morally passionate, passionately moral' fiction help free us from the prisons we make? To judge solely by his suicide, the experiment would seem to have failed. Then again, watching him loosed one last time upon the fields of language, we're apt to feel the way he felt at the end of his celebrated essay on Federer at Wimbledon: called to attention, called out of ourselves. Jesus, just look at him out there." New York

Wallace, Irving

The **man**; a novel. Simon & Schuster 1964 766p

This is the story of a black Senator who becomes the first black President of the United States after the deaths, in rapid succession, of first the Vice President and then both the President and the Speaker of the House

The portrayal of the "President as a man, an able, intelligent, politically moderate man who has never been to the fore but must take responsibility overnight, is excellent. With a huge cast of characters and one crisis after another in the plot, this makes an absorbing story." Publ Wkly

Wallace, Irving

The **prize**. Simon & Schuster 1962 768p

This novel is an "inquiry into the private lives of a batch of Nobel Prize winners. . . . The prize winners are . . . a French husband-and-wife team of chemists whose marriage is collapsing, a neurotic American heart surgeon broodingly resentful that he must share the award in medicine with an Italian doctor, a gentle German-born physicist from Atlanta who is being wooed by the Communists of East Germany, and an American novelist who is just coming out of a long alcoholic trance. Wallace . . . assembles them all in Stockholm and embarks them on the frenzied series of public and private events that surround Nobel award weeks in the Swedish capital." NY Her Trib Books

Wallace, Lew

★ **Ben**-Hur; a tale of the Christ. Harper 1880 552p

This novel "depicts the oppressive Roman occupation of ancient Palestine and the origins of Christianity. The Jew Judah Ben-Hur is wrongly accused by his former friend, the Roman Messala, of attempting to kill a Roman official. He is sent to be a slave and his mother and sister are imprisoned. Years later he returns, wins a chariot race against Messala, and is reunited with his now leprous mother and sister. Mother and daughter are cured on the day of the Crucifixion, and the family is converted to Christianity." Merriam-Webster's Ency of Lit

Wallace, Melanie

The **girl** in the garden; Melanie Wallace. Houghton Mifflin Harcourt 2017 232 p. (hardcover) $25.00

ISBN 9780544784208; 9780544784666

LC 2015043036

In this novel, by Melanie Wallace, "June is soon placed with Mabel's friend, Iris, in town, and her life becomes entwined with a number of locals who have known one another for decades: a wealthy recluse with a tragic past; a widow in mourning; a forsaken daughter returning for the first time in years, with a stranger in tow; a lawyer, whose longings he can never reveal; and a kindly World War II veteran who serves as the town's sage." (Publisher's note)

"Wallace's (The Housekeeper, 2006) poignant novel is, at once, a portrait of a small, coastal, New England town; a bit of a mystery; and a completely engaging study of an odd mix of characters whose lives become intricately intertwined." Booklist

Wallace, Stone

Montana dawn. Avalon Books 2010 231p $23.95

ISBN 978-0-8034-7770-4; 0-8034-7770-8

LC 2009-53848

When the remnants of a ruthless outlaw gang invade the peaceful desert setting Montana Dawn shares with her gentleman husband, little does the girl suspect that her long-dormant spirit for a life far removed from her domestic existence will be passionately re-ignited and that circumstances will soon brand her as the most wanted female criminal in the Southwest. With a bounty on their head and a determined posse hot in pursuit, Montana Dawn and her outlaw companion Walt Egan share romance and danger across the unrelenting Nevada terrain as they attempt to stay ahead of the law and escape into Mexico to start a new life.

"This unusual western mines some fairly fresh ground: female outlaws are in relatively short supply, as are love stories about pairs of outlaws. but the author sells it completely. The characters are quite well drawn—villains who capture our interest and compassion—and the plot is engaging in a Butch Cassidy and the Sundance Kid kind of way: exciting but with a colorful, light feel to it—until the end." Booklist

Wallace, Wendy

The **painted** bridge; Wendy Wallace. Simon & Schuster 2012 386 p. (hardcover) $25.00

ISBN 1451660820; 9780857209276; 9780857209306; 9781451660821

LC 2012453375

This historical novel, by Wendy Wallace, "is a story of family betrayals, illicit power, and a woman sent to an asylum against her will in Victorian England. Just outside London . . . lies Lake House, a private asylum for genteel women of a delicate nature. In the winter of 1859, Anna Palmer becomes its newest patient. . . . Confused and angry, Anna sets out to prove her sanity, but with her husband and doctors unwilling to listen, her freedom will not be won easily." (Publisher's note)

Wallant, Edward Lewis

The **pawnbroker**; {by} Edward L. Wallant. Harcourt, Brace & World 1961 279p

"Sol Nazerman is a survivor of the Holocaust. In the past he had been a university teacher in Poland; now he runs a pawnshop in Harlem in which Murillio, a ruthless racketeer, has a financial interest. Into Nazerman's shop come people who are sad, sick, or criminal. He also meets Marilyn Birchfield, a friendly social worker who tries to get past the frozen outward indifference of the pawnbroker. In flashbacks that describe the horror and torture suffered by Nazerman and his family, the reader begins to understand his withdrawal from humanity. The relationship between him and his young, ambitious, and confused assistant, Jesus Ortiz, provides the novel's shattering climax." Shapiro. Fic for Youth. 3d edition

Waller, Robert James

★ The **bridges** of Madison County. Warner Bks. 1992 171p il

LC 91-50416

"An erotic, bittersweet tale of lingering memories and forsaken possibilities." Publ Wkly

Walls, Jeannette

The **Silver** Star; a novel. Jeannette Walls. 1st Scribner hardcover ed. Simon & Schuster 2013 288 p. (hardcover) $26

ISBN 1451661509; 9781451661507

LC 2012050790

This novel, by Jeannette Walls, begins in "1970. . . . 'Bean' Holladay is twelve and her sister, Liz, is fifteen when their artistic mother, Charlotte . . . takes off to find herself, leaving her girls enough money to last a month or two. . . . She and Liz decide to take the bus to Virginia, where their Uncle Tinsley lives in the decaying mansion that's been in Charlotte's family for generations." (Publisher's note)

"[A] captivating, read-in-one-sitting, coming-of-age adventure." Booklist

Walser, Robert

The **assistant**; translated from the German by Susan Bernofsky. New Directions 2007 302p pa $16.95

ISBN 978-0-8112-1590-9; 0-8112-1590-3

LC 2007-6865

Original German edition, 1908

"Walser's clerks and layabouts are perhaps the nicest, most considerate people you can meet in modernist fiction, but they can also be cuttingly ironic in the way of only the very polite. . . . Susan Bernofsky reproduces this effect and others with impressive fluency and naturalness." New Yorker

Walsh, Helen

Brass. Canongate 2004 296p pa $14

ISBN 1-8419-5484-5 pa

LC 2005-415744

In this novel set in Liverpool, "nineteen-year-old university student Millie O'Reilley has not taken the news of the impending nuptials of her best mate, 28-year-old Jamie Keeley, very well. Drinking and drugging her way through the evenings, she usually ends up trolling the seedy section of town in search of female prostitutes (the 'brass' of the title). Jamie is growing increasingly impatient with and worried by Millie's behavior and is at a loss to explain their relationship to his dim-witted, social-climbing fiancee. What sets this first novel apart within a burgeoning subgenre is Walsh's lyrical prose. Her evocative phrasing both contains and stands in direct contrast to incredibly graphic scenes of depravity, and the result is both disturbing and compelling." Booklist

Walsh, M. O. (Milton O'Neal)

My sunshine away; M. O. Walsh. Amy Einhorn Books 2014 320 p. $26.95

ISBN 0399169520; 9780399169526

LC 2014003818

This book by M. O. Walsh "unfolds in a Baton Rouge neighborhood best known for cookouts on sweltering summer afternoons, cauldrons of spicy crawfish, and passionate football fandom. But in the summer of 1989, when fifteen-year-old Lindy Simpson--free spirit, track star, and belle of the block--experiences a horrible crime late one evening near her home, it becomes apparent that this idyllic stretch of Southern suburbia has a dark side, too." (Booklist)

"Suspenseful, compassionate, and absorbing, Walsh's word-perfect rendering of the doubts, insecurities, bravado, and idealism of teens deserves to be placed in the hands of readers of Tom Franklin, Hannah Pittard, and Jeffrey Eugenides." Booklist

Walsh, Therese

The **moon** sisters; a novel. Therese Walsh. Crown Publishers 2013 336 p. $25

ISBN 0307461602; 9780307461605

LC 2013018032

In this novel, by Therese Walsh, "after their mother's probable suicide, sisters Olivia and Jazz take steps to move on with their lives. Jazz, logical and forward-thinking, decides to get a new job, but spirited, strong-willed Olivia--who can see sounds, taste words, and smell sights--is determined to travel to the remote setting of their mother's unfinished novel to lay her spirit properly to rest." (Publisher's note)

"Both heartbreaking and hopeful, the Moon sisters' journey is no quixotic quest, and readers will find themselves completely immersed in their transformative search. This magical, moving tale is not to be missed." Booklist

Walter, Jess

★ **Beautiful** Ruins; A Novel. Jess Walter. Harper 2012 352 p.

ISBN 0061928127; 9780061928123

This book presents a "romance [story that] begins in April 1962, when a young innkeeper, Pasquale Tursi, puts up . . . American actress Dee Moray, who has arrived supposedly sick with stomach cancer at the remote Italian port of Vergogna. . . . Pasquale soon discovers that 20th Century-Fox's chief troubleshooter, the young Michael Deane, has in fact whisked Dee, pregnant with the married Burton's child, away from the public eye to avoid scandal. . . . Pasquale falls in love with the beleaguered, vulnerable Dee." (Publishers Weekly)

Walter, Jess

Citizen Vince; a novel. Jess Walter. Perennial 2008 293p (pbk.) $14.99; (acid-free paper) o.p.; o.p.

ISBN 9780061577659; 0060394412; 9780060394417

LC 2004046828

Edgar Allan Poe Award: Best Novel (2006)

This book, winner of the 2005 Edgar Allan Poe Award, begins "[a]t 1:59 a.m. in Spokane, Washington—eight days before the 1980 presidential election—[when] Vince Camden pockets his stash of stolen credit cards and drops by an all-night poker game before heading to his witness-protection job dusting crullers at Donut Make You Hungry. Along with a neurotic hooker girlfriend, this is the total sum of Vince's new life. But when a familiar face shows up in town, Vince realizes his sordid past is still too close behind him. During the next unforgettable week, he'll negotiate a coast-to-coast maze of obsessive cops, eager politicians, and assorted mobsters—only to find that redemption might exist, of all places, in the voting booth." (Publisher's note)

Walter, Jess

The **financial** lives of the poets; a novel. Harper 2009 290p $25.99

ISBN 978-0-06-191604-5; 0-06-191604-8

The protagonist of this novel is a "former financial journalist turned proprietor of poetfolio.com, an ill-conceived Web site featuring investment advice written in verse. Having gambled everything on this quixotic idea, he finds himself hobbled by debt and six days from losing his family home to a mortgage company. The only way out of his predicament, he decides, is to start dealing pot. The novel riffs (often in blank verse) on everything from balloon mortgages to thong-wearing suburban moms. Despite its unlikely conceit, the novel has warmth, and its protagonist emerges as a bourgeois Everyman of the downturn." New Yorker

Walter, Jess

★ **We** Live in Water; Stories. Jess Walter. HarperCollins 2013 192 p. (paperback) $14.99

ISBN 0061926620; 9780061926624

The short stories of this collection, by Jess Walter, "range from comic tales of love to social satire and suspenseful crime fiction. Traveling from hip Portland to once-hip Seattle to never-hip Spokane, to a condemned casino in Las Vegas and a bottomless lake in the dark woods of Idaho, this is a world of lost fathers and redemptive con men, of personal struggles and diminished dreams." (Publisher's note)

"Drug addicts and hard-luck cases abound here, but these stories aren't melodramatic or even dour. Walter's prose is straightforward and funny, and like Richard Russo, he knows his protagonists are concerned with their immediate predicaments, not the socioeconomic mechanisms that put them there. ... A witty and sobering snapshot of recession-era America." Kirkus

Walters, Minette

The **breaker**. Putnam 1999 351p $23.95
ISBN 0-399-14492-7

LC 98-51836

"Walters limits the suspects to two men with sufficient reason (and appropriate perversions) to have wanted the victim dead—the husband she betrayed and the lover she betrayed him with. Instead of making it easier to identify the killer, the narrow field only intensifies the challenge by demanding closer analysis." N Y Times Book Rev

Walters, Minette

★ The **dark** room. Putnam 1995 381p
LC 95-10616

"Motivation is at the heart of The Dark Room. Like all the best detective fiction it challenges readers to work out how a particular character would act faced with specific circumstances. . . . The quest for truth is punctuated by touches of humanity that lift this novel way above others of its genre." New Statesman Soc

Walters, Minette

The **devil's** feather. Alfred A. Knopf 2006 349p $24
ISBN 0-307-26462-9

LC 2006-41033

First published 2005 in the United Kingdom

In this "thriller, Connie Burns, a white Zimbabwean war correspondent for Reuters, investigates five gruesome murders in Sierra Leone and follows a hunch, convinced that a British mercenary is using the mayhem of war zones to disguise his taste for raping and killing women. After a mysterious assailant kidnaps her and holds her prisoner for three days in Iraq, she becomes convinced that her quarry is now hunting her. She flees to Dorset, rents an isolated house that turns out to have a troubled history, and is befriended by a reclusive neighbor who, some years before, lost her entire family in a car crash. Given the ultra-contemporary world of the early part of the novel, the scenes in Dorset . . . seem parochial, but this does not lessen Walters's ability to use horror-movie logic to terrifying effect." New Yorker

Walters, Minette

The **echo**. Putnam 1997 338p
LC 96-37485

"The discovery of a homeless man's body in the garage of a banker's wife leads her—and a journalist interested in the homeless—to find out more about the man. They also reinvestigate the disappearance, years ago, of the banker and a sizable sum of cash. . . . Well-crafted psychological suspense from a master." Libr J

Walters, Minette

The **sculptress**. St. Martin's Press 1993 308p
LC 93-21527

"Walters mesmerizes her readers with a sleek, exciting tale whose slick veneer disguises a sinister, menacing evil." Booklist

Walters, Minette

The **shape** of snakes. Putnam 2001 384p $24.95
ISBN 0-399-14733-0

LC 00-65319

The novel's protagonist "was traumatized in 1978 by the violent death of a London neighbor who suffered from Tourette's syndrome. 'I could never decide whether 'Mad Annie' was murdered because she was mad or because she was black,' she says. But the cruel nature of the woman's death and the torments she endured from prejudiced neighbors have haunted Mrs. Ranelagh for 20 years. And now it is time for the reckoning. Although the narrator obviously has a hidden agenda, the master manipulator here is Walters, whose commanding control over her inflammatory material—and her readers—distracts the eye from potential murder suspects and directs the mind to the everyday acts of casual inhumanity that are the real issue." N Y Times Book Rev

Walton, Jo

★ **Among** others. Tor 2011 302p $24.99
ISBN 978-0-7653-2153-4; 0-7653-2153-X

LC 2010-36108

2012 Hugo Award Winner, Best Novel

"Her mother half insane and her twin sister killed in a car accident, Morwenna Phelps finds herself in the custody of her estranged, feckless father, who almost immediately ships her off to boarding school. Used to conversing with the spirits of the woods in her Welsh hometown, Mori has a difficult time adjusting to a regimented place that seems almost devoid of magic. Even more daunting for her is the necessity to conform to school rules and make friends with girls who regard her with mistrust and envy. Desperate for companionship, Mori casts a spell that seems to bring her the support of a reading group of like-minded science fiction fans, but she fears that her supernatural meddling has attracted the attention of her mother. Despite her growing interest in one of the boys in the group, she must return to Wales to set everything right once and for all." San Francisco Chron

Walton, Jo

Farthing. Tor 2006 319p $25.95
ISBN 0-765-31421-5

LC 2005-34487

"In an alternate reality in which a group of English nobles overthrew Winston Churchill and made peace with Adolf Hitler in 1941, a murder is committed at the home of Lord and Lady Eversley, and suspicion falls on David Kahn, the Jewish husband of Lucy Eversley. Only Inspector Carmichael of Scotland Yard believes that something else might be at work and that the Kahns could, in fact, be victims themselves. . . . An excellent example of alternate history." Libr J

Walton, Jo

Ha'penny. Tor 2007 319p $25.95
ISBN 978-0-7653-1853-4; 0-7653-1853-9

LC 2007-21113

Sequel to: Farthing

This second volume of the author's Small Change trilogy "delves deeper into the intrigue and paranoia of 1940s fascist Great Britain. Denied help from the United States, England negotiated the Farthing Peace with the Nazis to end WWII, surrendering freedom for a narrow kind of safety. Eight years later, Scotland Yard investigators like Inspector Carmichael spend as much time monitoring the activities of gays, Jews and foreigners as they do hunting criminals. Carmichael, outed to his superiors as a homosexual and blackmailed into keeping deadly political secrets, plans to retire after his current case, a bombing at the country house of respected actress Lauria Gilmore. Meanwhile, Viola Lark is preparing for the role of her life as a female Hamlet when she's coerced into a plot to kill the prime minister and Hitler on opening night. World Fantasy Award-winner Walton masterfully illustrates how fear can overwhelm common sense." Publ Wkly

Walton, Jo

Half a crown. Tor 2008 316p $25.95
ISBN 978-0-7653-1621-9; 0-7653-1621-8

LC 2008-31019

Conclusion of the author's Small Change alternative-history trilogy; earlier titiles: Farthing and Ha'penny

"A difficult—and important—book to read about a world gone mad. The characterization is first-rate, the plot is compelling and most important of all, even in this world, there is hope." Romantic Times

Walton, Jo, 1964-

My real children; Jo Walton. First edition Tor 2014 320 p. (hardcover) $25.99

ISBN 0765332655; 9780765332653

LC 2013029673

Stonewall Honor Book - Literature (2015)

In this novel by Jo Walton, "Patricia Cowan is very old. 'Confused today,' read the notes clipped to the end of her bed. She forgets things she should know--what year it is, major events in the lives of her children. But she remembers things that don't seem possible. She remembers marrying Mark and having four children. . . . Jo Walton's 'My Real Children' is the tale of both of Patricia Cowan's lives . . . and of how every life means the entire world." (Publisher's note)

"Jo Walton's My Real Children is a bit like a novel written from the point of view of Schrödinger's cat, except that instead of a cat we have a smart, sympathetic Englishwoman named Patricia, and she's not alive and dead, she's alive twice—she lives two parallel lives, in two distinct worlds, both of which are apparently equally real...My Real Children is a quiet triumph, not least because whatever life Patricia happens to be living at any given moment, she remains deeply and recognizably herself. Good novels show us a character's destiny as an expression of who they fundamentally are. What most novels do only once, My Real Children does twice." PW

Walton, Jo, 1964-

★ **Necessity**; A Novel. by Jo Walton. St. Martin's Press 2016 336 p. (ebook) $60; (hardcover) $25.99

ISBN 9781466865709; 0765379023; 9780765379023

In this book by Jo Walton, part of the "Thessaly" series, "more than sixty-five years ago, Pallas Athena founded the Just City on an island in the eastern Mediterranean, . . . The Just City schismed into five cities, each devoted to a different version of the original vision. . . . Now, more than a generation has passed. The Cities are flourishing on Plato, . . . [then] two things happen. Pytheas dies as a human, returning immediately as Apollo in his full glory." (Publisher's note)

"As before, Walton has done a superb job of world building and character development, giving readers a novel that both stimulates and satisfies." Booklist

Wambaugh, Joseph

★ The **blue** knight. Little, Brown 1972 338p

"The caricature is deliberate; the author means to endow a stereotype with complexity and sentiment. Bumper has his own street ethics. . . . The book tends to be a bit ostentatious in such honesties, as if they established Bumper's credibility. In the end, Wambaugh sentimentalizes Bumper as a sort of repellently lovable super-cop who, whenever he is not strongarming 'pukepots,' is bantering in Yiddish, Spanish or Arabic with the ethnics on the beat." Time

Wambaugh, Joseph

Finnegan's week. Morrow 1993 348p

LC 93-24890

"There is a boyish excessiveness to Mr. Wambaugh's writing that produces an odd synergy with his carefully constructed plots and his colorful characters." N Y Times Book Rev

Wambaugh, Joseph

Floaters. Bantam Bks. 1996 293p

LC 95-26625

In this novel, "two clumsy conspirators try to fix the America's Cup race. A hot number named Blaze Duvall does the grunt work of seducing a dumb sailor into sabotaging the Black Magic, the formidable New Zealand contender. Blaze stands to make a buck from this scheme, but it is really a crime of passion devised by Ambrose Lutterworth, the keeper of the cup, who can't bear to give up his beloved charge. As a spy, the flame-haired Blaze is a bit conspicuous, catching the eye of Fortney and Leeds, a couple of calloused veterans with the harbor police unit that cruises Mission Bay in San Diego." N Y Times Book Rev

Wambaugh, Joseph

Harbor nocturne; Joseph Wambaugh. Grove/Atlantic 2012 320 p.

ISBN 9780802126108

In this book, "Sgt. Thaddeus Hawthorne of Hollywood Vice thinks he sees a way to put pressure on Hector Cozzo, an errand boy for a gang that's smuggling and prostituting illegals: Persuade [a] surfer officer . . . to use his amputated foot to ingratiate himself with a shadowy Russian associate with a fixation on amputations. . . . A fight among superhero panhandlers leads to the hot pursuit of a purse snatcher. A domestic violence call discloses a kinky sex contract gone wrong. A homeless man beds down in a dumpster that's already hosting a corpse. In the middle of this junkyard, a flower struggles to bloom: the unlikely romance between Lita Medina Flores, an incoming Mexican illegal hired to dance even though she's a terrible dancer, and Dinko Babich, the old school friend Hector pays to deliver her to Club Samara." (Kirkus)

Wambaugh, Joseph

Hollywood crows; a novel. Little, Brown 2008 343p $26.99

ISBN 978-0-316-02528-7; 0-316-02528-3

LC 2007-33059

"Wambaugh is an important writer not simply because he's ambitious and technically accomplished, but also because he 'owns' a critical slice of L.A.'s literary real estate: the Los Angeles Police Department not just its inner workings, but also its relationship to the city's political establishment and to its intricately enmeshed social classes." Los Angeles Times Book Rev

Wambaugh, Joseph

Hollywood Hills; a novel. Little, Brown and Co. 2010 356p il $26.99

ISBN 978-0-316-12950-3; 0-316-12950-X

LC 2010-26155

"The main event in this seriocomic production involves the collision of two separate but equally inept pairs of thieves: a sleazy art dealer who plans to defraud a movie producer's widow by making an accomplice of her butler, and an OxyContin addict who talks his druggie girlfriend into robbing mansions in the Hollywood Hills. While keeping these clowns busy tripping over their own shoelaces, Wambaugh salts the narrative with variously funny, sad and thoughtful anecdotes featuring a cast of characters we've come to treasure: handsome Hollywood Nate, the surfer cops Flotsam and Jetsam, and veterans like Viv Daley and Della Ravelle, burned by experience, but conscientiously training the next generation to face the fire." N Y Times Book Rev

Wambaugh, Joseph

★ **Hollywood** Station; a novel. Little, Brown and Co. 2006 340p $24.99

ISBN 9780316066143; 0-316-06614-1

LC 2006-15759

"Wambaugh has his finger on the pulse of today's police force in a way that most other authors simply can't match, and that makes his work a delight to read." Chicago Sun-Times

Wambaugh, Joseph

★ The **new** centurions. Little, Brown 1971 376p

"As a novel the book has lapses, it wears its exposition on its sleeve—necessarily, perhaps, in view of what it's trying to do—and the three protagonists, though very different in type, are perhaps not sufficiently different in sensibility. . . . But never mind that. What he knows Wambaugh tells truly, perceptively, and well." Book World

Wander, Fred

The **seventh** well; translated by Michael Hofmann. W.W. Norton & Co. 2008 160p $23.95; pa $13.95

ISBN 978-0-393-06538-1; 0-393-06538-3; 978-0-393-33362-6 pa; 0-393-33362-0 pa

LC 2007-28897

Original German edition, 1971

This is a "novel narrated by a young man who attempts to maintain his own sanity in the death camps by immersing himself in the lives of his fellow prisoners. Originally published in 1971, it is now available in a superb new translation by Michael Hofmann. Wander does not guide the reader on his own journey from boxcar to barbed wire, as Elie Wiesel and Primo Levi have done. Rather, his anonymous narrator undergoes a sort of spiritual education as he studies the doomed men and boys around him. The result is an indirect portrait of a man trying to grasp an unthinkable trauma." N Y Times Book Rev

Wang Anyi

The **song** of everlasting sorrow; a novel of Shanghai. translated by Michael Berry and Susan Chan Egan. Columbia University Press 2008 440p (Weatherhead books on Asia) $29.95

ISBN 0-231-14342-7; 978-0-231-14342-4

LC 2007-10812

Original Chinese edition, 1996

This novel "follows the adventures of Wang Qiyao, a girl born of the longtang, the crowded . . . alleys of Shanghai's working-class neighborhoods." (Publisher's note)

"Michael Berry and Susan Chang Egan's graceful translation, only rarely marred by jarring Americanisms ('grunt work,' 'deal breaker'), helps us understand why Wang Anyi is one of the most critically acclaimed writers in the Chinese-speaking world. . . . [As the novel] moves toward its violent, melodramatic and distressingly appropriate ending, readers may feel a Proustian nostalgia for the novel's lost time, a sadness that mirrors the melancholy that haunts Wang Qiyao and pervades the fascinating, mostly vanished longtang of Shanghai." N Y Times Book Rev

Includes bibliographical references

Ward, Amanda Eyre

Close your eyes; a novel. Random House 2010 249p $25

ISBN 978-0-345-49448-1

LC 2010-21115

"A captivating story of loss, forgiveness and ultimate redemption." Kirkus

Ward, Amanda Eyre

Forgive me; a novel. Random House 236p $23.95

ISBN 978-0-345-49446-7; 0-345-49446-6

LC 2006-50436

The protagonist of this novel is "Nadine, a fly-by-night journalist in her mid-30s who can't quite focus on anything beyond the next hot story. Continually jetting off for international trouble spots, Nadine is thoroughly unwilling to recognize just how utterly, and ultimately rather despicably, addicted she is to other peoples' misery. It doesn't help that she's also the kind of person who will harp on about troubles in faraway lands while remaining utterly blind to those existing right before her nose. After a troubled recovery in her home town of Nantucket (she got in over her head in Mexico, not surprisingly), Nadine heads off to South Africa, where she had once spent some time, to cover the Truth and Reconciliation Commission hearings on apartheid atrocities, and confronts some ugly truths about herself. Ward's plotting may not always be the best, this is a start-and-stop kind of book, but her sharp evocation of Nadine—newsgatherer as self-absorbed vampire—is one that's hard to forget." PopMatters

Ward, Jesmyn

Salvage the bones; Jesmyn Ward. Bloomsbury USA 2011 261p. $24

ISBN 978-1-608-19522-0; 1-608-19522-8; 9781608196265

LC 201053025

Alex Award (2012); National Book Award: Fiction (2011)

This book, a winner of the 2011 National Book Award, chronicles a family's experiences when a hurricane threatens their town.

"Ward uses fearless, toughly lyrical language to convey this family's close-knit tenderness [and] the sheer bloody-minded difficulty of rural African American life... It's an eye-opening heartbreaker that ends in hope... You owe it to yourself to read this book." Library Journal

Ward, Jesmyn

★ **Sing,** unburied, sing; a novel. Jesmyn Ward. Simon & Schuster 2017 304 p. hardcover $26

ISBN 9781501126062; 9781501126093; 1501126067

LC 2017039315

Kirkus Prize Finalist: Fiction (2017)
National Book Award: Fiction (2017)
Women's Prize for Fiction Longlist (2018)
National Book Critics Circle Award Finalist: Fiction (2017)
Carnegie Medal Finalist: Fiction (2018)

This novel, by Jesmyn Ward, presents "a journey through Mississippi's past and present that is both an intimate portrait of a family and an epic tale of hope and struggle. . . . Jojo and his toddler sister, Kayla, live with their grandparents . . . and the occasional presence of their drug-addicted mother, Leonie. . . . When the white father of Leonie's children is released from prison, she packs her kids and . . . sets out . . . on a journey rife with danger and promise." (Publisher's note)

"Lyrical yet tough, Ward's distilled language effectively captures the hard lives, fraught relationships, and spiritual depth of her characters." LJ

Ward, Liza

Outside valentine. Holt & Co. 2004 301p $23

ISBN 0-8050-7598-4

"A gifted writer, Ward uses simple imagery to chilling effect. A dog with a broken neck hiding under the bed after its owner has been murdered and a dead schoolgirl with her skirt pulled up—Starkweather says he just wanted to look—are as vivid as anything filmmakers have fashioned from the same raw material." Washington Post Book World

Ward, Mary Jane

The **snake** pit. Random House 1946 278p

Related in the first person, this tells of the experiences undergone by the patient, Virginia Cunningham, in a state mental hospital. It follows the course of her insanity from her commitment to her final release. It also takes the reader through mental hospital routine in all its reality

"Chronicled so quietly and unemphatically, the horrors of asylum life become infinitely more poignant than they appear in the hands of grimmer writers who are out to shock. Obviously an incomplete picture, but an extraordinarily moving one." New Yorker

Ware, Danie

Ecko Rising; Danie Ware. Random House Inc. 2013 480 p. (paperback) $14.95

ISBN 085768762X; 9780857687623

In this book, in "a tech-filled future London, Ecko is considered different. He's maxed out on body modifications and gleefully willing to do anything to take on Pilgrim, the organization bent on rendering society docile and compliant. While on a mission to infiltrate Pilgrim, he falls and comes to in a place without electricity, technology, or anything else that would make it resemble modern society. . . . Ecko is convinced it's a test, a program built to push him to his limits." (Library Journal)

Ware, Ruth

The **lying** game; Ruth Ware. Simon & Schuster 2017 370 p. (hardcover) $26.99

ISBN 9781501156199; 9781501156007; 0393285340

LC 2017943545

In this book, by Ruth Ware, "a woman is walking her dog in . . . a tidal estuary. . . . The dog charges into the water to retrieve what first appears to be a wayward stick, but . . . turns out to be something much more sinister. . . The next morning, three women in and around London--Fatima, Thea, and Isabel--receive the text they had always hoped would NEVER come, from the fourth in their formerly inseparable clique, Kate, that says only, 'I need you.'" (Publisher's note)

"Alternating between the past and present, Ware builds up a rock-solid cast of intriguing characters and spins a mystery that will keep readers turning pages to the end." Pub Wkly

Ware, Ruth

The **Woman** in Cabin Ten; by Ruth Ware. Simon & Schuster 2016 288 p. (ebook) $59.99; $26

ISBN 9781508217763; 1501132938; 9781501132933

LC 2016007713

Library Reads Favorite of Favorites (2016).

In this book, by Ruth Ware, "Lo Blacklock, a journalist who writes for a travel magazine, has just been given the assignment of a lifetime: a week on a luxury cruise with only a handful of cabins. The . . . Aurora, begins her voyage in the picturesque North Sea. At first, Lo's stay is nothing but pleasant. . . . But as the week wears on, frigid winds whip the deck, gray skies fall, and Lo witnesses what she can only describe as a dark and terrifying nightmare." (Publisher's note)

"Ware's follow-up to her best-selling debut, In a Dark, Dark Wood, is a gripping maritime psychological thriller that will keep readers spellbound. The intense final chapters just might induce heart palpitations." LJ

Warner, Kaki

Bride of the high country; Kaki Warner. Berkley Sensation 2012 390 p. $15

ISBN 0425247503; 9780425247501

LC 2012005041

In this novel by Kaki Warner, book 3 of the Runaway Brides series, "Margaret Hamilton escaped the Irish slums of Five Points as the ward of a wealthy Manhattan widow, but only marriage can make her future secure. Railroad mogul Doyle Kerrigan needs a well-connected wife. It seems a perfect match...until a shocking revelation sends her fleeing from the wedding reception. . . . Margaret takes on a new identity and heads West, finally stopping in Heartbreak Creek, Colorado. . . . But two men from Margaret's past are on her trail." (Publisher's note)

Warren, Diane

Juliet in August; Dianne Warren. 1st American ed. Penguin Group USA 2012 324 p. (paperback) $16.00; (hardcover) $25.95

ISBN 9780425261002; 0399157999; 9780399157998

LC 2012006196

Governor General's Award, 2010.

Author Dianne Warren tells the story of "the inhabitants of several households in Juliet (population 1,011). Lee Torgeson, 26, isn't sure he's capable of managing the farm left to him by his adoptive parents. Willard Shoenfeld and his brother's widow, Marian, [and] he can't admit to himself how much he loves her, [and] . . . Blaine Dolson has lost most of his family's farmland and faces bankruptcy. . . . Norval Birch . . . is also troubled by wife Lila's plans for an elaborate wedding for their pregnant daughter Rachelle." (Kirkus Reviews)

Warren, Robert Penn

★ **All** the king's men. Harcourt Brace Jovanovich 1990 531p $19

ISBN 0-15-104772-3

LC 90-36181

First published 1946

"In the South during the 1920s a young journalist, Jack Burden, becomes involved in the drive for political power by soon-to-be governor Willie Stark. The journey is a rocky, disillusioning one, and involves exploitation, deceit, and violence. When asked by Stark to uncover a scandal in the past of Judge Irwin, Jack must weigh the many consequences of such action." Shapiro. Fic for Youth. 3d edition

Warren, Robert Penn

★ **Band** of angels. Random House 1955 375p

"A lush, full-bodied Civil War story about a Kentucky plantation owner's daughter sold into slavery whose fight becomes an inquiry into the nature of freedom and the quest for individual identity." Oxford Companion to Am Lit. 6th edition

Warren, Robert Penn

★ **World** enough and time; a romantic novel. Random House 1950 512p

"The murder in Kentucky of Col. Solomon P. Sharp by Jeroboam O. Beauchamp, whose trial was the sensation of 1826, has been a popular theme for novelists ever since. Warren's version in this novel is based on The Confession, which Beauchamp published in 1826. Warren introduced many variations, however, and his quotations from documents are his own inventions." Benet's Reader's Ency of Am Lit

Warren, Susan May

Take a chance on me; Susan May Warren. Tyndale House Publishers, Inc. 2013 416 p. (Christiansen family) (paperback) $13.99

ISBN 1414378416; 9781414378411

LC 2012050809

This novel, by Susan May Warren, is part of the "Christiansen Family" series. "Darek Christiansen is almost a dream bachelor . . . but he's also wounded and angry since the tragic death of his wife, Felicity. . . . New assistant county attorney Ivy Madison . . . doesn't know . . . that . . . she . . . [released] the man responsible for Felicity's death. All Ivy knows is that the Christiansens feel like the family she's always longed for." (Publisher's note)

Warrington, Freda

Elfland. Tor 2009 464 p. (Aetherial tales)

ISBN 9780765318695; 0765318695

LC 2009012918

Romantic Times Reviewers' Choice Award: Best Science Fiction & Fantasy (2009)

When the passage to the Other World fails to open on the designated Night of the Summer Stars due to great danger in the realm, Aetherials Auberon and Rose form a forbidden alliance to breach the gates.

"Solid wordplay, great pacing and a thrilling conclusion." Pub Wkly

Warrington, Freda

Grail of the summer stars; Freda Warrington. 1st ed. Tor 2013 384 p. (Aetherial tales) (hardcover) $27.99

ISBN 0765318717; 9780765318718

LC 2012042626

This is the third installment in Freda Warrington's Aetherial Tales series. "When Stephanie Silverwood, curator of the Museum of Metalwork in Birmingham, England, receives a triptych . . . , she recognizes the work as belonging to her former friend and one-time lover, Daniel Manifold. At the same time, a man calling himself Mist, one of the ancient Aetherials, emerges from the sea to resume the search for his brother. The strange painting" leads both to an ancient, hidden faerie race. (Library Journal)

Warrington, Freda

Midsummer night; Freda Warrington. 1st ed. Tor 2010 412 p. (Aetherial tales.) (hardcover) $27.99

ISBN 0765318709; 9780765318701

LC 2010036680

This is the first in Freda Warrington's Aetherial Tales series. Decades ago, a deadly prank occurred at a place where the human and fairy worlds meet. Years later, the spot is home to an art museum. "One day, during a violent storm, a young woman studying art at the estate stumbles upon a portal to the Otherworld. A handsome young man comes through the portal and seeks shelter with her." He's charming, but others are suspicious. (Publisher's note)

Wascom, Kent, 1986-

★ The **Blood** of Heaven. Pgw 2013 432 p. $25

ISBN 0802121187; 9780802121189

This historical novel is Kent Wascom's debut. Set "mainly in West Florida (comprised of parts of current-day Florida, Alabama, Mississippi, and Louisiana) around 1800, the book follows Angel Woolsack through his transformation from preacher to robber to freedom fighter to hero for independence from Spanish rule as Angel joins his adopted brothers in the effort to free West Florida." (Library Journal)

Waters, Sarah, 1966-

Fingersmith. Riverhead Bks. 2002 511p

ISBN 1-573-22203-8

LC 2001-51053

"Sue Trinder, who also goes by a number of other names, appears to be a foundling, left for safekeeping at Mrs. Sucksby's baby farm by her thieving mother. . . . Raised by Mrs. Sucksby as her own, Sue picks up a few tricks from a crooked locksmith. . . . One day a young man, Richard Rivers, known as Gentleman, comes knocking at the door with a scheme to marry himself off to a lonely heiress, Maud Lilly, then have her shut up in a madhouse once her money is his. He enlists Sue to be the young woman's maid, promising her a cut of the proceeds. But having attached herself to Maud for the sake of the money, Sue finds herself drawn into an unexpected and fearful intimacy." N Y Times Book Rev

Waters, Sarah, 1966-

The **little** stranger. Riverhead Books 2009 466p $26.95

ISBN 978-1-59448-880-1; 1-59448-880-0

LC 2009-09338

"In post-World War II Britain, the financially struggling Dr. Faraday is called to Hundreds Hall, home of the upper-class Ayreses, now fallen on hard times. Ostensibly there to treat Roderick Ayres for a war injury, Faraday soon sees signs of mental decline—first in Roderick and later in his mother, Mrs. Ayres. Waters builds the suspense slowly, with the skeptical Faraday refusing to accept the explanations of Roderick or of the maid Betty, who believe that there is a supernatural presence in the house. Meanwhile, Faraday becomes enamored of Roderick's sister Caroline and begins to dream of building a family within the confines of the ruined Hundreds Hall. This spooky, satisfying read has the added pleasure of effectively detailing postwar village life, with its rationing, social strictures, and gossip." Libr J

Waters, Sarah, 1966-

The **night** watch. Riverhead Books 2006 450p $25.95

ISBN 1-59448-905-X

LC 2005-44927

"In the fall of 1947, an androgynous woman walks aimlessly through the scarred streets of London, adjusting her cufflinks. An ambulance driver during the Blitz, she now does nothing more dramatic than go to the cinema, arriving midway through a film and watching the second half first–'People's pasts, you know, being so much more interesting than their futures.' Likewise, this historical novel begins at the end and moves backward, tracing the lives of its characters from peacetime Britain to the early years of the war. The centerpiece of the book is set in 1944, when the characters come fully alive, creeping through blackout London–an apocalyptic landscape of rubble and ash, searchlights and fires. Waters, acclaimed for her Victorian-era romps, has done meticulous research, and renders wartime scenes with unnerving authenticity." New Yorker

Waters, Sarah, 1966-

The **Paying** Guests; Sarah Waters. Riverhead Books 2014 560 p. $28.95

ISBN 1594633118; 9781594633119

LC 2014016148

This novel, by Sarah Waters, is "about a widow and her daughter who take a young couple into their home in 1920s London. . . . [I]n a . . . Camberwell villa . . . life is about to be transformed as impoverished widow Mrs. Wray and her spinster daughter, Frances, are obliged to take in lodgers. With the arrival of Lilian and Leonard Barber, . . . the routines of the house will be shaken up. . . . Little do the Wrays know just how profoundly their new tenants will alter the course of Frances's life." (Publisher's note)

"Waters is a master of pacing, and her metaphor-laced prose is a delight. . . . As life-and-death questions are answered, new ones come up, and until the last page, the reader will have no idea what's going to happen." Kirkus

Waters, Sarah, 1966-

Tipping the velvet; A Novel. by Sarah Waters. Riverhead Books 2000 472 p. $16

ISBN 1573227889; 9781573227889

LC 9843836

In this novel, by Sarah Waters, "Nan King, an oyster girl, is captivated by the music hall phenomenon Kitty Butler, a male impersonator extraordinaire treading the boards in Canterbury. . . . Soon after, she becomes Kitty's dresser and the two head for the bright lights of Leicester Square where they begin a glittering career as music-hall stars. . . . At the same time, behind closed doors, they admit their attraction to each other and their affair begins." (Publisher's note)

"A perfect fictional equivalent to such eye-opening standard works as Frank Harris's My Life and Loves and Steven Marcus's The Other Victorians and a rather formidable debut." Kirkus

Watkins, Claire Vaye

Battleborn; Claire Vaye Watkins. Riverhead Books 2012 304 p. $25.95

ISBN 9781594488252

LC 2012009175

This collection of short stories, by Claire Vaye Watkins, set in "the author's home state, Nevada . . . cover[s] . . . a lot of ground, from the failed mining efforts of the forty-niners to Charles Manson's debauchery in his desert enclave . . . to the near-present with a legal brothel known as the Cherry Patch Ranch. The characters include small-town teenage girls looking for fun on a Vegas road trip . . . and a young Reno woman with a destructive streak." (Library Journal)

Watkins, Claire Vaye

★ **Gold** fame citrus; A Novel. Claire Vaye Watkins. Riverhead Books 2015 352 p. (hardback) $27.95

ISBN 1594634238; 9781594634239

LC 2015013564

"Unrelenting drought has transfigured Southern California. . . . In Los Angeles' Laurel Canyon, two young Mojavs—Luz, once a poster child for the Bureau of Conservation and its enemies, and Ray, a veteran of the "forever war" turned surfer—squat in a starlet's abandoned mansion. . . . But when they cross paths with a mysterious child, the thirst for a better future begins." (Publisher's note)

"In Margaret Atwood mode, Watkins spikes this fast-moving, high-tension, sexy, ecocrisis saga with caustic parodies and resounding allusions that cohere into a knowing and elegiac tale of scrappy adaptation and epic loss." Booklist

Watkins, Paul

★ The **forger**. Picador 2000 322p $25

ISBN 0-312-26593-X

LC 00-33631

"Watkins is an extremely facile writer. His novels are thrilling, fast-paced, intricately plotted and extraordinarily atmospheric. Cerebral in the manner of Graham Greene, . . . Watkins, like Greene, can create a wartime sensibility in which every footfall on the stairs has you holding your breath in anticipation. In 'The Forger', he has created a shifting—and shifty—cast of characters whose loyalties and alliances keep changing as the events of the war advance." N Y Times Book Rev

Watkins, Paul

The **ice** soldier. H. Holt 2006 341p $25

ISBN 0-8050-7867-3

LC 2005-46237

"Narrator William Bromley leads a quiet, isolated life in England circa 1950, socializing only with his similarly inclined friend and mountaineering partner Stanley Carton. Much to the dismay of Stanley's uncle Henry (who not only inspired them to become climbers but was also the first to climb a peak in the Italian Alps, which was named Carton Peak after him), both have given up mountaineering. When a former friend and mountaineer, Sturges, shows up, William begins having flashbacks to his mission as an ice soldier during World War II. The death of Uncle Henry forces both William and Stanley to confront their pasts in a dramatic fashion. With a narrative so strong in imagery and detail that the reader can almost feel the gusts of an Alpine blizzard, this adventurous tale builds to a final climax on Carton Peak, where William's horrific wartime experience occurred." Libr J

Watrous, Malena

If you follow me; a novel. Harper Perennial 2010 356p pa $14.99

ISBN 978-0-06-173285-0 pa; 0-06-173285-0 pa

LC 2009-18301

A "deft, funny, and emotionally acute first novel. . . . Watrous's book crackles with atmospheric detail and sharp dialogue, and tells a vivid story of an American confronting grief and self-knowledge in an unfamiliar place." Boston Globe

Watson, Brad

Aliens in the prime of their lives; stories. W. W. Norton 2010 268p $23.95

ISBN 978-0-393-05711-9; 0-393-05711-9

LC 2009-23469

"Domestic dramas, failed marriages, gunshots in the night and a dash of alien intrigue punctuate a collection of gothic tales. Returning to the pungent stories that represent his best work, . . . [the author], reaches new creative heights with some pieces and falls prey to literary navel-gazing in others. Fortunately, great works outnumber baffling ones in this mostly splendid collection." Kirkus

Watson, Brad

The **heaven** of Mercury. Norton 2002 333p $23.95

ISBN 0-393-04757-1

National Book Award Finalist: Fiction (2002)

In this "southern gothic tale, Finus Bates, an 89-year-old radio announcer, reflects on his thwarted love affair with Birdie Wells. As a child, Finus falls in love with the winsome Birdie when he spies her executing a naked cartwheel. Despite their mutual attraction, Birdie and Finus end up betrothed to others: Birdie to the lecherous son of one of the town's wealthiest families, and Finus to Birdie's best friend, a severe woman with unexpected reservoirs of strength. As Watson traces the lovers' sad histories, he flips to the present day, when Finus investigates the decades-old poisoning of Birdie's husband." Booklist

Watson, Brad

Miss Jane; A Novel. by Brad Watson. W W Norton & Co Inc 2016 224 p. (ebook) $50; $25.95

ISBN 9780393285444; 0393241734; 9780393241730

LC 2016011032

This novel, by Brad Watson, "explores the life of Miss Jane Chisolm, born in rural, early-twentieth-century Mississippi with a genital birth defect that would stand in the way of the central 'uses' for a woman in that time and place: sex and marriage. From the highly erotic world of nature around her to the hard tactile labor of farm life, from the country doctor who befriends her to the boy who loved but was forced to leave her, Miss Jane Chisolm and her world are anything but barren." (Publisher's note)

"As Watson arcs through the story of Jane's life in sensitive, beautifully precise prose, we are both absorbed and humbled. Highly recommended." LJ

Watson, Christie

Tiny sunbirds, far away; a novel. Christie Watson. Other Press 2011 438 p.

ISBN 1590514661; 159051467X; 9781590514665; 9781590514672

LC 2010054187

In this book, the winner of the 2011 Costa First Novel Award, "[w]hen their mother catches their father with another woman, twelve year-old Blessing and her fourteen-year-old brother, Ezikiel, are forced to leave their comfortable home in Lagos for a village in the Niger Delta, to live with their mother's family. . . . Blessing's grandmother . . . soon becomes a beloved mentor, teaching Blessing the ways of the midwife in rural Nigeria. Blessing is exposed to the horrors of genital mutilation and the devastation wrought on the environment by British and American oil companies. As Warri comes to feel like home, Blessing becomes . . . aware of the threats to its safety, both from its unshakable but dangerous traditions and the relentless carelessness of the modern world." (Publisher's note)

Watson, Jan Elizabeth

Asta in the wings. Tin House Books 2009 314p (Tin House new voice) pa $14

ISBN 978-0-9802436-1-1; 0-9802436-1-0

LC 2008-40525

This is the "story of what happens when the outside world discovers that a widowed mother in Maine has removed her two children, seven-year-old Asta and her nine-year-old brother, Orion, from any contact with the outside world. Unaware that their mother is delusional, the two children do not feel deprived under her care, appreciating her for what she is able to provide. When their isolated living situation is discovered, the children find themselves at the mercy of kind yet sometimes misguided adults. Asta emerges as the stronger, more communicative child. Bright and sometimes wily, she remains steadfastly devoted to her gifted yet now mute brother." Libr J

Watson, Larry

American boy. Milkweed Editions 2011 251p $24

ISBN 978-1-57131-078-1

LC 2011-21334

"The environment around Willow Falls—its heavy emptiness, its shadowy ground—looms over the story, sometimes ominous, sometimes hopeful. Watson paints it with a restrained vividness. . . . A soft but urgent rendering of a young man coming of age in a rural America that is recognizable even to those of us who were never there." Denver Post

Watson, Larry

As good as gone; A Novel. Larry Watson. Algonquin Books of Chapel Hill 2016 400 p. $26.95

ISBN 9781616205713

LC 2015034265

In this novel by Larry Watson, "Calvin Sidey, one of the last of the old cowboys, has long ago left his family to live a life of self-reliance out on the prairie. He's been a mostly absentee father and grandfather until his estranged son asks him to stay with his grandchildren, Ann and Will, for a week while he and his wife are away. . . . Trouble soon comes to the door . . . [and] Calvin knows only one way to solve problems: the Old West way, in which scores are settled." (Publisher's note)

"This is a very well done novel in which every character faces an individual conflict, resulting in a rich, suspenseful read." Pub Wkly

Watson, Larry

★ **Let** him go; a novel. Larry Watson. Milkweed Editions 2013 256 p. (hardcover : alk. paper) $24

ISBN 1571311025; 9781571311023

LC 2013006976

This book is set in 1950s rural North Dakota. "George Blackledge, a retired sheriff, returns home to find his wife Margaret packing to leave . . . on an honorable, valiant journey to reclaim her young grandson Jimmy from Lorna, the widow of her tragically deceased son, and Lorna's sketchy new husband, Donnie Weboy. . . . George joins his determined wife for the long road trip across the Dakota Badlands into Montana, where they become embroiled in the violence of the Weboy clan." (Publishers Weekly)

Watson, S. J.

Before I go to sleep. Harper 2011 360p $25.99

ISBN 978-0-06-206055-6; 0-06-206055-4

LC 2010-43159

British Book Awards (the Nibbies): Crime Thriller of the Year (2011)

Dagger Awards: CWA John Creasey (New Blood) Dagger (2011)

"Christine Lucas awakens each morning in London with no idea who she is or why she's in bed with a strange man, until he tells her that his name is Ben and they've been married for 22 years. Slowly, Christine learns that she has amnesia and is unable to remember her past or retain new memories: every night when she falls asleep, the slate is wiped clean. Dr. Nash, her therapist, has encouraged her to write in a journal that she keeps secret from Ben. Christine realizes how truly tangled-and dangerous-her life is after she sees the words 'don't trust Ben' written in her journal, whose contents reveal that the only person she can trust is herself." Publ Wkly

Watson, Sterling

Suitcase city; Sterling Watson. Akashic Books 2015 320 p. (trade pbk. original) $15.95

ISBN 161775319X; 9781617753190; 9781617753329

LC 2014938700

In this novel by Sterling Watson, "set in Tampa, Florida, in the late 1980s, . . . a man gets himself into a little bit of trouble, then a little bit more, then a lot. How does he get himself out of this mess of his own creation? The answer involves the end of an extramarital affair, reconciliation with a daughter he has neglected, and a deadly encounter with a man who comes out of the past bearing bad news and the keys to a new life." (Publisher's note)

"Each of ... [the] plot strands becomes a serpent's coil that winds around the willing reader and won't let go until the tension is released in the violent finale. Paranoia has been defined as 'seeing too much pattern.' Author Watson can make us sweaty victims of that madness, partaking of it, suffering from it, and loving every minute." Booklist

Watts, Peter

Blindsight. Tor 2006 384p $25.95

ISBN 978-0-7653-1218-1; 0-7653-1218-2

LC 2006-5917

Watts "remains one of the most exacting hard SF writers in the field, with a meticulous approach to the science in his works." Sci Fi Wkly

Watts, Peter

Starfish. Tor 1999 317p hardcover o.p. pa $14.95

ISBN 978-0-7653-1596-0; 0-7653-1596-3

LC 99-22967

First title in the author's Rifter's trilogy

"In the near future, energy comes from the geothermal waters of the deep ocean, but the cost of providing power for the surface has a price-the sanity of the physically modified humans ('rifters') who live in an alien and dangerous environment. Watts's first novel elegantly captures the isolation and claustrophobia of the lightless ocean depths, smoothly blending psychological suspense with high-tech sf adventure." Libr J

Followed by: Maelstrom (2001) and Behemoth (2004)

Waugh, Evelyn

★ **Brideshead** revisited; with an introduction by Frank Kermode. Knopf 1993 xxxvii, 315p $17

ISBN 0-679-42300-1

LC 93-1854

A reissue of the title first published 1945 by Little, Brown

"The novel, which takes the form of an extended flashback, is narrated by Charles Ryder, an army officer billeted at the eponymous country house, owned by an aristocratic Roman Catholic family headed by Lord and Lady Marchmain. Charles had visited Brideshead with Sebastian Flyte, the Marchmains' younger son, when both were Oxford undergraduates. In the course of the narrative Ryder conveys his fascination with the family, all of whom are eccentric or unhappy in some way." Oxford Companion to 20th Cent Lit in Engl

Waugh, Evelyn

★ The **complete** stories of Evelyn Waugh. Little, Brown 1999 535p $29.95

ISBN 0-316-92546-2

LC 99-20837

"These 39 stories span Waugh's writing career, and to a one they demonstrate his trademark wit and sophistication." Booklist

Waugh, Evelyn

Decline and fall. Doubleday, Doran 1929 293p

First published 1928 in the United Kingdom

This novel "recounts the chequered career of Paul Pennyfeather, sent down from Scone College, Oxford, for 'indecent behaviour', as the innocent victim of a drunken orgy. Thus forced to abandon a career in the church, he becomes a schoolmaster at Llanabba Castle, where he encounters headmaster Fagan and his daughters, the dubious, bigamous, and reappearing Captain Grimes, and young Beste-Chetwynde, whose glamorous mother Margot carries him off to the dangerous delight of high society. They are about to be married when Paul is arrested at the Ritz and subsequently imprisoned for Margot's activities in the white slave trade." Oxford Companion to Engl Lit. 6th edition

Waugh, Evelyn

The **loved** one; an Anglo-American tragedy. Little, Brown 1948 164p hardcover o.p. pa $13.95

ISBN 0-316-92608-6

"Depicting romance in a mortuary could be gruesome but the author succeeds both in poking satirical fun at the maudlin pretentiousness of the funeral industry and in delighting the reader with a hilarious love story." Shapiro. Fic for Youth. 3d edition

Waugh, Evelyn

★ **Vile** bodies. Little, Brown 1930 321p

"Set in England between the wars, the novel examines the frenetic but empty lives of the Bright Young Things, young people who indulge in constant party-going, heavy drinking, and promiscuous sex. At the novel's end, the realities of the world intrude, with Adam Fenwick-Symes, the protagonist, serving on a battlefield at the onset of another world war." Merriam-Webster's Ency of Lit

Wayne, Teddy

Loner; Teddy Wayne. Simon & Schuster 2016 224 p. (ebook) $19.99; (hardcover) $26

ISBN 9781501107917; 9781501107894; 9781501107900

LC 2015044742

In this book, by Teddy Wayne, "David Federman has never felt appreciated. An academically gifted yet painfully forgettable member of his New Jersey high school class, the withdrawn, mild-mannered freshman arrives at Harvard fully expecting to be embraced by a new tribe of high-achieving peers. Initially, however, his social prospects seem unlikely to change, sentencing him to a lifetime of anonymity. Then he meets Veronica Morgan Wells." (Publisher's note)

"Wayne (The Love Song of Jonny Valentine) offers a witty and fascinating peek into today's youth culture, and delivers an enthralling portrait of male narcissism and voyeuristic obsession through the literary device of an unreliable, though brilliant, narrator." LJ

Wayne, Teddy

★ The **Love** Song of Jonny Valentine; a novel. by Teddy Wayne. Free Press 2013 304 p. $24.99

ISBN 1476705852; 9781476705859

LC 2012038331

This book by Whiting Writers' Award-winning author Teddy Wayne follows "'tween sensation Jonny Valentine" whose bubblegum hits made him a superstar and whose mother Jane is micromanaging every piece of his life. Offered here are "the wholehearted yearnings of a conflicted 11-year-old: his obsession with getting a successful erection, a desire to be like his musical idols, and most of all a quest to reconnect with his father." (Publishers Weekly)

Weaver, Ashley

A **most** novel revenge; Ashley Weaver. Minotaur Books 2016 310 p. (Amory Ames mystery) (hardcover) $24.99

ISBN 9781466865686; 9781250060457

LC 2016010565

In this novel in the Amory Ames Mystery series, by Ashley Weaver, "Amory and Milo Ames intend to winter quietly in Italy when Amory receives an urgent summons to the English countryside from her cousin Laurel. . . . Isobel [van Allen] has returned to England to write a sequel to her scandalous first book. . . . [I]t's up to Amory and Milo to sort through a web of scandal and lies to uncover the truth, and the identity of a killer." (Publisher's note)

"Fascinating and stylish characters fill out a finely tuned traditional mystery." Pub Wkly

Webb, Jim

A **sense** of honor. Prentice-Hall 1981 308p

LC 80-25852

"In this powerful novel, Webb . . . a graduate of the Academy, pulls the reader right into the caldron of Annapolis for a vivid picture of heroes and martinets living according to their various interpretations of 'honor'; and he illuminates the mystique that makes men voluntarily stay in such a meat grinder." Publ Wkly

Weber, Carl

Man on the run; Carl Weber. Grand Central Publishing 2017 307 p. (hardback) $25

ISBN 9781455505272; 9781455579570

LC 2016035909

In this book, by Carl Weber, "Jay Crawford [was] locked up for a crime he never committed. Now, he's escaped prison and wants nothing more than to clear his name and protect his family. To get justice, he'll need the help of the three best friends who have always had his back--Wil, Kyle and Allan. But a man on the run requires absolute trust... and Jay may just be setting himself up for the ultimate betrayal." (Publisher's note)

Weber, David

By schism rent asunder; David Weber. Tor 2008 510p maps o.p.; o.p.; $8.99

ISBN 9780765315014; 0765315017; 9780765353986

LC 2008016957

In this science fiction novel, "[t]he mercantile kingdom of Charis has prevailed over the alliance designed to exterminate it. Armed with better sailing vessels, better guns and better devices of all sorts, Charis faced the combined navies of the rest of the world . . . and broke them. Despite the implacable hostility of the Church of God Awaiting, Charis . . . [is] still an island of innovation in a world in which the Church has worked for centuries to keep humanity locked at a medieval level of existence. But the powerful men who run the Church aren't going to take their defeat lying down. Charis may control the world's seas, but it barely has an army worthy of the name. And as King Cayleb knows, far too much of the kingdom's recent good fortune is due to the secret manipulations of the being that calls himself Merlin—a being that, the world must not find out too soon, is more than human." (Publisher's note)

Weber, David

Off Armageddon Reef; David Weber. Tor 2007 605p map (pbk.) $7.99

ISBN 9780765353979; 9780765315007; 0765315009

LC 2006025838

In this science fiction, "[h]umanity pushed its way to the stars—and encountered the Gbaba, a ruthless alien race that nearly wiped us out. . . . [The] few survivors have fled to distant, Earth-like Safehold, to try to rebuild. But the Gbaba can detect the emissions of an industrial civilization, so the human rulers of Safehold have taken extraordinary measures: with mind control and hidden high technology, they've built a . . . religion designed to keep Safehold society medieval forever. 800 years pass. In a hidden chamber on Safehold, an android from the far human past awakens. . . . Via automated recordings, 'Nimue' . . . is told her fate: she will emerge into Safeholdian society . . . and begin the process of provoking the technological progress which the Church of God Awaiting has worked for centuries to prevent." (Publisher's note)

The author launches an epic series with this far-future saga, "which springboards off the near-destruction of humanity in a massive war with the alien Gbaba. The survivors of the human race retreat to the planet Safehold, where they sacrifice basic human rights—and an accurate memory of the Gbaba—for the preservation of the species. The colony's founders psychologically program the colonists to prevent the re-emergence of scientific inquiry, higher mathematics or advanced technology, which the Gbaba would detect and destroy. Centuries later, cultural stagnation on this feudal but thriving planet is enforced by the all-powerful Church of God Awaiting. But one kingdom—with the aid of the war's last survivor, a cybernetic avatar that awakens to reinvent itself as a man named Merlin Athrawes—risks committing the ultimate heresy. Shifting effortlessly between battles among warp-speed starships and among oar-powered galleys, Weber brings the political maneuvering, past and future technologies, and vigorous protagonists together for a cohesive, engrossing whole." Publ Wkly

Weber, David, 1952-

Shadow of freedom; David Weber. Baen Books 2013 448 p. (hardcover) $25

ISBN 1451638698; 9781451638691

LC 2012047561

This entry in David Weber's Honor Harrington series retells some of the events from the previous book "Mission of Honor" from "the point of view of Michelle Henke, Harrington's best friend and the commanding officer of the troops stationed in the Talbott Quadrant. . . . Nearly all the action will be new to fans, including a great deal of unrest in the nearby sectors of the League, unrest that Mesan agents may be stirring up but that draws in Michelle's 10th Fleet." (Booklist)

Wecker, Helene

The **Golem** and the Jinni; Helene Wecker. HarperCollins 2013 496 p. (hardcover) $26.99

ISBN 0062110837; 9780062110831

This novel, by Helene Wecker, is set "in turn-of-the-century New York. Chava is a golem, a creature made of clay, brought to life to by a disgraced rabbi who dabbles in dark Kabbalistic magic and dies at sea on the voyage from Poland. . . . Ahmad is a jinni, a being of fire born in the ancient Syrian desert, trapped in an old copper flask, and released in New York City. . . . Ahmad and Chava become unlikely friends and soul mates with a mystical connection." (Publisher's note)

Weiner, Jennifer

Certain girls; a novel. Atria Books 2008 386p $26.95

ISBN 978-0-7432-9425-6; 0-7432-9425-4

LC 2007-38373

This is the "kind of book that gets under your skin, reminding you what it felt like to listen to your friend snap her retainer in the dark during a sleepover when you were 13 and capturing exactly what it feels like now, watching your child grow away from you and praying that someday she comes back." Washington Post Book World

Weiner, Jennifer

Good in bed; a novel. Pocket Books 2001 376p

ISBN 0-7434-1816-6

LC 00-68212

"Cannie Shapiro is in her late twenties, funny, independent, and a talented reporter for the Philadelphia Inquirer. After a 'temporary' breakup with her boyfriend of three years, she reads his debut column, 'Good in Bed,' in the women's magazine Moxie. Titled 'Loving a Larger Woman,' this very personal piece triggers events that completely transform her and those around her. Cannie's adventures will strike a chord with all young women struggling to find their place in the world, especially those larger than a size eight." Libr J

Weiner, Jennifer

In her shoes; a novel. Atria Books 2002 424p $25

ISBN 0-7434-1819-0

LC 2003-537614

"Meet plump, dependable Rose Feller and her gorgeous, out-of-control sister, Maggie. As children, they lost their mother and contact with grandmother Ella. Now, 20 years later, we follow their struggles to forgive the past, reclaim each other's love, and become their best selves. . . . Reworking the age-old theme that self-knowledge and acceptance are needed before love and happiness can be achieved, Weiner embroiders serious matters with threads of humor to produce a novel full of memorable characters and situations." Libr J

Weiner, Jennifer

Little earthquakes. Atria Bks. 2004 417p $26

ISBN 0-7434-7009-5

This is the "story of four women in Philadelphia who bond over pregnancy and motherhood. Becky, Kelly, and Ayinde meet in yoga class, and the three become friends when Ayinde's water breaks one day after class and they take her to the hospital. Becky is a chef with an adoring husband and an annoying mother-in-law; Kelly is frustrated when her husband loses his job and drags his feet looking for another; Ayinde's husband is a famous basketball player whom she suspects of infidelity. What brings the women together is their love for their newborns. The fourth woman, Lia, watches the group from afar; she's an actress who walked out on her husband after a devastating tragedy. Weiner seamlessly and gracefully weaves the four women's stories together." Booklist

Weiner, Jennifer, 1970-

The **next** best thing; a novel. Jennifer Weiner. Atria Books 2012 389 p.

ISBN 1451617755; 9781451617757; 9781451617771

LC 2012015557

In this novel, by Jennifer Weiner, "Ruth Saunders . . . headed west with her seventy-year-old grandma in tow, hoping to make it as a screenwriter. Six years later, she . . . gets The Call: the sitcom she wrote, 'The Next Best Thing,' has gotten the green light. . . . But her dreams of Hollywood happiness are threatened by demanding actors, number-crunching executives, an unrequited crush on her boss, and her grandmother's impending nuptials." (Publisher's note)

Weiner, Jennifer, 1970-

Then came you; a novel. Atria Books 2011 338p $26.99

ISBN 978-1-4516-1772-6

LC 2011-14411

This book "revolves around an unborn child with one hell of a potential extended family: a Princeton coed who's donated her eggs to a surgically enhanced gold digger and her millionaire husband, said husband's daughter, and a woman considering surrogacy to pay the bills. . . . Weiner's subject is topical, her characters richly drawn." People

Weinstein, Alexander

Children of the new world; stories. Alexander Weinstein. Picador 2016 240 p. (ebook) $60; (trade pbk.) $16

ISBN 9781250099006; 9781250098993

LC 2016019224

This short story collection, by Alexander Weinstein, "introduces readers to a near-future world of social media implants, memory manufacturers, dangerously immersive virtual reality games, and alarmingly intuitive robots. Many of these characters live in a utopian future of instant connection and technological gratification that belies an unbridgeable human distance, while others inhabit a post-collapse landscape made primitive by disaster." (Publisher's note)

"Complete with footnotes from fictional future publications and technology that is just one leap away, this is mind-bending stuff. Weinstein's collection is full of spot-on prose, wicked humor, and heart." Pub Wkly

Weir, Alison

A **dangerous** inheritance; a novel of Tudor rivals and the secret of the Tower. Alison Weir. Ballantine 2012 544 p. (hardcover : acid-free paper) $27

ISBN 0345511891; 9780345511898; 9780345535948

LC 2012027867

In this book, "[w]hen her older sister, Lady Jane Grey, the Nine Days' Queen, is executed in 1554 for unlawfully accepting the English crown, Lady Katherine Grey's world falls apart. Barely recovered from this tragic loss she risks all for love, only to incur the wrath of her formidable cousin Queen Elizabeth I, who sees Katherine as a rival for her insecure throne. Interlaced with Katherine's story is that of her distant kinswoman Kate Plantagenet, the bastard daughter of Richard III." (Publisher's note)

Weir, Alison

Innocent traitor; a novel of Lady Jane Grey. Ballantine Books 2007 402p $24.95

ISBN 0-345-49485-7

LC 2006-49860

"Lady Jane, known to history as the Nine Days Queen, is a tragic and appealing figure. Abused by her parents, this talented and intelligent girl was bullied into a hateful marriage and pushed into accepting the Crown after the death of King Edward VI. Edward's older sister, Princess Mary (later known as Bloody Mary, and for good reason), rightfully claimed the Crown as her own, and Jane was sent to the Tower of London and eventually executed. Weir tells the story of Jane's short life from multiple viewpoints, which might initially confuse readers unfamiliar with the history, but this is a small fault in an otherwise entertaining and moving novel." Libr J

Weir, Alison

The **Lady** Elizabeth; a novel. Ballantine Books 2008 480p $25

ISBN 978-0-345-49535-8; 0-345-49535-7

LC 2008-284

A novel about the life of the young Elizabeth Tudor before she ascended to the throne. "From the time of her mother's death when she was three to her inheritance of the throne in her twenties, danger always came at Elizabeth from some corner. Early in her life, she was stripped of her title of princess; later, she had to defend her virtue from the roving eyes and hands of her stepfather; and, finally, she had to navigate the deadly waters between her Protestant faith and her sister's fanatical Catholicism. Several times Elizabeth barely escaped alive; hers was not a life that could be borne by the average person. Weir successfully depicts this extraordinary young woman who beat the odds to become one of the world's greatest rulers." Libr J

Weir, Andy

Artemis; a novel. Andy Weir. Crown 2017 305 p. map (hardcover) $27

ISBN 0553448129; 9780553448139; 9780553448122

LC 2017478129

In this novel, by Andy Weir, "Jazz Bashara is a criminal. Well, sort of. Life on Artemis, the first and only city on the moon, is tough if you're not a rich tourist or an eccentric billionaire. So smuggling in the occasional harmless bit of contraband barely counts, right? . . . Everything changes when Jazz sees the chance to commit the perfect crime, with a reward too lucrative to turn down." (Publisher's note)

Weir, Andy

★ The **Martian**; a novel. Andy Weir. Random House Inc 2014 384 p. map $24

ISBN 0804139024; 9780804139021

LC 2013362514

Alex Award (2015)

"A dust storm strands astronaut Mark Watney on Mars and forces his landing crew to abandon the mission and return to Earth. . . . Watney, injured by flying debris and presumed dead, is alone on Mars with no communication and limited supplies. He is, however, the mission engineer, the fix-it guy, and with intelligence and grit he goes to work to stay alive. . . . Meanwhile, a desperate NASA team concocts a rescue plan on Earth." (Publishers Weekly)

"[A] tightly constructed and completely believable story of a man's ingenuity and strength in the face of seemingly insurmountable odds." Booklist

Weisgall, Deborah

The **world** before her. Houghton Mifflin 2008 278p $25

ISBN 978-0-618-74657-6; 0-618-74657-9

LC 2008-4734

"Mary Ann Evans, known to the world as George Eliot, the author of such great works as Middlemarch, is in Venice in 1880, to spend her honeymoon with Johnnie Cross, an uxorious American banker. Mary Ann had a long, passionate affair with philosopher and critic George Lewes, who was married to another woman. The two lived together until Lewes' death in 1878. . . . The other story is of Caroline Edgar Spingold, who arrives in Venice exactly a century after Evans, in 1980, on a business trip with her husband, Malcolm. He is 'commerce,' taking care of the finances, while she is 'art,' capricious and impulsive. Her views on marriage are tainted by her father's long-ago desertion of her mother. Describing the stories of Mary Ann and Caroline in alternate chapters, Weisgall draws parallel portraits of marital dissatisfaction and the attraction of the fleeting past to nullify the dreariness of the present. Her writing is tender, drowning you in its drunken energy, with the city of Venice providing a tasteful backdrop." St. Petersburg Times

Weisgarber, Ann

The **personal** history of Rachel Dupree; a novel. Viking 2010 321p $25.95

ISBN 978-0-670-02201-4; 0-670-02201-2

LC 2010-04713

"An eye-opening look at the little explored area of a black frontier woman in the American West." Chicago Sun-Times

Weiss, Leah

If the creek don't rise; a novel. Leah Weiss. Sourcebooks Landmark 2017 305 p. (pbk. : alk. paper) $15.99

ISBN 9781492647454; 9781492647461

LC 2017001928

In this novel, by Leah Weiss, "Sadie is desperate to make her own mark on the world, but in remote Appalachia, a ticket out of town is hard to come by, and hope often gets stomped out. When a stranger sweeps into Baines Creek and knocks things off kilter, Sadie finds herself with an unexpected lifeline...if she can just figure out how to use it." (Publisher's note)

"In this tender but powerful debut, Weiss paints both the bright and the dark in the lives of her fictional Appalachian community's denizens." Pub Wkly

Welch, James

★ The **heartsong** of Charging Elk; a novel. Doubleday 2000 440p $24.95

ISBN 0-385-49674-5

LC 99-58875

The author "estranges our vision. We have no choice but to feel, as we look through Charging Elk's eyes, what it is like to live in a no man's land forever." N Y Times Book Rev

Welch, James

★ The **Indian** lawyer. Norton 1990 349p

ISBN 0-393-02896-8

LC 90-6894

"The novel contains good, fast-paced action with succinct insight into our ordinary dilemmas." Nation

Weldon, Fay

Chalcot Crescent. Europa Editions 2010 269p pa $15

ISBN 978-1-933372-79-2; 1-933372-79-6

First published 2009 in the United Kingdom

"It's 2013. Fay Weldon's alter ego Frances, an 80-year-old novelist, sits waiting for the bailiffs (or the secret police of near-future dystopia) to break in, and muses on the greed-is-good decades of celebrity, cheery traffic jams and maxed-out credit cards that brought her to this pass. The house on Chalcot Crescent is very like the real house in London's Primrose Hill that Weldon occupied in the glory days of her generation. Frances's past, delivered in bite-sized chapters, is close to Weldon's. There is an ironic subplot about industrial-scale cannibalism, and a sketchy conspiracy to overthrow the brutal government but this is Orwellian nightmare recast for the Twittering classes. There is more skewed memoir than grim future or alternate universe, but you'll be entertained if you enjoy Weldon's trademark barbed frivolity." New Scientist

Weldon, Fay

★ The **life** and loves of a she-devil. Pantheon Bks. 1984 241p

LC 84-7070

First published 1983 in the United Kingdom

"A fable about female power and powerlessness, telling the story of Ruth, an ugly woman married to a philandering man, who transforms herself by sheer strength of will into the image of her hated rival." Oxford Companion to 20th-Century Lit in Engl

Weldon, Fay

Worst fears; a novel. Atlantic Monthly Press 1996 200p

LC 95-52367

Fay Weldon is the "quintessential anti-romance novelist and always will be. But she's filed down a few sharp edges in 'Worst Fears,' and that makes it one of her best novels yet." N Y Times Book Rev

Wellington, David

Positive; a novel. David Wellington. Harper Voyager 2015 448 p. (hardback) $26.99

ISBN 0062315374; 9780062315373; 9780062315397

LC 2014044675

In David Wellington's novel "the tattooed plus sign on Finnegan's hand marks him as a Positive. At any time, the zombie virus could explode in his body. His only chance of a normal life is to survive the last two years of the potential incubation period. But when the military caravan transporting him is attacked, Finn becomes separated. To make it to safety, he must embark on a perilous cross-country journey across an America transformed." (Publisher's note)

"Like The Walking Dead, the book uses the zombie apocalypse as a backdrop for a gripping story about the shattering of human society—the real villains here aren't the zombies but rather the road pirates, looters, religious cultists, and other groups that have sprung up in the 20 years since the 'crisis.' Wellington's most ambitious book is also his best, written with a maturity and compassion indicative of a writer who's found the story he was made to tell. Zombie groupies will eat this one up, but it should also be recommended to readers of all epic-scale fantasy, including Justin Cronin's best-selling epic vampire novel The Passage (2010)." Booklist

Wells, Dan

The **hollow** city; Dan Wells. 1st ed. St. Martin's Press 2012 333 p. (hardcover) $25.99

ISBN 0765331705; 9780765331700; 9781429950619

LC 2012011663

In this book by Dan Wells, "an amnesiac paranoid schizophrenic holds the key to a serial killer's motivation. . . . Michael Shipman is . . . tortured by his senses and afflicted with delusions about being pursued by Faceless Men. Now the authorities want to know whether Michael's

Faceless Men are involved with the Red Line Killer, whose de-faced victims were associated with the Children of the Earth, a cult based in the former home of notorious murderer Milos Cerny." (Publishers Weekly)

Wells, H. G. (Herbert George), 1866-1946

The **complete** short stories of H. G. Wells. St. Martin's Press 1987 1038p $19.95

ISBN 0-312-15855-6

LC 87-27478

First published 1927 in the United Kingdom with title: The short stories of H. G. Wells

A collection of 62 short stories and the complete work: The time machine, first published 1895

"A fat, heavy volume packed with humour, strangeness, horror and imaginative stimulus." Daily Telegraph

Wells, H. G. (Herbert George), 1866-1946

★ The **invisible** man. Penguin 2005 xxiv, 161p pa $6

ISBN 0-14-143998-X

First published 1897

"The story concerns the life and death of a scientist named Griffin who has gone mad. Having learned how to make himself invisible, Griffin begins to use his invisibility for nefarious purposes, including murder. When he is finally killed, his body becomes visible again." Merriam-Webster's Ency of Lit

Wells, H. G. (Herbert George), 1866-1946

★ The **island** of Doctor Moreau; edited by Patrick Parrinder; with an introduction by Margaret Atwood and notes by Steven McLean. Penguin Books 2005 xxxiv, 139p (Penguin classics)

ISBN 0-14-144102-X

First published 1896

This is "an evolutionary fantasy about a shipwrecked naturalist who becomes involved in an experiment to 'humanize' animals by surgery." Oxford Companion to Engl Lit. 6th edition

Wells, H. G. (Herbert George), 1866-1946

★ The **time** machine. Penguin 2005 xxviii, 104p pa $9

ISBN 0-14-143997-1

First published 1895

"Wells advanced his social and political ideas in this narrative of a nameless Time Traveller who is hurtled into the year 802,701 by his elaborate ivory, crystal, and brass contraption. The world he finds is peopled by two races: the decadent Eloi, fluttery and useless, are dependent for food, clothing, and shelter on the simian subterranean Morlocks, who prey on them. The two races—whose names are borrowed from the Biblical Eli and Moloch—symbolize Wells's vision of the eventual result of unchecked capitalism: a neurasthenic upper class that would eventually be devoured by a proletariat driven to the depths." Merriam-Webster's Ency of Lit

Wells, H. G. (Herbert George), 1866-1946

★ The **war** of the worlds; illustrated by Edward Gorey. New York Review Books 2005 251p il $16.95

ISBN 1-59017-158-6

LC 2005-3693

First published 1898

In this novel the author "introduced the 'Alien' being into the role which became a cliché—a monstrous invader of Earth, a competitor in a cosmic struggle for existence. Though the Martians were a ruthless and terrible enemy, HGW was careful to point out that Man had driven many animal species to extinction, and that human invaders of Tasmania had behaved no less callously in exterminating their cousins." Sci Fic Ency

Wells, Ken

Crawfish mountain; a novel. Random House 2007 364p $25.95

ISBN 978-0-375-50876-9; 0-375-50876-7

LC 2007-5612

A "cautionary tale about the environment, set five years before Hurricane Katrina. It's both a political satire and a page-turning mystery. Like the best jambalaya, it's liberally spiced. Readers can almost taste the boiled crawfish and oyster po' boys with extra pickles and mayonnaise (pronounced MY-Nez, by one character). Wells . . . makes the most of Louisiana's legendary political corruption and its roguish politicians." USA Today

Wells, Martha

All systems red; Martha Wells. Tor.com 2017 160 p. (The murderbot diaries) hardcover $14.99

ISBN 9780765397539; 9780765397522; 0765397536

Alex Award (2018)

Hugo Finalist: Best Novella (2018)

Nebula Finalist: Best Novella (2017)

In this novel in The Murderbot Diaries series, by Martha Wells, "on a distant planet, a team of scientists are conducting surface tests, shadowed by their Company-supplied 'droid-- a self-aware SecUnit that has hacked its own governor module, and refers to itself . . . as 'Murderbot.' . . . [A]ll it really wants is to be left alone long enough to figure out who it is. But when a neighboring mission goes dark, it's up to the scientists and their Murderbot to get to the truth." (Publisher's note)

Wells "gives depth to a rousing but basically familiar action plot by turning it into the vehicle by which SecUnit engages with its own rigorously denied humanity. The creepy panopticon of SecUnit's multiple interfaces allows a hybrid first-person/omniscient perspective that contextualizes its experience without ever giving center stage to the humans." Pub Wkly

Wells, Martha

Wheel of the infinite; Martha Wells. Eos 2000 355 p. $24.00

ISBN 0380973359 (alk. paper)

LC 00021726

This book is set in "the great Temple city of Duvalpore, [where every year] the image of the Wheel of the Infinite must be painstakingly remade to ensure another year of peace and harmony for the Celestial Empire. . . . But a black storm is spreading across the Wheel. Every night . . . the Wheel's constructors and caretakers brush the darkness away and repair the damage with brightly colored sands and potent magic. Each morning the storm reappears, bigger and darker than before. . . . A murderer and traitor, . . . Maskelle has been summoned back to help put the world right. . . . Now, in the company of Rian-a skilled and dangerously alluring swordsman-she must confront dread enemies old and new and a cold, stalking malevolence unlike any she has ever encountered." (Publisher's note)

Wells, Rebecca, 1952-

Divine secrets of the Ya-Ya Sisterhood; a novel. by Rebecca Wells. Harper 2011 357 p. (ebook) $12.99; $16.99

ISBN 9780061743368; 0062040359; 9780062040350

LC 2011012923

This novel, by Rebecca Wells, is "about a lifetime friendship between four Southern women. . . . [It] brilliantly explores the bonds of female friendship, the often-rocky relationship between mothers and daughters, and the healing power of humor and love, in a story as fresh and uplifting as when it was first published a decade and a half ago. If you haven't yet met the Ya-Yas, what are you waiting for?" (Publisher's note)

"She has written an entertaining and engrossing novel filled with humor and heartbreak." LJ

Welsh, Irvine

Porno. Norton 2002 483p $24.95

ISBN 0-393-05723-2

LC 2002-26362

Sequel to: Trainspotting (1994)

This novel "signals, if not a return to form, then at least a return to enthusiastic formlessness—to something like the raw, jagged energy of old." N Y Times Book Rev

Welsh, Irvine, 1958-

Skagboys; Irvine Welsh. W. W. Norton 2012 532 p. (hardcover) $26.95

ISBN 9780224087902; 9780393088731; 0393088731

LC 2012018043

This book a prequel to Irvine Welsch's "Transpotting," follows "Mark Renton, a philosophical young man who seems poised to rise above his lower-middle-class station until heroin (i.e., skag) implodes him. Not long after he starts using, he's dropped out of university and wants to quit drugs but not very badly. . . . Shifting among various characters' perspectives, Welsh shows how rapidly addiction sank Mark and his friends." (Kirkus Reviews)

Welsh, Irvine

Trainspotting. W.W. Norton 2002 343p $23.95

ISBN 0-393-05724-0

First published 1993 in the United Kingdom

This novel is set in a working class neighborhood in Edinburgh. Narrator Mark Renton tells the story "of young junkies in their 20s living on the dole, fending off adulthood and trying to escape from a world of AIDS, death and national despair." New Repub

Welsh, Louise

✓The **cutting** room. Canongate 2002 294p $24

ISBN 1-8419-5280-X

LC 2002-437974

"A remarkable first novel. Like all the best exponents of the genre, Louise Welsh sets up her template and then manipulates it, using the glamour of crime to examine more humdrum kinds of suffering and loss. She piles on atmosphere to produce a Glasgow that is predictably dark and yet still plausible." N Y Times Book Rev

Welty, Eudora

★ The **collected** stories of Eudora Welty. Harcourt Brace Jovanovich 1980 622p hardcover o.p. pa $16

ISBN 0-15-118994-3; 0-15-618921-6 pa

LC 80-7947

This volume contains four previously published collections: A curtain of green, and other stories; The wide net, and other stories; The golden apples and The bride of the Innisfallen, and other stories. Also included in this volume are two uncollected pieces: Where is the voice coming from? and The demonstrators.

Welty, Eudora

★ **Complete** novels. Library of Am. 1998 1009p $35

ISBN 1-883011-54-X

LC 97-46702

Includes bibliographical references (p. 1004-1009)

Contents: The robber bridegroom; Delta wedding; The Ponder heart; Losing battles; The optimist's daughter

Welty, Eudora

★ **Delta** wedding; a novel. Harcourt Brace & Co. 1946 247p

A "portrait of a Southern plantation family in 1923. Set in the context of the wedding of one of the daughters, the novel explores the relationships among members of the Fairchild family, most of whom have been sheltered from any contact with the world outside the Mississippi Delta. Although they quarrel among themselves, they also unite against any threats to the family's status, honoring the belief in the family as a sacred and unchanging entity." Merriam-Webster's Ency of Lit

Welty, Eudora

Losing battles. Random House 1970 436p il

"At a large family gathering in Banner, Mississippi, the Renfro and Beecham families have assembled to celebrate Granny's ninetieth birthday. They are also celebrating Jack Renfro's return from the prison farm. As one might expect, the day is made up of reminiscences and recountings of earlier events, so that the novel actually spans many years. One of the key figures is Gloria, an orphan. She is frequently teased about being the daughter of another orphan, Rachel Sojourner, and of one of the Beecham boys who died in World War I. Gloria, who had married Jack just prior to his imprisonment, feels that they must get away from the clan, all of whom seem proud of their ignorance in spite of Miss Julia Mortimer's lifelong struggle to teach them something. It was a losing battle, probably even for Gloria." Shapiro. Fic for Youth. 3d edition

Welty, Eudora

The **optimist's** daughter. Random House 1972 180p

"This novel is considered the high point of Welty's lengthy career. The strong character study examines 45-year-old Laurel McKelva Hand, who returns from Chicago to Mississippi, where her father is dying. She is forced to consider her complex and ambiguous emotions about her powerful and dynamic father, the impact of this relationship on her life, and her puzzlement at his late marriage to a coarse and shallow woman who is Laurel's own age." Shapiro. Fic for Youth. 3d edition

Welty, Eudora

★ The **Ponder** heart; drawings by Joe Krush. Harcourt Brace & Co. 1954 156p il

"Cast as a monologue, {this comic novella} is rich with colloquial speech and descriptive imagery. The narrator of the story is Miss Edna Earle Ponder, one of the last living members of a once-prominent family, who manages the Beulah Hotel in Clay, Miss. She tells a traveling salesman the history of her family and fellow townsfolk." Merriam-Webster's Ency of Lit

Welty, Eudora

★ The **robber** bridegroom; designed and illustrated by Barry Moser. Harcourt Brace Jovanovich 1987 134p il $19.95

ISBN 0-15-178318-7

LC 87-21195

A reissue of the title first published 1942 by Doubleday

"Miss Welty uses the magic of metaphor and simile like a lyric poet, and writes with a limpid purity, and exquisite sense of descriptive coloring that gives a warm glow of beauty to a fantastic, and unfortunately sometimes tiresome story." Springfield Repub

Welty, Eudora

Stories, essays & memoir; [selected and annotated by Richard Ford and Michael Kreyling] Library of Am. 1998 976p il $35

ISBN 1-88301-155-8

LC 97-46691

Includes bibliographical references

Werfel, Franz

★ The **forty** days of Musa Dagh. Viking 1934 824p

Original German edition, 1933; published in the United Kingdom with title: The forty days

"Gabriel Bagradian returns to his ancestral village in Syria, where he learns that the Turks are disarming the Armenians and sending them into exile. Gabriel plans the resistance to the Turks and directs the fortification of the mountain Musa Dagh. The Turks are successfully repulsed a number of times but at great cost in lives to the Armenians on the mountain. On the fortieth day the remnant of the Armenian force is rescued by the French." Shapiro. Fic for Youth. 3d edition

Werfel, Franz

The **song** of Bernadette; translated by Ludwig Lewisohn. Viking 1942 575p

Original German edition, 1941

A slightly fictionalized version of "the life of Saint Bernadette of Lourdes. While it is not exactly a religious work, it is truly reverent in its approach to the inscrutable, the unfathomable, the divine. There is an engrossing picture of emperor, bishops, priests, nuns, merchants and artisans. A living pageant of the second Empire in France." Ont Libr Rev

Wesley, Mary

Part of the furniture. Viking 1997 256p

LC 96-46226

"Wesley's skill with character development and her subtle, amusing dissection of that paramount British preoccupation, family background and breeding, endow this novel with the charm of a comedy of manners and the enduring appeal of a satisfying love story." Publ Wkly

The **Wesleyan** anthology of science fiction; edited by Arthur B. Evans . . . [et al.] Wesleyan University Press 2010 767p $85; pa $39.95

ISBN 978-0-8195-6954-7; 978-0-8195-6955-4 pa

LC 2009-53144

"This anthology offers an overview from the works of Nathaniel Hawthorne and Jules Verne to those of William Gibson—so thorough with its brief, informative analyses at the start of each story, reading this collection is like taking a course without the bother of tests." Washington City Paper

Wesselmann, Debbie Lee

Captivity. John F. Blair, Publisher 2008 295p $22.95

ISBN 978-089587-353-8; 0-89587-353-2

LC 2007-37816

"Primatologist Dana Armstrong is passionate about making a difference in the lives of the animals living at a South Carolina chimpanzee sanctuary. But a break-in resulting in the escape of numerous chimpanzees forces Dana to not only determine who was responsible for the vandalism but also deal with her traumatic memories of the past—for Dana is a survivor of a psychological experiment, raised as a child with a chimp named Annie. She now faces opposition from the local community, political pressure from her university, and a ghost from her past who is bent upon her destruction. . . . [The author combines] a riveting plot with exciting characters to hold you spellbound until the last page." Libr J

West, Dorothy

★ The **wedding**. Doubleday 1995 240p hardcover o.p. pa $12.95

ISBN 0-385-47143-2; 0-385-47144-0 pa

LC 94-27285

"Through the ancestral histories of the Coles family, West . . . subtly reveals the ways in which color can burden and codify behavior. The author makes her points with a delicate hand, maneuvering with confidence and ease through a sometimes incendiary subject." Publ Wkly

West, Jessamyn

★ The **friendly** persuasion. Harcourt 1945 214p hardcover o.p. pa $13

ISBN 0-15-133605-9; 0-15-602909-X pa

"The Birdwell family of Indiana led a quiet life until the Civil War came into their lives. They were Quakers and tried to live according to the teachings of William Penn. Jess Birdwell, a nurseryman, loved a fast horse as well as his trees and the people he knew. Eliza, his wife, was a Quaker minister and a gentle, albeit strict, soul. When the war reached Indiana, Josh, the oldest son, was torn between his Quaker upbringing and his belief in the rightness of the Union cause; Mattie was at that difficult age between childhood and womanhood; and Little Jess, the youngest, ran into trouble with Eliza's geese. This is a wonderful family chronicle, with the laughter, tears, and tenderness that can be found in many families." Shapiro. Fic for Youth. 3d edition

West, Morris L.

★ The **clowns** of God; [by] Morris West. St. Martin's Press 1990 370p $19.95

ISBN 0-312-04459-3

LC 89-70344

A reissue of the title first published 1981 by Morrow

"The fugitive ex-pope posits all the fearful questions about life that have perplexed us since Hiroshima. West's ultimate answers will disturb some and be dismissed by others, but no one will be left unmoved. The sheer power of his prose and his keen understanding of human nature make this novel a stunning accomplishment." Libr J

Followed by Lazarus

West, Morris L.

The **devil's** advocate. Morrow 1959 319p

"The characters all are firmly, brightly established. The writing, without fanciness or flourish, goes along with a fine, steady drive. There are no profound insights, no remarkable illuminations. But there is an engrossing story, expertly told, about a set of fascinating people whose lives are viewed as meaningful." Chicago Sunday Trib

West, Morris L.

Lazarus; {by} Morris West. St. Martin's Press 1990 293p

LC 89-77919

"A tense and exciting thriller, Lazarus also explores world crises and theological politics quite as fascinating to non-Catholics as to Catholics. . . . While the book can be read as a complement to the other two novels, it stands alone as a superb, absorbing novel." Libr J

West, Morris L.

The **shoes** of the fisherman; a novel. Morrow 1963 374p

In this first title in the author's Vatican trilogy, "a humble Ukrainian pope finds himself the central negotiator in an attempt to prevent the United States and the Soviet Union from starting World War III. During the negotiations, the pope must confront the Russian who once tortured him. The work, a popular and critical success, demonstrates West's concern with modern man's inability to communicate with his brother." McCormick and Fletcher. Spy Fic

Followed by The clowns of God

West, Nathanael

Novels and other writings. Library of Am. 1997 829p $35

ISBN 1-88301-128-0

LC 96-49007

"Each of West's novels is distinct in style and theme. In the Dada-inspired The Dream Life of Balso Snell (1931), he freely mixes high-flown literary and religious allusions with erotic and scatological humor. Miss Lonelyhearts (1933) presents, in a series of grotesque, starkly etched episodes, the spiritual breakdown of a newspaper columnist overwhelmed by his readers' suffering. By contrast, A Cool Million (1934) reduces the eternal optimism of Horatio Alger's novels to a brutal, cartoonish farce. In his last work, The Day of the Locust (1939), West renders with hallucinatory precision the reverse side of the Hollywood dream, as he choreographs a cast of failures, has-beens, and deluded glamour-seekers in what becomes an apocalyptic dance of death. Also included is a generous sampling of West's other surviving work, ranging from freewheeling improvisations and grotesque comic tales to more mainstream work written with Hollywood or Broadway in mind." Publisher's note

West, Rebecca

The **birds** fall down. Viking 1966 435p

LC 67-10214

"This is a great work of literature. . . . Rebecca West was fascinated by espionage and from her knowledge of Russian emigres she created a comprehensive picture of their preoccupations and torments at the turn of the century." McCormick and Fletcher. Spy Fic

Westerfeld, Scott

The **killing** of worlds. TOR Bks. 2003 336p (Succession) hardcover o.p. pa $14.95

ISBN 0-7653-0850-9; 0-7653-2052-5 pa

LC 2003-56304

Sequel to The risen empire

"Captain Laurent Zai demonstrates his strategic cleverness as well as an unusual amount of luck, when he unexpectedly defeats the Rix ship he was sent to destroy—an assignment intended to be a suicide mission. Meanwhile, in the imperial senate, Nara Oxham walks a fine line between treason and her party's agenda as she fights the emperor himself. . . . [This is] a rip-roaring space opera, with its strength residing in the characters, all of them involved in believable dilemmas." Booklist

Westerfeld, Scott

The **risen** empire. TOR Bks. 2003 304p (Succession) hardcover o.p. pa $14.95

ISBN 0-7653-0555-0; 0-7653-1998-5 pa

LC 2002-42952

"Westerfeld's speculations about the rise and fall of civilizations are appealingly quirky . . . and his action scenes have a breathless realism that does not gloss over the bloody nature of combat. Perhaps most important, his moral calculus never lapses into Q.E.D. As the narrative jumps from intimate glimpses of the Empire to the Rix Cult and back again, we grow less and less clear about whom we are rooting for." N Y Times Book Rev

Followed by The killing of worlds (2003)

Western Writers of America

American West: twenty new stories from the Western Writers of America; edited with an introduction by Loren D. Estleman. Forge 2001 367p $25.95

ISBN 0-312-87317-4

LC 00-48446

This collection of stories about the West includes works by Don Coldsmith, Jory Sherman, Elmer Kelton, Richard S. Wheeler, Johnny D. Boggs, and Max Evans

"Uniformly fine writing makes this a welcome addition to any western collection." Booklist

Western Writers of America

Westward; a fictional history of the American West: 28 original stories celebrating the 50th anniversary of the Western Writers of America. edited by Dale L. Walker. Forge 2003 432p $25.95

ISBN 0-7653-0451-1

LC 2002-45481

"The collection reveals both the vitality and the diversity of the western genre as well as the enduring appeal of the short story." Booklist

Westheimer, David

★ **Von** Ryan's Express. Doubleday 1964 327p

"Colonel Joseph Ryan is shot down over Italy and is sent to a prisoner-of-war camp, where he imposes military discipline upon the other prisoners. After Italy's surrender, when the prisoners are put on a train for Germany, Ryan plans a daring takeover of the train and gets the men to Switzerland." Shapiro. Fic for Youth. 2d edition

Followed by Von Ryan's return (1980)

Westlake, Donald E.

✓★ The **ax**. Mysterious Press 1997 273p

LC 96-52068

"As novels go, 'The Ax' is pretty much flawless, with a surprise ending that will unplug your expectations. Burke Devore is American Man at the millennium—as emblematic of his time as George F. Babbitt and Holden Caulfield and Capt. John Yossarian were of theirs. Westlake has written a remarkable book. If you can't relate to it, be thankful." N Y Times Book Rev

Westlake, Donald E.

✓ **Baby,** would I lie? a romance of the Ozarks. Mysterious Press 1994 291p

LC 93-40485

This comic mystery, featuring characters from the author's Trust me on this, "is set in 'the new Nashville': Branson, Missouri. Singer Ray Jones is accused of one murder and then of a second. Out on bail, he continues to entertain in this theater. Meanwhile, an army of troops from the sleazy tabloid Weekly Galaxy descends to bug offices, lie, infiltrate, and do anything else necessary to get some sort of story on the upcoming trial. Also arriving are reporters Sara and Jack, lovers and representatives of a trendy New York magazine called Trend: The Magazine for the Way We Live This Instant. The action is jet-fast, and the satiric commentary on country western stars and fans is wonderfully wicked." Libr J

Westlake, Donald E.

Bad news; by Donald Westlake. Mysterious Press 2001 342p $30

ISBN 0-89296-717-X

LC 00-45592

"Westlake has a genius for comic strategy, and the complications he devises when the casino operators initiate a counterplot to discredit Little Feather have a lunatic brilliance worthy of Abbott and Costello. But Westlake is also a card with characters, and he flashes that talent to terrific effect here." N Y Times Book Rev

Westlake, Donald E.

★ **Bank** shot. Simon & Schuster 1972 224p

It is Westlake's "triumph that whereas on one hand the reader knows he simply can't take the characters and situations seriously, those characters are so deftly drawn that they are eminently believable." N Y Times Book Rev

Westlake, Donald E.

Don't ask. Mysterious Press 1993 327p $18.95

ISBN 0-89296-469-3

LC 92-53721

"If the plot is of no great concern, it is the effortlessness, wit, and sheer good-heartedness of the telling that make 'Don't Ask' such a consistent delight." N Y Times Book Rev

Westlake, Donald E.

Drowned hopes. Mysterious Press 1990 422p

ISBN 0-89296-178-3

LC 89-35859

In this "comedy-mystery, ex-con John Dortmunder and his benevolent criminal cohorts are continuously frustrated in their attempts to recover $700,000 in stolen money from a 50-foot-deep reservoir in upper New York State." Booklist

Westlake, Donald E.

Get real. Grand Central Publishing 2009 278p $23.99

ISBN 978-0-446-17860-0; 0-446-17860-8

LC 2008-933234

"A rollicking crime caper that pulls the pants right off the reality TV industry." N Y Times Book Rev

Westlake, Donald E.

Good behavior. Mysterious Press 1985 244p

ISBN 0-89296-240-2

LC 85-43178

The author "manages to create characters who are a curious mixture of stereotypes and archetypes. If he is a master of the comic crime caper, and he is, he also does what the best comic writers throughout history have done—make a comment on society." N Y Times Book Rev

Westlake, Donald E.

The **hook**. Mysterious Press 2000 280p $30

ISBN 0-89296-588-6

LC 99-36273

"Westlake salts the stew with lots of fascinating publishing shoptalk, and his portrayal of the psychological unraveling of a writer is made all the more chilling by the quiet realism of its presentation. A fine thriller." Booklist

Westlake, Donald E.

★ The **hot** rock. Simon & Schuster 1970 249p

This novel "comes awesomely close to the ultimate in comic, big-caper novels; it's . . . filled with mocking style and action and imagination." N Y Times Book Rev

Westlake, Donald E.

★ **Memory**. Hard Case Crime 2010 366p pa $7.99

ISBN 0-8439-6375-1; 978-0-8439-6375-5

In this "novel that Westlake wrote in the early 1960s and never published, Paul Cole suffers from partial amnesia—his past is just beyond the reach of his mind. He keeps moving, like a fugitive, through a succession of working-class jobs; he falls in love; he gets in trouble with the law. Westlake never again dabbled in social realism, which is a shame: Memory is terse and bleak and low-key emotional, and as indelible as Westlake's other books." Entertainment Wkly

Westlake, Donald E.

Money for nothing. Mysterious Press 2003 294p $24.95

ISBN 0-89296-787-0

LC 2002-35888

"Although Westlake has written funnier books and his characters could use more dimension, 'Money for Nothing' has all of his trademarks: an ample supply of silliness and suspense wrapped up in a wacky plot." N Y Times Book Rev

Westlake, Donald E.

Put a lid on it. Mysterious Press 2002 247p $23.95

ISBN 0-89296-718-8

LC 2001-51435

This is a "crime caper that also gets some nice digs in as political satire. . . . Although Meehan isn't quite as ingenious a thief as some of Westlake's other criminal protagonists, he's a born philosopher." N Y Times Book Rev

Westlake, Donald E.

The **road** to ruin. Mysterious Press 2004 342p $25

ISBN 0-89296-801-X

LC 2003-65007

"Ingenuity fuels the plot, but what puts the match to the comedy is the moral outrage of the furiously funny characters." N Y Times Book Rev

Westlake, Donald E.

Smoke. Mysterious Press 1995 454p

ISBN 0-89296-534-7

LC 94-48254

"Though Mr. Westlake is a virtuoso plotter, the point of his books, here as ever, is to be found in the interstices. Wicked one-liners and testy miniature monologues about whatever happens to be on the author's mind are scattered generously throughout. The implications of invisibility are played for laughs with near-arrogant skill." N Y Times Book Rev

Westlake, Donald E.

Thieves' dozen. Mysterious Press 2004 183p pa $12.95

ISBN 0-446-69302-2 pa

LC 2003-70612

A collection of Dortmunder stories. "The swift succession of heists, getaways, scrapes, and screwups gathered in Thieves' Dozen epitomizes the venal joys of the comic caper. . . . The short-story form is well suited to Westlake's sly shenanigans, and he even finds room for snippets of the Runyonesque repartee that gives this inspired nonsense just the right touch of absurd panache." Booklist

Westlake, Donald E.

Trust me on this. Mysterious Press 1988 293p

LC 87-22098

"In between stories about space battles, 100-year-old twins, dead country music stars and bizarre medical happenings, Mr. Westlake has sandwiched a nice romance and a fairish murder mystery." N Y Times Book Rev

Westlake, Donald E.

Watch your back. Mysterious Press 2005 310p $24.95

ISBN 0-89296-802-8

LC 2004-61064

"Arnie Albright, a fence so obnoxious his family intervened and sent him to Club Med in hopes he'd become more likable, has returned from the resort minimally improved, but having met the man of his dreams Preston Fareweather, a millionaire who's as comically distasteful as Arnie and who, more importantly, plans to be away from his art-filled New York penthouse indefinitely, on the run from hordes of furious ex-wives. Albright calls in Dortmunder and his pals to take advantage of Fareweather's absence. . . . Events unfold in a delicious sequence, and every step is complemented by great writing." Publ Wkly

Westlake, Donald E.

What's so funny? Warner 2007 359p $24.99

ISBN 9780446582407; 0-446-58240-9

This caper has "an ending so laden with irony it almost has you thinking that crime doesn't pay. But of course it does pay, in those laughs that land on every page." N Y Times Book Rev

Westlake, Donald E.

What's the worst that could happen? Mysterious Press 1996 373p

LC 96-12770

"Although the gang's dirty tricks are wonderfully ingenious, the characters deliver the real razzle-dazzle. A grandiose guy like Max is cut to order for Mr. Westlake's droll comic style, which reflects a kind of gleeful horror at the schlocky esthetics of the rich and the morally damned." N Y Times Book Rev

Wharton, Edith

The **children**. Scribner 282p $25

ISBN 0-684-18453-2

First published 1928 by D. Appleton & Co.

Standing at the rail of the liner, Martin Boyne surveyed his fellow-passengers in the act of coming aboard. 'Not a soul I shall want to speak to—as usual!' was his comment. Then he saw Judy Wheater carrying a fat, rosy baby up the gang plank and he changed his mind. Judy was only sixteen, but there was nothing inexperienced in the way she herded her troupe of brothers and sisters and 'steps' over to Europe while her father and mother played at divorce and remarriage. For a whole summer, Martin, old bachelor that he was, joined forces with Judy in her gallant attempt to keep her flock together

Wharton, Edith

Collected stories, 1891-1910; [Maureen Howard selected the contents and wrote the notes for this volume] Library of Am. 2001 928p $35

ISBN 1-88301-193-0

LC 00-57596

Includes bibliographical references

Wharton, Edith

Collected stories, 1911-1937; edited by Maureen Howard. Library of Am. 2001 848p $35

ISBN 1-88301-194-9

LC 00-57595

Includes bibliographical references

Wharton, Edith

★ **Ethan** Frome. Scribner 1997 195p hardcover o.p. pa $13

ISBN 0-684-82591-0 pa

First published 1911

This is "an ironic tragedy of love, frustration, jealousy, and sacrifice. The scene is a New England village, where Ethan barely makes a living out of a stony farm and is at odds with his wife Zeena (short for Zenobia), a whining hypochondriac. Mattie, a cousin of Zeena's comes to live with them, and love develops between her and Ethan. They try to end their impossible lives by steering a bobsled into a tree; instead ending up crippled and tied for the rest of their unhappy time on earth to Zeena and the barren farm. Zeena, however, is transformed into a devoted nurse and Mattie becomes the nagging invalid." Benet's Reader's Ency of Am Lit

Wharton, Edith

New York novels; foreword by Louis Auchincloss. Modern Lib. 1998 xxi, 958p $27.95

ISBN 0-679-60302-6

LC 98-5465

Contents: The house of mirth (1905); The custom of the country (1913); The age of innocence (1920)

Wharton, Edith

Novellas and other writings. Library of Am. 1990 1137p il $45

ISBN 0-940450-53-4

LC 89-62930

In Madame de Treymes (1907), an American woman living in Paris tries to break her engagement with a local aristocrat. Ethan Frome is entered separately. Summer (1917) tells the story of Charity Royall, an adopted New England girl in a poor village who falls in love with a young architect from the city. Old New York (1924) is a collection of four novellas, each set in four different decades: False dawn, The old maid, The spark, and New Year's Day. In The mother's recompense (1925), a promiscuous mother moves in with her daughter only to discover her daughter's fiancee was once one of her own lovers. A backward glance (1934) is the author's autobiography.

Includes bibliographical references

Wharton, Edith

Novels. Library of America 1985 1328p $40

ISBN 0-940450-31-3

LC 85-191816

The house of mirth, The custom of the country, and the age of innocence are entered separately. In the reef (1912), the "action is confined almost exclusively to a chateau in France and the issue narrowed to a psychological struggle in the mind of the heroine, Anna Leath, who discovers that the man she has agreed to marry has had an affair with the young woman who is about to marry her stepson." Ref Guide to Am Lit. 2d edition

Wharton, Edith

The **selected** short stories of Edith Wharton; introduced and edited by R.W.B. Lewis. Scribner 1991 xxi, 390p $24.95

ISBN 0-684-19304-3

LC 91-11433

A "collection of 21 of the author's best stories. Lewis' excellent introduction explains Wharton's appeal and provides a brief overview of her life and prolific literary output." Booklist

Wharton, William

★ **Birdy**. Knopf 1979 309p

ISBN 0-394-42569-3

LC 77-28023

"Only the most rigorous imagination can make a story of this sort work for a reader who is generally indifferent to birds. Wharton has just such an imagination." Newsweek

Wharton, William

Dad; a novel. Knopf 1981 449p

LC 80-2725

"It's an old story, this man-in-the-middle business, but fresh in Wharton's telling because he lets experience—lunch, a crisis, baseball on TV—accumulate as naturally and surely as aging itself." Saturday Rev

Wheeler, Richard S.

The **canyon** of bones. Forge 2007 330p $24.95

ISBN 978-0-7653-1324-9; 0-7653-1324-3

LC 2006-102846

"Overall, this is genial, character-driven western writing with plenty of action and appreciation for Native American customs. Skye's foul-mouthed Crow wife, Victoria, is absolutely delightful, and even his cantankerous horse, Jawbone, has more personality than most western leads. Not just for fans of the series, this will appeal to anyone in search of solidly adventuresome tales." Booklist

Wheeler, Richard S.

Eclipse. Forge 2002 380p $27.95

ISBN 0-312-87846-X

LC 2001-58978

After returning home to a hero's welcome in 1806 "Meriwether Lewis floundered as the governor of the Louisiana Territory, Beset by financial and political difficulties, a depressed and despondent Lewis apparently either committed suicide or was murdered in the Tennessee backwoods in 1809. Wheeler ponders that puzzle, constructing a chilling scenario in which a delusional, syphilis-wracked Lewis feels duty bound to end his fife rather than bring shame upon his name, his family, and his beloved Corps of Discovery. A riveting re-creation of the tragic final years of an American legend." Booklist

Wheeler, Richard S.

North Star; a Barnaby Skye novel. Forge 2009 320p $25.95

ISBN 978-0-7653-1663-9; 0-7653-1663-3

LC 2009-278179

This novel in the author's series "featuring venerable mountain man Barnaby Skye, finds Skye—after more than 50 years of trapping beaver, hunting bear, fighting Indians and living outdoors—in constant rheumatic pain, losing his eyesight and wishing to live out his days in a house with a roof, a floor and a real bed. It is 1870, the fur business is dead and white men are taking all the Indian lands. His two Indian wives, Victoria and Mary, have different feelings about these changes. Victoria dreads leaving her Indian family for a white man's life, and Mary longs to see her son, Dirk, whom Skye had sent away to school several years earlier. There is little gun smoke, but plenty of suspense as Skye and Victoria confront brutal Texas cattlemen and cheating Indian agents, and Mary travels to St. Louis to find her son." Publ Wkly

Whitaker, Kayla Rae

The **animators**; a novel. Kayla Rae Whitaker. Random House Inc 2016 384 p. (ebook) $65; $27

ISBN 9780812989298; 9780812989281

LC 2015049662

In this novel, by Kayla Rae Whitaker, "in the male-dominated field of animation, Mel Vaught and Sharon Kisses are a dynamic duo. . . . After a decade of striving, the two are finally celebrating the release of their first full-length feature, which transforms Mel's difficult childhood into a provocative and visually daring work of art. . . . But with their success come doubt and destruction, cracks in their relationship threatening the delicate balance of their partnership." (Publisher's note)

White, Bailey

Quite a year for plums; a novel. Knopf 1998 220p $22

ISBN 0-679-44531-5

LC 97-41124

"The women in town are worried about Roger, the peanut virologist. Hilma and Meade discuss him at their weekly readings. Eula frets over his welfare—not to mention his appetite. And everyone else just seems to be content with giving opinions on his budding romance with the strange bird artist, Della. . . . {The author} will make the reader care about this nurturing gaggle of women and other community members in a small, sleepy town in southern Georgia." Libr J

White, Edmund

The **beautiful** room is empty. Knopf 1988 227p

LC 87-40495

In this sequel to A boy's own story, the author "follows our nameless hero from his final year at prep school in the mid-1950s through his cruisy but self-deprecating college years to the 'turning point' in his life—the famous Stonewall uprising of 1969 in which the clients of a New York gay bar stood up to the policemen trying to close it down. What emerges is the picture of a young man desperately struggling to come to terms with himself, a struggle that is a universal even if the context for every individual is different. Artfully constructed, this work clearly transcends its 'gay' theme." Libr J

Followed by The farewell symphony

White, Edmund

★ A **boy's** own story. Dutton 1982 217p hardcover o.p. pa $14

ISBN 978-0-14-311484-0

LC 82-9536

This first-person novel is "written with the flourish of a master stylist. . . . It is an endearing portrait of a child's longing to be charming, popular, powerful, and loved, and of his struggles with adults . . . {told with} sensitivity and elegance." Harpers

Followed by The beautiful room is empty (1988) and The farewell symphony (1997)

White, Edmund

Hotel de Dream; a New York novel. Ecco 2007 225p $23.95

ISBN 978-0-06-085225-2; 0-06-085225-9

LC 2007-29872

"The American novelist Stephen Crane, according to an unreliable contemporary, began a book about a male prostitute. As no such manuscript survives, White steps in with an artfully pulpy tale about Elliott, a teenage newsboy in New York, who is kept by a married banker. As frame and counterpoint, he shows us Crane, terminally tubercular, summoning his remaining strength to dictate "The Painted Boy" to his common-law wife, who transports him from England to the Black Forest in a vain search for a cure. White illuminates Crane's literary milieu, the urban gay subculture of his time, and the relationship of a writer's experience to his fiction." New Yorker

White, Edmund

Jack Holmes and his friend; Edmund White. Bloomsbury 2012

ISBN 1608197034; 9781608197033

LC 2011014728

'This "book maps . . . the friendship of a gay man and a heterosexual in the buttoned-up 1950s, the experimental '60s and, finally, to the first intimations of AIDS. . . . The young men meet in New York when they're both fresh from college. Jack, a Midwesterner with a 'Gothic horror novel' of a childhood, attended the University of Michigan; Will, a foxhunting Southerner of large lineage and small funds, attended Princeton. . . . Relatively early on, Jack introduces Will to Alex, the girl he will eventually marry, and the novel tracks the three of them through years of romantic strife." (Washington Post)

White, Edmund

The **married** man; a love story. Knopf 2000 321p $25

ISBN 0-375-40005-2

LC 99-53980

"A shrewd social observer with a great gift for dialogue, White composes quicksilver scenes bright with wit, then sets aside comedy-of-manners for the luster of tragedy." Booklist

White, Elle Katharine

Heartstone; Elle Katharine White. Harper Voyager 2016 352 p. (paperback) $15.99; (ebook) $14.99

ISBN 9780062451941; 9780062451958

LC 2016018398

This historical fantasy novel, by Elle Katharine White, "recasts Jane Austen's beloved 'Pride & Prejudice' in an imaginative world of wyverns, dragons, and the warriors who fight alongside them against the monsters that threaten the kingdom: gryphons, direwolves, lamias, banshees, and lindworms." (Publisher's note)

"Referencing Austen just enough to ground her characters, White fills her unusual fantasy world with plenty of interesting conflicts to fuel this tale of romance and heroism." Pub Wkly

White, Karen

The **night** the lights went out; Karen White. Berkley 2017 406 p. (hardcover) $26

ISBN 9780451488381; 9780451488398

LC 2016053299

In this book, by Karen White, "recently divorced, Merilee Talbot Dunlap moves with her two children to the Atlanta suburb of Sweet Apple, Georgia. . . . Merilee finds some measure of peace in the cottage she is renting from town matriarch Sugar Prescott. Though stubborn and irascible, Sugar sees something of herself in Merilee--something that allows her to open up about her own colorful past." (Publisher's note)

"An atmospheric and entertaining look at the friends who keep your secrets—and the friends who keep you guessing until it's too late." Kirkus

White, Kate

A **body** to die for. Warner Bks. 2003 294p $23.95

ISBN 0-446-53148-0

LC 2003-41081

"Once again, White's background as editor-in-chief of 'Cosmopolitan' shines through in her snappy dialog, tight plotting, and insider humor. . . . A breezy beach read for mystery fans." Libr J

White, Kate

Lethally blond. Warner Books 2007 323p $24.99

ISBN 978-0-446-57795-3; 0-446-57795-2

LC 2007-447

"White's flair for pop culture and affection for single career women make this trendy romantic suspense cocktail an addictive read." Publ Wkly

White, Randy Wayne

Black widow. G.P. Putnam's Sons 2008 337p $24.95

ISBN 978-0-399-15456-0; 0-399-15456-6

LC 2008-859

"Like Robert B. Parker and John D. MacDonald at their best, White draws readers into his world with characters you'd pay just to hang out with and then hooks us with straight-ahead action. It's an old-school combination, but it still works just fine." Booklist

White, Randy Wayne

Deep shadow. G.P. Putnam's Sons 2010 353p $25.95

ISBN 978-0-399-15626-7

LC 2009-51083

At the outset of this Doc Ford thriller, "two low-life ex-cons, King and Perry, are on the lam after killing a family of five in a burglary. They end up in Doc's neck of the woods, or rather his neck of the swamp, in central Florida. Doc; his boat-bum hipster pal, Tomlinson; troubled Indian teen Will Chaser, who played a key role in Dead Silence; and Arlis Futch, a crusty old fisherman, have arrived at a small lake, which they intend to search for Batista's treasure plane, which disappeared in 1958 while flying the ex-dictator's looted booty out of Cuba during the Castro takeover. King and Perry, who are as bad as they come, quickly take control of the others, forcing Doc and friends to continue diving in the lake, after which the pair plan to kill them all. Throw in a giant, mysterious swamp creature with an appetite for cattle, horses, and divers, and you've got a nail-biter that's virtually impossible to put down." Publ Wkly

White, Roseanna M.

A **lady** unrivaled; Roseanna M. White. Bethany House 2016 408 p. (Ladies of the Manor) (paperback) $14.99

ISBN 9780764213526; 9781441230539

LC 2016938542

In this book in the Ladies of the Manor series, by Roseanna M. White, "all her life everyone has tried to protect . . . [Lady Ella Myerston] from the realities of the world, but Ella knows . . . the danger that has haunted her brother and their friend. . . . Lord Cayton . . . [is] determined to live a better life. But that proves [to be] complicated when old friends arrive on the scene. . . . He does his best to remove . . . Ella from danger, but . . . [she] won't budge." (Publisher's note)

"Readers will be kept guessing through the final page, thrilled by the butterflies of Ella and Cayton's courtship and abuzz in the series' heart-pounding finale." Booklist

White, Stephen Walsh

Dry ice; a novel. Dutton 2007 401p $25.95

ISBN 978-0-525-94997-8

LC 2006-26771

Sequel to Kill me

"Contemporary cerebral thrillers don't get much better than . . . [this novel], which deftly combines complex characterization and intricate plotting." Publ Wkly

White, Stephen Walsh

Kill me; a novel. [by] Stephen White. Dutton 2006 402p $25.95

ISBN 0-525-94930-5

LC 2005-24296

"In this installment of the . . . series starring clinical psychologist Dr. Alan Gregory, the setting remains the picturesque Colorado countryside, but White sends Dr. Gregory to the background and instead features one of his patients, an unnamed, happily married businessman with an adventurous streak. After a near-fatal crash during a Canadian skiing expedition, coupled with a friend's accident, our hero begins to question his own mortality and vows never to be a burden to his family. When he gets word of an organization that, for a hefty fee, will end your life should you become 'a burden,' he rather hastily signs up.But what if you discover you have a slowly ticking time bomb in your head, and while death could come at any moment, it might not be right away? How do you say not quite yet" to your personal hit men?. . . . Bizarre, thrilling, and oh so much fun." Booklist

White, Stephen Walsh

Missing persons; [by] Stephen White. Dutton 2005 391p $25.95

ISBN 0-525-94859-7

LC 2004-27172

"Eight years to the day after JonBenet Ramsey was murdered, her childhood friend and neighbor, Mallory, winds up missing. At first, her disappearance seems unconnected to the disappearance of Diane, one of Boulder (Colorado) psychologist Alan Gregory's colleagues, or the apparent murder of Diane's friend Hannah. But nothing is coincidental in a White murder mystery, and once again, he expertly places the good doctor in the middle of one doozy of a whodunit." Booklist

White, T. H.

The **book** of Merlyn; the unpublished conclusion to The once and future king. prologue by Sylvia Townsend Warner; illustrated by Trevor Stubley. University of Tex. Press 1977 xx, 137p il

LC 77-3454

Sequel to The once and future king

"Writing during World War II, White vented his feelings about the futility of war with a fierceness that sometimes overwhelms the intriguing mixture of fantasy, humor, and rationality which pervaded the tetralogy." Booklist

White, T. H.

★ The **once** and future king. Putnam 1958 677p $25.95

ISBN 0-399-10597-2

LC 58-10760

"White's contemporary retelling of Malory's Le Morte d'Arthur is both romantic and exciting." Shapiro. Fic for Youth. 3d edition

White, T. H.

The **sword** in the stone; with decorations by the author and end papers by Robert Lawson. Putnam 1939

First published 1938 in the United Kingdom

"Delightful, fantastic, satirical nonsense, for the reader with a background of Arthurian legend." Wis Libr Bull

Followed by The witch in the wood

Whitehead, Colson

Apex hides the hurt. Doubleday 2006 212p $22.95

ISBN 0-385-50795-X

LC 2005-49391

"The protagonist of Apex Hides the Hurt is a nomenclature consultant. If you want just the right name for your new product, whether it be automobile or antidepressant, sneaker or spoon, he's the man to get the job done. . . . After leaving his job (following a mysterious misfortune), his expertise is called upon by the town of Winthrop. Once there, he meets the town council, who will try to sway his opinion over the coming days. Lucky Aberdeen, the millionaire software pioneer and hometown-boy-made-good, wants [Winthrop's] name changed to something that will reflect the town's capitalist aspirations, attracting new businesses and revitalizing the community. . . . Albie Winthrop, beloved son of the town's aristocracy, thinks Winthrop is a perfectly good name, and can't imagine what the fuss is about. Regina Goode, the mayor, is a descendent of the black settlers who founded the town, and has her own secret agenda for what the name should be." (Publisher's note)

"A secretive narrator often means the story is weak and has to be puffed up with mystery, but Whitehead's gorgeous, expertly crafted sentences help the reader past the novel's slow start. . . . We are slowly filled in on the limp, the misfortune, the meaning of the title–and we're treated to an eloquent novel about racial identity in America. . . . What could have been an academic exercise becomes a smart tale about who we are under our labels." Newsweek

Whitehead, Colson

The **intuitionist**; a novel. Anchor Bks. (NY) 1999 255p $19.95

ISBN 0-385-49299-5

LC 98-6756

This "novel follows the travails of the redoubtable Lila Mae Watson, the first black woman Elevator Inspector in a nameless city very much like New York. Caught between the political machinations of the two factions of the Elevator Guild (the Intuitionists, like Lila, inspect the elevators by a sort of sympathetic insight, whereas the Empiricists actually examine the cables and helical springs), Lila Mae finds herself in the midst of a murky underground war for control over the kingdom of Vertical Transport. Whitehead's prose is graceful and often lyrical and his elevator underworld is a complex, lovingly realized creation." New Yorker

Whitehead, Colson

John Henry Days; a novel. Doubleday 2001 389p $24.95

ISBN 0385498195

LC 00-43143

The protagonist of this novel is "a young freelance journalist named J. Sutter. . . . J. is black. . . . He is a 'junketeer,' an 'inveigler of invites,' an 'open bar opportunist.' . . . His love life consists of sterile biweekly couplings with a publicist named Monica. He has no discernible connection with his family. He lives in a bubble of educational privilege and ironic knowingness. . . . The novel's main action unfolds on a weekend in July 1996, when a Web site sends J. to Talcott, W.Va., to cover the unveiling of a John Henry postage stamp and the inauguration of a local festival called John Henry Days." (N Y Times Book Rev)

"Whitehead relishes slashing through the mindlessness of the age in a voice so intelligent and an idiom so imaginative that it can lift a reader right out of his chair. But he is not remorseless. He likes these people and respects their longings. They have no moral compass, but he has, so we can laugh at them but still grieve for the loss of so much possiblility." N Y Times Book Rev

Whitehead, Colson

Sag Harbor; a novel. Doubleday 2009 288p $24.95

ISBN 978-0-385-52765-1; 0-385-52765-9

LC 2008-13510

Benji, one of the only black kids at an elite prep school in Manhattan, tries desperately to fit in, but every summer, he and his brother, Reggie, escape to the East End of Sag Harbor, where a small community of African American professionals has built a world of its own.

The author "serves up whole sundaes worth of riffs on the quotidian, all hung on the skinny frame of a 15-year-old everyman virgin and his marginally less distinct friends, give or take a repressive father and a particularly evocative shoreline landscape." Village Voice

Whitehead, Colson

★ The **underground** railroad; a novel. Colson Whitehead. Doubleday 2016 336 p. (hardcover) $26.95

ISBN 9780385542364; 0385542364; 0385537034; 9780385537032

LC 2016000643

Carnegie Medal: Fiction (2017)
Pulitzer Prize: Fiction (2017)
National Book Award: Fiction (2016)
Kirkus Prize Finalist: Fiction (2016)

In this novel, by Colson Whitehead, "Cora is a slave on a cotton plantation in Georgia. Life is hell for all the slaves, but especially bad for Cora; an outcast even among her fellow Africans, she is coming into womanhood--where even greater pain awaits. When Caesar, a recent arrival from Virginia, tells her about the Underground Railroad, they decide to take a terrifying risk and escape." (Publisher's note)

"Everything Whitehead describes is vividly, often joltingly realistic, even the novel's most fantastic element, his vision of this secret transport network as an actual railroad running through tunnels dug beneath the blood-soaked fields of the South, a jolting and resounding embodiment of heroic efforts and colossal risks." Booklist

Whitehead, Colson

Zone one. Doubleday 2011 259p $25.95

ISBN 0385528078; 9780385528078

LC 2011-08339

The book, a novel, is a "meditation on the solitude of urban living, written through the dramatizing lens of a zombie movie. . . . The protagonist - 'they called him Mark Spitz nowadays' - is one of the few survivors of an unspecified apocalyptic event.

"It's a book you want to read rather than one you should read. Sure, there are familiar paradigms: the pandemic subsides behind a foreground of chase scenes, us-or-them admonitions, even the occasional bite sequence. But Zone One is mercilessly free of cookie-cutter social commentaries—office culture is for mindless drones; technology destroys our ability to connect—while still providing the chilling, fleshy pleasures of zombies who lurch, pursue, hunger." Esquire

Whittall, Zoe

Holding still for as long as possible; Zoe Whittall. Anansi 2009 301 p. (pbk.) $15.95

ISBN 9780887849640; 9780887842344

LC 2009510336

Lambda Literary Awards: Transgender/Bisexual/Gay (2010)

In this book, author "Zoe Whittall follows a group of twentysomethings struggling to cope with their complicated lives. Trapped somewhere between growing up and being grown-ups, these would-be adults hide behind excessive drinking and partying, and use text messages to relay their emotions. The story focuses on three troubled young people: Billy, a former teen pop starlet who suffers from severe panic attacks; Josh, a paramedic whose ability to patch up injured patients parallels his inability to repair his own emotional damages; and Amy, a rich kid trying to live the Bohemian indie girl life while dealing with her first broken heart." (Quill & Quire)

Whittle, Tina

Blood, Ash, and Bone; A Tai Randolph Series. Poisoned Pen Press 2013 250 p. (Tai Randolph mysteries) $14.95

ISBN 1464200955; 9781464200953

In this, Tina Whittle's third Tai Randolph mystery, Tai decides "to help an ex-boyfriend retrieve a missing Civil War relic. . . . Some collectors are simply obsessed with owning valuable things, but others—such as members of the spruced-up, squeaky-clean-looking Ku Klux Klan—feed on the racist rage that saturates certain historical memorabilia." Tai pursues her investigation at a Civil War expo in Georgia. (Publishers Weekly)

Whittle, Tina

★ The **Dangerous** Edge of Things; a Tai Randolph mystery. Poisoned Pen Press 2011 281 p. (Tai Randolph mysteries) $24.95

ISBN 1590588177; 9781590588178; 9781590588192

In this Tai Randolph mystery from Tina Whittle, "Tai Randolph thinks inheriting a Confederate-themed gun shop is her biggest headache—until she finds a murdered corpse in her brother's driveway. Even worse, her supposedly respectable brother begins behaving in decidedly non-innocent ways, like fleeing to the Bahamas and leaving her with both a homicide in her lap and the pointed suspicions of the Atlanta PD directed her way." (Publisher's note)

Whittle, Tina

Darker than any shadow; a Tai Randolph mystery. 1st ed. Poisoned Pen Press 2012 (hardcover) $24.95; (paperback) $14.95; (paperback) $22.95

ISBN 1590585488; 9781590585467; 9781590585481; 9781590585474 large print

LC 2011933442

This is the second of Tina Whittle's Tai Randolph mysteries. Here, "Atlanta's performance poetry scene is sizzling, and Tai Randolph's friends are preparing to debut their team in a major competition. But this hipster world goes decidedly cold when one of the team members is knifed to death. Then there is another killing; suddenly a 'Dead Poet Killer' panic sets in. Tai's friend Rico (one of the poets) is suspected of the murder and needs her help." (Library Journal)

Whittle, Tina

Deeper than the grave; a Tai Randolph mystery. Tina Whittle. Poisoned Pen Press 2014 294 p. (trade pbk : alk. paper) $14.95

ISBN 1464202648; 9781464202629; 9781464202643

LC 2014938569

In this mystery novel, by Tina Whittle, "Tai Randolph has her new life together. She's running a semisuccessful Atlanta gun shop catering to Civil War re-enactors. . . . Then a tornado blows by a Kennesaw Mountain cemetery, scattering the skeletal remains of a Confederate hero. . . . Does she hit the jackpot on discovering a jumble of bones in the underbrush? No. The bones reveal a more recent murder." (Publisher's note)

"Whittle skillfully intertwines Civil War relics with modern-day re-enactors and the Darknet, "like the Internet, only without the safeguards," in her intricate fourth mystery featuring Atlanta gun shop operator Tai Randolph (after 2013's Blood, Ash, and Bone)." Pub Wkly

Whyte, Jack

The **singing** sword. Forge 1996 383p

LC 96-19966

"As the novel progresses, and the Roman Empire continues to decay, the colony of Camulod flourishes. But the lives of the colony's main characters, Gaius Publius Varrus—ironsmith, innovator and soldier—and his brother-in-law, former Roman Senator Caius Britannicus, are not trouble-free, especially when their most bitter enemy, Claudius Seneca, reappears. . . . Whyte provides rich detail about the forging of superior weaponry, the breeding of horses, the training of cavalrymen, the growth of a lawmaking body within the community and the origins of the Round Table." Publ Wkly

Followed by The eagles' brood

Wibberley, Leonard

★ The **mouse** that roared. Little, Brown 1955 279p

LC 54-8294

"The 'Tiny Twenty' overtake the major powers of the world after plotting a bold maneuver to steal the atomic secrets of the United States. Centuries of industrialization and sophistication separate the tiny European nation from the enraged larger countries, who must acquiesce to the will of the former. Underneath this lighthearted tale is a serious warning about the dangers of nuclear power." Shapiro. Fic for Youth. 3d edition

Wickersham, Joan

The **news** from Spain; seven variations on a love story. Joan Wickersham. Alfred A. Knopf 2012 208 p. $24.95

ISBN 0307958884; 9780307958884

LC 2012005073

"Each of the seven stories in this . . . collection [by Joan Wickersham] is titled 'The News from Spain' and makes . . . use of that phrase somewhere in the narrative. A mother consigned to a nursing home and her adult daughter engage in an intricate dance of filial obligation after the mother's condition improves. At an all-boys school, a lone female student, 13, develops a friendship with her married Spanish teacher." (Publishers Weekly)

Wideman, John Edgar, 1941-

Fanon. Houghton Mifflin 2008 240p $24

ISBN 0618942637; 9780618942633

LC 2007-9420

This is a novel by the author of Brothers and Keepers (1984). The novel "weaves together fiction, biography, and memoir to evoke the life and message of Frantz Fanon, the . . . author of The Wretched of the Earth." (Publisher's note)

"This is Wideman's mulligan stew—on the one hand, the Homewood boy who went on scholarship to Penn, and from Penn to Oxford, and from Oxford to the Iowa Writers' Workshop, nods his head to Marx, Freud, Yeats, Sartre, Joyce, Nabokov, and Baudelaire; on the other, the novelist and college professor who still feels guilty about going to Europe instead of jail signifies his solidarity with W.E.B. DuBois, James Baldwin, and Frantz Fanon by riff, scat, and Igbo. How this mixture works is mysterious, but it always has." Harper's

Wideman, John Edgar

The **stories** of John Edgar Wideman. Pantheon Bks. 1992 432p

LC 91-50839

"The 25 stories pulled together here demonstrate {the author's} eloquence in picturing various elements in the constant friction between black and white societies in the U.S. Family and place are, thus, two prominent themes. He writes lushly, beautifully, yet loudly as well; his voice is deep, rich, booming." Booklist

Wiesel, Elie

A **beggar** in Jerusalem; a novel. translated from the French by Lily Edelman and the author. Random House 1970 211p

Original French edition, 1969

"Reading Elie Wiesel is not an easy experience. It is certainly by no means an act of escape, the traditional function of literary entertainment. His works touch all of one's fibers. . . . After we have listened to what Wiesel has to say, other literature seems meaningless." Saturday Rev

Wiesel, Elie

★ **Dawn**; translated from the French by Frances Frenaye. Hill & Wang 1961 89p

Original French edition, 1960

"Elisha, a young Jewish terrorist fighting for the creation of Israel in the 1940s, is faced with an agonizing moral dilemma. He is to be the executioner of a British officer in reprisal for the hanging of a captured terrorist. A survivor of the concentration camps and a victim all of his life, Elisha considers whether he is any different from his oppressors if he can execute a helpless prisoner in cold blood." Shapiro. Fic for Youth. 3d edition

Wiesel, Elie

The **forgotten**; translated by Stephen Becker. Summit Bks. 1992 237p

LC 91-46826

Original French edition, 1989

"Mr. Wiesel is a writer of contention and his characters, even when affectionate, speak with a bitter music. The most loving—and the saddest—of these sounds occur in the dark duets between father and son, especially as Elhanan admits to Malkiel that he 'cannot recall the essential thing that I want so much to pass on to you.' Elhanan's faith, his temptation to faith . . . is as stunning as the loss he confronts." N Y Times Book Rev

Wiesel, Elie

The **Golem**; the story of a legend. as told by Elie Wiesel and illustrated by Mark Podwal; translated by Anne Borchardt. Summit Bks. 1983 105p il

LC 83-9304

"This fable is eloquently presented through the combination of Wiesel's facile storytelling skills and Mark Podwal's evocative line drawings." Booklist

Wiesel, Elie

Hostage; Elie Wiesel; translated from the French by Catherine Temerson. 1st ed. Random House Inc. 2012 224 p. (hardcover) $25.95

ISBN 0307599582; 9780307599582

LC 2011050747

Author Elie Wiesel tells the story of "Shaltiel Feigenberg, who in 1975, is captured and imprisoned for 80 hours [by an Italian political revolutionary and a Palestinian advocate]. . . . This forced period of darkness ironically provides him with an extended period of enlightenment, as he has time to reflect on his life--the death of his grandmother at Auschwitz, his frequently absent but observant father, his initial meeting with Blanca (the woman who eventually becomes his wife), and the growing Communist sympathies of his older brother." (Kirkus Reviews)

Wiesel, Elie

The **judges**; a novel. translated from the French by Geoffrey Strachan. Knopf 2002 209p $24

ISBN 0-375-40909-2

LC 2002-25462

Original French edition, 1999

As the characters "talk about themselves and remember crucial turning points in their lives. Wiesel weaves in Jewish history and mysticism with the characters' personal memories, and he raises the big existential questions about life and death and memory and guilt and forgiveness, with lots of metaphors about scapegoat, fellow traveler, messenger, etc." Booklist

Wiesel, Elie

★ **Night,** Dawn, The accident: three tales. Hill & Wang 1972 318p hardcover o.p. pa $14

ISBN 0-374-52140-9

In Dawn, Elisha, a young Jewish terrorist fighting for the creation of Israel in the 1940s is faced with an agonizing moral dilemma. He is to be the executioner of a British officer in reprisal for the hanging of a captured terrorist. A survivor of the concentration camps and a victim all of his life, Elisha considers whether he is any different from his oppressors if he can execute a helpless prisoner in cold blood. Night is a memoir. The accident concerns a survivor of Auschwitz who, recovering from a near-fatal accident, questions the meaning of man's existence and purpose, and death

Wiesel, Elie

★ The **oath**; translated from the French by Marion Wiesel. Random House 1973 283p

ISBN 0-394-48779-6

A "powerful novel, interwoven with threads of Hasidic tales, cabalistic mysticism, Talmudic sayings, and pietistic folklore." Libr J

Wiesel, Elie

The **testament**; a novel. translated from the French by Marion Wiesel. Summit Bks. 1981 346p

ISBN 0-671-44833-1

LC 80-27251

Original French edition, 1980

"In none of Wiesel's earlier novels are the characters so earthy, so real, so finely chiseled, as in this one. Women advance more fully to center stage and play more dominant roles. . . . The almost photographic realism of the narrative gives it a cumulative power that is overwhelming." Christ Century

Wiggins, Marianne

Evidence of things unseen; a novel. Simon & Schuster 2003 383p $25

ISBN 0-684-86969-1

LC 2003-45611

National Book Award Finalist: Fiction (2003)

"Born in Kitty Hawk, where the Wright brothers first rose towards the sun, Ray Foster, or 'Fos', . . . is fascinated by radiance. A portrait photographer who deals with the dynamics of light, Fos . . . keeps a lump of phosphorous glowing in a fish tank by his bedside. . . . After signing on as an official photographer for the Tennessee Valley Authority–hence becoming complicit in kicking countless farmers off their ancestral lands to make way for hydroelectric dams–Fos assumes a similar recordkeeping role at the Oak Ridge Laboratory in Tennessee, one of three research sites for the Manhattan project." Economist

Wiggins, Marianne

The **shadow** catcher. Simon & Schuster 2007 323p il $25

ISBN 978-0-7432-6520--1; 0-7432-6520-3

LC 2007-11842

A fictionalization of the life of photographer Edward Sheriff Curtis. "Digging into the photographer's past in a parallel story line is the modern-day, fictional Marianne Wiggins, an Angeleno who has written a novel about Curtis and is resisting Hollywood's attempts to glamorize him. . . . This faux Wiggins—the real one thanks her sister in the acknowledgments for 'license to decorate our shared history'—stumbles into a mystery involving her family, but the personal developments are considerably less interesting than the detailed reconstruction of Curtis' wife Clara. . . . The beautifully rendered Clara gives resonant shape to Wiggins' musings on the enigmatic Curtis—wayward husband, absent father, acquaintance of Teddy Roosevelt, emblem of a great national restlessness—and leads the author to intriguing insights into sexual politics, the mythology of the West and the relationship between physical and emotional distance." PopMatters

Wiggs, Susan

The **Apple** Orchard; Susan Wiggs. Harlequin Books 2013 432 p. (hardcover) $24.95

ISBN 0778314936; 9780778314936

In this romance novel, by Susan Wiggs, "Tess's . . . history is filled with gaps: a father she never met, a mother who spent more time traveling than with her daughter. So Tess is shocked when she discovers the grandfather she never knew is in a coma. And that she has been named in his will to inherit half of Bella Vista, a hundred-acre apple orchard in the magical Sonoma town called Archangel. . . . Tess begins to discover a world filled with the simple pleasures of food and family." (Publisher's note)

Wiggs, Susan

The **ocean** between us. Mira 2004 382p $19.95

ISBN 0-7783-2035-9

LC 2004-557716

"Steve Bennett is a perfect navy officer with a perfect navy family, and he's confident that his world is just the way it should be. But his son wants to be an artist instead of attending the U.S. Naval Academy, and his stalwart and capable wife of 20 years, Grace, is tired of being the perfect navy wife. She wants her own home, and she wants her own career. She's feeling altogether unsettled, but nothing is more unsettling than the secret her husband has hidden from her their entire marriage. Nothing, that is, until the accident on the carrier. Wiggs has done an excellent job of depicting what lies beneath the surfaces of relationships—assumptions, misunderstandings, and expectations." Booklist

Wilde, Oscar

★ The **picture** of Dorian Gray. Modern Library 1992 254p $16.95

ISBN 0-679-60001-9

LC 92-11593

First published 1891 in the United Kingdom; first United States edition published 1895 by G. Munro's Sons

"An archetypal tale of a young man who purchases eternal youth at the expense of his soul, the novel was a romantic exposition of Wilde's Aestheticism. Dorian Gray is a wealthy Englishman who gradually sinks into a life of dissipation and crime. Despite his unhealthy behavior, his physical appearance remains youthful and unmarked by dissolution. Instead, a portrait of himself catalogues every evil deed by turning his once handsome features into a hideous mask." Merriam-Webster's Ency of Lit

Wilder, Thornton

The **bridge** of San Luis Rey and other novels 1926-1948; [edited by J. D. McClatchy] Library of America 2009 731p $35

ISBN 978-1-59853-045-2

The cabala (1926) is a tale of youthful enchantment with Rome in the form of a fictitious memoir of an American student. Set in 18th-century Peru, The bridge of San Luis Rey (1927), "is a kind of theological detective story concerning a friar's investigations into the lives of five individuals before they were killed in a bridge collapse. . . . The Woman of Andros [1930], based on the Andria of Roman writer Terence, is a consideration of the ancient world filtered through the sensibility of a meditative courtesan; Heaven's My Destination [1935], a departure from Wilder's historical themes, is a picaresque romp through Depression-era America; and The Ides of March [1948] takes up the story of Julius Caesar's assassination by imagining the exchange of letters among such prominent ancient figures as Catullus, Cleopatra, Cicero, and Caesar himself." Publisher's note

Wilder, Thornton

The **eighth** day. Harper & Row 1967 435p

"A chronicle of two early 20th-century Midwestern families and their involvement in a murder case raising serious questions about human nature." Oxford Companion to Am Lit. 6th edition

Wilder, Thornton

The **ides** of March. Harper 1948 246p

This novel offers "divergent views of Caesar's last months seen through letters and documents." Oxford Companion to Am Lit. 6th edition

Wilder, Thornton

★ **Theophilus** North. Harper & Row 1973 374p

"In the summer of 1926, a 30-year-old teacher named Theophilus North comes to Newport, R.I., to tutor the children of the fashionably rich and to read out loud. . . . In Newport he discovers nine separate cities differing in age and social class. In these stories of which this novel is composed, North marches through them all—careers and cities—healing the sick, repairing marriages, rescuing a damsel from injustice, restoring life and health to the old and frail, and freedom to the confined." Newsweek

Wildgen, Michelle

Bread and Butter; a novel. Michelle Wildgen. Doubleday 2013 336 p. (hardcover : alk. paper) $25.95

ISBN 0385537433; 9780385537438

LC 2013005474

"Britt and Leo have spent ten years running Winesap, the best restaurant in their small Pennsylvania town. They cater to their loyal customers; they don't sleep with the staff; and business is good, even if their temperamental pastry chef is bored with making the same chocolate cake night after night. But when their younger brother, Harry, opens his own restaurant—a hip little joint serving an aggressive lamb neck dish—Britt and Leo find their own restaurant thrown off-kilter. Britt becomes fascinated by a customer who arrives night after night, each time with a different dinner companion. Their pastry chef, Hector, quits, only to reappear at Harry's restaurant. And Leo finds himself falling for his executive chef-tempted to break the cardinal rule of restaurant ownership." (Publisher's note)

"Food journalist Wildgen has the professional chops to whip up a debut delicacy that's as complex as a rich cassoulet and as comforting as good ol' mac-and-cheese." Booklist

Includes bibliographical references and index

Wiles, Will

Care of wooden floors; a novel. Will Wiles. Houghton Mifflin Harcourt 2012 295 p. (hardcover) $24

ISBN 0547953569; 9780547953564

LC 2012014251

In author Will Wiles' book, a "nameless narrator is on a night to a foreign city, where he has been asked to look after an old friend's [or Oskar's] apartment. . . . The intrusion of an outside element upsets Oskar's ordered system . . . The crisis begins with what a landlord would call 'wear and tear' when what starts out as a small wine stain on the floor quickly complicates itself into a calamity of dead cats, broken glass, accidental stabbings and drunkenly demolished furniture." (Times Literary Supplement)

Wilhelm, Kate

The **best** defense. St. Martin's Press 1994 342p

LC 94-2039

In this legal thriller Barbara Holloway "defends Paula Kennerman, a battered wife accused of killing her daughter and burning down the safe house in which they had been sheltered. . . . The Holloways' crack team of private investigators assures that important clues are developed in time to use as evidence as Barbara skillfully conducts the defense in a suspenseful trial. The ambitious plot-subplot net threads together abortion rights, antifeminist backlash, and the inequities of legal aid for rich and poor." Libr J

Wilhelm, Kate

Death qualified; a mystery of chaos. St. Martin's Press 1991 438p

LC 90-27504

"It is difficult to describe the novel's many dimensions, ranging from tense courtroom scenes to the almost fantastic descriptions of the scientific study. Most astonishing is the author's ability to peel off one layer after another, revealing new ways of looking at the same facts." Libr J

Wilhelm, Kate

★ The **deepest** water. St. Martin's Minotaur 2000 279p $23.95

ISBN 0-312-26143-8

LC 00-31724

Wilhelm's "characters are well drawn, the setting is real, and the pace keeps the reader raptly involved to the last page." Libr J

Wilhelm, Kate

Defense for the devil. St. Martin's Press 1999 389p $24.95

ISBN 0-312-19854-X

LC 98-44576

"The nuances of courtroom procedure are compellingly presented, . . . including a sophisticated look at the complex psychology of a jury." Publ Wkly

Wilhelm, Kate

Desperate measures. St. Martin's Minotaur 2001 387p

ISBN 0-312-27663-X

Barbara Holloway's "latest client is a brilliant young man named Alex Feldman, who has been left hideously deformed by a birth defect. He is accused of killing his next-door neighbor, Gus Marchand, a tyrannical religious Zealot who saw Alex's deformity as the mark of the devil. There is little evidence against him, but Marchand has created such hostility and fear toward Alex in their small, rural community that it seems likely he will be convicted on the basis of his appearance alone. . . . Readers are given all the necessary facts and Alex is an excellent character. Wilhelm does a good job of conveying his anguish and isolation." Publ Wkly

Wilhelm, Kate

The **good** children. St. Martin's Press 1998 246p $22.95

ISBN 0-312-17914-6

LC 97-37101

"Brilliantly plotted, lyrically written, alluring and magical, mesmerizing, terrifying, and heartbreakingly funny, Wilhelm's story is a wrenching masterpiece about love, loyalty, and lies that will lodge itself in readers' psyches long after they've finished the last, stunning chapter." Booklist

Wilhelm, Kate

Justice for some. St. Martin's Press 1993 260p

LC 93-15046

"Heading for a family gathering at her father's home/water garden business in rural California, widowed Sarah Drexler anticipates a respite from her work as an Oregon state judge. Instead she finds her deductive skills challenged and the lives of those dearest to her threatened. Joining the tense family dinner is Fran Donatio, a woman whose presence Sarah's father Ralph does not explain. The next morning, after Ralph's body is pulled from a lily pond, police Lt. Arthur Fernandez arrives with questions on another matter. . . . This tale . . . offers a bonus in Fernandez who, running his own, equally intelligent investigation in the background, provides a welcome change from the expected solitary-sleuth plot structure." Publ Wkly

Wilhelm, Kate

Malice prepense. St. Martin's Press 1996 412p

LC 96-1190

"As Wilhelm spins her riveting tale, she not only makes the legal system comprehensible and compelling but also makes her readers care about her characters, particularly the efficient yet vulnerable Barbara." Publ Wkly

Wilhelm, Kate

No defense. St. Martin's Press 2000 376p $24.95

ISBN 0-312-20953-3

LC 99-56355

In this legal thriller Oregon attorney Barbara Holloway defends "Lara Jessup, a young widow accused of murdering her much older husband, Vinny, a man with a large insurance policy, a terminal case of cancer, and some very powerful enemies. Jessup's alibi begins to evaporate when her adolescent son contradicts her story, and Holloway is left with no way to defend her except to expose those powerful enemies. . . . Although there is nothing particularly original or surprising here, this well-written novel skillfully captures small-town life in a rural western community with all its benefits and drawbacks." Booklist

Wilhelm, Kate

★ **Where** late the sweet birds sang. Harper & Row 1976 251p

"Pollution and pestilence are the consequences of a war that destroys most of the earth and its inhabitants. The elder Sumners have created a scientific research center whose goal is to perfect a technique for cloning since, among the other results of the world disaster, men and women have become sterile. The younger Sumners are victimized by these clones, who perpetuate the form of humans but have no humaneness or humanity." Shapiro. Fic for Youth. 3d edition

Wilhide, Elizabeth

Ashenden; a novel. Elizabeth Wilhide. 1st Simon & Schuster ed. Simon & Schuster 2013 339 p. (hardcover) $24.99; (paperback) $16

ISBN 145168486X; 9781451684865; 9781451697896

LC 2012014720

This book tells the story of an 18th-century English estate house. "When Charlie Minton and his sister, Ros, inherit Ashenden Park (based on an actual estate in Berkshire, England) from their recently deceased aunt, they are forced to decide its fate. The house's history is revealed through chronologically ordered flashbacks, one per chapter." (Publishers Weekly)

Wilkins, Kim

Veil of gold. Tor 2008 495p $25.95

ISBN 978-0-7653-2006-3; 0-7653-2006-1

First published 2005 in Australia with title: Rosa and the veil of gold

"Wilkins's human characters are endearing and her mythic monsters spring into vibrant life. Adult fairy tales don't come any better than this." Publ Wkly

Willard, Tom

★ **Buffalo** soldiers. Forge 1996 331p $22.95

ISBN 0-312-86041-2

LC 95-53295

"Held captive by the Kiowa and then bartered to a white buffalo hunter, Augustus Sharps is freed in 1869 by troopers of the all-black Tenth U.S. Cavalry, in which he enlists. First in a series chronicling African American contributions to U.S. military history, Willard's . . . well-researched novel traces Augustus's soldiering from Fort Wallace, Kansas, until his retirement to an Arizona ranch." Libr J

Williams, Amanda Kyle

The **stranger** you seek; a novel. Bantam Books 2011 292p $25

ISBN 978-0-553-80807-0; 0-553-80807-9

LC 2010-53044

"Lt. Aaron Rauser needs help catching what seems to be a new serial killer in his Atlanta stomping ground. He knows that the woman for the job is his old friend and crime-solving compatriot Keye Street. Keye's not the kind of woman you mess around with, and while the folks on the force don't like that she's freelancing in their department, there's not much they can do about it. Keye was on track to be a well-respected FBI profiler before an inconvenient addiction to booze got in the way. Now that she's back on her feet, this tough and whip-smart investigator has opened her own small-time business. Although chasing bail jumpers keeps Keye and her hacker sidekick Neil in modest money, hunting down the deranged psychopath the Atlanta papers have dubbed the Wishbone Killer is just Keye's piece of pie. . . . [Williams] creates a frightening and occasionally witty novel, perfect for those who can sleep with one eye open. Think Mary Higgins Clark with an edge." Kirkus Rev

Williams, Ann Joslin

Down from Cascom Mountain; a novel. Bloomsbury USA 2011 325p $25

ISBN 978-1-60819-306-6; 1-60819-306-3

LC 2010-34477

"Ann Williams' novel contains a smaller world than her father's novels; more accessible, the problems more familiar. She follows her characters' moods more closely, with less of an emphasis on the cultural and historical context of her story. The reader is deeply invested, caught up in Mary's grieving, or in Tobin's failure to forgive his mother. Their stories are made memorable." Los Angeles Times

Williams, Charlie

★ **Stairway** to hell. Serpent's Tail 2010 281p pa $14.95

ISBN 978-1-84668-689-4; 184668689X

First published 2009 in the United Kingdom

"This is one of those rare books when, really, anything might happen in the next few pages. Rather than feeling contrived, Williams manages to create a milieu in which even the wackiest developments are both seamlessly logical and thoroughly unexpected, not to mention funny. Pop music, time travel, soul displacement? You bet!" PopMatters

Williams, Joy, 1944-

★ **99** stories of God; by Joy Williams. Tin House Books 2016 220 p. (hardcover) $19.95

ISBN 1941040357; 9781941040355

LC 2016006741

This book, by Joy Williams, offers a "series of short, fictional vignettes [that] explores our day-to-day interactions with an ever-elusive and arbitrary God. . . . The figures that haunt these stories range from Kafka . . . to the Aztecs, Tolstoy to Abraham and Sarah, O. J. Simpson to a pack of wolves. Most . . . are like the rest of us: anonymous strivers and bumblers who brush up against God in the least expected places or go searching for Him when He's standing right there." (Publisher's note)

"Each story is brief, with some less than a paragraph. Some amaze, some are quietly powerful, some gracefully absurd. Much like the divine, Williams' prose is simple and brutal, thoughtful and haunting." Booklist

Williams, Joy

Honored guest; stories. Knopf 2004 213p

ISBN 0-679-44647-8

LC 2004-44199

"The troubled characters in Williams' latest short stories, set in locales as diverse as Maine and Mexico, don't have the wherewithal to do anything but brood, with the exception of a forensic anthropologist who solves the mysteries of scattered bones, hair, and teeth, a feat not unlike the one Williams pulls off in these canny and dissecting tales of fractured lives." Booklist

Williams, Joy, 1944-

The **visiting** privilege; new and collected stories. Joy Williams. Alfred A. Knopf 2015 512 p. (hardcover) $30

ISBN 9781101873717; 9781101874899

LC 2014043360

This short story collection, by Joy Williams, features "thirty-three stories drawn from three much-lauded collections, and another thirteen appearing here for the first time in book form. Forty-six stories in all, . . . showcasing [the author's] crisp, elegant prose, her dark wit, and her uncanny ability to illuminate our world through characters and situations that feel at once peculiar and foreign and disturbingly familiar." (Publisher's note)

"Williams, to belabor the metaphor, isn't just a closer, but a utility player at the top of her game. If you want to see how the pros do it—or simply want to read some of the best stories being written today—you need look no further." Kirkus

Williams, Karen

Dirty to the grave. Urban Books 2010 216 p.

ISBN 1601622694; 9781601622693

This novel tells the story of "Cha, Goldie, and Red, who come together for fun, laughs, and sometimes treachery in Long Beach, California. For these three ladies, survival was always about . . . using lies, deceit, and sex. But when a plan goes dangerously wrong, Cha and Goldie take a step back out of the life. Cha desperately wants to rid herself of the demons of her past so she can at least feel normal enough to raise her son, Omari. Goldie . . . [is] tired of going from man to man, and knows her parents are rolling over in their graves at the life she chose for herself. Red craves the streets, and will cross anyone, friends included, to get what she wants. She . . . will betray both Cha and Goldie, leading to horrifying consequences." (Publisher's note)

Williams, Naomi J.

Landfalls; Naomi J. Williams. Farrar, Straus & Giroux 2015 336 p. map (hardcover) $26

ISBN 9780374183158; 0374183155

LC 2014039367

This novel, by Naomi J. Williams, long-listed for the NBCC's John Leonard Prize, "reimagines the historical Lapérouse expedition, a voyage of exploration that left Brest in 1785 with two frigates, more than two hundred men, and overblown Enlightenment ideals and expectations, in a brave attempt to circumnavigate the globe for science and the glory of France." (Publisher's note)

"Full of period sensibilities, particularly the Enlightenment-era urge to go forth and explore new domains, the novel is alternately charming, invigorating, and heartbreaking, and always thoughtful and humane." Booklist

Williams, Niall

John; a novel. Bloomsbury 2008 276p $24.95

ISBN 978-1-59691-467-4; 1-59691-467-X

LC 2007-25810

"This novel will appeal to readers who like imaginative and gritty sagas of the lives of key Christians in the early church as well as those who value lyricism." Publ Wkly

Williams, Tennessee

★ **Collected** stories; with an introduction by Gore Vidal. New Directions 1985 xxv, 574p

LC 85-10642

Contents: The angel in the alcove; Chronicle of a demise; Completed; Desire and the black masseur; Field of blue children; ¿Grand¿; Happy August the Tenth; The important thing; The inventory at Fontana Bella; The killer chicken and the closet queen; The kingdom of earth; The knightly quest; The malediction; Mama's old stucco house; Man bring this up road; The mattress by the tomato patch; Miss Coynte of Greene; The mysteries of the Joy Rio; The night of the Iguana; One arm; Oriflamme; The poet; Portrait of a girl in glass; Resemblance between a violin case and a coffin; Sabbatha and solitude; Three players of a summer game; Two on a party; The vengence of Nitocris; The vine; The yellow bird; A lady's beaded bag; Something by Tolstoi; Big Black; A Mississippi idyll; The accent of a coming foot; Twenty-seven wagons full of cotton; Sand; Ten minute stop; Gift of an apple; In memory of an aristocrat; The dark room; The interval; Tent worms; Something about him; Rubio y Morena; The coming of something to Widow Holly; Hard candy; A recluse and his guest; Das Wasser ist Kalt; Mother Yaws

Williams, Tennessee

★ The **Roman** spring of Mrs. Stone. New Directions 1950 148p

A wealthy widowed American ex-actress is the heroine of this short novel. At fifty Mrs. Stone is losing her beauty, her stage career is ended, and she finds herself just 'drifting' through an aimless existence in Rome. When an unscrupulous countess introduces a handsome young gigolo to Mrs. Stone it is the beginning of the end

"There are many superb moments, scenes which move with a dramatist's ease. There is a hard candor about Mrs. Stone, about all people who fail at real living and attempt a life of fantasy and fail at that, leaving them vulnerable to annihilation. . . . This different version of Mr. Williams' repeated theme has resulted in a sharp, witty and moving novel." Chicago Sunday Trib

Williams, Walter Jon, 1953-

The **fourth** wall; Walter Jon Williams. Orbit 2012 402 p.
ISBN 9780316133395

LC 2011022494

In this novel, "[f]ormer child actor Sean Makin finds himself reduced to taking gigs on the lowest type of reality television shows to make ends meet--and support his agent. A chance meeting with producer Dagmar Shaw, who is suspected of having connections with unsavory international cults and activist groups, lands him a starring role in a revolutionary film that is part reality TV and part scripted story. However, Sean discovers to his dismay that death seems to follow Dagmar, striking those close to her--thus making Sean a prime target." (Libr J)

Williamson, Penelope

Heart of the west; a novel. Simon & Schuster 1995 591p

LC 94-33487

"Williamson gives these characters convincing voices . . . and demonstrates how women could bond and find new identities on the frontier. Williamson tells her story with brio, if a little too much florid prose." Publ Wkly

Williamson, Penelope

The **outsider**. Simon & Schuster 1996 464p

LC 96-7291

"This is rich, wonderful reading sure to please any fan of good old-fashioned storytelling." Libr J

Willig, Lauren

The **Ashford** affair; Lauren Willig. St. Martin's Press 2013 368 p. (hardcover) $24.99
ISBN 1250014492; 9781250014498; 9781250027191; 9781250027863

LC 2012037787

In this historical romance, "Addie is 99 and beloved by her granddaughter, Clemmie, a lawyer looking to make partner. Clemmie sees the marriage between her grandmother and grandfather, Frederick, as her model for love and has recently ended an engagement because her fiancé did not measure up. After Addie dies, Clemmie, aided by her step-cousin, historian Jon, learns that their family's history is more complicated than she imagined." (Publishers Weekly)

Willig, Lauren

The **secret** history of the pink carnation; by Lauren Willig. Dutton 2005 388 p. (paperback) $7.99; (hardcover) $19.95
ISBN 9780451413185 reprint; 9780525948605 out of print

LC 2004021334

In this book, the first in Lauren Willig's Pink Carnation series, "American academic Eloise Kelly has come to London to uncover the identity of the Pink Carnation, a British spy who infiltrated Napoleonic France. Eloise . . . hits a vein of gold when she uncovers letters describing a love affair between the Purple Gentian, another famous spy, and Amy Balcourt, who may be the Pink Carnation." (Publishers Weekly)

Other titles in this series are:
The masque of the Black Tulip (2005)
The deception of the emerald ring (2006)
The seduction of the Crimson Rose (2008)
The temptation of the night jasmine (2009)
The betrayal of the blood lily (2010)
The mischief of the mistletoe (2010)
The orchid affair (2011)
The garden intrigue (2012)
The passion of the purple plumeria (2013)
The mark of the midnight manzanilla (2014)
The lure of the Moonflower (2015)

Willig, Lauren

The **seduction** of the crimson rose. Dutton 2008 385p $24.95; pa $15
ISBN 978-0-525-95033-2; 0-525-95033-8; 978-0-451-22441-5 pa; 0-451-22441-8 pa

LC 2007-43044

"The flower-named spies of Regency England return as Willig's smart, sassy style cleverly incorporates a modern-day historian's hunt for information with Regency characters and events. Willig switches from a historical voice to a modern tone with ease, drawing readers back and forth in time as they hold their breath to see what happens next." Romantic Times

Willis, Connie

Blackout. Spectra/Ballantine Books 2010 $26
ISBN 978-0-553-80319-8; 0-553-80319-0

LC 2009-44673

"Despite the conceit of time travel, the book shows the attention to period detail that defines historical novels." Cleveland Plain Dealer

Willis, Connie

Crosstalk; Connie Willis. Del Rey 2016 512 p. (hardback) $28; (ebook) $65
ISBN 9780345540676; 9780345540683

LC 2016022953

"Originally published in the United Kingdom [in 2016] by Gollancz, an imprint of The Orion Publishing Group, London"--Title-page verso.

In this novel, by Connie Willis, "in the not-too-distant future, a simple outpatient procedure to increase empathy between romantic partners has become all the rage. And Briddey Flannigan is delighted when her boyfriend, Trent, suggests undergoing the operation prior to a marriage proposal—to enjoy better emotional connection and a perfect relationship. . . . But things don't quite work out as planned, and Briddey finds herself connected to someone else entirely." (Publisher's note)

"In other hands this novel could have been mere cliché, but Willis' exuberant humor and warmhearted, fast-paced plotting transform it into a satisfying, if old-fashioned, romantic comedy." Kirkus

Willis, Connie

★ **Doomsday** book. Bantam Bks. 1992 445p
ISBN 0-553-08131-4

LC 91-42819

"Kivrin, a student of medieval history, is sent back in time to 14th-century Oxfordshire to do some hands-on study. Meanwhile, in the near-future present day of the book, an old disease comes back to smite Oxford. In the resultant chaos, no one realises that because of a slip-up, Kivrin has arrived bang in the middle of the Black Death." (New Statesman Soc)

"As much as I enjoyed [Willis's] story, . . . the time travel device is given no justification, and none of the paradoxical implications of time travel are explored. Doomsday Book is a historical novel with tenuous SF connections. . . . Warts and all, though, this is a cracking good story, and that is the bottom line criterion for any novel, SF or other." New Scientist

Willis, Connie

Passage. Bantam Bks. 2001 594p

ISBN 0-553-11124-8

LC 00-68052

This novel "concerns the scientific study of near death experiences (NDEs). . . . Psychologist Joanna Lander, an NDE specialist, joins neurologist Richard Wright in a research project employing a psychoactive drug to simulate NDEs. When most of the volunteer subjects drop out, Joanna agrees to go under and finds herself aboard the Titanic. She returns time after time to the ill-fated ship and becomes increasingly obsessed with the experience and why it seems so real and familiar. . . . With memorable characters, believable science, and convincing hospital ambiance, an initially slow-moving yarn turns into a page-turner whose explosive climax will rock readers back on their heels." Booklist

Willis, Connie

To say nothing of the dog; or, How we found the bishop's bird stump at last. Bantam Bks. 1998 434p hardcover o.p. pa $7.99

ISBN 0-553-09995-7; 0-553-57538-4 pa

LC 97-16002

"No one mixes scientific mumbo jumbo and comedy of manners with more panache than Willis." N Y Times Book Rev

Willocks, Tim

The **religion**. Sarah Crichton Books 2007 618p $26

ISBN 978-0-374-24865-9; 0-374-24865-6

LC 2006-30419

First published 2006 in the United Kingdom

The author is "especially convincing on the battle lust which overtakes both sides, and vividly places us among the besieged. If you don't mind a bit of romance tacked around the fighting, it is a gripping story with reliable factual underpinnings: history as heroics." Times Lit Suppl

Wilson, Adam

Flatscreen. Harper Perennial 2012 352 p.

ISBN 9780062090331

This book tells the story of "Eli Schwartz, the narrator, . . . [who] is the classic couch-bound failure-to-launch whiling away his 20s 'denying real time, like an anthropologist attempting to study a distant, extinct species, wondering what went wrong.' Eli's simple passions—pop culture, cooking, and watching the Food Network—render his life a pleasant stupor suddenly interrupted when his mother sells the house to one 'Seymour J. Kahn: actor, cripple.' The once accomplished and beloved but now elderly and wheelchair-bound Seymour acts as a time-lapsed version of Eli. . . . And under the old man's terrible tutelage, Eli awakens to a wholly incongruous lifestyle of hillbilly heroin and gunplay." (Publishers Weekly)

Wilson, Daniel H.

The **clockwork** dynasty; a novel. Daniel H. Wilson. Doubleday 2017 320 p. paperback $16.95; hardback $26.95

ISBN 9781101974087; 9780385541794; 9780385541787

LC 2016053069

Alex Award (2018)

This novel, by Daniel H. Wilson, is a "thriller that weaves a path through history, following a race of human-like machines that have been hiding among us for untold centuries. . . . Present day: When a young anthropologist specializing in ancient technology uncovers a terrible secret concealed in the workings of a three-hundred-year-old mechanical doll, she is thrown into a hidden world that lurks just under the surface of our own." (Publisher's note)

"This is science fiction at its best—thoughtful, challenging, beautifully written, and astonishing." Booklist

Wilson, Daniel H.

Robogenesis; a novel. Daniel H. Wilson. Doubleday 2014 384 p. $26.95

ISBN 0385537093; 9780385537094

LC 2014000720

Sequel to: Robopocalypse

An apocalyptic science fiction sequel to the novel "Robopocalypse," also by Daniel H. Wilson, "'Robogenesis' explores the fates of characters new and old, robotic and human, as they fight to build a new world in the wake of a devastating war. Readers will bear witness as survivors find one another, form into groups, and react to a drastically different (and deadly) technological landscape." (Publisher's note)

"This Hollywood-ready techno-thriller is packed to the brim with enough tough characters and brutal conflict to satisfy the most hardcore video gamers and action movie fans." Pub Wkly

Wilson, Daniel H.

Robopocalypse; Daniel H. Wilson. Doubleday 2011 347p. $25

ISBN 978-0-385-53385-0; 0-385-53385-3

LC 201043134

Alex Award (2012)

In this book by Daniel H. Wilson, Archos, a robot with "infinite processing power and cognitive power" kills his creator and "uses 'smart' toys, battlefield 'pacification' units, and pleasure dolls to evoke his dominion over the human world. What he doesn't plan for are the small pockets of human resistors." (Voice of Youth Advocates)

"In this story of a global robotic revolution, Wilson's malevolent machines have surprisingly nuanced motives, and a few of the vignettes, particularly one about the chilling fate of an Alaskan drill team, could even stand alone as great horror short fiction." Entertainment Wkly

Wilson, Edward O., 1929-

Anthill; a novel. [by] E. O. Wilson. W.W. Norton & Co. 2010 378p $24.95

ISBN 0-393-07119-7; 978-0-393-07119-1

LC 2009-52140

This novel follows the adventures of 15-year-old Raff Cody "whose improbable love of ants ends up transforming his own life and those around him. Alarmed by condo developers who are intent on destroying Alabama's endangered Nokobee tract, Raff idealistically heads off to law school. Returning home, he encounters the angry and corrupt ghosts of an old South he thought had disappeared. The sacred woods he must now travel through to save Lake Nokobee are teeming with [danger]." (Publisher's note)

Wilson indeed captures in Anthill the rapture of a boyhood amid the snakes and ants, pine and palmetto, of Alabama. He explores the simmering persistence of its painful history, the tensions between whites and blacks, rich and poor, men and women, as the Old South gave way to the New South a generation ago, sometimes languidly, sometimes not. The result is a charming and intriguing novel, elegant especially in a passage on warring ants, but a novel more impressive as advocacy than as artistry, more resonant in its views of nature and humanity than as fiction. Boston Globe

Wilson, F. Paul

Conspiracies; a Repairman Jack novel. Forge 2000 317p
ISBN 0-312-86797-2

LC 99-52372

"Jack, a fix-it man who specializes in problems that frequently require him to face powerful foes and slip into the world of the supernatural, is hired to locate the missing wife of a businessman. This time he must find a missing woman who happens to be one of the world's leading conspiracy theorists (she was preparing to reveal her Grand Unification Theory, which would explain the truth behind all manner of strange goings-on). To find her, Jack must attend a convention of conspiracy buffs, most of whom seem more than a little strange. . . . Those who look at conspiracy theories with a skeptical eye will have a great time, as will anyone who likes a well-plotted, spooky thriller. Wilson tells a great story." Booklist

Wilson, F. Paul

Deep as the marrow. Forge 1997 352p $24.95
ISBN 0-312-86264-4

LC 96-30502

"When President Thomas Winston announces a plan to attack the drug problem by making drugs legal, he's met first with public outrage, then with an assassination plot involving his boyhood friend and personal physician, Dr. John VanDuyne. In a plan masterminded by a Colombian drug lord, six-year-old Katie VanDuyne is kidnapped to persuade her father to give the president an antibiotic that will destroy his bone marrow. The kidnapping goes awry early on, because of the doctor's ethics and a kidnapper's attachment to Katie, but Wilson spins out the action to the last pages, making some persuasive arguments for drug legalization along the way." Libr J

Wilson, F. Paul

The **haunted** air; a Repairman Jack novel. Forge 2002 415p $24.95
ISBN 0-312-87868-0

LC 2002-72059

This Repairman Jack novel "teams the righteous urban mercenary with his strangest bedfellows yet: a pair of sham spirit mediums who openly operate their occult con game out of a brownstone in Queens. . . . Jack takes the case of brothers Lyle and Charlie Kenton, who've been threatened by other Big Apple pseudo-psychics for horning in on the lucrative seance scene. No sooner has Jack begun . . . than real ghosts begin popping up along with a secret cult of ritual child murderers. . . . Above all, the novel enhances the enigma of Jack, a hero who commands respect despite his curmudgeonly disdain for contemporary culture, his morally ambiguous work-for-hire ethic and his unsettling appeal to the vigilante in every reader." Publ Wkly

Wilson, F. Paul

Legacies. Forge 1998 381p $24.95
ISBN 0-312-86414-0

LC 98-14322

"Jack, a fix-it man who specializes in solving people's problems (and who, as far as the authorities are concerned, doesn't even exist), does a favor for a friend—he recovers some toys stolen from a hospital—and winds up helping a woman solve a deadly mystery from her past. Repairman Jack is a strong man whose moments of compassion don't seem forced, an enigma without being annoyingly mysterious." Booklist

Wilson, G. Willow, 1982-

★ **Alif** the unseen; G. Willow Wilson. Grove Press 2012 433 p. (hbk.) $25.00
ISBN 0802120202; 9780802120205

In this novel, by G. Willow Wilson, "a young Arab-Indian hacker shields his clients . . . from surveillance and tries to stay out of trouble. He goes by Alif. . . . When Alif discovers . . . the secret book of the jinn, which . . . he . . . suspect[s] may unleash a new level of information technology, the stakes are raised and Alif must struggle for life or death, aided by forces seen and unseen." (Publisher's note)

"Wilson skillfully weaves a story linking modern-day technologies and computer languages to the folklore and religion of the Middle East." LJ

Wilson, Kevin

The **family** Fang. Ecco 2011 309p $23.99
ISBN 978-0-06-157903-5; 0-06-157903-3

"Caleb and Camille Fang are gallery darlings of a particularly discomfiting sort, staging public confrontations to provoke an extreme reaction from unwitting bystanders—and recording the results for posterity. In a move that Dr. Spock would never endorse, they've raised their two young children to be accomplices in their work. They take their Santa-fearing daughter, Annie, to every mall they can find so she'll wail the moment she touches the jolly man's lap. They enter their son, Buster, in the Little Miss Crimson Clover pageant disguised as a girl. And so on. As you might imagine, the kids flee the first moment they can. Annie heads to Hollywood and takes up acting; Buster becomes a freelance writer and sometime novelist. But the Fang umbilical cord proves oddly bungee-like, and the offspring soon return for adult-size doses of psychological torment. Wilson writes with the studied quirkiness of George Saunders or filmmaker Wes Anderson, and there's some genuine warmth beneath all the surface eccentricity." Entertainment Wkly

Wilson, Robert

The **blind** man of Seville. Harcourt 2003 434p $26
ISBN 0-15-100835-3

LC 2002-68495

"Wilson . . . is able to hold reader interest at an almost unbearable pitch of excitement throughout this shocker with exquisite plot pacing and intriguing character revelations." Booklist

Wilson, Robert

Capital Punishment. Houghton Mifflin Harcourt 2013 416 p. (Charlie Boxer books) $28
ISBN 0547935196; 9780547935195

This is the first in Gold Dagger Award-winner Robert Wilson's Charles Boxer series. "When 25-year-old Alyshia D'Cruz, the daughter of a self-made Indian billionaire, is kidnapped after an evening out with her co-workers, Boxer is charged with getting Alyshia back alive. The kidnapper, who insists that the crime 'is not about money,' urges the family not to involve the press or the police." (Publishers Weekly)

Wilson, Robert

The **hidden** assassins. Harcourt 2006 453p $25
ISBN 978-0-15-101239-8; 0-15-101239-3

LC 2006-17507

"Falcón is smart and relentless and thoroughly decent, which makes him a capable, if less than captivating, guide through the complicated tangle of motives and suspects. . . . [The novel] is smart and challenging, a mystery that demonstrates the flexibility of a genre that is too often constrained by convention and stereotypes." Cleveland Plain Dealer

Wilson, Robert Charles

Blind Lake. TOR Bks. 2003 399p $24.95

ISBN 0-7653-0262-4

LC 2003-47345

"No one knows better than Wilson how to manipulate the language of science to suggest the essential unknowability of the universe. . . . The drama at Blind Like gradually expands to encompass humans and aliens in entirely unforeseen ways." N Y Times Book Rev

Wilson, Robert Charles

Julian Comstock; a story of 22nd-century America. Tor Bks. 2009 413p $25.95

ISBN 0765319713; 9780765319715

LC 2008-53400

This novel is set in a post-apocalyptic semifeudal America. "In Colorado Springs, the Dominion sees to the nation's spiritual needs. In Labrador, the Army wages war on the Dutch. America, unified, is rising once again. Then out of Labrador come tales of a . . . Captain Commongold, the Youthful Hero of the Saguenay. The ordinary people follow his adventures in the popular press. The Army adores him. The President is troubled. Especially when the dashing Captain turns out to be his nephew Julian, son of the falsely accused and executed Bryce. Treachery and intrigue dog Julian's footsteps." (Publisher's note)

The narrative is "beautifully written, populated with engaging and sympathetic, if conflicted, characters, and unlike anything else [Wilson's] done to date . . . . It's also a fascinating example of SF's ongoing negotiations with ideas of history and identity, and a good deal more complex than its faux-naif narrative voice and boys'- book adventure plotting would seem to suggest." Locus

Wilson, Robert Charles

Spin. Tor 2005 364p

ISBN 0-7653-0938-6

LC 2004-58862

"The narrative time oscillates effortlessly between Tyler Dupree's early adolescence and his near-future young manhood haunted by the impending death of the sun and the earth. Tyler's best friends, twins Diane and Jason Lawton, take two divergent paths: Diane into a troubling religious cult of the end, Jason into impassioned scientific research to discover the nature of the galactic Hypotheticals whose 'Spin' suddenly sealed Earth in a 'cosmic baggie,' making one of its days equal to a hundred million years in the universe beyond. As convincing as Wilson's scientific hypothesizing is—biological, astrophysical, medical—he excels even more dramatically with the infinitely intricate, minutely nuanced relationships among Jason, Diane and Tyler, whose older self tries to save them both with medicines from Mars, terraformed through Jason's genius into an incubator for new humanity." Publ Wkly

Wilson, Sloan

★ The **man** in the gray flannel suit. Simon & Schuster 1955 304p

The man of the title is the ordinary, upper middle class New York business employee, who at five o'clock heads for his home, wife, and children in Connecticut. Thomas Rath is his name in this book. Tom joins a large corporation, does an honest job, and is evidently headed for bigger money. As an undercurrent to his daily life Tom remembers his war service, the girl he met in Rome, and his illegitimate son

"Thoughtful, searching novel. . . . Sloan Wilson manages to hold the reader's interest and at the same time to solve Rath's problems without distorting his character." N Y Her Trib Books

Wilson, Susan

The **fortune** teller's daughter; Susan Wilson. Atria Books 2002 342 p. o.p.

ISBN 074344230X

LC 20020104271

This book follows Sabine Heartwood, who is "happy in her newly settled life until her flighty mother, Madame Ruby, starts proclaiming visions of a coming upheaval. Meanwhile, Danford Smith has returned from New York City to nurse his ailing grandmother through her final days and set his family's affairs in order before returning to a promising career as a filmmaker. Of course life has other plans, and Dan finds himself mired in . . . family loyalties and new obligations. As his long-distance relationship with rising starlet Karen Whitcomb unravels, Dan is increasingly drawn to the lovely and forthright Sabine, who seems to understand something about him that he himself does not. As for Sabine, the psychic gift she has long rejected awakens, intimating dark secrets in Dan's past and that of Moose River." (Publishers Weekly)

Wimberley, Darryl

The **king** of Colored Town. Toby 2007 353p $24.95

ISBN 978-1-59264-181-9; 1-59264-181-4

"An impassioned and eloquent piece of storytelling set in the last days of the Jim Crow South." Texas Monthly

Winawer, Melodie

The **scribe** of Siena; a novel. Melodie Winawer. Touchstone 2017 452 p. (hardback) $26.99

ISBN 9781501152252; 9781501152269; 9781501152276

LC 2016025826

In this novel, by Melodie Winawer, "accomplished neurosurgeon Beatrice Trovato knows that her deep empathy for her patients is starting to impede her work. So when her beloved brother passes away, she welcomes the unexpected trip to the Tuscan city of Siena to resolve his estate, even as she wrestles with grief. But as she delves deeper into her brother's affairs, she discovers intrigue she never imagined--a 700-year-old conspiracy to decimate the city." (Publisher's note)

"Winawer's debut is a detailed historical novel, a multifaceted mystery, and a moving tale of improbable love." Pub Wkly

Wind, Ruth

In the midnight rain; Ruth Wind. Harper Torch 2000 406p (pbk.) o.p.

ISBN 0061030120

LC 2001555211

RITA Awards: Top Ten Favorite Books (2000)

In this book, "[o]n a quest both professional and personal, biographer Ellie Connor accepts the invitation of experimental botanist and music lover Laurence 'Blue' Reynard and heads for Pine Bend, TX, to gather information on an obscure Thirties blues singer and, if she can, learn something about her unknown father. However, her search nets her far more than she expects, and Ellie is suddenly faced with a surprising family, the answer to a mysterious disappearance, and a love she never hoped to find." (Library Journal)

Windle, Jeanette

Congo dawn; Jeanette Windle. Tyndale House Publishers 2013 496 p. (sc) $12.99

ISBN 1414371586; 9781414371580

LC 2012036151

In this Christian novel, "Robin Duncan, member of a global security force for a precious metals mine, learns she is meant for more than providing security for a multinational corporation. She must also overcome her personal grief and betrayal by Michael Stewart if, together, the two are to help liberate people oppressed in once-beautiful, smoldering rain forests that the government and corporate greed have laid to waste." (Publishers Weekly)

Winer, Andrew

The **marriage** artist; a novel. Henry Holt and Company 2010 367p $26

ISBN 978-0-8050-9178-6; 0-8050-9178-5

LC 2009-52432

"As the two story lines converge, readers discern the central secret long before it's revealed, and Winer's prose flickers between ravishing and contrived. Yet structural flaws do not diminish the audacity and beauty of this elaborate psycho-political-sexual puzzle, with its hard truths, startling visions, and eerie insights into the mystical and memorializing powers of art, and that endless hunger we call love." Booklist

Wink, Callan

Dog run moon; stories. Callan Wink. The Dial Press 2016 256 p. (acid-free paper) $26

ISBN 9780812993776

LC 2015025025

This short story collection, by Callan Wink, features "a construction worker on the run from the shady local businessman whose dog he has stolen; a Custer's Last Stand reenactor engaged in a long-running affair with the Native American woman who slays him on the battlefield every year; a middle-aged high school janitor caught in a scary dispute over land and cattle with her former stepson." (Publisher's note)

"Wink doesn't deal in the romance of the Old West or dwell on the frontier past, yet both myth and history color these highly satisfying fictions about the way men and women struggle to shape their lives." Kirkus

Winkler, Anthony C.

Dog war. Akashic Books 2007 195p pa $14.95

ISBN 978-1-93335-428-6; 1-93335-428-3

LC 2006-936538

"Newly widowed, Precious, an upstanding Jamaican with practical ideas and a conversational relationship with Jesus, becomes a maid in a Miami mansion for a pampered dog, who soon develops overfond feelings for her person. The dog belongs to the spiritually questing Mistress Lucy, a multimillionaire among whose most pressing concerns is whether to have her Rolls 'decowed'—the leather removed on moral grounds. Winkler has a fine ear for patois and dialogue, and a love of language that makes bawdy jokes crackle." New Yorker

Winman, Sarah

When God was a rabbit; a novel. Bloomsbury 2011 296p $25

ISBN 978-1-60819-934-3; 1-60819-534-1

"Don't be fooled by When God Was a Rabbit, the existential-sounding title of Winman's debut novel. Her protagonist, Elly (whom we're introduced to as a child growing up in late-1960s England), simply has a pet rabbit named God. God the rabbit is a bit magical—he's able to speak with Elly—but that's par for the course in this eccentric coming-of-age story. Winman's prose is elegantly restrained as she sketches Elly's family life, touching lightly upon both good and bad moments. It's these little moments—some small, one monumental—that are the most affecting and poignant." Entertainment Wkly

Winslow, Don

★ The **cartel**; by Don Winslow. Alfred A. Knopf 2015 640 p. map $27.95

ISBN 1101874996; 9781101874998

LC 2015006233

Sequel to: The power of the dog

Los Angeles Times Book Prize: Mystery/Thriller (2015)

In this book, by Don Winslow, "after having put his onetime friend and eventual cartel king, Adán Barrera, in prison and killing his two brothers, [Art] Keller left the agency and took up tending bees in a monastery. But, in 2004, Barrera arranges his transfer to a Mexican prison, which leads quickly to his escape, and the war between competing cartels is ignited all over again. Reluctantly but inevitably, Keller joins the fight once more." (Booklist)

"The staggering body count will be a challenge for many readers to get past, but the payoffs for those who persevere are immense. Winslow's two-novel project about this still-raging conflict is entertaining, well researched, and difficult to process, a jarring glimpse into a reality about which many Americans remain blissfully unaware." LJ

Includes bibliographical references

Winslow, Don

The **Dawn** Patrol. Alfred A. Knopf 2008 303p $23.95

ISBN 978-0-307-26620-0; 0-307-26620-6

LC 2008-6531

"Winslow horses around early with a lightweight plot about San Diego cop turned PI Boone Daniels searching for an AWOL stripper scheduled to testify against a nightclub owner running an insurance scam. Riotous beach-rat banter abounds, and the 'endless summer' vibe is blissful. But a dreadful undercurrent emerges in which Winslow's amiable 'Dawn Patrol' (the day's earliest surfers) see their carefree lifestyle threatened by the modern virus of gangs, drugs and violence. Winslow transforms his blithe trifle into an elegiac riff on the Pacific Coast's paradise lost, and produces a classic. If you haven't read Winslow yet, get to it." San Francisco Chron

Winslow, Don

The **force**; Don Winslow. William Morrow 2017 482 p. (hardcover) $27.99

ISBN 0062664417; 9780062664419; 9780062664426

LC 2016053385

In this book, by Don Winslow, "Dennis Malone, a veteran NYPD detective sergeant, leads the Manhattan North Special Task Force, an elite unit established to combat drugs, gangs, and guns. . . . Malone and his crew have slipped over the edge, stealing millions in drugs and cash over the years . . . Now the feds have built a case against Malone, and they threaten to take him down if he doesn't help bring in bigger players in the criminal food chain." (Publisher's note)

"In an era rife with racially motivated police brutality, Winslow has created what will likely become our quintessential cop novel, looking both at what cops do right and wrong with clear-eyed realism and passionate humanity." Booklist

Winslow, Don

The **gentlemen's** hour. Simon & Schuster 2011 338p $25

ISBN 978-1-4391-8339-7; 1-4391-8339-2

LC 2011-10781

"Boone Daniels, underemployed private eye and obsessive surfer, ... [continues] his search for a simple life that he nonetheless complicates at every turn. Narrated in an omniscient third-person voice that is both smart-alecky and world-weary, the book finds Daniels in a conundrum when he is hired by a law firm to attempt to obtain mitigating evidence for the defense in a murder case. The problem is that the late victim,

Kelly Kuhio, is a local surfing icon revered by the community, including Daniels and his surfer buddies. . . . Winslow's matter-of-fact but dark narration is the key to this plot-driven work about the fragility and strength of friendships and principles." Bookreporter

Winslow, Don

The **kings** of cool; Don Winslow. Simon & Schuster 2012 322 p. (paperback) $15.00; (downloadable audio) $17.95; (hardcover) $25.00

ISBN 9781451665338; 9781442349803; 1451665326; 9781451665321

LC 2012010619

In this book by Don Winslow, the "prequel to 2010's 'Savages' . . . readers learn the blistering backstories of twentysomething buds Ben and Chon as well as O, the rebellious babe they both love. Beginning his tale in the 1960s, Winslow paints an unsettling portrait of the underbelly of Southern California, from pot- and coke-dealing hippie parents to Mexican gang leaders who compose messages with human entrails." (Booklist)

Winslow, Don

Satori. Grand Central Pub. 2010 504p $25.99

ISBN 978-0-446-56192-1; 0-446-56192-4

LC 2010-12415

"In this homage to Trevanian's cult classic Shibumi (1979), Winslow . . . fills in some of Trevanian's main character's back story. In Shibumi, Nicholai Hel was already an accomplished assassin, called out of retirement to perform one more job. Winslow takes the reader back a few decades to the early 1950s to explain how Hel got into the assassination business in the first place. He picks up the thread after Hel's three-year stint in an American jail for the murder of his mentor in the chaos of post–World War II Japan. The Americans recognize his unique abilities—including his mastery of several languages and thehoda korosumartial art—and offer him a deal: He can have his freedom and a chance to even the score with those who have mistreated him in prison if he will travel to Beijing under the guise of a French arms dealer and assassinate a Soviet official. . . . Perfect for Shibumi fans and anyone else who likes their espionage over the top." Kirkus

Winslow, Don

★ **Savages**. Simon & Schuster 2010 302p $25

ISBN 1-4391-8336-8; 978-1-4391-8336-6

LC 2010-16924

"Part-time environmentalist and philanthropist Ben and his ex-mercenary buddy Chon run a Laguna Beach-based marijuana operation, reaping significant profits from their loyal clientele. . . . Now they have come up against something that they can't handle—the Mexican Baja Cartel wants in, and sends them the message that a 'no' is unacceptable." (Publisher's note)

"Ben and Chon are two Americans running a lucrative marijuana operation out of ritzy Laguna Beach, California. Their business is buzzing along nicely until members of the Mexican Baja Cartel decide they want a piece of the action. Ben, a charitable, environmentally conscious Berkeley grad, doesn't want any trouble. Former Navy Seal Chon prefers peace as well but not if it means giving up primo weed. When Ben and Chon resist the Mexicans' demands, the cartel kidnaps 'O' (short for Ophelia), the boys' close confidante and frequent bedroom playmate. Ben and Chon conjure clever schemes to outwit their adversaries and win back O, using everything from improvised explosive devices to Letterman and Leno masks. . . . [Winslow] dispenses short chapters that drive his plot breathlessly forward. He also serves up plenty of savage wit." Booklist

Winslow, Don

The **winter** of Frankie Machine. Alfred A. Knopf 2006 299p $23.95

ISBN 1-4000-4498-7

LC 2006-45263

"Frank Machianno, a retired mob hit man known as Frankie Machine as a tribute to his efficiency, has put his past behind him and is living a tranquil life in San Diego running a bait shop and supplying restaurants with linens and seafood. When the son of a local mob boss asks for his backup in resolving a dispute with the Detroit mob, Frank agrees, only to find that he's been set up as the intended victim of a hit. Using his survival skills and street smarts, the executioner follows a trail of bodies to identify which of his past crimes has caught up with him. While the plot is familiar, Winslow has created plausible characters and taut scenes of suspense that will keep readers turning pages." Publ Wkly

Winspear, Jacqueline

Among the mad; a Maisie Dobbs novel. Henry Holt and Company 2009 303p $25

ISBN 978-0-8050-8216-6; 0-8050-8216-6

LC 2008-32576

Sequel to: An incomplete revenge (2008)

"The lamentation over economic crisis, terrorism and traumatized veterans feels both true to its setting and disquietingly contemporary. Well-crafted and well worth reading." Kirkus

Followed by The mapping of love and death (2010)

Winspear, Jacqueline

Birds of a feather; a novel. Soho Press 2004 311p $25

ISBN 1-569-47368-4

LC 2003-25732

Sequel to Maisie Dobbs (2003)

P.I. Maisie Dobbs "has been hired to find the missing daughter of a wealthy London magnate. As Maisie and her Cockney assistant, Billy Beale, try to track Charlotte Waite down, they discover that three of her old friends have been murdered-poisoned and then bayoneted." Libr J

Followed by Pardonable lies (2005)

Winspear, Jacqueline

A **Dangerous** Place; Jacqueline Winspear. HarperCollins 2015 320 p. $26.99

ISBN 0062220551; 9780062220554

LC 2014504287

This novel, by Jacqueline Winspear, is part of the Maisie Dobbs mystery series. "During an evening walk, Maisie finds the body of photographer Sebastian Babayoff. Feeling it's her responsibility to find the truth about the murder, she starts to work, which lifts her near-suicidal depression. Things become more complicated when she finds herself the object of investigation, then stumbles on dangerous activities that support the Spanish Republican forces." (Booklist)

"This eleventh entry in the Maisie Dobbs series, with enough backstory to stand alone, shows the same meticulous research that grounds these books so firmly in their time and place, along with moving life changes that further humanize the intrepid protagonist. Another winner from Winspear." Booklist

Winspear, Jacqueline

Elegy for Eddie; Jacqueline Winspear. Harper/HarperCollins 2012 352 pp. $25.99

ISBN 9780062049575

LC 2011278583

In this book, "[Maisie Dobbs, a] determined psychologist and private investigator looks into the death of Eddie, a gentle man who seemed to have no enemies, certainly not among the horses he charmed. . . . But she can never forget the poor neighborhood in which she was raised. So she doesn't hesitate when the costermongers of Covent Garden ask her to investigate Eddie's death after he's crushed by a roll of paper at the factory of wealthy Canadian newspaper baron John Otterburn. The more Maisie finds out, the more she's convinced that Otterburn is using his considerable influence to steer Britain toward a confrontation with a resurgent Germany led by Hitler. . . . Despite mounting danger, she continues to investigate while trying to put her own life in order." (Kirkus)

Winspear, Jacqueline

An **incomplete** revenge; a Maisie Dobbs novel. H. Holt 2008 306p $24; pa $14

ISBN 978-0-8050-8215-9; 0-8050-8215-8; 978-0-312-42818-1 pa; 0-312-42818-9 pa

LC 2007-40639

Sequel to Messenger of truth (2006)

Maisie Dobbs, the extraordinary psychologist and investigator, delves into a strange series of crimes in a small rural community involving mysterious fires, petty crimes, and the legacy of a wartime Zeppelin raid.

"Maisie is absolutely compelling not only as an investigator but also as a psychologist while she probes the hearts and minds of those she meets." Libr J

Followed by Among the mad (2009)

Winspear, Jacqueline

Leaving Everything Most Loved; a Maisie Dobbs Novel. Maisie Dobbs. HarperCollins 2013 352 p. (hardcover) $26.99

ISBN 0062049607; 9780062049605

This is the 10th Maisie Dobbs novel from Jacqueline Winspear. Here, in "the summer of 1933, a young Indian immigrant, Usha Pramal, is found dead in a London canal with a gunshot wound in her forehead. More than two months later, the victim's devastated brother, freshly arrived by boat from India, hires Daisy to solve his sister's murder. With the trail gone cold and the evidence thin, Maisie has her work cut out for her." (Publishers Weekly)

Winspear, Jacqueline

★ **Maisie** Dobbs; a novel. Soho Press 2003 294p pbk $16; hbk o.p.

ISBN 9780142004333; 9781569473306; 1569473307; 0142004332

LC 2002-44656

"For a clever and resourceful young woman who has just set herself up in business as a private investigator, Maisie seems a bit too sober and much too sad. Romantic readers sensing a story-within-a-story won't be disappointed. But first, they must prepare to be astonished at the sensitivity and wisdom with which Maisie resolves her first professional assignment." N Y Times Book Rev

Other titles about Maisie Dobbs are:
Birds of a feather (2004)
Pardonable lies (2005)
Messenger of truth (2006)
An incomplete revenge (2008)
Among the mad (2009)
The mapping of love and death (2010)
A lesson in secrets (2011)
Elegy for Eddie (2012)
Leaving everything most loved (2013)
A dangerous place (2015)
Journey to Munich (2016)
In this grave hour (2017)
To die but once (2018)

Winspear, Jacqueline

The **mapping** of love and death; a Maisie Dobbs novel. Harper 2010 338p $25.99; pa $14.99

ISBN 978-0-06-172766-5; 0-06-172766-0; 978-0-06-172768-9 pa; 0-06-172768-7 pa

LC 2009-49970

Sequel to Among the mad (2009)

London investigator Maisie Dobbs must unravel a case of wartime love and death—an investigation that leads her to a doomed affair between a young cartographer, listed as missing in action when World War I ends, and a mysterious nurse.

In this installment Maisie Dodds, a "private investigator and former World War I field nurse, tries to help the parents of an American soldier, missing since 1916, whose remains aren't recovered until 1932 on a farm in the Somme Valley. A mapmaker ('an adventurer with his feet on the ground'), Michael Clifton became a military cartographer and presumably perished in the same shelling that wiped out the rest of his unit. But when a necropsy shows he was murdered, Maisie must rely on his diary and the letters of an unknown English nurse to figure out how he died. Always the thorough researcher, Winspear surpasses herself in this absorbing novel by giving Maisie an exacting assignment: learning the skills cartographers bring into battle and then discovering why someone would want to kill one of them." N Y Times Book Rev

Followed by A lesson in secrets (2011)

Winspear, Jacqueline

Messenger of truth; a Maisie Dobbs novel. H. Holt 2006 322p $24; pa $14

ISBN 978-0-8050-7898-5; 0-8050-7898-3; 978-0-312-42685-9 pa; 0-312-42685-2 pa

LC 2006-43626

Sequel to Pardonable lies (2005)

This installment in the historical mystery series "finds our fearless psychologist/inquiry agent investigating the death of artist Nick Bassington-Hope. According to Detective Inspector Stratton, Nick's fall from a set of scaffolding was merely a tragic accident. Nick's twin sister, Georgina, however, insists he was murdered and hires Maisie to discover the truth. . . . The mystery itself is rather transparent, but what makes this book delightful is how Winspear shows Maisie's emotional development amid the bitter legacy of the Great War." Libr J

Followed by An incomplete revenge (2008)

Winspear, Jacqueline

Pardonable lies; a Maisie Dobbs novel. Henry Holt 2005 342p hardcover o.p. pa $15

ISBN 0-8050-7897-5; 0-312-42621-6 pa

LC 2005-46388

Sequel to Birds of a feather (2004)

In this installment, "British psychologist and investigator Maisie Dobbs, who attended university after serving as a nurse in France during World War I, tackles a trio of cases that ranges from the unsettling to the surreal. There's 13-year-old Avril Jarvis, accused of first-degree murder. And Sir Cecil Lawton, QC, who is attempting to honor his late wife's request to determine if their fighter-pilot son is living or dead. And Maisie's rich, trendy friend, Priscilla, desperate for details about her brother, who was killed in the Great War. Maisie pursues clues with the help of her Cockney assistant, Billy, and wisdom imparted by her elegant, if enigmatic, mentor, Maurice. . . . A trip to France reveals a startling connection between the cases but proves traumatic for the former nurse still haunted by her experiences tending to wounded soldiers during the war." Booklist

Followed by Messenger of truth (2006)

Winston, Lolly

Good grief. Warner Books 2004 344p $18

ISBN 0-446-53304-1

LC 2003-15207

After thirty-six-year-old Sophie Stanton's husband Ethan dies of cancer, she leaves her job with a technology company in Silicon Valley and winds up in Oregon where she reinvents herself as a baker and finds a new love interest

"Throughout this heartbreaking, gorgeous look at loss, Winston imbues her heroine and her narrative with the kind of grace, bitter humor and rapier-sharp realness that will dig deep into a reader's heart and refuse to let go. Sophie is wounded terribly, but she's also funny, fresh and utterly believable." Publ Wkly

Winter, Kathleen

Annabel; Kathleen Winter. Black Cat 2010 465p $14.95

ISBN 9780802170828

LC 2010481429

Writers' Federation of Nova Scotia Book Prizes: Thomas Head Raddall Atlantic Fiction Prize (2011)

In this book, which is set "[i]n 1968, into the beautiful, spare environment of remote coastal Labrador, a mysterious child is born: a baby who appears to be neither fully boy nor girl, but both at once. Only three people are privy to the secret—the baby's parents, Jacinta and Treadway, and a trusted neighbour, Thomasina. Together the adults make a difficult decision: to raise the child as a boy named Wayne. But as Wayne grows to adulthood within the hyper-masculine hunting culture of his father, his shadow-self—a girl he thinks of as 'Annabel'—is never entirely extinguished, and indeed is secretly nurtured by the women in his life." (Publisher's note)

Winters, Ben H.

Bedbugs. Quirk Books 2011 253p pa $14.95

ISBN 978-1-59474-523-2; 1-59474-523-4

LC 2011-922691

"The idea of supernatural bedbugs is a stroke of horror genius. Regular bedbugs are enough to inspire shuddering revulsion in most people, and stories abound about how hard they are to purge and how a bad case of them can cause enough strain to break up a stable relationship. Badbugs are bedbugs on steroids, and the death of the person who brought them into being is the only way they can be destroyed. The book sings when it sinks into the scary muck of this mythology." Los Angeles Times Book Rev

Winters, Ben H.

Countdown city; Ben H. Winters. Quirk Books 2013 320 p.

ISBN 9781594746260

LC 2013930159

This is the second book in Ben H. Winters' Last Policeman series. The Earth is due to be destroyed by an asteroid in 77 days. "An old family friend asks [former police officer Hank] to find her husband. Hank reluctantly agrees, but with so many people dropping out to pursue their bucket lists and no telephones or electricity, it won't be easy." (Library Journal)

Winters, Ben H.

The **last** policeman. Quirk Books 2012 316 p. (paperback) $14.95; (ebook) $14.95

ISBN 1594745765; 9781594745768; 9781594745775

LC 2012454509

In this detective novel by Ben H. Winters, "Hank Palace is investigating a suspicious death that may be a murder or might be part of an epidemic of suicides. Both the promotion and the suicides are rooted in the fact that an asteroid is on a collision course with Earth and will destroy all life in a few months. Palace faces indifference from many of his colleagues who don't see the point of solving one death when everyone is under the same sentence." (Library Journal)

Other titles in this series are:
Countdown city (2013)
World of trouble (2014)

Winters, Ben H.

World of trouble; Ben H. Winters. Quirk Books 2014 316 p. (Last policeman) (pbk.) $14.95

ISBN 9781594746857; 1594746850

LC 2014903377

"With the doomsday asteroid looming, Detective Hank Palace has found sanctuary in the woods of New England, secure in a well-stocked safe house with other onetime members of the Concord police force. But with time ticking away before the asteroid makes landfall, Hank's safety is only relative, and his only relative--his sister Nico--isn't safe." (Publisher's note)

"The bleak premise of this series could be too much, but, instead, it gives a certain clarity to the action of people who become their most real selves when the end of the world arrives." LJ

Winterson, Jeanette, 1959-

Oranges are not the only fruit. Grove Press 1997 176p pa $14

ISBN 0-8021-3516-1

First published 1985 in the United Kingdom

"Raised by an oppressively evangelical mother, Jeanette grows up a good little Christian soldier, even going so far as to stitch samplers whose apocalyptic themes terrify her classmates. . . . Jeanette would have remained in the fold but for her unconventional desires; though she can reconcile her love of women with her love of God, the church cannot. It could have been a grim tale, but this [novel] . . . is in fact a wry and tender telling of a young girl's triumphantly coming into her own." Libr J

Winterson, Jeanette, 1959-

The **Passion**; Jeanette Winterson. Grove Press 1997 176 p. (pbk.) $15

ISBN 0802135226; 9780802135223

This novel by Jeanette Winterson is set during the tumultuous years of the Napoleonic Wars. It "intertwines the destinies of two remarkable people: Henri, a simple French soldier, who follows Napoleon from glory to Russian ruin; and Villanelle, the red-haired, web-footed daughter of a Venetian boatman, whose husband has gambled away her heart. In Venice's compound of carnival, chance, and darkness, the pair meet their singular destiny." (Publisher's note)

Winthrop, Elizabeth Hartley

★ The **why** of things; by Elizabeth Hartley Winthrop. Simon & Schuster 2013 320 p. $24.99

ISBN 1451695756; 9781451695755

LC 2012041122

In this novel by Elizabeth Hartley Winthrop "since the tragic loss of her . . . daughter less than a year ago, Joan Jacobs has been working hard to keep her . . . family [together]. The Jacobses flee to their summer home in search of peace. That same evening a pickup truck had driven into the quarry in their backyard. The local police drag up the body of . . . James Favazza. As the Jacobs family learns more about the . . . events that led up to that . . . evening, each of them becomes increasingly tangled in . . . James' life and death." (Publisher's note)

Winton, Tim

Breath; a novel. Farrar, Straus and Giroux 2008 320p $23

ISBN 978-0-374-11634-7; 0-374-11634-2

LC 2007-47879

"The novel's complexity is poetic, psychological and ethical. Winton's descriptions of changing seas and changing seasons are outstanding. His insights into what motivates people like the bitter Eva or the profoundly irresponsible Sando disclose unsettling ethical implications with a sure hand." Sydney Morning Herald

Winton, Tim

Dirt music; a novel. Scribner 2002 411p $26

ISBN 0-7432-2802-2

LC 2002-17583

First published 2001 in Australia

"As well as offering nuanced portraits of three very different characters, [this] is a cracking page-turner which deftly splices together separate narrative threads without ever losing its headlong momentum. . . . Mr Winton comes from Western Australia, a vast state of exceptional natural beauty. . . . He brilliantly conjures its hostile desert spaces and its magnificent coastline. His characters, like the landscape they inhabit, are by turns callous and poetic, vulgar and seductive." Economist

Wiprud, Brian M.

Ringer. Minotaur Books 2011 338p $26.99

ISBN 978-0-312-60189-8; 0-312-60189-1

LC 2011-08724

Sequel to: Feelers (2009)

Morty Martinez pursues a sacred ring currently in the possession of a New York City billionaire, a situation that traps him between the billionaire and his tabloid-prone stepdaughter, all before Morty's sensational murder trial in Mexico.

"Told from Martinez's jail cell the night before he's to be executed, this relentlessly amusing novel is powered by a cast of decidedly quirky characters and its idiosyncratic narrator's frequent digressions (like his defense of breast implants). Fans of the comic crime fiction of Donald E. Westlake and Charles Willeford will find a lot to like." Publ Wkly

Wiseman, Beth

Plain paradise; a Daughters of the promise novel. Beth Wiseman. Thomas Nelson 2010 vi, 313p.p (soft cover) $15.99

ISBN 9781595548238

LC 2009052637

This novel tells the story of "Linda . . . [whose] Amish life seemed like paradise. Until she found out her family had been hiding a secret since the day of her birth. Josie was just a frightened teenager when she left her baby in the care of an Old Order Amish couple in Lancaster County. Since then, seventeen years have passed and while much has changed, one thing hasn't. Josie still longs to reconnect with her daughter Linda. But Linda is unaware of Josie--and living an idyllic life within the Amish community. The bishop's grandson, Stephen, is courting her and she hopes that he will propose soon. When her birth mother comes to Paradise, Linda finds herself unexpectedly drawn to Josie's world." (Publisher's note)

Wodehouse, P. G.

The **code** of the Woosters. Doubleday, Doran 1938 298p

"It was only the fact that Jeeves belonged to an exclusive club of gentlemen's personal gentlemen, where all the secrets in the lives of employers were filed for reference, that saved Bertie Wooster when the disappearance of an eighteenth-century silver cows-creamer threatened to land him in jail. Two rival collectors who coveted the piece of silver, and two pairs of bickering lovers, made Bertie's life a burden until Jeeves unearthed evidence that was a weapon." Booklist

Wodehouse, P. G.

The **inimitable** Jeeves; Autograph ed; British Bk. Centre 1956 192p

First published 1923 in the United Kingdom

The resourceful valet again takes command of a typical Wodehouse situation

Wodehouse, P. G.

Tales from the Drones Club. International Polygonics 1991 352p

LC 91-8386

First published 1982 in the United Kingdom

Contents: Jeeves takes charge; Jeeves in the springtime; Scoring off Jeeves; Sir Roderick comes to lunch; Aunt Agatha takes the count; The artistic career of Corky; Jeeves and Chump Cyril; Jeeves and the unbidden guest; Jeeves and the hard-boiled egg; The aunt and the sluggard; Comrade Bingo; The great sermon handicap; The purity of the turf; The metropolitan touch; The delayed exit of Claude and Eustace; Bingo and the little woman; The rummy affair of Old Biffy; Without the option; Fixing it for Freddie; Clustering round young Bingo; Jeeves and the impending doom; The inferiority complex of Old Sippy; Jeeves and the Yule-tide spirit; Jeeves and the song of songs; Episode of the dog Mcintosh; The spot of art; Jeeves and the kid Clementina; The love that purifies; Jeeves and the old school chum; Indian summer of an uncle; The ordeal of young Tuppy; Bertie changes his mind; Jeeves makes an omelette; Jeeves and the greasy bird

Wodehouse, P. G.

A **Wodehouse** bestiary; edited and with a preface by D.R. Bensen; foreword by Howard Phipps, Jr. Ticknor & Fields 1985 329p

LC 85-7999

"An anthology of tales featuring animals of all sorts wreaking havoc in the lives of Bertie Wooster, the indomitable Jeeves, Mr. Muliner's various relations, and other familiar characters from the madcap Wodehousian world. The numerous mishaps, involving snakes, pigs, gorillas, swans, dogs, and cats, prove as amusing as ever." Booklist

Wodehouse, P. G.

★ The **world** of Jeeves. Harper & Row 1988 654p

LC 88-45072

First published 1967 in the United Kingdom

Contents: Fate; Tried in the furnace; Trouble down at Tudsleigh; The amazing hat mystery; Goodbye to all cats; The luck of the Stiffhams; Noblesse oblige; Uncle Fred flits by; The masked troubadour; All's well with Bingo; Bingo and the Peke crisis; The editor regrets; Sonny boy; The shadow passes; Bramley is so bracing; The fat of the land; The word in season; Leave it to Algy; Oofy, Freddie and the beef trust; Bingo bans the bomb; Stylish stouts

Wolf, Christa, 1929-2011

City of angels or; The overcoat of Dr. Freud. Christa Wolf; translated from the German by Damion Searls. Farrar, Straus and Giroux 2013 336 p. (alk. paper) $27

ISBN 0374269351; 9780374269357

LC 2012018515

This novel is the last from the late author Christa Wolf, winner of the first Deutscher Bücherpress for lifetime achievement. The book "draws on an unsettling discovery she made while perusing her Stasi files: she herself had informed in the early 1960s--something she recalled not at all." (Library Journal)

Wolf, Joan

This scarlet cord; Joan Wolf. Thomas Nelson 2012 307 p. (trade paper) $15.99

ISBN 1595548777; 9781595548771

LC 2012010908

This novel, by Joan Wolf, revisits the Old Testament story of Rahab. "Rahab is the youngest daughter of a Canaanite farmer, taken to Jericho . . . so her father can find her a wealthy spouse. Sala, the Israelite boy who had once saved her from being kidnapped, is also in Jericho. When the two young people meet again they admit their love for one another, but . . . [i]t is only when the One True God of Israel comes into Rahab's life . . . that she and Sala can come together." (Publisher's note)

Wolfe, Gene

★ The **best** of Gene Wolfe; a definitive retrospective of his finest short fiction. Tor 2009 478p $27.95

ISBN 9780765321350; 0-7653-2135-1

LC 2009-12889

This "is a highly flattering career retrospective of a postmodern fabulist disguised as a mild-mannered SF writer." Publ Wkly

Wolfe, Gene

★ **Castleview**. Doherty Assocs. 1990 278p

LC 89-25712

Wolfe's "deceptively simple prose masks a wealth of complexity." Libr J

Wolfe, Gene

The **Citadel** of the Autarch. Timescape Bks. 1983 317p (Book of the new Sun)

LC 82-5964

"Wolfe plays with the language like a master wordsmith, yet never loses control of the multi-layered story he's weaving. His style is paradoxically both baroque and simple—the lush beauty of the words never renders the tale impenetrable." Best Sellers

Wolfe, Gene

The **claw** of the conciliator. Timescape Bks. 1981 303p (Book of the new Sun)

LC 80-20569

In this second volume of the series "Severian, a journeyman torturer, struggles to return the magical Claw of the Conciliator to its guardians. His quest is delayed when men under the leadership of the bandit Vodalus capture him to prevent the execution of a comrade. Severian and his companion Jonas win their freedom by agreeing to carry a message to an agent of Vodalus' at the Castle Absolute, seat of power for the ruling Autarch. Severian has no intention of carrying the promise through, in spite of his admiration for Vodalus. His intention to find his lover and continue his personal quest suffers a temporary setback at the hands of Castle guards." West Coast Rev Books

Followed by The sword of the Lictor

Wolfe, Gene

Home fires. Tor 2011 304p $24.99

ISBN 978-0-7653-2818-2; 0-7653-2818-6

LC 2010-36106

"With complications involving spies, murderers, cyborgs and pirates, Wolfe cross-examines his characters with a subtle, intelligent series of psychological and logical challenges. A somber, almost brooding tone permeates this compelling work from one of the genre's grandmasters." Kirkus

Wolfe, Gene

The **land** across; Gene Wolfe. Tor Books 2013 288 p. (hardback) $25.99

ISBN 0765335956; 9780765335951

LC 2013022126

In this fantasy novel, American writer Grafton "chooses to travel to a small and obscure Eastern European country. The moment Grafton crosses the border he is in trouble, much more than he could have imagined. His passport is taken by guards, and then he is detained for not having it. He is released into the custody of a family, but is again detained. It becomes evident that there are supernatural agencies at work." (Publisher's note)

Wolfe, Gene

Pirate freedom. Tor 2007 320p il $24.95

ISBN 978-0-7653-1878-7; 0-7653-1878-4

LC 2007-14348

"The one issue Wolfe tap-dances around is slavery. Chris treats slaves as fellow men and frees them whenever possible without anything more than the occasional light question from others. Wolfe's writing is reminiscent of Carol Emshwiller. . . . There's the same concrete level of detail mixed with an occasionally hazy sense of time and events. The novel is as simple as Wolfe's straightforward, lean prose and easily pulls the reader through to an enjoyable circular ending." BookPage

Wolfe, Gene

The **shadow** of the torturer. Simon & Schuster 1980 303p (Book of the new Sun)

LC 79-22371

"The book combines elements of fantasy and sf, and the slow pacing is balanced by the excellent characterization and the richly detailed, thoroughly compelling future world." Booklist

Followed by The claw of the conciliator

Wolfe, Gene

The **sorcerer's** house. Tor 2010 302p $24.99

ISBN 978-0-7653-2458-0; 0-7653-2458-X

LC 2009-40726

"Early on in the novel, Wolfe hints at a great darkness, and a world of tremendous power that may destroy Bax if he doesn't master it—but there's very little darkness in this book after the first hundred pages or so. It's almost as if Wolfe couldn't bear to have anything unpleasant happen to his main character, whose good fortune keeps getting better and better. It's a remarkably sunny version of fantasy literature, and though the novel runs out of narrative steam towards the end, by that point you're already drawn in by Wolfe's prodigious invention." io9

Wolfe, Gene

The **sword** of the Lictor. Timescape Bks. 1981 302p (Book of the new Sun)

LC 81-9427

In this third volume of the series "Severian, the torturer demoted to executioner, has reached Thrax, city of his exile, only to find that he can no longer do his work. He lets a prisoner escape rather than kill her (his original crime was to offer a prisoner the escape of death) and flees to the mountains. He meets the Alzabo, a terrifying creature in whom those eaten seem to live on, adopts a son and loses him, fights a revivified tyrant of the past and wins, helps the people of the floating islands, meets aliens and learns something of their true nature. The magical jewel called the Claw of the Conciliator is smashed, but Severian finds its essential heart, which is indeed a claw." Publ Wkly

Followed by The Citadel of the Autarch

Wolfe, Gene

The **Urth** of the new sun. Doherty Assocs. 1987 372p (Book of the new Sun)

LC 87-50478

For all its obvious unity, the book also has a strongly picaresque quality, with many episodes and characters developed as lovingly and skillfully as Wolfe can manage—which is very well indeed." Booklist

Wolfe, Inger Ash

The **calling**. Harcourt 2008 371p $24

ISBN 978-0-15-101347-0

LC 2007-29290

"An excellent literary thriller, both riveting and precise. The ending is a shocker." Libr J

Wolfe, Inger Ash

The **taken**. Houghton Mifflin Harcourt 2010 415p $25

ISBN 978-0-15-101353-1; 0-15-101353-5

LC 2010-05774

A "police procedural featuring Canadian Det. Insp. Hazel Micallef. . . . A bizarre case brings Micallef, who depends on her ex-husband and his new wife as she recovers from a serious back injury suffered in the line of duty, back into action sooner than planned. A body fishermen dredge up from the bottom of a lake in Port Dundas, Ont., turns out just to be a mannequin, but numbers on the dummy lead Micallef to a Web site streaming video that appears to show a man being tortured by his abductor. In a frantic search for clues, Micallef concludes that the kidnapping is somehow linked to a fictional story being run in installments in the local newspaper. It's a testament to Wolfe's storytelling gifts that her reveal of the criminal's identity about midway through heightens rather than diminishes the tension." Publ Wkly

Wolfe, Thomas

The **complete** short stories of Thomas Wolfe; edited by Francis E. Skipp; foreword by James Dickey. Scribner 1987 xxix, 621p hardcover o.p. pa $27.50

ISBN 0-02-040891-9 pa

LC 86-13782

"All 58 of Wolfe's short stories . . . have been edited by Skipp in a way that represents what Wolfe himself may have wanted his audience to read." Booklist

Wolfe, Thomas

★ **Look** homeward, angel; a story of the buried life. with an introduction by Maxwell E. Perkins. Scribner 563p $45; pa $14

ISBN 0-684-15158-8; 0-684-80443-3 pa

First published 1929

This novel, autobiographical in character, "describes the childhood and youth of Eugene Gant in the town of Altamont, state of Catawba (said to be Asheville, North Carolina). As Gant grows up, he becomes aware of the relations among his family, meets the eccentric people of the town, goes to college, discovers literature and ideas, has his first love affairs, and at last sets out alone on a mystic and romantic 'pilgrimage.'" Reader's Ency. 4th edition

Followed by Of time and the river (1935)

Wolfe, Thomas

O lost; a story of the buried life. text established by Arlyn and Matthew J. Bruccoli. Centenary ed; University of S.C. Press 2000 xli, 694p il $34.95

ISBN 1-57003-369-2

LC 00-9503

"The reinsertion of expurgated material puts the marrow back in the novel's bones, making for a richer reading experience." Libr J

Wolfe, Thomas

★ **Of** time and the river; a legend of man's hunger in his youth. Scribner 912p $35

ISBN 0-684-14739-4

First published 1935

In this sequel to Look homeward, angel, "Eugene Gant, the hero, spends two years as a graduate student at Harvard, returns home for the dramatic death of his father, and teaches literature in New York City at the 'School for Utility Culture' (New York University). Eventually he tours France, returning home financially and emotionally exhausted." Reader's Ency. 4th edition

Wolfe, Thomas

★ The **web** and the rock. Harper 1939 695p

"Wolfe's large scheme has the scope, massive detail and sense of space and time of an epic structure, but also the redundancy of its cyclic conception. The interest lies with the accurate dialogues, realistic descriptions and passages of poetic rhetoric sometimes of considerable power." Penguin Companion to Am Lit

Followed by You can't go home again

Wolfe, Thomas

★ **You** can't go home again. Harper 1940 743p

This sequel to The web and the rock "deals with George's life after his return to the U.S.: his continued unsatisfactory romance; his success in writing novels reminiscent of Wolfe's own; his kindly relation and later dissatisfaction with an internationally famous but disillusioned novelist and with his editor, who fatalistically accepts the sickness of civilization; his unsuccessful attempt to return to the roots of his hometown, whose morality has become shoddy during the prosperous decade of the '20s; and his horrid discovery of the destruction of the Germany he had once loved." Oxford Companion to Am Lit. 6th edition

Wolfe, Tom, 1931-2018

★ The **bonfire** of the vanities. Farrar, Straus & Giroux 1987 659p $25

ISBN 0-374-11534-6

LC 87-17691

In this book, "on a clandestine date with his mistress one night, top Wall Street investment banker and snobbish WASP Sherman McCoy misses his turn on the thruway and gets lost in the South Bronx; his Mercedes hits and seriously injures a young black man. The incident is inflated by a manipulative black leader, a district attorney seeking reelection and a sleazy tabloid reporter into a full-blown scandal. . . . The book . . . stand[s] as a[n] . . . evocation of New York's class, racial and political structure in the 1980s." (Publishers Weekly)

"The novel relates the fall of Sherman McCoy, an investment banker making a million a year who seems blind to everything except appearances, sex and money. He lives in the middle of New York City without knowing New York City. He seems barely to know his decorative wife, his decorative daughter or his libidinous mistress, to say nothing of himself. He's all surface is Sherman, and when he blunders off the expressway into the welfare jungle of the South Bronx in his $48,000 Mercedes, into the biggest trouble of his heretofore charmed life, he is without reserves of experience, imagination or moral awareness with which to guide himself." N Y Times Book Rev

Wolfe, Tom, 1931-2018

I am Charlotte Simmons. Farrar, Straus and Giroux 2004 676p $28.95

ISBN 0-374-28158-0

LC 2004-47131

Dupont University-the Olympian halls of learning housing the cream of America's youth, the roseate Gothic spires and manicured lawns suffused with tradition . . . Or so it appears to beautiful, brilliant Charlotte Simmons, a sheltered freshman from North Carolina. But Charlotte soon learns, to her mounting dismay, that for the uppercrust coeds of Dupont, sex, Cool, and kegs trump academic achievement every time. As Charlotte encounters Dupont's privileged elite . . . she gains a new, revelatory sense of her own power, that of her difference and of her very innocence, but little does she realize that she will act as a catalyst in all of their lives." Publisher's note

Wolfe, Tom, 1931-2018

★ **Back** to blood; a novel. Tom Wolfe. Little, Brown 2012 x, 704 p.p $30

ISBN 0316036315; 9780316036313; 9780316221795; 9780316224246

LC 2012019545

This novel by Tom Wolfe focuses on characters living in Miami, Florida including "the Cuban mayor, the black police chief, a . . . young journalist and his Yale-marinated editor; . . . a billionaire porn addict, crack dealers in the 'hoods, 'de-skilled' conceptual artists at the Miami Art Basel Fair, 'spectators' at the annual Biscayne Bay regatta looking only for that night's orgy, yenta-heavy ex-New Yorkers at an 'Active Adult' condo, and a nest of shady Russians." (Publisher's note)

"Wolfe is back to some old tricks, including an ever-shifting, sometimes untrustworthy point of view, dizzying pans from one actor to another and rat-a-tat prose...a welcome pleasure from an old master and the best from his pen in a long while." Kirkus

Wolfe, Tom, 1931-2018

★ A **man** in full; a novel. Farrar, Straus & Giroux 1998 742p $28.95

ISBN 0-374-27032-5

LC 98-29842

Wolfe's novel tells "the story of sixty-year-old Charlie Croker, an undereducated ex-college-football star who has developed much of the skyline of Atlanta, Georgia. . . . Along the way, he has picked up several businesses, a . . . 29,000-acre antebellum plantation (called 'Turpmtine') that he uses for quail hunting and writes off as an 'experimental farm,' and a wife who is less than half his age. Now he has plowed hundreds of millions of his own and other people's money into a 40-storey office building for which he cannot find tenants. . . . {As the novel opens}, the creditors are moving in. . . . {In a subplot}, Georgia Tech's star running back, a ghetto hoodlum named Fareek Fanon, has been accused of raping the daughter of one of Charlie's friends, a pillar of the good-'ol-boy establishment. But Atlanta's black mayor, facing reelection, needs to prevent racial unrest." (Commentary)

"Among all the animal appetites that are slaked or comically thwarted during the novel there appears one new to Wolfe's fiction. For all their affluence, or their pained lack of same, his chief characters hunger for a code of conduct or a framework of beliefs that will make sense of their lives right now, a blink before the millennium. At its heart, A Man in Full is a cliff-hanging morality tale." Time

Wolff, Isabel

A **vintage** affair; a novel. Bantam Books 2010 346p pa $15; $25

ISBN 055338662X; 0553807838; 9780553386622 pa; 9780553807837

LC 2010-1830

"Innocent, tidy and simple escapism, with frocks." Kirkus

Wolff, Tobias

★ **Old** school; a novel. Knopf 2003 195p $22

ISBN 0-375-40146-6

LC 2003-52930

"A fine offering, manly in spirit and style . . . Wolff displays exceptional skill in capturing the small sights and sensations that evoke the whole rarefied world he's taking us back to." Atl Mon (1993)

Wolff, Tobias

Our story begins; new and selected stories. Alfred A. Knopf 2008 379p $26.95

ISBN 978-1-4000-4459-7

LC 2007-44262

"It does not seem coincidental that Wolff's most protean narratives draw heavily upon his autobiographical experiences. Wolff, at his best, is truly a novelist of himself. His feats of self-invention offer a compelling rebuttal both to the fabulists whose stories fall so short of reality that they have to borrow the truth guarantee of memoir—if the lies rang truer, they could be published as fiction—and to those who denounce the faking of memoir as some sort of heinous crime, rather than the failed act of literature it is." Slate

Wolitzer, Hilma

★ **Hearts**. Farrar, Straus & Giroux 1980 342p

LC 80-18556

"This is a comedy about the heart-wrenching process of growth; it is written with great skill and no condescension. Few readers will fail to be moved." New Repub

Wolitzer, Meg

The **Interestings**; Meg Wolitzer. Penguin Group USA 2013 480 p. (hardcover) $27.95

ISBN 1594488398; 9781594488399

LC 2012050294

In this novel, by Meg Wolitzer, "the summer that [Richard] Nixon resigns, six teenagers at a summer camp for the arts become inseparable. Decades later the bond remains powerful, but so much else has changed. . . . Wolitzer follows these characters from the height of youth through middle age, as their talents, fortunes, and degrees of satisfaction diverge." (Publisher's note)

Wolitzer, Meg

The **position**; a novel. Meg Wolitzer. Scribner 2005 307p $24

ISBN 074326178X; 9780743261784

LC 2004056577

In this book, married couple "Paul and Roz Mellow . . . write a how-to sex book . . . that features illustrations of them in every imaginable position. The book becomes a runaway bestseller. When the children find the book and read it together, they're forever traumatized. . . . Flash forward 30 years: Paul and Roz are long divorced and remarried . . . [and] the grown children fumble through their lives on the eve of the publisher's reissue of the sex classic. The oldest, Holly, has settled into late motherhood after a lifetime of nomadic drug-taking; uptight Michael suffers from chronic depression; Dashiell, a gay Log Cabin Republican speechwriter, is diagnosed with Hodgkin's disease; and insecure late-bloomer Claudia returns to her Long Island hometown to finally figure out how to be a fully functioning adult." (Publishers Weekly)

Wolitzer, Meg

Surrender, Dorothy; a novel. Scribner 1999 224p $22

ISBN 0-684-84844-9

LC 98-47007

"Buried within this affecting novel is the troubling question of whether close friendships and close family ties can keep a person from finding romantic intimacy. Wolitzer's Sara didn't live long enough to explore that possibility; perhaps her survivors will be luckier." N Y Times Book Rev

Wolitzer, Meg

The **wife**; a novel. Scribner 2003 219p $23

ISBN 0-684-86940-3

LC 2002-36660

"Wolitzer's crisp pacing and dry wit carry us headlong into a devastating message about the price of love and fame." Publ Wkly

A **Woman's** eye; edited by Sara Paretsky. Delacorte Press 1991 448p

LC 90-28102

Stories included are: Lucky dip, by L. Cody; Murder without a text, by A. Cross; The puppet, by D. S. Davis; Death and diamonds, by S. Dunlap; Getting to know you, by A. Fraser; Full circle, by S. Grafton; Her good name, by C. G. Hart; That summer at Quichiquois, by D. B. Hughes; Discards, by F. Kellerman; Deborah's judgement, by M. Maron; Benny's space, by M. Muller; Where are you, Monica?, by M. A. Oliver; Settled score, by S. Paretsky; The scar, by N. Pickard; A man's home, by S. Singer; Looking for Thelma, by G. Slovo; A match made in hell, by J. Smith; The cutting edge, by M. Wallace; Ghost station, by C. Wheat; Theft of the poet, by B. Wilson; Kill the man for me, by M. Wings

Wong, David

★ **Futuristic** Violence and Fancy Suits; by David Wong. St. Martin's Press 2015 384 p. $26.99

ISBN 1250040191; 9781250040190

LC 2015025817

Alex Award (2016)

This novel by David Wong, takes place in "a world in which . . . human achievement soars to new heights while its depravity plunges to the blackest depths. . . . This is the world in which Zoey Ashe finds herself, navigating a futuristic city in which one can find elements of the fantastic, nightmarish and ridiculous on any street corner. Her only trusted advisor is . . . [a] cat, but even in the future, cats cannot give advice. At least not any that you'd want to follow." (Publisher's note)

"Well-timed humor and explosive thrills, a smart backbone, and witty wordsmithing make this new release by Cracked.com's pseudonym-wielding Jason Pargin (John Dies at the End, 2009) as fun as it gets. Steer this one toward readers of sf with a sense of humor, and fans of Max Barry's satirical futuristic novels." Booklist

Woo, Sung J.

Everything Asian. Thomas Dunne Books 2009 328p $23.95

ISBN 978-0-312-53885-9; 0-312-53885-5

LC 2008-37673

"A charming tale of family, community and the struggle for understanding. . . . Woo eschews immigrant clichés to focus on complicated familial relationships and surprising, sympathetic characters. Alternating between humor and melancholy, Woo's text strikes a true chord." Publ Wkly

Woo, Sung J.

Love love; a novel. Sung J. Woo. Soft Skull Press 2015 302 p. $15.95

ISBN 1593766173; 9781593766177

LC 2015009333

"Judy Lee's life has not turned out the way she'd imagined. She's divorced, she's broke, and her dreams of being a painter have fallen by the wayside. . . . Meanwhile, her brother Kevin, has decided to donate a kidney to their ailing father—until it turns out that he's not a genetic match. . . . Kevin's quest to learn the truth about his biological parents takes him across lines he never thought he'd cross:" (Publisher's note)

"Woo's narrative takes serendipitous turns--he has a knack for making these twists seem organic, like things that would happen in life. Scenes recounting memories of family and lost love are also skillfully interspersed." Pub Wkly

Wood, Barbara

The **dreaming**; a novel of Australia. Random House 1991 453p

LC 90-52883

"After her parents tragic deaths in 1871, Joanna Drury leaves her native India for Australia, to unlock the secret past that haunted her mother, Lady Emily, and led to her mysterious, sudden death at age 40. In Melbourne, Joanna meets dashing and sensitive frontiersman Hugh Westbrook, and together they build Hugh's sheep station into a thriving enterprise, all the while looking for the source of the 'curse' on Joanna's family that took hold in an ancient time the aborigines call 'the dreaming.' . . . Wood's soft-edged prose, likable characters, and period details are always a big hit with her many fans." Booklist

Wood, Barbara

Perfect Harmony; a novel. Little, Brown 1998 429p $23.95

ISBN 0-316-81653-1

LC 97-37623

"Charlotte Lee is the head of Harmony, a major player in the international herbal-medicine industry. Charlotte has taken the ancient Chinese remedies once concocted in her grandmother's kitchen and turned them into a multimillion-dollar business. But now three people have died after taking Harmony products, and when Charlotte receives a series of threatening e-mail messages, it's clear someone is out to ruin the company. Enter Jonathan Sutherland former FBI agent, computer whiz, and—coincidentally—the man Charlotte has loved since she was a teenager." Booklist

Wood, Barbara

★ **Vital** signs. Doubleday 1985 326p

LC 84-13639

"Wood's expert knowledge of medicine and her deft interplay of plot and character make this a richly textured and quite credible story that is delightfully unpredictable from the first page through the last." Booklist

Wood, Summer

Wrecker; a novel. Bloomsbury 2010 290p $20

ISBN 978-1-608-19280-9; 1-608-19280-6

LC 2010-20824

Wood "moves her characters gracefully through trying times, both cultural and personal." Kirkus

Wooding, Chris

Retribution falls; Chris Wooding. Ballantine Books 2011 461p. (pbk. : alk. paper) $16

ISBN 0345522516; 0345522583; 9780345522511; 9780345522580

LC 2010047793

In this book, "Dorian Frey's Ketty Jay is a hugely battered old freighter which just about runs. Frey keeps accepting jobs for himself and his crew in the hope of a big pay cheque. His current job turns out to be too good to be true. Suddenly Frey and his crew are running from the Navy Coalition and hired bounty hunters, as he is set up to take the fall after a freighter he is chasing explodes. Dorian Frey must outwit them all to prove his innocence and catch the real culprits." (Fantasy Book Review)

Woodrell, Daniel

★ The **death** of sweet mister; a novel. Putnam 2001 196p $23.95

ISBN 0-399-14751-9

LC 00-45972

Set in the Missouri hill country, this novel "presents one eventful summer in the life of Shug, a friendless, overweight 13-year-old living with his mother in the caretaker's cottage at the local cemetery. Glenda flirts incessantly, even with her son, who is becoming increasingly aware of her charms. Glenda's husband, Red (who may or may not be Shug's father), comes and goes, bringing money occasionally and strife a lot more often. . . . Shug's efforts to protect his mother from Red, from other admirers, and from her own rash decisions come to a head one hot summer night." Libr J

Woodrell, Daniel

★ **Give** us a kiss; a country noir. Holt & Co. 1996 237p

ISBN 0-8050-2298-8

LC 95-23458

A "novel set in the Missouri Ozarks, this is the . . . tale of tough-guy midlist novelist Doyle Redmond's transformation into the writer he only dreamed of being. Escaping from trendy California in his estranged wife's Volvo, Doyle reconnects with his roughneck heritage: gun-crazy grandpa and older brother, . . . marijuana farms, and a 50-year-old blood feud with the infamous Dolly clan." (Libr J)

The author creates a "vanishing South with an accuracy and understanding beyond any genre writer's capability. . . . If one is tempted to hear echoes of William Faulkner, Erskine Caldwell or Andrew Lytle in such themes, no matter. Mr. Woodrell isn't imitating any of them. He's only drawing from the same well they did, but with a different take, a different voice, a sharper sense of irony and satire." N Y Times Book Rev

Woodrell, Daniel

★ The **maid's** version; Daniel Woodrell. Little, Brown and Co. 2013 176 p. $25

ISBN 0316205850; 9780316205856

LC 2013937480

This book, loosely "based on the real-life West Plains Dance Hall Explosion of 1928, . . . centers on Alma DeGeer Dunahew, a maid with three children in fictional West Table, Mo. After years of bitter silence, Alma has chosen to unburden her story on her grandson, Alek." She explains that when her sister "Ruby [is] killed along with 42 other victims in the local Arbor Dance Hall, Alma [was] determined that the explosion was no accident." (Kirkus Reviews)

Woodrell, Daniel

The **outlaw** album; stories. by Daniel Woodrell. Little, Brown 2011 167p $24.99

ISBN 9780316057561; 0316057568

LC 2011-01107

This collection of short stories, by Dabniel Woodrell, presents "Ozarkian tales of those on the fringes of society. . . A husband cruelly avenges the killing of his wife's pet; an injured rapist is cared for by a young girl, until she reaches her breaking point; a disturbed veteran of Iraq is murdered for his erratic behavior. . . . There is also the tenderness and loyalty of the vulnerable in these stories--between spouses, parents and children, siblings, and comrades in arms." (Publisher's note)

"'Once Boshell finally killed his neighbor he couldn't seem to quit killing him.' That's the opening line of The Outlaw Album, a collection of country-noir stories by the author of Winter's Bone, and it's also a warning: People don't just die in the book. Instead, they go insane (as a Vietnam vet does in 'Night Stand') or get viciously tortured (as a rapist does in 'Uncle')—and then they die. At times, Woodrell seems too eager to punish his characters. But in his best tales, the human desperation behind the violence is gripping. If anyone understands what motivates a man to keep shooting a corpse with a squirrel rifle, it's Woodrell." Entertainment Wkly

Woodrell, Daniel

Winter's bone; a novel. Little, Brown and Co. 2006 193p $22.95

ISBN 0-316-05755-X

LC 2005-17349

"Like his characters, and especially his teen characters, Woodrell's prose mixes tough and tender so thoroughly yet so delicately that we never taste even a hint of false bravado, on the one hand, or sentimentality, on the other. And Ree is one of those heroines whose courage and vulnerability are both irresistible and completely believable—think of not just Mattie Ross in True Grit but also Scout in To Kill a Mockingbird or even Eliza Naumann in Bee Season. One runs out of superlatives to describe Woodrell's fiction." Booklist

Woodruff, Lee

Those we love most; Lee Woodruff. Voice/Hyperion 2012 305 p. (hardcover) $26.99

ISBN 1401341780; 9781401341787

LC 2011049422

In this novel, by Lee Woodruff, "[l]ife is good for Maura Corrigan. . . . Then one day, in a single turn of fate, that entire world comes crashing down and everything that she thought she knew changes. . . . [The novel] chronicles how these . . . characters confront their choices, examine their mistakes, fight for their most valuable relationships, and ultimately find their way back to each other." (Publisher's note)

Woods, Chavisa

Things to do when you're goth in the country; and other stories. Chavisa Woods. Seven Stories Press 2017 221 p. (hardcover) $23.95

ISBN 9781609807450; 9781609807467

LC 2016043180

In this book, by Chavisa Woods, "the eight stories vary in tone and in clip, but not will soon be forgotten. A transgender artist in Brooklyn wakes up one morning to find that a living diorama of the Gaza Strip has appeared on his head. Two twelve-year-old girls take care of a sweet, playful meth addict who has been living in a local mausoleum. A young woman and her schizophrenic girlfriend drop acid at a MENSA party thrown by the schizophrenic woman's parents." (Booklist)

"This book is tight, intelligent, and important, and sure to secure Woods a seat in the pantheon of critical twenty-first-century voices." Booklist

Woods, Stuart

★ **Chiefs**. Norton 1981 427p

ISBN 0-03-901461-4

LC 80-27350

"Set in the small town of Delano, Ga., the novel tells of three Delano police chiefs—a farmer, a sadistic racist and a black—who must deal with the same case: the disappearances and murders of a number of white, teenaged boys over the course of 40 years. The mystery—readers will discern the killer's identity quite early—is played against the South in transition as local politics acquire national prominence when the son of the first chief becomes a candidate for governor and is eyed by the JFK White House as a potential running mate in the reelection campaign." Publ Wkly

Woods, Stuart

Choke; a novel. HarperCollins Pubs. 1995 280p

LC 95-37300

"Mr. Woods knows how to keep the narrative pace in overdrive, and the twists of the plot, if not always surprising, are satisfactorily developed." N Y Times Book Rev

Woods, Stuart

Cold paradise. Putnam 2001 326p

ISBN 0-399-14736-5

LC 00-45974

When millionaire Thad Shames asks Stone Barrington "to go to Palm Beach to track down a mysterious woman he met at a party, Barrington sees the mission as little more than a wild goose chase. . . . To his surprise, it doesn't take long to find the woman, but it's an even bigger shock to him to discover that she is Allison Manning, now calling herself Liz, whom he helped when she was accused of killing her husband. . . . That husband is still very much alive, and Liz wants to pay him to leave her alone with some of the money from the insurance scam they pulled off together." Booklist

Woods, Stuart

Dead eyes. HarperCollins Pubs. 1994 303p

LC 93-14221

"Young Hollywood actress Chris Callaway is poised at the brink of stardom when her world collapses. Shortly after she begins receiving disquieting letters signed 'Admirer,' she is nearly blinded in a fall at the construction site of her new Malibu home. As Admirer becomes a menacing stalker, sending gifts and a gruesome photo and calling on the phone, Chris is stoutly guarded by her best friend and confidant, hairdresser Danny Devere. Also on duty is Beverly Hills police detective and stalker expert Jon Larsen. . . . Woods's style is lean and staccato, if unsubtle, and he's a pro at turning up the suspense." Publ Wkly

Woods, Stuart

Dead in the water; a novel. HarperCollins Pubs. 1997 325p

LC 97-14255

"This is a cleverly plotted, witty crime caper with a dash of sex, a likably roughish hero, and a surprising twist at the finish." Booklist

Woods, Stuart

Dirt; a novel. HarperCollins Pubs. 1996 272p

LC 96-199910

"Dripping with name-dropping, haute couture and pricey playthings, and spiced with hormonal aerobics as Stone trolls the siren-infested waters of upscale Manhattan, the narrative rockets toward an abrupt but absolutely stunning denouement." Publ Wkly

Woods, Stuart

Dirty work. Putnam 2003 322p $25.95

ISBN 0-399-14982-1

LC 2002-32975

"Suave cop-turned-lawyer Stone Barrington is asked to hire someone to take photos of Lawrence Fortescue, the husband of a wealthy socialite, with a woman who is presumably his mistress. Stone hires the nephew of an old friend, who proves to be grossly incompetent when he falls through the skylight onto the man he's supposed to be photographing. Fortescu ends up dead, the supposed mistress disappears, and the photographer is charged with manslaughter. As Stone digs deeper, he discovers that Fortescue wasn't killed by the photographer's fall, but by an injection of poison. Enter Carpenter, aka Felicity Devonshire, Stone's contact in British intelligence. Carpenter suspects the woman involved with Fortescue is actually . . . a trained assassin with a grudge." Booklist

Woods, Stuart

Doing hard time; Stuart Woods. G.P. Putnam's Sons 2013 320 p. (Stone Barrington series) (acid-free paper) $26.95

ISBN 0399164146; 9780399164149

LC 2013015375

This Edgar Award-winner Stuart Woods's 27th Stone Barrington novel "takes the New York City attorney to Los Angeles, where Stone's son, Peter; Peter's girlfriend, Hattie Patrick; and friend Dino Bacchetti's son, Benito, are headed to begin work on their first film . . . . Two assassins, dispatched by Yuri Majorov, a powerful Russian, are tailing the young people on their drive west, but fugitive and ex-CIA employee Teddy Fay . . . ensures the thugs do no harm." (Publishers Weekly)

Woods, Stuart

Grass roots; a novel. Simon & Schuster 1989 459p

ISBN 0-671-66739-4

LC 89-32198

"A consummate storyteller, Woods . . . demonstrates his narrative ability by intertwining contemporary southern politics and the murder trial into a most satisfying tale." Libr J

Woods, Stuart

Heat. HarperCollins Pubs. 1994 346p

ISBN 0-06-017776-4

LC 94-4175

"Despite a few momentary lapses into banal predictability, Woods has concocted a high-octane story filled with nail-biting suspense and enough unusual twists to keep even experienced puzzle-solvers guessing." Booklist

Woods, Stuart

Imperfect strangers. HarperCollins Pubs. 1995 269p
LC 94-34506

"Woods' 'imperfect' strangers meet on an airplane. Sandy Kinsolving is an attractive, well-dressed man of means. He's flying from London to New York because his father-in-law, who's bankrolled his lucrative wine-selling business, has just had a stroke. Sandy and his wife are far from close, and he's concerned that his father-in-law's death will have unpleasant financial consequences. His seatmate, Peter Martindale, also a well-dressed man of means, is a gallery owner based in San Francisco. It seems that he and his wife are also on the outs, and he, too, stands to lose his livelihood. . . . Peter proposes that they murder each other's wives. The trick here is to complicate matters, and Woods succeeds admirably." Booklist

Woods, Stuart

Kisser. G. P. Putnam's Sons 2010 291p $25.95
ISBN 978-0-399-15611-3; 0-399-15611-9
LC 2009-36934

At the start of this Stone Barrington novel, "the handsome New York lawyer smoothly picks up Carrie Cox, an aspiring actress who's recently moved from Georgia to New York City, at Elaine's, his favorite Manhattan restaurant. . . . Barrington manages to shield Carrie from her ex-husband, protect young heiress Hildy Parsons from a con artist/drug dealer, and plot to take down Ponzi scammer Sig Larsen. Too crafty to let Barrington sail unscathed through encounters with women or criminals, Woods devises plenty of snarls to provoke laughs and keep the action interesting in a series that excels at playing out male fantasies." Publ Wkly

Woods, Stuart

L.A. dead. Putnam 2000 338p
ISBN 0-399-14664-4
LC 00-28059

This Stone Barrington thriller "finds the lawyer/sleuth from New York back in Los Angeles on a murder case. . . . His ex-lover, Arrington Calder, stands accused of murdering her husband, movie star and renowned man-about-town Vance Calder, found dead of a gunshot wound in the couple's Bel Air mansion. Upon hearing the news, Barrington, in Italy for his imminent wedding to the lovely but unpredictable Dolce Bianchi, rushes to L.A. to take over Arrington's defense." Publ Wkly

Woods, Stuart

L.A. Times; a novel. HarperCollins Pubs. 1993 329p
LC 92-54724

"Vincente Michaele Callabrese works as a shakedown artist for the mob in New York City's Little Italy, but moviegoing is his passion. Early in the story, he changes his name to Michael Vincent and makes a break for L.A., where with the help of powerful studio head Leo Goldman he fulfills his dream of becoming a big-time producer. Vincent's cosa nostra connections keep in touch, particularly old pal Tommy Provenzano whose rise to power in New York parallels Vincent's in Hollywood. Eventually, Vincent's desire to bring a gentle turn-of-the-century novel to the screen leads him to employ the sorts of techniques and friends that served him in his mafia days." Publ Wkly

Woods, Stuart

Lucid intervals. G. P. Putnam's Sons 2010 291p $25.95
ISBN 978-0-399-15644-1; 0-399-15644-5
LC 2010-00527

This "Stone Barrington mystery features the charismatic lawyer juggling an unwanted new client and a hunt for a former British intelligence operative. Stone is less than thrilled when Herbie Fisher, the feckless nephew of his friend Bob Cantor, walks up to him at Elaine's and drops $1 million in his lap in exchange for representation. But Stone has bills to pay, so he helps Herbie with everything from a real-estate deal to a prenuptial agreement. But soon Stone has more pressing matters on his hands: Felicity Devonshire, a beautiful member of British intelligence, has need of his services, in and out of the bedroom. . . . Fans of Woods' long-running series will not be disappointed by this romp." Booklist

Woods, Stuart

New York dead. HarperCollins Pubs. 1991 303p
LC 90-56374

A mystery "set in Manhattan's Upper East Side, the stomping ground of Stone Barrington, a well-bred but unpretentious detective. . . . Late one evening, as Stone trudges home from Elaine's Restaurant, popular TV newscaster Sasha Nijinsky plummets 12 stories from her terrace and lands on a heap of dirt 20 yards away from him—remarkably, still alive. Stone fails to apprehend the person who flees Sasha's penthouse and, after the ambulance carrying her collides with a fire truck, Sasha herself disappears. Despite the fact that no corpse is in evidence, the baffled NYPD eagerly pins a murder rap on Sasha's distraught lesbian lover. Stone refuses to accept his colleagues' pat solution." Publ Wkly

Woods, Stuart

Orchid Beach. HarperCollins Pubs. 1998 325p $25
ISBN 0-06-019181-3
LC 98-23628

"The story gets extra bite from Holly's intriguing relationship with an inherited canine named Daisy, the clairvoyant Doberman that belonged to her mentor." Publ Wkly

Woods, Stuart

Palindrome. Harper & Row 1991 344p
ISBN 0-06-017911-2
LC 90-55587

"When Liz Barwick is beaten nearly to death by her steroid-crazed husband, Baker Ramsey, a star NFL running back, she quickly divorces him, takes a large cash settlement and disappears from public view. Liz, whose book of sports photographs has just been released, takes advantage of her publisher's offer to live in his cottage on an isolated private island off the Georgia coast. But when Ramsey goes on a murderous rampage, Liz's lawyer and publisher and his wife are among his victims. Meanwhile other events are unfolding on Cumberland Island, where Liz becomes involved with the Drummond family." Publ Wkly

Woods, Stuart

Reckless abandon. G.P. Putnam's Sons 2004 289p $25.95
ISBN 0-399-15151-6
LC 2003-64799

This thriller features cop-turned-lawyer Stone Barrington and Holly Barker, chief of the Orchid Beach, Florida, police department. "Holly's come to New York hot on the trail of Trini Rodriguez, a bad guy she thought she'd stabbed to death in an earlier adventure. He's currently wanted for (among other things) blowing up a dozen people by hiding bombs in the caskets of two of his earlier victims and detonating them at the funeral. But finding him won't be so simple: he's been placed in the FBI Witness Protection Program and is working with the Feds and the CIA to catch an Arab terrorist group trying to employ the Mafia in a money-laundering scheme. Shortly after Holly takes up residence in Stone's guest room, the two of them are hip deep in the dangerous case and likewise each other. . . . Cross-pollinating all these characters from various books makes for some heavyhanded background exposition at times, but readers with no previous experience will still enjoy this amusing, full-throttle sex and crime romp." Publ Wkly

Woods, Stuart

The **run**. HarperCollins Pubs. 2000 356p

ISBN 0-06-019187-2

Sequel to Grass roots (1989)

"A clever, well-constructed story of political ambition and behind-the-scenes skulduggery." Booklist

Woods, Stuart

Santa Fe rules. HarperCollins Pubs. 1992 303p

LC 91-58476

"You're a rich, successful Hollywood producer who awakens the morning before Thanksgiving in your Santa Fe home with no memory of the previous night. Ignoring your dog's attempts to get you to visit the guest wing of the house, you leave and fly your private plane to Los Angeles. But you never get there: a breakdown forces you to spend the holiday isolated in a small airport town. When you finally see the newspaper the next day, you read that the bodies of your wife, your business partner and a third man—assumed to be you—have been found in the guest room of the Santa Fe residence. . . . Wolf Willett decides to stay 'dead' for a while and finish work on his new film, then hires a top defense attorney and turns himself in." Publ Wkly

Woods, Stuart

The **short** forever. Putnam 2002 321p $24.95

ISBN 0-399-14868-X

LC 2001-48725

"Filling his story with enough twists and turns to dizzy even the most seasoned reader, Woods keeps the tension high until the last page." Booklist

Woods, Stuart

Short straw. G. P. Putnam's Sons 2006 289p $25.95

ISBN 0-399-15368-3

LC 2006-41643

When Santa Fe defense lawyer Ed Eagle "wakes up on the morning of his fiftieth birthday, he discovers his wife has left him and taken him for a cool million. The second shock Eagle receives is news that a local lawyer has blown his brains out in the courthouse, after murdering his wife and children. The plot races off in two directions: with two edgy characters, an ex-LAPD detective and an Apache Indian tracker, whom Eagle hires to find his wife in Mexico; and with Eagle's efforts to clear a man wrongly charged, he believes, with a triple homicide. Woods keeps the wattage high as the two plots intersect, and Eagle finds himself more and more entangled in a deadly criminal scheme. The homicidal desperation of Eagle's wife and the dodginess of the men he sends after her keep the surprises coming." Booklist

Woods, Stuart

Swimming to Catalina; a novel. HarperCollins Pubs. 1998 311p

LC 97-51173

Former NYPD cop turned lawyer Stone "Barrington's former girlfriend Arrington has married Barrington's friend Vance Calder, Hollywood's hottest actor. Three months into the marriage, Arrington's been kidnapped, and Vance calls Barrington to beg for his help. Barrington comes to L.A. only to find a hornet's nest. . . . Despite the fact that this book is definitely politically incorrect and Barrington has apparently never heard of safe sex, it's a highly entertaining read that's chock-full of slam-bang action, fast cars, beautiful women, fine wine, and tart, tongue-in-cheek humor." Booklist

Woods, Stuart

Two-dollar bill. G.P. Putnam's Sons 2005 298p $25.95

ISBN 0-399-15251-2

LC 2004-60068

Stone Barrington "becomes involved with a loud-talking Texan improbably named Billy Bob Barnstormer. It isn't long before Stone regrets ever being introduced to Billy Bob, especially when he leaves a dead body in Stone's guest room. But that is only the beginning of a tale that finds Stone, along with his best friend, Dino Bacchetti, following a twisted trail as they attempt to capture Billy Bob, who, it turns out, is much more dangerous than Stone could ever have imagined. Narrator Roberts slips comfortably into his performance, bringing a nice, down-to-earth quality to his portrayal of Stone." Publ Wkly

Woods, Stuart

Worst fears realized. HarperCollins Pubs. 1999 332p $25

ISBN 0-06-019182-1

LC 98-52924

In this Stone Barrington adventure, "the Manhattan lawyer turned investigator faces an indictment for the murder of a woman he's just met. When other brutal murders quickly pile up—all women connected to him or his best friend, Dino Bacchetti of the 19th Precinct—Stone knows that one of a cop's worst fears has been realized: a con with a grudge is bent on vengeance. While trying to save the lives of the women he cares about, Stone struggles to track down the killer and head off a DA who's out to get him for murder." Libr J

Woods, Teri

Alibi; Teri Woods. Grand Central Pub. 2009 257 p.

ISBN 0446581690; 9780446581691

LC 2008048145

This book "introduces 22-year-old Daisy Fothergill, a naive African-American stripper. Daisy accepts $2,000 from an organized crime rep to provide an alibi for Bernard "Nard" Guess after he shoots two thieves to death as well as a buddy by accident in a North Philly drug house. An innocent witness to the bloodbath identifies Nard to the police, but pays a fatal price. When Daisy arrives home to tell her mother, Abigail, of her windfall and finds Abigail dead of natural causes, she discovers the $2,000 barely covers funeral costs. Her life takes an even nastier turn once Daisy starts dating Reggie Carter, . . . who soon deserts her. Later, a pregnant Daisy flees to Murfreesboro, Tenn., to seek refuge with her aunt, but eventually she must return to Philly for a day of reckoning." (Publishers Wkly)

Woodson, Jacqueline

★ **Another** Brooklyn; a novel. Jacqueline Woodson. HarperCollins 2016 192 p. (hardcover) $22.99

ISBN 0062359983; 9780062359988

LC 2016296329

National Book Award Finalist: Fiction (2016)

This novel by Jacqueline Woodson "sets memory from the 1970s in motion for August, transporting her to a time and a place where friendship was everything. . . . For August and her girls, sharing confidences as they ambled through neighborhood streets, Brooklyn was a place where they believed that they were beautiful, talented, brilliant. . . . [But] there was another Brooklyn, a dangerous place where grown men reached for innocent girls." (Publisher's note)

"The novel's richness defies its slim page count. In her poet's prose, Woodson not only shows us backward-glancing August attempting to stave off growing up and the pains that betray youth, she also wonders how we dream of a life parallel to the one we're living." Booklist

Woolf, Virginia

Between the acts. Harcourt Brace & Co. 1941 219p

This novel "describes a pageant on English history, written and directed by Miss La Trobe, and its effects on the people who watch it. Most of the audience misunderstand it in various ways; a clergyman reduces its vision to a sermon. But, for a moment, Woolf implies art, has imposed order on the chaos of human life" Reader's Ency. 4th edition

Woolf, Virginia

The **complete** shorter fiction of Virginia Woolf; edited by Susan Dick. Harcourt Brace Jovanovich 1985 313p

"Woolf's 46 short stories demonstrate her fondness for experimenting with narrative forms and voices. Arranged chronologically, the pieces range from tales with traditional plot lines to denser interior monologues, and enable the reader to appreciate Woolf's development as a writer of fiction." Publ Wkly

Woolf, Virginia

Jacob's room. Harcourt Brace & Co. 1923 303p

First published 1922 in the United Kingdom

"The life story, character, and friends of Jacob Flanders are presented in a series of separate scenes and moments. The story of this sensitive, promising young man carries him from his childhood, through college at Cambridge, love affairs in London, and travels in Greece, to his death in the war. At the end, instead of describing his death, Virginia Woolf describes his empty room." Reader's Ency. 4th edition

Woolf, Virginia

★ **Mrs.** Dalloway. Knopf 1993 xxviii, 219p $16

ISBN 0-679-42042-8

LC 92-54300

A reissue of the title first published 1925 by Harcourt Brace & Co.

"In this stream-of-consciousness novel all action takes place on a single day. By probing the thoughts and memories of various characters, the author has encompassed several people's lives. Clarissa has a party planned for the evening and is thinking of her daughter's involvement with a religious fanatic. Also in her thoughts are old friends like Sally Seton, who drops by at the party, and Clarissa's former lover, Peter Walsh, who is drawn to Sally, much to Clarissa's chagrin. When a noted psychiatrist arrives late at the party because one of his patients, Septimus Smith, has committed suicide, Clarissa is affected, not because she knew the victim, but because suicide is tantamount to wastefulness." Shapiro. Fic for Youth. 3d edition

Woolf, Virginia

Orlando; a biography. Harcourt Brace & Co. 1928 333p il

"Orlando begins as a young Elizabethan nobleman and ends, three hundred years later, as a contemporary young woman, based on the author's friend Victoria Sackville-West. The novel contains a great deal of literary history and brilliant, ironic insights into the social history of the ages through which Orlando lives. Orlando starts life as a male poet and ends as an equally intense and able woman poet, in order to emphasize the author's belief that women are intellectually men's equals." Reader's Ency. 4th edition

Woolf, Virginia

★ **To** the lighthouse. Harcourt Brace & Co. 1927 310p $17; pa $9

ISBN 0-15-190737-4; 0-15-690739-9 pa

Arranged in three sections, the first "called 'The window,' describes a day during Mr. and Mrs. Ramsay's house party at their country home by the sea. Mr. Ramsay is a distinguished scholar . . . whose mind works rationally, heroically and rather icily. . . . The Ramsays have arranged to take a boat out to the lighthouse, the next morning, and their little son James is bitterly disappointed when a change in weather makes it impossible. The second section, called 'Time passes' describes the seasons and the house, unused and decaying, in the years after Mrs. Ramsay's death. In the third section, the 'Lighthouse,' Mr. Ramsay and his friends are back at the house. He takes the postponed trip to the lighthouse with his now 16-year-old son, who is at last able to communicate silently with him and forgive him for being different from his mother." Reader's Ency. 4th edition

Woolf, Virginia

The **voyage** out. Modern Lib. 2000 xliv, 473p $17.95

ISBN 0-679-64028-2

LC 99-54259

First published 1915 in the United Kingdom; first United States edition 1920 by Harcourt Brace & Co.

"The story concerns a young woman of 24, Rachel Vinrace, an innocent, 'unlicked' girl who voyages to South America on board her father's ship, the Euphrosyne. Accompanying her are her aunt, Helen Ambrose, and uncle Ridley, together with an assortment of English characters whose social interaction is delicately observed. In South America Rachel meets a young Englishman, Terence Hewet, an aspiring writer working on his first novel. . . . He and Rachel fall in love and become engaged, determined to establish their future marriage on a new basis of equality. However, during an expedition Rachel contracts an unspecified disease and is confined to her bed with a fever. After a fortnight's illness she dies." Camb Guide to Lit in Engl

Woolf, Virginia

★ The **waves**. Harcourt Brace & Co. 1931 297p $10.80

ISBN 9780199642922

"Highly original, unconventional, and poetic, it describes the characters, lives, and relationships of six persons living in England. The book is composed of interior monologues, spoken by the six characters in rotation, and of interludes describing the ascent and descent of the sun, the rise and fall of the waves, and the passing of the seasons. These natural cycles symbolize the progress of time, which carries the individual from birth to death." Reader's Ency. 4th edition

Woolf, Virginia

★ The **years**. Harcourt Brace & Co. 1937 435p

This novel "traces the history of a family, opening in 1880 as the children of Colonel and Mrs. Pargiter, living together in a large Victorian London house (later described by one of them as 'Hell') wait for their mother's death and the freedom it will bring; it takes them through several carefully dated and documented sections to the 'Present Day' of 1936, and a large family reunion, where two generations gather." Oxford Companion to Engl Lit. 6th edition

Worsley, Kate

She rises; by Kate Worsley. 1st U.S. ed. Bloomsbury USA 2013 432 p. (hardcover) $26

ISBN 1620400979; 9781620400975

LC 2012047087

Lambda Literary Awards Finalist (2014)

In this novel, by Kate Worsley, "It is 1740 and Louise Fletcher . . . is offered work in the bustling naval port of Harwich. . . . Intertwined with her story is fifteen-year-old Luke's: He is . . . sent to sea on board the warship Essex. . . . Louise navigates her new life among the streets and crooked alleys of Harwich. . . . Luke, aching for the girl he left behind and determined to one day find his way back to her, embarks on a long and perilous journey across the ocean." (Publisher's note)

Wortham, Reavis

The **rock** hole; Reavis Z. Wortham. Poisoned Pen Press 2011 250p.

ISBN 9781590588840; 9781590588864

LC 2011920305

This book is set "[i]n 1964, [when] farmer and part-time Constable Ned Parker combine forces with John Washington, the almost mythical black deputy sheriff from nearby Paris, to track down a disturbed individual who is rapidly becoming a threat to the entire small Texas community of Center Springs. When Ned is summoned to a hot cornfield one morning to examine the remains of a tortured bird dog, he finds a dark presence in their quiet community. A farmer by trade, Ned is usually confident when it comes to handling moonshiners, drunks and domestic disputes. But the animal atrocities turn to murder, and the investigation spins beyond his abilities." (Publisher's note)

Other titles in this series are:
Burrows (2012)
Right side of wrong (2013)
Vengeance is mine (2014)
Dark places (2015)
Unraveled (2016)

Wouk, Herman

★ The **Caine** mutiny; a novel of World War II. Doubleday 1951 494p

"The old American mine sweeper 'Caine' patrols the Pacific during World War II. The action shifts from the bridge of the ship to the wardroom and from scenes of petty tyranny on the part of the skipper to incidents of fierce action and heroism on the part of the men. Ensign Willie Keith is assigned to the ship and leads a mutiny against paranoid Captain Queeg, who is eventually brought to trial in a scene that poses the difficulty of weighing evidence to prove that the takeover by the men was justifiable." Shapiro. Fic for Youth. 3d edition

Wouk, Herman

A **hole** in Texas. Little, Brown 2004 278p $25

ISBN 0-316-52590-1

"The plot is busy but secondary to Carpenter's banter and romantic escapades. Occasionally corny but also playful, thoughtful and passionate." Publ Wkly

Wouk, Herman

The **lawgiver**; a novel. Herman Wouk. Simon & Schuster 2012 234 p. (hardcover : alk. paper) $25.99

ISBN 1451699387; 9781451699388; 9781451699395; 9781451699401

LC 2012038205

2013 Sophie Brody Medal Honor Book

This novel by Herman Wouk focuses on "Margo Solovei, a brilliant young writer-director who has rejected her rabbinical father's strict Jewish upbringing to pursue a career in the arts. When an Australian multibillionaire promises to finance a movie about Moses if the script meets certain standards, Margo does everything she can to land the job. . . . Herman Wouk himself and his wife . . . , Betty Sarah . . . almost against their will, find themselves entangled in the Moses movie." (Publisher's note)

Includes bibliographical references and index

Wouk, Herman

★ **Marjorie** Morningstar. Doubleday 1955 565p

"The story of a middle-class Jewish girl who temporarily rejects her upbringing in her infatuation with the world of show business." Reader's Ency. 4th edition

Wouk, Herman

★ **War** and remembrance; a novel. Little, Brown 1978 1042p

ISBN 0-316-95501-9

LC 78-17746

Sequel to The winds of war

Wouk's "work is a journey of extraordinary emotional riches. Quantity in time becomes quality, movement becomes scope, and history becomes human yearning." NY Times Book Rev

Wouk, Herman

★ The **winds** of war; a novel. Little, Brown 1971 885p hardcover o.p. pa $16.99

ISBN 0-316-95266-8

"On the broadest of tapestries, Wouk weaves the effect of the preparation and the actual outbreak of World War II upon the family of Commander 'Pug' Henry. The affairs of the Henry family became intertwined with those of others, in such varying scenes as Washington, Berlin, Rome, London, and Moscow. . . . Despite the novel's breadth, the development of Henry's character as the middle-class military leader America needed in the 1940's is surprisingly credible." Choice

Another title featuring the Henry family is:
War and remembrance (1978)

Wray, John

Canaan's tongue. Alfred A. Knopf 2005 341p $25

ISBN 1-400-04086-8

LC 2004-64902

"Loosely based on the story of pre-Civil War slave stealer John Murrell, a.k.a. 'The Redeemer,' and his 'Mystic Clan' gang, this novel centers on the relationship between gang member Virgil Ball and charismatic leader Thaddeus Morelle. Ball, the son of a Kansas preacher, is simultaneously captivated and repelled by the criminal Morelle. Though he quickly becomes part of the gang's inner circle, he finds himself deeply conflicted about his involvement, a tension that will eventually lead to a violent act of expiation. Yet, in the end, even murder will not free him from the sway of a power older and deeper than Morelle. Wray has crafted an ambitious and strongly allegorical tale about the ability of belief to structure reality." Libr J

Wray, John

Lowboy. Farrar, Straus and Giroux 2009 258p $25

ISBN 978-0-374-19416-1; 0-374-19416-5

LC 2008-17921

"Will Heller, aka Lowboy, is a brilliant but troubled 16-year-old paranoid schizophrenic in New York City. Recently escaped from a mental hospital and obsessed with the notion that the world is about to be destroyed by global warming, he boards the subway one morning seeking to save the world in the only way he believes it can be-by having sex with a woman. He attempts to locate former girlfriend Emily Wallace, whom he has not seen since he pushed her onto the subway tracks a year earlier, the act that led to his stay in a mental hospital. Throughout his daylong adventures in the tunnels and streets, he is pursued by police detective Ali Lateef and his mother, Violet, a woman with her own secrets, who seek to bring him home before he harms himself or others." Libr J

Wright, Alexis

★ **Carpentaria**; a novel. Atria Books 2009 517p $26

ISBN 978-1-4165-9310-2; 1-4165-9310-1

First published 2006 in Australia

"This book is a sprawling, surreal anti-Odyssey in which time and space contract and expand and experience takes place in the Dreamtime, on the sea, and on and under the continent of Australia. . . . [This novel]

will surely stand as a masterpiece of modern English-language literature." Libr J

Wright, John C.

The **golden** age; a romance of the far future. TOR Bks. 2002 336p

ISBN 0-312-84870-6

LC 2001-58468

In this future novel, the first of a projected two-volume saga, Phaethon Radamanthus, the 3,000 year-old scion of one of Earth's most powerful families begins a search for his lost memories

The author "chooses simple pulp-fiction plots to drive us through the technological complexities of Phaethon's world. The hero's quest to regain his lost memories, learn his true identity and reach the stars is undeniably compelling. As a result, having to wait for the next volume is frustrating. Wright's ornate and conceptually dense prose will not be to everyone's taste but, for those willing to be challenged, this is a rare and mind-blowing treat." Publ Wkly

Wright, Richard

Eight men. World Pub. 1961 250p

Contents: The man who was almost a man; The man who lived underground; Big black good man; The man who saw the flood; Man, God ain't like that . . .; The man who killed a shadow; The man who went to Chicago

Wright, Richard

★ **Native** son. Harper & Brothers 1940 359p

"Bigger Thomas is black. He is driven by anger, hate, and frustration, which are born out of the poverty that has dominated his life. When he gets a job with the Daltons, a white family, he is confused by their behavior and misinterprets their patronizing friendship. Tragedy follows when he accidentally kills Mary Dalton and escalates when Bigger murders his black girlfriend, Bessie." Shapiro. Fic for Youth. 3d edition

Wright, Richard

The **outsider**. Harper & Row 1953 440p

"Cross Damon, a black man who works in the Chicago post office, is caught in a subway accident but escapes without serious injury, though because of a mistaken identity his death is announced. He decides to take advantage of this error to start life anew and thus free himself of his entanglements with women and debts. He goes to New York to live under an assumed name and before long becomes enmeshed in the Communist party. By it he is used as a murderer, until he is himself killed by a Party member." Oxford Companion to Am Lit. 6th edition

Wright, Richard

Uncle Tom's children; five long stories. Harper & Row 1938 xxx, 384p hardcover o.p. pa $13.95

ISBN 0-06-058714-8 pa

The stories in this collection deal with conflicts between whites and blacks in the South.

Wright, Richard

Works. Library of Am. 1991 2v ea $35

ISBN 0-940450-66-6 v1; 0-940450-67-4 v2

LC 91-60540

This set contains the complete novels Native son; The outsider (1953); and Lawd today! (1963); the story collection Uncle Tom's children; and the memoir Black boy

Wright, Ronald

The **gold** eaters; a novel. Ronald Wright. Riverhead Books 2015 384 p. (hardcover) $28.95

ISBN 1594634629; 9781594634628

LC 2015014720

This book, by Ronald Wright, is an "epic historical novel of exploration and invasion. . . . Kidnapped at sea by conquistadors seeking the golden land of Peru, a young Inca boy named Waman is the everyman thrown into extraordinary circumstances. Forced to become Francisco Pizarro's translator, he finds himself caught up in one of history's great clashes of civilzations, the Spanish invasion of the Incan Empire of the 1530s." (Publisher's note)

"Wright displays his mastery of the historical fiction form with this terrific novel that will enlighten anyone interested in the conquest of Peru, the vision of Pizarro, and the fate of native Peruvian culture." LJ

Wrinkle, Margaret

Wash. Atlantic Monthly Press 2013 384 p. (hardcover) $25

ISBN 0802120660; 9780802120663

This historical novel focuses on "Revolutionary War veteran Gen. James Richardson and his slave, Wash. . . . Richardson had depended on slaves to 'carve out of nothing' a plantation on the Tennessee frontier. Though Richardson had wanted to leave slavery behind, he's driven by greed and still involved with it. . . . Imagining that the waves of settlers heading further west will need even more slaves, Richardson studs out Wash to neighboring plantations and fills the region with his visage." (Publishers Weekly)

Wroblewski, David

The **story** of Edgar Sawtelle; a novel. Ecco 2008 566p hardcover o.p. pa $16.99

ISBN 978-0-06-137422-7; 0-06-137422-9; 978-0-06-137423-4 pa; 0-06-137423-7 pa

"Set in rural nineteen-seventies Wisconsin, this loose retelling of Hamlet focusses on Edgar, a boy born mute and with a preternatural ability to commune with the dogs whose breeding and training is his family's business. Idyllic routine is threatened when Edgar's ne'er-do-well uncle comes to live with the family, and the menace persists even after his sudden departure. Soon afterward, Edgar's father dies of an apparent aneurysm; Edgar becomes convinced, but can't prove, that his uncle—who soon inserts himself back into the family—is to blame. . . . [The author] illustrates the relationship between man and canine (at times, from the dog's point of view) in a way that is both lyrical and unsentimental, and demonstrates an ability to create a coherent, captivating fictional world in which even supernatural elements feel entirely persuasive." New Yorker

Wu Ming-Yi

The **man** with the compound eyes; a novel. Wu Ming-Yi; Translated from Taiwanese by Darryl Sterk. Pantheon Books 2014 304 p. (hardback) $25.95

ISBN 0307907961; 9780307907967

LC 2013042177

"When a tsunami sends a massive island made entirely of trash crashing into the Taiwanese coast, two very different people--an outcast from a mythical island and a woman on the verge of suicide--are united in ways they never could have imagined." (Publisher's note)

"Wu's beautifully evocative language and multilayered ecological and cultural themes offer a richly satisfying reading experience." Booklist

Wu, Julie, 1967-

The **third** son; a novel. by Julie Wu. 1st ed. Algonquin Books of Chapel Hill 2013 320 p. (hardcover) $24.95

ISBN 1616200790; 9781616200794

LC 2012051161

In this book by Julie Wu, "growing up in Japanese-occupied Taiwan, Saburo feels rejected by his family. He finds love with Yoshiko, and, after their marriage, he leaves her and their baby son to find them a home in the U.S., but it takes years to get a college education and find work in Michigan, which will allow him to bring his loved ones to join him. The 1950s political history is always in the background." (Booklist)

Wuertz, Yoojin Grace

Everything belongs to us; A novel. Yoojin Grace Wuertz. Random House Inc 2016 368 p. $27; (ebook) $65

ISBN 9780812998542; 9780812998559

LC 2016012226

In this book, by Yoojin Grace Wuertz, "for childhood friends Jisun and Namin, the stakes couldn't be more different. . . . But everything changes when Jisun and Namin meet an ambitious, charming student named Sunam, whose need to please his family has led him to a prestigious club: the Circle. Under the influence of his mentor, Juno, a manipulative social climber, Sunam becomes entangled with both women, as they all make choices that will change their lives forever. (Publisher's note)

"Wuertz is an important new voice in American fiction." Kirkus

Wurlitzer, Rudolph

★ **Drop** edge of yonder; a novel. Two Dollar Radio 2008 304p pa $15

ISBN 978-0-9763895-5-2; 0-9763895-5-X

LC 2007-924062

"The novel tracks the wayward drift of a mountain man named Zebulon Shook, who is cursed by his dying Shoshone lover—named Not Here Not There—to 'drift like a blind man between the worlds, not knowing if you're dead or alive, or if the unseen world exists, or if you're dreaming.' With the collapse of the fur trade, Zebulon quits the mountains, crawls out of an arroyo after being shot in the heart and left for dead, and becomes an outlaw. In seedy Vera Cruz, he runs into a Russian count and his mysterious half-Abyssinian consort, Delilah, who pay him to sail with them to the gold fields of northern California. The story ends in the Pacific Northwest, at the Trail's End Saloon, but before we get there, we are treated to a Wunderkammer of western tropes and historical residues: wardens and wanted posters, rancheros and opium dens, freedom and fate, the Great Spirit and the Colt .45. Wurlitzer trots through this magic theater like a restless auteur. Chapters are short, the dialogue tangy and declarative, and scenes established and characters described with the visual fetishism of a Leone film." Bookforum

Wyld, Evie

After the fire, a still small voice. Pantheon Books 2009 296p $24

ISBN 978-0-307-37846-0; 0-307-37846-2

LC 2009-14832

"Frank last visited his family's shack, on a Queensland beach, as a gas-huffing teenager, battered by his mother's death and his father's abusive neglect. He returns an alcoholic man, . . . having lashed out at his girlfriend until she left. The shack has served as a retreat before: for Frank's grandfather, reeling from the Korean War, and for his father, who holed up there after serving in Vietnam. The stories of these wounded forebears are layered into Frank's tormented recovery, trauma seeping from one man into the next. Wyld has a feel both for beauty and for the ugliness of inherited pain. The mood is creepy—strange creatures in the sugar cane, grieving neighbors, a missing local girl—and the sentiment is plain." New Yorker

Wyman, Willard

Blue heaven. University of Nebraska Press 195p il $21.95

ISBN 978-0-8061-4218-0; 0-8061-4218-9

"Wyman's keen eye for landscape and his knowledge of pack and ranch animals enhance his prose style. He's a good, solid writer, too, a man of welcome sparseness and few fillers. . . . [The novel] has a philosophical edge in its story of friendship and constancy. It speaks to the resilience of humans, their ability to adapt, bend and accept change, or buckle and be sacrificed. Women and whiskey, music and camp meals pepper the pages, often with a bittersweet tone." Billings Gazette

Y

Yalom, Irvin David, 1931-

The **Schopenhauer** cure; a novel. Irvin D. Yalom. HarperCollins 2005 viii, 358p (alk. paper) $24.95; (pbk.) $13.99

ISBN 0066214416; 9780060938109

LC 2004047580

This book follows "Julius Hertzfeld, a successful therapist in San Francisco, [who] is shocked by the news that he suffers from terminal cancer. Moved to reassess his life's work, he contacts Philip Slate, whose three years of therapy for sexual addiction Julius describes as an 'old-time major-league failure.' Philip is now training to be a therapist himself, guided by the writings of Arthur Schopenhauer, and he offers to teach Julius about Schopenhauer as a way of helping him deal with his looming death. Julius and Philip strike a deal: Julius will serve as Philip's clinical supervisor, but only if Philip joins the ongoing therapy group Julius leads. To complicate matters further, Pam, a group member, is one of the hundreds of women Philip seduced and then rejected." (Publishers Weekly)

Includes bibliographical references (p. [347]-358).

Yanagihara, Hanya, 1975-

★ A **little** life; a novel. Hanya Yanagihara. Doubleday 2015 736 p. (hardcover) $30

ISBN 0385539258; 9780385539258; 9780804172707

LC 2014027379

Carnegie Medal Shortlist: Fiction (2016)
Man Booker Prize Shortlist (2015)
National Book Award Finalist: Fiction (2015)
Kirkus Prize: Fiction (2015)

In this novel, by Hanya Yanagihara, "when four classmates from a small Massachusetts college move to New York to make their way, they're broke, adrift, and buoyed only by their friendship and ambition. . . . Over the decades, their relationships deepen and darken, tinged by addiction, success, and pride. Yet their greatest challenge, each comes to realize, is Jude . . . , by midlife a terrifyingly talented litigator yet an increasingly broken man." (Publisher's note)

"This is a novel that values the everyday over the extraordinary, the push and pull of human relationships—and the book's effect is cumulative. There is real pleasure in following characters over such a long period, as they react to setbacks and successes, and, in some cases, change." Pub Wkly

Yanagihara, Hanya, 1975-

The **people** in the trees; Hanya Yanagihara. Doubleday 2013 384 p. (hardcover : alk. paper) $26.95

ISBN 0385536771; 9780385536776; 9780385536783

LC 2012034034

Hanya Yanagihara's novel "details the life of fictional doctor and Nobel Prize-winning scientist Dr. Abraham Norton Perina, who narrates his travels to the Micronesian islands of Ivu'ivu and U'ivu, where the secret to longevity is revealed to him. Perina learns that members of a primitive tribe who live to be 60 years old . . . are given the privilege . . . of consuming the meat of the opa'ivu'eke, a rare turtle." He discovers there is a dark side to longevity, however. (Library Journal)

Yang, J. Y.

The **black** tides of heaven; J.Y. Yang. Tor.com 2017 240 p. map (Tensorate series) $15.99

ISBN 076539541X; 9780765395412

Nebula Finalist: Best Novella (2017)

Hugo Finalist: Best Novella (2018)

In this book, by J.Y. Yang, "Mokoya and Akeha, the twin children of the Protector, were sold to the Grand Monastery as infants. While Mokoya developed her strange prophetic gift, Akeha was always the one who could see the strings that moved adults to action. While Mokoya received visions of what would be, Akeha realized what could be. What's more, they saw the sickness at the heart of their mother's Protectorate." (Publisher's note)

"Yang's world is imbued with magic, yet a burgeoning rebellion eschews that magic for technology. The other striking bit of worldbuilding is that children in this world do not have gender until they choose which sex they wish to be, and the stories are full of fascinating gender explorations." LJ

Other titles in this series are:

The red threads of forture (2017)

The descent of monsters (2018)

Yanique, Tiphanie

Land of love and drowning; Tiphanie Yanique. Riverhead Books 2014 368 p. (hardback) $27.95

ISBN 1594488339; 9781594488337

LC 2013044381

"Chronicling three generations of an island family from 1916 to the 1970s, 'Land of Love and Drowning' is a novel of love and magic, set against the emergence of Saint Thomas into the modern world. . . . Following the Bradshaw family through sixty years of fathers and daughters, mothers and sons, love affairs, curses, magical gifts, loyalties, births, deaths, and triumphs, 'Land of Love and Drowning' is a . . . debut by [a] young writer." (Publisher's note)

"This is a beautifully conceived and written tale of frustrated and forbidden love, beauty, aging, and family secrets." Booklist

Yarbrough, Steve

The **end** of California. Knopf 2006 303p $23.95

ISBN 1-4000-4438-3

LC 2005-57750

In this "novel, a 42-year-old doctor named Pete Barrington returns from California to his little home town in Mississippi. He started there as a poor farm boy, but brains, looks and football talent helped him advance to college, medical school and a good life out West. An adulterous affair with a patient ended that, and now he, his wife and their 15-year-old daughter are starting over back home. Yarbrough's story blends elements we have seen in other novels—the small-town South, the football hero grown up, passions that reach back to high school, a little incest and a lot of extramarital sex, racial tensions, hypocrisy among the pious—but it all works because Yarbrough knows his characters so well, cares for them so deeply and writes of them in prose that is graceful, precise and packed with surprises." Washington Post Book World

Yarbrough, Steve

★ **Prisoners** of war; a novel. Knopf 2004 287p $23

ISBN 0-375-41478-9

LC 2003-40071

"Yarbrough writes with quiet compassion about Loring's black population, its reluctance to fight for a country that has so consistently betrayed its democratic promise. To this combustible setting will come a peculiar prisoner, one with an 'angry purple stain, either a birthmark or a rash,' who speaks broken English and haunts one of the Loring natives assigned to guard him. It is the fate of this mysterious captive that once again forces the people of Loring to confront what it means to be American, and all the unexpected and often unwarranted sacrifices that identity might comprise." N Y Times Book Rev

Yarbrough, Steve

The **realm** of last chances; Steve Yarbrough. Alfred A. Knopf 2013 288 p. (hardback) $25.95

ISBN 0385349505; 9780345804884; 9780385349505

LC 2012050904

In this book, "Kristin has lost her job at a California university and has had to relocate to a less prestigious college in the northeast. She brings along her husband Cal, an unemployed woodworker and musician, and her troubled marriage. Kristin and Cal are both in their 50s, and Yarbrough focuses here primarily on how busy lives, past histories, and largely unexamined ideas about love and romance can threaten a marriage." (Library Journal)

Yarbrough, Steve

★ **Safe** from the neighbors. Alfred A. Knopf 2010 259p $25.95

ISBN 978-0-307-27170-9; 0-307-27170-6

LC 2009-22311

"The story is told from the point of view of Luke May, a high school teacher and history buff living in a small Mississippi River delta town where he and his wife carry on a passionless marriage. During Luke's childhood, a family friend killed his wife, and Luke never fully understood the circumstances. After Maggie, one of the slain mother's children, returns to town as the new high school French teacher, Luke begins to unravel the murder, which coincided with one of the key moments in the civil rights movement. He also begins an affair with Maggie." Publ Wkly

Yates, Alex

Moondogs; a novel. Doubleday 2011 339p $25.95

ISBN 978-0-385-53378-2; 0-385-53378-0

LC 2010-07947

"A cloud of exasperated doom hangs over the characters in this weird and weirdly affecting Philippines-set novel. The multiple story lines—involving an American businessman, his bumbling kidnappers, his estranged son, an embassy worker having an affair with a Filipino national hero, and an A-Team of supernaturally enhanced soldiers—languorously intertwine, thankfully without the soulless Swiss-watch efficiency that often governs books with such large casts." Entertainment Wkly

Yates, Christopher J.

★ **Grist** Mill Road; a novel. Christopher J. Yates. Picador 2017 342 p. (hardcover) $26

ISBN 9781250150288; 9781250150318

LC 2017028306

This book, by Christopher J. Yates, "is a dark, twisted, and expertly plotted 'Rashomon'-style tale. The year is 1982; the setting, an Edenic hamlet some ninety miles north of New York City. . . . Three friends--Patrick, Matthew, and Hannah--are bound together by a terrible and seemingly senseless crime. Twenty-six years later, in New York City, living lives their younger selves never could have predicted, the three meet again--with even more devastating results." (Publisher's note)

"Mesmerizing and impossible to put down, this novel demands full attention, full empathy, and full responsibility; in return it offers poignant insight into h u man fragility and resilience." Kirkus

Yates, Richard

★ The **collected** stories of Richard Yates; introduction by Richard Russo. Holt & Co. 2001 xx, 472p

ISBN 0-8050-6693-4

LC 00-61400

"Bitterness, loneliness and lack of fulfillment are the central themes of this grim posthumous collection." Publ Wkly

The **Year's** best fantasy and horror; 1st-21st annual collections. edited by Ellen Datlow and Kelly Link & Gavin J. Grant. St. Martin's Press 1988 21v

First two annual compilations published with title: The Year's best fantasy

Each annual collection includes short stories, poems, and essays. The nonfiction sections cover such topics as trends in fantasy and horror publishing; fantasy and horror films, television and comics; non-print media; and obituaries. Over the years contributors of stories have included Charles De Lint, Steve Rasnic Tem, Garry Kilworth, Angela Carter, Karel Capek, Isabel Allende, Stephen King, Jane Yolen, Thomas Ligotti and Clive Barker

The **year's** best science fiction; thirtieth annual collection. edited by Gardner Dozois. St. Martin's Griffin 2013 704 p. (hardcover) $40

ISBN 1250028051; 9781250028051; 9781250029133

LC 2013009319

In this collection of short stories, edited by Gardner Dozois, science fiction "authors explore ideas of a new world through their short stories. This venerable collection brings together award winning authors and masters of the field such as Robert Reed, Alastair Reynolds, Damien Broderick, Elizabeth Bear, Paul McAuley and John Barnes." (Publisher's note)

Year's best science fiction; 1st-26th annual collections. edited by Gardner Dozois. St. Martin's Press 1984

First three annual collections published by Bluejay Books

Each annual collection contains stories, a summation of developments in the field, and a list of honorable mentions. Over the years contributors have included Michael Swanwick, Maureen F. McHugh, Charles Sheffield, Cory Doctorow, Kage Baker, Brian Stableford, Gene Wolfe, Nancy Kress, Gregory Benford, Stephen Baxter, Elizabeth Bear, Paolo Bacigalupi, Jay Lake, and Mary Rosenblum

Year's Best SF 18; edited by David G. Hartwell. St. Martin's Press 2013 416 p. $15.99

ISBN 0765338203; 9780765338204

This collection of science fiction stories, edited by David G. Hartwell, "demonstrates the . . . depth and power of contemporary speculative fiction. . . . In this anthology, prepare to travel light years from the ordinary into a tomorrow at once . . . frightening and possible with . . . tales . . . published in 2012." (Publisher's note)

"A gender-balanced selection of 28 stories draws primarily on the talents of American authors, though authors from Britain, Canada, India, and France also appear. Hartwell acknowledges the emergence of a new crop of SF writers and does include relatively new talents like Yoon Ha Lee and Indrapramit Das, but the focus is on veterans with decades of experience, like Gene Wolfe, Megan Lindholm, and Pat Cadigan." Pub Wkly

Yezierska, Anzia, ca. 1880-1970

Bread givers; a novel. Anzia Yezierska; foreword and introduction by Alice Kessler-Harris with photographs. 3rd ed; Persea Books 2003 297 p. ill. $11.95

ISBN 0892552905; 9780892552900

LC 2003007187

This novel, by Anzia Yezierska, "is set in the 1920s on the Lower East Side of Manhattan and tells the story of Sara Smolinsky, the youngest daughter of an Orthodox rabbi, who rebels against her father's rigid conception of Jewish womanhood. Sarah's struggle towards independence and self-fulfillment resonates with a passion all can share. Beautifully redesigned page for page with the previous editions, Bread Givers is an essential historical work with enduring relevance." (Publisher's note)

Yiyun Li

A **thousand** years of good prayers; stories. Random House 2005 205p $21.95

ISBN 1-4000-6312-4

LC 2004-62891

This is the author's first collection of stories. "Many of the stories in 'A Thousand Years of Good Prayers' are set in the 1990's." (N Y Times Book Rev)

This collection is a "reminder that, at its best, the short story is the most elegant of literary forms. Each tale has a keen poignancy of its own, and assembled in a collection they give an impressively coherent sense of modern China. All melancholy, the stories are by turns angry and whimsical, and each bears the ugly imprint of Mao's China." Times Lit Suppl

Yiyun Li

The **vagrants**; a novel. Random House 2009 337p $25

ISBN 1-4000-6313-2; 978-1-4000-6313-0

LC 2008-23467

This novel "is set in China in the late 1970s. . . . A young woman, Gu Shan, . . . a follower of Chairman Mao, has renounced her faith in Communism. Now a political prisoner, she is set to be executed for her dissent." (Publisher's note)

This novel "begins and ends with an execution, in 1979, in a small city in China, where democratic reform movements are beginning to ripple through the nation. Gu Shan is a former Red Guard leader turned counter-revolutionary, whose execution, at the age of twenty-eight, devastates her parents and entwines their lives with those of a crippled twelve-year-old girl, the feckless nineteen-year-old son of a Communist hero, an elderly street-cleaning couple, and a radio announcer who comes to question her role in the spread of government propaganda. Li offers both a bleak view of a historical moment when 'people were the most dangerous animals in the world' and a meditation on the act of martyrdom, which is presented both as a duty and as a 'luxury that few could afford.'" New Yorker

Yocum, Robin

A **welcome** murder; Robin Yocum. Seventh Street Books, an imprint of Prometheus Books 2017 262 p. (paperback) $15.95

ISBN 9781633882638; 9781633882645

LC 2016051813

In this book, by Robin Yocum, "after his unspectacular professional baseball career ends with a knee injury in Toledo, Ohio, Johnny Earl gets busted for selling cocaine. After serving seven years in prison, all he wants to do is return to his hometown of Steubenville, retrieve the drug money he stashed before he went to jail. . . . However, before he can leave town with his money, Johnny is picked up for questioning in the murder of Rayce Daubner, the FBI informant who had set him up." (Publisher's note)

"Yocum (A Brilliant Death) has produced a rollicking tale sure to appeal to Donald Westlake and Elmore Leonard fans." Pub Wkly

Yoon, Paul

★ The **mountain**; stories. Paul Yoon. Simon & Schuster 2017 242 p. (hardcover) $25

ISBN 9781501154102; 1501154087; 9781501154089; 9781501154096

LC 2016054159

In this book, author Paul Yoon "displays his subtle, ethereal, and strikingly observant style with six thematically linked stories, taking place across several continents and time periods and populated with characters who are connected by their traumatic pasts, newly vagrant lives, and quests for solace in their futures." (Publisher's note)

Yoon, Paul

Once the shore; stories. Sarabande Books 2009 270p pa $15.95

ISBN 978-1-932511-70-3; 1-932511-70-9

LC 2008-19331

"Yoon's collection of eight richly textured stories explore the themes of family, lost love, silence, alienation and the effects of the Japanese occupation and the Korean War on the poor communities of a small South Korean island." Publ Wkly

Yoshida, Shuichi

Villain; translated from the Japanese by Philip Gabriel. Pantheon Books 2010 295p $25.95

ISBN 9780307378873; 0-307-37887-X

LC 2010-00159

"Villain can be confusing. Its many characters, multiple points of view and shifts in time require close attention. But that attention is rewarded. Each of Yoshida's characters, whether major or minor, is carefully defined. The title of the novel is finally ironic: No one villain can be separated out of the fabric of actions that led to Yoshino's death, and the line between villain and victim is almost translucent." Columbus Dispatch

Yoshimoto, Banana

Asleep; translated from the Japanese by Michael Emmerich. Grove Press 2000 177p

ISBN 0-8021-1669-8

LC 99-88699

This volume consists "of three novellas, each telling a somewhat mystical tale of haunted slumber. In the first story, a woman mourning a dead lover finds herself sleepwalking; in the next, a woman involved in a relationship with a man, whose wife is in a coma, realizes that she is unable to remain awake; and in the third, a woman finds her dreams inhabited by a dead woman, her former rival in a love triangle. The stories flow easily and quietly from one to the next, and while they have a lyrical, almost poetic, quality, they remain gripping, dramatic, intense, and real." Booklist

Yoshimoto, Banana

Goodbye Tsugumi; a novel. translated from the Japanese by Michael Emmerich. Grove Press 2002 186p $23

ISBN 0-8021-1638-8

LC 2001-58460

Original Japanese edition, 1999

"Maria Shirakawa is a thoughtful young woman thrown by family circumstance (her parents never married; with her mother, she is waiting for her father's divorce from his current wife) into growing up with her cousin, Tsugumi Yamamoto, in her aunt and uncle's small inn. Tsugumi, who is chronically ill, possesses a mischievous charm that both maddens and amuses her family. . . . Tsugumi's tenuous health seems to free her from the behavioral norms that govern Maria and Tsugumi's long-suffering older sister, Yoko, allowing her to curse, flirt with boys, concoct elaborate pranks and shock adults in a way Maria resents, envies and admires." Publ Wkly

Yoshimoto, Banana

★ **Kitchen**; translated from the Japanese by Megan Backus. Grove Press 1993 152p

LC 92-12871

Original Japanese edition, 1987

"In supple, precise prose Yoshimoto conveys her protagonists' emotional states by according them unusual sensitivity to the natural world; they share an enhanced vision that makes things shine with luminous clarity or emanate the gloom of mortality." Publ Wkly

Yoshimoto, Banana, 1964-

The **lake**; translated by Michael Emmerich. Melville House 2011 188p $15.95

ISBN 1-933633-77-8; 978-1-933633-77-0

LC 2011-06711

Original Japanese edition, 2005

This novel "tells the tale of a young woman who moves to Tokyo after the death of her mother, hoping to get over her grief and start a career as a graphic artist. She finds herself spending too much time staring out her window, though . . . until she realizes she's gotten used to seeing a young man across the street staring out his window, too." (Publisher's note)

"Chihiro, an artist, and Nakajima, a graduate student in genetics, finally meet after watching and waving to each other from their respective apartment windows across a Tokyo street. They're both unconventional and seemingly untethered souls; they've both lost their beloved mothers. They meander into a sweet, simple life together, although past secrets involving a mysterious brother and sister who live by an ethereal lake threaten to create an emotional divide. . . .Yoshimoto aficionados . . . will recognize her signature crisp, clipped style (thanks to exacting translator Emmerich's constancy) and revel in her latest cast of quirky characters." Libr J

Yoshimoto, Banana, 1964-

Moshi moshi; Banana Yoshimoto; translated by Asa Yoneda. Counterpoint 2016 206 p. illustrations (hardcover) $25

ISBN 1619027860; 9781619027862; 9781619028661

In this novel, by Banana Yoshimoto, translated by Asa Yoneda, "Yoshie's much-loved musician father has died in a suicide pact with an unknown woman. It is only when Yoshie and her mother move to Shimokitazawa . . . that they can finally start to put their painful past behind them. However, . . . Yoshie is haunted by nightmares in which her father is looking for the phone he left behind on the day he died, or on which she is trying--unsuccessfully--to call him." (Publisher's note)

"Prolific novelist Yoshimoto (The Lake, 2011, etc.) offers another story of youth, grief, and redemption in this ephemeral yet lovely portrait of an unformed woman." Kirkus

Young, Thomas W.

The **renegades**; Tom Young. G.P. Putnam's Sons 2012 336 p.

ISBN 0399158464; 9780399158469

LC 2012010954

This is the third novel with "Air Force Lt. Col. Michael Parson . . . . Now an adviser to a helicopter unit in Afghanistan, Parson requests that his interpreter friend, Sgt. Maj. Sophia Gold, be deployed back to Afghanistan." Parson and Gold have to deal with the actions of "a group called the Black Crescent"; they "get on the trail of the Crescent leader, Chaaku . . . , and in a last deadly battle bring a measure of justice to their corner of the war." (Publishers Weekly)

Yourcenar, Marguerite

★ **Memoirs** of Hadrian; translated from the French by Grace Frick in collaboration with the author. Farrar, Straus and Young 1954 313p

Original French edition, 1951

"The memoirs portray the emperor on the eve of his death and describe his reflections as he gazes out upon the city that seemed to him indestructible and that he now fears will fall. As with most of her work, the book is a minutely researched reconstruction of actual events in the distant past through which she develops penetrating and fully credible portraits of the people she describes." Reader's Ency. 4th edition

Yrsa Sigurdardottir

Last rituals; an Icelandic novel of secret symbols, medieval witchcraft, and modern murder. translated from the Icelandic by Bernard Scudder. HarperCollins Publishers 2007 314p (Thora Gudmundsdottir novels) $23.95

ISBN 978-0-06-114336-6; 0-06-114336-7

Original Icelandic edition, 2005

"Thóra is a thirtysomething divorcée, mother of two, and a partner in a small law firm. She is reluctantly drawn into a murder investigation when approached by the Guntlieb family, whose son, Harald, was killed at the university. With the pay at twice her usual rate and the assistance of Matthew Reich, the Guntlieb family representative, Thóra can't refuse, even though the gruesome murder appalls her. To find the murderer, Thóra and Matthew must delve into Harald's interests in witchcraft and witch burnings and investigate his university friends. Scudder provides such a smooth translation, right down to the slang used by Harald's college friends, that an engaged reader can easily forget this was originally written in Icelandic." Libr J

Other titles in this series are:
My soul to take (2009)
Ashes to dust (2012)
The day is dark (2013)
Someone to watch over me (2015)
Silence of the sea (2016)

Yu Hua

Brothers; translated from the Chinese by Eileen Chow and Carlos Rojas. Pantheon Books 2009 641p $29.95

ISBN 978-0-375-42499-1; 0-375-42499-7

LC 2008-21617

Original Chinese edition, 2005

This novel, "a family history documenting four decades of profound social and cultural transformation in China, begins on a toilet. In a sleepy rural outpost known as Liu Town, fourteen-year-old Baldy Li is caught peeping at women's bottoms in a latrine. He becomes known as a compulsive public masturbator, and his obsession continues into adulthood: he ends up hosting a beauty pageant for virgins (all of whom rely on doctored hymens to gain entrance). The book has sold more than a million copies in China, despite its irreverent take on everything from the Cultural Revolution to the capitalist boom." New Yorker

Yu, Charles, 1976-

★ **How** to live safely in a science fictional universe. Pantheon Books 2010 239p $24

ISBN 0-307-37920-5; 978-0-307-37920-7

LC 2010-01837

"Yu's protagonist, a time machine repairman also named Charles Yu, has lived the past decade of his life boxed up in a tiny TM-31 Recreational Time Travel Device. His two companions are TAMMY . . . and Ed, a nonexistent yet 'ontologically valid' dog." (N Y Times Book Rev)

"Our protagonist begins by explaining that he's gotten trapped in a time loop of his own making, caused when he thoughtlessly shot his own future self as he emerged from a time machine. As we ponder what it means, psychologically, to have murdered your future self, Yu takes us on a journey that gets progressively more emotionally intense. We learn about his protagonist's job as a time machine mechanic where his colleagues are mostly artificial intelligences who act more human than he does or who actually believe they are human. Yu effortlessly switches between comic vignettes about the fate of Luke Skywalker's less-famous son (who has messed up his time machine in a fictional universe), and his protagonist's painful memories of growing up at the center of a Venn diagram whose circles include the alien universes of Taiwan, America, and Tatooine. Yu is fond of meta-narrative, and packs the novel with adventures that take place entirely in theoretical universes, nostalgia-altered pasts, fictional worlds, and inside the protagonist's own time-looped mind." io9

Yunis, Alia

The **night** counter; a novel. Shaye Areheart Books 2009 365p $24

ISBN 978-0-307-45362-4; 0-307-45362-6

LC 2009-281269

This "novel, mixes equal parts of magical realism, social commentary, family drama and light-hearted humor to create a delicious and intriguing indulgence worth savoring." Minneapolis Star Trib

Z

Zahn, Timothy

The **last** command. Bantam Bks. 1993 407p (Star wars)

LC 92-43876

Earlier titles in the author's Thrawn trilogy: Heir to empire (1991); Dark force rising (1992)

In this concluding volume of the Star wars trilogy "Thrawn mounts a final siege against the Republic. While Han and Chewbacca struggle to form a wary alliance of smugglers in a last-ditch attack against the Empire, Leia keeps the Alliance together and prepares for the birth of her Jedi twins. But the Empire has too many ships and too many clones to combat. The Republic's only hope lies in sending a small force, led by Luke, into the very stronghold that houses Thrawn's terrible cloning machines." Publisher's note

Zailckas, Koren

Mother, mother; a novel. Koren Zailckas. Crown Publishers 2013 352 p. $24

ISBN 0385347235; 9780385347235

LC 2013010450

Alex Awards Winner (2014)

In this book, "Violet, the dysfunctional Hurst family's stoner middle child, cannot remember which family member slashed her 12-year-old brother Will the night she overdosed on some strange seeds. But her mother, Josephine, blames her, and has her committed to a psychiatric hospital. Violet has no idea who to turn to for help: her spineless, alcoholic father, Douglas; her runaway older sister, Rose; or Will, the homeschooled mama's boy." (Publishers Weekly)

Zamiatin, Evgenii Ivanovich

★ **We**; [by] Yevgeny Zamyatin; translated by Mirra Ginsburg. Viking 1972 204p

First translation published 1924

"The ultimate dystopian novel, presenting a vision of the United States: a society whose suppression of individuality in the cause of order proceeds to the logical limit of eliminating the imagination. Its origin, and the fact that it circulated surreptitiously in Russia as a samizdat publication, encourages a reading that construes it as an attack on Soviet communism, but it actually refers to a much more fundamental tendency in human nature towards conformity and autmatism. Not published in Russia until 1988." Anatomy of Wonder. 5th edition

Zan, Koethi

The **Never** List; Koethi Zan. Penguin Group USA 2013 320 p. $27.95

ISBN 0670026514; 9780670026517

LC 2013007348

In this novel by Koethi Zan "Sarah and Jennifer . . . accept a cab ride with grave . . . consequences. For . . . three years, they are held captive . . . by a connoisseur of sadism. Ten years later . . . Sarah [struggles] to resume a normal life . . . unable to come to grips with Jennifer['s death]. Sarah decides to confront her phobias and . . . goes on a cross-country chase that takes her into the perverse world of BDSM, secret cults, and the arcane study of torture, . . .unraveling a mystery.' (Publisher's note)

Zander, Joakim

The **Swimmer**; Joakim Zander. HarperCollins 2015 432 p. $27.99

ISBN 0062337246; 9780062337245

In this novel by Joakim Zander a "deep-cover CIA agent races across Europe to save the daughter he never knew. Klara Walldéen was raised by her grandparents on a remote archipelago in the Baltic Sea. Now, as an EU Parliament aide in Brussels . . . Klara has accidentally seen something she shouldn't have: a laptop containing information so sensitive that someone will kill to keep hidden. Meanwhile, in Virginia, an old spy hides from his past. Now, he is the only man who can save Klara." (Publisher's note)

"Skillfully moving between the past and the present, from Sweden to Syria to Washington and back again, Zander weaves an increasingly tight web of intrigue and suspense with Klara at the center. And if the novel occasionally veers toward spy-movie clichés, it's quickly reanchored by the strength of its characters. Beyond the blood-pumping chase sequences and requisite shootouts, there is real humanity here. A compulsively readable page-turner with unexpected heart." Kirkus

Zelazny, Roger

Blood of Amber. Arbor House 1986 215p

ISBN 0-87795-829-7

LC 86-3530

Sequel to Trumps of doom

In this seventh installment in the author's Amber fantasy series "the sorcerer Merlin of Amber—aka Merle Corey of San Francisco—learns the identities of two would-be assassins but makes a truce with one to pursue the greater, more dangerous power beyond them. Once again, the limited plot is enlivened by Zelazny's irony, his bravura sequences . . . and his laconic sense of the incongruous." Publ Wkly

Followed by Sign of chaos

Zelazny, Roger

The **courts** of chaos. Doubleday 1978 183p

ISBN 0-385-13685-4

LC 78-3263

Sequel to The hand of Oberon

This fifth title in the author's "Amber fantasy series answers many of the questions central to previous installments; the nature of the magical kingdom of Amber and the tangents it sometimes forms with the real world; the mystery behind the disappearance of Oberon the King—which forms the plot of the stories—and the machinations of Corwin, Prince of Amber, and his siblings, who thrive on intrigue." Booklist

Followed by Trumps of doom

Zelazny, Roger

The **dead** man's brother. Hard Case Crime 2009 256p pa $6.99

ISBN 978-0-8439-6115-7; 0-8439-6115-5

"The story follows Ovid Wiley, a former art smuggler turned respectable gallery owner who finds his former smuggling partner dead in his place of work. He is quickly picked up by the police, and then the CIA, which offers to make his trouble go away for a price. Wiley must track down a priest who has absconded with $3 million of the Vatican's dollars. This unwelcome assignment takes Wiley to Rome, where he meets up with his smuggling partner's ex-girlfriend, and then to Brazil, where he and Maria end up involved in local politics. The story is solid, but not spectacular. Zelazny keeps everything moving along nicely, but it's all territory that's been trod before. It's entertaining, and it shows Zelazny could have easily branched out into other genres, but The Dead Man's Brother is remarkable mainly for it's status as a forgotten novel." Independent Crime

Zelazny, Roger

Donnerjack; {by} Roger Zelazny, Jane Lindskold. Avon Bks. 1997 503p $24

ISBN 0-380-97326-X

LC 96-48705

"The late Zelazny's last novel, completed by Lindskold, is one of his largest and most ambitious. . . . All the mythic resonances we have come to expect from Zelazny are here in abundance." Booklist

Zelazny, Roger

The **guns** of Avalon. Doubleday 1972 180p (Amber)

Sequel to Nine princes in Amber

In this second volume of the author's Amber series Corwin "again walks the shadow worlds in search of his stolen birthright and encounters dreaded forces of evil conjured up by his own terrible curse." Booklist

Followed by Sign of the unicorn

Zelazny, Roger

The **hand** of Oberon. Doubleday 1976 181p

ISBN 0-385-08541-9

"Oberon, the royal leader of the land of Amber, is unexpectedly missing, and his large family of sons and daughters is engaged in searching for him, or else trying to keep him missing." Publ Wkly

Followed by The courts of chaos

Zelazny, Roger

Knight of shadows. Morrow 1989 251p (Amber)

LC 89-34658

Sequel to Sign of chaos

"The ninth book in Zelazny's Amber sagas. . . . Merlin, son of Corwin, escapes at the last minute from the Citadel of the FourWorlds. He is immediately plunged into intrigue and adventure. By book's end, it is apparent that his travels are not yet complete. Zelazny's pacing and the ingenious games he plays with magic continue to be rewarding." Booklist

Followed by Prince of chaos

Zelazny, Roger

★ **Lord** of light. Doubleday 1967 257p

This novel "describes a planet colonized by refugees from India who are tyrannized by a few of their fellow citizens who have assumed the guise and powers of the Hindu gods. Instead of easing his readers into the strange setting and unfamiliar mythology, Zelazny began the story in the middle, centuries after the initial landing; that the reader can absorb—and care to absorb—the complexities of the plot and setting is a tribute to the author's storytelling ability." New Ency of Sci Fic

Zelazny, Roger

★ **Nine** princes in Amber. Doubleday 1970 188p (Amber)

This tale, the first in the author's Amber series, is a fantasy and adventure story about Corwin, who, following an attack of amnesia, realizes that he is one of nine princes in the kingdom of Amber. Each one of the nine princes and four princesses wants the throne, and war breaks out between the brothers

Followed by The guns of Avalon

Zelazny, Roger

Prince of chaos. Morrow 1991 225p (Amber)

LC 91-17296

Sequel to Knight of shadows

The tenth book in the Amber sagas "takes Merlin Corey to the actual Courts of Chaos, which have figured as offstage presences in the series beginning with Trumps of Doom. We now see the Courts from the inside, and a certain amount of the mystery about Corey's world and future is dispelled, although not without the usual quota of intrigues and dangers. The finer nuances of the series are becoming a little hard to appreciate without having followed it from the beginning. The vivid imagination and high command of language, however, can still be enjoyed on a volume-by-volume basis." Booklist

Zelazny, Roger

Sign of chaos. Arbor House 1987 214p (Amber)

LC 87-14509

Sequel to Blood of Amber

In the eighth volume of the author's Amber fantasy series "Merlin Corey follows a confused trail to the Keep of Four Worlds, where he learns the secret of the involvement of the Courts of Chaos in all the intrigues and wars to which he is heir." Booklist

Followed by Knight of shadows

Zelazny, Roger

Sign of the unicorn. Doubleday 1975 186p (Amber)

Sequel to The guns of Avalon

"Third in a series of science fiction-fantasy adventures featuring Corwin, Prince of Amber. . . . Court intrigue is rampant among the surviving princes and princesses of Amber, all of whom weave in and out of Shadow, a multi-dimensional world they can manipulate, and unite to rescue a brother imprisoned by evil beings threatening the kingdom. This, though action packed, does not advance the fortunes of Corwin to any extent but does fill in background." Booklist

Followed by The hand of Oberon

Zelazny, Roger

Trumps of doom. Arbor House 1985 183p

ISBN 0-87795-718-5

LC 84-299

Sequel to The courts of chaos

"A new sequence {in the Amber fantasy series} begins in this sixth volume centering on Corwin's son Merlin, a sorcerer who has followed the father he barely knew from their powerful realm of Amber to an Earth that is one of Amber's many shadowy alternate worlds. Attempts on Merlin's life force him to return to Amber, where he becomes embroiled once more in family quarrels and finally confronts the man who has been stalking him. This fast-paced, colorful tale is enriched by Zelazny's literary analogs of his alternate worlds as he flips from one frame of reference to another (tarot, computers, lawyerly logic) and from one voice to another (hard-boiled detective, classical allusions, high fantasy)." Publ Wkly

Followed by Blood of Amber

Zeltserman, Dave

★ The **caretaker** of Lorne Field. Overlook Press 2010 237p $23.95

ISBN 1-59020-303-8; 978-1-59020-303-3

This novel "focuses on Jack Durkin, the ninth generation of firstborn sons in his family who have daily weeded Lorne Field to purge it of Aukowies, bloodthirsty plants that could overrun the world in weeks if not attended to. Though Jack takes his job seriously, no one else does: his oldest son doesn't want to follow in his footsteps; his wife is tired of living poorly on his caretaker's salary; and the townspeople who subsidize him are increasingly skeptical of purported menaces that no one has ever seen because Jack diligently nips them in the bud. With his support dwindling, Jack finds himself driven to desperate measures to prove that he's truly saving the world. Zeltserman . . . orchestrates events perfectly, making it impossible to tell if Jack is genuinely humankind's unsung hero or merely the latest descendant of a family of superstitious loonies." Publ Wkly

Zeltserman, Dave

Small crimes. Serpent's Tail 2008 263p pa $14.95

ISBN 978-1-85242-971-3; 1-85242-971-2

"This tale is told by one of fortune's fools: Joe Denton is a crooked ex-cop in Vermont who's just been released from jail after serving seven years for stabbing the local district attorney in the face. Since what's past is never truly past in crime noir, no sooner does Joe step out of the slammer than cosmic IOU's begin to rain down on his head. First, the disfigured DA cheerfully greets Joe outside the prison and announces that a local crime kingpin (and Joe's secret boss) is dying of cancer and has found religion. The kingpin's expected confession should send Joe straight back behind bars. Then, the local sheriff (also crooked) orders Joe to murder the DA before the crime kingpin can confess. The plot of Small Crimes ricochets out from this claustrophobic opening, and it's a thing of sordid beauty." NPR

Zevin, Gabrielle

The **hole** we're in; a novel. Black Cat 2010 283p pa $14

ISBN 978-0-8021-1923-0; 0-8021-1923-9

"All five Pomeroys—flawed, devoted, cranky, impetuous, utterly relatable—come blazingly alive on the page." Entertainment Wkly

Zevin, Gabrielle

The **storied** life of A. J. Fikry; a novel. by Gabrielle Zevin. Algonquin Books of Chapel Hill 2014 272 p. (alk. paper) $24.95

ISBN 1616203218; 9781616203214

LC 2013043144

In this book by Gabrielle Zevin, "A.J. Fikry, the . . . owner of Island Books, has recently endured some tough years: his wife has died, his bookstore is experiencing the worst sales in its history, and his prized possession--a rare edition of [Edgar Allan] Poe poems--has been stolen. Over time, he has given up on people. . . . Until a most unexpected occurrence gives him the chance to make his life over and see things anew." (Publisher's note)

"Filled with interesting characters, a deep knowledge of bookselling, wonderful critiques of classic titles, and very funny depictions of book clubs and author events, this will prove irresistible to book lovers everywhere." Booklist

Zimler, Richard

★ The **last** kabbalist of Lisbon. Overlook Press 1998 318p $24.95

ISBN 0-87951-834-0

LC 97-46184

This novel "first published in Portuguese, vividly re-creates the world of ancient Lisbon, presenting Berekiah's mysticism in graceful, albeit occasionally florid, prose. Zimler's portrait of the city (and the New Christians' uneasy place within it) enriches his many-layered narrative, in which a suitably complex cast of characters plays a dangerous game with fate." N Y Times Book Rev

Zimler, Richard

The **seventh** gate; a novel. Richard Zimler. Overlook Press 2012 577 p. ill., map (hardcover) $26.95

ISBN 1590207130; 9781590207130

LC 2007405815

This book by Richard Zimler presents a "coming-of-age epic set in Berlin at the start of the Nazi era. . . . Precocious 14-year-old Sophie Riedesel is adjusting to her changing body and desires, but she soon has other concerns as Hitler consolidates his power. . . . Although Sophie herself isn't Jewish, she's alarmed by the uptick in anti-Semitism and the threats posed to her Jewish friends." (Publishers Weekly)

Zimmer, Michael

The **long** hitch; a western story. Five Star 2011 364p $25.95

ISBN 978-1-43282-524-9; 1-43282-524-0

LC 2011-13162

"In 1874 Utah territory, young teamster Buck McCready becomes wagon boss for the Kavanaugh freight outfit after his mentor, old Mason Campbell, is murdered. With the Kavanaugh outfit engaged in a wagon train race that will decide whether Kavanaugh or a competitor lands a lucrative freight-hauling contract, Buck vows to find Campbell's killer. But first he must win the race, a difficult task considering there's a saboteur among his crew and a hired gun out to take him down, plus the possibility that Campbell's killer is after Buck, too. . . . Zimmer has put together a believable, gritty, and action-packed tale of the real Old West." Publ Wkly

Zimmer, Michael

Wild side of the river; a western story. Five Star 2011 216p $25.95

ISBN 978-1-59414-946-7; 1-59414-946-1

LC 2010-43349

"Ethan, eldest son of the Wilder clan, returns home after having been away only a couple of months. He finds his family near the point of self-destruction. One of his brothers is on the run, accused of beating a young girl. His father is warring with another brother, who is presently keeping his father locked up in the privy. As if that isn't enough, Ethan learns that local ranchers are being murdered by an unknown culprit, and when his own father becomes a victim, he puts everything he has on the line to make the killer pay. A man's single-minded quest for vengeance is a traditional western theme, but this one doesn't feel like a traditional western. It's darker, harder around the edges, a noir crime drama wearing western clothing." Booklist

Zimmerman, David

Sandbox; a novel. Soho Press 2010 350p $25

ISBN 978-1-56947-628-4

LC 2009-43994

"Set at a remote military base in the Iraqi desert, this debut novel unsparingly portrays the experience of fighting in the Iraq War. Private Toby Durrant is on a routine mission when his convoy gets ambushed. After the shooting has stopped, Durrant briefly leaves his vehicle to get sick. This seemingly minor infraction draws him into a complex conspiracy that involves the base's senior officers, an Iraqi translator, and many of his fellow soldiers." Libr J

Zimmerman, Jean

★ The **orphanmaster**; Jean Zimmerman. Viking 2012 418 p. maps $27.95

ISBN 0670023647; 9780670023646

LC 2011038593

In this historical thriller, a "feisty young Dutch woman, an English spy, and a local demon all cross paths in 1663 New Amsterdam. . . . Orphaned as a child, Blandine van Couvering now . . . looks out for the orphans around the small town . . . . But first one orphan disappears, and then another is found molested and murdered. Evidence of a witika, a fiend of Native American folklore, is found near the remains. . . . As the little bodies pile up, fears run wild." (Library Journal)

Zito, V. M.

The **return** man. Orbit 2012 400p (paperback) $9.99

ISBN 0316218286; 9780316218283

In this book, in the "desolate heat and haunting emptiness of the zombie-infested American Southwest, exneurologist Henry Marco is hired by the living to 'return' their undead loved ones, a euphemism for blowing their brains out. Marco also yearns to find and 'return' his own wife. Hired by the Department of Homeland Security to track down a scientist who may have developed a cure, Marco embarks on a journey across the desert." (Publishers Weekly)

Zola, Emile

★ **Germinal**; translated with an introduction and notes by Roger Pearson. Penguin Books 2004 xlv, 546p (Penguin classics) pa $10

ISBN 978-0-14-044742-2; 0-14-044742-3

Original French edition, 1885, one of the Rougon-Macquart series

"A study of life in the mines. . . . Étienne Lanier, a socialist, is forced to work in the mines. Low wages and fines cause a strike, of which Lanier is one of the leaders. He counsels moderation; but hunger drives the miners to desperation, and force is met by force. Several are killed, Lanier is deported, and the miners fall back into their old slavery." Keller. Reader's Dig of Books

Zola, Emile

★ **Nana**; translated with an introduction by Douglas Parmée. Oxford University Press 1998 xxix, 430p (Oxford world's classics)

ISBN 0-19-283670-6

Original French edition, 1880, one of the Rougon-Macquart series

"The title character grows up in the slums of Paris. She has a brief career as an untalented actress before finding success as a courtesan. Although vulgar and ignorant, she has a destructive sexuality that attracts many rich and powerful men. Cruelly contemptuous of her lovers' emotions, Nana wastes their fortunes, driving many of them to ruin and even suicide." Merriam-Webster's Ency of Lit

Zola, Emile

Three faces of love; especially translated for this volume by Roland Gant. Vanguard Press 1969 151p

These three early Zola stories explore different kinds of love. In For One Night of Love "Zola tells of a dullard whose passion leads to suicide through his having been accessory in the murder of his rival, killed by the girl, a marquise. 'Round Trip' is a lyric of youthful sensuality triumphing over middle-aged insensitivity. In 'Winkles for M. Chabre' Zola deals with a triangle (aging husband, young wife, young man); the husband has been told to expect a child if he follows a diet of shellfish; he gets the child, unaware that it is not because of winkles. Slight things, these stories, but welcome additions to the austere works usually associated with Zola." Libr J

Zuber, Isabel

Salt. Picador 2002 352p

ISBN 0-312-28133-1

LC 2001-54892

"Zuber gets the historical details right, and her characters' emotions (especially Anna's—romantic, tender and full of quiet desperation) are handled just as deftly." N Y Times Book Rev

Includes bibliographical references

Zumas, Leni

Red clocks; a novel. Leni Zumas. Little, Brown & Co. 2018 356 p. (hardcover) $26

ISBN 9780316510660; 9780316434812

LC 2017933411

In this novel, by Leni Zumas, "abortion is once again illegal in America, in-vitro fertilization is banned, and the Personhood Amendment grants rights of life, liberty, and property to every embryo. In a small Oregon fishing town, five very different women navigate these new barriers alongside age-old questions surrounding motherhood, identity, and freedom." (Publisher's note)

"Dark humor further enhances the novel, making this a thoroughly affecting and memorable political parable." Pub Wkly

NAME INDEX

This index of author names and pseudonyms provides a quick reference for finding authors who have written under multiple names. Included, also, are name listings that may require clarification with regard to accurate alphabetization (e.g. Honore de Balzac is filed under *Balzac, Honore de.*) The names are arranged alphabetically, and are listed according to Library of Congress name authority files. Furthermore, this list provides a two-way reference point for pseudonyms. For example, Mark Twain can be found under both *Twain, Mark, 1835-1910,* and *Clemens, Samuel Langhorne*. Works by authors included in this index may be found in Part 1 of this collection, listed under the name used in the responsibility statement of the work. As only authors listed in the *Fiction Core Collection* are included in this index, it should not be considered an exhaustive listing of current and past pseudonyms.

Abrahams, Peter, 1947-
See also Quinn, Spencer
Agnon, Shmuel Yosef, 1888-1970
See Czaczkes, Shmuel Josef
Ahmadou Kourouma
See Kourouma, Ahmadou
Ahndoril, Alexander
See also Kepler, Lars
Akunin, Boris, 1956-
See also Chkhartishvili, Grigory
Alba, Alicia Gaspar de
See Gaspar de Alba, Alicia, 1958-
Aleas, Richard
See also Ardai, Charles, 1969-
Alexander, Margaret Walker
See also Walker, Margaret, 1915-1998
Allen, Conrad, 1940-
See also Marston, Edward
Anatoli, A., 1929-1979
See also Kuznetsov, Anatolii Vasil'evich
Anderson, Sherwood, 1876-1941
See also Fever, Buck
Andrews, Cecily Isabel Fairfield
See also West, Rebecca, 1892-1983
Andrews, Colin
See also Wilson, F. Paul
Anthony, Evelyn, 1928-
See also Stephens, Eve
Ardai, Charles, 1969-
See also Aleas, Richard
Arends, Marthe
See also MacAlister, Katie
Aristides
See also Epstein, Joseph, 1937-
Armitage, G. E.
See also Edric, Robert, 1956-
Arouet, Francois Marie
See also Voltaire, 1694-1778
Arslan Veronese, Antonia
See Arslan, Antonia
Asimov, Isaac, 1920-1992
See also French, Paul
Aubert, Rosemary, 1946-
See also Snow, Lucy
Auster, Paul, 1947-
See also Benjamin, Paul
Awlinson, Richard
See Denning, Troy
Bachman, Richard
See also King, Stephen, 1947-
Baldwin, Margaret
See also Weis, Margaret, 1948-
Bales, Susan Ford Vance, 1957-
See also Ford, Susan
Balzac, Honore de, 1799-1850
See also Saint-Aubin, Horace de
Bancroft, Stephanie
See Bond, Stephanie; Hauck, Stephanie
Bannister, Patricia V., 1923-
See Veryan, Patricia
Banville, John
See also Black, Benjamin
Barbash, Thomas
See Barbash, Tom
Barger, Ralph
See also Barger, Sonny
Barger, Sonny
See also Barger, Ralph
Barlett, Alica Gimenez
See Gimenez Barlett, Alicia,1951-
Barnes, Djuna, 1892-1982
See also Steptoe, Lydia
Barnes, Julian, 1946-
See also Kavanagh, Dan
Bart, Andre Schwarz
See Schwarz-Bart, Andre, 1928-
Bayley, Iris
See also Murdoch, Iris
Beauman, Sally
See also James, Vanessa
Beaton, M.C.
See also Chesney, Marion; Tremaine, Jennie; Chesterton, G. K.
Becerra, Michael Jaime
See Jaime-Becerra, Michael
Bell, Acton

See also Bronte, Anne, 1820-1849
Bell, Currer
See also Bronte, Charlotte, 1816-1855
Bell, Ellis
See also Bronte, Emily, 1818-1848
Ben Jelloun, Tahar, 1944-
See Jelloun, Tahar ben
Benjamin, Paul
See also Auster, Paul, 1947-
Beyle, Marie Henri
See also Brulard, Henry; Stendhal, 1783-1842
Bienes, Nick
See also Gould, Judith
Birdwell, Cleo
See also DeLillo, Don
Black, Benjamin
See also Banville, John
Blair, Eric
See also Orwell, George, 1903-1950
Bleeck, Oliver, 1926-1995
See also Thomas, Ross
Block, Lawrence, 1938-
See also Kavanagh, Paul
Bolton, S. J.
See also Bolton, Sharon J.
Bolton, Sharon J.
See Bolton, S. J.
Bond, Stephanie
See also Bancroft, Stephanie; Hauck, Stephanie
Bostwick, Marie
See also Skinner, Marie Bostwick
Boucolon, Maryse
See also Conde, Maryse, 1937-
Bowen-Judd, Sara Hutton
See also Woods, Sara
Box, Edgar
See also Vidal, Gore, 1925-
Boyd, Jerry
See also Toole, F. X., 1930-2002
Boz
See also Dickens, Charles, 1812-1870; Sparks, Timothy
Bradley, Alan, 1938-
See Bradley, C. Alan
Bradley, C. Alan
See Bradley, Alan, 1938-
Bragi Olafsson, 1962-
See Olafsson, Bragi
Brand, Max, 1892-1944
See also Evans, Evan; Faust, Frederick
Braybrooke, June, 1920-1994
See also English, Isobel; Jolliffe, June
Brennan, John
See also Welcome, John, 1914-
Bronte, Anne, 1820-1849
See also Bell, Acton
Bronte, Charlotte, 1816-1855
See also Bell, Currer
Bronte, Charlotte, 1816-1855
See also Wellesley, Charles
Bronte, Emily, 1818-1848
See also Bell, Ellis
Brooks-Davies, Douglas
See Davies, Douglas Brooks-
Brown, Elizabeth Inness
See Inness-Brown, Elizabeth, 1954-
Brown, James Willie Jr.
See also Komunyakaa, Yusef
Brown, Sandra, 1948-
See also Jordan, Laura; Ryan, Rachel
Brulard, Henry
See also Stendhal, 1783-1842
Buchan, John, 1875-1940
See also Tweedsmuir, John Buchan
Buck, Pearl S. (Pearl Sydenstricker), 1892-1973
See also Hedge, John; Walsh, Pearl S.
Bulwer-Lytton, Edward
See Lytton, Edward Bulwer Lytton, 1803-1873
Buntline, Ned, 1822 or 3-1886
See also Judson, Edward Zane Carroll
Burgess, Anthony, 1917-1993
See also Wilson, John Anthony Burgess
Butler, Samuel, 1835-1902
See also Owen, John Pickard
Butters, Dorothy Gilman
See also Gilman, Dorothy, 1923-
Byatt, Antonia Susan
See Byatt, A. S., 1936-
Campbell, R. Wright, 1927-2000
See Campbell, Robert
Campbell, Robert
See Campbell, R. Wright, 1927-2000
Cannon, Curt, 1926-2005
See also Collins, Hunt, 1926-2005; Hannon, Ezra, 1926-2005; Hudson, Dean, 1926-2005; Hunter, Evan, 1926-2005 Marsten, Richard, 1926-2005; McBain, Ed, 1926-2005
Can Xue
See also Tsan-hsueh, 1953-; Deng Xiaohua
Carlyle, Liz, 1958-
See also Woodhouse, Susan T.
Carr, Alex
See also Siler, Jenny
Cary, Arthur Joyce Lunel
See also Cary, Joyce, 1888-1957
Cary, Joyce, 1888-1957
See Cary, Arthur Joyce Lunel
Cassirer, Nadine Gordimer
See Gordimer, Nadine, 1923-
Cauwelaert, Didier van, 1960-
See Van Cauwelaert, Didier
Cavallo, Evelyn
See also Spark, Muriel
Celine, Louis-Ferdinand, 1894-1961
See also Destouches, Henri-Louis
Challans, Mary

See also Renault, Mary, 1905-1983
Chekhonte, Antosha
See also Chekhov, Anton Pavlovich, 1860-1904
Chekhov, Anton Pavlovich, 1860-1904
See Chekhonte, Antosha
Chesney, Marion
See also Tremaine, Jennie; Beaton, M.C.; Chesterton, G. K.
Chesterton, G.K.
See also Chesney, Marion; Tremaine, Jennie; Beaton, M.C.
Chisholm, P. F., 1958-
See Patricia Finney
Chkhartishvili, Grigory
See also Akunin, Boris, 1956-
Chu, T'ien-Hsin, 1958-
See also Zhu Tianxin
Claudine, Sidonie Gabrielle
See also Colette, 1873-1954
Clemens, Samuel Langhorne
See Twain, Mark, 1835-1910
Clement, Hal, 1922-2003
See Stubbs, Harry Clement
Clezio, J.-M. G. le
See Le Clezio, J.-M. G., 1940-
Cohen, Janet
See also Neel, Janet, 1940-
Coleman, William Laurence
See Coleman, Lonnie, 1920-1982
Colette, 1873-1954
See also Claudine, Sidonie Gabrielle
Collins, Hunt, 1926-2005
See also Cannon, Curt, 1926-2005; Hunter, Evan, 1926-2005; Hannon, Ezra, 1926-2005; Hudson, Dean, 1926-2005; Marsten, Richard, 1926-2005; McBain, Ed, 1926-2005
Conde, Maryse, 1937-
See also Boucolon, Maryse
Conroy, Joseph Robert
See also Conroy, Robert, 1938-
Conroy, Robert, 1938-
See also Conroy, Joseph Robert
Cookson, Catherine
See also Marchant, Catherine
Cornwell, Bernard
See also Kells, Susannah
Cornwell, David John Moore
See also Le Carre, John, 1931-
Craig, Alisa
See also MacLeod, Charlotte
Crayencour, Marguerite De
See also Yourcenar, Marguerite
Crayon, Geoffrey
See also Irving, Washington, 1783-1859; Knickerbocker, Diedrich
Crichton, Michael, 1942-2008
See also Douglas, Michael; Hudson, Jeffery; Lange, John
Cross, Amanda, 1926-2003
See also Heilbrun, Carolyn G., 1926-2003
Cross, Mary Ann Evans
See Eliot, George, 1819-1880
Cunningham, E.V.
See also Fast, Howard, 1914-2003
Czaczkes, Shmuel Josef
See also Agnon, Shmuel Yosef, 1888-1970
Daniel, Margaret Truman
See also Truman, Margaret, 1924-2008
Dargatz, Gail Anderson-
See Anderson-Dargatz, Gail, 1963-
Davenport, Diana
See also Davenport, Kiana
Davenport, Kiana
See also Davenport, Diana
Davies, Douglas Brooks
See Brooks-Davies, Douglas
Davies, Robertson, 1913-1995
See Davies, William Robertson
Davies, William Robertson
See Davies, Robertson, 1913-1995
Dawlatabadi, Mahmud, 1940-
See Dowlatabadi, Mahmud
De Alba, Alicia Gaspar
See Gaspar de Alba, Alicia, 1958-
De Balzac, Honore
See Balzac, Honore de, 1799-1850
De Beauvoir, Simone
See Beauvoir, Simone de, 1908-1986
De Crayencour, Marguerite
See Yourcenar, Marguerite
De Hartog, Jan, 1914-2002
See Hartog, Jan de
De Heriz, Enrique
See Heriz, Enrique de, 1964-
De Jonge, Peter
See Jonge, Peter de
De Loo, Tessa
See Loo, Tessa de
De Moor, Margriet
See Moor, Margriet de
De Saint-Aubin, Horace
See also Balzac, Honore de, 1799-1850
De Saint-Exupery, Antoine
See Saint-Exupery, Antoine de, 1900-1944
Deane, Conor Fitzgerald
See also Fitzgerald, Conor
Deaver, Jeffery
See also Jefferies, William, 1950-
Defoe, Daniel, 1661?-1731
See also Foe, Daniel; Moreton, Andrew
DeLillo, Don
See also Birdwell, Cleo
Delinsky, Barbara
See also Douglass, Billie; Drake, Bonnie
Deng Xiaohua
See also Tsan-hsueh, 1953-; Can Xue
Denning, Troy

See also Awlinson, Richard
Dennis, Patrick, 1921-1976
See also Tanner, Edward Everett
Destouches, Henri-Louis
See Celine, Louis-Ferdinand, 1894-1961
Di Lampedusa, Giuseppe Tomasi
See Tomasi di Lampedusa, Giuseppe, 1896-1957
Diago, Evelio Rosero
See Rosero Diago, Evelio, 1958-
Dick, R. A.
See also Leslie, Josephine Aimee Campbell, 1898-1979
Dickens, Charles, 1812-1870
See also Boz; Sparks, Timothy
Dikty, Julian May
See May, Julian, 1931-
Ditzen, Rudolf
See also Fallada, Hans, 1893-1947
Dominic, R. B.
See also Lathen, Emma
Dos Passos, John
See Passos, John Dos
Dostoevskii, Fedor Mikhailovich
See Dostoyevsky, Fyodor, 1821-1881
Douglas, Michael
See also Crichton, Michael, 1942-2008; Hudson, Jeffery; Lange, John
Douglass, Billie
See Delinsky, Barbara; Drake, Bonnie
Doyle, Conan
See Doyle, Sir Arthur Conan, 1859-1930
Drabble, Margaret, 1939-
See also Swift, Margaret
Drake, Bonnie
See Delinsky, Barbara; Douglass, Billie
Drawcansir, Alexander
See also Fielding, Henry, 1707-1754
Ducornet, Rikki
See also Rikki
Dudevant, Amantine Lucile Aurore Dupin
See also Dudevant, Mme; Dupin, Amantine Aurore Lucile; Sand, George, 1804-1876; Sand, Jules
Dudevant, Mme
See also Dudevant, Amantine Lucile Aurore Dupin; Dupin, Amantine Aurore Lucile; Sand, George, 1804-1876; Sand, Jule
Dukes, Carol Muske, 1945-
See Muske-Dukes, Carol
Dunn, Kathleen
See also Fleming, Irene, 1939-
Dupin, Amantine Aurore Lucile, 1804-1876
See also Dudevant, Amantine Lucile Aurore Dupin; Dudevant, Mme; Sand, George; Sand, Jules
Eagles, Cynthia Harrod
See Harrod-Eagles, Cynthia
Echevarria, Roberto Gonzalez
See Gonzalez Echevarria, Roberto
Edric, Robert, 1956-
See also Armitage, G. E.
Eliot, Alice C.
See also Jewett, Sarah Orne, 1849-1909
Eliot, George, 1819-1880
See also Cross, Mary Ann Evans
Elliot, Jessie
See also Grodstein, Lauren
English, Isobel
See also Braybrooke, June, 1920-1994; Jolliffe, June
Ephron, Hallie
See also Touger, Hallie Ephron
Epstein, Joseph, 1937-
See also Aristides
Escobar, Marisol
See also Marisol, 1930-
Evanovich, Janet
See also Hall, Steffie
Evans, Evan
See also Brand, Max, 1892-1944; Faust, Frederick
Evelyn, John Michael
See also Underwood, Michael, 1916-
Exupery, Antoine de Saint
See Saint-Exupery, Antoine de, 1900-1944
Fair, A. A.
See also Gardner, Erle Stanley, 1889-1970; Kendrake, Carleton; Kenny, Charles J.
Fairbairn, Ann, 1901 or 2-1972
See also Tait, Dorothy
Fallada, Hans, 1893-1947
See also Ditzen, Rudolf
Fallon, Martin
See also Graham, James; Higgins, Jack, 1929-; Marlowe, Hugh; Patterson, Harry
Fast, Howard, 1914-2003
See also Cunningham, E. V.
Faust, Frederick
See also Brand, Max, 1892-1944; Evans, Evan
Feige, Hermann Albert Otto Max
See also Marut, Ret; Torsvan, Berick Traven; Torsvan, Traven; Traven, B.
Fever, Buck
See also Anderson, Sherwood, 1876-1941
Fielding, Henry, 1707-1754
See also Drawcansir, Alexander
Finlay, Peter Warren
See also Pierre, D. B. C.
Finney, Patricia
See also Chisholm, P. F., 1958-
Fitzgerald, Conor
See also Deane, Conor Fitzgerald
Fleming, Irene, 1939-
See also Dunn, Kathleen
Fleming, Oliver
See also Lawless, Anthony; Macdonald, Filip; MacDonald, Philip, 1899-1981; Porlock, Martin
Flying Officer X
See also Bates, H. E., 1905-1974

Foe, Daniel
See also Defoe, Daniel, 1661?-1731; Morton, Andrew
Ford, Ford Madox, 1873-1939
See also Hueffer, Ford Madox
Ford, Susan
See also Bales, Susan Ford Vance, 1957-
Frank, Pat, 1907-1964
See also Hart, HarryFranklin, Ariana
See also Norman, Diana
Franklin, Miles, 1879-1954
See also Franklin, Stella Maria Miles Lampe
Franklin, Stella Maria Miles Lampe
See also Franklin, Miles, 1879-1954
French, Paul
See also Asimov, Isaac, 1920-1992
Freundlich, Jeffry P.
See also Lindsay, Jeffry P., 1952-; Lindsay, Jeff
Fujiwara, Murasaki
See also Murasaki Shikibu, b. 978?; Shikibu, Murasaki
Fyfield, Frances, 1948-
See also Hegarty, Frances
Galbraith, Robert
See also Rowling, J.K.
Gallaher, Rhea
See also Gould, Judith
Gao Xingjian
See also Kao, Hsing-chien, 1940-
Gardner, Erle Stanley, 1889-1970
See also Fair, A. A.; Kendrake, Carleton; Kenny, Charles J.
Gardner, Lisa
See also Scott, Alicia
Gash, Joe
See also Granger, Bill; Griffith, Bill
Gash, Jonathan, 1933-
See also Grant, John
Gill, Bartholomew, 1943-2002
See also McGarrity, Mark
Gilman, Dorothy, 1923-
See also Butters, Dorothy Gilman
Goff, Annabel Davis
See Davis-Goff, Annabel
Goldsher, A. M.
See Goldsher, Alan, 1966-
Goodjohn, Bunny
See also Goodjohn, B. A.
GoodWeather, Hartley
See also King, Thomas, 1943-
Gopaleen, Myles
See also Knowall, George; Na Gopaleen, Myles; O'Brien, Flann, 1911-1966; O'Nolan, Brian
Gordimer, Nadine, 1923-
See also Cassirer, Nadine Gordimer
Gores, Joe
See Gores, Joseph N.
Gorky, Maksim, 1868-1936
See also Gorky, Maxim; Peshkov, Alexei Maximovich
Gorky, Maxim
See also Gorky, Maksim, 1868-1936; Peshkov, Alexei Maximovich
Gould, Judith
See also Bienes, Nick; Gallaher, Rhea
Graham, James
See also Fallon, Martin; Higgins, Jack, 1929-; Marlowe, Hugh; Patterson, Harry
Graham, Tom
See Lewis, Sinclair, 1885-1951
Granger, Bill
See also Gash, Joe; Griffith, Bill
Grant, John
See also Gash, Jonathan, 1933-
Grant, Linda
See also Williams, Linda Verlee
Grant, Mira
See also McGuire, Seanan
Green, Hannah
See also Greenberg, Joanne, 1932-
Greenberg, Joanne, 1932-
See also Green, Hannah
Griffith, Bill
See also Granger, Bill; Gash, Joe
Grodstein, Lauren
See also Elliot, Jessie
Hall, Oakley M.
See also Manor, Jason
Hall, Steffie
See also Evanovich, Janet
Hamilton, Clive
See also Lewis, C. S., 1898-1963
Hammett, Samuel Dashiell
See Hammett, Dashiell, 1894-1961
Hannon, Ezra, 1926-2005
See also Cannon, Curt, 1926-2005; Collins, Hunt, 1926-2005; Hannon, Ezra, 1926-2005; Hudson, Dean, 1926-2005; Hunter, Evan, 1926-2005; Marsten, Richard, 1926-2005; McBain, Ed, 1926-2005
Harding, John Wesley, 1965-
See also Stace, Wesley Harding
Harris, Mark, 1922-2007
See also Wiggen, Henry W.
Hart, Harry
See also Frank, Pat, 1907-1964
Hartog, Jan de
See De Hartog, Jan, 1914-2002
Harvey, Caroline
See also Trollope, Joanna
Harvey, Jack
See also Rankin, Ian, 1960-
Hauck, Stephanie
See also Bancroft, Stephanie; Bond, Stephanie
Hawk, Alex
See also Kelton, Elmer, 1926-2009; McElroy, Lee
Hawkins, Anthony Hope
See Hope, Anthony, 1863-1933
Haynes, Conrad

See also Haynes, Dana
Haynes, Dana
See also Haynes, Conrad
Haywood, Gar Anthony
See also Shannon, Ray
Head, Ann
See also Morse, Anne Christensen
Hedge, John
See also Buck, Pearl S., 1892-1973; Walsh, Pearl S.
Hegarty, Frances
See also Fyfield, Frances, 1948-
Heilbrun, Carolyn G., 1926-2003
See also Cross, Amanda, 1926-2003
Helgason, Hallgrimur
See Hallgrimur Helgason, 1959-
Henry, O., 1862-1910
See also Porter, William Sydney
Hervey, Evelyn
See also Keating, H. R. F., 1926-2011; Keating, Henry Reymond Fitzwalter
Higgins, Jack, 1929-
See also Fallon, Martin; Graham, James; Marlowe, Hugh; Patterson, Harry
Highet, Helen MacInnes
See also MacInnes, Helen, 1907-1985
Highsmith, Patricia, 1921-1995
See also Morgan, Claire
Hill, Joe
See also King, Joseph Hillstrom
Hill, John, 1945-
See also Koontz, Dean R.
Hill, Reginald, 1936-
See also Morland, Dick; Ruell, Patrick; Underhill, Charles
Hiraoka, Kimitake
See also Mishima, Yukio, 1925-1970
Hobb, Robin
See also Lindholm, Megan; Ogden, Margaret Astrid Lindholm
Holton, Leonard
See also O'Connor, Patrick; Wibberley, Leonard, 1915-1983
Hope, Anthony, 1863-1933
See also Hawkins, Anthony Hope
Horowitz, James
See also Salter, James
Hudson, Dean, 1926-2005
See also Cannon, Curt, 1926-2005; Collins, Hunt, 1926-2005; Hannon, Ezra, 1926-2005; Hunter, Evan, 1926-2005; Marsten, Richard, 1926-2005; McBain, Ed, 1926-2005
Hudson, Jeffery
See also Crichton, Michael, 1942-2008; Douglas, Michael; Lange, John
Hueffer, Ford Madox
See Ford, Ford Madox, 1873-1939
Hulme, Juliet
See also Perry, Anne, 1938-
Humphreys, C. C.
See also Humphreys, Chris
Humphreys, Chris
See also Humphreys, C. C.
Hunter, Evan, 1926-2005
See also Cannon, Curt, 1926-2005; Collins, Hunt, 1926-2005; Hannon, Ezra, 1926-2005; Hudson, Dean, 1926-2005; Marsten, Richard, 1926-2005; McBain, Ed, 1926-2005
Ibanez, Vicente Blasco
See Blasco Ibanez, Vicente, 1867-1928
Irving, Clifford
See also Luckless, John
Irving, Washington, 1783-1859
See also Crayon, Geoffrey; Knickerbocker, Diedrich
Isherwood, Christopher, 1904-1986
See also Bradshaw-Isherwood, Christopher William
Jaber, Diana Abu-
See Abu-Jaber, Diana
James, P. D.
See also White, Phyllis Dorothy James
James, Vanessa
See also Beauman, Sally
Jefferies, William, 1950-
See also Deaver, Jeffery
Jelloun, Taharben
See also Ben Jelloun, Tahar, 1944-
Jensen, Mrs. Oliver
See also Stafford, Jean, 1915-1979
Jewett, Sarah Orne, 1849-1909
See Eliot, Alice C.
Jiang Rong, 1946-
See also Lu Jiamin
Jin, Ha
See Ha Jin, 1956-
Jolliffe, June
See also Braybrooke, June, 1920-1994; English, Isobel
Jong, Erica
See also Mann, Erica
Jonge, Peter de
See also De Jonge, Peter
Jordan, Laura
See also Brown, Sandra, 1948-; Ryan, Rachel
Judson, Edward Zane Carroll
See also Buntline, Ned, 1822 or 3-1886
Kao, Hsing-chien
See also Gao Xingjian, 1940-
Katayev, Evgenii Petrovich
See also Petrov, Evgenii, 1903-1942
Kava, Alex
See also Kava, Sharon M.
Kava, Sharon M.
See also Kava, Alex
Kavanagh, Dan
See also Barnes, Julian, 1946-
Kavanagh, Paul
See also Block, Lawrence, 1938-
Keating, H. R. F., 1926-2011

See also Hervey, Evelyn; Keating, Henry Reymond Fitzwalter
Keating, Henry Reymond Fitzwalter
See Keating, H. R. F., 1926-2011; Hervey, Evelyn
Kells, Susannah
See Cornwell, Bernard
Kelman, Nic, 1971-
See also Kelman, Nicholas L.
Kelman, Nicholas L.
See also Kelman, Nic, 1971-
Kelton, Elmer, 1926-2009
See also Hawk, Alex; McElroy, Lee
Kendrake, Carleton
See also Gardner, Erle Stanley, 1889-1970; Fair, A. A.; Kenny, Charles J.
Kenny, Charles J.
See also Gardner, Erle Stanley, 1889-1970; Fair, A. A.; Kendrake, Carleton
Kepler, Lars
See also Ahndoril, Alexander
Kerouac, Jack, 1922-1969
See also Kerouac, Jean; Kerouac, Jeanlouis
Kerouac, Jean
See Kerouac, Jack, 1922-1969; Kerouac, Jeanlouis
Kerouac, Jeanlouis
See Kerouac, Jack, 1922-1969; Kerouac, Jean
Khadra, Yasmina
See also Moulessehoul, Mohammed, 1955-
Khoury, Elias
See also Khuri, Ilyas
Khuri, Ilyas
See also Khoury, Elias
King, Joseph Hillstrom
See also Hill, Joe
King, Stephen, 1947-
See also Bachman, Richard
King, Thomas, 1943-
See also GoodWeather, Hartley
Kinsella, Sophie
See also Wickham, Madeleine, 1969-
Knickerbocker, Diedrich
See also Irving, Washington, 1783-1859; Crayon, Geoffrey
Knowall, George
See also Gopaleen, Myles; Na Gopaleen, Myles; O'Brien, Flann, 1911-1966; O'Nolan, Brian
Komunyakaa, Yusef
See also Brown, James Willie Jr.
Koontz, Dean R., 1945-
See also Hill, John; North, Anthony
Kosinski, Jerzy N., 1933-1991
See also Novak, Joseph
Kourouma, Ahmadou
See also Ahmadou Kourouma
Krentz, Jayne Ann
See also Quick, Amanda
Kuznetsov, Anatolii Vasil'evich
See also Anatoli, A., 1929-1979
Lambrecht, Patricia
See Tracy, P. J.; Lambrecht, Traci
Lambrecht, Traci
See Tracy, P. J.; Lambrecht, Patricia
Lampedusa, Giuseppe Tomasi di
See Tomasi di Lampedusa, Giuseppe, 1896-1957
Lange, John
See also Crichton, Michael, 1942-2008; Douglas, Michael; Hudson, Jeffrey
Larminie, Margaret Beda
See also Nicholson, Margaret Beda; Yorke, Margaret
Lathen, Emma
See also Dominic, R. B.
Lawhead, Stephen R.
See Lawhead, Steve, 1950-
Lawless, Anthony
See also Fleming, Oliver; Macdonald, Filip; MacDonald, Philip, 1899-1981; Porlock, Martin
Lax, Andromeda Romano-
See Romano-Lax, Andromeda, 1971-
Le Carre, John, 1931-
See also Cornwell, David John Moore
Lear, Peter
See also Lovesey, Peter
Lee, Lilian
See also Li, Pi-hua
Lennon, J. Robert, 1970-
See also Lennon, John Robert
Lennon, John Robert
See also Lennon, J. Robert, 1970-
Leslie, Josephine Aimee Campbell, 1898-1979
See also Dick, R. A.
Lessing, Doris May, 1919-
See also Somers, Jane
Leventhal, Alice Walker
See also Walker, Alice, 1944-
Lewis, C. S. (Clive Staples), 1898-1963
See also Hamilton, Clive
Lewis, M. G. (Matthew Gregory), 1775-1818
See also Lewis, Monk
Lewis, Monk
See Lewis, M. G., 1775-1818
Lewis, Sinclair, 1885-1951
See also Graham, Tom
Li, Pi-hua
See also Lee, Lilian
Lindsay, Jeffry P., 1952-
See also Freundlich, Jeffry P.; Lindsay, Jeff
Lindsay, Jeff
See also Lindsay, Jeffry P., 1952-; Freundlich, Jeffry P.
Lindholm, Megan
See also Hobb, Robin; Ogden, Margaret Astrid Lindholm
Linmark, R. Zamora
See also Zamora Linmark, R.
Litwos
See also Sienkiewicz, Henryk, 1846-1916
Llosa, Mario Vargas

See Vargas Llosa, Mario, 1936-
Loo, Tessa de
See also De Loo, Tessa
Lovesey, Peter
See also Lear, Peter
Lu Jiamin
See also Jiang Rong, 1946-
Lucas, Victoria
See also Plath, Sylvia
Luckless, John
See also Irving, Clifford
Ludlum, Robert, 1927-2001
See also Ryder, Jonathan; Shepherd, Michael
Lynch, James Mitchell
See Lynch, Jim, 1961-
Lynch, Jim, 1961-
See also Lynch, James Mitchell
Lytton, Edward Bulwer Lytton, 1803-1873
See Bulwer-Lytton, Edward
MacAlister, Katie
See also Arends, Marthe; Maxwell, Katie
Macdonald, Filip
See MacDonald, Philip, 1899-1981
Lawless, Anthony; Porlock, Martin; Fleming, Oliver
Macdonald, John
See Macdonald, John Ross; Macdonald, Ross, 1915-1983; Millar, Kenneth
Macdonald, John Ross
See Macdonald, John; Macdonald, Ross, 1915-1983; Millar, Kenneth
Macdonald, Malcolm, 1932-
See also Ross-Macdonald, Malcolm
MacDonald, Philip, 1899-1981
See also Fleming, Oliver; Lawless, Anthony; Macdonald, Filip; Porlock, Martin
Macdonald, Ross, 1915-1983
See also Macdonald, John; Macdonald, John Ross; Millar, Kenneth
MacInnes, Helen, 1907-1985
See also Highet, Helen MacInnes
Mackintosh, Elizabeth
See also Tey, Josephine, 1896-1952
MacLean, Alistair, 1922-1987
See also Stuart, Ian
MacLeod, Charlotte
See also Craig, Alisa
MacNeil, Duncan
See also McCutchan, Philip, 1920-
Mahfouz, Naguib
See Mahfuz, Najib, 1911-2006
Malraux, Georges Andre
See Malraux, Andre, 1901-1976
Mandel, Emily St. John
See St. John Mandel, Emily, 1979-
Mankind (Wrestler)
See Foley, Mick, 1965-
Mann, Erica
See also Jong, Erica
Manor, Jason
See also Hall, Oakley M.
Mansfield, Kathleen Beauchamp
See Mansfield, Katherine, 1888-1923
Marchant, Catherine
See also Cookson, Catherine
Marisol, 1930-
See also Escobar, Marisol
Markandaya, Kamala, 1924-2004
See also Taylor, Kamala Purnaiya
Marlowe, Hugh
See also Fallon, Martin; Graham, James; Higgins, Jack, 1929-; Patterson, Harry
Marlowe, Ralph
See Manheim, Ralph, 1907-1992
Marquez, Gabriel Garcia
See Garcia Marquez, Gabriel, 1928-
Marshall, Sarah Catherine Wood
See Marshall, Catherine, 1914-1983
Marsten, Richard, 1926-2005
See also Cannon, Curt, 1926-2005; Collins, Hunt, 1926-2005; Hannon, Ezra, 1926-2005; Hudson, Dean, 1926-2005; Hunter, Evan, 1926-2005; Marsten, Richard, 1926-2005; McBain, Ed, 1926-2005
Marston, Edward
See also Allen, Conrad, 1940-
Martin, Peter
See Melville, James, 1931-; Martin, Roy Peter
Martin, Roy Peter
See Melville, James, 1931-; Martin, Peter
Marut, Ret
See also Feige, Hermann Albert Otto Max; Torsvan, Berick Traven; Torsvan, Traven; Traven, B.
Matas, Enrique Vila-
See Vila-Matas, Enrique, 1948-
Maugham, Somerset
See Maugham, W. Somerset (William Somerset), 1874-1965
Maxwell, Katie
See also MacAlister, Katie
May, Julian, 1931-
See also Dikty, Julian May
McBain, Ed, 1926-2005
See also Cannon, Curt, 1926-2005; Collins, Hunt, 1926-2005; Hannon, Ezra, 1926-2005; Hudson, Dean, 1926-2005; Hunter, Evan, 1926-2005; Marsten, Richard, 1926-2005; McBain, Ed, 1926-2005
McCall Smith, Alexander, 1948-
See also McCall Smith, R. A. (R. Alexander)
McCall Smith, R. A. (R. Alexander),
See also McCall Smith, Alexander, 1948-
McCutchan, Philip, 1920-
See also MacNeil, Duncan
McElroy, Lee
See also Kelton, Elmer, 1926-2009; Hawk, Alex
McGarrity, Mark

See also Gill, Bartholomew, 1943-2002
McGuire, Seanan
See also Grant, Mira
McMahon, Neil
See also Rhodes, Daniel
McPherson, Jessamyn West
See West, Jessamyn, 1902-1984; West, Mary Jessamyn
Melville, James, 1931-
See also Martin, Peter; Martin, Roy Peter
Mercado, Sergio Ramirez
See Ramirez Mercado, Sergio, 1942-
Mertz, Barbara Gross
See also Michaels, Barbara; Peters, Elizabeth, 1927-
Michaels, Barbara
See also Mertz, Barbara Gross; Peters, Elizabeth, 1927-
Millar, Kenneth
See also Macdonald, Ross, 1915-1983
Miller, A. D.
See Miller, Andrew, 1974-
Mishima, Yukio, 1925-1970
See also Hiraoka, Kimitake
Miss Read
See also Read, 1913-
Saint, Dora Jessie
Mo, Yen
See Mo Yan, 1956-
Moberg, Carl Artur Vilhelm
See Moberg, Vilhelm, 1898-1973
Molina, Antonio Munoz
See Munoz Molina, Antonio, 1956-
Morales, Adelaida Garcia
See Garcia Morales, Adelaida
Moravia, Alberto, 1907-1990
See also Pincherle, Alberto
Moreton, Andrew
See also Defoe, Daniel, 1661?-1731; Foe, Daniel
Morgan, Claire
See also Highsmith, Patricia, 1921-1995
Morland, Dick
See also Hill, Reginald, 1936-; Ruell, Patrick; Underhill, Charles
Morris, Roger N.
See Morris, R. N., 1960-
Morrison, Patricia Kennealy-
See Kennealy-Morrison, Patricia
Morse, Anne Christensen
See also Head, Ann
Moulessehoul, Mohammed, 1955-
See also Khadra, Yasmina
Moya, Horacio Castellanos
See Castellanos Moya, Horacio, 1957-
Munro, H. H.
See also Saki, 1870-1916
Murasaki Shikibu, b. 978?
See also Fujiwara, Murasaki; Shikibu, Murasaki
Murdoch, Iris
See also Bayley, Iris
Na Gopaleen, Myles
See also O'Brien, Flann, 1911-1966
Nahai, Gina Barkhordar-
See Barkhordar-Nahai, Gina
Neel, Janet, 1940-
See also Cohen, Janet
Nexo, Martin Andersen
See Andersen Nexo, Martin, 1869-1954
Nicholson, Margaret Beda
See also Yorke, Margaret; Larminie, Margaret Beda
Norman, Diana
See also Franklin, Ariana
Norris, Benjamin Franklin
See also Norris, Frank, 1870-1902
Norris, Frank, 1870-1902
See also Norris, Benjamin Franklin
North, Andrew
See also Norton, Andre, 1912-2005; Norton, Alice Mary
North, Anthony
See also Koontz, Dean R., 1945-
Norton, Alice Mary
See also North, Andrew; Norton, Andre, 1912-2005
Norton, Andre, 1912-2005
See also North, Andrew; Norton, Alice Mary
Norway, Nevil Shute
See Shute, Nevil, 1899-1960
Novack, Sandra
See Novack-Gottshall, Sandra
Novak, Joseph
See Kosinski, Jerzy N., 1933-1991
Noyes, Deborah, 1965-
See also Wayshak, Deborah
O'Brien, Flann, 1911-1966
See also Gopaleen, Myles; Knowall, George; Na Gopaleen, Myles; O'Nolan, Brian
O'Connor, Frank, 1903-1966
See also O'Donovan, Michael
O'Connor, Mary Flannery
See O'Connor, Flannery
O'Connor, Patrick
See also Holton, Leonard; Wibberley, Leonard, 1915-1983
O'Donovan, Michael
See also O'Connor, Frank, 1903-1966
Ogden, Margaret Astrid Lindholm
See Hobb, Robin; Lindholm, Megan
Okorafor, Nnedimma
See Okorafor-Mbachu, Nnedimma
Olafsson, Bragi
See Bragi Olafsson, 1962-
Oliver, Chad, 1928-1993
See also Oliver, Symmes Chadwick
Oliver, Symmes Chadwick
See also Oliver, Chad, 1928-1993
Olivieri, David
See also Wharton, Edith, 1862-1937
O'Nolan, Brian
See also Gopaleen, Myles; Knowall, George; Na Gopaleen,

Myles; O'Brien, Flann, 1911-1966
Orwell, George, 1903-1950
See also Blair, Eric
Owen, John Pickard
See also Butler, Samuel, 1835-1902
Parker, K. J.
See also Parker, Kenneth John
Parker, Kenneth John
See also Parker, K. J.
Passos, John Dos
See Dos Passos, John
Paterson, James Hamilton-
See Hamilton-Paterson, James
Patterson, Henry
See also Fallon, Martin; Graham, James; Higgins, Jack, 1929-; Marlowe, Hugh
Perry, Anne, 1938-
See also Hulme, Juliet
Peshkov, Alexei Maximovich
See also Gorky, Maksim, 1868-1936; Gorky, Maxim
Peters, Elizabeth, 1927-
See also Mertz, Barbara Gross; Michaels, Barbara
Petrov, David Shrayer-
See Shrayer-Petrov, David, 1936-
Pierre, D. B. C.
See also Finlay, Peter Warren
Pincherle, Alberto
See also Moravia, Alberto, 1907-1990
Plath, Sylvia
See also Lucas, Victoria
Porlock, Martin
See also MacDonald, Philip, 1899-1981; Fleming, Oliver; Lawless, Anthony; Macdonald, Filip
Porter, William Sydney
See Henry, O., 1862-1910
Pramoedya Ananta Toer
See Toer, Pramoedya Ananta, 1925-2006
Quick, Amanda
See also Krentz, Jayne Ann
Quinn, Spencer
See also Abrahams, Peter, 1947-
Quoirez, Francoise
See Sagan, Francoise, 1935-2004
Rabinovitch, Sholem
See Rabinowitz, Solomon; Sholem Aleichem, 1859-1916
Rabinowitz, Solomon
See Rabinovitch, Sholem; Sholem Aleichem, 1859-1916
Ramirez, Sergio
See Ramirez Mercado, Sergio, 1942-
Rampling, Anne
See also Rice, Anne, 1941-; Roquelaure, A. N.
Rankin, Ian, 1960-
See also Harvey, Jack
Read, 1913-
See also Miss Read; Saint, Dora Jessie
Reed, Ernesto Mestre-
See Mestre-Reed, Ernesto, 1964-
Reed, Kit, 1932-
See also Reed, Lillian Craig
Reed, Lillian Craig
See also Reed, Kit, 1932-
Renault, Mary, 1905-1983
See also Challans, Mary
Rendell, Ruth, 1930-
See also Vine, Barbara, 1930-
Reverte, Arturo Perez-
See Perez-Reverte, Arturo
Rhodes, Daniel
See also McMahon, Neil
Riboud, Barbara Chase-
See Chase-Riboud, Barbara, 1939-
Rice, Anne, 1941-
See also Rampling, Anne; Roquelaure, A. N.
Richardson, C. S.
See also Richardson, Charles Scott
Richardson, Charles Scott
See also Richardson, C. S.
Rikki
See also Ducornet, Rikki
Robb, J. D., 1950-
See also Roberts, Nora
Roberts, Nora
See also Robb, J.D., 1950-
Robertson, R. Garcia y
See Garcia y Robertson, R.
Rodriguez, Alisa Valdes-
See Valdes-Rodriguez, Alisa
Roquelaure, A. N.
See also Rampling, Anne; Rice, Anne, 1941-
Ross, Leonard Q.
See Rosten, Leo, 1908-1997
Ross-Macdonald, Malcolm
See also Macdonald, Malcom, 1932-
Rowling, J.K.
See also Galbraith, Robert
Roza, Luiz Alfredo Garcia-
See Garcia-Roza, Luiz Alfredo, 1936-
Ruell, Patrick
See also Hill, Reginald, 1936-; Morland, Dick; Underhill, Charles
Rule, Ann
See also Stack, Andy
Runyon, Damon, 1884-1946
See Runyon, Alfred Damon
Russell, Sean Thomas
See Russell, S. Thomas, 1952-
Ryan, Rachel
See also Brown, Sandra, 1948-; Jordan, Laura
Ryder, Jonathan
See also Ludlum, Robert, 1927-2001; Shepherd, Michael
Saavedra, Miguel de Cervantes
See Cervantes Saavedra, Miguel de, 1547-1616
Sagan, Francoise, 1935-2004
See also Quoirez, Francoise

Saint, Dora Jessie
See also Read, 1913-; Miss Read
Saint-Aubin, Horace de
See also Balzac, Honore de, 1799-1850
Saki, 1870-1916
See also Munro, H. H.
Salinger, Jerome David
See Salinger, J. D., 1919-2010
Salter, James
See also Horowitz, James
Samjatin, Jewgenij
See Samjatin, Jewgenij; Zamiatin, Evgenii Ivanovich, 1884-1937
Sand, George, 1804-1876
See also Dudevant, Amantine Lucile Aurore Dupin; Dudevant, Mme; Dupin, Amantine Aurore Lucile; Sand, Jules
Sand, Jules
See also Dudevant, Amantine Lucile Aurore Dupin; Dudevant, Mme; Dupin, Amantine Aurore Lucile; Sand, George, 1804-1876
Schmitz, Ettore
See also Svevo, Italo, 1861-1928
Scott, Alicia
See also Gardner, Lisa
Sears, Michael
See also Stanley, Michael; Trollip, Stanley
Sebald, Winfried Georg, 1944-2001
See Sebald, W. G.
Shan Sa, 1972-
See also Yan Ni
Shannon, Ray
See also Haywood, Gar Anthony
Shepherd, Michael
See also Ludlum, Robert, 1927-2001; Ryder, Jonathan
Shikibu, Murasaki
See Murasaki Shikibu, b. 978?; Fujiwara, Murasaki
Shraer, Maksim
See Shrayer, Maxim, 1967-
Shugaar, Tony
See Shugaar, Antony
Shute, Nevil, 1899-1960
See also Norway, Nevil Shute
Sienkiewicz, Henryk, 1846-1916
See also Litwos
Sigurdardottir, Yrsa
See also Yrsa Sigurdardottir
Siler, Jenny
See also Carr, Alex
Sjowall, Maj, 1935-
See also Wahloo, Maj Sjowall
Skinner, Marie Bostwick
See also Bostwick, Marie
Smith, Alexander McCall
See McCall Smith, Alexander, 1948-
Smith, B. J.
See also Smith, Brad, 1957-
Smith, Brad, 1957-
See also Smith, B. J.
Smith, Florence Margaret
See also Smith, Stevie, 1902-1971
Smith, Mary-Ann Tirone
See Tirone Smith, Mary-Ann, 1944-
Smith, R. A. McCall
See McCall Smith, Alexander, 1948-
Smith, Richard Liebmann-
See Liebmann-Smith, Richard, 1942-
Smith, Stevie, 1902-1971
See also Smith, Florence Margaret
Snow, Lucy
See also Aubert, Rosemary, 1946-
Soldan, Edmundo Paz
See Paz Soldan, Edmundo, 1967-
Somers, Jane
See also Lessing, Doris May, 1919-
Spark, Muriel
See also Cavallo, Evelyn
Sparks, Timothy
See also Dickens, Charles, 1812-1870; Boz
Spillane, Frank Morrison
See also Spillane, Mickey, 1918-2006
Spillane, Mickey, 1918-2006
See also Spillane, Frank Morrison
Stace, Wesley Harding
See also Harding, John Wesley, 1965-
Stack, Andy
See also Rule, Ann
Stafford, Jean, 1915-1979
See also Jensen, Mrs. Oliver
Stanley, Michael
See also Sears, Michael; Trollip, Stanley
Stendhal, 1783-1842
See also Beyle, Marie Henri; Brulard, Henry
Stephens, Eve
See Anthony, Evelyn, 1928-
Steptoe, Lydia
See Barnes, Djuna, 1892-1982
Stevens, Chevy
See also Unischewski, Rene
Stowe, Harriet Elizabeth
See Stowe, Harriet Beecher, 1811-1896
Stuart, Ian
See also MacLean, Alistair, 1922-1987
Stubbs, Harry Clement
See also Clement, Hal, 1922-2003
Sullivan, Vernon
See also Vian, Boris, 1920-1959
Sutherland, J. A.
See Sutherland, John, 1938-
Svevo, Italo, 1861-1928
See also Schmitz, Ettore
Swift, Margaret
See also Drabble, Margaret, 1939-
Tait, Dorothy
See Fairbairn, Ann, 1901 or 2-1972

Tan Twan Eng
See Eng, Tan Twan
Tanner, Edward Everett
See Dennis, Patrick, 1921-1976
Taylor, Kamala Purnaiya
See Markandaya, Kamala, 1924-2004
Templeton, Edith, 1916-
See also Walbrook, Louise
Tey, Josephine, 1896-1952
See also Mackintosh, Elizabeth
Thackeray, William Makepeace, 1811-1863
See also Titmarsh, Michael Angelo
Thomas, Ross, 1926-1995
See also Bleeck, Oliver
Thompson, Margaret Cezair
See Cezair-Thompson, Margaret
Titmarsh, Michael Angelo
See also Thackeray, William Makepeace, 1811-1863
Toer, Pramoedya Ananta, 1925-2006
See Pramoedya Ananta Toer
Toole, F. X., 1930-2002
See also Boyd, Jerry
Torsvan, Berick Traven
See also Feige, Hermann Albert Otto Max; Marut, Ret; Traven, B.; Torsvan, Traven
Torsvan, Traven
See also Feige, Hermann Albert Otto Max; Marut, Ret; Traven, B.; Torsvan, Berick Traven;
Touger, Hallie Ephron
See Ephron, Hallie
Tracy, P. J.
See also Lambrecht, Patricia; Lambrecht, Traci
Traven, B.
See also Feige, Hermann Albert Otto Max; Marut, Ret; Torsvan, Berick Traven; Torsvan, Traven
Traver, Robert, 1903-1991
See also Voelker, John Donaldson
Tremaine, Jennie
See also Chesney, Marion; Beaton, M.C.; Chesterton, G. K.
Trevanian
See also Whitaker, Rodney
Trollip, Stanley
See also Stanley, Michael; Sears, Michael
Trollope, Joanna
See also Harvey, Caroline
Truman, Margaret, 1924-2008
See also Daniel, Margaret Truman
Tsan-hsueh, 1953-
See also Can Xue; Deng Xiaohua
Twain, Mark, 1835-1910
See also Clemens, Samuel Langhorne
Tweedsmuir, John Buchan
See also Buchan, John, 1875-1940
Underhill, Charles
See also Hill, Reginald, 1936-
Underwood, Michael, 1916-
See also Evelyn, John Michael
Unischewski, Rene
See also Stevens, Chevy
Van Cauwelaert, Didier
See Cauwelaert, Didier van, 1960-
Van Gulik, Robert
See Gulik, Robert Hans van, 1910-1967
Vasilikos, Vasiles
See Vassilikos, Vassilis, 1934-
Veronese, Antonia Arslan
See Arslan, Antonia
Veryan, Patricia, 1923-
See also Bannister, Patricia V.
Vian, Boris, 1920-1959
See also Sullivan, Vernon
Vidal, Gore, 1925-
See also Box, Edgar
Vine, Barbara, 1930-
See also Rendell, Ruth, 1930-
Voelker, John Donaldson
See also Traver, Robert, 1903-1991
Voltaire, 1694-1778
See also Arouet, Francois Marie
Von Goethe, Johann Wolfgang
See Goethe, Johann Wolfgang von, 1749-1832
Wahloo, Maj Sjowall
See also Sjowall, Maj, , 1935-
Walbrook, Louise
See also Templeton, Edith, 1916-
Walker, Margaret, 1915-1998
See also Alexander, Margaret Walker
Walsh, Jill Paton
See Paton Walsh, Jill, 1937-
Walsh, Pearl S.
See Buck, Pearl S., 1892-1973; Hedge, John
Wayshak, Deborah
See Noyes, Deborah, 1965-
Webb, James H.
See also Webb, Jim
Webb, Jim
See also Webb, James H.
Weis, Margaret, 1948-
See also Baldwin, Margaret
Welcome, John, 1914-
See also Brennan, John
Wellesley, Charles
See also Bronte, Charlotte, 1816-1855
West, Bing
See also West, Francis J., 1940-
West, Francis J., 1940-
See also West, Bing;
West, Jessamyn, 1902-1984
See also McPherson, Jessamyn West; West, Mary Jessamyn
West, Mary Jessamyn
See also McPherson, Jessamyn West; West, Jessamyn, 1902-1984
West, Dame Rebecca, 1892-1983
See also Andrews, Cecily Isabel Fairfield

West, V. Sackville-
See Sackville-West, V., 1892-1962
Wharton, Edith, 1862-1937
See also Olivieri, David
Whetstone, Diane McKinney-
See McKinney-Whetstone, Diane
Whitaker, Rodney
See Trevanian
White, Phyllis Dorothy James
See James, P. D.
Wibberley, Leonard, 1915-1983
See also Holton, Leonard; O'Connor, Patrick
Wickham, Madeleine, 1969-
See also Kinsella, Sophie
Wiesel, Eliezer
See Wiesel, Elie, 1928-
Wiggen, Henry W.
See also Harris, Mark, 1922-2007
Wilder, Elly
See also Robb, J. D., 1950-; Roberts, Nora
Williams, Linda Verlee
See also Grant, Linda
Williams, Thomas Lanier
See Williams, Tennessee, 1911-1983
Wilson, John Anthony Burgess
See Burgess, Anthony, 1917-1993
Wolfe, J. Thomas
See Wolfe, Tom
Woodhouse, Susan T.
See Carlyle, Liz, 1958-
Woods, Sara
See also Bowen-Judd, Sara Hutton
Yan Ni
See also Shan Sa, 1972-
Yen, Ko-ling
See Yan, Geling, 1958-
Yorke, Margaret
See also Larminie, Margaret Beda; Nicholson, Margaret Beda
Yrsa Sigurdardottir
See also Sigurdardottir, Yrsa
Zafon, Carlos Ruiz
See Ruiz Zafon, Carlos, 1964-

TITLE AND SUBJECT INDEX

This index to the books listed in part 1 includes title and subject entries, arranged in one alphabet. Full information for each book is given in part 1 under the main entry, which is usually the author.

Title entries. Novels are listed under title. Analytical entries are made for novels published in omnibus editions and for novelettes. Such entries carry *In* or *also in* designations and usually include the page numbers in the book where the item is to be found.

Subject entries. Subject headings are printed in capital letters. The listing of a work under a subject indicates that a major portion of the work is about that subject. Under genre headings, such as SCIENCE FICTION or PHILOSOPHICAL NOVELS, works of that genre are listed. Under the heading DETECTIVES a list of individual fictional detectives makes reference to the authors of the detective novels in which they appear. Subdivisions under headings are given first by chronological period, then by topic, and then by place name.

& sons. Gilbert, D.
100 YEARS' WAR *See* Hundred Years' War, 1339-1453
101 Reykjavik. Hallgrimur Helgason
11/22/63. King, S.
13 ways of looking at a fat girl. Awad, M.
1356. Cornwell, B.
1861-1865
Gohlke, C. I have seen him in the watchfires
1876. Vidal, G.
1916. Llywelyn, M.
1919. Dos Passos, J.
1920S *See* Nineteen twenties
1921. Llywelyn, M.
1929. Turner, F. W.
1940. Neugeboren, J.
1949. Llywelyn, M.
1970S *See* Nineteen seventies
1980S *See* Nineteen eighties
The **19th** wife. Ebershoff, D.
1Q84. Murakami, H.
1st to die. Patterson, J.
2001: a space odyssey. Clarke, A. C.
22 Britannia Road. Hodgkinson, A.
2312. Robinson, K. S.
2666. Bolano, R.
30 Days. D'Abo, C.
36 arguments for the existence of God. Goldstein, R.
3: This gun for hire, The confidential agent, The ministry of fear. Greene, G.
4 3 2 1. Auster, P.
The **47th** samurai. Hunter, S.
4TH OF JULY *See* Fourth of July
82 Desire. Smith, J.
99 stories of God. Williams, J.

A

a + e 4ever. Merey, I.
A is for alibi. Grafton, S.
The **A.B.C.** murders. Christie, A.
A.D. 30. Dekker, T.
Abaddon's Gate. Corey, J. S. A.
ABANDONED CHILDREN
Sallis, J. The killer is dying
ABANDONED CHILDREN
See also Child welfare; Children
Bloom, A. Lucky us
Gaitskill, M. The mare
Oates, J. C. Mudwoman
ABBEYS -- ENGLAND
Austen, J. Northanger Abbey
Dean, A. A place of confinement
Dean, A. A woman of consequence
ABDUCTION *See* Kidnapping
ABDUCTION
Hayder, M. The treatment
Robards, K. Shiver
Stevens, C. Still missing
ABDUCTION -- TENNESSEE
Greene, A. Long Man
Abel (Biblical figure)
About
Maine, D. Fallen
ABERDEEN (SCOTLAND)
MacBride, S. Blind eye
MacBride, S. Cold granite
MacBride, S. Dying Light
ABNORMAL PSYCHOLOGY
Self, W. Shark
ABNORMAL PSYCHOLOGY
See also Mind and body; Nervous system
ABOLITION OF CAPITAL PUNISHMENT *See* Capital punishment
ABOLITION OF SLAVERY *See* Abolitionists; Slavery; Slaves -- Emancipation
ABOLITIONISTS
Leveen, L. The secrets of Mary Bowser
Stowe, H. B. Uncle Tom's cabin
Tryon, T. In the fire of spring
The **abominable.** Simmons, D.
ABORIGINAL AUSTRALIAN ART
See also Art
ABORIGINAL AUSTRALIANS
See also Australians; Indigenous peoples
Scott, K. That deadman dance
ABORIGINES *See* Indigenous peoples
ABORTION
Irving, J. The cider house rules
Jordan, H. When she woke
Manning, K. My notorious life

McKinney-Whetstone, D. Leaving Cecil Street
Patterson, R. N. No safe place
Patterson, R. N. Protect and defend
Zumas, L. Red clocks
ABORTION -- ETHICAL ASPECTS
See also Ethics
About a boy. Hornby, N.
About face. Leon, D.
About Schmidt. Begley, L.
Absalom, Absalom! Faulkner, W.
ABSAROKA RANGE (MONT. AND WYO.)
Hagy, A. Boleto
The **absent** one. Adler-Olsen, J.
ABSENTEE FATHERS
See also Absentee parents; Fathers
Grodstein, L. Our short history
Absolute friends. Le Carre, J.
An **absolute** gentleman. Kinder, R. M.
Absolution.
The **absolutist.** Boyne, J.
The **abstinence** teacher. Perrotta, T.
ABSTRACT ART
See also Art
ABSTRACT EXPRESSIONISM
Heller, P. The painter
Abundance. Naslund, S. J.
ABUSE OF ANIMALS *See* Animal welfare
ABUSE OF CHILDREN *See* Child abuse
Abuse of power. Rosenberg, N. T.
ABUSE OF WIVES *See* Wife abuse
ABUSED CHILDREN *See* Child abuse
ABUSED TEENAGERS
Yates, C. J. Grist Mill Road
ABUSED WIVES *See* Abused women; Wife abuse
ABUSED WOMEN
See also Victims of crimes; Women
Edwards, Y. A Cupboard full of coats
One thousand and one nights
Rice, L. Little night
Roberts, N. Dance upon the air
Abyss. Hagberg, D.
Acacia. Durham, D. A.
ACADEMIC ACHIEVEMENT
See also Success
ACADEMIC LIBRARIES
See also Libraries
ACADEMY AWARDS (MOTION PICTURES)
See also Motion pictures
ACADIANS -- LOUISIANA *See* Cajuns
Accelerando. Stross, C.
Acceptance. VanderMeer, J.
ACCIDENT VICTIMS
Cramer, W. D. Bad ground
Davidson, A. The gargoyle
Packer, A. The dive from Clausen's pier
Parkhurst, C. The dogs of Babel
Picoult, J. Lone wolf
ACCIDENT VICTIMS -- ENGLAND -- 20TH CENTURY
Jones, S. The uninvited guests
The **accidental.** Smith, A.
The **Accidental** Countess. Bowman, V.
An **accidental** man. Murdoch, I.
The **accidental** time machine. Haldeman, J. W.
The **accidental** tourist. Tyler, A.
ACCIDENTS
Brown, R. Tender mercies
Castillo, L. Her last breath
Carroll, J. The ghost in love
Erdrich, L. LaRose
Evans, N. The horse whisperer
Hamilton, J. When Madeline was young
Mawer, S. The fall
Minato, K. Confessions
Oates, J. C. American appetites
Packer, A. The dive from Clausen's pier
Pochoda, I. Visitation Street
Proulx, A. Postcards
Roy, A. The god of small things
Sears, M. Black Fridays
Trollope, J. The men and the girls
Vann, D. Goat Mountain
Vonnegut, K. Deadeye Dick
Wiles, W. Care of wooden floors
The **accomplice.** Robbins, C.
Accordion crimes. Proulx, A.
ACCORDIONISTS
Proulx, A. Accordion crimes
ACCOUNTANTS
Pronzini, B. The crimes of Jordan Wise
ACCOUNTING
See also Business; Business education; Business mathematics
ACCULTURATION
Momaday, N. S. House made of dawn
ACCULTURATION
See also Anthropology; Civilization; Culture; Ethnology
The **Accursed.** Oates, J. C.
The **accusation.** Bandi
Accused. Scottoline, L.
Achilles. Cook, E.
ACHILLES (GREEK MYTHOLOGY)
Cook, E. Achilles
Malouf, D. Ransom
Miller, M. The song of Achilles
ACHMED (FICTITIOUS CHARACTER : HAYDON)
Haydon, E. The Merchant Emperor
Haydon, E. Prophecy
Acorna. McCaffrey, A.
ACQUAINTANCE RAPE
Wolfe, T. A man in full
ACQUIRED IMMUNE DEFICIENCY SYNDROME *See* AIDS (Disease)
ACROBATS AND ACROBATICS

See also Circus
Act of revenge. Tanenbaum, R.
ACTORS
Abani, C. GraceLand
Alarcón, D. At Night We Walk in Circles
Atkins, A. Devil's garden
Baldwin, J. Tell me how long the train's been gone
Banville, J. Ancient light
Bernhard, T. Woodcutters
Estleman, L. D. The adventures of Johnny Vermillion
Everett, P. L. I am Not Sidney Poitier
Gold, G. D. Sunnyside
Hannah, K. Home again
Howrey, M. Blind sight
Isaacs, S. Almost paradise
L'Engle, M. Certain women
Leonard, E. Get Shorty
Lessing, D. M. Love, again
Mandel, E. S. J. Station eleven
Matheson, R. Hunted past reason
Miller, S. The Lake Shore Limited
Nehme, F. S. Missing reels
Oates, J. C. Blonde
O'Connor, J. Ghost light
Pearson, A. I think I love you
Phillips, C. Dancing in the dark
Pyne, D. Twentynine Palms
Rawn, M. Touchstone
Varley, J. The golden globe
Walter, J. Beautiful Ruins
Westlake, D. E. Money for nothing
Williams, W. J. The fourth wall
Wilson, A. Flatscreen
ACTORS
See also Entertainers
ACTORS -- UNITED STATES
See also Actors
ACTORS AND ACTRESSES *See* Actors
ACTRESSES
Bagshawe, T. Adored
Baldwin, J. Tell me how long the train's been gone
Blatty, W. P. The exorcist
Didion, J. Play it as it lays
Farrell, H. What ever happened to Baby Jane?
Ford, J. Songs of Willow Frost
Hornby, N. Funny girl
Leonard, E. LaBrava
Lipman, E. The family man
Lord, B. B. The middle heart
Oates, J. C. Blonde
O'Connor, J. Ghost light
Phillips, S. E. Heroes are my weakness
Pilcher, R. Winter solstice
Sontag, S. In America
Steel, D. Sunset in St. Tropez
Trollope, J. Second honeymoon
Walton, J. Ha'penny
Weldon, F. Worst fears
Williams, T. The Roman spring of Mrs. Stone
Wilson, K. The family Fang
ACTRESSES
See also Actors
Acts of faith. Caputo, P.
ACTUAL INNOCENCE
Chaon, D. Ill will
ACTUAL INNOCENCE
See also Criminal law
Ada. Nabokov, V. V.
Adam (Biblical figure)
About
Maine, D. Fallen
Adam and Eve and Pinch me. Rendell, R.
Adams, Abigail, 1744-1818
About
Hambly, B. Patriot hearts
Adams, John Quincy, 1767-1848
About
Pesci, D. Amistad
ADAPTATION (BIOLOGY)
See also Biology; Ecology; Genetics
ADDICTION
Palahniuk, C. Choke
ADDICTION TO ALCOHOL *See* Alcoholism
ADDICTION TO DRUGS *See* Drug abuse
ADDICTIVE BEHAVIOR *See* Compulsive behavior
ADDICTS *See* Drug addicts
Addie Pray. Brown, J. D.
ADIRONDACK MOUNTAINS (N.Y.)
Oates, J. C. Carthage
Robinson, R. Sweetwater
Unger, L. Heartbroken
ADMINISTRATION *See* Civil service; Management; Public administration
ADMINISTRATION OF CRIMINAL JUSTICE
See also Administration of justice; Criminal law
Admiral Hornblower in the West Indies. Forester, C. S.
ADMIRALS
Donoghue, E. The sealed letter
Nordhoff, C. Men against the sea
Nordhoff, C. Mutiny on the Bounty
O'Brian, P. The golden ocean
Sontag, S. The volcano lover
Unsworth, B. Losing Nelson
ADOLESCENCE
Aciman, A. A. Call me by your name
Alexie, S. Flight
Beard, J. A. In Zanesville
Berg, E. We are all welcome here
Betts, D. Souls raised from the dead
Bilenchi, R. The chill
Blume, J. Summer sisters
Bock, C. Beautiful children
Bognanni, P. The house of tomorrow
Brown, L. Joe

Campbell, B. J. Once upon a river
Coe, J. The Rotters' Club
Cooke, C. Daughters of the revolution
Dallas, S. Tallgrass
Dean, M. L. The time it takes to fall
Delaney, E. J. Broken Irish
Desai, K. The inheritance of loss
DeWoskin, R. Big girl small
Diaz, J. The brief wondrous life of Oscar Wao
Doctorow, E. L. Billy Bathgate
Doig, I. English Creek
Doig, I. The bartender's tale
Durham, D. A. Gabriel's story
Durrow, H. W. The girl who fell from the sky
Earley, T. The blue star
Earley, T. Jim the boy
The elegance of the hedgehog
Eugenides, J. Middlesex
Eugenides, J. The virgin suicides
Evison, J. All about Lulu
Fielding, J. Heartstopper
Fitch, J. White oleander
Fitzgerald, F. S. This side of paradise
Ford, J. The shadow year
Frame, R. The lantern bearers
Gardam, J. The flight of the maidens
Gay, W. Twilight
Gibbons, K. The life all around me by Ellen Foster
Gilb, D. The flowers
Godwin, G. The finishing school
Grant, S. Map of Ireland
Grass, G. Cat and mouse
Grossman, D. Someone to run with
Guene, F. Kiffe kiffe tomorrow
Guterson, D. Our Lady of the Forest
Hemingway, E. The Nick Adams stories
Henderson, E. Ten thousand saints
Hoeg, P. Borderliners
Hoffman, N. K. Catalyst
Hornby, N. About a boy
Howrey, M. Blind sight
Iles, G. Turning angel
Jones, T. Silver sparrow
Joyce, J. A portrait of the artist as a young man
Julavits, H. The uses of enchantment
Kidd, S. M. The secret life of bees
Kincaid, J. Annie John
King, S. Carrie
Klein, R. The moth diaries
Knowles, J. A separate peace
Kwok, J. Girl in translation
Lansdale, J. R. A fine dark line
Lee, G. China boy
Lee, H. To kill a mockingbird
Lethem, J. The fortress of solitude
Lodato, V. Mathilda Savitch
Louis, É. The end of Eddy
Makine, A. Dreams of my Russian summers
Mason, B. A. In country
Matar, H. Anatomy of a disappearance
McCammon, R. R. Boy's life
McCarthy, C. All the pretty horses
McDermott, A. Child of my heart
McDermott, A. That night
Meyers, K. The work of wolves
Miller, S. Lost in the forest
Mitcham, J. Sabbath Creek
Monaghan, N. The killing jar
Morris, W. Taps
Munro, A. Lives of girls & women
Murr, N. The perfect man
Murray, P. Skippy dies
Nadzam, B. Lamb
Noel, K. Halfway house
Nunez, S. Salvation city
Oates, J. C. Foxfire
O'Dell, T. Fragile beasts
Olmstead, R. Coal black horse
O'Nan, S. The night country
O'Nan, S. Snow angels
O'Nan, S. Songs for the missing
O'Neill, J. At swim, two boys
Oz, A. Panther in the basement
Palahniuk, C. Pygmy
Palliser, C. The quincunx
Parks, G. The learning tree
Parks Getting mother's body
Pearson, A. I think I love you
Pessl, M. Special topics in calamity physics
Picoult, J. Nineteen minutes
Pilcher, R. Coming home
Pittard, H. The fates will find their way
Powell, P. Edisto
Prose, F. Goldengrove
Quindlen, A. Object lessons
Riordan, R. Cold Springs
Rock, P. My abandonment
Rolvaag, O. E. Peder Victorious
Rosenberg, N. T. Interest of justice
Rossner, J. Perfidia
Roth, H. A diving rock on the Hudson
Roth, H. A star shines over Mt. Morris Park
Roth, P. Nemesis
Salinger, J. D. The catcher in the rye
Schulman, H. This beautiful life
Shange, N. Betsey Brown
Shreve, A. Testimony
Shriver, L. We need to talk about Kevin
Sittenfeld, C. Prep
Smith, A. The accidental
Smith, B. A tree grows in Brooklyn
Smith, D. I capture the castle
Sparks, N. A walk to remember
Strout, E. Amy and Isabelle

Swarthout, G. F. Bless the beasts and children
Tea, M. Rose of no man's land
Toews, M. A complicated kindness
Townsend, S. The Adrian Mole diaries
Tussing, J. The best people in the world
Ulinich, A. Petropolis
Updike, J. Terrorist
Vernon, O. Eden
Vernon, O. A killing in this town
Vlautin, W. Lean on Pete
Walton, J. Among others
Ward, J. Salvage the bones
Watson, L. American boy
Weiner, J. Certain girls
White, E. A boy's own story
Whitehead, C. Sag Harbor
Williams, A. J. Down from Cascom Mountain
Wimberley, D. The king of Colored Town
Winton, T. Breath
Wolff, T. Old school
Wolitzer, H. Hearts
Woo, S. J. Everything Asian
Woodrell, D. Winter's bone
Wray, J. Lowboy
Yoshimoto, B. Goodbye Tsugumi

ADOPTED CHILDREN
Mazzarella, N. This heavy silence
McCall Smith, A. The forgotten affairs of youth
Palwick, S. Mending the moon
Stedman, M. L. The light between oceans
Ullman, E. By blood
Woo, S. J. Love love

ADOPTED CHILDREN
See also Adoptees; Children

ADOPTEES
Parker, T. J. Silent Joe
Trollope, J. Brother and sister
Ullman, E. By blood

ADOPTION
Gaspar de Alba, A. Desert blood
Gilmore, J. The Mothers
Hood, A. An Italian Wife
Hood, A. The red thread
James, P. D. Innocent blood
Kingsolver, B. Pigs in heaven
Lee A gesture life
Lee, M. G. Somebody's daughter
Mishima, Y. The decay of the angel
Moore, L. A gate at the stairs
Morrison, T. A mercy
Parker, T. J. Silent Joe
Patchett, A. Run
Tevis, W. S. The queen's gambit
Trollope, J. Brother and sister
Tyler, A. Digging to America
Umrigar, T. N. The weight of heaven
Weiner, J. Then came you

ADOPTION -- CORRUPT PRACTICES
See also Criminal law

Adored. Bagshawe, T.
Adrian Mole. Townsend, S.
The **Adrian** Mole diaries. Townsend, S.
Adrian Mole: the lost years. Townsend, S.

ADULT CHILD ABUSE VICTIMS
See also Victims of crimes
I refuse

ADULT CHILDREN
St. Aubyn, E. At last

ADULTERY
Atwood, M. The Heart Goes Last
Choi, S. My education
Dubus, A. Dirty Love
Essbaum, J. A. Hausfrau
Green, J. Tempting fate
Hood, A. The Obituary Writer
Hughes, A. Market Street
In the wilderness
Kitamura, K. A separation
Levy, D. Swimming home
Lively, P. How it all began
McEwan, I. Nutshell
Park, P. Re Jane
Second person singular
Tóibín, C. House of Names
Walter, J. Beautiful Ruins
Watson, S. Suitcase city
What we become

Adulthood rites. Butler, O. E.

ADVENTURE
Allende, I. Daughter of fortune
Baker, K. The bird of the river
Ballard, J. G. The day of creation
Bates, H. E. Fair stood the wind for France
Benchley, P. Jaws
Berger, T. Little Big Man
The Big book of adventure stories
Birch, C. Jamrach's menagerie
Buchan, J. The thirty-nine steps
Caldwell, I. The rule of four
Cervantes Saavedra, M. d. Don Quixote de la Mancha
Clavell, J. Shogun
Conrad, J. Nostromo
Cooper, J. F. The last of the Mohicans
Cornwell, B. The archer's tale
Crichton, M. Pirate latitudes
Crichton, M. Sphere
Cussler, C. Fire ice
Cussler, C. The kingdom
Cussler, C. Lost city
Cussler, C. White death
Dickey, J. Deliverance
Du Maurier, D. Jamaica Inn
Dumas, A. The Count of Monte Cristo
Dumas, A. The three musketeers

Dunnett, D. Pawn in frankincense
Dunnett, D. To lie with lions
Eco, U. Baudolino
Forester, C. S. Admiral Hornblower in the West Indies
Forester, C. S. The African Queen
Forester, C. S. Beat to quarters
Forester, C. S. Commodore Hornblower
Forester, C. S. Flying colours
Forester, C. S. Hornblower and the Atropos
Forester, C. S. Hornblower and the Hotspur
Forester, C. S. Hornblower during the crisis, and two stories: Hornblower's temptation and The last encounter
Forester, C. S. Lieutenant Hornblower
Forester, C. S. Lord Hornblower
Forester, C. S. Ship of the line
Forsyth, F. The day of the jackal
Gear, K. O. People of the masks
Gear, K. O. People of the mist
Gear, W. M. People of the thunder
Ghosh, A. River of smoke
Ghosh, A. Sea of poppies
Gilman, D. The amazing Mrs. Pollifax
Gilman, D. The elusive Mrs. Pollifax
Gilman, D. The unexpected Mrs. Pollifax
Greene, G. Our man in Havana
Greene, G. Travels with my aunt
Haggard, H. R. King Solomon's mines
Haggard, H. R. She
Harrison, H. The Stainless Steel Rat joins the circus
Harrison, H. The Stainless Steel Rat sings the blues
Higgins, J. Flight of eagles
Hilton, J. Lost horizon
Hoffman, A. The probable future
Holland, C. Jerusalem
Hope, A. The prisoner of Zenda
Hughes, R. A. W. A high wind in Jamaica
Kelton, E. The way of the coyote
Lambdin, D. King's captain
L'Amour, L. Last of the breed
L'Amour, L. May there be a road
Lebbon, T. Fallen
London, J. The Sea-Wolf
Lowell, E. Pearl Cove
Ludlum, R. The Bourne identity
Ludlum, R. The Bourne supremacy
Ludlum, R. The Bourne ultimatum
Lustbader, E. V. Floating city
MacInnes, H. The Venetian affair
Martel, Y. Life of Pi
Martin, G. R. R. Hunter's run
Martin, W. Cape Cod
McDonald, R. Mr. Darwin's shooter
McMurtry, L. Comanche moon
McMurtry, L. Dead man's walk
McMurtry, L. Lonesome dove
McMurtry, L. Streets of Laredo
Michener, J. A. Caravans
Michener, J. A. Caribbean
Michener, J. A. Hawaii
Motion, A. Silver
Naslund, S. J. Ahab's wife; or, The star-gazer
Nordhoff, C. Botany Bay
Nordhoff, C. Pitcairn's Island
O'Brian, P. The unknown shore
O'Brian, P. Blue at the mizzen
O'Brian, P. The commodore
O'Brian, P. The golden ocean
O'Brian, P. The hundred days
O'Brian, P. The wine-dark sea
O'Brian, P. The yellow admiral
Orczy, E. The Scarlet Pimpernel
Parkhurst, C. Lost and found
Penney, S. The tenderness of wolves
Perez-Reverte, A. Captain Alatriste
Perez-Reverte, A. The nautical chart
Perez-Reverte, A. Purity of blood
Poyer, D. Black storm
Poyer, D. Fire on the waters
Poyer, D. The gulf
Preston, D. The codex
Pynchon, T. Against the day
Redfield, J. The celestine prophecy
Riley, J. M. In pursuit of the green lion
Sabatini, R. Captain Blood
Sabatini, R. Scaramouche
Scott, W. Rob Roy
Seton, A. Avalon
Sherwood, F. Night of sorrows
Silverberg, R. Lord Valentine's castle
Simmons, D. The terror
Smith, W. A. Birds of prey
Smith, W. A. Monsoon
Spark, M. The Mandelbaum Gate
Stendhal The charterhouse of Parma
Stewart, M. The ivy tree
Stone, R. Dog soldiers
Swarthout, G. F. Bless the beasts and children
Tinti, H. The good thief
Traven, B. The treasure of the Sierra Madre
Trevanian Shibumi
Vanderhaeghe, G. The last crossing
Varley, J. Titan
Varley, J. Wizard
Verne, J. Around the world in eighty days
Verne, J. The extraordinary journeys: Twenty thousand leagues under the sea
Verne, J. A journey to the centre of the earth
Verne, J. The mysterious island
Vollmann, W. T. The rifles
Watkins, P. The ice soldier
Westheimer, D. Von Ryan's Express
Whyte, J. The singing sword
Winslow, D. Satori
Wolfe, G. Pirate freedom

Zahn, T. The last command
Zelazny, R. The dead man's brother
ADVENTURE AND ADVENTURERS -- FICTION *See* Adventure fiction
ADVENTURE FICTION
Ahmad, A. X. The Caretaker
Boyle, T. C. The Terranauts
Brown, D. Inferno
Burke, J. L. House of the rising sun
Coben, H. Fool Me Once
Cussler, C. The Mayan secrets
DeSilva, B. Providence Rag
DeWitt, P. Undermajordomo Minor
Dickey, J. Deliverance
Doetsch, R. Half-past dawn
Dyachenko, M. The scar
Epperson, T. Sailor
Fay, K. The map of lost memories
Fleming, I. Casino Royale
Fleming, I. Doctor No
Fleming, I. From Russia, with love
Fleming, I. Goldfinger
Fleming, I. The man with the golden gun
Fleming, I. On Her Majesty's Secret Service
Fleming, I. You only live twice
Fortier, A. The lost sisterhood
Gerritsen, T. Playing with fire
Goldman, W. The princess bride
Grey, Z. Riders of the purple sage
Gunn, J. E. Transcendental
Guttridge, P. The thing itself
Hamilton, P. F. Great north road
Harkaway, N. Angelmaker
Harkaway, N. Tigerman
Harris, R. Pompeii
The healer
Hill, A. The good suicides
Hill, J. The fireman
Hodder, M. Expedition to the Mountains of the Moon
Hughes, R. A. W. A high wind in Jamaica
Hurwitz, G. The Nowhere Man
Hurwitz, G. Orphan X
Hurwitz, G. The survivor
Imperium
Jemisin, N. K. The killing moon
Karpyshyn, D. Children of fire
Koontz, D. R. The bad place
Lackberg, C. The hidden child
Lee, P. Signal
Levin, I. The boys from Brazil
Martel, Y. The high mountains of Portugal
Matthews, J. Red sparrow
Newman, S. The Country of Ice Cream Star
Parker, K. J. Sharps
Parkhurst, C. Lost and found
Perry, T. Poison flower
Roadside picnic
Robards, K. Shiver
Rollins, J. The blood Gospel
Rollins, J. The devil colony
Rollins, J. The eye of God
Rosenberg, J. C. Damascus Countdown
Sandford, J. Silken prey
Saylor, S. The seven wonders
Scalzi, J. Redshirts
Silva, D. The English Girl
Stabenow, D. Less than a treason
Steiner, P. The resistance
Steinhauer, O. The Cairo affair
Stevens, C. Always watching
Stevens, T. The informationist
Thomas, S. My Beautiful Enemy
Unger, L. Heartbroken
Wilson, G. W. Alif the unseen
Wooding, C. Retribution falls
ADVENTURE FILMS
See also Motion pictures
ADVENTURE GRAPHIC NOVELS
Henson, J. Jim Henson's tale of sand
ADVENTURE TRAVEL
See also Travel; Voyages and travels
ADVENTURERS
Vollmann, W. T. Argall
The **adventures** and the memoirs of Sherlock Holmes. Doyle, A. C. S.
Adventures of Arabella Ashby [series]
Levine, D. D. Arabella of Mars
The **adventures** of Augie March. Bellow, S.
The **adventures** of Johnny Vermillion. Estleman, L. D.
The **adventures** of Menahem-Mendl. Sholem Aleichem
The **adventures** of Mottel, the cantor's son. Sholem Aleichem
The **adventures** of Tom Sawyer, Tom Sawyer abroad, Tom Sawyer, detective. Twain, M.
Adverbs. Handler, D.
ADVERTISING
Kenney, J. Truth in advertising
Pohl, F. The space merchants
Roth, P. Everyman
Whitehead, C. Apex hides the hurt
ADVERTISING
See also Business; Retail trade
ADVERTISING AND CHILDREN
See also Advertising; Children
ADVERTISING COPY
See also Advertising; Authorship
ADVERTISING EXECUTIVES
Ballard, J. G. Kingdom come
Kenney, J. Truth in advertising
ADVERTISING LAYOUT AND TYPOGRAPHY
See also Advertising; Printing; Typography
AENEAS (LEGENDARY CHARACTER)
Graham, J. Black ships
AERIAL BOMBS *See* Bombs

AERIAL RECONNAISSANCE
See also Military aeronautics; Remote sensing
AERIALISTS
McCann, C. Let the great world spin
The **aeronaut's** windlass. Butcher, J.
AERONAUTICAL SPORTS
See also Aeronautics; Sports
AERONAUTICS
Faulkner, W. Pylon
Michener, J. A. Space
Aetherial tales [series]
Warrington, F. Elfland
Warrington, F. Grail of the summer stars
Warrington, F. Midsummer night
Affairs at Thrush Green. Read
Affairs by moonlight [series]
Gray, J. A Duke Never Yields
AFFECTION *See* Friendship; Love
AFFECTIVE DISORDERS
See also Abnormal psychology
Affliction. Banks, R.
AFFLICTION *See* Joy and sorrow; Suffering
AFGHAN WAR, 2001-
Hauck, R. How to catch a prince
The human body
Hunter, S. Dead zero
Klay, P. Redeployment
Roy-Bhattacharya, J. The watch
Young, T. W. The renegades
AFGHANISTAN
Ahmad, J. The wandering falcon
Aslam, N. The Blind Man's Garden
Aslam, N. The wasted vigil
Hosseini, K. The kite runner
Hosseini, K. A thousand splendid suns
Michener, J. A. Caravans
Moulessehoul, M. The swallows of Kabul
AFGHANISTAN -- RUSSIAN INVASION, 1979
Rahimi, A. A thousand rooms of dream and fear
AFRICA
Catling, B. The Erstwhile
Conrad, J. Heart of darkness
Due, T. Blood colony
Hoagland, E. Children are diamonds
Lessing, D. M. African stories
Levine, J. A. Bingo's Run
Maalouf, A. Leo Africanus
Naipaul, V. S. A bend in the river
Okorafor, N. Who fears death
Osondu, E. C. This house is not for sale
Schwartzman, A. Eddie Signwriter
Stevens, T. The informationist
Under African skies
AFRICA -- 17TH CENTURY
Smith, W. A. Birds of prey
Smith, W. A. Monsoon
AFRICA -- 19TH CENTURY
Haggard, H. R. King Solomon's mines
Haggard, H. R. She
AFRICA -- NATIVE PEOPLES
Bellow, S. Henderson the rain king
Hulme, K. The nun's story
AFRICA -- RACE RELATIONS
Gordimer, N. A guest of honor
AFRICA, CENTRAL -- DISCOVERY AND EXPLORATION
Hodder, M. Expedition to the Mountains of the Moon
AFRICA, NORTH
Davies, J. D. The mountain of gold
African stories. Lessing, D. M.
AFRICAN AMERICAN AUTHORS -- BIOGRAPHY
Miller, K. E. Q. An angry-ass black woman
Walker, A. The way forward is with a broken heart
AFRICAN AMERICAN BASEBALL PLAYERS
See also Baseball players
AFRICAN AMERICAN CHILDREN
Morrison, T. A mercy
AFRICAN AMERICAN CHILDREN
See also Black children; Children
AFRICAN AMERICAN DANCERS
See also African Americans; Dancers
AFRICAN AMERICAN DOMESTICS
Stockett, K. The help
AFRICAN AMERICAN EDUCATORS
See also African Americans; Educators
AFRICAN AMERICAN FAMILIES
Greenidge, K. We love you, Charlie Freeman
Hubbard, L. The talented Ribkins
Jones, T. An American marriage
Sexton, M. W. A kind of freedom
AFRICAN AMERICAN FAMILIES -- LOUISIANA -- NEW ORLEANS
Sexton, M. W. A kind of freedom
AFRICAN AMERICAN FAMILIES -- NEW YORK (STATE) -- NEW YORK
Miller, K. E. Q. An angry-ass black woman
AFRICAN AMERICAN FAMILIES -- PENNSYLVANIA -- PHILADELPHIA
Mathis, A. The twelve tribes of Hattie
AFRICAN AMERICAN GIRLS -- PENNSYLVANIA -- PHILADELPHIA
Solomon, A. Disgruntled
AFRICAN AMERICAN INVENTORS
See also African Americans; Inventors
AFRICAN AMERICAN JOURNALISTS
Whitehead, C. John Henry Days
AFRICAN AMERICAN LIBRARIANS
See also Black librarians; Librarians
AFRICAN AMERICAN MEN
See also Men
Everett, P. Erasure
Everett, P. God's country
Everett, P. Suder
Himes, C. B. Lonely crusade

Walker, A. The third life of Grange Copeland
AFRICAN AMERICAN MUSICIANS
See also Black musicians; Musicians
AFRICAN AMERICAN NEIGHBORHOODS
K'wan (Author) Section 8
K'wan (Author) Welfare wifeys
Naylor, G. The men of Brewster Place
AFRICAN AMERICAN OLDER PEOPLE
See also African Americans; Older people
AFRICAN AMERICAN POLICE
Locke, A. Bluebird, bluebird
Mullen, T. Lightning men
Patterson, J. Roses are red
AFRICAN AMERICAN SERVANTS
Watson, B. The heaven of Mercury
AFRICAN AMERICAN SINGERS
See also African Americans; Singers
AFRICAN AMERICAN SOLDIERS
Katzenbach, J. Hart's war
AFRICAN AMERICAN TEENAGERS
Bennett, B. The mothers
AFRICAN AMERICAN VETERANS
Morrison, T. Home
AFRICAN AMERICAN WOMEN
See also Black women; Women
AFRICAN AMERICAN WOMEN
Clotel, or, The president's daughter
Cole, A. An Extraordinary Union
Cooper, J. C. The future has a past
Hunt, L. The evening road
Hurston, Z. N. Their eyes were watching God
Johnson, D. Elsewhere, California
K'wan (Author) Section 8
Larsen, N. Passing
Marshall, P. Brown girl, brownstones
Miasha Chaser
Moore, E. K. The Supremes at Earl's all-you-can-eat
Morrison, T. Beloved
Southgate, M. The taste of salt
Stockett, K. The help
Swinson, K. Playing dirty
Turner, N. Heartbreak of a hustler's wife
Turner, N. Natural born hustler
Weisgarber, A. The personal history of Rachel Dupree
Williams, K. Dirty to the grave
Woods, T. Alibi
Woodson, J. Another Brooklyn
AFRICAN AMERICAN YOUTH
See also Youth
AFRICAN AMERICAN YOUTH -- WASHINGTON (D.C.)
Tucker, N. The ways of the dead
AFRICAN AMERICANS
Allen, J. R. Song of the shank
Baldwin, J. Early novels and stories
Baldwin, J. Going to meet the man
Bambara, T. C. Gorilla, my love
Barnett, L. K. Jam on the Vine
Barrett, W. E. The lilies of the field
Calling the wind
Campbell, B. M. Brothers and sisters
Carter, S. L. The emperor of Ocean Park
Carter, S. L. New England white
Carter, S. L. Palace council
Chesnutt, C. W. Stories, novels, & essay
Cooke, C. Daughters of the revolution
Cooper, J. C. Wild stars seeking midnight suns
Crafts, H. The bondswomans narrative
Diamond, D. A gangster and a gentleman
Doctorow, E. L. Ragtime
Durham, D. A. Gabriel's story
Durrow, H. W. The girl who fell from the sky
Everett, P. L. I am Not Sidney Poitier
Faulkner, W. The reivers
Gaines, E. J. The autobiography of Miss Jane Pittman
Gibbons, K. On the occasion of my last afternoon
Guinn, M. The scribe
Hamilton, J. When Madeline was young
Harlem Renaissance: five novels of the 1920s
Harlem Renaissance: four novels of the 1930s
Harris, E. L. And this too shall pass
Harris, E. L. If this world were mine
Harris, M. Bang the drum slowly
Himes, C. The collected stories of Chester Himes
Hughes, L. Not without laughter
Hughes, L. Short stories of Langston Hughes
Hughes, L. Simple speaks his mind
Hughes, L. Simple's Uncle Sam
Hurston, Z. N. The complete stories
Hurston, Z. N. Novels and stories
Jenkins, B. Forbidden
Jiles, P. The color of lightning
Johnson, M. Pym
Jones, E. All Aunt Hagar's children
Jones, T. An American marriage
Kidd, S. M. The secret life of bees
Lee, H. To kill a mockingbird
Marshall, P. Praisesong for the widow
Martin, V. Property
McCullers, C. The member of the wedding
McMillan, T. How Stella got her groove back
McMillan, T. A day late and a dollar short
McMillan, T. Waiting to exhale
Mitcham, J. Sabbath Creek
Morrison, T. Jazz
Morrison, T. Love
Morrison, T. Song of Solomon
Morrison, T. Tar baby
Mosley, W. The man in my basement
Mosley, W. RL's dream
Mullen, T. Darktown
Naylor, G. Mama Day
Naylor, G. Bailey's Cafe
Naylor, G. Linden Hills
Naylor, G. The men of Brewster Place

Naylor, G. The women of Brewster Place
Oates, J. C. Black girl/White girl
Parks, G. The learning tree
Parks Getting mother's body
Patchett, A. Run
Phillips, C. Dancing in the dark
Pitts, L. Freeman
Price, R. The good priest's son
Price, R. Clockers
Rawles, N. My Jim
Reed, I. Flight to Canada
Reed, I. Mumbo jumbo
Revoyr, N. Wingshooters
Roth, P. The human stain
Rush, N. Mortals
Rutland, E. No crystal stair
Sanders, D. Clover
Sexton, M. W. A kind of freedom
Shange, N. Sassafrass, Cypress & Indigo
The Sleeper wakes
Smith, L. E. Strange fruit
Southgate, M. The fall of Rome
Stowe, H. B. Uncle Tom's cabin
Styron, W. The confessions of Nat Turner
Swinson, K. Playing dirty
Three days before the shooting--
The Unforgetting heart: an anthology of short stories by African American women (1859-1993)
Unsworth, B. Sacred hunger
Vernon, O. Eden
Walker, A. By the light of my father's smile
Walker, A. Possessing the secret of joy
Walker, A. The temple of my familiar
Walker, A. The way forward is with a broken heart
Walker, A. You can't keep a good woman down
Walker, M. Jubilee
Wallace, D. Mr. Sebastian and the Negro magician
Wallace, I. The man
Weber, C. Man on the run
Whitehead, C. The intuitionist
Whitehead, C. John Henry Days
Whitehead, C. Sag Harbor
Wideman, J. E. The stories of John Edgar Wideman
Willard, T. Buffalo soldiers
Wolfe, T. A man in full
Wright, R. Eight men
Wright, R. Native son
Wright, R. The outsider
Wright, R. Uncle Tom's children
Wright, R. Works

AFRICAN AMERICANS

See also Blacks

AFRICAN AMERICANS -- CALIFORNIA

Straight, S. The gettin place

AFRICAN AMERICANS -- CIVIL RIGHTS

Berg, E. We are all welcome here
Naslund, S. J. Four spirits
Rutland, E. No crystal stair
Stockett, K. The help
Yarbrough, S. Safe from the neighbors

AFRICAN AMERICANS -- CONNECTICUT

Tryon, T. In the fire of spring

AFRICAN AMERICANS -- CRIMES AGAINST

Guinn, M. The scribe

AFRICAN AMERICANS -- CRIMES AGAINST -- MISSISSIPPI

McFadden, B. L. Gathering of waters

AFRICAN AMERICANS -- FAMILY LIFE

Mathis, A. The twelve tribes of Hattie
Straight, S. Take one candle light a room

AFRICAN AMERICANS -- FLORIDA

Hiaasen, C. Lucky you
Wimberley, D. The king of Colored Town

AFRICAN AMERICANS -- FOLKLORE

See also Blacks -- Folklore; Folklore

AFRICAN AMERICANS -- FRANCE

The Book of Harlan

AFRICAN AMERICANS -- GEORGIA

Bambara, T. C. The salt eaters
Jones, T. Silver sparrow
Woods, S. Chiefs

AFRICAN AMERICANS -- GERMANY

Beatty, P. Slumberland

AFRICAN AMERICANS -- LOUISIANA

Gaines, E. J. A gathering of old men
Gaines, E. J. A lesson before dying
Piazza, T. City of refuge
Rhodes, J. P. Voodoo dreams
Rhodes, J. P. Yellow moon
Tademy, L. Cane River

AFRICAN AMERICANS -- LOUISIANA -- NEW ORLEANS

Sexton, M. W. A kind of freedom

AFRICAN AMERICANS -- MARRIAGE

Jones, T. An American marriage

AFRICAN AMERICANS -- MARYLAND

McBride, J. Song yet sung

AFRICAN AMERICANS -- MASSACHUSETTS

Grant, S. Map of Ireland
West, D. The wedding

AFRICAN AMERICANS -- MICHIGAN

Cleage, P. What looks like crazy on an ordinary day--

AFRICAN AMERICANS -- MIGRATIONS -- HISTORY -- 20TH CENTURY

Mathis, A. The twelve tribes of Hattie

AFRICAN AMERICANS -- MISSISSIPPI

Faulkner, W. Light in August
Faulkner, W. Absalom, Absalom!
Faulkner, W. Intruder in the dust
Faulkner, W. Requiem for a nun
Faulkner, W. The sound and the fury
Franklin, T. Crooked letter, crooked letter
French, A. Billy
Grisham, J. A time to kill

Jordan, H. Mudbound
Nordan, L. Wolf whistle
Vernon, O. A killing in this town
Ward, J. Salvage the bones
Yarbrough, S. Prisoners of war
AFRICAN AMERICANS -- MISSOURI
Shange, N. Betsey Brown
AFRICAN AMERICANS -- NEW JERSEY
Price, R. Freedomland
AFRICAN AMERICANS -- NEW YORK (N.Y.)
Baker, D. Young man with a horn
Baker, K. Strivers Row
Baldwin, J. Another country
Baldwin, J. Go tell it on the mountain
Baldwin, J. If Beale Street could talk
Baldwin, J. Tell me how long the train's been gone
Ellison, R. Invisible man
Marshall, P. The fisher king
AFRICAN AMERICANS -- NEW YORK (STATE)
Oates, J. C. I lock my door upon myself
AFRICAN AMERICANS -- NORTH CAROLINA
Edgerton, C. The night train
Huyler, F. The laws of invisible things
AFRICAN AMERICANS -- OHIO
Morrison, T. Sula
AFRICAN AMERICANS -- OKLAHOMA
Morrison, T. Paradise
AFRICAN AMERICANS -- PENNSYLVANIA
McKinney-Whetstone, D. Leaving Cecil Street
AFRICAN AMERICANS -- RACE IDENTITY
Straight, S. Take one candle light a room
AFRICAN AMERICANS -- RELIGION
See also Blacks -- Religion; Religion
AFRICAN AMERICANS -- SAINT THOMAS (UNITED STATES VIRGIN ISLANDS)
Yanique, T. Land of love and drowning
AFRICAN AMERICANS -- SOCIAL CONDITIONS
See also Blacks -- Social conditions; Social conditions
AFRICAN AMERICANS -- SOCIAL CONDITIONS -- 20TH CENTURY
Howard, R. Driving the king
AFRICAN AMERICANS -- SOUTHERN STATES
Lester, J. Do Lord remember me
Walker, A. The color purple
AFRICAN AMERICANS -- TEXAS
Grisham, J. The confession
AFRICAN AMERICANS -- WASHINGTON (D.C.)
Pelecanos, G. P. Right as rain
Pelecanos, G. P. The turnaround
AFRICAN AMERICANS IN MOTION PICTURES
See also Blacks in motion pictures; Minorities in motion pictures; Motion pictures
AFRICAN AMERICANS ON TELEVISION
See also Television
AFRICAN ART
See also Art
AFRICAN MYTHOLOGY
See also Mythology
The **African** Queen. Forester, C. S.
AFRICANS -- ENGLAND
Phillips, C. A distant shore
AFRICANS -- ITALY
Leon, D. Blood from a stone
AFRICNA AMERICAN LAWYERS
Wolfe, T. A man in full
AFRIKAANERS *See* Afrikaners
AFRIKANERS
Michener, J. A. The covenant
AFRO-AMERICANS *See* African Americans
After Alice. Maguire, G.
After all these years. Isaacs, S.
After Birth. Albert, E.
After dark. Murakami, H.
After Hannibal. Unsworth, B.
After I'm gone. Lippman, L.
After Rome. Llywelyn, M.
After the apocalypse. McHugh, M. F.
After the earthquake. Murakami, H.
After the fall. Roberts, V.
After the Fall, Before the Fall, During the Fall. Kress, N.
After the fire, a still small voice. Wyld, E.
After the Parade. Ostlund, L.
After the war. Adams, A.
After this. McDermott, A.
Afterimage. Humphreys, H.
Afterlife. Monette, P.
AFTERLIFE *See* Future life
The **afterlife** and other stories. Updike, J.
Afterparty. Gregory, D.
Afterwards. Lupton, R.
Agaat. Van Niekerk, M.
Against the day. Pynchon, T.
AGAMEMNON (LEGENDARY CHARACTER)
Unsworth, B. The songs of the kings
Agape agape. Gaddis, W.
Agatha Raisin mysteries [series]
Beaton, M. C. Pushing up daisies
AGE -- PHYSIOLOGICAL EFFECT *See* Aging
The **age** of desire. Fields, J.
The **age** of miracles. Gilchrist, E.
The **age** of miracles. Walker, K. T.
The **age** of reason. Sartre, J. P.
The **age** of Shiva. Suri, M.
AGED WOMEN *See* Older women
AGEING *See* Aging
Agent 6. Smith, T. R.
AGING
Egan, J. A visit from the Goon Squad
Houellebecq, M. The possibility of an island
The immortalists
Lodge, D. Deaf sentence
Maupin, A. Michael Tolliver lives
Roth, P. Everyman
AGING

See also Age; Gerontology; Longevity; Middle age; Old age
AGNOSTICISM
Joyce, J. A portrait of the artist as a young man
AGNOSTICISM
See also Free thought; Religion
The **agony** and the ecstasy. Stone, I.
AGORAPHOBIA
Barnes, L. The Perfect Ghost
Reynolds, M. The Starlite Drive-in
AGRARIAN QUESTION *See* Agriculture -- Economic aspects; Agriculture -- Government policy; Land tenure
AGRICULTURAL LABORERS -- AUSTRALIA -- WESTERN AUSTRALIA
Coming rain
AGRICULTURE -- RESEARCH
See also Research
AGRICULTURE -- SOCIETIES
See also Associations; Country life; Societies
The **Aguero** sisters. Garcia, C.
Ah, but your land is beautiful. Paton, A.
Ah, treachery! Thomas, R.
Ahab's wife; or, The star-gazer. Naslund, S. J.
AI (ARTIFICIAL INTELLIGENCE) *See* Artificial intelligence
Aiding and abetting. Spark, M.
AIDS (DISEASE)
Brunt, C. R. Tell the wolves I'm home
Cleage, P. What looks like crazy on an ordinary day--
Cunningham, M. The hours
Due, T. Blood colony
Gaitskill, M. Veronica
Kramer, L. Search for My Heart
Lianke, Y. Dream of Ding Village
Monette, P. Afterlife
Peterson, P. W. Women in the grove
Samuel, B. No place like home
Self, W. Dorian
Tóibín, C. The blackwater lightship
White, E. Jack Holmes and his friend
White, E. The married man
AIDS (DISEASE)
See also Communicable diseases; Diseases
An Aimée Leduc investigation [series]
Black, C. Murder on the Champ de Mars
Ain't she sweet. Phillips, S. E.
AIR BASES
See also Airports; Military aeronautics
AIR CARGO *See* Commercial aeronautics
AIR DEFENSES
See also Military aeronautics
AIR FREIGHT *See* Commercial aeronautics
AIR MAIL SERVICE
Saint-Exupery, A. d. Night flight
AIR MAIL SERVICE
See also Commercial aeronautics; Postal service
AIR PILOTS
Bates, H. E. Fair stood the wind for France
Bohjalian, C. The night strangers
Bohjalian, C. A. Skeletons at the feast
Griffin, W. E. B. By order of the President
Heller, J. Catch-22
Higgins, J. Flight of eagles
L'Amour, L. Last of the breed
Michener, J. A. The bridges at Toko-ri
Mosher, H. F. On Kingdom Mountain
Novik, N. Blood of tyrants
Roth, P. The plot against America
Saint-Exupery, A. d. The little prince
Saint-Exupery, A. d. Night flight
Shreve, A. The pilot's wife
Torday, D. The Last Flight of Poxl West
Walls, J. Half broke horses
AIR PILOTS
See also Aeronautics
AIR PIRACY *See* Hijacking of airplanes
AIR POLLUTION
See also Environmental health; Pollution
AIR POWER
See also Military aeronautics
AIR ROUTES *See* Aeronautics
AIR TRANSPORT *See* Commercial aeronautics
AIR TRAVEL
Cusk, R. Outline
Miles, J. Dear American Airlines
AIR TRAVEL
See also Transportation; Travel; Voyages and travels
AIR WARFARE *See* Military aeronautics; Military airplanes
AIRCRAFT ACCIDENTS
See also Accidents
AIRCRAFT ACCIDENTS
Blume, J. In the unlikely event
Kelly, J. The fire baby
Stabenow, D. Restless in the grave
AIRCRAFT CARRIERS
Michener, J. A. The bridges at Toko-ri
AIRCRAFT CARRIERS
See also Military aeronautics; Warships
AIRLINE STEWARDS *See* Flight attendants
AIRLINES
See also Commercial aeronautics
AIRLINES -- HIJACKING *See* Hijacking of airplanes
AIRPLANE ACCIDENTS
Bohjalian, C. The night strangers
Haynes, D. Crashers
AIRPLANE CARRIERS *See* Aircraft carriers
AIRPLANE FACTORIES
Crowley, J. Four freedoms
Himes, C. B. Lonely crusade
AIRPLANE HIJACKING *See* Hijacking of airplanes
AIRPLANE INDUSTRY
Himes, C. B. Lonely crusade
AIRPLANE PILOTS *See* Air pilots
AIRPLANES

See also Aeronautics
AIRPLANES -- HIJACKING *See* Hijacking of airplanes
AIRPORTS
See also Aeronautics
Airs above the ground. Stewart, M.
AIRSHIPS
See also Aeronautics
Priest, C. Dreadnought
AIRSPACE LAW
See also Property
AIRWAYS *See* Aeronautics
AIX-EN-PROVENCE (FRANCE)
Kay, G. G. Ysabel
Longworth, M. L. Murder in the Rue Dumas
ALABAMA
Albert, S. W. The Darling Dahlias and the cucumber tree
Atkins, A. Wicked city
Childress, M. Crazy in Alabama
Flagg, F. Fried green tomatoes at the Whistle-Stop Cafe
Franklin, T. Hell at the breech
Henry, P. C. Coming up for air
Lee, H. Go set a watchman
Lee, H. To kill a mockingbird
McCammon, R. R. Boy's life
Wallace, D. The Watermelon King
Wilson, E. O. Anthill
ALABAMA -- BIRMINGHAM
Naslund, S. J. Four spirits
Alas, Babylon. Frank, P.
ALASKA
Brand, M. Chinook
Eggers, D. Heroes of the frontier
Hannah, K. The great alone
Heacox, K. Jimmy Bluefeather
Rice, L. The letters
Stabenow, D. Restless in the grave
Stabenow, D. Though not dead
Vann, D. Caribou Island
Vann, D. Legend of a suicide
ALASKA -- ANCHORAGE
Harrison, K. The seal wife
ALASKA -- HISTORY -- 1867-1959
Ivey, E. The snow child
Ivey, E. To the bright edge of the world
ALBANIA
Blatty, W. P. Dimiter
Gilman, D. The unexpected Mrs. Pollifax
Kadare, I. The general of the dead army
Kadare, I. The ghost rider
Kadare, I. The Successor
Kadare, I. The three-arched bridge
ALBANIANS -- UNITED STATES
Prose, F. My new American life
ALBANY (N.Y.)
Kennedy, W. Chango's beads and two-tone shoes
The **alchemist.**
ALCHEMY
Flyte, M. City of lost dreams
Harkness, D. E. A discovery of witches
Redfern, E. Auriel rising
Stott, R. Ghostwalk
ALCHEMY
See also Chemistry; Occultism
Alchemy of stone. Sedia, E.
The Alchemy Wars [series]
Tregillis, I. The Mechanical
ALCOHOL USE *See* Alcohol; Alcoholism; Drinking of alcoholic beverages
ALCOHOLICS
McDermott, A. Charming Billy
Moody, R. Right livelihoods
ALCOHOLISM
Allison, D. Bastard out of Carolina
Banks, R. Affliction
Bronte, A. The tenant of Wildfell Hall
Brown, L. Joe
Delaney, E. J. Broken Irish
Doyle, R. The woman who walked into doors
Erdrich, L. Four souls
Faulks, S. On Green Dolphin Street
French, T. Faithful Place
Goudge, E. Thorns of truth
Hannah, K. On Mystic lake
Harrison, J. The great leader
Hatoum, M. The brothers
Huneven, M. Blame
Jackson, C. The lost weekend
Jamison, L. The gin closet
Johnston, W. The colony of unrequited dreams
Kinder, C. Honeymooners
King, L. The father of the rain
Lowry, M. Under the volcano
McDermott, A. Charming Billy
McMurtry, L. Buffalo girls
Miles, J. Dear American Airlines
Moshfegh, O. Eileen
Moya, H. C. The dream of my return
O'Hara, J. Appointment in Samarra
Paretsky, S. Ghost country
Richler, M. Solomon Gursky was here
Rinehart, S. Built in a day
Rossner, J. Perfidia
Southgate, M. The taste of salt
Suri, M. The death of Vishnu
Tremain, R. Trespass
Turner, F. W. 1929
Van Booy, S. Everything beautiful began after
Woodrell, D. The death of sweet mister
Wyld, E. After the fire, a still small voice
ALCOHOLISM
See also Social problems
Alex Morrow [series]
Mina, D. The red road
Alex Verus [series]

Jacka, B. Fated
Alexander Pushkin: complete prose fiction. Pushkin, A. S.
Alexander VI, Pope, 1431-1503
About
Poole, S. The Borgia mistress
Alexander, the Great, 356 B.C.-323 B.C.
About
Renault, M. Funeral games
Renault, M. The Persian boy
Saylor, S. Raiders of the Nile
The **Alexandria** quartet: Justine; Balthazar; Mountolive {and} Clea. Durrell, L.
Alfred, King of England, 849-899
About
Cornwell, B. The last kingdom
ALGEBRA
See also Mathematical analysis; Mathematics
ALGERIA
The Meursault investigation
ALGERIA -- ORAN
Camus, A. The plague
ALGONQUIAN INDIANS
Gear, K. O. People of the mist
Alias Grace. Atwood, M.
Alibi. Woods, T.
Alice & Oliver. Bock, C.
Alice Adams. Tarkington, B.
Alice I have been. Benjamin, M.
Alice in exile. Read, P. P.
Alice in jeopardy. McBain, E.
An **alien** heat. Moorcock, M.
ALIENATION (PHILOSOPHY)
Rivers, F. Bridge to haven
ALIENATION (SOCIAL PSYCHOLOGY)
Antopol, M. The Unamericans
Burroughs, W. S. Naked lunch
Darnielle, J. Wolf in white van
Ford, R. Independence Day
Ford, R. The lay of the land
Grant, H. The vanishing of Katharina Linden
Hoeg, P. Borderliners
Hoffman, A. Skylight confessions
Koontz, D. R. Innocence
Lessing, D. M. The fifth child
Malae, P. N. What we are
Mengestu, D. How to read the air
Picoult, J. Nineteen minutes
Qashu, S. Dancing Arabs
Trevor, W. Felicia's journey
Vine, B. Grasshopper
Winton, T. Dirt music
The **alienist.** Carr, C.
ALIENS
Haig, M. The humans
ALIENS FROM OUTER SPACE *See* Extraterrestrial beings
Aliens in the prime of their lives. Watson, B.
ALIENS, ILLEGAL *See* Unauthorized immigrants
Alif the unseen. Wilson, G. W.
ALIMONY
See also Divorce
All about Lulu. Evison, J.
All Aunt Hagar's children. Jones, E.
All back full. Lopez, R.
All I did was shoot my man. Mosley, W.
All is forgotten, nothing is lost. Chang, L. S.
All is vanity. Schwarz, C.
All mortal flesh. Spencer-Fleming, J.
All my sins remembered. Thomas, R.
All other nights. Horn, D.
All our names. Mengestu, D.
All our wrong todays. Mastai, E.
All passion spent. Sackville-West, V.
All quiet on the western front. Remarque, E. M.
All she ever wanted. Austin, L.
All souls. Marias, J.
All souls trilogy [series]
Harkness, D. E. The Book of Life
All souls' rising. Bell, M. S.
All systems red. Wells, M.
All that followed. Urza, G.
All that I have. Freeman, C.
All that is. Salter, J.
All that is gone. Toer, P. A.
All that man is. Szalay, D.
All the birds in the sky. Anders, C. J.
All the days and nights. Maxwell, W.
All the dead lie down. Walker, M. W.
All the dead Yale men. Nova, C.
All the flowers are dying. Block, L.
All the king's men. Warren, R. P.
All the Land to Hold Us. Bass, R.
All the light we cannot see. Doerr, A.
All the lives he led. Pohl, F.
All the living. Morgan, C. E.
All the names. Saramago, J.
All the Old Knives. Steinhauer, O.
All the pretty horses. McCarthy, C.
All the sad young literary men. Gessen, K.
All the time in the world. Doctorow, E. L.
All the windwracked stars. Bear, E.
All things cease to appear. Brundage, E.
All this talk of love. Castellani, C.
ALLEGORIES
Abe, K. The woman in the dunes
Adams, R. Watership Down
Aira, C. Ghosts
The alchemist
Atwood, M. The Handmaid's tale
Auster, P. In the country of last things
Ballard, J. G. The day of creation
Barth, J. Giles goat-boy
Beagle, P. S. The last unicorn
Brooks, T. The sword of Shannara
Bunyan, J. The pilgrim's progress

Camus, A. The fall
Coetzee, J. M. The schooldays of Jesus
Coetzee, J. M. Life & times of Michael K.
Drabble, M. The witch of Exmoor
Faulkner, W. A fable
Flanagan, R. Gould's book of fish
García Márquez, G. One hundred years of solitude
Garcia Marquez, G. The autumn of the patriarch
Golding, W. Darkness visible
Golding, W. The inheritors
Golding, W. Lord of the flies
Grass, G. Cat and mouse
Grass, G. The flounder
Hesse, H. Siddhartha
Hoban, R. Riddley Walker
Irving, J. A prayer for Owen Meany
Johnson, M. Pym
Kafka, F. The castle
Kafka, F. The trial
King, S. The stand
Le Guin, U. K. The beginning place
Lessing, D. M. Shikasta
Lewis, C. S. Out of the silent planet
Lewis, C. S. Perelandra
Lewis, C. S. That hideous strength
Lewis, C. S. Till we have faces
Mahfouz, N. Children of the alley
Malamud, B. The natural
Martin, V. Mary Reilly
Murdoch, I. The green knight
Oates, J. C. Black water
O'Connor, F. The violent bear it away
Oe, K. Nip the buds, shoot the kids
Orwell, G. Animal farm
Percy, W. Lancelot
Perec, G. A void
Porter, K. A. Ship of fools
Robbins, T. Jitterbug perfume
Robbins, T. Still life with Woodpecker
Rushdie, S. Haroun and the sea of stories
Rushdie, S. Midnight's children
Saint-Exupery, A. d. The little prince
Saramago, J. All the names
Saramago, J. Blindness
Saramago, J. The cave
Silko, L. Gardens in the dunes
Stevenson, R. L. The strange case of Dr. Jekyll and Mr. Hyde
Tepper, S. S. The visitor
Theroux, P. The Mosquito Coast
Tolkien, J. R. R. The fellowship of the ring
Tolkien, J. R. R. The return of the king
Tolkien, J. R. R. The Silmarillion
Tolkien, J. R. R. The two towers
Updike, J. Brazil
Updike, J. The witches of Eastwick
Vernon, O. A killing in this town
Vollmann, W. T. The rifles
Whitehead, C. The intuitionist
Wilde, O. The picture of Dorian Gray
Allende Gossens, Salvador, 1908-1973
About
Ampuero, R. The Neruda case
Allgood, Molly, 1887-1952
About
O'Connor, J. Ghost light
ALLIANCES
Bear, E. Range of ghosts
ALLIGATORS
Russell, K. Swamplandia!
ALLON, GABRIEL (FICTITIOUS CHARACTER)
Silva, D. The English Girl
ALLOSAURUS
See also Dinosaurs
Almanac of the dead. Silko, L.
Almost criminal. Brown, E. R.
Almost Famous Women. Bergman, M. M.
The **almost** moon. Sebold, A.
Almost never. Sada, D.
Almost paradise. Isaacs, S.
An **almost** perfect moment. Kirshenbaum, B.
The **almost** sisters. Jackson, J.
ALMSHOUSES
Trollope, A. The warden
Aloft. Lee
Alone. Gardner, L.
Alone in the crowd. Garcia-Roza, L. A.
Along Came a Duke. Boyle, E.
Along came a spider. Patterson, J.
Alphabet of thorn. McKillip, P. A.
ALPS
Mann, T. The magic mountain
Mawer, S. The fall
Watkins, P. The ice soldier
Already dead. Huston, C.
Altered carbon. Morgan, R. K.
ALTERNATE HISTORIES *See* Alternative histories
ALTERNATIVE HISTORIES
Ciotta, B. Her Sky Cowboy
A clockwork orange
Connolly, T. Ironskin
Frei, M. The stranger's magic
Gailey, S. River of Teeth
Hodder, M. Expedition to the Mountains of the Moon
Kay, G. G. River of Stars
Masello, R. The Romanov cross
McFadden, B. L. Gathering of waters
Novik, N. Blood of tyrants
Numero Zero
Pearl, M. The technologists
Priest, C. Dreadnought
Shepherd, L. A fatal likeness
Tregillis, I. The Mechanical
Walton, J. My real children

Wilson, D. H. The clockwork dynasty
ALTERNATIVE HISTORIES
See also Fantasy fiction
ALTERNATIVE ROCK MUSIC
See also Rock music
ALTERNATIVE SCHOOLS
McPherson, C. The child garden
ALTRUISTS *See* Philanthropists
Always happy hour. Miller, M.
Always watching. Stevens, C.
Alys, always. Lane, H.
ALZHEIMER'S DISEASE
Laplante, A. Turn of mind
O'Farrell, M. The vanishing act of Esme Lennox
Robinson, R. Cost
Sparks, N. The notebook
Stuckey-French, E. Revenge of the radioactive lady
Amagansett. Mills, M.
AMATEUR FILMS
See also Motion pictures
The **amateur** marriage. Tyler, A.
The **amazing** adventures of Kavalier and Clay. Chabon, M.
The **amazing** Mrs. Pollifax. Gilman, D.
AMAZON RIVER VALLEY
Patchett, A. State of wonder
Walker, A. Now is the time to open your heart
AMAZONS
Fortier, A. The lost sisterhood
The **Ambassador's** Daughter. Jenoff, P.
AMBASSADORS
See also Diplomats
Amber [series]
Zelazny, R. The guns of Avalon
Zelazny, R. Knight of shadows
Zelazny, R. Nine princes in Amber
Zelazny, R. Prince of chaos
Zelazny, R. Sign of chaos
Zelazny, R. Sign of the unicorn
AMBITION
Abbott, M. E. You will know me
Adiga, A. The white tiger
Bradford, B. T. A woman of substance
Carter, S. L. The emperor of Ocean Park
Chang, L. S. All is forgotten, nothing is lost
Estleman, L. D. Gas City
Fuentes, C. The death of Artemio Cruz
Martin, S. An object of beauty
Millhauser, S. Martin Dressler
Rand, A. The fountainhead
Ross-Macdonald, M. The rich are with you always
Ross-Macdonald, M. Tamsin Harte
Ross-Macdonald, M. The world from rough stones
Schulberg, B. What makes Sammy run?
Stendhal The red and the black
Trollope, A. The Eustace diamonds
Vidal, G. Washington, D.C.
Warren, R. P. All the king's men
Woods, S. L.A. Times
Wuertz, Y. G. Everything belongs to us
AMERICA -- DISCOVERY AND EXPLORATION -- SPANISH
Lalami, L. The Moor's account
AMERICA -- EARLY ACCOUNTS TO 1600
Lalami, L. The Moor's account
AMERICA -- EXPLORATION
Ivey, E. To the bright edge of the world
Lalami, L. The Moor's account
America America. Canin, E.
American appetites. Oates, J. C.
AMERICAN ART
See also Art
AMERICAN AUTHORS
See also Authors
Irving, J. In one person
McCall Smith, A. The Limpopo Academy of Private Detection
American boy. Watson, L.
AMERICAN COMMUNIST PARTY
Lethem, J. Dissident Gardens
American dervish. Akhtar, A.
AMERICAN DIPLOMATIC AND CONSULAR SERVICE
Just, W. American romantic
AMERICAN DRAMATISTS
See also American authors; Dramatists
AMERICAN DREAM
Link, T. Denting the Bosch
Mbue, I. Behold the Dreamers
American elsewhere. Bennett, R. J.
AMERICAN ESPIONAGE
Hayes, T. I Am Pilgrim
Ignatius, D. Bloodmoney
AMERICAN FABLES
See also Fables
American fantastic tales: terror and the uncanny from Poe to the pulps.
American fantastic tales: terror and the uncanny from the 1940s to now.
AMERICAN FICTION -- 21ST CENTURY
Boyle, T. C. The relive box and other stories
Erdrich, L. Future home of the living god
Krauss, N. Forest dark
Prose, F. Mister Monkey
AMERICAN FICTION -- COLLECTIONS
The Oxford book of American detective stories
The Oxford book of American short stories
AMERICAN FICTION -- JEWISH AUTHORS
Englander, N. What we talk about when we talk about Anne Frank
AMERICAN FICTION -- WOMEN AUTHORS
Prose, F. Mister Monkey
American gods. Gaiman, N.
The **American** heiress. Goodwin, D.
An American Heiress in London [series]
Guhrke, L. L. How to lose a duke in ten days

AMERICAN HOSTAGES
See also Hostages
American housewife. Ellis, H.
American innovations. Galchen, R.
AMERICAN LITERATURE -- HISPANIC AMERICAN AUTHORS
Latin@ rising
The **American** Lover. Tremain, R.
AMERICAN LOYALISTS
Hill, L. Someone knows my name
An **American** marriage. Jones, T.
American masculine. Ray, S.
American meteor. Lock, N.
AMERICAN MUSEUM OF NATURAL HISTORY
Preston, D. The cabinet of curiosities
AMERICAN NOVELISTS
See also American authors; Novelists
American odysseys. Alarcón, D.
American pastoral. Roth, P.
AMERICAN POETS
See also American authors; Poets
AMERICAN PROPAGANDA
See also Propaganda
AMERICAN REVOLUTION BICENTENNIAL, 1776-1976 -- COLLECTIBLES
See also Collectors and collecting
American romantic. Just, W.
American rust. Meyer, P.
American salvage. Campbell, B. J.
AMERICAN SATIRE
Schumacher, J. Dear Committee Members
AMERICAN SATIRE
See also American literature; Satire
AMERICAN SHORT STORIES
Alvar, M. In the country
Beattie, A. The state we're in
Davis, L. Can't and Won't
Doctorow, E. L. Doctorow
Ellis, H. American housewife
Galchen, R. American innovations
In sunlight or in shadow
Johnson, D. The largesse of the sea maiden
McCormack, M. Forensic songs
McGuane, T. Crow fair
Miller, M. Always happy hour
Millhauser, S. Voices in the night
Nelson, A. Funny once
Pearlman, E. Honeydew
Quade, K. V. Night at the Fiestas
Rash, R. Something rich and strange
Urrea, L. A. The Water museum
Woods, C. Things to do when you're goth in the country
AMERICAN SHORT STORIES
See also Short stories
An **American** spy. Steinhauer, O.
American tabloid. Ellroy, J.
An **American** tragedy. Dreiser, T.
AMERICAN TRAVELERS
See also Travelers
The **American** trilogy, 1997-2000. Roth, P.
American war. El Akkad, O.
American West: twenty new stories from the Western Writers of America.
AMERICAN WIT AND HUMOR
Hudgins, A. The joker
AMERICAN WIT AND HUMOR
See also American literature; Wit and humor
AMERICANA
See also Collectors and collecting; Popular culture -- United States; United States -- Civilization; United States -- History
Americanah. Adichie, C. N.
AMERICANIZATION
Alvarez, J. How the Garcia girls lost their accents
Cather, W. My Antonia
Cather, W. O pioneers!
Jen, G. Mona in the promised land
Jen, G. Typical American
Rolvaag, O. E. Peder Victorious
AMERICANS -- AFGHANISTAN
Michener, J. A. Caravans
AMERICANS -- AFRICA
Bellow, S. Henderson the rain king
Hamilton, M. The camel bookmobile
Rush, N. Mating
Stevens, T. The informationist
AMERICANS -- ARGENTINA
Swann, M. The foreigners
AMERICANS -- AUSTRALIA
Nordhoff, C. Botany Bay
AMERICANS -- BELIZE
Millet, L. Ghost lights
AMERICANS -- BOTSWANA
McCall Smith, A. The Limpopo Academy of Private Detection
Rush, N. Mortals
AMERICANS -- BULGARIA
Greenwell, G. What belongs to you
AMERICANS -- BURMA
Tan, A. Saving fish from drowning
AMERICANS -- CAMBODIA
Long, J. The reckoning
AMERICANS -- CANADA
Ford, R. Canada
Freedman, B. Mrs. Mike
AMERICANS -- CARIBBEAN REGION
Marshall, P. Praisesong for the widow
AMERICANS -- CENTRAL AMERICA
Didion, J. A book of common prayer
AMERICANS -- CENTRAL EUROPE
Egan, J. The keep
AMERICANS -- CHINA
Jin, H. Nanjing requiem
AMERICANS -- CONGO (DEMOCRATIC REPUBLIC)

Kingsolver, B. The poisonwood Bible
Windle, J. Congo dawn

AMERICANS -- CUBA
Kennedy, W. Chango's beads and two-tone shoes

AMERICANS -- ECUADOR
Kunkel, B. Indecision

AMERICANS -- ENGLAND
Goodwin, D. The American heiress
Grant, L. We had it so good
Griesemer, J. Signal & noise
Hale, S. Austenland
Higgins, J. The eagle has landed
Hornby, N. Juliet, naked
James, H. The golden bowl
Leimbach, M. Daniel isn't talking
Lovett, C. The bookman's tale
Lurie, A. Foreign affairs
McMurtry, L. Buffalo girls
Murdoch, I. An accidental man
Perry, A. Slaves of obsession
Woods, S. The short forever
Willig, L. The secret history of the pink carnation

AMERICANS -- EUROPE
Hemingway, E. The sun also rises
Highsmith, P. The boy who followed Ripley
James, H. The portrait of a lady
James, H. The wings of the dove
Lewis, S. Dodsworth
Maugham, W. S. The razor's edge
McCarthy, M. Birds of America
McPhee, M. L'America
Pynchon, T. Gravity's rainbow
Wharton, E. The children
Wolfe, T. Of time and the river
Wolfe, T. The web and the rock
Wolfe, T. You can't go home again

AMERICANS -- FRANCE
Baldwin, J. Giovanni's room
Barnes, D. Nightwood
De Rosnay, T. Sarah's key
Johnson, D. Le divorce
Johnson, D. Le mariage
Just, W. S. Forgetfulness
Kay, G. G. Ysabel
Krantz, J. Mistral's daughter
Marshall, P. The fisher king
McLain, P. The Paris wife
Miller, H. Tropic of Cancer
Ozick, C. Foreign bodies
Steel, D. Sunset in St. Tropez
Truong, M. The book of salt
Watkins, P. The forger
Welch, J. The heartsong of Charging Elk
White, E. The married man

AMERICANS -- FRANCE -- PARIS
Avery, E. The last nude

AMERICANS -- GERMANY
Barnes, D. Nightwood
Belfer, L. And after the fire
Deaver, J. Garden of beasts
Just, W. S. The weather in Berlin
Katzenbach, J. Hart's war
Kennedy, D. The moment
O'Connor, R. Buffalo soldiers
Uris, L. Armageddon
Vonnegut, K. Slaughterhouse-five

AMERICANS -- GREAT BRITAIN
Alexander, V. The Scandalous Adventures of the Sister of the Bride
St. Aubyn, E. At last

AMERICANS -- GREECE
Murray, S. Forgery
Van Booy, S. Everything beautiful began after

AMERICANS -- HONDURAS
Theroux, P. The Mosquito Coast

AMERICANS -- HUNGARY
Phillips, A. Prague

AMERICANS -- INDIA
Sinha, I. Animal's people
Sundaresan, I. The splendor of silence
Umrigar, T. N. The weight of heaven

AMERICANS -- IRAQ
Gallagher, M. Youngblood
Unsworth, B. Land of marvels
Zimmerman, D. Sandbox

AMERICANS -- IRELAND
Carey, L. The stolen child
Lordan, B. But come ye back

AMERICANS -- ISLANDS OF THE PACIFIC
Melville, H. Omoo: a narrative of adventures in the South Seas

AMERICANS -- ISRAEL
Miller, R. Welcome to Heavenly Heights
Stone, R. Damascus Gate
Uris, L. Exodus

AMERICANS -- ITALY
Aciman, A. A. Call me by your name
Bausch, R. Peace
Fortier, A. Juliet
Goodman, C. The night villa
Gordon, M. The love of my youth
Grisham, J. Playing for pizza
Gruber, M. The forgery of Venus
Hayter, S. Bandit queen boogie
Hellenga, R. The Italian lover
Hemingway, E. A farewell to arms
James, H. Daisy Miller
Martin, V. Italian fever
Rabb, J. The book of Q
Rachman, T. The imperfectionists
Rice, L. The deep blue sea for beginners
Russo, R. Bridge of sighs
Scott, J. Tourmaline
Williams, T. The Roman spring of Mrs. Stone

AMERICANS -- IVORY COAST
D'Souza, T. Whiteman
AMERICANS -- JAPAN
Lee, D. Country of origin
Murakami, R. In the miso soup
Smith, M. C. December 6
Watrous, M. If you follow me
AMERICANS -- KENYA
Hoagland, E. Children are diamonds
AMERICANS -- KOREA
Limón, M. Mr. Kill
AMERICANS -- LUXEMBOURG
Pavone, C. The expats
AMERICANS -- MARQUESAS ISLANDS
Melville, H. Typee: a peep at Polynesian life
AMERICANS -- MEXICO
D'Erasmo, S. The Sky Below
Doerr, H. Stones for Ibarra
Fuentes, C. The old gringo
Gaspar de Alba, A. Desert blood
Hambly, B. Days of the dead
Johansen, I. And then you die--
Michener, J. A. Mexico
Olmstead, R. Far bright star
Portis, C. Gringos
Traven, B. The treasure of the Sierra Madre
AMERICANS -- NORTH AFRICA
Bowles, P. The sheltering sky
AMERICANS -- PERU
Lynn, A. Now you see it
AMERICANS -- PHILIPPINES
Yates, A. Moondogs
AMERICANS -- ROMANIA
Marks, J. Fangland
Wiesel, E. The forgotten
AMERICANS -- RUSSIA
Harris, R. Archangel
Krasikov, S. The patriots
L'Amour, L. Last of the breed
AMERICANS -- RWANDA
Leonard, E. Pagan babies
AMERICANS -- SICILY
Hersey, J. A bell for Adano
AMERICANS -- SINGAPORE
Kwan, K. Crazy rich Asians
AMERICANS -- SOUTH AFRICA
Ward, A. E. Forgive me
AMERICANS -- SOUTH SUDAN
Hoagland, E. Children are diamonds
AMERICANS -- SPAIN
Lerner, B. Leaving the Atocha Station
AMERICANS -- SUNDARBANS (BANGLADESH AND INDIA)
Ghosh, A. The hungry tide
AMERICANS -- SWEDEN
Between summer's longing and winter's end
AMERICANS -- SWITZERLAND
Ludlum, R. The Sigma protocol
AMERICANS -- TURKEY -- ISTANBUL
Kanon, J. Istanbul passage
AMERICANS -- UKRAINE
Foer, J. S. Everything is illuminated
AMERICANS -- URUGUAY
Cameron, P. The city of your final destination
AMERICANS -- VIETNAM
Greene, G. The quiet American
Johnson, D. Tree of smoke
Leimbach, M. The man from Saigon
Soli, T. The lotus eaters
AMERICANS -- WEST AFRICA
Patterson, R. N. Eclipse
AMERICANS -- ZAIRE
Kingsolver, B. The poisonwood Bible
AMISH
See also Christian sects; Mennonites
AMISH
Castillo, L. Breaking silence
Castillo, L. The dead will tell
Castillo, L. Her last breath
Castillo, L. Sworn to silence
Fisher, S. W. Anna's crossing
Harper, K. Fall from pride
Hoff, B. J. River of mercy
Lewis, B. The brethren
Lewis, B. The missing
Lewis, B. The preacher's daughter
Williamson, P. The outsider
Wiseman, B. Plain paradise
Amistad. Pesci, D.
AMISTAD (SCHOONER)
Pesci, D. Amistad
AMNESIA
Barr, N. The rope
Blame
Brown, S. The witness
Doetsch, R. Half-past dawn
Dreyer, E. Barely a lady
Eco, U. The mysterious flame of Queen Loana
Grimes, M. Dakota
Hall, S. The raw shark texts
Hilton, J. Random harvest
Kaufmann, N. Dying Is My Business
Livesey, M. The missing world
Ludlum, R. The Bourne identity
Moriarty, L. What Alice forgot
Putney, M. J. Loving a lost lord
Sakey, M. The two deaths of Daniel Hayes
Tyler, A. Noah's compass
Walters, M. The dark room
Watson, S. J. Before I go to sleep
Westlake, D. E. Memory
AMNESIA
See also Memory
Among others. Walton, J.

Among the living. Rabb, J.
Among the mad. Winspear, J.
Among the missing. Joss, M.
Among the ruins. Khan, A. Z.
Among the ten thousand things. Pierpont, J.
Among thieves. Clarkson, J.
Amory Ames mystery [series]
Weaver, A. A most novel revenge
Amos Walker. Estleman, L. D.
The **amount** to carry. Scholz, C.
AMPHIBIANS
See also Animals
Amsterdam. McEwan, I.
AMSTERDAM (NETHERLANDS)
The dinner
Keilson, H. Comedy in a minor key
The **Amsterdam** cops. Van de Wetering, J.
AMUSEMENT PARKS
Bradbury, R. Something wicked this way comes
Dunn, K. Geek love
Russell, K. Swamplandia!
Amy and Isabelle. Strout, E.
AMYOTROPHIC LATERAL SCLEROSIS
Harrison, J. Returning to earth
Redhill, M. Consolation
Ana of California. Teran, A.
The **analyst.** Katzenbach, J.
Anansi boys. Gaiman, N.
ANARCHISM AND ANARCHISTS
Lehane, D. The given day
Robbins, T. Still life with Woodpecker
ANARCHISTS
Smith, A. Judas horse
Anathem. Stephenson, N.
ANATOMISTS
Robertson, I. Anatomy of murder
Robertson, I. Instruments of darkness
The **anatomy** lesson. Roth, P.
Anatomy of a disappearance. Matar, H.
Anatomy of murder. Robertson, I.
Ancestor stones. Forna, A.
ANCESTOR WORSHIP
See also Religion
ANCESTRY *See* Genealogy; Heredity
ANCIENT ARCHITECTURE
See also Archeology; Architecture
ANCIENT ART
See also Art
The **ancient** child. Momaday, N. S.
Ancient evenings. Mailer, N.
Ancient light. Banville, J.
The **Ancient** Minstrel. Harrison, J.
The **ancient** rain. Stansberry, D.
Ancillary justice. Leckie, A.
Ancillary mercy. Leckie, A.
Ancillary sword. Leckie, A.
And after the fire. Belfer, L.
And quiet flows the Don. Sholokhov, M. A.
And sometimes I wonder about you. Mosley, W.
And the Mountains Echoed. Hosseini, K.
And then I found you. Henry, P. C.
And then there were none. Christie, A.
And then you die-- Johansen, I.
And thereby hangs a tale. Archer, J.
And this too shall pass. Harris, E. L.
And when she was good. Lippman, L.
Andersonville. Kantor, M.
ANDERSONVILLE PRISON
Groot, T. The sentinels of Andersonville
ANDES
Vargas Llosa, M. Death in the Andes
Andrew's Brain. Doctorow, E. L.
ANDROGYNY
Merey, I. a + e 4ever
The **android's** dream. Scalzi, J.
ANDROIDS
See also Robots
Stross, C. Neptune's brood
The **Andromeda** strain. Crichton, M.
Angel baby. Lange, R.
The **angel** maker. Pearson, R.
The **angel** of Montague Street. Green, N.
Angel time. Rice, A.
Angel's fall. Roberts, N.
The **angel's** game. Ruiz Zafon, C.
Angelina's bachelors. O'Reilly, B.
Angelmaker. Harkaway, N.
Angelology. Trussoni, D.
Angelopolis. Trussoni, D.
ANGELS
Ansay, A. M. River angel
De Bodard, A. The house of shattered wings
Hoffman, A. The third angel
Pettersson, V. The taken
Rice, A. Angel time
Rice, A. Of love and evil
Riley, J. M. The serpent garden
Trussoni, D. Angelology
Trussoni, D. Angelopolis
ANGELS
See also Heaven; Spirits
Angels & demons. Brown, D.
Angels Crest. Schwartz, L.
Anger. Sarton, M.
ANGER
See also Emotions
Anger, Kenneth

About

Lazar, Z. Sway
Angle of repose. Stegner, W. E.
ANGLICAN AND EPISCOPAL BISHOPS
Trollope, A. Barchester Towers
ANGLICAN AND EPISCOPAL CLERGY
Austen, J. Mansfield Park

Austen, J. Pride and prejudice
Bronte, C. Jane Eyre
Brooks, G. Year of wonders
Davies, R. The cunning man
Eliot, G. Middlemarch
Godwin, G. Evensong
Howatch, S. Glamorous powers
Howatch, S. Scandalous risks
Howatch, S. Ultimate prizes
Paton, A. Cry, the beloved country
Pym, B. An unsuitable attachment
Trollope, A. Barchester Towers
Trollope, A. Framley parsonage
Trollope, A. The last chronicle of Barset
ANGLICAN CHURCH *See* Church of England
ANGLO-SAXONS
Cornwell, B. The last kingdom
Griffiths, E. A Dying Fall
Sutcliff, R. Sword at sunset
An **angry-ass** black woman. Miller, K. E. Q.
Anil's ghost. Ondaatje, M.
Animal. K'wan (Author)
ANIMAL ABUSE *See* Animal welfare
ANIMAL BABIES
See also Animals
ANIMAL BEHAVIOR
See also Animals; Zoology
Animal crackers. Tinti, H.
ANIMAL EXPERIMENTATION
See also Research
ANIMAL EXPLOITATION *See* Animal welfare
Animal farm. Orwell, G.
ANIMAL HOUSING
See also Animals
ANIMAL INTELLIGENCE
Hale, B. The evolution of Bruno Littlemore
ANIMAL INTELLIGENCE
See also Animals
ANIMAL LOCOMOTION
See also Animals; Locomotion
ANIMAL MAGNETISM *See* Hypnotism
ANIMAL PARASITES *See* Parasites
ANIMAL PSYCHOLOGY *See* Animal intelligence; Comparative psychology
ANIMAL REPRODUCTION
See also Animals; Reproduction
ANIMAL RESCUE
See also Animal welfare
ANIMAL RIGHTS ACTIVISTS
Gruen, S. Ape house
Smith, A. Judas horse
ANIMAL WELFARE
Boyle, T. C. When the killing's done
Coetzee, J. M. Disgrace
Grimes, M. Dakota
Gruen, S. Ape house
Pelecanos, G. P. Drama city
Stott, R. Ghostwalk
Wesselmann, D. L. Captivity
Animal's people. Sinha, I.
ANIMALS
Bergman, M. M. Birds of a lesser paradise
Beukes, L. Zoo city
Broun, B. Night of the Animals
Dovey, C. Only the animals
Martel, Y. Beatrice and Virgil
Millet, L. How the dead dream
Orwell, G. Animal farm
Wells, H. G. The island of Doctor Moreau
White, T. H. The book of Merlyn
Wodehouse, P. G. A Wodehouse bestiary
ANIMALS -- COLOR
See also Color
ANIMALS -- DISEASES
See also Diseases
ANIMALS -- FOLKLORE
See also Folklore
ANIMALS -- FOOD
See also Animal behavior; Food
ANIMALS -- MISTREATMENT *See* Animal welfare
ANIMALS -- PROTECTION *See* Animal welfare
ANIMALS -- PSYCHOLOGICAL ASPECTS
Dovey, C. Only the animals
ANIMALS -- TREATMENT *See* Animal welfare
ANIMALS IN MOTION PICTURES
See also Motion pictures
ANIMALS IN POLICE WORK
See also Police; Working animals
ANIMALS, MYTHICAL
Perry, S. The Essex Serpent
ANIMATED FILMS
See also Cartoons and caricatures; Motion pictures
ANIMATED TELEVISION PROGRAMS
See also Television programs
The **animators.** Whitaker, K. R.
ANIMISM
See also Religion
Anna in-between. Nunez, E.
Anna Karenina. Tolstoy, L.
Anna Pigeon mysteries [series]
Barr, N. Destroyer angel
Anna's book. Vine, B.
Anna's crossing. Fisher, S. W.
Annabel. Winter, K.
Anne Boleyn, Queen, consort of Henry VIII, King of England, 1507-1536
About
Andersen, L. The Boleyn King
Gregory, P. The other Boleyn girl
Maxwell, R. The secret diary of Anne Boleyn
Plaidy, J. Murder most royal
Anne of Cleves, Queen, consort of Henry VIII, King of England, 1515-1557
About

Gregory, P. The Boleyn Inheritance
Anne, Queen, consort of Louis XIII, King of France, 1601-1666
About
Dumas, A. Twenty years after
Anne, Queen, consort of Richard III, King of England, 1456-1485
About
Gregory, P. The kingmaker's daughter
Annie John. Kincaid, J.
Annie's people [series]
Lewis, B. The preacher's daughter
Annihilation. VanderMeer, J.
The **Anniversary** Man. Ellory, R. J.
ANNUALS *See* Almanacs; Calendars; Periodicals; School yearbooks; Yearbooks
ANNUALS (PLANTS)
See also Cultivated plants; Flower gardening; Flowers
ANNUITIES
See also Investments; Retirement income
The **Anodyne** Necklace. Grimes, M.
Another Brooklyn. Woodson, J.
Another country. Baldwin, J.
Another life. Vachss, A. H.
Another man's moccasins. Johnson, C.
Another piece of my heart. Green, J.
Another time, another life.
Anson, George Anson, Baron, 1697-1762
About
O'Brian, P. The golden ocean
The **antagonist.** Coady, L.
ANTARCTIC REGIONS
Johnson, M. Pym
Robinson, K. S. Antarctica
Antarctica. Robinson, K. S.
ANTARCTICA
Robinson, K. S. Antarctica
Semple, M. Where'd you go, Bernadette
Anthem. Rand, A.
Anthill. Wilson, E. O.
ANTHOLOGIES
Alarcón, D. American odysseys
The big book of science fiction
Latin@ rising
A thousand forests in one acorn
ANTHOLOGIES
See also Books
The **anthologist.** Baker, N.
ANTHROPOLOGISTS
Barker, P. The eye in the door
Barker, P. The ghost road
Jackson, S. The haunting of Hill House
Johnson, A. Parasites like us
King, L. Euphoria
Ondaatje, M. Anil's ghost
Pym, B. An unsuitable attachment
Vanderbes, J. Easter Island
ANTHROPOMETRY
See also Anthropology; Ethnology; Human beings
ANTHROPOMORPHISM
Dovey, C. Only the animals
ANTI-CATHOLICISM
Brown, D. Angels & demons
ANTI-FASCIST MOVEMENTS
Lewis, S. It can't happen here
ANTI-UTOPIAS *See* Dystopias
ANTI-WAR STORIES *See* War stories
ANTICOMMUNIST MOVEMENTS
See also Communism
ANTIETAM (MD.), BATTLE OF, 1862
See also Battles; United States -- History -- 1861-1865, Civil War -- Campaigns
ANTIGUA AND BARBUDA
Kincaid, J. Annie John
Le Carre, J. Our kind of traitor
ANTIHEROES
Diaz, J. The brief wondrous life of Oscar Wao
Gibson, W. Spook country
Hill, J. Horns
Hilleman, A. World, chase me down
Hodgen, C. Elegies for the brokenhearted
Hynes, J. Kings of infinite space
Kunkel, B. Indecision
Leonard, E. Tishomingo blues
McGuane, T. Nothing but blue skies
ANTINUCLEAR MOVEMENT
See also Arms control; Nuclear weapons; Social movements
The **Antiquarian.** Faverón Patriau, G.
ANTIQUARIAN BOOKS *See* Rare books
ANTIQUARIANS
Sontag, S. The volcano lover
ANTIQUE AND CLASSIC CARS
See also Automobiles
ANTIQUE DEALERS
Krauss, N. Great house
Nevill, A. The house of small shadows
Pym, B. The sweet dove died
Tremain, R. Trespass
Welsh, L. The cutting room
ANTIQUES
Neville, K. The eight
Neville, K. The fire
ANTIQUES
See also Antiquities; Collectors and collecting; Decoration and ornament; Decorative arts
ANTIQUITIES
Rollins, J. The devil colony
ANTIQUITIES -- COLLECTION AND PRESERVATION
See also Collectors and collecting
Masello, R. The Romanov cross
ANTISEMITISM
Appelfeld, A. Until the dawn's light
Baxter, C. Saul and Patsy

Begley, L. About Schmidt
Black, C. Murder in the Marais
Franklin, A. Mistress of the art of death
Greenberg, J. I never promised you a rose garden
Hill, R. When all is said and done
Hobson, L. K. Z. Gentleman's agreement
Isaacs, S. Red, white and blue
Jacobson, H. The Finkler question
Lipman, E. The Inn at Lake Devine
Malamud, B. The fixer
Oates, J. C. The gravedigger's daughter
Orringer, J. The invisible bridge
Pears, I. The dream of Scipio
Pope, B. C. The blood of Lorraine
Rice, A. Angel time
Rice, A. Of love and evil
Richler, M. Solomon Gursky was here
Roth, P. The plot against America
Schwarz-Bart, A. The last of the just
Walton, J. Farthing
ANTISEMITISM
See also Prejudices
ANTISLAVERY *See* Abolitionists; Slavery; Slaves -- Emancipation
ANTISLAVERY MOVEMENTS
Hill, L. Someone knows my name
Kidd, S. M. The invention of wings
ANTISTALKING LAWS *See* Stalking
ANTS
See also Insects
Wilson, E. O. Anthill
Anvil of stars. Bear, G.
ANXIETY
See also Emotions; Neuroses; Stress (Psychology)
Whittall, Z. Holding still for as long as possible
The **anxiety** of everyday objects. Sheehan, A.
Any Duchess Will Do. Dare, T.
Any human heart. Boyd, W.
Anything for You. Higgins, K.
Anything is possible. Strout, E.
Anywhere but here. Simpson, M.
APACHE INDIANS
Fergus, J. The wild girl: the notebooks of Ned Giles, 1932
Rosenberg, R. This is not civilization
McLaren, K. The road to enchantment
APALACHICOLA (FLA.)
Morris, M. Man in the blue moon
APARTMENT HOUSES
Adiga, A. Last man in tower
Aira, C. Ghosts
The elegance of the hedgehog
Gilb, D. The flowers
Hegi, U. The vision of Emma Blau
Life
Marwood, A. The killer next door
McCall Smith, A. Love over Scotland
McCall Smith, A. The world according to Bertie
Nineveh
Saul, J. Midnight voices
Suri, M. The death of Vishnu
Wiles, W. Care of wooden floors
Winters, B. H. Bedbugs
APARTMENT HOUSES
See also Buildings; Domestic architecture; Houses; Housing
APARTMENTS
See also Apartment houses
Ape house. Gruen, S.
APES
Abu-Jaber, D. Origin
Boulle, P. Planet of the apes
Gruen, S. Ape house
Apex hides the hurt. Whitehead, C.
APOCALYPTIC FICTION
Anders, C. J. All the birds in the sky
Barnes, S. Domino Falls
Cronin, J. The city of mirrors
Cronin, J. The twelve
Doctorow, C. Walkaway
Haig, F. The fire sermon
Heller, P. The dog stars
Jemisin, N. K. The fifth season
Kazinski, A. J. The last good man
Malerman, J. Bird Box
Mandel, E. S. J. Station eleven
McHugh, M. F. After the apocalypse
Percy, B. The dead lands
Solomon, R. An unkindness of ghosts
This way to the end times
Wellington, D. Positive
Wilson, D. H. Robogenesis
Winters, B. H. Countdown city
Winters, B. H. The last policeman
APOCALYPTIC FILMS
See also Motion pictures
APOCALYPTIC LITERATURE
VanderMeer, J. Borne
APOLLO PROJECT
See also Life support systems (Space environment); Orbital rendezvous (Space flight); Space flight to the moon
The **Apostle.** Asch, S.
APOSTLES
Asch, S. The Apostle
Asch, S. The Nazarene
Kazantzakis, N. The last temptation of Christ
Tóibín, C. The testament of Mary
Williams, N. John
APPALACHIA *See* Appalachian Region
APPALACHIAN MOUNTAINS
McCrumb, S. The ballad of Frankie Silver
McCrumb, S. Foggy Mountain breakdown and other stories
McCrumb, S. She walks these hills
APPALACHIAN REGION
Greene, A. Bloodroot

Harman, P. The midwife of Hope River
Marshall, C. Christy
Rash, R. The cove
Rash, R. Something rich and strange
Scotton, C. The secret wisdom of the earth
Smith, L. Fair and tender ladies
Smith, L. Oral history
APPALACHIAN REGION, SOUTHERN
McCrumb, S. The ballad of Frankie Silver
Morgan, R. The road from Gap Creek
APPALACHIAN TRAIL
Doiron, P. The Precipice
Appaloosa. Parker, R. B.
APPARITIONS
See also Parapsychology; Spirits
APPEARANCE, PERSONAL *See* Personal appearance
An **appetite** for violets. Bailey, M.
The **Apple** Orchard. Wiggs, S.
APPLIED MECHANICS
See also Mechanics
Appointment in Samarra. O'Hara, J.
APPRAISAL OF BOOKS *See* Book reviewing; Books and reading; Criticism; Literature -- History and criticism
APPRENTICES
Modesitt, L. E. Imager's challenge
APPRENTICESHIP NOVELS *See* Bildungsromans
Aquarium. Vann, D.
AQUATIC ANIMALS
See also Animals
ARAB AMERICAN WOMEN
Abu-Jaber, D. Crescent
ARAB AMERICANS
Abu-Jaber, D. Crescent
Yunis, A. The night counter
ARAB COUNTRIES -- SOCIAL CONDITIONS -- 21ST CENTURY
Haddad, S. Guapa
ARAB REFUGEES
See also Refugees
ARAB-ISRAEL WAR, 1967 *See* Israel-Arab War, 1967
ARAB-JEWISH RELATIONS *See* Jewish-Arab relations
Arabella of Mars. Levine, D. D.
ARABIC LANGUAGE
See also Language and languages
ARABS
Higgins, J. Edge of danger
Spark, M. The Mandelbaum Gate
The Meursault investigation
ARABS -- PALESTINE *See* Palestinian Arabs
ARACHNIDS
See also Animals
ARBORICULTURE *See* Forests and forestry; Fruit culture; Trees
Arbuckle, Fatty, 1887-1933
About
Atkins, A. Devil's garden
Arcadia. Groff, L.
Arcadia Falls. Goodman, C.
Arch of triumph. Remarque, E. M.
ARCHAEOLOGISTS
Griffiths, E. The crossing places
Griffiths, E. A Dying Fall
Hart, E. The book of Killowen
Hart, E. Haunted ground
Hart, E. Lake of sorrows
Russell, M. D. Dreamers of the day
ARCHAEOLOGY *See* Archeology
ARCHAEOLOGY -- SCOTLAND
Graeme-Evans, P. The island house
ARCHAEOPTERYX
See also Dinosaurs
Archangel. Barrett, A.
Archangel. Harris, R.
ARCHBISHOPS
Penman, S. K. Time and chance
ARCHEOLOGISTS
Goodman, C. The night villa
Griffiths, E. The Janus stone
Long, J. The reckoning
Ondaatje, M. Anil's ghost
Unsworth, B. Land of marvels
Van Booy, S. Everything beautiful began after
ARCHEOLOGISTS
See also Historians
ARCHEOLOGY
Crichton, M. Timeline
Fay, K. The map of lost memories
Graeme-Evans, P. The island house
Rollins, J. The blood Gospel
The **archer's** tale. Cornwell, B.
ARCHERY
Cornwell, B. The archer's tale
ARCHERY
See also Martial arts; Shooting
Archform. Modesitt, L. E.
ARCHITECTS
Bognanni, P. The house of tomorrow
Boyle, T. C. The women
A Crack in the Wall
Delaney, J. P. The girl before
Dickens, C. Martin Chuzzlewit
Ferber, E. So Big
Hoffman, A. Skylight confessions
Horan, N. Loving Frank
Hunter, E. Candyland
Mawer, S. The glass room
O'Flynn, C. The news where you are
Orringer, J. The invisible bridge
Rand, A. The fountainhead
Stone, I. The agony and the ecstasy
Waldman, A. The submission
White, E. The married man
ARCHITECTS
See also Artists

ARCHITECTS -- FRANCE -- PARIS
Belfoure, C. The Paris Architect
ARCHITECTURAL DECORATION AND ORNAMENT
Gill, J. F. The gargoyle hunters
ARCHITECTURE
See also Art
ARCHIVAL MATERIALS -- DIGITIZATION
Lovett, C. The lost book of the Grail
The **archivist.** Cooley, M.
The **archivist's** story. Holland, T.
ARCHIVISTS
Holland, T. The archivist's story
Meltzer, B. The inner circle
ARCTIC REGIONS
Kiernan, S. P. The Curiosity
Mowat, F. The Snow Walker
Simmons, D. The terror
Vollmann, W. T. The rifles
ARDENNES (FRANCE), BATTLE OF THE, 1944-1945
Burke, J. L. Wayfaring Stranger
ARDENNES (FRANCE), BATTLE OF THE, 1944-1945
See also Battles; World War, 1939-1945 -- Campaigns
Argall. Vollmann, W. T.
Argall, Samuel Sir, ca. 1572-ca. 1626
About
Vollmann, W. T. Argall
ARGENTINA
Aira, C. The seamstress and the wind
De Robertis, C. The gods of tango
The fish child
Saer, J. J. The sixty-five years of Washington
ARGENTINA -- BUENOS AIRES
Aira, C. Ghosts
Cortazar, J. Hopscotch
Englander, N. The Ministry of Special Cases
Puig, M. Kiss of the spider woman
Restrepo, L. No place for heroes
Saint-Exupery, A. d. Night flight
Swann, M. The foreigners
ARGENTINA -- HISTORY -- DIRTY WAR, 1976-1983
De Robertis, C. Perla
ARGENTINA -- RURAL LIFE
Greene, G. The honorary consul
ARGENTINES -- FRANCE
Cortazar, J. Hopscotch
ARGONAUTS (GREEK MYTHOLOGY)
Greenwood, K. Medea
ARISTOCRACY (SOCIAL CLASS)
Ali, M. Untold story
Burrowes, G. Tremaine's True Love
Carey, P. Parrot and Olivier in America
Dare, T. Do you want to start a scandal
Goodwin, D. The American heiress
Raybourn, D. A perilous undertaking
Towles, A. A Gentleman in Moscow
White, R. M. A lady unrivaled
ARISTOCRACY (SOCIAL CLASS) -- GERMANY
Moore, S. The life of objects
ARISTOCRACY -- ENGLAND
Balogh, M. The secret mistress
Bowen, K. You're the Earl That I Want
Chase, L. L. Silk is for seduction
Goodwin, D. The American heiress
Kleypas, L. Cold-hearted Rake
Riley, J. M. The serpent garden
Sackville-West, V. The Edwardians
Wodehouse, P. G. The code of the Woosters
Wodehouse, P. G. Tales from the Drones Club
ARISTOCRACY -- FRANCE
Carey, P. Parrot and Olivier in America
Dickens, C. A tale of two cities
Haasse, H. S. In a dark wood wandering
Laker, R. To dance with kings
Orczy, E. The Scarlet Pimpernel
Proust, M. The Guermantes way
Proust, M. Sodom and Gomorrah
Riley, J. M. The serpent garden
Stendhal The red and the black
ARISTOCRACY -- GREAT BRITAIN
Dean, A. A gentleman of fortune, or, The suspicions of Miss Dido Kent
MacLean, S. The Rogue Not Taken
ARISTOCRACY -- ITALY
Stendhal The charterhouse of Parma
ARISTOCRACY -- JAPAN
Mishima, Y. Spring snow
Schwartz, J. B. The commoner
ARISTOCRACY -- RUSSIA
West, R. The birds fall down
ARISTOCRACY -- SICILY
Unsworth, B. The ruby in her navel
ARISTOCRACY -- WALES
James, E. When beauty tamed the beast
Aristotle
About
Lyon, A. The sweet girl
ARITHMETIC
See also Mathematics; Set theory
ARIZONA
Caputo, P. Crossers
Faust, C. Choke hold
Jance, J. A. Queen of the night
Krentz, J. A. White lies
Preston, D. Blasphemy
Rosenberg, R. This is not civilization
Walls, J. Half broke horses
ARIZONA -- 19TH CENTURY
Silko, L. Gardens in the dunes
Turner, N. E. These is my words
ARIZONA -- 20TH CENTURY
Kingsolver, B. The bean trees
Kingsolver, B. Pigs in heaven
ARIZONA -- PHOENIX
Abbott, M. E. Bury me deep

McMillan, T. Waiting to exhale
Sallis, J. The killer is dying
ARIZONA -- TUCSON
Kingsolver, B. Pigs in heaven
Ure, L. The fault tree
ARKANSAS
Hunter, S. Black light
ARKANSAS -- HOT SPRINGS
Hunter, S. Hot Springs
Armageddon. Uris, L.
Armageddon in retrospect. Vonnegut, K.
ARMAMENTS
Pears, I. Stone's fall
ARMENIAN AMERICANS
Bohjalian, C. The sandcastle girls
Shafak, E. The bastard of Istanbul
ARMENIAN MASSACRES, 1915-1923
Bohjalian, C. The sandcastle girls
Shafak, E. The bastard of Istanbul
Werfel, F. The forty days of Musa Dagh
ARMENIANS -- SYRIA
Werfel, F. The forty days of Musa Dagh
ARMENIANS -- TURKEY
Shafak, E. The bastard of Istanbul
The **armies.** Rosero Diago, E.
The **armies** of memory. Barnes, J.
Arms and the women. Hill, R.
ARMS CONTROL
See also International relations; International security; War
ARMY DESERTION *See* Military desertion
ARMY LIFE *See* Soldiers
ARMY OFFICERS
Dumas, A. The man in the iron mask
Dumas, A. Twenty years after
Jones, D. C. The court-martial of George Armstrong Custer
Parker, R. B. Double play
ARMY SCHOOLS *See* Military education
Around the world in eighty days. Verne, J.
ARRANGED MARRIAGE
Dev, S. A Bollywood affair
Harris, E. The Marrying of Chani Kaufman
Hood, A. An Italian Wife
Thomas, S. Ravishing the heiress
Arrowood. McHugh, L.
Arrowsmith; Elmer Gantry; Dodsworth. Lewis, S.
ARSON
Ball, J. How to set a fire and why
Clarke, B. An arsonist's guide to writers' homes in New England
Grant, S. Map of Ireland
Harper, K. Fall from pride
Haywood, G. A. Cemetery Road
Jones, S. Outcast
Lupton, R. Afterwards
MacBride, S. Dying Light
Spencer, S. Endless love
ARSON INVESTIGATION
DeSilva, B. Rogue island
Walker, M. The dark vineyard
An **arsonist's** guide to writers' homes in New England. Clarke, B.
ART
Dean, D. The madonnas of Leningrad
Martin, S. An object of beauty
Stone, I. The agony and the ecstasy
ART -- ATTRIBUTION
Conklin, T. The house girl
ART -- COLLECTORS AND COLLECTING -- NEW YORK (STATE) -- NEW YORK
Prentiss, M. Tuesday nights in 1980
ART
Sloin, H. Art on fire
Van Essen, T. The Center of the World
ART -- FORGERIES
See also Counterfeits and counterfeiting; Forgery
Amend, A. A nearly perfect copy
Gaddis, W. The recognitions
Smith, D. The last painting of Sara De Vos
ART -- PSYCHOLOGICAL ASPECTS
Van Essen, T. The Center of the World
ART AND MYTHOLOGY
See also Art; Mythology
ART AND RELIGION
See also Art; Religion
ART AND SOCIETY
See also Art
ART APPRECIATION
Levine, J. A. Bingo's Run
ART CATALOGS
See also Art
ART COLLECTORS
Murray, S. Forgery
ART CRITICS
O'Farrell, M. The hand that first held mine
Pears, I. The portrait
Winer, A. The marriage artist
ART CRITICS -- NEW YORK (STATE) -- NEW YORK
Prentiss, M. Tuesday nights in 1980
ART DEALERS
Amend, A. A nearly perfect copy
Boyd, W. Any human heart
Cunningham, M. By nightfall
MacInnes, H. Prelude to terror
Rothschild, H. The improbability of love
Woods, S. Imperfect strangers
ART DEALERS -- ENGLAND
Morgan-Jones, C. The jackal's share
ART FORGERIES *See* Art -- Forgeries
ART GALLERIES AND MUSEUMS
Kellerman, J. The genius
ART HISTORIANS
Pears, I. Death and restoration
Pears, I. The immaculate deception

Smith, D. The last painting of Sara De Vos
Trussoni, D. Angelopolis
Art in America. McLarty, R.
ART MUSEUMS
See also Museums
Aridjis, C. Asunder
ART OBJECTS
See also Antiques; Art; Decoration and ornament; Decorative arts
The **Art** of Crash Landing. Decarlo, M.
The **art** of deception. Pearson, R.
The **art** of fielding. Harbach, C.
The **art** of joy.
The **art** of racing in the rain. Stein, G.
Art on fire. Sloin, H.
Art Oveson [series]
Hunt, A. City of saints
ART RESTORERS
Silva, D. The English Girl
The **art** student's war. Leithauser, B.
ART THEFTS
See also Theft
Banville, J. The blue guitar
Morton, C. Stealing Mona Lisa
Artagnan, Charles de Batz-Castelmore, comte d', 1613?-1673
About
Dumas, A. The man in the iron mask
Dumas, A. Twenty years after
Artemis. Weir, A.
ARTHRITIS
See also Diseases
Arthur Rex. Berger, T.
Arthur, King
About
Berger, T. Arthur Rex
Bradley, M. Z. The mists of Avalon
Cornwell, B. Enemy of God
Cornwell, B. Excalibur
Cornwell, B. The winter king
Sutcliff, R. Sword at sunset
Twain, M. A Connecticut Yankee in King Arthur's court
White, T. H. The book of Merlyn
White, T. H. The once and future king
White, T. H. The sword in the stone
ARTIFICIAL FOODS
See also Food; Synthetic products
ARTIFICIAL INSEMINATION, HUMAN
Jewell, L. The making of us
ARTIFICIAL INTELLIGENCE
Anderson, P. Genesis
Chiang, T. The life cycle of software objects
Egan, G. Zendegi
Frankel, L. Goodbye for now
Hall, L. Speak
Harris, R. The fear index
Iles, G. The footprints of God
Kosmatka, T. The games
Palwick, S. Shelter
Powers, R. Galatea 2.2
Rucker, R. v. B. Postsingular
Stross, C. Accelerando
Tregillis, I. The Mechanical
Wells, M. All systems red
Westerfeld, S. The risen empire
Wilson, D. H. The clockwork dynasty
Wilson, D. H. Robopocalypse
Zelazny, R. Donnerjack
ARTIFICIAL LIFE
Chiang, T. The life cycle of software objects
Crichton, M. Prey
ARTIFICIAL ORGANS
See also Surgery
ARTIFICIAL REALITY *See* Virtual reality
ARTIST COLONIES
McCarthy, M. A charmed life
ARTIST LIFE
McCarthy, M. A charmed life
Sanders, L. The second deadly sin
Steinke, R. Holy skirts
Tyler, A. Celestial navigation
Updike, J. Seek my face
Vreeland, S. The passion of Artemesia
An **artist** of the floating world. Ishiguro, K.
ARTISTIC ANATOMY
See also Anatomy; Art; Drawing; Nude in art
ARTISTIC PHOTOGRAPHY
See also Art; Photography
ARTISTS
Avery, E. The last nude
Bialosky, J. The prize
Brown, D. The Da Vinci code
Chevalier, T. Girl with a pearl earring
D'Erasmo, S. The Sky Below
Erdrich, L. Shadow tag
Essex, K. Leonardo's swans
Flanagan, R. Gould's book of fish
Frayn, M. Headlong
Freudenberger, N. The dissident
Goodis, D. Nightfall
Grushin, O. The dream life of Sukhanov
Harding, G. Painter of silence
Harper, K. Fall from pride
Heller, P. The painter
Horn, D. The world to come
Jakeman, J. In the Kingdom of mists
Kellerman, J. The genius
Kincaid, J. Lucy
King, R. Domino
Kostova, E. The swan thieves
The lake
Lopez, B. H. Resistance
Makkai, R. The hundred-year house
The map and the territory

Maugham, W. S. The moon and sixpence
Munoz Molina, A. In her absence
My name is Red
Pears, I. The portrait
Prentiss, M. Tuesday nights in 1980
Powers, R. Plowing the dark
Raeder, L. Cam girl
Russo, R. Bridge of sighs
See, C. The handyman
Savage, S. The way of the dog
Sloin, H. Art on fire
Smith, A. How to be Both
Stone, I. The agony and the ecstasy
Stone, I. Lust for life
Urquhart, J. A map of glass
Vargas Llosa, M. The way to paradise
Vreeland, S. Clara and Mr. Tiffany
Vreeland, S. Girl in hyacinth blue
Vreeland, S. Luncheon of The Boating Party
Vreeland, S. The passion of Artemesia
Wilson, R. The blind man of Seville
Winer, A. The marriage artist
ARTISTS -- ITALY -- SIENA
Winawer, M. The scribe of Siena
ARTISTS -- NEW YORK (STATE) -- NEW YORK -- 20TH CENTURY
Shapiro, B. A. The muralist
ARTISTS' MODELS
Avery, E. The last nude
Buchanan, C. M. The painted girls
Chevalier, T. Girl with a pearl earring
Humphreys, H. Afterimage
ARTISTS' MODELS
See also Art
ARTS AND CRAFTS MOVEMENT
See also Art; Decoration and ornament; Decorative arts; Industrial arts
As chimney sweepers come to dust. Bradley, A.
As good as gone. Watson, L.
As husbands go. Isaacs, S.
As I lay dying. Faulkner, W.
As simple as snow. Galloway, G.
As we are now. Sarton, M.
ASCETICISM
See also Ethics; Religious life
ASEXUAL REPRODUCTION
Crichton, M. Jurassic Park
Houellebecq, M. The possibility of an island
Vinge, J. D. The Snow Queen
Wilhelm, K. Where late the sweet birds sang
The **ash** garden. Bock, D.
Ash Wednesday. Hawke, E.
ASHANTI (AFRICAN PEOPLE)
See also Africans; Indigenous peoples
Ashenden. Wilhide, E.
The **Ashford** affair. Willig, L.
ASIA -- CIVILIZATION
See also Civilization; East and West
ASIA MINOR
Renault, M. The Persian boy
ASIAN AMERICANS
Kwan, K. Crazy rich Asians
Tanenbaum, R. Act of revenge
ASIAN ART
See also Art
ASIAN REFUGEES
Dau, S. The book of Jonas
Asimov, Isaac, 1920-1992
About
Benford, G. Foundation's fear
The **ask.** Lipsyte, S.
Ask not. Collins, M. A.
Ask the parrot. Stark, R.
Asleep. Yoshimoto, B.
ASPERGER'S SYNDROME
Picoult, J. House rules
Simsion, G. The Rosie project
ASPERGER'S SYNDROME
See also Autism
Assassin's apprentice. Hobb, R.
The **assassin's** song. Vassanji, M. G.
ASSASSINATION
Block, L. Hit me
Block, L. Killing Castro
Buckley, W. F. Mongoose, R.I.P
Costello, M. Big if
Deaver, J. Garden of beasts
Ellroy, J. Blood's a rover
Ellroy, J. The cold six thousand
Forsyth, F. The day of the jackal
Grisham, J. The pelican brief
Havley, N. The good father
Higgins, J. The eagle has flown
Higgins, J. Edge of danger
Higgins, J. Eye of the storm
Higgins, J. Touch the devil
Higgins, J. The White House connection
Hunter, S. Havana
Hunter, S. I, sniper
Hunter, S. Time to hunt
James, M. A brief history of seven killings
Mishima, Y. Runaway horses
Murakami, H. 1Q84
Neville, S. The ghosts of Belfast
Stross, C. Neptune's brood
Trevanian The Eiger sanction
Trevanian Shibumi
Walton, J. Ha'penny
Westlake, D. E. Money for nothing
Winslow, D. Satori
Woods, S. Dirty work
Woods, S. The run
ASSASSINATION -- INVESTIGATION -- SWEDEN
Between summer's longing and winter's end

Free falling, as if in a dream
The **assassination** of Jesse James by the coward Robert Ford. Hansen, R.
The **assassination** of Margaret Thatcher. Mantel, H.
ASSASSINS
Block, L. Hit me
Eisler, B. The God's Eye View
Hurwitz, G. The Nowhere Man
Hurwitz, G. Orphan X
Knopf, C. Dead anyway
Kristoff, J. Nevernight
Nesbø, J. Blood on snow
Silva, D. The black widow
Singh, N. Shield of winter
Sternbergh, A. Shovel ready
Vachss, A. That's how I roll
Woods, S. Doing hard time
ASSAULT, SEXUAL *See* Rape
ASSIMILATION (SOCIOLOGY)
Yezierska, A. c. Bread givers
The **assistant.** Walser, R.
The **assistant.** Malamud, B.
ASSISTED SUICIDE
See also Suicide
The **association** of small bombs. Mahajan, K.
Asta in the wings. Watson, J. E.
ASTEROIDS
Harrington, M. J. The goliath stone
Pohl, F. Beyond the blue event horizon
Pohl, F. Gateway
Pohl, F. Heechee rendezvous
Winters, B. H. World of trouble
Astor Place Vintage. Lehmann, S.
ASTRAL PROJECTION
See also Parapsychology
Lupton, R. Afterwards
Astrid & Veronika. Olsson, L.
ASTROBIOLOGY *See* Life on other planets; Space biology
ASTROLOGY
See also Astronomy; Divination; Occultism
Extence, G. The Universe Versus Alex Woods
Leon, D. A question of belief
ASTRONAUTICS
See also Aeronautics
ASTRONAUTICS -- COMMUNICATION SYSTEMS
See also Interstellar communication; Telecommunication
ASTRONAUTS
Kiefer, C. The infinite tides
Michener, J. A. Space
Sher, I. Gentlemen of space
ASTRONAUTS
See also Air pilots; Space flight
ASTRONOMERS
Byers, M. Percival's planet
Grenville, K. The lieutenant
Hazzard, S. The transit of Venus
Pynchon, T. Mason & Dixon
Robinson, K. S. Galileo's dream
Sherwood, F. The book of splendor
ASTRONOMERS
See also Scientists
ASTRONOMY
Extence, G. The Universe Versus Alex Woods
ASTRONOMY -- MATHEMATICS
See also Mathematics
Asunder. Aridjis, C.
Asylum. McGrath, P.
ASYLUM
Guo, X. I am China
ASYLUMS
Sedgwick, M. Mister Memory
At home in Mitford. Karon, J.
At home in Thrush Green. Read
At last. St. Aubyn, E.
At Night We Walk in Circles. Alarcón, D.
AT RISK STUDENTS
See also Students
At swim, two boys. O'Neill, J.
At the mountains of madness, and other novels. Lovecraft, H. P.
At weddings and wakes. McDermott, A.
Atatürk, Kemal, 1881-1938
About
De Bernieres, L. Birds without wings
ATHEISM
Goldstein, R. 36 arguments for the existence of God
ATHEISM
See also Religion; Secularism; Theology
Athenian Mysteries [series]
Corby, G. The Marathon conspiracy
ATHENS (GREECE)
Corby, G. The Pericles Commission
ATHENS (GREECE) -- HISTORY
Corby, G. The Marathon conspiracy
ATHLETES
Coldsmith, D. The long journey home
Grisham, J. Playing for pizza
Karunatilaka, S. The legend of Pradeep Mathew
Patterson, J. Hide & seek
Phillips, S. E. Natural born charmer
ATHLETIC COACHING *See* Coaching (Athletics)
ATLANTA (GA.)
Boyce, T. N. Old bones
Guinn, M. The scribe
McIntosh, W. Hitchers
Mullen, T. Lightning men
ATLANTA (GA.) -- RACE RELATIONS
Mullen, T. Darktown
ATLANTIC OCEAN
See also Ocean
ATLANTIS (LEGENDARY PLACE)
Siegel, J. Prospero's children
An **atlas** of impossible longing. Roy, A.

Atlas shrugged. Rand, A.
Atmospheric disturbances. Galchen, R.
ATOMIC BOMB
Bock, D. The ash garden
Burdick, E. Fail-safe
Golding, W. Lord of the flies
Kanon, J. Los Alamos
Millet, L. Oh pure and radiant heart
Nesbit, T. The wives of Los Alamos
Vonnegut, K. Cat's cradle
Wibberley, L. The mouse that roared
Wiggins, M. Evidence of things unseen
ATOMIC BOMB
See also Bombs; Nuclear weapons
Atonement. McEwan, I.
ATONEMENT
Erdrich, L. LaRose
Greene, G. Brighton rock
Howatch, S. The heartbreaker
Pelecanos, G. P. The way home
Picoult, J. Change of heart
Seymour, G. Rat run
ATONEMENT -- CHRISTIANITY
See also Christianity; Sacrifice; Salvation
ATONEMENT -- JUDAISM
See also Judaism
ATROCITIES
Alarcon, D. Lost City Radio
De Robertis, C. Perla
Jin, H. Nanjing requiem
ATROCITIES
See also Crime; Cruelty
ATTEMPTED MURDER
Moore, C. The Serpent of Venice
ATTEMPTED SUICIDE *See* Suicide
ATTENTION
See also Apperception; Educational psychology; Memory; Psychology; Thought and thinking
ATTENTION DEFICIT DISORDER
See also Abnormal psychology
ATTITUDE (PSYCHOLOGY)
See also Emotions; Psychology
ATTORNEY AND CLIENT
Silver, E. L. The execution of Noa P. Singleton
ATTORNEYS *See* Lawyers
AU PAIRS
Kincaid, J. Lucy
Moore, L. A gate at the stairs
Prose, F. Primitive people
AUCTIONS
Welsh, L. The cutting room
AUDIENCES
See also Communication; Social psychology
AUDIO CASSETTES *See* Sound recordings
AUDIOBOOKS
See also Sound recordings
AUDIOTAPES *See* Sound recordings
Augustown. Miller, K.
Augustus, Emperor of Rome, 63 B.C.-14 A.D.
About
Graves, R. I, Claudius
Aunt Julia and the scriptwriter. Vargas Llosa, M.
AUNTS
Childress, M. Crazy in Alabama
Dean, A. A place of confinement
Dickens, C. David Copperfield
Frazier, C. Nightwoods
Gibbons, K. Divining women
Greene, G. Travels with my aunt
Hatcher, R. L. A promise kept
Heyer, G. Black sheep
Jamison, L. The gin closet
Lodge, D. Paradise news
McDermott, A. At weddings and wakes
O'Farrell, M. The vanishing act of Esme Lennox
Proulx, A. The shipping news
Rice, L. Little night
Vargas Llosa, M. Aunt Julia and the scriptwriter
Vernon, O. Eden
AUNTS
See also Family
AURICULAR CONFESSION *See* Confession
Auriel rising. Redfern, E.
Aurora. Robinson, K. S.
AUSCHWITZ (POLAND: CONCENTRATION CAMP)
See also Concentration camps
AUSCHWITZ (POLAND: CONCENTRATION CAMP)
Amis, M. The zone of interest
Gross, A. The one man
Konar, A. Mischling
Matthiessen, P. In Paradise
Tidhar, L. A man lies dreaming
Wander, F. The seventh well
AUSCHWITZ (POLAND: CONCENTRATION CAMP) -- BUILDINGS
Konar, A. Mischling
Austen, Jane, 1775-1817
About
Fowler, K. J. The Jane Austen book club
Hale, S. Austenland
White, E. K. Heartstone
Austenland. Hale, S.
Austerlitz.
AUSTRALIA
Coming rain
Flanagan, R. The unknown terrorist
Francis, D. Wedding Bush Road
Irwin, S. M. The dead path
Keneally, T. A family madness
Keneally, T. Woman of the inner sea
Malouf, D. The complete stories
McCullough, C. The thorn birds
McGahan, A. The white earth
Moriarty, L. What Alice forgot

Winton, T. Breath
Winton, T. Dirt music
Wyld, E. After the fire, a still small voice
AUSTRALIA -- 18TH CENTURY
Grenville, K. The lieutenant
AUSTRALIA -- 19TH CENTURY
Flanagan, R. Gould's book of fish
Franklin, M. My brilliant career
Grenville, K. The secret river
Holt, V. The black opal
Malouf, D. Remembering Babylon
Wood, B. The dreaming
AUSTRALIA -- HISTORY -- 20TH CENTURY
Keneally, T. Shame and the Captives
AUSTRALIA -- HISTORY
Kneale, M. English passengers
AUSTRALIA -- MELBOURNE
Garner, H. The spare room
Shute, N. On the beach
AUSTRALIA -- NEW SOUTH WALES
Grenville, K. The idea of perfection
Nordhoff, C. Botany Bay
AUSTRALIA -- OFFICIALS AND EMPLOYEES
Harper, J. The dry
AUSTRALIA -- QUEENSLAND
Carey, P. His illegal self
Wright, A. Carpentaria
AUSTRALIA -- RURAL LIFE
Franklin, M. My brilliant career
AUSTRALIAN ABORIGINES
Flanagan, R. Wanting
Grenville, K. The secret river
Grenville, K. The lieutenant
Keneally, T. Flying hero class
Malouf, D. Remembering Babylon
McGahan, A. The white earth
Wood, B. The dreaming
Wright, A. Carpentaria
AUSTRALIAN FICTION
Grenville, K. Sarah Thornhill
AUSTRALIAN FICTION -- 21ST CENTURY
Coming rain
AUSTRALIANS -- ENGLAND
Hazzard, S. The transit of Venus
Hill, R. The Stranger House
AUSTRALIANS -- MALAYSIA
Carey, P. My life as a fake
AUSTRIA -- HISTORY -- 1867-1918
Appelfeld, A. Until the dawn's light
AUSTRIA -- RURAL LIFE
Stewart, M. Airs above the ground
AUSTRIA -- VIENNA
Lightman, A. P. Einstein's dreams
MacInnes, H. Prelude to terror
Musil, R. The man without qualities
Skibell, J. A curable romantic
Winer, A. The marriage artist
AUSTRIANS -- ARGENTINA
Swann, M. The foreigners
AUSTRIANS -- ETHNIC IDENTITY
Gass, W. H. Middle C
AUTHORITARIANISM *See* Fascism; Totalitarianism
Authority. VanderMeer, J.
AUTHORS
Adrian, C. The great night
Aira, C. The literary conference
Atkins, A. Devil's garden
Auster, P. Invisible
Auster, P. Oracle night
Barker, P. The eye in the door
Barker, P. Regeneration
Barnes, L. The Perfect Ghost
Baxter, C. The feast of love
Bear, E. Ink and steel
Bellow, S. Humboldt's gift
Benford, G. Foundation's fear
Benjamin, M. Alice I have been
Berger, T. Being invisible
Bolano, R. 2666
Bolano, R. Monsieur Pain
Bolano, R. Nazi literature in the Americas
Boswell, R. Century's son
Boyd, W. Any human heart
Bulgakov, M. A. The master and Margarita
Cameron, P. The city of your final destination
Chabon, M. Wonder boys
Chesnutt, C. W. Stories, novels, & essay
Clarke, B. Exley
Clinch, J. Finn
Coetzee, J. M. Foe
Coetzee, J. M. Summertime
Cohen, J. Book of numbers
Cook, T. H. Instruments of night
Cooley, M. The archivist
Crowley, J. Lord Byron's novel
Cunningham, M. The hours
Cunningham, M. Specimen days
Delaney, E. J. Broken Irish
Dixon, S. Old friends
Dufresne, J. Requiem, Mass.
Dunne, D. Too much money
Durrell, L. Balthazar
Durrell, L. Clea
Egan, J. The keep
Ellis, B. E. Imperial bedrooms
Ellis, B. E. Lunar Park
Fairstein, L. Entombed
Faulks, S. Devil may care
Fitzgerald, P. The blue flower
Flanagan, R. Wanting
Foer, J. S. Everything is illuminated
Foulds, A. The quickening maze
Fowler, K. J. The Jane Austen book club
Fuentes, C. The old gringo

Furst, A. Blood of victory
Gaddis, W. A frolic of his own
Galbraith, R. The silkworm
Gessen, K. All the sad young literary men
Gide, A. The counterfeiters (Les faux-monnayeurs)
Godwin, G. The good husband
Goldman, F. Say her name
Gottlieb, E. Now you see him
Grass, G. The box
Greene, G. The end of the affair
Greene, G. The honorary consul
Gruber, M. The book of air and shadows
Haasse, H. S. In a dark wood wandering
Haig, M. The dead fathers club
Hale, S. Austenland
Hansen, R. Exiles
Harris, R. The ghost
Heller, J. Good as Gold
Higashino, K. Malice
Hockensmith, S. Holmes on the range
Hockensmith, S. On the wrong track
Holland, T. The archivist's story
Hollinghurst, A. The stranger's child
Horowitz, A. The House of Silk
Horowitz, A. Magpie murders
Hosseini, K. The kite runner
Hurwitz, G. The crime writer
I am the brother of XX
Iles, G. The devil's punchbowl
Irving, J. The world according to Garp
Jance, J. A. Queen of the night
Jio, S. The violets of March
Johnson, M. Pym
Jordan, H. When she woke
Kehlmann, D. Fame
Kennedy, D. The moment
Kinder, C. Honeymooners
King, L. R. The game
King, S. Misery
King, S. Salem's Lot
Kotzwinkle, W. The bear went over the mountain
Krauss, N. Great house
Krauss, N. The history of love
Lafferty, M. The shambling guide to New York City
Lashner, W. Kockroach
Littell, R. The Stalin epigram
Lodge, D. Thinks--
London, J. Martin Eden
Lopez, B. H. Resistance
Maguire, G. Son of a witch
Makine, A. The life of an unknown man
Malouf, D. Ransom
Mann, T. Death in Venice
Marks, J. Fangland
Markson, D. The last novel
Markson, D. Vanishing point
Marsh, N. Light thickens
Martel, Y. Beatrice and Virgil
Martin, V. Mary Reilly
Matheson, R. Hunted past reason
Maugham, W. S. Cakes and ale
McCann, C. Thirteen ways of looking
McEwan, I. The child in time
McLain, P. The Paris wife
McLarty, R. Art in America
Meyer, N. The seven-per-cent solution
Miller, A. Oxygen
Moore, G. The Sherlockian
Morrow, J. The last witchfinder
Mortimer, J. Felix in the underworld
Morton, B. Florence Gordon
Moses, K. Wintering
Munoz Molina, A. A manuscript of ashes
Murdoch, I. The book and the brotherhood
Murray, P. The mark and the void
My struggle
Nabokov, V. V. Look at the harlequins!
Nabokov, V. V. Novels and memoirs, 1941-1951
Naipaul, V. S. Half a life
Naipaul, V. S. Magic seeds
Naipaul, V. S. A way in the world
Naslund, S. J. Ahab's wife; or, The star-gazer
Naslund, S. J. The Fountain of St. James Court
Pearl, M. The Poe shadow
Peet, M. The Murdstone trilogy
Phillips, S. E. Heroes are my weakness
Oates, J. C. Jack of Spades
Oates, J. C. Wild nights!
O'Connor, J. Ghost light
Oe, K. The changeling
Ōe, K. Death by Water
Oe, K. A quiet life
Ondaatje, M. The cat's table
Parini, J. The passages of H.M.
Pearl, M. The Dante Club
Pearl, M. The last Dickens
Phillips, A. The tragedy of Arthur
Pipkin, J. Woodsburner
Pirie, D. The patient's eyes
Powell, J. The breaking of eggs
Powers, K. Capote in Kansas
Powers, R. Galatea 2.2
Price, N. Night woman
Price, R. Samaritan
Prose, F. Blue angel
Pyper, A. The killing circle
Reuss, F. Mohr
Reyn, I. What happened to Anna K.
Rich, N. The mayor's tongue
Richler, M. Barney's version
Roberts, N. Angel's fall
Robertson, M. The brothers of Baker Street
Rosales, G. The halfway house
Rose, J. Blackest bird

Rosenblatt, R. Lapham rising
Ross, A. Mr. Peanut
Roth, H. From bondage
Roth, H. Requiem for Harlem
Roth, P. Exit ghost
Roth, P. The anatomy lesson
Roth, P. The ghost writer
Roth, P. My life as a man
Roth, P. Zuckerman bound
Roth, P. Zuckerman unbound
Ruiz Zafon, C. The angel's game
Russell, M. D. Dreamers of the day
Schwarz, C. All is vanity
Self, W. Dorian
Sherwood, F. The book of splendor
Smith, A. The accidental
Spark, M. Loitering with intent
Steinke, R. Holy skirts
Straub, P. In the night room
Straub, P. Lost boy lost girl
Styron, W. Sophie's choice
Syjuco, M. Ilustrado
Tao Lin Taipei
Tearne, R. Mosquito
Theroux, P. My secret history
Tóibín, C. The master
Tournier, M. Friday
Truong, M. The book of salt
Tsypkin, L. Summer in Baden-Baden
Twain, M. The gilded age and later novels
Tyler, A. The accidental tourist
Updike, J. Gertrude and Claudius
Upson, N. Two for sorrow
Uris, L. QB VII
Vargas Llosa, M. Aunt Julia and the scriptwriter
Verissimo, L. F. Borges and the eternal orangutans
Vidal, G. Burr
Vine, B. The chimney sweeper's boy
Vonnegut, K. Breakfast of champions
Vonnegut, K. Timequake
Walker, A. The way forward is with a broken heart
Wallace, I. The prize
Weisgall, D. The world before her
Westlake, D. E. The hook
White, E. Hotel de Dream
Wideman, J. E. Fanon
Wilhelm, K. The deepest water
Wilson, K. The family Fang
Wind, R. In the midnight rain
Winslow, D. Satori
Wolfe, T. Of time and the river
Wolfe, T. The web and the rock
Wolfe, T. You can't go home again
Wolff, T. Old school
Wolitzer, M. The wife
Woodrell, D. Give us a kiss

AUTHORS -- CRIMES AGAINST
King, S. Finders Keepers

AUTHORS AND PUBLISHERS
See also Authorship; Contracts; Publishers and publishing

AUTHORS' SPOUSES
Fowler, T. A. Z
Wolitzer, M. The wife

AUTHORS, AMERICAN -- 19TH CENTURY -- DEATH
Pearl, M. The Poe shadow

AUTHORS, ENGLISH -- 19TH CENTURY
Jarvis, S. Death and Mr. Pickwick

AUTHORS, IRISH
The Short Fiction of Flann O'Brien

AUTHORS, SPANISH -- 20TH CENTURY -- INTERVIEWS
A thousand forests in one acorn

AUTHORSHIP
Auster, P. Oracle night
Carey, P. My life as a fake
Clarke, B. An arsonist's guide to writers' homes in New England
Currie, R. Flimsy little plastic miracles
Fishman, B. A replacement life
Fossum, K. Broken
Frame, J. In the memorial room
Hellenga, R. The Italian lover
Howard, M. The rags of time
Never any end to Paris
Oyeyemi, H. Mr. Fox
Peet, M. The Murdstone trilogy
Saramago, J. The history of the siege of Lisbon
Savage, S. The cry of the sloth
Savage, S. Glass
Vila-Matas, E. Montano's malady
White, E. Hotel de Dream

AUTISM
Cash, W. A land more kind than home
Dicks, M. Memoirs of an imaginary friend
Moon, E. The speed of dark
Gottlieb, E. Best boy

AUTISM IN ADOLESCENCE
Ludwig, B. Ginny Moon

AUTISM SPECTRUM DISORDERS *See* Autism

AUTISTIC CHILDREN
Haddon, M. The curious incident of the dog in the night-time
Leimbach, M. Daniel isn't talking
Ludwig, B. Ginny Moon
Perry, D. This is just exactly like you
Picoult, J. House rules
Rucker, R. v. B. Postsingular
Silver, M. The god of war
Stuckey-French, E. Revenge of the radioactive lady

AUTISTIC PEOPLE
See also People with mental disabilities
Gottlieb, E. Best boy

AUTISTIC SPECTRUM DISORDERS *See* Autism

AUTOBIOGRAPHICAL FICTION

Agee, J. Let us now praise famous men; A death in the family, and shorter fiction
The emigrants
Isherwood, C. The Berlin stories
Keilson, H. Life goes on
McMillan, T. How Stella got her groove back
Miller, K. E. Q. An angry-ass black woman
My struggle
Thelen, A. V. The island of second sight
Walls, J. Half broke horses
AUTOBIOGRAPHICAL FICTION
See also Biographical fiction
AUTOBIOGRAPHICAL GRAPHIC NOVELS
See also Graphic novels
AUTOBIOGRAPHICAL STORIES
Adler, H. G. Panorama
Baldwin, J. Go tell it on the mountain
Ballard, J. G. Empire of the Sun
Coetzee, J. M. Summertime
Colette The complete Claudine
Crafts, H. The bondswomans narrative
Dexter, P. Spooner
Dickens, C. David Copperfield
Dufresne, J. Requiem, Mass.
Eliot, G. Middlemarch
Ellis, B. E. Lunar Park
Gao Xingjian Soul mountain
Godwin, G. Queen of the underworld
Goldman, F. Say her name
Grass, G. The box
Guo Xiaolu Twenty fragments of a ravenous youth
Jhabvala, R. P. My nine lives
Joyce, J. A portrait of the artist as a young man
Kazantzakis, N. Zorba the Greek
Keilson, H. Comedy in a minor key
Kerouac, J. On the road
Kincaid, J. Autobiography of my mother
Kinder, C. Honeymooners
Lee, G. China boy
London, J. Martin Eden
Makine, A. Dreams of my Russian summers
Malraux, A. Man's hope
Maugham, W. S. Of human bondage
Melville, H. Omoo: a narrative of adventures in the South Seas
Melville, H. Typee: a peep at Polynesian life
Miller, H. Tropic of Cancer
Miller, H. Tropic of Capricorn
Nabokov, V. V. Look at the harlequins!
Naipaul, V. S. A way in the world
Oe, K. The changeling
Oe, K. A quiet life
Ondaatje, M. The cat's table
Plath, S. The bell jar
Powell, A. A dance to the music of time
Powers, R. Galatea 2.2
Proust, M. The captive [and] The fugitive
Proust, M. The Guermantes way
Proust, M. Remembrance of things past
Proust, M. Sodom and Gomorrah
Proust, M. Swann's way
Proust, M. Time regained
Proust, M. Within a budding grove
Roth, H. A diving rock on the Hudson
Roth, H. From bondage
Roth, H. Requiem for Harlem
Roth, H. A star shines over Mt. Morris Park
Roth, P. The anatomy lesson
Roth, P. The ghost writer
Roth, P. My life as a man
Roth, P. Zuckerman bound
Roth, P. Zuckerman unbound
Sand, G. Lelia
The sorrow of war
Stanisic, S. How the soldier repairs the gramophone
Styron, W. Sophie's choice
Svevo, I. Zeno's conscience
Theroux, P. My secret history
Tolstoy, L. Childhood, Boyhood and Youth
Tsypkin, L. Summer in Baden-Baden
Vann, D. Legend of a suicide
Vonnegut, K. Slaughterhouse-five
Vonnegut, K. Timequake
Ward, M. J. The snake pit
Whitehead, C. Sag Harbor
Wolfe, T. Look homeward, angel
Wolfe, T. O lost
Wolfe, T. Of time and the river
Wolfe, T. The web and the rock
AUTOBIOGRAPHIES
See also Biography
The **autobiography** of Fidel Castro. Fuentes, N.
The **autobiography** of Miss Jane Pittman. Gaines, E. J.
Autobiography of my mother. Kincaid, J.
The **autograph** man. Smith, Z.
AUTOGRAPHS
See also Biography; Writing
AUTOIMMUNE DISEASES
See also Diseases
AUTOMATA *See* Robots
AUTOMATIC MACHINERY *See* Automation
AUTOMATION
Vonnegut, K. Player piano
AUTOMATONS *See* Robots
AUTOMOBILE ACCIDENTS *See* Traffic accidents
AUTOMOBILE DRIVERS
Howard, R. Driving the king
Sallis, J. Drive
Sallis, J. Driven
AUTOMOBILE INDUSTRY
Johnson, D. E. Detroit shuffle
AUTOMOBILE RACES
Stein, G. The art of racing in the rain
AUTOMOBILE TRAVEL

See also Transportation; Travel; Voyages and travels
Doig, I. Last bus to wisdom
AUTOMOBILES
Boucher, C. How to keep your Volkswagen alive
Hawke, E. Ash Wednesday
AUTOMOBILES -- ACCIDENTS *See* Traffic accidents
AUTOMOBILES -- TOURING
Merullo, R. Breakfast with Buddha
AUTOMOTIVE INDUSTRY *See* Automobile industry
Autonomous. Newitz, A.
AUTOSUGGESTION *See* Hypnotism; Mental suggestion
Autumn. Smith, A.
Autumn bones. Carey, J.
The **Autumn** Bride. Gracie, A.
The **autumn** of the patriarch. Garcia Marquez, G.
Available dark. Hand, E.
Avalon. Seton, A.
AVARICE
Atwood, M. The blind assassin
Bialosky, J. The prize
Caputo, P. Acts of faith
Dickens, C. Our mutual friend
Estleman, L. D. Gas City
Frayn, M. Headlong
Goddard, R. Beyond recall
Green, G. D. Ravens
Grisham, J. The partner
Harrison, C. The finder
Haslett, A. Union Atlantic
Jen, G. Typical American
Johansen, I. And then you die--
Keesey, A. Little century
Lanchester, J. Fragrant Harbor
Lopez, B. H. Resistance
Mahfouz, N. Children of the alley
Martin, C. W. How to sell
McCarthy, C. No country for old men
Meyers, K. The work of wolves
Moore, C. The Serpent of Venice
Norman, H. The haunting of L
Palmer, M. Miracle cure
Phillips, A. Prague
Pronzini, B. The crimes of Jordan Wise
Rash, R. Serena
Richler, M. Solomon Gursky was here
Robbins, T. Half asleep in frog pajamas
Smith, S. A simple plan
Tremain, R. The color
Unsworth, B. Sacred hunger
Wolfe, T. A man in full
AVARICE
See also Sin
Avenger. Forsyth, F.
AVENTURE TRAVEL
Nevill, A. The ritual
Avenue of mysteries. Irving, J.
Avery and Blake novels [series]
Carter, M. J. The Strangler Vine
AVIATION *See* Aeronautics
The **aviator's** wife. Benjamin, M.
AVIATORS *See* Air pilots
Avon romance [series]
Chase, L. Dukes Prefer Blondes
Chase, L. L. Silk is for seduction
Dare, T. Do you want to start a scandal
Await your reply. Chaon, D.
The **awakening** land. Richter, C.
Away. Urquhart, J.
The **awkward** age. Segal, F.
Awp award series in the novel [series]
Motherlunge
The **ax.** Westlake, D. E.
AZTECS
Levack, S. Demon of the air
Sherwood, F. Night of sorrows

B

B is for burglar. Grafton, S.
Baalbergen, Sarah van, 1607- approximately 1638
About
Smith, D. The last painting of Sara De Vos
Babayaga. Barlow, T.
Babbitt. Lewis, S.
Babel-17 ; Empire star. Delany, S. R.
Babel, I. (Isaac), 1894-1940
About
Holland, T. The archivist's story
Babi Yar. Anatoli, A.
BABI YAR MASSACRE, 1941
Anatoli, A. Babi Yar
BABOONS
See also Apes
BABY SITTERS
Iles, G. Turning angel
Baby, would I lie? Westlake, D. E.
BABYLONIA
Anton, M. Rav Hisda's daughter, book I, apprentice
BACHELORS *See* Single men
Van Dyken, R. Cheater
Warren, S. M. Take a chance on me
Back of beyond. Box, C. J.
Back roads. O'Dell, T.
Back story. Parker, R. B.
Back to Back.
Back to blood. Wolfe, T.
Back when we were grownups. Tyler, A.
BACTERIA
See also Microorganisms; Parasites
BACTERIAL INFECTIONS
See also Diseases
Bad Blood. Dahl, A.
Bad Boy Brawly Brown. Mosley, W.
Bad company. Higgins, J.

Bad dirt. Proulx, A.
Bad dreams and other stories. Hadley, T.
The **bad** girl. Vargas Llosa, M.
Bad Girl Creek. Mapson
Bad ground. Cramer, W. D.
Bad intentions. Fossum, K.
Bad Little Falls. Doiron, P.
Bad monkey. Hiassen, C.
Bad moon rising. Gorman, E.
Bad news. Westlake, D. E.
The **bad** place. Koontz, D. R.
The **bad** seed. March, W.
Bad things happen. Dolan, H.
Badenheim 1939. Appelfeld, A.
Badger boy. Kelton, E.
Badlands. Box, C. J.
Badlands. Bowen, P.
BADLANDS (S.D.)
Weisgarber, A. The personal history of Rachel Dupree
BAGHDAD (IRAQ)
Robotham, M. The wreckage
Saadawi, A. Frankenstein in Baghdad
Bagombo snuff box: uncollected short fiction. Vonnegut, K.
Bahlmann, Anna Catherine, 1849-1916
About
Fields, J. The age of desire
BAIL
Leonard, E. Rum punch
A Bailey Ruth ghost novel [series]
Hart, C. Ghost gone wild
Bailey's Cafe. Naylor, G.
Baker towers. Haigh, J.
BAKERS
Picoult, J. The Storyteller
BALANCE OF NATURE *See* Ecology
Balance of power. Patterson, R. N.
BALDNESS
Kilpack, J. S. A heart revealed
BALKAN PENINSULA
McNally, T. M. The goat bridge
Obreht, T. The tiger's wife
BALL GAMES
See also Games
The **ballad** of Frankie Silver. McCrumb, S.
The **ballad** of Tom Dooley. McCrumb, S.
The **ballad** of Trenchmouth Taggart. Taylor, M. G.
BALLADS
See also Literature; Poetry; Songs
BALLERINAS
Roorbach, B. Life among giants
BALLET
Godden, R. Pippa passes
BALLET DANCERS
Buchanan, C. M. The painted girls
Stachniak, E. The chosen maiden
BALLET DANCERS
See also Dancers
BALLISTIC MISSILES
See also Guided missiles; Nuclear weapons; Rockets (Aeronautics)
BALLOONS
See also Aeronautics
BALLOT *See* Elections
Balthasar's odyssey. Maalouf, A.
Balthazar. Durrell, L.
BALTIMORE (MD.)
Criswell, M. What to do about Annie?
Lippman, L. After I'm gone
Bamboo and blood. Church, J.
Band of angels. Warren, R. P.
Bandbox. Mallon, T.
Bandit queen boogie. Hayter, S.
BANDITS *See* Thieves
BANDS (MUSIC)
Wimberley, D. The king of Colored Town
Banewreaker. Carey, J.
Bang the drum slowly. Harris, M.
BANGALORE (INDIA)
Mukherjee, B. Miss New India
Sankaran, L. The hope factory
Bangkok 8. Burdett, J.
BANGLADESH
Hensher, P. Scenes from early life
BANGLADESHIS -- ENGLAND
Ali, M. Brick lane
Banishing Verona. Livesey, M.
BANK ROBBERIES
See also Theft
Hurwitz, G. The survivor
Laukkanen, O. Criminal enterprise
Leonard, E. Raylan
BANK ROBBERIES -- UNITED STATES -- FICTION
Ford, R. Canada
BANK ROBBERS
Black, L. Takeover
Estleman, L. D. The adventures of Johnny Vermillion
Higgins, G. V. The friends of Eddie Coyle
Robotham, M. The wreckage
Tyler, A. Earthly possessions
Westlake, D. E. Bank shot
Bank shot. Westlake, D. E.
BANKERS
Haslett, A. Union Atlantic
Plain, B. Tapestry
Robotham, M. The wreckage
Sarton, M. Anger
Wolfe, T. The bonfire of the vanities
BANKS
Campbell, B. M. Brothers and sisters
Le Carre, J. A most wanted man
Le Carre, J. Our kind of traitor
BANKS AND BANKING
See also Business; Capital; Commerce; Finance
BANKS AND BANKING

Murray, P. The mark and the void
A **Banquet** of Consequences. George, E.
BANQUETS *See* Dining; Dinners
BAR *See* Lawyers
Barabbas. Lagerkvist, P.
Barabbas (Biblical figure)
About
Lagerkvist, P. Barabbas
BARBADOS
Jackson, N. The Star Side of Bird Hill
Barbara the slut and other people. Holmes, L.
The **barbarian** nurseries. Tobar, H.
Barber, Frank, d. 1801
About
Phillips, C. Foreigners
BARBERS
Berry, W. Jayber Crow
Dovey, C. Blood kin
BARCELONA (SPAIN)
Hill, A. The summer of dead toys
Ruiz Zafon, C. The prisoner of heaven
Barchester Towers. Trollope, A.
Bare bones. Reichs, K. J.
Barefoot dogs. Ruiz-Camacho, A.
Barely a lady. Dreyer, E.
Bark. Moore, L.
Barkskins. Proulx, A.
Barney's version. Richler, M.
Baron in the trees. Calvino, I.
BAROQUE ART
See also Art
BARRINGTON, STONE (FICTITIOUS CHARACTER)
Woods, S. Doing hard time
Woods, S. Cold paradise
Woods, S. Dirty work
Woods, S. L.A. dead
Woods, S. Reckless abandon
Woods, S. The short forever
BARRISTERS *See* Lawyers
BARS (DRINKING ESTABLISHMENTS)
Doig, I. The bartender's tale
Sáenz, B. A. Everything Begins and Ends at the Kentucky Club
BARS (DRINKING ESTABLISHMENTS) -- ITALY
Banner, C. The house at the edge of night
The **bartender's** tale. Doig, I.
BARTENDERS
Drury, T. The driftless area
Huston, C. Caught stealing
Koontz, D. R. Velocity
BASCOM, ERNIE (FICTITIOUS CHARACTER)
Limón, M. Mr. Kill
BASEBALL
Harbach, C. The art of fielding
Harris, M. Bang the drum slowly
Malamud, B. The natural
Parker, R. B. Double play
Ring around the bases
Roth, P. The great American novel
BASEBALL EXECUTIVES
Everett, P. L. I am Not Sidney Poitier
BASEBALL PLAYERS
See also Athletes
BASEBALL PLAYERS
Everett, P. Suder
Parker, R. B. Double play
Scottoline, L. One perfect lie
Yocum, R. A welcome murder
BASEBALL STORIES -- UNITED STATES
Sayers, V. The powers
BASEBALL TEAMS
See also Baseball; Sports teams
Basket case. Hiaasen, C.
BASQUE AMERICANS
Johnson, C. Death without company
BASQUES -- SPAIN
Urza, G. All that followed
The **bastard** of Istanbul. Shafak, E.
Bastard out of Carolina. Allison, D.
BASTILLE
Black, C. Murder in the Bastille
BASTOGNE, BATTLE OF *See* Ardennes (France), Battle of the, 1944-1945
The **Bat.**
BATH (ENGLAND)
Lovesey, P. Diamond dust
Lovesey, P. The vault
Bathing the Lion. Carroll, J.
The **bathing** women.
BATTERING OF WIVES *See* Wife abuse
Battle cry. Uris, L.
BATTLE OF THE BULGE *See* Ardennes (France), Battle of the, 1944-1945
The **battle** of the Villa Fiorita. Godden, R.
Battleborn. Watkins, C. V.
BATTLEFIELDS
See also Battles
BATTLES
See also Military art and science; Military history; War
Abercrombie, J. The heroes
Hurley, K. The Mirror Empire
Weber, D. By schism rent asunder
Baudolino. Eco, U.
Baum, L. Frank, 1856-1919
Adaptation
Maguire, G. Son of a witch
The **Bawdy** basket. Marston, E.
The **bay** of love and sorrows. Richards, D. A.
Bay of souls. Stone, R.
The **bazaar** of bad dreams. King, S.
BAZAARS *See* Fairs
Be cool. Leonard, E.
Be my knife. Grossman, D.
Be near me. O'Hagan, A.

Be safe I love you. Hoffman, C.
BEACHES
See also Seashore
The **bean** trees. Kingsolver, B.
The **bear** and the nightingale. Arden, K.
The **bear** went over the mountain. Kotzwinkle, W.
BEARS
King, S. The girl who loved Tom Gordon
Kotzwinkle, W. The bear went over the mountain
Pollen, B. The summer of the bear
The **Beast** in the Red Forest. Eastland, S.
Beast Master's ark. Norton, A.
Beastly Things. Leon, D.
BEASTS *See* Animals
BEAT GENERATION
See also American literature; Bohemianism
Beat to quarters. Forester, C. S.
Beatlebone. Barry, K.
BEATLES
Barry, K. Beatlebone
BEATLES
See also Bands (Music)
Beatrice
About
Jones, S. Four sisters, all queens
Beatrice and Virgil. Martel, Y.
Beaufort. Leshem, R.
The **beautiful** and damned. Fitzgerald, F. S.
A **beautiful** blue death. Finch, C.
The **beautiful** bureaucrat. Phillips, H.
Beautiful children. Bock, C.
Beautiful gravity. Hyatt, M.
Beautiful Maria of my soul. Hijuelos, O.
The **beautiful** mystery. Penny, L.
The **beautiful** room is empty. White, E.
Beautiful Ruins. Walter, J.
The **beautiful** things that heaven bears. Mengestu, D.
Beautiful you. Palahniuk, C.
BEAUTY CONTESTS
See also Contests
A **beauty** so rare. Alexander, T.
BEAUTY, PERSONAL *See* Personal appearance; Personal grooming
Because it is bitter, and because it is my heart. Oates, J. C.
Becoming Madame Mao. Min, A.
BED AND BREAKFAST ACCOMMODATIONS
Binchy, M. A week in winter
Bedbugs. Winters, B. H.
Bedding Lord Ned. MacKenzie, S.
Bedford Square. Perry, A.
Bedlam. Hollingshead, G.
The **bedlam** detective. Gallagher, S.
The **Bedlam** Stacks. Pulley, N.
BEDOUINS
See also Arabs
BEDTIME
See also Night; Sleep
Bee season. Goldberg, M.
The **beekeeper's** apprentice, or, on the segregation of the queen. King, L. R.
BEEKEEPING
The Blood of Angels
BEES
See also Insects
The **Beet** Queen. Erdrich, L.
Beethoven was one-sixteenth black. Gordimer, N.
BEETLES
See also Insects
Nineveh
Before and after. Brown, R.
Before I go to sleep. Watson, S. J.
Before the Fall. Hawley, N.
Before they are hanged. Abercrombie, J.
Before Versailles. Koen, K.
Before you suffocate your own fool self. Evans, D.
A **beggar** in Jerusalem. Wiesel, E.
The **beggar** king.
Beggarman, thief. Shaw, I.
The **beginner's** goodbye. Tyler, A.
The **beginning** place. Le Guin, U. K.
Beguiling the beauty. Thomas, S.
BEHAVIOR GENETICS
See also Genetics; Psychology
Behold the Dreamers. Mbue, I.
Beiderbecke, Bix, 1903-1931
About
Turner, F. W. 1929
Beijing coma.
Being dead. Crace, J.
Being invisible. Berger, T.
Being there. Kosinski, J. N.
BEL AIR (LOS ANGELES, CALIF.)
Woods, S. Doing hard time
Bel canto. Patchett, A.
BELGIUM
Gholson, C. A fish trapped inside the wind
BELGIUM -- 19TH CENTURY
Stone, I. Lust for life
BELGIUM -- FLANDERS
Dunnett, D. Niccolo rising
Belgrave Square. Perry, A.
Believing the lie. George, E.
The **bell.** Murdoch, I.
A **bell** for Adano. Hersey, J.
The **bell** jar. Plath, S.
The **bell** ringers. Porter, H.
Bell, Gertrude Margaret Lowthian, 1868-1926
About
Russell, M. D. Dreamers of the day
Bell, Vanessa, 1879-1961
About
Parmar, P. Vanessa and her sister
Bellefleur. Oates, J. C.
Bellevue Square. Redhill, M.

Bellfield Hall, or, The observations of Miss Dido Kent. Dean, A.
BELLS AND BELL RINGERS
Hersey, J. A bell for Adano
Hugo, V. The hunchback of Notre Dame
Bellweather rhapsody. Racculia, K.
A Belmont Mansion novel [series]
Alexander, T. A beauty so rare
BELONGING (SOCIAL PSYCHOLOGY)
Fridlund, E. History of wolves
Beloved. Morrison, T.
Beloved poison. Thomson, E. S.
Beluga. Pearson, T. R.
Ben-Hur. Wallace, L.
A **bend** in the river. Naipaul, V. S.
Bendigo Shafter. L'Amour, L.
Benediction. Haruf, K.
The **benediction** of Brother Cadfael. Peters, E.
BENEFICIAL INSECTS
See also Economic zoology; Insects
BENGALI LANGUAGE
See also Indian languages; Language and languages
Bent Road. Roy, L.
BEQUESTS *See* Gifts; Inheritance and succession; Wills
BEREAVEMENT
Adrian, C. The great night
Banks, R. The sweet hereafter
Boswell, R. Century's son
Clegg, B. Did you ever have a family
Cohen, L. H. The grief of others
Doughty, L. Whatever you love
Falling out of time
Fitch, J. Paint it black
Frankel, L. Goodbye for now
Goldman, F. Say her name
Gottlieb, E. Now you see him
Hadley, T. The London train
Hall, S. The raw shark texts
Hart, J. The truth about love
Henkin, J. The world without you
Hood, A. The knitting circle
Joss, M. The night following
The lake
Lasser, S. Say nice things about Detroit
Lodato, V. Mathilda Savitch
McCann, C. Let the great world spin
McIntosh, W. Hitchers
Miller, S. Lost in the forest
Monette, P. Afterlife
Moore, L. February
Morley, I. Come Sunday
Norman, H. Next life might be kinder
Odell, J. The healing
Petterson, P. In the wake
Pollen, B. The summer of the bear
Prose, F. Goldengrove
Pywell, S. L. What happened to Henry
Rice, L. Last kiss
Rice, L. The lemon orchard
Rice, L. The letters
Roy-Bhattacharya, J. The watch
Schwartz, J. B. Reservation Road
Sebold, A. The lovely bones
St. Aubyn, E. At last
Strayed, C. Torch
Swift, G. Wish you were here
Trollope, J. The other family
Tropper, J. How to talk to a widower
Tuck, L. I married you for happiness
Tyler, A. The beginner's goodbye
Umrigar, T. N. The weight of heaven
Walbert, K. The gardens of Kyoto
Waldman, A. Red Hook Road
Watrous, M. If you follow me
Williams, A. J. Down from Cascom Mountain
Winston, L. Good grief
Wolitzer, M. Surrender, Dorothy
Yoshimoto, B. Kitchen
BEREAVEMENT
See also Emotions
BEREAVEMENT IN YOUTH
Collins, C. The gamal
BERGEN-BELSEN (GERMANY: CONCENTRATION CAMP)
See also Concentration camps
BERKELEY (CALIF.)
Chabon, M. Telegraph Avenue
Berkley Sensation historical romance [series]
Thomas, S. The Luckiest Lady in London
BERLIN (GERMANY) -- FICTION
Isherwood, C. The Berlin stories
Zimler, R. The seventh gate
BERLIN (GERMANY) -- HISTORY -- 1918-1945
Edugyan, E. Half-blood blues
Gillham, D. R. City of women
Grossman, P. Children of wrath
Berlin game. Deighton, L.
The **Berlin** stories. Isherwood, C.
Bernadette, Saint, 1844-1879
About
Werfel, F. The song of Bernadette
Bernie Gunther [series]
Kerr, P. The lady from Zagreb
Kerr, P. Prussian blue
Berrybender narratives [series]
McMurtry, L. Sin killer
Berserker's star. Saberhagen, F.
Bertie and the seven bodies. Lovesey, P.
Bess Crawford mysteries [series]
Todd, C. A duty to the dead
Best American mystery stories [date]
The **Best** American mystery stories of the century.
The **best** American noir of the century.
The **Best** American short stories.

BEST BOOKS
See also Books
Best boy. Gottlieb, E.
The **best** defense. Wilhelm, K.
BEST FRIENDS -- DEATH
Harper, J. The dry
The **Best** from Fantasy & Science Fiction.
The **Best** from fantasy & science fiction: the fiftieth anniversary anthology.
Best kept secret. Archer, J.
The **Best** Man. Higgins, K.
The **best** of friends. Trollope, J.
The **best** of Gene Wolfe. Wolfe, G.
The **Best** of Larry Niven. Niven, L.
The **best** people in the world. Tussing, J.
BEST SELLERS (BOOKS)
See also Books and reading
The **best** short stories of Bret Harte. Harte, B.
The **best** short stories of Dostoevsky. Dostoyevsky, F.
The **best** short stories of O. Henry. Henry, O.
The **best** short stories of W. Somerset Maugham. Maugham, W. S.
Best staged plans. Cook, C.
The **best** western stories of John Jakes.
BESTIARIES
See also Books
BETHLEM ROYAL HOSPITAL (LONDON, ENGLAND)
Hollingshead, G. Bedlam
The **betrayal.** Dunmore, H.
BETRAYAL
Bezmozgis, D. The Betrayers
Dodd, C. The woman who couldn't scream
The **Betrayers.** Bezmozgis, D.
BETROTHAL
See also Courtship; Marriage
McCall Smith, A. The full cupboard of life
McKenzie, E. The portable Veblen
Betsey Brown. Shange, N.
A **Better** World. Sakey, M.
BETTING *See* Gambling
Between heaven and here. Straight, S.
Between love and honor. Lapierre, A.
Between my father and the king. Frame, J.
Between summer's longing and winter's end.
Between the acts. Woolf, V.
Between, Georgia. Jackson, J.
BEVERAGES
See also Diet; Food
Beyond recall. Goddard, R.
Beyond recognition. Pearson, R.
Beyond the blue event horizon. Pohl, F.
Beyond the outposts. Brand, M.
BIBLE -- O.T. -- GENESIS
Diamant, A. The red tent
BIBLE -- TRANSLATING -- GREAT BRITAIN
Vantrease, B. R. The illuminator
BIBLE FICTION
Mailer, N. The Gospel according to the Son
Wolf, J. This scarlet cord
BIBLE FILMS
See also Motion pictures
BIBLE GAMES AND PUZZLES
See also Games; Puzzles
The **Bible** salesman. Edgerton, C.
BIBLE STORIES, ENGLISH -- N.T. GOSPELS
Rice, A. Christ the Lord: the road to Cana
BIBLE. N.T. GOSPELS -- HISTORY OF BIBLICAL EVENTS
Rollins, J. The blood Gospel
BIBLICAL CHARACTERS
Cain
Diamant, A. The red tent
Halter, M. Sarah
Lagerkvist, P. Barabbas
Maine, D. Fallen
Maine, D. The preservationist
BIBLICAL STORIES
Asch, S. The Apostle
Asch, S. The Nazarene
Cain
Crace, J. Quarantine
Diamant, A. The red tent
Edghill, I. Queenmaker
Halter, M. Sarah
Kazantzakis, N. The last temptation of Christ
Lagerkvist, P. Barabbas
Mailer, N. The Gospel according to the Son
Maine, D. Fallen
Maine, D. The preservationist
Rice, A. Christ the Lord: the road to Cana
Rice, A. Christ the Lord: out of Egypt
Wallace, L. Ben-Hur
Williams, N. John
BIBLIOGRAPHY -- RARE BOOKS *See* Rare books
BICYCLE TOURING
See also Camping; Cycling; Travel
Bierce, Ambrose, 1842-1914?
About
Fuentes, C. The old gringo
The **big** bad city. McBain, E.
The **big** blowdown. Pelecanos, G. P.
The **Big** book of adventure stories.
The **big** book of science fiction.
The **big** book of Sherlock Holmes stories.
Big Cherry Holler. Trigiani, A.
BIG DATA
McCarthy, T. Satin Island
The **big** exit. Carnoy, D.
Big fish. Wallace, D.
BIG GAME HUNTING
See also Hunting
Big girl small. DeWoskin, R.
The **big** girls. Moore, S.
The **big** green tent.

Big if. Costello, M.
Big little lies. Moriarty, L.
Big Lonesome. Scapellato, J.
Big machine. LaValle, V. D.
The **big** picture. Kennedy, D.
The **Big** Rock Candy Mountain. Stegner, W. E.
The **big** sky. Guthrie, A. B.
The **big** sleep. Chandler, R.
Big Stone Gap. Trigiani, A.
A **big** storm knocked it over. Colwin, L.
BIGAMY
Haigh, J. Mrs. Kimble
A **bigger** life. Smith, A.
BIGHORN MOUNTAINS (WYO. AND MONT.)
Johnson, C. Death without company
BIGOTRY *See* Prejudices; Toleration
BILDUNGSROMANS
Adiga, A. Selection day
Akhtar, A. American dervish
Allende, I. Maya's Notebook
Ball, J. How to set a fire and why
Bank, M. The wonder spot
Batuman, E. The idiot
Bender, A. The particular sadness of lemon cake
Beverly, B. Dodgers
Brown, R. M. Rubyfruit jungle
Canin, E. A Doubter's Almanac
Clemmons, Z. What we lose
Crain, C. Necessary errors
Earley, T. The blue star
Everett, P. L. I am Not Sidney Poitier
The girl in the tower
Groff, L. Arcadia
Henry, P. C. And then I found you
It's fine by me
Jacobson, H. The mighty Walzer
Johnson, D. Elsewhere, California
Khadivi, L. A good country
Krueger, W. K. Ordinary grace
Leithauser, B. The art student's war
Lewis, B. The preacher's daughter
Lodato, V. Edgar and Lucy
Lovett, A. Everlasting Lane
McDermott, A. Someone
Merullo, R. The talk-funny girl
Moore, S. The life of objects
My struggle
O'Brien, E. The love object
O'Donnell, L. The death of bees
Ondaatje, M. The cat's table
Patchett, A. Commonwealth
Prose, F. Goldengrove
Romano-Lax, A. The Spanish bow
Schwartzman, A. Eddie Signwriter
Solomon, A. Disgruntled
Villarreal, J. A. Pocho
Walker, K. T. The age of miracles
Walsh, T. The moon sisters
Walton, J. Among others
Wayne, T. The Love Song of Jonny Valentine
Winter, K. Annabel
Wolitzer, M. The Interestings
Woodson, J. Another Brooklyn
Yanagihara, H. A little life
The Year of the Comet
BILINGUAL BOOKS
See also Books; Editions
BILINGUALISM
See also Language and languages
The Bill Hodges trilogy [series]
King, S. End of watch
Bill Slider mysteries [series]
Harrod-Eagles, C. Old bones
Billy. French, A.
Billy Bathgate. Doctorow, E. L.
Billy Boyle. Benn, J. R.
Billy Budd, sailor. Melville, H.
Billy Lynn's long halftime walk. Fountain, B.
Billy Straight. Kellerman, J.
Billy, the Kid
About
Momaday, N. S. The ancient child
BINARY SYSTEM (MATHEMATICS)
See also Mathematics; Numbers
Bingo's Run. Levine, J. A.
Binocular vision. Pearlman, E.
Binti. Okorafor, N.
Binti. Okorafor, N.
BIOCHEMISTS
Benford, G. Foundation's fear
BIOENGINEERING
Watts, P. Starfish
BIOETHICS
See also Ethics
BIOETHICS
Ishiguro, K. Never let me go
Picoult, J. My sister's keeper
BIOFEEDBACK TRAINING
See also Feedback (Psychology); Mind and body; Psychology of learning; Psychotherapy
BIOGEOGRAPHY
See also Ecology; Geography
BIOGRAPHERS
Absolution
Boyd, W. Any human heart
Cameron, P. The city of your final destination
Cohen, J. Book of numbers
Vargas Llosa, M. The way to paradise
Wind, R. In the midnight rain
BIOGRAPHERS -- ENGLAND
Palin, M. The truth
BIOGRAPHICAL FICTION
Alcott, K. A touch of stardust
Ampuero, R. The Neruda case

Benjamin, M. The aviator's wife
Boyle, T. C. The women
Craig, C. Miss Burma
The dream of the Celt
Fields, J. The age of desire
George, M. The confessions of young Nero
Gordon, M. The liar's wife
Gregory, P. The red queen
Hicks, R. The widow of the south
Horan, N. Loving Frank
Lalami, L. The Moor's account
Mailer, N. The castle in the forest
Mantel, H. Bring up the bodies
McCrea, G. Mrs. Engels
Moehringer, J. R. Sutton
Sharratt, M. Illuminations
Stachniak, E. The chosen maiden
Thu Huong Duong The zenith
Williams, N. John
BIOGRAPHY & AUTOBIOGRAPHY -- PERSONAL MEMOIRS
Hudgins, A. The joker
BIOGRAPHY -- COLLECTIVE
Jones, S. Four sisters, all queens
BIOGRAPHY -- DICTIONARIES
See also Encyclopedias and dictionaries
BIOGRAPHY AS A LITERARY FORM
See also Authorship; Literature
BIOLOGICAL ENGINEERING *See* Bioengineering
BIOLOGISTS
Crichton, M. Prey
Ledgard, J. M. Submergence
Steinbeck, J. Cannery Row
Steinbeck, J. Sweet Thursday
BIOLOGISTS
See also Naturalists; Scientists
BIOLOGY
Bergman, M. M. Birds of a lesser paradise
BIOLOGY -- ECOLOGY *See* Ecology
BIOLOGY IN LITERATURE
Bergman, M. M. Birds of a lesser paradise
BIOMATHEMATICS
See also Biology; Mathematics
BIOMEDICAL ENGINEERING
DeLillo, D. Zero K
BIONICS
Pohl, F. Man Plus
Westerfeld, S. The risen empire
BIOTECHNOLOGY -- ENVIRONMENTAL ASPECTS
VanderMeer, J. Borne
BIOTERRORISM
See also Terrorism
McIntosh, W. Hitchers
The **bird** artist. Norman, H.
Bird Box. Malerman, J.
The **bird** of the river. Baker, K.
BIRD REFUGES -- INDIA -- NĀGPUR
Festing, I. A. The birdkeeper
BIRD WATCHING
Rice, L. Little night
The **birdkeeper.** Festing, I. A.
Birdman. Hayder, M.
BIRDS
Drayson, N. Guide to the birds of East Africa
Wharton, W. Birdy
BIRDS
See also Animals
BIRDS -- COLOR
See also Color
BIRDS -- INDIA
Festing, I. A. The birdkeeper
The **birds** fall down. West, R.
Birds of a feather. Winspear, J.
Birds of a lesser paradise. Bergman, M. M.
Birds of America. McCarthy, M.
Birds of paradise. Abu-Jaber, D.
Birds of prey. Smith, W. A.
BIRDS OF PREY
See also Birds; Predatory animals
Birds of prey. Jance, J. A.
Birds without wings. De Bernieres, L.
Birdsong. Faulks, S.
Birdy. Wharton, W.
BIRTH ATTENDANTS *See* Midwives
BIRTH CONTROL -- ETHICAL ASPECTS
See also Ethics
BIRTH DEFECTS
Novak, C. Breed
The **birth** of Venus. Dunant, S.
BIRTH ORDER
See also Children; Family
BIRTHDAY BOOKS
See also Birthdays; Calendars
The **birthday** of the world and other stories. Le Guin, U. K.
BIRTHDAYS
Welty, E. Losing battles
BIRTHFATHERS
Thompson, V. Murder on Lenox Hill
BISEXUALITY
Baldwin, J. Giovanni's room
Barker, P. The eye in the door
Irving, J. In one person
White, E. The married man
BISEXUALITY
See also Sex
The **Bishop's** Wife. Harrison, M. I.
BISHOPS
See also Clergy
A **bit** on the side. Trevor, W.
Bitter Eden. Afrika, T.
Bitter in the mouth. Truong, M.
Bitter medicine. Paretsky, S.
Bitter Spirits. Bennett, J.
Bitter sweet. Spencer, L.

BLACK ACTORS
See also Actors
BLACK AMERICANS *See* African Americans
Black and blue. Rankin, I.
Black and blue. Quindlen, A.
Black Betty. Mosley, W.
Black cherry blues. Burke, J. L.
BLACK CHILDREN
See also Children
Black cross. Iles, G.
The **black** dahlia. Ellroy, J.
Black dahlia & white rose. Oates, J. C.
BLACK DEATH *See* Plague
BLACK DEATH -- ITALY -- SIENA
Winawer, M. The scribe of Siena
Black dogs. McEwan, I.
Black Fridays. Sears, M.
Black girl/White girl. Oates, J. C.
BLACK HAND (UNITED STATES) -- HISTORY -- 20TH CENTURY
Stewart, A. Girl waits with gun
The **black** hawk. Bourne, J.
Black hole. Burns, C.
The **black** hour. Rader-Day, L.
Black house. King, S.
BLACK HUMOR (LITERATURE)
See also Fiction; Literature; Wit and humor
Black iris. Raeder, L.
BLACK LIBRARIANS
See also Librarians
Black light. Hunter, S.
The **Black** Lizard big book of Black Mask stories.
BLACK MAGIC (WITCHCRAFT) *See* Magic; Witchcraft
Black maps. Spiegelman, P.
BLACK MARKET
Leonard, E. Raylan
BLACK MUSICIANS
See also Musicians
BLACK MUSLIM LEADERS
Baker, K. Strivers Row
Black Narcissus. Godden, R.
BLACK NATIONALISM
See also African Americans -- Political activity; African Americans -- Race identity; Blacks -- Political activity; Blacks -- Race identity
The **black** opal. Holt, V.
Black orchids; &, the silent speaker. Stout, R.
Black River. Hulse, S. M.
Black sheep. Heyer, G.
Black ships. Graham, J.
Black storm. Poyer, D.
The **black** swan. Mann, T.
Black swan green. Mitchell, D.
The **black** tides of heaven. Yang, J. Y.
The **black** tower. Bayard, L.
The **black** tower. James, P. D.
Black water. Parker, T. J.
Black water. Oates, J. C.
The **black** widow. Silva, D.
Black widow. White, R. W.
BLACK WOMEN
See also Women
BLACK WOMEN
Miller, K. E. Q. An angry-ass black woman
Black women writers series
Butler, O. E. Kindred
Blackbird house. Hoffman, A.
The **blackboard** jungle. Hunter, E.
Blackest bird. Rose, J.
The **Blackhouse.** May, P.
Blacklands. Bauer, B.
Blacklist. Paretsky, S.
BLACKMAIL
Clark, M. The legal limit
Goddard, R. Into the blue
Greene, G. The heart of the matter
Grisham, J. The brethren
Marlette, D. Magic time
Meltzer, B. The tenth justice
Richards, D. A. The bay of love and sorrows
Riordan, R. Cold Springs
Woods, S. Dirt
Blackout. Willis, C.
BLACKS
Bell, M. S. All souls' rising
Conde, M. I, Tituba, black witch of Salem
Hill, L. Someone knows my name
Kincaid, J. Autobiography of my mother
Nunez, E. Grace
Phillips, C. A distant shore
Sanders, D. Clover
Straight, S. Take one candle light a room
Walker, A. Possessing the secret of joy
BLACKS -- BIOGRAPHY
See also Biography
BLACKS -- ENGLAND
Phillips, C. Foreigners
BLACKS -- FOLKLORE
See also Folklore
BLACKS -- RELIGION
See also Religion
BLACKS -- SOCIAL CONDITIONS
See also Social conditions
BLACKS -- UNITED STATES *See* African Americans
BLACKS IN MOTION PICTURES
See also Minorities in motion pictures; Motion pictures
The **blackwater** lightship. Tóibín, C.
The **blade** itself. Abercrombie, J.
The **blade** itself. Sakey, M.
Blame.
Blame. Huneven, M.
BLANCHARD, URSULA (FICTITIOUS CHARACTER)
Buckley, F. The doublet affair
Buckley, F. The siren queen

Blank Canvas [series]
Anders, A. Under Her Skin
Blasphemy. Preston, D.
Blasphemy. Alexie, S.
The **blazing** world. Hustvedt, S.
BLEACHING
See also Cleaning; Industrial chemistry; Textile industry
Bleak House. Dickens, C.
Bleeding edge. Pynchon, T.
Bleeding Kansas. Paretsky, S.
Bleeding through. Parshall, S.
Bless the beasts and children. Swarthout, G. F.
BLESSING AND CURSING
López Barrio, C. The House of Impossible Loves
The **blessing** way. Hillerman, T.
Bligh, William, 1754-1817
About
Nordhoff, C. Men against the sea
Nordhoff, C. Mutiny on the Bounty
BLIND
Bronte, C. Jane Eyre
Doctorow, E. L. Homer & Langley
Doerr, A. All the light we cannot see
Flagg, F. Standing in the rainbow
London, J. The Sea-Wolf
Sheehan, A. The anxiety of everyday objects
Shreve, A. Eden Close
Ure, L. The fault tree
Wallace, C. The blind contessa's new machine
Woods, S. Dead eyes
BLIND
See also People with physical disabilities
BLIND -- BOOKS AND READING
See also Books and reading
Blind alley. Johansen, I.
The **blind** assassin. Atwood, M.
The **blind** contessa's new machine. Wallace, C.
Blind eye. MacBride, S.
Blind Lake. Wilson, R. C.
The **blind** man of Seville. Wilson, R.
The **Blind** Man's Garden. Aslam, N.
BLIND MEDICAL PERSONNEL
Raimondo, L. Dante's wood
Blind sight. Howrey, M.
Blind willow, sleeping woman. Murakami, H.
BLIND WOMEN
Ure, L. The fault tree
Blindness. Saramago, J.
The **blindness** of the heart. Franck, J.
Blindsight. Watts, P.
Bliss, remembered. Deford, F.
BLIZZARDS
See also Storms
Doiron, P. Bad Little Falls
Farrow, J. The Storm Murders
Bloch, Eduard
About
Neugeboren, J. 1940
BLOMKVIST MIKAEL (FICTITIOUS CHARACTER)
Lagercrantz, D. The girl who takes an eye for an eye
The **blond** baboon. Van de Wetering, J.
Blonde. Oates, J. C.
Blonde roots. Evaristo, B.
The **Blondes.** Schultz, E.
BLOOD -- DISEASES
See also Diseases
Blood and beauty. Dunant, S.
Blood and iron. Bear, E.
Blood canticle. Rice, A.
Blood colony. Due, T.
BLOOD DONORS
Lianke, Y. Dream of Ding Village
Blood from a stone. Leon, D.
The **blood** Gospel. Rollins, J.
Blood kin. Dovey, C.
Blood lines. Rendell, R.
Blood lines. Harrod-Eagles, C.
Blood memory. Coel, M.
Blood meridian. McCarthy, C.
Blood money. Perry, T.
Blood oath. Farnsworth, C.
Blood of Amber. Zelazny, R.
The **Blood** of Angels.
Blood of angels. Arvin, R.
The **Blood** of Heaven. Wascom, K.
The **blood** of Lorraine. Pope, B. C.
Blood of tyrants. Novik, N.
Blood of victory. Furst, A.
Blood on snow. Nesbø, J.
The **blood** oranges. Hawkes, J.
Blood oranges. Kiernan, C. R.
Blood rain. Dibdin, M.
Blood sins. Hooper, K.
Blood ties. Hooper, K.
Blood's a rover. Ellroy, J.
Blood, Ash, and Bone. Whittle, T.
Bloodland. Glynn, A.
Bloodmoney. Ignatius, D.
Bloodroot. Greene, A.
A **Bloodsmoor** romance. Oates, J. C.
Blooms of darkness. Appelfeld, A.
BLOOMSBURY GROUP
Parmar, P. Vanessa and her sister
Blue angel. Prose, F.
Blue at the mizzen. O'Brian, P.
The **blue** flower. Fitzgerald, P.
The **blue** fox.
The **blue** guitar. Banville, J.
Blue heaven. Wyman, W.
Blue Heron [series]
Higgins, K. Anything for You
Higgins, K. Waiting on You
The **blue** hour. Parker, T. J.
The **blue** knight. Wambaugh, J.

Blue light in the sky & other stories. Tsan-hsueh
Blue light Yokohama. Obregon, N.
Blue Mars. Robinson, K. S.
Blue Monday. French, N.
Blue moon. Rice, L.
Blue shoe. Lamott, A.
Blue shoes and happiness. McCall Smith, A.
The **blue** star. Earley, T.
Blue-eyed devil. Parker, R. B.
Bluebird, bluebird. Locke, A.
Bluegate Fields. Perry, A.
Blueprints for building better girls. Schappell, E.
BLUES MUSIC
Kunzru, H. White tears
BLUES MUSICIANS
Wind, R. In the midnight rain
The **bluest** eye. Morrison, T.
Blunt Impact. Black, L.
BOARD GAMES
Bolaño, R. The Third Reich
BOARD GAMES
See also Games
BOARDING HOUSES
Balzac, H. d. Pere Goriot (Old Goriot)
Doig, I. Work song
Koryta, M. The Cypress House
Levy, A. Small island
Naylor, G. Bailey's Cafe
Racculia, K. This must be the place
Ross-Macdonald, M. Tamsin Harte
Spark, M. A far cry from Kensington
Tyler, A. Celestial navigation
Waters, S. The Paying Guests
BOARDING SCHOOLS
Grant, M. Down Among the Sticks and Bones
Just, W. S. Rodin's debutante
Klein, R. The moth diaries
Shreve, A. Testimony
Southgate, M. The fall of Rome
Watkins, P. The ice soldier
BOARDING SCHOOLS -- CANADA
Bradley, A. As chimney sweepers come to dust
BOAT RACERS
Everett, P. L. I am Not Sidney Poitier
The **boat** rocker. Jin, H.
BOATS AND BOATING
George, N. The little Paris bookshop
Heacox, K. Jimmy Bluefeather
BODY AND MIND *See* Mind and body
Body Armor [series]
Foster, L. Under Pressure
Body double. Gerritsen, T.
BODY IMAGE
See also Human body; Mind and body; Personality; Self-perception
BODY IMAGE
Awad, M. 13 ways of looking at a fat girl
The **body** in the Big Apple. Page, K. H.
The **body** in the bog. Page, K. H.
The **body** in the bookcase. Page, K. H.
The **body** in the library. Christie, A.
The **body** of David Hayes. Pearson, R.
Body of lies. Ignatius, D.
BODY PIERCING
See also Personal appearance
A **body** to die for. White, K.
BODYGUARDS
Parker, R. B. Double play
Parker, T. J. Storm runners
Huston, C. Skinner
Jackson, B. Forged in desire
Sharp, Z. Die easy
Sharp, Z. Fourth Day
BOERS *See* Afrikaners
BOG BODIES
Hart, E. Lake of sorrows
BOHEMIANISM
Kerouac, J. On the road
Kerouac, J. The Dharma bums
Kerouac, J. Road novels 1957-1960
Maugham, W. S. Of human bondage
McCarthy, M. A charmed life
BOHEMIANISM
See also Counterculture; Manners and customs
Boleto. Hagy, A.
The **Boleyn** Inheritance. Gregory, P.
The **Boleyn** King. Andersen, L.
Boleyn, Jane, Viscountess Rochford, d. 1542
About
Gregory, P. The Boleyn Inheritance
Boleyn, Mary, 1508-1543
About
Gregory, P. The other Boleyn girl
Bolívar, Simón, 1783-1830
About
Garcia Marquez, G. The general and his labyrinth
A **Bollywood** affair. Dev, S.
BOLSHEVISM *See* Communism
Bolt. Francis, D.
BOMBINGS
See also Offenses against public safety; Political crimes and offenses; Terrorism
BOMBS
Crais, R. Demolition angel
Lutz, J. Final seconds
Veselka, V. Zazen
Bonanno, Joseph, 1905-2002
About
Latour, J. The Havana World Series
BONDAGE (SEXUAL BEHAVIOR)
Zan, K. The Never List
BONDS
See also Finance; Investments; Negotiable instruments; Securities; Stock exchanges

The **bondswomans** narrative. Crafts, H.
Bone. Ng, F. M.
Bone by bone. Matthiessen, P.
The **bone** clocks. Mitchell, D.
The **bone** people. Hulme, K.
The **bone** season. Shannon, S.
The **bone** tree. Iles, G.
Bones. Kellerman, J.
BONES
Van Eekhout, G. California bones
BONES -- DISEASES
See also Diseases
Bones and silence. Hill, R.
The **Bones** of Grace. Anam, T.
The **bones** of paradise. Agee, J.
Bones of the earth. Swanwick, M.
The **bonesetter's** daughter. Tan, A.
Boneshaker. Priest, C.
The **bonfire** of the vanities. Wolfe, T.
Bonita Avenue. Buwalda, P.
Bonjour tristesse. Sagan, F.
BONOBO
Gruen, S. Ape house
The **book** and the brotherhood. Murdoch, I.
BOOK CLUBS (DISCUSSION GROUPS)
See also Clubs
Majors, I. Love's winning plays
BOOK CLUBS
Barrows, A. The Guernsey Literary and Potato Peel Pie Society
BOOK COLLECTING
See also Book selection; Collectors and collecting
BOOK EDITORS
Horowitz, A. Magpie murders
The **book** of air and shadows. Gruber, M.
The **book** of Aron. Shepard, J.
A **book** of common prayer. Didion, J.
The **book** of Dahlia. Albert, E.
The **Book** of Dave. Self, W.
The **book** of Etta. Elison, M.
The **book** of evidence. Banville, J.
The **book** of fathers. Vamos, M.
The **Book** of Harlan.
The **book** of Jonas. Dau, S.
The **book** of Killowen. Hart, E.
The **book** of knowledge. Grumbach, D.
The **book** of lies. Horlock, M.
The **Book** of Life. Harkness, D. E.
The **book** of lost things. Connolly, J.
The **book** of Merlyn. White, T. H.
The **book** of Murdock. Estleman, L. D.
The **book** of night women. James, M.
Book of numbers. Cohen, J.
The **book** of Q. Rabb, J.
The **book** of salt. Truong, M.
The **book** of splendor. Sherwood, F.
The **Book** of Strange New Things. Faber, M.
Book of the new Sun [series]
Wolfe, G. The Citadel of the Autarch
Wolfe, G. The claw of the conciliator
Wolfe, G. The shadow of the torturer
Wolfe, G. The sword of the Lictor
Wolfe, G. The Urth of the new sun
The **Book** of the Unnamed Midwife. Elison, M.
The **book** of words. Erpenbeck, J.
BOOK RARITIES *See* Rare books
BOOK REVIEWING
See also Books and reading; Criticism
BOOK TRADE *See* Book industry; Booksellers and bookselling; Publishers and publishing
BOOKBINDING
See also Book industry; Books
Booked to die. Dunning, J.
BOOKKEEPERS *See* Accountants
BOOKKEEPING
See also Business; Business education; Business mathematics
BOOKMAKING (BETTING) *See* Gambling
The **bookman's** tale. Lovett, C.
The **bookman's** wake. Dunning, J.
BOOKS -- APPRAISAL *See* Book reviewing; Books and reading; Criticism; Literature -- History and criticism
BOOKS -- CONSERVATION AND RESTORATION
Brooks, G. People of the book
BOOKS -- LARGE PRINT *See* Large print books
BOOKS -- PRICES
See also Booksellers and bookselling; Prices
BOOKS AND READING
Alameddine, R. An Unnecessary Woman
Barrows, A. The Guernsey Literary and Potato Peel Pie Society
Brooks, G. People of the book
Connolly, J. The book of lost things
Fforde, J. The Eyre affair
Fforde, J. Lost in a good book
Fowler, K. J. The Jane Austen book club
Hamilton, M. The camel bookmobile
Maalouf, A. Balthasar's odyssey
Makkai, R. The borrower
Ruiz Zafon, C. The angel's game
Ruiz Zafon, C. The shadow of the wind
Savage, S. Firmin
Schlink, B. The reader
The slynx
Vila-Matas, E. Montano's malady
Walton, J. Among others
BOOKS AND READING
See also Communication; Education; Reading
King, S. Finders Keepers
BOOKS FOR SIGHT SAVING *See* Large print books
BOOKS FOR TEENAGERS *See* Young adult literature
BOOKS OF HOURS
See also Books
BOOKS, UPSIDE-DOWN *See* Upside-down books

BOOKSELLERS AND BOOKSELLING
Berry, S. The Charlemagne pursuit
Brookner, A. Undue influence
Cosse, L. A novel bookstore
Eco, U. The mysterious flame of Queen Loana
George, N. The little Paris bookshop
Glass, J. Three Junes
Goodman, A. The cookbook collector
Grossman, D. Be my knife
Gruber, M. The book of air and shadows
Lovett, C. The bookman's tale
Pipkin, J. Woodsburner
Reay, K. The Brontë plot
Schine, C. The love letter
Zevin, G. The storied life of A. J. Fikry
BOOKSELLERS' CATALOGS
See also Booksellers and bookselling
BOOKSTORES -- CALIFORNIA -- SAN FRANCISCO
Sloan, R. Mr. Penumbra's 24-hour bookstore
BOOKSTORES -- EMPLOYEES
Sloan, R. Mr. Penumbra's 24-hour bookstore
BOOKSTORES
McPherson, C. Quiet neighbors
Sloan, R. Mr. Penumbra's 24-hour bookstore
Zevin, G. The storied life of A. J. Fikry
Boone's Lick. McMurtry, L.
Bootlegger's daughter. Maron, M.
Borden, Lizzie, 1860-1927
About
Schmidt, S. See what I have done
Border child. Stone, M.
BORDER LIFE *See* Frontier and pioneer life
BORDER PATROL AGENTS
Lynch, J. Border songs
BORDER PATROLS
See also Police
Border songs. Lynch, J.
Borderliners. Hoeg, P.
Bordersnakes. Crumley, J.
BOREDOM
Aridjis, C. Asunder
Rourke, L. The canal
Wallace, D. F. The pale king
Borges and the eternal orangutans. Verissimo, L. F.
Borges, Jorge Luis, 1899-1986
About
Verissimo, L. F. Borges and the eternal orangutans
Borgia family
About
Dunant, S. Blood and beauty
Poole, S. The Borgia mistress
Puzo, M. The family
The **Borgia** mistress. Poole, S.
Borgia, Cesare, 1476?-1507
About
Poole, S. The Borgia mistress
Bormann, Martin, 1900-1945
About
Lindgren, T. Hash
Born on a Tuesday. John, E.
Born to run. Grippando, J.
Borne. VanderMeer, J.
The **borrower.** Makkai, R.
Bosch, Harry
About
Connelly, M. The crossing
BOSNIA AND HERCEGOVINA
Stanisic, S. How the soldier repairs the gramophone
BOSNIA AND HERCEGOVINA -- SARAJEVO
Hemon, A. Nowhere man
BOSNIAN AMERICANS
Prcic, I. Shards
BOSNIANS -- UNITED STATES
Hemon, A. Nowhere man
BOSSINESS
See also Personality
BOSTON (MASS.)
Diamant, A. The Boston girl
Higgins, G. V. The Digger's game
Lehane, D. Live by night
Moore, L. The Unseen World
Pearl, M. The technologists
The **Boston** girl. Diamant, A.
BOTANICAL ILLUSTRATION
See also Art; Illustration of books
BOTANISTS
Hay, E. A student of weather
Jio, S. The last camellia
Vanderbes, J. Easter Island
BOTANISTS
See also Naturalists
Botany Bay. Nordhoff, C.
Both ends of the night. Muller, M.
BOTSWANA -- FICTION
McCall Smith, A. The full cupboard of life
McCall Smith, A. The Kalahari typing school for men
McCall Smith, A. The Limpopo Academy of Private Detection
McCall Smith, A. The No. 1 Ladies' Detective Agency
McCall Smith, A. The Saturday big tent wedding party
McCall Smith, A. Tea time for the traditionally built
Stanley, M. Death of the mantis
The **bottoms.** Lansdale, J. R.
BOULDER (COLO.)
White, S. W. Dry ice
Bound. Nelson, A.
BOUNTY (SHIP)
Nordhoff, C. The Bounty trilogy
Nordhoff, C. Men against the sea
Nordhoff, C. Mutiny on the Bounty
The **Bounty** trilogy. Nordhoff, C.
The **Bourne** identity. Ludlum, R.
The **Bourne** supremacy. Ludlum, R.
The **Bourne** ultimatum. Ludlum, R.

BOWHUNTING
See also Hunting
Bowl of cherries. Kaufman, M.
Bowser, Mary Elizabeth, ca. 1840-
About
Leveen, L. The secrets of Mary Bowser
The **box.** Grass, G.
BOXERS (PERSONS)
Phillips, C. Foreigners
BOXERS (SPORTS)
Freeman, A. The fair fight
BOXES -- COLLECTORS AND COLLECTING
See also Collectors and collecting
BOXING
Lee, G. China boy
Toole, F. X. Pound for pound
The **boy** detective fails. Meno, J.
The **boy** on the bus. Schupack, D.
BOY SCOUTS
Butler, N. The Hearts of Men
BOY SCOUTS
See also Boys' clubs; Scouts and scouting
Boy still missing. Searles, J.
The **boy** who couldn't sleep and never had to. Pierson, D. C.
The **boy** who followed Ripley. Highsmith, P.
The **boy** who would live forever. Pohl, F.
Boy's life. McCammon, R. R.
A **boy's** own story. White, E.
Boy, snow, bird. Oyeyemi, H.
The **boyfriend.** Perry, T.
BOYS
Abani, C. GraceLand
Agawa, Y. The housekeeper and the professor
Ansay, A. M. River angel
Appelfeld, A. Blooms of darkness
Ballard, J. G. Empire of the Sun
Bauer, B. Blacklands
Bilenchi, R. The chill
Bradbury, R. Dandelion wine
Bradbury, R. Something wicked this way comes
Carey, P. His illegal self
Childress, M. Crazy in Alabama
Clarke, B. Exley
Clinch, J. Finn
Coe, J. The Rotters' Club
Connolly, J. The book of lost things
Couto, M. Sleepwalking land
Deane, S. Reading in the dark
Dickens, C. David Copperfield
Dickens, C. Dombey and Son
Dickens, C. Oliver Twist
Doyle, R. Paddy Clarke, ha ha ha
Earley, T. Jim the boy
Edgerton, C. The night train
Faulkner, W. The reivers
Flagg, F. Standing in the rainbow
Foer, J. S. Extremely loud & incredibly close
Ford, J. The shadow year
Frayn, M. Spies
French, A. Billy
Gaiman, N. The Ocean at the End of the Lane
George, E. What came before he shot her
Gilb, D. The flowers
Golding, W. Lord of the flies
Grisham, J. The client
Haddon, M. The curious incident of the dog in the night-time
Haig, M. The dead fathers club
Hart, J. Iron house
Hilton, J. Good-bye Mr. Chips
Hornby, N. About a boy
Hughes, L. Not without laughter
Huston, C. The shotgun rule
Kafka on the shore
Kneale, M. When we were Romans
Knowles, J. A separate peace
Kosinski, J. N. The painted bird
Lansdale, J. R. The bottoms
Lansdale, J. R. A fine dark line
Larsen, R. The selected works of T. S. Spivet
Lethem, J. The fortress of solitude
Lichtenstein, A. Lost
Lodato, V. Edgar and Lucy
Lourie, R. A hatred for tulips
Lovett, A. Everlasting Lane
Lychack, W. The wasp eater
Makkai, R. The borrower
Marshall, P. The fisher king
Martel, Y. Life of Pi
Matar, H. Anatomy of a disappearance
Matar, H. In the country of men
McCarthy, C. The crossing
McGahan, A. The white earth
McGowan, H. Duchess of nothing
Meyers, K. The work of wolves
Mitcham, J. Sabbath Creek
Morris, W. Taps
Murr, N. The perfect man
Murray, P. Skippy dies
Oe, K. Nip the buds, shoot the kids
Olmstead, R. Coal black horse
O'Nan, S. Snow angels
Ondaatje, M. The cat's table
O'Neill, J. At swim, two boys
Oz, A. Panther in the basement
Parker, R. B. Double play
Powell, P. Edisto
Richter, C. The light in the forest
Roth, H. Call it sleep
Roth, H. A star shines over Mt. Morris Park
Ruiz Zafon, C. The shadow of the wind
Sallis, J. The killer is dying
Saroyan, W. The human comedy
Schwartzman, A. Eddie Signwriter
Scott, J. Tourmaline

Searles, J. Boy still missing
Sharfeddin, H. Mineral spirits
Shepard, J. The book of Aron
Silver, M. The god of war
Slouka, M. Brewster
Southgate, M. The fall of Rome
Stanisic, S. How the soldier repairs the gramophone
Swarthout, G. F. Bless the beasts and children
Tinti, H. The good thief
Tobar, H. The barbarian nurseries
Torres, J. We the animals
Townsend, S. The Adrian Mole diaries
Tucker, T. Over and under
Vargas Llosa, M. The notebooks of Don Rigoberto
Vlautin, W. Lean on Pete
White, E. A boy's own story
Whitehead, C. Sag Harbor
Wilson, E. O. Anthill
Winton, T. Breath
Wolff, T. Old school
Woo, S. J. Everything Asian
Woodrell, D. The death of sweet mister
Woolf, V. Jacob's room
Wray, J. Lowboy
The Year of the Comet
BOYS
See also Children
The **boys** from Brazil. Levin, I.
BOYS' CLUBS
See also Clubs; Societies
BP DEEPWATER HORIZON EXPLOSION AND OIL SPILL, 2010
Cooper, T. The marauders
BRACHIOSAURUS
See also Dinosaurs
Bradbury stories. Bradbury, R.
The **Bradshaw** variations. Cusk, R.
Brahe, Tycho, 1546-1601
About
Sherwood, F. The book of splendor
BRAILLE BOOKS
See also Books
BRAIN
Powers, R. The echo maker
BRAIN -- DISEASES
See also Diseases
BRAIN -- WOUNDS AND INJURIES
Picoult, J. Lone wolf
BRAIN DEATH
See also Death
Brandling, Henry C. (Henry Charles), b. 1818
About
Carey, P. The chemistry of tears
BRANDT, SARAH (FICTITIOUS CHARACTER)
Thompson, V. Murder in Chinatown
Thompson, V. Murder on Fifth Avenue
Thompson, V. Murder on Lenox Hill
Brass. Aliu, X.
Brass. Walsh, H.
Brat Farrar. Tey, J.
Brave new world. Huxley, A.
Brave new worlds.
BRAVERY *See* Courage
Brazil. Updike, J.
BRAZIL
Hatoum, M. The brothers
Levin, I. The boys from Brazil
Peebles, F. d. P. The seamstress
Updike, J. Brazil
BRAZIL -- 19TH CENTURY
Vargas Llosa, M. The war of the end of the world
BRAZIL -- BAHIA
Amado, J. Dona Flor and her two husbands
Amado, J. Gabriela, clove and cinnamon
Breach of promise. O'Shaughnessy, P.
A **breach** of promise. Perry, A.
BREAD
See also Baking; Cooking; Food
Bread and Butter. Wildgen, M.
Bread and wine. Silone, I.
Bread givers. Yezierska, A. c.
Break no bones. Reichs, K. J.
Breakdown. Paretsky, S.
The **breaker.** Walters, M.
Breakfast at Tiffany's: a short novel and three stories. Capote, T.
Breakfast of champions. Vonnegut, K.
Breakfast with Buddha. Merullo, R.
The **breaking** of eggs. Powell, J.
Breaking point. Box, C. J.
Breaking silence. Castillo, L.
Breaking the tongue. Loh, V.
BREAKING UP (INTERPERSONAL RELATIONS)
Beach-Ferrara, J. Damn love
Breaking wild. Les Becquets, D.
Breakout. Stark, R.
BREAST CANCER
See also Cancer; Women -- Diseases
Breath. Winton, T.
Breath of fire. Bouchet, A.
A **breath** of snow and ashes. Gabaldon, D.
Breathing lessons. Tyler, A.
Breathless. Jenkins, B.
Brébeuf, Jean de, Saint, 1593-1649
About
Vollmann, W. T. Fathers and crows
Breed. Novak, C.
The **brethren.** Grisham, J.
The **brethren.** Lewis, B.
BREWERIES
See also Factories
Brewing up a storm. Lathen, E.
Brewster. Slouka, M.
Brick lane. Ali, M.

The **bride** of Lammermoor. Scott, W.
Bride of Pendorric. Holt, V.
Bride of the high country. Warner, K.
The **bride** sale. Hern, C.
The **bride** wore scarlet. Carlyle, L.
The **bridegroom.** Ha Jin
The **brides** of Rollrock Island. Lanagan, M.
Brideshead revisited. Waugh, E.
The **bridesmaid.** Rendell, R.
BRIDGE (GAME)
See also Card games
The **bridge** of San Luis Rey and other novels 1926-1948. Wilder, T.
Bridge of sighs. Russo, R.
The **Bridge** of Sighs. Steinhauer, O.
The **bridge** over the River Kwai. Boulle, P.
Bridge to haven. Rivers, F.
BRIDGES
Barton, E. Brookland
Boulle, P. The bridge over the River Kwai
Kadare, I. The three-arched bridge
The **bridges** at Toko-ri. Michener, J. A.
The **bridges** of Madison County. Waller, R. J.
Bridget Jones. Fielding, H.
Bridget Jones's diary. Fielding, H.
A **brief** history of seven killings. James, M.
The **brief** history of the dead. Brockmeier, K.
Brief interviews with hideous men. Wallace, D. F.
Brief lives. Brookner, A.
The **brief** wondrous life of Oscar Wao. Diaz, J.
BRIGANDS *See* Thieves
BRIGANDS AND ROBBERS
Blackmore, R. D. Lorna Doone
Brown, T. Fallen land
Lynch, S. The Republic of Thieves
Moehringer, J. R. Sutton
Puzo, M. The Sicilian
Urrea, L. A. Into the beautiful North
BRIGATE ROSSE
Kushner, R. The flamethrowers
Bright and distant shores. Smith, D.
BRIGHT CHILDREN *See* Gifted children
The **bright** forever. Martin, L.
Bright lights, big city. McInerney, J.
Brighton. Harvey, M.
BRIGHTON (ENGLAND)
Guttridge, P. The thing itself
Brighton rock. Greene, G.
Brilliance. Sakey, M.
The Brilliance Saga [series]
Sakey, M. A Better World
Brimstone. Preston, D.
Brimstone. Parker, R. B.
The **brimstone** wedding. Vine, B.
Bring up the bodies. Mantel, H.
BRISEIS (LEGENDARY CHARACTER)
Hauser, E. For the most beautiful
BRISTOL (ENGLAND) -- HISTORY -- 18TH CENTURY
Freeman, A. The fair fight
BRITAIN, BATTLE OF, 1940
See also Battles; World War, 1939-1945 -- Campaigns
BRITISH
Carter, M. J. The Strangler Vine
BRITISH -- AFRICA
Conrad, J. Heart of darkness
Gordimer, N. A guest of honor
BRITISH -- ARGENTINA
Greene, G. The honorary consul
BRITISH -- ASIA
Gardam, J. Old Filth
BRITISH -- AUSTRIA
Stewart, M. Airs above the ground
BRITISH -- BURMA
Ghosh, A. The glass palace
Mason, D. The piano tuner
BRITISH -- CHINA
Ballard, J. G. Empire of the Sun
Ishiguro, K. When we were orphans
BRITISH -- CRETE
Stewart, M. The moon-spinners
BRITISH -- CROATIA
Seymour, G. The heart of danger
BRITISH -- CYPRUS
Jones, S. Small wars
BRITISH -- DENMARK
Tremain, R. Music & silence
BRITISH -- EGYPT
Durrell, L. Mountolive
BRITISH -- ETHIOPIA
Gibb, C. Sweetness in the belly
BRITISH -- FOREIGN COUNTRIES
Boyd, W. Any human heart
BRITISH -- FRANCE
Bates, H. E. Fair stood the wind for France
Faulks, S. Birdsong
Godden, R. The greengage summer
Hemingway, E. The sun also rises
Mayle, P. Hotel Pastis
Orczy, E. The Scarlet Pimpernel
Rhys, J. Quartet
Stewart, M. Nine coaches waiting
Tremain, R. Trespass
BRITISH -- GERMANY
Hall, A. The Quiller memorandum
Le Carre, J. The spy who came in from the cold
BRITISH -- GREECE
Fowles, J. The magus
Goddard, R. Into the blue
BRITISH -- HONG KONG
Lanchester, J. Fragrant Harbor
Lee, J. Y. K. The piano teacher
Theroux, P. Kowloon Tong
BRITISH -- INDIA
Dyer, G. Jeff in Venice, death in Varanasi

Festing, I. A. The birdkeeper
Forster, E. M. A passage to India
Ghosh, A. The glass palace
Godden, R. Black Narcissus
Jhabvala, R. P. Heat and dust
Kaye, M. M. The far pavilions
Scott, P. The Raj quartet
Scott, P. Staying on
Todd, C. A question of honor
BRITISH -- IRAQ
Unsworth, B. Land of marvels
BRITISH -- IRELAND
Llywelyn, M. 1921
Uris, L. Redemption
Uris, L. Trinity
BRITISH -- ISRAEL
Spark, M. The Mandelbaum Gate
BRITISH -- ITALY
Amis, M. The pregnant widow
Dyer, G. Jeff in Venice, death in Varanasi
Forster, E. M. A room with a view
Godden, R. The battle of the Villa Fiorita
Godden, R. Pippa passes
Kneale, M. When we were Romans
Roberts, M. Reader, I married him
Scott, J. Tourmaline
Seymour, G. Killing ground
Watkins, P. The ice soldier
West, M. L. The devil's advocate
BRITISH -- JAPAN
Clavell, J. Shogun
Hazzard, S. The great fire
BRITISH -- MALAYSIA
Carey, P. My life as a fake
BRITISH -- MEXICO
Lowry, M. Under the volcano
BRITISH -- NEW YORK (STATE) -- NEW YORK
Coulter, C. The Final Cut
Lasdun, J. The horned man
BRITISH -- PALESTINE
Oz, A. Panther in the basement
Wiesel, E. Dawn
BRITISH -- PANAMA
Le Carre, J. The tailor of Panama
BRITISH -- RUSSIA
Read, P. P. Alice in exile
BRITISH -- SOUTH AFRICA
Francis, D. Smokescreen
Lessing, D. M. Children of violence
Michener, J. A. The covenant
BRITISH -- SPAIN
Hemingway, E. The sun also rises
O'Flynn, C. Mr. Lynch's holiday
Sansom, C. J. Winter in Madrid
BRITISH -- SWITZERLAND
Brookner, A. Hotel du Lac
BRITISH -- TAHITI
Maugham, W. S. The moon and sixpence
BRITISH -- TURKEY
Holt, V. Secret for a nightingale
BRITISH -- UNITED STATES
Dickens, C. Martin Chuzzlewit
Faulks, S. On Green Dolphin Street
Higgins, K. The Perfect Match
Lasdun, J. The horned man
Lodge, D. Paradise news
McMurtry, L. Sin killer
Pynchon, T. Mason & Dixon
Raban, J. Waxwings
Vanderhaeghe, G. The last crossing
Vollmann, W. T. Argall
Waugh, E. The loved one
BRITISH -- VIETNAM
Greene, G. The quiet American
BRITISH -- WEST AFRICA
Forester, C. S. The African Queen
Greene, G. The heart of the matter
BRITISH -- WEST INDIES
Naipaul, V. S. Guerrillas
BRITISH COLUMBIA
Haldane, S. The devil's making
BRITISH ESPIONAGE
Robertson, I. Anatomy of murder
BRITTANY (FRANCE)
Bannalec Death in Brittany
BROADBAND INTERNET
See also Internet; Internet access
BROADCAST JOURNALISM
See also Broadcasting; Journalism; Press
BROADCASTING EXECUTIVES
Everett, P. L. I am Not Sidney Poitier
Broadchurch. Kelly, E.
Broccoli and other tales of food and love. Vapnyar, L.
Broke heart blues. Oates, J. C.
Broken. Fossum, K.
Broken angels. Morgan, R. K.
The broken earth [series]
Jemisin, N. K. The fifth season
Jemisin, N. K. The obelisk gate
Jemisin, N. K. The stone sky
Broken for you. Kallos, S.
Broken Harbor. French, T.
Broken Irish. Delaney, E. J.
Broken monsters. Beukes, L.
The **broken** ones. Irwin, S. M.
Broken prey. Sandford, J.
The **broken** shore. Temple, P.
The **broken** teaglass. Arsenault, E.
The **Brontë** plot. Reay, K.
BRONX (NEW YORK, N.Y.)
Doctorow, E. L. World's fair
McDermott, A. Charming Billy
Neugeboren, J. 1940
Ozick, C. Heir to the glimmering world

BRONZES
See also Archeology; Art; Art metalwork; Decoration and ornament; Metalwork; Sculpture
Brookland. Barton, E.
Brooklyn. Tóibín, C.
BROOKLYN (NEW YORK, N.Y.)
K'wan (Author) Section 8
Huston, C. Half the blood of Brooklyn
McDermott, A. Someone
Woodson, J. Another Brooklyn
BROOKLYN (NEW YORK, N.Y.) -- SOCIAL LIFE AND CUSTOMS -- 20TH CENTURY
Loigman, L. C. The two-family house
The **Brooklyn** follies. Auster, P.
BROTHELS
Kent, K. The outcasts
Brother and sister. Trollope, J.
Brother Cadfael's penance. Peters, E.
Brother Odd. Koontz, D. R.
Brotherhood of war [series]
Griffin, W. E. B. Special ops
Brothers. Yu Hua
Brothers. Chen, D.
BROTHERS
Amis, M. House of meetings
Bakker, G. The twin
Baldwin, J. Tell me how long the train's been gone
Banks, R. Affliction
Barclay, L. Trust your eyes
Braffet, K. Save yourself
Burgess, M. Dogfight, a love story
Cash, W. A land more kind than home
Chaon, D. Await your reply
Chaon, D. Ill will
Clark, M. The legal limit
De la Roche, M. Jalna
DeWitt, P. The Sisters brothers
Doctorow, E. L. Homer & Langley
Doig, I. Bucking the sun
Dostoyevsky, F. The brothers Karamazov
Glass, J. Three Junes
Grisham, J. The client
Gross, A. Eyes wide open
Habila, H. Measuring time
Hart, J. Iron house
Hatoum, M. The brothers
Higgins, J. Flight of eagles
Hijuelos, O. Beautiful Maria of my soul
Hijuelos, O. The Mambo Kings play songs of love
Huston, C. The shotgun rule
Johnson, D. Tree of smoke
Kadare, I. The ghost rider
Kelton, E. Texas sunrise
Kerstan, L. Heart of the tiger
Lahiri, J. The lowland
Longworth, M. L. Death at the Chateau Bremont
Lourie, R. A hatred for tulips
Lundrigan, N. Glass boys
Martin, C. W. How to sell
Mathews, B. The world of tomorrow
McCann, C. Let the great world spin
McCarthy, C. The crossing
Miller, A. Oxygen
Mosley, W. Fortunate son
Murdoch, I. The green knight
Obioma, C. The fishermen
O'Dell, T. Fragile beasts
Orringer, J. The invisible bridge
Parker, T. J. California girl
Price, R. Clockers
Robertson, M. The brothers of Baker Street
Robinson, L. Water dogs
Rush, N. Mortals
Russo, R. Empire Falls
Shakar, A. Luminarium
Silver, M. The god of war
Singer, I. J. The brothers Ashkenazi
Smith, W. A. Monsoon
Strout, E. The burgess boys
Swift, G. Wish you were here
Torres, J. We the animals
Tsukiyama, G. The street of a thousand blossoms
Vanderhaeghe, G. The last crossing
Vachss, A. That's how I roll
Verghese, A. Cutting for stone
Vollmann, W. T. The royal family
Whitehead, C. Sag Harbor
Wildgen, M. Bread and Butter
The **brothers.** Hatoum, M.
BROTHERS
See also Men; Siblings
Brothers and sisters. Campbell, B. M.
BROTHERS AND SISTERS
Abu-Jaber, D. Birds of paradise
Atkinson, K. A God in Ruins
Auster, P. Invisible
Baker, K. The bird of the river
Barth, J. The sot-weed factor
Cohen, L. H. The grief of others
Conroy, P. The prince of tides
Cook, T. H. The cloud of unknowing
Cunningham, M. By nightfall
Doig, I. The whistling season
Eliot, G. The mill on the Floss
Enright, A. The gathering
Enright, A. The Green Road
Erdrich, L. The Beet Queen
Fay, J. The shortest way home
Flynn, G. Dark places
Ford, J. The shadow year
Gay, W. Twilight
George, E. What came before he shot her
Grant, S. Map of Ireland
Gregory, D. Raising Stony Mayhall

Haigh, J. The condition
Han, S. The enchantress
Hart, J. The king of lies
Hart, J. The reconstructionist
Harvey, J. Gone to ground
Hawthorne, N. The House of the Seven Gables
Hollinghurst, A. The stranger's child
Horn, D. The world to come
Hunter, E. The moment she was gone
Hustvedt, S. The sorrows of an American
The immortalists
Irving, J. Avenue of mysteries
Jen, G. Typical American
Kelly, E. The poison tree
Kelman, J. Mo said she was quirky
Kneale, M. When we were Romans
Lawson, M. Crow Lake
Lennon, J. R. Castle
Lipman, E. The dearly departed
Lively, P. Passing on
Livesey, M. Criminals
McBride, E. A girl is a half-formed thing
Meno, J. The boy detective fails
Merullo, R. Breakfast with Buddha
Miller, S. For love
Mitchard, J. A theory of relativity
Monaghan, N. The killing jar
Nabokov, V. V. Ada
Oates, J. C. Them
O'Brien, E. Wild Decembers
O'Dell, T. Back roads
Oe, K. A quiet life
Ozick, C. Foreign bodies
Packer, A. The Children's Crusade
Palaia, M. The given world
Perry, A. No graves as yet
Perry, A. Shoulder the sky
Phillips, J. A. Lark and Termite
Pollen, B. The summer of the bear
Powers, R. The echo maker
Pywell, S. L. What happened to Henry
Reiken, F. Day for night
Rice, A. The Feast of All Saints
Roy, A. The god of small things
Salinger, J. D. Franny & Zooey
Sanchez, T. King Bongo
Saunders, K. The Secrets of Wishtide
Schlink, B. The weekend
Settle, M. L. The killing ground
Southgate, M. The taste of salt
Spiotta, D. Stone Arabia
Strout, E. Anything is possible
Sung J. Woo Love love
Sweeney, C. D. The Nest
Tartt, D. The little friend
Theroux, P. Picture palace
Thompson, J. The year we left home
Toyne, S. Sanctus
Tremain, R. Trespass
Trevanian The summer of Katya
Tropper, J. How to talk to a widower
Vonnegut, K. Slapstick
Ward, J. Salvage the bones
Ward, J. Sing, unburied, sing
Watson, J. E. Asta in the wings
Wesselmann, D. L. Captivity
Wilhelm, K. The good children
Wilson, K. The family Fang
Winman, S. When God was a rabbit
Woodrell, D. Winter's bone
The **brothers** Ashkenazi. Singer, I. J.
The **brothers** Karamazov. Dostoyevsky, F.
Brothers Magnus [series]
Duncan, D. When the saints
The **brothers** of Baker Street. Robertson, M.
The Brothers Sinister [series]
Milan, C. The Duchess War
BROTHERS-IN-LAW
Oe, K. The changeling
Brown Dog. Harrison, J.
Brown girl, brownstones. Marshall, P.
BROWN UNIVERSITY
Eugenides, J. The marriage plot
Brown, John, 1800-1859
About
McBride, J. The good lord bird
Brown-Eyed Girl. Kleypas, L.
BROWNS (MUSICAL GROUP)
Bass, R. Nashville chrome
Brueghel, Pieter, the Elder, 1522?-1569
About
Frayn, M. Headlong
BRUNETTI, GUIDO (FICTITIOUS CHARACTER)
Leon, D. Blood from a stone
Leon, D. A question of belief
Bruno, chief of police. Walker, M.
Bruno, chief of police [series]
Walker, M. The Patriarch
Bruno, Giordano, 1548-1600
About
Parris, S. J. Sacrilege
Brush back. Paretsky, S.
BRUTALITY *See* Cruelty
Bryant & May. Fowler, C.
Bryant & May : Peculiar Crimes Unit mystery [series]
Fowler, C. Bryant & May
BRYANT, ARTHUR (FICTITIOUS CHARACTER)
Fowler, C. Bryant & May
BUBONIC PLAGUE *See* Plague
BUCCANEERS *See* Pirates
Buchanan, James, 1791-1868
About
Updike, J. Memories of the Ford Administration
BUCHENWALD (GERMANY: CONCENTRATION

CAMP)
The Book of Harlan
BUCHENWALD (GERMANY: CONCENTRATION CAMP)
See also Concentration camps
Bucking the sun. Doig, I.
Buckingham Palace gardens. Perry, A.
Buddenbrooks.
The **Buddha** in the attic. Otsuka, J.
BUDDHISM
Burdett, J. Bangkok 8
Endo, S. Deep river
Hesse, H. Siddhartha
Merullo, R. Breakfast with Buddha
Mishima, Y. The Temple of Dawn
Pattison, E. The skull mantra
Zelazny, R. Lord of light
BUDDHIST ART
See also Art
BUDDHIST LEADERS
Mishima, Y. The Temple of Dawn
BUDDHIST NUNS
Ozeki, R. L. A tale for the time being
BUENOS AIRES (ARGENTINA) -- HISTORY -- 20TH CENTURY
De Robertis, C. The gods of tango
BUFFALO BILL'S WILD WEST COMPANY
Welch, J. The heartsong of Charging Elk
Buffalo Bill, 1846-1917
About
McMurtry, L. Buffalo girls
Buffalo girls. McMurtry, L.
Buffalo soldiers. O'Connor, R.
Buffalo soldiers. Willard, T.
BUGGING, ELECTRONIC *See* Eavesdropping
BUILDING
Follett, K. The pillars of the earth
BUILDING INDUSTRY *See* Construction industry
BUILDINGS -- EARTHQUAKE EFFECTS
See also Earthquakes
Built in a day. Rinehart, S.
BULGARIA -- SOFIA
Gilman, D. The elusive Mrs. Pollifax
BULGE, BATTLE OF THE *See* Ardennes (France), Battle of the, 1944-1945
The **bull** from the sea. Renault, M.
Bullet Park. Cheever, J.
BULLFIGHTERS AND BULLFIGHTING
Garcia, C. The lady matador's hotel
Hemingway, E. The sun also rises
Michener, J. A. Mexico
O'Dell, T. Fragile beasts
Bullfighting and other stories. Doyle, R.
BULLIES
Lancaster, J. Here I go again
Minato, K. Confessions
Raeder, L. Black iris
The **bully** of order. Hart, B.
BULLYING
Picoult, J. Nineteen minutes
BUNGO CHANNEL (JAPAN)
Deutermann, P. T. The ghosts of Bungo Suido
BUNKER HILL (BOSTON, MASS.), BATTLE OF, 1775
See also Battles; United States -- History -- 1775-1783, Revolution -- Campaigns
Bunker, Chang, 1811-1874
About
Slouka, M. God's fool
Bunker, Eng, 1811-1874
About
Slouka, M. God's fool
The **burden** of proof. Turow, S.
BUREAUCRACY
Bulgakov, M. A. The master and Margarita
Grushin, O. The dream life of Sukhanov
Watkins, C. V. Gold fame citrus
Whitehead, C. The intuitionist
The **burgess** boys. Strout, E.
The **burglar** in the library. Block, L.
BURGLARS *See* Thieves
BURIAL
See also Archeology; Public health
Burial rites. Kent, H.
The **buried** giant. Ishiguro, K.
Buried prey. Sandford, J.
Buried secrets. Finder, J.
BURIED TREASURE
Conrad, J. Nostromo
DeMille, N. Plum Island
Fay, K. The map of lost memories
Forester, C. S. Hornblower and the Atropos
Mosher, H. F. On Kingdom Mountain
Motion, A. Silver
BURIED TREASURE
See also Archeology; Underwater exploration
BURLESQUE (LITERATURE)
See also Comedy; Parody; Satire
BURMA
Ghosh, A. The glass palace
Mason, D. The piano tuner
Tan, A. Saving fish from drowning
BURMA -- HISTORY -- 20TH CENTURY
Craig, C. Miss Burma
Burmese days; Keep the aspidistra flying; Coming up for air. Orwell, G.
Burn. Lutz, J.
BURN CARE UNITS
Davidson, A. The gargoyle
BURN OUT (PSYCHOLOGY)
See also Job satisfaction; Job stress; Mental health; Motivation (Psychology); Occupational health and safety; Stress (Psychology)
The **burning** air. Kelly, E.
Burning bright. Rash, R.

The **burning** point. Putney, M. J.
The **burning** room. Connelly, M.
The **burning** soul. Connolly, J.
Burning your boats. Carter, A.
Burr. Vidal, G.
Burr, Aaron, 1756-1836
About
Vidal, G. Burr
Burton, Richard Francis, Sir, 1821-1890
About
Hodder, M. Expedition to the Mountains of the Moon
Hodder, M. The strange affair of Spring Heeled Jack
Bury me deep. Abbott, M. E.
Bury your dead. Penny, L.
BURYING GROUNDS *See* Burial; Cemeteries
BUSES
See also Automobiles; Highway transportation; Local transit; Motor vehicles
BUSH SURVIVAL *See* Wilderness survival
BUSINESS
Dewitt, H. Lightning rods
Finder, J. Buried secrets
Finder, J. Vanished
Heffernan, W. The Dinosaur Club
Norris, F. The pit
O'Hara, J. From the terrace
Tarkington, B. The magnificent Ambersons
Theroux, P. Kowloon Tong
Vonnegut, K. Jailbird
Wilson, S. The man in the gray flannel suit
BUSINESS -- UNSCRUPULOUS METHODS
Goddard, R. Into the blue
Ignatius, D. A firing offense
Larsson, S. The girl with the dragon tattoo
Le Carre, J. The constant gardener
Martin, C. W. How to sell
Norris, F. The octopus
BUSINESS BUDGETS
See also Business
BUSINESS DEPRESSION, 1929
Adams, A. A southern exposure
Algren, N. A walk on the wild side
Brown, J. D. Addie Pray
Doig, I. Bucking the sun
Kennedy, W. Ironweed
Koryta, M. The Cypress House
BUSINESS ENTERPRISES
See also Business
BUSINESS ENTERPRISES -- CORRUPT PRACTICES
Gill, J. F. The gargoyle hunters
BUSINESS ETHICS
See also Ethics; Professional ethics
BUSINESS FAILURES
See also Business
BUSINESS INTELLIGENCE
Gibson, W. Pattern recognition
Morgan Jones, C. The silent oligarch
Stevens, T. The informationist
BUSINESS MATHEMATICS
See also Mathematics
The **Business** of Naming Things. Coffey, M.
BUSINESS WRITING
See also Authorship
BUSINESSMEN
Adiga, A. The white tiger
Atwood, M. The blind assassin
Boyle, T. C. When the killing's done
Dahl, A. Misterioso
The Discreet Hero
Eggers, D. A hologram for the king
Guinn, M. The scribe
Guterson, D. Ed King
Ignatius, D. The Sun King
Krentz, J. A. Trust no one
Lanchester, J. Fragrant Harbor
Lewis, S. Babbitt
Lightman, A. P. The diagnosis
McGuane, T. Nothing but blue skies
Millhauser, S. Martin Dressler
Percy, W. The moviegoer
Roth, P. American pastoral
Westlake, D. E. The ax
Yates, A. Moondogs
BUSINESSPEOPLE
See also Business
BUSINESSPEOPLE -- UNITED STATES
Moore, G. The last days of night
BUSINESSWOMEN
Bradford, B. T. A woman of substance
Campbell, B. M. Brothers and sisters
Dee, J. A thousand pardons
Goodman, A. The cookbook collector
Hill, R. When all is said and done
Lippman, L. And when she was good
McMillan, T. How Stella got her groove back
Vidal, G. Empire
Wood, B. Perfect Harmony
BUSINESSWOMEN
See also Businesspeople; Women
Busman's honeymoon. Sayers, D. L.
Busy bodies. Hess, J.
But come ye back. Lordan, B.
BUTLERS
Ishiguro, K. The remains of the day
McGrath, P. The grotesque
Wodehouse, P. G. The world of Jeeves
BUTTE (MONT.)
Doig, I. Work song
Butterfield 8. O'Hara, J.
BUTTERFLIES
See also Insects
Buying a fishing rod for my grandfather. Gao Xingjian
Buzz cut. Hall, J. W.
By blood. Ullman, E.

By blood we live. Duncan, G.
By Gaslight. Price, S.
By night in Chile. Bolano, R.
By nightfall. Cunningham, M.
By order of the President. Griffin, W. E. B.
By schism rent asunder. Weber, D.
By the lake. McGahern, J.
By the light of my father's smile. Walker, A.
By the waters of Manhattan. Reznikoff, C.
Byron, George Gordon Byron, 6th Baron, 1788-1824
About
Crowley, J. Lord Byron's novel
BYZANTINE ART
See also Ancient art; Art; Medieval art
BYZANTINE EMPIRE
Duffy, S. Theodora

C

C. McCarthy, T.
C is for corpse. Grafton, S.
CAB DRIVERS
O'Dell, T. Sister mine
Self, W. The Book of Dave
CABALA
See also Hebrew literature; Jewish literature; Judaism; Mysticism; Occultism
CABINET MEMBERS
Antunes, A. L. The inquisitors' manual
Holland, C. Valley of the Kings
Hunt, R. Mr. Chartwell
Russell, M. D. Dreamers of the day
The **cabinet** of curiosities. Preston, D.
CABLE RAILROADS
See also Railroads
CABLES, SUBMARINE
Griesemer, J. Signal & noise
CADAVERS *See* Dead
CÁDIZ (SPAIN) -- HISTORY -- SIEGE, 1810-1812
Pérez-Reverte, A. The siege
The **cadence** of grass. McGuane, T.
Caesar, Julius, 100-44 B.C.
About
Saylor, S. The triumph of Caesar
Wilder, T. The ides of March
CAGE BIRDS
See also Birds
CAGE, PENN (FICTITIOUS CHARACTER)
Iles, G. The bone tree
Iles, G. Mississippi blood
Iles, G. Natchez burning
Cain.
Cain (Biblical figure)
About
Cain
Maine, D. Fallen
Cain his brother. Perry, A.
The **Caine** mutiny. Wouk, H.
CAIRO (EGYPT)
Steinhauer, O. The Cairo affair
The **Cairo** affair. Steinhauer, O.
CAJUNS
Gaines, E. J. A gathering of old men
Wells, K. Crawfish mountain
Cakes and ale. Maugham, W. S.
Calamity Jane, 1852-1903
About
McMurtry, L. Buffalo girls
CALCULUS
See also Mathematical analysis; Mathematics
CALCUTTA (INDIA)
Mukherjee, A. A Rising Man
Caleb's crossing. Brooks, G.
CALENDARS
See also Time
Caliban's war. Corey, J. S. A.
CALIFORNIA
Bennett, B. The mothers
Boswell, R. Tumbledown
Cline, E. The girls
Darnielle, J. Wolf in white van
Huneven, M. Blame
Hurwitz, G. They're watching
Hurwitz, G. You're next
Huston, C. The shotgun rule
Johnson, D. Elsewhere, California
Kinder, C. Honeymooners
Klein, M. Con ed
Koontz, D. R. Brother Odd
Koontz, D. R. The darkest evening of the year
Koontz, D. R. The husband
Koontz, D. R. Velocity
Lazar, Z. Sway
Lee, C. Y. The flower drum song
Mapson Solomon's oak
Miller, S. Lost in the forest
Otto, W. How to make an American quilt
Packer, A. The Children's Crusade
Packer, A. Songs without words
Parker, T. J. California girl
Parker, T. J. Storm runners
Pronzini, B. The hidden
Puchner, E. Model home
Pyne, D. Twentynine Palms
Rosenberg, N. T. Abuse of power
Rosenberg, N. T. Interest of justice
Rosenberg, N. T. Mitigating circumstances
Saroyan, W. The human comedy
Saul, J. The homing
Schwartz, J. B. Northwest corner
Schwartz, L. Angels Crest
Silver, M. The god of war
Steinbeck, J. East of Eden
Straight, S. The gettin place

Straight, S. Highwire moon
Thomas, R. The fourth Durango
Tobar, H. The barbarian nurseries
Tsukiyama, G. Dreaming water
Van Eekhout, G. California bones
Villarreal, J. A. Pocho
Williams, K. Dirty to the grave
Winslow, D. Savages
Wood, S. Wrecker

CALIFORNIA -- 1846-1900
Allende, I. Daughter of fortune
DeWitt, P. The Sisters brothers
Norris, F. The octopus
Steinbeck, J. East of Eden

CALIFORNIA -- 19TH CENTURY
Holland, C. An ordinary woman
L'Amour, L. The Californios

CALIFORNIA -- 20TH CENTURY
Cunningham, M. The hours
Koontz, D. R. Intensity
Mapson Bad Girl Creek
Muller, M. Cyanide Wells
Otsuka, J. When the emperor was divine
Parker, T. J. Little Saigon
Parker, T. J. Silent Joe
Pronzini, B. In an evil time
Pynchon, T. The crying of lot 49
Pynchon, T. Vineland
Rosenberg, N. T. Abuse of power
Saul, J. The homing
Steinbeck, J. East of Eden
Steinbeck, J. The grapes of wrath
Steinbeck, J. In dubious battle
Steinbeck, J. The long valley
Steinbeck, J. Of mice and men
Woods, S. Dead eyes

CALIFORNIA -- BERKELEY
Goodman, A. The cookbook collector

CALIFORNIA -- BEVERLY HILLS
Martin, S. Shopgirl

CALIFORNIA -- GOLD DISCOVERIES
Allende, I. Daughter of fortune

CALIFORNIA -- HISTORY -- 1950-
Ullman, E. By blood

CALIFORNIA -- HOLLYWOOD
Barker, C. Coldheart Canyon
Didion, J. Play it as it lays
Erickson, S. Zeroville
Fitzgerald, F. S. The last tycoon
Gold, G. D. Sunnyside
Howrey, M. Blind sight
Leonard, E. Be cool
Leonard, E. Get Shorty
Puzo, M. The last Don
Schulberg, B. What makes Sammy run?
Vidal, G. Hollywood
Vidal, G. Myra Breckinridge [and] Myron
Wambaugh, J. Hollywood crows
Wambaugh, J. Hollywood Hills
Wambaugh, J. Hollywood Station
Waugh, E. The loved one
Woods, S. L.A. Times

CALIFORNIA -- LOS ANGELES
Abu-Jaber, D. Crescent
Albert, E. The book of Dahlia
Bender, A. The particular sadness of lemon cake
Boyle, T. C. The tortilla curtain
Campbell, B. M. Brothers and sisters
Connelly, M. The scarecrow
Crais, R. Demolition angel
Ellis, B. E. Imperial bedrooms
Ellroy, J. The black dahlia
Ellroy, J. Blood's a rover
Ellroy, J. L.A. confidential
Evison, J. All about Lulu
Fitch, J. Paint it black
Fitch, J. White oleander
Freudenberger, N. The dissident
Gilb, D. The flowers
Haywood, G. A. Cemetery Road
Hoag, T. Kill the messenger
Homes, A. M. This book will save your life
Hurwitz, G. The crime writer
Huston, C. The mystic arts of erasing all signs of death
Monette, P. Afterlife
Mosley, W. The last days of Ptolemy Grey
Parker, T. J. L.A. outlaws
Pynchon, T. Inherent vice
See, C. The handyman
See, C. There will never be another you
See, L. Shanghai girls
Simpson, M. Anywhere but here
Skyhorse, B. The Madonnas of Echo Park
Swierczynski, D. Fun and games
Toole, F. X. Pound for pound
Wambaugh, J. The blue knight
Wambaugh, J. The new centurions
Woods, S. Swimming to Catalina

CALIFORNIA -- MONTEREY
O'Shaughnessy, P. Unlucky in law
Steinbeck, J. Cannery Row
Steinbeck, J. Sweet Thursday
Steinbeck, J. Tortilla Flat

CALIFORNIA -- SAN DIEGO
Le, T. D. T. The gangster we are all looking for
Wambaugh, J. Finnegan's week
Wambaugh, J. Floaters
Winslow, D. The winter of Frankie Machine

CALIFORNIA -- SAN FRANCISCO
Adrian, C. The great night
Diffenbaugh, V. The language of flowers
Edgarian, C. Three stages of amazement
Egan, J. A visit from the Goon Squad
Gardiner, M. The Dirty Secrets Club

Greer, A. S. The story of a marriage
Jamison, L. The gin closet
Lee, C. Y. The flower drum song
Lee, G. China boy
Lescroart, J. T. The first law
Lescroart, J. T. Guilt
Lescroart, J. T. The hearing
Lescroart, J. T. Nothing but the truth
Lescroart, J. T. The oath
Maupin, A. Mary Ann in autumn
Maupin, A. Michael Tolliver lives
Mohr, J. Damascus
Moore, C. A dirty job
Ng, F. M. Bone
Norris, F. McTeague
Otsuka, J. The Buddha in the attic
Palwick, S. Shelter
Patterson, J. 1st to die
Richmond, M. No one you know
Shafak, E. The bastard of Istanbul
Tan, A. The Joy Luck Club
Tan, A. The bonesetter's daughter
Vollmann, W. T. The royal family
CALIFORNIA -- SAN JOSE
Malae, P. N. What we are
California bones. Van Eekhout, G.
California girl. Parker, T. J.
CALIFORNIA, SOUTHERN
Bennett, B. The mothers
Gavin, J. Middle men
Hagy, A. Boleto
Rice, L. The lemon orchard
The **Californios.** L'Amour, L.
The **call.** Murphy, Y.
Call it sleep. Roth, H.
Call me by your name. Aciman, A. A.
Call me irresistible. Phillips, S. E.
The **call** of the toad. Grass, G.
The **call** of the wild. London, J.
Callahan's con. Robinson, S.
The **calling.** Wolfe, I. A.
Calling Me Home. Kibler, J.
Calling the wind.
Calpurnia. Scott, A.
Calumet City. Newton, C.
CALVINISM
See also Reformation
Cam girl. Raeder, L.
CAMBODIA
Hall, A. Quiller Salamander
CAMBODIA -- HISTORY -- 1975-
Ratner, V. In the shadow of the banyan
CAMBODIANS -- CANADA
Echlin, K. The disappeared
CAMBODIANS -- UNITED STATES
Jen, G. World and town
CAMBRIDGE (ENGLAND)
Atkinson, K. Case histories
Cumming, C. The Trinity Six
Harris, R. Enigma
Stott, R. Ghostwalk
CAMBRIDGE (ENGLAND) -- SOCIAL LIFE AND CUSTOMS -- 19TH CENTURY
Friedman, D. Riot most uncouth
CAMBRIDGE (MASS.)
Aciman, A. Harvard Square
Goodman, A. The cookbook collector
Langton, J. The thief of Venice
CAMBRIDGESHIRE (ENGLAND)
Kelly, J. The fire baby
The **camel** bookmobile. Hamilton, M.
CAMEROONIANS -- UNITED STATES
Mbue, I. Behold the Dreamers
Camille. Dumas, A.
CAMPAIGN FUNDS
See also Elections; Politics
CAMPAIGNS, PRESIDENTIAL -- UNITED STATES *See* Presidents -- United States -- Election
CAMPING
Butler, N. The Hearts of Men
CAMPUS POLICE
Rodriguez, L. Every last secret
Camus, Albert, 1913-1960. Étranger
About
The Meursault investigation
Can't and Won't. Davis, L.
Canaan's tongue. Wray, J.
Canada. Ford, R.
CANADA
Adamson, G. The outlander
Atwood, M. The blind assassin
Braden, K. The Longest Night
Davies, R. The cunning man
Davies, R. Fifth business
Davies, R. Murther & walking spirits
Findley, T. The piano man's daughter
Ford, R. Canada
Itani, F. Remembering the bones
Itani, F. Requiem
Munro, A. Friend of my youth
Lewis, S. It can't happen here
Munro, A. Open secrets
Ondaatje, M. The cat's table
Ondaatje, M. In the skin of a lion
Pohl, F. Chernobyl
Reed, I. Flight to Canada
Shields, C. The stone diaries
Urquhart, J. Away
CANADA -- 19TH CENTURY
Atwood, M. Alias Grace
Brand, M. The Stingaree
Penney, S. The tenderness of wolves
CANADA -- BRITISH COLUMBIA
Stevens, C. Still missing

CANADA -- HALIFAX
Norman, H. The museum guard
CANADA -- MANITOBA
Norman, H. The haunting of L
Toews, M. A complicated kindness
CANADA -- MONTREAL
Echlin, K. The disappeared
Reichs, K. J. Deja dead
Ricci, N. The origin of species
Richler, M. Barney's version
Richler, M. Solomon Gursky was here
CANADA -- NEW BRUNSWICK
Richards, D. A. The bay of love and sorrows
CANADA -- NEWFOUNDLAND
Crummey, M. Galore
Johnston, W. The colony of unrequited dreams
Moore, L. February
Norman, H. The bird artist
Proulx, A. The shipping news
CANADA -- NORTHWEST TERRITORIES
Freedman, B. Mrs. Mike
Hay, E. Late nights on air
Patterson, K. Consumption
Vollmann, W. T. The rifles
CANADA -- NOVA SCOTIA
MacDonald Fall on your knees
Norman, H. What is left the daughter
CANADA -- ONTARIO
Davies, R. Fifth business
De la Roche, M. Jalna
Itani, F. Deafening
Lansens, L. The wife's tale
Lawson, M. Crow Lake
MacDonald The way the crow flies
Penney, S. The tenderness of wolves
Shields, C. Unless
Urquhart, J. A map of glass
CANADA -- QUÉBEC (PROVINCE)
Vollmann, W. T. Fathers and crows
CANADA -- ROYAL CANADIAN AIR FORCE
MacDonald The way the crow flies
CANADA -- RURAL LIFE
Munro, A. Lives of girls & women
CANADA -- SASKATCHEWAN
Hay, E. A student of weather
Stegner, W. E. The Big Rock Candy Mountain
CANADA -- TORONTO
Atwood, M. Cat's eye
Atwood, M. Life before man
Davies, R. The rebel angels
Gowdy, B. Helpless
Gowdy, B. The romantic
Michaels, A. Fugitive pieces
Pyper, A. The killing circle
Redhill, M. Consolation
Urquhart, J. A map of glass
CANADA -- WINNIPEG
Shields, C. The republic of love
Van Rooy, M. An ordinary decent criminal
Van Rooy, M. Your friendly neighborhood criminal
CANADA -- YUKON TERRITORY
London, J. The call of the wild
London, J. White Fang
CANADIANS -- EUROPE
Boyden, J. Three-day road
CANADIANS -- ITALY
Ondaatje, M. The English patient
CANADIANS -- UNITED STATES
Lansens, L. The wife's tale
The **canal.** Rourke, L.
CANARIES
See also Birds; Cage birds
CANASTA (GAME)
See also Card games
CANCER
Albert, E. The book of Dahlia
Bauermeister, E. Joy for beginners
D'Erasmo, S. The Sky Below
Garner, H. The spare room
Godwin, G. The good husband
Goodman, A. Intuition
Gordimer, N. Get a life
Hoffman, A. Skylight confessions
Keyes, M. Last Chance Saloon
Lee The surrendered
Lively, P. Moon tiger
Mann, T. The black swan
Maupin, A. Mary Ann in autumn
McPhee, M. Gorgeous lies
Mohr, J. Damascus
Nunez, E. Anna in-between
Petterson, P. I curse the river of time
Phillips, J. A. MotherKind
Robbins, T. Half asleep in frog pajamas
Sarton, M. A reckoning
Shriver, L. So much for that
Solzhenitsyn, A. Cancer ward
Strayed, C. Torch
Swarthout, G. F. The shootist
Vernon, O. Eden
West, M. L. The devil's advocate
CANCER
See also Diseases; Tumors
CANCER -- PATIENTS
Bock, C. Alice & Oliver
Brown, E. The weird sisters
Cunningham, M. The snow queen
Doyle, R. The Guts
Gordimer, N. Get a life
Like Family
Saunders, G. Tenth of December
CANCER -- SURGERY
See also Surgery
Cancer ward. Solzhenitsyn, A.

Candide and other stories. Voltaire
Candyland. Hunter, E.
Cane River. Tademy, L.
CANNABIS *See* Marijuana
Cannery Row. Steinbeck, J.
CANNIBALISM
Harris, T. Hannibal
Harris, T. Hannibal rising
CANNIBALISM
See also Ethnology; Human behavior
CANNIBALS
Melville, H. Omoo: a narrative of adventures in the South Seas
Melville, H. Typee: a peep at Polynesian life
CANOES AND CANOEING
Barr, N. Destroyer angel
Dickey, J. Deliverance
CANONIZATION
See also Christian saints; Rites and ceremonies
Canopus in Argos: archives [series]
Lessing, D. M. Shikasta
CANTERBURY (ENGLAND) -- HISTORY -- 16TH CENTURY
Parris, S. J. Sacrilege
A **canticle** for Leibowitz. Miller, W. M.
Canvey Island. Runcie, J.
The **canyon** of bones. Wheeler, R. S.
Capacity for murder. Pajer, B.
Cape Cod. Martin, W.
CAPE TOWN (SOUTH AFRICA)
Nineveh
Capital Punishment. Wilson, R.
CAPITAL PUNISHMENT
See also Criminal law; Punishment
CAPITAL PUNISHMENT
Dreiser, T. An American tragedy
Gaines, E. J. A lesson before dying
Grisham, J. The confession
Hellström, B. Cell 8
Mailer, N. The executioner's song
McCrumb, S. The ballad of Frankie Silver
Patterson, R. N. Conviction
Picoult, J. Change of heart
Silver, E. L. The execution of Noa P. Singleton
Turow, S. Reversible errors
CAPITALISTS AND FINANCIERS
Dickens, C. Dombey and Son
Durrell, L. Justine
Fuentes, C. The death of Artemio Cruz
Gordimer, N. The conservationist
Grippando, J. Money to burn
Gross, A. Reckless
Norris, F. The pit
Ondaatje, M. In the skin of a lion
O'Neill, J. Netherland
Pears, I. Stone's fall
Rand, A. Atlas shrugged
Singer, I. J. The brothers Ashkenazi
CAPITALS (CITIES)
See also Cities and towns
Capote in Kansas. Powers, K.
Capote, Truman, 1924-1984
About
Powers, K. Capote in Kansas
CAPRI
Goodman, C. The night villa
Rice, L. The deep blue sea for beginners
Captain Alatriste. Perez-Reverte, A.
The **captain** and the enemy. Greene, G.
Captain Blood. Sabatini, R.
Captain Newman, M.D. Rosten, L.
Captain Pantoja and the Special Service. Vargas Llosa, M.
The **captive** [and] The fugitive. Proust, M.
The **captive** Queen of Scots. Plaidy, J.
Captivity. Wesselmann, D. L.
CAR ACCIDENTS *See* Traffic accidents
CAR INDUSTRY *See* Automobile industry
CAR WRECKS *See* Traffic accidents
Caramba! Martinez, N. M.
Caravan of thieves. Rich, D.
Caravans. Michener, J. A.
CARCINOMA *See* Cancer
CARD GAMES
Stroby, W. Cold shot to the heart
CARD GAMES
See also Games
CARD TRICKS
See also Card games; Magic tricks; Tricks
CARDIFF (WALES)
Bingham, H. Talking to the dead
CARDINALS
Vallgren The horrific sufferings of the mind-reading monster Hercules Barefoot
Cardington Crescent. Perry, A.
CARE GIVERS *See* Caregivers
Care of wooden floors. Wiles, W.
Career of evil. Galbraith, R.
CAREGIVERS
Berg, E. We are all welcome here
Evison, J. The revised fundamentals of caregiving
Careless in red. George, E.
The **Caretaker.** Ahmad, A. X.
The **caretaker** of Lorne Field. Zeltserman, D.
Caribbean. Michener, J. A.
CARIBBEAN REGION
Allende, I. Island beneath the sea
Buffett, J. A salty piece of land
Crichton, M. Pirate latitudes
Kincaid, J. Autobiography of my mother
Matthiessen, P. Far Tortuga
Michener, J. A. Caribbean
Nunez, E. Anna in-between
Stone, R. Bay of souls
Vonnegut, K. Cat's cradle

Wolfe, G. Pirate freedom
Woods, S. Dead in the water
Caribou Island. Vann, D.
Carmen. Merimee, P.
Carnarvon, Henry Howard Molyneux Herbert, 4th Earl of, 1831-1890
About
Holland, C. Valley of the Kings
CARNIVAL
See also Festivals
CARNIVAL -- HAITI
Dépestre, R. Hadriana in all my dreams
CARNIVALS
See also Amusements; Festivals
Dunn, K. Geek love
CARNIVOROUS ANIMALS
See also Animals
CARPATHIAN MOUNTAINS
Wiesel, E. The oath
Carpentaria. Wright, A.
The **carpet** makers. Eschbach, A.
Carrie. King, S.
A **carrion** death. Stanley, M.
Carroll, Lewis, 1832-1898
About
Benjamin, M. Alice I have been
Carry the one. Anshaw, C.
CARS (AUTOMOBILES) *See* Automobiles
The **cartel.** Winslow, D.
Carter Ross mysteries [series]
Parks, B. The girl next door
Carter, Howard
About
Holland, C. Valley of the Kings
Carthage. Oates, J. C.
CARTOGRAPHERS
Humphreys, H. Afterimage
CARTOGRAPHY *See* Map drawing; Maps
CARTOONING
See also Cartoons and caricatures; Wit and humor
CARTOONISTS
Jacobson, H. Kalooki nights
CARTOONS AND COMICS
Pierson, D. C. The boy who couldn't sleep and never had to
CARVING, WOOD *See* Wood carving
The **case** has altered. Grimes, M.
Case histories. Atkinson, K.
The **case** of the deadly butter chicken. Hall, T.
The **case** of the love commandos. Hall, T.
Caselli and Torre [series]
Dazieri, S. Kill the father
Casement, Roger, Sir, 1864-1916
About
The dream of the Celt
Cashelmara. Howatch, S.
Casino Royale. Fleming, I.
CASINOS
Hilton, E. Dirty money Honey
The **Cassandra** project. McDevitt, J.
CASSETTE TAPES, AUDIO *See* Sound recordings
Cassidy, David
About
Pearson, A. I think I love you
CASTAWAYS *See* Survival after airplane accidents, shipwrecks, etc.
CASTE -- INDIA
Mistry, R. A fine balance
Roy, A. The god of small things
Viswanathan, P. The toss of a lemon
The **castle.** Kafka, F.
Castle. Lennon, J. R.
The **castle** in the forest. Mailer, N.
CASTLES
Egan, J. The keep
Holt, V. Bride of Pendorric
Nicholas, D. The wicked
Stewart, M. Nine coaches waiting
Castles ever after [series]
Dare, T. Romancing the duke
Castleview. Wolfe, G.
Castro, Fidel, 1926-2016
About
Block, L. Killing Castro
Fuentes, N. The autobiography of Fidel Castro
Hunter, S. Havana
The **casual** vacancy. Rowling, J. K.
CASUALTY INSURANCE
See also Insurance
Cat & mouse. Patterson, J.
Cat and mouse. Grass, G.
The **cat** who ate Danish modern. Braun, L. J.
The **cat** who went underground. Braun, L. J.
Cat's cradle. Vonnegut, K.
Cat's eye. Atwood, M.
The **cat's** table. Ondaatje, M.
CATACOMBS
See also Burial; Cemeteries; Christian antiquities; Tombs
Catalyst. Hoffman, N. K.
CATASTROPHES *See* Disasters
Catch me. Gardner, L.
Catch-22. Heller, J.
The **catcher** in the rye. Salinger, J. D.
Catching Katie. Hatcher, R. L.
Catharine Howard, Queen, consort of Henry VIII, King of England, d. 1542
About
Gregory, P. The Boleyn Inheritance
Plaidy, J. Murder most royal
Catharine Parr, Queen, consort of Henry VIII, King of England, 1512-1548
About
Gregory, P. The taming of the queen

Catharine, of Aragon, Queen, consort of Henry VIII, King of England, 1485-1536
About
Gregory, P. The constant princess
Gregory, P. The other Boleyn girl
CATHEDRAL LIFE
Dickens, C. The mystery of Edwin Drood
Hugo, V. The hunchback of Notre Dame
Palliser, C. The unburied
Trollope, A. Barchester Towers
CATHEDRALS
Dickens, C. The mystery of Edwin Drood
Follett, K. The pillars of the earth
Follett, K. World without end
Lovett, C. The lost book of the Grail
Steele, J. The watchers
Catherine, of Braganza, Queen, consort of Charles II, King of England, 1638-1705
About
Plaidy, J. The pleasures of love
Catherine, of Valois, Queen, consort of Henry V, King of England, 1401-1437
About
Bennett, V. The queen's lover
CATHOLIC BISHOPS
Cather, W. Death comes for the archbishop
CATHOLIC CHURCH
See also Christian sects; Christianity
CATHOLIC CHURCH -- CLERGY
See also Clergy; Priests
CATHOLIC CHURCH -- CLERGY
Bolano, R. By night in Chile
Erdrich, L. The last report on the miracles at Little No Horse
CATHOLIC CHURCH -- LITURGY
See also Liturgies; Rites and ceremonies
CATHOLIC CHURCH -- MISSIONS
Cather, W. Death comes for the archbishop
CATHOLIC EX-NUNS *See* Ex-nuns
CATHOLIC EX-PRIESTS *See* Ex-priests
CATHOLIC FAITH
Alexie, S. Reservation blues
Barrett, W. E. The lilies of the field
Boll, H. The clown
Cather, W. Death comes for the archbishop
Deane, S. Reading in the dark
Eco, U. The name of the rose
Endo, S. Deep river
Erdrich, L. The last report on the miracles at Little No Horse
Godwin, G. Unfinished desires
Gordon, M. The company of women
Gordon, M. Final payments
Grass, G. Cat and mouse
Greene, G. Brighton rock
Greene, G. The end of the affair
Greene, G. The heart of the matter
Greene, G. The power and the glory
Hansen, R. Mariette in ecstasy
Hulme, K. The nun's story
Lescroart, J. T. Guilt
McDermott, A. After this
McDermott, A. At weddings and wakes
McDermott, A. Charming Billy
Meloy, M. A family daughter
Meloy, M. Liars and saints
Percy, W. Love in the ruins
Powers, J. F. Wheat that springeth green
Prose, F. Household saints
Quindlen, A. Object lessons
Rabb, J. The book of Q
Rosero, E. Good offices
Stendhal The red and the black
Waugh, E. Brideshead revisited
Werfel, F. The song of Bernadette
West, M. L. The clowns of God
West, M. L. Lazarus
West, M. L. The shoes of the fisherman
CATHOLIC PRIESTS
Binchy, M. Whitethorn Woods
Blatty, W. P. The exorcist
Bolano, R. By night in Chile
Camus, A. The plague
Cather, W. Death comes for the archbishop
Cronin, A. J. The keys of the kingdom
Delaney, E. J. Broken Irish
Endo, S. Silence
Erdrich, L. The last report on the miracles at Little No Horse
Flynn, M. Eifelheim
Gordon, M. The company of women
Greene, G. The honorary consul
Greene, G. The power and the glory
Haigh, J. Faith
Higgins, J. Confessional
Kienzle, W. X. The rosary murders
McCullough, C. The thorn birds
O'Hagan, A. Be near me
Picoult, J. Change of heart
Powers, J. F. Wheat that springeth green
Rabb, J. The book of Q
Reimringer, J. Vestments
Roberts, M. Reader, I married him
Rosero, E. Good offices
Schulberg, B. Waterfront
Vargas Llosa, M. The Green House
West, M. L. The devil's advocate
Wolfe, G. Pirate freedom
Zelazny, R. The dead man's brother
CATHOLICS
Follett, K. A column of fire
CATS
Danielewski, M. Z. The familiar
Wong, D. Futuristic Violence and Fancy Suits
CATSKILL MOUNTAINS (N.Y.)
Goodman, A. Kaaterskill Falls
CATTLE DRIVERS

McMurtry, L. Lonesome dove
CAUCASUS, NORTHERN (RUSSIA)
Lapierre, A. Between love and honor
Caught. Coben, H.
Caught stealing. Huston, C.
CAUTIONARY TALES AND VERSES *See* Didactic fiction; Didactic poetry; Fables; Parables
The **cave.** Saramago, J.
CAVE ECOLOGY
See also Ecology
Caveat emptor. Downie, R.
CELEBRITIES
Hiaasen, C. Star Island
Rushdie, S. The ground beneath her feet
Wayne, T. The Love Song of Jonny Valentine
Williams, C. Stairway to hell
CELEBRITY *See* Fame
Celestial navigation. Tyler, A.
The **Celestials.** Shepard, K.
The **celestine** prophecy. Redfield, J.
CELIBACY
See also Clergy; Religious life
Celine. Heller, P.
Cell 8. Hellström, B.
CELL PHONE THEFT
Kinsella, S. I've got your number
CELLISTS
Romano-Lax, A. The Spanish bow
Celt and pepper. McInerny, R. M.
CELTS
Kay, G. G. Ysabel
CEMETERIES
King, S. Pet sematary
Miller, A. Pure
Reynolds, S. A gracious plenty
Cemetery Lake. Cleave, P.
Cemetery Road. Haywood, G. A.
CENSORSHIP
Absolution
The **centaur.** Updike, J.
Centennial. Michener, J. A.
The **center** of everything. Moriarty, L.
The **Center** of the World. Van Essen, T.
CENTRAL AFRICA
Ballard, J. G. The day of creation
CENTRAL AMERICA
Forester, C. S. Beat to quarters
CENTRAL EUROPE
Egan, J. The keep
CENTRAL PARK (NEW YORK, N.Y.)
Hallberg, G. R. City on fire
CENTRAL STATES *See* Middle West
Central Station. Tidhar, L.
Centuries of June. Donohue, K.
A **Century** of great Western stories.
Century's son. Boswell, R.
CERAMISTS
Vreeland, S. Clara and Mr. Tiffany
CEREBROVASCULAR DISEASE
Albert, E. The book of Dahlia
Ha Jin The crazed
CEREMONIES *See* Etiquette; Manners and customs; Rites and ceremonies
Ceremony. Silko, L.
Certain girls. Weiner, J.
A **certain** justice. James, P. D.
Certain prey. Sandford, J.
Certain women. L'Engle, M.
CERTIFIED PUBLIC ACCOUNTANTS *See* Accountants
Chagall, Marc, 1887-1985
About
Horn, D. The world to come
CHAIN STORES
See also Retail trade; Stores
Chalcot Crescent. Weldon, F.
Chalice of blood. Tremayne, P.
The **chalk** girl. O'Connell, C.
CHALLENGER (SPACE SHUTTLE)
Dean, M. L. The time it takes to fall
Champlain, Samuel de, 1574-1635
About
Penny, L. Bury your dead
Chance. Parker, R. B.
Chance Sisters [series]
Gracie, A. The Winter Bride
CHANCELLORSVILLE (VA.), BATTLE OF, 1863
Crane, S. The red badge of courage
CHANGE (PSYCHOLOGY)
Chiang, T. Stories of your life and others
Prose, F. A changed man
Change agent. Suárez, D.
Change of heart. Picoult, J.
A **changed** man. Prose, F.
The **changeling.** Oe, K.
Chango's beads and two-tone shoes. Kennedy, W.
CHANNEL ISLANDS
Goudge, E. Green Dolphin Street
CHANNEL ISLANDS (CALIF.)
Boyle, T. C. When the killing's done
CHAPBOOKS
See also Books; Folklore; Literature; Pamphlets; Periodicals; Wit and humor
CHAPLAINS
See also Clergy
Chaplin, Charlie, 1889-1977
About
Gold, G. D. Sunnyside
CHARACTER
See also Ethics; Personality
Charbonneau, Jean-Baptiste, 1805-1866
About
Sargent, C. Museum of human beings
CHARITY
Kubica, M. Pretty Baby

CHARITY
See also Ethics; Virtue
Charity girl. Lowenthal, M.
The **Charlemagne** pursuit. Berry, S.
Charles II, King of Great Britain, 1630-1685
About
Plaidy, J. The pleasures of love
Charles, d'Orléans, 1394-1465
About
Haasse, H. S. In a dark wood wandering
Charley Bland. Settle, M. L.
Charlie Boxer books [series]
Wilson, R. Capital Punishment
Charlie Martz and other stories. Leonard, E.
Charlotte Gray. Faulks, S.
The **Charlotte** Perkins Gilman reader. Gilman, C. P.
Charlotte Perkins Gilman's Utopian novels.
A **charmed** life. McCarthy, M.
Charming Billy. McDermott, A.
CHARMS
See also Folklore; Superstition
The **charterhouse** of Parma. Stendhal
Chaser. Miasha
CHASIDISM *See* Hasidism
Chasing darkness. Crais, R.
Chasing the king of hearts.
CHATEAUX *See* Castles
The **Chatham** School affair. Cook, T. H.
CHAUFFEURS
Adiga, A. The white tiger
Howard, R. Driving the king
Cheater. Van Dyken, R.
Cheating at solitaire. Haddam, J.
CHECHNIA (RUSSIA) -- HISTORY -- CIVIL WAR, 1994-
Marra, A. A constellation of vital phenomena
CHECKERS
See also Board games
CHEERFUL STORIES
Austen, J. Emma
Colwin, L. Happy all the time
Davies, V. Miracle on 34th Street
Read Affairs at Thrush Green
Read At home in Thrush Green
Read Farewell to Fairacre
Read Thrush Green
West, J. The friendly persuasion
White, B. Quite a year for plums
Wodehouse, P. G. The code of the Woosters
Wodehouse, P. G. The inimitable Jeeves
Wodehouse, P. G. Tales from the Drones Club
Wodehouse, P. G. A Wodehouse bestiary
Wodehouse, P. G. The world of Jeeves
CHEERLEADING -- COACHING
Abbott, M. E. Dare me
Cheeshahteaumuck, Caleb, ca. 1646-1666
About
Brooks, G. Caleb's crossing
CHEFS *See* Cooks
CHEMICAL INDUSTRY -- ACCIDENTS
See also Industrial accidents
CHEMICAL POLLUTION *See* Pollution
CHEMICAL WARFARE
See also Military art and science; War
CHEMISTRY -- DICTIONARIES
See also Encyclopedias and dictionaries
The **chemistry** of tears. Carey, P.
CHEMISTS
Levi, P. The monkey's wrench
Rubenfeld, J. The death instinct
Wallace, I. The prize
CHEMISTS
See also Scientists
CHEN, INSPECTOR (FICTITIOUS CHARACTER)
Qiu Xiaolong Shanghai redemption
Qiu Xiaolong Death of a red heroine
Cheney, Mamah Borthwick, d. 1914
About
Horan, N. Loving Frank
Chernobyl. Pohl, F.
CHERNOBYL NUCLEAR ACCIDENT, CHERNOBYL, UKRAINE, 1986
Pohl, F. Chernobyl
CHEROKEE INDIANS
Brown, D. A. Creek Mary's blood
Conley, R. J. Mountain windsong
Frazier, C. Thirteen moons
House, S. A parchment of leaves
Kingsolver, B. Pigs in heaven
McMurtry, L. Zeke and Ned
Chesapeake. Michener, J. A.
CHESAPEAKE BAY (MD. AND VA.)
Gear, K. O. People of the mist
Michener, J. A. Chesapeake
CHESS
Dunnett, D. Pawn in frankincense
Neville, K. The eight
Neville, K. The fire
Tevis, W. S. The queen's gambit
CHESS
See also Board games
CHEYENNE INDIANS
Berger, T. Little Big Man
CHICAGO (ILL.)
Newton, C. Start shooting
Paretsky, S. Breakdown
Paretsky, S. Brush back
Phillips, J. A. Quiet dell
Phillips, S. E. Match me if you can
Rotert, R. Last night at the blue angel
CHICAGO (ILL.) -- RACE RELATIONS
See also Race relations
CHICAGO (ILL.) -- SOCIAL CONDITIONS
See also Social conditions
The **Chicago** way. Harvey, M. T.

Chicana & Chicano visions of the Américas [series]
Anaya, R. A. The man who could fly and other stories
CHICANOS *See* Mexican Americans
CHICKENPOX
See also Diseases; Viruses
Chief Inspector Gamache [series]
Penny, L. Glass houses
Penny, L. The long way home
CHIEF JUSTICES *See* Judges
CHIEF OPERATING OFFICERS
Cohen, J. Book of numbers
CHIEFDOMS -- UGANDA -- HISTORY
Makumbi, J. N. Kintu
Chiefs. Woods, S.
The **child.** Barton, F.
Child 44. Smith, T. R.
CHILD ABUSE
Allison, D. Bastard out of Carolina
Newton, C. Calumet City
Oates, J. C. Daddy Love
O'Connell, C. The chalk girl
Revoyr, N. Wingshooters
Reynolds, M. The Starlite Drive-in
Rossner, J. Perfidia
CHILD ACTORS
See also Actors
CHILD ACTORS
Williams, W. J. The fourth wall
CHILD AND MOTHER *See* Mother-child relationship
CHILD ARTISTS
See also Artists; Gifted children
CHILD AUTHORS
See also Authors; Gifted children
CHILD CELEBRITIES
Wayne, T. The Love Song of Jonny Valentine
CHILD CUSTODY
Edwards, K. The memory keeper's daughter
Goodman, J. A place called home
Walker, A. The third life of Grange Copeland
CHILD DEATH *See* Children -- Death
CHILD DEVELOPMENT
See also Children
The **child** garden. McPherson, C.
The **child** goddess. Marley, L.
The **child** in time. McEwan, I.
CHILD LABOR
Dickens, C. Oliver Twist
CHILD LABOR
See also Age and employment; Child welfare; Labor; Social problems
CHILD MOLESTING *See* Child sexual abuse
CHILD NEGLECT *See* Child abuse
Child of my heart. McDermott, A.
CHILD SEXUAL ABUSE
Haigh, J. Faith
Hassman, T. Girlchild
MacDonald The way the crow flies
McBride, E. A girl is a half-formed thing
CHILD SEXUAL ABUSE
See also Child abuse; Incest; Sex crimes
CHILD SOLDIERS
See also Children; Soldiers
CHILD SOLDIERS -- AFRICA
Hoagland, E. Children are diamonds
The **child** who. Lelic, S.
CHILD-ADULT RELATIONSHIP
See also Children
CHILDBIRTH -- CHINA -- HISTORY -- 20TH CENTURY
Frog
CHILDHOOD DISEASES *See* Children -- Diseases
The **Childhood** of Jesus. Coetzee, J. M.
Childhood's end. Clarke, A. C.
Childhood, Boyhood and Youth. Tolstoy, L.
CHILDLESS MARRIAGE
Lynn, A. Now you see it
Moore, L. A gate at the stairs
Rosenfeld, L. I'm so happy for you
Ross, A. Mr. Peanut
Swift, G. Waterland
CHILDLESSNESS
See also Children; Family size
CHILDLESSNESS
Green, J. Another piece of my heart
Oates, J. C. I lock my door upon myself
The **children.** Wharton, E.
CHILDREN
Adrian, C. The children's hospital
Beattie, A. Picturing Will
Benjamin, M. Alice I have been
Doctorow, E. L. World's fair
Doyle, R. Paddy Clarke, ha ha ha
Garcia, C. A handbook to luck
Gibbons, K. Ellen Foster
Godden, R. The battle of the Villa Fiorita
Godden, R. The greengage summer
Hughes, R. A. W. A high wind in Jamaica
Ishiguro, K. Never let me go
Lee, H. To kill a mockingbird
Livesey, M. Criminals
Lourie, R. A hatred for tulips
McCullers, C. The member of the wedding
McDermott, A. At weddings and wakes
McEwan, I. The child in time
Morrison, T. God help the child
Pollen, B. The summer of the bear
Roth, H. Call it sleep
Walker, M. W. Under the beetle's cellar
CHILDREN
See also Age; Family
CHILDREN -- CONDUCT OF LIFE
Lambert, C. The children's home
CHILDREN -- CRIMES AGAINST
Ballantyne, L. The guilty one
Flint, E. Little deaths

CHILDREN -- CUSTODY *See* Child custody
CHILDREN -- DEATH
Erdrich, L. LaRose
Hemmings, K. H. The possibilities
Winthrop, E. H. The why of things
CHILDREN -- DEATH
See also Death
CHILDREN -- DISEASES
Newman, S. The Country of Ice Cream Star
CHILDREN -- DISEASES
See also Diseases
CHILDREN -- EMPLOYMENT *See* Child labor
CHILDREN -- INSTITUTIONAL CARE -- AUSTRIA
The chosen ones
CHILDREN -- LANGUAGE
See also Language and languages
CHILDREN -- MOLESTING *See* Child sexual abuse
CHILDREN -- MONTANA
Rock, P. The Shelter Cycle
CHILDREN -- NAZI PERSECUTION
The chosen ones
CHILDREN -- PLACING OUT *See* Adoption; Foster home care
CHILDREN -- SURGERY
See also Surgery
The **children** act. McEwan, I.
CHILDREN AND DEATH
See also Death
Children and fire. Hegi, U.
CHILDREN AND WAR
See also Children; War
CHILDREN AND WAR
Nović, S. Girl at war
Children are diamonds. Hoagland, E.
CHILDREN IN LITERATURE
Ivey, E. The snow child
Children in Reindeer Woods. Omarsdottir, K.
CHILDREN OF ALCOHOLICS
See also Children
CHILDREN OF ALCOHOLICS
Braffet, K. Save yourself
CHILDREN OF CLERGY
Lewis, B. The brethren
Lewis, B. The preacher's daughter
Sparks, N. A walk to remember
CHILDREN OF DISAPPEARED PERSONS
O'Farrell, M. Instructions for a heat wave
Schlink, B. Homecoming
CHILDREN OF DIVORCED PARENTS
See also Children; Divorce; Parent-child relationship
CHILDREN OF DIVORCED PARENTS
Stibbe, N. Man at the helm
Wolitzer, M. The position
CHILDREN OF DRUG ADDICTS
See also Children; Drug addicts
Children of earth and sky. Kay, G. G.
Children of fire. Karpyshyn, D.
CHILDREN OF GANGSTERS -- ENGLAND -- LONDON
Harkaway, N. Angelmaker
CHILDREN OF GAY PARENTS
See also Children
Children of God. Russell, M. D.
CHILDREN OF ILLEGAL ALIENS
Ko, L. The leavers
CHILDREN OF IMMIGRANTS
See also Children; Immigration and emigration
CHILDREN OF IMMIGRANTS
Villarreal, J. A. Pocho
CHILDREN OF MURDER VICTIMS
Black, S. The killing lessons
CHILDREN OF PRESIDENTS
Clotel, or, The president's daughter
Johansen, I. Final target
CHILDREN OF PRISONERS
Walker, A. The third life of Grange Copeland
CHILDREN OF PROMINENT PERSONS
Crowley, J. Lord Byron's novel
CHILDREN OF SINGLE PARENTS
See also Children; Single parents
Children of the alley. Mahfouz, N.
Children of the new world. Weinstein, A.
The **children** of the sky. Vinge, V.
Children of violence. Lessing, D. M.
CHILDREN OF WORKING PARENTS
See also Children; Parent-child relationship
Children of wrath. Grossman, P.
CHILDREN WITH DISABILITIES
See also Children; Exceptional children; People with disabilities
Drabble, M. The pure gold baby
CHILDREN WITH DISABILITIES -- INSTITUTIONAL CARE
Nussbaum, S. Good kings bad kings
CHILDREN WITH MENTAL DISABILITIES
See also Child psychiatry; Children with disabilities; People with mental disabilities
CHILDREN WITH MENTAL DISABILITIES
Edwards, K. The memory keeper's daughter
CHILDREN WITH PHYSICAL DISABILITIES
Phillips, J. A. Lark and Termite
CHILDREN WITH PHYSICAL DISABILITIES
See also Children with disabilities; People with physical disabilities
CHILDREN'S ART
See also Art
CHILDREN'S AUTHORS
Benford, G. Foundation's fear
Benjamin, M. Alice I have been
Faulks, S. Devil may care
Maguire, G. Son of a witch
The **children's** book. Byatt, A. S.
The **Children's** Crusade. Packer, A.
CHILDREN'S DISEASES *See* Children -- Diseases
The **children's** home. Lambert, C.

The **children's** hospital. Adrian, C.
CHILE
Allende, I. Maya's Notebook
Allende, I. The house of the spirits
Bolano, R. By night in Chile
CHILE -- 19TH CENTURY
Allende, I. Portrait in sepia
O'Brian, P. Blue at the mizzen
CHILE -- POLITICS AND GOVERNMENT -- 1970-1973
Ampuero, R. The Neruda case
CHILE -- VALPARAISO
Allende, I. Daughter of fortune
CHILEANS -- UNITED STATES
Allende, I. Daughter of fortune
The **chill.** Bilenchi, R.
Chilly scenes of winter. Beattie, A.
The **chimney** sweeper's boy. Vine, B.
CHIMPANZEES
Greenidge, K. We love you, Charlie Freeman
Hale, B. The evolution of Bruno Littlemore
Wesselmann, D. L. Captivity
CHIMPANZEES
See also Apes
CHIMPS *See* Chimpanzees
CHINA
Dai Sijie Once on a moonless night
Gao Xingjian Soul mountain
Garcia, C. Monkey hunting
Hood, A. The red thread
Lord, B. B. The middle heart
Tan, A. The Joy Luck Club
Yu Hua Brothers
CHINA -- 17TH CENTURY
See, L. Peony in love
CHINA -- 18TH CENTURY
Han, S. The enchantress
CHINA -- 1900-1949
Buck, P. S. The good earth
Cronin, A. J. The keys of the kingdom
Jin, H. Nanjing requiem
Lin Yutang Moment in Peking
Malraux, A. Man's fate (La condition humaine)
Shan, Sa The girl who played go
Tan, A. The kitchen god's wife
CHINA -- 1949-
Chen, D. Brothers
Gao Xingjian Buying a fishing rod for my grandfather
Ha Jin The bridegroom
Ha Jin The crazed
Ha Jin Waiting
Jiang Rong Wolf totem
Joinson, S. A lady cyclist's guide to Kashgar
Lin, J. The Dragon and the Pearl
Min, A. Becoming Madame Mao
Mo Yan Life and death are wearing me out
See, L. Dreams of joy
Steinhauer, O. An American spy
Tan, A. The bonesetter's daughter
Tan, A. The hundred secret senses
Thien, M. Do not say we have nothing
Yiyun Li A thousand years of good prayers
Yiyun Li The vagrants
CHINA -- 19TH CENTURY
Garcia, C. Monkey hunting
Min, A. Empress Orchid
CHINA -- 20TH CENTURY
Gao Xingjian Soul mountain
Garcia, C. Monkey hunting
Lianke, Y. Dream of Ding Village
Tan, A. The Joy Luck Club
CHINA -- BEIJING
Guo Xiaolu Twenty fragments of a ravenous youth
CHINA -- GUANGZHOU
Ghosh, A. River of smoke
CHINA -- HISTORY
Barker, S. The incarnations
The bathing women
Randel, W. D. The empress of bright moon
CHINA -- HISTORY -- TANG DYNASTY, 618-907
Randel, W. D. The empress of bright moon
CHINA -- HISTORY -- TIANAMEN SQUARE INCIDENT, 1989
Beijing coma
CHINA -- RELATIONS -- UNITED STATES
Jin, H. A map of betrayal
CHINA -- SHANGHAI
Ballard, J. G. Empire of the Sun
Ishiguro, K. When we were orphans
Malraux, A. Man's fate (La condition humaine)
Qiu Xiaolong Years of Red Dust
Reuss, F. Mohr
The song of everlasting sorrow
Stephenson, N. Reamde
CHINA -- SOCIAL CONDITIONS
Frog
CHINA -- SOCIAL LIFE AND CUSTOMS -- 21ST CENTURY
The bathing women
CHINA -- SOCIAL LIFE AND CUSTOMS
Thien, M. Do not say we have nothing
CHINA -- TIBET
Hilton, J. Lost horizon
Ma Jian Stick out your tongue
Pattison, E. The skull mantra
CHINA -- TO 1643
Kay, G. G. Under heaven
China boy. Lee, G.
China rich girlfriend. Kwan, K.
CHINATOWN (NEW YORK, N.Y.)
Lynch, K. Confucius Jane
Thompson, V. Murder in Chinatown
CHINESE
Bates, J. F. Midnight at the Dragon Café
Guo, X. I am China

CHINESE -- CUBA
Garcia, C. Monkey hunting
CHINESE -- ENGLAND
Guo Xiaolu A concise Chinese-English dictionary for lovers
CHINESE -- HAWAII
Michener, J. A. Hawaii
CHINESE -- MASSACHUSETTS
Shepard, K. The Celestials
CHINESE -- NEW YORK (STATE) -- NEW YORK
Kwok, J. Girl in translation
CHINESE -- NEW ZEALAND
Tremain, R. The color
CHINESE -- ONTARIO
Bates, J. F. Midnight at the Dragon Café
CHINESE -- SINGAPORE
Loh, V. Breaking the tongue
CHINESE -- UNITED STATES
Allende, I. Daughter of fortune
Fowler, K. J. Sarah Canary
Freudenberger, N. The dissident
Ha Jin A free life
Harrison, C. The finder
Jin, H. A good fall
Jin, H. The boat rocker
Kwok, J. Girl in translation
Lee, C. Y. The flower drum song
Raban, J. Waxwings
See, L. Shanghai girls
Steinbeck, J. Cannery Row
Williamson, P. Heart of the west
CHINESE AMERICAN TEENAGERS
Kwok, J. Girl in translation
CHINESE AMERICAN WOMEN
Lynch, K. Confucius Jane
CHINESE AMERICANS
Davies, P. H. The Fortunes
Jen, G. The love wife
Jen, G. Mona in the promised land
Jen, G. Typical American
Jen, G. Who's Irish?
Jen, G. World and town
Lee, G. China boy
Ng, F. M. Bone
Ng, C. Everything I never told you
Tan, A. The Joy Luck Club
Tan, A. The kitchen god's wife
Tan, A. The bonesetter's daughter
Tan, A. The hundred secret senses
Wood, B. Perfect Harmony
Yiyun Li A thousand years of good prayers
The **Chinese** bell murders. Gulik, R. H. v.
CHINESE FICTION -- TRANSLATIONS INTO ENGLISH
Beijing coma
Gao Xingjian Soul mountain
The song of everlasting sorrow
Yu Hua Brothers
CHINESE LANGUAGE
See also Language and languages
CHINESE MYTHOLOGY
See also Mythology
Chinook. Brand, M.
CHIPPEWA INDIANS
Erdrich, L. The plague of doves
Erdrich, L. Four souls
Erdrich, L. The last report on the miracles at Little No Horse
Erdrich, L. Love medicine
Erdrich, L. The painted drum
Erdrich, L. Tracks
CHIVALRY
Cervantes Saavedra, M. d. Don Quixote de la Mancha
Twain, M. A Connecticut Yankee in King Arthur's court
White, T. H. The once and future king
Chocolat. Harris, J.
CHOCOLATE
See also Food
CHOCOLATE
Harris, J. Peaches for Father Francis
CHOICE (PSYCHOLOGY)
Bennett, B. The mothers
Fridlund, E. History of wolves
Lijia Zhang Lotus
Silber, J. Fools
CHOICE OF BOOKS *See* Best books; Book selection; Books and reading
Choice of evil. Vachss, A. H.
Choke. Palahniuk, C.
Choke. Woods, S.
Choke hold. Faust, C.
CHOLERA
Roiphe, A. R. An imperfect lens
The **chosen** maiden. Stachniak, E.
The **chosen** ones.
Christ the Lord: out of Egypt. Rice, A.
Christ the Lord: the road to Cana. Rice, A.
CHRISTIAN ART
See also Art; Religious art
CHRISTIAN BIOGRAPHY
See also Biography; Religious biography
CHRISTIAN CIVILIZATION
See also Christianity; Civilization
CHRISTIAN ETHICS
See also Ethics
CHRISTIAN FICTION
Dekker, T. A.D. 30
Dekker, T. Mortal
Fisher, S. W. Anna's crossing
Groot, T. The sentinels of Andersonville
Lewis, B. The missing
Lewis, B. The preacher's daughter
Rosenberg, J. C. The twelfth Imam
Seitz, N. Trouble the water
Smith, A. A bigger life
Tatlock, A. Things we once held dear
Windle, J. Congo dawn

Wolf, J. This scarlet cord
CHRISTIAN FICTION
See also Fiction; Religious fiction
CHRISTIAN HERETICS
Parris, S. J. Sacrilege
CHRISTIAN LEGENDS
See also Legends
CHRISTIAN LIFE
Bunyan, J. The pilgrim's progress
Harper, K. Fall from pride
Kirkpatrick, J. A flickering light
Tyler, A. Saint maybe
CHRISTIAN MISSIONARIES
Joinson, S. A lady cyclist's guide to Kashgar
CHRISTIAN MISSIONS
See also Christianity; Church history; Church work
CHRISTIAN SAINTS
Urrea, L. A. The hummingbird's daughter
Williams, N. John
CHRISTIAN SAINTS
See also Saints
CHRISTIAN SAINTS -- ENGLAND -- NORTHUMBRIA (REGION)
Griffith, N. Hild
CHRISTIAN SCIENTISTS -- FICTION
Fridlund, E. History of wolves
CHRISTIAN SECTS
See also Christianity; Church history; Sects
CHRISTIAN SYMBOLISM
See also Symbolism
CHRISTIAN WOMEN
Jackson, N. Who do I talk to?
CHRISTIAN WOMEN SAINTS -- ENGLAND -- WHITBY
Griffith, N. Hild
CHRISTIANITY
Asch, S. The Apostle
Asch, S. The Nazarene
Brown, D. The Da Vinci code
De Bernieres, L. Birds without wings
Endo, S. Silence
L'Engle, M. Certain women
Sienkiewicz, H. Quo Vadis
Williams, N. John
CHRISTIANITY -- RELATIONS -- JUDAISM
See also Christianity and other religions; Judaism
CHRISTIANITY AND ECONOMICS
See also Christianity; Economics
CHRISTIANITY AND SCIENCE
See also Christianity; Religion and science
CHRISTIANS -- PERSECUTIONS
See also Church history; Persecution
Christiansen family [series]
Warren, S. M. Take a chance on me
Christine Falls. Banville, J.
CHRISTMAS
Johnson, C. Spirit of steamboat
A **Christmas** carol. Dickens, C.
CHRISTMAS STORIES
Davies, V. Miracle on 34th Street
Dickens, C. A Christmas carol
Faulks, S. A week in December
O'Nan, S. Last night at the Lobster
Pilcher, R. Winter solstice
Sedaris, D. Holidays on ice
CHRISTMAS TREES
See also Christmas decorations; Trees
Christy. Marshall, C.
CHROMOSOMES
See also Genetics; Heredity
Chronic city. Lethem, J.
CHRONIC DISEASES
See also Diseases
CHRONIC FATIGUE SYNDROME
See also Diseases
Chronicle of a death foretold. Garcia Marquez, G.
Chronicles of Barsetshire [series]
Trollope, A. Barchester Towers
Trollope, A. Doctor Thorne
Trollope, A. Framley parsonage
Trollope, A. The last chronicle of Barset
Trollope, A. The warden
Chronicles of Thomas Covenant, the Unbeliever [series]
Donaldson, S. R. The Illearth war
Donaldson, S. R. Lord Foul's bane
Donaldson, S. R. The power that preserves
Donaldson, S. R. The wounded Land
CHRONOLOGY
See also Astronomy; History; Time
CHURCH AND SOCIAL PROBLEMS
See also Church; Social problems
CHURCH AND STATE
Dunant, S. Blood and beauty
Poole, S. The Borgia mistress
CHURCH ARCHITECTURE
Follett, K. The pillars of the earth
CHURCH HISTORY -- 600-1500, MIDDLE AGES
See also Middle Ages
CHURCH HISTORY -- PRIMITIVE AND EARLY CHURCH
Sienkiewicz, H. Quo Vadis
CHURCH LIBRARIES
See also Libraries
CHURCH OF ENGLAND
Howatch, S. Glamorous powers
Howatch, S. The heartbreaker
Howatch, S. Scandalous risks
Howatch, S. Ultimate prizes
CHURCH SCHOOLS
Godwin, G. Unfinished desires
CHURCH UNIVERSAL AND TRIUMPHANT
Rock, P. The Shelter Cycle
CHURCH WORK WITH YOUTH
See also Church work; Youth
CHURCHES

Barrett, W. E. The lilies of the field
Churchill, Winston Sir, 1874-1965
About
Hunt, R. Mr. Chartwell
Russell, M. D. Dreamers of the day
CHURCHYARDS *See* Cemeteries
CIAMPI, MARLENE (FICTITIOUS CHARACTER)
Tanenbaum, R. K. Tragic
Tanenbaum, R. Act of revenge
Cibola burn. Corey, J. S. A.
The **cider** house rules. Irving, J.
CINEMA *See* Motion pictures
CINEMAS *See* Motion picture theaters
Cinnamon kiss. Mosley, W.
Cinnamon skin. MacDonald, J. D.
The **Circle.** Eggers, D.
Circle of friends. Binchy, M.
Circle of shadows. Robertson, I.
A **Circle** of Wives. Laplante, A.
Circling the Sun. McLain, P.
The **circular** staircase. Rinehart, M. R.
CIRCUS
Carter, A. Nights at the circus
Davis, A. Wonder when you'll miss me
Day, C. The circus in winter
Gruen, S. Water for elephants
Harrison, H. The Stainless Steel Rat joins the circus
Morgenstern, E. The night circus
Singer, I. B. The magician of Lublin
Stewart, M. Airs above the ground
Valentine, G. Mechanique
Wallace, D. Mr. Sebastian and the Negro magician
CIRCUS EXECUTIVES
McMurtry, L. Buffalo girls
The **circus** in winter. Day, C.
CIRCUS PERFORMERS
McMurtry, L. Buffalo girls
Morgenstern, E. The night circus
The **citadel.** Cronin, A. J.
The **Citadel** of the Autarch. Wolfe, G.
CITIES AND TOWNS
Acampora, L. The Wonder Garden
Barry, K. City of Bohane
Blackstock, T. Shadow in serenity
Veselka, V. Zazen
Warren, D. Juliet in August
Cities of the interior. Nin, A.
Cities of the plain. McCarthy, C.
Citizen Vince. Walter, J.
The **city** & the city. Mieville, C.
The **city** and the pillar. Vidal, G.
CITY AND TOWN LIFE
See also Cities and towns; Urban sociology
CITY AND TOWN LIFE
Canty, K. The underworld
Danler, S. Sweetbitter
Doctorow, E. L. Doctorow
Karon, J. At home in Mitford
Kendrick, B. New uses for old boyfriends
Martin, L. The bright forever
McCall Smith, A. The Kalahari typing school for men
Millhauser, S. Voices in the night
Moriarty, L. Big little lies
Perillo, L. Happiness is a chemical in the brain
Russo, R. Everybody's fool
Simonson, H. The summer before the war
Woodson, J. Another Brooklyn
CITY AND TOWN LIFE -- ALASKA
Moore, K. D. Piano tide
CITY AND TOWN LIFE -- ENGLAND
Rowling, J. K. The casual vacancy
CITY AND TOWN LIFE -- ENGLAND -- LONDON
McCall Smith, A. A conspiracy of friends
CITY AND TOWN LIFE -- HAITI
Danticat, E. Claire of the sea light
CITY AND TOWN LIFE -- IRELAND
Binchy, M. A week in winter
CITY AND TOWN LIFE -- NORTH CAROLINA
Karon, J. At home in Mitford
McCorkle, J. Life after life
CITY AND TOWN LIFE -- NORTH DAKOTA
Box, C. J. Badlands
CITY AND TOWN LIFE -- SWEDEN
Lackberg, C. The ice princess
CITY COUNCIL MEMBERS -- DEATH
Rowling, J. K. The casual vacancy
CITY LIFE *See* City and town life
City of angels or.
City of blades. Bennett, R. J.
City of Bohane. Barry, K.
The **city** of brass. Chakraborty, S. K.
City of dark magic. Flyte, M.
The **city** of Devi. Suri, M.
City of lost dreams. Flyte, M.
The **city** of mirrors. Cronin, J.
City of refuge. Piazza, T.
City of saints. Hunt, A.
City of stairs. Bennett, R. J.
City of the sun. Levien, D.
City of thieves. Benioff, D.
City of whispers. Muller, M.
City of women. Gillham, D. R.
The **city** of your final destination. Cameron, P.
City on fire. Hallberg, G. R.
The **city** who fought. Stirling, S. M.
CIVIL DISOBEDIENCE
See also Resistance to government
CIVIL RIGHTS ACTIVISTS
Baker, K. Strivers Row
CIVIL SERVANTS *See* Civil service
CIVIL SERVICE
Dickens, C. Little Dorrit
Greene, G. The heart of the matter
Civil to strangers and other writings. Pym, B.

CIVIL UNIONS
See also Rites and ceremonies
CIVIL WAR
Bear, E. Range of ghosts
CIVIL WAR -- UNITED STATES
El Akkad, O. American war
CIVILIZATION AND TECHNOLOGY *See* Technology and civilization
CIVILIZATION, MODERN *See* Modern civilization
Claire DeWitt and the city of the dead. Gran, S.
Claire of the sea light. Danticat, E.
CLAIRVOYANCE
Garcia, C. Dreaming in Cuban
Hoffman, A. The probable future
Sayers, V. The powers
CLAIRVOYANCE
See also Extrasensory perception; Occultism
Shannon, S. The bone season
Shannon, S. The mime order
The **Clan** of the Cave Bear. Auel, J. M.
CLANS
See also Family
Clara and Mr. Tiffany. Vreeland, S.
Clare, John, 1793-1864
About
Foulds, A. The quickening maze
Clarissa. Richardson, S.
Clark, William, 1770-1838
About
Sargent, C. Museum of human beings
A **clash** of kings. Martin, G. R. R.
CLASS CONSCIOUSNESS
See also Social classes; Social psychology
CLASS CONSCIOUSNESS
Hadley, T. Married love and other stories
CLASS DISTINCTION
Blume, J. Summer sisters
Chevalier, T. Girl with a pearl earring
Dreiser, T. An American tragedy
Forster, E. M. A room with a view
Greene, G. The tenth man
Ishiguro, K. The remains of the day
Rice, A. The Feast of All Saints
Richler, M. Solomon Gursky was here
Tarkington, B. Alice Adams
Towles, A. Rules of civility
Umrigar, T. N. The space between us
Wolff, T. Old school
CLASS DISTINCTION *See* Social classes
Class reunion. Jaffe, R.
The **classic** Philip Jose Farmer, 1952-1964--1964-1973. Farmer, P. J.
CLASSICAL DICTIONARIES
See also Ancient history; Encyclopedias and dictionaries
CLASSICAL DRAMA
See also Classical literature; Drama
CLASSICAL LITERATURE
Tóibín, C. House of Names
CLASSICAL MYTHOLOGY
See also Mythology
CLASSICAL MYTHOLOGY
Renault, M. The king must die
Claudius, Emperor of Rome, 10 B.C.-54
About
Graves, R. Claudius, the god and his wife Messalina
Graves, R. I, Claudius
Claudius, the god and his wife Messalina. Graves, R.
The **claw** of the conciliator. Wolfe, G.
Clea. Durrell, L.
CLEANING WOMEN
Hunt, S. The invention of everything else
Clear and present danger. Clancy, T.
Clear light of day. Desai, A.
Clementine. Priest, C.
Cleopatra's sister. Lively, P.
CLERGY
Baker, K. Strivers Row
Baldwin, J. Go tell it on the mountain
Bohjalian, C. A. Secrets of Eden
The elephant keepers' children
Estleman, L. D. The book of Murdock
Gardam, J. God on the rocks
Guterson, D. Our Lady of the Forest
Hawthorne, N. The scarlet letter
Jordan, H. When she woke
Lehrer, J. The special prisoner
Lewis, S. Elmer Gantry
Malliet, G. M. Pagan spring
Miller, S. While I was gone
Morgan, C. E. All the living
Morley, I. Come Sunday
Pipkin, J. Woodsburner
Price, R. The good priest's son
Robinson, M. Gilead
Robinson, M. Home
Robinson, M. Lila
Smith, M. C. Rose
Three days before the shooting--
Trollope, A. The warden
CLERGY -- NORTH CAROLINA
Karon, J. At home in Mitford
CLERGY -- SEXUAL BEHAVIOR
Alexander, V. S. The Magdalen girls
CLERICAL EMPLOYEES *See* Office workers
CLERICAL PERSONNEL *See* Office workers
CLERKS
Camus, A. The stranger
Kafka, F. The trial
Pym, B. Quartet in autumn
CLERKS *See* Office workers
CLERKS (RETAIL TRADE) *See* Sales personnel
Clever Girl. Hadley, T.
The **client.** Grisham, J.
CLIFF DWELLERS AND CLIFF DWELLINGS

See also Archeology; Native Americans -- Southwestern States
CLIMATE CHANGE
Hagberg, D. Abyss
Climates.
The **clinic.** Kellerman, J.
CLINICAL PSYCHOLOGISTS
White, S. W. Dry ice
CLIPPER SHIPS
See also Ships
CLIPPINGS (BOOKS, NEWSPAPERS, ETC.)
See also Newspapers
The **clock** winder. Tyler, A.
Clockers. Price, R.
CLOCKS AND WATCHES
See also Time
CLOCKS AND WATCHES
Pulley, N. The watchmaker of Filigree Street
CLOCKS AND WATCHES -- REPAIRING
Harkaway, N. Angelmaker
The **clockwork** dynasty. Wilson, D. H.
A **clockwork** orange.
CLONING
See also Genetic engineering
CLONING -- ETHICAL ASPECTS
See also Ethics
CLONING
Aira, C. The literary conference
Lafferty, M. Six wakes
Close quarters. Golding, W.
Close range. Proulx, A.
Close relations. Isaacs, S.
A **close** run thing. Mallinson, A.
Close to the Bone. MacBride, S.
Close your eyes. Ward, A. E.
CLOSED CAPTION TELEVISION
See also Deaf; Television
CLOSED CAPTION VIDEO RECORDINGS
See also Deaf; Video recordings
Closed Doors. O'Donnell, L.
CLOSED-CIRCUIT TELEVISION
See also Intercommunication systems; Microwave communication systems; Television
Clotel, or, The president's daughter.
CLOTHING TRADE
Steel, D. First sight
Cloud atlas. Mitchell, D.
Cloud chamber. Dorris, M.
The **cloud** of unknowing. Cook, T. H.
Clouds and eclipses. Vidal, G.
Clover. Sanders, D.
The **clown.** Boll, H.
CLOWNS
Boll, H. The clown
CLOWNS
See also Circus; Entertainers
The **clowns** of God. West, M. L.
The **Club** Dumas. Perez-Reverte, A.
CLUBS
Dickens, C. The posthumous papers of the Pickwick Club
Palahniuk, C. Fight Club
Spark, M. The girls of slender means
Tan, A. The Joy Luck Club
Wodehouse, P. G. Tales from the Drones Club
COACHING *See* Coaching (Athletics); Horsemanship
COACHING (ATHLETICS)
Perrotta, T. The abstinence teacher
Coal black horse. Olmstead, R.
COAL MINES AND MINING
Haigh, J. Baker towers
O'Dell, T. Coal Run
O'Dell, T. Sister mine
Pancake, A. Strange as this weather has been
Unsworth, B. The quality of mercy
COAL MINES AND MINING -- ENGLAND
Smith, M. C. Rose
COAL MINES AND MINING -- FRANCE
Zola, E. Germinal
COAL MINES AND MINING -- WALES
Llewellyn, R. How green was my valley
Coal Run. O'Dell, T.
COASTAL ECOLOGY
See also Ecology
COCAINE
McCann, C. Let the great world spin
Pelecanos, G. P. The sweet forever
Price, R. Clockers
Yocum, R. A welcome murder
COCKROACHES
Lashner, W. Kockroach
COCKROACHES
See also Insects
CODE DECIPHERING *See* Cryptography
CODE ENCIPHERING *See* Cryptography
The **code** of the Woosters. Wodehouse, P. G.
CODEPENDENCY
See also Abnormal psychology
CODES, PENAL *See* Criminal law
The **codex.** Preston, D.
Codrington, Henry John Sir, 1808-1877
About
Donoghue, E. The sealed letter
The **coffins** of Little Hope. Schaffert, T.
COGNITIVE THERAPY
See also Psychotherapy
COHABITATION *See* Unmarried couples
COINCIDENCE
Mason, J. Three graves full
COLD (DISEASE)
See also Communicable diseases; Diseases
Cold barrel zero. Quirk, M.
COLD CASES (CRIMINAL INVESTIGATION)
Adler-Olsen, J. The absent one
Adler-Olsen, J. The keeper of lost causes

Barton, F. The child
Connelly, M. The burning room
Eva's eye
Lansdale, J. R. Honky tonk samurai
Rankin, I. Rather be the devil
The shadow district
Spring Tide
Tucker, N. The ways of the dead
COLD CASES (CRIMINAL INVESTIGATION) -- SWEDEN
Free falling, as if in a dream
COLD CASES (CRIMINAL INVESTIGATIONS) -- ARIZONA
Chancellor, B. Sycamore
The **cold** cold ground. McKinty, A.
Cold cruel winter. Nickson, C.
The **cold** eye. Gilman, L. A.
Cold granite. MacBride, S.
Cold in hand. Harvey, J.
Cold is the grave. Robinson, P.
Cold light. Harvey, J.
Cold Mountain. Frazier, C.
Cold paradise. Woods, S.
Cold pursuit. Parker, T. J.
Cold service. Parker, R. B.
Cold shot to the heart. Stroby, W.
The **cold** six thousand. Ellroy, J.
Cold Springs. Riordan, R.
COLD WAR -- FICTION
Dunmore, H. Exposure
Kanon, J. Istanbul passage
Krasikov, S. The patriots
Powers, T. Declare
Cold-hearted Rake. Kleypas, L.
The **coldest** night.
Coldheart Canyon. Barker, C.
COLLAGE
See also Art; Handicraft
The **collapsing** empire. Scalzi, J.
Collected fictions. Borges, J. L.
Collected novellas. Garcia Marquez, G.
Collected novels. Hawthorne, N.
COLLECTED PAPERS (ANTHOLOGIES) *See* Anthologies
Collected stories. O'Connor, F.
The **collected** stories. Paley, G.
Collected stories. Carver, R.
Collected stories. Greene, G.
The **collected** stories. Thomas, D.
Collected stories. Kafka, F.
Collected stories. Dahl, R.
The **collected** stories. Michaels, L.
Collected stories. Lawrence, D. H.
Collected stories. Kipling, R.
Collected stories. McCullers, C.
Collected stories. Williams, T.
Collected stories. Garcia Marquez, G.
Collected stories & later writings. Bowles, P.
The **collected** stories of Amanda Cross. Cross, A.
The **collected** stories of Amy Hempel. Hempel, A.
The **collected** stories of Andre Maurois. Maurois, A.
The **collected** stories of Arthur C. Clarke. Clarke, A. C.
The **collected** stories of Chester Himes. Himes, C.
The **collected** stories of Colette. Colette
The **collected** stories of Deborah Eisenberg. Eisenberg, D.
The **collected** stories of Eudora Welty. Welty, E.
The **collected** stories of Greg Bear. Bear, G.
The **collected** stories of Hortense Calisher. Calisher, H.
The **collected** stories of Jack Schaefer. Schaefer, J. W.
The **collected** stories of Jean Stafford. Stafford, J.
Collected stories of John O'Hara. O'Hara, J.
The **collected** stories of Joseph Roth. Roth, J.
The **collected** stories of Katherine Anne Porter. Porter, K. A.
The **collected** stories of Lydia Davis. Davis, L.
The **collected** stories of Max Brand. Brand, M.
The **collected** stories of Philip K. Dick. Dick, P. K.
The **collected** stories of Richard Yates. Yates, R.
The **collected** stories of Sean O'Faolain. O'Faolain, S.
Collected stories of William Faulkner. Faulkner, W.
Collected stories, 1891-1910. Wharton, E.
Collected stories, 1911-1937. Wharton, E.
Collected stories: A friend of Kafka to Passions. Singer, I. B.
Collected stories: Gimpel the fool to The letter writer. Singer, I. B.
Collected stories: One night in Brazil to The death of Methuselah. Singer, I. B.
The **collected** tales and poems of Edgar Allan Poe. Poe, E. A.
The **collected** tales of E. M. Forster. Forster, E. M.
The **collected** tales of Nikolai Gogol. Gogol', N. V.
Collected works. O'Connor, F.
COLLECTED WORKS *See* Anthologies; Literature -- Collections; Storytelling -- Collections
COLLECTIVE SETTLEMENTS
Carey, P. His illegal self
McPhee, M. Gorgeous lies
Raymond, J. The half-life
Sontag, S. In America
Updike, J. S
COLLECTIVE SETTLEMENTS
See also Communism; Cooperation; Socialism
COLLECTORS AND COLLECTING
Bayard, L. The school of night
Chatwin, B. Utz
Doctorow, E. L. Homer & Langley
Hornby, N. High fidelity
Lazar, Z. Sway
Smith, D. Bright and distant shores
Smith, Z. The autograph man
COLLECTORS AND COLLECTING
See also Art; Hobbies
COLLEGE ADMINISTRATORS
Lipsyte, S. The ask
COLLEGE ALUMNI
Jaffe, R. Class reunion

COLLEGE AND SCHOOL JOURNALISM
See also Journalism; Student activities
COLLEGE FOOTBALL COACHES
Majors, I. Love's winning plays
COLLEGE FRESHMEN
Eugenides, J. Fresh complaint
COLLEGE LIFE
Barth, J. Giles goat-boy
COLLEGE LIFE *See* College students
COLLEGE LIFE -- CANADA
Davies, R. The rebel angels
COLLEGE LIFE -- ENGLAND
Amis, K. Lucky Jim
Lewis, C. S. That hideous strength
Lodge, D. Nice work
Lodge, D. Thinks--
Marias, J. All souls
COLLEGE LIFE -- FRANCE
McCarthy, M. Birds of America
COLLEGE LIFE -- IRELAND
Binchy, M. Circle of friends
COLLEGE LIFE -- UNITED STATES
Carter, S. L. New England white
Fitzgerald, F. S. This side of paradise
Godwin, G. The good husband
Harbach, C. The art of fielding
Jaffe, R. Class reunion
Kasischke, L. The raising
Lasdun, J. The horned man
McCarthy, M. The groves of Academe
Nabokov, V. V. Pnin
Nichols, J. T. The sterile cuckoo
Oates, J. C. Black girl/White girl
Perrotta, T. Joe College
Powers, R. Galatea 2.2
Prose, F. Blue angel
Roth, P. Indignation
Roth, P. Letting go
Russo, R. The straight man
Salinger, J. D. Franny & Zooey
Sarton, M. A small room
Smith, B. Joy in the morning
Tartt, D. The secret history
Theroux, A. Darconville's cat
Updike, J. Memories of the Ford Administration
Wolfe, T. Of time and the river
COLLEGE PRESIDENTS
Shaara, J. Gone for soldiers
Shaara, J. The last full measure
COLLEGE STUDENTS
Auster, P. Invisible
Caldwell, I. The rule of four
Cooley, M. The archivist
Eugenides, J. Fresh complaint
Finch, C. The last enchantments
Grossman, L. The magician's land
Grossman, L. The magicians
Harris, C. A secret rage
Johnson, T. G. Welcome to Braggsville
Kelly, E. The poison tree
Lavender, W. Dominance
Moore, L. A gate at the stairs
Nicholls, D. A question of attraction
Noel, K. Halfway house
Nunez, S. The last of her kind
Oates, J. C. Black girl/White girl
Ricci, N. The origin of species
Roth, H. Requiem for Harlem
Wayne, T. Loner
Wolfe, T. I am Charlotte Simmons
Wuertz, Y. G. Everything belongs to us
COLLEGE STUDENTS
See also Students
COLLEGE STUDENTS -- MASSACHUSETTS -- CAMBRIDGE
Pearl, M. The technologists
COLLEGE STUDENTS -- SEXUAL BEHAVIOR
See also Sex
COLLEGE TEACHERS
Allende, I. In the midst of winter
Byers, M. Percival's planet
Coetzee, J. M. Summertime
Goodman, C. River Road
Makkai, R. The hundred-year house
Millet, L. Oh pure and radiant heart
Nabokov, V. V. Novels and memoirs, 1941-1951
Pearl, M. The Dante Club
Rader-Day, L. The black hour
Schumacher, J. Dear Committee Members
Submission
Walker, A. The way forward is with a broken heart
COLLEGE TEACHERS *See* Colleges and universities -- Faculty; Educators; Teachers
COLLEGE TEACHERS -- AUSTRALIA
Simsion, G. The Rosie project
COLLEGES AND UNIVERSITIES -- ENDOWMENTS
See also Endowments
COLLEGES AND UNIVERSITIES -- FACULTY
See also Teachers
COLLEGES AND UNIVERSITIES -- FACULTY
Longworth, M. L. Murder in the Rue Dumas
Perlman, E. The street sweeper
COLLEGES AND UNIVERSITIES -- OFFICIALS AND EMPLOYEES
Oates, J. C. Mudwoman
COLLEGES AND UNIVERSITIES -- STUDENTS *See* College students
COLLIES
See also Dogs
Collyer, Homer, 1881-1947
About
Doctorow, E. L. Homer & Langley
Collyer, Langley, 1885-1947
About

Doctorow, E. L. Homer & Langley
COLOMBIA
Clancy, T. Clear and present danger
Garcia Marquez, G. The general and his labyrinth
Rosero Diago, E. The armies
COLOMBIA -- BOGOTA
Rosero, E. Good offices
COLOMBIA -- HISTORY
The sound of things falling
COLOMBIA -- RURAL LIFE
García Márquez, G. One hundred years of solitude
Garcia Marquez, G. Chronicle of a death foretold
Garcia Marquez, G. Collected novellas
Garcia Marquez, G. In evil hour
Garcia Marquez, G. Leaf storm, and other stories
COLOMBIANS -- ARGENTINA
Restrepo, L. No place for heroes
The **colonel.** Dowlatabadi, M.
COLONIAL ADMINISTRATORS
Nordhoff, C. Men against the sea
Nordhoff, C. Mutiny on the Bounty
Sherwood, F. Night of sorrows
Vollmann, W. T. Argall
COLONIALISM *See* Colonies; Imperialism
COLONIES
Imperium
Scott, K. That deadman dance
COLONIES
See also Imperialism
COLONIES, SPACE *See* Space colonies
COLONISTS
Vollmann, W. T. Argall
COLONIZATION
See also Imperialism; Land settlement
The **colony** of unrequited dreams. Johnston, W.
The **color.** Tremain, R.
COLOR
Fforde, J. Shades of grey
The **color** of lightning. Jiles, P.
The **color** of magic. Pratchett, T.
COLOR PRINTING
See also Printing
The **color** purple. Walker, A.
COLOR TELEVISION
See also Television
COLORADO
Cather, W. The song of the lark
Dallas, S. Tallgrass
Haruf, K. Eventide
Hemmings, K. H. The possibilities
McLarty, R. Art in America
Michener, J. A. Centennial
Overholser, W. D. Law at Angel's Landing
White, S. W. Dry ice
White, S. W. Missing persons
COLORADO -- 20TH CENTURY
Borland, H. When the legends die
Haruf, K. Plainsong
King, S. The shining
COLORADO -- DENVER
Coel, M. Blood memory
Colorless Tsukuru Tazaki and his years of pilgrimage.
COLOUR *See* Color
A **column** of fire. Follett, K.
COLUMNISTS *See* Journalists
Coma. Cook, R.
COMA
Beijing coma
Law, S. K. The paper marriage
Shakar, A. Luminarium
COMA -- PATIENTS -- BIOGRAPHY
Miller, K. E. Q. An angry-ass black woman
COMA -- PATIENTS
Beijing coma
Kelly, J. The fire baby
COMANCHE INDIANS
Kelton, E. Badger boy
Kelton, E. The way of the coyote
McMurtry, L. Comanche moon
Comanche moon. McMurtry, L.
Come home. Scottoline, L.
Come Sunday. Morley, I.
Come with me to Babylon. Levitt, P. M.
Comeback. Stark, R.
COMEDIANS
Ackroyd, P. The trial of Elizabeth Cree
Hornby, N. Funny girl
Houellebecq, M. The possibility of an island
McCracken, E. Niagara Falls all over again
Phillips, C. Dancing in the dark
COMEDIANS
See also Actors; Entertainers
COMEDIES
See also Drama; Wit and humor
COMEDY
Holt, T. Doughnut
COMEDY
See also Drama; Wit and humor
COMEDY FILMS
See also Comedies; Motion pictures
Comedy in a minor key. Keilson, H.
COMEDY RADIO PROGRAMS
See also Radio programs
COMEDY TELEVISION PROGRAMS
See also Comedies; Television programs
COMETS
Niven, L. Lucifer's hammer
COMFORT WOMEN
Lee A gesture life
The **comforts** of a muddy Saturday. McCall Smith, A.
COMIC BOOK NOVELS *See* Graphic novels
COMIC BOOKS, STRIPS, ETC.
Chabon, M. The amazing adventures of Kavalier and Clay
Cruse, H. The complete Wendel

McIntosh, W. Hitchers
COMIC BOOKS, STRIPS, ETC.
See also Wit and humor
The **coming.** Haldeman, J. W.
Coming home. Pilcher, R.
COMING OF AGE STORIES
Batuman, E. The idiot
Golden, A. Memoirs of a geisha
Groff, L. Arcadia
Makine, A. Dreams of my Russian summers
Oz, A. Panther in the basement
Powell, P. Edisto revisited
Reynolds, M. The Starlite Drive-in
Roth, H. From bondage
COMING OF AGE STORIES *See* Bildungsromans
COMING OUT (SEXUAL ORIENTATION)
Mootoo, S. Moving forward sideways like a crab
Coming rain.
Coming up for air. Henry, P. C.
The Commandant Camille Verhoeven Trilogy [series]
Lemaitre, P. Irene
COMMEDIA DELL'ARTE
See also Acting; Comedy; Farces
COMMERCIAL AERONAUTICS
Saint-Exupery, A. d. Night flight
Commissario Guido Brunetti mystery. [series]
Leon, D. A question of belief
The **commodore.** O'Brian, P.
Commodore Hornblower. Forester, C. S.
COMMON LAW MARRIAGE *See* Unmarried couples
The **commoner.** Schwartz, J. B.
Commonwealth. Patchett, A.
COMMUNAL LIVING
Atwood, M. Maddaddam
Dunn, M. Ella Minnow Pea
Groff, L. Arcadia
COMMUNAL LIVING -- CALIFORNIA
Cline, E. The girls
COMMUNICABLE DISEASES
See also Diseases; Public health
COMMUNICABLE DISEASES
Burns, C. Black hole
COMMUNICATION
Hall, L. Speak
Lem, S. Fiasco
Pynchon, T. The crying of lot 49
COMMUNICATION IN FAMILIES
Marcus, B. The flame alphabet
COMMUNICATION IN MARRIAGE
See also Marriage
COMMUNISM
Barnes, J. The noise of time
Makine, A. The life of an unknown man
McEwan, I. Black dogs
Oksanen, S. When the doves disappeared
Petterson, P. I curse the river of time
Powell, J. The breaking of eggs
Vollmann, W. T. Europe central
Wright, R. The outsider
COMMUNISM
See also Collectivism; Political science; Totalitarianism
COMMUNISM -- CHINA
Ha Jin The crazed
Ha Jin Waiting
Lord, B. B. The middle heart
Min, A. Becoming Madame Mao
See, L. Dreams of joy
COMMUNISM -- ENGLAND
Lessing, D. M. The golden notebook
COMMUNISM -- RUSSIA
Furnivall, K. The red scarf
Koestler, A. Darkness at noon
Littell, R. The Stalin epigram
Makine, A. Music of a life
Pasternak, B. L. Doctor Zhivago
Rand, A. We the living
Sholokhov, M. A. And quiet flows the Don
Sholokhov, M. A. The Don flows home to the sea
Solzhenitsyn, A. Cancer ward
Wiesel, E. The testament
COMMUNISM -- UNITED STATES
Roth, P. I married a communist
COMMUNISM -- VIETNAM
Greene, G. The quiet American
COMMUNIST LEADERS
Block, L. Killing Castro
Fuentes, N. The autobiography of Fidel Castro
Harris, R. Archangel
Hunter, S. Havana
Kadare, I. The Successor
Lawton, J. Old flames
Min, A. Becoming Madame Mao
COMMUNITIES, SPACE *See* Space colonies
COMMUNITY CHESTS *See* Fund raising
COMMUNITY LIFE
Carr, R. The Wanderer
Rhodes, D. Jewelweed
Snow White must die
COMMUTERS
Hawkins, P. The girl on the train
COMPACT CARS
See also Automobiles
COMPACT DISCS
See also Optical storage devices; Sound recordings
COMPANIONS
The man of feeling
Quick, A. I thee wed
Quick, A. The paid companion
The **company.** Littell, R.
The **company.** Parker, K. J.
The **company** man. Bennett, R. J.
The **company** of women. Gordon, M.
COMPASSION
See also Emotions

Compelling evidence. Martini, S. P.
COMPETITION (PSYCHOLOGY)
Cleave, C. Gold
Wildgen, M. Bread and Butter
COMPETITIONS *See* Awards; Contests
The **complaints.** Rankin, I.
The **complete** Claudine. Colette
The **complete** Drive-in. Lansdale, J. R.
Complete novels. Hammett, D.
Complete novels. Welty, E.
The **complete** novels. O'Brien, F.
Complete novels. McCullers, C.
Complete novels and stories. Chopin, K.
The **complete** novels of Stephen Crane. Crane, S.
The **complete** Patrick Melrose novels. St. Aubyn, E.
The **complete** Sherlock Holmes. Doyle, A. C.
The **complete** short fiction of Joseph Conrad.
Complete short stories.
The **complete** short stories. Stevenson, R. L.
Complete short stories. Maugham, W. S.
The **complete** short stories & sketches of Stephen Crane. Crane, S.
The **complete** short stories of Ambrose Bierce. Bierce, A.
The **complete** short stories of H. G. Wells. Wells, H. G.
The **complete** short stories of Jack London.
The **complete** short stories of Marcel Proust. Proust, M.
The **complete** short stories of Mark Twain. Twain, M.
Complete short stories of Nathaniel Hawthorne. Hawthorne, N.
The **complete** short stories of Thomas Wolfe.
The **complete** shorter fiction. Melville, H.
The **complete** shorter fiction of Virginia Woolf. Woolf, V.
The **complete** stories.
The **complete** stories. Malouf, D.
The **complete** stories. Malamud, B.
The **complete** stories. Asimov, I.
The **complete** stories. Hurston, Z. N.
The **complete** stories. O'Connor, F.
Complete stories and poems of Edgar Allan Poe. Poe, E. A.
The **complete** stories of Evelyn Waugh. Waugh, E.
The **complete** stories of J.G. Ballard. Ballard, J. G.
The **complete** stories of Truman Capote. Capote, T.
Complete stories, 1864-1874. James, H.
Complete stories, 1874-1884. James, H.
Complete stories, 1884-1891. James, H.
Complete stories, 1892-1898. James, H.
Complete stories, 1898-1910. James, H.
The **complete** tales of Washington Irving. Irving, W.
The **complete** Wendel. Cruse, H.
The **complete** Western stories of Elmore Leonard. Leonard, E.
The **complete** works of Isaac Babel. Babel', I.
The **complete** works of O. Henry. Henry, O.
A **complicated** kindness. Toews, M.
COMPOSERS
Bernhard, T. The loser
Frame, R. The lantern bearers
Grushin, O. The line
Hodgen, C. Elegies for the brokenhearted
Mann, T. Doctor Faustus
McEwan, I. Amsterdam
Oe, K. A quiet life
Powers, R. Orfeo
COMPOSERS
See also Musicians
COMPOSERS -- SOVIET UNION
Barnes, J. The noise of time
COMPOSITION (ART)
See also Art
Compromising positions. Isaacs, S.
Compulsion. Levin, M.
COMPULSION (PSYCHOLOGY) *See* Compulsive behavior
COMPULSIVE BEHAVIOR
Ferris, J. The unnamed
COMPUTER GAMES
Stephenson, N. Reamde
COMPUTER GAMES
See also Computer software; Games
COMPUTER HACKERS
Gibson, W. Neuromancer
Lagercrantz, D. The Girl in the Spider's Web
Lagercrantz, D. The girl who takes an eye for an eye
Larsson, S. The girl with the dragon tattoo
Larsson, S. The girl who kicked the hornets' nest
Larsson, S. The girl who played with fire
Stross, C. The Jennifer morgue
COMPUTER HACKERS
See also Computer crimes; Criminals
COMPUTER VIRUSES
Stephenson, N. Reamde
COMPUTER-HUMAN INTERACTION *See* Human-computer interaction
COMPUTERS
Brunner, J. Stand on Zanzibar
Costello, M. Big if
Heinlein, R. A. The moon is a harsh mistress
Iles, G. The footprints of God
Iles, G. Mortal fear
Powers, R. The gold bug variations
Stephenson, N. Cryptonomicon
Updike, J. Roger's version
Wilhelm, K. Death qualified
Wood, B. Perfect Harmony
COMPUTERS AND CHILDREN
See also Children; Computers
COMPUTERS AND CIVILIZATION
See also Civilization; Computers; Technology and civilization
COMPUTERS AND PEOPLE WITH DISABILITIES
See also Computers; People with disabilities
Comstock, Anthony, 1844-1915
About
Piercy, M. Sex wars

CON ARTISTS *See* Swindlers and swindling
Con ed. Klein, M.
CON GAME *See* Swindlers and swindling
CONCENTRATION CAMP INMATES
Amis, M. The zone of interest
Gross, A. The one man
Otsuka, J. When the emperor was divine
CONCENTRATION CAMPS
Gross, A. The one man
Iles, G. Black cross
Itani, F. Requiem
Kelly, M. H. Lilac girls
Otsuka, J. When the emperor was divine
Styron, W. Sophie's choice
Tidhar, L. A man lies dreaming
CONCENTRATION CAMPS -- POLAND
Konar, A. Mischling
A **concise** Chinese-English dictionary for lovers. Guo Xiaolu
Conclave. Harris, R.
CONCORD (MASS.), BATTLE OF, 1775
See also Battles; United States -- History -- 1775-1783, Revolution -- Campaigns
The **condition.** Haigh, J.
The **conditions** of love. Kushner, D. M.
CONDOMINIUMS
See also Apartment houses
CONDUCT OF LIFE
See also Ethics; Human behavior; Life skills
CONDUCT OF LIFE
Levine, S. Treasure Island!!!
Shumway, C. Ten girls to watch
CONDUCT OF LIFE -- GRAPHIC NOVELS
Moon, F. Daytripper
CONDUCTORS (MUSIC)
See also Musicians; Orchestra
CONDUCTORS (MUSIC)
Elias, G. Death and transfiguration
A **confederacy** of dunces. Toole, J. K.
CONFEDERATE STATES OF AMERICA
Kantor, M. Andersonville
CONFEDERATE STATES OF AMERICA -- ARMY
Bahr, H. The Judas Field
Leveen, L. The secrets of Mary Bowser
Shaara, J. Gods and generals
Shaara, J. The last full measure
The **confession.** Grisham, J.
CONFESSION
Banville, J. The book of evidence
Kelly, J. The fire baby
Rosero, E. Good offices
Confessional. Higgins, J.
Confessions. Minato, K.
The **confessions** of Nat Turner. Styron, W.
The **confessions** of young Nero. George, M.
The **confidant.**
CONFIDENCE GAME *See* Swindlers and swindling
The **confidence-man:** his masquerade. Melville, H.
CONFLICT OF CULTURES *See* Culture conflict
CONFLICT OF GENERATIONS
Austin, L. All she ever wanted
Bagshawe, T. Adored
Cunningham, M. Flesh and blood
Jen, G. Mona in the promised land
Lee, C. Y. The flower drum song
McDermott, A. That night
Meloy, M. Liars and saints
Read, P. P. The professor's daughter
Sankaran, L. The hope factory
Trollope, J. The men and the girls
Turgenev, I. S. Fathers and sons
Tyler, A. A slipping-down life
Vassanji, M. G. The assassin's song
West, D. The wedding
Wharton, W. Dad
Winslow, D. The kings of cool
Wolitzer, M. Surrender, Dorothy
CONFLICT OF GENERATIONS
See also Child-adult relationship; Interpersonal relations; Parent-child relationship; Social conflict
CONFORMITY
Berger, T. Neighbors
Hoeg, P. Borderliners
Karlsson, J. The room
Lewis, S. Babbitt
McCann, C. Zoli
Wilson, S. The man in the gray flannel suit
Confucius Jane. Lynch, K.
CONGLOMERATE CORPORATIONS
Wolfe, T. A man in full
CONGO (REPUBLIC)
Kingsolver, B. The poisonwood Bible
Congo dawn. Windle, J.
CONGREGATE HOUSING
Gottlieb, E. Best boy
CONGRESSIONAL INVESTIGATIONS *See* Governmental investigations
CONJOINED TWINS
Slouka, M. God's fool
CONNECTICUT
Hobson, L. K. Z. Gentleman's agreement
Hoffman, A. Skylight confessions
Lamb, W. We Are Water
O'Nan, S. Last night at the Lobster
O'Nan, S. The night country
Rice, L. Last kiss
Schine, C. The love letter
Schine, C. The three Weissmanns of Westport
Schwartz, J. B. Reservation Road
Tryon, T. The other
Westlake, D. E. The ax
CONNECTICUT -- 19TH CENTURY
Tryon, T. In the fire of spring
Tryon, T. The wings of the morning
CONNECTICUT -- NEW HAVEN

Perrotta, T. Joe College
A **Connecticut** Yankee in King Arthur's court. Twain, M.
CONQUERORS -- PERU
Wright, R. The gold eaters
The **conquest** of Lady Cassandra. Hunter, M.
Conquistadora. Santiago, E.
CONSCIENCE
Conrad, J. Lord Jim
Dostoyevsky, F. Crime and punishment
Hawthorne, N. The scarlet letter
CONSCIENCE
See also Christian ethics; Duty; Ethics
CONSCIENTIOUS OBJECTORS
Barker, P. The eye in the door
CONSCIOUSNESS
See also Apperception; Mind and body; Perception; Psychology
CONSCIOUSNESS
Bannon, J. I2
CONSCRIPT LABOR *See* Forced labor
Consequences. Lively, P.
The **conservationist.** Gordimer, N.
Consolation. Redhill, M.
CONSOLATION
See also Emotions; Human behavior
Conspiracies. Wilson, F. P.
CONSPIRACIES
Box, C. J. Force of nature
Buckley, F. The siren queen
Carter, S. L. Palace council
Church, J. A corpse in the Koryo
Cook, R. Marker
Cook, R. Vector
Costello, M. Big if
Crichton, M. Prey
Cussler, C. Fire ice
Cussler, C. White death
Dazieri, S. Kill the father
DeMille, N. Wild fire
Due, T. Blood colony
Eco, U. Foucault's pendulum
Ellroy, J. The cold six thousand
Geagley, B. Year of the hyenas
Grant, M. Deadline
Gross, A. Reckless
Harris, R. Fatherland
Harrison, C. The finder
Higgins, J. The eagle has flown
Higgins, J. The White House connection
Hoeg, P. Smilla's sense of snow
Hospital, J. T. Due preparations for the plague
Hunter, S. Pale horse coming
Ignatius, D. A firing offense
The Infatuations
Johansen, I. And then you die--
Kress, N. Dogs
Larsson, S. The girl who kicked the hornets' nest
Le Carre, J. Absolute friends
Le Carre, J. The tailor of Panama
Littell, R. The company
Ludlum, R. The Prometheus deception
Ludlum, R. The Sigma protocol
Lynch, S. The lies of Locke Lamora
McDevitt, J. The Cassandra project
Meltzer, B. The inner circle
Morgan, R. K. Broken angels
Newton, M. C. Nights of Villjamur
Niven, L. Saturn's race
O'Brien, T. L. The Lincoln conspiracy
Palmer, M. The fifth vial
Patterson, J. Four blind mice
Patterson, R. N. Eclipse
Porter, H. The bell ringers
Poyer, D. Down to a sunless sea
Pynchon, T. Bleeding edge
Rabb, J. The book of Q
Redfern, E. Auriel rising
Reich, C. Rules of deception
Ricks, T. E. A soldier's duty
Rollins, J. The devil colony
Silva, D. The mark of the assassin
Stephenson, N. Cryptonomicon
Sullivan, M. J. Theft of swords
Theroux, M. Strange bodies
Tolkien, S. Orders from Berlin
Toyne, S. Sanctus
Vinge, V. Rainbows end
Walton, J. Farthing
Walton, J. Ha'penny
Weir, A. Artemis
Weldon, F. Chalcot Crescent
Wiprud, B. M. Ringer
Wood, B. Perfect Harmony
Woods, S. Orchid Beach
A **Conspiracy** of Faith. Adler-Olsen, J.
A **conspiracy** of friends. McCall Smith, A.
The **constant** gardener. Le Carre, J.
The **constant** princess. Gregory, P.
A **constellation** of vital phenomena. Marra, A.
CONSTRUCTION INDUSTRY
Ondaatje, M. In the skin of a lion
Putney, M. J. The burning point
Trigiani, A. Big Cherry Holler
CONSTRUCTION WORKERS
Cramer, W. D. Bad ground
CONSULS
See also Diplomats
The **Consummata.** Spillane, M.
Consumption. Patterson, K.
CONSUMPTION (ECONOMICS) -- SOCIAL ASPECTS -- ENGLAND
Ballard, J. G. Kingdom come
Contact. Sagan, C.
CONTAMINATION OF ENVIRONMENT *See* Pollution

Contemporary classics [series]
Buck, P. S. The good earth
CONTESTS
Drayson, N. Guide to the birds of East Africa
Parkhurst, C. Lost and found
CONTESTS
Schwab, V. E. A gathering of shadows
CONTRABAND TRADE *See* Smuggling
The **contract** surgeon. O'Brien, D.
CONTRACTORS
Hurwitz, G. You're next
CONTROL (PSYCHOLOGY)
Delaney, J. P. The girl before
CONVENIENCE FOODS
See also Food
CONVENT LIFE
Godden, R. Black Narcissus
Hansen, R. Mariette in ecstasy
Hulme, K. The nun's story
Roberts, M. Reader, I married him
Westlake, D. E. Good behavior
CONVERSATION
Murdoch, I. A fairly honourable defeat
Segal, E. Love story
CONVERSATION
See also Communication; Language and languages
Conversation in the cathedral. Vargas Llosa, M.
CONVERSION
Baldwin, J. Go tell it on the mountain
Cooley, M. The archivist
CONVERTS
See also Conversion
CONVICT LABOR
See also Forced labor; Prisoners
Conviction. Dahl, J.
Conviction. Patterson, R. N.
CONVICTS *See* Criminals; Prisoners
The **cookbook** collector. Goodman, A.
COOKBOOKS
See also Books
COOKING
Esquivel, L. Like water for chocolate
Harris, J. Five quarters of the orange
Lanchester, J. The debt to pleasure
Norfolk, L. John Saturnall's feast
COOKS
Ali, M. In the kitchen
Desai, K. The inheritance of loss
Dovey, C. Blood kin
Faulkner, W. The sound and the fury
Glass, J. The whole world over
Handke, P. Don Juan
Lipman, E. The Inn at Lake Devine
McCullers, C. The member of the wedding
Morais, R. C. The hundred-foot journey
Mukherjee, N. A state of freedom
Norfolk, L. John Saturnall's feast
Raymond, J. The half-life
Roberts, N. Angel's fall
Thomas, S. Delicious
Townsend, S. Adrian Mole
Truong, M. The book of salt
COOPER, ALEXANDRA (FICTITIOUS CHARACTER)
Fairstein, L. Night watch
COOPERATIVE LIVING *See* Collective settlements; Communal living
COPENHAGEN (DENMARK)
Adler-Olsen, J. The absent one
Adler-Olsen, J. The keeper of lost causes
Hoeg, P. Borderliners
Hoeg, P. Smilla's sense of snow
COPPER MINES AND MINING
Doig, I. Work song
COPY ART
See also Art
Coral Glynn. Cameron, P.
CORAL REEF ECOLOGY
See also Ecology
CORAL REEFS AND ISLANDS
See also Geology; Islands
The **coral** thief. Stott, R.
Corduroy mansions. McCall Smith, A.
Cormoran Strike [series]
Galbraith, R. The silkworm
CORNET PLAYERS
Turner, F. W. 1929
The **coroner's** lunch. Cotterill, C.
CORONERS
Blake, R. A dark anatomy
Cotterill, C. The coroner's lunch
Cotterill, C. Slash and burn
Franklin, A. Mistress of the art of death
Franklin, A. The serpent's tale
CORPORATE LAWYERS -- NEW YORK (STATE) -- NEW YORK
Conklin, T. The house girl
CORPORATIONS
Flanery, P. Fallen land
CORPORATIONS -- CORRUPT PRACTICES
Clarkson, J. Among thieves
Dee, J. A thousand pardons
Le Carre, J. The constant gardener
Lee, P. Signal
Westlake, D. E. The road to ruin
A **corpse** in the Koryo. Church, J.
CORPSE REMOVALS
Guinn, M. The resurrectionist
CORPSES *See* Dead
CORPULENCE *See* Obesity
The **corrections.** Franzen, J.
CORRUPT PRACTICES
Atxaga, B. Seven houses in France
Clarkson, J. Among thieves
CORRUPTION (IN POLITICS)

Adams, H. Democracy
Atkins, A. Wicked city
Dovey, C. Blood kin
Ellroy, J. American tabloid
Ellroy, J. The cold six thousand
Estleman, L. D. Gas City
Goddard, R. Into the blue
Grisham, J. The pelican brief
Grisham, J. The brethren
Hiaasen, C. Strip tease
Meltzer, B. The zero game
Oates, J. C. The falls
Parker, T. J. The fallen
Patterson, R. N. Dark lady
Puzo, M. The godfather
Rogers, R. Devil's Cape
Roncagliolo, S. Red April
Rosenberg, N. T. Abuse of power
Silva, D. The mark of the assassin
Thomas, R. Ah, treachery!
Thomas, R. The fourth Durango
Turow, S. Presumed innocent
Vachss, A. H. Two trains running
Vassanji, M. G. The in-between world of Vikram Lall
Vidal, G. Hollywood
Vonnegut, K. Jailbird
Warren, R. P. All the king's men
Wells, K. Crawfish mountain
Wolfe, T. A man in full

CORRUPTION
Hunt, A. City of saints
Newton, C. Start shooting
Rash, R. Serena
Wolfe, G. The land across

CORRUPTION INVESTIGATION
Qiu Xiaolong Shanghai redemption

CORSAIRS *See* Pirates

CORSICA (FRANCE)
Silva, D. The English Girl

Cortés, Hernán, 1485-1547
About
Sherwood, F. Night of sorrows

COSMONAUTS *See* Astronauts

COSPLAY
See also Costume; Performance art

COSSACKS
Sholokhov, M. A. And quiet flows the Don
Sholokhov, M. A. The Don flows home to the sea

Cost. Robinson, R.

COST AND STANDARD OF LIVING
See also Economics; Home economics; Quality of life; Social conditions; Wealth

COSTUME
See also Decorative arts; Ethnology; Manners and customs

COSTUME DESIGN
Gibson, W. Zero history

COT DEATH *See* Sudden infant death syndrome

COTSWOLDS (ENGLAND)
Lively, P. Passing on
Pilcher, R. The shell seekers

Cotton comes to Harlem. Himes, C.

COTTON MANUFACTURE
See also Textile industry

COUNCILS AND SYNODS
See also Christianity; Church history

The **Count** of Monte Cristo. Dumas, A.

Countdown city. Winters, B. H.

COUNTER-REFORMATION
See also Christianity; Church history -- 1500- , Modern period

COUNTERCULTURE
Cline, E. The girls
Lazar, Z. Sway
Lessing, D. M. The good terrorist
Lopez, B. H. Resistance
Nunez, S. The last of her kind
Pynchon, T. Inherent vice
Pynchon, T. Vineland
Robbins, T. Still life with Woodpecker

COUNTERCULTURE
See also Lifestyles; Social conditions

The **counterfeiters** (Les faux-monnayeurs) Gide, A.

COUNTERFEITS AND COUNTERFEITING
Gaddis, W. The recognitions

COUNTERFEITS AND COUNTERFEITING
See also Coinage; Crime; Forgery; Impostors and imposture; Money; Swindlers and swindling

Counternarratives. Keene, J.

COUNTRY AND WESTERN MUSIC *See* Country music

The **country** doctor. Balzac, H. d.

The **country** girls trilogy and epilogue. O'Brien, E.

COUNTRY HOMES
Joss, M. Half broken things
Kelly, E. The burning air
Quick, A. Late for the wedding

COUNTRY HOMES -- ENGLAND
Dean, A. Bellfield Hall, or, The observations of Miss Dido Kent
Dean, A. A gentleman of fortune, or, The suspicions of Miss Dido Kent
Wilhide, E. Ashenden

COUNTRY LIFE
Allison, D. Bastard out of Carolina
The blue hour
Bouman, T. Dry bones in the valley
Crummey, M. Sweetland
Gloss, M. The hearts of horses
Hoff, B. J. River of mercy
Manfredi, V. M. A Winter's Night
Murphy, Y. The call
Pilcher, R. Winter solstice
Rhodes, D. Driftless
Roy, L. Bent Road

Stone upon stone
Taylor, M. G. The ballad of Trenchmouth Taggart
Taylor, A. The marble orchard
Wiggins, M. Evidence of things unseen
COUNTRY LIFE -- AUSTRALIA -- WESTERN AUSTRALIA
Coming rain
COUNTRY LIFE -- ENGLAND
Simonson, H. Major Pettigrew's last stand
COUNTRY LIFE -- FRANCE
Harris, J. Peaches for Father Francis
Walker, M. Bruno, chief of police
COUNTRY LIFE -- NIGERIA
Watson, C. Tiny sunbirds, far away
COUNTRY LIFE -- NORTH CAROLINA
Weiss, L. If the creek don't rise
COUNTRY MUSIC
Bass, R. Nashville chrome
Smith, L. The devil's dream
Spencer, L. Small town girl
Westlake, D. E. Baby, would I lie?
COUNTRY MUSICIANS
Earle, S. I'll never get out of this world alive
The **Country** of Ice Cream Star. Newman, S.
Country of origin. Lee, D.
A **country** of our own. Poyer, D.
The **country** of the pointed firs and other stories. Jewett, S. O.
COUPLES
Constantine, L. The Last Mrs. Parrish
Jemc, J. The grip of it
COUPONS (RETAIL TRADE)
See also Advertising
COUPS D'ÉTAT *See* Revolutions
COUPS D'ÉTAT
Dovey, C. Blood kin
COURAGE
Hemingway, E. The old man and the sea
Nordhoff, C. Men against the sea
Saint-Exupery, A. d. Night flight
Uris, L. Mila 18
The **courage** consort. Faber, M.
COUREURS DE BOIS
See also Fur trade; Fur trade -- Canada
COURT LIFE *See* Courts and courtiers
The **court-martial** of George Armstrong Custer. Jones, D. C.
COURTESANS
Dumas, A. Camille
Dunant, S. In the company of the courtesan
COURTIERS
Gregory, P. The Boleyn Inheritance
Naipaul, V. S. A way in the world
COURTIERS *See* Courts and courtiers
COURTING *See* Courtship
COURTS AND COURTIERS
Buckley, F. The doublet affair
Buckley, F. The siren queen
Hope, A. The prisoner of Zenda
Newton, M. C. Nights of Villjamur
COURTS AND COURTIERS -- DENMARK
Tremain, R. Music & silence
Updike, J. Gertrude and Claudius
COURTS AND COURTIERS -- ENGLAND
Bennett, V. The queen's lover
George, M. Elizabeth I
Mantel, H. Wolf Hall
Maxwell, R. The Queen's bastard
Maxwell, R. The secret diary of Anne Boleyn
Penman, S. K. Devil's brood
Penman, S. K. Falls the shadow
Penman, S. K. Here be dragons
Penman, S. K. The reckoning
Penman, S. K. The sunne in splendour
Penman, S. K. Time and chance
Penman, S. K. When Christ and his saints slept
Plaidy, J. The captive Queen of Scots
Plaidy, J. Murder most royal
Plaidy, J. The pleasures of love
Plaidy, J. William's wife
Riley, J. M. The serpent garden
Seton, A. Katherine
Weir, A. Innocent traitor
Weir, A. The Lady Elizabeth
COURTS AND COURTIERS -- FRANCE
Davis, K. Versailles
Dumas, A. The man in the iron mask
Dumas, A. The three musketeers
Haasse, H. S. In a dark wood wandering
Laker, R. To dance with kings
Naslund, S. J. Abundance
Riley, J. M. The serpent garden
COURTS AND COURTIERS -- ITALY
Sontag, S. The volcano lover
Stendhal The charterhouse of Parma
COURTS AND COURTIERS -- JAPAN
Mishima, Y. Spring snow
Murasaki Shikibu The tale of Genji
COURTS MARTIAL AND COURTS OF INQUIRY
See also Courts; Trials
The **courts** of chaos. Zelazny, R.
COURTS-MARTIAL
Jones, D. C. The court-martial of George Armstrong Custer
Nordhoff, C. Mutiny on the Bounty
COURTSHIP
Bowman, V. The Unexpected Duchess
Colwin, L. Happy all the time
James, H. Daisy Miller
Sittenfeld, C. Eligible
COURTSHIP
See also Love
Cousin Bette. Balzac, H. d.
COUSINS
Balzac, H. d. Cousin Bette
Chabon, M. The amazing adventures of Kavalier and Clay

Bowman, V. The Accidental Countess
Colwin, L. Happy all the time
Egan, J. The keep
Godwin, G. Flora
Hamilton, J. When Madeline was young
Krivak, A. The sojourn
McDermott, A. Child of my heart
Oksanen, S. When the doves disappeared
Robards, K. Ghost moon
Seton, A. Dragonwyck
St. John Mandel, E. The singer's gun
Thomas, R. All my sins remembered
Thompson, J. The year we left home
Walbert, K. The gardens of Kyoto
Yoshimoto, B. Goodbye Tsugumi
COUSINS
See also Family
Cousins' war [series]
Gregory, P. The red queen
The **cove.** Rash, R.
The **covenant.** Michener, J. A.
COVENS *See* Witches
COVERLETS *See* Bedspreads; Quilts
COVETOUSNESS *See* Avarice
Covington, Syms, 1813-1861
About
McDonald, R. Mr. Darwin's shooter
COWARDICE
Conrad, J. Lord Jim
COWBOYS
Clark, W. V. T. The Ox-bow incident
Durham, D. A. Gabriel's story
Evans, N. The horse whisperer
Houston, P. Cowboys are my weakness
Kittredge, W. The Willow Field
Lansdale, J. R. Paradise sky
McCarthy, C. All the pretty horses
McCarthy, C. The crossing
McMurtry, L. Lonesome dove
Paul, B. Under Tower Peak
Schaefer, J. W. Monte Walsh
Cowboys are my weakness. Houston, P.
COWHANDS
See also Frontier and pioneer life; Ranch life
COWRA (N.S.W.) -- HISTORY -- 20TH CENTURY
Keneally, T. Shame and the Captives
Coyote. Steele, A. M.
COZY MYSTERY STORIES
See also Mystery fiction
Crabwalk. Grass, G.
CRACK (DRUG)
See also Cocaine
A **Crack** in the Wall.
The **cradle** in the grave. Hannah, S.
CRAFT SHOWS
See also Exhibitions; Festivals
Crane, Cora Howarth Stewart Taylor, 1868-1910
About
White, E. Hotel de Dream
Crane, Stephen, 1871-1900
About
White, E. Hotel de Dream
Cranford. Gaskell, E. C.
CRANKS *See* Eccentrics and eccentricities
Crashed. Hallinan, T.
Crashers. Haynes, D.
Crawfish mountain. Wells, K.
CRAWFORD, BESS (FICTITIOUS CHARACTER) -- FICTION
Todd, C. A duty to the dead
Todd, C. A question of honor
Todd, C. An unmarked grave
The **crazed.** Ha Jin
Crazy Horse, Sioux Chief, ca. 1842-1877
About
O'Brien, D. The contract surgeon
Crazy in Alabama. Childress, M.
Crazy rich Asians. Kwan, K.
Crazybone. Pronzini, B.
Creation. Vidal, G.
CREATION (LITERARY, ARTISTIC, ETC.)
Ishiguro, K. The unconsoled
CREATION (LITERARY, ARTISTIC, ETC.)
See also Genius; Imagination; Intellect; Inventions
CREATION
Bennett, R. J. The troupe
CREATIVE ABILITY
Groff, L. Fates and furies
CREE INDIANS
Boyden, J. Three-day road
Creek Mary's blood. Brown, D. A.
CREOLES
Hambly, B. Days of the dead
Hambly, B. Dead water
Hambly, B. Die upon a kiss
Hambly, B. A free man of color
Hambly, B. Graveyard dust
Hambly, B. Sold down the river
Hambly, B. Wet grave
Tademy, L. Cane River
Crescent. Abu-Jaber, D.
Crescent City. Plain, B.
CRETE
Kazantzakis, N. Zorba the Greek
Renault, M. The king must die
Stewart, M. The moon-spinners
CRIB DEATH *See* Sudden infant death syndrome
CRICKET (SPORT)
Adiga, A. Selection day
Gunesekera, R. The match
Karunatilaka, S. The legend of Pradeep Mathew
O'Neill, J. Netherland
CRICKET STORIES
Adiga, A. Selection day

CRICKETS

See also Insects

CRIME

See also Administration of criminal justice; Social problems

CRIME

Atkins, A. The forsaken
Berney, L. The Long and Faraway Gone
Bouman, T. Dry bones in the valley
Box, C. J. Force of nature
Box, C. J. Free fire
Box, C. J. Vicious circle
Brookmyre, C. Where the bodies are buried
Connelly, M. The crossing
Connelly, M. The Gods of Guilt
DeSilva, B. Rogue island
Doetsch, R. Half-past dawn
Downie, R. Tabula Rasa
Ellory, R. J. A simple act of violence
Faletti, G. A pimp's notes
Farrow, J. The Storm Murders
Faverón Patriau, G. The Antiquarian
Faye, L. Jane Steele
Gardner, L. Catch me
Gardner, L. Find Her
Gruber, M. The return
Harvey, J. A darker shade of blue
Higashino, K. The devotion of suspect X
Jio, S. The last camellia
Kardos, M. The Three-Day Affair
Kelly, J. The fire baby
Kent, K. The Dime
Lansdale, J. R. Edge of dark water
Leonard, E. Raylan
Link, C. The Watcher
Mackintosh, C. I see you
Meyer, D. Trackers
Miasha Chaser
Mina, D. Field of blood
Newton, C. Start shooting
Paretsky, S. Brush back
Pettersson, V. The taken
Shepherd, L. The solitary house
The silence of the sea
The son
Speller, E. The strange fate of Kitty Easton
Spring Tide
Transgressions
Turner, N. Natural born hustler
Tursten, H. Night rounds
Walter, J. Citizen Vince
Walter, J. We Live in Water
Yates, C. J. Grist Mill Road

CRIME AND CRIMINALS

Abani, C. GraceLand
Atkins, A. White shadow
Atkins, A. Wicked city
Camus, A. The plague
Cheever, J. Falconer
Colfer, E. Plugged
Connelly, M. The Lincoln lawyer
Defoe, D. Moll Flanders
Dickens, C. Great expectations
Dickens, C. Oliver Twist
Dostoyevsky, F. Crime and punishment
Dreiser, T. An American tragedy
Drury, T. The driftless area
Ellroy, J. L.A. confidential
Faulkner, W. Intruder in the dust
Forsyth, F. The day of the jackal
Freeman, C. All that I have
George, E. What came before he shot her
Goodis, D. Nightfall
Greene, G. Brighton rock
Grisham, J. The brethren
Hage, R. De Niro's game
Harrison, C. The finder
Hart, J. Iron house
Hayter, S. Bandit queen boogie
Hemingway, E. To have and have not
Hiaasen, C. Lucky you
Hiaasen, C. Skin tight
Hiaasen, C. Skinny dip
Hiaasen, C. Strip tease
Higgins, G. V. The friends of Eddie Coyle
Highsmith, P. The boy who followed Ripley
Highsmith, P. The talented Mr. Ripley; Ripley under ground; Ripley's game
Hogan, C. Devils in exile
Hugo, V. Les miserables
Hunter, S. Black light
Hunter, S. Dirty white boys
Huston, C. Caught stealing
Huston, C. The mystic arts of erasing all signs of death
Isaacs, S. Lily White
James, P. D. Innocent blood
Johnson, D. Nobody move
Katzenbach, J. Just cause
Klein, M. Con ed
Latour, J. The Havana World Series
Leonard, E. Be cool
Leonard, E. Freaky Deaky
Leonard, E. Get Shorty
Leonard, E. The hot kid
Leonard, E. Killshot
Leonard, E. Mr. Paradise
Leonard, E. Pagan babies
Leonard, E. Rum punch
Leonard, E. Tishomingo blues
Levin, M. Compulsion
Livesey, M. Criminals
Ludlum, R. The Matlock paper
Mailer, N. The executioner's song
Marks, J. Fangland

Mayle, P. Hotel Pastis
McEwan, I. Saturday
Monaghan, N. The killing jar
Oates, J. C. Rape
Parker, B. Criminal justice
Parker, T. J. L.A. outlaws
Patterson, J. Along came a spider
Pelecanos, G. P. The big blowdown
Pelecanos, G. P. Drama city
Pelecanos, G. P. Shame the devil
Pelecanos, G. P. The sweet forever
Pelecanos, G. P. The turnaround
Pelecanos, G. The cut
Perry, T. Blood money
Perry, T. Dance for the dead
Perry, T. Vanishing act
Polansky, D. Low Town
Price, R. Clockers
Price, R. Freedomland
Price, R. Lush life
Puzo, M. The godfather
Puzo, M. The last Don
Rankin, I. The complaints
Rendell, R. Going wrong
Rendell, R. A judgment in stone
Rigosi, G. Night bus
Rogers, R. Devil's Cape
Rosenberg, N. T. Abuse of power
Rosenberg, N. T. First offense
Rosenberg, N. T. Mitigating circumstances
Sakey, M. The blade itself
Sanders, L. Sullivan's sting
Smith, R. Wake up dead
Spillane, M. The Consummata
St. John Mandel, E. The singer's gun
Stark, R. Ask the parrot
Stark, R. Breakout
Stark, R. Comeback
Stark, R. Dirty money
Stark, R. The hunter
Stark, R. The jugger
Stephenson, N. Reamde
Stroby, W. Cold shot to the heart
Tanenbaum, R. Act of revenge
Tolstoy, L. Resurrection
Vachss, A. H. Two trains running
Van Rooy, M. An ordinary decent criminal
Van Rooy, M. Your friendly neighborhood criminal
Vine, B. Grasshopper
Wambaugh, J. The blue knight
Wambaugh, J. Finnegan's week
Wambaugh, J. Hollywood crows
Wambaugh, J. Hollywood Hills
Wambaugh, J. Hollywood Station
Wambaugh, J. The new centurions
Welsh, I. Porno
Westlake, D. E. Bad news
Westlake, D. E. Bank shot
Westlake, D. E. Don't ask
Westlake, D. E. Drowned hopes
Westlake, D. E. Get real
Westlake, D. E. Good behavior
Westlake, D. E. The hot rock
Westlake, D. E. Put a lid on it
Westlake, D. E. The road to ruin
Westlake, D. E. Thieves' dozen
Westlake, D. E. Watch your back
Westlake, D. E. What's so funny?
Westlake, D. E. What's the worst that could happen?
Winslow, D. Savages
Woods, S. Grass roots
Woods, S. Reckless abandon
Woods, S. Two-dollar bill
Zelazny, R. The dead man's brother
Zeltserman, D. Small crimes
Crime and Mr. Campion. Allingham, M.
Crime and punishment. Dostoyevsky, F.
Crime novels: American noir of the 1930s and 40s.
Crime novels: American noir of the 1950s.
Crime of Privilege. Walker, W.
Crime school. O'Connell, C.
CRIME STORIES *See* Mystery fiction
CRIME VICTIMS *See* Victims of crimes
The **crime** writer. Hurwitz, G.
CRIME WRITING
Horowitz, A. Magpie murders
White, K. A body to die for
The **crimes** of Jordan Wise. Pronzini, B.
CRIMES WITHOUT VICTIMS
See also Crime; Criminal law
CRIMINAL DEFENSE LAWYERS
Grisham, J. Sycamore Row
Criminal enterprise. Laukkanen, O.
CRIMINAL INVESTIGATION
Andrew, S. Recipes for Love and Murder
Arsenault, E. In search of the Rose notes
Blake, R. A dark anatomy
Brandt, H. The Whites
Castillo, L. Her last breath
Catton, E. The luminaries
Clark, M. H. The sleeping beauty killer
Dahl, J. Conviction
Elias, G. Danse macabre
Finder, J. Buried secrets
Griffiths, E. A Dying Fall
Irwin, S. M. The broken ones
Johnson, D. E. Detroit shuffle
The leopard
Longworth, M. L. Murder on the Île Sordou
Malliet, G. M. A Demon Summer
Malliet, G. M. Pagan spring
Mark, D. The dark winter
Mark, D. Original skin
May, P. The Blackhouse

Mina, D. The red road
Mosley, W. Little Scarlet
Palliser, C. Rustication
Penny, L. The beautiful mystery
Pérez-Reverte, A. The siege
Qiu Xiaolong Shanghai redemption
The redeemer
Robertson, I. Circle of shadows
Smith, M. C. Tatiana
Tallis, F. Fatal lies
Todd, C. A question of honor
Tolkien, S. Orders from Berlin
Wells, D. The hollow city
Winthrop, E. H. The why of things
CRIMINAL INVESTIGATION -- ENGLAND -- LONDON
Hodder, M. The strange affair of Spring Heeled Jack
Criminal justice. Parker, B.
CRIMINAL LAW
De la Pava, S. A naked singularity
CRIMINAL PROFILERS
Grebe, C. The ice beneath her
Criminals. Livesey, M.
CRIMINALS
Bayard, L. The black tower
CRIMINALS -- ENGLAND -- LONDON
Lewis, T. GBH
CRIMINALS -- FAMILY RELATIONSHIPS
Turner, N. Heartbreak of a hustler's wife
CRIMINALS
Amis, M. Lionel Asbo
Beukes, L. Zoo city
Goldberg, T. Gangsterland
Hellström, B. Cell 8
Lewis, T. GBH
Pearson, T. R. Beluga
Sears, M. Black Fridays
Tran, V. Dragonfish
Turner, N. Heartbreak of a hustler's wife
CRIMINALS -- IDENTIFICATION
See also Criminal investigation; Identification
CRIMINALS -- NEVADA -- LAS VEGAS
Tran, V. Dragonfish
The **crimson** petal and the white. Faber, M.
Crippen. Boyne, J.
Crippen, Hawley Harvey, 1862-1910
About
Boyne, J. Crippen
Cripple Creek. Sallis, J.
CRIPPLED CHILDREN *See* Children with physical disabilities
CRIPPLED PEOPLE *See* People with physical disabilities
Crissa Stone [series]
Stroby, W. Shoot the woman first
CRITICS
Prentiss, M. Tuesday nights in 1980
CROATIA
Forna, A. The Hired Man
Seymour, G. The heart of danger
CROATIA -- HISTORY -- 1990-
Nović, S. Girl at war
CROATIAN AMERICANS
Martin, V. Trespass
The **Crocodile.** De Giovanni, M.
The **crocodile** bird. Rendell, R.
Cromwell, Thomas, Earl of Essex, 1485?-1540
About
Mantel, H. Bring up the bodies
Mantel, H. Wolf Hall
Crooked letter, crooked letter. Franklin, T.
Crooked Numbers. O'Mara, T.
Cross. Bruen, K.
Cross. Patterson, J.
CROSS CULTURAL CONFLICT *See* Culture conflict
CROSS-EXAMINATION *See* Witnesses
Crossbones. Farah, N.
Crossers. Caputo, P.
The **crossing.** Connelly, M.
The **crossing.** McCarthy, C.
The **crossing** places. Griffiths, E.
Crossing Purgatory. Schanbacher, G.
Crossing to safety. Stegner, W. E.
Crosstalk. Willis, C.
CROSSWORD PUZZLES
See also Puzzles; Word games
Crow fair. McGuane, T.
Crow Lake. Lawson, M.
The **crow** trap. Cleeves, A.
The **crowded** grave. Walker, M.
Crowe, Pat, 1869-1938
About
Hilleman, A. World, chase me down
A **crown** for cold silver. Marshall, A.
CROWS
Porter, M. Grief Is the Thing With Feathers
Crozier, Francis, 1796-1848
About
Simmons, D. The terror
Cruel as the grave. Penman, S. K.
Cruel mercy. Mark, D.
The **cruel** sea. Monsarrat, N.
The **cruelest** month. Penny, L.
CRUELTY
Kantor, M. Andersonville
Kosinski, J. N. The painted bird
Oe, K. Nip the buds, shoot the kids
Vallgren The horrific sufferings of the mind-reading monster Hercules Barefoot
CRUELTY
See also Ethics
CRUISE SHIPS
Ware, R. The Woman in Cabin Ten
CRUISES *See* Ocean travel
CRUSADES
Connell, E. S. Deus lo volt!

Eco, U. Baudolino
Holland, C. Jerusalem
Penman, S. K. Lionheart
Willocks, T. The religion
CRUSHES
See also Friendship; Love
Cry no more. Howard, L.
The **cry** of the sloth. Savage, S.
Cry, the beloved country. Paton, A.
The **crying** of lot 49. Pynchon, T.
CRYOSURGERY
See also Cold -- Therapeutic use; Surgery
CRYPTOGRAPHY
Brown, D. The Da Vinci code
Harris, R. Enigma
Stephenson, N. Cryptonomicon
Cryptonomicon. Stephenson, N.
The **crystal** cave. Stewart, M.
Crystal Cove. Kleypas, L.
The **crystal** frontier. Fuentes, C.
CUB SCOUTS *See* Boy Scouts
CUBA
Acevedo, C. The Distant Marvels
Block, L. Killing Castro
Fuentes, N. The autobiography of Fidel Castro
Garcia, C. The Aguero sisters
García, C. King of Cuba
Garcia, C. Monkey hunting
Hemingway, E. To have and have not
Hijuelos, O. Beautiful Maria of my soul
Kennedy, W. Chango's beads and two-tone shoes
Lehane, D. World gone by
CUBA
See also Islands
CUBA -- HAVANA
Garcia, C. Dreaming in Cuban
Greene, G. Our man in Havana
Hemingway, E. The old man and the sea
Hunter, S. Havana
Latour, J. The Havana World Series
Sanchez, T. King Bongo
CUBAN AMERICANS
Capó Crucet, J. Make Your Home Among Strangers
Garcia, C. A handbook to luck
Garcia, C. Monkey hunting
Parker, B. Suspicion of deceit
CUBANS
Acevedo, C. The Distant Marvels
CUBANS -- ENGLAND
Oyeyemi, H. The opposite house
CUBANS -- UNITED STATES
Atkins, A. White shadow
Garcia, C. The Aguero sisters
Garcia, C. Dreaming in Cuban
Hijuelos, O. The Mambo Kings play songs of love
Rosales, G. The halfway house
Spillane, M. The Consummata
CUBISM
See also Art
The **cuckoo's** calling. Rowling, J. K.
Cudahy, Edward Aloysius, Jr., 1885-1966
About
Hilleman, A. World, chase me down
Cudahy, Edward, 1859-1941
About
Hilleman, A. World, chase me down
Cujo. King, S.
CULLODEN, BATTLE OF, SCOTLAND, 1746
Gabaldon, D. Outlander
CULT MEMBERS -- CRIMES AGAINST
Krentz, J. A. Promise not to tell
CULTS
Atwood, M. The year of the flood
Barnes, S. Domino Falls
Bear, E. Range of ghosts
Cline, E. The girls
Goodman, C. The night villa
Harrison, J. The great leader
Hooper, K. Blood sins
Houellebecq, M. The possibility of an island
King, L. R. A darker place
LaValle, V. D. Big machine
Melamed, J. Gather the daughters
Merullo, R. The talk-funny girl
Mieville, C. Kraken
Murakami, H. 1Q84
Oe, K. Somersault
Parris, S. J. Sacrilege
Perrotta, T. The leftovers
Prose, F. Hunters and gatherers
Rabb, J. The book of Q
Rock, P. The Shelter Cycle
Sidor, S. Pitch dark
Stevens, C. Always watching
Vargas Llosa, M. The war of the end of the world
Walker, M. W. Under the beetle's cellar
Wilson, R. C. Spin
Woods, S. Heat
Zan, K. The Never List
CULTURE CONFLICT
Achebe, C. Things fall apart
Alvarez, J. How the Garcia girls lost their accents
Conde, M. I, Tituba, black witch of Salem
De Bernieres, L. Birds without wings
Doerr, H. Stones for Ibarra
D'Souza, T. The Konkans
Erdrich, L. Love medicine
Erdrich, L. Tracks
Garcia, C. Dreaming in Cuban
Gordimer, N. The pickup
Grenville, K. The secret river
Guo Xiaolu A concise Chinese-English dictionary for lovers
Ishiguro, K. An artist of the floating world
Jen, G. Mona in the promised land

Johnson, D. Le divorce
Kingsolver, B. Pigs in heaven
Kwok, J. Girl in translation
Lahiri, J. The namesake
Lee, C. Y. The flower drum song
Lee, D. Country of origin
Lee, G. China boy
Malouf, D. Remembering Babylon
Michener, J. A. Caribbean
Momaday, N. S. House made of dawn
Naipaul, V. S. A way in the world
Ng, F. M. Bone
Nunez, E. Anna in-between
Patterson, K. Consumption
Phillips, A. Prague
Power, S. The grass dancer
Richter, C. The light in the forest
Rosenberg, R. This is not civilization
Shafak, E. The bastard of Istanbul
Silko, L. Gardens in the dunes
Sundaresan, I. The splendor of silence
Tan, A. The Joy Luck Club
Thom, J. A. The red heart
Tyler, A. Digging to America
Updike, J. Terrorist
Watrous, M. If you follow me
Wright, R. The gold eaters
CULTURE CONFLICT
See also Ethnic relations; Ethnopsychology; Race relations
CULTURE CONFLICT -- PAKISTAN
Aslam, N. The golden legend
CULTURE CONTACT *See* Acculturation
CULTURE SHOCK *See* Culture conflict
The **cunning** man. Davies, R.
A **Cupboard** full of coats. Edwards, Y.
A **curable** romantic. Skibell, J.
CURATES *See* Clergy
A **cure** for suicide. Ball, J.
Curie, Marie, 1867-1934
About
Rubenfeld, J. The death instinct
CURIOSITIES AND WONDERS
Extence, G. The Universe Versus Alex Woods
The **Curiosity.** Kiernan, S. P.
The **curious** incident of the dog in the night-time. Haddon, M.
Curious liaisons [series]
Van Dyken, R. Cheater
The **current** that carries. Graley, L.
Curse of the Spellmans. Lutz, L.
CURSES
Bennett, J. Bitter Spirits
Diaz, J. The brief wondrous life of Oscar Wao
King, S. Thinner
Robbins, T. Fierce invalids home from hot climates
Curtain. Christie, A.
Curtis, Edward S., 1868-1952
About
Wiggins, M. The shadow catcher
Custer, George Armstrong, 1839-1876
About
Jones, D. C. The court-martial of George Armstrong Custer
CUSTODY OF CHILDREN
Edwards, K. The memory keeper's daughter
King, L. R. Keeping watch
Miller, S. The good mother
Mitchard, J. A theory of relativity
Picoult, J. Keeping Faith
Schwartz, L. Angels Crest
Shreve, A. Fortune's Rocks
Walker, A. The third life of Grange Copeland
CUSTODY OF CHILDREN *See* Child custody
CUSTOMER RELATIONS
See also Business; Public relations
The **cut.** Pelecanos, G.
Cutting for stone. Verghese, A.
The **cutting** room. Welsh, L.
The **cutting** season. Locke, A.
Cyanide Wells. Muller, M.
CYBERNETICS
See also Communication; Electronics; System theory
CYBERTERRORISM
See also Computer crimes; Terrorism
CYBERTERRORISM
Huston, C. Skinner
CYCLING
Cleave, C. Gold
Joinson, S. A lady cyclist's guide to Kashgar
CYCLONES
See also Meteorology; Storms; Winds
CYCLOPEDIAS *See* Encyclopedias and dictionaries
CYPERPUNK FICTION
See also Science fiction
Cypress Grove. Sallis, J.
The **Cypress** House. Koryta, M.
CYPRUS
Dunnett, D. Race of scorpions
Jones, S. Small wars
CZECH AMERICANS
Cather, W. My Antonia
Chabon, M. The amazing adventures of Kavalier and Clay
CZECH REPUBLIC -- PRAGUE
Adler, H. G. Panorama
Chatwin, B. Utz
Sherwood, F. The book of splendor
CZECHOSLOVAKIA
Hrabal, B. I served the King of England
Kundera, M. The unbearable lightness of being
Mawer, S. The glass room
CZECHS -- UNITED STATES
Cather, W. My Antonia
Cather, W. O pioneers!

D

D is for deadbeat. Grafton, S.
The **Da** Vinci code. Brown, D.
Dad. Wharton, W.
Daddy Love. Oates, J. C.
Daisy Miller. James, H.
Dakota. Grimes, M.
DAKOTA INDIANS
Harrison, J. The road home
Hill, R. B. Hanta yo
Power, S. The grass dancer
DALHOUSIE, ISABEL (FICTITIOUS CHARACTER)
McCall Smith, A. The forgotten affairs of youth
DALLAS (TEX.)
Ellroy, J. The cold six thousand
Kent, K. The Dime
Noire (Author) Natural born liar
DALZIEL, ANDREW (FICTITIOUS CHARACTER)
Hill, R. Death comes for the Fat Man
Damage. Hart, J.
Damascus. Mohr, J.
Damascus Countdown. Rosenberg, J. C.
Damascus Gate. Stone, R.
Damn love. Beach-Ferrara, J.
The **damned.** Pyper, A.
DAMS
Doig, I. Bucking the sun
Evison, J. West of here
Wiggins, M. Evidence of things unseen
DAMS -- TENNESSEE
Greene, A. Long Man
DANCE
Coetzee, J. M. The schooldays of Jesus
Dance for the dead. Perry, T.
Dance of the Jakaranda. Kimani, P.
A **dance** to the music of time. Powell, A.
Dance upon the air. Roberts, N.
A **dance** with dragons. Martin, G. R. R.
DANCERS
Durrell, L. Justine
Hamilton, J. The short history of a prince
Hiaasen, C. Strip tease
O'Neill, H. The Lonely Hearts Hotel
Smith, Z. Swing time
What we become
DANCERS
See also Entertainers
Dancers at the end of time [series]
Moorcock, M. An alien heat
Dancing Arabs. Qashu, S.
Dancing at the Rascal Fair. Doig, I.
Dancing in the dark. Kaminsky, S. M.
Dancing in the dark. Phillips, C.
Dandelion wine. Bradbury, R.
DANGEROUS ANIMALS
See also Animals
The **Dangerous** Edge of Things. Whittle, T.
DANGEROUS ENCOUNTERS
Row, J. Your face in mine
A **dangerous** inheritance. Weir, A.
Dangerous laughter. Millhauser, S.
A **dangerous** mourning. Perry, A.
A **Dangerous** Place. Winspear, J.
Dangerous women.
Daniel isn't talking. Leimbach, M.
The **Danish** Girl. Ebershoff, D.
DANISH LANGUAGE
See also Language and languages; Norwegian language; Scandinavian languages
DANISH LITERATURE
Karate chop
Danse macabre. Elias, G.
Dante Alighieri, 1265-1321
About
Pearl, M. The Dante Club
Dante Alighieri, 1265-1321. Inferno
About
Brown, D. Inferno
The **Dante** Club. Pearl, M.
Dante's equation. Jensen, J.
Dante's wood. Raimondo, L.
The **Danzig** trilogy. Grass, G.
Darconville's cat. Theroux, A.
Dare me. Abbott, M. E.
Daredevils. Vestal, S.
The **dark.**
DARK AGES *See* Middle Ages
A **dark** anatomy. Blake, R.
Dark at the Crossing. Ackerman, E.
Dark currents. Carey, J.
The **dark** dark. Hunt, S.
The **dark** design. Farmer, P. J.
The **dark** flood rises. Drabble, M.
The **dark** forest. Liu Cixin
The **dark** horse. Johnson, C.
Dark horse. Hoag, T.
Dark lady. Patterson, R. N.
Dark legacy of Shannara [series]
Brooks, T. Wards of Faerie
Dark lies the island. Barry, K.
Dark lightning. Varley, J.
Dark matter. Crouch, B.
A **dark** matter. Straub, P.
DARK NIGHT OF THE SOUL *See* Mysticism
Dark orbit. Gilman, C. I.
Dark places. Flynn, G.
The **dark** room. Walters, M.
Dark Rooms. Anolik, L.
Dark tide. Haynes, E.
The **dark** vineyard. Walker, M.
Dark voyage. Furst, A.
The **dark** winter. Mark, D.
A **darker** place. King, L. R.

A **darker** shade of blue. Harvey, J.
A **Darker** Shade of Magic. Schwab, V. E.
Darker than any shadow. Whittle, T.
The **darkest** evening of the year. Koontz, D. R.
A **Darkling** Sea. Cambias, J. L.
Darkly dreaming Dexter. Lindsay, J. P.
Darkmans. Barker, N.
Darkness and light. Harvey, J.
Darkness at noon. Koestler, A.
A **darkness** forged in fire. Evans, C.
Darkness visible. Golding, W.
Darkness, Darkness. Harvey, J.
Darkside. Bauer, B.
Darktown. Mullen, T.
The **Darling** Dahlias and the cucumber tree. Albert, S. W.
Darling Dahlias mysteries [series]
Albert, S. W. The Darling Dahlias and the cucumber tree
The **dart** league king. Morris, K. L.
DARTS PLAYERS
Morris, K. L. The dart league king
Darwin, Charles, 1809-1882
About
McDonald, R. Mr. Darwin's shooter
DATING (SOCIAL CUSTOMS)
See also Courtship; Etiquette; Manners and customs
DATING (SOCIAL CUSTOMS)
Dubus, A. Dirty Love
Fielding, H. Bridget Jones
Higgins, K. Waiting on You
Kendrick, B. New uses for old boyfriends
Moore, L. Bark
Phillips, S. E. Match me if you can
Tropper, J. How to talk to a widower
The wedding date
DATING ETIQUETTE *See* Dating (Social customs)
DATING SERVICES
Phillips, S. E. Match me if you can
Daughter of fortune. Allende, I.
Daughter of the forest. Marillier, J.
The **daughter** of time. Tey, J.
DAUGHTERS
López Barrio, C. The House of Impossible Loves
DAUGHTERS
See also Family; Women
DAUGHTERS -- DEATH
Doughty, L. Whatever you love
DAUGHTERS AND MOTHERS *See* Mother-daughter relationship
The **daughters** of Cain. Dexter, C.
The **Daughters** of Mars. Keneally, T.
Daughters of the revolution. Cooke, C.
Daughters of the Witching Hill. Sharratt, M.
DAVENPORT, LUCAS (FICTITIOUS CHARACTER)
Sandford, J. Silken prey
Sandford, J. Naked prey
David Copperfield. Dickens, C.
David, King of Israel
About
Edghill, I. Queenmaker
L'Engle, M. Certain women
DAW Book Collectors ; no. 1487 [series]
Grant, M. Rosemary and Rue
Dawn. Wiesel, E.
Dawn. Butler, O. E.
The **Dawn** Patrol. Winslow, D.
The **Dawson** pedigree. Sayers, D. L.
DAY
See also Chronology; Time
Day for night. Reiken, F.
The **day** I died. Rader-Day, L.
A **day** in the life of a smiling woman. Drabble, M.
A **day** late and a dollar short. McMillan, T.
The **day** of creation. Ballard, J. G.
Day of reckoning. Higgins, J.
The **day** of the jackal. Forsyth, F.
Day out of days. Shepard, S.
Days of awe. Fox, L.
Days of the dead. Hambly, B.
Days Without End. Barry, S.
Daytripper. Moon, F.
DE LUCE, FLAVIA (FICTITIOUS CHARACTER)
Bradley, A. As chimney sweepers come to dust
De Niro's game. Hage, R.
De Quincey, Thomas, 1785-1859
About
Morrell, D. Murder as a fine art
DEAD
Blake, R. A dark anatomy
Buehlman, C. The Necromancer's house
Keilson, H. Comedy in a minor key
King, S. Pet sematary
Murphy, S. F. The possessions
Reynolds, S. A gracious plenty
Stross, C. The Jennifer morgue
DEAD
See also Burial; Cremation; Death; Funeral rites and ceremonies; Obituaries
Dead and gone. Vachss, A. H.
Dead anyway. Knopf, C.
Dead eyes. Woods, S.
The **dead** fathers club. Haig, M.
The **dead** fish museum. D'Ambrosio, C.
The **dead** hand of history. Spencer, S.
The **dead** hour. Mina, D.
Dead in the water. Woods, S.
The **dead** lands. Percy, B.
The **dead** man's brother. Zelazny, R.
Dead man's ransom. Peters, E.
Dead man's walk. McMurtry, L.
Dead midnight. Muller, M.
The **dead** path. Irwin, S. M.
Dead reckoning. Harris, C.
The **dead** republic. Doyle, R.
Dead ringer. Scottoline, L.

The **dead** sit round in a ring. Lawrence, D.
Dead souls. Gogol', N. V.
Dead water. Marsh, N.
Dead water. Hambly, B.
The **dead** will tell. Castillo, L.
Dead winter. Tapply, W. G.
Dead zero. Hunter, S.
Deadeye Dick. Vonnegut, K.
Deadline. Sandford, J.
Deadline. Grant, M.
Deadly Harvest. Stanley, M.
Deadwood. Dexter, P.
DEAF
Eisler, B. The God's Eye View
Greenberg, J. In this sign
Itani, F. Deafening
Lodge, D. Deaf sentence
McCullers, C. The heart is a lonely hunter
Seth, V. An equal music
DEAF
See also Hearing impaired; People with physical disabilities
DEAF -- MEANS OF COMMUNICATION
See also Communication
Deaf sentence. Lodge, D.
Deafening. Itani, F.
Deal with the dead. Standiford, L.
Dear American Airlines. Miles, J.
Dear Committee Members. Schumacher, J.
Dear husband, Oates, J. C.
Dear life. Munro, A.
The **dearly** departed. Lipman, E.
Dearly devoted Dexter. Lindsay, J. P.
DEATH
Agee, J. A death in the family
Banks, R. The sweet hereafter
Bausch, R. Peace
Betts, D. Souls raised from the dead
Brockmeier, K. The brief history of the dead
Cohen, L. H. The grief of others
Crace, J. Being dead
Davies, R. The cunning man
The death of Ivan Ilyich and Confession
Dekker, T. Mortal
DeLillo, D. Zero K
Doctorow, C. Walkaway
Duncan, G. Death of an ordinary man
Garner, H. The spare room
Glass, J. Three Junes
Godwin, G. The good husband
Goldman, F. Say her name
Greer, A. S. The Impossible Lives of Greta Wells
Griffith, M. Trophy
Harrison, J. Returning to earth
Hart, J. Damage
Haruf, K. Benediction
Hoffman, A. Skylight confessions
Horn, D. Eternal life
Johnson, D. Train dreams
Jones, D. Second grave on the left
Kawabata, Y. The sound of the mountain
Klein, R. The moth diaries
Krauss, N. Great house
Lively, P. Moon tiger
Lively, P. Passing on
Lodato, V. Mathilda Savitch
Lupton, R. Sister
Mann, T. Death in Venice
Maynard, J. The usual rules
McDermott, A. At weddings and wakes
Monette, P. Afterlife
Moore, C. A dirty job
Morgan, R. K. Altered carbon
Morley, I. Come Sunday
Morrison, T. Love
Ng, C. Everything I never told you
Oates, J. C. Middle age
Ōe, K. Death by Water
O'Flynn, C. The news where you are
Okuizumi, H. The stones cry out
Petterson, P. In the wake
Pollen, B. The summer of the bear
Poore, M. Reincarnation Blues
Pyper, A. The damned
Rice, L. Home fires
Rice, L. The letters
Ross, A. Mr. Peanut
Roth, P. Sabbath's theater
Roth, P. Everyman
Roy, A. The god of small things
Saramago, J. Death with interruptions
Sarton, M. A reckoning
Schwartz, J. B. Reservation Road
Searles, J. Boy still missing
Settle, M. L. The killing ground
Spark, M. Memento mori
Strayed, C. Torch
Suri, M. The death of Vishnu
Swift, G. Last orders
Swift, G. Wish you were here
Tóibín, C. The blackwater lightship
Trevor, W. Death in summer
Trollope, J. Next of kin
Tuck, L. I married you for happiness
Tyler, A. Saint maybe
Tyler, A. The tin can tree
Vollmann, W. T. Last stories and other stories
Wallace, D. Big fish
Wilhelm, K. The good children
Wolitzer, M. Surrender, Dorothy
Yoshimoto, B. Kitchen
Death and Mr. Pickwick. Jarvis, S.
Death and restoration. Pears, I.
Death and transfiguration. Elias, G.

Death at the Chateau Bremont. Longworth, M. L.
Death benefits. Perry, T.
Death by the light of the moon. Hess, J.
Death by Water. Ōe, K.
The **death** collectors. Kerley, J.
Death comes for the archbishop. Cather, W.
Death comes for the Fat Man. Hill, R.
Death comes to Pemberley. James, P. D.
Death in Brittany. Bannalec
Death in holy orders. James, P. D.
Death in paradise. Parker, R. B.
Death in summer. Trevor, W.
Death in the Andes. Vargas Llosa, M.
A **death** in the family. Agee, J.
Death in Venice. Mann, T.
The **death** instinct. Rubenfeld, J.
Death of a cattle king. Overholser, W. D.
Death of a literary widow. Barnard, R.
Death of a macho man. Beaton, M. C.
Death of a nationalist. Pawel, R.
Death of a red heroine. Qiu Xiaolong
Death of a stranger. Perry, A.
Death of an expert witness. James, P. D.
Death of an ordinary man. Duncan, G.
The **death** of Artemio Cruz. Fuentes, C.
The **death** of bees. O'Donnell, L.
The **death** of Ivan Ilyich and Confession.
Death of kings. Cornwell, B.
The **death** of sweet mister. Woodrell, D.
Death of the mantis. Stanley, M.
The **death** of Vishnu. Suri, M.
DEATH PENALTY *See* Capital punishment
Death qualified. Wilhelm, K.
DEATH ROW INMATES
Grisham, J. The confession
McCrumb, S. The ballad of Frankie Silver
Picoult, J. Change of heart
Silver, E. L. The execution of Noa P. Singleton
Vachss, A. That's how I roll
Death to go. Harrod-Eagles, C.
Death to the landlords! Peters, E.
Death walked in. Hart, C. G.
Death watch. Harrod-Eagles, C.
Death with interruptions. Saramago, J.
Death without company. Johnson, C.
Death's End.
DEATHBED SCENES
Fuentes, C. The death of Artemio Cruz
Debris. Anderton, J.
The **debt** to pleasure. Lanchester, J.
DEBTS
Zevin, G. The hole we're in
The **decay** of the angel. Mishima, Y.
DECEASED *See* Dead
DECEIT *See* Deception; Fraud
December 6. Smith, M. C.
December heat. Garcia-Roza, L. A.
DECEPTION
See also Truthfulness and falsehood
DECEPTION
Brockway, C. The golden season
Coben, H. Fool Me Once
DECEPTIVE ADVERTISING
See also Advertising; Business ethics
DECLAMATIONS *See* Monologues; Recitations
Declare. Powers, T.
Decline and fall. Waugh, E.
DECORATION AND ORNAMENT
See also Art; Decorative arts
DECORATION AND ORNAMENT, ARCHITECTURAL
Gill, J. F. The gargoyle hunters
DECOYS (HUNTING)
See also Hunting; Shooting
The **deeds** of the disturber. Peters, E.
DEEJAYS *See* Disc jockeys
Deep as the marrow. Wilson, F. P.
The **deep** blue sea for beginners. Rice, L.
DEEP DIVING
See also Underwater exploration; Water sports
Deep down true. Fay, J.
The **deep** end of the ocean. Mitchard, J.
Deep in the shade of paradise. Dufresne, J.
Deep river. Endo, S.
Deep shadow. White, R. W.
Deeper than the grave. Whittle, T.
The **deepest** water. Wilhelm, K.
A **deepness** in the sky. Vinge, V.
DEFECTORS
Clancy, T. The hunt for Red October
Kanon, J. Istanbul passage
Le Carre, J. Our kind of traitor
Defend and betray. Perry, A.
Defending Jacob. Landay, W.
DEFENSE CONTRACTS
Gibson, W. Zero history
Defense for the devil. Wilhelm, K.
DEFENSE INFORMATION, CLASSIFIED -- SOVIET UNION
Eastland, S. Shadow pass
Defoe, Daniel, 1661?-1731
About
Coetzee, J. M. Foe
Tournier, M. Friday
DEFORMITIES
Dalton, J. The inverted forest
Golding, W. Darkness visible
Grass, G. Cat and mouse
Vallgren The horrific sufferings of the mind-reading monster Hercules Barefoot
Wilhelm, K. Desperate measures
DEGENERATION
Algren, N. A walk on the wild side
Caldwell, E. Tobacco road
Dickey, J. Deliverance

Faulkner, W. Absalom, Absalom!
Faulkner, W. As I lay dying
Faulkner, W. The hamlet
Faulkner, W. Sanctuary
Faulkner, W. The sound and the fury
Gide, A. The immoralist
Herlihy, J. L. Midnight cowboy
Kennedy, W. Ironweed
Kosinski, J. N. The devil tree
Norris, F. McTeague
Proulx, A. Postcards
Rossner, J. Looking for Mr. Goodbar
Styron, W. Lie down in darkness
Wilde, O. The picture of Dorian Gray
Zola, E. Nana
DEISM
See also Religion; Theology
Deja dead. Reichs, K. J.
DELAWARE INDIANS
Richter, C. The light in the forest
DELHI (INDIA)
Mahajan, K. The association of small bombs
Delicate edible birds and other stories. Groff, L.
A **Delicate** Truth. Le Carré, J.
Delicious. Thomas, S.
Delicious Foods. Hannaham, J.
DELINQUENCY, JUVENILE *See* Juvenile delinquency
DELINQUENTS *See* Criminals
Deliverance. Dickey, J.
DELTA (MISS. : REGION)
Morris, W. Taps
Pearson, T. R. Beluga
Yarbrough, S. Prisoners of war
Delta wedding. Welty, E.
DELUSIONS *See* Hallucinations and illusions
DEMENTIA
Healey, E. Elizabeth is missing
Lichtenstein, A. Lost
Democracy. Adams, H.
Demolition angel. Crais, R.
Demon. Varley, J.
Demon of the air. Levack, S.
A **Demon** Summer. Malliet, G. M.
DEMONIAC POSSESSION
Gregory, D. Pandemonium
Seton, A. Green darkness
DEMONOLOGY
See also Occultism
DEMONOLOGY
Searles, J. Help for the Haunted
Deng, Valentino Achak
About
Eggers, D. What is the what
DENMARK
Adler-Olsen, J. The absent one
Adler-Olsen, J. The keeper of lost causes
Hoeg, P. Borderliners
Hoeg, P. The history of Danish dreams
Kazinski, A. J. The last good man
Ramsland, M. Doghead
DENMARK -- 17TH CENTURY
Tremain, R. Music & silence
DENMARK -- 19TH CENTURY
Dinesen, I. Winter's tales
DENMARK -- COPENHAGEN
Hoeg, P. Smilla's sense of snow
DENMARK -- TO 1241
Anderson, P. War of the Gods
DENOMINATIONAL SCHOOLS *See* Church schools
Denting the Bosch. Link, T.
DENTISTS
Ferris, J. To Rise Again at a Decent Hour
Norris, F. McTeague
Russell, M. D. Doc
DEPARTMENT STORES
Bradford, B. T. A woman of substance
Davies, V. Miracle on 34th Street
Martin, S. Shopgirl
DEPARTMENT STORES
See also Business; Retail trade; Stores
DEPENDENCIES *See* Colonies
DEPORTATION
Ko, L. The leavers
DEPRESSED PERSONS
Hoffman, C. Be safe I love you
DEPRESSION (PSYCHOLOGY)
See also Abnormal psychology; Affective disorders; Neuroses
DEPRESSION (PSYCHOLOGY)
Haslett, A. Imagine me gone
Hoffman, C. Be safe I love you
DEPRESSION IN WOMEN
Greer, A. S. The Impossible Lives of Greta Wells
DEPRESSIONS -- 1929
Silver, M. Mary Coin
Dept. of speculation. Offill, J.
The **Dervish** House. McDonald, I.
DESCENT *See* Genealogy; Heredity
DESERT ANIMALS
See also Animals; Deserts
Desert blood. Gaspar de Alba, A.
Desert boys. McCormick, C.
DESERT ECOLOGY
See also Ecology
DESERT PLANTS
See also Deserts; Plant ecology; Plants
DESERTED HOUSES
Rayne, S. Property of a lady
The **deserter.** Langton, J.
DESERTS
Aira, C. The seamstress and the wind
Bolano, R. 2666
Pyne, D. Twentynine Palms
Silko, L. Gardens in the dunes

DESERTS -- GRAPHIC NOVELS
Henson, J. Jim Henson's tale of sand
DESIGNED GENETIC CHANGE *See* Genetic engineering
DESIGNER DRUGS
See also Drugs
DESIGNERS
Lively, P. How it all began
DESIGNERS
See also Artists
DESIRE (PHILOSOPHY)
Aciman, A. Enigma variations
Choi, S. My education
DESKS
Krauss, N. Great house
Desperate duchesses by the numbers [series]
James, E. Seven minutes in heaven
James, E. Three Weeks With Lady X
Desperate measures. Wilhelm, K.
DESTINY *See* Fate and fatalism
Destiny and desire. Fuentes, C.
Destiny: child of the sky. Haydon, E.
DESTITUTION *See* Poverty
Destroyer angel. Barr, N.
DESTROYERS (WARSHIPS) -- UNITED STATES -- HISTORY -- 20TH CENTURY
Sundin, S. Through waters deep
DETECTIVE AND MYSTERY STORIES
Abrahams, P. Dog on it
Atkinson, K. Case histories
Atkinson, K. When will there be good news?
Bauer, B. Darkside
Bayard, L. The pale blue eye
Block, L. A drop of the hard stuff
Box, C. J. Vicious circle
Bradley, A. A red herring without mustard
Bradley, A. The sweetness at the bottom of the pie
Bradley, A. The weed that strings the hangman's bag
Cain, C. Heartsick
Carter, S. L. New England white
Chabon, M. The Yiddish policemen's union
Chancellor, B. Sycamore
Child, L. One shot
Cotterill, C. Killed at the whim of a hat
Crais, R. First rule
Doiron, P. The poacher's son
Elkins, A. J. Unnatural selection
Faye, L. The whole art of detection
French, T. Faithful Place
French, T. In the woods
Grafton, S. T is for trespass
Gran, S. Claire DeWitt and the city of the dead
Grant, H. The glass demon
Grimes, M. The Old Wine Shades
Gruber, M. Valley of bones
Gundar-Goshen, A. Waking lions
Hart, J. The king of lies
Heller, P. Celine
Herron, M. Spook street
Hiaasen, C. Nature girl
Horowitz, A. Magpie murders
James, P. D. The private patient
Kellerman, J. Therapy
Koryta, M. The ridge
Kunzru, H. White tears
Lavender, W. Dominance
Leon, D. Drawing conclusions
Leon, D. The girl of his dreams
Lippman, L. What the dead know
Locke, A. Bluebird, bluebird
Mankell, H. The troubled man
McCall Smith, A. The Double Comfort Safari Club
McCall Smith, A. The good husband of Zebra Drive
McCall Smith, A. In the company of cheerful ladies
Mills, M. Amagansett
Mina, D. The long drop
Mina, D. The dead hour
Mina, D. Still midnight
Mosley, W. Little Scarlet
Mukherjee, A. A Rising Man
O'Loughlin, E. Minds of winter
Paretsky, S. Fallout
Paretsky, S. Fire sale
Paretsky, S. Hardball
Parker, R. B. Sixkill
Parker, T. J. California girl
Parker, T. J. The fallen
Peace, D. Tokyo year zero
Pearl, M. The last Dickens
Pearl, M. The Poe shadow
Pears, I. The portrait
Pears, I. Stone's fall
Pelecanos, G. P. The night gardener
Penny, L. Glass houses
Perry, T. Nightlife
Pessl, M. Special topics in calamity physics
Peters, E. Guardian of the horizon
The play of death
Read, C. Invisible boy
The red-haired woman
Rendell, R. The water's lovely
Robertson, I. Instruments of darkness
Robinson, P. Piece of my heart
Ross, A. Mr. Peanut
Sager, R. Final girls
Sallis, J. The killer is dying
Smith, M. C. Stalin's ghost
Smith, M. C. Wolves eat dogs
Swierczynski, D. Fun and games
Turow, S. Innocent
Winslow, D. The force
Yocum, R. A welcome murder
DETECTIVE AND MYSTERY STORIES *See* Mystery fiction
DETECTIVE AND MYSTERY STORIES, AMERICAN

Crime novels: American noir of the 1930s and 40s
Crime novels: American noir of the 1950s
Hammett, D. Complete novels
Highsmith, P. The talented Mr. Ripley; Ripley under ground; Ripley's game
Mosley, W. Six easy pieces
Spillane, M. The Mike Hammer collection [v1]
Spillane, M. The Mike Hammer collection [v2]
Transgressions
Van de Wetering, J. The Amsterdam cops
Westlake, D. E. Thieves' dozen

DETECTIVE AND MYSTERY STORIES, ENGLISH
Doyle, A. C. S. The adventures and the memoirs of Sherlock Holmes

Detective D.D. Warren [series]
Gardner, L. Find Her

DETECTIVE FICTION *See* Mystery fiction

Detective Galileo mysteries [series]
Higashino, K. The devotion of suspect X

Detective Kubu mysteries [series]
Stanley, M. A carrion death

Detective Mollel [series]
Crompton, R. Hell's gate
Crompton, R. Hour of the Red God

Detective Sarah Alt [series]
Boyce, T. N. Old bones

Detective Sergeant McAvoy [series]
Mark, D. Cruel mercy
Mark, D. Sorrow bound

DETECTIVE STORIES *See* Mystery fiction

DETECTIVES
Abrahams, P. Dog on it
Allingham, M. Crime and Mr. Campion
Allingham, M. Three cases for Mr. Campion
Andrews, M. K. Every crooked nanny
Andrews, M. K. Irish eyes
Atkinson, K. Case histories
Atkinson, K. When will there be good news?
Ball, J. D. In the heat of the night
Banville, J. Christine Falls
Barnard, R. A fall from grace
Bayard, L. The black tower
Beaton, M. C. Death of a macho man
Benn, J. R. Billy Boyle
Black, C. Murder in Passy
Black, C. Murder in the Sentier
Block, L. All the flowers are dying
Block, L. The burglar in the library
Block, L. A drop of the hard stuff
Block, L. Eight million ways to die
Block, L. The sins of the fathers
Block, L. A ticket to the boneyard
Block, L. When the sacred ginmill closes
Bowen, P. Badlands
Box, C. J. Back of beyond
Box, C. J. Nowhere to run
Bradley, A. A red herring without mustard
Braun, L. J. The cat who ate Danish modern
Braun, L. J. The cat who went underground
Brett, S. Murder unprompted
Brett, S. The torso in the town
Brown, R. M. Murder at Monticello; or, Old sins
Brown, R. M. Wish you were here
Bruen, K. Cross
Bruen, K. The guards
Buchanan, E. Love kills
Buchanan, E. You only die twice
Burke, J. L. Black cherry blues
Burke, J. L. Heaven's prisoners
Chandler, R. The big sleep
Chandler, R. The long goodbye
Child, L. One shot
Christie, A. The A.B.C. murders
Christie, A. The body in the library
Christie, A. Curtain
Christie, A. The Hollow
Christie, A. Mrs. McGinty's dead
Christie, A. The murder at the vicarage
Christie, A. A murder is announced
Christie, A. The murder of Roger Ackroyd
Christie, A. Murder on the Orient Express
Christie, A. Towards zero
Connolly, J. The burning soul
Cotterill, C. Killed at the whim of a hat
Craig, P. R. A shoot on Martha's Vineyard
Craig, P. R. Third strike
Craig, P. R. A vineyard killing
Crais, R. Chasing darkness
Crais, R. First rule
Crombie, D. Water like a stone
Cross, A. The collected stories of Amanda Cross
Crumley, J. Bordersnakes
Crumley, J. The final country
Crumley, J. The last good kiss
Crumley, J. The wrong case
Dexter, C. The daughters of Cain
Dexter, C. The remorseful day
Dexter, C. The way through the woods
Dibdin, M. Blood rain
Downie, R. Caveat emptor
Downie, R. Medicus
Downie, R. Terra incognita
Doyle, A. C. The complete Sherlock Holmes
Dunning, J. Booked to die
Dunning, J. The bookman's wake
Elkins, A. J. Good blood
Elkins, A. J. Unnatural selection
Estleman, L. D. Amos Walker
Estleman, L. D. Frames
Estleman, L. D. Infernal angels
Estleman, L. D. A smile on the face of the tiger
Faulks, S. Devil may care
Finch, C. The September Society
Fleming, I. Casino Royale

Fleming, I. Doctor No
Fleming, I. From Russia, with love
Fleming, I. Goldfinger
Fleming, I. The man with the golden gun
Fleming, I. On Her Majesty's Secret Service
Fleming, I. You only live twice
Fossum, K. Bad intentions
Francis, D. Bolt
Garcia-Roza, L. A. Alone in the crowd
Gardner, L. Love you more
Gash, J. Prey dancing
Gash, J. The rich and the profane
George, E. Careless in red
George, E. This body of death
Gilman, D. The amazing Mrs. Pollifax
Gilman, D. The elusive Mrs. Pollifax
Gilman, D. Kaleidoscope
Gilman, D. Mrs. Pollifax and the whirling dervish
Gilman, D. Mrs. Pollifax pursued
Gilman, D. Mrs. Pollifax, innocent tourist
Gilman, D. The unexpected Mrs. Pollifax
Gorman, E. Bad moon rising
Gorman, E. Fools rush in
Gorman, E. Save the last dance for me
Gorman, E. Sleeping dogs
Gorman, E. Ticket to ride
Grafton, S. B is for burglar
Grafton, S. C is for corpse
Grafton, S. D is for deadbeat
Grafton, S. E is for evidence
Grafton, S. F is for fugitive
Grafton, S. G is for gumshoe
Grafton, S. H is for homicide
Grafton, S. I is for innocent
Grafton, S. A is for alibi
Grafton, S. J is for judgment
Grafton, S. K is for killer
Grafton, S. N is for noose
Grafton, S. O is for outlaw
Grafton, S. P is for peril
Grafton, S. Q is for quarry
Grafton, S. S is for Silence
Grafton, S. T is for trespass
Gran, S. Claire DeWitt and the city of the dead
Greenleaf, S. False conception
Greenleaf, S. Strawberry Sunday
Greer, R. O. First of state
Grimes, M. The Anodyne Necklace
Grimes, M. The case has altered
Grimes, M. The five bells and bladebone
Grimes, M. Help the poor struggler
Grimes, M. The Horse You Came In On
Grimes, M. I am the only running footman
Grimes, M. The Old Contemptibles
Grimes, M. The old fox deceiv'd
Grimes, M. The Old Silent
Grimes, M. The Old Wine Shades
Grimes, M. Rainbow's end
Grimes, M. The Stargazey
Grimes, M. The winds of change
Gulik, R. H. v. The Chinese bell murders
Gulik, R. H. v. The haunted monastery
Gulik, R. H. v. The lacquer screen
Gulik, R. H. v. The Red Pavilion
Gulik, R. H. v. The willow pattern
Haddam, J. Cheating at solitaire
Haddam, J. Hardscrabble road
Haddam, J. True believers
Hall, J. W. Buzz cut
Hall, J. W. Off the chart
Hall, J. W. Red sky at night
Hammett, D. The glass key
Hammett, D. The Maltese falcon
Hammett, D. The thin man
Harper, K. The Poyson garden
Harrod-Eagles, C. Blood lines
Harrod-Eagles, C. Death to go
Harrod-Eagles, C. Death watch
Harrod-Eagles, C. Game over
Harrod-Eagles, C. Grave music
Harrod-Eagles, C. Killing time
Harrod-Eagles, C. Orchestrated death
Harrod-Eagles, C. Shallow grave
Hart, C. G. Death walked in
Hart, C. G. Murder walks the plank
Hart, C. G. Resort to murder
Hart, C. G. White elephant dead
Hart, C. G. Yankee Doodle dead
Harvey, J. Cold in hand
Harvey, J. Cold light
Harvey, J. Darkness and light
Harvey, J. Easy meat
Harvey, J. Last rites
Harvey, J. Still waters
Harvey, J. Wasted years
Harvey, M. T. The Chicago way
Harvey, M. T. The Fifth Floor
Harvey, M. T. We all fall down
Hayder, M. Gone
Hayder, M. Ritual
Hess, J. Busy bodies
Hess, J. Death by the light of the moon
Hess, J. Madness in Maggody
Hess, J. Maggody and the moonbeams
Hess, J. Mischief in Maggody
Hess, J. Misery loves Maggody
Hess, J. Murder@maggody.com
Hewson, D. The garden of evil
Hewson, D. A season for the dead
Hill, R. Arms and the women
Hill, R. Bones and silence
Hill, R. Death comes for the Fat Man
Hill, R. Singing the sadness
Hill, S. The pure in heart

Hill, S. The various haunts of men
Hillerman, T. The blessing way
Hillerman, T. Hunting badger
Hillerman, T. The Jim Chee mysteries
Hillerman, T. Listening woman
Hillerman, T. Sacred clowns
Hillerman, T. The shape shifter
Hillerman, T. The sinister pig
Hillerman, T. Skinwalkers
Hillerman, T. Talking God
Hillerman, T. A thief of time
Hillerman, T. The wailing wind
Himes, C. Cotton comes to Harlem
Hockensmith, S. Holmes on the range
Hockensmith, S. On the wrong track
Horowitz, A. The House of Silk
Hunter, E. The moment she was gone
Huston, C. Already dead
Huston, C. Every last drop
Huston, C. Half the blood of Brooklyn
James, P. D. The black tower
James, P. D. A certain justice
James, P. D. Death in holy orders
James, P. D. Death of an expert witness
James, P. D. Devices and desires
James, P. D. The lighthouse
James, P. D. Original sin
James, P. D. The private patient
James, P. D. The skull beneath the skin
James, P. D. A taste for death
James, P. D. An unsuitable job for a woman
Jance, J. A. Birds of prey
Jance, J. A. Devil's claw
Jance, J. A. Skeleton canyon
Johnson, C. The dark horse
Jungstedt, M. The inner circle
Kaminsky, S. M. Dancing in the dark
Kaminsky, S. M. A fatal glass of beer
Kaminsky, S. M. Murder on the Trans-Siberian Express
Kaminsky, S. M. To catch a spy
Kaminsky, S. M. Tomorrow is another day
Kava, A. Hotwire
Kellerman, F. The forgotten
Kellerman, F. Jupiter's bones
Kellerman, F. Milk and honey
Kellerman, F. Prayers for the dead
Kellerman, F. Serpent's tooth
Kellerman, J. Bones
Kellerman, J. The clinic
Kellerman, J. Devil's waltz
Kellerman, J. Gone
Kellerman, J. Monster
Kellerman, J. Private eyes
Kellerman, J. Self-defense
Kellerman, J. Therapy
Kellerman, J. Time bomb
Kemelman, H. Monday the rabbi took off
Kemelman, H. One fine day the rabbi bought a cross
Kemelman, H. Thursday the rabbi walked out
Kerr, P. Field gray
Kienzle, W. X. The rosary murders
King, L. R. The game
Knopf, C. The last refuge
Krueger, W. K. Vermilion drift
Lackberg, C. The preacher
Langton, J. The deserter
Langton, J. Murder at Monticello
Langton, J. The thief of Venice
Lansdale, J. R. Devil red
Lansdale, J. R. Vanilla Ride
Larsson, A. Until thy wrath be past
Lathen, E. Brewing up a storm
Lathen, E. East is east
Lathen, E. Something in the air
Lehane, D. Prayers for rain
Lehane, D. Sacred
Leon, D. About face
Leon, D. Drawing conclusions
Leon, D. The girl of his dreams
Leon, D. Uniform justice
Lippman, L. No good deeds
Liss, D. A spectacle of corruption
Lovesey, P. Bertie and the seven bodies
Lovesey, P. Diamond dust
Lovesey, P. Diamond solitaire
Lovesey, P. The house sitter
Lovesey, P. The last detective
Lovesey, P. Skeleton Hill
Lovesey, P. Upon a dark night
Lovesey, P. The vault
Lovesey, P. Waxwork
Lutz, J. Burn
Lutz, J. Lightning
MacBride, S. Flesh house
MacDonald, J. D. Cinnamon skin
MacDonald, J. D. The green ripper
MacDonald, J. D. The lonely silver rain
MacDonald, J. D. The long lavender look
MacDonald, J. D. A purple place for dying
MacDonald, J. D. The scarlet ruse
MacDonald, J. D. The turquoise lament
MacDonald, P. The list of Adrian Messenger
Macdonald, R. The drowning pool
Macdonald, R. The far side of the dollar
Macdonald, R. The Galton case
Macdonald, R. The goodbye look
Macdonald, R. Sleeping beauty
Macdonald, R. The underground man
Malliet, G. M. Wicked autumn
Mankell, H. One step behind
Mankell, H. Dogs of Riga
Mankell, H. Firewall
Mankell, H. The man who smiled
Mankell, H. The troubled man

Maron, M. Bootlegger's daughter
Maron, M. High country fall
Maron, M. Shooting at loons
Maron, M. Storm track
Maron, M. Uncommon clay
Maron, M. Up jumps the Devil
Marsh, N. Dead water
Marsh, N. False scent
Marsh, N. Grave mistake
Marsh, N. Last ditch
Marsh, N. Light thickens
Marsh, N. When in Rome
Marston, E. The Bawdy basket
Marston, E. The Devil's apprentice
Marston, E. The roaring boy
Marston, E. The vagabond clown
Marston, E. The wanton angel
Mayor, A. Red herring
Mayor, A. The sniper's wife
Mayor, A. Tag man
McBain, E. The big bad city
McBain, E. Fat Ollie's book
McBain, E. The frumious Bandersnatch
McBain, E. Hark!
McBain, E. The last dance
McBain, E. Nocturne
McCall Smith, A. Blue shoes and happiness
McCall Smith, A. The comforts of a muddy Saturday
McCall Smith, A. The Double Comfort Safari Club
McCall Smith, A. The good husband of Zebra Drive
McCall Smith, A. In the company of cheerful ladies
McCall Smith, A. The lost art of gratitude
McClure, J. The steam pig
McCrumb, S. If I'd killed him when I met him
Mcdonald, G. Fletch
McGarrity, M. Everyone dies
McGown, J. Murder at the old vicarage
McGown, J. Verdict unsafe
McInerny, R. M. Celt and pepper
McInerny, R. M. Irish coffee
McInerny, R. M. Requiem for a realtor
Meyer, D. Devil's peak
Meyer, N. The seven-per-cent solution
Mina, D. The dead hour
Mina, D. Slip of the knife
Mosley, W. Devil in a blue dress
Mosley, W. When the thrill is gone
Mosley, W. Bad Boy Brawly Brown
Mosley, W. Black Betty
Mosley, W. Cinnamon kiss
Mosley, W. Gone fishin'
Mosley, W. Known to evil
Mosley, W. A little yellow dog
Mosley, W. The long fall
Mosley, W. A red death
Mosley, W. Six easy pieces
Mosley, W. White butterfly
Muller, M. Both ends of the night
Muller, M. City of whispers
Muller, M. Dead midnight
Muller, M. A walk through the fire
Muller, M. Where echoes live
Muller, M. While other people sleep
Muller, M. A wild and lonely place
Muller, M. Wolf in the shadows
Nabb, M. Some bitter taste
Nesbo, J. The devil's star
Newman, S. Strong as death
O'Connell, C. Crime school
O'Connell, C. Killing critics
O'Connell, C. Stone angel
O'Donovan, G. The priest
Page, K. H. The body in the Big Apple
Page, K. H. The body in the bog
Page, K. H. The body in the bookcase
Pajer, B. A spark of death
Paretsky, S. Bitter medicine
Paretsky, S. Blacklist
Paretsky, S. Fire sale
Paretsky, S. Guardian angel
Paretsky, S. Hard time
Paretsky, S. Hardball
Paretsky, S. Total recall
Paretsky, S. Tunnel vision
Paretsky, S. Windy City blues
Parker, R. B. Back story
Parker, R. B. Chance
Parker, R. B. Cold service
Parker, R. B. Death in paradise
Parker, R. B. Double Deuce
Parker, R. B. Hugger mugger
Parker, R. B. Hush money
Parker, R. B. Melancholy baby
Parker, R. B. Now and then
Parker, R. B. Painted ladies
Parker, R. B. Potshot
Parker, R. B. Rough weather
Parker, R. B. School days
Parker, R. B. Sea change
Parker, R. B. Shrink rap
Parker, R. B. Sixkill
Parker, R. B. Small vices
Parker, R. B. Thin air
Parker, R. B. Trouble in Paradise
Parker, R. B. Walking shadow
Parker, R. B. Widow's walk
Pears, I. Death and restoration
Pears, I. The immaculate deception
Pears, I. The last judgment
Pearson, R. Killer summer
Pelecanos, G. P. Hard revolution
Pelecanos, G. P. Hell to pay
Pelecanos, G. P. Soul circus
Penman, S. K. Cruel as the grave

Penman, S. K. Dragon's lair
Penny, L. Bury your dead
Penny, L. The cruelest month
Penny, L. Still life
Penny, L. A trick of the light
Perry, A. Bedford Square
Perry, A. Belgrave Square
Perry, A. Bluegate Fields
Perry, A. A breach of promise
Perry, A. Buckingham Palace gardens
Perry, A. Cain his brother
Perry, A. Cardington Crescent
Perry, A. A dangerous mourning
Perry, A. Death of a stranger
Perry, A. Defend and betray
Perry, A. The face of a stranger
Perry, A. Farriers' Lane
Perry, A. Funeral in blue
Perry, A. Half Moon Street
Perry, A. Highgate rise
Perry, A. The Hyde Park headsman
Perry, A. Paragon Walk
Perry, A. Pentecost Alley
Perry, A. Resurrection row
Perry, A. Seven dials
Perry, A. The silent cry
Perry, A. The sins of the wolf
Perry, A. Slaves of obsession
Perry, A. Southampton Row
Perry, A. Traitor's gate
Perry, A. The twisted root
Perry, A. Weighed in the balance
Perry, A. The Whitechapel conspiracy
Peters, E. The deeds of the disturber
Peters, E. The golden one
Peters, E. Guardian of the horizon
Peters, E. He shall thunder in the sky
Peters, E. The hippopotamus pool
Peters, E. The last camel died at noon
Peters, E. Lion in the valley
Peters, E. The mummy case
Peters, E. Night train to Memphis
Peters, E. Seeing a large cat
Peters, E. The snake, the crocodile, and the dog
Peters, E. The benediction of Brother Cadfael
Peters, E. Brother Cadfael's penance
Peters, E. Dead man's ransom
Peters, E. Death to the landlords!
Peters, E. Fallen into the pit
Peters, E. The hermit of Eyton Forest
Peters, E. Monk's-hood
Peters, E. The potter's field
Peters, E. A rare Benedictine
Peters, E. The rose rent
Peters, E. Saint Peter's Fair
Peters, E. The sanctuary sparrow
Peters, E. The summer of the Danes
Peters, E. The virgin in the ice
Pintoff, S. In the shadow of Gotham
Qiu Xiaolong Red mandarin dress
Qiu Xiaolong When red is black
Rankin, I. Black and blue
Rankin, I. Exit music
Rankin, I. The falls
Rankin, I. The naming of the dead
Rankin, I. A question of blood
Rankin, I. Resurrection men
Rankin, I. Set in darkness
Read, C. Invisible boy
The redbreast
Reichs, K. J. Bare bones
Reichs, K. J. Break no bones
Reichs, K. J. Grave secrets
Rendell, R. Harm done
Rendell, R. Kissing the gunner's daughter
Rendell, R. Not in the flesh
Rendell, R. Simisola
Rendell, R. A sleeping life
Rinehart, M. R. The circular staircase
Rinehart, M. R. Miss Pinkerton: adventures of a nurse detective
Robb, J. D. Naked in death
Robinson, L. S. Murder at the feast of rejoicing
Robinson, L. S. Murder at the God's gate
Robinson, P. Cold is the grave
Robinson, P. Innocent grave
Robinson, P. Piece of my heart
Roosevelt, E. The Hyde Park murder
Roosevelt, E. Murder and the First Lady
Roosevelt, E. Murder at midnight
Roosevelt, E. Murder in the map room
Roosevelt, E. Murder in the Oval Office
Russell, S. This insane train
Sallis, J. Cripple Creek
Sallis, J. Cypress Grove
Sallis, J. Salt River
Sanders, L. The fourth deadly sin
Sanders, L. McNally's dilemma
Sanders, L. McNally's gamble
Sanders, L. McNally's puzzle
Sanders, L. Timothy's game
Sandford, J. Broken prey
Sandford, J. Buried prey
Sandford, J. Certain prey
Sandford, J. Mind prey
Sandford, J. Naked prey
Sandford, J. Night prey
Sandford, J. Rules of prey
Sandford, J. Shock wave
Sandford, J. Winter prey
Sayers, D. L. Busman's honeymoon
Sayers, D. L. The Dawson pedigree
Sayers, D. L. The documents in the case
Sayers, D. L. The five red herrings

Sayers, D. L. Gaudy Night
Sayers, D. L. Lord Peter
Sayers, D. L. Murder must advertise
Sayers, D. L. The nine tailors
Sayers, D. L. Strong poison
Sayers, D. L. Thrones, dominations
Sayers, D. L. The unpleasantness at the Bellona Club
Sayers, D. L. Whose body?
Saylor, S. The house of the Vestals
Saylor, S. The judgment of Caesar
Saylor, S. A mist of prophecies
Saylor, S. Rubicon
Saylor, S. The triumph of Caesar
Schlink, B. Self's punishment
See, L. Dragon bones
Simenon, G. Maigret and the madwoman
Simenon, G. Maigret and the Saturday caller
Simenon, G. Maigret goes home
Sjowall, M. The laughing policeman
Smith, J. 82 Desire
Smith, M. C. Gorky Park
Smith, M. C. Havana Bay
Smith, M. C. Stalin's ghost
Smith, M. C. Wolves eat dogs
The snowman
Spencer-Fleming, J. All mortal flesh
Spiegelman, P. Black maps
Spillane, M. The Goliath bone
Spillane, M. The Mike Hammer collection [v1]
Spillane, M. The Mike Hammer collection [v2]
Stabenow, D. Hunter's moon
Stabenow, D. Killing grounds
Stabenow, D. Whisper to the blood
Standiford, L. Deal with the dead
Stanley, M. A carrion death
Stansberry, D. The ancient rain
Stone, N. The king of swords
Stout, R. Black orchids; &, the silent speaker
Stout, R. The doorbell rang
Stout, R. Fer-de-lance; &, The league of frightened men
Stout, R. Gambit
Stout, R. The rubber band & The red box
Stout, R. Some buried Caesar & The golden spiders
Stout, R. Too many cooks; & champagne for one
Tapply, W. G. Dead winter
Temple, P. The broken shore
Tey, J. The daughter of time
Tey, J. The man in the queue
Todd, C. The red door
Tremayne, P. Chalice of blood
Truman, M. Murder at Ford's Theatre
Vachss, A. H. Another life
Vachss, A. H. Choice of evil
Vachss, A. H. Dead and gone
Vachss, A. H. Down here
Vachss, A. H. Down in the zero
Vachss, A. H. Footsteps of the hawk
Vachss, A. H. Hard candy
Vachss, A. H. Pain management
Vachss, A. H. Sacrifice
Vachss, A. H. Safe house
Van de Wetering, J. The Amsterdam cops
Van de Wetering, J. The blond baboon
Van de Wetering, J. The hollow-eyed angel
Van de Wetering, J. Just a corpse at twilight
Van de Wetering, J. The perfidious parrot
Verdon, J. Shut your eyes tight
Walker, M. The dark vineyard
Walker, M. W. All the dead lie down
Wall, K. R. The Mercy Oak
White, K. A body to die for
White, K. Lethally blond
White, R. W. Black widow
White, R. W. Deep shadow
Williams, A. K. The stranger you seek
Wilson, F. P. Conspiracies
Wilson, F. P. The haunted air
Wilson, F. P. Legacies
Winslow, D. The Dawn Patrol
Winslow, D. The gentlemen's hour
Winspear, J. Among the mad
Winspear, J. Birds of a feather
Winspear, J. An incomplete revenge
Winspear, J. Maisie Dobbs
Winspear, J. The mapping of love and death
Winspear, J. Messenger of truth
Winspear, J. Pardonable lies
Wolfe, I. A. The taken

DETECTIVES

See also Police

DETECTIVES -- CRIMES AGAINST

Moore, J. The night market

DETECTIVES -- DENMARK

Kazinski, A. J. The last good man

DETECTIVES -- ENGLAND

Bradley, A. Speaking from among the bones

DETECTIVES

Abani, C. The secret history of Las Vegas
Atkinson, K. Started early, took my dog
Boyce, T. N. Old bones
Bradley, A. The weed that strings the hangman's bag
Butcher, J. Proven guilty
Cain, C. Let me go
Cleeves, A. Thin air
Coben, H. Stay close
Conlon, E. Red on red
Connelly, M. The crossing
Cross, N. Luther
Dahl, A. Bad Blood
De la Pava, S. Personae
Dugoni, R. My sister's grave
Eastland, S. Shadow pass
Fielding, J. Someone Is Watching
Freeman, B. Goodbye to the dead

French, T. The secret place
Galbraith, R. The silkworm
Gallagher, S. The bedlam detective
Gardner, L. Live to tell
George, E. Believing the lie
George, E. Just one evil act
Grossman, P. Children of wrath
Hall, T. The case of the love commandos
Harvey, J. A darker shade of blue
Harvey, J. Darkness, Darkness
Hayder, M. Poppet
Higashino, K. The devotion of suspect X
Horowitz, A. Moriarty
Kelly, E. Broadchurch
Kerley, J. The death collectors
Koryta, M. The prophet
Krentz, J. A. River road
Lackberg, C. The stonecutter
MacBride, S. Cold granite
Mark, D. Cruel mercy
Mark, D. Sorrow bound
Mina, D. The red road
Mosley, W. All I did was shoot my man
Mukherjee, A. A Rising Man
Nadel, B. The Ottoman cage
Obregon, N. Blue light Yokohama
Paretsky, S. Fallout
Pearl, M. The Poe shadow
Penney, S. The invisible ones
Price, S. By Gaslight
Ridgway, K. Hawthorn & child
Smith, M. C. Tatiana
Tidhar, L. A man lies dreaming
Tolkien, S. The king of diamonds
Walker, M. The Patriarch
Wambaugh, J. Harbor nocturne

DETECTIVES -- FRANCE
Syndrome E

DETECTIVES -- IRELAND -- DUBLIN
French, T. The secret place
O'Donovan, G. Dublin dead

DETECTIVES -- NORTHERN IRELAND
McKinty, A. In the Morning I'll Be Gone

DETECTIVES -- NORWAY
Brekke, J. The fifth element

DETECTIVES -- SWEDEN
Lackberg, C. The stonecutter

DETECTIVES, PRIVATE
Barnes, J. The somnambulist
Coover, R. Noir
Hughes, M. Hespira
Ishiguro, K. When we were orphans
Jones, D. Second grave on the left
Koontz, D. R. The bad place
Lethem, J. Motherless Brooklyn
Levien, D. City of the sun
Lutz, L. Curse of the Spellmans
Lutz, L. Revenge of the Spellmans
Lutz, L. The Spellman files
McPhee, J. No ordinary matter
Meno, J. The boy detective fails
Pelecanos, G. P. Right as rain
Pelecanos, G. The cut
Perry, T. Nightlife
Pronzini, B. Crazybone
Pronzini, B. Fever
Pronzini, B. Mourners
Pronzini, B. Nightcrawlers
Pronzini, B. Savages
Pronzini, B. Spook
Pynchon, T. Inherent vice
Richardson, K. Greywalker
Rickards, J. Winter's end
Seymour, G. The heart of danger
Vollmann, W. T. The royal family

DETROIT (MICH.)
Beukes, L. Broken monsters
Lasser, S. Say nice things about Detroit

Detroit shuffle. Johnson, D. E.
Deus lo volt! Connell, E. S.
DEVELOPMENT *See* Embryology; Evolution; Growth disorders; Modernization (Sociology)
Devereaux, Robert

About

Maxwell, R. The wild Irish

Devices and desires. James, P. D.
Devices and desires. Parker, K. J.
DEVIL
Benet, S. V. The Devil and Daniel Webster
Bulgakov, M. A. The master and Margarita
Hill, J. Horns
Gilman, L. A. The cold eye
Gilman, L. A. Silver on the Road
Oates, J. C. The Accursed
Peet, M. The Murdstone trilogy
Wallace, D. Mr. Sebastian and the Negro magician

The **devil** all the time. Pollock, D. R.
The **Devil** and Daniel Webster. Benet, S. V.
The **devil** colony. Rollins, J.
Devil in a blue dress. Mosley, W.
The **devil** in silver. LaValle, V. D.
Devil may care. Faulks, S.
Devil red. Lansdale, J. R.
The **devil** tree. Kosinski, J. N.
The **devil's** advocate. West, M. L.
The **devil's** alphabet. Gregory, D.
The **Devil's** apprentice. Marston, E.
Devil's brood. Penman, S. K.
Devil's Cape. Rogers, R.
Devil's claw. Jance, J. A.
The **devil's** daughter. Robert, K.
The **devil's** dream. Smith, L.
The **devil's** feather. Walters, M.
Devil's garden. Atkins, A.

The **devil's** making. Haldane, S.
Devil's peak. Meyer, D.
The **devil's** punchbowl. Iles, G.
The **devil's** star. Nesbo, J.
Devil's waltz. Kellerman, J.
Devils in exile. Hogan, C.
The **devotion** of suspect X. Higashino, K.
The **dew** breaker. Danticat, E.
The **Dewey** Decimal system. Larson, N.
DHARMA
Kerouac, J. The Dharma bums
The **Dharma** bums. Kerouac, J.
DIABETES
See also Diseases
The **diagnosis.** Lightman, A. P.
DIALECTICAL MATERIALISM
See also Communism; Socialism
The **diamond** age. Stephenson, N.
Diamond dust. Lovesey, P.
Diamond solitaire. Lovesey, P.
DIAMOND, PETER (FICTITIOUS CHARACTER)
Lovesey, P. Diamond dust
Lovesey, P. The house sitter
Lovesey, P. The tooth tattoo
Lovesey, P. The vault
DIAMONDS
Coulter, C. The Final Cut
Haggard, H. R. King Solomon's mines
Trollope, A. The Eustace diamonds
White, R. M. A lady unrivaled
Diana, Princess of Wales, 1961-1997
About
Ali, M. Untold story
DIARIES (STORIES ABOUT)
Brockmeier, K. The Illumination
Cooley, M. The archivist
Couto, M. Sleepwalking land
Erdrich, L. Shadow tag
Higgins, J. Bad company
Hustvedt, S. The sorrows of an American
Maxwell, R. The secret diary of Anne Boleyn
Moore, G. The Sherlockian
Van Booy, S. Everything beautiful began after
DIARIES (STORIES IN DIARY FORM)
Boyd, W. Any human heart
Bronte, A. The tenant of Wildfell Hall
Cheever, J. The Wapshot chronicle
Collins, W. The woman in white
Fielding, H. Bridget Jones's diary
Golding, W. Close quarters
Golding, W. Fire down below
Golding, W. Rites of passage
Guo Xiaolu A concise Chinese-English dictionary for lovers
Horlock, M. The book of lies
Ivey, E. To the bright edge of the world
Jio, S. The violets of March
Kaufman, S. Diary of a mad housewife
Keyes, D. Flowers for Algernon
Klein, R. The moth diaries
Leshem, R. Beaufort
Lessing, D. M. The golden notebook
Lodge, D. Deaf sentence
Moore, M. M. So far away
Oe, K. A quiet life
Ozeki, R. L. A tale for the time being
Palahniuk, C. Diary
Sams, F. Down town
Sarton, M. As we are now
Shields, C. The stone diaries
Smith, L. On Agate Hill
Stabenow, D. Though not dead
Townsend, S. Adrian Mole
Townsend, S. The Adrian Mole diaries
Townsend, S. Adrian Mole: the lost years
Turner, N. E. These is my words
Updike, J. Toward the end of time
Vine, B. Anna's book
Walton, J. Among others
Watson, S. J. Before I go to sleep
DIARISTS
Lourie, R. A hatred for tulips
Diary. Palahniuk, C.
Diary of a mad housewife. Kaufman, S.
Dick Francis's Damage. Francis, F.
Dickens, Charles, 1812-1870
About
Flanagan, R. Wanting
Jarvis, S. Death and Mr. Pickwick
Pearl, M. The last Dickens
Dictation. Ozick, C.
DICTATORS
The Feast of the Goat
Garcia Marquez, G. The autumn of the patriarch
Orwell, G. Animal farm
DICTATORS
See also Heads of state; Totalitarianism
DICTATORS -- CUBA
García, C. King of Cuba
DICTIONARIES *See* Encyclopedias and dictionaries
Did you ever have a family. Clegg, B.
DIDACTIC FICTION
Aciman, A. Enigma variations
Dido Kent mystery [series]
Dean, A. A place of confinement
Dean, A. A woman of consequence
Die easy. Sharp, Z.
Die upon a kiss. Hambly, B.
Dies the fire. Stirling, S. M.
DIESEL AUTOMOBILES
See also Automobiles
DIETETIC FOODS
See also Diet; Food
Dietland. Walker, S.
DIFFERENCE (PSYCHOLOGY)

Ruby, I. The salt god's daughter
Different seasons. King, S.
Difficult women. Gay, R.
The **Digger's** game. Higgins, G. V.
Digging to America. Tyler, A.
DIGITAL LIBRARIES
See also Information systems; Libraries
DIGITAL MEDIA
See also Mass media
DiMaggio, Joe, 1914-1999
About
Sayers, V. The powers
The **Dime.** Kent, K.
Dimiter. Blatty, W. P.
Dinah (Biblical figure)
About
Diamant, A. The red tent
DINERS (RESTAURANTS)
Martinez, A. L. Gil's All Fright Diner
Moore, E. K. The Supremes sing the happy heartache blues
DINING
See also Food
The **dinner.**
Dinner at the Homesick Restaurant. Tyler, A.
DINNERS
Bernhard, T. Woodcutters
Smith, A. There but for the
The dinner
DINNERS AND DINING *See* Dining; Dinners
The **Dinosaur** Club. Heffernan, W.
DINOSAURS
Crichton, M. Jurassic Park
Preston, D. Tyrannosaur Canyon
Swanwick, M. Bones of the earth
Diotima (Legendary character)
About
Corby, G. The Marathon conspiracy
DIPHTHERIA
See also Diseases
DIPLODOCUS
See also Dinosaurs
DIPLOMACY
Corey, J. S. A. Caliban's war
DIPLOMATIC LIFE
Durrell, L. Mountolive
Faulks, S. On Green Dolphin Street
Greene, G. The honorary consul
Le Carre, J. The constant gardener
Michener, J. A. Caravans
Rushdie, S. Shalimar the clown
Sontag, S. The volcano lover
Wouk, H. The winds of war
DIPLOMATS
Just, W. American romantic
Morrow, J. The last witchfinder
Roosevelt, E. Murder at midnight
Wideman, J. E. Fanon
DIPLOMATS
See also Diplomacy; International relations; Statesmen
Dirt. Woods, S.
Dirt music. Winton, T.
The **dirty** dozen. Nathanson, E. M.
Dirty girls on top. Valdes-Rodriguez, A.
A **dirty** job. Moore, C.
Dirty Love. Dubus, A.
Dirty money. Stark, R.
Dirty money Honey. Hilton, E.
The **Dirty** Secrets Club. Gardiner, M.
Dirty to the grave. Williams, K.
Dirty white boys. Hunter, S.
Dirty work. Woods, S.
DISABILITIES
See also Diseases; Wounds and injuries
DISABILITY INSURANCE
See also Insurance
Disappearance at Devil's Rock. Tremblay, P.
The **Disappeared.**
The **disappeared.** Echlin, K.
DISAPPOINTMENT
See also Emotions
DISASTER PREPAREDNESS *See* Disaster relief
DISASTER RELIEF
Ford, R. Let Me Be Frank With You
Young, T. W. The renegades
DISASTERS
The healer
Lessing, D. M. The memoirs of a survivor
Mahajan, K. The association of small bombs
McHugh, M. F. After the apocalypse
Moor, M. d. The storm
DISASTERS -- FINLAND
The healer
DISASTERS -- PSYCHOLOGICAL ASPECTS
Canty, K. The underworld
DISC JOCKEYS
Beatty, P. Slumberland
A **discovery** of witches. Harkness, D. E.
The **Discreet** Hero.
DISCRIMINATION
See also Ethnic relations; Interpersonal relations; Prejudices; Race relations; Social problems; Social psychology
DISCUSSION *See* Conversation; Debates and debating; Negotiation
DISCUSSION GROUPS
See also Conversation
DISEASES
Ferris, J. The unnamed
Gregory, D. The devil's alphabet
Huyler, F. The laws of invisible things
Layton, E. To wed a stranger
Marks, J. Fangland
Palahniuk, C. Rant
Percy, B. The dead lands

DISEASES AND PESTS *See* Agricultural bacteriology; Agricultural pests; Fungi; Household pests; Insect pests; Parasites; Plant diseases
DISEASES OF CHILDREN *See* Children -- Diseases
DISFIGURED PERSONS
Darnielle, J. Wolf in white van
Disgrace. Coetzee, J. M.
The Disgraceful Dukes [series]
Bell, L. How the Duke Was Won
Disgruntled. Solomon, A.
DISGUISE
Gracie, A. To catch a bride
Thomas, S. Beguiling the beauty
DISK JOCKEYS *See* Disc jockeys
Disobedience. Hamilton, J.
DISPLACED PERSONS *See* Political refugees; Refugees
The **dispossessed.** Le Guin, U. K.
DISSENTERS
Holland, T. The archivist's story
DISSERTATIONS
See also Research
The **dissident.** Freudenberger, N.
Dissident Gardens. Lethem, J.
The **distant** echo. McDermid, V.
The **distant** hours. Morton, K.
The **Distant** Marvels. Acevedo, C.
A **distant** shore. Phillips, C.
DISTILLERIES
Barton, E. Brookland
DISTRIBUTION OF WEALTH *See* Economics; Wealth
The **dive** from Clausen's pier. Packer, A.
A **divided** spy. Cumming, C.
DIVINATION
See also Occultism
Jacka, B. Fated
Divine and human and other stories. Tolstoy, L.
The Divine Cities [series]
Bennett, R. J. City of blades
Divine secrets of the Ya-Ya Sisterhood. Wells, R.
The **diviner.** Rawn, M.
A **diving** rock on the Hudson. Roth, H.
Divining women. Gibbons, K.
DIVORCE
Banks, R. Affliction
De los Santos, M. The Precious One
Donoghue, E. The sealed letter
Doughty, L. Whatever you love
Glass, J. The widower's tale
Godden, R. The battle of the Villa Fiorita
Haigh, J. The condition
Isaacs, S. Close relations
Johnson, D. Le divorce
Meloy, M. A family daughter
Mengestu, D. How to read the air
Miller, S. The good mother
Nicholls, D. Us
Nichols, P. The rocks
O'Nan, S. Snow angels
O'Nan, S. The odds
Petterson, P. I curse the river of time
Robinson, R. Cost
Trollope, J. Other people's children
Tyler, A. The amateur marriage
Wakefield, D. Starting over
DIVORCE
See also Family
DIVORCED FATHERS
Smith, A. A bigger life
DIVORCED MEN
Ford, R. Let Me Be Frank With You
DIVORCED MOTHERS
See also Divorced parents; Divorced people; Mothers
DIVORCED MOTHERS
Eggers, D. Heroes of the frontier
Fay, J. Deep down true
Samuel, B. No place like home
Scottoline, L. Come home
DIVORCED PERSONS
Barnes, J. The sense of an ending
Beattie, A. Picturing Will
Berg, E. Once upon a time, there was you
Betts, D. Souls raised from the dead
DeLillo, D. Falling man
Dreyer, E. Barely a lady
Ferrante, E. The lost daughter
Ford, R. Independence Day
Ford, R. The lay of the land
Grenville, K. The idea of perfection
Hall, B. The music teacher
Harrison, J. The English major
Hart, J. The reconstructionist
Hiaasen, C. Strip tease
Higgins, K. My one and only
Hoffman, A. Turtle Moon
Lamott, A. Blue shoe
Lipman, E. The family man
McMillan, T. How Stella got her groove back
Miller, S. Lost in the forest
Miyamoto, T. Kinshu: Autumn brocade
Morris, M. M. Songs in ordinary time
Muller, M. Cyanide Wells
Nadzam, B. Lamb
O'Brien, E. Time and tide
Ozick, C. Foreign bodies
Perrotta, T. The abstinence teacher
Picoult, J. Sing you home
Putney, M. J. The burning point
Roth, P. Everyman
Schwartz, L. Angels Crest
Shields, C. The republic of love
Spencer, L. That Camden summer
Tran, V. Dragonfish
Tyler, A. Noah's compass
Tyler, A. A patchwork planet

Woods, S. Palindrome
DIVORCED WOMEN
See also Divorced people; Single women
DIVORCED WOMEN
Dee, J. A thousand pardons
Higgins, K. In Your Dreams
Jones, L. The Dixie Belle's Guide to Love
Kendrick, B. New uses for old boyfriends
White, K. The night the lights went out
The **Dixie** Belle's Guide to Love. Jones, L.
Dixon, Jeremiah, 1733-1779
About
Pynchon, T. Mason & Dixon
Djibouti. Leonard, E.
DJS (DISC JOCKEYS) *See* Disc jockeys
Do androids dream of electric sheep? Dick, P. K.
Do Lord remember me. Lester, J.
Do not become alarmed. Meloy, M.
Do not say we have nothing. Thien, M.
Do you want to start a scandal. Dare, T.
The **do-right.** Sandlin, L.
Doc. Russell, M. D.
Doctor (Fictitious Character)
Gaiman, N. Trigger warning
Doctor Faustus. Mann, T.
Doctor No. Fleming, I.
DOCTOR NOVELS *See* Medical novels
Doctor Sleep. King, S.
Doctor Thorne. Trollope, A.
Doctor Zhivago. Pasternak, B. L.
Doctorow. Doctorow, E. L.
DOCTORS *See* Physicians
DOCUMENTARY FILMS
See also Motion pictures
DOCUMENTARY FILMS
Spiotta, D. Innocents and others
Valente, C. M. Radiance
DOCUMENTARY FILMS -- PRODUCTION AND DIRECTION
DeLillo, D. Point Omega
Leonard, E. Djibouti
DOCUMENTARY TELEVISION PROGRAMS
See also Television programs
The **documents** in the case. Sayers, D. L.
Dodgers. Beverly, B.
Dodsworth. Lewis, S.
DOG *See* Dogs
The **dog** of the South. Portis, C.
Dog on it. Abrahams, P.
DOG PARKS
See also Dogs; Parks
Dog run moon. Wink, C.
The **dog** said bow-wow. Swanwick, M.
DOG SHOWS
See also Dogs
Dog soldiers. Stone, R.
The **dog** stars. Heller, P.
Dog war. Winkler, A. C.
Dog years. Grass, G.
Dogfight, a love story. Burgess, M.
Doghead. Ramsland, M.
Dogs. Kress, N.
DOGS
Abrahams, P. Dog on it
Agnon, S. Y. Only yesterday
Carroll, J. The ghost in love
Danielewski, M. Z. The familiar
Desai, K. The inheritance of loss
Haddon, M. The curious incident of the dog in the night-time
Haslett, A. Union Atlantic
Hunt, R. Mr. Chartwell
King, S. Cujo
Koontz, D. R. The darkest evening of the year
Koontz, D. R. Watchers
Kress, N. Dogs
London, J. The call of the wild
London, J. White Fang
McCall Smith, A. A conspiracy of friends
Parkhurst, C. The dogs of Babel
Rosenblatt, R. Lapham rising
Schine, C. The New Yorkers
Spencer, S. Man in the woods
Stein, G. The art of racing in the rain
Ward, J. Salvage the bones
Winkler, A. C. Dog war
Wroblewski, D. The story of Edgar Sawtelle
DOGS -- PSYCHOLOGY
See also Animal intelligence; Comparative psychology; Psychology
The **dogs** of Babel. Parkhurst, C.
Dogs of Riga. Mankell, H.
Doing hard time. Woods, S.
Doing harm. Parsons, K.
The **Doll** Collection.
The **Doll-Master** and Other Tales of Terror. Oates, J. C.
Dollface. Rosen, R.
The **dollmaker.** Arnow, H. L. S.
DOLLS
The Doll Collection
Dolores Claiborne. King, S.
DOLPHINS
Ghosh, A. The hungry tide
Dombey and Son. Dickens, C.
DOMESTIC ANIMALS
See also Animals
DOMESTIC FICTION
Clemmons, Z. What we lose
Ellis, H. American housewife
Hadley, T. Bad dreams and other stories
Han, K. The vegetarian
Jackson, J. The opposite of everyone
Krasikov, S. The patriots
Lee, M. J. Pachinko
Loigman, L. C. The two-family house

McDermott, A. The ninth hour
Ng, C. Little fires everywhere
Senna, D. New People
Stone, M. Border child
Straub, E. Modern lovers
Ties
Ward, J. Sing, unburied, sing
Weiss, L. If the creek don't rise
DOMESTIC RELATIONS
Chung, C. Forgotten country
Cook, C. Best staged plans
Jackson, J. A grown up kind of pretty
Jensen, N. The sisters
McNeal, T. To be sung underwater
Merullo, R. The talk-funny girl
DOMESTIC VIOLENCE
In the wilderness
Moshfegh, O. Eileen
Straight, S. Take one candle light a room
DOMESTIC WORKERS *See* Household employees
DOMESTICS
Phillips, C. Foreigners
Dominance. Lavender, W.
DOMINICA
Kincaid, J. Autobiography of my mother
DOMINICAN AMERICANS
Alvarez, J. How the Garcia girls lost their accents
Alvarez, J. Yo!
Diaz, J. The brief wondrous life of Oscar Wao
DOMINICAN REPUBLIC
Danticat, E. The farming of bones
The Feast of the Goat
DOMINICAN-HAITIAN CONFLICT, 1937
Danticat, E. The farming of bones
DOMINICANS (DOMINICAN REPUBLIC)
Coster, N. Halsey Street
Domino. King, R.
Domino Falls. Barnes, S.
The **Don** flows home to the sea. Sholokhov, M. A.
Don Juan. Handke, P.
DON JUAN (LEGENDARY CHARACTER)
Handke, P. Don Juan
Don Quixote de la Mancha. Cervantes Saavedra, M. d.
Don't ask. Westlake, D. E.
Don't call it night. Oz, A.
Don't cry. Gaitskill, M.
Don't ever get old. Friedman, D.
Don't Go. Scottoline, L.
Don't tell a soul. Rosenfelt, D.
Dona Flor and her two husbands. Amado, J.
Donnerjack. Zelazny, R.
Doomsday book. Willis, C.
The **doorbell** rang. Stout, R.
DOPPELGÄNGERS
Redhill, M. Bellevue Square
DORDOGNE (FRANCE)
Walker, M. Bruno, chief of police
Walker, M. The crowded grave
Walker, M. The dark vineyard
Dorian. Self, W.
Dostoyevsky, Fyodor, 1821-1881
About
Tsypkin, L. Summer in Baden-Baden
The **Double** Comfort Safari Club. McCall Smith, A.
Double Deuce. Parker, R. B.
Double happiness. Hughes
The **Double** Life of Liliane. Tuck, L.
Double play. Parker, R. B.
The **doublet** affair. Buckley, F.
A **Doubter's** Almanac. Canin, E.
Doughnut. Holt, T.
The **dovekeepers.** Hoffman, A.
Down Among the Sticks and Bones. Grant, M.
Down and out in the Magic Kindgom. Doctorow, C.
Down from Cascom Mountain. Williams, A. J.
Down here. Vachss, A. H.
Down in the zero. Vachss, A. H.
Down river. Hart, J.
DOWN SYNDROME
The blue fox
Edwards, K. The memory keeper's daughter
Down to a sunless sea. Poyer, D.
Down town. Sams, F.
Downtown Owl. Klosterman, C.
DOWRY
James, E. The ugly duchess
Doyle, Arthur Conan Sir, 1859-1930
About
Faye, L. The whole art of detection
Hockensmith, S. Holmes on the range
Hockensmith, S. On the wrong track
Horowitz, A. The House of Silk
King, L. R. The game
Meyer, N. The seven-per-cent solution
Moore, G. The Sherlockian
Pirie, D. The patient's eyes
Robertson, M. The brothers of Baker Street
Dracula. Stoker, B.
DRACULA, COUNT (FICTIONAL CHARACTER)
See also Fictional characters
The new annotated Dracula
DRAG CULTURE
See also Counterculture
The **Dragon** and the Pearl. Lin, J.
Dragon bones. See, L.
Dragon's Kin. McCaffrey, A.
Dragon's lair. Penman, S. K.
Dragonfish. Tran, V.
Dragonflight. McCaffrey, A.
Dragonriders of Pern [series]
McCaffrey, A. Dragonflight
McCaffrey, A. The white dragon
DRAGONS
Brennan, M. A natural history of dragons

Cross, J. Touched by venom
Lackey, M. Joust
Martin, G. R. R. A storm of swords
McCaffrey, A. Dragonflight
McCaffrey, T. Dragonsblood
McCaffrey, A. Dragon's Kin
McCaffrey, A. The white dragon
Norton, A. The elvenbane
Norton, A. Elvenblood
Novik, N. Blood of tyrants
Novik, N. His majesty's dragon
Novik, N. League of Dragons
DRAGONS
See also Animals -- Folklore; Folklore; Monsters; Mythical animals
Dragonsblood. McCaffrey, T.
Dragonwyck. Seton, A.
Drake's Rakes [series]
Dreyer, E. Once a Rake
DRAMA -- TECHNIQUE
See also Authorship
Drama city. Pelecanos, G. P.
DRAMATIC MUSIC *See* Musicals; Opera; Operetta
DRAMATISTS
Adrian, C. The great night
Aira, C. The literary conference
Barber, R. The Marlowe papers
Bear, E. Ink and steel
Cooley, M. The archivist
Gruber, M. The book of air and shadows
Haig, M. The dead fathers club
Hazzard, S. The transit of Venus
Holland, T. The archivist's story
Lessing, D. M. Love, again
Maguire, G. Son of a witch
Marsh, N. Light thickens
Murdoch, I. The sea, the sea
O'Connor, J. Ghost light
Phillips, A. The tragedy of Arthur
Reyn, I. What happened to Anna K.
Self, W. Dorian
Updike, J. Gertrude and Claudius
Upson, N. London rain
DRAMATISTS
See also Authors; Drama
DRAPER (UTAH)
Harrison, M. I. The Bishop's Wife
DRAWING
See also Art; Graphic arts
Drawing conclusions. Leon, D.
Dreadnought. Priest, C.
Dream eyes. Krentz, J. A.
DREAM INTERPRETATION *See* Dreams
The **dream** life of Sukhanov. Grushin, O.
Dream of Ding Village. Lianke, Y.
The **dream** of my return. Moya, H. C.
The **dream** of perpetual motion. Palmer, D. C.
The **dream** of Scipio. Pears, I.
The **dream** of the Celt.
The **Dream-Quest** of Vellitt Boe. Johnson, K.
Dreamers of the day. Russell, M. D.
The **dreaming.** Wood, B.
DREAMING *See* Dreams
Dreaming in Cuban. Garcia, C.
The **dreaming** void. Hamilton, P. F.
Dreaming water. Tsukiyama, G.
DREAMS
Carroll, J. Bathing the Lion
Irving, J. Avenue of mysteries
O'Brien, T. Going after Cacciato
Sallis, J. The killer is dying
DREAMS
See also Visions
Dreams and Shadows. Cargill, C. R.
Dreams of joy. See, L.
Dreams of my Russian summers. Makine, A.
Dreamsnake. McIntyre, V. N.
The **dreamthief's** daughter. Moorcock, M.
DRESDEN, HARRY (FICTITIOUS CHARACTER)
Butcher, J. Proven guilty
DRESSMAKERS
Aira, C. The seamstress and the wind
Chase, L. L. Silk is for seduction
Peebles, F. d. P. The seamstress
Wolff, I. A vintage affair
Dressmakers [series]
Chase, L. Vixen in Velvet
DRESSMAKING
Chase, L. Scandal wears satin
DRIED FOODS
See also Food
Drifting house. Lee, K.
Driftless. Rhodes, D.
The **driftless** area. Drury, T.
Drinking coffee elsewhere. Packer, Z.
DRINKING PROBLEM *See* Alcoholism; Drinking of alcoholic beverages
Driscoll, Clara, 1861-1944
About
Vreeland, S. Clara and Mr. Tiffany
Drive. Sallis, J.
DRIVE-IN THEATERS
Lansdale, J. R. The complete Drive-in
Lansdale, J. R. A fine dark line
Driven. Sallis, J.
The **driver's** seat. Spark, M.
Driving the king. Howard, R.
Drop edge of yonder. Wurlitzer, R.
A **drop** of Chinese blood. Church, J.
A **drop** of the hard stuff. Block, L.
DROPOUTS
See also Students; Youth
DROUGHTS
Bacigalupi, P. The water knife

Meadows, R. I will send rain
Watkins, C. V. Gold fame citrus
Drowned hopes. Westlake, D. E.
The **drowned** life. Ford, J.
DROWNING
Grimes, M. Hotel Paradise
Hamilton, J. A map of the world
Ng, C. Everything I never told you
Oates, J. C. Black water
O'Nan, S. Snow angels
Schwarz, C. Drowning Ruth
The **drowning** house. Black, E.
Drowning lessons. Selgin, P.
The **drowning** pool. Macdonald, R.
Drowning Ruth. Schwarz, C.
DRUG ABUSE
See also Social problems; Substance abuse
Braden, K. The Longest Night
Gregory, D. Afterparty
Welsh, I. Porno
Welsh, I. Skagboys
Zailckas, K. Mother, mother
DRUG ADDICTION
Cheever, J. Falconer
Grossman, D. Someone to run with
Hoffman, A. Skylight confessions
Mahfouz, N. Midaq Alley
Meyer, N. The seven-per-cent solution
Monaghan, N. The killing jar
Mrazek, R. J. Unholy fire
O'Connor, R. Buffalo soldiers
Robinson, R. Cost
Southgate, M. The taste of salt
Wallace, D. F. Infinite jest
DRUG ADDICTION *See* Drug abuse
DRUG ADDICTS
Burroughs, W. S. Naked lunch
Cunningham, M. The snow queen
Earle, S. I'll never get out of this world alive
Harding, P. Enon
Lamott, A. Imperfect birds
LaValle, V. D. Big machine
McGregor, J. Even the dogs
Phantom
The son
St. Aubyn, E. The complete Patrick Melrose novels
Welsh, I. Trainspotting
DRUG ADDICTS -- SCOTLAND
Welsh, I. Skagboys
DRUG DEALERS
Burgess, M. Uncle Janice
Lange, R. Angel baby
VanderMeer, J. Borne
Woods, T. Alibi
DRUG TRADE
Rosero Diago, E. The armies
DRUG TRADE, ILLICIT *See* Drug traffic
DRUG TRAFFIC
Burdett, J. Bangkok 8
Burgess, M. Dogfight, a love story
Caputo, P. Crossers
Clancy, T. Clear and present danger
Clement, J. Prayers for the stolen
D'Souza, T. Mule
Dugoni, R. Murder one
Ellroy, J. Blood's a rover
Ellroy, J. The cold six thousand
Faulks, S. Devil may care
George, E. What came before he shot her
Huston, C. The shotgun rule
Land, J. Strong at the break
Lange, R. Angel baby
Leonard, E. Rum punch
Ludlum, R. The Matlock paper
O'Donovan, G. Dublin dead
Palmer, D. Helpless
Parker, B. Criminal justice
Pelecanos, G. P. The sweet forever
Pelecanos, G. The cut
Poyer, D. Down to a sunless sea
Price, R. Clockers
Robards, K. Shiver
Robbins, T. Villa incognito
Seymour, G. Killing ground
Seymour, G. Rat run
Silko, L. Almanac of the dead
Stewart, M. Airs above the ground
Stone, R. Dog soldiers
Stroby, W. Shoot the woman first
Waite, U. The terror of living
Wilson, F. P. Deep as the marrow
Winslow, D. The cartel
Winslow, D. The kings of cool
Winslow, D. Savages
Woodrell, D. Winter's bone
DRUG TRAFFIC -- COLOMBIA
The sound of things falling
DRUG TRAFFIC -- INVESTIGATION
Burgess, M. Uncle Janice
DRUG TRAFFIC -- KENYA
Levine, J. A. Bingo's Run
DRUG TRAFFIC -- NORTH DAKOTA
Box, C. J. Badlands
DRUG USE *See* Drug abuse; Drugs
DRUGS
A clockwork orange
Cohen, J. Four new messages
Ellis, B. E. Lunar Park
Gaitskill, M. Veronica
Hagedorn, J. T. Toxicology
Henderson, E. Ten thousand saints
Hiaasen, C. Star Island
Hogan, C. Devils in exile
Kunkel, B. Indecision

Lazar, Z. Sway
Martin, C. W. How to sell
Richards, D. A. The bay of love and sorrows
Robbins, T. Fierce invalids home from hot climates
Tao Lin Taipei
Tea, M. Rose of no man's land
Vollmann, W. T. The royal family
Walker, A. Now is the time to open your heart
Walsh, H. Brass
DRUGS -- ABUSE *See* Drug abuse
DRUGS -- MISUSE *See* Drug abuse
DRUGS -- SIDE EFFECTS
Newitz, A. Autonomous
DRUGS AND CRIME
See also Crime; Drugs
DRUGSTORES
See also Retail trade; Stores
The **druid** of Shannara. Brooks, T.
DRUIDS AND DRUIDISM
See also Celts; Religions
DRUIDS AND DRUIDISM
Rose, M. J. Seduction
DRUM MAJORING
See also Bands (Music)
DRUMMERS
Sanchez, T. King Bongo
Drums along the Mohawk. Edmonds, W. D.
DRUNKENNESS
Rosero, E. Good offices
DRUNKENNESS *See* Alcoholism; Temperance
The **dry.** Harper, J.
Dry bones. Quinn, P.
Dry bones in the valley. Bouman, T.
Dry ice. White, S. W.
DRYDEN, PHILIP (FICTITIOUS CHARACTER)
Kelly, J. The fire baby
Kelly, J. The moon tunnel
DS Aector McAvoy [series]
Mark, D. Original skin
DUAL PERSONALITY
Hesse, H. Steppenwolf
Martin, V. Mary Reilly
Stevenson, R. L. The strange case of Dr. Jekyll and Mr. Hyde
DUAL-CAREER FAMILIES
See also Family
DUBLIN (IRELAND)
Lally, C. Eggshells
O'Donovan, G. Dublin dead
Dublin dead. O'Donovan, G.
Dubliners. Joyce, J.
Duchess of nothing. McGowan, H.
The **Duchess** War. Milan, C.
DUCHIES
James, E. The ugly duchess
DUCKS
See also Birds; Poultry
Due preparations for the plague. Hospital, J. T.
DUELING
See also Manners and customs; Martial arts
DUELING
Kushner, E. Swordspoint
The **Duke.** Byrne, K.
A **Duke** Never Yields. Gray, J.
Duke of Midnight. Hoyt, E.
The **Duke's** Guide to Correct Behavior. Frampton, M.
The Duke's sons [series]
Ashford, J. What the duke doesn't know
Dukes Prefer Blondes. Chase, L.
Dula, Tom, 1843 or 4-1868
About
McCrumb, S. The ballad of Tom Dooley
DUNCAN, EVE (FICTITIOUS CHARACTER)
Johansen, I. Taking Eve
Dune. Herbert, F.
Dune [series]
Herbert, F. Dune messiah
Dune messiah. Herbert, F.
Dune: House Atreides. Herbert, B.
Dune: House Corrino. Herbert, B.
Dune: The Butlerian jihad. Herbert, B.
The **Dunwich** horror, and others. Lovecraft, H. P.
Duplex. Davis, K.
DURHAM (ENGLAND: COUNTY) -- HISTORY
Unsworth, B. The quality of mercy
DUST BOWL ERA, 1931-1939
Meadows, R. I will send rain
DUST STORMS
See also Droughts; Erosion; Storms
The **dust** that falls from dreams. De Bernières, L.
Dust to dust. Hoag, T.
DUTY
See also Ethics; Human behavior
A **duty** to the dead. Todd, C.
DWARF TREES
See also Trees
DWARFS
DeWoskin, R. Big girl small
Dickens, C. The old curiosity shop
Dunant, S. In the company of the courtesan
Dunn, K. Geek love
Grass, G. The tin drum
Hegi, U. Stones from the river
Swift, J. Gulliver's travels
Vallgren The horrific sufferings of the mind-reading monster Hercules Barefoot
DWELLINGS *See* Domestic architecture; Houses; Housing
DWELLINGS
Delaney, J. P. The girl before
Hoffman, A. Blackbird house
DYES AND DYEING
See also Color; Pigments; Textile chemistry; Textile industry
The **dying** animal. Roth, P.

A **Dying** Fall. Griffiths, E.
The **Dying** Grass. Vollmann, W. T.
Dying Is My Business. Kaufmann, N.
Dying Light. MacBride, S.
Dying on the vine. Elkins, A. J.
DYNAMICS
See also Mathematics; Mechanics
DYSFUNCTIONAL FAMILIES
Ball, J. How to set a fire and why
Foer, J. S. Here I am
Kenney, J. Truth in advertising
McKenzie, E. The portable Veblen
Millet, L. Sweet Lamb of Heaven
O'Farrell, M. Instructions for a heat wave
Schmidt, S. See what I have done
Silent house
Strout, E. The burgess boys
Zailckas, K. Mother, mother
DYSLEXIA
Charlton, B. Spellwright
DYSTOPIAN FICTION
Alderman, N. The power
Atwood, M. The year of the flood
Baggott, J. Pure
Ballard, J. G. Kingdom come
Barry, M. Lexicon
Bell, A. The reapers are the angels
Brown, P. Golden Son
Brown, P. Red Rising
A clockwork orange
Elison, M. The book of Etta
Elison, M. The Book of the Unnamed Midwife
Graedon, A. The word exchange
Haig, F. The fire sermon
Haig, F. The map of bones
Jemisin, N. K. The obelisk gate
Kress, N. After the Fall, Before the Fall, During the Fall
Lee On such a full sea
Lelic, S. The facility
McDevitt, J. Odyssey
Okorafor, N. Who fears death
Palmer, D. C. The dream of perpetual motion
Romano, S. Resurrection Express
Saintcrow, L. Trailer park fae
Shteyngart, G. Super sad true love story
Sternbergh, A. Shovel ready
Stirling, S. M. Dies the fire
Theroux, M. Far north
VanderMeer, J. Authority
VanderMeer, J. Borne
Ware, D. Ecko Rising
Watkins, C. V. Gold fame citrus
Wilson, R. C. Julian Comstock
Winters, B. H. World of trouble
DYSTOPIAN FICTION
See also Fantasy fiction; Science fiction
DYSTOPIAS
Atwood, M. Maddaddam

E

E is for evidence. Grafton, S.
The **eagle** has flown. Higgins, J.
The **eagle** has landed. Higgins, J.
The **eagle's** throne. Fuentes, C.
EAGLES
See also Birds; Birds of prey
EARLY CHRISTIANS
Asch, S. The Apostle
Asch, S. The Nazarene
Lagerkvist, P. Barabbas
Sienkiewicz, H. Quo Vadis
Williams, N. John
Early novels and stories. Baldwin, J.
EARLY PRINTED BOOKS
See also Books
Early short stories, 1883-1888.
Early warning. Smiley, J.
Earp, Wyatt, 1848-1929
About
Parker, R. B. Gunman's rhapsody
Russell, M. D. Doc
EARTH
This way to the end times
Earth abides. Stewart, G. R.
EARTH SHELTERED HOUSES
See also House construction; Houses; Underground architecture
Earth's children [series]
Auel, J. M. The Clan of the Cave Bear
Auel, J. M. The land of painted caves
EARTH, DESTRUCTION OF
Bear, G. Anvil of stars
Bear, G. The forge of God
Hoban, R. Riddley Walker
Niven, L. Lucifer's hammer
Earthly possessions. Tyler, A.
EARTHQUAKES
Gardiner, M. The Dirty Secrets Club
Rosenberg, R. This is not civilization
Walker, K. T. The age of miracles
Young, T. W. The renegades
EARTHWORKS (ART)
See also Art
EAST AND WEST
Clavell, J. Shogun
Endo, S. Silence
Forster, E. M. A passage to India
Hair, D. Mage's blood
Mitchell, D. The thousand autumns of Jacob de Zoet
Osborne, L. The forgiven
Rushdie, S. The ground beneath her feet

Tan, A. The Joy Luck Club
EAST EUROPEANS -- ENGLAND
Tremain, R. The road home
EAST INDIAN AMERICANS
Mehta, R. Quarantine
Satyal, R. No one can pronounce my name
Sidhu, R. S. Good Indian Girls
EAST INDIANS
Sanghera, S. Marriage Material
EAST INDIANS -- AFRICA
Naipaul, V. S. A bend in the river
Naipaul, V. S. Half a life
EAST INDIANS -- CANADA
Vassanji, M. G. The assassin's song
EAST INDIANS -- ENGLAND
Kunzru, H. The impressionist
Naipaul, V. S. Half a life
Naipaul, V. S. Magic seeds
Seton, A. Green darkness
EAST INDIANS -- ENGLAND -- LONDON
Chaudhuri, A. Odysseus Abroad
EAST INDIANS -- FRANCE
Morais, R. C. The hundred-foot journey
EAST INDIANS -- GUYANA
Bhattacharya, R. The sly company of people who care
EAST INDIANS -- ITALY
Ondaatje, M. The English patient
EAST INDIANS -- MALAYSIA
Samarasan, P. Evening is the whole day
EAST INDIANS -- TRINIDAD AND TOBAGO
Naipaul, V. S. A house for Mr. Biswas
EAST INDIANS -- UNITED STATES
D'Souza, T. The Konkans
Sharma, A. Family Life
Sidhu, R. S. Good Indian Girls
East into Upper East. Jhabvala, R. P.
East is east. Lathen, E.
East of Eden. Steinbeck, J.
East, west. Rushdie, S.
EASTER
See also Christian holidays; Holy Week
Easter Island. Vanderbes, J.
EASTER ISLAND
Vanderbes, J. Easter Island
EASTERN CHURCHES
See also Christian sects; Christianity
EASTERN EUROPE
Kostova, E. The historian
Powell, J. The breaking of eggs
Easy meat. Harvey, J.
Eat the document. Spiotta, D.
EATING DISORDERS
See also Abnormal psychology
EAVESDROPPING
Ullman, E. By blood
EAVESDROPPING
See also Criminal investigation; Right of privacy
ECCENTRICS AND ECCENTRICITIES
Barker, N. Darkmans
Binchy, M. Whitethorn Woods
Boyle, T. C. Road to Wellville
Cadwalladr, C. The family tree
Childress, M. Crazy in Alabama
Crews, H. A feast of snakes
Cusk, R. In the fold
Dallas, S. The Persian Pickle Club
Darnielle, J. Wolf in white van
Diamant, A. Last days of Dogtown
Doctorow, E. L. Homer & Langley
Drabble, M. The witch of Exmoor
D'Souza, T. The Konkans
Dufresne, J. Deep in the shade of paradise
Dufresne, J. Requiem, Mass.
Echenoz, J. Lightning
Erdrich, L. The Beet Queen
Gallagher, S. The bedlam detective
Gay, W. Twilight
Goldberg, M. Bee season
Hiaasen, C. Nature girl
Irving, J. A widow for one year
Jackson, J. Between, Georgia
Kallos, S. Broken for you
Lansdale, J. R. Sunset and sawdust
Larsen, R. The selected works of T. S. Spivet
Lindgren, T. Hash
Marias, J. All souls
Martin, S. The pleasure of my company
Martinez, N. M. Caramba!
McGahern, J. By the lake
McMurtry, L. Sin killer
Mosher, H. F. On Kingdom Mountain
Murakami, H. The wind-up bird chronicle
Ozick, C. Heir to the glimmering world
Pearson, T. R. A short history of a small place
Pessl, M. Special topics in calamity physics
Portis, C. The dog of the South
Portis, C. Gringos
Portis, C. Masters of Atlantis
Racculia, K. This must be the place
Ramsland, M. Doghead
Roberts, V. After the fall
Robbins, T. Villa incognito
Rosenblatt, R. Lapham rising
Schaffert, T. The coffins of Little Hope
Smith, D. I capture the castle
Spark, M. A far cry from Kensington
Spark, M. Loitering with intent
Spiotta, D. Stone Arabia
Steinke, R. Holy skirts
Toole, J. K. A confederacy of dunces
Townsend, S. Number 10
Tyler, A. Back when we were grownups
Tyler, A. Morgan's passing
Unsworth, B. Losing Nelson

Vine, B. King Solomon's carpet
Wilson, K. The family Fang
Wood, S. Wrecker
ECCENTRICS AND ECCENTRICITIES
See also Curiosities and wonders; Personality
ECCLESIASTICAL RITES AND CEREMONIES *See* Rites and ceremonies
The **echo.** Walters, M.
An **echo** in the bone. Gabaldon, D.
The **echo** maker. Powers, R.
Echoes from the dead. Theorin, J.
Echoes of the dead. Spencer, S.
Ecko Rising. Ware, D.
Eclipse. Patterson, R. N.
Eclipse. Wheeler, R. S.
ECOLOGICAL DISTURBANCES
Boyle, T. C. When the killing's done
Ghosh, A. The hungry tide
ECOLOGISTS
Gordimer, N. Get a life
ECOLOGY
Boyle, T. C. When the killing's done
Michener, J. A. Chesapeake
Robinson, K. S. Antarctica
ECOTERRORISM
Glass, J. The widower's tale
ECOTOURISM
See also Tourist trade
Ed King. Guterson, D.
The edda of burdens [series]
Bear, E. All the windwracked stars
EDDAS
See also Old Norse literature; Poetry; Scandinavian literature
Eddie Signwriter. Schwartzman, A.
Eden. Vernon, O.
Eden. Lem, S.
Eden Close. Shreve, A.
EDGAR ALLAN POE AWARDS
See also Literary prizes; Mystery fiction
Edgar and Lucy. Lodato, V.
Edge. Deaver, J.
Edge of danger. Higgins, J.
Edge of dark water. Lansdale, J. R.
Edge of Eternity. Follett, K.
The **Edge** of the Earth. Schwarz, C.
EDIBLE PLANTS
See also Economic botany; Food; Plants
EDINBURGH (SCOTLAND) -- FICTION
McCall Smith, A. The forgotten affairs of youth
Rankin, I. Rather be the devil
Rankin, I. Black and blue
Rankin, I. The falls
Rankin, I. A question of blood
Rankin, I. Set in darkness
Welsh, I. Skagboys
Edison, Thomas A. (Thomas Alva), 1847-1931
About
Echenoz, J. Lightning
Moore, G. The last days of night
Edisto. Powell, P.
Edisto revisited. Powell, P.
EDITING
See also Authorship; Publishers and publishing
EDITORS
Cleave, C. Little Bee
Cooley, M. The archivist
Dolan, H. Bad things happen
Dolan, H. Very bad men
Nunez, E. Anna in-between
Rosenfeld, L. I'm so happy for you
Walker, A. The way forward is with a broken heart
EDMONTOSAURUS
See also Dinosaurs
EDUCATIONAL FUND RAISING
Lipsyte, S. The ask
EDUCATIONAL GAMES
See also Education; Games
Edward I, King of England, 1239-1307
About
Penman, S. K. The reckoning
Edward IV, King of England, 1442-1483
About
Penman, S. K. The sunne in splendour
Edward V, King of England, 1470-1483
About
Gregory, P. The red queen
The **Edwardians.** Sackville-West, V.
EGGS
See also Food
Eggshells. Lally, C.
EGO (PSYCHOLOGY)
See also Personality; Psychoanalysis; Psychology; Self
EGOISM
Self, W. Dorian
Wilde, O. The picture of Dorian Gray
EGYPT
Gracie, A. To catch a bride
Greenwood, K. Out of the black land
EGYPT -- 20TH CENTURY
Mahfouz, N. Children of the alley
EGYPT -- ALEXANDRIA
Durrell, L. The Alexandria quartet: Justine; Balthazar; Mountolive {and} Clea
Durrell, L. Balthazar
Durrell, L. Clea
Durrell, L. Justine
Durrell, L. Mountolive
Roiphe, A. R. An imperfect lens
EGYPT -- CAIRO
Mahfouz, N. Midaq Alley
Mahfouz, N. Palace of desire
Mahfouz, N. Palace walk
Mahfouz, N. Sugar Street

Matar, H. Anatomy of a disappearance
Russell, M. D. Dreamers of the day
EGYPT -- HISTORY
Davis, L. Master and God
Geagley, B. Year of the hyenas
EGYPT -- HISTORY -- 332-30 B.C.
Saylor, S. Raiders of the Nile
Saylor, S. Wrath of the furies
EGYPT -- TO 640
Holland, C. Valley of the Kings
Mailer, N. Ancient evenings
EGYPTIAN MYTHOLOGY
See also Mythology
EGYPTIANS -- MASSACHUSETTS -- CAMBRIDGE
Aciman, A. Harvard Square
Eifelheim. Flynn, M.
The **Eiger** sanction. Trevanian
The **eight.** Neville, K.
Eight girls taking pictures. Otto, W.
Eight men. Wright, R.
Eight million ways to die. Block, L.
The **eighth** day. Wilder, T.
Eileen. Moshfegh, O.
Einstein's dreams. Lightman, A. P.
Einstein, Albert, 1879-1955
About
Lightman, A. P. Einstein's dreams
Powers, T. Three days to never
El Paso. Groom, W.
EL PASO (TEX.)
Gaspar de Alba, A. Desert blood
Groom, W. El Paso
EL SALVADOR
Castellanos Moya, H. Tyrant memory
Garcia, C. A handbook to luck
Elantris. Sanderson, B.
Eleanor, of Aquitaine, Queen, consort of Henry II, King of England, 1122?-1204
About
Franklin, A. The serpent's tale
Penman, S. K. Cruel as the grave
Penman, S. K. Devil's brood
Penman, S. K. Dragon's lair
Penman, S. K. The queen's man
Penman, S. K. Time and chance
Eleanor, of Provence, Queen, consort of Henry III, King of England
About
Jones, S. Four sisters, all queens
ELECTION *See* Elections
ELECTION (THEOLOGY) *See* Predestination
ELECTIONS
Lynch, J. Truth like the sun
Rowling, J. K. The casual vacancy
Vidal, G. 1876
ELECTORAL COLLEGE *See* Presidents -- United States -- Election
ELECTRIC AUTOMOBILES
See also Automobiles
ELECTRIC LIGHTING
Moore, G. The last days of night
ELECTRIC POWER FAILURES
Stirling, S. M. Dies the fire
ELECTRIC RAILROADS
See also Railroads
ELECTRIC SHOCK THERAPY
Greer, A. S. The Impossible Lives of Greta Wells
ELECTRIC SIGNS
See also Advertising; Signs and signboards
ELECTRICAL ENGINEERS
Echenoz, J. Lightning
Hunt, S. The invention of everything else
ELECTRONIC MAIL MESSAGES
Hamilton, J. Disobedience
ELECTRONIC PUBLISHING
See also Information services; Publishers and publishing
ELECTRONIC SURVEILLANCE
Eisler, B. The God's Eye View
Hurwitz, G. They're watching
Raban, J. Surveillance
ELECTROTYPING
See also Electrochemistry; Printing
The **elegance** of the hedgehog.
ELEGIAC POETRY
See also Poetry
Elegies for the brokenhearted. Hodgen, C.
Elegy for Eddie. Winspear, J.
ELEMENTARY SCHOOL TEACHERS
Messud, C. The woman upstairs
The **elephant** keeper. Nicholson, C.
The **elephant** keepers' children.
The **elephant's** journey.
ELEPHANTS
The elephant's journey
Gruen, S. Water for elephants
Nicholson, C. The elephant keeper
ELEVATORS
Whitehead, C. The intuitionist
The **eleventh** man. Doig, I.
Elfland. Warrington, F.
Eligible. Sittenfeld, C.
Eliot, George, 1819-1880
About
Weisgall, D. The world before her
Eliot, T. S. (Thomas Stearns), 1888-1965
About
Cooley, M. The archivist
ELITE (SOCIAL SCIENCES)
See also Leadership; Power (Social sciences); Social classes; Social groups
ELIXIRS
Clark, G. The regulars
Elizabeth I. George, M.
Elizabeth I, Queen of England, 1533-1603

About
Buckley, F. The siren queen
George, M. Elizabeth I
Harper, K. The Poyson garden
Maxwell, R. The Queen's bastard
Maxwell, R. The secret diary of Anne Boleyn
Maxwell, R. The wild Irish
Plaidy, J. The captive Queen of Scots
Weir, A. The Lady Elizabeth
ELIZABETH II, 1926- (QUEEN OF GREAT BRITAIN)
See also Queens
Elizabeth is missing. Healey, E.
Elizabeth, Queen, consort of Edward IV, King of England, 1437?-1492
About
Gregory, P. The red queen
Elizabeth, Queen, Consort of Henry VII, King of England, 1465-1503
Gregory, P. The white princess
Ella Minnow Pea. Dunn, M.
Ellen Foster. Gibbons, K.
Ellen Gilchrist: collected stories. Gilchrist, E.
Elmer Gantry. Lewis, S.
Elsewhere, California. Johnson, D.
The **elusive** Mrs. Pollifax. Gilman, D.
The **elvenbane.** Norton, A.
Elvenblood. Norton, A.
ELVES
See also Folklore
ELVES
Evans, C. A darkness forged in fire
EMBASSY BUILDINGS
Patchett, A. Bel canto
Embassytown. Mieville, C.
EMBEZZLEMENT
Eugenides, J. Fresh complaint
Johnson, D. Nobody move
Perry, T. Dance for the dead
Pronzini, B. The crimes of Jordan Wise
EMERALDS
Westlake, D. E. The hot rock
EMERGENCIES *See* Accidents; Disasters; First aid
EMERGENCY MEDICAL TECHNICIANS
Whittall, Z. Holding still for as long as possible
Emerson, Ralph Waldo, 1803-1882
About
Pearl, M. The Dante Club
The **emigrants.**
EMIGRANTS *See* Immigrants
EMIGRATION AND IMMIGRATION
Bezmozgis, D. The free world
Bulawayo, N. We need new names
Cleave, C. Little Bee
Wolfe, T. Back to blood
Emile Cinq-Mars [series]
Farrow, J. The Storm Murders
Emily, alone. O'Nan, S.
EMINENT DOMAIN
See also Constitutional law; Land use; Property
Emissary. Locke, T.
Emma. Austen, J.
Emma. Bronte, C.
Emma, Queen, consort of Canute I, King of England, d. 1052
About
Bracewell, P. Shadow on the crown
Emmeline. Rossner, J.
EMOTIONALLY DISTURBED CHILDREN
See also Exceptional children; Mentally ill
EMOTIONS
Bender, A. The particular sadness of lemon cake
Gaiman, N. Trigger warning
EMOTIONS IN CHILDREN
See also Child psychology; Emotions
EMPATHY
See also Attitude (Psychology); Emotions; Social psychology
The **emperor** of Ocean Park. Carter, S. L.
The **emperor's** children. Messud, C.
EMPERORS
See also Kings and rulers
EMPERORS
Levack, S. Demon of the air
EMPERORS -- ROME
George, M. The confessions of young Nero
Empire. Vidal, G.
Empire Falls. Russo, R.
Empire games. Stross, C.
Empire games [series]
Stross, C. Empire games
The **empire** of ice cream. Ford, J.
Empire of the Sun. Ballard, J. G.
EMPLOYMENT REFERENCES
Schumacher, J. Dear Committee Members
The **empress** of bright moon. Randel, W. D.
Empress Orchid. Min, A.
EMPRESSES
Eastland, S. Eye of the Red Tsar
Graves, R. I, Claudius
Min, A. Empress Orchid
Penman, S. K. When Christ and his saints slept
EMPRESSES -- CHINA
Randel, W. D. The empress of bright moon
The **empty** family. Tóibín, C.
EMPTY NESTERS
Green, J. Tempting fate
Link, T. Denting the Bosch
The **Empty** Throne. Cornwell, B.
EMTS (MEDICINE) *See* Emergency medical technicians
The **enchanted** wanderer and other stories. Leskov, N. S.
Enchantments. Harrison, K.
The **enchantress.** Han, S.
The **enchantress** of Florence. Rushdie, S.
ENCOURAGEMENT
See also Courage; Helping behavior

ENCYCLOPEDIAS *See* Encyclopedias and dictionaries
ENCYCLOPEDIAS AND DICTIONARIES
Levithan, D. The lover's dictionary
The **end** game. Coulter, C.
The **End** of All Things. Scalzi, J.
The **end** of California. Yarbrough, S.
The **end** of Eddy. Louis, É.
The **end** of the affair. Greene, G.
The **end** of the alphabet. Richardson, C. S.
End of the drive. L'Amour, L.
END OF THE EARTH *See* End of the world
The **end** of the wasp season. Mina, D.
END OF THE WORLD
Adrian, C. The children's hospital
Butler, O. E. Adulthood rites
Butler, O. E. Dawn
Butler, O. E. Imago
Cronin, J. The twelve
Currie, R. Everything matters!
Gaiman, N. Good omens
Harkaway, N. Angelmaker
Heller, P. The dog stars
Percy, W. Love in the ruins
McCarthy, C. The road
Shute, N. On the beach
This way to the end times
Updike, J. Toward the end of time
West, M. L. The clowns of God
Whitehead, C. Zone one
Wilson, R. C. Spin
END OF THE WORLD (ASTRONOMY) *See* End of the world
End of watch. King, S.
END-OF-THE-WORLD FICTION *See* Apocalyptic fiction
ENDANGERED SPECIES
Millet, L. How the dead dream
Ender's game. Card, O. S.
Endless love. Spencer, S.
Endless night. Christie, A.
ENDOWED CHARITIES *See* Charities; Endowments
ENDOWMENTS
Vonnegut, K. God bless you, Mr. Rosewater
Endurance. Lake, J.
Endymion. Simmons, D.
Enemies, a love story. Singer, I. B.
Enemy of God. Cornwell, B.
Enemy women. Jiles, P.
Engelhardt, August, 1877-1919
About
Imperium
Engineer trilogy [series]
Parker, K. J. Devices and desires
ENGINEERING, BIOLOGICAL *See* Bioengineering
ENGINEERING, GENETIC *See* Genetic engineering
ENGINEERS
Griesemer, J. Signal & noise
Harris, R. Pompeii
Levi, P. The monkey's wrench
Vonnegut, K. Player piano
ENGLAND
Bragg, M. A son of war
Byrne, K. The Duke
Cadwalladr, C. The family tree
Cleeves, A. Thin air
Dare, T. Do you want to start a scandal
De Bernières, L. The dust that falls from dreams
Drabble, M. The sea lady
Forster, E. M. Maurice
Gardam, J. The flight of the maidens
Gardam, J. God on the rocks
George, E. A Banquet of Consequences
Haig, M, The Radleys
Hensher, P. King of the badgers
Hodgson, A. The last confession of Thomas Hawkins
Hollinghurst, A. The stranger's child
Horowitz, A. Magpie murders
Howatch, S. Scandalous risks
Howatch, S. Ultimate prizes
Jones, S. Outcast
Kunzru, H. My revolutions
Lawton, J. Old flames
Lessing, D. M. The memoirs of a survivor
Lodge, D. Deaf sentence
Moody, D. Hater
Moore, A. Jerusalem
Mukherjee, N. A life apart
Nicholls, D. One day
Porter, H. The bell ringers
Pym, B. Quartet in autumn
Reay, K. The Brontë plot
Rendell, R. Tigerlily's orchids
Robinson, P. The first cut
Runcie, J. Canvey Island
Rutherfurd, E. Sarum
Sahota, S. The year of the runaways
Sanghera, S. Marriage Material
Saunders, K. The Secrets of Wishtide
Simonson, H. The summer before the war
Swift, G. England and other stories
St. Aubyn, E. The complete Patrick Melrose novels
Sykes, S. D. Plague Land
Thomas, R. Other people's marriages
Townsend, S. Number 10
Tremain, R. Sacred country
Trollope, J. The best of friends
Trollope, J. Other people's children
Trollope, J. A Spanish lover
Uris, L. QB VII
Vine, B. The brimstone wedding
Vyleta, D. Smoke
Walters, M. The sculptress
Walton, J. Ha'penny
Waugh, E. Decline and fall
Weldon, F. Chalcot Crescent

Williams, C. Stairway to hell
Willig, L. The seduction of the crimson rose
Winterson, J. Oranges are not the only fruit
Wodehouse, P. G. The code of the Woosters
Wodehouse, P. G. The inimitable Jeeves
Wodehouse, P. G. Tales from the Drones Club
Woolf, V. Jacob's room
Woolf, V. Orlando

ENGLAND -- 12TH CENTURY

Follett, K. The pillars of the earth
Franklin, A. Mistress of the art of death
Franklin, A. The serpent's tale
Penman, S. K. Devil's brood
Penman, S. K. Lionheart
Penman, S. K. Time and chance
Penman, S. K. When Christ and his saints slept
Rice, A. Angel time
Scott, W. Ivanhoe

ENGLAND -- 13TH CENTURY

Penman, S. K. Falls the shadow
Penman, S. K. Here be dragons
Penman, S. K. The reckoning
White, T. H. The once and future king
White, T. H. The sword in the stone

ENGLAND -- 14TH CENTURY

Follett, K. World without end
Riley, J. M. In pursuit of the green lion
Riley, J. M. A vision of light
Seton, A. Katherine
Unsworth, B. Morality play

ENGLAND -- 15TH CENTURY

Bennett, V. The queen's lover
Penman, S. K. The sunne in splendour

ENGLAND -- 16TH CENTURY

Baker, K. In the garden of Iden
Bayard, L. The school of night
Bear, E. Ink and steel
George, M. Elizabeth I
Gregory, P. The other Boleyn girl
Gregory, P. The Boleyn Inheritance
L'Amour, L. To the far blue mountains
Mantel, H. Wolf Hall
Maxwell, R. The Queen's bastard
Maxwell, R. The secret diary of Anne Boleyn
Maxwell, R. The wild Irish
Plaidy, J. The captive Queen of Scots
Plaidy, J. Murder most royal
Riley, J. M. The serpent garden
Seton, A. Green darkness
Weir, A. Innocent traitor
Weir, A. The Lady Elizabeth

ENGLAND -- 17TH CENTURY

Barth, J. The sot-weed factor
Blackmore, R. D. Lorna Doone
Brooks, G. Year of wonders
Defoe, D. Moll Flanders
Du Maurier, D. Frenchman's Creek
Dumas, A. Twenty years after
Morrow, J. The last witchfinder
Pears, I. An instance of the fingerpost
Plaidy, J. The pleasures of love
Plaidy, J. William's wife

ENGLAND -- 18TH CENTURY

Bronte, C. Emma
Fielding, H. The history of Tom Jones, a foundling
Fielding, H. Joseph Andrews and Shamela
Koen, K. Through a glass darkly
Nicholson, C. The elephant keeper
Richardson, S. Pamela
Robertson, I. Instruments of darkness
Thackeray, W. M. The Virginians

ENGLAND -- 19TH CENTURY

Austen, J. Emma
Austen, J. Mansfield Park
Austen, J. Northanger Abbey
Austen, J. Persuasion
Austen, J. Pride and prejudice
Balogh, M. More than a mistress
Balogh, M. The secret mistress
Balogh, M. Seducing an angel
Birch, C. Jamrach's menagerie
Chase, L. L. The last hellion
Cornwell, B. The archer's tale
Cox, M. The glass of time
Cox, M. The meaning of night
Dickens, C. Bleak House
Dickens, C. A Christmas carol
Dickens, C. David Copperfield
Dickens, C. Dombey and Son
Dickens, C. Great expectations
Dickens, C. Little Dorrit
Dickens, C. Nicholas Nickleby
Dickens, C. The old curiosity shop
Dickens, C. The posthumous papers of the Pickwick Club
Donoghue, E. The sealed letter
Eliot, G. Middlemarch
Eliot, G. The mill on the Floss
Forester, C. S. Commodore Hornblower
Forester, C. S. Lord Hornblower
Foulds, A. The quickening maze
Fowles, J. The French lieutenant's woman
Gaskell, E. C. Cranford
Goodwin, D. The American heiress
Heyer, G. Black sheep
Holt, V. The black opal
Holt, V. Secret for a nightingale
Humphreys, H. Afterimage
Kowal, M. R. Shades of milk and honey
Lofts, N. Gad's Hall
Mallinson, A. A close run thing
Palliser, C. The unburied
Quick, A. I thee wed
Quick, A. Late for the wedding
Quick, A. The paid companion

Richler, M. Solomon Gursky was here
Ross-Macdonald, M. For they shall inherit
Ross-Macdonald, M. The rich are with you always
Ross-Macdonald, M. The Trevarton inheritance
Ross-Macdonald, M. The world from rough stones
Smith, M. C. Rose
Thackeray, W. M. Vanity fair
Thomas, S. Private arrangements
Trollope, A. Barchester Towers
Trollope, A. Doctor Thorne
Trollope, A. The Eustace diamonds
Trollope, A. Framley parsonage
Trollope, A. The last chronicle of Barset
Trollope, A. The prime minister
Trollope, A. The warden
Willig, L. The seduction of the crimson rose
Willis, C. To say nothing of the dog; or, How we found the bishop's bird stump at last
Woolf, V. The years

ENGLAND -- 20TH CENTURY

Binchy, M. Silver wedding
Bradford, B. T. A woman of substance
Cadwalladr, C. The family tree
Drabble, M. The radiant way
Drabble, M. The witch of Exmoor
Forster, E. M. A room with a view
Frayn, M. Headlong
Goddard, R. Into the blue
Hart, J. Damage
Howatch, S. Glamorous powers
James, P. D. Innocent blood
Kunzru, H. The impressionist
Lessing, D. M. The fifth child
Lively, P. Moon tiger
Lively, P. Passing on
Lodge, D. Nice work
Lodge, D. Thinks--
McGrath, P. Asylum
McGrath, P. The grotesque
Miller, A. Oxygen
Murdoch, I. The book and the brotherhood
Nicholls, D. A question of attraction
Perry, A. No graves as yet
Powell, A. A dance to the music of time
Rendell, R. The crocodile bird
Robinson, P. The first cut
Self, W. Dorian
Sillitoe, A. The loneliness of the long-distance runner
Sillitoe, A. Saturday night and Sunday morning
Spark, M. Memento mori
Speller, E. The strange fate of Kitty Easton
Swift, G. Waterland
Swift, G. Last orders
Townsend, S. Adrian Mole
Townsend, S. The Adrian Mole diaries
Townsend, S. Adrian Mole: the lost years
Trevor, W. Felicia's journey
Trollope, J. The best of friends
Trollope, J. Other people's children
Trollope, J. A Spanish lover
Uris, L. QB VII
Waugh, E. Brideshead revisited
Weldon, F. Worst fears
Wesley, M. Part of the furniture
Woolf, V. The years

ENGLAND -- ANGLO-SAXON PERIOD, 449-1066

Berger, T. Arthur Rex
Bradley, M. Z. The mists of Avalon
Cornwell, B. Enemy of God
Cornwell, B. Excalibur
Cornwell, B. The winter king
Seton, A. Avalon
Stewart, M. The crystal cave
Stewart, M. The hollow hills
Stewart, M. The last enchantment
Sutcliff, R. Sword at sunset
Twain, M. A Connecticut Yankee in King Arthur's court

ENGLAND -- BIRMINGHAM

Coe, J. The Rotters' Club
O'Flynn, C. The news where you are

ENGLAND -- BRIGHTON

Greene, G. Brighton rock

ENGLAND -- BRISTOL

Archer, J. Only time will tell

ENGLAND -- CAMBRIDGE

Franklin, A. Mistress of the art of death
Harris, R. Enigma
Harvey, J. Far cry
Harvey, J. Gone to ground
Stott, R. Ghostwalk

ENGLAND -- CHESHIRE

Gaskell, E. C. Cranford

ENGLAND -- CORNWALL

Du Maurier, D. Frenchman's Creek
Du Maurier, D. Jamaica Inn
Du Maurier, D. Rebecca
Goddard, R. Beyond recall
Holt, V. Bride of Pendorric
Pilcher, R. Coming home
Ross-Macdonald, M. Tamsin Harte
Ross-Macdonald, M. The Trevarton inheritance

ENGLAND -- CUMBRIA

Hill, R. The woodcutter

ENGLAND -- DERBYSHIRE

Brooks, G. Year of wonders
Lawrence, D. H. Lady Chatterley's lover

ENGLAND -- DEVON

Blackmore, R. D. Lorna Doone
Vine, B. The chimney sweeper's boy

ENGLAND -- DORSET

Fowles, J. The French lieutenant's woman
Gardam, J. Old Filth
Hardy, T. Far from the madding crowd
Hardy, T. Jude the obscure

Hardy, T. The return of the native
Hardy, T. Tess of the D'Urbervilles
McEwan, I. On Chesil Beach
Murdoch, I. The nice and the good
Walters, M. The breaker
Walters, M. The devil's feather

ENGLAND -- ESSEX
Trevor, W. Death in summer
Vine, B. The minotaur
Winman, S. When God was a rabbit

ENGLAND -- HAMPSHIRE
Drabble, M. The witch of Exmoor

ENGLAND -- HISTORY *See* Great Britain -- History

ENGLAND -- KENT
Barker, N. Darkmans
Dickens, C. The mystery of Edwin Drood

ENGLAND -- KINGS AND RULERS
Gregory, P. The other Boleyn girl
Gregory, P. The Boleyn Inheritance

ENGLAND -- LANCASHIRE
Sharratt, M. Daughters of the Witching Hill
Smith, M. C. Rose

ENGLAND -- LIVERPOOL
Walsh, H. Brass

ENGLAND -- LONDON
Ali, M. In the kitchen
Amis, M. London fields
Ballard, J. G. Millennium people
Balogh, M. Seducing an angel
Barnes, J. The somnambulist
Barrows, A. The Guernsey Literary and Potato Peel Pie Society
Birch, C. Jamrach's menagerie
Blake, S. The postmistress
Bolton, S. J. Now you see me
Brookner, A. Family and friends
Brookner, A. Undue influence
Chase, L. L. Silk is for seduction
Cox, M. The meaning of night
De Bernieres, L. A partisan's daughter
Donoghue, E. The sealed letter
Faulks, S. Engleby
Faulks, S. A week in December
Foulds, A. The quickening maze
George, E. What came before he shot her
Gibb, C. Sweetness in the belly
Gibson, W. Zero history
Grant, L. We had it so good
Guo X. A concise Chinese-English dictionary for lovers
Hadley, T. The London train
Hart, J. The reconstructionist
Hilton, J. Random harvest
Hoban, R. Her name was Lola
Hoffman, A. The third angel
Hornby, N. How to be good
Hornby, N. A long way down
Howatch, S. The heartbreaker
Hunt, R. Mr. Chartwell
Kelly, E. The poison tree
Keyes, M. Last Chance Saloon
Lebrecht, N. The song of names
Levy, A. Small island
Lively, P. Consequences
Livesey, M. Banishing Verona
Livesey, M. The house on Fortune Street
Lurie, A. Foreign affairs
Marias, J. Your face tomorrow: volume one: Fever and spear
Marias, J. Your face tomorrow: volume two: Dance and dream
Mawer, S. The fall
McCall Smith, A. Corduroy mansions
McEwan, I. Saturday
Mieville, C. Kraken
Mortimer, J. Felix in the underworld
Niffenegger, A. Her fearful symmetry
O'Brien, E. Time and tide
O'Farrell, M. The hand that first held mine
Pearl, M. The last Dickens
Pym, B. Excellent women
Pym, B. The sweet dove died
Robertson, M. The brothers of Baker Street
Rourke, L. The canal
Rutherfurd, E. London
Sackville-West, V. All passion spent
Self, W. The Book of Dave
Seymour, G. Rat run
Shriver, L. The post-birthday world
Smith, A. There but for the
Spark, M. Loitering with intent
Templeton, E. Gordon
Thomas, R. All my sins remembered
Tremain, R. The road home
Trevanian The Loo sanction
Trollope, J. Second honeymoon
Unsworth, B. Losing Nelson
Vargas Llosa, M. The bad girl
Vine, B. Grasshopper
Vine, B. The house of stairs
Vine, B. King Solomon's carpet
Walters, M. The shape of snakes
Waters, S. Fingersmith
Waters, S. The night watch
Willig, L. The seduction of the crimson rose
Willis, C. Blackout

ENGLAND -- LONDON -- 17TH CENTURY
Redfern, E. Auriel rising

ENGLAND -- LONDON -- 18TH CENTURY
Dickens, C. A tale of two cities
Donoghue, E. Slammerkin
Hollingshead, G. Bedlam
King, R. Domino
Richardson, S. Clarissa

ENGLAND -- LONDON -- 19TH CENTURY
Ackroyd, P. The trial of Elizabeth Cree

Austen, J. Sense and sensibility
Dickens, C. Little Dorrit
Dickens, C. Martin Chuzzlewit
Dickens, C. Oliver Twist
Dickens, C. Our mutual friend
Faber, M. The crimson petal and the white
Griesemer, J. Signal & noise
Hill, T. The love of stones
Jakeman, J. In the Kingdom of mists
James, H. The golden bowl
Martin, V. Mary Reilly
Moorcock, M. An alien heat
Palliser, C. The quincunx
Quick, A. Slightly shady
Quick, A. Wicked widow
Smith, Z. White teeth
Stevenson, R. L. The strange case of Dr. Jekyll and Mr. Hyde
Wilde, O. The picture of Dorian Gray

ENGLAND -- LONDON -- 20TH CENTURY

Ali, M. Brick lane
Amis, K. The Russian girl
Amis, M. London fields
Beckett, S. Murphy
Bowen, E. The heat of the day
Brookner, A. Family and friends
Brookner, A. Undue influence
Byatt, A. S. Possession
Cronin, A. J. The citadel
Fielding, H. Bridget Jones's diary
Frayn, M. Spies
Greene, G. The end of the affair
Greene, G. The human factor
Hornby, N. About a boy
Hornby, N. How to be good
Lessing, D. M. The good terrorist
Lessing, D. M. Love, again
Lessing, D. M. The sweetest dream
Livesey, M. The missing world
Maugham, W. S. Of human bondage
McEwan, I. Amsterdam
McGrath, P. Spider
Murdoch, I. An accidental man
Murdoch, I. A fairly honourable defeat
Murdoch, I. The green knight
Murdoch, I. The nice and the good
Murdoch, I. Nuns and soldiers
Naipaul, V. S. Half a life
O'Brien, E. Time and tide
Pym, B. An unsuitable attachment
Pynchon, T. Gravity's rainbow
Rendell, R. Adam and Eve and Pinch me
Rendell, R. The bridesmaid
Rendell, R. Going wrong
Rendell, R. The keys to the street
Rendell, R. The tree of hands
Spark, M. Aiding and abetting
Spark, M. A far cry from Kensington
Spark, M. The girls of slender means
Taylor, E. Mrs. Palfrey at the Claremont
Vine, B. Anna's book
Vine, B. The house of stairs
Waugh, E. Vile bodies
Woolf, V. Mrs. Dalloway

ENGLAND -- LONDON -- 21ST CENTURY

Gibson, W. Pattern recognition
Steel, D. The kiss

ENGLAND -- MANCHESTER

Noon, J. Vurt

ENGLAND -- MIDLANDS

Pietroni, A. L. Ruby's spoon

ENGLAND -- NORFOLK

Smith, A. The accidental

ENGLAND -- NORTHUMBERLAND

Stewart, M. The ivy tree

ENGLAND -- NOTTINGHAM

Monaghan, N. The killing jar
Sillitoe, A. Saturday night and Sunday morning

ENGLAND -- NOTTINGHAMSHIRE

Haig, M. The dead fathers club
Lawrence, D. H. The rainbow
Lawrence, D. H. Women in love

ENGLAND -- OXFORD

Benjamin, M. Alice I have been
Marias, J. All souls
Trollope, J. The men and the girls
Willis, C. Doomsday book

ENGLAND -- RACE RELATIONS

Levy, A. Small island
Phillips, C. Foreigners
Walters, M. The shape of snakes

ENGLAND -- ROMAN PERIOD, 55 B.C.-449 A.D.

Graves, R. Claudius, the god and his wife Messalina
Whyte, J. The singing sword

ENGLAND -- RURAL LIFE

Austen, J. Emma
Austen, J. Mansfield Park
Austen, J. Persuasion
Austen, J. Pride and prejudice
Austen, J. Sense and sensibility
Bauer, B. Darkside
Blackmore, R. D. Lorna Doone
Bragg, M. The soldier's return
Cusk, R. In the fold
Eliot, G. The mill on the Floss
Forster, E. M. Howards End
Gaskell, E. C. Cranford
Golding, W. Darkness visible
Hill, R. The Stranger House
Hoban, R. Riddley Walker
Ishiguro, K. The remains of the day
Joyce, G. The limits of enchantment
Lawrence, D. H. Sons and lovers
Lofts, N. Gad's Hall

McEwan, I. Atonement
Morton, K. The house at Riverton
Murdoch, I. The bell
Murdoch, I. The philosopher's pupil
Murdoch, I. The sea, the sea
Pilcher, R. The shell seekers
Pym, B. Jane and Prudence
Read Affairs at Thrush Green
Read At home in Thrush Green
Read Farewell to Fairacre
Read Thrush Green
Sackville-West, V. The Edwardians
Simonson, H. Major Pettigrew's last stand
Snow, C. P. Strangers and brothers
Trollope, J. Next of kin
Woolf, V. Between the acts
ENGLAND -- SHROPSHIRE
Dean, A. A gentleman of fortune, or, The suspicions of Miss Dido Kent
Freeman, A. The fair fight
Morrell, D. Murder as a fine art
Rayne, S. Property of a lady
ENGLAND -- SOCIAL LIFE AND CUSTOMS -- 16TH CENTURY
Barber, R. The Marlowe papers
ENGLAND -- SOCIAL LIFE AND CUSTOMS -- 18TH CENTURY
Bailey, M. An appetite for violets
Freeman, A. The fair fight
Heyer, G. These old shades
ENGLAND -- SOCIAL LIFE AND CUSTOMS -- 19TH CENTURY
Bowen, K. You're the Earl That I Want
Dean, A. Bellfield Hall, or, The observations of Miss Dido Kent
Dean, A. A gentleman of fortune, or, The suspicions of Miss Dido Kent
Dean, A. A place of confinement
Dean, A. A woman of consequence
Heyer, G. The grand Sophy
Kilpack, J. S. A heart revealed
Kowal, M. R. Without a summer
Quinn, J. An offer from a gentleman
ENGLAND -- SOCIAL LIFE AND CUSTOMS -- 20TH CENTURY
Fitzgerald, P. The means of escape
Jones, S. The uninvited guests
Lovett, A. Everlasting Lane
Stibbe, N. Man at the helm
Waugh, E. The complete stories of Evelyn Waugh
ENGLAND -- SOMERSET
Bauer, B. Blacklands
Blackmore, R. D. Lorna Doone
Fielding, H. Joseph Andrews and Shamela
Trollope, A. Barchester Towers
Trollope, A. Doctor Thorne
Trollope, A. Framley parsonage
Trollope, A. The last chronicle of Barset
ENGLAND -- SURREY
Forster, E. M. A room with a view
ENGLAND -- SUSSEX
Robertson, I. Instruments of darkness
White, E. Hotel de Dream
ENGLAND -- WARWICKSHIRE
Eliot, G. Middlemarch
Eliot, G. Silas Marner
Waters, S. The little stranger
ENGLAND -- WILTSHIRE
Dickens, C. Martin Chuzzlewit
ENGLAND -- YORKSHIRE
Bronte, A. The tenant of Wildfell Hall
Bronte, C. Jane Eyre
Bronte, E. Wuthering Heights
England and other stories. Swift, G.
ENGLAND, CHURCH OF *See* Church of England
ENGLAND, SOUTHERN
Lelic, S. The child who
Ware, R. The lying game
Engleby. Faulks, S.
ENGLISH -- AFRICA
Ballard, J. G. The day of creation
ENGLISH -- FRANCE
Todd, C. An unmarked grave
ENGLISH -- INDIA -- NĀGPUR
Festing, I. A. The birdkeeper
ENGLISH -- MOROCCO
Osborne, L. The forgiven
ENGLISH -- SIERRA LEONE
Forna, A. The memory of love
ENGLISH -- UNITED STATES
Ali, M. Untold story
ENGLISH AUTHORS
See also Authors
English Creek. Doig, I.
ENGLISH FICTION -- IRISH AUTHORS -- 21ST CENTURY
McCormack, M. Solar bones
The **English** Girl. Silva, D.
The **English** major. Harrison, J.
ENGLISH NOVELISTS
See also Novelists
ENGLISH NOVELISTS
McEwan, I. Sweet tooth
English passengers. Kneale, M.
The **English** patient. Ondaatje, M.
ENGLISH PERIODICALS
See also Periodicals
ENGLISH POETRY
See also English literature; Poetry
ENGLISH POETS
See also Poets
ENGLISH SATIRE
See also English literature; Satire
ENGLISH TEACHERS

Cusk, R. Outline
Cusk, R. Transit
ENGLISH WIT AND HUMOR
See also English literature; Wit and humor
English, August. Chatterjee, U.
ENGRAVERS
See also Artists
ENGRAVING
See also Art; Graphic arts; Illustration of books; Pictures
Enigma. Harris, R.
Enigma variations. Aciman, A.
ENLIGHTENMENT
See also Modern civilization; Modern philosophy; Rationalism
ENLIGHTENMENT
Gilbert, E. The Signature of All Things
Morrow, J. The last witchfinder
Enon. Harding, P.
ENSEMBLES (MUSIC)
See also Music; Musical form; Musicians
ENTERTAINERS
Ackroyd, P. The trial of Elizabeth Cree
Gruen, S. Water for elephants
The hall of singing caryatids
McMurtry, L. Buffalo girls
Nicholls, D. One day
Phillips, C. Dancing in the dark
Roth, P. I married a communist
Singer, I. B. The magician of Lublin
Turner, F. W. 1929
Tyler, A. A slipping-down life
Waters, S. Tipping the velvet
Entombed. Fairstein, L.
ENTOMOLOGISTS
Abe, K. The woman in the dunes
Saul, J. The homing
ENTOZOA *See* Parasites
ENTREPRENEURSHIP
See also Business; Capitalism; Small business
ENVIRONMENTAL DISASTERS
Hall, J. W. Going Dark
ENVIRONMENTAL ETHICS
See also Ethics
ENVIRONMENTAL MOVEMENT
Hall, J. W. Going Dark
ENVIRONMENTAL POLLUTION *See* Pollution
ENVIRONMENTAL PROTECTION
See also Ecology; Environment
ENVIRONMENTAL PROTECTION
Carr, R. The Wanderer
Windle, J. Congo dawn
ENVIRONMENTALISTS
Cussler, C. White death
Glass, J. The widower's tale
Palin, M. The truth
Pancake, A. Strange as this weather has been
Rash, R. Serena
ENVIRONMENTALISTS
See also Activists; Scientists
ENVY
Eugenides, J. Fresh complaint
Ephron, Nora
About
Willis, C. Crosstalk
EPIC FILMS
See also Motion pictures
EPIDEMICS
Abbott, M. E. The fever
Cronin, J. The city of mirrors
Gibbons, K. Divining women
Goldberg, M. Wickett's remedy
Hill, J. The fireman
King, S. The stand
Marcus, B. The flame alphabet
Nunez, S. Salvation city
Roiphe, A. R. An imperfect lens
Saintcrow, L. Trailer park fae
Scalzi, J. Lock in
Willis, C. Blackout
EPIDEMICS
See also Diseases; Public health
EPIGRAMS
See also Wit and humor
EPISTOLARY FICTION
Barrows, A. The Guernsey Literary and Potato Peel Pie Society
Dunn, M. Ella Minnow Pea
Grossman, D. Be my knife
Joyce, R. The Love Song of Miss Queenie Hennessy
Updike, J. S
EPISTOLARY NOVELS *See* Epistolary fiction
EPISTOLARY POETRY
See also Poetry
Epitaph. Russell, M. D.
EPITAPHS
See also Biography; Cemeteries; Inscriptions; Tombs
EPIZOA *See* Parasites
An **equal** music. Seth, V.
Equal of the sun. Amirrezvani, A.
EQUALITY
Solomon, R. An unkindness of ghosts
EQUATIONS
See also Mathematics
Erasure. Everett, P.
ERLENDUR SVEINSSON (FICTITIOUS CHARACTER)
Indridason, A. Outrage
EROTIC ART
See also Art; Erotica
EROTIC FILMS
See also Motion pictures
EROTIC POETRY
See also Erotic literature; Poetry
EROTIC STORIES

Baker, N. House of holes
Erotic stories for Punjabi widows. Jaswal, B. K.
The **Erstwhile.** Catling, B.
The **escape.** Balogh, M.
ESCAPED CONVICTS
Hunter, S. Dirty white boys
Maynard, J. Labor Day
McCrumb, S. She walks these hills
ESCAPED PRISONERS
Friedman, D. Don't ever get old
Norton, C. What doesn't kill her
Weber, C. Man on the run
ESCAPES
Bates, H. E. Fair stood the wind for France
Dumas, A. The Count of Monte Cristo
Forester, C. S. Flying colours
Forester, C. S. Hornblower and the Atropos
Hostage
Lee, P. Runner
Sallis, J. Driven
Stark, R. Breakout
Westheimer, D. Von Ryan's Express
ESCAPES -- AUSTRALIA -- COWRA (N.S.W.)
Keneally, T. Shame and the Captives
ESKIMOS *See* Inuit
ESP *See* Extrasensory perception
ESPERANTO
Skibell, J. A curable romantic
ESPIONAGE
See also Intelligence service; Secret service; Subversive activities
Cumming, C. A divided spy
Dunmore, H. Exposure
Eastland, S. The Beast in the Red Forest
Furst, A. A Hero of France
Herron, M. Spook street
Jin, H. A map of betrayal
Priest, C. Fiddlehead
Putney, M. J. Not quite a wife
Quinn, P. Dry bones
Silva, D. The black widow
Steinhauer, O. The Cairo affair
ESPIONAGE STORIES *See* Spy stories
ESPIONAGE, AMERICAN *See* American espionage
ESPIONAGE, AMERICAN -- HISTORY -- 20TH CENTURY
Groot, T. Flame of resistance
ESQUIMAUX *See* Inuit
ESSAYISTS
Aira, C. The literary conference
Bayard, L. The pale blue eye
Clinch, J. Finn
Coetzee, J. M. Foe
Coetzee, J. M. Summertime
Cooley, M. The archivist
Cunningham, M. The hours
Cunningham, M. Specimen days
Fairstein, L. Entombed
Fuentes, C. The old gringo
Johnson, M. Pym
Martin, V. Mary Reilly
Nabokov, V. V. Novels and memoirs, 1941-1951
Oates, J. C. Wild nights!
Pearl, M. The Dante Club
Pearl, M. The Poe shadow
Pipkin, J. Woodsburner
Powers, K. Capote in Kansas
Rose, J. Blackest bird
Tournier, M. Friday
Truong, M. The book of salt
Twain, M. The gilded age and later novels
Vargas Llosa, M. The way to paradise
Verissimo, L. F. Borges and the eternal orangutans
Walker, A. The way forward is with a broken heart
Weisgall, D. The world before her
ESSENES
See also Jews
The **Essex** Serpent. Perry, S.
ESTONIA
Oksanen, S. When the doves disappeared
ESTRANGEMENT (SOCIAL PSYCHOLOGY) *See* Alienation (Social psychology)
ETCHERS
See also Artists; Engravers
ETCHING
See also Art; Pictures
Eternal life. Horn, D.
ETERNAL LIFE *See* Eternity; Future life; Immortality
ETERNAL PUNISHMENT *See* Hell
Eternal sky [series]
Bear, E. Shattered pillars
Ethan Frome. Wharton, E.
Ethelred II, King of England, 968?-1016
About
Bracewell, P. Shadow on the crown
ETHICAL PROBLEMS
Bialosky, J. The prize
ETHICS
Canin, E. America America
Clark, M. The legal limit
Franzen, J. Freedom
Horn, D. All other nights
Reuland, R. Semiautomatic
Steinbeck, J. The winter of our discontent
ETHIOPIA
Gibb, C. Sweetness in the belly
Verghese, A. Cutting for stone
ETHIOPIANS -- UNITED STATES
Mengestu, D. The beautiful things that heaven bears
Mengestu, D. How to read the air
ETHNIC ART
See also Art; Ethnic groups
ETHNIC CONFLICT -- SOUTH ASIA
Suri, M. The city of Devi

ETHNIC GROUPS
See also Ethnology
ETHNIC RELATIONS
See also Acculturation; Ethnology; Sociology
Desai, K. The inheritance of loss
Gordimer, N. The pickup
Smith, Z. White teeth
ETHNOHISTORY -- UGANDA
Makumbi, J. N. Kintu
ETHNOLOGY
McCarthy, T. Satin Island
ETIQUETTE
Jones, S. The uninvited guests
ETRUSCAN ART
See also Art
Etta and Otto and Russell and James. Hooper, E.
EUGENICS
See also Genetics; Population
EUNUCHS
Amirrezvani, A. Equal of the sun
King, R. Domino
Euphoria. King, L.
EUROPE
Ishiguro, K. The unconsoled
Pynchon, T. Gravity's rainbow
Sartre, J. P. The reprieve
Szalay, D. All that man is
Tournier, M. The ogre
West, R. The birds fall down
Winterson, J. The Passion
EUROPE -- 12TH CENTURY
Eco, U. Baudolino
EUROPE -- 15TH CENTURY
Dunnett, D. Niccolo rising
Dunnett, D. Race of scorpions
Dunnett, D. To lie with lions
EUROPE -- 17TH CENTURY
Maalouf, A. Balthasar's odyssey
EUROPE -- 19TH CENTURY
James, H. The portrait of a lady
Vallgren The horrific sufferings of the mind-reading monster Hercules Barefoot
EUROPE -- HISTORY -- 20TH CENTURY
Follett, K. Fall of giants
EUROPE -- HISTORY -- 476-1492
Jones, S. Four sisters, all queens
Europe central. Vollmann, W. T.
EUROPEAN UNION
Marr, A. Head of State
EUROPEAN WAR, 1914-1918 *See* World War, 1914-1918
EUROPEAN WAR, 1939-1945 *See* World War, 1939-1945
EUROPEANS -- UNITED STATES
Echenoz, J. Lightning
The **Eustace** diamonds. Trollope, A.
EUTHANASIA
White, S. W. Kill me
EUTHANASIA
See also Homicide; Medical ethics
EUTHANASIA -- AUSTRIA -- VIENNA
The chosen ones
Eva Luna. Allende, I.
Eva moves the furniture. Livesey, M.
Eva's eye.
EVACUATION OF CIVILIANS
See also Civil defense; Disaster relief
EVALUATION OF LITERATURE *See* Best books; Books and reading; Criticism; Literature -- History and criticism
EVANGELISTS
Lester, J. Do Lord remember me
Lewis, S. Elmer Gantry
Perrotta, T. The abstinence teacher
Eve (Biblical figure)
About
Maine, D. Fallen
Even money. Francis, D.
Even the dogs. McGregor, J.
Evening. Minot, S.
Evening is the whole day. Samarasan, P.
The **evening** road. Hunt, L.
The **evening** star. McMurtry, L.
Eveningland. Knight, M.
Evensong. Godwin, G.
EVENT TOURISM
See also Tourist trade
Eventide. Haruf, K.
EVEREST, MOUNT (CHINA AND NEPAL)
Simmons, D. The abominable
EVERGLADES (FLA.)
Matthiessen, P. Bone by bone
Matthiessen, P. Shadow country
Russell, K. Swamplandia!
Evergreen. Plain, B.
EVERGREENS
See also Landscape gardening; Shrubs; Trees
Everlasting Enchantment. Kennedy, K.
Everlasting Lane. Lovett, A.
Every broken trust. Rodriguez, L.
Every crooked nanny. Andrews, M. K.
Every day is for the thief. Cole, T.
Every fifteen minutes. Scottoline, L.
Every Heart a Doorway. Grant, M.
Every hidden fear. Rodriguez, L.
Every last cuckoo. Maloy, K.
Every last drop. Huston, C.
Every last one. Quindlen, A.
Every last secret. Rodriguez, L.
Every man for himself. Bainbridge, B.
Everybody Has Everything. Onstad, K.
Everybody loves somebody. Scott, J.
Everybody's fool. Russo, R.
EVERYDAY LIFE
Lopez, R. Good People
Everyman. Roth, P.
Everyman's library [series]

Cain, J. M. The postman always rings twice, double indemnity, Mildred Pierce and selected stories
Ford, F. M. The good soldier
Orwell, G. Burmese days; Keep the aspidistra flying; Coming up for air
Everyman's library children's classics [series]
Orczy, E. The Scarlet Pimpernel
Everyone dies. McGarrity, M.
Everything Asian. Woo, S. J.
Everything beautiful began after. Van Booy, S.
Everything Begins and Ends at the Kentucky Club. Sáenz, B. A.
Everything belongs to us. Wuertz, Y. G.
Everything I never told you. Ng, C.
Everything is illuminated. Foer, J. S.
Everything matters! Currie, R.
Everything that rises must converge. O'Connor, F.
Evidence of things unseen. Wiggins, M.
EVIL *See* Good and evil
Evil Eye. Oates, J. C.
EVIL IN MOTION PICTURES
Syndrome E
EVOLUTION
Erdrich, L. Future home of the living god
McDonald, R. Mr. Darwin's shooter
Stott, R. The coral thief
Vonnegut, K. Galapagos
The **evolution** of Bruno Littlemore. Hale, B.
EX-CONCENTRATION CAMP INMATES
Edugyan, E. Half-blood blues
EX-CONVICTS
Banks, R. Lost memory of skin
Burgess, M. Dogfight, a love story
Carnoy, D. The big exit
Clarke, B. An arsonist's guide to writers' homes in New England
Hamilton, S. The second life of Nick Mason
Hart, B. Then came the evening
Heinlein, R. A. The moon is a harsh mistress
Higgins, G. V. The Digger's game
Hill, R. The woodcutter
Huneven, M. Blame
James, P. D. Innocent blood
Jones, S. Outcast
Joss, M. Among the missing
Klein, M. Con ed
Le Carre, J. The tailor of Panama
Lehane, D. Mystic river
Leonard, E. Glitz
Leonard, E. Pagan babies
Leonard, E. Rum punch
McEwan, I. Atonement
Mortimer, J. Quite honestly
Oates, J. C. Missing mom
Pekearo, N. T. The wolfman
Pelecanos, G. P. Drama city
Richards, D. A. The bay of love and sorrows
Sakey, M. The blade itself
Schlink, B. The weekend
Schwartz, J. B. Northwest corner
Spencer, L. Morning glory
Stroby, W. Cold shot to the heart
Van Rooy, M. An ordinary decent criminal
Van Rooy, M. Your friendly neighborhood criminal
Waite, U. The terror of living
Wolfe, G. The sorcerer's house
Yocum, R. A welcome murder
Zeltserman, D. Small crimes
EX-NAZIS
Picoult, J. The Storyteller
EX-NUNS
Murdoch, I. Nuns and soldiers
EX-NUNS
See also Nuns
EX-POLICE OFFICERS
Bennett, R. J. American elsewhere
Friedman, D. Don't ever get old
Hoag, T. Dark horse
King, S. Black house
Lansdale, J. R. A fine dark line
O'Mara, T. Crooked Numbers
Pattison, E. The lord of death
Stroby, W. Shoot the woman first
EX-PRIESTS
Criswell, M. What to do about Annie?
Lodge, D. Paradise news
Wells, M. Wheel of the infinite
EX-PRIESTS
See also Catholic Church -- Clergy; Priests
Excalibur. Cornwell, B.
EXCAVATIONS (ARCHEOLOGY)
See also Archeology
EXCAVATIONS (ARCHEOLOGY)
Kelly, J. The moon tunnel
Unsworth, B. Land of marvels
Excellent women. Pym, B.
EXCEPTIONAL CHILDREN
See also Children; Elementary education
EXCHANGE OF PRISONERS OF WAR *See* Prisoners of war
The **execution** of Noa P. Singleton. Silver, E. L.
The **executioner's** song. Mailer, N.
EXECUTIONS AND EXECUTIONERS
The beggar king
Estleman, L. D. The master executioner
French, A. Billy
Mailer, N. The executioner's song
Wiesel, E. Dawn
EXECUTIONS AND EXECUTIONERS
See also Criminal law; Criminal procedure
EXHUMATION
Miller, A. Pure
Exiles. Hansen, R.
EXILES -- FICTION

Adler, H. G. The wall
Bennett, R. J. City of blades
Cortazar, J. Hopscotch
García, C. King of Cuba
Moya, H. C. The dream of my return
Palwick, S. The necessary beggar
Rosales, G. The halfway house
Wells, M. Wheel of the infinite
EXILES -- FLORIDA -- MIAMI
García, C. King of Cuba
EXILES -- GERMANY
The emigrants
Exiles in the garden. Just, W. S.
Existence. Brin, D.
EXISTENTIALISM
Banville, J. The book of evidence
Beauvoir, S. d. The mandarins
Camus, A. The fall
Sartre, J. P. The age of reason
Sartre, J. P. Nausea
Sartre, J. P. The reprieve
Sartre, J. P. Troubled sleep
Exit ghost. Roth, P.
Exit music. Rankin, I.
Exit West. Hamid, M.
Exley. Clarke, B.
Exley, Frederick
About
Clarke, B. Exley
Exodus. Uris, L.
EXORCISM
Blatty, W. P. The exorcist
Tremblay, P. A Head Full of Ghosts
The **exorcist.** Blatty, W. P.
The Expanse [series]
Corey, J. S. A. Cibola burn
Corey, J. S. A. Leviathan Wakes
EXPATRIATION
Crain, C. Necessary errors
McLain, P. Circling the Sun
The **expats.** Pavone, C.
Expedition to the Mountains of the Moon. Hodder, M.
EXPERIMENTAL FICTION
Aira, C. Ghosts
Aira, C. The literary conference
Auster, P. Sunset Park
Coady, L. The antagonist
Egan, J. A visit from the Goon Squad
Garcia, C. The lady matador's hotel
Kehlmann, D. Fame
Lashner, W. Kockroach
Munoz Molina, A. In her absence
Powell, P. The interrogative mood
Pynchon, T. Against the day
Pynchon, T. Inherent vice
Robson, J. Living next door to the god of love
Sorokin, V. Ice
Syjuco, M. Ilustrado
Unferth, D. O. Vacation
Walser, R. The assistant
Wiggins, M. The shadow catcher
EXPERIMENTAL FILMS
See also Motion pictures
EXPERIMENTAL STORIES
Aira, C. The seamstress and the wind
Amis, M. Time's arrow
Barnes, J. A history of the world in 10 1/2 chapters
Bolano, R. Nazi literature in the Americas
Boucher, C. How to keep your Volkswagen alive
Calvino, I. If on a winter's night a traveler
Cortazar, J. Hopscotch
Danielewski, M. Z. Only revolutions
Dixon, S. Interstate
The emigrants
Foer, J. S. Extremely loud & incredibly close
Gaddis, W. Agape agape
Gaddis, W. A frolic of his own
Garcia Marquez, G. The autumn of the patriarch
Grass, G. My century
Gray, A. Poor things
Hoban, R. Her name was Lola
Howard, M. The rags of time
Joyce, J. Finnegans wake
Joyce, J. Ulysses
Lashner, W. Kockroach
Levithan, D. The lover's dictionary
Life
Markson, D. The last novel
Markson, D. Vanishing point
McGregor, J. Even the dogs
Mitchell, D. Cloud atlas
Naipaul, V. S. A way in the world
Oz, A. The same sea
Perec, G. A void
Perez-Reverte, A. The Club Dumas
Pessl, M. Special topics in calamity physics
Powell, P. The interrogative mood
Powers, R. The gold bug variations
Pynchon, T. Against the day
Pynchon, T. Gravity's rainbow
Ramirez Mercado, S. A thousand deaths plus one
Saramago, J. The history of the siege of Lisbon
Silko, L. Almanac of the dead
Silko, L. Gardens in the dunes
Syjuco, M. Ilustrado
Tsypkin, L. Summer in Baden-Baden
Unferth, D. O. Vacation
Vila-Matas, E. Montano's malady
Vollmann, W. T. The ice-shirt
Walker, A. The temple of my familiar
Wallace, D. F. Infinite jest
An **expert** in murder. Upson, N.
EXPERT SYSTEMS (COMPUTER SCIENCE)
See also Artificial intelligence; Data processing; Infor-

mation systems
EXPLORERS
Flanagan, R. Wanting
Gilman, C. P. Herland
Maalouf, A. Leo Africanus
McDonald, R. Mr. Darwin's shooter
Naipaul, V. S. A way in the world
Nordhoff, C. Men against the sea
Nordhoff, C. Mutiny on the Bounty
Russell, M. D. Dreamers of the day
Sargent, C. Museum of human beings
Sherwood, F. Night of sorrows
Simmons, D. The terror
Vollmann, W. T. Argall
Vollmann, W. T. The rifles
Wheeler, R. S. Eclipse
With her in Ourland
EXPLORERS -- SOUTH AMERICA
Wright, R. The gold eaters
Exposure. Dunmore, H.
EXTORTION
Dickens, C. Our mutual friend
The Discreet Hero
Greaves, C. Hush money
Gruber, M. The forgery of Venus
Leonard, E. Freaky Deaky
Leonard, E. LaBrava
Trevanian The Loo sanction
The **extraordinary** journeys: Twenty thousand leagues under the sea. Verne, J.
An **Extraordinary** Union. Cole, A.
EXTRASENSORY PERCEPTION
Greene, A. Bloodroot
King, S. Carrie
King, S. The shining
Koontz, D. R. The bad place
Krentz, J. A. Running hot
Le Guin, U. K. The left hand of darkness
Stewart, M. Touch not the cat
Wilson, R. C. Blind Lake
EXTRASENSORY PERCEPTION
See also Parapsychology
EXTRATERRESTRIAL BEINGS
See also Life on other planets
EXTRATERRESTRIAL BEINGS
Baxter, S. Manifold
Brin, D. Existence
Chu, W. The Lives of Tao
Corey, J. S. A. Abaddon's Gate
Liu Cixin The dark forest
Omarsdottir, K. Children in Reindeer Woods
Saint-Exupery, A. d. The little prince
EXTRATERRESTRIAL COMMUNICATION *See* Interstellar communication
EXTRATERRESTRIAL LIFE *See* Life on other planets
EXTRAVEHICULAR ACTIVITY (SPACE FLIGHT)
See also Space flight
Extremely loud & incredibly close. Foer, J. S.
The **eye** in the door. Barker, P.
The **eye** of God. Rollins, J.
The **eye** of the leopard. Mankell, H.
Eye of the needle. Follett, K.
Eye of the Red Tsar. Eastland, S.
Eye of the storm. Higgins, J.
The **eye** of the world. Jordan, R.
Eyes wide open. Gross, A.
The **Eyre** affair. Fforde, J.

F

F is for fugitive. Grafton, S.
A **fable.** Faulkner, W.
FABLES
Ozick, C. The Puttermesser papers
Rushdie, S. Haroun and the sea of stories
Tan, A. Saving fish from drowning
Walker, A. The temple of my familiar
The **fabulous** riverboat. Farmer, P. J.
The **face** of a stranger. Perry, A.
The **face** of trespass. Rendell, R.
The **face-changers.** Perry, T.
FACETIAE *See* Anecdotes; Wit and humor
FACIAL RECONSTRUCTION (ANTHROPOLOGY)
Johansen, I. Taking Eve
The **facility.** Lelic, S.
FACTORIES
Crowley, J. Four freedoms
Lodge, D. Nice work
Pietroni, A. L. Ruby's spoon
Theroux, P. Kowloon Tong
FACULTY (EDUCATION) *See* Colleges and universities -- Faculty; Educators; Teachers
Fahrenheit 451. Bradbury, R.
Fail-safe. Burdick, E.
FAILURE
Hall, B. The music teacher
Miles, J. Dear American Airlines
Scott, J. Tourmaline
Wheeler, R. S. Eclipse
Fair and tender ladies. Smith, L.
The **fair** fight. Freeman, A.
Fair stood the wind for France. Bates, H. E.
FAIRIES
See also Folklore
FAIRIES
Adrian, C. The great night
Grant, M. Rosemary and Rue
Saintcrow, L. Trailer park fae
Warrington, F. Grail of the summer stars
Warrington, F. Midsummer night
A **fairly** honourable defeat. Murdoch, I.
FAIRS
Read Thrush Green
Updike, J. The poorhouse fair

The **fairy** godmother. Lackey, M.
FAIRY TALES
Allen, S. A. The sugar queen
Dare, T. Romancing the duke
Goodman, C. Arcadia Falls
Hesse, H. The fairy tales of Hermann Hesse
Joyce, G. Some kind of fairy tale
The Oxford book of modern fairy tales
Saint-Exupery, A. d. The little prince
FAIRY TALES -- ADAPTATIONS
Balaskovits, A. A. Magic for unlucky girls
The **fairy** tales of Hermann Hesse. Hesse, H.
Faith. Haigh, J.
FAITH
Ansay, A. M. River angel
Cooley, M. The archivist
Cutter, K. The maid
Davies, R. The cunning man
Endo, S. Deep river
Godwin, G. Evensong
Guterson, D. Our Lady of the Forest
Hansen, R. Mariette in ecstasy
Haslett, A. Imagine me gone
Hoffman, A. The third angel
Howatch, S. Glamorous powers
Howatch, S. Scandalous risks
Howatch, S. Ultimate prizes
L'Engle, M. Certain women
Maine, D. The preservationist
Markovits, A. I am forbidden
McDonald, R. Mr. Darwin's shooter
Picoult, J. Keeping Faith
Robinson, M. Home
Russell, M. D. Children of God
Russell, M. D. The sparrow
FAITH
See also Religion; Salvation; Spiritual life; Theology; Virtue
FAITH CURE
Bambara, T. C. The salt eaters
Faithful Place. French, T.
Faithfull, Emily, 1835-1895
About
Donoghue, E. The sealed letter
Faithless. Oates, J. C.
Falconer. Cheever, J.
FALCONRY
See also Game and game birds; Hunting
The **fall.** Camus, A.
The **fall.** Mawer, S.
A **fall** from grace. Barnard, R.
Fall from pride. Harper, K.
The **fall** guy. Lasdun, J.
Fall of giants. Follett, K.
The **fall** of Hyperion. Simmons, D.
The **fall** of Rome. Southgate, M.
Fall on your knees. MacDonald
Fallen. Lebbon, T.
The **fallen.** Parker, T. J.
Fallen. Maine, D.
Fallen into the pit. Peters, E.
Fallen land. Flanery, P.
Fallen land. Brown, T.
Falling in Love. Leon, D.
Falling man. DeLillo, D.
Falling out of time.
Fallout. Paretsky, S.
The **falls.** Oates, J. C.
The **falls.** Rankin, I.
Falls the shadow. Penman, S. K.
FALSE ACCUSATION
Baldwin, J. If Beale Street could talk
Coben, H. Caught
Eliot, G. Silas Marner
Gaines, E. J. A lesson before dying
Grippando, J. Money to burn
Grisham, J. The confession
Hamilton, J. A map of the world
Haywood, G. A. Cemetery Road
Holt, V. The black opal
Katzenbach, J. Hart's war
Lee, H. To kill a mockingbird
Malamud, B. The fixer
McEwan, I. Atonement
Palmer, D. Helpless
Parker, B. Suspicion of vengeance
Patterson, R. N. Eclipse
Picoult, J. House rules
Rankin, I. The complaints
Richmond, M. No one you know
Rosenfelt, D. Don't tell a soul
Tey, J. The Franchise affair
Wilder, T. The eighth day
False conception. Greenleaf, S.
FALSE IMPRISONMENT
Jones, T. An American marriage
Lelic, S. The facility
Scottoline, L. Accused
FALSE MEMORY SYNDROME
See also Memory
FALSE PERSONATION
Noire (Author) Natural born liar
Quick, A. The paid companion
False scent. Marsh, N.
FALSEHOOD *See* Truthfulness and falsehood
Fame. Kehlmann, D.
FAME
Bloom, A. Lucky us
Gold, G. D. Sunnyside
Hawley, N. Before the Fall
Leonard, E. The hot kid
Oates, J. C. Blonde
FAME -- PSYCHOLOGICAL ASPECTS
Wayne, T. The Love Song of Jonny Valentine

Familiar. Lennon, J. R.
The **familiar.** Danielewski, M. Z.
FAMILIES
Frankel, L. This is how it always is
Hadley, T. Bad dreams and other stories
Jackson, J. The almost sisters
Kwan, K. Rich people problems
Meloy, M. Do not become alarmed
Mootoo, S. Moving forward sideways like a crab
Segal, F. The awkward age
Shamsie, K. Home fire
Stone, M. Border child
FAMILIES -- AUSTRALIA
Francis, D. Wedding Bush Road
FAMILIES -- BURMA
Craig, C. Miss Burma
FAMILIES -- CALIFORNIA
Walker, K. T. The age of miracles
FAMILIES -- CHINA
Thien, M. Do not say we have nothing
FAMILIES -- COLORADO
Haruf, K. Benediction
FAMILIES -- CRIMES AGAINST
Dahl, J. Conviction
FAMILIES -- ENGLAND
Butler, S. Ten things I've learnt about love
Lane, H. Alys, always
FAMILIES -- ENGLAND -- HISTORY -- 20TH CENTURY
Archer, J. Best kept secret
FAMILIES -- GREAT BRITAIN
Baker, J. Longbourn
Baker, J. The undertow
FAMILIES -- HISTORY
Hart, B. The bully of order
FAMILIES -- INDIA
Ghachar ghochar
Taseer, A. The way things were
FAMILIES -- INDIA -- NĀGPUR
Festing, I. A. The birdkeeper
FAMILIES -- IRELAND
McCormack, M. Solar bones
Riley, L. The girl on the cliff
FAMILIES -- ITALY
Banner, C. The house at the edge of night
FAMILIES -- KENTUCKY
Morgan, C. E. The sport of kings
Roy, L. Let me die in his footsteps
Scotton, C. The secret wisdom of the earth
FAMILIES -- KOREA
Lee, M. J. Pachinko
FAMILIES -- MASSACHUSETTS
Greenidge, K. We love you, Charlie Freeman
FAMILIES -- MEXICO
Stone, M. Border child
FAMILIES -- MINNESOTA
Krueger, W. K. Ordinary grace
Treuer, D. Prudence
FAMILIES -- NEBRASKA
Agee, J. The bones of paradise
FAMILIES -- NETHERLANDS
The dinner
FAMILIES -- NEW YORK (STATE) -- NEW YORK
Finn, A. J. The woman in the window
Gilbert, D. & sons
Hacker, C. The Morels
FAMILIES -- NIGERIA
Watson, C. Tiny sunbirds, far away
FAMILIES -- PALESTINE
Alyan, H. Salt houses
FAMILIES -- PENNSYLVANIA
Braffet, K. Save yourself
FAMILIES -- RELIGIOUS LIFE
The elephant keepers' children
FAMILIES -- RUSSIA (FEDERATION) -- MOSCOW
Krasikov, S. The patriots
FAMILIES -- UGANDA
Makumbi, J. N. Kintu
FAMILIES -- UNITED STATES
Krasikov, S. The patriots
FAMILIES -- VIETNAM
Barry, Q. She weeps each time you're born
FAMILIES -- WASHINGTON (STATE) -- SOCIAL LIFE AND CUSTOMS
Hart, B. The bully of order
FAMILIES -- ZIMBABWE
Bulawayo, N. We need new names
FAMILIES OF SOLDIERS
See also Family
Krivak, A. The signal flame
FAMILIES OF TERMINALLY ILL
Bock, C. Alice & Oliver
Haruf, K. Benediction
FAMILIES SECRETS
McHugh, L. Arrowood
The **family.** Puzo, M.
FAMILY
See also Interpersonal relations; Sociology
FAMILY
Abbott, M. E. You will know me
Agee, J. The bones of paradise
Aslam, N. The Blind Man's Garden
Austin, L. All she ever wanted
Banner, C. The house at the edge of night
Bates, J. F. Midnight at the Dragon Café
Brkic, C. A. The First Rule of Swimming
Butler, S. Ten things I've learnt about love
DeLillo, D. Zero K
Doyle, R. The Guts
Duffy, B. House of echoes
Flournoy, A. c. The Turner house
Foroutan, P. The girl from the garden
Gilbert, D. & sons
Griffith, M. Trophy
Haddon, M. The red house

Harrison, J. Returning to earth
Hart, B. The bully of order
Haslett, A. Imagine me gone
Herrin, L. Fractures
Hood, A. An Italian Wife
Hosseini, K. And the Mountains Echoed
Like Family
Manfredi, V. M. A Winter's Night
Markovits, A. I am forbidden
Morgan, C. E. The sport of kings
Nadler, S. The inseparables
O'Farrell, M. This must be the place
Osondu, E. C. This house is not for sale
Palliser, C. Rustication
Picoult, J. Lone wolf
Rushdie, S. The golden house
Schanbacher, G. Crossing Purgatory
See, L. The tea girl of hummingbird lane
Sharma, A. Family Life
Smiley, J. Some luck
Solomon, A. Leaving Lucy Pear
Strout, E. Anything is possible
Thien, M. Do not say we have nothing
Treuer, D. Prudence
Tuck, L. The Double Life of Liliane
Turner, N. Heartbreak of a hustler's wife
Tyler, A. A spool of blue thread
Vanderbes, J. Strangers at the feast
Walsh, M. O. My sunshine away
Winthrop, E. H. The why of things
Family and friends. Brookner, A.
FAMILY CAREGIVERS *See* Caregivers
FAMILY CHRONICLES
Allende, I. The house of the spirits
Allison, D. Bastard out of Carolina
Archer, J. Only time will tell
Baldwin, J. Go tell it on the mountain
Boyle, T. C. World's end
Brown, D. A. Creek Mary's blood
Buddenbrooks
Carter, S. L. The emperor of Ocean Park
Cheever, J. The Wapshot chronicle
Cheever, J. The Wapshot scandal
Conroy, P. The prince of tides
Cunningham, M. Flesh and blood
Davidar, D. The house of blue mangoes
Davies, R. Murther & walking spirits
De la Roche, M. Jalna
Doig, I. Bucking the sun
Dorris, M. Cloud chamber
Dorris, M. A yellow raft in blue water
Dunnett, D. Niccolo rising
Dunnett, D. Race of scorpions
Galsworthy, J. The Forsyte saga
García Márquez, G. One hundred years of solitude
Garcia, C. The Aguero sisters
Garcia, C. Dreaming in Cuban
Garcia, C. Monkey hunting
Gilmore, J. Golden country
Grau, S. A. The keepers of the house
Greene, A. Bloodroot
Harrison, J. The road home
Hatoum, M. The brothers
Hawthorne, N. The House of the Seven Gables
Hegi, U. The vision of Emma Blau
Hill, R. B. Hanta yo
Hoeg, P. The history of Danish dreams
Howatch, S. Cashelmara
Isaacs, S. Almost paradise
Isaacs, S. Red, white and blue
Jakes, J. Love and war
Jakes, J. North and South
Kittredge, W. The Willow Field
Krantz, J. Mistral's daughter
Laker, R. To dance with kings
Lawrence, D. H. The rainbow
L'Engle, M. Certain women
Lessing, D. M. The sweetest dream
MacDonald Fall on your knees
Mahfouz, N. Palace of desire
Mahfouz, N. Palace walk
Mahfouz, N. Sugar Street
Manicka, R. The rice mother
Martin, W. Cape Cod
McCullough, C. The thorn birds
McDermott, A. At weddings and wakes
Michener, J. A. Chesapeake
Michener, J. A. Mexico
Morrison, T. Jazz
Morrison, T. Song of Solomon
Nabokov, V. V. Ada
Naylor, G. Linden Hills
Ng, F. M. Bone
Oates, J. C. Bellefleur
Pilcher, R. September
Pilcher, R. The shell seekers
Plain, B. Evergreen
Plain, B. The golden cup
Plain, B. Harvest
Plain, B. Random winds
Plain, B. Tapestry
Puzo, M. The family
Rice, A. The witching hour
Richler, M. Solomon Gursky was here
Ross-Macdonald, M. For they shall inherit
Ross-Macdonald, M. The rich are with you always
Ross-Macdonald, M. The world from rough stones
Rushdie, S. The Moor's last sigh
Rutherfurd, E. Russka
Rutherfurd, E. Sarum
Scott, W. The bride of Lammermoor
Seth, V. A suitable boy
Shange, N. Betsey Brown
Shaw, I. Beggarman, thief

Shaw, I. Rich man, poor man
Simpson, M. Anywhere but here
Singer, I. B. The family Moskat
Smith, L. The devil's dream
Smith, L. Family linen
Smith, L. Oral history
Smith, Z. White teeth
Stegner, W. E. Angle of repose
Steinbeck, J. East of Eden
Tademy, L. Cane River
Tarkington, B. The magnificent Ambersons
Thackeray, W. M. The Virginians
Trevor, W. Fools of fortune
Tryon, T. In the fire of spring
Tryon, T. The wings of the morning
Tyler, A. Dinner at the Homesick Restaurant
Tyler, A. Searching for Caleb
Undset, S. Kristin Lavransdatter
Updike, J. In the beauty of the lilies
Uris, L. Trinity
Urquhart, J. Away
Vamos, M. The book of fathers
Welty, E. Losing battles
West, D. The wedding
Woolf, V. The years
Yunis, A. The night counter
FAMILY CURSES
Hawthorne, N. The House of the Seven Gables
Holt, V. Bride of Pendorric
Smith, L. Oral history
Wood, B. The dreaming
A **family** daughter. Meloy, M.
The **family** Fang. Wilson, K.
FAMILY FARMS
Mazzarella, N. This heavy silence
Smiley, J. Early warning
Family furnishings. Munro, A.
Family happiness. Colwin, L.
FAMILY HISTORIES *See* Genealogy
Family honor. Parker, R. B.
Family Life. Sharma, A.
FAMILY LIFE
Adams, A. After the war
Adams, A. A southern exposure
Agee, J. A death in the family
Aira, C. Ghosts
Allen, S. A. The girl who chased the moon
Allende, I. The house of the spirits
Allende, I. Portrait in sepia
Allison, D. Bastard out of Carolina
Alvarez, J. How the Garcia girls lost their accents
Antopol, M. The Unamericans
Archer, J. Best kept secret
Attenberg, J. The Middlesteins
Austen, J. Emma
Austen, J. Mansfield Park
Austen, J. Northanger Abbey
Austen, J. Sense and sensibility
Auster, P. The Brooklyn follies
Baker, J. The undertow
Balzac, H. d. Cousin Bette
Banville, J. The infinities
Barry, S. On Canaan's side
Bellow, S. Henderson the rain king
Bellow, S. Mr. Sammler's planet
Bender, A. The particular sadness of lemon cake
Betts, D. Souls raised from the dead
Bezmozgis, D. The free world
Binchy, M. Silver wedding
The blue hour
Bradbury, R. Dandelion wine
Bronsky, A. The Hottest Dishes of the Tartar Cuisine
Brookner, A. Family and friends
Brown, E. The weird sisters
Brown, R. Before and after
Buck, P. S. The good earth
Butler, R. O. Perfume River
Buwalda, P. Bonita Avenue
Byatt, A. S. The children's book
Cadwalladr, C. The family tree
Cheever, J. Bullet Park
Clegg, B. Did you ever have a family
Cohen, L. H. The grief of others
Colwin, L. A big storm knocked it over
Colwin, L. Family happiness
Connell, E. S. Mrs. Bridge
Conroy, P. The prince of tides
Cook, C. Best staged plans
Cook, T. H. The cloud of unknowing
Cunningham, M. Flesh and blood
Cusk, R. The Bradshaw variations
Cusk, R. In the fold
De la Roche, M. Jalna
De los Santos, M. The Precious One
Dean, M. L. The time it takes to fall
Deane, S. Reading in the dark
Dee, J. The privileges
Desai, A. Clear light of day
Diaz, J. The brief wondrous life of Oscar Wao
The dinner
Doig, I. Dancing at the Rascal Fair
Doig, I. English Creek
Doig, I. Last bus to wisdom
Doyle, R. Paddy Clarke, ha ha ha
Doyle, R. Smile
Doyle, R. The woman who walked into doors
Drabble, M. The witch of Exmoor
D'Souza, T. The Konkans
Dufresne, J. Deep in the shade of paradise
Dufresne, J. Requiem, Mass.
Dunmore, H. The betrayal
Dunn, K. Geek love
Eggers, D. Heroes of the frontier
The elephant keepers' children

Eliot, G. The mill on the Floss
Ellis, B. E. Lunar Park
Enright, A. The gathering
Enright, A. The Green Road
Faulkner, W. As I lay dying
Faulkner, W. The sound and the fury
Fay, J. Deep down true
Fay, J. The shortest way home
Ferber, E. So Big
Ferris, J. The unnamed
Flynn, G. Sharp objects
Follett, K. Edge of Eternity
Forman, G. Leave Me
Forster, E. M. Howards End
Fowler, K. J. We Are All Completely Beside Ourselves
Franck, J. The blindness of the heart
Franzen, J. Freedom
Franzen, J. The corrections
Franzen, J. Purity
French, T. Faithful Place
Freudenberger, N. The dissident
Freudenberger, N. The newlyweds
Gaitskill, M. The mare
Galsworthy, J. The Forsyte saga
Gibbons, K. Sights unseen
Gilmore, J. Something red
Goddard, R. Beyond recall
Godwin, G. A mother and two daughters
Goldberg, M. Bee season
Goodman, A. Kaaterskill Falls
Grant, H. The glass demon
Grant, L. We had it so good
Greenberg, J. In this sign
Grenville, K. The secret river
Grey, Z. Woman of the frontier
Grushin, O. The line
Guest, J. Ordinary people
Haddon, M. A spot of bother
Haig, M. The Radleys
Haigh, J. Baker towers
Haigh, J. The condition
Hamilton, J. Disobedience
Hamilton, J. A map of the world
Hamilton, J. The short history of a prince
Hamilton, J. When Madeline was young
Hannah, K. The great alone
Harrison, J. Returning to earth
Hart, B. Then came the evening
Hart, J. Down river
Hart, J. The truth about love
Haruf, K. Plainsong
Hassman, T. Girlchild
Hatoum, M. The brothers
Heller, J. Good as Gold
Henkin, J. The world without you
Hill, N. The Nix
Hill, R. When all is said and done
Hilton, J. Random harvest
Holmes, L. Barbara the slut and other people
Hooper, K. Finding Laura
Hosseini, K. A thousand splendid suns
Hughes, L. Not without laughter
Irving, J. The world according to Garp
It's fine by me
Jackson, J. The opposite of everyone
Jacobson, H. Kalooki nights
Jen, G. The love wife
Johnson, D. Le divorce
Kafka, F. Metamorphosis
Kaufman, S. Diary of a mad housewife
King, S. Pet sematary
Kingsolver, B. Flight behavior
Kingsolver, B. The poisonwood Bible
Krueger, W. K. Ordinary grace
Lamb, W. We Are Water
Le, T. D. T. The gangster we are all looking for
Lee, C. Y. The flower drum song
Lee, K. Drifting house
Lee Aloft
Levitt, P. M. Come with me to Babylon
Lightman, A. P. The diagnosis
Lin Yutang Moment in Peking
Llewellyn, R. How green was my valley
MacDonald Fall on your knees
MacDonald The way the crow flies
Maine, D. The preservationist
Marshall, P. Brown girl, brownstones
Marshall, P. The fisher king
Martin, V. Trespass
Mason, B. A. In country
Mbue, I. Behold the Dreamers
McCullers, C. The member of the wedding
McCullough, C. The thorn birds
McDermott, A. After this
McDermott, A. At weddings and wakes
McDermott, A. Charming Billy
McEwan, I. Saturday
McGuane, T. The cadence of grass
McMillan, T. A day late and a dollar short
McMillan, T. I Almost Forgot About You
McMurtry, L. Boone's Lick
McPhee, M. Gorgeous lies
Meek, J. The heart broke in
Meloy, M. A family daughter
Meloy, M. Liars and saints
Meyer, P. The Son
Miller, R. Welcome to Heavenly Heights
Mitchard, J. The deep end of the ocean
Mitchard, J. No time to wave goodbye
Mitchell, D. Black swan green
Moore, L. February
Morris, M. M. Songs in ordinary time
Morrison, T. Song of Solomon
Morton, B. Florence Gordon

Mukherjee, N. The Lives of Others
Murdoch, I. A fairly honourable defeat
My struggle
Naipaul, V. S. A house for Mr. Biswas
Nelson, A. Funny once
Never let you go
Noel, K. Halfway house
Oates, J. C. A Bloodsmoor romance
Oates, J. C. The falls
Oates, J. C. The gravedigger's daughter
Oates, J. C. Them
Oates, J. C. We were the Mulvaneys
Oe, K. A quiet life
O'Brien, E. The love object
O'Farrell, M. The vanishing act of Esme Lennox
Offill, J. Dept. of speculation
O'Flynn, C. The news where you are
O'Hara, J. Ten North Frederick
O'Nan, S. Snow angels
Orner, P. Love and shame and love
Otsuka, J. When the emperor was divine
Packer, A. The Children's Crusade
Pancake, A. Strange as this weather has been
Parks Getting mother's body
Patchett, A. Commonwealth
Paton, A. Too late the phalarope
Perrotta, T. The leftovers
Phillips, J. A. Lark and Termite
Picoult, J. My sister's keeper
Pierpont, J. Among the ten thousand things
Plain, B. Evergreen
Plain, B. Harvest
Plain, B. Tapestry
Pollen, B. The summer of the bear
Porter, M. Grief Is the Thing With Feathers
Potok, C. My name is Asher Lev
Prose, F. Household saints
Proulx, A. Barkskins
Proulx, A. Postcards
Puchner, E. Model home
Pywell, S. L. What happened to Henry
Quade, K. V. Night at the Fiestas
Quindlen, A. Every last one
Quindlen, A. Object lessons
Ramsland, M. Doghead
The red-haired woman
Reisman, N. The first desire
Reynolds, M. The Starlite Drive-in
Rice, L. Blue moon
Rice, L. Home fires
Richter, C. The awakening land
Riley, L. The girl on the cliff
Roberts, V. After the fall
Robinson, R. Cost
Rolvaag, O. E. Giants in the earth
Rolvaag, O. E. Peder Victorious
Rossner, J. Emmeline
Roth, H. Call it sleep
Roth, H. A star shines over Mt. Morris Park
Rowell, R. Landline
Roy, A. An atlas of impossible longing
Roy, A. The god of small things
Ruby, I. The salt god's daughter
Runcie, J. Canvey Island
Russo, R. Nobody's fool
Salinger, J. D. Franny & Zooey
Salinger, J. D. Raise high the roof beam, carpenters, and Seymour: an introduction
Samarasan, P. Evening is the whole day
Saroyan, W. The human comedy
Schwartz, J. B. Reservation Road
Scott, J. Tourmaline
Searles, J. Boy still missing
Sebold, A. The lovely bones
Segal, F. The awkward age
Settle, M. L. Charley Bland
Shafak, E. The bastard of Istanbul
Shamsie, K. Home fire
Shreve, A. The weight of water
Singer, I. B. The family Moskat
Smiley, J. A thousand acres
Smiley, J. Early warning
Smiley, J. Golden age
Smith, A. The accidental
Smith, B. A tree grows in Brooklyn
Smith, D. I capture the castle
Smith, Z. On beauty
Sofer, D. The Septembers of Shiraz
Spencer, S. Endless love
St. John Mandel, E. The singer's gun
Stead, C. The man who loved children
Stegner, W. E. The Big Rock Candy Mountain
Stein, G. The art of racing in the rain
Steinbeck, J. The grapes of wrath
Straight, S. The gettin place
Straub, E. The vacationers
Strayed, C. Torch
Styron, W. Lie down in darkness
Tanizaki, J. The Makioka sisters
Tarkington, B. Alice Adams
Tartt, D. The little friend
Taseer, A. The way things were
Tatlock, A. Things we once held dear
Taylor, P. H. A summons to Memphis
Thomas, M. We are not ourselves
Thompson, J. The year we left home
Thompson, J. Wide blue yonder
Tóibín, C. The blackwater lightship
Tóibín, C. The heather blazing
Torres, J. We the animals
Townsend, S. The Adrian Mole diaries
Trollope, J. Brother and sister
Trollope, J. Marrying the mistress
Trollope, J. The men and the girls

Trollope, J. Next of kin
Trollope, J. The other family
Trollope, J. Other people's children
Trollope, J. Second honeymoon
Tryon, T. The other
Turow, S. The burden of proof
Tyler, A. The amateur marriage
Tyler, A. Back when we were grownups
Tyler, A. The beginner's goodbye
Tyler, A. Breathing lessons
Tyler, A. The clock winder
Tyler, A. Digging to America
Tyler, A. Dinner at the Homesick Restaurant
Tyler, A. Earthly possessions
Tyler, A. Ladder of years
Tyler, A. Morgan's passing
Tyler, A. Saint maybe
Tyler, A. The tin can tree
Udall, B. The lonely polygamist
Vernon, O. Eden
Viswanathan, P. The toss of a lemon
Waldman, A. Red Hook Road
Walker, K. T. The age of miracles
Watson, L. As good as gone
Ward, A. E. Close your eyes
Ward, J. Salvage the bones
Weiner, J. Then came you
Weiner, J. In her shoes
Welty, E. Delta wedding
Welty, E. Losing battles
Welty, E. The optimist's daughter
West, J. The friendly persuasion
Wharton, E. The children
Wiggs, S. The ocean between us
Wilder, T. The eighth day
Wilhelm, K. The good children
Wilson, K. The family Fang
Wind, R. In the midnight rain
Winterson, J. Oranges are not the only fruit
Wolfe, T. Look homeward, angel
Wolfe, T. O lost
Wolitzer, M. The position
Woo, S. J. Everything Asian
Woodrell, D. The death of sweet mister
Woodson, J. Another Brooklyn
Woolf, V. To the lighthouse
Wouk, H. Marjorie Morningstar
Yanique, T. Land of love and drowning
Zevin, G. The hole we're in

FAMILY LIFE
See also Family

FAMILY LIFE -- GRAPHIC NOVELS
Moon, F. Daytripper

FAMILY LIFE -- HISTORY
Gyasi, Y. Homegoing

FAMILY LIFE -- LOUISIANA
Walsh, M. O. My sunshine away

Family linen. Smith, L.
A **family** madness. Keneally, T.
The **family** man. Lipman, E.
The **family** Moskat. Singer, I. B.
The **Family** Plot. Priest, C.

FAMILY RELATIONS *See* Domestic relations; Family life

FAMILY REUNIONS
Hadley, T. The past

FAMILY SECRETS
Archer, J. Best kept secret
Belfer, L. And after the fire
Bennett, R. J. American elsewhere
Black, E. The drowning house
Buwalda, P. Bonita Avenue
Cao, L. The lotus and the storm
Chabon, M. Moonglow
Coben, H. Fool Me Once
Decarlo, M. The Art of Crash Landing
Divakaruni, C. B. Oleander girl
Farrell, H. What ever happened to Baby Jane?
Frankel, L. This is how it always is
Gilbert, D. & sons
Hartnett, A. Rabbit cake
Hepworth, S. The Secrets of Midwives
Hill, N. The Nix
Hoffman, A. The rules of magic
Jacob, M. The sleepwalker's guide to dancing
Jewell, L. The making of us
Jin, H. A map of betrayal
Lundrigan, N. Glass boys
Macmillan, G. The perfect girl
Makkai, R. The hundred-year house
Matthiessen, P. In Paradise
McHugh, L. Arrowood
Mitchell, J. C. A reunion of ghosts
Nadler, S. Wise men
Ndiaye, M. Ladivine
Netzer, L. Shine shine shine
Ng, C. Everything I never told you
Nova, C. All the dead Yale men
O'Donnell, L. Closed Doors
Ohanesian, A. Orhan's inheritance
O'Loughlin, E. Minds of winter
Patchett, A. Commonwealth
Riley, L. The girl on the cliff
Robertson, I. Island of bones
Roy, L. Let me die in his footsteps
Solomon, A. Leaving Lucy Pear
Strout, E. My name is Lucy Barton
Vann, D. Aquarium
Wallace, M. The girl in the garden
Woodruff, L. Those we love most

FAMILY SIZE
See also Family

FAMILY THERAPY
See also Counseling; Psychotherapy

FAMILY TRADITIONS

See also Family life; Manners and customs
The **family** tree. Cadwalladr, C.
FAMILY TREES *See* Genealogy
FAMILY VACATIONS
Meloy, M. Do not become alarmed
FAMINES
Buck, P. S. The good earth
FAMOUS PEOPLE *See* Celebrities
A **fanatic** heart. O'Brien, E.
FANATICISM
Boyle, T. C. Road to Wellville
Meek, J. The people's act of love
Moulessehoul, M. The swallows of Kabul
FANATICISM
See also Emotions
Fangland. Marks, J.
Fanon. Wideman, J. E.
Fanon, Frantz, 1925-1961
About
Wideman, J. E. Fanon
FANS (PERSONS)
King, S. Finders Keepers
Pearson, A. I think I love you
FANTASIES
Abercrombie, J. Before they are hanged
Abercrombie, J. The blade itself
Adrian, C. The children's hospital
Adrian, C. The great night
Aiken, J. The monkey's wedding, and other stories
Aira, C. Ghosts
American fantastic tales: terror and the uncanny from Poe to the pulps
American fantastic tales: terror and the uncanny from the 1940s to now
Anderson, P. War of the Gods
Baker, K. The bird of the river
Baker, K. The house of the stag
Baker, N. House of holes
Ballard, J. G. The day of creation
Barker, C. Imajica
Barker, C. Weaveworld
Beagle, P. S. The last unicorn
Bear, E. Blood and iron
Bear, E. Ink and steel
Berger, T. Being invisible
The Best from fantasy & science fiction: the fiftieth anniversary anthology
Bledsoe, A. The hum and the shiver
Bradbury, R. Something wicked this way comes
Bradley, M. Z. The mists of Avalon
Brockmeier, K. The brief history of the dead
Brockmeier, K. The Illumination
Brooks, T. The druid of Shannara
Brooks, T. First king of Shannara
Brooks, T. The measure of the magic
Brooks, T. The sword of Shannara
Bujold, L. M. The paladin of souls
Calvino, I. Baron in the trees
Calvino, I. Invisible cities
Capote, T. The grass harp
Card, O. S. Keeper of dreams
Card, O. S. Seventh son
Carey, J. Kushiel's dart
Carroll, J. The ghost in love
Carter, A. Nights at the circus
Charlton, B. Spellbound
Charlton, B. Spellwright
Connolly, J. The book of lost things
Dark matter
Davies, R. Murther & walking spirits
Davies, V. Miracle on 34th Street
De Lint, C. Widdershins
Donaldson, S. R. The Illearth war
Donaldson, S. R. Lord Foul's bane
Donaldson, S. R. The power that preserves
Donaldson, S. R. The runes of the earth
Donaldson, S. R. The wounded Land
Donohue, K. The stolen child
Durham, D. A. Acacia
Fforde, J. The Eyre affair
Fforde, J. Lost in a good book
Fforde, J. Shades of grey
Ford, J. The empire of ice cream
Gaiman, N. Anansi boys
Gaiman, N. Stardust
Gilman, C. P. Herland
Gilman, F. The half-made world
Gilman, L. A. Hard magic
Graham, J. Black ships
Grass, G. The flounder
Gregory, D. The devil's alphabet
Gregory, D. Pandemonium
Grossman, A. Soon I will be invincible
Grossman, L. The magician king
Grossman, L. The magicians
Haggard, H. R. She
Hall, S. The raw shark texts
Hamill, P. Forever
Harkness, D. E. A discovery of witches
Haydon, E. Destiny: child of the sky
Haydon, E. Prophecy
Helprin, M. Winter's tale
Hesse, H. The fairy tales of Hermann Hesse
Hilton, J. Lost horizon
Hobb, R. Assassin's apprentice
Houellebecq, M. The possibility of an island
Hughes, M. Hespira
Hunt, R. Mr. Chartwell
Jemisin, N. K. The hundred thousand kingdoms
Jones, D. W. A sudden wild magic
Kay, G. G. Ysabel
Kiernan, C. R. The red tree
King, S. The stand
Kowal, M. R. Shades of milk and honey

Lackey, M. The fairy godmother
Lackey, M. Joust
Lackey, M. Winds of fate
Lake, J. Endurance
Le Guin, U. K. The other wind
Le Guin, U. K. The beginning place
Le Guin, U. K. Orsinian tales
Levin, I. The Stepford wives
Lewis, C. S. Out of the silent planet
Lewis, C. S. Perelandra
Lewis, C. S. That hideous strength
Lord, K. Redemption in indigo
Lustbader, E. V. Mistress of the pearl
Lynch, S. The lies of Locke Lamora
Maguire, G. Wicked
Maguire, G. Son of a witch
Marillier, J. Daughter of the forest
Marks, L. J. Fire logic
Martin, G. R. R. A dance with dragons
Martin, G. R. R. A clash of kings
Martin, G. R. R. A feast for crows
Martin, G. R. R. A game of thrones
McCaffrey, A. Acorna
McCaffrey, A. Dragonflight
McCaffrey, A. Dragon's Kin
McCaffrey, A. The white dragon
McKillip, P. A. Alphabet of thorn
Mieville, C. The city & the city
Mieville, C. Kraken
Mieville, C. Perdido Street Station
Miller, W. M. A canticle for Leibowitz
Millhauser, S. Martin Dressler
Moorcock, M. An alien heat
Moorcock, M. The dreamthief's daughter
Nabokov, V. V. Pale fire
Nathan, R. Portrait of Jennie
Norton, A. The elvenbane
Norton, A. Elvenblood
Norton, A. Golden Trillium
Novik, N. His majesty's dragon
Orwell, G. Animal farm
The Oxford book of modern fairy tales
Oyeyemi, H. Mr. Fox
Palmer, D. C. The dream of perpetual motion
Parker, K. J. The company
Parker, K. J. Devices and desires
Piercy, M. Woman on the edge of time
Polansky, D. Low Town
Powers, T. Three days to never
Pratchett, T. The color of magic
Pratchett, T. The fifth elephant
Pratchett, T. Going postal
Pratchett, T. Monstrous regiment
Pratchett, T. Thief of time
Pratchett, T. Thud!
Pratchett, T. The truth
Putney, M. J. A kiss of fate
Rand, A. Atlas shrugged
Rawn, M. The diviner
Riley, J. M. The serpent garden
Robbins, T. Jitterbug perfume
Robbins, T. Villa incognito
Robson, J. Keeping it real
Rothfuss, P. The name of the wind
Rothfuss, P. The wise man's fear
Ruiz Zafon, C. The angel's game
Ruiz Zafon, C. The shadow of the wind
Rushdie, S. The satanic verses
Rushdie, S. The Moor's last sigh
Ryman, G. Paradise tales
Saberhagen, F. The fifth book of lost swords: Coinspinner's story
Saberhagen, F. The first book of lost swords: Woundhealer's story
Saberhagen, F. The fourth book of lost swords: Farslayer's story
Saberhagen, F. The last book of swords: Shieldbreaker's story
Saberhagen, F. The second book of lost swords: Sightblinder's story
Saberhagen, F. The seventh book of lost swords: Wayfinder's story
Saberhagen, F. The sixth book of lost swords: Mindsword's story
Saberhagen, F. The third book of lost swords: Stonecutter's story
Saint, H. F. Memoirs of an invisible man
Saint-Exupery, A. d. The little prince
Sanderson, B. Elantris
Sanderson, B. The final empire
Savage, S. Firmin
Sedia, E. Alchemy of stone
Silverberg, R. Lord Valentine's castle
Swift, J. Gulliver's travels
Tolkien, J. R. R. The fellowship of the ring
Tolkien, J. R. R. The return of the king
Tolkien, J. R. R. The Silmarillion
Tolkien, J. R. R. The two towers
Trussoni, D. Angelology
Turtledove, H. Into the darkness
Turtledove, H. Rulers of the darkness
Twain, M. A Connecticut Yankee in King Arthur's court
Valentine, G. Mechanique
VanderMeer, J. Finch
Vinge, J. D. The Snow Queen
Vinge, J. D. The Summer Queen
Vonnegut, K. Cat's cradle
Vonnegut, K. Slapstick
Wallace, D. The Watermelon King
Walton, J. Among others
Warrington, F. Elfland
Welty, E. The robber bridegroom
The white people and other weird stories
White, T. H. The book of Merlyn

White, T. H. The once and future king
White, T. H. The sword in the stone
Wibberley, L. The mouse that roared
Wilkins, K. Veil of gold
With her in Ourland
Wolfe, G. The best of Gene Wolfe
Wolfe, G. Castleview
Wolfe, G. The Citadel of the Autarch
Wolfe, G. The claw of the conciliator
Wolfe, G. Pirate freedom
Wolfe, G. The shadow of the torturer
Wolfe, G. The sorcerer's house
Wolfe, G. The sword of the Lictor
Wolfe, G. The Urth of the new sun
Woolf, V. Orlando
The Year's best fantasy and horror
Zelazny, R. Blood of Amber
Zelazny, R. The courts of chaos
Zelazny, R. The guns of Avalon
Zelazny, R. The hand of Oberon
Zelazny, R. Knight of shadows
Zelazny, R. Nine princes in Amber
Zelazny, R. Prince of chaos
Zelazny, R. Sign of chaos
Zelazny, R. Sign of the unicorn
Zelazny, R. Trumps of doom

FANTASTIC FICTION *See* Fantasy fiction

FANTASY

See also Dreams; Imagination

FANTASY FICTION

Abercrombie, J. Half a King
Abercrombie, J. Half a war
Abercrombie, J. Half the world
Abercrombie, J. The heroes
Abercrombie, J. Red country
Addison, K. The Goblin Emperor
Anders, C. J. All the birds in the sky
Atkinson, K. Life After Life
Atwood, M. The Handmaid's tale
Balaskovits, A. A. Magic for unlucky girls
Ballard, J. G. The day of creation
Barnes, S. Domino Falls
Beagle, P. S. The last unicorn
Bear, E. Range of ghosts
Bear, E. Shattered pillars
Bear, E. Steles of the sky
Bennett, R. J. City of blades
Bennett, R. J. City of stairs
Bennett, R. J. The troupe
The Best from fantasy & science fiction: the fiftieth anniversary anthology
Bouchet, A. Breath of fire
Bowen, L. Wake of vultures
Bradbury, R. Something wicked this way comes
Bradley, M. Z. The mists of Avalon
Brennan, M. A natural history of dragons
Brooks, T. Wards of Faerie
Broun, B. Night of the Animals
Buehlman, C. The suicide motor club
Butcher, J. The aeronaut's windlass
Butcher, J. Proven guilty
Callihan, K. Firelight
Card, O. S. Seventh son
Carey, J. Banewreaker
Carey, J. Dark currents
Carey, J. Kushiel's Scion
Cargill, C. R. Dreams and Shadows
Carroll, J. Bathing the Lion
Carter, A. Nights at the circus
Catling, B. The Erstwhile
Charlton, B. Spellbreaker
Charlton, B. Spellwright
Cho, Z. Sorcerer to the crown
Cline, E. Ready player one
Connolly, T. Ironskin
Cooper, I. No proper lady
Cross, J. Touched by venom
Czerneda, J. E. A Turn of Light
De Lint, C. Widdershins
Donohue, K. The stolen child
Duncan, D. When the saints
Dyachenko, M. The scar
Engelmann, K. The Stockholm Octavo
Evans, C. A darkness forged in fire
Fforde, J. The Eyre affair
Finney, J. From time to time
Flyte, M. City of dark magic
The Future Is Japanese
Gaiman, N. American gods
Gaiman, N. Good omens
Gaiman, N. The Ocean at the End of the Lane
Gaiman, N. Anansi boys
Gaiman, N. Fragile things
Gaiman, N. Stardust
Gilman, L. A. Silver on the Road
Gilman, L. A. Flesh and fire
Goldman, W. The princess bride
Grant, M. Down Among the Sticks and Bones
Grant, M. Every Heart a Doorway
Grant, M. Rosemary and Rue
Griffin, K. Stray souls
Grimes, L. In a fix
Grimes, L. Quick fix
Grossman, A. Soon I will be invincible
Grossman, L. The magician king
Grossman, L. The magician's land
Grossman, L. The magicians
Harkness, D. E. The Book of Life
Hawkins, S. The Library at Mount Char
Haydon, E. The Merchant Emperor
Hoffman, A. The rules of magic
Hurley, K. The Mirror Empire
Ishiguro, K. The buried giant
Jacka, B. Fated

Jemisin, N. K. The fifth season
Jemisin, N. K. The killing moon
Jemisin, N. K. The obelisk gate
Jemisin, N. K. The stone sky
Johnson, K. The Dream-Quest of Vellitt Boe
Jordan, R. The eye of the world
Joyce, G. Some kind of fairy tale
Kay, G. G. River of Stars
King, S. The stand
Kristoff, J. Nevernight
Kushner, E. Swordspoint
Lackey, M. Joust
Lafferty, M. The shambling guide to New York City
Lambert, C. The children's home
Lanagan, M. The brides of Rollrock Island
Lancaster, J. Here I go again
Lee, Y. H. Raven Stratagem
Lewis, C. S. That hideous strength
Link, K. Get in trouble
Liu, K. The grace of kings
Liu, K. The wall of storms
Locke, T. Emissary
Logan, K. The gracekeepers
Lynch, S. The lies of Locke Lamora
Lynch, S. Red seas under red skies
Maguire, G. Wicked
Maguire, G. Son of a witch
Marillier, J. Daughter of the forest
Marshall, A. A crown for cold silver
Martin, G. R. R. A dance with dragons
Martin, G. R. R. A storm of swords
Martinez, N. M. Caramba!
McCaffrey, A. Dragonflight
McClellan, B. Promise of blood
McKillip, P. A. Ombria in shadow
Miéville, C. Three moments of an explosion
Mieville, C. Kraken
Miller, R. Jacob's folly
Millhauser, S. Martin Dressler
Modesitt, L. E. Imager's battalion
Modesitt, L. E. Imager's intrigue
Modesitt, L. E. Scholar
Moore, A. Jerusalem
Mott, J. The Returned
New Cthulhu
Newton, M. C. Nights of Villjamur
Nicholas, D. The wicked
Norton, A. Golden Trillium
Novik, N. League of Dragons
Novik, N. Uprooted
Orullian, P. V. The unremembered
Palwick, S. The necessary beggar
Parker, K. J. Sharps
Pulley, N. The Bedlam Stacks
Putney, M. J. Stolen magic
Rawn, M. Touchstone
Rogues
Ruby, I. The salt god's daughter
Rushdie, S. The satanic verses
Rushdie, S. Two years eight months and twenty-eight nights
Saintcrow, L. Trailer park fae
Saint-Exupery, A. d. The little prince
Schwab, V. E. A gathering of shadows
Siegel, J. Prospero's children
Singh, N. Shield of winter
Sisters of the Revolution
Stephenson, N. The rise and fall of D.O.D.O.
Sullivan, M. J. Theft of swords
Swift, J. Gulliver's travels
Tolkien, J. R. R. The hobbit, or, There and back again
Tolkien, J. R. R. The lord of the rings
Tolkien, J. R. R. The Silmarillion
Vyleta, D. Smoke
Walton, J. Among others
Warrington, F. Grail of the summer stars
Warrington, F. Midsummer night
Wecker, H. The Golem and the Jinni
Wells, M. Wheel of the infinite
White, E. K. Heartstone
White, T. H. The once and future king
Wolfe, G. The land across
Wolfe, G. The Urth of the new sun
Wooding, C. Retribution falls
Woods, C. Things to do when you're goth in the country

FANTASY GRAPHIC NOVELS
Henson, J. Jim Henson's tale of sand

FANTASY GRAPHIC NOVELS
See also Graphic novels

FANTASY LITERATURE, AMERICAN
Latin@ rising

Far bright star. Olmstead, R.
Far cry. Harvey, J.
A **far** cry from Kensington. Spark, M.
Far from the madding crowd. Hardy, T.
Far north. Theroux, M.
The **far** pavilions. Kaye, M. M.
The **far** side of the dollar. Macdonald, R.
Far Tortuga. Matthiessen, P.

FARCE
Wiles, W. Care of wooden floors

A **farewell** to arms. Hemingway, E.
Farewell to Fairacre. Read
A Fargo adventure [series]
Cussler, C. The Mayan secrets

FARM FAMILIES
See also Family

FARM FAMILIES
Meadows, R. I will send rain

FARM LIFE
Bakker, G. The twin
Dallas, S. Tallgrass
Hoover, M. The quickening
Kingsolver, B. Flight behavior
Markandaya, K. Nectar in a sieve

Meno, J. Marvel and a wonder
Smiley, J. Golden age
Smiley, J. Some luck
FARM LIFE
See also Country life; Farmers
FARM LIFE -- ALABAMA -- HISTORY -- 20TH CENTURY
Agee, J. Let us now praise famous men; A death in the family, and shorter fiction
FARM LIFE -- CALIFORNIA
Mapson Bad Girl Creek
Norris, F. The octopus
FARM LIFE -- CANADA
Lawson, M. Crow Lake
FARM LIFE -- CHINA
Buck, P. S. The good earth
FARM LIFE -- ENGLAND
Hardy, T. Far from the madding crowd
Trollope, J. Next of kin
FARM LIFE -- ILLINOIS
Ferber, E. So Big
FARM LIFE -- IOWA
Smiley, J. A thousand acres
Waller, R. J. The bridges of Madison County
FARM LIFE -- IRELAND
O'Brien, E. Wild Decembers
FARM LIFE -- KANSAS
Roy, L. Bent Road
FARM LIFE -- KENTUCKY
Morgan, C. E. All the living
FARM LIFE -- MISSISSIPPI
Jordan, H. Mudbound
FARM LIFE -- NEBRASKA
Cather, W. O pioneers!
FARM LIFE -- NEW ENGLAND
Wharton, E. Ethan Frome
FARM LIFE -- NEW HAMPSHIRE
Benet, S. V. The Devil and Daniel Webster
FARM LIFE -- NORTH CAROLINA
Frazier, C. Cold Mountain
FARM LIFE -- NORWAY
Undset, S. Kristin Lavransdatter
FARM LIFE -- OKLAHOMA
Meadows, R. I will send rain
FARM LIFE -- SOUTH AFRICA
Lessing, D. M. The grass is singing
FARM LIFE -- SOUTH DAKOTA
Rolvaag, O. E. Giants in the earth
Rolvaag, O. E. Peder Victorious
FARM LIFE -- TEXAS
Proulx, A. That old ace in the hole
FARM LIFE -- VERMONT
Proulx, A. Postcards
FARM LIFE -- WESTERN STATES
Stegner, W. E. The Big Rock Candy Mountain
FARM LIFE -- WISCONSIN
Hamilton, J. A map of the world
Schwarz, C. Drowning Ruth
FARM LIFE -- ZAMBIA
Mankell, H. The eye of the leopard
FARM PRODUCE
See also Food; Raw materials
FARM TENANCY
See also Farms; Land tenure
FARMERS
McCall Smith, A. The Saturday big tent wedding party
The **farming** of bones. Danticat, E.
FARMS
See also Land use; Real estate
FARMS
Chanter, C. The well
Teran, A. Ana of California
Warren, D. Juliet in August
Farriers' Lane. Perry, A.
Farthing. Walton, J.
FASCISM
Furst, A. The foreign correspondent
Roth, P. The plot against America
Walton, J. Half a crown
Walton, J. Ha'penny
FASCISM
See also Totalitarianism
FASCISM -- ITALY
Silone, I. Bread and wine
FASCISM -- UNITED STATES
Lewis, S. It can't happen here
FASHION
Steel, D. First sight
FASHION DESIGNERS
See also Designers
FASHION DESIGNERS
Steel, D. First sight
FASHION INDUSTRY AND TRADE
Gibson, W. Zero history
FASHION MODELS
Gaitskill, M. Veronica
Rowling, J. K. The cuckoo's calling
FASHION MODELS
See also Advertising
FASTING
Donoghue, E. The wonder
Fat Ollie's book. McBain, E.
A **fatal** glass of beer. Kaminsky, S. M.
Fatal induction. Pajer, B.
Fatal lies. Tallis, F.
A **fatal** likeness. Shepherd, L.
A **fatal** winter. Malliet, G. M.
Fatale. Manchette
FATE AND FATALISM
Browne, S. G. Lucky bastard
Garcia Marquez, G. Chronicle of a death foretold
Garcia, C. A handbook to luck
Guterson, D. Ed King
Lively, P. How it all began

Locke, T. Emissary
The **fate** of Katherine Carr. Cook, T. H.
Fated. Jacka, B.
Fates and furies. Groff, L.
The **fates** will find their way. Pittard, H.
The **father** of the rain. King, L.
FATHER-CHILD RELATIONSHIP
See also Children; Fathers; Parent-child relationship
Nichols, J. On top of Spoon Mountain
Thompson, J. The humanity project
FATHER-DAUGHTER RELATIONSHIP
See also Daughters; Father-child relationship; Fathers
Arimah, L. N. What it means when a man falls from the sky
Begley, L. About Schmidt
Box, C. J. Open season
Butler, S. Ten things I've learnt about love
Cash, W. This dark road to mercy
Danielewski, M. Z. The familiar
De los Santos, M. The Precious One
Divakaruni, C. B. Oleander girl
Ephron, H. Night Night, Sleep Tight
Gaige, A. Schroder
Handler, D. We are pirates
Hannah, K. Home front
Hartnett, A. Rabbit cake
Jin, H. A map of betrayal
Joinson, S. The Photographer's Wife
Lee, H. Go set a watchman
Lyon, A. The sweet girl
McLain, P. Circling the Sun
Moore, L. The Unseen World
Morrell, D. Murder as a fine art
Moshfegh, O. Eileen
Pessl, M. Night Film
Ratner, V. In the shadow of the banyan
Roberts, N. The obsession
Solomon, A. Disgruntled
Tinti, H. The twelve lives of Samuel Hawley
Tirza
Tropper, J. One last thing before I go
Turner, N. Natural born hustler
Tyler, A. Vinegar girl
Watson, S. Suitcase city
Yezierska, A. c. Bread givers
Zander, J. The Swimmer
FATHER-SON RELATIONSHIP
See also Father-child relationship; Fathers; Sons
FATHER-SON RELATIONSHIP
Beatty, P. The sellout
Bialosky, J. The prize
The Blood of Angels
Boyle, T. C. The Harder They Come
Burke, J. L. House of the rising sun
DeLillo, D. Zero K
Enger, L. The high divide
Everett, P. Percival Everett by Virgil Russell
Gill, J. F. The gargoyle hunters
Hall, J. W. Going Dark
Havley, N. The good father
Heacox, K. Jimmy Bluefeather
Hostage
Iles, G. Natchez burning
Irving, J. In one person
Kenney, J. Truth in advertising
Lam, V. The headmaster's wager
Landay, W. Defending Jacob
The leopard
Little, T. Where there's smoke
Malik, T. Three bargains
Mansbach, A. Rage is back
McNally, T. M. The goat bridge
My struggle
Ōe, K. Death by Water
O'Flynn, C. Mr. Lynch's holiday
Porter, M. Grief Is the Thing With Feathers
Rich, D. Caravan of thieves
Robinson, M. Gilead
Waite, U. Sometimes the wolf
Fatherland. Harris, R.
FATHERLESS FAMILIES
Ruby, I. The salt god's daughter
FATHERS
Banks, R. Affliction
Bijan, D. The last days of Café Leila
Ford, R. The lay of the land
Foroutan, P. The girl from the garden
Grass, G. The box
Greenfeld, K. T. Triburbia
Hustvedt, S. The sorrows of an American
Porter, M. Grief Is the Thing With Feathers
Restrepo, L. No place for heroes
Simsion, G. The Rosie effect
FATHERS
See also Family; Men
FATHERS -- CARE
Coster, N. Halsey Street
FATHERS -- DEATH
Bijan, D. The last days of Café Leila
Campbell, B. J. Once upon a river
Parker, T. J. Silent Joe
Watrous, M. If you follow me
Wilhelm, K. The deepest water
Wroblewski, D. The story of Edgar Sawtelle
Fathers and crows. Vollmann, W. T.
FATHERS AND DAUGHTERS
Balzac, H. d. Pere Goriot (Old Goriot)
The beggar king
Begley, L. About Schmidt
Bellow, S. Mr. Sammler's planet
Betts, D. Souls raised from the dead
Bourne, J. My lord and spymaster
Box, C. J. Open season
Brown, J. D. Addie Pray
Butler, S. Ten things I've learnt about love

Cash, W. This dark road to mercy
Coetzee, J. M. Disgrace
Danticat, E. The dew breaker
Dickens, C. Dombey and Son
Divakaruni, C. B. Oleander girl
Dixon, S. Interstate
Doctorow, C. Walkaway
Erpenbeck, J. The book of words
Fforde, J. The Eyre affair
Freeman, B. Spilled blood
French, T. Faithful Place
Gaddis, W. Agape agape
Gaige, A. Schroder
Glass, J. The widower's tale
Gordon, M. Final payments
Green, J. Another piece of my heart
Hadley, T. The London train
Hannah, K. On Mystic lake
Hartnett, A. Rabbit cake
Ishiguro, K. An artist of the floating world
James, H. The golden bowl
Jones, T. Silver sparrow
Kay, G. G. River of Stars
King, L. The father of the rain
Larsson, S. The girl who kicked the hornets' nest
Le, T. D. T. The gangster we are all looking for
Lee, H. To kill a mockingbird
L'Engle, M. Certain women
Lipman, E. The family man
Livesey, M. The house on Fortune Street
Lyon, A. The sweet girl
Malone, M. The four corners of the sky
McPhee, M. Gorgeous lies
Miles, J. Dear American Airlines
Moore, C. A dirty job
Morrell, D. Murder as a fine art
Norman, H. What is left the daughter
Oates, J. C. Black girl/White girl
Pears, I. Stone's fall
Pessl, M. Night Film
Pessl, M. Special topics in calamity physics
Picoult, J. Vanishing acts
Pronzini, B. In an evil time
Proulx, A. The shipping news
Read, P. P. The professor's daughter
Rendell, R. Heartstones
Reuss, F. Mohr
Roberts, N. The obsession
Robinson, M. Home
Rock, P. My abandonment
Roth, P. American pastoral
Russo, R. Empire Falls
Sagan, F. Bonjour tristesse
Saramago, J. The cave
Scottoline, L. Don't Go
Scottoline, L. Moment of truth
See, L. Dreams of joy
Segal, E. Love story
Smiley, J. A thousand acres
Tinti, H. The twelve lives of Samuel Hawley
Toews, M. A complicated kindness
Trevor, W. Death in summer
Trollope, J. Next of kin
Tyler, A. Noah's compass
Ulinich, A. Petropolis
Vidal, G. 1876
Vine, B. The chimney sweeper's boy
Walker, A. By the light of my father's smile
Walton, J. Among others
Wiggins, M. The shadow catcher
Wilhelm, K. The deepest water
Woodrell, D. Winter's bone
Yezierska, A. c. Bread givers
Fathers and sons. Turgenev, I. S.
FATHERS AND SONS *See* Father-son relationship
FATHERS AND SONS
Abani, C. GraceLand
Archer, J. Only time will tell
Bakker, G. The twin
Banville, J. The infinities
Barker, N. Darkmans
Berry, S. The Charlemagne pursuit
Boucher, C. How to keep your Volkswagen alive
Bradbury, R. Something wicked this way comes
Bragg, M. The soldier's return
Bragg, M. A son of war
Burke, J. L. House of the rising sun
Chaon, D. Await your reply
Clarke, B. Exley
Coady, L. The antagonist
Coetzee, J. M. Summertime
Cook, T. H. Master of the delta
Cusk, R. In the fold
Deb, S. The point of return
Dexter, P. Spooner
Dickens, C. Dombey and Son
Doig, I. The bartender's tale
Doiron, P. The poacher's son
Dostoyevsky, F. The brothers Karamazov
Ellis, B. E. Lunar Park
Enger, L. Undiscovered country
Foer, J. S. Extremely loud & incredibly close
Ford, R. Independence Day
Forsyth, F. Avenger
Garcia, C. A handbook to luck
Garey, J. Too bright to hear too loud to see
Gill, J. F. The gargoyle hunters
Glass, J. Three Junes
Gordimer, N. The conservationist
Gordimer, N. My son's story
Grippando, J. Born to run
Grodstein, L. A friend of the family
Gunesekera, R. The match
Habila, H. Measuring time

Haig, M. The dead fathers club
Hall, J. W. Going Dark
Harding, P. Tinkers
Harkaway, N. Angelmaker
Hart, B. Then came the evening
Hart, J. Down river
Hart, J. The king of lies
Hart, J. Damage
Havley, N. The good father
Homes, A. M. This book will save your life
Howrey, M. Blind sight
Hunter, S. Black light
Just, W. S. Exiles in the garden
Just, W. S. An unfinished season
Klein, M. Con ed
Lansdale, J. R. The bottoms
Lee, C. Y. The flower drum song
Lodge, D. Deaf sentence
Lodge, D. Paradise news
Lychack, W. The wasp eater
Machart, B. The wake of forgiveness
Malik, T. Three bargains
Malouf, D. Ransom
Mansbach, A. Rage is back
Marias, J. A heart so white
Marlette, D. Magic time
Matar, H. Anatomy of a disappearance
Maxwell, R. The Queen's bastard
McCarthy, C. The road
McNally, T. M. The goat bridge
Mosley, W. Gone fishin'
Murdoch, I. The good apprentice
Naipaul, V. S. Half a life
Nicholls, D. Us
O'Flynn, C. Mr. Lynch's holiday
Okuizumi, H. The stones cry out
Olmstead, R. Coal black horse
O'Nan, S. The names of the dead
Parker, T. J. Silent Joe
Pattison, E. The lord of death
Pelecanos, G. P. The way home
Percy, B. The wilding
Perry, D. This is just exactly like you
Phillips, A. The tragedy of Arthur
Potok, C. My name is Asher Lev
Poyer, D. Down to a sunless sea
Preston, D. The codex
Price, R. The good priest's son
Pyper, A. The killing circle
Ramsland, M. Doghead
Rice, L. Summer light
Richter, C. The sea of grass
Robinson, M. Gilead
Robinson, M. Home
Roth, H. Call it sleep
Roth, P. Portnoy's complaint
Russo, R. Nobody's fool
Russo, R. The risk pool
Schlink, B. Homecoming
Schwartz, L. Angels Crest
Schwartz, J. B. Northwest corner
Schwartz, J. B. Reservation Road
Segal, E. Love story
Sharma, A. Family Life
Sher, I. Gentlemen of space
Smith, W. A. Birds of prey
Smith, W. A. Monsoon
Stone, R. Bay of souls
Straub, P. Mr. X
Townsend, S. Adrian Mole
Tucker, T. Over and under
Turow, S. Ordinary heroes
Updike, J. The centaur
Vamos, M. The book of fathers
Vanderhaeghe, G. The last crossing
Vargas Llosa, M. The notebooks of Don Rigoberto
Vassanji, M. G. The assassin's song
Verghese, A. Cutting for stone
Vanderhaeghe, G. The last crossing
Waite, U. Sometimes the wolf
Wallace, D. Big fish
Wharton, W. Dad
Wiesel, E. The forgotten
Wilson, R. The blind man of Seville
Wyld, E. After the fire, a still small voice
Yates, A. Moondogs
Yu, C. How to live safely in a science fictional universe
FATHERS-IN-LAW
Plain, B. Looking back
FATNESS *See* Obesity
The **Faulkner** reader. Faulkner, W.
The **fault** tree. Ure, L.
FAUNA *See* Animals; Zoology
FAUST LEGEND
Mann, T. Doctor Faustus
FEAR
Du Maurier, D. Rebecca
King, S. The girl who loved Tom Gordon
See, C. There will never be another you
FEAR
See also Emotions
FEAR IN CHILDREN
See also Child psychology; Fear
The **fear** index. Harris, R.
FEAR OF DEATH
Maloy, K. Every last cuckoo
Fear of Dying. Jong, E.
Fear of flying. Jong, E.
FEAR OF OPEN SPACES *See* Agoraphobia
FEAR OF THE DARK
See also Fear; Fear in children
Fearless Jones. Mosley, W.
A **feast** for crows. Martin, G. R. R.
The **Feast** of All Saints. Rice, A.

The **feast** of love. Baxter, C.
A **feast** of snakes. Crews, H.
The **Feast** of the Goat.
February. Moore, L.
Feed. Grant, M.
Feedback. Grant, M.
FEEDBACK CONTROL SYSTEMS
See also Automation
FEELINGS *See* Emotions
Felicia's journey. Trevor, W.
Felix in the underworld. Mortimer, J.
Fellow travelers. Mallon, T.
The **fellowship** of the ring. Tolkien, J. R. R.
FEMALE ACTORS *See* Actresses
FEMALE CIRCUMCISION
Cross, J. Touched by venom
FEMALE FRIENDSHIP
See also Friendship
FEMALE FRIENDSHIP
Abbott, M. E. Dare me
Andrews, M. K. Summer rental
The bathing women
Berg, E. Tapestry of fortunes
Buntin, J. Marlena
Clark, G. The regulars
Cleave, C. Gold
Delinsky, B. Sweet salt air
Fay, J. Deep down true
Ferrante, E. My brilliant friend
Ferrante, E. The Story of a New Name
Ferrante, E. The Story of the Lost Child
Ferrante, E. Those Who Leave and Those Who Stay
Fields, J. The age of desire
Gould, E. Friendship
Hannah, K. Fly Away
Higgins, K. The Perfect Match
In the wilderness
Jackson, N. Who do I talk to?
Lansdale, J. R. Edge of dark water
Lutz, L. How to start a fire
Martinusen-Coloma, C. The salt garden
Moore, E. K. The Supremes at Earl's all-you-can-eat
Moore, E. K. The Supremes sing the happy heartache blues
Moriarty, L. Big little lies
Otto, W. Eight girls taking pictures
Seitz, N. Trouble the water
Spiotta, D. Innocents and others
Umrigar, T. The world we found
Urquhart, R. The Visionist
Ware, R. The lying game
Whitaker, K. R. The animators
Williams, K. Dirty to the grave
FEMALE OFFENDERS
Stroby, W. Shoot the woman first
FEMALE SUPERHERO GRAPHIC NOVELS
See also Graphic novels
FEMINISM
Cooke, C. Daughters of the revolution
Donoghue, E. The sealed letter
Drabble, M. The sea lady
Franklin, M. My brilliant career
French, M. The women's room
Gilman, C. P. Herland
Horan, N. Loving Frank
Irving, J. The world according to Garp
Isaacs, S. Close relations
Jong, E. Fear of flying
Kidd, S. M. The invention of wings
Lessing, D. M. The golden notebook
Lessing, D. M. The sweetest dream
Martinez, N. M. Caramba!
Naslund, S. J. Ahab's wife; or, The star-gazer
Paretsky, S. Ghost country
Prose, F. Hunters and gatherers
Roiphe, A. R. Lovingkindness
Rush, N. Mating
Sisters of the Revolution
Tepper, S. S. The gate to Women's Country
Tepper, S. S. Singer from the sea
Walker, A. Possessing the secret of joy
With her in Ourland
FEMINIST ETHICS
See also Ethics; Feminism
FEMINIST THEORY *See* Feminism
FEMINISTS
Donoghue, E. The sealed letter
Ebershoff, D. The 19th wife
Horan, N. Loving Frank
Piercy, M. Sex wars
Walker, S. Dietland
FEMMES FATALES
Spiotta, D. Innocents and others
FENCING
Parker, K. J. Sharps
Perez-Reverte, A. The fencing master
The **fencing** master. Perez-Reverte, A.
FENS, THE (ENGLAND)
Kelly, J. The fire baby
Fer-de-lance; &, The league of frightened men. Stout, R.
FERMENTED FOODS
See also Food
Fermi, Enrico, 1901-1954
About
Millet, L. Oh pure and radiant heart
FERTILIZATION IN VITRO
Shattuck, J. Perfect life
FESTIVALS
Crews, H. A feast of snakes
FETAL ALCOHOL SYNDROME
See also Social problems
FETISHISM (SEXUAL BEHAVIOR)
See also Sex
FEUDALISM
Clavell, J. Shogun

FEUDALISM
See also Land tenure; Medieval civilization
FEUDS
Fortier, A. Juliet
Jackson, J. Between, Georgia
Paretsky, S. Bleeding Kansas
Swerling, B. Shadowbrook
Tryon, T. In the fire of spring
Tryon, T. The wings of the morning
Woodrell, D. Give us a kiss
Fever. Pronzini, B.
The **fever.** Abbott, M. E.
Fever. Keane, M. B.
Fever dream.
FIANCÉES
Divakaruni, C. B. Oleander girl
Kwan, K. China rich girlfriend
Kwan, K. Crazy rich Asians
Fiasco. Lem, S.
FICTION -- 20TH CENTURY
Flash fiction international
FICTION -- 21ST CENTURY
Flash fiction international
FICTION -- AUTHORSHIP
Everett, P. Erasure
FICTION -- TECHNIQUE
See also Authorship
FICTIONAL CHARACTERS
Frame, R. Havisham
Lemaitre, P. Irene
Fiddlehead. Priest, C.
Fidelity. Perry, T.
FIEFS *See* Feudalism; Land tenure
Field gray. Kerr, P.
Field of blood. Mina, D.
Field study. Seiffert, R.
Fields where they lay. Hallinan, T.
Fierce invalids home from hot climates. Robbins, T.
Fierce kingdom. Phillips, G.
A **fierce** radiance. Belfer, L.
The **fiery** cross. Gabaldon, D.
FIESTAS *See* Festivals
FIFTH AVENUE (NEW YORK, N.Y.)
Thompson, V. Murder on Fifth Avenue
The **fifth** book of lost swords: Coinspinner's story. Saberhagen, F.
Fifth business. Davies, R.
FIFTH CENTURY, B.C.
Vidal, G. Creation
The **fifth** child. Lessing, D. M.
The **fifth** element. Brekke, J.
The **fifth** elephant. Pratchett, T.
The **Fifth** Floor. Harvey, M. T.
The **Fifth** Gospel. Caldwell, I.
The **fifth** season. Jemisin, N. K.
The **fifth** vial. Palmer, M.
Fight Club. Palahniuk, C.
FIGHTER PILOTS -- UNITED STATES
Groot, T. Flame of resistance
FIGHTING *See* Battles; Boxing; Bullfights; Dueling; Fencing; Gladiators; Military art and science; Naval art and science; Self-defense; Self-defense for women; War
FIGURES OF SPEECH
See also Rhetoric; Symbolism
FILICIDE
Moore, S. The big girls
FILIPINO AMERICANS
Alvar, M. In the country
Fima. Oz, A.
The **final** country. Crumley, J.
The **Final** Cut. Coulter, C.
The **final** empire. Sanderson, B.
Final girls. Sager, R.
The **final** martyrs. Endo, S.
Final payments. Gordon, M.
Final seconds. Lutz, J.
Final target. Johansen, I.
Finale. Mallon, T.
FINANCE
Harris, R. The fear index
FINANCE -- CORRUPT PRACTICES
Sears, M. Black Fridays
The **financial** lives of the poets. Walter, J.
FINANCIAL RISK
See also Finance; Risk
FINANCIERS *See* Capitalists and financiers
Finch. VanderMeer, J.
Find Her. Gardner, L.
The **finder.** Harrison, C.
Finders Keepers. King, S.
Finding Laura. Hooper, K.
Finding Nouf. Ferraris, Z.
A **fine** balance. Mistry, R.
A **fine** dark line. Lansdale, J. R.
Fine just the way it is. Proulx, A.
FINGERPRINTS
See also Anthropometry; Criminal investigation; Criminals -- Identification; Identification
Fingersmith. Waters, S.
The **finishing** school. Godwin, G.
The **Finkler** question. Jacobson, H.
FINLAND
Hand, E. Available dark
Finn. Clinch, J.
Finnegan's week. Wambaugh, J.
Finnegans wake. Joyce, J.
The **fire.** Neville, K.
The **fire** baby. Kelly, J.
Fire down below. Golding, W.
FIRE ECOLOGY
See also Ecology
FIRE FIGHTING
See also Fire prevention; Fires
Fire ice. Cussler, C.

FIRE IN MYTHOLOGY
See also Mythology
Fire in the blood. Nemirovsky, I.
FIRE INSURANCE
See also Insurance
Fire logic. Marks, L. J.
Fire on the waters. Poyer, D.
FIRE PREVENTION
See also Fires
Fire sale. Paretsky, S.
The **fire** sermon. Haig, F.
Fire sermon [series]
Haig, F. The map of bones
A **fire** upon the deep. Vinge, V.
FIREARMS
Patterson, R. N. Balance of power
FIREARMS *See* Guns
The **Firebird.** Kearsley, S.
FIREFIGHTERS
Harrison, C. The finder
Firelight. Callihan, K.
The **fireman.** Hill, J.
FIRES
Canty, K. The underworld
Johnson, D. Train dreams
Pipkin, J. Woodsburner
FIRES
See also Accidents; Disasters; Fire
Firestarter. King, S.
Firewall. Mankell, H.
A **firing** offense. Ignatius, D.
The **firm.** Grisham, J.
Firmin. Savage, S.
The **first** book of lost swords: Woundhealer's story. Saberhagen, F.
The **first** cut. Robinson, P.
The **first** deadly sin. Sanders, L.
The **first** desire. Reisman, N.
First Edition [series]
Aslam, N. The Blind Man's Garden
First Frost. Allen, S. A.
First king of Shannara. Brooks, T.
FIRST LADIES
Chiaverini, J. Mrs. Lincoln's dressmaker
First lady. Phillips, S. E.
The **first** law. Lescroart, J. T.
First love and other stories. Turgenev, I. S.
FIRST LOVES
Abercrombie, J. Half the world
Gordon, M. The love of my youth
Higgins, K. Waiting on You
Lytal, B. A map of Tulsa
Walsh, M. O. My sunshine away
The **first** man in Rome. McCullough, C.
First of state. Greer, R. O.
First offense. Rosenberg, N. T.
First rule. Crais, R.
The **First** Rule of Swimming. Brkic, C. A.
First sight. Steel, D.
First Star I See Tonight. Phillips, S. E.
The **first** victim. Pearson, R.
FIRST WORLD WAR *See* World War, 1914-1918
FISH *See* Fish as food; Fishes
FISH AS FOOD
See also Cooking; Fishes; Food
The **fish** child.
A **fish** trapped inside the wind. Gholson, C.
The **fisher** king. Marshall, P.
The **fishermen.** Obioma, C.
FISHERMEN
Grass, G. The flounder
Guterson, D. Snow falling on cedars
Mills, M. Amagansett
Rice, L. Blue moon
Winton, T. Dirt music
FISHES
Gholson, C. A fish trapped inside the wind
Grass, G. The flounder
FISHES -- ECOLOGY
See also Ecology
FISHING
Edwardson, Å. Sail of stone
FISHING VILLAGES -- SWEDEN
Lackberg, C. The ice princess
Fitzgerald, F. Scott (Francis Scott), 1896-1940
About
Fowler, T. A. Z
Fitzgerald, Zelda, 1900-1948
About
Fowler, T. A. Z
The **five** bells and bladebone. Grimes, M.
Five minutes alone. Cleave, P.
Five novels of the 1960s & 70s. Dick, P. K.
Five quarters of the orange. Harris, J.
The **five** red herrings. Sayers, D. L.
Five skies. Carlson, R.
Five Star standard print romance series
Chase, L. L. The last hellion
Five-carat soul. McBride, J.
FIXED IDEAS *See* Obsessive-compulsive disorder
The **fixed** stars. Conn, B.
The **fixer.** Malamud, B.
The **flame** alphabet. Marcus, B.
Flame of resistance. Groot, T.
The **flamethrowers.** Kushner, R.
Flannery O'Connor Award for Short Fiction [series]
Graley, L. The current that carries
Flannigan, Katherine Mary O'Fallon
About
Freedman, B. Mrs. Mike
Flash fiction international.
FLASH MOBS
See also Crowds; Performance art
FLATS *See* Apartments

Flatscreen. Wilson, A.
Flavia Albia mysteries [series]
Davis, L. The Ides of April
Flavia de Luce [series]
Bradley, A. As chimney sweepers come to dust
Bradley, A. The sweetness at the bottom of the pie
FLAVORING ESSENCES
See also Cooking; Essences and essential oils; Food
Fledgling. Butler, O. E.
Fleming, Ian, 1908-1964
About
Faulks, S. Devil may care
Flesh and blood. Harvey, J.
Flesh and blood. Cunningham, M.
Flesh and fire. Gilman, L. A.
Flesh house. MacBride, S.
Fletch. Mcdonald, G.
A **flickering** light. Kirkpatrick, J.
FLIES
See also Household pests; Insects; Pests
Flight. Alexie, S.
FLIGHT ATTENDANTS
Leonard, E. Rum punch
Flight behavior. Kingsolver, B.
Flight of eagles. Higgins, J.
The **flight** of Gemma Hardy. Livesey, M.
The **flight** of the maidens. Gardam, J.
Flight to Canada. Reed, I.
FLIGHT TO THE MOON *See* Space flight to the moon
Flights of angels. Gilchrist, E.
Flimsy little plastic miracles. Currie, R.
Floaters. Wambaugh, J.
Floating city. Lustbader, E. V.
Flood of fire. Ghosh, A.
FLOODS
Atwood, M. Maddaddam
Cheng, B. Southern Cross the Dog
Runcie, J. Canvey Island
FLOORS
Wiles, W. Care of wooden floors
Flora. Godwin, G.
FLORENCE (ITALY)
Brown, D. Inferno
Nabb, M. Some bitter taste
FLORENCE (ITALY) -- HISTORY -- 1421-1737
Dunant, S. The birth of Venus
Florence Gordon. Morton, B.
FLORIDA
Banks, R. Lost memory of skin
Daniel, S. Stiltsville
Dean, M. L. The time it takes to fall
Dubus, A. The garden of last days
Due, T. Ghost summer
Fielding, J. Heartstopper
Frank, P. Alas, Babylon
Hagberg, D. Abyss
Haldeman, J. W. The coming
Hiassen, C. Bad monkey
Hiaasen, C. Nature girl
Hiaasen, C. Skinny dip
Hiaasen, C. Star Island
Hiaasen, C. Strip tease
Hoffman, A. Turtle Moon
Hurston, Z. N. Their eyes were watching God
Koryta, M. The Cypress House
Lehane, D. World gone by
Matthiessen, P. Shadow country
McBain, E. Alice in jeopardy
Poyer, D. Down to a sunless sea
Reiken, F. Day for night
Sanders, L. Sullivan's sting
Sher, I. Gentlemen of space
Stroby, W. Cold shot to the heart
Stuckey-French, E. Revenge of the radioactive lady
Wascom, K. The Blood of Heaven
Weiner, J. In her shoes
Wimberley, D. The king of Colored Town
Winkler, A. C. Dog war
FLORIDA -- 18TH CENTURY
Unsworth, B. Sacred hunger
FLORIDA -- 19TH CENTURY
Matthiessen, P. Bone by bone
Matthiessen, P. Killing Mister Watson
FLORIDA -- 20TH CENTURY
Hiaasen, C. Basket case
Hiaasen, C. Lucky you
Hiaasen, C. Skin tight
Hiaasen, C. Strip tease
Hoffman, A. Turtle Moon
Leonard, E. LaBrava
Leonard, E. Rum punch
Quindlen, A. Black and blue
Woods, S. Orchid Beach
FLORIDA -- KEY WEST
Hemingway, E. To have and have not
Robinson, S. Callahan's con
Woods, S. Choke
FLORIDA -- MIAMI
Abu-Jaber, D. Birds of paradise
Godwin, G. Queen of the underworld
Grippando, J. Born to run
Leonard, E. LaBrava
Lindsay, J. P. Darkly dreaming Dexter
Lindsay, J. P. Dearly devoted Dexter
Parker, B. Criminal justice
Parker, B. Suspicion of betrayal
Parker, B. Suspicion of deceit
Parker, B. Suspicion of vengeance
Rosales, G. The halfway house
Spillane, M. The Consummata
Stone, N. The king of swords
FLORIDA -- PALM BEACH
Hoag, T. Dark horse
FLORIDA -- TAMPA

Atkins, A. White shadow
FLORIDA KEYS (FLA.)
Hall, J. W. Going Dark
FLORISTS
Diffenbaugh, V. The language of flowers
The **flounder.** Grass, G.
FLOWER ARRANGEMENT
See also Decoration and ornament; Flowers; Table setting and decoration
The **flower** drum song. Lee, C. Y.
Flowering Judas and other stories. Porter, K. A.
The **flowers.** Gilb, D.
FLOWERS
Diffenbaugh, V. The language of flowers
FLOWERS -- ENGLAND
Jio, S. The last camellia
Flowers for Algernon. Keyes, D.
Flowers in the rain & other stories. Pilcher, R.
FLOWERS, VIRGIL (FICTITIOUS CHARACTER)
Sandford, J. Deadline
Sandford, J. Storm Front
FLU *See* Influenza
FLUID MECHANICS
See also Mechanics
Fly Away. Hannah, K.
Flying colours. Forester, C. S.
Flying hero class. Keneally, T.
FOALS *See* Horses; Ponies
Fobbit. Abrams, D.
FOCUS GROUPS
See also Research; Social groups
Foe. Coetzee, J. M.
Foggy Mountain breakdown and other stories. McCrumb, S.
FOLKLORE
Maguire, G. Hiddensee
FOLKLORE
See also Ethnology; Fiction; Manners and customs
FOLKLORE -- CAMBODIA
Ratner, V. In the shadow of the banyan
FOLKLORE -- PARAGUAY
The fish child
FOLKLORE -- RUSSIA
Buehlman, C. The Necromancer's house
The girl in the tower
Follies. Beattie, A.
Follow me. Scott, J.
Folly Beach. Frank, D. B.
FOOD
Lanchester, J. The debt to pleasure
O'Reilly, B. Angelina's bachelors
Fool Me Once. Coben, H.
Fools. Silber, J.
FOOLS AND JESTERS
See also Comedians; Courts and courtiers; Entertainers
Fools of fortune. Trevor, W.
Fools rush in. Gorman, E.
FOOTBALL
Bachelder, C. The throwback special
Fountain, B. Billy Lynn's long halftime walk
Grisham, J. Playing for pizza
Harris, E. L. And this too shall pass
Phillips, S. E. It had to be you
FOOTBALL -- COACHING
See also Coaching (Athletics)
FOOTBALL -- COACHING
Majors, I. Love's winning plays
FOOTBALL PLAYERS
Phillips, S. E. First Star I See Tonight
The **footprints** of God. Iles, G.
Footsteps of the hawk. Vachss, A. H.
For love. Miller, S.
For the most beautiful. Hauser, E.
For they shall inherit. Ross-Macdonald, M.
For whom the bell tolls. Hemingway, E.
Forbidden. Jenkins, B.
The **force.** Winslow, D.
Force of nature. Box, C. J.
FORCED LABOR
Solzhenitsyn, A. One day in the life of Ivan Denisovich
FORD AUTOMOBILE
See also Automobiles
Ford County. Grisham, J.
Ford, Gerald R., 1913-2006
About
Updike, J. Memories of the Ford Administration
Ford, Robert, 1862-1892
About
Hansen, R. The assassination of Jesse James by the coward Robert Ford
Foreign affairs. Lurie, A.
FOREIGN AUTOMOBILES
See also Automobiles
Foreign bodies. Ozick, C.
The **foreign** correspondent. Furst, A.
FOREIGN INVESTMENTS
See also Investments; Multinational corporations
FOREIGN POPULATION *See* Immigrants; Immigration and emigration; Minorities; Noncitizens; Population
Foreign soil and other stories. Clarke, M. B.
FOREIGN STUDENTS
See also Students
FOREIGN VISITORS
Palahniuk, C. Pygmy
Silber, J. The size of the world
FOREIGN WORKERS
Unnikrishnan, D. Temporary people
Foreigner. Cherryh, C. J.
The **foreigners.** Swann, M.
Foreigners. Phillips, C.
FOREIGNERS *See* Immigrants; Noncitizens
FORENSIC ANTHROPOLOGISTS
Elkins, A. J. Dying on the vine
FORENSIC SCIENCES
Griffiths, E. The house at sea's end

Robertson, I. Anatomy of murder
FORENSIC SCIENTISTS
Abu-Jaber, D. Origin
Black, L. Takeover
Gardiner, M. The Dirty Secrets Club
Hart, E. Lake of sorrows
Lindsay, J. P. Dearly devoted Dexter
Forensic songs. McCormack, M.
FOREORDINATION *See* Predestination
The **forest.** Rutherfurd, E.
FOREST ANIMALS
See also Animals
FOREST CONSERVATION -- SOUTH AFRICA
Mason, R. Who killed Piet Barol?
Forest dark. Krauss, N.
FOREST ECOLOGY
See also Ecology
FOREST FIRES
See also Fires
FORESTS AND FORESTRY
Catling, B. The Erstwhile
Mason, R. Who killed Piet Barol?
Proulx, A. Barkskins
Forever. Hamill, P.
Forever free. Haldeman, J. W.
Forever peace. Haldeman, J. W.
The **forever** war. Haldeman, J. W.
Forever Your Earl. Leigh, E.
Forever, interrupted. Reid, T. J.
The **forge** of God. Bear, G.
Forged in desire. Jackson, B.
The **forger.** Watkins, P.
Forgery. Murray, S.
FORGERY
See also Crime; Fraud; Impostors and imposture
Theroux, M. Strange bodies
The **forgery** of Venus. Gruber, M.
FORGERY OF WORKS OF ART
Goddard, R. Long time coming
Gruber, M. The forgery of Venus
Watkins, P. The forger
FORGERY OF WORKS OF ART *See* Art -- Forgeries
Forgetfulness. Just, W. S.
FORGETFULNESS
See also Memory; Personality
Forgive me. Ward, A. E.
The **forgiven.** Osborne, L.
FORGIVENESS
Woodruff, L. Those we love most
The **forgotten.** Kellerman, F.
The **forgotten.** Wiesel, E.
The **forgotten** affairs of youth. McCall Smith, A.
Forgotten country. Chung, C.
The forgotten gods [series]
Pinborough, S. A matter of blood
The **forgotten** waltz. Enright, A.
FORMER NUNS *See* Ex-nuns
FORMER PRIESTS *See* Ex-priests
The **forsaken.** Atkins, A.
The **Forsyte** saga. Galsworthy, J.
FORT HOOD (TEX.)
Fallon, S. You know when the men are gone
The **fortress** of solitude. Lethem, J.
Fortunate son. Mosley, W.
FORTUNE *See* Fate and fatalism; Probabilities; Success
FORTUNE
Browne, S. G. Lucky bastard
Livesey, M. The house on Fortune Street
FORTUNE HUNTERS
Brockway, C. The golden season
Fortune smiles. Johnson, A.
The **fortune** teller's daughter. Wilson, S.
FORTUNE TELLING
Bishop, A. Written in red
Engelmann, K. The Stockholm Octavo
Fortune's Rocks. Shreve, A.
FORTUNE-TELLERS
The immortalists
The **Fortunes.** Davies, P. H.
FORTUNES *See* Income; Wealth
The **forty** days of Musa Dagh. Werfel, F.
Forward the Foundation. Asimov, I.
FOSSIL HOMINIDS
See also Archeology; Fossils
FOSTER CHILDREN
Alexie, S. Flight
Austen, J. Mansfield Park
Diffenbaugh, V. The language of flowers
Eliot, G. Silas Marner
Fagan, J. The panopticon
Fitch, J. White oleander
Gibbons, K. Ellen Foster
Hurwitz, G. You're next
Mapson Solomon's oak
March, W. The bad seed
Rinehart, S. Built in a day
Teran, A. Ana of California
FOSTER CHILDREN
See also Children
FOSTER GRANDPARENTS
See also Grandparents; Volunteer work
FOSTER HOME CARE
Gibbons, K. Ellen Foster
Gibbons, K. The life all around me by Ellen Foster
FOTONOVELAS
See also Comic books, strips, etc.
Foucault's pendulum. Eco, U.
Foundation. Asimov, I.
Foundation [series]
Asimov, I. Forward the Foundation
Asimov, I. Foundation
Asimov, I. Foundation and earth
Asimov, I. Foundation and empire
Asimov, I. Foundation's edge

Asimov, I. Prelude to Foundation
Asimov, I. Second Foundation
Foundation and earth. Asimov, I.
Foundation and empire. Asimov, I.
Foundation's edge. Asimov, I.
Foundation's fear. Benford, G.
FOUNDATIONS (ENDOWMENTS) *See* Endowments
FOUNDLINGS *See* Orphans
FOUNDLINGS
Grey, Z. Woman of the frontier
Stedman, M. L. The light between oceans
The **Fountain** of St. James Court. Naslund, S. J.
The **fountainhead.** Rand, A.
Four blind mice. Patterson, J.
The **four** corners of the sky. Malone, M.
Four freedoms. Crowley, J.
Four new messages. Cohen, J.
Four Nights With the Duke. James, E.
Four novels of the 1960s. Dick, P. K.
Four past midnight. King, S.
Four sisters, all queens. Jones, S.
Four souls. Erdrich, L.
Four spirits. Naslund, S. J.
Four ways to forgiveness. Le Guin, U. K.
The **fourth** book of lost swords: Farslayer's story. Saberhagen, F.
Fourth Day. Sharp, Z.
The **fourth** deadly sin. Sanders, L.
FOURTH DIMENSION
See also Mathematics
The **fourth** Durango. Thomas, R.
The **fourth** hand. Irving, J.
FOURTH OF JULY
Lockridge, R. Raintree County
The **fourth** wall. Williams, W. J.
FOX HUNTING
The blue fox
Foxfire. Oates, J. C.
The **fractal** prince. Rajaniemi, H.
FRACTIONS
See also Arithmetic; Mathematics
FRACTURED FAIRY TALES
See also Fairy tales; Parodies
Fractures. Herrin, L.
Fragile beasts. O'Dell, T.
Fragile things. Gaiman, N.
Fragrant Harbor. Lanchester, J.
Frames. Estleman, L. D.
Framley parsonage. Trollope, A.
FRANCE
Black, C. Murder below Montparnasse
Black, C. Murder in the rue de Paradis
Black, C. Murder on the Champ de Mars
Bourne, J. The black hawk
George, N. The little Paris bookshop
Guene, F. Kiffe kiffe tomorrow
Handke, P. Don Juan
Hannah, K. The nightingale
Lanchester, J. The debt to pleasure
Manchette Fatale
The map and the territory
Morais, R. C. The hundred-foot journey
Pope, B. C. The blood of Lorraine
Submission
Three strong women
Tremain, R. Trespass
Walker, M. The crowded grave
FRANCE -- 12TH CENTURY
Rice, A. Angel time
FRANCE -- 14TH CENTURY
Pears, I. The dream of Scipio
FRANCE -- 15TH CENTURY
Cutter, K. The maid
Haasse, H. S. In a dark wood wandering
Twain, M. Personal recollections of Joan of Arc
FRANCE -- 16TH CENTURY
Riley, J. M. The serpent garden
FRANCE -- 1789-1799
Dickens, C. A tale of two cities
Forester, C. S. Lord Hornblower
Orczy, E. The Scarlet Pimpernel
Sabatini, R. Scaramouche
FRANCE -- 1799-1815
Forester, C. S. Lord Hornblower
FRANCE -- 17TH CENTURY
Dumas, A. The man in the iron mask
Dumas, A. The three musketeers
Dumas, A. Twenty years after
Laker, R. To dance with kings
FRANCE -- 1815-1848
Stendhal The red and the black
Stott, R. The coral thief
FRANCE -- 1848-1870
Werfel, F. The song of Bernadette
FRANCE -- 1870-1940
Celine Journey to the end of the night
Faulkner, W. A fable
FRANCE -- 18TH CENTURY
Davis, K. Versailles
Dickens, C. A tale of two cities
Koen, K. Through a glass darkly
Laker, R. To dance with kings
Naslund, S. J. Abundance
Suskind, P. Perfume: the story of a murderer
FRANCE -- 1940-1945
Bates, H. E. Fair stood the wind for France
Faulks, S. Charlotte Gray
Follett, K. Jackdaws
Greene, G. The tenth man
Nemirovsky, I. Suite Francaise
Pears, I. The dream of Scipio
Sartre, J. P. Troubled sleep
FRANCE -- 19TH CENTURY
Flaubert, G. Sentimental education

Hugo, V. Les miserables
Sand, G. Lelia
Sand, G. Marianne
Vreeland, S. Luncheon of The Boating Party
FRANCE -- 20TH CENTURY
Colette The complete Claudine
Harris, J. Chocolat
Proust, M. The captive [and] The fugitive
Proust, M. The Guermantes way
Proust, M. Remembrance of things past
Proust, M. Sodom and Gomorrah
Proust, M. Time regained
Sartre, J. P. The reprieve
FRANCE -- AIX-EN-PROVENCE
Kay, G. G. Ysabel
FRANCE -- BRITTANY
Stewart, M. The crystal cave
FRANCE -- GASCONY
Dumas, A. The three musketeers
FRANCE -- HISTORY -- 1589-1789, BOURBONS
Koen, K. Before Versailles
FRANCE -- HISTORY -- 1789-1799, REVOLUTION
See also Revolutions
FRANCE -- HISTORY -- 1789-1799, REVOLUTION
Miller, A. Pure
FRANCE -- HISTORY -- 1799-1815
Moore, C. Sacre bleu
Putney, M. J. No longer a gentleman
Willig, L. The secret history of the pink carnation
FRANCE -- HISTORY -- 1815-1914
Stendhal The red and the black
FRANCE -- HISTORY -- GERMAN OCCUPATION, 1940-1945
Belfoure, C. The Paris Architect
The Book of Harlan
De Rosnay, T. Sarah's key
Doerr, A. All the light we cannot see
Faulks, S. Charlotte Gray
Follett, K. Jackdaws
Steiner, P. The resistance
FRANCE -- KINGS AND RULERS
Koen, K. Before Versailles
FRANCE -- PARIS
Bolano, R. Monsieur Pain
Cosse, L. A novel bookstore
Dumas, A. Camille
The elegance of the hedgehog
Johnson, D. Le mariage
Kostova, E. The swan thieves
Krantz, J. Mistral's daughter
MacInnes, H. The Venetian affair
McLain, P. The Paris wife
Never any end to Paris
Orringer, J. The invisible bridge
Ozick, C. Foreign bodies
Powell, J. The breaking of eggs
Truong, M. The book of salt
Vargas Llosa, M. The bad girl
Watkins, P. The forger
White, E. The married man
FRANCE -- PARIS -- 15TH CENTURY
Hugo, V. The hunchback of Notre Dame
FRANCE -- PARIS -- 18TH CENTURY
Dickens, C. A tale of two cities
Sabatini, R. Scaramouche
FRANCE -- PARIS -- 19TH CENTURY
Balzac, H. d. Cousin Bette
Balzac, H. d. Pere Goriot (Old Goriot)
Dumas, A. The Count of Monte Cristo
Zola, E. Nana
FRANCE -- PARIS -- 20TH CENTURY
Baldwin, J. Giovanni's room
Barnes, D. Nightwood
Beauvoir, S. d. The mandarins
Cortazar, J. Hopscotch
Dumas, A. Camille
Gide, A. The counterfeiters (Les faux-monnayeurs)
Hemingway, E. The sun also rises
Makine, A. Dreams of my Russian summers
Marshall, P. The fisher king
McCarthy, M. Birds of America
Miller, A. Oxygen
Miller, H. Tropic of Cancer
Remarque, E. M. Arch of triumph
Rhys, J. Quartet
Richler, M. Barney's version
Sartre, J. P. The age of reason
Truong, M. The book of salt
Watkins, P. The forger
FRANCE -- PROVENCE
Mayle, P. Hotel Pastis
Pears, I. The dream of Scipio
FRANCE -- RURAL LIFE
Balzac, H. d. The country doctor
Bates, H. E. Fair stood the wind for France
Godden, R. The greengage summer
Harris, J. Chocolat
Harris, J. Five quarters of the orange
Nemirovsky, I. Fire in the blood
Proust, M. Swann's way
Proust, M. Within a budding grove
Sartre, J. P. Nausea
Stewart, M. The crystal cave
Stewart, M. Nine coaches waiting
Texier, C. Victorine
Trevanian The summer of Katya
FRANCE -- SAINT-TROPEZ
Steel, D. Sunset in St. Tropez
FRANCE -- VERSAILLES
Davis, K. Versailles
Laker, R. To dance with kings
Naslund, S. J. Abundance
FRANCE, SOUTHERN
Longworth, M. L. Murder in the Rue Dumas

Frances and Bernard. Bauer, C.
FRANCHISE *See* Citizenship; Elections; Suffrage
The **Franchise** affair. Tey, J.
FRANCISCANS
See also Monasticism and religious orders
Frank Bascombe [series]
Ford, R. Let Me Be Frank With You
Frank, Anne, 1929-1945
About
Lourie, R. A hatred for tulips
Frankenstein in Baghdad. Saadawi, A.
FRANKENSTEIN'S MONSTER (FICTIONAL CHARACTER)
See also Fictional characters
Sheck, L. A monster's notes
Frankenstein; or, The modern Prometheus. Shelley, M. W.
FRANKLIN, BATTLE OF, FRANKLIN, TENN., 1864
Hicks, R. The widow of the south
Franklin, Benjamin, 1706-1790
About
Morrow, J. The last witchfinder
Franklin, Jane Griffin, Lady, 1792-1875
About
Flanagan, R. Wanting
Franklin, John Sir, 1786-1847
About
Flanagan, R. Wanting
Simmons, D. The terror
Vollmann, W. T. The rifles
Franny & Zooey. Salinger, J. D.
FRATRICIDE
Cheever, J. Falconer
Wroblewski, D. The story of Edgar Sawtelle
FRAUD
Greaves, C. Hush money
Hart, B. The bully of order
Iles, G. Third degree
Freaky Deaky. Leonard, E.
Frederick I, Holy Roman Emperor, ca. 1123-1190
About
Eco, U. Baudolino
FREE AFRICAN AMERICANS -- NEW YORK (STATE) -- NEW YORK
Faye, L. Seven for a secret
Free falling, as if in a dream.
Free fire. Box, C. J.
A **free** life. Ha Jin
A **free** man of color. Hambly, B.
FREE VERSE
See also Poetry
The **free** world. Bezmozgis, D.
FREEDMEN
Jiles, P. The color of lightning
Leveen, L. The secrets of Mary Bowser
Pitts, L. Freeman
Rawles, N. My Jim
Freedom. Franzen, J.
FREEDOM OF CONSCIENCE
See also Conscience; Freedom; Toleration
FREEDOM OF INFORMATION -- UNITED STATES -- HANDBOOKS, MANUALS, ETC.
Intellectual Freedom Manual
Freedom's landing. McCaffrey, A.
Freedomland. Price, R.
Freeman. Pitts, L.
FREEMASONS
See also Secret societies
Freida Klein [series]
French, N. Waiting for Wednesday
FREIGHT
See also Maritime law; Materials handling; Railroads; Transportation
FRENCH -- ALGERIA
Camus, A. The stranger
FRENCH -- EGYPT
Roiphe, A. R. An imperfect lens
FRENCH -- ENGLAND
Du Maurier, D. Frenchman's Creek
FRENCH -- INDOCHINA
Texier, C. Victorine
FRENCH -- IRELAND
Flanagan, T. The year of the French
FRENCH -- POLAND
Furst, A. The spies of Warsaw
FRENCH -- RUSSIA
Makine, A. Dreams of my Russian summers
FRENCH -- UNITED STATES
Carey, P. Parrot and Olivier in America
Cather, W. Death comes for the archbishop
FRENCH FICTION -- TRANSLATIONS INTO ENGLISH
Conde, M. I, Tituba, black witch of Salem
Dumas, A. The three musketeers
The elegance of the hedgehog
Flaubert, G. Madame Bovary
Houellebecq, M. The possibility of an island
Life
Maalouf, A. Balthasar's odyssey
Makine, A. Dreams of my Russian summers
Makine, A. Music of a life
Makine, A. The woman who waited
Makine, A. The life of an unknown man
Manchette Fatale
Moulessehoul, M. The swallows of Kabul
Nemirovsky, I. Fire in the blood
Nemirovsky, I. Suite Francaise
Perec, G. A void
FRENCH LANGUAGE
See also Language and languages; Romance languages
FRENCH LANGUAGE -- DICTIONARIES -- ENGLISH
See also Encyclopedias and dictionaries
The **French** lieutenant's woman. Fowles, J.
FRENCH LITERATURE
Modiano, P. Suspended sentences
FRENCH POETRY

See also French literature; Poetry
Frenchman's Creek. Du Maurier, D.
The **frenzy** way. Lamberson, G.
Fresh complaint. Eugenides, J.
FRESHWATER ECOLOGY
See also Ecology
Freud, Sigmund, 1856-1939
About
Meyer, N. The seven-per-cent solution
Rubenfeld, J. The death instinct
Skibell, J. A curable romantic
Thomas, D. M. The white hotel
Freytag-Loringhoven, Elsa von, Baroness, 1874-1927
About
Steinke, R. Holy skirts
Friday. Tournier, M.
Friday nights. Trollope, J.
Fried green tomatoes at the Whistle-Stop Cafe. Flagg, F.
Frieda Klein mysteries [series]
French, N. Blue Monday
French, N. Thursday's children
A **friend** of Mr. Lincoln. Harrigan, S.
Friend of my youth. Munro, A.
A **friend** of the family. Grodstein, L.
The **friendly** persuasion. West, J.
FRIENDS *See* Friendship
The **friends** of Eddie Coyle. Higgins, G. V.
Friendship. Gould, E.
FRIENDSHIP
Arsenault, E. In search of the Rose notes
Barnes, J. The sense of an ending
Bauermeister, E. Joy for beginners
Beard, J. A. In Zanesville
The big green tent
Binchy, M. Circle of friends
Blume, J. Summer sisters
Brookner, A. Brief lives
Brunt, C. R. Tell the wolves I'm home
Burke, S. Into the Savage Country
Butler, N. The Hearts of Men
Carey, P. Parrot and Olivier in America
Cargill, C. R. Dreams and Shadows
Carlson, R. Five skies
Chabon, M. Telegraph Avenue
Chang, L. S. All is forgotten, nothing is lost
Chaudhuri, A. Odysseus Abroad
Cleave, C. Little Bee
Coe, J. The Rotters' Club
Colwin, L. A big storm knocked it over
The confidant
Conlon, E. Red on red
Conroy, P. South of Broad
Dallas, S. The Persian Pickle Club
Dixon, S. Old friends
Doig, I. The bartender's tale
Doig, I. Dancing at the Rascal Fair
Edgerton, C. The night train
Ellis, B. E. Imperial bedrooms
Erdrich, L. The Beet Queen
Evison, J. The revised fundamentals of caregiving
Faverón Patriau, G. The Antiquarian
Feldman, E. Next to love
Franklin, T. Crooked letter, crooked letter
Frayn, M. Spies
Fuentes, C. Destiny and desire
Gaitskill, M. Veronica
Gardam, J. The flight of the maidens
Garner, H. The spare room
Giordano, P. The solitude of prime numbers
Goddard, R. Into the blue
Gordimer, N. No time like the present
Gordon, M. Final payments
Gottlieb, E. Now you see him
Gould, E. Friendship
Gowdy, B. The romantic
Grant, L. We had it so good
Grumbach, D. The book of knowledge
Gurganus, A. Local souls
Guterson, D. The other
Hage, R. De Niro's game
Harris, E. L. If this world were mine
Harvey, M. Brighton
Herlihy, J. L. Midnight cowboy
Higashino, K. Malice
Highsmith, P. The boy who followed Ripley
Hilderbrand, E. Silver girl
Hollinghurst, A. The stranger's child
Horlock, M. The book of lies
Hosseini, K. The kite runner
I refuse
Iles, G. Turning angel
Jacobson, H. The Finkler question
Jakes, J. North and South
John, E. Born on a Tuesday
Johnson, B. More of this world or maybe another
Joyce, R. The unlikely pilgrimage of Harold Fry
Just, W. S. Rodin's debutante
Kardos, M. The Three-Day Affair
Keyes, M. Last Chance Saloon
Kiefer, C. The infinite tides
Kimani, P. Dance of the Jakaranda
Klein, R. The moth diaries
Knowles, J. A separate peace
Kutsukake, L. The translation of love
Lally, C. Eggshells
Larsen, N. Passing
Lebrecht, N. The song of names
Lehane, D. Mystic river
Lethem, J. The fortress of solitude
Lippman, L. The most dangerous thing
Lord, B. B. The middle heart
The man with the compound eyes
Mapson Bad Girl Creek
Matheson, R. Hunted past reason

Mawer, S. The fall
McCormick, C. Desert boys
McCracken, E. Niagara Falls all over again
McDermid, V. The distant echo
McEwan, I. Amsterdam
McMillan, T. Waiting to exhale
Medlicott, J. A. The ladies of Covington send their love
Miller, S. The senator's wife
Monette, P. Afterlife
Moore, L. Bark
Moriarty, L. Truly madly guilty
Morrison, T. Sula
Mosley, W. RL's dream
Murdoch, I. The book and the brotherhood
Murr, N. The perfect man
Noble, K. The Game and the Governess
Nunez, S. The last of her kind
Oe, K. The changeling
Olsson, L. Astrid & Veronika
O'Neill, J. At swim, two boys
Packer, A. Songs without words
Palwick, S. Mending the moon
Pearson, A. I think I love you
Pelecanos, G. P. The big blowdown
Phillips, C. A distant shore
Picoult, J. The Storyteller
Pierson, D. C. The boy who couldn't sleep and never had to
Pilcher, R. Coming home
Pilcher, R. Winter solstice
Plain, B. Looking back
Powers, K. The yellow birds
Pym, B. Jane and Prudence
Raeder, L. Black iris
Raeder, L. Cam girl
Raymond, J. The half-life
Rich, N. The mayor's tongue
Romano-Lax, A. The Spanish bow
Rosenfeld, L. I'm so happy for you
Ross-Macdonald, M. For they shall inherit
Row, J. Your face in mine
Rush, N. Subtle bodies
Russo, R. Bridge of sighs
Samuel, B. No place like home
Schlink, B. The weekend
Schwarz, C. All is vanity
Smith, A. Autumn
Smith, Z. Swing time
The sound of things falling
Steel, D. Sunset in St. Tropez
Stegner, W. E. Crossing to safety
Steinbeck, J. Of mice and men
Steinbeck, J. Tortilla Flat
Swift, G. Last orders
Taylor, E. Mrs. Palfrey at the Claremont
Trollope, J. The best of friends
Trollope, J. The men and the girls
Tucker, T. Over and under
Two she-bears
Tyler, A. Digging to America
Umrigar, T. The world we found
Valdes-Rodriguez, A. Dirty girls on top
Weiner, J. Little earthquakes
Wells, R. Divine secrets of the Ya-Ya Sisterhood
Wharton, W. Birdy
White, E. Jack Holmes and his friend
Wiggins, M. Evidence of things unseen
Williams, A. J. Down from Cascom Mountain
Wilson, A. Flatscreen
Winman, S. When God was a rabbit
Winslow, D. The kings of cool
Wolitzer, M. Surrender, Dorothy
Woodson, J. Another Brooklyn
Wuertz, Y. G. Everything belongs to us
Yanagihara, H. A little life

FRIENDSHIP -- GRAPHIC NOVELS
Merey, I. a + e 4ever

FRIENDSHIP IN YOUTH
Collins, C. The gamal

Frog.
Frog music. Donoghue, E.
A **frolic** of his own. Gaddis, W.
From bondage. Roth, H.
From here to eternity. Jones, J.
From Russia, with love. Fleming, I.
From the earth to the moon, and Round the moon. Verne, J.
From the terrace. O'Hara, J.
From time to time. Finney, J.

FRONTIER AND PIONEER LIFE
Evison, J. West of here
Groom, W. El Paso
Ivey, E. The snow child
Keesey, A. Little century
Kirkpatrick, J. This road we traveled
Pynchon, T. Mason & Dixon
Richter, C. The light in the forest
Sargent, C. Museum of human beings
Schanbacher, G. Crossing Purgatory
Thom, J. A. The red heart
Wheeler, R. S. Eclipse

FRONTIER AND PIONEER LIFE -- ALASKA
Brand, M. Chinook
Ivey, E. The snow child
Ivey, E. To the bright edge of the world

FRONTIER AND PIONEER LIFE -- ARIZONA
Grey, Z. Woman of the frontier
Turner, N. E. These is my words

FRONTIER AND PIONEER LIFE -- AUSTRALIA
Grenville, K. The secret river
Malouf, D. Remembering Babylon
Nordhoff, C. Botany Bay

FRONTIER AND PIONEER LIFE -- CANADA
Adamson, G. The outlander
Freedman, B. Mrs. Mike
Urquhart, J. Away

Vanderhaeghe, G. The last crossing
FRONTIER AND PIONEER LIFE -- COLORADO
Michener, J. A. Centennial
FRONTIER AND PIONEER LIFE -- KANSAS
Durham, D. A. Gabriel's story
FRONTIER AND PIONEER LIFE -- MONTANA
Williamson, P. Heart of the west
Williamson, P. The outsider
FRONTIER AND PIONEER LIFE -- NEBRASKA
Cather, W. My Antonia
Cather, W. O pioneers!
FRONTIER AND PIONEER LIFE -- NEW YORK (STATE)
Cooper, J. F. The last of the Mohicans
Edmonds, W. D. Drums along the Mohawk
FRONTIER AND PIONEER LIFE -- NEW ZEALAND
Goudge, E. Green Dolphin Street
FRONTIER AND PIONEER LIFE -- OHIO
Richter, C. The awakening land
Swerling, B. Shadowbrook
FRONTIER AND PIONEER LIFE -- OHIO RIVER VALLEY
Settle, M. L. O Beulah Land
FRONTIER AND PIONEER LIFE -- PENNSYLVANIA
Liss, D. The whiskey rebels
FRONTIER AND PIONEER LIFE -- SOUTH DAKOTA
Dexter, P. Deadwood
Rolvaag, O. E. Giants in the earth
Rolvaag, O. E. Peder Victorious
FRONTIER AND PIONEER LIFE -- SOUTHWEST, NEW
Groom, W. El Paso
FRONTIER AND PIONEER LIFE -- VIRGINIA
L'Amour, L. To the far blue mountains
FRONTIER AND PIONEER LIFE -- WESTERN STATES
Berger, T. Little Big Man
Coldsmith, D. Tallgrass
Guthrie, A. B. The big sky
Guthrie, A. B. The way West
Holland, C. An ordinary woman
Johnson, D. Train dreams
L'Amour, L. End of the drive
McMurtry, L. Boone's Lick
McMurtry, L. Buffalo girls
McMurtry, L. Comanche moon
McMurtry, L. Dead man's walk
McMurtry, L. Lonesome dove
McMurtry, L. Zeke and Ned
Portis, C. True grit
Schaefer, J. W. The collected stories of Jack Schaefer
Vanderhaeghe, G. The last crossing
Willard, T. Buffalo soldiers
FRONTIER AND PIONEER LIFE -- WYOMING
L'Amour, L. Bendigo Shafter
Frontier justice. Brooks, B.
FROZEN FOODS
See also Food
FROZEN HUMAN EMBRYOS
Picoult, J. Sing you home
FRUIT
See also Food; Plants
FRUIT CULTURE
See also Agriculture; Fruit; Gardening; Horticulture; Trees
FRUIT GROWERS
Coplin, A. The orchardist
The **frumious** Bandersnatch. McBain, E.
FRUSTRATION
See also Attitude (Psychology); Emotions
Fugate, Caril Ann
About
Ward, L. Outside valentine
Fugitive pieces. Michaels, A.
FUGITIVE SLAVES
See also Slaves
FUGITIVE SLAVES
Conklin, T. The house girl
Crafts, H. The bondswomans narrative
Deón, N. Grace
McBride, J. The good lord bird
McBride, J. Song yet sung
Perkins-Valdez, D. Wench
Priest, C. Clementine
Reed, I. Flight to Canada
Tryon, T. In the fire of spring
Whitehead, C. The underground railroad
FUGITIVES
Doiron, P. The poacher's son
Furnivall, K. The red scarf
Meek, J. The people's act of love
Piercy, M. Vida
Reiken, F. Day for night
Riordan, R. Cold Springs
Saint, H. F. Memoirs of an invisible man
Spark, M. Aiding and abetting
Spiotta, D. Eat the document
Woodrell, D. Winter's bone
Wray, J. Canaan's tongue
FUGITIVES FROM JUSTICE
See also Criminals
FUGITIVES FROM JUSTICE
Dreyer, E. Once a Rake
Lutz, L. The Passenger
Powers, R. Orfeo
Taylor, A. The marble orchard
The **full** cupboard of life. McCall Smith, A.
Full dark, no stars. King, S.
Fuller, R. Buckminster, 1895-1983
About
Bognanni, P. The house of tomorrow
Fun and games. Swierczynski, D.
Fun with problems. Stone, R.
FUNCTIONS
See also Differential equations; Mathematical analysis; Mathematics; Set theory
FUND RAISING

Lipsyte, S. The ask
FUNDAMENTALISM
Atwood, M. The Handmaid's tale
Hamid, M. The reluctant fundamentalist
Nunez, S. Salvation city
FUNDAMENTALISTS
Cash, W. A land more kind than home
Nunez, S. Salvation city
Paretsky, S. Bleeding Kansas
Winterson, J. Oranges are not the only fruit
FUNERAL CUSTOMS AND RITES *See* Funeral rites and ceremonies
FUNERAL DIRECTORS *See* Undertakers and undertaking
Funeral games. Renault, M.
Funeral in blue. Perry, A.
FUNERAL RITES AND CEREMONIES
Agee, J. A death in the family
Duncan, G. Death of an ordinary man
Faulkner, W. As I lay dying
Lipman, E. The dearly departed
Rojstaczer, S. The Mathematician's Shiva
St. Aubyn, E. At last
Styron, W. Lie down in darkness
Tyler, A. Breathing lessons
Waugh, E. The loved one
Welty, E. Losing battles
Welty, E. The optimist's daughter
FUNERAL RITES AND CEREMONIES
See also Manners and customs; Rites and ceremonies
FUNNIES *See* Comic books, strips, etc.
Funny girl. Hornby, N.
Funny once. Nelson, A.
FUR TRADE
Guthrie, A. B. The big sky
FUR TRADERS
Sargent, C. Museum of human beings
FURBEARING ANIMALS
See also Animals; Economic zoology
FUTURE
Amis, M. London fields
Anderson, P. Genesis
Asaro, C. Primary inversion
Asimov, I. Forward the Foundation
Asimov, I. Foundation
Asimov, I. Foundation and earth
Asimov, I. Foundation and empire
Asimov, I. Foundation's edge
Asimov, I. Prelude to Foundation
Asimov, I. Second Foundation
Atwood, M. The Handmaid's tale
Atwood, M. The year of the flood
Auster, P. In the country of last things
Bacigalupi, P. The windup girl
Banks, I. Matter
Barnes, J. The armies of memory
Bear, G. Anvil of stars
Bear, G. The forge of God
Benford, G. Foundation's fear
Benford, G. Timescape
Brunner, J. Stand on Zanzibar
Cherryh, C. J. Foreigner
Cline, E. Ready player one
Conn, B. The fixed stars
Crace, J. The pesthouse
Cunningham, M. Specimen days
Delany, S. R. Stars in my pocket like grains of sand
Doctorow, C. Down and out in the Magic Kindgom
Egan, G. Zendegi
Fuentes, C. The eagle's throne
Gibson, W. Neuromancer
Goonan, K. A. Light music
Grant, M. Feed
Haldeman, J. W. The coming
Haldeman, J. W. Forever free
Haldeman, J. W. Forever peace
Haldeman, J. W. The forever war
Hamilton, P. F. The dreaming void
Heinlein, R. A. The moon is a harsh mistress
Helprin, M. Winter's tale
Herbert, F. Dune
Herbert, F. Dune messiah
Hoban, R. Riddley Walker
Hughes, M. Hespira
Huxley, A. Brave new world
Jordan, H. When she woke
Larson, N. The Dewey Decimal system
Lessing, D. M. The memoirs of a survivor
Lessing, D. M. Shikasta
Marion, I. Warm bodies
McCarthy, C. The road
McDonald, I. The Dervish House
McDonald, I. River of gods
McHugh, M. F. Nekropolis
McMullen, S. Souls in the great machine
Miller, W. M. A canticle for Leibowitz
Moon, E. The speed of dark
Morgan, R. K. Altered carbon
Morgan, R. K. Broken angels
Niven, L. The Mote in God's Eye
Niven, L. Saturn's race
Noon, J. Vurt
Nunez, S. Salvation city
Okorafor, N. Who fears death
Palwick, S. Shelter
Percy, W. Love in the ruins
Pohl, F. All the lives he led
Pohl, F. Beyond the blue event horizon
Pohl, F. The boy who would live forever
Pohl, F. Gateway
Pohl, F. Heechee rendezvous
Pohl, F. Man Plus
Pohl, F. The space merchants
Porter, H. The bell ringers
Raban, J. Surveillance

Robinson, K. S. Antarctica
Robson, J. Keeping it real
Rucker, R. v. B. Hylozoic
Rucker, R. v. B. Postsingular
Russell, M. D. Children of God
Russell, M. D. The sparrow
Sagan, C. Contact
Self, W. The Book of Dave
Shteyngart, G. Super sad true love story
Simmons, D. Endymion
Simmons, D. The rise of Endymion
The slynx
Stephenson, N. The diamond age
Sterling, B. Holy fire
Stross, C. Accelerando
Stross, C. Glasshouse
Stross, C. Saturn's children
Tepper, S. S. The gate to Women's Country
Tepper, S. S. The visitor
Theroux, M. Far north
Updike, J. Toward the end of time
Varley, J. Rolling thunder
Vinge, V. Rainbows end
Vonnegut, K. Cat's cradle
Vonnegut, K. Galapagos
Vonnegut, K. Hocus pocus
Wallace, D. F. Infinite jest
Weber, D. Off Armageddon Reef
Weldon, F. Chalcot Crescent
West, M. L. The clowns of God
West, M. L. Lazarus
Wilhelm, K. Where late the sweet birds sang
Willis, C. To say nothing of the dog; or, How we found the bishop's bird stump at last
Wilson, D. H. Robopocalyse
Wilson, R. C. Julian Comstock
Wolfe, G. The Citadel of the Autarch
Wolfe, G. The claw of the conciliator
Wolfe, G. Home fires
Wolfe, G. The shadow of the torturer
Wolfe, G. The sword of the Lictor
Wolfe, G. The Urth of the new sun
Zamiatin, E. I. We
Zelazny, R. Lord of light
The **future** has a past. Cooper, J. C.
Future home of the living god. Erdrich, L.
The **Future** Is Japanese.
FUTURE LIFE
Brockmeier, K. The brief history of the dead
Farmer, P. J. The fabulous riverboat
Maguire, G. Hiddensee
Pyper, A. The damned
FUTURE LIFE
See also Death; Eschatology
FUTURE SHOCK *See* Culture conflict
FUTURES
See also Investments; Securities
FUTURISM (ART)
See also Art
FUTURISM
Kushner, R. The flamethrowers
Futuristic Violence and Fancy Suits. Wong, D.

G

G is for gumshoe. Grafton, S.
Gable, Clark, 1901-1960
About
Alcott, K. A touch of stardust
Gabriel's story. Durham, D. A.
Gabriela, clove and cinnamon. Amado, J.
Gad's Hall. Lofts, N.
GAELS *See* Celts
GAIA HYPOTHESIS
See also Biology; Earth; Ecology; Life (Biology)
Gaius Ruso [series]
Downie, R. Tabula Rasa
Galapagos. Vonnegut, K.
GALAPAGOS ISLANDS
Vonnegut, K. Galapagos
Galatea 2.2. Powers, R.
Galilei, Galileo, 1564-1642
About
Robinson, K. S. Galileo's dream
Galileo's dream. Robinson, K. S.
Gallatin Canyon. McGuane, T.
Gallow and Ragged [series]
Saintcrow, L. Trailer park fae
GALLOWAY, RUTH (FICTITIOUS CHARACTER)
Griffiths, E. The crossing places
Griffiths, E. A Dying Fall
Griffiths, E. The house at sea's end
Gallowglass. Vine, B.
Galore. Crummey, M.
The **Galton** case. Macdonald, R.
GALVESTON (TEX.)
Black, E. The drowning house
GAMACHE, ARMAND (FICTITIOUS CHARACTER)
Penny, L. The beautiful mystery
Penny, L. Bury your dead
Penny, L. Glass houses
Penny, L. A great reckoning
Penny, L. How the light gets in
Penny, L. The long way home
Penny, L. The nature of the beast
The **gamal.** Collins, C.
Gambit. Stout, R.
GAMBLERS
Russell, M. D. Doc
GAMBLING
Amado, J. Dona Flor and her two husbands
Atkins, A. White shadow
Dickens, C. The old curiosity shop
Fleming, I. Casino Royale

Francis, D. Even money
Higgins, G. V. The Digger's game
Iles, G. The devil's punchbowl
Johnson, D. Nobody move
Latour, J. The Havana World Series
O'Nan, S. The odds
Rigosi, G. Night bus
Westlake, D. E. Bad news
GAMBLING
See also Games
GAMBLING -- RHODE ISLAND
DeSilva, B. A Scourge of Vipers
The **game.** King, L. R.
GAME AND GAME BIRDS
See also Animals; Birds; Wildlife
The **Game** and the Governess. Noble, K.
A **game** of thrones. Martin, G. R. R.
Game over. Harrod-Eagles, C.
GAME PROTECTION
Box, C. J. Open season
Doiron, P. The poacher's son
GAME PROTECTION
See also Game and game birds; Hunting; Wildlife conservation
GAME RESERVES
See also Hunting; Wildlife conservation
GAME THEORY
See also Mathematical models; Mathematics; Probabilities
GAME WARDENS *See* Game protection
GAME WARDENS
Box, C. J. Force of nature
Box, C. J. Free fire
Box, C. J. Open season
Doiron, P. Bad Little Falls
Doiron, P. The poacher's son
The **games.** Kosmatka, T.
GAMES
Shan S. The girl who played go
GAMIFICATION
See also Games
GAMING *See* Gambling
GANGS
See also Criminals; Juvenile delinquency; Organized crime
GANGS
Barry, K. City of Bohane
Beverly, B. Dodgers
Coleman, R. F. Where it hurts
Grossman, D. Someone to run with
K'wan (Author) Animal
Mark, D. Original skin
Oates, J. C. Foxfire
Rosen, R. Dollface
Wray, J. Canaan's tongue
GANGS -- NIGERIA
John, E. Born on a Tuesday
A **gangster** and a gentleman. Diamond, D.
GANGSTER FILMS
See also Motion pictures
The **gangster** we are all looking for. Le, T. D. T.
Gangsterland. Goldberg, T.
GANGSTERS
Atkins, A. White shadow
Doctorow, E. L. Billy Bathgate
Faust, C. Choke hold
Gilmore, J. Golden country
Gruber, M. The book of air and shadows
Hallinan, T. Fields where they lay
Hunter, S. Hot Springs
Lashner, W. Kockroach
Leonard, E. Get Shorty
Parker, R. B. Double play
Shteyngart, G. The Russian debutante's handbook
Tanenbaum, R. Act of revenge
Turner, F. W. 1929
GANGSTERS *See* Gangs
GARDEN ECOLOGY
See also Ecology
Garden of beasts. Deaver, J.
A **garden** of earthly delights. Oates, J. C.
The **Garden** of Evening Mists. Tan, T. E.
The **garden** of evil. Hewson, D.
The **garden** of last days. Dubus, A.
Garden of lies. Goudge, E.
Garden of Lies. Quick, A.
The **Garden** of Rama. Clarke, A. C.
GARDEN ROOMS
See also Houses; Rooms
Garden Spells. Allen, S. A.
GARDENERS
Coetzee, J. M. Life & times of Michael K.
Kosinski, J. N. Being there
Visitation
GARDENS
Allen, S. A. Garden Spells
Tan, T. E. The Garden of Evening Mists
Gardens in the dunes. Silko, L.
The **gardens** of Kyoto. Walbert, K.
The **gargoyle.** Davidson, A.
The **gargoyle** hunters. Gill, J. F.
GARGOYLES
Gill, J. F. The gargoyle hunters
Gas City. Estleman, L. D.
A gaslight mystery [series]
Thompson, V. Murder on Fifth Avenue
A **gate** at the stairs. Moore, L.
Gate of the sun. Khoury, E.
The **gate** to Women's Country. Tepper, S. S.
Gateway. Pohl, F.
Gather the daughters. Melamed, J.
The **gathering.** Enright, A.
A **gathering** of old men. Gaines, E. J.
A **gathering** of shadows. Schwab, V. E.

Gathering of waters. McFadden, B. L.
Gaudy Night. Sayers, D. L.
Gauguin, Paul, 1848-1903
About
Maugham, W. S. The moon and sixpence
Vargas Llosa, M. The way to paradise
Gaulle, Charles de, 1890-1970
About
Forsyth, F. The day of the jackal
Gautama Buddha
About
Mishima, Y. The Temple of Dawn
GAY AUTHORS
See also Authors; Gay men
GAY LIBERATION MOVEMENT
See also Homosexuality
GAY MEN
Alenyikov, M. Ivan and Misha
Beach-Ferrara, J. Damn love
Boyne, J. The absolutist
Brunt, C. R. Tell the wolves I'm home
Crain, C. Necessary errors
Evaristo, B. Mr. Loverman
Greenwell, G. What belongs to you
Jones, J. S. The silence
Kramer, L. Search for My Heart
Mehta, R. Quarantine
Ostlund, L. After the Parade
White, E. Jack Holmes and his friend
GAY MEN
See also Gays; LGBT people; Men
GAY MEN -- ARAB COUNTIES
Haddad, S. Guapa
GAY MEN -- COMIC BOOKS, STRIPS, ETC
Cruse, H. The complete Wendel
GAY MEN -- CRIMES AGAINST
Harvey, J. Gone to ground
McGarrity, M. Everyone dies
McKinty, A. The cold cold ground
GAY MEN -- INDIA -- NĀGPUR
Festing, I. A. The birdkeeper
GAY TEENAGERS
Aciman, A. A. Call me by your name
Yates, C. J. Grist Mill Road
GAY YOUTH
See also Youth
GAY YOUTH
Cruse, H. The complete Wendel
GAYS
McCormick, C. Desert boys
GBH. Lewis, T.
Geek love. Dunn, K.
GEESE
See also Birds; Poultry
GEISHAS
Golden, A. Memoirs of a geisha
GEISHAS
See also Entertainers
The **Gemini** contenders. Ludlum, R.
GEMINI PROJECT
See also Orbital rendezvous (Space flight); Space flight
GEMS
See also Archeology; Art; Decoration and ornament; Engraving; Minerals
GENDER IDENTITY
See also Identity (Psychology)
GENDER IDENTITY
De Robertis, C. The gods of tango
Louis, É. The end of Eddy
GENDER ROLE
See also Sex; Sex differences (Psychology); Social role
GENDER ROLE
Winter, K. Annabel
GENEALOGY
Groff, L. The monsters of Templeton
The **general** and his labyrinth. Garcia Marquez, G.
The **general** of the dead army. Kadare, I.
GENERAL STORES
See also Retail trade; Stores
GENERALS
Bell, M. S. All souls' rising
Castellanos Moya, H. Tyrant memory
Charyn, J. Johnny One-Eye
De Bernieres, L. Birds without wings
Doctorow, E. L. The march
The Feast of the Goat
Forsyth, F. The day of the jackal
Gingrich, N. Grant comes east
Jakes, J. Savannah; or, A gift for Mr. Lincoln
Jones, D. C. The court-martial of George Armstrong Custer
McBride, J. Five-carat soul
McCullough, C. The first man in Rome
Mrazek, R. J. Unholy fire
Naipaul, V. S. A way in the world
Penman, S. K. Falls the shadow
Ricks, T. E. A soldier's duty
Roth, P. The plot against America
Shaara, J. Gods and generals
Shaara, J. Gone for soldiers
Shaara, J. The last full measure
GENERATION GAP *See* Conflict of generations
Generation loss. Hand, E.
GENERIC DRUGS
See also Drugs; Generic products
Generosity. Powers, R.
Genesis. Anderson, P.
GENETIC ENGINEERING
Bacigalupi, P. The windup girl
Gonzales, L. Lucy
Kosmatka, T. The games
Morgan, R. K. Thirteen
Newitz, A. Autonomous
Scalzi, J. The ghost brigades
Suárez, D. Change agent

Willis, C. Crosstalk
GENETIC INTERVENTION *See* Genetic engineering
GENETIC SURGERY *See* Genetic engineering
GENETICS
Crichton, M. Jurassic Park
DeMille, N. Plum Island
Herbert, F. Dune
Herbert, F. Dune messiah
Johansen, I. Long after midnight
Koontz, D. R. Watchers
Powers, R. Generosity
GENETICS -- RESEARCH
Simsion, G. The Rosie project
GENIES
Wecker, H. The Golem and the Jinni
The **genius.** Kellerman, J.
GENIUS
Bernhard, T. The loser
Macmillan, G. The perfect girl
Pessl, M. Special topics in calamity physics
Rand, A. The fountainhead
GENIUSES *See* Gifted people
GENOCIDE
Okorafor, N. Who fears death
GENOMES
See also Genetics
Gentileschi, Artemisia, 1593-ca. 1652
About
Vreeland, S. The passion of Artemesia
Gentleman Bastard [series]
Lynch, S. The lies of Locke Lamora
Lynch, S. Red seas under red skies
Gentleman captain. Davies, J. D.
A **Gentleman** in Moscow. Towles, A.
A **gentleman** of fortune, or, The suspicions of Miss Dido Kent. Dean, A.
Gentleman's agreement. Hobson, L. K. Z.
Gentlemen of space. Sher, I.
The **gentlemen's** hour. Winslow, D.
GENTRIFICATION
Coster, N. Halsey Street
GEOGRAPHICAL MYTHS
See also Mythology
GEOGRAPHICAL MYTHS
Siegel, J. Prospero's children
GEOGRAPHY -- DICTIONARIES
See also Encyclopedias and dictionaries
GEOLOGISTS
Hoeg, P. Smilla's sense of snow
Unsworth, B. Land of marvels
Verne, J. A journey to the centre of the earth
GEOLOGISTS
See also Scientists
GEOMETRY
See also Mathematics
The **geometry** of sisters. Rice, L.
GEORGIA
Child, L. Killing floor
Crews, H. A feast of snakes
Green, G. D. Ravens
Jackson, J. Between, Georgia
Mitcham, J. Sabbath Creek
Sams, F. Down town
Spencer, L. Morning glory
Walker, A. The third life of Grange Copeland
White, B. Quite a year for plums
GEORGIA -- 19TH CENTURY
Doctorow, E. L. The march
GEORGIA -- 20TH CENTURY
Bambara, T. C. The salt eaters
Caldwell, E. Tobacco road
Dexter, P. Paris Trout
McCullers, C. The member of the wedding
Siddons, A. R. Heartbreak Hotel
Smith, L. E. Strange fruit
Woods, S. Grass roots
Woods, S. Palindrome
GEORGIA -- ATLANTA
Ha Jin A free life
Hooper, K. Finding Laura
Jones, T. Silver sparrow
Wolfe, T. A man in full
GEORGIA -- SAVANNAH
Jakes, J. Savannah; or, A gift for Mr. Lincoln
GEORGIA -- SOCIAL LIFE AND CUSTOMS -- 19TH CENTURY
Rabb, J. Among the living
GERMAN AMERICANS
Erdrich, L. The Master Butchers Singing Club
Hegi, U. The vision of Emma Blau
The **German** bride. Hershon, J.
GERMAN FICTION -- 20TH CENTURY
Thelen, A. V. The island of second sight
GERMAN FICTION -- TRANSLATIONS INTO ENGLISH
Adler, H. G. Panorama
Bernhard, T. The loser
Bernhard, T. Woodcutters
Boll, H. The silent angel
The emigrants
Grass, G. The box
Grass, G. The call of the toad
Handke, P. Don Juan
Kehlmann, D. Fame
Keilson, H. Comedy in a minor key
Musil, R. The man without qualities
Schlink, B. Homecoming
Schlink, B. The reader
Schlink, B. The weekend
Schulze, I. New lives
Sebald, W. G. Vertigo
Stanisic, S. How the soldier repairs the gramophone
Walser, R. The assistant
GERMAN LANGUAGE
See also Language and languages

GERMAN REFUGEES
Remarque, E. M. Arch of triumph
Remarque, E. M. The night in Lisbon
GERMANS
Thelen, A. V. The island of second sight
GERMANS -- BRAZIL
Levin, I. The boys from Brazil
GERMANS -- CANADA
Norman, H. What is left the daughter
GERMANS -- CHINA
Reuss, F. Mohr
GERMANS -- DENMARK
Follett, K. Hornet flight
GERMANS -- ENGLAND
Follett, K. Eye of the needle
Higgins, J. The eagle has landed
GERMANS -- FRANCE
Remarque, E. M. Arch of triumph
GERMANS -- GREAT BRITAIN
Griffiths, E. The house at sea's end
GERMANS -- ISLANDS OF THE PACIFIC
Conrad, J. Victory
GERMANS -- NAMIBIA
Brink, A. P. The other side of silence
GERMANS -- POLAND
Uris, L. Mila 18
GERMANS -- RUSSIA
Anatoli, A. Babi Yar
Robbins, D. L. War of the rats
GERMANS -- SPAIN
Bolaño, R. The Third Reich
GERMANS -- UNITED STATES
Hershon, J. The German bride
Oates, J. C. The gravedigger's daughter
Yarbrough, S. Prisoners of war
GERMANY
Gillham, D. R. City of women
Grant, H. The vanishing of Katharina Linden
Hegi, U. Stones from the river
Hesse, H. Steppenwolf
Keilson, H. Life goes on
Schlink, B. Homecoming
Schlink, B. The weekend
Schulze, I. New lives
Traveler of the century
Visitation
Vollmann, W. T. Europe central
GERMANY -- 14TH CENTURY
Davidson, A. The gargoyle
Flynn, M. Eifelheim
GERMANY -- 18TH CENTURY
Fitzgerald, P. The blue flower
GERMANY -- 1918-1945
Bohjalian, C. A. Skeletons at the feast
Deaver, J. Garden of beasts
Franck, J. The blindness of the heart
Grass, G. Crabwalk
Grass, G. Dog years
Grass, G. The tin drum
Hegi, U. Children and fire
Remarque, E. M. The night in Lisbon
Remarque, E. M. The road back
Remarque, E. M. A time to love and a time to die
Reuss, F. Mohr
GERMANY -- 1945-
Forsyth, F. The Odessa file
Grass, G. The call of the toad
Grass, G. Dog years
Grass, G. Too far afield
Harris, R. Fatherland
Schlink, B. The reader
Uris, L. Armageddon
GERMANY -- 19TH CENTURY
Buddenbrooks
GERMANY -- 20TH CENTURY
Boll, H. The clown
Grass, G. My century
Hesse, H. Steppenwolf
Mann, T. Doctor Faustus
Remarque, E. M. The night in Lisbon
Remarque, E. M. The road back
Remarque, E. M. A time to love and a time to die
Vollmann, W. T. Europe central
GERMANY -- ARMY
Anatoli, A. Babi Yar
GERMANY -- BERLIN
Barnes, D. Nightwood
Beatty, P. Slumberland
Deaver, J. Garden of beasts
Deighton, L. Berlin game
Deighton, L. London match
Grass, G. Too far afield
Just, W. S. The weather in Berlin
Kennedy, D. The moment
McEwan, I. The innocent
Nabokov, V. V. King, queen, knave
Oe, K. The changeling
Uris, L. Armageddon
GERMANY -- BONN
Boll, H. The clown
GERMANY -- COLOGNE
Boll, H. The silent angel
GERMANY -- COLONIES -- OCEANIA
Imperium
GERMANY -- DRESDEN
Vonnegut, K. Slaughterhouse-five
GERMANY -- DÜSSELDORF
Mann, T. The black swan
GERMANY -- HAMBURG
Le Carre, J. A most wanted man
GERMANY -- HISTORY
Belfer, L. And after the fire
GERMANY -- HISTORY -- 1648-1740
The play of death

GERMANY -- HISTORY -- 17TH CENTURY
The beggar king
GERMANY -- HISTORY -- 1918-1933
Keilson, H. Life goes on
GERMANY -- HISTORY -- 1933-1945
Edugyan, E. Half-blood blues
Kerr, P. The lady from Zagreb
GERMANY -- HISTORY -- 1945-1990
Back to Back
Germinal. Zola, E.
GERMS *See* Bacteria; Germ theory of disease; Microorganisms
Gertrude and Claudius. Updike, J.
A **gesture** life. Lee
Get a life. Gordimer, N.
Get in trouble. Link, K.
Get real. Westlake, D. E.
Get Shorty. Leonard, E.
The **gettin** place. Straight, S.
Getting mother's body. Parks
Gettysburg. Gingrich, N.
GETTYSBURG (PA.), BATTLE OF, 1863
See also Battles; United States -- History -- 1861-1865, Civil War -- Campaigns
GETTYSBURG (PA.), BATTLE OF, 1863
Gingrich, N. Gettysburg
Olmstead, R. Coal black horse
Shaara, M. The killer angels
Ghachar ghochar.
GHANA
Gyasi, Y. Homegoing
The **ghost.** Harris, R.
The **ghost** brigades. Scalzi, J.
Ghost country. Paretsky, S.
Ghost gone wild. Hart, C.
The **ghost** in love. Carroll, J.
Ghost light. O'Connor, J.
Ghost lights. Millet, L.
Ghost moon. Robards, K.
The **ghost** rider. Kadare, I.
The **Ghost** Riders of Ordebec.
The **ghost** road. Barker, P.
GHOST STORIES
Aaronovitch, B. Midnight riot
Aira, C. Ghosts
Bledsoe, A. The hum and the shiver
Bohjalian, C. The night strangers
Carroll, J. The ghost in love
The dark
Davies, R. Murther & walking spirits
De Robertis, C. Perla
Dickens, C. A Christmas carol
Due, T. Ghost summer
Earle, S. I'll never get out of this world alive
Ellis, B. E. Lunar Park
Goodman, C. River Road
Haig, M. The dead fathers club
Harwood, J. The ghost writer
Hill, J. Heart-shaped box
Hill, J. Strange Weather
Hoffman, A. The third angel
Hunt, S. Mr. Splitfoot
Irwin, S. M. The broken ones
Irwin, S. M. The dead path
Jackson, S. The haunting of Hill House
James, H. The turn of the screw
Kallos, S. Broken for you
Livesey, M. Eva moves the furniture
Lofts, N. Gad's Hall
McGregor, J. Even the dogs
Murphy, S. F. The possessions
Neville, S. The ghosts of Belfast
Niffenegger, A. Her fearful symmetry
O'Nan, S. The night country
The Oxford book of English ghost stories
The Oxford book of twentieth-century ghost stories
Powers, T. Hide me among the graves
Priest, C. The Family Plot
Rayne, S. Property of a lady
Saint James, S. The haunting of Maddy Clare
Saul, J. Second child
See, L. Peony in love
Straub, P. Ghost story
Straub, P. In the night room
Tan, A. The hundred secret senses
Tursten, H. Night rounds
Tyler, A. The beginner's goodbye
Vollmann, W. T. Last stories and other stories
GHOST STORIES
See also Fantasy fiction; Horror fiction; Paranormal fiction
Ghost story. Straub, P.
Ghost summer. Due, T.
The **ghost** writer. Harwood, J.
The **ghost** writer. Roth, P.
Ghosts. Aira, C.
GHOSTS
See also Apparitions; Folklore; Spirits
GHOSTS -- FICTION *See* Ghost stories
The **ghosts** of Belfast. Neville, S.
The **ghosts** of Bungo Suido. Deutermann, P. T.
Ghostwalk. Stott, R.
The **giant's** house. McCracken, E.
GIANTS
Baker, T. The little giant of Aberdeen County
McCracken, E. The giant's house
Swift, J. Gulliver's travels
GIANTS
See also Folklore; Monsters
Giants in the earth. Rolvaag, O. E.
The **gift** of Asher Lev. Potok, C.
The **gift** of rain. Eng, T. T.
GIFTED CHILDREN
Larsen, R. The selected works of T. S. Spivet

Potok, C. My name is Asher Lev
GIFTED CHILDREN
See also Exceptional children; Gifted people
GIFTED PEOPLE
Canin, E. A Doubter's Almanac
Wolitzer, M. The Interestings
Gil's All Fright Diner. Martinez, A. L.
The **gilded** age and later novels. Twain, M.
Gilead. Robinson, M.
Giles goat-boy. Barth, J.
Gilman, Laura Anne. Devil's West [series]
Gilman, L. A. The cold eye
Gilman, L. A. Silver on the Road
Gilmore, Gary
About
Mailer, N. The executioner's song
The **gin** closet. Jamison, L.
Ginny Moon. Ludwig, B.
Giovanni's room. Baldwin, J.
GIPSIES *See* Romanies
Girl at war. Nović, S.
The **girl** before. Delaney, J. P.
The **girl** from the coast. Toer, P. A.
The **girl** from the garden. Foroutan, P.
The **girl** in green. Miller, D. B.
Girl in hyacinth blue. Vreeland, S.
The **girl** in the garden. Wallace, M.
The **girl** in the red coat. Hamer, K.
The **Girl** in the Spider's Web. Lagercrantz, D.
The **girl** in the tower.
Girl in translation. Kwok, J.
A **girl** is a half-formed thing. McBride, E.
The **girl** next door. Parks, B.
The **girl** of his dreams. Leon, D.
The **girl** on the cliff. Riley, L.
The **girl** on the train. Hawkins, P.
GIRL SCOUTS
See also Girls' clubs; Scouts and scouting
The **girl** she used to be. Cristofano, D.
Girl waits with gun. Stewart, A.
The **girl** who chased the moon. Allen, S. A.
The **girl** who fell from the sky. Durrow, H. W.
The **girl** who kicked the hornets' nest. Larsson, S.
The **girl** who knew too much. Quick, A.
The **girl** who loved Tom Gordon. King, S.
The **girl** who played go. Shan S.
The **girl** who played with fire. Larsson, S.
The **girl** who takes an eye for an eye. Lagercrantz, D.
Girl with a pearl earring. Chevalier, T.
The **girl** with the dragon tattoo. Larsson, S.
The **girl** you left behind. Moyes, J.
Girlchild. Hassman, T.
The **girls.** Cline, E.
GIRLS
Abbott, M. E. Dare me
Aira, C. Ghosts
Allison, D. Bastard out of Carolina
Awad, M. 13 ways of looking at a fat girl
Balaskovits, A. A. Magic for unlucky girls
Barnes, J. The sky so big and black
Beard, J. A. In Zanesville
Bender, A. The particular sadness of lemon cake
Berg, E. Once upon a time, there was you
Berg, E. We are all welcome here
Betts, D. Souls raised from the dead
Blume, J. Summer sisters
Bronte, C. Emma
Campbell, B. J. Once upon a river
Cisneros, S. The house on Mango Street
Cline, E. The girls
Dallas, S. Tallgrass
Davis, K. The thin place
Dean, M. L. The time it takes to fall
Desai, K. The inheritance of loss
DeWoskin, R. Big girl small
Dickens, C. The old curiosity shop
Durrow, H. W. The girl who fell from the sky
The elegance of the hedgehog
Erpenbeck, J. The book of words
Fitch, J. White oleander
Gibbons, K. Ellen Foster
Gibbons, K. The life all around me by Ellen Foster
Gibbons, K. Sights unseen
Godwin, G. Unfinished desires
Goldberg, M. Bee season
Golden, A. Memoirs of a geisha
Gowdy, B. Helpless
Grant, H. The vanishing of Katharina Linden
Grimes, M. Hotel Paradise
Guene, F. Kiffe kiffe tomorrow
Guterson, D. Our Lady of the Forest
Hannah, K. On Mystic lake
Hassman, T. Girlchild
Hoffman, A. Illumination night
Jen, G. Mona in the promised land
Johansen, I. Final target
Jones, T. Silver sparrow
Julavits, H. The uses of enchantment
Kidd, S. M. The secret life of bees
King, S. The girl who loved Tom Gordon
Kirshenbaum, B. An almost perfect moment
Klein, R. The moth diaries
Krauss, N. The history of love
Kwok, J. Girl in translation
Lawson, M. Crow Lake
Le, T. D. T. The gangster we are all looking for
Lodato, V. Mathilda Savitch
Lukas, M. D. The Oracle of Stamboul
MacDonald The way the crow flies
Mapson Solomon's oak
March, W. The bad seed
Maynard, J. The usual rules
McDermott, A. Child of my heart
McEwan, I. Atonement

Melamed, J. Gather the daughters
Merullo, R. The talk-funny girl
Miller, S. Lost in the forest
Monaghan, N. The killing jar
Moore, M. M. So far away
Moriarty, L. The center of everything
Nadzam, B. Lamb
Oates, J. C. Foxfire
Oates, J. C. Rape
O'Connell, C. Judas child
Ozeki, R. L. A tale for the time being
Paretsky, S. Breakdown
Pearson, A. I think I love you
Pessl, M. Special topics in calamity physics
Picoult, J. My sister's keeper
Picoult, J. Keeping Faith
Pietroni, A. L. Ruby's spoon
Pilcher, R. Coming home
Powell, S. The Mushroom Man
Prose, F. Goldengrove
Raymond, J. The half-life
Revoyr, N. Wingshooters
Reynolds, M. The Starlite Drive-in
Riordan, R. Cold Springs
Rock, P. My abandonment
Roy, L. Bent Road
Russell, K. Swamplandia!
Samarasan, P. Evening is the whole day
Sanders, D. Clover
Sebold, A. The lovely bones
Sittenfeld, C. Prep
Smith, D. I capture the castle
Spark, M. The prime of Miss Jean Brodie
Tarkington, B. Alice Adams
Tartt, D. The little friend
Tea, M. Rose of no man's land
Tepper, S. S. The Margarets
Toews, M. A complicated kindness
Ulinich, A. Petropolis
Urrea, L. A. Queen of America
Vernon, O. Eden
Walton, J. Among others
Watson, J. E. Asta in the wings
Weiner, J. Certain girls
Wilson, R. C. Blind Lake
Woodrell, D. Winter's bone
Yoshimoto, B. Goodbye Tsugumi

GIRLS
See also Children

GIRLS -- CRIMES AGAINST
Corby, G. The Marathon conspiracy
Danticat, E. Claire of the sea light
Martin, L. The bright forever

GIRLS -- INSTITUTIONAL CARE -- IRELAND -- DUBLIN
Alexander, V. S. The Magdalen girls

GIRLS -- JAPAN
Kutsukake, L. The translation of love

GIRLS -- PSYCHOLOGY
Kushner, D. M. The conditions of love

GIRLS -- ZIMBABWE
Bulawayo, N. We need new names

The **girls** of slender means. Spark, M.

GIRLS' CLUBS
See also Clubs; Societies

Give us a kiss. Woodrell, D.
The **given** day. Lehane, D.
The **given** world. Palaia, M.

GLADIATORS
Kane, B. Spartacus
Lytton, E. B. L. The last days of Pompeii
Sienkiewicz, H. Quo Vadis

GLADNESS *See* Happiness
Glamorous powers. Howatch, S.
Glamourist histories [series]
Kowal, M. R. Shades of milk and honey

GLASGOW (SCOTLAND)
Brookmyre, C. Where the bodies are buried

Glass. Savage, S.

GLASS ARTISTS
Vreeland, S. Clara and Mr. Tiffany

GLASS BLOWING AND WORKING
Vreeland, S. Clara and Mr. Tiffany

Glass boys. Lundrigan, N.
The **glass** demon. Grant, H.
Glass God. Griffin, K.
Glass houses. Penny, L.
The **glass** key. Hammett, D.
The **glass** lake. Binchy, M.
The **Glass** Ocean. Baker, L.
The **glass** of time. Cox, M.
The **glass** palace. Ghosh, A.
The **glass** room. Mawer, S.
Glasshouse. Stross, C.

GLEN CANYON NATIONAL RECREATION AREA (UTAH AND ARIZ.)
Barr, N. The rope

GLIDERS (AERONAUTICS)
See also Aeronautics; Airplanes

GLIDING AND SOARING
See also Aeronautics

Glitz. Leonard, E.

GLOBAL FINANCIAL CRISIS, 2008-2009
Mbue, I. Behold the Dreamers

The **Glorious** Heresies. McInerney, L.
GLOSSARIES *See* Encyclopedias and dictionaries

GLOUCESTERSHIRE (ENGLAND)
St. Aubyn, E. The complete Patrick Melrose novels

GNOMES
See also Folklore

Go down, Moses. Faulkner, W.
Go set a watchman. Lee, H.
Go tell it on the mountain. Baldwin, J.
Go with me. Freeman, C.

The **goat** bridge. McNally, T. M.
Goat Mountain. Vann, D.
The **Goblin** Emperor. Addison, K.
GOBLINS
See also Folklore
GOD
Williams, J. 99 stories of God
God bless you, Mr. Rosewater. Vonnegut, K.
God help the child. Morrison, T.
A **God** in Ruins. Atkinson, K.
The **god** of small things. Roy, A.
The **god** of small things. Roy, A.
The **god** of war. Silver, M.
God on the rocks. Gardam, J.
God's country. Everett, P.
The **God's** Eye View. Eisler, B.
God's fool. Slouka, M.
GODDESS RELIGION
See also Paganism
The **godfather.** Puzo, M.
GODS
Gaiman, N. American gods
Jemisin, N. K. The hundred thousand kingdoms
Lake, J. Endurance
Gods and beasts. Mina, D.
Gods and generals. Shaara, J.
GODS AND GODDESSES
Bennett, R. J. City of blades
Bennett, R. J. City of stairs
Carey, J. Banewreaker
Greenwood, K. Out of the black land
Walton, J. Necessity
The **gods** of Gotham. Faye, L.
The **Gods** of Guilt. Connelly, M.
Gods of Riverworld. Farmer, P. J.
The **gods** of tango. De Robertis, C.
The **gods** themselves. Asimov, I.
Gods without men. Kunzru, H.
Gogh, Vincent van, 1853-1890
About
Stone, I. Lust for life
Going after Cacciato. O'Brien, T.
Going Dark. Hall, J. W.
Going postal. Pratchett, T.
Going to meet the man. Baldwin, J.
Going wrong. Rendell, R.
Gold. Cleave, C.
GOLD
Brand, M. Chinook
Fleming, I. Goldfinger
Friedman, D. Don't ever get old
L'Amour, L. The Californios
Stephenson, N. Cryptonomicon
The **gold** bug variations. Powers, R.
The **gold** eaters. Wright, R.
Gold fame citrus. Watkins, C. V.
GOLD MINES AND MINING
Overholser, W. D. Law at Angel's Landing
Traven, B. The treasure of the Sierra Madre
Tremain, R. The color
GOLD, SOPHIA (FICTITIOUS CHARACTER)
Young, T. W. The renegades
The **golden** age. Vidal, G.
The **Golden** Age. London, J.
Golden age. Smiley, J.
The **golden** age. Wright, J. C.
The **golden** bowl. James, H.
Golden country. Gilmore, J.
The **golden** cup. Plain, B.
The **Golden** Egg. Leon, D.
GOLDEN GATE BRIDGE (SAN FRANCISCO, CALIF.)
See also Bridges
The **golden** globe. Varley, J.
Golden Hill. Spufford, F.
The **golden** house. Rushdie, S.
The **golden** legend. Aslam, N.
The **golden** leopard. Kerstan, L.
The **golden** notebook. Lessing, D. M.
The **golden** ocean. O'Brian, P.
The **golden** one. Peters, E.
GOLDEN RULE
See also Ethics
The **golden** season. Brockway, C.
Golden Son. Brown, P.
Golden Trillium. Norton, A.
Goldengrove. Prose, F.
The **goldfinch.** Tartt, D.
Goldfinger. Fleming, I.
The **Golem.** Wiesel, E.
GOLEM
See also Jewish legends; Mysticism -- Judaism
GOLEM
Wecker, H. The Golem and the Jinni
Wiesel, E. The Golem
The **Golem** and the Jinni. Wecker, H.
The **Goliath** bone. Spillane, M.
The **goliath** stone. Harrington, M. J.
Gone. Hayder, M.
Gone. Kellerman, J.
Gone fishin' Mosley, W.
Gone for soldiers. Shaara, J.
Gone girl. Flynn, G.
Gone to ground. Harvey, J.
Gone to soldiers. Piercy, M.
Gone with the wind. Mitchell, M.
GONE WITH THE WIND (MOTION PICTURE : 1939)
Alcott, K. A touch of stardust
The **gone-away** world. Harkaway, N.
GOOD AND EVIL
Arden, K. The bear and the nightingale
Barker, C. Imajica
Barker, C. Weaveworld
Brooks, T. The druid of Shannara
Brooks, T. First king of Shannara

Brooks, T. The measure of the magic
Brooks, T. The sword of Shannara
Bulgakov, M. A. The master and Margarita
De la Cruz, M. Witches of East End
Dickey, J. Deliverance
Garcia Marquez, G. In evil hour
Gay, W. Twilight
Greene, G. The captain and the enemy
James, H. The turn of the screw
Jordan, R. The eye of the world
Karpyshyn, D. Children of fire
Kaufmann, N. Dying Is My Business
King, S. The stand
Lewis, C. S. Out of the silent planet
Lewis, C. S. Perelandra
Lewis, C. S. That hideous strength
Lewis, C. S. Till we have faces
Locke, T. Emissary
Mailer, N. The castle in the forest
McCammon, R. R. Boy's life
McEwan, I. Black dogs
Melville, H. Billy Budd, sailor
Murdoch, I. The green knight
Murdoch, I. The nice and the good
Picoult, J. The Storyteller
Rice, A. The witching hour
Rogers, R. Devil's Cape
Rushdie, S. The satanic verses
Saul, J. Second child
Steinbeck, J. East of Eden
Straub, P. A dark matter
Straub, P. Ghost story
Tartt, D. The secret history
Wiesel, E. The judges
Wright, R. The outsider

GOOD AND EVIL

See also Ethics; Philosophy; Theology

The **good** apprentice. Murdoch, I.
Good as Gold. Heller, J.
Good as gone. Corleone, D.
Good behavior. Westlake, D. E.
Good blood. Elkins, A. J.
The **good** children. Wilhelm, K.
A **good** country. Khadivi, L.
The **good** earth. Buck, P. S.
A **good** fall. Jin, H.
The **good** father. Havley, N.

GOOD FRIDAY

See also Christian holidays; Holy Week; Lent

Good grief. Winston, L.
The **good** husband. Godwin, G.
The **good** husband of Zebra Drive. McCall Smith, A.
Good in bed. Weiner, J.
Good Indian Girls. Sidhu, R. S.
Good kings bad kings. Nussbaum, S.
The **good** life. McInerney, J.
The **good** lord bird. McBride, J.
Good man Friday. Hambly, B.
The **good** mother. Miller, S.
Good offices. Rosero, E.
Good omens. Gaiman, N.
Good People. Lopez, R.
The **good** priest's son. Price, R.
A **good** scent from a strange mountain. Butler, R. O.
The **good** soldier. Ford, F. M.
The **good** son. Gruber, M.
The **good** suicides. Hill, A.
The **good** terrorist. Lessing, D. M.
The **good** thief. Tinti, H.
The **good** wife. O'Nan, S.
Good-bye Mr. Chips. Hilton, J.
Goodbye for now. Frankel, L.
The **goodbye** look. Macdonald, R.
Goodbye to the dead. Freeman, B.
Goodbye Tsugumi. Yoshimoto, B.
Goodbye without leaving. Colwin, L.
Goodbye, Columbus, and five short stories. Roth, P.

GORDIANUS THE FINDER (FICTITIOUS CHARACTER)

Saylor, S. The judgment of Caesar
Saylor, S. Raiders of the Nile
Saylor, S. The seven wonders
Saylor, S. Wrath of the furies

Gordon. Templeton, E.
Gorgeous lies. McPhee, M.
Gorilla, my love. Bambara, T. C.

GORILLAS

See also Apes

Gorky Park. Smith, M. C.
The **Gospel** according to the Son. Mailer, N.

GOSSIP

See also Journalism; Libel and slander

GOSSIP

Leigh, E. Forever Your Earl
Raeder, L. Black iris

GOTHIC FICTION *See* Gothic novels

GOTHIC NOVELS

Red Spectres

GOTHIC NOVELS

See also Historical fiction; Horror fiction; Paranormal fiction

GOTHIC REVIVAL (ART)

See also Art

GOTHIC ROMANCES

Austen, J. Northanger Abbey
Bronte, C. Emma
Bronte, C. Jane Eyre
Bronte, E. Wuthering Heights
Holt, V. The black opal
Holt, V. Bride of Pendorric
Holt, V. The Judas kiss
Holt, V. Secret for a nightingale
Hooper, K. Finding Laura
Michaels, B. Stitches in time

Ogilvie, E. When the music stopped
The Oxford book of gothic tales
Quick, A. I thee wed
Quick, A. Wicked widow
Radcliffe, A. W. The mysteries of Udolpho
Seton, A. Dragonwyck
Shelley, M. W. Frankenstein; or, The modern Prometheus
Stewart, M. The ivy tree
Stewart, M. Nine coaches waiting
Stewart, M. Touch not the cat
Stewart, M. Wildfire at midnight
Stoker, B. Dracula
Trevanian The summer of Katya
Wood, B. The dreaming
Gould's book of fish. Flanagan, R.
Gould, Glenn, 1932-1982
About
Bernhard, T. The loser
Gould, William Buelow, 1803-1853
About
Flanagan, R. Gould's book of fish
GOVERNESSES
Bronte, C. Jane Eyre
Connolly, T. Ironskin
Faber, M. The crimson petal and the white
James, H. The turn of the screw
McLaughlin, E. The nanny diaries
Noble, K. The Game and the Governess
Read, P. P. Alice in exile
Seton, A. Dragonwyck
Stewart, M. Nine coaches waiting
GOVERNMENT EMPLOYEES *See* Civil service
GOVERNMENT INVESTIGATIONS *See* Governmental investigations
GOVERNMENT INVESTIGATORS
Harris, T. Red Dragon
Higgins, J. Day of reckoning
Isaacs, S. Red, white and blue
King, L. R. A darker place
Laukkanen, O. Criminal enterprise
Ludlum, R. The Sigma protocol
Perry, T. The informant
Rush, N. Mortals
GOVERNMENT INVESTIGATORS -- MINNESOTA
Sandford, J. Deadline
Sandford, J. Storm Front
GOVERNMENT OFFICIALS
Donoghue, E. Slammerkin
Millet, L. Oh pure and radiant heart
Nordhoff, C. Men against the sea
Nordhoff, C. Mutiny on the Bounty
GOVERNMENT OWNERSHIP
See also Economic policy; Industrial policy; Socialism
GOVERNMENT SERVICE *See* Civil service
GOVERNMENT, RESISTANCE TO *See* Resistance to government
GOVERNMENT, RESISTANCE TO
Brown, P. Golden Son
Brown, P. Red Rising
Lopez, B. H. Resistance
Solomon, R. An unkindness of ghosts
GOVERNMENTAL INVESTIGATIONS
Porter, H. The bell ringers
The **governor's** wife. Harvey, M.
Grace. Deón, N.
Grace. Nunez, E.
The **grace** of kings. Liu, K.
The **gracekeepers.** Logan, K.
GraceLand. Abani, C.
A **gracious** plenty. Reynolds, S.
GRADUATE STUDENTS
Choi, S. My education
GRAFFITI
Mansbach, A. Rage is back
GRAIL
Burke, J. L. House of the rising sun
Cornwell, B. The archer's tale
Eco, U. Baudolino
Lovett, C. The lost book of the Grail
GRAIL
See also Folklore
Grail of the summer stars. Warrington, F.
GRAMMAR
See also Language and languages; Linguistics
GRAMMY AWARDS
See also Sound recordings
The **grand** Sophy. Heyer, G.
GRANDCHILDREN
McMurtry, L. The evening star
Tyler, A. The amateur marriage
GRANDDAUGHTERS
Desai, K. The inheritance of loss
Walker, A. The third life of Grange Copeland
GRANDFATHERS
Allen, S. A. The girl who chased the moon
Bilenchi, R. The chill
Dickens, C. Martin Chuzzlewit
Dickens, C. The old curiosity shop
Dreyer, E. Twice tempted
Foer, J. S. Everything is illuminated
Foer, J. S. Extremely loud & incredibly close
McIntosh, W. Hitchers
Obreht, T. The tiger's wife
Paretsky, S. Ghost country
Revoyr, N. Wingshooters
Stanisic, S. How the soldier repairs the gramophone
Toole, F. X. Pound for pound
Watson, L. As good as gone
GRANDFATHERS
See also Grandparents
GRANDFATHERS -- FAMILY RELATIONSHIPS
Watson, L. As good as gone
The **grandmother's** tale and selected stories. Narayan, R. K.
GRANDMOTHERS

Allende, I. Portrait in sepia
Bognanni, P. The house of tomorrow
De la Roche, M. Jalna
Durrow, H. W. The girl who fell from the sky
Greene, A. Bloodroot
Isaacs, S. As husbands go
Jackson, J. The almost sisters
Jackson, N. The Star Side of Bird Hill
Jhabvala, R. P. Heat and dust
Makine, A. Dreams of my Russian summers
Read Thrush Green
Robinson, K. S. 2312
Ross-Macdonald, M. The Trevarton inheritance
Scott, J. Follow me
Tóibín, C. The blackwater lightship
Tryon, T. The other
Watson, C. Tiny sunbirds, far away
Weiner, J. In her shoes
GRANDMOTHERS
See also Grandparents
GRANDMOTHERS -- DEATH
Backman, F. My grandmother asked me to tell you she's sorry
GRANDPARENT AND CHILD
Chabon, M. Moonglow
Walker, A. The third life of Grange Copeland
GRANDPARENT AND CHILD -- NIGERIA
Watson, C. Tiny sunbirds, far away
GRANDPARENT-GRANDCHILD RELATIONSHIP
See also Family; Grandparents
GRANDPARENT-GRANDCHILD RELATIONSHIP
Backman, F. My grandmother asked me to tell you she's sorry
Meno, J. Marvel and a wonder
GRANDPARENTING
See also Grandparents; Parenting
GRANDPARENTS
Benioff, D. City of thieves
Mitchard, J. A theory of relativity
GRANDPARENTS
See also Family
GRANDPARENTS AS PARENTS
See also Grandparents; Parenting
GRANDSONS
Glass, J. The widower's tale
GRANDSONS -- FICTION
Harding, P. Enon
Grant comes east. Gingrich, N.
Grant, Ulysses S. (Ulysses Simpson), 1822-1885
About
Gingrich, N. Grant comes east
Shaara, J. The last full measure
The **grapes** of wrath. Steinbeck, J.
GRAPHIC NOVELS
Moon, F. Daytripper
GRAPHIC NOVELS
See also Comic books, strips, etc.; Fiction
GRAPHOLOGISTS
Rader-Day, L. The day I died
Grass. Tepper, S. S.
GRASS (DRUG) *See* Marijuana
The **grass** dancer. Power, S.
The **grass** harp. Capote, T.
The **grass** is singing. Lessing, D. M.
Grass roots. Woods, S.
Grasshopper. Vine, B.
GRASSLAND ECOLOGY
See also Ecology
GRATITUDE
See also Emotions; Virtue
Grave mistake. Marsh, N.
Grave music. Harrod-Eagles, C.
Grave secrets. Reichs, K. J.
The **gravedigger's** daughter. Oates, J. C.
GRAVES *See* Burial; Cemeteries; Epitaphs; Funeral rites and ceremonies; Mounds and mound builders; Tombs
Graveyard dust. Hambly, B.
GRAVEYARDS *See* Cemeteries
Gravity's rainbow. Pynchon, T.
Gray man [series]
Greaney, M. Gunmetal gray
Gray, Henry Judd, 1892-1928
About
Hansen, R. A wild surge of guilty passion
The **great** alone. Hannah, K.
The **great** American novel. Roth, P.
GREAT BRITAIN
Bourne, J. The black hawk
Bradley, A. The sweetness at the bottom of the pie
Bradley, A. The weed that strings the hangman's bag
Dare, T. A night to surrender
Dean, A. A woman of consequence
Gallagher, S. The bedlam detective
Hodder, M. Expedition to the Mountains of the Moon
Kelly, J. The fire baby
Kelly, J. The moon tunnel
Swift, G. Wish you were here
Winspear, J. Elegy for Eddie
GREAT BRITAIN -- ARMY
Kaye, M. M. The far pavilions
GREAT BRITAIN -- ARMY -- OFFICERS
Boulle, P. The bridge over the River Kwai
Forester, C. S. Hornblower and the Atropos
Forester, C. S. Ship of the line
Mallinson, A. A close run thing
GREAT BRITAIN -- COLONIES
See also Colonies
GREAT BRITAIN -- COURT AND COURTIERS
Weir, A. A dangerous inheritance
GREAT BRITAIN -- HISTORY
Franklin, A. The Siege Winter
GREAT BRITAIN -- HISTORY -- 0-1066
Bracewell, P. Shadow on the crown
Cornwell, B. Death of kings

Cornwell, B. The last kingdom
Ishiguro, K. The buried giant
Llywelyn, M. After Rome
GREAT BRITAIN -- HISTORY -- 1066-1485, MEDIEVAL PERIOD
Nicholas, D. The wicked
GREAT BRITAIN -- HISTORY -- 1154-1399, PLANTAGENETS
Follett, K. The pillars of the earth
Vantrease, B. R. The illuminator
GREAT BRITAIN -- HISTORY -- 1455-1485, WARS OF THE ROSES
Gregory, P. The lady of the rivers
Gregory, P. The red queen
GREAT BRITAIN -- HISTORY -- 1485-1603, TUDORS
Andersen, L. The Boleyn King
Buckley, F. The doublet affair
Buckley, F. The siren queen
Clements, R. Revenger
Gregory, P. The constant princess
Gregory, P. The taming of the queen
Gregory, P. The white princess
Mantel, H. Bring up the bodies
GREAT BRITAIN -- HISTORY -- 14TH CENTURY
Vantrease, B. R. The illuminator
GREAT BRITAIN -- HISTORY -- 1714-1837
Blake, R. A dark anatomy
Brockway, C. The golden season
Hern, C. The bride sale
Hern, C. Once a gentleman
Putney, M. J. The marriage spell
GREAT BRITAIN -- HISTORY -- 1800-1837
Motion, A. Silver
GREAT BRITAIN -- HISTORY -- 18TH CENTURY
Robertson, I. Island of bones
GREAT BRITAIN -- HISTORY -- 1945-1952
Cameron, P. Coral Glynn
GREAT BRITAIN -- HISTORY -- 19TH CENTURY
Dean, A. A gentleman of fortune, or, The suspicions of Miss Dido Kent
Hodder, M. The strange affair of Spring Heeled Jack
Shepherd, L. The solitary house
GREAT BRITAIN -- HISTORY -- 20TH CENTURY
Baker, J. The undertow
GREAT BRITAIN -- HISTORY -- ALFRED, 871-899
Cornwell, B. The last kingdom
GREAT BRITAIN -- HISTORY -- CHARLES II, 1660-1685
Brooks, G. Year of wonders
Davies, J. D. Gentleman captain
Davies, J. D. The mountain of gold
Pears, I. An instance of the fingerpost
GREAT BRITAIN -- HISTORY -- EDWARD IV, 1461-1483
Gregory, P. The kingmaker's daughter
Gregory, P. The red queen
GREAT BRITAIN -- HISTORY -- ELIZABETH, 1558-1603
Buckley, F. The doublet affair
Buckley, F. The siren queen
Follett, K. A column of fire
Marston, E. The Devil's apprentice
Marston, E. The wanton angel
Maxwell, R. The Queen's bastard
Maxwell, R. The wild Irish
GREAT BRITAIN -- HISTORY -- ETHELRED II, 979-1016
Bracewell, P. Shadow on the crown
GREAT BRITAIN -- HISTORY -- GEORGE II, 1727-1760
Worsley, K. She rises
GREAT BRITAIN -- HISTORY -- GEORGE VI, 1936-1952
Nicholson, W. Motherland
GREAT BRITAIN -- HISTORY -- HENRY VIII, 1509-1547
Andersen, L. The Boleyn King
Gregory, P. The constant princess
Gregory, P. The other Boleyn girl
Gregory, P. The taming of the queen
Mantel, H. Bring up the bodies
Mantel, H. Wolf Hall
GREAT BRITAIN -- HISTORY -- RICHARD I, 1189-1199
Penman, S. K. Cruel as the grave
Penman, S. K. Dragon's lair
Penman, S. K. A King's Ransom
GREAT BRITAIN -- HISTORY -- RICHARD III, 1483-1485
Gregory, P. The red queen
GREAT BRITAIN -- HISTORY -- STEPHEN, 1135-1154
Follett, K. The pillars of the earth
GREAT BRITAIN -- HISTORY -- VICTORIA, 1837-1901
Perry, S. The Essex Serpent
Raybourn, D. A perilous undertaking
Shepherd, L. The solitary house
Thomson, E. S. Beloved poison
Wallace, W. The painted bridge
GREAT BRITAIN -- HISTORY -- WARS OF THE ROSES, 1455-1485
Gregory, P. The lady of the rivers
Gregory, P. The red queen
GREAT BRITAIN -- HISTORY, NAVAL -- 17TH CENTURY
Davies, J. D. Gentleman captain
Davies, J. D. The mountain of gold
GREAT BRITAIN -- KINGS AND RULERS
See also Kings and rulers
GREAT BRITAIN -- KINGS AND RULERS
Andersen, L. The Boleyn King
Cornwell, B. Death of kings
GREAT BRITAIN -- POLITICS AND GOVERNMENT
Marr, A. Head of State
GREAT BRITAIN -- ROYAL AIR FORCE
Goddard, R. Never go back
GREAT BRITAIN -- SOCIAL CONDITIONS -- 19TH CENTURY
Hodder, M. The strange affair of Spring Heeled Jack
GREAT BRITAIN -- SOCIAL LIFE AND CUSTOMS
Amis, M. Lionel Asbo
Dean, A. A woman of consequence
GREAT BRITAIN -- SOCIAL LIFE AND CUSTOMS -- 20TH CENTURY

Baker, J. Longbourn
Baker, J. The undertow
GREAT BRITAIN. ARMY -- OFFICERS -- CRIMES AGAINST
Todd, C. An unmarked grave
GREAT BRITAIN. METROPOLITAN POLICE OFFICE. CRIMINAL INVESTIGATION DEPARTMENT
Coulter, C. The Final Cut
GREAT BRITAIN. MI5 -- OFFICIALS AND EMPLOYEES
Herron, M. Spook street
GREAT BRITAIN. MI6
Cumming, C. A divided spy
GREAT BRITAIN. ROYAL NAVY
Forester, C. S. Admiral Hornblower in the West Indies
Forester, C. S. Beat to quarters
Forester, C. S. Flying colours
Forester, C. S. Mr. Midshipman Hornblower
Lambdin, D. King's captain
Monsarrat, N. The cruel sea
O'Brian, P. The unknown shore
O'Brian, P. The hundred days
O'Brian, P. The yellow admiral
Unsworth, B. Losing Nelson
GREAT BRITAIN. ROYAL NAVY -- OFFICERS
Davies, J. D. The mountain of gold
Forester, C. S. Hornblower and the Hotspur
Forester, C. S. Hornblower during the crisis, and two stories: Hornblower's temptation and The last encounter
Forester, C. S. Lieutenant Hornblower
Novik, N. Blood of tyrants
Novik, N. His majesty's dragon
O'Brian, P. Blue at the mizzen
O'Brian, P. The commodore
O'Brian, P. The wine-dark sea
GREAT DEPRESSION, 1929-1939
Lansdale, J. R. Edge of dark water
Silver, M. Mary Coin
Great dream of heaven. Shepard, S.
The **great** escape. Phillips, S. E.
Great expectations. Dickens, C.
The **great** fire. Hazzard, S.
The **great** Gatsby. Fitzgerald, F. S.
Great house. Krauss, N.
Great illustrated classics [series]
Verne, J. From the earth to the moon, and Round the moon
The **great** leader. Harrison, J.
The **great** night. Adrian, C.
Great north road. Hamilton, P. F.
GREAT POWERS
Alderman, N. The power
A **great** reckoning. Penny, L.
GREAT SMOKY MOUNTAINS (N.C. AND TENN.)
Bledsoe, A. Wisp of a thing
Godwin, G. Evensong
Great stories of the American West.
Greatest hits.
GRECO-TURKISH WAR, 1921-1922
Karnezis, P. The maze
GREECE
Cook, E. Achilles
Fowles, J. The magus
Glass, J. Three Junes
Goddard, R. Into the blue
Malouf, D. Ransom
Michaels, A. Fugitive pieces
Murray, S. Forgery
Renault, M. The bull from the sea
Renault, M. Funeral games
Renault, M. The king must die
Unsworth, B. The songs of the kings
GREECE -- ATHENS
Renault, M. The last of the wine
Van Booy, S. Everything beautiful began after
Vidal, G. Creation
GREECE -- BIOGRAPHY
See also Biography
GREECE -- HISTORY -- ATHENIAN SUPREMACY, 479-431 B.C.
Corby, G. The Marathon conspiracy
GREECE -- HISTORY -- TO 146 B.C.
Lyon, A. The sweet girl
Miller, M. The song of Achilles
GREECE -- SALONIKA
Furst, A. Spies of the Balkans
GREED
Bass, R. All the Land to Hold Us
Keller, J. Last Ragged Breath
Swinson, K. Playing dirty
GREEK AMERICANS
Cunningham, M. Flesh and blood
Eugenides, J. Middlesex
Pelecanos, G. P. The big blowdown
GREEK ART
See also Ancient art; Art; Classical antiquities
GREEK LANGUAGE
See also Language and languages
GREEK MYTHOLOGY
Banville, J. The infinities
Hauser, E. For the most beautiful
GREEKS -- TURKEY
Miller, M. The song of Achilles
Green darkness. Seton, A.
Green Dolphin Street. Goudge, E.
The **Green** House. Vargas Llosa, M.
The **green** knight. Murdoch, I.
The **green** ripper. MacDonald, J. D.
The **Green** Road. Enright, A.
The **greengage** summer. Godden, R.
GREENLAND
The prophets of eternal fjord
Vollmann, W. T. The ice-shirt
Grey, Jane Lady, 1537-1554
About
Weir, A. Innocent traitor

Greywalker. Richardson, K.
GRIEF
See also Emotions
Doctorow, E. L. Andrew's Brain
Falling out of time
Harding, P. Enon
Hemmings, K. H. The possibilities
Henkin, J. The world without you
Itani, F. Requiem
Krueger, W. K. Ordinary grace
Moshi moshi
Ng, C. Everything I never told you
Palwick, S. Mending the moon
Pochoda, I. Visitation Street
Porter, M. Grief Is the Thing With Feathers
Saunders, G. Lincoln in the bardo
Smith, A. How to be Both
GRIEF IN WOMEN
Rose, M. J. Seduction
Grief Is the Thing With Feathers. Porter, M.
The **grief** of others. Cohen, L. H.
Grimke, Sarah Moore, 1792-1873
About
Kidd, S. M. The invention of wings
Gringos. Portis, C.
The **grip** of it. Jemc, J.
Grist Mill Road. Yates, C. J.
GROCERS
Malamud, B. The assistant
Steinbeck, J. The winter of our discontent
GROSS NATIONAL PRODUCT
See also Economics; Statistics; Wealth
The **grotesque.** McGrath, P.
The **ground** beneath her feet. Rushdie, S.
The **group.** McCarthy, M.
GROUP IDENTITY
See also Identity (Psychology)
GROUP LIVING *See* Communal living
GROUP PSYCHOTHERAPY -- FICTION
Yalom, I. D. The Schopenhauer cure
GROUP RELATIONS TRAINING
See also Interpersonal relations
GROUP THEORY
See also Algebra; Mathematics; Number theory
GROUP TRAVEL *See* Travel
The **groves** of Academe. McCarthy, M.
A **grown** up kind of pretty. Jackson, J.
GRUNTHOR (FICTITIOUS CHARACTER : HAYDON)
Haydon, E. The Merchant Emperor
Haydon, E. Prophecy
Gryphon. Baxter, C.
Guapa. Haddad, S.
GUARDIAN AND WARD
Amis, M. Lionel Asbo
Coetzee, J. M. The Childhood of Jesus
Edgerton, C. Walking across Egypt
Godwin, G. Flora
Kingsolver, B. The bean trees
Guardian angel. Paretsky, S.
Guardian of the horizon. Peters, E.
GUARDIANS
Gracie, A. The Winter Bride
The **guards.** Bruen, K.
GUERILLAS *See* Guerrillas
The **Guermantes** way. Proust, M.
GUERNSEY (CHANNEL ISLANDS)
Barrows, A. The Guernsey Literary and Potato Peel Pie Society
Horlock, M. The book of lies
The **Guernsey** Literary and Potato Peel Pie Society. Barrows, A.
GUERRILLA WARFARE
See also Insurgency; Military art and science; Tactics; War
Guerrillas. Naipaul, V. S.
GUERRILLAS
Levi, P. If not now, when?
Naipaul, V. S. Guerrillas
Nathanson, E. M. The dirty dozen
Rosero Diago, E. The armies
A **guest** of honor. Gordimer, N.
GUESTS
Waters, S. The Paying Guests
Guevara, Ernesto, 1928-1967
About
Griffin, W. E. B. Special ops
Guide to the birds of East Africa. Drayson, N.
GUIDED MISSILES
See also Bombs; Projectiles; Rocketry; Rockets (Aeronautics)
GUIDES (PERSONS)
Sargent, C. Museum of human beings
Guilt. Lescroart, J. T.
GUILT
Amis, M. House of meetings
Ballantyne, L. The guilty one
Bohjalian, C. The night strangers
Camus, A. The fall
Canin, E. America America
Coben, H. The woods
Cook, T. H. The Chatham School affair
Cooley, M. The archivist
Edwards, Y. A Cupboard full of coats
Egan, J. The keep
Frame, R. The lantern bearers
Goddard, R. Beyond recall
Greene, G. The tenth man
Hamilton, J. A map of the world
Hart, J. Damage
Hatoum, M. The brothers
Haywood, G. A. Cemetery Road
Highsmith, P. The boy who followed Ripley
Hodgkinson, A. 22 Britannia Road
Hosseini, K. The kite runner

Huneven, M. Blame
Irwin, S. M. The dead path
Joss, M. The night following
Kallos, S. Broken for you
Kennedy, W. Ironweed
Koryta, M. The prophet
LaValle, V. D. Big machine
Lehrer, J. The special prisoner
Lourie, R. A hatred for tulips
McEwan, I. Atonement
McEwan, I. The innocent
Morrison, T. Jazz
Neville, S. The ghosts of Belfast
Nordan, L. Wolf whistle
Oates, J. C. The gravedigger's daughter
O'Dell, T. Coal Run
Petterson, P. In the wake
Robinson, L. Water dogs
Rossner, J. Looking for Mr. Goodbar
Schlink, B. The reader
Schwartz, J. B. Reservation Road
Schwarz, C. Drowning Ruth
Shreve, A. The weight of water
Smith, S. A simple plan
Spencer, S. Man in the woods
Styron, W. Sophie's choice
Tyler, A. Saint maybe
Ward, A. E. Forgive me
GUILT
See also Conscience; Emotions; Ethics; Good and evil; Sin
Guilt by association. Clark, M.
Guilty as sin. Hoag, T.
The **guilty** one. Ballantyne, L.
GUITARISTS
Long, J. A. Wild at Whiskey Creek
GUITARS -- METHODS (JAZZ)
See also Jazz music
The **gulf.** Poyer, D.
GULF COAST (LA.) -- HISTORY -- 19TH CENTURY
Kent, K. The outcasts
GULF OF ADEN
Leonard, E. Djibouti
GULF STREAM
Hemingway, E. The old man and the sea
Gulliver's travels. Swift, J.
Gunman's rhapsody. Parker, R. B.
Gunmetal gray. Greaney, M.
GUNPOWDER
See also Explosives; Guns
GUNS
Patterson, R. N. Balance of power
Russell, M. D. Epitaph
The **guns** of Avalon. Zelazny, R.
GUNTHER, BERNHARD (FICTITIOUS CHARACTER)
Kerr, P. The lady from Zagreb
Kerr, P. A Man Without Breath
Kerr, P. March violets
Kerr, P. Prussian blue
The **guru** of love. Upadhyay, S.
Gutenberg's apprentice. Christie, A.
Gutenberg, Johann, 1397?-1468
About
Christie, A. Gutenberg's apprentice
The **Guts.** Doyle, R.
Gutshot. Gray, A.
GUYANA
Bhattacharya, R. The sly company of people who care
GYMNASTICS
Abbott, M. E. You will know me
GYPSIES
King, S. Thinner
GYPSIES *See* Romanies

H

H is for homicide. Grafton, S.
H. P. Lovecraft. Lovecraft, H. P.
Ha'penny. Walton, J.
HABITAT (ECOLOGY)
See also Ecology
HACKERS
Lagercrantz, D. The girl who takes an eye for an eye
HACKNEY (LONDON, ENGLAND) -- SOCIAL LIFE AND CUSTOMS
Evaristo, B. Mr. Loverman
HADES *See* Hell
Hadrian, Emperor of Rome, 76-138
About
Yourcenar, M. Memoirs of Hadrian
Hadriana in all my dreams. Dépestre, R.
HAIKU
See also Poetry
HAIR -- DISEASES
Kilpack, J. S. A heart revealed
HAITI
Danticat, E. Claire of the sea light
Dépestre, R. Hadriana in all my dreams
Gay, R. An Untamed State
Shacochis, B. The Woman Who Lost Her Soul
HAITI -- 20TH CENTURY
Danticat, E. Krik? Krak!
HAITI -- REVOLUTION, 1791-1804
Allende, I. Island beneath the sea
Bell, M. S. All souls' rising
HAITIANS -- DOMINICAN REPUBLIC
Danticat, E. The farming of bones
HAITIANS -- UNITED STATES
Danticat, E. The dew breaker
Danticat, E. Krik? Krak!
Prose, F. Primitive people
Swinson, K. Playing dirty
Half a crown. Walton, J.
Half a heart. Brown, R.

Half a King. Abercrombie, J.
Half a life. Naipaul, V. S.
Half a war. Abercrombie, J.
Half asleep in frog pajamas. Robbins, T.
Half broke horses. Walls, J.
Half broken things. Joss, M.
Half Moon Street. Perry, A.
Half of a yellow sun. Adichie, C. N.
Half the blood of Brooklyn. Huston, C.
Half the world. Abercrombie, J.
Half-blood blues. Edugyan, E.
HALF-BROTHERS
Murdoch, I. The good apprentice
The **half-life.** Raymond, J.
The **half-made** world. Gilman, F.
Half-past dawn. Doetsch, R.
HALF-SISTERS
Garcia, C. The Aguero sisters
Halfblood chronicles [series]
Norton, A. The elvenbane
Norton, A. Elvenblood
Halfway house. Noel, K.
The **halfway** house. Rosales, G.
The **hall** of singing caryatids.
The **hall** of singing caryatids. Pelevin, V.
Hallet, Elizabeth Fones Winthrop Feake, b. 1610
About
Seton, A. The Winthrop woman
HALLEY'S COMET
See also Comets
HALLUCINATIONS AND ILLUSIONS
Tyler, A. The beginner's goodbye
HALLUCINATIONS AND ILLUSIONS
See also Abnormal psychology; Parapsychology; Subconsciousness; Visions
HALLUCINOGENS
See also Drugs; Psychotropic drugs; Stimulants
Halsey Street. Coster, N.
The **Hamilton** case. De Kretser, M.
Hamilton, Alexander, 1757-1804
About
Liss, D. The whiskey rebels
Hamilton, Emma Lady, 1761?-1815
About
Sontag, S. The volcano lover
Hamilton, William Sir, 1730-1803
About
Sontag, S. The volcano lover
The **hamlet.** Faulkner, W.
Hammett, Dashiell, 1894-1961
About
Atkins, A. Devil's garden
HAND
Irving, J. The fourth hand
The **hand** of Oberon. Zelazny, R.
The **hand** that first held mine. O'Farrell, M.
A **handbook** to luck. Garcia, C.
HANDGUNS
See also Guns
The **Handmaid's** tale. Atwood, M.
The **handyman.** See, C.
HANGING *See* Capital punishment
Hanging hill. Hayder, M.
Hangman's daughter tales [series]
The play of death
Hannibal. Harris, T.
Hannibal rising. Harris, T.
Hanta yo. Hill, R. B.
A Hap and Leonard novel [series]
Lansdale, J. R. Honky tonk samurai
HAPPENING (ART) *See* Performance art
HAPPINESS
Powers, R. Generosity
HAPPINESS
See also Emotions
Happiness is a chemical in the brain. Perillo, L.
Happiness, Like Water. Okparanta, C.
Happy all the time. Colwin, L.
Happy now? Shonk, K.
HARASSMENT, SEXUAL *See* Sexual harassment
Harbor nocturne. Wambaugh, J.
Hard candy. Vachss, A. H.
Hard magic. Gilman, L. A.
Hard revolution. Pelecanos, G. P.
Hard time. Paretsky, S.
Hard twisted. Greaves, C. J.
Hardball. Paretsky, S.
The **Harder** They Come. Boyle, T. C.
Hardly knew her. Lippman, L.
Hardscrabble road. Haddam, J.
Hargreaves, Alice Pleasance Liddell, 1852-1934
About
Benjamin, M. Alice I have been
HARISTEEN, HARRY (FICTITIOUS CHARACTER)
Brown, R. M. The litter of the law
Hark! McBain, E.
HARLAN COUNTY (KY.)
Leonard, E. Raylan
HARLEM (NEW YORK, N.Y.)
Miller, K. E. Q. An angry-ass black woman
Reed, I. Mumbo jumbo
Harlem Renaissance: five novels of the 1920s.
Harlem Renaissance: four novels of the 1930s.
Harm done. Rendell, R.
Haroun and the sea of stories. Rushdie, S.
HARPERS FERRY (W. VA.) -- HISTORY -- JOHN BROWN'S RAID, 1859
McBride, J. The good lord bird
HARRINGTON, HONOR (FICTITIOUS CHARACTER)
Weber, D. Shadow of freedom
Harry Hole [series]
The Bat
Nesbø, J. The thirst
Hart's war. Katzenbach, J.

Harvard Square. Aciman, A.
HARVARD UNIVERSITY
Aciman, A. Harvard Square
Brooks, G. Caleb's crossing
Vassanji, M. G. The assassin's song
Wolfe, T. Of time and the river
Harvest. Crace, J.
Harvest. Plain, B.
A **harvest** of thorns. Addison, C.
HARWICH (ENGLAND)
Worsley, K. She rises
Hash. Lindgren, T.
HASHISH *See* Marijuana
HASIDIM
See also Jews
HASIDISM
Lebrecht, N. The song of names
Mirvis, T. The outside world
Potok, C. The gift of Asher Lev
Potok, C. My name is Asher Lev
HASIDISM
See also Judaism
HASSIDISM *See* Hasidism
HASTINGS (EAST SUSSEX, ENGLAND), BATTLE OF, 1066
See also Battles; Great Britain -- History -- 1066-1154, Norman period
HATE
See also Emotions
HATE CRIMES
See also Crime; Discrimination; Violence
Hater. Moody, D.
Hateship, friendship, courtship, loveship, marriage. Munro, A.
A **hatred** for tulips. Lourie, R.
Haunted. Oates, J. C.
The **haunted** air. Wilson, F. P.
Haunted ground. Hart, E.
HAUNTED HOUSES
See also Houses
HAUNTED HOUSES
Danielewski, M. Z. House of leaves
Jemc, J. The grip of it
Priest, C. The Family Plot
The **haunted** monastery. Gulik, R. H. v.
HAUNTED PLACES
Dean, A. A woman of consequence
The **haunting** of Hill House. Jackson, S.
The **haunting** of L. Norman, H.
The **haunting** of Maddy Clare. Saint James, S.
Hausfrau. Essbaum, J. A.
Havana. Hunter, S.
HAVANA (CUBA)
García, C. King of Cuba
Garcia, C. Dreaming in Cuban
Havana Bay. Smith, M. C.
The **Havana** World Series. Latour, J.
HAVERS, BARBARA (FICTITIOUS CHARACTER)
George, E. Believing the lie
George, E. Just one evil act
Havisham. Frame, R.
Hawaii. Michener, J. A.
HAWAII
Goodman, A. Paradise park
Jones, J. From here to eternity
Lodge, D. Paradise news
Michener, J. A. Hawaii
Robbins, T. Still life with Woodpecker
HAWAII -- HONOLULU
Morley, I. Come Sunday
Hawk quest. Lyndon, R.
Hawthorn & child. Ridgway, K.
Hawthorne, Nathaniel, 1804-1864
About
Jordan, H. When she woke
Hays, Jacob
About
Rose, J. Blackest bird
He shall thunder in the sky. Peters, E.
A **Head** Full of Ghosts. Tremblay, P.
Head of State. Marr, A.
The **headhunters.** Nesbo, J.
Headlong. Frayn, M.
The **headmaster's** wager. Lam, V.
HEADS OF STATE
Antunes, A. L. The inquisitors' manual
Harris, R. Archangel
Harris, R. Fatherland
Lawton, J. Old flames
Mailer, N. The castle in the forest
Neugeboren, J. 1940
HEADS OF STATE
See also Executive power; Statesmen
The **healer.**
The **healing.** Odell, J.
HEALTH INSURANCE
See also Insurance
HEALTH RESORTS
Boyle, T. C. Road to Wellville
Murdoch, I. The philosopher's pupil
HEALTH RESORTS, SPAS, ETC. *See* Health resorts
HEALTH SPAS *See* Health resorts; Physical fitness centers
HEALTH TEACHERS
Boyle, T. C. Road to Wellville
The **hearing.** Lescroart, J. T.
HEARING IMPAIRED
See also People with physical disabilities
The **heart.** Kerangal, M. d.
HEART -- SURGERY
See also Surgery
HEART -- TRANSPLANTATION
Kerangal, M. d. The heart
HEART -- TRANSPLANTATION
See also Transplantation of organs, tissues, etc.

The **heart** broke in. Meek, J.
HEART DISEASES
See also Diseases
The **Heart** Goes Last. Atwood, M.
The **heart** is a lonely hunter. McCullers, C.
The **heart** of danger. Seymour, G.
Heart of darkness. Conrad, J.
Heart of the hunter. Meyer, D.
The **heart** of the matter. Greene, G.
Heart of the matter. Giffin, E.
Heart of the tiger. Kerstan, L.
Heart of the west. Williamson, P.
Heart of war. Truscott, L. K.
A **heart** revealed. Kilpack, J. S.
A **heart** so white. Marias, J.
Heart-shaped box. Hill, J.
Heartbreak Hotel. Siddons, A. R.
Heartbreak of a hustler's wife. Turner, N.
The **heartbreaker.** Howatch, S.
Hearts. Wolitzer, H.
Hearts and bones. Lawrence, M. K.
The **hearts** of horses. Gloss, M.
The **Hearts** of Men. Butler, N.
Heartsick. Cain, C.
The **heartsong** of Charging Elk. Welch, J.
Heartstone. White, E. K.
Heartstones. Rendell, R.
Heartstopper. Fielding, J.
Heat. Woods, S.
Heat and dust. Jhabvala, R. P.
The **heat** of the day. Bowen, E.
The **heather** blazing. Tóibín, C.
HEAVEN
Sebold, A. The lovely bones
HEAVEN
See also Eschatology; Future life
The **heaven** of Mercury. Watson, B.
Heaven's prisoners. Burke, J. L.
The **heavens** may fall. Eskens, A.
HEAVY METAL (MUSIC)
See also Rock music
HEBREW FICTION -- TRANSLATIONS INTO ENGLISH
Appelfeld, A. Blooms of darkness
Grossman, D. Someone to run with
Leshem, R. Beaufort
Oz, A. Panther in the basement
Oz, A. The same sea
Scenes from village life
To the end of the land
HEBREW LANGUAGE
See also Language and languages
HEBREWS *See* Jews
HEBRIDES (SCOTLAND)
Pollen, B. The summer of the bear
Woolf, V. To the lighthouse
HEDGE FUNDS
Harris, R. The fear index
HEDONISM
Kazantzakis, N. Zorba the Greek
See, C. The handyman
HEDSTRÖM, PATRIK (FICTITIOUS CHARACTER)
Lackberg, C. The hidden child
Heechee rendezvous. Pohl, F.
The **Heights.** Hedges, P.
The **heir.** Burrowes, G.
Heir to the glimmering world. Ozick, C.
HEIRESSES
Duran, M. A lady's code of misconduct
Hughes, A. Market Street
HEIRS *See* Inheritance and succession
Helen of Troy. George, M.
HELEN OF TROY (LEGENDARY CHARACTER)
George, M. Helen of Troy
HELICOPTERS
See also Aeronautics; Airplanes
Hell. Butler, R. O.
HELL
See also Eschatology; Future life
HELL
Butler, R. O. Hell
Hell at the breech. Franklin, T.
Hell is empty. Johnson, C.
Hell or high water. Castro, J.
Hell or Richmond. Peters, R.
Hell to pay. Pelecanos, G. P.
Hell's gate. Crompton, R.
Hellcat Canyon series
Long, J. A. Hot in Hellcat Canyon
HELLER, NATHAN (FICTITIOUS CHARACTER)
Collins, M. A. Ask not
Helliconia spring. Aldiss, B. W.
Helliconia summer. Aldiss, B. W.
Helliconia winter. Aldiss, B. W.
The **help.** Stockett, K.
Help for the Haunted. Searles, J.
Help the poor struggler. Grimes, M.
HELPING BEHAVIOR
See also Human behavior; Interpersonal relations
Helpless. Palmer, D.
Helpless. Gowdy, B.
HELPLESSNESS (PSYCHOLOGY)
See also Emotions
HELSINKI (FINLAND) -- FICTION
Hand, E. Available dark
Hemings, Sally, 1773-1835
About
Hambly, B. Patriot hearts
Hemingway, Ernest, 1899-1961
About
McLain, P. The Paris wife
Hemingway, Hadley
About
McLain, P. The Paris wife
Henderson the rain king. Bellow, S.

Henry and Rachel. Saville, L.
Henry II, King of England, 1133-1189
About
Franklin, A. Mistress of the art of death
Franklin, A. The serpent's tale
Penman, S. K. Devil's brood
Penman, S. K. Time and chance
Penman, S. K. When Christ and his saints slept
Henry III, King of England, 1207-1272
About
Penman, S. K. Falls the shadow
Henry VIII, King of England, 1491-1547
About
Andersen, L. The Boleyn King
Gregory, P. The constant princess
Gregory, P. The other Boleyn girl
Gregory, P. The taming of the queen
Gregory, P. The Boleyn Inheritance
Mantel, H. Wolf Hall
Maxwell, R. The secret diary of Anne Boleyn
Plaidy, J. Murder most royal
Her body and other parties. Machado, C. M.
Her every fear. Swanson, P.
Her fearful symmetry. Niffenegger, A.
Her last breath. Castillo, L.
Her name was Lola. Hoban, R.
Her Sky Cowboy. Ciotta, B.
HERALDRY
See also Archeology; Signs and symbols; Symbolism
HERBIVORES
See also Animals
HERCULANEUM (ANCIENT CITY)
Goodman, C. The night villa
Here be dragons. Penman, S. K.
Here Comes the Sun. Dennis-Benn, N. Y.
Here I am. Foer, J. S.
Here I go again. Lancaster, J.
HEREDITARY SUCCESSION *See* Inheritance and succession
HERESY
See also Religion
The **heretic's** daughter. Kent, K.
Heritage of Shannara [series]
Brooks, T. The druid of Shannara
Herland. Gilman, C. P.
HERMETIC ART AND PHILOSOPHY *See* Alchemy; Astrology; Occultism
The **hermit** of Eyton Forest. Peters, E.
HERMITAGE (SAINT PETERSBURG, RUSSIA)
Dean, D. The madonnas of Leningrad
HERMITS
Alameddine, R. An Unnecessary Woman
Finn, A. J. The woman in the window
Guterson, D. The other
Johnson, D. Train dreams
HERMITS
See also Eccentrics and eccentricities
Hernández Martínez, Maximiliano, 1882-1966
About
Castellanos Moya, H. Tyrant memory
A **Hero** of France. Furst, A.
The **heroes.** Abercrombie, J.
HEROES
Grossman, A. Soon I will be invincible
Rogers, R. Devil's Cape
Heroes are my weakness. Phillips, S. E.
HEROES IN MASS MEDIA
Chabon, M. The amazing adventures of Kavalier and Clay
Heroes of the frontier. Eggers, D.
HEROIN
Nadel, B. The Ottoman cage
Robbins, T. Villa incognito
Robinson, R. Cost
Welsh, I. Skagboys
HEROISM
Keneally, T. Flying hero class
HEROISM *See* Courage; Heroes and heroines
Hespira. Hughes, M.
Heydrich, Reinhard, 1904-1942
About
Binet, L. HHhH
HHhH. Binet, L.
Hickok, Wild Bill, 1837-1876
About
Dexter, P. Deadwood
The **hidden.** Pronzini, B.
The **hidden** assassins. Wilson, R.
The **hidden** child. Lackberg, C.
HIDDEN TREASURE *See* Buried treasure
Hiddensee. Maguire, G.
Hide & seek. Patterson, J.
Hide me among the graves. Powers, T.
High country fall. Maron, M.
HIGH DEFINITION TELEVISION
See also Television
The **high** divide. Enger, L.
High fidelity. Hornby, N.
High lonesome. Oates, J. C.
The **high** mountains of Portugal. Martel, Y.
HIGH SCHOOL GIRLS -- SWEDEN -- STOCKHOLM
Giolito, M. P. Quicksand
HIGH SCHOOL GRADUATES
Hilderbrand, E. Summerland
HIGH SCHOOL STUDENTS
See also Students
HIGH SCHOOL STUDENTS
Burns, C. Black hole
Galloway, G. As simple as snow
Giolito, M. P. Quicksand
Johnson, L. L. The most dangerous place on earth
Nadol, J. This is how it ends
Racculia, K. Bellweather rhapsody
Rodriguez, L. Every hidden fear
HIGH SCHOOL TEACHERS

Johnson, L. L. The most dangerous place on earth
Scottoline, L. One perfect lie
HIGH SCHOOLS
Pierson, D. C. The boy who couldn't sleep and never had to
HIGH SPEED AERONAUTICS
See also Aeronautics
HIGH TECHNOLOGY
Pynchon, T. Bleeding edge
HIGH TECHNOLOGY INDUSTRIES
Cohen, J. Book of numbers
HIGH TREASON *See* Treason
A **high** wind in Jamaica. Hughes, R. A. W.
Highgate rise. Perry, A.
The Highland grooms [series]
London, J. Wild Wicked Scot
HIGHLANDS (SCOTLAND)
London, J. Wild Wicked Scot
The **highway.** Box, C. J.
HIGHWAY ACCIDENTS *See* Traffic accidents
HIGHWAYMEN *See* Thieves
Highwire moon. Straight, S.
HIJACKING OF AIRCRAFT *See* Hijacking of airplanes
HIJACKING OF AIRPLANES
Griffin, W. E. B. By order of the President
Hospital, J. T. Due preparations for the plague
Keneally, T. Flying hero class
HIKING
Nevill, A. The ritual
Hild. Griffith, N.
Hilda, of Whitby, Saint, 614-680
About
Griffith, N. Hild
Hildegard, Saint, 1098-1179
About
Sharratt, M. Illuminations
HILLBILLY MUSIC *See* Country music
HIMALAYA MOUNTAINS
Godden, R. Black Narcissus
HINDI LANGUAGE
See also Indian languages; Language and languages
HINDUS
Kaye, M. M. The far pavilions
Seth, V. A suitable boy
HIP-HOP FICTION *See* Urban fiction
Hippias, -490 B.C.
About
Corby, G. The Marathon conspiracy
HIPPIES
Carey, P. His illegal self
McPhee, M. L'America
HIPPIES
See also Bohemianism
Groff, L. Arcadia
HIPPOPOTAMUS
Gailey, S. River of Teeth
The **hippopotamus** pool. Peters, E.
Hirasawa, Sadamichi, 1892-1987
About
Peace, D. Occupied city
HIRED KILLERS
DeWitt, P. The Sisters brothers
Estleman, L. D. Something borrowed, something black
Gay, W. Twilight
Greatest hits
Hunter, S. Havana
Leonard, E. Mr. Paradise
Manchette Fatale
McCarthy, C. No country for old men
Neville, S. The ghosts of Belfast
Perry, T. Fidelity
Perry, T. The informant
Perry, T. Pursuit
Perry, T. Runner
Perry, T. Shadow woman
Rice, A. Angel time
Rice, A. Of love and evil
Sallis, J. The killer is dying
Silva, D. The mark of the assassin
Stroby, W. Cold shot to the heart
Vachss, A. H. Two trains running
Waite, U. The terror of living
Westlake, D. E. The hook
Winslow, D. The winter of Frankie Machine
The **Hired** Man. Forna, A.
HIRED MEN
Malamud, B. The fixer
See, C. The handyman
Tyler, A. A patchwork planet
HIRED WOMEN
Tyler, A. The clock winder
His Bloody Project. Burnet, G. M.
His cowboy heart. Ryan, J.
His illegal self. Carey, P.
His majesty's dragon. Novik, N.
His Master's Voice. Lem, S.
HISPANIC AMERICAN LITERATURE (SPANISH) -- TRANSLATIONS INTO ENGLISH
Latin@ rising
HISPANIC AMERICANS
Burgess, M. Dogfight, a love story
Valdes-Rodriguez, A. Dirty girls on top
HISPANIC AMERICANS *See* Latinos (U.S.)
The **historian.** Kostova, E.
HISTORIANS
Bayard, L. The school of night
Coetzee, J. M. Foe
Flynn, M. Eifelheim
Harris, R. Archangel
Hunt, R. Mr. Chartwell
Lively, P. How it all began
Martin, V. Trespass
McEwan, I. On Chesil Beach
Naipaul, V. S. A way in the world
Palliser, C. The unburied

Russell, M. D. Dreamers of the day
Saylor, S. The triumph of Caesar
Scott, J. Tourmaline
Tournier, M. Friday
Wilder, T. The ides of March

HISTORIANS
See also Authors

HISTORIC SITES
See also Archeology; History

HISTORICAL FICTION
Abdul-Jabbar, K. Mycroft Holmes
Aciman, A. Harvard Square
Ampuero, R. The Neruda case
The art of joy
Atkinson, K. Life After Life
Atlee, A. The typewriter girl
Atxaga, B. Seven houses in France
Ausubel, R. No one is here except all of us
Avery, E. The last nude
Bailey, M. An appetite for violets
Baker, J. The undertow
Baker, L. The Glass Ocean
Balogh, M. The escape
Balogh, M. Only a Promise
Barber, R. The Marlowe papers
Barlow, T. Babayaga
Barnes, J. The noise of time
Barrett, A. Archangel
Barrett, A. Ship fever and other stories
Barry, Q. She weeps each time you're born
Barry, S. Days Without End
Bauer, C. Frances and Bernard
The beggar king
Belfoure, C. The Paris Architect
Bell, L. How the Duke Was Won
Bennett, R. J. The company man
Bergman, M. M. Almost Famous Women
Bourne, J. The black hawk
Bourne, J. Rogue Spy
Boyden, J. Three-day road
Boyle, E. Along Came a Duke
Boyne, J. The house of special purpose
Bradley, A. I am half-sick of shadows
Brill, A. The movement of stars
Brink, A. P. Philida
Brookmyre, C. When the Devil Drives
Brown, K. The longings of wayward girls
Burrowes, G. Lady Maggie's secret scandal
Byatt, A. S. Ragnarok
Cameron, P. Coral Glynn
Carlyle, L. The bride wore scarlet
Chase, L. Dukes Prefer Blondes
Chase, L. Scandal wears satin
Chee, A. The queen of the night
Cheng, B. Southern Cross the Dog
Chevalier, T. The last runaway
Chiaverini, J. Mrs. Lincoln's dressmaker
Christie, A. Gutenberg's apprentice
Clarke, S. Jonathan Strange & Mr. Norrell
Clements, R. Revenger
Clinch, J. Finn
Cole, A. An Extraordinary Union
Cole, A. A hope divided
Collins, M. A. Ask not
Cooper, I. No proper lady
Coplin, A. The orchardist
Corby, G. The Marathon conspiracy
Corby, G. The Pericles Commission
Cornwell, B. 1356
Cornwell, B. Death of kings
Cornwell, B. The Empty Throne
Cornwell, B. The last kingdom
Crace, J. Harvest
Crichton, M. Pirate latitudes
Czepiel, K. L. A violet season
Dare, T. Any Duchess Will Do
Davies, J. D. Gentleman captain
Davies, J. D. The mountain of gold
Davis, L. Master and God
Dean, A. Bellfield Hall, or, The observations of Miss Dido Kent
Dean, M. I, Hogarth
Dekker, T. A.D. 30
Delaney, F. The matchmaker of Kenmare
Diamant, A. The Boston girl
Doerr, A. All the light we cannot see
Doig, I. Sweet thunder
Donoghue, E. Frog music
Dowlatabadi, M. The colonel
Downie, R. Semper Fidelis
Downie, R. Tabula Rasa
Druon, M. The Iron King
Duenas, M. The time in between
Duffy, S. Theodora
Duncan, D. When the saints
Duran, M. Luck Be a Lady
Egan, J. Manhattan Beach
Faulks, S. Jeeves and the Wedding Bells
Faye, L. Jane Steele
Ferrante, E. The Story of a New Name
Finch, C. A beautiful blue death
Fisher, S. W. Anna's crossing
Follett, K. Winter of the world
Ford, J. Songs of Willow Frost
Frampton, M. Put Up Your Duke
Franklin, A. The Siege Winter
Furst, A. Mission to Paris
Gabaldon, D. The fiery cross
Gardam, J. Last Friends
Gilbert, E. The Signature of All Things
Gillham, D. R. City of women
Godwin, G. Flora
Gohlke, C. I have seen him in the watchfires
Gohlke, C. Promise me this

Goldberg, P. The Yid
Gordon, M. The liar's wife
Gracie, A. The Autumn Bride
Gray, J. A Duke Never Yields
Greenwood, K. Out of the black land
Greenwood, K. Unnatural Habits
Gregory, P. The constant princess
Gregory, P. The kingmaker's daughter
Gregory, P. The lady of the rivers
Gregory, P. The red queen
Grenville, K. Sarah Thornhill
Grindle, L. Villa triste
Groot, T. Flame of resistance
Hambly, B. Good man Friday
Han, K. Human Acts
Harkness, D. E. Shadow of night
Harman, P. The midwife of Hope River
Harrison, K. Enchantments
Hatcher, R. L. Catching Katie
Hauser, E. For the most beautiful
Hensher, P. Scenes from early life
Hern, C. The bride sale
Heyns, M. The typewriter's tale
Higley, T. L. Pompeii
Hijuelos, O. Twain and Stanley Enter Paradise
Hilleman, A. World, chase me down
Hodder, M. Expedition to the Mountains of the Moon
Hood, A. The Obituary Writer
Hoyt, E. Duke of Midnight
Hoyt, E. Thief of Shadows
Hunt, L. The evening road
Hunter, M. The conquest of Lady Cassandra
Ivey, E. The snow child
James, E. The Lady Most Willing
James, E. Seven minutes in heaven
James, E. When beauty tamed the beast
James, M. A brief history of seven killings
James, P. D. Death comes to Pemberley
Jensen, N. The sisters
Joinson, S. The Photographer's Wife
Jones, E. P. The known world
Jones, J. S. The silence
Jones, S. The uninvited guests
Jones, S. Four sisters, all queens
Joyce, R. The Love Song of Miss Queenie Hennessy
Kane, B. Spartacus
Keane, M. B. Fever
Keene, J. Counternarratives
Kent, K. The outcasts
Kerr, P. A Man Without Breath
Kerstan, L. The golden leopard
Kibler, J. Calling Me Home
Kidd, S. M. The invention of wings
Kimani, P. Dance of the Jakaranda
Kirkpatrick, J. A flickering light
Kneale, M. English passengers
Koen, K. Before Versailles
Kowal, M. R. Without a summer
Kramer, L. Search for My Heart
Krivak, A. The signal flame
Lambdin, D. Hostile Shores
Lawton, J. Then We Take Berlin
Leavitt, D. The Two Hotels Francfort
Lehmann, S. Astor Place Vintage
Lent, J. A slant of light
Lethem, J. Dissident Gardens
Lin, J. The Dragon and the Pearl
Linden, C. Love and other scandals
Livesey, M. The flight of Gemma Hardy
Locke, A. The cutting season
Loigman, L. C. The two-family house
London, L. The windflower
Lyndon, R. Hawk quest
MacLean, S. No Good Duke Goes Unpunished
MacLean, S. One Good Earl Deserves a Lover
Majmudar, A. Partitions
Makumbi, J. N. Kintu
Mallon, T. Watergate
Manfredi, V. M. A Winter's Night
Manning, K. My notorious life
Mantel, H. Bring up the bodies
The map of time
McCann, C. Transatlantic
McGuire, I. The North water
Medeiros, T. The Temptation of Your Touch
Meyer, P. The Son
Moore, A. Jerusalem
Moore, S. The life of objects
Morgan, R. The road from Gap Creek
Morgenstern, E. The night circus
Morris, M. Man in the blue moon
Morrow, J. The last witchfinder
Morton, C. Stealing Mona Lisa
Moyes, J. The girl you left behind
Naslund, S. J. The Fountain of St. James Court
Nicholas, D. Something red
Nicholson, W. Motherland
Nickson, C. Cold cruel winter
Norfolk, L. John Saturnall's feast
Oates, J. C. The Accursed
O'Brien, T. L. The Lincoln conspiracy
Odell, J. The healing
O'Loughlin, E. Minds of winter
Pajer, B. Capacity for murder
Pajer, B. Fatal induction
Parris, S. J. Sacrilege
Pearl, M. The last Dickens
Perry, A. A sunless sea
Perry, S. The Essex Serpent
Pitts, L. Freeman
The Poisoned Pilgrim
Powers, T. Hide me among the graves
Powning, B. The sea captain's wife
Preston, C. The scrapbook of Frankie Pratt

Proulx, A. Barkskins
Pulley, N. The Bedlam Stacks
Putney, M. J. Nowhere near respectable
Rabb, J. Among the living
Rash, R. The cove
Rice, A. Prince Lestat
Rindell, S. The Other Typist
Roberts, M. Ignorance
Robertson, I. Island of bones
Roy, L. Let me die in his footsteps
Roy, L. Until she comes home
Ruiz Zafon, C. The prisoner of heaven
Russell, M. D. Epitaph
Saint James, S. The haunting of Maddy Clare
Salter, J. All that is
Saylor, S. Raiders of the Nile
Saylor, S. Roma
Saylor, S. The seven wonders
Schwarz, C. The Edge of the Earth
Scott, K. That deadman dance
Sharratt, M. Illuminations
Shepard, K. The Celestials
Shepherd, L. A fatal likeness
Shepherd, L. The solitary house
Shreve, A. Fortune's Rocks
Silver, M. Mary Coin
Smith, D. The last painting of Sara De Vos
Smith, Z. Swing time
Sontag, S. The volcano lover
Speller, E. The strange fate of Kitty Easton
Spencer, S. The dead hand of history
Spencer, S. Echoes of the dead
Spufford, F. Golden Hill
Stachniak, E. The Winter Palace
Stedman, M. L. The light between oceans
Stott, R. The coral thief
Sykes, S. D. Plague Land
Tallis, F. Vienna blood
Tan, A. The Valley of Amazement
Tan, T. E. The Garden of Evening Mists
Thomas, S. Beguiling the beauty
Thomas, S. Delicious
Thomas, S. Ravishing the heiress
Thomas, S. Tempting the bride
Thompson, V. Murder on Fifth Avenue
Todd, C. An unmarked grave
Traveler of the century
Unsworth, B. The quality of mercy
Urrea, L. A. The hummingbird's daughter
Urrea, L. A. Queen of America
Van Booy, S. The illusion of separateness
Vollmann, W. T. The Dying Grass
Wallace, W. The painted bridge
Warner, K. Bride of the high country
Wascom, K. The Blood of Heaven
Watson, L. Let him go
Wilhide, E. Ashenden
Williams, N. J. Landfalls
Willig, L. The Ashford affair
Willig, L. The secret history of the pink carnation
Winspear, J. Elegy for Eddie
Winspear, J. Leaving Everything Most Loved
Woodrell, D. The maid's version
Worsley, K. She rises
Wrinkle, M. Wash
Zimmerman, J. The orphanmaster
HISTORICAL NOVELS *See* Historical fiction
HISTORICAL REENACTMENTS
Whittle, T. Blood, Ash, and Bone
Historical romances. Twain, M.
The **history** of Danish dreams. Hoeg, P.
The **history** of love. Krauss, N.
The **history** of the siege of Lisbon. Saramago, J.
A **history** of the world in 10 1/2 chapters. Barnes, J.
The **history** of Tom Jones, a foundling. Fielding, H.
History of wolves. Fridlund, E.
HISTORY, MODERN -- 20TH CENTURY *See* World history -- 20th century
HIT AND RUN DRIVERS
Joss, M. The night following
Hit me. Block, L.
HIT-AND-RUN DRIVERS
Goodman, C. River Road
Schwartz, J. B. Reservation Road
Hitchers. McIntosh, W.
The **hitchhiker's** guide to the galaxy. Adams, D.
Hitler's peace. Kerr, P.
Hitler, Adolf, 1889-1945
About
Harris, R. Fatherland
Mailer, N. The castle in the forest
Neugeboren, J. 1940
HIV DISEASE *See* AIDS (Disease)
HMONG (ASIAN PEOPLE)
See also Indigenous peoples
HOAXES
Carey, P. My life as a fake
Pynchon, T. The crying of lot 49
The **hobbit,** or, There and back again. Tolkien, J. R. R.
HOCKEY
Rice, L. Summer light
Hocus pocus. Vonnegut, K.
HODGKIN'S DISEASE
Harris, M. Bang the drum slowly
HOGARTH, WILLIAM, 1697-1764
Dean, M. I, Hogarth
Hold tight. Coben, H.
Holding still for as long as possible. Whittall, Z.
A **hole** in Texas. Wouk, H.
The **hole** we're in. Zevin, G.
HOLE, HARRY (FICTITIOUS CHARACTER)
The leopard
Phantom
HOLIDAYS

Sedaris, D. Holidays on ice
Holidays on ice. Sedaris, D.
Holliday, John Henry, 1851-1887
About
Russell, M. D. Doc
The **Hollow.** Christie, A.
The **hollow** city. Wells, D.
The **hollow** hills. Stewart, M.
The **hollow-eyed** angel. Van de Wetering, J.
Hollywood. Vidal, G.
HOLLYWOOD (CALIF.)
Alcott, K. A touch of stardust
Bagshawe, T. Adored
Ephron, H. Night Night, Sleep Tight
Erickson, S. Zeroville
Ford, J. Songs of Willow Frost
Gold, G. D. Sunnyside
Oates, J. C. Blonde
Kaminsky, S. M. To catch a spy
Quick, A. The girl who knew too much
Rivers, F. Bridge to haven
Sallis, J. Drive
Vidal, G. Hollywood
Wambaugh, J. Harbor nocturne
Wambaugh, J. Hollywood Hills
Wambaugh, J. Hollywood Station
Weiner, J. The next best thing
Wouk, H. The lawgiver
Hollywood crows. Wambaugh, J.
Hollywood Hills. Wambaugh, J.
Hollywood Station. Wambaugh, J.
Holmes on the range. Hockensmith, S.
Holmes, Oliver Wendell, 1809-1894
About
Pearl, M. The Dante Club
HOLMES, SHERLOCK (FICTIONAL CHARACTER)
Doyle, A. C. S. The adventures and the memoirs of Sherlock Holmes
Faye, L. The whole art of detection
Gaiman, N. Trigger warning
King, L. R. The beekeeper's apprentice, or, on the segregation of the queen
King, L. R. The game
Moore, G. The Sherlockian
HOLMES, SHERLOCK (FICTIONAL CHARACTER)
See also Fictional characters
HOLOCAUST DENIAL
See also Holocaust, 1939-1945
HOLOCAUST SURVIVORS
Adler, H. G. Panorama
Adler, H. G. The wall
Auslander, S. Hope
Bellow, S. Mr. Sammler's planet
Chatwin, B. Utz
Krauss, N. The history of love
Michaels, A. Fugitive pieces
Ozick, C. The shawl
Perlman, E. The street sweeper
Prose, F. A changed man
Rosen, J. Joy comes in the morning
Wallant, E. L. The pawnbroker
Wiesel, E. The forgotten
Winer, A. The marriage artist
HOLOCAUST SURVIVORS
See also Holocaust, 1939-1945
HOLOCAUST VICTIMS
Lourie, R. A hatred for tulips
HOLOCAUST, 1933-1945 *See* Holocaust, 1939-1945
HOLOCAUST, 1939-1945
See also Antisemitism; Germany -- History -- 1933-1945; Jews -- Persecutions
HOLOCAUST, 1933-1945
Amis, M. Time's arrow
Appelfeld, A. Badenheim 1939
Appelfeld, A. Blooms of darkness
Austerlitz
The Book of Harlan
Chasing the king of hearts
Cooley, M. The archivist
De Rosnay, T. Sarah's key
Drndić, D. Trieste
The emigrants
Harris, R. Fatherland
Iles, G. Black cross
Jensen, J. Dante's equation
Keneally, T. Schindler's list
Konar, A. Mischling
Krauss, N. Great house
Lebrecht, N. The song of names
Martel, Y. Beatrice and Virgil
Matthiessen, P. In Paradise
Norman, H. The museum guard
Ozick, C. The shawl
Reich, T. My Holocaust
Russell, M. D. A thread of grace
Shepard, J. The book of Aron
Uris, L. Mila 18
Wander, F. The seventh well
Wiesel, E. The forgotten
Zimler, R. The seventh gate
HOLOCAUST, (1939-1945) -- HUNGARY
Waldman, A. Love and treasure
HOLOCAUST, JEWISH (1939-1945) *See* Holocaust, 1939-1945
A **hologram** for the king. Eggers, D.
Holy fire. Sterling, B.
Holy skirts. Steinke, R.
HOLY WEEK
Faulkner, W. A fable
Home. Robinson, M.
Home. Morrison, T.
HOME
Chanter, C. The well
Lee, H. Go set a watchman

Palmer, L. Nowhere but home
HOME -- PSYCHOLOGICAL ASPECTS
Bennett, R. J. American elsewhere
HOME ACCIDENTS
See also Accidents
Home again. Hannah, K.
HOME BUILDING INDUSTRY *See* Construction industry
HOME DETENTION
Towles, A. A Gentleman in Moscow
HOME EXCHANGING
Swanson, P. Her every fear
Home fire. Shamsie, K.
Home fires. Rice, L.
Home fires. Wolfe, G.
Home front. Hannah, K.
HOME LIFE *See* Family life
HOME VIDEO SYSTEMS
See also Television
HOME-BASED BUSINESS
See also Business; Self-employed; Small business
Homecoming. Schlink, B.
HOMECOMING
Butler, S. Ten things I've learnt about love
Groff, L. Arcadia
Harper, J. The dry
Harris, J. Peaches for Father Francis
Lasser, S. Say nice things about Detroit
HOMECOMINGS
Settle, M. L. The killing ground
Homegoing. Gyasi, Y.
HOMELESS *See* Homeless persons; Homelessness
HOMELESS PEOPLE *See* Homeless persons
HOMELESS PERSONS
Auster, P. In the country of last things
Banks, R. Lost memory of skin
Bock, C. Beautiful children
Jackson, N. Who do I talk to?
Kennedy, W. Ironweed
Kubica, M. Pretty Baby
Rendell, R. The keys to the street
Robinson, M. Lila
Rock, P. My abandonment
Vlautin, W. Lean on Pete
Walters, M. The echo
HOMELESSNESS
See also Housing; Poverty; Social problems
HOMEMAKERS
Ellis, H. American housewife
Shepard, J. The world to come
HOMEOPATHIC PHYSICIANS
Boyne, J. Crippen
Homer
About
Malouf, D. Ransom
Homer & Langley. Doctorow, E. L.
HOMES *See* Houses
HOMESTEADING
Doig, I. Dancing at the Rascal Fair
Stegner, W. E. The Big Rock Candy Mountain
HOMICIDE
See also Crime; Criminal law; Offenses against the person
Anolik, L. Dark Rooms
Aslam, N. Maps for lost lovers
Barclay, L. Trust your eyes
Bell, A. The reapers are the angels
Black, C. Murder in the Bastille
Black, C. Murder in the Marais
Box, C. J. Breaking point
Box, C. J. Force of nature
Box, C. J. Free fire
Bradley, A. I am half-sick of shadows
Burns, C. Black hole
Cain, C. Kill you twice
Callihan, K. Firelight
Carey, J. Dark currents
Church, J. A corpse in the Koryo
Clark, M. Guilt by association
Cleave, P. Cemetery Lake
Coben, H. Stay close
Cotterill, C. Slash and burn
Dean, A. A place of confinement
Edwards, Y. A Cupboard full of coats
Elias, G. Danse macabre
Elkins, A. J. Dying on the vine
Ellis, D. In the company of liars
Faletti, G. A pimp's notes
Flynn, G. Gone girl
Freeman, B. Spilled blood
French, N. Tuesday's gone
French, T. Broken Harbor
Gardner, L. Catch me
Gardner, L. Live to tell
Gaspar de Alba, A. Desert blood
Geagley, B. Year of the hyenas
Greaves, C. J. Hard twisted
Griffiths, E. The Janus stone
Hambly, B. Ran away
Hamilton, P. F. Great north road
Harrod-Eagles, C. Old bones
Hart, E. Haunted ground
Haynes, E. Dark tide
Higashino, K. The devotion of suspect X
Hunt, A. City of saints
The Infatuations
James, P. D. Death comes to Pemberley
Jensen, L. The uninvited
Johnson, C. Hell is empty
Johnson, C. Death without company
Kerley, J. The death collectors
Klaussmann, L. Tigers in red weather
Knopf, C. Dead anyway
Lackberg, C. The stonecutter
Lemaitre, P. Irene

Leon, D. Blood from a stone
Levack, S. Demon of the air
Link, C. The other child
Longworth, M. L. Death at the Chateau Bremont
Malliet, G. M. A fatal winter
Martin, L. The bright forever
May, P. The Blackhouse
The Meursault investigation
Mogford, T. Shadow of the rock
Mosley, W. The last days of Ptolemy Grey
Newton, M. C. Nights of Villjamur
Nickson, C. Cold cruel winter
O'Connell, C. The chalk girl
Palmer, D. Helpless
Paretsky, S. Breakdown
Parks, B. The girl next door
Parshall, S. Bleeding through
Penny, L. How the light gets in
Pessl, M. Night Film
Priest, C. The islanders
Raimondo, L. Dante's wood
The redeemer
Robertson, I. Circle of shadows
Robotham, M. Suspect
Rodriguez, L. Every broken trust
Searles, J. Help for the Haunted
Sears, M. Black Fridays
Sedgwick, M. Mister Memory
Shafak, E. Honor
Snow White must die
Stabenow, D. Less than a treason
Sullivan, M. J. Theft of swords
Thompson, J. Lucifer's tears
Thompson, V. Murder in Chinatown
Thompson, V. Murder on Lenox Hill
Tolkien, S. The king of diamonds
Upson, N. Two for sorrow
Walker, W. Crime of Privilege
Wortham, R. The rock hole

HOMICIDE INVESTIGATION
Harper, J. The dry

HOMICIDE TRIALS *See* Trials (Homicide)

The **homing.** Saul, J.

HOMO SAPIENS *See* Human beings

HOMOPHOBIA
Kramer, L. Search for My Heart

HOMOSEXUALITY
Aciman, A. A. Call me by your name
Adrian, C. The great night
Baldwin, J. Tell me how long the train's been gone
Barker, P. The eye in the door
Cunningham, M. Flesh and blood
D'Erasmo, S. The Sky Below
Durrell, L. Clea
Forster, E. M. Maurice
Frame, R. The lantern bearers
Gide, A. The counterfeiters (Les faux-monnayeurs)
Gide, A. The immoralist
Glass, J. Three Junes
Glass, J. The whole world over
Glass, J. The widower's tale
Grant, S. Map of Ireland
Greer, A. S. The story of a marriage
Grumbach, D. The book of knowledge
Haddon, M. A spot of bother
Hamilton, J. The short history of a prince
Harris, E. L. And this too shall pass
Haslett, A. Union Atlantic
Hodgen, C. Elegies for the brokenhearted
Howrey, M. Blind sight
Keyes, M. Last Chance Saloon
Lessing, D. M. The good terrorist
Lipman, E. The family man
Mallon, T. Fellow travelers
Mann, T. Death in Venice
Maupin, A. Mary Ann in autumn
Maupin, A. Michael Tolliver lives
Monette, P. Afterlife
Murdoch, I. The bell
Murdoch, I. A fairly honourable defeat
O'Neill, J. At swim, two boys
Parkhurst, C. Lost and found
Penguin book of gay short fiction
Puig, M. Kiss of the spider woman
Pym, B. The sweet dove died
Renault, M. The Persian boy
Rush, N. Mortals
Self, W. Dorian
Tóibín, C. The blackwater lightship
Trollope, J. The best of friends
Truong, M. The book of salt
Truscott, L. K. Heart of war
Vidal, G. The city and the pillar
Vine, B. No night is too long
Waugh, E. Brideshead revisited
Welsh, L. The cutting room
White, E. The beautiful room is empty
White, E. A boy's own story
White, E. Hotel de Dream
White, E. The married man

HOMOSEXUALITY
See also Sex

HOMOSEXUALITY -- INDIA
Festing, I. A. The birdkeeper

HONDURAS
Theroux, P. The Mosquito Coast

HONESTY
See also Ethics; Human behavior

HONEY
See also Food

Honeydew. Pearlman, E.

Honeymooners. Kinder, C.

HONEYMOONS
McEwan, I. On Chesil Beach

HONG KONG
Gardam, J. The man in the wooden hat
Lanchester, J. Fragrant Harbor
Lee, J. Y. K. The piano teacher
Theroux, P. Kowloon Tong
Honky tonk samurai. Lansdale, J. R.
Honor. Shafak, E.
HONOR
Eng, T. T. The gift of rain
Shafak, E. Honor
The **honorary** consul. Greene, G.
Honored guest. Williams, J.
HONOUR *See* Honor
The **honourable** schoolboy. Le Carre, J.
Hood rat novel. [series]
K'wan (Author) Welfare wifeys
HOODLUMS
Amis, M. Lionel Asbo
The **hook.** Westlake, D. E.
Hooker, Joseph, 1814-1879
About
Mrazek, R. J. Unholy fire
HOOVER DAM (ARIZ. AND NEV.)
See also Dams
Hope. Auslander, S.
HOPE
See also Emotions; Spiritual life; Virtue
HOPE
Maguire, G. Hiddensee
Sankaran, L. The hope factory
A **hope** divided. Cole, A.
The **hope** factory. Sankaran, L.
Hopkins, Gerard Manley, 1844-1889
About
Hansen, R. Exiles
Hopper, Edward, 1882-1967
About
In sunlight or in shadow
Hopscotch. Cortazar, J.
Hornblower and the Atropos. Forester, C. S.
Hornblower and the Hotspur. Forester, C. S.
Hornblower during the crisis, and two stories: Hornblower's temptation and The last encounter. Forester, C. S.
The **horned** man. Lasdun, J.
Hornet flight. Follett, K.
Horns. Hill, J.
HOROLOGY *See* Clocks and watches; Sundials; Time
The **horrific** sufferings of the mind-reading monster Hercules Barefoot. Vallgren
HORROR FICTION
Danielewski, M. Z. The familiar
Danielewski, M. Z. House of leaves
Darnielle, J. Universal harvester
Deborde, R. Portlandtown
Flanery, P. Fallen land
Gaiman, N. Trigger warning
Gaiman, N. Fragile things
Grant, M. Deadline
Gray, A. Gutshot
Hayder, M. Poppet
Hill, J. The fireman
Jensen, L. The uninvited
King, S. The bazaar of bad dreams
King, S. Carrie
King, S. Cujo
King, S. Different seasons
King, S. Doctor Sleep
King, S. Firestarter
King, S. Four past midnight
King, S. It
King, S. Night shift
King, S. Pet sematary
King, S. Salem's Lot
King, S. Skeleton crew
King, S. The stand
Koontz, D. R. The bad place
Koontz, D. R. Watchers
LaValle, V. D. The devil in silver
Levin, I. Rosemary's baby
Levin, I. The Stepford wives
Little star
The living dead
Lovecraft, H. P. H. P. Lovecraft
Malerman, J. Bird Box
Matheson, R. I am legend
Mott, J. The Returned
Nevill, A. The house of small shadows
Nevill, A. The ritual
The new annotated Dracula
New Cthulhu
Nightmares
Oates, J. C. The Accursed
Oates, J. C. Lovely, Dark, Deep
Reid, I. I'm thinking of ending things
Saadawi, A. Frankenstein in Baghdad
Sisters of the Revolution
HORROR FILMS
See also Motion pictures
Pessl, M. Night Film
HORROR GRAPHIC NOVELS
See also Graphic novels
The **horror** in the museum, and other revisions.
HORROR NOVELS *See* Horror fiction
HORROR RADIO PROGRAMS
See also Radio programs
HORROR STORIES
American fantastic tales: terror and the uncanny from Poe to the pulps
American fantastic tales: terror and the uncanny from the 1940s to now
Barker, C. Coldheart Canyon
Bradbury, R. Something wicked this way comes
Due, T. Blood colony
Gallagher, S. The kingdom of bones

Grant, H. The glass demon
Grant, M. Feed
Gregory, D. Pandemonium
Gregory, D. Raising Stony Mayhall
Hill, J. Heart-shaped box
Hill, J. Horns
Hooper, T. Midnight movie
The horror in the museum, and other revisions
Irwin, S. M. The dead path
James, H. The turn of the screw
Kasischke, L. The raising
King, S. Black house
King, S. The shining
King, S. Thinner
Koryta, M. The ridge
Koryta, M. So cold the river
Lamberson, G. The frenzy way
Lansdale, J. R. The complete Drive-in
Lebbon, T. Fallen
March, W. The bad seed
Marks, J. Fangland
Martin, V. Mary Reilly
McCammon, R. R. Boy's life
Moody, D. Hater
O'Connor, F. The violent bear it away
The Oxford book of gothic tales
Pekearo, N. T. The wolfman
Poe's children
Preston, D. Reliquary
Pyper, A. The killing circle
Rayne, S. Property of a lady
Rice, A. The queen of the damned
Rice, A. The vampire Lestat
Rice, A. Blood canticle
Rice, A. Interview with the vampire
Rice, A. The tale of the body thief
Rice, A. The vampire Armand
Rice, A. The witching hour
Saul, J. The homing
Saul, J. Midnight voices
Saul, J. Second child
Shelley, M. W. Frankenstein; or, The modern Prometheus
Simmons, D. The terror
Stevenson, R. L. The strange case of Dr. Jekyll and Mr. Hyde
Stoker, B. Dracula
Straub, P. A dark matter
Straub, P. Ghost story
Straub, P. In the night room
Straub, P. Lost boy lost girl
Straub, P. Mr. X
Strieber, W. The hunger
Stross, C. The Jennifer morgue
Tryon, T. The other
The white people and other weird stories
Whitehead, C. Zone one
Winters, B. H. Bedbugs
The Year's best fantasy and horror
Zeltserman, D. The caretaker of Lorne Field
HORROR STORIES *See* Horror fiction
HORROR TALES
Grant, M. Down Among the Sticks and Bones
Harris, T. Hannibal rising
Hill, J. Strange Weather
HORROR TALES *See* Horror fiction
HORROR TELEVISION PROGRAMS
See also Television programs
HORSE BREEDING
Machart, B. The wake of forgiveness
HORSE FARMS
Hoag, T. Dark horse
Horse heaven. Smiley, J.
HORSE RACING
Francis, D. Bolt
Francis, D. Even money
Francis, D. Longshot
Francis, D. Nerve
Francis, D. Smokescreen
Francis, D. Whip hand
Francis, F. Dick Francis's Damage
Gordon, J. Lord of Misrule
Morgan, C. E. The sport of kings
Smiley, J. Horse heaven
HORSE RACING -- ENGLAND
Francis, F. Dick Francis's Damage
HORSE TRAINERS
Hagy, A. Boleto
The **horse** whisperer. Evans, N.
The **Horse** You Came In On. Grimes, M.
HORSEMANSHIP
Hagy, A. Boleto
HORSES
Evans, N. The horse whisperer
Gaitskill, M. The mare
Gloss, M. The hearts of horses
Gordon, J. Lord of Misrule
Greaves, C. Hush money
Hagy, A. Boleto
McCarthy, C. All the pretty horses
Meno, J. Marvel and a wonder
Meyers, K. The work of wolves
Olmstead, R. Coal black horse
Vlautin, W. Lean on Pete
HORSES -- BREEDING
Morgan, C. E. The sport of kings
HOSIERY
See also Clothing and dress; Textile industry
HOSPITAL ADMINISTRATORS
Boyle, T. C. Road to Wellville
HOSPITAL LIBRARIES
See also Libraries
HOSPITAL SHIPS
See also Hospitals; Ships
HOSPITALITY

Waters, S. The Paying Guests

HOSPITALS
Parsons, K. Doing harm

HOSPITALS -- RUSSIA
Marra, A. A constellation of vital phenomena

HOSPITALS AND SANATORIUMS
Adrian, C. The children's hospital
Barker, P. The eye in the door
Barker, P. The ghost road
Barker, P. Regeneration
Blatty, W. P. Dimiter
Cook, R. Coma
Hemingway, E. A farewell to arms
Hooker, R. MASH
Hulme, K. The nun's story
Jackson, C. The lost weekend
Kesey, K. One flew over the cuckoo's nest
Mann, T. The magic mountain
McCullough, C. An indecent obsession
Rosten, L. Captain Newman, M.D.
Sanders, L. The sixth commandment
See, C. There will never be another you
Solzhenitsyn, A. Cancer ward
Wharton, W. Birdy
Willis, C. Passage

Hostage.

HOSTAGE ESCAPES *See* Escapes

HOSTAGE NEGOTIATION
See also Hostages; Negotiation

Hostage taker. Pintoff, S.

HOSTAGES
Black, L. Takeover
Dovey, C. Blood kin
Green, G. D. Ravens
Greene, G. The tenth man
Gruber, M. The good son
Hunter, S. Soft target
Iles, G. Third degree
King, S. Misery
Lively, P. Cleopatra's sister
O'Brien, E. House of splendid isolation
Palmer, M. The patient
Patchett, A. Bel canto
Patterson, J. Roses are red
Pintoff, S. Hostage taker
Powers, R. Plowing the dark
Tyler, A. Earthly possessions
Wiesel, E. Dawn
Wiesel, E. The judges

HOSTAGES
See also Terrorism

Hostile Shores. Lambdin, D.
Hot in Hellcat Canyon. Long, J. A.
The **hot** kid. Leonard, E.
Hot Milk. Levy, D.
The **hot** rock. Westlake, D. E.
Hot Springs. Hunter, S.
Hotel de Dream. White, E.
Hotel du Lac. Brookner, A.
Hotel Paradise. Grimes, M.
Hotel Pastis. Mayle, P.

HOTELS -- RUSSIA
Towles, A. A Gentleman in Moscow

HOTELS AND MOTELS
Binchy, M. A week in winter
Dickey, E. J. One night
Racculia, K. Bellweather rhapsody
Walter, J. Beautiful Ruins

HOTELS, TAVERNS, ETC.
Ali, M. In the kitchen
Amado, J. Gabriela, clove and cinnamon
Brookner, A. Hotel du Lac
Conrad, J. Victory
Du Maurier, D. Jamaica Inn
Egan, J. The keep
Garcia, C. The lady matador's hotel
Godden, R. The greengage summer
Grimes, M. Hotel Paradise
Haig, M. The dead fathers club
Hoffman, A. The third angel
Hunt, S. The invention of everything else
King, S. The shining
Koryta, M. So cold the river
Lent, J. Lost nation
Mayle, P. Hotel Pastis
Mehta, G. A river Sutra
Mohr, J. Damascus
Robinson, S. Callahan's con
Taylor, E. Mrs. Palfrey at the Claremont

The **Hottest** Dishes of the Tartar Cuisine. Bronsky, A.
Hotwire. Kava, A.
Hour of the Red God. Crompton, R.
The **hours.** Cunningham, M.
The **house** at Riverton. Morton, K.
The **house** at sea's end. Griffiths, E.
The **house** at the edge of night. Banner, C.
A **house** for Mr. Biswas. Naipaul, V. S.
The **house** girl. Conklin, T.
House made of dawn. Momaday, N. S.
The **house** of blue mangoes. Davidar, D.
House of echoes. Duffy, B.
House of holes. Baker, N.
The **House** of Impossible Loves. López Barrio, C.
House of leaves. Danielewski, M. Z.
House of meetings. Amis, M.
House of Names. Tóibín, C.

House of Niccolò [series]
Dunnett, D. Niccolo rising
Dunnett, D. Race of scorpions
Dunnett, D. To lie with lions

House of Romanov
About
Eastland, S. Eye of the Red Tsar

The **house** of rumour. Arnott, J.

The **house** of shattered wings. De Bodard, A.
The **House** of Silk. Horowitz, A.
The **house** of small shadows. Nevill, A.
The **house** of special purpose. Boyne, J.
House of splendid isolation. O'Brien, E.
The **house** of stairs. Vine, B.
House of the rising sun. Burke, J. L.
The **House** of the Seven Gables. Hawthorne, N.
The **house** of the spirits. Allende, I.
The **house** of the stag. Baker, K.
The **house** of the Vestals. Saylor, S.
The **house** of tomorrow. Bognanni, P.
The **house** of Wolfe. Blake, J. C.
The **house** on Fortune Street. Livesey, M.
The **house** on Mango Street. Cisneros, S.
House rules. Picoult, J.
The **house** sitter. Lovesey, P.
HOUSEBOATS
Haynes, E. Dark tide
HOUSEHOLD EMPLOYEES
Burrowes, G. The heir
Like Family
Ozick, C. Heir to the glimmering world
Park, P. Re Jane
Swift, G. Mothering Sunday
Umrigar, T. N. The space between us
Van Niekerk, M. Agaat
HOUSEHOLD EMPLOYEES -- ENGLAND -- SOCIAL CONDITIONS -- 18TH CENTURY
Bailey, M. An appetite for violets
Household saints. Prose, F.
The **housekeeper** and the professor. Agawa, Y.
HOUSEKEEPERS
Adams, A. After the war
Agawa, Y. The housekeeper and the professor
Doig, I. The whistling season
McBain, E. Alice in jeopardy
Stein, G. Three lives
Tobar, H. The barbarian nurseries
Winkler, A. C. Dog war
HOUSEMAIDS *See* Household employees
HOUSES
De la Roche, M. Jalna
Delaney, J. P. The girl before
Flournoy, A. c. The Turner house
Forna, A. The Hired Man
Forster, E. M. Howards End
Hawthorne, N. The House of the Seven Gables
Howatch, S. Cashelmara
Lofts, N. Gad's Hall
Makkai, R. The hundred-year house
Mawer, S. The glass room
Morris, M. Man in the blue moon
Naipaul, V. S. A house for Mr. Biswas
Rosenblatt, R. Lapham rising
Scott, A. Calpurnia
Speller, E. The strange fate of Kitty Easton
Stewart, M. Touch not the cat
Swerling, B. Shadowbrook
Unsworth, B. After Hannibal
Visitation
Wilhide, E. Ashenden
Wolfe, G. The sorcerer's house
HOUSES -- BUYING AND SELLING
See also Real estate business
Houses of stone. Michaels, B.
HOUSESITTING
Joss, M. Half broken things
HOUSEWIVES
Hood, A. The Obituary Writer
HOUSING
See also Houses; Landlord and tenant
HOUSTON (TEX.)
Kleypas, L. Brown-Eyed Girl
How far is the ocean from here. Shearn, A.
How green was my valley. Llewellyn, R.
How it all began. Lively, P.
How Stella got her groove back. McMillan, T.
How the dead dream. Millet, L.
How the Duke Was Won. Bell, L.
How the Garcia girls lost their accents. Alvarez, J.
How the light gets in. Penny, L.
How the soldier repairs the gramophone. Stanisic, S.
How to be Both. Smith, A.
How to be good. Hornby, N.
How to catch a prince. Hauck, R.
How to Get Filthy Rich in Rising Asia. Hamid, M.
How to keep your Volkswagen alive. Boucher, C.
How to live safely in a science fictional universe. Yu, C.
How to lose a duke in ten days. Guhrke, L. L.
How to make an American quilt. Otto, W.
How to read the air. Mengestu, D.
How to School Your Scoundrel. Gray, J.
How to sell. Martin, C. W.
How to set a fire and why. Ball, J.
How to start a fire. Lutz, L.
How to talk to a widower. Tropper, J.
How to Tame Your Duke. Gray, J.
How we are hungry. Eggers, D.
Howards End. Forster, E. M.
Hudgins, Andrew
About
Hudgins, A. The joker
HUDSON RIVER VALLEY (N.Y. AND N.J.) -- HISTORY -- 19TH CENTURY
Czepiel, K. L. A violet season
Hugger mugger. Parker, R. B.
Hughes, Ted, 1930-1998
About
Moses, K. Wintering
HUGO AWARD
See also Literary prizes; Science fiction
The **Hugo** winners.
Hugo, Victor, 1802-1885

About
Rose, M. J. Seduction
HUGUENOTS
See also Christian sects; Reformation
HULL (ENGLAND)
Mark, D. Original skin
The **hum** and the shiver. Bledsoe, A.
Human Acts. Han, K.
HUMAN BEHAVIOR
Novak, C. Breed
HUMAN BEINGS
Haig, M. The humans
HUMAN BEINGS -- PHILOSOPHY
Bell, A. The reapers are the angels
HUMAN BEINGS -- SEXUAL BEHAVIOR *See* Sex
The **human** body.
HUMAN BODY
See also Human beings; Self
HUMAN CLONING -- ETHICAL ASPECTS
See also Ethics
HUMAN CLONING
Lafferty, M. Six wakes
The **human** comedy. Saroyan, W.
The **human** division. Scalzi, J.
HUMAN ECOLOGY
Ghosh, A. The hungry tide
HUMAN EXPERIMENTATION IN MEDICINE
See also Medical ethics; Medicine -- Research
HUMAN EXPERIMENTATION IN MEDICINE
Cronin, J. The twelve
The **human** factor. Greene, G.
HUMAN REMAINS (ARCHEOLOGY)
Barton, F. The child
Whittle, T. Deeper than the grave
HUMAN RIGHTS
Allende, I. In the midst of winter
HUMAN SACRIFICE
Levack, S. Demon of the air
HUMAN SEXUALITY *See* Sex
The **human** stain. Roth, P.
HUMAN TRAFFICKING
Coplin, A. The orchardist
HUMAN-ALIEN ENCOUNTERS
Brin, D. Existence
Cambias, J. L. A Darkling Sea
Death's End
Haig, M. The humans
Hamilton, P. F. Great north road
Okorafor, N. Binti
Scalzi, J. The End of All Things
The three-body problem
HUMAN-ANIMAL COMMUNICATION
Johansen, I. No easy target
HUMAN-ANIMAL RELATIONSHIPS
See also Animals; Human beings
HUMAN-ANIMAL RELATIONSHIPS
Bergman, M. M. Birds of a lesser paradise
Dovey, C. Only the animals
Fowler, K. J. We Are All Completely Beside Ourselves
Geni, A. The last animal
Hagy, A. Boleto
HUMAN-COMPUTER INTERACTION
Hall, L. Speak
HUMANE TREATMENT OF ANIMALS *See* Animal welfare
HUMANITARIAN ASSISTANCE -- AFRICA
Hoagland, E. Children are diamonds
HUMANITARIAN INTERVENTION
Hoagland, E. Children are diamonds
HUMANITARIANS
Keneally, T. Schindler's list
Roosevelt, E. Murder at midnight
HUMANITARIANS *See* Philanthropists
The **humanity** project. Thompson, J.
The **humans.** Haig, M.
HUMANS IN SPACE *See* Space flight
Humboldt's gift. Bellow, S.
HUMIDITY
See also Meteorology; Weather
The **hummingbird's** daughter. Urrea, L. A.
HUMOR
Adams, D. The hitchhiker's guide to the galaxy
Adams, D. Life, the universe, and everything
Adams, D. The restaurant at the end of the universe
Adams, D. So long, and thanks for all the fish
Aira, C. The literary conference
Alvarez, J. How the Garcia girls lost their accents
Alvarez, J. Yo!
Amis, K. Lucky Jim
Beatty, P. Slumberland
Bellow, S. Henderson the rain king
Bellow, S. Mr. Sammler's planet
Berger, T. Little Big Man
Boucher, C. How to keep your Volkswagen alive
Browne, S. G. Lucky bastard
Capote, T. The grass harp
Cheever, J. The Wapshot chronicle
Cheever, J. The Wapshot scandal
Claudel, P. The investigation
Colfer, E. Plugged
Davies, V. Miracle on 34th Street
Dickens, C. The posthumous papers of the Pickwick Club
Dobyns, S. Is fat Bob dead yet?
Edgerton, C. The Bible salesman
Faulkner, W. The reivers
Fielding, H. Bridget Jones's diary
Flagg, F. Fried green tomatoes at the Whistle-Stop Cafe
Flagg, F. Standing in the rainbow
Frayn, M. Headlong
Goldstein, R. 36 arguments for the existence of God
Goodman, A. Paradise park
Greene, G. Travels with my aunt
Guo Xiaolu A concise Chinese-English dictionary for lovers
Harrison, J. The English major

Heffernan, W. The Dinosaur Club
Heller, J. Catch-22
Hiaasen, C. Lucky you
Hiaasen, C. Skinny dip
Hill, N. The Nix
Hooker, R. MASH
Hornby, N. How to be good
Hughes, L. Simple speaks his mind
Hughes, L. Simple's Uncle Sam
Jones, S. The uninvited guests
Kingsolver, B. The bean trees
Kotzwinkle, W. The bear went over the mountain
Kwan, K. China rich girlfriend
Levi, P. The monkey's wrench
Levine, S. Treasure Island!!!
Life
Lipman, E. The Inn at Lake Devine
Lodato, V. Mathilda Savitch
Lutz, L. Curse of the Spellmans
Lutz, L. Revenge of the Spellmans
Lutz, L. The Spellman files
Makkai, R. The borrower
Martin, S. The pleasure of my company
McCall Smith, A. Corduroy mansions
McCall Smith, A. Love over Scotland
McCall Smith, A. The world according to Bertie
McInerney, J. Bright lights, big city
McLarty, R. Art in America
McLaughlin, E. The nanny diaries
McMurtry, L. The evening star
McMurtry, L. Rhino Ranch
McMurtry, L. Terms of endearment
Miles, J. Dear American Airlines
Millet, L. Ghost lights
Murdoch, I. The nice and the good
Nabokov, V. V. Pnin
O'Brien, F. The complete novels
Parameswaran, R. I am an executioner
Pearson, T. R. A short history of a small place
Perry, D. This is just exactly like you
Phillips, S. E. First Star I See Tonight
Portis, C. The dog of the South
Portis, C. Gringos
Portis, C. Masters of Atlantis
Portis, C. True grit
Pratchett, T. The fifth elephant
Pratchett, T. The truth
Puchner, E. Model home
Pym, B. Jane and Prudence
Ramsland, M. Doghead
Rinehart, S. Built in a day
Roth, P. Sabbath's theater
Roth, P. My life as a man
Roth, P. Portnoy's complaint
Rushdie, S. Midnight's children
Saint, H. F. Memoirs of an invisible man
Schaffert, T. The coffins of Little Hope
Schine, C. The love letter
Sholem Aleichem The adventures of Menahem-Mendl
Sholem Aleichem The adventures of Mottel, the cantor's son
Sinha, I. Animal's people
Spark, M. The prime of Miss Jean Brodie
Steinbeck, J. Cannery Row
Steinbeck, J. Sweet Thursday
Stephenson, N. Snow Crash
Straub, E. Modern lovers
Stuckey-French, E. Revenge of the radioactive lady
Svevo, I. Zeno's conscience
Swarthout, G. F. Bless the beasts and children
Toole, J. K. A confederacy of dunces
Townsend, S. Adrian Mole
Townsend, S. The Adrian Mole diaries
Townsend, S. Adrian Mole: the lost years
Tropper, J. How to talk to a widower
Wallace, D. Big fish
Walter, J. The financial lives of the poets
Waugh, E. Decline and fall
Waugh, E. The loved one
Weiner, J. Good in bed
Weiner, J. In her shoes
Welsh, I. Trainspotting
Welty, E. The Ponder heart
West, J. The friendly persuasion
Westlake, D. E. Bad news
Westlake, D. E. Bank shot
Westlake, D. E. Don't ask
Westlake, D. E. Drowned hopes
Westlake, D. E. Get real
Westlake, D. E. Good behavior
Westlake, D. E. The hot rock
Westlake, D. E. Money for nothing
Westlake, D. E. Put a lid on it
Westlake, D. E. The road to ruin
Westlake, D. E. Smoke
Westlake, D. E. Thieves' dozen
Westlake, D. E. Watch your back
Westlake, D. E. What's so funny?
Westlake, D. E. What's the worst that could happen?
White, B. Quite a year for plums
Wibberley, L. The mouse that roared
Williams, C. Stairway to hell
Winkler, A. C. Dog war
Wodehouse, P. G. The code of the Woosters
Wodehouse, P. G. The inimitable Jeeves
Wodehouse, P. G. Tales from the Drones Club
Wodehouse, P. G. A Wodehouse bestiary
Yunis, A. The night counter
HUMOR *See* Wit and humor
HUMOR -- FORM -- ESSAYS
Hudgins, A. The joker
HUMORISTS
Clinch, J. Finn
Oates, J. C. Wild nights!

Twain, M. The gilded age and later novels
HUMORISTS
See also Wit and humor
HUMOROUS FICTION
See also Fiction; Wit and humor
HUMOROUS GRAPHIC NOVELS
See also Graphic novels
HUMOROUS PICTURES *See* Comic books, strips, etc.
HUMOROUS POETRY
See also Poetry; Wit and humor
HUMOROUS STORIES
Cadwalladr, C. The family tree
Harrison, J. The English major
Hiaasen, C. Nature girl
Hiaasen, C. Star Island
Hodgen, C. Elegies for the brokenhearted
Kunkel, B. Indecision
Mortimer, J. Quite honestly
Sedaris, D. Holidays on ice
Stuckey-French, E. Revenge of the radioactive lady
Walter, J. The financial lives of the poets
HUMOROUS STORIES *See* Humorous fiction
The **hunchback** of Notre Dame. Hugo, V.
HUNCHBACKS
Hugo, V. The hunchback of Notre Dame
Rosero, E. Good offices
The **hundred** days. O'Brian, P.
The **hundred** secret senses. Tan, A.
The **hundred** thousand kingdoms. Jemisin, N. K.
HUNDRED YEARS' WAR, 1339-1453
Cornwell, B. The archer's tale
Druon, M. The Iron King
Haasse, H. S. In a dark wood wandering
The **hundred-foot** journey. Morais, R. C.
The **hundred-year** house. Makkai, R.
HUNGARIANS -- FRANCE
Miller, A. Oxygen
HUNGARY
Vamos, M. The book of fathers
HUNGARY -- BUDAPEST
Orringer, J. The invisible bridge
Phillips, A. Prague
HUNGARY -- HISTORY -- 1956, REVOLUTION
See also Revolutions
The **hunger.** Strieber, W.
HUNGER
The hunger angel
The **hunger** angel.
HUNGER STRIKES
See also Demonstrations; Fasting; Nonviolence; Passive resistance; Resistance to government
The **hungry** tide. Ghosh, A.
The **hunt** for Red October. Clancy, T.
Hunted past reason. Matheson, R.
The **hunter.** Stark, R.
Hunter's moon. Stabenow, D.
Hunter's run. Martin, G. R. R.
HUNTERS
McMurtry, L. Buffalo girls
HUNTERS -- ICELAND -- 19TH CENTURY
The blue fox
Hunters and gatherers. Prose, F.
HUNTING
Erdrich, L. LaRose
Guthrie, A. B. The big sky
Percy, B. The wilding
Vann, D. Goat Mountain
HUNTING ACCIDENTS
Erdrich, L. LaRose
Murphy, Y. The call
Hunting badger. Hillerman, T.
HUNTINGTON'S CHOREA
Fay, J. The shortest way home
HUNTINGTON'S DISEASE -- PATIENTS
Genova, L. Inside the O'Briens
HURON, LAKE (MICH. AND ONT.)
Munro, A. Dear life
HURRICANE KATRINA, 2005
Piazza, T. City of refuge
Ward, J. Salvage the bones
HURRICANES
See also Cyclones; Storms; Winds
HURRICANES
Acevedo, C. The Distant Marvels
Ford, R. Let Me Be Frank With You
Johnson, A. Fortune smiles
The **husband.** Koontz, D. R.
HUSBAND AND WIFE
Crace, J. Being dead
Gardam, J. The man in the wooden hat
Hodgkinson, A. 22 Britannia Road
Hollingshead, G. Bedlam
Krauss, N. Great house
Lewis, S. Dodsworth
Lichtenstein, A. Lost
McCabe, E. L. I shall be near to you
McEwan, I. On Chesil Beach
Moriarty, L. The husband's secret
Nicholls, D. Us
Oates, J. C. American appetites
Oyeyemi, H. Mr. Fox
Pronzini, B. The hidden
Putney, M. J. Loving a lost lord
Rash, R. Serena
Reuss, F. Mohr
Richardson, C. S. The end of the alphabet
Sparks, N. The notebook
Tremain, R. The color
Tuck, L. I married you for happiness
Unferth, D. O. Vacation
Watson, S. J. Before I go to sleep
Wiggins, M. Evidence of things unseen
Wiggins, M. The shadow catcher
Wolitzer, M. The wife

The **husband's** secret. Moriarty, L.
HUSBANDS
Flynn, G. Gone girl
HUSBANDS
See also Family; Marriage; Married people; Men
HUSBANDS -- CRIMES AGAINST
Kent, C. The loving husband
Hush hush. Lippman, L.
Hush money. Parker, R. B.
Hush money. Greaves, C.
HYBRID AUTOMOBILES
See also Automobiles
The **Hyde** Park headsman. Perry, A.
The **Hyde** Park murder. Roosevelt, E.
HYDRAULIC FRACTURING
Herrin, L. Fractures
The **hydrogen** sonata. Banks, I.
Hylozoic. Rucker, R. v. B.
HYPERACTIVITY
See also Diseases
Hyperion. Simmons, D.
HYPNEROTOMACHIA POLIPHILI
Caldwell, I. The rule of four
HYPNOSIS *See* Hypnotism
HYPNOTISM
Kepler, L. The hypnotist
Moya, H. C. The dream of my return
Stoker, B. Dracula
The **hypnotist.** Kepler, L.
HYPOCRISY
Dickens, C. Martin Chuzzlewit
Rosero, E. Good offices
Hystopia. Means, D.

I

I Almost Forgot About You. McMillan, T.
I am an executioner. Parameswaran, R.
I am Charlotte Simmons. Wolfe, T.
I am China. Guo, X.
I am forbidden. Markovits, A.
I am half-sick of shadows. Bradley, A.
I am legend. Matheson, R.
I am no one you know. Oates, J. C.
I am Not Sidney Poitier. Everett, P. L.
I Am Pilgrim. Hayes, T.
I Am Radar. Larsen, R.
I am the brother of XX.
I am the only running footman. Grimes, M.
I capture the castle. Smith, D.
I curse the river of time. Petterson, P.
I hate to see that evening sun go down. Gay, W.
I have seen him in the watchfires. Gohlke, C.
I is for innocent. Grafton, S.
I let you go. Mackintosh, C.
I lock my door upon myself. Oates, J. C.
I married a communist. Roth, P.
I married you for happiness. Tuck, L.
I never promised you a rose garden. Greenberg, J.
I refuse.
I sailed with Magellan. Dybek, S.
I see you. Mackintosh, C.
I see you everywhere. Glass, J.
I served the King of England. Hrabal, B.
I shall be near to you. McCabe, E. L.
I thee wed. Quick, A.
I Thee Wed. Bradley, C.
I think I love you. Pearson, A.
I will send rain. Meadows, R.
I'd know you anywhere. Lippman, L.
I'll never get out of this world alive. Earle, S.
I'm so happy for you. Rosenfeld, L.
I'm thinking of ending things. Reid, I.
I've got your number. Kinsella, S.
I, Alex Cross. Patterson, J.
I, Claudius. Graves, R.
I, Hogarth. Dean, M.
I, robot. Asimov, I.
I, sniper. Hunter, S.
I, Tituba, black witch of Salem. Conde, M.
I2. Bannon, J.
IBO (AFRICAN PEOPLE)
Achebe, C. Things fall apart
Ice. Sorokin, V.
The **ice** beneath her. Grebe, C.
The **Ice** Cream Queen of Orchard Street. Gilman, S. J.
ICE CREAM, ICES, ETC.
Gilman, S. J. The Ice Cream Queen of Orchard Street
ICE HOCKEY *See* Hockey
The **ice** princess. Lackberg, C.
The **ice** queen. Hoffman, A.
The **ice** soldier. Watkins, P.
The **ice-shirt.** Vollmann, W. T.
ICEBERGS
See also Ice; Ocean; Physical geography
ICELAND -- 10TH CENTURY
Seton, A. Avalon
ICELAND
Hand, E. Available dark
The silence of the sea
ICELAND -- REYKJAVIK
Hallgrimur Helgason 101 Reykjavik
Yrsa Sigurdardottir Last rituals
ICELANDIC LANGUAGE
See also Language and languages; Scandinavian languages
ICHTHYOLOGY *See* Fishes
ICHTHYOSAURUS
See also Dinosaurs
Idaho. Ruskovich, E.
IDAHO
Carlson, R. Five skies
Hatcher, R. L. Catching Katie
Hart, B. Then came the evening

Woods, S. Heat
IDEA (PHILOSOPHY)
Horn, D. Eternal life
The **idea** of perfection. Grenville, K.
IDEAL STATES *See* Utopian fiction; Utopias
Ideas of heaven. Silber, J.
IDENTITY *See* Identity (Psychology); Individuality; Personality
IDENTITY (PSYCHOLOGY)
Alarcón, D. American odysseys
Coady, L. The antagonist
Cole, T. Every day is for the thief
Cole, T. Open city
Divakaruni, C. B. Oleander girl
Ferris, J. The unnamed
Gaige, A. Schroder
Gass, W. H. Middle C
Harding, P. Tinkers
Joss, M. Among the missing
Kunzru, H. My revolutions
Larsen, N. Passing
Lutz, L. The Passenger
Mehta, R. Quarantine
Row, J. Your face in mine
Saunders, G. Tenth of December
Smith, A. How to be Both
Smith, A. There but for the
Theroux, M. Strange bodies
Vida, V. Let the Northern Lights erase your name
Watson, S. J. Before I go to sleep
IDENTITY (PSYCHOLOGY)
See also Personality; Psychology; Self
IDENTITY THEFT
See also Offenses against the person; Theft
IDENTITY THEFT
Chaon, D. Await your reply
Ferris, J. To Rise Again at a Decent Hour
The **Ides** of April. Davis, L.
The **ides** of March. Wilder, T.
The **idiot.** Batuman, E.
If Beale Street could talk. Baldwin, J.
If ever I return, pretty Peggy-O. McCrumb, S.
If I'd killed him when I met him. McCrumb, S.
If not now, when? Levi, P.
If on a winter's night a traveler. Calvino, I.
If the creek don't rise. Weiss, L.
If this world were mine. Harris, E. L.
If you follow me. Watrous, M.
IGBO (AFRICAN PEOPLE)
Achebe, C. Things fall apart
IGLOOS
See also Houses; Inuit
Ignorance. Roberts, M.
Ignorance. Roberts, M.
IGUANODON
See also Dinosaurs
Ill will. Chaon, D.
The **Illearth** war. Donaldson, S. R.
ILLEGAL ALIENS *See* Unauthorized immigrants
ILLEGAL ALIENS
Gordimer, N. The pickup
Ko, L. The leavers
Pearson, R. The first victim
Sekaran, S. Lucky boy
Straight, S. Highwire moon
ILLEGAL ARMS TRANSFERS
Le Carré, J. A Delicate Truth
ILLEGITIMACY
Allison, D. Bastard out of Carolina
Brown, R. Half a heart
Cheever, J. Bullet Park
Chen, D. Brothers
Dickens, C. Bleak House
Dunnett, D. Pawn in frankincense
Faulkner, W. The sound and the fury
Fielding, H. The history of Tom Jones, a foundling
Findley, T. The piano man's daughter
Guterson, D. Ed King
Hawthorne, N. The scarlet letter
Krantz, J. Mistral's daughter
Kunzru, H. The impressionist
Lofts, N. Gad's Hall
Maxwell, R. The Queen's bastard
Oates, J. C. A garden of earthly delights
Rash, R. Serena
Rossner, J. Emmeline
Strout, E. Amy and Isabelle
Tryon, T. In the fire of spring
Vida, V. Let the Northern Lights erase your name
Vine, B. Anna's book
ILLEGITIMATE CHILDREN *See* Illegitimacy
ILLEGITIMATE CHILDREN
Brown, R. Half a heart
Kunzru, H. The impressionist
Thompson, V. Murder on Lenox Hill
Urrea, L. A. The hummingbird's daughter
Vida, V. Let the Northern Lights erase your name
ILLINOIS
Beard, J. A. In Zanesville
Bradbury, R. Dandelion wine
Bradbury, R. Something wicked this way comes
Hamilton, J. When Madeline was young
Straub, P. Mr. X
Thompson, J. Wide blue yonder
Turow, S. Limitations
Wilder, T. The eighth day
ILLINOIS -- 19TH CENTURY
Dickens, C. Martin Chuzzlewit
ILLINOIS -- CHICAGO
Algren, N. The man with the golden arm
Bellow, S. The adventures of Augie March
Bellow, S. Humboldt's gift
Cisneros, S. The house on Mango Street
Dreiser, T. Sister Carrie

D'Souza, T. The Konkans
Dybek, S. I sailed with Magellan
Farrell, J. T. Studs Lonigan
Hamilton, J. Disobedience
Harris, E. L. And this too shall pass
Hemon, A. Nowhere man
Just, W. S. Rodin's debutante
Just, W. S. An unfinished season
Mitchard, J. The deep end of the ocean
Newton, C. Calumet City
Norris, F. The pit
Paretsky, S. Ghost country
Phillips, S. E. It had to be you
Powers, R. Generosity
Sakey, M. The blade itself
Shonk, K. Happy now?
Sinclair, U. The jungle
Smith, D. Bright and distant shores
Spencer, S. Endless love
Turner, F. W. 1929
Wright, R. Native son
Wright, R. The outsider

ILLNESS

Betts, D. Souls raised from the dead
James, H. The wings of the dove
Klein, R. The moth diaries
Lightman, A. P. The diagnosis
Martin, V. Italian fever
Sarton, M. A reckoning

ILLNESS *See* Diseases

ILLUMINATI

Brown, D. Angels & demons

The **Illumination.** Brockmeier, K.

Illumination night. Hoffman, A.

ILLUMINATION OF BOOKS AND MANUSCRIPTS

See also Art; Books; Decoration and ornament; Illustration of books; Manuscripts; Medieval art

Vantrease, B. R. The illuminator

Illuminations. Sharratt, M.

The **illuminator.** Vantrease, B. R.

The **illusion** of separateness. Van Booy, S.

ILLUSIONS *See* Hallucinations and illusions; Optical illusions

The **illustrated** man. Bradbury, R.

ILLUSTRATION OF BOOKS

See also Art; Books; Color printing; Decoration and ornament

ILLUSTRATORS

Bock, C. Beautiful children
Martin, V. Trespass
Neugeboren, J. 1940
Norman, H. The bird artist
Shriver, L. The post-birthday world

ILLUSTRATORS

See also Artists

Ilustrado. Syjuco, M.

Imager's battalion. Modesitt, L. E.

Imager's challenge. Modesitt, L. E.

Imager's intrigue. Modesitt, L. E.

IMAGERY (PSYCHOLOGY)

Modesitt, L. E. Imager's battalion
Modesitt, L. E. Imager's intrigue
Modesitt, L. E. The one-eyed man

IMAGINARY BATTLES *See* Imaginary wars and battles

IMAGINARY CITIES

Calvino, I. Invisible cities

IMAGINARY HISTORIES (FICTION) *See* Alternative histories

IMAGINARY KINGDOMS

Barker, C. Weaveworld
Brooks, T. The druid of Shannara
Brooks, T. First king of Shannara
Brooks, T. The measure of the magic
Brooks, T. The sword of Shannara
Hope, A. The prisoner of Zenda
Pohl, F. Beyond the blue event horizon
Silverberg, R. Lord Valentine's castle
Swift, J. Gulliver's travels
Tolkien, J. R. R. The return of the king
Tolkien, J. R. R. The Silmarillion
Tolkien, J. R. R. The two towers
Vinge, J. D. The Snow Queen
Vinge, J. D. The Summer Queen
Vinge, J. D. World's end

IMAGINARY PLACES

Chakraborty, S. K. The city of brass
Dickinson, S. The traitor Baru Cormorant
Hair, D. Scarlet tides

IMAGINARY PLAYMATES

Dicks, M. Memoirs of an imaginary friend

IMAGINARY VOYAGES

See also Fantasy fiction; Science fiction

The **imaginary** voyages: The narrative of Arthur Gordon Pym; The unparalleled adventure of one Hans Pfaall; The journal of Julius Rodman. Poe, E. A.

IMAGINARY WARS AND BATTLES

See also Alternative histories

IMAGINARY WARS AND BATTLES

Death's End
Dickinson, S. The traitor Baru Cormorant
Duncan, D. When the saints
Gilman, C. I. Dark orbit
Kay, G. G. Under heaven
Mitchell, D. The bone clocks
Modesitt, L. E. Imager's battalion
Modesitt, L. E. The one-eyed man
Yang, J. Y. The black tides of heaven

IMAGINATION

Hill, J. Nos4a2
O'Malley, T. This magnificent desolation
Tuck, L. The Double Life of Liliane

Imagine me gone. Haslett, A.

Imago. Butler, O. E.

Imajica. Barker, C.

The **immaculate** deception. Pears, I.
IMMIGRANT FAMILIES
Nahai, G. B. The luminous heart of Jonah S.
IMMIGRANTS
Aciman, A. Harvard Square
Adichie, C. N. Americanah
Ali, M. Brick lane
Bezmozgis, D. The free world
Boyle, T. C. The tortilla curtain
Bronsky, A. The Hottest Dishes of the Tartar Cuisine
Cather, W. My Antonia
Cleave, C. Little Bee
Coetzee, J. M. The Childhood of Jesus
Cunningham, M. Flesh and blood
De la Pava, S. A naked singularity
Doctorow, E. L. Ragtime
D'Souza, T. The Konkans
Edwards, Y. A Cupboard full of coats
Gaige, A. Schroder
Gilmore, J. Golden country
Gilman, S. J. The Ice Cream Queen of Orchard Street
Hegi, U. The vision of Emma Blau
Hemon, A. Nowhere man
Hershon, J. The German bride
Jen, G. Typical American
Johnson, A. D. Moonshine
Kwok, J. Girl in translation
Lee, M. J. Pachinko
Levitt, P. M. Come with me to Babylon
Levy, A. Small island
Lish, A. Preparation for the Next Life
Manseau, P. Songs for the butcher's daughter
McCann, C. Let the great world spin
Mengestu, D. The beautiful things that heaven bears
Mengestu, D. How to read the air
Mukherjee, N. A life apart
Nguyen, V. T. The Refugees
Ondaatje, M. The cat's table
O'Neill, J. Netherland
Oyeyemi, H. The opposite house
Piercy, M. Sex wars
Pipkin, J. Woodsburner
Powers, R. Generosity
Prcic, I. Shards
Prose, F. My new American life
Proulx, A. Accordion crimes
Raban, J. Waxwings
Reyn, I. What happened to Anna K.
Reznikoff, C. By the waters of Manhattan
Rice, L. The lemon orchard
Roth, H. A star shines over Mt. Morris Park
Sahota, S. The year of the runaways
Samarasan, P. Evening is the whole day
Sanghera, S. Marriage Material
Shepard, K. The Celestials
See, L. Shanghai girls
Sinclair, U. The jungle
Smith, Z. White teeth
Tan, A. The bonesetter's daughter
Tóibín, C. Brooklyn
Tremain, R. The road home
Ulinich, A. Petropolis
Unnikrishnan, D. Temporary people
Vapnyar, L. Broccoli and other tales of food and love
IMMIGRANTS -- CRIMES AGAINST
Ray, K. No country
IMMIGRANTS -- ENGLAND
Mukherjee, N. A life apart
IMMIGRANTS -- LITERARY COLLECTIONS
Alarcón, D. American odysseys
IMMIGRANTS -- NEW YORK (STATE) -- NEW YORK -- 20TH CENTURY
McDermott, A. The ninth hour
IMMIGRANTS -- NEW YORK (STATE) -- NEW YORK
Alenyikov, M. Ivan and Misha
IMMIGRANTS -- UNITED STATES
Bulawayo, N. We need new names
Castellani, C. All this talk of love
Faye, L. The gods of Gotham
Freudenberger, N. The newlyweds
Gohlke, C. Promise me this
Kolpan, G. Magic words
Lee, K. Drifting house
Ray, K. No country
Yezierska, A. c. Bread givers
IMMIGRANTS IN LITERATURE
Chung, C. Forgotten country
IMMIGRANTS' WRITINGS, AMERICAN
Alarcón, D. American odysseys
IMMIGRATION AND EMIGRATION
Mbue, I. Behold the Dreamers
Mukherjee, N. A state of freedom
Rao, S. An Unrestored Woman
The **immoralist.** Gide, A.
The **immortalists.**
Immortality. Kundera, M.
IMMORTALITY
See also Eschatology; Soul; Theology
IMMORTALITY
Doctorow, C. Down and out in the Magic Kindgom
Due, T. Blood colony
Hamill, P. Forever
Horn, D. Eternal life
Kundera, M. Immortality
Marley, L. The child goddess
Robbins, T. Jitterbug perfume
Saramago, J. Death with interruptions
Sterling, B. Holy fire
Westerfeld, S. The killing of worlds
Westerfeld, S. The risen empire
Yanagihara, H. The people in the trees
Impact. Preston, D.
Imperfect birds. Lamott, A.
An **imperfect** lens. Roiphe, A. R.

Imperfect strangers. Woods, S.
The **imperfectionists.** Rachman, T.
Imperial bedrooms. Ellis, B. E.
Imperial Radch [series]
Leckie, A. Ancillary mercy
Leckie, A. Ancillary sword
IMPERIALISM
De Kretser, M. The Hamilton case
Ghosh, A. The glass palace
Kingsolver, B. The poisonwood Bible
Lapierre, A. Between love and honor
Naipaul, V. S. A way in the world
Silverberg, R. Roma eterna
Vassanji, M. G. The in-between world of Vikram Lall
Westerfeld, S. The killing of worlds
Westerfeld, S. The risen empire
Imperium.
IMPERSONATIONS
Allende, I. Daughter of fortune
Dickens, C. Our mutual friend
Dickens, C. A tale of two cities
Erdrich, L. The last report on the miracles at Little No Horse
Greene, G. The tenth man
Grimes, L. In a fix
Higgins, J. Night of the fox
Hope, A. The prisoner of Zenda
Leonard, E. Pagan babies
Mason, R. Who killed Piet Barol?
McCabe, E. L. I shall be near to you
Rice, A. Angel time
Stewart, M. The ivy tree
Tey, J. Brat Farrar
Townsend, S. Number 10
Twain, M. Pudd'nhead Wilson;
The **impossible** dead. Rankin, I.
The **Impossible** Lives of Greta Wells. Greer, A. S.
IMPOSTORS
Kunzru, H. The impressionist
Makine, A. Music of a life
IMPOSTORS AND IMPOSTURE
See also Crime; Criminals
IMPOTENCE
See also Diseases
IMPRESSIONISM (ART)
See also Art
The **impressionist.** Kunzru, H.
IMPRISONMENT
Barr, N. The rope
The **improbability** of love. Rothschild, H.
In a dark wood wandering. Haasse, H. S.
In a fix. Grimes, L.
In America. Sontag, S.
In an evil time. Pronzini, B.
In country. Mason, B. A.
In dubious battle. Steinbeck, J.
In evil hour. Garcia Marquez, G.
In her absence. Munoz Molina, A.
In her shoes. Weiner, J.
In one person. Irving, J.
In other rooms, other wonders. Mueenuddin, D.
In Paradise. Matthiessen, P.
In persuasion nation. Saunders, G.
In pinelight. Rayfiel, T.
In pursuit of the green lion. Riley, J. M.
In search of Klingsor. Volpi, J.
In search of lost time [series]
Proust, M. The captive [and] The fugitive
Proust, M. The Guermantes way
Proust, M. Sodom and Gomorrah
Proust, M. Swann's way
Proust, M. Time regained
Proust, M. Within a budding grove
In search of the Rose notes. Arsenault, E.
In sunlight and in shadow. Helprin, M.
In sunlight or in shadow.
In the beauty of the lilies. Updike, J.
In the bleak midwinter. Spencer-Fleming, J.
In the company of cheerful ladies. McCall Smith, A.
In the company of liars. Ellis, D.
In the company of the courtesan. Dunant, S.
In the Convent of Little Flowers. Sundaresan, I.
In the country. Alvar, M.
In the country of last things. Auster, P.
In the country of men. Matar, H.
In the fire of spring. Tryon, T.
In the first circle. Solzhenitsyn, A.
In the fold. Cusk, R.
In the forest. O'Brien, E.
In the garden of Iden. Baker, K.
In the heat of the night. Ball, J. D.
In the Kingdom of mists. Jakeman, J.
In the kitchen. Ali, M.
In the Lake of the Woods. O'Brien, T.
In the Lion's Mouth. Flynn, M.
In the memorial room. Frame, J.
In the midnight rain. Wind, R.
In the midst of winter. Allende, I.
In the miso soup. Murakami, R.
In the Morning I'll Be Gone. McKinty, A.
In the night room. Straub, P.
In the shadow of Gotham. Pintoff, S.
In the shadow of the banyan. Ratner, V.
In the shadow of the law. Roosevelt, K.
In the skin of a lion. Ondaatje, M.
In the unlikely event. Blume, J.
In the wake. Petterson, P.
In the wilderness.
In the wolf's mouth. Foulds, A.
In the woods. French, T.
In this light. Thon, M. R.
In this sign. Greenberg, J.
IN VITRO FERTILIZATION *See* Fertilization in vitro
In war times. Goonan, K. A.
In Your Dreams. Higgins, K.

In Zanesville. Beard, J. A.
The **in-between** world of Vikram Lall. Vassanji, M. G.
The **incarnations.** Barker, S.
INCAS
Wright, R. The gold eaters
INCENDIARY BOMBS
See also Bombs; Incendiary weapons
INCEST
Grumbach, D. The book of knowledge
Hacker, C. The Morels
Hatoum, M. The brothers
Lewis, M. G. The monk
Meloy, M. A family daughter
Noon, J. Vurt
O'Dell, T. Back roads
Rossner, J. Emmeline
Roth, H. A diving rock on the Hudson
Shreve, A. The weight of water
Theroux, P. Picture palace
Vachss, A. That's how I roll
Incident at Twenty Mile. Trevanian
INCOME
See also Economics; Finance; Property; Wealth
An **incomplete** revenge. Winspear, J.
The **increment.** Ignatius, D.
INCUNABULA
See also Books
An **indecent** obsession. McCullough, C.
Indecision. Kunkel, B.
Independence Day. Ford, R.
INDEPENDENCE DAY (UNITED STATES) *See* Fourth of July
INDEPENDENT FILMS
See also Motion pictures
INDIA
Adiga, A. Selection day
Carter, M. J. The Strangler Vine
Davidar, D. The house of blue mangoes
D'Souza, T. The Konkans
Ghachar ghochar
Ghosh, A. River of smoke
Hall, T. The case of the love commandos
Hesse, H. Siddhartha
Jacob, M. The sleepwalker's guide to dancing
Majmudar, A. Partitions
Malik, T. Three bargains
Markandaya, K. Nectar in a sieve
McDonald, I. River of gods
Mehta, G. A river Sutra
Mukherjee, N. The Lives of Others
Narayan, R. K. Mr. Sampath--the printer of Malgudi, The financial expert, Waiting for the Mahatma
Roy, A. An atlas of impossible longing
Sahota, S. The year of the runaways
Sinha, I. Animal's people
Taseer, A. The way things were
Viswanathan, P. The toss of a lemon
Zelazny, R. Lord of light
INDIA -- 1947-
Adiga, A. Last man in tower
Adiga, A. The white tiger
Chatterjee, U. English, August
Deb, S. The point of return
Desai, A. Clear light of day
Dyer, G. Jeff in Venice, death in Varanasi
Endo, S. Deep river
Jhabvala, R. P. Out of India
Mukherjee, B. Miss New India
Naipaul, V. S. Magic seeds
Narayan, R. K. Under the banyan tree and other stories
Roy, A. The god of small things
Rushdie, S. Midnight's children
Rushdie, S. Shalimar the clown
Scott, P. Staying on
Seth, V. A suitable boy
Sundaresan, I. In the Convent of Little Flowers
Suri, M. The age of Shiva
Vassanji, M. G. The assassin's song
INDIA -- BENARES
Mishima, Y. The Temple of Dawn
INDIA -- BOMBAY
Joseph, M. Serious men
Mistry, R. A fine balance
Rushdie, S. The ground beneath her feet
Rushdie, S. Midnight's children
Rushdie, S. The Moor's last sigh
Suri, M. The death of Vishnu
Umrigar, T. N. The space between us
INDIA -- BRITISH OCCUPATION, 1765-1947
Forster, E. M. A passage to India
Ghosh, A. The glass palace
Godden, R. Black Narcissus
Jhabvala, R. P. Heat and dust
Kaye, M. M. The far pavilions
Kunzru, H. The impressionist
Mehta, G. Raj
Narayan, R. K. Swami and friends, The bachelor of arts, The dark room, The English teacher
Scott, P. The Raj quartet
Sundaresan, I. The splendor of silence
INDIA -- CALCUTTA
Ghosh, A. Sea of poppies
INDIA -- DELHI
Desai, A. Clear light of day
INDIA -- HISTORY -- 1765-1947, BRITISH OCCUPATION
Ghosh, A. Flood of fire
Kerstan, L. The golden leopard
Moran, M. Rebel queen
INDIA -- HISTORY -- 1947-
Lahiri, J. The lowland
INDIA -- HISTORY -- 19TH CENTURY
Ghosh, A. Flood of fire
INDIA -- HISTORY -- 20TH CENTURY
Rao, S. An Unrestored Woman

INDIA -- HISTORY -- BRITISH OCCUPATION, 1765-1947
Moran, M. Rebel queen
Mukherjee, A. A Rising Man
INDIA -- POLITICS AND GOVERNMENT -- 1947-
Festing, I. A. The birdkeeper
INDIA -- RACE RELATIONS
Forster, E. M. A passage to India
INDIA -- RURAL LIFE
Jhabvala, R. P. Heat and dust
Narayan, R. K. The grandmother's tale and selected stories
Narayan, R. K. Malgudi days
INDIA -- SOCIAL CONDITIONS -- 20TH CENTURY
Festing, I. A. The birdkeeper
Taseer, A. The way things were
INDIA-PAKISTAN CONFLICT, 1971
Hensher, P. Scenes from early life
INDIAN ART
See also Art
INDIAN CHIEFS
O'Brien, D. The contract surgeon
Thom, J. A. Panther in the sky
INDIAN FAMILIES
Erdrich, L. LaRose
Erdrich, L. The round house
Indian killer. Alexie, S.
INDIAN LANGUAGES
See also Language and languages
The **Indian** lawyer. Welch, J.
INDIAN LEADERS
McMurtry, L. Zeke and Ned
Vollmann, W. T. Argall
INDIAN OCEAN
See also Ocean
INDIAN POETRY
See also Indian literature; Poetry
INDIAN RESERVATIONS
Erdrich, L. The round house
Erdrich, L. The last report on the miracles at Little No Horse
INDIAN RESERVATIONS -- NEW MEXICO
McLaren, K. The road to enchantment
INDIAN WOMEN -- CRIMES AGAINST
Erdrich, L. The round house
INDIANA
Day, C. The circus in winter
Martin, L. The bright forever
Moore, E. K. The Supremes sing the happy heartache blues
Nunez, S. Salvation city
Reynolds, M. The Starlite Drive-in
Tarkington, B. Alice Adams
Tucker, T. Over and under
Vonnegut, K. God bless you, Mr. Rosewater
West, J. The friendly persuasion
INDIANA -- 19TH CENTURY
Lockridge, R. Raintree County
Tarkington, B. The magnificent Ambersons
West, J. The friendly persuasion
INDIANS OF MEXICO
Levack, S. Demon of the air
INDIANS OF NORTH AMERICA
Alexie, S. Flight
Brand, M. Beyond the outposts
Brown, D. A. Creek Mary's blood
Coel, M. Blood memory
Coldsmith, D. The long journey home
Coldsmith, D. Tallgrass
Cooper, J. F. The last of the Mohicans
Erdrich, L. The red convertible
Gear, K. O. People of the masks
Gear, W. M. People of the thunder
Guthrie, A. B. The big sky
Guthrie, A. B. The way West
Hill, R. B. Hanta yo
Humphreys, J. Nowhere else on earth
L'Amour, L. Last of the breed
McCarthy, C. Blood meridian
McMurtry, L. Buffalo girls
Meyers, K. The work of wolves
Michener, J. A. Centennial
Momaday, N. S. House made of dawn
Overholser, W. D. Death of a cattle king
Perry, T. Blood money
Perry, T. Dance for the dead
Perry, T. The face-changers
Perry, T. Runner
Perry, T. Shadow woman
Perry, T. Vanishing act
Silko, L. Almanac of the dead
Silko, L. Gardens in the dunes
Sosin, D. The long-shining waters
Treuer, D. The translation of Dr Apelles
Vanderhaeghe, G. The last crossing
Welch, J. The Indian lawyer
Westlake, D. E. Bad news
Wheeler, R. S. The canyon of bones
Wheeler, R. S. North Star
Wyman, W. Blue heaven
INDIANS OF NORTH AMERICA -- ALASKA
Ivey, E. To the bright edge of the world
INDIANS OF NORTH AMERICA -- CALIFORNIA
L'Amour, L. The Californios
INDIANS OF NORTH AMERICA -- CANADA
Vollmann, W. T. Fathers and crows
INDIANS OF NORTH AMERICA -- CAPTIVITIES
Berger, T. Little Big Man
Jiles, P. The color of lightning
McCrumb, S. She walks these hills
Richter, C. The light in the forest
Thom, J. A. The red heart
INDIANS OF NORTH AMERICA
Silko, L. Almanac of the dead
INDIANS OF NORTH AMERICA -- FOLKLORE *See* Native Americans -- Folklore
INDIANS OF NORTH AMERICA -- MASSACHUSETTS
Brooks, G. Caleb's crossing

INDIANS OF NORTH AMERICA -- MONTANA
Dorris, M. A yellow raft in blue water
INDIANS OF NORTH AMERICA -- NEW MEXICO
Cather, W. Death comes for the archbishop
INDIANS OF NORTH AMERICA -- NORTH DAKOTA
Erdrich, L. The plague of doves
Erdrich, L. The last report on the miracles at Little No Horse
Erdrich, L. Love medicine
Erdrich, L. Tracks
Power, S. The grass dancer
INDIANS OF NORTH AMERICA -- RESERVATIONS
Rosenberg, R. This is not civilization
INDIANS OF NORTH AMERICA -- SOUTHWESTERN STATES
Jance, J. A. Queen of the night
INDIANS OF NORTH AMERICA -- UTAH
Rollins, J. The devil colony
INDIANS OF NORTH AMERICA -- VIRGINIA
Vollmann, W. T. Argall
INDIANS OF NORTH AMERICA -- WARS
Cooper, J. F. The last of the Mohicans
Edmonds, W. D. Drums along the Mohawk
O'Brien, D. The contract surgeon
INDIANS OF NORTH AMERICA -- WASHINGTON (STATE)
Alexie, S. Indian killer
Alexie, S. Reservation blues
INDIGENOUS PEOPLES
Stanley, M. Death of the mantis
INDIGENOUS PEOPLES
See also Ethnology
Indignation. Roth, P.
INDIVIDUALISM
Orwell, G. Nineteen eighty-four
Pasternak, B. L. Doctor Zhivago
Rand, A. Anthem
Rand, A. Atlas shrugged
Rand, A. The fountainhead
INDIVIDUALITY
Backman, F. My grandmother asked me to tell you she's sorry
INDONESIA
Toer, P. A. The girl from the coast
INDOOR GAMES
See also Games
INDUCED ABORTION *See* Abortion
INDUSTRIAL ACCIDENTS
Sinha, I. Animal's people
INDUSTRIAL CONDITIONS
Singer, I. J. The brothers Ashkenazi
INDUSTRIAL REVOLUTION
Gilbert, E. The Signature of All Things
INDUSTRIAL ROBOTS
See also Automation; Industrial equipment; Robots
INDUSTRIALISTS
Sankaran, L. The hope factory
INDUSTRIES
Lodge, D. Nice work
INFANT SUDDEN DEATH *See* Sudden infant death syndrome
INFANTICIDE
Abu-Jaber, D. Origin
Morrison, T. Beloved
INFANTS
Larsen, R. I Am Radar
INFANTS -- DEATH
Barton, F. The child
INFANTS -- DISEASES
See also Diseases
The **Infatuations.**
Infernal angels. Estleman, L. D.
Inferno. Brown, D.
INFERTILITY
Gilmore, J. The Mothers
Weiner, J. Then came you
INFINITE
See also Mathematics
Infinite jest. Wallace, D. F.
The **infinite** tides. Kiefer, C.
The **infinities.** Banville, J.
INFLUENCE (LITERARY, ARTISTIC, ETC.)
Hacker, C. The Morels
INFLUENCE (PSYCHOLOGY)
Buntin, J. Marlena
INFLUENZA
Goldberg, M. Wickett's remedy
Masello, R. The Romanov cross
INFLUENZA
See also Communicable diseases; Diseases
INFLUENZA EPIDEMIC, 1918-1919 -- FICTION
Todd, C. An unmarked grave
The **informant.** Perry, T.
INFORMATION TECHNOLOGY -- MORAL AND ETHICAL ASPECTS
Cohen, J. Book of numbers
INFORMATION THEORY
See also Communication
The **informationist.** Stevens, T.
INFORMERS
Bayard, L. The black tower
Perry, T. The informant
Inherent vice. Pynchon, T.
INHERITANCE AND SUCCESSION
Addison, K. The Goblin Emperor
Balogh, M. Someone to Love
Bear, E. Range of ghosts
Boyle, E. Along Came a Duke
Cheever, J. The Wapshot chronicle
Cox, M. The meaning of night
Decarlo, M. The Art of Crash Landing
Dickens, C. Bleak House
Dickens, C. Great expectations
Dickens, C. Our mutual friend
Duran, M. A lady's code of misconduct

Gracie, A. The Autumn Bride
Grisham, J. Sycamore Row
Guhrke, L. L. How to lose a duke in ten days
Guhrke, L. L. When the Marquess Met His Match
James, H. The wings of the dove
Kleypas, L. Cold-hearted Rake
McGahan, A. The white earth
McGuane, T. The cadence of grass
Merullo, R. Breakfast with Buddha
Morrison, T. Love
Ohanesian, A. Orhan's inheritance
Palliser, C. The quincunx
Perry, T. Dance for the dead
Phillips, S. E. Match me if you can
Preston, D. The codex
Renault, M. Funeral games
Scott, A. Calpurnia
Stewart, M. The ivy tree
Sweeney, C. D. The Nest
Trollope, J. The other family
Vine, B. The minotaur
Wiggs, S. The Apple Orchard
Woods, S. Imperfect strangers

INHERITANCE AND SUCCESSION
See also Wealth

INHERITANCE AND SUCCESSION -- CALIFORNIA
Millet, L. Magnificence

INHERITANCE AND TRANSFER TAX
See also Estate planning; Inheritance and succession; Internal revenue; Taxation

The **inheritance** of loss. Desai, K.

Inheritance trilogy [series]
Jemisin, N. K. The hundred thousand kingdoms

The **inheritors.** Golding, W.

The **inimitable** Jeeves. Wodehouse, P. G.

INITIATION RITES
See also Rites and ceremonies

INJUNCTIONS
See also Constitutional law; Labor unions

INJURIES *See* Accidents; First aid; Wounds and injuries

Ink and steel. Bear, E.

The **Inn** at Lake Devine. Lipman, E.

The **inner** circle. Jungstedt, M.

The **inner** circle. Meltzer, B.

INNER CITIES
See also Cities and towns

Innocence. Koontz, D. R.

The **innocent.** McEwan, I.

Innocent. Turow, S.

Innocent blood. James, P. D.

Innocent grave. Robinson, P.

Innocent traitor. Weir, A.

Innocents and others. Spiotta, D.

INNUIT *See* Inuit

INQUISITION
Lewis, M. G. The monk

The **Inquisitor.** Smith, M. A.

The **inquisitors'** manual. Antunes, A. L.

INSANE *See* Mentally ill

INSANE, CRIMINAL AND DANGEROUS
Crais, R. Demolition angel
Donoghue, E. Room
Harris, T. Hannibal
Harris, T. Hannibal rising
Harris, T. Red Dragon
Harris, T. The silence of the lambs
Katzenbach, J. The analyst
Katzenbach, J. Just cause
King, S. Misery
Koontz, D. R. Intensity
Koontz, D. R. Velocity
Lehane, D. Shutter Island
Leonard, E. Glitz
O'Brien, E. In the forest
Palmer, M. The last surgeon
Patterson, J. Along came a spider
Patterson, J. Cat & mouse
Patterson, J. Cross
Patterson, J. I, Alex Cross
Patterson, J. Jack and Jill
Patterson, J. Kiss the girls
Patterson, J. Roses are red
Perry, T. Fidelity
Rendell, R. Live flesh

INSANITY
Bohjalian, C. The night strangers
Bronte, C. Jane Eyre
Cheever, J. Bullet Park
Faulkner, W. The sound and the fury
Jackson, S. We have always lived in the castle
Keneally, T. A family madness
McGrath, P. Asylum
Rendell, R. Adam and Eve and Pinch me
Ward, M. J. The snake pit
West, M. L. The clowns of God

INSANITY DEFENSE
See also Criminal law

INSCRIPTIONS
See also Ancient history; Archeology

INSECT PESTS
See also Economic zoology; Insects; Pests

INSECTS
Kafka, F. Metamorphosis
Saul, J. The homing

INSECTS
See also Animals

The **inseparables.** Nadler, S.

Inside the O'Briens. Genova, L.

Inspector Armand Gamache [series]
Penny, L. A great reckoning

Inspector Chen Cao [series]
Qiu Xiaolong Shanghai redemption
Qiu, Xiaolong Death of a red heroine

Inspector Lynley [series]

George, E. Just one evil act
Inspector Rebus novel [series]
Rankin, I. Rather be the devil
INSPIRATION *See* Creation (Literary, artistic, etc.)
INSTALLMENT PLAN
See also Business; Consumer credit; Credit; Purchasing
An **instance** of the fingerpost. Pears, I.
INSTITUTIONAL CARE -- EMPLOYEES
Nussbaum, S. Good kings bad kings
INSTRUCTIONAL MATERIALS CENTERS
See also Libraries
Instructions for a heat wave. O'Farrell, M.
INSTRUMENTALISTS
See also Musicians
INSTRUMENTATION AND ORCHESTRATION
See also Bands (Music); Composition (Music); Music; Orchestra
Instruments of darkness. Robertson, I.
Instruments of night. Cook, T. H.
INSURANCE
Greaves, C. Hush money
Shriver, L. So much for that
INSURGENCY
See also Revolutions
INSURGENCY -- SOUTH AMERICA -- HISTORY -- 16TH CENTURY
Wright, R. The gold eaters
INTEGRATION, RACIAL *See* Race relations
Intellectual Freedom Manual.
INTELLECTUAL PROPERTY
See also Property
INTELLECTUALS
Davies, R. The cunning man
Oz, A. Fima
INTELLECTUALS
See also Persons; Social classes
INTELLIGENCE AGENTS *See* Spies
INTELLIGENCE AGENTS
Kanon, J. Istanbul passage
INTELLIGENCE OF ANIMALS *See* Animal intelligence
INTELLIGENCE OFFICERS
Coulter, C. The end game
Cumming, C. A divided spy
Higgins, J. Midnight runner
Huston, C. Skinner
King, L. R. The game
Le Carre, J. A most wanted man
Littell, R. The company
Ludlum, R. The Prometheus deception
McCarry, C. Old boys
Silva, D. The English Girl
Silva, D. The mark of the assassin
INTELLIGENCE OFFICERS -- GREAT BRITAIN
Morgan Jones, C. The silent oligarch
INTELLIGENCE OFFICERS -- UNITED STATES
Rosenberg, J. C. Damascus Countdown
Rosenberg, J. C. The Tehran initiative
Rosenberg, J. C. The twelfth Imam
INTELLIGENCE SERVICE
See also Public administration; Research
INTELLIGENCE SERVICE
Coulter, C. The end game
INTELLIGENCE SERVICE -- GERMANY (EAST)
City of angels or
INTELLIGENCE SERVICE -- GREAT BRITAIN
Cumming, C. A divided spy
Herron, M. Spook street
INTELLIGENCE SERVICE -- UNITED STATES
Hayes, T. I Am Pilgrim
Kanon, J. Istanbul passage
INTELLIGENCE SERVICE AGENTS
Faulks, S. Devil may care
INTELLIGENTSIA *See* Intellectuals
INTEMPERANCE *See* Alcoholism; Temperance
Intensity. Koontz, D. R.
INTERACTION, HUMAN-COMPUTER *See* Human-computer interaction
Interest of justice. Rosenberg, N. T.
The **Interestings.** Wolitzer, M.
INTERFAITH MARRIAGE
Roth, P. Letting go
INTERGENERATIONAL RELATIONS
Smith, A. Autumn
Thien, M. Do not say we have nothing
Waldman, A. Love and treasure
Winslow, D. The kings of cool
INTERIOR DESIGN
See also Art; Decoration and ornament; Design; Home economics
INTERIOR DESIGNERS
Vreeland, S. Clara and Mr. Tiffany
INTERNATIONAL CRIMINAL POLICE ORGANIZATION
Suárez, D. Change agent
INTERNATIONAL INTRIGUE
Buchan, J. The thirty-nine steps
Buckley, W. F. Mongoose, R.I.P
Clancy, T. Clear and present danger
Clancy, T. The hunt for Red October
Clancy, T. Patriot games
Cumming, C. The Trinity Six
Cussler, C. Fire ice
Deighton, L. Berlin game
Deighton, L. The Ipcress file
Deighton, L. London match
Durrell, L. Mountolive
Fleming, I. Casino Royale
Fleming, I. Doctor No
Fleming, I. From Russia, with love
Fleming, I. Goldfinger
Fleming, I. The man with the golden gun
Fleming, I. On Her Majesty's Secret Service
Fleming, I. You only live twice
Forsyth, F. The day of the jackal

Furst, A. The spies of Warsaw
Gilman, D. The amazing Mrs. Pollifax
Gilman, D. The elusive Mrs. Pollifax
Gilman, D. The unexpected Mrs. Pollifax
Goldman, W. Marathon man
Grady, J. Six days of the condor
Greene, G. 3: This gun for hire, The confidential agent, The ministry of fear
Greene, G. The captain and the enemy
Greene, G. Our man in Havana
Greene, G. The quiet American
Greene, G. Travels with my aunt
Hall, A. The Quiller memorandum
Hall, A. Quiller Salamander
Hall, A. Quiller solitaire
Harris, R. Fatherland
Higgins, J. The eagle has flown
Higgins, J. The eagle has landed
Higgins, J. Edge of danger
Higgins, J. Eye of the storm
Higgins, J. Rough justice
Higgins, J. Touch the devil
Hunter, S. Havana
Ignatius, D. A firing offense
Le Carre, J. Absolute friends
Le Carre, J. The honourable schoolboy
Le Carre, J. The little drummer girl
Le Carre, J. A perfect spy
Le Carre, J. The secret pilgrim
Le Carre, J. Smiley's people
Le Carre, J. The spy who came in from the cold
Le Carre, J. The tailor of Panama
Le Carre, J. Tinker, tailor, soldier, spy
Littell, R. The company
Ludlum, R. The Bourne identity
Ludlum, R. The Bourne supremacy
Ludlum, R. The Bourne ultimatum
Ludlum, R. The Gemini contenders
Ludlum, R. The Rhinemann exchange
Lustbader, E. V. Floating city
MacInnes, H. Prelude to terror
MacInnes, H. Ride a pale horse
MacInnes, H. The Venetian affair
Neville, K. The eight
Neville, K. The fire
The Oxford book of spy stories
Reich, C. Rules of deception
Robinson, P. Kilo class
Robinson, P. Nimitz class
Steinhauer, O. The nearest exit
Steinhauer, O. The tourist
Westlake, D. E. Money for nothing

INTERNATIONAL MARRIAGES
Gordimer, N. The pickup
James, H. The golden bowl
Just, W. S. Exiles in the garden

INTERNATIONAL POLITICS *See* World politics

INTERNATIONAL RELATIONS
Cussler, C. Fire ice
Littell, R. The company
Rosenberg, J. C. Damascus Countdown
Rosenberg, J. C. The Tehran initiative

INTERNET
Coben, H. Hold tight

INTERNET (COMPUTER NETWORK) *See* Internet

INTERNET -- SOCIAL ASPECTS
Cohen, J. Book of numbers

INTERNET INDUSTRY
Eggers, D. The Circle

INTERPERSONAL RELATIONS
Acampora, L. The Wonder Garden
Anshaw, C. Carry the one
Arimah, L. N. What it means when a man falls from the sky
Atwood, M. The Heart Goes Last
Atwood, M. Stone mattress
Boyle, T. C. The Harder They Come
Bronsky, A. The Hottest Dishes of the Tartar Cuisine
Danielewski, M. Z. The familiar
Eggers, D. How we are hungry
Forna, A. The memory of love
Francis, D. Wedding Bush Road
Geni, A. The lightkeepers
George, E. Believing the lie
Green, J. Another piece of my heart
Haddad, S. Guapa
Hallberg, G. R. City on fire
Higley, T. L. Pompeii
Hodgson, A. The last confession of Thomas Hawkins
Holmes, L. Barbara the slut and other people
Hoover, C. November 9
I refuse
Jio, S. The violets of March
Joss, M. Half broken things
Kay, G. G. Children of earth and sky
Keesey, A. Little century
Lasser, S. Say nice things about Detroit
Lively, P. How it all began
Lopez, R. All back full
Manual of painting & calligraphy
McCall Smith, A. The forgotten affairs of youth
McCorkle, J. Life after life
Moore, K. D. Piano tide
Moore, L. Bark
Morris, M. Man in the blue moon
North, A. The Life and Death of Sophie Stark
O'Brien, E. The love object
O'Nan, S. The odds
Pearlman, E. Honeydew
Perlman, E. The street sweeper
Phillips, S. E. Call me irresistible
Phillips, S. E. First Star I See Tonight
Robinson, K. S. New York 2140
Roy, A. The ministry of utmost happiness
Ruskovich, E. Idaho

Scenes from village life
Sherrill, S. The minotaur takes his own sweet time
Simonson, H. The summer before the war
Smith, G. B. The maze at Windermere
Steel, D. First sight
Steele, J. The watchers
Summer lies
White, K. The night the lights went out
INTERPERSONAL RELATIONS -- ENGLAND -- LONDON
Hodgson, A. The last confession of Thomas Hawkins
INTERPERSONAL RELATIONS -- GRAPHIC NOVELS
Willis, C. Crosstalk
INTERPLANETARY COMMUNICATION *See* Interstellar communication
INTERPLANETARY VISITORS
Bear, G. Anvil of stars
Bear, G. The forge of God
Clarke, A. C. Rendezvous with Rama
Emshwiller, C. The secret city
Flynn, M. Eifelheim
Haldeman, J. W. The coming
Rucker, R. v. B. Hylozoic
Saint-Exupery, A. d. The little prince
Watts, P. Blindsight
Wells, H. G The war of the worlds
INTERPLANETARY VISITORS *See* Extraterrestrial beings
INTERPLANETARY VOYAGES
Adams, D. The hitchhiker's guide to the galaxy
Adams, D. Life, the universe, and everything
Adams, D. The restaurant at the end of the universe
Adams, D. So long, and thanks for all the fish
Baxter, S. Manifold
Clarke, A. C. 2001: a space odyssey
Eschbach, A. The carpet makers
Faber, M. The Book of Strange New Things
Gilman, C. I. Dark orbit
Haldeman, J. W. Starbound
Heinlein, R. A. Variable star
Lafferty, M. Six wakes
Levine, D. D. Arabella of Mars
Lewis, C. S. Out of the silent planet
Lewis, C. S. Perelandra
Okorafor, N. Binti
Scalzi, J. The collapsing empire
Simmons, D. Endymion
Stephenson, N. Seveneves
Valente, C. M. Radiance
Verne, J. From the earth to the moon, and Round the moon
Vonnegut, K. The sirens of Titan
Wells, M. All systems red
INTERPLANETARY WARFARE *See* Space warfare
INTERPLANETARY WARS
Card, O. S. Ender's game
Haldeman, J. W. The forever war
Saberhagen, F. Berserker's star
Scalzi, J. The ghost brigades
Scalzi, J. Old man's war
Wells, H. G. The war of the worlds
Interpreter of maladies. Lahiri, J.
INTERPRETERS
Sargent, C. Museum of human beings
Sherwood, F. Night of sorrows
INTERPRETING AND TRANSLATING *See* Translating and interpreting
INTERRACIAL ADOPTION
See also Adoption; Race relations
INTERRACIAL ADOPTION
Lee, M. G. Somebody's daughter
INTERRACIAL DATING
Brill, A. The movement of stars
Grenville, K. Sarah Thornhill
Kibler, J. Calling Me Home
Mengestu, D. All our names
Nadler, S. Wise men
INTERRACIAL FRIENDSHIP
Nadler, S. Wise men
INTERRACIAL MARRIAGE
Grau, S. A. The keepers of the house
Greene, G. The human factor
House, S. A parchment of leaves
Jen, G. The love wife
Smith, Z. On beauty
Warren, R. P. Band of angels
West, D. The wedding
INTERRACIAL RELATIONS *See* Race relations
The **interrogative** mood. Powell, P.
INTERSEX PEOPLE
Eugenides, J. Middlesex
Winter, K. Annabel
Interstate. Dixon, S.
INTERSTELLAR COMMUNICATION
Lem, S. His Master's Voice
Sagan, C. Contact
Interview with the vampire. Rice, A.
INTERVIEWING
Updike, J. Seek my face
INTIFADA, 2000-
Dabbagh, S. Out of It
INTIMACY (PSYCHOLOGY)
See also Emotions; Interpersonal relations; Love; Psychology
Intimacy, and other stories. Sartre, J. P.
INTIMIDATION
Freeman, C. Go with me
Into the beautiful North. Urrea, L. A.
Into the blue. Goddard, R.
Into the darkness. Turtledove, H.
Into the Savage Country. Burke, S.
INTOLERANCE *See* Fanaticism; Toleration
INTOXICATION *See* Alcoholism; Temperance
Intruder in the dust. Faulkner, W.
Intuition. Goodman, A.
The **intuitionist.** Whitehead, C.

INUIT
Mowat, F. The Snow Walker
Patterson, K. Consumption
Simmons, D. The terror
Vollmann, W. T. The rifles
INUIT
See also Indigenous peoples
INUIT -- FOLKLORE
See also Folklore
INUIT ARTISTS
See also Artists; Inuit
INVALIDS
Dickens, C. Dombey and Son
Wharton, E. Ethan Frome
Invasion of privacy. O'Shaughnessy, P.
INVECTIVE
See also Satire
The **invention** of everything else. Hunt, S.
The **invention** of wings. Kidd, S. M.
INVENTIONS
Echenoz, J. Lightning
INVENTORS
Bognanni, P. The house of tomorrow
Echenoz, J. Lightning
Hunt, S. The invention of everything else
Moore, G. The last days of night
Morrow, J. The last witchfinder
Priest, C. Fiddlehead
Tesla
Theroux, P. The Mosquito Coast
Varley, J. Dark lightning
Wallace, C. The blind contessa's new machine
INVERTEBRATES
See also Animals
The **inverted** forest. Dalton, J.
The **investigation.**
The **investigation.** Claudel, P.
INVESTIGATIVE REPORTING
Jin, H. The boat rocker
Pessl, M. Night Film
INVESTMENTS
Finder, J. Buried secrets
INVISIBILITY
Berger, T. Being invisible
Klosterman, C. The visible man
Saint, H. F. Memoirs of an invisible man
Westlake, D. E. Smoke
Invisible. Auster, P.
Invisible boy. Read, C.
The **invisible** bridge. Orringer, J.
Invisible cities. Calvino, I.
The **invisible** library. Cogman, G.
The invisible library novel [series]
Cogman, G. The invisible library
Invisible man. Ellison, R.
The **invisible** man. Wells, H. G.
The **invisible** ones. Penney, S.
Invisible planets.
The **invisibles.** Sheehy, H.
IOWA
Bognanni, P. The house of tomorrow
Darnielle, J. Universal harvester
Drury, T. The driftless area
Robinson, M. Gilead
Robinson, M. Lila
Smiley, J. Some luck
Smiley, J. A thousand acres
Thompson, J. The year we left home
Waller, R. J. The bridges of Madison County
The **Ipcress** file. Deighton, L.
IPHIGENIA (LEGENDARY CHARACTER)
Unsworth, B. The songs of the kings
IRAN
Dowlatabadi, M. The colonel
Egan, G. Zendegi
Rosenberg, J. C. The twelfth Imam
IRAN -- EMIGRATION AND IMMIGRATION
Bijan, D. The last days of Café Leila
IRAN -- TEHRAN
Garcia, C. A handbook to luck
Ignatius, D. The increment
Sofer, D. The Septembers of Shiraz
IRAN -- TO 640 A.D.
Vidal, G. Creation
IRANIAN AMERICAN TEENAGERS
Khadivi, L. A good country
IRANIAN AMERICAN WOMEN
Bijan, D. The last days of Café Leila
IRANIAN AMERICANS
Bijan, D. The last days of Café Leila
Tyler, A. Digging to America
IRAQ
Unsworth, B. Land of marvels
IRAQ -- BAGHDAD
Robotham, M. The wreckage
IRAQ -- HISTORY -- 2003-2011 , ANGLO-AMERICAN INVASION *See* Iraq War, 2003-2011
IRAQ WAR, 2003-2011
Abrams, D. Fobbit
DeLillo, D. Point Omega
Fountain, B. Billy Lynn's long halftime walk
Gallagher, M. Youngblood
Haslett, A. Union Atlantic
Hoffman, C. Be safe I love you
Klay, P. Redeployment
Mohr, J. Damascus
Paretsky, S. Bleeding Kansas
Powers, K. The yellow birds
The road ahead
Zimmerman, D. Sandbox
IRAQ WAR, 2003-2011 -- VETERANS
Clarke, B. Exley
Hamill, P. Tabloid city
Hogan, C. Devils in exile

Lennon, J. R. Castle
Pelecanos, G. The cut
Percy, B. The wilding
Robinson, R. Sparta
IRELAND
Banville, J. The infinities
Banville, J. The sea
Barrett, C. Young skins
Barry, K. City of Bohane
Barry, K. Dark lies the island
Binchy, M. A week in winter
Carey, L. The stolen child
Delaney, F. The matchmaker of Kenmare
Doyle, R. Bullfighting and other stories
Doyle, R. The dead republic
Enright, A. The forgotten waltz
French, T. Broken Harbor
French, T. In the woods
French, T. The likeness
Hart, J. The truth about love
Hart, E. The book of Killowen
Hart, E. Lake of sorrows
Higgins, J. Confessional
Llywelyn, M. 1921
Llywelyn, M. 1949
Mathews, B. The world of tomorrow
McInerney, L. The Glorious Heresies
Murray, P. The mark and the void
O'Brien, E. House of splendid isolation
O'Brien, E. Lantern slides
O'Brien, F. The complete novels
O'Faolain, S. The collected stories of Sean O'Faolain
The Oxford book of Irish short stories
Ray, K. No country
Riley, L. The girl on the cliff
Rutherfurd, E. The princes of Ireland
Rutherfurd, E. The rebels of Ireland
Tóibín, C. Nora Webster
Trevor, W. Fools of fortune
IRELAND -- 19TH CENTURY
Flanagan, T. The tenants of time
Howatch, S. Cashelmara
Mallinson, A. A close run thing
Uris, L. Trinity
IRELAND -- 20TH CENTURY
Banville, J. The book of evidence
Binchy, M. Circle of friends
Binchy, M. The glass lake
Doyle, R. A star called Henry
Joyce, J. Dubliners
Joyce, J. Finnegans wake
Joyce, J. Ulysses
Llywelyn, M. 1949
O'Connor, F. Collected stories
Tóibín, C. The blackwater lightship
Uris, L. Redemption
Uris, L. Trinity
IRELAND -- DUBLIN
Beckett, S. Murphy
Doyle, R. Paddy Clarke, ha ha ha
Doyle, R. The woman who walked into doors
Enright, A. The gathering
French, T. Faithful Place
Joyce, J. Dubliners
Joyce, J. Finnegans wake
Joyce, J. A portrait of the artist as a young man
Joyce, J. Ulysses
Llywelyn, M. 1916
Murray, P. Skippy dies
O'Neill, J. At swim, two boys
Tóibín, C. The heather blazing
IRELAND -- FRENCH INVASION, 1798
Flanagan, T. The year of the French
IRELAND -- GALWAY
Lordan, B. But come ye back
IRELAND -- HISTORY -- FAMINE, 1845-1852
Ray, K. No country
IRELAND -- MAYO
Flanagan, T. The year of the French
IRELAND -- RURAL LIFE
Binchy, M. Whitethorn Woods
McGahern, J. By the lake
O'Brien, E. In the forest
O'Brien, E. Wild Decembers
Trevor, W. Love and summer
IRELAND -- SINN FEIN REBELLION, 1916
Llywelyn, M. 1916
O'Neill, J. At swim, two boys
IRELAND -- SOCIAL LIFE AND CUSTOMS -- 20TH CENTURY
Carey, L. The stolen child
Irene. Lemaitre, P.
IRISH -- AUSTRALIA
McCullough, C. The thorn birds
IRISH -- CANADA
Urquhart, J. Away
IRISH -- EGYPT
Durrell, L. Balthazar
Durrell, L. Justine
IRISH -- ENGLAND
Beckett, S. Murphy
Keyes, M. Last Chance Saloon
O'Brien, E. Time and tide
Trevor, W. Felicia's journey
IRISH -- NEW ZEALAND
Uris, L. Redemption
IRISH -- UNITED STATES
Barry, S. Days Without End
Barry, S. On Canaan's side
Colfer, E. Plugged
Farrell, J. T. Studs Lonigan
L'Amour, L. The Californios
Mathews, B. The world of tomorrow
McCann, C. Let the great world spin

McDermott, A. At weddings and wakes
Tóibín, C. Brooklyn
IRISH AMERICANS
Barry, S. On Canaan's side
Delaney, E. J. Broken Irish
Dorris, M. Cloud chamber
Faye, L. The gods of Gotham
Goldberg, M. Wickett's remedy
McDermott, A. After this
McDermott, A. Charming Billy
McDermott, A. Child of my heart
Quindlen, A. Object lessons
Thomas, M. We are not ourselves
Irish coffee. McInerny, R. M.
Irish eyes. Andrews, M. K.
IRISH LITERATURE
The Short Fiction of Flann O'Brien
IRISH REPUBLICAN ARMY
Doyle, R. A star called Henry
Higgins, J. Confessional
Neville, S. The ghosts of Belfast
O'Brien, E. House of splendid isolation
Iron house. Hart, J.
The **Iron** King. Druon, M.
Ironskin. Connolly, T.
Ironweed. Kennedy, W.
The **irresistible** Henry House. Grunwald, L.
Is fat Bob dead yet? Dobyns, S.
ISLAM
Robinson, K. S. The years of rice and salt
Rushdie, S. The satanic verses
Snow
Submission
ISLAM -- CUSTOMS AND PRACTICES
See also Rites and ceremonies
ISLAM -- RELATIONS -- JUDAISM
See also Islam; Judaism
ISLAM AND POLITICS -- TURKEY
Snow
ISLAMOPHOBIA
See also Prejudices
The **island.** Hilderbrand, E.
Island beneath the sea. Allende, I.
ISLAND ECOLOGY
See also Ecology
Island girls. Thayer, N.
The **island** house. Graeme-Evans, P.
Island of bones. Robertson, I.
The **island** of Doctor Moreau. Wells, H. G.
The **island** of second sight. Thelen, A. V.
The **island** of the day before. Eco, U.
The **islanders.** Priest, C.
ISLANDS
Banner, C. The house at the edge of night
Defoe, D. Robinson Crusoe
Glass, J. Three Junes
Guterson, D. Snow falling on cedars
Hand, E. Generation loss
Melamed, J. Gather the daughters
Naylor, G. Mama Day
Nichols, P. The rocks
Palahniuk, C. Diary
Parker, K. J. The company
Pollen, B. The summer of the bear
Priest, C. The islanders
Runcie, J. Canvey Island
Shreve, A. The weight of water
Theorin, J. Echoes from the dead
Tournier, M. Friday
Urquhart, J. A map of glass
Verne, J. The mysterious island
Wells, H. G. The island of Doctor Moreau
Yanique, T. Land of love and drowning
ISLANDS OF THE PACIFIC
Barker, P. The ghost road
Nordhoff, C. The Bounty trilogy
Smith, D. Bright and distant shores
The man with the compound eyes
ISLANDS OF THE PACIFIC
See also Islands
ISRAEL
Bezmozgis, D. The Betrayers
Brooks, G. The Secret Chord
Grossman, D. Be my knife
Kemelman, H. Monday the rabbi took off
Kemelman, H. One fine day the rabbi bought a cross
Miller, R. Welcome to Heavenly Heights
Oz, A. Don't call it night
Oz, A. Fima
Oz, A. The same sea
Reiken, F. Day for night
Roiphe, A. R. Lovingkindness
Sandford, J. Storm Front
Scenes from village life
To the end of the land
Uris, L. Exodus
ISRAEL-ARAB WAR, 1967
Wiesel, E. A beggar in Jerusalem
ISRAELI FICTION
Second person singular
ISRAELIS
See also Jews
ISRAELITES *See* Jews
ISTANBUL (TURKEY)
Nadel, B. The Ottoman cage
The red-haired woman
A strangeness in my mind
ISTANBUL (TURKEY) -- HISTORY
Kanon, J. Istanbul passage
ISTANBUL (TURKEY) -- SOCIAL CONDITIONS
A strangeness in my mind
Istanbul passage. Kanon, J.
It. King, S.
It can't happen here. Lewis, S.

It had to be you. Phillips, S. E.
It's beginning to hurt. Lasdun, J.
It's fine by me.
It's getting later all the time. Tabucchi, A.
ITALIAN AMERICAN FAMILIES
Castellani, C. All this talk of love
Hood, A. An Italian Wife
Samuel, B. No place like home
ITALIAN AMERICANS
Castellani, C. All this talk of love
Criswell, M. What to do about Annie?
Lee Aloft
Pelecanos, G. P. The big blowdown
Puzo, M. The last Don
Quindlen, A. Object lessons
Samuel, B. No place like home
Scottoline, L. Killer smile
Trigiani, A. Very Valentine
Italian fever. Martin, V.
ITALIAN FICTION -- TRANSLATIONS INTO ENGLISH
Eco, U. The name of the rose
Eco, U. Baudolino
Eco, U. The island of the day before
Eco, U. The mysterious flame of Queen Loana
Giordano, P. The solitude of prime numbers
The **Italian** lover. Hellenga, R.
An **Italian** Wife. Hood, A.
ITALIANS -- AFGHANISTAN
The human body
ITALIANS -- NEW YORK (N.Y.)
Prose, F. Household saints
ITALIANS -- RUSSIA
Levi, P. The monkey's wrench
ITALIANS -- SOUTH AMERICA
Conrad, J. Nostromo
ITALIANS -- UNITED STATES
Malamud, B. The assistant
Puzo, M. The godfather
Waller, R. J. The bridges of Madison County
ITALY
Aciman, A. A. Call me by your name
Banner, C. The house at the edge of night
Dibdin, M. Ratking
Eco, U. The mysterious flame of Queen Loana
Ferrante, E. The lost daughter
Ferrante, E. The Story of a New Name
Furst, A. The foreign correspondent
Godden, R. The battle of the Villa Fiorita
Godden, R. Pippa passes
Heller, J. Catch-22
Kushner, R. The flamethrowers
Martin, V. Italian fever
McPhee, M. L'America
Rich, N. The mayor's tongue
Roberts, M. Reader, I married him
Seymour, G. Killing ground
Silone, I. Bread and wine
Unsworth, B. After Hannibal
Walter, J. Beautiful Ruins
ITALY -- 14TH CENTURY
Eco, U. The name of the rose
ITALY -- 15TH CENTURY
Dunant, S. The birth of Venus
Essex, K. Leonardo's swans
Puzo, M. The family
Rice, A. Of love and evil
Stone, I. The agony and the ecstasy
ITALY -- 16TH CENTURY
Dunant, S. In the company of the courtesan
Rushdie, S. The enchantress of Florence
Stone, I. The agony and the ecstasy
ITALY -- 17TH CENTURY
Vreeland, S. The passion of Artemesia
ITALY -- 18TH CENTURY
Stendhal The charterhouse of Parma
ITALY -- 19TH CENTURY
Calvino, I. Baron in the trees
James, H. Daisy Miller
Wallace, C. The blind contessa's new machine
ITALY -- BOLOGNA
Rigosi, G. Night bus
ITALY -- CALABRIA
West, M. L. The devil's advocate
ITALY -- ELBA
Scott, J. Tourmaline
ITALY -- FLORENCE
Dunant, S. The birth of Venus
Forster, E. M. A room with a view
Hellenga, R. The Italian lover
Rushdie, S. The enchantress of Florence
Stone, I. The agony and the ecstasy
ITALY -- HISTORY -- 0-1559
Dunant, S. Blood and beauty
ITALY -- HISTORY -- 1492-1559
Dunant, S. Blood and beauty
Puzo, M. The family
ITALY -- HISTORY -- 20TH CENTURY
Ferrante, E. My brilliant friend
ITALY -- HISTORY -- ALLIED OCCUPATION, 1943-1947
Foulds, A. In the wolf's mouth
ITALY -- HISTORY -- GERMAN OCCUPATION, 1943-1945
Drndić, D. Trieste
ITALY -- MILAN
Eco, U. Foucault's pendulum
Essex, K. Leonardo's swans
King, R. Domino
ITALY -- NAPLES
Sontag, S. The volcano lover
ITALY -- PARMA
Grisham, J. Playing for pizza
Stendhal The charterhouse of Parma
ITALY -- ROME
Bezmozgis, D. The free world

Gordon, M. The love of my youth
Kneale, M. When we were Romans
McGowan, H. Duchess of nothing
Rabb, J. The book of Q
Rachman, T. The imperfectionists
Rice, A. Of love and evil
Stone, I. The agony and the ecstasy
West, M. L. The shoes of the fisherman
Williams, T. The Roman spring of Mrs. Stone
ITALY -- SIENA
Fortier, A. Juliet
ITALY -- TUSCANY
Bilenchi, R. The chill
Ondaatje, M. The English patient
ITALY -- VENICE
Chase, L. Your scandalous ways
Dunant, S. In the company of the courtesan
Dyer, G. Jeff in Venice, death in Varanasi
Godden, R. Pippa passes
MacInnes, H. The Venetian affair
Mann, T. Death in Venice
Weisgall, D. The world before her
Wharton, E. The children
ITALY -- VESUVIUS
Pohl, F. All the lives he led
Ivan and Misha. Alenyikov, M.
Ivanhoe. Scott, W.
IVORY COAST
D'Souza, T. Whiteman
The **ivy** tree. Stewart, M.

J

J is for judgment. Grafton, S.
Jack and Jill. Patterson, J.
Jack Holmes and his friend. White, E.
Jack of Spades. Oates, J. C.
Jack Reacher [series]
Child, L. Killing floor
JACK THE RIPPER MURDERS, LONDON, ENGLAND, 1888
See also Serial killers
The **jackal's** share. Morgan-Jones, C.
Jackdaws. Follett, K.
Jackson, Stonewall, 1824-1863
About
Shaara, J. Gods and generals
JACMEL (HAITI)
Dépestre, R. Hadriana in all my dreams
Jacob's folly. Miller, R.
Jacob's room. Woolf, V.
JACOBITE REBELLION, 1745-1746
Gabaldon, D. Outlander
Jacquetta, Duchess of Bedford, 1416?-1472
About
Gregory, P. The lady of the rivers
Jailbird. Vonnegut, K.
Jalna. De la Roche, M.
Jam on the Vine. Barnett, L. K.
JAMAICA
Dennis-Benn, N. Y. Here Comes the Sun
Fleming, I. The man with the golden gun
James, M. The book of night women
Levy, A. The long song
McMillan, T. How Stella got her groove back
Miller, K. Augustown
Jamaica Inn. Du Maurier, D.
JAMAICANS -- ENGLAND
Levy, A. Small island
JAMAICANS -- UNITED STATES
Winkler, A. C. Dog war
James, Henry, 1843-1916
About
Heyns, M. The typewriter's tale
Tóibín, C. The master
James, Jesse, 1847-1882
About
Hansen, R. The assassination of Jesse James by the coward Robert Ford
Jamrach's menagerie. Birch, C.
Jane and Prudence. Pym, B.
The **Jane** Austen book club. Fowler, K. J.
Jane Eyre. Bronte, C.
Jane Ryland mysteries [series]
Ryan, H. P. The other woman
Jane Steele. Faye, L.
The **Janson** directive. Ludlum, R.
The **January** dancer. Flynn, M.
January thaw. Lourey, J.
The **Janus** stone. Griffiths, E.
JAPAN
Agawa, Y. The housekeeper and the professor
The Future Is Japanese
Higashino, K. The devotion of suspect X
Higashino, K. Malice
Kirk, D. Sword of honor
Kutsukake, L. The translation of love
Oe, K. The changeling
Watrous, M. If you follow me
JAPAN -- 11TH CENTURY
Murasaki Shikibu The tale of Genji
JAPAN -- 1787-1868
Mitchell, D. The thousand autumns of Jacob de Zoet
JAPAN -- 17TH CENTURY
Clavell, J. Shogun
Endo, S. Silence
JAPAN -- 1867-1945
Kawabata, Y. Snow country, and Thousand cranes
Mishima, Y. Runaway horses
Mishima, Y. Spring snow
Tanizaki, J. The Makioka sisters
JAPAN -- 1945-
Hazzard, S. The great fire
Kafka on the shore

Kawabata, Y. The sound of the mountain
Mishima, Y. The decay of the angel
Miyamoto, T. Kinshu: Autumn brocade
Murakami, H. South of the border, west of the sun
Oe, K. A quiet life
Oe, K. Somersault
Okuizumi, H. The stones cry out
Peace, D. Occupied city
Schwartz, J. B. The commoner
Yoshida, S. Villain
Yoshimoto, B. Goodbye Tsugumi
Yoshimoto, B. Kitchen
JAPAN -- 20TH CENTURY
Golden, A. Memoirs of a geisha
Ishiguro, K. An artist of the floating world
Mishima, Y. The Temple of Dawn
Murakami, H. The wind-up bird chronicle
Oe, K. Nip the buds, shoot the kids
JAPAN -- HIROSHIMA
Bock, D. The ash garden
Pywell, S. L. What happened to Henry
JAPAN -- KAMAKURA
Kawabata, Y. The sound of the mountain
JAPAN -- KYOTO
Walbert, K. The gardens of Kyoto
JAPAN -- NAGASAKI
Mitchell, D. The thousand autumns of Jacob de Zoet
JAPAN -- RURAL LIFE
Abe, K. The woman in the dunes
JAPAN -- TOKYO
Hill, T. The love of stones
Hunter, S. The 47th samurai
Kawabata, Y. The sound of the mountain
The lake
Lee, D. Country of origin
Mishima, Y. Spring snow
Murakami, H. After dark
Murakami, R. In the miso soup
Peace, D. Occupied city
Peace, D. Tokyo year zero
Smith, M. C. December 6
Tsukiyama, G. The street of a thousand blossoms
Vargas Llosa, M. The bad girl
JAPANESE -- CALIFORNIA
Otsuka, J. The Buddha in the attic
JAPANESE -- CANADA
Itani, F. Requiem
JAPANESE -- CHINA
Ballard, J. G. Empire of the Sun
Shan S. The girl who played go
JAPANESE -- GERMANY
Oe, K. The changeling
JAPANESE -- HAWAII
Michener, J. A. Hawaii
JAPANESE -- INDIA
Endo, S. Deep river
JAPANESE -- UNITED STATES
Allende, I. The Japanese Lover
JAPANESE AMERICAN WOMEN
Uchida, Y. Picture bride
JAPANESE AMERICANS
Guterson, D. Snow falling on cedars
Lee A gesture life
Revoyr, N. Wingshooters
JAPANESE AMERICANS -- EVACUATION AND RELOCATION, 1942-1945
Dallas, S. Tallgrass
Ellroy, J. Perfidia
Otsuka, J. When the emperor was divine
JAPANESE FICTION -- TRANSLATIONS INTO ENGLISH
Agawa, Y. The housekeeper and the professor
Colorless Tsukuru Tazaki and his years of pilgrimage
Endo, S. Deep river
Endo, S. The final martyrs
The lake
Minato, K. Confessions
Murakami, H. The wind-up bird chronicle
Murakami, H. After dark
Murakami, R. In the miso soup
Oe, K. The changeling
Oe, K. Nip the buds, shoot the kids
Oe, K. A quiet life
Yoshimoto, B. Asleep
Yoshimoto, B. Kitchen
JAPANESE LANGUAGE
See also Language and languages
The **Japanese** Lover. Allende, I.
Jaws. Benchley, P.
Jayber Crow. Berry, W.
Jazz. Morrison, T.
JAZZ MUSIC
Baker, D. Young man with a horn
Faulks, S. On Green Dolphin Street
Goonan, K. A. In war times
Marshall, P. The fisher king
Turner, F. W. 1929
JAZZ MUSICIANS
The Book of Harlan
Edugyan, E. Half-blood blues
Rotert, R. Last night at the blue angel
Turner, F. W. 1929
JEALOUSY
Balzac, H. d. Cousin Bette
Barker, N. Darkmans
Chevalier, T. Girl with a pearl earring
Eliot, G. Middlemarch
Essex, K. Leonardo's swans
Green, J. Another piece of my heart
Hatoum, M. The brothers
Hawkes, J. The blood oranges
Iles, G. Third degree
Klein, R. The moth diaries
Lebrecht, N. The song of names

Munoz Molina, A. In her absence
Norman, H. The haunting of L
Oates, J. C. The falls
Rendell, R. Going wrong
Rosenfeld, L. I'm so happy for you
Shreve, A. The weight of water
JEALOUSY
See also Emotions
JEEVES (FICTITIOUS CHARACTER)
Faulks, S. Jeeves and the Wedding Bells
Jeeves and the Wedding Bells. Faulks, S.
Jeff in Venice, death in Varanasi. Dyer, G.
Jefferson, Thomas, 1743-1826
About
Clotel, or, The president's daughter
Jem Flockhart mystery [series]
Thomson, E. S. Beloved poison
Jenna Starborn. Shinn, S.
The **Jennifer** morgue. Stross, C.
JERICHO
Wolf, J. This scarlet cord
Jerusalem. Moore, A.
Jerusalem. Holland, C.
JERUSALEM
Blatty, W. P. Dimiter
Bulgakov, M. A. The master and Margarita
Grossman, D. Be my knife
Grossman, D. Someone to run with
Holland, C. Jerusalem
Joinson, S. The Photographer's Wife
Oz, A. Fima
Oz, A. Panther in the basement
Qashu, S. Dancing Arabs
Spark, M. The Mandelbaum Gate
Stone, R. Damascus Gate
Wiesel, E. A beggar in Jerusalem
JESUITS
Blatty, W. P. The exorcist
Eco, U. The island of the day before
Hansen, R. Exiles
Russell, M. D. Children of God
Russell, M. D. The sparrow
Vollmann, W. T. Fathers and crows
Jesus Christ
About
Asch, S. The Nazarene
Bulgakov, M. A. The master and Margarita
Crace, J. Quarantine
Kazantzakis, N. The last temptation of Christ
Mailer, N. The Gospel according to the Son
Rice, A. Christ the Lord: the road to Cana
Rice, A. Christ the Lord: out of Egypt
Rollins, J. The blood Gospel
Tóibín, C. The testament of Mary
Wallace, L. Ben-Hur
JESUS CHRIST -- PARABLES
See also Parables
Jesus' son. Johnson, D.
The **Jew** of Home Depot and other stories. Apple, M.
JEWELERS
Martin, C. W. How to sell
JEWELRY
Hill, T. The love of stones
Parks Getting mother's body
Tolkien, J. R. R. The Silmarillion
Trollope, A. The Eustace diamonds
JEWELS *See* Gems; Jewelry; Precious stones
Jewelweed. Rhodes, D.
JEWISH CARTOONISTS
Jacobson, H. Kalooki nights
JEWISH CHILDREN IN THE HOLOCAUST
See also Holocaust, 1939-1945
JEWISH CHILDREN IN THE HOLOCAUST -- POLAND
Shepard, J. The book of Aron
JEWISH DIASPORA
See also Human geography; Jews
JEWISH ETHICS
See also Ethics
JEWISH FAMILIES -- FICTION
Auster, P. 4 3 2 1
Goodman, A. Kaaterskill Falls
Jacobson, H. Kalooki nights
Rabb, J. Among the living
JEWISH HOLIDAYS
See also Judaism; Religious holidays
JEWISH HOLOCAUST (1933-1945) *See* Holocaust, 1939-1945
JEWISH LEGENDS
Kazinski, A. J. The last good man
JEWISH LEGENDS
See also Legends
JEWISH MEN
See also Men
Appelfeld, A. The man who never stopped sleeping
JEWISH PROPERTY -- HUNGARY
Waldman, A. Love and treasure
JEWISH REFUGEES
Appelfeld, A. The man who never stopped sleeping
Bellow, S. Mr. Sammler's planet
The emigrants
Uris, L. Exodus
JEWISH RELIGION *See* Judaism
JEWISH RELIGIOUS FICTION
See also Fiction; Jewish literature; Religious fiction
JEWISH TEACHERS
Rojstaczer, S. The Mathematician's Shiva
JEWISH WIT AND HUMOR
See also Wit and humor
JEWISH WOMEN
Anton, M. Rav Hisda's daughter, book I, apprentice
Bank, M. The wonder spot
Diamant, A. The Boston girl
Ozick, C. The Puttermesser papers
Sherwood, F. The book of splendor

Yezierska, A. c. Bread givers
JEWISH WOMEN
See also Women
JEWISH YOUTH
Appelfeld, A. The man who never stopped sleeping
JEWISH-ARAB RELATIONS
Littell, R. Vicious circle
JEWISH-ARAB RELATIONS
See also Arabs; Jews
JEWS
Albert, E. The book of Dahlia
Appelfeld, A. The man who never stopped sleeping
Auslander, S. Hope
Ausubel, R. No one is here except all of us
Bezmozgis, D. The Betrayers
Bezmozgis, D. The free world
Diamant, A. The red tent
The emigrants
Goodman, A. Paradise park
Hershon, J. The German bride
Higley, T. L. Pompeii
Horn, D. The world to come
Isaacs, S. Red, white and blue
Krauss, N. Great house
London, J. The Golden Age
Markovits, A. I am forbidden
Matthiessen, P. In Paradise
Michaels, A. Fugitive pieces
Nahai, G. B. The luminous heart of Jonah S.
Neugeboren, J. 1940
Oz, A. Fima
Oz, A. Panther in the basement
Ozick, C. Foreign bodies
Ozick, C. The shawl
Pears, I. The dream of Scipio
Reiken, F. Day for night
Reisman, N. The first desire
Sholem Aleichem Tevye the dairyman and The railroad stories
Skibell, J. A curable romantic
Spark, M. The Mandelbaum Gate
Stern, S. The pinch
Two she-bears
Unsworth, B. The ruby in her navel
Weiner, J. Certain girls
Wiesel, E. A beggar in Jerusalem
Wiesel, E. The forgotten
Wiesel, E. Night, Dawn, The accident: three tales
Winer, A. The marriage artist
JEWS -- AFGHANISTAN
Michener, J. A. Caravans
JEWS -- ARGENTINA
Englander, N. The Ministry of Special Cases
Ludlum, R. The Rhinemann exchange
JEWS -- AUSTRIA
Appelfeld, A. Until the dawn's light
Appelfeld, A. Badenheim 1939
JEWS -- CANADA
Norman, H. The museum guard
Richler, M. Barney's version
Richler, M. Solomon Gursky was here
JEWS -- CONNECTICUT
Hill, R. When all is said and done
JEWS -- CZECH REPUBLIC
Adler, H. G. Panorama
JEWS -- CZECHOSLOVAKIA
Mawer, S. The glass room
JEWS -- DENMARK
Follett, K. Hornet flight
JEWS -- EGYPT
Durrell, L. Justine
Durrell, L. Mountolive
JEWS -- ENCYCLOPEDIAS
See also Encyclopedias and dictionaries
JEWS -- ENGLAND
Franklin, A. Mistress of the art of death
Jacobson, H. The Finkler question
Jacobson, H. Kalooki nights
Lebrecht, N. The song of names
Scott, W. Ivanhoe
Walton, J. Farthing
Walton, J. Half a crown
JEWS -- EUROPE
Wiesel, E. The oath
JEWS -- FOLKLORE
See also Folklore
JEWS -- FRANCE
De Rosnay, T. Sarah's key
JEWS -- FRANCE -- HISTORY
Belfoure, C. The Paris Architect
JEWS -- GERMANY
Bohjalian, C. A. Skeletons at the feast
Franck, J. The blindness of the heart
Grass, G. Dog years
Grossman, P. Children of wrath
Keilson, H. Life goes on
Schwarz-Bart, A. The last of the just
Zimler, R. The seventh gate
JEWS -- GREAT BRITAIN
Harris, E. The Marrying of Chani Kaufman
Jacobson, H. Kalooki nights
JEWS -- HUNGARY
Orringer, J. The invisible bridge
JEWS -- IDENTITY
Englander, N. What we talk about when we talk about Anne Frank
JEWS -- IRAN
Sofer, D. The Septembers of Shiraz
JEWS -- ITALY
Drndić, D. Trieste
JEWS -- LEGENDS *See* Jewish legends
JEWS -- MICHIGAN
Baxter, C. Saul and Patsy
JEWS -- NETHERLANDS

Keilson, H. Comedy in a minor key
JEWS -- NEW JERSEY
Roth, P. Nemesis
Roth, P. American pastoral
JEWS -- NEW YORK (N.Y.)
Bellow, S. Mr. Sammler's planet
Chabon, M. The amazing adventures of Kavalier and Clay
Colwin, L. Family happiness
Kirshenbaum, B. An almost perfect moment
Malamud, B. The assistant
Mirvis, T. The outside world
Ozick, C. Heir to the glimmering world
Ozick, C. The Puttermesser papers
Plain, B. The golden cup
Potok, C. The gift of Asher Lev
Potok, C. My name is Asher Lev
Reyn, I. What happened to Anna K.
Reznikoff, C. By the waters of Manhattan
Rosen, J. Joy comes in the morning
Roth, H. Call it sleep
Roth, H. A diving rock on the Hudson
Roth, H. From bondage
Roth, H. Requiem for Harlem
Roth, H. A star shines over Mt. Morris Park
Sholem Aleichem The adventures of Mottel, the cantor's son
Styron, W. Sophie's choice
Wallant, E. L. The pawnbroker
Wouk, H. Marjorie Morningstar
JEWS -- NEW YORK (STATE)
Goodman, A. Kaaterskill Falls
Reisman, N. The first desire
JEWS -- PALESTINE
Asch, S. The Apostle
Wallace, L. Ben-Hur
Wiesel, E. Dawn
JEWS -- PERSECUTIONS
Anatoli, A. Babi Yar
Appelfeld, A. Badenheim 1939
Belfoure, C. The Paris Architect
Keneally, T. Schindler's list
Levi, P. If not now, when?
Lourie, R. A hatred for tulips
Malamud, B. The fixer
Schwarz-Bart, A. The last of the just
Uris, L. Exodus
Uris, L. QB VII
Wiesel, E. The oath
Wiesel, E. The testament
Zimler, R. The last kabbalist of Lisbon
JEWS -- PERSECUTIONS
See also Antisemitism; Persecution
JEWS -- POLAND
Chasing the king of hearts
JEWS -- PORTUGAL
Zimler, R. The last kabbalist of Lisbon
JEWS -- RELIGION *See* Judaism
JEWS -- ROME
Asch, S. The Apostle
JEWS -- RUSSIA
Amis, M. House of meetings
Anatoli, A. Babi Yar
Malamud, B. The fixer
Richler, N. Your mouth is lovely
Sholem Aleichem The adventures of Menahem-Mendl
Sholem Aleichem The nightingale
Sholem Aleichem Tevye's daughters
Wiesel, E. The testament
JEWS -- SEGREGATION
Uris, L. Mila 18
JEWS -- SOCIAL CONDITIONS
See also Social conditions
JEWS -- SOUTH AFRICA
Gordimer, N. No time like the present
JEWS -- SOVIET UNION
Goldberg, P. The Yid
JEWS -- UNITED STATES
Bellow, S. The adventures of Augie March
Bellow, S. Mr. Sammler's planet
Chabon, M. The Yiddish policemen's union
Criswell, M. What to do about Annie?
Doctorow, E. L. Ragtime
Epstein, J. The love song of A. Jerome Minkoff and other stories
Gilmore, J. Golden country
Gilmore, J. Something red
Goldberg, M. Bee season
Heller, J. Good as Gold
Hobson, L. K. Z. Gentleman's agreement
Horn, D. All other nights
Kolpan, G. Magic words
Levitt, P. M. Come with me to Babylon
Lipman, E. The Inn at Lake Devine
Manseau, P. Songs for the butcher's daughter
Plain, B. Crescent City
Plain, B. Evergreen
Plain, B. Harvest
Plain, B. Tapestry
Reich, T. My Holocaust
Roth, P. Indignation
Roth, P. The anatomy lesson
Roth, P. The ghost writer
Roth, P. Goodbye, Columbus, and five short stories
Roth, P. I married a communist
Roth, P. Letting go
Roth, P. My life as a man
Roth, P. The plot against America
Roth, P. Portnoy's complaint
Roth, P. The professor of desire
Roth, P. Zuckerman bound
Roth, P. Zuckerman unbound
Styron, W. Sophie's choice
JEWS, RUSSIAN -- UNITED STATES
Fishman, B. A replacement life

Levitt, P. M. Come with me to Babylon
JHANSI (INDIA : DISTRICT) -- HISTORY -- 19TH CENTURY
Moran, M. Rebel queen
Jiang Qing, 1914-1991
About
Min, A. Becoming Madame Mao
JIGSAW PUZZLES
See also Puzzles
JIHAD
See also International relations; Islam
The **Jim** Chee mysteries. Hillerman, T.
Jim Henson's tale of sand. Henson, J.
Jim the boy. Earley, T.
Jimmy Bluefeather. Heacox, K.
JINN
Chakraborty, S. K. The city of brass
Johnson, A. D. Moonshine
Rushdie, S. Two years eight months and twenty-eight nights
Jitterbug perfume. Robbins, T.
JIU-JITSU
See also Martial arts; Self-defense
Joan, of Arc, Saint, 1412-1431
About
Cutter, K. The maid
Twain, M. Personal recollections of Joan of Arc
JOB INTERVIEWS
See also Applications for positions; Interviewing
JOBLESS PEOPLE *See* Unemployed
JOCKEYS
Francis, D. Bolt
Francis, D. Nerve
Francis, D. Whip hand
Joe. Brown, L.
Joe College. Perrotta, T.
Joe Pickett novel [series]
Box, C. J. Force of nature
Box, C. J. Vicious circle
John. Williams, N.
JOHN HENRY (LEGENDARY CHARACTER)
Whitehead, C. John Henry Days
A John Henry Cole story [series]
Brooks, B. Winter kill
John Henry Days. Whitehead, C.
John Saturnall's feast. Norfolk, L.
John simmons short fiction award [series]
Founds, K. When mystical creatures attack!
John, King of England, 1167-1216
About
Penman, S. K. Here be dragons
John, of Gaunt, Duke of Lancaster, 1340-1399
About
Seton, A. Katherine
John, the Apostle, Saint
About
Williams, N. John
Johnny got his gun. Trumbo, D.
Johnny One-Eye. Charyn, J.
JOINT CUSTODY OF CHILDREN *See* Child custody; Part-time parenting
The **joker.** Hudgins, A.
JOKES
See also Wit and humor
Jonathan Strange & Mr. Norrell. Clarke, S.
A Jonathan Stride novel [series]
Freeman, B. Goodbye to the dead
JONES, BRIDGET (FICTITIOUS CHARACTER)
Fielding, H. Bridget Jones
JORDAN
Spark, M. The Mandelbaum Gate
Joseph Andrews and Shamela. Fielding, H.
Josephine Tey [series]
Upson, N. An expert in murder
Upson, N. London rain
JOURNALING
See also Authorship; Diaries
JOURNALISM
DeSilva, B. A Scourge of Vipers
Numero Zero
Westlake, D. E. Trust me on this
JOURNALISM
See also Authorship; Literature
JOURNALISTS
Addison, C. A harvest of thorns
Bacigalupi, P. The water knife
Barton, F. The child
Belfer, L. A fierce radiance
Bhattacharya, R. The sly company of people who care
Bolano, R. 2666
Camus, A. The plague
Carr, C. The alienist
Connelly, M. The scarecrow
Cook, T. H. The fate of Katherine Carr
Dahl, J. Conviction
DeSilva, B. Providence Rag
DeSilva, B. Rogue island
Doctorow, E. L. The waterworks
Doig, I. The eleventh man
Doig, I. Sweet thunder
Dolan, H. Very bad men
Downing, D. Potsdam station
Dyer, G. Jeff in Venice, death in Varanasi
Egan, G. Zendegi
Estleman, L. D. Gas City
Farah, N. Crossbones
Faulks, S. Devil may care
Faulks, S. On Green Dolphin Street
Flanagan, R. The unknown terrorist
Flint, E. Little deaths
Fuentes, C. The old gringo
Furst, A. The foreign correspondent
Gibson, W. Spook country
Glass, J. Three Junes
Glynn, A. Bloodland

Grant, M. Feed
Grass, G. Crabwalk
Greene, G. The quiet American
Grisham, J. The pelican brief
Grisham, J. The last juror
Guterson, D. Snow falling on cedars
Hamill, P. Tabloid city
Harris, R. Archangel
Harvey, M. Brighton
Hiaasen, C. Basket case
Hiaasen, C. Lucky you
Hobson, L. K. Z. Gentleman's agreement
Ignatius, D. A firing offense
Ignatius, D. The Sun King
Irving, J. The fourth hand
Jin, H. The boat rocker
Johnson, A. D. Moonshine
Johnson, D. Le mariage
Karunatilaka, S. The legend of Pradeep Mathew
Katzenbach, J. Just cause
Kelly, J. The fire baby
Kelly, J. The moon tunnel
Kennedy, W. Chango's beads and two-tone shoes
Lanchester, J. Fragrant Harbor
Larsson, S. The girl with the dragon tattoo
Larsson, S. The girl who kicked the hornets' nest
Larsson, S. The girl who played with fire
Leonard, E. The hot kid
Lindgren, T. Hash
Littell, R. Vicious circle
Llywelyn, M. 1921
Lynn, A. Now you see it
MacInnes, H. The Venetian affair
Maguire, G. Son of a witch
Mallon, T. Bandbox
Marlette, D. Magic time
McEwan, I. Amsterdam
Meltzer, B. The tenth justice
Messud, C. The emperor's children
Michener, J. A. Mexico
Miller, D. B. The girl in green
Moya, H. C. The dream of my return
Murray, S. Forgery
Naipaul, V. S. A house for Mr. Biswas
Palahniuk, C. Lullaby
Palin, M. The truth
Parks, B. The girl next door
Pears, I. Stone's fall
Piazza, T. City of refuge
Plath, S. The bell jar
Pratchett, T. The truth
Preston, D. The cabinet of curiosities
Proulx, A. The shipping news
Rachman, T. The imperfectionists
Robotham, M. The wreckage
Salak, K. The white Mary
Schaffert, T. The coffins of Little Hope
Stone, R. Damascus Gate
Toyne, S. Sanctus
Vidal, G. 1876
Waldman, A. The submission
Walters, M. The echo
Westlake, D. E. Baby, would I lie?
White, E. Hotel de Dream
Whitehead, C. John Henry Days
Wilson, R. C. Blind Lake
JOURNALISTS
See also Authors
JOURNALISTS -- SWEDEN
Lagercrantz, D. The girl who takes an eye for an eye
JOURNALISTS -- WASHINGTON (DC)
Tucker, N. The ways of the dead
JOURNALS *See* Periodicals
A **journey** to the centre of the earth. Verne, J.
Journey to the end of the night. Celine
JOURNEYS *See* Travel; Voyages and travels
Joust. Lackey, M.
JOY AND SORROW
See also Emotions
Joy comes in the morning. Rosen, J.
Joy for beginners. Bauermeister, E.
Joy in the morning. Smith, B.
The **Joy** Luck Club. Tan, A.
Jubilee. Walker, M.
Judah Loew ben Bezalel, ca. 1525-1609
About
Sherwood, F. The book of splendor
Wiesel, E. The Golem
JUDAISM
Agnon, S. Y. Only yesterday
Brooks, G. People of the book
Goodman, A. Kaaterskill Falls
Jen, G. Mona in the promised land
Mirvis, T. The outside world
Potok, C. The gift of Asher Lev
Potok, C. My name is Asher Lev
Roiphe, A. R. Lovingkindness
Singer, I. B. The magician of Lublin
Wiesel, E. The Golem
Zimler, R. The last kabbalist of Lisbon
JUDAISM -- CUSTOMS AND PRACTICES
See also Rites and ceremonies
JUDAISM -- RELATIONS -- CHRISTIANITY
See also Christianity and other religions; Judaism
JUDAISM -- RELATIONS -- ISLAM
See also Islam; Judaism
Judas child. O'Connell, C.
The **Judas** Field. Bahr, H.
Judas horse. Smith, A.
Judas Iscariot
About
Asch, S. The Nazarene
Kazantzakis, N. The last temptation of Christ
The **Judas** kiss. Holt, V.

Jude the obscure. Hardy, T.
The **judges.** Wiesel, E.
JUDGES
See also Lawyers
JUDGES
Carter, S. L. The emperor of Ocean Park
The death of Ivan Ilyich and Confession
Desai, K. The inheritance of loss
Grisham, J. The brethren
Longworth, M. L. Death at the Chateau Bremont
Mankell, H. The man from Beijing
Marlette, D. Magic time
McCann, C. Thirteen ways of looking
McEwan, I. The children act
Parks, B. Say nothing
Patterson, R. N. Protect and defend
Picoult, J. Nineteen minutes
Rosenberg, N. T. Interest of justice
Schwartz, L. Angels Crest
Tóibín, C. The heather blazing
Trollope, J. Marrying the mistress
Turow, S. Innocent
Turow, S. Limitations
JUDGMENT DAY
See also End of the world; Second Advent
A **judgment** in stone. Rendell, R.
The **judgment** of Caesar. Saylor, S.
JUDICIAL ERROR
Grisham, J. The confession
JUDICIAL INVESTIGATIONS *See* Governmental investigations
JUDO
See also Martial arts; Self-defense
The **jugger.** Stark, R.
Julian Comstock. Wilson, R. C.
Juliet. Fortier, A.
Juliet in August. Warren, D.
Juliet, naked. Hornby, N.
JULY FOURTH *See* Fourth of July
July's people. Gordimer, N.
The **jungle.** Sinclair, U.
JUNGLE ANIMALS
See also Animals; Forest animals
JUNGLE ECOLOGY
See also Ecology; Forest ecology
JUNGLES
Conrad, J. Heart of darkness
Forester, C. S. The African Queen
Millet, L. Ghost lights
Patchett, A. State of wonder
Salak, K. The white Mary
Junior Bender [series]
Hallinan, T. Fields where they lay
Jupiter's bones. Kellerman, F.
Jurassic Park. Crichton, M.
JURISTS *See* Lawyers
JURY
See also Courts; Criminal law
JURY
Doctorow, C. Rapture of the nerds
Just a corpse at twilight. Van de Wetering, J.
Just cause. Katzenbach, J.
Just one evil act. George, E.
Just What Kind of Mother Are You? Daly, P.
JUSTICE
Gruber, M. The return
Spark, M. Aiding and abetting
JUSTICE
See also Ethics; Law; Virtue
Justice for some. Wilhelm, K.
JUSTICE LEAGUE (FICTIONAL CHARACTERS)
See also Fictional characters; Superheroes
Justine. Durrell, L.
JUVENILE DELINQUENCY
Edgerton, C. Walking across Egypt
Fagan, J. The panopticon
Hunter, E. The blackboard jungle
Lelic, S. The child who
Levin, M. Compulsion
Oe, K. Nip the buds, shoot the kids
JUVENILE DELINQUENCY
See also Crime; Social problems
JUVENILE DELINQUENTS *See* Juvenile delinquency
JUVENILE PROSTITUTION
See also Juvenile delinquency; Prostitution
JUVENILE PROSTITUTION
Coplin, A. The orchardist

K

K is for killer. Grafton, S.
Kaaterskill Falls. Goodman, A.
KABUL (AFGHANISTAN)
Hosseini, K. The kite runner
Moulessehoul, M. The swallows of Kabul
Kafka on the shore.
Kafka, Franz, 1883-1924
About
Lashner, W. Kockroach
The **Kalahari** typing school for men. McCall Smith, A.
Kaleidoscope. Gilman, D.
Kalooki nights. Jacobson, H.
KANCHENJUNGA (NEPAL AND INDIA)
Desai, K. The inheritance of loss
KANSAS
Byers, M. Percival's planet
Dallas, S. The Persian Pickle Club
Flynn, G. Dark places
Hughes, L. Not without laughter
Moriarty, L. The center of everything
Nelson, A. Bound
Paretsky, S. Bleeding Kansas
Paretsky, S. Fallout
Parks, G. The learning tree

Preston, D. Still life with crows
Roy, L. Bent Road
Russell, M. D. Doc
KANSAS -- 19TH CENTURY
Durham, D. A. Gabriel's story
Parker, R. B. Gunman's rhapsody
KARATE
See also Judo; Martial arts; Self-defense
Karate chop.
KAREN (SOUTHEAST ASIAN PEOPLE)
Craig, C. Miss Burma
KARP, BUTCH (FICTITIOUS CHARACTER)
Tanenbaum, R. K. Tragic
Tanenbaum, R. Act of revenge
KASHI (CHINA)
Joinson, S. A lady cyclist's guide to Kashgar
Kate Burkholder thrillers [series]
Castillo, L. Breaking silence
Castillo, L. The dead will tell
Castillo, L. Sworn to silence
Kate Shugak [series]
Stabenow, D. Less than a treason
Stabenow, D. Restless in the grave
Stabenow, D. Though not dead
Katherine. Seton, A.
Katherine, Duchess of Lancaster, 1350-1403
About
Seton, A. Katherine
KATRINA, HURRICANE, 2005 *See* Hurricane Katrina, 2005
KAYAKING
See also Canoes and canoeing
Keckley, Elizabeth, ca. 1818-1907
About
Chiaverini, J. Mrs. Lincoln's dressmaker
The **keep.** Egan, J.
Keeper of dreams. Card, O. S.
The **keeper** of lost causes. Adler-Olsen, J.
The **keeper's** son. Hickam, H. H.
The **keepers** of the house. Grau, S. A.
Keeping Faith. Picoult, J.
Keeping it real. Robson, J.
Keeping watch. King, L. R.
Keilson, Hans, 1909-2011
About
Keilson, H. Life goes on
KELLER, JOHN (FICTITIOUS CHARACTER)
Block, L. Hit me
Kellogg, John Harvey, 1852-1943
About
Boyle, T. C. Road to Wellville
Kelsey, Nancy, 1823 or 4-1896
About
Holland, C. An ordinary woman
KENKEN
See also Puzzles
Kennedy, John F. (John Fitzgerald), 1917-1963
About
Buckley, W. F. Mongoose, R.I.P
Ellroy, J. American tabloid
King, S. 11/22/63
KENT (ENGLAND)
Haynes, E. Dark tide
KENTUCKY
Arnow, H. L. S. The dollmaker
Berry, W. Jayber Crow
Berry, W. That distant land
House, S. A parchment of leaves
Koryta, M. The ridge
Mason, B. A. In country
Morgan, C. E. All the living
Morgan, C. E. The sport of kings
Taylor, A. The marble orchard
KENTUCKY -- 19TH CENTURY
Warren, R. P. World enough and time
KENTUCKY -- SOCIAL LIFE AND CUSTOMS -- 20TH CENTURY
Roy, L. Let me die in his footsteps
KENYA
Crompton, R. Hell's gate
Crompton, R. Hour of the Red God
McLain, P. Circling the Sun
Vassanji, M. G. The in-between world of Vikram Lall
KENYA -- HISTORY -- 1895-1963
Kimani, P. Dance of the Jakaranda
KENYA -- NAIROBI
Drayson, N. Guide to the birds of East Africa
Le Carre, J. The constant gardener
KENYANS -- CANADA
Vassanji, M. G. The in-between world of Vikram Lall
The **kept.** Scott, J.
KEYS *See* Locks and keys
The **keys** of the kingdom. Cronin, A. J.
The **keys** to the street. Rendell, R.
Khrushchev, Nikita Sergeevich, 1894-1971
About
Lawton, J. Old flames
KIBERA (KENYA)
Levine, J. A. Bingo's Run
KIDNAPPING
Aira, C. The seamstress and the wind
Barr, N. Destroyer angel
Blake, J. C. The house of Wolfe
Cain, C. One Kick
Carey, J. Banewreaker
Carey, P. His illegal self
Corleone, D. Good as gone
Deaver, J. The October list
Dibdin, M. Ratking
Dicks, M. Memoirs of an imaginary friend
Donoghue, E. Room
Duncan, G. Talulla rising
Farah, N. Links
Faye, L. Seven for a secret
Fergus, J. The wild girl: the notebooks of Ned Giles, 1932

Fielding, J. Heartstopper
Finder, J. Buried secrets
Flynn, M. On the razor's edge
French, N. Blue Monday
Gardner, L. Find Her
Gay, R. An Untamed State
George, E. Just one evil act
Gowdy, B. Helpless
Grant, D. The Protector
Grant, H. The vanishing of Katharina Linden
Greene, G. The honorary consul
Groom, W. El Paso
Gruber, M. The good son
Hiaasen, C. Star Island
Highsmith, P. The boy who followed Ripley
Hill, J. Nos4a2
Hoag, T. Dark horse
Hoag, T. Guilty as sin
Hoag, T. Night sins
Howard, L. Cry no more
Johansen, I. Taking Eve
Julavits, H. The uses of enchantment
Kardos, M. The Three-Day Affair
Kelton, E. The way of the coyote
King, L. R. Keeping watch
Koontz, D. R. The husband
Land, J. Strong at the break
Lansdale, J. R. The thicket
Laukkanen, O. The professionals
Lehane, D. Mystic river
Levin, M. Compulsion
Lippman, L. I'd know you anywhere
Lippman, L. What the dead know
Littell, R. Vicious circle
Ludlum, R. The Janson directive
Matar, H. Anatomy of a disappearance
McBain, E. Alice in jeopardy
McEwan, I. The child in time
McHugh, L. Arrowood
Miller, D. B. Norwegian by night
Mitchard, J. The deep end of the ocean
Norton, C. What doesn't kill her
Oates, J. C. Daddy Love
O'Connell, C. Judas child
Parker, T. J. Little Saigon
Parks, B. Say nothing
Patterson, J. Along came a spider
Peebles, F. d. P. The seamstress
Rader-Day, L. The day I died
Rendell, R. The tree of hands
Ruiz-Camacho, A. Barefoot dogs
Sakey, M. The blade itself
Saylor, S. Raiders of the Nile
Searles, J. Boy still missing
Silva, D. The secret servant
Stephenson, N. Reamde
Stevens, C. Still missing
Trevor, W. Death in summer
Vine, B. Gallowglass
Walker, M. W. Under the beetle's cellar
Walters, M. The devil's feather
Westerfeld, S. The risen empire
Wilson, F. P. Deep as the marrow
Wilson, R. Capital Punishment
Winslow, D. Savages
Woods, S. Swimming to Catalina
Yates, A. Moondogs
Zan, K. The Never List

KIDNAPPING

See also Criminal law; Offenses against the person

KIDNAPPING VICTIMS

Cain, C. One Kick
Swanson, P. Her every fear

KIDNAPPING -- INVESTIGATION

George, E. Just one evil act
Rader-Day, L. The day I died

KIDNAPPING -- ITALY -- ROME

Dazieri, S. Kill the father

KIDNAPPING -- NEBRASKA -- OMAHA

Hilleman, A. World, chase me down

KIDNAPPING -- SCOTLAND

MacBride, S. Shatter the bones

Kiffe kiffe tomorrow. Guene, F.
Kill me. White, S. W.
Kill the father. Dazieri, S.
Kill the messenger. Hoag, T.
Kill you twice. Cain, C.,
Killed at the whim of a hat. Cotterill, C.
The **killer** angels. Shaara, M.
The **killer** inside me. Thompson, J.
The **killer** is dying. Sallis, J.
The **killer** next door. Marwood, A.
Killer smile. Scottoline, L.
Killer summer. Pearson, R.
A **killer's** kiss. Lashner, W.
Killing Castro. Block, L.
The **killing** circle. Pyper, A.
Killing critics. O'Connell, C.
Killing floor. Child, L.
The **killing** ground. Settle, M. L.
Killing ground. Seymour, G.
Killing grounds. Stabenow, D.
A **killing** in the hills. Keller, J.
A **killing** in this town. Vernon, O.
The **killing** jar. Monaghan, N.
The **killing** lessons. Black, S.
Killing Mister Watson. Matthiessen, P.
The **killing** moon. Jemisin, N. K.
The **killing** of worlds. Westerfeld, S.
Killing time. Harrod-Eagles, C.
Killing Trail. Mizushima, M.
Killshot. Leonard, E.
Kilo class. Robinson, P.
A **kind** of freedom. Sexton, M. W.

Kindred. Butler, O. E.
Kinds of love. Sarton, M.
KINETIC ART
See also Art
King Bongo. Sanchez, T.
The **king** must die. Renault, M.
The **king** of Colored Town. Wimberley, D.
King of Cuba. García, C.
The **king** of diamonds. Tolkien, S.
The **king** of lies. Hart, J.
The **king** of swords. Stone, N.
King of the badgers. Hensher, P.
King Solomon's carpet. Vine, B.
King Solomon's mines. Haggard, H. R.
King's captain. Lambdin, D.
A **King's** Ransom. Penman, S. K.
King, queen, knave. Nabokov, V. V.
The **kingdom.** Cussler, C.
Kingdom come. Ballard, J. G.
The **kingdom** of bones. Gallagher, S.
Kingdom of strangers. Ferraris, Z.
The Kingmaker chronicles [series]
Bouchet, A. Breath of fire
The **kingmaker's** daughter. Gregory, P.
KINGS
Berger, T. Arthur Rex
Bradley, M. Z. The mists of Avalon
Calvino, I. Invisible cities
Cornwell, B. Enemy of God
Cornwell, B. Excalibur
Cornwell, B. The winter king
Dumas, A. The man in the iron mask
Eco, U. Baudolino
Edghill, I. Queenmaker
Franklin, A. Mistress of the art of death
Franklin, A. The serpent's tale
Gregory, P. The other Boleyn girl
Gregory, P. The Boleyn Inheritance
Holland, C. Valley of the Kings
Laker, R. To dance with kings
L'Engle, M. Certain women
Mantel, H. Wolf Hall
Maxwell, R. The secret diary of Anne Boleyn
Penman, S. K. Devil's brood
Penman, S. K. Falls the shadow
Penman, S. K. Here be dragons
Penman, S. K. Lionheart
Penman, S. K. The reckoning
Penman, S. K. The sunne in splendour
Penman, S. K. Time and chance
Penman, S. K. When Christ and his saints slept
Plaidy, J. Murder most royal
Plaidy, J. The pleasures of love
Plaidy, J. William's wife
Puzo, M. The family
Renault, M. Funeral games
Renault, M. The Persian boy
Scott, W. Ivanhoe
Sutcliff, R. Sword at sunset
Tey, J. The daughter of time
Twain, M. A Connecticut Yankee in King Arthur's court
White, T. H. The book of Merlyn
White, T. H. The once and future king
White, T. H. The sword in the stone
KINGS AND RULERS
Abercrombie, J. Half a King
Abercrombie, J. Half a war
Anderson, P. War of the Gods
Greenwood, K. Out of the black land
Koen, K. Before Versailles
Leigh, E. Forever Your Earl
Liu, K. The grace of kings
Liu, K. The wall of storms
McClellan, B. Promise of blood
McKillip, P. A. Ombria in shadow
Penman, S. K. A King's Ransom
Tremain, R. Music & silence
KINGS AND RULERS
See also Heads of state
KINGS AND RULERS -- SUCCESSION
Abercrombie, J. Half a war
Carey, J. Kushiel's Scion
The **kings** of cool. Winslow, D.
Kings of infinite space. Hynes, J.
KINGS, QUEENS, RULERS, ETC. *See* Kings and rulers
Kingsbridge [series]
Follett, K. A column of fire
KINSHIP
See also Ethnology; Family
Kinshu: Autumn brocade. Miyamoto, T.
Kintu. Makumbi, J. N.
KIOWA INDIANS
Jiles, P. News of the world
Momaday, N. S. The ancient child
The **kiss.** Steel, D.
A **kiss** before dying. Levin, I.
A **kiss** of fate. Putney, M. J.
Kiss of the spider woman. Puig, M.
Kiss the girls. Patterson, J.
Kisser. Woods, S.
Kissing the gunner's daughter. Rendell, R.
Kitchen. Yoshimoto, B.
The **kitchen** god's wife. Tan, A.
KITCHENS
See also Houses; Rooms
The **kite** runner. Hosseini, K.
KITES
See also Aeronautics
KLOSTER ANDECHS (ANDECHS, GERMANY)
The Poisoned Pilgrim
Knight of shadows. Zelazny, R.
KNIGHTHOOD *See* Knights and knighthood
KNIGHTS AND KNIGHTHOOD
Berger, T. Arthur Rex

Cervantes Saavedra, M. d. Don Quixote de la Mancha
Connell, E. S. Deus lo volt!
Cornwell, B. Enemy of God
Cornwell, B. Excalibur
Cornwell, B. The winter king
Follett, K. World without end
Holland, C. Jerusalem
Martin, G. R. R. A storm of swords
Scott, W. Ivanhoe
White, T. H. The once and future king
KNIGHTS AND KNIGHTHOOD
See also Middle Ages; Nobility
KNIGHTS OF MALTA
Willocks, T. The religion
KNITTING
Hood, A. The knitting circle
The **knitting** circle. Hood, A.
Knockemstiff. Pollock, D. R.
Knollys, Lettice
About
George, M. Elizabeth I
Knots. Farah, N.
Known to evil. Mosley, W.
The **known** world. Jones, E. P.
Kockroach. Lashner, W.
KOKNA (INDIC PEOPLE)
D'Souza, T. The Konkans
KOLKATA (INDIA)
Divakaruni, C. B. Oleander girl
Mukherjee, A. A Rising Man
The **Konkans.** D'Souza, T.
KOREA
Han, K. Human Acts
The investigation
Lee, K. Drifting house
Lee, M. G. Somebody's daughter
Lee, M. J. Pachinko
Park, S. This burns my heart
KOREA (NORTH)
Bandi The accusation
Church, J. Bamboo and blood
Johnson, A. The orphan master's son
KOREA (NORTH) -- OFFICIALS AND EMPLOYEES
Church, J. A corpse in the Koryo
KOREA (SOUTH)
Han, K. The vegetarian
Limón, M. Mr. Kill
Yoon, P. Once the shore
KOREAN AMERICAN WOMEN
Chung, C. Forgotten country
KOREAN AMERICANS
Lee, K. Drifting house
Lee, M. G. Somebody's daughter
Shteyngart, G. Super sad true love story
KOREAN WAR, 1950-1953
Griffin, W. E. B. Under fire
Ha Jin War trash
Hooker, R. MASH
Lee The surrendered
Michener, J. A. The bridges at Toko-ri
Morris, W. Taps
Roth, P. Indignation
KOREAN WAR, 1950-1953 -- CASUALTIES
Phillips, J. A. Lark and Termite
KOREAN WAR, 1950-1953 -- VETERANS
Morrison, T. Home
KOREANS
Lee, K. Drifting house
Woo, S. J. Love love
KOREANS -- UNITED STATES
Lee The surrendered
Woo, S. J. Everything Asian
Kowloon Tong. Theroux, P.
Kraken. Mieville, C.
Krik? Krak! Danticat, E.
Kristin Lavransdatter. Undset, S.
KU KLUX KLAN
Ellroy, J. The cold six thousand
Iles, G. The bone tree
Marlette, D. Magic time
Vernon, O. A killing in this town
KU KLUX KLAN
See also Secret societies
Kublai Khan, 1216-1294
About
Calvino, I. Invisible cities
KUNG FU
See also Martial arts
KURDS
Shafak, E. Honor
KURSK, BATTLE OF, RUSSIA, 1943
Robbins, D. L. The last citadel
Kushiel's dart. Carey, J.
Kushiel's Scion. Carey, J.
KYRGYZSTAN
Rosenberg, R. This is not civilization

L

L'America. McPhee, M.
L.A. confidential. Ellroy, J.
L.A. dead. Woods, S.
L.A. outlaws. Parker, T. J.
L.A. Times. Woods, S.
LABOR
See also Economics; Social conditions; Sociology
LABOR -- ACCIDENTS *See* Industrial accidents
LABOR AND LABORING CLASSES -- ENGLAND
Sillitoe, A. Saturday night and Sunday morning
Swift, G. Last orders
LABOR AND LABORING CLASSES -- FRANCE
Zola, E. Germinal
LABOR AND LABORING CLASSES -- PENNSYLVANIA
Poyer, D. Thunder on the mountain

LABOR AND LABORING CLASSES -- POLAND
Singer, I. J. The brothers Ashkenazi
LABOR AND LABORING CLASSES -- UNITED STATES
Doig, I. Bucking the sun
Lehane, D. The given day
Steinbeck, J. In dubious battle
LABOR AND LABORING CLASSES -- WALES
Llewellyn, R. How green was my valley
LABOR CAMPS
The hunger angel
Labor Day. Maynard, J.
LABOR DISPUTES
Tucker, T. Over and under
LABOR ORGANIZATIONS *See* Labor unions
LABOR UNIONS
Bennett, R. J. The company man
Doig, I. Work song
Himes, C. B. Lonely crusade
Lehane, D. The given day
Poyer, D. Thunder on the mountain
Schulberg, B. Waterfront
LABOR UNIONS -- CORRUPT PRACTICES
Tanenbaum, R. K. Tragic
LABOR UNIONS -- MASSACHUSETTS
Shepard, K. The Celestials
LABORATORY ANIMAL WELFARE *See* Animal welfare
LABORATORY FERTILIZATION *See* Fertilization in vitro
LABORERS
Eschbach, A. The carpet makers
LaBrava. Leonard, E.
The **lace** reader. Barry, B.
The **lacquer** screen. Gulik, R. H. v.
Ladder of years. Tyler, A.
Ladies and gentlemen. Ross, A.
The **ladies** of Covington send their love. Medlicott, J. A.
Ladies of the Manor [series]
White, R. M. A lady unrivaled
Ladivine. Ndiaye, M.
Lady Chatterley's lover. Lawrence, D. H.
A **lady** cyclist's guide to Kashgar. Joinson, S.
The **Lady** Elizabeth. Weir, A.
The **lady** from Zagreb. Kerr, P.
Lady Maggie's secret scandal. Burrowes, G.
The **lady** matador's hotel. Garcia, C.
The **Lady** Most Willing. James, E.
A **lady** never lies. Gray, J.
The **lady** of the rivers. Gregory, P.
The **lady** travelers guide to scoundrels & other gentlemen. Alexander, V.
A **lady** unrivaled. White, R. M.
A **lady's** code of misconduct. Duran, M.
LADY'S MAIDS
Worsley, K. She rises
LAGUNA BEACH (CALIF.)
Khadivi, L. A good country
Winslow, D. The kings of cool
Winslow, D. Savages
LAGUNA INDIANS
Silko, L. Ceremony
The **lake.**
LAKE DISTRICT (ENGLAND)
Robertson, I. Island of bones
LAKE ECOLOGY
See also Ecology
Lake of sorrows. Hart, E.
The **Lake** Shore Limited. Miller, S.
LAKE SUPERIOR
Sosin, D. The long-shining waters
LAKE TAHOE (CALIF. AND NEV.)
O'Shaughnessy, P. Breach of promise
O'Shaughnessy, P. Invasion of privacy
O'Shaughnessy, P. Motion to suppress
O'Shaughnessy, P. Obstruction of justice
O'Shaughnessy, P. Writ of execution
Pronzini, B. Step to the graveyard easy
Lakshmibai, Rani of Jhansi, 1828-1858
About
Moran, M. Rebel queen
LAMAS
Hilton, J. Lost horizon
Lamb. Nadzam, B.
LAMBS *See* Sheep
Lancelot. Percy, W.
The **land** across. Wolfe, G.
A **land** more kind than home. Cash, W.
The **Land** of Dreams.
Land of love and drowning. Yanique, T.
Land of marvels. Unsworth, B.
The **land** of painted caves. Auel, J. M.
LAND QUESTION *See* Land tenure
LAND SETTLEMENT
See also Colonies; Land use
LAND TENURE
Mazzarella, N. This heavy silence
McGahan, A. The white earth
McLarty, R. Art in America
O'Brien, E. Wild Decembers
Landfalls. Williams, N. J.
Landline. Rowell, R.
LANDLORD AND TENANT
See also Commercial law; Land tenure; Real estate
Lands of memory. Hernandez, F.
LANGDON, ROBERT (FICTITIOUS CHARACTER)
Brown, D. Inferno
LANGUAGE *See* Language and languages
LANGUAGE ACQUISITION
See also Language and languages
LANGUAGE AND CULTURE
See also Culture; Language and languages
LANGUAGE AND LANGUAGES
Barker, N. Darkmans
Delany, S. R. Babel-17 ; Empire star
The elegance of the hedgehog
Hoban, R. Riddley Walker

Mieville, C. Embassytown
LANGUAGE AND LANGUAGES
See also Anthropology; Communication; Ethnology
LANGUAGE ARTS
See also Communication
The **language** of flowers. Diffenbaugh, V.
LANGUAGES *See* Language and languages
Lannan translation series
Petterson, P. I curse the river of time
Petterson, P. Out stealing horses
Lansky, Meyer, 1902-1983
About
Latour, J. The Havana World Series
The **lantern** bearers. Frame, R.
Lantern slides. O'Brien, E.
LAOS
Cotterill, C. Slash and burn
Lapham rising. Rosenblatt, R.
LAPLAND
Vida, V. Let the Northern Lights erase your name
LARCENY *See* Theft
LARGE DATA SETS *See* Big data
LARGE PRINT BOOKS
Allende, I. Portrait in sepia
Bradbury, R. The illustrated man
Crichton, M. Timeline
Erdrich, L. The last report on the miracles at Little No Horse
Gaiman, N. Stardust
García Márquez, G. One hundred years of solitude
King, S. Different seasons
Knowles, J. A separate peace
McCullers, C. The heart is a lonely hunter
Mitchell, M. Gone with the wind
Russo, R. Empire Falls
Steinbeck, J. Cannery Row
Tademy, L. Cane River
Tyler, A. Saint maybe
Waugh, E. The loved one
LARGE TYPE BOOKS
George, E. Believing the lie
LARGE TYPE BOOKS *See* Large print books
The **largesse** of the sea maiden. Johnson, D.
Lark and Termite. Phillips, J. A.
LaRose. Erdrich, L.
LAS VEGAS (NEV.)
Abani, C. The secret history of Las Vegas
Goldberg, T. Gangsterland
Hilton, E. Dirty money Honey
Watkins, C. V. Battleborn
LASERS IN AERONAUTICS
See also Aeronautics; Lasers
The **last** alibi. Ellis, D.
The **last** animal. Geni, A.
The **last** book of swords: Shieldbreaker's story. Saberhagen, F.
Last bus to wisdom. Doig, I.
The **last** camel died at noon. Peters, E.
The **last** camellia. Jio, S.
Last Chance Saloon. Keyes, M.
The **last** child. Hart, J.
The **last** chronicle of Barset. Trollope, A.
Last chronicles of Thomas Covenant [series]
Donaldson, S. R. The runes of the earth
The **last** citadel. Robbins, D. L.
The **last** command. Zahn, T.
The **last** confession of Thomas Hawkins. Hodgson, A.
The **last** crossing. Vanderhaeghe, G.
The **last** dance. McBain, E.
The **last** days of Café Leila. Bijan, D.
Last days of Dogtown. Diamant, A.
The **last** days of night. Moore, G.
The **last** days of Pompeii. Lytton, E. B. L.
The **last** days of Ptolemy Grey. Mosley, W.
The **last** detective. Lovesey, P.
The **last** Dickens. Pearl, M.
Last ditch. Marsh, N.
The **last** Don. Puzo, M.
The **last** enchantment. Stewart, M.
The **last** enchantments. Finch, C.
Last evenings on Earth. Bolano, R.
The **Last** Flight of Poxl West. Torday, D.
Last Friends. Gardam, J.
The **last** full measure. Shaara, J.
The **last** gentleman. Percy, W.
The **last** good kiss. Crumley, J.
The **last** good man. Kazinski, A. J.
The **last** hellion. Chase, L. L.
Last Hundred Years Trilogy [series]
Smiley, J. Early warning
Smiley, J. Golden age
Smiley, J. Some luck
The **last** judgment. Pears, I.
The **last** juror. Grisham, J.
The **last** kabbalist of Lisbon. Zimler, R.
The **last** kingdom. Cornwell, B.
Last kiss. Rice, L.
Last man in tower. Adiga, A.
The **Last** Mrs. Parrish. Constantine, L.
The **last** Nazi. Pottinger, S.
The **last** Neanderthal. Cameron, C.
Last night. Salter, J.
Last night at the blue angel. Rotert, R.
Last night at the Lobster. O'Nan, S.
The **last** novel. Markson, D.
The **last** nude. Avery, E.
The **last** of her kind. Nunez, S.
Last of the breed. L'Amour, L.
The **last** of the just. Schwarz-Bart, A.
The **last** of the Mohicans. Cooper, J. F.
The **last** of the wine. Renault, M.
Last orders. Swift, G.
The **last** painting of Sara De Vos. Smith, D.
The **last** policeman. Winters, B. H.
Last policeman [series]

Winters, B. H. World of trouble
Last Ragged Breath. Keller, J.
The **last** refuge. Knopf, C.
The **last** report on the miracles at Little No Horse. Erdrich, L.
Last rites. Harvey, J.
Last rituals. Yrsa Sigurdardottir
The **last** runaway. Chevalier, T.
Last stories and other stories. Vollmann, W. T.
The **last** surgeon. Palmer, M.
The **last** temptation of Christ. Kazantzakis, N.
The **last** time they met. Shreve, A.
The **last** tycoon. Fitzgerald, F. S.
The **last** unicorn. Beagle, P. S.
The **last** werewolf. Duncan, G.
The **last** witchfinder. Morrow, J.
The **last** word. Lutz, L.
The **last** word and other stories. Greene, G.
Late for the wedding. Quick, A.
Late nights on air. Hay, E.
Later short stories, 1888-1903.
The **lathe** of heaven. Le Guin, U. K.
LATIN AMERICA
Allende, I. Eva Luna
Garcia Marquez, G. Love in the time of cholera
Garcia, C. The lady matador's hotel
Naipaul, V. S. A way in the world
The Oxford book of Latin American short stories
LATIN AMERICAN ART
See also Art
LATIN AMERICANS
The Oxford book of Latin American short stories
LATIN AMERICANS -- EUROPE
Garcia Marquez, G. Strange pilgrims
LATIN LANGUAGE
See also Language and languages
Latin@ rising.
LATINO AUTHORS
Latin@ rising
LATINOS (U.S.)
Burgess, M. Dogfight, a love story
Valdes-Rodriguez, A. Dirty girls on top
The **laughing** policeman. Sjowall, M.
LAUGHTER
See also Emotions
Laveau, Marie, 1794-1881
About
Rhodes, J. P. Voodoo dreams
LAW *See* Legal stories
LAW AND LAWYERS
Banks, R. The sweet hereafter
Camus, A. The fall
Carter, S. L. The emperor of Ocean Park
Clark, M. The legal limit
Connell, E. S. Mrs. Bridge
Connelly, M. The Lincoln lawyer
De Kretser, M. The Hamilton case
DeLillo, D. Falling man
Dickens, C. Bleak House
Dickens, C. The posthumous papers of the Pickwick Club
Dugoni, R. Murder one
Ferris, J. The unnamed
Forsyth, F. Avenger
Gaddis, W. A frolic of his own
Gardam, J. The man in the wooden hat
Gardam, J. Old Filth
Greene, G. The tenth man
Grippando, J. Born to run
Grippando, J. Lying with strangers
Grisham, J. The client
Grisham, J. The confession
Grisham, J. The pelican brief
Grisham, J. The firm
Grisham, J. The last juror
Grisham, J. The partner
Grisham, J. A time to kill
Gruber, M. The book of air and shadows
Hart, J. The king of lies
Hoag, T. Guilty as sin
Iles, G. Turning angel
Katzenbach, J. Hart's war
Kaufman, S. Diary of a mad housewife
Kennedy, D. The big picture
King, S. Thinner
Lashner, W. A killer's kiss
Lee, H. To kill a mockingbird
Lescroart, J. T. The first law
Lescroart, J. T. Guilt
Lescroart, J. T. The hearing
Lescroart, J. T. Nothing but the truth
Lescroart, J. T. The oath
Lipman, E. The family man
Martini, S. P. Compelling evidence
Meltzer, B. The tenth justice
Miller, S. The good mother
Mishima, Y. The decay of the angel
Mishima, Y. Runaway horses
Mishima, Y. The Temple of Dawn
Mortimer, J. Rumpole's return
Parker, B. Criminal justice
Parker, B. Suspicion of betrayal
Parker, B. Suspicion of deceit
Parker, B. Suspicion of vengeance
Patchett, A. Run
Patterson, R. N. Balance of power
Patterson, R. N. Conviction
Patterson, R. N. Dark lady
Patterson, R. N. Eclipse
Patterson, R. N. Silent witness
Picoult, J. My sister's keeper
Picoult, J. Change of heart
Reuland, R. Semiautomatic
Robertson, M. The brothers of Baker Street
Roosevelt, K. In the shadow of the law
Sams, F. Down town

Schlink, B. The reader
Scottoline, L. Dead ringer
Scottoline, L. Killer smile
Scottoline, L. Moment of truth
Sheehan, A. The anxiety of everyday objects
Snow, C. P. Strangers and brothers
Tanenbaum, R. Act of revenge
Tey, J. The Franchise affair
Turow, S. Presumed innocent
Turow, S. The burden of proof
Turow, S. Innocent
Turow, S. The laws of our fathers
Turow, S. Limitations
Turow, S. Personal injuries
Turow, S. Reversible errors
Unsworth, B. After Hannibal
Warren, R. P. All the king's men
Warren, R. P. World enough and time
Welch, J. The Indian lawyer
Wilhelm, K. The best defense
Wilhelm, K. Defense for the devil
Woods, S. Cold paradise
Woods, S. Dead in the water
Woods, S. Dirty work
Woods, S. Grass roots
Woods, S. Kisser
Woods, S. L.A. dead
Woods, S. Lucid intervals
Woods, S. Orchid Beach
Woods, S. Reckless abandon
Woods, S. The short forever
Woods, S. Short straw
Woods, S. Swimming to Catalina
Woods, S. Two-dollar bill
Woods, S. Worst fears realized
Law at Angel's Landing. Overholser, W. D.
LAW CLERKS
Stone, N. The Verdict
LAW ENFORCEMENT
Leonard, E. Raylan
Mullen, T. Darktown
LAW FIRMS
Stone, N. The Verdict
The **lawgiver.** Wouk, H.
LAWN TENNIS *See* Tennis
Lawrence, T. E. (Thomas Edward), 1888-1935
About
Russell, M. D. Dreamers of the day
The **laws** of invisible things. Huyler, F.
The **laws** of our fathers. Turow, S.
LAWYERS
Benet, S. V. The Devil and Daniel Webster
Vidal, G. Lincoln
LAWYERS *See* Legal stories
LAWYERS -- GREAT BRITAIN
Ballantyne, L. The guilty one
LAWYERS -- MASSACHUSETTS -- BOSTON
Nova, C. All the dead Yale men
The **lay** of the land. Ford, R.
Lazarus. West, M. L.
LAZINESS
See also Personality
Le divorce. Johnson, D.
Le mariage. Johnson, D.
LEADERSHIP
See also Ability; Executive ability; Social groups; Success
LEADERSHIP IN WOMEN
See also Leadership; Women
Leaf storm, and other stories. Garcia Marquez, G.
League of Dragons. Novik, N.
Lean on Pete. Vlautin, W.
The **leaning** tower, and other stories. Porter, K. A.
LEARNING AND SCHOLARSHIP
Markovits, A. I am forbidden
Modesitt, L. E. Scholar
The **learning** tree. Parks, G.
Leave Me. Forman, G.
The **leavers.** Ko, L.
Leaving Cecil Street. McKinney-Whetstone, D.
Leaving Everything Most Loved. Winspear, J.
Leaving Lucy Pear. Solomon, A.
Leaving the Atocha Station. Lerner, B.
Leaving Time. Picoult, J.
LEBANESE -- BRAZIL
Hatoum, M. The brothers
LEBANON
Leshem, R. Beaufort
LEBANON -- BEIRUT
Hage, R. De Niro's game
Powers, R. Plowing the dark
LECTURERS
Self, W. Dorian
LEDUC, AIMEE (FICTITIOUS CHARACTER)
Black, C. Murder below Montparnasse
Black, C. Murder in the Bastille
Black, C. Murder in the rue de Paradis
Black, C. Murder on the Champ de Mars
Lee, Harper, 1926-2016
About
Powers, K. Capote in Kansas
Lee, Robert E. (Robert Edward), 1807-1870
About
Shaara, J. Gone for soldiers
Shaara, J. The last full measure
LEECH LAKE INDIAN RESERVATION (MINN.) -- SOCIAL LIFE AND CUSTOMS
Treuer, D. Prudence
The **left** hand of darkness. Le Guin, U. K.
The **leftovers.** Perrotta, T.
Legacies. Wilson, F. P.
The **legal** limit. Clark, M.
LEGAL NOVELS *See* Legal stories
LEGAL PROFESSION *See* Lawyers

LEGAL STORIES
Ackroyd, P. The trial of Elizabeth Cree
Arvin, R. Blood of angels
Ballantyne, L. The guilty one
Clark, M. Guilt by association
Connelly, M. The Lincoln lawyer
Cook, T. H. Sandrine's Case
De la Pava, S. A naked singularity
Ellis, D. The last alibi
Fairstein, L. Night watch
Gaddis, W. A frolic of his own
Grisham, J. Sycamore Row
Grisham, J. Ford County
Grisham, J. The last juror
Hamilton, J. A map of the world
Hoag, T. Guilty as sin
Iles, G. The bone tree
Isaacs, S. Lily White
Keller, J. A killing in the hills
Landay, W. Defending Jacob
Lelic, S. The child who
Lippman, L. Wilde Lake
Lutz, L. The last word
Massey, S. The widows of Malabar Hill
Meltzer, B. The tenth justice
Mina, D. The red road
Nova, C. All the dead Yale men
O'Shaughnessy, P. Motion to suppress
Perry, A. A sunless sea
Roberts, N. Whiskey Beach
Rogan, C. The lifeboat
Roosevelt, K. In the shadow of the law
Rosenberg, N. T. Mitigating circumstances
Scottoline, L. Accused
Stone, N. The Verdict
Tanenbaum, R. K. Tragic
Turow, S. Presumed innocent
Turow, S. The burden of proof
Turow, S. Innocent
Unsworth, B. The quality of mercy
Unsworth, B. After Hannibal
Walker, W. Crime of Privilege
Welch, J. The Indian lawyer
Wilhelm, K. The best defense
Legal tender. Scottoline, L.
Legend of a suicide. Vann, D.
The **legend** of Pradeep Mathew. Karunatilaka, S.
LEGENDARY CHARACTERS
See also Legends; Mythology
LEGENDS
Earley, T. Mr. Tall
The Ghost Riders of Ordebec
LEGENDS -- EUROPE
Obreht, T. The tiger's wife
LEGENDS AND FOLK TALES
Benet, S. V. The Devil and Daniel Webster
Berger, T. Arthur Rex
Bradley, M. Z. The mists of Avalon
Lewis, C. S. Till we have faces
Mailer, N. Ancient evenings
Mehta, G. A river Sutra
Renault, M. The bull from the sea
Renault, M. The king must die
Schwarz-Bart, A. The last of the just
Steinbeck, J. The pearl
Stewart, M. The hollow hills
Stewart, M. The last enchantment
Sutcliff, R. Sword at sunset
Updike, J. The centaur
Welty, E. The robber bridegroom
White, T. H. The once and future king
White, T. H. The sword in the stone
Wiesel, E. The Golem
LEGENDS AND FOLK TALES -- AFRICA
Lord, K. Redemption in indigo
Legends of the realm [series]
Locke, T. Emissary
LEGENDS, JEWISH *See* Jewish legends
LEGISLATIVE INVESTIGATIONS *See* Governmental investigations
LEGISLATORS
See also Statesmen
LEGITIMACY (LAW) *See* Illegitimacy
Leicester, Robert Dudley, Earl of, 1532?-1588
About
George, M. Elizabeth I
Maxwell, R. The Queen's bastard
LEICESTERSHIRE (ENGLAND)
Stibbe, N. Man at the helm
Lelia. Sand, G.
The **lemon** orchard. Rice, L.
Lempicka, Tamara de, 1898-1980
About
Avery, E. The last nude
Leno, Dan, 1860-1904
About
Ackroyd, P. The trial of Elizabeth Cree
LENOX, CHARLES (FICTITIOUS CHARACTER)
Finch, C. A beautiful blue death
Leo Africanus. Maalouf, A.
Leo Africanus, ca. 1492-ca. 1550
About
Maalouf, A. Leo Africanus
Leonardo's swans. Essex, K.
Leonardo, da Vinci, 1452-1519
About
Brown, D. The Da Vinci code
Essex, K. Leonardo's swans
The **leopard.**
Leopold, Nathan Freundenthal, 1904 or 5-1971
About
Levin, M. Compulsion
LEPROSY
See also Diseases

Les miserables. Hugo, V.
LESBIANISM
Barnes, D. Nightwood
Brown, R. M. Rubyfruit jungle
Dennis-Benn, N. Y. Here Comes the Sun
The fish child
Gaspar de Alba, A. Desert blood
Grant, S. Map of Ireland
Grumbach, D. The book of knowledge
Hagedorn, J. T. Toxicology
Hall, R. The well of loneliness
Hallgrimur Helgason 101 Reykjavik
Humphreys, H. Afterimage
Merey, I. a + e 4ever
Muller, M. Cyanide Wells
Naylor, G. The women of Brewster Place
Parks Getting mother's body
The Penguin book of lesbian short stories
Picoult, J. Sing you home
Schwartz, L. Angels Crest
Tea, M. Rose of no man's land
Tremain, R. Trespass
Truong, M. The book of salt
Vine, B. The house of stairs
Walsh, H. Brass
Waters, S. Fingersmith
Waters, S. Tipping the velvet
Watrous, M. If you follow me
Winterson, J. Oranges are not the only fruit
LESBIANISM
See also Homosexuality
LESBIANS
See also Gays; LGBT people; Women
Less than a treason. Stabenow, D.
A **lesson** before dying. Gaines, E. J.
Let him go. Watson, L.
Let Me Be Frank With You. Ford, R.
Let me die in his footsteps. Roy, L.
Let me go. Cain, C.
Let the great world spin. McCann, C.
Let the Northern Lights erase your name. Vida, V.
Let us now praise famous men; A death in the family, and shorter fiction. Agee, J.
Lethally blond. White, K.
Letter from home. Hart, C. G.
LETTER WRITING
The confidant
Gohlke, C. Promise me this
Kilpack, J. S. The vicar's daughter
The **letters.** Rice, L.
LETTERS (STORIES ABOUT)
Kostova, E. The swan thieves
Schine, C. The love letter
LETTERS (STORIES IN LETTER FORM)
Adiga, A. The white tiger
Barrows, A. The Guernsey Literary and Potato Peel Pie Society
Bohjalian, C. The sandcastle girls
Davies, R. Fifth business
Founds, K. When mystical creatures attack!
Fuentes, C. The eagle's throne
Grass, G. Dog years
Grossman, D. Be my knife
Kingsolver, B. The poisonwood Bible
Miles, J. Dear American Airlines
Miyamoto, T. Kinshu: Autumn brocade
Murdoch, I. An accidental man
Norman, H. What is left the daughter
Rice, L. The letters
Richardson, S. Clarissa
Richardson, S. Pamela
Richler, N. Your mouth is lovely
Robinson, E. The true and outstanding adventures of the Hunt sisters
Robinson, M. Gilead
Savage, S. The cry of the sloth
Schulze, I. New lives
Sholem Aleichem The adventures of Menahem-Mendl
Shriver, L. We need to talk about Kevin
Smith, L. Fair and tender ladies
Tabucchi, A. It's getting later all the time
Updike, J. S
Walker, A. The color purple
Wolfe, G. The sorcerer's house
Letting go. Roth, P.
LEUKEMIA
Doerr, H. Stones for Ibarra
Picoult, J. My sister's keeper
Reiken, F. Day for night
Robinson, E. The true and outstanding adventures of the Hunt sisters
Segal, E. Love story
LEUKEMIA
See also Blood -- Diseases; Cancer
Levi's will. Cramer, W. D.
Leviathan Wakes. Corey, J. S. A.
LEWIS AND CLARK EXPEDITION (1804-1806)
Sargent, C. Museum of human beings
Wheeler, R. S. Eclipse
LEWIS WITH HARRIS ISLAND (SCOTLAND)
May, P. The Blackhouse
Lewis, Meriwether, 1774-1809
About
Wheeler, R. S. Eclipse
LEXICOGRAPHERS
Arsenault, E. The broken teaglass
Graedon, A. The word exchange
LEXICOGRAPHY
See also Encyclopedias and dictionaries
Lexicon. Barry, M.
LEXINGTON (MASS.), BATTLE OF, 1775
See also Battles; United States -- History -- 1775-1783, Revolution -- Campaigns
LGBT COMIC BOOKS, STRIPS, ETC.

See also Comic books, strips, etc.
Liam Mulligan [series]
DeSilva, B. Providence Rag
The **liar's** wife. Gordon, M.
Liars and saints. Meloy, M.
LIBEL AND SLANDER
See also Journalism
LIBERIA
Maksik, A. A marker to measure drift
LIBERTY
Coetzee, J. M. Life & times of Michael K.
Sartre, J. P. The age of reason
LIBRARIANS
Cogman, G. The invisible library
Cooley, M. The archivist
Doig, I. Work song
Glass, J. The widower's tale
Hamilton, M. The camel bookmobile
Hegi, U. Stones from the river
Hoffman, A. The ice queen
Makkai, R. The borrower
McCracken, E. The giant's house
Millet, L. Oh pure and radiant heart
Pym, B. An unsuitable attachment
Schwartz, L. S. The writing on the wall
LIBRARIANS' UNIONS
See also Labor unions
LIBRARIES
Hawkins, S. The Library at Mount Char
Larson, N. The Dewey Decimal system
Treuer, D. The translation of Dr Apelles
LIBRARIES -- AUTOMATION
See also Automation
LIBRARIES -- CENSORSHIP -- UNITED STATES -- HANDBOOKS, MANUALS, ETC.
Intellectual Freedom Manual
The **Library** at Mount Char. Hawkins, S.
LIBRARY CATALOGS
See also Libraries
LIBRARY COOPERATION
See also Libraries
library of America [series]
Alcott, L. M. Little women; Little men; Jo's boys
Dos Passos, J. Novels, 1920-1925
Farrell, J. T. Studs Lonigan
Nabokov, V. V. Novels and memoirs, 1941-1951
Twain, M. Historical romances
LIBRARY OF CONGRESS
Truman, M. Murder at the Library of Congress
LIBYA
Matar, H. In the country of men
Licks of love. Updike, J.
The **lie.** Dunmore, H.
LIE DETECTORS AND DETECTION
See also Criminal investigation; Medical jurisprudence; Truthfulness and falsehood
Lie down in darkness. Styron, W.
LIEBERMANN, MAX (FICTITIOUS CHARACTER)
Tallis, F. Fatal lies
Tallis, F. Vienna Twilight
The **lies** of Locke Lamora. Lynch, S.
The **lieutenant.** Grenville, K.
Lieutenant Hornblower. Forester, C. S.
Life & times of Michael K. Coetzee, J. M.
LIFE (PHILOSOPHY OF LIFE)
Merullo, R. Breakfast with Buddha
LIFE
Bell, A. The reapers are the angels
LIFE -- ORIGIN
See also Evolution
LIFE AFTER DEATH *See* Future life; Immortality
Life after life. McCorkle, J.
Life After Life. Atkinson, K.
The **life** all around me by Ellen Foster. Gibbons, K.
Life among giants. Roorbach, B.
Life and death are wearing me out. Mo Yan
The **Life** and Death of Sophie Stark. North, A.
The **life** and loves of a she-devil. Weldon, F.
The **life** and opinions of Tristram Shandy, gentleman and A sentimental journey through France and Italy. Sterne, L.
A **life** apart. Mukherjee, N.
Life before man. Atwood, M.
LIFE CHANGE EVENTS
Ballantyne, L. The guilty one
Buchanan, C. M. The painted girls
Chiang, T. Stories of your life and others
Cole, T. Every day is for the thief
Cusk, R. Transit
Delinsky, B. Sweet salt air
Fowler, K. J. We Are All Completely Beside Ourselves
Graeme-Evans, P. The island house
Hadley, T. Clever Girl
Hannah, K. Fly Away
Jong, E. Fear of Dying
Kinsella, S. My not so perfect life
Lutz, L. How to start a fire
Mackintosh, C. I let you go
McMillan, T. I Almost Forgot About You
Miller, D. B. The girl in green
Millet, L. Magnificence
Ostlund, L. After the Parade
Quindlen, A. Still life with bread crumbs
Raeder, L. Cam girl
Roberts, V. After the fall
Ruskovich, E. Idaho
Slouka, M. Brewster
The **life** cycle of software objects. Chiang, T.
Life goes on. Keilson, H.
LIFE HISTORIES *See* Biography
LIFE INSURANCE
See also Insurance
The **life** of an unknown man. Makine, A.
The **life** of objects. Moore, S.
Life of Pi. Martel, Y.

LIFE ON OTHER PLANETS
Aldiss, B. W. Helliconia spring
Aldiss, B. W. Helliconia summer
Aldiss, B. W. Helliconia winter
Banks, I. Matter
Barnes, J. The armies of memory
Butler, O. E. Adulthood rites
Butler, O. E. Dawn
Butler, O. E. Imago
Cherryh, C. J. Foreigner
Delany, S. R. Babel-17 ; Empire star
Flynn, M. The January dancer
Hamilton, P. F. The dreaming void
Hoffman, N. K. Catalyst
Le Guin, U. K. Four ways to forgiveness
Le Guin, U. K. The telling
Lem, S. Eden
Lem, S. Fiasco
Lem, S. Solaris
Martin, G. R. R. Hunter's run
McCaffrey, A. Dragonflight
McCaffrey, T. Dragonsblood
McCaffrey, A. Dragon's Kin
McCaffrey, A. The white dragon
Mieville, C. Embassytown
Niven, L. The Mote in God's Eye
Norton, A. Beast Master's ark
Reynolds, A. The prefect
Robinson, K. S. Blue Mars
Robinson, K. S. The Martians
Robinson, K. S. Red Mars
Russell, M. D. Children of God
Russell, M. D. The sparrow
Sagan, C. Contact
Scalzi, J. The android's dream
Scalzi, J. The collapsing empire
Scalzi, J. Old man's war
Steele, A. M. Coyote
Tepper, S. S. Grass
Tepper, S. S. Singer from the sea
Varley, J. Demon
Varley, J. Titan
Vinge, V. The children of the sky
Vinge, V. A deepness in the sky
Vinge, V. A fire upon the deep
Weber, D. Off Armageddon Reef
Wells, M. All systems red
Westerfeld, S. The killing of worlds
Westerfeld, S. The risen empire
Wilson, R. C. Blind Lake
LIFE SKILLS
See also Interpersonal relations; Success
LIFE SPAN PROLONGATION *See* Longevity
Life times. Gordimer, N.
LIFE, FUTURE *See* Future life
Life, the universe, and everything. Adams, D.
The **lifeboat.** Rogan, C.
LIFTS *See* Elevators; Hoisting machinery
The **light** between oceans. Stedman, M. L.
Light in August. Faulkner, W.
The **light** in the forest. Richter, C.
Light music. Goonan, K. A.
Light thickens. Marsh, N.
The **Lighthouse.** Moore, A.
The **lighthouse.** James, P. D.
LIGHTHOUSE KEEPERS
Schwarz, C. The Edge of the Earth
LIGHTHOUSES
Koryta, M. The ridge
The **lightkeepers.** Geni, A.
Lightless. Higgins, C. A.
Lightning. Echenoz, J.
LIGHTNING
Hoffman, A. The ice queen
Lightning. Lutz, J.
Lightning men. Mullen, T.
Lightning rods. Dewitt, H.
LIGHTSHIPS
See also Lighthouses; Ships
Like Family.
Like water for chocolate. Esquivel, L.
Like you'd understand, anyway. Shepard, J.
The **likeness.** French, T.
Lila. Robinson, M.
Lilac girls. Kelly, M. H.
The **lilies** of the field. Barrett, W. E.
Lillian Boxfish Takes a Walk. Rooney, K.
Lily White. Isaacs, S.
Limitations. Turow, S.
The **limits** of enchantment. Joyce, G.
The **Limpopo** Academy of Private Detection. McCall Smith, A.
Lincoln. Vidal, G.
The **Lincoln** conspiracy. O'Brien, T. L.
Lincoln in the bardo. Saunders, G.
The **Lincoln** lawyer. Connelly, M.
Lincoln Lawyer [series]
Connelly, M. The Gods of Guilt
Lincoln Perry [series]
Koryta, M. Tonight I said goodbye
Lincoln, Abraham, 1809-1865
About
Harrigan, S. A friend of Mr. Lincoln
O'Brien, T. L. The Lincoln conspiracy
Saunders, G. Lincoln in the bardo
Vidal, G. Lincoln
Lincoln, Mary Todd, 1818-1882
About
Chiaverini, J. Mrs. Lincoln's dressmaker
Newman, J. C. Mary
O'Brien, T. L. The Lincoln conspiracy
Lindbergh, Anne Morrow, 1906-2001
About
Benjamin, M. The aviator's wife

Lindbergh, Charles A. (Charles Augustus), 1902-1974
About
Benjamin, M. The aviator's wife
Roth, P. The plot against America
Linden Hills. Naylor, G.
The **line.** Grushin, O.
LINGUISTICS
See also Language and languages
LINGUISTS
Barry, M. Lexicon
Karinthy, F. Metropole
Links. Farah, N.
LINOLEUM BLOCK PRINTING
See also Printing; Prints
LINOTYPE
See also Printing; Type and type-founding; Typesetting
Lion in the valley. Peters, E.
Lionel Asbo. Amis, M.
Lionheart. Penman, S. K.
LIPPIZANER HORSES
Stewart, M. Airs above the ground
LIQUOR PROBLEM *See* Alcoholism; Drinking of alcoholic beverages
LIQUOR TRAFFIC
Francis, D. Proof
The **list** of Adrian Messenger. MacDonald, P.
LISTENING DEVICES *See* Eavesdropping
Listening woman. Hillerman, T.
LITERARY COLLECTIONS *See* Anthologies; Literature -- Collections
The **literary** conference. Aira, C.
LITERARY CRITICS
Coetzee, J. M. Summertime
Cooley, M. The archivist
Nabokov, V. V. Novels and memoirs, 1941-1951
Truong, M. The book of salt
Verissimo, L. F. Borges and the eternal orangutans
LITERARY FORGERIES
See also Counterfeits and counterfeiting; Forgery
LITERARY LIFE
Barnes, D. Nightwood
Bernhard, T. Woodcutters
Bolano, R. By night in Chile
Byatt, A. S. Possession
Chabon, M. Wonder boys
Gessen, K. All the sad young literary men
Martin, V. Italian fever
McInerney, J. Bright lights, big city
Powell, A. A dance to the music of time
Savage, S. The cry of the sloth
Wolitzer, M. The wife
LITERARY PRIZES
Frame, J. In the memorial room
LITERATURE -- COLLECTIONS
The mammoth book of steampunk
LITHOGRAPHY
See also Color printing; Printing; Prints
LITHUANIANS -- UNITED STATES
Sinclair, U. The jungle
The **litter** of the law. Brown, R. M.
Little Bee. Cleave, C.
Little Big Man. Berger, T.
Little bird of heaven. Oates, J. C.
Little century. Keesey, A.
Little children. Perrotta, T.
Little deaths. Flint, E.
Little Dorrit. Dickens, C.
The **little** drummer girl. Le Carre, J.
Little earthquakes. Weiner, J.
Little fires everywhere. Ng, C.
The **little** friend. Tartt, D.
The **little** giant of Aberdeen County. Baker, T.
Little green. Mosley, W.
LITTLE ITALY (BALTIMORE, MD.)
Criswell, M. What to do about Annie?
LITTLE LEAGUE BASEBALL
See also Baseball
A **little** life. Yanagihara, H.
LITTLE MAGAZINES
See also Periodicals
Little night. Rice, L.
The **little** Paris bookshop. George, N.
The **little** prince. Saint-Exupery, A. d.
Little Saigon. Parker, T. J.
Little Scarlet. Mosley, W.
Little star.
The **little** stranger. Waters, S.
Little women; Little men; Jo's boys. Alcott, L. M.
A **little** yellow dog. Mosley, W.
LITURGIES
See also Public worship; Rites and ceremonies
Live by night. Lehane, D.
Live flesh. Rendell, R.
Live to tell. Gardner, L.
Lives of girls & women. Munro, A.
The **Lives** of Others. Mukherjee, N.
The **Lives** of Tao. Chu, W.
Livia, Empress, consort of Augustus, Emperor of Rome, 58? B.C.-29
About
Graves, R. I, Claudius
The **living** dead.
Living next door to the god of love. Robson, J.
LIVING TOGETHER *See* Unmarried couples
Llewelyn ap Iorwerth, d. 1240
About
Penman, S. K. Here be dragons
Llywelyn ap Gruffydd, d. 1282
About
Penman, S. K. The reckoning
LOANS
Higgins, G. V. The Digger's game
LOBBYING
See also Politics; Propaganda

LOCAL ELECTIONS
Rowling, J. K. The casual vacancy
Local girls. Hoffman, A.
Local souls. Gurganus, A.
LOCH NESS MONSTER
See also Monsters
The **lock** artist. Hamilton, S.
Lock in. Scalzi, J.
LOCK PICKING
Hamilton, S. The lock artist
LOCKS AND KEYS
Hamilton, S. The lock artist
LOCOMOTIVES
See also Railroads
Locus solus.
LOCUSTS
See also Insect pests; Insects
Loeb, Richard A., 1905-1936
About
Levin, M. Compulsion
LOG CABINS AND HOUSES
See also House construction; Houses
LOGGERS
Guterson, D. Our Lady of the Forest
Rash, R. Serena
Urquhart, J. A map of glass
LOGGING
Hart, B. The bully of order
Proulx, A. Barkskins
Loitering with intent. Spark, M.
Lolita. Nabokov, V. V.
Lombard, Carole, 1908-1942
About
Alcott, K. A touch of stardust
London. Rutherfurd, E.
LONDON (ENGLAND)
Adler, H. G. The wall
Brockway, C. No Place for a Dame
Burrowes, G. The heir
Chase, L. Dukes Prefer Blondes
Chaudhuri, A. Odysseus Abroad
Cumming, C. A divided spy
Cusk, R. Transit
Dare, T. When a Scot Ties the Knot
Drabble, M. The pure gold baby
Dunmore, H. Exposure
French, N. Blue Monday
Griffin, K. Stray souls
Guo, X. I am China
Hawkins, P. The girl on the train
Hayder, M. Birdman
Hodgson, A. The last confession of Thomas Hawkins
Jacka, B. Fated
Joinson, S. A lady cyclist's guide to Kashgar
Leigh, E. Forever Your Earl
Lewis, T. GBH
MacLean, S. Never Judge a Lady by Her Cover
MacLean, S. No Good Duke Goes Unpunished
MacLean, S. The Rogue Not Taken
McCall Smith, A. A conspiracy of friends
Price, S. By Gaslight
Quick, A. 'Til death do us part
Ridgway, K. Hawthorn & child
Robertson, I. Anatomy of murder
Schwab, V. E. A Darker Shade of Magic
Shannon, S. The mime order
Smith, Z. NW
Thomas, S. The Luckiest Lady in London
Waters, S. The Paying Guests
LONDON (ENGLAND) -- HISTORY -- 16TH CENTURY
Parris, S. J. Sacrilege
LONDON (ENGLAND) -- HISTORY -- 1800-1950
Perry, A. A sunless sea
LONDON (ENGLAND) -- HISTORY -- 18TH CENTURY
Donoghue, E. Slammerkin
Hodgson, A. The last confession of Thomas Hawkins
King, R. Domino
Liss, D. A spectacle of corruption
Robertson, I. Anatomy of murder
Unsworth, B. The quality of mercy
LONDON (ENGLAND) -- HISTORY -- 19TH CENTURY
Atlee, A. The typewriter girl
LONDON (ENGLAND) -- INTELLECTUAL LIFE -- 20TH CENTURY
Parmar, P. Vanessa and her sister
LONDON (ENGLAND) -- SOCIAL CONDITIONS -- 19TH CENTURY
Morrell, D. Murder as a fine art
Quick, A. 'Til death do us part
Shepherd, L. The solitary house
LONDON (ENGLAND) -- SOCIAL LIFE AND CUSTOMS
Ridgway, K. Hawthorn & child
LONDON (ENGLAND) -- SOCIAL LIFE AND CUSTOMS -- 20TH CENTURY
Joinson, S. A lady cyclist's guide to Kashgar
London bridges. Patterson, J.
London fields. Amis, M.
London match. Deighton, L.
London rain. Upson, N.
The **London** train. Hadley, T.
Lone wolf. Picoult, J.
LONELINESS
Bakker, G. The twin
Brookner, A. Undue influence
Harrison, K. The seal wife
Haruf, K. Our souls at night
Heller, Z. What was she thinking?
Hornby, N. Juliet, naked
Martin, S. Shopgirl
Moore, B. The lonely passion of Judith Hearne
Phillips, A. The song is you
Pym, B. Excellent women
Pym, B. Quartet in autumn
Pym, B. The sweet dove died

Rossner, J. Looking for Mr. Goodbar
Schine, C. The New Yorkers
Taylor, E. Mrs. Palfrey at the Claremont
Tyler, A. The accidental tourist
Vann, D. Caribou Island
LONELINESS
See also Emotions
LONELINESS IN CHILDREN
O'Malley, T. This magnificent desolation
The **loneliness** of the long-distance runner. Sillitoe, A.
Lonely crusade. Himes, C. B.
The **Lonely** Hearts Hotel. O'Neill, H.
The **lonely** passion of Judith Hearne. Moore, B.
The **lonely** polygamist. Udall, B.
The **lonely** silver rain. MacDonald, J. D.
Loner. Wayne, T.
Lonesome dove. McMurtry, L.
Long after midnight. Johansen, I.
The **Long** and Faraway Gone. Berney, L.
LONG BEACH (CALIF.)
Ruby, I. The salt god's daughter
Long Black Veil. Boylan, J. F.
The **long** drop. Mina, D.
The **long** fall. Mosley, W.
The **long** goodbye. Chandler, R.
The **long** hitch. Zimmer, M.
LONG ISLAND (N.Y.)
Benchley, P. Jaws
Bollen, C. Orient
De la Cruz, M. Witches of East End
DeMille, N. Plum Island
Fitzgerald, F. S. The great Gatsby
Isaacs, S. After all these years
Isaacs, S. As husbands go
Isaacs, S. Close relations
Isaacs, S. Lily White
Lee Aloft
McDermott, A. After this
McDermott, A. Charming Billy
McDermott, A. Child of my heart
McDermott, A. That night
Mills, M. Amagansett
Puzo, M. The last Don
Rosenblatt, R. Lapham rising
Steinbeck, J. The winter of our discontent
Westlake, D. E. Bank shot
Whitehead, C. Sag Harbor
Wolitzer, M. Surrender, Dorothy
The **long** journey home. Coldsmith, D.
The **long** lavender look. MacDonald, J. D.
LONG LIFE *See* Longevity
Long Man. Greene, A.
The **long** song. Levy, A.
Long time coming. Goddard, R.
The **long** valley. Steinbeck, J.
A **long** way down. Hornby, N.
The **long** way home. Penny, L.
The **long-shining** waters. Sosin, D.
Longbourn. Baker, J.
Longer stories from the last decade. Chekhov, A. P.
The **Longest** Night. Braden, K.
LONGEVITY
Hilton, J. Lost horizon
Sanders, L. The sixth commandment
The **longings** of wayward girls. Brown, K.
Longmire [series]
Johnson, C. Spirit of steamboat
LONGMIRE, WALT (FICTITIOUS CHARACTER)
Johnson, C. Another man's moccasins
Johnson, C. Spirit of steamboat
Johnson, C. Death without company
LONGSHORE WORKERS
Schulberg, B. Waterfront
Longshot. Francis, D.
The **Loo** sanction. Trevanian
Look at the birdie. Vonnegut, K.
Look at the harlequins! Nabokov, V. V.
Look homeward, angel. Wolfe, T.
Looking back. Plain, B.
Looking for Mr. Goodbar. Rossner, J.
Loot, and other stories. Gordimer, N.
Lord Byron's novel. Crowley, J.
Lord Foul's bane. Donaldson, S. R.
Lord Hornblower. Forester, C. S.
Lord Jim. Conrad, J.
The **lord** of death. Pattison, E.
Lord of light. Zelazny, R.
Lord of Misrule. Gordon, J.
Lord of the flies. Golding, W.
The **lord** of the rings. Tolkien, J. R. R.
Lord Peter. Sayers, D. L.
Lord Valentine's castle. Silverberg, R.
Lorna Doone. Blackmore, R. D.
Los Alamos. Kanon, J.
LOS ANGELES (CALIF.)
Clark, M. Guilt by association
Ellroy, J. Perfidia
Hallinan, T. Crashed
Mosley, W. Little green
Mosley, W. Little Scarlet
Watkins, C. V. Gold fame citrus
The **loser.** Bernhard, T.
Losing battles. Welty, E.
Losing Nelson. Unsworth, B.
LOSS (PSYCHOLOGY)
Adebayo, A. Stay with me
Brunt, C. R. Tell the wolves I'm home
Castellani, C. All this talk of love
Ford, R. Canada
Fox, L. Days of awe
Hilderbrand, E. Summerland
Joss, M. Half broken things
Lansdale, J. R. Edge of dark water
McCormick, C. Desert boys

Moore, E. K. The Supremes sing the happy heartache blues
LOSS (PSYCHOLOGY) IN CHILDREN
O'Malley, T. This magnificent desolation
Lost. Lichtenstein, A.
Lost and found. Parkhurst, C.
LOST AND FOUND POSSESSIONS
See also Property
LOST AND FOUND POSSESSIONS
Kinsella, S. I've got your number
The **lost** art of gratitude. McCall Smith, A.
The **lost** book of the Grail. Lovett, C.
The **lost** boy. Lackberg, C.
Lost boy lost girl. Straub, P.
LOST CHILDREN *See* Missing children
Lost city. Cussler, C.
Lost City Radio. Alarcon, D.
The **lost** daughter. Ferrante, E.
Lost horizon. Hilton, J.
Lost in a good book. Fforde, J.
Lost in the forest. Miller, S.
Lost in Uttar Pradesh. Connell, E. S.
Lost memory of skin. Banks, R.
Lost nation. Lent, J.
The **lost** order. Berry, S.
The **lost** sisterhood. Fortier, A.
LOST TRIBES OF ISRAEL
See also Jews
The **lost** weekend. Jackson, C.
LOTTERIES
Green, G. D. Ravens
Hiaasen, C. Lucky you
LOTTERIES
See also Gambling
The **lottery** and other stories. Jackson, S.
LOTTERY WINNERS
Amis, M. Lionel Asbo
Lotus. Lijia Zhang
The **lotus** and the storm. Cao, L.
The **lotus** eaters. Soli, T.
Louis XIV, King of France, 1638-1715
About
Dumas, A. The man in the iron mask
Laker, R. To dance with kings
Louis XV, King of France, 1710-1774
About
Laker, R. To dance with kings
Louis XVI, King of France, 1754-1793
About
Laker, R. To dance with kings
LOUISIANA
Butler, R. O. A good scent from a strange mountain
Dufresne, J. Deep in the shade of paradise
Gailey, S. River of Teeth
Gaines, E. J. A gathering of old men
Harris, C. Dead reckoning
Hyatt, M. Beautiful gravity
Locke, A. The cutting season
Martin, V. Property
Robards, K. Ghost moon
Rogers, R. Devil's Cape
Tademy, L. Cane River
Walsh, M. O. My sunshine away
Wells, K. Crawfish mountain
LOUISIANA -- 19TH CENTURY
Chopin, K. Complete novels and stories
Gaines, E. J. The autobiography of Miss Jane Pittman
Straight, S. A million nightingales
LOUISIANA -- NEW ORLEANS
Algren, N. A walk on the wild side
Allende, I. Island beneath the sea
Hambly, B. Dead water
Hambly, B. Die upon a kiss
Hambly, B. A free man of color
Hambly, B. Graveyard dust
Hambly, B. Sold down the river
Hambly, B. Wet grave
Percy, W. Lancelot
Percy, W. The moviegoer
Piazza, T. City of refuge
Plain, B. Crescent City
Rhodes, J. P. Voodoo dreams
Rhodes, J. P. Yellow moon
Rice, A. The Feast of All Saints
Roberts, N. Midnight Bayou
Toole, J. K. A confederacy of dunces
Warren, R. P. Band of angels
LOUISIANA -- SOCIAL LIFE AND CUSTOMS
Chopin, K. Complete novels and stories
Love. Morrison, T.
LOVE
See also Emotions; Human behavior
LOVE
Adrian, C. The great night
Allende, I. The Japanese Lover
Anam, T. The Bones of Grace
Beach-Ferrara, J. Damn love
Brockway, C. No Place for a Dame
D'Abo, C. 30 Days
Dare, T. When a Scot Ties the Knot
Dreyer, E. Once a Rake
Gray, J. How to Tame Your Duke
Greer, A. S. The Impossible Lives of Greta Wells
Hamid, M. Exit West
Hamid, M. How to Get Filthy Rich in Rising Asia
Hauck, R. How to catch a prince
Higgins, K. Anything for You
Holmes, L. Barbara the slut and other people
Hosseini, K. And the Mountains Echoed
James, E. My American Duchess
Jenkins, B. Breathless
Jong, E. Fear of Dying
Just, W. American romantic
Kleypas, L. Cold-hearted Rake
Kleypas, L. Rainshadow road

London, J. The Golden Age
MacLean, S. The Rogue Not Taken
MacLean, S. A Scot in the dark
McCall Smith, A. Trains and Lovers
McCormick, C. Desert boys
McLain, P. Circling the Sun
O'Neill, H. The Lonely Hearts Hotel
Reid, T. J. Forever, interrupted
Sarton, M. Kinds of love
Smith, G. B. The maze at Windermere
Sundin, S. Through waters deep
Thomas, S. The Luckiest Lady in London

LOVE -- GRAPHIC NOVELS

Merey, I. a + e 4ever

LOVE AFFAIRS

Abbott, M. E. Bury me deep
Adams, A. After the war
Alvarez, J. How the Garcia girls lost their accents
Amis, K. The Russian girl
Atwood, M. The blind assassin
Atwood, M. Life before man
Baker, N. The anthologist
Baldwin, J. Another country
Betts, D. Souls raised from the dead
Bowen, E. The heat of the day
Boyle, T. C. The women
Chang, L. S. All is forgotten, nothing is lost
Colwin, L. Family happiness
Cook, T. H. The Chatham School affair
Eco, U. The mysterious flame of Queen Loana
Enright, A. The forgotten waltz
Faulks, S. Birdsong
Faulks, S. On Green Dolphin Street
Fielding, H. The history of Tom Jones, a foundling
Findley, T. The piano man's daughter
Franck, J. The blindness of the heart
French, M. The women's room
Giffin, E. Heart of the matter
Goodman, A. The cookbook collector
Gordimer, N. The conservationist
Gordimer, N. A guest of honor
Gordimer, N. My son's story
Gordon, M. The company of women
Gordon, M. Final payments
Gottlieb, E. Now you see him
Greene, G. The end of the affair
Griesemer, J. Signal & noise
Grossman, D. Be my knife
Ha Jin Waiting
Hadley, T. The London train
Hamilton, J. Disobedience
Hannah, S. The wrong mother
Hansen, R. A wild surge of guilty passion
Hazzard, S. The transit of Venus
Hellenga, R. The Italian lover
Heller, Z. What was she thinking?
Hogan, C. Devils in exile
Horan, N. Loving Frank
Hornby, N. Juliet, naked
Howatch, S. Scandalous risks
Howatch, S. Ultimate prizes
Hunter, E. Privileged conversation
Irving, J. A widow for one year
Isaacs, S. Close relations
Jen, G. Typical American
Jhabvala, R. P. Heat and dust
Jones, J. From here to eternity
Jordan, H. When she woke
Keneally, T. A family madness
Keyes, M. Last Chance Saloon
Kostova, E. The swan thieves
Krantz, J. Mistral's daughter
Kundera, M. Immortality
Kundera, M. The unbearable lightness of being
LeCraw, H. The swimming pool
Lee, J. Y. K. The piano teacher
Lescroart, J. T. Guilt
Lipman, E. The dearly departed
Llywelyn, M. 1949
Lodge, D. Thinks--
Lurie, A. Foreign affairs
Mallon, T. Fellow travelers
The man of feeling
Marias, J. All souls
Martin, V. Italian fever
Martini, S. P. Compelling evidence
McEwan, I. Amsterdam
McEwan, I. The innocent
McGrath, P. Asylum
McGuane, T. Nothing but blue skies
McInerney, J. The good life
McMillan, T. Waiting to exhale
McMurtry, L. The evening star
McMurtry, L. Rhino Ranch
McMurtry, L. Terms of endearment
McPhee, M. L'America
Miller, S. The good mother
Miller, S. Lost in the forest
Miller, S. The senator's wife
Moore, L. A gate at the stairs
Morton, K. The house at Riverton
Murdoch, I. An accidental man
Murdoch, I. The nice and the good
Naipaul, V. S. Magic seeds
Nelson, A. Bound
Nichols, J. T. The sterile cuckoo
Nin, A. Cities of the interior
Norman, H. The museum guard
Oates, J. C. I lock my door upon myself
Oates, J. C. Missing mom
O'Brien, E. Time and tide
O'Connor, J. Ghost light
O'Dell, T. Back roads
O'Hara, J. From the terrace

Ondaatje, M. In the skin of a lion
Ostermiller, D. Outside the ordinary world
Oz, A. Fima
Packer, A. The dive from Clausen's pier
Perrotta, T. Little children
Piercy, M. Vida
Plain, B. Looking back
Pyne, D. Twentynine Palms
Rendell, R. The bridesmaid
Reyn, I. What happened to Anna K.
Reynolds, M. The Starlite Drive-in
Rosenberg, N. T. First offense
Ross-Macdonald, M. For they shall inherit
Roth, H. From bondage
Roth, H. Requiem for Harlem
Roth, P. Sabbath's theater
Roth, P. The dying animal
Rush, N. Mortals
Schlink, B. The reader
Settle, M. L. Charley Bland
Shreve, A. Fortune's Rocks
Shreve, A. The last time they met
Shreve, A. The weight of water
Shriver, L. The post-birthday world
Sillitoe, A. Saturday night and Sunday morning
Singer, I. B. Enemies, a love story
Skibell, J. A curable romantic
Sontag, S. In America
Sontag, S. The volcano lover
Steel, D. Sunset in St. Tropez
Stone, R. Bay of souls
Templeton, E. Gordon
Texier, C. Victorine
Thomas, R. Other people's marriages
Thomas, S. Private arrangements
Tolstoy, L. Anna Karenina
Trollope, J. The best of friends
Trollope, J. A Spanish lover
Trueblood, V. Seven loves
Tryon, T. In the fire of spring
Upadhyay, S. The guru of love
Updike, J. Gertrude and Claudius
Valdes-Rodriguez, A. Dirty girls on top
Wakefield, D. Starting over
Walbert, K. The gardens of Kyoto
Wall, P. S. The Wilde women
Weldon, F. Worst fears
Westlake, D. E. Trust me on this
White, E. The married man
Wilson, R. C. Blind Lake
Winer, A. The marriage artist
Woods, S. Choke
Woods, S. Palindrome
Yarbrough, S. Safe from the neighbors

Love among the particles & other stories. Lock, N.
Love and other scandals. Linden, C.
Love and shame and love. Orner, P.
Love and summer. Trevor, W.
Love and treasure. Waldman, A.
Love and war. Jakes, J.
Love in the ruins. Percy, W.
Love in the time of cholera. Garcia Marquez, G.
Love is power, or something like that. Barrett, A. I.
Love kills. Buchanan, E.
The **love** letter. Schine, C.
A **love** like blood. Sedgwick, M.
Love love. Woo, S.J.
Love medicine. Erdrich, L.
The **love** object. O'Brien, E.
The **love** of a good woman. Munro, A.
The **love** of my youth. Gordon, M.
The **love** of stones. Hill, T.
Love over Scotland. McCall Smith, A.

LOVE POETRY
See also Poetry

The **love** song of A. Jerome Minkoff and other stories. Epstein, J.
The **Love** Song of Jonny Valentine. Wayne, T.
The **Love** Song of Miss Queenie Hennessy. Joyce, R.

LOVE STORIES
Abu-Jaber, D. Crescent
Aciman, A. A. Call me by your name
Agnon, S. Y. Only yesterday
Allen, S. A. The sugar queen
Allende, I. Daughter of fortune
Allende, I. Eva Luna
Amis, K. The Russian girl
Amis, M. House of meetings
Austen, J. Emma
Austen, J. Mansfield Park
Austen, J. Persuasion
Austen, J. Sense and sensibility
Bagshawe, T. Adored
Baker, K. In the garden of Iden
Baldwin, J. If Beale Street could talk
Balogh, M. More than a mistress
Balogh, M. The secret mistress
Balogh, M. Seducing an angel
Baxter, C. The feast of love
Belfer, L. A fierce radiance
Benjamin, M. Alice I have been
Bennett, V. The queen's lover
Berry, W. Jayber Crow
Binchy, M. The glass lake
Binchy, M. Whitethorn Woods
Blake, S. The postmistress
Bolano, R. Monsieur Pain
Boll, H. The silent angel
Bourne, J. My lord and spymaster
Bourne, J. The spymaster's lady
Bronte, A. The tenant of Wildfell Hall
Bronte, C. Jane Eyre
Bronte, E. Wuthering Heights
Brookner, A. Brief lives

Burgess, M. Dogfight, a love story
Byatt, A. S. Possession
Cameron, P. The city of your final destination
Carroll, J. The ghost in love
Chase, L. L. The last hellion
Chase, L. L. Silk is for seduction
Chase, L. Your scandalous ways
Chen, D. Brothers
Colwin, L. Happy all the time
Conley, R. J. Mountain windsong
Cosse, L. A novel bookstore
Crace, J. The pesthouse
Dai Sijie Once on a moonless night
Danielewski, M. Z. Only revolutions
Davidson, A. The gargoyle
Davies, P. H. The Welsh girl
Dickens, C. Great expectations
Diffenbaugh, V. The language of flowers
Doig, I. Dancing at the Rascal Fair
Drabble, M. The sea lady
Drayson, N. Guide to the birds of East Africa
Dreyer, E. Barely a lady
Du Maurier, D. Frenchman's Creek
Dunant, S. The birth of Venus
Earley, T. The blue star
Echlin, K. The disappeared
Esquivel, L. Like water for chocolate
Eugenides, J. The marriage plot
Evans, N. The horse whisperer
Faulks, S. Charlotte Gray
Feldman, E. Next to love
Finney, J. Time and again
Fitch, J. Paint it black
Fitzgerald, P. The blue flower
Fortier, A. Juliet
Fowles, J. The French lieutenant's woman
Frazier, C. Cold Mountain
Frazier, C. Thirteen moons
Furnivall, K. The red scarf
Garcia Marquez, G. Love in the time of cholera
George, M. Helen of Troy
Gibb, C. Sweetness in the belly
Giordano, P. The solitude of prime numbers
Glass, J. The widower's tale
Godden, R. Pippa passes
Golden, A. Memoirs of a geisha
Goldman, F. Say her name
Goodwin, D. The American heiress
Gordon, M. The love of my youth
Goudge, E. Garden of lies
Goudge, E. Green Dolphin Street
Gowdy, B. The romantic
Grass, G. The call of the toad
Grenville, K. The idea of perfection
Groot, T. Flame of resistance
Grossman, D. Be my knife
Gruen, S. Water for elephants
Gunning, S. The rebellion of Jane Clarke
Guo Xiaolu A concise Chinese-English dictionary for lovers
Handler, D. Adverbs
Hannah, K. On Mystic lake
Harkness, D. E. A discovery of witches
Harper, K. Fall from pride
Harris, E. L. And this too shall pass
Harrison, J. The English major
Harrison, K. The seal wife
Hawke, E. Ash Wednesday
Hay, E. A student of weather
Hazzard, S. The great fire
Heinlein, R. A. Variable star
Hemingway, E. A farewell to arms
Henry, P. C. Coming up for air
Heyer, G. Black sheep
Hilderbrand, E. Silver girl
Hilton, J. Random harvest
Hoban, R. Her name was Lola
Hoffman, A. The dovekeepers
Hoffman, A. The ice queen
Hoffman, A. The third angel
Hoffman, A. Turtle Moon
Hollinghurst, A. The stranger's child
Holt, V. The black opal
Holt, V. Secret for a nightingale
Hornby, N. High fidelity
House, S. A parchment of leaves
Humphreys, J. Nowhere else on earth
Ignatius, D. The Sun King
Irving, J. The fourth hand
Isaacs, S. Red, white and blue
Itani, F. Deafening
James, E. When beauty tamed the beast
Jiles, P. Enemy women
Jones, D. Second grave on the left
Jones, S. Outcast
Kaye, M. M. The far pavilions
Kennedy, D. The moment
Kittredge, W. The Willow Field
Koen, K. Through a glass darkly
Krauss, N. The history of love
Krentz, J. A. Running hot
Leithauser, B. The art student's war
Lessing, D. M. Love, again
Levithan, D. The lover's dictionary
Lightman, A. P. Reunion
Lipman, E. The Inn at Lake Devine
Lipman, E. The pursuit of Alice Thrift
Lively, P. Cleopatra's sister
Lively, P. Consequences
Lively, P. Moon tiger
Livesey, M. Banishing Verona
Livesey, M. The house on Fortune Street
Llywelyn, M. 1921
Lodge, D. Nice work
Lodge, D. Paradise news

Lord, B. B. The middle heart
Lowell, E. Pearl Cove
Makine, A. The woman who waited
Manseau, P. Songs for the butcher's daughter
Marion, I. Warm bodies
Martin, V. Trespass
Martin, W. Cape Cod
Mawer, S. The fall
McCarthy, C. Cities of the plain
McCracken, E. The giant's house
McCrumb, S. The ballad of Tom Dooley
McCullough, C. An indecent obsession
McDermott, A. At weddings and wakes
McDermott, A. Charming Billy
McDermott, A. That night
McGuane, T. Nothing but blue skies
McMillan, T. How Stella got her groove back
McMillan, T. Waiting to exhale
McMurtry, L. Sin killer
McPhee, M. L'America
Mda, Z. The whale caller
Messud, C. The emperor's children
Miller, S. For love
Mills, M. Amagansett
Minot, S. Evening
Mirvis, T. The outside world
Mishima, Y. Spring snow
Moggach, D. Tulip fever
Momaday, N. S. The ancient child
Moore, C. You suck
Morrison, T. Love
Mosher, H. F. On Kingdom Mountain
Munoz Molina, A. In her absence
Munoz Molina, A. A manuscript of ashes
Murakami, H. South of the border, west of the sun
Murdoch, I. Nuns and soldiers
Murdoch, I. The sea, the sea
The museum of innocence
My mistress's sparrow is dead
Nabokov, V. V. Ada
Nathan, R. Portrait of Jennie
Naylor, G. Mama Day
Nicholls, D. One day
Niffenegger, A. The time traveler's wife
Norman, H. The bird artist
Norman, H. What is left the daughter
Oates, J. C. A Bloodsmoor romance
O'Farrell, M. The hand that first held mine
O'Nan, S. Snow angels
Orringer, J. The invisible bridge
Oz, A. Don't call it night
Pears, I. The dream of Scipio
Penman, S. K. Here be dragons
Percy, W. The last gentleman
Percy, W. The second coming
Phillips, A. The song is you
Phillips, S. E. Ain't she sweet
Phillips, S. E. It had to be you
Phillips, S. E. Natural born charmer
Pilcher, R. Coming home
Pilcher, R. September
Plain, B. Random winds
Powers, R. Galatea 2.2
Powers, R. The gold bug variations
Powning, B. The sea captain's wife
Putney, M. J. Loving a lost lord
Pym, B. An unsuitable attachment
Quick, A. I thee wed
Quick, A. The paid companion
Quick, A. Slightly shady
Quick, A. Wicked widow
Rand, A. The fountainhead
Rand, A. We the living
Read, P. P. Alice in exile
Reimringer, J. Vestments
Remarque, E. M. The night in Lisbon
Remarque, E. M. A time to love and a time to die
Reuss, F. Mohr
Reynolds, M. The Starlite Drive-in
Rice, L. Home fires
Rice, L. Last kiss
Richter, C. The sea of grass
Robards, K. Ghost moon
Roberts, N. Angel's fall
Roberts, N. Midnight Bayou
Robinson, E. The true and outstanding adventures of the Hunt sisters
Roiphe, A. R. An imperfect lens
Ross-Macdonald, M. Tamsin Harte
Ross-Macdonald, M. The Trevarton inheritance
Roy, A. An atlas of impossible longing
Rush, N. Mating
Rushdie, S. The ground beneath her feet
Russell, M. D. Dreamers of the day
Saint, H. F. Memoirs of an invisible man
Sand, G. Marianne
Saramago, J. The history of the siege of Lisbon
Sayers, D. L. Busman's honeymoon
Schickler, D. Sweet and vicious
Schine, C. The love letter
Schine, C. The New Yorkers
Schine, C. The three Weissmanns of Westport
Schlink, B. The reader
Schwartz, J. B. The commoner
Schwartzman, A. Eddie Signwriter
Scott, W. Rob Roy
See, L. Peony in love
Segal, E. Love story
Seth, V. An equal music
Settle, M. L. Charley Bland
Shan, S. The girl who played go
Sherwood, F. The book of splendor
Shields, C. The republic of love
Sholem Aleichem The nightingale

Shreve, A. Eden Close
Shteyngart, G. Super sad true love story
Simonson, H. Major Pettigrew's last stand
Smith, M. C. Rose
Soli, T. The lotus eaters
Sparks, N. The notebook
Sparks, N. A walk to remember
Spencer, L. Bitter sweet
Spencer, L. Morning glory
Spencer, L. Small town girl
Spencer, L. That Camden summer
Spencer, S. Endless love
Steel, D. The kiss
Stott, R. The coral thief
Styron, W. Sophie's choice
Sundaresan, I. The splendor of silence
Tabucchi, A. It's getting later all the time
Tanner, H. Vaclav and Lena
Tearne, R. Mosquito
Theroux, A. Darconville's cat
Thomas, R. All my sins remembered
Tremain, R. Music & silence
Treuer, D. The translation of Dr Apelles
Trevanian The summer of Katya
Trevor, W. Love and summer
Trigiani, A. Very Valentine
Trollope, J. Friday nights
Trueblood, V. Seven loves
Tryon, T. The wings of the morning
Turgenev, I. S. First love and other stories
Turgenev, I. S. The torrents of spring
Turner, N. E. These is my words
Tussing, J. The best people in the world
Updike, J. Brazil
Uris, L. Redemption
Urquhart, J. Away
Urquhart, J. A map of glass
Vallgren The horrific sufferings of the mind-reading monster Hercules Barefoot
Van Booy, S. Everything beautiful began after
Vargas Llosa, M. Aunt Julia and the scriptwriter
Vargas Llosa, M. The bad girl
Villars, E. The Normandie affair
Vine, B. The brimstone wedding
Wall, P. S. The Wilde women
Wallace, C. The blind contessa's new machine
Wallace, S. Montana dawn
Waller, R. J. The bridges of Madison County
Watson, B. The heaven of Mercury
Weiner, J. Good in bed
Wesley, M. Part of the furniture
Williamson, P. Heart of the west
Williamson, P. The outsider
Willig, L. The seduction of the crimson rose
Wood, B. Perfect Harmony
Wood, B. Vital signs
Wouk, H. A hole in Texas
Yoshimoto, B. Asleep
LOVE STORIES *See* Romance fiction
LOVE STORIES, AMERICAN
Soli, T. The lotus eaters
LOVE STORIES, ENGLISH
Hollinghurst, A. The stranger's child
Love story. Segal, E.
The **love** wife. Jen, G.
Love you more. Gardner, L.
Love's winning plays. Majors, I.
Love, again. Lessing, D. M.
LOVE-LETTERS
Brockmeier, K. The Illumination
Rose, M. J. Seduction
The **loved** one. Waugh, E.
Lovelace, Ada King, Countess of, 1815-1852
About
Crowley, J. Lord Byron's novel
The **lovely** bones. Sebold, A.
Lovely, Dark, Deep. Oates, J. C.
The **lover's** dictionary. Levithan, D.
LOVERS
McGowan, H. Duchess of nothing
Trueblood, V. Seven loves
Loving a lost lord. Putney, M. J.
Loving Frank. Horan, N.
The **loving** husband. Kent, C.
Lovingkindness. Roiphe, A. R.
Low Town. Polansky, D.
Lowboy. Wray, J.
LOWER EAST SIDE (NEW YORK, N.Y.)
Mosley, W. RL's dream
Price, R. Lush life
Yezierska, A. c. Bread givers
The **lowland.** Lahiri, J.
Loyal League [series]
Cole, A. An Extraordinary Union
Cole, A. A hope divided
LOYALTY
See also Ethics; Virtue
Lucan, Richard John Bingham, Earl of, 1934-
About
Spark, M. Aiding and abetting
Luciano's luck. Higgins, J.
Luciano, Lucky, 1897-1962
About
Higgins, J. Luciano's luck
Lucid intervals. Woods, S.
Lucifer's hammer. Niven, L.
Lucifer's tears. Thompson, J.
Luck Be a Lady. Duran, M.
The **Luck** of Roaring Camp, and other tales. Harte, B.
The **Luckiest** Lady in London. Thomas, S.
Lucky bastard. Browne, S. G.
Lucky boy. Sekaran, S.
Lucky Jim. Amis, K.
Lucky us. Bloom, A.

Lucky you. Hiaasen, C.
LUCUMI (RELIGION) *See* Santeria
Lucy. Kincaid, J.
Lucy. Gonzales, L.
The **Ludwig** Conspiracy.
Ludwig II, King of Bavaria, 1845-1886
About
The Ludwig Conspiracy
Lullaby. Palahniuk, C.
LUMBER AND LUMBERING
See also Forest products; Forests and forestry; Trees; Wood
LUMBER INDUSTRY
Rash, R. Serena
The **luminaries.** Catton, E.
Luminarium. Shakar, A.
The **luminous** heart of Jonah S. Nahai, G. B.
LUNAR EXPEDITIONS *See* Space flight to the moon
Lunar Park. Ellis, B. E.
LUNAR PROBES
See also Space probes
Luncheon of The Boating Party. Vreeland, S.
LUNG CANCER
See also Cancer; Lungs -- Diseases
LUNGS -- DISEASES
See also Diseases
Lush life. Price, R.
Lust for life. Stone, I.
Luther. Cross, N.
LYING *See* Truthfulness and falsehood
The **lying** game. Ware, R.
Lying with strangers. Grippando, J.
LYME DISEASE
See also Diseases
LYNCHING
Atkins, A. The forsaken
Clark, W. V. T. The Ox-bow incident
Lansdale, J. R. The bottoms
Nordan, L. Wolf whistle
Smith, L. E. Strange fruit
Vernon, O. A killing in this town
LYNLEY, THOMAS (FICTITIOUS CHARACTER)
George, E. Believing the lie
George, E. Just one evil act
LYRICISTS
See also Poets

M

MAASAI (AFRICAN PEOPLE)
Crompton, R. Hell's gate
Crompton, R. Hour of the Red God
MACHINE INTELLIGENCE *See* Artificial intelligence
Machineries of empire [series]
Lee, Y. H. Raven Stratagem
MACINTOSH (COMPUTER)
See also Computers
Madame Bovary. Flaubert, G.
Maddaddam. Atwood, M.
Madison, Dolley, 1768-1849
About
Hambly, B. Patriot hearts
Madness in Maggody. Hess, J.
The **Madonna** of Excelsior. Mda, Z.
The **Madonnas** of Echo Park. Skyhorse, B.
The **madonnas** of Leningrad. Dean, D.
MADRID (SPAIN)
Lewis, M. G. The monk
Maestra. Hilton, L. S.
MAFIA
Coleman, R. F. Where it hurts
Cristofano, D. The girl she used to be
Ellroy, J. American tabloid
Ellroy, J. The cold six thousand
Estleman, L. D. Gas City
Foulds, A. In the wolf's mouth
Goldberg, T. Gangsterland
Green, N. The angel of Montague Street
Grisham, J. The client
Grisham, J. The firm
Harkaway, N. Angelmaker
Higgins, J. Day of reckoning
Higgins, J. Luciano's luck
Latour, J. The Havana World Series
Patterson, R. N. Dark lady
Perry, T. Blood money
Perry, T. The informant
Puzo, M. The godfather
Puzo, M. The last Don
Puzo, M. The Sicilian
Robinson, S. Callahan's con
Seymour, G. Killing ground
Swinson, K. Playing dirty
Tanenbaum, R. Act of revenge
Vachss, A. H. Two trains running
Winslow, D. The winter of Frankie Machine
Woods, S. L.A. Times
Woods, S. Reckless abandon
MAGAZINES *See* Periodicals
The **Magdalen** girls. Alexander, V. S.
Mage winds [series]
Lackey, M. Winds of fate
Mage's blood. Hair, D.
Maggie: a girl of the streets (a story of New York) Crane, S.
Maggody and the moonbeams. Hess, J.
MAGI
Hair, D. Mage's blood
MAGIC
Adrian, C. The great night
The alchemist
Allen, S. A. First Frost
Anders, C. J. All the birds in the sky
Andrews, I. White Hot
Anton, M. Rav Hisda's daughter, book I, apprentice

Arden, K. The bear and the nightingale
Baker, K. The house of the stag
Barry, K. Beatlebone
Bear, E. All the windwracked stars
Bear, E. Steles of the sky
Bledsoe, A. Wisp of a thing
Buehlman, C. The Necromancer's house
Butcher, J. Proven guilty
Card, O. S. Seventh son
Carey, L. The stolen child
Chakraborty, S. K. The city of brass
Charlton, B. Spellbound
Charlton, B. Spellwright
Clarke, S. Jonathan Strange & Mr. Norrell
De Bodard, A. The house of shattered wings
De Robertis, C. Perla
Dépestre, R. Hadriana in all my dreams
Duncan, D. When the saints
Esquivel, L. Like water for chocolate
Evans, C. A darkness forged in fire
Flyte, M. City of lost dreams
Frei, M. The stranger's magic
Gilman, L. A. The cold eye
Gilman, L. A. Flesh and fire
Gilman, L. A. Hard magic
Gilman, L. A. Silver on the Road
Grant, M. Down Among the Sticks and Bones
Griffin, K. Glass God
Griffin, K. Stray souls
Grossman, L. The magician king
Grossman, L. The magicians
Hair, D. Scarlet tides
Harkness, D. E. A discovery of witches
Hill, J. Nos4a2
Hoffman, A. The rules of magic
Jacka, B. Fated
Jemisin, N. K. The killing moon
Jordan, R. The eye of the world
Karpyshyn, D. Children of fire
Keene, J. Counternarratives
Kennedy, K. Everlasting Enchantment
Kowal, M. R. Shades of milk and honey
Lake, J. Endurance
Lanagan, M. The brides of Rollrock Island
Lynch, S. The Republic of Thieves
Mailer, N. Ancient evenings
McKillip, P. A. Ombria in shadow
Mieville, C. Kraken
Nordan, L. Wolf whistle
Okorafor, N. Who fears death
Putney, M. J. The marriage spell
Putney, M. J. Stolen magic
Rawn, M. The diviner
Rawn, M. Touchstone
Roberts, N. Dance upon the air
Rushdie, S. Two years eight months and twenty-eight nights
Schwab, V. E. A Darker Shade of Magic
Schwab, V. E. A gathering of shadows
Tolkien, J. R. R. The fellowship of the ring
Tolkien, J. R. R. The return of the king
Tolkien, J. R. R. The two towers
Updike, J. The widows of Eastwick
Updike, J. The witches of Eastwick
Van Eekhout, G. California bones
Walton, J. Among others
Wilkins, K. Veil of gold
Wolfe, G. The sorcerer's house
Yanique, T. Land of love and drowning

MAGIC
See also Occultism
Magic for beginners. Link, K.
Magic for unlucky girls. Balaskovits, A. A.
The **magic** labyrinth. Farmer, P. J.
The **magic** mountain. Mann, T.
The **Magic** of Saida. Vassanji, M. G.
MAGIC REALISM (LITERATURE)
Beagle, P. S. Summerlong
The girl in the tower
MAGIC REALISM (LITERATURE)
See also Fantasy fiction; Surrealism
Magic seeds. Naipaul, V. S.
Magic time. Marlette, D.
Magic words. Kolpan, G.
The **magician** king. Grossman, L.
The **magician** of Lublin. Singer, I. B.
The **magician's** land. Grossman, L.
The **magicians.** Grossman, L.
MAGICIANS
Barnes, J. The somnambulist
Garcia, C. A handbook to luck
Grossman, L. The magician's land
Kolpan, G. Magic words
Morgenstern, E. The night circus
Stewart, M. The crystal cave
Stewart, M. The hollow hills
Stewart, M. The last enchantment
Tanner, H. Vaclav and Lena
Wallace, D. Mr. Sebastian and the Negro magician
White, T. H. The book of Merlyn
Magicians trilogy [series]
Grossman, L. The magician's land
Magnificence. Millet, L.
The **magnificent** Ambersons. Tarkington, B.
Magpie murders. Horowitz, A.
The **magus.** Fowles, J.
Mahmood, Zaved, 1970-
About
Hensher, P. Scenes from early life
MAIASAURA
See also Dinosaurs
The **maid.** Cutter, K.
The **maid's** version. Woodrell, D.
MAIDEN AUNTS
Dean, A. Bellfield Hall, or, The observations of Miss Dido

Kent
Dean, A. A place of confinement
Dean, A. A woman of consequence
Maiden Lane [series]
Hoyt, E. Duke of Midnight
MAIDS (SERVANTS)
Chevalier, T. Girl with a pearl earring
Cox, M. The glass of time
Danticat, E. The farming of bones
Humphreys, H. Afterimage
Richardson, S. Pamela
Maigret and the madwoman. Simenon, G.
Maigret and the Saturday caller. Simenon, G.
Maigret goes home. Simenon, G.
MAIL SERVICE *See* Postal service
MAIL-ORDER BUSINESS
See also Business; Direct selling; Selling
Main Street. Lewis, S.
MAINE
Beattie, A. The state we're in
Currie, R. Everything matters!
Doiron, P. The poacher's son
Hand, E. Generation loss
Harding, P. Tinkers
Irving, J. The cider house rules
Jewett, S. O. The country of the pointed firs and other stories
King, S. Carrie
King, S. Cujo
King, S. Dolores Claiborne
King, S. It
King, S. Pet sematary
King, S. Salem's Lot
Ogilvie, E. When the music stopped
Rickards, J. Winter's end
Robinson, L. Water dogs
Robinson, R. Cost
Russo, R. Empire Falls
Spencer, L. That Camden summer
Strout, E. Olive Kitteridge
Waldman, A. Red Hook Road
Watson, J. E. Asta in the wings
MAINE -- 18TH CENTURY
Lawrence, M. K. Hearts and bones
MAINE -- 19TH CENTURY
Rossner, J. Emmeline
Maisie Dobbs. Winspear, J.
Major Pettigrew's last stand. Simonson, H.
MAJORCA (SPAIN)
Nichols, P. The rocks
Straub, E. The vacationers
Make Your Home Among Strangers. Capó Crucet, J.
The **making** of us. Jewell, L.
The **Makioka** sisters. Tanizaki, J.
MALARIA
See also Diseases
MALAYA
Eng, T. T. The gift of rain
Tan, T. E. The Garden of Evening Mists
MALAYSIA
Carey, P. My life as a fake
Conrad, J. Lord Jim
Manicka, R. The rice mother
Samarasan, P. Evening is the whole day
Malcolm X, 1925-1965
About
Baker, K. Strivers Row
MALE ACTORS
See also Actors
MALE CLIMACTERIC
See also Aging
MALE DANCERS
What we become
MALE FRIENDSHIP -- SOVIET UNION
The big green tent
MALE FRIENDSHIP -- UNITED STATES
Bachelder, C. The throwback special
MALE HOMOSEXUALITY
White, E. Jack Holmes and his friend
Malgudi days. Narayan, R. K.
Malice. Higashino, K.
Malice prepense. Wilhelm, K.
MALIGNANT TUMORS *See* Cancer
Mallory's oracle. O'Connell, C.
MALLORY, KATHLEEN (FICTITIOUS CHARACTER)
O'Connell, C. The chalk girl
O'Connell, C. Crime school
MALLOY, FRANK (FICTITIOUS CHARACTER)
Thompson, V. Murder in Chinatown
Thompson, V. Murder on Fifth Avenue
MALPRACTICE INSURANCE
See also Insurance
MALTA
Willocks, T. The religion
The **Maltese** falcon. Hammett, D.
Mama Day. Naylor, G.
The **Mambo** Kings play songs of love. Hijuelos, O.
MAMMALS
See also Animals
The **mammoth** book of steampunk.
The **man.** Wallace, I.
MAN *See* Human beings
Man at the helm. Stibbe, N.
A **man** called Ove. Backman, F.
The **man** from Beijing. Mankell, H.
The **man** from Saigon. Leimbach, M.
A **man** in full. Wolfe, T.
The **man** in my basement. Mosley, W.
MAN IN SPACE *See* Space flight
Man in the blue moon. Morris, M.
The **man** in the gray flannel suit. Wilson, S.
The **man** in the high castle. Dick, P. K.
The **man** in the iron mask. Dumas, A.
Man in the Iron Mask
About

Dumas, A. The man in the iron mask
The **man** in the queue. Tey, J.
The **man** in the wooden hat. Gardam, J.
Man in the woods. Spencer, S.
A **man** lies dreaming. Tidhar, L.
The **man** of feeling.
Man on the run. Weber, C.
Man Plus. Pohl, F.
The **man** who could fly and other stories. Anaya, R. A.
The **man** who loved children. Stead, C.
The **man** who never stopped sleeping. Appelfeld, A.
The **man** who smiled. Mankell, H.
The **man** with the compound eyes.
The **man** with the golden arm. Algren, N.
The **man** with the golden gun. Fleming, I.
A **Man** Without Breath. Kerr, P.
The **man** without qualities. Musil, R.
Man's fate (La condition humaine) Malraux, A.
Man's hope. Malraux, A.
MAN-WOMAN RELATIONSHIP
See also Interpersonal relations
MAN-WOMAN RELATIONSHIP
Alexander, V. The lady travelers guide to scoundrels & other gentlemen
Anam, T. The Bones of Grace
Anders, A. Under Her Skin
Ball, J. A cure for suicide
Boswell, R. Tumbledown
Bowen, K. You're the Earl That I Want
Byrne, K. The Duke
Carey, J. Kushiel's Scion
Cole, A. An Extraordinary Union
Dare, T. Romancing the duke
Dee, J. A thousand pardons
Dickey, E. J. One night
The Disappeared
Dodd, C. The woman who couldn't scream
Duran, M. A lady's code of misconduct
Duran, M. Luck Be a Lady
Foster, L. Under Pressure
Grant, D. The Protector
Gray, J. A lady never lies
Guhrke, L. L. When the Marquess Met His Match
Hauck, R. How to catch a prince
Hern, C. Once a gentleman
Higgins, K. Anything for You
James, E. My American Duchess
James, E. Three Weeks With Lady X
Jenkins, B. Breathless
Jones, T. An American marriage
Kinsella, S. My not so perfect life
Kleypas, L. Brown-Eyed Girl
Krentz, J. A. River road
Krentz, J. A. When all the girls have gone
Leavitt, D. The Two Hotels Francfort
Lynch, K. Confucius Jane
Machado, C. M. Her body and other parties
MacLean, S. A Scot in the dark
Moore, E. K. The Supremes sing the happy heartache blues
Murphy, S. F. The possessions
Oates, J. C. Evil Eye
Otto, W. Eight girls taking pictures
Palahniuk, C. Beautiful you
Quick, A. 'Til death do us part
Rabb, J. Among the living
Roberts, N. The obsession
Rowell, R. Landline
Ruskovich, E. Idaho
Ryan, J. His cowboy heart
Sada, D. Almost never
Singh, N. Shield of winter
Smith, G. B. The maze at Windermere
Summer lies
Thus bad begins
Turner, N. Natural born hustler
Van Dyken, R. Cheater
Wallace, D. F. Brief interviews with hideous men
Wayne, T. Loner
Whittall, Z. Holding still for as long as possible
Winawer, M. The scribe of Siena
Zevin, G. The storied life of A. J. Fikry
MANAGEMENT
See also Business; Industries
MANCHESTER (ENGLAND)
Jacobson, H. Kalooki nights
Jacobson, H. The mighty Walzer
Noon, J. Vurt
The **mandarins.** Beauvoir, S. d.
The **Mandelbaum** Gate. Spark, M.
Mandelstam, Osip, 1891-1938
About
Littell, R. The Stalin epigram
MANGA
See also Graphic novels
MANHATTAN (NEW YORK, N.Y.)
Haimoff, M. These days are ours
Lehmann, S. Astor Place Vintage
McLaughlin, E. The nanny diaries
Winslow, D. The force
Manhattan Beach. Egan, J.
Manhattan transfer. Dos Passos, J.
MANHUNTS
Forsyth, F. The Odessa file
MANHWA
See also Comic books, strips, etc.
MANIC-DEPRESSIVE ILLNESS
See also Affective disorders; Mental illness
MANIC-DEPRESSIVE ILLNESS
Alenyikov, M. Ivan and Misha
Garey, J. Too bright to hear too loud to see
Manifold. Baxter, S.
MANIKINS (FASHION MODELS) *See* Fashion models
MANIPULATIVE BEHAVIOR
Constantine, L. The Last Mrs. Parrish

MANNERS AND CUSTOMS
Calisher, H. The collected stories of Hortense Calisher
MANORS -- ENGLAND -- 20TH CENTURY
Jones, S. The uninvited guests
Mansfield Park. Austen, J.
MANSIONS
Lambert, C. The children's home
Millet, L. Magnificence
Manson, Charles, 1934-2017
About
Lazar, Z. Sway
A **manual** for cleaning women. Berlin, L.
Manual of painting & calligraphy.
Manuel, Peter, 1927-1958
About
Mina, D. The long drop
MANUFACTURING EXECUTIVES
Keneally, T. Schindler's list
A **manuscript** of ashes. Munoz Molina, A.
MANUSCRIPTS
Belfer, L. And after the fire
Caldwell, I. The rule of four
Crowley, J. Lord Byron's novel
Dai Sijie Once on a moonless night
Durrell, L. Balthazar
Gruber, M. The book of air and shadows
Harkness, D. E. Shadow of night
Holland, T. The archivist's story
Kiernan, C. R. The red tree
Lovett, C. The lost book of the Grail
Ludlum, R. The Gemini contenders
McCarry, C. Old boys
Michaels, B. Houses of stone
Redfield, J. The celestine prophecy
Silko, L. Almanac of the dead
MANUSCRIPTS
See also Archives; Bibliography; Books
MAORIS
Hulme, K. The bone people
Tremain, R. The color
MAORIS
See also Indigenous peoples
The **map** and the territory.
MAP DRAWING
Larsen, R. The selected works of T. S. Spivet
A **map** of betrayal. Jin, H.
The **map** of bones. Haig, F.
A **map** of glass. Urquhart, J.
Map of Ireland. Grant, S.
The **map** of lost memories. Fay, K.
A **map** of the world. Hamilton, J.
The **map** of time.
Map of time [series]
The map of time
The **map** of true places. Barry, B.
A **map** of Tulsa. Lytal, B.
The **mapping** of love and death. Winspear, J.
MAPS
Penny, L. A great reckoning
Maps for lost lovers. Aslam, N.
Maps in a mirror. Card, O. S.
MARAIS (PARIS, FRANCE)
Black, C. Murder in the Marais
The **Marathon** conspiracy. Corby, G.
Marathon man. Goldman, W.
The **marauders.** Cooper, T.
The **marble** orchard. Taylor, A.
The **march.** Doctorow, E. L.
March violets. Kerr, P.
MARDI GRAS
Faulkner, W. Pylon
The **mare.** Gaitskill, M.
The **Margarets.** Tepper, S. S.
The Margellos World Republic of Letters [series]
Modiano, P. Suspended sentences
Marguerite, Queen, consort of Louis IX, King of France
About
Jones, S. Four sisters, all queens
Marianne. Sand, G.
Marie Antoinette, Queen, consort of Louis XVI, King of France, 1755-1793
About
Davis, K. Versailles
Naslund, S. J. Abundance
Mariette in ecstasy. Hansen, R.
MARIHUANA *See* Marijuana
MARIJUANA
Brown, E. R. Almost criminal
Leonard, E. Raylan
Walter, J. The financial lives of the poets
Winslow, D. Savages
MARIJUANA INDUSTRY
Brown, E. R. Almost criminal
Winslow, D. Savages
Marina, ca. 1505-ca. 1530
About
Sherwood, F. Night of sorrows
MARINAS
See also Boats and boating; Harbors; Yachts and yachting
MARINE BIOLOGY
Drabble, M. The sea lady
Southgate, M. The taste of salt
MARINES
Hunter, S. Dead zero
MARIONETTES *See* Puppets and puppet plays
MARITAL CONFLICT
Fox, L. Days of awe
Kitamura, K. A separation
McEwan, I. Nutshell
Marius, Gaius, ca. 157-86 B.C.
About
McCullough, C. The first man in Rome
Marjorie Morningstar. Wouk, H.

The **mark** and the void. Murray, P.
Mark Angelotti novels [series]
Raimondo, L. Dante's wood
The **mark** of the assassin. Silva, D.
Marker. Cook, R.
A **marker** to measure drift. Maksik, A.
Market Street. Hughes, A.
Marks, Grace
About
Atwood, M. Alias Grace
MARKSMANSHIP
Cain, C. One Kick
Marlena. Buntin, J.
The **Marlowe** papers. Barber, R.
Marlowe, Christopher, 1564-1593
About
Barber, R. The Marlowe papers
Bear, E. Ink and steel
MARQUESAS ISLANDS
Melville, H. Omoo: a narrative of adventures in the South Seas
Melville, H. Typee: a peep at Polynesian life
MARRIAGE
Ali, M. Brick lane
The art of joy
Baxter, C. Saul and Patsy
Belle, K. The marriage lie
Bialosky, J. The prize
Bowman, V. The Accidental Countess
Bowman, V. The Unexpected Duchess
Bragg, M. The soldier's return
Bragg, M. A son of war
Burrowes, G. The heir
Cadwalladr, C. The family tree
Carter, S. L. New England white
Colwin, L. A big storm knocked it over
Colwin, L. Goodbye without leaving
Colwin, L. Happy all the time
Connell, E. S. Mrs. Bridge
Cunningham, M. By nightfall
Cusk, R. The Bradshaw variations
Daniel, S. Stiltsville
Dare, T. When a Scot Ties the Knot
Doerr, H. Stones for Ibarra
Dunant, S. The birth of Venus
Duran, M. Luck Be a Lady
Ebershoff, D. The Danish Girl
Edgarian, C. Three stages of amazement
Egan, E. A window opens
Erdrich, L. Four souls
Erdrich, L. The Master Butchers Singing Club
Essbaum, J. A. Hausfrau
Essex, K. Leonardo's swans
Ferrante, E. The Story of a New Name
Ford, F. M. The good soldier
Franzen, J. Freedom
Franzen, J. The corrections
Galchen, R. Atmospheric disturbances
Gardam, J. The man in the wooden hat
Gibbons, K. On the occasion of my last afternoon
Gilmore, J. The Mothers
Goodwin, D. The American heiress
Goolrick, R. A reliable wife
Grant, L. We had it so good
Groff, L. Fates and furies
Guhrke, L. L. How to lose a duke in ten days
Guhrke, L. L. When the Marquess Met His Match
Hamilton, J. When Madeline was young
Hannah, K. Home front
Harris, E. The Marrying of Chani Kaufman
Hedges, P. The Heights
Higgins, K. Anything for You
Higgins, K. My one and only
Higgins, K. The Perfect Match
Hill, R. When all is said and done
Hoffman, A. Skylight confessions
Hornby, N. How to be good
Isaacs, S. As husbands go
Itani, F. Tell
Jaffe, R. Class reunion
James, E. Four Nights With the Duke
James, E. Three Weeks With Lady X
James, E. When beauty tamed the beast
James, H. The wings of the dove
Jones, S. Small wars
Joss, M. The night following
Kinder, C. Honeymooners
Kittredge, W. The Willow Field
Koen, K. Through a glass darkly
Lamb, W. We Are Water
Lodge, D. Deaf sentence
Lordan, B. But come ye back
Marias, J. A heart so white
Mawer, S. The glass room
Mbue, I. Behold the Dreamers
McEwan, I. Black dogs
McEwan, I. On Chesil Beach
McLain, P. The Paris wife
Meloy, M. Liars and saints
Miller, S. The senator's wife
Moore, A. The Lighthouse
Morgan, R. The road from Gap Creek
Morley, I. Come Sunday
Nelson, A. Bound
Netzer, L. Shine shine shine
Nicholls, D. Us
Norman, H. Next life might be kinder
Nunez, E. Anna in-between
Oates, J. C. The falls
Offill, J. Dept. of speculation
O'Nan, S. The good wife
O'Nan, S. The odds
Otsuka, J. The Buddha in the attic
Park, S. This burns my heart

Phillips, S. E. Call me irresistible
Price, R. Roxanna Slade
Putney, M. J. Not quite a wife
Rice, L. Blue moon
Robinson, M. Lila
Ross, A. Mr. Peanut
Rush, N. Subtle bodies
Russo, R. Bridge of sighs
Russo, R. That old Cape magic
Sanghera, S. Marriage Material
Sarton, M. Anger
Savage, S. Glass
Saville, L. Henry and Rachel
Seth, V. A suitable boy
Shreve, A. Sea glass
Shriver, L. So much for that
Stegner, W. E. Crossing to safety
Stone, R. Outerbridge Reach
Suri, M. The age of Shiva
Swift, G. Tomorrow
Theroux, P. My secret history
Thomas, S. The Luckiest Lady in London
Ties
Toer, P. A. The girl from the coast
Trollope, J. The men and the girls
Trollope, J. Next of kin
Tuck, L. I married you for happiness
Tyler, A. The amateur marriage
Tyler, A. Breathing lessons
Vidal, G. 1876
Warner, K. Bride of the high country
Weiner, J. Little earthquakes
Winer, A. The marriage artist
Wood, B. The dreaming
Yarbrough, S. The realm of last chances
MARRIAGE
See also Family; Sacraments
The **marriage** artist. Winer, A.
MARRIAGE BROKERS
Pym, B. Jane and Prudence
MARRIAGE COUNSELING
Gideon, M. Wife 22
MARRIAGE CUSTOMS AND RITES
See also Manners and customs; Marriage; Rites and ceremonies; Weddings
The **marriage** lie. Belle, K.
Marriage Material. Sanghera, S.
The **marriage** plot. Eugenides, J.
MARRIAGE PROBLEMS
Climates
Haddon, M. The red house
Higgins, K. My one and only
The **marriage** spell. Putney, M. J.
MARRIAGE, INTERRACIAL *See* Interracial marriage
MARRIED LIFE *See* Marriage
Married love and other stories. Hadley, T.
The **married** man. White, E.
MARRIED PEOPLE
See also Family; Marriage
MARRIED PEOPLE
Adebayo, A. Stay with me
Arudpragasam, A. The story of a brief marriage
Atwood, M. The Heart Goes Last
Flynn, G. Gone girl
Gideon, M. Wife 22
James, E. The ugly duchess
Johnson, A. Fortune smiles
Layton, E. To wed a stranger
Link, T. Denting the Bosch
McEwan, I. Nutshell
Moriarty, L. The husband's secret
Moriarty, L. Truly madly guilty
Palmer, D. Version control
Phillips, H. The beautiful bureaucrat
Pierpont, J. Among the ten thousand things
Rowell, R. Landline
Simsion, G. The Rosie effect
Thus bad begins
Woodruff, L. Those we love most
MARRIED WOMEN
Aslam, N. Maps for lost lovers
Bock, C. Alice & Oliver
Essbaum, J. A. Hausfrau
Hornby, N. How to be good
King, L. R. The game
Kitamura, K. A separation
Law, S. K. The paper marriage
McEwan, I. Nutshell
Min, A. Becoming Madame Mao
Morgan, R. The road from Gap Creek
O'Dell, T. Back roads
Palmer, D. Version control
Plain, B. Looking back
Sekaran, S. Lucky boy
Trigiani, A. Big Cherry Holler
Wilhelm, K. The deepest water
Wolitzer, M. The wife
The **Marrowbone** Marble Company. Taylor, M. G.
The **Marrying** of Chani Kaufman. Harris, E.
Marrying the mistress. Trollope, J.
Mars. Bova, B.
MARS (PLANET)
Barnes, J. The sky so big and black
Bova, B. Mars
Bradbury, R. The Martian chronicles
Brown, P. Red Rising
Haldeman, J. W. Marsbound
Levine, D. D. Arabella of Mars
Lewis, C. S. Out of the silent planet
Pohl, F. Man Plus
Preston, D. Impact
Robinson, K. S. Blue Mars
Robinson, K. S. The Martians
Robinson, K. S. Red Mars

Tepper, S. S. The Margarets
Varley, J. Red lightning
Varley, J. Rolling thunder
Weir, A. The Martian
MARS PROBES
See also Mars (Planet); Space probes
Marsbound. Haldeman, J. W.
MARSH ECOLOGY
See also Ecology
MARTHA'S VINEYARD (MASS.)
Blume, J. Summer sisters
Brooks, G. Caleb's crossing
Carter, S. L. The emperor of Ocean Park
Harris, R. The ghost
Hoffman, A. Illumination night
Klaussmann, L. Tigers in red weather
West, D. The wedding
MARTIAL ARTS
Faust, C. Choke hold
The **Martian.** Weir, A.
The **Martian** chronicles. Bradbury, R.
The **Martians.** Robinson, K. S.
MARTIANS
Haldeman, J. W. Starbound
Heinlein, R. A. Stranger in a strange land
Martin Chuzzlewit. Dickens, C.
Martin Dressler. Millhauser, S.
Martin Eden. London, J.
MARTYRS
Penman, S. K. Time and chance
Marvel and a wonder. Meno, J.
Mary. Newman, J. C.
MARY (BLESSED VIRGIN, SAINT) -- ART
See also Art
Mary Ann in autumn. Maupin, A.
Mary Coin. Silver, M.
Mary I, Queen of England, 1516-1558
About
Harper, K. The Poyson garden
Mary II, Queen of Great Britain, 1662-1694
About
Plaidy, J. William's wife
Mary Reilly. Martin, V.
Mary Russell and Sherlock Holmes mysteries [series]
King, L. R. The beekeeper's apprentice, or, on the segregation of the queen
Mary, Blessed Virgin, Saint
About
Guterson, D. Our Lady of the Forest
Kirshenbaum, B. An almost perfect moment
Tóibín, C. The testament of Mary
Mary, Queen of Scots, 1542-1587
About
Plaidy, J. The captive Queen of Scots
Marya. Oates, J. C.
MARYLAND
Lippman, L. I'd know you anywhere
Lippman, L. The most dangerous thing
McBride, J. Song yet sung
Michener, J. A. Chesapeake
Tyler, A. Searching for Caleb
Walbert, K. The gardens of Kyoto
MARYLAND -- 17TH CENTURY
Barth, J. The sot-weed factor
MARYLAND -- BALTIMORE
Lippman, L. What the dead know
Palmer, M. The last surgeon
Tyler, A. The amateur marriage
Tyler, A. Back when we were grownups
Tyler, A. Celestial navigation
Tyler, A. The clock winder
Tyler, A. Digging to America
Tyler, A. Dinner at the Homesick Restaurant
Tyler, A. Ladder of years
Tyler, A. Morgan's passing
Tyler, A. Noah's compass
Tyler, A. A patchwork planet
Tyler, A. Saint maybe
MASADA SITE (ISRAEL)
Hoffman, A. The dovekeepers
MASAI (AFRICAN PEOPLE)
See also Africans; Indigenous peoples
Masaryk Station. Down, D.
MASCULINITY
Bachelder, C. The throwback special
MASH. Hooker, R.
MASKS (PLAYS)
See also Drama; Pageants; Theater
MASOCHISM
Templeton, E. Gordon
Mason & Dixon. Pynchon, T.
MASON (OHIO)
Tatlock, A. Things we once held dear
Mason, Charles, 1730-1787
About
Pynchon, T. Mason & Dixon
MASS COMMUNICATION *See* Communication; Mass media; Telecommunication
MASS MEDIA
Hawley, N. Before the Fall
MASS MEDIA
See also Communication
MASS MURDER
Mankell, H. The man from Beijing
MASS MURDER -- SWEDEN -- STOCKHOLM
Giolito, M. P. Quicksand
MASSACHUSETTS
Arsenault, E. The broken teaglass
Blake, S. The postmistress
Dufresne, J. Requiem, Mass.
Giffin, E. Heart of the matter
Glass, J. The widower's tale
Haigh, J. The condition
Harvey, M. Brighton

Haslett, A. Union Atlantic
Hoffman, A. The red garden
Lahiri, J. The namesake
Pipkin, J. Woodsburner
Sittenfeld, C. Prep
Smith, Z. On beauty
Tea, M. Rose of no man's land
Updike, J. Toward the end of time
Urquhart, R. The Visionist
MASSACHUSETTS -- 17TH CENTURY
Brooks, G. Caleb's crossing
MASSACHUSETTS -- 18TH CENTURY
Gunning, S. The rebellion of Jane Clarke
MASSACHUSETTS -- 19TH CENTURY
Diamant, A. Last days of Dogtown
MASSACHUSETTS -- 20TH CENTURY
Cook, T. H. The Chatham School affair
Hoffman, A. Practical magic
Hoffman, A. The river king
Lightman, A. P. The diagnosis
Updike, J. Roger's version
MASSACHUSETTS -- BOSTON
Delaney, E. J. Broken Irish
Finder, J. Buried secrets
Grant, S. Map of Ireland
Grippando, J. Lying with strangers
Haigh, J. Faith
Hawthorne, N. The scarlet letter
Hogan, C. Devils in exile
Lehane, D. The given day
Lehane, D. Mystic river
Lehane, D. Shutter Island
Lipman, E. The pursuit of Alice Thrift
Livesey, M. Banishing Verona
Lowenthal, M. Charity girl
Palmer, M. Miracle cure
Patchett, A. Run
Pearl, M. The Dante Club
Read, P. P. The professor's daughter
Sarton, M. Anger
Shattuck, J. Perfect life
MASSACHUSETTS -- BOSTON -- 20TH CENTURY
Cook, R. Coma
Higgins, G. V. The friends of Eddie Coyle
Wakefield, D. Starting over
MASSACHUSETTS -- CAMBRIDGE
Goodman, A. The cookbook collector
Miller, S. For love
MASSACHUSETTS -- CAPE COD
LeCraw, H. The swimming pool
Martin, W. Cape Cod
McCracken, E. The giant's house
Russo, R. That old Cape magic
Theroux, P. Picture palace
MASSACHUSETTS -- HISTORY -- 19TH CENTURY
Shepard, K. The Celestials
MASSACHUSETTS -- LOWELL
Rossner, J. Emmeline
MASSACHUSETTS -- MARBLEHEAD
Howe, K. The physick book of Deliverance Dane
MASSACHUSETTS -- PROVINCETOWN
Dillard, A. The Maytrees
MASSACHUSETTS -- SALEM
Barry, B. The lace reader
Barry, B. The map of true places
Conde, M. I, Tituba, black witch of Salem
Hawthorne, N. The House of the Seven Gables
Howe, K. The physick book of Deliverance Dane
Julavits, H. The uses of enchantment
Kent, K. The heretic's daughter
Morrow, J. The last witchfinder
MASSACHUSETTS INSTITUTE OF TECHNOLOGY
Pearl, M. The technologists
MASSACHUSETTS INSTITUTE OF TECHNOLOGY -- HISTORY -- 19TH CENTURY
Pearl, M. The technologists
MASSACRES
Danticat, E. The farming of bones
Mankell, H. The man from Beijing
O'Brien, T. In the Lake of the Woods
Stanisic, S. How the soldier repairs the gramophone
Zimler, R. The last kabbalist of Lisbon
MASSACRES
See also Atrocities; History; Persecution
The **master.** Tóibín, C.
Master and God. Davis, L.
The **master** and Margarita. Bulgakov, M. A.
MASTER AND SERVANT
Carey, P. Parrot and Olivier in America
Osborne, L. The forgiven
Umrigar, T. N. The space between us
The **Master** Butchers Singing Club. Erdrich, L.
The **master** executioner. Estleman, L. D.
Master of the delta. Cook, T. H.
Masters of Atlantis. Portis, C.
Mata Hari, 1876-1917
About
Murphy, Y. Signed, Mata Hari
The **match.** Gunesekera, R.
Match me if you can. Phillips, S. E.
The **matchmaker** of Kenmare. Delaney, F.
MATE SELECTION
Shriver, L. The post-birthday world
The wedding date
MATERNAL DEPRIVATION
Gowdy, B. The romantic
Kidd, S. M. The secret life of bees
Livesey, M. Eva moves the furniture
Wallace, D. The Watermelon King
The **Mathematician's** Shiva. Rojstaczer, S.
MATHEMATICIANS
Agawa, Y. The housekeeper and the professor
Banville, J. The infinities
Benjamin, M. Alice I have been

Crowley, J. Lord Byron's novel
Goodman, C. The night villa
Morrow, J. The last witchfinder
Rojstaczer, S. The Mathematician's Shiva
Rucker, R. v. B. Mathematicians in love
Stott, R. Ghostwalk
Zamiatin, E. I. We
MATHEMATICIANS
See also Scientists
Mathematicians in love. Rucker, R. v. B.
MATHEMATICS
Richmond, M. No one you know
Mathew, Pradeep Sivanathan, 1965-
About
Karunatilaka, S. The legend of Pradeep Mathew
Mathilda Savitch. Lodato, V.
Matilda, Empress, consort of Henry V, Holy Roman Emperor, 1102-1167
About
Penman, S. K. When Christ and his saints slept
Mating. Rush, N.
The **Matlock** paper. Ludlum, R.
MATRIMONY *See* Marriage
Matter. Banks, I.
A **matter** of blood. Pinborough, S.
Matterhorn. Marlantes, K.
MATURATION (PSYCHOLOGY)
Bognanni, P. The house of tomorrow
Howrey, M. Blind sight
Just, W. S. Rodin's debutante
Maurice. Forster, E. M.
Max Brand's best western stories. Brand, M.
Max Tudor mysteries [series]
Malliet, G. M. A Demon Summer
Malliet, G. M. Pagan spring
Malliet, G. M. Wicked autumn
MAY DAY
Read Thrush Green
May there be a road. L'Amour, L.
MAY, JOHN (FICTITIOUS CHARACTER)
Fowler, C. Bryant & May
Maya's Notebook. Allende, I.
The **Mayan** secrets. Cussler, C.
MAYO (IRELAND : COUNTY)
Barrett, C. Young skins
The **mayor's** tongue. Rich, N.
MAYORS
Iles, G. The devil's punchbowl
The **Maytrees.** Dillard, A.
The **maze.** Karnezis, P.
The **maze** at Windermere. Smith, G. B.
MAZE PUZZLES
See also Puzzles
Mazzarella, Nicole
About
Mazzarella, N. This heavy silence
McGavock, Caroline E. Winder, 1829-1905
About
Hicks, R. The widow of the south
MCGILL, LEONID (FICTITIOUS CHARACTER)
Mosley, W. All I did was shoot my man
Mosley, W. And sometimes I wonder about you
McNally's dilemma. Sanders, L.
McNally's gamble. Sanders, L.
McNally's puzzle. Sanders, L.
MCRAE, LOGAN (FICTITIOUS CHARACTER)
MacBride, S. Blind eye
MacBride, S. Cold granite
MacBride, S. Dying Light
MacBride, S. Shatter the bones
McTeague. Norris, F.
Me before you. Moyes, J.
MEALS *See* Breakfasts; Dinners; Luncheons
MEANING (PHILOSOPHY)
Ford, R. Canada
The **meaning** of night. Cox, M.
The **means** of escape. Fitzgerald, P.
The **measure** of the magic. Brooks, T.
MEASUREMENT
See also Mathematics
Measuring time. Habila, H.
MEAT
See also Food
MEAT INDUSTRY
Leon, D. Beastly Things
Sinclair, U. The jungle
The **Mechanical.** Tregillis, I.
MECHANICAL ENGINEERS
Bognanni, P. The house of tomorrow
MECHANICAL MOVEMENTS
See also Kinematics; Mechanical engineering; Mechanics; Motion
MECHANICS
Ulfelder, S. Purgatory chasm
MECHANICS (PERSONS)
Franklin, T. Crooked letter, crooked letter
Mechanique. Valentine, G.
Medea. Greenwood, K.
MEDEA (GREEK MYTHOLOGY)
Greenwood, K. Medea
MEDIA *See* Mass media
MEDICAL CARE -- ETHICAL ASPECTS *See* Medical ethics
MEDICAL CARE
Grant, M. Parasite
MEDICAL COLLEGES
Guinn, M. The resurrectionist
MEDICAL ETHICS
Iles, G. The footprints of God
Lescroart, J. T. The oath
Moon, E. The speed of dark
Picoult, J. My sister's keeper
MEDICAL ETHICS
See also Bioethics; Ethics; Professional ethics

MEDICAL EXAMINERS
Cook, R. Marker
Patterson, J. 1st to die
MEDICAL FICTION
Thomson, E. S. Beloved poison
MEDICAL FICTION *See* Medical novels
MEDICAL GENETICS
See also Genetics; Pathology
MEDICAL NOVELS
Elison, M. The Book of the Unnamed Midwife
Kellerman, J. Devil's waltz
Thomson, E. S. Beloved poison
Winawer, M. The scribe of Siena
Yanagihara, H. The people in the trees
MEDICAL SCHOOLS *See* Medical colleges
MEDICAL STUDENTS
Guinn, M. The resurrectionist
MEDICINE -- RESEARCH
Mosley, W. The last days of Ptolemy Grey
Palmer, M. The fifth vial
Patchett, A. State of wonder
Sanders, L. The sixth commandment
Uris, L. QB VII
MEDICINE -- RESEARCH
See also Research
Patchett, A. State of wonder
MEDICINE, PEDIATRIC *See* Children -- Diseases
MEDICINES, PATENT, PROPRIETARY, ETC.
Capote, T. The grass harp
Medicus. Downie, R.
Medicus investigation [series]
Downie, R. Medicus
MEDIEVAL ART
See also Art; Medieval civilization
MEDIEVAL TOURNAMENTS
See also Chivalry; Medieval civilization; Pageants
MEDITERRANEAN REGION
Dunnett, D. Pawn in frankincense
MEDIUMS
Hunt, S. Mr. Splitfoot
MEEHAN, PADDY (FICTITIOUS CHARACTER)
Mina, D. Field of blood
MEGALITHIC MONUMENTS
See also Antiquities; Archeology; Monuments
MELANCHOLY
See also Emotions; Mood (Psychology)
Melancholy baby. Parker, R. B.
Melmoth the wanderer. Maturin, C. R.
Melville, Herman, 1819-1891
About
Naslund, S. J. Ahab's wife; or, The star-gazer
Parini, J. The passages of H.M.
The **member** of the wedding. McCullers, C.
MEMBERS OF CONGRESS
Buckley, W. F. Mongoose, R.I.P
Ellroy, J. American tabloid
Morrow, J. The last witchfinder
Pesci, D. Amistad
Updike, J. Memories of the Ford Administration
Vidal, G. Lincoln
MEMBERS OF PARLIAMENT
Holland, C. Valley of the Kings
Hunt, R. Mr. Chartwell
Kadare, I. The Successor
Russell, M. D. Dreamers of the day
Sontag, S. The volcano lover
Memento mori. Spark, M.
MEMOIRISTS
Clinch, J. Finn
Doctorow, E. L. The march
Eggers, D. What is the what
Hunt, R. Mr. Chartwell
Jakes, J. Savannah; or, A gift for Mr. Lincoln
Nabokov, V. V. Novels and memoirs, 1941-1951
Oates, J. C. Wild nights!
Roth, P. The plot against America
Russell, M. D. Dreamers of the day
Truong, M. The book of salt
Twain, M. The gilded age and later novels
MEMOIRS *See* Autobiographies; Autobiography; Biography
Memoirs of a geisha. Golden, A.
The **memoirs** of a survivor. Lessing, D. M.
Memoirs of an ex-prom queen. Shulman, A. K.
Memoirs of an imaginary friend. Dicks, M.
Memoirs of an invisible man. Saint, H. F.
Memoirs of Hadrian. Yourcenar, M.
Memories of my melancholy whores. García Márquez, G.
Memories of the Ford Administration. Updike, J.
Memory. Westlake, D. E.
MEMORY
Agawa, Y. The housekeeper and the professor
Alarcón, D. American odysseys
Amis, M. House of meetings
Anolik, L. Dark Rooms
Austerlitz
Ball, J. A cure for suicide
Banville, J. Ancient light
Banville, J. The sea
Blume, J. In the unlikely event
Carroll, J. The ghost in love
Dean, D. The madonnas of Leningrad
Doctorow, E. L. Andrew's Brain
Drabble, M. The sea lady
Enright, A. The forgotten waltz
Flynn, G. Dark places
Frame, J. In the memorial room
Griffith, M. Trophy
Harding, P. Tinkers
Harrison, J. Returning to earth
I refuse
Irving, J. Avenue of mysteries
Itani, F. Remembering the bones
Katzenbach, J. What comes next
Krauss, N. Great house

Laplante, A. Turn of mind
Lightman, A. P. Reunion
Lourie, R. A hatred for tulips
Makine, A. Dreams of my Russian summers
Maksik, A. A marker to measure drift
Michaels, A. Fugitive pieces
Miller, D. B. Norwegian by night
Minot, S. Evening
Moriarty, L. What Alice forgot
Morton, K. The house at Riverton
Murakami, H. South of the border, west of the sun
Norton, C. What doesn't kill her
O'Brien, E. House of splendid isolation
Rayfiel, T. In pinelight
Robinson, M. Home
Romano, S. Resurrection Express
Sedgwick, M. Mister Memory
Smith, A. Autumn
Stone upon stone
Taylor, M. G. The ballad of Trenchmouth Taggart
Trueblood, V. Seven loves
Tsukiyama, G. Dreaming water
Tuck, L. I married you for happiness
Tyler, A. Noah's compass
Watson, S. J. Before I go to sleep
Westlake, D. E. Memory
Wiesel, E. The forgotten
MEMORY
See also Brain; Educational psychology; Intellect; Psychology; Psychophysiology; Thought and thinking
MEMORY DISORDERS
Agawa, Y. The housekeeper and the professor
The **memory** keeper's daughter. Edwards, K.
The **memory** of love. Forna, A.
Memory wall. Doerr, A.
MEMPHIS (TENN.)
Stern, S. The pinch
MEN
Backman, F. A man called Ove
Carlson, R. Five skies
Gavin, J. Middle men
Naylor, G. The men of Brewster Place
O'Farrell, M. This must be the place
Szalay, D. All that man is
Wallace, D. F. Brief interviews with hideous men
MEN -- BIOGRAPHY
See also Biography
MEN -- DISEASES
See also Diseases
MEN -- GREAT BRITAIN
Joyce, R. The unlikely pilgrimage of Harold Fry
MEN -- PSYCHOLOGY
Nadzam, B. Lamb
MEN -- SEXUAL BEHAVIOR
Roth, G. The unknowns
MEN -- SOCIAL CONDITIONS
See also Social conditions
MEN -- SOCIETIES
See also Clubs; Societies
MEN -- SOCIETIES
Brockway, C. No Place for a Dame
Men against the sea. Nordhoff, C.
The **men** and the girls. Trollope, J.
MEN IN BUSINESS *See* Businessmen
The **men** of Brewster Place. Naylor, G.
Mending. Bingham, S.
Mending the moon. Palwick, S.
MENNONITES
Toews, M. A complicated kindness
MENOPAUSE
See also Aging
MENTAL DEPRESSION
Hall, B. The music teacher
MENTAL DISEASES *See* Abnormal psychology; Mental illness
MENTAL HEALING
George, N. The little Paris bookshop
MENTAL HEALTH
Lennon, J. R. Familiar
MENTAL HEALTH
See also Happiness; Health
MENTAL HYGIENE *See* Mental health
MENTAL ILLNESS
Alexie, S. Indian killer
Banville, J. The book of evidence
Barry, B. The lace reader
Bauer, C. Frances and Bernard
Beattie, A. Chilly scenes of winter
Bulgakov, M. A. The master and Margarita
Cooley, M. The archivist
Didion, J. Play it as it lays
Findley, T. The piano man's daughter
Frame, J. Between my father and the king
Gibbons, K. Sights unseen
Gross, A. Eyes wide open
Guest, J. Ordinary people
Matheson, R. Hunted past reason
McGrath, P. Spider
Meno, J. The boy detective fails
Murr, N. The perfect man
Neugeboren, J. 1940
Noel, K. Halfway house
O'Farrell, M. The vanishing act of Esme Lennox
Percy, W. The moviegoer
Percy, W. The second coming
Plath, S. The bell jar
Price, N. Night woman
Pyper, A. The killing circle
Rendell, R. Going wrong
Rhys, J. Wide Sargasso Sea
Rock, P. The Shelter Cycle
Roth, P. When she was good
Schupack, D. The boy on the bus
Spark, M. The driver's seat

Vonnegut, K. Breakfast of champions
Vonnegut, K. Slaughterhouse-five
Walker, A. Possessing the secret of joy
MENTAL ILLNESS
See also Abnormal psychology; Diseases
MENTALLY HANDICAPPED
Steinbeck, J. Of mice and men
MENTALLY HANDICAPPED *See* People with mental disabilities
MENTALLY ILL
Banasky, C. The suicide of Claire Bishop
Hayder, M. Poppet
LaValle, V. D. The devil in silver
Matheson, R. Hunted past reason
Meno, J. The boy detective fails
Scottoline, L. Every fifteen minutes
Wallace, W. The painted bridge
MENTALLY ILL -- CARE AND TREATMENT
Foulds, A. The quickening maze
Greenberg, J. I never promised you a rose garden
Hollingshead, G. Bedlam
Kesey, K. One flew over the cuckoo's nest
LaValle, V. D. The devil in silver
Lehane, D. Shutter Island
McCullough, C. An indecent obsession
McGrath, P. Asylum
Newman, J. C. Mary
Piercy, M. Woman on the edge of time
Plath, S. The bell jar
Rosten, L. Captain Newman, M.D.
Self, W. Umbrella
Wallace, W. The painted bridge
Ward, M. J. The snake pit
Wharton, W. Birdy
MENTALLY RETARDED *See* People with mental disabilities
MERCEDES AUTOMOBILES
King, S. Mr. Mercedes
MERCENARY SOLDIERS
See also Military personnel; Soldiers
The **Merchant** Emperor. Haydon, E.
MERCHANT MARINE
See also Maritime law; Sailors; Ships; Transportation
MERCHANTS
Butcher, J. The aeronaut's windlass
Dunnett, D. Niccolo rising
Dunnett, D. Race of scorpions
Maalouf, A. Balthasar's odyssey
Naipaul, V. S. A bend in the river
MERCURY (PLANET)
Robinson, K. S. 2312
A **mercy.** Morrison, T.
MERCY
See also Ethics; Kindness
MERCY KILLING *See* Euthanasia
The **Mercy** Oak. Wall, K. R.
Mercy of a rude stream [series]
Roth, H. A diving rock on the Hudson
Roth, H. From bondage
Roth, H. Requiem for Harlem
Roth, H. A star shines over Mt. Morris Park
MERLIN (LEGENDARY CHARACTER)
Stewart, M. The crystal cave
Stewart, M. The hollow hills
Stewart, M. The last enchantment
White, T. H. The book of Merlyn
MERMAIDS
Shields, C. The republic of love
MESMERISM
Bolano, R. Monsieur Pain
MESMERISM *See* Hypnotism
Messalina, Valeria, d. 48
About
Graves, R. Claudius, the god and his wife Messalina
The **messenger.** Silva, D.
Messenger of truth. Winspear, J.
MESSENGERS
Hoag, T. Kill the messenger
METABOLIC DISORDERS
See also Diseases
Metamorphosis. Kafka, F.
METAPHYSICS
DeLillo, D. Point Omega
METEOROLOGISTS
Galchen, R. Atmospheric disturbances
Harrison, K. The seal wife
METEOROLOGY IN AERONAUTICS
See also Aeronautics; Meteorology
METRIC SYSTEM
See also Arithmetic; Mathematics
Metropole. Karinthy, F.
The **Meursault** investigation.
MEXICAN AMERICAN AUTHORS
See also Latino authors
MEXICAN AMERICAN BORDER REGION
Gaspar de Alba, A. Desert blood
MEXICAN AMERICAN WOMEN
See also Mexican Americans; Women
MEXICAN AMERICANS
Anaya, R. A. The man who could fly and other stories
Boyle, T. C. The tortilla curtain
Cisneros, S. The house on Mango Street
Gilb, D. The flowers
Martinez, N. M. Caramba!
Nichols, J. T. The Milagro beanfield war
Piercy, M. Woman on the edge of time
Skyhorse, B. The Madonnas of Echo Park
Tobar, H. The barbarian nurseries
Toole, F. X. Pound for pound
Villarreal, J. A. Pocho
Wiprud, B. M. Ringer
MEXICAN AMERICANS
See also Americans; Ethnic groups; Immigrants -- United States; Latinos (U.S.); Minorities

MEXICAN-AMERICAN BORDER REGION
Caputo, P. Crossers
Olmstead, R. Far bright star
Stone, M. Border child
MEXICANS
Irving, J. Avenue of mysteries
MEXICANS -- NEW YORK (N.Y.)
Wiprud, B. M. Ringer
MEXICANS -- UNITED STATES
Sekaran, S. Lucky boy
Urrea, L. A. Into the beautiful North
Mexico. Barkan, J.
Mexico. Michener, J. A.
MEXICO
Barkan, J. Mexico
Blake, J. C. The house of Wolfe
Bolano, R. 2666
Clement, J. Prayers for the stolen
Doerr, H. Stones for Ibarra
Esquivel, L. Like water for chocolate
Fuentes, C. Destiny and desire
Fuentes, C. The eagle's throne
Fuentes, C. The old gringo
Fuentes, C. The years with Laura Diaz
Gaspar de Alba, A. Desert blood
Greene, G. The power and the glory
Howard, L. Cry no more
Johansen, I. And then you die--
Lowry, M. Under the volcano
Luiselli, V. The story of my teeth
McCarthy, C. All the pretty horses
Michener, J. A. Mexico
Moya, H. C. The dream of my return
Portis, C. Gringos
Ruiz-Camacho, A. Barefoot dogs
Urrea, L. A. The hummingbird's daughter
Urrea, L. A. Into the beautiful North
Winslow, D. The cartel
MEXICO -- 16TH CENTURY
Sherwood, F. Night of sorrows
MEXICO -- 19TH CENTURY
Fuentes, C. The death of Artemio Cruz
Hambly, B. Days of the dead
MEXICO -- BAJA CALIFORNIA
Steinbeck, J. The pearl
MEXICO -- EMIGRATION AND IMMIGRATION
Stone, M. Border child
MEXICO -- HISTORY -- 1910-1920, REVOLUTION
Urrea, L. A. Queen of America
MEXICO -- JUAREZ
McCarthy, C. Cities of the plain
MEXICO -- MEXICO CITY
Gilman, D. The unexpected Mrs. Pollifax
MIAMI (FLA.)
Fielding, J. Someone Is Watching
Swinson, K. Playing dirty
Wolfe, T. Back to blood
MIAMI INDIANS
Thom, J. A. The red heart
Michael Tolliver lives. Maupin, A.
Michal
About
Edghill, I. Queenmaker
Michelangelo Buonarroti, 1475-1564
About
Stone, I. The agony and the ecstasy
MICHIGAN
Baxter, C. Saul and Patsy
Buntin, J. Marlena
Campbell, B. J. Once upon a river
Harrison, J. The great leader
Harrison, J. Returning to earth
Kasischke, L. The raising
MICHIGAN -- 20TH CENTURY
Cleage, P. What looks like crazy on an ordinary day--
Eugenides, J. The virgin suicides
MICHIGAN -- ANN ARBOR
Baxter, C. The feast of love
Dolan, H. Bad things happen
Dolan, H. Very bad men
MICHIGAN -- BATTLE CREEK
Boyle, T. C. Road to Wellville
MICHIGAN -- DETROIT
Arnow, H. L. S. The dollmaker
Bolano, R. 2666
Eugenides, J. Middlesex
Leithauser, B. The art student's war
Leonard, E. Freaky Deaky
Leonard, E. Mr. Paradise
Leonard, E. Pagan babies
Oates, J. C. Them
Yunis, A. The night counter
MICHIGAN, LAKE, REGION
Harbach, C. The art of fielding
MICROBES *See* Bacteria; Germ theory of disease; Microorganisms; Viruses
MICROORGANISMS
Crichton, M. The Andromeda strain
MICROPROCESSORS
See also Computers
MICROSCOPIC ORGANISMS *See* Microorganisms
Midaq Alley. Mahfouz, N.
Middle age. Oates, J. C.
MIDDLE AGE
Barnes, J. The sense of an ending
Connell, E. S. Mrs. Bridge
Ellis, B. E. Imperial bedrooms
Enright, A. The forgotten waltz
Ford, R. The lay of the land
Gordon, M. The love of my youth
Greenfeld, K. T. Triburbia
Harrison, J. The English major
Lessing, D. M. The memoirs of a survivor
Lewis, S. Dodsworth

Mann, T. The black swan
Nadzam, B. Lamb
Oates, J. C. Middle age
Phillips, A. The song is you
Price, R. The good priest's son
Savage, S. The cry of the sloth
Smith, A. There but for the
Spark, M. The prime of Miss Jean Brodie
Straub, E. Modern lovers
Tyler, A. The accidental tourist
Tyler, A. Breathing lessons
Tyler, A. Ladder of years
Williams, T. The Roman spring of Mrs. Stone
MIDDLE AGED MEN
Ferris, J. To Rise Again at a Decent Hour
Tyler, A. The beginner's goodbye
MIDDLE AGED PERSONS
Link, T. Denting the Bosch
MIDDLE AGED WOMEN
Green, J. Tempting fate
Seitz, N. Trouble the water
MIDDLE AGES
Anderson, P. War of the Gods
Connell, E. S. Deus lo volt!
Cornwell, B. Enemy of God
Cornwell, B. Excalibur
Cornwell, B. The winter king
Crichton, M. Timeline
Cutter, K. The maid
Follett, K. The pillars of the earth
Follett, K. World without end
Haasse, H. S. In a dark wood wandering
Holland, C. Jerusalem
Jones, S. Four sisters, all queens
Riley, J. M. In pursuit of the green lion
Riley, J. M. A vision of light
Twain, M. Personal recollections of Joan of Arc
Undset, S. Kristin Lavransdatter
Unsworth, B. The ruby in her navel
White, T. H. The once and future king
White, T. H. The sword in the stone
MIDDLE AGES -- HISTORY *See* Middle Ages
Middle C. Gass, W. H.
MIDDLE CLASS
See also Social classes
MIDDLE CLASSES
Ballard, J. G. Millennium people
Berger, T. Neighbors
Cheever, J. Bullet Park
Connell, E. S. Mrs. Bridge
Eliot, G. Middlemarch
Franzen, J. Freedom
Lewis, S. Babbitt
Tanizaki, J. The Makioka sisters
Wilson, S. The man in the gray flannel suit
Wouk, H. Marjorie Morningstar
MIDDLE EAST
Ignatius, D. Body of lies
Poyer, D. The gulf
Silva, D. The messenger
Silva, D. Prince of Fire
Wilson, G. W. Alif the unseen
The **middle** heart. Lord, B. B.
Middle men. Gavin, J.
Middle of nowhere. Pearson, R.
Middle passage. Johnson, C. R.
MIDDLE SCHOOL
Minato, K. Confessions
MIDDLE WEST
McGuane, T. Crow fair
Scapellato, J. Big Lonesome
MIDDLE WESTERN STATES
Boswell, R. Century's son
Hoover, M. The quickening
Moore, L. A gate at the stairs
Patterson, R. N. Dark lady
Powers, J. F. Wheat that springeth green
Roth, P. When she was good
Simpson, M. Anywhere but here
MIDDLE-AGED MEN
Begley, L. About Schmidt
Ford, R. Let Me Be Frank With You
Nicholls, D. Us
Tyler, A. The beginner's goodbye
MIDDLE-AGED PERSONS
Link, T. Denting the Bosch
MIDDLE-AGED WOMEN
Fielding, H. Bridget Jones
Green, J. Tempting fate
Seitz, N. Trouble the water
Middlemarch. Eliot, G.
Middlesex. Eugenides, J.
The **Middlesteins.** Attenberg, J.
MIDLIFE CRISIS
See also Middle age
Midnight at the Dragon Café. Bates, J. F.
Midnight Bayou. Roberts, N.
Midnight cowboy. Herlihy, J. L.
Midnight movie. Hooper, T.
Midnight riot. Aaronovitch, B.
Midnight runner. Higgins, J.
Midnight voices. Saul, J.
Midnight's children. Rushdie, S.
MIDSHIPMEN
Webb, J. A sense of honor
Midsummer night. Warrington, F.
MIDWEST *See* Middle West
The **midwife** of Hope River. Harman, P.
MIDWIFERY *See* Midwives
MIDWIVES -- FICTION
Elison, M. The Book of the Unnamed Midwife
Frog
Harman, P. The midwife of Hope River
Hepworth, S. The Secrets of Midwives

Joyce, G. The limits of enchantment
Riley, J. M. A vision of light
Watson, C. Tiny sunbirds, far away
MIDWIVES -- NEW YORK (STATE) -- NEW YORK
Thompson, V. Murder on Fifth Avenue
The **mighty** Walzer. Jacobson, H.
MIGRANT LABOR
Guterson, D. Our Lady of the Forest
Oates, J. C. A garden of earthly delights
Steinbeck, J. The grapes of wrath
Steinbeck, J. In dubious battle
Steinbeck, J. Of mice and men
Straight, S. Highwire moon
MIGRATION, INTERNAL -- INDIA
Mukherjee, N. A state of freedom
MIGRATORY WORKERS *See* Migrant labor
Mike Bowditch Mysteries [series]
Doiron, P. The Precipice
The **Mike** Hammer collection [v1] Spillane, M.
The **Mike** Hammer collection [v2] Spillane, M.
Mila 18. Uris, L.
The **Milagro** beanfield war. Nichols, J. T.
MILITARY AERONAUTICS
Heller, J. Catch-22
Malraux, A. Man's hope
MILITARY DESERTION
Frazier, C. Cold Mountain
Hemingway, E. A farewell to arms
O'Brien, T. Going after Cacciato
MILITARY EDUCATION
Vargas Llosa, M. The time of the hero
Webb, J. A sense of honor
MILITARY OCCUPATION
See also War
MILITARY OFFENSES
See also Criminal law; Military law
MILITARY PERSONNEL
See also Armed forces; War
MILITARY PERSONNEL
Atxaga, B. Seven houses in France
Dowlatabadi, M. The colonel
Limón, M. Mr. Kill
Omarsdottir, K. Children in Reindeer Woods
MILITARY PERSONNEL -- UNITED STATES
Rich, D. Caravan of thieves
Scottoline, L. Don't Go
MILITARY RESEARCH
See also Research
MILITARY RESEARCH -- SOVIET UNION
Eastland, S. Shadow pass
MILITARY SCHOOLS *See* Military education
MILITARY SPOUSES
Fallon, S. You know when the men are gone
Hannah, K. Home front
Itani, F. Tell
Portrait of the mother as a young woman
MILITARY TRAINING *See* Military education
MILITARY TRAINING CAMPS
McCullers, C. Reflections in a golden eye
MILITARY TRAINING CAMPS
See also Military education
MILITARY WEAPONS
Eastland, S. Shadow pass
MILITIA MOVEMENTS
Isaacs, S. Red, white and blue
Land, J. Strong at the break
MILITIAS *See* Militia movements
MILK
See also Dairy products; Dairying; Food
Milk and honey. Kellerman, F.
MILL AND FACTORY BUILDINGS *See* Factories
The **mill** on the Floss. Eliot, G.
MILLENNIALISM
Palahniuk, C. Fight Club
Millennium [series]
Lagercrantz, D. The Girl in the Spider's Web
Millennium people. Ballard, J. G.
Millennium series
Lagercrantz, D. The girl who takes an eye for an eye
Miller, Karen E. Quinones
About
Miller, K. E. Q. An angry-ass black woman
MILLHONE, KINSEY (FICTITIOUS CHARACTER)
Grafton, S. X
Grafton, S. N is for noose
Grafton, S. P is for peril
Grafton, S. Q is for quarry
A **million** nightingales. Straight, S.
MILLIONAIRES
Bellow, S. Henderson the rain king
Fowles, J. The magus
Guterson, D. Ed King
Palahniuk, C. Beautiful you
Vonnegut, K. God bless you, Mr. Rosewater
Wiprud, B. M. Ringer
The **mime** order. Shannon, S.
MIMES
Ackroyd, P. The trial of Elizabeth Cree
MIND AND BODY
Lightman, A. P. The diagnosis
MIND AND BODY
See also Brain; Medicine; Parapsychology; Philosophy
MIND AND REALITY
Hosking, J. Three years with the rat
McCarthy, T. Satin Island
Mind prey. Sandford, J.
MIND READING *See* Telepathy
Minds of winter. O'Loughlin, E.
MINE RESCUE WORK
Doig, I. Work song
Mineral spirits. Sharfeddin, H.
MINERALS IN HUMAN NUTRITION
See also Food; Minerals; Nutrition
MINERS -- FICTION

Cramer, W. D. Bad ground
Doig, I. Work song
MINES AND MINING
Stegner, W. E. Angle of repose
MINING ENGINEERING
See also Civil engineering; Coal mines and mining; Engineering; Mines and mineral resources
MINISTERS (DIPLOMATIC AGENTS) *See* Diplomats
MINISTERS OF THE GOSPEL *See* Clergy
The **Ministry** of Special Cases. Englander, N.
The **ministry** of utmost happiness. Roy, A.
MINNEAPOLIS (MINN.)
Hoag, T. Dust to dust
Sandford, J. Silken prey
Sandford, J. Naked prey
Tracy, P. J. Monkeewrench
MINNESOTA
Enger, L. Undiscovered country
Hoag, T. Guilty as sin
Hoag, T. Night sins
Hustvedt, S. The sorrows of an American
The Land of Dreams
Lewis, S. Main Street
Lourey, J. January thaw
O'Brien, T. In the Lake of the Woods
Sidor, S. Pitch dark
Strayed, C. Torch
Treuer, D. Prudence
Watson, L. American boy
MINNESOTA -- ST. PAUL
Franzen, J. Freedom
Reimringer, J. Vestments
Minnesota trilogy [series]
The Land of Dreams
MINOR LEAGUE BASEBALL
See also Baseball
MINOR PLANETS *See* Asteroids
MINORITIES
Unnikrishnan, D. Temporary people
The **minority** report. Dick, P. K.
The **minotaur.** Vine, B.
MINOTAUR (GREEK MYTHOLOGY)
Sherrill, S. The minotaur takes his own sweet time
The **minotaur** takes his own sweet time. Sherrill, S.
MINSTRELS
See also Poets
Miracle cure. Palmer, M.
Miracle on 34th Street. Davies, V.
MIRACLES
Paretsky, S. Ghost country
Werfel, F. The song of Bernadette
Miranda, Francisco de, 1750-1816
About
Naipaul, V. S. A way in the world
The **Mirror** Empire. Hurley, K.
The **mirror** thief. Seay, M.
MIRRORS
Seay, M. The mirror thief
MISCARRIAGE
See also Pregnancy
MISCEGENATION
Paton, A. Too late the phalarope
Tademy, L. Cane River
Mischief in Maggody. Hess, J.
Mischling. Konar, A.
MISCONDUCT IN OFFICE
See also Conflict of interests; Criminal law
MISDEMEANORS (LAW) *See* Criminal law
MISERS
Dickens, C. A Christmas carol
Eliot, G. Silas Marner
Misery. King, S.
Misery loves Maggody. Hess, J.
Miss Burma. Craig, C.
Miss Jane. Watson, B.
Miss New India. Mukherjee, B.
Miss Pinkerton: adventures of a nurse detective. Rinehart, M. R.
The **missing.** Lewis, B.
MISSING CHILDREN
Bock, C. Beautiful children
Brown, K. The longings of wayward girls
Cain, C. One Kick
Coben, H. Hold tight
Corleone, D. Good as gone
Danticat, E. Claire of the sea light
Dazieri, S. Kill the father
French, N. Blue Monday
Grant, H. The vanishing of Katharina Linden
Greene, A. Long Man
Griffiths, E. The crossing places
Grossman, P. Children of wrath
Hamer, K. The girl in the red coat
Hart, J. The last child
Harvey, J. Far cry
Hayder, M. The treatment
Hensher, P. King of the badgers
Howard, L. Cry no more
Irwin, S. M. The dead path
Kunzru, H. Gods without men
Lelic, S. The child who
Levien, D. City of the sun
Martin, L. The bright forever
McDermid, V. A place of execution
McEwan, I. The child in time
Meloy, M. Do not become alarmed
Mitchard, J. The deep end of the ocean
Mitchard, J. No time to wave goodbye
Oates, J. C. Carthage
Oates, J. C. Daddy Love
Ohlsson, K. Unwanted
Penny, L. The nature of the beast
Powell, S. The Mushroom Man
Roy, L. Bent Road

Schaffert, T. The coffins of Little Hope
Schwartz, L. Angels Crest
Stone, M. Border child
Theorin, J. Echoes from the dead
MISSING CHILDREN
See also Children; Missing persons
MISSING IN ACTION
See also Prisoners of war; Soldiers
Missing mom. Oates, J. C.
Missing persons. White, S. W.
MISSING PERSONS
Alarcon, D. Lost City Radio
Alexander, V. The lady travelers guide to scoundrels & other gentlemen
Atkinson, K. Started early, took my dog
Bauer, B. Blacklands
Black, C. Murder in the Sentier
Bolaño, R. The Third Reich
Bolano, R. 2666
Box, C. J. The highway
Brkic, C. A. The First Rule of Swimming
Carter, M. J. The Strangler Vine
Chancellor, B. Sycamore
Church, J. A drop of Chinese blood
Coben, H. Caught
Coben, H. Stay close
Coetzee, J. M. The Childhood of Jesus
Cook, T. H. The fate of Katherine Carr
Delaney, F. The matchmaker of Kenmare
Dickens, C. The mystery of Edwin Drood
Doiron, P. Bad Little Falls
Doiron, P. The Precipice
Dugoni, R. My sister's grave
Edugyan, E. Half-blood blues
Enger, L. The high divide
Englander, N. The Ministry of Special Cases
Ferraris, Z. Kingdom of strangers
Finder, J. Buried secrets
Finder, J. Vanished
Flynn, G. Gone girl
Flynn, M. In the Lion's Mouth
Franklin, T. Crooked letter, crooked letter
French, T. Faithful Place
Galloway, G. As simple as snow
Gardner, L. The neighbor
Gaspar de Alba, A. Desert blood
George, E. Just one evil act
Goddard, R. Into the blue
Gracie, A. To catch a bride
Griffin, K. Glass God
Gross, G. When she was gone
Hambly, B. Good man Friday
Harvey, M. The governor's wife
Healey, E. Elizabeth is missing
Hill, S. Shadows in the street
Hosking, J. Three years with the rat
Hunter, E. The moment she was gone
Indridason, A. Outrage
Ishiguro, K. When we were orphans
Joyce, G. Some kind of fairy tale
Kelly, E. The burning air
Krentz, J. A. When all the girls have gone
Larsson, S. The girl with the dragon tattoo
Le Carre, J. A perfect spy
Lebrecht, N. The song of names
Lee On such a full sea
Lee, D. Country of origin
Les Becquets, D. Breaking wild
Lichtenstein, A. Lost
Liss, D. The whiskey rebels
Livesey, M. Banishing Verona
Lynn, A. Now you see it
MacBride, S. Close to the Bone
Matar, H. Anatomy of a disappearance
McCall Smith, A. The No. 1 Ladies' Detective Agency
McCann, C. Thirteen ways of looking
McMahon, J. The One I Left Behind
Michener, J. A. Caravans
Mosley, W. Little Scarlet
Muller, M. Cyanide Wells
O'Brien, T. In the Lake of the Woods
O'Farrell, M. Instructions for a heat wave
O'Nan, S. Songs for the missing
Ondaatje, M. In the skin of a lion
Palaia, M. The given world
Penney, S. The invisible ones
Picoult, J. Leaving Time
Picoult, J. Vanishing acts
Pittard, H. The fates will find their way
Reisman, N. The first desire
Robinson, L. Water dogs
Robotham, M. Say you're sorry
Romano, S. Resurrection Express
Roy, L. Until she comes home
Salak, K. The white Mary
Sanchez, T. King Bongo
Scott, J. Tourmaline
Semple, M. Where'd you go, Bernadette
Shapiro, B. A. The muralist
Simmons, D. The abominable
Smith, M. C. Rose
The snowman
Spark, M. Aiding and abetting
Speller, E. The strange fate of Kitty Easton
Stevens, T. The informationist
Straub, P. Lost boy lost girl
Sundaresan, I. The splendor of silence
Tan, A. Saving fish from drowning
Tremblay, P. Disappearance at Devil's Rock
Tyler, A. Searching for Caleb
Vanderhaeghe, G. The last crossing
Walters, M. The echo
White, S. W. Missing persons
MISSING PERSONS

See also Criminal investigation
MISSING PERSONS -- DRAMA
Edwardson, Å. Sail of stone
MISSING PERSONS -- INVESTIGATION
Adler-Olsen, J. The keeper of lost causes
Dean, A. Bellfield Hall, or, The observations of Miss Dido Kent
Grant, H. The vanishing of Katharina Linden
Krentz, J. A. When all the girls have gone
Missing reels. Nehme, F. S.
The **missing** world. Livesey, M.
Mission to Paris. Furst, A.
MISSIONARIES
Achebe, C. Things fall apart
Cather, W. Death comes for the archbishop
Cronin, A. J. The keys of the kingdom
Endo, S. Silence
Forester, C. S. The African Queen
Jin, H. Nanjing requiem
Kingsolver, B. The poisonwood Bible
Lee The surrendered
Marks, J. Fangland
Marshall, C. Christy
Melville, H. Omoo: a narrative of adventures in the South Seas
Michener, J. A. Hawaii
Vollmann, W. T. Fathers and crows
MISSISSIPPI
Atkins, A. The forsaken
Atkins, A. The ranger
Berg, E. We are all welcome here
Brown, L. Joe
Cheng, B. Southern Cross the Dog
Cook, T. H. Master of the delta
Faulkner, W. Light in August
Faulkner, W. Go down, Moses
Faulkner, W. The hamlet
Faulkner, W. Intruder in the dust
Faulkner, W. Requiem for a nun
Faulkner, W. Sanctuary
Faulkner, W. The sound and the fury
Franklin, T. Crooked letter, crooked letter
French, A. Billy
Grisham, J. Ford County
Grisham, J. The last juror
Grisham, J. A time to kill
Hunter, S. Pale horse coming
Iles, G. The bone tree
Iles, G. The devil's punchbowl
Iles, G. Third degree
Logan, C. South of Shiloh
Marlette, D. Magic time
Morris, W. Taps
Nordan, L. Wolf whistle
Phillips, S. E. Ain't she sweet
Spencer, E. The stories of Elizabeth Spencer
Tartt, D. The little friend
Vernon, O. Eden
Vernon, O. A killing in this town
Ward, J. Salvage the bones
Ward, J. Sing, unburied, sing
Watson, B. The heaven of Mercury
Welty, E. Delta wedding
Welty, E. Losing battles
Welty, E. The optimist's daughter
Welty, E. The Ponder heart
Yarbrough, S. The end of California
Yarbrough, S. Prisoners of war
Yarbrough, S. Safe from the neighbors
MISSISSIPPI -- 19TH CENTURY
Faulkner, W. Absalom, Absalom!
MISSISSIPPI -- JACKSON
Stockett, K. The help
MISSISSIPPI -- NATCHEZ
Iles, G. Turning angel
MISSISSIPPI -- RACE RELATIONS
Jordan, H. Mudbound
McFadden, B. L. Gathering of waters
Stockett, K. The help
Mississippi blood. Iles, G.
MISSISSIPPI RIVER
Clinch, J. Finn
Twain, M. Mississippi writings
Welty, E. The robber bridegroom
Mississippi writings. Twain, M.
MISSOURI
Clinch, J. Finn
Dalton, J. The inverted forest
Flagg, F. Standing in the rainbow
Flynn, G. Sharp objects
Kinder, R. M. An absolute gentleman
Murr, N. The perfect man
Spencer, L. Small town girl
Twain, M. Pudd'nhead Wilson;
Woodrell, D. The death of sweet mister
Woodrell, D. Give us a kiss
MISSOURI -- 19TH CENTURY
Jiles, P. Enemy women
MISSOURI -- KANSAS CITY
Connell, E. S. Mrs. Bridge
MISSOURI -- SAINT LOUIS
Shange, N. Betsey Brown
MISSOURI RIVER
McMurtry, L. Sin killer
A **mist** of prophecies. Saylor, S.
Mistaken identity. Scottoline, L.
MISTAKEN IDENTITY
Collins, W. The woman in white
Putney, M. J. Loving a lost lord
Quirk, M. Cold barrel zero
Stewart, M. The ivy tree
Wiprud, B. M. Ringer
Mistborn [series]
Sanderson, B. The final empire

Mister Memory. Sedgwick, M.
Mister monkey. Prose, F.
Mister Roberts. Heggen, T.
Misterioso. Dahl, A.
Mistral's daughter. Krantz, J.
Mistress of the art of death. Franklin, A.
Mistress of the pearl. Lustbader, E. V.
MISTRESSES
Cameron, P. The city of your final destination
Faber, M. The crimson petal and the white
Gregory, P. The other Boleyn girl
Hambly, B. Patriot hearts
King, R. Domino
Martin, V. Property
Trollope, J. Marrying the mistress
The **mists** of Avalon. Bradley, M. Z.
MITFORD (N.C. : IMAGINARY PLACE)
Karon, J. At home in Mitford
Mitigating circumstances. Rosenberg, N. T.
MIXED BLOODS
Alexie, S. Flight
Eng, T. T. The gift of rain
Erdrich, L. The Beet Queen
Humphreys, J. Nowhere else on earth
Murr, N. The perfect man
MIXED MARRIAGE *See* Interfaith marriage; Intermarriage
Mo said she was quirky. Kelman, J.
MOBILE (ALA.)
Kerley, J. The death collectors
MOBSTERS
Higgins, J. Luciano's luck
Latour, J. The Havana World Series
Moby-Dick; or, The whale. Melville, H.
MOCK-HEROIC LITERATURE
See also Literature; Wit and humor
Model home. Puchner, E.
MODELS *See* Artists' models; Fashion models; Mathematical models; Models and modelmaking
MODELS (PERSONS) *See* Artists' models; Fashion models
MODELS (PERSONS)
Bagshawe, T. Adored
Gaitskill, M. Veronica
MODELS, ARTISTS' *See* Artists' models
MODERN CIVILIZATION
Numero Zero
MODERN GREEK LANGUAGE
See also Language and languages
MODERN HISTORY -- 1900-1999 (20TH CENTURY) *See* World history -- 20th century
MODERN LANGUAGES
See also Language and languages
The Modern Library classics [series]
Cooper, J. F. The last of the Mohicans
Larsen, N. Passing
Twain, M. Pudd'nhead Wilson;
Modern lovers. Straub, E.
MODERNISM IN ART
See also Art; Modernism (Aesthetics)
Modiano, Patrick, 1945-
About
Modiano, P. Suspended sentences
MOGUL EMPIRE
Rushdie, S. The enchantress of Florence
MOHAWK VALLEY (N.Y.)
Edmonds, W. D. Drums along the Mohawk
MOHEGAN INDIANS
Cooper, J. F. The last of the Mohicans
Mohr. Reuss, F.
Mohr, Max, 1891-1937
About
Reuss, F. Mohr
MOJAVE DESERT (CALIF.)
Kunzru, H. Gods without men
McCormick, C. Desert boys
MOLECULAR CLONING
See also Cloning; Genetic engineering
MOLECULAR TECHNOLOGY *See* Nanotechnology
MOLES (SPIES)
Jin, H. A map of betrayal
MOLESTING OF CHILDREN *See* Child sexual abuse
Moll Flanders. Defoe, D.
Molloy, Malone dies, The unnamable. Beckett, S.
The **moment.** Kennedy, D.
Moment in Peking. Lin Yutang
A **moment** in the sun. Sayles, J.
Moment of truth. Scottoline, L.
The **moment** she was gone. Hunter, E.
Mona in the promised land. Jen, G.
MONARCHS *See* Kings and rulers
MONASTERIES
Penny, L. The beautiful mystery
MONASTICISM AND RELIGIOUS ORDERS
Gulik, R. H. v. The haunted monastery
Miller, W. M. A canticle for Leibowitz
Monday the rabbi took off. Kemelman, H.
Monet, Claude, 1840-1926
About
Jakeman, J. In the Kingdom of mists
MONEY
Bender, K. E. Refund
Money for nothing. Westlake, D. E.
MONEY LAUNDERING
Pearson, T. R. Beluga
MONEY RAISING *See* Fund raising
Money shot. Faust, C.
Money to burn. Grippando, J.
MONEYLENDERS
Dickens, C. Nicholas Nickleby
MONGOLIA
Jiang Rong Wolf totem
Mongoose, R.I.P. Buckley, W. F.
Monika Paniatowski mysteries [series]
Spencer, S. The dead hand of history
Spencer, S. Echoes of the dead

The **monk.** Lewis, M. G.
Monk's-hood. Peters, E.
MONK, WILLIAM (FICTITIOUS CHARACTER)
Perry, A. A sunless sea
Perry, A. Funeral in blue
Perry, A. Slaves of obsession
Monkeewrench. Tracy, P. J.
Monkey hunting. Garcia, C.
The **monkey's** wedding, and other stories. Aiken, J.
The **monkey's** wrench. Levi, P.
MONKS
Eco, U. The name of the rose
Kadare, I. The three-arched bridge
Lewis, M. G. The monk
McCann, C. Let the great world spin
Pattison, E. The skull mantra
Penny, L. The beautiful mystery
The Poisoned Pilgrim
Preston, D. The wheel of darkness
Toyne, S. Sanctus
Unsworth, B. Morality play
MONKS -- SPAIN -- MADRID -- SEXUAL BEHAVIOR
Lewis, M. G. The monk
MONMOUTH'S REBELLION, 1685
Blackmore, R. D. Lorna Doone
MONMOUTHSHIRE (WALES)
Putney, M. J. Stolen magic
MONOLOGUES
Hamid, M. The reluctant fundamentalist
Monroe, Marilyn, 1926-1962
About
Oates, J. C. Blonde
Monsieur Pain. Bolano, R.
Monsoon. Smith, W. A.
Monster. Kellerman, J.
A **monster's** notes. Sheck, L.
MONSTERS
See also Animals -- Folklore; Curiosities and wonders; Folklore; Mythology
MONSTERS
Frei, M. The stranger's magic
Groff, L. The monsters of Templeton
Kosmatka, T. The games
Lafferty, M. The shambling guide to New York City
Nicholas, D. Something red
Perry, S. The Essex Serpent
Saadawi, A. Frankenstein in Baghdad
White, E. K. Heartstone
The **monsters** of Templeton. Groff, L.
Monstrous regiment. Pratchett, T.
MONTANA
Doig, I. Work song
Doig, I. Bucking the sun
Doig, I. Dancing at the Rascal Fair
Doig, I. The eleventh man
Doig, I. English Creek
Doig, I. The whistling season
Evans, N. The horse whisperer
Kennedy, D. The big picture
Kittredge, W. The Willow Field
McGuane, T. The cadence of grass
McGuane, T. Nothing but blue skies
Ray, S. American masculine
Ryan, J. His cowboy heart
Sharfeddin, H. Mineral spirits
Welch, J. The Indian lawyer
MONTANA -- 19TH CENTURY
Williamson, P. Heart of the west
Williamson, P. The outsider
Montana dawn. Wallace, S.
Montana men [series]
Ryan, J. His cowboy heart
Montano's malady. Vila-Matas, E.
Monte Walsh. Schaefer, J. W.
Montezuma II, Emperor of Mexico, ca. 1480-1520
About
Levack, S. Demon of the air
Montfort, Simon de, Earl of Leicester, 1208?-1265
About
Penman, S. K. Falls the shadow
MONTMARTRE (PARIS, FRANCE)
The Book of Harlan
MOON
Heinlein, R. A. The moon is a harsh mistress
Verne, J. From the earth to the moon, and Round the moon
Weir, A. Artemis
MOON -- EXPLORATION
See also Space flight to the moon
The **moon** and sixpence. Maugham, W. S.
The **moon** is a harsh mistress. Heinlein, R. A.
The **moon** sisters. Walsh, T.
Moon tiger. Lively, P.
The **moon** tunnel. Kelly, J.
MOON WORSHIP
See also Religion
MOON, VOYAGES TO *See* Space flight to the moon
The **moon-spinners.** Stewart, M.
Moondogs. Yates, A.
Moonglow. Chabon, M.
Moonshine. Johnson, A. D.
MOONSHINERS
Faulkner, W. Sanctuary
The **moonstone.** Collins, W.
The **Moor's** account. Lalami, L.
The **Moor's** last sigh. Rushdie, S.
MORALITY
Morrow, J. The philosopher's apprentice
MORALITY *See* Ethics
Morality play. Unsworth, B.
MORALITY STORIES *See* Didactic fiction
MORALITY TALES *See* Parables
MORALS *See* Conduct of life; Ethics; Human behavior; Moral conditions
More of this world or maybe another. Johnson, B.

More than a mistress. Balogh, M.
The **Morels.** Hacker, C.
Morgan's passing. Tyler, A.
MORGON, LOUIS (FICTITIOUS CHARACTER)
Steiner, P. The resistance
Moriarty. Horowitz, A.
MORMONS AND MORMONISM
Ebershoff, D. The 19th wife
Grey, Z. Riders of the purple sage
Harrison, M. I. The Bishop's Wife
Udall, B. The lonely polygamist
Morning glory. Spencer, L.
Morning Star. Brown, P.
MOROCCO
Duenas, M. The time in between
McHugh, M. F. Nekropolis
MOROCCO -- RACE RELATIONS
Osborne, L. The forgiven
Mortal. Dekker, T.
Mortal fear. Iles, G.
Mortals. Rush, N.
MORTICIANS *See* Undertakers and undertaking
MORTUARY CUSTOMS *See* Cremation; Funeral rites and ceremonies
MOSAIC DESIGNERS
Vreeland, S. Clara and Mr. Tiffany
MOSCOW (RUSSIA) -- HISTORY
Towles, A. A Gentleman in Moscow
Moses (Biblical leader)
About
Wouk, H. The lawgiver
Moshi moshi.
MOSLEMS *See* Muslims
MOSQUE OFFICERS
See also Muslims
Mosquito. Tearne, R.
The **Mosquito** Coast. Theroux, P.
MOSQUITOES
See also Insects
MOSQUITOES -- CONTROL
See also Pest control
The **most** dangerous place on earth. Johnson, L. L.
The **most** dangerous thing. Lippman, L.
A **most** novel revenge. Weaver, A.
A **most** wanted man. Le Carre, J.
Mostly harmless. Adams, D.
The **Mote** in God's Eye. Niven, L.
The **moth** diaries. Klein, R.
MOTHER AND CHILD *See* Mother-child relationship
MOTHER AND CHILD
Donoghue, E. Room
Drabble, M. The pure gold baby
Ford, J. Songs of Willow Frost
Moshi moshi
A **mother** and two daughters. Godwin, G.
Mother, mother. Zailckas, K.
MOTHER-CHILD RELATIONSHIP
See also Children; Mothers; Parent-child relationship
MOTHER-CHILD RELATIONSHIP
Back to Back
Eggers, D. Heroes of the frontier
Enright, A. The Green Road
Ford, J. Songs of Willow Frost
Gurganus, A. Local souls
Lackberg, C. The lost boy
Malerman, J. Bird Box
Mathis, A. The twelve tribes of Hattie
Moshi moshi
Solomon, A. Leaving Lucy Pear
Zailckas, K. Mother, mother
MOTHER-DAUGHTER RELATIONSHIP
See also Daughters; Mother-child relationship; Mothers
MOTHER-DAUGHTER RELATIONSHIP
Absolution
Aliu, X. Brass
Austin, L. All she ever wanted
Campbell, B. J. Mothers, tell your daughters
Conrad, H. Toured to Death
Czepiel, K. L. A violet season
Decarlo, M. The Art of Crash Landing
Evison, J. This is your life, Harriet Chance!
Fox, L. Days of awe
Hamer, K. The girl in the red coat
Hassman, T. Girlchild
Jackson, J. A grown up kind of pretty
Jackson, J. The opposite of everyone
Jemisin, N. K. The obelisk gate
Keller, J. A killing in the hills
Kent, K. The heretic's daughter
Kingsolver, B. Pigs in heaven
Kirkpatrick, J. This road we traveled
Lange, R. Angel baby
Levy, D. Hot Milk
Lewis, B. The missing
Lupton, R. Afterwards
Mazzarella, N. This heavy silence
McLaren, K. The road to enchantment
McMahon, J. The One I Left Behind
Morrison, T. Beloved
Nadler, S. The inseparables
Ndiaye, M. Ladivine
Picoult, J. Leaving Time
Rotert, R. Last night at the blue angel
Semple, M. Where'd you go, Bernadette
Strout, E. Anything is possible
Strout, E. My name is Lucy Barton
Tan, A. The Valley of Amazement
Vann, D. Aquarium
Wells, R. Divine secrets of the Ya-Ya Sisterhood
Wiseman, B. Plain paradise
MOTHER-SON RELATIONSHIP
See also Mother-child relationship; Mothers; Sons
MOTHER-SON RELATIONSHIP
Coetzee, J. M. The Childhood of Jesus

Donoghue, E. Room
Erdrich, L. Four souls
Everett, P. Erasure
Grodstein, L. Our short history
Hannaham, J. Delicious Foods
Hill, N. The Nix
Jeffries, S. 'Twas the night after Christmas
Ko, L. The leavers
Lodato, V. Edgar and Lucy
Maguire, G. Son of a witch
O'Malley, T. This magnificent desolation
Palahniuk, C. Choke
Phillips, G. Fierce kingdom
Rojstaczer, S. The Mathematician's Shiva
Samuel, B. No place like home

MOTHERHOOD

Bergman, M. M. Birds of a lesser paradise
Motherlunge
Onstad, K. Everybody Has Everything

Mothering Sunday. Swift, G.
MotherKind. Phillips, J. A.
Motherland. Nicholson, W.
Motherless Brooklyn. Lethem, J.
Motherlunge.
The **mothers.** Bennett, B.

MOTHERS

Albert, E. After Birth
Arnow, H. L. S. The dollmaker
Colwin, L. A big storm knocked it over
Colwin, L. Goodbye without leaving
Doughty, L. Whatever you love
Edgarian, C. Three stages of amazement
Egan, E. A window opens
Giffin, E. Heart of the matter
Goudge, E. Thorns of truth
Grunwald, L. The irresistible Henry House
Hannah, S. The cradle in the grave
Hannah, S. The wrong mother
Hood, A. The red thread
Lee, M. G. Somebody's daughter
Lippman, L. Hush hush
McCann, C. Thirteen ways of looking
Morrison, T. God help the child
Moses, K. Wintering
Oates, J. C. Them
O'Farrell, M. The hand that first held mine
Pilcher, R. The shell seekers
Quindlen, A. Every last one
Smith, L. Family linen
Tóibín, C. Nora Webster
Trollope, J. Second honeymoon
Trueblood, V. Seven loves
Weiner, J. Then came you
Weiner, J. Little earthquakes

MOTHERS

See also Family; Women

The **Mothers.** Gilmore, J.

MOTHERS -- DEATH

Hartnett, A. Rabbit cake
Harwood, J. The ghost writer
Lipman, E. The dearly departed
Macmillan, G. The perfect girl
Robards, K. Ghost moon
Searles, J. Boy still missing

MOTHERS AND DAUGHTERS

Allen, S. A. The sugar queen
Berg, E. We are all welcome here
Berg, E. What we keep
Bijan, D. The last days of Café Leila
Binchy, M. The glass lake
Blatty, W. P. The exorcist
Brown, R. Half a heart
Coster, N. Halsey Street
Didion, J. A book of common prayer
Dorris, M. A yellow raft in blue water
Dubus, A. The garden of last days
Erdrich, L. The painted drum
Evans, N. The horse whisperer
Ferrante, E. The lost daughter
Fitch, J. White oleander
Garcia, C. Dreaming in Cuban
Gardam, J. God on the rocks
Gibbons, K. Sights unseen
Godwin, G. A mother and two daughters
Goodman, C. Arcadia Falls
Goudge, E. Garden of lies
Gowdy, B. Helpless
Greene, A. Bloodroot
Gregory, D. Raising Stony Mayhall
Griesemer, J. Signal & noise
Hagedorn, J. T. Toxicology
Hannah, K. Winter garden
Harris, J. Chocolat
Harris, J. Five quarters of the orange
Hilderbrand, E. The island
Hodgen, C. Elegies for the brokenhearted
Hoffman, A. The probable future
Hoffman, A. The story sisters
Hood, A. The knitting circle
Jackson, J. Between, Georgia
Jakes, J. Savannah; or, A gift for Mr. Lincoln
James, P. D. Innocent blood
Jemisin, N. K. The stone sky
Jones, T. Silver sparrow
Joyce, G. The limits of enchantment
Kadare, I. The ghost rider
Kent, K. The heretic's daughter
Kincaid, J. Annie John
Kincaid, J. Autobiography of my mother
Kingsolver, B. Pigs in heaven
Kirshenbaum, B. An almost perfect moment
Krantz, J. Mistral's daughter
Kwok, J. Girl in translation
Lamott, A. Blue shoe

Leroy, M. Postcards from Berlin
Lippman, L. I'd know you anywhere
Lively, P. Consequences
Lively, P. Passing on
Manicka, R. The rice mother
Maxwell, R. The secret diary of Anne Boleyn
McCann, C. Let the great world spin
McMurtry, L. Buffalo girls
McMurtry, L. Terms of endearment
Miller, S. The good mother
Moriarty, L. The center of everything
Morley, I. Come Sunday
Morrison, T. A mercy
Nunez, E. Anna in-between
Oates, J. C. Marya
Oates, J. C. Missing mom
Oates, J. C. Rape
Ostermiller, D. Outside the ordinary world
Packer, A. Songs without words
Parkhurst, C. Lost and found
Phillips, J. A. MotherKind
Picoult, J. Keeping Faith
Powell, S. The Mushroom Man
Quindlen, A. Object lessons
Racculia, K. This must be the place
Reiken, F. Day for night
Rendell, R. The crocodile bird
Rendell, R. The water's lovely
Rice, L. The deep blue sea for beginners
Rice, L. The geometry of sisters
Rice, L. Home fires
Rice, L. Summer light
Richler, N. Your mouth is lovely
Robards, K. Ghost moon
Roiphe, A. R. Lovingkindness
Rosenberg, N. T. Mitigating circumstances
Ross-Macdonald, M. Tamsin Harte
Rossner, J. Perfidia
Schine, C. The three Weissmanns of Westport
Schwarz, C. Drowning Ruth
Sebold, A. The almost moon
See, L. Dreams of joy
Shields, C. Unless
Shreve, A. Eden Close
Shreve, A. The pilot's wife
Simpson, M. Anywhere but here
Spencer, L. Bitter sweet
Spencer, L. That Camden summer
Straight, S. Highwire moon
Straight, S. A million nightingales
Strout, E. Amy and Isabelle
Tan, A. The Joy Luck Club
Tan, A. The kitchen god's wife
Tan, A. The bonesetter's daughter
Tóibín, C. The blackwater lightship
Truong, M. Bitter in the mouth
Tsukiyama, G. Dreaming water
Urquhart, J. Away
Vine, B. Anna's book
Walbert, K. The gardens of Kyoto
Walsh, T. The moon sisters
Walton, J. Among others
Watson, J. E. Asta in the wings
Weiner, J. Certain girls
Wolitzer, M. Surrender, Dorothy
MOTHERS AND DAUGHTERS *See* Mother-daughter relationship
Mothers and sons. Tóibín, C.
MOTHERS AND SONS *See* Mother-son relationship
MOTHERS AND SONS
Agawa, Y. The housekeeper and the professor
Bauer, B. Blacklands
Beattie, A. Chilly scenes of winter
Carey, P. His illegal self
Clarke, B. Exley
Coetzee, J. M. Life & times of Michael K.
Delaney, E. J. Broken Irish
Donoghue, E. Room
Erdrich, L. Four souls
Everett, P. Erasure
Ferber, E. So Big
Findley, T. The piano man's daughter
Fitch, J. Paint it black
Flagg, F. Standing in the rainbow
Glass, J. The whole world over
Greer, A. S. The story of a marriage
Gruber, M. The good son
Hallgrimur Helgason 101 Reykjavik
Hamilton, J. Disobedience
Harrison, J. The road home
Harwood, J. The ghost writer
Hoffman, A. Turtle Moon
Howrey, M. Blind sight
Irving, J. The world according to Garp
Isaacs, S. As husbands go
Kneale, M. When we were Romans
Lawrence, D. H. Sons and lovers
Leimbach, M. Daniel isn't talking
Letts, B. Shoot the moon
Levy, A. The long song
Lively, P. Passing on
Maguire, G. Son of a witch
Martin, S. The pleasure of my company
Martin, V. Trespass
Maupin, A. Michael Tolliver lives
Maynard, J. Labor Day
McGrath, P. Spider
Miller, A. Oxygen
Millet, L. How the dead dream
Mitcham, J. Sabbath Creek
Miyamoto, T. Kinshu: Autumn brocade
Neugeboren, J. 1940
Oates, J. C. Broke heart blues
Oates, J. C. A garden of earthly delights

O'Brien, E. Time and tide
Parkhurst, C. The nobodies album
Penney, S. The tenderness of wolves
Petterson, P. I curse the river of time
Picoult, J. House rules
Price, R. Freedomland
Priest, C. Boneshaker
Quindlen, A. Black and blue
Rader-Day, L. The day I died
Restrepo, L. No place for heroes
Rice, L. Last kiss
Rolvaag, O. E. Peder Victorious
Rosenberg, N. T. First offense
Roth, H. Call it sleep
Roth, P. Portnoy's complaint
Schupack, D. The boy on the bus
Shriver, L. We need to talk about Kevin
Spiotta, D. Eat the document
Suri, M. The age of Shiva
To the end of the land
Tóibín, C. Mothers and sons
Toole, J. K. A confederacy of dunces
Wallace, M. The girl in the garden
Williamson, P. The outsider

Mothers, tell your daughters. Campbell, B. J.

MOTHERS-IN-LAW
Jen, G. The love wife
Naipaul, V. S. A house for Mr. Biswas
Trevor, W. Death in summer

MOTHS
See also Insects

MOTION PICTURE ACTORS AND ACTRESSES
Alcott, K. A touch of stardust
Atkins, A. Devil's garden
Barker, C. Coldheart Canyon
Francis, D. Smokescreen
Gold, G. D. Sunnyside
Harvey, J. Gone to ground
Oates, J. C. Blonde
Swierczynski, D. Fun and games
Woods, S. Dead eyes

MOTION PICTURE ACTORS AND ACTRESSES *See* Actors

MOTION PICTURE DIRECTORS
Atkins, A. Devil's garden
Everett, P. L. I am Not Sidney Poitier
Gold, G. D. Sunnyside
Lazar, Z. Sway

MOTION PICTURE DIRECTORS *See* Motion picture producers and directors

MOTION PICTURE INDUSTRY
Alcott, K. A touch of stardust
Bagshawe, T. Adored
Williams, W. J. The fourth wall

MOTION PICTURE PRODUCERS
Gold, G. D. Sunnyside

MOTION PICTURE PRODUCERS *See* Motion picture producers and directors

MOTION PICTURE PRODUCERS AND DIRECTORS
DeLillo, D. Point Omega
Hagedorn, J. T. Toxicology
Hooper, T. Midnight movie
Just, W. S. The weather in Berlin
Leonard, E. Be cool
Leonard, E. Djibouti
North, A. The Life and Death of Sophie Stark
Oe, K. The changeling
Robinson, E. The true and outstanding adventures of the Hunt sisters
Welsh, I. Porno
Wilson, S. The fortune teller's daughter
Woods, S. L.A. Times
Woods, S. Santa Fe rules
Wouk, H. The lawgiver

MOTION PICTURE SERIALS
See also Motion pictures

MOTION PICTURE THEATERS
Reynolds, M. The Starlite Drive-in

MOTION PICTURES
Davies, R. Murther & walking spirits
Erickson, S. Zeroville
Fitzgerald, F. S. The last tycoon
Gibson, W. Pattern recognition
Gold, G. D. Sunnyside
Hellenga, R. The Italian lover
Leonard, E. Get Shorty
Oates, J. C. Blonde
Percy, W. The moviegoer
Raymond, J. The half-life
Schulberg, B. What makes Sammy run?
Sheehan, A. The anxiety of everyday objects
Updike, J. In the beauty of the lilies
Vidal, G. Hollywood
Vidal, G. Myra Breckinridge [and] Myron

MOTION PICTURES AND CHILDREN
See also Children; Motion pictures

MOTION PICTURES IN EDUCATION
See also Audiovisual education; Motion pictures; Teaching -- Aids and devices

Motion to suppress. O'Shaughnessy, P.

MOTIVATION (PSYCHOLOGY)
Wuertz, Y. G. Everything belongs to us

MOTOR CARS *See* Automobiles

MOTOR VEHICLE INDUSTRY *See* Automobile industry

MOTORCYCLES
Kushner, R. The flamethrowers

MOUNDS AND MOUND BUILDERS
See also Archeology; Burial; Tombs

MOUNT EVEREST (CHINA AND NEPAL)
Simmons, D. The abominable

The **mountain.** Yoon, P.

MOUNTAIN ANIMALS
See also Animals

MOUNTAIN CLIMBING *See* Mountaineering
MOUNTAIN ECOLOGY
See also Ecology
MOUNTAIN LIFE
House, S. A parchment of leaves
Morgan, R. The road from Gap Creek
Pancake, A. Strange as this weather has been
Trigiani, A. Big Cherry Holler
Trigiani, A. Big Stone Gap
Woodrell, D. Give us a kiss
Woodrell, D. Winter's bone
MOUNTAIN LIFE
See also Country life
MOUNTAIN LIFE -- APPALACHIAN REGION
Scotton, C. The secret wisdom of the earth
MOUNTAIN LIFE -- SOUTHERN STATES
Arnow, H. L. S. The dollmaker
Marshall, C. Christy
Smith, L. Fair and tender ladies
Smith, L. Oral history
The **mountain** of gold. Davies, J. D.
MOUNTAIN PEOPLE
See also Ethnology
Mountain windsong. Conley, R. J.
MOUNTAINEERING
Mawer, S. The fall
Nichols, J. On top of Spoon Mountain
Simmons, D. The abominable
Trevanian The Eiger sanction
Watkins, P. The ice soldier
MOUNTAINS
The blue hour
Mountolive. Durrell, L.
Mourners. Pronzini, B.
MOURNING *See* Bereavement
MOURNING CUSTOMS *See* Funeral rites and ceremonies
MOURNUNG CUSTOMS
Rojstaczer, S. The Mathematician's Shiva
The **mouse** that roared. Wibberley, L.
MOUTH -- DISEASES
See also Diseases
The **movement** of stars. Brill, A.
MOVIE THEATERS *See* Motion picture theaters
The **moviegoer.** Percy, W.
MOVIES *See* Motion pictures
Moving forward sideways like a crab. Mootoo, S.
MOVING, HOUSEHOLD
Duffy, B. House of echoes
MOZAMBIQUE
Couto, M. Sleepwalking land
Mr. Chartwell. Hunt, R.
Mr. Darwin's shooter. McDonald, R.
Mr. Fox. Oyeyemi, H.
Mr. Kill. Limón, M.
Mr. Loverman. Evaristo, B.
Mr. Lynch's holiday. O'Flynn, C.
Mr. Mercedes. King, S.
Mr. Midshipman Hornblower. Forester, C. S.
Mr. Paradise. Leonard, E.
Mr. Peanut. Ross, A.
Mr. Penumbra's 24-hour bookstore. Sloan, R.
Mr. Sammler's planet. Bellow, S.
Mr. Sampath--the printer of Malgudi, The financial expert, Waiting for the Mahatma. Narayan, R. K.
Mr. Sebastian and the Negro magician. Wallace, D.
Mr. Splitfoot. Hunt, S.
Mr. Tall. Earley, T.
Mr. X. Straub, P.
Mrs Pargeter Mysteries [series]
Brett, S. Mrs Pargeter's Principle
Mrs Pargeter's Principle. Brett, S.
Mrs. Bridge. Connell, E. S.
Mrs. Dalloway. Woolf, V.
Mrs. Darcy and the blue-eyed stranger. Smith, L.
Mrs. Engels. McCrea, G.
Mrs. Kimble. Haigh, J.
Mrs. Lincoln's dressmaker. Chiaverini, J.
Mrs. McGinty's dead. Christie, A.
Mrs. Mike. Freedman, B.
Mrs. Palfrey at the Claremont. Taylor, E.
Mrs. Pollifax and the whirling dervish. Gilman, D.
Mrs. Pollifax pursued. Gilman, D.
Mrs. Pollifax, innocent tourist. Gilman, D.
Ms. Hempel chronicles. Bynum, S.
Mudbound. Jordan, H.
Mudwoman. Oates, J. C.
MULATTOES
Allende, I. Island beneath the sea
Brown, R. Half a heart
Durrow, H. W. The girl who fell from the sky
Larsen, N. Passing
Mda, Z. The Madonna of Excelsior
Rice, A. The Feast of All Saints
Straight, S. A million nightingales
Walker, M. Jubilee
Warren, R. P. Band of angels
The **Mulberry** Bush. McCarry, C.
Mule. D'Souza, T.
MULTIPLE PERSONALITY
Flynn, M. In the Lion's Mouth
MULTIPLE PREGNANCY
See also Pregnancy
MULTIPLE SCLEROSIS
Price, R. The good priest's son
A **multitude** of sins. Ford, R.
MUMBAI (INDIA)
Adiga, A. Selection day
Massey, S. The widows of Malabar Hill
Suri, M. The city of Devi
Mumbo jumbo. Reed, I.
MUMMIES
See also Archeology; Burial; Human remains (Archeology)
The **mummy** case. Peters, E.

Mundo cruel.
MUNICIPAL ART
See also Art; Cities and towns
MUNICIPAL OFFICIALS AND EMPLOYEES
See also Civil service
MUNICIPALITIES *See* Cities and towns; Municipal government
The **muralist.** Shapiro, B. A.
MURDER
Abani, C. The secret history of Las Vegas
Agee, J. The bones of paradise
Andrew, S. Recipes for Love and Murder
Beukes, L. Broken monsters
Black, C. Murder on the Champ de Mars
Black, S. The killing lessons
Caldwell, I. The Fifth Gospel
Castillo, L. The dead will tell
Chaon, D. Ill will
Clark, M. H. The sleeping beauty killer
Cleeves, A. Thin air
Coleman, R. F. Where it hurts
Connelly, M. The burning room
Connelly, M. The Gods of Guilt
Conrad, H. Toured to Death
Corby, G. The Pericles Commission
Crompton, R. Hell's gate
Dickey, E. J. One night
The Disappeared
Doiron, P. The Precipice
Dugoni, R. My sister's grave
Ellroy, J. Perfidia
Ephron, H. Night Night, Sleep Tight
Farrow, J. The Storm Murders
Faverón Patriau, G. The Antiquarian
Fowler, C. Bryant & May
Freeman, B. Goodbye to the dead
French, N. Thursday's children
French, N. Waiting for Wednesday
French, T. The secret place
Friedman, D. Riot most uncouth
Galbraith, R. The silkworm
George, E. A Banquet of Consequences
Gilman, C. I. Dark orbit
Giolito, M. P. Quicksand
Goodman, C. River Road
Grant, M. Rosemary and Rue
Haldane, S. The devil's making
Hallberg, G. R. City on fire
Hallinan, T. Fields where they lay
Harrison, M. I. The Bishop's Wife
Hart, B. The bully of order
Harvey, J. Darkness, Darkness
Harvey, M. Brighton
Hayes, T. I Am Pilgrim
Higashino, K. Malice
Iles, G. The bone tree
Iles, G. Natchez burning
The investigation
Kelly, E. Broadchurch
Khan, A. Z. The unquiet dead
King, S. End of watch
King, S. Finders Keepers
Koenig, M. Nine days
Koryta, M. Those who wish me dead
Krentz, J. A. River road
Lackberg, C. The hidden child
The Land of Dreams
Laplante, A. A Circle of Wives
Link, C. The Watcher
Locke, A. Bluebird, bluebird
Longworth, M. L. Murder on the Île Sordou
Lourey, J. January thaw
Malliet, G. M. A Demon Summer
Mark, D. Sorrow bound
McInerney, L. The Glorious Heresies
Mina, D. The long drop
Minato, K. Confessions
Nadol, J. This is how it ends
Nesbø, J. The thirst
Norman, H. Next life might be kinder
Paretsky, S. Brush back
Parshall, S. Poisoned ground
Penny, L. The nature of the beast
Pérez-Reverte, A. The siege
The play of death
Quick, A. Garden of Lies
Racculia, K. Bellweather rhapsody
Rodriguez, L. Every hidden fear
Sandford, J. Deadline
Schultz, E. The Blondes
Scott, J. The kept
Spring Tide
Sykes, S. D. Plague Land
Thomas, S. A study in scarlet women
Thomson, E. S. Beloved poison
Upson, N. An expert in murder
Urza, G. All that followed
Walker, M. The Patriarch
MURDER -- INVESTIGATION
The Bat
Beaton, M. C. Pushing up daisies
Boyce, T. N. Old bones
Brekke, J. The fifth element
Brundage, E. All things cease to appear
Cleeves, A. The crow trap
Faye, L. The whole art of detection
Fowler, C. Bryant & May
Grebe, C. The ice beneath her
Harper, J. The dry
Hart, J. Redemption road
Khan, A. Z. Among the ruins
Mark, D. Cruel mercy
Moore, J. The night market
Mukherjee, A. A Rising Man

Obregon, N. Blue light Yokohama
Penny, L. Glass houses
The play of death
Pronzini, B. The violated
Rader-Day, L. The day I died
Rankin, I. Rather be the devil
Raybourn, D. A perilous undertaking
Robert, K. The devil's daughter
The shadow district
Swanson, P. Her every fear
Weaver, A. A most novel revenge
Yocum, R. A welcome murder
MURDER -- INVESTIGATION -- ENGLAND -- PENNINE CHAIN
Cleeves, A. The crow trap
MURDER -- INVESTIGATION -- GERMANY -- OBERAMMERGAU
The play of death
MURDER -- INVESTIGATION -- ICELAND
The shadow district
MURDER -- INVESTIGATION -- ITALY -- ROME
Dazieri, S. Kill the father
MURDER -- INVESTIGATION -- JAPAN
Higashino, K. Malice
MURDER -- INVESTIGATION -- MINNESOTA
Sandford, J. Deadline
MURDER -- INVESTIGATION -- SAUDI ARABIA
Ferraris, Z. Kingdom of strangers
MURDER -- INVESTIGATION -- SWEDEN
Tursten, H. Night rounds
MURDER -- MINNESOTA
Krueger, W. K. Ordinary grace
Murder and the First Lady. Roosevelt, E.
Murder as a fine art. Morrell, D.
Murder at Ford's Theatre. Truman, M.
Murder at midnight. Roosevelt, E.
Murder at Monticello. Langton, J.
Murder at Monticello; or, Old sins. Brown, R. M.
Murder at the feast of rejoicing. Robinson, L. S.
Murder at the God's gate. Robinson, L. S.
Murder at the Library of Congress. Truman, M.
Murder at the old vicarage. McGown, J.
The **murder** at the vicarage. Christie, A.
Murder below Montparnasse. Black, C.
Murder in Chinatown. Thompson, V.
Murder in Passy. Black, C.
Murder in the Bastille. Black, C.
Murder in the map room. Roosevelt, E.
Murder in the Marais. Black, C.
Murder in the Oval Office. Roosevelt, E.
Murder in the rue de Paradis. Black, C.
Murder in the Rue Dumas. Longworth, M. L.
Murder in the Sentier. Black, C.
Murder in the White House. Truman, M.
A **murder** is announced. Christie, A.
Murder most royal. Plaidy, J.
Murder must advertise. Sayers, D. L.
MURDER MYSTERIES *See* Mystery and detective plays; Mystery fiction; Mystery films; Mystery radio programs; Mystery television programs
The **murder** of Roger Ackroyd. Christie, A.
Murder on Capitol Hill. Truman, M.
Murder on Fifth Avenue. Thompson, V.
Murder on Lenox Hill. Thompson, V.
Murder on the Champ de Mars. Black, C.
Murder on the Île Sordou. Longworth, M. L.
Murder on the Orient Express. Christie, A.
Murder on the Trans-Siberian Express. Kaminsky, S. M.
Murder one. Dugoni, R.
MURDER STORIES
Abbott, M. E. Bury me deep
Ackroyd, P. The trial of Elizabeth Cree
Adiga, A. The white tiger
Alexie, S. Indian killer
Amis, M. London fields
Arsenault, E. The broken teaglass
Arsenault, E. In search of the Rose notes
Atkins, A. The ranger
Atkins, A. White shadow
Atkins, A. Wicked city
Atwood, M. Alias Grace
Banville, J. The book of evidence
Barry, B. The lace reader
Bauer, B. Darkside
Bohjalian, C. A. Secrets of Eden
Bolano, R. 2666
Bolton, S. J. Now you see me
Brown, D. The Da Vinci code
Brown, R. Before and after
Brown, S. The witness
Burdett, J. Bangkok 8
Cain, C. Heartsick
Camus, A. The stranger
Carr, C. The alienist
Carter, S. L. New England white
Carver, T. The surrogate
Childress, M. Crazy in Alabama
Clark, M. The legal limit
Coben, H. Hold tight
Colfer, E. Plugged
Connelly, M. The scarecrow
Cook, T. H. The Chatham School affair
Cook, T. H. Instruments of night
Cosse, L. A novel bookstore
Coulter, C. Split second
Cox, M. The glass of time
Crace, J. Being dead
Dahl, A. Misterioso
Dallas, S. The Persian Pickle Club
Dallas, S. Tallgrass
Davies, R. Murther & walking spirits
De Kretser, M. The Hamilton case
DeMille, N. Plum Island
Dickey, J. Deliverance

Dolan, H. Bad things happen
Dolan, H. Very bad men
Donoghue, E. Slammerkin
Donohue, K. Centuries of June
Dostoyevsky, F. The brothers Karamazov
Dostoyevsky, F. Crime and punishment
Dreiser, T. An American tragedy
Du Maurier, D. Rebecca
Dugoni, R. Murder one
Eastland, S. Eye of the Red Tsar
Ebershoff, D. The 19th wife
Ellory, R. J. The Anniversary Man
Ellroy, J. The black dahlia
Enger, L. Undiscovered country
Erdrich, L. The plague of doves
Fairstein, L. Entombed
Faulkner, W. Requiem for a nun
Faulkner, W. Sanctuary
Faulks, S. Engleby
Flynn, G. Sharp objects
Flynn, G. Dark places
Franklin, A. Mistress of the art of death
Franklin, A. The serpent's tale
French, A. Billy
French, T. In the woods
French, T. The likeness
Gaines, E. J. A gathering of old men
Gallagher, S. The kingdom of bones
Garcia Marquez, G. Chronicle of a death foretold
Gardiner, M. The Dirty Secrets Club
Gerritsen, T. Body double
Gilman, L. A. Hard magic
Goddard, R. Beyond recall
Goddard, R. Into the blue
Goddard, R. Never go back
Gottlieb, E. Now you see him
Greene, G. Brighton rock
Gregory, D. The devil's alphabet
Grippando, J. Lying with strangers
Grisham, J. A time to kill
Gross, A. Reckless
Gruber, M. The book of air and shadows
Gruber, M. Valley of bones
Guterson, D. Snow falling on cedars
Haddon, M. The curious incident of the dog in the night-time
The hall of singing caryatids
Hambly, B. A free man of color
Hambly, B. Graveyard dust
Hamill, P. Tabloid city
Hand, E. Generation loss
Hansen, R. A wild surge of guilty passion
Harris, R. Fatherland
Harris, R. The ghost
Harris, T. Red Dragon
Harris, T. The silence of the lambs
Hart, C. G. Letter from home
Hart, J. Down river
Hart, J. Iron house
Hart, J. The king of lies
Harvey, J. Gone to ground
Haywood, G. A. Cemetery Road
Hiaasen, C. Basket case
Hill, J. Horns
Hoag, T. Dust to dust
Hoag, T. Kill the messenger
Hoeg, P. Smilla's sense of snow
Hoffman, A. The probable future
Hoffman, A. The river king
Hoffman, A. Turtle Moon
Holt, V. The black opal
Holt, V. The Judas kiss
Hooper, K. Blood sins
Hooper, K. Blood ties
Hooper, K. Finding Laura
Hunter, E. Candyland
Hunter, S. The 47th samurai
Hunter, S. Dirty white boys
Hurwitz, G. The crime writer
Iles, G. The devil's punchbowl
Iles, G. Mortal fear
Iles, G. Turning angel
Irwin, S. M. The dead path
Isaacs, S. After all these years
Isaacs, S. As husbands go
Isaacs, S. Lily White
Jakeman, J. In the Kingdom of mists
Jance, J. A. Queen of the night
Johansen, I. And then you die--
Johansen, I. Blind alley
Kanon, J. Los Alamos
Katzenbach, J. Hart's war
Katzenbach, J. Just cause
Kellerman, J. The genius
Kelly, E. The poison tree
Kennedy, D. The big picture
Kepler, L. The hypnotist
King, S. Dolores Claiborne
King, S. Misery
Koontz, D. R. Intensity
Koontz, D. R. Velocity
Lamberson, G. The frenzy way
Lansdale, J. R. The bottoms
Lansdale, J. R. A fine dark line
Lansdale, J. R. Sunset and sawdust
Laplante, A. Turn of mind
Larsson, S. The girl who kicked the hornets' nest
Larsson, S. The girl who played with fire
Lashner, W. A killer's kiss
Lawrence, M. K. Hearts and bones
Le Carre, J. The constant gardener
LeCraw, H. The swimming pool
Lehane, D. Mystic river
Lescroart, J. T. The first law
Lescroart, J. T. Guilt

Lescroart, J. T. The hearing
Lescroart, J. T. Nothing but the truth
Lescroart, J. T. The oath
Letts, B. Shoot the moon
Levin, I. A kiss before dying
Lewis, M. G. The monk
Logan, C. South of Shiloh
Ludlum, R. The Sigma protocol
Lupton, R. Sister
Lustbader, E. V. Floating city
Lutz, J. Final seconds
Mailer, N. The executioner's song
Mankell, H. The man from Beijing
March, W. The bad seed
Margolin, P. Wild justice
Matthiessen, P. Bone by bone
Matthiessen, P. Killing Mister Watson
Matthiessen, P. Shadow country
McCammon, R. R. Boy's life
McCrumb, S. The ballad of Tom Dooley
McCrumb, S. If ever I return, pretty Peggy-O
McDermid, V. The distant echo
McEwan, I. The innocent
McGrath, P. The grotesque
Meyer, P. American rust
Mieville, C. The city & the city
Miller, S. While I was gone
Mills, M. Amagansett
Moore, G. The Sherlockian
Morrison, T. Jazz
Mortimer, J. Felix in the underworld
Mosley, W. The last days of Ptolemy Grey
Muller, M. Cyanide Wells
Munoz Molina, A. A manuscript of ashes
Murdoch, I. The green knight
Murray, S. Forgery
My name is Red
Nabokov, V. V. King, queen, knave
Norman, H. The bird artist
Norman, H. What is left the daughter
Norris, F. McTeague
Oates, J. C. Because it is bitter, and because it is my heart
Oates, J. C. Broke heart blues
Oates, J. C. Little bird of heaven
Oates, J. C. Missing mom
Ogilvie, E. When the music stopped
O'Hara, J. Butterfield 8
O'Nan, S. Snow angels
O'Shaughnessy, P. Invasion of privacy
O'Shaughnessy, P. Motion to suppress
O'Shaughnessy, P. Unlucky in law
Palliser, C. The unburied
Palmer, M. The society
Parker, B. Suspicion of vengeance
Parker, T. J. Black water
Parker, T. J. California girl
Parker, T. J. Cold pursuit
Parker, T. J. The fallen
Parker, T. J. Silent Joe
Parkhurst, C. The nobodies album
Patterson, J. 1st to die
Patterson, J. Cat & mouse
Patterson, J. Cross
Patterson, J. Four blind mice
Patterson, J. Hide & seek
Patterson, J. I, Alex Cross
Patterson, J. Jack and Jill
Patterson, J. Kiss the girls
Patterson, R. N. Dark lady
Patterson, R. N. Silent witness
Pattison, E. The skull mantra
Pawel, R. Death of a nationalist
Peace, D. Occupied city
Peace, D. Tokyo year zero
Pearl, M. The Dante Club
Pearl, M. The last Dickens
Pears, I. An instance of the fingerpost
Pearson, R. The angel maker
Pearson, R. Beyond recognition
Pearson, R. The first victim
Pearson, R. Undercurrents
Pelecanos, G. P. The night gardener
Pelecanos, G. P. Shame the devil
Pelevin, V. The hall of singing caryatids
Penney, S. The tenderness of wolves
Perez-Reverte, A. The fencing master
Pessl, M. Special topics in calamity physics
Picoult, J. House rules
Pope, B. C. The blood of Lorraine
Poyer, D. Down to a sunless sea
Poyer, D. Thunder on the mountain
Preston, D. Brimstone
Preston, D. The cabinet of curiosities
Preston, D. Reliquary
Preston, D. The wheel of darkness
Price, R. Clockers
Pronzini, B. In an evil time
Pronzini, B. Step to the graveyard easy
Quick, A. Late for the wedding
Rankin, I. The impossible dead
Rankin, I. The complaints
Reichs, K. J. Deja dead
Rendell, R. Adam and Eve and Pinch me
Rendell, R. The crocodile bird
Rendell, R. The face of trespass
Rendell, R. A judgment in stone
Rendell, R. The keys to the street
Rendell, R. A sight for sore eyes
Rendell, R. Tigerlily's orchids
Rendell, R. The water's lovely
Reuland, R. Semiautomatic
Reynolds, M. The Starlite Drive-in
Richards, D. A. The bay of love and sorrows
Richler, M. Barney's version

Richmond, M. No one you know
Rickards, J. Winter's end
Rigosi, G. Night bus
Riordan, R. Cold Springs
Robards, K. Ghost moon
Roberts, N. Angel's fall
Robertson, I. Instruments of darkness
Robertson, M. The brothers of Baker Street
Roncagliolo, S. Red April
Rose, J. Blackest bird
Rosenberg, N. T. Interest of justice
Rosenberg, N. T. Sullivan's law
Rosenfelt, D. Don't tell a soul
Roy, L. Bent Road
Sakey, M. The two deaths of Daniel Hayes
Sanders, L. The first deadly sin
Sanders, L. The second deadly sin
Sanders, L. The third deadly sin
Saul, J. The homing
Scottoline, L. Dead ringer
Scottoline, L. Legal tender
Scottoline, L. Mistaken identity
Sebold, A. The lovely bones
Seton, A. Dragonwyck
Sharfeddin, H. Mineral spirits
Shreve, A. The weight of water
Shriver, L. We need to talk about Kevin
Smith, L. E. Strange fruit
Smith, R. Wake up dead
Smith, S. A simple plan
Spark, M. The driver's seat
Spencer, S. Man in the woods
Spiegelman, P. Thick as thieves
Steinhauer, O. The Bridge of Sighs
Stewart, M. Nine coaches waiting
Stewart, M. Wildfire at midnight
Straight, S. The gettin place
Straub, P. In the night room
Straub, P. Lost boy lost girl
Suskind, P. Perfume: the story of a murderer
Syjuco, M. Ilustrado
Tartt, D. The secret history
Tartt, D. The little friend
Tracy, P. J. Monkeewrench
Truscott, L. K. Heart of war
Turow, S. The laws of our fathers
Turow, S. Reversible errors
Unsworth, B. Morality play
Ure, L. The fault tree
Verdon, J. Think of a number
Verissimo, L. F. Borges and the eternal orangutans
Vine, B. Anna's book
Vine, B. No night is too long
Walters, M. The breaker
Walters, M. The dark room
Walters, M. The sculptress
Walters, M. The shape of snakes
Walton, J. Farthing
Wambaugh, J. Floaters
Ward, L. Outside valentine
Warren, R. P. World enough and time
Welsh, L. The cutting room
Welty, E. The Ponder heart
Westlake, D. E. The hook
Wilhelm, K. Death qualified
Wilhelm, K. The deepest water
Wilhelm, K. Defense for the devil
Wilhelm, K. Desperate measures
Wilhelm, K. Malice prepense
Wilhelm, K. No defense
Wilson, R. The blind man of Seville
Woods, S. Chiefs
Woods, S. Choke
Woods, S. Dead in the water
Woods, S. Dirt
Woods, S. Grass roots
Woods, S. Imperfect strangers
Woods, S. L.A. dead
Woods, S. Orchid Beach
Woods, S. Palindrome
Woods, S. Santa Fe rules
Woods, S. Short straw
Woods, S. Worst fears realized
Yoshida, S. Villain
Yrsa Sigurdardottir Last rituals
Zimler, R. The last kabbalist of Lisbon
MURDER TRIALS *See* Trials (Homicide)
Murder unprompted. Brett, S.
MURDER VICTIMS
Dean, A. Bellfield Hall, or, The observations of Miss Dido Kent
Hansen, R. The assassination of Jesse James by the coward Robert Ford
Khan, A. Z. The unquiet dead
Norman, H. Next life might be kinder
O'Brien, E. In the forest
Palwick, S. Mending the moon
Rose, J. Blackest bird
MURDER VICTIMS -- IRAN
Morgan-Jones, C. The jackal's share
MURDER VICTIMS' FAMILIES
Aslam, N. Maps for lost lovers
LeCraw, H. The swimming pool
Sebold, A. The lovely bones
MURDER VICTIMS' FAMILIES -- CONNECTICUT
Roorbach, B. Life among giants
Murder walks the plank. Hart, C. G.
A Murder-by-Month mystery [series]
Lourey, J. January thaw
Murder@maggody.com. Hess, J.
The murderbot diaries [series]
Wells, M. All systems red
MURDERERS
Adamson, G. The outlander

Bauer, B. Blacklands
Boyne, J. Crippen
Cook, T. H. Master of the delta
Cox, M. The meaning of night
Egan, J. The keep
Fitch, J. White oleander
Frazier, C. Nightwoods
Grisham, J. The last juror
Hansen, R. The assassination of Jesse James by the coward Robert Ford
Hansen, R. A wild surge of guilty passion
Harris, T. Hannibal
Harris, T. Hannibal rising
Jacobson, H. Kalooki nights
Joss, M. Half broken things
Joss, M. The night following
Kinder, R. M. An absolute gentleman
King, S. Black house
Lanchester, J. The debt to pleasure
Lavender, W. Dominance
Lazar, Z. Sway
Lehane, D. Shutter Island
Levin, M. Compulsion
Lindsay, J. P. Darkly dreaming Dexter
Mailer, N. The executioner's song
Mason, J. Three graves full
Matthiessen, P. Shadow country
McCrumb, S. The ballad of Frankie Silver
McCrumb, S. The ballad of Tom Dooley
Moody, D. Hater
Moore, S. The big girls
Murakami, R. In the miso soup
Nunez, S. The last of her kind
O'Brien, E. In the forest
O'Connell, C. Judas child
Parker, T. J. The blue hour
Parker, T. J. Where serpents lie
Peace, D. Occupied city
Perry, T. Nightlife
Picoult, J. Change of heart
Richler, N. Your mouth is lovely
Scottoline, L. Rough justice
Spark, M. Aiding and abetting
Swierczynski, D. Fun and games
Swinson, K. Playing dirty
Trevor, W. Felicia's journey
Ure, L. The fault tree
Walters, M. The devil's feather
Ward, L. Outside valentine
Westlake, D. E. The ax
The **Murdstone** trilogy. Peet, M.
Murphy. Beckett, S.
MURPHY, MRS. (FICTITIOUS CHARACTER)
Brown, R. M. The litter of the law
Murther & walking spirits. Davies, R.
The **museum** guard. Norman, H.
Museum of human beings. Sargent, C.
The **museum** of innocence.
MUSEUMS
DeLillo, D. Point Omega
Mieville, C. Kraken
MUSEUMS AND SCHOOLS
See also Museums; Schools
The **Mushroom** Man. Powell, S.
Music & silence. Tremain, R.
MUSIC
Gass, W. H. Middle C
Gerritsen, T. Playing with fire
MUSIC -- HUMOR
See also Wit and humor
MUSIC -- PUBLISHING
See also Publishers and publishing
MUSIC -- QUOTATIONS, MAXIMS, ETC.
Powers, R. Orfeo
MUSIC FANS
Doyle, R. The Guts
MUSIC FESTIVALS
See also Festivals
MUSIC INDUSTRY
K'wan (Author) Section 8
Music of a life. Makine, A.
MUSIC STUDENTS
Flyte, M. City of dark magic
The **music** teacher. Hall, B.
MUSIC TEACHERS
Gass, W. H. Middle C
Hall, B. The music teacher
Lee, J. Y. K. The piano teacher
MUSICAL FICTION
Powers, R. Orfeo
MUSICAL FILMS
See also Motion pictures
MUSICAL THEATER
Prose, F. Mister monkey
MUSICIANS
Baldwin, J. Another country
Bass, R. Nashville chrome
Beatty, P. Slumberland
Bledsoe, A. Wisp of a thing
Doyle, R. The Guts
Edgerton, C. The night train
Elias, G. Death and transfiguration
Flagg, F. Standing in the rainbow
Franzen, J. Freedom
Hijuelos, O. Beautiful Maria of my soul
Hijuelos, O. The Mambo Kings play songs of love
Hornby, N. High fidelity
Hyatt, M. Beautiful gravity
Kalotay, D. Sight Reading
MacDonald Fall on your knees
McEwan, I. On Chesil Beach
Mosley, W. RL's dream
Murakami, H. After dark
Reiken, F. Day for night

Romano-Lax, A. The Spanish bow
Sarton, M. Anger
Seth, V. An equal music
Smith, L. The devil's dream
Spiotta, D. Stone Arabia
Taylor, M. G. The ballad of Trenchmouth Taggart
Tremain, R. Music & silence
Turner, F. W. 1929
Tyler, A. Searching for Caleb
Tyler, A. A slipping-down life
Wimberley, D. The king of Colored Town
MUSICIANS -- BIOGRAPHY
See also Biography
MUSICOLOGY
See also Research
MUSLIM FAMILIES
Akhtar, A. American dervish
Smith, Z. White teeth
MUSLIM WOMEN
Amirrezvani, A. Equal of the sun
Aslam, N. The golden legend
Aslam, N. Maps for lost lovers
MUSLIM WOMEN
See also Muslims; Women
MUSLIMS
Akhtar, A. American dervish
Caputo, P. Acts of faith
De Bernieres, L. Birds without wings
D'Souza, T. Whiteman
Gibb, C. Sweetness in the belly
Guene, F. Kiffe kiffe tomorrow
Khadivi, L. A good country
Lapierre, A. Between love and honor
My name is Red
Seth, V. A suitable boy
Unsworth, B. The ruby in her navel
Updike, J. Terrorist
Waldman, A. The submission
MUSLIMS -- FRANCE
Harris, J. Peaches for Father Francis
MUTATION (BIOLOGY)
Gregory, D. The devil's alphabet
MUTATION (BIOLOGY) *See* Evolution; Variation (Biology)
MUTE PERSONS
Barnes, J. The somnambulist
Hamilton, S. The lock artist
Harding, G. Painter of silence
Harrison, K. The seal wife
Reuss, F. The wasties
Wroblewski, D. The story of Edgar Sawtelle
MUTINY
Faulkner, W. A fable
Nordhoff, C. Mutiny on the Bounty
Pesci, D. Amistad
Unsworth, B. Sacred hunger
Wouk, H. The Caine mutiny
Mutiny on the Bounty. Nordhoff, C.
MUTUAL FUNDS
See also Investments
My abandonment. Rock, P.
My American Duchess. James, E.
My Antonia. Cather, W.
My Beautiful Enemy. Thomas, S.
My brilliant career. Franklin, M.
My brilliant friend. Ferrante, E.
My century. Grass, G.
My education. Choi, S.
My father's tears and other stories. Updike, J.
My grandmother asked me to tell you she's sorry. Backman, F.
My Holocaust. Reich, T.
My Jim. Rawles, N.
My life as a fake. Carey, P.
My life as a man. Roth, P.
My lord and spymaster. Bourne, J.
My mistress's sparrow is dead.
My name is Asher Lev. Potok, C.
My name is Lucy Barton. Strout, E.
My name is Red.
My name is Resolute. Turner, N. E.
My new American life. Prose, F.
My nine lives. Jhabvala, R. P.
My not so perfect life. Kinsella, S.
My notorious life. Manning, K.
My one and only. Higgins, K.
My real children. Walton, J.
My revolutions. Kunzru, H.
My secret history. Theroux, P.
My sister's grave. Dugoni, R.
My sister's keeper. Picoult, J.
My son's story. Gordimer, N.
My struggle.
My sunshine away. Walsh, M. O.
Mycroft Holmes. Abdul-Jabbar, K.
Myra Breckinridge [and] Myron. Vidal, G.
MYSTERIES *See* Mysteries and miracle plays; Mystery and detective plays; Mystery fiction; Mystery films; Mystery radio programs; Mystery television programs
MYSTERIES AND MIRACLE PLAYS
See also Bible plays; English drama; Pageants; Religious drama; Theater
The **mysteries** of Udolpho. Radcliffe, A. W.
The **mysterious** flame of Queen Loana. Eco, U.
The **mysterious** island. Verne, J.
The **Mysterious** West.
Mystery. Straub, P.
MYSTERY AND DETECTIVE STORIES
Best American mystery stories [date]
The Black Lizard big book of Black Mask stories
Christie, A. Murder on the Orient Express
Coover, R. Noir
Grimes, M. Rainbow's end
Lovesey, P. Diamond solitaire

McCrumb, S. Foggy Mountain breakdown and other stories
Meyer, N. The seven-per-cent solution
Mosley, W. White butterfly
Muller, M. A wild and lonely place
Neville, K. The eight
Neville, K. The fire
Pears, I. The last judgment
Pears, I. Stone's fall
Perez-Reverte, A. The Club Dumas
Poe, E. A. Complete stories and poems of Edgar Allan Poe
Rendell, R. Blood lines
Straub, P. Mystery
Van de Wetering, J. The hollow-eyed angel
Van de Wetering, J. The perfidious parrot
VanderMeer, J. Finch
The vicious circle
A Woman's eye
MYSTERY AND DETECTIVE STORIES *See* Mystery fiction
MYSTERY AND DETECTIVE STORIES -- AUSTRALIA
Temple, P. The broken shore
MYSTERY AND DETECTIVE STORIES -- BAHAMAS
Hart, C. G. Resort to murder
MYSTERY AND DETECTIVE STORIES -- BOTSWANA
McCall Smith, A. Blue shoes and happiness
McCall Smith, A. The Double Comfort Safari Club
McCall Smith, A. The good husband of Zebra Drive
McCall Smith, A. In the company of cheerful ladies
Stanley, M. A carrion death
MYSTERY AND DETECTIVE STORIES -- BRAZIL
Garcia-Roza, L. A. Alone in the crowd
Garcia-Roza, L. A. December heat
MYSTERY AND DETECTIVE STORIES -- CANADA
Penny, L. Bury your dead
Penny, L. The cruelest month
Penny, L. Still life
Penny, L. A trick of the light
Reichs, K. J. Deja dead
Wolfe, I. A. The taken
MYSTERY AND DETECTIVE STORIES -- CARIBBEAN REGION
White, R. W. Black widow
MYSTERY AND DETECTIVE STORIES -- CHINA
Gulik, R. H. v. The Chinese bell murders
Gulik, R. H. v. The haunted monastery
Gulik, R. H. v. The lacquer screen
Gulik, R. H. v. The Red Pavilion
Gulik, R. H. v. The willow pattern
Qiu Xiaolong Red mandarin dress
Qiu Xiaolong When red is black
See, L. Dragon bones
MYSTERY AND DETECTIVE STORIES -- CUBA
Smith, M. C. Havana Bay
MYSTERY AND DETECTIVE STORIES -- EGYPT
Peters, E. The golden one
Peters, E. Guardian of the horizon
Peters, E. He shall thunder in the sky
Peters, E. The hippopotamus pool
Peters, E. Lion in the valley
Peters, E. The mummy case
Peters, E. Night train to Memphis
Peters, E. Seeing a large cat
Peters, E. The snake, the crocodile, and the dog
Robinson, L. S. Murder at the feast of rejoicing
Robinson, L. S. Murder at the God's gate
MYSTERY AND DETECTIVE STORIES -- ENGLAND
Allingham, M. Crime and Mr. Campion
Allingham, M. Three cases for Mr. Campion
Atkinson, K. Case histories
Atkinson, K. Started early, took my dog
Barnard, R. Death of a literary widow
Barnard, R. A fall from grace
Bradley, A. A red herring without mustard
Brett, S. Murder unprompted
Brett, S. The torso in the town
Carver, T. The surrogate
Christie, A. The A.B.C. murders
Christie, A. And then there were none
Christie, A. The body in the library
Christie, A. Curtain
Christie, A. Endless night
Christie, A. The Hollow
Christie, A. Mrs. McGinty's dead
Christie, A. The murder at the vicarage
Christie, A. A murder is announced
Christie, A. The murder of Roger Ackroyd
Christie, A. The pale horse
Christie, A. Three blind mice and other stories
Christie, A. Towards zero
Collins, W. The moonstone
Collins, W. The woman in white
Crombie, D. Water like a stone
Dexter, C. The daughters of Cain
Dexter, C. The remorseful day
Dexter, C. The way through the woods
Dickens, C. Bleak House
Dickens, C. The mystery of Edwin Drood
Dickinson, P. The yellow room conspiracy
Doyle, A. C. The complete Sherlock Holmes
Elkins, A. J. Unnatural selection
Francis, D. Bolt
Francis, D. Even money
Francis, D. Longshot
Francis, D. Nerve
Francis, D. Proof
Francis, D. Whip hand
Gash, J. Prey dancing
George, E. Careless in red
George, E. This body of death
Grimes, M. The Anodyne Necklace
Grimes, M. The case has altered
Grimes, M. The five bells and bladebone
Grimes, M. Help the poor struggler
Grimes, M. I am the only running footman

Grimes, M. The Old Contemptibles
Grimes, M. The old fox deceiv'd
Grimes, M. The Old Silent
Grimes, M. The Old Wine Shades
Grimes, M. The Stargazey
Grimes, M. The winds of change
Harper, K. The Poyson garden
Harrod-Eagles, C. Blood lines
Harrod-Eagles, C. Death to go
Harrod-Eagles, C. Death watch
Harrod-Eagles, C. Game over
Harrod-Eagles, C. Grave music
Harrod-Eagles, C. Killing time
Harrod-Eagles, C. Orchestrated death
Harrod-Eagles, C. Shallow grave
Harvey, J. Cold in hand
Harvey, J. Cold light
Harvey, J. Darkness and light
Harvey, J. Easy meat
Harvey, J. Flesh and blood
Harvey, J. Last rites
Harvey, J. Still waters
Harvey, J. Wasted years
Hayder, M. Gone
Hayder, M. Ritual
Hill, R. Arms and the women
Hill, R. Bones and silence
Hill, R. Death comes for the Fat Man
Hill, R. Singing the sadness
Hill, S. The pure in heart
Hill, S. The various haunts of men
Horowitz, A. The House of Silk
James, P. D. The black tower
James, P. D. A certain justice
James, P. D. Devices and desires
James, P. D. The lighthouse
James, P. D. Original sin
James, P. D. The private patient
James, P. D. The skull beneath the skin
James, P. D. A taste for death
James, P. D. An unsuitable job for a woman
Keating, H. R. F. The soft detective
Lawrence, D. The dead sit round in a ring
Liss, D. A spectacle of corruption
Lovesey, P. Bertie and the seven bodies
Lovesey, P. Diamond dust
Lovesey, P. The house sitter
Lovesey, P. The last detective
Lovesey, P. Upon a dark night
Lovesey, P. The vault
Lovesey, P. Waxwork
MacDonald, P. The list of Adrian Messenger
Macdonald, R. The drowning pool
Malliet, G. M. Wicked autumn
Marsh, N. Dead water
Marsh, N. False scent
Marsh, N. Grave mistake
Marsh, N. Last ditch
Marsh, N. Light thickens
Marston, E. The Bawdy basket
Marston, E. The Devil's apprentice
Marston, E. The roaring boy
Marston, E. The vagabond clown
Marston, E. The wanton angel
McGown, J. Murder at the old vicarage
McGown, J. Verdict unsafe
Mina, D. The end of the wasp season
Penman, S. K. Cruel as the grave
Penman, S. K. The queen's man
Perry, A. Bedford Square
Perry, A. Belgrave Square
Perry, A. Bluegate Fields
Perry, A. A breach of promise
Perry, A. Buckingham Palace gardens
Perry, A. Cain his brother
Perry, A. Cardington Crescent
Perry, A. A dangerous mourning
Perry, A. Death of a stranger
Perry, A. Defend and betray
Perry, A. The face of a stranger
Perry, A. Farriers' Lane
Perry, A. Funeral in blue
Perry, A. Half Moon Street
Perry, A. Highgate rise
Perry, A. The Hyde Park headsman
Perry, A. Paragon Walk
Perry, A. Pentecost Alley
Perry, A. Resurrection row
Perry, A. Seven dials
Perry, A. The silent cry
Perry, A. The sins of the wolf
Perry, A. Slaves of obsession
Perry, A. Southampton Row
Perry, A. Traitor's gate
Perry, A. The twisted root
Perry, A. Weighed in the balance
Perry, A. The Whitechapel conspiracy
Peters, E. The deeds of the disturber
Peters, E. The last camel died at noon
Peters, E. The benediction of Brother Cadfael
Peters, E. Brother Cadfael's penance
Peters, E. Dead man's ransom
Peters, E. Fallen into the pit
Peters, E. The hermit of Eyton Forest
Peters, E. Monk's-hood
Peters, E. The potter's field
Peters, E. A rare Benedictine
Peters, E. The rose rent
Peters, E. Saint Peter's Fair
Peters, E. The sanctuary sparrow
Peters, E. The summer of the Danes
Peters, E. The virgin in the ice
Pirie, D. The patient's eyes
Rendell, R. Harm done

Rendell, R. Kissing the gunner's daughter
Rendell, R. Not in the flesh
Rendell, R. Simisola
Rendell, R. A sleeping life
Robinson, P. Cold is the grave
Robinson, P. Innocent grave
Robinson, P. Piece of my heart
Sayers, D. L. Busman's honeymoon
Sayers, D. L. The Dawson pedigree
Sayers, D. L. The documents in the case
Sayers, D. L. Gaudy Night
Sayers, D. L. Lord Peter
Sayers, D. L. Murder must advertise
Sayers, D. L. The nine tailors
Sayers, D. L. Strong poison
Sayers, D. L. Thrones, dominations
Sayers, D. L. The unpleasantness at the Bellona Club
Sayers, D. L. Whose body?
Tey, J. Brat Farrar
Tey, J. The daughter of time
Tey, J. The Franchise affair
Tey, J. The man in the queue
Todd, C. The red door
Winspear, J. Among the mad
Winspear, J. Birds of a feather
Winspear, J. An incomplete revenge
Winspear, J. Maisie Dobbs
Winspear, J. The mapping of love and death
Winspear, J. Messenger of truth
Winspear, J. Pardonable lies

MYSTERY AND DETECTIVE STORIES -- FRANCE
Bayard, L. The black tower
Black, C. Murder in Passy
Black, C. Murder in the Sentier
Newman, S. Strong as death
Simenon, G. Maigret and the madwoman
Simenon, G. Maigret and the Saturday caller
Simenon, G. Maigret goes home
Walker, M. The dark vineyard

MYSTERY AND DETECTIVE STORIES -- GERMANY
Grant, H. The glass demon
Kerr, P. March violets
Kerr, P. Field gray
Schlink, B. Self's punishment

MYSTERY AND DETECTIVE STORIES -- GUATEMALA
Reichs, K. J. Grave secrets

MYSTERY AND DETECTIVE STORIES -- GUERNSEY (CHANNEL ISLANDS)
Gash, J. The rich and the profane

MYSTERY AND DETECTIVE STORIES -- INDIA
King, L. R. The game
Peters, E. Death to the landlords!

MYSTERY AND DETECTIVE STORIES -- IRELAND
Banville, J. Christine Falls
Bruen, K. Cross
Bruen, K. The guards
O'Donovan, G. The priest
Tremayne, P. Chalice of blood

MYSTERY AND DETECTIVE STORIES -- ISRAEL
Kemelman, H. Monday the rabbi took off
Kemelman, H. One fine day the rabbi bought a cross

MYSTERY AND DETECTIVE STORIES -- ITALY
Dibdin, M. Blood rain
Eco, U. The name of the rose
Eco, U. Foucault's pendulum
Elkins, A. J. Good blood
Hewson, D. The garden of evil
Hewson, D. A season for the dead
Langton, J. The thief of Venice
Leon, D. About face
Leon, D. Drawing conclusions
Leon, D. The girl of his dreams
Leon, D. Uniform justice
Marsh, N. When in Rome
Nabb, M. Some bitter taste
Pears, I. Death and restoration
Pears, I. The immaculate deception

MYSTERY AND DETECTIVE STORIES -- JAPAN
Lathen, E. East is east

MYSTERY AND DETECTIVE STORIES -- JORDAN
Gilman, D. Mrs. Pollifax, innocent tourist

MYSTERY AND DETECTIVE STORIES -- MOROCCO
Gilman, D. Mrs. Pollifax and the whirling dervish

MYSTERY AND DETECTIVE STORIES -- NETHERLANDS
Van de Wetering, J. The Amsterdam cops
Van de Wetering, J. The blond baboon

MYSTERY AND DETECTIVE STORIES -- NORWAY
Benn, J. R. Billy Boyle
Fossum, K. Bad intentions
The redbreast
The snowman

MYSTERY AND DETECTIVE STORIES -- ROME
Downie, R. Caveat emptor
Downie, R. Medicus
Downie, R. Terra incognita
Saylor, S. The house of the Vestals
Saylor, S. The judgment of Caesar
Saylor, S. A mist of prophecies
Saylor, S. Rubicon
Saylor, S. The triumph of Caesar

MYSTERY AND DETECTIVE STORIES -- RUSSIA
Kaminsky, S. M. Murder on the Trans-Siberian Express
Smith, M. C. Gorky Park
Smith, M. C. Stalin's ghost
Smith, M. C. Wolves eat dogs

MYSTERY AND DETECTIVE STORIES -- SAUDI ARABIA
Ferraris, Z. Finding Nouf

MYSTERY AND DETECTIVE STORIES -- SCOTLAND
Atkinson, K. When will there be good news?
Beaton, M. C. Death of a macho man
MacBride, S. Flesh house
McCall Smith, A. The comforts of a muddy Saturday

McCall Smith, A. The lost art of gratitude
Mina, D. The dead hour
Mina, D. Slip of the knife
Mina, D. Still midnight
Rankin, I. Black and blue
Rankin, I. Exit music
Rankin, I. The falls
Rankin, I. The naming of the dead
Rankin, I. A question of blood
Rankin, I. Resurrection men
Rankin, I. Set in darkness
Sayers, D. L. The five red herrings

MYSTERY AND DETECTIVE STORIES -- SOUTH AFRICA

Francis, D. Smokescreen
McClure, J. The steam pig
Meyer, D. Devil's peak

MYSTERY AND DETECTIVE STORIES -- SWEDEN

Eriksson, K. The princess of Burundi
Jungstedt, M. The inner circle
Lackberg, C. The preacher
Larsson, A. Until thy wrath be past
Mankell, H. One step behind
Mankell, H. Dogs of Riga
Mankell, H. Firewall
Mankell, H. The man who smiled
Mankell, H. The return of the dancing master
Mankell, H. The troubled man
Nesbo, J. The devil's star
Sjowall, M. The laughing policeman

MYSTERY AND DETECTIVE STORIES -- THAILAND

Cotterill, C. Killed at the whim of a hat

MYSTERY AND DETECTIVE STORIES -- UNITED STATES

Abrahams, P. Dog on it
Andrews, M. K. Every crooked nanny
Andrews, M. K. Irish eyes
Arsenault, E. In search of the Rose notes
Ball, J. D. In the heat of the night
Bayard, L. The pale blue eye
The Best American mystery stories of the century
The best American noir of the century
Block, L. All the flowers are dying
Block, L. The burglar in the library
Block, L. A drop of the hard stuff
Block, L. Eight million ways to die
Block, L. The sins of the fathers
Block, L. A ticket to the boneyard
Block, L. When the sacred ginmill closes
Bowen, P. Badlands
Box, C. J. Back of beyond
Box, C. J. Nowhere to run
Braun, L. J. The cat who ate Danish modern
Braun, L. J. The cat who went underground
Brown, R. M. Murder at Monticello; or, Old sins
Brown, R. M. Wish you were here
Buchanan, E. Love kills
Buchanan, E. You only die twice
Burke, J. L. Black cherry blues
Burke, J. L. Heaven's prisoners
Carr, C. The alienist
Chabon, M. The Yiddish policemen's union
Chandler, R. The big sleep
Chandler, R. The long goodbye
Child, L. One shot
Connolly, J. The burning soul
Craig, P. R. A shoot on Martha's Vineyard
Craig, P. R. Third strike
Craig, P. R. A vineyard killing
Crais, R. Chasing darkness
Crais, R. First rule
Cross, A. The collected stories of Amanda Cross
Crumley, J. Bordersnakes
Crumley, J. The final country
Crumley, J. The last good kiss
Crumley, J. The wrong case
Dunning, J. Booked to die
Dunning, J. The bookman's wake
Estleman, L. D. Amos Walker
Estleman, L. D. Frames
Estleman, L. D. Infernal angels
Estleman, L. D. A smile on the face of the tiger
Evanovich, J. One for the money
Finch, C. The September Society
Gardner, L. Love you more
Gilman, D. Kaleidoscope
Gilman, D. Mrs. Pollifax pursued
Gilman, D. Thale's Folly
Gorman, E. Bad moon rising
Gorman, E. Fools rush in
Gorman, E. Save the last dance for me
Gorman, E. Sleeping dogs
Gorman, E. Ticket to ride
Grafton, S. B is for burglar
Grafton, S. C is for corpse
Grafton, S. D is for deadbeat
Grafton, S. E is for evidence
Grafton, S. F is for fugitive
Grafton, S. G is for gumshoe
Grafton, S. H is for homicide
Grafton, S. I is for innocent
Grafton, S. A is for alibi
Grafton, S. J is for judgment
Grafton, S. K is for killer
Grafton, S. N is for noose
Grafton, S. O is for outlaw
Grafton, S. P is for peril
Grafton, S. Q is for quarry
Grafton, S. S is for Silence
Grafton, S. T is for trespass
Gran, S. Claire DeWitt and the city of the dead
Greenleaf, S. False conception
Greenleaf, S. Strawberry Sunday
Greer, R. O. First of state

Grimes, M. The Horse You Came In On
Grimes, M. Hotel Paradise
Haddam, J. Cheating at solitaire
Haddam, J. Hardscrabble road
Haddam, J. True believers
Hall, J. W. Buzz cut
Hall, J. W. Off the chart
Hall, J. W. Red sky at night
Hammett, D. Complete novels
Hammett, D. The glass key
Hammett, D. The Maltese falcon
Hammett, D. The thin man
Harris, C. A secret rage
Hart, C. G. Death walked in
Hart, C. G. Murder walks the plank
Hart, C. G. White elephant dead
Hart, C. G. Yankee Doodle dead
Harvey, M. T. The Chicago way
Harvey, M. T. The Fifth Floor
Harvey, M. T. We all fall down
Hess, J. Busy bodies
Hess, J. Death by the light of the moon
Hess, J. Madness in Maggody
Hess, J. Maggody and the moonbeams
Hess, J. Mischief in Maggody
Hess, J. Misery loves Maggody
Hess, J. Murder@maggody.com
Hiaasen, C. Skin tight
Hillerman, T. The blessing way
Hillerman, T. Hunting badger
Hillerman, T. The Jim Chee mysteries
Hillerman, T. Listening woman
Hillerman, T. Sacred clowns
Hillerman, T. The shape shifter
Hillerman, T. The sinister pig
Hillerman, T. Skinwalkers
Hillerman, T. Talking God
Hillerman, T. A thief of time
Hillerman, T. The wailing wind
Himes, C. Cotton comes to Harlem
Hockensmith, S. Holmes on the range
Hockensmith, S. On the wrong track
Hunter, E. The moment she was gone
Huston, C. Already dead
Huston, C. Every last drop
Huston, C. Half the blood of Brooklyn
Isaacs, S. Compromising positions
James, P. D. Death in holy orders
James, P. D. Death of an expert witness
Jance, J. A. Birds of prey
Jance, J. A. Devil's claw
Jance, J. A. Skeleton canyon
Johnson, C. The dark horse
Kaminsky, S. M. Dancing in the dark
Kaminsky, S. M. A fatal glass of beer
Kaminsky, S. M. To catch a spy
Kaminsky, S. M. Tomorrow is another day
Kava, A. Hotwire
Kellerman, F. The forgotten
Kellerman, F. Jupiter's bones
Kellerman, F. Milk and honey
Kellerman, F. Prayers for the dead
Kellerman, F. Serpent's tooth
Kellerman, J. Billy Straight
Kellerman, J. Bones
Kellerman, J. The clinic
Kellerman, J. Devil's waltz
Kellerman, J. Gone
Kellerman, J. Monster
Kellerman, J. Private eyes
Kellerman, J. Self-defense
Kellerman, J. Therapy
Kellerman, J. Time bomb
Kemelman, H. Thursday the rabbi walked out
Kienzle, W. X. The rosary murders
Knopf, C. The last refuge
Koryta, M. Tonight I said goodbye
Krueger, W. K. Vermilion drift
Langton, J. The deserter
Langton, J. Murder at Monticello
Lansdale, J. R. Devil red
Lansdale, J. R. Vanilla Ride
Lathen, E. Brewing up a storm
Lathen, E. Something in the air
Lavender, W. Dominance
Lehane, D. Prayers for rain
Lehane, D. Sacred
Leonard, E. When the women come out to dance, and other stories
Lethem, J. Motherless Brooklyn
Lippman, L. Hardly knew her
Lippman, L. No good deeds
Lovesey, P. Skeleton Hill
Lutz, J. Burn
Lutz, J. Lightning
Lutz, L. Curse of the Spellmans
Lutz, L. Revenge of the Spellmans
Lutz, L. The Spellman files
MacDonald, J. D. Cinnamon skin
MacDonald, J. D. The green ripper
MacDonald, J. D. The lonely silver rain
MacDonald, J. D. The long lavender look
MacDonald, J. D. A purple place for dying
MacDonald, J. D. The scarlet ruse
MacDonald, J. D. The turquoise lament
Macdonald, R. The far side of the dollar
Macdonald, R. The Galton case
Macdonald, R. The goodbye look
Macdonald, R. Sleeping beauty
Macdonald, R. The underground man
Maron, M. Bootlegger's daughter
Maron, M. High country fall
Maron, M. Shooting at loons
Maron, M. Storm track

Maron, M. Uncommon clay
Maron, M. Up jumps the Devil
Mayor, A. Red herring
Mayor, A. The sniper's wife
Mayor, A. Tag man
McBain, E. The big bad city
McBain, E. Fat Ollie's book
McBain, E. The frumious Bandersnatch
McBain, E. Hark!
McBain, E. The last dance
McBain, E. Nocturne
McCrumb, S. If I'd killed him when I met him
Mcdonald, G. Fletch
McGarrity, M. Everyone dies
McInerny, R. M. Celt and pepper
McInerny, R. M. Irish coffee
McInerny, R. M. Requiem for a realtor
Mosley, W. Devil in a blue dress
Mosley, W. When the thrill is gone
Mosley, W. Bad Boy Brawly Brown
Mosley, W. Black Betty
Mosley, W. Cinnamon kiss
Mosley, W. Fearless Jones
Mosley, W. Gone fishin'
Mosley, W. Known to evil
Mosley, W. A little yellow dog
Mosley, W. The long fall
Mosley, W. A red death
Mosley, W. Six easy pieces
Muller, M. Both ends of the night
Muller, M. City of whispers
Muller, M. Dead midnight
Muller, M. A walk through the fire
Muller, M. Where echoes live
Muller, M. While other people sleep
Muller, M. Wolf in the shadows
The Mysterious West
O'Connell, C. Crime school
O'Connell, C. Killing critics
O'Connell, C. Mallory's oracle
O'Connell, C. Stone angel
The Oxford book of American detective stories
Page, K. H. The body in the Big Apple
Page, K. H. The body in the bog
Page, K. H. The body in the bookcase
Pajer, B. A spark of death
Paretsky, S. Bitter medicine
Paretsky, S. Blacklist
Paretsky, S. Fire sale
Paretsky, S. Guardian angel
Paretsky, S. Hard time
Paretsky, S. Hardball
Paretsky, S. Total recall
Paretsky, S. Tunnel vision
Paretsky, S. Windy City blues
Parker, R. B. Back story
Parker, R. B. Chance
Parker, R. B. Cold service
Parker, R. B. Death in paradise
Parker, R. B. Double Deuce
Parker, R. B. Family honor
Parker, R. B. Hugger mugger
Parker, R. B. Hush money
Parker, R. B. Melancholy baby
Parker, R. B. Now and then
Parker, R. B. Painted ladies
Parker, R. B. Potshot
Parker, R. B. Rough weather
Parker, R. B. School days
Parker, R. B. Sea change
Parker, R. B. Shrink rap
Parker, R. B. Sixkill
Parker, R. B. Small vices
Parker, R. B. Thin air
Parker, R. B. Trouble in Paradise
Parker, R. B. Walking shadow
Parker, R. B. Widow's walk
Parker, T. J. Pacific beat
Pearson, R. Killer summer
Pelecanos, G. P. Hard revolution
Pelecanos, G. P. Hell to pay
Pelecanos, G. P. Soul circus
Perry, T. Death benefits
Pintoff, S. In the shadow of Gotham
Pronzini, B. Crazybone
Pronzini, B. Fever
Pronzini, B. Mourners
Pronzini, B. Nightcrawlers
Pronzini, B. Savages
Pronzini, B. Spook
Read, C. Invisible boy
Reichs, K. J. Bare bones
Reichs, K. J. Break no bones
Rinehart, M. R. The circular staircase
Rinehart, M. R. Miss Pinkerton: adventures of a nurse detective
Roosevelt, E. The Hyde Park murder
Roosevelt, E. Murder and the First Lady
Roosevelt, E. Murder at midnight
Roosevelt, E. Murder in the map room
Roosevelt, E. Murder in the Oval Office
Russell, S. This insane train
Sallis, J. Cripple Creek
Sallis, J. Cypress Grove
Sallis, J. Salt River
Sanders, L. The fourth deadly sin
Sanders, L. McNally's dilemma
Sanders, L. McNally's gamble
Sanders, L. McNally's puzzle
Sanders, L. Timothy's game
Sandford, J. Broken prey
Sandford, J. Buried prey
Sandford, J. Certain prey
Sandford, J. Mind prey

Sandford, J. Naked prey
Sandford, J. Night prey
Sandford, J. Rules of prey
Sandford, J. Shock wave
Sandford, J. Winter prey
Smith, J. 82 Desire
Spencer-Fleming, J. All mortal flesh
Spencer-Fleming, J. In the bleak midwinter
Spiegelman, P. Black maps
Spillane, M. The Goliath bone
Spillane, M. The Mike Hammer collection [v1]
Spillane, M. The Mike Hammer collection [v2]
Stabenow, D. Hunter's moon
Stabenow, D. Killing grounds
Stabenow, D. Whisper to the blood
Standiford, L. Deal with the dead
Stansberry, D. The ancient rain
Stone, N. The king of swords
Stout, R. Black orchids; &, the silent speaker
Stout, R. The doorbell rang
Stout, R. Fer-de-lance; &, The league of frightened men
Stout, R. Gambit
Stout, R. The rubber band & The red box
Stout, R. Some buried Caesar & The golden spiders
Stout, R. Too many cooks; & champagne for one
Tapply, W. G. Dead winter
Truman, M. Murder at Ford's Theatre
Truman, M. Murder at the Library of Congress
Truman, M. Murder in the White House
Truman, M. Murder on Capitol Hill
Vachss, A. H. Another life
Vachss, A. H. Choice of evil
Vachss, A. H. Dead and gone
Vachss, A. H. Down here
Vachss, A. H. Down in the zero
Vachss, A. H. Footsteps of the hawk
Vachss, A. H. Hard candy
Vachss, A. H. Pain management
Vachss, A. H. Sacrifice
Vachss, A. H. Safe house
Van de Wetering, J. Just a corpse at twilight
Verdon, J. Shut your eyes tight
Walker, M. W. All the dead lie down
Wall, K. R. The Mercy Oak
Westlake, D. E. Baby, would I lie?
Westlake, D. E. Memory
Westlake, D. E. Trust me on this
White, K. A body to die for
White, K. Lethally blond
White, R. W. Deep shadow
Wilhelm, K. Justice for some
Williams, A. K. The stranger you seek
Wilson, F. P. Conspiracies
Wilson, F. P. The haunted air
Wilson, F. P. Legacies
Winslow, D. The Dawn Patrol
Winslow, D. The gentlemen's hour
Woods, S. Chiefs
Woods, S. New York dead
MYSTERY AND DETECTIVE STORIES -- WALES
Penman, S. K. Dragon's lair
MYSTERY COMIC BOOKS, STRIPS, ETC.
See also Comic books, strips, etc.
MYSTERY FICTION
Aaronovitch, B. Midnight riot
Abani, C. The secret history of Las Vegas
Abdul-Jabbar, K. Mycroft Holmes
Adler-Olsen, J. The absent one
Adler-Olsen, J. A Conspiracy of Faith
Adler-Olsen, J. The keeper of lost causes
Ahmad, A. X. The Caretaker
Albert, S. W. The Darling Dahlias and the cucumber tree
Ampuero, R. The Neruda case
Andrew, S. Recipes for Love and Murder
Another time, another life
Atkinson, K. Started early, took my dog
Bannalec Death in Brittany
Barclay, L. Trust your eyes
Barr, N. Destroyer angel
Barr, N. The rope
The Bat
The beggar king
The Best American mystery stories of the century
Between summer's longing and winter's end
Beukes, L. Broken monsters
Beukes, L. Zoo city
The big book of Sherlock Holmes stories
Bingham, H. Talking to the dead
Black, C. Murder below Montparnasse
Black, C. Murder in the rue de Paradis
Black, C. Murder on the Champ de Mars
Black, L. Blunt Impact
Black, S. The killing lessons
Blake, R. A dark anatomy
Bollen, C. Orient
Box, C. J. Breaking point
Box, C. J. Vicious circle
Bradley, A. As chimney sweepers come to dust
Bradley, A. I am half-sick of shadows
Bradley, A. Speaking from among the bones
Bradley, A. The sweetness at the bottom of the pie
Bradley, A. The weed that strings the hangman's bag
Brekke, J. The fifth element
Brett, S. Mrs Pargeter's Principle
Brookmyre, C. When the Devil Drives
Brookmyre, C. Where the bodies are buried
Brooks, B. Winter kill
Brown, D. Inferno
Brown, E. R. Almost criminal
Brown, R. M. The litter of the law
Brown, R. Before and after
Browne, S. G. Lucky bastard
Brundage, E. All things cease to appear
Buckley, F. The siren queen

Burrowes, G. Lady Maggie's secret scandal
Butcher, J. Proven guilty
Cain, C. Kill you twice
Caldwell, I. The Fifth Gospel
Carey, J. Autumn bones
Carnoy, D. The big exit
Carr, C. The alienist
Carter, M. J. The Strangler Vine
Castillo, L. Breaking silence
Castro, J. Hell or high water
Catton, E. The luminaries
Chancellor, B. Sycamore
Child, L. Killing floor
Christie, A. The A.B.C. murders
Christie, A. And then there were none
Church, J. Bamboo and blood
Church, J. A drop of Chinese blood
Clark, M. Guilt by association
Claudel, P. The investigation
Cleave, P. Cemetery Lake
Cleave, P. Five minutes alone
Cleeves, A. Thin air
Clements, R. Revenger
Coben, H. Stay close
Coco, G. Shadows on the lake
Cole, D. Ragdoll
Coleman, R. F. Where it hurts
Conlon, E. Red on red
Connelly, M. The burning room
Connelly, M. The Gods of Guilt
Conrad, H. Toured to Death
Cook, T. H. Sandrine's Case
Corby, G. The Marathon conspiracy
Corby, G. The Pericles Commission
Corey, J. S. A. Leviathan Wakes
Cotterill, C. Slash and burn
Crompton, R. Hell's gate
Crompton, R. Hour of the Red God
Cross, N. Luther
Crumley, J. Bordersnakes
Cussler, C. The Mayan secrets
Davis, L. The Ides of April
De Giovanni, M. The Crocodile
Dean, A. Bellfield Hall, or, The observations of Miss Dido Kent
Dean, A. A gentleman of fortune, or, The suspicions of Miss Dido Kent
Dean, A. A woman of consequence
Deaver, J. The October list
DeSilva, B. Rogue island
Dibdin, M. Ratking
Dickinson, P. The yellow room conspiracy
The Disappeared
Dobyns, S. Is fat Bob dead yet?
Doiron, P. Bad Little Falls
Doiron, P. The Precipice
Donoghue, E. Frog music
Downie, R. Semper Fidelis
Doyle, A. C. S. The adventures and the memoirs of Sherlock Holmes
Doyle, A. C. The complete Sherlock Holmes
Dunning, J. The bookman's wake
Eastland, S. The Beast in the Red Forest
Eastland, S. Shadow pass
Edwardson, Å. Sail of stone
The elephant keepers' children
Elias, G. Death and transfiguration
Elkins, A. J. Dying on the vine
Ellis, D. In the company of liars
Ellory, R. J. A simple act of violence
Ephron, H. Night Night, Sleep Tight
Eriksson, K. The princess of Burundi
Eskens, A. The heavens may fall
Evanovich, J. One for the money
Fairstein, L. Night watch
Farrow, J. The Storm Murders
Faverón Patriau, G. The Antiquarian
Faye, L. The gods of Gotham
Faye, L. The whole art of detection
Ferraris, Z. Kingdom of strangers
Fielding, J. Someone Is Watching
Finch, C. A beautiful blue death
Flanery, P. Fallen land
Flynn, G. Gone girl
Flyte, M. City of dark magic
Fowler, C. Bryant & May
Francis, F. Dick Francis's Damage
Free falling, as if in a dream
Freeman, B. Spilled blood
Frei, M. The stranger's magic
French, N. Blue Monday
French, N. Thursday's children
French, N. Tuesday's gone
French, N. Waiting for Wednesday
French, T. Broken Harbor
Friedman, D. Don't ever get old
Friedman, D. Riot most uncouth
Galbraith, R. Career of evil
Galbraith, R. The silkworm
Gallagher, S. The bedlam detective
Gardner, L. Catch me
Gardner, L. Find Her
Gardner, L. Live to tell
Gardner, L. The neighbor
George, E. A Banquet of Consequences
George, E. Believing the lie
Glynn, A. Bloodland
Gorman, E. Riders on the Storm
Grafton, S. G is for gumshoe
Grafton, S. J is for judgment
Grafton, S. K is for killer
Grafton, S. O is for outlaw
Greaves, C. J. Hard twisted
Greaves, C. Hush money

Grebe, C. The ice beneath her
Greenwood, K. Unnatural Habits
Griffiths, E. The house at sea's end
Griffiths, E. The Janus stone
Grimes, M. The case has altered
Grimes, M. The Horse You Came In On
Grimes, M. Hotel Paradise
Grimes, M. Rainbow's end
Grindle, L. Villa triste
Grossman, P. Children of wrath
Guinn, M. The scribe
Guttridge, P. The thing itself
Hall, T. The case of the deadly butter chicken
Hallberg, G. R. City on fire
Hambly, B. Good man Friday
Hambly, B. Ran away
Hand, E. Available dark
Harper, J. The dry
Harris, C. A secret rage
Harrod-Eagles, C. Death to go
Harrod-Eagles, C. Death watch
Harrod-Eagles, C. Grave music
Hart, C. Ghost gone wild
Hart, E. The book of Killowen
Hart, E. Haunted ground
Hart, E. Lake of sorrows
Hart, J. Redemption road
Harvey, J. Cold light
Harvey, J. A darker shade of blue
Harvey, J. Still waters
Hayder, M. Birdman
Hayder, M. Hanging hill
Hayder, M. Skin
Hayder, M. The treatment
Heller, P. Celine
Hellström, B. Cell 8
Hiassen, C. Bad monkey
Higashino, K. Malice
Hill, A. The good suicides
Hill, A. The summer of dead toys
Hill, S. The risk of darkness
Hill, S. Shadows in the street
Hillerman, T. Hunting badger
Hillerman, T. Sacred clowns
Hillerman, T. The sinister pig
Hillerman, T. Skinwalkers
Hillerman, T. A thief of time
Horowitz, A. Moriarty
Iles, G. Mississippi blood
Iles, G. Natchez burning
Indridason, A. Outrage
Irwin, S. M. The broken ones
Jackson, J. A grown up kind of pretty
James, P. D. Death comes to Pemberley
James, P. D. Devices and desires
Jenkins, V. An unattended death
Jin, H. The boat rocker
Jio, S. The violets of March
Johansen, I. Taking Eve
Johnson, C. Another man's moccasins
Johnson, C. Hell is empty
Johnson, C. Spirit of steamboat
Johnson, C. Death without company
Jones, J. S. The silence
Kazinski, A. J. The last good man
Kellerman, F. Prayers for the dead
Kellerman, J. The clinic
Kellerman, J. Devil's waltz
Kelly, E. Broadchurch
Kelly, E. The burning air
Kelly, J. The fire baby
Kelly, J. The moon tunnel
Kerley, J. The death collectors
Kerr, P. The lady from Zagreb
Kerr, P. A Man Without Breath
Kerr, P. Prussian blue
Khan, A. Z. Among the ruins
Khan, A. Z. The unquiet dead
King, L. R. The beekeeper's apprentice, or, on the segregation of the queen
Koontz, D. R. The bad place
Koryta, M. The prophet
Krentz, J. A. Dream eyes
Krentz, J. A. River road
Krentz, J. A. Secret sisters
Kunzru, H. White tears
Lackberg, C. The lost boy
Lackberg, C. The ice princess
Lackberg, C. The stonecutter
Lagercrantz, D. The Girl in the Spider's Web
Lagercrantz, D. The girl who takes an eye for an eye
The Land of Dreams
Laplante, A. A Circle of Wives
Lehane, D. Sacred
Lehane, D. Since we fell
Lelic, S. The child who
Leon, D. Beastly Things
Leon, D. Blood from a stone
Leon, D. The Golden Egg
Leon, D. A question of belief
Leonard, E. Charlie Martz and other stories
The leopard
Levack, S. Demon of the air
Lewis, T. GBH
Limón, M. Mr. Kill
Link, C. The other child
Link, C. The Watcher
Lippman, L. After I'm gone
Lippman, L. Hush hush
Locke, A. Bluebird, bluebird
Locke, A. The cutting season
Longworth, M. L. Murder in the Rue Dumas
Lovesey, P. The tooth tattoo
The Ludwig Conspiracy

Lupton, R. Afterwards
Lutz, L. The last word
MacBride, S. Blind eye
MacBride, S. Close to the Bone
MacBride, S. Cold granite
MacBride, S. Dying Light
MacBride, S. Shatter the bones
Mackintosh, C. I see you
Malliet, G. M. A fatal winter
Malliet, G. M. Pagan spring
The map and the territory
Mark, D. The dark winter
Mark, D. Sorrow bound
Maron, M. Shooting at loons
Marwood, A. The killer next door
Mason, R. Who killed Piet Barol?
Massey, S. The widows of Malabar Hill
McCall Smith, A. The forgotten affairs of youth
McCall Smith, A. The full cupboard of life
McCall Smith, A. The Kalahari typing school for men
McCall Smith, A. The Limpopo Academy of Private Detection
McCall Smith, A. The No. 1 Ladies' Detective Agency
McCall Smith, A. The Saturday big tent wedding party
McCall Smith, A. Tea time for the traditionally built
McHugh, L. Arrowood
McKinty, A. In the Morning I'll Be Gone
McMahon, J. The One I Left Behind
Mina, D. Gods and beasts
Mina, D. The red road
Mizushima, M. Killing Trail
Mizushima, M. Stalking Ground
Mogford, T. Shadow of the rock
Moore, C. Sacre bleu
Moore, L. The Unseen World
Morgan-Jones, C. The jackal's share
Morton, C. Stealing Mona Lisa
Mosley, W. All I did was shoot my man
Mosley, W. And sometimes I wonder about you
Mosley, W. Devil in a blue dress
Mosley, W. Little green
Mosley, W. Black Betty
Mosley, W. Gone fishin'
Mosley, W. A little yellow dog
Mosley, W. A red death
Mukherjee, A. A Rising Man
Mullen, T. Lightning men
Nadel, B. The Ottoman cage
Newton, C. Start shooting
Nichols, P. The rocks
Nickson, C. Cold cruel winter
Obregon, N. Blue light Yokohama
O'Brien, T. L. The Lincoln conspiracy
O'Connell, C. The chalk girl
O'Connell, C. Mallory's oracle
O'Donovan, G. Dublin dead
Ohlsson, K. Unwanted
O'Loughlin, E. Minds of winter
O'Mara, T. Crooked Numbers
The Oxford book of American detective stories
Pajer, B. Capacity for murder
Pajer, B. Fatal induction
Palliser, C. Rustication
Palmer, D. Helpless
Paretsky, S. Breakdown
Paretsky, S. Fallout
Paretsky, S. Hard time
Paretsky, S. Tunnel vision
Parker, R. B. Walking shadow
Parks, B. The girl next door
Parris, S. J. Sacrilege
Parshall, S. Poisoned ground
Patterson, J. Cat & mouse
Pavone, C. The expats
Pearl, M. The Poe shadow
Pears, I. The portrait
Penman, S. K. The queen's man
Penney, S. The invisible ones
Penny, L. The beautiful mystery
Penny, L. A great reckoning
Penny, L. How the light gets in
Penny, L. The long way home
Penny, L. The nature of the beast
Perec, G. A void
Perez-Reverte, A. The Club Dumas
Perry, A. A sunless sea
Perry, A. Half Moon Street
Perry, A. The silent cry
Perry, T. The boyfriend
Perry, T. Poison flower
Perry, T. Shadow woman
Phantom
Picoult, J. Leaving Time
Pinborough, S. A matter of blood
Pintoff, S. Hostage taker
The play of death
The Poisoned Pilgrim
Price, S. By Gaslight
Priest, C. The islanders
Pynchon, T. Bleeding edge
Qiu Xiaolong Shanghai redemption
Qiu Xiaolong Death of a red heroine
Quick, A. Garden of Lies
Quick, A. The girl who knew too much
Racculia, K. Bellweather rhapsody
Rankin, I. Rather be the devil
Rankin, I. Black and blue
Rendell, R. The bridesmaid
Rendell, R. Simisola
Richmond, M. No one you know
Robbins, C. The accomplice
Robertson, I. Anatomy of murder
Robertson, I. Island of bones
Robinson, L. S. Murder at the feast of rejoicing

Robinson, P. Innocent grave
Robotham, M. Say you're sorry
Robotham, M. Suspect
Rodriguez, L. Every broken trust
Rodriguez, L. Every hidden fear
Rodriguez, L. Every last secret
Rollins, J. The eye of God
Romano, S. Resurrection Express
Roorbach, B. Life among giants
Rosenberg, J. C. The Tehran initiative
Rosenberg, N. T. Mitigating circumstances
Rowling, J. K. The cuckoo's calling
Runcie, J. Sidney Chambers and the Forgiveness of Sins
Ryan, H. P. The other woman
Sandford, J. Deadline
Sandford, J. Silken prey
Sandlin, L. The do-right
Saunders, K. The Secrets of Wishtide
Saylor, S. Raiders of the Nile
Saylor, S. The seven wonders
Scalzi, J. Lock in
Scottoline, L. Come home
Scottoline, L. Don't Go
Sedgwick, M. Mister Memory
The shadow district
Sharp, Z. Die easy
Sharp, Z. Fourth Day
Shepherd, L. The solitary house
The silence of the sea
Silva, D. The English Girl
Slaughter, K. Pretty Girls
Sloan, R. Mr. Penumbra's 24-hour bookstore
Smith, M. A. The Inquisitor
Smith, T. R. Agent 6
Snow White must die
The snowman
Speller, E. The strange fate of Kitty Easton
Spencer, S. The dead hand of history
Spencer, S. Echoes of the dead
Spring Tide
Stabenow, D. Less than a treason
Stabenow, D. Restless in the grave
Stabenow, D. Though not dead
Stanley, M. Deadly Harvest
Stanley, M. Death of the mantis
Steele, J. The watchers
Steiner, P. The resistance
Steinhauer, O. An American spy
Straight, S. Between heaven and here
Straight, S. The gettin place
Sundin, S. Through waters deep
Sykes, S. D. Plague Land
Syndrome E
Tallis, F. Fatal lies
Tallis, F. Vienna blood
Tey, J. The daughter of time
Thomas, S. A study in scarlet women
Thompson, J. Lucifer's tears
Thompson, V. Murder on Fifth Avenue
Thomson, E. S. Beloved poison
Todd, C. A duty to the dead
Todd, C. An unmarked grave
Tolkien, S. The king of diamonds
Transgressions
Tremblay, P. Disappearance at Devil's Rock
Tucker, N. The ways of the dead
Turow, S. Presumed innocent
Turow, S. The burden of proof
Tursten, H. Night rounds
Ulfelder, S. Purgatory chasm
Unger, L. The red hunter
Upson, N. An expert in murder
Upson, N. London rain
Upson, N. Two for sorrow
Vine, B. No night is too long
Walker, M. Bruno, chief of police
Walker, M. The crowded grave
Walker, M. The Patriarch
Walter, J. Citizen Vince
Walters, M. The echo
Westlake, D. E. The hook
Westlake, D. E. What's the worst that could happen?
Whittle, T. Blood, Ash, and Bone
Whittle, T. The Dangerous Edge of Things
Whittle, T. Darker than any shadow
Whittle, T. Deeper than the grave
Williams, W. J. The fourth wall
Wilson, R. Capital Punishment
Winspear, J. Among the mad
Winspear, J. Birds of a feather
Winspear, J. A Dangerous Place
Winspear, J. Elegy for Eddie
Winspear, J. An incomplete revenge
Winspear, J. Leaving Everything Most Loved
Winspear, J. Maisie Dobbs
Winspear, J. The mapping of love and death
Winspear, J. Messenger of truth
Winspear, J. Pardonable lies
Winters, B. H. Countdown city
Winters, B. H. The last policeman
Woodrell, D. The maid's version
Woods, S. Doing hard time
Wortham, R. The rock hole
Yates, C. J. Grist Mill Road
Yocum, R. A welcome murder
Zimmerman, J. The orphanmaster
MYSTERY FILMS
See also Motion pictures
MYSTERY GRAPHIC NOVELS
See also Graphic novels
The **mystery** of Edwin Drood. Dickens, C.
MYSTERY RADIO PROGRAMS
See also Radio programs
MYSTERY STORIES *See* Mystery fiction

MYSTERY TELEVISION PROGRAMS
See also Television programs
MYSTERY WRITERS
Atkins, A. Devil's garden
Faulks, S. Devil may care
Hockensmith, S. Holmes on the range
Hockensmith, S. On the wrong track
Horowitz, A. The House of Silk
King, L. R. The game
Meyer, N. The seven-per-cent solution
Moore, G. The Sherlockian
Pirie, D. The patient's eyes
Robertson, M. The brothers of Baker Street
The **mystic** arts of erasing all signs of death. Huston, C.
Mystic river. Lehane, D.
MYSTICAL THEOLOGY *See* Mysticism
MYSTICISM
Bennett, R. J. The troupe
Erdrich, L. Four souls
Hesse, H. Siddhartha
McEwan, I. Black dogs
Zimler, R. The last kabbalist of Lisbon
MYSTICISM -- ISLAM
See also Islam
MYSTICISM -- JUDAISM
See also Judaism
MYTHICAL ANIMALS
See also Mythology
MYTHOLOGY
Fortier, A. The lost sisterhood
Gaiman, N. American gods
Hauser, E. For the most beautiful
Lewis, C. S. Till we have faces
Momaday, N. S. The ancient child
Murdoch, I. The green knight
Tóibín, C. House of Names
MYTHOLOGY, GREEK *See* Greek mythology
MYTHOLOGY, NORSE
Byatt, A. S. Ragnarok
MYTHS *See* Mythology

N

N is for noose. Grafton, S.
Nabokov, Vladimir Vladimirovich, 1899-1977
About
Nabokov, V. V. Novels and memoirs, 1941-1951
NAIROBI (KENYA)
Crompton, R. Hell's gate
Crompton, R. Hour of the Red God
The **naked** and the dead. Mailer, N.
Naked in death. Robb, J. D.
Naked lunch. Burroughs, W. S.
Naked prey. Sandford, J.
A **naked** singularity. De la Pava, S.
The **name** of the rose. Eco, U.
The **name** of the wind. Rothfuss, P.
NAMES
Whitehead, C. Apex hides the hurt
The **names** of the dead. O'Nan, S.
The **namesake.** Lahiri, J.
NAMIBIA
Brink, A. P. The other side of silence
The **naming** of the dead. Rankin, I.
Nana. Zola, E.
Nanjing requiem. Jin, H.
NANNIES
Livesey, M. The flight of Gemma Hardy
The **nanny** diaries. McLaughlin, E.
NANOTECHNOLOGY
Harrington, M. J. The goliath stone
Stross, C. Accelerando
NANTUCKET ISLAND (MASS.)
Hilderbrand, E. The island
Hilderbrand, E. Silver girl
Thayer, N. Island girls
NANTUCKET ISLAND (MASS.) -- HISTORY -- 19TH CENTURY
Brill, A. The movement of stars
NAPLES (ITALY)
Ferrante, E. The Story of the Lost Child
NAPOLEONIC WARS, 1800-1815
Bowman, V. The Accidental Countess
Dreyer, E. Barely a lady
Mallinson, A. A close run thing
Novik, N. His majesty's dragon
O'Brian, P. The commodore
O'Brian, P. The hundred days
O'Brian, P. The wine-dark sea
O'Brian, P. The yellow admiral
Putney, M. J. No longer a gentleman
Unsworth, B. Losing Nelson
Winterson, J. The Passion
NARCISSISM
Cusk, R. In the fold
NARCISSISM
See also Neuroses; Personality disorders
NARCISSISTS -- FAMILY RELATIONSHIPS
Zailckas, K. Mother, mother
NARCOTICS
See also Drugs; Materia medica; Psychotropic drugs
NARCOTICS DEALERS
Burgess, M. Dogfight, a love story
Pelecanos, G. P. The sweet forever
Winslow, D. Savages
The **narrow** road to the deep north. Flanagan, R.
Narváez, Pánfilo de, -1528
About
Lalami, L. The Moor's account
NASHVILLE (TENN.)
Arvin, R. Blood of angels
Nashville chrome. Bass, R.
NATCHEZ (MISS.)
Iles, G. Mississippi blood

Natchez burning. Iles, G.
Natchez Burning [series]
Iles, G. Mississippi blood
Nathan Heller mysteries [series]
Collins, M. A. Ask not
NATIONAL BOOK WEEK
See also Books and reading
NATIONAL CHARACTERISTICS
See also Anthropology; Nationalism; Social psychology
NATIONAL CHARACTERISTICS, AMERICAN
Gaiman, N. American gods
NATIONAL CONSCIOUSNESS *See* Nationalism
NATIONAL FOOTBALL LEAGUE
See also Football
NATIONAL LIBERATION MOVEMENTS
See also Nationalism; Revolutions
NATIONAL PARKS AND RESERVES -- UNITED STATES
Barr, N. The rope
NATIONAL RESOURCES *See* Economic conditions; Natural resources; United States -- Economic conditions
NATIONAL SECURITY
Eisler, B. The God's Eye View
Lagercrantz, D. The Girl in the Spider's Web
NATIONAL SECURITY -- CHINA
Church, J. A drop of Chinese blood
NATIONAL SECURITY -- KOREA (NORTH)
Church, J. A drop of Chinese blood
NATIONAL SELF-DETERMINATION
See also Nationalism
NATIONAL SOCIALISM
Amis, M. Time's arrow
Bolano, R. Nazi literature in the Americas
Deaver, J. Garden of beasts
Dick, P. K. The man in the high castle
Faulks, S. Charlotte Gray
Forsyth, F. The Odessa file
Grass, G. Dog years
Hall, A. The Quiller memorandum
Harris, R. Fatherland
Hegi, U. Children and fire
Hegi, U. Stones from the river
Iles, G. Black cross
Keneally, T. Schindler's list
Lourie, R. A hatred for tulips
Pottinger, S. The last Nazi
Ramirez Mercado, S. A thousand deaths plus one
Schlink, B. The reader
The chosen ones
Tournier, M. The ogre
Ullman, E. By blood
Uris, L. Mila 18
Vollmann, W. T. Europe central
Volpi, J. In search of Klingsor
NATIONAL SOCIALISM
See also Fascism; World War, 1939-1945 -- Causes
NATIONAL SOCIALISTS
Back to Back
Black, C. Murder in the Marais
Kelly, M. H. Lilac girls
Picoult, J. The Storyteller
NATIONALISM
Grass, G. The call of the toad
Werfel, F. The forty days of Musa Dagh
NATIONALISM -- TURKEY
Silent house
NATIONALISM AND COMMUNISM
Barnes, J. The noise of time
NATIVE AMERICAN WOMEN
Perry, T. Poison flower
NATIVE AMERICANS
See also Indigenous peoples
NATIVE AMERICANS -- CAPTIVITIES
See also Frontier and pioneer life
NATIVE AMERICANS
Agee, J. The bones of paradise
Alexie, S. Blasphemy
Boyden, J. Three-day road
Brooks, G. Caleb's crossing
Erdrich, L. LaRose
Harrison, J. Brown Dog
Kolpan, G. Magic words
NATIVE AMERICANS -- FOLKLORE
Haldane, S. The devil's making
NATIVE AMERICANS -- RESERVATIONS
Erdrich, L. The round house
NATIVE AMERICANS -- WYOMING
Johnson, C. Another man's moccasins
NATIVE PEOPLES *See* Indigenous peoples
Native son. Wright, R.
NATIVES *See* Indigenous peoples
The **natural.** Malamud, B.
Natural born charmer. Phillips, S. E.
Natural born hustler. Turner, N.
Natural born liar. Noire (Author)
NATURAL DISASTERS
See also Disasters
The Blood of Angels
Faber, M. The Book of Strange New Things
Walker, K. T. The age of miracles
NATURAL FOODS
See also Food
NATURAL HISTORY -- ICELAND -- 19TH CENTURY
The blue fox
A **natural** history of dragons. Brennan, M.
NATURAL LAW
See also Ethics; Law
NATURAL SELECTION
See also Genetics; Variation (Biology)
NATURALISTS
Garcia, C. The Aguero sisters
McDonald, R. Mr. Darwin's shooter
Pipkin, J. Woodsburner
Stott, R. The coral thief
Wells, H. G. The island of Doctor Moreau

Wilson, E. O. Anthill
NATURALISTS
See also Scientists
NATURE
Bergman, M. M. Birds of a lesser paradise
McCarthy, M. Birds of America
Wilson, E. O. Anthill
NATURE AND NURTURE
See also Genetics; Heredity
Nature girl. Hiaasen, C.
The **nature** of the beast. Penny, L.
Nausea. Sartre, J. P.
The **nautical** chart. Perez-Reverte, A.
NAVAHO INDIANS *See* Navajo Indians
NAVAJO CHILDREN
See also Native American children; Navajo Indians
NAVAJO INDIANS
Hillerman, T. The blessing way
Hillerman, T. Hunting badger
Hillerman, T. The Jim Chee mysteries
Hillerman, T. Listening woman
Hillerman, T. Sacred clowns
Hillerman, T. The shape shifter
Hillerman, T. Skinwalkers
Hillerman, T. Talking God
Hillerman, T. A thief of time
Hillerman, T. The wailing wind
Silko, L. Ceremony
NAVAJO WOMEN
See also Native American women; Navajo Indians
NAVAL AERONAUTICS *See* Military aeronautics
NAVAL BATTLES
Forester, C. S. Beat to quarters
Forester, C. S. Commodore Hornblower
Forester, C. S. Hornblower and the Atropos
Forester, C. S. Ship of the line
NAVAL BATTLES
See also Battles
NAVAL OFFICERS
Flanagan, R. Wanting
Simmons, D. The terror
Vollmann, W. T. The rifles
NAVAL OFFICERS -- ITALY -- VENICE
Moore, C. The Serpent of Venice
NAXALITE MOVEMENT
Lahiri, J. The lowland
The **Nazarene.** Asch, S.
NAZI LEADERS
Harris, R. Fatherland
Lindgren, T. Hash
Mailer, N. The castle in the forest
Neugeboren, J. 1940
Nazi literature in the Americas. Bolano, R.
NAZIS
Gillham, D. R. City of women
Konar, A. Mischling
NAZIS -- EUROPE
Kelly, M. H. Lilac girls
NAZISM *See* National socialism
NEANDERTHAL RACE
Golding, W. The inheritors
NEANDERTHALS
Cameron, C. The last Neanderthal
Neapolitan Novels [series]
Ferrante, E. The Story of the Lost Child
Ferrante, E. Those Who Leave and Those Who Stay
NEAR-DEATH EXPERIENCES
Davis, K. The thin place
Urrea, L. A. The hummingbird's daughter
Willis, C. Passage
NEAR-DEATH EXPERIENCES
See also Death
The **nearest** exit. Steinhauer, O.
A **nearly** perfect copy. Amend, A.
NEBRASKA
Agee, J. The bones of paradise
Harrison, J. The road home
Powers, R. The echo maker
Schaffert, T. The coffins of Little Hope
Ward, L. Outside valentine
NEBRASKA -- 19TH CENTURY
Cather, W. My Antonia
Cather, W. O pioneers!
NEBULA AWARD
See also Literary prizes; Science fiction
The **necessary** beggar. Palwick, S.
Necessary errors. Crain, C.
Necessity. Walton, J.
The **Necromancer's** house. Buehlman, C.
NECROMANCY *See* Divination; Magic
Nectar in a sieve. Markandaya, K.
NEGRO LEAGUES
See also Baseball
NEGROES *See* African Americans; Blacks
The **neighbor.** Gardner, L.
NEIGHBORHOOD
Greenfeld, K. T. Triburbia
McCall Smith, A. A conspiracy of friends
Osondu, E. C. This house is not for sale
Neighbors. Berger, T.
NEIGHBORS
Backman, F. A man called Ove
Baxter, C. The feast of love
Berger, T. Neighbors
Cheever, J. Bullet Park
D'Abo, C. 30 Days
De Bernières, L. The dust that falls from dreams
Gowdy, B. The romantic
Hagedorn, J. T. Toxicology
Hamilton, J. A map of the world
Haslett, A. Union Atlantic
Hedges, P. The Heights
Hoffman, A. Illumination night
Hoover, M. The quickening

McCall Smith, A. Corduroy mansions
McKinney-Whetstone, D. Leaving Cecil Street
Mengestu, D. The beautiful things that heaven bears
Miller, S. For love
Parker, T. J. California girl
Rendell, R. Tigerlily's orchids
Schine, C. The New Yorkers
Shreve, A. Eden Close
Simonson, H. Major Pettigrew's last stand
Stuckey-French, E. Revenge of the radioactive lady
Unsworth, B. After Hannibal
Nekropolis. McHugh, M. F.
Nelson, Horatio Nelson, Viscount, 1758-1805
About
Sontag, S. The volcano lover
Unsworth, B. Losing Nelson
Nemesis. Roth, P.
NEO-FASCISM *See* Fascism; Neo-Nazis
NEO-NAZIS
See also Fascism
NEPAL
Desai, K. The inheritance of loss
NEPAL -- KATHMANDU
Upadhyay, S. The guru of love
NEPHEWS
Gross, A. Eyes wide open
Nabokov, V. V. King, queen, knave
Ozick, C. Foreign bodies
Rosenberg, N. T. Interest of justice
Wood, S. Wrecker
Neptune's brood. Stross, C.
Nero, Emperor of Rome, 37-68
About
George, M. The confessions of young Nero
Sienkiewicz, H. Quo Vadis
The **Neruda** case. Ampuero, R.
Neruda, Pablo, 1904-1973
About
Ampuero, R. The Neruda case
Nerve. Francis, D.
NERVOUS BREAKDOWN
Marlette, D. Magic time
Wilson, R. The blind man of Seville
NERVOUS SYSTEM -- DISEASES
See also Diseases
The **Nest.** Sweeney, C. D.
Netherland. O'Neill, J.
NETHERLANDS
Bakker, G. The twin
Keilson, H. Comedy in a minor key
Moor, M. d. The storm
Vreeland, S. Girl in hyacinth blue
NETHERLANDS -- 17TH CENTURY
Chevalier, T. Girl with a pearl earring
Moggach, D. Tulip fever
NETHERLANDS -- AMSTERDAM
Camus, A. The fall
Lourie, R. A hatred for tulips
Moggach, D. Tulip fever
NEURASTHENIA
See also Mental illness
Lehane, D. Since we fell
NEUROLOGISTS
Barker, P. The eye in the door
Barker, P. The ghost road
Powers, R. The echo maker
Willis, C. Passage
Neuromancer. Gibson, W.
NEVADA
Crichton, M. Prey
Kittredge, W. The Willow Field
Udall, B. The lonely polygamist
Wallace, S. Montana dawn
Watkins, C. V. Battleborn
NEVADA -- 19TH CENTURY
Clark, W. V. T. The Ox-bow incident
NEVADA -- LAS VEGAS
Bock, C. Beautiful children
Ellroy, J. Blood's a rover
Faust, C. Choke hold
Garcia, C. A handbook to luck
Puzo, M. The last Don
NEVADA -- RENO
Vlautin, W. Northline
Never any end to Paris.
Never breathe a word. Blackwood, C.
Never go back. Goddard, R.
Never Judge a Lady by Her Cover. MacLean, S.
Never let me go. Ishiguro, K.
Never let you go.
The **Never** List. Zan, K.
Neverhome. Hunt, L.
Nevernight. Kristoff, J.
NEW AGE MOVEMENT
See also Cults; Occultism; Social movements
The **new** annotated Dracula.
The **new** centurions. Wambaugh, J.
New Cthulhu.
New Directions paperbook [series]
Moya, H. C. The dream of my return
NEW ENGLAND
Brown, R. Tender mercies
Carroll, J. Bathing the Lion
Carter, S. L. New England white
Cheever, J. The Wapshot chronicle
Cheever, J. The Wapshot scandal
Clarke, B. An arsonist's guide to writers' homes in New England
Cooke, C. Daughters of the revolution
Erdrich, L. The painted drum
Hoffman, A. The probable future
Irving, J. In one person
Jackson, S. We have always lived in the castle
Jen, G. World and town

Knowles, J. A separate peace
Levin, I. The Stepford wives
McCarthy, M. A charmed life
Miller, S. The senator's wife
Murphy, Y. The call
Rice, L. Home fires
Sarton, M. A small room
Strout, E. Amy and Isabelle
Theroux, P. Picture palace
NEW ENGLAND -- 17TH CENTURY
Seton, A. The Winthrop woman
NEW ENGLAND -- 19TH CENTURY
Naslund, S. J. Ahab's wife; or, The star-gazer
Tinti, H. The good thief
Wharton, E. Ethan Frome
New England white. Carter, S. L.
NEW FOREST (ENGLAND)
Rutherfurd, E. The forest
NEW GUINEA
King, L. Euphoria
NEW HAMPSHIRE
Banks, R. Affliction
Bohjalian, C. The night strangers
Brown, R. Before and after
Costello, M. Big if
Hegi, U. The vision of Emma Blau
Irving, J. A prayer for Owen Meany
Lent, J. Lost nation
Lipman, E. The dearly departed
Maynard, J. Labor Day
Perry, T. Death benefits
Picoult, J. Keeping Faith
Picoult, J. Nineteen minutes
Sarton, M. Kinds of love
Shreve, A. Sea glass
Updike, J. Memories of the Ford Administration
Williams, A. J. Down from Cascom Mountain
Winters, B. H. World of trouble
NEW HAMPSHIRE -- 19TH CENTURY
Benet, S. V. The Devil and Daniel Webster
Lent, J. Lost nation
Shreve, A. Fortune's Rocks
NEW JERSEY
Caldwell, I. The rule of four
Coben, H. Caught
Coben, H. The woods
Colfer, E. Plugged
Diaz, J. The brief wondrous life of Oscar Wao
Evanovich, J. One for the money
Ford, R. Independence Day
Ford, R. The lay of the land
Ford, R. Let Me Be Frank With You
Grodstein, L. A friend of the family
Levitt, P. M. Come with me to Babylon
Meno, J. The boy detective fails
Perrotta, T. Joe College
Price, R. Clockers
Price, R. Freedomland
Price, R. Samaritan
Prose, F. My new American life
Rosenfelt, D. Don't tell a soul
Roth, P. American pastoral
Roth, P. The plot against America
Updike, J. The poorhouse fair
Updike, J. Terrorist
Woo, S. J. Everything Asian
NEW JERSEY -- ATLANTIC CITY
Leonard, E. Glitz
NEW JERSEY -- HISTORY -- 20TH CENTURY
Stewart, A. Girl waits with gun
NEW JERSEY -- NEWARK
Roth, P. Indignation
Roth, P. Nemesis
Roth, P. The human stain
Roth, P. I married a communist
Roth, P. The plot against America
New lives. Schulze, I.
NEW MEXICO
Bennett, R. J. American elsewhere
Heller, P. The painter
McCarthy, C. Cities of the plain
McCarthy, C. The crossing
Nesbit, T. The wives of Los Alamos
Nichols, J. T. The Milagro beanfield war
Quade, K. V. Night at the Fiestas
Schaefer, J. W. Monte Walsh
Valdes-Rodriguez, A. Dirty girls on top
NEW MEXICO -- 19TH CENTURY
Cather, W. Death comes for the archbishop
NEW MEXICO -- LOS ALAMOS
Kanon, J. Los Alamos
NEW MEXICO -- SANTA FE
Glass, J. The whole world over
Hershon, J. The German bride
Rossner, J. Perfidia
Woods, S. Santa Fe rules
Woods, S. Short straw
NEW ORLEANS (LA.)
Johnson, B. More of this world or maybe another
New People. Senna, D.
NEW SOUTH WALES (AUSTRALIA)
Grenville, K. The secret river
The **new** space opera.
New stories from the South: the year's best [date]
New uses for old boyfriends. Kendrick, B.
NEW YORK (N.Y.)
Baker, D. Young man with a horn
Baldwin, J. Another country
Bellow, S. Mr. Sammler's planet
Burgess, M. Uncle Janice
Chabon, M. The amazing adventures of Kavalier and Clay
Cole, T. Every day is for the thief
Colwin, L. A big storm knocked it over
Colwin, L. Family happiness

Conroy, P. The prince of tides
Cook, R. Marker
Cunningham, M. The snow queen
Cunningham, M. Specimen days
Danler, S. Sweetbitter
Davies, V. Miracle on 34th Street
Dos Passos, J. Manhattan transfer
Dreiser, T. Sister Carrie
Faulks, S. On Green Dolphin Street
Fitzgerald, F. S. The great Gatsby
Foer, J. S. Extremely loud & incredibly close
Gill, J. F. The gargoyle hunters
Goudge, E. Garden of lies
Hallberg, G. R. City on fire
Hamill, P. Forever
Hamill, P. Tabloid city
Heller, P. Celine
Helprin, M. In sunlight and in shadow
Helprin, M. Winter's tale
Hobson, L. K. Z. Gentleman's agreement
Hunter, E. The blackboard jungle
Hunter, E. Candyland
Jackson, C. The lost weekend
Jen, G. Typical American
Keane, M. B. Fever
Larsen, N. Passing
Larson, N. The Dewey Decimal system
Mallon, T. Bandbox
Marshall, P. Brown girl, brownstones
Mathews, B. The world of tomorrow
Martin, S. An object of beauty
McInerney, J. Bright lights, big city
Miller, H. Tropic of Capricorn
Mosley, W. All I did was shoot my man
Nathan, R. Portrait of Jennie
O'Hara, J. Butterfield 8
O'Mara, T. Crooked Numbers
O'Neill, J. Netherland
Ozick, C. The Puttermesser papers
Plath, S. The bell jar
Prentiss, M. Tuesday nights in 1980
Preston, D. Reliquary
Rand, A. The fountainhead
Robb, J. D. Naked in death
Roberts, V. After the fall
Rooney, K. Lillian Boxfish Takes a Walk
Ross, A. Mr. Peanut
Roth, H. A diving rock on the Hudson
Roth, H. From bondage
Roth, H. Requiem for Harlem
Roth, P. The dying animal
Saint, H. F. Memoirs of an invisible man
Salinger, J. D. The catcher in the rye
Salinger, J. D. Franny & Zooey
Salinger, J. D. Raise high the roof beam, carpenters, and Seymour: an introduction
Sanders, L. The sixth commandment
Shakar, A. Luminarium
Shapiro, B. A. The muralist
Shumway, C. Ten girls to watch
Singer, I. B. Enemies, a love story
Sternbergh, A. Shovel ready
Tanenbaum, R. Act of revenge
Thompson, V. Murder on Lenox Hill
Towles, A. Rules of civility
Trigiani, A. Very Valentine
Westlake, D. E. Don't ask
Westlake, D. E. Good behavior
Westlake, D. E. The hook
Westlake, D. E. Money for nothing
Westlake, D. E. Smoke
Wolfe, T. The web and the rock
Wolfe, T. You can't go home again
Wolfe, T. The bonfire of the vanities
Wray, J. Lowboy
Wright, R. The outsider
Zimmerman, J. The orphanmaster

NEW YORK (N.Y.) -- 18TH CENTURY
Charyn, J. Johnny One-Eye
Liss, D. The whiskey rebels

NEW YORK (N.Y.) -- 19TH CENTURY
Carr, C. The alienist
Crane, S. Maggie: a girl of the streets (a story of New York)
Doctorow, E. L. The waterworks
Finney, J. Time and again
Millhauser, S. Martin Dressler
Piercy, M. Sex wars
Rose, J. Blackest bird
Vidal, G. 1876

NEW YORK (N.Y.) -- BRONX
Doctorow, E. L. Billy Bathgate
McCann, C. Let the great world spin
Neugeboren, J. 1940
Ozick, C. Foreign bodies
Verghese, A. Cutting for stone

NEW YORK (N.Y.) -- BROOKLYN
Auster, P. The Brooklyn follies
Auster, P. Sunset Park
Barton, E. Brookland
Danticat, E. The dew breaker
Garcia, C. Dreaming in Cuban
Gilmore, J. Golden country
Green, N. The angel of Montague Street
Hedges, P. The Heights
Kirshenbaum, B. An almost perfect moment
Kwok, J. Girl in translation
Lethem, J. The fortress of solitude
Malamud, B. The assistant
Marshall, P. The fisher king
Maynard, J. The usual rules
McDermott, A. At weddings and wakes
Miller, H. Tropic of Capricorn
Mirvis, T. The outside world
Nunez, E. Grace

Potok, C. The gift of Asher Lev
Potok, C. My name is Asher Lev
Reuland, R. Semiautomatic
Reznikoff, C. By the waters of Manhattan
Rosenfeld, L. I'm so happy for you
Schwartz, L. S. The writing on the wall
Singer, I. B. Enemies, a love story
Smith, B. A tree grows in Brooklyn
Styron, W. Sophie's choice
Tanner, H. Vaclav and Lena
Tóibín, C. Brooklyn
Winters, B. H. Bedbugs

NEW YORK (N.Y.) -- GREENWICH VILLAGE

Cunningham, M. The hours
Glass, J. The whole world over
Henderson, E. Ten thousand saints
Steinke, R. Holy skirts
White, E. The beautiful room is empty
Wolitzer, M. The wife

NEW YORK (N.Y.) -- HARLEM

Baker, K. Strivers Row
Baldwin, J. Go tell it on the mountain
Baldwin, J. If Beale Street could talk
Baldwin, J. Tell me how long the train's been gone
Hughes, L. Simple speaks his mind
Hughes, L. Simple's Uncle Sam
Morrison, T. Jazz
Roth, H. A star shines over Mt. Morris Park
Wallant, E. L. The pawnbroker

NEW YORK (N.Y.) -- HISTORY -- 1775-1865

Faye, L. The gods of Gotham

NEW YORK (N.Y.) -- HISTORY -- 1898-1951

Mathews, B. The world of tomorrow
Rindell, S. The Other Typist

NEW YORK (N.Y.) -- HISTORY -- 21ST CENTURY

Bohjalian, C. The sandcastle girls

NEW YORK (N.Y.) -- HISTORY

Carr, C. The alienist

NEW YORK (N.Y.) -- LOWER EAST SIDE

Crane, S. Maggie: a girl of the streets (a story of New York)
Huston, C. Caught stealing
Johnson, A. D. Moonshine
Mosley, W. RL's dream
Price, R. Lush life
Roth, H. Call it sleep

NEW YORK (N.Y.) -- MANHATTAN

Colwin, L. Happy all the time
Cunningham, M. By nightfall
Davies, V. Miracle on 34th Street
Dee, J. The privileges
DeLillo, D. Falling man
D'Erasmo, S. The Sky Below
Doctorow, E. L. Homer & Langley
Dunne, D. Too much money
Fairstein, L. Entombed
Faulks, S. On Green Dolphin Street
Fitzgerald, F. S. The beautiful and damned
Fitzgerald, F. S. The great Gatsby
Gaitskill, M. Veronica
Glass, J. Three Junes
Goldman, W. Marathon man
Goodis, D. Nightfall
Hagedorn, J. T. Toxicology
Harrison, C. The finder
Heller, J. Good as Gold
Herlihy, J. L. Midnight cowboy
Hijuelos, O. The Mambo Kings play songs of love
Howard, M. The rags of time
Hunt, S. The invention of everything else
Hunter, E. The moment she was gone
Hunter, E. Privileged conversation
Kaufman, B. Up the down staircase
Kaufman, S. Diary of a mad housewife
Kellerman, J. The genius
Krauss, N. The history of love
Lethem, J. Chronic city
Levin, I. Rosemary's baby
Lipman, E. The family man
Lynn, A. Now you see it
Mallon, T. Bandbox
McCann, C. Let the great world spin
McInerney, J. The good life
McLaughlin, E. The nanny diaries
McPhee, J. No ordinary matter
Messud, C. The emperor's children
O'Hara, J. Butterfield 8
O'Neill, J. Netherland
Packer, A. The dive from Clausen's pier
Percy, W. The last gentleman
Preston, D. The cabinet of curiosities
Price, R. The good priest's son
Prose, F. Household saints
Robinson, R. Sweetwater
Rosen, J. Joy comes in the morning
Roth, P. Exit ghost
Saul, J. Midnight voices
Schine, C. The New Yorkers
Schulberg, B. Waterfront
Schulman, H. This beautiful life
Schwarz, C. All is vanity
Waldman, A. The submission
Westlake, D. E. Good behavior
White, E. Hotel de Dream
Whitehead, C. Zone one
Woods, S. Dirt
Woods, S. Kisser
Woods, S. Lucid intervals
Woods, S. Two-dollar bill
Wouk, H. Marjorie Morningstar

NEW YORK (N.Y.) -- QUEENS

Burgess, M. Dogfight, a love story
Hansen, R. A wild surge of guilty passion
Isaacs, S. Close relations
Jin, H. A good fall

McDermott, A. Charming Billy
Reyn, I. What happened to Anna K.
NEW YORK (N.Y.) -- SOCIAL LIFE AND CUSTOMS -- 20TH CENTURY
Bauer, C. Frances and Bernard
Shapiro, B. A. The muralist
NEW YORK (STATE)
Baker, T. The little giant of Aberdeen County
Canin, E. America America
Clarke, B. Exley
Clarkson, J. Among thieves
Dreiser, T. An American tragedy
Gaitskill, M. The mare
Goodman, C. Arcadia Falls
Gottlieb, E. Now you see him
Groff, L. Arcadia
Groff, L. The monsters of Templeton
Hill, J. Heart-shaped box
Lennon, J. R. Castle
Oates, J. C. The falls
Oates, J. C. The gravedigger's daughter
Oates, J. C. Little bird of heaven
Oates, J. C. Missing mom
O'Connell, C. Judas child
Perry, T. Dance for the dead
Perry, T. The face-changers
Perry, T. Vanishing act
Prose, F. Goldengrove
Racculia, K. This must be the place
Ray, K. No country
Robinson, K. S. New York 2140
Russo, R. Bridge of sighs
Scott, J. The kept
Shriver, L. We need to talk about Kevin
Spencer, S. Man in the woods
Spufford, F. Golden Hill
Torres, J. We the animals
NEW YORK (STATE) -- 18TH CENTURY
Cooper, J. F. The last of the Mohicans
NEW YORK (STATE) -- 19TH CENTURY
Seton, A. Dragonwyck
NEW YORK (STATE) -- 20TH CENTURY
Banks, R. The sweet hereafter
Cheever, J. Bullet Park
Cook, T. H. Instruments of night
Dreiser, T. An American tragedy
Godwin, G. The finishing school
Hansen, R. Mariette in ecstasy
Lee A gesture life
Oates, J. C. Because it is bitter, and because it is my heart
Oates, J. C. Broke heart blues
Oates, J. C. Foxfire
Oates, J. C. I lock my door upon myself
Oates, J. C. Middle age
Oates, J. C. We were the Mulvaneys
Perry, T. Shadow woman
Prose, F. Primitive people
Puzo, M. The godfather
Quindlen, A. Object lessons
Russo, R. Nobody's fool
Russo, R. The risk pool
Shreve, A. Eden Close
Straub, P. Ghost story
Westlake, D. E. Drowned hopes
NEW YORK (STATE) -- 21ST CENTURY
Shriver, L. We need to talk about Kevin
NEW YORK (STATE) -- ALBANY
Kennedy, W. Chango's beads and two-tone shoes
Kennedy, W. Ironweed
NEW YORK (STATE) -- BUFFALO
Reisman, N. The first desire
NEW YORK (STATE) -- HISTORY -- COLONIAL PERIOD, CA. 1600-1775
Spufford, F. Golden Hill
NEW YORK (STATE) -- ITHACA
O'Nan, S. The names of the dead
NEW YORK (STATE) -- NIAGARA FALLS
Oates, J. C. The falls
Oates, J. C. Rape
NEW YORK (STATE) -- SYRACUSE
Abu-Jaber, D. Origin
NEW YORK (STATE) -- WESTCHESTER COUNTY
Boyle, T. C. World's end
Jen, G. Mona in the promised land
New York 2140. Robinson, K. S.
New York dead. Woods, S.
New York novels. Wharton, E.
New York Review Books classics [series]
Chatterjee, U. English, August
The **New** Yorker stories. Beattie, A.
The **New** Yorkers. Schine, C.
NEW ZEALAND
Catton, E. The luminaries
Cleave, P. Five minutes alone
Hulme, K. The bone people
Tremain, R. The color
Uris, L. Redemption
NEW ZEALAND -- 19TH CENTURY
Goudge, E. Green Dolphin Street
NEW ZEALANDERS -- ENGLAND
Frame, J. Towards another summer
NEWARK (N.J.)
Parks, B. The girl next door
Roth, P. Nemesis
Roth, P. The human stain
NEWFOUNDLAND
Crummey, M. Sweetland
Lundrigan, N. Glass boys
Norman, H. The bird artist
The **newlyweds.** Freudenberger, N.
NEWLYWEDS
Freudenberger, N. The newlyweds
NEWPORT (R.I.)
Smith, G. B. The maze at Windermere

The **news** from Spain. Wickersham, J.
News of the world. Jiles, P.
NEWS PHOTOGRAPHERS
Belfer, L. A fierce radiance
Just, W. S. Exiles in the garden
Leimbach, M. The man from Saigon
Soli, T. The lotus eaters
The **news** where you are. O'Flynn, C.
Newsflesh [series]
Grant, M. Feedback
NEWSLETTERS
See also Journalism; Newspapers
NEWSPAPER ADVERTISING
See also Advertising; Newspapers
NEWSPAPER EDITORS
Doig, I. Sweet thunder
Lewis, S. It can't happen here
Rachman, T. The imperfectionists
NEWSPAPERS
Barnett, L. K. Jam on the Vine
Hamill, P. Tabloid city
Rachman, T. The imperfectionists
Rand, A. The fountainhead
Schulberg, B. What makes Sammy run?
Vidal, G. Empire
NEWSPAPERS
See also Mass media; Serial publications
Newton, Isaac Sir, 1642-1727
About
Morrow, J. The last witchfinder
Stott, R. Ghostwalk
Next. Hynes, J.
The **next** best thing. Weiner, J.
Next life might be kinder. Norman, H.
Next of kin. Trollope, J.
Next to love. Feldman, E.
NEZ PERCE INDIANS
Vollmann, W. T. The Dying Grass
NEZ PERCE WAR, 1877
Vollmann, W. T. The Dying Grass
NIAGARA FALLS (N.Y. AND ONT.)
Oates, J. C. The falls
Niagara Falls all over again. McCracken, E.
NICARAGUA
Ramirez Mercado, S. A thousand deaths plus one
Niccolo rising. Dunnett, D.
The **nice** and the good. Murdoch, I.
Nice work. Lodge, D.
Nicholas Nickleby. Dickens, C.
The **Nick** Adams stories. Hemingway, E.
NICOLAOS (FICTITIOUS CHARACTER : CORBY)
Corby, G. The Pericles Commission
NIECES
Rice, L. Little night
NIGER RIVER DELTA REGION (NIGERIA) -- SOCIAL CONDITIONS
Watson, C. Tiny sunbirds, far away
NIGERIA
Adebayo, A. Stay with me
Barrett, A. I. Love is power, or something like that
Cole, T. Every day is for the thief
Habila, H. Measuring time
Obioma, C. The fishermen
Okparanta, C. Happiness, Like Water
Okparanta, C. Under the udala trees
Osondu, E. C. Voice of America
Watson, C. Tiny sunbirds, far away
NIGERIA -- 19TH CENTURY
Achebe, C. Things fall apart
NIGERIA -- CIVIL WAR, 1967-1970
Adichie, C. N. Half of a yellow sun
NIGERIA -- LAGOS
Abani, C. GraceLand
NIGERIANS -- ENGLAND
Adichie, C. N. Americanah
Cleave, C. Little Bee
NIGERIANS
Cleave, C. Little Bee
Cole, T. Open city
NIGERIANS -- UNITED STATES
Adichie, C. N. Americanah
Cole, T. Open city
Osondu, E. C. Voice of America
NIGHT
Murakami, H. After dark
NIGHT
See also Chronology; Time
Night at the Fiestas. Quade, K. V.
Night bus. Rigosi, G.
The **night** circus. Morgenstern, E.
NIGHT CLUBS
The hall of singing caryatids
Hiaasen, C. Strip tease
Pelevin, V. The hall of singing caryatids
Smith, M. C. December 6
The **night** counter. Yunis, A.
The **night** country. O'Nan, S.
Night Film. Pessl, M.
Night flight. Saint-Exupery, A. d.
The **night** following. Joss, M.
The **night** gardener. Pelecanos, G. P.
The **night** guest. McFarlane, F.
The **night** in Lisbon. Remarque, E. M.
The **night** market. Moore, J.
Night Night, Sleep Tight. Ephron, H.
Night of sorrows. Sherwood, F.
Night of the Animals. Broun, B.
Night of the fox. Higgins, J.
Night prey. Sandford, J.
Night rounds. Tursten, H.
Night shift. King, S.
Night sins. Hoag, T.
The **Night** Stages. Urquhart, J.
The **night** strangers. Bohjalian, C.

The **night** the lights went out. White, K.
A **night** to surrender. Dare, T.
The **night** train. Edgerton, C.
Night train to Memphis. Peters, E.
The **night** villa. Goodman, C.
The **night** watch. Waters, S.
Night watch. Fairstein, L.
Night woman. Price, N.
Night, Dawn, The accident: three tales. Wiesel, E.
Nightcrawlers. Pronzini, B.
Nightfall. Goodis, D.
The **nightingale.** Hannah, K.
The **nightingale.** Sholem Aleichem
Nightlife. Perry, T.
Nightmares.
Nightmares & dreamscapes. King, S.
NIGHTMARES
Bowen, L. Wake of vultures
Carey, J. Poison fruit
Nights at the circus. Carter, A.
Nights of Villjamur. Newton, M. C.
Nightwood. Barnes, D.
Nightwoods. Frazier, C.
Nijinska, Bronislava, 1891-1972
About
Stachniak, E. The chosen maiden
Nijinsky, Vaslaw, 1890-1950
About
Stachniak, E. The chosen maiden
Nimitz class. Robinson, P.
Nine coaches waiting. Stewart, M.
Nine days. Koenig, M.
Nine princes in Amber. Zelazny, R.
Nine stories. Salinger, J. D.
The **nine** tailors. Sayers, D. L.
Ninefox gambit. Lee, Y. H.
NINETEEN EIGHTIES
Prentiss, M. Tuesday nights in 1980
Rooney, K. Lillian Boxfish Takes a Walk
Watson, S. Suitcase city
NINETEEN EIGHTIES
See also World history -- 20th century
Nineteen eighty-four. Orwell, G.
NINETEEN FIFTIES
See also World history -- 20th century
Blume, J. In the unlikely event
NINETEEN FORTIES
See also World history -- 20th century
Nineteen minutes. Picoult, J.
NINETEEN NINETIES
See also World history -- 20th century
Senna, D. New People
NINETEEN SEVENTIES
Mengestu, D. All our names
Wuertz, Y. G. Everything belongs to us
NINETEEN SEVENTIES
See also World history -- 20th century
NINETEEN SIXTIES
See also World history -- 20th century
Cline, E. The girls
Groff, L. Arcadia
NINETEEN THIRTIES
See also World history -- 20th century
NINETEEN TWENTIES
Bennett, J. Bitter Spirits
Lehane, D. Live by night
Rosen, R. Dollface
NINETEEN TWENTIES
See also World history -- 20th century
Nineveh.
The **ninth** hour. McDermott, A.
The **ninth** step. Jerkins, G.
Nip the buds, shoot the kids. Oe, K.
NISEI *See* Japanese Americans
The **Nix.** Hill, N.
NIXON, RICHARD M. (RICHARD MILHOUS), 1913-1994
Self, W. Shark
No country. Ray, K.
No country for old men. McCarthy, C.
No crystal stair. Rutland, E.
No defense. Wilhelm, K.
No easy target. Johansen, I.
No good deeds. Lippman, L.
No Good Duke Goes Unpunished. MacLean, S.
No graves as yet. Perry, A.
No longer a gentleman. Putney, M. J.
No night is too long. Vine, B.
No one belongs here more than you. July, M.
No one can pronounce my name. Satyal, R.
No one is here except all of us. Ausubel, R.
No one you know. Richmond, M.
No ordinary matter. McPhee, J.
No Place for a Dame. Brockway, C.
No place for heroes. Restrepo, L.
No place like home. Samuel, B.
No proper lady. Cooper, I.
No safe place. Patterson, R. N.
No time like the present. Gordimer, N.
No time to wave goodbye. Mitchard, J.
No. 1 Ladies' Detective Agency [series]
McCall Smith, A. The Limpopo Academy of Private Detection
McCall Smith, A. The good husband of Zebra Drive
McCall Smith, A. The No. 1 Ladies' Detective Agency
The **No.** 1 Ladies' Detective Agency. McCall Smith, A.
NO. 1 LADIES' DETECTIVE AGENCY (IMAGINARY ORGANIZATION)
McCall Smith, A. The Limpopo Academy of Private Detection
McCall Smith, A. The No. 1 Ladies' Detective Agency
McCall Smith, A. The Saturday big tent wedding party
McCall Smith, A. Tea time for the traditionally built
Noah (Biblical figure)
About

Maine, D. The preservationist
Noah's compass. Tyler, A.
NOBEL LAUREATES FOR LITERATURE
Coetzee, J. M. Summertime
Cooley, M. The archivist
Hunt, R. Mr. Chartwell
McLain, P. The Paris wife
Oates, J. C. Wild nights!
Russell, M. D. Dreamers of the day
NOBEL LAUREATES FOR PHYSICS
Lightman, A. P. Einstein's dreams
Powers, T. Three days to never
Rubenfeld, J. The death instinct
NOBEL PRIZES
Wallace, I. The prize
NOBILITY
Bowen, K. You're the Earl That I Want
Bowman, V. The Unexpected Duchess
Boyle, E. Along Came a Duke
Butcher, J. The aeronaut's windlass
Byrne, K. The Duke
Chase, L. Vixen in Velvet
Dare, T. Say Yes to the Marquess
Dreyer, E. Once a Rake
Dreyer, E. Twice tempted
Guhrke, L. L. How to lose a duke in ten days
James, E. My American Duchess
James, E. Three Weeks With Lady X
Kleypas, L. Cold-hearted Rake
MacKenzie, S. Bedding Lord Ned
MacLean, S. A Scot in the dark
Michels, E. The rebel heir
Milan, C. The Duchess War
Putney, M. J. Loving a lost lord
Putney, M. J. Not quite a wife
Robertson, I. Circle of shadows
NOBILITY -- ENGLAND
Jeffries, S. 'Twas the night after Christmas
NOBILITY -- PAPAL STATES
Dunant, S. Blood and beauty
The **nobodies** album. Parkhurst, C.
Nobody move. Johnson, D.
Nobody's fool. Russo, R.
Nocturne. McBain, E.
Noir. Coover, R.
NOIR FICTION
Mosley, W. And sometimes I wonder about you
Sandlin, L. The do-right
Waite, U. Sometimes the wolf
The **noise** of time. Barnes, J.
NOISE POLLUTION
See also Pollution
NOMADS
Ahmad, J. The wandering falcon
NONCONFORMITY *See* Conformity; Counterculture; Dissent
None to accompany me. Gordimer, N.
NONFICTION WRITERS
Boyle, T. C. Road to Wellville
Boyle, T. C. The women
Horan, N. Loving Frank
Pipkin, J. Woodsburner
Powers, K. Capote in Kansas
NONVERBAL COMMUNICATION
Lopez, R. All back full
Nora Webster. Tóibín, C.
NORFOLK (ENGLAND)
Griffiths, E. The house at sea's end
James, P. D. Devices and desires
NORMANDIE (STEAMSHIP)
Villars, E. The Normandie affair
The **Normandie** affair. Villars, E.
NORMANS -- ENGLAND
Lyndon, R. Hawk quest
NORMANS -- GREAT BRITAIN
Bracewell, P. Shadow on the crown
NORSE LEGENDS
See also Legends
Norse mythology. Gaiman, N.
NORSE MYTHOLOGY
See also Mythology
NORSE MYTHOLOGY
Gaiman, N. Norse mythology
NORSEMEN *See* Vikings
NORTH ADAMS (MASS.)
Shepard, K. The Celestials
North and South. Jakes, J.
NORTH CAROLINA
Adams, A. After the war
Adams, A. A southern exposure
Allen, S. A. Garden Spells
Allen, S. A. The girl who chased the moon
Allen, S. A. The sugar queen
Betts, D. Souls raised from the dead
Earley, T. The blue star
Earley, T. Jim the boy
Edgerton, C. The Bible salesman
Edgerton, C. The night train
Edgerton, C. Walking across Egypt
Frazier, C. Nightwoods
Gabaldon, D. The fiery cross
Gibbons, K. Divining women
Gibbons, K. Sights unseen
Godwin, G. Evensong
Godwin, G. A mother and two daughters
Godwin, G. Unfinished desires
Gurganus, A. Local souls
Gurganus, A. The oldest living Confederate widow tells all
Hart, J. Down river
Hart, J. Iron house
Hart, J. The king of lies
Hart, J. The last child
Hickam, H. H. The keeper's son
Hooper, K. Blood sins

Huyler, F. The laws of invisible things
Karon, J. At home in Mitford
Kostova, E. The swan thieves
Malone, M. The four corners of the sky
McCrumb, S. The ballad of Tom Dooley
Medlicott, J. A. The ladies of Covington send their love
Patterson, J. Four blind mice
Pearson, T. R. A short history of a small place
Percy, W. The second coming
Pessl, M. Special topics in calamity physics
Price, R. The good priest's son
Price, R. Roxanna Slade
Rash, R. Serena
Smith, L. On Agate Hill
Sparks, N. The notebook
Sparks, N. A walk to remember
Truong, M. Bitter in the mouth
Tyler, A. A slipping-down life
Tyler, A. The tin can tree
Wolfe, T. The web and the rock
Zuber, I. Salt
NORTH CAROLINA -- 18TH CENTURY
Gabaldon, D. A breath of snow and ashes
Gabaldon, D. An echo in the bone
NORTH CAROLINA -- 19TH CENTURY
Crafts, H. The bondswomans narrative
Humphreys, J. Nowhere else on earth
Slouka, M. God's fool
NORTH CENTRAL STATES *See* Middle West
NORTH DAKOTA
Box, C. J. Badlands
Erdrich, L. The plague of doves
Erdrich, L. The Beet Queen
Erdrich, L. The last report on the miracles at Little No Horse
Erdrich, L. The Master Butchers Singing Club
Erdrich, L. Tracks
Grimes, M. Dakota
Klosterman, C. Downtown Owl
Power, S. The grass dancer
North Star. Wheeler, R. S.
The **North** water. McGuire, I.
Northanger Abbey. Austen, J.
NORTHEAST PASSAGE
See also Arctic regions; Exploration; Voyages and travels
NORTHERN IRELAND
The dream of the Celt
McKinty, A. In the Morning I'll Be Gone
NORTHERN IRELAND -- BELFAST
Moore, B. The lonely passion of Judith Hearne
Rankin, I. Watchman
NORTHERN IRELAND -- HISTORY -- 1969-1994
McKinty, A. The cold cold ground
Northline. Vlautin, W.
NORTHMEN *See* Vikings
Northwest corner. Schwartz, J. B.
NORTHWEST, PACIFIC
Lowell, E. Pearl Cove
Perillo, L. Happiness is a chemical in the brain
Raymond, J. The half-life
The **Norton** book of science fiction.
NORWAY
Brekke, J. The fifth element
My struggle
Petterson, P. In the wake
NORWAY -- OSLO
Nesbo, J. The headhunters
NORWAY -- RURAL LIFE
Undset, S. Kristin Lavransdatter
NORWAY -- TO 1397
Undset, S. Kristin Lavransdatter
Norwegian by night. Miller, D. B.
NORWEGIAN LANGUAGE
See also Language and languages; Scandinavian languages
NORWEGIANS -- UNITED STATES
Rolvaag, O. E. Giants in the earth
Rolvaag, O. E. Peder Victorious
NORWICH (ENGLAND)
Griffiths, E. The Janus stone
Nos4a2. Hill, J.
NOSTALGIA
Castellani, C. All this talk of love
Nostromo. Conrad, J.
Not in the flesh. Rendell, R.
Not quite a wife. Putney, M. J.
Not So Much, Said the Cat. Swanwick, M.
Not without laughter. Hughes, L.
The **notebook.** Sparks, N.
NOTEBOOKS
See also Books
The **notebooks** of Don Rigoberto. Vargas Llosa, M.
Notes from underground. Dostoyevsky, F.
Nothing but blue skies. McGuane, T.
Nothing but the truth. Lescroart, J. T.
NOVA SCOTIA
MacDonald Fall on your knees
Norman, H. The museum guard
Norman, H. What is left the daughter
Nova swing. Harrison, M. J.
Novalis, 1772-1801
About
Fitzgerald, P. The blue flower
A **novel** bookstore. Cosse, L.
Novel of Empress Wu [series]
Randel, W. D. The empress of bright moon
NOVELETTES
Aira, C. Ghosts
Aira, C. The literary conference
Aira, C. The seamstress and the wind
Appelfeld, A. Badenheim 1939
Barrett, W. E. The lilies of the field
Benet, S. V. The Devil and Daniel Webster
Bilenchi, R. The chill

Bolano, R. By night in Chile
Bolano, R. Monsieur Pain
Capote, T. Breakfast at Tiffany's: a short novel and three stories
Chiang, T. The life cycle of software objects
Cisneros, S. The house on Mango Street
Colette Six novels
Conrad, J. Heart of darkness
Cook, E. Achilles
Crane, S. The complete novels of Stephen Crane
Davies, V. Miracle on 34th Street
DeLillo, D. Point Omega
Dickens, C. A Christmas carol
Dostoyevsky, F. Notes from underground
Erpenbeck, J. The book of words
Faber, M. The courage consort
Ferrante, E. The lost daughter
Gaddis, W. Agape agape
Garcia Marquez, G. Chronicle of a death foretold
Garcia Marquez, G. Collected novellas
Gibbons, K. Ellen Foster
Gurganus, A. The practical heart
The hall of singing caryatids
Handke, P. Don Juan
Hilton, J. Good-bye Mr. Chips
The Hugo winners
James, H. Complete stories, 1864-1874
James, H. Complete stories, 1874-1884
James, H. Complete stories, 1884-1891
James, H. Complete stories, 1892-1898
James, H. Complete stories, 1898-1910
Johnson, D. Train dreams
Kafka, F. Metamorphosis
Kawabata, Y. Snow country, and Thousand cranes
Keilson, H. Comedy in a minor key
King, S. Different seasons
King, S. Four past midnight
King, S. Full dark, no stars
Le Guin, U. K. Four ways to forgiveness
Lessing, D. M. The fifth child
Levin, I. The Stepford wives
London, J. The call of the wild
Makine, A. Music of a life
Manchette Fatale
Mann, T. The black swan
Mann, T. Death in Venice
Martin, S. The pleasure of my company
Martin, S. Shopgirl
McEwan, I. Black dogs
Melville, H. Billy Budd, sailor
Merimee, P. Carmen
Minot, S. Rapture
Moody, R. Right livelihoods
Munoz Molina, A. In her absence
Nemirovsky, I. Fire in the blood
Nin, A. Cities of the interior
Oates, J. C. Black water
Oates, J. C. I lock my door upon myself
Oates, J. C. Rape
Otsuka, J. The Buddha in the attic
Otsuka, J. When the emperor was divine
Oz, A. Panther in the basement
Pelevin, V. The hall of singing caryatids
Poe, E. A. The imaginary voyages: The narrative of Arthur Gordon Pym; The unparalleled adventure of one Hans Pfaall; The journal of Julius Rodman
Porter, K. A. Pale horse, pale rider: three short novels
Rand, A. Anthem
Rendell, R. Heartstones
Richardson, C. S. The end of the alphabet
Rosales, G. The halfway house
Rosero, E. Good offices
Roth, P. The dying animal
Sagan, F. Bonjour tristesse
Salinger, J. D. Franny & Zooey
Salinger, J. D. Raise high the roof beam, carpenters, and Seymour: an introduction
Sand, G. Marianne
Savage, S. Firmin
Segal, E. Love story
Simenon, G. Maigret and the Saturday caller
Simenon, G. Maigret goes home
Spark, M. The driver's seat
Steinbeck, J. Of mice and men
Steinbeck, J. The pearl
Stevenson, R. L. The strange case of Dr. Jekyll and Mr. Hyde
Torres, J. We the animals
Tsypkin, L. Summer in Baden-Baden
Turgenev, I. S. First love and other stories
Turow, S. Limitations
Vann, D. Legend of a suicide
Verissimo, L. F. Borges and the eternal orangutans
Visitation
Welty, E. The Ponder heart
Wiesel, E. Dawn
Wiesel, E. Night, Dawn, The accident: three tales
Williams, T. The Roman spring of Mrs. Stone
Yoshimoto, B. Asleep

NOVELISTS

Aira, C. The literary conference
Atkins, A. Devil's garden
Barker, P. The eye in the door
Barker, P. Regeneration
Benford, G. Foundation's fear
Benjamin, M. Alice I have been
Bolano, R. Monsieur Pain
Chesnutt, C. W. Stories, novels, & essay
Clarke, B. Exley
Clinch, J. Finn
Coetzee, J. M. Foe
Coetzee, J. M. Summertime
Cunningham, M. The hours
Everett, P. Erasure

Faulks, S. Devil may care
Fitzgerald, P. The blue flower
Flanagan, R. Wanting
Fowler, K. J. The Jane Austen book club
Hacker, C. The Morels
Hale, S. Austenland
Hockensmith, S. Holmes on the range
Hockensmith, S. On the wrong track
Hoover, C. November 9
Horowitz, A. The House of Silk
Jordan, H. When she woke
King, L. R. The game
Lashner, W. Kockroach
Marks, J. Fangland
Martin, V. Mary Reilly
McLain, P. The Paris wife
Meyer, N. The seven-per-cent solution
Moore, G. The Sherlockian
Moses, K. Wintering
Nabokov, V. V. Novels and memoirs, 1941-1951
Naslund, S. J. Ahab's wife; or, The star-gazer
Oates, J. C. Wild nights!
Parini, J. The passages of H.M.
Pearl, M. The last Dickens
Pirie, D. The patient's eyes
Powers, K. Capote in Kansas
Priest, C. The islanders
Reyn, I. What happened to Anna K.
Robertson, M. The brothers of Baker Street
Russell, M. D. Dreamers of the day
Self, W. Dorian
Tóibín, C. The master
Tournier, M. Friday
Truong, M. The book of salt
Tsypkin, L. Summer in Baden-Baden
Twain, M. The gilded age and later novels
Vargas Llosa, M. The way to paradise
Verissimo, L. F. Borges and the eternal orangutans
Walker, A. The way forward is with a broken heart
Weisgall, D. The world before her
White, E. Hotel de Dream
Winslow, D. Satori

NOVELISTS
See also Authors

Novellas and other writings. Wharton, E.
Novels. Wharton, E.
Novels & stories, 1963-1979. Vonnegut, K.
Novels and essays. Norris, F.
Novels and memoirs, 1941-1951. Nabokov, V. V.
Novels and other writings. West, N.
Novels and stories. Jackson, S.
Novels and stories. Hurston, Z. N.
Novels and stories, 1920-1922. Fitzgerald, F. S.
NOVELS IN LETTERS *See* Epistolary fiction

Novels of ancient Rome [series]
Saylor, S. Raiders of the Nile
Saylor, S. Wrath of the furies

Novels, 1920-1925. Dos Passos, J.
Novels, 1926-1929. Faulkner, W.
Novels, 1930-1935. Faulkner, W.
Novels, 1936-1940. Faulkner, W.
Novels, 1942-1954. Faulkner, W.
Novels, 1944-1953. Bellow, S.
Novels, 1955-1962. Nabokov, V. V.
Novels, 1956-1964. Bellow, S.
Novels, 1957-1962. Faulkner, W.
Novels, 1969-1974. Nabokov, V. V.
Novels, 1970-1982. Bellow, S.
Novels, 1993-1995. Roth, P.
November 9. Hoover, C.
Now and then. Parker, R. B.
Now is the time to open your heart. Walker, A.
Now you see him. Gottlieb, E.
Now you see it. Lynn, A.
Now you see me. Bolton, S. J.
Nowhere but home. Palmer, L.
Nowhere else on earth. Humphreys, J.
Nowhere man. Hemon, A.
The **Nowhere** Man. Hurwitz, G.
Nowhere near respectable. Putney, M. J.
Nowhere to run. Box, C. J.

Núñez Cabeza de Vaca, Alvar, active 16th century
About
Lalami, L. The Moor's account

NUCLEAR PHYSICISTS
Millet, L. Oh pure and radiant heart

NUCLEAR POWER PLANTS
Pohl, F. Chernobyl

NUCLEAR POWER PLANTS -- FIRES AND FIRE PREVENTION
See also Fire prevention; Fires

NUCLEAR POWER PLANTS -- FLORIDA
Hall, J. W. Going Dark

NUCLEAR SUBMARINES
Clancy, T. The hunt for Red October

NUCLEAR SUBMARINES
See also Nuclear propulsion; Submarines

NUCLEAR WARFARE
Burdick, E. Fail-safe
Frank, P. Alas, Babylon
Rosenberg, J. C. The twelfth Imam
Shute, N. On the beach
Suri, M. The city of Devi
West, M. L. The clowns of God

NUCLEAR WARFARE
See also War

NUCLEAR WARFARE -- PREVENTION
Rosenberg, J. C. Damascus Countdown
Rosenberg, J. C. The Tehran initiative
Rosenberg, J. C. The twelfth Imam

NUCLEAR WEAPONS
DeMille, N. Wild fire
Ignatius, D. The increment
Robinson, P. Nimitz class

Scholz, C. Radiance
Number 10. Townsend, S.
NUMBER THEORY
See also Algebra; Mathematics; Set theory
Numbers don't lie. Bisson, T.
Numero Zero.
NUMEROLOGY
See also Occultism; Symbolism of numbers
NUMISMATICS
See also Ancient history; Archeology; History
The **nun's** story. Hulme, K.
NUNS
Barrett, W. E. The lilies of the field
Cross, J. Touched by venom
Godden, R. Black Narcissus
Godwin, G. Unfinished desires
Hulme, K. The nun's story
Lanchester, J. Fragrant Harbor
McCann, C. Thirteen ways of looking
Robbins, T. Fierce invalids home from hot climates
Roberts, M. Reader, I married him
Sharratt, M. Illuminations
Tremayne, P. Chalice of blood
Trussoni, D. Angelology
NUNS
See also Women
Nuns and soldiers. Murdoch, I.
NURSE MIDWIVES *See* Midwives
NURSERY SCHOOLS
Glass, J. The widower's tale
NURSES
Cameron, P. Coral Glynn
Donoghue, E. The wonder
Keneally, T. The Daughters of Mars
MacKall, D. D. With love, wherever you are
Todd, C. An unmarked grave
NURSES -- CRIMES AGAINST
Robotham, M. Suspect
Tursten, H. Night rounds
NURSES -- ENGLAND
Todd, C. A duty to the dead
Todd, C. A question of honor
NURSES AND NURSING
Hamilton, J. A map of the world
Hemingway, E. A farewell to arms
Holt, V. Secret for a nightingale
Hulme, K. The nun's story
Kesey, K. One flew over the cuckoo's nest
McCullough, C. An indecent obsession
McEwan, I. Atonement
Ondaatje, M. The English patient
Rinehart, M. R. Miss Pinkerton: adventures of a nurse detective
Vine, B. The minotaur
NURSING HOMES
Lindgren, T. Hash
McCorkle, J. Life after life
NUTS
See also Food; Seeds
Nutshell. McEwan, I.
NW. Smith, Z.
NYUNGA (AUSTRALIAN PEOPLE)
Scott, K. That deadman dance

O

O Beulah Land. Settle, M. L.
O is for outlaw. Grafton, S.
O lost. Wolfe, T.
O pioneers! Cather, W.
O'Malley, Grace, 1530?-1603?
About
Maxwell, R. The wild Irish
OAK
See also Trees; Wood
OAKLAND (CALIF.)
Chabon, M. Telegraph Avenue
The **oath.** Wiesel, E.
The **oath.** Lescroart, J. T.
The **obelisk** gate. Jemisin, N. K.
OBELISKS
See also Archeology; Architecture; Monuments
OBESITY
Attenberg, J. The Middlesteins
Walker, S. Dietland
Walters, M. The sculptress
Weiner, J. Good in bed
OBESITY -- SURGERY
Walker, S. Dietland
OBITUARIES
See also Biography
OBITUARIES -- GRAPHIC NOVELS
Moon, F. Daytripper
The **Obituary** Writer. Hood, A.
Object lessons. Quindlen, A.
Object lessons.
An **object** of beauty. Martin, S.
Oblivion. Wallace, D. F.
OBSCENE MATERIALS *See* Obscenity (Law); Pornography
OBSCENITY (LAW)
See also Criminal law
The **obsession.** Roberts, N.
OBSESSION (PSYCHOLOGY) *See* Obsessive-compulsive disorder
OBSESSIONS
Erickson, S. Zeroville
Klosterman, C. The visible man
Kostova, E. The swan thieves
The museum of innocence
Phillips, A. The song is you
Vargas Llosa, M. The bad girl
OBSESSIVE-COMPULSIVE DISORDER
Lally, C. Eggshells

Martin, S. The pleasure of my company
Scottoline, L. Every fifteen minutes
OBSESSIVE-COMPULSIVE NEUROSES *See* Obsessive-compulsive disorder
Obstruction of justice. O'Shaughnessy, P.
OCCULT FICTION
Aira, C. Ghosts
Bolano, R. Monsieur Pain
King, S. Pet sematary
Michaels, B. Stitches in time
Naylor, G. Mama Day
Rice, A. The queen of the damned
Rice, A. The tale of the body thief
Rice, A. The witching hour
OCCULT FICTION *See* Paranormal fiction
OCCULT SCIENCES *See* Occultism
OCCULTISM
Bolano, R. Monsieur Pain
Eco, U. Foucault's pendulum
Gallagher, S. The kingdom of bones
Howe, K. The physick book of Deliverance Dane
King, S. Firestarter
LaValle, V. D. Big machine
Williams, C. Stairway to hell
Occupied city. Peace, D.
OCEAN
Verne, J. The extraordinary journeys: Twenty thousand leagues under the sea
The **Ocean** at the End of the Lane. Gaiman, N.
The **ocean** between us. Wiggs, S.
OCEAN LINERS
Rogan, C. The lifeboat
OCEAN TRAVEL
Davies, J. D. The mountain of gold
Evison, J. This is your life, Harriet Chance!
Golding, W. Close quarters
Golding, W. Fire down below
Golding, W. Rites of passage
Meloy, M. Do not become alarmed
Ondaatje, M. The cat's table
Porter, K. A. Ship of fools
Preston, D. The wheel of darkness
Villars, E. The Normandie affair
Woolf, V. The voyage out
OCEAN TRAVEL
See also Transportation; Travel; Voyages and travels
OCEAN WAVES
See also Ocean; Waves
OCEANOGRAPHY -- RESEARCH
See also Research
OCEANS *See* Ocean
October Daye novel. [series]
Grant, M. Rosemary and Rue
The **October** list. Deaver, J.
The **octopus.** Norris, F.
Odd Thomas series
Koontz, D. R. Brother Odd
The **odds.** O'Nan, S.
Odds against tomorrow. Rich, N.
The **Odessa** file. Forsyth, F.
Odysseus Abroad. Chaudhuri, A.
Odyssey. McDevitt, J.
Of human bondage. Maugham, W. S.
Of love and evil. Rice, A.
Of mice and men. Steinbeck, J.
Of time and the river. Wolfe, T.
Off Armageddon Reef. Weber, D.
Off the chart. Hall, J. W.
An **offer** from a gentleman. Quinn, J.
OFFICE EMPLOYEES *See* Office workers
OFFICE MANAGEMENT
See also Business; Factory management; Industrial efficiency; Management
OFFICE WORKERS
Hynes, J. Kings of infinite space
Karlsson, J. The room
Phillips, H. The beautiful bureaucrat
Moon, E. The speed of dark
Wallace, D. F. The pale king
OFFICIAL SECRETS
DeLillo, D. Point Omega
OGLALA INDIANS
O'Brien, D. The contract surgeon
Welch, J. The heartsong of Charging Elk
The **ogre.** Tournier, M.
Oh pure and radiant heart. Millet, L.
OHIO
Castillo, L. Breaking silence
Castillo, L. Sworn to silence
Morrison, T. Sula
O'Nan, S. Songs for the missing
Patterson, R. N. Silent witness
Perkins-Valdez, D. Wench
Pollock, D. R. The devil all the time
Pollock, D. R. Knockemstiff
Roth, P. Indignation
Satyal, R. No one can pronounce my name
Smith, S. A simple plan
Vonnegut, K. Deadeye Dick
OHIO -- 18TH CENTURY
Richter, C. The awakening land
OHIO -- 19TH CENTURY
Anderson, S. Winesburg, Ohio
Richter, C. The awakening land
OHIO -- BIOGRAPHY
See also Biography
OHIO -- CLEVELAND
Southgate, M. The taste of salt
OHIO -- HISTORY -- 1787-1865
Perkins-Valdez, D. Wench
OHIO RIVER VALLEY
Settle, M. L. O Beulah Land
OIL INDUSTRY *See* Petroleum industry
OIL SPILLS -- CLEANUP -- GULF STATES

Cooper, T. The marauders
OIL WELL DRILLING
See also Drilling and boring (Earth and rocks); Petroleum industry
OIL WELLS
See also Petroleum industry
OJIBWA INDIANS
Erdrich, L. Four souls
OJIBWA INDIANS -- NORTH DAKOTA
Erdrich, L. LaRose
Erdrich, L. The round house
OKLAHOMA
Berney, L. The Long and Faraway Gone
Crowley, J. Four freedoms
Decarlo, M. The Art of Crash Landing
Hart, C. G. Letter from home
Hunter, S. Dirty white boys
Letts, B. Shoot the moon
Meadows, R. I will send rain
Morrison, T. Paradise
OKLAHOMA -- TULSA
Straight, S. The gettin place
OLD AGE
Dean, D. The madonnas of Leningrad
Dixon, S. Old friends
Drabble, M. The dark flood rises
Edgerton, C. Walking across Egypt
García Márquez, G. Memories of my melancholy whores
Gilman, S. J. The Ice Cream Queen of Orchard Street
Gordon, M. Final payments
Gurganus, A. The oldest living Confederate widow tells all
Harding, P. Tinkers
Hemingway, E. The old man and the sea
Hilton, J. Good-bye Mr. Chips
Itani, F. Remembering the bones
Kawabata, Y. The sound of the mountain
Krauss, N. The history of love
Lindgren, T. Hash
Maloy, K. Every last cuckoo
McMurtry, L. The evening star
Medlicott, J. A. The ladies of Covington send their love
Miller, D. B. Norwegian by night
Mosley, W. RL's dream
O'Flynn, C. The news where you are
Olsson, L. Astrid & Veronika
O'Nan, S. Emily, alone
Price, R. The good priest's son
Roth, P. Exit ghost
Roth, P. Sabbath's theater
Sackville-West, V. All passion spent
Sarton, M. As we are now
Sarton, M. Kinds of love
Scott, A. Calpurnia
Scott, P. Staying on
Spark, M. Memento mori
Sparks, N. The notebook
Stuckey-French, E. Revenge of the radioactive lady
Taylor, E. Mrs. Palfrey at the Claremont
Taylor, M. G. The ballad of Trenchmouth Taggart
Trollope, J. The men and the girls
Trueblood, V. Seven loves
Tyler, A. A patchwork planet
Updike, J. The poorhouse fair
Updike, J. Seek my face
Updike, J. The widows of Eastwick
Van Niekerk, M. Agaat
Wharton, W. Dad
Wiesel, E. The forgotten
OLD AGE HOMES
Sarton, M. As we are now
Updike, J. The poorhouse fair
Old bones. Harrod-Eagles, C.
Old bones. Boyce, T. N.
Old boys. McCarry, C.
The **Old** Contemptibles. Grimes, M.
The **old** curiosity shop. Dickens, C.
Old Filth. Gardam, J.
Old Filth trilogy [series]
Gardam, J. Last Friends
Old flames. Lawton, J.
The **old** fox deceiv'd. Grimes, M.
Old friends. Dixon, S.
The **old** gringo. Fuentes, C.
The **old** man and the sea. Hemingway, E.
Old man's war. Scalzi, J.
OLD NORSE LANGUAGE
See also Language and languages; Scandinavian languages
Old school. Wolff, T.
The **Old** Silent. Grimes, M.
OLD SOUTHWEST
Richter, C. The sea of grass
The **Old** Wine Shades. Grimes, M.
OLDER GAY MEN
Evaristo, B. Mr. Loverman
OLDER MEN
See also Men; Older people
OLDER MEN
Evaristo, B. Mr. Loverman
Friedman, D. Don't ever get old
Mosley, W. The last days of Ptolemy Grey
Rayfiel, T. In pinelight
Savage, S. The way of the dog
OLDER MEN -- CRIMES AGAINST
Keller, J. A killing in the hills
Mina, D. Gods and beasts
OLDER PEOPLE -- DISEASES
See also Diseases
OLDER PEOPLE
Cotterill, C. The coroner's lunch
Cotterill, C. Slash and burn
McCorkle, J. Life after life
OLDER WOMEN
Drabble, M. The dark flood rises

Maloy, K. Every last cuckoo
Morton, B. Florence Gordon
Walton, J. My real children
OLDER WOMEN
See also Older people; Women
The **oldest** living Confederate widow tells all. Gurganus, A.
Oleander girl. Divakaruni, C. B.
Olive Kitteridge. Strout, E.
Oliver Twist. Dickens, C.
OLIVER, GIDEON (FICTITIOUS CHARACTER)
Elkins, A. J. Dying on the vine
Elkins, A. J. Good blood
Oluwale, David, 1930 or 1-1969
About
Phillips, C. Foreigners
OLYMPIC ATHLETES
See also Athletes
OLYMPIC GAMES
See also Athletics; Contests; Games; Sports
OLYMPIC GAMES
Kosmatka, T. The games
OLYMPIC GAMES, 2012 (LONDON, ENGLAND)
Cleave, C. Gold
OLYMPIC PENINSULA (WASH.)
Evison, J. West of here
OMAHA (NEB.)
Hilleman, A. World, chase me down
Ombria in shadow. McKillip, P. A.
Omoo: a narrative of adventures in the South Seas. Melville, H.
On Agate Hill. Smith, L.
On beauty. Smith, Z.
On Canaan's side. Barry, S.
On Chesil Beach. McEwan, I.
On Green Dolphin Street. Faulks, S.
On Her Majesty's Secret Service. Fleming, I.
On Kingdom Mountain. Mosher, H. F.
On Mystic lake. Hannah, K.
On secret service. Jakes, J.
On such a full sea. Lee
On the beach. Shute, N.
On the occasion of my last afternoon. Gibbons, K.
On the razor's edge. Flynn, M.
On the road. Kerouac, J.
On the wrong track. Hockensmith, S.
On top of Spoon Mountain. Nichols, J.
Once a gentleman. Hern, C.
Once a hero. Moon, E.
Once a Rake. Dreyer, E.
The **once** and future king. White, T. H.
Once on a moonless night. Dai Sijie
Once the shore. Yoon, P.
Once upon a river. Campbell, B. J.
Once upon a time, there was you. Berg, E.
One day. Nicholls, D.
One day in the life of Ivan Denisovich. Solzhenitsyn, A.
One fine day the rabbi bought a cross. Kemelman, H.
One flew over the cuckoo's nest. Kesey, K.
One for the money. Evanovich, J.
One Good Earl Deserves a Lover. MacLean, S.
One hundred years of solitude. García Márquez, G.
The **One** I Left Behind. McMahon, J.
One Kick. Cain, C.
One last thing before I go. Tropper, J.
The **one** man. Gross, A.
One night. Dickey, E. J.
One perfect lie. Scottoline, L.
One Plus One. Moyes, J.
One shot. Child, L.
One step behind. Mankell, H.
One thousand and one nights.
The **one-eyed** man. Modesitt, L. E.
ONLINE CHAT GROUPS
See also Conversation; Social media
ONLINE DATING
See also Dating (Social customs)
ONLINE DATING
Raeder, L. Cam girl
ONLINE JOURNALISM
See also Journalism
Only a Promise. Balogh, M.
ONLY CHILD
See also Children; Family size
Tuck, L. The Double Life of Liliane
Only revolutions. Danielewski, M. Z.
Only the animals. Dovey, C.
Only time will tell. Archer, J.
Only yesterday. Agnon, S. Y.
ONTARIO
Bates, J. F. Midnight at the Dragon Café
Itani, F. Deafening
Itani, F. Requiem
Lawson, M. Crow Lake
Munro, A. Friend of my youth
Shields, C. Unless
OPEN AND CLOSED SHOP
See also Labor; Labor contract; Labor unions
Open city. Cole, T.
Open season. Box, C. J.
Open secrets. Munro, A.
Open to the public. Spark, M.
OPERA
Hambly, B. Die upon a kiss
Leon, D. Falling in Love
The man of feeling
Parker, B. Suspicion of deceit
See, L. Peony in love
OPIUM TRADE
Ghosh, A. Flood of fire
Ghosh, A. River of smoke
Ghosh, A. Sea of poppies
The **opposite** house. Oyeyemi, H.
The **opposite** of everyone. Jackson, J.
OPTICAL ILLUSIONS

See also Hallucinations and illusions; Psychophysiology; Vision
The **optimist's** daughter. Welty, E.
Oracle night. Auster, P.
The **Oracle** of Stamboul. Lukas, M. D.
ORACLES
Graham, J. Black ships
Lukas, M. D. The Oracle of Stamboul
ORACLES
See also Occultism
ORAL COMMUNICATION
Lopez, R. All back full
Oral history. Smith, L.
Oranges are not the only fruit. Winterson, J.
ORBITAL RENDEZVOUS (SPACE FLIGHT)
See also Space flight; Space stations; Space vehicles
The **orchard** of lost souls. Mohamed, N.
The **orchardist.** Coplin, A.
ORCHARDS -- NORTHWEST, PACIFIC
Coplin, A. The orchardist
ORCHESTRA
Racculia, K. Bellweather rhapsody
Orchestrated death. Harrod-Eagles, C.
Orchid Beach. Woods, S.
Orders from Berlin. Tolkien, S.
ORDERS, MONASTIC *See* Monasticism and religious orders
The **ordinary.** Grimsley, J.
An **ordinary** decent criminal. Van Rooy, M.
Ordinary grace. Krueger, W. K.
Ordinary heroes. Turow, S.
Ordinary people. Guest, J.
An **ordinary** woman. Holland, C.
ORDINATION
See also Rites and ceremonies; Sacraments
ORDINATION OF WOMEN
Merullo, R. Vatican waltz
OREGON
Carr, R. The Wanderer
Gloss, M. The hearts of horses
Percy, B. The wilding
Rock, P. My abandonment
Smith, A. Judas horse
Wilhelm, K. The deepest water
Wilhelm, K. The good children
Winston, L. Good grief
OREGON -- PORTLAND
Cain, C. Heartsick
Durrow, H. W. The girl who fell from the sky
Margolin, P. Wild justice
Vlautin, W. Lean on Pete
OREGON TERRITORY -- HISTORY
Kirkpatrick, J. This road we traveled
OREGON TRAIL
See also Overland journeys to the Pacific; United States
Orfeo. Powers, R.
ORGAN DONORS
Kerangal, M. d. The heart
ORGAN TRANSPLANTS *See* Transplantation of organs, tissues, etc.
ORGANIZED CRIME
Banks, I. Stonemouth
Clarkson, J. Among thieves
DeSilva, B. A Scourge of Vipers
Diamond, D. A gangster and a gentleman
Epperson, T. Sailor
Hamilton, S. The second life of Nick Mason
Haynes, E. Dark tide
Higgins, G. V. The Digger's game
Johansen, I. The perfect witness
Knopf, C. Dead anyway
Laukkanen, O. The professionals
Lehane, D. Live by night
Lehane, D. World gone by
North, C. The Sudden Appearance of Hope
O'Donovan, G. Dublin dead
Sallis, J. Drive
Sallis, J. Driven
Stewart, A. Girl waits with gun
Swinson, K. Playing dirty
Tanenbaum, R. K. Tragic
Vachss, A. That's how I roll
Walter, J. Citizen Vince
Wambaugh, J. Harbor nocturne
Winslow, D. The cartel
Woods, T. Alibi
ORGANIZED CRIME -- ENGLAND -- LONDON
Haynes, E. Dark tide
ORGANIZED CRIME -- ILLINOIS -- CHICAGO
Rosen, R. Dollface
ORGANIZED CRIME -- ITALY
De Giovanni, M. The Crocodile
ORGANIZED CRIME -- NEW JERSEY
Stewart, A. Girl waits with gun
ORGANIZED CRIME -- SWEDEN
Nesbø, J. Blood on snow
ORGANIZED LABOR *See* Labor unions
Orhan's inheritance. Ohanesian, A.
Orient. Bollen, C.
ORIENTALISM
See also East and West
Origin. Abu-Jaber, D.
The **origin** of species. Ricci, N.
ORIGIN OF SPECIES *See* Evolution
Original sin. James, P. D.
Original skin. Mark, D.
ORISKANY, BATTLE OF, 1777
Edmonds, W. D. Drums along the Mohawk
Orlando. Woolf, V.
ORNITHOLOGISTS
Drayson, N. Guide to the birds of East Africa
ORPHAN DRUGS
See also Drugs
The **orphan** master's son. Johnson, A.
Orphan train. Kline, C. B.

ORPHAN TRAINS
Kline, C. B. Orphan train
Orphan X. Hurwitz, G.
ORPHANAGES
Grant, M. Every Heart a Doorway
The **orphanmaster.** Zimmerman, J.
ORPHANS
Alexie, S. Flight
Allende, I. Eva Luna
Baker, K. The bird of the river
Balogh, M. Someone to Love
Berry, W. Jayber Crow
Bohjalian, C. A. Secrets of Eden
Boyle, E. Along Came a Duke
Brockway, C. The golden season
Bronte, C. Emma
Bronte, C. Jane Eyre
Bronte, E. Wuthering Heights
Brown, J. D. Addie Pray
Capote, T. The grass harp
Cox, M. The glass of time
Cramer, W. D. Bad ground
Desai, K. The inheritance of loss
Dickens, C. Great expectations
Dickens, C. The old curiosity shop
Dickens, C. Oliver Twist
Ford, J. Songs of Willow Frost
Fuentes, C. Destiny and desire
Goodman, J. A place called home
Grant, M. Down Among the Sticks and Bones
Grant, M. Every Heart a Doorway
Grunwald, L. The irresistible Henry House
Hart, J. Iron house
Hoeg, P. Borderliners
Holt, V. The black opal
Holt, V. The Judas kiss
Hoyt, E. Thief of Shadows
Hunt, S. Mr. Splitfoot
Irving, J. The cider house rules
Jiles, P. News of the world
Keesey, A. Little century
Lansdale, J. R. The thicket
Lawson, M. Crow Lake
Lee The surrendered
Livesey, M. The flight of Gemma Hardy
Lynch, S. The lies of Locke Lamora
Lyon, A. The sweet girl
Mitchard, J. A theory of relativity
Moore, L. The Unseen World
Norman, H. The museum guard
Norman, H. What is left the daughter
Nunez, S. Salvation city
Obreht, T. The tiger's wife
O'Donnell, L. The death of bees
O'Malley, T. This magnificent desolation
Omarsdottir, K. Children in Reindeer Woods
O'Neill, H. The Lonely Hearts Hotel
Orullian, P. V. The unremembered
Ozick, C. Heir to the glimmering world
Ross-Macdonald, M. The Trevarton inheritance
Roy, A. An atlas of impossible longing
Sholem Aleichem The adventures of Mottel, the cantor's son
Smith, L. On Agate Hill
Stedman, M. L. The light between oceans
Taylor, M. G. The Marrowbone Marble Company
Tevis, W. S. The queen's gambit
Tinti, H. The good thief
Wallace, D. The Watermelon King
Ward, L. Outside valentine
Wilhelm, K. The good children
Wood, B. The dreaming
Zimmerman, J. The orphanmaster
ORPHANS
See also Children
ORPHANS -- ENGLAND
Mukherjee, N. A life apart
Orsinian tales. Le Guin, U. K.
ORTHOPEDICS
See also Medicine; Surgery
Osgood, James R., 1836-1892
About
Pearl, M. The last Dickens
OSLO (NORWAY)
The leopard
Phantom
The **other.** Guterson, D.
The **other.** Tryon, T.
The **other** Boleyn girl. Gregory, P.
The **other** child. Link, C.
The **other** family. Trollope, J.
Other people's children. Trollope, J.
Other people's marriages. Thomas, R.
The **other** side of silence. Brink, A. P.
Corby, G. The Pericles Commission
The **Other** Typist. Rindell, S.
The **other** wind. Le Guin, U. K.
The **other** woman. Ryan, H. P.
OTTAWA (ONT.)
Itani, F. Requiem
The **Ottoman** cage. Nadel, B.
Our kind of traitor. Le Carre, J.
Our Lady of the Forest. Guterson, D.
Our man in Havana. Greene, G.
Our mutual friend. Dickens, C.
Our short history. Grodstein, L.
Our souls at night. Haruf, K.
Our story begins. Wolff, T.
Out of India. Jhabvala, R. P.
Out of It. Dabbagh, S.
Out of the black land. Greenwood, K.
Out of the silent planet. Lewis, C. S.
Out stealing horses. Petterson, P.
OUT-OF-WORK PEOPLE *See* Unemployed

Outcast. Jones, S.
The **outcasts.** Kent, K.
OUTCASTS
Lovett, A. Everlasting Lane
OUTER SPACE
Leckie, A. Ancillary justice
Provenance
OUTER SPACE -- EXPLORATION
Corey, J. S. A. Abaddon's Gate
Corey, J. S. A. Cibola burn
Howrey, M. The wanderers
McDevitt, J. The Cassandra project
McDevitt, J. Odyssey
Robinson, K. S. Aurora
Outerbridge Reach. Stone, R.
The **outlander.** Adamson, G.
Outlander [series]
Gabaldon, D. Written in my own heart's blood
Outlander. Gabaldon, D.
The **outlaw** album. Woodrell, D.
OUTLAWS
Brooks, B. Winter kill
Estleman, L. D. The book of Murdock
Groom, W. El Paso
Hansen, R. The assassination of Jesse James by the coward Robert Ford
Hilleman, A. World, chase me down
Humphreys, J. Nowhere else on earth
Lynch, S. The lies of Locke Lamora
McMurtry, L. Streets of Laredo
Momaday, N. S. The ancient child
Olmstead, R. Far bright star
Resnick, M. The return of Santiago
Scott, W. Rob Roy
Wallace, S. Montana dawn
Williamson, P. The outsider
OUTLAWS *See* Criminals; Thieves
Outline. Cusk, R.
Outrage. Indridason, A.
Outside the ordinary world. Ostermiller, D.
Outside valentine. Ward, L.
The **outside** world. Mirvis, T.
The **outsider.** Wright, R.
The **outsider.** Williamson, P.
OUTSIDER ART
See also Art
Over and under. Tucker, T.
Overclocked. Doctorow, C.
The **overcoat,** and other tales of good and evil. Gogol', N. V.
OVERLAND JOURNEYS
Holland, C. An ordinary woman
Wolitzer, H. Hearts
OVERLAND JOURNEYS TO THE PACIFIC
Guthrie, A. B. The way West
Priest, C. Dreadnought
Vanderhaeghe, G. The last crossing
OVERLAND JOURNEYS TO THE PACIFIC
See also Frontier and pioneer life; Voyages and travels
OVERWEIGHT *See* Obesity
OWNERSHIP *See* Property
The **Ox-bow** incident. Clark, W. V. T.
OXFORD (ENGLAND)
Benjamin, M. Alice I have been
Murdoch, I. The book and the brotherhood
Pears, I. An instance of the fingerpost
Willis, C. Doomsday book
The **Oxford** book of American detective stories.
The **Oxford** book of American short stories.
The **Oxford** book of English ghost stories.
The **Oxford** book of English short stories.
The **Oxford** book of gothic tales.
The **Oxford** book of Irish short stories.
The **Oxford** book of Latin American short stories.
The **Oxford** book of modern fairy tales.
The **Oxford** book of science fiction stories.
The **Oxford** book of short stories.
The **Oxford** book of spy stories.
The **Oxford** book of twentieth-century ghost stories.
Oxford world's classics [series]
Blackmore, R. D. Lorna Doone
Bunyan, J. The pilgrim's progress
Cather, W. O pioneers!
Defoe, D. Robinson Crusoe
Fielding, H. Joseph Andrews and Shamela
Gaskell, E. C. Cranford
Grey, Z. Riders of the purple sage
Lewis, M. G. The monk
Richardson, S. Pamela
Thackeray, W. M. Vanity fair
Trollope, A. The prime minister
Verne, J. Around the world in eighty days
Zola, E. Nana
Oxygen. Miller, A.
OZ (IMAGINARY PLACE)
Maguire, G. Wicked
Maguire, G. Son of a witch
OZARK MOUNTAINS
McMurtry, L. Zeke and Ned
Woodrell, D. Give us a kiss
Woodrell, D. The outlaw album
OZARK MOUNTAINS REGION
Woodrell, D. The outlaw album
Woodrell, D. Winter's bone

P

P is for peril. Grafton, S.
Pachinko. Lee, M. J.
PACHYCEPHALOSAURUS
See also Dinosaurs
Pacific beat. Parker, T. J.
Pacific glory. Deutermann, P. T.
PACIFIC NORTHWEST
Evison, J. West of here

Fowler, K. J. Sarah Canary
Perillo, L. Happiness is a chemical in the brain
Priest, C. Boneshaker
Raymond, J. The half-life
PACIFIC OCEAN
Smith, D. Bright and distant shores
Watts, P. Starfish
PACIFIC OCEAN
See also Ocean
PACIFISTS
Pipkin, J. Woodsburner
PACKAGING
See also Advertising; Retail trade
PACKING INDUSTRY *See* Meat industry
Paddy Clarke, ha ha ha. Doyle, R.
Pagan babies. Leonard, E.
Pagan spring. Malliet, G. M.
PAGANISM
Renault, M. The king must die
Sienkiewicz, H. Quo Vadis
PAGEANTS
Woolf, V. Between the acts
PAIBOUN, SIRI, DOCTOR (FICTITIOUS CHARACTER)
Cotterill, C. The coroner's lunch
Cotterill, C. Slash and burn
The **paid** companion. Quick, A.
PAIN
See also Diagnosis; Emotions; Psychophysiology; Senses and sensation
Pain management. Vachss, A. H.
Paint it black. Fitch, J.
The **painted** bird. Kosinski, J. N.
The **painted** bridge. Wallace, W.
The **painted** drum. Erdrich, L.
The **painted** girls. Buchanan, C. M.
Painted ladies. Parker, R. B.
The **painter.** Heller, P.
The **painter** of battles.
Painter of silence. Harding, G.
PAINTERS
Banville, J. The blue guitar
Brown, D. The Da Vinci code
Chevalier, T. Girl with a pearl earring
Colwin, L. Family happiness
Dovey, C. Blood kin
Durrell, L. Clea
Essex, K. Leonardo's swans
Flanagan, R. Gould's book of fish
Frayn, M. Headlong
Gruber, M. The forgery of Venus
Horn, D. The world to come
Ishiguro, K. An artist of the floating world
Jakeman, J. In the Kingdom of mists
Just, W. S. Forgetfulness
Krantz, J. Mistral's daughter
Life
Manual of painting & calligraphy
Maugham, W. S. The moon and sixpence
Momaday, N. S. The ancient child
Moore, C. Sacre bleu
Murdoch, I. Nuns and soldiers
Nathan, R. Portrait of Jennie
Pears, I. The portrait
Potok, C. The gift of Asher Lev
Potok, C. My name is Asher Lev
Smith, D. The last painting of Sara De Vos
Stone, I. The agony and the ecstasy
Stone, I. Lust for life
Stonich, S. Vacationland
Vargas Llosa, M. The way to paradise
Vreeland, S. Clara and Mr. Tiffany
Vreeland, S. Girl in hyacinth blue
Vreeland, S. Luncheon of The Boating Party
Vreeland, S. The passion of Artemesia
Wharton, W. Dad
PAINTERS
See also Artists
PAINTERS -- NEW YORK (STATE) -- NEW YORK
Prentiss, M. Tuesday nights in 1980
PAINTING
See also Art; Graphic arts
PAINTING
Vreeland, S. Luncheon of The Boating Party
Warrington, F. Grail of the summer stars
PAINTING -- COLLECTORS AND COLLECTING
Rothschild, H. The improbability of love
PAINTING, DUTCH -- 17TH CENTURY
Smith, D. The last painting of Sara De Vos
PAINTINGS
Frayn, M. Headlong
Horn, D. The world to come
Johnson, D. Le divorce
Nesbo, J. The headhunters
Norman, H. The museum guard
Price, R. The good priest's son
Vreeland, S. Girl in hyacinth blue
Watkins, P. The forger
PAKISTAN
Ahmad, J. The wandering falcon
Gruber, M. The good son
Hall, T. The case of the deadly butter chicken
Majmudar, A. Partitions
Mueenuddin, D. In other rooms, other wonders
PAKISTAN -- HISTORY -- 20TH CENTURY
Rao, S. An Unrestored Woman
PAKISTAN -- LAHORE
Hamid, M. The reluctant fundamentalist
PAKISTAN -- SOCIAL LIFE AND CUSTOMS
Aslam, N. The golden legend
PAKISTANI AMERICANS
Gruber, M. The good son
PAKISTANIS -- AFGHANISTAN
Aslam, N. The Blind Man's Garden
PAKISTANIS -- ENGLAND

Aslam, N. Maps for lost lovers
Simonson, H. Major Pettigrew's last stand
PAKISTANIS -- UNITED STATES
Akhtar, A. American dervish
Hamid, M. The reluctant fundamentalist
Palace council. Carter, S. L.
Palace of desire. Mahfouz, N.
Palace of treason. Matthews, J.
Palace walk. Mahfouz, N.
The **paladin** of souls. Bujold, L. M.
The **pale** blue eye. Bayard, L.
Pale fire. Nabokov, V. V.
The **pale** horse. Christie, A.
Pale horse coming. Hunter, S.
Pale horse, pale rider: three short novels. Porter, K. A.
The **pale** king. Wallace, D. F.
PALEONTOLOGISTS
Lively, P. Cleopatra's sister
Preston, D. Tyrannosaur Canyon
Swanwick, M. Bones of the earth
Vine, B. No night is too long
PALESTINE
Agnon, S. Y. Only yesterday
Dabbagh, S. Out of It
Joinson, S. The Photographer's Wife
Khoury, E. Gate of the sun
Oz, A. Panther in the basement
Shabtai, Y. Uncle Peretz takes off
Uris, L. Exodus
Wiesel, E. Dawn
PALESTINE -- TO 70 A.D.
Asch, S. The Apostle
Asch, S. The Nazarene
Edghill, I. Queenmaker
Wallace, L. Ben-Hur
PALESTINIAN ARABS
Alyan, H. Salt houses
Dabbagh, S. Out of It
Keneally, T. Flying hero class
Khoury, E. Gate of the sun
Littell, R. Vicious circle
Qashu, S. Dancing Arabs
PALESTINIAN ARABS
See also Arabs
PALESTINIANS *See* Palestinian Arabs
Palindrome. Woods, S.
Palme, Olof, 1927-1986
About
Between summer's longing and winter's end
Free falling, as if in a dream
PALMISTRY
See also Divination; Fortune telling; Occultism
Pamela. Richardson, S.
PAMPHLETEERS
Coetzee, J. M. Foe
Tournier, M. Friday
PANAMA
Le Carre, J. The tailor of Panama
Pandemonium. Gregory, D.
Pandora's star. Hamilton, P. F.
PANIC DISORDERS
See also Abnormal psychology; Neuroses
The **panopticon.** Fagan, J.
Panorama. Adler, H. G.
PANTHEISM
See also Philosophy; Religion
Panther in the basement. Oz, A.
Panther in the sky. Thom, J. A.
PAPAL VISITS
See also Voyages and travels
The **paper** marriage. Law, S. K.
PAPERBACK BOOKS
See also Books; Editions
PAPUA NEW GUINEA
Salak, K. The white Mary
PARABLES
Baker, T. The little giant of Aberdeen County
Emshwiller, C. The secret city
Grass, G. Dog years
Han, S. The enchantress
Hemingway, E. The old man and the sea
Hrabal, B. I served the King of England
Kadare, I. The three-arched bridge
Kosinski, J. N. Being there
Kotzwinkle, W. The bear went over the mountain
Le Guin, U. K. The telling
Oates, J. C. I lock my door upon myself
Paretsky, S. Ghost country
Roth, P. Everyman
Saramago, J. Death with interruptions
Steinbeck, J. East of Eden
Steinbeck, J. The pearl
Vonnegut, K. Deadeye Dick
Vonnegut, K. Galapagos
Weldon, F. The life and loves of a she-devil
PARACHUTE TROOPS
See also Military aeronautics; Parachutes
PARACHUTES
See also Aeronautics
Parade's end. Ford, F. M.
PARADES
See also Festivals; Pageants
Paradise. Morrison, T.
PARADISE
See also Future life
Paradise news. Lodge, D.
Paradise park. Goodman, A.
Paradise sky. Lansdale, J. R.
Paradise tales. Ryman, G.
Paragon Walk. Perry, A.
PARAGUAY
The fish child
PARALLEL UNIVERSES
Schwab, V. E. A Darker Shade of Magic

PARALYSIS
Moyes, J. Me before you
PARANOIA
Chaon, D. Await your reply
Galchen, R. Atmospheric disturbances
Gibson, W. Pattern recognition
Gibson, W. Spook country
Gibson, W. Zero history
Goodis, D. Nightfall
Lazar, Z. Sway
Lethem, J. Chronic city
Pynchon, T. Vineland
Winters, B. H. Bedbugs
PARANOID SCHIZOPHRENIA
Wells, D. The hollow city
PARANORMAL FICTION
Aira, C. Ghosts
Andrews, I. White Hot
Barry, M. Lexicon
Beagle, P. S. Summerlong
Bear, E. Shattered pillars
Belcher, R. S. The six-gun tarot
Bishop, A. Written in red
Bolano, R. Monsieur Pain
Carey, J. Autumn bones
Carey, J. Dark currents
Cargill, C. R. Dreams and Shadows
Czerneda, J. E. A Turn of Light
Gilman, L. A. Silver on the Road
Grant, M. Rosemary and Rue
Gregory, D. We Are All Completely Fine
Grimes, L. Quick fix
Hart, C. Ghost gone wild
Hill, J. Strange Weather
Jemisin, N. K. The killing moon
Kiernan, C. R. Blood oranges
King, S. The bazaar of bad dreams
King, S. Doctor Sleep
King, S. Pet sematary
Kleypas, L. Crystal Cove
Kowal, M. R. Without a summer
Krentz, J. A. Dream eyes
Michaels, B. Stitches in time
Modesitt, L. E. Imager's challenge
Modesitt, L. E. Imager's intrigue
Naylor, G. Mama Day
Nightmares
Percy, B. Red moon
Poore, M. Reincarnation Blues
Rice, A. The queen of the damned
Rice, A. The tale of the body thief
Rice, A. The witching hour
Stanley, M. Deadly Harvest
Trussoni, D. Angelopolis
Wolfe, G. The land across
Zimmerman, J. The orphanmaster
PARANORMAL PHENOMENA *See* Parapsychology
PARAPSYCHOLOGY
Carey, J. Poison fruit
Krentz, J. A. White lies
PARAPSYCHOLOGY
See also Psychology; Research; Supernatural
PARASAUROLOPHUS
See also Dinosaurs
Parasite. Grant, M.
PARASITES
Grant, M. Parasite
Parasites like us. Johnson, A.
Parasitology [series]
Grant, M. Parasite
PARCEL POST *See* Postal service
A **parchment** of leaves. House, S.
Pardonable lies. Winspear, J.
PARENT AND ADULT CHILD
Gaddis, W. Agape agape
Lamb, W. We Are Water
Meloy, M. Liars and saints
Mootoo, S. Moving forward sideways like a crab
Picoult, J. Lone wolf
Pronzini, B. In an evil time
Wilson, K. The family Fang
Wolitzer, M. The position
PARENT AND CHILD
Abu-Jaber, D. Birds of paradise
Adebayo, A. Stay with me
Aira, C. The seamstress and the wind
Banks, R. Affliction
Beattie, A. Picturing Will
Berg, E. Once upon a time, there was you
Bock, C. Beautiful children
Bohjalian, C. The night strangers
Braffet, K. Save yourself
Brookner, A. Family and friends
Brown, R. Before and after
Byatt, A. S. The children's book
Carter, S. L. New England white
Coben, H. Hold tight
Cohen, L. H. The grief of others
Cunningham, M. By nightfall
Dallas, S. Tallgrass
Dillard, A. The Maytrees
Duncan, G. Death of an ordinary man
Edwards, K. The memory keeper's daughter
Englander, N. The Ministry of Special Cases
Erdrich, L. Shadow tag
Fielding, J. Heartstopper
Franck, J. The blindness of the heart
Garcia, C. The Aguero sisters
Godden, R. The battle of the Villa Fiorita
Gordimer, N. Get a life
Grass, G. The box
Greene, G. The captain and the enemy
Haddon, M. The curious incident of the dog in the night-time
Haddon, M. A spot of bother

Haigh, J. The condition
Hamilton, J. When Madeline was young
Henderson, E. Ten thousand saints
Hodgkinson, A. 22 Britannia Road
Hoffman, A. Skylight confessions
Huston, C. The shotgun rule
Hustvedt, S. The sorrows of an American
Ishiguro, K. When we were orphans
Krauss, N. Great house
Krauss, N. The history of love
Lamott, A. Blue shoe
Lamott, A. Imperfect birds
Laplante, A. Turn of mind
Lee The surrendered
Lessing, D. M. The fifth child
Levien, D. City of the sun
Lodato, V. Mathilda Savitch
Marcus, B. The flame alphabet
Matar, H. In the country of men
Maynard, J. The usual rules
McDermott, A. Child of my heart
McEwan, I. The child in time
Meloy, M. Liars and saints
Mengestu, D. How to read the air
Miller, S. Lost in the forest
Mirvis, T. The outside world
Murphy, Y. The call
Oates, J. C. Middle age
O'Nan, S. Emily, alone
O'Nan, S. Songs for the missing
Palwick, S. Shelter
Patchett, A. Run
Perrotta, T. Little children
Picoult, J. Nineteen minutes
Powell, P. Edisto
Price, R. Roxanna Slade
Quindlen, A. Every last one
Rice, L. The letters
Robinson, R. Cost
Roth, P. Everyman
Schulman, H. This beautiful life
Schwartz, L. Angels Crest
See, C. There will never be another you
Shattuck, J. Perfect life
Sundaresan, I. The splendor of silence
Swift, G. Tomorrow
Tarkington, B. Alice Adams
Trollope, J. The best of friends
Trollope, J. Other people's children
Trollope, J. Second honeymoon
Trueblood, V. Seven loves
Turow, S. The laws of our fathers
Tyler, A. The clock winder
Tyler, A. Dinner at the Homesick Restaurant
Vida, V. Let the Northern Lights erase your name
Weiner, J. Little earthquakes
Wilson, E. O. Anthill
Wilson, K. The family Fang
Wolitzer, H. Hearts

PARENT-ADULT CHILD RELATIONSHIP
Mootoo, S. Moving forward sideways like a crab
Straub, E. Modern lovers

PARENT-CHILD RELATIONSHIP
See also Child-adult relationship; Children; Family; Parents

PARENT-CHILD RELATIONSHIP
Adebayo, A. Stay with me
Edwards, K. The memory keeper's daughter
Frankel, L. This is how it always is
Gaitskill, M. The mare
Lennon, J. R. Familiar
Marcus, B. The flame alphabet
Moore, A. The Lighthouse
Moore, L. Bark
Ng, C. Everything I never told you
O'Donnell, L. Closed Doors
Picoult, J. Lone wolf
Powers, T. Hide me among the graves
St. Aubyn, E. At last

PARENTAL CUSTODY *See* Child custody

PARENTAL KIDNAPPING
See also Child custody

PARENTAL KIDNAPPING
Jackson, N. Who do I talk to?

PARENTAL RELOCATION (CHILD CUSTODY)
Watson, L. Let him go

PARENTHOOD
See also Family

PARENTHOOD
Novak, C. Breed

PARENTING
Nova, C. All the dead Yale men

PARENTS
See also Family

PARENTS
Nova, C. All the dead Yale men
Onstad, K. Everybody Has Everything
Stedman, M. L. The light between oceans

PARENTS -- DEATH
St. Aubyn, E. At last

PARENTS OF AUTISTIC CHILDREN
Netzer, L. Shine shine shine

PARENTS OF MURDER VICTIMS
Johansen, I. Taking Eve

PARENTS OF PRESIDENTS
Hambly, B. Patriot hearts

PARENTS, UNMARRIED *See* Unmarried fathers; Unmarried mothers

Paris. Rutherfurd, E.

PARIS (FRANCE)
Black, C. Murder in the Bastille
Black, C. Murder in the Marais
Black, C. Murder in the Sentier
De Bodard, A. The house of shattered wings

Furst, A. Mission to Paris
Modiano, P. Suspended sentences
Robertson, I. The Paris winter
PARIS (FRANCE) -- HISTORY
Miller, A. Pure
Rutherfurd, E. Paris
PARIS (FRANCE) -- HISTORY -- 1789-1900
Sedgwick, M. Mister Memory
PARIS (FRANCE) -- HISTORY -- 1870-1940
Buchanan, C. M. The painted girls
Robertson, I. The Paris winter
PARIS (FRANCE) -- HISTORY -- 1940-1944
Belfoure, C. The Paris Architect
Edugyan, E. Half-blood blues
The **Paris** Architect. Belfoure, C.
Paris Trout. Dexter, P.
The **Paris** wife. McLain, P.
The **Paris** winter. Robertson, I.
PARKINSONISM
Franzen, J. The corrections
PARKS
See also Cities and towns; Landscape architecture
PAROCHIAL SCHOOLS *See* Church schools
PARODIES
Berger, T. Arthur Rex
Coover, R. Noir
Fielding, H. Joseph Andrews and Shamela
Nabokov, V. V. Lolita
North, R. Romeo And/Or Juliet
PARODY
See also Literature; Satire; Wit and humor
PAROLE
Hulse, S. M. Black River
PAROLEES
Sandlin, L. The do-right
PARRICIDE
Rossner, J. Perfidia
Sebold, A. The almost moon
Parrot and Olivier in America. Carey, P.
PARSON, MICHAEL (FICTITIOUS CHARACTER)
Young, T. W. The renegades
Part of the furniture. Wesley, M.
The **particular** sadness of lemon cake. Bender, A.
PARTIES
Jones, S. The uninvited guests
Pilcher, R. September
Rendell, R. Tigerlily's orchids
PARTIES -- ENGLAND -- 20TH CENTURY
Jones, S. The uninvited guests
A **partisan's** daughter. De Bernieres, L.
PARTISANS *See* Guerrillas
Partitions. Majmudar, A.
The **partner.** Grisham, J.
PASCOE, PETER (FICTITIOUS CHARACTER)
Hill, R. Death comes for the Fat Man
Passage. Willis, C.
The **passage.** Cronin, J.
A **passage** to India. Forster, E. M.
Passage trilogy [series]
Cronin, J. The city of mirrors
Cronin, J. The twelve
The **passages** of H.M. Parini, J.
The **Passenger.** Lutz, L.
Passing. Larsen, N.
Passing on. Lively, P.
The **Passion.** Winterson, J.
The **passion** of Artemesia. Vreeland, S.
PASSIONS *See* Emotions
PASSIVE RESISTANCE
See also Resistance to government
The **past.** Hadley, T.
PATAGONIA (ARGENTINA AND CHILE)
Aira, C. The seamstress and the wind
O'Brian, P. The unknown shore
A **patchwork** planet. Tyler, A.
PATCHWORK QUILTS *See* Quilts
PATENTS
Moore, G. The last days of night
PATHOLOGICAL PSYCHOLOGY *See* Abnormal psychology
The **patient.** Palmer, M.
The **patient's** eyes. Pirie, D.
The **Patriarch.** Walker, M.
Patricia Highsmith: selected novels and short stories. Highsmith, P.
Patriot games. Clancy, T.
Patriot hearts. Hambly, B.
PATRIOTISM
Doyle, R. A star called Henry
Mishima, Y. Runaway horses
The **patriots.** Krasikov, S.
PATROCLUS (GREEK MYTHOLOGY)
Miller, M. The song of Achilles
Pattern recognition. Gibson, W.
PATTERNS (MATHEMATICS)
See also Mathematics
Paul of Dune. Herbert, B.
Paul, the Apostle, Saint
About
Asch, S. The Apostle
PAUPERISM *See* Poverty
Pawn in frankincense. Dunnett, D.
The **pawnbroker.** Wallant, E. L.
PAWNBROKERS
Wallant, E. L. The pawnbroker
PAWNEE INDIANS
Coldsmith, D. Tallgrass
The **Paying** Guests. Waters, S.
Peace. Bausch, R.
PEACE
Vonnegut, K. Armageddon in retrospect
PEACE CORPS (U.S.)
Rosenberg, R. This is not civilization
Peaches for Father Francis. Harris, J.

PEACOCKS
See also Birds
The **pearl.** Steinbeck, J.
Pearl Cove. Lowell, E.
PEARL FISHING
Steinbeck, J. The pearl
PEARLS
Lowell, E. Pearl Cove
Steinbeck, J. The pearl
PEASANT LIFE -- CHINA
Buck, P. S. The good earth
PEASANT LIFE -- IRELAND
Uris, L. Trinity
PEASANT LIFE -- ITALY
Silone, I. Bread and wine
PEASANT LIFE -- RUSSIA
Sholokhov, M. A. The Don flows home to the sea
PEASANT LIFE -- SICILY
Puzo, M. The Sicilian
PEASANTRY
See also Feudalism; Labor
PEDDLERS
Miller, R. Jacob's folly
PEDDLERS AND PEDDLING
See also Direct selling; Sales personnel
Peder Victorious. Rolvaag, O. E.
PEDIATRICS *See* Children -- Diseases; Children -- Health and hygiene; Infants -- Diseases; Infants -- Health and hygiene
PEDIGREES *See* Genealogy; Heraldry
The **pelican** brief. Grisham, J.
PENAL CODES *See* Criminal law
PENAL COLONIES
See also Colonies; Correctional institutions
The **penal** colony: stories and short pieces. Kafka, F.
PENAL LAW *See* Criminal law
Penguin book of gay short fiction.
The **Penguin** book of lesbian short stories.
Penguin classics [series]
Dumas, A. The man in the iron mask
Greene, G. The heart of the matter
Radcliffe, A. W. The mysteries of Udolpho
Tolstoy, L. Resurrection
Wells, H. G. The island of Doctor Moreau
The white people and other weird stories
Zola, E. Germinal
Penguin twentieth-century classics [series]
Forster, E. M. A room with a view
PENGUINS
See also Birds
PENICILLIN
Belfer, L. A fierce radiance
PENINSULAR WAR, 1807-1814
Forester, C. S. Commodore Hornblower
Forester, C. S. Hornblower and the Hotspur
Forester, C. S. Lieutenant Hornblower
Forester, C. S. Ship of the line
Penn Cage series ; 4 [series]
Iles, G. Natchez burning
PENNINE CHAIN (ENGLAND) -- 13TH CENTURY
Nicholas, D. Something red
PENNSYLVANIA
Haigh, J. Baker towers
Hornby, N. Juliet, naked
Meyer, P. American rust
O'Dell, T. Back roads
O'Dell, T. Coal Run
O'Dell, T. Fragile beasts
O'Dell, T. Sister mine
O'Hara, J. From the terrace
O'Hara, J. Ten North Frederick
O'Nan, S. Snow angels
Poyer, D. Thunder on the mountain
Russo, R. The straight man
Scott, J. Follow me
PENNSYLVANIA -- 18TH CENTURY
Liss, D. The whiskey rebels
PENNSYLVANIA -- 19TH CENTURY
Jakes, J. Love and war
Jakes, J. North and South
PENNSYLVANIA -- 20TH CENTURY
Updike, J. The centaur
Updike, J. Rabbit Angstrom
Wharton, W. Birdy
PENNSYLVANIA -- PHILADELPHIA
Gallagher, S. The kingdom of bones
Lashner, W. A killer's kiss
Liss, D. The whiskey rebels
McKinney-Whetstone, D. Leaving Cecil Street
Morrow, J. The last witchfinder
Scott, A. Calpurnia
Scottoline, L. Dead ringer
Scottoline, L. Legal tender
Scottoline, L. Mistaken identity
Scottoline, L. Rough justice
Weiner, J. Certain girls
Weiner, J. Good in bed
Weiner, J. Little earthquakes
PENNSYLVANIA -- PITTSBURGH
Chabon, M. Wonder boys
O'Nan, S. Emily, alone
PENTAGON (VA.) TERRORIST ATTACK, 2001 *See* September 11 terrorist attacks, 2001
Pentecost Alley. Perry, A.
PENTECOSTALISM
See also Christianity
PEONAGE
See also Forced labor
Peony in love. See, L.
PEOPLE *See* Ethnic groups; Indigenous peoples; Persons
PEOPLE IN SPACE *See* Space flight
The **people** in the trees. Yanagihara, H.
People of the book. Brooks, G.
People of the masks. Gear, K. O.

People of the mist. Gear, K. O.
People of the thunder. Gear, W. M.
The **people** on Privilege Hill and other stories. Gardam, J.
PEOPLE WITH DISABILITIES
Darnielle, J. Wolf in white van
Leon, D. The Golden Egg
Vachss, A. That's how I roll
PEOPLE WITH DISABILITIES -- INSTITUTIONAL CARE
Nussbaum, S. Good kings bad kings
PEOPLE WITH DISABILITIES -- NAZI PERSECUTION
See also Persecution; World War, 1939-1945 -- Atrocities
PEOPLE WITH DISABILITIES -- TRAVEL
See also Travel
PEOPLE WITH MENTAL DISABILITIES
Dalton, J. The inverted forest
Faulkner, W. The sound and the fury
Gaines, E. J. A lesson before dying
Hamilton, J. When Madeline was young
Hunter, S. Dirty white boys
Kafka on the shore
Keyes, D. Flowers for Algernon
Moon, E. The speed of dark
Oe, K. A quiet life
Raimondo, L. Dante's wood
Steinbeck, J. Of mice and men
Welty, E. The Ponder heart
PEOPLE WITH PHYSICAL DISABILITIES
Brown, R. Tender mercies
Crowley, J. Four freedoms
Dunn, K. Geek love
Evans, N. The horse whisperer
MacDonald Fall on your knees
Mapson Bad Girl Creek
Maugham, W. S. Of human bondage
McCracken, E. The giant's house
Rendell, R. Live flesh
Reynolds, S. A gracious plenty
Stewart, M. Nine coaches waiting
Trumbo, D. Johnny got his gun
The **people's** act of love. Meek, J.
Percival Everett by Virgil Russell. Everett, P.
Percival's planet. Byers, M.
Perdido Street Station. Mieville, C.
Pere Goriot (Old Goriot) Balzac, H. d.
Perelandra. Lewis, C. S.
PERENNIALS
See also Cultivated plants; Flower gardening; Flowers
PEREZ, JIMMY (FICTITIOUS CHARACTER)
Cleeves, A. Thin air
The **Perfect** Ghost. Barnes, L.
The **perfect** girl. Macmillan, G.
Perfect Harmony. Wood, B.
Perfect life. Shattuck, J.
The **perfect** man. Murr, N.
The **Perfect** Match. Higgins, K.
A **perfect** spy. Le Carre, J.
A **perfect** stranger. Robinson, R.
The **perfect** witness. Johansen, I.
PERFECTIONISM (PERSONALITY TRAIT)
See also Personality
Perfidia. Ellroy, J.
Perfidia. Rossner, J.
The **perfidious** parrot. Van de Wetering, J.
PERFORMANCE ART
DeLillo, D. Falling man
Wilson, K. The family Fang
PERFORMANCE ART
See also Art; Performing arts
PERFORMANCE ARTISTS
Steinke, R. Holy skirts
Wilson, K. The family Fang
PERFORMING ARTS
Alarcón, D. At Night We Walk in Circles
Perfume River. Butler, R. O.
Perfume: the story of a murderer. Suskind, P.
PERFUMES
Faber, M. The crimson petal and the white
The **Pericles** Commission. Corby, G.
A **perilous** undertaking. Raybourn, D.
PERIODICALS
Dolan, H. Bad things happen
Mallon, T. Bandbox
PERIODICALS
See also Mass media; Serial publications
The **Peripatetic** Coffin and other stories. Rutherford, E.
The **peripheral.** Gibson, W.
Perla. De Robertis, C.
PERN (IMAGINARY PLACE)
McCaffrey, T. Dragonsblood
PERSECUTION
Vallgren The horrific sufferings of the mind-reading monster Hercules Barefoot
The **Persian** boy. Renault, M.
The **Persian** Pickle Club. Dallas, S.
PERSISTENCE
See also Personality
Personae. De la Pava, S.
PERSONAL APPEARANCE
Walker, S. Dietland
The **personal** history of Rachel Dupree. Weisgarber, A.
Personal injuries. Turow, S.
PERSONAL NARRATIVES *See* Autobiographies; Biography
Personal recollections of Joan of Arc. Twain, M.
PERSONAL SPACE
See also Interpersonal relations; Nonverbal communication; Space and time
PERSONALITY
De la Pava, S. Personae
Kehlmann, D. Fame
Ludlum, R. The Bourne identity
Ludlum, R. The Bourne supremacy

Moon, E. The speed of dark
Tyler, A. Morgan's passing
PERSONALITY DISORDERS
Conroy, P. The prince of tides
Faulks, S. Engleby
Percy, W. Lancelot
Rendell, R. A sight for sore eyes
Thomas, D. M. The white hotel
Unsworth, B. Losing Nelson
PERSONALITY DISORDERS
See also Abnormal psychology
PERSONS
See also Human beings
Persuasion. Austen, J.
PERSUASION (PSYCHOLOGY)
See also Communication; Conformity
PERSUASION (PSYCHOLOGY)
Barry, M. Lexicon
PERU
Redfield, J. The celestine prophecy
Roncagliolo, S. Red April
Vargas Llosa, M. Captain Pantoja and the Special Service
Vargas Llosa, M. Conversation in the cathedral
Vargas Llosa, M. Death in the Andes
Vargas Llosa, M. The Green House
Wright, R. The gold eaters
PERU -- ARMY -- OFFICERS
Vargas Llosa, M. Captain Pantoja and the Special Service
PERU -- LIMA
Vargas Llosa, M. Aunt Julia and the scriptwriter
Vargas Llosa, M. The notebooks of Don Rigoberto
Vargas Llosa, M. The time of the hero
PEST CONTROL
Nineveh
PEST EXTERMINATION *See* Pest control
The **pesthouse.** Crace, J.
Pet sematary. King, S.
Peter Decker/Rina Lazarus Series
Kellerman, F. The forgotten
Kellerman, F. Jupiter's bones
Kellerman, F. Milk and honey
Kellerman, F. Prayers for the dead
Petit, Philippe, 1949-
About
McCann, C. Let the great world spin
PETROLEUM INDUSTRY
Burke, J. L. Wayfaring Stranger
Estleman, L. D. Gas City
Furst, A. Blood of victory
Patterson, R. N. Eclipse
Poyer, D. Thunder on the mountain
Unsworth, B. Land of marvels
Wells, K. Crawfish mountain
Petropolis. Ulinich, A.
PETS
See also Animals
PETTING ZOOS
See also Zoos
Phantom.
PHARISEES
Asch, S. The Nazarene
PHARMACEUTICAL INDUSTRY
Belfer, L. A fierce radiance
Le Carre, J. The constant gardener
Palmer, M. Miracle cure
Patchett, A. State of wonder
Preston, D. The codex
Wood, B. Perfect Harmony
PHARMACEUTICALS *See* Drugs
PHARMACISTS
Amado, J. Dona Flor and her two husbands
Redhill, M. Consolation
PHEASANTS
See also Birds; Game and game birds
PHILADELPHIA (PA.)
Gabaldon, D. Written in my own heart's blood
Woods, T. Alibi
PHILADELPHIA (PA.) -- HISTORY -- 20TH CENTURY
Solomon, A. Disgruntled
PHILANTHROPISTS
Everett, P. L. I am Not Sidney Poitier
Philida. Brink, A. P.
Philip Dryden [series]
Kelly, J. The fire baby
Philip IV, King of France, 1268-1314
About
Druon, M. The Iron King
PHILIPPINES
Syjuco, M. Ilustrado
Yates, A. Moondogs
PHILIPPINES -- MANILA
Holthe, T. U. When the elephants dance
PHILOLOGY *See* Language and languages; Linguistics
The **philosopher's** apprentice. Morrow, J.
The **philosopher's** pupil. Murdoch, I.
PHILOSOPHERS
Goldstein, R. 36 arguments for the existence of God
Goodman, C. The night villa
Mishima, Y. The Temple of Dawn
Morrow, J. The philosopher's apprentice
Murdoch, I. The philosopher's pupil
Parris, S. J. Sacrilege
Pearl, M. The Dante Club
Renault, M. The last of the wine
PHILOSOPHERS' STONE *See* Alchemy
PHILOSOPHICAL FICTION
Allende, I. The house of the spirits
Eco, U. The name of the rose
Eco, U. The island of the day before
Hoeg, P. Borderliners
Life
Lightman, A. P. Einstein's dreams
Marias, J. A heart so white
McEwan, I. The child in time

Murdoch, I. The book and the brotherhood
Murdoch, I. The green knight
Robbins, T. Skinny legs and all
Sebald, W. G. Vertigo
Stone, R. Outerbridge Reach
PHILOSOPHICAL NOVELS
Amis, M. House of meetings
Amis, M. Time's arrow
Austerlitz
Barker, P. The eye in the door
Barker, P. The ghost road
Barker, P. Regeneration
Barnes, J. A history of the world in 10 1/2 chapters
Beauvoir, S. d. The mandarins
Bellow, S. Henderson the rain king
Bellow, S. Mr. Sammler's planet
Brooks, G. Year of wonders
Bulgakov, M. A. The master and Margarita
Calvino, I. If on a winter's night a traveler
Camus, A. The fall
Coetzee, J. M. Foe
Cooley, M. The archivist
Crace, J. Being dead
Cunningham, M. By nightfall
Cunningham, M. Specimen days
Davies, R. The cunning man
Davies, R. The rebel angels
DeLillo, D. Point Omega
Doctorow, E. L. The waterworks
Dostoyevsky, F. Notes from underground
Drabble, M. The witch of Exmoor
Eco, U. Baudolino
Eco, U. The island of the day before
The emigrants
Endo, S. Deep river
Fuentes, C. Destiny and desire
Gaddis, W. Agape agape
Gao Xingjian Soul mountain
Garcia Marquez, G. The general and his labyrinth
Golding, W. Close quarters
Golding, W. Fire down below
Golding, W. The inheritors
Golding, W. Rites of passage
Grass, G. Crabwalk
Guterson, D. The other
Hale, B. The evolution of Bruno Littlemore
Handke, P. Don Juan
Hansen, R. Mariette in ecstasy
Harrison, J. The English major
Hazzard, S. The great fire
Hoban, R. Riddley Walker
Hoeg, P. Borderliners
Hulme, K. The bone people
Ishiguro, K. Never let me go
Johnson, C. R. Middle passage
Kadare, I. The Successor
Kehlmann, D. Fame
Kundera, M. Immortality
Kundera, M. The unbearable lightness of being
Le Guin, U. K. The dispossessed
Lehrer, J. The special prisoner
Lem, S. Solaris
Lewis, C. S. Out of the silent planet
Lewis, C. S. Perelandra
Lewis, C. S. That hideous strength
Lightman, A. P. The diagnosis
Lightman, A. P. Einstein's dreams
Lodge, D. Thinks--
Mahfouz, N. Children of the alley
Mahfouz, N. Palace of desire
Mahfouz, N. Sugar Street
Malouf, D. Remembering Babylon
The man of feeling
Mann, T. The magic mountain
Maugham, W. S. The razor's edge
McCarthy, C. The road
McCarthy, C. All the pretty horses
McCarthy, C. Cities of the plain
McCarthy, M. Birds of America
McEwan, I. Atonement
McEwan, I. Black dogs
Meek, J. The people's act of love
Michaels, A. Fugitive pieces
Mitchell, D. Cloud atlas
Morrow, J. The last witchfinder
Mosley, W. The man in my basement
Murakami, H. The wind-up bird chronicle
Murdoch, I. The book and the brotherhood
Murdoch, I. The good apprentice
Murdoch, I. The green knight
Murdoch, I. The philosopher's pupil
My name is Red
Naylor, G. Linden Hills
Norman, H. The museum guard
Oe, K. Nip the buds, shoot the kids
Ondaatje, M. The English patient
Ondaatje, M. Anil's ghost
Percy, W. The last gentleman
Percy, W. The moviegoer
Percy, W. The second coming
Perez-Reverte, A. The nautical chart
Petterson, P. In the wake
Powers, R. The echo maker
Powers, R. Generosity
Powers, R. The gold bug variations
Powers, R. Plowing the dark
Pywell, S. L. What happened to Henry
Robbins, T. Skinny legs and all
Roth, P. Everyman
Russell, M. D. Children of God
Russell, M. D. The sparrow
Saint-Exupery, A. d. The little prince
Saramago, J. All the names
Saramago, J. The cave

Saramago, J. The history of the siege of Lisbon
Sartre, J. P. Nausea
Savage, S. Firmin
Schlink, B. Homecoming
Scott, J. Tourmaline
Sebald, W. G. Vertigo
Shields, C. Unless
Spark, M. Aiding and abetting
Stephenson, N. Anathem
Stone, R. Bay of souls
Stone, R. Outerbridge Reach
Suri, M. The death of Vishnu
Tournier, M. Friday
Tournier, M. The ogre
Updike, J. Roger's version
Vidal, G. Creation
Vonnegut, K. Galapagos
Whitehead, C. The intuitionist
Wiesel, E. The forgotten
Wiesel, E. The judges
Zimler, R. The last kabbalist of Lisbon
PHILOSOPHY -- ENCYCLOPEDIAS
See also Encyclopedias and dictionaries
PHILOSOPHY
Hustvedt, S. The blazing world
PHILOSOPHY AND RELIGION
See also Philosophy; Religion
PHOBIAS
See also Fear; Neuroses
PHOBIAS
Semple, M. Where'd you go, Bernadette
PHOENIX (ARIZ.)
Bacigalupi, P. The water knife
Sallis, J. Driven
PHONETICS
See also Language and languages; Sound
PHONOGRAPH RECORDS *See* Sound recordings
The **Photographer's** Wife. Joinson, S.
PHOTOGRAPHERS
Beattie, A. Picturing Will
Fergus, J. The wild girl: the notebooks of Ned Giles, 1932
Grass, G. The box
Groff, L. Arcadia
Just, W. S. Exiles in the garden
Kennedy, D. The big picture
Kirkpatrick, J. A flickering light
Leimbach, M. The man from Saigon
McNally, T. M. The goat bridge
Norman, H. The haunting of L
The painter of battles
Ramirez Mercado, S. A thousand deaths plus one
Rushdie, S. The ground beneath her feet
Theroux, P. Picture palace
Trevor, W. Love and summer
Waller, R. J. The bridges of Madison County
Wiggins, M. Evidence of things unseen
Wiggins, M. The shadow catcher
PHOTOGRAPHERS
See also Artists
PHOTOGRAPHIC MEMORY
Sedgwick, M. Mister Memory
PHOTOGRAPHS
Redhill, M. Consolation
PHOTOGRAPHY -- GENERAL
Otto, W. Eight girls taking pictures
PHOTOJOURNALISM
See also Commercial photography; Journalism; Photography
PHOTOJOURNALISM -- UNITED STATES -- HISTORY -- 20TH CENTURY
Silver, M. Mary Coin
PHOTOS *See* Photographs
PHRENOLOGY
See also Brain; Head; Psychology
Phryne Fisher Mysteries [series]
Greenwood, K. Unnatural Habits
PHYSICAL ANTHROPOLOGY
See also Anthropology; Ethnology
PHYSICAL APPEARANCE *See* Personal appearance
PHYSICALLY HANDICAPPED
Mapson Bad Girl Creek
Reynolds, S. A gracious plenty
PHYSICIAN-PATIENT RELATIONSHIP
Iles, G. Natchez burning
Self, W. Umbrella
PHYSICIANS
Forna, A. The memory of love
Guinn, M. The resurrectionist
Havley, N. The good father
Laplante, A. A Circle of Wives
Levy, D. Hot Milk
PHYSICISTS
Benford, G. Timescape
Bock, D. The ash garden
Flynn, M. Eifelheim
Jensen, J. Dante's equation
Le Guin, U. K. The dispossessed
Lightman, A. P. Einstein's dreams
Millet, L. Oh pure and radiant heart
Morrow, J. The last witchfinder
Palmer, D. Version control
Powers, T. Three days to never
Preston, D. Blasphemy
Rubenfeld, J. The death instinct
Scholz, C. Radiance
Stott, R. Ghostwalk
Wallace, I. The prize
Wouk, H. A hole in Texas
PHYSICISTS
See also Scientists
PHYSICISTS -- CRIMES AGAINST
Brown, D. Angels & demons
The **physick** book of Deliverance Dane. Howe, K.
PHYSICS

Holt, T. Doughnut
Rajaniemi, H. The fractal prince
PHYSIOLOGICAL PSYCHOLOGY
Keyes, D. Flowers for Algernon
PHYSIOLOGISTS
Barker, P. The eye in the door
Barker, P. The ghost road
PIANISTS
Bernhard, T. The loser
Hambly, B. Die upon a kiss
Hambly, B. A free man of color
Hamilton, J. Disobedience
Ishiguro, K. The unconsoled
Macmillan, G. The perfect girl
Makine, A. Music of a life
Morgan, C. E. All the living
O'Neill, H. The Lonely Hearts Hotel
Romano-Lax, A. The Spanish bow
The **piano** man's daughter. Findley, T.
The **piano** teacher. Lee, J. Y. K.
Piano tide. Moore, K. D.
The **piano** tuner. Mason, D.
PIANO TUNERS
Mason, D. The piano tuner
PICARDY (FRANCE)
Louis, É. The end of Eddy
PICARESQUE LITERATURE
Hrabal, B. I served the King of England
Portis, C. Gringos
PICARESQUE NOVELS
Adamson, G. The outlander
Barth, J. The sot-weed factor
Bellow, S. The adventures of Augie March
Berger, T. Little Big Man
Bolano, R. The savage detectives
Brown, J. D. Addie Pray
Cervantes Saavedra, M. d. Don Quixote de la Mancha
Charyn, J. Johnny One-Eye
Crace, J. The pesthouse
Defoe, D. Moll Flanders
Dexter, P. Spooner
Dickens, C. The posthumous papers of the Pickwick Club
Doctorow, E. L. Billy Bathgate
Dunn, K. Geek love
Eco, U. Baudolino
Edgerton, C. The Bible salesman
Fielding, H. The history of Tom Jones, a foundling
Fowler, K. J. Sarah Canary
Gogol', N. V. Dead souls
Grossman, D. Someone to run with
Harrison, J. The English major
Hrabal, B. I served the King of England
Kafka on the shore
Kaufman, M. Bowl of cherries
Keneally, T. Woman of the inner sea
Kerouac, J. On the road
Kunzru, H. The impressionist
Lynch, S. The lies of Locke Lamora
Maalouf, A. Balthasar's odyssey
Manseau, P. Songs for the butcher's daughter
Portis, C. The dog of the South
Portis, C. Gringos
Proulx, A. Accordion crimes
Proulx, A. Postcards
Rushdie, S. The Moor's last sigh
Smith, Z. The autograph man
Sontag, S. In America
Stendhal The red and the black
Tan, A. Saving fish from drowning
Taylor, M. G. The ballad of Trenchmouth Taggart
Tinti, H. The good thief
Toole, J. K. A confederacy of dunces
Urrea, L. A. Into the beautiful North
Vallgren The horrific sufferings of the mind-reading monster Hercules Barefoot
Wallace, D. Mr. Sebastian and the Negro magician
PICARESQUE NOVELS *See* Picaresque literature
PICARESQUE STORIES
DeWitt, P. The Sisters brothers
PICKETT, JOE (FICTITIOUS CHARACTER)
Box, C. J. Force of nature
Box, C. J. Free fire
Box, C. J. Open season
The **pickup.** Gordimer, N.
PICNICS
See also Dining; Dinners; Luncheons; Outdoor recreation
Picture bride. Uchida, Y.
The **picture** of Dorian Gray. Wilde, O.
Picture palace. Theroux, P.
PICTURE PUZZLES
See also Puzzles
PICTURES
See also Art
Picturing Will. Beattie, A.
Piece of my heart. Robinson, P.
Pierre; or, The ambiquities, Israel Potter: his fifty years of exile, The piazza tales, The confidence-man: his masquerade, Uncollected prose, Billy Budd, Sailor: (an inside narrative) Melville, H.
Pigeon feathers, and other stories. Updike, J.
PIGEON, ANNA (FICTITIOUS CHARACTER)
Barr, N. Destroyer angel
Barr, N. The rope
Pigs in heaven. Kingsolver, B.
The **pilgrim.** Nissenson, H.
The **pilgrim's** progress. Bunyan, J.
PILGRIMS (NEW ENGLAND COLONISTS)
See also Puritans; United States -- History -- 1600-1775, Colonial period
PILGRIMS (NEW PLYMOUTH COLONY)
Nissenson, H. The pilgrim
PILGRIMS AND PILGRIMAGES
Endo, S. Deep river

Mehta, G. A river Sutra
PILGRIMS AND PILGRIMAGES
See also Voyages and travels
The **pillars** of the earth. Follett, K.
The **pilot's** wife. Shreve, A.
PILOTS *See* Air pilots; Ship pilots
PIMLICO (LONDON, ENGLAND) -- SOCIAL LIFE AND CUSTOMS
McCall Smith, A. A conspiracy of friends
A **pimp's** notes. Faletti, G.
The **pinch.** Stern, S.
PING-PONG *See* Table tennis
PIONEER LIFE *See* Frontier and pioneer life
PIONEERS
McMurtry, L. Buffalo girls
Pippa passes. Godden, R.
PIRACY *See* Pirates
Pirate freedom. Wolfe, G.
Pirate latitudes. Crichton, M.
PIRATES
Baker, K. The bird of the river
Crichton, M. Pirate latitudes
Davies, J. D. The mountain of gold
Du Maurier, D. Frenchman's Creek
Farah, N. Crossbones
Handler, D. We are pirates
Hughes, R. A. W. A high wind in Jamaica
Leonard, E. Djibouti
Levine, S. Treasure Island!!!
London, L. The windflower
Maxwell, R. The wild Irish
Reynolds, A. Revenger
Sabatini, R. Captain Blood
Smith, W. A. Birds of prey
Smith, W. A. Monsoon
Stross, C. Neptune's brood
Wolfe, G. Pirate freedom
Wooding, C. Retribution falls
PIRATES
See also Criminals; International law; Maritime law; Naval history
The **pit.** Norris, F.
PITCAIRN ISLAND
Nordhoff, C. Pitcairn's Island
Pitcairn's Island. Nordhoff, C.
Pitch dark. Sidor, S.
Pizarro, Francisco, approximately 1475-1541
About
Wright, R. The gold eaters
A **place** called home. Goodman, J.
A **place** of confinement. Dean, A.
A **place** of execution. McDermid, V.
PLAGIARISM
Sarton, M. A small room
PLAGIARISM
See also Authorship; Offenses against property
Oates, J. C. Jack of Spades
The **plague.** Camus, A.
PLAGUE
Brooks, G. Year of wonders
Camus, A. The plague
Conn, B. The fixed stars
Crace, J. The pesthouse
Flynn, M. Eifelheim
Follett, K. World without end
Johnson, A. Parasites like us
Mann, T. Death in Venice
Newman, S. The Country of Ice Cream Star
Oe, K. Nip the buds, shoot the kids
Pears, I. The dream of Scipio
Robinson, K. S. The years of rice and salt
Sykes, S. D. Plague Land
Willis, C. Doomsday book
PLAGUE
See also Communicable diseases; Epidemics
Plague Land. Sykes, S. D.
The **plague** of doves. Erdrich, L.
Plain paradise. Wiseman, B.
Plainsong. Haruf, K.
Planet of the apes. Boulle, P.
PLANETOIDS *See* Asteroids
PLANNED COMMUNITIES -- ENGLAND -- LONDON
Smith, Z. NW
PLANTATION LIFE
Allende, I. Island beneath the sea
Bell, M. S. All souls' rising
Crafts, H. The bondswomans narrative
Faulkner, W. Absalom, Absalom!
Gaines, E. J. The autobiography of Miss Jane Pittman
Jones, E. P. The known world
Levy, A. The long song
Martin, V. Property
Mitchell, M. Gone with the wind
Santiago, E. Conquistadora
Smith, L. On Agate Hill
Stowe, H. B. Uncle Tom's cabin
Straight, S. A million nightingales
Walker, M. Jubilee
PLANTATION LIFE
See also Country life
PLANTATION LIFE -- AFRICA
Forna, A. Ancestor stones
PLANTATION OWNERS
Matthiessen, P. Bone by bone
Matthiessen, P. Killing Mister Watson
Matthiessen, P. Shadow country
Slouka, M. God's fool
PLANTATION OWNERS' SPOUSES
Crafts, H. The bondswomans narrative
Hicks, R. The widow of the south
Martin, V. Property
PLANTS -- COLLECTION AND PRESERVATION
See also Collectors and collecting
PLANTS -- FOLKLORE

See also Folklore
PLANTS, INDUSTRIAL *See* Factories
PLASTIC SURGERY
See also Surgery
Plath, Sylvia
About
Moses, K. Wintering
Play it as it lays. Didion, J.
The **play** of death.
Player piano. Vonnegut, K.
Playing dirty. Swinson, K.
Playing for pizza. Grisham, J.
Playing with fire. Gerritsen, T.
PLAYWRIGHTS *See* Dramatists
PLEASURE
See also Emotions; Joy and sorrow; Senses and sensation
The **pleasure** of my company. Martin, S.
The **pleasures** of love. Plaidy, J.
The **plot** against America. Roth, P.
Plowing the dark. Powers, R.
Plugged. Colfer, E.
Plum Island. DeMille, N.
Plume contemporary fiction [series]
Jen, G. Typical American
PLUTO (PLANET)
Byers, M. Percival's planet
Pnin. Nabokov, V. V.
The **poacher's** son. Doiron, P.
POACHING
Doiron, P. The poacher's son
Winton, T. Dirt music
Pocahontas, d. 1617
About
Vollmann, W. T. Argall
Pocho. Villarreal, J. A.
The **Poe** shadow. Pearl, M.
Poe's children.
Poe, Edgar Allan, 1809-1849
About
Bayard, L. The pale blue eye
Fairstein, L. Entombed
Johnson, M. Pym
Pearl, M. The Poe shadow
Rose, J. Blackest bird
POETICS
See also Poetry
POETRY -- AUTHORSHIP
Baker, N. The anthologist
Chang, L. S. All is forgotten, nothing is lost
Gibbons, K. The life all around me by Ellen Foster
POETS
Adams, A. A southern exposure
Adrian, C. The great night
Auster, P. Invisible
Baker, N. The anthologist
Barker, P. The eye in the door
Barker, P. Regeneration
Barry, K. Dark lies the island
Bear, E. Ink and steel
Bolano, R. Monsieur Pain
Bolano, R. The savage detectives
Byatt, A. S. Possession
Carey, P. My life as a fake
Chang, L. S. All is forgotten, nothing is lost
Cooley, M. The archivist
Crowley, J. Lord Byron's novel
Cunningham, M. Specimen days
Dillard, A. The Maytrees
Eugenides, J. Fresh complaint
Fairstein, L. Entombed
Fitzgerald, P. The blue flower
Foulds, A. The quickening maze
Graham, J. Black ships
Gruber, M. The book of air and shadows
Ha Jin A free life
Haasse, H. S. In a dark wood wandering
Haig, M. The dead fathers club
Hansen, R. Exiles
Hollinghurst, A. The stranger's child
Johnson, M. Pym
Krauss, N. Great house
Lashner, W. Kockroach
Lerner, B. Leaving the Atocha Station
Littell, R. The Stalin epigram
Malae, P. N. What we are
Malouf, D. Ransom
Manseau, P. Songs for the butcher's daughter
Marsh, N. Light thickens
Martin, V. Mary Reilly
McCann, C. Zoli
McLain, P. The Paris wife
Michaels, A. Fugitive pieces
Miles, J. Dear American Airlines
Morton, K. The house at Riverton
Moses, K. Wintering
Nabokov, V. V. Novels and memoirs, 1941-1951
Nabokov, V. V. Pale fire
Naipaul, V. S. A way in the world
Oates, J. C. Wild nights!
Pearl, M. The Dante Club
Pearl, M. The Poe shadow
Pears, I. The dream of Scipio
Phillips, A. The tragedy of Arthur
Reznikoff, C. By the waters of Manhattan
Rose, J. Blackest bird
Salinger, J. D. Raise high the roof beam, carpenters, and Seymour: an introduction
Self, W. Dorian
Sherwood, F. The book of splendor
Shreve, A. The last time they met
Snow
Spark, M. The girls of slender means
Steinke, R. Holy skirts

Truong, M. The book of salt
Updike, J. Gertrude and Claudius
Verissimo, L. F. Borges and the eternal orangutans
Walker, A. The way forward is with a broken heart
Waugh, E. The loved one
Wiesel, E. The testament
POETS
See also Authors
POETS LAUREATE
Foulds, A. The quickening maze
Moses, K. Wintering
POETS, AMERICAN -- 20TH CENTURY -- BIOGRAPHY
Hudgins, A. The joker
POETS, ENGLISH -- 19TH CENTURY
Shepherd, L. A fatal likeness
POETS, FINNISH
The healer
The **point** of return. Deb, S.
Point Omega. DeLillo, D.
Poison flower. Perry, T.
Poison fruit. Carey, J.
The **poison** tree. Kelly, E.
Poisoned ground. Parshall, S.
The **Poisoned** Pilgrim.
POISONING
Bradley, A. The sweetness at the bottom of the pie
Hall, T. The case of the deadly butter chicken
Peace, D. Occupied city
Robertson, I. Circle of shadows
Watson, B. The heaven of Mercury
POISONOUS ANIMALS
See also Animals; Dangerous animals; Economic zoology; Poisons and poisoning
POISONS
Rendell, R. Heartstones
POISONS AND POISONING
See also Accidents; Hazardous substances; Homicide; Medical jurisprudence
POISONS AND POISONING
Lynch, S. The Republic of Thieves
Moore, J. The night market
Poole, S. The Borgia mistress
The **poisonwood** Bible. Kingsolver, B.
Poitier, Sidney
About
Everett, P. L. I am Not Sidney Poitier
POKER
See also Card games
POKER (GAME)
Pronzini, B. Step to the graveyard easy
POLAND
Allende, I. The Japanese Lover
Shepard, J. The book of Aron
Stone upon stone
POLAND -- 19TH CENTURY
Singer, I. B. The magician of Lublin
POLAND -- 20TH CENTURY
Kosinski, J. N. The painted bird
POLAND -- GDANSK
Grass, G. The call of the toad
Grass, G. Cat and mouse
Grass, G. The Danzig trilogy
Grass, G. Dog years
Grass, G. The tin drum
POLAND -- HISTORY -- OCCUPATION, 1939-1945
Kelly, M. H. Lilac girls
POLAND -- LODZ
Singer, I. J. The brothers Ashkenazi
POLAND -- WARSAW
Furst, A. The spies of Warsaw
Singer, I. B. The family Moskat
Skibell, J. A curable romantic
Uris, L. Mila 18
POLAR REGIONS -- DISCOVERY AND EXPLORATION
O'Loughlin, E. Minds of winter
POLES -- ENGLAND
Murdoch, I. Nuns and soldiers
POLES -- FRANCE
Powell, J. The breaking of eggs
Rhys, J. Quartet
POLES -- ITALY
Mann, T. Death in Venice
POLES -- UNITED STATES
Powell, J. The breaking of eggs
Sontag, S. In America
Styron, W. Sophie's choice
POLICE
Box, C. J. The highway
Castillo, L. Sworn to silence
Dibdin, M. Ratking
Estleman, L. D. Gas City
Eva's eye
Genova, L. Inside the O'Briens
The Ghost Riders of Ordebec
Guinn, M. The scribe
Haldane, S. The devil's making
Higashino, K. Malice
Hunt, A. City of saints
Johnson, C. Hell is empty
Katzenbach, J. What comes next
Koenig, M. Nine days
Laukkanen, O. Criminal enterprise
Leon, D. Blood from a stone
Mark, D. Cruel mercy
Mieville, C. The city & the city
Mizushima, M. Stalking Ground
Mullen, T. Darktown
Penny, L. Glass houses
Penny, L. A great reckoning
Penny, L. The nature of the beast
Pérez-Reverte, A. The siege
Rendell, R. Live flesh
Rodriguez, L. Every broken trust
Sandford, J. Storm Front

Spring Tide
Winslow, D. The force
Winters, B. H. World of trouble
POLICE -- ALABAMA -- MOBILE
Kerley, J. The death collectors
POLICE -- ARIZONA
Sallis, J. The killer is dying
POLICE -- ARKANSAS
Hunter, S. Pale horse coming
POLICE -- ATLANTA (GA.)
Johansen, I. Blind alley
POLICE -- AUSTRIA -- VIENNA
Tallis, F. Fatal lies
Tallis, F. Vienna blood
Tallis, F. Vienna Twilight
POLICE -- BALTIMORE (MD.)
Lippman, L. What the dead know
POLICE -- BANGKOK (THAILAND)
Burdett, J. Bangkok 8
POLICE -- BOSTON (MASS.)
Gerritsen, T. Body double
Lehane, D. The given day
Lehane, D. Mystic river
Palmer, M. The society
POLICE -- BRITISH COLUMBIA
Haldane, S. The devil's making
POLICE -- CALIFORNIA
Parker, T. J. Black water
Parker, T. J. The blue hour
Parker, T. J. California girl
Parker, T. J. Where serpents lie
Rosenberg, N. T. Abuse of power
Rosenberg, N. T. Interest of justice
Wambaugh, J. Finnegan's week
Woods, S. Dead eyes
POLICE -- CANADA
Van Rooy, M. An ordinary decent criminal
Wolfe, I. A. The calling
POLICE -- CHICAGO (ILL.)
Harris, E. L. And this too shall pass
Newton, C. Calumet City
POLICE -- CHINA -- SHANGHAI
Qiu Xiaolong Shanghai redemption
Qiu Xiaolong Death of a red heroine
POLICE -- CLEVELAND (OHIO)
Black, L. Takeover
POLICE -- DENMARK
Adler-Olsen, J. The absent one
Adler-Olsen, J. The keeper of lost causes
POLICE -- DETROIT (MICH.)
Leonard, E. Freaky Deaky
Leonard, E. Mr. Paradise
POLICE -- EASTERN EUROPE
Steinhauer, O. The Bridge of Sighs
POLICE -- EDINBURGH (SCOTLAND)
Rankin, I. The impossible dead
Rankin, I. The complaints
POLICE -- ENGLAND
Bauer, B. Darkside
Bolton, S. J. Now you see me
Boyne, J. Crippen
Carver, T. The surrogate
Grimes, M. The Stargazey
Harvey, J. Far cry
Harvey, J. Gone to ground
Mark, D. Cruel mercy
Mark, D. Original skin
McDermid, V. A place of execution
Rendell, R. Harm done
Robotham, M. The wreckage
Townsend, S. Number 10
Walton, J. Farthing
Walton, J. Half a crown
Walton, J. Ha'penny
POLICE -- ENGLAND -- BATH
Lovesey, P. Diamond dust
Lovesey, P. The tooth tattoo
Lovesey, P. The vault
POLICE -- ENGLAND -- CAMBRIDGESHIRE
Malliet, G. M. A Demon Summer
POLICE -- ENGLAND -- LONDON
Harrod-Eagles, C. Old bones
POLICE -- ENGLAND -- YORKSHIRE
Hill, R. Death comes for the Fat Man
POLICE -- FLORIDA
Atkins, A. White shadow
Hoffman, A. Turtle Moon
Leonard, E. Rum punch
Woods, S. Choke
Woods, S. Orchid Beach
Woods, S. Reckless abandon
POLICE -- GEORGIA
Woods, S. Chiefs
POLICE -- GEORGIA -- ATLANTA
Guinn, M. The scribe
POLICE -- GREAT BRITAIN
Harvey, J. Gone to ground
Walton, J. Ha'penny
POLICE -- IRELAND
French, T. Faithful Place
French, T. In the woods
French, T. The likeness
POLICE -- IRELAND -- DUBLIN
French, T. Broken Harbor
POLICE -- ITALY
Coco, G. Shadows on the lake
POLICE -- ITALY -- VENICE
Leon, D. A question of belief
Leon, D. Blood from a stone
POLICE -- JAPAN
Higashino, K. Malice
POLICE -- LAS VEGAS (NEV.)
Ellroy, J. The cold six thousand
POLICE -- LONDON (ENGLAND)

Forsyth, F. The day of the jackal
Gallagher, S. The kingdom of bones

POLICE -- LOS ANGELES (CALIF.)
Crais, R. Demolition angel
Ellroy, J. The black dahlia
Ellroy, J. L.A. confidential
Hoag, T. Kill the messenger
Parker, T. J. L.A. outlaws
Wambaugh, J. The blue knight
Wambaugh, J. Hollywood crows
Wambaugh, J. Hollywood Hills
Wambaugh, J. Hollywood Station
Wambaugh, J. The new centurions

POLICE -- MASSACHUSETTS
Gardner, L. Alone
Genova, L. Inside the O'Briens
Hoffman, A. The river king
Parker, R. B. Death in paradise

POLICE -- MASSACHUSETTS -- BOSTON
Lehane, D. Mystic river
Ryan, H. P. The other woman

POLICE -- MIAMI (FLA.)
Gruber, M. Valley of bones
Leonard, E. Glitz

POLICE -- MICHIGAN
Harrison, J. The great leader

POLICE -- MINNESOTA
Hoag, T. Dust to dust
Hoag, T. Night sins
Tracy, P. J. Monkeewrench

POLICE -- MISSISSIPPI
Franklin, T. Crooked letter, crooked letter
Logan, C. South of Shiloh

POLICE -- NEW JERSEY
Price, R. Clockers
Price, R. Freedomland
Price, R. Samaritan
Rosenfelt, D. Don't tell a soul

POLICE -- NEW YORK (N.Y.)
Brandt, H. The Whites
Carr, C. The alienist
DeMille, N. Plum Island
DeMille, N. Wild fire
Doctorow, E. L. The waterworks
Ellory, R. J. The Anniversary Man
Fairstein, L. Entombed
Faye, L. Seven for a secret
Goodis, D. Nightfall
Hamill, P. Tabloid city
Hunter, E. Candyland
Lamberson, G. The frenzy way
Preston, D. Reliquary
Price, R. Lush life
Quindlen, A. Black and blue
Ross, A. Mr. Peanut
Rubenfeld, J. The death instinct
Sanders, L. The first deadly sin
Sanders, L. The second deadly sin
Sanders, L. The third deadly sin

POLICE -- NEW YORK (STATE)
Faye, L. The gods of Gotham
Faye, L. Seven for a secret
Hunter, E. Candyland
Mark, D. Cruel mercy
Mills, M. Amagansett
O'Connell, C. The chalk girl
O'Connell, C. Crime school
O'Connell, C. Judas child
Thompson, V. Murder in Chinatown
Thompson, V. Murder on Fifth Avenue
Verdon, J. Think of a number
Winslow, D. The force

POLICE -- NORTH CAROLINA
Betts, D. Souls raised from the dead

POLICE -- NORTHERN IRELAND
McKinty, A. The cold cold ground

POLICE -- NORWAY -- OSLO
The leopard
Phantom

POLICE -- OKLAHOMA
Hunter, S. Dirty white boys

POLICE -- OREGON -- PORTLAND
Cain, C. Kill you twice

POLICE -- PARIS (FRANCE)
Forsyth, F. The day of the jackal

POLICE -- PENNSYLVANIA
Bouman, T. Dry bones in the valley

POLICE -- PHILADELPHIA (PA.)
Scottoline, L. Legal tender
Scottoline, L. Mistaken identity

POLICE -- PHILIPPINES
Yates, A. Moondogs

POLICE -- PORTLAND (ORE.)
Cain, C. Heartsick
Perry, T. Nightlife

POLICE -- QUÉBEC (PROVINCE)
Penny, L. Bury your dead
Penny, L. Glass houses
Penny, L. A great reckoning
Penny, L. How the light gets in
Penny, L. The long way home
Penny, L. The nature of the beast

POLICE -- SAN DIEGO (CALIF.)
Parker, T. J. Cold pursuit
Parker, T. J. The fallen
Wambaugh, J. Floaters

POLICE -- SAN FRANCISCO (CALIF.)
Gardiner, M. The Dirty Secrets Club
Lescroart, J. T. The first law
Lescroart, J. T. Guilt
Lescroart, J. T. The hearing
Patterson, J. 1st to die

POLICE -- SCOTLAND -- ABERDEEN
MacBride, S. Blind eye

MacBride, S. Cold granite
MacBride, S. Dying Light
MacBride, S. Shatter the bones
POLICE -- SCOTLAND -- EDINBURGH
Rankin, I. Rather be the devil
Rankin, I. The falls
Rankin, I. A question of blood
Rankin, I. Set in darkness
POLICE -- SCOTLAND -- SHETLAND
Cleeves, A. Thin air
POLICE -- SEVILLE (SPAIN)
Wilson, R. The blind man of Seville
Wilson, R. The hidden assassins
POLICE -- SHANGHAI (CHINA)
Qiu Xiaolong Shanghai redemption
Qiu Xiaolong Death of a red heroine
POLICE -- SOUTH AFRICA
Paton, A. Too late the phalarope
POLICE -- SWEDEN
Dahl, A. Misterioso
Lackberg, C. The stonecutter
Ohlsson, K. Unwanted
POLICE -- SWEDEN -- STOCKHOLM
Dahl, A. Bad Blood
POLICE -- TEXAS
Lansdale, J. R. The bottoms
Lansdale, J. R. Sunset and sawdust
POLICE -- TOKYO (JAPAN)
Lee, D. Country of origin
Peace, D. Tokyo year zero
POLICE -- TURKEY -- ISTANBUL -- FICTION
Nadel, B. The Ottoman cage
POLICE -- WASHINGTON (D.C.)
Patterson, J. Four blind mice
Patterson, J. London bridges
Patterson, J. Roses are red
Pelecanos, G. P. The night gardener
Pelecanos, G. P. Right as rain
POLICE -- WASHINGTON (STATE)
Pearson, R. The angel maker
Pearson, R. The art of deception
Pearson, R. Beyond recognition
Pearson, R. The body of David Hayes
Pearson, R. The first victim
Pearson, R. Middle of nowhere
Pearson, R. Undercurrents
Waite, U. The terror of living
POLICE -- WASHINGTON (STATE) -- SPOKANE
Walter, J. Citizen Vince
POLICE -- WISCONSIN
Tracy, P. J. Monkeewrench
POLICE BRUTALITY
See also Police
POLICE CHIEFS -- FRANCE, SOUTHWEST
Walker, M. The crowded grave
POLICE CORRUPTION
See also Misconduct in office; Police
POLICE CORRUPTION -- NEW YORK (STATE) -- NEW YORK
Winslow, D. The force
POLICE DOGS
Mizushima, M. Stalking Ground
Woods, S. Orchid Beach
POLICE OFFICERS *See* Police
POLICE OFFICERS
Hiassen, C. Bad monkey
POLICE STATIONS -- NEW YORK (STATE) -- NEW YORK
Rindell, S. The Other Typist
POLICEMEN *See* Police
POLICEWOMEN
Bingham, H. Talking to the dead
Bolton, S. J. Now you see me
Burgess, M. Uncle Janice
Castillo, L. The dead will tell
Dolan, H. Bad things happen
Dolan, H. Very bad men
Hart, J. Redemption road
Mina, D. The end of the wasp season
Mina, D. Still midnight
Newton, C. Calumet City
Robb, J. D. Naked in death
Rodriguez, L. Every hidden fear
Wolfe, I. A. The calling
POLICEWOMEN
See also Police; Women
POLICEWOMEN -- NEW JERSEY -- HACKENSACK
Stewart, A. Girl waits with gun
POLICEWOMEN -- NORTH DAKOTA
Box, C. J. Badlands
POLIO *See* Poliomyelitis
POLIOMYELITIS
Berg, E. We are all welcome here
London, J. The Golden Age
Roth, P. Nemesis
POLIOMYELITIS
See also Diseases
POLISH FICTION -- TRANSLATIONS INTO ENGLISH
Lem, S. Eden
Stone upon stone
POLITICAL ACTIVISTS
The dream of the Celt
POLITICAL AND SOCIAL PHILOSOPHERS
Wideman, J. E. Fanon
POLITICAL CORRUPTION
Glynn, A. Bloodland
Lelic, S. The facility
Marr, A. Head of State
POLITICAL CORRUPTION -- GREAT BRITAIN
Le Carré, J. A Delicate Truth
POLITICAL CRIMES AND OFFENSES
See also Criminal law; Political ethics; Subversive activities
POLITICAL DEFECTORS *See* Defectors

POLITICAL ETHICS
See also Ethics; Political science; Politics; Social ethics
POLITICAL FICTION
Berry, S. The lost order
Han, K. Human Acts
Rushdie, S. The golden house
POLITICAL LEADERS
Harris, R. Archangel
Johnston, W. The colony of unrequited dreams
Lawton, J. Old flames
Min, A. Becoming Madame Mao
POLITICAL PARTY LEADERS
Kadare, I. The Successor
POLITICAL PRISONERS
Eastland, S. Eye of the Red Tsar
Haasse, H. S. In a dark wood wandering
Holland, T. The archivist's story
Hostage
Lelic, S. The facility
Lord, B. B. The middle heart
Solzhenitsyn, A. In the first circle
Solzhenitsyn, A. One day in the life of Ivan Denisovich
POLITICAL PRISONERS
See also Political crimes and offenses; Prisoners
POLITICAL REFUGEES
See also Asylum; International law; International relations; Refugees
POLITICAL SATIRE
Maguire, G. Wicked
Numero Zero
POLITICAL SATIRE
See also Satire
POLITICAL SCIENTISTS
Carey, P. Parrot and Olivier in America
POLITICAL VIOLENCE *See* Sabotage; Terrorism
POLITICAL VIOLENCE -- ZIMBABWE
Bulawayo, N. We need new names
POLITICIANS
See also Statesmen
POLITICIANS -- CRIMES AGAINST -- CHINA
Pattison, E. The lord of death
POLITICIANS -- SEXUAL BEHAVIOR
Mark, D. Original skin
POLITICIANS -- UNITED STATES
Lewis, S. It can't happen here
Lynch, J. Truth like the sun
POLITICS
Chiaverini, J. Mrs. Lincoln's dressmaker
Dowlatabadi, M. The colonel
Ignatius, D. Bloodmoney
Johnson, A. Fortune smiles
Robbins, C. The accomplice
Shacochis, B. The Woman Who Lost Her Soul
POLITICS -- AFRICA
Gordimer, N. A guest of honor
Naipaul, V. S. A bend in the river
POLITICS -- BRAZIL
Amado, J. Gabriela, clove and cinnamon
POLITICS -- CANADA
Johnston, W. The colony of unrequited dreams
POLITICS -- CENTRAL AMERICA
Didion, J. A book of common prayer
POLITICS -- CHILE
Allende, I. The house of the spirits
POLITICS -- CHINA
Min, A. Becoming Madame Mao
POLITICS -- EGYPT
Durrell, L. Mountolive
POLITICS -- ENGLAND
Drabble, M. The radiant way
Goddard, R. Into the blue
Hart, J. Damage
Maxwell, R. The secret diary of Anne Boleyn
McEwan, I. Amsterdam
Penman, S. K. Devil's brood
Penman, S. K. Time and chance
Penman, S. K. When Christ and his saints slept
Trollope, A. The Eustace diamonds
Trollope, A. The prime minister
POLITICS -- EUROPE
Dunnett, D. Niccolo rising
Dunnett, D. Race of scorpions
Sartre, J. P. The reprieve
POLITICS -- FRANCE
Beauvoir, S. d. The mandarins
POLITICS -- HAWAII
Michener, J. A. Hawaii
POLITICS -- INDIA
Mehta, G. Raj
Mistry, R. A fine balance
Rushdie, S. Shalimar the clown
POLITICS -- IRELAND
Uris, L. Redemption
Uris, L. Trinity
POLITICS -- ITALY
Silone, I. Bread and wine
POLITICS -- KENTUCKY
Warren, R. P. World enough and time
POLITICS -- LATIN AMERICA
Allende, I. Eva Luna
Garcia Marquez, G. The autumn of the patriarch
POLITICS -- MASSACHUSETTS
Martin, W. Cape Cod
POLITICS -- MEXICO
Fuentes, C. The eagle's throne
POLITICS -- MIDDLE WESTERN STATES
Patterson, R. N. Dark lady
POLITICS -- NEW YORK (STATE)
Isaacs, S. Close relations
POLITICS -- NIGERIA
Adichie, C. N. Half of a yellow sun
POLITICS -- ROME
McCullough, C. The first man in Rome
POLITICS -- RUSSIA

Koestler, A. Darkness at noon
Pasternak, B. L. Doctor Zhivago
POLITICS -- SOUTH AFRICA
Gordimer, N. My son's story
Gordimer, N. None to accompany me
Paton, A. Ah, but your land is beautiful
POLITICS -- SOUTH AMERICA
Conrad, J. Nostromo
POLITICS -- SOUTHERN STATES
Warren, R. P. All the king's men
Woods, S. Grass roots
POLITICS -- SPAIN
Romano-Lax, A. The Spanish bow
POLITICS -- UNITED STATES -- 1900-
Canin, E. America America
Ellroy, J. American tabloid
Gorman, E. Sleeping dogs
Heller, J. Good as Gold
Klein, J. Primary colors
Mallon, T. Fellow travelers
O'Brien, T. In the Lake of the Woods
Patterson, R. N. No safe place
Patterson, R. N. Protect and defend
Roth, P. I married a communist
Thomas, R. Ah, treachery!
Vidal, G. The golden age
Vidal, G. Hollywood
Vidal, G. Washington, D.C.
Vonnegut, K. Jailbird
Wallace, I. The man
Woods, S. The run
POLITICS -- UNITED STATES -- TO 1900
Adams, H. Democracy
Jakes, J. Love and war
Lockridge, R. Raintree County
Vidal, G. 1876
Vidal, G. Burr
Vidal, G. Empire
Vidal, G. Lincoln
POLITICS -- WEST INDIES
Naipaul, V. S. Guerrillas
POLITICS IN LITERATURE
Modesitt, L. E. Scholar
POLITICS, PRACTICAL
Wolfe, T. A man in full
POLLEN AS FOOD
See also Food
POLLS *See* Elections; Public opinion polls
POLLUTION
Benford, G. Timescape
Oates, J. C. The falls
POLO
Hagy, A. Boleto
Polo, Marco, 1254-1323?
About
Calvino, I. Invisible cities
POLYGAMY
Ebershoff, D. The 19th wife
Jones, T. Silver sparrow
Laplante, A. A Circle of Wives
Udall, B. The lonely polygamist
POLYGAMY
See also Marriage
POLYNESIANS
Michener, J. A. Hawaii
Nordhoff, C. Pitcairn's Island
POLYTHEISM
See also Religion; Theism
Pompeii. Harris, R.
Pompeii. Higley, T. L.
POMPEII (ANCIENT CITY)
Harris, R. Pompeii
Lytton, E. B. L. The last days of Pompeii
POND ECOLOGY
See also Ecology
The **Ponder** heart. Welty, E.
POOR
See also Poverty; Public welfare
POOR
Guene, F. Kiffe kiffe tomorrow
Poor things. Gray, A.
The **poorhouse** fair. Updike, J.
POP ART
See also Art
POPES
West, M. L. The clowns of God
West, M. L. Lazarus
West, M. L. The shoes of the fisherman
POPES -- ELECTION
Harris, R. Conclave
Poppet. Hayder, M.
POPULAR CULTURE
See also Communication; Culture; Intellectual life; Recreation
Porno. Welsh, I.
PORNOGRAPHIC FILM INDUSTRY
Hallinan, T. Crashed
PORNOGRAPHY
Banks, R. Lost memory of skin
Cohen, J. Four new messages
Faust, C. Money shot
Hallinan, T. Crashed
Hayder, M. Hanging hill
Rosenberg, N. T. Interest of justice
Welsh, I. Porno
Welsh, L. The cutting room
PORTABLE COMPUTERS
See also Computers
The **portable** Stephen Crane. Crane, S.
The **portable** Veblen. McKenzie, E.
PORTLAND (OR.)
Cain, C. Heartsick
Cain, C. Kill you twice
Deborde, R. Portlandtown

Durrow, H. W. The girl who fell from the sky
Perry, T. Nightlife
Vachss, A. H. Pain management
Portlandtown. Deborde, R.
Portnoy's complaint. Roth, P.
The **portrait.** Pears, I.
Portrait in sepia. Allende, I.
The **portrait** of a lady. James, H.
Portrait of Jennie. Nathan, R.
A **portrait** of the artist as a young man. Joyce, J.
Portrait of the mother as a young woman.
PORTRAIT PAINTERS
Modesitt, L. E. Imager's challenge
Modesitt, L. E. Imager's intrigue
Pears, I. The portrait
PORTRAIT PAINTING
Manual of painting & calligraphy
PORTRAITS
See also Art; Biography; Pictures
PORTRAITS
Wilde, O. The picture of Dorian Gray
PORTUGAL
Antunes, A. L. The inquisitors' manual
Martel, Y. The high mountains of Portugal
PORTUGAL -- LISBON
Saramago, J. The history of the siege of Lisbon
Zimler, R. The last kabbalist of Lisbon
PORTUGUESE -- JAPAN
Endo, S. Silence
PORTUGUESE FICTION -- TRANSLATIONS INTO ENGLISH
The alchemist
Couto, M. Sleepwalking land
Hatoum, M. The brothers
Saramago, J. Death with interruptions
The **position.** Wolitzer, M.
Positive. Wellington, D.
The **possessed.** Dostoyevsky, F.
Possessing the secret of joy. Walker, A.
Possession. Byatt, A. S.
The **possessions.** Murphy, S. F.
The **possibilities.** Hemmings, K. H.
The **possibility** of an island. Houellebecq, M.
POST OFFICE *See* Postal service
The **post-birthday** world. Shriver, L.
POST-TRAUMATIC STRESS DISORDER
Cain, C. One Kick
Lish, A. Preparation for the Next Life
Robinson, R. Sparta
POSTAGE STAMPS
See also Postal service
POSTAL SERVICE
Blake, S. The postmistress
POSTAL SERVICE
See also Communication; Transportation
Postcards. Proulx, A.
Postcards from Berlin. Leroy, M.
POSTERS
See also Advertising; Commercial art
The **posthumous** papers of the Pickwick Club. Dickens, C.
POSTIMPRESSIONISM (ART)
See also Art
The **postman** always rings twice, double indemnity, Mildred Pierce and selected stories. Cain, J. M.
The **postmistress.** Blake, S.
Postsingular. Rucker, R. v. B.
POT (DRUG) *See* Marijuana
POTPOURRI
See also Herbs; Nature craft; Perfumes
Potsdam station. Downing, D.
Potshot. Parker, R. B.
The **potter's** field. Peters, E.
Pound for pound. Toole, F. X.
POVERTY
Adiga, A. The white tiger
Allison, D. Bastard out of Carolina
Boyle, T. C. The tortilla curtain
Bragg, M. A son of war
Brown, L. Joe
Caldwell, E. Tobacco road
Cisneros, S. The house on Mango Street
Dickens, C. Little Dorrit
Donoghue, E. Slammerkin
DuPree, K. Silenced
Garcia, C. A handbook to luck
George, E. What came before he shot her
Hardy, T. Jude the obscure
Hugo, V. Les miserables
Lawson, M. Crow Lake
Mahfouz, N. Children of the alley
Mahfouz, N. Midaq Alley
Morris, M. M. Songs in ordinary time
Morrison, T. Sula
Norris, F. McTeague
Oates, J. C. A garden of earthly delights
Oates, J. C. Them
Parks Getting mother's body
Piercy, M. Sex wars
Robertson, I. The Paris winter
Sankaran, L. The hope factory
Sinclair, U. The jungle
Smith, Z. White teeth
Vernon, O. Eden
Ward, J. Salvage the bones
Welty, E. Losing battles
Woodrell, D. The death of sweet mister
Wright, R. Native son
POVERTY
See also Economic conditions; Social problems
The powder mage [series]
McClellan, B. Promise of blood
The **power.** Alderman, N.
POWER (MECHANICS)
See also Mechanical engineering; Mechanics

POWER (SOCIAL SCIENCES)
Canin, E. America America
Carter, S. L. The emperor of Ocean Park
Clavell, J. Shogun
Dovey, C. Blood kin
Estleman, L. D. Gas City
The Feast of the Goat
Min, A. Becoming Madame Mao
Mosley, W. The man in my basement
Puzo, M. The family
Rand, A. Atlas shrugged
Vidal, G. Empire
The **power** and the glory. Greene, G.
POWER PLANTS, NUCLEAR *See* Nuclear power plants
POWER RESOURCES
Watts, P. Starfish
The **power** that preserves. Donaldson, S. R.
The **powers.** Sayers, V.
POWS *See* Prisoners of war
POWWOWS
See also Festivals; Native Americans -- Rites and ceremonies; Native Americans -- Social life and customs
The **Poyson** garden. Harper, K.
The **practical** heart. Gurganus, A.
PRACTICAL JOKES
See also Jokes; Wit and humor
Practical magic. Hoffman, A.
Prague. Phillips, A.
PRAGUE (CZECH REPUBLIC)
Adler, H. G. The wall
Crain, C. Necessary errors
PRAIRIE ECOLOGY
See also Ecology; Grassland ecology
PRAIRIE LIFE
Cather, W. My Antonia
Cather, W. O pioneers!
Praisesong for the widow. Marshall, P.
A **prayer** for Owen Meany. Irving, J.
Prayers for rain. Lehane, D.
Prayers for the dead. Kellerman, F.
Prayers for the stolen. Clement, J.
The **preacher.** Lackberg, C.
The **preacher's** daughter. Lewis, B.
PREACHERS *See* Clergy
The **Precious** One. De los Santos, M.
The **Precipice.** Doiron, P.
PRECIPITATION (METEOROLOGY)
See also Meteorology; Water; Weather
PRECOCIOUS CHILDREN *See* Gifted children
PREDATORY ANIMALS
See also Animals
PREDESTINATION
Irving, J. A prayer for Owen Meany
PREDICTIONS *See* Forecasting; Prophecies
PREFABRICATED HOUSES
See also Domestic architecture; House construction; Houses; Prefabricated buildings
The **prefect.** Reynolds, A.
PREGNANCY
Albert, E. After Birth
Burgess, M. Dogfight, a love story
Erdrich, L. Future home of the living god
Gould, E. Friendship
Hallgrimur Helgason 101 Reykjavik
Hannah, K. On Mystic lake
Haruf, K. Plainsong
Hawke, E. Ash Wednesday
Joss, M. Among the missing
McPhee, J. No ordinary matter
Novak, C. Breed
Parks Getting mother's body
Pottinger, S. The last Nazi
Read, P. P. Alice in exile
Ward, J. Salvage the bones
Weiner, J. Little earthquakes
PREGNANT TEENAGERS
Coplin, A. The orchardist
The **pregnant** widow. Amis, M.
PREGNANT WOMEN -- CRIMES AGAINST
Gaspar de Alba, A. Desert blood
PREGNANT WOMEN
Cameron, C. The last Neanderthal
McEwan, I. Nutshell
McLaren, K. The road to enchantment
Schultz, E. The Blondes
PREHISTORIC ANIMALS
See also Animals; Fossils
PREHISTORIC ART
See also Art
PREHISTORIC MAN
Auel, J. M. The Clan of the Cave Bear
Auel, J. M. The land of painted caves
Gear, W. M. People of the thunder
Golding, W. The inheritors
PREHISTORIC PEOPLES
See also Antiquities; Archeology; Human beings
PREHISTORIC PEOPLES
Cameron, C. The last Neanderthal
PREHISTORIC TIMES
Auel, J. M. The Clan of the Cave Bear
Auel, J. M. The land of painted caves
PREHISTORY *See* Archeology; Fossil hominids; Prehistoric peoples
PREJUDICE *See* Prejudices
PREJUDICES
Brown, S. The witness
Coldsmith, D. The long journey home
Dallas, S. Tallgrass
Dexter, P. Paris Trout
Grau, S. A. The keepers of the house
Guterson, D. Snow falling on cedars
Katzenbach, J. Hart's war
Lee, D. Country of origin
Morrison, T. Tar baby

Paretsky, S. Bleeding Kansas
See, L. Shanghai girls
Straight, S. Highwire moon
Waldman, A. The submission
West, D. The wedding
PREJUDICES
See also Attitude (Psychology); Emotions; Interpersonal relations
Prelude to Foundation. Asimov, I.
Prelude to terror. MacInnes, H.
PREMONITIONS
King, S. The shining
PRENATAL CARE
See also Pregnancy
Prep. Sittenfeld, C.
Preparation for the Next Life. Lish, A.
PREPARATORY SCHOOLS
Cooke, C. Daughters of the revolution
Schulman, H. This beautiful life
PREPARED CEREALS
See also Breakfasts; Food
PRESCHOOL CHILDREN *See* Children
PRESCHOOLS
Glass, J. The widower's tale
PRESERVATION OF SPECIMENS *See* Taxidermy
The **preservationist.** Maine, D.
PRESIDENTIAL CAMPAIGNS -- UNITED STATES *See* Presidents -- United States -- Election
PRESIDENTIAL CANDIDATES
Piercy, M. Sex wars
PRESIDENTS
Block, L. Killing Castro
Buckley, W. F. Mongoose, R.I.P
Castellanos Moya, H. Tyrant memory
Charyn, J. Johnny One-Eye
De Bernieres, L. Birds without wings
Dovey, C. Blood kin
Ellroy, J. American tabloid
The Feast of the Goat
Forsyth, F. The day of the jackal
Fuentes, N. The autobiography of Fidel Castro
Gingrich, N. Grant comes east
Hunter, S. Havana
Pesci, D. Amistad
Shaara, J. The last full measure
Updike, J. Memories of the Ford Administration
Vidal, G. Lincoln
PRESIDENTS
See also Heads of state
PRESIDENTS -- UNITED STATES
Burdick, E. Fail-safe
Farnsworth, C. Blood oath
Johansen, I. Final target
Lewis, S. It can't happen here
Mallon, T. Finale
Patterson, R. N. Balance of power
Patterson, R. N. Protect and defend
Saunders, G. Lincoln in the bardo
Vonnegut, K. Slapstick
Wallace, I. The man
Wilson, F. P. Deep as the marrow
PRESIDENTS -- UNITED STATES -- ASSASSINATION
See also Assassination
PRESIDENTS -- UNITED STATES -- CHILDREN
Clotel, or, The president's daughter
PRESIDENTS -- UNITED STATES -- ELECTION
Robbins, C. The accomplice
Lewis, S. It can't happen here
PRESIDENTS -- UNITED STATES -- ELECTION
See also Elections
PRESIDENTS' SPOUSES -- UNITED STATES
Phillips, S. E. First lady
Presley, Elvis, 1935-1977
About
Abani, C. GraceLand
PRESS
See also Journalism; Propaganda; Publicity
Prester John
About
Eco, U. Baudolino
PRESTON (LANCASHIRE, ENGLAND)
Blake, R. A dark anatomy
Presumed innocent. Turow, S.
Pretty Baby. Kubica, M.
Pretty Girls. Slaughter, K.
PREVENTION OF CRUELTY TO ANIMALS *See* Animal welfare
Prey. Crichton, M.
Prey [series]
Sandford, J. Silken prey
Prey dancing. Gash, J.
PRIAM (GREEK MYTHOLOGY)
Malouf, D. Ransom
Pride and prejudice. Austen, J.
PRIDE AND VANITY
See also Conduct of life; Sin
The **priest.** O'Donovan, G.
PRIESTS
Caldwell, I. The Fifth Gospel
Hansen, R. Exiles
Malliet, G. M. A fatal winter
Marley, L. The child goddess
The prophets of eternal fjord
Runcie, J. Sidney Chambers and the Forgiveness of Sins
Vollmann, W. T. Fathers and crows
PRIESTS
See also Clergy
PRIESTS -- FRANCE
Harris, J. Peaches for Father Francis
PRIESTS -- ICELAND -- 19TH CENTURY
The blue fox
PRIMARIES
See also Elections; Political conventions; Politics
Primary colors. Klein, J.

Primary inversion. Asaro, C.
PRIMATOLOGISTS
Gonzales, L. Lucy
Wesselmann, D. L. Captivity
The **prime** minister. Trollope, A.
PRIME MINISTERS
Antunes, A. L. The inquisitors' manual
Forsyth, F. The day of the jackal
Harris, R. The ghost
Hunt, R. Mr. Chartwell
Kadare, I. The Successor
Russell, M. D. Dreamers of the day
Townsend, S. Number 10
PRIME MINISTERS -- ASSASSINATION
Walton, J. Ha'penny
PRIME MINISTERS -- SWEDEN -- ASSASSINATION
Another time, another life
Between summer's longing and winter's end
Free falling, as if in a dream
The **prime** of Miss Jean Brodie. Spark, M.
Primitive people. Prose, F.
PRIMITIVE SOCIETIES
See also Civilization; Ethnology
Prince Lestat. Rice, A.
Prince of chaos. Zelazny, R.
Prince of Fire. Silva, D.
The **prince** of tides. Conroy, P.
PRINCES
Bear, E. Steles of the sky
Hauck, R. How to catch a prince
Morgan, J. The royal we
Penman, S. K. The reckoning
Saint-Exupery, A. d. The little prince
Seton, A. Katherine
PRINCES
See also Courts and courtiers
PRINCES AND PRINCESSES *See* Princes; Princesses
The **princes** of Ireland. Rutherfurd, E.
The **princess** bride. Goldman, W.
The **princess** of Burundi. Eriksson, K.
PRINCESSES
Ali, M. Untold story
Amirrezvani, A. Equal of the sun
Gray, J. How to School Your Scoundrel
Gray, J. How to Tame Your Duke
Mehta, G. Raj
Mishima, Y. The Temple of Dawn
Penman, S. K. When Christ and his saints slept
Putney, M. J. Nowhere near respectable
Seton, A. Katherine
Sherwood, F. Night of sorrows
Vollmann, W. T. Argall
PRINCESSES
See also Courts and courtiers
PRINCETON (N.J.)
Oates, J. C. The Accursed
PRINCETON UNIVERSITY
Caldwell, I. The rule of four
Prine, Sarah Agnes
About
Turner, N. E. These is my words
PRINTERS
Donoghue, E. The sealed letter
PRINTING
Christie, A. Gutenberg's apprentice
PRINTING
See also Bibliography; Book industry; Graphic arts; Industrial arts; Publishers and publishing
PRINTING -- SPECIMENS
See also Advertising; Initials
PRISON ESCAPES *See* Escapes
PRISON REFORM
See also Social problems
PRISON WARDENS -- GREAT BRITAIN
Lelic, S. The facility
The **prisoner** of heaven. Ruiz Zafon, C.
The **prisoner** of Zenda. Hope, A.
PRISONER-OF-WAR ESCAPES
Groot, T. The sentinels of Andersonville
PRISONERS
Flanagan, R. Gould's book of fish
Hodgson, A. The last confession of Thomas Hawkins
Hulse, S. M. Black River
Lazar, Z. Sway
Lyndon, R. Hawk quest
Silver, E. L. The execution of Noa P. Singleton
The son
Ward, L. Outside valentine
Weber, C. Man on the run
PRISONERS
See also Criminals
PRISONERS -- AUSTRALIA
Grenville, K. The secret river
PRISONERS -- ENGLAND -- LONDON
Hodgson, A. The last confession of Thomas Hawkins
PRISONERS AND PRISONS
Blatty, W. P. Dimiter
Egan, J. The keep
Fitch, J. White oleander
Hope, A. The prisoner of Zenda
Koestler, A. Darkness at noon
London, J. The star rover
Palmer, D. C. The dream of perpetual motion
PRISONERS AND PRISONS *See* Prisoners; Prisoners of war; Prisons
PRISONERS AND PRISONS -- ARGENTINA
Puig, M. Kiss of the spider woman
PRISONERS AND PRISONS -- AUSTRALIA
Flanagan, R. Gould's book of fish
Grenville, K. The lieutenant
PRISONERS AND PRISONS -- CHINA
Pattison, E. The skull mantra
PRISONERS AND PRISONS -- ENGLAND
Defoe, D. Moll Flanders

Dickens, C. Little Dorrit
Dickens, C. The posthumous papers of the Pickwick Club
Walters, M. The sculptress
PRISONERS AND PRISONS -- FRANCE
Dumas, A. The Count of Monte Cristo
PRISONERS AND PRISONS -- IRAN
Sofer, D. The Septembers of Shiraz
PRISONERS AND PRISONS -- RUSSIA
Furnivall, K. The red scarf
Solzhenitsyn, A. In the first circle
PRISONERS AND PRISONS -- SIBERIA (RUSSIA)
Amis, M. House of meetings
Solzhenitsyn, A. One day in the life of Ivan Denisovich
PRISONERS AND PRISONS -- UNITED STATES
Baldwin, J. If Beale Street could talk
Cain, C. Heartsick
Cheever, J. Falconer
Clark, M. The legal limit
Fitch, J. White oleander
Gaines, E. J. A lesson before dying
Grisham, J. The confession
Grisham, J. The brethren
Huneven, M. Blame
Hunter, S. Pale horse coming
Jordan, H. When she woke
Kantor, M. Andersonville
Katzenbach, J. Just cause
Lowenthal, M. Charity girl
Mailer, N. The executioner's song
Moore, S. The big girls
O'Nan, S. The good wife
Picoult, J. Change of heart
Turow, S. Reversible errors
Vonnegut, K. Jailbird
Woods, S. Heat
PRISONERS OF CONSCIENCE *See* Political prisoners
Prisoners of war. Yarbrough, S.
PRISONERS OF WAR
Afrika, T. Bitter Eden
Braden, K. The Longest Night
Ha Jin War trash
Kantor, M. Andersonville
Keneally, T. Shame and the Captives
Vonnegut, K. Slaughterhouse-five
PRISONERS OF WAR
See also War
PRISONERS OF WAR -- AUSTRALIA
Keneally, T. Shame and the Captives
PRISONERS OF WAR -- BURMA
Flanagan, R. The narrow road to the deep north
PRISONERS OF WAR -- GEORGIA
Groot, T. The sentinels of Andersonville
PRISONERS OF WAR -- JAPAN
Keneally, T. Shame and the Captives
PRISONS
The investigation
Moshfegh, O. Eileen
Shannon, S. The bone season
The son
Private arrangements. Thomas, S.
PRIVATE EYE STORIES *See* Mystery and detective plays; Mystery fiction; Mystery films; Mystery radio programs; Mystery television programs
Private eyes. Kellerman, J.
PRIVATE INVESTIGATORS
Bacigalupi, P. The water knife
Black, C. Murder on the Champ de Mars
Cleave, P. Five minutes alone
Francis, F. Dick Francis's Damage
Galbraith, R. Career of evil
George, E. A Banquet of Consequences
Gorman, E. Riders on the Storm
Grafton, S. X
Hallinan, T. Crashed
Harvey, M. The governor's wife
Heller, P. Celine
Kerr, P. Prussian blue
Krentz, J. A. When all the girls have gone
Lansdale, J. R. Honky tonk samurai
Lutz, L. The Spellman files
Mosley, W. And sometimes I wonder about you
Paretsky, S. Brush back
Sandford, J. Deadline
PRIVATE INVESTIGATORS -- CALIFORNIA -- LOS ANGELES
Hallinan, T. Crashed
Kaminsky, S. M. To catch a spy
Mosley, W. Little green
PRIVATE INVESTIGATORS -- ENGLAND
The big book of Sherlock Holmes stories
Doyle, A. C. S. The adventures and the memoirs of Sherlock Holmes
Friedman, D. Riot most uncouth
Gallagher, S. The bedlam detective
PRIVATE INVESTIGATORS -- ENGLAND -- LONDON
Weaver, A. A most novel revenge
PRIVATE INVESTIGATORS -- GERMANY
Kerr, P. The lady from Zagreb
Kerr, P. A Man Without Breath
PRIVATE INVESTIGATORS -- GERMANY -- BERLIN
Kerr, P. March violets
PRIVATE INVESTIGATORS -- GREECE -- ATHENS
Corby, G. The Marathon conspiracy
PRIVATE INVESTIGATORS -- INDIA
Hall, T. The case of the deadly butter chicken
Hall, T. The case of the love commandos
PRIVATE INVESTIGATORS -- MINNESOTA -- MINNEAPOLIS
Sandford, J. Silken prey
Sandford, J. Naked prey
PRIVATE INVESTIGATORS -- NEW YORK (STATE) -- NEW YORK
Lethem, J. Motherless Brooklyn
Mosley, W. All I did was shoot my man

Quinn, P. Dry bones
Vachss, A. H. Choice of evil
Vachss, A. H. Down here
Woods, S. Cold paradise
Woods, S. Dirty work
Woods, S. Reckless abandon
Woods, S. The short forever
PRIVATE INVESTIGATORS -- NEW ZEALAND -- CHRISTCHURCH
Cleave, P. Cemetery Lake
PRIVATE INVESTIGATORS -- ROME
Davis, L. The Ides of April
The **private** patient. James, P. D.
PRIVATE SCHOOLS
Vyleta, D. Smoke
PRIVATE SECRETARIES
Fields, J. The age of desire
Truong, M. The book of salt
PRIVATE SECURITY SERVICES
Foster, L. Under Pressure
PRIVATEERING
See also International law; Naval art and science; Naval history; Pirates
Privileged conversation. Hunter, E.
The **privileges.** Dee, J.
The **prize.** Wallace, I.
The **prize.** Bialosky, J.
PRIZE FIGHTING *See* Boxing
Prizes. Frame, J.
PROBABILITIES
See also Algebra; Logic; Mathematics; Statistics
The **probable** future. Hoffman, A.
PROBATE LAW AND PRACTICE
See also Civil procedure; Inheritance and succession
PROBATION
See also Corrections; Criminal law; Prisons; Punishment; Reformatories; Social case work
PROBATION OFFICERS
Pelecanos, G. P. Drama city
Rosenberg, N. T. First offense
Rosenberg, N. T. Sullivan's law
PROBIOTICS
See also Dietary supplements; Microorganisms
PROBLEM DRINKING *See* Alcoholism
PROBLEM FAMILIES
Franzen, J. Freedom
Haig, M. The Radleys
King, L. The father of the rain
Lawson, M. Crow Lake
Lundrigan, N. Glass boys
O'Dell, T. Back roads
Woodrell, D. The death of sweet mister
Proctor, Ezekiel, 1831-1907
About
McMurtry, L. Zeke and Ned
PRODIGAL SON (PARABLE)
See also Parables
PRODIGIES *See* Gifted people
PROFESSIONAL ETHICS
See also Ethics
The **professionals.** Laukkanen, O.
The **professor** of desire. Roth, P.
The **professor's** daughter. Read, P. P.
PROFESSORS *See* Educators; Teachers
PROFIT
See also Business; Capital; Economics; Wealth
PROGRAMMING (COMPUTERS)
Tracy, P. J. Monkeewrench
PROHIBITION
Lehane, D. Live by night
Rosen, R. Dollface
PROLETARIAN NOVELS
Nichols, J. T. The Milagro beanfield war
Steinbeck, J. The grapes of wrath
Steinbeck, J. In dubious battle
Zola, E. Germinal
PROLETARIAT
See also Labor; Socialism; Working class
The **Prometheus** deception. Ludlum, R.
A **promise** kept. Hatcher, R. L.
Promise me this. Gohlke, C.
Promise not to tell. Krentz, J. A.
Promise of blood. McClellan, B.
PROMISES
See also Ethics
PROMISES
Vassanji, M. G. The Magic of Saida
Proof. Francis, D.
PROOFREADING
See also Printing
PROPAGANDA
Johnson, A. The orphan master's son
Proper romance [series]
Kilpack, J. S. The vicar's daughter
Property. Martin, V.
PROPERTY
Haslett, A. Union Atlantic
Property of a lady. Rayne, S.
PROPHECIES
Carey, J. Banewreaker
Charlton, B. Spellbreaker
Currie, R. Everything matters!
Gaiman, N. Good omens
The immortalists
Kazinski, A. J. The last good man
Rawn, M. Touchstone
Yang, J. Y. The black tides of heaven
PROPHECIES -- ISLAM
Rosenberg, J. C. The Tehran initiative
Rosenberg, J. C. The twelfth Imam
Prophecy. Haydon, E.
PROPHECY *See* Prophecies
The **prophet.** Koryta, M.
The **prophets** of eternal fjord.

Prose and poetry. Crane, S.
PROSE POETRY
See also Poetry
PROSPECTING
See also Gold mines and mining; Mines and mineral resources; Silver mines and mining
Prospero's children. Siegel, J.
PROSTITUTES
Appelfeld, A. Blooms of darkness
Charyn, J. Johnny One-Eye
Crane, S. Maggie: a girl of the streets (a story of New York)
De Bernieres, L. A partisan's daughter
Defoe, D. Moll Flanders
Dunant, S. In the company of the courtesan
Faber, M. The crimson petal and the white
Faulkner, W. Sanctuary
Hambly, B. Wet grave
Howatch, S. The heartbreaker
Isaacs, S. As husbands go
Lent, J. Lost nation
Lijia Zhang Lotus
Lowenthal, M. Charity girl
Mahfouz, N. Midaq Alley
McCann, C. Let the great world spin
McCarthy, C. Cities of the plain
McMurtry, L. Buffalo girls
McMurtry, L. Dead man's walk
Murakami, H. After dark
O'Hara, J. Butterfield 8
Parker, T. J. The fallen
Russell, M. D. Doc
White, E. Hotel de Dream
Williamson, P. Heart of the west
Yates, A. Moondogs
PROSTITUTES -- CRIMES AGAINST
Hayder, M. Birdman
Hunter, E. Candyland
MacBride, S. Dying Light
PROSTITUTION
Atkins, A. White shadow
Bock, C. Beautiful children
Burdett, J. Bangkok 8
Connelly, M. The Gods of Guilt
Donoghue, E. Slammerkin
Faletti, G. A pimp's notes
García Márquez, G. Memories of my melancholy whores
George, E. What came before he shot her
Gruber, M. Valley of bones
Lippman, L. And when she was good
Martini, S. P. Compelling evidence
Perry, T. The boyfriend
Sada, D. Almost never
Vargas Llosa, M. Captain Pantoja and the Special Service
Vargas Llosa, M. The Green House
Vollmann, W. T. The royal family
Watkins, C. V. Battleborn
PROSTITUTION
See also Sexual ethics; Social problems; Women -- Social conditions
Protect and defend. Patterson, R. N.
PROTECTION OF ANIMALS *See* Animal welfare
PROTECTION OF GAME *See* Game protection
The **Protector.** Grant, D.
The protectors [series]
Jackson, B. Forged in desire
PROTESTANT REFORMATION *See* Reformation
PROTESTANTISM
See also Christianity; Church history
PROTESTANTS
Follett, K. A column of fire
PROTOZOA
See also Microorganisms
Proven guilty. Butcher, J.
Provenance.
PROVERBS
See also Folklore; Quotations
PROVIDENCE (R.I.)
DeSilva, B. Providence Rag
DeSilva, B. Rogue island
Providence Rag. DeSilva, B.
Prudence. Treuer, D.
PRUNING
See also Forests and forestry; Fruit culture; Gardening; Trees
Prussian blue. Kerr, P.
PSI (PARAPSYCHOLOGY) *See* Parapsychology
Psy-Changeling [series]
Singh, N. Shield of winter
PSYCHE (GODDESS)
Lewis, C. S. Till we have faces
PSYCHIATRIC HOSPITAL PATIENTS
Kesey, K. One flew over the cuckoo's nest
LaValle, V. D. The devil in silver
Lehane, D. Shutter Island
PSYCHIATRISTS
Barker, P. The eye in the door
Barker, P. The ghost road
Barker, P. Regeneration
Galchen, R. Atmospheric disturbances
Glass, J. The whole world over
Greenberg, J. I never promised you a rose garden
Guest, J. Ordinary people
Hart, J. The reconstructionist
Hunter, E. Privileged conversation
Hustvedt, S. The sorrows of an American
Jong, E. Fear of flying
Kostova, E. The swan thieves
McGrath, P. Asylum
Moore, S. The big girls
Raimondo, L. Dante's wood
Robotham, M. Suspect
Rosten, L. Captain Newman, M.D.
Tallis, F. Fatal lies
Templeton, E. Gordon

Wideman, J. E. Fanon
PSYCHIATRISTS
See also Psychologists
PSYCHIC ABILITY
Barry, Q. She weeps each time you're born
Haig, F. The map of bones
Sittenfeld, C. Sisterland
PSYCHIC PHENOMENA *See* Parapsychology
PSYCHIC TRAUMA
Adler, H. G. The wall
PSYCHICAL RESEARCH *See* Parapsychology
PSYCHICS
See also Parapsychology; Persons
PSYCHICS
Barry, Q. She weeps each time you're born
Jacka, B. Fated
Kearsley, S. The Firebird
Krentz, J. A. Dream eyes
Mitchell, D. The bone clocks
Odell, J. The healing
Shannon, S. The mime order
Singh, N. Shield of winter
Sittenfeld, C. Sisterland
Wilson, S. The fortune teller's daughter
PSYCHO (MOTION PICTURE: 1960)
DeLillo, D. Point Omega
PSYCHOANALYSIS
Roth, P. My life as a man
Roth, P. Portnoy's complaint
Rubenfeld, J. The death instinct
Thomas, D. M. The white hotel
PSYCHOANALYSTS
Clarke, B. Exley
Katzenbach, J. The analyst
Klosterman, C. The visible man
Meyer, N. The seven-per-cent solution
Rubenfeld, J. The death instinct
Tallis, F. Fatal lies
Tallis, F. Vienna blood
Tallis, F. Vienna Twilight
Thomas, D. M. The white hotel
PSYCHOKINESIS
King, S. Carrie
King, S. Firestarter
PSYCHOKINESIS
See also Parapsychology; Spiritualism
PSYCHOLOGICAL FICTION
Ball, J. A cure for suicide
Black, S. The killing lessons
Carey, P. The chemistry of tears
Chaon, D. Ill will
Claudel, P. The investigation
Constantine, L. The Last Mrs. Parrish
Cunningham, M. The snow queen
Doyle, R. Smile
Finn, A. J. The woman in the window
Franzen, J. Purity
Gaiman, N. Trigger warning
Hill, J. The fireman
Hill, J. Strange Weather
Jemc, J. The grip of it
McCormack, M. Solar bones
Millet, L. Sweet Lamb of Heaven
Moshfegh, O. Eileen
Never let you go
Nevill, A. The house of small shadows
Park, P. Re Jane
Reid, I. I'm thinking of ending things
Roy-Bhattacharya, J. The watch
Sager, R. Final girls
Second person singular
Smith, A. Autumn
Unger, L. Heartbroken
PSYCHOLOGICAL FICTION, AMERICAN
Eggers, D. How we are hungry
Ford, R. A multitude of sins
Lopez, B. H. Resistance
PSYCHOLOGICAL WARFARE
See also Applied psychology; Military art and science; Morale; Propaganda; War
PSYCHOLOGISTS
Ballard, J. G. Millennium people
Carr, C. The alienist
French, N. Blue Monday
Freudenberger, N. The dissident
Gruber, M. The good son
Gruber, M. Valley of bones
Julavits, H. The uses of enchantment
O'Connell, C. Judas child
Robotham, M. Say you're sorry
Tallis, F. Vienna blood
White, S. W. Dry ice
White, S. W. Missing persons
Willis, C. Passage
PSYCHOLOGY
See also Brain; Philosophy; Soul
PSYCHOLOGY
Atwood, M. Stone mattress
Doctorow, E. L. Andrew's Brain
PSYCHOLOGY OF LEARNING
See also Animal intelligence; Child psychology; Education; Educational psychology; Memory
PSYCHOPATHS
King, S. End of watch
PSYCHOPATHY *See* Abnormal psychology
PSYCHOPHYSICS
Hosking, J. Three years with the rat
PSYCHOSES *See* Mental illness
PSYCHOSOMATIC MEDICINE
See also Abnormal psychology; Medicine; Mind and body; Psychoanalysis
PSYCHOTHERAPIST AND PATIENT
Katzenbach, J. The analyst
Paretsky, S. Ghost country

Robotham, M. Suspect
PSYCHOTHERAPY
Barry, B. The map of true places
Dau, S. The book of Jonas
Paretsky, S. Ghost country
Spark, M. Aiding and abetting
Yalom, I. D. The Schopenhauer cure
PSYCHOTHERAPY PATIENTS
Collins, C. The gamal
Theroux, M. Strange bodies
PUBLIC HOUSING
DuPree, K. Silenced
PUBLIC LIBRARIES
See also Libraries
PUBLIC PROSECUTORS
Arvin, R. Blood of angels
Coben, H. The woods
Fairstein, L. Night watch
Landay, W. Defending Jacob
Patterson, R. N. Dark lady
Reuland, R. Semiautomatic
Turow, S. Innocent
Vachss, A. H. Down here
PUBLIC SPEAKING
See also Communication
PUBLISHERS AND PUBLISHING
Canin, E. America America
Colwin, L. A big storm knocked it over
Eco, U. Foucault's pendulum
Ignatius, D. The Sun King
Jarvis, S. Death and Mr. Pickwick
Kotzwinkle, W. The bear went over the mountain
Pearl, M. The last Dickens
Saramago, J. The history of the siege of Lisbon
Schaffert, T. The coffins of Little Hope
Spark, M. A far cry from Kensington
Vidal, G. Empire
Vidal, G. The golden age
Vidal, G. Washington, D.C.
PUBLISHING EXECUTIVES
Pearl, M. The last Dickens
Pudd'nhead Wilson; Twain, M.
PUERTO RICO
Mundo cruel
Santiago, E. Conquistadora
Puffin classics [series]
Crane, S. The red badge of courage
PUFFINS
See also Birds
PUGET SOUND (WASH.)
Beagle, P. S. Summerlong
PUGILISM *See* Boxing
Pulse. Barnes, J.
PUNCTUALITY
See also Time; Virtue
PUNISHMENT
Crace, J. Harvest
PUNK CULTURE
See also Counterculture
PUNK ROCK MUSIC
Bognanni, P. The house of tomorrow
Egan, J. A visit from the Goon Squad
PUNS
See also Wit and humor
PUPPETS AND PUPPET PLAYS
Tyler, A. Morgan's passing
PUPPIES *See* Dogs
Pure. Baggott, J.
Pure. Miller, A.
The **pure** gold baby. Drabble, M.
The **pure** in heart. Hill, S.
Purgatory chasm. Ulfelder, S.
PURITANISM
Seton, A. The Winthrop woman
PURITANS
Conde, M. I, Tituba, black witch of Salem
Hawthorne, N. The House of the Seven Gables
Hawthorne, N. The scarlet letter
Nissenson, H. The pilgrim
Purity. Franzen, J.
Purity of blood. Perez-Reverte, A.
A **purple** place for dying. MacDonald, J. D.
Pursuit. Perry, T.
The **pursuit** of Alice Thrift. Lipman, E.
The **pursuit** of love & Love in a cold climate. Mitford, N.
Pushing up daisies. Beaton, M. C.
Put a lid on it. Westlake, D. E.
Put Up Your Duke. Frampton, M.
The **Puttermesser** papers. Ozick, C.
PUZZLES
Cline, E. Ready player one
Pygmy. Palahniuk, C.
Pylon. Faulkner, W.
Pym. Johnson, M.
PYRAMIDS
See also Ancient architecture; Archeology; Monuments
PYROMANIA
Ball, J. How to set a fire and why
Pythagoras
About
Goodman, C. The night villa

Q

Q is for quarry. Grafton, S.
QAIDA (ORGANIZATION)
See also Terrorism
QB VII. Uris, L.
QUACKS AND QUACKERY
See also Impostors and imposture; Medicine; Swindlers and swindling
QUADRIPLEGICS
Brown, R. Tender mercies
QUAKERS -- DEATH

Lansdale, J. R. Edge of dark water
QUALITY OF LIFE
See also Economic conditions; Social conditions
The **quality** of mercy. Unsworth, B.
QUANTUM THEORY
Palmer, D. Version control
The **quantum** thief. Rajaniemi, H.
Quarantine. Crace, J.
Quarantine. Mehta, R.
QUARTERBACKS (FOOTBALL)
Roorbach, B. Life among giants
Quartet. Rhys, J.
Quartet in autumn. Pym, B.
QUÉBEC (PROVINCE)
Penny, L. The beautiful mystery
Penny, L. Bury your dead
Penny, L. Glass houses
Penny, L. The long way home
Queen of America. Urrea, L. A.
The **queen** of blood. Durst, S. B.
The **queen** of the damned. Rice, A.
Queen of the night. Jance, J. A.
The **queen** of the night. Chee, A.
Queen of the underworld. Godwin, G.
The **Queen's** bastard. Maxwell, R.
The **queen's** gambit. Tevis, W. S.
The **queen's** lover. Bennett, V.
The **queen's** man. Penman, S. K.
Queenmaker. Edghill, I.
QUEENS
Bennett, V. The queen's lover
Bouchet, A. Breath of fire
Davis, K. Versailles
Dumas, A. Twenty years after
Durst, S. B. The queen of blood
Franklin, A. The serpent's tale
George, M. Elizabeth I
Gregory, P. The other Boleyn girl
Gregory, P. The Boleyn Inheritance
Harper, K. The Poyson garden
Jones, S. Four sisters, all queens
Maxwell, R. The Queen's bastard
Maxwell, R. The secret diary of Anne Boleyn
Maxwell, R. The wild Irish
Naslund, S. J. Abundance
Penman, S. K. Cruel as the grave
Penman, S. K. Devil's brood
Penman, S. K. Dragon's lair
Penman, S. K. The queen's man
Penman, S. K. Time and chance
Plaidy, J. The captive Queen of Scots
Plaidy, J. Murder most royal
Plaidy, J. The pleasures of love
Plaidy, J. William's wife
Weir, A. Innocent traitor
Weir, A. The Lady Elizabeth
QUEENS (NEW YORK, N.Y.) -- HISTORY -- 20TH CENTURY
Thomas, M. We are not ourselves
QUEENS (NEW YORK, N.Y.) -- SOCIAL LIFE AND CUSTOMS -- 20TH CENTURY
Flint, E. Little deaths
QUEENS -- GREAT BRITAIN
Gregory, P. The constant princess
Gregory, P. The taming of the queen
The queens of Renthia [series]
Durst, S. B. The queen of blood
A **question** of attraction. Nicholls, D.
A **question** of belief. Leon, D.
A **question** of blood. Rankin, I.
A **question** of honor. Todd, C.
QUESTS (EXPEDITIONS)
Durst, S. B. The queen of blood
Quick fix. Grimes, L.
The **quickening.** Hoover, M.
The **quickening** maze. Foulds, A.
Quicksand. Giolito, M. P.
The **quiet** American. Greene, G.
Quiet dell. Phillips, J. A.
A **quiet** life. Oe, K.
Quiet neighbors. McPherson, C.
Quiller Balalaika. Hall, A.
The **Quiller** memorandum. Hall, A.
Quiller Salamander. Hall, A.
Quiller solitaire. Hall, A.
QUILTS
Dallas, S. The Persian Pickle Club
Michaels, B. Stitches in time
Otto, W. How to make an American quilt
The **quincunx.** Palliser, C.
Quinn Colson [series]
Atkins, A. The forsaken
Quite a year for plums. White, B.
Quite honestly. Mortimer, J.
Quo Vadis. Sienkiewicz, H.
QUR'AN
See also Islam; Sacred books

R

RABBIS
Anton, M. Rav Hisda's daughter, book I, apprentice
Goodman, A. Kaaterskill Falls
Harris, E. The Marrying of Chani Kaufman
Jensen, J. Dante's equation
Kemelman, H. Monday the rabbi took off
Kemelman, H. One fine day the rabbi bought a cross
Kemelman, H. Thursday the rabbi walked out
Littell, R. Vicious circle
Rosen, J. Joy comes in the morning
Sherwood, F. The book of splendor
Wiesel, E. The Golem
RABBIS

See also Clergy; Judaism
Rabbit Angstrom. Updike, J.
Rabbit cake. Hartnett, A.
RABBITS
Adams, R. Watership Down
RABIES
King, S. Cujo
RACE
See also Ethnology
Clarke, M. B. Foreign soil and other stories
RACE AWARENESS
See also Race relations
RACE DISCRIMINATION -- UNITED STATES -- HISTORY
Howard, R. Driving the king
RACE HORSES
Gordon, J. Lord of Misrule
Race of scorpions. Dunnett, D.
RACE PROBLEMS *See* Race relations
RACE RELATIONS
See also Acculturation; Ethnology; Sociology
RACE RELATIONS
Arvin, R. Blood of angels
Everett, P. God's country
Beatty, P. Slumberland
D'Souza, T. Whiteman
Evaristo, B. Blonde roots
Grisham, J. Sycamore Row
Hubbard, L. The talented Ribkins
Hunt, L. The evening road
Johnson, T. G. Welcome to Braggsville
Kimani, P. Dance of the Jakaranda
Lansdale, J. R. Edge of dark water
Lee, H. Go set a watchman
Locke, A. Bluebird, bluebird
Mullen, T. Lightning men
Oyeyemi, H. Boy, snow, bird
Row, J. Your face in mine
Vassanji, M. G. The in-between world of Vikram Lall
RACE RELATIONS -- UNITED STATES
Howard, R. Driving the king
RACERS (PERSONS)
Simmons, D. The abominable
RACES OF PEOPLE *See* Ethnology
Rachel Getty and Esa Khattak novels [series]
Khan, A. Z. Among the ruins
Khan, A. Z. The unquiet dead
Rachel Goddard Mysteries [series]
Parshall, S. Poisoned ground
RACIAL INTEGRATION *See* Race relations
RACIAL INTERMARRIAGE *See* Interracial marriage
RACIALLY MIXED CHILDREN
Thompson, V. Murder in Chinatown
RACIALLY MIXED FAMILIES -- BURMA
Craig, C. Miss Burma
RACIALLY MIXED PEOPLE
Bowen, L. Wake of vultures
Clotel, or, The president's daughter
Thompson, V. Murder in Chinatown
RACISM
See also Attitude (Psychology); Prejudices; Race awareness; Race relations
Chaudhuri, A. Odysseus Abroad
Morgan, C. E. The sport of kings
RADAR
See also Navigation; Radio; Remote sensing
Radiance. Scholz, C.
Radiance. Valente, C. M.
Radiance of tomorrow. Beah, I.
The **radiant** way. Drabble, M.
RADIATION -- PHYSIOLOGICAL EFFECT
Hill, R. When all is said and done
Shute, N. On the beach
Wiggins, M. Evidence of things unseen
RADICALISM
See also Political science; Revolutions; Right and left (Political science)
RADICALISM
Kushner, R. The flamethrowers
RADICALIZATION
Khadivi, L. A good country
RADICALS
Hall, J. W. Going Dark
RADICALS AND RADICALISM
Carey, P. His illegal self
Kunzru, H. My revolutions
Leonard, E. Freaky Deaky
Lessing, D. M. The good terrorist
Lessing, D. M. The sweetest dream
Meek, J. The people's act of love
Nunez, S. The last of her kind
Piercy, M. Vida
Plain, B. Harvest
Read, P. P. The professor's daughter
Spiotta, D. Eat the document
Turow, S. The laws of our fathers
RADIO BROADCASTING
Alarcon, D. Lost City Radio
Hay, E. Late nights on air
Jacobson, H. The Finkler question
Shields, C. The republic of love
Vargas Llosa, M. Aunt Julia and the scriptwriter
RADIO PROGRAMS
Strayed, C. Torch
The **Radleys.** Haig, M.
Ragdoll. Cole, D.
Rage is back. Mansbach, A.
Ragnarok. Byatt, A. S.
RAGPICKERS
Elison, M. The book of Etta
The **rags** of time. Howard, M.
Ragtime. Doctorow, E. L.
Rahab (Biblical figure)
About

Wolf, J. This scarlet cord
Raiders of the Nile. Saylor, S.
RAILROAD ACCIDENTS
See also Accidents; Disasters
RAILROAD CONSTRUCTION WORKERS -- KENYA
Kimani, P. Dance of the Jakaranda
RAILROAD CONSTRUCTION WORKERS -- UNITED STATES
Johnson, D. Train dreams
RAILROAD ENGINEERING
See also Civil engineering; Engineering; Railroads
RAILROAD TRAVEL
See also Transportation; Travel; Voyages and travels
RAILROAD TRAVEL
Hawkins, P. The girl on the train
RAILROADS
Lock, N. American meteor
McCall Smith, A. Trains and Lovers
Norris, F. The octopus
Rand, A. Atlas shrugged
Ross-Macdonald, M. The rich are with you always
Ross-Macdonald, M. The world from rough stones
RAILROADS -- TRAVEL
West, R. The birds fall down
RAILWAYS *See* Railroads
RAIN FOREST ECOLOGY
See also Ecology
The **rainbow.** Lawrence, D. H.
Rainbow's end. Grimes, M.
Rainbows end. Vinge, V.
Rainmaker translations [series]
Khoury, E. Gate of the sun
Rainshadow road. Kleypas, L.
Raintree County. Lockridge, R.
Raise high the roof beam, carpenters, and Seymour: an introduction. Salinger, J. D.
RAISIN, AGATHA (FICTITIOUS CHARACTER)
Beaton, M. C. Pushing up daisies
The **raising.** Kasischke, L.
Raising Stony Mayhall. Gregory, D.
Raj. Mehta, G.
The **Raj** quartet. Scott, P.
Raleigh, Walter Sir, 1552?-1618
About
Naipaul, V. S. A way in the world
Rama [series]
Clarke, A. C. The Garden of Rama
Clarke, A. C. Rendezvous with Rama
RAMOTSWE, PRECIOUS (FICTITIOUS CHARACTER)
McCall Smith, A. The full cupboard of life
McCall Smith, A. The Kalahari typing school for men
McCall Smith, A. The Limpopo Academy of Private Detection
McCall Smith, A. The No. 1 Ladies' Detective Agency
McCall Smith, A. The Saturday big tent wedding party
McCall Smith, A. Tea time for the traditionally built
Ramses III, King of Egypt
About
Geagley, B. Year of the hyenas
Ran away. Hambly, B.
RANCH LIFE
Caputo, P. Crossers
Doig, I. English Creek
Grey, Z. Woman of the frontier
Keesey, A. Little century
Kittredge, W. The Willow Field
L'Amour, L. The Californios
Larsen, R. The selected works of T. S. Spivet
McCarthy, C. All the pretty horses
McCarthy, C. Cities of the plain
McCullough, C. The thorn birds
Meyers, K. The work of wolves
Overholser, W. D. Death of a cattle king
Richter, C. The sea of grass
Schaefer, J. W. Monte Walsh
Schaefer, J. W. Shane
Steinbeck, J. Of mice and men
Turner, N. E. These is my words
Walls, J. Half broke horses
Weisgarber, A. The personal history of Rachel Dupree
Williamson, P. The outsider
Zimmer, M. Wild side of the river
RANCH LIFE
See also Farm life; Frontier and pioneer life
RANCHERS
Ryan, J. His cowboy heart
Walls, J. Half broke horses
Random harvest. Hilton, J.
Random winds. Plain, B.
Range of ghosts. Bear, E.
RANGELANDS -- OREGON
Keesey, A. Little century
The **ranger.** Atkins, A.
RANK *See* Social classes
Ransom. Malouf, D.
Rant. Palahniuk, C.
Rape. Oates, J. C.
RAPE
Brink, A. P. The other side of silence
Coetzee, J. M. Disgrace
Dallas, S. Tallgrass
Davis, A. Wonder when you'll miss me
Donoghue, E. Room
Erdrich, L. The round house
Grisham, J. A time to kill
Indridason, A. Outrage
Lawrence, M. K. Hearts and bones
Lewis, M. G. The monk
Limón, M. Mr. Kill
Oates, J. C. Rape
Oates, J. C. We were the Mulvaneys
Pronzini, B. The violated
Rendell, R. Live flesh
Rosenberg, N. T. Mitigating circumstances

Stevens, C. Still missing
Turow, S. Limitations
Wolfe, T. A man in full
RAPE VICTIMS
Cleave, P. Five minutes alone
Czepiel, K. L. A violet season
French, N. Thursday's children
O'Donnell, L. Closed Doors
Rappe, Virginia, 1895-1921
About
Atkins, A. Devil's garden
RAPTOREX
See also Dinosaurs
Rapture. Minot, S.
Rapture of the nerds. Doctorow, C.
RARE ANIMALS
See also Animals
A **rare** Benedictine. Peters, E.
RARE BOOKS
Cogman, G. The invisible library
Goodman, A. The cookbook collector
Perez-Reverte, A. The Club Dumas
RARE BOOKS
See also Books
RASTAFARI MOVEMENT
Miller, K. Augustown
Rat run. Seymour, G.
Rather be the devil. Rankin, I.
RATIONALISM
See also Philosophy; Religion; Secularism; Theory of knowledge
Ratking. Dibdin, M.
RATS
Savage, S. Firmin
RATTLESNAKES
See also Poisonous animals; Snakes
Rav Hisda's daughter, book I, apprentice. Anton, M.
Raven Stratagem. Lee, Y. H.
The Ravenels [series]
Kleypas, L. Cold-hearted Rake
Ravens. Green, G. D.
RAVENSBRÜCK (CONCENTRATION CAMP)
Kelly, M. H. Lilac girls
Ravishing the heiress. Thomas, S.
The **raw** shark texts. Hall, S.
RAWLINS, EASY (FICTITIOUS CHARACTER)
Mosley, W. Little green
Mosley, W. Six easy pieces
Raylan. Leonard, E.
Raymond Donne mysteries [series]
O'Mara, T. Crooked Numbers
The **razor's** edge. Maugham, W. S.
Re Jane. Park, P.
REACHER, JACK (FICTIONAL CHARACTER)
Child, L. Killing floor
The **reader.** Schlink, B.
Reader, I married him. Roberts, M.
READING
Brown, E. The weird sisters
Reading in the dark. Deane, S.
READING INTERESTS *See* Books and reading
READINGS (ANTHOLOGIES) *See* Anthologies
Ready player one. Cline, E.
Reagan, Ronald
About
Mallon, T. Finale
REAL ESTATE
Ford, R. Independence Day
Ford, R. The lay of the land
Lennon, J. R. Castle
Puchner, E. Model home
REAL ESTATE
See also Land use; Property
REAL ESTATE BUSINESS
Millet, L. How the dead dream
REAL ESTATE BUSINESS
See also Business; Real estate
REAL ESTATE DEVELOPMENT
Adiga, A. Last man in tower
Flanery, P. Fallen land
REAL ESTATE DEVELOPMENT
See also Real estate business
REALITY
Mastai, E. All our wrong todays
REALITY TELEVISION PROGRAMS
See also Television programs
Tremblay, P. A Head Full of Ghosts
Williams, W. J. The fourth wall
The **realm** of last chances. Yarbrough, S.
REALTY *See* Real estate
Reamde. Stephenson, N.
The **reapers** are the angels. Bell, A.
Rebecca. Du Maurier, D.
Rebekah Roberts [series]
Dahl, J. Conviction
The **rebel** angels. Davies, R.
The **rebel** heir. Michels, E.
Rebel queen. Moran, M.
REBELLION
Liu, K. The grace of kings
The **rebellion** of Jane Clarke. Gunning, S.
REBELLIONS *See* Insurgency; Revolutions
REBELS (SOCIAL PSYCHOLOGY) *See* Alienation (Social psychology)
The **rebels** of Ireland. Rutherfurd, E.
REBIRTH *See* Reincarnation
REBUSES
See also Literary recreations; Puzzles; Riddles
RECESSIONS
Eggers, D. A hologram for the king
Recipes for Love and Murder. Andrew, S.
Reckless. Gross, A.
Reckless abandon. Woods, S.
The **reckoning.** Penman, S. K.

The **reckoning.** Long, J.
A **reckoning.** Sarton, M.
RECLUSES
Doctorow, E. L. Homer & Langley
Guterson, D. The other
King, S. Finders Keepers
Mosley, W. The last days of Ptolemy Grey
RECLUSES *See* Hermits
RECLUSES -- NEW YORK (STATE) -- NEW YORK
Finn, A. J. The woman in the window
The **recognitions.** Gaddis, W.
RECOMBINANT DNA
See also DNA; Genetic engineering; Genetic recombination
RECONCILIATION
Jeffries, S. 'Twas the night after Christmas
Pelecanos, G. P. The turnaround
RECONSTRUCTION
Mitchell, M. Gone with the wind
Smith, L. On Agate Hill
RECONSTRUCTION (1939-1951) -- SICILY
Hersey, J. A bell for Adano
RECONSTRUCTION (U.S. HISTORY, 1865-1877)
Pitts, L. Freeman
The **reconstructionist.** Hart, J.
RECOVERING ALCOHOLICS
Jerkins, G. The ninth step
Ulfelder, S. Purgatory chasm
RECTORS *See* Clergy
RED
See also Color
The **red** and the black. Stendhal
Red April. Roncagliolo, S.
RED ARMY FACTION
Schlink, B. The weekend
The **red** badge of courage. Crane, S.
Red clocks. Zumas, L.
The **red** convertible. Erdrich, L.
Red country. Abercrombie, J.
A **red** death. Mosley, W.
The **red** door. Todd, C.
Red Dragon. Harris, T.
The **red** garden. Hoffman, A.
The **red** heart. Thom, J. A.
Red herring. Mayor, A.
A **red** herring without mustard. Bradley, A.
Red Hook Road. Waldman, A.
The **red** house. Haddon, M.
The **red** hunter. Unger, L.
Red lightning. Varley, J.
Red mandarin dress. Qiu Xiaolong
Red Mars. Robinson, K. S.
Red moon. Percy, B.
Red on red. Conlon, E.
The **Red** Pavilion. Gulik, R. H. v.
The **red** queen. Gregory, P.
Red Rising. Brown, P.
Red Rising trilogy [series]
Brown, P. Morning Star
The **red** road. Mina, D.
The **red** scarf. Furnivall, K.
Red seas under red skies. Lynch, S.
Red sky at night. Hall, J. W.
Red sparrow. Matthews, J.
Red Spectres.
The **red** tent. Diamant, A.
The **red** thread. Hood, A.
Red thunder. Varley, J.
The **red** tree. Kiernan, C. R.
Red, white and blue. Isaacs, S.
The **red-haired** woman.
The **redbreast.**
Redburn, his first voyage; White-jacket, or, The world in a man-of-war; Moby-Dick, or, The whale. Melville, H.
The **redeemer.**
Redemption. Uris, L.
REDEMPTION
Warrington, F. Midsummer night
Redemption in indigo. Lord, K.
Redemption road. Hart, J.
Redeployment. Klay, P.
Redline the stars. Norton, A.
Redshirts. Scalzi, J.
REEF ECOLOGY
See also Ecology; Marine ecology
Reeve LeClaire series
Norton, C. What doesn't kill her
Reflections in a golden eye. McCullers, C.
REFORM, SOCIAL *See* Social problems
REFORMATION
Maxwell, R. The secret diary of Anne Boleyn
Norfolk, L. John Saturnall's feast
REFORMATION
See also Christianity; Church history -- 1500- , Modern period
REFORMATORIES FOR WOMEN
Alexander, V. S. The Magdalen girls
The **Refugees.** Nguyen, V. T.
REFUGEES
Alyan, H. Salt houses
Brookner, A. Family and friends
Couto, M. Sleepwalking land
Dau, S. The book of Jonas
Hamid, M. Exit West
Jen, G. World and town
Kosinski, J. N. The painted bird
Le, T. D. T. The gangster we are all looking for
Lee The surrendered
Ozick, C. Foreign bodies
Ozick, C. Heir to the glimmering world
Palwick, S. The necessary beggar
REFUGEES
See also Homeless persons; Immigration and emigration; Noncitizens

REFUGEES -- CAMBODIA
Ratner, V. In the shadow of the banyan
REFUGEES -- SUDAN
Eggers, D. What is the what
REFUGEES -- UNITED STATES
Eggers, D. What is the what
REFUGEES, JEWISH
Neugeboren, J. 1940
Refund. Bender, K. E.
REFUSE COLLECTORS
VanderMeer, J. Borne
REGENCY NOVELS
Bell, L. How the Duke Was Won
Bradley, C. I Thee Wed
Burrowes, G. The heir
Dare, T. Any Duchess Will Do
Dare, T. A week to be wicked
Heyer, G. The grand Sophy
Heyer, G. These old shades
Hunter, M. The conquest of Lady Cassandra
James, E. The ugly duchess
Kilpack, J. S. A heart revealed
Leigh, E. Temptations of a Wallflower
MacKenzie, S. Bedding Lord Ned
MacLean, S. The Rogue Not Taken
REGENCY NOVELS
See also Historical fiction
Regeneration. Barker, P.
Regensberg, Izoldą
About
Chasing the king of hearts
REGENTS
Dumas, A. Twenty years after
Min, A. Empress Orchid
REGISTERS OF BIRTHS, ETC.
See also Genealogy
REGRESSION (CIVILIZATION)
Cline, E. Ready player one
Haig, F. The map of bones
Hoban, R. Riddley Walker
Lee On such a full sea
Stirling, S. M. Dies the fire
REGRET
Hood, A. The Obituary Writer
The **regulars.** Clark, G.
REINCARNATION
Barker, S. The incarnations
Davidson, A. The gargoyle
Hooper, K. Finding Laura
In the wilderness
Mailer, N. Ancient evenings
Miller, R. Jacob's folly
Mishima, Y. The decay of the angel
Mo Yan Life and death are wearing me out
Seton, A. Green darkness
Zelazny, R. Lord of light
Reincarnation Blues. Poore, M.
The **reivers.** Faulkner, W.
REJUVENATION
Haggard, H. R. She
A **reliable** wife. Goolrick, R.
RELICS
Kearsley, S. The Firebird
Kennedy, K. Everlasting Enchantment
Sandford, J. Storm Front
Wiprud, B. M. Ringer
RELICS AND RELIQUARIES *See* Relics
The **religion.** Willocks, T.
RELIGION
Baker, K. In the garden of Iden
Baldwin, J. Go tell it on the mountain
Bunyan, J. The pilgrim's progress
The death of Ivan Ilyich and Confession
Dostoyevsky, F. The brothers Karamazov
Goodman, A. Paradise park
Hansen, R. Mariette in ecstasy
Iles, G. The footprints of God
Irving, J. A prayer for Owen Meany
Kafka, F. The castle
Lewis, S. Elmer Gantry
Mahfouz, N. Children of the alley
Marshall, C. Christy
Meek, J. The people's act of love
Murdoch, I. The bell
Murdoch, I. The green knight
O'Connor, F. Wise blood
Picoult, J. Sing you home
Preston, D. Blasphemy
Robbins, T. Skinny legs and all
Salinger, J. D. Franny & Zooey
Self, W. The Book of Dave
Sorokin, V. Ice
Spark, M. The Mandelbaum Gate
Stone, R. Damascus Gate
Updike, J. In the beauty of the lilies
Updike, J. S
Vidal, G. Creation
West, M. L. The devil's advocate
RELIGION AND LAW
McEwan, I. The children act
RELIGIOUS EDUCATORS
Brown, D. Angels & demons
RELIGIOUS FICTION
Merullo, R. Vatican waltz
RELIGIOUS FUNDAMENTALISM
John, E. Born on a Tuesday
RELIGIOUS TOLERANCE
The elephant keepers' children
Reliquary. Preston, D.
The **relive** box and other stories. Boyle, T. C.
The **reluctant** fundamentalist. Hamid, M.
The **remains** of the day. Ishiguro, K.
REMARRIAGE
Robinson, R. Sweetwater

Trollope, J. Marrying the mistress
Trollope, J. Other people's children
REMARRIAGE
See also Marriage
Remembering Babylon. Malouf, D.
Remembering the bones. Itani, F.
Remembrance of things past. Proust, M.
REMINISCING IN OLD AGE
Banville, J. Ancient light
Benioff, D. City of thieves
Gilman, S. J. The Ice Cream Queen of Orchard Street
Harding, P. Tinkers
Rawles, N. My Jim
Waldman, A. Love and treasure
The **remorseful** day. Dexter, C.
RENAISSANCE
Poole, S. The Borgia mistress
Rendezvous with Rama. Clarke, A. C.
The **renegades.** Young, T. W.
Renoir, Auguste, 1841-1919
About
Vreeland, S. Luncheon of The Boating Party
RENOWN *See* Fame
REPARATIONS FOR HISTORICAL INJUSTICES
Conklin, T. The house girl
The **repeat** year. Lochen, A.
A **replacement** life. Fishman, B.
REPORT WRITING
See also Authorship
REPORTERS AND REPORTING
See also Journalism; Newspapers
REPORTERS AND REPORTING
Grant, M. Feedback
Lohmann, J. Winning Ruby Heart
Quick, A. The girl who knew too much
REPORTERS AND REPORTING -- RHODE ISLAND
DeSilva, B. A Scourge of Vipers
The **reprieve.** Sartre, J. P.
REPRINTS (PUBLICATIONS)
See also Books; Editions
REPTILES
See also Animals
The **republic** of love. Shields, C.
The **Republic** of Thieves. Lynch, S.
Requiem. Itani, F.
Requiem for a nun. Faulkner, W.
Requiem for a realtor. McInerny, R. M.
Requiem for Harlem. Roth, H.
Requiem, Mass. Dufresne, J.
Rescue missions. Busch, F.
RESCUE WORK
Cash, W. This dark road to mercy
RESCUES
Cash, W. This dark road to mercy
RESEARCH
Goodman, A. Intuition
Michener, J. A. Space
Reservation blues. Alexie, S.
Reservation Road. Schwartz, J. B.
RESIDENCES *See* Domestic architecture; Houses
Resistance. Lopez, B. H.
The **resistance.** Steiner, P.
Resistance. Sheers, O.
RESISTANCE TO GOVERNMENT
Brown, P. Golden Son
Brown, P. Red Rising
Shannon, S. The mime order
Westerfeld, S. The risen empire
Resort to murder. Hart, C. G.
RESORTS
Longworth, M. L. Murder on the Île Sordou
RESORTS -- OHIO -- 19TH CENTURY
Perkins-Valdez, D. Wench
RESPONSIBILITY
See also Ethics
The **restaurant** at the end of the universe. Adams, D.
RESTAURANTS
Jones, L. The Dixie Belle's Guide to Love
Leon, D. Beastly Things
Martinez, A. L. Gil's All Fright Diner
Wildgen, M. Bread and Butter
RESTAURANTS, LUNCHROOMS, ETC.
Ali, M. In the kitchen
Ha Jin A free life
Harris, J. Five quarters of the orange
Morais, R. C. The hundred-foot journey
Naylor, G. Bailey's Cafe
O'Nan, S. Last night at the Lobster
Rice, L. Blue moon
Russo, R. Empire Falls
Steinbeck, J. Sweet Thursday
RESTAURATEURS
Harris, J. Five quarters of the orange
Martinez, A. L. Gil's All Fright Diner
Russo, R. Empire Falls
Wildgen, M. Bread and Butter
Restless in the grave. Stabenow, D.
Resurrection. Tolstoy, L.
RESURRECTION
Amado, J. Dona Flor and her two husbands
Farmer, P. J. The dark design
Farmer, P. J. The fabulous riverboat
Farmer, P. J. Gods of Riverworld
Farmer, P. J. The magic labyrinth
Farmer, P. J. To your scattered bodies go
RESURRECTION *See* Future life
Resurrection Express. Romano, S.
Resurrection men. Rankin, I.
Resurrection row. Perry, A.
The **resurrectionist.** Guinn, M.
RETAIL STORES *See* Stores
RETIRED MILITARY PERSONNEL
Lee, P. Runner
Lee, P. Signal

RETIREES
Begley, L. About Schmidt
Friedman, D. Don't ever get old
RETIREMENT
Begley, L. About Schmidt
Glass, J. The widower's tale
Lee A gesture life
Pym, B. Quartet in autumn
Tyler, A. Noah's compass
RETIREMENT
See also Leisure; Old age
RETIREMENT COMMUNITIES
McCorkle, J. Life after life
RETIREMENT INCOME
See also Income; Retirement
RETIREMENT PLANNING
See also Retirement
Retribution falls. Wooding, C.
RETROSPECTIVE STORIES
Gardam, J. Old Filth
The **return.** Gruber, M.
The **return** man. Zito, V. M.
The **return** of Santiago. Resnick, M.
The **return** of the dancing master. Mankell, H.
The **return** of the king. Tolkien, J. R. R.
The **return** of the native. Hardy, T.
The **Returned.** Mott, J.
Returning to earth. Harrison, J.
Reunion. Lightman, A. P.
A **reunion** of ghosts. Mitchell, J. C.
REUNIONS
Cole, T. Every day is for the thief
Drabble, M. The sea lady
Edugyan, E. Half-blood blues
Goddard, R. Never go back
Jaffe, R. Class reunion
McCrumb, S. If ever I return, pretty Peggy-O
Rush, N. Subtle bodies
REVENGE
Alexie, S. Flight
Amis, K. The Russian girl
Baker, K. The house of the stag
Balzac, H. d. Cousin Bette
Banks, I. Stonemouth
Bear, G. Anvil of stars
Blatty, W. P. Dimiter
Brandt, H. The Whites
Brink, A. P. The other side of silence
Bronte, E. Wuthering Heights
Brooks, B. Frontier justice
Brown, P. Morning Star
Carter, S. L. The emperor of Ocean Park
Chen, D. Brothers
Conrad, J. Victory
Cox, M. The meaning of night
Deaver, J. Edge
Dickens, C. Great expectations
Dickens, C. A tale of two cities
Dickinson, S. The traitor Baru Cormorant
Dolan, H. Very bad men
Dumas, A. The Count of Monte Cristo
Enger, L. Undiscovered country
Estleman, L. D. Gas City
Faust, C. Money shot
Frame, R. The lantern bearers
Franklin, T. Hell at the breech
French, A. Billy
Garcia Marquez, G. Chronicle of a death foretold
George, E. What came before he shot her
Goddard, R. Beyond recall
Goodman, C. Arcadia Falls
Grisham, J. The last juror
Grisham, J. A time to kill
Gruber, M. The return
Haig, M. The dead fathers club
Harris, T. Hannibal rising
Hart, J. Redemption road
Haywood, G. A. Cemetery Road
Heffernan, W. The Dinosaur Club
Hiaasen, C. Skinny dip
Higgins, J. Bad company
Higgins, J. Day of reckoning
Higgins, J. Edge of danger
Higgins, J. Midnight runner
Hill, J. Heart-shaped box
Hill, J. Horns
Hill, R. The woodcutter
Hunter, S. The 47th samurai
Hunter, S. Black light
Hunter, S. Time to hunt
Huston, C. The shotgun rule
James, P. D. Innocent blood
Jiles, P. The color of lightning
Just, W. S. Forgetfulness
Katzenbach, J. The analyst
Kay, G. G. Children of earth and sky
Kelly, E. The burning air
Kerstan, L. Heart of the tiger
Knopf, C. Dead anyway
Koryta, M. So cold the river
Kristoff, J. Nevernight
K'wan (Author) Animal
K'wan (Author) Welfare wifeys
Lansdale, J. R. Paradise sky
Lebrecht, N. The song of names
Lehane, D. Mystic river
Lehrer, J. The special prisoner
Leonard, E. Glitz
Lippman, L. The most dangerous thing
Little star
Machart, B. The wake of forgiveness
Martin, L. The bright forever
McCarry, C. The Mulberry Bush
McDermid, V. The distant echo

McEwan, I. Amsterdam
Melville, H. Moby-Dick; or, The whale
Michels, E. The rebel heir
Minato, K. Confessions
Murdoch, I. The green knight
Murphy, Y. The call
Neville, S. The ghosts of Belfast
Norman, H. The haunting of L
Parker, T. J. Silent Joe
Pelecanos, G. P. Drama city
Pelecanos, G. P. Shame the devil
Percy, W. Lancelot
Perry, T. Pursuit
Pyne, D. Twentynine Palms
Rawn, M. The diviner
Robertson, I. The Paris winter
Robinson, P. The first cut
Robotham, M. Suspect
Rosenberg, N. T. Mitigating circumstances
Savage, S. The cry of the sloth
Schwartz, J. B. Reservation Road
Shaw, I. Beggarman, thief
Smith, W. A. Birds of prey
Stanley, M. Deadly Harvest
Stuckey-French, E. Revenge of the radioactive lady
Tartt, D. The little friend
Theroux, A. Darconville's cat
Thomas, S. Beguiling the beauty
Unger, L. The red hunter
Van Dyken, R. Cheater
Wall, P. S. The Wilde women
Warren, R. P. World enough and time
Weldon, F. The life and loves of a she-devil
Westlake, D. E. What's the worst that could happen?
Woods, S. Dirty work
Woods, S. Palindrome
Woods, S. Worst fears realized
Yarbrough, S. The end of California
Zimmer, M. Wild side of the river

Revenge of the radioactive lady. Stuckey-French, E.
Revenge of the Spellmans. Lutz, L.
Revenger. Reynolds, A.
Revenger. Clements, R.
REVERSIBLE BOOKS *See* Upside-down books
Reversible errors. Turow, S.
The **revised** fundamentals of caregiving. Evison, J.

REVOLUTIONARIES
Bell, M. S. All souls' rising
Garcia Marquez, G. The general and his labyrinth
Griffin, W. E. B. Special ops
McCarry, C. The Mulberry Bush
Naipaul, V. S. A way in the world
Olmstead, R. Far bright star
Penman, S. K. Falls the shadow
Styron, W. The confessions of Nat Turner
Wideman, J. E. Fanon

REVOLUTIONISTS
Alarcon, D. Lost City Radio
Allende, I. Eva Luna
Ballard, J. G. Millennium people
Beijing coma
Castellanos Moya, H. Tyrant memory
Naipaul, V. S. Magic seeds
Naipaul, V. S. A way in the world
Olmstead, R. Far bright star
Puig, M. Kiss of the spider woman
Rush, N. Mortals
Sanchez, T. King Bongo
West, R. The birds fall down

REVOLUTIONS
Bell, M. S. All souls' rising
Didion, J. A book of common prayer
Flanagan, T. The tenants of time
Flynn, M. On the razor's edge
Gordimer, N. July's people
Heinlein, R. A. The moon is a harsh mistress
Liu, K. The grace of kings
Rajaniemi, H. The fractal prince

REYKJAVÍK (ICELAND)
Indridason, A. Outrage
The silence of the sea

RHAPSODY (FICTITIOUS CHARACTER : HAYDON)
Haydon, E. The Merchant Emperor
Haydon, E. Prophecy

RHETORIC
See also Language and languages

RHEUMATISM
See also Diseases

The **Rhinemann** exchange. Ludlum, R.
Rhino Ranch. McMurtry, L.

RHODE ISLAND
DeSilva, B. A Scourge of Vipers
Kiernan, C. R. The red tree
Rice, L. Blue moon
Smith, G. B. The maze at Windermere
Updike, J. The widows of Eastwick
Updike, J. The witches of Eastwick

RHODE ISLAND -- NEWPORT
Rice, L. The deep blue sea for beginners
Rice, L. The geometry of sisters
Wilder, T. Theophilus North

RHODE ISLAND -- PROVIDENCE
Hood, A. The knitting circle
Hood, A. The red thread

The **rice** mother. Manicka, R.

RICH
See also Social classes
Gallagher, S. The bedlam detective
Gay, R. An Untamed State
Gilbert, D. & sons
Haimoff, M. These days are ours
Jenkins, V. An unattended death
Klaussmann, L. Tigers in red weather
Kwan, K. China rich girlfriend

Kwan, K. Crazy rich Asians
Kwan, K. Rich people problems
Laukkanen, O. The professionals
Stone, N. The Verdict
The **rich** and the profane. Gash, J.
The **rich** are with you always. Ross-Macdonald, M.
Rich boy. Pomerantz, S.
Rich man, poor man. Shaw, I.
RICH PEOPLE
Dee, J. The privileges
Doctorow, C. Walkaway
Everett, P. L. I am Not Sidney Poitier
Koryta, M. So cold the river
Kwan, K. Crazy rich Asians
Kwan, K. Rich people problems
McLaughlin, E. The nanny diaries
Schulman, H. This beautiful life
Thompson, V. Murder on Fifth Avenue
RICH PEOPLE -- CHINA -- SHANGHAI
Kwan, K. China rich girlfriend
RICH PEOPLE -- ENGLAND
Gallagher, S. The bedlam detective
RICH PEOPLE -- NEW YORK (STATE) -- NEW YORK
Gilbert, D. & sons
Rich people problems. Kwan, K.
Richard I, King of England, 1157-1199
About
Penman, S. K. A King's Ransom
Penman, S. K. Lionheart
Scott, W. Ivanhoe
Richard III, King of England, 1452-1485
About
Gregory, P. The red queen
Penman, S. K. The sunne in splendour
Tey, J. The daughter of time
Richard, Duke of York, 1472-1483
About
Gregory, P. The red queen
RICHES *See* Wealth
RICHMOND (VA.)
Turner, N. Heartbreak of a hustler's wife
Riddley Walker. Hoban, R.
Ride a pale horse. MacInnes, H.
Riders of the purple sage. Grey, Z.
Riders on the Storm. Gorman, E.
The **ridge.** Koryta, M.
The **rifles.** Vollmann, W. T.
RIFLES
See also Guns
Right as rain. Pelecanos, G. P.
Right livelihoods. Moody, R.
RIGHT OF PROPERTY
See also Civil rights; Property
Morris, M. Man in the blue moon
RIGHT TO DIE
See also Death; Medical ethics; Medicine -- Law and legislation
RIGHTEOUS GENTILES IN THE HOLOCAUST
See also Holocaust, 1939-1945; World War, 1939-1945 -- Jews -- Rescue
Ring around the bases.
Ringer. Wiprud, B. M.
RINGS
Tolkien, J. R. R. The fellowship of the ring
Tolkien, J. R. R. The return of the king
Tolkien, J. R. R. The two towers
Ringworld. Niven, L.
The **Ringworld** engineers. Niven, L.
The **Ringworld** throne. Niven, L.
Ringworld's children. Niven, L.
Riot most uncouth. Friedman, D.
RIOTS
Mosley, W. Little Scarlet
RIPOFFS *See* Fraud
The **rise** and fall of D.O.D.O. Stephenson, N.
The **rise** of Endymion. Simmons, D.
The **risen** empire. Westerfeld, S.
A **Rising** Man. Mukherjee, A.
The **rising** tide. Shaara, J.
RISK
Thomas, S. My Beautiful Enemy
RISK ASSESSMENT
See also Evaluation; Risk
The **risk** of darkness. Hill, S.
The **risk** pool. Russo, R.
A **risk** worth taking. Pilcher, R.
RITES AND CEREMONIES
Conn, B. The fixed stars
Straub, P. A dark matter
Wallace, D. The Watermelon King
RITES AND CEREMONIES -- CARIBBEAN REGION
Marshall, P. Praisesong for the widow
Rites of passage. Golding, W.
The **ritual.** Nevill, A.
RITUAL *See* Liturgies; Rites and ceremonies
Ritual. Hayder, M.
River angel. Ansay, A. M.
RIVER ECOLOGY
See also Ecology
The **river** king. Hoffman, A.
River of gods. McDonald, I.
River of mercy. Hoff, B. J.
The **river** of no return. Ridgway, B.
River of smoke. Ghosh, A.
River of Stars. Kay, G. G.
River of Teeth. Gailey, S.
River Road. Goodman, C.
River road. Krentz, J. A.
A **river** Sutra. Mehta, G.
RIVERS
Ballard, J. G. The day of creation
Campbell, B. J. Once upon a river
Scott, J. Follow me
Rivers of London [series]

Aaronovitch, B. Midnight riot
Rivers, W. H. R. (William Halse Rivers), 1864-1922
About
Barker, P. The eye in the door
Barker, P. The ghost road
Riverworld [series]
Farmer, P. J. The dark design
Farmer, P. J. Gods of Riverworld
Farmer, P. J. The magic labyrinth
Farmer, P. J. To your scattered bodies go
RIVIERA FRANCE
Levy, D. Swimming home
Sagan, F. Bonjour tristesse
RL's dream. Mosley, W.
ROACHES (INSECTS) *See* Cockroaches
The **road.** McCarthy, C.
The **road** ahead.
The **road** back. Remarque, E. M.
The **road** from Gap Creek. Morgan, R.
The **road** home. Harrison, J.
The **road** home. Tremain, R.
Road novels 1957-1960. Kerouac, J.
The **road** to enchantment. McLaren, K.
The road to Nowhere [series]
Elison, M. The book of Etta
Elison, M. The Book of the Unnamed Midwife
The **road** to ruin. Westlake, D. E.
Road to Wellville. Boyle, T. C.
ROADS -- MONTANA
Box, C. J. The highway
Roads to freedom [series]
Sartre, J. P. The age of reason
Sartre, J. P. The reprieve
Sartre, J. P. Troubled sleep
Roadside picnic.
The **roaring** boy. Marston, E.
Roaring Twenties [series]
Bennett, J. Bitter Spirits
Rob Roy. Scott, W.
Rob Roy, 1671-1734
About
Scott, W. Rob Roy
The **robber** bridegroom. Welty, E.
ROBBERS *See* Thieves
ROBBERY
Hilton, E. Dirty money Honey
Latour, J. The Havana World Series
Malamud, B. The assistant
Pelecanos, G. P. Shame the devil
Spiegelman, P. Thick as thieves
Stark, R. Comeback
Westlake, D. E. The hot rock
Westlake, D. E. Put a lid on it
Westlake, D. E. What's the worst that could happen?
Woods, T. Alibi
A **Robert** Silverberg omnibus. Silverberg, R.
ROBINS
See also Birds
Robinson Crusoe. Defoe, D.
Robinson, Jackie, 1919-1972
About
Parker, R. B. Double play
ROBINSONADES
See also Adventure fiction; Imaginary voyages
Robogenesis. Wilson, D. H.
Robopocalypse. Wilson, D. H.
Robot series
Asimov, I. I, robot
Roboteer. Lamb, A.
ROBOTICS *See* Robots
ROBOTS
Asimov, I. I, robot
Carey, P. The chemistry of tears
Davis, K. Duplex
Lamb, A. Roboteer
Newitz, A. Autonomous
Sedia, E. Alchemy of stone
Stross, C. Neptune's brood
Stross, C. Saturn's children
Tregillis, I. The Mechanical
Wilson, D. H. Robogenesis
Wilson, D. H. Robopocalypse
The **rock** hole. Wortham, R.
ROCK MUSIC
Alexie, S. Reservation blues
Bognanni, P. The house of tomorrow
Egan, J. A visit from the Goon Squad
Hiaasen, C. Basket case
Hill, J. Heart-shaped box
Hornby, N. High fidelity
Hornby, N. Juliet, naked
Lazar, Z. Sway
Parker, B. Criminal justice
Rushdie, S. The ground beneath her feet
Spiotta, D. Stone Arabia
Williams, C. Stairway to hell
ROCK MUSICIANS
Abani, C. GraceLand
Long, J. A. Hot in Hellcat Canyon
Tropper, J. One last thing before I go
The **rocks.** Nichols, P.
ROCKY MOUNTAINS
Rollins, J. The devil colony
RODEOS
Borland, H. When the legends die
Rodin's debutante. Just, W. S.
Roger's version. Updike, J.
Rogers, Mary, 1820-1841
About
Rose, J. Blackest bird
Rogue island. DeSilva, B.
The **Rogue** Not Taken. MacLean, S.
Rogue Spy. Bourne, J.
Rogues.

ROGUES AND VAGABONDS
Brown, J. D. Addie Pray
Kerouac, J. On the road
Kerouac, J. The Dharma bums
Rogues
Steinbeck, J. Cannery Row
Steinbeck, J. Sweet Thursday
Steinbeck, J. Tortilla Flat
Tinti, H. The good thief
ROGUES AND VAGABONDS *See* Picaresque literature
ROLAND (LEGENDARY CHARACTER)
See also Folklore
ROLE PLAYING
Darnielle, J. Wolf in white van
ROLLING STONES
Lazar, Z. Sway
Rolling thunder. Varley, J.
Roma. Saylor, S.
Roma eterna. Silverberg, R.
ROMAN ART
See also Ancient art; Art; Classical antiquities
The **Roman** spring of Mrs. Stone. Williams, T.
ROMANCE FICTION
Abu-Jaber, D. Crescent
Aciman, A. A. Call me by your name
Adichie, C. N. Americanah
Agnon, S. Y. Only yesterday
Alexander, T. A beauty so rare
Alexander, V. The Scandalous Adventures of the Sister of the Bride
Allen, S. A. The sugar queen
Allende, I. In the midst of winter
Allende, I. Daughter of fortune
Allende, I. Eva Luna
Amis, K. The Russian girl
Amis, M. The zone of interest
Amis, M. House of meetings
Anders, A. Under Her Skin
Andrews, I. White Hot
Andrews, M. K. Summer rental
Ashford, J. What the duke doesn't know
Atlee, A. The typewriter girl
Austen, J. Emma
Austen, J. Mansfield Park
Austen, J. Persuasion
Austen, J. Sense and sensibility
Avery, E. The last nude
Bagshawe, T. Adored
Baker, K. In the garden of Iden
Baker, L. The Glass Ocean
Baldwin, J. If Beale Street could talk
Balogh, M. The escape
Balogh, M. More than a mistress
Balogh, M. Only a Promise
Balogh, M. The secret mistress
Balogh, M. Seducing an angel
Banks, I. Stonemouth
Bannon, J. I2
Baxter, C. The feast of love
Belfer, L. A fierce radiance
Benjamin, M. Alice I have been
Bennett, J. Bitter Spirits
Bennett, V. The queen's lover
Berry, W. Jayber Crow
Binchy, M. The glass lake
Binchy, M. Whitethorn Woods
Blackstock, T. Shadow in serenity
Blake, S. The postmistress
Bohjalian, C. The sandcastle girls
Bolano, R. Monsieur Pain
Boll, H. The silent angel
Bouchet, A. Breath of fire
Bourne, J. The black hawk
Bourne, J. My lord and spymaster
Bourne, J. Rogue Spy
Bourne, J. The spymaster's lady
Bowen, K. You're the Earl That I Want
Bowman, V. The Unexpected Duchess
Boyle, E. Along Came a Duke
Braden, K. The Longest Night
Bradley, C. I Thee Wed
Brill, A. The movement of stars
Bronte, A. The tenant of Wildfell Hall
Bronte, C. Jane Eyre
Bronte, E. Wuthering Heights
Brookner, A. Brief lives
Burgess, M. Dogfight, a love story
Burrowes, G. The heir
Burrowes, G. Lady Maggie's secret scandal
Burrowes, G. Tremaine's True Love
Byatt, A. S. Possession
Byrne, K. The Duke
Callihan, K. Firelight
Cameron, P. The city of your final destination
Cameron, P. Coral Glynn
Carlyle, L. The bride wore scarlet
Carroll, J. The ghost in love
Chase, L. L. The last hellion
Chase, L. L. Silk is for seduction
Chase, L. Dukes Prefer Blondes
Chase, L. Scandal wears satin
Chase, L. Vixen in Velvet
Chase, L. Your scandalous ways
Chen, D. Brothers
Ciotta, B. Her Sky Cowboy
Climates
Cole, A. An Extraordinary Union
Colwin, L. Happy all the time
Conley, R. J. Mountain windsong
Cooper, I. No proper lady
Cosse, L. A novel bookstore
Crace, J. The pesthouse
Criswell, M. What to do about Annie?
Currie, R. Flimsy little plastic miracles

Dai Sijie Once on a moonless night
Danielewski, M. Z. Only revolutions
Dare, T. Any Duchess Will Do
Dare, T. Do you want to start a scandal
Dare, T. A night to surrender
Dare, T. Romancing the duke
Dare, T. Say Yes to the Marquess
Dare, T. A week to be wicked
Davidson, A. The gargoyle
Davies, P. H. The Welsh girl
Davis, L. Master and God
Delaney, F. The matchmaker of Kenmare
Deutermann, P. T. Pacific glory
Dev, S. A Bollywood affair
Diamond, D. A gangster and a gentleman
Díaz, J. This is how you lose her
Dickens, C. Great expectations
Diffenbaugh, V. The language of flowers
Doig, I. Dancing at the Rascal Fair
Drabble, M. The sea lady
Drayson, N. Guide to the birds of East Africa
Dreyer, E. Barely a lady
Dreyer, E. Twice tempted
Du Maurier, D. Frenchman's Creek
Dunant, S. The birth of Venus
Duncan, G. By blood we live
Duran, M. A lady's code of misconduct
Duran, M. Luck Be a Lady
Dyachenko, M. The scar
Earley, T. The blue star
Echlin, K. The disappeared
Esquivel, L. Like water for chocolate
Eugenides, J. The marriage plot
Evans, N. The horse whisperer
Faulks, S. Charlotte Gray
Fay, J. The shortest way home
Feldman, E. Next to love
Finch, C. The last enchantments
Finney, J. Time and again
Fitch, J. Paint it black
Fitzgerald, P. The blue flower
Flanagan, R. The narrow road to the deep north
Flyte, M. City of dark magic
Fortier, A. Juliet
Foster, L. Under Pressure
Fountain, B. Billy Lynn's long halftime walk
Fowles, J. The French lieutenant's woman
Frampton, M. Put Up Your Duke
Frankel, L. Goodbye for now
Frazier, C. Cold Mountain
Frazier, C. Thirteen moons
Furnivall, K. The red scarf
Gabaldon, D. Outlander
Garcia Marquez, G. Love in the time of cholera
George, M. Helen of Troy
Gibb, C. Sweetness in the belly
Gilbert, E. The Signature of All Things
Giordano, P. The solitude of prime numbers
Glass, J. The widower's tale
Godden, R. Pippa passes
Gohlke, C. Promise me this
Golden, A. Memoirs of a geisha
Goldman, F. Say her name
Goldman, W. The princess bride
Goodman, J. A place called home
Goodwin, D. The American heiress
Gordon, M. The love of my youth
Goudge, E. Garden of lies
Goudge, E. Green Dolphin Street
Gowdy, B. The romantic
Gracie, A. The Autumn Bride
Gracie, A. To catch a bride
Gracie, A. The Winter Bride
Grant, D. The Protector
Grass, G. The call of the toad
Gray, J. A Duke Never Yields
Gray, J. How to School Your Scoundrel
Gray, J. A lady never lies
Green, J. Another piece of my heart
Grenville, K. Sarah Thornhill
Grenville, K. The idea of perfection
Groot, T. Flame of resistance
Grossman, D. Be my knife
Gruen, S. Water for elephants
Guhrke, L. L. How to lose a duke in ten days
Guhrke, L. L. When the Marquess Met His Match
Gunning, S. The rebellion of Jane Clarke
Guo Xiaolu A concise Chinese-English dictionary for lovers
Hall, T. The case of the love commandos
Handler, D. Adverbs
Hannah, K. On Mystic lake
Harkness, D. E. A discovery of witches
Harper, K. Fall from pride
Harris, E. L. And this too shall pass
Harrison, J. The English major
Harrison, K. The seal wife
Haruf, K. Our souls at night
Hatcher, R. L. Catching Katie
Hawke, E. Ash Wednesday
Hay, E. A student of weather
Hazzard, S. The great fire
Heinlein, R. A. Variable star
Helprin, M. In sunlight and in shadow
Hemingway, E. A farewell to arms
Henry, P. C. And then I found you
Henry, P. C. Coming up for air
Hern, C. The bride sale
Hern, C. Once a gentleman
Heyer, G. Black sheep
Heyer, G. The grand Sophy
Heyer, G. These old shades
Higgins, K. The Best Man
Higgins, K. In Your Dreams
Higgins, K. Waiting on You

Hilderbrand, E. Silver girl
Hilton, J. Random harvest
Hoban, R. Her name was Lola
Hoff, B. J. River of mercy
Hoffman, A. The dovekeepers
Hoffman, A. The ice queen
Hoffman, A. The third angel
Hoffman, A. Turtle Moon
Hollinghurst, A. The stranger's child
Holt, V. The black opal
Holt, V. Secret for a nightingale
Hood, A. The Obituary Writer
Hooper, E. Etta and Otto and Russell and James
Hornby, N. High fidelity
House, S. A parchment of leaves
Hoyt, E. Duke of Midnight
Hoyt, E. Thief of Shadows
Hughes, A. Market Street
Humphreys, J. Nowhere else on earth
Ignatius, D. The Sun King
Irving, J. The fourth hand
Isaacs, S. Red, white and blue
Itani, F. Deafening
Jackson, B. Forged in desire
James, E. The Lady Most Willing
James, E. Seven minutes in heaven
James, E. Three Weeks With Lady X
James, E. The ugly duchess
James, E. When beauty tamed the beast
Jeffries, S. 'Twas the night after Christmas
Jenkins, B. Forbidden
Jiles, P. Enemy women
Jio, S. The violets of March
Jones, D. Second grave on the left
Jones, L. The Dixie Belle's Guide to Love
Jones, S. Outcast
Kaye, M. M. The far pavilions
Kennedy, D. The moment
Kerstan, L. The golden leopard
Kerstan, L. Heart of the tiger
Kilpack, J. S. A heart revealed
Kilpack, J. S. The vicar's daughter
Kinsella, S. I've got your number
Kittredge, W. The Willow Field
Kleypas, L. Brown-Eyed Girl
Kleypas, L. Crystal Cove
Kleypas, L. Rainshadow road
Koen, K. Through a glass darkly
Koontz, D. R. Innocence
Krauss, N. The history of love
Krentz, J. A. Dream eyes
Krentz, J. A. Trust no one
Krentz, J. A. Running hot
Kushner, D. M. The conditions of love
Law, S. K. The paper marriage
Layton, E. To wed a stranger
Ledgard, J. M. Submergence
Leithauser, B. The art student's war
Lessing, D. M. Love, again
Levithan, D. The lover's dictionary
Levy, D. Swimming home
Lewis, B. The brethren
Lewis, B. The missing
Lightman, A. P. Reunion
Lin, J. The Dragon and the Pearl
Linden, C. Love and other scandals
Lipman, E. The Inn at Lake Devine
Lipman, E. The pursuit of Alice Thrift
Lish, A. Preparation for the Next Life
Lively, P. Cleopatra's sister
Lively, P. Consequences
Lively, P. Moon tiger
Livesey, M. Banishing Verona
Livesey, M. The house on Fortune Street
Llywelyn, M. 1921
Lodge, D. Nice work
Lodge, D. Paradise news
Lohmann, J. Winning Ruby Heart
London, J. Wild Wicked Scot
London, L. The windflower
Long, J. A. Hot in Hellcat Canyon
Long, J. A. Wild at Whiskey Creek
López Barrio, C. The House of Impossible Loves
Lord, B. B. The middle heart
Lowell, E. Pearl Cove
Lytal, B. A map of Tulsa
MacKenzie, S. Bedding Lord Ned
MacLean, S. Never Judge a Lady by Her Cover
MacLean, S. No Good Duke Goes Unpunished
MacLean, S. One Good Earl Deserves a Lover
Makine, A. The woman who waited
Manseau, P. Songs for the butcher's daughter
Marion, I. Warm bodies
Martin, V. Trespass
Martin, W. Cape Cod
Mawer, S. The fall
McCarthy, C. Cities of the plain
McCracken, E. The giant's house
McCrumb, S. The ballad of Tom Dooley
McCullough, C. An indecent obsession
McDermott, A. At weddings and wakes
McDermott, A. Charming Billy
McDermott, A. That night
McEwan, I. Sweet tooth
McFadden, B. L. Gathering of waters
McGuane, T. Nothing but blue skies
McMillan, T. How Stella got her groove back
McMillan, T. Waiting to exhale
McMurtry, L. Sin killer
McNeal, T. To be sung underwater
McPhee, M. L'America
Mda, Z. The whale caller
Medeiros, T. The Temptation of Your Touch
Messud, C. The emperor's children

Schine, C. The three Weissmanns of Westport
Schlink, B. The reader
Schwartz, J. B. The commoner
Schwartzman, A. Eddie Signwriter
Scott, W. Rob Roy
See, L. Peony in love
Segal, E. Love story
Segal, F. The awkward age
Seth, V. An equal music
Settle, M. L. Charley Bland
Shalvis, J. Sweet little lies
Shan, S. The girl who played go
Sherwood, F. The book of splendor
Shields, C. The republic of love
Shinn, S. Jenna Starborn
Sholem Aleichem The nightingale
Shreve, A. Eden Close
Shteyngart, G. Super sad true love story
Simonson, H. Major Pettigrew's last stand
Simsion, G. The Rosie project
Smith, A. A bigger life
Smith, M. C. Rose
Soli, T. The lotus eaters
Sparks, N. The notebook
Sparks, N. A walk to remember
Spencer, L. Bitter sweet
Spencer, L. Morning glory
Spencer, L. Small town girl
Spencer, L. That Camden summer
Spencer, S. Endless love
Steel, D. The kiss
Steinhauer, O. All the Old Knives
Stott, R. The coral thief
Styron, W. Sophie's choice
Sundaresan, I. The splendor of silence
Swift, G. Mothering Sunday
Tabucchi, A. It's getting later all the time
Tanner, H. Vaclav and Lena
Tearne, R. Mosquito
Theroux, A. Darconville's cat
Thomas, R. All my sins remembered
Thomas, S. Beguiling the beauty
Thomas, S. Delicious
Thomas, S. My Beautiful Enemy
Thomas, S. Ravishing the heiress
Thomas, S. Tempting the bride
Thus bad begins
Tremain, R. Music & silence
Treuer, D. The translation of Dr Apelles
Trevanian The summer of Katya
Trevor, W. Love and summer
Trigiani, A. Very Valentine
Trollope, J. Friday nights
Trueblood, V. Seven loves
Tryon, T. The wings of the morning
Turgenev, I. S. First love and other stories
Turgenev, I. S. The torrents of spring
Turner, N. E. These is my words
Tussing, J. The best people in the world
Updike, J. Brazil
Uris, L. Redemption
Urquhart, J. Away
Urquhart, J. A map of glass
Vallgren The horrific sufferings of the mind-reading monster Hercules Barefoot
Van Booy, S. Everything beautiful began after
Van Dyken, R. Cheater
Vargas Llosa, M. Aunt Julia and the scriptwriter
Vargas Llosa, M. The bad girl
Vassanji, M. G. The Magic of Saida
Villars, E. The Normandie affair
Vine, B. The brimstone wedding
Wall, P. S. The Wilde women
Wallace, C. The blind contessa's new machine
Wallace, S. Montana dawn
Waller, R. J. The bridges of Madison County
Walter, J. We Live in Water
Walton, L. The strange and beautiful sorrows of Ava Lavender
Warner, K. Bride of the high country
Warren, S. M. Take a chance on me
Warrington, F. Midsummer night
Waters, S. The Paying Guests
Watkins, C. V. Gold fame citrus
Watson, B. The heaven of Mercury
The wedding date
Weiner, J. Good in bed
Wesley, M. Part of the furniture
White, R. M. A lady unrivaled
Wiggs, S. The Apple Orchard
Williamson, P. Heart of the west
Williamson, P. The outsider
Willig, L. The Ashford affair
Willig, L. The seduction of the crimson rose
Wilson, S. The fortune teller's daughter
Wind, R. In the midnight rain
Winspear, J. Elegy for Eddie
Wiseman, B. Plain paradise
Wolf, J. This scarlet cord
Wood, B. Perfect Harmony
Wood, B. Vital signs
Worsley, K. She rises
Wouk, H. A hole in Texas
Yarbrough, S. The realm of last chances
Yoshimoto, B. Asleep

ROMANCE FICTION -- TECHNIQUE
See also Authorship

Romancing the duke. Dare, T.

ROMANIA
Ausubel, R. No one is here except all of us
Furst, A. Blood of victory
Harding, G. Painter of silence
King, S. Thinner
Marks, J. Fangland

Wiesel, E. The forgotten
ROMANIES
Hugo, V. The hunchback of Notre Dame
McCann, C. Zoli
Merimee, P. Carmen
Penney, S. The invisible ones
The **Romanov** cross. Masello, R.
ROMANS -- EGYPT
Saylor, S. Raiders of the Nile
The **romantic.** Gowdy, B.
ROMANTIC FICTION *See* Romance fiction
ROMANTIC STORIES *See* Romance fiction
ROMANTIC SUSPENSE FICTION
O'Loughlin, E. Minds of winter
ROMANTIC SUSPENSE NOVELS
The Infatuations
Krentz, J. A. White lies
Sedgwick, M. A love like blood
ROMANTIC SUSPENSE NOVELS
See also Adventure fiction
ROMANTICISM IN ART
See also Art
ROME
Davis, L. The Ides of April
Downie, R. Tabula Rasa
Portrait of the mother as a young woman
Saylor, S. Raiders of the Nile
Saylor, S. Roma
Silverberg, R. Roma eterna
ROME -- 30 B.C.-476 A.D.
Asch, S. The Nazarene
Downie, R. Caveat emptor
Downie, R. Medicus
Downie, R. Terra incognita
Graves, R. Claudius, the god and his wife Messalina
Graves, R. I, Claudius
Harris, R. Pompeii
Lytton, E. B. L. The last days of Pompeii
Pears, I. The dream of Scipio
Sienkiewicz, H. Quo Vadis
Wallace, L. Ben-Hur
Yourcenar, M. Memoirs of Hadrian
ROME -- 510-30 B.C.
Downie, R. Medicus
McCullough, C. The first man in Rome
Saylor, S. The house of the Vestals
Saylor, S. The judgment of Caesar
Saylor, S. A mist of prophecies
Saylor, S. Rubicon
Saylor, S. The triumph of Caesar
Wilder, T. The ides of March
ROME -- BIOGRAPHY
See also Biography
ROME -- HISTORY -- DOMITIAN, 81-96
Davis, L. Master and God
ROME -- HISTORY
Downie, R. Semper Fidelis
Saylor, S. Wrath of the furies
ROME -- HISTORY -- NERO, 54-68
George, M. The confessions of young Nero
ROME -- HISTORY -- REPUBLIC, 265-30 B.C.
Saylor, S. Raiders of the Nile
Saylor, S. The seven wonders
Saylor, S. Wrath of the furies
ROME -- HISTORY -- SERVILE WARS, 135-71 B.C.
Kane, B. Spartacus
Romeo And/Or Juliet. North, R.
The **rook.** O'Malley, D.
The **room.** Karlsson, J.
Room. Donoghue, E.
A **room** with a view. Forster, E. M.
A **room** with a view. Forster, E. M.
ROOMMATES
Hodgen, C. Elegies for the brokenhearted
ROOMS
See also Buildings; Houses
Roosevelt, Eleanor, 1884-1962
About
Roosevelt, E. Murder at midnight
The **rope.** Barr, N.
ROPE SKIPPING
See also Games
The **rosary** murders. Kienzle, W. X.
ROSATO & ASSOCIATES (IMAGINARY ORGANIZATION)
Scottoline, L. Accused
Scottoline, L. Killer smile
Rose. Smith, M. C.
Rose of no man's land. Tea, M.
The **rose** rent. Peters, E.
Rosemary and Rue. Grant, M.
Rosemary's baby. Levin, I.
ROSES
See also Flowers
Roses are red. Patterson, J.
The **Rosie** effect. Simsion, G.
The **Rosie** project. Simsion, G.
ROSS, CARTER (FICTITIOUS CHARACTER)
Parks, B. The girl next door
The **Rotters'** Club. Coe, J.
Rough justice. Scottoline, L.
Rough justice. Higgins, J.
Rough weather. Parker, R. B.
The **round** house. Erdrich, L.
Roxanna Slade. Price, R.
ROYAL CANADIAN MOUNTED POLICE
Freedman, B. Mrs. Mike
The **royal** family. Vollmann, W. T.
ROYAL FAVORITES
Gregory, P. The other Boleyn girl
ROYAL HOUSES *See* Kings and rulers; Monarchy
The **royal** we. Morgan, J.
Royal wedding series
Hauck, R. How to catch a prince

ROYAL WEDDINGS
Morgan, J. The royal we
ROYALTY *See* Kings and rulers; Monarchy; Princes; Princesses; Queens
The **rubber** band & The red box. Stout, R.
RUBBER STAMP PRINTING
See also Handicraft; Printing
Rubicon. Saylor, S.
The **ruby** in her navel. Unsworth, B.
Ruby's spoon. Pietroni, A. L.
Rubyfruit jungle. Brown, R. M.
Rudolf II, Holy Roman Emperor, 1552-1612
About
Sherwood, F. The book of splendor
RUGBY FOOTBALL
See also Football
The **rule** of four. Caldwell, I.
RULERS *See* Emperors; Heads of state; Kings and rulers; Queens
Rulers of the darkness. Turtledove, H.
Rules for the reckless [series]
Duran, M. A lady's code of misconduct
Duran, M. Luck Be a Lady
Rules of civility. Towles, A.
Rules of deception. Reich, C.
The **rules** of magic. Hoffman, A.
Rules of prey. Sandford, J.
Rules of Scoundrels [series]
MacLean, S. Never Judge a Lady by Her Cover
MacLean, S. No Good Duke Goes Unpunished
MacLean, S. One Good Earl Deserves a Lover
Rum punch. Leonard, E.
Rumpole's return. Mortimer, J.
The **run.** Woods, S.
Run. Patchett, A.
Run silent, run deep. Beach, E. L.
Runaway. Munro, A.
RUNAWAY ADULTS
See also Desertion and nonsupport; Missing persons
RUNAWAY ADULTS
Saville, L. Henry and Rachel
RUNAWAY CHILDREN
See also Children; Homeless persons; Missing children
RUNAWAY CHILDREN
Walls, J. The Silver Star
Runaway horses. Mishima, Y.
RUNAWAY SLAVES *See* Fugitive slaves
RUNAWAY TEENAGERS
See also Homeless persons; Missing persons; Teenagers
RUNAWAY TEENAGERS
Katzenbach, J. What comes next
RUNAWAY WIVES
Lange, R. Angel baby
RUNAWAY WOMEN
Alexander, V. S. The Magdalen girls
RUNAWAYS (YOUTH)
Abu-Jaber, D. Birds of paradise
Byatt, A. S. The children's book
Chaon, D. Await your reply
Davis, A. Wonder when you'll miss me
Grossman, D. Someone to run with
Guterson, D. Our Lady of the Forest
Pyne, D. Twentynine Palms
The **runes** of the earth. Donaldson, S. R.
Runner. Perry, T.
Runner. Lee, P.
RUNNING
Benaron, N. Running the rift
Running hot. Krentz, J. A.
Running the rift. Benaron, N.
RURAL DEVELOPMENT
Parshall, S. Poisoned ground
RURAL FAMILIES
Lawson, M. Crow Lake
Slouka, M. God's fool
Trollope, J. Next of kin
Vernon, O. Eden
Warren, D. Juliet in August
RURAL FAMILIES -- IOWA
Smiley, J. Early warning
Smiley, J. Golden age
RURAL FAMILIES -- KENTUCKY
Taylor, A. The marble orchard
RURAL FAMILIES -- OKLAHOMA
Meadows, R. I will send rain
RURAL LIFE *See* Country life; Farm life; Outdoor life
RURAL LIFE -- PENNSYLVANIA
Bouman, T. Dry bones in the valley
RURAL POOR
Ghosh, A. The hungry tide
Silver, M. Mary Coin
RUSSIA
Arden, K. The bear and the nightingale
Furnivall, K. The red scarf
Grushin, O. The dream life of Sukhanov
Grushin, O. The line
The hall of singing caryatids
Hall, A. Quiller Balalaika
Harris, R. Archangel
Harrison, K. Enchantments
Holland, T. The archivist's story
Littell, R. The Stalin epigram
Makine, A. Dreams of my Russian summers
Malamud, B. The fixer
Marra, A. The tsar of love and techno
Morgan Jones, C. The silent oligarch
Pelevin, V. The hall of singing caryatids
Pohl, F. Chernobyl
Read, P. P. Alice in exile
Richler, N. Your mouth is lovely
Sholem Aleichem The adventures of Mottel, the cantor's son
Sholem Aleichem Tevye's daughters
Sholokhov, M. A. And quiet flows the Don

Sholokhov, M. A. The Don flows home to the sea
The slynx
Smith, T. R. Child 44
Smith, T. R. The secret speech
Smith, M. C. Tatiana
Solzhenitsyn, A. Cancer ward
Solzhenitsyn, A. In the first circle
Solzhenitsyn, A. One day in the life of Ivan Denisovich
Sorokin, V. Ice
Vollmann, W. T. Europe central
Wiesel, E. The testament
Wilkins, K. Veil of gold
The Year of the Comet
RUSSIA -- 1917-1945
Amis, M. House of meetings
Anatoli, A. Babi Yar
Eastland, S. Eye of the Red Tsar
Koestler, A. Darkness at noon
Makine, A. Music of a life
Pasternak, B. L. Doctor Zhivago
Rand, A. We the living
Sholokhov, M. A. And quiet flows the Don
Sholokhov, M. A. The Don flows home to the sea
RUSSIA -- ARMY -- OFFICERS
Uris, L. Armageddon
RUSSIA -- COURT AND COURTIERS
Boyne, J. The house of special purpose
RUSSIA -- HISTORY -- 1689-1801
Stachniak, E. The Winter Palace
RUSSIA -- HISTORY -- 1801-1917
Boyne, J. The house of special purpose
RUSSIA -- HISTORY -- 1900-1917
Boyne, J. The house of special purpose
RUSSIA -- HISTORY -- 1917-1921, REVOLUTION
See also Revolutions
RUSSIA -- HISTORY -- 1917-1925
Harrison, K. Enchantments
RUSSIA -- HISTORY -- 1917-1991, SOVIET UNION
Eastland, S. Shadow pass
RUSSIA -- KINGS AND RULERS
Lapierre, A. Between love and honor
RUSSIA -- MOSCOW
Bulgakov, M. A. The master and Margarita
Tolstoy, L. Childhood, Boyhood and Youth
RUSSIA -- NAVY
Clancy, T. The hunt for Red October
RUSSIA -- RURAL LIFE
Makine, A. The woman who waited
Rutherfurd, E. Russka
Sholokhov, M. A. And quiet flows the Don
Sholokhov, M. A. The Don flows home to the sea
Solzhenitsyn, A. Cancer ward
RUSSIA -- ST. PETERSBURG
Benioff, D. City of thieves
Dean, D. The madonnas of Leningrad
Dostoyevsky, F. Crime and punishment
Dunmore, H. The betrayal
RUSSIAN AMERICANS
Boswell, R. Century's son
Dean, D. The madonnas of Leningrad
Hannah, K. Winter garden
Shteyngart, G. The Russian debutante's handbook
Shteyngart, G. Super sad true love story
Tanner, H. Vaclav and Lena
The **Russian** debutante's handbook. Shteyngart, G.
The **Russian** girl. Amis, K.
RUSSIAN LANGUAGE
See also Language and languages
RUSSIAN LITERATURE
Red Spectres
RUSSIAN REFUGEES
Nabokov, V. V. Look at the harlequins!
Nabokov, V. V. Pnin
RUSSIAN SCIENCE FICTION
Roadside picnic
RUSSIANS -- AUSTRALIA
Keneally, T. A family madness
RUSSIANS -- ENGLAND
Amis, K. The Russian girl
Boyne, J. The house of special purpose
Lawton, J. Old flames
RUSSIANS -- GERMANY
Turgenev, I. S. The torrents of spring
Uris, L. Armageddon
RUSSIANS -- ITALY
Bezmozgis, D. The free world
RUSSIANS -- NEW YORK (STATE) -- NEW YORK
Alenyikov, M. Ivan and Misha
RUSSIANS -- UNITED STATES
Alenyikov, M. Ivan and Misha
Russka. Rutherfurd, E.
Rustication. Palliser, C.
Ruth Galloway mysteries [series]
Griffiths, E. The crossing places
Griffiths, E. The house at sea's end
RWANDA
Benaron, N. Running the rift
RYE (ENGLAND)
Heyns, M. The typewriter's tale

S

S. Updike, J.
S is for Silence. Grafton, S.
SABBATH
See also Judaism
Sabbath Creek. Mitcham, J.
Sabbath's theater. Roth, P.
SABOTAGE
Banks, I. The hydrogen sonata
Vonnegut, K. Player piano
SABOTAGE
See also Offenses against public safety; Strikes; Subversive activities; Terrorism

Sacagawea, b. 1786
About
Sargent, C. Museum of human beings
SACRAMENTS
See also Church; Grace (Theology); Rites and ceremonies
Sacre bleu. Moore, C.
Sacred. Lehane, D.
SACRED BOOKS
Jensen, J. Dante's equation
Sacred clowns. Hillerman, T.
Sacred country. Tremain, R.
Sacred hearts. Dunant, S.
Sacred hunger. Unsworth, B.
Sacrifice. Vachss, A. H.
Sacrilege. Parris, S. J.
SADISM
Templeton, E. Gordon
SAFARIS
See also Adventure and adventurers; Outdoor recreation; Scientific expeditions; Travel
Safe from the neighbors. Yarbrough, S.
Safe house. Vachss, A. H.
Sag Harbor. Whitehead, C.
SAGAS
Baker, J. The undertow
SAGAS
See also Folklore; Literature; Old Norse literature; Scandinavian literature
SAHARA
Bowles, P. The sheltering sky
Sail of stone. Edwardson, Å.
SAILING
See also Ships; Water sports
SAILING VESSELS
Stone, R. Outerbridge Reach
Sailor. Epperson, T.
SAILORS
Nordhoff, C. Men against the sea
SAILORS *See* Sea stories
SAILORS -- GREAT BRITAIN
Worsley, K. She rises
SAILORS' LIFE *See* Sailors; Seafaring life
SAINT BARTHOLOMEW'S DAY, MASSACRE OF, 1572
See also France -- History -- 1328-1589, House of Valois; Huguenots; Massacres
SAINT LOUIS (MO.)
Robards, K. Shiver
Saint maybe. Tyler, A.
SAINT PAUL (MINN.)
Franzen, J. Freedom
Saint Peter's Fair. Peters, E.
SAINT PETERSBURG (RUSSIA)
Makine, A. The life of an unknown man
SAINT THOMAS (UNITED STATES VIRGIN ISLANDS)
Yanique, T. Land of love and drowning
SAINTS
Asch, S. The Apostle
Cutter, K. The maid
Guterson, D. Our Lady of the Forest
Kirshenbaum, B. An almost perfect moment
Penman, S. K. Time and chance
Twain, M. Personal recollections of Joan of Arc
Vollmann, W. T. Fathers and crows
Werfel, F. The song of Bernadette
West, M. L. The devil's advocate
Williams, N. John
Saints and sinners. O'Brien, E.
SALANDER, LISBETH (FICTITIOUS CHARACTER)
Lagercrantz, D. The girl who takes an eye for an eye
Salazar, Antonio de Oliveira, 1889-1970
About
Antunes, A. L. The inquisitors' manual
SALE OF ORGANS, TISSUES, ETC.
Leonard, E. Raylan
SALEM (MASS.)
Barry, B. The lace reader
Kent, K. The heretic's daughter
Salem's Lot. King, S.
SALES AGENTS *See* Sales personnel
SALES PERSONNEL
Hansen, R. A wild surge of guilty passion
SALES PERSONNEL AND SELLING
Dewitt, H. Lightning rods
Edgerton, C. The Bible salesman
Flagg, F. Standing in the rainbow
Kafka, F. Metamorphosis
Vonnegut, K. Breakfast of champions
SALMON
See also Fishes
Salt. Zuber, I.
The **salt** eaters. Bambara, T. C.
The **salt** garden. Martinusen-Coloma, C.
The **salt** god's daughter. Ruby, I.
Salt houses. Alyan, H.
SALT LAKE CITY (UTAH)
Hunt, A. City of saints
Salt River. Sallis, J.
A **salty** piece of land. Buffett, J.
SALVAGE
Priest, C. The Family Plot
Salvage the bones. Ward, J.
Salvation city. Nunez, S.
Sam Acquillo mysteries [series]
Knopf, C. The last refuge
Sam Dryden novels [series]
Lee, P. Runner
Lee, P. Signal
Samaritan. Price, R.
The **same** sea. Oz, A.
SAME-SEX MARRIAGE
See also Marriage
SAME-SEX MARRIAGE
Lamb, W. We Are Water

SAMOAN AMERICANS
Malae, P. N. What we are
SAMURAI
Clavell, J. Shogun
Kirk, D. Sword of honor
Mishima, Y. Runaway horses
SAN FRANCISCO (CALIF.)
Allende, I. The Japanese Lover
Ostlund, L. After the Parade
SAN FRANCISCO (CALIF.) -- 19TH CENTURY
Donoghue, E. Frog music
SAN FRANCISCO BAY AREA (CALIF.)
Handler, D. We are pirates
San Francisco novels [series]
Moore, J. The night market
Sancha, of Provence, Queen, consort of Richard, King of the Romans
About
Jones, S. Four sisters, all queens
Sanctuary. Faulkner, W.
The **sanctuary** sparrow. Peters, E.
Sanctus. Toyne, S.
SAND DUNES
See also Seashore
Sandbox. Zimmerman, D.
The **sandcastle** girls. Bohjalian, C.
Sandrine's Case. Cook, T. H.
SANSKRIT LANGUAGE
See also Indian languages; Language and languages
SANTA CLAUS
Davies, V. Miracle on 34th Street
SANTA FE (N.M.)
McGarrity, M. Everyone dies
Millet, L. Oh pure and radiant heart
Santa Fe rules. Woods, S.
SANTERIA
Oyeyemi, H. The opposite house
SANTERIA
See also Religion
SANTURCE (SAN JUAN, P.R.)
Mundo cruel
Sarah. Halter, M.
Sarah (Biblical figure)
About
Halter, M. Sarah
Sarah Canary. Fowler, K. J.
Sarah Thornhill. Grenville, K.
Sarah's key. De Rosnay, T.
SARAJEVO (BOSNIA AND HERCEGOVINA)
McNally, T. M. The goat bridge
SARCOSUCHUS IMPERATOR
See also Dinosaurs
Sarum. Rutherfurd, E.
SASKATCHEWAN
Ford, R. Canada
Hay, E. A student of weather
Warren, D. Juliet in August
SASQUATCH
See also Monsters; Mythical animals
Sassafrass, Cypress & Indigo. Shange, N.
Sassoon, Siegfried, 1886-1967
About
Barker, P. The eye in the door
Barker, P. Regeneration
SATAN *See* Devil
The **satanic** verses. Rushdie, S.
SATANISM
Sidor, S. Pitch dark
Satin Island. McCarthy, T.
SATIRE
Abrams, D. Fobbit
Adams, D. The hitchhiker's guide to the galaxy
Adams, D. Life, the universe, and everything
Adams, D. The restaurant at the end of the universe
Adams, D. So long, and thanks for all the fish
Adiga, A. The white tiger
Amis, K. The Russian girl
Austen, J. Northanger Abbey
Austen, J. Sense and sensibility
Ballard, J. G. Millennium people
Barth, J. Giles goat-boy
Barth, J. The sot-weed factor
Begley, L. About Schmidt
Bellow, S. Humboldt's gift
Berger, T. Arthur Rex
Berger, T. Neighbors
Bernhard, T. Woodcutters
Bolano, R. Nazi literature in the Americas
Boulle, P. The bridge over the River Kwai
Boulle, P. Planet of the apes
Boyle, T. C. Road to Wellville
Brooks, M. World War Z
Cervantes Saavedra, M. d. Don Quixote de la Mancha
Chabon, M. Wonder boys
Chabon, M. The Yiddish policemen's union
Chatterjee, U. English, August
Cheever, J. The Wapshot chronicle
Cheever, J. The Wapshot scandal
Clarke, B. An arsonist's guide to writers' homes in New England
Claudel, P. The investigation
Coe, J. The Rotters' Club
Cusk, R. In the fold
Davies, R. Murther & walking spirits
Dewitt, H. Lightning rods
Diaz, J. The brief wondrous life of Oscar Wao
Dickens, C. Bleak House
Dickens, C. Little Dorrit
Dos Passos, J. 1919
Dos Passos, J. U.S.A.
Drabble, M. The sea lady
Drabble, M. The witch of Exmoor
Dunn, K. Geek love
Dunne, D. Too much money

Eco, U. Foucault's pendulum
Egan, J. A visit from the Goon Squad
Everett, P. L. I am Not Sidney Poitier
Fielding, H. The history of Tom Jones, a foundling
Fielding, H. Joseph Andrews and Shamela
The fish child
Fowler, K. J. Sarah Canary
Franzen, J. The corrections
Fuentes, C. The eagle's throne
Fuentes, N. The autobiography of Fidel Castro
Gaddis, W. A frolic of his own
García Márquez, G. One hundred years of solitude
Garcia Marquez, G. In evil hour
Gessen, K. All the sad young literary men
Gilman, C. P. Herland
Gogol', N. V. Dead souls
Golding, W. The inheritors
Grass, G. The call of the toad
Grass, G. Dog years
Grass, G. The tin drum
Gray, A. Poor things
Greene, G. Our man in Havana
Guterson, D. Ed King
Haldeman, J. W. The coming
Harris, R. The ghost
Heinlein, R. A. The moon is a harsh mistress
Heinlein, R. A. Stranger in a strange land
Heller, J. Good as Gold
Hensher, P. King of the badgers
Hiaasen, C. Nature girl
Hiaasen, C. Star Island
Hiaasen, C. Strip tease
Hoeg, P. The history of Danish dreams
Homes, A. M. This book will save your life
Hornby, N. About a boy
Houellebecq, M. The possibility of an island
Hrabal, B. I served the King of England
Hughes, R. A. W. A high wind in Jamaica
Huxley, A. Brave new world
Hynes, J. Kings of infinite space
Irving, J. A prayer for Owen Meany
Irving, J. The world according to Garp
Isaacs, S. After all these years
Isaacs, S. Close relations
Ishiguro, K. The remains of the day
Jacobson, H. The Finkler question
Jacobson, H. Kalooki nights
Jen, G. Mona in the promised land
Johnson, A. Parasites like us
Johnson, M. Pym
Joseph, M. Serious men
Kaufman, B. Up the down staircase
Kaufman, M. Bowl of cherries
Keilson, H. Comedy in a minor key
Klein, J. Primary colors
Kosinski, J. N. Being there
Kotzwinkle, W. The bear went over the mountain
Krauss, N. The history of love
Kunkel, B. Indecision
Lasdun, J. The horned man
Le Carre, J. The tailor of Panama
Lethem, J. Chronic city
Lewis, C. S. That hideous strength
Lewis, S. Babbitt
Lewis, S. Dodsworth
Lewis, S. Elmer Gantry
Lewis, S. Main Street
Lipsyte, S. The ask
Lodge, D. Nice work
Lodge, D. Paradise news
Maguire, G. Son of a witch
Marias, J. All souls
Martin, C. W. How to sell
Martin, V. Italian fever
Maugham, W. S. Cakes and ale
Mayle, P. Hotel Pastis
McCarthy, M. Birds of America
McCarthy, M. A charmed life
McCarthy, M. The group
McCarthy, M. The groves of Academe
McEwan, I. Amsterdam
McGrath, P. The grotesque
McLaughlin, E. The nanny diaries
Melville, H. The confidence-man: his masquerade
Messud, C. The emperor's children
Miéville, C. Three moments of an explosion
Mo Yan Life and death are wearing me out
Moore, C. The Serpent of Venice
Moore, C. A dirty job
Moore, C. You suck
Morrow, J. The philosopher's apprentice
Mortimer, J. Felix in the underworld
Mortimer, J. Quite honestly
Murakami, H. The wind-up bird chronicle
Murdoch, I. The book and the brotherhood
Murdoch, I. A fairly honourable defeat
Nabokov, V. V. Lolita
Nabokov, V. V. Pale fire
Nabokov, V. V. Pnin
Naipaul, V. S. A house for Mr. Biswas
Orwell, G. Animal farm
Orwell, G. Nineteen eighty-four
Palahniuk, C. Lullaby
Palahniuk, C. Rant
Parkhurst, C. Lost and found
Percy, W. Love in the ruins
Perrotta, T. The abstinence teacher
Perrotta, T. Joe College
Perrotta, T. The leftovers
Perrotta, T. Little children
Phillips, A. The tragedy of Arthur
Phillips, A. Prague
Pohl, F. The space merchants
Portis, C. Gringos

Powell, A. A dance to the music of time
Powers, J. F. Wheat that springeth green
Prose, F. Blue angel
Prose, F. A changed man
Prose, F. Household saints
Prose, F. Hunters and gatherers
Prose, F. My new American life
Prose, F. Primitive people
Pynchon, T. Against the day
Pynchon, T. The crying of lot 49
Pynchon, T. V.
Pynchon, T. Vineland
Raban, J. Waxwings
Reich, T. My Holocaust
Richler, M. Barney's version
Richler, M. Solomon Gursky was here
Robbins, T. Fierce invalids home from hot climates
Robbins, T. Half asleep in frog pajamas
Robbins, T. Jitterbug perfume
Robbins, T. Skinny legs and all
Robbins, T. Still life with Woodpecker
Robbins, T. Villa incognito
Roberts, M. Reader, I married him
Rosenblatt, R. Lapham rising
Rosenfeld, L. I'm so happy for you
Rosero, E. Good offices
Roth, P. The great American novel
Roth, P. The human stain
Rucker, R. v. B. Mathematicians in love
Russo, R. The straight man
Savage, S. The cry of the sloth
Savage, S. Firmin
Scalzi, J. The android's dream
Schaffert, T. The coffins of Little Hope
Scholz, C. Radiance
Shteyngart, G. The Russian debutante's handbook
Shteyngart, G. Super sad true love story
Skibell, J. A curable romantic
The slynx
Smith, Z. White teeth
Spark, M. Aiding and abetting
Spark, M. A far cry from Kensington
Spark, M. The girls of slender means
Spark, M. Loitering with intent
Spark, M. Memento mori
Spiotta, D. Eat the document
Stross, C. Glasshouse
Svevo, I. Zeno's conscience
Swift, J. Gulliver's travels
Tan, A. Saving fish from drowning
Thackeray, W. M. Vanity fair
Theroux, A. Darconville's cat
Tolkien, J. R. R. The fellowship of the ring
Tolkien, J. R. R. The return of the king
Tolkien, J. R. R. The two towers
Toole, J. K. A confederacy of dunces
Townsend, S. Number 10
Trumbo, D. Johnny got his gun
Twain, M. A Connecticut Yankee in King Arthur's court
Updike, J. S
Vargas Llosa, M. Captain Pantoja and the Special Service
Veselka, V. Zazen
Vidal, G. Hollywood
Vidal, G. Myra Breckinridge [and] Myron
Voltaire Voltaire's Candide, Zadig, and selected stories
Vonnegut, K. Breakfast of champions
Vonnegut, K. Cat's cradle
Vonnegut, K. Deadeye Dick
Vonnegut, K. God bless you, Mr. Rosewater
Vonnegut, K. Hocus pocus
Vonnegut, K. Jailbird
Vonnegut, K. Player piano
Vonnegut, K. Slapstick
Vonnegut, K. Timequake
Waugh, E. Brideshead revisited
Waugh, E. Decline and fall
Waugh, E. The loved one
Waugh, E. Vile bodies
Weldon, F. Chalcot Crescent
Weldon, F. The life and loves of a she-devil
Wells, K. Crawfish mountain
Westlake, D. E. Baby, would I lie?
Westlake, D. E. Trust me on this
White, T. H. The sword in the stone
Whitehead, C. Apex hides the hurt
Wibberley, L. The mouse that roared
With her in Ourland
Wolfe, T. A man in full
Wolfe, T. The bonfire of the vanities
Wolfe, T. I am Charlotte Simmons
Wolitzer, M. The wife
Woodrell, D. Give us a kiss
Yu Hua Brothers
SATIRE
See also Literature; Rhetoric; Wit and humor
SATIRE, AMERICAN *See* American satire
SATIRICAL FICTION
Adams, D. Mostly harmless
Gaiman, N. Good omens
Rushdie, S. The golden house
Townsend, S. Adrian Mole: the lost years
SATIRISTS
Clinch, J. Finn
Oates, J. C. Wild nights!
Twain, M. The gilded age and later novels
Satori. Winslow, D.
Saturday. McEwan, I.
The **Saturday** big tent wedding party. McCall Smith, A.
Saturday night and Sunday morning. Sillitoe, A.
Saturn's children. Stross, C.
Saturn's race. Niven, L.
SAUDI ARABIA
Ferraris, Z. Kingdom of strangers
SAUDI ARABIANS -- UNITED STATES

Dubus, A. The garden of last days
Saul and Patsy. Baxter, C.
Saunders, Mary
About
Donoghue, E. Slammerkin
The **savage** detectives. Bolano, R.
Savages. Pronzini, B.
Savages. Winslow, D.
Savannah; or, A gift for Mr. Lincoln. Jakes, J.
SAVANTS (SAVANT SYNDROME)
Hamilton, S. The lock artist
Save the last dance for me. Gorman, E.
Save yourself. Braffet, K.
SAVING AND INVESTMENT
See also Capital; Economics; Personal finance; Wealth
Saving fish from drowning. Tan, A.
SAVINGS AND LOAN ASSOCIATIONS
See also Banks and banking; Cooperation; Cooperative societies; Investments; Loans; Personal loans; Saving and investment
Say her name. Goldman, F.
Say nice things about Detroit. Lasser, S.
Say nothing. Parks, B.
Say Yes to the Marquess. Dare, T.
Say you're sorry. Robotham, M.
SCANDAL
Burrowes, G. Lady Maggie's secret scandal
Dare, T. A week to be wicked
Haigh, J. Faith
O'Hagan, A. Be near me
Schulman, H. This beautiful life
Shreve, A. Testimony
Walter, J. Beautiful Ruins
Scandal & scoundrel [series]
MacLean, S. The Rogue Not Taken
MacLean, S. A Scot in the dark
Scandal wears satin. Chase, L.
The **Scandalous** Adventures of the Sister of the Bride. Alexander, V.
Scandalous risks. Howatch, S.
SCANDINAVIA
Nevill, A. The ritual
SCANDINAVIAN LANGUAGES
See also Language and languages
SCANDINAVIAN MYTHOLOGY *See* Norse mythology
The **scar.** Dyachenko, M.
Scaramouche. Sabatini, R.
SCARBOROUGH (ENGLAND)
Link, C. The other child
The **scarecrow.** Connelly, M.
The **scarlet** letter. Hawthorne, N.
The **Scarlet** Pimpernel. Orczy, E.
The **scarlet** ruse. MacDonald, J. D.
Scarlet tides. Hair, D.
SCENERY *See* Landscape protection; Natural monuments; Views; Wilderness areas
Scenes from early life. Hensher, P.
Scenes from village life.
SCHEHERAZADE (LEGENDARY CHARACTER)
Yunis, A. The night counter
Scheherazade (Legendary character)
About
Yunis, A. The night counter
Schild's ladder. Egan, G.
Schindler's list. Keneally, T.
Schindler, Oskar, 1908-1974
About
Keneally, T. Schindler's list
Schismatrix plus. Sterling, B.
SCHIZOPHRENIA
Banasky, C. The suicide of Claire Bishop
Chaon, D. Await your reply
Cook, T. H. The cloud of unknowing
Greenberg, J. I never promised you a rose garden
Hunter, E. The moment she was gone
Moore, S. The big girls
Rosales, G. The halfway house
Tremblay, P. A Head Full of Ghosts
Vine, B. The minotaur
Wells, D. The hollow city
Wray, J. Lowboy
SCHIZOPHRENIA
See also Mental illness
SCHIZOPHRENICS
Banasky, C. The suicide of Claire Bishop
SCHMIDT, ALBERT (FICTITIOUS CHARACTER)
Begley, L. About Schmidt
Scholar. Modesitt, L. E.
SCHOLARS
Aciman, A. A. Call me by your name
Amis, K. The Russian girl
Bulgakov, M. A. The master and Margarita
Cumming, C. The Trinity Six
Davies, R. The rebel angels
Drabble, M. The sea lady
Eco, U. Foucault's pendulum
Frayn, M. Headlong
Gruber, M. The book of air and shadows
Hill, R. The Stranger House
Marias, J. All souls
Michaels, B. Houses of stone
Moore, G. The Sherlockian
Powers, R. Galatea 2.2
Redhill, M. Consolation
Stott, R. Ghostwalk
Updike, J. Roger's version
Verissimo, L. F. Borges and the eternal orangutans
White, E. The married man
School days. Parker, R. B.
SCHOOL LIFE -- DENMARK
Hoeg, P. Borderliners
SCHOOL LIFE -- ENGLAND
Bronte, C. Emma
Dickens, C. David Copperfield

Dickens, C. Nicholas Nickleby
Faulks, S. Engleby
Hilton, J. Good-bye Mr. Chips
Ishiguro, K. Never let me go
Swift, G. Waterland
Walton, J. Among others
SCHOOL LIFE -- FRANCE
Flaubert, G. Sentimental education
SCHOOL LIFE -- GERMANY
Hegi, U. Children and fire
SCHOOL LIFE -- IRELAND
Murray, P. Skippy dies
SCHOOL LIFE -- SCOTLAND
Spark, M. The prime of Miss Jean Brodie
SCHOOL LIFE -- UNITED STATES
Beard, J. A. In Zanesville
Bynum, S. Ms. Hempel chronicles
Cook, T. H. The Chatham School affair
Cooke, C. Daughters of the revolution
DeWoskin, R. Big girl small
Earley, T. The blue star
Goodman, C. Arcadia Falls
Hoffman, A. The river king
Hunter, E. The blackboard jungle
Just, W. S. Rodin's debutante
Kaufman, B. Up the down staircase
Klein, R. The moth diaries
Knowles, J. A separate peace
Pessl, M. Special topics in calamity physics
Picoult, J. Nineteen minutes
Rice, L. The geometry of sisters
Schulman, H. This beautiful life
Shreve, A. Testimony
Sittenfeld, C. Prep
Southgate, M. The fall of Rome
Sparks, N. A walk to remember
Wolff, T. Old school
The **school** of night. Bayard, L.
SCHOOL PRINCIPALS *See* School superintendents and principals
SCHOOL PSYCHOLOGISTS
See also Psychologists
SCHOOL SPORTS
Majors, I. Love's winning plays
SCHOOL STORIES
Bradley, A. As chimney sweepers come to dust
Capó Crucet, J. Make Your Home Among Strangers
Ishiguro, K. Never let me go
Knowles, J. A separate peace
McPherson, C. The child garden
Nicholls, D. A question of attraction
O'Mara, T. Crooked Numbers
Sittenfeld, C. Prep
Southgate, M. The fall of Rome
SCHOOL SUPERINTENDENTS AND PRINCIPALS
Cooke, C. Daughters of the revolution
Godwin, G. Evensong
Lam, V. The headmaster's wager
SCHOOL VIOLENCE
See also Juvenile delinquency; Violence
SCHOOL VIOLENCE
Picoult, J. Nineteen minutes
The **schooldays** of Jesus. Coetzee, J. M.
SCHOOLS
Bynum, S. Ms. Hempel chronicles
Grant, M. Down Among the Sticks and Bones
Ishiguro, K. Never let me go
Pierson, D. C. The boy who couldn't sleep and never had to
SCHOOLS -- FICTION *See* School stories
SCHOOLS, MILITARY *See* Military education
The **Schopenhauer** cure. Yalom, I. D.
Schopenhauer, Arthur, 1788-1860
About
Yalom, I. D. The Schopenhauer cure
Schroder. Gaige, A.
SCIENCE -- EXPERIMENTS
Locus solus
MacLean, S. One Good Earl Deserves a Lover
SCIENCE -- SOCIAL ASPECTS -- HISTORY -- 19TH CENTURY
Barrett, A. Archangel
SCIENCE -- SOCIAL ASPECTS -- HISTORY -- 20TH CENTURY
Barrett, A. Archangel
SCIENCE AND MAGIC
Grimsley, J. The ordinary
Harkness, D. E. The Book of Life
SCIENCE FICTION
See also Adventure fiction; Fiction
SCIENCE FICTION -- 20TH CENTURY
The big book of science fiction
SCIENCE FICTION -- 21ST CENTURY
The big book of science fiction
SCIENCE FICTION COMIC BOOKS, STRIPS, ETC.
See also Comic books, strips, etc.
SCIENCE FICTION FILMS
See also Motion pictures
SCIENCE FICTION GRAPHIC NOVELS
VanderMeer, J. Borne
SCIENCE FICTION WRITERS
Benford, G. Foundation's fear
SCIENCE FICTION, AMERICAN
The Best from fantasy & science fiction: the fiftieth anniversary anthology
Bradbury, R. Bradbury stories
Cronin, J. The passage
Dark matter
Dick, P. K. VALIS and later novels
Latin@ rising
Robinson, K. S. The Martians
The time traveler's almanac
Wolfe, G. The best of Gene Wolfe
The year's best science fiction
SCIENCE FICTION, ENGLISH

The time traveler's almanac
SCIENCE FICTION, RUSSIAN
Roadside picnic
Science in the Capital [series]
Robinson, K. S. New York 2140
SCIENTIFIC EXPEDITIONS
See also Voyages and travels
SCIENTIFIC EXPEDITIONS -- ALASKA
Ivey, E. To the bright edge of the world
SCIENTIFIC EXPEDITIONS
Kiernan, S. P. The Curiosity
Shepard, J. The world to come
VanderMeer, J. Acceptance
VanderMeer, J. Annihilation
VanderMeer, J. Authority
Williams, N. J. Landfalls
SCIENTIFIC EXPERIMENTS
Benford, G. Timescape
Doctorow, E. L. The waterworks
Hoeg, P. Smilla's sense of snow
Lem, S. His Master's Voice
Wells, H. G. The island of Doctor Moreau
Wilhelm, K. Death qualified
SCIENTIFIC JOURNALISM
See also Journalism
SCIENTISTS
Bradley, C. I Thee Wed
Brown, D. The Da Vinci code
Crichton, M. Jurassic Park
Crichton, M. The Andromeda strain
Crichton, M. Sphere
Doiron, P. The Precipice
Essex, K. Leonardo's swans
Goodman, A. Intuition
Gruen, S. Ape house
Haigh, J. The condition
Harris, R. The fear index
Kanon, J. Los Alamos
Klosterman, C. The visible man
Lem, S. His Master's Voice
Locus solus
Lodge, D. Thinks--
Morrow, J. The last witchfinder
Newitz, A. Autonomous
Patchett, A. State of wonder
Powers, R. The gold bug variations
Preston, D. Blasphemy
Rich, N. Odds against tomorrow
Roiphe, A. R. An imperfect lens
Rucker, R. v. B. Postsingular
Volpi, J. In search of Klingsor
Wiggins, M. Evidence of things unseen
SCIENTOLOGY
See also Cults
SCIPIONYX
See also Dinosaurs
A **Scot** in the dark. MacLean, S.
SCOTLAND
Cronin, A. J. The keys of the kingdom
Gabaldon, D. Outlander
Glass, J. Three Junes
Joss, M. Among the missing
Livesey, M. Criminals
MacBride, S. Blind eye
MacBride, S. Cold granite
May, P. The Blackhouse
Mina, D. Field of blood
McDermid, V. The distant echo
McPherson, C. Quiet neighbors
O'Donnell, L. Closed Doors
O'Farrell, M. The vanishing act of Esme Lennox
O'Hagan, A. Be near me
Pilcher, R. A risk worth taking
Pilcher, R. September
SCOTLAND -- 16TH CENTURY
Plaidy, J. The captive Queen of Scots
SCOTLAND -- 18TH CENTURY
Scott, W. The bride of Lammermoor
Scott, W. Rob Roy
SCOTLAND -- EDINBURGH
McCall Smith, A. Love over Scotland
McCall Smith, A. The world according to Bertie
Rankin, I. The impossible dead
Rankin, I. The complaints
Spark, M. The prime of Miss Jean Brodie
Welsh, I. Porno
Welsh, I. Trainspotting
SCOTLAND -- GLASGOW
Gray, A. Poor things
Mina, D. The end of the wasp season
Mina, D. Still midnight
Welsh, L. The cutting room
SCOTLAND -- HISTORY -- 18TH CENTURY
Gabaldon, D. Outlander
SCOTLAND -- HISTORY -- 19TH CENTURY
Dare, T. A week to be wicked
SCOTLAND -- RURAL LIFE
Buchan, J. The thirty-nine steps
Livesey, M. Eva moves the furniture
Pilcher, R. Winter solstice
SCOTS -- FRANCE
Faulks, S. Charlotte Gray
SCOTS -- UNITED STATES
Doig, I. Dancing at the Rascal Fair
Glass, J. Three Junes
Scott, Winfield, 1786-1866
About
Shaara, J. Gone for soldiers
SCOTTISH AMERICANS
Gabaldon, D. Written in my own heart's blood
A **Scourge** of Vipers. DeSilva, B.
SCOUTS
Dexter, P. Deadwood
McMurtry, L. Buffalo girls

SCOUTS AND SCOUTING
Berger, T. Little Big Man
Cooper, J. F. The last of the Mohicans
SCOUTS AND SCOUTING
See also Clubs; Community life
The **scrapbook** of Frankie Pratt. Preston, C.
SCREENWRITERS
Lazar, Z. Sway
Weiner, J. The next best thing
The **scribe.** Guinn, M.
The **scribe** of Siena. Winawer, M.
SCRIBES
Vantrease, B. R. The illuminator
SCULPTORS
Davidson, A. The gargoyle
Murray, S. Forgery
Pierpont, J. Among the ten thousand things
Stone, I. The agony and the ecstasy
Weisgall, D. The world before her
SCULPTORS
See also Artists
The **sculptress.** Walters, M.
SCULPTURE
See also Art; Decoration and ornament
The **sea.** Banville, J.
The **sea** captain's wife. Powning, B.
Sea change. Parker, R. B.
Sea glass. Shreve, A.
The **sea** lady. Drabble, M.
SEA LIFE *See* Marine biology; Navies; Sailors; Seafaring life
SEA MONSTERS
Groff, L. The monsters of Templeton
Sea of fertility [series]
Mishima, Y. The decay of the angel
Mishima, Y. Runaway horses
Mishima, Y. Spring snow
Mishima, Y. The Temple of Dawn
The **sea** of grass. Richter, C.
Sea of poppies. Ghosh, A.
The **Sea** of Tranquility. Millay, K.
SEA POETRY
See also Poetry
SEA STORIES
Beach, E. L. Run silent, run deep
Conrad, J. Lord Jim
Crichton, M. Pirate latitudes
Forester, C. S. Admiral Hornblower in the West Indies
Forester, C. S. Beat to quarters
Forester, C. S. Commodore Hornblower
Forester, C. S. Flying colours
Forester, C. S. Hornblower and the Atropos
Forester, C. S. Hornblower and the Hotspur
Forester, C. S. Hornblower during the crisis, and two stories: Hornblower's temptation and The last encounter
Forester, C. S. Lieutenant Hornblower
Forester, C. S. Lord Hornblower
Forester, C. S. Mr. Midshipman Hornblower
Forester, C. S. Ship of the line
Heggen, T. Mister Roberts
Lambdin, D. Hostile Shores
Lambdin, D. King's captain
Leonard, E. Djibouti
London, J. The Sea-Wolf
Martel, Y. Life of Pi
Matthiessen, P. Far Tortuga
Melville, H. Billy Budd, sailor
Melville, H. Moby-Dick; or, The whale
Melville, H. Omoo: a narrative of adventures in the South Seas
Melville, H. Redburn, his first voyage; White-jacket, or, The world in a man-of-war; Moby-Dick, or, The whale
Monsarrat, N. The cruel sea
Nordhoff, C. The Bounty trilogy
Nordhoff, C. Men against the sea
Nordhoff, C. Mutiny on the Bounty
Nordhoff, C. Pitcairn's Island
O'Brian, P. The unknown shore
O'Brian, P. Blue at the mizzen
O'Brian, P. The commodore
O'Brian, P. The golden ocean
O'Brian, P. The hundred days
O'Brian, P. The wine-dark sea
O'Brian, P. The yellow admiral
Perez-Reverte, A. The nautical chart
Poyer, D. Black storm
Poyer, D. The gulf
Poyer, D. The Whiteness of the Whale
Sabatini, R. Captain Blood
Smith, W. A. Birds of prey
Smith, W. A. Monsoon
Stone, R. Outerbridge Reach
Unsworth, B. Sacred hunger
Verne, J. The extraordinary journeys: Twenty thousand leagues under the sea
Verne, J. The mysterious island
Williams, N. J. Landfalls
Wolfe, G. Pirate freedom
Worsley, K. She rises
SEA STORIES
See also Adventure and adventurers; Adventure fiction; Fiction
SEA TRAVEL *See* Ocean travel
The **sea,** the sea. Murdoch, I.
SEA-SHORE *See* Seashore
The **Sea-Wolf.** London, J.
SEAFARING LIFE
See also Adventure and adventurers; Manners and customs; Voyages and travels
Kneale, M. English passengers
Powning, B. The sea captain's wife
SEAFOOD
See also Food; Marine resources
The **seal** wife. Harrison, K.

The **sealed** letter. Donoghue, E.
SEAMEN
Beach, E. L. Run silent, run deep
Birch, C. Jamrach's menagerie
Forester, C. S. Ship of the line
Ghosh, A. River of smoke
Ghosh, A. Sea of poppies
Heggen, T. Mister Roberts
Lambdin, D. King's captain
London, J. The Sea-Wolf
Matthiessen, P. Far Tortuga
Melville, H. Billy Budd, sailor
Melville, H. Moby-Dick; or, The whale
Monsarrat, N. The cruel sea
Nordhoff, C. Men against the sea
O'Brian, P. The unknown shore
O'Brian, P. Blue at the mizzen
O'Brian, P. The commodore
O'Brian, P. The golden ocean
O'Brian, P. The hundred days
O'Brian, P. The wine-dark sea
O'Brian, P. The yellow admiral
Poyer, D. Black storm
Poyer, D. The gulf
Smith, W. A. Birds of prey
Smith, W. A. Monsoon
Wouk, H. The Caine mutiny
SEAMEN *See* Sailors
The **seamstress.** Peebles, F. d. P.
The **seamstress** and the wind. Aira, C.
SEANCES
Rose, M. J. Seduction
SEARCH AND RESCUE OPERATIONS
Lichtenstein, A. Lost
Search for My Heart. Kramer, L.
Searching for Caleb. Tyler, A.
SEASHORE
Ferrante, E. The lost daughter
SEASHORE ECOLOGY
See also Ecology
SEASIDE RESORTS
Gholson, C. A fish trapped inside the wind
A **season** for the dead. Hewson, D.
Seasonal (Ali Smith) [series]
Winter
SEATTLE (WASH.)
Everett, P. Suder
Jacob, M. The sleepwalker's guide to dancing
Lynch, J. Truth like the sun
Semple, M. Where'd you go, Bernadette
SECLUSION *See* Solitude
SECLUSION
Rutherford, E. The Peripatetic Coffin and other stories
SECOND ADVENT
Silko, L. Almanac of the dead
The **second** book of lost swords: Sightblinder's story. Saberhagen, F.
Second child. Saul, J.
The **second** coming. Percy, W.
The **second** deadly sin. Sanders, L.
Second Foundation. Asimov, I.
Second Foundation trilogy [series]
Benford, G. Foundation's fear
Second grave on the left. Jones, D.
Second honeymoon. Trollope, J.
The **second** life of Nick Mason. Hamilton, S.
Second person singular.
SECOND WORLD WAR *See* World War, 1939-1945
SECRECY
Bates, J. F. Midnight at the Dragon Café
Belle, K. The marriage lie
Bennett, A. Smut
Fridlund, E. History of wolves
Gardner, L. The neighbor
Hunt, A. City of saints
Jerkins, G. The ninth step
Kent, C. The loving husband
Martinusen-Coloma, C. The salt garden
Oates, J. C. Evil Eye
O'Farrell, M. Instructions for a heat wave
Yates, C. J. Grist Mill Road
The **secret** between us. Delinsky, B.
The **Secret** Chord. Brooks, G.
The **secret** city. Emshwiller, C.
The **secret** diary of Anne Boleyn. Maxwell, R.
Secret for a nightingale. Holt, V.
The **secret** goldfish. Means, D.
The **secret** history. Tartt, D.
The **secret** history of Las Vegas. Abani, C.
The **secret** history of the pink carnation. Willig, L.
The **secret** life of bees. Kidd, S. M.
The **Secret** Life of William Shakespeare. Morgan, J.
The **secret** mistress. Balogh, M.
The **secret** pilgrim. Le Carre, J.
The **secret** place. French, T.
A **secret** rage. Harris, C.
The **secret** river. Grenville, K.
The **secret** servant. Silva, D.
SECRET SERVICE
Buchan, J. The thirty-nine steps
Cole, A. An Extraordinary Union
Deighton, L. Berlin game
Deighton, L. The Ipcress file
Deighton, L. London match
Downing, D. Potsdam station
Faulks, S. Devil may care
Fleming, I. Casino Royale
Fleming, I. Doctor No
Fleming, I. From Russia, with love
Fleming, I. Goldfinger
Fleming, I. The man with the golden gun
Fleming, I. On Her Majesty's Secret Service
Fleming, I. You only live twice
Forsyth, F. The Odessa file

Greene, G. The human factor
Greene, G. Our man in Havana
Hall, A. Quiller Balalaika
Hall, A. The Quiller memorandum
Hall, A. Quiller Salamander
Hall, A. Quiller solitaire
Harris, R. Enigma
Higgins, J. Confessional
Higgins, J. The eagle has landed
Higgins, J. Eye of the storm
Higgins, J. Night of the fox
Higgins, J. Rough justice
Higgins, J. Touch the devil
Ignatius, D. The increment
Lawton, J. Old flames
Le Carre, J. The honourable schoolboy
Le Carre, J. The little drummer girl
Le Carre, J. A most wanted man
Le Carre, J. Smiley's people
Le Carre, J. The spy who came in from the cold
Le Carre, J. The tailor of Panama
Le Carre, J. Tinker, tailor, soldier, spy
Ludlum, R. The Janson directive
Ludlum, R. The Prometheus deception
MacInnes, H. Ride a pale horse
Sansom, C. J. Winter in Madrid
Smith, T. R. Agent 6
Smith, T. R. Child 44
Smith, T. R. The secret speech
Stewart, M. Airs above the ground
Stross, C. The Jennifer morgue
SECRET SERVICE
See also Police
SECRET SERVICE -- GREAT BRITAIN
Cumming, C. The Trinity Six
Sansom, C. J. Winter in Madrid
Secret sisters. Krentz, J. A.
SECRET SOCIETIES
Bayard, L. The school of night
Bear, E. Ink and steel
Cogman, G. The invisible library
Neville, K. The eight
Neville, K. The fire
O'Malley, D. The rook
Portis, C. Masters of Atlantis
Ridgway, B. The river of no return
Rollins, J. The devil colony
SECRET SOCIETIES
See also Rites and ceremonies; Societies
The **secret** speech. Smith, T. R.
The **secret** wisdom of the earth. Scotton, C.
SECRET WRITING *See* Cryptography
SECRETARIES
Rindell, S. The Other Typist
Sheehan, A. The anxiety of everyday objects
SECRETARIES OF STATE
Benet, S. V. The Devil and Daniel Webster
Pesci, D. Amistad
Updike, J. Memories of the Ford Administration
SECRETARIES OF THE TREASURY
Liss, D. The whiskey rebels
SECRETARIES OF WAR
Doctorow, E. L. The march
Jakes, J. Savannah; or, A gift for Mr. Lincoln
SECRETS
Abbott, M. E. The fever
Addison, C. A harvest of thorns
Arango, S. The truth and other lies
Beagle, P. S. Summerlong
Cash, W. A land more kind than home
Dare, T. When a Scot Ties the Knot
DeWitt, P. Undermajordomo Minor
Gross, G. When she was gone
Harper, J. The dry
Karlsson, J. The room
Lackberg, C. The lost boy
Lamb, W. We Are Water
Lutz, L. The Passenger
MacLean, S. Never Judge a Lady by Her Cover
Milan, C. The Duchess War
Millay, K. The Sea of Tranquility
Moore, L. The Unseen World
Moriarty, L. The husband's secret
O'Farrell, M. This must be the place
Urza, G. All that followed
VanderMeer, J. Annihilation
Secrets of Eden. Bohjalian, C. A.
The **secrets** of Mary Bowser. Leveen, L.
The **Secrets** of Midwives. Hepworth, S.
The **Secrets** of Wishtide. Saunders, K.
SECTARIAN CONFLICT
Cornwell, B. The Empty Throne
Section 8. K'wan (Author)
Seducing an angel. Balogh, M.
Seduction. Rose, M. J.
SEDUCTION
Handke, P. Don Juan
Mawer, S. The fall
Nabokov, V. V. Lolita
Tolstoy, L. Resurrection
The **seduction** of the crimson rose. Willig, L.
See what I have done. Schmidt, S.
Seeing a large cat. Peters, E.
Seek my face. Updike, J.
SEGREGATION
See also Race relations
Barnett, L. K. Jam on the Vine
SEISMOGRAPHY *See* Earthquakes
SEISMOLOGY *See* Earthquakes
Seize the day. Bellow, S.
The **selected** short stories of Edith Wharton.
Selected stories. Munro, A.
The **selected** works of T. S. Spivet. Larsen, R.
Selection day. Adiga, A.

SELF
See also Consciousness; Individuality; Personality
SELF IMAGE *See* Personal appearance
SELF REALIZATION
Mastai, E. All our wrong todays
Self's punishment. Schlink, B.
SELF-ACCEPTANCE
Shumway, C. Ten girls to watch
SELF-ACTUALIZATION (PSYCHOLOGY)
Banville, J. The blue guitar
Bynum, S. Ms. Hempel chronicles
Eugenides, J. The marriage plot
Goodman, A. The cookbook collector
Grodstein, L. Our short history
Haddad, S. Guapa
Ko, L. The leavers
Lansens, L. The wife's tale
McCarthy, T. C
Mukherjee, B. Miss New India
Sears, M. Black Fridays
Shumway, C. Ten girls to watch
Walker, A. Now is the time to open your heart
SELF-ACTUALIZATION (PSYCHOLOGY) IN ADOLESCENCE
Gill, J. F. The gargoyle hunters
Walls, J. The Silver Star
SELF-ACTUALIZATION (PSYCHOLOGY) IN WOMEN
Buntin, J. Marlena
Lijia Zhang Lotus
Schwarz, C. The Edge of the Earth
SELF-CONFIDENCE
See also Emotions
Self-defense. Kellerman, J.
SELF-MADE MEN
Pomerantz, S. Rich boy
SELF-MUTILATION
See also Abnormal psychology
SELF-PERCEPTION
Lennon, J. R. Familiar
SELF-PRESENTATION
Gass, W. H. Middle C
SELF-PUBLISHING
See also Publishers and publishing
SELF-REALIZATION
Aciman, A. Enigma variations
Adler, H. G. The wall
Amend, A. A nearly perfect copy
Berg, E. Tapestry of fortunes
Haddad, S. Guapa
Haimoff, M. These days are ours
Kleypas, L. Rainshadow road
Ko, L. The leavers
Krauss, N. Forest dark
Lijia Zhang Lotus
Mastai, E. All our wrong todays
McEwan, I. The children act
Messud, C. The woman upstairs
Phillips, S. E. The great escape
Roy, A. The ministry of utmost happiness
Shumway, C. Ten girls to watch
Three strong women
Weiner, J. The next best thing
Wolitzer, M. The Interestings
Wu, J. The third son
SELF-REALIZATION IN WOMEN
Clark, G. The regulars
SELF-SACRIFICE
Dickens, C. A tale of two cities
Tolstoy, L. Resurrection
Wolitzer, M. The wife
SELFISHNESS
Balzac, H. d. Pere Goriot (Old Goriot)
SELFISHNESS
See also Personality
SELKIES
Lanagan, M. The brides of Rollrock Island
Ruby, I. The salt god's daughter
SELLING
See also Business; Retail trade
The **sellout.** Beatty, P.
SEMANTICS
See also Language and languages; Linguistics
Semiautomatic. Reuland, R.
SEMITIC PEOPLES
See also Ethnology
Semper Fidelis. Downie, R.
The **senator's** wife. Miller, S.
SENATORS
Buckley, W. F. Mongoose, R.I.P
Ellroy, J. American tabloid
Pesci, D. Amistad
Updike, J. Memories of the Ford Administration
SENATORS -- ITALY -- VENICE
Moore, C. The Serpent of Venice
SENECA INDIANS
Perry, T. Poison flower
SENEGAL
Three strong women
SENESCENCE *See* Aging
SENILE DEMENTIA
Healey, E. Elizabeth is missing
Sense and sensibility. Austen, J.
The **sense** of an ending. Barnes, J.
A **sense** of honor. Webb, J.
SENTIER (PARIS, FRANCE)
Black, C. Murder in the Sentier
Sentimental education. Flaubert, G.
The **sentinels** of Andersonville. Groot, T.
SEOUL (KOREA)
Wuertz, Y. G. Everything belongs to us
A **separate** peace. Knowles, J.
A **separation.** Kitamura, K.
SEPARATION (LAW)
See also Divorce; Marriage

SEPARATION (PSYCHOLOGY)
See also Interpersonal relations; Loss (Psychology)
SEPARATION (PSYCHOLOGY)
Edwards, K. The memory keeper's daughter
O'Nan, S. The good wife
Rice, L. The lemon orchard
September. Pilcher, R.
SEPTEMBER 11 TERRORIST ATTACKS, 2001
DeLillo, D. Falling man
Foer, J. S. Extremely loud & incredibly close
Maynard, J. The usual rules
McInerney, J. The good life
McPhee, M. L'America
Messud, C. The emperor's children
Price, R. The good priest's son
Schwartz, L. S. The writing on the wall
Tirza
Waldman, A. The submission
The **September** Society. Finch, C.
The **Septembers** of Shiraz. Sofer, D.
SEQUENCES (MATHEMATICS)
See also Algebra; Mathematics
SERBIANS -- ENGLAND
De Bernieres, L. A partisan's daughter
Serena. Rash, R.
SERIAL KILLERS
Abu-Jaber, D. Origin
Bauer, B. Blacklands
Bauer, B. Darkside
Black, C. Murder in the Bastille
Bolton, S. J. Now you see me
Box, C. J. The highway
Cain, C. Heartsick
Cain, C. Kill you twice
Cain, C. Let me go
Castillo, L. Sworn to silence
Coben, H. The woods
Cole, D. Ragdoll
Connelly, M. The scarecrow
Coulter, C. Split second
Dahl, A. Bad Blood
Dahl, A. Misterioso
DeSilva, B. Providence Rag
Ellory, R. J. The Anniversary Man
Ellory, R. J. A simple act of violence
Estleman, L. D. Gas City
Faye, L. The gods of Gotham
Ferraris, Z. Kingdom of strangers
Fielding, J. Heartstopper
Grafton, S. X
Hand, E. Available dark
Hayder, M. Birdman
The healer
Kerley, J. The death collectors
King, S. Mr. Mercedes
Koontz, D. R. Velocity
Koryta, M. Those who wish me dead
Lavender, W. Dominance
Lemaitre, P. Irene
Lindsay, J. P. Dearly devoted Dexter
Lippman, L. I'd know you anywhere
MacBride, S. Cold granite
Mark, D. The dark winter
Marwood, A. The killer next door
McKinty, A. The cold cold ground
McMahon, J. The One I Left Behind
Mina, D. The long drop
Moore, G. The Sherlockian
Morgan, R. K. Thirteen
Morrell, D. Murder as a fine art
Murakami, R. In the miso soup
Nelson, A. Bound
Nesbø, J. The thirst
Norton, C. What doesn't kill her
O'Brien, E. In the forest
Ohlsson, K. Unwanted
Palahniuk, C. Rant
Palmer, M. The last surgeon
Peace, D. Tokyo year zero
Pekearo, N. T. The wolfman
Perry, T. The boyfriend
Phillips, J. A. Quiet dell
Pinborough, S. A matter of blood
Pronzini, B. The hidden
Pyper, A. The killing circle
Ryan, H. P. The other woman
Smith, T. R. Child 44
The snowman
Tallis, F. Vienna blood
Thompson, J. The killer inside me
Verdon, J. Think of a number
Wells, D. The hollow city
Wolfe, I. A. The calling
Wortham, R. The rock hole
SERIAL KILLERS
See also Criminals; Homicide
SERIAL MURDER INVESTIGATION
Box, C. J. The highway
Cleave, P. Cemetery Lake
Faye, L. The gods of Gotham
Grafton, S. X
Guinn, M. The scribe
SERIAL MURDER INVESTIGATION -- ENGLAND -- LONDON
Cole, D. Ragdoll
Pinborough, S. A matter of blood
SERIAL MURDER INVESTIGATION -- SWEDEN
Dahl, A. Bad Blood
SERIAL MURDERERS *See* Serial killers
SERIAL MURDERS
Schmidt, S. See what I have done
SERIAL MURDERS -- SAUDI ARABIA
Ferraris, Z. Kingdom of strangers
SERIAL PUBLICATIONS

See also Bibliography; Publishers and publishing
SERIAL RAPE INVESTIGATION
Indridason, A. Outrage
Serious men. Joseph, M.
The **serpent** garden. Riley, J. M.
The **Serpent** of Venice. Moore, C.
The **serpent's** tale. Franklin, A.
Serpent's tooth. Kellerman, F.
SERPENTS *See* Snakes
SERVANTS
Amado, J. Gabriela, clove and cinnamon
Baker, J. Longbourn
Brooks, G. Year of wonders
Carey, P. Parrot and Olivier in America
Dickens, C. The posthumous papers of the Pickwick Club
Faulkner, W. Requiem for a nun
Faulks, S. Jeeves and the Wedding Bells
Gordimer, N. July's people
Morton, K. The house at Riverton
Scott, W. The bride of Lammermoor
Verne, J. Around the world in eighty days
SERVANTS *See* Household employees
Set in darkness. Rankin, I.
SET THEORY
See also Mathematics
Seven dials. Perry, A.
Seven for a secret. Faye, L.
Seven Gothic tales. Dinesen, I.
Seven houses in France. Atxaga, B.
Seven loves. Trueblood, V.
Seven minutes in heaven. James, E.
The **seven** wonders. Saylor, S.
SEVEN WONDERS OF THE WORLD
Saylor, S. The seven wonders
The **seven-per-cent** solution. Meyer, N.
Seveneves. Stephenson, N.
The **seventh** book of lost swords: Wayfinder's story. Saberhagen, F.
The **seventh** gate. Zimler, R.
Seventh son. Card, O. S.
The **seventh** well. Wander, F.
Sevenwaters trilogy [series]
Marillier, J. Daughter of the forest
SEWING
Duenas, M. The time in between
SEX
Amis, M. London fields
Amis, M. The pregnant widow
Auster, P. Invisible
Baker, N. House of holes
Baldwin, J. Another country
Barker, C. Imajica
Barnes, D. Nightwood
Beatty, P. Slumberland
Bock, C. Beautiful children
Burdett, J. Bangkok 8
Dewitt, H. Lightning rods
Eugenides, J. The virgin suicides
Faust, C. Money shot
Gaitskill, M. Veronica
García Márquez, G. Memories of my melancholy whores
Gray, A. Poor things
The hall of singing caryatids
Harrison, J. The great leader
Harrison, K. The seal wife
Hart, J. Damage
Herlihy, J. L. Midnight cowboy
Hoffman, N. K. Catalyst
Holmes, L. Barbara the slut and other people
Houellebecq, M. The possibility of an island
Hunter, E. Candyland
Irving, J. The fourth hand
Irving, J. A widow for one year
Jen, G. Mona in the promised land
Johnson, D. Nobody move
Johnson, D. Le divorce
Jong, E. Fear of flying
Lewis, M. G. The monk
Lowell, E. Pearl Cove
Martin, C. W. How to sell
McDermott, A. Child of my heart
McEwan, I. On Chesil Beach
McMillan, T. How Stella got her groove back
McMillan, T. Waiting to exhale
Minot, S. Rapture
Mishima, Y. The Temple of Dawn
Mundo cruel
Murakami, R. In the miso soup
Norman, H. The haunting of L
Oates, J. C. Blonde
Oates, J. C. Foxfire
O'Dell, T. Back roads
Palahniuk, C. Pygmy
Patterson, J. Along came a spider
Perrotta, T. The abstinence teacher
Perrotta, T. Little children
Prose, F. Goldengrove
Reynolds, M. The Starlite Drive-in
Richards, D. A. The bay of love and sorrows
Rinehart, S. Built in a day
Robbins, T. Fierce invalids home from hot climates
Roberts, M. Reader, I married him
Rossner, J. Perfidia
Roth, H. Requiem for Harlem
Roth, P. Indignation
Roth, P. Sabbath's theater
Roth, P. Everyman
Roth, P. The professor of desire
Schlink, B. The reader
Schulman, H. This beautiful life
Self, W. Dorian
Shreve, A. Testimony
Strout, E. Amy and Isabelle
Tea, M. Rose of no man's land

Templeton, E. Gordon
Theroux, P. My secret history
Updike, J. Memories of the Ford Administration
Updike, J. Roger's version
Vargas Llosa, M. The bad girl
Vargas Llosa, M. The notebooks of Don Rigoberto
Vidal, G. Myra Breckinridge [and] Myron
Vollmann, W. T. The royal family
Wallace, D. The Watermelon King
Walsh, H. Brass
Winton, T. Breath
Wolfe, T. I am Charlotte Simmons
Woods, S. Dirt
Woods, S. Reckless abandon
Yarbrough, S. The end of California
Yu Hua Brothers
SEX -- HANDBOOKS, MANUALS, ETC. -- AUTHORSHIP
Wolitzer, M. The position
SEX ADDICTS
Palahniuk, C. Choke
SEX BIAS *See* Sexism
SEX CRIMES
See also Crime; Sex
SEX CUSTOMS
Wolitzer, M. The position
SEX DISCRIMINATION
See also Discrimination; Sexism
SEX EDUCATION
Wolitzer, M. The position
SEX IN LITERATURE
Jacobson, H. The mighty Walzer
SEX IN MASS MEDIA
See also Mass media
SEX IN THE WORKPLACE
See also Sex
SEX OFFENDERS
Banks, R. Lost memory of skin
Castro, J. Hell or high water
Pronzini, B. The violated
SEX PROBLEMS
Hawkes, J. The blood oranges
Nabokov, V. V. Lolita
Rossner, J. Looking for Mr. Goodbar
Roth, P. My life as a man
Roth, P. Portnoy's complaint
Thomas, D. M. The white hotel
Tremain, R. Sacred country
Woolf, V. The voyage out
SEX REASSIGNMENT SURGERY
See also Surgery
SEX THERAPY
See also Psychotherapy
SEX TOYS
Palahniuk, C. Beautiful you
Sex wars. Piercy, M.
SEX-ORIENTED BUSINESSES
Dubus, A. The garden of last days
SEXISM
Hustvedt, S. The blazing world
Oates, J. C. Mudwoman
SEXISM
See also Attitude (Psychology); Prejudices
SEXOLOGISTS -- FAMILY RELATIONSHIPS
Wolitzer, M. The position
SEXUAL HARASSMENT
Prose, F. Blue angel
SEXUAL HARASSMENT
See also Sex; Sexual ethics
SEXUAL INSTINCT
Bilenchi, R. The chill
SEXUAL INTERCOURSE *See* Sex
SEXUAL ORIENTATION
Mootoo, S. Moving forward sideways like a crab
SEXUAL PERVERSION
Gay, W. Twilight
SEXUALLY TRANSMITTED DISEASES
Lowenthal, M. Charity girl
Seymour, Robert, 1798-1836
About
Jarvis, S. Death and Mr. Pickwick
Shades of grey. Fforde, J.
Shades of magic [series]
Schwab, V. E. A gathering of shadows
Shades of Magic [series]
Schwab, V. E. A Darker Shade of Magic
Shades of milk and honey. Kowal, M. R.
The **shadow** catcher. Wiggins, M.
Shadow country. Matthiessen, P.
The **shadow** district.
Shadow in serenity. Blackstock, T.
Shadow of freedom. Weber, D.
Shadow of night. Harkness, D. E.
Shadow of the rock. Mogford, T.
The **shadow** of the torturer. Wolfe, G.
The **shadow** of the wind. Ruiz Zafon, C.
Shadow on the crown. Bracewell, P.
SHADOW PANTOMIMES AND PLAYS
See also Amateur theater; Pantomimes; Puppets and puppet plays; Shadow pictures; Theater
Shadow pass. Eastland, S.
Shadow tag. Erdrich, L.
Shadow woman. Perry, T.
The **shadow** year. Ford, J.
Shadowbrook. Swerling, B.
SHADOWPACT (FICTIONAL CHARACTERS)
See also Fictional characters; Superheroes
Shadows in the street. Hill, S.
Shadows on the lake. Coco, G.
SHAKER HEIGHTS (OHIO)
Ng, C. Little fires everywhere
SHAKERS
Urquhart, R. The Visionist
Shakespeare's kitchen. Segal, L. G.
Shakespeare, William, 1564-1616

About
Adrian, C. The great night
Barber, R. The Marlowe papers
Bear, E. Ink and steel
Gruber, M. The book of air and shadows
Haig, M. The dead fathers club
Lovett, C. The bookman's tale
Marsh, N. Light thickens
Moore, C. The Serpent of Venice
Morgan, J. The Secret Life of William Shakespeare
North, R. Romeo And/Or Juliet
Phillips, A. The tragedy of Arthur
Tyler, A. Vinegar girl
Updike, J. Gertrude and Claudius
SHALE GAS INDUSTRY
Herrin, L. Fractures
Shalimar the clown. Rushdie, S.
Shallow grave. Harrod-Eagles, C.
SHAMANS
Griffin, K. Glass God
The **shambling** guide to New York City. Lafferty, M.
SHAME
See also Emotions
Shame and the Captives. Keneally, T.
Shame the devil. Pelecanos, G. P.
SHAN, TAO YUN (FICTITIOUS CHARACTER)
Pattison, E. The lord of death
Pattison, E. The skull mantra
Shane. Schaefer, J. W.
SHANGHAI (CHINA)
Kwan, K. China rich girlfriend
Shanghai girls. See, L.
Shanghai redemption. Qiu Xiaolong
SHANNARA (IMAGINARY PLACE)
Brooks, T. Wards of Faerie
The **shape** of snakes. Walters, M.
The **shape** shifter. Hillerman, T.
SHAPESHIFTING
Grimes, L. Quick fix
Shards. Prcic, I.
SHARED CUSTODY *See* Child custody
SHARED HOUSING
Millet, L. Magnificence
Shark. Self, W.
SHARKS
Benchley, P. Jaws
Sharp objects. Flynn, G.
Sharps. Parker, K. J.
Shatter the bones. MacBride, S.
Shattered pillars. Bear, E.
Shattered Sea [series]
Abercrombie, J. Half a King
Shattered sea [series]
Abercrombie, J. Half a war
The **shawl.** Ozick, C.
SHAWNEE INDIANS
Thom, J. A. Panther in the sky
She. Haggard, H. R.
She rises. Worsley, K.
She walks these hills. McCrumb, S.
She weeps each time you're born. Barry, Q.
SHEEP
Hardy, T. Far from the madding crowd
Shehu, Mehmet, 1913-1981
About
Kadare, I. The Successor
The **shell** seekers. Pilcher, R.
Shelley family
About
Shepherd, L. A fatal likeness
Shelley, Percy Bysshe, 1792-1822
About
Shepherd, L. A fatal likeness
Shelter. Palwick, S.
The **Shelter** Cycle. Rock, P.
The **sheltering** sky. Bowles, P.
The **sheltering** sky; Let it come down; The spider's house. Bowles, P.
SHELTERS FOR THE HOMELESS
Jackson, N. Who do I talk to?
SHENZHEN SHI (CHINA)
Lijia Zhang Lotus
Sheppard, Sam, 1923-1970
About
Ross, A. Mr. Peanut
SHERIDAN, ARCHIE (FICTITIOUS CHARACTER)
Cain, C. Kill you twice
Cain, C. Let me go
SHERIFFS
Freeman, C. All that I have
Grimes, M. Hotel Paradise
Johnson, C. Another man's moccasins
Letts, B. Shoot the moon
McCarthy, C. No country for old men
McCrumb, S. The ballad of Frankie Silver
McCrumb, S. If ever I return, pretty Peggy-O
McCrumb, S. She walks these hills
McLarty, R. Art in America
Meyer, P. American rust
Overholser, W. D. Law at Angel's Landing
Parker, R. B. Appaloosa
Parker, R. B. Brimstone
Parker, R. B. Gunman's rhapsody
Rickards, J. Winter's end
Russell, M. D. Doc
Sharfeddin, H. Mineral spirits
Thompson, J. The killer inside me
Wimberley, D. The king of Colored Town
SHERIFFS -- NEW JERSEY -- PATERSON
Stewart, A. Girl waits with gun
SHERLOCK HOLMES FILMS
See also Motion pictures; Mystery films
The **Sherlockian.** Moore, G.
Sherman, William T. (William Tecumseh), 1820-1891

About
Doctorow, E. L. The march
Jakes, J. Savannah; or, A gift for Mr. Lincoln
Shibumi. Trevanian
Shield of winter. Singh, N.
Shikasta. Lessing, D. M.
Shiloh and other stories. Mason, B. A.
Shine shine shine. Netzer, L.
The **shining.** King, S.
SHIP CAPTAINS
Ashford, J. What the duke doesn't know
Davies, J. D. Gentleman captain
Shalvis, J. Sweet little lies
SHIP CAPTAINS -- GREAT BRITAIN
Davies, J. D. Gentleman captain
Davies, J. D. The mountain of gold
Ship fever and other stories. Barrett, A.
Ship of fools. Porter, K. A.
Ship of the line. Forester, C. S.
SHIP PILOTS
See also Sailors
SHIPMASTERS
Clavell, J. Shogun
Furst, A. Dark voyage
Melville, H. Billy Budd, sailor
Simmons, D. The terror
Unsworth, B. Sacred hunger
The **shipping** news. Proulx, A.
SHIPS
Baker, K. The bird of the river
Butcher, J. The aeronaut's windlass
Davies, J. D. Gentleman captain
Grass, G. Crabwalk
McGuire, I. The North water
SHIPWRECK SURVIVAL
Martinusen-Coloma, C. The salt garden
Rogan, C. The lifeboat
SHIPWRECKS
See also Accidents; Adventure and adventurers; Disasters; Navigation; Voyages and travels
Gohlke, C. Promise me this
Martinusen-Coloma, C. The salt garden
SHIPWRECKS AND CASTAWAYS
Clavell, J. Shogun
Conrad, J. Lord Jim
Defoe, D. Robinson Crusoe
Eco, U. The island of the day before
Hansen, R. Exiles
Tournier, M. Friday
Wells, H. G. The island of Doctor Moreau
Shiver. Robards, K.
Shock wave. Sandford, J.
SHOEMAKERS
Trigiani, A. Very Valentine
The **shoes** of the fisherman. West, M. L.
Shogun. Clavell, J.
A **shoot** on Martha's Vineyard. Craig, P. R.
Shoot the moon. Letts, B.
Shoot the woman first. Stroby, W.
Shooting at loons. Maron, M.
The **shootist.** Swarthout, G. F.
Shopgirl. Martin, S.
SHOPLIFTING
See also Theft
Hallinan, T. Fields where they lay
SHOPS *See* Stores
The **Short** Fiction of Flann O'Brien.
SHORT FILMS
See also Motion pictures
The **short** forever. Woods, S.
The **short** history of a prince. Hamilton, J.
A **short** history of a small place. Pearson, T. R.
The **short** stories. Hemingway, E.
Short stories. Pirandello, L.
Short stories. Tolstoy, L.
SHORT STORIES
Adams, A. The stories of Alice Adams
Adichie, C. N. The thing around your neck
Agee, J. Let us now praise famous men; A death in the family, and shorter fiction
Aiken, J. The monkey's wedding, and other stories
Alenyikov, M. Ivan and Misha
Alexie, S. Blasphemy
American fantastic tales: terror and the uncanny from Poe to the pulps
American fantastic tales: terror and the uncanny from the 1940s to now
American West: twenty new stories from the Western Writers of America
Amsterdam, S. Things we didn't see coming
Anaya, R. A. The man who could fly and other stories
Anderson, S. Winesburg, Ohio
Antopol, M. The Unamericans
Apple, M. The Jew of Home Depot and other stories
Archer, J. And thereby hangs a tale
Asimov, I. The complete stories
Asimov, I. I, robot
Atwood, M. Stone mattress
Baldwin, J. Going to meet the man
Ballard, J. G. The complete stories of J.G. Ballard
Bambara, T. C. Gorilla, my love
Bandi The accusation
Bank, M. The wonder spot
Barnes, J. Pulse
Barrett, A. I. Love is power, or something like that
Barrett, A. Archangel
Barrett, A. Ship fever and other stories
Barry, K. Dark lies the island
Barthelme, D. Sixty stories
Bausch, R. Something is out there
Bausch, R. The stories of Richard Bausch
Baxter, C. Gryphon
Baxter, C. There's something I want you to do
Bear, G. The collected stories of Greg Bear

Beattie, A. The New Yorker stories
Beattie, A. Follies
Bellow, S. Seize the day
Bennett, A. Smut
Berry, W. That distant land
Best American mystery stories [date]
The Best American mystery stories of the century
The best American noir of the century
The Best American short stories
The Best from Fantasy & Science Fiction
The Best from fantasy & science fiction: the fiftieth anniversary anthology
The best western stories of John Jakes
Bierce, A. The complete short stories of Ambrose Bierce
The Big book of adventure stories
Bingham, S. Mending
The Black Lizard big book of Black Mask stories
Blackwood, C. Never breathe a word
Borges, J. L. Collected fictions
Bowles, P. Collected stories & later writings
Bowles, P. The stories of Paul Bowles
Boyle, T. C. The relive box and other stories
Boyle, T. C. Wild child
Bradbury, R. Bradbury stories
Bradbury, R. The illustrated man
Bradbury, R. The Martian chronicles
Brand, M. The collected stories of Max Brand
Brand, M. Max Brand's best western stories
Brave new worlds
Brockmeier, K. The view from the seventh layer
Busch, F. Rescue missions
Calisher, H. The collected stories of Hortense Calisher
Calling the wind
Campbell, B. J. American salvage
Capote, T. The complete stories of Truman Capote
Capote, T. Breakfast at Tiffany's: a short novel and three stories
Card, O. S. Keeper of dreams
Card, O. S. Maps in a mirror
Carter, A. Burning your boats
Carver, R. Collected stories
Carver, R. What we talk about when we talk about love
A Century of great Western stories
Chekhov, A. P. Longer stories from the last decade
Chesnutt, C. W. Stories, novels, & essay
Chopin, K. Complete novels and stories
Christie, A. Three blind mice and other stories
Clarke, A. C. The collected stories of Arthur C. Clarke
Cohen, J. Four new messages
Colette The collected stories of Colette
The complete short stories of Jack London
The complete short stories of Thomas Wolfe
The complete stories
Connell, E. S. Lost in Uttar Pradesh
Cooper, J. C. The future has a past
Cooper, J. C. Wild stars seeking midnight suns
Crane, E. You must be this happy to enter
Crane, S. The complete short stories & sketches of Stephen Crane
Crane, S. The portable Stephen Crane
Crane, S. Prose and poetry
Cross, A. The collected stories of Amanda Cross
Dahl, R. Collected stories
D'Ambrosio, C. The dead fish museum
Danticat, E. Krik? Krak!
The dark
Dark matter
Davis, L. The collected stories of Lydia Davis
Day, C. The circus in winter
Díaz, J. This is how you lose her
Dinesen, I. Seven Gothic tales
Dinesen, I. Winter's tales
Doctorow, C. Overclocked
Doctorow, E. L. All the time in the world
Doctorow, E. L. Sweet land stories
Doerr, A. Memory wall
Donoghue, E. Touchy subjects
Dostoyevsky, F. The best short stories of Dostoevsky
Doyle, A. C. The complete Sherlock Holmes
Doyle, R. Bullfighting and other stories
Drabble, M. A day in the life of a smiling woman
Dubus, A. Dirty Love
Due, T. Ghost summer
Dybek, S. I sailed with Magellan
Early short stories, 1883-1888
Eggers, D. How we are hungry
Eisenberg, D. The collected stories of Deborah Eisenberg
Eisenberg, D. Twilight of the superheroes
Endo, S. The final martyrs
Englander, N. What we talk about when we talk about Anne Frank
Enright, A. Yesterday's weather
Epstein, J. The love song of A. Jerome Minkoff and other stories
Erdrich, L. The red convertible
Estleman, L. D. Amos Walker
Eugenides, J. Fresh complaint
Evans, D. Before you suffocate your own fool self
Fallon, S. You know when the men are gone
Farmer, P. J. The classic Philip Jose Farmer, 1952-1964--1964-1973
Faulkner, W. Collected stories of William Faulkner
Faulkner, W. The Faulkner reader
Faulkner, W. Go down, Moses
Faulkner, W. Uncollected stories of William Faulkner
Fitzgerald, F. S. The short stories of F. Scott Fitzgerald
Fitzgerald, F. S. Six tales of the jazz age, and other stories
Fitzgerald, P. The means of escape
Flash fiction international
Ford, J. The drowned life
Ford, J. The empire of ice cream
Ford, R. A multitude of sins
Forester, C. S. Mr. Midshipman Hornblower
Forster, E. M. The collected tales of E. M. Forster

Fowler, K. J. What I didn't see and other stories
Frame, J. Between my father and the king
Frame, J. Prizes
Fuentes, C. The crystal frontier
The Future Is Japanese
Gaiman, N. Trigger warning
Gaiman, N. Fragile things
Gaitskill, M. Don't cry
Gao Xingjian Buying a fishing rod for my grandfather
Garcia Marquez, G. Collected stories
Garcia Marquez, G. Leaf storm, and other stories
Garcia Marquez, G. Strange pilgrims
Gardam, J. The people on Privilege Hill and other stories
Gavin, J. Middle men
Gay, W. I hate to see that evening sun go down
Geni, A. The last animal
Gifford, B. The stars above Veracruz
Gilchrist, E. The age of miracles
Gilchrist, E. Ellen Gilchrist: collected stories
Gilchrist, E. Flights of angels
Gilman, C. P. The Charlotte Perkins Gilman reader
Gogol', N. V. The collected tales of Nikolai Gogol
Gogol', N. V. The overcoat, and other tales of good and evil
Gordimer, N. Beethoven was one-sixteenth black
Gordimer, N. Life times
Gordimer, N. Loot, and other stories
Gray, A. Gutshot
Great stories of the American West
Greatest hits
Greene, G. Collected stories
Greene, G. The last word and other stories
Grisham, J. Ford County
Groff, L. Delicate edible birds and other stories
Gurganus, A. White people
Ha Jin The bridegroom
Hadley, T. Married love and other stories
Hadley, T. Sunstroke and other stories
Harte, B. The best short stories of Bret Harte
Harte, B. The Luck of Roaring Camp, and other tales
Harvey, J. A darker shade of blue
Hawthorne, N. Complete short stories of Nathaniel Hawthorne
Heathcock, A. Volt
Heiny, K. Single, carefree, mellow
Hemingway, E. The Nick Adams stories
Hemingway, E. The short stories
Hemingway, E. The snows of Kilimanjaro and other stories
Hempel, A. The collected stories of Amy Hempel
Henry, O. The best short stories of O. Henry
Henry, O. The complete works of O. Henry
Hernandez, F. Lands of memory
Hesse, H. The fairy tales of Hermann Hesse
Himes, C. The collected stories of Chester Himes
Hoffman, A. Local girls
Hoffman, A. The red garden
The horror in the museum, and other revisions
Houston, P. Cowboys are my weakness
Hughes, L. Short stories of Langston Hughes
Hughes, L. Simple's Uncle Sam
Hughes Double happiness
The Hugo winners
Hurston, Z. N. The complete stories
Hurston, Z. N. Novels and stories
I am the brother of XX
Irving, W. The complete tales of Washington Irving
Jackson, S. The lottery and other stories
James, H. Complete stories, 1864-1874
James, H. Complete stories, 1874-1884
James, H. Complete stories, 1884-1891
James, H. Complete stories, 1892-1898
James, H. Complete stories, 1898-1910
Jen, G. Who's Irish?
Jewett, S. O. The country of the pointed firs and other stories
Jhabvala, R. P. East into Upper East
Jhabvala, R. P. Out of India
Jin, H. A good fall
Johnson, B. More of this world or maybe another
Johnson, D. Jesus' son
Jones, E. All Aunt Hagar's children
Joyce, J. Dubliners
July, M. No one belongs here more than you
Kafka, F. Collected stories
Kafka, F. The penal colony: stories and short pieces
Karate chop
Kelly, J. P. The wreck of the Godspeed
Kennedy, A. L. What becomes
King, S. Different seasons
King, S. Four past midnight
King, S. Night shift
King, S. Nightmares & dreamscapes
King, S. Skeleton crew
Kipling, R. Collected stories
Lahiri, J. Interpreter of maladies
L'Amour, L. End of the drive
L'Amour, L. May there be a road
Lasdun, J. It's beginning to hurt
Later short stories, 1888-1903
Lawrence, D. H. Collected stories
Le Guin, U. K. The birthday of the world and other stories
Le Guin, U. K. Four ways to forgiveness
Le Guin, U. K. Orsinian tales
Lee, K. Drifting house
Leonard, E. Charlie Martz and other stories
Leonard, E. The complete Western stories of Elmore Leonard
Leonard, E. When the women come out to dance, and other stories
Leskov, N. S. The enchanted wanderer and other stories
Lessing, D. M. African stories
Leung, B. World famous love acts
Link, K. Get in trouble
Link, K. Magic for beginners
Lippman, L. Hardly knew her
The living dead

Lock, N. Love among the particles & other stories
London, J. South Sea tales
Lovecraft, H. P. At the mountains of madness, and other novels
Lovecraft, H. P. The Dunwich horror, and others
Lovecraft, H. P. H. P. Lovecraft
Ma Jian Stick out your tongue
Machado, C. M. Her body and other parties
Malamud, B. The complete stories
Malouf, D. The complete stories
The mammoth book of steampunk
Mann, T. Six early stories
Mantel, H. The assassination of Margaret Thatcher
Mason, B. A. Shiloh and other stories
Matheson, R. I am legend
Maugham, W. S. The best short stories of W. Somerset Maugham
Maugham, W. S. Complete short stories
Maurois, A. The collected stories of Andre Maurois
Maxwell, W. All the days and nights
McBride, J. Five-carat soul
McCrumb, S. Foggy Mountain breakdown and other stories
McCullers, C. Collected stories
McGuane, T. Gallatin Canyon
McHugh, M. F. After the apocalypse
Means, D. The secret goldfish
Mehta, R. Quarantine
Melville, H. The complete shorter fiction
Michaels, L. The collected stories
Miéville, C. Three moments of an explosion
Millhauser, S. Dangerous laughter
Mosley, W. Six easy pieces
Mowat, F. The Snow Walker
Mueenuddin, D. In other rooms, other wonders
Mundo cruel
Munro, A. Dear life
Munro, A. Family furnishings
Munro, A. Friend of my youth
Munro, A. Hateship, friendship, courtship, loveship, marriage
Munro, A. The love of a good woman
Munro, A. Open secrets
Munro, A. Runaway
Munro, A. Selected stories
Munro, A. Too much happiness
Munro, A. The view from Castle Rock
Murakami, H. Blind willow, sleeping woman
My mistress's sparrow is dead
The Mysterious West
Nabokov, V. V. The stories of Vladimir Nabokov
Narayan, R. K. The grandmother's tale and selected stories
Narayan, R. K. Malgudi days
Narayan, R. K. Under the banyan tree and other stories
New Cthulhu
The new space opera
New stories from the South: the year's best [date]
Niven, L. The Best of Larry Niven
The Norton book of science fiction
Oates, J. C. Black dahlia & white rose
Oates, J. C. Dear husband,
Oates, J. C. Faithless
Oates, J. C. Haunted
Oates, J. C. High lonesome
Oates, J. C. I am no one you know
Oates, J. C. Sourland
Oates, J. C. Wild nights!
Oates, J. C. Will you always love me? and other stories
Object lessons
O'Brien, E. Saints and sinners
O'Brien, E. A fanatic heart
O'Brien, E. Lantern slides
O'Brien, T. The things they carried
O'Connor, F. Collected works
O'Connor, F. The complete stories
O'Connor, F. Everything that rises must converge
O'Connor, F. Collected stories
O'Faolain, S. The collected stories of Sean O'Faolain
O'Hara, J. Collected stories of John O'Hara
Olsen, T. Tell me a riddle
One thousand and one nights
Osondu, E. C. Voice of America
The Oxford book of American detective stories
The Oxford book of American short stories
The Oxford book of English ghost stories
The Oxford book of English short stories
The Oxford book of gothic tales
The Oxford book of Irish short stories
The Oxford book of Latin American short stories
The Oxford book of modern fairy tales
The Oxford book of science fiction stories
The Oxford book of short stories
The Oxford book of spy stories
The Oxford book of twentieth-century ghost stories
Ozick, C. Dictation
Packer, A. Swim back to me
Packer, Z. Drinking coffee elsewhere
Paley, G. The collected stories
Paretsky, S. Windy City blues
Paton, A. Tales from a troubled land
Pearlman, E. Binocular vision
Penguin book of gay short fiction
The Penguin book of lesbian short stories
Perillo, L. Happiness is a chemical in the brain
Peters, E. A rare Benedictine
Peterson, P. W. Women in the grove
Petrushevskaya, L. There once lived a woman who tried to kill her neighbor's baby
Pilcher, R. Flowers in the rain & other stories
Pirandello, L. Short stories
Poe, E. A. Complete stories and poems of Edgar Allan Poe
Poe's children
Pollock, D. R. Knockemstiff
Porter, K. A. The collected stories of Katherine Anne Porter
Porter, K. A. Flowering Judas and other stories

Porter, K. A. The leaning tower, and other stories
Proulx, A. Bad dirt
Proulx, A. Close range
Proulx, A. Fine just the way it is
Proust, M. The complete short stories of Marcel Proust
Pushkin, A. S. Alexander Pushkin: complete prose fiction
Pym, B. Civil to strangers and other writings
Qiu Xiaolong Years of Red Dust
Rash, R. Burning bright
Ray, S. American masculine
Rendell, R. Blood lines
Ring around the bases
Robinson, K. S. The Martians
Robinson, R. A perfect stranger
Ross, A. Ladies and gentlemen
Roth, J. The collected stories of Joseph Roth
Roth, P. Goodbye, Columbus, and five short stories
Ruiz-Camacho, A. Barefoot dogs
Runcie, J. Sidney Chambers and the Forgiveness of Sins
Rushdie, S. East, west
Russell, K. St. Lucy's home for girls raised by wolves
Russell, K. Vampires in the lemon grove
Russo, R. The whore's child
Rutherford, E. The Peripatetic Coffin and other stories
Ryman, G. Paradise tales
Saki The short stories of Saki
Salinger, J. D. Nine stories
Salter, J. Last night
Sartre, J. P. Intimacy, and other stories
Saunders, G. In persuasion nation
Saunders, G. Tenth of December
Sayers, D. L. Lord Peter
Saylor, S. The house of the Vestals
Scenes from village life
Schaefer, J. W. The collected stories of Jack Schaefer
Schappell, E. Blueprints for building better girls
Scholz, C. The amount to carry
Scott, J. Everybody loves somebody
Sedaris, D. Holidays on ice
Segal, L. G. Shakespeare's kitchen
Seiffert, R. Field study
The selected short stories of Edith Wharton
Selgin, P. Drowning lessons
Shabtai, Y. Uncle Peretz takes off
Shaw, I. Short stories: five decades
Sheehy, H. The invisibles
Shepard, J. Like you'd understand, anyway
Shepard, J. You think that's bad
Shepard, S. Day out of days
Shepard, S. Great dream of heaven
Sholem Aleichem Tevye the dairyman and The railroad stories
Sholem Aleichem Tevye's daughters
Sidhu, R. S. Good Indian Girls
Silber, J. Fools
Silber, J. Ideas of heaven
Sillitoe, A. The loneliness of the long-distance runner
Singer, I. B. Collected stories: A friend of Kafka to Passions
Singer, I. B. Collected stories: Gimpel the fool to The letter writer
Singer, I. B. Collected stories: One night in Brazil to The death of Methuselah
The Sleeper wakes
Smith, L. Mrs. Darcy and the blue-eyed stranger
Spark, M. Open to the public
Spencer, E. The southern woman
Spencer, E. The stories of Elizabeth Spencer
Stafford, J. The collected stories of Jean Stafford
Steinbeck, J. The long valley
Stevenson, R. L. The complete short stories
Stone, R. Fun with problems
Stories
Strout, E. Olive Kitteridge
Summer lies
Sundaresan, I. In the Convent of Little Flowers
Swanwick, M. The dog said bow-wow
Swift, G. England and other stories
Szalay, D. All that man is
Thomas, D. The collected stories
Thon, M. R. In this light
Tinti, H. Animal crackers
Toer, P. A. All that is gone
Tóibín, C. The empty family
Tóibín, C. Mothers and sons
Tolkien, J. R. R. The Silmarillion
Tolstoy, L. Divine and human and other stories
Tolstoy, L. Short stories
Transgressions
Tremain, R. The American Lover
Trevor, W. A bit on the side
Tsan-hsueh Blue light in the sky & other stories
Twain, M. The complete short stories of Mark Twain
Under African skies
The Unforgetting heart: an anthology of short stories by African American women (1859-1993)
Updike, J. The afterlife and other stories
Updike, J. Licks of love
Updike, J. My father's tears and other stories
Updike, J. Pigeon feathers, and other stories
Updike, J. Trust me
Van de Wetering, J. The Amsterdam cops
VanderMeer, J. The third bear
Vann, D. Legend of a suicide
Vapnyar, L. Broccoli and other tales of food and love
The vicious circle
Vidal, G. Clouds and eclipses
Vollmann, W. T. Last stories and other stories
Voltaire Candide and other stories
Voltaire Voltaire's Candide, Zadig, and selected stories
Vonnegut, K. Armageddon in retrospect
Vonnegut, K. Bagombo snuff box: uncollected short fiction
Vonnegut, K. Look at the birdie
Vonnegut, K. Welcome to the monkey house
Vonnegut, K. While mortals sleep

Walker, A. The way forward is with a broken heart
Walker, A. You can't keep a good woman down
Wallace, D. F. Oblivion
Walter, J. We Live in Water
Watkins, C. V. Battleborn
Watson, B. Aliens in the prime of their lives
Waugh, E. The complete stories of Evelyn Waugh
Wells, H. G. The complete short stories of H. G. Wells
Welty, E. The collected stories of Eudora Welty
We're flying
The Wesleyan anthology of science fiction
West, J. The friendly persuasion
Westlake, D. E. Thieves' dozen
Westward
Wharton, E. Collected stories, 1891-1910
Wharton, E. Collected stories, 1911-1937
While the women are sleeping
The white people and other weird stories
Wickersham, J. The news from Spain
Wideman, J. E. The stories of John Edgar Wideman
Williams, J. 99 stories of God
Williams, J. Honored guest
Williams, T. Collected stories
Wodehouse, P. G. Tales from the Drones Club
Wodehouse, P. G. A Wodehouse bestiary
Wodehouse, P. G. The world of Jeeves
Wolfe, G. The best of Gene Wolfe
Wolff, T. Our story begins
A Woman's eye
Woodrell, D. The outlaw album
Woolf, V. The complete shorter fiction of Virginia Woolf
Wright, R. Eight men
Wright, R. Uncle Tom's children
Yates, R. The collected stories of Richard Yates
The Year's best fantasy and horror
Year's best science fiction
Year's Best SF 18
Yiyun Li A thousand years of good prayers
Yoon, P. The mountain
Yoon, P. Once the shore
Yoshimoto, B. Asleep
Zola, E. Three faces of love

SHORT STORIES -- BY INDIVIDUAL AUTHORS

Adichie, C. N. The thing around your neck
Agee, J. Let us now praise famous men; A death in the family, and shorter fiction
Amsterdam, S. Things we didn't see coming
Anaya, R. A. The man who could fly and other stories
Apple, M. The Jew of Home Depot and other stories
Ballard, J. G. The complete stories of J.G. Ballard
Bank, M. The wonder spot
Barrett, A. Ship fever and other stories
Bausch, R. Something is out there
Bausch, R. The stories of Richard Bausch
Baxter, C. Gryphon
Beattie, A. The New Yorker stories
Beattie, A. Follies
Bingham, S. Mending
Bolano, R. Last evenings on Earth
Boyle, T. C. Wild child
Busch, F. Rescue missions
Butler, R. O. A good scent from a strange mountain
Capote, T. The complete stories of Truman Capote
Carter, A. Burning your boats
Carver, R. Collected stories
Complete short stories
Danticat, E. Krik? Krak!
Davis, L. The collected stories of Lydia Davis
Doctorow, E. L. All the time in the world
Doctorow, E. L. Sweet land stories
Doerr, A. Memory wall
Donoghue, E. Touchy subjects
Drabble, M. A day in the life of a smiling woman
Eisenberg, D. The collected stories of Deborah Eisenberg
Eisenberg, D. Twilight of the superheroes
Endo, S. The final martyrs
Enright, A. Yesterday's weather
Erdrich, L. The red convertible
Estleman, L. D. Amos Walker
Evans, D. Before you suffocate your own fool self
Faber, M. The courage consort
Fallon, S. You know when the men are gone
Fuentes, C. The crystal frontier
Gaiman, N. Fragile things
Gaitskill, M. Don't cry
Garcia Marquez, G. Strange pilgrims
Gardam, J. The people on Privilege Hill and other stories
Gilchrist, E. The age of miracles
Gordimer, N. Beethoven was one-sixteenth black
Gordimer, N. Life times
Grisham, J. Ford County
Gurganus, A. White people
Heathcock, A. Volt
Hempel, A. The collected stories of Amy Hempel
Houston, P. Cowboys are my weakness
Hughes Double happiness
Jackson, S. Novels and stories
Jin, H. A good fall
Johnson, D. Jesus' son
Jones, E. All Aunt Hagar's children
July, M. No one belongs here more than you
King, S. Full dark, no stars
Link, K. Magic for beginners
Lovecraft, H. P. H. P. Lovecraft
Malamud, B. The complete stories
Mann, T. Six early stories
McCrumb, S. Foggy Mountain breakdown and other stories
McGuane, T. Gallatin Canyon
Means, D. The secret goldfish
Michaels, L. The collected stories
Millhauser, S. Dangerous laughter
Munro, A. Friend of my youth
Munro, A. Hateship, friendship, courtship, loveship, marriage

Munro, A. Open secrets
Munro, A. Runaway
Munro, A. Too much happiness
Munro, A. The view from Castle Rock
Oates, J. C. Dear husband,
Oates, J. C. High lonesome
Oates, J. C. I am no one you know
Oates, J. C. Sourland
Oates, J. C. Wild nights!
Oates, J. C. Will you always love me? and other stories
O'Brien, E. Saints and sinners
O'Connor, F. Collected works
Osondu, E. C. Voice of America
Ozick, C. Dictation
Packer, A. Swim back to me
Paley, G. The collected stories
Pearlman, E. Binocular vision
Petrushevskaya, L. There once lived a woman who tried to kill her neighbor's baby
Pollock, D. R. Knockemstiff
Proulx, A. Bad dirt
Proulx, A. Fine just the way it is
Pym, B. Civil to strangers and other writings
Qiu Xiaolong Years of Red Dust
Rash, R. Burning bright
Robinson, R. A perfect stranger
Ross, A. Ladies and gentlemen
Salter, J. Last night
Saunders, G. In persuasion nation
Scenes from village life
Schappell, E. Blueprints for building better girls
Scott, J. Everybody loves somebody
Segal, L. G. Shakespeare's kitchen
The selected short stories of Edith Wharton
Selgin, P. Drowning lessons
Shepard, J. You think that's bad
Shepard, S. Day out of days
Silber, J. Ideas of heaven
Singer, I. B. Collected stories: A friend of Kafka to Passions
Smith, L. Mrs. Darcy and the blue-eyed stranger
Spark, M. Open to the public
Stevenson, R. L. The complete short stories
Stone, R. Fun with problems
Tóibín, C. The empty family
Trevor, W. A bit on the side
Updike, J. The afterlife and other stories
Updike, J. My father's tears and other stories
Vann, D. Legend of a suicide
Vapnyar, L. Broccoli and other tales of food and love
Vonnegut, K. Look at the birdie
Wallace, D. F. Brief interviews with hideous men
Watson, B. Aliens in the prime of their lives
Wharton, E. Collected stories, 1891-1910
Wharton, E. Novellas and other writings
While the women are sleeping
Williams, J. Honored guest
Wolfe, G. The best of Gene Wolfe
Wolff, T. Our story begins
Woodrell, D. The outlaw album
Yiyun Li A thousand years of good prayers
Yoon, P. Once the shore

SHORT STORIES -- COLLECTIONS
Acampora, L. The Wonder Garden
Barkan, J. Mexico
Bergman, M. M. Birds of a lesser paradise
Berlin, L. A manual for cleaning women
Butler, R. O. A good scent from a strange mountain
Coffey, M. The Business of Naming Things
The Doll Collection
Earley, T. Mr. Tall
Faye, L. The whole art of detection
Founds, K. When mystical creatures attack!
Gay, R. Difficult women
Gustine, A. You should pity us instead
Harrison, J. The Ancient Minstrel
Holmes, L. Barbara the slut and other people
Hunt, S. The dark dark
Invisible planets
Johnson, A. Fortune smiles
Johnson, D. The largesse of the sea maiden
Knight, M. Eveningland
Marra, A. The tsar of love and techno
McCann, C. Thirteen ways of looking
Nguyen, V. T. The Refugees
O'Brien, E. The love object
Parameswaran, R. I am an executioner
Rogues
Shepard, J. The world to come
Swanwick, M. Not So Much, Said the Cat
Wallace, D. F. Brief interviews with hideous men
Williams, J. The visiting privilege
Wink, C. Dog run moon

The **short** stories of F. Scott Fitzgerald. Fitzgerald, F. S.
Short stories of Langston Hughes. Hughes, L.
The **short** stories of Saki. Saki

SHORT STORIES, ENGLISH
Guo, X. I am China

Short stories: five decades. Shaw, I.

SHORT STORY -- AUTHORSHIP
Object lessons

SHORT STORY WRITERS
Aira, C. The literary conference
Atkins, A. Devil's garden
Bayard, L. The pale blue eye
Benford, G. Foundation's fear
Chesnutt, C. W. Stories, novels, & essay
Clinch, J. Finn
Cunningham, M. The hours
Fairstein, L. Entombed
Fuentes, C. The old gringo
Holland, T. The archivist's story
Johnson, M. Pym
Jordan, H. When she woke
Lashner, W. Kockroach

Marks, J. Fangland
Martin, V. Mary Reilly
McLain, P. The Paris wife
Moore, G. The Sherlockian
Nabokov, V. V. Novels and memoirs, 1941-1951
Oates, J. C. Wild nights!
Pearl, M. The Poe shadow
Powers, K. Capote in Kansas
Reyn, I. What happened to Anna K.
Rose, J. Blackest bird
Tsypkin, L. Summer in Baden-Baden
Twain, M. The gilded age and later novels
Verissimo, L. F. Borges and the eternal orangutans
Walker, A. The way forward is with a broken heart
Short straw. Woods, S.
The **shortest** way home. Fay, J.
SHORTWAVE RADIO
See also Radio; Radio frequency modulation
Shostakovich, Dmitriĭ Dmitrievich, 1906-1975
About
Barnes, J. The noise of time
The **shotgun** rule. Huston, C.
SHOTGUNS
See also Guns
Shoulder the sky. Perry, A.
Shovel ready. Sternbergh, A.
SHOW JUMPING
Greaves, C. Hush money
SHOW WINDOWS
See also Advertising; Decoration and ornament; Windows
SHOWERS (PARTIES)
See also Parties
SHRINES
Vassanji, M. G. The assassin's song
Shrink rap. Parker, R. B.
SHRUBS
See also Plants; Trees
SHUGAK, KATE (FICTITIOUS CHARACTER)
Stabenow, D. Hunter's moon
Stabenow, D. Killing grounds
Stabenow, D. Restless in the grave
Stabenow, D. Though not dead
Shut your eyes tight. Verdon, J.
Shutter Island. Lehane, D.
SHYNESS
See also Emotions
SIAMESE TWINS
Slouka, M. God's fool
SIBERIA (RUSSIA)
L'Amour, L. Last of the breed
Meek, J. The people's act of love
Pasternak, B. L. Doctor Zhivago
Richler, N. Your mouth is lovely
Theroux, M. Far north
SIBLING RIVALRY
Chung, C. Forgotten country
SIBLINGS
See also Family
Anshaw, C. Carry the one
Haddon, M. The red house
Hosking, J. Three years with the rat
I am the brother of XX
Jewell, L. The making of us
Meek, J. The heart broke in
Morrison, T. Home
Shamsie, K. Home fire
The **Sicilian.** Puzo, M.
SICILY
Hersey, J. A bell for Adano
Higgins, J. Luciano's luck
Puzo, M. The Sicilian
Unsworth, B. The ruby in her navel
SICK
Ondaatje, M. The English patient
Shriver, L. So much for that
Wharton, E. Ethan Frome
SICK CHILDREN
Donoghue, E. The wonder
Leroy, M. Postcards from Berlin
SICKNESS *See* Diseases
Siddhartha. Hesse, H.
Sidney Chambers and the Forgiveness of Sins. Runcie, J.
SIDS (DISEASE) *See* Sudden infant death syndrome
The **siege.** Pérez-Reverte, A.
The **Siege** Winter. Franklin, A.
SIEGES *See* Battles
SIERRA LEONE
Hill, L. Someone knows my name
SIERRA LEONE -- HISTORY -- CIVIL WAR, 1991-
Beah, I. Radiance of tomorrow
Forna, A. The memory of love
SIERRA MADRE (MEXICO)
Groom, W. El Paso
SIERRA MADRE MOUNTAINS (MEXICO)
Traven, B. The treasure of the Sierra Madre
A **sight** for sore eyes. Rendell, R.
Sight Reading. Kalotay, D.
SIGHT SAVING BOOKS *See* Large print books
Sights unseen. Gibbons, K.
A Sigma Force novel [series]
Rollins, J. The eye of God
The **Sigma** protocol. Ludlum, R.
SIGN LANGUAGE
See also Language and languages
Greenidge, K. We love you, Charlie Freeman
Sign of chaos. Zelazny, R.
Sign of the unicorn. Zelazny, R.
SIGN PAINTING
See also Advertising; Industrial painting
Signal. Lee, P.
Signal & noise. Griesemer, J.
The **signal** flame. Krivak, A.
SIGNALS AND SIGNALING

See also Communication; Military art and science; Naval art and science; Navigation; Signs and symbols
The **Signature** of All Things. Gilbert, E.
Signed, Mata Hari. Murphy, Y.
SIGNS AND SYMBOLS
Brown, D. Angels & demons
Krentz, J. A. Promise not to tell
Silas Marner. Eliot, G.
The **silence.** Jones, J. S.
Silence. Endo, S.
The **silence** of the lambs. Harris, T.
The **silence** of the sea.
Silenced. DuPree, K.
The **silent** angel. Boll, H.
The **silent** cry. Perry, A.
SILENT FILMS
Nehme, F. S. Missing reels
SILENT FILMS
See also Motion pictures
Silent house.
Silent Joe. Parker, T. J.
SILENT MOTION PICTURES *See* Silent films
The **silent** oligarch. Morgan Jones, C.
Silent witness. Patterson, R. N.
Silk is for seduction. Chase, L. L.
SILK WORKERS' STRIKE, PATERSON, N.J., 1913
Stewart, A. Girl waits with gun
Silken prey. Sandford, J.
The **silkworm.** Galbraith, R.
SILKWORMS
See also Beneficial insects; Insects; Moths
The **Silmarillion.** Tolkien, J. R. R.
Silver. Motion, A.
Silver girl. Hilderbrand, E.
SILVER MINES AND MINING
Conrad, J. Nostromo
Trevanian Incident at Twenty Mile
SILVER MINES AND MINING -- ACCIDENTS -- IDAHO
Canty, K. The underworld
Silver on the Road. Gilman, L. A.
Silver sparrow. Jones, T.
The **Silver** Star. Walls, J.
Silver wedding. Binchy, M.
Simisola. Rendell, R.
A **simple** act of violence. Ellory, R. J.
SIMPLE MACHINES
See also Machinery; Mechanical movements; Mechanics
A **simple** plan. Smith, S.
Simple speaks his mind. Hughes, L.
Simple's Uncle Sam. Hughes, L.
SIN
Greene, G. Brighton rock
SIN
See also Ethics; Good and evil; Theology
Sin killer. McMurtry, L.
Since we fell. Lehane, D.
Sing you home. Picoult, J.
Sing, unburied, sing. Ward, J.
SINGAPORE
Boulle, P. The bridge over the River Kwai
Kwan, K. Crazy rich Asians
Loh, V. Breaking the tongue
Singer from the sea. Tepper, S. S.
The **singer's** gun. St. John Mandel, E.
SINGERS
Abani, C. GraceLand
Cather, W. The song of the lark
Earle, S. I'll never get out of this world alive
Erdrich, L. The Master Butchers Singing Club
Grossman, D. Someone to run with
Hiaasen, C. Star Island
King, R. Domino
Little star
The man of feeling
McCrumb, S. If ever I return, pretty Peggy-O
Patchett, A. Bel canto
Patterson, J. Hide & seek
Pearson, A. I think I love you
Phillips, A. The song is you
Phillips, C. Dancing in the dark
Pynchon, T. The crying of lot 49
Rotert, R. Last night at the blue angel
Rushdie, S. The ground beneath her feet
Sarton, M. Anger
Smith, L. The devil's dream
Spencer, L. Small town girl
Thomas, D. M. The white hotel
Tyler, A. A slipping-down life
Weiner, J. In her shoes
Williams, C. Stairway to hell
SINGERS
See also Musicians
SINGING GAMES
See also Games
The **singing** sword. Whyte, J.
Singing the sadness. Hill, R.
SINGLE FATHERS
Tinti, H. The twelve lives of Samuel Hawley
SINGLE MEN
Doig, I. Work song
Hornby, N. About a boy
Lee A gesture life
Pym, B. Quartet in autumn
Sams, F. Down town
Woo, S. J. Love love
SINGLE MEN
See also Men; Single people
SINGLE MOTHERS
Black, C. Murder on the Champ de Mars
Ferrante, E. Those Who Leave and Those Who Stay
Flint, E. Little deaths
Hadley, T. Clever Girl
Jenkins, V. An unattended death

Moyes, J. One Plus One
Robards, K. Shiver
Sekaran, S. Lucky boy
Stibbe, N. Man at the helm
SINGLE PARENT FAMILY
Moriarty, L. The center of everything
SINGLE PARENTS
See also Parents; Unmarried couples
SINGLE PARENTS
Scottoline, L. One perfect lie
Smith, A. A bigger life
SINGLE WOMEN
Abu-Jaber, D. Crescent
Albert, E. The book of Dahlia
Allen, S. A. The sugar queen
Balzac, H. d. Cousin Bette
Brookner, A. Hotel du Lac
Brookner, A. Undue influence
Bynum, S. Ms. Hempel chronicles
Burrowes, G. Lady Maggie's secret scandal
Capote, T. The grass harp
Cox, M. The glass of time
Dare, T. A night to surrender
Davies, P. H. The Welsh girl
Delaney, J. P. The girl before
Diffenbaugh, V. The language of flowers
Dreyer, E. Barely a lady
The elegance of the hedgehog
Faulkner, W. Intruder in the dust
Fielding, H. Bridget Jones
Fielding, H. Bridget Jones's diary
Fitch, J. Paint it black
Forester, C. S. The African Queen
Freeman, C. Go with me
Gaskell, E. C. Cranford
Gloss, M. The hearts of horses
Goodman, A. Paradise park
Gordon, M. Final payments
Groff, L. The monsters of Templeton
Gunning, S. The rebellion of Jane Clarke
Guo X. A concise Chinese-English dictionary for lovers
Guo X. Twenty fragments of a ravenous youth
Hale, S. Austenland
The hall of singing caryatids
Hayter, S. Bandit queen boogie
Heller, Z. What was she thinking?
Hiaasen, C. Strip tease
Hoffman, A. The ice queen
Jamison, L. The gin closet
Kallos, S. Broken for you
Keyes, M. Last Chance Saloon
Kinsella, S. My not so perfect life
The lake
Lurie, A. Foreign affairs
Makkai, R. The borrower
Martin, S. Shopgirl
Moore, B. The lonely passion of Judith Hearne
Moore, L. A gate at the stairs
Mortimer, J. Quite honestly
Mosher, H. F. On Kingdom Mountain
Mukherjee, B. Miss New India
Oates, J. C. Black water
Oates, J. C. Missing mom
O'Dell, T. Fragile beasts
O'Farrell, M. The vanishing act of Esme Lennox
Packer, A. The dive from Clausen's pier
Phillips, S. E. Ain't she sweet
Pym, B. Excellent women
Pym, B. Jane and Prudence
Pym, B. Quartet in autumn
Pym, B. The sweet dove died
Pym, B. An unsuitable attachment
Robinson, E. The true and outstanding adventures of the Hunt sisters
Rosenberg, N. T. Interest of justice
Rossner, J. Looking for Mr. Goodbar
Rothschild, H. The improbability of love
Russell, M. D. Dreamers of the day
Sand, G. Marianne
Schine, C. The New Yorkers
Schine, C. The three Weissmanns of Westport
Shalvis, J. Sweet little lies
Sheehan, A. The anxiety of everyday objects
Shields, C. The republic of love
Spark, M. The driver's seat
Spark, M. Loitering with intent
Tóibín, C. Brooklyn
Trigiani, A. Big Stone Gap
Urrea, L. A. Into the beautiful North
Vida, V. Let the Northern Lights erase your name
Vlautin, W. Northline
Walsh, H. Brass
Watrous, M. If you follow me
Woo, S. J. Love love
SINGLE WOMEN
See also Single people; Women
Single, carefree, mellow. Heiny, K.
SINGLE-PARENT FAMILIES
See also Family
SINGLE-PARENT FAMILY
Boucher, C. How to keep your Volkswagen alive
Moriarty, L. The center of everything
The **sinister** pig. Hillerman, T.
The **sins** of the fathers. Block, L.
The **sins** of the wolf. Perry, A.
The **siren** queen. Buckley, F.
The **sirens** of Titan. Vonnegut, K.
Sister. Lupton, R.
Sister Carrie. Dreiser, T.
Sister Carrie; Jennie Gerhardt; Twelve men. Dreiser, T.
Sister mine. O'Dell, T.
Sisterland. Sittenfeld, C.
The **sisters.** Jensen, N.
SISTERS

Adichie, C. N. Half of a yellow sun
Alexander, V. The Scandalous Adventures of the Sister of the Bride
Allen, S. A. First Frost
Allen, S. A. Garden Spells
Alvarez, J. How the Garcia girls lost their accents
Alvarez, J. Yo!
Atwood, M. The blind assassin
Austen, J. Pride and prejudice
Austen, J. Sense and sensibility
Barton, E. Brookland
Berg, E. What we keep
Bloom, A. Lucky us
Brown, E. The weird sisters
Buchanan, C. M. The painted girls
Capote, T. The grass harp
Cash, W. This dark road to mercy
Chung, C. Forgotten country
Cleage, P. What looks like crazy on an ordinary day--
De los Santos, M. The Precious One
Dennis-Benn, N. Y. Here Comes the Sun
Desai, A. Clear light of day
Dreyer, E. Twice tempted
Essex, K. Leonardo's swans
Eugenides, J. The virgin suicides
Farrell, H. What ever happened to Baby Jane?
Forna, A. Ancestor stones
Forster, E. M. Howards End
Franck, J. The blindness of the heart
Glass, J. I see you everywhere
Golding, W. Darkness visible
Goodman, A. The cookbook collector
Goudge, E. Green Dolphin Street
Gracie, A. The Winter Bride
Gregory, P. The kingmaker's daughter
Hannah, K. The nightingale
Hannah, K. Winter garden
Hansen, R. Mariette in ecstasy
Hartnett, A. Rabbit cake
Hay, E. A student of weather
Hazzard, S. The transit of Venus
Hilderbrand, E. The island
Hodgen, C. Elegies for the brokenhearted
Hoffman, A. Practical magic
Hoffman, A. The story sisters
Jackson, N. The Star Side of Bird Hill
Jackson, S. We have always lived in the castle
Jensen, N. The sisters
Jones, T. Silver sparrow
Keneally, T. The Daughters of Mars
Kilpack, J. S. The vicar's daughter
Kowal, M. R. Shades of milk and honey
Krentz, J. A. Secret sisters
Kutsukake, L. The translation of love
Lawrence, D. H. Women in love
Lin Yutang Moment in Peking
Lupton, R. Sister
MacDonald Fall on your knees
Markovits, A. I am forbidden
McPhee, J. No ordinary matter
Mitchell, J. C. A reunion of ghosts
Moor, M. d. The storm
Morton, K. The house at Riverton
Motherlunge
Murakami, H. After dark
Ng, F. M. Bone
Niffenegger, A. Her fearful symmetry
Nunez, S. The last of her kind
Oates, J. C. A Bloodsmoor romance
O'Dell, T. Sister mine
O'Donnell, L. The death of bees
Parmar, P. Vanessa and her sister
Parshall, S. Bleeding through
Peebles, F. d. P. The seamstress
Picoult, J. My sister's keeper
Powell, S. The Mushroom Man
Prose, F. Goldengrove
Rendell, R. The water's lovely
Rice, L. The geometry of sisters
Rice, L. Home fires
Rice, L. Little night
Richmond, M. No one you know
Robinson, E. The true and outstanding adventures of the Hunt sisters
Schine, C. The three Weissmanns of Westport
See, L. Shanghai girls
Shange, N. Sassafrass, Cypress & Indigo
Silko, L. Gardens in the dunes
Sittenfeld, C. Eligible
Sittenfeld, C. Sisterland
Slaughter, K. Pretty Girls
Smiley, J. A thousand acres
Suri, M. The age of Shiva
Tan, A. The hundred secret senses
Tanizaki, J. The Makioka sisters
Tea, M. Rose of no man's land
Thayer, N. Island girls
Trollope, J. A Spanish lover
Vanderbes, J. Easter Island
Walker, A. By the light of my father's smile
Walker, A. The color purple
Wall, P. S. The Wilde women
Walls, J. The Silver Star
Walsh, T. The moon sisters
Weiner, J. In her shoes
Weldon, F. Chalcot Crescent

SISTERS

See also Siblings; Women

SISTERS (RELIGIOUS) *See* Nuns

SISTERS -- ENGLAND

Gregory, P. The kingmaker's daughter

SISTERS -- FRANCE

Buchanan, C. M. The painted girls

The **Sisters** brothers. DeWitt, P.

Sisters of the Revolution.
SISTERS-IN-LAW
O'Nan, S. Emily, alone
SIX DAY WAR, 1967 *See* Israel-Arab War, 1967
Six days of the condor. Grady, J.
Six early stories. Mann, T.
Six easy pieces. Mosley, W.
Six novels. Colette
Six tales of the jazz age, and other stories. Fitzgerald, F. S.
Six wakes. Lafferty, M.
The **six-gun** tarot. Belcher, R. S.
Sixkill. Parker, R. B.
The **sixth** book of lost swords: Mindsword's story. Saberhagen, F.
The **sixth** commandment. Sanders, L.
Sixty stories. Barthelme, D.
The **sixty-five** years of Washington. Saer, J. J.
The **size** of the world. Silber, J.
Skagboys. Welsh, I.
Skeleton canyon. Jance, J. A.
Skeleton crew. King, S.
Skeleton Hill. Lovesey, P.
Skeletons at the feast. Bohjalian, C. A.
Skin. Hayder, M.
SKIN -- DISEASES
See also Diseases
Skin tight. Hiaasen, C.
SKINHEADS
Prose, F. A changed man
Skinner. Huston, C.
Skinny dip. Hiaasen, C.
Skinny legs and all. Robbins, T.
Skinwalkers. Hillerman, T.
Skippy dies. Murray, P.
The **skull** beneath the skin. James, P. D.
The **skull** mantra. Pattison, E.
The **Sky** Below. D'Erasmo, S.
The **sky** so big and black. Barnes, J.
SKYE (SCOTLAND)
Stewart, M. Wildfire at midnight
Skylight confessions. Hoffman, A.
SKYSCRAPERS -- EARTHQUAKE EFFECTS
See also Buildings -- Earthquake effects; Earthquakes
Slammerkin. Donoghue, E.
Slan. Van Vogt, A. E.
A **slant** of light. Lent, J.
Slapstick. Vonnegut, K.
Slash and burn. Cotterill, C.
Slaughterhouse-five. Vonnegut, K.
SLAVE NARRATIVES
See also Autobiography; Slavery
SLAVE REVOLTS
See also Revolutions
SLAVE TRADE
Elison, M. The book of Etta
Evaristo, B. Blonde roots
Johnson, C. R. Middle passage
Unsworth, B. The quality of mercy
Unsworth, B. Sacred hunger
Wray, J. Canaan's tongue
SLAVE TRADE
See also International law; Slavery
SLAVE TRADE -- UNITED STATES -- HISTORY 19TH CENTURY
Faye, L. Seven for a secret
SLAVE TRADERS
Elison, M. The book of Etta
SLAVERY
Allende, I. Island beneath the sea
Bell, M. S. All souls' rising
Butler, O. E. Kindred
Caputo, P. Acts of faith
Conde, M. I, Tituba, black witch of Salem
Crafts, H. The bondswomans narrative
Gaines, E. J. The autobiography of Miss Jane Pittman
Garcia, C. Monkey hunting
Gibbons, K. On the occasion of my last afternoon
Gyasi, Y. Homegoing
Hambly, B. Sold down the river
Hannaham, J. Delicious Foods
Hill, L. Someone knows my name
James, M. The book of night women
Kidd, S. M. The invention of wings
Levy, A. The long song
Martin, V. Property
Morrison, T. A mercy
Odell, J. The healing
Pesci, D. Amistad
Plain, B. Crescent City
Rhodes, J. P. Voodoo dreams
Santiago, E. Conquistadora
Stowe, H. B. Uncle Tom's cabin
Straight, S. A million nightingales
Stross, C. Saturn's children
Styron, W. The confessions of Nat Turner
Tademy, L. Cane River
Twain, M. Pudd'nhead Wilson;
Unsworth, B. The quality of mercy
Walker, M. Jubilee
Warren, R. P. Band of angels
Wrinkle, M. Wash
SLAVERY -- UNITED STATES
Jones, E. P. The known world
Leveen, L. The secrets of Mary Bowser
Morrison, T. Beloved
Pitts, L. Freeman
Rawles, N. My Jim
Turner, N. E. My name is Resolute
Whitehead, C. The underground railroad
SLAVES
Clotel, or, The president's daughter
Conde, M. I, Tituba, black witch of Salem
Guinn, M. The resurrectionist
Hambly, B. Patriot hearts

Kane, B. Spartacus
Lalami, L. The Moor's account
McBride, J. The good lord bird
Perkins-Valdez, D. Wench
Sherwood, F. Night of sorrows
Styron, W. The confessions of Nat Turner
SLAVES
See also Slavery
SLAVES -- EMANCIPATION -- SOUTH AFRICA
Brink, A. P. Philida
Slaves of obsession. Perry, A.
SLEEP
See also Health; Hygiene; Mind and body; Psychophysiology; Rest; Subconsciousness
SLEEP
Pierson, D. C. The boy who couldn't sleep and never had to
SLEEP DISORDERS
Pierson, D. C. The boy who couldn't sleep and never had to
The **Sleeper** wakes.
Sleeping beauty. Macdonald, R.
SLEEPING BEAUTY (TALE)
See also Fairy tales
The **sleeping** beauty killer. Clark, M. H.
Sleeping dogs. Gorman, E.
A **sleeping** life. Rendell, R.
Sleeping with the enemy. Price, N.
The **sleepwalker's** guide to dancing. Jacob, M.
Sleepwalking land. Couto, M.
Slightly shady. Quick, A.
Slip of the knife. Mina, D.
A **slipping-down** life. Tyler, A.
Slough house [series]
Herron, M. Spook street
SLOVAKIA
McCann, C. Zoli
SLUM LIFE
Abani, C. GraceLand
Algren, N. A walk on the wild side
Bellow, S. The adventures of Augie March
Crane, S. Maggie: a girl of the streets (a story of New York)
Dickens, C. Oliver Twist
Farrell, J. T. Studs Lonigan
Naylor, G. The men of Brewster Place
Naylor, G. The women of Brewster Place
Oates, J. C. Them
Sinha, I. Animal's people
Smith, B. A tree grows in Brooklyn
Wright, R. Native son
Slumberland. Beatty, P.
The **sly** company of people who care. Bhattacharya, R.
The **slynx.**
SMALL ARMS *See* Guns
SMALL BUSINESS
See also Business
Chabon, M. Telegraph Avenue
Small crimes. Zeltserman, D.
SMALL HOUSES
See also Houses
Small island. Levy, A.
A **small** room. Sarton, M.
Small town girl. Spencer, L.
SMALL TOWN LIFE
Adams, A. After the war
Adams, A. A southern exposure
Allen, S. A. The girl who chased the moon
Anderson, S. Winesburg, Ohio
Ansay, A. M. River angel
Baker, T. The little giant of Aberdeen County
Bambara, T. C. The salt eaters
Banks, R. Affliction
Banks, R. The sweet hereafter
Baxter, C. Saul and Patsy
Berry, W. Jayber Crow
Binchy, M. Whitethorn Woods
Bradbury, R. Dandelion wine
Brown, L. Joe
Capote, T. The grass harp
Cheever, J. The Wapshot chronicle
Cheever, J. The Wapshot scandal
Cleage, P. What looks like crazy on an ordinary day--
Cook, T. H. Master of the delta
Dallas, S. The Persian Pickle Club
Dallas, S. Tallgrass
Davis, K. The thin place
Dexter, P. Paris Trout
Diamant, A. Last days of Dogtown
Dufresne, J. Deep in the shade of paradise
Earley, T. The blue star
Edgerton, C. Walking across Egypt
Enger, L. Undiscovered country
Erdrich, L. The Master Butchers Singing Club
Faulkner, W. The hamlet
Flagg, F. Fried green tomatoes at the Whistle-Stop Cafe
Flagg, F. Standing in the rainbow
Flynn, G. Sharp objects
Ford, J. The shadow year
Franklin, T. Crooked letter, crooked letter
Freeman, C. All that I have
Grimes, M. Hotel Paradise
Haigh, J. Baker towers
Hamilton, J. A map of the world
Hamilton, J. The short history of a prince
Hart, C. G. Letter from home
Hart, J. Down river
Haruf, K. Eventide
Haruf, K. Plainsong
Hoffman, A. Turtle Moon
Jackson, J. Between, Georgia
Jackson, S. We have always lived in the castle
Jen, G. World and town
King, S. Carrie
Klosterman, C. Downtown Owl
Lansdale, J. R. The bottoms
Lansdale, J. R. A fine dark line

Lee, H. To kill a mockingbird
Letts, B. Shoot the moon
Lewis, S. Main Street
Lipman, E. The dearly departed
Lockridge, R. Raintree County
Marlette, D. Magic time
Mason, B. A. In country
McCammon, R. R. Boy's life
McCrumb, S. If ever I return, pretty Peggy-O
McCrumb, S. She walks these hills
McCullers, C. The heart is a lonely hunter
McLarty, R. Art in America
McMurtry, L. Rhino Ranch
Medlicott, J. A. The ladies of Covington send their love
Miller, S. While I was gone
Morris, K. L. The dart league king
Morris, M. M. Songs in ordinary time
Morris, W. Taps
Mosher, H. F. On Kingdom Mountain
Murr, N. The perfect man
Naylor, G. Mama Day
Nichols, J. T. The Milagro beanfield war
Nordan, L. Wolf whistle
Oates, J. C. Broke heart blues
Oates, J. C. Little bird of heaven
Oates, J. C. Missing mom
Oates, J. C. Rape
O'Dell, T. Back roads
O'Dell, T. Coal Run
O'Dell, T. Sister mine
O'Hara, J. Ten North Frederick
O'Nan, S. Snow angels
Otto, W. How to make an American quilt
Parks, G. The learning tree
Pearson, T. R. A short history of a small place
Phillips, S. E. Ain't she sweet
Picoult, J. Nineteen minutes
Pollock, D. R. Knockemstiff
Poyer, D. Thunder on the mountain
Price, R. Roxanna Slade
Revoyr, N. Wingshooters
Reynolds, S. A gracious plenty
Richards, D. A. The bay of love and sorrows
Rinehart, S. Built in a day
Roth, P. When she was good
Roy, L. Bent Road
Russo, R. Bridge of sighs
Russo, R. Empire Falls
Russo, R. Nobody's fool
Russo, R. The risk pool
Sams, F. Down town
Saroyan, W. The human comedy
Sarton, M. Kinds of love
Schaffert, T. The coffins of Little Hope
Schupack, D. The boy on the bus
Schwartz, J. B. Reservation Road
Settle, M. L. Charley Bland
Sholem Aleichem The nightingale
Sidor, S. Pitch dark
Smith, L. Family linen
Spencer, L. Bitter sweet
Spencer, L. Morning glory
Spencer, L. That Camden summer
Steinbeck, J. East of Eden
Strout, E. Amy and Isabelle
Strout, E. Olive Kitteridge
Tarkington, B. Alice Adams
Thomas, R. The fourth Durango
Trigiani, A. Big Cherry Holler
Trigiani, A. Big Stone Gap
Tryon, T. In the fire of spring
Tryon, T. The wings of the morning
Twain, M. Pudd'nhead Wilson;
Vernon, O. A killing in this town
Wallace, D. The Watermelon King
Watson, B. The heaven of Mercury
Watson, L. American boy
Welty, E. Losing battles
Welty, E. The optimist's daughter
White, B. Quite a year for plums
Whitehead, C. Apex hides the hurt
Williams, A. J. Down from Cascom Mountain
Wolfe, T. Look homeward, angel
Wolfe, T. O lost
Woods, S. Chiefs
Yarbrough, S. The end of California
Yarbrough, S. Prisoners of war
Zuber, I. Salt
Small vices. Parker, R. B.
Small wars. Jones, S.
Smallwood, Joseph R., 1900-1991
About
Johnston, W. The colony of unrequited dreams
Smile. Doyle, R.
A **smile** on the face of the tiger. Estleman, L. D.
Smiley's people. Le Carre, J.
Smilla's sense of snow. Hoeg, P.
Smith, John, 1580-1631
About
Vollmann, W. T. Argall
Smith, Lily Casey, 1901-1968
About
Walls, J. Half broke horses
Smoke. Vyleta, D.
Smoke. Westlake, D. E.
Smokescreen. Francis, D.
SMUGGLING
Du Maurier, D. Jamaica Inn
Hemingway, E. To have and have not
Howard, L. Cry no more
Meyer, D. Trackers
Stone, R. Dog soldiers
Weir, A. Artemis
SMUGGLING OF DRUGS *See* Drug traffic

Smut. Bennett, A.
SNACK FOODS
See also Food
The **snake** pit. Ward, M. J.
The **snake,** the crocodile, and the dog. Peters, E.
SNAKES
Parker, T. J. Where serpents lie
SNAKES AS PETS
See also Pets; Snakes
SNAPSHOTS *See* Photographs
The **sniper's** wife. Mayor, A.
SNIPERS
Hunter, S. Soft target
Snopes. Faulkner, W.
Snow.
SNOW
The snowman
Snow angels. O'Nan, S.
The **snow** child. Ivey, E.
Snow country, and Thousand cranes. Kawabata, Y.
Snow Crash. Stephenson, N.
Snow falling on cedars. Guterson, D.
The **snow** queen. Cunningham, M.
The **Snow** Queen. Vinge, J. D.
The **Snow** Walker. Mowat, F.
Snow White must die.
The **snowman.**
The **snows** of Kilimanjaro and other stories. Hemingway, E.
Snyder, Ruth, 1895-1928
About
Hansen, R. A wild surge of guilty passion
So Big. Ferber, E.
So cold the river. Koryta, M.
So far away. Moore, M. M.
So long, and thanks for all the fish. Adams, D.
So much for that. Shriver, L.
SŎUL TAEHAKKYO
Wuertz, Y. G. Everything belongs to us
SOCCER
See also Ball games; Football; Sports
SOCCER
McCall Smith, A. Tea time for the traditionally built
SOCIAL CHANGE
Doctorow, C. Walkaway
SOCIAL CHANGE -- INDIA
Festing, I. A. The birdkeeper
SOCIAL CHANGE -- UNITED STATES -- HISTORY -- 20TH CENTURY
Smiley, J. Early warning
Smiley, J. Golden age
Smiley, J. Some luck
SOCIAL CLASSES
Archer, J. Only time will tell
Bellow, S. The adventures of Augie March
Boyle, T. C. The tortilla curtain
Canin, E. America America
The fish child
Doctorow, E. L. Ragtime
Ghosh, A. River of smoke
Ghosh, A. Sea of poppies
Hosseini, K. The kite runner
James, H. The portrait of a lady
Lee On such a full sea
Lodge, D. Nice work
Malik, T. Three bargains
Oates, J. C. Because it is bitter, and because it is my heart
O'Brien, E. The love object
O'Hara, J. Ten North Frederick
Taylor, P. H. A summons to Memphis
Waugh, E. Decline and fall
Wilder, T. Theophilus North
Wolfe, T. I am Charlotte Simmons
SOCIAL CONDITIONS
Bender, K. E. Refund
SOCIAL CONFLICT
Kwan, K. Crazy rich Asians
Waldman, A. Red Hook Road
SOCIAL CONFLICT -- PENNSYLVANIA
Bouman, T. Dry bones in the valley
SOCIAL HISTORY *See* Social conditions
SOCIAL INTEGRATION
See also Interpersonal relations; Sociology
SOCIAL ISOLATION
Bognanni, P. The house of tomorrow
Koontz, D. R. Innocence
Smith, Z. NW
Watson, J. E. Asta in the wings
SOCIAL JUSTICE
Keller, J. Last Ragged Breath
SOCIAL JUSTICE
See also Equality; Justice
SOCIAL MEDIA
See also Communication
Johnson, L. L. The most dangerous place on earth
SOCIAL MOVEMENTS
See also Social conditions; Social psychology
SOCIAL MOVEMENTS -- UNITED STATES
Mengestu, D. All our names
SOCIAL NETWORKING
See also Communication
Fielding, H. Bridget Jones
Gideon, M. Wife 22
SOCIAL POLICY
See also Planning; Social conditions
SOCIAL PROBLEMS
Calvino, I. Invisible cities
Cronin, A. J. The citadel
Doctorow, E. L. Ragtime
Dos Passos, J. 1919
Dos Passos, J. Manhattan transfer
Dos Passos, J. U.S.A.
Drabble, M. The radiant way
Dreiser, T. An American tragedy
Forster, E. M. A passage to India

Hugo, V. Les miserables
Mahfouz, N. Midaq Alley
Momaday, N. S. House made of dawn
Morrison, T. Sula
Musil, R. The man without qualities
Naylor, G. The men of Brewster Place
Oates, J. C. Foxfire
Rossner, J. Looking for Mr. Goodbar
Sinclair, U. The jungle
Smith, B. A tree grows in Brooklyn
Smith, L. E. Strange fruit
Smith, M. C. Rose
Steinbeck, J. The grapes of wrath
Tolstoy, L. Childhood, Boyhood and Youth
Turgenev, I. S. Fathers and sons
Wouk, H. Marjorie Morningstar
Wright, R. Native son
Wright, R. The outsider
SOCIAL PROBLEMS
See also Social conditions; Sociology
SOCIAL REFORM *See* Social problems
SOCIAL REFORMERS
Piercy, M. Sex wars
Vargas Llosa, M. The way to paradise
SOCIAL RESPONSIBILITY OF BUSINESS
See also Business; Business ethics
SOCIAL SKILLS
See also Interpersonal relations; Life skills
SOCIAL STRATIFICATION
Haig, F. The map of bones
Lee On such a full sea
SOCIAL WELFARE *See* Charities; Public welfare; Social problems; Social work
SOCIAL WORKERS
Coben, H. Caught
Martin, S. The pleasure of my company
SOCIALISM
Zola, E. Germinal
SOCIALIST LEADERS
Vargas Llosa, M. The way to paradise
SOCIALITES -- CRIMES AGAINST
Hunt, A. City of saints
SOCIALITES -- SINGAPORE
Kwan, K. China rich girlfriend
SOCIALIZATION
See also Acculturation; Child rearing; Education; Sociology
The **society.** Palmer, M.
SOCIETY NOVELS
Dunne, D. Too much money
Musil, R. The man without qualities
Powell, A. A dance to the music of time
Proust, M. The Guermantes way
Sackville-West, V. The Edwardians
Thackeray, W. M. Vanity fair
Tolstoy, L. Anna Karenina
Trollope, A. Framley parsonage
Trollope, A. The prime minister
Vidal, G. 1876
Waugh, E. Brideshead revisited
Waugh, E. Vile bodies
Wharton, E. The children
SOCIETY OF FRIENDS
Jiles, P. The color of lightning
West, J. The friendly persuasion
SOCIOLINGUISTICS
See also Language and languages; Linguistics; Sociology
SOCIOLOGISTS
Banks, R. Lost memory of skin
Socrates
About
Renault, M. The last of the wine
Sodom and Gomorrah. Proust, M.
The **soft** detective. Keating, H. R. F.
Soft target. Hunter, S.
The **sojourn.** Krivak, A.
Solar bones. McCormack, M.
SOLAR HOMES
See also Domestic architecture; Houses; Solar heating
SOLAR SYSTEM
Robinson, K. S. 2312
Solaris. Lem, S.
Sold down the river. Hambly, B.
A **soldier's** duty. Ricks, T. E.
The **soldier's** return. Bragg, M.
SOLDIERS
Boyne, J. The absolutist
Cameron, P. Coral Glynn
Carter, M. J. The Strangler Vine
Dare, T. A night to surrender
Evans, C. A darkness forged in fire
Gallagher, M. Youngblood
Ghosh, A. Flood of fire
Gohlke, C. I have seen him in the watchfires
Habila, H. Measuring time
The human body
Hunter, S. Dead zero
Kadare, I. The general of the dead army
Kane, B. Spartacus
Karnezis, P. The maze
MacKall, D. D. With love, wherever you are
Meek, J. The people's act of love
Miller, D. B. The girl in green
Powers, K. The yellow birds
Russell, M. D. Dreamers of the day
Scalzi, J. Old man's war
Stone upon stone
Weber, D. By schism rent asunder
Winterson, J. The Passion
Young, T. W. The renegades
SOLDIERS -- AUSTRALIA
McCullough, C. An indecent obsession
SOLDIERS -- AUSTRIA

Krivak, A. The sojourn
SOLDIERS -- ENGLAND
Jones, S. Small wars
SOLDIERS -- FRANCE
Balzac, H. d. The country doctor
Faulkner, W. A fable
Flanagan, T. The year of the French
SOLDIERS -- GERMANY
Boll, H. The silent angel
Friedman, D. Don't ever get old
Higgins, J. The eagle has landed
Remarque, E. M. A time to love and a time to die
Robbins, D. L. War of the rats
SOLDIERS -- GREAT BRITAIN
Barker, P. The eye in the door
Barker, P. The ghost road
Barker, P. Regeneration
Boulle, P. The bridge over the River Kwai
Mallinson, A. A close run thing
Ondaatje, M. The English patient
Swift, G. Wish you were here
SOLDIERS -- HISTORY -- 19TH CENTURY
McCabe, E. L. I shall be near to you
SOLDIERS -- ISRAEL
Leshem, R. Beaufort
Reiken, F. Day for night
To the end of the land
SOLDIERS -- JAPAN
Shan, S. The girl who played go
SOLDIERS -- UNITED STATES
Bausch, R. Peace
Fountain, B. Billy Lynn's long halftime walk
Gold, G. D. Sunnyside
Goonan, K. A. In war times
Griffin, W. E. B. Special ops
Hawke, E. Ash Wednesday
Hersey, J. A bell for Adano
Higgins, J. Night of the fox
Hooker, R. MASH
Johnson, D. Tree of smoke
Jones, J. From here to eternity
Jones, J. The thin red line
Klay, P. Redeployment
Lee The surrendered
Leimbach, M. The man from Saigon
Mailer, N. The naked and the dead
Nathanson, E. M. The dirty dozen
O'Brien, T. Going after Cacciato
Olmstead, R. Far bright star
Ricks, T. E. A soldier's duty
Shaara, J. Gone for soldiers
Sundaresan, I. The splendor of silence
Willard, T. Buffalo soldiers
Zimmerman, D. Sandbox
SOLDIERS -- VIETNAM
The sorrow of war
SOLDIERS OF FORTUNE
Walters, M. The devil's feather
SOLDIERS' LIFE *See* Soldiers
SOLICITORS *See* Lawyers
SOLILOQUIES
See also Drama; Monologues
SOLITAIRE (GAME)
See also Card games
The **solitary** house. Shepherd, L.
SOLITUDE
Giordano, P. The solitude of prime numbers
The **solitude** of prime numbers. Giordano, P.
Solomon Gursky was here. Richler, M.
SOLOMON ISLANDS
London, J. South Sea tales
Solomon's oak. Mapson
SOLVENT ABUSE
See also Social problems; Substance abuse
SOMALI AMERICANS
Strout, E. The burgess boys
SOMALIA
Farah, N. Crossbones
Farah, N. Knots
Farah, N. Links
Mohamed, N. The orchard of lost souls
Some bitter taste. Nabb, M.
Some buried Caesar & The golden spiders. Stout, R.
Some kind of fairy tale. Joyce, G.
Some luck. Smiley, J.
Somebody's daughter. Lee, M. G.
Someone. McDermott, A.
Someone Is Watching. Fielding, J.
Someone knows my name. Hill, L.
Someone to Love. Balogh, M.
Someone to run with. Grossman, D.
Somersault. Oe, K.
Something borrowed, something black. Estleman, L. D.
Something in the air. Lathen, E.
Something is out there. Bausch, R.
Something red. Nicholas, D.
Something red. Gilmore, J.
Something rich and strange. Rash, R.
Something wicked this way comes. Bradbury, R.
Sometimes the wolf. Waite, U.
The **somnambulist.** Barnes, J.
The **Son.** Meyer, P.
Son of a witch. Maguire, G.
A **son** of war. Bragg, M.
The **song** is you. Phillips, A.
The **song** of Achilles. Miller, M.
The **song** of Bernadette. Werfel, F.
The **song** of everlasting sorrow.
Song of ice and fire [series]
Martin, G. R. R. A dance with dragons
Martin, G. R. R. A storm of swords
Martin, G. R. R. A clash of kings
Martin, G. R. R. A feast for crows
Martin, G. R. R. A game of thrones

The **song** of names. Lebrecht, N.
Song of Solomon. Morrison, T.
The **song** of the lark. Cather, W.
Song of the shank. Allen, J. R.
Song yet sung. McBride, J.
SONGS
See also Poetry; Vocal music
Bennett, R. J. The troupe
Songs for the butcher's daughter. Manseau, P.
Songs for the missing. O'Nan, S.
Songs in ordinary time. Morris, M. M.
The **songs** of the kings. Unsworth, B.
The songs of the seraphim [series]
Rice, A. Angel time
Songs of Willow Frost. Ford, J.
Songs without words. Packer, A.
SONGWRITERS
Earle, S. I'll never get out of this world alive
Pearson, A. I think I love you
SONGWRITERS *See* Composers; Lyricists
SONNETS
See also Poetry
SONS
See also Family; Men
SONS -- DEATH
Hemmings, K. H. The possibilities
SONS AND FATHERS *See* Father-son relationship
Sons and lovers. Lawrence, D. H.
SONS AND MOTHERS *See* Mother-son relationship
The **sons** of heaven. Baker, K.
Sons of Texas [series]
Grant, D. The Protector
SONS-IN-LAW
Saramago, J. The cave
Soon I will be invincible. Grossman, A.
Sophie's choice. Styron, W.
Sorcerer Royal [series]
Cho, Z. Sorcerer to the crown
Sorcerer to the crown. Cho, Z.
The **sorcerer's** house. Wolfe, G.
SORCERY *See* Magic; Occultism; Witchcraft
SORROW *See* Bereavement; Grief; Joy and sorrow
Sorrow bound. Mark, D.
The **sorrow** of war.
The **sorrows** of an American. Hustvedt, S.
The **sorrows** of young Werther, and Novella. Goethe, J. W. v.
The **sot-weed** factor. Barth, J.
SOUL
Williams, C. Stairway to hell
SOUL
See also Future life; Human beings (Theology); Philosophy
Bannon, J. I2
Soul circus. Pelecanos, G. P.
Soul mountain. Gao Xingjian
Souls in the great machine. McMullen, S.
Souls raised from the dead. Betts, D.
The **sound** and the fury. Faulkner, W.
The **sound** of the mountain. Kawabata, Y.
The **sound** of things falling.
SOUND RECORDING EXECUTIVES AND PRODUCERS
Kunzru, H. White tears
SOUND RECORDINGS
Egan, J. A visit from the Goon Squad
Sourland. Oates, J. C.
SOUTH AFRICA
Absolution
Andrew, S. Recipes for Love and Murder
Beukes, L. Zoo city
Coetzee, J. M. Summertime
Gordimer, N. The conservationist
Gordimer, N. Get a life
Gordimer, N. July's people
Gordimer, N. Life times
Gordimer, N. None to accompany me
Gordimer, N. The pickup
Lessing, D. M. Children of violence
Lessing, D. M. The grass is singing
Mason, R. Who killed Piet Barol?
Mda, Z. The whale caller
Meyer, D. Trackers
Michener, J. A. The covenant
Morley, I. Come Sunday
Paton, A. Ah, but your land is beautiful
Paton, A. Cry, the beloved country
Paton, A. Tales from a troubled land
Ward, A. E. Forgive me
SOUTH AFRICA -- CAPE TOWN
Meyer, D. Heart of the hunter
Smith, R. Wake up dead
SOUTH AFRICA -- COMMISSION FOR TRUTH AND RECONCILIATION
Ward, A. E. Forgive me
SOUTH AFRICA -- HISTORY -- 19TH CENTURY
Brink, A. P. Philida
SOUTH AFRICA -- JOHANNESBURG
Paton, A. Too late the phalarope
SOUTH AFRICA -- NATIVE PEOPLES
Coetzee, J. M. Life & times of Michael K.
SOUTH AFRICA -- RACE RELATIONS
Coetzee, J. M. Disgrace
Gordimer, N. The conservationist
Gordimer, N. July's people
Gordimer, N. My son's story
Gordimer, N. None to accompany me
Gordimer, N. No time like the present
Lessing, D. M. The grass is singing
Mda, Z. The Madonna of Excelsior
Michener, J. A. The covenant
Paton, A. Ah, but your land is beautiful
Paton, A. Cry, the beloved country
Paton, A. Too late the phalarope
Van Niekerk, M. Agaat
SOUTH AFRICA -- RACE RELATIONS

See also Race relations
SOUTH AFRICA -- SOCIAL LIFE AND CUSTOMS -- 20TH CENTURY
Mason, R. Who killed Piet Barol?
SOUTH AFRICAN DUTCH *See* Afrikaners
SOUTH AFRICANS -- MIDDLE EAST
Gordimer, N. The pickup
SOUTH AFRICANS -- WEST INDIES
Naipaul, V. S. Guerrillas
SOUTH AFRICANS, AFRIKAANS-SPEAKING *See* Afrikaners
SOUTH AMERICA
Alarcon, D. Lost City Radio
Allende, I. Eva Luna
Conrad, J. Nostromo
Erpenbeck, J. The book of words
Patchett, A. Bel canto
Woolf, V. The voyage out
SOUTH AMERICA -- DISCOVERY AND EXPLORATION -- SPANISH
Wright, R. The gold eaters
SOUTH AMERICA -- HISTORY -- 16TH CENTURY
Wright, R. The gold eaters
SOUTH AMERICAN ART
See also Art
SOUTH CAROLINA
Allison, D. Bastard out of Carolina
Brown, S. The witness
Conroy, P. The prince of tides
Doctorow, E. L. The march
Dunn, M. Ella Minnow Pea
Frank, D. B. Folly Beach
Hart, C. G. Murder walks the plank
Hart, C. G. White elephant dead
Hart, C. G. Yankee Doodle dead
Kidd, S. M. The secret life of bees
Powell, P. Edisto
Powell, P. Edisto revisited
Sanders, D. Clover
Wesselmann, D. L. Captivity
SOUTH CAROLINA -- 19TH CENTURY
Jakes, J. Love and war
Jakes, J. North and South
SOUTH CAROLINA -- CHARLESTON
Conroy, P. South of Broad
Shange, N. Sassafrass, Cypress & Indigo
SOUTH DAKOTA
Meyers, K. The work of wolves
Weisgarber, A. The personal history of Rachel Dupree
SOUTH DAKOTA -- 19TH CENTURY
Rolvaag, O. E. Giants in the earth
Rolvaag, O. E. Peder Victorious
South of Broad. Conroy, P.
South of Shiloh. Logan, C.
South of the border, west of the sun. Murakami, H.
South Sea tales. London, J.
SOUTHAMPTON INSURRECTION, 1831
Styron, W. The confessions of Nat Turner
Southampton Row. Perry, A.
Southern Cross the Dog. Cheng, B.
A **southern** exposure. Adams, A.
Southern Reach Trilogy [series]
VanderMeer, J. Acceptance
VanderMeer, J. Authority
VanderMeer, J. Annihilation
SOUTHERN STATES
Adams, A. A southern exposure
Allison, D. Bastard out of Carolina
Bambara, T. C. The salt eaters
Brown, J. D. Addie Pray
Brown, L. Joe
Capote, T. The grass harp
Childress, M. Crazy in Alabama
Conroy, P. The prince of tides
Dexter, P. Paris Trout
Dickey, J. Deliverance
Faulkner, W. Light in August
Faulkner, W. As I lay dying
Faulkner, W. Pylon
Flagg, F. Fried green tomatoes at the Whistle-Stop Cafe
Gaines, E. J. A gathering of old men
Gay, W. I hate to see that evening sun go down
Gibbons, K. Ellen Foster
Grau, S. A. The keepers of the house
Johnson, T. G. Welcome to Braggsville
Lee, H. To kill a mockingbird
Lester, J. Do Lord remember me
McCullers, C. The heart is a lonely hunter
McCullers, C. Reflections in a golden eye
Morgan, C. E. The sport of kings
O'Connor, F. Everything that rises must converge
Pearson, T. R. A short history of a small place
Percy, W. The last gentleman
Percy, W. Love in the ruins
Powell, P. Edisto revisited
Price, R. Roxanna Slade
Reynolds, S. A gracious plenty
Siddons, A. R. Heartbreak Hotel
Smith, L. The devil's dream
Smith, L. Mrs. Darcy and the blue-eyed stranger
Smith, L. Oral history
Spencer, E. The southern woman
Tyler, A. Earthly possessions
Walker, A. The color purple
Wallace, D. Mr. Sebastian and the Negro magician
White, B. Quite a year for plums
Woods, S. Chiefs
SOUTHERN STATES -- 19TH CENTURY
Gibbons, K. On the occasion of my last afternoon
Mitchell, M. Gone with the wind
Walker, M. Jubilee
SOUTHERN STATES -- HISTORY -- 1865-1877
Alexander, T. A beauty so rare
Pitts, L. Freeman

SOUTHERN STATES -- SOCIAL LIFE AND CUSTOMS
Welty, E. Complete novels
Welty, E. Stories, essays & memoir
The **southern** woman. Spencer, E.
SOUTHWESTERN STATES
Anaya, R. A. The man who could fly and other stories
Barrett, W. E. The lilies of the field
Hillerman, T. Sacred clowns
Hillerman, T. A thief of time
McCarthy, C. All the pretty horses
McCarthy, C. The crossing
SOUTHWESTERN STATES -- GRAPHIC NOVELS
Henson, J. Jim Henson's tale of sand
SOVEREIGNS *See* Emperors; Kings and rulers; Monarchy; Queens
SOVIET LITERATURE *See* Russian literature
SOVIET UNION
Barnes, J. The noise of time
The big green tent
Bronsky, A. The Hottest Dishes of the Tartar Cuisine
Eastland, S. The Beast in the Red Forest
Marra, A. The tsar of love and techno
Smith, T. R. Agent 6
SOVIET UNION -- HISTORY -- 20TH CENTURY
Goldberg, P. The Yid
SOVIET UNION -- INTELLECTUAL LIFE
The big green tent
SOVIET UNION -- POLITICS AND GOVERNMENT -- 20TH CENTURY
Barnes, J. The noise of time
Space. Michener, J. A.
SPACE AND TIME
Benford, G. Timescape
Donohue, K. Centuries of June
Hosking, J. Three years with the rat
Murakami, H. 1Q84
Scalzi, J. The collapsing empire
Yu, C. How to live safely in a science fictional universe
SPACE AND TIME
See also Fourth dimension; Metaphysics; Space sciences; Time
The **space** between us. Umrigar, T. N.
SPACE COLONIES
Corey, J. S. A. Cibola burn
Haldeman, J. W. Marsbound
Hamilton, P. F. The dreaming void
Heinlein, R. A. The moon is a harsh mistress
Howrey, M. The wanderers
Lamb, A. Roboteer
Levine, D. D. Arabella of Mars
Martin, G. R. R. Hunter's run
McCaffrey, A. Freedom's landing
Mieville, C. Embassytown
Niven, L. Ringworld
Niven, L. The Ringworld engineers
Niven, L. The Ringworld throne
Niven, L. Ringworld's children
Pohl, F. Man Plus
Robinson, K. S. 2312
Robinson, K. S. Blue Mars
Robinson, K. S. Galileo's dream
Robinson, K. S. The Martians
Robinson, K. S. Red Mars
Scalzi, J. The human division
Scalzi, J. Old man's war
Steele, A. M. Coyote
Varley, J. Rolling thunder
SPACE COMMUNICATION *See* Astronautics -- Communication systems; Interstellar communication
SPACE DEBRIS
See also Pollution; Space environment
SPACE FLIGHT
Adams, D. Mostly harmless
Flynn, M. In the Lion's Mouth
Pohl, F. Beyond the blue event horizon
Pohl, F. Gateway
Pohl, F. Heechee rendezvous
Reynolds, A. Revenger
Sher, I. Gentlemen of space
SPACE FLIGHT *See* Imaginary voyages; Science fiction
SPACE FLIGHT TO MARS
Varley, J. Red thunder
Weir, A. The Martian
SPACE FLIGHT TO THE MOON
Michener, J. A. Space
Netzer, L. Shine shine shine
SPACE FLIGHT TO THE MOON
See also Astronautics; Space flight
The **space** merchants. Pohl, F.
SPACE PROBES
Crichton, M. The Andromeda strain
SPACE SHIPS
Clarke, A. C. The Garden of Rama
Clarke, A. C. Rendezvous with Rama
Crichton, M. Sphere
Lamb, A. Roboteer
Lem, S. Fiasco
McDevitt, J. Odyssey
Stirling, S. M. The city who fought
Varley, J. Red thunder
Westerfeld, S. The killing of worlds
SPACE TELECOMMUNICATION *See* Interstellar communication
SPACE TRAVEL *See* Interplanetary voyages; Space flight
SPACE TRAVELERS
Higgins, C. A. Lightless
SPACE VEHICLE ACCIDENTS
See also Accidents
SPACE VEHICLES
Higgins, C. A. Lightless
Lamb, A. Roboteer
Leckie, A. Ancillary justice
McDevitt, J. Odyssey
Varley, J. Dark lightning

SPACE VEHICLES -- PILOTING
See also Astronauts; Navigation (Astronautics)
SPACE WARFARE
See also Outer space; War
SPACE WARFARE
Banks, I. The hydrogen sonata
Corey, J. S. A. Leviathan Wakes
Gunn, J. E. Transcendental
Leckie, A. Ancillary justice
Scalzi, J. The End of All Things
Scalzi, J. Redshirts
Weber, D. Off Armageddon Reef
SPACE WARS *See* Space warfare
SPACE WEAPONS
See also Military weapons; Space warfare
SPAIN
Hemingway, E. The sun also rises
Levy, D. Hot Milk
O'Flynn, C. Mr. Lynch's holiday
Malraux, A. Man's hope
Merimee, P. Carmen
Munoz Molina, A. In her absence
Munoz Molina, A. A manuscript of ashes
Urza, G. All that followed
SPAIN -- 16TH CENTURY
Cervantes Saavedra, M. d. Don Quixote de la Mancha
SPAIN -- 17TH CENTURY
Perez-Reverte, A. Captain Alatriste
Perez-Reverte, A. Purity of blood
SPAIN -- 19TH CENTURY
Perez-Reverte, A. The fencing master
SPAIN -- BARCELONA
Perez-Reverte, A. The nautical chart
Ruiz Zafon, C. The angel's game
Ruiz Zafon, C. The shadow of the wind
SPAIN -- COSTA BRAVA
Bolaño, R. The Third Reich
SPAIN -- HISTORY
Pérez-Reverte, A. The siege
Ruiz Zafon, C. The prisoner of heaven
SPAIN -- HISTORY -- 1936-1939, CIVIL WAR
Follett, K. Winter of the world
Pawel, R. Death of a nationalist
Sansom, C. J. Winter in Madrid
Winspear, J. A Dangerous Place
SPAIN -- MADRID
Lerner, B. Leaving the Atocha Station
Lewis, M. G. The monk
Marias, J. Your face tomorrow: volume three: Poison, shadow and farewell
Perez-Reverte, A. The Club Dumas
Romano-Lax, A. The Spanish bow
Vargas Llosa, M. The bad girl
SPAIN -- SEVILLE
Wilson, R. The blind man of Seville
Wilson, R. The hidden assassins
SPANIARDS -- ENGLAND
Hill, R. The Stranger House
Marias, J. All souls
Marias, J. Your face tomorrow: volume one: Fever and spear
Marias, J. Your face tomorrow: volume two: Dance and dream
SPANIARDS -- MEXICO
Sherwood, F. Night of sorrows
The **Spanish** bow. Romano-Lax, A.
SPANISH FICTION -- 20TH CENTURY
A thousand forests in one acorn
SPANISH FICTION -- TRANSLATIONS INTO ENGLISH
Aira, C. Ghosts
Allende, I. Island beneath the sea
Bolano, R. 2666
Bolano, R. Last evenings on Earth
Bolano, R. Monsieur Pain
Bolano, R. Nazi literature in the Americas
Castellanos Moya, H. Tyrant memory
Fuentes, C. Destiny and desire
Fuentes, N. The autobiography of Fidel Castro
Marias, J. A heart so white
Marias, J. Your face tomorrow: volume two: Dance and dream
Munoz Molina, A. In her absence
Munoz Molina, A. A manuscript of ashes
The painter of battles
Perez-Reverte, A. Captain Alatriste
Perez-Reverte, A. The Club Dumas
Perez-Reverte, A. The nautical chart
Perez-Reverte, A. Purity of blood
Ruiz Zafon, C. The angel's game
Ruiz Zafon, C. The shadow of the wind
Saer, J. J. The sixty-five years of Washington
Vargas Llosa, M. The bad girl
While the women are sleeping
SPANISH LANGUAGE
See also Language and languages; Romance languages
SPANISH LITERATURE
A thousand forests in one acorn
Traveler of the century
A **Spanish** lover. Trollope, J.
SPANISH MAIN
Sabatini, R. Captain Blood
Spare heirs [series]
Michels, E. The rebel heir
The **spare** room. Garner, H.
A **spark** of death. Pajer, B.
SPARRING *See* Boxing
The **sparrow.** Russell, M. D.
Sparta. Robinson, R.
Spartacus. Kane, B.
Spartacus, d. 71 B.C.
About
Kane, B. Spartacus
SPAS *See* Health resorts; Physical fitness centers
Speak. Hall, L.
Speaking from among the bones. Bradley, A.

SPECIAL FORCES (MILITARY SCIENCE)
Le Carré, J. A Delicate Truth
Lee, P. Runner
SPECIAL LIBRARIES
See also Libraries
SPECIAL OPERATIONS (MILITARY SCIENCE)
Quirk, M. Cold barrel zero
Special ops. Griffin, W. E. B.
The **special** prisoner. Lehrer, J.
Special topics in calamity physics. Pessl, M.
Specimen days. Cunningham, M.
SPECIMENS, PRESERVATION OF *See* Plants -- Collection and preservation; Taxidermy; Zoological specimens -- Collection and preservation
A **spectacle** of corruption. Liss, D.
SPECULATION
Moggach, D. Tulip fever
Norris, F. The pit
SPEECH -- HEALTH ASPECTS
Marcus, B. The flame alphabet
SPEECH DISORDERS
Mitchell, D. Black swan green
Wroblewski, D. The story of Edgar Sawtelle
The **speed** of dark. Moon, E.
Spellbound. Charlton, B.
Spellbreaker. Charlton, B.
SPELLING BEES
See also Language and languages
The **Spellman** files. Lutz, L.
SPELLMAN, ISABEL (FICTITIOUS CHARACTER)
Lutz, L. The last word
SPELLS *See* Charms; Magic
Spellwright. Charlton, B.
Spellwright Trilogy [series]
Charlton, B. Spellbreaker
SPERM BANKS
Jewell, L. The making of us
Sphere. Crichton, M.
SPICES
See also Food
Spider. McGrath, P.
SPIDER-MAN (FICTIONAL CHARACTER)
See also Fictional characters; Superheroes
SPIEGELGRUND (CHILDREN'S INSTITUTION)
The chosen ones
Spies. Frayn, M.
SPIES
Berry, S. The lost order
Blatty, W. P. Dimiter
Bourne, J. My lord and spymaster
Bourne, J. The spymaster's lady
Bowen, E. The heat of the day
Boyd, W. Any human heart
Buchan, J. The thirty-nine steps
Buckley, W. F. Mongoose, R.I.P
Charyn, J. Johnny One-Eye
Chase, L. Your scandalous ways
City of angels or
Clancy, T. The hunt for Red October
Cumming, C. A divided spy
Cumming, C. The Trinity Six
Deaver, J. Garden of beasts
Deighton, L. Berlin game
Deighton, L. The Ipcress file
Deighton, L. London match
Faulks, S. Devil may care
Fleming, I. Casino Royale
Fleming, I. Doctor No
Fleming, I. From Russia, with love
Fleming, I. Goldfinger
Fleming, I. The man with the golden gun
Fleming, I. On Her Majesty's Secret Service
Fleming, I. You only live twice
Follett, K. Eye of the needle
Follett, K. Hornet flight
Furst, A. Dark voyage
Furst, A. Spies of the Balkans
Furst, A. The spies of Warsaw
Gilman, D. The amazing Mrs. Pollifax
Gilman, D. The elusive Mrs. Pollifax
Gilman, D. The unexpected Mrs. Pollifax
Goldman, W. Marathon man
Grady, J. Six days of the condor
Greene, G. 3: This gun for hire, The confidential agent, The ministry of fear
Greene, G. The human factor
Greene, G. Our man in Havana
Hall, A. Quiller Balalaika
Hall, A. The Quiller memorandum
Hall, A. Quiller Salamander
Hall, A. Quiller solitaire
Higgins, J. The eagle has flown
Higgins, J. The eagle has landed
Horn, D. All other nights
Ignatius, D. Body of lies
Ignatius, D. The increment
Jakes, J. On secret service
Johnson, D. Tree of smoke
Kennedy, D. The moment
Kerr, P. Hitler's peace
Koontz, D. R. Watchers
Le Carre, J. Absolute friends
Le Carre, J. The honourable schoolboy
Le Carre, J. The little drummer girl
Le Carre, J. Our kind of traitor
Le Carre, J. A perfect spy
Le Carre, J. The secret pilgrim
Le Carre, J. Smiley's people
Le Carre, J. The spy who came in from the cold
Le Carre, J. The tailor of Panama
Le Carre, J. Tinker, tailor, soldier, spy
Littell, R. The company
Ludlum, R. The Bourne identity
Ludlum, R. The Bourne supremacy

Ludlum, R. The Bourne ultimatum
MacInnes, H. Prelude to terror
MacInnes, H. Ride a pale horse
Marias, J. Your face tomorrow: volume one: Fever and spear
Marias, J. Your face tomorrow: volume three: Poison, shadow and farewell
Marias, J. Your face tomorrow: volume two: Dance and dream
McCarry, C. The Mulberry Bush
McCarry, C. Old boys
McEwan, I. The innocent
Murphy, Y. Signed, Mata Hari
Ondaatje, M. The English patient
The Oxford book of spy stories
Powers, T. Declare
Rankin, I. Watchman
Sansom, C. J. Winter in Madrid
Spillane, M. The Consummata
Steiner, P. The terrorist
Steinhauer, O. The nearest exit
Steinhauer, O. The tourist
Sundaresan, I. The splendor of silence
Trevanian The Eiger sanction
Trevanian The Loo sanction
West, R. The birds fall down
Willig, L. The seduction of the crimson rose

Spies of the Balkans. Furst, A.
The **spies** of Warsaw. Furst, A.
Spilled blood. Freeman, B.
Spin. Wilson, R. C.
SPINNING
See also Textile industry
SPINOSAURUS
See also Dinosaurs
SPIRIT *See* Soul
Spirit of steamboat. Johnson, C.
SPIRITISM *See* Spiritualism
SPIRITS
Arden, K. The bear and the nightingale
Durst, S. B. The queen of blood
SPIRITUAL WARFARE
Gaiman, N. American gods
SPIRITUALISM
Griesemer, J. Signal & noise
Jackson, S. The haunting of Hill House
Paretsky, S. Ghost country
Vargas Llosa, M. Death in the Andes
SPIRITUALISM
See also Occultism; Supernatural
The **splendor** of silence. Sundaresan, I.
SPLICING OF GENES *See* Genetic engineering
Split second. Coulter, C.
SPOKANE (WASH.)
Walter, J. Citizen Vince
SPOKANE INDIANS
Alexie, S. Reservation blues
Spook. Pronzini, B.
Spook country. Gibson, W.
Spook street. Herron, M.
A **spool** of blue thread. Tyler, A.
Spooner. Dexter, P.
The **sport** of kings. Morgan, C. E.
SPORTS
Hagy, A. Boleto
SPORTS -- CORRUPT PRACTICES
See also Criminal law
SPORTS -- GRAPHIC NOVELS
See also Graphic novels
SPORTS AGENTS
Phillips, S. E. Match me if you can
A **spot** of bother. Haddon, M.
SPOUSES
Belle, K. The marriage lie
Kent, C. The loving husband
SPOUSES -- CRIMES AGAINST
Ross, A. Mr. Peanut
SPOUSES OF PRESIDENTS
Hambly, B. Patriot hearts
Newman, J. C. Mary
Roosevelt, E. Murder at midnight
SPOUSES OF PROMINENT PERSONS
Ebershoff, D. The 19th wife
Flanagan, R. Wanting
McLain, P. The Paris wife
Min, A. Becoming Madame Mao
Sontag, S. The volcano lover
Steinke, R. Holy skirts
White, E. Hotel de Dream
Wiggins, M. The shadow catcher
Spring snow. Mishima, Y.
Spring Tide.
SPRING-HEELED JACK (LEGENDARY CHARACTER)
Hodder, M. The strange affair of Spring Heeled Jack
SPY FILMS
See also Motion pictures
SPY MASTERS
Bennett, R. J. City of stairs
SPY NOVELS *See* Spy stories
SPY RADIO PROGRAMS
See also Radio programs
SPY STORIES
Arnott, J. The house of rumour
Bennett, R. J. City of stairs
Between summer's longing and winter's end
Bourne, J. The black hawk
Bourne, J. Rogue Spy
Boyd, W. Waiting for sunrise
Charyn, J. Johnny One-Eye
Cole, A. An Extraordinary Union
Collins, M. A. Ask not
Cumming, C. The Trinity Six
Furst, A. Dark voyage
Furst, A. Mission to Paris
Furst, A. The spies of Warsaw

Harkaway, N. Angelmaker
Ignatius, D. Bloodmoney
Ignatius, D. A firing offense
Kanon, J. Istanbul passage
Lawton, J. Then We Take Berlin
Le Carre, J. Absolute friends
Le Carre, J. Our kind of traitor
Le Carre, J. The tailor of Panama
Marias, J. Your face tomorrow: volume two: Dance and dream
Matthews, J. Palace of treason
Matthews, J. Red sparrow
McCarry, C. Old boys
McEwan, I. Sweet tooth
Morgan Jones, C. The silent oligarch
Nguyen, V. T. The Sympathizer
Pavone, C. The expats
Priest, C. Clementine
Rosenberg, J. C. Damascus Countdown
Rosenberg, J. C. The twelfth Imam
Smith, T. R. Agent 6
Steinhauer, O. All the Old Knives
Steinhauer, O. An American spy
Steinhauer, O. The nearest exit
Steinhauer, O. The tourist
Zander, J. The Swimmer
SPY STORIES
See also Adventure fiction
SPY TELEVISION PROGRAMS
See also Television programs
The **spy** who came in from the cold. Le Carre, J.
SPYING *See* Espionage; Spies
The **spymaster's** lady. Bourne, J.
Spymasters [series]
Bourne, J. Rogue Spy
SQUATTERS
Auster, P. Sunset Park
SQUIDS
Mieville, C. Kraken
SRI LANKA
De Kretser, M. The Hamilton case
Karunatilaka, S. The legend of Pradeep Mathew
Ondaatje, M. Anil's ghost
Tearne, R. Mosquito
SRI LANKA -- HISTORY -- CIVIL WAR, 1983-2009
Arudpragasam, A. The story of a brief marriage
SRI LANKANS -- ENGLAND
Gunesekera, R. The match
St. Lucy's home for girls raised by wolves. Russell, K.
STABLEMEN
Nicholson, C. The elephant keeper
STAINED GLASS ARTISTS
Vreeland, S. Clara and Mr. Tiffany
The **Stainless** Steel Rat joins the circus. Harrison, H.
The **Stainless** Steel Rat sings the blues. Harrison, H.
Stairway to hell. Williams, C.
The **Stalin** epigram. Littell, R.
Stalin's ghost. Smith, M. C.
Stalin, Joseph, 1879-1953
About
Harris, R. Archangel
STALINGRAD, BATTLE OF, 1942-1943
Robbins, D. L. War of the rats
STALKERS
Leon, D. Falling in Love
Parshall, S. Bleeding through
Percy, B. The wilding
Quick, A. 'Til death do us part
STALKING
Freeman, C. Go with me
Hurwitz, G. They're watching
Krentz, J. A. Trust no one
STALKING -- LAW AND LEGISLATION *See* Stalking
Stalking Ground. Mizushima, M.
STALKING VICTIMS
Never let you go
Stamm, Peter, 1963-
About
We're flying
STAMP COLLECTING
See also Collectors and collecting
Block, L. Hit me
Bradley, A. The sweetness at the bottom of the pie
The **stand.** King, S.
Stand on Zanzibar. Brunner, J.
STANDARD TIME *See* Time
Standing in the rainbow. Flagg, F.
STANLEY CUP (HOCKEY)
See also Awards; Hockey; Sports tournaments
A **star** called Henry. Doyle, R.
Star Island. Hiaasen, C.
The **star** rover. London, J.
A **star** shines over Mt. Morris Park. Roth, H.
The **Star** Side of Bird Hill. Jackson, N.
Star wars [series]
Zahn, T. The last command
STAR WARS FILMS
See also Motion pictures; Science fiction films
Starbound. Haldeman, J. W.
Stardust. Gaiman, N.
Starfish. Watts, P.
The **Stargazey.** Grimes, M.
Starkweather, Charles, 1938-1959
About
Ward, L. Outside valentine
The **Starlite** Drive-in. Reynolds, M.
The **stars** above Veracruz. Gifford, B.
Stars in my pocket like grains of sand. Delany, S. R.
Starship troopers. Heinlein, R. A.
Start shooting. Newton, C.
Started early, took my dog. Atkinson, K.
Starting over. Wakefield, D.
STATE BIRDS
See also Birds; State emblems

STATE FLOWERS
See also Flowers; State emblems
STATE LEGISLATORS
Vidal, G. Lincoln
A **state** of freedom. Mukherjee, N.
State of wonder. Patchett, A.
STATE POLICE
See also Police
The **state** we're in. Beattie, A.
STATE, HEADS OF *See* Heads of state
STATESMEN
Benet, S. V. The Devil and Daniel Webster
Carey, P. Parrot and Olivier in America
Forsyth, F. The day of the jackal
Garcia Marquez, G. The general and his labyrinth
Holland, C. Valley of the Kings
Hunt, R. Mr. Chartwell
Liss, D. The whiskey rebels
Mantel, H. Wolf Hall
McCullough, C. The first man in Rome
Morrow, J. The last witchfinder
Penman, S. K. Falls the shadow
Russell, M. D. Dreamers of the day
Saylor, S. The triumph of Caesar
Wilder, T. The ides of March
STATICS
See also Mechanics; Physics
Station eleven. Mandel, E. S. J.
Stay close. Coben, H.
Stay with me. Adebayo, A.
Staying on. Scott, P.
STEALING *See* Theft
Stealing Mona Lisa. Morton, C.
The **steam** pig. McClure, J.
STEAMBOATS
Forester, C. S. The African Queen
STEAMBOATS
See also Boats and boating; Naval architecture; Ocean travel; Shipbuilding; Ships
STEAMPUNK CULTURE
See also Counterculture
STEAMPUNK FICTION
The mammoth book of steampunk
Priest, C. Clementine
Priest, C. Dreadnought
Pulley, N. The watchmaker of Filigree Street
STEAMPUNK FICTION
See also Science fiction
STEAMSHIPS *See* Steamboats
The **steel** wave. Shaara, J.
Stefania Valenti mystery [series]
Coco, G. Shadows on the lake
STEGOSAURUS
See also Dinosaurs
Stein, Gertrude, 1874-1946
About
Truong, M. The book of salt
Steles of the sky. Bear, E.
Step to the graveyard easy. Pronzini, B.
STEPBROTHERS
Chen, D. Brothers
Haigh, J. Faith
Yu Hua Brothers
STEPCHILDREN
McPhee, M. Gorgeous lies
Trollope, J. Other people's children
STEPCHILDREN
See also Children; Parent-child relationship
STEPDAUGHTERS
Amis, M. House of meetings
Green, J. Another piece of my heart
Lipman, E. The family man
STEPFAMILIES
See also Family
Hulse, S. M. Black River
Robards, K. Ghost moon
Segal, F. The awkward age
Trollope, J. Other people's children
STEPFATHERS
Abercrombie, J. Red country
Dexter, P. Spooner
Dickens, C. David Copperfield
Saul, J. Midnight voices
STEPFATHERS
See also Fathers; Stepparents
The **Stepford** wives. Levin, I.
STEPMOTHERS
Green, J. Another piece of my heart
Lee, G. China boy
Matar, H. Anatomy of a disappearance
Oyeyemi, H. Boy, snow, bird
Phillips, J. A. MotherKind
Sanders, D. Clover
Vargas Llosa, M. The notebooks of Don Rigoberto
Wolitzer, H. Hearts
STEPMOTHERS
See also Mothers; Stepparents
Steppenwolf. Hesse, H.
STEPSISTERS
Evison, J. All about Lulu
STEPSONS
Tropper, J. How to talk to a widower
The **sterile** cuckoo. Nichols, J. T.
STERILITY IN ANIMALS *See* Infertility
STERILITY IN HUMANS *See* Infertility
STEROIDS
See also Biochemistry; Drugs
STEVEDORES -- FICTION
Tanenbaum, R. K. Tragic
Stevenson, Robert Louis, 1850-1894
About
Martin, V. Mary Reilly
STEWARDESSES, AIRLINE *See* Flight attendants
STEWARDS, AIRLINE *See* Flight attendants

Stick out your tongue. Ma Jian
Still life. Penny, L.
Still life with bread crumbs. Quindlen, A.
Still life with crows. Preston, D.
Still life with Woodpecker. Robbins, T.
Still midnight. Mina, D.
Still missing. Stevens, C.
Still waters. Harvey, J.
Stiltsville. Daniel, S.
STIMULANTS
See also Drugs; Psychotropic drugs
The **Stingaree.** Brand, M.
Stitches in time. Michaels, B.
STOCK EXCHANGE
Robbins, T. Half asleep in frog pajamas
STOCKHOLM (SWEDEN)
Dahl, A. Bad Blood
Lagercrantz, D. The girl who takes an eye for an eye
Larsson, S. The girl with the dragon tattoo
The **Stockholm** Octavo. Engelmann, K.
STOCKYARDS
See also Meat industry
STOICS
See also Ancient philosophy; Ethics
Stoker, Bram, 1847-1912
About
Marks, J. Fangland
Moore, G. The Sherlockian
The **stolen** child. Donohue, K.
The **stolen** child. Carey, L.
Stolen magic. Putney, M. J.
Stone angel. O'Connell, C.
Stone Arabia. Spiotta, D.
Stone Barrington series
Woods, S. Doing hard time
STONE CARVING
Davidson, A. The gargoyle
The **stone** diaries. Shields, C.
Stone mattress. Atwood, M.
The **stone** sky. Jemisin, N. K.
Stone upon stone.
Stone's fall. Pears, I.
STONE, CRISSA (FICTITIOUS CHARACTER)
Stroby, W. Shoot the woman first
The **stonecutter.** Lackberg, C.
Stonemouth. Banks, I.
The **stones** cry out. Okuizumi, H.
Stones for Ibarra. Doerr, H.
Stones from the river. Hegi, U.
STORES
Russo, R. Bridge of sighs
The **storied** life of A. J. Fikry. Zevin, G.
Stories.
STORIES *See* Anecdotes; Bible stories; Fairy tales; Fiction; Legends; Romances; Short stories; Stories in rhyme; Stories without words; Storytelling
The **stories** of Alice Adams. Adams, A.
The **stories** of Elizabeth Spencer. Spencer, E.
The **stories** of John Edgar Wideman. Wideman, J. E.
The **stories** of Paul Bowles. Bowles, P.
The **stories** of Richard Bausch. Bausch, R.
The **stories** of Vladimir Nabokov. Nabokov, V. V.
Stories of your life and others. Chiang, T.
STORIES WITHIN A NOVEL
Atwood, M. The blind assassin
Barnes, J. A history of the world in 10 1/2 chapters
Baxter, C. The feast of love
Conley, R. J. Mountain windsong
Fowles, J. The magus
Harwood, J. The ghost writer
King, S. Misery
Roth, P. The ghost writer
Tan, A. The Joy Luck Club
Vargas Llosa, M. Aunt Julia and the scriptwriter
Vidal, G. Burr
Wallace, D. Big fish
Waller, R. J. The bridges of Madison County
Wiesel, E. The testament
Stories, essays & memoir. Welty, E.
Stories, novels, & essay. Chesnutt, C. W.
The **storm.** Moor, M. d.
Storm Front. Sandford, J.
The **Storm** Murders. Farrow, J.
A **storm** of swords. Martin, G. R. R.
Storm runners. Parker, T. J.
Storm track. Maron, M.
STORMS
Pronzini, B. The hidden
STORMS
See also Meteorology; Natural disasters; Weather
The **story** of a brief marriage. Arudpragasam, A.
The **story** of a marriage. Greer, A. S.
The **Story** of a New Name. Ferrante, E.
The **story** of Edgar Sawtelle. Wroblewski, D.
The **story** of my teeth. Luiselli, V.
The **Story** of the Lost Child. Ferrante, E.
The **story** sisters. Hoffman, A.
STORY WITHIN A STORY
Egan, J. The keep
Treuer, D. The translation of Dr Apelles
The **Storyteller.** Picoult, J.
STORYTELLING
Ausubel, R. No one is here except all of us
Backman, F. My grandmother asked me to tell you she's sorry
De Bernieres, L. A partisan's daughter
Donohue, K. Centuries of June
Erdrich, L. Tracks
Everett, P. Percival Everett by Virgil Russell
Faulks, S. Engleby
Gurganus, A. The oldest living Confederate widow tells all
Holthe, T. U. When the elephants dance
Khoury, E. Gate of the sun
Mehta, G. A river Sutra

Naylor, G. Bailey's Cafe
Obreht, T. The tiger's wife
Oyeyemi, H. Mr. Fox
Phillips, A. The tragedy of Arthur
Rich, N. The mayor's tongue
Rushdie, S. Haroun and the sea of stories
Rushdie, S. The enchantress of Florence
Sáenz, B. A. Everything Begins and Ends at the Kentucky Club
Treuer, D. The translation of Dr Apelles
Tyler, A. A spool of blue thread
Yunis, A. The night counter
The **straight** man. Russo, R.
STRAINS AND STRESSES
See also Mechanics; Statics; Structural analysis (Engineering)
The **strange** affair of Spring Heeled Jack. Hodder, M.
The **strange** and beautiful sorrows of Ava Lavender. Walton, L.
Strange as this weather has been. Pancake, A.
Strange bodies. Theroux, M.
The **strange** case of Dr. Jekyll and Mr. Hyde. Stevenson, R. L.
The **strange** fate of Kitty Easton. Speller, E.
Strange fruit. Smith, L. E.
Strange pilgrims. Garcia Marquez, G.
Strange Weather. Hill, J.
A **strangeness** in my mind.
The **stranger.** Camus, A.
The **Stranger** House. Hill, R.
Stranger in a strange land. Heinlein, R. A.
The **stranger** you seek. Williams, A. K.
The **stranger's** child. Hollinghurst, A.
The **stranger's** magic. Frei, M.
STRANGERS
Hawkins, P. The girl on the train
Kubica, M. Pretty Baby
See, L. The tea girl of hummingbird lane
Strangers and brothers. Snow, C. P.
Strangers and brothers [series]
Snow, C. P. Strangers and brothers
Strangers at the feast. Vanderbes, J.
The **Strangler** Vine. Carter, M. J.
STRATEGIC DEFENSE INITIATIVE
See also Military policy -- United States; Space warfare; United States -- Defenses
Strawberry Sunday. Greenleaf, S.
Stray souls. Griffin, K.
STREAM ANIMALS
See also Animals; Rivers
STREAM ECOLOGY
See also Ecology; Freshwater ecology
STREAM OF CONSCIOUSNESS
Antunes, A. L. The inquisitors' manual
Barnes, D. Nightwood
Bolano, R. By night in Chile
Boll, H. The clown
Faulkner, W. As I lay dying
Gaddis, W. Agape agape
Garcia Marquez, G. The autumn of the patriarch
Joyce, J. Finnegans wake
Joyce, J. Ulysses
Lessing, D. M. The golden notebook
Lowry, M. Under the volcano
Percy, W. Lancelot
Proust, M. The captive [and] The fugitive
Proust, M. The Guermantes way
Proust, M. Remembrance of things past
Proust, M. Sodom and Gomorrah
Proust, M. Swann's way
Proust, M. Time regained
Proust, M. Within a budding grove
Pynchon, T. Gravity's rainbow
Savage, S. Glass
Styron, W. Lie down in darkness
Tsypkin, L. Summer in Baden-Baden
Woolf, V. Jacob's room
Woolf, V. Mrs. Dalloway
Woolf, V. To the lighthouse
Woolf, V. The waves
Woolf, V. The years
STREET ART
See also Art
STREET CHILDREN
Harkaway, N. Tigerman
STREET GANGS *See* Gangs
STREET LIFE
See also City and town life
STREET LIFE
K'wan (Author) Section 8
Little, T. Where there's smoke
Miasha Chaser
Turner, N. Heartbreak of a hustler's wife
Turner, N. Natural born hustler
Williams, K. Dirty to the grave
The **street** of a thousand blossoms. Tsukiyama, G.
STREET PEOPLE *See* Homeless persons
STREET RAILROADS
See also Local transit; Railroads
The **street** sweeper. Perlman, E.
STREET VENDORS -- CRIMES AGAINST
Leon, D. Blood from a stone
STREET VENDORS -- TURKEY -- ISTANBUL
A strangeness in my mind
STREETS
See also Cities and towns; Civil engineering; Transportation
Streets of Laredo. McMurtry, L.
STRENGTH OF MATERIALS
See also Mechanics; Structural analysis (Engineering)
STRESS (PSYCHOLOGY)
See also Mental health; Psychology
STRIKES
See also Industrial relations; Labor disputes

STRIKES
Harvey, J. Darkness, Darkness
STRIKES AND LOCKOUTS
Poyer, D. Thunder on the mountain
Shreve, A. Sea glass
Steinbeck, J. In dubious battle
Strip tease. Hiaasen, C.
STRIPTEASERS
Bock, C. Beautiful children
Dubus, A. The garden of last days
Flanagan, R. The unknown terrorist
STRIPTEASERS -- CRIMES AGAINST
Hayder, M. Birdman
Strivers Row. Baker, K.
STROLLING PLAYERS
Sabatini, R. Scaramouche
Strong as death. Newman, S.
Strong at the break. Land, J.
Strong poison. Sayers, D. L.
STUBBORNNESS
See also Personality
STUDENT ACTIVITIES
See also Students
STUDENT LIFE *See* College students; Students
A **student** of weather. Hay, E.
STUDENTS
Cook, R. Coma
Eggers, D. What is the what
Goldman, W. Marathon man
Haslett, A. Union Atlantic
Palahniuk, C. Pygmy
Rahimi, A. A thousand rooms of dream and fear
STUDENTS' MILITARY TRAINING CAMPS *See* Military training camps
STUDENTS, FOREIGN -- UNITED STATES
Mengestu, D. All our names
Studs Lonigan. Farrell, J. T.
A **study** in scarlet women. Thomas, S.
STUNT PERFORMERS
See also Actors
STUNT PERFORMERS
Sallis, J. Drive
Sallis, J. Driven
STYLE MANIKINS *See* Fashion models
SUBCONSCIOUSNESS
See also Parapsychology; Psychology
SUBCULTURE *See* Counterculture
SUBCULTURE
Pessl, M. Night Film
SUBJECT DICTIONARIES *See* Encyclopedias and dictionaries
SUBLIMINAL PERCEPTION
Syndrome E
SUBMARINE WARFARE
Deutermann, P. T. The ghosts of Bungo Suido
SUBMARINES
Beach, E. L. Run silent, run deep
Robinson, P. Kilo class
Robinson, P. Nimitz class
Verne, J. The extraordinary journeys: Twenty thousand leagues under the sea
Submergence. Ledgard, J. M.
Submission.
The **submission.** Waldman, A.
SUBSTANCE ABUSE
See also Social problems
Subtle bodies. Rush, N.
SUBURBAN LIFE
Berger, T. Neighbors
Cheever, J. Bullet Park
Coben, H. Caught
Coben, H. Hold tight
Cohen, L. H. The grief of others
Connell, E. S. Mrs. Bridge
Ford, R. Independence Day
Gordimer, N. No time like the present
Grodstein, L. A friend of the family
Hamilton, J. When Madeline was young
Hill, R. When all is said and done
Isaacs, S. As husbands go
Johnson, D. Elsewhere, California
Just, W. S. An unfinished season
Kiefer, C. The infinite tides
Levin, I. The Stepford wives
McDermott, A. That night
Ng, C. Little fires everywhere
Oates, J. C. American appetites
Oates, J. C. Middle age
Oates, J. C. Missing mom
Perrotta, T. The abstinence teacher
Perrotta, T. The leftovers
Perrotta, T. Little children
Perry, D. This is just exactly like you
Powers, J. F. Wheat that springeth green
Roth, P. American pastoral
Scottoline, L. Come home
Stead, C. The man who loved children
Tropper, J. How to talk to a widower
Tyler, A. The amateur marriage
Walter, J. The financial lives of the poets
White, K. The night the lights went out
Wilson, S. The man in the gray flannel suit
SUBURBAN LIFE -- ENGLAND
Ballard, J. G. Kingdom come
SUBURBS
Ballard, J. G. Kingdom come
Davis, K. Duplex
SUBURBS -- ILLINOIS -- CHICAGO
Lancaster, J. Here I go again
SUBWAYS
Preston, D. Reliquary
Vine, B. King Solomon's carpet
Wray, J. Lowboy
SUBWAYS

See also Local transit; Railroads
SUCCESS
Adiga, A. The white tiger
Bradford, B. T. A woman of substance
Fitzgerald, F. S. The great Gatsby
Lee Aloft
Millhauser, S. Martin Dressler
O'Hara, J. Ten North Frederick
Spiotta, D. Innocents and others
SUCCESS
See also Business ethics; Wealth
Succession [series]
Westerfeld, S. The killing of worlds
Westerfeld, S. The risen empire
The **Successor.** Kadare, I.
SUDAN
Caputo, P. Acts of faith
Eggers, D. What is the what
SUDAN -- HISTORY -- CIVIL WAR, 1983-2005
Eggers, D. What is the what
The **Sudden** Appearance of Hope. North, C.
SUDDEN DEATH IN INFANTS *See* Sudden infant death syndrome
SUDDEN INFANT DEATH SYNDROME
Hannah, S. The cradle in the grave
Palahniuk, C. Lullaby
A **sudden** wild magic. Jones, D. W.
Suder. Everett, P.
SUDOKU
See also Puzzles
SUENO, GEORGE (FICTITIOUS CHARACTER)
Limón, M. Mr. Kill
SUFFERING
Brockmeier, K. The Illumination
SUFFRAGE
See also Citizenship; Constitutional law; Democracy; Elections; Political science
SUFFRAGETTES *See* Suffragists
SUFFRAGISTS
Hatcher, R. L. Catching Katie
Piercy, M. Sex wars
SUGAR
See also Food
The **sugar** queen. Allen, S. A.
Sugar Street. Mahfouz, N.
SUICIDE
See also Medical jurisprudence; Social problems
Banasky, C. The suicide of Claire Bishop
Elias, G. Death and transfiguration
Elkins, A. J. Dying on the vine
George, E. A Banquet of Consequences
Hayder, M. Skin
Jones, J. S. The silence
King, S. End of watch
Lackberg, C. The ice princess
McDermott, A. The ninth hour
McPherson, C. The child garden
Moore, C. Sacre bleu
Moyes, J. Me before you
O'Donovan, G. Dublin dead
Palwick, S. The necessary beggar
Two she-bears
Winters, B. H. The last policeman
SUICIDE ATTEMPTS *See* Suicide
SUICIDE BOMBERS
See also Terrorism
The **suicide** motor club. Buehlman, C.
The **suicide** of Claire Bishop. Banasky, C.
SUICIDE VICTIMS
Boswell, R. Century's son
Hill, A. The good suicides
Palwick, S. Mending the moon
A **suitable** boy. Seth, V.
Suitcase city. Watson, S.
Suite Francaise. Nemirovsky, I.
Sula. Morrison, T.
SULFONAMIDES
See also Drugs
Sulla, Lucius Cornelius
About
McCullough, C. The first man in Rome
Sullivan's law. Rosenberg, N. T.
Sullivan's sting. Sanders, L.
SUMMER
Bradbury, R. Dandelion wine
Cline, E. The girls
The **summer** before the war. Simonson, H.
SUMMER CAMPS
Dalton, J. The inverted forest
Swarthout, G. F. Bless the beasts and children
Summer in Baden-Baden. Tsypkin, L.
Summer lies.
Summer light. Rice, L.
The **summer** of dead toys. Hill, A.
The **summer** of Katya. Trevanian
The **summer** of the bear. Pollen, B.
The **summer** of the Danes. Peters, E.
The **Summer** Queen. Vinge, J. D.
Summer rental. Andrews, M. K.
SUMMER RESORTS
Appelfeld, A. Badenheim 1939
Benchley, P. Jaws
Hensher, P. King of the badgers
Morrison, T. Love
Summer sisters. Blume, J.
SUMMER SOLSTICE
Adrian, C. The great night
Summerland. Hilderbrand, E.
Summerlong. Beagle, P. S.
Summertime. Coetzee, J. M.
A **summons** to Memphis. Taylor, P. H.
The **sun** also rises. Hemingway, E.
The **Sun** King. Ignatius, D.
SUN WORSHIP

See also Religion
SUNDARBANS (BANGLADESH AND INDIA)
Ghosh, A. The hungry tide
SUNDIALS
See also Clocks and watches; Garden ornaments and furniture; Time
SUNKEN TREASURE *See* Buried treasure
A **sunless** sea. Perry, A.
The **sunne** in splendour. Penman, S. K.
Sunnyside. Gold, G. D.
Sunset and sawdust. Lansdale, J. R.
Sunset in St. Tropez. Steel, D.
Sunset Park. Auster, P.
Sunstroke and other stories. Hadley, T.
SUPER BOWL (GAME)
See also Football; Sports tournaments
Super sad true love story. Shteyngart, G.
SUPERNATURAL
Bennett, R. J. American elsewhere
Browne, S. G. Lucky bastard
Extence, G. The Universe Versus Alex Woods
Kaufmann, N. Dying Is My Business
Kay, G. G. Ysabel
King, S. End of watch
Kunzru, H. Gods without men
Mitchell, D. The bone clocks
Nevill, A. The ritual
North, C. The Sudden Appearance of Hope
O'Malley, D. The rook
Pettersson, V. The taken
Powers, T. Declare
Powers, T. Hide me among the graves
Saint James, S. The haunting of Maddy Clare
Sakey, M. Brilliance
Tremblay, P. Disappearance at Devil's Rock
Walton, L. The strange and beautiful sorrows of Ava Lavender
Wilson, G. W. Alif the unseen
SUPERNATURAL GRAPHIC NOVELS
See also Graphic novels
SUPERNATURAL PHENOMENA
Adrian, C. The children's hospital
Allen, S. A. The sugar queen
Allende, I. The house of the spirits
Baker, T. The little giant of Aberdeen County
Barry, B. The lace reader
Bradbury, R. Something wicked this way comes
Drury, T. The driftless area
Farnsworth, C. Blood oath
Ford, J. The drowned life
Gregory, D. Pandemonium
Hill, R. The Stranger House
Hooper, K. Blood sins
Hooper, K. Blood ties
Johansen, I. Final target
Johnson, A. D. Moonshine
Jones, D. Second grave on the left
Kasischke, L. The raising
King, S. Carrie
King, S. Firestarter
King, S. Salem's Lot
Koontz, D. R. Brother Odd
Koontz, D. R. The darkest evening of the year
Koryta, M. The Cypress House
Koryta, M. The ridge
LaValle, V. D. Big machine
Levin, I. Rosemary's baby
Lewis, M. G. The monk
Lofts, N. Gad's Hall
Lord, K. Redemption in indigo
Lovecraft, H. P. At the mountains of madness, and other novels
Lovecraft, H. P. The Dunwich horror, and others
Michaels, B. Stitches in time
Naylor, G. Mama Day
Picoult, J. Change of heart
Power, S. The grass dancer
Powers, T. Three days to never
Preston, D. The wheel of darkness
Rayne, S. Property of a lady
Reynolds, S. A gracious plenty
Rice, A. The witching hour
Richardson, K. Greywalker
Riley, J. M. In pursuit of the green lion
Roberts, N. Midnight Bayou
Rogers, R. Devil's Cape
Stoker, B. Dracula
Stott, R. Ghostwalk
Straub, P. Ghost story
Straub, P. Mr. X
Wallace, D. The Watermelon King
Waters, S. The little stranger
Wilde, O. The picture of Dorian Gray
Wolfe, G. Castleview
Wolfe, G. The sorcerer's house
SUPERSTITION
Carey, L. The stolen child
Kadare, I. The ghost rider
Naylor, G. Mama Day
SUPERSTITION
See also Folklore
The **Supremes** at Earl's all-you-can-eat. Moore, E. K.
The **Supremes** sing the happy heartache blues. Moore, E. K.
SURFERS
Winslow, D. The Dawn Patrol
Winslow, D. The gentlemen's hour
Winton, T. Breath
SURGEONS
Gundar-Goshen, A. Waking lions
Hiaasen, C. Skin tight
Irving, J. The fourth hand
Jacob, M. The sleepwalker's guide to dancing
Kundera, M. The unbearable lightness of being
Laplante, A. Turn of mind

Palmer, M. The last surgeon
Parsons, K. Doing harm
Uris, L. QB VII
SURGEONS
See also Physicians
SURGERY
Cook, R. Coma
Cook, R. Marker
Palmer, M. The patient
SURREALISM
Aira, C. The literary conference
Bolano, R. By night in Chile
Burroughs, W. S. Naked lunch
Childress, M. Crazy in Alabama
Donohue, K. Centuries of June
Ellis, B. E. Lunar Park
Erickson, S. Zeroville
Foer, J. S. Everything is illuminated
Garcia Marquez, G. The autumn of the patriarch
Gholson, C. A fish trapped inside the wind
Grushin, O. The dream life of Sukhanov
The hall of singing caryatids
Harkaway, N. The gone-away world
Ishiguro, K. The unconsoled
Ishiguro, K. When we were orphans
Kafka on the shore
Lethem, J. Chronic city
Lethem, J. The fortress of solitude
Munoz Molina, A. In her absence
Murakami, H. The wind-up bird chronicle
Murakami, H. 1Q84
Murakami, H. South of the border, west of the sun
Saramago, J. Blindness
Shteyngart, G. The Russian debutante's handbook
Surrender, Dorothy. Wolitzer, M.
The **surrendered.** Lee
SURREY (ENGLAND)
Dean, A. A gentleman of fortune, or, The suspicions of Miss Dido Kent
The **surrogate.** Carver, T.
SURROGATE MOTHERS
The confidant
Shearn, A. How far is the ocean from here
Weiner, J. Then came you
SURROGATE MOTHERS
See also Mothers
Surveillance. Raban, J.
SURVEILLANCE, ELECTRONIC *See* Electronic surveillance
SURVEYORS
Pynchon, T. Mason & Dixon
SURVEYS
See also Research
SURVIVAL (AFTER AIRPLANE ACCIDENTS, SHIPWRECKS, ETC.)
Defoe, D. Robinson Crusoe
Frank, P. Alas, Babylon
Golding, W. Lord of the flies
Hawley, N. Before the Fall
Martel, Y. Life of Pi
McCarthy, C. The road
O'Brian, P. The unknown shore
Putney, M. J. Loving a lost lord
Rogan, C. The lifeboat
Simmons, D. The terror
Tournier, M. Friday
Vonnegut, K. Galapagos
SURVIVAL
Bell, A. The reapers are the angels
Brown, T. Fallen land
Cronin, J. The city of mirrors
Cronin, J. The twelve
Elison, M. The book of Etta
Elison, M. The Book of the Unnamed Midwife
Heller, P. The dog stars
Newman, S. The Country of Ice Cream Star
Phillips, G. Fierce kingdom
Smith, G. B. The maze at Windermere
This way to the end times
SURVIVAL -- PSYCHOLOGICAL ASPECTS
Sager, R. Final girls
SURVIVAL SKILLS
Heller, P. The dog stars
Johansen, I. No easy target
The **survivor.** Hurwitz, G.
Survivors' Club [series]
Balogh, M. The escape
Suspect. Robotham, M.
Suspended sentences. Modiano, P.
SUSPENSE FICTION
Addison, C. A harvest of thorns
Arango, S. The truth and other lies
Blame
Bollen, C. Orient
Box, C. J. Badlands
Boylan, J. F. Long Black Veil
Buckley, W. F. Mongoose, R.I.P
Caldwell, I. The rule of four
Carter, S. L. Palace council
Clancy, T. Clear and present danger
Clancy, T. Patriot games
Coben, H. Stay close
Coleman, R. F. Where it hurts
Cox, M. The meaning of night
Crouch, B. Dark matter
Cumming, C. A divided spy
Darnielle, J. Universal harvester
Deaver, J. Edge
Dodd, C. The woman who couldn't scream
Dovey, C. Blood kin
Down, D. Masaryk Station
Eastland, S. The Beast in the Red Forest
Eastland, S. Shadow pass
Eggers, D. The Circle

Ellroy, J. Blood's a rover
Epperson, T. Sailor
Evans, J. The white devil
Faulks, S. Devil may care
Finn, A. J. The woman in the window
Furst, A. The spies of Warsaw
Gibson, W. Spook country
Glynn, A. Bloodland
Gowdy, B. Helpless
Grisham, J. The client
Grisham, J. The pelican brief
Grisham, J. Ford County
Gundar-Goshen, A. Waking lions
Hall, J. W. Buzz cut
Hall, S. The raw shark texts
Harris, R. Conclave
Harris, R. The fear index
Harrison, C. The finder
Hart, J. Redemption road
Hayder, M. Hanging hill
Hiaasen, C. Lucky you
Hiaasen, C. Skinny dip
Hill, J. Heart-shaped box
Hilton, L. S. Maestra
Hoeg, P. Smilla's sense of snow
Hunter, S. Dead zero
Hunter, S. Soft target
Ignatius, D. A firing offense
Iles, G. Mississippi blood
Isaacs, S. After all these years
Jackson, B. Forged in desire
Johansen, I. No easy target
Katzenbach, J. What comes next
King, S. Finders Keepers
King, S. Mr. Mercedes
Knopf, C. Dead anyway
Koryta, M. The Cypress House
Krentz, J. A. Promise not to tell
Krentz, J. A. Secret sisters
Lane, H. Alys, always
Larsson, S. The girl who kicked the hornets' nest
Lasdun, J. The fall guy
Le Carre, J. A most wanted man
Leon, D. Falling in Love
Les Becquets, D. Breaking wild
Limón, M. Mr. Kill
Littell, R. Vicious circle
Lutz, L. The Passenger
Mackintosh, C. I see you
Macmillan, G. The perfect girl
McCormack, M. Solar bones
McGuire, I. The North water
Meltzer, B. The tenth justice
Meyer, D. Trackers
Morgan Jones, C. The silent oligarch
Mosley, W. The man in my basement
Never let you go
Nicholas, D. Something red
O'Flynn, C. The news where you are
Parris, S. J. Sacrilege
Patterson, J. Along came a spider
Patterson, J. Cat & mouse
Pearl, M. The technologists
Penney, S. The invisible ones
Perry, T. Shadow woman
Peters, E. Guardian of the horizon
Phillips, G. Fierce kingdom
Picoult, J. Vanishing acts
Redhill, M. Bellevue Square
Reich, C. Rules of deception
Reid, I. I'm thinking of ending things
Rendell, R. The keys to the street
Rice, A. Angel time
Rosenberg, J. C. The twelfth Imam
Roy, L. Let me die in his footsteps
Schickler, D. Sweet and vicious
Scottoline, L. Every fifteen minutes
Shreve, A. The weight of water
Smith, M. A. The Inquisitor
Smith, M. C. Rose
Smith, T. R. Child 44
Smith, T. R. The secret speech
Steiner, P. The terrorist
Steinhauer, O. The nearest exit
Stott, R. The coral thief
Tartt, D. The secret history
Tran, V. Dragonfish
Tursten, H. Night rounds
Verdon, J. Think of a number
Vine, B. Anna's book
Vine, B. Gallowglass
Vine, B. No night is too long
Waite, U. The terror of living
Ware, R. The Woman in Cabin Ten
Weaver, A. A most novel revenge
Winslow, D. The cartel
Winslow, D. The force
Wouk, H. A hole in Texas

SUSPENSE NOVELS

Ackroyd, P. The trial of Elizabeth Cree
Atkins, A. Wicked city
Barry, B. The lace reader
Berry, S. The Charlemagne pursuit
Black, L. Takeover
Block, L. Killing Castro
Brown, D. The Da Vinci code
Brown, S. The witness
Byatt, A. S. Possession
Cain, C. Heartsick
Caldwell, I. The rule of four
Carr, C. The alienist
Carter, S. L. The emperor of Ocean Park
Carter, S. L. Palace council
Clancy, T. Clear and present danger

Clancy, T. The hunt for Red October
Clancy, T. Patriot games
Clark, M. The legal limit
Coben, H. Hold tight
Coben, H. The woods
Coel, M. Blood memory
Cook, R. Marker
Cook, R. Vector
Cook, T. H. Instruments of night
Costello, M. Big if
Cox, M. The meaning of night
Crais, R. Demolition angel
Crichton, M. Prey
Cussler, C. Fire ice
Cussler, C. Lost city
Cussler, C. White death
Deaver, J. Garden of beasts
Deighton, L. Berlin game
Deighton, L. The Ipcress file
Deighton, L. London match
DeMille, N. Plum Island
DeMille, N. Wild fire
Dickey, J. Deliverance
D'Souza, T. Whiteman
Estleman, L. D. Something borrowed, something black
Fairstein, L. Entombed
Faulks, S. Devil may care
Fielding, J. Heartstopper
Finder, J. Vanished
Flanagan, R. The unknown terrorist
Fleming, I. Casino Royale
Fleming, I. Doctor No
Fleming, I. From Russia, with love
Fleming, I. Goldfinger
Fleming, I. The man with the golden gun
Fleming, I. On Her Majesty's Secret Service
Fleming, I. You only live twice
Flynn, G. Sharp objects
Flynn, G. Dark places
Follett, K. Eye of the needle
Follett, K. Hornet flight
Follett, K. Jackdaws
Forsyth, F. Avenger
Forsyth, F. The day of the jackal
Forsyth, F. The Odessa file
Freeman, C. Go with me
French, T. Faithful Place
French, T. In the woods
French, T. The likeness
Furst, A. The foreign correspondent
Gallagher, S. The kingdom of bones
Gardiner, M. The Dirty Secrets Club
Gardner, L. Alone
Gerritsen, T. Body double
Gibson, W. Spook country
Gilman, D. The amazing Mrs. Pollifax
Gilman, D. The elusive Mrs. Pollifax
Goddard, R. Into the blue
Goddard, R. Never go back
Goldman, W. Marathon man
Gowdy, B. Helpless
Grady, J. Six days of the condor
Green, G. D. Ravens
Griffin, W. E. B. By order of the President
Grippando, J. Born to run
Grippando, J. Lying with strangers
Grisham, J. The client
Grisham, J. The pelican brief
Grisham, J. The brethren
Grisham, J. The firm
Grisham, J. The last juror
Grisham, J. The partner
Gruber, M. The book of air and shadows
Gruber, M. The forgery of Venus
Gruber, M. Valley of bones
Hall, A. Quiller Balalaika
Hall, A. The Quiller memorandum
Hall, A. Quiller Salamander
Hall, A. Quiller solitaire
Hall, S. The raw shark texts
Hambly, B. Days of the dead
Hambly, B. Dead water
Hambly, B. Die upon a kiss
Hambly, B. A free man of color
Hambly, B. Graveyard dust
Hambly, B. Sold down the river
Hambly, B. Wet grave
Hand, E. Generation loss
Hannah, S. The wrong mother
Harris, R. Archangel
Harris, R. Enigma
Harris, R. Fatherland
Harris, R. The ghost
Harris, R. Pompeii
Harris, T. Hannibal
Harris, T. Hannibal rising
Harris, T. Red Dragon
Harris, T. The silence of the lambs
Harrison, C. The finder
Hart, J. The king of lies
Hart, J. The last child
Hiaasen, C. Lucky you
Higgins, J. Bad company
Higgins, J. Confessional
Higgins, J. Day of reckoning
Higgins, J. Edge of danger
Higgins, J. Eye of the storm
Higgins, J. Luciano's luck
Higgins, J. Midnight runner
Higgins, J. Night of the fox
Higgins, J. Rough justice
Higgins, J. Touch the devil
Higgins, J. The White House connection
Highsmith, P. The boy who followed Ripley

Highsmith, P. The talented Mr. Ripley; Ripley under ground; Ripley's game
Hill, R. The Stranger House
Hoag, T. Dark horse
Hoag, T. Dust to dust
Hoag, T. Guilty as sin
Hoag, T. Kill the messenger
Hoag, T. Night sins
Hoeg, P. Smilla's sense of snow
Hooper, K. Blood sins
Hooper, K. Finding Laura
Hospital, J. T. Due preparations for the plague
Hunter, E. Privileged conversation
Hunter, S. The 47th samurai
Hunter, S. Black light
Hunter, S. Dirty white boys
Hunter, S. Havana
Hunter, S. Time to hunt
Huston, C. Caught stealing
Huston, C. The shotgun rule
Huyler, F. The laws of invisible things
Ignatius, D. A firing offense
Iles, G. Black cross
Iles, G. The devil's punchbowl
Iles, G. The footprints of God
Iles, G. Mortal fear
Iles, G. Third degree
Iles, G. Turning angel
Johansen, I. And then you die--
Johansen, I. Blind alley
Johansen, I. Final target
Johansen, I. Long after midnight
Kanon, J. Los Alamos
Katzenbach, J. The analyst
Katzenbach, J. Just cause
Kellerman, J. The genius
Kinder, R. M. An absolute gentleman
King, L. R. A darker place
King, L. R. Keeping watch
King, S. Dolores Claiborne
King, S. Misery
Koontz, D. R. The bad place
Koontz, D. R. Brother Odd
Koontz, D. R. The darkest evening of the year
Koontz, D. R. The husband
Koontz, D. R. Intensity
Koontz, D. R. Velocity
Krentz, J. A. Running hot
Kress, N. Dogs
Kunzru, H. My revolutions
Larsson, S. The girl with the dragon tattoo
Larsson, S. The girl who played with fire
Lashner, W. A killer's kiss
Lawton, J. Old flames
Le Carre, J. The constant gardener
Le Carre, J. The honourable schoolboy
Le Carre, J. The little drummer girl
Le Carre, J. A perfect spy
Le Carre, J. Smiley's people
Le Carre, J. The spy who came in from the cold
Le Carre, J. Tinker, tailor, soldier, spy
Lehane, D. Shutter Island
Leonard, E. Freaky Deaky
Leonard, E. Glitz
Leonard, E. Killshot
Leonard, E. LaBrava
Leonard, E. Mr. Paradise
Leroy, M. Postcards from Berlin
Lescroart, J. T. The first law
Lescroart, J. T. Guilt
Lescroart, J. T. The hearing
Lescroart, J. T. Nothing but the truth
Lescroart, J. T. The oath
Levien, D. City of the sun
Levin, I. The boys from Brazil
Lindsay, J. P. Dearly devoted Dexter
Littell, R. Vicious circle
Logan, C. South of Shiloh
Long, J. The reckoning
Lowell, E. Pearl Cove
Ludlum, R. The Bourne identity
Ludlum, R. The Bourne supremacy
Ludlum, R. The Bourne ultimatum
Ludlum, R. The Gemini contenders
Ludlum, R. The Janson directive
Ludlum, R. The Matlock paper
Ludlum, R. The Prometheus deception
Ludlum, R. The Rhinemann exchange
Ludlum, R. The Sigma protocol
Lustbader, E. V. Floating city
Lutz, J. Final seconds
MacInnes, H. Prelude to terror
MacInnes, H. Ride a pale horse
MacInnes, H. The Venetian affair
Margolin, P. Wild justice
Matheson, R. Hunted past reason
McBain, E. Alice in jeopardy
McCammon, R. R. Boy's life
McCarry, C. Old boys
McCrumb, S. The ballad of Frankie Silver
McCrumb, S. If ever I return, pretty Peggy-O
McCrumb, S. She walks these hills
McDermid, V. The distant echo
McDermid, V. A place of execution
McEwan, I. Black dogs
McEwan, I. The innocent
Meltzer, B. The tenth justice
Meltzer, B. The zero game
Meyer, D. Heart of the hunter
Michaels, B. Houses of stone
Mrazek, R. J. Unholy fire
Muller, M. Cyanide Wells
Neville, K. The eight
Neville, K. The fire

Newton, C. Calumet City
O'Connell, C. Judas child
Ogilvie, E. When the music stopped
O'Nan, S. The names of the dead
O'Shaughnessy, P. Breach of promise
O'Shaughnessy, P. Invasion of privacy
O'Shaughnessy, P. Motion to suppress
O'Shaughnessy, P. Obstruction of justice
O'Shaughnessy, P. Unlucky in law
O'Shaughnessy, P. Writ of execution
Palmer, M. The fifth vial
Palmer, M. Miracle cure
Palmer, M. The patient
Palmer, M. The society
Parker, B. Criminal justice
Parker, B. Suspicion of betrayal
Parker, B. Suspicion of deceit
Parker, B. Suspicion of vengeance
Parker, T. J. Black water
Parker, T. J. The blue hour
Parker, T. J. California girl
Parker, T. J. Cold pursuit
Parker, T. J. The fallen
Parker, T. J. L.A. outlaws
Parker, T. J. Little Saigon
Parker, T. J. Silent Joe
Parker, T. J. Storm runners
Parker, T. J. Where serpents lie
Patterson, J. Along came a spider
Patterson, J. 1st to die
Patterson, J. Cat & mouse
Patterson, J. Cross
Patterson, J. Four blind mice
Patterson, J. Hide & seek
Patterson, J. Jack and Jill
Patterson, J. Kiss the girls
Patterson, J. London bridges
Patterson, J. Roses are red
Patterson, R. N. Balance of power
Patterson, R. N. Conviction
Patterson, R. N. Dark lady
Patterson, R. N. Eclipse
Patterson, R. N. No safe place
Patterson, R. N. Silent witness
Pattison, E. The skull mantra
Pearl, M. The Dante Club
Pearson, R. The angel maker
Pearson, R. The art of deception
Pearson, R. Beyond recognition
Pearson, R. The body of David Hayes
Pearson, R. The first victim
Pearson, R. Middle of nowhere
Pelecanos, G. P. Shame the devil
Pelecanos, G. P. The sweet forever
Perez-Reverte, A. The nautical chart
Perry, T. Blood money
Perry, T. Dance for the dead
Perry, T. The face-changers
Perry, T. Fidelity
Perry, T. Nightlife
Perry, T. Pursuit
Perry, T. Runner
Perry, T. Shadow woman
Perry, T. Vanishing act
Picoult, J. Vanishing acts
Pottinger, S. The last Nazi
Poyer, D. Down to a sunless sea
Preston, D. Blasphemy
Preston, D. Brimstone
Preston, D. The cabinet of curiosities
Preston, D. The codex
Preston, D. Reliquary
Preston, D. Still life with crows
Preston, D. Tyrannosaur Canyon
Preston, D. The wheel of darkness
Price, N. Night woman
Pronzini, B. The crimes of Jordan Wise
Pronzini, B. In an evil time
Pronzini, B. Step to the graveyard easy
Pyper, A. The killing circle
Quick, A. I thee wed
Quick, A. Late for the wedding
Quick, A. Slightly shady
Quick, A. Wicked widow
Rabb, J. The book of Q
Rankin, I. Watchman
Redfern, E. Auriel rising
Reich, C. Rules of deception
Reichs, K. J. Deja dead
Rendell, R. The bridesmaid
Rendell, R. Heartstones
Rendell, R. A judgment in stone
Rendell, R. The keys to the street
Rendell, R. Live flesh
Rendell, R. A sight for sore eyes
Rendell, R. The water's lovely
Reuland, R. Semiautomatic
Rigosi, G. Night bus
Riordan, R. Cold Springs
Robards, K. Ghost moon
Robbins, D. L. War of the rats
Roberts, N. Angel's fall
Roberts, N. Midnight Bayou
Robinson, P. Kilo class
Robinson, P. Nimitz class
Robinson, P. The first cut
Rosenberg, N. T. First offense
Rosenberg, N. T. Interest of justice
Rosenberg, N. T. Sullivan's law
Rosenfelt, D. Don't tell a soul
Ruiz Zafon, C. The shadow of the wind
Sanchez, T. King Bongo
Sanders, L. The first deadly sin
Sanders, L. The second deadly sin

Sanders, L. The sixth commandment
Sanders, L. Sullivan's sting
Sanders, L. The third deadly sin
Sansom, C. J. Winter in Madrid
Schickler, D. Sweet and vicious
Scottoline, L. Legal tender
Scottoline, L. Mistaken identity
Scottoline, L. Moment of truth
Scottoline, L. Rough justice
Seymour, G. Killing ground
Seymour, G. Rat run
Shreve, A. Testimony
Shreve, A. The weight of water
Silva, D. The mark of the assassin
Silva, D. The messenger
Silva, D. Prince of Fire
Silva, D. The secret servant
Smith, A. Judas horse
Smith, M. C. December 6
Smith, S. A simple plan
Smith, T. R. Child 44
Smith, T. R. The secret speech
Stark, R. Ask the parrot
Stark, R. Breakout
Stark, R. Dirty money
Stark, R. The hunter
Stark, R. The jugger
Steinhauer, O. The Bridge of Sighs
Steinhauer, O. The tourist
Stephenson, N. Cryptonomicon
Stewart, M. Airs above the ground
Stewart, M. The moon-spinners
Stone, R. Damascus Gate
Tanenbaum, R. Act of revenge
Tartt, D. The secret history
Theorin, J. Echoes from the dead
Thomas, R. Ah, treachery!
Thomas, R. The fourth Durango
Tracy, P. J. Monkeewrench
Trevanian The Eiger sanction
Trevanian The Loo sanction
Trevor, W. Felicia's journey
Truscott, L. K. Heart of war
Turow, S. The laws of our fathers
Turow, S. Personal injuries
Turow, S. Reversible errors
Ure, L. The fault tree
Vargas Llosa, M. Death in the Andes
Vine, B. Gallowglass
Vine, B. Grasshopper
Vine, B. King Solomon's carpet
Vine, B. The minotaur
Vine, B. No night is too long
Volpi, J. In search of Klingsor
Walker, M. W. Under the beetle's cellar
Wallace, I. The man
Walters, M. The breaker
Walters, M. The dark room
Walters, M. The devil's feather
Walters, M. The echo
Walters, M. The sculptress
Walters, M. The shape of snakes
Watkins, P. The forger
West, M. L. The clowns of God
Westlake, D. E. Money for nothing
White, S. W. Dry ice
White, S. W. Kill me
White, S. W. Missing persons
Wilhelm, K. The best defense
Wilhelm, K. The deepest water
Wilhelm, K. Defense for the devil
Wilhelm, K. Desperate measures
Wilhelm, K. Malice prepense
Wilhelm, K. No defense
Wilson, F. P. Deep as the marrow
Wilson, R. The blind man of Seville
Wilson, R. The hidden assassins
Winslow, D. The winter of Frankie Machine
Wolfe, I. A. The calling
Wood, B. Perfect Harmony
Woods, S. Choke
Woods, S. Cold paradise
Woods, S. Dead eyes
Woods, S. Dead in the water
Woods, S. Dirt
Woods, S. Dirty work
Woods, S. Grass roots
Woods, S. Heat
Woods, S. Imperfect strangers
Woods, S. L.A. dead
Woods, S. L.A. Times
Woods, S. Orchid Beach
Woods, S. Reckless abandon
Woods, S. The run
Woods, S. Santa Fe rules
Woods, S. The short forever
Woods, S. Short straw
Woods, S. Swimming to Catalina
Woods, S. Two-dollar bill
Woods, S. Worst fears realized
Wouk, H. A hole in Texas
SUSPENSE NOVELS *See* Adventure fiction; Mystery fiction; Romantic suspense novels
SUSPENSE STORIES
Abbott, M. E. Bury me deep
Bayard, L. The school of night
Blatty, W. P. Dimiter
Bolton, S. J. Now you see me
Boyle, T. C. When the killing's done
Caputo, P. Crossers
Coben, H. Caught
Coulter, C. Split second
Doiron, P. The poacher's son
Dolan, H. Very bad men

Donoghue, E. Room
Downing, D. Potsdam station
Eastland, S. Eye of the Red Tsar
Finder, J. Buried secrets
Frazier, C. Nightwoods
Gibson, W. Zero history
Goddard, R. Long time coming
Grippando, J. Money to burn
Grisham, J. The confession
Gross, A. Eyes wide open
Gross, A. Reckless
Gruber, M. The good son
Hagberg, D. Abyss
Hannah, S. The cradle in the grave
Harper, K. Fall from pride
Haynes, D. Crashers
Hill, R. The woodcutter
Hogan, C. Devils in exile
Hooper, K. Blood ties
Hunter, S. I, sniper
Hurwitz, G. They're watching
Hurwitz, G. You're next
Jance, J. A. Queen of the night
Joss, M. Among the missing
Kelly, E. The poison tree
Kepler, L. The hypnotist
Koryta, M. The Cypress House
Koryta, M. So cold the river
Larsson, S. The girl who kicked the hornets' nest
Lupton, R. Sister
Meltzer, B. The inner circle
Nesbo, J. The headhunters
Palmer, M. The last surgeon
Patterson, J. I, Alex Cross
Perry, T. The informant
Polansky, D. Low Town
Pollock, D. R. The devil all the time
Preston, D. Impact
Pronzini, B. The hidden
Rice, A. Angel time
Rice, A. Of love and evil
Robotham, M. The wreckage
Rollins, J. The devil colony
Sakey, M. The two deaths of Daniel Hayes
Sallis, J. The killer is dying
Sidor, S. Pitch dark
Smith, R. Wake up dead
Spiegelman, P. Thick as thieves
Steiner, P. The terrorist
Steinhauer, O. The nearest exit
Stephenson, N. Reamde
Straub, P. A dark matter
Stroby, W. Cold shot to the heart
Swierczynski, D. Fun and games
Toyne, S. Sanctus
Trussoni, D. Angelology
Turow, S. Innocent
Verdon, J. Think of a number
Waite, U. The terror of living
Wilson, D. H. Robopocalypse
Winters, B. H. Bedbugs
Suspicion of betrayal. Parker, B.
Suspicion of deceit. Parker, B.
Suspicion of vengeance. Parker, B.
Sutton. Moehringer, J. R.
Sutton, Willie
About
Moehringer, J. R. Sutton
SWAGGER, BOB LEE (FICTITIOUS CHARACTER)
Hunter, S. Dead zero
Hunter, S. Hot Springs
Hunter, S. Pale horse coming
The **swallows** of Kabul. Moulessehoul, M.
Swami and friends, The bachelor of arts, The dark room, The English teacher. Narayan, R. K.
SWAMP ANIMALS
See also Animals
SWAMP ECOLOGY
See also Ecology; Wetland ecology
Swamplandia! Russell, K.
The **swan** thieves. Kostova, E.
Swann's way. Proust, M.
SWASHBUCKLERS *See* Adventure fiction; Adventure films
Sway. Lazar, Z.
SWEDEN
Another time, another life
Between summer's longing and winter's end
Dahl, A. Bad Blood
Edwardson, Å. Sail of stone
Kepler, L. The hypnotist
Lackberg, C. The ice princess
Larsson, S. The girl with the dragon tattoo
Larsson, S. The girl who kicked the hornets' nest
Larsson, S. The girl who played with fire
Lindgren, T. Hash
Mankell, H. The man from Beijing
Olsson, L. Astrid & Veronika
Theorin, J. Echoes from the dead
SWEDEN -- SOCIAL LIFE AND CUSTOMS
Lackberg, C. The hidden child
SWEDEN -- STOCKHOLM
Dahl, A. Misterioso
SWEDES -- ENGLAND
Vine, B. The minotaur
SWEDES -- ISLANDS OF THE PACIFIC
Conrad, J. Victory
SWEDES -- ZAMBIA
Mankell, H. The eye of the leopard
SWEDISH AMERICANS
Cather, W. O pioneers!
Cather, W. The song of the lark
SWEDISH FICTION -- TRANSLATIONS INTO ENGLISH
Larsson, S. The girl with the dragon tattoo
Larsson, S. The girl who kicked the hornets' nest

Mankell, H. The man from Beijing
Mankell, H. One step behind
SWEDISH LANGUAGE
See also Language and languages; Scandinavian languages
Sweet and vicious. Schickler, D.
Sweet Caress. Boyd, W.
The **sweet** dove died. Pym, B.
The **sweet** forever. Pelecanos, G. P.
The **sweet** girl. Lyon, A.
The **sweet** hereafter. Banks, R.
Sweet Lamb of Heaven. Millet, L.
Sweet land stories. Doctorow, E. L.
Sweet little lies. Shalvis, J.
Sweet salt air. Delinsky, B.
Sweet thunder. Doig, I.
Sweet Thursday. Steinbeck, J.
Sweet tooth. McEwan, I.
Sweetbitter. Danler, S.
The **sweetest** dream. Lessing, D. M.
Sweetland. Crummey, M.
The **sweetness** at the bottom of the pie. Bradley, A.
Sweetness in the belly. Gibb, C.
Sweetwater. Robinson, R.
Swim back to me. Packer, A.
The **Swimmer.** Zander, J.
SWIMMERS
Deford, F. Bliss, remembered
Swimming home. Levy, D.
The **swimming** pool. LeCraw, H.
Swimming to Catalina. Woods, S.
Swinburne, Algernon Charles, 1837-1909
About
Hodder, M. Expedition to the Mountains of the Moon
Hodder, M. The strange affair of Spring Heeled Jack
SWINDLERS AND SWINDLING
Blackstock, T. Shadow in serenity
Brown, J. D. Addie Pray
Cooper, T. The marauders
Dickens, C. Martin Chuzzlewit
Green, G. D. Ravens
Haigh, J. Mrs. Kimble
Joss, M. Half broken things
Lynch, S. The lies of Locke Lamora
Lynch, S. Red seas under red skies
Manchette Fatale
Melville, H. The confidence-man: his masquerade
Michels, E. The rebel heir
Noire (Author) Natural born liar
Palahniuk, C. Choke
Phillips, A. The tragedy of Arthur
Rich, D. Caravan of thieves
Tinti, H. The good thief
SWINDLERS AND SWINDLING
See also Crime; Criminals
SWINDLERS AND SWINDLING -- VIOLENCE AGAINST
French, N. Tuesday's gone
Swing time. Smith, Z.
SWITZERLAND
Brookner, A. Hotel du Lac
Reich, C. Rules of deception
Steele, J. The watchers
Wharton, E. The children
SWITZERLAND -- GENEVA
Ludlum, R. The Sigma protocol
Sword at sunset. Sutcliff, R.
The **sword** in the stone. White, T. H.
Sword of honor. Kirk, D.
The **sword** of Shannara. Brooks, T.
The **sword** of the Lictor. Wolfe, G.
SWORDS
Hunter, S. The 47th samurai
Swordspoint. Kushner, E.
Sworn to silence. Castillo, L.
Sycamore. Chancellor, B.
Sycamore Row. Grisham, J.
SYMBIOSIS
See also Biology; Ecology
SYMBOLIC LOGIC
See also Logic; Mathematics
SYMBOLISM
Ballard, J. G. The day of creation
Barth, J. Giles goat-boy
Bellow, S. Henderson the rain king
Coetzee, J. M. Foe
Faulkner, W. A fable
Fowles, J. The magus
Garcia, C. The Aguero sisters
Gordimer, N. The conservationist
Grass, G. Cat and mouse
Grass, G. The Danzig trilogy
Grass, G. Dog years
Grass, G. The tin drum
Grushin, O. The line
Hawthorne, N. The scarlet letter
Hesse, H. Steppenwolf
Hoeg, P. The history of Danish dreams
Hulme, K. The bone people
Irving, J. A prayer for Owen Meany
Joyce, J. Ulysses
Kafka, F. Metamorphosis
Kafka, F. The trial
Krauss, N. Great house
Mann, T. The black swan
Mann, T. Death in Venice
Mann, T. The magic mountain
Martel, Y. Beatrice and Virgil
Mawer, S. The glass room
Melville, H. Billy Budd, sailor
Melville, H. Moby-Dick; or, The whale
Momaday, N. S. The ancient child
Morrison, T. Beloved
Murakami, H. The wind-up bird chronicle
Murdoch, I. Nuns and soldiers

Nabokov, V. V. Ada
Nabokov, V. V. Pale fire
O'Brien, T. In the Lake of the Woods
Okuizumi, H. The stones cry out
Percy, W. Lancelot
Porter, K. A. Ship of fools
Pynchon, T. V.
Roy, A. The god of small things
Rushdie, S. The satanic verses
Rushdie, S. The ground beneath her feet
Tan, A. The bonesetter's daughter
Theroux, P. The Mosquito Coast
Thomas, D. M. The white hotel
Updike, J. Roger's version
Vargas Llosa, M. The Green House
Walbert, K. The gardens of Kyoto
Wiesel, E. A beggar in Jerusalem
Woolf, V. Between the acts
Woolf, V. The waves
SYMBOLISM
See also Art; Mythology
SYMBOLISM IN LITERATURE
See also Literature; Symbolism
SYMBOLISM OF NUMBERS
See also Symbolism
The **Sympathizer.** Nguyen, V. T.
SYMPATHY
See also Conduct of life; Emotions
The symphony of ages [series]
Haydon, E. The Merchant Emperor
Syndrome E.
SYNDROMES
See also Diseases; Pathology
Synge, J. M. (John Millington), 1871-1909
About
O'Connor, J. Ghost light
SYPHILIS
See also Sexually transmitted diseases
SYRIA
Ackerman, E. Dark at the Crossing
Werfel, F. The forty days of Musa Dagh
SYRIA -- HISTORY -- CIVIL WAR, 2011-
Khadivi, L. A good country
SYRIANS -- BRAZIL
Amado, J. Gabriela, clove and cinnamon
SYSTEMS ENGINEERING
See also Automation; Cybernetics; Engineering; Industrial design; System analysis; System theory
Szilard, Leo
About
Millet, L. Oh pure and radiant heart

T

T is for trespass. Grafton, S.
TABLE TALK *See* Conversation
TABLE TENNIS
Jacobson, H. The mighty Walzer
Tabloid city. Hamill, P.
Tabula Rasa. Downie, R.
TAE KWON DO
See also Karate; Martial arts; Self-defense
Tag man. Mayor, A.
TAHITI
Maugham, W. S. The moon and sixpence
Melville, H. Omoo: a narrative of adventures in the South Seas
TAI CHI
See also Exercise; Martial arts
Tai Randolph mysteries [series]
Whittle, T. Blood, Ash, and Bone
Whittle, T. The Dangerous Edge of Things
The **tailor** of Panama. Le Carre, J.
Taipei. Tao Lin
TAIWAN -- HISTORY -- 1895-1945
Wu, J. The third son
Take a chance on me. Warren, S. M.
Take one candle light a room. Straight, S.
The **taken.** Wolfe, I. A.
The **taken.** Pettersson, V.
Takeover. Black, L.
Taking Eve. Johansen, I.
A **tale** for the time being. Ozeki, R. L.
The **tale** of Genji. Murasaki Shikibu
The **tale** of the body thief. Rice, A.
A **tale** of two cities. Dickens, C.
TALENT *See* Ability; Genius
The **talented** Mr. Ripley; Ripley under ground; Ripley's game. Highsmith, P.
The **talented** Ribkins. Hubbard, L.
TALES *See* Fables; Fairy tales; Folklore; Legends
Tales from a troubled land. Paton, A.
Tales from the Drones Club. Wodehouse, P. G.
Tales of Alvin Maker [series]
Card, O. S. Seventh son
TALIBAN
Hosseini, K. The kite runner
Young, T. W. The renegades
TALK SHOWS
See also Interviewing; Radio programs; Television programs
The **talk-funny** girl. Merullo, R.
TALKING *See* Conversation
Talking God. Hillerman, T.
Talking to the dead. Bingham, H.
TALL TALES
See also Folklore; Legends; Wit and humor
Tallgrass. Coldsmith, D.
Tallgrass. Dallas, S.
TALMUD
See also Hebrew literature; Jewish literature; Judaism
Talulla rising. Duncan, G.
The **taming** of the queen. Gregory, P.
Tamsin Harte. Ross-Macdonald, M.

TANK WARFARE
See also War
Tannie Maria Mystery [series]
Andrew, S. Recipes for Love and Murder
TANZANIA
Vassanji, M. G. The Magic of Saida
TAPE RECORDINGS, AUDIO *See* Sound recordings
Tapestry. Plain, B.
Tapestry of fortunes. Berg, E.
Taps. Morris, W.
Tar baby. Morrison, T.
TAROT
See also Card games; Fortune telling; Playing cards
Engelmann, K. The Stockholm Octavo
TASMANIA (AUSTRALIA)
Flanagan, R. Wanting
TASTE
Bender, A. The particular sadness of lemon cake
A **taste** for death. James, P. D.
The **taste** of salt. Southgate, M.
Tatiana. Smith, M. C.
TATTOOING
See also Manners and customs; Personal appearance
Lovesey, P. The tooth tattoo
TAX EVASION
See also Criminal law; White collar crimes
TAXICAB DRIVERS
O'Dell, T. Sister mine
TAXIDERMY
Martel, Y. Beatrice and Virgil
Millet, L. Magnificence
TEA
See, L. The tea girl of hummingbird lane
The **tea** girl of hummingbird lane. See, L.
Tea time for the traditionally built. McCall Smith, A.
TEACHER-STUDENT RELATIONSHIP
See also Child-adult relationship; Interpersonal relations; Teaching
Abbott, M. E. Dare me
Chang, L. S. All is forgotten, nothing is lost
Choi, S. My education
Godwin, G. Unfinished desires
Hall, B. The music teacher
Messud, C. The woman upstairs
Rader-Day, L. The black hour
Roth, P. The dying animal
Southgate, M. The fall of Rome
Tussing, J. The best people in the world
TEACHERS
Abe, K. The woman in the dunes
Adiga, A. Last man in tower
Amis, K. Lucky Jim
Banks, R. Lost memory of skin
Baxter, C. Saul and Patsy
Boswell, R. Century's son
Bynum, S. Ms. Hempel chronicles
Carter, S. L. The emperor of Ocean Park
Chabon, M. Wonder boys
Chang, L. S. All is forgotten, nothing is lost
Chaon, D. Await your reply
Cheever, J. Falconer
Coetzee, J. M. Disgrace
Cook, T. H. The Chatham School affair
Cook, T. H. Master of the delta
Cusk, R. Outline
Cusk, R. Transit
Davies, R. Fifth business
Dickens, C. Nicholas Nickleby
Doig, I. The whistling season
Durrell, L. Balthazar
Durrell, L. Clea
Durrell, L. Justine
Fielding, J. Heartstopper
Founds, K. When mystical creatures attack!
Fowles, J. The magus
Gaines, E. J. A lesson before dying
Godwin, G. The good husband
Godwin, G. Unfinished desires
Goldstein, R. 36 arguments for the existence of God
Goodman, C. Arcadia Falls
Goodman, C. The night villa
Gordimer, N. My son's story
Gordimer, N. No time like the present
Gordon, M. The company of women
Grant, S. Map of Ireland
Grunwald, L. The irresistible Henry House
Guterson, D. The other
Ha Jin The crazed
Haldeman, J. W. The coming
Hamilton, J. The short history of a prince
Harrison, J. The English major
Haruf, K. Plainsong
Haslett, A. Union Atlantic
Hegi, U. Children and fire
Heller, J. Good as Gold
Heller, Z. What was she thinking?
Hilton, J. Good-bye Mr. Chips
Huneven, M. Blame
Hunter, E. The blackboard jungle
Jacobson, H. The Finkler question
Johnson, M. Pym
Kaufman, B. Up the down staircase
Kinder, R. M. An absolute gentleman
Kirshenbaum, B. An almost perfect moment
Knowles, J. A separate peace
Lasdun, J. The horned man
Lavender, W. Dominance
Lightman, A. P. Reunion
Little, T. Where there's smoke
Lockridge, R. Raintree County
Lodge, D. Nice work
Lodge, D. Deaf sentence
Lodge, D. Thinks--
Ludlum, R. The Matlock paper

Lurie, A. Foreign affairs
MacDonald The way the crow flies
Marshall, C. Christy
McCarthy, M. The groves of Academe
Nabokov, V. V. Ada
Nabokov, V. V. Pale fire
Nabokov, V. V. Pnin
Nunez, E. Grace
Ozick, C. Foreign bodies
Parker, T. J. L.A. outlaws
Powers, R. Generosity
Price, N. Night woman
Prose, F. Blue angel
Read, P. P. The professor's daughter
Reuss, F. The wasties
Revoyr, N. Wingshooters
Rice, L. The geometry of sisters
Rosero Diago, E. The armies
Rossner, J. Looking for Mr. Goodbar
Roth, P. The dying animal
Roth, P. The human stain
Roth, P. Letting go
Roth, P. The professor of desire
Rush, N. Mortals
Russell, M. D. Dreamers of the day
Russo, R. The straight man
Russo, R. That old Cape magic
Sarton, M. As we are now
Sarton, M. A small room
Sartre, J. P. The age of reason
Smith, Z. On beauty
Southgate, M. The fall of Rome
Spark, M. The prime of Miss Jean Brodie
Stone, R. Bay of souls
Strout, E. Amy and Isabelle
Swift, G. Waterland
Tartt, D. The secret history
Theroux, A. Darconville's cat
Trollope, J. The men and the girls
Trueblood, V. Seven loves
Tussing, J. The best people in the world
Tyler, A. Noah's compass
Upadhyay, S. The guru of love
Updike, J. The centaur
Updike, J. Memories of the Ford Administration
Vassanji, M. G. The assassin's song
Walls, J. Half broke horses
Watkins, P. The ice soldier
Watrous, M. If you follow me
Yarbrough, S. Safe from the neighbors
TEACHERS' ASSISTANTS
Rader-Day, L. The black hour
TECHNOLOGICAL INNOVATIONS
See also Inventions; Technology
TECHNOLOGICAL INNOVATIONS
Weinstein, A. Children of the new world
The **technologists.** Pearl, M.
TECHNOLOGY
Anders, C. J. All the birds in the sky
Doctorow, C. Rapture of the nerds
TECHNOLOGY -- SOCIAL ASPECTS
Weinstein, A. Children of the new world
TECHNOLOGY AND CIVILIZATION
Burdick, E. Fail-safe
Graedon, A. The word exchange
Huxley, A. Brave new world
Percy, W. Love in the ruins
Vonnegut, K. Cat's cradle
Vonnegut, K. Player piano
Vonnegut, K. The sirens of Titan
TECHNOLOGY TRANSFER
See also Inventions; Technology
Tecumseh, Shawnee Chief, 1768-1813
About
Thom, J. A. Panther in the sky
TEEN AGE *See* Adolescence
TEENAGE BOYS
See also Boys; Teenagers
Abani, C. GraceLand
Aciman, A. A. Call me by your name
A clockwork orange
Coe, J. The Rotters' Club
Cooke, C. Daughters of the revolution
Cramer, W. D. Bad ground
Earley, T. The blue star
Edgerton, C. The Bible salesman
Follett, K. Hornet flight
Ford, R. Canada
Galloway, G. As simple as snow
Gilb, D. The flowers
Gohlke, C. I have seen him in the watchfires
Kafka on the shore
Kay, G. G. Ysabel
McMurtry, L. Boone's Lick
Mitchell, D. Black swan green
O'Dell, T. Back roads
O'Neill, J. At swim, two boys
Searles, J. Boy still missing
Shriver, L. We need to talk about Kevin
Slouka, M. Brewster
Sparks, N. A walk to remember
Wilson, E. O. Anthill
TEENAGE GIRLS
Abercrombie, J. Half the world
Ball, J. How to set a fire and why
Buntin, J. Marlena
French, N. Thursday's children
Fridlund, E. History of wolves
Gilman, L. A. The cold eye
Smith, A. How to be Both
TEENAGE GIRLS -- CRIMES AGAINST
French, N. Thursday's children
Sebold, A. The lovely bones
TEENAGE GIRLS -- CRIMES AGAINST -- MINNESOTA

Freeman, B. Spilled blood
TEENAGE GIRLS -- DEATH
Buntin, J. Marlena
TEENAGE GIRLS -- FAMILY RELATIONSHIPS
Teran, A. Ana of California
TEENAGE GIRLS -- NIGERIA
Watson, C. Tiny sunbirds, far away
TEENAGE PARENTS
Kingsolver, B. Flight behavior
TEENAGE PREGNANCY
See also Pregnancy
Bennett, B. The mothers
Hadley, T. Clever Girl
Thompson, V. Murder on Lenox Hill
TEENAGERS
See also Age; Youth
TEENAGERS -- BOOKS AND READING
See also Books and reading
TEENAGERS -- CRIMES AGAINST
Tucker, N. The ways of the dead
TEENAGERS -- DEVELOPMENT *See* Adolescence
TEENAGERS -- DRUG USE
Little, T. Where there's smoke
TEENAGERS -- FAMILY RELATIONSHIPS
Segal, F. The awkward age
TEENAGERS
Bradley, A. As chimney sweepers come to dust
Burns, C. Black hole
Dau, S. The book of Jonas
Ford, R. Canada
Galloway, G. As simple as snow
Grant, H. The glass demon
Kerangal, M. d. The heart
Khadivi, L. A good country
Little star
Pierson, D. C. The boy who couldn't sleep and never had to
Scotton, C. The secret wisdom of the earth
Walton, L. The strange and beautiful sorrows of Ava Lavender
Woods, C. Things to do when you're goth in the country
TEENAGERS -- GRAPHIC NOVELS
Merey, I. a + e 4ever
TEENAGERS -- LITERATURE *See* Young adult literature
TEENAGERS -- PENNSYLVANIA
Braffet, K. Save yourself
TEENAGERS -- SUICIDE
See also Suicide
Palwick, S. Mending the moon
TEETH -- DISEASES
See also Diseases
The **Tehran** initiative. Rosenberg, J. C.
TEL AVIV (ISRAEL)
Krauss, N. Forest dark
TELECOMMUNICATION
See also Communication
TELECOMMUTING
See also Automation; Telecommunication
Telegraph Avenue. Chabon, M.
TELEKINESIS *See* Psychokinesis
TELEPATHY
Irving, J. Avenue of mysteries
Johansen, I. The perfect witness
Le Guin, U. K. The left hand of darkness
Lee, P. Runner
Liu Cixin The dark forest
Rucker, R. v. B. Hylozoic
Vallgren The horrific sufferings of the mind-reading monster Hercules Barefoot
Willis, C. Crosstalk
TELEPATHY
See also Extrasensory perception
TELEVANGELISTS
See also Clergy; Television personalities
TELEVISION
Gilmore, J. Golden country
Irving, J. The fourth hand
Kosinski, J. N. Being there
O'Flynn, C. The news where you are
TELEVISION PRODUCERS AND DIRECTORS
Clark, M. H. The sleeping beauty killer
Hannah, S. The cradle in the grave
Marks, J. Fangland
TELEVISION PROGRAMS
Clark, M. H. The sleeping beauty killer
Gruen, S. Ape house
McPhee, J. No ordinary matter
Nicholls, D. A question of attraction
Parkhurst, C. Lost and found
Westlake, D. E. Get real
TELEVISION SERIALS
See also Television programs
Tell. Itani, F.
Tell me a riddle. Olsen, T.
Tell me how long the train's been gone. Baldwin, J.
Tell the wolves I'm home. Brunt, C. R.
The **telling.** Le Guin, U. K.
Telling stories! [series]
Roy, A. The god of small things
Temeraire [series]
Novik, N. Blood of tyrants
Novik, N. His majesty's dragon
Novik, N. League of Dragons
TEMPER TANTRUMS
See also Emotions; Human behavior
TEMPERAMENT
See also Mind and body; Psychology; Psychophysiology
TEMPLARS
Holland, C. Jerusalem
The **Temple** of Dawn. Mishima, Y.
The **temple** of my familiar. Walker, A.
TEMPORARY EMPLOYEES
Barr, N. The rope
Temporary people. Unnikrishnan, D.

The **Temptation** of Your Touch. Medeiros, T.
Temptations of a Wallflower. Leigh, E.
Tempting fate. Green, J.
Tempting the bride. Thomas, S.
Ten girls to watch. Shumway, C.
Ten North Frederick. O'Hara, J.
Ten things I've learnt about love. Butler, S.
Ten thousand saints. Henderson, E.
The **tenant** of Wildfell Hall. Bronte, A.
The **tenants** of time. Flanagan, T.
Tender mercies. Brown, R.
The **tenderness** of wolves. Penney, S.
TENEMENT HOUSES
See also Apartment houses
TENNESSEE
Bahr, H. The Judas Field
Bledsoe, A. The hum and the shiver
Greene, A. Bloodroot
Greene, A. Long Man
Gregory, D. The devil's alphabet
Hooper, K. Blood ties
McCrumb, S. The ballad of Frankie Silver
McCrumb, S. If ever I return, pretty Peggy-O
McCrumb, S. She walks these hills
O'Connor, F. The violent bear it away
O'Connor, F. Wise blood
Pekearo, N. T. The wolfman
Wall, P. S. The Wilde women
Wiggins, M. Evidence of things unseen
TENNESSEE -- HISTORY -- CIVIL WAR, 1861-1865 -- CASUALTIES
Hicks, R. The widow of the south
TENNESSEE -- KNOXVILLE
Agee, J. A death in the family
TENNESSEE -- MEMPHIS
Faulkner, W. The reivers
Faulkner, W. Sanctuary
Grisham, J. The firm
Taylor, P. H. A summons to Memphis
TENNESSEE -- NASHVILLE
Bass, R. Nashville chrome
TENNIS
Wallace, D. F. Infinite jest
Woods, S. Choke
Tennyson, Alfred Tennyson, Baron, 1809-1892
About
Foulds, A. The quickening maze
Tensorate series
Yang, J. Y. The black tides of heaven
The **tenth** justice. Meltzer, B.
The **tenth** man. Greene, G.
Tenth of December. Saunders, G.
TENURE OF LAND *See* Land tenure
TENURE OF OFFICE *See* Civil service
TEREZIN (CZECHOSLOVAKIA: CONCENTRATION CAMP)
See also Concentration camps
TERMINAL CARE
Smith, A. A bigger life
TERMINAL CARE -- DECISION MAKING
Picoult, J. Lone wolf
TERMINAL ILLNESS
Albert, E. The book of Dahlia
Banville, J. The infinities
Gaddis, W. Agape agape
L'Engle, M. Certain women
McPhee, M. Gorgeous lies
Miller, A. Oxygen
Miller, S. The Lake Shore Limited
Minot, S. Evening
Richardson, C. S. The end of the alphabet
Sallis, J. The killer is dying
Tóibín, C. The blackwater lightship
Tsukiyama, G. Dreaming water
TERMINALLY ILL
Bannon, J. I2
Bock, C. Alice & Oliver
Chabon, M. Moonglow
Evison, J. The revised fundamentals of caregiving
Genova, L. Inside the O'Briens
Haruf, K. Benediction
Hurwitz, G. The survivor
Russo, R. Everybody's fool
Tropper, J. One last thing before I go
Yalom, I. D. The Schopenhauer cure
TERMINALLY ILL PARENTS
Grodstein, L. Our short history
TERMINATION OF PREGNANCY *See* Abortion
Terms of endearment. McMurtry, L.
TERNS
See also Birds; Water birds
Terra incognita. Downie, R.
The **Terranauts.** Boyle, T. C.
TERRIERS
McCall Smith, A. A conspiracy of friends
TERRITORIAL GOVERNORS
Sargent, C. Museum of human beings
Wheeler, R. S. Eclipse
The **terror.** Simmons, D.
The **terror** of living. Waite, U.
TERROR TALES *See* Ghost stories; Horror fiction
TERRORISM
Aslam, N. The wasted vigil
Ballard, J. G. Millennium people
Clancy, T. Patriot games
Cook, R. Vector
DeLillo, D. Falling man
DeMille, N. Wild fire
Dubus, A. The garden of last days
Ellis, D. In the company of liars
Farah, N. Crossbones
Flanagan, R. The unknown terrorist
Glass, J. The widower's tale
Griffin, W. E. B. By order of the President

Gruber, M. The good son
Hagberg, D. Abyss
Hamid, M. The reluctant fundamentalist
Hamill, P. Tabloid city
Hayes, T. I Am Pilgrim
Higgins, J. Confessional
Higgins, J. Edge of danger
Higgins, J. Eye of the storm
Higgins, J. Midnight runner
Higgins, J. Touch the devil
Higgins, J. The White House connection
Huston, C. Skinner
Hynes, J. Next
Ignatius, D. Body of lies
Johansen, I. And then you die--
Just, W. S. Forgetfulness
Keneally, T. Flying hero class
Kress, N. Dogs
Le Carre, J. The little drummer girl
Leonard, E. Djibouti
Lessing, D. M. The good terrorist
Littell, R. Vicious circle
Ludlum, R. The Bourne ultimatum
Ludlum, R. The Janson directive
Ludlum, R. The Prometheus deception
MacInnes, H. Prelude to terror
McCarry, C. Old boys
Meyer, D. Heart of the hunter
Miller, S. The Lake Shore Limited
O'Brien, E. House of splendid isolation
Oe, K. Somersault
Palahniuk, C. Pygmy
Palmer, M. The patient
Patchett, A. Bel canto
Patterson, J. London bridges
Piercy, M. Vida
Pohl, F. All the lives he led
Porter, H. The bell ringers
Pottinger, S. The last Nazi
Reich, C. Rules of deception
Robinson, K. S. Antarctica
Roncagliolo, S. Red April
Rosenberg, J. C. The Tehran initiative
Rosenfelt, D. Don't tell a soul
Roth, P. American pastoral
Rubenfeld, J. The death instinct
Rushdie, S. Shalimar the clown
Sakey, M. A Better World
Schlink, B. The weekend
See, C. There will never be another you
Silva, D. The black widow
Silva, D. The mark of the assassin
Silva, D. The messenger
Silva, D. Prince of Fire
Silva, D. The secret servant
Smith, A. Judas horse
Steiner, P. The terrorist
Stone, R. Damascus Gate
Trevanian Shibumi
Updike, J. Terrorist
Wallace, D. F. Infinite jest
West, M. L. Lazarus
West, R. The birds fall down
Wilson, R. The hidden assassins
Woods, S. Reckless abandon

TERRORISM -- PREVENTION
Coulter, C. The end game
Le Carré, J. A Delicate Truth

Terrorist. Updike, J.

The **terrorist.** Steiner, P.

TERRORISTS
Sakey, M. Brilliance

Tesla.

Tesla, Nikola, 1856-1943

About
Echenoz, J. Lightning
Hunt, S. The invention of everything else

A Tess Monaghan Novel [series]
Lippman, L. Hush hush

Tess of the D'Urbervilles. Hardy, T.

TEST PILOTS *See* Air pilots; Airplanes -- Testing

TEST TUBE BABIES *See* Fertilization in vitro

TEST TUBE FERTILIZATION *See* Fertilization in vitro

The **testament.** Wiesel, E.

The **testament** of Mary. Tóibín, C.

Testimony. Shreve, A.

Tevye the dairyman and The railroad stories. Sholem Aleichem

Tevye's daughters. Sholem Aleichem

TEXAS
Bass, R. All the Land to Hold Us
Estleman, L. D. The book of Murdock
Founds, K. When mystical creatures attack!
Grisham, J. The confession
Hunter, S. Dirty white boys
Jordan, H. When she woke
Kelton, E. Texas sunrise
Kent, K. The Dime
Koenig, M. Nine days
Land, J. Strong at the break
Lansdale, J. R. A fine dark line
Machart, B. The wake of forgiveness
Martin, C. W. How to sell
McCarthy, C. No country for old men
McMurtry, L. Rhino Ranch
Meyer, P. The Son
Palmer, L. Nowhere but home
Parks Getting mother's body
Proulx, A. That old ace in the hole
Riordan, R. Cold Springs
Thompson, J. The killer inside me
Walker, M. W. Under the beetle's cellar
Zevin, G. The hole we're in

TEXAS -- 19TH CENTURY

Jiles, P. The color of lightning
Kelton, E. Badger boy
Kelton, E. The way of the coyote
TEXAS -- AUSTIN
Hynes, J. Next
Klosterman, C. The visible man
TEXAS -- HOUSTON
Brown, R. Half a heart
McMurtry, L. The evening star
McMurtry, L. Terms of endearment
TEXAS -- SAN ANTONIO
Earle, S. I'll never get out of this world alive
TEXAS RANGERS
Burke, J. L. House of the rising sun
Kelton, E. Texas vendetta
Kelton, E. The way of the coyote
McMurtry, L. Comanche moon
Texas sunrise. Kelton, E.
Texas vendetta. Kelton, E.
TEXAS, EAST
Lansdale, J. R. The thicket
Lansdale, J. R. The bottoms
Lansdale, J. R. Sunset and sawdust
Locke, A. Bluebird, bluebird
TEXAS, WEST
Bass, R. All the Land to Hold Us
TEXTBOOKS
See also Books
TEXTILE CHEMISTRY
See also Industrial chemistry; Textile industry
TEXTILE INDUSTRY
Singer, I. J. The brothers Ashkenazi
TEXTILE PRINTING
See also Printing; Textile industry
Tey, Josephine, 1896 or 1897-1952
About
Upson, N. An expert in murder
Upson, N. London rain
THAILAND
Boulle, P. The bridge over the River Kwai
Cotterill, C. Killed at the whim of a hat
THAILAND -- 18TH CENTURY
Han, S. The enchantress
THAILAND -- BANGKOK
Bacigalupi, P. The windup girl
Burdett, J. Bangkok 8
Mishima, Y. The Temple of Dawn
Thale's Folly. Gilman, D.
THANKSGIVING DAY
Ford, R. The lay of the land
Vanderbes, J. Strangers at the feast
That Camden summer. Spencer, L.
That deadman dance. Scott, K.
That distant land. Berry, W.
That hideous strength. Lewis, C. S.
That night. McDermott, A.
That old ace in the hole. Proulx, A.
That old Cape magic. Russo, R.
That's how I roll. Vachss, A.
the Darktown series
Mullen, T. Lightning men
THEATER
Alarcón, D. At Night We Walk in Circles
Goldberg, P. The Yid
Rawn, M. Touchstone
Upson, N. An expert in murder
THEATER LIFE
Dickens, C. Nicholas Nickleby
Dreiser, T. Sister Carrie
Gallagher, S. The kingdom of bones
L'Engle, M. Certain women
Lessing, D. M. Love, again
O'Connor, J. Ghost light
Singer, I. B. The magician of Lublin
Unsworth, B. Morality play
Zola, E. Nana
THEFT
Eliot, G. Silas Marner
Hilton, E. Dirty money Honey
Hunter, M. The conquest of Lady Cassandra
Morgan-Jones, C. The jackal's share
Nesbo, J. The headhunters
Perez-Reverte, A. The fencing master
Stott, R. The coral thief
Westlake, D. E. Don't ask
Theft of swords. Sullivan, M. J.
Their eyes were watching God. Hurston, Z. N.
THEISM
See also Philosophy; Religion; Theology
Thelen, Albert Vigoleis, 1903-1989
About
Thelen, A. V. The island of second sight
Them. Oates, J. C.
THEME PARKS *See* Amusement parks
Then came the evening. Hart, B.
Then came you. Weiner, J.
Then We Take Berlin. Lawton, J.
Theodora. Duffy, S.
Theodora, Empress, consort of Justinian I, Emperor of the East, d. 548
About
Duffy, S. Theodora
Theophilus North. Wilder, T.
A **theory** of relativity. Mitchard, J.
THEOSOPHY
See also Mysticism; Religions
Therapy. Kellerman, J.
THERAPY, PSYCHOLOGICAL *See* Psychotherapy
There but for the. Smith, A.
There once lived a woman who tried to kill her neighbor's baby. Petrushevskaya, L.
There will never be another you. See, C.
There's something I want you to do. Baxter, C.
These days are ours. Haimoff, M.

These is my words. Turner, N. E.
These old shades. Heyer, G.
THESEUS (GREEK MYTHOLOGY)
Renault, M. The bull from the sea
Renault, M. The king must die
They're watching. Hurwitz, G.
Thick as thieves. Spiegelman, P.
The **thicket.** Lansdale, J. R.
Thief of Shadows. Hoyt, E.
Thief of time. Pratchett, T.
A **thief** of time. Hillerman, T.
The **thief** of Venice. Langton, J.
THIEVES
Ashford, J. What the duke doesn't know
Banville, J. The blue guitar
Brown, T. Fallen land
Defoe, D. Moll Flanders
Dickens, C. Oliver Twist
Edwardson, Å. Sail of stone
Hansen, R. The assassination of Jesse James by the coward Robert Ford
Herlihy, J. L. Midnight cowboy
Horn, D. The world to come
Lynch, S. The Republic of Thieves
Moehringer, J. R. Sutton
Noire (Author) Natural born liar
Parker, T. J. L.A. outlaws
Rajaniemi, H. The fractal prince
Roadside picnic
Sallis, J. Drive
Schickler, D. Sweet and vicious
Smith, S. A simple plan
Waters, S. Fingersmith
Westlake, D. E. Smoke
Woodrell, D. The death of sweet mister
THIEVES
See also Criminals
THIEVES -- CALIFORNIA
Hallinan, T. Crashed
Thieves' dozen. Westlake, D. E.
Thin air. Parker, R. B.
Thin air. Cleeves, A.
The **thin** man. Hammett, D.
The **thin** place. Davis, K.
The **thin** red line. Jones, J.
The **thing** around your neck. Adichie, C. N.
The **thing** itself. Guttridge, P.
Things fall apart. Achebe, C.
The **things** they carried. O'Brien, T.
Things to do when you're goth in the country. Woods, C.
Things we didn't see coming. Amsterdam, S.
Things we once held dear. Tatlock, A.
Think of a number. Verdon, J.
Thinks-- Lodge, D.
Thinner. King, S.
The **third** angel. Hoffman, A.
The **third** bear. VanderMeer, J.
The **third** book of lost swords: Stonecutter's story. Saberhagen, F.
The **third** deadly sin. Sanders, L.
Third degree. Iles, G.
The **third** life of Grange Copeland. Walker, A.
The **Third** Reich. Bolaño, R.
The **third** son. Wu, J.
Third strike. Craig, P. R.
The **thirst.** Nesbø, J.
Thirteen. Morgan, R. K.
Thirteen moons. Frazier, C.
Thirteen ways of looking. McCann, C.
The **thirty-nine** steps. Buchan, J.
This beautiful life. Schulman, H.
This body of death. George, E.
This book will save your life. Homes, A. M.
This burns my heart. Park, S.
This dark road to mercy. Cash, W.
This heavy silence. Mazzarella, N.
This house is not for sale. Osondu, E. C.
This insane train. Russell, S.
This is how it always is. Frankel, L.
This is how it ends. Nadol, J.
This is how you lose her. Díaz, J.
This is just exactly like you. Perry, D.
This is not civilization. Rosenberg, R.
This is your life, Harriet Chance! Evison, J.
This magnificent desolation. O'Malley, T.
This must be the place. Racculia, K.
This must be the place. O'Farrell, M.
This road we traveled. Kirkpatrick, J.
This scarlet cord. Wolf, J.
This side of paradise. Fitzgerald, F. S.
This way to the end times.
THÓRA GUDMUNDSDÓTTIR (FICTITIOUS CHARACTER)
The silence of the sea
Thomas Kell novels [series]
Cumming, C. A divided spy
Thomas, à Becket, Saint, Archbishop of Canterbury, 1118?-1170
About
Penman, S. K. Time and chance
Thora Gudmundsdottir novels [series]
Yrsa Sigurdardottir Last rituals
Thoreau, Henry David, 1817-1862
About
Pipkin, J. Woodsburner
The **thorn** birds. McCullough, C.
Thorn P.I. [series]
Hall, J. W. Going Dark
Thorns of truth. Goudge, E.
Those we love most. Woodruff, L.
Those Who Leave and Those Who Stay. Ferrante, E.
Those who wish me dead. Koryta, M.
Though not dead. Stabenow, D.
A **thousand** acres. Smiley, J.

The **thousand** autumns of Jacob de Zoet. Mitchell, D.
A **thousand** deaths plus one. Ramirez Mercado, S.
A **thousand** forests in one acorn.
A **thousand** pardons. Dee, J.
A **thousand** rooms of dream and fear. Rahimi, A.
A **thousand** splendid suns. Hosseini, K.
A **thousand** years of good prayers. Yiyun Li
A **thread** of grace. Russell, M. D.
THREATENED SPECIES *See* Endangered species
THREATS
Shepherd, L. The solitary house
Three bargains. Malik, T.
Three blind mice and other stories. Christie, A.
Three cases for Mr. Campion. Allingham, M.
Three days before the shooting--
Three days to never. Powers, T.
Three faces of love. Zola, E.
Three graves full. Mason, J.
Three Junes. Glass, J.
Three lives. Stein, G.
Three moments of an explosion. Miéville, C.
The **three** musketeers. Dumas, A.
Three Pines mystery [series]
Penny, L. Glass houses
Three stages of amazement. Edgarian, C.
THREE STOOGES FILMS
See also Comedy films; Motion pictures
Three strong women.
Three Weeks With Lady X. James, E.
The **three** Weissmanns of Westport. Schine, C.
Three years with the rat. Hosking, J.
The **three-arched** bridge. Kadare, I.
The **three-body** problem.
Three-body trilogy [series]
Death's End
The **Three-Day** Affair. Kardos, M.
Three-day road. Boyden, J.
THREE-DIMENSIONAL PRINTING
See also Printing
THRIFT SHOPS
See also Secondhand trade; Stores
THRILLERS *See* Adventure fiction; Adventure films
THRILLERS
Constantine, L. The Last Mrs. Parrish
Thrones, dominations. Sayers, D. L.
Through a glass darkly. Koen, K.
Through waters deep. Sundin, S.
The **throwback** special. Bachelder, C.
Thrush Green. Read
Thud! Pratchett, T.
Thunder and lightning [series]
Varley, J. Dark lightning
Thunder on the mountain. Poyer, D.
THUNDERSTORMS
See also Meteorology; Storms
Thursday the rabbi walked out. Kemelman, H.
Thursday's children. French, N.
Thus bad begins.
TIBET AUTONOMOUS REGION (CHINA)
Pattison, E. The lord of death
Ticket to ride. Gorman, E.
A **ticket** to the boneyard. Block, L.
TIDE POOL ECOLOGY
See also Ecology
TIDES
See also Ocean
Ghosh, A. The hungry tide
Ties.
TIFFANY & CO.
Vreeland, S. Clara and Mr. Tiffany
Tiffany, Louis Comfort, 1848-1933
About
Vreeland, S. Clara and Mr. Tiffany
The **tiger's** wife. Obreht, T.
Tigerlily's orchids. Rendell, R.
Tigerman. Harkaway, N.
TIGERS
Martel, Y. Life of Pi
Tigers in red weather. Klaussmann, L.
TIJUANA (MEXICO)
Lange, R. Angel baby
'Til death do us part. Quick, A.
Till we have faces. Lewis, C. S.
Till, Emmett, 1941-1955
About
McFadden, B. L. Gathering of waters
TIMBER *See* Forests and forestry; Lumber and lumbering; Trees; Wood
Timber Creek K-9 mysteries [series]
Mizushima, M. Killing Trail
Mizushima, M. Stalking Ground
TIME
Amis, M. Time's arrow
Hoeg, P. Borderliners
Lightman, A. P. The diagnosis
Stern, S. The pinch
Time and again. Finney, J.
Time and chance. Penman, S. K.
TIME AND SPACE *See* Space and time
Time and tide. O'Brien, E.
Time bomb. Kellerman, J.
The **time** in between. Duenas, M.
The **time** it takes to fall. Dean, M. L.
The **time** machine. Wells, H. G.
TIME MANAGEMENT
See also Management; Time
The **time** of the hero. Vargas Llosa, M.
Time regained. Proust, M.
Time to hunt. Hunter, S.
A **time** to kill. Grisham, J.
A **time** to love and a time to die. Remarque, E. M.
TIME TRAVEL
Alexie, S. Flight
Baker, K. In the garden of Iden

Baker, K. The sons of heaven
Butler, O. E. Kindred
Crichton, M. Timeline
Danielewski, M. Z. Only revolutions
Finney, J. From time to time
Finney, J. Time and again
Flyte, M. City of dark magic
Gabaldon, D. A breath of snow and ashes
Gabaldon, D. An echo in the bone
Gabaldon, D. The fiery cross
Gabaldon, D. Outlander
Gabaldon, D. Written in my own heart's blood
Greer, A. S. The Impossible Lives of Greta Wells
Haldeman, J. W. The accidental time machine
Harkness, D. E. The Book of Life
Harkness, D. E. Shadow of night
Helprin, M. Winter's tale
Lancaster, J. Here I go again
Lee, P. Signal
Lochen, A. The repeat year
The map of time
Mastai, E. All our wrong todays
McCaffrey, T. Dragonsblood
Millet, L. Oh pure and radiant heart
Moorcock, M. An alien heat
Niffenegger, A. The time traveler's wife
Piercy, M. Woman on the edge of time
Powers, T. Three days to never
Rice, A. Angel time
Rice, A. Of love and evil
Ridgway, B. The river of no return
Stephenson, N. The rise and fall of D.O.D.O.
Stross, C. Empire games
Swanwick, M. Bones of the earth
The time traveler's almanac
Vonnegut, K. Slaughterhouse-five
Wells, H. G. The time machine
Willis, C. Blackout
Willis, C. Doomsday book
Willis, C. To say nothing of the dog; or, How we found the bishop's bird stump at last
Wolfe, G. Pirate freedom
Yu, C. How to live safely in a science fictional universe

TIME TRAVEL
See also Fourth dimension; Space and time
The **time** traveler's almanac.
The **time** traveler's wife. Niffenegger, A.
Time's arrow. Amis, M.
Timeline. Crichton, M.
Timequake. Vonnegut, K.
Timescape. Benford, G.
TIMESHARING (REAL ESTATE)
See also Condominiums; Housing; Property; Real estate business
Timothy's game. Sanders, L.
The **tin** can tree. Tyler, A.
The **tin** drum. Grass, G.
Tin House new voice [series]
Watson, J. E. Asta in the wings
Tinker, tailor, soldier, spy. Le Carre, J.
Tinkers. Harding, P.
Tiny sunbirds, far away. Watson, C.
Tipping the velvet. Waters, S.
Tirza.
Tishomingo blues. Leonard, E.
TISSUES -- TRANSPLANTATION *See* Transplantation of organs, tissues, etc.
Titan. Varley, J.
TITANIC (STEAMSHIP)
Bainbridge, B. Every man for himself
Finney, J. From time to time
Willis, C. Passage
Tituba
About
Conde, M. I, Tituba, black witch of Salem
To be sung underwater. McNeal, T.
To catch a bride. Gracie, A.
To catch a spy. Kaminsky, S. M.
To dance with kings. Laker, R.
To have and have not. Hemingway, E.
To kill a mockingbird. Lee, H.
To lie with lions. Dunnett, D.
To Rise Again at a Decent Hour. Ferris, J.
To say nothing of the dog; or, How we found the bishop's bird stump at last. Willis, C.
To the bright edge of the world. Ivey, E.
To the end of the land.
To the far blue mountains. L'Amour, L.
To the lighthouse. Woolf, V.
To wed a stranger. Layton, E.
To your scattered bodies go. Farmer, P. J.
TOBACCO FARMS
Morgan, C. E. All the living
TOBACCO INDUSTRY
Morgan, C. E. All the living
Tobacco road. Caldwell, E.
Tocqueville, Alexis de
About
Carey, P. Parrot and Olivier in America
Toklas, Alice B.
About
Truong, M. The book of salt
TOKYO (JAPAN)
Moshi moshi
Tokyo year zero. Peace, D.
TOLERATION
See also Interpersonal relations
Tolstoy, Leo, graf, 1828-1910
About
Reyn, I. What happened to Anna K.
Tombaugh, Clyde, 1906-1997
About
Byers, M. Percival's planet
TOMBS

See also Archeology; Architecture; Burial; Monuments; Shrines
TOMBS -- EGYPT -- ALEXANDRIA
Saylor, S. Raiders of the Nile
Tomorrow. Swift, G.
Tomorrow is another day. Kaminsky, S. M.
Tonight I said goodbye. Koryta, M.
Too bright to hear too loud to see. Garey, J.
Too far afield. Grass, G.
Too late the phalarope. Paton, A.
Too many cooks; & champagne for one. Stout, R.
Too much happiness. Munro, A.
Too much money. Dunne, D.
The **tooth** tattoo. Lovesey, P.
Torch. Strayed, C.
TORNADOES
See also Meteorology; Storms; Winds
TORONTO (ONT.)
Redhill, M. Bellevue Square
The **torrents** of spring. Turgenev, I. S.
The **torso** in the town. Brett, S.
The **tortilla** curtain. Boyle, T. C.
Tortilla Flat. Steinbeck, J.
TORTURE
Danticat, E. The dew breaker
Lehrer, J. The special prisoner
Katzenbach, J. What comes next
Smith, M. A. The Inquisitor
Zan, K. The Never List
TORTURE
See also Criminal procedure; Cruelty; Punishment
The **toss** of a lemon. Viswanathan, P.
Total recall. Paretsky, S.
TOTALITARIANISM
Antunes, A. L. The inquisitors' manual
Bolano, R. By night in Chile
Chatwin, B. Utz
Danticat, E. The dew breaker
Dunn, M. Ella Minnow Pea
Englander, N. The Ministry of Special Cases
Erpenbeck, J. The book of words
Farah, N. Links
Hrabal, B. I served the King of England
Kadare, I. The Successor
Koestler, A. Darkness at noon
Matar, H. In the country of men
McCann, C. Zoli
Moulessehoul, M. The swallows of Kabul
Orwell, G. Animal farm
Orwell, G. Nineteen eighty-four
Porter, H. The bell ringers
Saramago, J. The cave
Smith, T. R. Child 44
Sorokin, V. Ice
Steele, A. M. Coyote
Vargas Llosa, M. Conversation in the cathedral
Vollmann, W. T. Europe central
Zamiatin, E. I. We
TOTEMS AND TOTEMISM
See also Ethnology; Mythology
Touch not the cat. Stewart, M.
A **touch** of stardust. Alcott, K.
Touch the devil. Higgins, J.
Touched by venom. Cross, J.
Touchstone. Rawn, M.
Touchy subjects. Donoghue, E.
Toured to Death. Conrad, H.
TOURETTE SYNDROME -- PATIENTS
Lethem, J. Motherless Brooklyn
TOURISM *See* Tourist trade; Travel
The **tourist.** Steinhauer, O.
TOURIST INDUSTRY *See* Tourist trade
TOURIST TRADE
Lodge, D. Paradise news
Tan, A. Saving fish from drowning
TOURISTS *See* Tourist trade; Travelers
Tourmaline. Scott, J.
Toussaint Louverture, 1743?-1803
About
Bell, M. S. All souls' rising
Toward the end of time. Updike, J.
Towards another summer. Frame, J.
Towards zero. Christie, A.
TOWER OF LONDON (LONDON, ENGLAND)
Weir, A. A dangerous inheritance
TOWN LIFE *See* City and town life
TOWNS *See* Cities and towns
Toxicology. Hagedorn, J. T.
TOYS
McBride, J. Five-carat soul
Tracey Crosswhite [series]
Dugoni, R. My sister's grave
Trackers. Meyer, D.
TRACKING AND TRAILING
See also Hunting
Tracks. Erdrich, L.
TRADE *See* Business; Commerce
TRADE SHOWS
See also Exhibitions; Fairs
TRADE-UNIONS *See* Labor unions
TRADING POSTS
Mitchell, D. The thousand autumns of Jacob de Zoet
TRADITIONS *See* Folklore; Legends; Manners and customs; Rites and ceremonies; Superstition
TRAFFIC ACCIDENTS
Agee, J. A death in the family
Banks, R. The sweet hereafter
Blame
Goodman, C. River Road
Gundar-Goshen, A. Waking lions
Hilderbrand, E. Summerland
Huneven, M. Blame
Itani, F. Remembering the bones
Kasischke, L. The raising

Kerangal, M. d. The heart
Lane, H. Alys, always
Livesey, M. The missing world
Mackintosh, C. I let you go
McEwan, I. Saturday
Miasha Chaser
Mitchard, J. A theory of relativity
Oates, J. C. Black water
O'Nan, S. The night country
Osborne, L. The forgiven
Powers, R. The echo maker
Reiken, F. Day for night
Steel, D. The kiss
Thompson, J. The year we left home
Waldman, A. Red Hook Road
TRAFFIC ACCIDENTS
See also Accidents
TRAFFICKING IN DRUGS *See* Drug traffic
TRAFFICKING IN NARCOTICS *See* Drug traffic
The **tragedy** of Arthur. Phillips, A.
Tragic. Tanenbaum, R. K.
TRAILER CAMPS
Hassman, T. Girlchild
Trailer park fae. Saintcrow, L.
TRAILER PARKS
Hassman, T. Girlchild
Train dreams. Johnson, D.
TRAINING CAMPS, MILITARY *See* Military training camps
TRAINS *See* Railroads
Trains and Lovers. McCall Smith, A.
Trainspotting. Welsh, I.
The **traitor** Baru Cormorant. Dickinson, S.
Traitor's gate. Perry, A.
TRAMPS
See also Homeless persons; Poor
TRANSACTIONAL ANALYSIS
See also Psychotherapy
Transatlantic. McCann, C.
TRANSATLANTIC VOYAGES
McCann, C. Transatlantic
Transcendental. Gunn, J. E.
TRANSCONTINENTAL JOURNEYS (AMERICAN CONTINENT) *See* Overland journeys to the Pacific
TRANSGENDER PEOPLE
Ebershoff, D. The Danish Girl
Frankel, L. This is how it always is
TRANSGENICS *See* Genetic engineering
Transgressions.
Transit. Cusk, R.
The **transit** of Venus. Hazzard, S.
TRANSLATING AND INTERPRETING
Alameddine, R. An Unnecessary Woman
TRANSLATING AND INTERPRETING
See also Language and languages
The **translation** of Dr Apelles. Treuer, D.
The **translation** of love. Kutsukake, L.
TRANSLATORS
Coetzee, J. M. Summertime
Dai Sijie Once on a moonless night
Horan, N. Loving Frank
Kennedy, D. The moment
Littell, R. The Stalin epigram
Manseau, P. Songs for the butcher's daughter
Marias, J. A heart so white
McKillip, P. A. Alphabet of thorn
Miller, A. Oxygen
Nabokov, V. V. Novels and memoirs, 1941-1951
Sherwood, F. Night of sorrows
Treuer, D. The translation of Dr Apelles
Van Booy, S. Everything beautiful began after
Vargas Llosa, M. The bad girl
Verissimo, L. F. Borges and the eternal orangutans
TRANSMIGRATION
London, J. The star rover
Theroux, M. Strange bodies
TRANSMISSION OF TEXTS
Graedon, A. The word exchange
TRANSMUTATION OF METALS *See* Alchemy; Transmutation (Chemistry)
TRANSPLANTATION *See* Transplantation of organs, tissues, etc.
TRANSPLANTATION OF ORGANS, TISSUES, ETC.
Cook, R. Coma
Irving, J. The fourth hand
Palmer, M. The fifth vial
Picoult, J. My sister's keeper
Picoult, J. Change of heart
TRANSPLANTATION OF ORGANS, TISSUES, ETC.
See also Surgery
TRANSSEXUALS
Tremain, R. Sacred country
Vidal, G. Myra Breckinridge [and] Myron
TRANSYLVANIA (ROMANIA)
The new annotated Dracula
TRAPPERS AND TRAPPING
Guthrie, A. B. The big sky
Penney, S. The tenderness of wolves
Raymond, J. The half-life
Sargent, C. Museum of human beings
TRAVEL
Bhattacharya, R. The sly company of people who care
Conrad, H. Toured to Death
Higgins, K. My one and only
Kerouac, J. On the road
Luiselli, V. The story of my teeth
Maugham, W. S. The razor's edge
McCall Smith, A. Trains and Lovers
Priest, C. Dreadnought
Richardson, C. S. The end of the alphabet
Simpson, M. Anywhere but here
TRAVEL BOOKS *See* Voyages and travels; Voyages around the world
TRAVEL IN LITERATURE

See also Literature -- Themes; Travel
TRAVEL INDUSTRY *See* Tourist trade
TRAVEL WRITERS
Calvino, I. Invisible cities
Clinch, J. Finn
Flanagan, R. Wanting
Martin, V. Mary Reilly
McDonald, R. Mr. Darwin's shooter
Naipaul, V. S. A way in the world
Oates, J. C. Wild nights!
Russell, M. D. Dreamers of the day
Simmons, D. The terror
Twain, M. The gilded age and later novels
Vollmann, W. T. Argall
Vollmann, W. T. The rifles
Wolfe, G. The land across
TRAVEL WRITING
See also Authorship
Traveler of the century.
TRAVELERS
Alexander, V. The lady travelers guide to scoundrels & other gentlemen
Calvino, I. Invisible cities
Ghosh, A. Sea of poppies
Maalouf, A. Leo Africanus
Russell, M. D. Dreamers of the day
TRAVELERS
See also Voyages and travels
TRAVELERS -- WEST (U.S) -- HISTORY -- 19TH CENTURY
Kent, K. The outcasts
TRAVELING SALES PERSONNEL *See* Sales personnel
TRAVELING THEATER -- SOUTH AMERICA
Alarcón, D. At Night We Walk in Circles
TRAVELS *See* Voyages and travels
Travels with Charley and later novels, 1947-1962. Steinbeck, J.
Travels with my aunt. Greene, G.
TREASON
Bowen, E. The heat of the day
Treasure Island!!! Levine, S.
The **treasure** of the Sierra Madre. Traven, B.
TREASURE TROVE *See* Buried treasure
Albert, S. W. The Darling Dahlias and the cucumber tree
Cussler, C. The Mayan secrets
Davies, J. D. The mountain of gold
Fortier, A. The lost sisterhood
Handler, D. We are pirates
Kelly, J. The moon tunnel
The **treatment.** Hayder, M.
A **tree** grows in Brooklyn. Smith, B.
The **tree** of hands. Rendell, R.
Tree of smoke. Johnson, D.
TREES
Kiernan, C. R. The red tree
Tremaine's True Love. Burrowes, G.
Trespass. Tremain, R.
Trespass. Martin, V.
Trevanian
About
Winslow, D. Satori
The **Trevarton** inheritance. Ross-Macdonald, M.
The **trial.** Kafka, F.
TRIAL MARRIAGE *See* Unmarried couples
The **trial** of Elizabeth Cree. Ackroyd, P.
TRIALS
Ackroyd, P. The trial of Elizabeth Cree
Atkins, A. Devil's garden
Atwood, M. Alias Grace
Benet, S. V. The Devil and Daniel Webster
Camus, A. The stranger
Connelly, M. The Lincoln lawyer
Dexter, P. Paris Trout
Dickens, C. Bleak House
Dickens, C. The posthumous papers of the Pickwick Club
Dickens, C. A tale of two cities
Donoghue, E. The sealed letter
Dostoyevsky, F. The brothers Karamazov
Dreiser, T. An American tragedy
Faulkner, W. Requiem for a nun
French, A. Billy
Grisham, J. The partner
Grisham, J. A time to kill
Guterson, D. Snow falling on cedars
Hamilton, J. A map of the world
Hansen, R. A wild surge of guilty passion
Hoag, T. Guilty as sin
Howe, K. The physick book of Deliverance Dane
Iles, G. Turning angel
Jones, D. C. The court-martial of George Armstrong Custer
Kafka, F. The trial
Katzenbach, J. Hart's war
Kent, K. The heretic's daughter
Koestler, A. Darkness at noon
Lawrence, M. K. Hearts and bones
Lehrer, J. The special prisoner
Lescroart, J. T. The hearing
Levin, M. Compulsion
Marlette, D. Magic time
Martini, S. P. Compelling evidence
Miller, S. The good mother
Morrow, J. The last witchfinder
Oates, J. C. American appetites
O'Shaughnessy, P. Breach of promise
O'Shaughnessy, P. Invasion of privacy
O'Shaughnessy, P. Motion to suppress
O'Shaughnessy, P. Obstruction of justice
O'Shaughnessy, P. Writ of execution
Patterson, J. Hide & seek
Patterson, R. N. Silent witness
Pesci, D. Amistad
Picoult, J. My sister's keeper
Scottoline, L. Mistaken identity
Scottoline, L. Rough justice

Sharratt, M. Daughters of the Witching Hill
Turow, S. Presumed innocent
Turow, S. Innocent
Turow, S. The laws of our fathers
Turow, S. Limitations
Uris, L. QB VII
Warren, R. P. World enough and time
Welty, E. The Ponder heart
Wilhelm, K. The best defense
Wilhelm, K. Death qualified
Wilhelm, K. Defense for the devil
Wilhelm, K. Desperate measures
Wilhelm, K. Malice prepense
Wilhelm, K. No defense
Wiprud, B. M. Ringer
Woods, S. Dead in the water
Woods, S. Grass roots
TRIALS
See also Criminal law
TRIALS (HOMICIDE)
See also Homicide; Trials
TRIALS (HOMICIDE)
Burnet, G. M. His Bloody Project
Connelly, M. The crossing
Ellis, D. The last alibi
Keller, J. A killing in the hills
Keller, J. Last Ragged Breath
Landay, W. Defending Jacob
Lelic, S. The child who
Phillips, J. A. Quiet dell
Silver, E. L. The execution of Noa P. Singleton
TRIALS (MURDER) *See* Trials (Homicide)
TRIALS (MURDER) -- ENGLAND
Stone, N. The Verdict
TRIALS (MURDER)
Connelly, M. The Gods of Guilt
De Kretser, M. The Hamilton case
Iles, G. Natchez burning
Mina, D. The long drop
Reuland, R. Semiautomatic
TRIALS (MURDER) -- SWEDEN -- STOCKHOLM
Giolito, M. P. Quicksand
TRIALS -- FICTION *See* Legal stories
TRIANGLES (INTERPERSONAL RELATIONS)
Beach-Ferrara, J. Damn love
Bennett, B. The mothers
Collins, C. The gamal
Deford, F. Bliss, remembered
Helprin, M. In sunlight and in shadow
James, E. Four Nights With the Duke
Jenoff, P. The Ambassador's Daughter
Kalotay, D. Sight Reading
Levy, D. Swimming home
Nicholson, W. Motherland
Suri, M. The city of Devi
TRIATHLETES
See also Athletes
TRIBECA (NEW YORK, N.Y.)
Greenfeld, K. T. Triburbia
TRIBES
See also Clans; Family
Triburbia. Greenfeld, K. T.
TRICERATOPS
See also Dinosaurs
A **trick** of the light. Penny, L.
Trieste. Drndić, D.
Trigger warning. Gaiman, N.
TRIGONOMETRY
See also Geometry; Mathematics
Trillium [series]
Norton, A. Golden Trillium
TRINIDAD
Mootoo, S. Moving forward sideways like a crab
TRINIDAD AND TOBAGO
Abdul-Jabbar, K. Mycroft Holmes
Naipaul, V. S. A house for Mr. Biswas
Naipaul, V. S. A way in the world
Trinity. Uris, L.
The **Trinity** Six. Cumming, C.
TRIPLETS
Powell, S. The Mushroom Man
Tristan, Flora, 1803-1844
About
Vargas Llosa, M. The way to paradise
The **triumph** of Caesar. Saylor, S.
TROJAN WAR
George, M. Helen of Troy
Miller, M. The song of Achilles
Unsworth, B. The songs of the kings
TROJAN WAR
See also Greek mythology; Troy (Extinct city)
TROODON
See also Dinosaurs
Trophy. Griffith, M.
Tropic of Cancer. Miller, H.
Tropic of Capricorn. Miller, H.
TROPICAL FISH
See also Fishes
TROPICAL JUNGLES *See* Jungles
Trouble in Paradise. Parker, R. B.
Trouble the water. Seitz, N.
The **troubled** man. Mankell, H.
Troubled sleep. Sartre, J. P.
The Troubles Trilogy [series]
McKinty, A. In the Morning I'll Be Gone
The **troupe.** Bennett, R. J.
TROY (ANCIENT CITY)
Cook, E. Achilles
George, M. Helen of Troy
Hauser, E. For the most beautiful
Miller, M. The song of Achilles
TRUCKS
See also Automobiles; Highway transportation; Motor vehicles

The **true** and outstanding adventures of the Hunt sisters. Robinson, E.
True believers. Haddam, J.
True grit. Portis, C.
Trujillo Molina, Rafael Leónidas, 1891-1961
About
The Feast of the Goat
Truly madly guilty. Moriarty, L.
TRUMPET PLAYERS
Baker, D. Young man with a horn
Trumps of doom. Zelazny, R.
TRUST
See also Attitude (Psychology); Emotions
McFarlane, F. The night guest
TRUST COMPANIES
See also Business; Corporations
Trust me. Updike, J.
Trust me on this. Westlake, D. E.
Trust no one. Krentz, J. A.
Trust your eyes. Barclay, L.
The **truth.** Palin, M.
The **truth.** Pratchett, T.
The **truth** about love. Hart, J.
The **truth** and other lies. Arango, S.
Truth in advertising. Kenney, J.
Truth like the sun. Lynch, J.
TRUTHFULNESS AND FALSEHOOD
Dunmore, H. The lie
Eco, U. Baudolino
Harper, J. The dry
Horlock, M. The book of lies
Johnson, A. The orphan master's son
Smith, A. The accidental
Smith, M. A. The Inquisitor
Ware, R. The lying game
The **tsar** of love and techno. Marra, A.
TUBERCULOSIS
Gide, A. The immoralist
Mann, T. The magic mountain
Patterson, K. Consumption
Tudor, Owen, ca. 1400-1461
About
Bennett, V. The queen's lover
Tuesday nights in 1980. Prentiss, M.
Tuesday's gone. French, N.
Tulip fever. Moggach, D.
TULIP MANIA, 17TH CENTURY
Moggach, D. Tulip fever
TULSA (OKLA.)
Lytal, B. A map of Tulsa
Tumbledown. Boswell, R.
TUNDRA ECOLOGY
See also Ecology
Tunnel vision. Paretsky, S.
TUNNELS
Kelly, J. The moon tunnel
TURKEY
Ackerman, E. Dark at the Crossing
De Bernieres, L. Birds without wings
Karnezis, P. The maze
Snow
TURKEY -- ISTANBUL
Gilman, D. The amazing Mrs. Pollifax
Hill, T. The love of stones
Lukas, M. D. The Oracle of Stamboul
McDonald, I. The Dervish House
The museum of innocence
My name is Red
Rosenberg, R. This is not civilization
Shafak, E. The bastard of Istanbul
TURKEYS
See also Birds; Poultry
TURKISH AMERICANS
Batuman, E. The idiot
TURKISH FICTION -- TRANSLATIONS INTO ENGLISH
The museum of innocence
My name is Red
Snow
TURKS
Hambly, B. Ran away
A **Turn** of Light. Czerneda, J. E.
Turn of mind. Laplante, A.
The **turn** of the screw. James, H.
The **turnaround.** Pelecanos, G. P.
TURNCOATS *See* Defectors
The **Turner** house. Flournoy, A. c.
TURNER'S SYNDROME
Haigh, J. The condition
Turner, J. M. W. (Joseph Mallord William), 1775-1851
About
Van Essen, T. The Center of the World
Turner, Nat, 1800?-1831
About
Styron, W. The confessions of Nat Turner
Turner, Ted, 1938-
About
Everett, P. L. I am Not Sidney Poitier
Turning angel. Iles, G.
Turpin, Randy, 1928-1966
About
Phillips, C. Foreigners
The **turquoise** lament. MacDonald, J. D.
Turtle Moon. Hoffman, A.
TUSCANY (ITALY)
Elkins, A. J. Dying on the vine
Tutankhamen, King of Egypt
About
Holland, C. Valley of the Kings
TUTORS
Barth, J. The sot-weed factor
Desai, K. The inheritance of loss
Mann, T. The black swan
Upadhyay, S. The guru of love
Wilder, T. Theophilus North

TUTSI (AFRICAN PEOPLE)
See also Africans; Indigenous peoples
TUTSI (AFRICAN PEOPLE)
Benaron, N. Running the rift
TV *See* Television
Twain and Stanley Enter Paradise. Hijuelos, O.
Twain, Mark, 1835-1910
About
Clinch, J. Finn
'Twas the night after Christmas. Jeffries, S.
The **twelfth** Imam. Rosenberg, J. C.
The **twelve.** Cronin, J.
The **twelve** lives of Samuel Hawley. Tinti, H.
The **twelve** tribes of Hattie. Mathis, A.
TWENTIETH CENTURY *See* World history -- 20th century
TWENTIETH CENTURY
Follett, K. Winter of the world
Twenty fragments of a ravenous youth. Guo Xiaolu
Twenty years after. Dumas, A.
TWENTY-SECOND CENTURY
Robinson, K. S. New York 2140
Twentynine Palms. Pyne, D.
Twice tempted. Dreyer, E.
Twilight. Gay, W.
Twilight of the superheroes. Eisenberg, D.
The **twin.** Bakker, G.
TWIN BROTHERS
Alenyikov, M. Ivan and Misha
TWIN SISTERS
Konar, A. Mischling
TWINS
Adichie, C. N. Half of a yellow sun
Alenyikov, M. Ivan and Misha
Bakker, G. The twin
Barth, J. The sot-weed factor
Bohjalian, C. The night strangers
Chaon, D. Await your reply
Frazier, C. Nightwoods
Golding, W. Darkness visible
Habila, H. Measuring time
Haig, F. The fire sermon
Haig, F. The map of bones
Hart, J. The last child
Hatoum, M. The brothers
Higgins, J. Flight of eagles
Hunter, E. The moment she was gone
Konar, A. Mischling
Niffenegger, A. Her fearful symmetry
Pyper, A. The damned
Roy, A. The god of small things
Shakar, A. Luminarium
Singer, I. J. The brothers Ashkenazi
Thackeray, W. M. The Virginians
Trevanian The summer of Katya
Trollope, J. A Spanish lover
Tryon, T. The other
Verghese, A. Cutting for stone
Woods, S. Palindrome
Yang, J. Y. The black tides of heaven
The **twisted** root. Perry, A.
The **two** deaths of Daniel Hayes. Sakey, M.
Two for sorrow. Upson, N.
The **Two** Hotels Francfort. Leavitt, D.
Two she-bears.
The **two** towers. Tolkien, J. R. R.
Two trains running. Vachss, A. H.
Two years eight months and twenty-eight nights. Rushdie, S.
Two-dollar bill. Woods, S.
The **two-family** house. Loigman, L. C.
TYPE AND TYPE-FOUNDING
See also Founding; Printing
Typee: a peep at Polynesian life. Melville, H.
Typee: a peep at Polynesian life; Omoo: a narrative of adventures in the South Seas; Mardi: and a voyager thither. Melville, H.
TYPESETTING
See also Printing
The **typewriter** girl. Atlee, A.
The **typewriter's** tale. Heyns, M.
TYPHOID FEVER
See also Diseases
Keane, M. B. Fever
Typhoid Mary, -1938
About
Keane, M. B. Fever
TYPHOONS
See also Cyclones; Storms; Winds
Typical American. Jen, G.
TYPISTS
Rindell, S. The Other Typist
TYPOGRAPHY
See also Graphic arts; Printing
TYPOLOGY (PSYCHOLOGY)
See also Personality; Psychology; Temperament
Tyrannosaur Canyon. Preston, D.
TYRANNOSAURUS REX
See also Dinosaurs
Tyrant memory. Castellanos Moya, H.
Tzu-hsi, Empress dowager of China, 1835-1908
About
Min, A. Empress Orchid

U

U.S.A. Dos Passos, J.
UGANDA
Makumbi, J. N. Kintu
The **ugly** duchess. James, E.
UKRAINE
Foer, J. S. Everything is illuminated
UKRAINE -- KIEV
Anatoli, A. Babi Yar
Malamud, B. The fixer
UKRAINIANS -- UNITED STATES

Kiefer, C. The infinite tides
Ultimate prizes. Howatch, S.
Ulysses. Joyce, J.
Umbrella. Self, W.
The **Unamericans.** Antopol, M.
An **unattended** death. Jenkins, V.
UNAUTHORIZED IMMIGRANTS
Allende, I. In the midst of winter
Ko, L. The leavers
Sekaran, S. Lucky boy
Wambaugh, J. Harbor nocturne
The **unbearable** lightness of being. Kundera, M.
The **unburied.** Palliser, C.
Uncle Janice. Burgess, M.
Uncle Peretz takes off. Shabtai, Y.
Uncle Tom's cabin. Stowe, H. B.
Uncle Tom's children. Wright, R.
UNCLES
Abu-Jaber, D. Crescent
Amis, M. Lionel Asbo
Chaudhuri, A. Odysseus Abroad
Cramer, W. D. Bad ground
Dickens, C. Nicholas Nickleby
Enger, L. Undiscovered country
Haig, M. The dead fathers club
Hodgen, C. Elegies for the brokenhearted
Jackson, S. We have always lived in the castle
McGahan, A. The white earth
Meloy, M. A family daughter
Mitchard, J. A theory of relativity
Norman, H. The bird artist
Norman, H. The museum guard
Stabenow, D. Though not dead
Trollope, J. The men and the girls
Welty, E. The Ponder heart
Wood, S. Wrecker
Wroblewski, D. The story of Edgar Sawtelle
UNCLES
See also Family
Uncollected stories of William Faulkner. Faulkner, W.
Uncommon clay. Maron, M.
The **unconsoled.** Ishiguro, K.
Under African skies.
Under fire. Griffin, W. E. B.
Under heaven. Kay, G. G.
Under Her Skin. Anders, A.
Under Pressure. Foster, L.
Under suspicion novel [series]
Clark, M. H. The sleeping beauty killer
Under the banyan tree and other stories. Narayan, R. K.
Under the beetle's cellar. Walker, M. W.
Under the udala trees. Okparanta, C.
Under the volcano. Lowry, M.
Under Tower Peak. Paul, B.
UNDERACHIEVERS
See also Students
UNDERCOVER OPERATIONS
Burgess, M. Uncle Janice
Crompton, R. Hell's gate
Gross, A. The one man
Ledgard, J. M. Submergence
Robert, K. The devil's daughter
Smith, A. Judas horse
Undercurrents. Pearson, R.
UNDERGRADUATES *See* College students
The **underground** man. Macdonald, R.
The **underground** railroad. Whitehead, C.
UNDERGROUND RAILROAD
Chevalier, T. The last runaway
Faye, L. Seven for a secret
Stowe, H. B. Uncle Tom's cabin
Whitehead, C. The underground railroad
UNDERGROUND RAILROADS *See* Subways
Undermajordomo Minor. DeWitt, P.
UNDERSEA EXPLORATION *See* Underwater exploration
UNDERSEA RESEARCH STATIONS
See also Oceanography -- Research; Underwater exploration
UNDERTAKERS AND UNDERTAKING
Gay, W. Twilight
Logan, K. The gracekeepers
The **undertow.** Baker, J.
UNDERWATER EXPLORATION
Cambias, J. L. A Darkling Sea
Underworld. DeLillo, D.
UNDERWORLD
Algren, N. The man with the golden arm
Dickens, C. Oliver Twist
Dos Passos, J. U.S.A.
Ellroy, J. American tabloid
Ellroy, J. Blood's a rover
Ellroy, J. The cold six thousand
Ellroy, J. L.A. confidential
Faust, C. Choke hold
Faust, C. Money shot
Johansen, I. Final target
Mieville, C. Kraken
Mortimer, J. Felix in the underworld
Pelecanos, G. P. The big blowdown
Polansky, D. Low Town
Puzo, M. The godfather
Puzo, M. The last Don
Sanchez, T. King Bongo
Steinbeck, J. Cannery Row
Wambaugh, J. Hollywood crows
Wambaugh, J. Hollywood Hills
Wambaugh, J. Hollywood Station
The **underworld.** Canty, K.
Undiscovered country. Enger, L.
UNDOCUMENTED ALIENS
Boyle, T. C. The tortilla curtain
Cleave, C. Little Bee
Glass, J. The widower's tale
Prose, F. Primitive people

Straight, S. Highwire moon
Tobar, H. The barbarian nurseries
UNDOCUMENTED ALIENS *See* Unauthorized immigrants
Undue influence. Brookner, A.
UNEMPLOYED
Atwood, M. The Heart Goes Last
Austin, L. All she ever wanted
Laukkanen, O. The professionals
Link, C. The Watcher
Pilcher, R. A risk worth taking
Steinbeck, J. Cannery Row
Steinbeck, J. The grapes of wrath
Steinbeck, J. Sweet Thursday
Walter, J. The financial lives of the poets
Westlake, D. E. The ax
UNEMPLOYMENT
See also Employment; Labor supply; Social problems
Thompson, J. The humanity project
UNEMPLOYMENT INSURANCE
See also Insurance
The **Unexpected** Duchess. Bowman, V.
The **unexpected** Mrs. Pollifax. Gilman, D.
Unfinished desires. Godwin, G.
UNFINISHED NOVELS
Dickens, C. The mystery of Edwin Drood
Fitzgerald, F. S. The last tycoon
Forester, C. S. Hornblower during the crisis, and two stories: Hornblower's temptation and The last encounter
Kafka, F. The castle
Kafka, F. The trial
Musil, R. The man without qualities
Three days before the shooting--
Wallace, D. F. The pale king
An **unfinished** season. Just, W. S.
The **Unforgetting** heart: an anthology of short stories by African American women (1859-1993)
Unholy fire. Mrazek, R. J.
UNICORNS
Beagle, P. S. The last unicorn
UNIDENTIFIED FLYING OBJECTS
See also Aeronautics; Astronautics
Uniform justice. Leon, D.
The **uninvited.** Jensen, L.
The **uninvited** guests. Jones, S.
Union Atlantic. Haslett, A.
UNIONS, LABOR *See* Labor unions
UNITED ARAB EMIRATES
Unnikrishnan, D. Temporary people
UNITED STATES
Kerouac, J. On the road
Kosinski, J. N. Being there
Roth, P. The American trilogy, 1997-2000
Sayers, D. L. Busman's honeymoon
Sayers, D. L. The unpleasantness at the Bellona Club
Sayles, J. A moment in the sun
Vonnegut, K. Hocus pocus
Wilson, R. C. Julian Comstock
UNITED STATES -- 1783-1815
Hambly, B. Patriot hearts
UNITED STATES -- 1815-1861
Stowe, H. B. Uncle Tom's cabin
Updike, J. Memories of the Ford Administration
UNITED STATES -- 18TH CENTURY
Thackeray, W. M. The Virginians
Thom, J. A. The red heart
Vidal, G. Burr
UNITED STATES -- 19TH CENTURY
Carey, P. Parrot and Olivier in America
Hill, R. B. Hanta yo
Kantor, M. Andersonville
Lockridge, R. Raintree County
Mitchell, M. Gone with the wind
Oates, J. C. A Bloodsmoor romance
Plain, B. Crescent City
Sontag, S. In America
Thom, J. A. The red heart
Vidal, G. 1876
Vidal, G. Burr
Vidal, G. Empire
Vidal, G. Lincoln
UNITED STATES -- BIOGRAPHY
See also Biography
UNITED STATES -- CIVIL WAR, 1861-1865 -- CAMPAIGNS
Crane, S. The red badge of courage
UNITED STATES -- CIVIL WAR, 1861-1865 -- NAVAL OPERATIONS
Poyer, D. A country of our own
UNITED STATES -- ECONOMIC CONDITIONS
Eggers, D. A hologram for the king
UNITED STATES -- EMIGRATION AND IMMIGRATION
Fishman, B. A replacement life
UNITED STATES -- EXPLORING EXPEDITIONS
See also Explorers
UNITED STATES -- FOREIGN POLICY *See* United States -- Foreign relations
UNITED STATES -- FOREIGN RELATIONS
Shacochis, B. The Woman Who Lost Her Soul
UNITED STATES -- FOREIGN RELATIONS
See also Diplomacy; International relations; World politics
UNITED STATES -- FOREIGN RELATIONS -- RUSSIA
Matthews, J. Palace of treason
UNITED STATES -- HISTORY
Bloom, A. Lucky us
Burke, J. L. Wayfaring Stranger
Mallon, T. Finale
Rollins, J. The devil colony
Self, W. Shark
UNITED STATES -- HISTORY -- 1600-1775, COLONIAL PERIOD
Brooks, G. Caleb's crossing
Defoe, D. Moll Flanders
Gabaldon, D. A breath of snow and ashes

Gabaldon, D. The fiery cross
L'Amour, L. To the far blue mountains
Morrison, T. A mercy
Pynchon, T. Mason & Dixon
Richter, C. The light in the forest
Spufford, F. Golden Hill
Turner, N. E. My name is Resolute
UNITED STATES -- HISTORY -- 1755-1763, FRENCH AND INDIAN WAR
Cooper, J. F. The last of the Mohicans
Swerling, B. Shadowbrook
UNITED STATES -- HISTORY -- 1775-1783, REVOLUTION
Charyn, J. Johnny One-Eye
Edmonds, W. D. Drums along the Mohawk
Gabaldon, D. An echo in the bone
Gabaldon, D. Written in my own heart's blood
Hambly, B. Patriot hearts
Hill, L. Someone knows my name
UNITED STATES -- HISTORY -- 1775-1783, REVOLUTION
See also Revolutions
UNITED STATES -- HISTORY -- 1783-1865
Perkins-Valdez, D. Wench
Rawles, N. My Jim
UNITED STATES -- HISTORY -- 1861-1865, CIVIL WAR -- BIOGRAPHY
See also Biography
UNITED STATES -- HISTORY -- 1861-1865, CIVIL WAR
Alexander, T. A beauty so rare
Bahr, H. The Judas Field
Barry, S. Days Without End
Cole, A. An Extraordinary Union
Cole, A. A hope divided
Doctorow, E. L. The march
Frazier, C. Cold Mountain
Gibbons, K. On the occasion of my last afternoon
Gingrich, N. Gettysburg
Gingrich, N. Grant comes east
Gohlke, C. I have seen him in the watchfires
Griesemer, J. Signal & noise
Gurganus, A. The oldest living Confederate widow tells all
Hicks, R. The widow of the south
Horn, D. All other nights
Humphreys, J. Nowhere else on earth
Hunt, L. Neverhome
Jakes, J. Love and war
Jakes, J. North and South
Jakes, J. On secret service
Jakes, J. Savannah; or, A gift for Mr. Lincoln
Jiles, P. Enemy women
Kantor, M. Andersonville
Lent, J. A slant of light
Lock, N. American meteor
Logan, C. South of Shiloh
McCabe, E. L. I shall be near to you
Mitchell, M. Gone with the wind
Mrazek, R. J. Unholy fire
Olmstead, R. Coal black horse
Plain, B. Crescent City
Poyer, D. Fire on the waters
Peters, R. Hell or Richmond
Priest, C. Clementine
Priest, C. Dreadnought
Priest, C. Fiddlehead
Reed, I. Flight to Canada
Shaara, J. Gods and generals
Shaara, J. The last full measure
Shaara, M. The killer angels
Vidal, G. Lincoln
Warren, R. P. Band of angels
Wray, J. Canaan's tongue
UNITED STATES -- HISTORY -- 1861-1865, CIVIL WAR -- PERSONAL NARRATIVES
See also Autobiographies; Biography
UNITED STATES -- HISTORY -- 1861-1865, CIVIL WAR -- PRISONERS AND PRISONS
Groot, T. The sentinels of Andersonville
UNITED STATES -- HISTORY -- 1861-1865, CIVIL WAR -- PRISONERS AND PRISONS
See also Prisoners of war; Prisons
UNITED STATES -- HISTORY -- 1861-1865, CIVIL WAR -- WOMEN
Alexander, T. A beauty so rare
UNITED STATES -- HISTORY -- 1865-1898
Allen, J. R. Song of the shank
UNITED STATES -- HISTORY -- 18TH CENTURY
Fisher, S. W. Anna's crossing
UNITED STATES -- HISTORY -- 1919-1933
Albert, S. W. The Darling Dahlias and the cucumber tree
UNITED STATES -- HISTORY -- 19TH CENTURY
Enger, L. The high divide
Jiles, P. News of the world
UNITED STATES -- HISTORY -- 20TH CENTURY
Celine Journey to the end of the night
DeLillo, D. Underworld
Didion, J. Play it as it lays
Doctorow, E. L. Ragtime
Dos Passos, J. 1919
Dos Passos, J. U.S.A.
Ellroy, J. American tabloid
Ellroy, J. The cold six thousand
Fitzgerald, F. S. The beautiful and damned
Fitzgerald, F. S. The great Gatsby
Franzen, J. The corrections
Gaddis, W. A frolic of his own
Kerouac, J. On the road
Kerouac, J. The Dharma bums
Kosinski, J. N. Being there
Lewis, S. Babbitt
Means, D. Hystopia
Nabokov, V. V. Lolita
Piercy, M. Vida
Proulx, A. Accordion crimes

Proulx, A. Postcards
Roth, P. The great American novel
Shaw, I. Rich man, poor man
Thomas, M. We are not ourselves
Turner, F. W. 1929
Updike, J. In the beauty of the lilies
Updike, J. Memories of the Ford Administration
Vonnegut, K. Jailbird
Wiggins, M. Evidence of things unseen
Wouk, H. War and remembrance
Wouk, H. The winds of war

UNITED STATES -- HISTORY -- CIVIL WAR, 1861-1865 -- PARTICIPATION, FEMALE

Cole, A. An Extraordinary Union

UNITED STATES -- HISTORY -- CIVIL WAR, 1861-1865 -- SECRET SERVICE

Jakes, J. On secret service
Leveen, L. The secrets of Mary Bowser

UNITED STATES -- HISTORY -- REVOLUTION, 1775-1783

Charyn, J. Johnny One-Eye
Gabaldon, D. Written in my own heart's blood
Turner, N. E. My name is Resolute

UNITED STATES -- IMMIGRATION AND EMIGRATION

See also Americanization; Immigration and emigration

UNITED STATES -- IMMIGRATION AND EMIGRATION -- HISTORY

Wu, J. The third son

UNITED STATES -- NATIONAL PARKS AND RESERVES

See National parks and reserves -- United States

UNITED STATES -- POLITICS AND GOVERNMENT

Sakey, M. A Better World

UNITED STATES -- RACE RELATIONS

Alexie, S. Indian killer
Baker, K. Strivers Row
Baldwin, J. Another country
Baldwin, J. If Beale Street could talk
Bambara, T. C. The salt eaters
Berg, E. We are all welcome here
Brown, R. Half a heart
Brown, S. The witness
Campbell, B. M. Brothers and sisters
Chesnutt, C. W. Stories, novels, & essay
Childress, M. Crazy in Alabama
Clinch, J. Finn
Cole, T. Open city
Cooke, C. Daughters of the revolution
Dexter, P. Paris Trout
Doctorow, E. L. Ragtime
Durrow, H. W. The girl who fell from the sky
Edgerton, C. The night train
Ellison, R. Invisible man
Everett, P. L. I am Not Sidney Poitier
Faulkner, W. Light in August
Faulkner, W. Intruder in the dust
Fowler, K. J. Sarah Canary
French, A. Billy
Gaines, E. J. A gathering of old men
Gaines, E. J. A lesson before dying
Gibbons, K. Divining women
Gilb, D. The flowers
Grant, S. Map of Ireland
Grau, S. A. The keepers of the house
Greer, A. S. The story of a marriage
Grisham, J. A time to kill
Hambly, B. A free man of color
Harlem Renaissance: five novels of the 1920s
Harlem Renaissance: four novels of the 1930s
Hughes, L. Not without laughter
Hughes, L. Simple speaks his mind
Hughes, L. Simple's Uncle Sam
Jordan, H. Mudbound
Kennedy, W. Chango's beads and two-tone shoes
Kidd, S. M. The secret life of bees
Lansdale, J. R. The bottoms
Lansdale, J. R. A fine dark line
Lansdale, J. R. Sunset and sawdust
Lee, H. To kill a mockingbird
Lehane, D. The given day
Lethem, J. The fortress of solitude
Marlette, D. Magic time
Matthiessen, P. Bone by bone
Matthiessen, P. Shadow country
Mengestu, D. The beautiful things that heaven bears
Michener, J. A. Chesapeake
Morrison, T. A mercy
Morrison, T. Tar baby
Mosley, W. Fortunate son
Naslund, S. J. Four spirits
Nordan, L. Wolf whistle
Oates, J. C. Because it is bitter, and because it is my heart
Oates, J. C. Black girl/White girl
Parker, R. B. Double play
Parks, G. The learning tree
Parks Getting mother's body
Pelecanos, G. P. The night gardener
Pelecanos, G. P. Right as rain
Pelecanos, G. P. The turnaround
Phillips, C. Dancing in the dark
Powell, P. Edisto
Price, R. Freedomland
Reed, I. Mumbo jumbo
Revoyr, N. Wingshooters
Rhodes, J. P. Voodoo dreams
Rice, A. The Feast of All Saints
Robinson, M. Gilead
Roth, P. The human stain
Silko, L. Almanac of the dead
Smith, L. E. Strange fruit
Southgate, M. The fall of Rome
Straight, S. The gettin place
Straight, S. A million nightingales
Styron, W. The confessions of Nat Turner
Tademy, L. Cane River

Taylor, M. G. The Marrowbone Marble Company
Three days before the shooting--
Vachss, A. H. Two trains running
Vernon, O. Eden
Vernon, O. A killing in this town
Wallace, I. The man
Warren, R. P. Band of angels
West, D. The wedding
Whitehead, C. Apex hides the hurt
Whitehead, C. The intuitionist
Wimberley, D. The king of Colored Town
Wolfe, T. A man in full
Woods, S. Chiefs
Wright, R. Native son
Yarbrough, S. Prisoners of war
UNITED STATES -- RACE RELATIONS
See also Race relations
UNITED STATES -- RELATIONS -- CHINA
Jin, H. A map of betrayal
UNITED STATES -- RELIGION
See also Religion
UNITED STATES -- RURAL CONDITIONS
Rhodes, D. Jewelweed
UNITED STATES -- SOCIAL CONDITIONS
See also Social conditions
UNITED STATES -- SOCIAL LIFE AND CUSTOMS -- 20TH CENTURY
Fitzgerald, F. S. Novels and stories, 1920-1922
Gurganus, A. The practical heart
Jen, G. Who's Irish?
Klaussmann, L. Tigers in red weather
Oates, J. C. Faithless
Updike, J. Licks of love
Vonnegut, K. Bagombo snuff box: uncollected short fiction
UNITED STATES -- SOCIAL LIFE AND CUSTOMS
Bachelder, C. The throwback special
Hood, A. The Obituary Writer
Yates, R. The collected stories of Richard Yates
UNITED STATES -- WAR WITH MEXICO, 1845-1848
Shaara, J. Gone for soldiers
UNITED STATES MARSHALS
Lehane, D. Shutter Island
Leonard, E. Raylan
Parker, R. B. Gunman's rhapsody
UNITED STATES MILITARY ACADEMY
Bayard, L. The pale blue eye
UNITED STATES NATIONAL ARCHIVES
Meltzer, B. The inner circle
UNITED STATES NAVAL ACADEMY
Webb, J. A sense of honor
UNITED STATES. AIR FORCE
Heller, J. Catch-22
Rosten, L. Captain Newman, M.D.
UNITED STATES. AIR FORCE -- OFFICERS
L'Amour, L. Last of the breed
Westheimer, D. Von Ryan's Express
UNITED STATES. ARMY
Jones, J. From here to eternity
Jones, J. The thin red line
McCullers, C. Reflections in a golden eye
O'Connor, R. Buffalo soldiers
Shaara, J. Gods and generals
Shaara, J. The last full measure
Truscott, L. K. Heart of war
Willard, T. Buffalo soldiers
UNITED STATES. ARMY -- BIOGRAPHY
See also Biography
UNITED STATES. ARMY -- COMMANDO TROOPS
Atkins, A. The forsaken
UNITED STATES. ARMY CRIMINAL INVESTIGATION COMMAND
Limón, M. Mr. Kill
UNITED STATES. ARMY -- MILITARY LIFE
See also Military personnel; Soldiers
UNITED STATES. ARMY -- OFFICERS
Hersey, J. A bell for Adano
Nathanson, E. M. The dirty dozen
Pynchon, T. Gravity's rainbow
Uris, L. Armageddon
UNITED STATES. ARMY -- OFFICERS
See also Military personnel; Soldiers
UNITED STATES. ARMY -- SPECIAL FORCES
Griffin, W. E. B. Special ops
UNITED STATES. ARMY -- SURGEONS
Scottoline, L. Don't Go
UNITED STATES. CENTRAL INTELLIGENCE AGENCY
Buckley, W. F. Mongoose, R.I.P
Ellroy, J. American tabloid
Gilman, D. The amazing Mrs. Pollifax
Gilman, D. The elusive Mrs. Pollifax
Gilman, D. The unexpected Mrs. Pollifax
Grady, J. Six days of the condor
Greaney, M. Gunmetal gray
Griffin, W. E. B. Special ops
Griffin, W. E. B. Under fire
Grisham, J. The brethren
Harris, R. The ghost
Hospital, J. T. Due preparations for the plague
Huston, C. Skinner
Ignatius, D. Body of lies
Jin, H. A map of betrayal
Johansen, I. And then you die--
Johnson, D. Tree of smoke
Littell, R. The company
Palmer, M. The patient
Robbins, T. Fierce invalids home from hot climates
Rush, N. Mortals
Silva, D. The mark of the assassin
Steiner, P. The terrorist
Steinhauer, O. The nearest exit
Steinhauer, O. The tourist
Thomas, R. Ah, treachery!
UNITED STATES. CENTRAL INTELLIGENCE AGENCY -- EMPLOYEES

Johansen, I. No easy target
UNITED STATES. COAST GUARD
Hickam, H. H. The keeper's son
UNITED STATES. CONGRESS -- SENATE
Oates, J. C. Black water
Three days before the shooting--
Vidal, G. Washington, D.C.
UNITED STATES. FEDERAL BUREAU OF INVESTIGATION
Coulter, C. The end game
Coulter, C. The Final Cut
Coulter, C. Split second
DeMille, N. Wild fire
Hooper, K. Blood sins
Hooper, K. Blood ties
Isaacs, S. Red, white and blue
King, L. R. A darker place
Pottinger, S. The last Nazi
Preston, D. Brimstone
Preston, D. The cabinet of curiosities
Preston, D. Reliquary
Preston, D. Still life with crows
Preston, D. The wheel of darkness
Reiken, F. Day for night
Rosenfelt, D. Don't tell a soul
Smith, A. Judas horse
Turow, S. Personal injuries
UNITED STATES. FEDERAL BUREAU OF INVESTIGATION -- OFFICIALS AND EMPLOYEES
Robert, K. The devil's daughter
UNITED STATES. INTERNAL REVENUE SERVICE
Wallace, D. F. The pale king
UNITED STATES. MARINE CORPS
Grant, D. The Protector
Griffin, W. E. B. Under fire
Marlantes, K. Matterhorn
Uris, L. Battle cry
Webb, J. A sense of honor
UNITED STATES. NATIONAL AERONAUTICS AND SPACE ADMINISTRATION
Dean, M. L. The time it takes to fall
McDevitt, J. The Cassandra project
Michener, J. A. Space
UNITED STATES. NATIONAL SECURITY COUNCIL
Clancy, T. Clear and present danger
UNITED STATES. NATIONAL TRANSPORTATION SAFETY BOARD
Haynes, D. Crashers
UNITED STATES. NAVY
Heggen, T. Mister Roberts
Michener, J. A. The bridges at Toko-ri
Poyer, D. Black storm
Poyer, D. A country of our own
Poyer, D. Fire on the waters
Poyer, D. The gulf
Robinson, P. Kilo class
Wambaugh, J. Finnegan's week
Wiggs, S. The ocean between us
Wouk, H. The Caine mutiny
UNITED STATES. NAVY -- OFFICERS
Wouk, H. War and remembrance
UNITED STATES. SECRET SERVICE
Costello, M. Big if
UNITED STATES. SUPREME COURT
Meltzer, B. The tenth justice
Patterson, R. N. Protect and defend
Universal harvester. Darnielle, J.
UNIVERSAL LANGUAGE
See also Language and languages; Linguistics
The **Universe** Versus Alex Woods. Extence, G.
UNIVERSITIES AND COLLEGES
Carter, S. L. New England white
Lipsyte, S. The ask
UNIVERSITY OF NOTRE DAME
McInerny, R. M. Celt and pepper
McInerny, R. M. Irish coffee
UNIVERSITY OF OXFORD
Marias, J. All souls
Sayers, D. L. Gaudy Night
UNIVERSITY STUDENTS *See* College students
An **unkindness** of ghosts. Solomon, R.
The **unknown** shore. O'Brian, P.
The **unknown** terrorist. Flanagan, R.
The **unknowns.** Roth, G.
Unless. Shields, C.
The **unlikely** pilgrimage of Harold Fry. Joyce, R.
Unlucky in law. O'Shaughnessy, P.
An **unmarked** grave. Todd, C.
UNMARRIED COUPLES
Hawke, E. Ash Wednesday
Levithan, D. The lover's dictionary
Morgan, C. E. All the living
Reiken, F. Day for night
Shriver, L. The post-birthday world
Spencer, S. Man in the woods
Walker, A. Now is the time to open your heart
UNMARRIED FATHERS
See also Fathers; Single parents
UNMARRIED FATHERS
Law, S. K. The paper marriage
Little, T. Where there's smoke
UNMARRIED MEN *See* Single men
UNMARRIED MOTHERS
DuPree, K. Silenced
Gordon, M. The company of women
Hannah, K. Home again
K'wan (Author) Section 8
K'wan (Author) Welfare wifeys
Lippman, L. And when she was good
Llywelyn, M. 1949
Richler, N. Your mouth is lovely
Shreve, A. Fortune's Rocks
Upadhyay, S. The guru of love
Wallace, M. The girl in the garden

UNMARRIED MOTHERS
See also Mothers; Single parents
The **unnamed.** Ferris, J.
Unnatural Habits. Greenwood, K.
Unnatural selection. Elkins, A. J.
An **Unnecessary** Woman. Alameddine, R.
The **unpleasantness** at the Bellona Club. Sayers, D. L.
The **unquiet** dead. Khan, A. Z.
The **unremembered.** Orullian, P. V.
An **Unrestored** Woman. Rao, S.
The **Unseen** World. Moore, L.
UNSOLVED MYSTERIES
Berney, L. The Long and Faraway Gone
King, S. End of watch
An **unsuitable** attachment. Pym, B.
An **unsuitable** job for a woman. James, P. D.
An **Untamed** State. Gay, R.
Until she comes home. Roy, L.
Until the dawn's light. Appelfeld, A.
Until thy wrath be past. Larsson, A.
Untold story. Ali, M.
UNTRUTH *See* Truthfulness and falsehood
Unwanted. Ohlsson, K.
UNWED MOTHERS *See* Unmarried mothers
Up jumps the Devil. Maron, M.
Up the down staircase. Kaufman, B.
Upon a dark night. Lovesey, P.
UPPER CLASS
Alexander, T. A beauty so rare
Balogh, M. Someone to Love
Walker, W. Crime of Privilege
UPPER CLASS
See also Social classes
UPPER CLASS -- ENGLAND
Dean, A. A gentleman of fortune, or, The suspicions of Miss Dido Kent
Dean, A. A woman of consequence
Lane, H. Alys, always
UPPER CLASS -- ENGLAND -- SOCIAL LIFE AND CUSTOMS -- 18TH CENTURY
Bailey, M. An appetite for violets
UPPER CLASS -- UNITED STATES
Mbue, I. Behold the Dreamers
UPPER CLASS FAMILIES -- ENGLAND
Dean, A. Bellfield Hall, or, The observations of Miss Dido Kent
St. Aubyn, E. The complete Patrick Melrose novels
UPPER CLASS FAMILIES
Benjamin, M. Alice I have been
Kelly, E. The burning air
Samarasan, P. Evening is the whole day
UPPER EAST SIDE (NEW YORK, N.Y.)
Gilbert, D. & sons
Uprooted. Novik, N.
UPSIDE-DOWN BOOKS
Delany, S. R. Babel-17 ; Empire star
UPSTATE NEW YORK (N.Y.)
Duffy, B. House of echoes
URBAN AREAS *See* Cities and towns; Metropolitan areas
URBAN ECOLOGY
See also Cities and towns; Ecology
URBAN FICTION
Diamond, D. A gangster and a gentleman
DuPree, K. Silenced
K'wan (Author) Animal
K'wan (Author) Welfare wifeys
Williams, K. Dirty to the grave
Woods, T. Alibi
URBAN FOLKLORE
See also Folklore
URBAN LIFE *See* City and town life
URBAN POLICY
See also City and town life; Economic policy; Social policy; Urban sociology
URBANIZATION
See also Cities and towns; Rural sociology; Social change; Social conditions; Urban sociology
Urrea, Teresa
About
Urrea, L. A. The hummingbird's daughter
The **Urth** of the new sun. Wolfe, G.
URUGUAY
Cameron, P. The city of your final destination
Us. Nicholls, D.
The **uses** of enchantment. Julavits, H.
The **usual** rules. Maynard, J.
UTAH
Ebershoff, D. The 19th wife
Grey, Z. Riders of the purple sage
Mailer, N. The executioner's song
Udall, B. The lonely polygamist
UTAH -- SALT LAKE CITY
Reiken, F. Day for night
UTE INDIANS
Borland, H. When the legends die
UTILITARIANISM
See also Ethics
UTOPIAN FICTION
Charlotte Perkins Gilman's Utopian novels
Cline, E. Ready player one
Gilman, C. P. Herland
Hilton, J. Lost horizon
Huxley, A. Brave new world
Le Guin, U. K. The dispossessed
Mastai, E. All our wrong todays
Murdoch, I. The bell
Niven, L. Saturn's race
Piercy, M. Woman on the edge of time
Rush, N. Mating
Unsworth, B. Sacred hunger
With her in Ourland
UTOPIAN FICTION
See also Fantasy fiction; Science fiction
UTOPIAN LITERATURE *See* Utopian fiction; Utopias

UTOPIAS
See also Political science; Socialism
UTOPIAS -- FICTION *See* Utopian fiction
Utz. Chatwin, B.
UXORICIDE
Walker, A. The third life of Grange Copeland

V

V. Pynchon, T.
V.I. Warshawski [series]
Paretsky, S. Fallout
Vacation. Unferth, D. O.
VACATION HOMES
See also Houses
Hadley, T. The past
Stonich, S. Vacationland
Thayer, N. Island girls
The **vacationers.** Straub, E.
Vacationland. Stonich, S.
VACATIONS
Andrews, M. K. Summer rental
Brookner, A. Hotel du Lac
Fairstein, L. Night watch
Haddon, M. The red house
Hilderbrand, E. The island
Spark, M. The driver's seat
Steel, D. Sunset in St. Tropez
Straub, E. The vacationers
Vaclav and Lena. Tanner, H.
The **vagabond** clown. Marston, E.
The **vagrants.** Yiyun Li
Valentino mysteries [series]
Estleman, L. D. Frames
VALETS
Faulks, S. Jeeves and the Wedding Bells
Verne, J. Around the world in eighty days
Wodehouse, P. G. The code of the Woosters
Wodehouse, P. G. The inimitable Jeeves
VALIS and later novels. Dick, P. K.
Vallejo, César Abraham, 1892-1938
About
Bolano, R. Monsieur Pain
The **Valley** of Amazement. Tan, A.
Valley of bones. Gruber, M.
Valley of the Kings. Holland, C.
VALUES
See also Aesthetics; Ethics; Psychology
The **vampire** Armand. Rice, A.
The vampire chronicles [series]
Rice, A. Prince Lestat
Rice, A. The queen of the damned
Rice, A. The vampire Lestat
Rice, A. Blood canticle
Rice, A. The tale of the body thief
Rice, A. The vampire Armand
VAMPIRE FILMS
See also Horror films; Motion pictures
The **vampire** Lestat. Rice, A.
VAMPIRES
Buehlman, C. The suicide motor club
Butler, O. E. Fledgling
Cronin, J. The passage
Duncan, G. By blood we live
Duncan, G. Talulla rising
Farnsworth, C. Blood oath
Haig, M. The Radleys
Harkness, D. E. The Book of Life
Harkness, D. E. A discovery of witches
Harkness, D. E. Shadow of night
Harris, C. Dead reckoning
Huston, C. Already dead
Huston, C. Every last drop
Huston, C. Half the blood of Brooklyn
Johnson, A. D. Moonshine
Kiernan, C. R. Blood oranges
King, S. Salem's Lot
Klein, R. The moth diaries
Kostova, E. The historian
Marks, J. Fangland
Martinez, A. L. Gil's All Fright Diner
Matheson, R. I am legend
Moore, C. You suck
The new annotated Dracula
Rhodes, J. P. Yellow moon
Rice, A. The queen of the damned
Rice, A. The vampire Lestat
Rice, A. Blood canticle
Rice, A. Interview with the vampire
Rice, A. Prince Lestat
Rice, A. The tale of the body thief
Rice, A. The vampire Armand
Russell, K. Vampires in the lemon grove
Sedgwick, M. A love like blood
Stoker, B. Dracula
Strieber, W. The hunger
VAMPIRES
See also Folklore
Vampires in the lemon grove. Russell, K.
VANCOUVER ISLAND (B.C.)
Ozeki, R. L. A tale for the time being
Vanessa and her sister. Parmar, P.
Vanilla Ride. Lansdale, J. R.
Vanished. Finder, J.
Vanishing act. Perry, T.
The **vanishing** act of Esme Lennox. O'Farrell, M.
Vanishing acts. Picoult, J.
The **vanishing** of Katharina Linden. Grant, H.
Vanishing point. Markson, D.
VANISHING SPECIES *See* Endangered species
Vanity fair. Thackeray, W. M.
Variable star. Heinlein, R. A.
The **various** haunts of men. Hill, S.
VASSALS *See* Feudalism

VASSAR COLLEGE
McCarthy, M. The group
VATICAN
Puzo, M. The family
Rabb, J. The book of Q
West, M. L. Lazarus
VATICAN CITY
Caldwell, I. The Fifth Gospel
Harris, R. Conclave
Merullo, R. Vatican waltz
Vatican waltz. Merullo, R.
VAUDEVILLE
Bennett, R. J. The troupe
McCracken, E. Niagara Falls all over again
The **vault.** Lovesey, P.
Vautrin, Wilhelmina, d. 1941
About
Jin, H. Nanjing requiem
VD *See* Sexually transmitted diseases
Vector. Cook, R.
VEGETABLES
See also Food; Plants
The **vegetarian.** Han, K.
Veil of gold. Wilkins, K.
Veiled worlds trilogy [series]
Anderton, J. Debris
VELOCIRAPTORS
See also Dinosaurs
Velocity. Koontz, D. R.
VENDETTA
Brown, D. Angels & demons
Higgins, J. Edge of danger
Kelton, E. Texas vendetta
Machart, B. The wake of forgiveness
VENEREAL DISEASES *See* Sexually transmitted diseases
The **Venetian** affair. MacInnes, H.
VENGENCE *See* Revenge
VENICE (ITALY)
Chase, L. Your scandalous ways
Leon, D. Beastly Things
Leon, D. Blood from a stone
Leon, D. A question of belief
Seay, M. The mirror thief
VENUS (PLANET)
Lewis, C. S. Perelandra
Pohl, F. The space merchants
Vera Stanhope [series]
Cleeves, A. The crow trap
VERBAL LEARNING
See also Language and languages; Psychology of learning
The **Verdict.** Stone, N.
Verdict unsafe. McGown, J.
Vermeer, Johannes, 1632-1675
About
Chevalier, T. Girl with a pearl earring
Vreeland, S. Girl in hyacinth blue
Vermilion drift. Krueger, W. K.
VERMONT
Bohjalian, C. A. Secrets of Eden
Freeman, C. All that I have
Freeman, C. Go with me
Henderson, E. Ten thousand saints
Lewis, S. It can't happen here
Lipman, E. The Inn at Lake Devine
Maloy, K. Every last cuckoo
Morris, M. M. Songs in ordinary time
Mosher, H. F. On Kingdom Mountain
Prose, F. Blue angel
Proulx, A. Postcards
Schupack, D. The boy on the bus
Shreve, A. Testimony
Tartt, D. The secret history
Tussing, J. The best people in the world
Updike, J. Seek my face
Zeltserman, D. Small crimes
Veronica. Gaitskill, M.
Veronica Speedwell mystery [series]
Raybourn, D. A perilous undertaking
Versailles. Davis, K.
VERSIFICATION
See also Authorship; Poetics; Rhythm
Version control. Palmer, D.
VERTEBRATES
See also Animals
Vertigo. Sebald, W. G.
Very bad men. Dolan, H.
Very Valentine. Trigiani, A.
VESSELS (SHIPS) *See* Ships
Vestments. Reimringer, J.
VETERAN REINTEGRATION
Hoffman, C. Be safe I love you
VETERANS
Atkins, A. The ranger
Boyle, T. C. The Harder They Come
Dunmore, H. The lie
Harkaway, N. Tigerman
Hoffman, C. Be safe I love you
Itani, F. Tell
Liss, D. The whiskey rebels
Means, D. Hystopia
Morrison, T. Home
Oates, J. C. Carthage
Parker, K. J. The company
Quirk, M. Cold barrel zero
The road ahead
Robinson, R. Sparta
Salter, J. All that is
Saunders, G. Tenth of December
Wyld, E. After the fire, a still small voice
VETERANS (AMERICAN CIVIL WAR, 1861-1865)
Bahr, H. The Judas Field
VETERANS (KOREAN WAR, 1950-1953)
Hill, R. When all is said and done

Percy, W. The moviegoer
Walbert, K. The gardens of Kyoto
VETERANS (VIETNAMESE WAR, 1961-1975)
Forsyth, F. Avenger
Green, N. The angel of Montague Street
Hunter, S. I, sniper
Hunter, S. Time to hunt
King, L. R. Keeping watch
Mason, B. A. In country
O'Brien, T. In the Lake of the Woods
O'Nan, S. The names of the dead
Pekearo, N. T. The wolfman
Stone, R. Dog soldiers
Thomas, R. Ah, treachery!
Thompson, J. The year we left home
Vonnegut, K. Hocus pocus
Walker, M. W. Under the beetle's cellar
Webb, J. A sense of honor
VETERANS (WORLD WAR, 1914-1918)
Erdrich, L. The Master Butchers Singing Club
Koryta, M. The Cypress House
Remarque, E. M. The road back
Rubenfeld, J. The death instinct
Wiggins, M. Evidence of things unseen
VETERANS (WORLD WAR, 1939-1945)
Algren, N. The man with the golden arm
Boll, H. The silent angel
Bragg, M. The soldier's return
Bragg, M. A son of war
Greer, A. S. The story of a marriage
Guterson, D. Snow falling on cedars
Hazzard, S. The great fire
Hunter, S. Hot Springs
Jordan, H. Mudbound
Lee A gesture life
Lehrer, J. The special prisoner
Levy, A. Small island
McEwan, I. Atonement
Okuizumi, H. The stones cry out
Taylor, M. G. The Marrowbone Marble Company
Turow, S. Ordinary heroes
Watkins, P. The ice soldier
Wharton, W. Birdy
Wilson, S. The man in the gray flannel suit
VETERANS -- CRIMES AGAINST
Griffiths, E. The house at sea's end
VETERANS -- TEXAS
Fountain, B. Billy Lynn's long halftime walk
VETERINARIANS
The blue hour
Deb, S. The point of return
Gruen, S. Water for elephants
Leon, D. Beastly Things
Miller, S. While I was gone
Murphy, Y. The call
Reiken, F. Day for night
Stewart, M. Airs above the ground
VIADUCTS *See* Bridges
VIBRATION
See also Mechanics; Sound
The **vicar's** daughter. Kilpack, J. S.
VICARS, PAROCHIAL -- ENGLAND
Malliet, G. M. A fatal winter
Malliet, G. M. Pagan spring
VICE
See also Conduct of life; Ethics; Human behavior
VICE
Baxter, C. There's something I want you to do
VICE-PRESIDENTS
Updike, J. Memories of the Ford Administration
Vidal, G. Burr
VICE-PRESIDENTS
See also Presidents
Vicious circle. Littell, R.
Vicious circle. Box, C. J.
The **vicious** circle.
VICTIMS OF CRIME *See* Victims of crimes
VICTIMS OF CRIMES
Ellory, R. J. A simple act of violence
Gardner, L. Find Her
Phillips, C. Foreigners
Rader-Day, L. The black hour
Sager, R. Final girls
Walsh, M. O. My sunshine away
VICTIMS OF TERRORISM
Johansen, I. Final target
Miller, S. The Lake Shore Limited
Patchett, A. Bel canto
Victoria, Queen of Great Britain, 1819-1901
About
Hodder, M. The strange affair of Spring Heeled Jack
Victorian Rebels [series]
Byrne, K. The Duke
VICTORIANA
See also Antiques; Collectibles
Victorine. Texier, C.
Victory. Conrad, J.
Vida. Piercy, M.
VIDEO GAMES
Gibson, W. The peripheral
Tracy, P. J. Monkeewrench
VIDEO GAMES
See also Electronic toys; Games
VIDEO TELEPHONE
See also Data transmission systems; Telephone; Television
VIDEOTAPES
Darnielle, J. Universal harvester
Vidocq, Eugène Francois, 1775-1857
About
Bayard, L. The black tower
VIENNA (AUSTRIA)
Boyd, W. Waiting for sunrise
The chosen ones

Jones, J. S. The silence
Vienna blood. Tallis, F.
Vienna Twilight. Tallis, F.
VIETNAM
The sorrow of war
VIETNAM -- HISTORY
Barry, Q. She weeps each time you're born
VIETNAM -- HO CHI MINH CITY
Greene, G. The quiet American
Soli, T. The lotus eaters
VIETNAM WAR, 1961-1975
Butler, R. O. A good scent from a strange mountain
Butler, R. O. Perfume River
Cao, L. The lotus and the storm
Gorman, E. Riders on the Storm
Johnson, D. Tree of smoke
Krivak, A. The signal flame
Lam, V. The headmaster's wager
Leimbach, M. The man from Saigon
Long, J. The reckoning
Marlantes, K. Matterhorn
Mason, B. A. In country
McCann, C. Let the great world spin
McDermott, A. After this
Means, D. Hystopia
Nguyen, V. T. The Sympathizer
O'Brien, T. The things they carried
O'Brien, T. Going after Cacciato
O'Nan, S. The names of the dead
Palaia, M. The given world
Robbins, T. Villa incognito
Soli, T. The lotus eaters
The sorrow of war
VIETNAM WAR, 1961-1975 -- VETERANS
Boyle, T. C. The Harder They Come
O'Malley, T. This magnificent desolation
Palaia, M. The given world
VIETNAMESE -- FRANCE
Truong, M. The book of salt
VIETNAMESE -- UNITED STATES
Johnson, C. Another man's moccasins
Nguyen, V. T. The Sympathizer
Parker, T. J. Little Saigon
VIETNAMESE AMERICANS
Butler, R. O. A good scent from a strange mountain
Cao, L. The lotus and the storm
Le, T. D. T. The gangster we are all looking for
VIETNAMESE DIASPORA
Cao, L. The lotus and the storm
VIETNAMESE REFUGEES
See also Refugees
The **view** from Castle Rock. Munro, A.
The **view** from the seventh layer. Brockmeier, K.
VIGILANCE COMMITTEES *See* Vigilantes
VIGILANTES
Franklin, T. Hell at the breech
Peebles, F. d. P. The seamstress
VIGILANTES
See also Crime; Criminal law
Mosley, W. The last days of Ptolemy Grey
VIKINGS
Anderson, P. War of the Gods
Cornwell, B. The last kingdom
Grimes, L. In a fix
Seton, A. Avalon
Vollmann, W. T. The ice-shirt
VIKINGS -- SCOTLAND
Graeme-Evans, P. The island house
Vile bodies. Waugh, E.
Villa incognito. Robbins, T.
Villa triste. Grindle, L.
Villa, Pancho, 1878-1923
About
Groom, W. El Paso
Olmstead, R. Far bright star
VILLAGE COMMUNITIES
Stibbe, N. Man at the helm
VILLAGES
See also Cities and towns
VILLAGES
Arden, K. The bear and the nightingale
Beah, I. Radiance of tomorrow
Collins, C. The gamal
DeWitt, P. Undermajordomo Minor
Falling out of time
Harris, J. Peaches for Father Francis
See, L. The tea girl of hummingbird lane
Walker, M. The crowded grave
VILLAGES -- ENGLAND
Crace, J. Harvest
VILLAGES -- SIERRA LEONE
Beah, I. Radiance of tomorrow
Villain. Yoshida, S.
Vinegar girl. Tyler, A.
Vineland. Pynchon, T.
A **vineyard** killing. Craig, P. R.
VINEYARDS
Gilman, L. A. Flesh and fire
Higgins, K. Anything for You
A **vintage** affair. Wolff, I.
VINTAGE CLOTHING
Lehmann, S. Astor Place Vintage
The **violated.** Pronzini, B.
VIOLENCE
Alexie, S. Flight
Ballard, J. G. Millennium people
Banks, R. Affliction
Barker, C. Imajica
Bell, M. S. All souls' rising
Brink, A. P. The other side of silence
Brown, L. Joe
Coetzee, J. M. Disgrace
Coetzee, J. M. Life & times of Michael K.
Conn, B. The fixed stars

Cornwell, B. The Empty Throne
Crews, H. A feast of snakes
Dalton, J. The inverted forest
Deane, S. Reading in the dark
Deb, S. The point of return
The dinner
Dixon, S. Interstate
Doig, I. Bucking the sun
D'Souza, T. Whiteman
Ellroy, J. Blood's a rover
Franklin, T. Hell at the breech
Gunning, S. The rebellion of Jane Clarke
Hage, R. De Niro's game
Hart, J. Down river
Heller, P. The painter
Hoagland, E. Children are diamonds
Hunter, S. Black light
Hunter, S. Dirty white boys
Huston, C. The shotgun rule
Jen, G. World and town
Jiles, P. The color of lightning
Johnson, D. Nobody move
Jones, S. Outcast
Jordan, H. Mudbound
Karate chop
Lansdale, J. R. Sunset and sawdust
Lazar, Z. Sway
Lehrer, J. The special prisoner
Lessing, D. M. The memoirs of a survivor
Llywelyn, M. 1916
Mankell, H. The eye of the leopard
Martin, V. Trespass
Matar, H. In the country of men
Matthiessen, P. Bone by bone
Matthiessen, P. Shadow country
McCarthy, C. The road
McCarthy, C. Blood meridian
McCarthy, C. No country for old men
Miller, R. Welcome to Heavenly Heights
Monaghan, N. The killing jar
Naslund, S. J. Four spirits
Oates, J. C. Black girl/White girl
Oates, J. C. The gravedigger's daughter
O'Dell, T. Back roads
Palahniuk, C. Rant
Patterson, J. Hide & seek
Pawel, R. Death of a nationalist
Pelecanos, G. P. The big blowdown
Pelecanos, G. P. Drama city
Pelecanos, G. P. Shame the devil
Pelecanos, G. P. The sweet forever
Pelecanos, G. P. The turnaround
Picoult, J. Nineteen minutes
Pollock, D. R. The devil all the time
Poyer, D. Thunder on the mountain
Price, R. Samaritan
Quindlen, A. Every last one
Rader-Day, L. The black hour
Rash, R. Serena
Richards, D. A. The bay of love and sorrows
Rosero Diago, E. The armies
Rushdie, S. Shalimar the clown
Salak, K. The white Mary
Scott, J. The kept
Scotton, C. The secret wisdom of the earth
Shriver, L. We need to talk about Kevin
Straight, S. The gettin place
Urza, G. All that followed
Vachss, A. H. Two trains running
Vanderbes, J. Strangers at the feast
Vargas Llosa, M. Death in the Andes
Vargas Llosa, M. The war of the end of the world
Vernon, O. Eden
Vine, B. King Solomon's carpet
Vonnegut, K. Armageddon in retrospect
Walker, A. Possessing the secret of joy
Wimberley, D. The king of Colored Town
Woods, S. L.A. Times
VIOLENCE AGAINST WOMEN
See also Violence; Women
The **violent** bear it away. O'Connor, F.
VIOLENT CRIMES
Lange, R. Angel baby
Robards, K. Shiver
A **violet** season. Czepiel, K. L.
The **violets** of March. Jio, S.
VIOLIN PLAYERS *See* Violinists
VIOLIN TEACHERS
Elias, G. Death and transfiguration
VIOLINISTS
De Robertis, C. The gods of tango
Elias, G. Danse macabre
Hall, B. The music teacher
Lebrecht, N. The song of names
VIPERS *See* Snakes
Virgil
About
Graham, J. Black ships
Virgil Flowers [series]
Sandford, J. Storm Front
The **virgin** in the ice. Peters, E.
VIRGIN ISLANDS OF THE UNITED STATES
Pronzini, B. The crimes of Jordan Wise
The **virgin** suicides. Eugenides, J.
VIRGINIA
Clark, M. The legal limit
Jones, E. P. The known world
Parshall, S. Poisoned ground
Michaels, B. Stitches in time
Smith, L. Fair and tender ladies
Smith, L. Family linen
Smith, L. Oral history
Styron, W. Lie down in darkness
Theroux, A. Darconville's cat

Trigiani, A. Big Cherry Holler
Trigiani, A. Big Stone Gap
VIRGINIA -- 18TH CENTURY
Settle, M. L. O Beulah Land
VIRGINIA -- 19TH CENTURY
Jones, E. P. The known world
Styron, W. The confessions of Nat Turner
VIRGINIA -- HISTORY -- 1775-1865
Peters, R. Hell or Richmond
VIRGINIA -- TO 1800
L'Amour, L. To the far blue mountains
Thackeray, W. M. The Virginians
Vollmann, W. T. Argall
The **Virginians.** Thackeray, W. M.
VIRTUAL REALITY
Cline, E. Ready player one
Egan, G. Zendegi
Niven, L. Saturn's race
Noon, J. Vurt
Powers, R. Plowing the dark
Rucker, R. v. B. Postsingular
Shakar, A. Luminarium
Stephenson, N. Reamde
Stephenson, N. Snow Crash
Zelazny, R. Donnerjack
VIRTUE
See also Conduct of life; Ethics; Human behavior
Baxter, C. There's something I want you to do
Virtue Falls series
Dodd, C. The woman who couldn't scream
VIRUS DISEASES
Cronin, J. The twelve
Grant, M. Feedback
VIRUSES
Cronin, J. The passage
DeMille, N. Plum Island
Grant, M. Feed
Kress, N. Dogs
Pottinger, S. The last Nazi
Whitehead, C. Zone one
VIRUSES
See also Microorganisms
VISCOSITY
See also Hydrodynamics; Mechanics
The **visible** man. Klosterman, C.
The **vision** of Emma Blau. Hegi, U.
A **vision** of light. Riley, J. M.
The **Visionist.** Urquhart, R.
VISIONS
The Ghost Riders of Ordebec
McBride, J. Song yet sung
McCarthy, T. Satin Island
Nadol, J. This is how it ends
VISIONS
See also Parapsychology; Religion; Spiritual gifts
A **visit** from the Goon Squad. Egan, J.
Visitation.
VISITATION RIGHTS (DOMESTIC RELATIONS)
See also Domestic relations
Watson, L. Let him go
Visitation Street. Pochoda, I.
The **visiting** privilege. Williams, J.
The **visitor.** Tepper, S. S.
VISITORS, FOREIGN -- MOROCCO
Osborne, L. The forgiven
VISUAL COMMUNICATION
See also Communication
Vital signs. Wood, B.
Vixen in Velvet. Chase, L.
VOCABULARY
See also Language and languages
Levithan, D. The lover's dictionary
VOCATION
See also Duty; Ethics; Occupations; Work
VODOU
Dépestre, R. Hadriana in all my dreams
VODUN *See* Voodooism
VOICE
See also Language and languages; Throat
Voice of America. Osondu, E. C.
Voices in the night. Millhauser, S.
A **void.** Perec, G.
The **volcano** lover. Sontag, S.
VOLCANOES
Harris, R. Pompeii
Lytton, E. B. L. The last days of Pompeii
Verne, J. A journey to the centre of the earth
Volt. Heathcock, A.
Voltaire's Candide, Zadig, and selected stories. Voltaire
VOLUNTEER WORKERS
See, C. There will never be another you
Von Ryan's Express. Westheimer, D.
VOODOO *See* Voodooism
Voodoo dreams. Rhodes, J. P.
VOODOOISM
Rhodes, J. P. Voodoo dreams
Rhodes, J. P. Yellow moon
Stone, R. Bay of souls
The **voyage** out. Woolf, V.
VOYAGERS *See* Explorers; Travelers
VOYAGES AND TRAVELS
The alchemist
Campbell, B. J. Once upon a river
Carey, P. Parrot and Olivier in America
Cornwell, B. 1356
Dare, T. A week to be wicked
Dunnett, D. To lie with lions
The elephant's journey
Garey, J. Too bright to hear too loud to see
Ghosh, A. Flood of fire
Ghosh, A. River of smoke
Ghosh, A. Sea of poppies
Golding, W. Close quarters
Golding, W. Fire down below

Golding, W. Rites of passage
Grossman, L. The magician king
Hall, T. The case of the deadly butter chicken
Harrison, J. Brown Dog
Hooper, E. Etta and Otto and Russell and James
Johnson, C. R. Middle passage
Johnson, M. Pym
Joyce, R. The unlikely pilgrimage of Harold Fry
Kay, G. G. Children of earth and sky
Larsen, R. The selected works of T. S. Spivet
Lodge, D. Paradise news
McCann, C. Transatlantic
McCarthy, C. The road
McGuire, I. The North water
Modesitt, L. E. The one-eyed man
Morrison, T. Home
Motion, A. Silver
O'Brian, P. The golden ocean
Orullian, P. V. The unremembered
Poe, E. A. The imaginary voyages: The narrative of Arthur Gordon Pym; The unparalleled adventure of one Hans Pfaall; The journal of Julius Rodman
Preston, C. The scrapbook of Frankie Pratt
Schwartzman, A. Eddie Signwriter
Seton, A. Avalon
Stone, R. Outerbridge Reach
Thomas, S. Beguiling the beauty
Verne, J. Around the world in eighty days
Villars, E. The Normandie affair
Vollmann, W. T. The ice-shirt

VOYAGES AROUND THE WORLD
See also Travel; Voyages and travels
Silko, L. Gardens in the dunes
Verne, J. Around the world in eighty days

VOYAGES TO THE MOON *See* Imaginary voyages; Space flight to the moon

VOYEURS
Klosterman, C. The visible man

VULNERABILITY (PERSONALITY TRAIT)
Gaiman, N. Trigger warning

Vurt. Noon, J.

W

WAGON TRAINS
Guthrie, A. B. The way West

The **wailing** wind. Hillerman, T.

WAITERS AND WAITRESSES
Long, J. A. Hot in Hellcat Canyon
Murray, P. The mark and the void

Waiting. Ha Jin
Waiting for sunrise. Boyd, W.
Waiting for Wednesday. French, N.
Waiting on You. Higgins, K.
Waiting to exhale. McMillan, T.

WAITRESSES
Beagle, P. S. Summerlong
O'Nan, S. Last night at the Lobster
Robbins, T. Skinny legs and all
Schwartz, L. Angels Crest
Vlautin, W. Northline

The **wake** of forgiveness. Machart, B.
Wake of vultures. Bowen, L.
Wake up dead. Smith, R.
Waking lions. Gundar-Goshen, A.

WALES
Cronin, A. J. The citadel
Haddon, M. The red house
Mawer, S. The fall
Pearson, A. I think I love you
Sheers, O. Resistance

WALES -- 5TH CENTURY
Stewart, M. The crystal cave

WALES -- 13TH CENTURY
Penman, S. K. Here be dragons
Penman, S. K. The reckoning

WALES -- 18TH CENTURY
Putney, M. J. Stolen magic

WALES -- 19TH CENTURY
Llewellyn, R. How green was my valley

WALES -- CARDIFF
Hadley, T. The London train

WALES -- RURAL LIFE
Davies, P. H. The Welsh girl
Powell, S. The Mushroom Man
Sheers, O. Resistance

A **walk** on the wild side. Algren, N.
A **walk** through the fire. Muller, M.
A **walk** to remember. Sparks, N.
Walkaway. Doctorow, C.

Walker, Alice, 1944-

About

Walker, A. The way forward is with a broken heart

WALKING
Joyce, R. The unlikely pilgrimage of Harold Fry

Walking across Egypt. Edgerton, C.
Walking shadow. Parker, R. B.
The **wall.** Adler, H. G.
The **wall** of storms. Ken Liu

WALL STREET (NEW YORK, N.Y.)
Rubenfeld, J. The death instinct
Sears, M. Black Fridays
Towles, A. Rules of civility

WALT DISNEY WORLD (FLA.)
Doctorow, C. Down and out in the Magic Kindgom

WALT DISNEY WORLD (FLA.)
See also Amusement parks

WAMPANOAG INDIANS
Brooks, G. Caleb's crossing

The **Wanderer.** Carr, R.
The **wanderers.** Howrey, M.
The **wandering** falcon. Ahmad, J.
Wanting. Flanagan, R.
The **wanton** angel. Marston, E.

The **Wapshot** chronicle. Cheever, J.
The **Wapshot** scandal. Cheever, J.
WAR
Alarcon, D. Lost City Radio
Aslam, N. The Blind Man's Garden
Aslam, N. The wasted vigil
Barker, P. The eye in the door
Barker, P. The ghost road
Barker, P. Regeneration
Brooks, M. World War Z
Caputo, P. Acts of faith
Couto, M. Sleepwalking land
Faulkner, W. A fable
Faulks, S. Birdsong
Flynn, M. On the razor's edge
Follett, K. World without end
Forsyth, F. Avenger
Franklin, A. The Siege Winter
Goonan, K. A. In war times
Haldeman, J. W. Forever peace
Jin, H. Nanjing requiem
Kadare, I. The general of the dead army
Karnezis, P. The maze
Leshem, R. Beaufort
Lopez, B. H. Resistance
Moulessehoul, M. The swallows of Kabul
Olmstead, R. Coal black horse
The painter of battles
Prcic, I. Shards
Seymour, G. The heart of danger
Sheers, O. Resistance
The sorrow of war
Stanisic, S. How the soldier repairs the gramophone
Tearne, R. Mosquito
The three-body problem
Tolkien, J. R. R. The Silmarillion
Turtledove, H. Into the darkness
Turtledove, H. Rulers of the darkness
White, T. H. The book of Merlyn
WAR -- RELIGIOUS ASPECTS
See also Religion; War
Weber, D. By schism rent asunder
WAR -- SIMULATION GAMES *See* War games
WAR AND CIVILIZATION
See also Civilization; War
WAR AND EMERGENCY POWERS
See also Constitutional law; Executive power; Legislative bodies; War
War and peace. Tolstoy, L.
War and peace. Tolstoy, L.
War and remembrance. Wouk, H.
WAR CASUALTIES
See also War
WAR CRIME TRIALS
Schlink, B. The reader
WAR CRIME TRIALS
See also Trials
WAR CRIMES
Thompson, J. Lucifer's tears
WAR CRIMES
See also Crimes against humanity; International law; War
WAR CRIMINALS
Forsyth, F. The Odessa file
Khan, A. Z. The unquiet dead
Levin, I. The boys from Brazil
Ondaatje, M. Anil's ghost
Seymour, G. The heart of danger
Uris, L. QB VII
WAR FILMS
See also Historical drama; Motion pictures
WAR GAMES
Bolaño, R. The Third Reich
The **war** of the end of the world. Vargas Llosa, M.
War of the Gods. Anderson, P.
War of the rats. Robbins, D. L.
The **war** of the worlds. Wells, H. G.
WAR ON TERRORISM, 2001-
Harris, R. The ghost
Le Carré, J. A Delicate Truth
Le Carre, J. A most wanted man
WAR PHOTOGRAPHERS
The painter of battles
WAR RADIO PROGRAMS
See also Radio programs
WAR STORIES
Abercrombie, J. The heroes
Bausch, R. Peace
Boll, H. The silent angel
Boyden, J. Three-day road
Brown, P. Morning Star
Byatt, A. S. Ragnarok
Corey, J. S. A. Caliban's war
Cornwell, B. 1356
Delaney, F. The matchmaker of Kenmare
Deutermann, P. T. Pacific glory
El Akkad, O. American war
Groot, T. Flame of resistance
Gurganus, A. The oldest living Confederate widow tells all
Harris, R. Enigma
Haydon, E. The Merchant Emperor
Hicks, R. The widow of the south
Hunter, S. Dead zero
Larsen, R. I Am Radar
Leckie, A. Ancillary mercy
Leckie, A. Ancillary sword
Marra, A. A constellation of vital phenomena
Marshall, A. A crown for cold silver
McClellan, B. Promise of blood
Modesitt, L. E. Imager's battalion
Oe, K. Nip the buds, shoot the kids
Olmstead, R. Coal black horse
Ondaatje, M. The English patient
Rash, R. The cove

Roberts, M. Ignorance
Vollmann, W. T. The Dying Grass
Vonnegut, K. Armageddon in retrospect
Weber, D. Shadow of freedom
Young, T. W. The renegades
WAR STORIES
See also Fiction; Historical fiction
WAR TELEVISION PROGRAMS
See also Television programs
War trash. Ha Jin
WAR VETERANS *See* Veterans
WARD, SUSAN (FICTITIOUS CHARACTER)
Cain, C. Let me go
The **warden.** Trollope, A.
Wards of Faerie. Brooks, T.
WARGAMES *See* War games
Warlord chronicles [series]
Cornwell, B. Enemy of God
Cornwell, B. Excalibur
Cornwell, B. The winter king
Warm bodies. Marion, I.
WARRIORS
Marshall, A. A crown for cold silver
WARS *See* Military history; Naval history; War
WARSHAWSKI, V. I. (FICTITIOUS CHARACTER)
Paretsky, S. Breakdown
Paretsky, S. Brush back
Paretsky, S. Fallout
Paretsky, S. Total recall
WARSHIPS
See also Naval architecture; Naval art and science; Sea power; Ships
Wash. Wrinkle, M.
WASHINGTON (D.C.)
Bayard, L. The school of night
Carter, S. L. The emperor of Ocean Park
Carter, S. L. Palace council
DuPree, K. Silenced
Everett, P. Erasure
Faulks, S. On Green Dolphin Street
Grisham, J. The pelican brief
Heller, J. Good as Gold
Ignatius, D. The Sun King
Jones, E. All Aunt Hagar's children
Mallon, T. Fellow travelers
Meltzer, B. The inner circle
Meltzer, B. The tenth justice
Meltzer, B. The zero game
Mengestu, D. The beautiful things that heaven bears
Patterson, J. Along came a spider
Patterson, J. Cat & mouse
Patterson, J. I, Alex Cross
Patterson, J. Jack and Jill
Patterson, J. Kiss the girls
Patterson, J. Roses are red
Patterson, R. N. Balance of power
Pelecanos, G. P. The big blowdown
Pelecanos, G. P. Drama city
Pelecanos, G. P. The night gardener
Pelecanos, G. P. Right as rain
Pelecanos, G. P. Shame the devil
Pelecanos, G. P. The sweet forever
Pelecanos, G. P. The turnaround
Pelecanos, G. P. The way home
Pelecanos, G. The cut
Roosevelt, K. In the shadow of the law
Stead, C. The man who loved children
Tucker, N. The ways of the dead
Vidal, G. The golden age
Vidal, G. Hollywood
Vidal, G. Washington, D.C.
Wilson, F. P. Deep as the marrow
WASHINGTON (D.C.) -- 19TH CENTURY
Adams, H. Democracy
Jakes, J. On secret service
Mrazek, R. J. Unholy fire
Vidal, G. 1876
Vidal, G. Empire
Vidal, G. Lincoln
WASHINGTON (D.C.) -- GEORGETOWN
Blatty, W. P. The exorcist
WASHINGTON (STATE)
Alexie, S. Reservation blues
Dugoni, R. Murder one
Guterson, D. The other
Guterson, D. Our Lady of the Forest
Guterson, D. Snow falling on cedars
Hannah, K. On Mystic lake
Hart, B. The bully of order
Lynch, J. Border songs
Perillo, L. Happiness is a chemical in the brain
Waite, U. The terror of living
WASHINGTON (STATE) -- SEATTLE
Alexie, S. Indian killer
Bauermeister, E. Joy for beginners
Guterson, D. Ed King
Kallos, S. Broken for you
Pearson, R. The angel maker
Pearson, R. The art of deception
Pearson, R. Beyond recognition
Pearson, R. The body of David Hayes
Pearson, R. The first victim
Pearson, R. Middle of nowhere
Pearson, R. Undercurrents
Powers, R. Plowing the dark
Raban, J. Surveillance
Raban, J. Waxwings
Robbins, T. Half asleep in frog pajamas
Washington, D.C. Vidal, G.
Washington, George, 1732-1799
About
Charyn, J. Johnny One-Eye
Washington, Martha, 1731-1802
About

Hambly, B. Patriot hearts
The **wasp** eater. Lychack, W.
WASPS
See also Insects
The **wasted** vigil. Aslam, N.
Wasted years. Harvey, J.
The **wasties.** Reuss, F.
The **watch.** Roy-Bhattacharya, J.
Watch your back. Westlake, D. E.
The **Watcher.** Link, C.
Watchers. Koontz, D. R.
The **watchers.** Steele, J.
The **watchmaker** of Filigree Street. Pulley, N.
Watchman. Rankin, I.
WATER
Bacigalupi, P. The water knife
WATER BIRDS
See also Birds
Water dogs. Robinson, L.
Water for elephants. Gruen, S.
The **water** knife. Bacigalupi, P.
Water like a stone. Crombie, D.
The **Water** museum. Urrea, L. A.
WATER POLLUTION
See also Environmental health; Pollution; Public health
WATER POWER
See also Energy resources; Hydraulics; Power (Mechanics); Renewable energy resources; Rivers; Water resources development
WATER RIGHTS
Bacigalupi, P. The water knife
The **water's** lovely. Rendell, R.
WATER-SUPPLY
Chanter, C. The well
Waterfront. Schulberg, B.
Watergate. Mallon, T.
WATERGATE AFFAIR, 1972-1974
Mallon, T. Watergate
WATERING PLACES *See* Health resorts
Waterland. Swift, G.
The **Watermelon** King. Wallace, D.
WATERMELONS
Wallace, D. The Watermelon King
Watership Down. Adams, R.
The **waterworks.** Doctorow, E. L.
Watson, Edgar J., 1855-1910
About
Matthiessen, P. Bone by bone
Matthiessen, P. Killing Mister Watson
Matthiessen, P. Shadow country
WATSON, JOHN H. (FICTITIOUS CHARACTER)
Faye, L. The whole art of detection
WAVE MECHANICS
See also Mechanics; Quantum theory; Waves
The **waves.** Woolf, V.
Waxwings. Raban, J.
Waxwork. Lovesey, P.
The **way** forward is with a broken heart. Walker, A.
The **way** home. Pelecanos, G. P.
A **way** in the world. Naipaul, V. S.
The **way** of the coyote. Kelton, E.
The **way** of the dog. Savage, S.
The **way** the crow flies. MacDonald
The **way** things were. Taseer, A.
The **way** through the woods. Dexter, C.
The **way** to paradise. Vargas Llosa, M.
The **way** West. Guthrie, A. B.
Wayfaring Stranger. Burke, J. L.
The **ways** of the dead. Tucker, N.
Wayward Children [series]
Grant, M. Down Among the Sticks and Bones
We. Zamiatin, E. I.
We all fall down. Harvey, M. T.
We Are All Completely Beside Ourselves. Fowler, K. J.
We Are All Completely Fine. Gregory, D.
We are all welcome here. Berg, E.
We are not ourselves. Thomas, M.
We are pirates. Handler, D.
We Are Water. Lamb, W.
We had it so good. Grant, L.
We have always lived in the castle. Jackson, S.
We Live in Water. Walter, J.
We love you, Charlie Freeman. Greenidge, K.
We need new names. Bulawayo, N.
We need to talk about Kevin. Shriver, L.
We the animals. Torres, J.
We the living. Rand, A.
We were the Mulvaneys. Oates, J. C.
We're flying.
WEALTH
Adichie, C. N. Half of a yellow sun
Atwood, M. The blind assassin
Boyle, T. C. The tortilla curtain
Canin, E. America America
Cusk, R. In the fold
Dee, J. The privileges
Dickens, C. Great expectations
Doctorow, E. L. The waterworks
Dunne, D. Too much money
Everett, P. L. I am Not Sidney Poitier
Fitzgerald, F. S. The beautiful and damned
Fitzgerald, F. S. The great Gatsby
Hamid, M. How to Get Filthy Rich in Rising Asia
Ignatius, D. The Sun King
Isaacs, S. After all these years
Klein, M. Con ed
Koryta, M. So cold the river
Kosinski, J. N. The devil tree
McLaughlin, E. The nanny diaries
McPhee, M. L'America
Morrison, T. Love
O'Hara, J. From the terrace
Pears, I. Stone's fall
Pilcher, R. September

Pomerantz, S. Rich boy
Prose, F. Primitive people
Rosenblatt, R. Lapham rising
Steel, D. Sunset in St. Tropez
Tyler, A. A patchwork planet
Vonnegut, K. God bless you, Mr. Rosewater
Wilder, T. Theophilus North
Winkler, A. C. Dog war
Wolfe, T. A man in full
Wood, B. The dreaming
Woods, S. Imperfect strangers
WEAPONS SYSTEMS -- SOVIET UNION
Eastland, S. Shadow pass
WEAPONS, ATOMIC *See* Nuclear weapons
WEAPONS, NUCLEAR *See* Nuclear weapons
WEATHER
Hay, E. A student of weather
Thompson, J. Wide blue yonder
WEATHER -- FOLKLORE
See also Folklore; Meteorology; Weather forecasting
WEATHER CONTROL
See also Meteorology; Weather
WEATHER FORECASTING
See also Forecasting; Meteorology; Weather
The **weather** in Berlin. Just, W. S.
Weatherhead books on Asia [series]
The song of everlasting sorrow
WEAVERS
Eliot, G. Silas Marner
Singer, I. J. The brothers Ashkenazi
Weaveworld. Barker, C.
WEAVING
See also Handicraft; Textile industry
The **web** and the rock. Wolfe, T.
WEBSITES
Jong, E. Fear of Dying
Webster, Daniel, 1782-1852
About
Benet, S. V. The Devil and Daniel Webster
The **wedding.** West, D.
Wedding Bush Road. Francis, D.
The **wedding** date.
WEDDINGS
Alexander, V. The Scandalous Adventures of the Sister of the Bride
Anshaw, C. Carry the one
Dare, T. Say Yes to the Marquess
Haddon, M. A spot of bother
Higgins, K. The Best Man
Johnson, D. Le mariage
Kinsella, S. I've got your number
Kleypas, L. Brown-Eyed Girl
Mapson Solomon's oak
McCall Smith, A. The Saturday big tent wedding party
McCullers, C. The member of the wedding
Morgan, J. The royal we
Waldman, A. Red Hook Road
Warren, D. Juliet in August
Welty, E. Delta wedding
West, D. The wedding
WEDDINGS
See also Marriage
The **weed** that strings the hangman's bag. Bradley, A.
A **week** in December. Faulks, S.
A **week** in winter. Binchy, M.
A **week** to be wicked. Dare, T.
The **weekend.** Schlink, B.
Weighed in the balance. Perry, A.
WEIGHT LOSS
Awad, M. 13 ways of looking at a fat girl
The **weight** of heaven. Umrigar, T. N.
The **weight** of water. Shreve, A.
The **weird** sisters. Brown, E.
A **welcome** murder. Yocum, R.
Welcome to Braggsville. Johnson, T. G.
Welcome to Heavenly Heights. Miller, R.
Welcome to the monkey house. Vonnegut, K.
Welfare wifeys. K'wan (Author)
The **well.** Chanter, C.
The **well** of loneliness. Hall, R.
The **Welsh** girl. Davies, P. H.
Wench. Perkins-Valdez, D.
WEREWOLVES
Duncan, G. By blood we live
Duncan, G. The last werewolf
Duncan, G. Talulla rising
Harris, C. Dead reckoning
Hodder, M. The strange affair of Spring Heeled Jack
Kiernan, C. R. Blood oranges
Lamberson, G. The frenzy way
Martinez, A. L. Gil's All Fright Diner
Pekearo, N. T. The wolfman
Percy, B. Red moon
WEREWOLVES
See also Folklore
WERNER'S SYNDROME
Tsukiyama, G. Dreaming water
The **Wesleyan** anthology of science fiction.
WEST (U.S.)
Gilman, L. A. Silver on the Road
Greaves, C. J. Hard twisted
Lansdale, J. R. Paradise sky
Lock, N. American meteor
Russell, M. D. Epitaph
Scapellato, J. Big Lonesome
Watkins, C. V. Battleborn
Watson, L. As good as gone
WEST (U.S.) -- HISTORY -- 19TH CENTURY
Burke, S. Into the Savage Country
WEST AFRICA
Celine Journey to the end of the night
Forna, A. Ancestor stones
Greene, G. The heart of the matter
Patterson, R. N. Eclipse

WEST AFRICANS -- FRANCE
Three strong women
WEST INDIAN AMERICANS
Marshall, P. Brown girl, brownstones
Marshall, P. The fisher king
WEST INDIANS -- ENGLAND
Walters, M. The shape of snakes
WEST INDIANS -- UNITED STATES
Conde, M. I, Tituba, black witch of Salem
Kincaid, J. Lucy
Nunez, E. Anna in-between
WEST INDIES
Forester, C. S. Admiral Hornblower in the West Indies
Marshall, P. Praisesong for the widow
Morrison, T. Tar baby
Naipaul, V. S. Guerrillas
Rhys, J. Wide Sargasso Sea
Saville, L. Henry and Rachel
West of here. Evison, J.
West of the Pecos. Grey, Z.
WEST VIRGINIA
Gordon, J. Lord of Misrule
Keller, J. A killing in the hills
Pancake, A. Strange as this weather has been
Phillips, J. A. Lark and Termite
Settle, M. L. Charley Bland
Settle, M. L. The killing ground
Taylor, M. G. The ballad of Trenchmouth Taggart
Taylor, M. G. The Marrowbone Marble Company
Whitehead, C. John Henry Days
WESTCHESTER COUNTY (N.Y.)
Robinson, R. Sparta
A Westcott novel [series]
Balogh, M. Someone to Love
WESTERN AUSTRALIA -- SOCIAL LIFE AND CUSTOMS
Scott, K. That deadman dance
WESTERN CIVILIZATION
See also Civilization; East and West
WESTERN COMIC BOOKS, STRIPS, ETC.
See also Comic books, strips, etc.
WESTERN FILMS
See also Adventure films; Historical drama; Motion pictures
WESTERN STATES
Dexter, P. Deadwood
Frazier, C. Thirteen moons
Guthrie, A. B. The big sky
McMurtry, L. Buffalo girls
McMurtry, L. Comanche moon
McMurtry, L. Dead man's walk
McMurtry, L. Lonesome dove
McMurtry, L. Streets of Laredo
Michener, J. A. Centennial
Momaday, N. S. The ancient child
The Mysterious West
Wiggins, M. The shadow catcher
Willard, T. Buffalo soldiers
WESTERN STORIES
American West: twenty new stories from the Western Writers of America
Belcher, R. S. The six-gun tarot
Berger, T. Little Big Man
The best western stories of John Jakes
Brand, M. Beyond the outposts
Brand, M. Chinook
Brand, M. Max Brand's best western stories
Brand, M. The Stingaree
Brooks, B. Frontier justice
Brooks, B. Winter kill
Burke, S. Into the Savage Country
A Century of great Western stories
Clark, W. V. T. The Ox-bow incident
Coldsmith, D. Tallgrass
Deborde, R. Portlandtown
DeWitt, P. The Sisters brothers
Doig, I. The whistling season
Estleman, L. D. The adventures of Johnny Vermillion
Estleman, L. D. The book of Murdock
Estleman, L. D. The master executioner
Everett, P. God's country
Fergus, J. The wild girl: the notebooks of Ned Giles, 1932
Gilman, F. The half-made world
Great stories of the American West
Grey, Z. Riders of the purple sage
Grey, Z. West of the Pecos
Grey, Z. Woman of the frontier
Guthrie, A. B. The way West
Hansen, R. The assassination of Jesse James by the coward Robert Ford
Hershon, J. The German bride
Hockensmith, S. Holmes on the range
Hockensmith, S. On the wrong track
Houston, P. Cowboys are my weakness
Jenkins, B. Forbidden
Jiles, P. The color of lightning
Kelton, E. Badger boy
Kelton, E. Texas sunrise
Kelton, E. Texas vendetta
Kelton, E. The way of the coyote
Kent, K. The outcasts
Kittredge, W. The Willow Field
Kolpan, G. Magic words
L'Amour, L. Bendigo Shafter
L'Amour, L. The Californios
L'Amour, L. End of the drive
Leonard, E. The complete Western stories of Elmore Leonard
McCarthy, C. Blood meridian
McMurtry, L. Boone's Lick
McMurtry, L. Comanche moon
McMurtry, L. Sin killer
O'Brien, D. The contract surgeon
Olmstead, R. Far bright star

Overholser, W. D. Death of a cattle king
Overholser, W. D. Law at Angel's Landing
Parker, R. B. Appaloosa
Parker, R. B. Blue-eyed devil
Parker, R. B. Brimstone
Parker, R. B. Gunman's rhapsody
Paul, B. Under Tower Peak
Portis, C. True grit
Russell, M. D. Doc
Sargent, C. Museum of human beings
Schaefer, J. W. The collected stories of Jack Schaefer
Schaefer, J. W. Monte Walsh
Schaefer, J. W. Shane
Sharfeddin, H. Mineral spirits
Stegner, W. E. Angle of repose
Swarthout, G. F. The shootist
Trevanian Incident at Twenty Mile
Wallace, S. Montana dawn
Walls, J. Half broke horses
Watson, L. Let him go
Westward
Wheeler, R. S. The canyon of bones
Wheeler, R. S. North Star
Williamson, P. Heart of the west
Williamson, P. The outsider
Wurlitzer, R. Drop edge of yonder
Wyman, W. Blue heaven
Zimmer, M. The long hitch
Zimmer, M. Wild side of the river
Westinghouse, George, 1846-1914
About
Moore, G. The last days of night
WESTMINSTER ABBEY
See also Abbeys; Church buildings
Westward.
Wet grave. Hambly, B.
WET NURSES -- FICTION
Czepiel, K. L. A violet season
WETLAND ECOLOGY
See also Ecology
The **whale** caller. Mda, Z.
WHALES
Mda, Z. The whale caller
Melville, H. Moby-Dick; or, The whale
WHALING
Poyer, D. The Whiteness of the Whale
Wharton, Edith, 1862-1937
About
Fields, J. The age of desire
What Alice forgot. Moriarty, L.
What becomes. Kennedy, A. L.
What belongs to you. Greenwell, G.
What came before he shot her. George, E.
What comes next. Katzenbach, J.
What doesn't kill her. Norton, C.
What ever happened to Baby Jane? Farrell, H.
What happened to Anna K. Reyn, I.
What happened to Henry. Pywell, S. L.
What I didn't see and other stories. Fowler, K. J.
What is left the daughter. Norman, H.
What is the what. Eggers, D.
What it means when a man falls from the sky. Arimah, L. N.
What looks like crazy on an ordinary day-- Cleage, P.
What makes Sammy run? Schulberg, B.
What the dead know. Lippman, L.
What the duke doesn't know. Ashford, J.
What to do about Annie? Criswell, M.
What was she thinking? Heller, Z.
What we are. Malae, P. N.
What we become.
What we keep. Berg, E.
What we lose. Clemmons, Z.
What we talk about when we talk about Anne Frank. Englander, N.
What we talk about when we talk about love. Carver, R.
What's eating Gilbert Grape. Hedges, P.
What's so funny? Westlake, D. E.
What's the worst that could happen? Westlake, D. E.
Whatever you love. Doughty, L.
WHEAT
Norris, F. The octopus
Norris, F. The pit
Wheat that springeth green. Powers, J. F.
The **wheel** of darkness. Preston, D.
Wheel of the infinite. Wells, M.
The Wheel of Time [series]
Jordan, R. The eye of the world
When a Scot Ties the Knot. Dare, T.
When all is said and done. Hill, R.
When all the girls have gone. Krentz, J. A.
When beauty tamed the beast. James, E.
When Christ and his saints slept. Penman, S. K.
When God was a rabbit. Winman, S.
When in Rome. Marsh, N.
When Madeline was young. Hamilton, J.
When mystical creatures attack! Founds, K.
When red is black. Qiu Xiaolong
When she was gone. Gross, G.
When she was good. Roth, P.
When she woke. Jordan, H.
When the Devil Drives. Brookmyre, C.
When the doves disappeared. Oksanen, S.
When the elephants dance. Holthe, T. U.
When the emperor was divine. Otsuka, J.
When the killing's done. Boyle, T. C.
When the legends die. Borland, H.
When the Marquess Met His Match. Guhrke, L. L.
When the music stopped. Ogilvie, E.
When the sacred ginmill closes. Block, L.
When the saints. Duncan, D.
When the thrill is gone. Mosley, W.
When the women come out to dance, and other stories. Leonard, E.
When we were orphans. Ishiguro, K.

When we were Romans. Kneale, M.
When will there be good news? Atkinson, K.
Where echoes live. Muller, M.
Where it hurts. Coleman, R. F.
Where late the sweet birds sang. Wilhelm, K.
Where serpents lie. Parker, T. J.
Where the bodies are buried. Brookmyre, C.
Where there's smoke. Little, T.
Where'd you go, Bernadette. Semple, M.
While I was gone. Miller, S.
While mortals sleep. Vonnegut, K.
While other people sleep. Muller, M.
While the women are sleeping.
Whip hand. Francis, D.
Whiskey Beach. Roberts, N.
WHISKEY REBELLION, PA., 1794
Liss, D. The whiskey rebels
The **whiskey** rebels. Liss, D.
Whisper to the blood. Stabenow, D.
WHISTLE BLOWING
Eisler, B. The God's Eye View
The **whistling** season. Doig, I.
WHITBY (ENGLAND)
The new annotated Dracula
White butterfly. Mosley, W.
White death. Cussler, C.
The **white** devil. Evans, J.
The **white** dragon. McCaffrey, A.
The **white** earth. McGahan, A.
White elephant dead. Hart, C. G.
White Fang. London, J.
White Hot. Andrews, I.
The **white** hotel. Thomas, D. M.
The **White** House connection. Higgins, J.
White lies. Krentz, J. A.
The **white** Mary. Salak, K.
White oleander. Fitch, J.
White people. Gurganus, A.
The **white** people and other weird stories.
The **white** princess. Gregory, P.
White shadow. Atkins, A.
WHITE SUPREMACY MOVEMENTS
See also Race relations; Racism; Social movements
White tears. Kunzru, H.
White teeth. Smith, Z.
The **white** tiger. Adiga, A.
The **Whitechapel** conspiracy. Perry, A.
Whiteman. D'Souza, T.
The **Whiteness** of the Whale. Poyer, D.
The **Whites.** Brandt, H.
Whitethorn Woods. Binchy, M.
Whitman, Walt, 1819-1892
About
Cunningham, M. Specimen days
WHITTLING *See* Wood carving
Who do I talk to? Jackson, N.
Who fears death. Okorafor, N.
Who killed Piet Barol? Mason, R.
Who's Irish? Jen, G.
WHODUNITS *See* Mystery and detective plays; Mystery fiction; Mystery films; Mystery radio programs; Mystery television programs
The **whole** art of detection. Faye, L.
The **whole** world over. Glass, J.
The **whore's** child. Russo, R.
Whose body? Sayers, D. L.
The **why** of things. Winthrop, E. H.
WICCA
See also Paganism
Wicked. Maguire, G.
The **wicked.** Nicholas, D.
Wicked autumn. Malliet, G. M.
Wicked city. Atkins, A.
The wicked quills of London [series]
Leigh, E. Forever Your Earl
Leigh, E. Temptations of a Wallflower
Wicked widow. Quick, A.
The wicked Worthingtons series
Bradley, C. I Thee Wed
WICKEDNESS *See* Good and evil
Wickett's remedy. Goldberg, M.
Widdershins. De Lint, C.
Wide blue yonder. Thompson, J.
Wide Sargasso Sea. Rhys, J.
A **widow** for one year. Irving, J.
The **widow** of the south. Hicks, R.
Widow's walk. Parker, R. B.
The **widower's** tale. Glass, J.
WIDOWERS
Adiga, A. Last man in tower
Banville, J. The sea
Begley, L. About Schmidt
Caputo, P. Crossers
Cooley, M. The archivist
De Bernieres, L. A partisan's daughter
Doig, I. The whistling season
Drayson, N. Guide to the birds of East Africa
Gardam, J. Old Filth
Glass, J. Three Junes
Glass, J. The widower's tale
Goldman, F. Say her name
Hoffman, A. Skylight confessions
Hulse, S. M. Black River
Irwin, S. M. The dead path
Johnson, D. Train dreams
Joss, M. The night following
Kawabata, Y. The sound of the mountain
Lane, H. Alys, always
Moore, C. A dirty job
Norman, H. Next life might be kinder
Parkhurst, C. The dogs of Babel
Pilcher, R. Winter solstice
Proulx, A. The shipping news
Racculia, K. This must be the place

Reid, T. J. Forever, interrupted
Rinehart, S. Built in a day
Sagan, F. Bonjour tristesse
Saramago, J. The cave
Simonson, H. Major Pettigrew's last stand
Tatlock, A. Things we once held dear
Tremain, R. The road home
Trevor, W. Death in summer
Trollope, J. Next of kin
Tropper, J. How to talk to a widower
Ward, J. Salvage the bones
Wesley, M. Part of the furniture
Zevin, G. The storied life of A. J. Fikry

WIDOWERS

See also Men

WIDOWS

Abe, K. The woman in the dunes
Adamson, G. The outlander
Atwood, M. The blind assassin
Bennett, A. Smut
Boll, H. The silent angel
Bowen, E. The heat of the day
Brett, S. Mrs Pargeter's Principle
Brooks, G. Year of wonders
Byrne, K. The Duke
Cleage, P. What looks like crazy on an ordinary day--
Cleave, C. Little Bee
D'Abo, C. 30 Days
Doig, I. Work song
Edgerton, C. Walking across Egypt
Evison, J. This is your life, Harriet Chance!
Frank, D. B. Folly Beach
Goldberg, M. Wickett's remedy
Goudge, E. Thorns of truth
Gray, J. A lady never lies
Gurganus, A. The oldest living Confederate widow tells all
Harris, J. Chocolat
Harris, J. Five quarters of the orange
Howatch, S. The heartbreaker
Hunt, R. Mr. Chartwell
Hustvedt, S. The sorrows of an American
Irving, J. The fourth hand
Isaacs, S. As husbands go
Jaswal, B. K. Erotic stories for Punjabi widows
Jen, G. World and town
Kleypas, L. Cold-hearted Rake
Koenig, M. Nine days
Lessing, D. M. Love, again
Lodge, D. Thinks--
Maloy, K. Every last cuckoo
Mann, T. The black swan
Mapson Solomon's oak
Marshall, P. Praisesong for the widow
Mawer, S. The fall
McBain, E. Alice in jeopardy
McFarlane, F. The night guest
McMurtry, L. The evening star
McMurtry, L. Terms of endearment
Medlicott, J. A. The ladies of Covington send their love
Miller, S. The Lake Shore Limited
Millet, L. Magnificence
Moore, L. February
Moore, M. M. So far away
Murdoch, I. Nuns and soldiers
Oates, J. C. The falls
O'Brien, E. House of splendid isolation
O'Nan, S. Emily, alone
O'Reilly, B. Angelina's bachelors
Perry, S. The Essex Serpent
Perry, T. Fidelity
Phillips, S. E. First lady
Powell, S. The Mushroom Man
Quick, A. Garden of Lies
Quick, A. Wicked widow
Redhill, M. Consolation
Riley, J. M. The serpent garden
Roberts, M. Reader, I married him
Robinson, R. Sweetwater
Russo, R. Empire Falls
Sackville-West, V. All passion spent
Sarton, M. A reckoning
Saunders, K. The Secrets of Wishtide
Savage, S. Glass
See, C. There will never be another you
Shonk, K. Happy now?
Shreve, A. The pilot's wife
Simonson, H. Major Pettigrew's last stand
Spark, M. A far cry from Kensington
Spencer, L. Bitter sweet
Spencer, L. Morning glory
Tóibín, C. Nora Webster
Trueblood, V. Seven loves
Tuck, L. I married you for happiness
Tyler, A. Back when we were grownups
Tyler, A. The clock winder
Updike, J. Seek my face
Updike, J. The widows of Eastwick
Vantrease, B. R. The illuminator
Viswanathan, P. The toss of a lemon
Waters, S. The Paying Guests
Weldon, F. Worst fears
Welty, E. The optimist's daughter
Williams, A. J. Down from Cascom Mountain
Williams, T. The Roman spring of Mrs. Stone
Williamson, P. The outsider
Winkler, A. C. Dog war
Winston, L. Good grief
Wolitzer, H. Hearts

WIDOWS

See also Women

The **widows** of Eastwick. Updike, J.
The **widows** of Malabar Hill. Massey, S.
The **wife.** Wolitzer, M.
Wife 22. Gideon, M.

WIFE ABUSE
Adler-Olsen, J. A Conspiracy of Faith
Bohjalian, C. A. Secrets of Eden
Doyle, R. The woman who walked into doors
King, S. Dolores Claiborne
Oates, J. C. The gravedigger's daughter
Price, N. Sleeping with the enemy
Quindlen, A. Black and blue
Wilhelm, K. The best defense
WIFE BATTERING *See* Wife abuse
WIFE BEATING *See* Wife abuse
The **wife's** tale. Lansens, L.
A **wild** and lonely place. Muller, M.
WILD ANIMALS *See* Animals; Wildlife
Wild at Whiskey Creek. Long, J. A.
Wild child. Boyle, T. C.
Wild Decembers. O'Brien, E.
Wild fire. DeMille, N.
WILD FLOWERS
See also Flowers
The **wild** girl: the notebooks of Ned Giles, 1932. Fergus, J.
The **wild** Irish. Maxwell, R.
Wild justice. Margolin, P.
Wild nights! Oates, J. C.
Wild side of the river. Zimmer, M.
Wild stars seeking midnight suns. Cooper, J. C.
A **wild** surge of guilty passion. Hansen, R.
Wild Wicked Scot. London, J.
Wilde Lake. Lippman, L.
The **Wilde** women. Wall, P. S.
Wilde, Oscar, 1854-1900
About
Self, W. Dorian
WILDERNESS AREAS
Barr, N. Destroyer angel
Doiron, P. The poacher's son
Lent, J. Lost nation
Les Becquets, D. Breaking wild
McCarthy, C. The crossing
VanderMeer, J. Acceptance
WILDERNESS AREAS -- MAINE
Doiron, P. Bad Little Falls
WILDERNESS SURVIVAL
Barnes, J. The sky so big and black
Brockmeier, K. The brief history of the dead
Brown, T. Fallen land
Campbell, B. J. Once upon a river
Eggers, D. Heroes of the frontier
King, S. The girl who loved Tom Gordon
Koryta, M. Those who wish me dead
Long, J. The reckoning
Matheson, R. Hunted past reason
Paul, B. Under Tower Peak
Perry, T. Vanishing act
Riordan, R. Cold Springs
Schwartz, L. Angels Crest
Stirling, S. M. Dies the fire
Wildfire at midnight. Stewart, M.
WILDFIRES
See also Fires
The **wilding.** Percy, B.
WILDLIFE REFUGES
Festing, I. A. The birdkeeper
Will you always love me? and other stories. Oates, J. C.
William III, King of Great Britain, 1650-1702
About
Plaidy, J. William's wife
William's wife. Plaidy, J.
Williams, Bert, 1874-1922
About
Phillips, C. Dancing in the dark
Williams, Hank, 1923-1953
About
Earle, S. I'll never get out of this world alive
WILLIAMSON COUNTY (TENN.)
Hicks, R. The widow of the south
The **Willow** Field. Kittredge, W.
The **willow** pattern. Gulik, R. H. v.
WILLS
See also Genealogy; Registers of births, etc.
The **wind-up** bird chronicle. Murakami, H.
The **windflower.** London, L.
A **window** opens. Egan, E.
WINDOWS
Grant, H. The glass demon
WINDS
See also Meteorology; Navigation; Physical geography; Weather
The **winds** of change. Grimes, M.
Winds of fate. Lackey, M.
The **winds** of war. Wouk, H.
The **windup** girl. Bacigalupi, P.
Windy City blues. Paretsky, S.
WINE AND WINE MAKING
Francis, D. Proof
Woods, S. Imperfect strangers
The **wine-dark** sea. O'Brian, P.
Winesburg, Ohio. Anderson, S.
The **wings** of the dove. James, H.
The **wings** of the morning. Tryon, T.
Wingshooters. Revoyr, N.
Winning Ruby Heart. Lohmann, J.
Winter.
WINTER
Hannah, K. The great alone
Lourey, J. January thaw
The **Winter** Bride. Gracie, A.
Winter garden. Hannah, K.
Winter in Madrid. Sansom, C. J.
Winter kill. Brooks, B.
The **winter** king. Cornwell, B.
The **winter** of Frankie Machine. Winslow, D.
The **winter** of our discontent. Steinbeck, J.
Winter of the world. Follett, K.

The **Winter** Palace. Stachniak, E.
Winter prey. Sandford, J.
Winter solstice. Pilcher, R.
Winter's bone. Woodrell, D.
Winter's end. Rickards, J.
A **Winter's** Night. Manfredi, V. M.
Winter's tale. Helprin, M.
Winter's tales. Dinesen, I.
Wintering. Moses, K.
Winternight trilogy [series]
The girl in the tower
The **Winthrop** woman. Seton, A.
WIRELESS *See* Radio
WIRETAPPING
See also Criminal investigation; Right of privacy
WISCONSIN
Ansay, A. M. River angel
Beverly, B. Dodgers
Goolrick, R. A reliable wife
Hamilton, J. A map of the world
Hamilton, J. The short history of a prince
Harbach, C. The art of fielding
King, S. Black house
Packer, A. The dive from Clausen's pier
Revoyr, N. Wingshooters
Rhodes, D. Driftless
Spencer, L. Bitter sweet
Straub, P. A dark matter
Wroblewski, D. The story of Edgar Sawtelle
Wise blood. O'Connor, F.
The **wise** man's fear. Rothfuss, P.
Wise men. Nadler, S.
Wish you were here. Brown, R. M.
Wish you were here. Swift, G.
Wisp of a thing. Bledsoe, A.
WIT AND HUMOR
Adams, D. The hitchhiker's guide to the galaxy
Adams, D. The restaurant at the end of the universe
Adams, D. So long, and thanks for all the fish
Lopez, R. Good People
Sedaris, D. Holidays on ice
Waugh, E. The loved one
The **witch** of Exmoor. Drabble, M.
WITCHCRAFT
Barry, B. The lace reader
Brooks, T. The sword of Shannara
Conde, M. I, Tituba, black witch of Salem
De la Cruz, M. Witches of East End
Gaiman, N. Good omens
Harkness, D. E. A discovery of witches
Hoffman, A. Practical magic
Howe, K. The physick book of Deliverance Dane
Jones, D. W. A sudden wild magic
Kent, K. The heretic's daughter
King, S. Thinner
Kleypas, L. Crystal Cove
Levin, I. Rosemary's baby
Morrow, J. The last witchfinder
Pietroni, A. L. Ruby's spoon
Rice, A. The witching hour
Sharratt, M. Daughters of the Witching Hill
Updike, J. The widows of Eastwick
Updike, J. The witches of Eastwick
Yrsa Sigurdardottir Last rituals
WITCHCRAFT
See also Folklore; Occultism
WITCHES
Barlow, T. Babayaga
Conde, M. I, Tituba, black witch of Salem
Harkness, D. E. The Book of Life
Harkness, D. E. Shadow of night
Maguire, G. Wicked
Rhodes, J. P. Voodoo dreams
WITCHES
See also Witchcraft
Witches of East End. De la Cruz, M.
The **witches** of Eastwick. Updike, J.
The **witching** hour. Rice, A.
With her in Ourland.
With love, wherever you are. MacKall, D. D.
Within a budding grove. Proust, M.
Without a summer. Kowal, M. R.
The **witness.** Brown, S.
WITNESSES
Black, L. Blunt Impact
Cristofano, D. The girl she used to be
Faust, C. Choke hold
Koryta, M. Those who wish me dead
Leonard, E. Killshot
WITNESSES
See also Litigation; Trials
WITNESSES -- PROTECTION
Deaver, J. Edge
Johansen, I. The perfect witness
Koenig, M. Nine days
WIVES
Bock, C. Alice & Oliver
Kitamura, K. A separation
London, J. Wild Wicked Scot
Nesbit, T. The wives of Los Alamos
Turner, N. Heartbreak of a hustler's wife
WIVES
See also Family; Marriage; Married people; Women
WIVES -- CRIMES AGAINST
Flynn, G. Gone girl
Sedgwick, M. Mister Memory
WIVES -- DEATH
Tyler, A. The beginner's goodbye
The **wives** of Los Alamos. Nesbit, T.
Wizard. Varley, J.
WIZARDS
Cho, Z. Sorcerer to the crown
Modesitt, L. E. Imager's battalion
Modesitt, L. E. Imager's challenge

Novik, N. Uprooted
A **Wodehouse** bestiary. Wodehouse, P. G.
Wolf Hall. Mantel, H.
Wolf in the shadows. Muller, M.
Wolf in white van. Darnielle, J.
Wolf totem. Jiang Rong
Wolf whistle. Nordan, L.
The **wolfman.** Pekearo, N. T.
WOLVES
Jiang Rong Wolf totem
McCarthy, C. The crossing
Wolves eat dogs. Smith, M. C.
WOMAN *See* Women
The **Woman** in Cabin Ten. Ware, R.
The **woman** in the dunes. Abe, K.
The **woman** in the window. Finn, A. J.
The **woman** in white. Collins, W.
A **woman** of consequence. Dean, A.
A **woman** of substance. Bradford, B. T.
Woman of the frontier. Grey, Z.
Woman of the inner sea. Keneally, T.
Woman on the edge of time. Piercy, M.
The **woman** upstairs. Messud, C.
The **woman** who couldn't scream. Dodd, C.
The **Woman** Who Lost Her Soul. Shacochis, B.
The **woman** who waited. Makine, A.
The **woman** who walked into doors. Doyle, R.
A **Woman's** eye.
The **women.** Boyle, T. C.
WOMEN
Acevedo, C. The Distant Marvels
Ali, M. Brick lane
Allende, I. Daughter of fortune
Baker, T. The little giant of Aberdeen County
Bambara, T. C. The salt eaters
Barton, E. Brookland
Bergman, M. M. Almost Famous Women
Berlin, L. A manual for cleaning women
Blackwood, C. Never breathe a word
Blake, S. The postmistress
Brookner, A. Brief lives
Campbell, B. J. Mothers, tell your daughters
Castillo, L. Sworn to silence
Cook, C. Best staged plans
Dallas, S. The Persian Pickle Club
Dangerous women
Diamant, A. The red tent
Dorris, M. Cloud chamber
Dorris, M. A yellow raft in blue water
Dovey, C. Blood kin
Egan, E. A window opens
Esquivel, L. Like water for chocolate
Faulks, S. Charlotte Gray
Faye, L. Jane Steele
Ferrante, E. Those Who Leave and Those Who Stay
Flagg, F. Fried green tomatoes at the Whistle-Stop Cafe
Fowler, K. J. The Jane Austen book club
Freudenberger, N. The newlyweds
Fuentes, C. The years with Laura Diaz
Gardam, J. The flight of the maidens
Gay, R. Difficult women
Gibbons, K. Divining women
Godwin, G. A mother and two daughters
Gordon, M. The company of women
Goudge, E. Garden of lies
Goudge, E. Thorns of truth
Greene, A. Bloodroot
Gideon, M. Wife 22
Gilman, S. J. The Ice Cream Queen of Orchard Street
Goodman, A. Kaaterskill Falls
Graeme-Evans, P. The island house
Haigh, J. Mrs. Kimble
Halter, M. Sarah
Harrison, J. The road home
Healey, E. Elizabeth is missing
Heiny, K. Single, carefree, mellow
Hilderbrand, E. The island
Hilton, L. S. Maestra
Hoffman, A. The dovekeepers
Hoffman, A. Practical magic
Hoffman, A. The probable future
Hoffman, A. The third angel
Holland, C. An ordinary woman
Holmes, L. Barbara the slut and other people
Hoover, M. The quickening
Howatch, S. Scandalous risks
Isaacs, S. Close relations
Itani, F. Remembering the bones
Jackson, J. The almost sisters
Jemisin, N. K. The fifth season
Jhabvala, R. P. My nine lives
Joyce, R. The Love Song of Miss Queenie Hennessy
Jong, E. Fear of Dying
Keneally, T. Woman of the inner sea
Kline, C. B. Orphan train
Laker, R. To dance with kings
L'Engle, M. Certain women
Lively, P. Consequences
Lively, P. Moon tiger
Lutz, L. How to start a fire
Lutz, L. The Passenger
Machado, C. M. Her body and other parties
Manicka, R. The rice mother
Maupin, A. Mary Ann in autumn
McDermott, A. At weddings and wakes
McDermott, A. Someone
McInerney, L. The Glorious Heresies
McMillan, T. How Stella got her groove back
McMillan, T. I Almost Forgot About You
McNeal, T. To be sung underwater
Mehta, G. Raj
Mohamed, N. The orchard of lost souls
Momaday, N. S. The ancient child
Moriarty, L. Big little lies

Morrison, T. Paradise
Munro, A. Open secrets
Naylor, G. The women of Brewster Place
Nin, A. Cities of the interior
Nineveh
Okparanta, C. Happiness, Like Water
Otto, W. How to make an American quilt
Oyeyemi, H. The opposite house
Palmer, D. Version control
Paretsky, S. Ghost country
Pilcher, R. September
Pilcher, R. The shell seekers
Pym, B. Excellent women
Read, P. P. Alice in exile
Rindell, S. The Other Typist
Rooney, K. Lillian Boxfish Takes a Walk
Rushdie, S. The enchantress of Florence
Santiago, E. Conquistadora
Scott, J. Follow me
See, L. Peony in love
Senna, D. New People
Shields, C. The stone diaries
Sosin, D. The long-shining waters
Strout, E. Olive Kitteridge
Swann, M. The foreigners
Three strong women
Towles, A. Rules of civility
Trueblood, V. Seven loves
Turner, N. E. These is my words
Updike, J. S
Vine, B. The brimstone wedding
Walbert, K. The gardens of Kyoto
Walker, A. Possessing the secret of joy
Walker, S. Dietland
Watson, B. Miss Jane
Wells, R. Divine secrets of the Ya-Ya Sisterhood
Williamson, P. Heart of the west
Wolff, I. A vintage affair
Zumas, L. Red clocks

WOMEN -- BIOGRAPHY
See also Biography

WOMEN -- CALIFORNIA -- SAN FRANCISCO
Hughes, A. Market Street

WOMEN -- CHINA
The bathing women

WOMEN -- CONNECTICUT
Brown, K. The longings of wayward girls

WOMEN -- CRIMES AGAINST
Dodd, C. The woman who couldn't scream
The leopard

WOMEN -- CRIMES AGAINST -- SAUDI ARABIA
Ferraris, Z. Kingdom of strangers

WOMEN -- DISEASES
See also Diseases

WOMEN -- EMPLOYMENT
Crowley, J. Four freedoms

WOMEN -- ENGLAND
Cleeves, A. The crow trap
Freeman, A. The fair fight

WOMEN -- ENGLAND -- LONDON
Thomas, S. A study in scarlet women

WOMEN -- ENGLAND -- PENNINE CHAIN
Cleeves, A. The crow trap

WOMEN -- FRANCE
Three strong women

WOMEN -- GERMANY -- BERLIN
Gillham, D. R. City of women

WOMEN -- GREAT BRITAIN
Hadley, T. Clever Girl

WOMEN -- GREECE
Greenwood, K. Medea

WOMEN -- HISTORY
See also Feminism; History

WOMEN -- HISTORY -- MIDDLE AGES, 500-1500
Griffith, N. Hild

WOMEN -- IDENTITY
See also Identity (Psychology)
Machado, C. M. Her body and other parties
Oates, J. C. Mudwoman
Traveler of the century

WOMEN -- INDIA
Umrigar, T. The world we found

WOMEN -- IRAN
Amirrezvani, A. Equal of the sun

WOMEN -- JAPAN
Schwartz, J. B. The commoner

WOMEN -- MENTAL HEALTH
See also Mental health; Women -- Health and hygiene

WOMEN -- NEW YORK (STATE) -- ADIRONDACK MOUNTAINS REGION
Unger, L. Heartbroken

WOMEN -- NEW YORK (STATE) -- NEW YORK
Gould, E. Friendship
McPhee, J. No ordinary matter
Rindell, S. The Other Typist

WOMEN -- NIGERIA
Okparanta, C. Happiness, Like Water

WOMEN -- PSYCHOLOGY
Alarcon, D. Lost City Radio
Appelfeld, A. Until the dawn's light
Berg, E. What we keep
Cleage, P. What looks like crazy on an ordinary day--
Colwin, L. Goodbye without leaving
Cristofano, D. The girl she used to be
Cunningham, M. The hours
De Bernieres, L. A partisan's daughter
Doyle, R. The woman who walked into doors
Enright, A. The forgotten waltz
Enright, A. The gathering
Erdrich, L. Four souls
Ferrante, E. The lost daughter
Findley, T. The piano man's daughter
Gibbons, K. On the occasion of my last afternoon
Giffin, E. Heart of the matter

Godwin, G. Evensong
Gowdy, B. The romantic
Greer, A. S. The story of a marriage
Hall, B. The music teacher
Hamilton, J. A map of the world
Hannah, K. On Mystic lake
Hannah, S. The wrong mother
Hansen, R. Mariette in ecstasy
Hegi, U. Stones from the river
Hill, R. When all is said and done
Hoeg, P. Smilla's sense of snow
Hoffman, A. Skylight confessions
Huneven, M. Blame
Isaacs, S. Lily White
Joss, M. The night following
Kallos, S. Broken for you
Kincaid, J. Autobiography of my mother
Kincaid, J. Lucy
King, L. The father of the rain
King, S. Dolores Claiborne
Lamott, A. Blue shoe
Lansens, L. The wife's tale
Lessing, D. M. The good terrorist
Lessing, D. M. Love, again
Lipman, E. The pursuit of Alice Thrift
Lippman, L. I'd know you anywhere
Livesey, M. Criminals
Livesey, M. Eva moves the furniture
MacDonald Fall on your knees
Martin, V. Italian fever
Martin, V. Trespass
McGowan, H. Duchess of nothing
Miller, S. For love
Miller, S. While I was gone
Minot, S. Evening
Morgan, C. E. All the living
Morley, I. Come Sunday
Nelson, A. Bound
Oates, J. C. Blonde
Oates, J. C. The falls
Oates, J. C. The gravedigger's daughter
Oates, J. C. I lock my door upon myself
O'Brien, E. House of splendid isolation
O'Brien, E. Time and tide
O'Farrell, M. The vanishing act of Esme Lennox
O'Nan, S. The good wife
Ostermiller, D. Outside the ordinary world
Ozick, C. Foreign bodies
Packer, A. The dive from Clausen's pier
Patterson, J. Hide & seek
Patterson, K. Consumption
Pearson, A. I think I love you
Phillips, C. A distant shore
Phillips, J. A. MotherKind
Price, N. Night woman
Price, R. Roxanna Slade
Quindlen, A. Black and blue
Reynolds, S. A gracious plenty
Rice, L. Home fires
Robinson, R. Sweetwater
Rosen, J. Joy comes in the morning
Rosenberg, N. T. Abuse of power
Rush, N. Mating
Schwartz, L. S. The writing on the wall
Sebold, A. The almost moon
Shields, C. Unless
Shreve, A. The pilot's wife
Shriver, L. The post-birthday world
Stevens, C. Still missing
Swift, G. Tomorrow
Texier, C. Victorine
Trevor, W. Felicia's journey
Truong, M. Bitter in the mouth
Tyler, A. Back when we were grownups
Tyler, A. Ladder of years
Updike, J. Seek my face
Urquhart, J. A map of glass
Vanderbes, J. Easter Island
Walker, A. Now is the time to open your heart
Waller, R. J. The bridges of Madison County
Weldon, F. Worst fears
Winton, T. Dirt music
Wolitzer, M. The wife

WOMEN -- RELATION TO OTHER WOMEN

Abbott, M. E. Bury me deep
Allen, S. A. The sugar queen
Bauermeister, E. Joy for beginners
Binchy, M. Circle of friends
Blume, J. Summer sisters
Cleave, C. Little Bee
Furnivall, K. The red scarf
Gaitskill, M. Veronica
Garner, H. The spare room
Golden, A. Memoirs of a geisha
Hagedorn, J. T. Toxicology
Heller, Z. What was she thinking?
Hilderbrand, E. Silver girl
Hood, A. The knitting circle
Hosseini, K. A thousand splendid suns
Keyes, M. Last Chance Saloon
Kingsolver, B. The bean trees
Laplante, A. Turn of mind
Livesey, M. The house on Fortune Street
Mapson Bad Girl Creek
Martinez, N. M. Caramba!
McMillan, T. Waiting to exhale
Medlicott, J. A. The ladies of Covington send their love
Miller, S. The senator's wife
Nunez, S. The last of her kind
Oates, J. C. Black girl/White girl
Packer, A. Songs without words
Plain, B. Looking back
Prose, F. Hunters and gatherers
Pym, B. Jane and Prudence

Rosenfeld, L. I'm so happy for you
Schwarz, C. All is vanity
Trollope, J. Friday nights
Umrigar, T. N. The space between us
Updike, J. The widows of Eastwick
Updike, J. The witches of Eastwick
Valdes-Rodriguez, A. Dirty girls on top
Van Niekerk, M. Agaat
Vine, B. The house of stairs
Weiner, J. Little earthquakes
Wood, B. Vital signs
WOMEN -- RELIGIOUS LIFE
Merullo, R. Vatican waltz
WOMEN -- SENEGAL
Three strong women
WOMEN -- SOCIAL CONDITIONS
Oates, J. C. Mudwoman
WOMEN -- SOCIAL CONDITIONS
See also Social conditions
WOMEN -- SOCIAL CONDITIONS -- 20TH CENTURY
Joinson, S. A lady cyclist's guide to Kashgar
WOMEN -- SOCIETIES
See also Clubs; Societies
WOMEN -- VIOLENCE AGAINST
Black, S. The killing lessons
Sager, R. Final girls
WOMEN ACTORS *See* Actresses
WOMEN AIR PILOTS
Grant, D. The Protector
Malone, M. The four corners of the sky
WOMEN AIR PILOTS
See also Air pilots; Women
WOMEN ANIMATORS
Whitaker, K. R. The animators
WOMEN ARCHAEOLOGISTS
Cameron, C. The last Neanderthal
Griffiths, E. The crossing places
Griffiths, E. The Janus stone
Hart, E. Lake of sorrows
Peters, E. The golden one
Peters, E. He shall thunder in the sky
WOMEN ARCHEOLOGISTS
Preston, D. The cabinet of curiosities
WOMEN ARCHITECTS -- WASHINGTON (STATE) -- SEATTLE
Semple, M. Where'd you go, Bernadette
WOMEN ARTISTS
Atwood, M. Cat's eye
Dunant, S. The birth of Venus
Hooper, K. Finding Laura
Hustvedt, S. The blazing world
Krentz, J. A. Promise not to tell
Kushner, R. The flamethrowers
Lewis, B. The brethren
Messud, C. The woman upstairs
Mohr, J. Damascus
Palahniuk, C. Diary
Riley, J. M. The serpent garden
Smith, D. The last painting of Sara De Vos
Tearne, R. Mosquito
Updike, J. Seek my face
Weisgall, D. The world before her
WOMEN ARTISTS
See also Artists; Women
WOMEN ARTISTS -- ENGLAND -- 20TH CENTURY
Parmar, P. Vanessa and her sister
WOMEN ARTISTS -- NETHERLANDS
Smith, D. The last painting of Sara De Vos
WOMEN ASTRONAUTS
See also Astronauts; Women
WOMEN ATHLETES
See also Athletes; Women
WOMEN ATHLETES
Cleave, C. Gold
Lohmann, J. Winning Ruby Heart
WOMEN AUTHORS
Absolution
Alvarez, J. Yo!
Atwood, M. The blind assassin
Barrows, A. The Guernsey Literary and Potato Peel Pie Society
Bohjalian, C. A. Secrets of Eden
Brookner, A. Hotel du Lac
Byatt, A. S. The children's book
De Rosnay, T. Sarah's key
Doig, I. Bucking the sun
Drabble, M. The witch of Exmoor
Ferrante, E. Those Who Leave and Those Who Stay
Fossum, K. Broken
Frame, J. Towards another summer
Hagedorn, J. T. Toxicology
Howard, M. The rags of time
Irving, J. A widow for one year
Lessing, D. M. The golden notebook
Martinusen-Coloma, C. The salt garden
McEwan, I. Atonement
Meloy, M. A family daughter
Nicholls, D. One day
Oates, J. C. Marya
Ogilvie, E. When the music stopped
Olsson, L. Astrid & Veronika
Ozeki, R. L. A tale for the time being
Parkhurst, C. The nobodies album
Preston, C. The scrapbook of Frankie Pratt
Robinson, P. The first cut
Settle, M. L. Charley Bland
Settle, M. L. The killing ground
Shields, C. Unless
Stegner, W. E. Angle of repose
Thomas, R. All my sins remembered
Watson, S. J. Before I go to sleep
Weiner, J. Certain girls
Weldon, F. Chalcot Crescent
Wiggins, M. The shadow catcher

WOMEN AUTHORS
See also Authors; Women
WOMEN AUTHORS, AMERICAN -- 20TH CENTURY -- BIOGRAPHY
Welty, E. Stories, essays & memoir
WOMEN AUTHORS, ENGLISH -- 20TH CENTURY
Parmar, P. Vanessa and her sister
WOMEN BIOLOGISTS
Boyle, T. C. When the killing's done
Kingsolver, B. Flight behavior
WOMEN BOTANISTS
Gilbert, E. The Signature of All Things
Vanderbes, J. Easter Island
WOMEN BOTANISTS -- ENGLAND
Jio, S. The last camellia
WOMEN BOXERS
Freeman, A. The fair fight
WOMEN CLERGY
See also Clergy; Women
WOMEN COLLEGE GRADUATES
See also College graduates; Women
WOMEN COLLEGE GRADUATES
Shumway, C. Ten girls to watch
WOMEN COLLEGE PRESIDENTS
Oates, J. C. Mudwoman
WOMEN COLLEGE STUDENTS
Batuman, E. The idiot
Capó Crucet, J. Make Your Home Among Strangers
WOMEN COLLEGE TEACHERS
Goodman, C. River Road
King, L. R. A darker place
WOMEN CRIMINALS
Hilton, E. Dirty money Honey
Stroby, W. Shoot the woman first
WOMEN DANCERS
Donoghue, E. Frog music
WOMEN DETECTIVES
Beaton, M. C. Pushing up daisies
Beukes, L. Broken monsters
Black, C. Murder on the Champ de Mars
Brookmyre, C. When the Devil Drives
Castillo, L. Breaking silence
Coco, G. Shadows on the lake
Dean, A. Bellfield Hall, or, The observations of Miss Dido Kent
Dean, A. A gentleman of fortune, or, The suspicions of Miss Dido Kent
Dean, A. A woman of consequence
The Disappeared
Ferraris, Z. Kingdom of strangers
Greenwood, K. Unnatural Habits
Hayder, M. Hanging hill
Kent, K. The Dime
Khan, A. Z. The unquiet dead
Laplante, A. A Circle of Wives
Lippman, L. Hush hush
McCall Smith, A. The full cupboard of life
McCall Smith, A. The Kalahari typing school for men
McCall Smith, A. The Limpopo Academy of Private Detection
McCall Smith, A. The No. 1 Ladies' Detective Agency
McCall Smith, A. The Saturday big tent wedding party
McCall Smith, A. Tea time for the traditionally built
Mina, D. Gods and beasts
Mizushima, M. Stalking Ground
Ohlsson, K. Unwanted
Phillips, S. E. First Star I See Tonight
Pintoff, S. Hostage taker
Raybourn, D. A perilous undertaking
Robertson, I. Anatomy of murder
Rodriguez, L. Every last secret
Sharp, Z. Fourth Day
The silence of the sea
Spencer, S. The dead hand of history
Stabenow, D. Restless in the grave
Stabenow, D. Though not dead
Syndrome E
Whittle, T. The Dangerous Edge of Things
Whittle, T. Darker than any shadow
WOMEN DETECTIVES -- ENGLAND
Brett, S. The torso in the town
Buckley, F. The doublet affair
Buckley, F. The siren queen
George, E. Believing the lie
George, E. Just one evil act
WOMEN DETECTIVES -- NEW YORK (STATE) -- NEW YORK
Thompson, V. Murder in Chinatown
Thompson, V. Murder on Lenox Hill
WOMEN DETECTIVES -- SAUDI ARABIA
Ferraris, Z. Kingdom of strangers
WOMEN DETECTIVES -- SWEDEN
Tursten, H. Night rounds
WOMEN DETECTIVES -- VIRGINIA
Brown, R. M. The litter of the law
WOMEN DETECTIVES -- WASHINGTON (STATE)
Jenkins, V. An unattended death
WOMEN DRAMATISTS
Miller, S. The Lake Shore Limited
WOMEN DRAMATISTS -- SCOTLAND
Upson, N. London rain
WOMEN DRESSMAKERS
Chiaverini, J. Mrs. Lincoln's dressmaker
WOMEN EDITORS
Carey, P. My life as a fake
Evans, N. The horse whisperer
Lafferty, M. The shambling guide to New York City
Spark, M. A far cry from Kensington
WOMEN ENGINEERS
Higgins, C. A. Lightless
WOMEN EX-CONVICTS
Rice, L. Little night
WOMEN EXECUTIVES
Steel, D. First sight

WOMEN FARMERS
Mazzarella, N. This heavy silence
WOMEN FORENSIC ANTHROPOLOGISTS
Griffiths, E. A Dying Fall
Griffiths, E. The house at sea's end
Ondaatje, M. Anil's ghost
WOMEN FORENSIC PATHOLOGISTS
Franklin, A. The serpent's tale
WOMEN GENEALOGISTS
Groff, L. The monsters of Templeton
WOMEN GRADUATE STUDENTS
Willig, L. The secret history of the pink carnation
WOMEN HISTORIANS
Harkness, D. E. The Book of Life
Willig, L. The secret history of the pink carnation
WOMEN HOUSEHOLD EMPLOYEES -- CRIMES AGAINST
Finch, C. A beautiful blue death
WOMEN IMMIGRANTS
Kwok, J. Girl in translation
Tan, A. The bonesetter's daughter
Yezierska, A. c. Bread givers
WOMEN IN BUSINESS *See* Businesswomen
WOMEN IN CHRISTIANITY
See also Christianity; Women
WOMEN IN ISLAM
See also Islam; Women
Women in love. Lawrence, D. H.
WOMEN IN MEDICINE
See also Medical personnel; Women
WOMEN IN MOTION PICTURES
See also Motion pictures
WOMEN IN POLITICS
Didion, J. A book of common prayer
WOMEN IN THE BIBLE
Edghill, I. Queenmaker
Wolf, J. This scarlet cord
Women in the grove. Peterson, P. W.
WOMEN IN THE MILITARY
See also Military personnel; Women
WOMEN IN THE MOTION PICTURE INDUSTRY
See also Motion picture industry; Women
WOMEN JOURNALISTS
Andrew, S. Recipes for Love and Murder
Barnett, L. K. Jam on the Vine
Cain, C. Heartsick
Castro, J. Hell or high water
Coben, H. Caught
Coel, M. Blood memory
Cotterill, C. Killed at the whim of a hat
Flynn, G. Sharp objects
Godwin, G. Queen of the underworld
Hart, C. G. Letter from home
Isaacs, S. Red, white and blue
Johnston, W. The colony of unrequited dreams
Lehane, D. Since we fell
Leimbach, M. The man from Saigon
Lively, P. Cleopatra's sister
MacInnes, H. Ride a pale horse
Mina, D. Field of blood
Patterson, J. 1st to die
Price, R. Freedomland
Raban, J. Surveillance
Ryan, H. P. The other woman
Salak, K. The white Mary
Soli, T. The lotus eaters
Updike, J. Seek my face
Villars, E. The Normandie affair
Walker, M. W. Under the beetle's cellar
Walters, M. The devil's feather
Walters, M. The sculptress
Ward, A. E. Forgive me
Ware, R. The Woman in Cabin Ten
Weiner, J. Good in bed
Woods, S. Dirt
WOMEN JUDGES
See also Judges; Women
WOMEN LAWYERS
Brown, S. The witness
Gordimer, N. None to accompany me
Harris, E. L. And this too shall pass
Isaacs, S. Lily White
Lippman, L. Wilde Lake
Margolin, P. Wild justice
O'Shaughnessy, P. Breach of promise
O'Shaughnessy, P. Invasion of privacy
O'Shaughnessy, P. Motion to suppress
O'Shaughnessy, P. Obstruction of justice
O'Shaughnessy, P. Unlucky in law
O'Shaughnessy, P. Writ of execution
Pottinger, S. The last Nazi
Rosenberg, N. T. Interest of justice
Rosenberg, N. T. Mitigating circumstances
Scottoline, L. Accused
Scottoline, L. Legal tender
Scottoline, L. Mistaken identity
Scottoline, L. Rough justice
Swinson, K. Playing dirty
Truscott, L. K. Heart of war
Warren, S. M. Take a chance on me
Weiner, J. In her shoes
Wilhelm, K. The best defense
Wilhelm, K. Death qualified
Wilhelm, K. Defense for the devil
Wilhelm, K. Desperate measures
Wilhelm, K. Malice prepense
Wilhelm, K. No defense
Yrsa Sigurdardottir Last rituals
WOMEN LAWYERS -- INDIA
Massey, S. The widows of Malabar Hill
WOMEN LIBRARIANS
Millet, L. Oh pure and radiant heart
WOMEN MARINE BIOLOGISTS
Ledgard, J. M. Submergence

WOMEN MEDIUMS
Murphy, S. F. The possessions
WOMEN MIGRANT LABOR
Silver, M. Mary Coin
WOMEN MISSIONARIES
Joinson, S. A lady cyclist's guide to Kashgar
WOMEN MOTION PICTURE PRODUCERS AND DIRECTORS
Spiotta, D. Innocents and others
Whitaker, K. R. The animators
Wouk, H. The lawgiver
WOMEN MURDERERS
Kent, H. Burial rites
Perry, T. Nightlife
WOMEN MUSEUM CURATORS
Carey, P. The chemistry of tears
WOMEN MYSTICS
Urquhart, R. The Visionist
WOMEN NOVELISTS
Atwood, M. The blind assassin
Martinusen-Coloma, C. The salt garden
Parkhurst, C. The nobodies album
The **women** of Brewster Place. Naylor, G.
WOMEN ON TELEVISION
See also Television
WOMEN PAINTERS
Avery, E. The last nude
O'Farrell, M. The hand that first held mine
Updike, J. Seek my face
Vreeland, S. The passion of Artemesia
WOMEN PARK RANGERS
Barr, N. Destroyer angel
WOMEN PATHOLOGISTS
Hart, E. The book of Killowen
Hart, E. Haunted ground
WOMEN PHILOSOPHERS
McCall Smith, A. The forgotten affairs of youth
WOMEN PHOTOGRAPHERS
Allende, I. Portrait in sepia
Belfer, L. A fierce radiance
Black, E. The drowning house
Boyd, W. Sweet Caress
Geni, A. The lightkeepers
Hand, E. Available dark
Hand, E. Generation loss
Humphreys, H. Afterimage
Johansen, I. And then you die--
Kirkpatrick, J. A flickering light
Quindlen, A. Still life with bread crumbs
Shreve, A. The weight of water
Trollope, J. Next of kin
Woods, S. Palindrome
WOMEN PHYSICIANS
Adrian, C. The children's hospital
Glass, J. The widower's tale
Grippando, J. Lying with strangers
Hannah, K. Home again
Hornby, N. How to be good
Laplante, A. Turn of mind
Lessing, D. M. The sweetest dream
Lipman, E. The pursuit of Alice Thrift
Obreht, T. The tiger's wife
Palmer, M. The patient
Rhodes, J. P. Yellow moon
Winawer, M. The scribe of Siena
Wood, B. Vital signs
WOMEN PHYSICIANS
See also Physicians; Women
WOMEN POETS
Amis, K. The Russian girl
Conroy, P. The prince of tides
Fitch, J. White oleander
Michaels, B. Houses of stone
Phillips, J. A. MotherKind
Steinke, R. Holy skirts
WOMEN POISONERS
Poole, S. The Borgia mistress
WOMEN POLICE CHIEFS
Castillo, L. The dead will tell
Rodriguez, L. Every broken trust
WOMEN POLICE OFFICERS *See* Policewomen
WOMEN PRISONERS
Lagercrantz, D. The girl who takes an eye for an eye
Moore, S. The big girls
Silver, E. L. The execution of Noa P. Singleton
WOMEN PRIVATE INVESTIGATORS -- ALASKA
Stabenow, D. Hunter's moon
Stabenow, D. Killing grounds
Stabenow, D. Less than a treason
Stabenow, D. Restless in the grave
Stabenow, D. Though not dead
WOMEN PRIVATE INVESTIGATORS -- BOTSWANA
McCall Smith, A. The full cupboard of life
McCall Smith, A. The Kalahari typing school for men
McCall Smith, A. The Limpopo Academy of Private Detection
McCall Smith, A. The No. 1 Ladies' Detective Agency
McCall Smith, A. The Saturday big tent wedding party
McCall Smith, A. Tea time for the traditionally built
WOMEN PRIVATE INVESTIGATORS -- CALIFORNIA
Grafton, S. X
Grafton, S. N is for noose
Grafton, S. P is for peril
Grafton, S. Q is for quarry
WOMEN PRIVATE INVESTIGATORS -- ENGLAND -- COTSWOLD HILLS
Beaton, M. C. Pushing up daisies
WOMEN PRIVATE INVESTIGATORS -- ENGLAND -- LONDON
Gibson, W. Pattern recognition
Weaver, A. A most novel revenge
Winspear, J. Birds of a feather
Winspear, J. Maisie Dobbs
WOMEN PRIVATE INVESTIGATORS

Heller, P. Celine
Krentz, J. A. River road
Lutz, L. The last word
Pynchon, T. Bleeding edge
Raybourn, D. A perilous undertaking
WOMEN PRIVATE INVESTIGATORS -- FRANCE -- PARIS
Black, C. Murder below Montparnasse
Black, C. Murder in the Bastille
Black, C. Murder in the Marais
Black, C. Murder in the rue de Paradis
Black, C. Murder on the Champ de Mars
WOMEN PRIVATE INVESTIGATORS -- ILLINOIS -- CHICAGO
Paretsky, S. Breakdown
Paretsky, S. Brush back
Paretsky, S. Fallout
Paretsky, S. Total recall
WOMEN PSYCHOTHERAPISTS
French, N. Tuesday's gone
French, N. Waiting for Wednesday
WOMEN SCHOLARS
Fortier, A. The lost sisterhood
WOMEN SCIENTISTS
Ghosh, A. The hungry tide
Hagberg, D. Abyss
Johansen, I. Long after midnight
Southgate, M. The taste of salt
Vanderbes, J. Easter Island
Wilson, R. C. Blind Lake
WOMEN SCREENWRITERS
Weiner, J. The next best thing
WOMEN SCULPTORS
Johansen, I. Taking Eve
WOMEN SERIAL MURDERERS
Cain, C. Heartsick
Cain, C. Kill you twice
WOMEN SINGERS
Chee, A. The queen of the night
Leon, D. Falling in Love
WOMEN SLAVES
Allende, I. Island beneath the sea
Clotel, or, The president's daughter
Martin, V. Property
Morrison, T. Beloved
Morrison, T. A mercy
Rawles, N. My Jim
WOMEN SLAVES -- OHIO -- SOCIAL CONDITIONS
Perkins-Valdez, D. Wench
WOMEN SLAVES -- SOUTH AFRICA
Brink, A. P. Philida
WOMEN SOLDIERS
Bledsoe, A. The hum and the shiver
Hunt, L. Neverhome
McCabe, E. L. I shall be near to you
WOMEN SPIES
Cole, A. An Extraordinary Union
McEwan, I. Sweet tooth
Putney, M. J. No longer a gentleman
WOMEN STATISTICIANS
Suri, M. The city of Devi
WOMEN TEACHERS
Simonson, H. The summer before the war
WOMEN'S MOVEMENT
See also Women -- Social conditions; Women's rights
WOMEN'S RIGHTS
Kidd, S. M. The invention of wings
Massey, S. The widows of Malabar Hill
The **women's** room. French, M.
WOMEN, SOMALI
Mohamed, N. The orchard of lost souls
WOMEN-OWNED BUSINESS ENTERPRISES
Lehmann, S. Astor Place Vintage
The **wonder.** Donoghue, E.
Wonder boys. Chabon, M.
The **Wonder** Garden. Acampora, L.
The **wonder** spot. Bank, M.
Wonder when you'll miss me. Davis, A.
WONDER WOMAN (FICTIONAL CHARACTER)
See also Fictional characters; Superheroes
WOOD
See also Building materials; Forest products; Fuel; Trees
WOOD CARVING
Arnow, H. L. S. The dollmaker
The **woodcutter.** Hill, R.
Woodcutters. Bernhard, T.
Woodhull, Victoria C., 1838-1927
About
Piercy, M. Sex wars
The **woods.** Coben, H.
Woodsburner. Pipkin, J.
Woolf, Virginia, 1882-1941
About
Cunningham, M. The hours
Parmar, P. Vanessa and her sister
WOOSTER, BERTIE (FICTITIOUS CHARACTER)
Faulks, S. Jeeves and the Wedding Bells
The **word** exchange. Graedon, A.
WORD GAMES
See also Games; Literary recreations
WORD PROBLEMS (MATHEMATICS)
See also Mathematics
WORK
Eggers, D. The Circle
WORK AND FAMILY
See also Family; Work
WORK ETHIC
See also Ethics; Work
The **work** of wolves. Meyers, K.
Work song. Doig, I.
WORK-LIFE BALANCE
Egan, E. A window opens
WORKAHOLISM

See also Compulsive behavior
WORKHOUSES -- IRELAND -- DUBLIN
Alexander, V. S. The Magdalen girls
WORKING ANIMALS
See also Animals; Domestic animals; Economic zoology
WORKING CHILDREN *See* Child labor
WORKING CLASS
See also Social classes
WORKING CLASS
Campbell, B. J. Mothers, tell your daughters
WORKING DOGS
See also Dogs; Working animals
Mizushima, M. Killing Trail
Mizushima, M. Stalking Ground
WORKING MOTHERS
See also Mothers; Women -- Employment
Forman, G. Leave Me
WORKING POOR
Gilb, D. The flowers
Louis, É. The end of Eddy
Works. Wright, R.
The **world** according to Bertie. McCall Smith, A.
The **world** according to Garp. Irving, J.
World and town. Jen, G.
The **world** at the end of time. Pohl, F.
The **world** before her. Weisgall, D.
World enough and time. Warren, R. P.
World famous love acts. Leung, B.
The **world** from rough stones. Ross-Macdonald, M.
World gone by. Lehane, D.
WORLD HISTORY -- 20TH CENTURY
Atkinson, K. A God in Ruins
Follett, K. Edge of Eternity
Follett, K. Winter of the world
The **world** of Jeeves. Wodehouse, P. G.
The **world** of tomorrow. Mathews, B.
World of trouble. Winters, B. H.
WORLD POLITICS
Church, J. Bamboo and blood
Kerr, P. Hitler's peace
West, M. L. The clowns of God
West, M. L. The shoes of the fisherman
WORLD SERIES (BASEBALL)
See also Baseball; Sports tournaments
The **world** to come. Horn, D.
The **world** to come. Shepard, J.
WORLD TRADE CENTER (NEW YORK, N.Y.) TERRORIST ATTACK, 2001 *See* September 11 terrorist attacks, 2001
WORLD WAR I *See* World War, 1914-1918
WORLD WAR II *See* World War, 1939-1945
WORLD WAR III
See also War; World politics
World War Z. Brooks, M.
WORLD WAR, 1914-1918
Boyd, W. Waiting for sunrise
Boyden, J. Three-day road
Boyne, J. The absolutist
De Bernières, L. The dust that falls from dreams
Ford, F. M. Parade's end
Itani, F. Deafening
Keneally, T. The Daughters of Mars
Krivak, A. The sojourn
McCarthy, T. C
Perry, A. Shoulder the sky
Rash, R. The cove
Sholokhov, M. A. And quiet flows the Don
Todd, C. A duty to the dead
Trumbo, D. Johnny got his gun
WORLD WAR, 1914-1918
See also Europe -- History -- 1871-1918; World history -- 20th century; World politics
WORLD WAR, 1914-1918 -- AFRICA
Forester, C. S. The African Queen
WORLD WAR, 1914-1918 -- CAMPAIGNS -- WESTERN FRONT
Boyne, J. The absolutist
WORLD WAR, 1914-1918 -- CONSCIENTIOUS OBJECTORS
Boyne, J. The absolutist
WORLD WAR, 1914-1918 -- ENGLAND
Barker, P. The eye in the door
Barker, P. The ghost road
Barker, P. Regeneration
Byatt, A. S. The children's book
Hilton, J. Random harvest
Morton, K. The house at Riverton
Perry, A. No graves as yet
Todd, C. A duty to the dead
Winspear, J. The mapping of love and death
WORLD WAR, 1914-1918 -- FRANCE
Celine Journey to the end of the night
Faulkner, W. A fable
Faulks, S. Birdsong
Proust, M. Time regained
Todd, C. A question of honor
WORLD WAR, 1914-1918 -- GERMANY
Franck, J. The blindness of the heart
Remarque, E. M. The road back
WORLD WAR, 1914-1918 -- ITALY
Hemingway, E. A farewell to arms
WORLD WAR, 1914-1918 -- LITERATURE AND THE WAR
Dunmore, H. The lie
WORLD WAR, 1914-1918 -- MIDDLE EAST
Werfel, F. The forty days of Musa Dagh
WORLD WAR, 1914-1918 -- PEACE
See also Peace
WORLD WAR, 1914-1918 -- SECRET SERVICE
Murphy, Y. Signed, Mata Hari
WORLD WAR, 1914-1918 -- TREATIES
Jenoff, P. The Ambassador's Daughter
WORLD WAR, 1914-1918 -- TURKEY

De Bernieres, L. Birds without wings

WORLD WAR, 1914-1918 -- UNITED STATES

Dos Passos, J. 1919
Dos Passos, J. Manhattan transfer
Gold, G. D. Sunnyside

WORLD WAR, 1939-1945

Allende, I. The Japanese Lover
Appelfeld, A. Blooms of darkness
Appelfeld, A. The man who never stopped sleeping
Belfer, L. And after the fire
Bock, D. The ash garden
Byatt, A. S. Ragnarok
Deutermann, P. T. The ghosts of Bungo Suido
Deutermann, P. T. Pacific glory
Doig, I. The eleventh man
Doerr, A. All the light we cannot see
Down, D. Masaryk Station
Downing, D. Potsdam station
Flanagan, R. The narrow road to the deep north
Follett, K. Winter of the world
Furst, A. A Hero of France
Gillham, D. R. City of women
Grindle, L. Villa triste
Higgins, J. The eagle has flown
Itani, F. Requiem
Jones, J. The thin red line
Keneally, T. Shame and the Captives
Kerr, P. Hitler's peace
Kerr, P. A Man Without Breath
Lee A gesture life
London, J. The Golden Age
MacKall, D. D. With love, wherever you are
Moore, S. The life of objects
Nesbit, T. The wives of Los Alamos
Ōe, K. Death by Water
Orringer, J. The invisible bridge
Piercy, M. Gone to soldiers
Quinn, P. Dry bones
Roberts, M. Ignorance
Shepard, J. The book of Aron
Sundin, S. Through waters deep
Tolkien, S. Orders from Berlin
Torday, D. The Last Flight of Poxl West
Treuer, D. Prudence
Turow, S. Ordinary heroes
Van Booy, S. The illusion of separateness
Volpi, J. In search of Klingsor
Walbert, K. The gardens of Kyoto
Waldman, A. Love and treasure
Wouk, H. War and remembrance
Wouk, H. The winds of war

WORLD WAR, 1939-1945

See also Europe -- History -- 1918-1945; World history -- 20th century; World politics

WORLD WAR, 1939-1945 -- AERIAL OPERATIONS

Torday, D. The Last Flight of Poxl West

WORLD WAR, 1939-1945 -- ATLANTIC OCEAN

Monsarrat, N. The cruel sea

WORLD WAR, 1939-1945 -- ATROCITIES

Anatoli, A. Babi Yar
Uris, L. QB VII

WORLD WAR, 1939-1945 -- ATROCITIES

See also Atrocities

WORLD WAR, 1939-1945 -- AUSTRALIA

McCullough, C. An indecent obsession

WORLD WAR, 1939-1945 -- BATTLES, SIEGES, ETC.

See World War, 1939-1945 -- Aerial operations; World War, 1939-1945 -- Campaigns; World War, 1939-1945 -- Naval operations

WORLD WAR, 1939-1945 -- BELGIUM

Hulme, K. The nun's story

WORLD WAR, 1939-1945 -- BIOGRAPHY

See also Biography

WORLD WAR, 1939-1945 -- CANADA

Norman, H. The museum guard
Norman, H. What is left the daughter

WORLD WAR, 1939-1945 -- CHILDREN -- AUSTRIA -- VIENNA

The chosen ones

WORLD WAR, 1939-1945 -- COLLABORATIONISTS

Eng, T. T. The gift of rain

WORLD WAR, 1939-1945 -- CONFISCATIONS AND CONTRIBUTIONS -- HUNGARY

Waldman, A. Love and treasure

WORLD WAR, 1939-1945 -- CONSCIENTIOUS OBJECTORS

See also Conscientious objectors

WORLD WAR, 1939-1945 -- DENMARK

Follett, K. Hornet flight

WORLD WAR, 1939-1945 -- DESERTIONS

See also Military desertion

WORLD WAR, 1939-1945 -- EGYPT

Mahfouz, N. Sugar Street

WORLD WAR, 1939-1945 -- ENGLAND

Blake, S. The postmistress
Bowen, E. The heat of the day
Follett, K. Eye of the needle
Follett, K. Hornet flight
Frayn, M. Spies
Goddard, R. Long time coming
Greene, G. The end of the affair
Griffiths, E. The house at sea's end
Harris, R. Enigma
Higgins, J. The eagle has landed
Horlock, M. The book of lies
Lebrecht, N. The song of names
Lively, P. Consequences
McEwan, I. Atonement
Pilcher, R. Coming home
Spark, M. The girls of slender means
Waters, S. The night watch
Wesley, M. Part of the furniture
Willis, C. Blackout

WORLD WAR, 1939-1945 -- ENGLAND -- KENT

Morton, K. The distant hours
WORLD WAR, 1939-1945 -- ETHICAL ASPECTS
See also Ethics
WORLD WAR, 1939-1945 -- EUROPE
Appelfeld, A. The man who never stopped sleeping
WORLD WAR, 1939-1945 -- EVACUATION OF CIVILIANS
Morton, K. The distant hours
WORLD WAR, 1939-1945 -- FRANCE
Bates, H. E. Fair stood the wind for France
Faulks, S. Charlotte Gray
Greene, G. The tenth man
Hannah, K. The nightingale
Harris, J. Five quarters of the orange
Nemirovsky, I. Suite Francaise
Pears, I. The dream of Scipio
Remarque, E. M. Arch of triumph
Sartre, J. P. Troubled sleep
Shaara, J. The steel wave
Watkins, P. The forger
Wolff, I. A vintage affair
WORLD WAR, 1939-1945 -- FRANCE -- ANNIVERSARIES, ETC.
De Rosnay, T. Sarah's key
WORLD WAR, 1939-1945 -- GERMANY
Binet, L. HHhH
Bohjalian, C. A. Skeletons at the feast
Boll, H. The silent angel
Franck, J. The blindness of the heart
Grass, G. Crabwalk
Grass, G. Dog years
Gross, A. The one man
Iles, G. Black cross
Remarque, E. M. A time to love and a time to die
WORLD WAR, 1939-1945 -- HONG KONG
Lee, J. Y. K. The piano teacher
WORLD WAR, 1939-1945 -- HUMOR
See also Wit and humor
WORLD WAR, 1939-1945 -- ICELAND
The shadow district
WORLD WAR, 1939-1945 -- ITALY
Bausch, R. Peace
Drndić, D. Trieste
Foulds, A. In the wolf's mouth
Ondaatje, M. The English patient
Portrait of the mother as a young woman
Russell, M. D. A thread of grace
Watkins, P. The ice soldier
WORLD WAR, 1939-1945 -- JAPAN
Smith, M. C. December 6
Tsukiyama, G. The street of a thousand blossoms
WORLD WAR, 1939-1945 -- JERSEY (CHANNEL ISLANDS)
Higgins, J. Night of the fox
WORLD WAR, 1939-1945 -- JEWS
Keneally, T. Schindler's list
Levi, P. If not now, when?
Remarque, E. M. The night in Lisbon
Wander, F. The seventh well
WORLD WAR, 1939-1945 -- JEWS
See also Jews
WORLD WAR, 1939-1945 -- JOURNALISTS
See also Journalists
WORLD WAR, 1939-1945 -- MISSING IN ACTION
See also Missing in action; World War, 1939-1945 -- Prisoners and prisons
WORLD WAR, 1939-1945 -- MOTION PICTURES AND THE WAR
See also Motion pictures; War films
WORLD WAR, 1939-1945 -- MUSEUMS
See also Museums
WORLD WAR, 1939-1945 -- NAVAL OPERATIONS
Furst, A. Dark voyage
Heggen, T. Mister Roberts
Hickam, H. H. The keeper's son
WORLD WAR, 1939-1945 -- NAVAL OPERATIONS -- SUBMARINE
Beach, E. L. Run silent, run deep
WORLD WAR, 1939-1945 -- NETHERLANDS
Lourie, R. A hatred for tulips
WORLD WAR, 1939-1945 -- NORTH AFRICA
Afrika, T. Bitter Eden
Foulds, A. In the wolf's mouth
WORLD WAR, 1939-1945 -- NORWAY
Benn, J. R. Billy Boyle
WORLD WAR, 1939-1945 -- PACIFIC OCEAN
Beach, E. L. Run silent, run deep
Heggen, T. Mister Roberts
Mailer, N. The naked and the dead
Uris, L. Battle cry
Wouk, H. The Caine mutiny
WORLD WAR, 1939-1945 -- PEACE
Kerr, P. Hitler's peace
WORLD WAR, 1939-1945 -- PERSONAL NARRATIVES
See also Autobiographies; Biography
WORLD WAR, 1939-1945 -- PHILIPPINES
Holthe, T. U. When the elephants dance
WORLD WAR, 1939-1945 -- POLAND
Hodgkinson, A. 22 Britannia Road
Keneally, T. Schindler's list
Kosinski, J. N. The painted bird
Shepard, J. The book of Aron
Uris, L. Mila 18
WORLD WAR, 1939-1945 -- PORTUGAL
Leavitt, D. The Two Hotels Francfort
WORLD WAR, 1939-1945 -- PRISONERS AND PRISONS
Afrika, T. Bitter Eden
Friedman, D. Don't ever get old
The hunger angel
Kelly, J. The moon tunnel
WORLD WAR, 1939-1945 -- PRISONERS AND PRISONS
See also Concentration camps; Prisoners of war; Prisons
WORLD WAR, 1939-1945 -- PRISONERS AND PRISONS, AUSTRALIAN

Keneally, T. Shame and the Captives
WORLD WAR, 1939-1945 -- PRISONERS AND PRISONS, GERMAN
Katzenbach, J. Hart's war
Tidhar, L. A man lies dreaming
WORLD WAR, 1939-1945 -- PRISONERS AND PRISONS, JAPANESE
Keneally, T. Shame and the Captives
WORLD WAR, 1939-1945 -- PROPAGANDA
See also Propaganda
WORLD WAR, 1939-1945 -- REFUGEES
Leavitt, D. The Two Hotels Francfort
WORLD WAR, 1939-1945 -- ROMANIA
Furst, A. Blood of victory
WORLD WAR, 1939-1945 -- RUSSIA
Benioff, D. City of thieves
Keneally, T. A family madness
Makine, A. Music of a life
Robbins, D. L. The last citadel
Robbins, D. L. War of the rats
WORLD WAR, 1939-1945 -- SECRET SERVICE
Follett, K. Eye of the needle
Follett, K. Jackdaws
Iles, G. Black cross
Ludlum, R. The Rhinemann exchange
WORLD WAR, 1939-1945 -- SECRET SERVICE
See also Secret service
WORLD WAR, 1939-1945 -- SICILY
Hersey, J. A bell for Adano
Higgins, J. Luciano's luck
Shaara, J. The rising tide
WORLD WAR, 1939-1945 -- SINGAPORE
Loh, V. Breaking the tongue
WORLD WAR, 1939-1945 -- UNDERGROUND MOVEMENTS
Faulks, S. Charlotte Gray
Follett, K. Hornet flight
Follett, K. Jackdaws
Furst, A. Blood of victory
Furst, A. The foreign correspondent
Furst, A. Spies of the Balkans
Uris, L. Mila 18
WORLD WAR, 1939-1945 -- UNDERGROUND MOVEMENTS -- CZECHOSLOVAKIA
Binet, L. HHhH
Groot, T. Flame of resistance
Kelly, M. H. Lilac girls
Zimler, R. The seventh gate
WORLD WAR, 1939-1945 -- UNDERGROUND MOVEMENTS -- FRANCE
Groot, T. Flame of resistance
WORLD WAR, 1939-1945 -- UNDERGROUND MOVEMENTS -- FRANCE -- PARIS
Belfoure, C. The Paris Architect
WORLD WAR, 1939-1945 -- UNITED STATES
Adams, A. After the war
Belfer, L. A fierce radiance
Blake, S. The postmistress
Crowley, J. Four freedoms
Earley, T. The blue star
Ellroy, J. Perfidia
Guterson, D. Snow falling on cedars
Hickam, H. H. The keeper's son
Leithauser, B. The art student's war
Otsuka, J. When the emperor was divine
Rutland, E. No crystal stair
Wouk, H. War and remembrance
Yarbrough, S. Prisoners of war
WORLD WAR, 1939-1945 -- VETERANS
Johnson, C. Spirit of steamboat
Silko, L. Ceremony
WORLD WAR, 1939-1945 -- VETERANS
See also Veterans
WORLD WAR, 1939-1945 -- WALES
Davies, P. H. The Welsh girl
Sheers, O. Resistance
WORLD WAR, 1939-1945 -- WOMEN
See also Women
WORLD WAR, 1939-1945 -- WOMEN
Kelly, M. H. Lilac girls
The **world** we found. Umrigar, T.
WORLD WIDE WEB
See also Internet
World without end. Follett, K.
The **world** without you. Henkin, J.
World's end. Vinge, J. D.
World's end. Boyle, T. C.
World's fair. Doctorow, E. L.
WORLD'S FAIRS *See* Exhibitions; Fairs
World, chase me down. Hilleman, A.
Worldbreaker saga [series]
Hurley, K. The Mirror Empire
Worst fears. Weldon, F.
Worst fears realized. Woods, S.
Wouk, Herman, 1915-
About
Wouk, H. The lawgiver
The **wounded** Land. Donaldson, S. R.
WOUNDS AND INJURIES
See also Accidents
Wrath of the furies. Saylor, S.
The **wreck** of the Godspeed. Kelly, J. P.
The **wreckage.** Robotham, M.
Wrecker. Wood, S.
WRECKS *See* Accidents
Wright, Frank Lloyd, 1867-1959
About
Boyle, T. C. The women
Horan, N. Loving Frank
Writ of execution. O'Shaughnessy, P.
WRITER'S BLOCK
My struggle
WRITERS *See* Authors
WRITERS

Currie, R. Flimsy little plastic miracles
WRITERS ON FILM
Lazar, Z. Sway
WRITERS ON MEDICINE
Boyle, T. C. Road to Wellville
Meyer, N. The seven-per-cent solution
Pearl, M. The Dante Club
Rubenfeld, J. The death instinct
Thomas, D. M. The white hotel
Wideman, J. E. Fanon
WRITERS ON NATURE
Pipkin, J. Woodsburner
WRITERS ON POLITICS
Carey, P. Parrot and Olivier in America
Coetzee, J. M. Foe
Tournier, M. Friday
WRITERS ON RELIGION
Asch, S. The Apostle
Reyn, I. What happened to Anna K.
WRITERS ON SCIENCE
Benford, G. Foundation's fear
Benjamin, M. Alice I have been
Bognanni, P. The house of tomorrow
Brown, D. The Da Vinci code
Essex, K. Leonardo's swans
McDonald, R. Mr. Darwin's shooter
Morrow, J. The last witchfinder
Robinson, K. S. Galileo's dream
Stott, R. Ghostwalk
WRITING
See also Communication; Language and languages; Language arts
WRITING (AUTHORSHIP) *See* Authorship; Creative writing
WRITING
Binet, L. HHhH
The **writing** on the wall. Schwartz, L. S.
Written in my own heart's blood. Gabaldon, D.
Written in red. Bishop, A.
The **wrong** case. Crumley, J.
The **wrong** mother. Hannah, S.
WRONGFUL CONVICTION *See* Actual innocence
WROXETER (ENGLAND) -- HISTORY
Llywelyn, M. After Rome
Wu hou, Empress of China, 624-705
About
Randel, W. D. The empress of bright moon
Wuthering Heights. Bronte, E.
WYOMING
Box, C. J. Force of nature
Box, C. J. Free fire
Box, C. J. Open season
Isaacs, S. Red, white and blue
Johnson, C. Another man's moccasins
Johnson, C. Hell is empty
Roberts, N. Angel's fall
WYOMING -- 19TH CENTURY
L'Amour, L. Bendigo Shafter
Schaefer, J. W. Shane
Trevanian Incident at Twenty Mile

X

X. Grafton, S.
Xenogenesis [series]
Butler, O. E. Adulthood rites
Butler, O. E. Dawn
Butler, O. E. Imago

Y

YA LITERATURE *See* Young adult literature
YACHTING *See* Yachts and yachting
YACHTS AND YACHTING
Wambaugh, J. Floaters
YACHTS AND YACHTING
See also Boatbuilding; Boats and boating; Ocean travel; Ships; Voyages and travels; Water sports
Yankee Doodle dead. Hart, C. G.
The **Year** of the Comet.
The **year** of the flood. Atwood, M.
The **year** of the French. Flanagan, T.
Year of the hyenas. Geagley, B.
The **year** of the runaways. Sahota, S.
Year of wonders. Brooks, G.
The **year** we left home. Thompson, J.
The **Year's** best fantasy and horror.
Year's best science fiction.
The **year's** best science fiction.
Year's Best SF 18.
The **years.** Woolf, V.
Years of Red Dust. Qiu Xiaolong
The **years** of rice and salt. Robinson, K. S.
The **years** with Laura Diaz. Fuentes, C.
The **yellow** admiral. O'Brian, P.
The **yellow** birds. Powers, K.
Yellow moon. Rhodes, J. P.
A **yellow** raft in blue water. Dorris, M.
The **yellow** room conspiracy. Dickinson, P.
YELLOWSTONE NATIONAL PARK
Box, C. J. Back of beyond
Yesterday's weather. Enright, A.
YETI
See also Monsters; Mythical animals
The **Yid.** Goldberg, P.
YIDDISH LANGUAGE
See also Language and languages
The **Yiddish** policemen's union. Chabon, M.
Yo! Alvarez, J.
YORKSHIRE (ENGLAND)
Hill, R. Death comes for the Fat Man
YORUBA (AFRICAN PEOPLE)
See also Africans; Indigenous peoples
YOSEMITE NATIONAL PARK (CALIF.)

See also National parks and reserves -- United States
You can't go home again. Wolfe, T.
You can't keep a good woman down. Walker, A.
You know when the men are gone. Fallon, S.
You must be this happy to enter. Crane, E.
You only die twice. Buchanan, E.
You only live twice. Fleming, I.
You should pity us instead. Gustine, A.
You suck. Moore, C.
You think that's bad. Shepard, J.
You will know me. Abbott, M. E.
You're next. Hurwitz, G.
You're the Earl That I Want. Bowen, K.
YOUNG ADULT AUTHORS
Benford, G. Foundation's fear
Faulks, S. Devil may care
YOUNG ADULT LITERATURE
Adams, R. Watership Down
Bradley, A. The sweetness at the bottom of the pie
Brown, P. Red Rising
Card, O. S. Ender's game
Cisneros, S. The house on Mango Street
Erdrich, L. The last report on the miracles at Little No Horse
Gordimer, N. My son's story
Lanagan, M. The brides of Rollrock Island
Lee, H. To kill a mockingbird
Lessing, D. M. The sweetest dream
Marillier, J. Daughter of the forest
Marshall, C. Christy
McCaffrey, A. Dragonflight
Millay, K. The Sea of Tranquility
Moriarty, L. The center of everything
Obreht, T. The tiger's wife
Walton, L. The strange and beautiful sorrows of Ava Lavender
YOUNG ADULTS *See* Teenagers; Youth
YOUNG ADULTS' LITERATURE *See* Young adult literature
Young man with a horn. Baker, D.
YOUNG MEN
See also Men; Youth
YOUNG MEN -- CONDUCT OF LIFE
Levine, J. A. Bingo's Run
YOUNG MEN -- ENGLAND -- LONDON
Chaudhuri, A. Odysseus Abroad
YOUNG MEN
Akhtar, A. American dervish
Appelfeld, A. The man who never stopped sleeping
Chaudhuri, A. Odysseus Abroad
Colorless tsukuru tazaki and his years of pilgrimage
Louis, É. The end of Eddy
Mastai, E. All our wrong todays
Palahniuk, C. Fight Club
Swift, G. England and other stories
Villarreal, J. A. Pocho
Wilson, A. Flatscreen
YOUNG MEN -- INDIA -- MUMBAI
Adiga, A. Selection day
YOUNG MEN -- IRELAND -- MAYO (COUNTY)
Barrett, C. Young skins
YOUNG MEN -- KENTUCY
Taylor, A. The marble orchard
YOUNG MEN -- SCOTLAND
Welsh, I. Skagboys
YOUNG PEOPLE *See* Teenagers; Youth
YOUNG PERSONS *See* Teenagers; Youth
Young skins. Barrett, C.
YOUNG WOMEN
Arden, K. The bear and the nightingale
Banasky, C. The suicide of Claire Bishop
Bank, M. The wonder spot
Bell, A. The reapers are the angels
Clement, J. Prayers for the stolen
A Crack in the Wall
Danler, S. Sweetbitter
Frame, R. Havisham
Freeman, C. Go with me
Haimoff, M. These days are ours
Kelman, J. Mo said she was quirky
Mackintosh, C. I see you
McLain, P. Circling the Sun
Miller, M. Always happy hour
Palaia, M. The given world
Rivers, F. Bridge to haven
Rogan, C. The lifeboat
Shinn, S. Jenna Starborn
Simonson, H. The summer before the war
Tyler, A. Vinegar girl
YOUNG WOMEN
See also Women; Youth
YOUNG WOMEN -- CRIMES AGAINST
Albert, S. W. The Darling Dahlias and the cucumber tree
Brooks, B. Winter kill
Winspear, J. Birds of a feather
YOUNG WOMEN -- ENGLAND -- LONDON
Atlee, A. The typewriter girl
YOUNG WOMEN -- GREECE
Lyon, A. The sweet girl
YOUNG WOMEN -- ILLINOIS -- CHICAGO
Rosen, R. Dollface
YOUNG WOMEN -- IRELAND -- MAYO (COUNTY)
Barrett, C. Young skins
YOUNG WOMEN -- NEW YORK (STATE) -- NEW YORK
Clark, G. The regulars
Egan, J. Manhattan Beach
YOUNG WOMEN -- UNITED STATES
El Akkad, O. American war
Young, Ann Eliza, b. 1844
About
Ebershoff, D. The 19th wife
Youngblood. Gallagher, M.
Your face in mine. Row, J.

Your face tomorrow: volume one: Fever and spear. Marias, J.
Your face tomorrow: volume three: Poison, shadow and farewell. Marias, J.
Your face tomorrow: volume two: Dance and dream. Marias, J.
Your friendly neighborhood criminal. Van Rooy, M.
Your mouth is lovely. Richler, N.
Your scandalous ways. Chase, L.
YOUTH
Barrett, C. Young skins
Fitzgerald, F. S. The beautiful and damned
Fitzgerald, F. S. This side of paradise
Gardam, J. The flight of the maidens
Gessen, K. All the sad young literary men
Godden, R. Pippa passes
Guest, J. Ordinary people
Guo X. Twenty fragments of a ravenous youth
Huston, C. The shotgun rule
It's fine by me
Jones, S. Outcast
Kay, G. G. Ysabel
McCarthy, M. Birds of America
Nichols, J. T. The sterile cuckoo
O'Hagan, A. Be near me
Salinger, J. D. The catcher in the rye
Schwartzman, A. Eddie Signwriter
Siddons, A. R. Heartbreak Hotel
Sillitoe, A. Saturday night and Sunday morning
Smith, B. Joy in the morning
Sparks, N. A walk to remember
Spencer, S. Endless love
Tarkington, B. Alice Adams
Townsend, S. Adrian Mole: the lost years
Turgenev, I. S. Fathers and sons
Tyler, A. A slipping-down life
Updike, J. Brazil
Whittall, Z. Holding still for as long as possible
Wolfe, T. Of time and the river
Wolfe, T. The web and the rock
Woolf, V. Jacob's room
YOUTH -- PSYCHOLOGY
Collins, C. The gamal
YOUTH WITH DISABILITIES
Nussbaum, S. Good kings bad kings
YOUTH WITH MENTAL DISABILITIES
Raimondo, L. Dante's wood
YOUTHS' WRITINGS
Collins, C. The gamal
Ysabel. Kay, G. G.
YUGOSLAV WAR, 1991-1995
Prcic, I. Shards
Nović, S. Girl at war
YUGOSLAVIA
Seymour, G. The heart of danger
YUKON RIVER VALLEY (YUKON AND ALASKA)
London, J. The call of the wild
London, J. White Fang

Z

Z. Fowler, T. A.
ZAIRE
Griffin, W. E. B. Special ops
Hulme, K. The nun's story
Kingsolver, B. The poisonwood Bible
ZAMBIA -- RACE RELATIONS
Mankell, H. The eye of the leopard
Zamenhof, L. L., 1859-1917
About
Skibell, J. A curable romantic
Zazen. Veselka, V.
Zeke and Ned. McMurtry, L.
ZEN BUDDHISM
Kerouac, J. The Dharma bums
ZEN BUDDHISM
See also Buddhism
ZEN, AURELIO (FICTITIOUS CHARACTER)
Dibdin, M. Ratking
Zendegi. Egan, G.
The **zenith.** Thu Huong Duong
Zeno's conscience. Svevo, I.
The **zero** game. Meltzer, B.
Zero history. Gibson, W.
Zero K. DeLillo, D.
Zeroville. Erickson, S.
ZIMBABWE
Bulawayo, N. We need new names
ZIONISM
Agnon, S. Y. Only yesterday
Iles, G. Black cross
Uris, L. Exodus
ZIP CODE
See also Postal service
Zoli. McCann, C.
ZOMBIES
Bell, A. The reapers are the angels
Brooks, M. World War Z
Cronin, J. The twelve
Deborde, R. Portlandtown
Dépestre, R. Hadriana in all my dreams
Grant, M. Deadline
Grant, M. Feed
Grant, M. Feedback
Gregory, D. Raising Stony Mayhall
Hooper, T. Midnight movie
Hynes, J. Kings of infinite space
The living dead
Marion, I. Warm bodies
Martinez, A. L. Gil's All Fright Diner
Priest, C. Boneshaker
Wellington, D. Positive
Whitehead, C. Zone one
Zito, V. M. The return man
ZOMBIES
See also Dead; Folklore

The **zone** of interest. Amis, M.
Zone one. Whitehead, C.
Zones of thought [series]
Vinge, V. The children of the sky
Zoo city. Beukes, L.
ZOOLOGICAL GARDENS *See* Zoos
ZOOLOGICAL SPECIMENS -- COLLECTION AND PRESERVATION
See also Collectors and collecting
ZOOLOGISTS
Lawson, M. Crow Lake
ZOOS
Martel, Y. Life of Pi
Phillips, G. Fierce kingdom
ZOOS -- EMPLOYEES
Grimes, L. Quick fix
Zorba the Greek. Kazantzakis, N.
Zuckerman bound. Roth, P.
Zuckerman unbound. Roth, P.
ZULU (AFRICAN PEOPLE)
See also Africans; Indigenous peoples
ZULUS (AFRICAN PEOPLE)
Paton, A. Cry, the beloved country

Ref